HAMMOND®
WORLD ATLAS

HAMMOND® AMBASSADOR WORLD

ATLAS

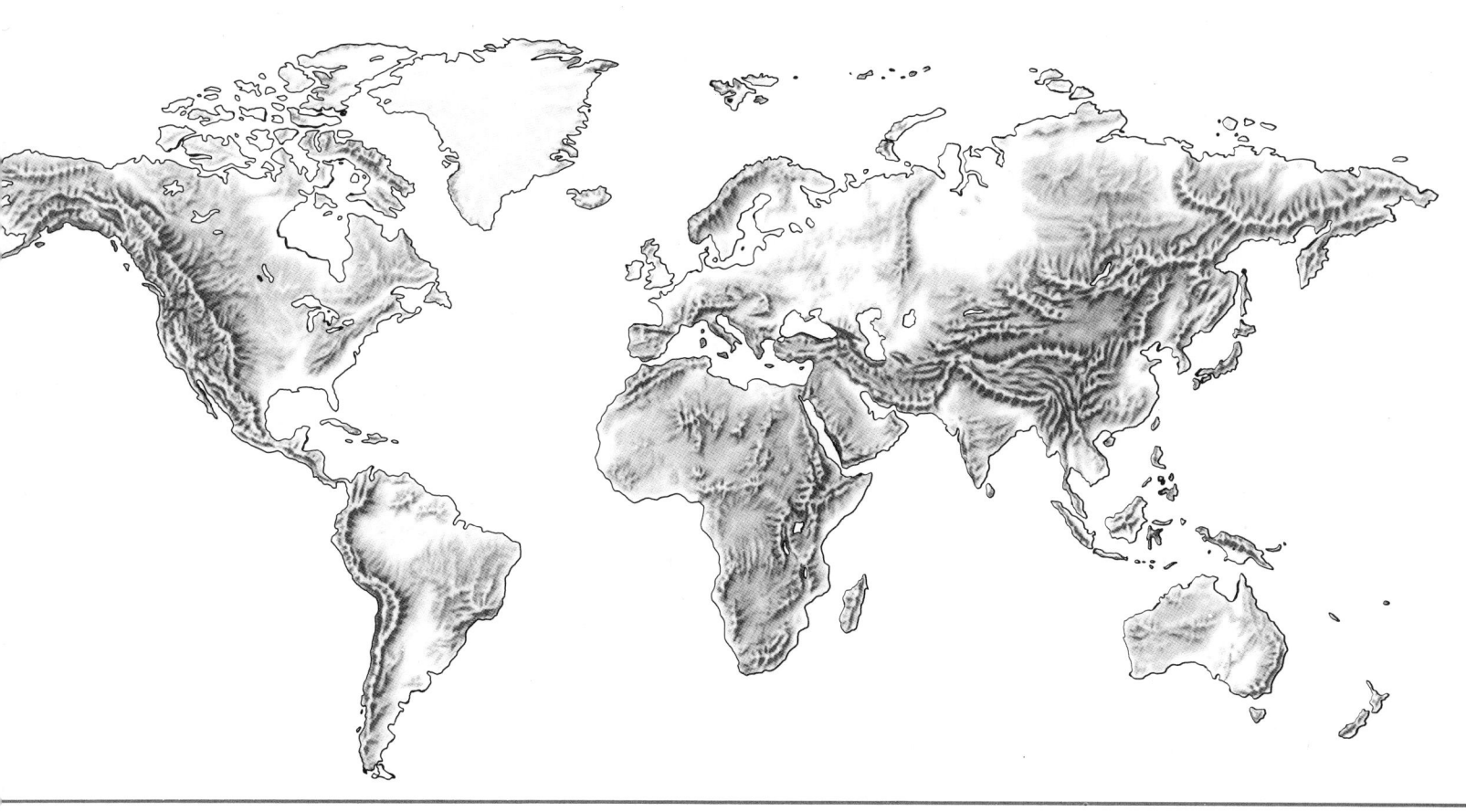

HAMMOND INCORPORATED   MAPLEWOOD, NEW JERSEY 07040

Library of Congress Cataloging in Publication Data
Hammond Incorporated.
  Hammond ambassador world atlas.
  Includes indexes.
  1. Atlases.   I. Title.   II. Title: Ambassador world
atlas.
G1021.H265 1982   912   82-81114
ISBN 0-8437-1251-1   AACR2

Hammond Publications Advisory Board

Contents

Introduction to the World Atlas

As in previous editions, this Hammond World Atlas is organized to make the retrieval of information as simple and quick as possible. The guiding principle in organizing the atlas material has been to present separate subjects on *separate* maps. In this way, each individual map topic is shown with the greatest degree of clarity, unencumbered with extraneous information that is best revealed on separate maps. Of equal importance from the standpoint of good atlas design is the treatment of all current information on a given country or state as a single atlas unit. Thus, the basic reference map of an area is accompanied on adjacent pages by all supplementary information pertaining to that area. For example, the detailed index for a given map always appears on the same page as, or on the pages immediately following, the reference map. This same map index provides population data for the many cities, towns and villages shown on the map. Highlight information on the area, i.e., the total population and area, the capital, the highest point, is listed in the summary fact listings accompanying each unit. An adjacent locator map relates the subject area to the larger world beyond. A three-dimensional picture of the area is exhibited by means of the accompanying full-color topographic map. A separate economic map defines the vital agricultural, industrial and mineral resources of the area. In the case of the foreign maps, the flag of each independent nation appears on the appropriate page. Finally, certain country units contain special subject maps dealing with the history, climate, demography and vegetation of the area.

An outstanding feature of the atlas is the addition of ZIP codes to the index entries for each of the legion of communities shown on the state maps. With the exception of the U.S. Postal Service directories of limited availability, the ZIP code listings herein are the most extensive published. In addition to listing ZIP codes for the communities possessing post offices, ZIP codes of the nearest post offices are listed for communities without postal facilities. It may be said with a fair degree of certainty that this innovation in atlas content doubles the value of the work for home, office and school.

The back of the book contains a second type of index. This is a multi-paged "A-to-Z" index of all the world's places that appear on the maps. The use of this map index is essential when the name of a place is known but its country, state, or province is unknown. ZIP codes also are given here for each U.S. city, town, or community entry.

The numerous geographical changes of the decade are all recorded in the Hammond World Atlas. Over 8,000 changes, which occurred throughout the world since the last major revision, were entered on the maps. The state maps now reveal the many new towns and cities that have developed in the recent past. The majority of these are burgeoning suburbs on the fringes of our larger cities. On the other hand, large numbers of abandoned and defunct rural hamlets have been removed from the maps and map indexes. Hundreds of other changes are also recorded on the state maps: new national parks and monuments, new dams, new reservoirs, name changes, etc.

Of course, the maps of foreign areas have been thoroughly updated. These revisions echo the new nations, shifting boundaries and the fluid internal divisions of many countries. New communities generated by the opening up of resources in the developing nations are also noted.

In closing it may be said that the atlas has truly been designed for contemporary use. Just as the information presented on the following pages is as current and up to date as the editors and cartographers could issue it, so the design and organization has been as well planned as possible to create a work useful to present generations.

President
HAMMOND INCORPORATED

Gazetteer-Index of the World

This alphabetical list of continents, countries, states, colonial possessions and other major geographical areas provides a quick reference to their area in square miles and square kilometers, population, capital or chief town, map page number and index key thereon. The last name indicates the square on the respective page in which the name may be found. An indication of the population sources used is also included, and refers both to the total figures given in this Gazetteer-Index and to the populations appearing in greater detail with the maps throughout the atlas. The population figures used in each case are the latest reliable figures obtainable. A glance at the sources will show that the dates vary considerably throughout the world. In certain areas where no census has ever been taken, we must rely on official estimates. In other areas where censuses have been taken at infrequent intervals, we again rely on estimates. The key to the abbreviations used in the Gazetteer-Index follows:

aut = autonomous	est = estimates	reg = regions
boro = boroughs	excl = excluding	rep = republics
cap = capital	FC = final census	S.S.R. = Soviet Socialist Republic
CE = census (undetermined)	gov = governorates	terr = territories; territory
CIA = U.S. Central Intelligence Agency	incl = including	TP = total population
	isl = islands	U.K. = United Kingdom
cit = cities	met = metropolitan	UN = United Nations
co = counties	OE = official estimate	U.S.A. = United States of America
com = communes	oth = other populations	U.S.S.R. = Union of Soviet Socialist Republics
dept = departments	par = parishes	
dist = districts	PC = preliminary census	ws = with suburbs
div = divisions	prov = provinces; provincial	

Country	Area Square Miles	Area Square Kilometers	Population	Capital or Chief Town	Page and Index Ref.	Sources of Population Data
*Afghanistan	250,775	649,507	15,540,000	Kabul	68/A 2	79 PC
Africa	11,707,000	30,321,130	469,000,000	....	102/......	80 UN est
Alabama, U.S.A.	51,705	133,916	3,893,888	Montgomery	195/......	80 FC & OE
Alaska, U.S.A.	591,004	1,530,700	401,851	Juneau	196/......	80 FC & OE
*Albania	11,100	28,749	2,590,600	Tiranë	45/E 5	TP—79 PC; cit over 6,000—70 OE; oth—63 OE
Alberta, Canada	255,285	661,185	2,207,856	Edmonton	182/......	TP—81 PC; oth—76 FC
*Algeria	919,591	2,381,740	17,422,000	Algiers	106/D 3	77 PC
American Samoa	77	199	32,395	Pago Pago	87/J 7; 86/......	TP—80 PC
Andorra	188	487	31,000	Andorra la Vella	33/G 1	TP—79 OE; cap—75 OE
*Angola	481,351	1,246,700	7,078,000	Luanda	114/C 6	TP—80 UN est; oth—70 FC
Anguilla	35	91	6,519	The Valley	156/F 3	74 FC
Antarctica	5,500,000	14,245,000	....	....	5/......	....
*Antigua and Barbuda	171	443	72,000	St. John's	161/E11; 156/G 3	TP—77 OE; oth—70 FC
*Argentina	1,072,070	2,776,661	27,862,771	Buenos Aires	143/......	TP, prov—80 PC; cap (ws)—78 OE; oth—70 PC
Arizona, U.S.A.	114,000	295,260	2,718,425	Phoenix	198/......	80 FC & OE
Arkansas, U.S.A.	53,187	137,754	2,286,435	Little Rock	202/......	80 FC & OE
Armenian S.S.R., U.S.S.R.	11,506	29,800	3,031,000	Erivan	52/F 6	TP, cit over 50,000—79 PC; oth—70 FC
Aruba, Neth. Antilles	70	181	55,148	Oranjestad	161/E 9	TP—71 FC; cap—72 est
Ascension Island, St. Helena	34	88	719	Georgetown	102/A 5	76 FC
Ashmore & Cartier Islands, Australia	61	159	....	(Canberra, Austr.)	88/C 2	....
Asia	17,128,500	44,362,815	2,633,000,000	....	54/......	80 est
*Australia	2,966,136	7,682,300	13,548,448	Canberra	88/......	76 FC
Australian Capital Territory	927	2,400	203,300	Canberra	96/E 4	76 FC
*Austria	32,375	83,851	7,507,000	Vienna	40/B 3	TP—80 OE; cap, cit over 100,000—73 OE; oth—71 FC
Azerbaidzhan S.S.R., U.S.S.R.	33,436	86,600	6,028,000	Baku	52/G 6	TP, cit over 50,000—79 PC; oth—70 FC
Azores Islands, Portugal	902	2,335	264,400	Ponta Delgada; Angra do Heroísmo; Horta	32/......	TP—77 OE; oth—70 FC & PC
*Bahamas	5,382	13,939	223,455	Nassau	156/C 1	TP—80 PC; oth—70 FC
*Bahrain	240	622	358,857	Manama	58/F 4	TP—81 PC; oth—71 FC
Baker Island, U.S.A.	1	2.6	....	....	87/J 5	....
Balearic Islands, Spain	1,936	5,014	558,287	Palma	33/H 3	70 FC
*Bangladesh	55,126	142,776	87,052,024	Dacca	68/G 4	TP—81 PC; oth—74 FC
*Barbados	166	430	249,000	Bridgetown	161/B 8	TP—80 PC; oth—70 PC
Belau (Palau)	188	487	12,177	Koror	86/D 5	TP—80 PC
*Belgium	11,781	30,513	9,855,110	Brussels	27/E 7	TP—80 OE; oth—70 FC (com)
*Belize	8,867	22,966	144,857	Belmopan	154/C 2	TP, cap, cit over 1,000—80 PC; oth—70 PC
*Benin	43,483	112,620	3,338,240	Porto-Novo	106/E 6	TP—79 PC; cap, Cotonou—75 OE; oth—73 OE
Bermuda	21	54	67,761	Hamilton	156/H 3	TP—80 PC; oth—70 FC
*Bhutan	18,147	47,000	1,298,000	Thimphu	68/G 3	TP—80 UN est; oth—70 OE
*Bolivia	424,163	1,098,582	5,600,000	La Paz; Sucre	136/......	TP—80 OE; cap, dept, dept cap—76 FC; oth—50 FC
Bonaire, Neth. Antilles	112	291	8,087	Kralendijk	161/E 9	TP—71 FC; cap—72 est
Bophuthatswana (rep.), South Africa	15,570	40,326	1,200,000	Mmabatho	119/D 5	TP—78 est; oth—70 FC
*Botswana	224,764	582,139	819,000	Gaborone	119/C 4	TP—80 OE; cap, Francistown—74 OE; Selebi-Pikwe—75 FC; oth—71 FC
Bouvet Island	22	57	....	....	5/D 1	....
*Brazil	3,284,426	8,506,663	119,024,600	Brasília	132/......	TP, cap, cit over 1,000,000 (incl Belém)—80 PC; oth—70 PC
British Columbia, Canada	366,253	948,596	2,716,301	Victoria	184/......	TP—81 PC; oth—76 FC
British Indian Ocean Terr.	29	75	2,000	(London, U.K.)	54/L10	78 est
British Virgin Islands	59	153	12,000	Road Town	157/H 1	TP—76 OE; oth—70 FC
Brunei	2,226	5,765	212,840	Bandar Seri Begawan	85/E 4	TP—79 OE; cap—71 FC
*Bulgaria	42,823	110,912	8,862,000	Sofia	45/F 4	TP—80 OE; oth—75 PC
*Burma	261,789	678,034	32,913,000	Rangoon	72/B 2	TP—79 OE; states, div. cit over 100,000—73 PC; oth—53 FC
*Burundi	10,747	27,835	4,021,910	Bujumbura	114/E 4	79 PC
*Byelorussian S.S.R. (White Russian S.S.R.), U.S.S.R.	80,154	207,600	9,560,000	Minsk	52/C 4	TP, cit over 50,000—79 PC; oth—70 FC
California, U.S.A.	158,706	411,049	23,667,565	Sacramento	204/......	80 FC & OE
*Cambodia (Kampuchea)	69,898	181,036	5,200,000	Phnom Penh	72/E 4	TP—79 CIA est; cap—80 est
*Cameroon	183,568	475,441	8,503,000	Yaoundé	114/B 2	TP—80 OE; cit over 21,000—76 FC; Ebolowa, oth—70 OE
*Canada	3,851,787	9,976,139	24,105,163	Ottawa	162/......	TP, prov, terr—81 PC; oth—76 FC
Canary Islands, Spain	2,808	7,273	1,170,224	Las Palmas; Santa Cruz	32/B 4	70 FC
Cape of Good Hope, South Africa	261,705	677,816	5,543,506	Cape Town	118/C 6	TP—80 PC; oth—70 FC
*Cape Verde	1,557	4,033	324,000	Praia	106/B 8	TP—80 UN est; oth—70 PC
Cayman Islands	100	259	16,677	Georgetown	156/B 3	79 FC

*Member of the United Nations.

Gazetteer-Index of the World

Country	Area Square Miles	Area Square Kilometers	Population	Capital or Chief Town	Page and Index Ref.	Sources of Population Data
Celebes, Indonesia	72,986	189,034	7,732,383	Ujung Pandang	85/G 6	71 PC
*Central African Republic	242,000	626,780	2,284,000	Bangui	114/C 2	TP—79 est; oth—75 FC
Central America	197,480	511,475	21,000,000	....	154/......	79 OE
Ceylon, see Sri Lanka						
*Chad	495,752	1,283,998	4,309,000	N'Djamena	111/C 4	TP—78 OE; oth—72 OE
Channel Islands	75	194	133,000	St. Helier; St. Peter Port	13/E 8	TP—81 OE; oth—71 FC
*Chile	292,257	756,946	11,198,789	Santiago	138/......	TP—80 OE; cap (ws)—78 OE; oth—70 FC & PC
*China, People's Rep. of	3,691,000	9,559,690	958,090,000	Peking (Beijing)	77/......	TP, prov, Peking, Shanghai, Tianjin—78 OE; oth—70 est
China, Republic of (Taiwan)	13,971	36,185	16,609,961	Taipei	77/K 7	TP, cap, Penghu Isl., cit over 300,000—77 OE; oth—70 OE
Christmas Island, Australia	52	135	3,184	Flying Fish Cove	54/O11	80 OE
Ciskei (rep.), S. Africa	2,988	7,740	635,631	Bisho	119/D 6	80 PC
Clipperton Island	2	5.2	....	....	146/H 8	....
Cocos (Keeling) Islands, Australia	5.4	14	555	West Island	54/N11	81 PC
*Colombia	439,513	1,138,339	27,520,000	Bogotá	126/......	TP—80 OE; oth—73 PC
Colorado, U.S.A.	104,091	269,596	2,889,735	Denver	208/......	80 FC & OE
*Comoros	719	1,862	290,000	Moroni	119/G 2	TP—78 est; cap—75 OE; oth—66 FC
*Congo	132,046	342,000	1,537,000	Brazzaville	114/B 4	TP—80 UN est; cap—74 FC; oth—74 PC
Connecticut, U.S.A.	5,018	12,997	3,107,576	Hartford	210/......	80 FC & OE
Cook Islands	91	236	18,128	Avarua	87/K 3	76 FC
Coral Sea Islands, Australia	8.5	22	....	....	88/J 3	....
Corsica, France	3,352	8,682	289,842	Ajaccio; Bastia	28/B 6	75 FC
*Costa Rica	19,575	50,700	2,245,000	San José	154/E 5	TP—80 OE; oth—73 FC
*Cuba	44,206	114,494	9,706,369	Havana	158/......	TP—81 PC; prov, cap—76 OE; cit over 80,000—75 OE; oth—70 PC
Curaçao, Neth. Antilles	178	462	145,430	Willemstad	161/G 7	TP—71 FC; cap—75 OE
*Cyprus	3,473	8,995	629,000	Nicosia	62/E 5	TP—80 OE; oth—73 FC, 72 OE
*Czechoslovakia	49,373	127,876	15,276,799	Prague	41/C 2	TP—80 PC; cap, cit over 100,000—75 OE; rep, reg—74 OE; oth—75 OE, 70 FC
Delaware, U.S.A.	2,044	5,294	594,317	Dover	245/R 3	80 FC & OE
*Denmark	16,629	43,069	5,124,000	Copenhagen	21/......	TP—80 OE; oth—75 OE, 71 OE, 70 FC
District of Columbia, U.S.A.	69	179	638,432	Washington	244/F 5	80 FC
*Djibouti	8,880	23,000	386,000	Djibouti	111/H 5	TP—79 est; cap—73 OE
*Dominica	290	751	74,089	Roseau	161/E 7	TP—80 PC; oth—70 FC
*Dominican Republic	18,704	48,443	5,431,000	Santo Domingo	158/D 6	TP—80 OE; prov, cap—70 FC; oth—70 FC, 60 PC
*East Germany (German Democratic Republic)	41,768	108,179	16,737,000	Berlin (East)	22/......	TP—80 OE; oth—75 OE
*Ecuador	109,483	283,561	8,354,000	Quito	128/C 3	TP—80 OE; oth—74 FC
*Egypt	386,659	1,001,447	41,572,000	Cairo	110/E 2	TP—79 OE; oth—76 PC
*El Salvador	8,260	21,393	4,813,000	San Salvador	154/C 4	TP—80 OE; oth—71 FC
England, U.K.	50,516	130,836	46,220,955	London	13/......	TP—81 PC; co, cap (boro & ws)—76 OE; cit—76 & 73 OE; oth—71 FC
*Equatorial Guinea	10,831	28,052	244,000	Malabo	114/A 3	TP—79 est; terr—68 OE; oth—60 FC
Estonian S.S.R., U.S.S.R.	17,413	45,100	1,466,000	Tallinn	52/C 3; 53/......	TP, cit over 50,000—79 PC; oth—70 FC
*Ethiopia	471,776	1,221,900	31,065,000	Addis Ababa	110/G 5	TP—80 OE; cap, Asmara—78 OE; prov—72 OE; oth—72 & 71 OE
Europe	4,057,000	10,507,630	676,000,000	....	7/......	80 est
Faerøe Islands, Denmark	540	1,399	41,969	Tórshavn	21/B 2	77 FC
Falkland Islands & Dependencies	6,198	16,053	1,855	Stanley	120/E 8; 143/D 7	80 FC
*Fiji	7,055	18,272	588,068	Suva	87/H 8; 86/......	76 FC
*Finland	130,128	337,032	4,788,000	Helsinki	18/O 6	TP—80 OE; prov—75 OE; oth—75 OE, 70 FC
Florida, U.S.A.	58,664	151,940	9,746,342	Tallahassee	212/......	80 FC & OE
*France	210,038	543,998	53,788,000	Paris	28/......	TP—80 OE; oth—75 FC
French Guiana	35,135	91,000	64,000	Cayenne	131/E 3	TP—80 OE; oth—74 FC
French Polynesia	1,544	4,000	137,382	Papeete	87/L 8	77 FC
*Gabon	103,346	267,666	551,000	Libreville	114/B 4	TP—80 UN est; oth—70 FC
*Gambia	4,127	10,689	601,000	Banjul	106/A 6	TP—80 OE; oth—73 FC
Gaza Strip	139	360	400,000	Gaza	65/A 4	TP—76 OE; oth—67 CE
Georgia, U.S.A.	58,910	152,577	5,463,105	Atlanta	217/......	80 FC & OE
Georgian S.S.R., U.S.S.R.	26,911	69,700	5,015,000	Tbilisi	52/F 6	TP, cit over 50,000—79 PC; oth—70 FC
*Germany, East (German Democratic Republic)	41,768	108,179	16,737,000	Berlin (East)	22/......	TP—80 OE; oth—75 OE
*Germany, West (Federal Republic)	95,985	248,601	61,658,000	Bonn	22/......	TP—80 OE; states, cap—76 OE; oth—76 OE, 70 FC
*Ghana	92,099	238,536	11,450,000	Accra	106/D 7	TP—80 OE; oth—70 FC
Gibraltar	2.28	5.91	29,760	Gibraltar	33/D 4	79 OE
*Great Britain & Northern Ireland (United Kingdom)	94,399	244,493	55,672,000	London	10/......	TP—81 OE (see England, Wales, Scotland, Northern Ireland)
*Greece	50,944	131,945	9,599,000	Athens	45/F 6	TP—80 OE; oth—71 FC
Greenland	840,000	2,175,600	49,773	Nûk (Godthåb)	4/B12	TP—80 OE
*Grenada	133	344	110,000	St. George's	161/D 9; 156/G 4	TP—79 OE; oth—70 FC
Guadeloupe & Dependencies	687	1,779	319,000	Basse-Terre	161/A 5; 156/F 4	TP—80 OE; oth—74 FC
Guam	209	541	105,821	Agaña	87/E 4; 86/......	TP—80 PC
*Guatemala	42,042	108,889	7,262,419	Guatemala	154/B 3	TP—80 OE; oth—73 FC
*Guinea	94,925	245,856	5,143,284	Conakry	106/B 6	TP, cap (ws), Kankan, Kindia, Labé—72 FC; oth—67 OE
*Guinea-Bissau	13,948	36,125	777,214	Bissau	106/A 6	79 PC
*Guyana	83,000	214,970	820,000	Georgetown	131/B 3	TP—80 OE; cap, cit over 10,000—70 FC; oth—60 FC
*Haiti	10,694	27,697	5,009,000	Port-au-Prince	158/C 5	TP—80 OE; oth—71 FC
Hawaii, U.S.A.	6,471	16,760	964,691	Honolulu	218/......	80 FC & OE
Heard & McDonald Islands, Australia	113	293	....	....	2/N 8	....
Holland, see Netherlands						
*Honduras	43,277	112,087	3,691,000	Tegucigalpa	154/D 3	TP—80 OE; oth—74 FC
Hong Kong	403	1,044	5,022,000	Victoria	77/H 7; 78/......	TP—81 PC; oth—76 FC
Howland Island, U.S.A.	1	2.6	....	....	87/J 5	....
*Hungary	35,919	93,030	10,709,536	Budapest	41/D 3	TP, cap, co—80 PC; oth—80 PC, 70 FC
*Iceland	39,768	103,000	228,785	Reykjavík	21/B 1	TP—80 PC; oth—70 FC
Idaho, U.S.A.	83,564	216,431	944,038	Boise	220/......	80 FC & OE

Country	Area Square Miles	Square Kilometers	Population	Capital or Chief Town	Page and Index Ref.	Sources of Population Data
Illinois, U.S.A.	56,345	145,934	11,426,596	Springfield	222/	80 FC & OE
*India	1,269,339	3,287,588	683,810,051	New Delhi	68/D 4	TP & states—81 PC; oth—71 FC
Indiana, U.S.A.	36,185	93,719	5,490,260	Indianapolis	227/	80 FC & OE
*Indonesia	788,430	2,042,034	147,383,075	Jakarta	85/D 7	TP—80 PC; cit, isl—71 PC; Timor—71 PC (Indon.) + 70 PC (Port.)
Iowa, U.S.A.	56,275	145,752	2,913,808	Des Moines	229/	80 FC & OE
*Iran	636,293	1,648,000	37,447,000	Tehran	66/F 4	TP—80 OE; div, cit over 50,000—76 PC; oth—66 FC & PC, 56 FC
*Iraq	172,476	446,713	12,767,000	Baghdad	66/C 4	TP—79 OE; oth—65 & 57 FC
*Ireland	27,136	70,282	3,440,427	Dublin	17/	TP—81 PC; oth—71 FC
Ireland, Northern, U.K.	5,452	14,121	1,543,000	Belfast	17/F 2	TP—81 OE; dist—76 OE; cap, Londonderry—73 OE; oth—71 FC
Isle of Man	227	588	64,000	Douglas	13/C 3	TP—80 OE; oth—71 FC
*Israel	7,847	20,324	3,878,000	Jerusalem	65/B 4	TP—80 OE; cap, cit over 100,000—77 OE; dist, cit over 5,000—72 PC; oth—61 FC
*Italy	116,303	301,225	57,140,000	Rome	34/	TP—80 OE; oth—71 FC
*Ivory Coast	124,504	322,465	7,920,000	Abidjan	106/C 7	TP—79 OE; oth—75 PC
*Jamaica	4,411	11,424	2,161,000	Kingston	158/	TP—79 OE; oth—70 & 60 FC
Jan Mayen	144	373	....	....	6/D 1	....
*Japan	145,730	377,441	117,057,485	Tokyo	81/	TP—80 PC; oth—75 FC
Jarvis Island, U.S.A.	1	2.6	....	....	87/K 6	....
Java, Indonesia	48,842	126,500	73,712,411	Jakarta	85/J 2	71 PC
Johnston Atoll	.91	2.4	327	....	87/K 4	80 FC
*Jordan	35,000	90,650	2,152,273	Amman	65/D 3	TP—79 PC; cap, cit over 100,000—77 OE; gov, cit 9,000-100,000—73 OE; oth—61 FC
*Kampuchea (Cambodia)	69,898	181,036	5,200,000	Phnom Penh	72/E 4	TP—79 CIA est; cap—80 est
Kansas, U.S.A.	82,277	213,097	2,364,236	Topeka	232/	80 FC & OE
Kazakh S.S.R., U.S.S.R.	1,048,300	2,715,100	14,684,000	Alma-Ata	48/G 5	TP, cit over 50,000—79 PC; oth—70 FC
Kentucky, U.S.A.	40,409	104,659	3,660,257	Frankfort	237/	80 FC & OE
*Kenya	224,960	582,646	15,327,061	Nairobi	115/G 3	TP—79 PC; oth—69 FC
Kermadec Islands	13	33	11	....	87/J 9	76 FC
Kingman Reef	0.1	0.26	....	....	87/K 5	....
Kirgiz S.S.R., U.S.S.R.	76,641	198,500	3,529,000	Frunze	48/H 5	TP, cit over 50,000—79 PC; oth—70 FC
Kiribati	291	754	56,213	Bairiki	87/J 6	TP—78 FC; oth—73 FC
Korea, North	46,540	120,539	17,914,000	P'yŏngyang	80/D 3	TP—80 UN est; cap—76 OE; Hamhŭng—72 OE; oth—70 OE
Korea, South	38,175	98,873	37,448,836	Seoul	80/D 5	TP—80 PC; oth—75 FC & PC
*Kuwait	6,532	16,918	1,355,827	Al Kuwait	58/E 4	80 PC
*Laos	91,428	236,800	3,721,000	Vientiane	72/D 3	TP—80 UN est; cap—66 FC; oth—58 OE
Latvian S.S.R., U.S.S.R.	24,595	63,700	2,521,000	Riga	52/B 3; 53/	TP, cit over 50,000—79 PC; oth—70 FC
*Lebanon	4,015	10,399	3,161,000	Beirut	62/F 6	TP—80 UN est; cap—70 FC; Tarabulus—64 OE; oth—61 OE
*Lesotho	11,720	30,355	1,339,000	Maseru	119/D 5	TP—80 OE; oth—80 est
*Liberia	43,000	111,370	1,873,000	Monrovia	106/C 7	TP—80 OE; oth—74 FC
*Libya	679,358	1,759,537	2,856,000	Tripoli	110/B 2	TP—79 OE; oth—73 FC & PC
Liechtenstein	61	158	25,220	Vaduz	39/J 2	80 PC
Lithuanian S.S.R., U.S.S.R.	25,174	65,200	3,398,000	Vilna	52/B 3; 53/	TP, cit over 50,000—79 PC; oth—70 FC
Louisiana, U.S.A.	47,752	123,678	4,206,312	Baton Rouge	238/	80 FC & OE
*Luxembourg	999	2,587	364,000	Luxembourg	27/J 9	TP—79 OE; cap—74 OE; oth—70 FC
Macau	6	16	271,000	Macau	77/H 7	TP—78 OE; cap—70 FC
*Madagascar	226,657	587,041	8,742,000	Antananarivo	119/H 3	TP—80 UN est; prov, cap, cit over 40,000—75 PC; oth—71 OE
Madeira Islands, Portugal	307	796	262,800	Funchal	32/A 2	TP—77 OE; oth—70 FC & PC
Maine, U.S.A.	33,265	86,156	1,125,027	Augusta	243/	80 FC & OE
*Malawi	45,747	118,485	5,968,000	Lilongwe	114/F 6	TP—80 OE; oth—77 PC
Malaya, Malaysia	50,806	131,588	11,138,227	Kuala Lumpur	72/D 6	TP, states, Kuala Lumpur—80 PC; cit over 100,000—70 FC; oth—70 PC
*Malaysia	128,308	332,318	13,435,588	Kuala Lumpur	72/D 6; 85/E 4	TP, states, Kuala Lumpur—80 PC; Kuching, Kota Kinabalu, cit over 100,000—70 FC; oth—70 FC
*Maldives	115	298	143,046	Male	54/L 9	78 FC
*Mali	464,873	1,204,021	6,906,000	Bamako	106/C 6	TP—80 OE; oth—76 PC
*Malta	122	316	343,970	Valletta	34/E 7	TP, cit—79 OE; oth—73 OE
Man, Isle of	227	588	64,000	Douglas	13/C 3	TP—80 OE; oth—71 FC
Manitoba, Canada	250,999	650,087	1,017,323	Winnipeg	179/	TP—81 PC; oth—76 PC
Marquesas Islands, French Polynesia	492	1,274	5,419	Atuona	87/N 6	77 FC
Marshall Islands	70	181	31,042	Majuro	87/G 4	TP—80 PC
Martinique	425	1,101	308,000	Fort-de-France	161/D 5	TP—80 OE; oth—74 FC
Maryland, U.S.A.	10,460	27,091	4,216,975	Annapolis	245/	80 FC & OE
Massachusetts, U.S.A.	8,284	21,456	5,737,037	Boston	249/	80 FC & OE
*Mauritania	419,229	1,085,803	1,634,000	Nouakchott	106/B 5	TP—80 UN est; oth—76 PC
*Mauritius	790	2,046	959,000	Port Louis	119/G 5	TP—80 OE; cap—77 OE; Curepipe, Quatre Bornes—74 OE; oth—72 PC
Mayotte	144	373	47,300	Dzaoudzi	119/G 2	TP—78 CE; cap—66 FC
*Mexico	761,601	1,972,546	67,395,826	Mexico City	150/	TP, states, cap—80 PC; cap (ws), Guadalajara (ws), Monterrey (ws)—78 OE; oth—70 PC
Michigan, U.S.A.	58,527	151,585	9,262,078	Lansing	250/	80 FC & OE
Micronesia, Federated States of	....	....	73,755	Kolonia	87/E 5	TP—80 PC
Midway Islands	1.9	4.9	468	....	87/J 3	80 FC
Minnesota, U.S.A.	84,402	218,601	4,075,970	St. Paul	255/	80 FC & OE
Mississippi, U.S.A.	47,689	123,515	2,520,638	Jackson	256/	80 FC & OE
Missouri, U.S.A.	69,697	180,515	4,916,759	Jefferson City	261/	80 FC & OE
Moldavian S.S.R., U.S.S.R.	13,012	33,700	3,947,000	Kishinev	52/C 5	TP, cit over 50,000—79 PC; oth—70 FC
Monaco	368 acres	149 hectares	25,029	Monaco	28/G 6	75 FC
*Mongolia	606,163	1,569,962	1,594,800	Ulaanbaatar	77/E 2	TP—79 PC; prov, cap, Darhan—77 OE; oth—69 FC
Montana, U.S.A.	147,046	380,849	786,690	Helena	262/	80 FC & OE
Montserrat	40	104	12,073	Plymouth	157/G 3	80 PC
*Morocco	172,414	446,550	20,242,000	Rabat	106/C 2	TP—80 OE; oth—71 FC
*Mozambique	303,769	786,762	12,130,000	Maputo	119/E 4	TP, prov, cap—80 PC; oth—70 FC
Namibia (South-West Africa)	317,827	823,172	1,200,000	Windhoek	118/B 3	TP—74 est; oth—70 PC
Natal, South Africa	33,578	86,967	5,722,215	Pietermaritzburg	119/E 5	TP—80 PC; oth—70 PC
Nauru	7.7	20	7,254	Yaren (district)	87/G 6	77 PC
Navassa Island	2	5	....	....	156/C 3	....
Nebraska, U.S.A.	77,355	200,349	1,569,825	Lincoln	264/	80 FC & OE
*Nepal	54,663	141,577	14,179,301	Kathmandu	68/E 3	TP—81 PC; oth—71 FC
*Netherlands	15,892	41,160	14,227,000	The Hague; Amsterdam	27/F 5	TP—81 OE; oth—76 OE (com)

Gazetteer-Index of the World

Country	Square Miles	Square Kilometers	Population	Capital or Chief Town	Page and Index Ref.	Sources of Population Data
Netherlands Antilles	390	1,010	246,000	Willemstad	156/E 4	TP—78 OE
Nevada, U.S.A.	110,561	286,353	800,493	Carson City	266/......	80 FC & OE
New Brunswick, Canada	28,354	73,437	688,926	Fredericton	170/......	TP—81 PC; oth—76 FC
New Caledonia & Dependencies	7,335	18,998	133,233	Nouméa	87/G 8	76 FC
Newfoundland, Canada	156,184	404,517	561,996	St. John's	166/......	TP—81 PC; oth—76 FC
New Hampshire, U.S.A.	9,279	24,033	920,610	Concord	268/......	80 FC & OE
New Hebrides, see Vanuatu						
New Jersey, U.S.A.	7,787	20,168	7,364,823	Trenton	273/......	80 FC & OE
New Mexico, U.S.A.	121,593	314,926	1,302,981	Santa Fe	274/......	80 FC & OE
New South Wales, Australia	309,498	801,600	4,914,300	Sydney	96/B 2	76 FC
New York, U.S.A.	49,108	127,190	17,558,072	Albany	276/......	80 FC & OE
*New Zealand	103,736	268,676	3,167,357	Wellington	100/......	TP—81 PC; oth—76 FC
*Nicaragua	45,698	118,358	2,703,000	Managua	154/D 4	TP—80 OE; oth—71 PC
*Niger	489,189	1,267,000	5,098,427	Niamey	106/F 5	TP, cap, Maradi, Tahoua, Zinder—77 PC; oth—72 OE
*Nigeria	357,000	924,630	82,643,000	Lagos	106/F 6	TP—79 OE; prov—63 FC; oth—75 & 71 OE
Niue	100	259	3,843	Alofi	87/K 7	76 FC
Norfolk Island, Australia	13.4	34.6	2,180	Kingston	88/L 5	79 OE
North America	9,363,000	24,250,170	370,000,000	....	146/......	80 UN est
North Carolina, U.S.A.	52,669	136,413	5,881,813	Raleigh	281/......	80 FC & OE
North Dakota, U.S.A.	70,702	183,118	652,717	Bismarck	282/......	80 FC & OE
Northern Ireland, U.K.	5,452	14,121	1,543,000	Belfast	17/F 2	TP—81 OE; dist—76 OE; cap, Londonderry—73 OE; oth—71 FC
Northern Marianas	184	477	16,758	Capitol Hill	87/E 4	80 PC
Northern Territory, Australia	519,768	1,346,200	97,090	Darwin	93/......	76 FC
North Korea	46,540	120,539	17,914,000	P'yŏngyang	80/D 3	TP—80 UN est; cap—76 OE; Hamhŭng—72 OE; oth—70 OE
Northwest Territories, Canada	1,304,896	3,379,683	44,684	Yellowknife	187/G 3	TP—81 PC; oth—76 FC
*Norway	125,053	323,887	4,092,000	Oslo	18/F 7	TP—80 OE; co, Svalbard—76 OE; oth—76 OE, 70 FC
Nova Scotia, Canada	21,425	55,491	837,789	Halifax	168/......	TP—81 PC; oth—76 FC
Oceania	3,292,000	8,526,280	23,000,000	....	87/......	80 UN est
Ohio, U.S.A.	41,330	107,045	10,797,624	Columbus	284/......	80 FC & OE
Oklahoma, U.S.A.	69,956	181,186	3,025,290	Oklahoma City	288/......	80 FC & OE
*Oman	120,000	310,800	891,000	Muscat	58/G 6	TP—80 UN est; cap, Matrah—66 OE; Salala—68 OE
Ontario, Canada	412,580	1,068,582	8,551,733	Toronto	175, 177/......	TP—81 PC; oth—76 FC
Orange Free State, South Africa	49,866	129,153	1,833,216	Bloemfontein	119/D 5	TP—80 PC; oth—70 FC
Oregon, U.S.A.	97,073	251,419	2,633,149	Salem	291/......	80 FC & OE
Orkney Islands, Scotland	376	974	17,675	Kirkwall	15/E 1	TP—76 OE; oth—71 FC
Pacific Islands, Territory of the	533	1,380	133,732	Saipan	87/F 5	80 PC
*Pakistan	310,403	803,944	83,782,000	Islamabad	68/B 3	TP—81 PC; Abbottabad, Bannu, cit over 50,000—72 PC; oth—61 FC
Palau (Belau)	188	487	12,177	Koror	86/D 5	TP—80 PC
Palmyra Atoll	3.85	1	....		87/K 5	....
*Panama	29,761	77,082	1,830,175	Panamá	154/G 6	TP, cit over 1,600—80 PC; oth—70 FC
*Papua New Guinea	183,540	475,369	3,006,799	Port Moresby	85/B 7; 87/E 6	TP—80 PC; oth—80 PC, 71 FC
Paracel Islands	....	....	....		85/E 2	
*Paraguay	157,047	406,752	2,973,000	Asunción	144/......	TP—79 OE; oth—72 PC
Pennsylvania, U.S.A.	45,308	117,348	11,863,895	Harrisburg	294/......	80 FC & OE
Persia, see Iran						
*Peru	496,222	1,285,215	17,031,221	Lima	128/......	TP—81 PC; oth—72 PC
*Philippines	115,707	299,681	47,914,017	Manila	82/......	TP, prov—80 PC; oth—80 PC, 70 FC
Pitcairn Islands	18	47	61	Adamstown	87/O 8	78 FC
*Poland	120,725	312,678	35,815,000	Warsaw	47/......	TP—81 OE; prov, cap, Cracow, Łódź—75 OE; oth—70 F
*Portugal	35,549	92,072	9,933,000	Lisbon	32/B 3	TP—80 OE; cap (ws)—76 OE; oth—70 FC & PC
Prince Edward Island, Canada	2,184	5,657	121,328	Charlottetown	168/E 2	TP—81 OE; oth—76 FC
Puerto Rico	3,515	9,104	3,186,076	San Juan	161/......	80 PC
*Qatar	4,247	11,000	220,000	Doha	58/F 4	TP—80 UN est; cap—79 OE
Québec, Canada	594,857	1,540,680	6,377,518	Québec	172, 174/......	TP—81 PC; oth—76 FC
Queensland, Australia	666,872	1,727,200	2,111,700	Brisbane	95/......	76 FC
Réunion	969	2,510	491,000	St-Denis	119/F 5	TP—80 OE; oth—74 OE
Rhode Island, U.S.A.	1,212	3,139	947,154	Providence	249/H 5	80 FC & OE
Rhodesia, see Zimbabwe						
*Romania	91,699	237,500	22,048,305	Bucharest	45/F 3	79 OE
Russian S.F.S.R., U.S.S.R.	6,592,812	17,075,400	137,551,000	Moscow	48/D 4	TP, cit over 50,000—79 PC; oth—70 FC
*Rwanda	10,169	26,337	4,819,317	Kigali	114/E 4	78 PC
Sabah, Malaysia	29,300	75,887	1,002,608	Kota Kinabalu	85/F 4	TP—80 PC; Kota Kinabalu—70 FC; oth—70 PC
Saint Christopher (St. Kitts)-Nevis	104	269	44,404	Basseterre	156/F 3; 161/C11	TP, isl, cap—80 PC; oth—70 FC
Saint Helena & Dependencies	162	420	5,147	Jamestown	102/B 6	76 FC
*Saint Lucia	238	616	115,783	Castries	161/G 6	80 PC
*Saint Pierre & Miquelon	93.5	242	5,840	Saint-Pierre	166/C 4	74 FC
*Saint Vincent & the Grenadines	150	388	124,000	Kingstown	161/A 8; 157/G 4	TP—80 OE; oth—70 FC
Sakhalin, U.S.S.R.	29,500	76,405	655,000	Yuzhno-Sakhalinsk	48/P 4	TP, cit over 50,000—79 PC; oth—70 FC
*Salvador, El	8,260	21,393	4,813,000	San Salvador	154/C 4	TP—80 OE; oth—71 FC
San Marino	23.4	60.6	19,149	San Marino	34/D 3	TP—76 FC; oth—77 OE
*São Tomé e Príncipe	372	963	85,000	São Tomé	106/F 8	TP—80 UN est; oth—70 PC
Sarawak, Malaysia	48,202	124,843	1,294,753	Kuching	85/E 5	TP—80 PC; Kuching—70 FC; oth—70 PC
Sardinia, Italy	9,301	24,090	1,450,483	Cagliari	34/B 4	71 FC
Saskatchewan, Canada	251,699	651,900	957,025	Regina	181/......	TP—81 PC; oth—76 FC
*Saudi Arabia	829,995	2,149,687	8,367,000	Riyadh	58/D 4	TP—80 UN est; oth—74 OE
Scotland, U.K.	30,414	78,772	5,117,146	Edinburgh	15/......	TP—81 PC; reg—75 OE; cit—75 & 73 OE, 71 FC; oth—71 FC
*Senegal	75,954	196,720	5,508,000	Dakar	106/A 5	TP—79 OE; oth—76 FC
*Seychelles	145	375	63,000	Victoria	119/H 5	TP—79 OE; oth—77 FC
Shetland Islands, Scotland	552	1,430	18,494	Lerwick	15/G 2	TP—76 OE; oth—73 OE & 71 FC
Siam, see Thailand						
Sicily, Italy	9,926	25,708	4,628,918	Palermo	34/D 6	71 FC
*Sierra Leone	27,925	72,325	3,470,000	Freetown	106/B 7	TP—80 UN est; cap, Bo, Kenema, Makeni—74 PC; oth—63 FC
*Singapore	226	585	2,413,945	Singapore	72/F 6	80 FC
Society Islands, French Polynesia	677	1,753	117,703	Papeete	87/L 7	77 FC
*Solomon Islands	11,500	29,785	221,000	Honiara	87/G 6; 86/......	TP—79 OE; oth—76 FC
*Somalia	246,200	637,658	3,645,000	Mogadishu	115/H 3	TP—80 UN est; prov, cap—75 PC; oth—69, 68, 67, 63 & 62 OE

Gazetteer-Index of the World

Country	Area Square Miles	Area Square Kilometers	Population	Capital or Chief Town	Page and Index Ref.	Sources of Population Data
*South Africa	455,318	1,179,274	23,771,970	Cape Town; Pretoria	118/C 5	TP (excl Transkei, Bophuthatswana, Venda), prov—80 PC; Transkei, Bophuthatswana—78 est; Venda—79 est; oth—70 FC
South America	6,875,000	17,806,250	245,000,000	....	120/......	80 UN est
South Australia, Australia	379,922	984,000	1,261,600	Adelaide	94/......	76 FC
South Carolina, U.S.A.	31,113	80,583	3,121,833	Columbia	296/......	80 FC & OE
South Dakota, U.S.A.	77,116	199,730	690,768	Pierre	298/......	80 FC & OE
South Korea	38,175	98,873	37,448,836	Seoul	80/D 5	TP—80 PC; oth—75 FC & PC
South-West Africa (Namibia)	317,827	823,172	1,200,000	Windhoek	118/B 3	TP—74 est; oth—70 PC
*Spain	194,881	504,742	37,430,000	Madrid	33/......	TP—80 OE; met areas—75 OE; oth—70 FC
Spratly Island	....	....	....		85/E 4	....
*Sri Lanka	25,332	65,610	14,850,001	Colombo	68/E 7	TP—81 PC; cap, Jaffna—73 OE; oth—71 FC
*Sudan	967,494	2,505,809	18,691,000	Khartoum	110/E 4	TP—80 OE; cap, prov, prov cap—73 PC; oth—73 PC, 72 OE
Sumatra, Indonesia	164,000	424,760	19,360,400	Medan	84/B 5	71 PC
*Suriname	55,144	142,823	352,041	Paramaribo	131/C 3	TP—80 PC; dist, cap—71 PC; oth—64 FC
Svalbard, Norway	23,957	62,049	3,431	Longyearbyen	18/C 2	76 OE
*Swaziland	6,705	17,366	547,000	Mbabane	119/E 5	TP—80 OE; oth—76 FC
*Sweden	173,665	449,792	8,320,000	Stockholm	18/J 8	TP—81 OE; oth—75 FC
Switzerland	15,943	41,292	6,365,960	Bern	39/......	TP—80 FC; cantons—78 OE; cap, cit over 100,000 (& ws)—74 OE; cit (com) over 30,000 (& ws)—73 OE; oth—70 FC
*Syria	71,498	185,180	8,979,000	Damascus	62/G 5	TP—80 OE; oth—70 FC
Tadzhik S.S.R., U.S.S.R.	55,251	143,100	3,801,000	Dushanbe	48/G 6	TP, cit over 50,000—79 PC; oth—70 FC
Tahiti, French Polynesia	402	1,041	95,604	Papeete	87/L 7	77 FC
Taiwan	13,971	36,185	16,609,961	Taipei	77/K 7	TP, cap, Penghu Isl., cit over 300,000—77 OE; oth—70 OE
*Tanzania	363,708	942,003	17,527,560	Dar es Salaam	114/F 5	TP—78 PC; div, cap, cit over 17,000—78 PC; oth—67 FC
Tasmania, Australia	26,178	67,800	402,866	Hobart	99/......	76 FC
Tennessee, U.S.A.	42,144	109,153	4,591,120	Nashville	237/......	80 FC & OE
Texas, U.S.A.	266,807	691,030	14,229,288	Austin	303/......	80 FC & OE
*Thailand	198,455	513,998	46,455,000	Bangkok	72/D 3	TP—80 OE; oth—70 FC
Tibet, China	463,320	1,200,000	1,790,000	Lhasa	76/C 5	TP—78 OE; oth—70 est
*Togo	21,622	56,000	2,472,000	Lomé	106/E 7	TP—79 OE; oth—70 FC
Tokelau	3.9	10	1,575	Fakaofo	87/J 6	TP—76 FC; oth—72 FC
Tonga	270	699	90,128	Nuku'alofa	87/J 8	76 FC
Transkei (rep.), South Africa	16,910	43,797	2,000,000	Umtata	119/D 6	TP—80 est; oth—70 FC
Transvaal, South Africa	109,621	283,918	10,673,033	Pretoria	119/D 4	TP—80 PC; oth—70 FC
*Trinidad and Tobago	1,980	5,128	1,067,108	Port-of-Spain	157/G 5; 161/A10	TP—80 PC; oth—70 FC
Tristan da Cunha, St. Helena	38	98	251	Edinburgh	2/J 7	79 OE
Tuamotu Archipelago, French Polynesia	341	883	9,052	Apataki	87/M 7	77 FC
*Tunisia	63,378	164,149	6,367,000	Tunis	106/F 1	TP—79 OE; oth—75 FC
*Turkey	300,946	779,450	45,217,556	Ankara	62/D 3	TP—80 PC; oth—75 FC
Turkmen S.S.R., U.S.S.R.	188,455	488,100	2,759,000	Ashkhabad	48/F 6	TP, cit over 50,000—79 PC; oth—70 FC
Turks and Caicos Islands	166	430	7,436	Cockburn Town, Grand Turk	156/D 2	80 PC
Tuvalu	9.78	25.33	7,349	Fongafale, Funafuti	87/H 6	79 FC
*Uganda	91,076	235,887	12,630,076	Kampala	114/F 3	TP, cap—80 PC; oth—69 FC
*Ukrainian S.S.R., U.S.S.R.	233,089	603,700	49,755,000	Kiev	52/D 5	TP, cit over 50,000—79 PC; oth—70 FC
*Union of Soviet Socialist Republics	8,649,490	22,402,179	262,436,227	Moscow	48/......	TP, S.S.R., cit over 50,000—79 PC; oth—70 FC
*United Arab Emirates	32,278	83,600	1,040,275	Abu Dhabi	58/F 5	TP—80 PC; oth—79 OE
*United Kingdom	94,399	244,493	55,672,000	London	10/......	TP—81 OE (see England, Wales, Scotland, Northern Ireland)
*United States of America	3,623,420	9,384,658	226,504,825	Washington	188/......	80 FC & OE
*Upper Volta	105,869	274,200	6,908,000	Ouagadougou	106/D 6	TP—80 UN est; oth—75 FC, 73 OE
*Uruguay	72,172	186,925	2,899,000	Montevideo	145/......	TP—80 OE; oth—75 PC
Utah, U.S.A.	84,899	219,888	1,461,037	Salt Lake City	304/......	80 FC & OE
Uzbek S.S.R., U.S.S.R.	173,591	449,600	15,391,000	Tashkent	48/G 5	TP, cit over 50,000—79 PC; oth—70 FC
*Vanuatu	5,700	14,763	112,596	Vila	87/G 7	79 FC
Vatican City	108.7 acres	44 hectares	728	....	34/B 6	78 OE
Venda (rep.), South Africa	2,510	6,501	450,000	Thohoyandou	119/E 4	79 est
*Venezuela	352,143	912,050	13,913,000	Caracas	124/......	TP—80 OE; oth—71 FC
Vermont U.S.A.	9,614	24,900	511,456	Montpelier	268/......	80 FC & OE
Victoria, Australia	87,876	227,600	3,746,000	Melbourne	96/B 5	76 FC
*Vietnam	128,405	332,569	52,741,766	Hanoi	72/E 3	TP—79 FC; cap, Haiphong, Ho Chi Minh City—79 PC; oth cit over 100,000 (north)—70 est, (south)—73 & 71 OE; oth—69 OE, 60 FC
Virginia, U.S.A.	40,767	105,587	5,346,818	Richmond	307/......	80 FC & OE
Virgin Islands, British	59	153	12,000	Road Town	157/H 1	TP—76 OE; oth—70 FC
Virgin Islands, U.S.A.	132	342	95,591	Charlotte Amalie	161/A 4	80 PC
Wake Island	2.5	6.5	302	Wake Islet	87/G 4	80 FC
Wales, U.K.	8,017	20,764	2,790,462	Cardiff	13/D 5	TP—81 PC; co—76 OE; cit—76 & 73 OE; par—71 FC
Wallis and Futuna	106	275	9,192	Mata Utu	87/J 7	76 FC
Washington, U.S.A.	68,139	176,480	4,132,180	Olympia	310/......	80 FC & OE
West Bank	2,100	5,439	c. 800,000	....	65/C 3	TP—81 est; oth—67 CE & 61 FC
Western Australia, Australia	975,096	2,525,500	1,169,800	Perth	92/......	76 FC
Western Sahara	102,703	266,000	76,425	....	106/B 3	70 FC
*Western Samoa	1,133	2,934	151,983	Apia	87/J 7	76 FC
*West Germany (Federal Republic)	95,985	248,601	61,658,000	Bonn	22/......	TP—80 OE; states, cap—76 OE; oth—76 OE, 70 FC
West Virginia, U.S.A.	24,231	62,758	1,950,279	Charleston	312/......	80 FC & OE
*White Russian S.S.R. (Byelorussian S.S.R.), U.S.S.R.	80,154	207,600	9,560,000	Minsk	52/C 4	TP, cit over 50,000—79 PC; oth—70 FC
Wisconsin, U.S.A.	56,153	145,436	4,705,521	Madison	317/......	80 FC & OE
World	(land) 57,970,000	150,142,300	4,415,000,000	....	1, 2/......	80 UN est
Wyoming, U.S.A.	97,809	253,325	469,557	Cheyenne	319/......	80 FC & OE
*Yemen, People's Democratic Republic of	111,101	287,752	1,969,000	Aden	58/E 7	TP—81 PC; oth—75 FC
*Yemen Arab Republic	77,220	200,000	6,456,189	San a	58/D 6	TP—80 OE; Mukalla, Seiyun—76 OE; cap—73 OE; Saihut—60 OE
*Yugoslavia	98,766	255,804	22,471,000	Belgrade	45/C 3	TP—81 OE; oth—71 FC
Yukon Territory, Canada	207,075	536,324	22,684	Whitehorse	186/E 3	TP—81 PC; oth—76 FC
*Zaire	905,063	2,344,113	28,291,000	Kinshasa	114/D 4	TP—80 OE; prov, cap—70 FC; oth—70 FC & PC
*Zambia	290,586	752,618	5,679,808	Lusaka	114/E 7	80 PC
*Zimbabwe	150,803	390,580	7,360,000	Harare (Salisbury)	119/D 3	TP—80 OE; cap, cit over 12,000—77 OE; oth—69 FC

Introduction to the Maps and Indexes

The following notes have been added to aid the reader in making the best use of this atlas. Though he may be familiar with maps and map indexes, the publisher believes that a quick review of the material below will add to his enjoyment of this reference work.

Arrangement — The Plan of the Atlas. The atlas has been designed with maximum convenience for the user as its objective. All geographically related information pertaining to a country or region appears on adjacent pages, eliminating the task of searching throughout the entire volume for data on a given area. Thus, the reader will find, conveniently assembled, political, topographic, economic and special maps of a political area or region, accompanied by detailed map indexes, statistical data, and illustrations of the national flags of the area.

The sequence of country units in this American-designed atlas is international in arrangement. Units on the world as a whole are followed by a section on the polar regions which, in turn, is followed by pages devoted to Europe and its countries. Every continent map is accompanied by special population distribution, climatic and vegetation maps of that continent. Following the maps of the European continent and its countries, the geographic sequence plan proceeds as follows: Asia, the Pacific and Australia, Africa, South America, North America, and ends with detailed coverage on the United States.

Political Maps — The Primary Reference Tool. The most detailed maps in each country unit are the *political maps.* It is our feeling that the reader is likely to refer to these maps more often than to any other in the book when confronted by such questions as — Where? How big? What is it near? Answering these common queries is the function of the political maps. Each political map stresses *political* phenomena — countries, internal political divisions, boundaries, cities and towns. The major political unit or units, shown on the map, are banded in distinctive colors for easy identification and delineation. First-order political subdivisions (states, provinces, counties on the state maps) are shown, scale permitting.

The reader is advised to make use of the *legend* appearing under the title on each political map. Map *symbols,* the special "language" of maps, are explained in the legend. Each variety of dot, circle, star or interrupted line has a special meaning which should be clearly understood by the user so that he may interpret the map data correctly.

Each country has been portrayed at a *scale* commensurate with its political, areal, economic or tourist importance. In certain cases, a whole map unit may be devoted to a single nation if that nation is considered to be of prime interest to most atlas users. In other cases, several nations will be shown on a single map if, as separate entities, they are of lesser relative importance. Areas of dense settlement and important significance within a country have been enlarged and portrayed in inset maps inserted on the margins of the main map. The scale of each map is indicated as a fractional representation (1:1,000,000). The reader is advised to refer to the linear or "bar" scale appearing on each map or map inset in order to determine the distance between points.

The *projection* system used for each map is noted near the title of the map. Map projections are the special graphic systems used by cartographers to render the curved three-dimensional surface of the globe on a flat surface. Optimum map projections determined by the attributes of the area have been used by the publishers for each map in the atlas.

A word here as to the choice of place names on the maps. Throughout the atlas names appear, with a few exceptions, in their local official spellings. However, conventional Anglicized spellings are used for major geographical divisions and for towns and topographic features for which English forms exist; i.e., "Spain" instead of "España" or "Munich" instead of "München." Names of this type are normally followed by the local official spelling in parentheses. As an aid to the user the indexes are cross-referenced for all current and most former spellings of such names.

Names of cities and towns in the United States follow the forms listed in the *Post Office Directory* of the United States Postal Service. Domestic physical names follow the decisions of the Board on Geographic Names, U.S. Department of the Interior, and of various state geographic name boards.

It is the belief of the publishers that the boundaries shown in a general reference atlas should reflect current geographic and political realities. This policy has been followed consistently in the atlas. The presentation of *de facto* boundaries in cases of territorial dispute between various nations does not imply the political endorsement of such boundaries by the publisher, but simply the honest representation of boundaries as they exist at the time of the printing of the atlas maps.

Indexes — Pinpointing a Location. Each political map is accompanied by a comprehensive index of the place names appearing on the map. If you are unfamiliar with the location of a particular geographical place and wish to find its position within the confines of the subject area of the map, consult the map index as your first step. The name of the feature sought will be found in its proper alphabetical sequence with a key reference letter-number combination corresponding to its location on the map. After noting the key reference letter-number combination for the place name, turn to the map. The place name will be found within the square formed by the two lines of latitude and the two lines of longitude which enclose the co-ordinates — i.e., the marginal letters and numbers. The diagram below illustrates the system of indexing.

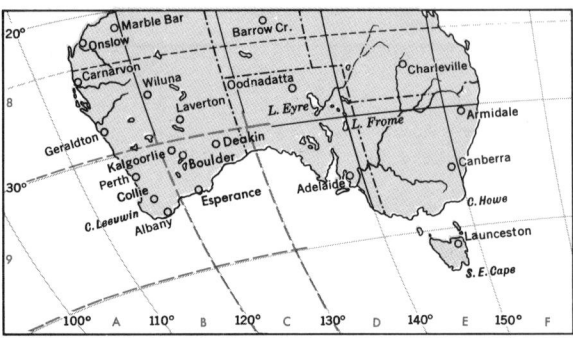

In the case of maps consisting entirely of insets, the place name is found near the intersection point of the imaginary lines connecting the co-ordinates at right angles. See below.

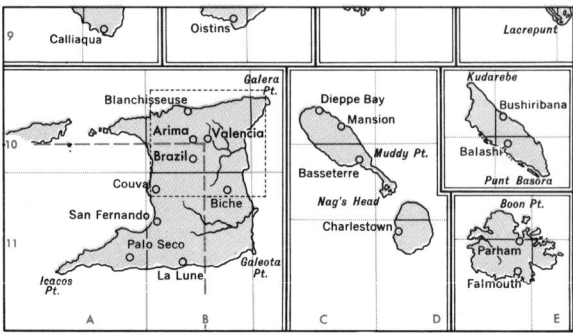

Where space on the map has not permitted giving the complete form of the place name, the complete form is shown in the index. Where a place is known by more than one name or by various spellings of the same name, the different forms have been included in the index. Physical features are listed under their proper names and not according to their generic terms; that is to say, Rio Negro will be found under Negro and not under Rio Negro. On the other hand, Rio Grande will be found under Rio Grande. Accompanying most index entries for cities and towns, and for other political units, are *population figures* for the particular entries. The large number of population figures in the atlas makes this work one of the most comprehensive statistical sources available to the public today. The population figures have been taken from the latest official censuses and estimates of the various nations. Dates and sources for the population figures are listed in the Gazetteer-Index of the World preceding this section.

Population and area figures for countries and major political units are listed in bold type *fact lists* on the margins of the indexes. In addition, the capital, largest city, highest point, monetary unit, principal languages and the prevailing religions of the country concerned are also listed. The Gazetteer-Index of the World on the preceding pages provides a quick reference index for countries and other important areas. Though population and area figures for each major unit area also found in the map section, the Gazetteer-Index provides a conveniently arranged statistical comparison contained in five pages. As mentioned, dates and sources of the population figures appearing in the country indexes are also listed in this section.

All index entries for cities and towns in the United States are preceded by a five-digit postal ZIP code number applying to the community. This useful feature permits the reader to address his mail so that it will be routed and delivered more efficiently and quickly by the U.S. Postal Service. A dagger (†) designates those places that do not possess a post office. The ZIP code number listed in such cases refers to that of the nearest post office. An asterisk (*) marks those larger cities which are divided into multiple ZIP code areas. Using the single ZIP code number listed in such cases will direct your letter to the proper city with dispatch. However, if the precise ZIP code number of the address within the city is needed, it is suggested that the reader refer to the latest National ZIP Code Directory at his local post office. This detailed guide lists every street in a multiple ZIP code city with the proper ZIP code for the street.

Relief Maps. Accompanying each political map is a relief map of the area. The purpose of the relief map is to illustrate the surface configuration (TOPOGRAPHY) of the region. A shading technique in color simulates the relative ruggedness of the terrain — plains, plateaus, valleys, hills and mountains. Graded colors, ranging from greens for lowlands, yellows for intermediate elevations to browns in the highlands, indicate the height above sea level of each part of the land. A vertical scale at the margin of the map shows the approximate height in meters and feet represented by each color.

Economic Maps — Agriculture, Industry and Resources. One of the most interesting features that will be found in each country unit is the economic map. From this map one can determine the basic activities of a nation as expressed through its economy. A perusal of the map yields a full understanding of the area's economic geography and natural resources.

The agricultural economy is manifested in two ways: color bands and commodity names. The color bands express broad categories of *dominant land use,* such as, cereal belts, forest lands, livestock range lands, nonagricultural wastes. The red commodity names, on the other hand, pinpoint the areas of production of *specific* crops; i.e., wheat, cotton, sugar beets, etc.

Major mineral occurrences are denoted by standard letter symbols appearing in blue. The relative size of the letter symbols signifies the relative importance of the deposit.

The manufacturing sector of the economy is presented by means of diagonal line patterns expressing the various *industrial areas* of consequence within a country.

The fishing industry is represented by names of commercial fish species appearing offshore in blue letters. Major waterpower sites are designated by blue symbols.

The publishers have tried to make this work the most comprehensive and useful atlas available, and it is hoped that it will prove a valuable reference work. Any constructive suggestions from the reader will be welcomed.

Sources and Acknowledgments

A multitude of sources goes into the making of a large-scale reference work such as this. To list them all would take many pages and would consume space better devoted to the maps and reference materials themselves. However, certain general sources were very useful in preparing this work and are listed below.

STATISTICAL OFFICE OF THE UNITED NATIONS.
Demographic Yearbook. New York. Issued annually.

STATISTICAL OFFICE OF THE UNITED NATIONS.
Statistical Yearbook. New York. Issued annually.

THE GEOGRAPHER, U.S. DEPARTMENT OF STATE.
International Boundary Study papers. Washington. Various dates.

THE GEOGRAPHER, U.S. DEPARTMENT OF STATE.
Geographic Notes. Washington. Various dates.

UNITED STATES BOARD ON GEOGRAPHIC NAMES.
Decisions on Geographic Names in the United States. Washington. Various dates.

UNITED STATES BOARD ON GEOGRAPHIC NAMES.
Official Standard Names Gazetteers. Washington. Various dates.

CANADIAN PERMANENT COMMITTEE ON GEOGRAPHICAL NAMES.
Gazetteer of Canada series. Ottawa. Various dates.

UNITED STATES POSTAL SERVICE.
National Five Digit ZIP Code and Post Office Directory. Washington. 1982.

UNITED STATES POSTAL SERVICE.
Postal Bulletin. Washington. Issued weekly.

UNITED STATES DEPARTMENT OF THE INTERIOR. BUREAU OF MINES.
Minerals Yearbook. 4 vols. Washington. Various dates.

UNITED STATES GEOLOGICAL SURVEY.
Elevations and distances in the United States. Reston, Va. 1980.

CARTACTUAL.
Cartactual — Topical Map Service. Budapest. Issued bimonthly.

AMERICAN GEOGRAPHICAL SOCIETY.
Focus. New York. Issued ten times a year.

THE AMERICAN UNIVERSITY.
Foreign Area Studies. Washington. Various dates.

CENTRAL INTELLIGENCE AGENCY.
General reference maps. Washington. Various dates.

A sample list of sources used for specific countries follows:

Afghanistan
CENTRAL STATISTICS OFFICE.
Preliminary Results of the First Afghan Population Census 1979. Kabul.

Albania
DREJTORIA E STATISTIKËS.
1979 Census. Tiranë.

Burundi
SERVICE NATIONAL DES ÉTUDES ET STATISTIQUES.
1979 Census. Bujumbura.

French Polynesia
INSTITUT NATIONAL DE LA STATISTIQUE ET DES ÉTUDES ÉCONOMIQUES.
Recensement Général de la Population 1977. Papeete.

Guinea-Bissau
DEPARTAMENTO CENTRAL DE RECENSEAMENTO.
Recenseamento Geral da População 1979. Bissau.

Hungary
HUNGARIAN CENTRAL STATISTICAL OFFICE.
1980 Census. Budapest.

Kuwait
CENTRAL OFFICE OF STATISTICS.
1980 Census. Al Kuwait.

Malawi
NATIONAL STATISTICAL OFFICE.
Population Census 1977. Zomba.

Panama
DIRECCIÓN DE ESTADISTICA Y CENSO.
Censos Nacionales de 1980. Panamá.

Papua New Guinea
BUREAU OF STATISTICS.
National Population Census 1980. Port Moresby.

Philippines
NATIONAL CENSUS AND STATISTICS OFFICE.
1980 Census of Population. Manila.

Romania
DIRECTIA CENTRALĂ DE STATISTICĂ.
1979 Estimates. Bucharest.

Rwanda
BUREAU NATIONAL DE RECENSEMENT.
Recensement Général de la Population 1978. Kigali.

Saint Lucia
CENSUS OFFICE.
1980 Population Census. Castries.

Singapore
DEPARTMENT OF STATISTICS.
Census of Population 1980. Singapore.

Tanzania
BUREAU OF STATISTICS.
1978 Population Census. Dar es Salaam.

U.S.S.R.
CENTRAL STATISTICAL ADMINISTRATION.
1979 Census. Moscow.

United States
BUREAU OF THE CENSUS.
1980 Census of Population. Washington.

Vanuatu
CENSUS OFFICE.
1979 Population Census. Port Vila.

Zambia
CENTRAL STATISTICAL OFFICE.
1980 Census of Population and Housing. Lusaka.

Glossary of Abbreviations

A

A. A. F. — Army Air Field
Acad. — Academy
A. C. T. — Australian Capital Territory
adm. — administration; administrative
A. F. B. — Air Force Base
Afgh., Afghan. — Afghanistan
Afr. — Africa
Ala. — Alabama
Alb. — Albania
Alg. — Algeria
Alta. — Alberta
Amer. — American
Amer. Samoa — American Samoa
And. — Andorra
Ant., Antarc. — Antarctica
Ant. & Bar. — Antigua and Barbuda
Ar. — Arabia
arch. — archipelago
Arg. — Argentina
Ariz. — Arizona
Ark. — Arkansas
A. S. S. R. — Autonomous Soviet
　　　　Socialist Republic
Aust. — Austria
Aust. Cap. Terr. — Australian Capital
　　　　Territory
Austr., Austral. — Australian, Australia
aut. — autonomous
Aut. Obl. — Autonomous Oblast

B

B. — bay
Bah. — Bahamas
Barb. — Barbados
Battlef. — Battlefield
Bch. — Beach
Belg. — Belgium
Berm. — Bermuda
Bol. — Bolivia
Bots. — Botswana
Br. — Branch
Br. — British
Braz. — Brazil
Br. Col. — British Columbia
Br. Ind. Oc. Terr. — British Indian
　　　　Ocean Territory
Bulg. — Bulgaria

C

C. — cape
Calif. — California
Can. — Canada
can. — canal
cap. — capital
Cent. Afr. Rep. — Central African
　　　　Republic
Cent. Amer. — Central America
C. G. Sta. — Coast Guard Station
C. H. — Court House
chan. — channel
Chan. Is. — Channel Islands
Chem. Ctr. — Chemical Center
co. — county
C. of G. H. — Cape of Good Hope
Col. — Colombia
Colo. — Colorado
comm. — commissary
Conn. — Connecticut
cont. — continent
cord. — cordillera (mountain range)
C. Rica — Costa Rica
C. S. — County Seat
C. Verde — Cape Verde
Czech. — Czechoslovakia

D

D. C. — District of Columbia
Del. — Delaware
Dem. — Democratic
Den. — Denmark
depr. — depression
dept. — department
des. — desert
dist., dist's — district, districts
div. — division
Dom. Rep. — Dominican Republic

E

E. — East
Ec., Ecua. — Ecuador
E. Ger. — East Germany
elec. div. — electoral division
El Salv. — El Salvador
Eng. — England
Equat. Guinea, Eq. Guin — Equatorial
　　　　Guinea

escarp. — escarpment
est. — estuary
Eth. — Ethiopia

F

Falk. Is. — Falkland Islands
Fin. — Finland
Fk., Fks. — Fork, Forks
Fla. — Florida
for. — forest
Fr. — France, French
Fr. Gui. — French Guiana
Fr. Poly. — French Polynesia
Ft. — Fort

G

G. — gulf
Ga. — Georgia
Game Res. — Game Reserve
Ger. — Germany
geys. — geyser
Gibr. — Gibraltar
glac. — glacier
gov. — governorate
Gr. — Group
Greenl. — Greenland
Gren. — Grenada
Gt. Brit. — Great Britain
Guad. — Guadeloupe
Guat. — Guatemala
Guinea-Biss. — Guinea-Bissau
Guy. — Guyana

H

har., harb., hbr. — harbor
hd. — head
highl. — highland, highlands
Hist. — Historic, Historical
Hond. — Honduras
Hts. — Heights
Hung. — Hungary

I

i., isl. — island, isle
I. C. — independent city
Ice., Icel. — Iceland
Ida. — Idaho
Ill. — Illinois
Ind. — Indiana
ind. city — independent city
Indon. — Indonesia
Ind. Res. — Indian Reservation
int. div. — internal division
inten. — intendency
Int'l — International
Ire. — Ireland
is., isls. — islands
Isr. — Israel
isth. — isthmus
Iv. Coast — Ivory Coast

J

Jam. — Jamaica
Jct. — Junction

K

Kans. — Kansas
Ky. — Kentucky

L

L. — Lake, Loch, Lough
La. — Louisiana
Lab. — Laboratory
lag. — lagoon
Ld. — Land
Leb. — Lebanon
Les. — Lesotho
Liecht. — Liechtenstein
Lux. — Luxembourg

M

Mad., Madag. — Madagascar
Man. — Manitoba
Mart. — Martinique
Mass. — Massachusetts
Maur. — Mauritania
Md. — Maryland
met. area — metropolitan area
Mex. — Mexico
Mich. — Michigan
Minn. — Minnesota
Miss. — Mississippi
Mo. — Missouri
Mon. — Monument
Mong. — Mongolia
Mont. — Montana
Mor. — Morocco

Moz., Mozamb. — Mozambique
mt. — mount
mtn. — mountain

N

N., No., North. — North, Northern
N. Amer. — North America
Nam., Namib. — Namibia
N. A. S. — Naval Air Station
Nat'l — National
Nat'l Cem. — National Cemetery
Nat'l Mem. Park — National Memorial
　　　　Park
Nat'l Mil. Park — National Military
　　　　Park
Nat'l Pkwy. — National Parkway
Nav. Base — Naval Base
Nav. Sta. — Naval Station
N. B., N. Br. — New Brunswick
N. C. — North Carolina
N. Dak. — North Dakota
Nebr. — Nebraska
Neth. — Netherlands
Neth. Ant. — Netherlands Antilles
Nev. — Nevada
New Bruns. — New Brunswick
New Cal., New Caled. — New Caledonia
Newf. — Newfoundland
New Hebr. — New Hebrides
N. H. — New Hampshire
Nic. — Nicaragua
N. Ire. — Northern Ireland
N. J. — New Jersey
N. Mex. — New Mexico
Nor. — Norway, Norwegian
North. — Northern
North. Terr., No. Terr. — Northern
　　　　Territory
　　　　(Australia)
N. S. — Nova Scotia
N. S. W., N.S. Wales — New South Wales
N. W. T., N. W. Terrs. — Northwest
　　　　Territories
　　　　(Canada)
N. Y. — New York
N. Z., N. Zealand — New Zealand

O

Obl. — Oblast
O. F. S. — Orange Free State
Okla. — Oklahoma
Okr. — Okrug
Ont. — Ontario
Ord. Depot — Ordnance Depot
Oreg. — Oregon

P

Pa. — Pennsylvania
Pac. Is. — Pacific Islands,
　　　　Territory of the
Pak. — Pakistan
Pan. — Panama
Papua N. G. —Papua New Guinea
Par. — Paraguay
par. — parish
passg. — passage
P.D.R. Yemen — People's Democratic
　　　　Republic of Yemen
P. E. I. — Prince Edward Island
pen. — peninsula
Phil., Phil. Is. — Philippines
Pk. — Park
pk. — peak
plat. — plateau
P. N. G. — Papua New Guinea
Pol. — Poland
Port. — Portugal, Portuguese
Pr. Edward I. — Prince Edward Island
pref. — prefecture
P. Rico — Puerto Rico
prom. — promontory
prov. — province, provincial
pt. — point

Q

Que. — Quebec
Queens. — Queensland

R

R. — River
ra. — range
Rec., Recr. — Recreation, Recreational
reg. — region
Rep. — Republic
res. — reservoir
Res. — Reservation, Reserve
R. i. — Rhode Island

riv. — river
Rom. — Romania

S

S. — South
Sa. — Sierra, Serra
S. Afr., S. Africa — South Africa
salt dep. — salt deposit
salt des. — salt desert
S. Amer. — South America
São T. & Pr. — São Tomé
　　　　and Príncipe
Sask. — Saskatchewan
Saudi Ar. — Saudi Arabia
S. Aust., S. Austral. — South Australia
S. C. — South Carolina
Scot. — Scotland
Sd. — Sound
S. Dak. — South Dakota
Sen. — Senegal
sen. dist. — senatorial district
Seych. — Seychelles
S. F. S. R. — Soviet Federated Socialist
　　　　Republic
Sing. — Singapore
S. Leone — Sierra Leone
S. Marino — San Marino
Sol. Is. — Solomon Islands
Sp. — Spanish
Spr., Sprs. — Spring, Springs
S. S. R. — Soviet Socialist Republic
St., Ste. — Saint, Sainte
Sta. — Station
St. Chris.-Nevis — Saint Christopher-
　　　　Nevis
St. P. & M. — Saint Pierre and
　　　　Miquelon
St. Vin. & Grens. — St. Vincent & The
　　　　Grenadines
str., strs. — strait, straits
Sur. — Suriname
S. W. Afr. — South-West Africa
Swaz. — Swaziland
Switz. — Switzerland

T

Tanz. — Tanzania
Tas. — Tasmania
Tenn. — Tennessee
terr., terrs. — territory, territories
Tex. — Texas
Thai. — Thailand
trad. — traditional
Trin. & Tob. — Trinidad and Tobago
Tun. — Tunisia
twp. — township

U

U.A.E. — United
　　　　Arab Emirates
U. K. — United Kingdom
Upp. Volta — Upper Volta
urb. area — urban area
Urug. — Uruguay
U. S. — United States
U. S. S. R. — Union of Soviet Socialist
　　　　Republics

V

Va. — Virginia
Ven., Venez. — Venezuela
V. I. (Br.) — Virgin Islands (British)
V. I. (U. S.) — Virgin Islands (U. S.)
Vic. — Victoria
Viet. — Vietnam
Vill. — Village
vol. — volcano
Vt. — Vermont

W

W. — West, Western
Wash. — Washington
W. Aust., W. Austral. — Western
　　　　Australia
W. Ger. — West Germany
W. Indies — West Indies
Wis. — Wisconsin
W. Samoa — Western Samoa
W. Va. — West Virginia
Wyo. — Wyoming

Y

Yugo. — Yugoslavia
Yukon — Yukon Territory

Z

Zim. — Zimbabwe

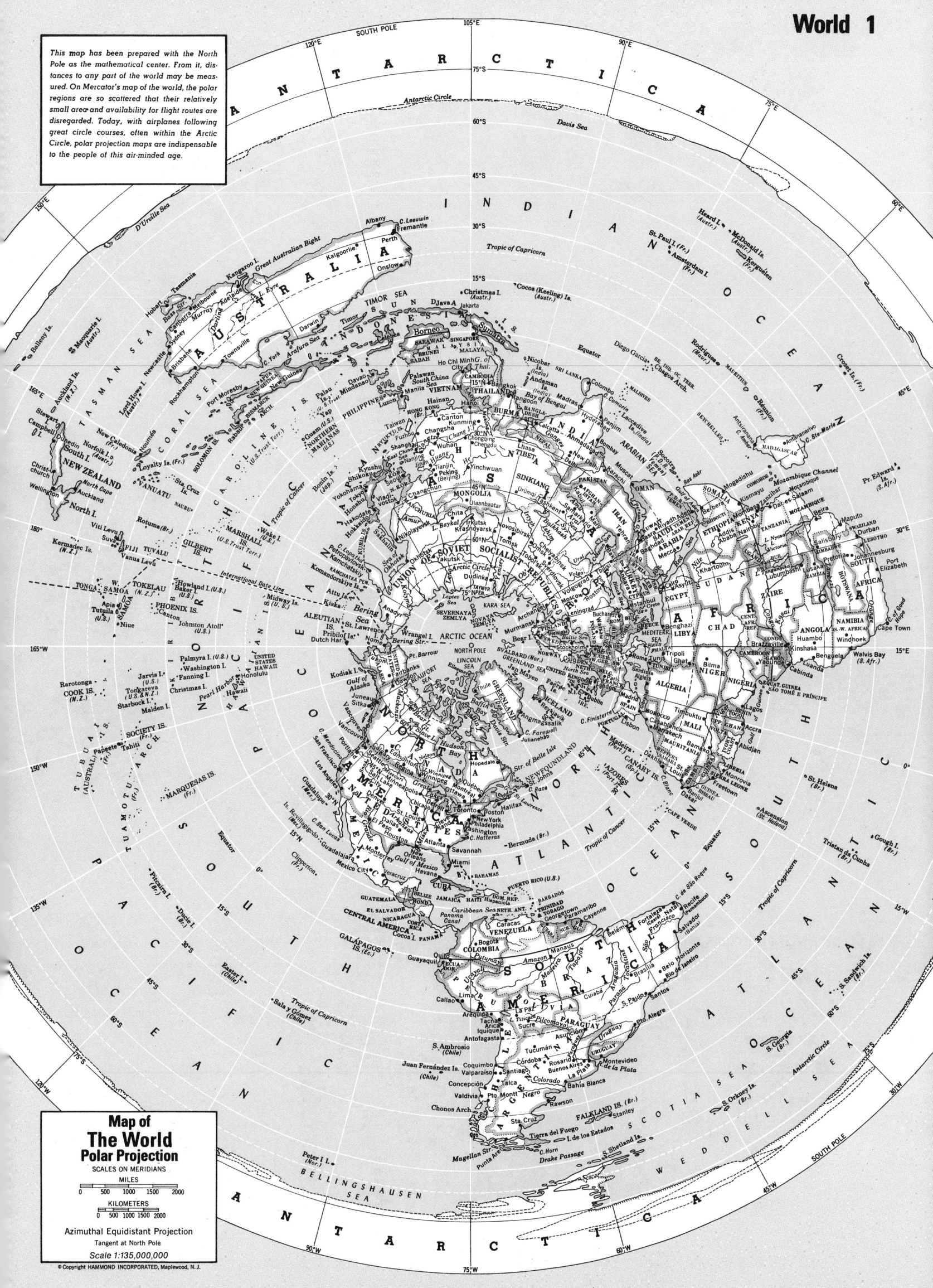

World 1

This map has been prepared with the North Pole as the mathematical center. From it, distances to any part of the world may be measured. On Mercator's map of the world, the polar regions are so scattered that their relatively small area and availability for flight routes are disregarded. Today, with airplanes following great circle courses, often within the Arctic Circle, polar projection maps are indispensable to the people of this air-minded age.

Map of
The World
Polar Projection
SCALES ON MERIDIANS

MILES
0   500   1000   1500   2000

KILOMETERS
0   500   1000   1500   2000

Azimuthal Equidistant Projection
Tangent at North Pole
Scale 1:135,000,000

© Copyright HAMMOND INCORPORATED, Maplewood, N.J.

The World

BRIESEMEISTER ELLIPTICAL
EQUAL-AREA PROJECTION

Capitals of Countries ....⊛
Other Capitals...........................⊛
International Boundaries..... – – –

Scale 1:80,000,000

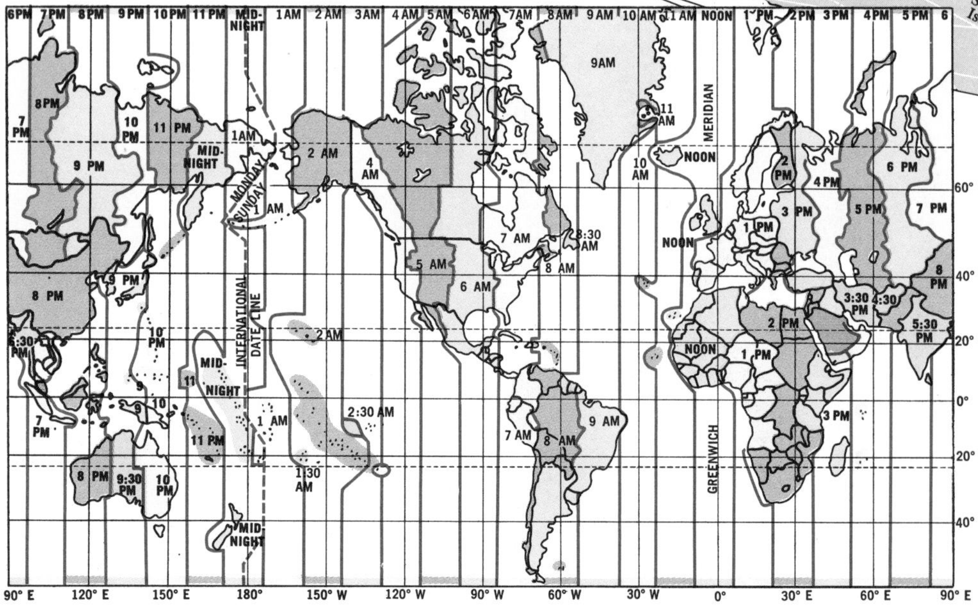

NORTH PACIFIC OCEAN

NORTH AMERICA

UNITED STATES

Honolulu
HAWAII

Whitehorse
Juneau
Anchorage
Fairbanks
Pt. Barrow
UNITED STATES
ALASKA
Yukon

Vancouver I.
Vancouver
Portland
Seattle
San Francisco
Los Angeles
Calgary
Edmonton
Yellowknife
Banks I.
Queen
Elizabeth
Islands
Victoria
Mackenzie

Lower California
UNITED STATES
Colo.
Denver
El Paso
Arkansas
Rio Grande
Missouri
Minneapolis
Winnipeg
Sask.
Hudson
Bay
Thule
GREENLAND
(Den.)
Great
Lakes
Baffin I.
Baffin B.
Davis Str.

Is. Revillagigedo
(Mex.) C. San Lucas
MEXICO
CANADA
Dallas
Houston
New
Orleans
St. Louis
Chicago
Detroit
Toronto
Ottawa
Montréal
Québec
Labrador
C. Farewell
Julianehåb
Arctic Circle
60° N

Guadalajara
Monterrey
Mexico City
Veracruz
GULF OF MEXICO
Havana
CUBA
Miami
C. Canaveral
Savannah
Atlanta
Washington
Philadelphia
New York
Boston
Halifax
St. Lawrence
Newfoundland
St. John's
Str. of Belle I.
NId. (Goathåb)
ICELAND
Reykjavik

Clipperton
(Fr.)
CENTRAL AMERICA
EL SALV. HON.
BELIZE
NIC.
JAM.
HAITI
DOM. REP.
BAHAMAS
Bermuda
(Br.)
C. Hatteras
Azores
(Port.)
40° N
NORTH ATLANTIC OCEAN

Palmyra I.
(U.S.)
Fanning I.
KIRIBATI
Vostok I.
Line Is.
160° W
140° W
120° W
100° W
80° W
60° W
40° W
20° W

Niue
(N.Z.)
Cook Is.
(N.Z.)
Papeete
Tahiti
(Fr. Poly.)
Marquesas Is.
(Fr. Poly.)
Tuamotu Arch.
(Fr. Poly.)
FRENCH POLYNESIA
AUSTRALIS.
(Fr. Poly.)
Equator
Tropic of Capricorn

SOUTH PACIFIC OCEAN

Easter I.
(Chile)
Sala y Gómez
(Chile)
Pitcairn I.
(Br.)
Galápagos Is.
(Ec.)
Panama Can.
ECUADOR
Guayaquil
Quito
COLOMBIA
Bogotá
VENEZUELA
Orinoco
Caracas
TRIN. & TOB.
BARBADOS
Georgetown
GUY.
SUR.
Paramaribo
FR. GUI.
Cayenne
PUERTO RICO
WEST INDIES
CARIBBEAN SEA
ST. VINC.
GRENADA
DOMINICA
ST. LUCIA
Tropic of Cancer
20° N

PERU
Lima
Callao
Ucayali
SOUTH AMERICA
Madeira
Manaus
Amazon
Negro
BRAZIL
Belém
CAPE VERDE
C. Blanc
Dakar
SEN.
GAMBIA
GUINEA-BISSAU
Nouakchott
MAURITANIA
MALI
Bamako

Arequipa
Antofagasta
Titicaca
La Paz
Sucre
BOLIVIA
Tapajós
Tocantins
São Francisco
Equator
SIERRA LEONE
GUINEA
Monrovia
LIBERIA
IVORY COAST
UPP. VOLTA
Niamey
Abidjan
Accra
GHANA
TOGO
BENIN

Juan Fernández Is.
(Chile)
Valparaíso
Santiago
Valdivia
CHILE
ARGENTINA
Córdoba
Colorado
PARAGUAY
Asunción
Paraná
URUGUAY
Brasília
São Paulo
Belo Horizonte
Fortaleza
C. de São Roque
Natal
Recife
Salvador
Ghana
Gulf of Guinea

Antarctic Circle
Str. of Magellan
Tierra del Fuego
Cape Horn
Buenos Aires
Bahía Blanca
Montevideo
R. de la Plata
Porto Alegre
Santos
Río de Janeiro
Ascension
(St. Hel.)
20° S
SOUTH ATLANTIC OCEAN

MARIE BYRD LAND
Drake Passage
Falkland Is.
(Br.)
SCOTIA SEA
S. Orkney Is.
(Br.)
S. Georgia
(Br.)
60° S
St. Helena
(Br.)
Tropic of Capricorn
ANTARCTICA
Ronne Ice Shelf
Antarctic Pen.
Larsen Ice Shelf
Berkner I.
COATS LAND
S. Sandwich Is.
(Br.)
Tristan da Cunha
(St. Hel.)
Gough I.
(St. Hel.)
40° S
80° S

UNITED KINGDOM
IRELAND
London
Paris
B. of Biscay
SPAIN
Lisbon
Madrid
Gibraltar
PORT.
Str. of Gibraltar
Madeira
(Port.)
Canary Is.
(Sp.)
Rabat
MOROCCO
Casablanca
WESTERN SAHARA
ALGERIA
SAHARA

Time Zones

| 6PM | 7PM | 8PM | 9PM | 10PM | 11PM | MID-NIGHT | 1AM | 2AM | 3AM | 4AM | 5AM | 6AM | 7AM | 8AM | 9AM | 10AM | 11AM | NOON | 1PM | 2PM | 3PM | 4PM | 5PM | 6 |

9AM
8 PM
7 PM
10 PM
11 PM
9 PM
MID-NIGHT
1 AM
2 AM
11 AM
10 AM
NOON
4 PM
6 PM
7 PM
MID-NIGHT
SUNDAY
MONDAY
INTERNATIONAL DATE LINE
7 AM
8:30 AM
3 AM
5 PM
7 PM
60° N
8 PM
10 PM
1 PM
NOON
8 AM
6 AM
5 AM
4 AM
3:30 PM 4:30 PM
40° N
MID-NIGHT
11
2 AM
2:30 AM
7 AM
8 AM
9 AM
NOON
1 PM
2 PM
5:30 PM
MERIDIAN
20° N
GREENWICH
0°
7 PM
11 PM
10
1 AM
1 AM
3 PM
20° S
8 PM
9:30 PM
10 PM
1:30 AM
MID-NIGHT
40° S

| 90° E | 120° E | 150° E | 180° | 150° W | 120° W | 90° W | 60° W | 30° W | 0° | 30° E | 60° E | 90° E |

	Areas using half hour deviations.
STANDARD	
TIME	Areas not using zone system.
ZONES	

NOTE: Standard time zones in the U.S.S.R. are always advanced one hour.

LAND AREA 57,970,000 sq. mi.
(150,142,300 sq. km.)
WATER AREA 139,781,000 sq. mi.
(362,032,790 sq. km.)
TOTAL SURFACE AREA 197,751,000 sq.mi.
(512,175,090 sq. km.)
POPULATION 4,415,000,000

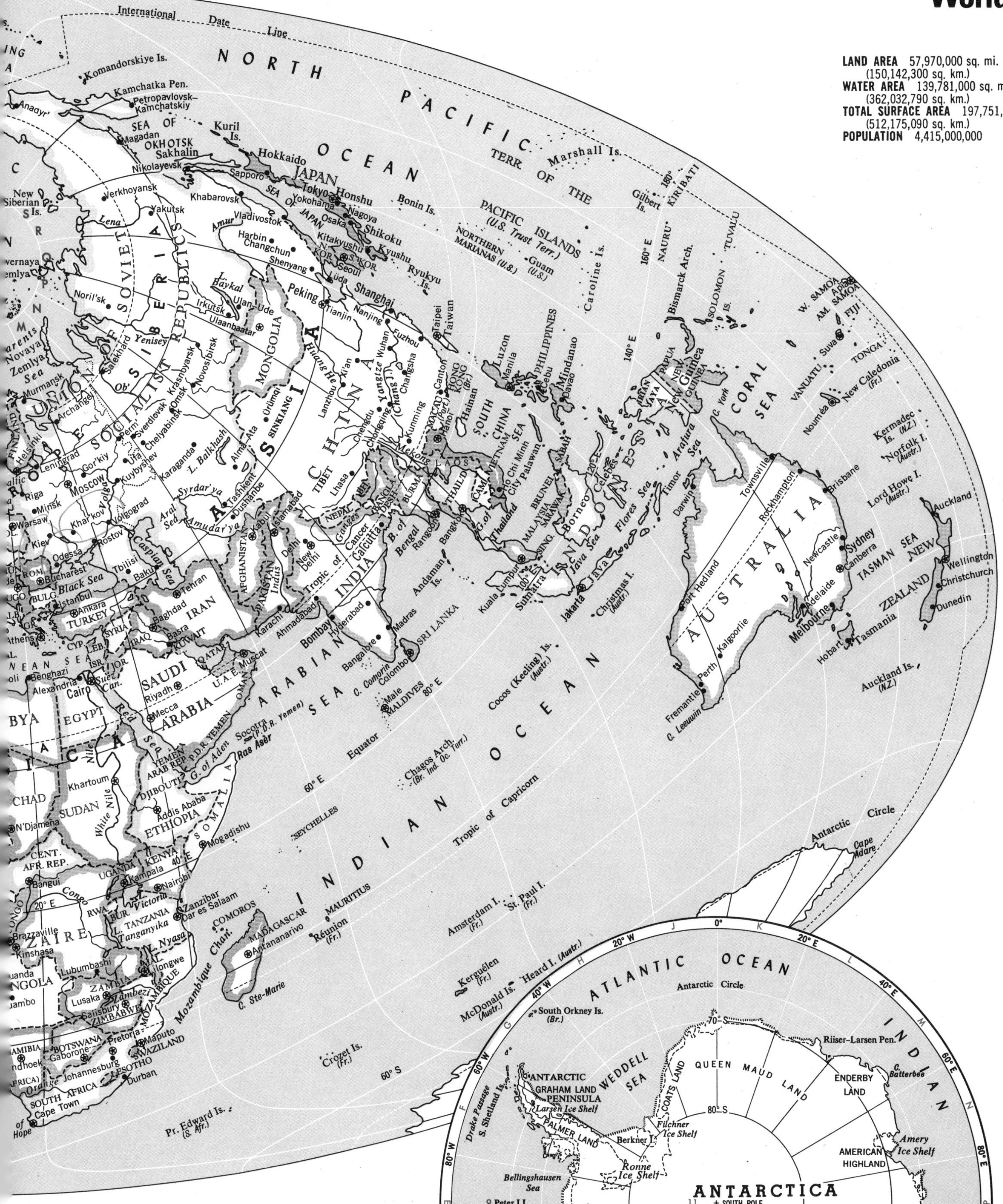
International Date Line
NORTH PACIFIC OCEAN
TERR. OF THE PACIFIC ISLANDS (U.S. Trust Terr.)
UNION OF SOVIET SOCIALIST REPUBLICS
SIBERIA
ASIA
CHINA
MONGOLIA
JAPAN
INDIA
INDONESIA
AUSTRALIA
NEW ZEALAND
CORAL SEA
TASMAN SEA
SOUTH CHINA SEA
ARABIAN SEA
INDIAN OCEAN
SAUDI ARABIA
IRAN
TURKEY
EGYPT
SUDAN
ETHIOPIA
ZAIRE
TANZANIA
MADAGASCAR
SOUTH AFRICA
Equator
Tropic of Cancer
Tropic of Capricorn
Antarctic Circle

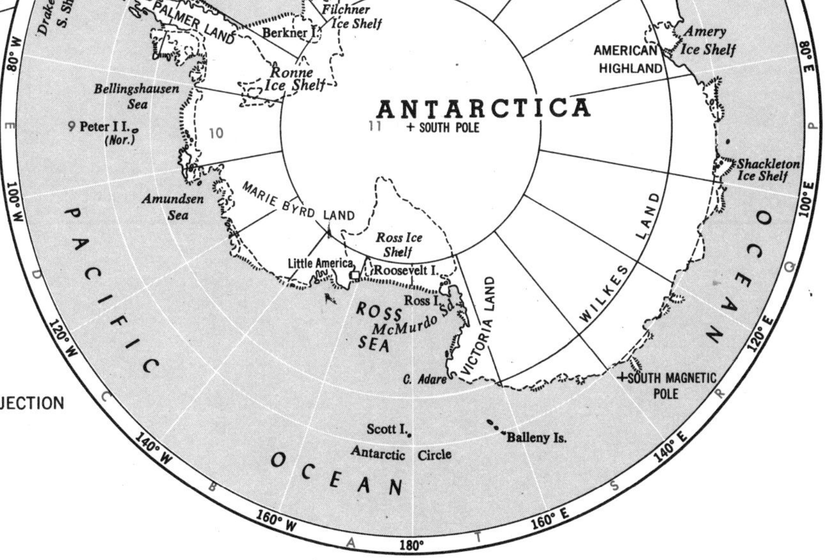
ATLANTIC OCEAN
INDIAN OCEAN
PACIFIC OCEAN
ANTARCTICA
+ SOUTH POLE
QUEEN MAUD LAND
ENDERBY LAND
AMERICAN HIGHLAND
WILKES LAND
VICTORIA LAND
MARIE BYRD LAND
WEDDELL SEA
ROSS SEA
ANTARCTIC PENINSULA
Ross Ice Shelf
Ronne Ice Shelf
Amery Ice Shelf
Antarctic Circle

Antarctica
AZIMUTHAL EQUIDISTANT PROJECTION
Scale 1:62,000,000

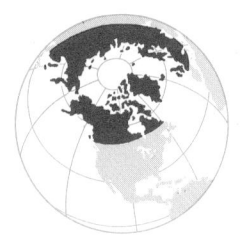

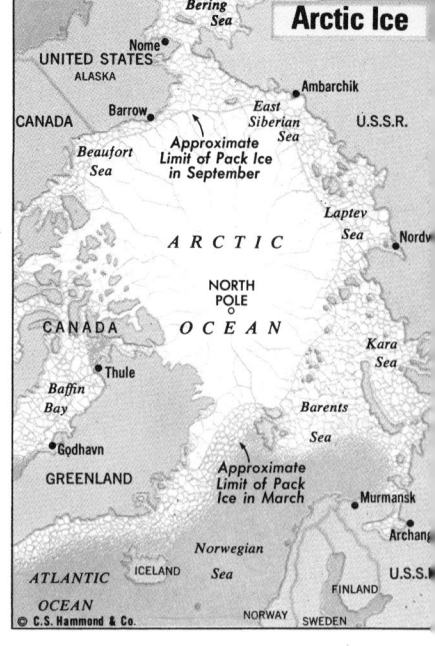

Arctic Ice

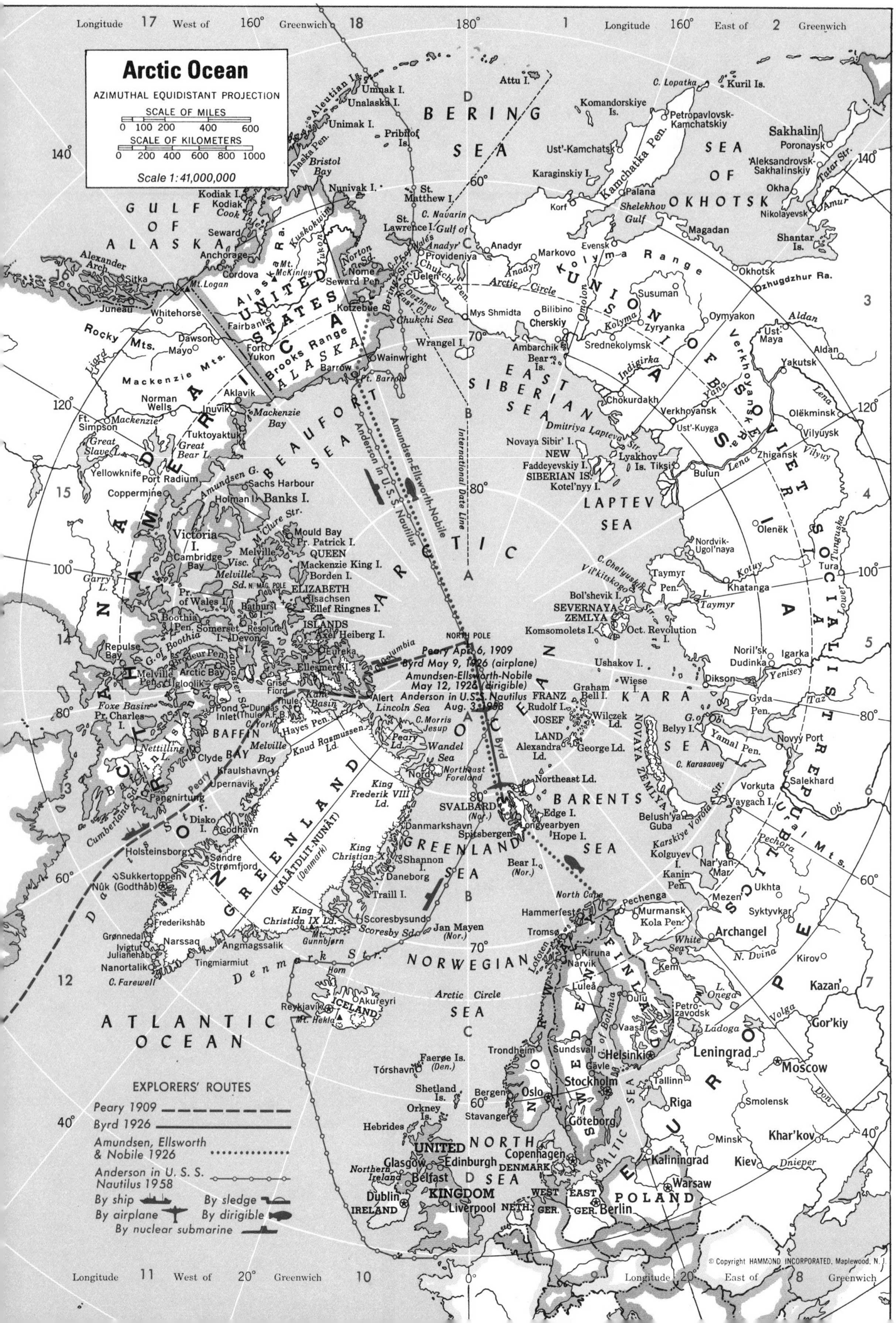

Arctic Ocean

AZIMUTHAL EQUIDISTANT PROJECTION

SCALE OF MILES
0 100 200 400 600

SCALE OF KILOMETERS
0 200 400 600 800 1000

Scale 1:41,000,000

EXPLORERS' ROUTES

Peary 1909
Byrd 1926
Amundsen, Ellsworth & Nobile 1926
Anderson in U.S.S. Nautilus 1958

By ship
By sledge
By airplane
By dirigible
By nuclear submarine

Peary April 6, 1909
Byrd May 9, 1926 (airplane)
Amundsen-Ellsworth-Nobile May 12, 1926 (dirigible)
Anderson in U.S.S. Nautilus Aug. 3, 1958

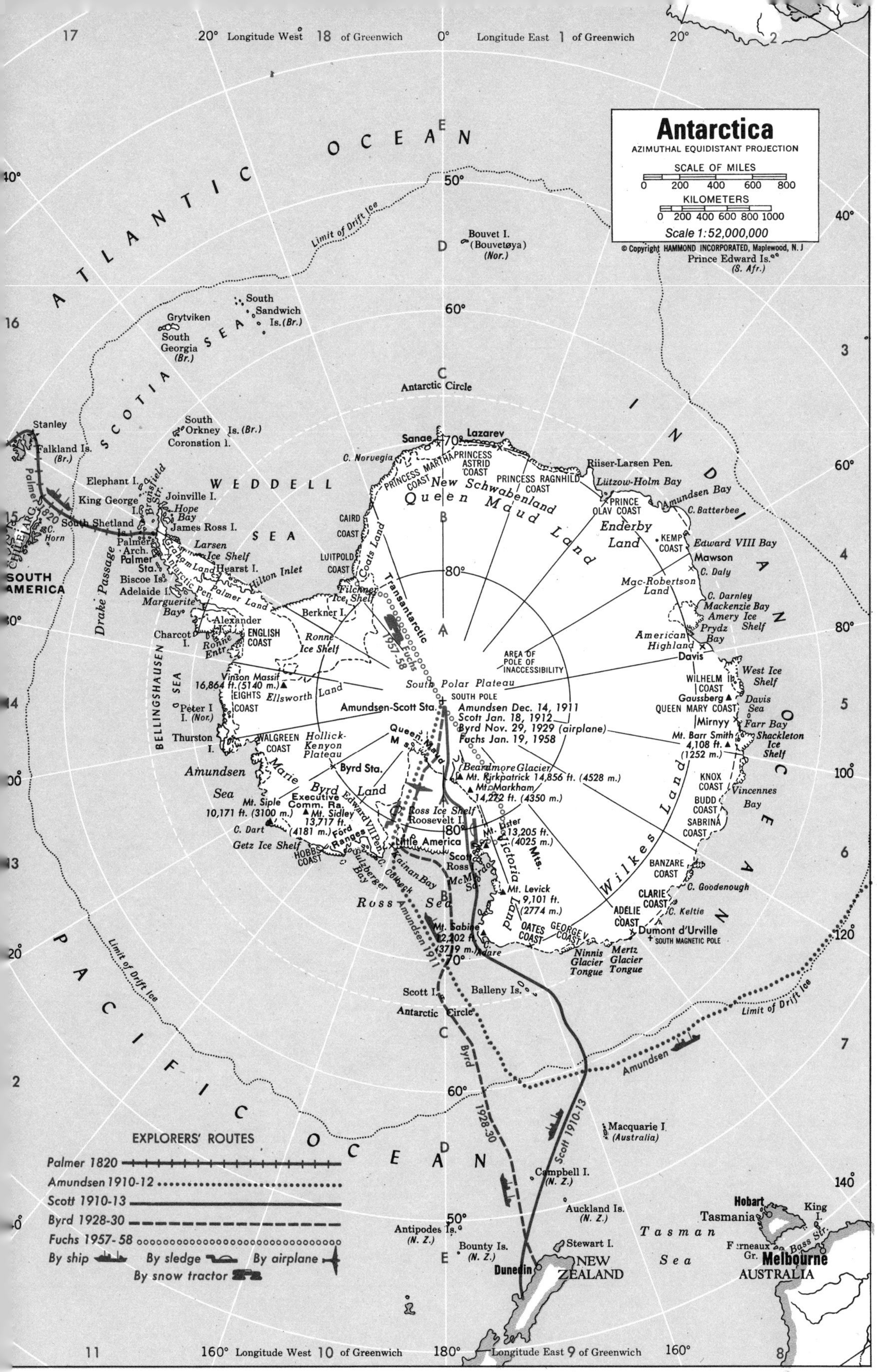

Antarctica
AZIMUTHAL EQUIDISTANT PROJECTION

SCALE OF MILES
0 200 400 600 800

KILOMETERS
0 200 400 600 800 1000

Scale 1:52,000,000

© Copyright HAMMOND INCORPORATED, Maplewood, N.J.

EXPLORERS' ROUTES

Palmer 1820
Amundsen 1910-12
Scott 1910-13
Byrd 1928-30
Fuchs 1957-58
By ship   By sledge   By airplane
By snow tractor

Weddell Sea

Traverse of Cross Section Shown Below

SOUTH POLE

ANTARCTICA

Ross Sea

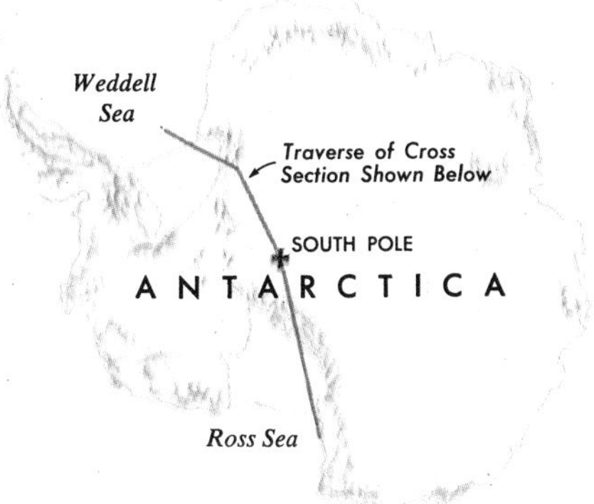

Antarctic Cross Section: Weddell Sea to Ross Sea

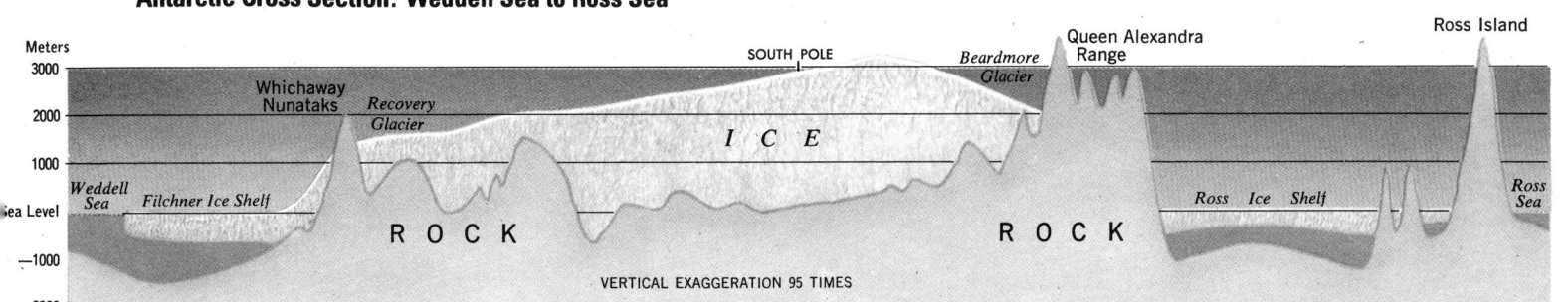

VERTICAL EXAGGERATION 95 TIMES

Information Based on American Geographical Society's "Antarctic Map Folio Series"

Europe

POLYCONIC PROJECTION

SCALE OF MILES

0 100 200 300 400

KILOMETERS

0 100 200 300 400

Capitals of Countries...............⊛
Other Capitals........................⊛
International Boundaries .... ▬ ▪ ▬ ▪
Internal Boundaries .... ▬ ▪ ▬
Canals................................... ⊣⊢⊣⊢⊣

Scale 1:20,800,000

AREA 4,057,000 sq. mi.
(10,507,630 sq. km.)
POPULATION 676,000,000
LARGEST CITY Paris
HIGHEST POINT El'brus 18,510 ft.
(5,642 m.)
LOWEST POINT Caspian Sea -92 ft.
(-28 m.)

Population Distribution

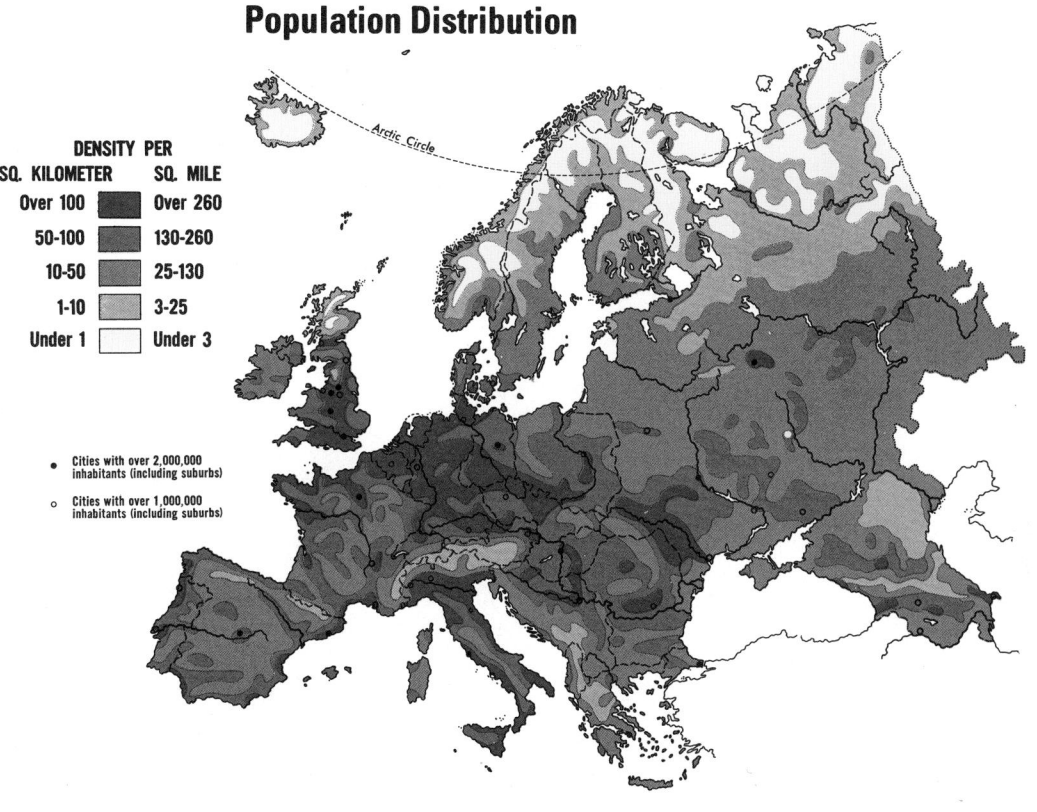

DENSITY PER

SQ. KILOMETER	SQ. MILE
Over 100	Over 260
50-100	130-260
10-50	25-130
1-10	3-25
Under 1	Under 3

• Cities with over 2,000,000
inhabitants (including suburbs)

○ Cities with over 1,000,000
inhabitants (including suburbs)

Vegetation

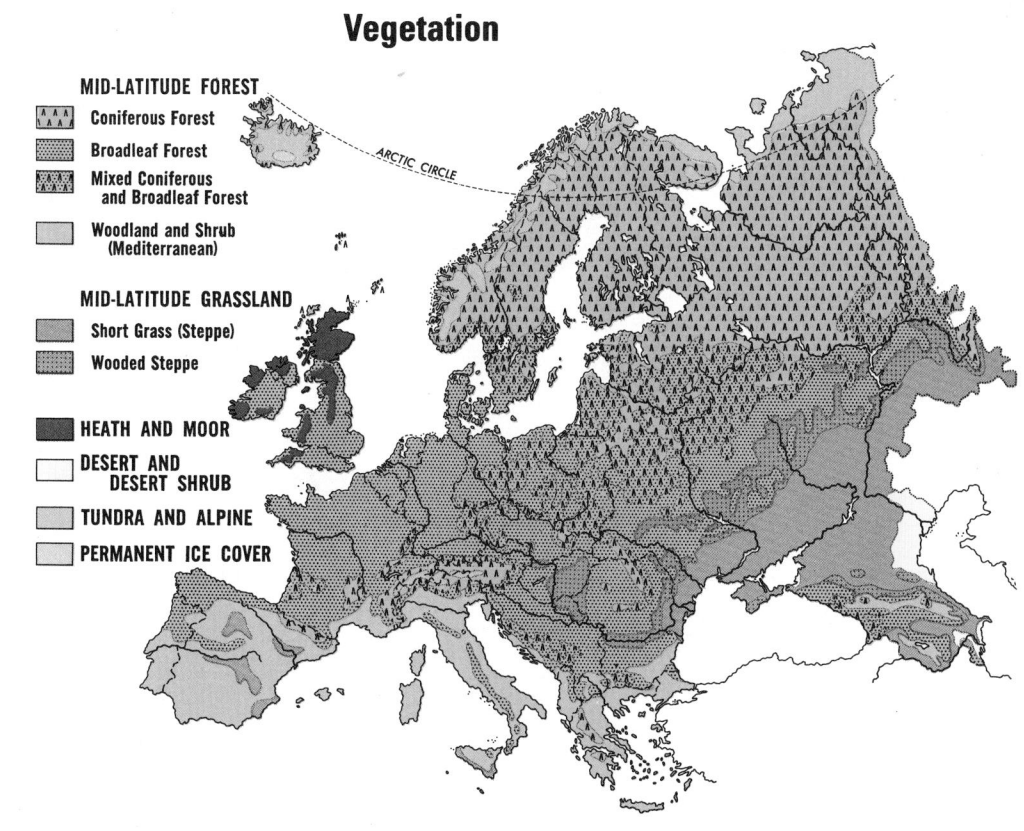

MID-LATITUDE FOREST

- Coniferous Forest
- Broadleaf Forest
- Mixed Coniferous and Broadleaf Forest
- Woodland and Shrub (Mediterranean)

MID-LATITUDE GRASSLAND

- Short Grass (Steppe)
- Wooded Steppe

HEATH AND MOOR

DESERT AND DESERT SHRUB

TUNDRA AND ALPINE

PERMANENT ICE COVER

© Copyright HAMMOND INCORPORATED, Maplewood, N.J.

ICELAND
Reykjavík

Hammerfest
Nordkapp
Søroy
BARENTS SEA
Kolguyev I.
Kanin Pen.
Chesha Bay

Faeroe Is.
(Den.)

NORWEGIAN SEA

Vesterålen
Lofoten
Vestfjord
Kiruna
Murmansk
Kola Pen.
WHITE SEA
Archangel
Northern Dvina

Shetland Is.

Trondheim
Glittertind
8,110 ft.
(2,470 m.)
Sundsvall
Oulu
FINLAND
Lake Onega

Hebrides
Orkney Is.
Moray Firth
Hardangerfjord
Bergen
Oslo
Vänern
Tampere
Åland Is.
Helsinki
Leningrad
Lake Ladoga
Volga
SOVIET UNION

Ben Nevis
4,406 ft.
(1,343 m.)
Aberdeen
Glasgow
UNITED
KINGDOM
NORTH SEA
Skagerrak
Göteborg
Västerås
Stockholm
Hiiumaa
Saaremaa
Gotland
Riga
Moscow
Gor'kiy
SOCIA

UK
Belfast
Dublin
IRELAND
IRISH SEA
Liverpool
Birmingham
DENMARK
Copenhagen
Rügen
Bornholm
BALTIC SEA
Gdańsk
Minsk
Western Dvina

C. Clear
St. George's Chan.
Land's End
London
NETHERLANDS
Amsterdam
Hamburg
Elbe
EAST
Berlin
POLAND
Vistula
Warsaw
Bug
Kiev
Khar'kov
Don

ATLANTIC OCEAN
English Channel
Channel Is.
(U.K.)
Le Havre
BELGIUM
Brussels
Cologne
Bonn
WEST
GERMANY
Leipzig
Oder
Łódź
Cracow
Prague
L'vov
Dnieper
Donetsk

Seine
Paris
LUX
GERMANY
Stuttgart
CZECHOSLOVAKIA
Brno
Carpathian Mts.
Prut
Odessa
SEA OF AZOV
Krasnodar

Nantes
Loire
FRANCE
Rhine
Munich
AUSTRIA
Vienna
Budapest
Cluj-Napoca
HUNGARY
ROMANIA
Crimea
BLACK SEA

Bay of Biscay
Finisterre
Bordeaux
Dordogne
Lyon
SWITZ.
Bern
Graz
Zagreb
Sava
Belgrade
Danube
Bucharest

Garonne
Pyrenees
Mt. Blanc
Turin
Milan
Genoa
MONACO
Venice
YUGOSLAVIA
Balkan Mts.
Sofia
BULGARIA

Porto
SPAIN
Zaragoza
Ebro
Gulf of Lions
Marseille
San Marino
ADRIATIC SEA
Skopje
Istanbul
Bosporus
Ankara
TURKEY

Lisbon
PORTUGAL
Madrid
Tagus
Guadiana
Barcelona
Corsica
VATICAN CITY
Rome
Naples
Tirana
Thessaloniki
Dardanelles
Lésvos

C. de São Vicente
Guadalquivir
Valencia
Balearic Is.
Minorca
Majorca
Ibiza
Sardinia
TYRRHENIAN SEA
IONIAN SEA
Évvoia
Izmir
Athens

Málaga
Strait of Gibraltar
Cádiz
Tangier
GIBRALTAR
(U.K.)
Oran
Algiers
C. Teulada
C. Bon
Palermo
Sicily
Etna
11,053 ft.
(3,369 m.)
C. Passero
Crete
Rhodes
CYPRUS
Nicosia
LEBANON
Beirut

Rabat
Casablanca
MOROCCO
ALGERIA
Constantine
Tunis
TUNISIA
MALTA
Valletta
MEDITERRANEAN SEA
C. Tainaron
AFRICA

Vegetation/Relief

Longitude West of   Greenwich   0°   Longitude East of   Greenwich

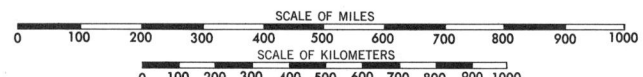

Capitals of Countries .... ⊛
International Boundaries .... —··—
Canals ....
Depths in Fathoms

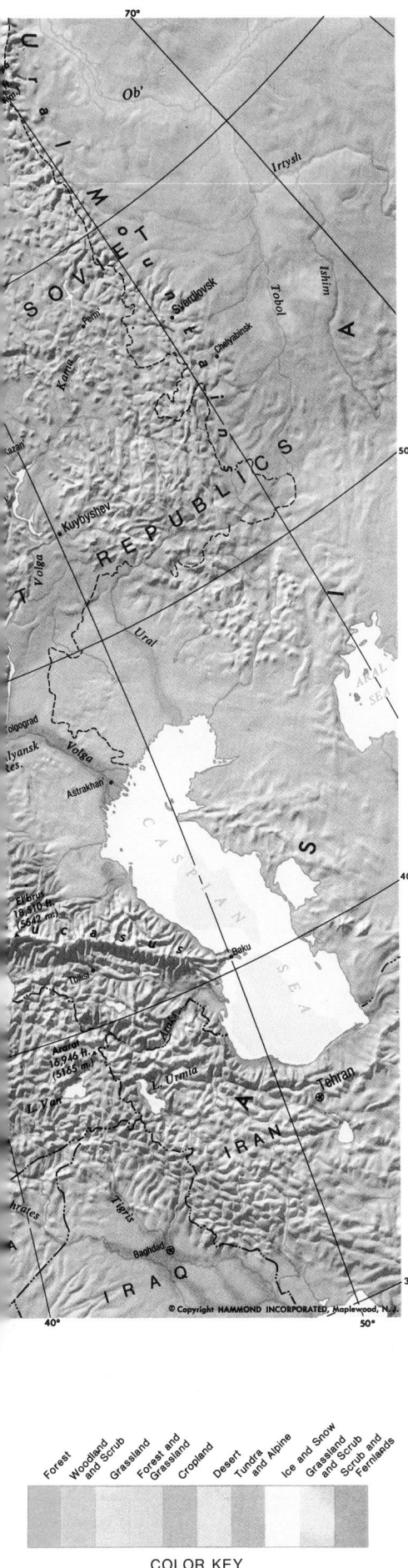

COLOR KEY

Forest | Woodland and Scrub | Grassland | Forest and Grassland | Cropland | Desert | Tundra and Alpine | Ice and Snow | Grassland and Scrub | Scrub and Fernlands

Rainfall

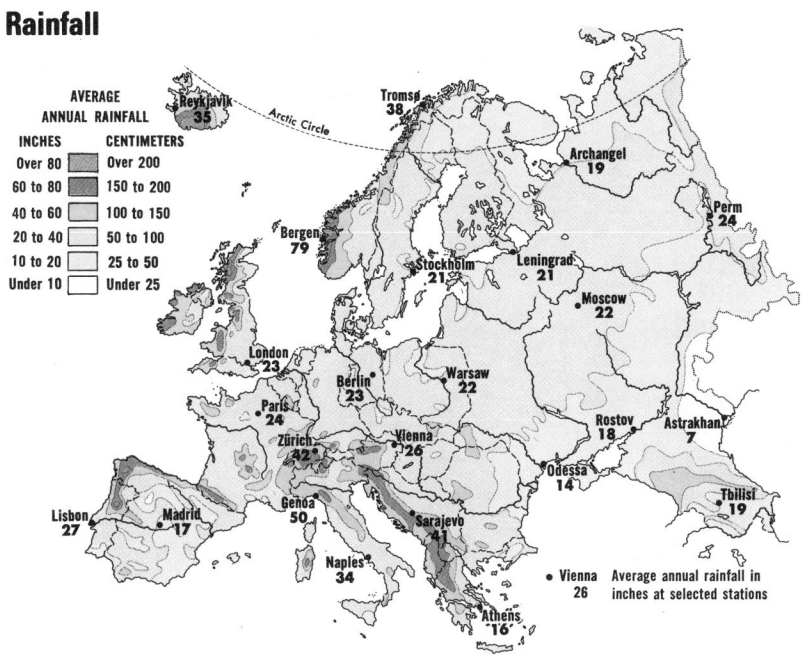

AVERAGE ANNUAL RAINFALL

INCHES	CENTIMETERS
Over 80	Over 200
60 to 80	150 to 200
40 to 60	100 to 150
20 to 40	50 to 100
10 to 20	25 to 50
Under 10	Under 25

Reykjavík 35
Tromsø 38
Archangel 19
Perm 24
Bergen 79
Stockholm 21
Leningrad 21
Moscow 22
London 23
Warsaw 22
Berlin 23
Paris 24
Rostov 18
Astrakhan 7
Vienna 26
Zürich 32
Odessa 14
Tbilisi 19
Lisbon 27
Madrid 17
Genoa 50
Sarajevo 41
Naples 34
Athens 16

• Vienna 26 — Average annual rainfall in inches at selected stations

Average January Temperature

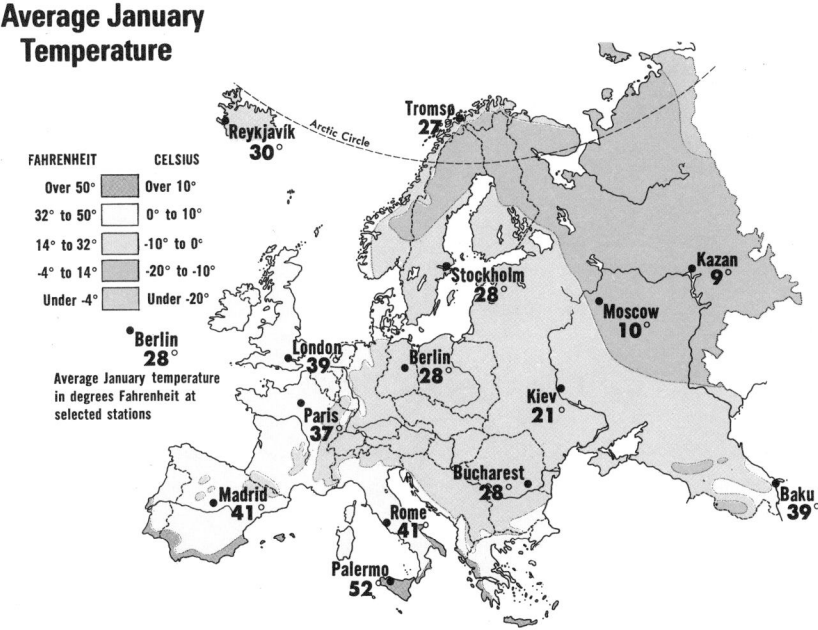

FAHRENHEIT	CELSIUS
Over 50°	Over 10°
32° to 50°	0° to 10°
14° to 32°	-10° to 0°
-4° to 14°	-20° to -10°
Under -4°	Under -20°

Tromsø 27°
Reykjavík 30°
Kazan 9°
Stockholm 28°
Moscow 10°
• Berlin 28°
London 39°
Berlin 28°
Kiev 21°

Average January temperature in degrees Fahrenheit at selected stations

Paris 37°
Bucharest 28°
Madrid 41°
Rome 41°
Baku 39°
Palermo 52°

Average July Temperature

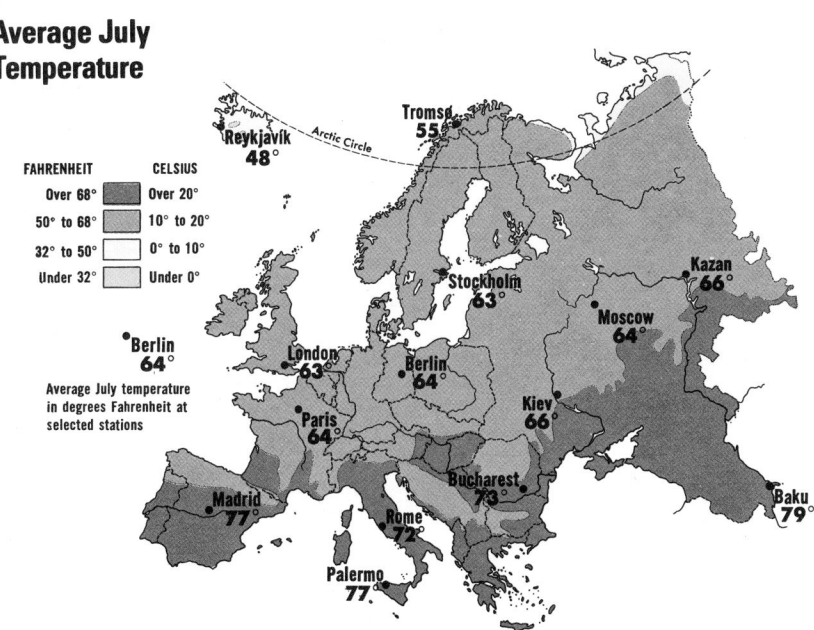

FAHRENHEIT	CELSIUS
Over 68°	Over 20°
50° to 68°	10° to 20°
32° to 50°	0° to 10°
Under 32°	Under 0°

Tromsø 55°
Reykjavík 48°
Kazan 66°
Stockholm 63°
Moscow 64°
• Berlin 64°
London 63°
Berlin 64°
Kiev 66°

Average July temperature in degrees Fahrenheit at selected stations

Paris 64°
Bucharest 73°
Madrid 77°
Rome 72°
Baku 79°
Palermo 77°

United Kingdom and Ireland

BONNE PROJECTION

SCALE OF MILES

SCALE OF KILOMETERS

Capitals of Countries .... ☆
International Boundaries ....
Other Boundaries ....
Canals ....

Scale 1 : 4,200,000

Shetland Islands

Same scale as main map.

UNITED KINGDOM
AREA 94,399 sq. mi. (244,493 sq. km.)
POPULATION 55,672,000
CAPITAL London
LARGEST CITY London
HIGHEST POINT Ben Nevis 4,406 ft. (1,343 m.)
MONETARY UNIT pound sterling
MAJOR LANGUAGES English, Gaelic, Welsh
MAJOR RELIGIONS Protestantism, Roman Catholicism

IRELAND
AREA 27,136 sq. mi. (70,282 sq. km.)
POPULATION 3,440,427
CAPITAL Dublin
LARGEST CITY Dublin
HIGHEST POINT Carrantuohill 3,415 ft. (1,041 m.)
MONETARY UNIT Irish pound
MAJOR LANGUAGES English, Gaelic (Irish)
MAJOR RELIGION Roman Catholicism

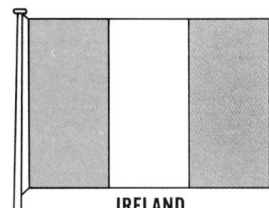

UNITED KINGDOM

IRELAND

ENGLAND
AREA 50,516 sq. mi. (130,836 sq. km.)
POPULATION 46,220,955
CAPITAL London
LARGEST CITY London
HIGHEST POINT Scafell Pike 3,210 ft. (978 m.)

WALES
AREA 8,017 sq. mi. (20,764 sq. km.)
POPULATION 2,790,462
LARGEST CITY Cardiff
HIGHEST POINT Snowdon 3,560 ft. (1,085 m.)

SCOTLAND
AREA 30,414 sq. mi. (78,772 sq. km.)
POPULATION 5,117,146
CAPITAL Edinburgh
LARGEST CITY Glasgow
HIGHEST POINT Ben Nevis 4,406 ft. (1,343 m.)

NORTHERN IRELAND
AREA 5,452 sq. mi. (14,121 sq. km.)
POPULATION 1,543,000
CAPITAL Belfast
LARGEST CITY Belfast
HIGHEST POINT Slieve Donard 2,796 ft. (852 m.)

(continued on following page)

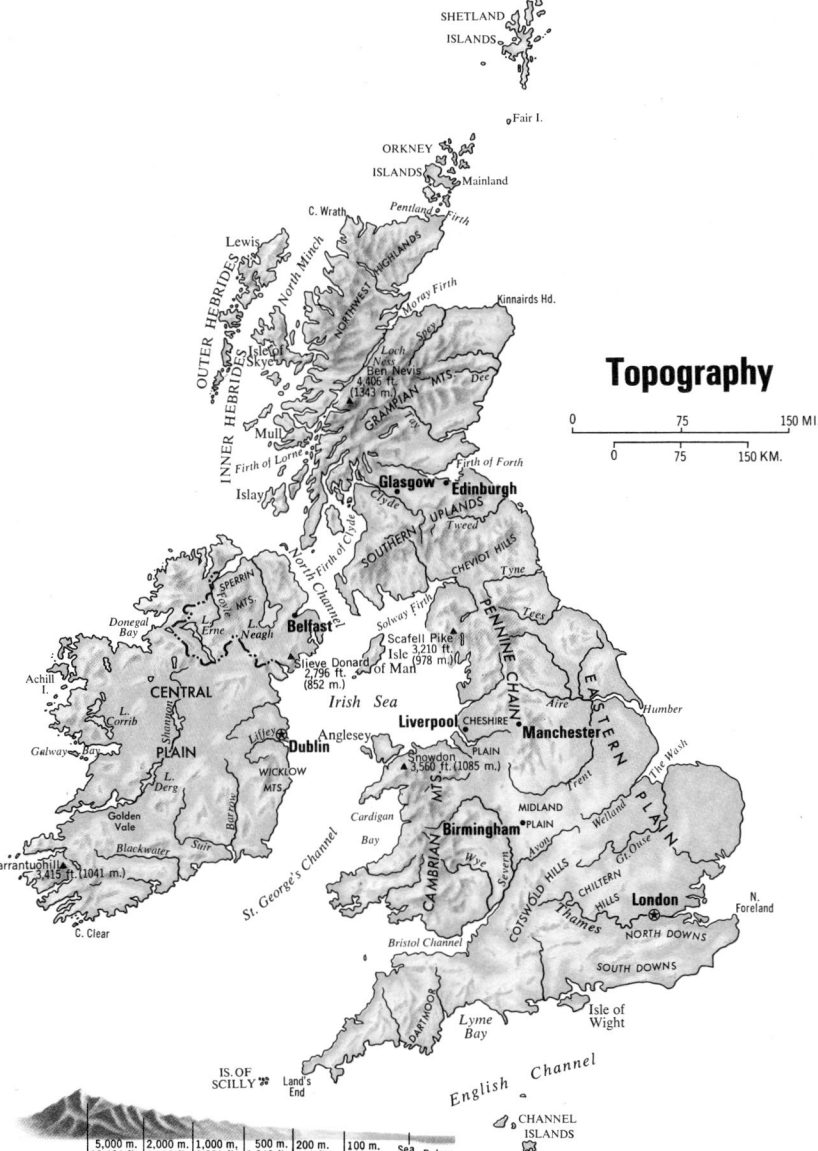

Topography

0   75   150 MI.

0   75   150 KM.

5,000 m. 16,404 ft.   2,000 m. 6,562 ft.   1,000 m. 3,281 ft.   500 m. 1,640 ft.   200 m. 656 ft.   100 m. 328 ft.   Sea Level   Below

12 United Kingdom and Ireland
(continued)

Liverpool, 539,700 G 2
Loftus, 7,850 G 3
London (cap.), 7,028,200 H 8
London, ★12,332,900 H 8
Long Eaton, 33,560 F 5
Longbenton, 50,120 J 3
Looe, 4,060 C 7
Loughborough, 49,010 F 5
Lowestoft, 53,260 J 5
Ludlow, ⊙7,466 E 5
Luton, 164,500 G 6
Lydd, 4,670 H 7
Lyme Regis, 3,460 E 7
Lymington, 36,780 F 7
Lynton, 1,770 D 6
Lytham Saint Anne's, 42,120 G 1
Mablethorpe and Sutton, 6,750 H 4
Macclesfield, 45,420 H 2
Maidenhead, 48,210 G 8
Maidstone, 72,110 J 8
Maldon, 14,350 H 6
Malmesbury, 2,550 E 6
Malton, 4,010 G 3
Malvern, 30,420 E 5
Manchester, 490,000 H 2
Mangotsfield, 23,000 E 6
Mansfield, 58,450 K 2
Mansfield Woodhouse, 25,400 F 4
March, 14,560 H 5
Margate, 50,290 J 6
Market Harborough, 15,230 G 5
Marlborough, 6,370 F 6
Matlock, 20,300 J 2
Melton Mowbray, 20,680 G 5
Merton, 169,400 H 8
Middlesbrough, 153,900 F 3
Middleton, 53,340 H 2
Middlewich, 7,600 H 2
Mildenhall, ⊙9,269 H 5
Millom, ⊙7,101 D 3
Milton Keynes, 89,900 F 5
Minehead, 8,230 D 6
Moretonhampstead, ⊙1,440 C 7
Morpeth, 14,450 F 2
Mundesley, ⊙1,536 J 5
Nelson, 31,220 H 1
Neston, 18,210 G 2
Newark, 24,760 G 4
Newbury, 24,850 F 6
Newcastle upon Tyne, 295,800 H 3
Newcastle-under-Lyme, 75,940 E 4
Newham, 228,900 H 8
Newhaven, 9,970 H 7
Newport, 22,430 F 7
New Romney, 3,830 J 7
Newton Abbot, 19,940 D 7
Newton-le-Willows, 21,780 H 2
New Windsor, 29,660 G 8
Northallerton F 3
Northam, 8,310 C 6
Northampton, 128,290 F 5
Northfleet, 27,150 J 8
North Sunderland, ⊙1,725 F 2
Northwich, 17,710 H 2
Norton, 5,580 G 3
Norton-Radstock, 15,900 E 6
Norwich, 119,200 J 5
Nottingham, 280,300 F 5
Nuneaton, 69,210 F 5
Oadby, 20,700 F 5
Oakham, 7,280 G 5
Okehampton, 4,000 D 7
Oldham, 103,690 H 2
Ormskirk, 28,860 G 2
Oswaldtwistle, 14,270 H 1
Oxford, 117,400 F 6
Padstow, ⊙2,802 B 7
Penryn, 5,660 B 7
Penzance, 19,360 B 7
Peterborough, 118,900 G 5
Peterlee, ⊙21,846 J 3
Plymouth, 259,100 C 7
Polperro, ⊙1,491 C 7
Poole, 110,600 E 7
Porlock, ⊙1,290 D 6
Portishead, 9,680 E 6
Portland, 14,860 E 7
Portslade-by-Sea, 18,040 G 7
Portsmouth, 198,500 F 7
Potters Bar, 24,670 H 7
Poulton-le-Fylde, 16,340 G 1
Preston, 94,760 G 1
Prestwich, 32,850 H 2
Queenborough, 31,550 H 6
Radcliffe, 29,630 H 2
Ramsbottom, 16,710 H 2
Ramsgate, 40,090 J 6
Rawtenstall, 20,950 H 1
Rayleigh, 26,740 J 8
Reading, 131,200 G 8
Redbridge, 231,600 H 8
Redcar, ⊙46,325 F 3
Redditch, 44,750 E 5
Reigate, 55,600 H 8
Richmond upon Thames, 166,800 H 8
Rickmansworth, 29,030 G 8
Ripley, 18,060 F 4
Rochdale, 93,780 H 2
Rochester, 56,030 J 8
Rothbury, ⊙1,818 E 2
Rotherham, 84,770 K 2
Royal Leamington Spa, 44,950 F 5
Royal Tunbridge Wells, 44,800 H 6
Rugby, 60,380 F 5
Rugeley, 24,440 E 5
Runcorn, 42,730 G 2
Rushden, 21,840 G 5
Ryde, 23,170 F 7
Rye, 4,530 H 7
Ryton, 15,170 H 3
Saddleworth, 21,340 J 2
Saint Agnes, ⊙4,747 B 7
Saint Albans, 123,800 H 7
Saint Austell-with-Fowey, 32,710 C 7
Saint Columb Major, ⊙3,953 B 7
Saint Helens, 104,890 G 2
Saint Ives, Cornwall, 9,760 B 7
Saint Neots, 17,940 G 5
Salcombe, 2,370 D 7
Sale, 59,060 H 2
Salford, 261,100 H 2
Salisbury, 35,460 F 6
Saltburn and Marske-by-the-Sea, 21,170 G 3
Sandbach, 14,280 H 2
Sandown-Shanklin, 14,800 F 7
Sandwich, 4,420 J 6
Saxmundham, 1,820 J 5
Scarborough, 43,300 G 3
Scunthorpe, 68,100 G 4
Seaford, 18,020 H 7
Seaham, 22,470 J 3
Seascale, ⊙2,106 D 3
Seaton, 4,500 D 7
Seaton Valley, 35,880 J 3
Sedbergh, ⊙2,741 E 3
Selsey, ⊙6,491 G 7
Sevenoaks, 18,160 J 8
Shaftesbury, 4,180 E 7
Sheffield, 558,000 J 2
Sherborne, 9,230 E 7
Sheringham, 4,940 J 5
Shildon, 15,360 F 3
Shoreham-by-Sea, 19,620 G 7
Shrewsbury, 56,120 E 5
Silloth, ⊙2,662 D 3
Sittingbourne and Milton, 32,830 H 6
Skelmersdale, 35,850 G 2
Skelton and Brotton, 15,930 G 3
Sleaford, 8,050 G 5
Slough, 89,060 G 8
Solihull, 108,230 F 5
Southampton, 213,700 F 7
Southend-on-Sea, 159,300 H 6
Southport, 86,030 G 1
South Shields, 96,900 J 3
Southwark, 224,900 H 8
Southwold, 1,960 J 5
Sowerby Bridge, 15,700 H 1
Spalding, 17,040 G 5
Spenborough, 41,460 J 1
Spennymoor, 19,050 F 3
Stafford, 54,860 E 5
Staines, 56,380 G 8
Stamford, 14,980 G 5
Stanley, 42,280 H 3
Staveley, 17,620 K 2
Stevenage, 72,600 G 6
Stockport, 138,350 H 2
Stockton-on-Tees, 165,400 F 3
Stoke-on-Trent, 256,200 E 4
Stourbridge, 56,530 E 5
Stourport-on-Severn, 19,430 E 5
Stowmarket, 9,020 J 5
Stratford-upon-Avon, 20,080 F 5
Stretford, 52,450 H 2
Stroud, 19,600 E 6
Sudbury, 8,860 H 5
Sunbury-on-Thames, 40,070 G 8
Sunderland, 214,820 J 3
Sutton, 166,700 H 8
Sutton Bridge, ⊙3,113 H 5
Sutton in Ashfield, 40,330 K 2
Swadlincote, 21,060 F 5
Swanage, 8,000 E 7
Swindon, 90,680 F 6
Tamworth, 46,960 F 5
Taunton, 37,570 D 6
Tavistock, ⊙7,620 C 7
Telford, ⊙79,451 E 5
Tenbury, ⊙2,151 E 5
Tewkesbury, 9,210 E 6
Thetford, 15,690 H 5
Thirsk, ⊙2,884 F 3
Thornaby-on-Tees, ⊙42,385 F 3
Thorne, ⊙16,694 F 4
Thornton Cleveleys, 27,090 G 1
Thurrock, 127,700 J 8
Tiverton, 16,190 D 7
Todmorden, 14,540 H 1
Tonbridge, 31,410 H 8
Torbay, 109,900 D 7
Torpoint, 6,840 C 7
Tower Hamlets, 146,100 H 8
Tow Law, 2,460 H 4
Trowbridge, 20,120 E 6
Truro, 15,690 B 7
Turton, 22,800 H 2
Tynemouth, 67,090 J 3
Upton upon Severn, ⊙2,048 E 5
Urmston, 44,130 H 2
Uttoxeter, 9,100 E 5
Ventnor, 6,980 F 7
Wainfleet All Saints, ⊙1,116 H 4
Wakefield, 306,500 J 2
Wallasey, 94,520 G 2
Wallsend, 45,490 J 3
Walsall, 182,430 E 5
Waltham Forest, 223,700 H 8
Waltham Holy Cross, 14,810 H 7
Walton and Weybridge, 51,270 G 8
Walton-le-Dale, 27,660 G 1
Wandsworth, 284,600 H 8
Wantage, 8,490 F 6
Ware, 14,900 H 7
Wareham, 4,630 E 7
Warley, 161,260 E 5
Warminster, 14,440 E 6
Warrington, 65,320 G 2
Warwick, 17,870 F 5
Washington, 27,720 J 3
Watchet, 2,980 D 6
Watford, 77,000 H 7
Wellingborough, 39,570 G 5
Wells, 8,960 E 6
Wells-next-the-Sea, 2,450 H 5
Welwyn, 39,900 H 7
Wem, ⊙3,411 E 5
West Bridgford, 28,340 F 5
West Bromwich, 162,740 F 5
West Mersea, 4,730 H 6
Westminster, 216,100 H 8
Weston-super-Mare, 51,960 D 6
Weymouth and Melcombe Regis, 41,080 E 7
Whickham, 29,710 J 3
Whitchurch, ⊙7,142 E 5
Whitehaven, 26,260 D 3
Whitley Bay, 37,010 J 3
Widnes, 58,330 G 2
Wigan, 80,920 G 2
Wigston, 31,650 F 5
Wilmslow, 31,250 H 2
Wilton, 4,090 F 6
Winchester, 88,900 F 6
Windermere, 7,860 E 3
Winsford, 26,920 G 2
Wirral, 27,510 G 2
Wisbech, 16,990 H 5
Witham, 19,730 H 6
Withernsea, 6,300 H 4
Wivenhoe, 5,630 J 6
Woking, 79,300 G 8
Wokingham, 22,390 G 8
Wolverhampton, 266,400 E 5
Wombwell, 17,850 K 2
Woodhall Spa, 2,420 G 4
Woodley and Sandford, ⊙24,581 G 8
Woodstock, 2,070 F 6
Wooler, ⊙1,833 F 2
Worcester, 73,900 E 5
Workington, 28,260 D 3
Worksop, 36,590 F 4
Worsbrough, 15,180 J 2
Worsley, 49,530 H 2
Worthing, 89,100 G 7
Wymondham, 9,390 J 5
Yateley, ⊙16,505 G 8
Yeovil, 26,180 E 7
York, 101,900 F 4

OTHER FEATURES

Aire (riv.) F 4
Atlantic Ocean A 7
Avon (riv.) F 5
Avon (riv.) F 7
Axe Edge (mt.) H 2
Barnstaple (bay) C 6
Beachy (head) H 7
Bigbury (bay) C 7
Blackwater (riv.) H 6
Bristol (chan.) C 6
Brown Willy (mt.) C 7
Cheviot (hills) E 2
Cheviot, The (mt.) E 2
Chiltern (hills) G 6
Cleveland (hills) F 3
Colne (riv.) G 8
Cornwall (cape) B 7
Cotswold (hills) E 6
Cross Fell (mt.) E 3
Cumbrian (mts.) D 3
Dart (riv.) D 7
Dartmoor National Park C 7
Dee (riv.) D 4
Derwent (riv.) G 3
Derwent (riv.) H 3
Don (riv.) F 4
Dorset Heights (hills) E 7
Dove (riv.) J 2
Dover (str.) J 7
Dungeness (prom.) J 7
Dunkery (hill) D 6
Eddystone (rocks) C 7
Eden (riv.) E 3
English (chan.) D 8
Esk (riv.) D 2
Exe (riv.) D 7
Exmoor National Park D 6
Fens, The (reg.) G 5
Flamborough (head) G 3
Formby (head) G 2
Foulness Island (pen.) J 6
Gibraltar (pt.) H 4
Great Ouse (riv.) H 5
Hartland (pt.) C 6
High Willhays (mt.) C 7
Hodder (riv.) H 1
Holderness (pen.), 43,900 G 4
Holy (isl.), 189 F 2
Humber (riv.) G 4
Irish (sea) B 4
Kennet (riv.) F 6
Lake District National Park D 3
Land's End (prom.) B 7
Lea (riv.) G 6
Lincoln Wolds (hills) G 4
Lindisfarne (Holy) (isl.), 189 F 2
Liverpool (bay) D 4
Lizard, The (pen.), 7,371 B 8
Lundy (isl.), 49 C 6
Lune (riv.) E 3
Lyme (bay) D 7
Manacle (pt.) C 7
Medway (riv.) H 6
Mendip (hills) E 6
Mersea (isl.), 4,423 J 6
Mersey (riv.) G 2
Morecambe (bay) D 3
Mounts (bay) B 7
Naze, The (prom.) J 6
Nene (riv.) H 5
New (for.) F 6
North (sea) J 4
North Downs (hills) G 6
North Foreland (prom.) J 6
Northumberland National Park E 2
North York Moors National Park G 3
Orford Ness (prom.) J 5
Ouse (riv.) G 4
Ouse (riv.) G 6
Parrett (riv.) E 6
Peak District National Park F 4
Peak, The (mt.) J 2
Peel Fell (mt.) E 2
Pennine Chain (range) E 3
Plymouth (sound) C 7
Portland, Bill of (pt.) E 7
Prawle (pt.) D 7
Purbeck, Isle of (pen.), 39,500 F 7
Ribble (riv.) E 4
Saint Alban's (head) F 7
Saint Bees (head) D 3
Saint Martin's (isl.), 106 A 8
Saint Mary's (isl.), 1,958 A 8
Scafell Pike (mt.) D 3
Scilly (isls.), 1,900 A 7
Selsey Bill (prom.) G 7
Severn (riv.) E 6
Sheppey (isl.), 31,550 J 6
Sherwood (for.) F 4
Skiddaw (mt.) D 3
Solent (chan.) F 7
Solway (firth) D 3
South Downs (hills) G 7
Spithead (chan.) F 7
Spurn (head) H 4
Stonehenge (ruins) F 6
Stour (riv.) E 7
Stour (riv.) H 6
Stour (riv.) J 6
Swale (riv.) F 3
Tamar (riv.) C 7
Taw (riv.) D 7
Tees (riv.) F 3
Test (riv.) F 6
Thames (riv.) H 6
Tintagel (head) C 7
Torridge (riv.) C 7
Trent (riv.) G 4
Tresco (isl.), 246 A 8
Tweed (riv.) E 2
Tyne (riv.) F 3
Ure (riv.) F 3
Ver (riv.) H 7
Walney, Isle of (isl.), 11,241 D 3
Wash, The (bay) H 5
Weald, The (reg.) H 6
Wear (riv.) F 3
Weaver (riv.) G 2
Welland (riv.) G 5
Wey (riv.) G 6
Wharfe (riv.) E 3
Wirral (pen.), 432,900 G 2
Witham (riv.) G 4
Wolds, The (hills) G 4
Wye (riv.) D 5
Wyre (riv.) F 2
Yare (riv.) J 5
Yorkshire Dales National Park E 3

CHANNEL ISLANDS

CITIES and TOWNS

Saint Anne E 8
Saint Helier (cap.), Jersey, ⊙28,135 E 8
Saint Peter Port (cap.), Guernsey, ⊙16,303 E 8
Saint Sampson's, ⊙6,534 E 8

OTHER FEATURES

Alderney (isl.), 1,686 E 8
Guernsey (isl.), 51,351 E 8
Herm (isl.), 96 E 8
Jersey (isl.), 72,629 E 8
Sark (isl.), 590 E 8

ISLE of MAN

CITIES and TOWNS

Castletown, 2,620 C 3
Douglas (cap.), 20,389 C 3
Laxey, 1,170 C 3
Michael, 408 C 3
Onchan, 4,807 C 3
Peel, 3,081 C 3
Port Erin, 1,714 C 3
Port Saint Mary, 1,508 C 3
Ramsey, 5,048 C 3

OTHER FEATURES

Ayre (pt.) C 3
Calf of Man (isl.) C 3
Langness (prom.) C 3
Snaefell (mt.) C 3
Spanish (head) C 3

WALES

COUNTIES

Clwyd, 376,000 D 4
Dyfed, 323,100 C 6
Gwent, 439,600 D 6
Gwynedd, 225,100 C 4
Mid Glamorgan, 540,400 D 6
Powys, 101,500 D 5
South Glamorgan, 389,200 A 7
West Glamorgan, 371,900 D 6

CITIES and TOWNS

Aberaeron, 1,340 C 5
Abercarn, 18,370 B 6
Aberdare, 38,030 A 6
Abertillery, 20,550 B 6
Amlwch, 3,630 C 4
Bala, 1,650 D 5
Bangor, 16,030 C 4
Barmouth, 2,070 C 5
Barry, 42,780 B 7
Beaumaris, 2,090 C 4
Bedwellty, 25,460 B 6
Bethesda, 4,180 D 4
Betws-y-Coed, 720 D 4
Brecknock (Brecon), 6,460 D 6
Brecon, 6,460 D 6
Bridgend, 14,690 A 7
Brynmawr, 5,970 B 6
Builth Wells, 1,480 D 5
Burry Port, 5,990 C 6
Caernarfon, 8,840 C 4
Caerphilly, 42,190 B 6
Cardiff, 281,500 B 7
Cardigan, 3,830 C 5
Chepstow, 8,260 E 6
Chirk, ⊙3,564 D 5
Colwyn Bay, 25,370 D 4
Criccieth, 1,590 C 5
Cwmamman, 3,950 D 6
Cwmbran, 32,980 B 6
Denbigh, 8,420 D 4
Dolgellau, 2,430 D 5
Ebbw Vale, 25,670 B 6
Ffestiniog, 5,510 D 5
Fishguard and Goodwick, 5,020 B 5
Flint, 15,070 G 2
Gelligaer, 33,820 A 6
Harlech, ⊙332 C 5
Haverfordwest, 8,930 B 6
Hawarden, ⊙20,389 G 2
Hay, 1,200 D 5
Holywell, 8,570 G 2
Kidwelly, 3,090 C 6
Knighton, 2,190 D 5
Llandeilo, 1,780 C 6
Llandovery, 2,040 D 5
Llandrindod Wells, 3,460 D 5
Llandudno, 17,700 D 4
Llanelli, 25,870 C 6
Llanfairfechan, 3,800 D 4
Llangefni, 4,070 C 4
Llangollen, 3,050 D 5
Llanguicke, ⊙15,029 D 6
Llanidloes, 2,390 D 5
Llantrisant, ⊙27,490 A 7
Llanwrtyd Wells, 460 D 5
Llwchwr, 27,530 D 6
Machynlleth, 1,830 D 5
Maesteg, 21,100 D 6
Menai Bridge, 2,730 C 4
Merthyr Tydfil, 61,500 A 6
Milford Haven, 13,960 B 6
Mold, 8,700 G 2
Montgomery, 1,000 D 5
Mountain Ash, 27,710 A 6
Mynyddislwyn, 15,590 B 6
Narberth, 970 C 6
Neath, 27,280 D 6
Nefyn, ⊙2,086 C 5
Newcastle Emlyn, 690 C 5
Newport, Dyfed, ⊙1,062 C 5
Newport, Gwent, 110,090 B 6
New Quay, 760 C 5
Newtown, 6,400 D 5
Neyland, 2,690 B 6
Ogmore and Garw, 19,680 A 6
Pembroke, 14,570 C 6
Penarth, 24,180 B 7
Penmaenmawr, 4,050 C 4
Pontypool, 36,710 B 6
Pontypridd, 34,180 A 6
Porthcawl, 14,980 D 6
Porthmadog, 3,900 C 5
Port Talbot, 58,200 D 6
Prestatyn, 15,480 D 4
Presteigne, 1,330 D 5
Pwllheli, 4,020 C 5
Rhondda, 85,400 A 6
Rhyl, 22,150 D 4
Risca, 15,780 B 6
Ruthin, 4,780 D 4
Saint David's, ⊙1,638 B 6
Swansea, 190,800 C 6
Tenby, 4,930 C 6
Tredegar, 17,450 B 6
Tywyn, 3,850 C 5
Welshpool, 7,370 D 5
Wrexham, 39,530 E 4

OTHER FEATURES

Anglesey (isl.), 64,500 C 4
Aran Fawddwy (mt.) C 5
Bardsey (isl.), 9 C 5
Berwyn (mts.) D 5
Black (mts.) D 6
Braich-y-Pwll (prom.) C 5
Brecon Beacons (mt.) D 6
Brecon Beacons National Park D 6
Caldy (isl.), 70 C 6
Cambrian (mts.) D 5
Cardigan (bay) C 5
Carmarthen (bay) C 6
Cemmaes (head) C 5
Dee (riv.) D 4
Dovey (riv.) D 5
Ely (riv.) B 7
Gower (pen.), 17,220 C 6
Great Ormes (head) C 4
Holy (isl.), 13,715 C 4
Lleyn (pen.), 25,800 C 5
Menai (str.) C 4
Milford Haven (inlet) B 6
Pembrokeshire Coast National Park C 6
Plynlimon (mt.) D 5
Preseli (mts.) C 6
Radnor (for.) D 5
Rhymney (riv.) B 6
Saint Brides (bay) B 6
Saint David's (head) B 6
Saint George's (chan.) B 5
Saint Gowans (head) C 6
Severn (riv.) E 5
Snowdon (mt.) D 4
Snowdonia National Park D 4
Taff (riv.) B 7
Teifi (riv.) C 5
Towy (riv.) D 6
Tremadoc (bay) C 5
Usk (riv.) B 6
Wye (riv.) D 5
Ynys Môn (Anglesey) (isl.), 64,500 C 4

★Population of met. area.
⊙Population of parish.

SCOTLAND
(map on page 15)

REGIONS

Borders, 99,409 E 5
Central, 269,281 D 4
Dumfries and Galloway, 143,667 E 5
Fife, 336,339 E 4
Grampian, 448,772 F 3
Highland, 182,044 D 3
Lothian, 754,008 E 5
Orkney (islands area), 17,675 E 1
Shetland (islands area), 18,494 F 2
Strathclyde, 2,504,909 C 4
Tayside, 401,987 E 4
Western Isles (islands area), 29,615 A 3

CITIES and TOWNS

Aberchirder, 877 F 3
Aberdeen, 210,362 F 3
Aberdour, 1,576 D 1
Aberfeldy, 1,552 E 4
Aberfoyle, 793 D 4
Aberlady, 737 F 4
Aberlour, 842 E 3
Abernethy, 776 E 4
Aboyne, 1,040 F 3
Acharacle, ⊙764 C 4
Achiltibuie, ⊙1,564 C 3
Achnasheen, ⊙1,078 C 3
Ae, 239 E 5
Airdrie, 38,491 C 2
Alexandria, 9,758 A 1
Alford, 764 F 3
Alloa, 13,558 C 1
Alness, 2,560 D 3
Altnaharra, ⊙1,227 D 2
Alva, 4,593 C 1
Alyth, 1,738 E 4
Ancrum, 266 F 5
Annan, 6,250 E 6
Annat, ⊙550 C 3
Annbank Station, 2,530 D 5
Applecross, ⊙550 C 3
Arbroath, 22,706 F 4
Ardavasar, ⊙449 B 3
Ardersier, 942 E 3
Ardgay, 193 D 3
Ardrishaig, 946 C 4
Ardrossan, 11,072 D 5
Armadale, 7,200 C 2
Arrochar, 543 D 4
Ascog, 230 A 2
Auchenblae, 339 F 4
Auchencairn, 215 E 6
Auchinleck, 4,883 D 5
Auchterarder, 1,738 E 4
Auchtermuchty, 1,426 E 4
Auldearn, 405 E 3
Aviemore, 1,224 E 3
Avoch, 776 D 3
Ayr, 47,990 D 5
Ayton, 410 F 5
Bailivanish, 347 A 3
Baillieston, 7,671 B 2
Balallan, 283 B 2
Balerno, 3,576 D 2
Balfron, 1,149 B 1
Ballantrae, 262 C 5
Ballater, 981 F 3
Ballingry, 4,332 D 1
Ballinluig, 188 E 4
Balloch, Highland, 572 D 3
Balloch, Strathclyde, 1,484 B 1
Baltasound, 246 G 2
Banchory, 2,435 F 3
Banff, 3,832 F 3
Bankfoot, 868 E 4
Bankhead, 1,492 F 3
Bannockburn, 5,889 C 1
Barrhead, 18,736 B 2
Barrhill, 236 D 5
Barvas, 279 B 2
Bathgate, 14,038 C 2
Bayble, 543 B 2
Bearsden, 25,128 B 2
Beattock, 309 E 5
Beauly, 1,141 D 3
Beith, 5,859 D 5
Bellsbank, 3,066 D 5
Bellshill, 18,166 C 2
Berriedale, ⊙1,927 E 2
Bieldside, 1,137 F 3
Biggar, 1,718 E 5
Birnam, 659 E 4
Bishopbriggs, 21,570 B 2
Bishopton, 2,931 B 2
Blackburn, 7,636 C 2
Blackford, 529 E 4
Blair Atholl, 437 E 4
Blairgowrie and Rattray, 5,681 E 4
Blanefield, 835 B 1
Blantyre, 13,992 B 2
Blyth Bridge, ⊙441 E 5
Bo'ness, 12,959 C 1
Boat of Garten, 406 E 3
Boddam, 1,429 G 3
Bonar Bridge, 519 D 3
Bonhill, 4,385 B 1
Bonnybridge, 5,701 C 1
Bonnyrigg and Lasswade, 7,429 D 2
Bowmore, 947 B 5
Braemar, 394 E 3
Breasclete, 234 B 2
Brechin, 6,759 F 4
Bridge of Allan, 4,638 C 1
Bridge of Don, 4,086 F 3
Bridge of Weir, 4,724 A 2
Brightons, 3,106 C 1
Broadford, 310 B 3
Brodick, 630 C 5
Brora, 1,436 E 2
Broxburn, 7,776 D 1
Buchlyvie, 412 B 1
Buckhaven and Methil, 17,930 F 4
Buckie, 8,145 E 3
Bucksburn, 6,567 F 3
Bunessan, ⊙585 B 4
Burghead, 1,321 E 3
Burnmouth, 300 F 5
Burntisland, 5,626 D 1
Cairndow, ⊙874 D 4
Cairnryan, 199 D 6
Callander, 1,805 D 4
Cambuslang, 14,607 B 2
Campbeltown, 6,428 C 5
Cannich, 203 D 3
Canonbie, 234 F 5
Caol, 3,719 C 4
Carbost, ⊙772 B 3
Cardenden, 6,802 D 1
Carloway, 178 B 2
Carluke, 8,864 E 5
Carnoustie, 6,838 F 4
Carnwath, 1,246 E 5
Carradale, 262 C 5
Carrbridge, 416 E 3
Carron, 2,626 C 1
Carsphairn, 186 D 5
Castlebay, 284 A 4
Castle Douglas, 3,384 E 6
Castle Kennedy, 307 D 6
Castletown, 902 E 2
Catrine, 2,681 D 5
Cawdor, 111 E 3
Chirnside, 888 F 5
Chryston, 8,322 C 2
Clackmannan, 3,248 C 1
Clarkston, 8,404 B 2
Closeburn, 225 E 5
Clovulin, ⊙315 C 4
Clydebank, 47,538 B 2
Coalburn, 1,460 E 5
Coatbridge, 50,806 C 2
Cockburnspath, 233 F 5
Cockenzie and Port Seton, 3,539 D 1
Coldingham, 423 F 5
Coldstream, 1,393 F 5
Coll, 305 B 2
Colmonell, 218 D 5
Comrie, 1,119 E 4
Connel, 300 C 4
Cononbridge, 914 D 3
Corpach, 1,296 C 4
Coupar Angus, 2,010 E 4
Cove and Kilcreggan, 1,402 A 1
Cove Bay, 765 F 3
Cowdenbeath, 10,215 D 1
Cowie, 2,751 C 1
Craigellachie, 382 E 3
Craignure, ⊙544 C 4
Crail, 1,033 F 4
Crawford, 384 E 5
Creetown, 769 D 6
Crieff, 5,718 E 4
Crimond, 313 G 3
Crinan, ⊙462 C 4
Cromarty, 492 E 3
Crosshill, 535 D 5
Crossmichael, 317 D 6
Cruden Bay, 528 G 3
Cullen, 1,199 F 3
Culross, 504 C 1
Cults, 3,336 F 3
Cumbernauld, 41,200 C 1
Cumnock and Holmhead, 6,298 D 5
Cupar, 6,607 E 4
Currie, 6,764 D 2
Dailly, 1,258 D 5
Dalbeattie, 3,659 E 6
Daliburgh, 261 A 3
Dalkeith, 9,713 D 2
Dalmally, 283 D 4
Dalmellington, 1,949 D 5
Dalry, 5,833 D 5
Dalrymple, 1,336 D 5
Darvel, 3,177 D 5
Daviot, ⊙513 D 3
Denholm, 581 F 5
Denny and Dunipace, 10,424 C 1
Dervaig, ⊙1,081 B 4
Dingwall, 4,275 D 3
Dollar, 2,573 E 4
Dornoch, 880 D 3
Douglas, 1,843 E 5
Doune, 859 D 4
Drongan, 3,609 D 5
Drumbeg, ⊙833 C 2
Drummore, 336 D 6
Drumnadrochit, 359 D 3
Drymen, 659 B 1
Dufftown, 1,481 E 3
Dumbarton, 25,469 B 1
Dumfries, 29,259 E 5
Dunbar, 4,609 F 4
Dunbeath, 161 E 2
Dunbeg, 939 C 4
Dunblane, 5,222 E 4
Dundee, 194,732 F 4
Dundonald, 2,256 D 5
Dunfermline, 52,098 D 1
Dunkeld, 273 E 4
Dunning, 564 E 4
Dunoon, 8,759 A 2
Dunragit, 323 D 6
Duns, 1,812 F 5
Duntocher, 3,532 B 2
Dunure, 452 D 5
Dunvegan, 301 B 3
Dyce, 2,733 F 3
Eaglesfield, 581 E 5
Eaglesham, 2,788 D 5
Earlston, 1,415 F 5
East Calder, 2,690 D 2
East Kilbride, 71,200 B 2
East Linton, 882 F 5
Eastriggs, 1,455 E 5
Ecclefechan, 844 E 5
Edinburgh (cap.), 470,085 D 1
Edzell, 658 F 4
Elderslie, 5,204 B 2
Elgin, 17,042 E 3
Elie and Earlsferry, 807 F 4
Ellon, 2,855 F 3
Embo, 260 E 3
Errol, 762 E 4
Evanton, 562 D 3
Eyemouth, 2,704 F 5
Fairlie, 1,029 D 5
Falkirk, 36,901 C 1
Falkland, 998 E 4
Fallin, 3,159 C 1
Fauldhouse, 5,247 C 2
Ferness, ⊙287 E 3
Ferryden, 740 F 4
Findhorn, 664 E 3
Findochty, 1,229 E 3
Fintry, 296 B 1
Fochabers, 1,238 E 3
Forfar, 11,179 F 4
Forres, 5,317 E 3
Fort Augustus, 670 D 3
Forth, 2,929 C 2
Fortrose, 1,150 D 3
Fort William, 4,370 C 4
Foyers, 276 D 3
Fraserburgh, 10,930 G 3
Friockheim, 807 F 4
Furnace, 220 C 4
Fyvie, 405 F 3
Gairloch, 125 C 3
Galashiels, 12,808 F 5
Galston, 4,256 D 5
Gardenstown, 892 F 3
Garelochhead, 1,552 A 1
Gargunnock, 457 B 1
Garlieston, 385 D 6
Garmouth, 352 E 3
Garrabost, 307 B 2
Gartmore, 253 B 1
Gatehouse-of-Fleet, 835 D 6
Giffnock, 10,987 B 2
Gifford, 575 F 5
Girvan, 7,597 D 5
Glamis, 190 F 4
Glasgow, 880,617 B 2
Glasgow, ★1,674,789 B 2
Glenbarr, ⊙691 C 5
Glencaple, 275 E 5
Glencoe, 195 C 4
Glenelg, ⊙1,468 C 3
Glenluce, 725 D 6
Glenrothes, 31,400 E 4
Golspie, 1,374 E 3
Gordon, 320 F 5
Gorebridge, 3,426 D 2
Gourock, 11,192 A 1
Grangemouth, 24,430 C 1
Grantown-on-Spey, 1,578 E 3
Greenlaw, 574 F 5
Greenock, 67,275 A 2
Gretna, 1,907 E 5
Gullane, 1,701 F 4
Haddington, 6,767 F 5
Halkirk, 679 E 2
Hamilton, 45,495 C 2
Hamnavoe, 307 G 2
Harthill, 4,712 C 2
Hatton, 315 G 3
Hawick, 16,484 F 5
Heathhall, 1,365 E 5
Helensburgh, 13,327 A 1
Helmsdale, 727 E 2
Hill of Fearn, 233 D 3
Hillside, 692 F 4
Hillswick, ⊙696 G 2
Hopeman, 1,248 E 3
Huntly, 4,078 F 3
Hurlford, 4,294 D 5
Inchnadamph, ⊙833 D 2
Innellan, 922 A 2
Innerleithen, 2,293 E 5
Insch, 881 F 3
Inveraray, 473 C 4
Inverbervie, 853 F 4
Invercassley, ⊙1,067 D 3
Invergordon, 2,385 D 3
Invergowrie, 1,389 E 4
Inverie, ⊙1,468 C 3
Inverkeithing, 6,102 D 1
Inverness, 35,801 D 3
Inverurie, 5,534 F 3
Irvine, 48,500 D 5
Isle of Whithorn, 222 D 6
Jedburgh, 3,953 F 5
John O'Groats, 195 E 2
Johnshaven, 544 F 4
Johnstone, 23,251 B 2
Kames, 230 C 5
Keiss, 344 E 2
Keith, 4,192 F 3
Kelso, 4,934 F 5
Kelty, 6,573 D 1
Kemnay, 1,042 F 3
Kenmore, 211 E 4
Kilbarchan, 2,669 A 2
Kilbirnie, 8,259 A 2
Kilchoan, ⊙764 B 4
Kildonan, ⊙1,105 E 2
Killearn, 1,086 B 1
Killin, 600 D 4
Kilmacolm, 3,348 A 2
Kilmarnock, 50,175 D 5
Kilmaurs, 2,518 D 5
Kilninver, ⊙247 C 4
Kilrenny and Anstruther, 2,951 F 4
Kilsyth, 10,210 B 1
Kilwinning, 8,460 D 5
Kinbrace, ⊙1,105 E 2
Kincardine, 3,278 C 1
Kinghorn, 2,163 D 1
Kingussie, 1,036 D 3
Kinlochewe, ⊙1,794 C 3
Kinlochleven, 1,243 D 4
Kinloch Rannoch, 241 D 4
Kinloss, 2,378 E 3
Kinross, 2,829 E 4
Kintore, 970 F 3
Kippen, 529 B 1
Kirkcaldy, 50,207 D 1
Kirkcolm, 346 C 6
Kirkconnel, 3,318 E 5
Kirkcowan, 354 D 6
Kirkcudbright, 2,690 E 6
Kirkhill, 210 D 3
Kirkintilloch, 26,664 B 2
Kirkmuirhill, 2,575 E 5
Kirkton of Glenisla, ⊙331 E 4
Kirkwall, 4,777 E 2
Kirriemuir, 4,295 E 4
Kyleakin, 268 C 3
Kyle of Lochalsh, 687 C 3
Kylestrome, ⊙745 D 2
Ladybank, 1,216 E 4
Laggan, 393 D 3
Lairg, 572 D 2
Lamlash, 613 C 5
Lanark, 8,842 E 5
Langholm, 2,509 E 5
Larbert, 4,922 C 1
Largs, 9,461 A 2
Larkhall, 15,926 E 5
Lauder, 639 F 5
Laurencekirk, 1,416 F 4

(continued)

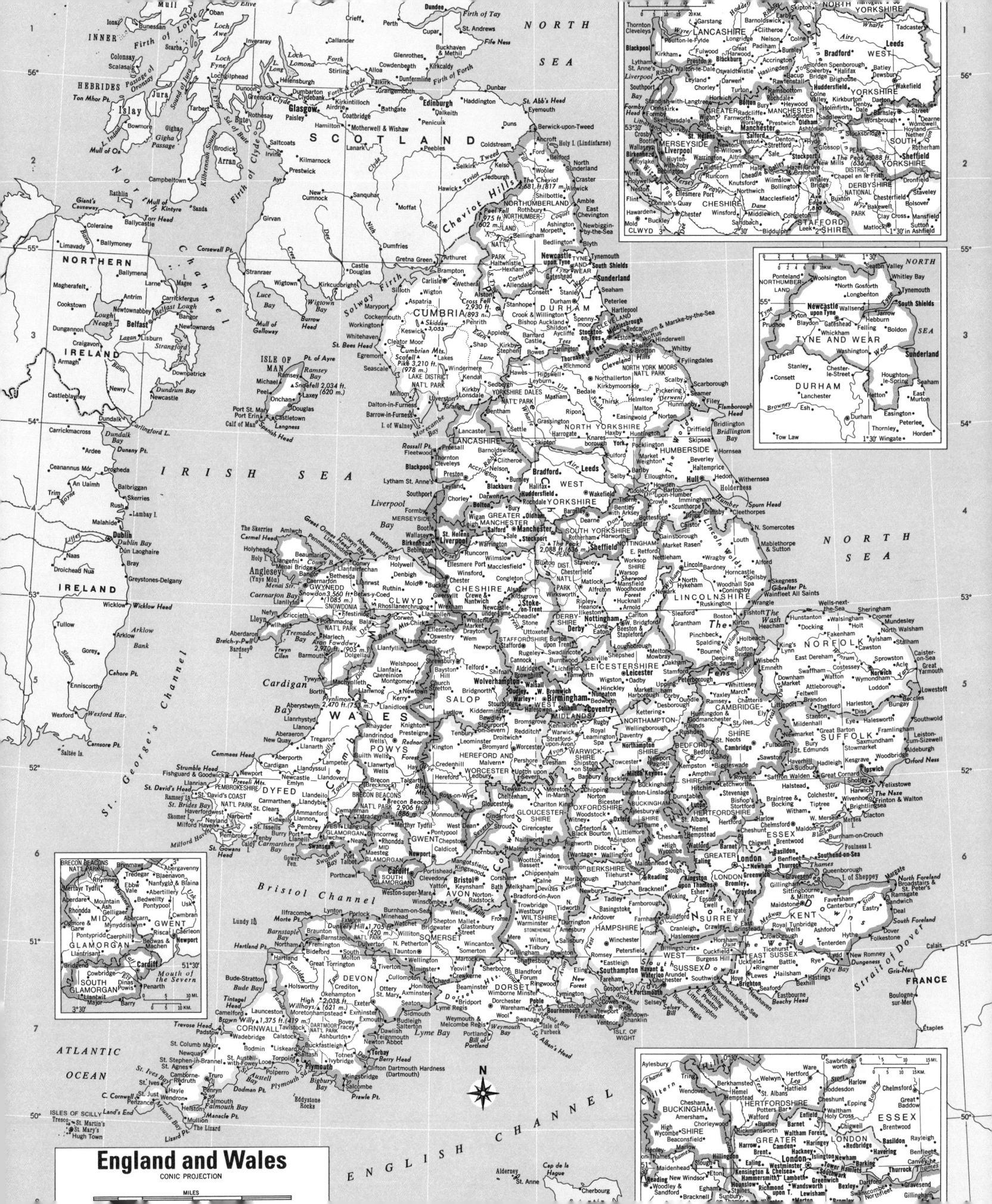

England and Wales

CONIC PROJECTION

MILES

Lennoxtown, 3,070 B 1
Lerwick, 6,195 G 2
Leslie, 3,303 E 4
Lesmahagow, 3,906 E 5
Leswalt, 237 C 6
Letham, 804 F 4
Leuchars, 2,482 F 4
Leurbost, 461 B 2
Leven, 9,507 F 4
Leverburgh, 223 B 3
Lhanbryde, 1,184 E 3
Lilliesleaf, 212 F 5
Limekilns, 812 D 1
Linlithgow, 6,098 C 1
Linwood, 10,510 B 2
Lionel, 187 B 2
Livingston, 21,900 C 2
Loanhead, 5,971 D 2
Lochailort, ⊙673 C 4
Lochaline, 213 C 4
Lochans, 355 D 6
Locharbriggs, 2,561 E 5
Lochawe, 200 C 4
Lochboisdale, 382 A 3
Lochcarron, 204 C 3
Lochgelly, 7,754 D 1
Lochgilphead, 1,217 C 4
Lochgoilhead, 216 D 4
Lochinver, 283 C 2
Lochmaben, 1,304 E 5
Lochmaddy, 307 A 3
Lochore, 2,994 D 1
Lochwinnoch, 2,064 A 2
Lockerbie, 3,135 E 5
Lossiemouth and Branderburgh, 5,817 E 3
Lumsden, 248 F 3
Luncarty, 584 E 4
Lybster, 554 E 2
Lyness, ⊙454 E 2
Macduff, 3,682 F 3
Machrihanish, 212 C 5
Maidens, 536 D 5
Mallaig, 903 C 4
Markinch, 2,366 E 4
Mauchline, 3,612 D 5
Maud, 634 F 3
Maybole, 4,703 D 5
Mayfield, 8,232 D 2
Meigle, 357 E 4
Melrose, 2,197 F 5
Melvaig, ⊙1,794 C 3
Methlick, 315 F 3
Methven, 806 E 4
Mid Yell, 220 G 2
Millport, 1,161 A 2
Milnathort, 1,099 E 4
Milngavie, 10,846 B 1
Minnigaff, 658 D 6
Mintlaw, 657 F 3
Moffat, 2,041 E 5
Moniaive, 342 E 5
Monifieth, 7,100 F 4
Montrose, 4,704 F 4
Morar, 184 C 4
Motherwell and Wishaw, 72,991 C 2
Muirkirk, 2,607 E 5
Muir of Ord, 1,339 D 3
Musselburgh, 17,045 D 2
Muthill, 672 E 4
Nairn, 5,821 E 3
Neilston, 4,358 B 2
Nethy Bridge, 431 E 3
New Abbey, 339 E 6
Newarthill, 7,003 C 2
Newburgh, Fife, 2,124 E 4
Newburgh, Grampian, 447 G 3
Newcastleton, 903 F 5
New Cumnock, 5,077 D 5
New Deer, 601 F 3
New Galloway, 337 D 5
Newmains, 6,847 C 2
Newmarket, 613 B 2
Newmill, 449 E 3
Newmilns and Greenholm, 3,509 D 5
New Pitsligo, 1,125 F 3
Newport-on-Tay, 3,762 F 4
New Scone, 3,830 E 4
Newtongrange, 4,555 D 2
Newton Mearns, 6,901 B 2
Newtonmore, 894 D 3
Newton Stewart, 1,983 D 6
Newtown Saint Boswells, 1,101 F 5
Newtyle, 664 E 4
North Berwick, 4,317 F 4
North Tolsta, 527 B 2
Oakley, 3,499 C 1
Oban, 6,515 C 4
Old Kilpatrick, 3,256 B 2
Oldmeldrum, 1,103 F 3
Oykel Bridge, ⊙742 D 3
Paisley, 94,833 B 2
Palnackie, 225 E 6
Patna, 2,867 D 5
Peebles, 6,049 E 5
Penicuik, 10,476 D 2
Penpont, 364 E 5
Perth, 43,098 E 4
Peterculter, 3,226 F 3
Peterhead, 14,846 G 3
Pierowall, ⊙735 E 1
Pitlochry, 2,468 E 4
Pitmedden, 313 F 3
Pittenweem, 1,548 F 4
Plockton, 288 C 3
Poolewe, ⊙1,794 C 3
Port Appin, ⊙2,172 C 4
Port Askaig, ⊙1,795 B 5
Port Bannatyne, 730 A 2
Port Charlotte, 240 B 5
Port Ellen, 932 B 5
Port Glasgow, 22,189 A 2
Portgordon, 814 F 3
Portknockie, 1,217 F 3
Portmahomack, 226 E 3
Portpatrick, 643 C 6
Portree, 1,374 B 3
Portsoy, 1,717 F 3
Port William, 517 D 6
Prestonpans, 3,272 D 1
Prestwick, 13,218 D 5
Queensferry, 5,339 D 1
Reay, 283 E 2
Renfrew, 18,880 B 2
Renton, 3,443 A 1
Rhu, 1,540 A 1
Rhynie, 333 F 3
Rigside, 1,195 E 5
Rosehearty, 1,220 F 3
Rosneath, 946 A 1
Rothes, 1,240 E 3
Rothesay, 6,285 A 2
Rutherglen, 24,091 B 2
Saint Abbs, 203 F 5
Saint Andrews, 12,837 F 4
Saint Combs, 738 G 3
Saint Cyrus, 340 F 4
Saint Margaret's Hope, 210 F 2
Saint Monance, 1,205 F 4
Saline, 831 C 1
Saltcoats, 14,861 D 5
Sandbank, 850 A 1
Sandhead, 248 D 6
Sandwick, 603 B 2
Sanquhar, 2,030 D 5
Sauchie, 6,082 C 1
Scalasaig, ⊙137 B 4
Scalloway, 896 G 2
Scarinish, ⊙875 B 4
Scourie, ⊙745 C 2
Scrabster, 273 E 2
Selkirk, 5,635 F 5
Shader, 258 B 2
Shawbost, 458 B 2
Shieldaig, ⊙550 C 3
Shotts, 9,512 C 2
Skateraw, 674 F 3
Skelmorlie, 1,535 A 2
Skipness, ⊙765 C 5
Slamannan, 1,584 C 2
Spean Bridge, 235 D 4
Springholm, 340 E 5
Stanley, 1,385 E 4
Stenhousemuir, 8,203 C 1
Stevenston, 11,786 D 5
Stewarton, 5,165 D 5
Stirling, 29,799 C 1
Stonehaven, 4,837 F 4
Stonehouse, 7,900 D 5
Stornoway, 5,371 B 2
Stow, 485 F 5
Strachan, ⊙390 F 3
Strachur Bay, ⊙678 C 4
Stranraer, 10,174 C 6
Strathaven, 5,464 D 5
Strathpeffer, 874 D 3
Strichen, 962 F 3
Stromeferry, ⊙1,724 C 3
Stromness, 1,680 E 2
Strontian, ⊙764 C 4
Struan, ⊙772 B 3
Swinton, 235 F 5
Tain, 2,057 D 3
Tarbert, Strathclyde, 1,391 C 5
Tarbert, W. Isles, 479 B 3
Tarbolton, 2,224 D 5
Tarland, 452 F 3
Tayport, 2,848 F 4
Thornhill, Central, 443 D 4
Thornhill, Dumf. & Gall., 1,510 E 5
Thurso, 9,113 E 2
Tillicoultry, 4,320 C 1
Tobermory, 652 B 4
Tolob, ⊙2,033 G 2
Tomatin, 214 D 3
Tomintoul, 306 E 3
Torphins, 499 F 3
Tradespark, 425 E 3
Tranent, 7,212 F 5
Troon, 11,656 D 5
Tullibody, 6,082 C 1
Turriff, 3,051 F 3
Tweedsmuir, ⊙105 E 5
Twynholm, 274 D 6
Tyndrum, ⊙1,153 D 4
Uddingston, 5,278 B 2
Uig, Highland, 103 B 3
Uig, W. Isles, ⊙1,948 A 2
Ullapool, 807 C 3
Uphall, 3,035 C 2
Viewpark, 9,812 C 2
Walkerburn, 842 F 5
Watten, 347 E 2
Wemyss Bay, 323 A 2
West Barns, 659 F 5
West Calder, 2,005 C 2
West Kilbride, 3,883 D 5
West Linton, 705 D 2
Whitburn, 11,647 C 2
Whitehills, 875 F 3
Whithorn, 990 D 6
Whiting Bay, 352 C 5
Wick, 7,804 E 2
Wigtown, 1,118 D 6
Winchburgh, 2,409 D 1
Yetholm, 435 F 5

OTHER FEATURES

A'Chralaig (mt.) C 3
Ailsa Craig (isl.), 3 C 5
Almond (riv.) E 4
Annan (riv.) E 5
Appin (dist.), 2,006 C 4
Ardgour (dist.), 315 C 4
Ardle (riv.) E 4
Ardnamurchan (pen.), 764 B 4
Argyll (dist.), 4,940 C 4
Arkaig, Loch (lake) C 4
Arran (isl.), 3,564 C 5
Askival (mt.) B 4
Assynt (dist.), 833 C 2
Athol (dist.), 1,082 D 4
Atlantic Ocean B 2
Avon (riv.) C 1
Avon (riv.) E 3
Awe, Loch (lake) C 4
Ayr (riv.) D 5
Ayr, Heads of (cape) D 5
Badenoch (dist.), 2,717 D 4
Baleshare (isl.), 64 A 3
Balmoral Castle E 3
Barra (sound) A 3
Barra (isl.), 1,005 A 4
Barra (head) A 4
Barra Isles (isls.), 1,092 A 4
Battock (mt.) F 4
Beauly (riv.) D 3
Beinn Dearg (mt.) D 3
Beinn a Ghlo (mt.) E 4
Bell Rock (isl.), 3 F 4
Ben Alder (mt.) D 4
Ben Avon (mt.) E 3
Benbecula (isl.), 1,355 A 3
Ben Cruachan (mt.) C 4
Ben Lawers (mt.) D 4
Ben Lui (mt.) D 4
Ben Macdhui (mt.) E 3
Ben Mhor (mt.) A 3
Ben More (mt.) B 4
Ben More (mt.) D 4
Ben More Assynt (mt.) D 2
Ben Nevis (mt.) D 4
Bernera (isl.), 276 B 2
Berneray (isl.), 131 A 3
Berneray (isl.), 6 A 4
Bidean nam Bian (mt.) D 4
Black Isle (pen.), 7,209 D 3
Blackwater (res.) D 4
Boisdale, Loch (inlet) A 3
Bracadale, Loch (inlet) B 3
Braemar (dist.), 7,624 E 3
Breadalbane (dist.), 3,649 D 4
Bressay (isl.), 248 G 2
Broad (bay) B 2
Broad Law (mt.) E 5
Broom, Loch (inlet) C 3
Brough Ness (prom.) F 2
Buchan (dist.), 40,089 F 3
Buddon Ness (prom.) F 4
Burray (isl.), 209 F 2
Burrow (head) D 6
Bute (isl.), 8,423 C 5
Bute (sound) C 5
Butt of Lewis (prom.) B 2
Cairn Gorm (mt.) E 3
Cairngorm (mts.) E 3
Cairn Toul (mt.) E 3
Caledonian (canal) D 3
Canna (isl.), 22 B 3
Carn Ban (mt.) D 3
Carn Eige (mt.) C 3
Carrick (dist.), 21,425 D 5
Carron (riv.) C 1
Carron (riv.) C 3
Cheviot (hills) F 5
Cheviot, The (mt.) F 5
Clisham (mt.) B 3
Clyde (riv.) D 5
Clyde (firth) D 5
Coll (isl.), 144 B 4
Colonsay (isl.), 137 B 4
Copinsay (isl.), 3 F 2
Cowal (dist.), 15,548 C 4
Creag Meagaidh (mt.) D 4
Cromarty (firth) D 3
Cuillin (hills) B 3
Cuillin (sound) B 3
Dee (riv.) D 5
Dee (riv.) F 3
Dennis (head) F 1
Deveron (riv.) F 3
Don (riv.) F 3
Doon (riv.) D 5
Dornoch (firth) E 3
Duirinish (dist.), 1,085 B 3
Duncansby (head) F 2
Dunnet (head) E 2
Earn (riv.) E 4
Earn, Loch (lake) D 4
Eday (isl.), 179 F 1
Eddrachillis (bay) C 2
Eden (riv.) F 4
Egilsay (isl.), 39 F 1
Eigg (isl.), 69 B 4
Eil, Loch (lake) C 4
Eishort, Loch (inlet) B 3
Enard (bay) C 2
Eriboll, Loch (inlet) D 2
Ericht, Loch (lake) D 4
Eriskay (isl.), 219 A 3
Erisort, Loch (inlet) B 2
Esk (riv.) F 5
Etive, Loch (inlet) C 4
Ewe, Loch (inlet) C 3
Eye (pen.), 850 B 2
Fair Isle (isl.), 65 F 3
Fetlar (isl.), 88 G 2
Fife Ness (prom.) F 4
Findhorn (riv.) E 3
Flannan (isls.), 3 A 2
Formartine (dist.), 10,768 F 3
Forth (riv.) B 1
Forth (firth) F 4
Forth and Clyde (canal) B 2
Foula (isl.), 33 F 2
Fyne, Loch (inlet) C 5
Galloway (dist.), 54,972 D 5
Galloway, Mull of (prom.) D 6
Gare Loch (inlet) A 1
Garioch (dist.), 6,863 F 3
Garry, Loch (lake) D 3
Gigha (isl.), 174 C 5
Girdle Ness (prom.) G 3
Glass (riv.) D 3
Glen More (dist.), 55,035 D 3
Goat Fell (mt.) C 5
Gometra (isl.), 10 B 4
Grampian (mts.) D 4
Great Cumbrae (isl.), 1,296 A 2
Gruinard (bay) C 3
Hallandale (riv.) E 2
Harris (sound) A 3
Harris (dist.), 2,175 B 3
Hebrides (sea) B 3
Hebrides, Inner (isls.), 14,881 B 4
Hebrides, Outer (isls.), 29,615 A 3
Helmsdale (riv.) E 2
Herma Ness (prom.) G 2
Holy (isl.), 10 C 5
Holy Loch (inlet) A 1
Hoy (isl.), 419 E 2
Inchcape (Bell Rock) (isl.), 3 F 4
Inchkeith (isl.), 3 D 1
Indaal, Loch (inlet) B 5
Inner (sound) C 3
Inner Hebrides (isls.), 14,881 B 4
Iona (isl.), 145 B 4
Isla (riv.) E 4
Islay (isl.), 3,816 B 5
Jura (isl.), 210 C 5
Jura (sound) C 5
Katrine, Loch (lake) D 4
Kerrera (isl.), 27 C 4
Kilbrannan (sound) C 5
Kinnairds (head) G 3
Kintyre (pen.), 10,077 C 5
Kintyre, Mull of (prom.) C 5
Knapdale (dist.), 4,082 C 5
Kyle of Tongue (inlet) D 2
Laggan (bay) B 5
Lammermuir (hills) F 5
Lennox (hills) B 1
Leven (lake) E 4
Leven, Loch (inlet) D 4
Lewis (dist.), 20,047 B 2
Liddel Water (riv.) F 5
Linnhe, Loch (inlet) C 4
Lismore (isl.), 166 C 4
Little Minch (sound) B 3
Lochaber (dist.), 13,813 D 4
Lochnagar (mt.) E 4
Lochy, Loch (lake) D 3
Lomond, Loch (lake) D 4
Long, Loch (inlet) D 4
Lorne (dist.), 12,162 C 4
Lorne (firth) C 4
Loyal, Loch (lake) D 2
Luce (bay) D 6
Luing (isl.), 151 C 4
Lyon (riv.) D 4
Machers, The (pen.), 6,192 D 6
Mainland (isl.), 12,747 E 1
Mainland (isl.), 12,944 G 2
Mar (dist.), 23,931 F 3
Maree, Loch (lake) C 3
May, Isle of (isl.), 10 F 4
Merrick (mt.) D 5
Minginish (dist.), 772 B 3
Moidart (dist.), 155 C 4
Monach (sound) A 3
Monadhliath (mts.) D 3
Moorfoot (hills) E 5
Moray (firth) E 3
Moriston (riv.) D 3
Morven (dist.), 398 C 4
Morven (mt.) E 2
Muck (isl.), 24 B 4
Muckle Flugga (isl.), 3 G 2
Mull (isl.), 2,024 C 4
Mull (head) F 1
Mull (sound) C 4
Nairn (riv.) D 3
na Keal, Loch (inlet) B 4
Naver (riv.) D 2
Ness, Loch (lake) D 3
Nevis, Loch (inlet) C 3
Nith (riv.) E 5
North (chan.) C 5
North (sound) F 1
North (sound) G 4
North Esk (riv.) F 4
North Minch (sound) B 3
North Ronaldsay (isl.), 134 F 1
North Uist (isl.), 1,469 A 3
Oa, Mull of (prom.) B 5
Ochil (hills) E 4
Oich (riv.) D 3
Orchy (riv.) D 4
Orkney (isls.), 17,675 F 1
Oronsay (isl.), 2 B 4
Outer Hebrides (isls.), 29,615 A 3
Oykel (riv.) D 3
Pabbay (isl.), 4 A 3
Papa Stour (isl.), 24 F 2
Papa Westray (isl.), 106 F 1
Paps of Jura (mt.) C 5
Park (dist.), 210 B 2
Peel Fell (mt.) F 5
Pentland (hills) D 2
Pentland (firth) E 2
Pladda (isl.), 2 C 5
Quoich, Loch (lake) C 3
Raasay (isl.), 163 C 3
Rannoch (dist.), 1,177 D 4
Rannoch, Loch (lake) D 4
Rhinns, The (pen.), 8,295 C 6
Roag, Loch (inlet) B 2
Rona (isl.), 3 B 3
Ross of Mull (pen.), 585 B 4
Rousay (isl.), 181 E 1
Rudha Hunish (cape) B 3
Rudh Re (cape) C 3
Rum (isl.), 40 B 3
Ryan, Loch (inlet) C 5
Saint Kilda (isl.), 65 A 2
Saint Magnus (bay) F 2
Sanda (isl.), 9 C 5
Sanday (isl.), 11 B 3
Sanday (isl.), 592 F 1
Scalpay (isl.), 483 B 3
Scalpay (isl.), 5 C 3
Scapa Flow (chan.) E 2
Scarp (isl.), 12 A 2
Scridain, Loch (inlet) B 4
Scurdie Ness (prom.) F 4
Seaforth, Loch (inlet) B 3
Seil (isl.), 326 C 4
Sgurr a'Choire Ghlais (mt.) D 3
Sgurr Alasdair (mt.) B 3
Sgurr Mor (mt.) C 3
Sgurr na Lapaich (mt.) C 3
Shapinsay (isl.), 346 F 1
Shetland (isls.), 18,494 G 2
Shiant (sound) B 3
Shiel, Loch (lake) C 4
Shin (falls) D 3
Shin, Loch (lake) D 2
Shona (isl.), 17 C 4
Sidlaw (hills) E 4
Sinclair's (bay) E 2
Skye, Isle of (isl.), 7,183 B 3
Sleat (pt.) B 4
Sleat (dist.), 449 C 3
Small Isles (isls.), 171 B 4
Snizort, Loch (inlet) B 3
Soay (isl.), 5 B 3
Solway (firth) E 6
South Esk (riv.) F 4
South Ronaldsay (isl.), 776 F 2
South Uist (isl.), 2,281 A 3
Spean (riv.) D 4
Spey (riv.) E 3
Start (pt.) F 1
Stinchar (riv.) D 5
Strathbogie (dist.), 7,959 F 3
Strathmore (valley) E 4
Strathspey (dist.), 6,668 E 3
Strathy (pt.) E 2
Stroma (isl.), 8 E 2
Stronsay (isl.), 436 F 1
Sumburgh (head) G 2
Sunart, Loch (inlet) C 4
Swona (isl.), 3 E 2
Taransay (isl.), 5 A 3
Tarbat Ness (prom.) E 3
Tarbert, East Loch (inlet) B 3
Tarbert, Loch (inlet) B 5
Tarbert, West Loch (inlet) A 3
Tay (riv.) E 4
Tay (firth) F 4
Tay, Loch (lake) D 4
Teith (riv.) D 4
Teviot (riv.) F 5
Thurso (riv.) E 2
Tiree (isl.), 875 B 4
Tolsta (head) B 2
Tor Ness (prom.) E 2
Torridon, Loch (inlet) C 3
Trossachs, The (valley) D 4
Trotternish (dist.), 1,948 B 3
Tweed (riv.) F 5
Tyne (riv.) F 5
Ulva (isl.), 23 B 4
Unst (isl.), 1,124 G 2
Vaternish (dist.), 162 B 3
Vatersay (isl.), 77 A 4
West Burra (isl.), 501 G 2
Westray (firth) E 1
Westray (isl.), 735 E 1
Whalsay (isl.), 870 G 2
White Coomb (mt.) E 5
Wigtown (bay) D 6
Wrath (cape) C 2
Wyre (isl.), 36 F 1
Yarrow (riv.) E 5
Yell (isl.), 1,143 G 2
Ythan (riv.) F 3

★Population of met. area
⊙Population of parish.

Agriculture, Industry and Resources

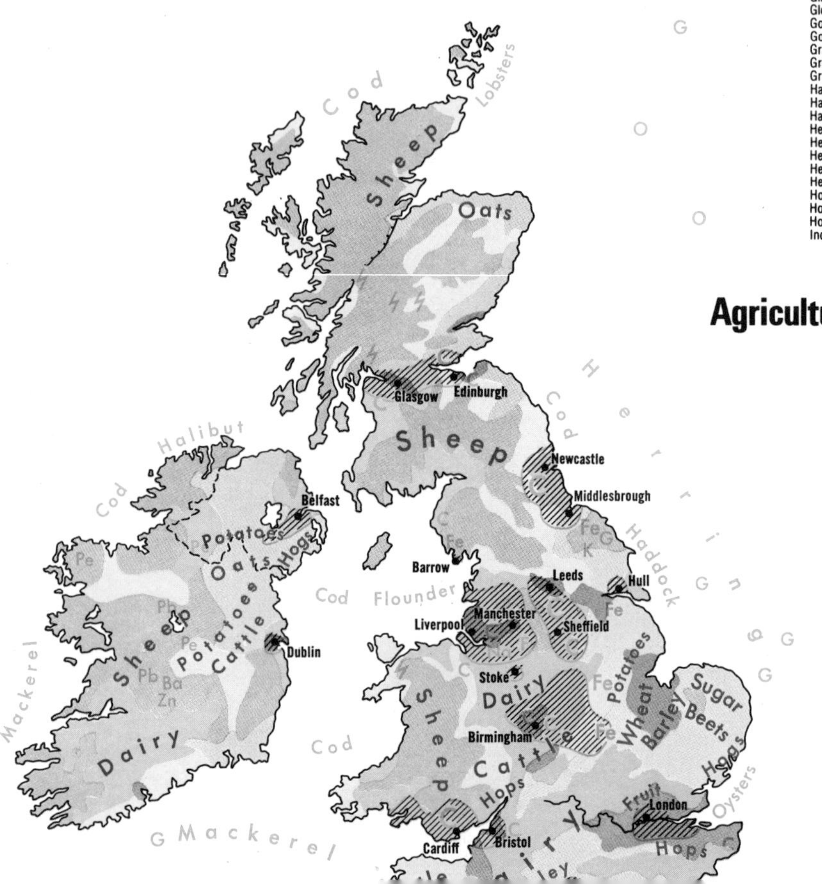

DOMINANT LAND USE

- Cereals (chiefly oats, barley)
- Truck Farming, Horticulture
- Dairy, Mixed Farming
- Livestock, Mixed Farming
- Pasture Livestock

MAJOR MINERAL OCCURRENCES

Ba Barite	Na Salt
C Coal	O Petroleum
F Fluorspar	Pb Lead
Fe Iron Ore	Pe Peat
G Natural Gas	Sn Tin

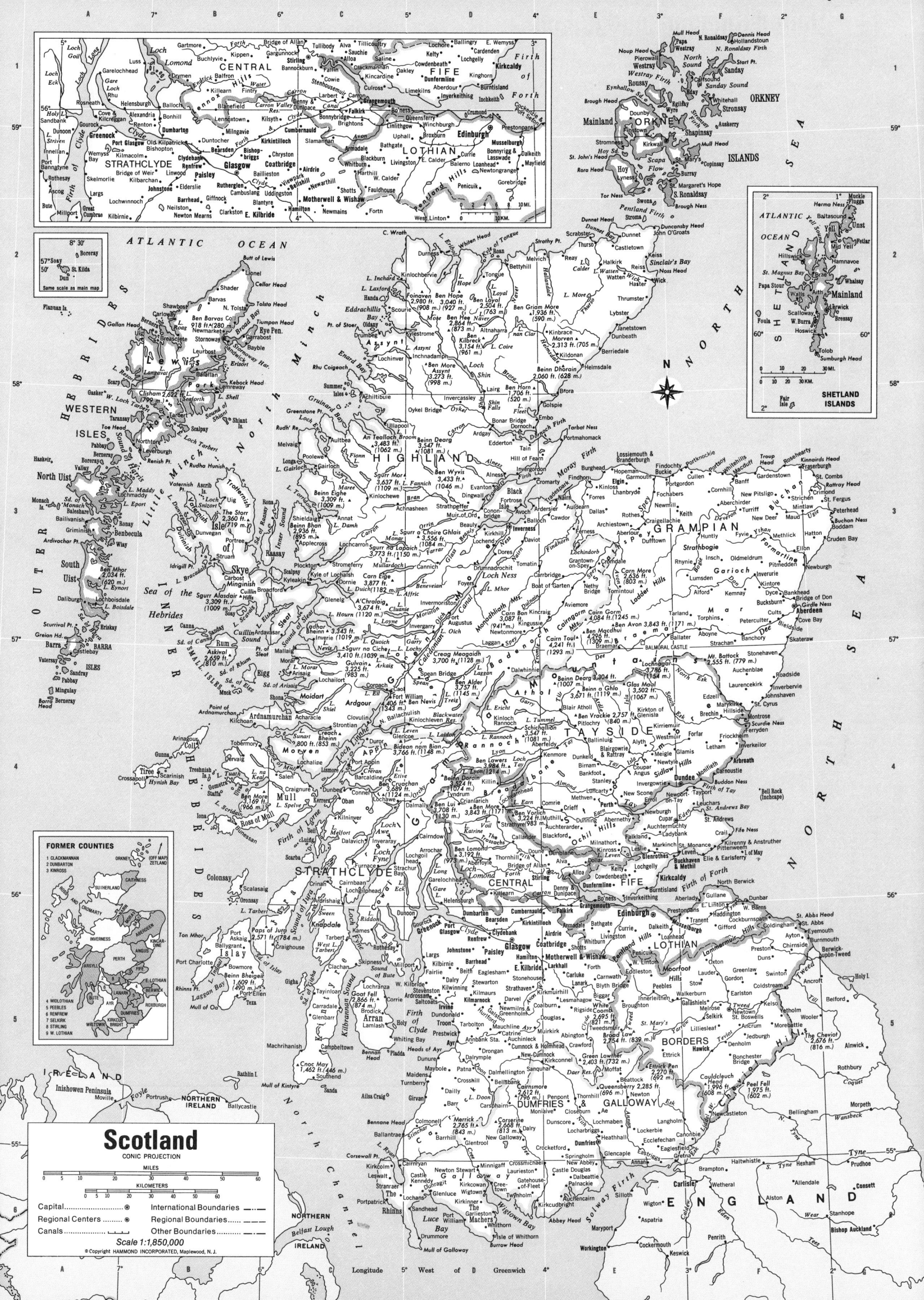

Scotland

CONIC PROJECTION

Scale 1:1,850,000

© Copyright HAMMOND INCORPORATED, Maplewood, N.J.

Capital ⊛
Regional Centers ⊚
Canals ⎯⎯⎯
International Boundaries ⎯ ⎯
Regional Boundaries ⎯ ⎯
Other Boundaries ⎯⎯⎯

FORMER COUNTIES

1 CLACKMANNAN
2 DUNBARTON
3 KINROSS
4 MIDLOTHIAN
5 PEEBLES
6 RENFREW
7 SELKIRK
8 STIRLING
9 W. LOTHIAN

IRELAND

COUNTIES

Carlow, 34,237 H 6
Cavan, 52,618 G 4
Clare, 75,008 D 6
Cork, 352,883 D 7
Donegal, 108,344 K 2
Dublin, 852,219 J 5
Galway, 149,223 D 5
Kerry, 112,772 B 7
Kildare, 71,977 H 5
Kilkenny, 61,473 G 6
Laoighis, 45,259 G 6
Leitrim, 28,360 E 3
Leix (Laoighis), 45,259 G 6
Limerick, 140,459 D 7
Longford, 28,250 F 4
Louth, 74,951 J 4
Mayo, 109,525 C 4
Meath, 71,729 H 4
Monaghan, 46,242 H 3
Offaly, 51,829 F 5
Roscommon, 53,519 E 4
Sligo, 50,275 D 3
Tipperary, 123,565 F 6
Waterford, 77,315 F 7
Westmeath, 53,570 G 5
Wexford, 86,351 H 7
Wicklow, 66,295 J 5

CITIES and TOWNS

Abbeydorney, 188 B 7
Abbeyfeale, 1,337 C 7
Abbeylara, ‡290 F 4
Abbeyleix, 1,033 G 6
Achill Sound, ‡1,163 B 4
Aclare, ‡336 D 3
Adare, 545 D 6
Aghada-Farsid-Rostellan, 461 E 8
Aghadoe, ‡497 B 7
Aghagower, ‡693 C 4
Ahascragh, 221 E 5
Annagry, 201 E 1
Annascaul, 236 B 7
An Uaimh, 4,605 H 4
An Uaimh, *6,665 H 4
Ardagh, Limerick, 213 C 7
Ardagh, Longford, ‡974 F 4
Ardara, 683 E 2
Ardee, *3,183 H 4
Ardee, 3,096 H 4
Ardfert, 286 B 7
Ardfinnan, 510 F 7
Ardmore, 233 F 8
Ardrahan, ‡239 D 5
Arklow, 6,948 J 6
Arthurstown, 1,188 H 7
Arva, 370 F 4
Ashford, 341 J 5
Askeaton, 844 D 6
Athboy, 705 H 4
Athea, 328 C 7
Athenry, 1,240 D 5
Athleague, ‡955 E 4
Athlone, 9,825 F 5
Athlone, *11,611 F 5
Athy, 4,270 H 6
Athy, *4,654 H 6
Aughrim, 451 J 6
Avoca, ‡620 J 6
Bagenalstown (Muinebeag), 2,321 H 6
Baile Átha Cliath (Dublin) (cap.), 567,866 K 5
Bailieborough, 1,293 G 4
Balbriggan, 3,741 J 4
Balla, 293 C 4
Ballaghaderreen, 1,121 E 4
Ballina, Mayo, 6,063 C 3
Ballina, *6,369 C 3
Ballina, Tipperary, 336 E 6
Ballinagh, 459 G 4
Ballinakill, 300 G 6
Ballineen D 8
Ballinamore, 808 F 3
Ballinasloe, 5,969 E 5
Ballincollig-Carrigrohane, 2,110 D 8
Ballindine, 232 C 4
Ballingarry, Limerick, 422 D 7
Ballingarry, Tipperary, ‡574 F 6
Ballinlough, 242 D 4
Ballinrobe, 1,272 C 4
Ballintober, ‡867 E 4
Ballintra, 197 E 2
Ballisodare, 486 E 3
Ballivor, 287 H 4
Ballybay, 754 G 3
Ballybay, *1,159 G 3
Ballybofey-Stranorlar, 2,214 F 2
Ballybunion, 1,287 B 7
Ballycanew, ‡460 J 6
Ballycarney, ‡294 J 6
Ballycastle, ‡724 C 3
Ballyconnell, 421 F 3
Ballycotton, 389 F 8
Ballydehob, 253 C 8
Ballyduff, 406 B 7
Ballygar, 359 E 4
Ballygeary, 726 J 7
Ballyhaise, 274 G 3
Ballyhaunis, 1,093 D 4
Ballyheigue, 450 B 7
Ballyjamesduff, 673 G 4
Ballylanders, 266 E 7
Ballylongford, 504 B 6
Ballymahon, 707 F 4
Ballymakeery, 272 C 8
Ballymore, ‡447 F 5
Ballymore Eustace, 433 J 5
Ballymote, 952 D 3
Ballyporeen, ‡810 E 7
Ballyragget, 519 G 6
Ballyroan, ‡478 G 6
Ballyshannon, 2,325 E 3
Ballytore, ‡580 H 5
Baltimore, 200 C 9
Baltinglass, 909 H 6
Baltray, 236 J 4
Banagher, 1,052 F 5
Bandon, 2,257 D 8
Bandon, *4,071 D 8
Bannow, ‡798 H 7
Bansha, 184 E 7
Bantry, 2,579 C 8
Barna, ‡1,734 C 5
Belmullet, 744 B 3
Belturbet, 1,092 G 3
Bennettsbridge, 367 G 6
Birr, 3,319 F 5
Birr, *3,881 F 5
Blanchardstown, 3,279 H 5
Blarney, 1,128 D 8
Blessington, 637 J 5
Boherbue, 372 C 7
Borris, 430 H 6
Borris-in-Ossory, 276 F 6
Borrisokane, 769 E 6
Borrisoleigh, 471 E 6
Boyle, 1,727 E 4
Boyle, *1,939 E 4
Bray, 14,467 K 5
Bray, *15,841 K 5
Brí Chualann (Bray), 14,467 K 5
Broadford, 226 C 7
Brosna, 250 C 7
Bruff, 547 D 7
Bruree, 243 D 7
Bunbeg-Derrybeg, 878 E 1
Bunclody-Carrickduff, 929 H 6
Buncrana, 2,955 G 1
Buncrana, *3,334 G 1
Bundoran, 1,337 E 3
Burtonport, ‡1,288 E 2
Buttevant, 1,045 D 7
Cahir, 1,747 F 7
Cahirciveen, 1,547 A 8
Callan, 1,283 G 7
Camolin, 306 J 6
Campile, 231 H 7
Cappamore, 567 E 6
Cappawhite, 305 E 6
Cappoquin, 872 F 7
Carbury, ‡894 H 5
Carlingford, 559 J 3
Carlow, 9,588 H 6
Carlow, *10,399 H 6
Carndonagh, 1,146 G 1
Carnew, 570 H 6
Carrickmacross, 2,100 H 4
Carrickmacross, *2,475 H 4
Carrick-on-Shannon, 1,854 F 4
Carrick-on-Suir, 5,006 F 7
Carrigaholt, ‡493 B 6
Carrigaline, 951 E 8
Carrigallen, 230 F 4
Carrigart, ‡753 F 1
Carrigtwohill, 622 E 8
Carrowkeel, ‡326 G 1
Cashel, 2,692 F 7
Castlebar, 5,979 C 4
Castlebar, *6,476 C 4
Castlebellingham, 407 J 4
Castleblayney, 2,118 H 3
Castleblayney, *2,395 H 3
Castlecomer-Donaguile, 1,244 G 6
Castledermot, 583 H 6
Castlefin, 610 F 2
Castlegregory, 216 A 7
Castleisland, 1,929 B 7
Castlemartyr, 491 E 8
Castlepollard, 693 G 4
Castlerea, 1,752 D 4
Castletown, ‡504 F 6
Castletownbere, 812 B 8
Castletownroche, 399 D 7
Castletownshend, 170 C 9
Causeway, 215 B 7
Cavan, 3,273 G 3
Cavan, *4,312 G 3
Ceanannus Mór, 2,391 G 4
Ceanannus Mór, *2,653 G 4
Celbridge, 1,568 H 5
Charlestown-Bellahy, 677 D 4
Charleville (Rathluirc), 2,232 D 7
Clara, 2,156 F 5
Claregalway, ‡594 D 5
Claremorris, 1,718 C 4
Clashmore, ‡379 F 8
Clifden, 790 B 5
Cloghan, 404 F 5
Clogh-Chatsworth, 324 G 6
Clogheen, 530 F 7
Clogherhead, 649 J 4
Clonakilty, 2,430 D 8
Clonaslee, 285 F 5
Clondalkin, 7,009 J 5
Clonegal, 202 H 6
Clones, 2,164 G 3
Clonfert, ‡430 E 5
Clonmany, ‡936 G 1
Clonmel, 11,622 F 7
Clonmel, *12,291 F 7
Clonmellon, 328 H 4
Clonroche, 222 H 7
Clontuskert, 351 E 4
Cloone, ‡460 F 4
Cloughjordan, 480 E 6
Cloyne, 654 E 8
Coachford, 290 D 8
Cóbh, 6,076 E 8
Cóbh, *7,141 E 8
Coill Dubh, 920 H 5
Collon, 262 J 4
Collooney, 546 E 3
Cong, 233 C 4
Convoy, 654 F 2
Coolaney, ‡352 D 3
Coolgreany, ‡603 J 6
Cootehill, 1,415 G 3
Cootehill, *1,542 G 3
Cork, 128,645 E 8
Cork, *134,430 E 8
Corofin, 342 C 6
Courtmacsherry, 210 D 8
Courtown Harbour, 291 J 6
Creeslough, 269 F 1
Crookhaven, ‡400 B 9
Croom, 756 D 6
Crosshaven, 1,222 E 8
Crossmolina, 1,077 C 3
Crusheen, ‡405 D 6
Culdaff, ‡621 G 1
Daingean, 492 G 5
Delvin, 223 G 4
Dingle, 1,401 A 7
Doaghbeg, ‡701 F 1
Donabate, 426 J 5
Donegal, 1,725 F 2
Doneraile, 799 D 7
Dooagh-Keel, 649 A 4
Doon, 387 E 6
Douglas, ‡4,448 D 8
Drimoleague, 415 C 8
Drishane, ‡1,548 C 7
Drogheda, 19,762 J 4
Drogheda, *20,095 J 4
Droichead Nua, 5,053 H 5
Droichead Nua, *6,444 H 5
Dromahair, 177 E 3
Drumcar, ‡1,215 J 4
Drumconrath, ‡1,044 H 4
Drumkeerin, ‡467 E 3
Drumlish, 205 F 4
Drumshanbo, 576 E 3
Dublin (cap.), 567,866 K 5
Dublin, *679,748 K 5
Duleek, 658 J 4
Duncannon, 228 H 7
Dundalk, 21,672 H 3
Dundalk, *23,816 H 3
Dunfanaghy, 303 F 1
Dungarvan, 5,583 F 7
Dungloe, 940 E 2
Dunkineely, 288 E 2
Dún Laoghaire, 53,171 K 5
Dún Laoghaire, *98,379 K 5
Dunlavin, 423 H 5
Dunleer, 855 J 4
Dunmanway, 1,392 C 8
Dunmore, 522 D 4
Dunmore East, 656 G 7
Dunshaughlin, ‡283 H 5
Durrow, Laoighis, 596 G 6
Durrow, Offaly, ‡441 F 5
Easky, 184 D 3
Edenderry, 2,953 G 5
Edenderry, *3,116 G 5
Elphin, 489 E 4
Emyvale, 281 G 3
Ennis, 5,972 D 6
Ennis, *10,840 D 6
Enniscorthy, 5,704 J 7
Enniscorthy, *6,642 J 7
Enniskerry, 772 J 5
Ennistymon, 1,013 C 6
Eyrecourt, 314 E 5
Fahan, ‡1,023 G 1
Falcarragh, 506 E 1
Feakle, ‡398 D 6
Fenit, 360 B 7
Ferbane, 1,064 F 5
Fermoy, 3,237 E 7
Fermoy, *4,033 E 7
Ferns, 712 J 6
Fethard, Tipperary, 1,064 F 7
Fethard, Wexford, ‡637 H 7
Foxford, 868 C 4
Foynes, 624 C 6
Frankford (Kilcormac), 1,089 F 5
Frenchpark, ‡693 E 4
Freshford, 585 G 6
Galbally, 258 E 7
Galway, 27,726 C 5
Galway, *29,375 C 5
Geashill, ‡751 G 5
Glandore, ‡695 C 8
Glanmire-Riverstown, 1,113 E 8
Glanworth, 335 E 7
Glenamaddy, 315 D 4
Glenbeigh, 266 B 7
Glencolumbkille, ‡787 D 2
Glengarriff, 244 C 8
Glenties, 734 E 2
Glenville, ‡264 D 7
Glin, 623 C 6
Golden, ‡640 F 7
Gorey, 2,946 J 6
Gorey, *3,024 J 6
Gormanston, ‡1,384 J 4
Gort, 975 D 5
Gowran, 402 G 6
Graiguenamanagh-Tinnahinch, 1,303 H 6
Granard, 1,054 F 4
Greencastle, 322 H 1
Greenore, 882 J 4
Greystones-Delgany, 4,517 K 5
Gurteen, 165 D 3
Hacketstown, 574 H 6
Headford, 673 C 5
Holycross, ‡902 F 6
Hospital, 525 E 7
Inchigeelagh, ‡516 C 8
Inishannon, 190 D 8
Inistioge, 179 G 7
Inniscrone, 582 C 3
Johnstown, 303 G 6
Kanturk, 2,063 D 7
Keel-Dooagh, 649 A 4
Kells, ‡423 G 6
Kells (Ceanannus Mór), 2,391 G 4
Kenmare, 903 B 8
Kilbaha, ‡471 B 6
Kilbeggan, 635 G 5
Kilcar, 273 D 2
Kilcock, 827 H 5
Kilconnell, ‡629 E 5
Kilcoole, 679 K 5
Kilcormac, 1,089 F 5
Kilcullen, 880 H 5
Kildare, 3,137 H 5
Kildysart, 239 C 6
Kilfenora, ‡441 C 6
Kilfinane, 561 D 7
Kilgarvan, 228 B 8
Kilkee, 1,287 B 6
Kilkelly, 225 D 4
Kilkenny, 9,838 G 6
Kilkenny, *13,306 G 6
Killala, 368 C 3
Killaloe, 871 D 6
Killarney, 7,184 C 7
Killarney, *7,541 C 7
Killavullen, 221 D 7
Killenaule, 592 F 6
Killeshandra, 432 F 3
Killimor, 221 E 5
Killinaboy, ‡297 C 6
Killorglin, 1,150 B 7
Killucan-Rathwire, 290 G 4
Killybegs, 1,094 E 2
Kilmacrennan, 274 F 1
Kilmacthomas, 396 G 7
Kilmallock, 1,170 D 7
Kilmeadan, ‡262 G 7
Kilmihill, 284 C 6
Kilmoganny, 181 G 7
Kilmore Quay, 273 H 7
Kilmurry, ‡387 C 6
Kilnaleck, 273 G 4
Kilronan, 243 B 5
Kilrush, 2,671 C 6
Kilsheelan, ‡665 F 7
Kiltimagh, 978 C 4
Kilworth, 360 E 7
Kingscourt, 1,016 H 4
Kingstown (Dún Laoghaire), 53,171 K 5
Kinlough, 160 E 3
Kinnegad, 362 G 5
Kinnitty, ‡420 F 5
Kinsale, 1,622 D 8
Kinsale, *1,989 D 8
Kinvara, 293 D 5
Knightstown, 236 A 8
Knock, ‡1,202 D 4
Knocklong, 248 D 7
Knocknagashel, 168 C 7
Labasheeda, ‡468 C 6
Laghey, ‡625 E 2
Lahinch, 455 C 6
Lanesborough-Ballyleague, 906 E 4
Laracor, ‡404 H 4
Laytown-Bettystown-Mornington, 1,882 J 4
Leenane, ‡271 B 4
Leighlindridge, 379 H 6
Leitrim, ‡544 F 3
Leixlip, 2,402 H 5
Letterkenny, 4,930 F 2
Letterkenny, *5,207 F 2
Lifford, 1,121 F 2
Limerick, 57,161 D 6
Limerick, *63,002 D 6
Liscarroll, 231 D 7
Lisdoonvarna, 459 C 5
Lismore, 884 F 7
Lismore, *1,041 F 7
Listowel, 3,021 C 7
Littleton, 322 F 6
Longford, 3,876 F 4
Longford, *4,791 F 4
Lorrha, ‡685 E 5
Loughrea, 3,075 E 5
Louisburgh, 310 B 4
Louth, 208 J 4
Lucan-Doddsborough, 4,245 J 5
Luimneach (Limerick), 57,161 D 6
Lusk, 553 J 4
Macroom, 2,256 C 8
Malahide, 3,834 J 5
Malin, ‡552 G 1
Mallow, 5,901 D 7
Mallow, *6,506 D 7
Manorhamilton, 858 E 3
Manulla, ‡660 C 4
Maryborough (Portlaoighise), 3,902 G 5
Maynooth, 1,296 H 5
Meathas Truim, 546 G 4
Midleton, 3,075 E 8
Midleton, *4,666 E 8
Milford, 763 F 1
Millstreet, 1,319 D 7
Milltown, 260 A 7
Miltown-Malbay, 677 C 6
Minard, ‡397 A 7
Mitchelstown, 2,783 E 7
Moate, 1,378 F 5
Mohill, 868 F 4
Monaghan, 5,256 G 3
Monasterevan, 1,619 H 5
Moneygall, 282 F 6
Monivea, ‡405 D 5
Mooncoin, 413 G 7
Mount Bellew, 275 D 5
Mountcharles, 445 E 2
Mountmellick, 2,595 G 5
Mountmellick, *2,864 G 5
Mountrath, 1,098 F 5
Moville, 1,089 G 1
Moycullen, ‡498 C 5
Moynalty, ‡583 H 4
Muff, 240 G 1
Muinebeag, 2,321 H 6
Mullagh, 293 H 4
Mullaghmore, ‡629 D 3
Mullinahone, 262 F 7
Mullinavat, 343 G 7
Mullingar, 6,790 G 4
Mullinger, *9,245 G 4
Naas, 5,078 H 5
Navan (An Uaimh), 4,605 H 4
Nenagh, 5,085 E 6
Nenagh, *5,174 E 6
Newbliss, ‡547 G 3
Newbridge (Droichead Nua), 5,053 H 5
Newcastle, 2,549 D 7
Newcastle, *2,680 D 7
Newmarket, 886 C 7
Newmarket-on-Fergus, 1,052 D 6
New Pallas, ‡1,271 E 6
Newport, Mayo, 420 C 4
Newport, Tipperary, 582 E 6
New Ross, 4,775 H 7
New Ross, *5,153 H 7
Newtownforbes, ‡495 F 4
Newtownmountkennedy, 882 J 5
Newtownsandes, 268 C 6
O'Briensbridge-Montpelier, 237 D 6
Oldcastle, 759 G 4
Old Leighlin, ‡309 G 6
Oola, 348 E 6
Oranmore, 440 D 5
Oughterard, 628 C 5
Passage East, 408 G 7
Passage West, 2,709 E 8
Patrickswell, 415 D 6
Pettigo, 332 F 2
Piltown, 456 G 7
Portarlington, 3,117 G 5
Portlaoighise, 3,902 G 5
Portlaoighise, *6,470 G 5
Portlaw, 1,166 G 7
Portmarnock, 1,726 J 5
Portumna, 913 E 5
Queenstown (Cóbh), 6,076 E 8
Rahan, ‡531 F 5
Ramelton, 807 F 1
Raphoe, 945 F 2
Rathangan, 868 G 5
Rathcoole, 1,740 J 5
Rathcormac, 191 E 7
Rathdowney, 892 F 6
Rathdrum, 1,141 J 6
Rathgormuck, ‡231 F 7
Rathkeale, 1,543 D 7
Rathluirc, 2,232 D 7
Rathmore, 437 J 5
Rathmullen, 486 F 1
Rathnew-Merrymeeting, 954 J 6
Rathowen, ‡294 F 4
Rathvilly, 230 H 6
Ratoath, 300 J 5
Riverstown, 236 E 3
Rockcorry, 233 H 3
Rosapenna, ‡822 F 1
Roscommon, 1,556 E 4
Roscommon, *2,821 E 4
Roscrea, 3,855 F 6
Rosscarbery, 309 C 8
Rosses Point, 464 D 3
Rosslare, 588 J 7
Rosslare Harbour (Ballygeary), 725 J 7
Roundstone, 204 A 5
Roundwood, 260 J 5
Rush, 2,633 J 4
Saint Johnston, 463 F 2
Scarriff, 619 E 6
Schull, 457 B 8
Scotstown, 264 H 3
Shanagolden, 231 C 6
Shannon Airport, 3,657 D 6
Shannon Bridge, 188 F 5
Shercock, 313 G 4
Shillelagh, 246 J 6
Shinrone, 365 F 5
Shrule, 288 C 4
Sixmilebridge, 567 D 6
Skerries, 3,044 J 4
Skibbereen, 2,104 C 8
Slane, 483 H 4
Sligo, 14,080 E 3
Sligo, *14,456 E 3
Sneem, 285 B 8
Spiddal, ‡819 C 5
Stepaside, 748 J 5
Stradbally, Laoighis, 891 G 5
Stradbally, Waterford, 158 F 7
Strokestown, 563 E 4
Swanlinbar, 257 F 3
Swinford, 1,105 C 4
Swords, 4,133 J 5
Taghmon, 369 H 7
Tallaght, 6,174 J 5
Tallow, 883 F 7
Tarbert, 485 C 6
Teltown, ‡739 H 4
Templemore, 2,174 F 6
Templetuohy, 197 F 6
Termonfeckin, 328 J 4
Thomastown, 1,270 G 7
Thurles, 6,840 F 6
Thurles, *7,087 F 6
Timoleague, 257 D 8
Tinahely, 450 H 6
Tipperary, 4,631 E 7
Tipperary, *4,717 E 7
Toomevara, 272 E 6
Tralee, 12,287 B 7
Tralee, *13,263 B 7
Tramore, 3,792 G 7
Trim, 1,700 H 4
Trim, *2,255 H 4
Tuam, 3,808 D 4
Tuam, *4,952 D 4
Tubbercurry, 959 D 3
Tulla, 415 D 6
Tullamore, 6,809 G 5
Tullamore, *7,474 G 5
Tullaroan, ‡301 G 6
Tullow, 1,838 H 6
Tullow, *1,945 H 6
Tynagh, ‡452 E 5
Tyrrellspass, 289 G 5
Urlingford, 652 F 6
Virginia, 583 G 4
Waterford, 31,968 G 7
Waterford, *33,676 G 7
Waterville, 547 A 8
Westport, 3,023 C 4
Wexford, 11,849 H 7
Wexford, *13,293 H 7
Whitegate, 370 E 8
Wicklow, 3,786 K 6
Wicklow, *3,915 K 6
Woodenbridge, ‡620 J 6
Woodford, 198 E 5
Youghal, 5,445 F 8
Youghal, *5,626 F 8

OTHER FEATURES

Achill (isl.), 3,129 A 4
Allen (lake) E 3
Allen, Bog of (marsh) H 5
Aran (isl.), 773 D 2
Aran (isls.), 1,499 B 5
Arklow (bank) K 6
Arrow (lake) E 3
Awbeg (riv.) D 7
Ballinskelligs (bay) A 8
Ballycotton (bay) F 8
Ballyheige (bay) B 7
Ballyhoura (hills) E 7
Ballyteige (bay) H 7
Bandon (riv.) D 8
Bann (riv.) J 6
Bantry (bay) B 8
Barrow (riv.) H 7
Baurtregaum (mt.) A 7
Bear (isl.), 288 B 8
Blacksod (bay) A 3
Blackstairs (mt.) H 6
Blackwater (riv.) D 7
Blackwater (riv.) H 4
Blasket (isls.) A 7
Bloody Foreland (prom.) E 1
Blue Stack (mts.) E 2
Boderg (lake) E 4
Boggeragh (mts.) D 7
Boyne (riv.) J 4
Brandon (head) A 7
Bride (riv.) E 7
Broad Haven (harb.) B 3
Brosna (riv.) F 5
Bull, The (isl.), 5 A 8
Caha (mts.) B 8
Carlingford (inlet) J 3
Carnsore (pt.) J 7
Carrantuohill (mt.) B 7
Clare (riv.) D 5
Clare (isls.), 168 A 4
Clear (cape) B 9
Clear (isl.), 192 C 9
Clew (bay) B 4
Comeragh (mts.) F 7
Conn (lake) C 3
Connacht (prov.), 390,902 C 4
Connemara (dist.), 7,599 B 5
Cork (harb.) E 8
Corrib (lake) C 5
Courtmacsherry (bay) D 8
Curragh, The H 5
Dee (riv.) H 4
Deel (riv.) D 7
Deele (riv.) F 2
Derg (lake) E 6
Derravaragh (lake) G 4
Derryveagh (mts.) E 2
Dingle (bay) A 7
Donegal (bay) D 3
Drum (hills) F 7
Dublin (bay) J 5
Dundalk (bay) J 4
Dunmanus (bay) B 8
Dursey (isl.), 38 A 8
Ennell (lake) G 5
Erne (riv.) E 3
Errigal (mt.) E 1
Erris (head) A 3
Fanad (head) F 1
Fastnet Rock (isl.), 3 B 9
Feale (riv.) C 7
Fergus (riv.) D 6
Finn (riv.) F 2
Finn (riv.) G 3
Flesk (riv.) C 7
Foyle (inlet) G 1
Foyle (riv.) G 2
Galley (head) D 9
Galtee (mts.) E 7
Galtymore (mt.) E 7
Galway (bay) C 5
Gara (lake) D 4
Garadice (lake) F 3
Gill (lake) E 3
Glyde (riv.) H 4
Golden Vale (plain) E 7
Gorumna (isl.), 1,108 B 5
Gowna (lake) G 4
Grand (canal) G 5
Greenore (pt.) J 7
Gweebarra (bay) D 2
Hags (head) B 6
Helvick (head) G 7
Hook (head) H 7
Horn (head) E 1
Iar Connacht (dist.), 10,774 C 5
Inishbofin (isl.), 236 A 4
Inishbofin (isl.), 103 E 1
Inisheer (isl.), 313 B 5
Inishmaan (isl.), 319 C 5
Inishmore (isl.), 864 B 5
Inishowen (head) H 1
Inishowen (pen.), 24,109 G 1
Inishtrahull (isl.), 3 G 1
Inishturk (isls.), 83 A 4
Inny (riv.) A 8
Inny (riv.) F 4
Inver (bay) E 2
Ireland's Eye (isl.) K 5
Irish (sea) K 4
Joyce's Country (dist.), 2,021 B 4
Kenmare (riv.) A 8
Kerry (head) A 7
Key (lake) E 3
Kilkieran (bay) B 5
Killala (bay) C 3
Killary (harb.) A 4
Kinsale (harb.) E 8
Kippure (mt.) J 5
Knockboy (mt.) B 8
Knockmealdown (mts.) F 7
Lady's Island Lake (inlet) J 7
Lambay (isl.), 24 K 4
Laune (riv.) B 7
Leane (lake) B 7
Leane (lake) G 4
Lee (riv.) D 8
Leinster (mt.) H 6
Leinster (prov.), 1,498,140 G 5
Lettermullan (isl.), 221 B 5
Liffey (riv.) H 5
Liscannor (bay) B 6
Long Island (bay) B 9
Loop (head) A 6
Lugnaquillia (mt.) J 5
Macgillicuddy's Reeks (mts.) B 7
Macnean (lake) F 3
Maigue (riv.) D 6
Maine (riv.) C 7
Malin (head) F 1
Mask (lake) C 4
Maumturk (mts.) B 5
Melvin (lake) E 3
Mizen (head) B 9
Moher (cliffs) B 6
Monavullagh (mts.) F 7
Moy (riv.) C 3
Mulkear (riv.) E 6
Mullaghareirk (mts.) C 7
Mulroy (bay) F 1
Munster (prov.), 882,002 D 7
Mweelrea (mt.) B 4
Mweenish (isl.), 198 B 5
Nagles (mts.) E 7
Nenagh (riv.) E 6
Nephin (mt.) C 3
Nore (riv.) G 7
North (sound) B 5
Omey (isl.), 34 A 5
Oughter (lake) G 3
Ovoca (riv.) J 6
Owenmore (riv.) D 3
Owey (isl.), 51 D 1
Paps, The (mt.) C 7
Partry (mts.) C 4
Pollaphuca (res.) J 5
Punchestown H 5
Rathlin O'Birne (isl.), 3 C 2
Ree (lake) F 5
Roaringwater (bay) B 9
Rosses (bay) D 1
Rosskeeragh (pt.) D 3
Royal (canal) G 4
Saint Finan's (bay) A 8
Saint George's (chan.) K 7
Saint John's (pt.) D 2
Saltee (isls.) H 7
Seven (heads) D 8
Seven Hogs, The (isls.) A 7
Shannon (riv.) E 6
Sheeffry (hills) B 4
Sheelin (lake) G 4
Sheep Haven (harb.) F 1
Sheeps (head) B 8
Sherkin (isl.), 82 C 9
Silvermine (mts.) E 6
Slaney (riv.) H 7
Slieve Aughty (mts.) D 5
Slieve Bloom (mts.) F 5
Slieve Gamph (mts.) D 3
Slievenaman (mt.) F 7
Sligo (bay) D 3
Slyne (head) A 5
South (sound) C 5
Stacks (mts.) B 7
Suck (riv.) E 5
Suir (riv.) G 7
Swilly (inlet) F 1
Tara (hill) H 4
Tory (isl.), 273 E 1
Tory (sound) E 1
Tralee (bay) B 7
Trawbreaga (bay) F 1
Ulster (part) (prov.), 207,204 G 2
Valencia (Valentia) (isl.), 770 A 8
Valentia (isl.), 770 A 8
Waterford (harb.) G 7
Wexford (bay) J 7
Wicklow (head) K 6
Wicklow (mts.) J 6
Youghal (bay) F 8

NORTHERN IRELAND

DISTRICTS

Antrim, 37,600 J 2
Ards, 52,100 K 2
Armagh, 47,500 H 3
Ballymena, 52,200 J 2
Ballymoney, 22,700 J 1
Bainbridge, 28,800 J 3
Belfast, 368,200 J 2
Carrickfergus, 27,500 K 2
Castlereagh, 63,600 K 2
Coleraine, 44,900 H 1
Cookstown, 27,500 H 2
Craigavon, 71,200 J 3
Down, 48,800 K 3
Dungannon, 43,000 H 3
Fermanagh, 50,900 F 3
Larne, 29,000 K 2
Limavady, 25,000 H 1
Lisburn, 80,800 J 2
Londonderry, 86,600 G 2
Magherafelt, 32,200 H 2
Mourne (Newry and Mourne), 75,300 J 3
Moyle, 13,400 J 1
Newtownabbey, 71,500 J 2
North Down, 59,600 K 2
Omagh, 41,800 G 2
Strabane, 35,500 G 2

CITIES and TOWNS

Ahoghill, ‡1,929 J 2
Annalong, 1,001 K 3
Antrim, 8,351 J 2
Ardglass, 1,052 K 3
Armagh, 13,606 H 3
Armoy, ‡1,051 J 1
Augher, ‡1,986 G 3
Aughnacloy, ‡1,885 H 3
Ballycastle, 2,899 J 1
Ballyclare, 5,155 J 2
Ballygawley, ‡2,165 G 3
Ballykelly, 1,116 G 1
Ballymena, 23,386 J 2
Ballymoney, 5,697 J 1
Ballynahinch, 3,485 J 3
Banbridge, 7,968 J 3
Bangor, 35,260 K 2
Belfast (cap.), 353,700 J 2
Belfast, *551,940 J 2
Bellaghy, ‡2,265 H 2
Belleek, ‡2,487 E 3
Beragh, ‡2,137 G 2
Bessbrook, 2,619 J 3
Brookeborough, ‡2,534 G 3
Broughshane, 1,288 J 2
Bushmills, 1,288 J 1
Caledon, ‡1,828 H 3
Carnlough, 1,416 J 2
Carrickfergus, 16,603 K 2
Carrowdore, 2,548 K 2
Castledawson, 1,162 H 2
Castlederg, 1,766 F 2
Castlewellan, 1,488 K 3
Claudy, ‡2,507 G 2
Clogher, ‡1,888 G 3
Coalisland, 3,614 H 2
Coleraine, 16,354 H 1
Comber, 5,575 K 2
Cookstown, 6,965 H 2
Craigavon, 12,740 J 3
Crossgar, 1,098 K 3
Crossmaglen, 1,085 H 3
Crumlin, 1,450 J 2
Cullybackey, 1,649 J 2
Derrygonnelly, ‡2,539 F 3
Dervock, ‡1,191 J 1
Donaghadee, 4,008 K 2
Downpatrick, 7,918 K 3
Draperstown, ‡2,247 H 2
Dromore, Bainbridge, 2,848 J 3
Dromore, Omagh, ‡2,224 G 3
Drumquin, ‡1,982 F 2
Dundrum, ‡2,245 K 3
Dungannon, 8,190 H 3
Dungiven, 1,536 H 2
Dunnamanagh, ‡2,242 G 2
Ederny and Kesh, ‡2,497 F 2
Enniskillen, 9,679 F 3
Feeny, ‡1,459 H 2
Fintona, 1,190 G 3
Fivemiletown, ‡1,649 G 3
Garvagh, ‡2,363 H 2
Gilford, 1,592 J 3
Glenarm, ‡1,728 J 2
Glenavy, ‡2,360 J 2
Glynn, ‡1,872 K 2
Gortin, ‡2,033 G 2
Greyabbey, ‡2,646 K 2
Hillsborough, 1,021 J 3
Holywood, 9,892 K 2
Irvinestown, 1,457 F 3
Keady, 2,145 H 3
Kells, ‡2,560 J 2
Kesh, ‡2,497 F 3
Kilkeel, 4,090 K 3
Killough, ‡3,295 K 3
Killyleagh, 2,359 K 3
Kilrea, 1,196 H 2
Kircubbin, 1,075 K 3
Larne, 18,482 K 2
Limavady, 6,004 H 1
Lisburn, 31,836 J 2
Lisnaskea, 1,443 G 3
Londonderry, 51,200 G 2
Loughbrickland, ‡2,056 J 3
Maghera, 2,085 H 2
Magherafelt, 4,704 H 2
Markethill, ‡2,352 H 3
Millisle, 1,172 K 2
Moneymore, 1,178 H 2
Moy, ‡2,349 H 3
Moygashel, 1,086 H 3
Newcastle, 4,647 J 3
Newry, 20,279 J 3
Newtownabbey, 58,114 K 2
Newtownards, 15,484 K 2
Newtownbutler, ‡2,663 G 3
Newtownhamilton, ‡1,936 H 3
Newtownstewart, 1,433 G 2
Omagh, 14,594 G 2
Pomeroy, ‡1,786 H 2
Portaferry, 1,730 K 3
Portavogie, 1,310 K 3
Portglenone, ‡2,061 H 2
Portrush, 5,376 H 1
Portstewart, 5,085 H 1
Randalstown, 2,799 J 2
Rathfriland, 1,886 J 3
Rostrevor, 1,617 J 3
Saintfield, ‡2,198 K 3
Sion Mills, 1,588 G 2
Sixmilecross, ‡1,980 G 2
Stewartstown, ‡1,759 H 2
Strabane, 9,413 G 2
Strangford, ‡1,987 K 3
Tandragee, 1,725 J 3
Tempo, ‡2,282 G 3
Trillick, ‡2,167 G 3
Warrenpoint, 4,291 J 3
Whitehead, 2,642 K 2

OTHER FEATURES

Bann (riv.) H 2
Belfast (inlet) K 2
Blackwater (riv.) H 3
Bush (riv.) H 1
Derg (riv.) F 2
Divis (mt.) J 2
Dundrum (bay) K 3
Erne (lake) F 3
Foyle (inlet) G 1
Foyle (riv.) G 2
Giant's Causeway H 1
Lagan (riv.) K 2
Larne (inlet) K 2
Magee, Island (pen.), 1,581 K 2
Magilligan (pt.) H 1
Main (riv.) J 2
Mourne (mts.) J 3
Mourne (riv.) G 2
Neagh (lake) J 2
North (chan.) K 1
Rathlin (isl.), 109 J 1
Red (bay) K 1
Roe (riv.) H 1
Saint John's (pt.) K 3
Slieve Donard (mt.) K 3
Sperrin (mts.) G 2
Strangford (inlet) K 3
Torr (head) K 1
Ulster (part) (prov.), 1,537,200 G 2
Upper Lough Erne (lake) F 3

*City and suburbs.
‡Population of district.

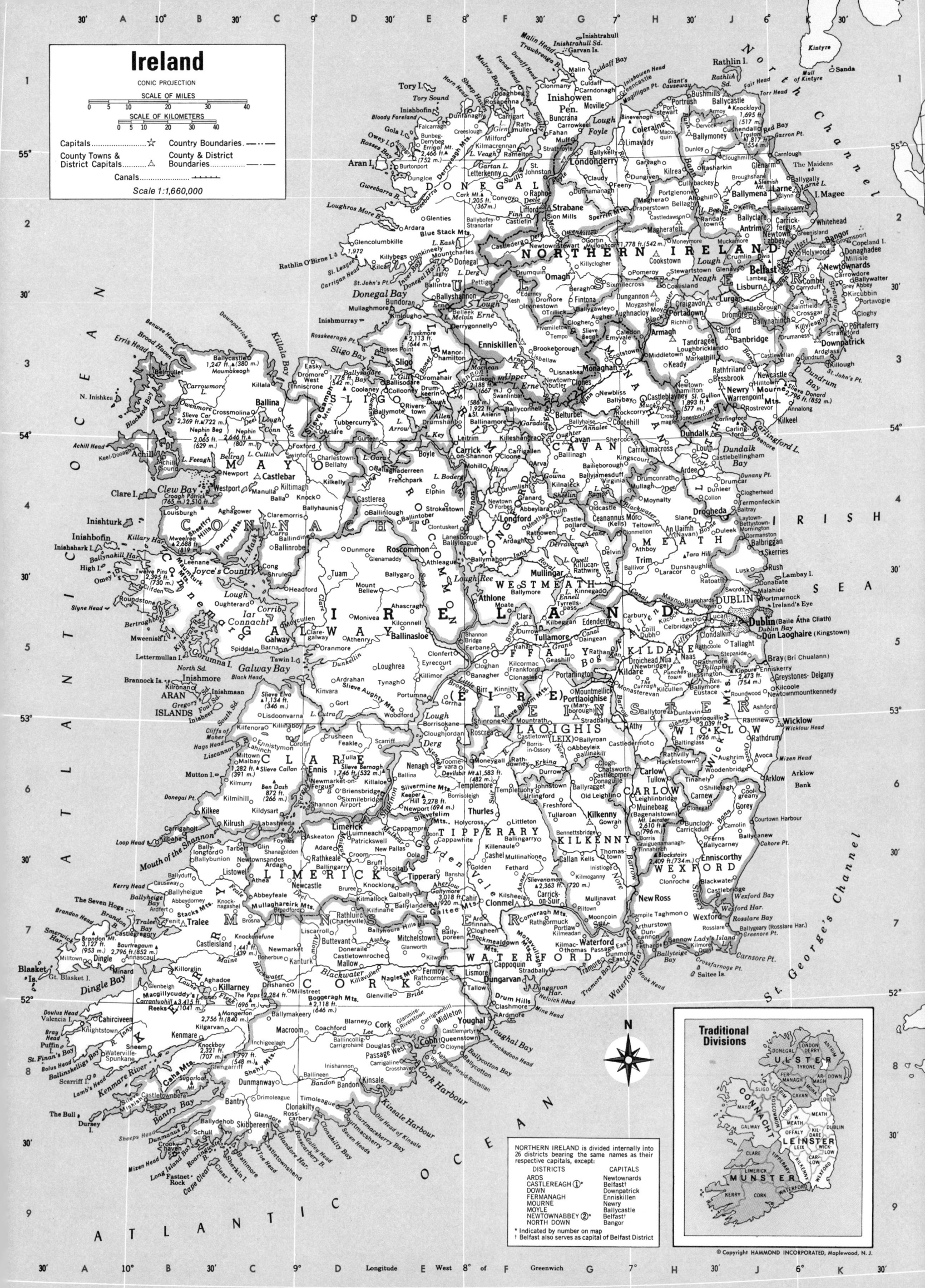

Svalbard

Norway, Sweden, Finland and Denmark

CONIC PROJECTION

SCALE OF MILES
0   50   100   150

SCALE OF KILOMETERS
0   50   100   150   200

Capitals of Countries .... ☆
Administrative Centers .... △
International Boundaries ....
Internal Boundaries ....
Canals ....

Scale 1:7,440,000

SUBDIVISIONS
Indicated by Numbers

Counties in NORWAY
1 Akershus   G 6
2 Vestfold   G 7
3 Østfold   G 7
4 Oslo   G 7

Oslo is the administrative
center for Akershus and
Oslo County.

Counties in SWEDEN
5 Göteborg och
   Bohus   G 7
6 Västmanland   G 7
7 Södermanland   K 7
8 Östergötland   H 7
9 Malmöhus   H 9
10 Kristianstad   J 8

© Copyright HAMMOND INCORPORATED, Maplewood, N.J.

AREA 125,053 sq. mi.
(323,887 sq. km.)
POPULATION 4,092,000
CAPITAL Oslo
LARGEST CITY Oslo
HIGHEST POINT Glittertinden
8,110 ft. (2,472 m.)
MONETARY UNIT krone
MAJOR LANGUAGE Norwegian
MAJOR RELIGION Protestantism

AREA 173,665 sq. mi.
(449,792 sq. km.)
POPULATION 8,320,000
CAPITAL Stockholm
LARGEST CITY Stockholm
HIGHEST POINT Kebnekaise 6,946 ft.
(2,117 m.)
MONETARY UNIT krona
MAJOR LANGUAGE Swedish
MAJOR RELIGION Protestantism

AREA 130,128 sq. mi.
(337,032 sq. km.)
POPULATION 4,788,000
CAPITAL Helsinki
LARGEST CITY Helsinki
HIGHEST POINT Haltiatunturi
4,343 ft. (1,324 m.)
MONETARY UNIT markka
MAJOR LANGUAGES Finnish, Swedish
MAJOR RELIGION Protestantism

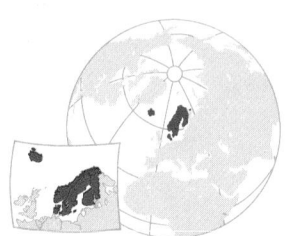

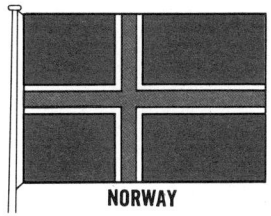

NORWAY

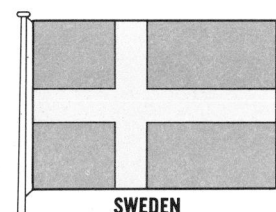

SWEDEN

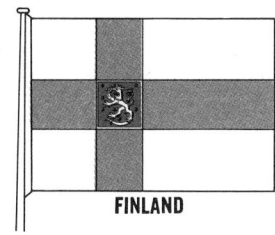

FINLAND

FINLAND

PROVINCES

Ahvenanmaa 22,380	L6
Åland (Ahvenanmaa) 22,380	L6
Häme 662,500	O6
Keski-Suomi 241,770	O5
Kuopio 252,023	P5
Kymi 346,478	O6
Lappi 196,792	P3
Mikkeli 211,453	P6
Oulu 406,309	P4
Pohjois-Karjala 179,065	Q5
Turku ja Pori 697,988	N6
Uusimaa 1,085,625	O6
Vaasa 425,283	N5

CITIES and TOWNS

Äänekoski 10,725	O5
Åbo (Turku) 164,857	N6
Alavus 10,285	N5
Borgaå 18,740	O6
Ekenäs 7,391	N6
Espoo 117,090	O6
Forssa 18,442	N6
Haapajärvi 7,791	O5
Hämeenlinna 40,761	O6
Hamina 11,055	O6
Hangö 10,374	N7
Hanko (Hangö) 10,374	N7
Harjavalta 8,445	M6
Heinola 15,350	P6
Helsinki (cap.) 502,961	O6
Helsinki* 794,746	O6
Huutokoski† 6,458	P5
Hyvinkää 35,865	O6
Iisalmi 21,159	P5
Ikaalinen 8,364	N6
Imatra 35,590	Q6
Ivalo 2,661	P2
Jakobstad 20,397	N5
Jämsä 12,526	O6
Järvenpää 16,259	O6
Joensuu 41,429	R5
Jyväskylä 61,209	O5
Jyväskylä* 84,185	O5
Kajaani 20,583	P4
Kalajoki 3,624	N4
Kankaanpää 12,564	M6
Karhula 21,834	O6
Karis 8,152	N6
Karjaa (Karis) 8,152	N6
Karkkila 8,678	N6
Kauniainen 6,219	O6
Kauttua 3,297	M6
Kelloselkä† 8,200	Q3
Kemi 27,893	O4
Kemijärvi 12,951	P3
Kerava 19,966	O6
Kokemäki 10,188	N6
Kokkola 22,096	N5
Kotka 34,026	P6
Kotka* 60,235	P6
Kouvola 29,383	P6
Kouvola* 59,507	P6
Kristiinankaupunki	
(Kristinestad) 9,331	N5
Kristinestad 9,331	N5
Kuhmo 4,150	Q4
Kuopio 71,684	P5
Kurikka 11,177	M5
Kuusamo 4,449	Q4
Kuusankoski 22,342	P6
Lahti 94,864	O6
Lahti* 112,129	O6
Pudasjärvi† 12,594	P4
Raahe 15,379	O4
Raisio 14,271	M6
Rauma 29,081	M6
Riihimäki 24,106	O6
Rovaniemi 28,411	O3
Saarijärvi 2,714	O5
Salo 19,176	N6
Savonlinna 28,336	Q6
Seinäjoki 22,123	N5
Sodankylä 3,304	P3
Sotkamo 2,316	Q4
Suolahti 5,936	O5
Suonenjoki 9,286	P5
Tammisaari (Ekenäs) 7,391	N6
Tampere 168,118	N6
Tampere* 220,920	N6
Toijala 8,080	N6
Tornio 19,971	O4
Turku 164,857	N6
Turku* 217,423	N6
Turtola† 5,852	O3
Ulvila† 8,040	N6
Uusikaarlepyy	
(Nykarleby) 7,408	N5
Uusikaupunki 11,915	M6
Vaasa 54,402	M5
Vaasa* 58,224	M5
Valkeakoski 22,588	N6
Vammala 16,363	N6
Varkaus 24,450	Q5
Vasa (Vaasa) 54,402	M5
Vuotso† 10,186	P2
Ylivieska 10,827	O4

OTHER FEATURES

Åland (isls.)	L6
Baltic (sea)	K9
Bothnia (gulf)	M5
Finland (gulf)	P7
Hailuoto (isl.)	O4
Haltiatunturi (mt.)	M2
Hangöudd (prom.)	N7
Haukivesi (lake)	Q5
Iijoki (riv.)	O4
Inari (lake)	P2
Ivalojoki (riv.)	P2
Juojärvi (lake)	Q5
Kalajoki (riv.)	N4
Kallavesi (lake)	P5
Karlö (Hailuoto) (isl.)	O4
Keitele (lake)	O5
Kemijärvi (lake)	Q3
Kemijoki (riv.)	O3
Kiantajärvi (lake)	Q4
Kilpisjärvi (lake)	M2
Kitinen (riv.)	P3
Kivijärvi (lake)	O5
Koitere (lake)	R5
Kuusamojärvi (lake)	Q4
Längelmävesi (lake)	O6
Lapland (reg.)	O2
Lappajärvi (lake)	O5
Lestijärvi (lake)	N5
Lokka (res.)	O3
Muojärvi (lake)	R4
Muonio (riv.)	M2
Näsijärvi (lake)	N6
Onkivesi (lake)	P5
Orihvesi (lake)	Q5
Oulujärvi (lake)	P4
Oulujoki (riv.)	O4
Ounasjoki (riv.)	O3
Päijänne (lake)	O6
Pielinen (lake)	Q5
Puruvesi (lake)	Q6
Puulavesi (lake)	P5
Pyhäjärvi (lake)	O5
Pyhäjärvi (lake)	M6
Saimaa (lake)	Q6
Siikajoki (riv.)	O4
Simojärvi (lake)	P3
Simojoki (riv.)	O4
Tana (riv.)	P2
Tornio (riv.)	O3
Valigrund (isl.)	M5
Ylikitka (lake)	Q3

NORWAY

COUNTIES

Akershus 355,196	G6
Aust-Agder 86,216	E7
Buskerud 209,684	F6
Finnmark 79,373	O2
Hedmark 183,465	G6
Hordaland 386,492	E6
Møre og Romsdal 231,944	E5
Nordland 243,233	F4
Nord-Trøndelag 122,886	H4
Oppland 178,250	F6
Oslo (city) 462,732	D3
Østfold 228,546	G7
Rogaland 287,653	E7
Sogn og Fjordane 103,135	E6
Sør-Trøndelag 241,361	G5
Telemark 158,853	F7
Troms 144,111	L2
Vest-Agder 131,659	E7
Vestfold 182,433	G7

CITIES and TOWNS

Ålesund 40,868	D5
Ålgård 2,322	D7
Alta 5,582	N2
Åndalsnes 2,574	F5
Årdalstangen 2,360	F6
Arendal 11,701	E7
Arendal* 21,228	F7
Årnes 2,267	G6
Askim 8,413	E4
Bamble† 7,031	F7
Bergen 213,434	D6
Bodø 31,077	J3
Borge† 3,294	H2
Brønnøysund 3,130	G4
Dombås 1,114	F5
Drammen 50,777	C4
Drammen* 56,521	C4
Egersund 6,805	D7
Eidsvoll 2,906	D4
Eigersund 11,379	D7
Elverum 7,391	G6
Farsund 8,908	E7
Flekkefjord 8,750	E7
Florø 8,822	D6
Fredrikstad 29,024	D4
Fredrikstad* 51,141	D4
Gjøvik 25,963	G6
Grimstad 13,091	F7
Halden 27,087	G6
Hamar 16,418	G6
Hamar* 25,138	G6
Hammerfest 7,610	N1
Hammerfest* 8,005	N1
Harstad 21,125	K2
Haugesund 27,386	P7
Haugesund* 29,277	D7
Hermansverk 706	E6
Holmestrand 8,246	C4
Holmsbu 273	D4
Honningsvåg 3,780	N1
Horten 13,746	D4
Horten* 17,246	D4
Kirkenes 4,466	Q2
Kongsberg 19,854	C4
Kongsvinger 16,146	H6
Kopervik 4,221	D7
Kornsjøt 6,079	G7
Kragerø 5,249	F7
Kristiansand 59,488	F8
Kristiansund 18,847	E5
Kvinnherad† 2,898	E6
Larvik 9,907	C4
Larvik* 19,202	D4
Lenvik† 11,098	L2
Levanger 5,066	G5
Lillehammer 21,248	C3
Lillesand 3,028	F7
Lillestrøm† 11,550	D3
Lysaker† 81,612	D3
Mandal 11,579	E7
Meråker† 2,907	G5
Mo 21,033	J3
Molde 20,334	E5
Mosjøen 9,341	H4
Moss 25,786	D4
Moss* 27,430	D4
Mysen 3,760	D4
Namsos 11,452	G4
Narvik 19,582	K2
Nesttun† 11,519	D6
Nittedal† 8,889	D3
Notodden 12,970	F7
Nøtterøy 11,944	C4
Ny-Ålesund	C2
Odda 7,401	E6
Oppdal 2,173	F5
Oslo (cap.) 462,732	D3
Oslo* 645,413	D3
Porsgrunn 31,709	C4
Rakkestad 2,392	D4
Ringerike 30,156	C4
Risør 6,089	F7
Rjukan 5,334	F7
Røros 3,041	G5
Sandefjord 33,350	C4
Sandnes 33,934	D7
Sandvika† 34,337	C3
Sarpsborg 12,889	D4
Sarpsborg* 36,449	D4
Seljet 3,386	D5
Ski 9,081	D4
Skien 47,105	F7
Stavanger 86,639	D7
Stavern 2,604	D4
Steinkjer 20,553	G4
Stor-Elvdal† 2,993	G6
Sunndalsøra 5,114	F5
Svolvær 3,942	J2
Tønsberg 9,964	C4
Tønsberg* 36,374	D4
Tromsø 43,830	L2
Trondheim 134,910	F5
Ullensvang† 2,326	E6
Vadsø 6,019	Q1
Vardø 3,875	R1
Vik 1,019	E6
Volda 3,511	E5
Voss 5,944	E6

OTHER FEATURES

Alsten (isl.)	H4
Andøya (isl.)	J2
Barduelv (riv.)	L2
Bellsund	C2
Bjørnafjorden (fjord)	D6
Bjørnøya (isl.)	D3
Boknafjord (fjord)	D7
Bremanger (isl.)	D6
Dønna (isl.)	H3
Dovrefjell (hills)	F5
Edgeøya (isl.)	E2
Femundsjø (lake)	G6
Folda (fjord)	G4
Folda (fjord)	J3
Frohavet (bay)	F5
Frøya (isl.)	F5
Glittertinden (mt.)	F6
Hardangervidda (plat.)	E6
Hardangerfjord (fjord)	D7
Hinlopenstreten (str.)	C1
Hinnøya (isl.)	K2
Hitra (isl.)	F5
Hopen (isl.)	E2
Isfjorden (fjord)	C2
Jostedalsbreen (glac.)	E6
Kjølen (mts.)	K3
Kongsfjorden (fjord)	B2
Kvaløya (isl.)	O1
Lågen (riv.)	G6
Laksefjorden (fjord)	P1
Langøy (isl.)	J2
Lapland (reg.)	G4
Leka (isl.)	G4
Lofoten (isls.)	H2
Lopphavet (bay)	M1
Magerøya (isl.)	P1
Moskenesøya (isl.)	H3
Namsen (riv.)	H4
Nordaustlandet (isl.)	D1
Nordfjord (fjord)	E6
Nordkapp (pt.)	C1
Nordkinn (headland)	P1
Nordkinn (pen.)	P1
North Cape (Nordkapp) (pt.)	P1
Norwegian (sea)	F3
Ofotfjorden (fjord)	K2
Oslofjord (fjord)	D4
Otra (riv.)	E7
Otterøya (isl.)	E5
Pasvikelv (riv.)	Q2
Platen, Kapp (pt.)	D1
Porsangen (fjord)	O1
Rana (fjord)	H3
Rauma (riv.)	F5
Ringvassøy (isl.)	L2
Romsdalsfjorden (fjord)	E5
Saltfjorden (fjord)	J3
Seiland (isl.)	N1
Senja (isl.)	K2
Skagerrak (str.)	F8
Smøla (isl.)	E5
Sognafjorden (fjord)	D6
Sørkapp (pt.)	C2
Sørøya (isl.)	N1
Spitsbergen (isl.)	C2
Storfjorden (fjord)	D2
Sulitjelma (mt.)	J3
Svalbard (isls.)	C3
Tana (riv.)	P1
Tanafjord (fjord)	P1
Tokke (riv.)	F7
Trondheimsfjorden (fjord)	G5
Tyrifjorden (fjord)	C3
Vaerøy (isl.)	H3
Vågavatn (lake)	F6
Vannøy (isl.)	L1
Varangerhalvøya (pen.)	Q1
Varangerfjord (fjord)	Q1
Vega (isl.)	G4
Vesterålen (isls.)	J2
Vestfjord (fjord)	H3
Vestvågøya (isl.)	H3
Vikna (isls.)	G4

SWEDEN

COUNTIES

Älvsborg 418,150	H7
Blekinge 155,391	J8
Gävleborg 294,595	K6
Göteborg och Bohus 714,660	G7
Gotland 54,447	L8
Halland 219,767	H8
Jämtland 133,559	J5
Jönköping 301,905	H8
Kalmar 240,768	K8
Kopparberg 281,082	J6
Kristianstad 272,090	J8

(continued on following page)

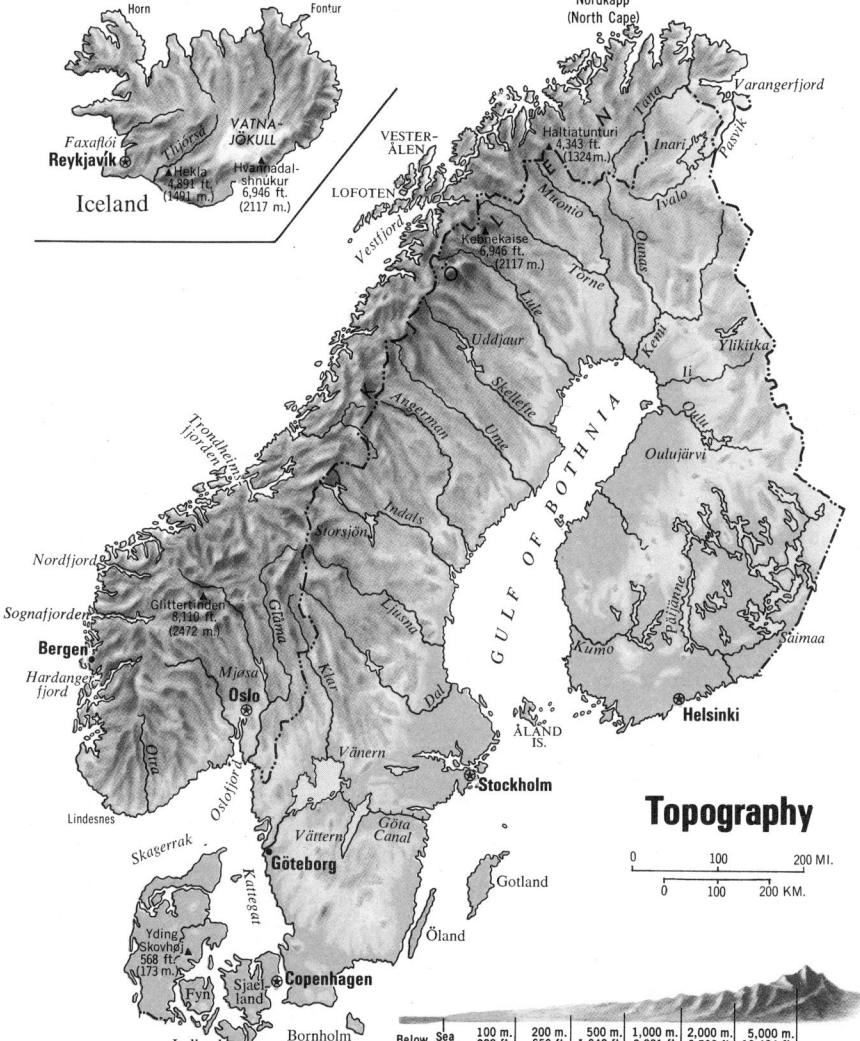

Topography

0 100 200 MI.
0 100 200 KM.

	Below Sea Level	100 m. 328 ft.	200 m. 656 ft.	500 m. 1,640 ft.	1,000 m. 3,281 ft.	2,000 m. 6,562 ft.	5,000 m. 16,404 ft.

(continued)

Kronoberg 169,454 .... J8
Malmöhus 740,137 .... H9
Norrbotten 264,215 .... L3
Örebro 273,994 .... J7
Östergötland 387,104 .... J7
Skaraborg 263,382 .... H7
Södermanland 252,030 .... K7
Stockholm 1,493,052 .... L7
Uppsala 229,879 .... K7
Värmland 284,442 .... H7
Västerbotten 236,367 .... K4
Västernorrland 268,202 .... K5
Västmanland 259,872 .... K7

CITIES and TOWNS

Åhus 6,125 .... J9
Alingsås 18,892 .... H7
Älmhult 7,390 .... H8
Alvesta 7,261 .... J8
Älvsbyn 4,707 .... M4
Åmål 9,556 .... H7
Ånge 3,760 .... J5
Ängelholm 16,016 .... H8
Arboga 11,819 .... J7
Arbrå 2,734 .... K6
Årjäng† 2,596 .... H7
Arvidsjaur 4,194 .... L4
Arvika 13,934 .... H7
Åseda 2,465 .... J8
Askim 17,609 .... G8
Åtvidaberg 8,436 .... K7
Avesta 19,095 .... J6
Bålsta 8,243 .... G1
Båstad 2,452 .... H8
Bengtsfors 3,535 .... H7
Boden 19,590 .... M4
Bollnäs 13,305 .... K6
Bollstabruk 3,548 .... L5
Borås 67,537 .... H8
Borås* 187,710 .... H8
Borgholm 2,789 .... K8
Borlänge 40,158 .... J6
Brunflo 3,460 .... J5
Dalby† 4,013 .... H6
Danderyd† 36,596 .... H1
Dannemora 291 .... K6
Edsbyn 4,388 .... J6
Eksjö 9,686 .... J8
Emmaboda 5,652 .... J8
Enköping 18,541 .... G1
Eskilstuna 66,409 .... K7
Eslöv 13,629 .... H9
Fagersta† 14,778 .... J6
Falkenberg 14,148 .... H8
Falköping 15,126 .... H7
Falun 30,073 .... J6
Färjestaden 2,995 .... K8
Filipstad 7,835 .... H7
Finspång 16,346 .... J7
Flen 6,770 .... K7
Forshaga 6,000 .... H7
Frösö 10,274 .... J5
Frövi 2,583 .... J7
Gällivare 8,669 .... M3
Gamleby 3,666 .... J8
Gävle 67,454 .... K6
Gimo 3,154 .... K6
Gislaved 8,564 .... H8
Gnesta 3,835 .... G2
Göteborg 444,540 .... G8
Göteborg* 690,767 .... G8
Hagfors 8,060 .... H6
Hällefors 7,862 .... J7
Hallsberg 6,799 .... J7
Hallstahammar 13,583 .... K7
Hallstavik 5,162 .... L6
Halmstad 49,558 .... H8
Haparanda 5,031 .... N4
Härnösand 18,971 .... L5
Hässleholm 16,813 .... H8
Hedemora 7,039 .... K6
Helsingborg 80,986 .... H8
Helsingborg* 215,894 .... H8
Hjo 4,615 .... J7
Hofors 11,459 .... K6
Höganäs 10,866 .... H8
Holmsund 5,467 .... M5
Hörnefors 2,441 .... L5
Huddinge 48,339 .... H1
Hudiksvall 15,004 .... K6
Hultsfred 5,763 .... K8
Husum 2,517 .... L5
Hyltebruk 3,469 .... H8
Iggesund 4,448 .... K6
Järna 6,237 .... G2
Jokkmokk 3,186 .... L3
Jönköping 78,650 .... H8
Jönköping* 131,499 .... H8
Kalix 7,668 .... N4
Kalmar 32,049 .... K8
Karlshamn 17,447 .... J8
Karlskoga† 35,425 .... J7
Karlskrona 33,414 .... J8
Karlstad 51,243 .... H7
Katrineholm 22,884 .... K7
Kinna 13,676 .... H8
Kiruna 25,410 .... L3
Kisa 4,323 .... J7
Köping 20,059 .... J7
Kopparberg 3,942 .... J7
Kramfors 7,719 .... L5
Kristianstad 30,780 .... J9
Kristinehamn 21,146 .... H7
Kumla 11,451 .... J7
Kungälv† 12,764 .... G8
Kungsbacka† 11,986 .... G8
Kvissleby 3,413 .... K5
Laholm 3,898 .... H8
Landskrona 29,486 .... H9
Långshyttan 2,744 .... K6
Laxå 5,166 .... J7
Leksand 4,410 .... J6
Lessebo 2,991 .... J8
Lidingö 30,098 .... H1
Lidköping 21,001 .... H7
Lindesberg 8,247 .... J7
Linköping 80,274 .... K7
Linköping* 132,839 .... K7
Ljungby 12,969 .... J8
Ljusdal 7,075 .... J6
Ljusne 3,578 .... K6
Ludvika 18,217 .... J6
Luleå 42,139 .... N4
Lund 55,047 .... H9
Lycksele 8,586 .... L4
Lysekil 7,815 .... G7
Malmberget 10,239 .... M3
Malmö 241,191 .... H9
Malmö* 453,339 .... H9
Malung 6,211 .... H6
Mariefred 2,553 .... F1
Mariestad 16,454 .... H7
Markaryd 4,266 .... H8
Märsta 17,066 .... K7
Marstrand 1,168 .... G8
Mellerud 3,579 .... H7
Mjölby 12,488 .... J7
Mölndal† 47,248 .... H8
Mönsterås 5,005 .... K8
Mora 8,772 .... J6
Motala 29,454 .... J7
Nacka 19,708 .... H1
Nässjö 18,634 .... J8
Nora 5,515 .... J7
Norberg 5,438 .... K6
Norrköping 85,244 .... K7
Norrköping* 163,206 .... K7
Norrtälje 12,784 .... L7
Nybro 13,010 .... J8
Nyköping 30,352 .... K7
Nynäshamn 11,070 .... L7
Ockelbo 2,810 .... K6
Olofström 10,096 .... J8
Örebro 117,877 .... J7
Örebro* 171,440 .... J7
Örnsköldsvik 29,514 .... L5
Orrefors 919 .... J8
Orsa 5,099 .... J6
Oskarshamn 19,021 .... K8
Östersund 40,056 .... J5
Östhammar 1,783 .... L6
Oxelösund 13,862 .... K7
Piteå 16,169 .... M4
Rättvik 4,087 .... J6
Rimbo 3,404 .... L7
Ronneby 12,086 .... J8
Säffle 11,428 .... H7
Sala 11,216 .... K7
Saltsjöbaden 8,113 .... J1
Sandviken 27,994 .... K6
Säter 4,297 .... J6
Sävsjö 4,913 .... J8
Sigtuna 4,780 .... H1
Simrishamn 5,834 .... J9
Skanör med Falsterbo 4,909 .... H9
Skara 10,138 .... H7
Skellefteå 29,353 .... M4
Skövde 29,945 .... H7
Skutskär 7,174 .... K6
Smedjebacken 8,418 .... J6
Söderhamn 14,673 .... K6
Söderköping 5,310 .... K7
Södertälje 58,408 .... G1
Sollefteå 8,923 .... K5
Sollentuna† 40,905 .... H1
Solna† 53,992 .... H1
Sölvesborg 7,292 .... J9
Stenungsund 8,361 .... G7
Stockholm (cap.) 665,550 .... G1
Stockholm* 1,357,183 .... G1
Storuman 2,587 .... K4
Storvik 2,748 .... K6
Strängnäs 10,255 .... F1
Strömstad 4,735 .... G7
Strömsund 4,119 .... K5
Sundbyberg† 27,058 .... G1
Sundsvall 52,268 .... K5
Sunne 4,273 .... H7
Surahammar 6,509 .... J7
Sveg 2,608 .... J5
Svenljunga 3,189 .... H8
Täby† 41,285 .... H1
Tibro 8,476 .... J7
Tidaholm 8,039 .... J7
Tierp 5,005 .... K6
Timrå 11,416 .... K5
Tomelilla 5,371 .... J9
Torsby 3,632 .... H6
Torshälla 8,231 .... K7
Tranås 14,854 .... J7
Trelleborg 22,559 .... H9
Trollhättan 42,499 .... H7
Trosa 3,128 .... K7
Uddevalla 32,700 .... G7
Ulricehamn 7,827 .... H8
Umeå 49,715 .... M5
Uppsala 101,850 .... K7
Uppsala* 157,202 .... L7
Vadstena 5,294 .... J7
Vaggeryd 3,974 .... J8
Valdemarsvik 3,558 .... K7
Vallentuna 10,477 .... H1
Vänersborg 20,510 .... G7
Vännäs 3,876 .... L5
Vansbro 2,708 .... H6
Vara 3,049 .... H7
Varberg 19,467 .... G8
Värnamo 15,726 .... J8
Västerås 98,858 .... K7
Västerås* 147,508 .... K7
Västerhaninge 14,125 .... H1
Västervik 21,239 .... K8
Vaxholm† 3,744 .... J1
Växjö 40,328 .... J8
Vetlanda 12,358 .... J8
Vilhelmina 4,060 .... K4
Vimmerby 7,405 .... J8
Virserum 2,495 .... J8
Visby 19,886 .... L8
Ystad 14,286 .... H9

OTHER FEATURES

Ångermanälven (riv.) K5
Åsnen (lake) J8
Baltic (sea) K9
Bolmen (lake) H8
Bothnia (gulf) N4
Dalälven (riv.) K6
Fårö (isl.) L8
Göta (canal) J7
Göta (riv.) H7
Gotland (isl.) L8
Gräsö (isl.) L6
Hanöbukten (bay) J9
Hjälmaren (lake) J7
Hoburgen (cliff) L8
Hornslandet (pen.) K6
Indalsälven (riv.) H5
Kalixälv (riv.) N3
Kalmarsund (sound) K8
Kattegat (str.) G8
Kebnekaise (mt.) L3
Kölen (mts.) K3
Klarälv (riv.) H6
Lapland (reg.) M2
Ljusnan (riv.) H5
Luleälv (riv.) M4
Mälaren (lake) G1
Muonioälv (riv.) M2
Öland (isl.) K8
Öresund (sound) H9
Ornö (isl.) J2
Österdalälven (riv.) H6
Piteälv (riv.) M4
Siljan (lake) J6
Skagerrak (str.) F8
Sommen (lake) J8
Stora Lulevatten (lake) L3
Storsjön (lake) J5
Sulitelma (mt.) K3
Torneälv (riv.) M3
Uddjaur (lake) L4
Umeälv (riv.) L4
Vänern (lake) H7
Västerdalälven (riv.) H6
Vättern (lake) J7

*City and suburbs.
†Population of commune.
†Population of parish.

DENMARK

COUNTIES

Århus 534,333 .... D5
Bornholm 47,241 .... F9
Copenhagen (commune) 622,612 .... F6
Faerøe Islands 41,969 .... B2
Frederiksberg (commune) 101,874 .... F6
Frederiksborg 260,825 .... E5
Fyn 433,765 .... D7
København (Copenhagen) (commune) 622,612 .... F6
Københaven 616,571 .... F6
Nordjylland 457,165 .... D4
Ribe 198,153 .... B7
Ringkøbing 242,006 .... B5
Roskilde 154,314 .... E6
Sønderjylland 238,502 .... C7
Storstrøm 252,780 .... E7
Vejle 306,809 .... C6
Vestsjaelland 259,484 .... E6
Viborg 221,002 .... C4

CITIES and TOWNS

Åbenrå 15,196 .... C7
Åbybro 2,897 .... C3
Åkirkeby 2,001 .... F9
Ålborg 154,582 .... D4
Ålestrup 1,926 .... C4
Århus 245,941 .... D5
Års 4,266 .... C4
Årup 1,675 .... D7
AErøskøbing 1,223 .... D8
Agerbaek 935 .... B6
Allingaåbro 1,385 .... D5
Allinge-Sandvig 1,991 .... F8
Ansager 1,157 .... B6
Arden 1,303 .... C4
Asaå 1,344 .... D3
Askov 904 .... C7
Asnaes 1,413 .... E6
Assens, Århus 1,341 .... D4
Assens, Fyn 5,139 .... D7
Augustenborg 2,628 .... D8
Auning 1,516 .... D5
Avlum 1,729 .... B5
Baelum 1,169 .... D4
Bagenkop 776 .... D8
Ballerup 50,673 .... F6
Bandholm 693 .... E8
Bedsted 965 .... B4
Birkerød 13,663 .... F6
Bjerringbro 4,761 .... C5
Bogense 2,861 .... D6
Bolderslev 774 .... C8
Børkop 1,410 .... C6
Borup 1,591 .... E7
Braedstrup 2,163 .... C6
Bramming 3,678 .... B7
Brande 4,784 .... B6
Bredebro 1,173 .... B7
Broager 2,143 .... C8
Brønderslev 10,247 .... C3
Brørup 2,584 .... C7
Brovst 4,200 .... C3
Bryrup 579 .... C5
Christiansfeld 1,994 .... C7
Copenhagen (cap.) 603,368 .... F6
Copenhagen* 1,327,940 .... F6
Dronninglund 4,661 .... D3
Dybvad 805 .... D3
Ebeltoft 3,017 .... D5
Egernsund 1,323 .... C8
Egtved 1,311 .... C6
Ejby 1,372 .... C7
Esbjerg 68,097 .... B7
Faåborg 6,495 .... D7
Fakse 2,720 .... F7
Fakse Ladeplads 1,799 .... F7
Farsø 2,821 .... C4
Farum 9,936 .... F6
Fjerritslev 2,134 .... C3
Fredensborg 4,709 .... F6
Fredericia 36,157 .... C6
Frederiksberg 101,874 .... F6
Frederikshavn 24,846 .... D3
Frederikssund 11,272 .... E6
Frederiksvaerk 8,903 .... E6
Fuglebjerg 1,094 .... E7
Gedser 1,200 .... F8
Gedsted 1,006 .... C4
Gelsted 1,307 .... C7
Gentofte 77,744 .... F6
Gilleleje 2,943 .... F5
Give 2,366 .... C6
Glamsbjerg 2,226 .... D7
Glostrup 28,326 .... F6
Glumsø 1,027 .... E7
Glyngøre 1,071 .... C4
Gørding 1,261 .... B7
Gørlev 1,542 .... E7
Graested 1,654 .... F5
Gram 2,061 .... C7
Graåsten 2,947 .... C8
Grenaå 12,569 .... D5
Grindsted 7,558 .... B6
Haårby 1,506 .... D7
Haderslev 20,042 .... C7
Hadsten 3,914 .... C5
Hadsund 3,652 .... D4
Hals 1,654 .... D3
Hammel 3,247 .... C5
Hammerum 3,227 .... C5
Hanstholm 1,716 .... B3
Harboør 1,359 .... B4
Haårlev 1,228 .... F7
Hasle 18
Haslev 6,925 .... E7
Havdrup 1,833 .... F6
Hedensted 2,659 .... C6
Hellebaek 2,911 .... F5
Helsinge 3,613 .... F6
Helsingør 42,425 .... F6
Herning 32,973 .... B5
Hillerød 23,963 .... F6
Hinnerup 2,061 .... D5
Hirtshals 6,861 .... C2
Hjallerup 1,573 .... C3
Hjerm 647 .... B5
Hjørring 19,692 .... C3
Hobro 8,737 .... C4
Højer 1,416 .... B8
Højslev 1,641 .... C4
Holbaek 19,485 .... E6
Holeby 1,434 .... E8
Holstebro 25,006 .... B5
Holsted 1,390 .... B6
Høng 2,488 .... E7
Hornslet 2,561 .... D5
Horsens 44,120 .... C6
Hørsholm 19,346 .... F6
Hørve 1,139 .... E6
Hov 635 .... D6
Humlum 546 .... B4
Hundested 5,443 .... E6
Hurup 2,287 .... B4
Hvidbjerg 994 .... B4
Hvide Sande 2,129 .... A6
Ikast 9,222 .... C5
Jelling 1,540 .... C6
Jerslev 798 .... D3
Juelsminde 1,991 .... D6
Jyderup 2,901 .... E6
Kalundborg 12,248 .... D6
Karise 1,184 .... F7
Karup 1,694 .... C5
Kastrup† 17,391 .... F6
Kerteminde 5,007 .... D7
Kibaek 1,279 .... B5
Kjellerup 3,245 .... C5
Klitmøller 542 .... B3
København (Copenhagen) (cap.) 603,368 .... F6
Køge 18,608 .... F7
Kolding 41,602 .... C7
Kolind 1,036 .... D5
Korsør 15,502 .... E7
Kvaerndrup 891 .... D7
Langaå 2,320 .... C5
Lem 1,026 .... B5
Lemvig 6,448 .... B4
Løgstør 3,633 .... C4
Løgumkloster 2,091 .... B7
Lohals 580 .... D7
Løjt Kirkeby 1,203 .... C7
Løkken 1,345 .... C3
Løsning 1,967 .... C6
Lundby 747 .... E7
Lunderskov 1,494 .... C7
Lyngby 61,516 .... F6
Malling 1,584 .... D5
Mariager 1,692 .... D4
Maribo 5,287 .... E8
Marstal 4,124 .... D8
Middelfart 13,315 .... C7

Agriculture, Industry and Resources

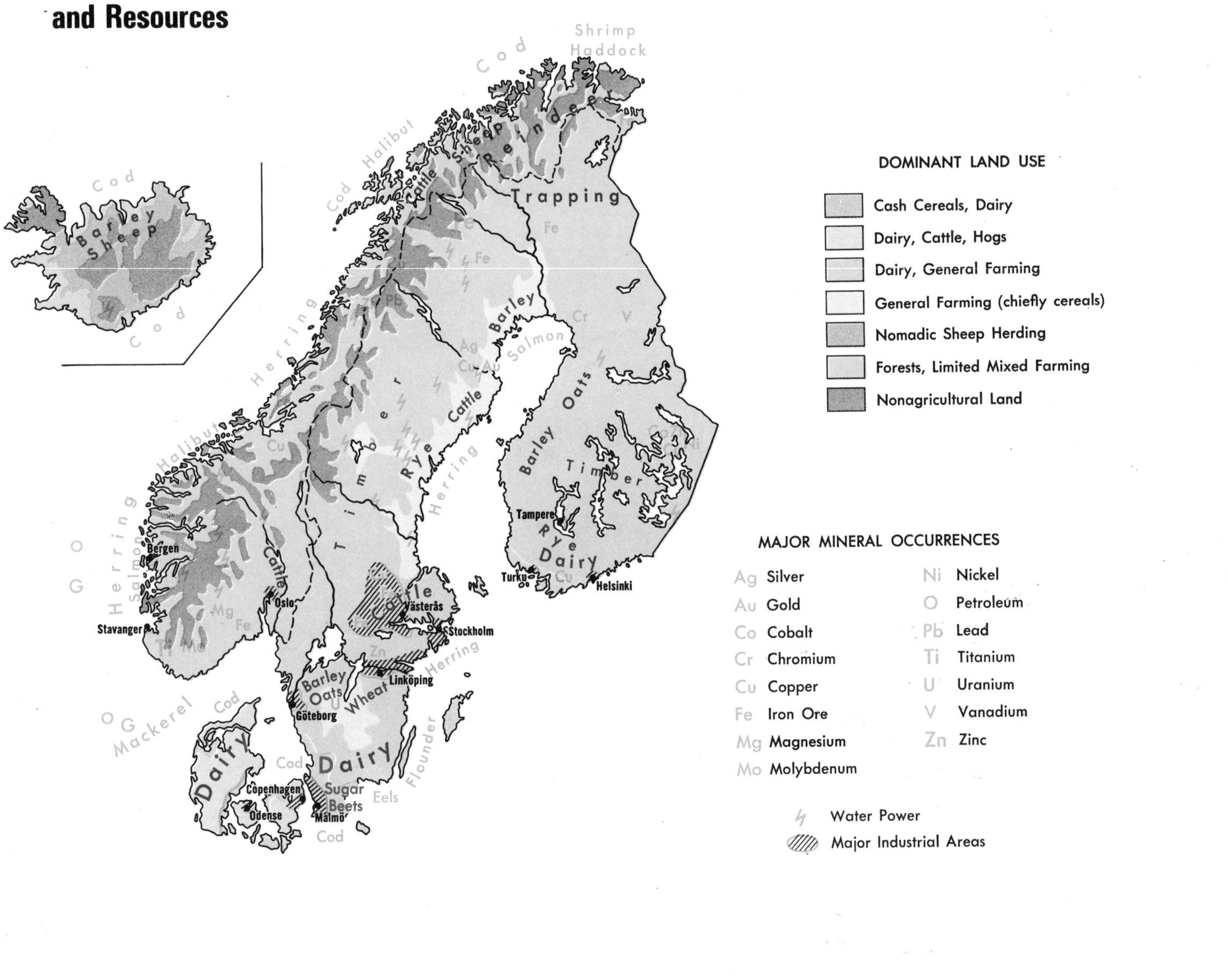

Shrimp
Haddock
Cod
Halibut
Cattle
Sheep
Reindeer
Trapping
Barley
Herring
Salmon
Oats
Timber
Rye
Dairy
Tampere
Turku
Helsinki
Bergen
Oslo
Stavanger
Västerås
Stockholm
Linköping
Göteborg
Wheat
Mackerel
Copenhagen
Odense
Sugar Beets
Malmö
Eels
Flounder
DOMINANT LAND USE
Cash Cereals, Dairy
Dairy, Cattle, Hogs
Dairy, General Farming
General Farming (chiefly cereals)
Nomadic Sheep Herding
Forests, Limited Mixed Farming
Nonagricultural Land
MAJOR MINERAL OCCURRENCES
Ag Silver
Au Gold
Co Cobalt
Cr Chromium
Cu Copper
Fe Iron Ore
Mg Magnesium
Mo Molybdenum
Ni Nickel
O Petroleum
Pb Lead
Ti Titanium
U Uranium
V Vanadium
Zn Zinc
Water Power
Major Industrial Areas

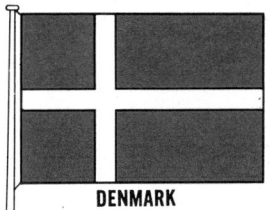

DENMARK

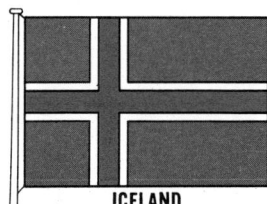

ICELAND

DENMARK

AREA 16,629 sq. mi. (43,069 sq. km.)
POPULATION 5,124,000
CAPITAL Copenhagen
LARGEST CITY Copenhagen
HIGHEST POINT Yding Skovhøj
568 ft. (173 m.)
MONETARY UNIT krone
MAJOR LANGUAGE Danish
MAJOR RELIGION Protestantism

ICELAND

AREA 39,768 sq. mi. (103,000 sq. km.)
POPULATION 228,785
CAPITAL Reykjavík
LARGEST CITY Reykjavík
HIGHEST POINT Hvannadalshnúkur
6,952 ft. (2,119 m.)
MONETARY UNIT króna
MAJOR LANGUAGE Icelandic
MAJOR RELIGION Protestantism

Denmark and Iceland

CONIC PROJECTION

SCALE OF MILES
0 10 20 30 40 50

SCALE OF KILOMETERS
0 10 20 30 40 50

Capitals of Countries _____ ☆
Capitals of Counties (amter) ____ ⌂
International Boundaries _____
Internal Boundaries _____

Scale 1:2,300,000

Denmark is divided into fourteen Counties plus Copenhagen and Frederiksberg communes.

© Copyright HAMMOND INCORPORATED, Maplewood, N.J.

Faerøe Islands

Streymoy
Klaksvík
Eysturoy
Tórshavn
Sandoy
Sudhuroy
(Den.)

0 15 30 MI.
0 15 30 KM.

Longitude 19° West of Greenwich

Longitude 10° East of Greenwich

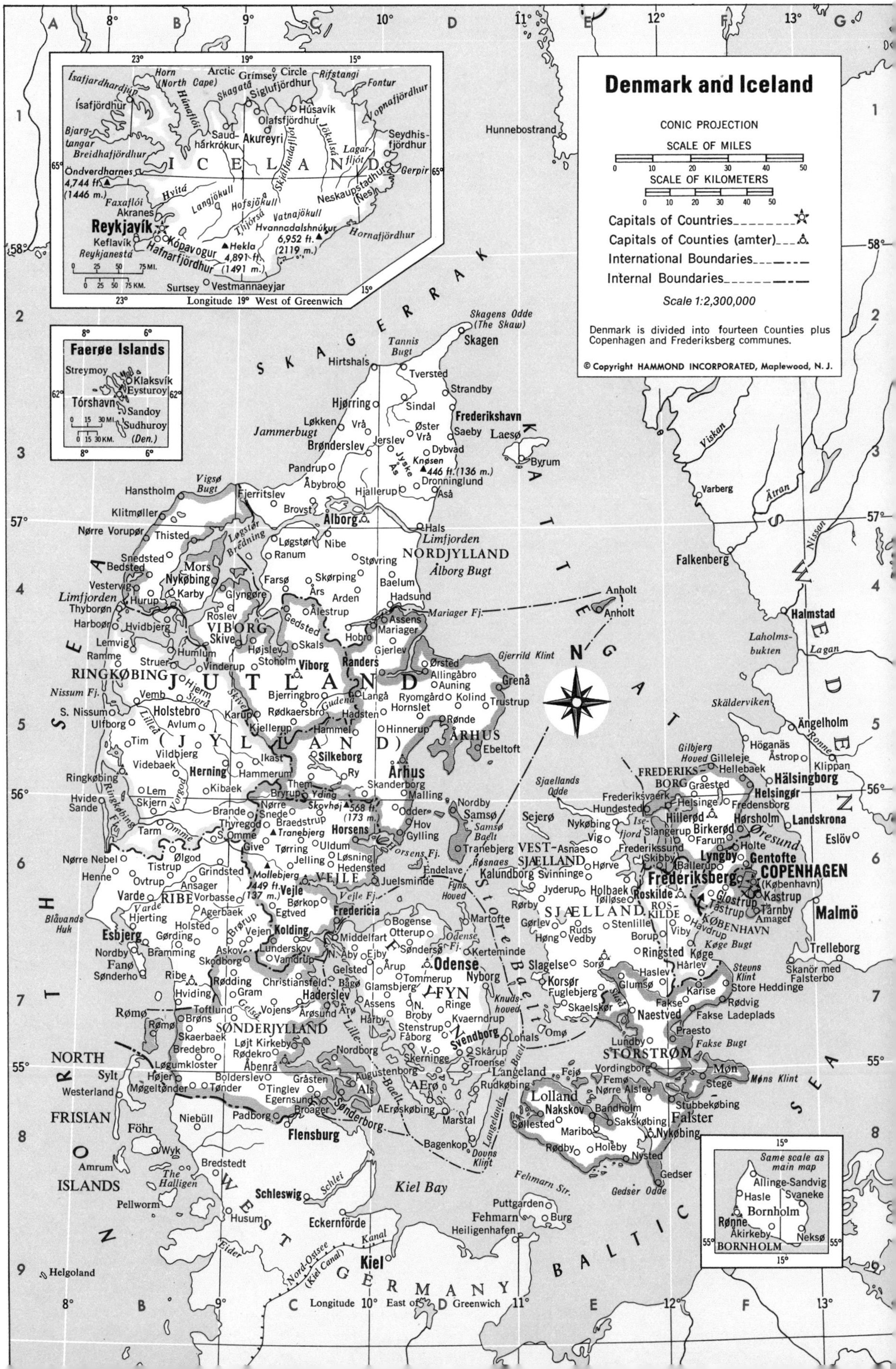

Germany

CONIC PROJECTION
SCALE OF MILES

SCALE OF KILOMETERS

Capitals of Countries .... ★
State and District Capitals ...... ◉
International Boundaries ....
State and District Boundaries ...
Canals ....

Scale 1:3,040,000

East Germany is divided into districts bearing the same name as their respective capitals.

© Copyright HAMMOND INCORPORATED, Maplewood, N.J.

Berlin

Longitude East 10° of Greenwich

AREA 95,985 sq. mi. (248,601 sq. km.)
POPULATION 61,658,000
CAPITAL Bonn
LARGEST CITY Berlin (West)
HIGHEST POINT Zugspitze 9,718 ft. (2,962 m.)
MONETARY UNIT Deutsche mark
MAJOR LANGUAGE German
MAJOR RELIGIONS Protestantism, Roman Catholicism

AREA 41,768 sq. mi. (108,179 sq. km.)
POPULATION 16,737,000
CAPITAL Berlin (East)
LARGEST CITY Berlin (East)
HIGHEST POINT Fichtelberg 3,983 ft. (1,214 m.)
MONETARY UNIT East German mark
MAJOR LANGUAGE German
MAJOR RELIGIONS Protestantism, Roman Catholicism

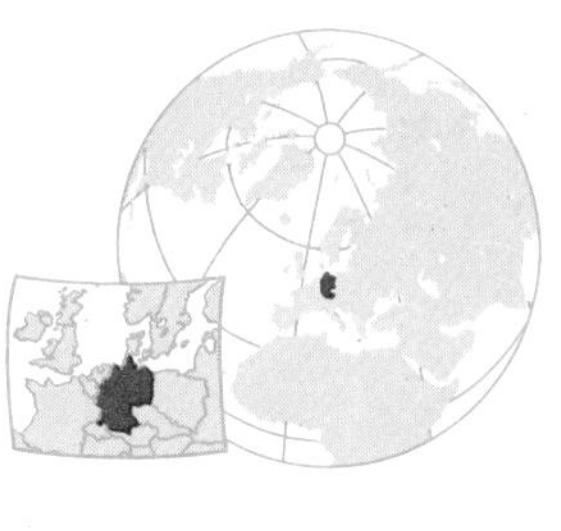

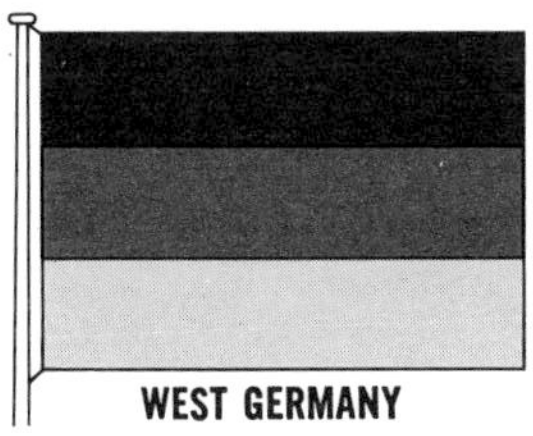

WEST GERMANY

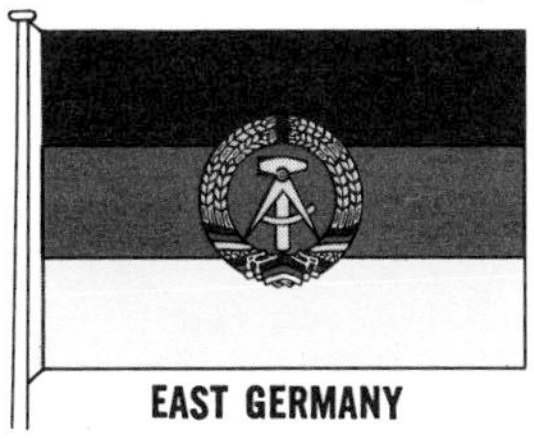

EAST GERMANY

Topography

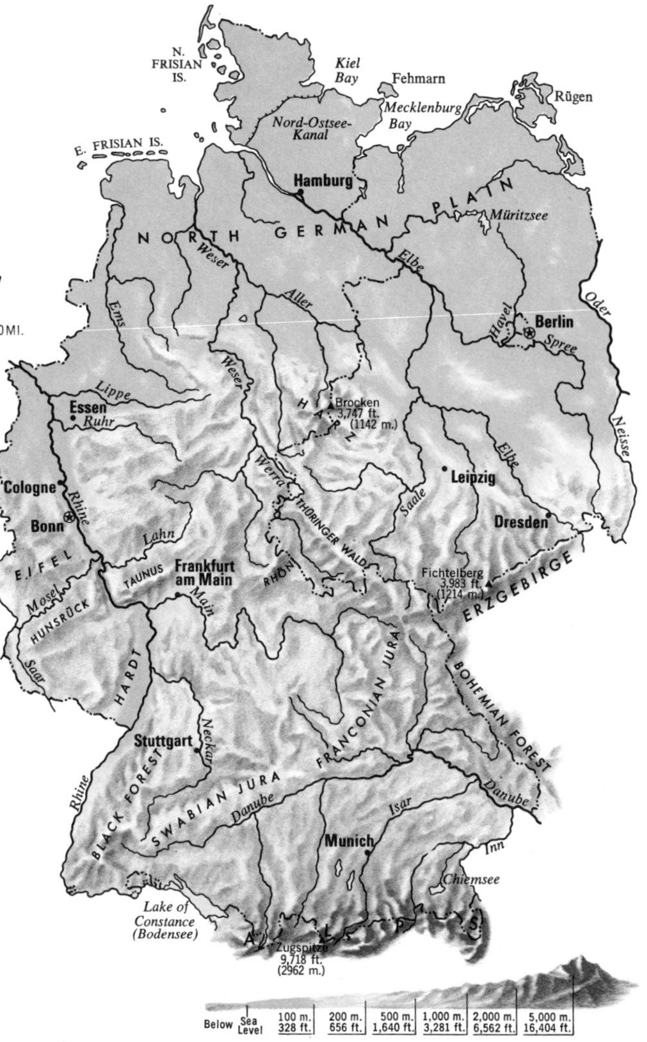
0 50 100 MI.
0 50 100 KM.
N. FRISIAN IS.
E. FRISIAN IS.
Kiel Bay
Fehmarn
Rügen
Mecklenburg Bay
Nord-Ostsee-Kanal
Hamburg
NORTH GERMAN PLAIN
Müritzsee
Weser
Elbe
Aller
Ems
Havel
Berlin
Spree
Oder
Lippe
Essen
Ruhr
HARZ
Brocken 3,747 ft. (1142 m.)
Neisse
Leipzig
Werra
Saale
Cologne
Rhine
Bonn
Lahn
THÜRINGER WALD
Dresden
EIFEL
TAUNUS
Frankfurt am Main
RHÖN
Fichtelberg 3,983 ft. (1214 m.)
ERZGEBIRGE
Mosel
HUNSRÜCK
Main
Saar
HARDT
FRANCONIAN JURA
BOHEMIAN FOREST
Stuttgart
Neckar
BLACK FOREST
SWABIAN JURA
Danube
Isar
Munich
Inn
Chiemsee
Lake of Constance (Bodensee)
ALPS
Zugspitze 9,718 ft. (2962 m.)
Below Sea Level
100 m. 328 ft.
200 m. 656 ft.
500 m. 1,640 ft.
1,000 m. 3,281 ft.
2,000 m. 6,562 ft.
5,000 m. 16,404 ft.

EAST GERMANY

DISTRICTS

Berlin 1,094,147 .... F4
Cottbus 872,242 .... F3
Dresden 1,845,459 .... E3
Erfurt 1,247,213 .... D3
Frankfurt 688,637 .... F2
Gera 738,847 .... D3
Halle 1,890,187 .... D3
Karl-Marx-Stadt 1,994,115 .... E3
Leipzig 1,457,817 .... E3
Magdeburg 1,297,881 .... D2
Neubrandenburg 628,686 .... E2
Potsdam 1,124,892 .... E2
Rostock 867,806 .... E1
Schwerin 592,334 .... D2
Suhl 550,497 .... D3

CITIES and TOWNS

Aken 11,742 .... D3
Altenburg 51,193 .... E3
Angermünde 11,786 .... E2
Anklam 19,099 .... E2
Annaberg-Buchholz 26,561 .... E3
Apolda 28,649 .... D3
Arnstadt 29,462 .... D3
Aschersleben 36,674 .... D3
Aue 32,622 .... E3
Auerbach 18,168 .... E3
Bad Doberan 12,541 .... D1
Bad Dürrenberg 15,192 .... D3
Bad Langensalza 166,282 .... D3
Bad Salzungen 17,277 .... C3
Barth 12,069 .... E1
Bautzen 45,851 .... F3
Bergen 13,244 .... E1
Berlin, East (cap.) 1,094,147 .... F4
Bernau bei Berlin 15,749 .... E2
Bernburg 44,428 .... D3
Bischofswerda 11,540 .... F3
Bitterfeld 27,062 .... E3
Blankenburg am Harz 18,784 .... D3
Boizenburg an der Elbe 12,428 .... D2
Borna 21,807 .... E3
Brandenburg 94,071 .... E2
Burg bei Magdeburg 29,027 .... D2
Calbe 15,976 .... D3
Chemnitz
 (Karl-Marx-Stadt) 303,811 .... E3
Coswig, Dresden 22,149 .... E3
Coswig, Halle 12,473 .... E3
Cottbus 94,293 .... F3
Crimmitschau 28,845 .... E3
Delitzsch 24,076 .... E3
Demmin 17,270 .... E2
Dessau 100,820 .... E3
Döbeln 27,624 .... E3
Dresden 507,692 .... E3
Ebersbach 12,694 .... F3
Eberswalde-Finow 47,141 .... E2
Eilenburg 22,245 .... E3
Eisenach 49,954 .... D3
Eisenberg 13,450 .... D3
Eisenhüttenstadt 46,455 .... F2
Eisleben 29,297 .... D3
Erfurt 202,979 .... D3
Falkensee 25,295 .... E3
Falkenstein 14,367 .... E3
Finsterwalde 22,466 .... E3
Forst 28,084 .... F3
Frankfurt an der Oder 70,817 .... F2
Freiberg 50,815 .... E3
Freital 46,061 .... E3
Friedland E2
Fürstenwalde 31,065 .... F2
Gardelegen 12,987 .... D2
Genthin 15,916 .... E2
Gera 113,108 .... E3
Glauchau 30,927 .... E3
Görlitz 84,658 .... F3
Gotha 59,243 .... D3
Greifswald 53,940 .... E1
Greiz 37,612 .... E3
Grevesmühlen 12,005 .... D2
Grimma 17,100 .... E3
Grimmen 14,571 .... E1
Grossenhain 18,712 .... E3
Grossräschen 12,889 .... E3
Guben
 (Wilhelm-Pieck-Stadt) 32,731 .... F3
Güstrow 36,824 .... E2
Halberstadt 46,669 .... D3
Haldensleben 19,194 .... D2
Halle 241,425 .... D3
Halle-Neustadt 67,956 .... D3
Havelberg D2
Heidenau 21,315 .... E3
Heiligenstadt 13,931 .... D3
Hennigsdorf bei Berlin 24,853 .... E3
Hettstedt 20,291 .... D3
Hildburghausen 11,372 .... D3
Hoyerswerda 64,904 .... F3
Ilmenau 22,021 .... D3
Jena 99,431 .... D3
Johanngeorgenstadt 10,328 .... E3
Jüterbog 13,477 .... E3
Kamenz 18,221 .... F3
Karl-Marx-Stadt 303,811 .... E3
Kleinmachnow 14,059 .... E4
Klingenthal 13,614 .... E3
Königs Wusterhausen 11,825 .... E2
Köpenick 130,987 .... F4
Köthen 35,451 .... E3
Kühlungsborn D1
Lauchhammer 26,939 .... E3
Leipzig 570,972 .... E3
Lichtenberg 192,063 .... F4
Limbach-Oberfrohna 25,706 .... E3
Löbau 18,077 .... F3
Lübben 14,224 .... E3
Lübbenau 22,350 .... F3
Luckenwalde 28,544 .... E2
Ludwigslust 13,280 .... D2
Magdeburg 276,089 .... D2
Markkleeberg 22,380 .... E3
Meerane 25,037 .... E3
Meiningen 26,134 .... D3
Meissen 43,561 .... E3
Merseburg 54,269 .... D3
Meuselwitz 13,585 .... E3
Mittweida 19,259 .... E3
Mühlhausen
 (Thomas-Müntzer-Stadt) 44,106 .... D3
Nauen 11,940 .... E2
Naumburg 36,358 .... D3
Neubrandenburg 59,971 .... E2
Neuenhagen bei Berlin 12,603 .... F4
Neuruppin 24,888 .... E2
Neustrelitz 27,074 .... E2
Nordhausen 44,442 .... D3
Oelsnitz 15,084 .... E3
Oelsnitz im Erzgebirge 16,063 .... E3
Olbernhau 13,479 .... E3
Oranienburg 24,452 .... E2
Oschatz 18,974 .... E3
Oschersleben 17,377 .... D2
Pankow 136,527 .... F3
Parchim 22,927 .... D2
Pasewalk 15,099 .... F2
Peenemünde E1
Perleberg 15,029 .... D2
Pirna 49,771 .... E3
Plauen 80,353 .... E3
Pössneck 18,648 .... D3
Potsdam 117,236 .... E2
Prenzlau 22,738 .... E2
Pritzwalk 11,887 .... E2
Quedlinburg 29,796 .... D3
Radeberg 18,528 .... E3
Radebeul 38,383 .... E3
Rathenow 32,011 .... E2
Reichenbach 27,440 .... E3
Ribnitz-Damgarten 17,254 .... E1
Riesa 49,989 .... E3
Rosslau 16,520 .... E3
Rostock 210,167 .... E1
Rudolstadt 31,698 .... D3
Saalfeld 33,648 .... D3
Salzwedel 21,741 .... D2
Sangerhausen 32,721 .... D3
Sassnitz 13,857 .... E1
Schkeuditz 15,585 .... E3
Schmalkalden 15,017 .... D3
Schmölln 13,406 .... E3
Schneeberg 20,376 .... E3
Schönebeck 45,197 .... D2
Schwedt 45,729 .... F2
Schwerin 104,984 .... D2
Sebnitz 13,470 .... F3
Senftenberg 29,953 .... F3
Sömmerda 20,712 .... D3
Sondershausen 23,383 .... D3
Sonneberg 29,193 .... D3
Spremberg 22,862 .... F3
Stassfurt 26,225 .... D3
Stendal 39,647 .... D2
Stralsund 72,167 .... E1
Strausberg 21,334 .... F2
Suhl 36,642 .... D3
Tangermünde 12,898 .... D2
Teltow 16,171 .... E4
Templin 11,718 .... E2
Thale 17,248 .... D3
Thomas-Müntzer-Stadt 44,106 .... D3
Torgau 21,613 .... E3
Torgelow 14,320 .... F2
Treptow 127,448 .... F4
Ueckermünde 11,423 .... F2
Waldheim 11,925 .... E3
Waltershausen 13,893 .... D3
Waren 22,921 .... E2
Weida 11,816 .... D3
Weimar 63,144 .... D3
Weissenfels 43,191 .... D3
Weissensee 78,451 .... F3
Weisswasser 25,910 .... F3
Werdau 22,249 .... E3
Wernigerode 34,658 .... D3
Wilhelm-Pieck-Stadt 32,731 .... F3
Wismar 56,765 .... D2
Wittenberg 51,364 .... E3
Wittenberge 32,907 .... D2
Wolfen 27,570 .... E3
Wolgast 16,384 .... E1
Wurzen 20,501 .... E3
Zehdenick 12,651 .... E2
Zeitz 44,582 .... E3
Zella-Mehlis 16,301 .... D3
Zerbst 19,356 .... E3
Zeulenroda 13,452 .... D3
Zittau 42,298 .... F3
Zwickau 123,069 .... E3

OTHER FEATURES

Altmark (reg.) D2
Arkona (cape) E1
Baltic (sea) E1
Black Elster (riv.) E3
Brandenburg (reg.) E2
Elbe (riv.) D2
Elde (riv.) D2
Elster, Black (riv.) E3
Elster, White (riv.) E3
Erzgebirge (mts.) E3
Fichtelberg (mt.) E3
Harz (mts.) D3
Havel (riv.) E2
Lusatia (reg.) F3
Mecklenburg (bay) D1
Mecklenburg (reg.) E2
Mulde (riv.) E3
Neisse (riv.) F3
Oder (riv.) F2
Peene (riv.) E2
Pomerania (reg.) E2
Pomeranian (bay) F1
Rhön (mts.) D3
Rügen (isl.) E1
Saale (riv.) D3
Saxony (reg.) E3
Spree (riv.) F3
Spreewald (for.) F3
Thüringer Wald (for.) D3
Thuringia (reg.) D3
Ücker (riv.) E2
Unstrut (riv.) D3
Usedom (isl.) F1
Warnow (riv.) D2
Werra (riv.) D3
White Elster (riv.) E3

WEST GERMANY

STATES

Baden-Württemberg 9,152,700 .... C4
Bavaria 10,810,400 .... D4
Berlin (West) (free
 city) 1,984,800 .... E4
Bremen 716,800 .... C2
Hamburg 1,717,400 .... D2
Hesse 5,549,800 .... C3
Lower Saxony 7,238,500 .... C2
North
 Rhine-Westphalia 17,129,600 .... B3
Rhineland-Palatinate 3,665,800 .... B4
Saarland 1,096,300 .... B4
Schleswig-Holstein 2,582,400 .... C1

CITIES and TOWNS

Aachen 242,453 .... B3
Aalen 64,735 .... D4
Ahaus 27,126 .... B2
Ahlen 54,214 .... B3
Ahrensburg 24,964 .... D2
Alfeld 24,273 .... C2
Alsdorf 47,473 .... B3
Alsfeld 18,091 .... C3
Altena 26,753 .... B3
Altona C2
Alzey 15,190 .... C4
Amberg 46,934 .... D4
Andernach 27,132 .... B3
Ansbach 39,117 .... D4
Arnsberg 80,287 .... C3
Arolsen 15,619 .... C3
Aschaffenburg 55,398 .... C4
Augsburg 249,943 .... D4
Aurich 34,194 .... B2
Backnang 29,614 .... C4
Bad Berleburg 20,415 .... C3
Bad Driburg 17,478 .... C3
Bad Dürkheim 16,133 .... C4
Bad Ems 10,487 .... B3
Baden-Baden 49,718 .... C4
Bad Gandersheim 11,614 .... D3
Bad Harzburg 25,786 .... D3
Bad Hersfeld 29,248 .... C3
Bad Homburg vor der
 Höhe 51,196 .... C3
Bad Honnef 20,903 .... B3
Bad Kissingen 22,279 .... D3
Bad Kreuznach 42,588 .... B4
Bad Lauterberg im Harz 14,715 .... D3
Bad Mergentheim 19,895 .... C4
Bad Münstereifel 14,340 .... B3
Bad Nauheim 25,916 .... C3
Bad Neuenahr-Ahrweiler 26,371 .... B3
Bad Oldesloe 19,640 .... D2
Bad Pyrmont 21,896 .... C3
Bad Reichenhall 13,048 .... E5
Bad Salzuflen 50,924 .... C2
Bad Schwartau 18,696 .... D2
Bad Segeberg 13,320 .... D2
Bad Tölz 12,458 .... D5
Bad Vilbel 25,012 .... C3
Bad Waldsee 14,296 .... C5
Bad Wildungen 15,418 .... C3
Bad Wimpfen 5,536 .... C4
Baiersbronn 14,845 .... C4
Balingen 29,310 .... C4
Bamberg 74,236 .... D4
Barsinghausen 32,873 .... C2
Bassum 14,113 .... C2
Bayreuth 67,035 .... D4
Bayrischzell 1,639 .... E5
Bebra 15,740 .... C3
Bendorf 15,943 .... B3
Bensheim 32,653 .... C4
Bentheim 13,681 .... B2
Berchtesgaden 8,558 .... E5
Bergisch Gladbach 99,517 .... B3
Berleburg (Bad
 Berleburg) 20,415 .... C3
Berlin (West) 1,984,837 .... E4
Biberach an der Riss 28,891 .... C4
Bielefeld 316,058 .... C2
Bietigheim-Bissingen 34,042 .... C4
Bingen 24,541 .... B4
Birkenfeld 5,883 .... B4
Blaubeuren 11,652 .... C4
Böblingen 40,547 .... C4
Bocholt 65,460 .... B3
Bochum 414,842 .... B3
Bonn (cap.) 283,711 .... B3
Boppard 16,888 .... B3
Borghorst 17,238 .... B2
Borken 30,212 .... B3
Bornheim 32,847 .... B3
Bottrop 101,495 .... B3
Brake 18,089 .... C2
Bramsche 24,119 .... B2
Braunschweig
 (Brunswick) 268,519 .... D2
Breisach am Rhein 9,230 .... B4
Bremen 572,969 .... C2
Bremerhaven 143,836 .... C2
Bremervörde 17,565 .... C2
Bretten 22,140 .... C4
Brilon 24,595 .... C3
Bruchsal 38,929 .... C4
Brühl 44,305 .... B3
Brunsbüttel 11,451 .... C2
Brunswick 268,519 .... D2
Buchholz in der
 Nordheide 25,713 .... C2
Bückeburg 21,393 .... C2
Büdingen 16,845 .... C3
Bühl 21,596 .... C4
Bünde 40,021 .... C2
Büren 17,352 .... C3
Burg auf Fehmarn 5,874 .... D1
Burghausen 16,892 .... E4
Burgsteinfurt 31,367 .... B2
Butzbach 20,592 .... C3
Buxtehude 30,249 .... C2
Castrop-Rauxel 82,373 .... B3
Celle 74,347 .... D2
Cham 12,423 .... E4
Charlottenburg 201,732 .... E4
Clausthal-Zellerfeld 16,690 .... D3
Cloppenburg 19,757 .... B2
Coburg 46,244 .... D3
Coesfeld 30,617 .... B3
Cologne 1,013,771 .... B3
Crailsheim 24,506 .... D4
Cuxhaven 60,353 .... C2
Dachau 33,207 .... D4
Dahlem E4
Darmstadt 137,018 .... C4
Deggendorf 25,188 .... E4
Delmenhorst 71,488 .... C2
Detmold 65,629 .... C3
Diepholz 14,201 .... C2
Dillenburg 14,068 .... C3
Dillingen 21,369 .... B4
Dillingen an der Donau 11,601 .... D4
Dingolfing 13,325 .... E4
Dinkelsbühl 10,034 .... D4
Donaueschingen 17,578 .... C5
Donauwörth 17,077 .... D4
Dorsten 65,718 .... B3
Dortmund 630,609 .... B3
Duderstadt 23,255 .... D3
Dudweiler 27,877 .... B4
Duisburg 591,635 .... B3
Dülmen 37,013 .... B3
Düren 87,774 .... B3
Düsseldorf 664,336 .... B3
Eberbach 15,834 .... C4
Ebingen 22,594 .... C4
Eckernförde 22,938 .... D1
Ehingen 21,600 .... C4
Eichstätt 13,080 .... D4
Einbeck 29,821 .... C3
Eiserfeld 22,346 .... C3
Ellwangen 21,994 .... D4
Elmshorn 41,355 .... C2
Emden 53,509 .... B2
Emmendingen 24,722 .... B4
Emmerich 29,113 .... B3
Emsdetten 30,195 .... B2
Erlangen 100,671 .... D4
Eschwege 24,882 .... C3
Eschweiler 53,603 .... B3
Espelkamp 22,670 .... C2
Essen 677,568 .... B3
Esslingen am Neckar 95,298 .... C4
Ettlingen 35,159 .... C4
Euskirchen 43,558 .... B3
Eutin 17,701 .... D1
Fellbach 42,501 .... C4
Flensburg 93,213 .... C1
Forchheim 23,430 .... D4
Frankenberg-Eder 15,337 .... C3
Frankenthal 43,684 .... C4
Frankfurt am Main 636,157 .... C3
Frechen 41,453 .... B3
Freiburg im Breisgau 175,371 .... B5
Freising 31,524 .... D4
Freudenstadt 19,454 .... C4
Friedberg 24,762 .... C3
Friedrichshafen 51,544 .... C5
Fritzlar 15,079 .... C3
Fulda 58,976 .... C3
Fürstenfeldbruck 27,194 .... D4
Fürth 101,639 .... D4
Füssen 10,506 .... D5
Gaggenau 28,846 .... C4
Garbsen 56,337 .... C2
Garmisch-Partenkirchen 26,831 .... D5
Gatow E4
Geesthacht 24,745 .... D2
Geislingen an der
 Steige 28,693 .... C4
Geldern 24,082 .... B3
Gelnhausen 17,889 .... C3
Gelsenkirchen 322,584 .... B3
Georgsmarienhütte 30,259 .... B2
Geretsried 17,330 .... D5
Germersheim 12,041 .... C4
Gerolstein 6,857 .... B3
Gifhorn 31,635 .... D2
Glückstadt 12,159 .... C2
Goch 28,213 .... B3
Göggingen 15,980 .... D4
Göppingen 54,365 .... C4
Goslar 53,957 .... D3
Göttingen 123,797 .... D3
Greven 27,479 .... B2
Grevenbroich 56,392 .... B3
Griesheim 18,548 .... C4
Gronau 40,527 .... B2
Gummersbach 49,316 .... B3
Günzburg 13,528 .... D4
Gunzenhausen 13,565 .... D4
Gütersloh 77,128 .... C3
Haar 18,824 .... D4
Hagen 229,224 .... B3
Haltern 29,750 .... B3
Hamburg 1,717,383 .... D2
Hameln 61,066 .... C2
Hamm 172,210 .... B3
Hammelburg 12,350 .... C3
Hanau 86,676 .... C3
Hannover 552,955 .... C2
Harburg-Wilhelmsburg C2
Hassloch 17,752 .... C4
Haunstetten 21,810 .... D4
Hechingen 15,926 .... C4
Heide 21,918 .... C1
Heidelberg 129,368 .... C4
Heidenheim an der Brenz 49,943 .... D4
Heilbronn 113,177 .... C4
Helmstedt 28,095 .... D2
Hennef 27,815 .... B3
Herford 64,385 .... C2
Herne 190,561 .... B3
Hildesheim 105,290 .... D2
Hockenheim 16,890 .... C4
Hof 54,357 .... D3
Hofgeismar 13,380 .... C3
Holzminden 23,650 .... C3
Homburg 41,861 .... B4
Horn-Bad Meinberg 16,927 .... C3
Höxter 32,759 .... C3
Hückelhoven 34,865 .... B3
Hünfeld 13,873 .... C3
Hürth 51,692 .... B3
Husum 24,984 .... C1
Hüttental 39,561 .... C3
Ibbenbüren 42,202 .... B2
Idar-Oberstein 37,179 .... B4
Immenstadt im Allgäu 13,720 .... C5
Ingolstadt 88,500 .... D4
Iserlohn 96,174 .... B3
Isny im Allgäu 12,367 .... D5
Itzehoe 35,077 .... C2
Jever 12,096 .... B2
Jülich 31,564 .... B3
Kaiserslautern 100,886 .... B4
Karlsruhe 280,448 .... C4
Kassel 205,534 .... C3
Kaufbeuren 42,224 .... D5
Kehl 29,861 .... B4
Kelheim 11,996 .... D4
Kempten 56,944 .... D5
Kevelaer 20,971 .... B3
Kiel 262,164 .... D1
Kirchheim unter Teck 31,666 .... C4
Kitzingen 19,116 .... C4
Kleve 44,043 .... B3
Koblenz 118,394 .... B3
Köln (Cologne) 1,013,771 .... B3
Königswinter 34,586 .... B3
Konstanz 70,152 .... C5
Korbach 22,998 .... C3
Kornwestheim 27,771 .... C4
Krefeld 228,463 .... B3
Kreutztal 30,473 .... C3
Kronach 11,538 .... D3
Kulmbach 25,711 .... D3
Lage 31,724 .... C3
Lahnstein 19,725 .... B3
Lahr 35,570 .... B4
Lampertheim 31,993 .... C4
Landau in der Pfalz 37,661 .... C4
Landsberg am Lech 15,862 .... D4
Landshut 55,858 .... E4
Langen 30,227 .... C4
Langenhagen 47,092 .... C2
Lauenburg an der Elbe 11,077 .... D2
Lauf an der Pegnitz 19,443 .... D4
Lauingen 8,778 .... D4
Lauterbach 15,007 .... C3
Leer 32,785 .... B2
Lehrte 38,272 .... D2
Lemgo 39,664 .... C2
Lengerich 20,836 .... B2
Leverkusen 165,947 .... B3
Lichtenfels 13,719 .... D3
Limburg an der Lahn 28,606 .... C3
Lindau 23,930 .... C5

(continued on following page)

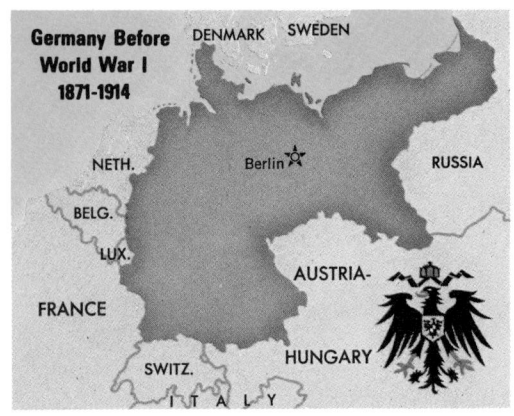

Germany Before World War I 1871-1914

Germany Between Wars 1919-1937

Occupied Germany 1945-1949

Agriculture, Industry and Resources

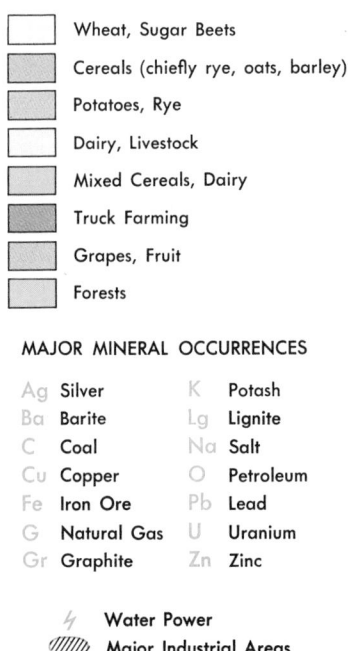

DOMINANT LAND USE

- Wheat, Sugar Beets
- Cereals (chiefly rye, oats, barley)
- Potatoes, Rye
- Dairy, Livestock
- Mixed Cereals, Dairy
- Truck Farming
- Grapes, Fruit
- Forests

MAJOR MINERAL OCCURRENCES

Ag	Silver	K	Potash
Ba	Barite	Lg	Lignite
C	Coal	Na	Salt
Cu	Copper	O	Petroleum
Fe	Iron Ore	Pb	Lead
G	Natural Gas	U	Uranium
Gr	Graphite	Zn	Zinc

⚡ Water Power

▨ Major Industrial Areas

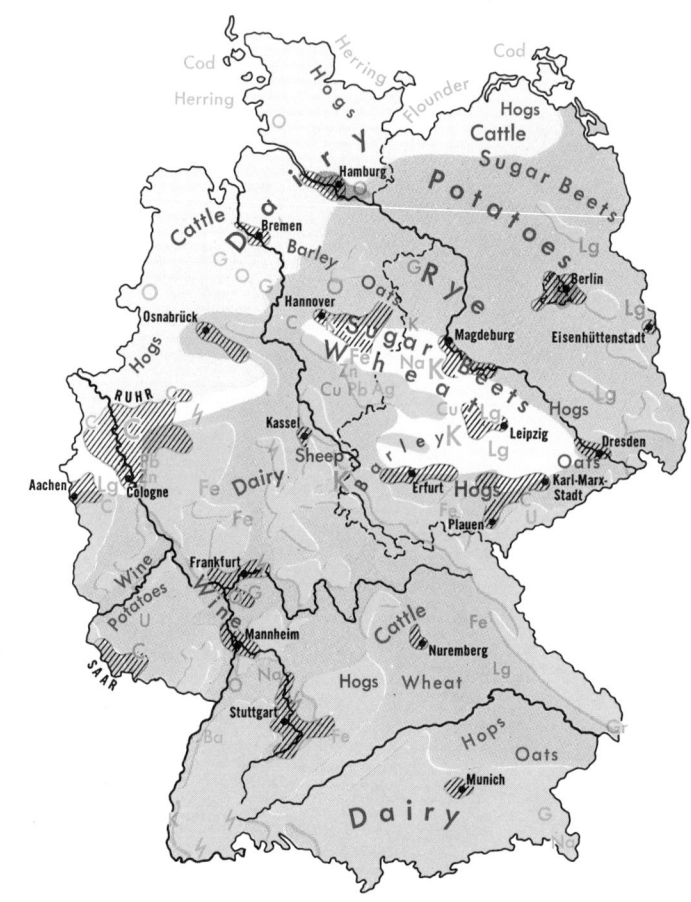

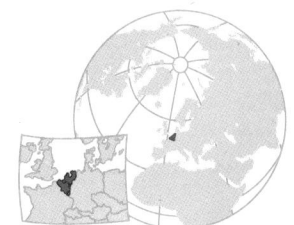

AREA 15,892 sq. mi. (41,160 sq. km.)
POPULATION 14,227,000
CAPITALS The Hague, Amsterdam
LARGEST CITY Amsterdam
HIGHEST POINT Vaalserberg 1,056 ft. (322 m.)
MONETARY UNIT guilder (florin)
MAJOR LANGUAGE Dutch
MAJOR RELIGIONS Protestantism, Roman Catholicism

AREA 11,781 sq. mi. (30,513 sq. km.)
POPULATION 9,855,110
CAPITAL Brussels
LARGEST CITY Brussels (greater)
HIGHEST POINT Botrange 2,277 ft. (694 m.)
MONETARY UNIT Belgian franc
MAJOR LANGUAGES French (Walloon), Flemish
MAJOR RELIGION Roman Catholicism

AREA 999 sq. mi. (2,587 sq. km.)
POPULATION 364,000
CAPITAL Luxembourg
LARGEST CITY Luxembourg
HIGHEST POINT Ardennes Plateau 1,825 ft. (556 m.)
MONETARY UNIT Luxembourg franc
MAJOR LANGUAGES Luxembourgeois (Letzeburgisch), French, German
MAJOR RELIGION Roman Catholicism

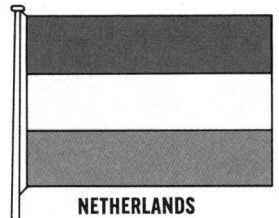

NETHERLANDS

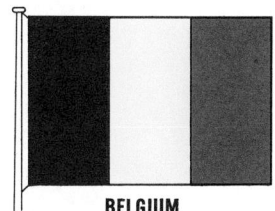

BELGIUM

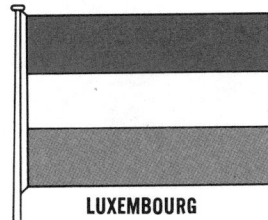

LUXEMBOURG

BELGIUM

PROVINCES

Antwerp 1,533,249 ....F6
Brabant 2,176,373 ....F7
East Flanders 1,310,117 ....D7
Hainaut 1,317,453 ....D7
Liège 1,008,905 ....H7
Limburg 652,547 ....G7
Luxembourg 217,310 ....G9
Namur 380,561 ....F8
West Flanders 1,054,429 ....B7

CITIES and TOWNS†

Aalst 46,659 ....D7
Aalter 9,173 ....C6
Aarlen (Arlon) 13,745 ....H9
Aarschot 12,474 ....F7
Aat (Ath) 11,842 ....D7
Aiken 8,677 ....G7
Alost (Aalst) 46,659 ....D7
Amay 7,617 ....G7
Andenne 8,091 ....G8
Anderlecht 103,796 ....B9

Anderlues 12,176 ....E8
Ans H7
Antoing 3,426 ....C7
Antwerp 224,543 ....E6
Antwerp* 928,000 ....E6
Antwerpen (Antwerp) 224,543 ....E6
Ardooie 7,081 ....C7
Arendonk 9,919 ....G6
Arlon 13,745 ....H9
As 5,496 ....H6
Asse 6,583 ....E7
Ath 11,842 ....D7
Attert H9
Aubange 3,761 ....D7
Audenarde (Oudenaarde) 26,615 ....D7
Auderghem 34,546 ....C9
Auvelais 8,287 ....F8
Aywaille 3,850 ....H8
Baerle-Hertog F6
Balen 15,110 ....G6
Basse-Sambre F8
Bastenaken (Bastogne) 6,816 ....H9
Bastogne 6,816 ....H9
Beernem C6
Beloeil D7
Berchem 50,241 ....F6

Berchem-Sainte-Agathe 19,087 ....B9
Bergen (Mons) 59,362 ....E8
Beringen G7
Bertogne H8
Bertrix 4,562 ....G9
Beveren 15,913 ....E6
Bilzen 7,178 ....G7
Binche 10,098 ....E8
Blankenberge 13,969 ....C6
Bocholt 6,497 ....H6
Boom 16,584 ....E6
Borgerhout 49,002 ....E6
Borgloon 3,412 ....G7
Borgworm (Waremme) 10,956 ....G7
Bourg-Léopold (Leopoldsburg) 9,593 ....G6
Boussu 11,474 ....D8
Braine-l'Alleud 18,531 ....E7
Braine-le-Comte 11,957 ....E7
Brecht F6
Bredene 9,244 ....B6
Bree 10,389 ....H6
Bruges 117,220 ....C6
Brugge (Bruges) 117,220 ....C6
Brussels (cap.)* 1,054,970 ....C9
Bruxelles (Brussels)

(cap.)* 1,054,970 ....C9
Certfontaine E8
Charleroi 23,689 ....E8
Charleroi* 458,000 ....E8
Chastre F7
Châtelet 14,752 ....F8
Chièvres 3,283 ....D7
Chimay 3,288 ....E8
Chiny G9
Ciney 7,536 ....G8
Comblain-au-Pont 3,582 ....E7
Comines 8,192 ....B7
Courcelles 17,015 ....E8
Courtrai (Kortrijk) 44,961 ....C7
Couvin 4,234 ....F8
Damme C6
De Haan B6
Deinze 16,711 ....D7
Denderleeuw 9,925 ....E7
Dendermonde 22,119 ....E6
De Panne 8,985 ....B6
Dessel 7,505 ....G6
Destelbergen D6
Deurne 80,766 ....F6
Diest 10,799 ....F7
Diksmuide 6,669 ....B6

Dilbeek 15,108 ....B9
Dilsen H6
Dinant 9,747 ....G8
Dison 8,466 ....H7
Dixmude (Diksmuide) 6,669 ....B6
Doische F8
Doornik (Tournai) 32,794 ....C7
Dour 10,059 ....D8
Drogenbos 4,840 ....B10
Duffel 13,802 ....F6
Durbuy H8
Ecaussinnes 6,630 ....E7
Edingen (Enghien) 4,115 ....D7
Eeklo 19,144 ....D6
Éghezée F7
Eigenbrakel (Braine-l'Alleud) 18,531 ....E7
Ekeren 27,648 ....E6
Ellezelles 3,556 ....D7
Enghien 4,115 ....D7
Érezée G8
Erquelinnes 4,471 ....E8
Esneux 6,183 ....H7
Essen 10,795 ....F6
Estampuis D7
Etterbeek 51,030 ....B9

Eupen 14,879 ....J7
Evere 26,957 ....C9
Evergem 12,886 ....D6
Farciennes E8
Fernelmont F7
Ferrières H8
Flémalle 8,135 ....G7
Fleurus 8,523 ....E8
Florennes 4,107 ....F8
Forest 55,135 ....B9
Fosses-La-Ville 3,972 ....F8
Frameries 11,224 ....D8
Froidchapelle E8
Furnes (Veurne) 9,496 ....B6
Ganshoren 21,147 ....B9
Geel 29,346 ....F6
Geldenaken (Jodoigne) 4,132 ....F7
Gembloux-sur-Orneau 11,249 ....F7
Genk 57,913 ....H7
Gent (Ghent) 148,860 ....D6
Geraardsbergen 17,533 ....D7
Gerpinnes F8
Ghent 148,860 ....D6
Ghent* 477,000 ....D6
Gistel B6
Gooik E7
Gouvy H8
Grammont (Geraardsbergen) 17,533 ....D7
Grez-Doiceau F7
Grimbergen E7
Haacht 4,436 ....F7
Habay H9
Hal (Halle) 20,017 ....D8
Halen 5,322 ....G7
Halle 20,017 ....E7
Hamme 17,559 ....E6
Hamois G8
Hamont-Achel 6,893 ....H6
Hannuit (Hannut) 7,232 ....G7
Hannut 7,232 ....G7
Harelbeke 18,498 ....C7
Hasselt 39,663 ....G7
Hastière G8
Heist-Knokke 27,582 ....C6
Heist-op-den-Berg 13,472 ....F6
Hensies D8
Herentals 18,639 ....F6
Herne E7
Herselt 7,412 ....F6
Herstal 29,600 ....H7
Herve 4,118 ....H7
Heuvelland B7
Hoboken 33,693 ....E6
Hoei (Huy) 12,736 ....G7
Hoeselt 6,884 ....G7
Honnelles D8
Hoogstraten 4,381 ....F6
Hotton G8
Huy 12,736 ....G7
Ichtegem B6
Ieper 20,825 ....B7
Ingelmunster 10,245 ....C7
Ittre E7
Ixelles 86,450 ....C9
Izegem 22,928 ....C7
Jabbeke C6
Jemappes 18,632 ....D8
Jette 40,013 ....B9
Jodoigne 4,132 ....F7
Kalmthout 12,724 ....E6
Kapellen 13,352 ....E6
Kasterlee F6
Kinrooi H6
Knokke-Heist 27,582 ....C6
Koekelare 7,807 ....B6
Koekelberg 17,570 ....B9
Koksijde B6
Kontich 14,432 ....E6
Kortemark 5,904 ....C6
Kortrijk 44,961 ....C7
Kraainem 11,390 ....C9
La Louvière 23,310 ....E8
La Louvière* 113,259 ....E8
Lanaken 6,659 ....H7
Landen 5,740 ....G7
Langemark-Poelkapelle 5,457 ....B7
Lasne F7
Lede 10,316 ....D7
Léglise H9
Leopoldsburg 9,593 ....G6
Le Roeulx E8
Lessen (Lessines) 8,906 ....D7
Lessines 8,906 ....D7
Leuze-en-Hainaut 7,185 ....D7
Leuven 30,623 ....F7
Libin G9
Libramont-Chevigny 2,975 ....G9
Lichtervelde 7,459 ....C6
Liedekerke 10,482 ....E7
Liège 145,573 ....H7
Liège* 622,000 ....H7
Lier 28,416 ....F6
Lierre (Lier) 28,416 ....F6
Limbourg 3,762 ....J7
Limburg (Limbourg) 3,762 ....J7
Linkebeek 4,265 ....C10

Linter G7
Lochristi D6
Lokeren 26,740 ....E6
Lommel 21,984 ....G6
Lontzen H9
Looz (Borgloon) 3,412 ....G7
Lo-Reninge B7
Louvain (Leuven) 30,623 ....F7
Luik (Liège) 145,573 ....H7
Lummen G7
Maaseik 8,622 ....H6
Maasmechelen H7
Machelen 7,057 ....C9
Maldegem 14,474 ....C6
Malines (Mechelen) 65,466 ....F6
Malmédy 6,464 ....J8
Manage E7
Manhay H8
Marche-en-Famenne 4,567 ....G8
Marchin 4,206 ....G8
Mechelen 65,466 ....F6
Meerhout 8,567 ....G6
Meise E7
Menen 22,037 ....C7
Menin (Menen) 22,037 ....C7
Merchtem 8,998 ....E7
Merelbeke 13,837 ....D7
Merksem 39,768 ....E6
Merksplas 5,065 ....F6
Messancy 3,150 ....H9
Mettet 3,372 ....F8
Meulebeke 10,458 ....C7
Middelkerke B6
Moeskroen (Mouscron) 37,311 ....C7
Mol 28,823 ....G6
Molenbeek-Saint-Jean 68,411 ....B9
Momignies E8
Mons 59,362 ....E8
Montigny-le-Tilleul E8
Moorslede B7
Mortsel 28,012 ....E6
Mouscron 37,311 ....C7
Namen (Namur) 32,269 ....F8
Namur 32,269 ....F8
Nassogne G8
Nazareth D7
Neerpelt 8,771 ....G6
Neufchâteau 2,670 ....G9
Nevele D6
Nieuport (Nieuwpoort) 8,273 ....B6
Nieuwpoort 8,273 ....B6
Nijvel (Nivelles) 16,126 ....E7
Ninove 12,428 ....D7
Nivelles 16,126 ....E7
Ohey G8
Onhaye F8
Oostende (Ostend) 71,227 ....B6
Oostkamp 8,999 ....C6
Opwijk 9,699 ....E7
Ostend 71,227 ....B6
Oudenaarde 26,615 ....D7
Oudenburg B6
Oud-Turnhout 9,245 ....F6
Oupeye H7
Overijse 16,181 ....F7
Overpelt 10,470 ....G6
Paliseul G9
Peer 7,201 ....G6
Péruwelz 7,878 ....D8
Philippeville 2,076 ....E8
Plombières F7
Pont-à-Celles E8
Poperinge 12,671 ....B7
Profondeville F8
Putte 6,953 ....F6
Quaregnon 17,688 ....D8
Quévy D8
Quiévrain 5,510 ....D8
Raeren 3,655 ....J7
Ravels G6
Rebecq 3,744 ....E7
Renaix (Ronse) 25,056 ....D7
Rendeux H8
Retie 6,619 ....G6
Rochefort 4,357 ....G8
Roeselare 40,428 ....C7
Ronse 25,056 ....D7
Roulers (Roeselare) 40,428 ....C7
Rouvroy G9
Ruiselede C6
Sainte-Ode H8
Saint-Georges-sur-Meuse 6,003 ....G7
Saint-Gilles 55,055 ....B9
Saint-Hubert 3,091 ....G8
Saint-Josse-ten-Noode 23,633 ....C9
Saint-Nicolas
Saint-Trond (Sint-Truiden) 21,473 ....G7
Saint-Vith (Sankt Vith) 3,001 ....J8
Sankt Vith 3,001 ....J8
Schaerbeek 118,950 ....C9
Schoten 29,914 ....F6
Seraing 40,545 ....G7
's-Gravenbrakel (Braine-le-Comte) 11,957 ....D7
Sint-Laureins D6
Sint-Niklaas 49,214 ....E6

(continued on following page)

Agriculture, Industry and Resources

DOMINANT LAND USE

- Dairy, Truck Farming
- Cash Crops, Livestock
- Mixed Cereals, Dairy
- Specialized Horticulture
- Grapes, Wine
- Forests
- Sand Dunes

MAJOR MINERAL OCCURRENCES

C   Coal
Fe   Iron Ore
G   Natural Gas
Na   Salt
O   Petroleum

/////   Major Industrial Areas

Land from the Sea

NORTH SEA — WEST FRISIAN ISLANDS — WADDENZEE — Leeuwarden — Enclosing Dam 1932 — Wieringermeer Polder 1930 — IJSSELMEER (ZUIDER ZEE) — North East Polder 1942 — Markerwaard (planned) — East Flevoland 1957 — South Flevoland 1969 — Amsterdam — Haarlemmer Lake 1852

1600, 1400, 1280, 1242, 1427, 1200, 1847, 1824, 1599, 1610, 1456, 1844, 1927, 1564, 1631, 1608, 1635, 1683, 1612, 1626, 1872, 1622, 1628

Reclaimed Land and Dates of Completion
Future Polders
☐ =10 Square Miles

For centuries the Dutch have been renowned for the drainage of marshes and the construction of polders, i.e., arable land reclaimed from the sea. Future projects will convert much of the present IJsselmeer to agricultural land.

Topography

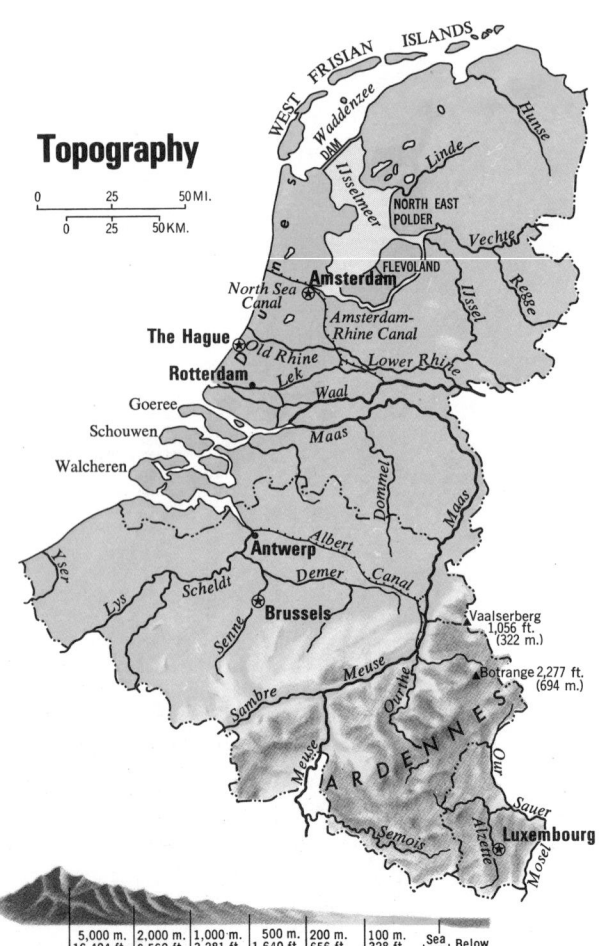

0   25   50 MI.

0   25   50 KM.

WEST FRISIAN ISLANDS — Waddenzee — IJsselmeer — NORTH EAST POLDER — FLEVOLAND — Linde — Hunse — Vechte — Regge — IJssel — Amsterdam — North Sea Canal — Amsterdam-Rhine Canal — The Hague — Old Rhine — Lower Rhine — Rotterdam — Lek — Waal — Goeree — Maas — Schouwen — Walcheren — Yser — Lys — Scheldt — Senne — Dommel — Maas — Antwerp — Demer — Albert Canal — Brussels — Sombre — Ourthe — Meuse — Meuse — Semois — Sauer — Alzette — Moxel — ARDENNES — Luxembourg

Vaalserberg 1,056 ft. (322 m.)

Botrange 2,277 ft. (694 m.)

5,000 m. 16,404 ft. | 2,000 m. 6,562 ft. | 1,000 m. 3,281 ft. | 500 m. 1,640 ft. | 200 m. 656 ft. | 100 m. 328 ft. | Sea Level | Below

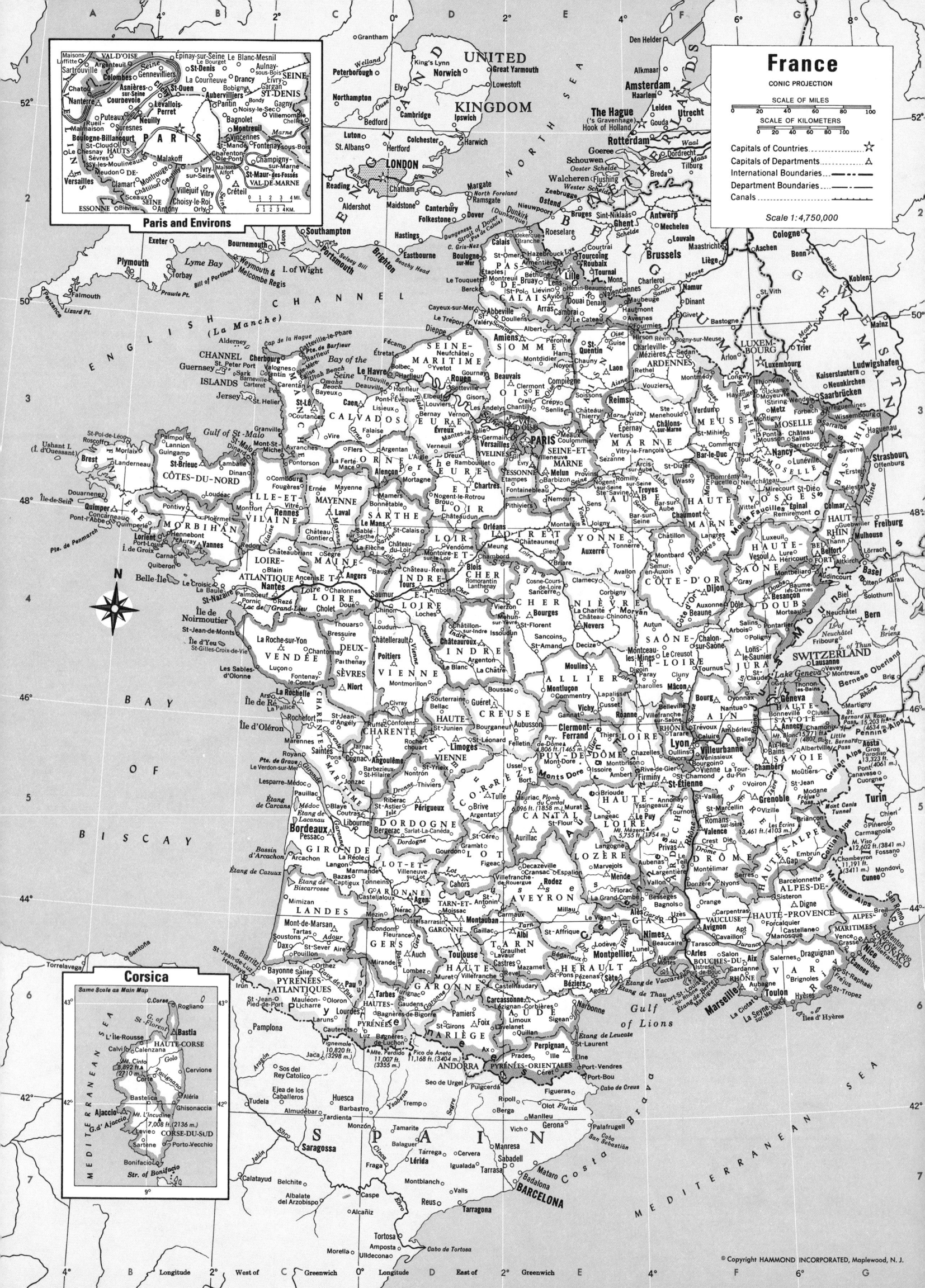

DEPARTMENTS

Ain 376,477 .... F4
Aisne 533,862 .... E3
Allier 378,406 .... E4
Alpes-de-Haute-Provence 112,178 .... G5
Alpes-Maritimes 816,681 .... G6
Ardèche 257,065 .... F5
Ardennes 309,306 .... F3
Ariège 137,857 .... D6
Aube 284,823 .... E3
Aude 272,366 .... E6
Aveyron 278,306 .... E5
Bas-Rhin 882,121 .... G3
Belfort (terr.) 128,125 .... G4
Bouches-du-Rhône 1,632,974 .... F6
Calvados 560,967 .... C3
Cantal 166,549 .... E5
Charente 337,064 .... D5
Charente-Maritime 497,859 .... C5
Cher 316,350 .... E4
Corrèze 240,363 .... D5
Corse du Sud 128,634 .... B6
Côte-d'Or 456,070 .... F4
Côtes-du-Nord 525,556 .... B3
Creuse 146,214 .... D4
Deux-Sèvres 335,829 .... C4
Dordogne 373,179 .... D5
Doubs 471,082 .... G4
Drôme 361,847 .... F5
Essonne 923,063 .... E3
Eure 422,952 .... D3
Eure-et-Loir 335,151 .... D3
Finistère 804,088 .... A3
Gard 494,575 .... F6
Gers 175,366 .... D6
Gironde 1,061,480 .... C5
Haute-Corse 161,208 .... B6
Haute-Garonne 777,431 .... D6
Haute-Loire 205,491 .... E5
Haute-Marne 212,304 .... F3
Hautes-Alpes 97,358 .... G5
Haute-Saône 222,254 .... G4
Haute-Savoie 447,795 .... G5
Hautes-Pyrénées 227,222 .... D6
Haute-Vienne 352,149 .... D5
Haut-Rhin 635,209 .... G4
Hauts-de-Seine 1,438,930 .... A2
Hérault 648,202 .... E6
Ille-et-Vilaine 702,199 .... C3
Indre 248,523 .... D4
Indre-et-Loire 478,601 .... D4
Isère 860,339 .... F5
Jura 238,856 .... F4
Landes 288,323 .... C5
Loire 742,396 .... F5
Loire-Atlantique 934,499 .... C4
Loiret 490,189 .... E4
Loir-et-Cher 283,686 .... D4
Lot 150,778 .... D5
Lot-et-Garonne 292,616 .... D5
Lozère 74,825 .... E5
Maine-et-Loire 629,849 .... C4
Manche 451,662 .... C3
Marne 530,399 .... F3
Mayenne 261,789 .... C3
Meurthe-et-Moselle 722,588 .... G3
Meuse 203,904 .... F3
Morbihan 563,588 .... B4
Moselle 1,006,373 .... G3
Nièvre 245,212 .... E4
Nord 2,510,738 .... E2
Oise 606,320 .... E3
Orne 293,523 .... C3
Paris (city) 2,299,830 .... B2
Pas-de-Calais 1,403,035 .... E2
Puy-de-Dôme 580,033 .... E5
Pyrénées-Atlantiques 534,748 .... C6
Pyrénées-Orientales 299,506 .... E6
Rhône 1,429,647 .... F5
Saône-et-Loire 569,810 .... F4
Sarthe 490,385 .... D3
Savoie 305,118 .... G5
Seine-et-Marne 755,762 .... E3
Seine-Saint-Denis 1,322,127 .... C1
Somme 538,462 .... E3
Tarn 338,024 .... E6
Tarn-et-Garonne 183,314 .... D5
Val-de-Marne 1,215,713 .... C1
Val-d'Oise 840,885 .... E3
Var 626,093 .... G6
Vaucluse 390,446 .... F6
Vendée 450,641 .... C4
Vienne 357,366 .... D4
Vosges 397,957 .... G3
Yonne 299,851 .... E4
Yvelines 1,082,255 .... D3

CITIES and TOWNS

Abbeville 25,252 .... D2
Agde 9,856 .... E6
Agen 33,763 .... D5
Aix-en-Provence 91,665 .... F6
Aix-les-Bains 21,884 .... G5
Ajaccio 47,065 .... B7
Albert 11,746 .... E2
Albertville 16,630 .... G5
Albi 43,942 .... E6
Alençon 32,917 .... D3
Alès 33,315 .... E5
Ambérieu-en-Bugey 9,294 .... F5
Amboise 10,498 .... D4
Amiens 129,453 .... D3
Ancenis 6,689 .... C4
Angers 136,603 .... C4
Angoulême 46,293 .... D5
Annecy 53,058 .... G5
Annonay 19,234 .... F5
Antibes 44,226 .... G6
Antony 57,450 .... B2
Apt 9,735 .... F6
Arcachon 13,856 .... C5
Argentan 16,063 .... D3
Argenteuil 101,542 .... A1
Arles 37,337 .... F6
Armentières 23,850 .... E2
Arras 45,804 .... E2
Asnières-sur-Seine 75,328 .... A1
Aubagne 26,145 .... F6
Aubenas 11,967 .... F5
Aubervilliers 72,859 .... B1
Auch 18,767 .... D6
Audincourt 18,570 .... G4
Aulnay-sous-Bois 77,982 .... B1
Auray 10,006 .... B4
Aurignac 744 .... D6
Aurillac 29,458 .... E5
Autun 19,441 .... F4
Auxerre 36,039 .... E4
Auxonne 6,414 .... F4
Avallon 8,518 .... E4
Avignon 73,482 .... F6
Avion 22,860 .... E2
Avranches 10,128 .... C3
Ax-les-Thermes 1,456 .... D6
Bagnères-de-Bigorre 9,080 .... D6
Bagnolet 35,858 .... B2
Bagnols-sur-Cèze 13,111 .... F5
Barbizon 1,189 .... E3
Barcelonnette 2,523 .... G5
Barfleur 701 .... C3
Bar-le-Duc 19,188 .... F3
Bar-sur-Aube 7,227 .... F3
Bastia 45,387 .... B6
Bayeux 13,381 .... C3
Bayonne 41,281 .... C6
Beaucaire 10,189 .... F6
Beaune 16,386 .... F4
Beauvais 53,493 .... E3
Belfort 54,469 .... G4
Belley 6,612 .... F5
Berck 14,104 .... D2
Bergerac 25,488 .... D5
Bernay 9,928 .... D3
Besançon 119,803 .... G4
Béthune 26,208 .... E2
Béziers 79,213 .... E6
Biarritz 27,453 .... C6
Blois 49,134 .... D4
Bobigny 43,041 .... B1
Bogny-sur-Meuse 6,845 .... F3
Bolbec 12,347 .... D3
Bondy 48,285 .... B1
Bonneville 6,717 .... G4
Bordeaux 220,830 .... C5
Boulogne-Billancourt 103,527 .... A2
Boulogne-sur-Mer 48,309 .... D2
Bourg-en-Bresse 40,052 .... F4
Bourges 75,200 .... E4
Bourgoin-Jallieu 18,504 .... F5
Bressuire 9,778 .... C4
Brest 163,940 .... A3
Briançon 8,523 .... G5

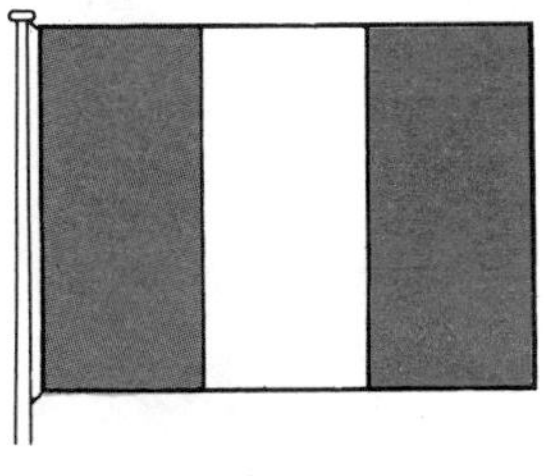

Brignoles 8,784 .... G6
Brioude 7,756 .... E5
Brive-la-Gaillarde 49,276 .... D5
Bruay-en-Artois 25,544 .... E2
Caen 116,987 .... C3
Cahors 19,288 .... D5
Calais 73,009 .... D2
Caluire-et-Cuire 43,024 .... F5
Cambrai 38,706 .... E2
Cannes 70,226 .... G6
Carcassonne 38,887 .... D6
Carmaux 11,970 .... E5
Carpentras 20,169 .... F5
Castelnaudary 8,947 .... E6
Castelsarrasin 6,562 .... D6
Castres 41,037 .... E6
Cavaillon 17,383 .... F6
Châlons-sur-Marne 50,870 .... F3
Chalon-sur-Saône 55,495 .... F4
Chambéry 52,286 .... F5
Chambord 166 .... D4
Chamonix-Mont-Blanc 6,246 .... G5
Champigny-sur-Marne 80,189 .... C2
Chantilly 10,517 .... E3
Charenton-le-Pont 20,383 .... B2
Charleville-Mézières 59,513 .... F3
Chartres 38,574 .... D3
Châteaubriant 12,417 .... C4
Château-du-Loir 5,598 .... D4
Châteaudun 14,634 .... D3
Château-Gontier 8,301 .... C4
Châteauroux 53,166 .... D4
Château-Thierry 13,379 .... E3
Châtellerault 33,811 .... D4
Châtillon 26,562 .... B2
Châtillon-sur-Seine 7,367 .... F4
Chatou 26,415 .... A1
Chaumont 26,568 .... F3
Chauny 14,324 .... E3
Chelles 24,192 .... C1
Cherbourg 31,333 .... C3
Chinon 5,378 .... D4
Choisy-le-Roi 38,629 .... B2
Cholet 49,887 .... C4
Clamart 52,881 .... A2
Clermont 7,834 .... E3
Clermont-Ferrand 153,379 .... E5
Clichy 47,731 .... B1
Cluny 4,335 .... F4
Cluses 12,713 .... G4
Cognac 21,567 .... C5
Colmar 58,585 .... G3
Colombes 83,241 .... A1
Commentry 8,074 .... E4
Commercy 6,918 .... F3
Compiègne 37,009 .... E3
Concarneau 15,096 .... A4
Cosne-Cours-sur-Loire 9,768 .... E4
Coudekerque-Branche 24,702 .... E2
Coulommiers 11,363 .... E3
Courbevoie 54,391 .... A1
Coutances 8,286 .... C3
Creil 31,893 .... E3
Crépy-en-Valois 10,661 .... E3
Créteil 58,665 .... B2
Cusset 13,672 .... E4
Dax 18,019 .... C6
Deauville 5,655 .... C3
Decazeville 9,318 .... E5
Decize 6,853 .... E4
Denain 26,096 .... E2
Dieppe 25,607 .... D3

AREA 210,038 sq. mi. (543,998 sq. km.)
POPULATION 53,788,000
CAPITAL Paris
LARGEST CITY Paris
HIGHEST POINT Mont Blanc 15,771 ft. (4,807 m.)
MONETARY UNIT franc
MAJOR LANGUAGE French
MAJOR RELIGION Roman Catholicism

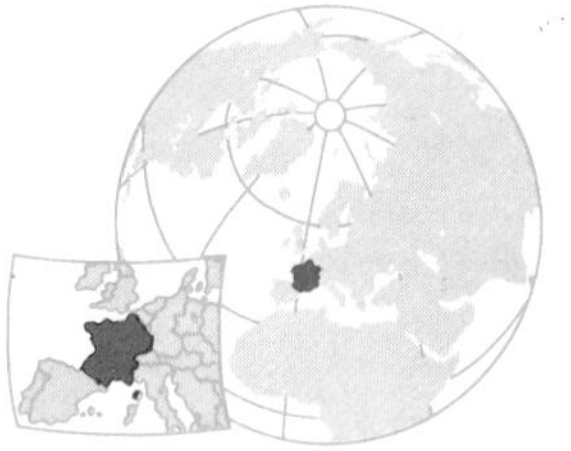

Topography

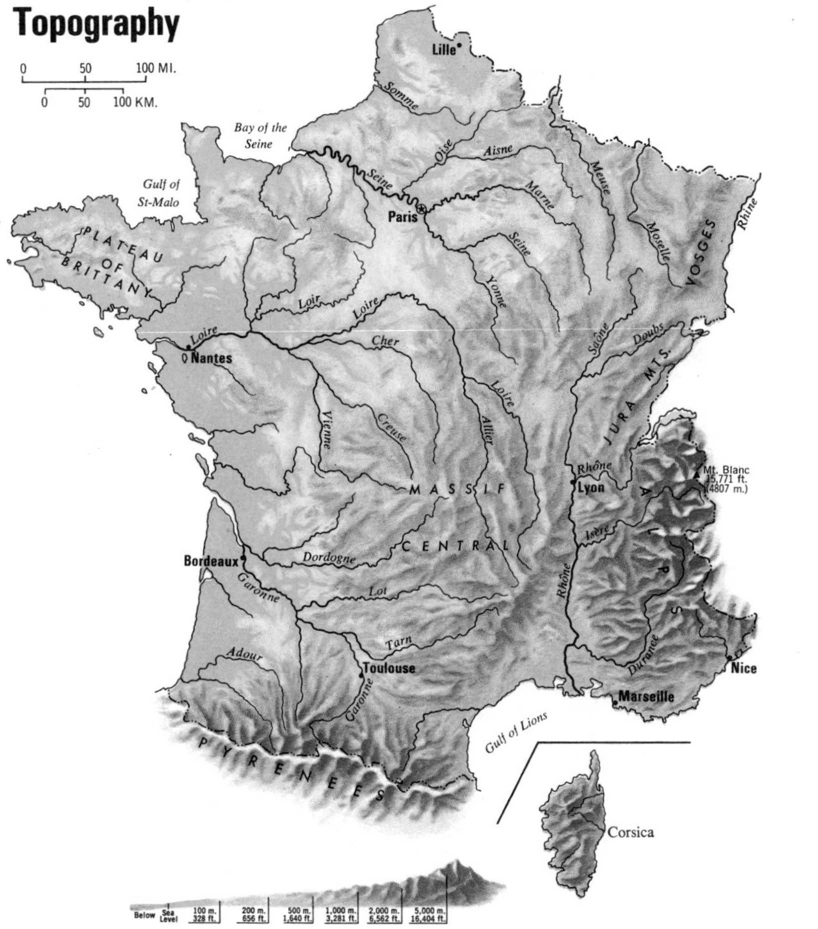

Historic Provinces

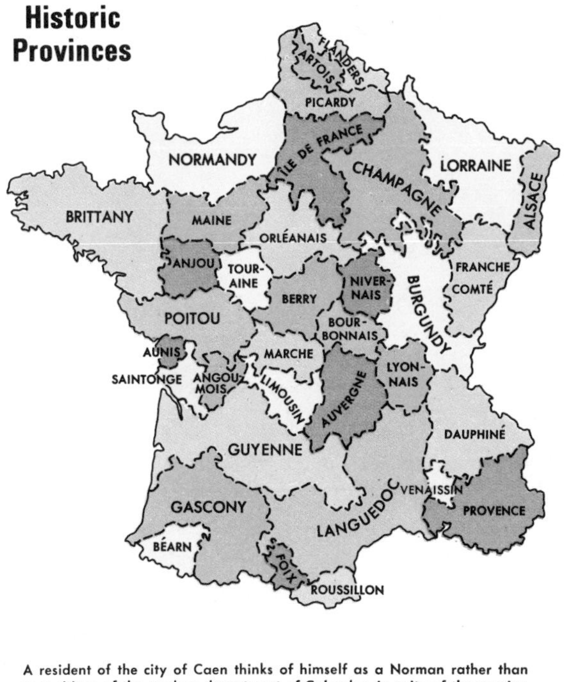

A resident of the city of Caen thinks of himself as a Norman rather than as a citizen of the modern department of Calvados. In spite of the passing of nearly two centuries, the historic provinces which existed before 1790 command the local patriotism of most Frenchmen.

Digne 13,140 .... G5
Digoin 10,449 .... F4
Dijon 149,899 .... F4
Dinan 13,303 .... B3
Dinard 9,211 .... B3
Dôle 28,109 .... F4
Domrémy-la-Pucelle 190 .... F3
Douai 43,954 .... E2
Douarnenez 17,851 .... A3
Doullens 6,806 .... E2
Draguignan 19,653 .... G6
Drancy 64,258 .... B1
Dreux 31,503 .... D3
Dunkirk (Dunkerque) 78,171 .... E2
Elbeuf 18,642 .... D3
Épernay 29,286 .... E3
Épinal 39,000 .... G3
Épinay-sur-Seine 46,458 .... B1
Erstein 6,494 .... G3
Étampes 18,810 .... E3
Étaples 10,423 .... D2
Eu 8,349 .... D3
Évreux 46,181 .... D3
Évry 15,300 .... E3
Falaise 8,133 .... C3
Fécamp 20,835 .... D3
Figeac 8,675 .... D5
Firminy 23,776 .... F5
Flers 18,590 .... C3
Foix 9,569 .... D6
Fontainebleau 16,436 .... E3
Fontenay-le-Comte 12,301 .... C4
Fontenay-sous-Bois 46,200 .... C2
Forbach 24,812 .... G3
Fougères 26,260 .... C3
Fourmies 15,318 .... F2
Fréjus 27,805 .... G6
Gagny 36,714 .... C1
Gaillac 7,653 .... D6
Gap 24,962 .... G5
Gardanne 8,175 .... F6
Gennevillers 50,154 .... B1
Gentilly 16,843 .... B2
Gex 3,959 .... G4
Gien 13,817 .... E4
Gif 10,866 .... E3
Gisors 7,591 .... D3
Givet 7,787 .... F2
Givors 19,356 .... F5
Granville 12,869 .... C3
Grasse 24,260 .... G6
Graulhet 11,099 .... E6
Gray 8,718 .... F4
Grenoble 165,431 .... F5
Guebwiller 10,477 .... G4
Guéret 14,418 .... D4
Guingamp 9,269 .... B3
Guise 6,642 .... E3
Haguenau 23,023 .... G3
Harfleur 9,857 .... D3
Hautmont 19,130 .... F2
Hayange 8,479 .... F3
Hazebrouck 18,867 .... E2
Hendaye 9,404 .... C6
Hénin-Beaumont 26,296 .... E2
Hennebont 8,978 .... B4
Héricourt 8,481 .... G4
Hirson 11,909 .... F3
Honfleur 8,995 .... D3
Hyères 29,366 .... G6
Issoire 13,560 .... E5
Issoudun 15,065 .... D4
Issy-les-Moulineaux 47,355 .... A2
Istres 10,127 .... F6
Ivry-sur-Seine 62,804 .... B2
Joigny 10,825 .... E3
La Baule-Escoublac 13,854 .... B4
La Ciotat 29,290 .... F6
La Courneuve 37,917 .... B1
La Flèche 12,743 .... C4
La Grand-Combe 9,406 .... E5
L'Aigle 9,198 .... D3
Landerneau 13,983 .... B3
Langres 10,745 .... F4
Lannion 13,692 .... B3
Laon 27,420 .... E3
La Pallice C4
La Rochelle 72,936 .... C4
La Roche-sur-Yon 40,789 .... C4
La Seyne-sur-Mer 50,059 .... F6
Laval 50,734 .... C3
Lavelanet 9,278 .... E6
Le Blanc 7,431 .... D4
Le Blanc-Mesnil 49,062 .... B1
Le Bourget 10,520 .... B1
Le Cateau 8,680 .... E2
Le Chesnay 24,590 .... A2
Le Creusot 31,643 .... F4
Le Havre 216,917 .... C3
Le Mans 150,289 .... C3
Lens 39,973 .... E2
Le Puy 24,793 .... F5
Les Andelys 7,524 .... D3
Les Sables-d'Olonne 17,157 .... B4
Le Teil 7,993 .... F5
Le Tréport 6,463 .... D2
Levallois-Perret 52,460 .... A1
Lézignan-Corbières 6,929 .... E6
Libourne 21,265 .... C5
Liévin 33,040 .... E2
Lille 171,010 .... E2
Limoges 136,059 .... D5
Limoux 9,595 .... E6
Lisieux 24,972 .... D3
Livry-Gargan 32,879 .... C1
Lodève 7,131 .... E6
Longwy 20,107 .... F3
Lons-le-Saunier 20,897 .... F4
Lorient 68,655 .... B4
Loudéac 7,173 .... B3
Loudun 7,060 .... D4
Lourdes 17,685 .... C6
Louviers 17,919 .... D3
Luçon 8,834 .... C4
Lunel 12,392 .... E6
Lunéville 22,438 .... G3
Lure 8,538 .... G4
Luxeuil-les-Bains 10,061 .... G4
Lyon 454,265 .... F5
Mâcon 39,130 .... F4
Maisons-Alfort 53,963 .... B2
Maisons-Laffitte 23,465 .... A1
Malakoff 34,100 .... A2
Manosque 17,256 .... G6
Mantes-la-Jolie 42,408 .... D3
Marmande 13,223 .... C5
Marseille 901,421 .... F6
Martigues 26,850 .... F6
Maubeuge 34,152 .... F2
Mayenne 11,278 .... C3
Mazamet 13,148 .... E6
Meaux 41,831 .... E3
Mehun-sur-Yèvre 6,533 .... E4
Melun 36,913 .... E3
Mende 10,040 .... E5
Menton 24,736 .... G6
Metz 110,939 .... G3
Meudon 31,294 .... A2
Millau 20,401 .... E5
Mimizan 6,826 .... C5
Mirecourt 7,160 .... G3
Moissac 7,403 .... D5
Montargis 18,021 .... E3
Montauban 35,344 .... D5
Montbard 7,477 .... F4
Montbéliard 29,968 .... G4
Montbrison 9,945 .... E5
Montceau-les-Mines 28,093 .... F4
Mont-de-Marsan 24,812 .... C6
Mont-Dore 2,074 .... E5
Montélimar 25,422 .... F5
Montfort 2,701 .... C3
Montigny-les-Metz 24,208 .... G3
Montluçon 56,337 .... E4
Montmédy 1,859 .... F3
Montpellier 178,136 .... E6
Montreuil, Seine-Saint-Denis 96,441 .... B2
Montrouge 40,189 .... B2
Mont-Saint-Michel 88 .... C3
Morlaix 15,919 .... B3
Morteau 6,515 .... G4
Moulins 25,856 .... E4
Moyeuvre-Grande 12,448 .... G3
Mulhouse 116,494 .... G4
Muret 13,041 .... D6
Nancy 106,906 .... G3
Nanterre 94,441 .... A1
Nantes 252,537 .... C4
Narbonne 36,525 .... E6
Nemours 11,159 .... E3
Neufchâteau 8,582 .... F3
Neuilly-sur-Seine 65,941 .... A1
Nevers 45,122 .... E4
Nice 331,002 .... G6
Nîmes 123,914 .... F6
Niort 59,297 .... C4
Nogent-le-Rotrou 12,284 .... D3
Noisy-le-Sec 37,674 .... B1
Noyon 13,784 .... E3
Oloron-Sainte-Marie 11,616 .... C6
Orange 19,847 .... F5
Orléans 88,503 .... D3
Orly 26,090 .... B2
Orthez 9,639 .... C6
Oullins 27,731 .... F5
Oyonnax 22,548 .... F4
Pamiers 12,906 .... D6
Pantin 42,651 .... B1
Paray-le-Monial 11,523 .... F4
Paris (cap.) 2,291,554 .... B2
Parthenay 12,549 .... C4
Pau 81,560 .... C6
Périgueux 34,779 .... D5
Péronne 8,358 .... E3
Perpignan 101,198 .... E6
Pessac 50,333 .... C5
Pézenas 6,768 .... E6
Pithiviers 9,976 .... E3
Poitiers 78,739 .... D4
Pont-à-Mousson 14,461 .... G3
Pontarlier 17,778 .... G4
Pontivy 9,478 .... B3
Pont-l'Abbe 6,618 .... A4
Pontoise 26,702 .... E3
Port-de-Bouc 20,448 .... F6
Port-Saint-Louis-du-Rhône 9,649 .... F6
Port-Vendres 5,448 .... E6
Privas 9,385 .... F5
Provins 12,281 .... E3
Puteau 35,366 .... A2
Quimper 50,856 .... A4
Quimperlé 9,783 .... B4
Rambouillet 18,446 .... D3
Redon 9,528 .... C4
Reims 177,320 .... E3
Remiremont 10,250 .... G3
Rennes 194,094 .... C3

(continued on following page)

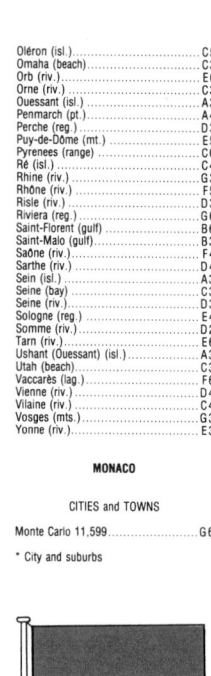
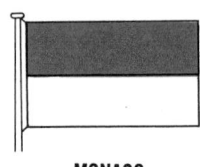

MONACO

AREA   368 acres
(149 hectares)
POPULATION   25,029

Wine Regions

CALVADOS (distilled from cider)

CHAMPAGNE · ALSACE · Colmar · Reims · Caen

Chablis · BURGUNDY · Côte-d'Or · Beaune · JURA · Mâcon · Beaujolais · Mâconnais

Anjou · Touraine · POUILLY SANCERRE · QUINCY REUILLY · LOIRE VALLEY · Angers · Tours

COGNAC · Cognac

BORDEAUX · Bordeaux · Bergerac · Médoc · Graves · Sauternes · CÔTES DE DURAS · Valence · CÔTES DU RHÔNE · Avignon · PROVENCE · Toulon

ARMAGNAC · Auch · GAILLAC · LANGUEDOC · Béziers · JURANÇON · Pau · LIMOUX · ROUSSILLON

Climate, soil and variety of grape planted determine the quality of wine. Long, hot and fairly dry summers with cool, humid nights constitute an ideal climate. The nature of the soil is such a determining influence that identical grapes planted in Bordeaux, Burgundy and Champagne, will yield wines of widely different types.

Agriculture, Industry and Resources

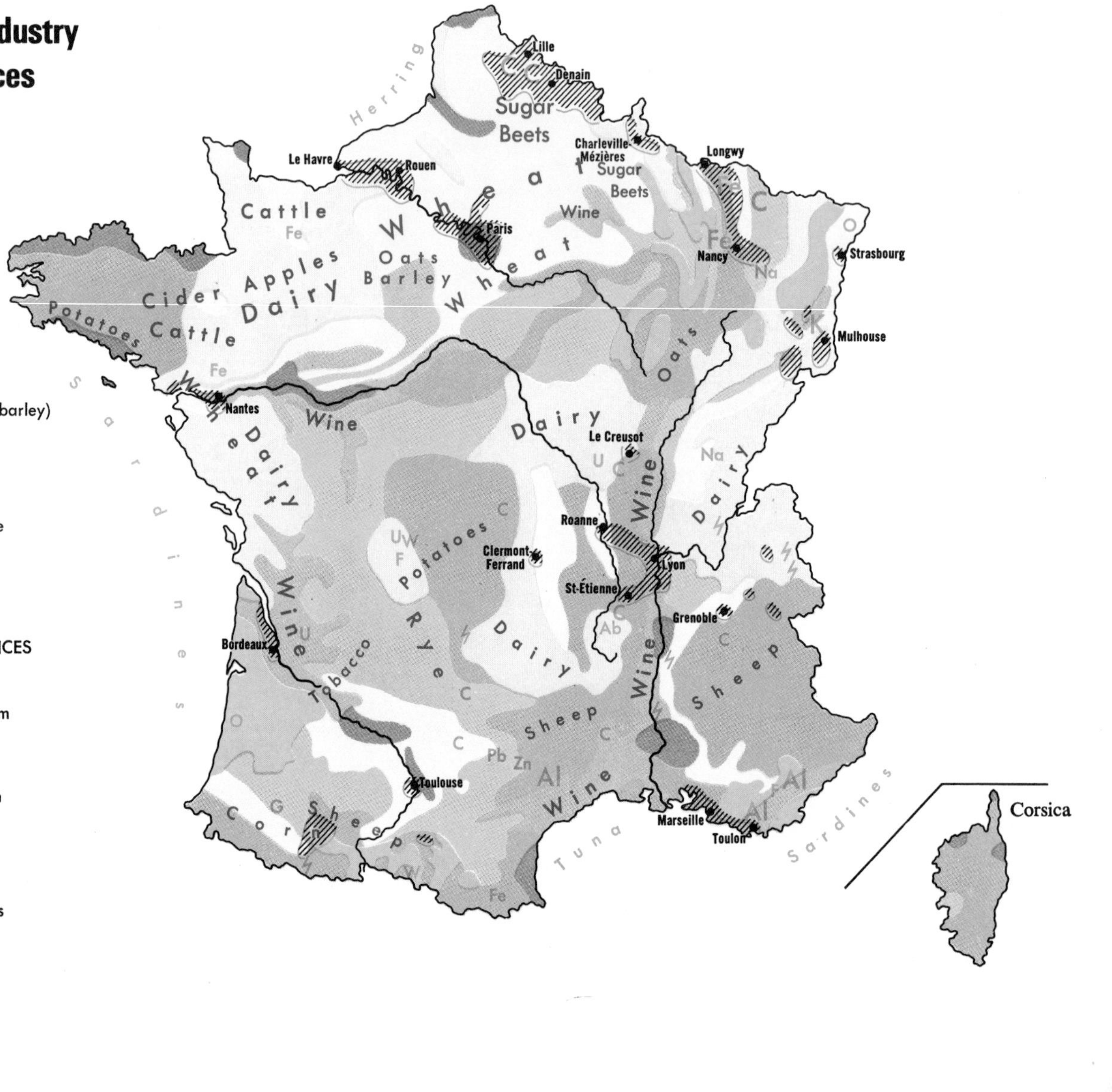

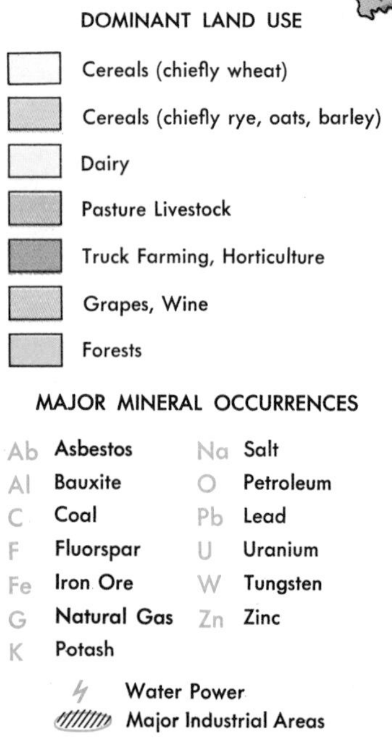

DOMINANT LAND USE

- Cereals (chiefly wheat)
- Cereals (chiefly rye, oats, barley)
- Dairy
- Pasture Livestock
- Truck Farming, Horticulture
- Grapes, Wine
- Forests

MAJOR MINERAL OCCURRENCES

Ab	Asbestos	Na	Salt
Al	Bauxite	O	Petroleum
C	Coal	Pb	Lead
F	Fluorspar	U	Uranium
Fe	Iron Ore	W	Tungsten
G	Natural Gas	Zn	Zinc
K	Potash		

⚡ Water Power

▨ Major Industrial Areas

Corsica

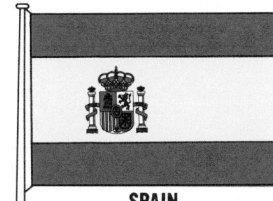

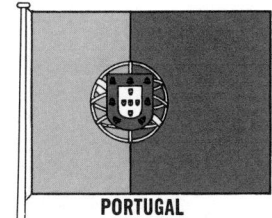

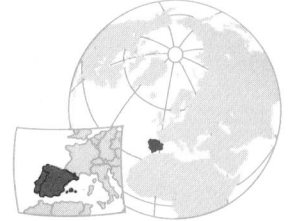

ANDORRA **SPAIN** **PORTUGAL**

Agriculture, Industry and Resources

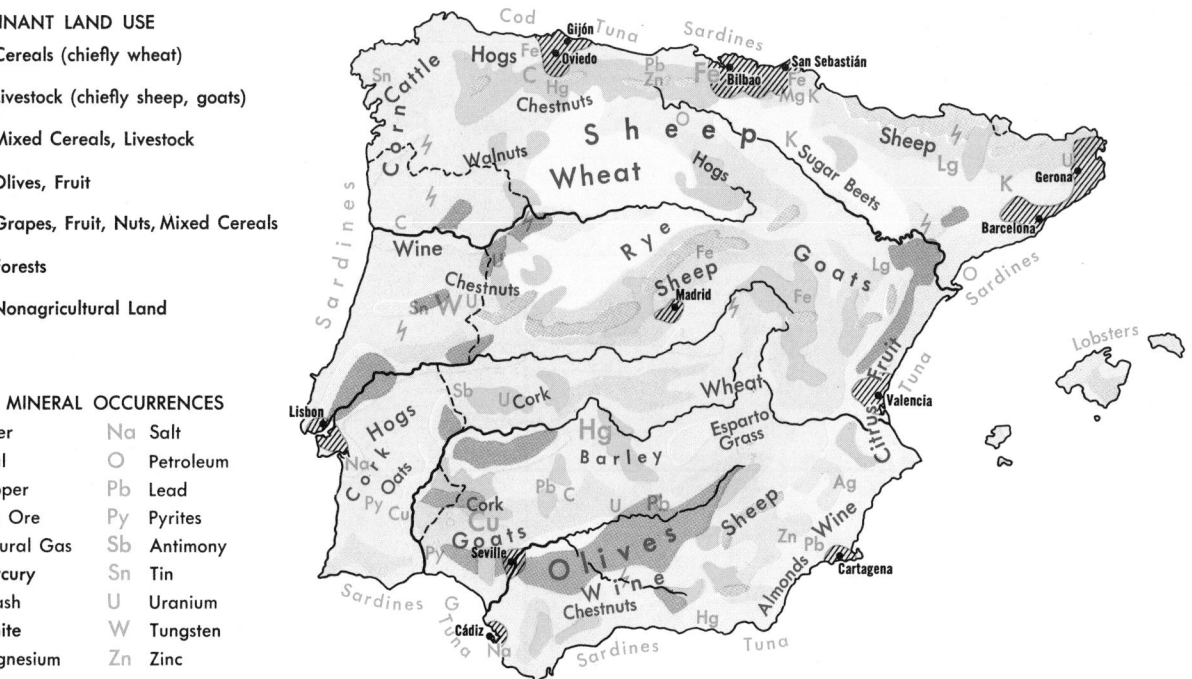

(continued on following page)

Topography

Below Sea Level | 100 m. 328 ft. | 200 m. 656 ft. | 500 m. 1,640 ft. | 1,000 m. 3,281 ft. | 2,000 m. 6,562 ft. | 5,000 m. 16,404 ft.

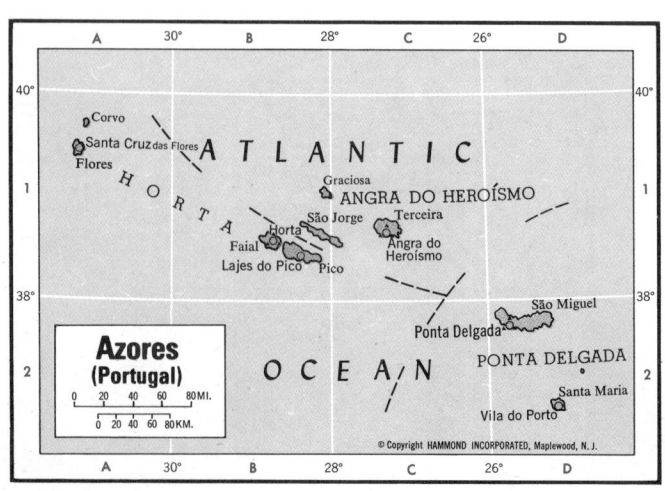

Azores (Portugal)

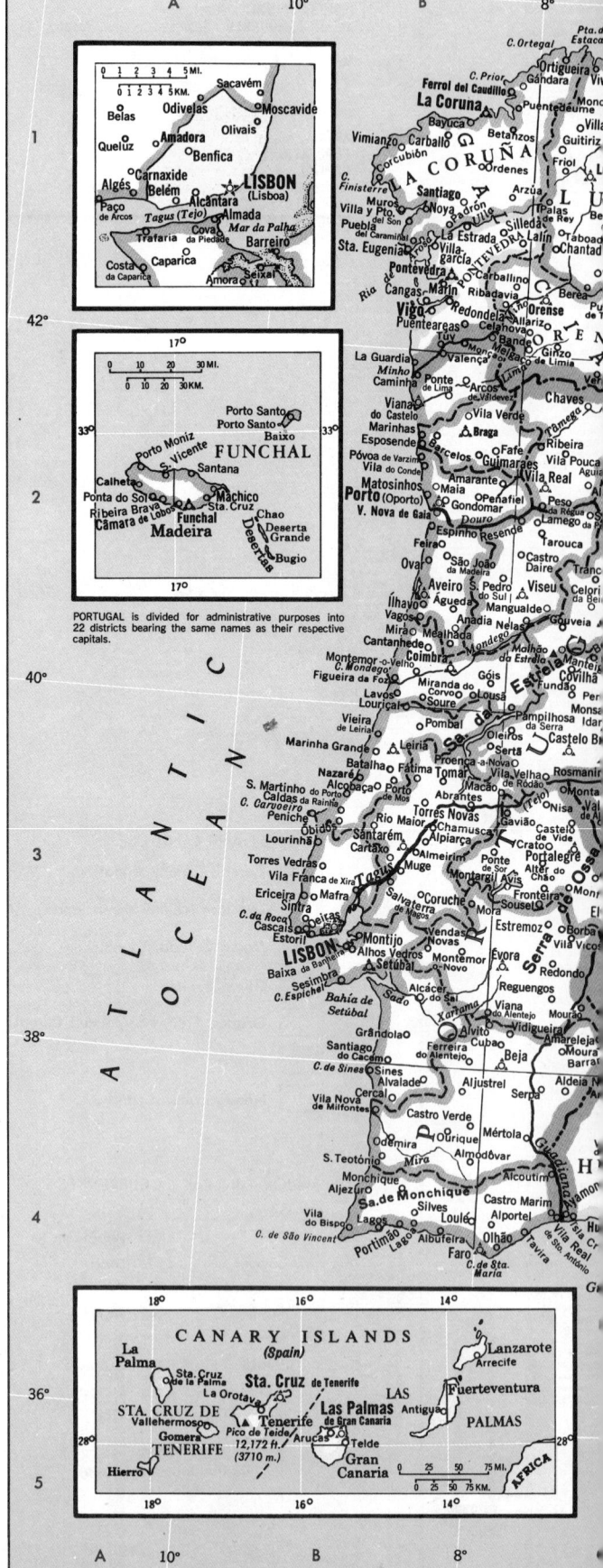

PORTUGAL is divided for administrative purposes into 22 districts bearing the same names as their respective capitals.

Alcobaça 4,799 ...... B3
Aldeia Nova de São
Bento 5,228 ...... C4
Algés 18,010 ...... A1
Alhos Vedros 7,915 ...... A3
Aljustrel 7,473 ...... B4
Almada 38,990 ...... A3
Almeirim 8,780 ...... B3
Alpiarça 7,623 ...... B3
Alportel 7,632 ...... C2
Amadora 65,870 ...... A1
Amarante 6,067 ...... C2
Amora 10,330 ...... A1
Aveiro 19,905 ...... C3
Avis 1,686 ...... B3
Baixa da Banheira 18,550 ...... A3
Barreiro 53,690 ...... B1
Batalha 6,673 ...... B3
Beja 14,760 ...... C3
Belas 12,001 ...... A1
Belém 19,043 ...... A1
Benfica 39,459 ...... A1
Borba 4,879 ...... C3
Braga 48,735 ...... B2
Bragança 9,310 ...... C2
Caldas da Rainha 13,070 ...... B3
Câmara de Lobos 14,068 ...... A2

Campo Maior 7,405 ...... C3
Canhede 6,734 ...... C3
Caparica 13,315 ...... A1
Carnaxide 38,309 ...... A1
Cartaxo 6,628 ...... B3
Cascais 14,925 ...... A3
Castelo Branco 18,740 ...... C3
Cercal 5,021 ...... B4
Chaves 11,465 ...... C2
Coimbra 55,985 ...... B3
Coruche 17,461 ...... B3
Cova da Piedade 21,000 ...... A1
Covilhã 26,530 ...... C2
Elvas 10,305 ...... C3
Espinho 11,745 ...... B2
Estremoz 9,565 ...... C3
Évora 23,665 ...... C3
Fafe 8,142 ...... C2
Faro 20,470 ...... B4
Fátima 6,433 ...... B3
Feira 5,222 ...... B2
Ferreira do Alentejo 6,153 ...... B4
Figueira da Foz 10,485 ...... B3
Funchal 38,340 ...... A2
Fundão 5,081 ...... C2
Gondomar 14,105 ...... B2

Grândola 9,698 ...... B3
Guarda 9,735 ...... C2
Guimarães 24,280 ...... B2
Ílhavo 11,083 ...... B2
Lagoa 5,694 ...... B4
Lagos 10,359 ...... B4
Lamego 10,350 ...... C2
Lavos 5,051 ...... B3
Leiria 7,540 ...... B3
Lisbon (Lisboa) (cap.) 769,410 ...... A1
Lisbon‡ 1,100,000 ...... A1
Loulé 12,777 ...... B4
Lourical 6,087 ...... B3
Lourinhã 7,340 ...... A3
Lousã 7,341 ...... B3
Machico 10,905 ...... A2
Mafra 7,149 ...... A3
Manguale 4,839 ...... C2
Marinha Grande 18,548 ...... B3
Matosinhos 22,505 ...... B2
Mira 12,740 ...... B2
Mirandela 5,203 ...... C2
Monchique 8,155 ...... B4
Montemor-o-Novo 9,284 ...... B3
Montijo 26,730 ...... A3
Moscavide 21,765 ...... A1

Moura 9,351 ...... C3
Nazaré 8,553 ...... A3
Odemira 6,793 ...... B4
Odivelas 26,020 ...... A1
Oeiras 14,880 ...... A3
Olhão 15,155 ...... B4
Olivais 55,138 ...... A1
Oporto (Porto) 300,925 ...... B2
Ovar 16,004 ...... B2
Paço de Arcos 11,791 ...... A1
Penafiel 6,463 ...... B2
Peniche 12,555 ...... A3
Peso da Régua 5,376 ...... C2
Pombal 12,508 ...... B3
Ponta do Sol 5,599 ...... A2
Ponte de Sor 9,951 ...... B3
Portalegre 10,970 ...... C3
Portimão 10,300 ...... B4
Porto 300,925 ...... B2
Póvoa de Varzim 17,415 ...... B2
Proença-a-Nova 4,792 ...... B3
Queluz 25,845 ...... A1
Redondo 6,858 ...... C3
Reguengos de Monsaraz 5,806 ...... C3
Ribeira Brava 7,416 ...... A2
Rio Maior 10,206 ...... B3
Sacavém 12,625 ...... A1

Salvaterra de Magos 6,265 ...... B3
Santa Cruz 6,348 ...... A2
Santarém 16,850 ...... B3
Santiago do Cacém 5,887 ...... B3
São Brás de Alportel 7,632 ...... C4
São João da Madeira 14,225 ...... B2
São Teotónio 6,146 ...... B4
São Vicente 5,147 ...... A2
Serpa 7,991 ...... C4
Sertã 5,043 ...... B3
Sesimbra 16,614 ...... A3
Setúbal 49,670 ...... B3
Silves 9,493 ...... B4
Sines 6,996 ...... B4
Sintra 15,994 ...... A3
Soure 7,620 ...... B3
Tavira 10,263 ...... C4
Tomar 10,905 ...... B3
Torres Novas 13,806 ...... B3
Torres Vedras 14,833 ...... A3
Trafaria 6,145 ...... A1
Vagos 5,088 ...... B2
Vendas Novas 8,979 ...... B3
Viana do Castelo 12,510 ...... B2
Vila do Conde 16,485 ...... B2
Vila Franca de Xira 13,070 ...... B3

Vila Nova de Gaia
Gaia 50,805 ...... B2
Vila Real Real 10,050 ...... C2
Vila Real de Santo
Antonio 10,320 ...... C4
Viseu 16,190 ...... C2

OTHER FEATURES

Atlantic Ocean A3
Carvoeiroeiro (cape) B3
Desertasrtas (isls.) A2
Douro (riv.) B2
Espichel (cape) A3
Estrela, Serra da (mts.) C2
Guadiana (riv.) C4
Lima (riv.) B2
Madeira (isl.) A2
Madeira (isls.) A2
Minho (riv.) B2
Mira (riv.) B4
Monchique, Serra de (mts.) B4
Mondego (riv.) B2
Monsanto (mt.) B3
Porto Santo (isl.) A1

Sado (riv.) B3
São Vincent (cape) B4
Santa Marla (cape) C4
Setúbal (bay) B3
Tagus (riv.) B3
Tâmega (riv.) B2
Tejo (Tagus) (riv.) B3
Xarrama (riv.) B3

ANDORRA

CITIES and TOWNS

Andorra la Vella (cap.) 12,000 ...... G1

GIBRALTAR

Gibraltar 29,760 ...... D4

PHYSICAL FEATURES

Europa (pt.) D4

‡Population of metropolitan area.

Spain and Portugal

CONIC PROJECTION

SCALE OF MILES
0 20 40 60 80 100

KILOMETERS
0 20 40 60 80 100

Capitals of Countries .... ☆
Provincial and District Capitals .... △
International Boundaries .... ▬▬▬▬
Provincial & District Boundaries ____

Scale 1:4,240,000

In SPAIN, following the referenda of October 29, 1979, autonomous status was granted to CATALONIA and the BASQUE COUNTRY (*País Vasco*). Catalonia consists of the provinces of Barcelona, Gerona, Lerida and Tarragona; the Basque Country consists of Alava, Guipuzcoa and Vizcaya.

© Copyright HAMMOND INCORPORATED, Maplewood, N.J.

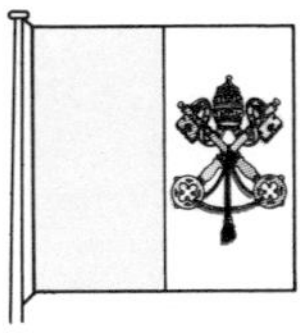

VATICAN CITY

AREA 108.7 acres (44 hectares)
POPULATION 728

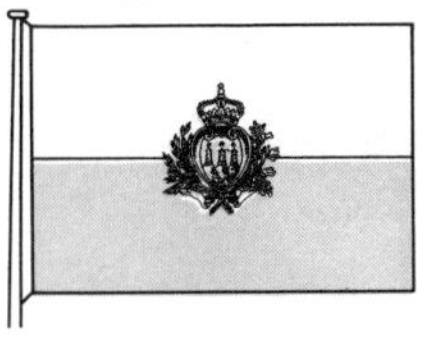

SAN MARINO

AREA 23.4 sq. mi. (60.6 sq. km.)
POPULATION 19,149

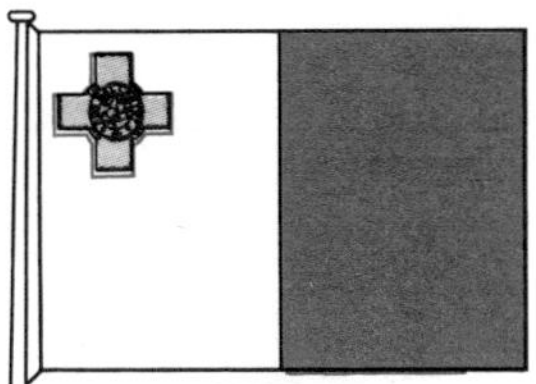

MALTA

AREA 122 sq. mi. (316 sq. km.)
POPULATION 343,970
CAPITAL Valletta
LARGEST CITY Sliema
HIGHEST POINT 787 ft. (240 m.)
MONETARY UNIT Maltese pound
MAJOR LANGUAGES Maltese, English
MAJOR RELIGION Roman Catholicism

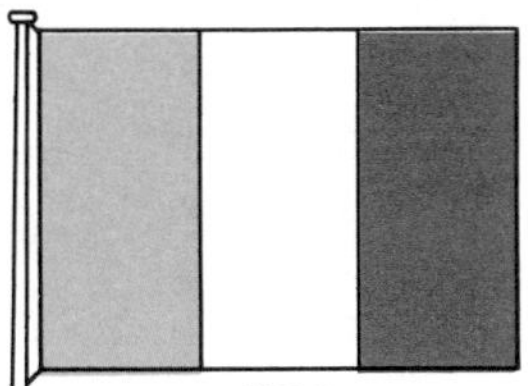

ITALY

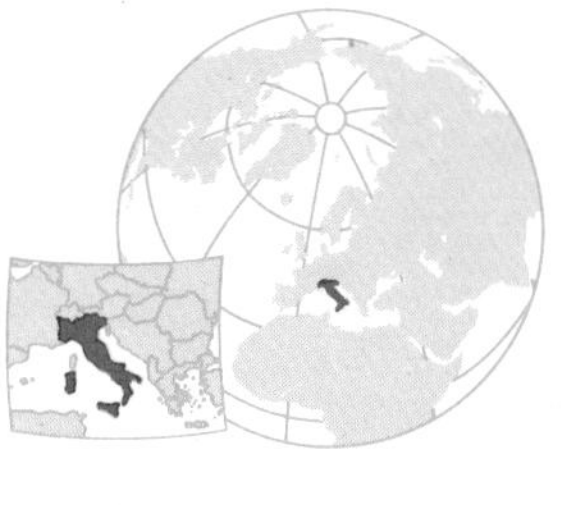

AREA 116,303 sq. mi. (301,225 sq. km.)
POPULATION 57,140,000
CAPITAL Rome
LARGEST CITY Rome
HIGHEST POINT Dufourspitze (Mte. Rosa) 15,203 ft. (4,634 m.)
MONETARY UNIT lira
MAJOR LANGUAGE Italian
MAJOR RELIGION Roman Catholicism

ITALY

REGIONS

Abruzzi 1,166,664 D3
Aosta 109,150 A2
Apulia (Puglia) 3,582,787 F4
Basilicata 603,064 F4
Calabria 1,988,051 F5
Campania 5,059,348 E4
Emilia-Romagna 3,846,755 C2
Friuli-Venezia Giulia 1,213,532 D1
Latium (Lazio) 4,689,482 D3
Liguria 1,853,578 B2
Lombardy 8,543,657 B2
Marche 1,359,907 D3
Molise 319,807 E4
Piedmont 4,432,313 A2
Sardinia 1,473,800 B4
Sicily 4,680,715 D6
Trentino-Alto Adige 841,886 C1
Tuscany 3,473,097 C3
Umbria 775,783 D3
Veneto 2,109,502 D3

PROVINCES

Agrigento 454,045 D6
Alessandria 483,183 B2
Ancona 416,611 D3
Aosta 109,150 A2
Arezzo 306,340 C3
Ascoli Piceno 340,758 D3
Asti 218,547 B2
Avellino 427,509 E4
Bari 1,351,288 F4
Belluno 221,155 D1
Benevento 286,499 E4
Bergamo 829,019 B2
Bologna 918,844 C2
Bolzano-Bozen 414,041 C1
Brescia 957,686 C2
Brindisi 366,027 G4
Cagliari 802,888 B5
Caltanissetta 282,069 D6
Campobasso 227,641 E4
Caserta 677,959 E4
Catania 938,273 E6
Catanzaro 718,069 F5
Chieti 351,567 E3
Como 720,463 B2
Cosenza 691,659 F5
Cremona 334,281 B2
Cuneo 540,504 A2
Enna 202,131 E6
Ferrara 383,639 C2
Florence 1,146,367 C3
Foggia 657,292 E4
Forlì 565,470 D2
Frosinone 422,630 D4
Genoa 1,087,973 B2
Gorizia 142,412 D2
Grosseto 216,315 C3
Imperia 225,127 B3
Isernia 92,166 E4
L'Aquila 293,066 D3
La Spezia 244,435 B2
Latina 376,238 D4
Lecce 696,503 G4
Leghorn 335,265 C3
Lucca 380,356 C3
Macerata 286,155 D3
Mantua 376,892 C2
Massa-Carrara 200,955 C2
Matera 194,629 F4
Messina 654,703 E5
Milan 3,903,685 B2
Modena 553,852 C2
Naples 2,709,929 E4
Novara 496,811 B2
Nuoro 273,021 B4
Padua 762,998 C2
Palermo 1,124,015 D5
Parma 395,497 C2
Pavia 526,389 B2
Perugia 552,936 D3
Pesaro e Urbino 316,383 D3
Pescara 264,981 E3
Piacenza 284,881 B2
Pisa 375,933 C3
Pistoia 254,335 C2
Pordenone 253,906 D2
Potenza 408,435 E4
Ragusa 255,047 E6
Ravenna 351,876 D2
Reggio di Calabria 578,323 E5
Reggio nell'Emilia 392,696 C2
Rieti 143,162 D3
Rome 3,490,377 F6
Rovigo 251,908 C2
Salerno 957,452 E4
Sassari 397,891 B4
Savona 296,043 B2
Siena 257,221 C3
Sondrio 169,149 B1
Syracuse 365,039 E6
Taranto 511,677 F4
Teramo 257,080 D3
Terni 222,847 D3
Trapani 405,393 D5
Trento 427,845 C1
Treviso 668,620 D2
Trieste 300,304 E2
Turin 2,287,016 A2
Udine 516,910 D1
Varese 725,823 B2
Venice 807,251 D2
Vercelli 406,252 B2
Verona 733,595 C2
Vicenza 677,884 C2
Viterbo 257,075 C3

CITIES and TOWNS

Acireale 34,081 E6
Acqui Terme 20,099 B2
Acri 8,150 F5
Adrano 31,988 E6
Adria 11,951 D2
Agira 11,262 E6
Agnone 3,965 E4
Agrigento 40,513 D6
Agropoli 9,413 E4
Alassio 13,512 A2
Alatri 5,710 D4
Alba 23,522 B2
Albano Laziale 15,561 F7
Albenga 13,397 B3
Albino 8,837 B2
Alcamo 41,448 D6
Alessandria 78,644 B2
Alghero 28,454 B4
Altamura 44,879 F4
Amalfi 4,205 E4
Amantea 6,132 E5
Amelia 4,331 D3
Ancona 88,427 D3
Andria 76,405 F4
Anguillara Sabazia 3,241 F6
Anzio 14,966 D4
Aosta 35,053 A2
Aprilia 18,412 D4
Aragona 11,213 D6
Arezzo 56,693 C3
Argenta 6,682 D2
Ariano Irpino 9,796 E4
Ariccia 7,287 F7
Artena 5,034 F7
Ascoli Piceno 43,041 D3
Assisi 4,630 D3
Asti 62,277 B2
Atessa 3,079 E3
Atri 4,686 D3
Augusta 32,501 E6
Avellino 44,750 E4
Aversa 46,536 E4
Avezzano 26,456 D3
Avigliano 5,400 E4
Avola 29,089 E6
Bagheria 32,465 D5
Barcellona Pozzo di Gotto 25,280 E5
Bari 339,110 F4
Barletta 75,116 F4
Bassano del Grappa 33,002 C2
Bellagio 3,258 B2
Belluno 22,180 D1
Benevento 48,523 E4
Bergamo 127,553 B2
Biancavilla 18,743 E6
Biella 46,453 B2
Bisceglie 45,014 F4
Bitonto 39,714 F4
Bitti 4,606 B4
Bologna 493,282 C2
Bolzano (Bolzen) 102,806 C1
Bondeno 7,451 C2
Bonorva 5,232 B4
Bordighera 8,994 A3
Borgo 4,013 C1
Borgomanero 16,655 B2
Bórgo San Lorenzo 7,699 C2
Bosa 8,045 B4
Boves 3,896 A2
Bra 18,399 A2
Bracciano 7,681 C3
Brescia 189,092 C2
Bressanone 12,261 C1
Brindisi 76,612 G4
Bronte 17,823 E6
Brunico 5,175 D1
Budrio 5,635 C2
Busto Arsizio 72,400 B2
Cagli 4,356 D3
Cagliari 211,015 B5
Caltagirone 34,444 E6
Caltanissetta 52,838 D6
Camaiore 8,578 C3
Camerino 4,644 D3
Campobasso 35,551 E4
Campo Tures 1,325 C1
Canicatti 28,761 E6
Canosa di Puglia 30,263 E4
Cantù 28,617 B2
Capua 13,938 E4
Caravaggio 11,298 B2
Carbonia 23,031 B5
Carini 14,255 D5
Carloforte 6,671 B5
Carmagnola 16,469 A2
Carpi 41,789 C2
Carrara 56,236 C2
Casale Monferrato 35,156 B2
Casalmaggiore 6,374 C2
Cascina-Navacchio 28,263 C3
Caserta 51,621 E4
Cassano allo Ionio 9,661 F5
Cassino 14,747 D4
Castelfranco Veneto 16,042 D2
Castel Gandolfo 2,965 F7
Castellammare del Golfo 13,144 D5
Castellammare di Stabia 64,341 E4
Castel San Pietro Terme 6,985 C2
Castelvetrano 29,167 D6
Castiglion Fiorentino 3,797 C3
Castrovillari 15,207 F5
Catania 403,390 E6
Catanzaro 52,054 F5
Caulonia 3,402 F5
Cava de'Tirreni 33,868 E4
Cavarzere 7,917 D2
Cecina 19,415 C3
Cefalù 11,043 E5
Ceglie Messapico 17,512 F4
Celano 9,531 D3
Cerignola 44,648 E4
Cernobbio 8,026 B2
Cerveteri 5,239 E6
Cesano 2,883 F6
Cesena 49,915 D2
Cesenatico 12,805 D2
Chiari 12,017 C2
Chiavari 29,950 B2
Chieri 27,548 A2
Chieti 31,895 E3
Chioggia 24,044 D2
Chivasso 21,369 A2
Ciampino 36,728 F7
Cittadella 9,321 C2
Città di Castello 18,880 C3
Cittanova 11,045 F5
Cividale del Friuli 8,345 D1
Civitavecchia 41,305 C3
Clusone-Fiorine 6,428 C2
Codroipo 6,117 D2
Colle di Val d'Elsa 8,657 C3
Comacchio 10,437 D2
Comiso 24,508 E6
Como 73,257 B2
Conegliano 28,635 D2
Conversano 16,805 F4
Corato 38,163 F4
Cori 6,829 F7
Corigliano Calabro 14,518 F5
Corleone 11,057 D6
Correggio 11,415 C2
Cortina d'Ampezzo 7,285 D1
Cortona 3,482 C3
Cosenza 94,565 F5
Courmayeur 1,401 A2
Crema 26,061 B2
Cremona 75,988 B2
Crotone 44,081 F5
Cuneo 41,633 A2
Cuorgnè 6,752 A2
Desenzano del Garda 14,624 C2
Diano Marina 6,001 B3
Domodossola 18,562 A1
Dorgali 6,714 B4
Eboli 19,787 E4
Edolo 3,707 C1
Empoli 30,526 C3
Enna 27,351 E6
Este 12,992 C2
Fabriano 18,355 D3
Faenza 36,241 D2
Fano 31,238 D3
Fasano 21,247 F4
Favara 27,940 D6
Feltre 11,806 C1
Fermo 17,521 D3
Ferrandina 8,372 F4
Ferrara 97,507 C2
Fidenza 18,064 B2
Fiesole 3,772 C3
Finale Emilia 7,474 C2
Finale Ligure 11,461 B2
Firenze (Florence) 441,654 C3
Fiumicino 13,180 F7
Florence 441,654 C3
Floridia 16,562 E6
Foggia 136,436 E4
Foligno 26,887 D3
Fondi 16,472 D4
Forlì 83,303 D2
Formia 18,978 D4
Fossano 15,857 A2
Fossombrone 5,882 D3
Francavilla Fontana 30,347 F4
Frascati 14,217 F7
Frosinone 34,066 D4
Gaeta 21,973 D4
Galatina 22,137 G4
Galatone 13,880 F4
Gallarate 43,773 B2
Gallipoli 16,878 F4
Garessio 3,359 A2
Gela 66,845 E6
Gemona 6,863 D1
Genoa 787,011 B2
Genova (Genoa) 787,011 B2
Genzano di Roma 14,147 F7
Giarre 18,233 E6
Gioia del Colle 23,299 F4
Gioiosa Ionica 3,811 F5
Giovinazzo 17,768 F4
Giulianova 17,926 E3
Gorizia 35,912 D2
Gravina in Puglia 32,006 F4
Grosseto 48,309 C3
Grottaferrata 10,639 F7
Grottaglie 23,556 F4
Guardiagrele 4,122 E3
Guastalla 7,639 C2
Gubbio 12,371 D3
Guidonia 8,413 F6
Iglesias 24,472 B5
Imola 42,111 C2
Imperia 37,585 B3
Isernia 12,290 E4
Ivrea 26,530 B2
Jesi 33,011 D3
Ladispoli 6,625 E6
Lagonegro 5,613 E4
La Maddalena 10,405 B4
Lanciano 19,652 E3
Lanusei 5,508 B5
Lanuvio 2,970 F7
L'Aquila 36,233 D3
Larino 5,166 E4
La Spezia 121,254 B2
Latina 53,003 D4
Lauria 4,927 E4
Lavello 11,486 E4
Lecce 80,114 G4
Lecco 53,165 B2
Leghorn 170,369 C3
Legnago 15,534 C2
Lendinara 7,079 C2
Lentini 31,429 E6
Leonforte 16,317 E6
Lerici 5,407 B2
Licata 40,997 D6
Lido di Ostia 61,492 F7
Lido di Venezia 18,794 D2
Lipari 3,886 E5
Livigno 2,135 C1
Livorno (Leghorn) 170,369 C3
Lodi 42,489 B2
Lonigo 6,368 C2
Lucca 54,280 C3
Lucera 29,355 E4
Lugo 19,497 D2
Macerata 33,470 D3
Macomer 9,433 B4
Maglie 13,326 G4
Manduria 25,194 F4
Manfredonia 44,463 F4
Mantua 59,529 C2
Marino 12,135 F7
Marsala 34,150 D6
Marsciano 5,372 D3
Martina Franca 31,811 F4
Massa 56,591 C2
Massafra 22,610 F4
Massa Marittima 6,438 C3
Matera 43,026 F4
Mazara del Vallo 37,441 D6
Mazzarino 14,981 E6
Melfi 13,355 E4
Menfi 12,386 D6
Merano 30,951 C1
Mesagne 26,955 G4
Messina 203,937 E5
Mestre 184,818 D2
Milan 1,724,557 B2
Milazzo 18,576 E5
Minturno 2,428 D4
Mirandola 11,551 C2
Mira Taglio 10,194 D2
Mistretta 6,631 E6
Modena 149,029 C2
Modica 31,074 E6
Mola di Bari 23,778 F4
Molfetta 63,250 F4
Moncalieri 49,953 A2
Mondovì Breo 12,524 A2
Monfalcone 29,589 D2
Monopoli 29,776 F4
Monreale 19,348 D5
Monselice 9,047 C2
Montalto Uffugo 3,173 E5
Montebelluna 9,573 D2
Montefiascone 6,885 D3
Montepulciano 4,069 C3
Monterotondo 15,869 F6
Monte Sant'Angelo 17,756 F4
Montevarchi 16,849 C3
Monza 110,735 B2
Mortara 13,929 B2
Naples 1,214,775 E4
Nardò 24,142 F4
Narni 6,213 D3
Naro 13,171 D6
Nettuno 20,927 D4
Nicastro 27,206 F5
Nicosia 13,982 E6
Niscemi 23,925 E6
Nizza Monferrato 7,532 B2
Nocera Inferiore 44,415 E4
Noto 21,606 E6
Novara 92,634 B2
Novi Ligure 29,944 B2
Nuoro 30,551 B4
Olbia 20,998 B4
Oliena 7,030 B4
Orbetello 6,884 C3
Oristano 20,966 B5
Ortona 11,966 E3
Orvieto 8,813 D3
Osimo 12,034 D3
Ostia Antica 2,583 F7
Ostuni 27,241 F4
Otranto 3,707 G4
Ozieri 9,149 B4
Pachino 20,427 E6
Padua 210,950 C2
Palazzolo Acreide 8,981 E6
Palermo 556,374 D5
Palestrina 9,239 F7
Palma di Montechiaro 22,381 D6
Palmi 14,405 E5
Palombara Sabina 5,292 F6
Pantelleria 3,116 C6
Paola 11,330 E5
Parma 151,967 C2
Partanna 10,303 D6
Partinico 25,447 D6
Paterno 41,504 E6
Patti 7,500 E5
Pavia 80,639 B2
Pavullo nel Frignano 5,026 C2
Penne 5,889 D3
Pergine Valsugana 6,248 C1
Pergola 3,866 D3
Perugia 65,975 D3
Pesaro 72,104 D3
Pescara 125,391 E3
Pescia 9,918 C3
Piacenza 100,001 B2
Piazza Armerina 21,754 E6
Pietrasanta 6,620 B3
Pinerolo 33,935 A2
Piombino 35,641 C3
Piove di Sacco 7,035 C2
Pisa 91,156 C3
Pisticci 11,239 F4
Pistoia 55,403 C2
Poggibonsi 21,271 C3
Pomezia 11,915 F7
Pont Canavese 4,075 A2
Pontecorvo 5,986 D4
Pontinia 3,166 D4
Pontremoli 5,222 B2
Popoli 5,372 E3
Pordenone 43,230 D2
Portocivitanova 25,773 D3
Porto Empedocle 15,986 D6
Portoferraio 7,579 C3
Portofino 720 B2
Portogruaro 12,258 D2
Portomaggiore 6,343 C2
Porto Recanati 5,389 D3
Porto Torres 15,422 B4
Potenza 46,869 E4
Pozzallo 12,199 E6
Pozzuoli 53,546 D4
Prato 108,385 C3
Prima Porta 11,393 F6
Priverno 9,950 D4
Putignano 19,290 F4
Quartu Sant'Elena 29,715 B5
Ragusa 55,751 E6
Rapallo 22,272 B2
Ravenna 75,153 D2
Recanati 10,176 D3
Reggio di Calabria 110,291 E5
Reggio nell'Emilia 102,337 C2
Rho 39,206 B2
Riesi 15,855 E6
Rieti 26,775 D3
Rimini 101,579 D2
Rionero in Vulture 11,230 E4
Riva del Garda 8,513 C2
Roccastrada 2,629 C3
Rome (cap.) 2,535,018 F6
Ronciglione 5,900 C3
Rossano 12,119 F5
Rovereto 26,827 C2
Rovigo 31,124 C2
Ruvo di Puglia 23,133 F4

(continued on following page)

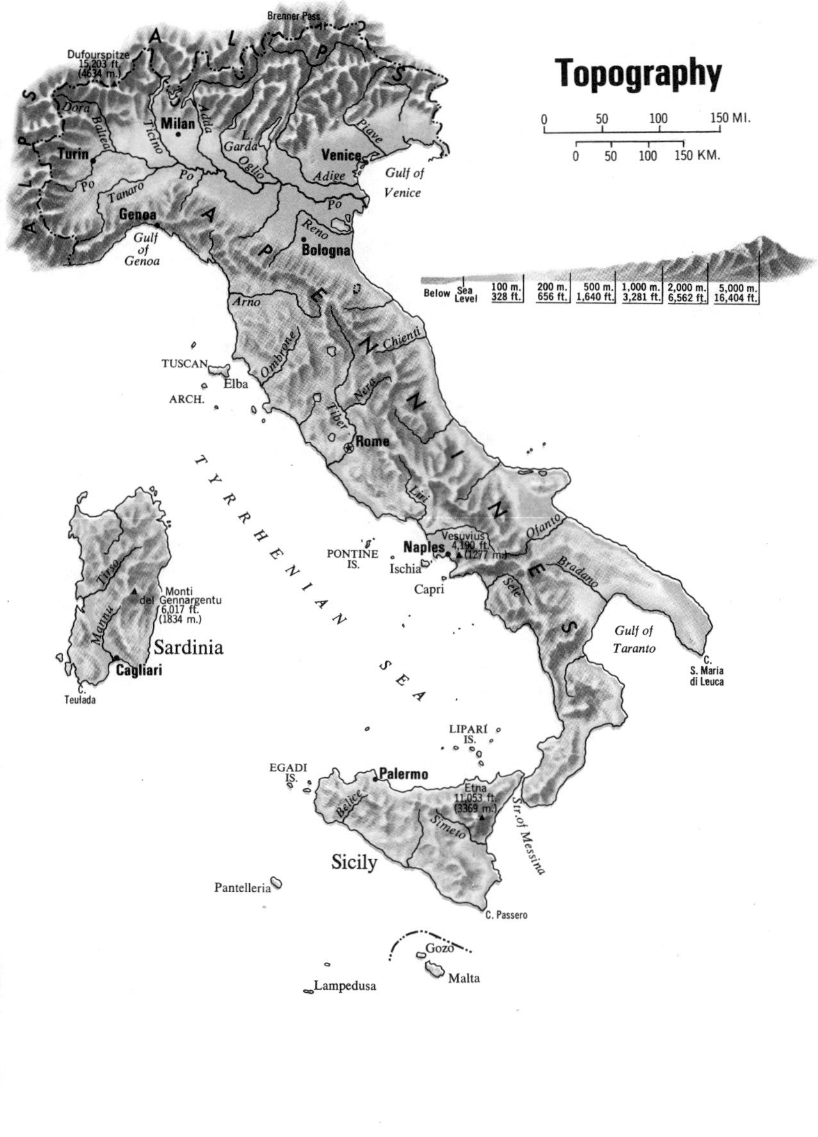

Topography
0 50 100 150 MI.
0 50 100 150 KM.
Below Sea Level
100 m. 328 ft.
200 m. 656 ft.
500 m. 1,640 ft.
1,000 m. 3,281 ft.
2,000 m. 6,562 ft.
5,000 m. 16,404 ft.
Brenner Pass
Dufourspitze 15,203 ft. (4634 m.)
A L P S
Dora Baltea
Ticino
Adda
Milan
Garda
Oglio
Piave
Venice
Adige
Gulf of Venice
Turin
Po
Tanaro
Genoa
Gulf of Genoa
Reno
Bologna
A P P E N N I N E S
Arno
Ombrone
Chienti
Tiber
Nera
Rome
TUSCAN ARCH.
Elba
Liri
PONTINE IS.
Naples
Ischia
Capri
Vesuvius 4,190 ft. (1277 m.)
Ofanto
Bradano
Sele
Gulf of Taranto
C. S. Maria di Leuca
TYRRHENIAN SEA
Tirso
Monti del Gennargentu 6,017 ft. (1834 m.)
Sardinia
Cagliari
C. Teulada
LIPARI IS.
EGADI IS.
Palermo
Etna 11,053 ft. (3369 m.)
Belice
Simeto
Str. of Messina
Sicily
Pantelleria
C. Passero
Gozo
Malta
Lampedusa

Agriculture, Industry and Resources

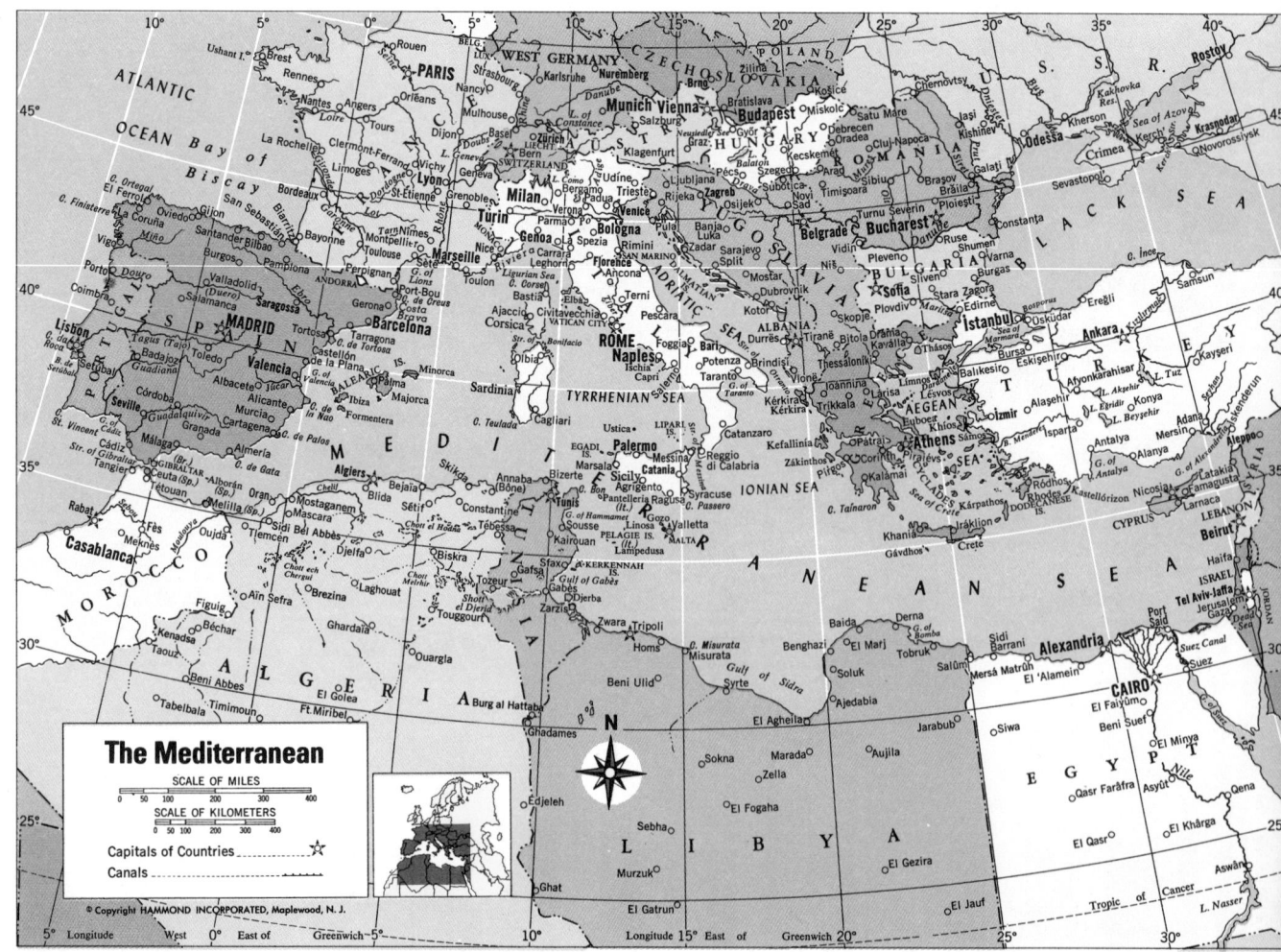

DOMINANT LAND USE

- Wheat, Rice, Dairy
- Pasture Livestock
- Cereals, Livestock
- Fruit, Truck and Mixed Farming
- Grapes, Wine
- Forests
- Nonagricultural Land

MAJOR MINERAL OCCURRENCES

Ab	Asbestos	K	Potash	Pb	Lead
Al	Bauxite	Lg	Lignite	Py	Pyrites
C	Coal	Mr	Marble	S	Sulfur
Fe	Iron Ore	Na	Salt	Sb	Antimony
G	Natural Gas	O	Petroleum	Zn	Zinc
Hg	Mercury				

⚡ Water Power

▨ Major Industrial Areas

The Mediterranean

SCALE OF MILES
0 50 100 200 300 400

SCALE OF KILOMETERS
0 50 100 200 300 400

Capitals of Countries .... ☆

Canals

© Copyright HAMMOND INCORPORATED, Maplewood, N.J.

SWITZERLAND

AREA 15,943 sq. mi. (41,292 sq. km.)
POPULATION 6,365,960
CAPITAL Bern
LARGEST CITY Zürich
HIGHEST POINT Dufourspitze
  (Mte. Rosa) 15,203 ft. (4,634 m.)
MONETARY UNIT Swiss franc
MAJOR LANGUAGES German, French,
  Italian, Romansch
MAJOR RELIGIONS Protestantism,
  Roman Catholicism

LIECHTENSTEIN

AREA 61 sq. mi. (158 sq. km.)
POPULATION 25,220
CAPITAL Vaduz
LARGEST CITY Vaduz
HIGHEST POINT Grauspitze 8,527 ft.
  (2,599 m.)
MONETARY UNIT Swiss franc
MAJOR LANGUAGE German
MAJOR RELIGION Roman Catholicism

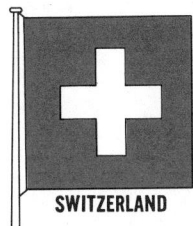

SWITZERLAND

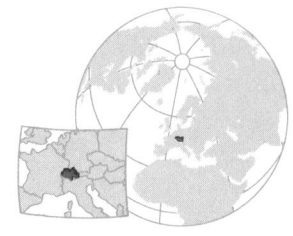

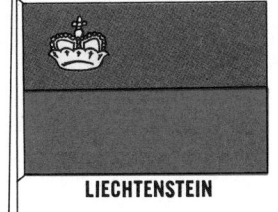

LIECHTENSTEIN

Languages

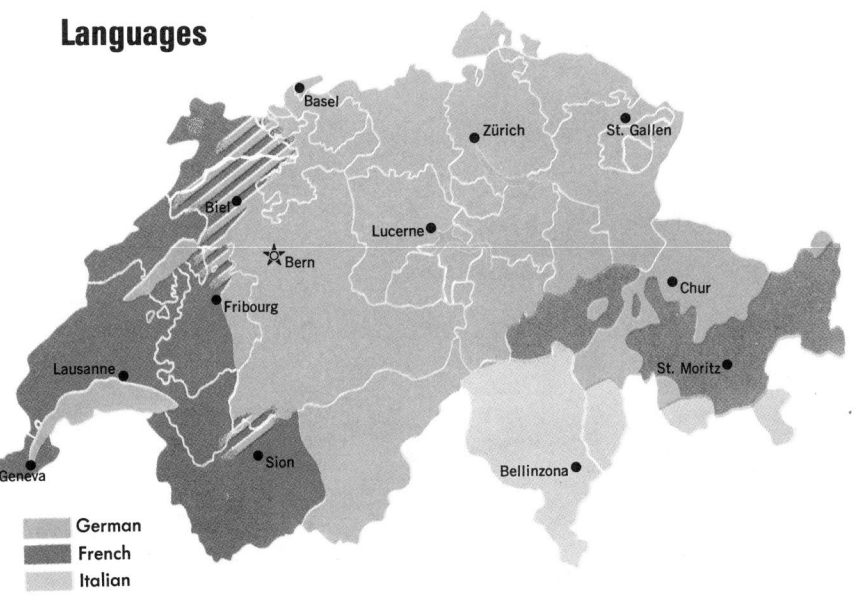

- German
- French
- Italian
- Romansch

Switzerland is a multilingual nation with four official languages. 70% of the people speak German, 19% French, 10% Italian and 1% Romansch.

Agriculture, Industry and Resources

DOMINANT LAND USE

- Cereals, Dairy
- Pasture Livestock
- General Farming, Livestock
- Fruit, Truck, Mixed Farming
- Forests
- Nonagricultural Land

⚡ Water Power
▨ Major Industrial Areas

SWITZERLAND
CANTONS

Aargau 442,400 ....F2
Appenzell, Ausser
  Rhoden 46,700 ....H2
Appenzell, Inner Rhoden 13,500 ...H2
Baselland 219,500 ....E2
Baselstadt 209,700 ....E1
Bern 920,900 ....D2
Fribourg 181,600 ....D3
Geneva (Genève) 338,600 .....B4
Glarus 35,700 ....H3
Graubünden (Grisons) 164,300 ...H3
Grisons (Graubünden) 164,300 ...H3
Jura 67,200 ....D2
Lucerne (Luzern) 292,900 .....F2
Luzern 292,900 ....F2
Neuchâtel 162,200 ....C3
Nidwalden 26,900 ....F3
Obwalden 25,400 ....F3
Sankt Gallen 385,000 ....H2
Schaffhausen 69,300 ....G1
Schwyz 93,100 ....F2
Soleure (Solothurn) 221,800 ...E2
Solothurn 221,800 ....E2
Thurgau 183,500 ....H1
Ticino 264,400 ....G4
Uri 34,000 ....G3
Valais 214,000 ....D4
Vaud 523,500 ....B3
Zug 73,600 ....G2
Zürich 1,117,300 ....G2

CITIES and TOWNS

Aadorf 3,022 ....G2
Aarau 16,881 ....F2
Aarau* 51,800 ....F2
Aarberg 3,122 ....D2
Aarburg 5,943 ....E2
Adelboden 3,326 ....E3
Adliswil 15,920 ....F2
Aeschi bei Spiez 1,402 .....E3
Affoltern am Albis 7,363 ...F2
Affoltern im Emmental 1,223 ...E2
Aigle 6,532 ....C4
Airolo 2,140 ....G4
Alle 1,615 ....D2
Allschwil 17,638 ....D1
Alpnach 3,277 ....F3
Altdorf 8,647 ....G3
Altstätten 9,084 ....J2
Amriswil 7,601 ....H1
Andelfingen 1,453 ....G1
Andermatt 1,589 ....G3
Appenzell 5,217 ....H2
Arbedo-Castione 2,456 .....G4
Arbon 12,227 ....H1
Arbon* 15,400 ....H1
Ardon 1,498 ....D4
Arosa 2,717 ....J3
Arth 7,580 ....F2
Ascona 4,086 ....G4
Attalens 1,116 ....C3
Au 4,944 ....J2
Aubonne 1,983 ....B4
Avenches 2,235 ....D3
Baar 14,074 ....F2
Baden 14,115 ....F2
Baden* 66,800 ....F2
Bad Ragaz 3,713 ....H2
Balerna 3,885 ....G5
Balsthal 5,607 ....E2
Bäretswil 2,733 ....G2
Basel 199,600 ....E1
Basel* 379,700 ....E1
Bassecourt 2,985 ....D2
Bätterkinden 1,757 ....E2

Bauma 3,159 ....G2
Beatenberg 1,263 ....E3
Beinwil am See 2,520 .....F2
Belfaux 1,075 ....D3
Bellinzona 16,979 ....H4
Bellinzona* 31,000 ....H4
Belp 6,981 ....D3
Berg 1,039 ....H1
Bern (cap.) 154,700 ......D3
Bern* 285,300 ....D3
Beromünster 1,552 ....F2
Bettlach 4,046 ....D2
Bex 5,069 ....D4
Biasca 4,696 ....H4
Biberist 7,769 ....D2
Biel 63,400 ....D2
Biel**89,900 ....D2
Bière 1,252 ....B3
Binningen 15,344 ....D1
Bischofszell 4,233 ....H1
Blumenstein 1,049 ....E3
Bodio 1,425 ....G4
Bolligen 26,121 ....E3
Boltigen 1,519 ....D3
Bonaduz 1,289 ....H3
Boncourt 1,528 ....D2
Bönigen 1,738 ....E3
Boswil 1,904 ....F2
Boudry 4,372 ....C3
Bourg Saint-Pierre 236 ...D5
Breil-Brigels 1,215 ......H3
Breitenbach 2,455 ....E2
Bremgarten 4,873 ....F2
Brienz 2,796 ....F3
Brig 5,191 ....F4
Brissago 2,120 ....G4
Brissago 2,120 ....G4
Brittnau 2,888 ....E2
Broc 1,842 ....D3
Brugg 8,635 ....F2
Brusio 1,344 ....K4
Bubendorf 2,070 ....E2
Bubikon 3,244 ....G2
Buchs 8,454 ....H2
Bülach 11,043 ....G1
Bulle 7,556 ....D3
Buochs 3,232 ....F3
Büren an der Aare 3,085 ...D2
Burgdorf 15,888 ....E2
Burgdorf* 18,400 ....E2
Bürglen, Thurgau 1,920 ...H1
Bürglen, Uri 3,401 ....G3
Bussigny-près-Lausanne 4,509 ...B3
Bütschwil 3,270 ....H2
Carouge 14,055 ....B4
Castagnola 4,430 ....G4
Cazis 1,687 ....H3
Cernier 1,717 ....C2
Chalais 1,651 ....E4
Cham 8,209 ....F2
Chamoson 2,049 ....D4
Charmey 1,155 ....D3
Château-d'Oex 3,203 ......D4
Châtel-Saint-Denis 2,842 ...C3
Chêne-Bougeries 8,670 ....B4
Chavornay 1,521 ....C3
Chexbres 1,607 ....C4
Chiasso 8,868 ....G5
Chippis 1,561 ....E4
Chur 32,400 ....J3
Churwalden 1,052 ....J3
Claro 1,143 ....G4
Collombey-Muraz 2,279 ....C4
Collonge-Bellerive 3,541 ...B4
Conthey 4,259 ....D4
Coppet 1,097 ....B4
Corcelles-près-Payerne 1,256 ...C3
Corgémont 1,645 ....D2
Cossonay 1,529 ....B3
Courgenay 1,954 ....D2
Courrendlin 2,656 ....D2
Courroux 1,788 ....D2
Courtelary 1,462 ....C2
Courtételle 1,864 ....D2
Couvet 3,481 ....C3
Cully 1,535 ....C4
Davos 10,238 ....J3
Degersheim 3,400 ....H2
Delémont 11,797 ....D2
Derendingen 4,917 ....E2
Dielsdorf 2,691 ....F1
Diemtigen 1,913 ....D3
Diepoldsau 3,311 ....J2
Diessenhofen 2,532 ....G1
Dietikon 22,705 ....F2
Disentis-Mustér 2,319 ....G3
Domat-Ems 5,701 ....H3
Dombresson 1,109 ....C2
Dornach 5,258 ....E2
Döttingen 3,380 ....F1
Dübendorf 19,639 ....G2
Düdingen 4,932 ....D3
Dürnten 4,820 ....G2
Dürrenroth 1,084 ....E2
Ebnat-Kappel 5,131 ....H2
Echallens 1,643 ....C3
Ecublens 6,379 ....B3
Egg 5,250 ....G2
Eggiwil 2,391 ....E3
Eglisau 2,160 ....G1
Egnach 3,466 ....H1

(continued on following page)

Topography

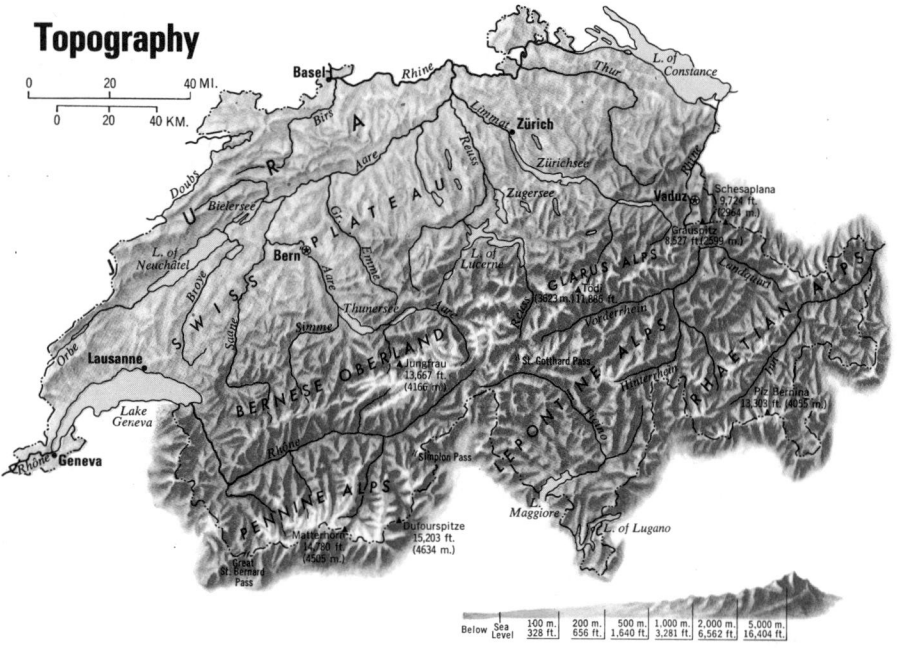

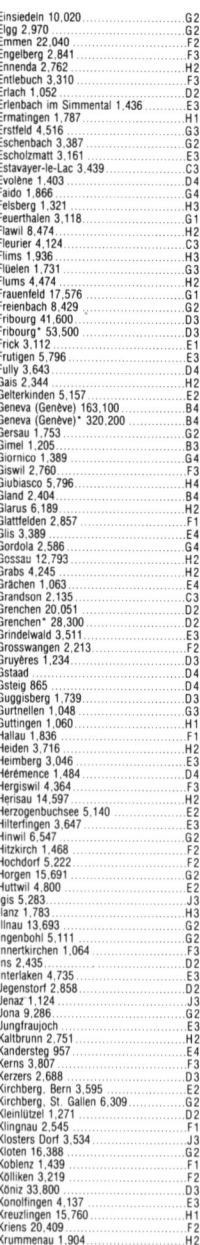

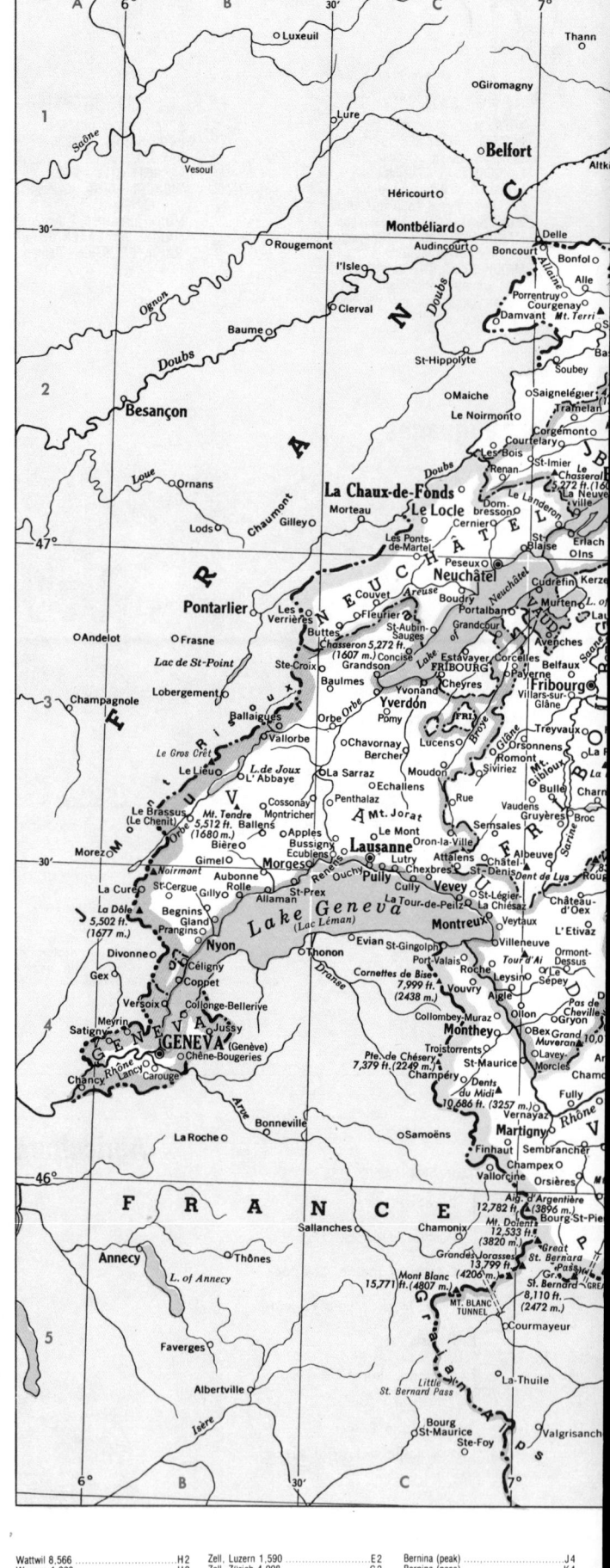

Einsiedeln 10,020 G2
Elgg 2,970 G2
Emmen 22,040 F2
Engelberg 2,841 F3
Ennenda 2,762 H2
Entlebuch 3,310 F3
Erlach 1,052 D2
Erlenbach im Simmental 1,436 E3
Ermatingen 1,787 H1
Erstfeld 4,516 G3
Eschenbach 3,387 G2
Escholzmatt 3,161 E3
Estavayer-le-Lac 3,439 C3
Evolène 1,403 D4
Faido 1,866 G4
Felsberg 1,321 H3
Feuerthalen 3,118 G1
Flawil 8,474 H2
Fleurier 4,124 C3
Flims 1,936 H3
Flüelen 1,731 G3
Flums 4,474 H2
Frauenfeld 17,576 G1
Freienbach 8,429 G2
Fribourg 41,600 D3
Fribourg* 53,500 D3
Frick 3,112 E1
Frutigen 5,796 E3
Fully 3,643 D4
Gais 2,344 H2
Gelterkinden 5,157 E2
Geneva (Genève) 163,100 B4
Geneva (Genève)* 320,200 B4
Gersau 1,753 G2
Gimel 1,205 B3
Giornico 1,389 G4
Giswil 2,760 F3
Giubiasco 5,796 H4
Gland 2,404 B4
Glarus 6,189 H2
Glattfelden 2,857 F1
Glis 3,389 E4
Gordola 2,586 G4
Gossau 12,793 H2
Grabs 4,245 H2
Grächen 1,063 E4
Grandson 2,135 C3
Grenchen 20,051 D2
Grenchen* 28,300 D2
Grindelwald 3,511 E3
Grosswangen 2,213 F2
Gruyères 1,234 D3
Gstaad D4
Gsteig 865 D4
Guggisberg 1,739 D3
Gurtnellen 1,048 G3
Guttingen 1,060 H1
Hallau 1,836 F1
Heiden 3,716 H2
Heimberg 3,046 E3
Hérémence 1,484 D4
Hergiswil 4,364 F3
Herisau 14,597 H2
Herzogenbuchsee 5,140 E2
Hilterfingen 3,647 E3
Hinwil 6,547 G2
Hitzkirch 1,468 F2
Hochdorf 5,222 F2
Horgen 15,691 G2
Huttwil 4,800 E2
Igis 5,283 J3
Ilanz 1,783 H3
Illnau 13,693 G2
Ingenbohl 5,111 G2
Innertkirchen 1,064 F3
Ins 2,435 D2
Interlaken 4,735 E3
Jegenstorf 2,858 D2
Jenaz 1,124 J3
Jona 9,286 G2
Jungfraujoch E3
Kaltbrunn 2,751 H2
Kandersteg 957 E4
Kerns 3,807 F3
Kerzers 2,688 D3
Kirchberg, Bern 3,595 E2
Kirchberg, St. Gallen 6,309 G2
Kleinlützel 1,271 D2
Klingnau 2,545 F1
Klosters Dorf 3,534 J3
Kloten 16,388 G2
Koblenz 1,439 F1
Kölliken 3,219 F2
Köniz 33,800 D3
Konolfingen 4,137 E3
Kreuzlingen 15,760 H1
Kriens 20,409 F2
Krummenau 1,904 H2
Küsnacht 12,193 G2
Küssnacht am Rigi 7,956 F2
Küttigen 4,181 F2
L'Abbaye 1,319 B3
La Chaux-de-Fonds 42,500 C2
Lachen 4,914 G2
Lancy 20,523 B4
La Neuveville 3,917 D2
Langenthal 13,077 E2
Langenthal* 22,100 E2
Langnau am Albis 4,879 G2
Langnau in Emmental 8,950 E3
La Roche 1,069 D3
La Sarraz 1,190 C3
La Tour-de-Peilz 8,864 C4
Läufelfingen 1,243 E2
Laufen 4,723 D2
Laufenburg 2,128 F1
Laupen 2,139 D3
Lauperswil 2,542 E3
Lausanne 136,100 C3
Lausanne* 228,700 C3
Lauterbrunnen 3,431 E3
Le Brassus 5,465 B3
Le Châble 4,541 D4
Le Chenit (Le Brassus) 5,465 B3
Le Landeron 2,768 C2
Le Locle 14,452 C2
Le Mont-sur-Lausanne 2,692 C3
Lengau 4,736 D2
Lenk 1,876 D4
Le Noirmont 1,516 C2
Lens 2,052 D4
Lenzburg 7,594 F2
Les Bois 1,110 C2
Les Ponts-de-Martel 1,327 C2
Leuk 2,796 E4
Leukerbad 1,056 E4
Leysin 2,752 C4
Liechtensteig 2,131 H2
Liestal 12,500 E2
Liestal-Sissach* 40,800 E2
Linthal 1,458 H3
Littau 13,495 F2
Locarno 14,143 G4
Locarno* 39,200 G4
Lodrino 1,075 G4
Lotzwil 2,323 E2
Lucens 2,144 C3
Lucerne 70,200 F2
Lucerne* 158,600 F2
Lugano 22,280 G4
Lugano* 64,200 G4
Lungern 1,813 F3
Luthern 1,706 E2
Lutry 4,994 C3
Lützelflüh 3,842 E3
Luzern (Lucerne) 70,200 F2
Lyss 8,131 D2
Maienfeld 1,542 J2
Malans 1,294 J3
Malleray 1,969 D2
Malters 5,100 F2
Malvaglia 1,099 H4
Männedorf 7,419 G2
Marbach 1,265 E3
Martigny 10,478 C4
Meilen 9,881 G2
Meiringen 3,759 F3
Melide 1,315 G5
Mellingen 3,211 F2
Mels 5,969 H2
Mendrisio 6,223 G5
Menzingen 3,483 G2
Menznau 2,185 E2
Mesocco 1,376 H4
Meyrin 14,255 B4
Minusio 5,027 G4
Möhlin 6,003 E1
Mollis 2,628 H2
Montana 1,725 D4
Monthey 10,114 C4
Montreux 20,421 C4
Morges 11,931 B3
Morges* 17,200 B3
Moudon 3,773 C3
Moutier 8,794 D2
Müllheim 1,620 G1
Mümliswil-Ramiswil 2,702 E2
Münchenbuchsee 6,459 E2
Münsingen 8,350 E3
Muotathal 2,763 G3
Muri 4,853 F2
Muri bei Bern 3,057 E3
Mürren E3
Murten 4,256 D3
Muttenz 15,518 E1
Näfels 3,739 H2
Naters 5,517 E4
Nebikon 1,378 F2
Nendaz 4,051 D4
Nesslau 1,934 H2
Netstal 2,771 H2
Neuchâtel 38,400 C3
Neuchâtel* 61,700 C3
Neuenegg 3,452 D3
Neuhausen am Rheinfall 12,103 G1
Neunkirch 1,239 F1
Nidau 7,962 D2
Niederbipp 3,293 E2
Niederurnen 3,354 G2
Nunningen 1,450 E2
Nyon 11,424 B4
Oberägeri 2,992 G2
Oberburg 3,015 E2
Oberdiessbach 2,145 E3
Oberdorf 1,953 E2
Oberriet 6,123 J2
Obersiggenthal 6,623 F1
Oberzwil 4,659 H2
Oensingen 3,387 E2
Oftringen 9,189 E2
Ollon 4,470 D4
Olten 21,209 E2
Olten* 49,000 E2
Opfikon 11,115 G2
Orbe 4,522 C3
Orsières 2,470 D4
Ouchy C4
Paradiso 3,101 G5
Payerne 6,899 C3
Penthalaz 1,701 C3
Péry 1,486 D2
Peseux 5,578 C3
Pfaffnau 2,584 E2
Pieterlen 3,485 D2
Plaffeien 1,448 D3
Pontresina 1,646 J3
Porrentruy 7,827 C2
Port-Valais 1,363 C4
Poschiavo 3,563 J4
Prangins 1,466 B4
Pratteln 15,127 E1
Pully 15,917 C4
Quinto 1,490 G3
Rafz 2,215 G1
Ramsen 1,217 G1
Rapperswil 8,713 G2
Raron 1,257 E4
Regensdorf 8,566 F2
Reichenbach im Kandertal 2,900 E3
Reiden 3,275 F2
Reinach in Aargau 5,862 F2
Reinach in Baselland 13,419 E2
Renan 1,094 C2
Renens 17,391 C3
Rheinau 2,075 G1
Rheineck 3,275 J2
Rheinfelden 6,866 E1
Richterswil 7,380 G2
Riehen 21,026 E1
Riggisberg 2,193 E3
Riva San Vitale 1,607 G5
Rivera 1,146 G4
Roggwil 3,403 E2
Rolle 3,658 B4
Romanshorn 8,329 H1
Romont 3,276 C3
Rorschach 11,963 H2
Rorschach* 24,200 H2
Rosenlaui F3
Rothrist 5,883 E2
Roveredo 2,037 H4
Rüeggisberg 1,857 E3
Rumlang 5,677 G2
Rüschegg 1,346 D3
Ruswil 4,756 F2
Rüthi 1,493 J2
Rüti, Zürich 9,546 G2
Saanen 5,840 D4
Sachseln 3,059 F3
Saignelégier 1,745 D2
Saint-Aubin-Sauges 2,058 C3
Saint-Blaise 2,586 D2
Sainte-Croix 6,240 B3
Saint-Imier 6,740 D2
Saint-Légier-La Chiésaz 2,230 C4
Saint-Martin 1,120 E4
Saint-Maurice 3,808 C4
Saint Moritz 5,699 J3
Saint Niklaus 2,043 E4
Saint-Prex 2,306 B4
Saint Stephan 1,213 D3
Saint-Ursanne 1,073 D2
Samedan 2,574 J3
Sankt Gallen 81,900 H2
Sankt Gallen* 90,400 H2
Sankt Margrethen 5,101 J2
Sargans 4,058 H2
Sarnen 6,952 F3
Satigny 1,877 A4
Savièse 3,585 D4
Saxon 2,409 D4
Schaffhausen 36,800 G1
Schaffhausen* 55,800 G1
Schänis 2,355 H2
Schattdorf 3,292 G3
Scherzingen 1,420 H1
Schiers 2,342 J3
Schinznach-Dorf 1,154 F2
Schleitheim 1,544 G1
Schlieren 11,869 F2
Schönenwerd 4,793 E2
Schübelbach 4,395 G2
Schüpfheim 3,773 F3
Schwanden 2,823 H2
Schwyz 12,194 G2
Scuol 1,686 K3
Sempach 1,619 F2
Seon 3,628 F2
Seuzach 3,258 G1
Sevelen 2,742 H2
Sierre 11,017 D4
Signau 2,642 E3
Sigriswil 3,540 E3
Silenen 2,338 G3
Sils im Domleschg 762 H3
Silvaplana 714 J4
Sins 2,435 F2
Sion 21,925 D4
Sirnach 3,706 G2
Sissach 4,938 E2
Solothurn (Soleure) 17,708 E2
Solothurn* 35,600 E2
Somvix 1,555 G3
Sonvico 1,129 G4
Spiez 9,911 E3
Stäfa 9,937 G2
Stalden 1,121 E4
Stans 5,180 F3
Steckborn 3,752 G1
Steffisburg 12,621 E3
Stein 1,763 E1
Stein am Rhein 2,751 G1
Suhr 7,223 F2
Sulgen 1,834 H1
Sumiswald 5,334 E2
Sursee 7,052 F2
Tafers 2,021 D3
Täuffelen 1,761 D2
Tavannes 3,869 D2
Tavetsch 1,273 G3
Teufen 5,300 H2
Thal 4,919 J2
Thalwil 13,591 G2
Thayngen 3,640 G1
Therwil 5,412 E1
Thun 37,000 E3
Thun* 63,600 E3
Thunstetten 2,483 E2
Thusis 2,381 H3
Trachselwald 1,199 E2
Tramelan 5,549 D2
Trimmis 1,109 J3
Troistorrents 2,208 C4
Trub 1,833 E3
Trun 1,607 G3
Turbenthal 2,939 G2
Uetendorf 3,132 E3
Unterägeri 4,671 G2
Unteriberg 1,344 G2
Unterkulm 2,596 F2
Unterseen 4,192 E3
Untervaz 1,230 H3
Urnäsch 2,313 H2
Uster 21,819 G2
Utzenstorf 3,193 E2
Uznach 3,984 H2
Uzwil 9,133 H2
Vallorbe 4,028 B3
Vaz-Obervaz 2,003 J3
Vechigen 3,595 E3
Vernayaz 1,356 D4
Versoix 5,627 B4
Vevey 17,957 C4
Vevey-Montreux* 62,300 C4
Villeneuve 3,705 C4
Visp 5,252 E4
Vouvry 1,851 C4
Vuadens 1,278 C3
Wädenswil 15,695 G2
Wahlern 4,832 D3
Wald 8,185 G2
Waldenburg 1,449 E2
Waldkirch 2,669 H2
Walenstadt 3,446 H2
Wallisellen 10,415 G2
Walzenhausen 2,082 J2
Wangen an der Aare 2,013 E2
Wängi 2,730 H1
Wartau 3,604 H2
Wattwil 8,566 H2
Weesen 1,308 H2
Weggis 2,517 F2
Weinfelden 8,621 H1
Wettingen 19,900 F2
Wetzikon 13,469 G2
Wil 14,646 H2
Wil* 20,500 H2
Wilchingen 1,066 F1
Wilderswil 1,666 E3
Wildhaus 1,104 H2
Willisau 2,728 F2
Wimmis 1,833 E3
Windisch 7,444 F1
Winterthur 93,500 G1
Winterthur* 110,100 G1
Wohlen 12,024 F2
Wohlen* 16,000 F2
Wohlen bei Bern 4,190 D3
Wolfenschiessen 1,470 F3
Wolhusen 3,556 F2
Worb 9,526 E3
Wünnewil 3,652 D3
Wynigen 1,986 E2
Yverdon 20,538 C3
Yvonand 1,321 C3
Zell, Luzern 1,590 E2
Zell, Zürich 4,008 G2
Zermatt 3,101 E4
Zizers 1,913 J3
Zofingen 9,292 F2
Zollikofen 9,069 E3
Zollikon 12,117 G2
Zug 22,972 G2
Zug* 51,300 G2
Zuoz 1,165 J3
Zürich 401,600 F2
Zürich* 718,100 F2
Zurzach 3,098 F1
Zweisimmen 2,738 D3

OTHER FEATURES

Aa (riv.) F3
Aare (riv.) E3
Ägerisee (lake) G2
Aiguille d'Argentière (mt.) C5
Aletschhorn (mt.) F4
Aroser Rothorn (mt.) J3
Ault (peak) H3
Balmhorn (mt.) E4
Bernese Oberland (reg.) E3
Bernina (peak) J4
Bernina (pass) K4
Bielersee (lake) D2
Bietschhorn (mt.) E4
Birs (riv.) D2
Blinnenhorn (mt.) F4
Blümlisalp (mt.) E3
Bodensee (Constance) (lake) H1
Borgne (riv.) D4
Breithorn (mt.) E5
Breithorn (mt.) E4
Brienzer Rothorn (mt.) F3
Brienzersee (lake) F3
Broye (riv.) C3
Buchegg (mts.) D2
Buin (peak) K3
Campo Tencia (peak) G4
Chasseron (mt.) C3
Churfirsten (mt.) H2
Clariden (mt.) G3
Constance (lake) H1
Cornettes de Bise (mts.) C4
Dammastock (mt.) F3
Davos (valley) J3
Dent Blanche (mt.) E4
Dent de Lys (mt.) D4

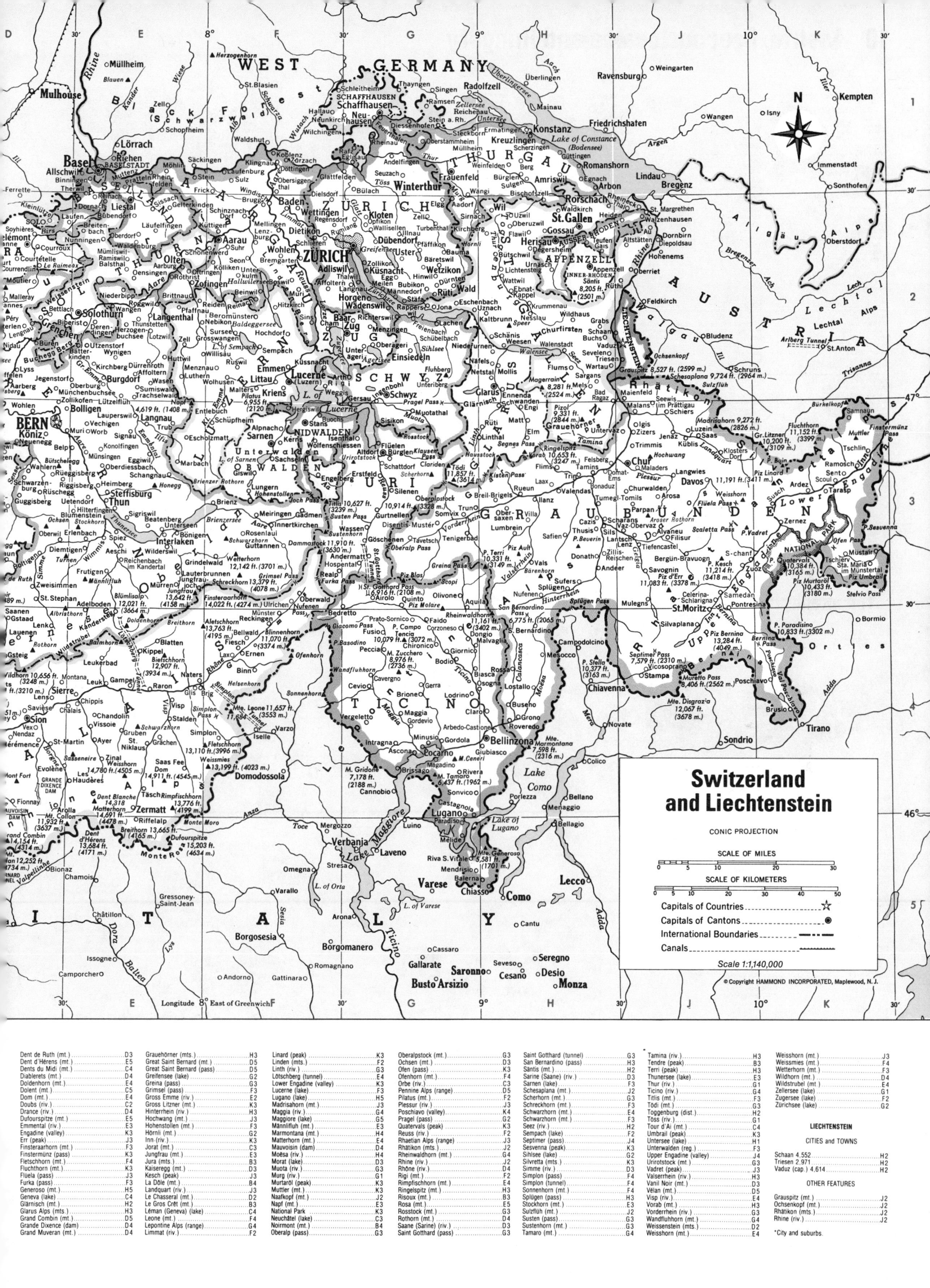

Switzerland and Liechtenstein

CONIC PROJECTION

SCALE OF MILES

SCALE OF KILOMETERS

Capitals of Countries .... ☆
Capitals of Cantons .... ◉
International Boundaries _____ ___ ___
Canals ....

Scale 1:1,140,000

© Copyright HAMMOND INCORPORATED, Maplewood, N.J.

Dent de Ruth (mt.)	D3	Grauehörner (mts.)	H3	Linard (peak)	K3	Oberalpstock (mt.)	G3	Saint Gotthard (tunnel)	G3	Tamina (riv.)	H3	Weisshorn (mt.)	J3
Dent d'Hèrens (mt.)	E5	Great Saint Bernard (mt.)	D5	Linden (mts.)	F2	Ochsen (riv.)	D3	San Bernardino (pass)	H3	Tendre (peak)	B3	Weissmies (mt.)	F4
Dents du Midi (mt.)	C4	Great Saint Bernard (pass)	D5	Linth (riv.)	G3	Ofen (pass)	K3	Säntis (mt.)	H2	Terri (mt.)	H3	Wetterhorn (mt.)	F3
Diablerets (mt.)	D4	Greifensee (lake)	G2	Lötschberg (tunnel)	E4	Ofenhorn (mt.)	F4	Sarine (Saane) (riv.)	D3	Thunersee (lake)	E3	Wildhorn (mt.)	D4
Doldenhorn (mt.)	D4	Greina (pass)	G3	Lower Engadine (valley)	K3	Orbe (riv.)	C3	Schesaplana (mt.)	J2	Thur (riv.)	F2	Wildstrubel (mt.)	E4
Dolent (mt.)	C5	Grimsel (pass)	F3	Lucerne (lake)	F3	Pennine Alps (range)	D5	Schorhorn (mt.)	J3	Ticino (riv.)	G4	Zellersee (lake)	G1
Dom (mt.)	E4	Gross Emme (riv.)	E3	Lugano (lake)	H5	Pilatus (mt.)	F3	Schreckhorn (mt.)	F3	Titlis (mt.)	F3	Zugersee (lake)	F2
Doubs (riv.)	C2	Gross Litzner (mt.)	J2	Madrisahorn (mt.)	J2	Plessur (riv.)	J3	Schwarzhorn (mt.)	F3	Tödi (mt.)	G3	Zürichsee (lake)	G2
Drance (riv.)	C4	Hinterrhein (riv.)	H3	Maggia (riv.)	G4	Poschiavo (valley)	K4	Schwarzhorn (mt.)	F4	Toggenburg (dist.)	H2		
Dufourspitze (mt.)	E5	Hochwang (mt.)	J3	Maggiore (lake)	G5	Pragel (pass)	G2	Seez (riv.)	H2	Töss (riv.)	G1		
Emmental (riv.)	E3	Hohenstollen (mt.)	F3	Männlifluh (mt.)	E3	Quatervals (peak)	K3	Septimer (pass)	J4	Tour d'Aï (mt.)	C4	**LIECHTENSTEIN**	
Engadine (valley)	K3	Hörnli (mt.)	G2	Martmartinhorn (mt.)	H4	Reuss (riv.)	F2	Sesvenna (peak)	K3	Umbrail (pass)	K3		
Err (peak)	J3	Inn (riv.)	J3	Matterhorn (mt.)	E4	Rhaetian Alps (range)	J3	Silhorn (mt.)	G2	Untersee (lake)	H1	CITIES and TOWNS	
Finsteraarhorn (mt.)	F3	Jungfrau (mt.)	E3	Moesa (riv.)	H4	Rhätikon (mts.)	J2	Silvretta (mts.)	K3	Unterwalden (can.)	F3		
Finstermünz (pass)	K3	Jura (mts.)	B3	Morat (lake)	D3	Rheinwaldhorn (mt.)	G4	Simme (riv.)	D4	Upper Engadine (valley)	J3	Schaan 4,552	H2
Fletschhorn (mt.)	E4	Kaiseregg (mt.)	D3	Muota (riv.)	G3	Rhine (riv.)	J2	Simplon (pass)	E4	Urirotstock (mt.)	F3	Triesen 2,971	H2
Fluchthorn (mt.)	K3	Kesch (peak)	J3	Murg (riv.)	G1	Rhône (riv.)	D4	Simplon (tunnel)	E4	Vadret (peak)	J3	Vaduz (cap.) 4,614	H2
Flüela (pass)	J3	La Dôle (mt.)	B4	Murtaröl (peak)	K3	Rigi (mt.)	F2	Sonnenhorn (mt.)	F4	Valserrhein (riv.)	H3		
Furka (pass)	F3	Landquart (riv.)	J3	Muttler (mt.)	K3	Rimpfischhorn (mt.)	E4	Splügen (pass)	H3	Vanil Noir (mt.)	D4	OTHER FEATURES	
Generoso (mt.)	H5	Le Chasseral (mt.)	C3	Naafkopf (mt.)	J2	Ringelspitz (mt.)	H3	Septimer (pass)	J4	Vélan (mt.)	D5		
Geneva (lake)	C4	Le Gros Crêt (mt.)	B3	Napf (mt.)	E3	Risoux (mt.)	B3	Spügen (pass)	E3	Visp (riv.)	E4	Grauspitz (mt.)	J2
Glärnisch (mt.)	G2	Léman (Geneva) (lake)	C4	National Park	K3	Rosstock (mt.)	F3	Stelvio (pass)	K3	Vorab (mt.)	H3	Ochsenkopf (mt.)	J2
Glarus Alps (mts.)	H3	Leone (mt.)	E4	Neuchâtel (lake)	C3	Rothorn (mt.)	D4	Susten (pass)	F3	Vorderrhein (riv.)	G3	Rhätikon (mts.)	J2
Grand Combin (mt.)	D5	Lepontine Alps (range)	G4	Noirmont (mt.)	B4	Saane (Sarine) (riv.)	D4	Sustenhorn (mt.)	F3	Wandfluhhorn (mt.)	F4	Rhine (riv.)	J2
Grande Dixence (dam)	D4	Limmat (riv.)	F2	Oberalp (pass)	G3	Saint Gotthard (pass)	G4	Tamaro (mt.)	G4	Weissenstein (mts.)	D2		
Grand Muveran (mt.)	D4											Weisshorn (mt.)	E4	*City and suburbs	

AUSTRIA

PROVINCES

Burgenland 272,119 ..... D3
Carinthia 525,728 ..... B3
Lower Austria 1,414,161 ..... C2
Salzburg 401,766 ..... B3
Styria 1,192,442 ..... C3
Tirol 540,771 ..... A3
Upper Austria 1,223,444 ..... B2
Vienna (city) 1,614,841 ..... D2
Vorarlberg 271,473 ..... A3

CITIES and TOWNS†

Admont 3,126 ..... C3
Allentsteig 2,783 ..... C2
Altheim 4,766 ..... B2
Althofen 3,886 ..... C3
Amstetten 13,330 ..... C2
Andau 3,058 ..... D3
Arnoldstein 6,740 ..... B3
Aspang Markt 2,316 ..... D3
Attnang-Puchheim 7,837 ..... B2
Bad Aussee 5,039 ..... B3
Baden 22,631 ..... D2
Badgastein 5,228 ..... B3
Bad Goisern 6,360 ..... B3
Bad Hofgastein 5,525 ..... B3
Bad Ischl 12,740 ..... B3
Bad Leonfelden 2,712 ..... C2
Bad Sankt-Leonhard im Lavanttal 4,882 ..... C3
Berndorf 8,371 ..... C3
Bischofshofen 9,417 ..... B3
Bludenz 12,050 ..... A3
Bramberg am Wildkogel 3,129 ..... B3
Braunau am Inn 16,432 ..... B2
Bregenz 22,839 ..... A3
Bruck an der Leitha 7,506 ..... D2
Bruck an der Mur 16,359 ..... C3
Deutsch Feistritz 3,820 ..... C3
Deutschkreutz 3,673 ..... D3
Deutsch Landsberg 6,614 ..... C3
Deutsch Wagram 4,481 ..... D2
Dornbirn 33,810 ..... A3
Ebenfurth 2,272 ..... D3
Ebensee 9,413 ..... B3
Eferding 3,014 ..... B2
Eggenburg 3,730 ..... C2
Ehrwald 2,198 ..... A3
Horn 6,264 ..... C2
Hüttenberg 3,251 ..... C3
Imst 5,855 ..... A3
Innsbruck 115,800 ..... A3
Innsbruck* 167,200 ..... A3
Jenbach 5,868 ..... A3
Jennersdorf 4,210 ..... C3
Judenburg 11,346 ..... C3
Kapfenberg 26,001 ..... C3
Kappl 2,156 ..... A3
Kaprun 2,604 ..... B3
Kindberg 6,128 ..... C3
Kirchdorf an der Krems 3,471 ..... C3
Kitzbühel 7,995 ..... B3
Klagenfurt 74,326 ..... C3
Klagenfurt* 112,600 ..... C3
Klosterneuburg 21,912 ..... D2
Knittelfeld 14,517 ..... C3
Köflach 12,612 ..... C3
Königswiesen 2,921 ..... C2
Korneuburg 8,892 ..... D2
Kössen 2,764 ..... B3
Kötschach-Mauthen 3,740 ..... B3
Krems an der Donau 21,733 ..... C2
Kufstein 12,766 ..... A3
Kundl 3,020 ..... A3
Laa an der Thaya 5,455 ..... D2
Laakirchen 7,664 ..... B3
Lambach 3,301 ..... C2
Landeck 7,388 ..... A3
Längenfeld 2,838 ..... A3
Langenlois 4,957 ..... C2
Langenwang 4,071 ..... C3
Lavamünd 4,120 ..... C3
Leibnitz 6,646 ..... C3
Lenzing 5,385 ..... B3
Leoben 35,153 ..... C3
Lienz 11,696 ..... B3
Liezen 6,244 ..... C3
Lilienfeld 3,126 ..... C3
Linz 205,700 ..... C2
Linz* 356,500 ..... C2
Lustenau 15,239 ..... A3
Mannersdorf am Leithagebirge 4,012 ..... D3
Marchegg 2,678 ..... D2
Mariazell 2,298 ..... C3
Matrei in Osttirol 4,003 ..... B3
Mattersburg 5,417 ..... D3
Mattighofen 4,344 ..... B2
Mauerkirchen 2,237 ..... B2
Mautern in Steiermark 2,536 ..... C3
Sankt Valentin 8,715 ..... C2
Sankt Veit an der Glan 11,047 ..... C3
Sankt Wolfgang im Salzkammergut 2,746 ..... B3
Schärding 5,874 ..... B2
Scheibbs 4,419 ..... C2
Schladming 3,460 ..... B3
Schrems 3,393 ..... C2
Schruns 3,607 ..... A3
Schwarzach im Pongau 3,616 ..... B3
Schwaz 10,253 ..... A3
Schwechat 14,997 ..... D2
Schwertberg 3,881 ..... C2
Sierning 8,162 ..... C2
Sillian 1,988 ..... B3
Solbad Hall in Tirol 12,335 ..... A3
Spital am Pyhrn 2,315 ..... C3
Spittal an der Drau 13,690 ..... B3
Steinach 2,698 ..... A3
Steyr 40,578 ..... C2
Stockerau 12,634 ..... D2
Strassburg 2,850 ..... C3
Tamsweg 5,060 ..... B3
Telfs 6,589 ..... A3
Ternitz 10,287 ..... D3
Traiskirchen 8,878 ..... D2
Traun 20,843 ..... C2
Trieben 4,639 ..... C3
Trofaiach 8,731 ..... C3
Tulln 7,705 ..... D2
Velden am Wörthersee 7,306 ..... C3
Vienna (cap.) 1,700,000 ..... D2
Vienna* 1,858,700 ..... D2
Villach 50,979 ..... B3
Vöcklabruck 10,627 ..... B2
Voitsberg 11,094 ..... C3
Völkermarkt 10,772 ..... C3
Vordernberg 2,508 ..... C3
Waidhofen an der Thaya 4,200 ..... C2
Waidhofen an der Ybbs 5,218 ..... C3
Weitensfeld-Flattnitz 5,206 ..... B3
Weitra 3,250 ..... C2
Weiz 8,241 ..... C3
Wels 47,279 ..... C2
Weyer Markt 2,518 ..... C3
Wien (Vienna) (cap.) 1,700,000 ..... D2
Wiener Neustadt 34,774 ..... D3
Wildon 2,002 ..... C3
Wilhelmsburg 6,307 ..... C2
Wolfsberg 31,176 ..... C3
Wörgl 7,811 ..... A3
Ybbs an der Donau 6,422 ..... C2
Zams 3,120 ..... A3
Zell am See 7,456 ..... B3
Zell am Ziller 1,882 ..... A3
Zeltweg 8,431 ..... C3
Zirl 4,157 ..... A3
Zistersdorf 3,412 ..... D2
Zwettl-Niederösterreich 11,624 ..... C2

OTHER FEATURES

AllgÄu Alps (mts.) A3
Bavarian Alps (mts.) A3
Bodensee (Constance) (lake) A3
Brenner (pass) A3
Carnic Alps (mts.) B3
Constance (lake) A3
Danube (riv.) C2
Donau (Danube) (riv.) D2
Drau (riv.) C3
Enns (riv.) C3
Grossglockner (mt.) B3
Hohe Tauern (range) B3
Inn (riv.) B2
Karawanken (range) C3
March (riv.) D2
Mühlviertel (reg.) C2
Mur (riv.) C3
Neusiedler See (lake) D3
Niedere Tauern (range) B3
Ötztal Alps (mts.) A3
Raab (riv.) C3
Rhine (riv.) A3
Salzach (riv.) B2
Salzkammergut (reg.) B3
Semmering (pass) C3
Thaya (riv.) C2
Traun (riv.) C2
Wildspitze (mt.) A3
Zugspitze (mt.) A3

CZECHOSLOVAKIA

REPUBLICS

Czech Socialist Rep. 9,964,338 ..... B1
Slovak Socialist Rep. 4,670,409 ..... E2

REGIONS

Bratislava (city) 333,000 ..... D2
Jihočeský 662,002 ..... C2
Jihomoravský 1,966,850 ..... D2
Praha (city) 1,161,200 ..... C1
Severočeský 1,122,035 ..... C1
Severomoravský 1,849,286 ..... D2
Středočeský 1,193,041 ..... C2
Středoslovenský 1,436,351 ..... E2
Východočeský 1,214,581 ..... C1
Východoslovenský 1,298,481 ..... F2
Západočeský 865,094 ..... B2
Západoslovenský 1,610,542 ..... D2

CITIES and TOWNS

Aš 120,000 ..... B1
Austerlitz (Slavkov) D2
Bánovce nad Bebravou 11,400 ..... E2
Banská Bystrica 53,000 ..... E2
Banská štiavnica 7,486 ..... E2
Bardejov 17,400 ..... F2
Benešov 11,100 ..... C2
Beroun 17,600 ..... B2
Bílina 17,800 ..... B1
Blansko 13,800 ..... D2
Boskovice 8,531 ..... D2
Brandýs nad Labem-Stará Boleslavv 333,000 ..... C1
Bratislava 333,000 ..... D2
Břeclav 21,100 ..... D2
Brezno 14,800 ..... E2
Brno 335,700 ..... D2
Broumov 7,782 ..... D1
Bruntál 12,300 ..... D2
Bystřice nad Pernštejnem 6,471 ..... D2
Bystřice pod Hostýnem 6,681 ..... D2
Bytča 6,922 ..... E2
Čadca 16,800 ..... E2
Čalovo 6,591 ..... D3
Čáslav 10,200 ..... C2
Česká Lípa 18,600 ..... C1
Česká Třebová 14,700 ..... D2
České Budějovice 80,800 ..... C2
Český Brod 6,640 ..... C1
Český Krumlov 12,000 ..... C2
Český Těšín 17,200 ..... E2
Cheb 27,000 ..... B1
Choceň 8,198 ..... D1
Chodov 14,400 ..... B1
Chomutov 44,200 ..... B1
Chotěboř 6,692 ..... C2
Chrudim 18,800 ..... C2
Čierny Balog 6,435 ..... E2
Děčín 46,500 ..... C1
Detva 13,100 ..... E2
Dobříš 6,378 ..... C2
Dobruška 5,779 ..... D1
Dolný Kubín 9,900 ..... E2
Domažlice 9,100 ..... B2
Dubnica nad Váhom 11,300 ..... E2
Duchcov 9,712 ..... B1
Dunajská Streda 13,000 ..... D3
Dvory nad Žitavou 5,847 ..... E3
Dvů Králové nad Labem 16,800 ..... C1
Falknov (Sokolov) 23,900 ..... B1
Fil'akovo 7,822 ..... E2
Frenštát pod Radhoštěm 8,516 ..... E2
Frýdek-Místek 43,800 ..... E2
Frýdlant v. Čechách 5,948 ..... C1
Frýdlant nad Ostravicí 6,250 ..... E2
Galanta 12,300 ..... D2
Gottwaldov 84,300 ..... D2
Handlová 16,200 ..... E2
Havířov 85,000 ..... E2
Havlíčkův Brod 19,200 ..... C2
Hlinsko 8,890 ..... D2
Hlohovec 15,200 ..... D2
Hlučín 15,300 ..... E2
Hnúšt'a-Likier E2
Hodonín 22,600 ..... D2
Holešov 9,091 ..... D2
Holíč 7,602 ..... D2
Holice 6,151 ..... C1
Horažd'ovice B2
Hořice v Podkrkonoší 7,715 ..... C1
Horná Štubňa E2
Horní Benešov D2
Horní Libina D2
Hořovice 5,665 ..... C2
Horšovský Týn B2
Hostinné C1
Hradec Králové 85,600 ..... C1
Hranice 13,300 ..... D2
Hrinova 7,800 ..... E2
Hronov 9,767 ..... D1
Hrušovany D2
Humenné 22,200 ..... G2
Humpolec 7,810 ..... C2
Hurbanovo E3
Hustopeče D2
Ilava E2
Ivančice 7,314 ..... D2

Topography

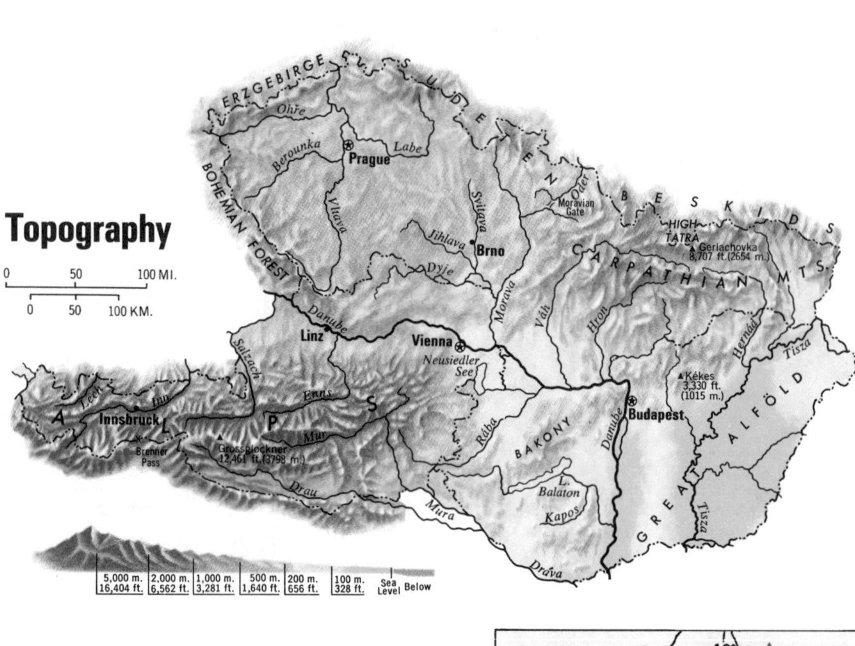

Eisenerz 11,563 ..... C3
Eisenkappel-Vellach 3,761 ..... C3
Eisenstadt 10,059 ..... D3
Enns 9,622 ..... C2
Feldbach 3,887 ..... C3
Feldkirch 21,214 ..... A3
Feldkirchen in Kärnten 11,188 ..... B3
Ferlach 7,621 ..... C3
Fieberbrunn 3,651 ..... B3
Fohnsdorf 11,169 ..... C3
Frankenmarkt 2,960 ..... B3
Frauenkirchen 2,749 ..... D3
Freistadt 5,956 ..... C2
Freidberg 2,504 ..... D3
Friesach 7,257 ..... C3
Frohnleiten 5,081 ..... C3
Fulpmes 2,553 ..... A3
Fürstenfeld 6,054 ..... C3
Gaming 4,181 ..... C3
Gänserndorf 4,211 ..... D2
Gleisdorf 4,921 ..... C3
Gloggnitz 7,078 ..... D3
Gmünd, Carinthia 2,267 ..... B3
Gmünd, Lower Austria 6,323 ..... C2
Gmunden 12,270 ..... B3
Golling an der Salzach 3,089 ..... B3
Götzis 7,931 ..... A3
Gratwein 2,747 ..... C3
Graz 251,900 ..... C3
Graz* 314,200 ..... C3
Grein 2,767 ..... C2
f21Grieskirchen 4,519 ..... B2
Grosssiegharts 3,288 ..... C2
Grünburg 3,775 ..... C3
Güssing 3,675 ..... D3
Haag 5,060 ..... C2
Hainburg an der Donau 6,009 ..... D2
Hainfeld 3,897 ..... C2
Hallein 14,371 ..... B3
Hallstatt 1,303 ..... B3
Hartberg 5,702 ..... C3
Haslach an der Mühl 2,636 ..... C2
Heidenreichstein 4,340 ..... C2
Heiligenblut 1,324 ..... B3
Hermagor-Preseggersee 7,531 ..... B3
Herzogenburg 7,299 ..... C2
Hohenau an der March 3,591 ..... D2
Hohenberg 2,016 ..... C3
Hohenems 11,487 ..... A3
Hollabrunn 6,563 ..... D2
Hopfgarten in Nordtirol 4,784 ..... B3
Mauthausen 4,419 ..... C2
Mauthen-Kötschach 3,750 ..... B3
Mayrhofen 3,174 ..... A3
Melk 5,108 ..... C2
Mistelbach an der Zaya 6,306 ..... D2
Mittersill 4,361 ..... B3
Mödling 18,712 ..... D2
Mondsee 2,141 ..... B3
Murau 2,710 ..... C3
Mürzzuschlag 11,564 ..... C3
Neuberg an der Mürz 2,183 ..... C3
Neumarkt am Wallersee 3,267 ..... B3
Neunkirchen 10,922 ..... C3
Neusiedl am See 3,999 ..... D3
Neustift im Stubaital 2,789 ..... A3
Ober Grafendorf 4,109 ..... C2
Oberndorf bei Salzburg 3,293 ..... B3
Obervellach 2,420 ..... B3
Oberwart 5,661 ..... D3
Paternion 5,805 ..... B3
Perg 4,872 ..... C2
Peuerbach 2,161 ..... B2
Pfunds 2,043 ..... A3
Pinkafeld 4,610 ..... C3
Pöchlarn 3,199 ..... C2
Pörtschach am Wörthersee 2,511 ..... C3
Poysdorf 5,774 ..... D2
Pregarten 3,249 ..... C2
Raabs an der Thaya 4,194 ..... C2
Radenthein 6,847 ..... B3
Radkersburg 2,000 ..... C3
Radstadt 3,585 ..... B3
Rankweil 8,440 ..... A3
Rechnitz 3,412 ..... D3
Reichenau an der Rax 4,053 ..... C3
Retz 4,780 ..... D2
Ried im Innkreis 10,534 ..... B2
Rottenmann 4,781 ..... C3
Saalfelden am Steinernen Meer 10,172 ..... B3
Salzburg 122,100 ..... B3
Salzburg* 213,430 ..... B3
Sankt Aegyd am Neuwalde 3,165 ..... C3
Sankt Anton am Arlberg 2,086 ..... A3
Sankt Johann in Tirol 5,942 ..... B3
Sankt Michael im Lungau 2,839 ..... B3
Sankt Michael in Obersteiermark 3,717 ..... C3
Sankt Michael im Lungau 2,839 ..... B3
Sankt Paul im Lavanttal 6,721 ..... C3
Sankt Pölten 43,300 ..... C2

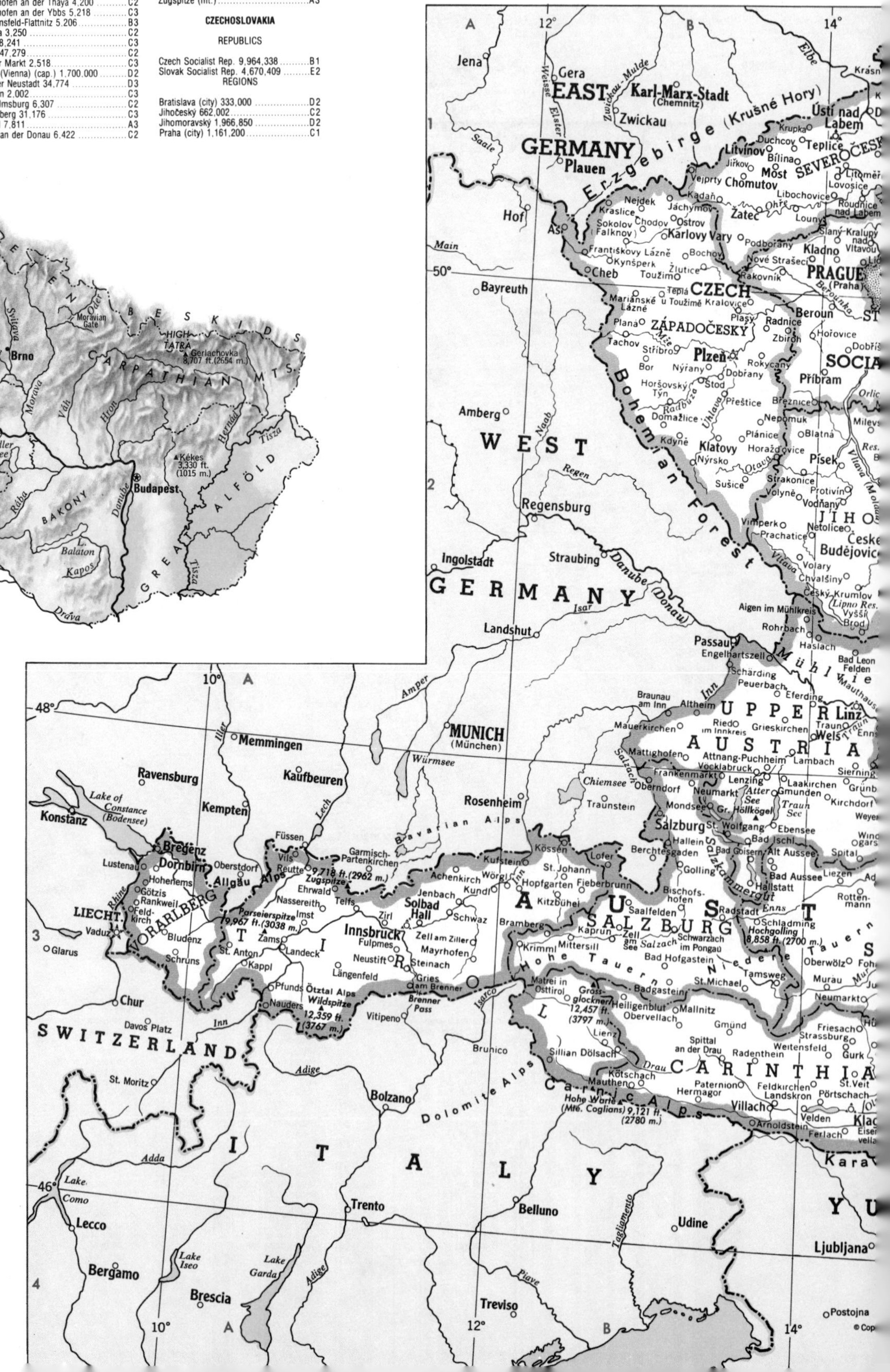

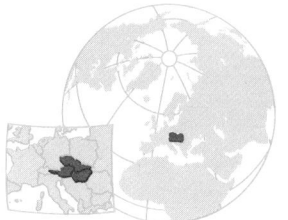

AREA 32,375 sq. mi. (83,851 sq. km.)
POPULATION 7,507,000
CAPITAL Vienna
LARGEST CITY Vienna
HIGHEST POINT Grossglockner 12,457 ft. (3,797 m.)
MONETARY UNIT schilling
MAJOR LANGUAGE German
MAJOR RELIGION Roman Catholicism

AREA 49,373 sq. mi. (127,876 sq. km.)
POPULATION 15,276,799
CAPITAL Prague
LARGEST CITY Prague
HIGHEST POINT Gerlachovka 8,707 ft. (2,654 m.)
MONETARY UNIT koruna
MAJOR LANGUAGES Czech, Slovak
MAJOR RELIGIONS Roman Catholicism, Protestantism

AREA 35,919 sq. mi. (93,030 sq. km.)
POPULATION 10,709,536
CAPITAL Budapest
LARGEST CITY Budapest
HIGHEST POINT Kékes 3,330 ft. (1,015 m.)
MONETARY UNIT forint
MAJOR LANGUAGE Hungarian
MAJOR RELIGIONS Roman Catholicism, Protestantism

AUSTRIA

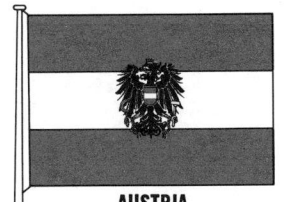

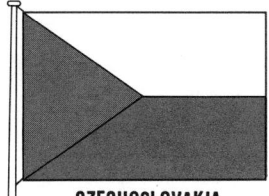

CZECHOSLOVAKIA

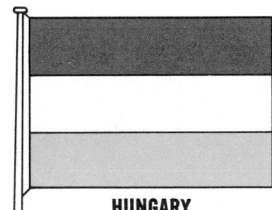

HUNGARY

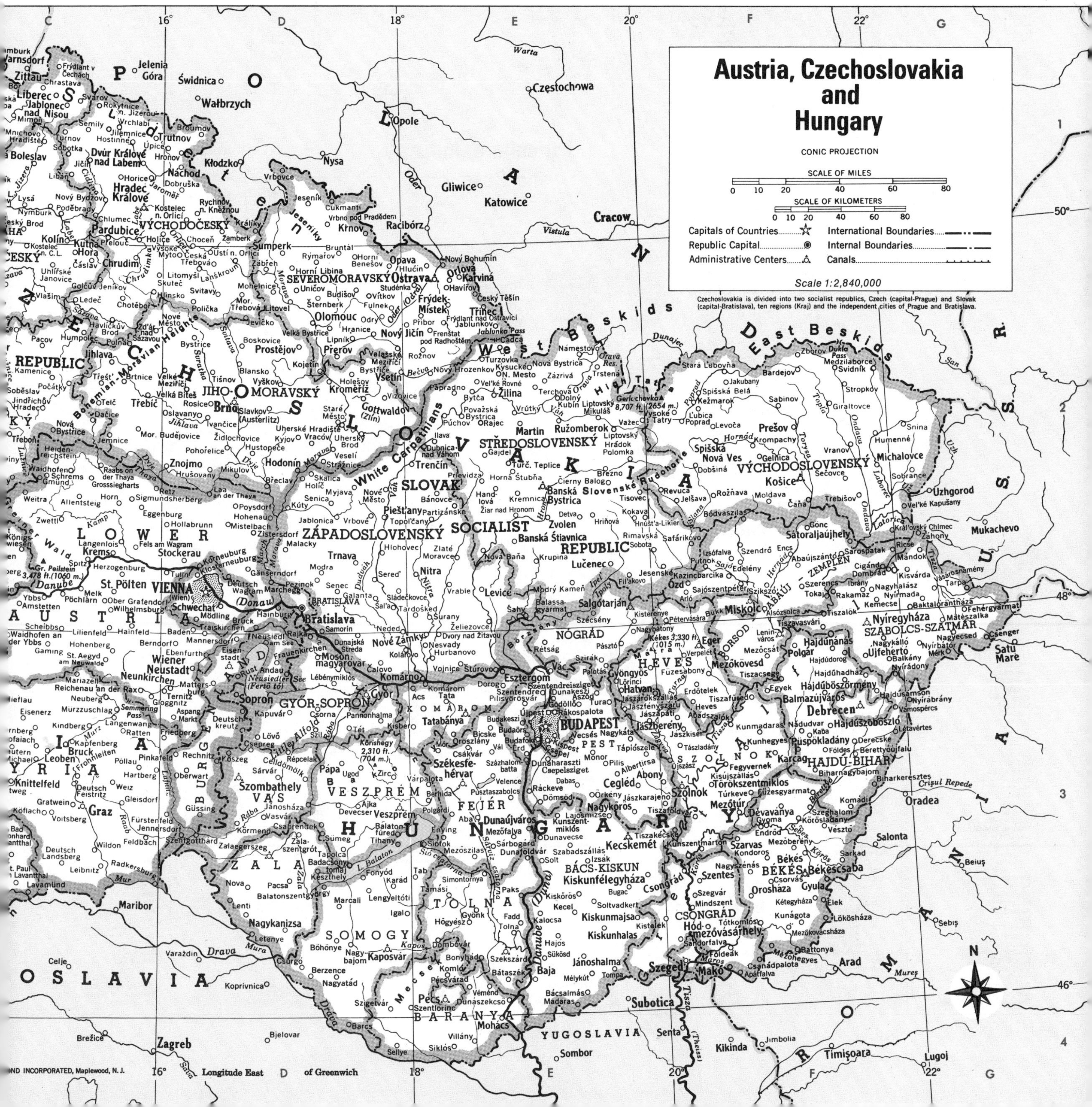

Austria, Czechoslovakia and Hungary
CONIC PROJECTION
SCALE OF MILES
0 10 20 40 60 80
SCALE OF KILOMETERS
0 10 20 40 60 80
Capitals of Countries
Republic Capital
Administrative Centers
International Boundaries
Internal Boundaries
Canals
Scale 1:2,840,000
Czechoslovakia is divided into two socialist republics, Czech (capital-Prague) and Slovak (capital-Bratislava), ten regions (Kraj) and the independent cities of Prague and Bratislava.
Longitude East of Greenwich
POLAND
CZECH SOCIALIST REPUBLIC
SLOVAK SOCIALIST REPUBLIC
LOWER AUSTRIA
HUNGARY
YUGOSLAVIA
RUMANIA
U.S.S.R.
VIENNA
BUDAPEST
Bratislava
Brno
Ostrava
Katowice
Cracow
Wrocław
Košice
Debrecen
Szeged
Pécs
Graz
Zagreb
West Beskids
East Beskids
High Tatra
White Carpathians
Danube
Tisza
Drava
L. Balaton

42 Austria, Czechoslovakia and Hungary
(continued)

Jablonec nad Nisou 36,300 C1
Jablonica D2
Jablunkov 9,405 E2
Jáchymov B1
Jakubany F2
Jaroměř 11,600 C1
Jelšava F2
Jemnice C2
Jeseník 10,900 D1
Jesenské F2
Jevíčko D2
Jičín 13,200 C1
Jihlava 44,500 C2
Jilemnice C1
Jindřichův Hradec 15,700 C2
Jiřkov 11,400 B1
Kadaň 18,100 B1
Kamenice C2
Kaplice C2
Karlovy Vary 43,300 B1
Karviná 79,100 E2
Kdyně B2
Kežmarok 11,000 F2
Kladno 61,200 B1
Klatovy 18,500 B2
Kojetín 5,852 D2
Kokava nad Rimavicou 5,391 E2
Kolárovo 10,500 D3
Kolín 29,100 C1
Komárno 28,200 D3
Košice 169,100 F2
Kostelec nad Orlicí 5,575 D1
Král'ovský Chlmec 5,329 G2
Kralupy nad Vltavou 16,900 C1
Kraslice 6,733 B1
Kremnica 5,941 E2
Krnov 25,000 D1
Kroměříž 23,200 D2
Krompachy 6,332 F2
Krupina 6,627 E2
Krupka 8,301 B1
Kutná Hora 19,200 C2
Kyjov 10,700 D2
Kynšperk 5,524 B1
Kysucké Nové Mesto 11,700 E2
Lanškroun 8,683 D2
Levice 19,000 E2
Levoča 10,100 F2
Libáň C1
Liberec 75,600 C1
Lidice C1
Lipník nad Bečvou 7,358 D2
Liptovský Mikuláš 19,400 E2
Litoměřice 19,700 C1
Litomyšl 8,112 D2
Litovel 5,805 D2
Litvínov 23,300 B1
Lomnice C2
Louny 15,200 B1
Lovosice 9,323 C1
L'ubica F2
Lučenec 23,300 E2
Lysá nad Labem 9,920 C1
Malacky 13,200 D2
Mariánské Lázně 14,600 B2
Martin 47,800 E2
Medzilaborce F2
Měln'k 17,800 C1
Michalovce 23,600 G2
Mikulov 6,267 D2
Milevsko 7,091 C2
Mimoň 6,773 C1
Mladá Boleslav 36,900 C1
Mladá Vožice C2
Mnichovo Hradiště 5,239 C1
Modra 7,219 D2
Modrý Kameň 6,200 E2
Mohelnice 6,050 D2
Moldava nad Bodvou 5,397 F2
Moravská Třebová 9,052 D2
Moravské Budějovice 5,576 D2
Most 59,400 B1
Myjava 6,657 D2
Náchod 19,300 D1
Námestovo E2
Neded D2
Nejdek 8,187 B1
Nepomuk B2
Nesvady 5,453 E3
Netolice C2
Nitra 50,000 E2
Nová Baňa 6,218 E2
Nová Bystrica E2
Nová Bystřice C2
Nové Hrady C2
Nové Město na Moravě 6,581 D2
Nové Město nad Váhom 15,900 D2
Nové Strašecí B1
Nové Zámky 27,300 D3
Nový Bohumín 16,700 E2
Nový Bor 7,621 C1
Nový Bydžov 6,824 C1
Nový Hrozenkov E2
Nový Jičín 21,400 E2
Nymburk 13,600 C1
Nýřany 6,204 B2
Nýrsko B2
Odry D2
Olomouc 82,800 D2
Opava 53,800 E2
Orlová 25,500 E2
Ostrava 293,500 E2
Ostrov 18,200 B1
Pardubice 78,500 C1
Partizánske 15,100 E2
Pelhřimov 11,900 C2
Pezinok 13,100 D2
Piešt'any 25,400 D2
Písek 25,100 C2
Plzeň 155,000 B2
Počátky C2
Podbořany B1
Poděbrady 13,400 C1
Pohořelice D2
Polička 6,529 D2
Polná C2
Polomka E2
Poprad 25,800 F2
Považská Bystrica 19,300 E2
Prachatice 7,900 B2
Prague (Praha) (cap.) 1,161,200 C1
Přelouč 6,251 C1
Přerov 43,500 D2
Prešov 61,000 F2
Přeštice B2
Příbor 7,726 E2
Příbram 31,300 B2
Prievidza 30,900 E2
Prostějov 44,200 D2
Protivín C2
Púchov 9,306 E2
Radnice B2
Rajec E2
Rakovník 14,200 B1
Revúca 5,901 F2
Říčany u Prahy 8,407 C2
Rimavská Sobota 5,800 E2
Rokycany 12,800 B2
Rokytnice nad Jizerou C1
Rosice D2
Roudnice nad Labem 11,800 C1
Rožňava 12,400 F2
Rožnov pod Radhoštěm 11,600 E2
Rumburk C1
Ružomberok 22,600 E2
Rychnov nad Kněžnou 7,500 D1
Rýmařov 7,522 D2
Sabinov 5,473 F2
Šafárikovo F2
Šahy 5,049 E2
Šal'a 15,200 D2
Samorín 8,287 D2
Sečovce 5,744 F2
Sedlčany C2
Semily 8,200 C1
Senec 8,544 D2
Senica 12,300 D2
Sereď 12,500 D2
Skalica 11,100 D2
Skuteč D2
Sládečkovce 5,598 D2
Slaný 13,200 C1
Slavkov D2
Snina 10,900 G2
Soběslav 6,140 C2
Sobotka C1
Sobrance G2
Sokolov 23,900 B1
Spišská Belá F2
Spišská Nová Ves 26,100 F2
Stará L'ubovňa 5,800 F2
Staré Město 6,293 D2
Šternberk 13,700 D2
Stod B2
Strakonice 19,000 B2
Strážnice 5,482 D2
Stříbro B2
Stropkov 5,645 F2
Studénka 9,744 D2
Štúrovo 8,287 E3
Šumperk 25,900 D1
Šurany 6,693 E2
Sušice 10,300 B2
Svárov C1
Svidník 4,600 F2
Svitavy 15,000 D2
Tábor 28,100 C2
Tachov 11,400 B2
Telč 5,285 C2
Teplice 52,300 B1
Tišnov 8,263 D2
Topol'čany 17,500 D2
Třebíč 23,900 C2
Trebišov 13,700 F2
Třeboň 6,068 C2
Trenčín 38,800 E2
Třešť 5,053 C2
Třinec 32,000 E2
Trnava 48,600 D2
Trutnov 24,500 D1
Turnov 13,600 C1
Turzovka 6,107 E2
Uherské Hradiště 32,100 D2
Uherský Brod 12,800 D2
Uničov 10,800 D2
Úpice 6,323 C1
Ústí nad Labem 74,900 C1
Ústí nad Orlicí 13,700 D2
Valašské Meziříčí 19,400 D2
Varnsdorf 14,700 C1
Važec E2
Vejprty B1
Velká Bíteš D2
Velká Bystřice D2
Vel'ké Kapušany G2
Velké Meziříčí 7,590 D2
Vel'ké Rovné E2
Veselí nad Lužnicí C2
Veselí nad Moravou 11,500 D2
Vimperk 5,749 B2
Vítkov 5,138 D2
Vizovice D2
Vlašim 8,873 C2
Vodňany 5,620 C2
Vojnice E3
Volary B2
Volyně B2
Votice C2
Vráble E2
Vracov D2
Vranov nad Teplou 14,700 F2
Vrbno pod Pradědem 5,594 D1
Vrbovce D1
Vrbové D2
Vrchlabí 11,700 C1
Vrútky 5,756 E2
Vsetín 24,100 D2
Vyškov 15,100 D2
Vysoké Mýto 8,830 D2
Vysoké Tatry F2
Vyšší Brod C2
Zábřeh 11,300 D2
Žamberk 5,040 D1
Žatec 17,400 B1
Zázrivá E2
Zbiroh B2
Zborov F2
Žďár nad Sázavou 17,800 C2
Želiezovce 5,478 E2
Žiar nad Hronom 14,800 E2
Židlochovice D2
Žilina 56,000 E2
Zlaté Moravce 10,300 E2
Zlín (Gottwaldov) 84,300 D2
Žlutice B1
Znojmo 28,500 D2
Zvolen 29,000 E2

OTHER FEATURES

Berounka (riv.) C2
Beskids, East (mts.) F1
Beskids, West (mts.) E2
Bohemian (for.) B2
Bohemian-Moravian Heights (hills) C2
Danube (riv.) C2
Dunajec (riv.) F2
Dyje (riv.) D2
Erzgebirge (mts.) B1
Gerlachovka (mt.) E2
Hornád (riv.) F2
Hron (riv.) E2
Ipel' (riv.) E2
Jablunka (pass) E2
Jeseníky (mts.) D1
Jihlava (riv.) D2
Krušné Hory (Erzgebirge) (mts.) B1
Labe (riv.) C1
Lipno (res.) C2
Lužnice (riv.) C2
Moldau (Vltava) (riv.) C2
Morava (riv.) D2
Nitra (riv.) E2
Oder (Odra) (riv.) D2
Ohře (riv.) B1
Ondava (riv.) F2
Orava (riv.) E2
Orlická (res.) C2
Sázava (riv.) C2
Slovenské Rudohorie (mts.) E2
Sudeten (mts.) C1
Svitava (riv.) D2
Svratka (riv.) D2
Tatra, High (mts.) E2
Torysa (riv.) F2
Úhlava (riv.) B2
Váh (riv.) D2
Vltava (riv.) C2
White Carpathians (mts.) E2

HUNGARY

COUNTIES

Bács-Kiskun 568,532 E3
Baranya 434,030 E4
Békés 436,987 F3
Borsod-Abaúj-Zemplén 808,924 F2
Budapest (city) 2,060,170 E3
Csongrád 456,862 F3
Fejér 421,568 E3
Győr-Sopron 428,476 D3
Hajdú-Bihar 552,417 F3
Heves 350,874 F3
Komárom 321,579 E3
Nógrád 239,907 E3
Pest 973,486 E3
Somogy 360,308 D3
Szabolcs-Szatmár 593,746 G3
Szolnok 446,379 F3
Tolna 266,414 E3
Vas 285,527 D3
Veszprém 386,740 D3
Zala 316,610 D3

CITIES and TOWNS

Aba 4,271 E3
Abádszalók 6,386 F3
Abaújszántó 4,209 F2
Abony 15,624 E3
Ács 8,423 E3
Ajka 29,601 D3
Albertirsa 11,252 E3
Alsózsolca 5,045 F2
Arló 4,203 F2
Aszód 6,218 E3
Bácsalmás 9,025 E3
Badacsonytomaj 2,933 D3
Baja 38,456 E3
Baktalórántháza 3,736 G2
Balassagyarmat 18,534 E2
Balatonfüred 12,599 D3
Balkány 7,667 G3
Balmazújváros 17,371 F3
Barcs 11,448 D4
Bátaszék 7,274 E3
Battonya 9,324 F3
Békés 22,287 F3
Békéscsaba 67,266 F3
Berettyóújfalu 16,406 F3
Berzence 3,406 D3
Bicske 10,720 E3
Biharkeresztes 4,788 F3
Biharnagybajom 4,093 F3
Böhönye 3,215 D3
Bonyhád 14,841 E3
Budafok 40,623 E3
Budaörs 13,958 E3
Budakeszi 10,429 E3
Budapest (cap.) 2,060,170 E3
Bugak 4,989 E3
Cegléd 40,567 E3
Celldömölk 12,533 D3
Cigánd 4,767 F2
Csabrendek 3,045 D3
Csákvár 5,238 E3
Csanádpalota 4,642 F3
Csenger 4,792 G3
Csepel 71,693 E3
Csepreg 4,079 D3
Csongrád 22,202 E3
Csorna 12,131 D3
Csorvás 6,826 F3
Csurgó 5,463 D3
Dabas 13,075 E3
Debrecen 192,484 F3
Derecske 9,579 F3
Dévaványa 11,208 F3
Devecser 5,482 D3
Dombóvár 19,917 E3
Dombrád 6,328 F2
Dömsöd 6,545 E3
Dorog 10,754 E3
Dunaföldvár 10,318 E3
Dunaharaszti 15,788 E3
Dunakeszi 25,187 E3
Dunaszekcső 2,999 E3
Dunaújváros 60,694 E3
Dunavecse 4,521 E3
Edelény 9,559 F2
Eger 61,283 F3
Egyek 7,956 F3
Elek 6,032 F3
Enes 2,565 F2
Endrőd 8,136 F3
Enying 7,518 E3
Érd 41,210 E3
Erdőtelek 4,250 F3
Esztergom 30,476 E3
Fadd 4,805 E3
Fegyvernek 8,421 F3
Fehérgyarmat 6,729 G3
Földeák 3,855 F3
Földes 5,293 F2
Fonyód 3,957 D3
Füzesabony 6,965 F3
Füzesgyarmat 7,097 F3
Gödöllő 28,057 E3
Gönc 2,875 F2
Gyoma 10,392 F3
Gyöngyös 36,927 E3
Gyönk 2,507 E3
Győr 123,618 D3
Gyula 34,514 F3
Hajdúböszörmény 32,145 F3
Hajdúdorog 10,118 F3
Hajdúhadház 13,626 F3
Hajdúnánás 18,146 F3
Hajdúsámson 7,492 F3
Hajdúszoboszló 23,374 F3
Hajós 5,113 E3
Hatvan 24,790 E3
Heves 10,943 F3
Hódmezővásárhely 54,481 F3
Hőgyész 3,534 E3
Ibrány 7,037 F2
Izsák 7,686 E3
Izsófalva 6,816 F2
Jánoshalma 12,534 E3
Jánosháza 3,274 D3
Jászapáti 10,424 E3
Jászárokszállás 10,139 E3
Jászberény 31,347 E3
Jászfényszaru 6,869 E3
Jászkarajenő 4,101 E3
Jászkisér 6,816 F3
Jászladány 7,823 F3
Kaba 6,654 F2
Kalocsa 18,613 E3
Kaposvár 72,330 D3
Kapuvár 11,243 D3
Karád 2,754 D3
Karcag 25,264 F3
Kazincbarcika 37,481 F2
Kecel 10,493 E3
Kecskemét 91,929 E3
Kemecse 4,583 F2
Keszthely 21,671 D3
Kétegyháza 4,728 F3
Kisbér 4,562 D3
Kiskőrös 15,499 E3
Kiskunfélegyháza 35,339 E3
Kiskunhalas 30,552 E3
Kiskunmajsa 14,439 E3
Kispest 65,106 E3
Kistelek 8,544 E3
Kisterenye 6,844 E2
Kisújszállás 13,699 F3
Kisvárda 17,828 G2
Komádi 8,765 F3
Komárom 19,955 E3
Komló 30,301 E3
Kondoros 7,319 F3
Körmend 11,787 D3
Körösladány 6,565 F3
Kőszeg 12,705 D3
Kunágota 4,622 F3
Kunhegyes 10,116 F3
Kunmadaras 7,343 F3
Kunszentmárton 11,103 F3
Kunszentmiklós 7,952 E3
Lajosmizse 12,872 E3
Lébénymiklós 6,190 D3
Lengyeltóti 3,389 D3
Leninváros 18,667 F3
Lenti 8,106 D3
Létavértes 9,106 G3
Letenye 4,395 D3
Lőkösháza 2,514 F3
Lőrinci 10,679 E3
Madaras 4,519 E3
Makó 29,943 F3
Mándok 5,093 G2
Marcali 12,485 D3
Mátészalka 17,709 G3
Mélykút 7,640 E3
Mérk 3,211 G3
Mezőberény 12,702 F3
Mezőcsát 6,729 F3
Mezőfalva 5,008 E3
Mezőhegyes 8,631 F3
Mezőkovácsháza 7,473 F3
Mezőkövesd 18,435 F3
Mezőszilas 2,792 E3
Mezőtúr 22,018 F3
Mindszent 8,730 F3
Miskolc 206,727 F2
Mohács 21,385 E4
Monor 16,838 E3
Mór 12,066 E3
Mosonmagyaróvár 29,732 D3
Nádudvar 9,447 F3
Nagyatád 12,946 D3
Nagybajom 4,402 D3
Nagyecsed 8,225 G3
Nagyhalász 6,437 F2
Nagykálló 11,282 F3
Nagykanizsa 48,494 D3
Nagykáta 11,922 E3
Nagykőrös 27,900 E3
Nagyszénás 7,124 F3
Nyírábrány 4,509 G3
Nyíradony 7,146 G3
Nyírbátor 13,388 G3
Nyíregyháza 108,156 F3
Nyírmada 4,744 F2
Örkény 5,013 E3
Orosháza 36,243 F3
Oroszlány 20,604 E3
Ózd 48,521 F2
Pacsa 1,984 D3
Paks 19,514 E3
Pannonhalma 3,731 D3
Pápa 32,202 D3
Pásztó 7,962 E3
Pécs 168,788 E3
Pécsvárad 3,672 E3
Pétervására 2,753 F3
Pilis 9,055 E3
Pilisvörösvár 10,217 E3
Polgár 9,429 F3
Polgárdi 5,767 E3
Püspökladány 15,730 F3
Pusztaszabolcs 5,794 E3
Putnok 7,103 F2
Ráckeve 7,534 E3
Rajka 2,448 D3
Rakamaz 5,407 F2
Rákospalota 60,983 E3
Répcelak 1,997 D3
Ricse 2,992 G2
Sajószentpéter 13,992 F2
Salgótarján 49,320 E2
Sándorfalva 5,949 F3
Sárbogárd 11,178 E3
Sarkad 11,937 F3
Sárospatak 15,316 F2
Sárvár 15,126 D3
Sátoraljaújhely 19,252 F2
Sellye 2,804 D4
Siklós 10,567 E4
Simontornya 4,892 E3
Siófok 20,084 E3
Solt 6,911 E3
Soltvadkert 7,934 E3
Sopron 53,930 D3
Sükösd 4,430 E3
Sümeg 6,229 D3
Szabadszállás 8,223 E3
Szarvas 20,598 F3
Szécsény 5,690 E2
Százhalombatta 13,963 E3
Szeged 171,342 E3
Szeghalom 9,736 F3
Szegvár 6,395 F3
Székesfehérvár 103,197 E3
Szekszárd 34,592 E3
Szendrő 4,098 F2
Szentendre 16,844 E3
Szentes 35,326 F3
Szentgotthárd 5,837 D3
Szentlőrinc 3,926 E3
Szerencs 8,612 F2
Szigetvár 12,114 D3
Szikszó 6,419 F2
Szil 2,073 D3
Szolnok 75,203 F3
Szombathely 82,830 D3
Tab 3,922 E3
Tamási 7,602 E3
Tápiószele 5,575 E3
Tapolca 17,161 D3
Tarpa 3,436 G2
Tata 24,114 E3
Tatabánya 75,942 E3
Tét 4,441 D3
Tiszacsege 6,263 F3
Tiszaföldvár 12,560 F3
Tiszafüred 12,259 F3
Tiszakécske 12,378 E3
Tiszalök 6,230 F2
Tiszavasvári 13,292 F3
Tokaj 4,845 F2
Tolna 8,997 E3
Tompa 5,365 E3
Törökszentmiklós 25,551 F3
Tótkomlós 8,803 F3
Tura 8,235 E3
Túrkeve 11,393 F3
Újfehértó 14,412 F3
Újpest 80,384 E3
Újszász 7,098 F2
Vác 34,837 E3
Vál 2,488 E3
Vámospércs 5,213 F3
Várpalota 28,293 E3
Vásárosnamény 8,637 G2
Vasvár 4,275 D3
Vecsés 19,193 E3
Velence 3,463 E3
Vémend 2,293 E3
Verpelét 4,622 F2
Veszprém 54,898 D3
Vésztő 9,815 F3
Villány 2,764 E4
Záhony 3,049 G2
Zalaegerszeg 39,671 D3
Zalaszentgrót 5,346 D3
Zirc 5,980 D3

OTHER FEATURES

Bakony (mts.) D3
Balaton (lake) D3
Berettyó (riv.) F3
Bükk (mts.) F2
Csepelsziget (isl.) E3
Danube (riv.) E3
Dráva (riv.) D3
Duna (Danube) (riv.) E3
Fertő tó (Neusiedler See) (lake) D3
Great Alföld (plain) F3
Hernád (riv.) F2
Kapos (riv.) D3
Kékes (mt.) E3
Körös (riv.) F3
Maros (riv.) F3
Mátra (mts.) E3
Mecsek (mts.) D3
Mura (riv.) D3
Rába (riv.) D3
Sajó (riv.) F2
Sárviz csatorna (canal) E3
Sió csatorna (canal) E3
Szentendreisziget (isl.) E3
Tisza (riv.) F3
Zala (riv.) D3

*City and suburbs.
†Population of Austrian cities are communes.

Agriculture, Industry and Resources

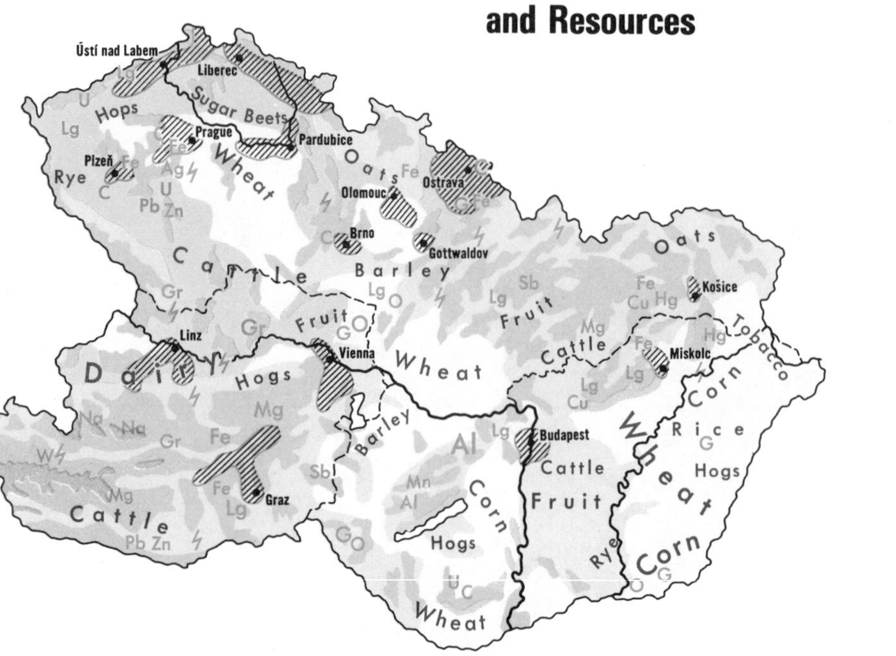

DOMINANT LAND USE

- Cereals (chiefly wheat, corn)
- Other Cereals, Livestock, Dairy
- General Farming, Livestock
- General Farming, Truck Farming
- Pasture Livestock
- Grapes, Wine
- Forests
- Nonagricultural Land

MAJOR MINERAL OCCURRENCES

- Ag Silver
- Al Bauxite
- C Coal
- Cu Copper
- Fe Iron Ore
- G Natural Gas
- Gr Graphite
- Hg Mercury
- Lg Lignite
- Mg Magnesium
- Mn Manganese
- Na Salt
- O Petroleum
- Pb Lead
- Sb Antimony
- U Uranium
- W Tungsten
- Zn Zinc

- Water Power
- Major Industrial Areas

YUGOSLAVIA

AREA 98,766 sq. mi. (255,804 sq. km.)
POPULATION 22,471,000
CAPITAL Belgrade
LARGEST CITY Belgrade
HIGHEST POINT Triglav 9,393 ft. (2,863 m.)
MONETARY UNIT Yugoslav dinar
MAJOR LANGUAGES Serbo-Croatian, Slovenian, Macedonian, Montenegrin, Albanian
MAJOR RELIGIONS Eastern Orthodoxy, Roman Catholicism, Islam

ALBANIA

AREA 11,100 sq. mi. (28,749 sq. km.)
POPULATION 2,590,600
CAPITAL Tiranë
LARGEST CITY Tiranë
HIGHEST POINT Korab 9,026 ft. (2,751 m.)
MONETARY UNIT lek
MAJOR LANGUAGE Albanian
MAJOR RELIGIONS Islam, Eastern Orthodoxy, Roman Catholicism

ROMANIA

AREA 91,699 sq. mi. (237,500 sq. km.)
POPULATION 22,048,305
CAPITAL Bucharest
LARGEST CITY Bucharest
HIGHEST POINT Moldoveanul 8,343 ft. (2,543 m.)
MONETARY UNIT leu
MAJOR LANGUAGES Romanian, Hungarian
MAJOR RELIGION Eastern Orthodoxy

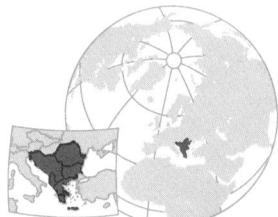

BULGARIA

AREA 42,823 sq. mi. (110,912 sq. km.)
POPULATION 8,862,000
CAPITAL Sofia
LARGEST CITY Sofia
HIGHEST POINT Musala 9,597 ft. (2,925 m.)
MONETARY UNIT lev
MAJOR LANGUAGE Bulgarian
MAJOR RELIGION Eastern Orthodoxy

GREECE

AREA 50,944 sq. mi. (131,945 sq. km.)
POPULATION 9,599,000
CAPITAL Athens
LARGEST CITY Athens
HIGHEST POINT Olympus 9,570 ft. (2,917 m.)
MONETARY UNIT drachma
MAJOR LANGUAGE Greek
MAJOR RELIGION Eastern (Greek) Orthodoxy

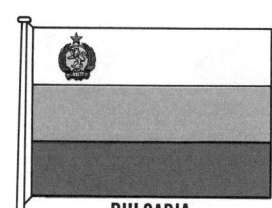
BULGARIA

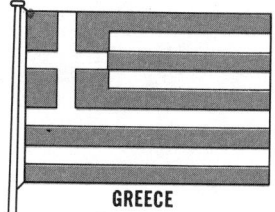
GREECE

YUGOSLAVIA

ALBANIA

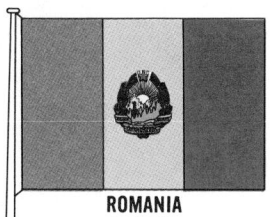
ROMANIA

Agriculture, Industry and Resources

DOMINANT LAND USE

	Cereals (chiefly wheat, corn)
	Mixed Farming, Horticulture
	Pasture Livestock
	Tobacco, Cotton
	Grapes, Wine
	Forests
	Nonagricultural Land

MAJOR MINERAL OCCURRENCES

Ab	Asbestos	Mg	Magnesium
Ag	Silver	Mn	Manganese
Al	Bauxite	Mr	Marble
C	Coal	Na	Salt
Cr	Chromium	Ni	Nickel
Cu	Copper	O	Petroleum
Fe	Iron Ore	Pb	Lead
G	Natural Gas	Sb	Antimony
Hg	Mercury	U	Uranium
Lg	Lignite	Zn	Zinc

⚡ Water Power
▨ Major Industrial Areas

ALBANIA

CITIES and TOWNS

Berat 25,700	D5
Çorovodë	D5
Burrel	D5
Delvinë 6,000	D6
Durrës (Durazzo) 53,800	D5
Elbasan 41,700	E5
Ersekë	E5
Fier 23,000	D5
Gjirokastër 17,100	D5
Kavajë 18,700	D5
Korçë 47,300	E5
Krujë 7,900	D5
Kuçovë (Stalin) 14,000	D5
Kukës 6,100	E4
Leskovik	E5
Lezhë	D5
Lushnje 18,900	D5
Memaliaj	D5
Peqin	D5
Përmet	E5
Peshkopi 6,600	E5
Pogradec 10,100	E5
Pukë	E4
Sarandë 8,700	E6
Shëngjin	D5
Shijak 6,200	D5
Shkodër 55,300	D5
Stalin 14,000	D5
Tepelenë	D5
Tiranë (Tirana) (cap.) 171,300	E5
Vlorë 50,000	D5

OTHER FEATURES

Adriatic (sea)	B4
Drin (riv.)	E4
Korab (mt.)	E5
Ohrid (lake)	E5
Otranto (str.)	E5
Prespa (lake)	E5
Sazan (isl.)	D5
Scutari (lake)	D4
Vijosë (riv.)	D5

BULGARIA

CITIES and TOWNS

Akhtopol 938	H4
Alfatar 3,249	H4
Ardino 5,080	G5
Asenovgrad 43,049	G5
Aytos 20,967	H4
Balchik 11,070	J4
Bansko 10,011	F5
Belogradchik 6,892	F4
Berkovitsa 16,253	F4
Blagoevgrad 50,043	F5
Botevgrad 17,789	F4
Bregovo 5,567	F3
Breznik 4,699	F4
Burgas 144,449	H4
Byala 10,564	G4
Byala Slatina 15,788	F4
Chirpan 20,595	G4
Devin 7,120	G5
Dimitrovgrad 45,596	G4
Dobrich (Tolbukhin) 86,184	H4
Dryanovo 9,804	G4
Elena 7,008	G4
Elin Pelin 5,499	F4
Elkhovo 12,397	H4
Gabrovo 75,034	G4
General-Toshevo 8,928	H4
Godech 5,225	F4
Gorna Oryakhovitsa 34,157	G4
Gotse Delchev 17,015	F5
Grudovo 9,871	H4
Ikhtiman 11,482	F4
Isperikh 10,500	H4
Ivaylovgrad 3,900	H5
Karapelit	H4
Karlovo 25,472	G4
Karnobat 21,480	H4
Kavarna 10,872	J4
Kazanlŭk 53,607	G4
Kharmanli 19,240	H5
Khaskovo 75,031	G4
Kotel 8,229	H4
Krumovgrad 5,211	G5
Kubrat 9,826	H4
Kula 5,667	F4
Kŭrdzhali 47,757	G5
Kyustendil 48,239	F4
Lom 30,538	F4
Lovech 43,858	G4
Lukovit 10,400	G4
Malko Tŭrnovo 4,233	H4
Maritsa 8,664	H4
Michurin 4,434	H4
Mikhaylovgrad 40,064	F4
Momchilgrad 8,185	G5
Nesebŭr 6,768	H4
Nikopol 5,563	G4
Nova Zagora 21,872	H4
Novi Pazar 15,751	H4
Omurtag 9,067	H4
Oryakhovo 14,012	F4
Panagyurishte 20,649	G4
Pazardzhik 65,577	G4
Pernik 87,432	F4
Peshtera 16,882	G4
Petrich 24,381	F5
Pirdop 8,248	G4
Pleven 107,567	G4
Plovdiv 300,242	G4
Pomorie 11,960	H4
Popina	H3
Popovo 19,428	H4
Provadiya 15,143	H4
Radomir 10,436	F4
Razgrad 42,486	H4
Razlog 13,690	F5
Rositsa	H4
Ruse 160,351	H4
Samokov 25,763	F4
Sandanski 19,003	F5
Sevlievo 24,421	G4
Shabla 4,471	J4
Shumen 83,525	H4
Silistra 58,270	H3
Simeonovgrad (Maritsa) 8,664	H4
Sliven 90,137	H4
Smolyan 29,032	G5
Smyadovo 5,020	H4
Sofia (cap.) 965,728	F4
Sozopol 3,877	H4
Stanke Dimitrov 42,034	F4
Stara Zagora 122,200	G4
Svilengrad 15,150	G5
Svishtov 29,412	G4
Teteven 12,555	G4
Tolbukhin 86,184	H4
Topolovgrad 7,230	H4
Troyan 23,692	G4
Tŭrn 3,435	F4
Tŭrgovishte 38,796	H4
Tutrakan 11,447	H4
Varna 251,654	J4
Veliko Tŭrnovo 56,497	G4
Vidin 53,030	F4
Vratsa 61,265	F4
Yambol 75,861	H4
Zimnitsa	H4
Zlatograd 7,732	G5

OTHER FEATURES

Balkan (mts.)	G4
Black (sea)	J4
Danube (riv.)	H4
Dunav (Danube) (riv.)	H4
Emine (cape)	J4
Iskŭr (riv.)	G4
Kaliakra (cape)	J4
Maritsa (riv.)	H4
Mesta (riv.)	F5
Midzhur (mt.)	F4
Musala (mt.)	F4
Osŭm (riv.)	G4
Rhodope (mts.)	F5
Rujen (mt.)	F4
Struma (riv.)	F5
Timok (riv.)	F3
Tundzha (riv.)	H4
Vit (riv.)	G4

GREECE

REGIONS

Aegean Islands 417,813	G6
Athens, Greater 2,566,775	F7
Ayion Óros (aut. dist.) 1,732	G5
Central Greece and Euboea 966,543	F6
Crete 456,642	G8
Epirus 310,334	E6
Ionian Islands 184,443	D6
Macedonia 1,888,952	F5
Peloponnisos 986,912	F6
Thessaly 659,913	F6
Thrace 329,582	G5

CITIES and TOWNS

Agrínion 30,973	E6
Aíyina 5,704	F7
Aíyion 18,829	F6
Alexandroúpolis 22,995	H5
Alivérion 4,414	G6
Almirós 5,680	F6
Amaliás 14,177	E7
Amfilokhía 4,668	E6
Ámfissa 6,605	F6
Andíssa 1,762	H6
Andravídha 3,046	E7
Ándros 1,827	G7
Áno Viánnos 1,431	G8
Anóyia 2,750	G8
Ardhéa 3,555	F5
Areópolis 674	F7
Árgalastí 1,621	F6
Árgos 18,890	F7
Argostólion 7,060	E6
Arkhángelos 3,016	J7
Árnaia 2,424	F5
Árta 19,498	E6
Astipálaia 787	H7
Atalándi 4,581	F6
Athens (cap.) 867,023	F7
Athens' 2,566,775	F7
Ayiá 3,241	F6
Áyioi Kírikos 1,083	H7
Áyios Matthaíos 1,596	D6
Áyios Nikólaos 5,002	G8
Candia (Iráklion) 77,506	G8
Canea (Khaniá) 40,564	G8
Corinth 20,773	F7
Delfí 1,185	F6
Delvinákion 1,067	E6
Dhidhimótikhon 8,388	H5
Dhíkaia 1,222	H5
Dhimitsána 996	F7
Dhomokós 1,991	F6
Dráma 29,692	F5
Edhessa 13,967	F5
Elassón 7,200	F6
Elevtheroúpolis 4,888	G5
Ermoúpolis 13,502	G7
Fársala 6,967	F6
Filiátes 2,579	E6
Filiatrá 5,919	E7
Filippiás 3,248	E6
Flórina 11,164	E5
Gargaliánoi 5,888	E7
Grevená 8,106	E5
Ídhra 2,381	F7
Ierápetra 7,055	G8
Igoumenítsa 4,109	E6
Ioánnina 40,130	E6
Íos 1,270	G7
Iráklion 77,506	G8
Istíaia 4,059	F6
Itháki 2,293	E6
Kalámai 39,133	F7
Kalampáka 5,453	F6
Kalávrita 1,948	F6
Kálimnos 6,492	H7
Kándanos 403	F8
Kardhítsa 25,685	F6
Kará 1,350	G4
Karíaí 301	G5
Káristos 3,550	G6
Kárpathos 1,363	H8
Karpenísion 4,414	E6
Kastéllion (Kíssamos) 2,996	F8
Kastéllion 1,152	G8
Kastoría 15,407	E5
Katákolon 697	E7
Kateríni 28,808	F5
Kavália 46,234	G5
Kéa 693	G7
Kérkira 28,630	D6
Khalkís 36,300	F6
Khaniá 40,564	G8
Khíos 24,084	G6
Khóra Sfakíon 246	G8
Kíaton 7,392	F6
Kilkís 10,538	F5
Kími 2,772	G6
Kiparissía 3,882	E7
Kíssamos 2,996	G8
Kíthira 349	F7
Komotiní 28,896	G5
Kónitsa 3,150	E5
Koropí 9,367	F7
Kos 7,828	H7
Kozáni 23,240	F5
Kranídhion 3,657	F7
Lagkadá 1,350	E7
Lamía 37,872	F6
Langadhás 6,707	F5
Langádhia	F7
Lárisa 72,336	F6
Lávrion 8,283	G7
Leonídhion 3,181	F7
Levádhia 15,445	F6
Levkás 6,818	E6
Liménaria 1,507	G5

(continued on following page)

Hg Hg Al O Oats
Fruit Wheat Sugar Beets Corn Na G G Na Oats
Zagreb Hunedoara Brașov Galati
Fruit Co
Belgrade Fruit Ploiești
Zenica Fe Al Sb Lg Cu Wheat Bucharest
Sarajevo Pb C Cu
Sugar Beets
Cattle Hogs
Barley
Ag Goats Sofia Cu Tobacco
Tuna Tobacco Pb Tobacco
Cr Cu
Cr Sheep Lg Ab
Olives Sardines Athens
Sponges
Goats Sardines
Wine Sponges
Olives Al
Sponges
Olives

44 Balkan States

(continued)

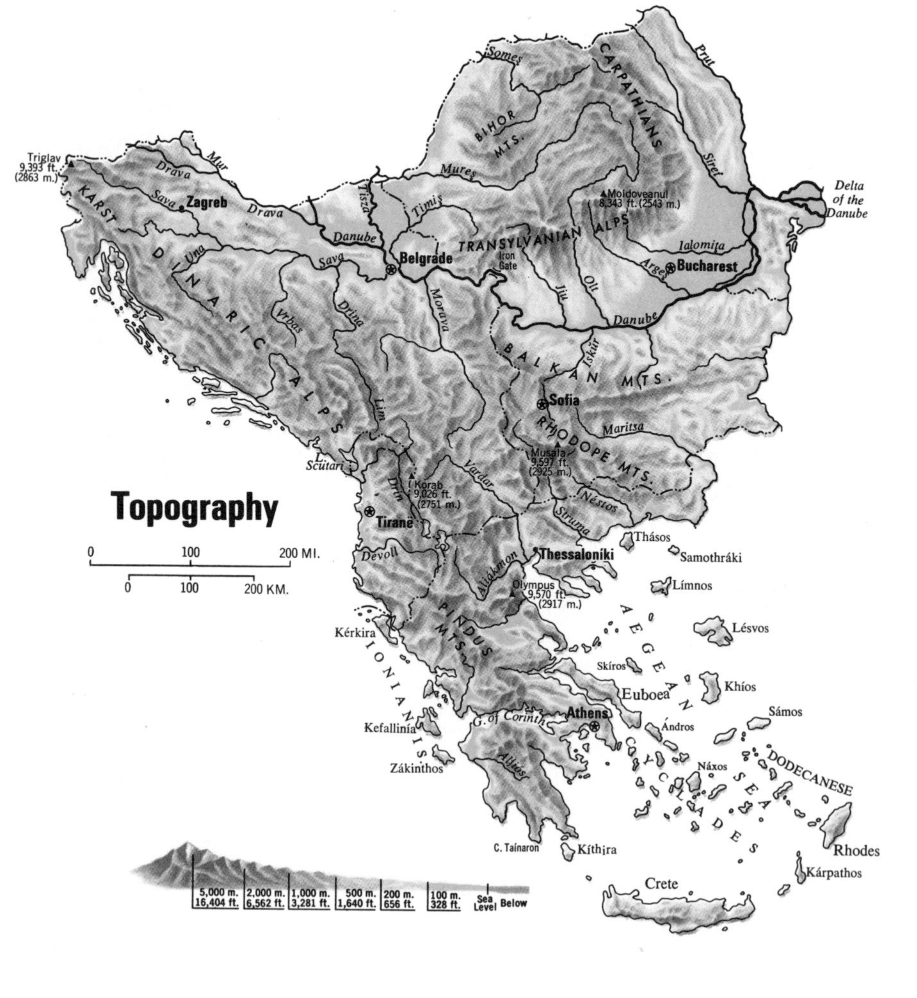

Topography
Triglav 9,393 ft. (2863 m.)
Drava
Mur
Sava
Zagreb
KARST
Una
DINARIC ALPS
Vrbas
Drina
Danube
Tisza
Mureș
Someș
BIHOR MTS.
CARPATHIANS
Prut
Siret
Delta of the Danube
Timiș
Belgrade
Iron Gate
TRANSYLVANIAN ALPS
Moldoveanul 8,343 ft. (2543 m.)
Ialomița
Argeș
Bucharest
Olt
Jiu
Morava
Danube
Iskur
BALKAN MTS.
Sofia
Maritsa
RHODOPE MTS.
Musala 9,597 ft. (2925 m.)
Lim
Scutari
Drin
Korab 9,026 ft. (2751 m.)
Tirane
Vardar
Néstos
Struma
Thásos
Samothráki
Thessaloníki
Devoll
Aliákmon
Olympus 9,570 ft. (2917 m.)
Límnos
PINDUS MTS.
AEGEAN SEA
Lésvos
Kérkira
IONIAN SEA
Skíros
Euboea
Khíos
Sámos
G. of Corinth
Athens
Kefallinía
Ándros
Zákinthos
Náxos
CYCLADES
DODECANESE
Alfiós
C. Taínaron
Kíthira
Rhodes
Kárpathos
Crete
0 100 200 MI.
0 100 200 KM.
5,000 m. 16,404 ft.
2,000 m. 6,562 ft.
1,000 m. 3,281 ft.
500 m. 1,640 ft.
200 m. 656 ft.
100 m. 328 ft.
Sea Level
Below

Límni 2,394 ..... F6
Líndos 700 ..... J7
Litókhoron 5,561 ..... F5
Lixoúrion 3,364 ..... E6
Loutrá Aidhipsoú 2,195 ..... F6
Marathón 1,976 ..... G6
Megalópolis 3,357 ..... E7
Mégara 17,294 ..... F6
Meligalá 1,724 ..... F7
Mesolóngion 11,614 ..... E6
Messíni 6,625 ..... E7
Métsovon 2,823 ..... E6
Mikínai 390 ..... F7
Mílos 850 ..... G7
Mírina 3,982 ..... G6
Míthimna 1,414 ..... G6
Mitilíni 23,426 ..... H6
Moîrai 2,948 ..... G8
Moláoi 2,484 ..... F7
Monólithos 247 ..... H7
Moúdhros 1,024 ..... G6
Náousa 17,375 ..... F5
Návpaktos 8,170 ..... F6
Návplion 9,281 ..... F7
Náxos 2,892 ..... G7
Neápolis 3,070 ..... F7
Neméa 4,356 ..... F7
Néon Karlóvasi 4,401 ..... H7
Nestórion 1,143 ..... E5
Nigríta 7,301 ..... F5
Oinóï 188 ..... F6
Orestías 10,727 ..... H5
Paramithía 2,747 ..... E6
Pátrai 111,607 ..... E6
Pérdika 1,198 ..... E6
Péta 2,116 ..... E6
Pílos 2,258 ..... E7
Piraiévs (Piraeus) 187,362 ..... F7
Pírgos 20,599 ..... E7
Pirýí 1,455 ..... G6
Píthion 1,047 ..... H5
Plomárion 4,353 ..... H6
Políkastron 5,279 ..... F5
Políkhnitos 4,152 ..... G6
Políyiros 3,707 ..... F5
Póros 4,051 ..... F7
Préveza 11,439 ..... E6
Psakhná 4,650 ..... F6
Psári 622 ..... E7
Ptolemaís 16,588 ..... E5
Réthimnon 14,969 ..... G8
Rhodes (Ródhos) 32,092 ..... J7
Salamís 18,256 ..... F6
Salonika (Thessaloníki) 345,799 ..... F5
Sámi 957 ..... E6
Sámos 5,146 ..... H7
Samothráki 508 ..... G5
Sápai 2,456 ..... G5
Sérrai 39,897 ..... F5
Sérvia 3,834 ..... F5
Siátista 4,852 ..... E5
Sidhirókastron 6,363 ..... F5
Sími 2,344 ..... H7
Sitía 6,167 ..... H8
Skíathos 3,707 ..... F6
Skíros 1,925 ..... G6
Skópelos 2,545 ..... F6
Souflíon 5,637 ..... H5
Sparta 10,549 ..... F7
Spétsai 3,427 ..... F7
Spíli 789 ..... G8
Stavrós 1,700 ..... F5
Stílís 4,427 ..... F6
Thásos 2,052 ..... G5
Thessaloníki 345,799 ..... F5
Thessaloníki* 482,361 ..... F5
Thíra 1,322 ..... G7
Thívai 15,971 ..... F6
Timbákion 3,229 ..... G8
Tínos 3,423 ..... G7
Tírnavos 10,451 ..... F6
Tríkkala 34,794 ..... E6
Trípolis 20,209 ..... F7
Vámos 652 ..... F8
Vartholomión 3,015 ..... E7
Vathí 2,491 ..... H7
Velvendós 4,063 ..... F5
Vérroia 29,528 ..... F5
Vólos 51,290 ..... F6
Vónitsa 3,324 ..... E6
Vrondádhes 4,253 ..... G6
Xánthi 24,867 ..... G5
Yerolimín 73 ..... F7
Yiannitsá 18,151 ..... F5
Yíthion 4,915 ..... F7
Zákinthos 9,339 ..... E7
Zante (Zákinthos) 9,339 ..... E7

OTHER FEATURES

Aegean (sea) G6
Akrítas (cape) E7
Aktí (pen.) G5
Amorgós (isl.) G7
Anáfi (isl.) G7
Andikíthira (isl.) F8
Ándros (isl.) G7
Arda (riv.) G5
Argolís (gulf) F7
Astipálaia (isl.) H7
Áthos (mt.) G5
Áyios Evstrátios (isl.) G6
Áyios Yeóryios (cape) G5
Cephalonia (Kefallinía) (isl.) E6
Corfu (Kérkira) (isl.) D6
Corinth (gulf) F6
Crete (isl.) G8
Crete (sea) G7
Cyclades (isls.) G7
Día (isl.) G8
Dodecanese (isls.) H8
Euboea (Évvoia) (isl.) G6
Évros (riv.) H5
Évvoia (isl.) G6
Gávdhos (isl.) F8
Ídhi (mt.) G8
Ikaría (isl.) G7
Ionian (sea) D7
Íos (isl.) G7
Itháki (Ithaca) (isl.) E6
Kafirévs (cape) G6
Kálimnos (isl.) H7
Kárpathos (isl.) H8
Kásos (isl.) H8
Kassándra (pen.) F6
Kéa (isl.) G7
Kefallinía (isl.) E6
Kérkira (isl.) D6
Khálki (isl.) H7
Khaniá (gulf) G8
Khíos (isl.) G6
Kímolos (isl.) G7
Kiparissía (gulf) E7
Kíthira (isl.) F7
Kíthnos (isl.) G7
Kos (isl.) H7
Kriós (cape) F8
Kríti (Crete) (isl.) G8
Lakonía (gulf) F7
Léros (isl.) H7
Lésvos (isl.) G6
Levítha (isl.) H7
Levkás (isl.) E6
Límnos (isl.) G6
Maléa (cape) F7
Matapan (Taínaron) (cape) F7
Merabéllou (gulf) H8
Mesará (gulf) G8
Messíni (gulf) E7
Míkonos (isl.) G7
Mílos (isl.) G7
Mirtóön (sea) F7
Náxos (isl.) G7
Néstos (riv.) G5
Nísiros (isl.) H7
Northern Sporades (isls.) F6
Olympia (isls.) E7
Olympus (mt.) F5
Parnassus (mt.) F6
Páros (isl.) G7
Pátmos (isl.) H7
Paxoí (isl.) D6
Pindus (mts.) E6
Piniós (riv.) E6
Prespa (lake) E5
Psará (isl.) G6
Psevdhókavos (cape) G6
Rhodes (isl.) H7
Rhodope (mts.) G5
Salonika (Thermaic) (gulf) F6
Sámos (isl.) H7
Samothráki (isl.) G5
Saría (isl.) H8
Saronic (gulf) F7
Sérifos (isl.) G7
Sídheros (cape) H8
Sífnos (isl.) G7
Sími (isl.) H7
Síros (isl.) G7
Sithoniá (pen.) F5
Skíros (isl.) G6
Spátha (cape) F8
Strimón (gulf) G5
Strofádhes (isls.) E7
Taínaron (cape) F7
Thásos (isl.) G5
Thermaic (gulf) F6
Thíra (isl.) G7
Tílos (isl.) H7
Tínos (isl.) G7
Toronaic (gulf) F5
Vardar (riv.) E5
Voïvís (lake) F6
Vólvi (lake) F5
Voúxa (cape) F8
Zákinthos (Zante) (isl.) E7

ROMANIA

CITIES and TOWNS

Aiud 25,173 ..... F2
Alba Iulia 44,552 ..... F2
Alexandria 38,296 ..... G3
Anina 11,594 ..... E3
Arad 161,568 ..... E2
Babadag 8,423 ..... J3
Bacău 131,413 ..... H2
Baia de Aramă 5,065 ..... F3
Baia Mare 112,893 ..... F2
Băile Herculane 4,606 ..... F3
Băilești 21,246 ..... F3
Balș 16,091 ..... G3
Beiuș 9,992 ..... F2
Berești Tîrg H2
Bicaz 9,490 ..... G2
Bîrlad 59,059 ..... H2
Bistrița 47,562 ..... G2
Bivolari H2
Blaj 21,678 ..... F2
Borșa 25,287 ..... G2
Botoșani 69,881 ..... H2
Brad 18,391 ..... F2
Brăila 203,983 ..... H3
Brașov 259,108 ..... G3
Bucharest (București) (cap.) 1,832,015 ..... G3
Bucharest* 1,960,097 ..... G3
Buhuși 20,204 ..... H2
Buzău 106,738 ..... H3
Buziaș 8,310 ..... E3
Calafat 16,421 ..... F3
Călărași 58,960 ..... H3
Caracal 31,159 ..... G3
Caransebeș 27,429 ..... F3
Carei 24,496 ..... F2
Cernavodă 14,686 ..... J3
Chișineu Criș 9,344 ..... E2
Cîmpeni 7,722 ..... F2
Cîmpia Turzii 23,745 ..... F2
Cîmpina 33,259 ..... H3
Cîmpulung 33,448 ..... G3
Cîmpulung Moldovenesc 19,270 ..... G2
Cisnădie 21,114 ..... G3
Cluj-Napoca 274,095 ..... F2
Cogealac J3
Comanești 18,177 ..... H2
Constanța 279,308 ..... J3
Corabia 20,454 ..... G4
Costești 10,446 ..... G3
Craiova 220,893 ..... F3
Cujmir F3
Curtea de Argeș 23,555 ..... G3
Dăbuleni F4
Dăeni J3
Darabani 12,207 ..... H1
Dej 35,396 ..... F2
Deta 6,956 ..... E3
Deva 68,290 ..... F3
Dorohoi 23,121 ..... H2
Drăgănești Olt 11,606 ..... G3
Drăgășani 16,290 ..... F3
Drobeta-Turnu Severin 80,114 ..... F3
Făgăraș 34,762 ..... G3
Fălciu J2
Fălticeni 22,463 ..... H2
Făurei 3,620 ..... H3
Fetești 28,730 ..... H3
Focșani 62,275 ..... H3
Foltești H3
Găești 13,384 ..... G3
Galați 252,884 ..... H3
Gheorghe Gheorghiu-Dej 41,297 ..... H2
Gheorghieni 20,592 ..... G2
Gherla 19,303 ..... G2
Giurgiu 53,241 ..... G3
Hațeg 9,706 ..... F3
Hîrlău 8,135 ..... H2
Hîrșova 8,434 ..... J3
Huedin 8,557 ..... F2
Hunedoara 83,159 ..... F3
Huși 24,329 ..... J2
Iași 262,493 ..... H2
Ineu 10,414 ..... E2
Isaccea 5,283 ..... J3
Jibou F2
Jimbolia 15,325 ..... E3
Lipova 12,427 ..... E2
Luduș 15,771 ..... G2
Lugoj 48,558 ..... F3
Lupeni 28,251 ..... F3
Mangalia 27,263 ..... J4
Medgidia 43,691 ..... J3
Mediaș 68,442 ..... G2
Miercurea Ciuc 38,097 ..... G2
Mizil 14,294 ..... H3
Mociu G2
Moinești 21,015 ..... H2
Moldova Nouă 18,498 ..... E3
Moreni 17,743 ..... G3
Nădlac 8,407 ..... E2
Năsăud 8,646 ..... G2
Negrești 7,435 ..... H2
Ocna Mureș 16,381 ..... G2
Odobești 8,440 ..... H3
Odorheiu Secuiesc 33,392 ..... G2
Oltenița 25,536 ..... H3
Oradea 175,400 ..... E2
Orăștie 18,769 ..... F3
Oravița 13,628 ..... E3
Orșova 14,873 ..... F3
Panciu 7,772 ..... H3
Pașcani 26,937 ..... H2
Pătulele F3
Pechea H3
Pecica E2
Periam E2
Petrila 25,087 ..... F3
Petroșeni 42,316 ..... F3
Piatra Neamț 84,192 ..... G2
Pincota 7,494 ..... E2
Pitești 125,029 ..... G3
Plenița F3
Ploiești 207,009 ..... H3
Poenari Burchi G3
Poiana Mare F4
Pucioasa 14,056 ..... G3
Rădăuți 24,222 ..... G2
Reghin 31,948 ..... G2
Reșița 90,698 ..... E3
Rîmnicu Sărat 29,815 ..... H3
Rîmnicu Vîlcea 75,070 ..... G3
Roman 56,466 ..... H2
Roșiori de Vede 28,832 ..... G3
Săcele 29,391 ..... G3
Salonta 19,698 ..... E2
Satu Mare 108,152 ..... F2
Săveni 7,913 ..... H1
Sebeș 27,448 ..... F3
Sebiș 6,401 ..... F2
Segarcea 8,783 ..... F3
Sfîntu Gheorghe 51,210 ..... G3
Sfîntu Gheorghe J3
Sibiu 156,854 ..... G3
Sighetu Marmației 38,879 ..... F2
Sighișoara 32,296 ..... G2
Șimleul Silvaniei 14,780 ..... F2
Sinaia 14,215 ..... G3
Sînnicolaul Mare 13,565 ..... E2
Siret 6,677 ..... G1
Slănic 8,017 ..... G3
Slatina 54,954 ..... G3
Slobozia 35,207 ..... H3
Solca 4,835 ..... G2
Sovata 10,745 ..... G2
Ștefănești H2
Strehaia 11,431 ..... F3
Suceava 66,857 ..... G2
Sulina 5,240 ..... J3
Tășnad 10,441 ..... F2
Techirghiol 11,228 ..... J3
Tecuci 37,928 ..... H3
Timișoara 281,320 ..... E3
Tinca F2
Tîrgoviște 71,533 ..... G3
Tîrgu Cărbunești 7,536 ..... F3
Tîrgu Frumos 6,428 ..... H2
Tîrgu Jiu 70,629 ..... F3
Tîrgu Mureș 129,284 ..... G2
Tîrgu Neamț 15,756 ..... G2
Tîrgu Ocna 12,960 ..... H2
Tîrgu Secuiesc 18,265 ..... H2
Tîrnăveni 27,799 ..... F2
Toplița 14,347 ..... G2
Tulcea 67,091 ..... J3
Turda 57,972 ..... F2
Turnu Măgurele 30,003 ..... G4
Urlața 10,900 ..... H3
Urziceni 13,500 ..... H3
Vasile Roaită J3
Vaslui 44,134 ..... H2
Vatra Dornei 16,748 ..... G2
Videle 11,323 ..... G3
Vișeul de Sus 20,697 ..... F2
Viziru H3
Zalău 36,158 ..... F2
Zărnești 23,378 ..... G3
Zimnicea 15,111 ..... G4

OTHER FEATURES

Argeș (riv.) G3
Bîrlad (riv.) H2
Black (sea) J4
Brăila (marshes) H3
Buzău (riv.) H3
Carpathian (mts.) G2
Crișul Alb (riv.) F2
Crișul Repede (riv.) F2
Danube (delta) J3
Danube (riv.) H4
Ialomița (marshes) J3
Ialomița (riv.) H3
Jijia (riv.) H2
Jiu (riv.) F3
Moldoveanul (mt.) G3
Mureș (riv.) E2
Olt (riv.) G3
Peleaga (mt.) F3
Pietrosul (mt.) G2
Prut (riv.) J2
Siret (riv.) H2
Someș (riv.) F2
Timiș (riv.) E3
Tîrnava Mare (riv.) G2
Transylvanian Alps (mts.) G3

YUGOSLAVIA

INTERNAL DIVISIONS

Bosnia and Hercegovina (rep.) 3,710,965 ..... C3
Croatia (rep.) 4,396,397 ..... C3
Kosovo (aut. reg.) 1,240,919 ..... E4
Macedonia (rep.) 1,623,598 ..... E5
Montenegro (rep.) 527,207 ..... D4
Serbia (rep.) 8,401,673 ..... E3
Slovenia (rep.) 1,697,068 ..... B2
Vojvodina (aut. prov.) 1,953,980 ..... D3

CITIES and TOWNS

Aleksinac 11,943 ..... E4
Apatin 17,501 ..... D3
Arendjelovac 15,659 ..... E3
Bačka Topola 16,028 ..... D3
Bakar B3
Banja Luka 85,786 ..... C3
Bar 3,594 ..... D4
Bečej 26,616 ..... E3
Bela Crkva 11,137 ..... E3
Belgrade (cap.) 727,945 ..... E3
Beli Manastir 7,325 ..... D3
Beograd (Belgrade) (cap.) 727,945 ..... E3
Berovo 5,053 ..... F5
Bihać 24,155 ..... B3
Bijeljina 24,888 ..... D3
Bijelo Polje 9,298 ..... D4
Bileća 4,083 ..... D4
Biograd 3,595 ..... B4
Bitola 64,467 ..... E5
Bjelovar 21,019 ..... C3
Blato 5,591 ..... C4
Bled 4,710 ..... A2
Bor 27,520 ..... E3
Bosanska Dubica 9,191 ..... C3
Bosanska Gradiška 9,742 ..... C3
Bosanska Kostajnica 2,535 ..... B3
Bosanska Krupa 8,947 ..... C3
Bosanski Brod 10,113 ..... D3
Bosanski Novi 9,861 ..... C3
Bosanski Petrovac 4,113 ..... C3
Bosanski Šamac 4,949 ..... D3
Brčko 25,575 ..... D3
Brežice 3,271 ..... B3
Budva 2,483 ..... D4
Bugojno 9,079 ..... C3
Čačak 38,890 ..... E4
Čakovec 11,766 ..... C2
Čapljina 4,677 ..... C4
Caribrod (Dimitrovgrad) 5,449 ..... F4
Cazin 1,213 ..... B3
Celje 30,827 ..... B2
Cetinje 12,089 ..... D4
Ćuprija 17,691 ..... E4
Daruvar 8,478 ..... C3
Debar 8,597 ..... E5
Derventa 11,887 ..... C3
Dimitrovgrad 5,449 ..... F4
Djakovica 29,499 ..... E4
Djakovo 15,833 ..... D3
Doboj 18,073 ..... C3
Donji Vakuf 4,928 ..... C3
Drvar 6,237 ..... C3
Dubrovnik 31,213 ..... C4
Fiume (Rijeka) 128,883 ..... B3
Foča 9,370 ..... D4
Gacko 1,641 ..... D4
Gevgelija 9,319 ..... F5
Glamoč 2,627 ..... C3
Gnjilane 21,359 ..... E4
Gornji Milanovac 11,114 ..... D3
Gornji Vakuf 2,429 ..... C4
Gospić 8,238 ..... B3
Gostivar 18,805 ..... E5
Gračac 3,228 ..... B3
Gračanica 9,302 ..... D3
Gradačac 7,571 ..... D3
Grubišno Polje 2,771 ..... C3
Gusinje 2,616 ..... D4
Herceg Novi 6,645 ..... D4
Ivangrad 11,373 ..... E4
Ivanjica 5,719 ..... E4
Jajce 9,221 ..... C3
Jesenice 16,163 ..... A2
Kanjiža 11,348 ..... D2
Karlovac 47,046 ..... B3
Kavadarci 17,974 ..... E5
Kičevo 14,189 ..... E5
Kikinda 37,392 ..... E3
Kladanj 3,255 ..... D3
Ključ 3,466 ..... C3
Knin 7,279 ..... C3
Knjaževac 11,734 ..... F4
Kočani 16,611 ..... F5
Kočevje 7,277 ..... B3
Kolašin 2,111 ..... D4
Konjic 9,161 ..... D4
Koper 16,683 ..... A3
Koprivnica 16,398 ..... C2
Kosovska Mitrovica 42,526 ..... E4
Kostajnica 9,161 ..... C3
Kotor 5,728 ..... D4
Kragujevac 72,080 ..... E3
Kraljevo 28,065 ..... E4
Kranj 26,341 ..... B2
Križevci 8,501 ..... C2
Krk 1,500 ..... B3
Krško 4,451 ..... B3
Kruševac 29,902 ..... E4
Kulen Vakuf 1,078 ..... B3
Kumanovo 44,791 ..... E4
Kutina 10,892 ..... C3
Leskovac 46,050 ..... E4
Livno 7,223 ..... C4
Ljubinje 785 ..... D4
Ljubljana 169,064 ..... B3
Ljubuški 2,891 ..... C4
Loznica 13,513 ..... D3
Maglaj 5,869 ..... D3
Makarska 6,589 ..... C4
Maribor 94,976 ..... B2
Modriča 7,406 ..... D3
Mostar 47,821 ..... D4
Murska Sobota 9,665 ..... C2
Našice 5,836 ..... C3
Negotin 11,325 ..... F3
Nevesinje 3,077 ..... D4
Nikšić 28,940 ..... D4
Nin 1,782 ..... B3
Niš 128,231 ..... F4
Nova Gorizia A2
Nova Gradiška 11,765 ..... C3
Novi 2,682 ..... B3
Novi Pazar 28,696 ..... E4
Novi Sad 143,591 ..... D3
Novo Mesto 9,553 ..... B3
Novska 5,168 ..... C3
Ogulin 9,975 ..... B3
Ohrid 26,352 ..... E5
Omiš 3,515 ..... C4
Opatija 9,238 ..... A3
Osijek 94,989 ..... D3
Pag 2,318 ..... B3
Pančevo 53,979 ..... E3
Paraćin 21,555 ..... E4
Peć 41,783 ..... E4
Petrinja 12,296 ..... B3
Piran 5,485 ..... A3
Pirot 29,658 ..... F4
Plav 3,072 ..... D4
Pljevlja 14,459 ..... D4
Plŏce 4,257 ..... C4
Pola (Pula) 47,117 ..... A3
Poreč 4,512 ..... A3
Postojna 6,085 ..... B3
Požarevac 33,336 ..... E3
Preševo 7,634 ..... E4
Priboj 12,556 ..... D4
Prijedor 22,379 ..... C3
Prijepolje 7,960 ..... D4
Prilep 48,045 ..... E5
Priština 71,264 ..... E4
Prizren 41,875 ..... E4
Prokuplje 20,617 ..... E4
Prozor 1,420 ..... C4
Ptuj 9,245 ..... C2
Pula 47,117 ..... A3
Rab 1,675 ..... B3
Radoviš 9,373 ..... F5
Ragusa (Dubrovnik) 31,213 ..... C4
Raška 3,935 ..... E4
Ravne na Koroškem 6,529 ..... B2
Rijeka 128,883 ..... B3
Rogatica 4,801 ..... D4
Rovinj 8,998 ..... A3
Rožaj E4
Ruma 24,180 ..... D3
Šabac 43,539 ..... D3
Samobor 7,821 ..... B3
Sanski Most 8,718 ..... C3
Sarajevo 245,058 ..... D4
Senj 4,927 ..... B3
Senta 24,694 ..... D3
Šibenik 29,619 ..... C4
Šid 11,867 ..... D3
Sinj 4,705 ..... C4
Sisak 37,215 ..... C3
Sjenica 9,118 ..... E4
Škofja Loka 4,971 ..... A2
Skopje 308,117 ..... E5
Skradin 893 ..... B4
Slavonska Požega 18,160 ..... C3
Slavonski Brod 38,829 ..... D3
Smederevo 39,200 ..... E3
Smederevska Palanka 18,837 ..... E3
Sombor 44,210 ..... D3
Split 150,739 ..... C4
Srebrenica 3,101 ..... D3
Sremska Mitrovica 32,569 ..... D3
Štip 27,218 ..... F5
Stolac 3,862 ..... D4
Ston 407 ..... C4
Struga 11,369 ..... E5
Strumica 22,770 ..... F5
Subotica 89,476 ..... D2
Surdulica 7,048 ..... F4
Svetozarevo 27,812 ..... E4
Svilajnac 7,848 ..... E3
Teslić 4,940 ..... C3
Tetovo 35,293 ..... E5
Titograd 54,639 ..... D4
Titovo Užice 35,465 ..... D4
Titov Veles 35,583 ..... E5
Travnik 12,745 ..... C3
Trbovlje 16,393 ..... B2
Trebinje 3,553 ..... D4
Trogir 6,162 ..... C4
Trstenik 7,167 ..... E4
Tržič 4,435 ..... B2
Tuzla 53,836 ..... D3
Ub 3,785 ..... E3
Ulcinj 7,472 ..... D5
Umag 3,228 ..... A3
Uroševac E4
Valjevo 26,655 ..... D3
Varaždin 34,662 ..... B2
Vareš 7,632 ..... D3
Velenje 11,225 ..... B2
Velika Plana E3
Veliki Bečkerek (Zrenjanin) 60,201 ..... E3
Vinkovci 29,257 ..... D3
Virovitica 16,389 ..... C3
Višegrad 4,753 ..... D4
Visoko 9,365 ..... D4
Vlasenica 4,033 ..... D3
Vranje 25,909 ..... F4
Vrbas 22,502 ..... D3
Vršac 33,573 ..... E3
Vučitrn 11,701 ..... E4
Vukovar 29,500 ..... D3
Žabljak 1,023 ..... D4
Zadar 43,588 ..... B3
Zagreb 561,773 ..... C3
Zaječar 27,724 ..... E4
Zara (Zadar) 43,588 ..... B3
Zenica 49,522 ..... C3
Žepče 3,177 ..... D3
Zrenjanin 60,201 ..... E3
Zvornik 8,498 ..... D3

OTHER FEATURES

Adriatic (sea) B4
Bobotov Kuk (mt.) D4
Bosna (riv.) D3
Brač (isl.) C4
Cazma (riv.) C3
Cres (isl.) B3
Čvrsnica (mt.) C4
Dalmatia (reg.) C4
Danube (riv.) E3
Dinaric Alps (mts.) B3
Drava (riv.) C3
Drina (riv.) D3
Dugi Otok (isl.) B3
Hvar (isl.) C4
Ibar (riv.) E4
Istria (pen.) A3
Kamenjak (cape) A3
Kladovo F3
Korab (mt.) E5
Korčula (isl.) C4
Kornat (isl.) B4
Krk (isl.) B3
Kupa (riv.) B3
Kvarner (gulf) B3
Lastovo (Lagosta) (isl.) C4
Lim (riv.) D4
Lošinj (isl.) B3
Midzhur (mt.) F4
Mljet (isl.) C4
Morava (riv.) E3
Mur (riv.) B2
Neretva (riv.) D4
Ohrid (lake) E5
Pag (isl.) B3
Palagruža (Pelagosa) (isl.) C4
Prespa (lake) E5
Rab (isl.) B3
Rujen (mt.) F4
Sava (riv.) D3
Scutari (lake) D4
Slavonia (reg.) C3
Šolta (isl.) C4
Tara (riv.) D4
Timok (riv.) F3
Tisa (riv.) E3
Triglav (mt.) A2
Una (riv.) C3
Vardar (riv.) E5
Vis (isl.) C4
Vrbas (riv.) C3
Žirje (isl.) B4

*City and suburbs.

The Balkan States

CONIC PROJECTION

SCALE OF MILES

0 25 50 75 100 125 150 175

SCALE OF KILOMETERS

0 25 50 75 100 125 150 175

Capitals of Countries .... ☆
Administrative Centers .... △
International Boundaries _____
Major Internal Boundaries __ __ __
Minor Internal Boundaries _ _ _ _
Canals ....

Scale 1:6,150,000

BULGARIA and GREECE are divided into counties and departments, respectively. Because of the scale no attempt has been made to delimit and name these subdivisions; their administrative centers have, however, been designated.

The larger divisions named in Greece are well-known geographical regions, without administrative function.

ROMANIA consists of thirty-nine counties and three cities of regional status, Bucharest, Constanţa and Petroşeni. Scale does not permit delimiting these counties.

ALBANIA is divided into twenty-seven districts. Scale does not permit the delimitation of these divisions.

YUGOSLAVIA is a federation of six republics. The Serbian republic includes an autonomous province (Vojvodina), and an autonomous region (Kosovo).

© Copyright HAMMOND INCORPORATED, Maplewood, N.J.

Topography

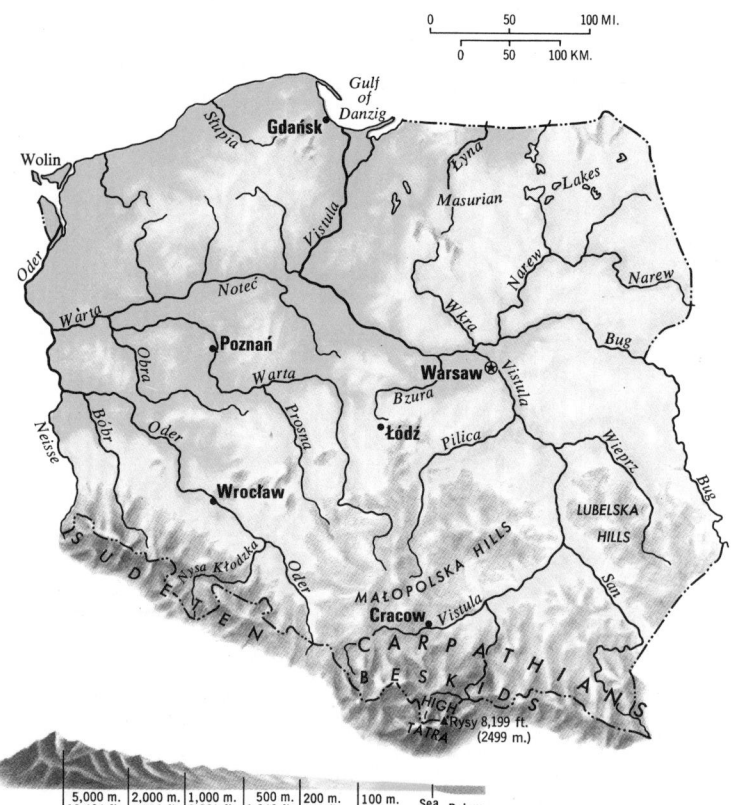

Agriculture, Industry and Resources

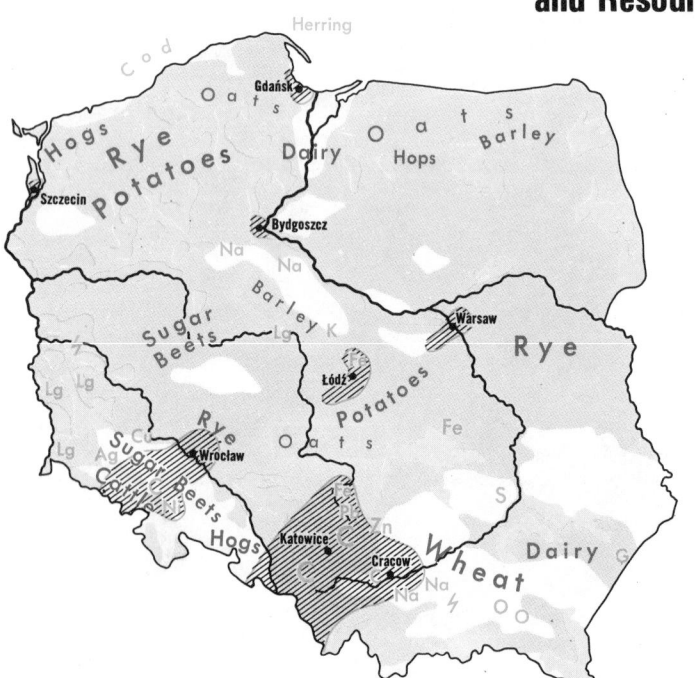

MAJOR MINERAL OCCURRENCES

Ag	Silver	Na	Salt
C	Coal	Ni	Nickel
Cu	Copper	O	Petroleum
Fe	Iron Ore	Pb	Lead
G	Natural Gas	S	Sulfur
K	Potash	Zn	Zinc
Lg	Lignite		

 Water Power

 Major Industrial Areas

DOMINANT LAND USE

 Cereals (chiefly wheat)

 Rye, Oats, Barley, Potatoes

 General Farming, Livestock

 Forests

PROVINCES		
Biała Podlaska 283,200	F3	
Białystok 613,800	F2	
Bielsko 765,500	D4	
Bydgoszcz 982,100	C2	
Chełm 221,000	F3	
Ciechanów 398,500	E2	
Cracow (Kraków) 1,097,600	E4	
Cracow (city) 651,300	E4	
Częstochowa 723,200	D3	
Elbląg 419,800	D1	
Gdańsk 1,312,300	D1	
Gorzów 428,700	B2	
Jelenia Góra 483,400	B3	
Kalisz 640,300	D3	
Katowice 3,439,700	D3	
Kielce 1,030,400	E3	
Konin 423,700	D2	
Koszalin 428,500	C1	
Krosno 418,000	E4	
Legnica 405,600	C4	
Leszno 340,600	C3	
Łódź 1,063,700	D3	
Łódź (city) 777,800	D3	
Łomża 320,600	F2	
Lublin 875,300	F3	
Nowy Sącz 600,300	E4	
Olsztyn 654,400	E2	
Opole 961,600	C3	
Ostrołęka 360,700	E2	
Piła 414,000	C2	
Piotrków 581,900	D3	
Płock 479,700	D2	
Poznań 1,156,500	C2	
Przemyśl 373,100	F4	
Radom 674,400	E3	
Rzeszów 602,200	F4	
Siedlce 602,100	F2	
Sieradz 388,000	D3	
Skierniewice 388,300	E3	
Słupsk 352,900	C1	
Suwałki 412,700	F1	
Szczecin 841,400	B2	
Tarnobrzeg 532,200	E3	
Tarnów 573,900	E4	
Toruń 580,500	D2	
Wałbrzych 709,600	C3	
Warsaw 2,117,700	E2	
Warsaw (city) 1,377,100	E2	
Włocławek 402,000	D2	
Wrocław 1,014,600	C3	
Zamość 472,300	F3	
Zielona Góra 575,000	B3	

CITIES and TOWNS	
Aleksandrów Kujawski 9,600	D2
Aleksandrów	
Łódzki 14,400	D3
Allenstein (Olsztyn) 94,119	E2
Andrespol 12,400	D3
Andrychów 14,300	D4
Augustów 19,784	F2
Auschwitz	
(Oświęcim) 39,600	D3
Bartoszyce 15,500	E1
Będzin 42,787	D3
Beuthen (Bytom) 186,993	D3
Biała Podlaska 26,100	F3
Białogard 20,500	C1
Białystok 166,619	F2
Bielawa 30,900	C3
Bielsk Podlaski 14,000	F2
Bielsko-Biała 105,601	D4
Biłgoraj 12,888	F3
Błonie 11,800	E2
Bochnia 14,500	E4
Bogatynia 11,800	B3
Boguszów-Gorce 11,900	B3
Bolesławiec 30,500	B3

Poland 1938

Poland 1945

Poland 47

aniewo 12,100 D1
eslau (Wrocław) 461,900 C3
ieg (Brzeg) 30,780 C3
odnica 17,300 D2
zeg 30,780 C3
zeg Dolny 10,800 C3
zesko 9,701 E3
sko Zdrój 11,100 E3
dgoszcz 280,460 C2
tom 186,993 A3
tów 10,642 C1
ełm 38,789 F3
ełmno 17,906 D2
ełmza 14,200 D2
odziez 14,100 C2
ojnice 23,500 C2
ojnów 11,000 B3
orzów 151,338 B4
oszczno 9,800 B2
rzanów 29,300 B4
echanów 28,500 E2
eplice
Śląskie-Zdrój 15,400 B3
eszyn 25,234 D4
racow 651,300 E4
echowice-Dziedzice 25,400 D4
eladź 31,843 B4
ęstochowa 187,613 D3
ąbrowa Górnicza 61,660 B3
anzig (Gdańsk) 364,285 D1
arłowo 11,200 C1
ębica 22,900 E3
ęblin 14,600 E3
ębno 10,700 B2
ziałdowo 10,100 E2
zierzoniów 32,800 C3
bing (Elblag) 89,835 D1
k 27,188 F2
dańsk 364,285 D1
dynia 190,125 D1
izycko 18,200 E1
leiwitz (Gliwice) 170,912 A4
ogów (Glogau) 20,226 C3
owno 12,800 D2
ubczyce 11,300 C3
ucholazy 13,200 C3
niezno 50,643 C2
oleniów 14,600 B2
orlice 15,200 E4
orzów Wielkopolski 74,267 B2
ostyń 13,000 C3
ostynin 12,000 D2
rajewo 11,200 F2
rodzisk Mazowiecki 20,400 E2
rójec 10,300 E3
rudziądz 75,511 D2
rünberg (Zielona
Góra) 59,700 B3
ryfice 13,200 B2
uben (Gubin) 14,600 B3
ajnowka m4,345 F2
indenburg (Zabrze) 199,400 A4
irschberg (Jelenia
Góra) 55,720 B3
rubieszów 14,999 F3
awa 16,400 D2
owrocław 54,817 D2

Jarocin 18,100 C3
Jarosław 29,000 F4
Jaslo 17,025 E4
Jastrzębie Zdroj 34,400 D3
Jaworzno 63,271 B4
Jędrzejów 13,264 E3
Jelenia Góra 55,720 B3
Kalisz 81,227 D3
Kamienna Góra 21,000 B3
Kartuzy 10,558 C1
Katowice 303,264 B4
Kedzierzyn-Koźle 45,600 C3
Kępno 10,151 C3
Kętrzyn 19,300 E1
Kielce 125,952 E3
Kłobuck 12,600 D3
Kłodzko 26,000 C3
Kluczbork 18,000 D3
Knurów 28,400 A4
Kolberg (Kołobrzeg) 25,419 B1
Koło 13,100 D2
Kołobrzeg 25,419 B1
Konin 40,600 D2
Końskie 13,100 E3
Konstantynów
Łódzki 12,800 D3
Kościan 18,700 C2
Kościerzyna 18,914 C1
Köslin (Koszalin) 64,414 C1
Kostrzyń 11,200 B2
Koszalin 64,414 C1
Kraków (Cracow) 651,300 E4
Krapkowice 13,800 D3
Kraśnik Fabryczny 14,600 F3
Krasnystaw 12,495 F3
Krosno 26,500 E4
Krotoszyn 21,900 C3
Krynica 10,200 E4
Küstrin 11,200 B2
Kutno 30,000 D2
Kwidzin 23,104 D2
Łancut 12,049 F3
Landsberg (Gorzów
Wielkepolski) 74,267 B2
Łaziska Górne 10,800 A4
Lębork 25,000 C1
Łęczyca 13,900 D2
Legionowo 20,800 E2
Legnica 75,843 C3
Leszcyny 12,200 A4
Leszno 33,890 C3
Libiaz 10,600 D3
Lidzbark Warmiński 12,900 E1
Liegnitz (Legnica) 75,843 C3
Lipno 10,900 D2
Łódź 777,800 D3
Łomza 25,500 F2
Łowicz 20,400 D2
Lubań 17,200 B3
Lubartów 10,000 F3
Lubin 28,400 C3
Lublin 235,937 F3
Lubliniec 19,800 D3
Luboń 16,400 C2
Lubsko 12,600 B3
Łuków 15,500 F3
Malbork (Marienburg) 30,900 D1

Międzyrzec Podlaski 13,500 F3
Międzyrzecz 14,900 B2
Mielec 26,800 E3
Mikłów 21,300 B4
Mińsk Mazowiecki 24,200 E2
Mława 20,007 E2
Mońki 9,560 F2
Morąg 9,681 E2
Mrągowo 13,400 E2
Myślenice 12,100 E4
Mysłowice 44,737 C4
Myszków 18,000 D3
Nakło nad Notecia 16,800 C2
Namysłów 11,076 C3
Neisse (Nysa) 31,837 C3
Nidzica 9,642 E2
Nisko 10,000 E3
Nowa Ruda 18,100 C3
Nowa Sól 33,300 B3
Nowy Dwór Mazowiecki 16,900 E2
Nowy Sącz 41,103 E4
Nowy Targ 21,900 E4
Nysa 31,837 C3
Oborniki 10,200 C2
Oława 17,746 C3
Oleśnica 27,500 C3
Olkusz 15,800 D3
Olsztyn 94,119 E2
Opoczno 12,168 E3
Opole 86,510 C3
Oppeln 86,510 C3
Orzesze 9,600 A4
Ostróda 21,300 D2
Ostrołęka 21,981 E2
Ostrów Mazowiecka 15,000 E2
Ostrów Wielkopolski 49,530 C3
Ostrowiec
Świętokrzyski 49,958 E3
Oświęcim 39,600 D3
Otwock 39,863 E2
Ozorków 18,200 D3
Pabianice 62,275 D3
Piekary Śląskie 36,300 B4
Piła 43,778 C2

Pionki 13,600 E3
Piotrków Trybunalski 59,683 D3
Pisz 11,100 E2
Pleszew 13,348 C3
Płock 71,727 D2
Płońsk 11,619 E2
Police 12,700 B2
Poznań 469,085 C2
Prudnik 20,300 C3
Pruszcz Gdanski 13,000 D1
Pruszków 42,961 E2
Przasnysz 11,100 E2
Przemyśl 53,228 F4
Puck 9,500 D1
Puławy 34,800 F3
Pułtusk 12,600 E2
Rabka 10,700 D4
Racibórz 40,418 C3
Radom 158,640 E3
Radomsko 31,179 D3
Ratibor (Racibórz) 40,418 C3
Rawa Mazowiecka 9,800 E3
Rawicz 14,100 C3
Ruda Śląska 142,407 B4
Rumia 23,300 D1
Rybnik 43,415 D3
Rypin 10,029 D2
Rzeszów 82,192 F4
Sandomierz 16,800 E3
Sanok 21,600 F4
Schneidemühl (Piła) 36,600 C2
Schweidnitz
(Świdnica) 47,542 C3
Siedlce 38,983 F2
Siemianowice
Śląskie 67,278 B4
Sieradz 18,500 D3
Sierpc 12,700 D2
Skarzysko-Kamienna 39,194 E3
Skawina 15,900 D4
Skierniewice 25,590 E2
Sławno 10,700 C1
Słubice 12,000 B2
Słupsk 68,311 C1

Sochaczew 20,500 E2
Sokółka 10,023 F2
Sokołów Podlaski 9,569 F2
Sopot 47,573 D1
Sosnowiec 144,652 B4
Śrem 15,600 C2
Środa Śląska 10,259 C3
Środa Wielkopolska 14,800 C2
Stalowa Wola 29,768 F3
Starachowice 42,807 E3
Stargard Szceciński 44,400 B2
Starogard Gdański 33,400 D2
Stary Sacz 57,400 E4
Stettin (Szczecin) 337,294 B2
Stolp (Słupsk) 68,311 C1
Strzegom 14,000 C3
Strzelce Opolskie 14,700 D3
Strzelin 9,800 C3
Sulechów 10,200 B2
Suwałki 25,360 F1
Swarzędz 12,100 C2
Świdnica 47,542 C3
Świdnik 21,900 F3
Świdwin 12,500 B2
Świebodzice 18,500 C3
Świebodzin 14,900 B2
Świecie 17,900 D2
Świętochłowice 57,633 A4
Świnoujście
(Swinemünde) 27,900 B1
Szamotuły 14,600 C2
Szczecin 337,204 B2
Szczecinek 28,600 C2
Szczytno 17,371 E2
Szprotawa 11,200 B3
Tarnobrzeg 18,800 E3
Tarnów 85,514 E4
Tarnowskie Góry 34,200 A3
Tczew 40,794 D1
Tomaszów Lubelski 12,329 F3
Tomaszów Mazowiecki 54,911 E3
Toruń 129,152 D2
Trzcianka 10,900 C2
Trzebinia-Siersza C4

Turek 18,500 D2
Tychy 71,384 B4
Ustka 9,900 C1
Wąbrzeźno 11,800 D2
Wadowice 11,700 D4
Wągrowiec 15,600 C2
Wałbrzych 125,048 C3
Wałcz 18,900 C2
Waldenburg
(Wałbrzych) 125,048 C3
Warsaw (Warszawa)
(cap.) 1,377,100 E2
Wejherowo 33,600 D1
Wieliczka 13,600 E3
Wieluń 14,300 D3
Wisła 9,800 D4
Włocławek 77,169 D2
Wodzisław Śląski 25,600 D4
Wolin 35,458 B2
Wołomin 24,000 E2
Wołów 10,500 C3
Wrocław 523,318 C3
Września 17,800 C2
Wschowa 10,000 C3
Wyszków E2
Ząbki 16,000 E2
Ząbkowice Śląskie 13,800 C3
Zabrze 197,214 A4
Żagań 21,400 B3
Zakopane 27,039 D4
Zambrów 14,082 E2
Zamość 34,734 F3
Żary 28,300 B3
Zawiercie 39,410 D3
Zduńska Wola 29,066 D3
Zgierz 42,838 D3
Zgorzelec 28,400 B3
Ziębice 9,700 C3
Zielona Góra 73,156 B3
Złocieniec 10,100 C2
Złotoryja 12,200 C3
Złotów 11,600 C2
Znin 9,600 C2
Zyrardów 33,196 E2

Zywiec 22,400 D4

OTHER FEATURES

Baltic (sea) B1
Beskids (range) D4
Brda (riv.) C2
Brynica (riv.) B4
Bug (riv.) F2
Danzig (Gdańsk) (gulf) D1
Dukla (pass) E4
Dunajec (riv.) E4
Gwda (riv.) C2
Hel (pen.) D1
High Tatra (range) D4
Kłodnica (riv.) A4
Łyna (riv.) E1
Mamry, Jezioro (lake) E1
Masurian (lkes) E2
Narew (riv.) E2
Neisse (riv.) B3
Noteć (riv.) B2
Nysa Kłodzka (riv.) C3
Nysa Łuzycka (Neisse)
(riv.) B3
Oder (riv.) B2
Orava (res.) D4
Pilica (riv.) D3
Pomeranian (bay) B1
Prosna (riv.) C3
Przemsza (riv.) B4
Rysy (mt.) D4
San (riv.) F3
Słupia (riv.) C1
Śniardwy, Jezioro (lake) E2
Sudeten (range) B3
Uznam (Usedom) (isl.) B1
Vistula (riv.) D2
Warmia (reg.) D1
Warta (riv.) B2
Wieprz (riv.) F3
Wisła (Vistula) (riv.) D2
Wkra (riv.) E2
Wolin (Wollin) (isl.) B2

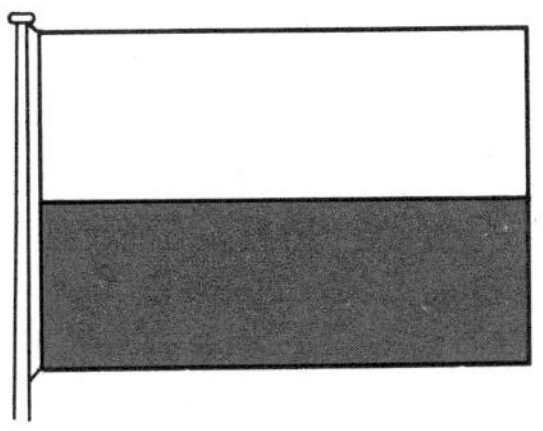

AREA 120,725 sq. mi. (312,678 sq. km.)
POPULATION 35,815,000
CAPITAL Warsaw
LARGEST CITY Warsaw
HIGHEST POINT Rysy 8,199 ft. (2,499 m.)
MONETARY UNIT zloty
MAJOR LANGUAGE Polish
MAJOR RELIGION Roman Catholicism

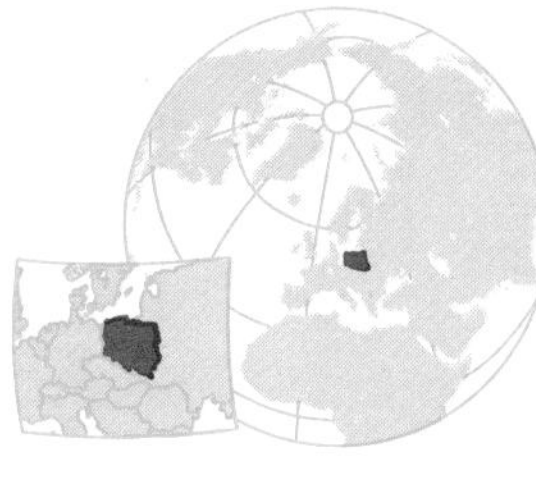

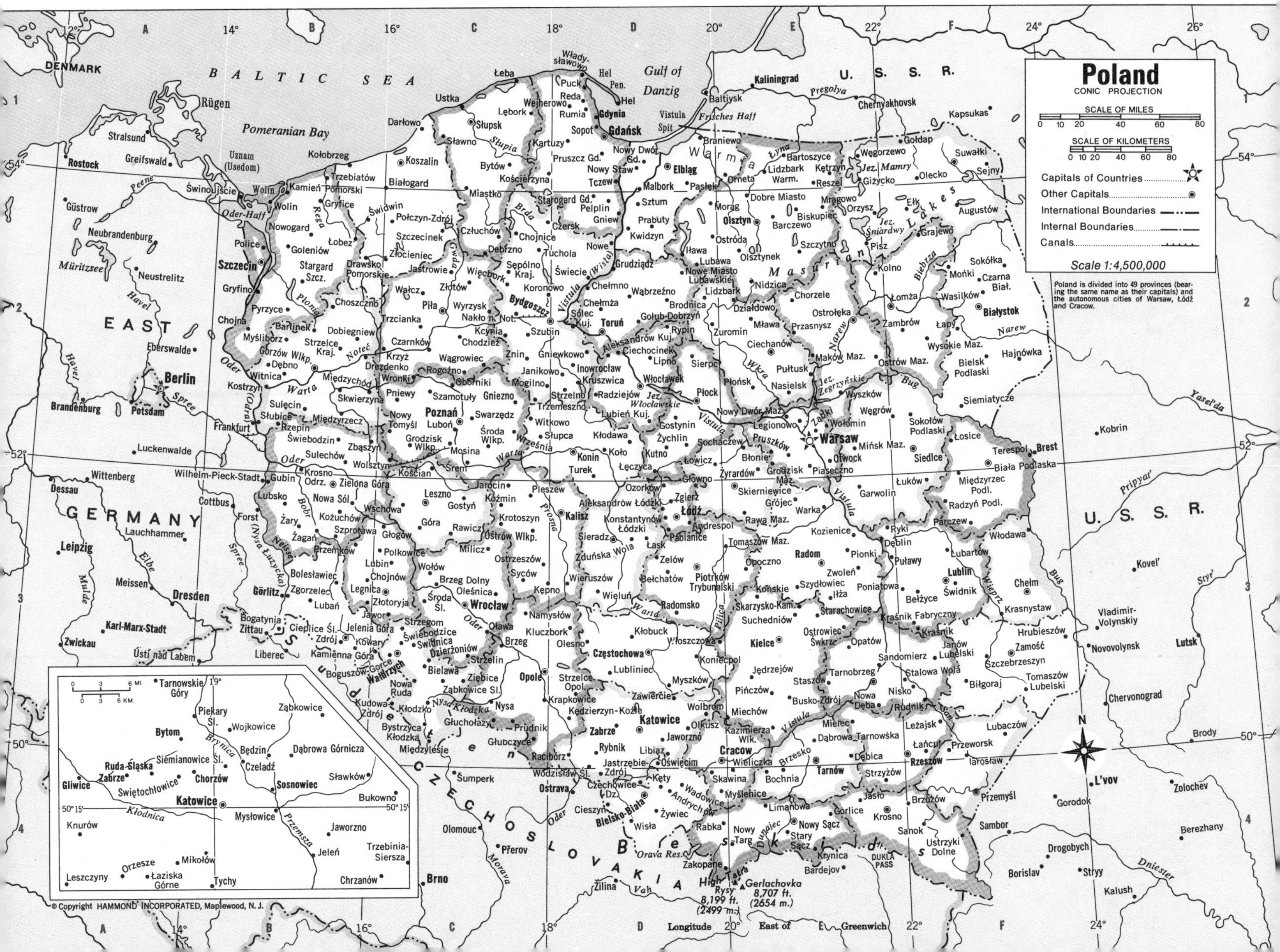
Poland
CONIC PROJECTION
SCALE OF MILES
SCALE OF KILOMETERS
Capitals of Countries
Other Capitals
International Boundaries
Internal Boundaries
Canals
Scale 1:4,500,000
Poland is divided into 49 provinces (bearing the same name as their capitals) and the autonomous cities of Warsaw, Łódź and Cracow.
BALTIC SEA
Pomeranian Bay
Gulf of Danzig
U.S.S.R.
EAST GERMANY
CZECHOSLOVAKIA
Warsaw
Longitude East of Greenwich
© Copyright HAMMOND INCORPORATED, Maplewood, N.J.

UNION REPUBLICS

Armenian S.S.R. 3,031,000 .... E6
Azerbaidzhan S.S.R. 6,028,000 .... E5
Estonian S.S.R. 1,466,000 .... C4
Georgian S.S.R. 5,015,000 .... D5
Kazakh S.S.R. 14,684,000 .... G5
Kirgiz S.S.R. 3,529,000 .... H5
Latvian S.S.R. 2,521,000 .... C4
Lithuanian S.S.R. 3,398,000 .... C4
Moldavian S.S.R. 3,947,000 .... C5
Russian S.F.S.R. 137,551,000 .... D4
Tadzhik S.S.R. 3,801,000 .... H6
Turkmen S.S.R. 2,759,000 .... F5
Ukrainian S.S.R. 49,755,000 .... C5
Uzbek S.S.R. 15,391,000 .... G5
White Russian S.S.R. 9,560,000 .... C4

INTERNAL DIVISIONS

Abkhaz A.S.S.R. 505,000 .... E5
Adygey Aut. Obl. 405,000 .... D5
Adzhar A.S.S.R. 354,000 .... E5
Aginsk Buryat Aut. Okr. 69,000 .... M4
Bashkir A.S.S.R. 3,849,000 .... F4
Buryat A.S.S.R. 900,000 .... M4
Chechen-Ingush
  A.S.S.R. 1,154,000 .... E5
Chukchi Aut. Okr. 133,000 .... R3
Chuvash A.S.S.R. 1,292,000 .... E4
Dagestan A.S.S.R. 1,628,000 .... E5
Evenki Aut. Okr. 16,000 .... K3
Gorno-Altay Aut. Obl. 172,000 .... J4
Gorno-Badakhshan Aut.
  Obl. 127,000 .... H6
Jewish Aut. Obl. 190,000 .... O5
Kabardin-Balkar

A.S.S.R. 674,000 .... E5
Kalmuck A.S.S.R. 294,000 .... E5
Karachay-Cherkess Aut.
  Obl. 368,000 .... E5
Karakalpak A.S.S.R. 904,000 .... G5
Karelian A.S.S.R. 736,000 .... D3
Khakass Aut. Obl. 500,000 .... J4
Khanty-Mansi Aut. Okr. 569,000 .... H3
Komi A.S.S.R. 1,119,000 .... F3
Komi-Permyak Aut. Okr. 173,000 .... F4
Koryak Aut. Okr. 34,000 .... R3
Mari A.S.S.R. 703,000 .... E4
Mordvinian A.S.S.R. 991,000 .... E4
Nagorno-Karabakh Aut.
  Obl. 161,000 .... E5
Nakhichevan' A.S.S.R. 239,000 .... E6
Nenets Aut. Okr. 47,000 .... F3
North Ossetian
  A.S.S.R. 597,000 .... E5
South Ossetian Aut.
  Obl. 98,000 .... E5
Tatar A.S.S.R. 3,436,000 .... F4
Taymyr Aut. Okr. 44,000 .... K2
Tuvinian A.S.S.R. 267,000 .... K4
Udmurt A.S.S.R. 1,494,000 .... F4
Ust'-Ordynskiy Buryat Aut.
  Okr. 133,000 .... L4
Yakut A.S.S.R. 839,000 .... N3
Yamal-Nenets Aut. Okr. 158,000 .... H3

CITIES and TOWNS

Abakan 128,000 .... K4
Abay 34,245 .... H5
Abaza 15,202 .... J4
Achinsk 117,000 .... K4

Agata K3
Aginskoye 7,922 .... M4
Akmolinsk
  (Tselinograd) 234,000 .... H4
Aksay 10,010 .... F4
Aktas G5
Aktash J4
Aktyubinsk 191,000 .... F4
Aldan 17,689 .... N4
Aleksandrovsk-Sakhalinskiy
  20,342 .... P5
Alekseyevka 18,041 .... H4
Aleysk 32,487 .... J4
Alga 12,000 .... F4
Aliskerovo R3
Allakh-Yun' O3
Alma-Ata 910,000 .... H5
Almaznyy M3
Ambarchik F3
Amderma F3
Amursk 24,010 .... O4
Anadyr' 7,703 .... S3
Andizhan 230,000 .... H5
Angarsk 239,000 .... L4
Angren H5
Anzhero-Sudzhensk 105,000 .... J4
Aral'sk 37,722 .... G5
Archangel
  (Arkhangel'sk) 385,000 .... E3
Arkalyk 15,108 .... G4
Armavir 162,000 .... D5
Arsen'yev 60,000 .... O5
Artem 69,000 .... O5
Artemovskiy M4
Arys' 26,414 .... G5
Arzamas 93,000 .... E4
Asbest 79,000 .... F4

Ashkhabad 312,000 .... F6
Asino 29,395 .... J4
Astrakhan' 461,000 .... F5
Atbasar 37,228 .... H4
Atka Q3
Ayaguz 35,827 .... J5
Aykhal M3
Bagdarin M4
Baku 1,022,000 .... E5
Balakovo 152,000 .... F4
Balashov 93,000 .... E4
Baley 27,215 .... M4
Balkhash 78,000 .... H5
Balykshi 22,397 .... F5
Bam N2
Barabinsk 37,274 .... H4
Baranovichi 131,000 .... C4
Barnaul 533,000 .... J4
Batagay 10,000 .... O3
Batumi 123,000 .... E5
Baykonyr G5
Bayram-Ali 31,987 .... G6
Belgorod 240,000 .... D5
Belogorsk 63,000 .... O4
Belomorsk 16,595 .... D3
Beloretsk 71,000 .... F4
Belovo 112,000 .... J4
Berdsk 67,000 .... J4
Berdyansk 122,000 .... D5
Berezniki 185,000 .... F4
Berezovo 6,000 .... G3
Beringovskiy T3
Bikin 17,473 .... O5
Bira O5

Birobidzhan 69,000 .... O5
Biruni G5
Biysk 212,000 .... J4
Bobrovka N4
Bobruysk 192,000 .... D4
Bodaybo 19,000 .... M4
Borisoglebsk 68,000 .... E4
Borzya 27,815 .... M4
Bratsk 214,000 .... L4
Brest 177,000 .... C4
Brindakit O4
Bryansk 394,000 .... D4
Bugul'ma 80,000 .... F4
Bugurslan 54,000 .... F4
Bukachacha 10,000 .... M4
Bukhara 185,000 .... G5
Bulun N2
Buzuluk 76,000 .... F4
Chadan K4
Chapayevsk 85,000 .... F4
Chardzhou 140,000 .... G6
Charsk 10,100 .... J5
Cheboksary 308,000 .... E4
Chegdomyn 16,499 .... O4
Chelkar 19,377 .... F5
Chelyabinsk 1,030,000 .... F4
Cheremkhovo 77,000 .... L4
Cherepovets 266,000 .... D4
Cherkessk 91,000 .... E5
Chernigov 238,000 .... D4
Chernogorsk 71,000 .... K4
Chernovtsy 219,000 .... C5
Chernyshevsk 10,000 .... M4
Chersk Q3
Chimbay 18,899 .... G5
Chimkent 322,000 .... H5
Chirchik 132,000 .... H5

Chita 303,000 .... M4
Chokurdakh P2
Chumikan O4
Dal'negorsk 33,506 .... O5
Dal'nerechensk 28,224 .... O5
Daugavpils 116,000 .... C4
Denau G6
Dikson J2
Dimitrovgrad 106,000 .... F4
Dnepropetrovsk 1,066,000 .... D5
Donetsk 1,021,000 .... D5
Drogobych 66,000 .... C5
Druzhba J5
Druzhina P3
Dudinka 19,701 .... J3
Dushanbe 494,000 .... G6
Dzerzhinsk 257,000 .... E4
Dzhalal-Abad 55,000 .... H5
Dzhalinda N4
Dzhambul 264,000 .... H5
Dzhetygara 32,169 .... G4
Dzhezkazgan 89,000 .... G5
Dzhusaly 20,658 .... G5
Egvekinot S3
Ekibastuz 66,000 .... H4
Ekimchan O4
El'dikan O3
Elista 70,000 .... E5
Emba 17,820 .... F5
Engel's 161,000 .... E4
Erivan 1,019,000 .... E6
Evensk Q3
Fergana 176,000 .... H5
Fort-Shevchenko 12,000 .... F5
Frolovo 33,398 .... E5
Frunze 533,000 .... H5

Gasan-Kuli F6
Gol'chikha J2
Gomel 383,000 .... D4
Gor'kiy 1,344,000 .... E4
Gorno-Altaysk 34,413 .... J4
Gornyak 16,643 .... J4
Grodno 195,000 .... C4
Groznyy 375,000 .... E5
Gubakha 33,243 .... F4
Gulistan 30,879 .... H5
Gur'yev 131,000 .... F5
Gusinoozersk 10,000 .... L4
Gyda J2
Igarka 15,624 .... J3
Igrim G3
Iianskiy 22,852 .... K4
Indiga F3
Inta 51,000 .... F3
Iolotan' 10,000 .... G6
Irkutsk 550,000 .... L4
Ishim 63,000 .... G4
Isil'kul' 25,958 .... H4
Iul'tin S3
Ivano-Frankovsk 150,000 .... C5
Ivanovo 465,000 .... E4
Ivdel 15,308 .... F4
Izhevsk 549,000 .... F4
Izmail 83,000 .... C5
Kagan 34,117 .... G6
Kalachinsk 20,809 .... H4
Kalakan M4
Kalinin 412,000 .... D4
Kaliningrad 355,000 .... B4
Kalmykovo F5
Kaluga 265,000 .... D4
Kamen'-na-Obi 35,604 .... J4

ADMINISTRATIVE DIVISIONS NOT NAMED ON MAP

Division	Ref.	Division	Ref.
1. Abkhaz A.S.S.R.	E5	13. Khakass Aut. Oblast	J4
2. Adygey Aut. Oblast	D5	14. Komi-Permyak Aut. Okrug	F4
3. Adzhar A.S.S.R.	E5	15. Mari A.S.S.R.	E4
4. Aginsk Buryat		16. Mordvinian A.S.S.R.	E4
Autonomous Okrug	M4	17. Nagorno-Karabakh Aut. Oblast	E5
5. Chechen-Ingush A.S.S.R.	E5	18. Nakhichevan' A.S.S.R.	E6
6. Chuvash A.S.S.R.	E4	19. North Ossetian A.S.S.R.	E5
7. Gorno-Altay Aut. Oblast	J4	20. South Ossetian Aut. Oblast	E5
8. Gorno-Badakhshan Aut. Oblast	H6	21. Tatar A.S.S.R.	F4
9. Jewish Aut. Oblast	O5	22. Tuvinian A.S.S.R.	K4
10. Kabardin-Balkar A.S.S.R.	E5	23. Udmurt A.S.S.R.	F4
11. Karachay-Cherkess Aut. Oblast	E5	24. Ust'-Ordynsk Buryat	
12. Karakalpak A.S.S.R.	G5	Autonomous Okrug	L4

Union of Soviet Socialist Republics

CONIC PROJECTION

SCALE OF MILES
0 100 200 300 400 500 600

SCALE OF KILOMETERS
0 100 200 300 400 500 600

Capitals | Boundaries
★ National
☆ Union Republic
◎ A.S.S.R.
◎ Autonomous Oblast
○ Autonomous Okrug

Scale 1:30,400,000

AREA 8,649,490 sq. mi. (22,402,179 sq. km.)
POPULATION 262,436,227
CAPITAL Moscow
LARGEST CITY Moscow
HIGHEST POINT Communism Peak 24,599 ft. (7,498 m.)
MONETARY UNIT ruble
MAJOR LANGUAGES Russian, Ukrainian, White Russian, Uzbek,
Azerbaidzhani, Tatar, Georgian, Lithuanian, Armenian, Yiddish,
Latvian, Mordvinian, Kirgiz, Tadzhik, Estonian, Kazakh, Moldavian
(Romanian), German, Chuvash, Turkmenian, Bashkir
MAJOR RELIGIONS Eastern (Russian) Orthodoxy, Islam, Judaism,
Protestantism (Baltic States)

Kamenskoye		R3
Kamensk-Ural'skiy 187,000		G4
Kamyshin 112,000		E4
Kandalaksha 42,656		C3
Kansk 101,000		K4
Kapchagay		H5
Kara		G3
Karaganda 572,000		H5
Karasuk 22,637		H4
Karatau 26,962		H5
Karazhal 17,702		H5
Kargasok		J4
Karpinsk		F4
Karshi 108,000		G6
Kartaly 42,801		G4
Katangli		P4
Kattakurgan 53,000		G5
Kaunas 370,000		C4
Kavalerovo 16,415		O5
Kazan' 993,000		F4
Kem' 21,025		D3
Kemerovo 471,000		J4
Kentau 52,000		G5
Kerki 10,000		G6
Khabarovsk 528,000		O5
Khandyga		O3
Khanty-Mansiysk 24,754		H3
Khar'kov 1,444,000		D4
Khatanga		L2
Kherson 319,000		D5
Khilok 17,000		M4
Khiva 24,139		F5
Khodzheyli 36,435		F5
Kholmsk 37,412		P5
Khorog 12,295		H6
Kiev 2,144,000		D4

UNION REPUBLICS

	AREA (sq. mi.)	AREA (sq. km.)	POPULATION	CAPITAL and LARGEST CITY
RUSSIAN S.F.S.R.	6,592,812	17,075,400	137,551,000	Moscow 7,831,000
KAZAKH S.S.R.	1,048,300	2,715,100	14,684,000	Alma-Ata 910,000
UKRAINIAN S.S.R.	233,089	603,700	49,755,000	Kiev 2,144,000
TURKMEN S.S.R.	188,455	488,100	2,759,000	Ashkhabad 312,000
UZBEK S.S.R.	173,591	449,600	15,391,000	Tashkent 1,780,000
WHITE RUSSIAN S.S.R.	80,154	207,600	9,560,000	Minsk 1,262,000
KIRGIZ S.S.R.	76,641	198,500	3,529,000	Frunze 533,000
TADZHIK S.S.R.	55,251	143,100	3,801,000	Dushanbe 494,000
AZERBAIDZHAN S.S.R.	33,436	86,600	6,028,000	Baku 1,022,000
GEORGIAN S.S.R.	26,911	69,700	5,015,000	Tbilisi 1,066,000
LITHUANIAN S.S.R.	25,174	65,200	3,398,000	Vilna 481,000
LATVIAN S.S.R.	24,595	63,700	2,521,000	Riga 835,000
ESTONIAN S.S.R.	17,413	45,100	1,466,000	Tallinn 430,000
MOLDAVIAN S.S.R.	13,012	33,700	3,947,000	Kishinev 503,000
ARMENIAN S.S.R.	11,506	29,800	3,031,000	Erivan 1,019,000

Kirensk 10,000	L4	Krasnokamsk 56,000	F4	Leninakan 207,000	E5
Kirov 390,000	E4	Krasnotur'insk 61,000	G3	Leningrad 4,073,000	D4
Kirovabad 232,000	E5	Krasnoural'sk 39,743	G4	Leningrad* 4,588,000	D4
Kirovograd 237,000	D5	Krasnovodsk 53,000	F5	Leningorsk 54,000	J5
Kirovskiy	H5	Krasnoyarsk 796,000	K4	Leninsk	G5
Kiselevsk 122,000	J4	Kremenchug 210,000	D5	Leninsk 16,000	K4
Kishinev 503,000	C5	Krivoy Rog 650,000	D5	Leninsk-Kuznetskiy 132,000	J4
Kizel 46,264	F4	Kudymkar 26,350	F4	Leninskoye	G5
Kizyl-Arvat 21,671	F6	Kul'sary 16,427	F5	Lenkoran' 35,505	E6
Klaipeda 176,000	B4	Kulunda 15,264	H4	Lensk 16,758	M3
Kokand 153,000	H5	Kulyab 55,000	H6	Lesosibirsk	K4
Kokchetav 103,000	H4	Kum-Dag 10,000	F6	Lesozavodsk 34,957	O5
Kolomna 147,000	D4	Kungur 80,000	F4	Liepāja 108,000	B4
Kolpashevo 24,911	J4	Kupino 20,799	H4	Lipetsk 396,000	E4
Komsomol'sk 15,385	G4	Kurgan 310,000	G4	Luga 31,905	C4
Komsomol'sk-na-Amure 264,000	O4	Kurgan-Tyube 34,620	G6	Lutsk 137,000	C4
Kondopoga 27,908	D3	Kursk 375,000	D4	L'vov 667,000	C4
Kopeysk 146,000	G4	Kushka	G6	Lys'va 75,000	F4
Korf	R3	Kustanay 165,000	G4	Magadan 121,000	P4
Korsakov 38,210	P5	Kutaisi 194,000	E5	Magdagachi 15,059	N4
Koslan	E3	Kuybyshev 1,216,000	F4	Magnitogorsk 406,000	G4
Kostroma 255,000	E4	Kuybyshev 40,166	H4	Makhachkala 251,000	E5
Kotlas 61,000	E3	Kyakhta 15,316	L4	Makinsk 22,850	H4
Kovel' 33,351	C4	Kyusyur	N2	Mama	L4
Kovrov 143,000	E4	Kyzyl 66,000	K4	Markovo	S3
Kozhevnikovo	L2	Kzyl-Orda 156,000	G5	Mary (Merv) 74,000	G6
Krasino	F2	Labytnangi	G3	Maykop 128,000	D5
Krasnodar 560,000	E5	Lebedinyy	N4	Mednogorsk 38,024	F4
Krasnokamensk 51,000	M4	Leninabad 130,000	G5	Medvezh'yegorsk 17,465	D3
				Mezen'	E3
Miass 150,000	G4	Nazarovo 54,000	K4
Michurinsk 101,000	E4	Nazyvayevsk 15,792	H4
Millerovo 34,627	E5	Nebit-Dag 71,000	F6
Minsk 1,262,000	C4	Neftegugansk 52,000	H3
Minsk* 1,276,000	C4	Nel'kan	O4
Minusinsk 56,000	K4	Nepa	L4
Mirnyy 23,826	M3	Neryungri	N4
Mogilev 290,000	D4	Nevel'sk 20,726	P5
Mogocha 17,884	N4	Nevel' 440,000	D5
Molodechno 73,000	C4	Nikolayev 440,000	D5
Monchegorsk 51,000	C3	Nikolayevsk-na-Amure 30,082	P4
Moscow (cap.) 7,831,000	D4	Nikol'skoye	R4
Moscow* 8,011,000	D4	Nizhneudinsk 39,743	K4
Motygino 10,000	K4	Nizhnevartovsk 109,000	H3
Mozyr' 73,000	C4	Nizhneyansk	O3
Murgab	H6	Nizhniy Tagil 398,000	G4
Murmansk 381,000	D3	Nordvik-Ugol'naya	M2
Muynak 12,000	F5	Noril'sk 180,000	J3
Mys Shmidta	T3	Novaya Kazanka	F5
Nadym	H3	Novgorod 186,000	D4
Nagornyy	N4	Novokazalinsk 34,815	G5
Nakhichevan' 33,279	E6	Novokuznetsk 541,000	J4
Nakhodka 133,000	O5	Novomoskovsk 147,000	E4
Nal'chik 207,000	E5	Novorossiysk 159,000	D5
Namangan 227,000	H5	Novosibirsk 1,312,000	J4
Naminga	M4	Novozybkov 34,433	D4
Nar'yan-Mar 16,864	F3	Novyy Port	G3
Naryn 21,098	H5	Novyy Uzen' 18,073	F5
Navoi 84,000	G6	Novyy Urengoy	H3
		Nukus 109,000	G5

Topography

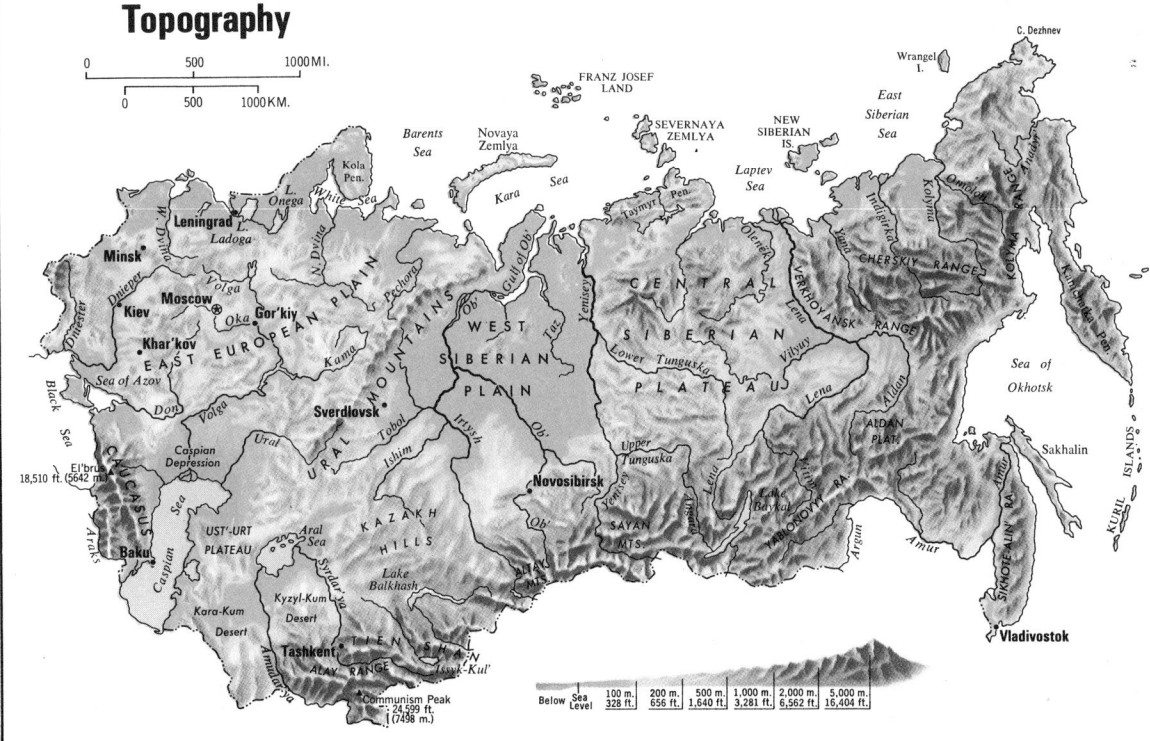

Below Sea Level	100 m. 328 ft.	200 m. 656 ft.	500 m. 1,640 ft.	1,000 m. 3,281 ft.	2,000 m. 6,562 ft.	5,000 m. 16,404 ft.

© Copyright HAMMOND INCORPORATED, Maplewood, N.J.

(continued)

Nyandoma 23,366 .... E3
Nyurba M3
Obluch'ye 17,000 .... N5
Odessa 1,046,000 .... D5
Okha 30,890 .... P4
Okhotsk P4
Olëkminsk N3
Olënek M3
Omsk 1,014,000 .... H4
Omsukchan Q3
Omutninsk 28,777 .... F4
Onega 25,047 .... D3
Ordzhonikidze 279,000 .... E5
Orel 305,000 .... D4
Orenburg 459,000 .... F4
Orotukan Q3
Orsk 247,000 .... F4
Osh 169,000 .... H5
Ostrogozhsk 29,921 .... D4
Oymyakon O3
Ozernovskiy Q4
Palana 2,735 .... R4
Panfilov 19,173 .... H5
Pärnu 51,000 .... C4
Partizansk 48,345 .... O5
Pavlodar 273,000 .... H4
Pechenga D2
Pechora 56,000 .... F3
Peleduy M4
Penza 483,000 .... E4
Perkatkin T2
Perm' 999,000 .... F4
Pervoural'sk 129,000 .... F4
Petropavlovsk 207,000 .... G4
Petropavlovsk-Kamchatskiy 215,000 .... R4
Petrovsk-Zabaykal'skiy 28,313 .... L4
Petrozavodsk 234,000 .... D3
Pevek S3
Pikol'skiy 32,862 .... G5
Pinsk 90,000 .... C4
Plastun O5
Podol'sk 202,000 .... D4
Pokrovsk N3
Poligus K3
Poltava 279,000 .... D5
Polyarnyy 15,321 .... D3
Ponoy E3
Poronaysk 23,610 .... P5
Prikumsk 35,768 .... E5
Progress 10,000 .... O5
Prokop'yevsk 266,000 .... J4
Provideniya T3
Przheval'sk 51,000 .... H5
Pskov 176,000 .... C4
Pushkin 90,000 .... C4
Raychikhinsk 25,157 .... N5
Riga 835,000 .... C4
Rostov-na-Donu 934,000 .... E5
Rovno 179,000 .... C4
Rubtsovsk 157,000 .... J4
Ruch'i E3
Rudnyy 110,000 .... G4
Ryazan' 453,000 .... E4
Rybach'ye H5
Rybinsk 239,000 .... D4
Rzhev 69,000 .... D4
Saksaul'skiy F5
Salekhard 21,929 .... G3
Sal'sk 57,000 .... E5
Samagaltay K4
Samarkand 477,000 .... G6
Sangar N3
Saran' 55,000 .... H5
Saransk 263,000 .... E4
Sarapul 107,000 .... F4
Saratov 856,000 .... E4
Sarkand 18,296 .... J5
Segezha 28,810 .... D3
Semipalatinsk 283,000 .... H4
Serakhs G6
Serov 101,000 .... G4
Serpukhov 140,000 .... D4
Sevastopol' 301,000 .... D5
Severobaykal'sk M4
Severodvinsk 197,000 .... E3
Severo-Kuril'sk 8,000 .... Q4
Severoural'sk 29,880 .... G3
Severo-Yeniseysk K3
Shadrinsk 82,000 .... G4
Shakhtinsk 50,000 .... H5
Shakhty 209,000 .... E5
Shar'ya 25,788 .... E4
Shchuchinsk 40,432 .... H4
Shenkursk E3
Shevchenko 111,000 .... F5
Shilka 16,065 .... M4
Shimanovsk 16,880 .... N4
Shushenskoye 10,000 .... K4
Šiauliai 118,000 .... C4
Siktyakh N3
Simferopol' 302,000 .... D5
Skovorodino 10,000 .... N4
Slavgorod 32,908 .... H4
Slobodskoy 34,374 .... E4
Slyudyanka 20,639 .... L4
Smolensk 276,000 .... D4
Snezhnogorsk J3
Sochi 287,000 .... D5
Sokol 48,253 .... E4
Solikamsk 101,000 .... F3
Sortavala 22,188 .... C3
Sosnogorsk 24,688 .... F3
Sosnovo-Ozerskoye M4
Sovetskaya Gavan' 28,455 .... P5
Spassk-Dal'niy 53,000 .... O5
Srednekolymsk Q3
Sretensk 16,000 .... M4
Stalingrad (Volgograd) 929,000 .... E5
Stavropol' 258,000 .... E5
Stepanakert 30,293 .... E6
Sterlitamak 220,000 .... F4
Strezhevoy H3
Sukhana M3
Sukhumi 114,000 .... D5
Sumy 228,000 .... D4
Suntar M3
Surgut 107,000 .... H3
Susuman 12,000 .... P3
Sverdlovsk 1,211,000 .... F4
Svobodnyy 75,000 .... N4
Syktyvkar 171,000 .... F3
Syzran' 178,000 .... E4
Taganrog 276,000 .... D5
Takhiatash F5
Takhta-Bazar G6
Taksimo M4
Taldy-Kurgan 88,000 .... H5
Talgar 31,273 .... H5
Tallinn 430,000 .... C4
Tambey G2
Tambov 270,000 .... E4
Tara 22,358 .... H4
Tarko-Sale H3
Tartu 105,000 .... C4
Tashauz 84,000 .... F5
Tashkent 1,780,000 .... G5
Tatarsk 29,589 .... H4
Tavda G4
Tayshet 34,232 .... K4
Tazovskiy J3
Tbilisi 1,066,000 .... E5
Tedzhen 25,708 .... F6
Tekeli 29,846 .... H5
Temirtau 213,000 .... H4
Termez 57,000 .... G6
Ternopol' 144,000 .... C5
Tiksi N2
Tobol'sk 62,000 .... G4
Togliatti (Tol'yatti) 502,000 .... F4
Tokmak 59,000 .... H5
Tommot 8,000 .... N4
Tomsk 421,000 .... J4
Tot'ma E4
Troitsk 88,000 .... G4
Tselinograd 234,000 .... H4
Tskhinvali 30,311 .... E5
Tula 514,000 .... D4
Tulun 52,000 .... L4
Tura 3,528 .... L3
Turan K4
Turgay G5
Turkestan 67,000 .... G5
Tynda N4
Tyumen' 359,000 .... G4
Uelen T3
Ufa 969,000 .... F4
Uglegorsk 17,921 .... P5
Ukhta 87,000 .... F3
Ulan-Ude 300,000 .... L4
Ul'yanovsk 464,000 .... E4
Ural'sk 167,000 .... F4
Uray 17,385 .... G3
Urgench 100,000 .... G5
Ushtobe 24,484 .... H5
Usol'ye-Sibirskoye 103,000 .... L4
Ussuriysk 147,000 .... O5
Ust'-Ilimsk 69,000 .... L4
Ust'-Kamchatsk 10,000 .... R4
Ust'-Kamenogorsk 274,000 .... J5
Ust'-Kut 50,000 .... L4
Ust'-Kuyga O3
Ust'-Maya O3
Ust'-Nera P3
Ust'-Omchug P3
Ust'-Olenëk M2
Ust'-Ordynskiy 10,693 .... L4
Ust'-Port J2
Vanavara L3
Vanino 15,401 .... P5
Velikiye Luki 102,000 .... D4
Velikiy Ustyug 36,737 .... E3
Vel'sk 21,899 .... E3
Ventspils 40,467 .... B4
Verkhnevilyuysk N3
Verkniy At-Uryakh Q3
Verkhoyansk 2,000 .... N3
Vilna (Vilnius) 481,000 .... C4
Vilyuysk N3
Vinnitsa 314,000 .... C5
Vitebsk 297,000 .... D4
Vitimskiy M4
Vladimir 296,000 .... D4
Vladivostok 550,000 .... O5
Volgograd 929,000 .... E5
Volochanka K2
Vologda 237,000 .... E4
Vorkuta 100,000 .... G3
Voronezh 783,000 .... E4
Voroshilovgrad 463,000 .... E5
Vostochnyy O5
Votkinsk 90,000 .... F4
Voy-Vozh 10,000 .... F3
Vyazemskiy 18,365 .... O5
Vyborg 76,000 .... C3
Vyshniy Volochek 72,000 .... D4
Yakutsk 152,000 .... N3
Yalutorsk 25,426 .... G4
Yamsk Q4
Yaroslavl' 597,000 .... D4
Yartsevo J4
Yelets 112,000 .... D4
Yelizovo 10,000 .... Q4
Yeniseysk 19,880 .... K4
Yermak 28,133 .... H4
Yermentau 15,276 .... H4
Yesil' 15,000 .... G4
Yessey L3
Yoshkar-Ola 201,000 .... E4
Yurga 78,000 .... J4
Yuzhno-Sakhalinsk 140,000 .... P5
Zabaykal'sk M5
Zakamensk 10,000 .... L4
Zaozernyy 27,216 .... K4
Zaporozh'ye 781,000 .... D5
Zarafshan G5
Zavitinsk 19,009 .... O4
Zaysan 10,000 .... J5
Zeya 16,684 .... N4
Zhatay O3
Zhdanov 503,000 .... D5
Zheleznogorsk-Ilimskiy 22,179 .... L4
Zhigalovo L4
Zhigansk N3
Zhitomir 244,000 .... C4
Zima 41,567 .... L4
Zlatoust 198,000 .... F4
Zyryanka Q3

OTHER FEATURES

Alakol' (lake) J5
Alazeya (riv.) Q3
Aldan (plat.) N4
Aldan (riv.) O3
Alexandra Land (isl.) E1
Altay (mts.) J5
Amga (riv.) O3
Amgun' (riv.) O4
Amudar'ya (riv.) G5
Amur (riv.) O4
Anabar (riv.) M2
Anadyr' (gulf) T3
Anadyr' (range) S3
Anadyr' (riv.) S3
Angara (riv.) K4
Aniva (cape) P5
Aral (sea) F5
Arctic Ocean K1
Argun' (riv.) M4
Arkticheskiy Institut (isls.) H2
Atrek (riv.) F6
Ayon (isl.) R2
Azov (sea) D5
Balkhash (lake) H5
Baltic (sea) B4
Barents (sea) D2
Baykal (lake) L4
Baykal (mts.) L4
Beloye (lake) D3
Belyy (isl.) G2
Bering (isl.) R4
Bering (sea) S4
Bering (str.) U3
Bet-Pak-Dala (des.) H5
Black (sea) D5
Bol'shevik (isl.) K2
Bol'shoy Lyakhovskiy (isl.) P2
Bolvanskiy Nos (cape) G2
Bratsk (res.) L4
Caspian (sea) F6
Caucasus (mts.) E5
Chelyuskin (cape) M2
Cherskiy (range) P3
Chu (riv.) H5
Chukchi (pen.) T3
Chukchi (sea) T2
Chulym (riv.) J4
Chuna (riv.) K4
Chunya (riv.) K3
Communism (peak) H6
Crimea (pen.) D5
Dezhnev (cape) T3
Dmitriya Lapteva (str.) O2
Dnieper (riv.) D5
Dniester (riv.) C5
Don (riv.) E5
Donets (riv.) D5
Dulgalakh (riv.) O3
Dvina, Northern (riv.) E3
Dvina, Western (riv.) C4

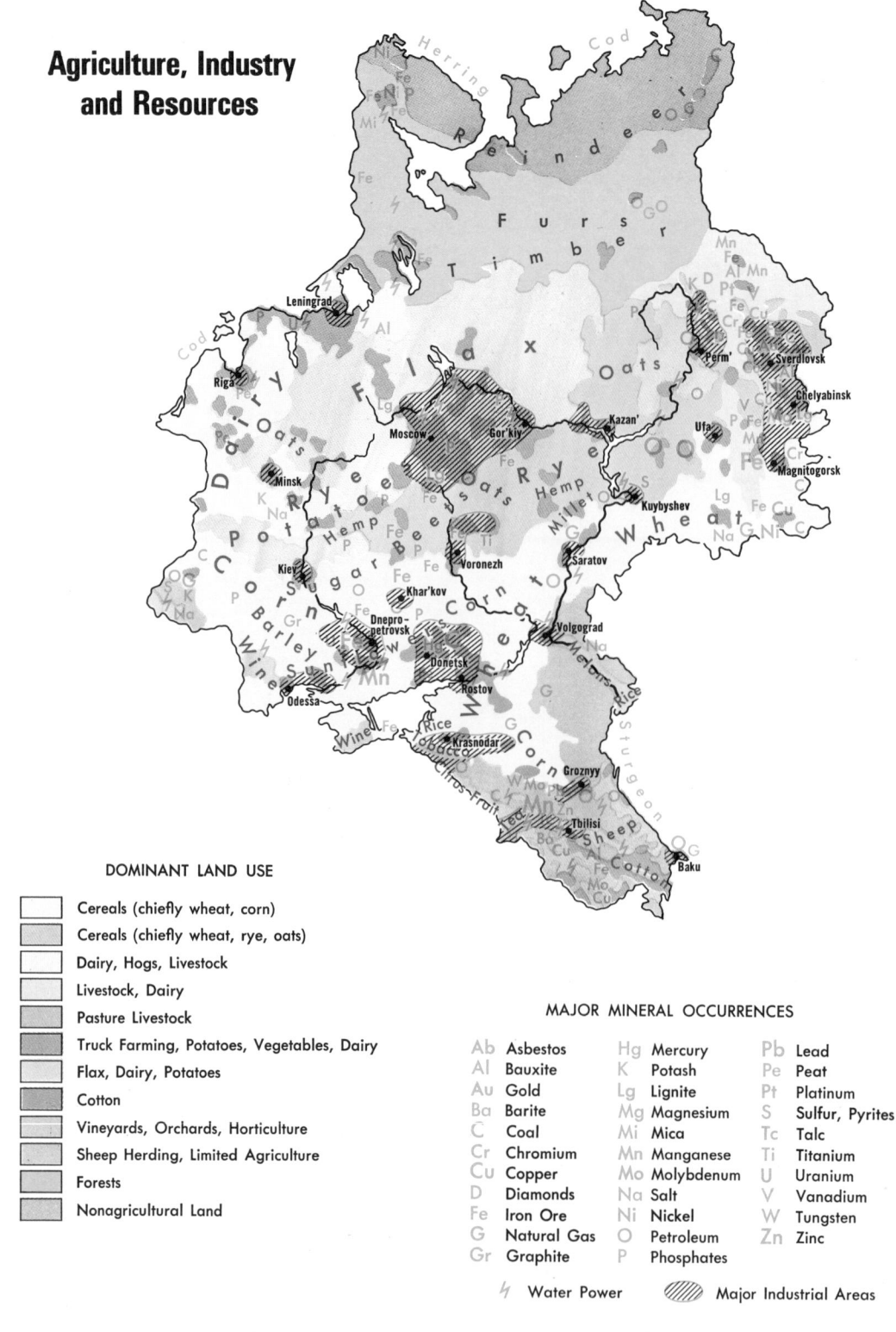

Agriculture, Industry and Resources

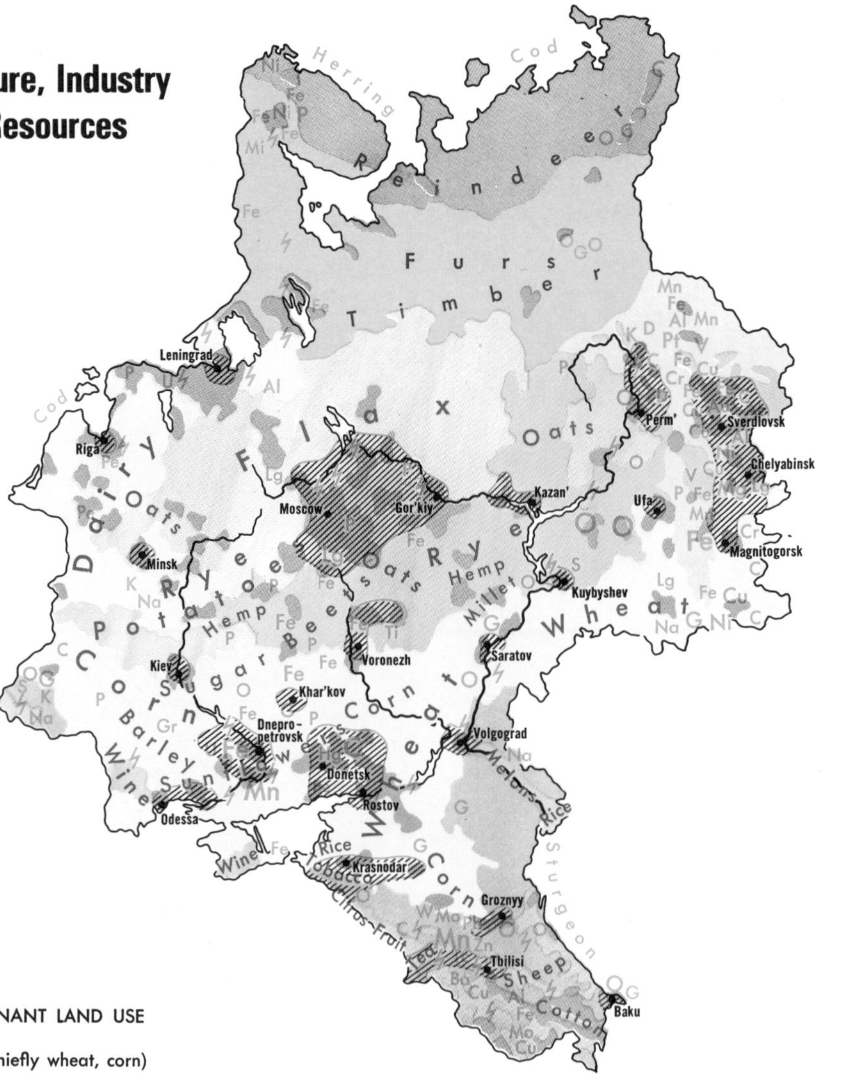

DOMINANT LAND USE

- Cereals (chiefly wheat, corn)
- Cereals (chiefly wheat, rye, oats)
- Dairy, Hogs, Livestock
- Livestock, Dairy
- Pasture Livestock
- Truck Farming, Potatoes, Vegetables, Dairy
- Flax, Dairy, Potatoes
- Cotton
- Vineyards, Orchards, Horticulture
- Sheep Herding, Limited Agriculture
- Forests
- Nonagricultural Land

MAJOR MINERAL OCCURRENCES

Ab	Asbestos	Hg	Mercury	Pb	Lead
Al	Bauxite	K	Potash	Pe	Peat
Au	Gold	Lg	Lignite	Pt	Platinum
Ba	Barite	Mg	Magnesium	S	Sulfur, Pyrites
C	Coal	Mi	Mica	Tc	Talc
Cr	Chromium	Mn	Manganese	Ti	Titanium
Cu	Copper	Mo	Molybdenum	U	Uranium
D	Diamonds	Na	Salt	V	Vanadium
Fe	Iron Ore	Ni	Nickel	W	Tungsten
G	Natural Gas	O	Petroleum	Zn	Zinc
Gr	Graphite	P	Phosphates		

Water Power — Major Industrial Areas

Dzhugdzhur (range) O4
East Siberian (sea) S2
Emba (riv.) F5
Faddeyevskiy (isl.) P2
Finland (gulf) C4
Franz Josef Land (isls.) F1
George Land (isl.) E1
Gizhiga (bay) Q3
Govena (cape) R4
Graham Bell (isl.) G1
Gyda (pen.) H2
Gydan (Kolyma) (range) Q3
Hiiumaa (isl.) C4
Ili (riv.) H5
Imandra (lake) D3
Indigirka (riv.) P3
Irtysh (riv.) H4
Ishim (riv.) G4
Issyk-Kul' (lake) H5
Iturup (isl.) P5
Japan (sea) O6
Kakhovka (res.) D5
Kamchatka (pen.) Q4
Kanin (pen.) E3
Kanin Nos (cape) E3
Kara (sea) G2
Kara-Bogaz-Gol (gulf) F5
Karaginskiy (isl.) R4
Kara-Kum (canal) F6
Kara-Kum (des.) F5
Karskiye Vorota (str.) F2
Khanka (lake) O5
Kharasavey (cape) G2
Kheta (riv.) K2
Klyuchevskaya Sopka (vol.) Q4
Kola (pen.) D3
Kolguyev (isl.) E3
Kolyma (range) Q3
Kolyma (riv.) Q3
Komandorskiye (isls.) R4
Komsomolets (isl.) L1
Koni (pen.) Q4
Koryak (range) S3
Kotel'nyy (isl.) O2
Kotuy (riv.) L3
Kuma (riv.) E5
Kura (riv.) E6
Kuril (isls.) P5
Kuybyshev (res.) F4
Kyzyl-Kum (des.) G5
Ladoga (lake) D3
La Pérouse (str.) P5
Laptev (sea) N2
Lena (riv.) N3
Little Yenisey (riv.) K4
Long (str.) S2
Lopatka (cape) Q4
Lower Tunguska (riv.) K3
Lyatkhovskiye (isls.) O2
Mangyshlak (pen.) F5
Markha (riv.) M3
Matochkin Shar (str.) F2
Maya (riv.) O4
Mezen' (riv.) E3
Murgab (riv.) G6
Nadym (riv.) H3
Narodnaya (mt.) G3
Navarin (cape) T3
New Siberian (isls.) P2
Northern Dvina (riv.) E3
Novaya Sibir' (isl.) Q2
Novaya Zemlya (isls.) F2
Ob' (gulf) H3
Ob' (riv.) G3
October Revolution (isl.) L2
Oka (riv.) L4
Okhotsk (sea) P4
Olëkma (riv.) N4
Olënek (bay) N2
Olënek (riv.) M3
Oloy (range) R3
Olyutorskiy (cape) S4
Omolon (riv.) Q3
Omoloy (riv.) O3
Onega (lake) D3
Onega (riv.) D3
Ozernoy (cape) R4
Paramushir (isl.) Q4
Pechora (riv.) F3
Peipus (lake) C4
Penzhina (bay) R3
Pioner (isl.) J2
Pobeda (peak) J5
Pur (riv.) H3
Pyasina (riv.) J2
Riga (gulf) C4
Rybachiy (pen.) D2
Rybinsk (res.) D4
Saaremaa (isl.) B4
Sakhalin (gulf) P4
Sakhalin (isl.) P4
Sannikova (str.) O2
Sary Su (riv.) H5
Sayan (mts.) K4
Selemdzha (riv.) O4
Sergeya Kirova (isls.) J2
Severnaya Zemlya (isls.) L1
Shantar (isls.) O4
Shelagskiy (cape) R2
Shelekhov (gulf) Q4
Siberia (reg.) 38,524,000 .... M3
Sikhote-Alin' (range) O5
Stanovoy (range) N4
Stony Tunguska (riv.) K3
Syrdar'ya (riv.) G5
Tannu-Ola (range) K5
Tatar (str.) P4
Taymyr (lake) K2
Taymyr (pen.) L2
Taymyr (riv.) K2
Taz (riv.) J3
Tengiz (lake) G4
Terpeniye (cape) P5
Tobol (riv.) G4
Tsimlyansk (res.) E5
Tym (riv.) J3
Tyung (riv.) M3
Uda (riv.) O4
Ulutau (mts.) G5
Ural (mts.) F4
Ural (riv.) F5
Urup (isl.) Q5
Ussuri (riv.) O5
Ust'-Urt (plat.) F5
Vakh (riv.) J3
Velikaya (riv.) S3
Verkhoyansk (range) N3
Vil'kitskogo (str.) L2
Vilyuy (range) M3
Vilyuy (res.) M3
Vilyuy (riv.) L3
Vitim (riv.) M4
Volga (riv.) E5
Western Dvina (riv.) C4
White (sea) D3
Wiese (isl.) H2
Wilczek Land (isl.) G1
Wrangel (isl.) T2
Yablonovyy (range) M4
Yamal (pen.) G2
Yana (riv.) O3
Yelizavety (cape) P4
Yenisey (riv.) J3
Zaysan (lake) J5
Zeya (riv.) N4
Zhelaniye (cape) H2

*City and suburbs.

Agriculture, Industry and Resources

DOMINANT LAND USE

- Cereals (chiefly wheat, corn)
- Livestock, Dairy
- Truck Farming, Potatoes, Vegetables, Dairy
- Cotton
- Sheep Herding, Limited Agriculture
- Forests
- Nonagricultural Land

Omsk · Novosibirsk · Krasnoyarsk · Komsomol'sk · Khabarovsk · Irkutsk · Ulan-Ude · Vladivostok · Karaganda · Tashkent · Alma-Ata

Cattle · Corn · Wheat · Flax · Oats · Cu · Rice · Cotton · Camels · Sheep · Timber · Furs · Reindeer · Walrus · Cod · Salmon · Herring

MAJOR MINERAL OCCURRENCES

Ab	Asbestos	Cu	Copper	Mi	Mica	Pt	Platinum
Ag	Silver	D	Diamonds	Mn	Manganese	S	Sulfur, Pyrites
Al	Bauxite	F	Fluorspar	Mo	Molybdenum	Sb	Antimony
Au	Gold	Fe	Iron Ore	Na	Salt	Sn	Tin
Be	Beryl	G	Natural Gas	Ni	Nickel	U	Uranium
C	Coal	Hg	Mercury	O	Petroleum	W	Tungsten
Co	Cobalt	Ka	Kaolin	P	Phosphates	Zn	Zinc
Cr	Chromium	Lg	Lignite	Pb	Lead		

⚡ Water Power   ▨ Major Industrial Areas

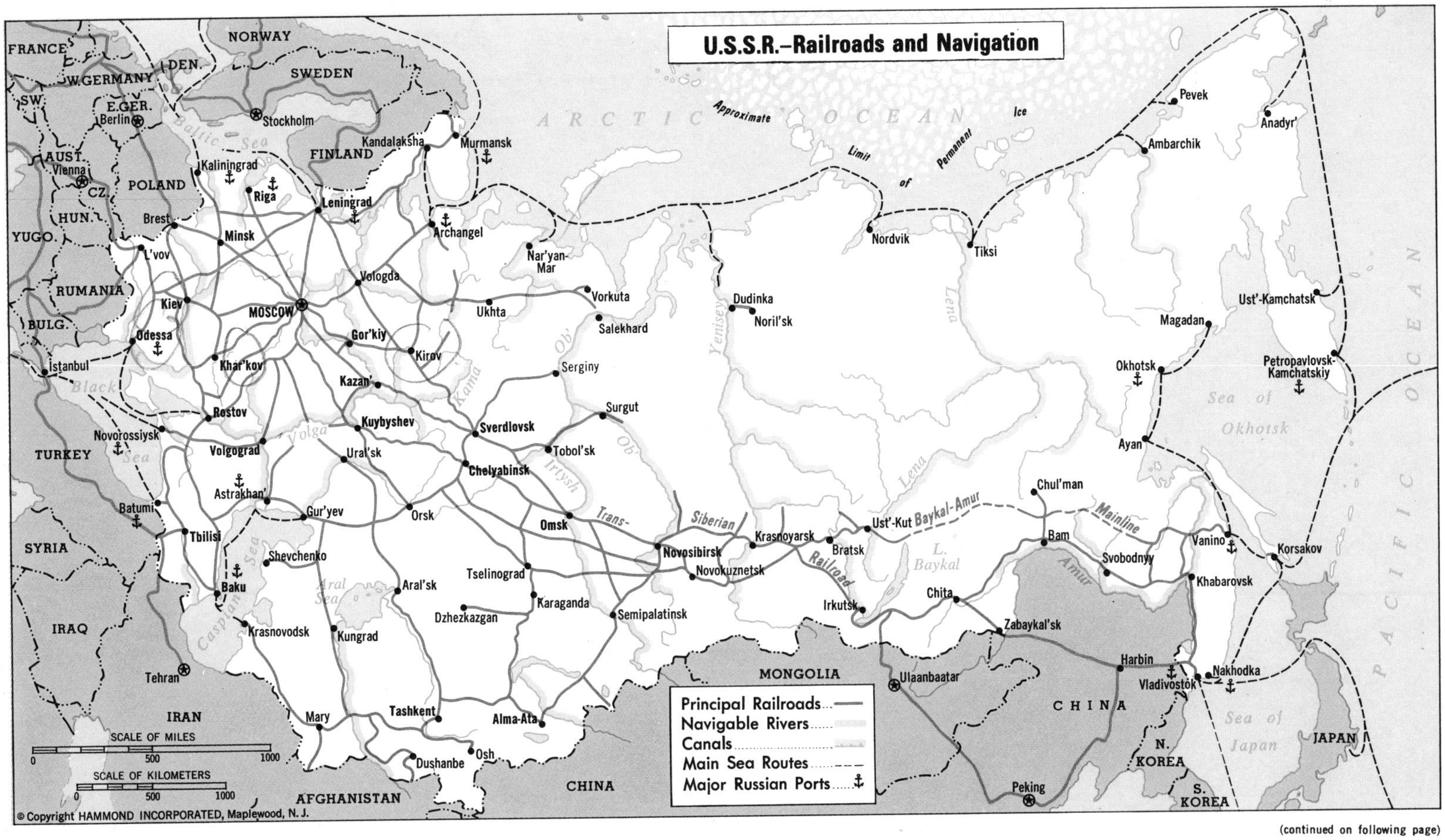

U.S.S.R.–Railroads and Navigation

FRANCE · NORWAY · DEN. · SWEDEN · W.GERMANY · SW. · E.GER. · Berlin · AUST. · Vienna · CZ. · POLAND · HUN. · YUGO. · RUMANIA · BULG. · Istanbul · TURKEY · SYRIA · IRAQ · IRAN · Tehran · AFGHANISTAN · CHINA · MONGOLIA · Ulaanbaatar · Peking · N. KOREA · S. KOREA · JAPAN

Stockholm · Kaliningrad · Riga · Kandalaksha · Murmansk · FINLAND · Leningrad · Archangel · Brest · Minsk · L'vov · Kiev · MOSCOW · Vologda · Nar'yan-Mar · Vorkuta · Ukhta · Odessa · Khar'kov · Gor'kiy · Kirov · Serginy · Surgut · Dudinka · Noril'sk · Nordvik · Tiksi · Pevek · Anadyr' · Ambarchik · Ust'-Kamchatsk · Kazan' · Kuybyshev · Sverdlovsk · Tobol'sk · Magadan · Rostov · Volgograd · Ural'sk · Chelyabinsk · Petropavlovsk-Kamchatskiy · Novorossiysk · Astrakhan' · Gur'yev · Orsk · Okhotsk · Batumi · Tbilisi · Shevchenko · Omsk · Novosibirsk · Novokuznetsk · Krasnoyarsk · Bratsk · Ust'-Kut · Bam · Chul'man · Ayan · Baku · Aral'sk · Tselinograd · Semipalatinsk · Irkutsk · Chita · Zabaykal'sk · Svobodnyy · Vanino · Korsakov · Khabarovsk · Krasnovodsk · Kungrad · Dzhezkazgan · Karaganda · Harbin · Nakhodka · Vladivostok · Mary · Tashkent · Alma-Ata · Dushanbe · Osh

ARCTIC OCEAN · Approximate Limit of Permanent Ice · PACIFIC OCEAN · Baltic Sea · Black Sea · Caspian Sea · Aral Sea · Sea of Okhotsk · Sea of Japan · L. Baykal · Ob' · Yenisey · Lena · Amur · Volga · Kama · Irtysh · Trans-Siberian Railroad · Baykal-Amur Mainline

Legend:
- Principal Railroads
- Navigable Rivers
- Canals
- Main Sea Routes
- Major Russian Ports ⚓

SCALE OF MILES 0 – 500 – 1000
SCALE OF KILOMETERS 0 – 500 – 1000

(continued on following page)

Union of Soviet Socialist Republics
European Part

CONIC PROJECTION
SCALE OF MILES
0 50 100   200   300
SCALE OF KILOMETERS
0 50 100 200   300

National Capitals ☆
Capitals of Union Republics ⬡
Administrative Centers △
International boundaries
Union Republic boundaries
A.S.S.R., Oblast, Kray boundaries
Autonomous Oblast boundaries
Autonomous Okrug boundaries

Scale 1:13,250,000

The government of the United States has not recognized the incorporation of Estonia, Latvia and Lithuania into the Soviet Union.

Administrative Divisions bear same names as their respective Capitals or Centers, except:

Abkhaz A.S.S.R.	Sukhumi	F6
Adygey Aut. Oblast	Maykop	F6
Adzhar A.S.S.R.	Batumi	F6
Bashkir A.S.S.R.	Ufa	J4
Chechen-Ingush A.S.S.R.	Groznyy	G6
Chuvash A.S.S.R.	Cheboksary	G3
Crimean Oblast	Simferopol'	D6
Dagestan A.S.S.R.	Makhachkala	G6
Kabardin-Balkar A.S.S.R.	Nal'chik	F6
Kalmuck A.S.S.R.	Elista	F5
Karachay-Cherkess Aut. Obl.	Cherkessk	F6
Karelian A.S.S.R.	Petrozavodsk	D2
Komi A.S.S.R.	Syktyvkar	H2
Komi-Permyak Aut. Okrug	Kudymkar	H3
Mari A.S.S.R.	Yoshkar-Ola	G3
Mordvinian A.S.S.R.	Saransk	G4
Nagorno-Karabakh Aut. Obl.	Stepanakert	G7
Nenets Aut. Okrug	Nar'yan-Mar	H1
North Ossetian A.S.S.R.	Ordzhonikidze	F6
South Ossetian Aut. Obl.	Tskhinvali	F6
Tatar A.S.S.R.	Kazan'	G3
Trans-Carpathian Oblast	Uzhgorod	B5
Udmurt A.S.S.R.	Izhevsk	H3
Volyn Oblast	Lutsk	C4

© Copyright HAMMOND INCORPORATED, Maplewood, N.J.

U.S.S.R. — EUROPEAN

UNION REPUBLICS

Armenian S.S.R. 3,031,000 ....F6
Azerbaidzhan S.S.R. 6,028,000 ....G6
Estonian S.S.R. 1,466,000 ....C3
Georgian S.S.R. 5,015,000 ....F6
Latvian S.S.R. 2,521,000 ....C3
Lithuanian S.S.R. 3,398,000 ....B3
Moldavian S.S.R. 3,947,000 ....C5
Russian S.F.S.R. 137,551,000 ....F3
Ukrainian S.S.R. 49,755,000 ....D5
White Russian S.S.R. 9,560,000 ....C4

INTERNAL DIVISIONS

Abkhaz A.S.S.R. 505,000 ....F6
Adygei Aut. Obl. 405,000 ....F6
Adzhar A.S.S.R. 354,000 ....F6
Bashkir A.S.S.R. 3,849,000 ....J4
Chechen-Ingush
  A.S.S.R. 1,154,000 ....G6
Chuvash A.S.S.R. 1,292,000 ....G3
Crimean Oblast 2,183,000 ....G6
Dagestan A.S.S.R. 1,628,000 ....G6
Kabardin-Balkar
  A.S.S.R. 674,000 ....F6
Kalmuck A.S.S.R. 294,000 ....F5
Karachev-Cherkess Aut. Obl. 368,000 ..F6
Karelian A.S.S.R. 736,000 ....D2
Komi A.S.S.R. 1,119,000 ....H2
Komi-Permyak Aut. Okr. 173,000 ....H3
Mari A.S.S.R. 703,000 ....G3
Mordvinian A.S.S.R. 991,000 ....G4
Nagorno-Karabakh Aut.
  Obl. 161,000 ....G7
Nakhichevan' A.S.S.R. 239,000 ....F7
Nenets Aut. Okr. 47,000 ....H1
North Ossetian
  A.S.S.R. 597,000 ....F6
South Ossetian Aut.
  Obl. 98,000 ....F6
Tatar A.S.S.R. 3,436,000 ....G3
Trans-Carpathian
  Oblast 1,155,000 ....B5
Udmurt A.S.S.R. 1,494,000 ....H3
Volyn Oblast 1,015,000 ....C4

CITIES and TOWNS

Abdulino 26,010 ....H4
Agdam 21,277 ....G6
Agryz 19,267 ....H3
Akhaltsikhe 18,972 ....F6
Akhtubinsk 43,466 ....G5
Akhty G6
Akhtyrka 41,354 ....E4
Akkerman
  (Belgorod-Dnestrovskiy) 32,928 ....D5
Alagir 18,161 ....F6
Alatyr' 43,499 ....G4
Alaverdi 21,311 ....F6
Aleksandriya 82,000 ....D5
Aleksandrovsk 18,286 ....J3
Alekseyevka 25,562 ....E4
Aleksin 67,000 ....E4
Ali-Bayramly 33,828 ....G7
Al'met'yevsk 110,000 ....H3
Alushta 22,016 ....D6
Amderma K1
Anapa 29,900 ....E6
Apatity 62,000 ....D1
Apsheronsk 32,867 ....F6
Archangel
  (Arkhangel'sk) 385,000 ....F2
Armavir 162,000 ....F5
Arzamas 93,000 ....F3
Astara G7
Astrakhan' 461,000 ....G5
Atkarsk 28,881 ....G4
Azov 75,000 ....E5
Bakhchisaray 15,912 ....D6
Baku 1,022,000 ....H6
Baku' 1,550,000 ....H6
Balakhna 96,542 ....F3
Balaklava D6
Balakovo 152,000 ....G4
Balashov 93,000 ....F4
Baltiysk 20,300 ....A4
Baranovichi 131,000 ....C4
Barysh 20,792 ....G4
Batamay 55,000 ....F4
Batumi 123,000 ....F6
Belaya Tserkov' 151,000 ....C5
Belebey 32,460 ....H4
Belev 17,733 ....E4
Belgorod 240,000 ....E4
Belgorod-Dnestrovskiy 32,928 ....D5
Belomorsk 16,595 ....D2
Belorechensk 35,970 ....F6
Beloretsk 71,000 ....J4
Belozersk E3
Bel'tsy 125,000 ....C5
Belush'ya Guba H1
Bendery 101,000 ....C5
Berdichev 80,000 ....C5
Berdyansk 122,000 ....E5
Beregovo 27,308 ....B5
Berezniki 185,000 ....J3
Beslan 26,893 ....F6
Bezhetsk 30,030 ....E3
Birsk 29,607 ....J3
Bobrov 17,977 ....F4
Bobruysk 192,000 ....D4
Bologoye 33,949 ....D3
Bor 63,000 ....F3
Borislav 33,800 ....B5
Borisoglebsk 68,000 ....F4
Borisov 112,000 ....C4
Borovichi 60,000 ....D3
Brest 177,000 ....B4
Bryansk 394,000 ....D4
Bugul'ma 80,000 ....H4
Buguruslan 54,000 ....H4
Buturlinovka 21,643 ....F4
Buy 29,960 ....F3
Buynaksk 37,946 ....G6
Buzuluk 76,000 ....H4
Bykhov 17,371 ....C4
Cěsis 17,696 ....C3
Chadyr-Lunga 20,474 ....C5
Chapayevsk 85,000 ....G4
Chausy 48,034 ....H3
Cheboksary 308,000 ....G3
Cherdyn' J2
Cherepovets 266,000 ....E3
Cherkassy 228,000 ....D5
Cherkessk 91,000 ....F6
Chernigov 238,000 ....D4
Chernivtsy 219,000 ....C5
Chernushka 33,230 ....J3
Chervonograd 55,000 ....B4
Chiatura 25,474 ....F6
Chistopol' 64,000 ....H3
Chortkov 19,183 ....B5
Chudovo D3
Danilov 20,030 ....F3
Daugavpils 116,000 ....C3
Davlekanovo 20,123 ....H4
Derbent 70,000 ....G6
Dimitrovgrad 106,000 ....G4
Dneprodzerzhinsk 250,000 ....D5
Dnepropetrovsk 1,066,000 ....D5
Dobrush 16,809 ....D4
Dobryanka 18,349 ....J3
Donetsk 1,021,000 ....E5
Drogobych 66,000 ....B5
Dubna 55,000 ....E3
Dubna E4

Dubno 25,442 ....C4
Dvinsk (Daugavpils) 116,000 ....C3
Dyat'kovo 26,825 ....D4
Dzerzhinsk 257,000 ....F3
Dzhankoy 43,459 ....D5
Dzhul'fa G7
Echmiadzin 31,819 ....F6
Elektrostal' 139,000 ....E3
Elista 70,000 ....G5
El'ton G4
Engel's 161,000 ....G4
Erivan 1,019,000 ....F6
Fastov 51,000 ....C4
Feodosiya 76,000 ....D5
Frolovo 33,398 ....F5
Furmanov 40,155 ....F3
Gagra 23,025 ....F6
Galich 19,374 ....F3
Gandzha (Kirovabad) 232,000 ....G6
Garibaldovka 75,000 ....C3
Gay 28,250 ....J4
Gaysin 23,741 ....C5
Gdov C3
Gelendzhik 29,086 ....E6
Genichesk 20,031 ....E4
Georgiu-Dezh 52,000 ....E4
Glazov 81,000 ....H3
Glubokoye C3
Glukhov 27,096 ....D4
Gomel' 383,000 ....D4
Gori 56,000 ....F6
Gor'kiy 1,344,000 ....F3
Gorlovka 336,000 ....E5
Gorodets 34,229 ....F3
Gremikha E1
Gremyachinsk 29,975 ....J3
Groznyy 375,000 ....G6
Gryazi 41,292 ....F4
Gubakha 33,243 ....J3
Gudkin 65,000 ....J4
Gudauta F6
Gudermes 32,445 ....G6
Gukovo 68,000 ....F5
Gus'-Khrustal'nyy 72,000 ....F3
Imishli 17,839 ....G7
Inta 51,000 ....K1
Inza 19,060 ....G4
Ishimbay 57,000 ....J4
Ivano-Frankovsk 150,000 ....B5
Ivanovo 465,000 ....E3
Izberbash 17,299 ....G6
Izhevsk 549,000 ....H3
Izmail 83,000 ....C5
Izyum 61,000 ....E5
Jēkabpils 22,440 ....C3
Jelgava 63,000 ....C3
Jurmala 61,000 ....B3
Kadyevka (Stakhanov) 108,000 ......E5
Kafan 29,916 ....G7
Kagul 26,249 ....C5
Kakhovka 28,472 ....D5
Kalach 18,475 ....F4
Kalach-na-Donu 20,795 ....F5
Kalinin 412,000 ....E3
Kaliningrad,
  Kaliningrad 355,000 ....B4
Kaliningrad, Moscow
  Oblast 133,000 ....E3
Kalinkovichi 23,918 ....C4
Kaluga 265,000 ....E4
Kalush 60,000 ....B5
Kamenets-Podol'skiy 81,000 ....C5
Kamenka, Penza 30,067 ....F4
Kamensk-Shakhtinskiy 72,000 ....F5
Kamyshin 112,000 ....F4
Kanash 40,682 ....G3
Kandalaksha 42,656 ....D1
Kapsukas 28,763 ....B3
Karachayevsk F6
Karachev 15,372 ....E4
Kashin 17,678 ....E3
Kasimov 33,066 ....F4
Kaspiysk 38,990 ....G6
Kaunas 370,000 ....B4
Kazan' 993,000 ....G3
Kazatin 26,649 ....C5
Kem' 21,025 ....D2
Kerch' 157,000 ....E5
Keret' D1
Khachmas 22,313 ....G6
Khadyzhensk 17,856 ....E6
Khar'kov 1,444,000 ....E5
Khasavyurt 65,000 ....G6
Khashuri 24,469 ....F6
Kherson 319,000 ....D5
Khmel'nitskiy 172,000 ....C5
Khotin C5
Khust 23,810 ....B5
Khvalynsk 16,249 ....G4
Kiev 2,144,000 ....D4
Kiliya 24,276 ....C5
Kimovsk 44,490 ....E4
Kimry 58,000 ....E3
Kinel' 39,373 ....H4
Kineshma 101,000 ....F3
Kirishi 27,252 ....D3
Kirov, Kaluga 29,355 ....D4
Kirov, Kirov 390,000 ....G3
Kirovabad 232,000 ....G6
Kirovakan 146,000 ....G6
Kirovo-Chepetsk 71,000 ....H3
Kirovograd 237,000 ....D5
Kirovsk 38,464 ....D1
Kirsanov 21,795 ....F4
Kishinev 503,000 ....C5
Kislovodsk 101,000 ....F6
Kizel 46,264 ....J3
Kizlyar 29,745 ....G6
Klaipeda 176,000 ....B3
Klintsy 67,000 ....D4
Kohtla-Järve 73,000 ....C3
Kolomiya 52,000 ....B5
Kolomna 147,000 ....E4
Kolpino 114,000 ....D3
Kommunarsk 120,000 ....E5
Komrat 21,369 ....C5
Komsomol'skiy 17,078 ....K1
Kondopoga 27,908 ....D2
Königsberg
  (Kaliningrad) 355,000 ....B4
Konotop 82,000 ....D4
Konstantinovka 112,000 ....E5
Korenovsk 26,323 ....E5
Korosten' 65,000 ....C4
Korostyshev 21,153 ....C4
Koryazhma 33,230 ....G2
Kostopol' 17,548 ....C4
Kostroma 255,000 ....F3
Kotel'nich 29,184 ....G3
Kotel'nikovo 19,063 ....F5
Kotlas 61,000 ....G2
Kotovo 20,553 ....G4
Kotovsk, Odessa 36,463 ....C5
Kotovsk, Tambov 33,347 ....F4
Kovel' 33,351 ....C4
Kovrov 143,000 ....F3
Kovylkino 17,300 ....F4
Kramatorsk 178,000 ....E5
Krasnoarmeysk 60,000 ....G4
Krasnodar 560,000 ....E6
Krasnograd 18,386 ....E5
Krasnokamsk 56,000 ....J3
Krasnoslobodsk 17,749 ....G4
Krasnovishersk J2
Krasnyy Kut 17,087 ....G4
Krasnyy Luch 106,000 ....E5

Krasnyy Sulin 41,684 ....F5
Kremenchug 210,000 ....D5
Krichev 25,682 ....D4
Krivoy Rog 650,000 ....D5
Krolevets 18,000 ....D4
Kronshtadt 39,477 ....C3
Kropotkin 70,000 ....E5
Krymsk 41,430 ....E6
Kuba 18,871 ....G6
Kudymkar 26,350 ....H3
Kulebaki 46,252 ....F3
Kumertau 52,000 ....J4
Kunda C3
Kungur 80,000 ....J3
Kupyansk 30,055 ....E5
Kuressaare 12,140 ....B3
Kurgan 20,374 ....C4
Kursk 375,000 ....E4
Kutaisi 194,000 ....F6
Kuvandyk 22,914 ....J4
Kuybyshev 1,216,000 ....G4
Kuznetsk 94,000 ....G4
Kuzomen' E1
Labinsk 54,000 ....F6
Lakhdenpoh'ya C2
Lebedin 29,240 ....D4
Leningrad 4,073,000 ....D3
Leningrad' 4,588,000 ....D3
Leninogorsk 54,000 ....H4
Lenkoran' 35,505 ....G7
Lida 66,000 ....C4
Liepāja 108,000 ....B3
Likhoslavl' E3
Lipetsk 396,000 ....E4
Lisichansk 119,000 ....E5
Lozovaya 53,000 ....E5
Lubny 54,000 ....D4
Lodeynoye Pole 19,632 ....D2
Luga 31,905 ....D3
Lutsk 134,000 ....C4
L'vov (Lwów) 667,000 ....B5
Lys'va 75,000 ....J3
Lyubertsy 160,000 ....E4
Lyubotin 33,324 ....E5
Lyudinovo 33,871 ....D4
Makeyevka 436,000 ....E5
Makhachkala 251,000 ....G6
Makharadze 21,679 ....F6
Malaya Vishera 15,381 ....D3
Malgobek 20,548 ....F6
Manturovo 21,510 ....F3
Marganets 50,000 ....D5
Mariupol' (Zhdanov) 503,000 ....E5
Marks 31,122 ....G4
Maykop 128,000 ....F6
Mednogorsk 38,420 ....J4
Medvezh'yegorsk 17,465 ....D2
Melenki 18,545 ....F3
Meleuz 24,851 ....J4
Melitopol' 161,000 ....E5
Memel (Klaipeda) 176,000 ....B3
Merefa 29,865 ....E5
Mezen' F1
Michurinsk 101,000 ....F4
Mikhaylovka 58,000 ....F4
Millerovo 34,627 ....F5
Mineral'nye Vody 67,000 ....F6
Mingechaur 60,000 ....G6
Minsk 1,262,000 ....C4
Minsk' 1,276,000 ....C4
Mirgorod 28,407 ....D4
Mogilev 290,000 ....D4
Mogilev-Podol'skiy 26,051 ....C5
Molodechno 73,000 ....C4
Molotov (Perm') 999,000 ....J3
Monchegorsk 51,000 ....D1
Morshansk 44,245 ....F4
Moscow (Moskva)
  (cap.) 7,831,000 ....E3
Moscow' 8,011,000 ....E3
Mozhaysk 20,321 ....E3
Mozhga 38,930 ....H3
Mtsensk 27,833 ....E4
Mukachevo 72,000 ....B5
Murmansk 381,000 ....D1
Murom 114,000 ....F3
Mytishchi 141,000 ....E3
Naberezhnye Chelny 301,000 ....H3
Nadvoitsy D2
Nal'chik 207,000 ....F6
Nar'yan-Mar 16,864 ....H1
Narkhov B5
Naro-Fominsk 58,000 ....E3
Nartkala 27,000 ....F6
Nazran' F6
Neftekamsk 70,000 ....H3
Nelidovo 29,813 ....D3
Nerekhta 25,722 ....F3
Nevel' 17,804 ....C3
Nevinnomyssk 104,000 ....F6

Nezhin 70,000 ....D4
Nikel' 21,299 ....C1
Nikolayev 440,000 ....D5
Nikol'sk 20,740 ....G4
Nikopol' 146,000 ....D5
Nizhnekamsk 134,000 ....H3
Nizhniy Lomov 17,460 ....F4
Nizhniy Novgorod
  (Gor'kiy) 1,344,000 ....F3
Nosovka 19,430 ....D4
Novaya Kakhovka 52,000 ....D5
Novgorod 186,000 ....D3
Novgorod-Severskiy D4
Novoanninskiy 20,461 ....F4
Novocherkassk 183,000 ....F5
Novograd-Volynskiy 41,194 ....C4
Novogrudok 19,374 ....C4
Novokuybyshevsk 109,000 ....G4
Novomoskovsk 147,000 ....E4
Novopolotsk 67,000 ....C3
Novorossiysk 159,000 ....E6
Novoshakhtinsk 104,000 ....E5
Novotroitsk 95,000 ....J4
Novoukrainka 19,554 ....D5
Novouzensk G4
Novovolynsk 41,187 ....B4
Novovyatsk 26,408 ....G3
Novozybkov 34,433 ....D4
Nurlat 17,533 ....H4
Nyandoma 23,366 ....F2
Nytva 17,491 ....H3
Nyuvchim H2
Obninsk 73,000 ....E3
Ochamchira 18,718 ....F6
Odessa 1,046,000 ....D5
Oktyabr'sk 33,981 ....G4
Oktyabr'skiy 88,000 ....H4
Olekma 19,194 ....D3
Olenegorsk 21,485 ....D1
Omsk 54,000 ....D4
Omutninsk 28,777 ....H3
Onega 25,047 ....E2
Ordzhonikidze 279,000 ....F6
Orel 305,000 ....E4
Orenburg 459,000 ....J4
Orgeyev 25,798 ....C5
Orsha 112,000 ....C4
Orsk 247,000 ....J4
Osa 15,038 ....J3
Osipenko (Berdyansk) 122,000 ....E5
Osipovichi 71,705 ....C4
Ostashkov 23,419 ....D3
Ostrogozhsk 39,921 ....E4
Ostrov 22,369 ....C3
Otradnyy 44,426 ....H4
Panevėžys 102,000 ....B3
Pärnu 51,000 ....C3
Pavlograd 107,000 ....E5
Pavlovo 68,000 ....F3
Pechenga D1
Pechora 56,000 ....J1
Penza 483,000 ....G4
Perm' 999,000 ....J3
Pervomaysk 72,000 ....D5
Petrokrepost' D3
Petrovsk 30,953 ....G4
Petrozavodsk 234,000 ....D2
Petsamo (Pechenga) D1
Podol'sk 202,000 ....E3
Podporozh'ye 21,545 ....D2
Pokrovskoye 26,125 ....H4
Polonnoye 22,484 ....C4
Polotsk 71,000 ....C3
Poltava 279,000 ....D5
Polyarnyy 15,321 ....D1
Ponoy F1
Povenets D2
Povorino 20,591 ....F4
Priluki 65,000 ....D4
Primorsk C3
Primorsko-Akhtarsk 25,981 ....E5
Priozersk 18,000 ....D2
Privolzhskiy 23,041 ....G4
Prokhladnyy 40,074 ....F6
Pskov 176,000 ....C3
Pushkin 90,000 ....D3
Pyatigorsk 110,000 ....F6
Rabochostrov D2
Rakhov B5
Rakvere 17,891 ....C3
Rasskazovo 40,038 ....F4
Razdan 26,833 ....F6
Rechitsa 60,000 ....D4
Reni 19,625 ....C5
Revel (Tallinn) 430,000 ....B3

Rēzekne 30,803 ....C3
Riga 835,000 ....B3
Romny 53,000 ....D4
Roslavl' 56,000 ....D4
Rossosh' 36,438 ....E4
Rostov 30,815 ....E3
Rostov-na-Donu 934,000 ....F5
Rovno 179,000 ....C4
Rtishchevo 37,146 ....F4
Rubezhnoye 66,000 ....E5
Rustavi 129,000 ....G6
Ruzayevka 41,084 ....F4
Ryazan' 453,000 ....F4
Ryazhsk 25,425 ....F4
Rybinsk 239,000 ....E3
Rybnitsa 32,266 ....C5
Rzhev 69,000 ....D3
Safonovo 53,000 ....D3
Saki 24,208 ....D5
Salavat 137,000 ....J4
Sal'sk 57,000 ....F5
Sal'yany 24,223 ....G7
Samara (Kuybyshev) 1,216,000 ......H4
Sambor 29,253 ....B5
Saransk 263,000 ....G4
Sarapul 107,000 ....H3
Saratov 856,000 ....G4
Sasovo 27,228 ....F4
Segezha 28,810 ....D2
Semenov 23,633 ....F3
Semলuki 18,221 ....E4
Sengiley G4
Serdobol (Sortavala) 22,188 ....D2
Serdobsk 33,783 ....F4
Sergach 22,509 ....F3
Serpukhov 140,000 ....E4
Sevastopol' 301,000 ....D6
Severodonetsk 113,000 ....E5
Severodvinsk 197,000 ....E2
Severomorsk 50,000 ....D1
Shakhty 209,000 ....F5
Shakhun'ya 20,000 ....G3
Shar'ya 25,788 ....G3
Shchekino 70,000 ....E4
Shchigry 17,133 ....E4
Shebekino 37,000 ....E4
Shemakha 17,986 ....G6
Shepetovka 38,707 ....C4
Shostka 82,000 ....D4
Shpola 19,806 ....D5
Shumerlya 33,816 ....G3
Shuya 72,000 ....F3
Siauliai 118,000 ....B3
Sibay 37,648 ....J4
Simferopol' 302,000 ....D6
Skadovsk D5
Skopin 24,429 ....F4
Slantsy 41,146 ....C3
Slavuta 25,573 ....C4
Slavyansk 140,000 ....E5
Slavyansk-na-Kubani 54,000 ....E5
Slobodskoy 34,374 ....H3
Slonim 30,279 ....C4
Slutsk 35,609 ....C4
Smela 62,000 ....D5
Smolensk 276,000 ....D4
Sochi 287,000 ....F6
Sokol 48,243 ....F3
Soligorsk 65,000 ....C4
Solikamsk 101,000 ....J3
Sol'-Iletsk 22,227 ....J4
Sorochinsk 23,235 ....H4
Soroki 21,924 ....C5
Sortavala 22,188 ....D2
Sosnogorsk 24,688 ....H2
Sovetsk (Tilsit) 38,456 ....B3
Sovetsk 17,027 ....G3
Sovetskaya Gavan' Q5
Staraya Russa 34,577 ....D3
Staryy Oskol 115,000 ....E4
Stavropol' 258,000 ....F6
Stepanakert 30,293 ....G7
Sterlitamak 220,000 ....J4
Stupino 70,000 ....E4
Sudak D6
Sukhumi 114,000 ....F6
Sumgait 190,000 ....G6
Sumy 228,000 ....E4
Suzdal 23,963 ....F3
Svetlograd 40,265 ....F5
Syktyvkar 171,000 ....H2
Syzran' 178,000 ....G4
Taganrog 291,000 ....E5
Taldom E3
Tallinn (cap.) 430,000 ....B3
Tambov 270,000 ....F4
Tartu 105,000 ....C3
Taurage 19,461 ....B3
Tbilisi 1,066,000 ....F6
Telavi 21,179 ....G6

Telšiai 20,220 ....B3
Temryuk 23,172 ....E5
Ternopol' 144,000 ....C5
Teykovo 41,607 ....E3
Tiflis (Tbilisi) 1,066,000 ....F6
Tighina (Bendery) 101,000 ....C5
Tikhoretsk 64,000 ....F5
Tikhvin 59,000 ....D3
Tilsit (Sovetsk) 38,456 ....B4
Timashevsk 29,055 ....E5
Tiraspol' 139,000 ....C5
Togliatti (Tol'yatti) 502,000 ....G4
Tokmak 59,000 ....E5
Toropets 16,863 ....D3
Torzhok 45,443 ....D3
Troitsko-Pechorsk J2
Tskhinvali 30,311 ....F6
Tuapse 60,000 ....E6
Tukums 14,800 ....B3
Tula 514,000 ....E4
Tutayev 16,839 ....E3
Tuymazy 37,021 ....H4
Tver (Kalinin) 412,000 ....E3
Tyrnyauz 18,253 ....F6
Uchaly 21,808 ....J4
Ufa 969,000 ....J4
Uglich 35,483 ....E3
Ukmerge 21,663 ....C3
Ul'yanovsk 464,000 ....G4
Uman' 79,000 ....D5
Unecha 21,749 ....D4
Ungeny 17,228 ....C5
Uryupinsk 38,192 ....F4
Usinsk J1
Usman' 20,150 ....E4
Uvarovo 24,946 ....F4
Uzhgorod 91,000 ....B5
Uzlovaya 65,000 ....E4
Valga 16,795 ....C3
Valmiera 20,331 ....C3
Valuyki 29,093 ....E4
Vasil'kov 26,741 ....D4
Velikiye Luki 102,000 ....D3
Velikiy Ustyug 36,737 ....F2
Vel'sk 21,899 ....F2
Ventspils 40,467 ....B3
Vereshchagino 23,585 ....H3
Vichuga 52,000 ....F3
Viipuri (Vyborg) 76,000 ....C2
Vileyka C4
Vilna (Vilnius) 481,000 ....C4
Vinnitsa 314,000 ....C5
Vinogradov 20,580 ....B5
Vitebsk 297,000 ....C3
Vladimir 296,000 ....F3
Vladimir-Volynskiy 28,412 ....B4
Vlodogdonsk 91,000 ....F5
Volgograd 929,000 ....F5
Volkhov 47,025 ....D3
Volkovysk 28,266 ....B4
Vologda 237,000 ....E3
Vol'sk 66,000 ....G4
Volzhsk 52,000 ....G3
Volzhskiy 209,000 ....G5
Vorkuta 100,000 ....K1
Voronezh 783,000 ....E4
Voroshilovgrad 463,000 ....E5
Voskresensk 76,000 ....E3
Votkinsk 90,000 ....H3
Voznesensk 36,453 ....D5
Vyatskiye Polyany 32,729 ....H3
Vyaz'ma 52,000 ....D3
Vyborg 76,000 ....C2
Vyksa 76,000 ....F3
Vyshniy Volochek 72,000 ....D3
Yalta 80,000 ....D6
Yanaul 20,115 ....J3
Yaroslavl' 597,000 ....E3
Yartsevo 36,662 ....D3
Yefremov 53,000 ....E4
Yelabuga 31,728 ....H3
Yelets 112,000 ....E4
Yenakiyevo 114,000 ....E5
Yershov 21,731 ....G4
Yessentuki 78,000 ....F6
Yevlakh 29,462 ....G6
Yevpatoria 93,000 ....D5
Yeysk 71,000 ....E5
Yoshkar-Ola 201,000 ....G3
Yur'yevets 20,144 ....F3
Zagorsk 107,000 ....E3
Zapolyarnyy 22,286 ....D1
Zaporozh'ye 781,000 ....E5
Zelenodol'sk 85,000 ....G3
Zelenogradsk 29,691 ....A4
Zernograd 20,324 ....F5
Zheleznodorozhnyy 29,061 ....H2
Zheleznogorsk 65,000 ....E4
Zhigulevsk 52,130 ....G4

Zhitomir 244,000 ....C4
Zhlobin 25,359 ....D4
Zhmerinka 36,195 ....C5
Zhodino 22,083 ....C4
Zhovtnevoye 31,102 ....D5
Zmeinogorsk 27,393 ....D5
Zolotonosha 27,639 ....D5
Zugdidi 39,896 ....F6
Zuyevka 17,001 ....H3

OTHER FEATURES

Apsheron (pen.) H6
Araks (riv.) G7
Azov (sea) E5
Baltic (sea) B3
Barents (sea) E1
Belaya (riv.) J4
Beloye (lake) E2
Black (sea) D6
Bug (riv.) B4
Bug (riv.) D5
Caspian (sea) G6
Caucasus (mts.) F6
Crimea (pen.) D5
Desna (riv.) D4
Dnieper (riv.) D5
Dniester (riv.) C5
Don (riv.) F5
Donets (riv.) E5
Dvina (bay) E2
Dvina, Northern (riv.) F2
Dvina, Western (riv.) C3
Dykh-Tau (mt.) F6
El'brus (mt.) F6
Finland (gulf) C3
Hiiumaa (isl.) B3
Il'men' (lake) D3
Imandra (lake) D1
Kakhovka (res.) D5
Kama (riv.) H2
Kandalaksha (gulf) D1
Kanin (pen.) G1
Kara (sea) K1
Karskiye Vorota (str.) J1
Kazbek (mt.) F6
Khopér (riv.) F4
Kola (pen.) E1
Kolguyev (isl.) G1
Kuban' (riv.) E5
Kura (riv.) G6
Kuybyshev (res.) G4
Ladoga (lake) D2
Lapland (reg.) D1
Mezen' (riv.) G1
Moksha (riv.) F4
Narodnaya (mt.) J1
Niemen (riv.) B4
Novaya Zemlya (isls.) H1
Oka (riv.) E4
Onega (bay) E2
Onega (lake) E2
Onega (riv.) E2
Pechora (riv.) H1
Peipus (lake) C3
Pripet (marshes) C4
Pripyat' (riv.) C4
Prut (riv.) C5
Rybachiy (pen.) D1
Rybinsk (res.) E3
Saaremaa (isl.) B3
Samara (riv.) H4
Sevan (lake) G6
Seym (riv.) D4
Svir' (riv.) D2
Timan (ridge) G1
Tsil'ma (riv.) H1
Tsimlyansk (res.) F5
Tuloma (riv.) D1
Ural (mts.) J2
Ural (riv.) J4
Ussuri K1
Vaalak (hills) C1
Vaygach (isl.) K1
Velikaya (riv.) C3
Volga (riv.) G5
Volga-Don (canal) F5
Volgograd (res.) G4
Volkhov (riv.) D3
Vychegda (riv.) H2
Vyg (lake) D2
White (sea) E1
Yamantau (mt.) J4
Yugorskiy (pen.) K1

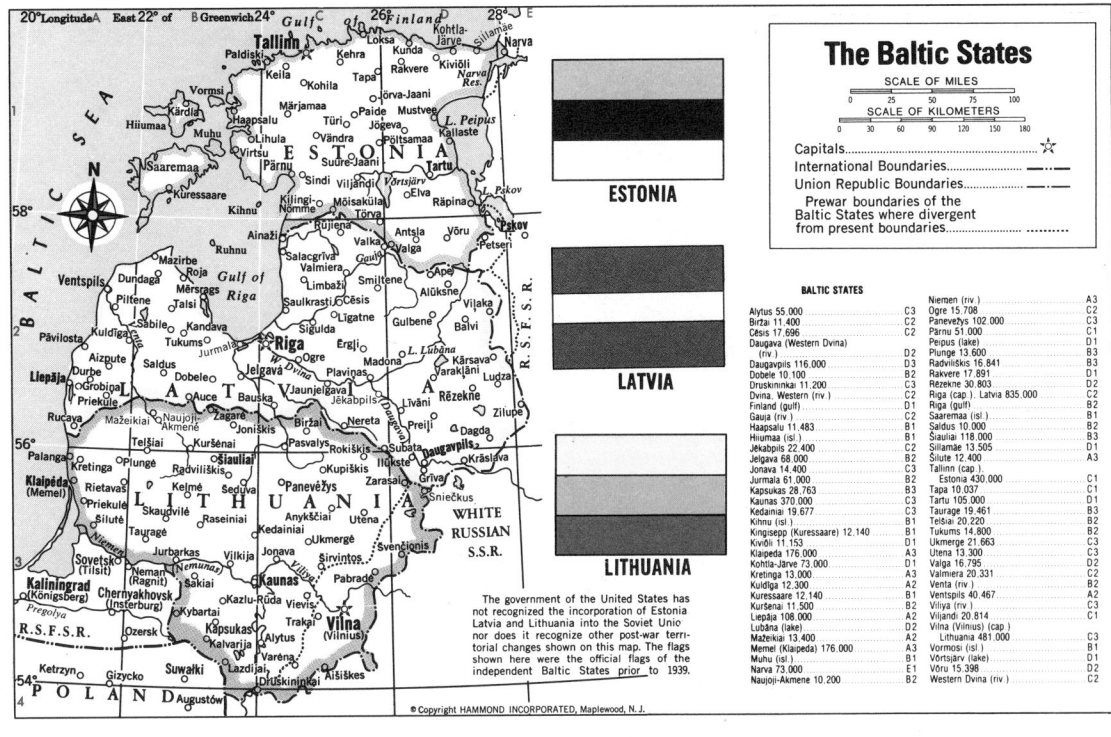

The Baltic States

SCALE OF MILES
0   25   50   75   100
SCALE OF KILOMETERS
0   30   60   90   120 150 180

Capitals...☆
International Boundaries..............━ ━ ━
Union Republic Boundaries...........━ ━ ━
Prewar boundaries of the
Baltic States where divergent
from present boundaries.........................

ESTONIA

LATVIA

LITHUANIA

The government of the United States has
not recognized the incorporation of Estonia
Latvia and Lithuania into the Soviet Unio
nor does it recognize other post-war territorial changes shown on this map. The flags
shown here were the official flags of the
independent Baltic States prior to 1939.

© Copyright HAMMOND INCORPORATED, Maplewood, N.J.

BALTIC STATES

Alytus 55,000 ....C3
Biržai 11,400 ....C2
Cēsis 17,696 ....C2
Daugava (Western Dvina)
  (riv.) D2
Dobele 10,100 ....B2
Druskininkai 11,200 ....C3
Dvina, Western (riv.) C2
Finland (gulf) C1
Gauja (riv.) C2
Haapsalu 11,483 ....B1
Hiiumaa (isl.) B1
Jēkabpils 22,400 ....C2
Jelgava 63,000 ....B2
Jonava 14,400 ....C3
Jurmala 61,000 ....B2
Kapsukas 28,763 ....B3
Kaunas 370,000 ....C3
Kedainiai 19,677 ....C3
Keila B1
Kingisepp (Kuressaare) 12,140 ....B1
Kivõli 11,153 ....D1
Klaipeda 176,000 ....B2
Kohtla-Järve 73,000 ....D1
Kretinga 13,000 ....A3
Kretinga 13,000 ....A3
Kuldīga 12,300 ....A2
Kuressaare 12,140 ....B1
Kuršėnai 11,500 ....B2
Liepāja 108,000 ....A2
Lubāna (lake) D2
Mažeikiai 13,400 ....A2
Memel (Klaipeda) 176,000 ....B2

Niemen (riv.) A3
Ogre 15,708 ....C2
Panevėžys 102,000 ....C2
Pärnu 51,000 ....C1
Peipus (lake) D1
Plunge 13,600 ....B3
Radviliskis 16,841 ....B3
Rakvere 17,891 ....D1
Rēzekne 30,803 ....D2
Riga (cap.), Latvia 835,000 ....C2
Riga (gulf) B1
Saaremaa (isl.) B1
Saldus 10,000 ....B2
Siauliai 118,000 ....B3
Siliamäe 13,505 ....D1
Sindi 12,400 ....C1
Tallinn (cap.) C1
Estonia 430,000 ....C1
Tapa 10,037 ....C1
Tartu 105,000 ....D1
Tauragė 19,461 ....B3
Telšiai 20,220 ....B3
Tukums 14,800 ....B2
Ukmerge 21,663 ....C3
Utena 13,300 ....C3
Valga 16,795 ....D2
Valmiera 20,331 ....C2
Venta (riv.) B2
Ventspils 40,467 ....A2
Viljandi 20,814 ....C1
Viļani (riv.) (cap.) C4
Vōrtsjarv (lake) C1
Vōru 15,398 ....D2
Western Dvina (riv.) C2

*City and suburbs.

Asia

LAMBERT AZIMUTHAL EQUAL-AREA PROJECTION

SCALE OF MILES

0 100 200   400   600   800   1000   1200

SCALE OF KILOMETERS

0   200 400 600 800 1000 1200

Capitals of Countries .... ⊛

Other Capitals .... ⊛

International Boundaries .... —·—·—

Other Boundaries.................. —·—··—

Canals .... ⊢⊣⊢⊣⊢

Scale 1: 46,500,000

© Copyright HAMMOND INCORPORATED, Maplewood, N.J.

Population Distribution

AREA 17,128,500 sq. mi.
(44,362,815 sq. km.)
POPULATION 2,633,000,000
LARGEST CITY Tokyo
HIGHEST POINT Mt. Everest 29,028 ft.
(8,848 m.)
LOWEST POINT Dead Sea -1,296 ft.
(-395 m.)

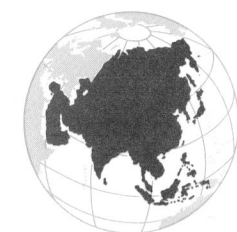

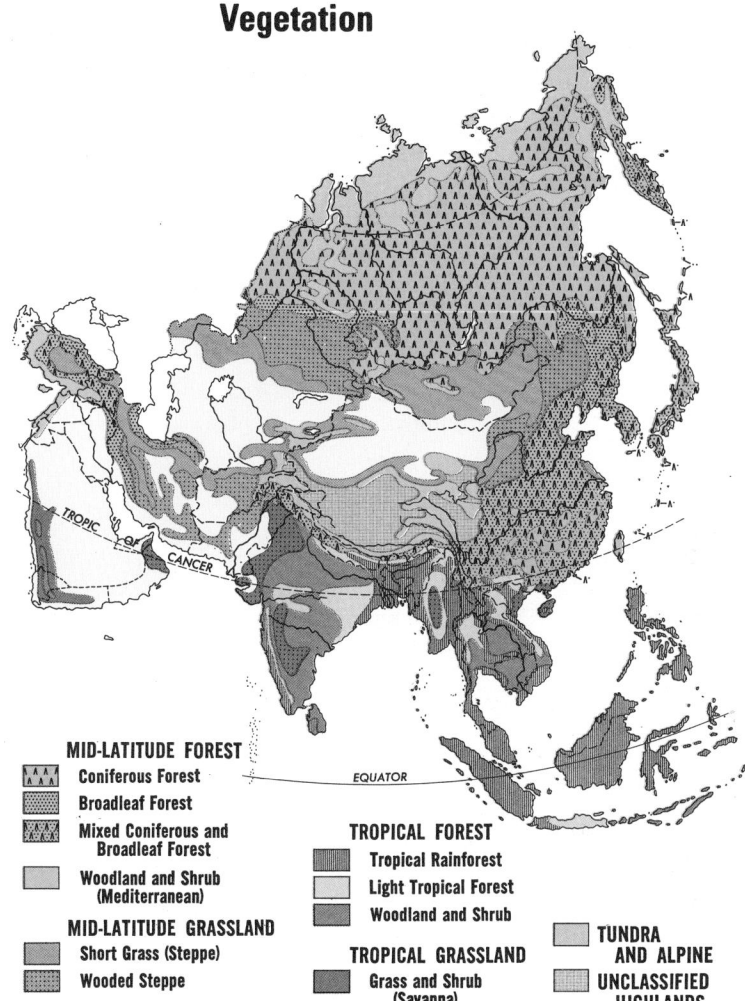

DENSITY PER

SQ. KILOMETER	SQ. MILE
Over 100	Over 260
50-100	130-260
10-50	25-130
1-10	3-25
Under 1	Under 3

• Cities with over 2,000,000 inhabitants (including suburbs)

○ Cities with over 1,000,000 inhabitants (including suburbs)

Vegetation

MID-LATITUDE FOREST
Coniferous Forest
Broadleaf Forest
Mixed Coniferous and Broadleaf Forest
Woodland and Shrub (Mediterranean)

MID-LATITUDE GRASSLAND
Short Grass (Steppe)
Wooded Steppe

DESERT AND DESERT SHRUB

TROPICAL FOREST
Tropical Rainforest
Light Tropical Forest
Woodland and Shrub

TROPICAL GRASSLAND
Grass and Shrub (Savanna)
Wooded Savanna

TUNDRA AND ALPINE

UNCLASSIFIED HIGHLANDS

Average January Temperature

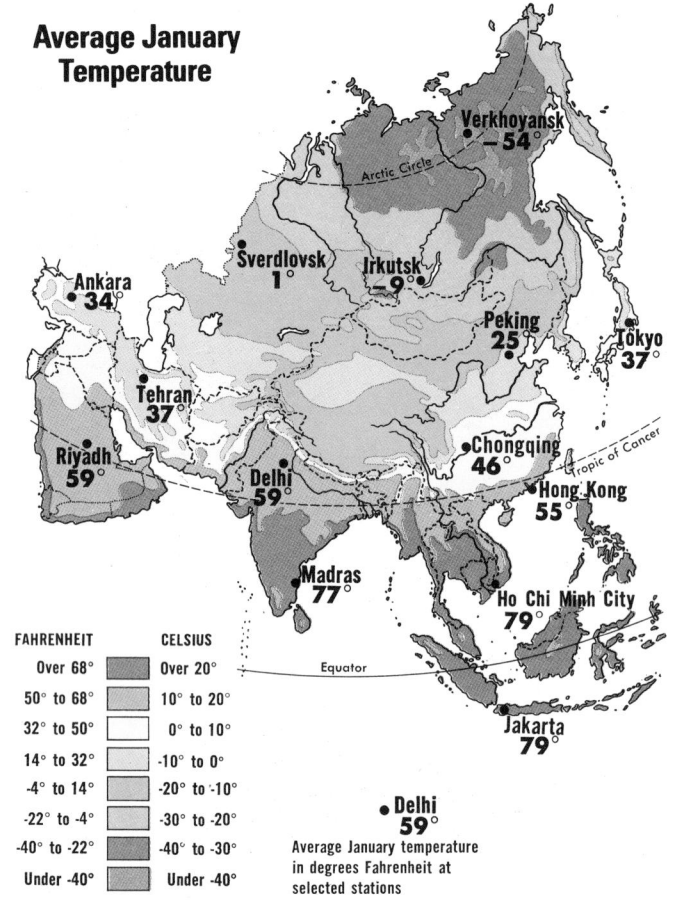

Verkhoyansk −54°
Sverdlovsk 1°
Irkutsk −9°
Ankara 34°
Peking 25°
Tokyo 37°
Tehran 37°
Chongqing 46°
Riyadh 59°
Delhi 59°
Hong Kong 55°
Madras 77°
Ho Chi Minh City 79°
Jakarta 79°

Arctic Circle
Tropic of Cancer
Equator

FAHRENHEIT	CELSIUS
Over 68°	Over 20°
50° to 68°	10° to 20°
32° to 50°	0° to 10°
14° to 32°	−10° to 0°
−4° to 14°	−20° to −10°
−22° to −4°	−30° to −20°
−40° to −22°	−40° to −30°
Under −40°	Under −40°

• Delhi 59°
Average January temperature in degrees Fahrenheit at selected stations

Average July Temperature

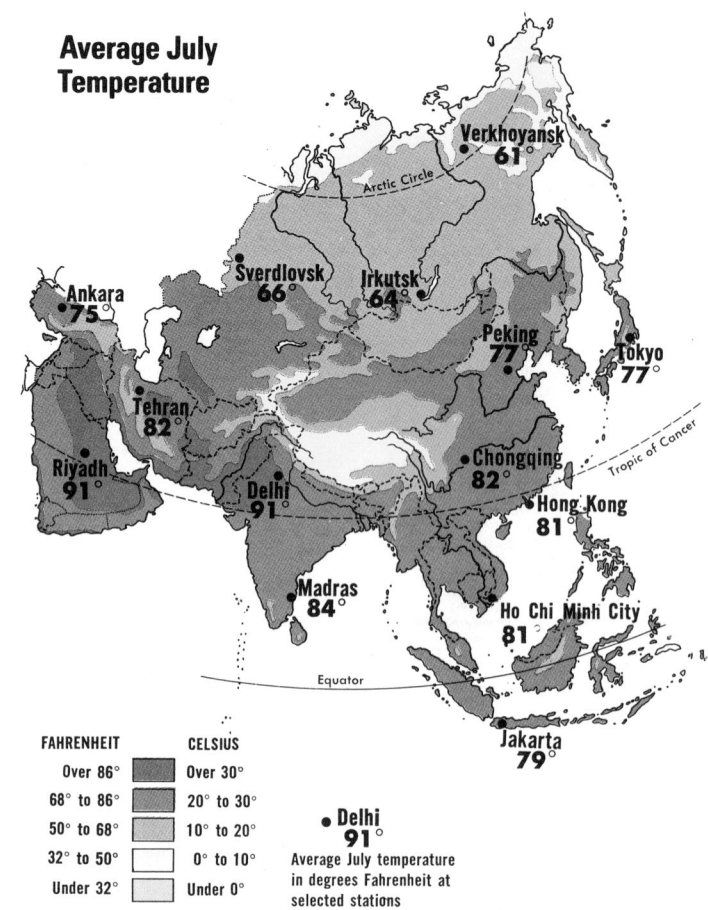

Verkhoyansk 61°
Sverdlovsk 66°
Irkutsk 64°
Ankara 75°
Peking 77°
Tokyo 77°
Tehran 82°
Chongqing 82°
Riyadh 91°
Delhi 91°
Hong Kong 81°
Madras 84°
Ho Chi Minh City 81°
Jakarta 79°

Arctic Circle
Tropic of Cancer
Equator

FAHRENHEIT	CELSIUS
Over 86°	Over 30°
68° to 86°	20° to 30°
50° to 68°	10° to 20°
32° to 50°	0° to 10°
Under 32°	Under 0°

• Delhi 91°
Average July temperature in degrees Fahrenheit at selected stations

Rainfall

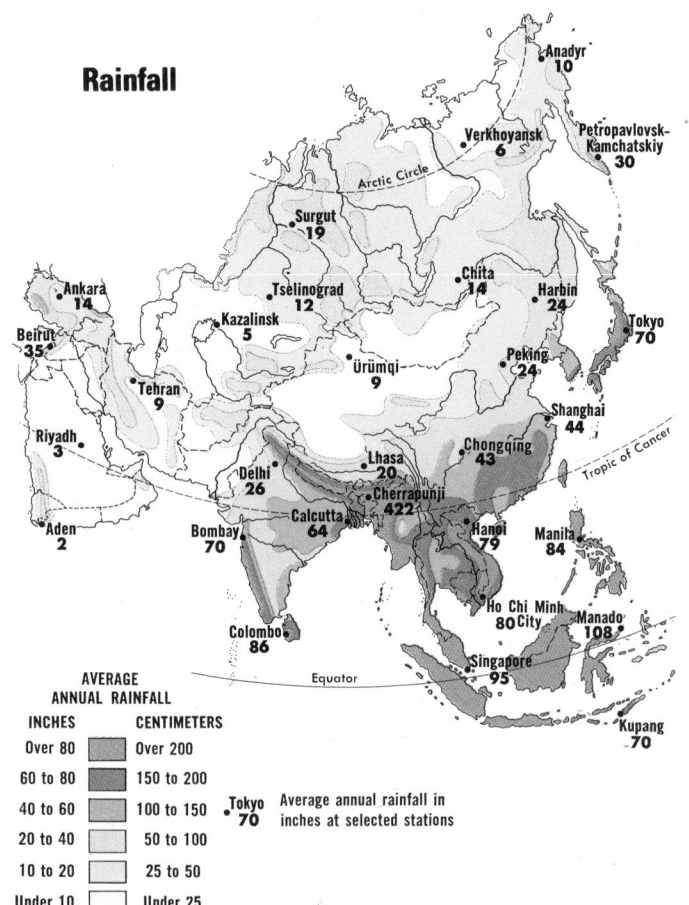

Anadyr 10
Verkhoyansk 6
Petropavlovsk-Kamchatskiy 30
Surgut 19
Chita 14
Harbin 24
Tselinograd 12
Tokyo 70
Ankara 14
Kazalinsk 5
Peking 24
Beirut 35
Ürümqi 9
Shanghai 44
Tehran 9
Riyadh 3
Lhasa 20
Chongqing 43
Delhi 26
Cherrapunji 422
Aden 2
Calcutta 64
Hanoi 79
Manila 84
Bombay 70
Ho Chi Minh City 80
Manado 108
Colombo 86
Singapore 95
Kupang 70

Arctic Circle
Tropic of Cancer
Equator

AVERAGE ANNUAL RAINFALL

INCHES	CENTIMETERS
Over 80	Over 200
60 to 80	150 to 200
40 to 60	100 to 150
20 to 40	50 to 100
10 to 20	25 to 50
Under 10	Under 25

• Tokyo 70
Average annual rainfall in inches at selected stations

Vegetation/Relief

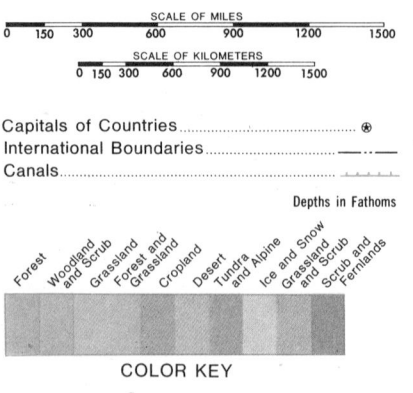

SCALE OF MILES
0 150 300 600 900 1200 1500

SCALE OF KILOMETERS
0 150 300 600 900 1200 1500

Capitals of Countries .... ⊛
International Boundaries ....
Canals ....

Depths in Fathoms

Forest
Woodland and Scrub
Grassland
Forest and Grassland
Cropland
Desert
Tundra and Alpine
Ice and Snow
Grassland and Scrub
Scrub and Fernlands

COLOR KEY

Longitude 70° East of Greenwich

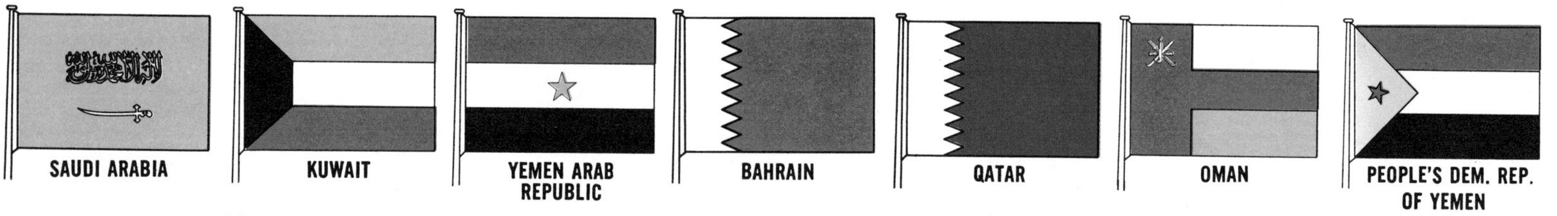

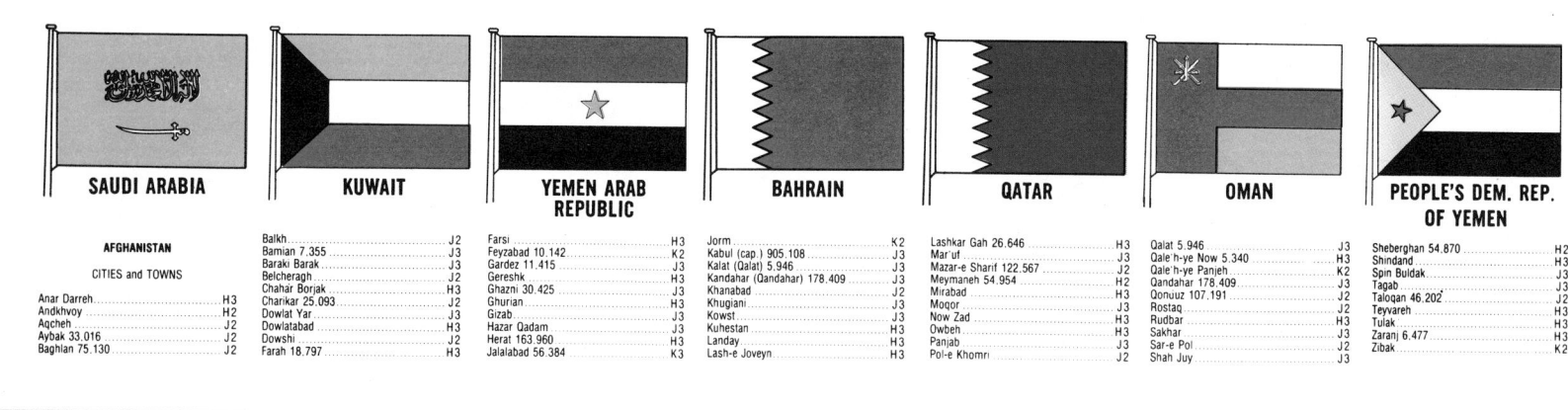

AFGHANISTAN

CITIES and TOWNS

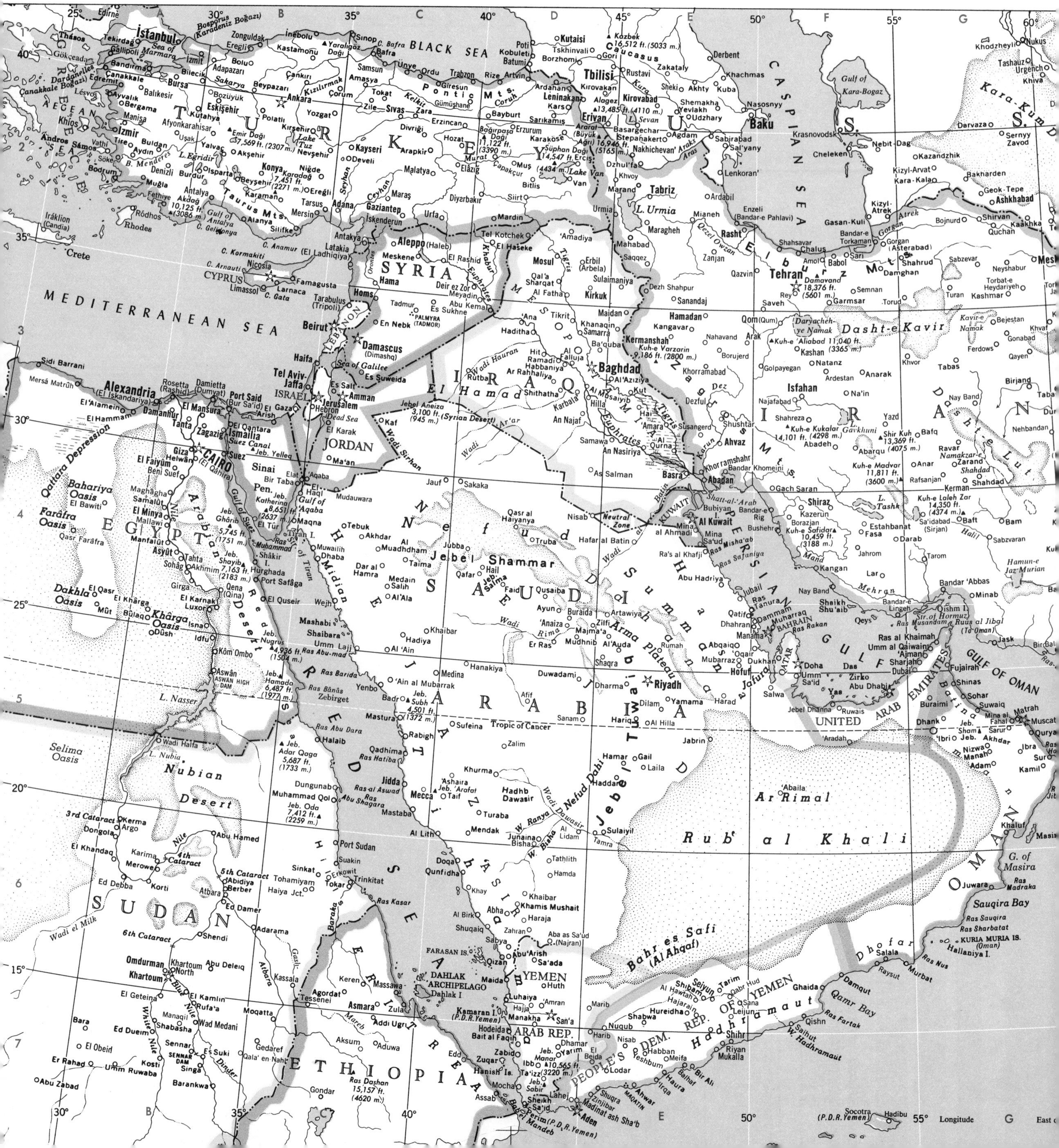

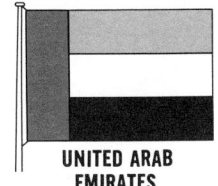

UNITED ARAB EMIRATES

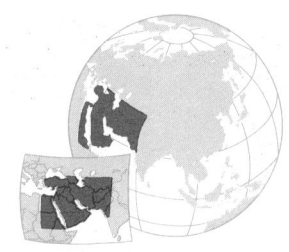

OTHER FEATURES

Farah Rud (riv.)	H3
Gowd-e Zerreh (depr.)	H4
Harirud (riv.)	H3
Helmand (riv.)	J3
Hindu Kush (mts.)	J2
Kabul (riv.)	K3
Konar (riv.)	K2
Lurah (riv.)	J3

Märgow, Dasht-e (des.)	H3
Murghab (riv.)	H2
Namakzar (salt lake)	H3
Paropamisus (mts.)	H3
Rigestan (reg.)	H3

BAHRAIN

CITIES and TOWNS

Manama (cap.) 88,785	F4
Muharraq 37,732	F4

GAZA STRIP

CITIES and TOWNS

Gaza* 118,272	B3

IRAN

CITIES and TOWNS

Abadan 296,081	E3
Abadeh 16,000	F3
Abarqu 8,000	F3
Ahvaz 329,006	E3

Amol 68,782	F2
Anar 463	G3
Anarak 2,038	F3
Arak 114,507	E3
Ardabil 147,404	E2
Ardestan 5,868	F3
Asterabad (Gorgan) 88,348	F2
Babol 67,790	F2
Bafq 5,000	G3
Baft 6,000	G4

(continued on following page)

SAUDI ARABIA

AREA 829,995 sq. mi.
(2,149,687 sq. km.)
POPULATION 8,367,000
CAPITAL Riyadh
MONETARY UNIT Saudi riyal
MAJOR LANGUAGE Arabic
MAJOR RELIGION Islam

YEMEN ARAB REPUBLIC

AREA 77,220 sq. mi. (200,000 sq. km.)
POPULATION 6,456,189
CAPITAL San'a
MONETARY UNIT Yemeni rial
MAJOR LANGUAGE Arabic
MAJOR RELIGION Islam

QATAR

AREA 4,247 sq. mi. (11,000 sq. km.)
POPULATION 220,000
CAPITAL Doha
MONETARY UNIT Qatari riyal
MAJOR LANGUAGE Arabic
MAJOR RELIGION Islam

PEOPLE'S DEM. REP. OF YEMEN

AREA 111,101 sq. mi. (287,752 sq. km.)
POPULATION 1,969,000
CAPITAL Aden
MONETARY UNIT Yemeni dinar
MAJOR LANGUAGE Arabic
MAJOR RELIGION Islam

KUWAIT

AREA 6,532 sq mi. (16,918 sq. km.)
POPULATION 1,355,827
CAPITAL Al Kuwait
MONETARY UNIT Kuwaiti dinar
MAJOR LANGUAGE Arabic
MAJOR RELIGION Islam

BAHRAIN

AREA 240 sq. mi. (622 sq. km.)
POPULATION 358,857
CAPITAL Manama
MONETARY UNIT Bahraini dinar
MAJOR LANGUAGE Arabic
MAJOR RELIGION Islam

OMAN

AREA 120,000 sq. mi. (310,800 sq. km.)
POPULATION 891,000
CAPITAL Muscat
MONETARY UNIT Omani rial
MAJOR LANGUAGE Arabic
MAJOR RELIGION Islam

UNITED ARAB EMIRATES

AREA 32,278 sq. mi. (83,600 sq. km.)
POPULATION 1,040,275
CAPITAL Abu Dhabi
MONETARY UNIT dirham
MAJOR LANGUAGE Arabic
MAJOR RELIGION Islam

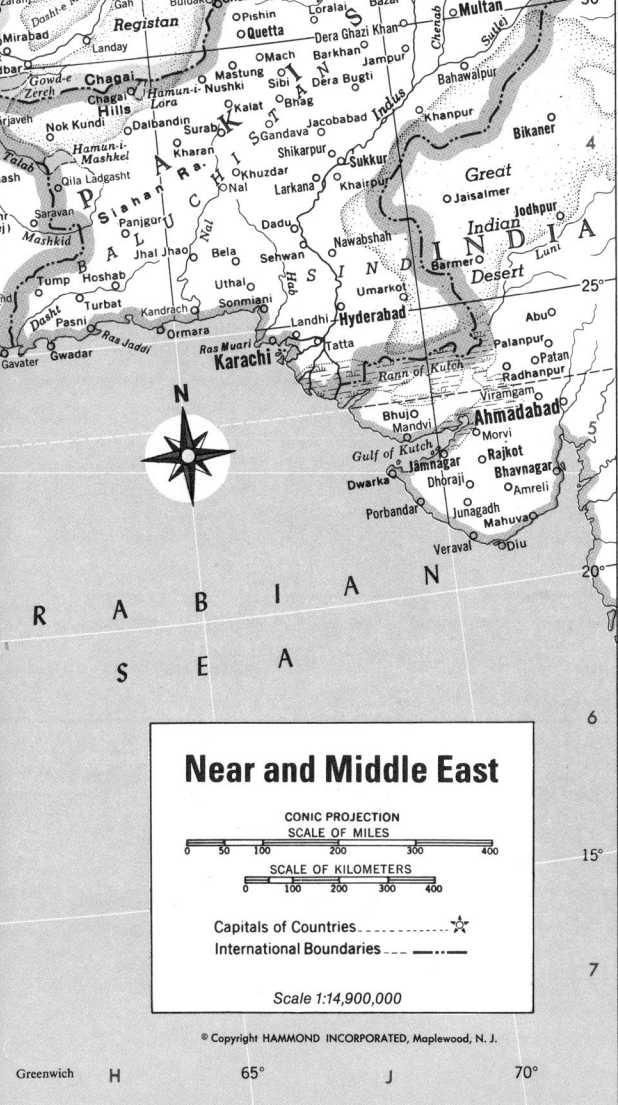

Near and Middle East

CONIC PROJECTION
SCALE OF MILES
0 50 100 200 300 400

SCALE OF KILOMETERS
0 100 200 300 400

Capitals of Countries ⭐
International Boundaries

Scale 1:14,900,000

© Copyright HAMMOND INCORPORATED, Maplewood, N.J.

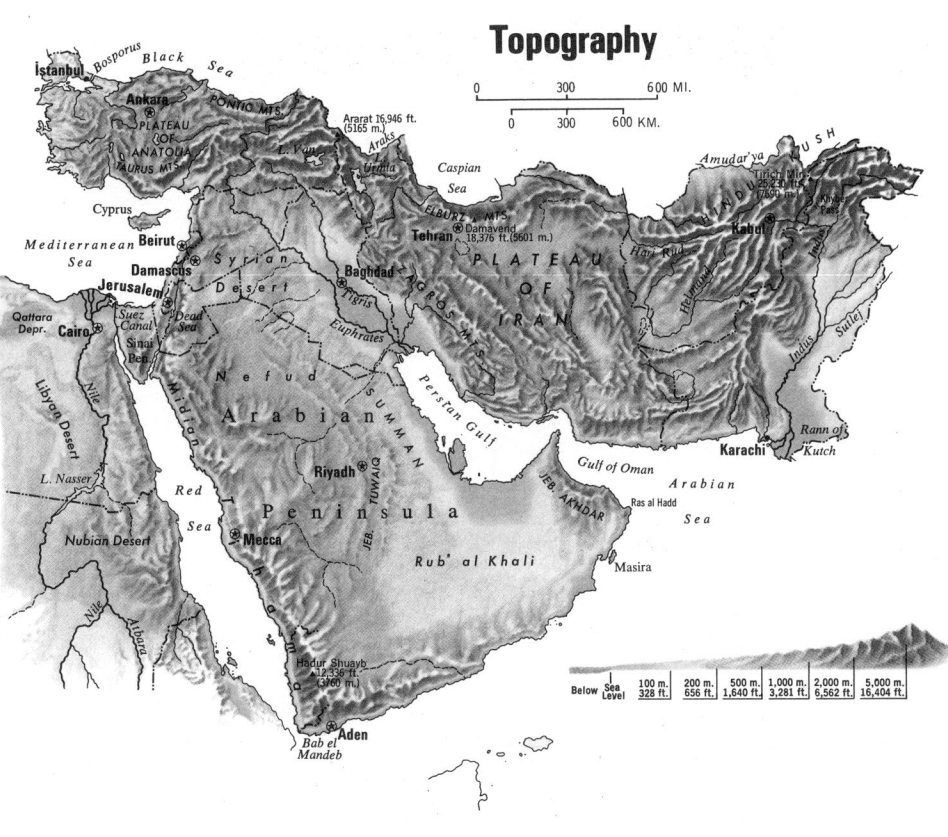

Topography

0 300 600 MI.
0 300 600 KM.

Below Sea Level	100 m. 328 ft.	200 m. 656 ft.	500 m. 1,640 ft.	1,000 m. 3,281 ft.	2,000 m. 6,562 ft.	5,000 m. 16,404 ft.

Agriculture, Industry and Resources

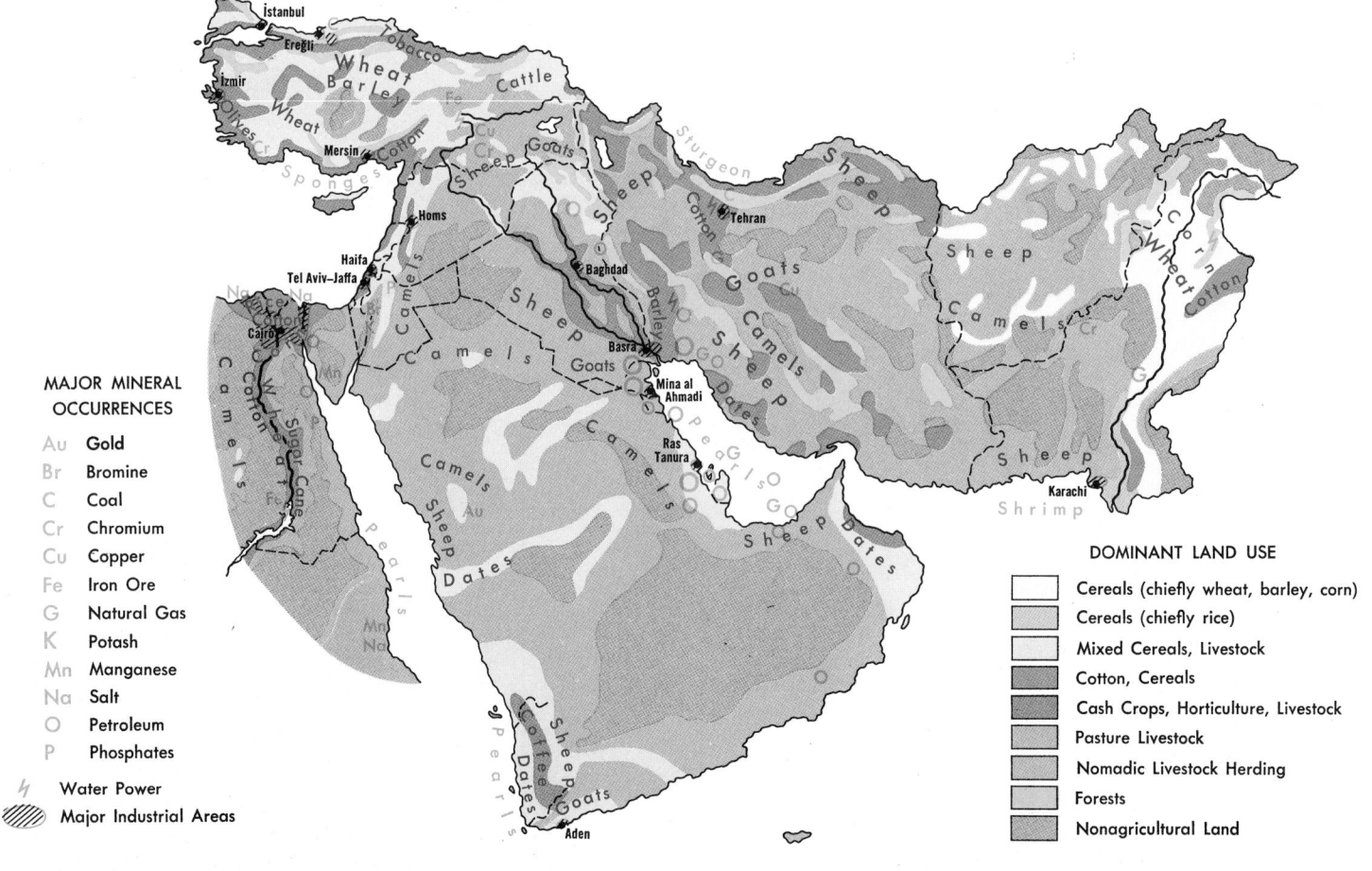

MAJOR MINERAL OCCURRENCES

- Au Gold
- Br Bromine
- C Coal
- Cr Chromium
- Cu Copper
- Fe Iron Ore
- G Natural Gas
- K Potash
- Mn Manganese
- Na Salt
- O Petroleum
- P Phosphates
- ⚡ Water Power
- ▨ Major Industrial Areas

DOMINANT LAND USE

- Cereals (chiefly wheat, barley, corn)
- Cereals (chiefly rice)
- Mixed Cereals, Livestock
- Cotton, Cereals
- Cash Crops, Horticulture, Livestock
- Pasture Livestock
- Nomadic Livestock Herding
- Forests
- Nonagricultural Land

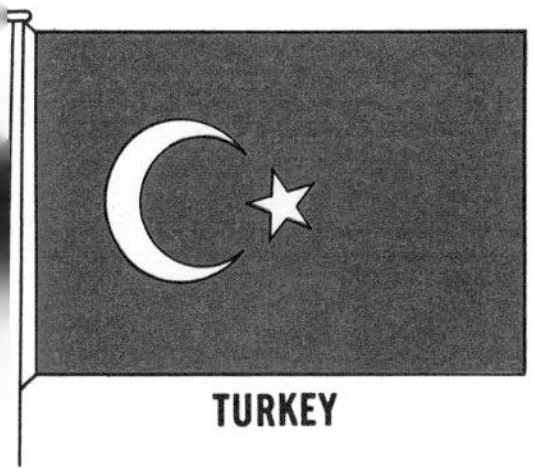
TURKEY

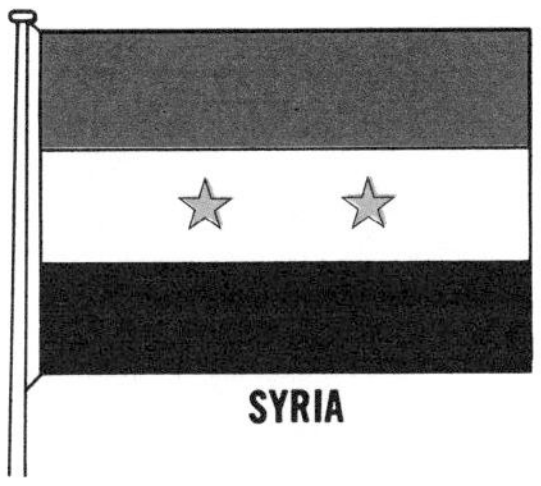
SYRIA

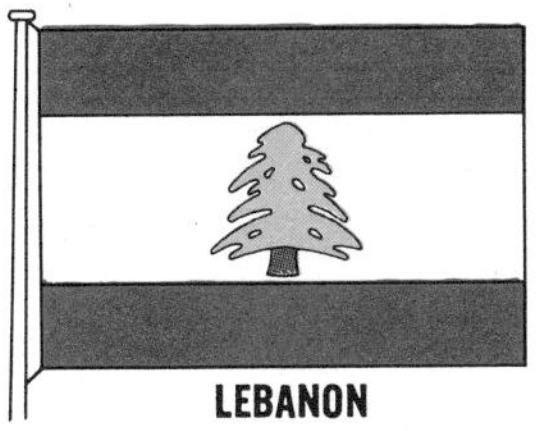
LEBANON

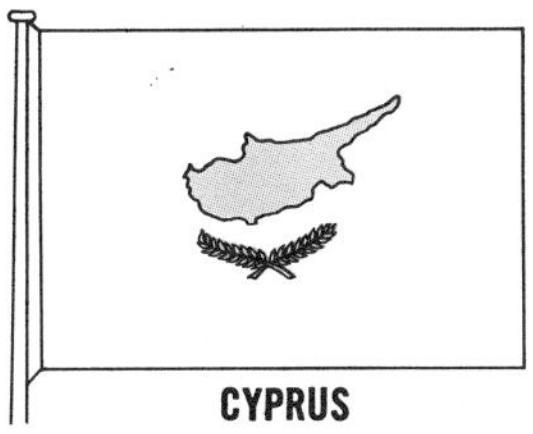
CYPRUS

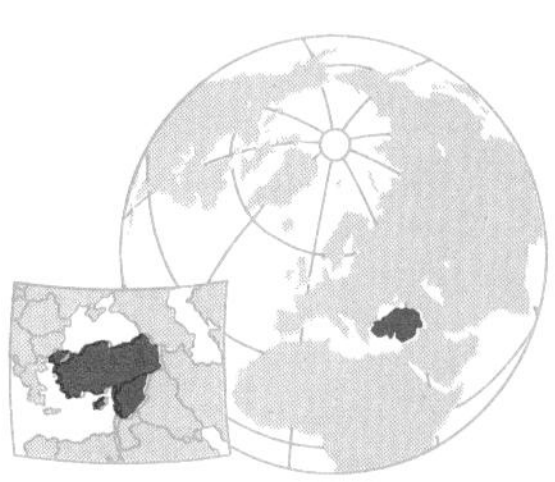

AREA 300,946 sq. mi. (779,450 sq. km.)
POPULATION 45,217,556
CAPITAL Ankara
LARGEST CITY Istanbul
HIGHEST POINT Ararat 16,946 ft. (5,165 m.)
MONETARY UNIT Turkish lira
MAJOR LANGUAGE Turkish
MAJOR RELIGION Islam

AREA 71,498 sq. mi. (185,180 sq. km.)
POPULATION 8,979,000
CAPITAL Damascus
LARGEST CITY Damascus
HIGHEST POINT Hermon 9,232 ft. (2,814 m.)
MONETARY UNIT Syrian pound
MAJOR LANGUAGES Arabic, French, Kurdish, Armenian
MAJOR RELIGIONS Islam, Christianity

AREA 4,015 sq. mi. (10,399 sq. km.)
POPULATION 3,161,000
CAPITAL Beirut
LARGEST CITY Beirut
HIGHEST POINT Qurnet es Sauda 10,131 ft. (3,088 m.)
MONETARY UNIT Lebanese pound
MAJOR LANGUAGES Arabic, French
MAJOR RELIGIONS Christianity, Islam

AREA 3,473 sq. mi. (8,995 sq. km.)
POPULATION 629,000
CAPITAL Nicosia
LARGEST CITY Nicosia
HIGHEST POINT Troödos 6,406 ft. (1,953 m.)
MONETARY UNIT Cypriot pound
MAJOR LANGUAGES Greek, Turkish, English
MAJOR RELIGIONS Eastern (Greek) Orthodoxy, Islam

CYPRUS

CITIES and TOWNS

Dhali 2,970 .... E5
Episkopi 2,150 .... E5
Famagusta 38,960 .... F5
Ktima E5
Kyrenia 3,892 .... E5
Kythrea 3,400 .... E5
Lapithos 3,600 .... E5
Larnaca 19,608 .... E5
Lefka 3,650 .... E5
Limassol 79,641 .... E5
Morphou 9,040 .... E5
Nicosia (cap.) 115,718 .... E5
Paphos 8,984 .... E5
Polis 2,200 .... E5
Rizokarpasso 3,600 .... F5
Yialousa 2,750 .... E5

OTHER FEATURES

Andreas (cape) F5
Arnauti (cape) E5
Gata (cape) E5
Greco (cape) F5
Kormakiti (cape) E5
Troodos (mt.) E5

LEBANON

CITIES and TOWNS

A'leih 18,630 .... F6
Amyun 7,926 .... F5
Baa'lbek 15,560 .... G5
Batrun 5,976 .... F5
Beirut (cap.) 474,870 .... F6
Beirut* 938,940 .... F6
Hermil 2,652 .... G5
Merj U'yun 9,318 .... F6
Rasheiya 6,731 .... F6
Rayak 1,480 .... G6
Saida 32,200 .... F6
Sidon (Saida) 32,200 .... F6
Sur 16,483 .... F6
Tripoli (Tarabulus) 127,611 .... F5
Tyre (Sur) 16,483 .... F6
Zahle 53,121 .... F6
Zegharta 18,210 .... G5

OTHER FEATURES

Lebanon (mts.) F6
Leontes (Litani) (riv.) F6
Litani (riv.) F6
Sauda, Qurnet es (mt.) G5

SYRIA

PROVINCES

Aleppo 1,316,872 .... G4
Damascus 1,457,934 .... G6
Deir ez Zor 292,780 .... H5
Dera' 230,481 .... G6
El Quneitra 16,490 .... F6
Es Suweida 139,650 .... G6
Hama 514,748 .... G5
Haseke 468,506 .... J4
Homs 546,176 .... G5
Idlib 383,695 .... G5
Latakia 389,552 .... G5
Rashid 243,736 .... H5
Tartus 302,065 .... G5

CITIES and TOWNS

Abu Kemal 6,907 .... J5
A'in el A'rab 4,529 .... H4
Aleppo 639,428 .... G4
Azaz 13,923 .... G4
Baniyas 8,537 .... F5
Busra G6
Damascus (cap.) 836,668 .... G6
Damascus* 923,253 .... G6
Deir ez Zor 66,164 .... H5
Dera' 27,651 .... G6
Dimashq (Damascus) (cap.) 836,668 .... G6
Duma 30,050 .... G6
El Bab 27,366 .... G4
El Haseke 32,746 .... J4
El Ladhiqiya (Latakia) 125,716 .... F5
El Quryatein G5
El Quneitra 17,752 .... F6
El Rashid 37,151 .... H5
En Nebk 16,334 .... G5
Es Suweide 29,524 .... G6
Et Tell el Abyad H4
Haffe 4,656 .... G5
Haleb (Aleppo) 639,428 .... G4
Hama 137,421 .... G5
Harim 6,837 .... G4
Homs 215,423 .... G5
Idlib 34,515 .... G5
Izra 3,226 .... G6
Jeble 15,715 .... F5
Jerablus 8,610 .... G4
Jisr esh Shughur 13,131 .... G5
Khan Sheikhun G5
Latakia 125,716 .... F5
Masyaf 7,058 .... G5
Membij 13,796 .... G4
Meskene H5
Meyadin 12,515 .... J5
Qala't es Salihiye J5
Qamishliye 31,448 .... J4
Quteife 4,993 .... G6
Raqqa (El Rashid) 37,151 .... H5
Sabkha 3,375 .... H5
Safita 9,650 .... G5
Selemiya 21,677 .... G5
Tadmur 10,670 .... H5
Tartus 29,842 .... F5
Telkalakh 6,242 .... F5
Zebdani 10,010 .... G6

OTHER FEATURES

A'mrit (ruins) F5
Arwad (Ruad) (isl.) F5
A'si (Orontes) (riv.) G5
Druz, Jebel ed (mts.) G6
El Furat (riv.) H4
Euphrates (El Furat) (riv.) H4
Hermon (mt.) F6
Khabur (riv.) J5
Orontes (riv.) G5
Palmyra (Tadmor) (ruins) H5
Ruwaq, Jebel er (mts.) G5

TURKEY

PROVINCES

Adana 1,240,475 .... F4
Adiyaman 346,892 .... H4
Afyonkarahisar 579,171 .... D3
Ağri 330,201 .... K3
Amasya 322,806 .... F2
Ankara 2,585,293 .... E3
Antalya 669,357 .... D4
Artvin 228,026 .... J2
Aydin 609,869 .... B4
Balikesir 789,255 .... B3
Bilecik 137,120 .... D2
Bingöl 210,804 .... J3
Bitlis 218,305 .... J3
Bolu 428,704 .... D2
Burdur 222,896 .... D4
Bursa 961,639 .... C2
Çanakkale 369,385 .... B2
Çankiri 265,468 .... E2
Çorum 547,580 .... F2
Denizli 560,916 .... C4
Diyarbakir 651,233 .... H4
Edirne 340,732 .... B2
Elâzığ 417,924 .... H3
Erzincan 283,683 .... H3
Erzurum 746,666 .... J3
Eskişehir 495,097 .... D3
Gaziantep 715,939 .... G4
Giresun 463,587 .... H2
Gümüşhane 293,673 .... H2
Hakkâri 126,036 .... K4
Hatay 744,113 .... G4
Içel 714,817 .... F4
Isparta 322,685 .... D4
Istanbul 3,904,588 .... C2
Izmir 1,673,966 .... B3
Kahramanmaraş 641,480 .... G4
Kars 707,398 .... K2
Kastamonu 438,243 .... E2
Kayseri 676,809 .... F3
Kirklareli 268,399 .... B2
Kirşehir 232,853 .... F3
Kocaeli 477,736 .... C2
Konya 1,422,461 .... E4
Kütahya 470,423 .... C3
Malatya 574,558 .... H3
Manisa 872,375 .... B3
Mardin 519,687 .... J4
Muğla 400,796 .... C4
Muş 267,203 .... J3
Nevşehir 249,308 .... F3
Niğde 463,121 .... F4
Ordu 664,290 .... G2
Rize 336,278 .... J2
Sakarya 495,649 .... D2
Samsun 906,381 .... F2
Siirt 381,503 .... J4
Sinop 267,605 .... F2
Sivas 741,713 .... G3
Tekirdağ 319,987 .... B2
Tokat 599,166 .... G2
Trabzon 719,008 .... H2
Tunceli 164,591 .... H3
Urfa 597,277 .... H4
Uşak 229,679 .... C3
Van 386,314 .... K3
Yozgat 500,371 .... F3
Zonguldak 836,156 .... D2

CITIES and TOWNS

Acigöl 3,934 .... F3
Acipayam 5,046 .... C4
Adalia (Antalya) 130,774 .... D4
Adana 475,384 .... F4
Adapazari 114,130 .... D2
Adilcevaz 9,022 .... K3
Adiyaman 43,782 .... H4
Afşin 18,231 .... G3
Afyonkarahisar 60,150 .... D3
Ağlasun 4,288 .... D4
Ağli 3,399 .... E2
Ağri (Karaköse) 35,284 .... K3
Ahlat 7,995 .... K3
Akçaabat 10,756 .... H2
Akçadağ 7,366 .... G3
Akçakoca 9,066 .... D2
Akdağmadeni 7,909 .... F3
Akhisar 53,357 .... B3
Aksaray 45,564 .... F3
Akşehir 35,544 .... D3
Akseki 5,141 .... D4
Akviran 3,799 .... E4
Akyazi 12,438 .... D2
Alaca 12,552 .... F2
Alacahan 2,321 .... G3
Alaçam 10,013 .... F2
Alanya 18,520 .... D4
Alaşehir 23,243 .... C3
Alexandretta (Iskenderun) 107,437 .... G4
Aliağa 5,727 .... B3
Alibeyköyü 33,387 .... D6
Almus 4,225 .... G2
Alpu 3,718 .... D3
Altindağ 512,392 .... E2
Altinova 6,980 .... B3
Altintaş 3,386 .... C3
Altinözü 5,158 .... G4
Alucra 7,070 .... H2
Amasra 4,369 .... E2
Amasya 41,496 .... G2
Anamur 21,475 .... E4
Andirin 5,018 .... G4
Ankara (cap.) 1,701,004 .... E3
Antakya 77,518 .... G4
Antalya 130,774 .... D4
Antioch (Antakya) 77,518 .... G4
Araç 3,594 .... E2
Aralik 4,155 .... L3
Arapkir 8,436 .... H3
Ardahan 16,285 .... K2
Ardeşen 7,980 .... J2
Ardanuç 2,942 .... K2
Arguvan 2,461 .... H3
Arhavi 6,311 .... J2
Arpaçay 2,651 .... K2
Arsin 6,557 .... H2
Artova 2,813 .... G2
Artvin 13,390 .... J2
Aşkale 10,817 .... J3
Avanos 8,635 .... F3
Ayancik 7,202 .... F1
Ayaş 4,575 .... E2
Aybasti 13,180 .... G2
Aydin 59,579 .... B4
Aydincik 6,739 .... E4
Ayranci 2,664 .... E4
Ayvacik 3,120 .... B3
Ayvalik 18,041 .... B3
Babadağ 5,890 .... C4
Babaeski 17,090 .... B2
Bafra 34,288 .... F2
Bahçe 10,212 .... G4
Bakirköy 200,942 .... D6
Baklan 3,327 .... C4
Balâ 4,107 .... E3
Balikesir 99,443 .... B3
Balya 2,362 .... B3
Banaz 6,264 .... C3
Bandirma 45,752 .... B2
Bartin 18,409 .... E2
Başkale 8,558 .... K3
Başmakçi 5,925 .... C4
Batman 64,384 .... J4
Bayat 4,671 .... F2
Bayburt 20,156 .... J2
Bayindir 14,078 .... B3
Baykan 2,690 .... J3
Bayramiç 6,385 .... B3
Bergama 29,749 .... B3
Beşiktaş 174,931 .... D6
Beşiri 4,165 .... J4
Besni 16,313 .... G4
Beykoz 76,804 .... D5
Beyoğlu 230,532 .... D6
Beypazari 14,963 .... D2
Beyşehir 15,060 .... D4
Beytüşşebap 2,766 .... K4
Biga 15,188 .... B2
Bigadiç 7,535 .... C3
Bilecik 11,269 .... D2
Bingöl (Çapakçur) 22,047 .... J3
Birecik 20,104 .... H4
Bismil 12,775 .... J4
Bitlis 25,054 .... J3
Bodrum 7,858 .... B4
Boğazliyan 10,329 .... F3
Bolu 32,812 .... D2
Bolvadin 29,218 .... D3
Bor 16,560 .... F4
Borçka 4,636 .... J2
Bornova 45,096 .... B3
Boyabat 13,139 .... F2
Bozdoğan 7,218 .... C4
Bozkir 5,294 .... E4
Bozkurt 2,948 .... F2
Bozova 5,462 .... H4
Bozüyük 15,197 .... C3
Bucak 15,090 .... D4
Bulancak 14,153 .... H2
Bulanik 8,296 .... K3
Buldan 11,115 .... C3
Bünyan 12,277 .... G3
Burdur 36,633 .... D4
Burhaniye 12,800 .... B3
Bursa 346,103 .... C2
Büyükada D6
Büyükdere D5
Çal 3,274 .... C3
Çala 2,450 .... K2
Caldiran 3,366 .... K3

(continued on following page)

Agriculture, Industry and Resources

DOMINANT LAND USE

- Cereals (chiefly wheat, barley), Livestock
- Cash Crops, Horticulture, Livestock
- Pasture Livestock
- Nomadic Livestock Herding
- Forests
- Nonagricultural Land

MAJOR MINERAL OCCURRENCES

Ab	Asbestos	Na	Salt
Al	Bauxite	O	Petroleum
C	Coal	P	Phosphates
Cr	Chromium	Pb	Lead
Cu	Copper	Py	Pyrites
Fe	Iron Ore	Sb	Antimony
Hg	Mercury	Zn	Zinc
Mg	Magnesium		

Water Power
Major Industrial Areas

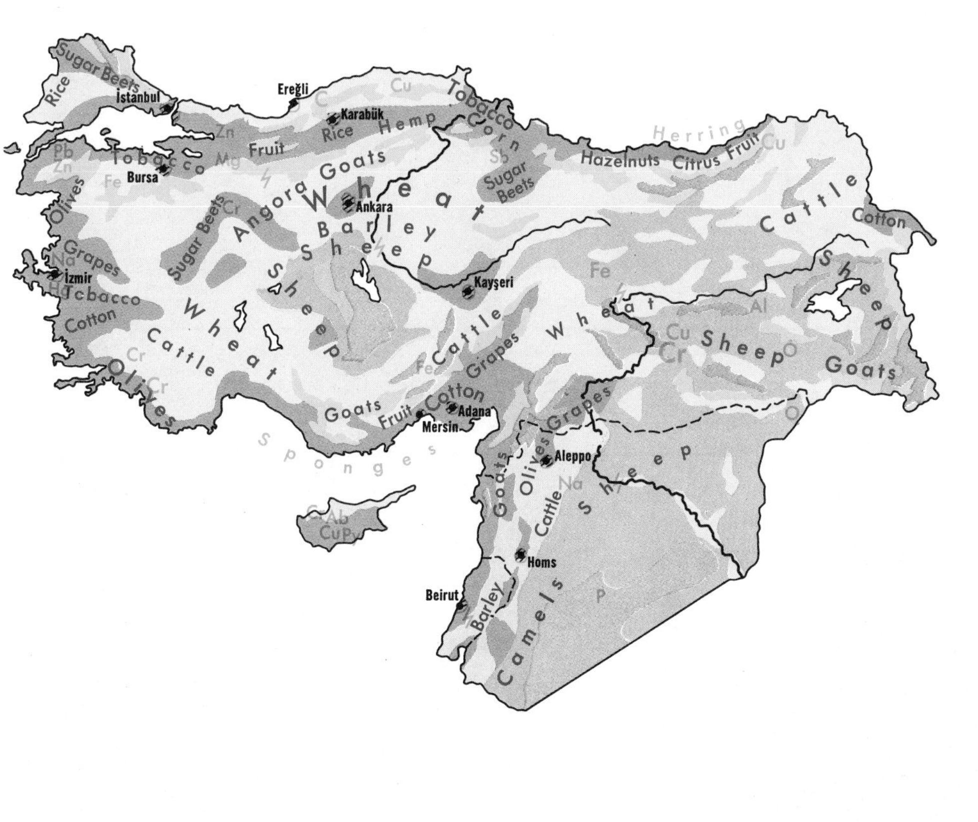
Sugar Beets
Rice
Istanbul
Ereğli
Cu
Tobacco
Karabük
Rice
Hemp
Corn
Herring
Hazelnuts
Citrus Fruit
Pb
Zn
Tobacco
Mg
Fruit
Angora Goats
Wheat
Ankara
Sugar Beets
Sb
Fe
Bursa
Olives
Cr
Sugar Beets
Barley
Sheep
Cattle
Cotton
Grapes
Izmir
Tobacco
Cotton
Kayseri
Wheat
Cattle
Sheep
Goats
Olives
Fruit
Cotton
Adana
Mersin
Sponges
Grapes
Aleppo
Na
Homs
Beirut
Barley
Camels

Hayrabolu 12,331	B2	İslâhiye 20,683	G4
Hazro 4,896	J3	Isparta 62,870	D4
Hekimhan 11,818	G3	Ispir 3,929	H2
Hendek 15,291	D2	İstanbul 2,547,364	D6
Hilvan 6,473	H4	İvrindi 3,730	B3
Hinis 10,226	J3	İzmir 636,834	B3
Hisarönü 4,485	E2	İzmit 165,483	D2
Hizan 2,545	K3	İznik 11,614	C2
Hopa 9,089	J2	Kadıköy 354,957	D6
Horasan 7,724	J3	Kadınhanı 11,802	E3
Hozat 5,796	H3	Kadirli 34,779	F4
İçel (Mersin) 152,236	F4	Kağızman 11,517	K2
İdil 4,862	J4	Kâhta 15,602	H4
İğdir 29,862	K3	Kalan 11,637	H3
Ilgaz 6,624	E2	Kale 3,399	C4
Ilgın 11,830	D3	Kalecik 4,707	E2
İlıca 8,947	J3	Kaman 16,516	E3
İmranli 5,667	H2	Kandıra 10,187	D2
İncesu 7,089	F3	Kangal 5,937	G3
İnebolu 6,824	E1	Karabük 69,182	E2
İnegöl 37,805	C2	Karacabey 21,648	C2
İnönü 4,152	D3	Karaçalı 5,539	C3
İpsala 6,829	B2	Karaisalı 2,316	F4
İpsile 2,328	G2	Karakoçan 5,604	H3
İskenderun 107,437	G4	Karaköse (Ağrı) 35,284	K3
İskilip 16,588	F2		

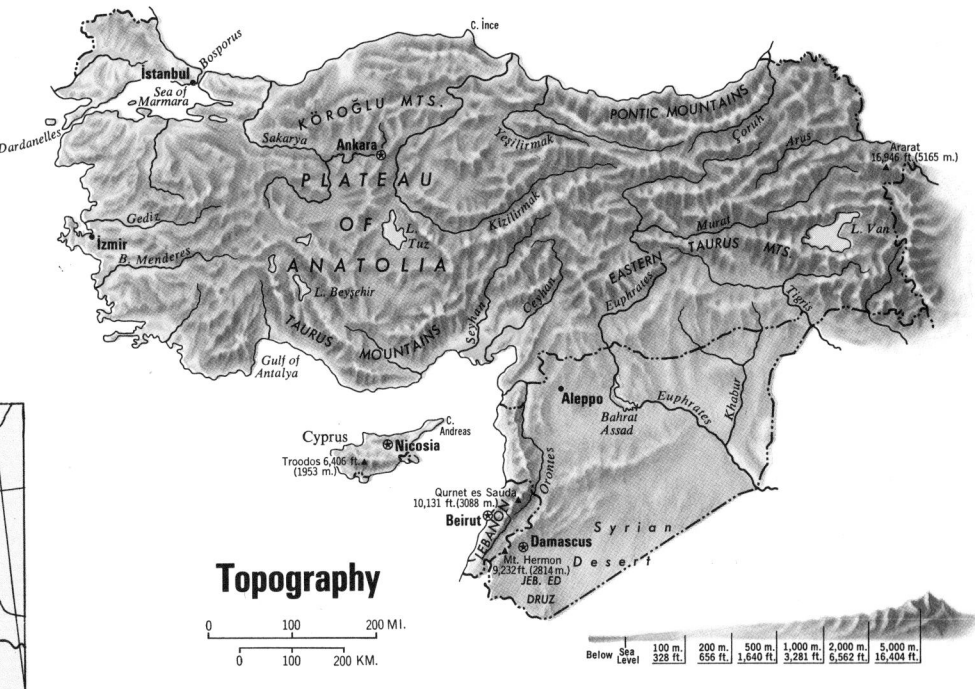

Topography

0   100   200 MI.

0   100   200 KM.

| Below Sea Level | 100 m. 328 ft. | 200 m. 656 ft. | 500 m. 1,640 ft. | 1,000 m. 3,281 ft. | 2,000 m. 6,562 ft. | 5,000 m. 16,404 ft. |

Karaman 43,759	E4	Muğla 24,178	C4
Karamanlı 5,904	C4	Muradiye 6,334	K3
Karapinar 19,589	E4	Muş 27,761	J3
Karasu 11,600	D2	Mustafakemalpaşa 27,706	C3
Karataş 5,598	F4	Mut 11,466	E4
Karayaka 4,242	G2	Mutki 2,815	J3
Karayazı 3,595	J3	Muttalip 3,917	D3
Kargı 5,021	F2	Nallıhan 7,883	D2
Karlıova 3,631	J3	Narman 4,607	J2
Kars 54,892	K2	Nazilli 52,001	C4
Karşıyaka 171,600	B3	Nevşehir 30,203	F3
Kartal 53,073	D6	Niğde 31,844	F4
Kaş 2,493	C4	Niksar 19,156	G2
Kastamonu 29,993	E2	Nizip 36,190	G4
Kavak, Çanakkale 3,932	C5	Nurhak 5,330	G4
Kavak, Samsun 3,964	G2	Nusaybin 23,684	J4
Kayseri 207,037	F3	Ödemiş 37,364	C3
Kazanlı 4,461	F4	Of 10,376	J2
Kazımkarabekir 4,086	E4	Oğuzeli 7,194	G4
Keban 5,800	H3	Oltu 10,093	J2
Keçiborlu 7,096	C3	Ömerli 4,738	J4
Keles 2,423	C3	Ordu 47,481	G2
Kelkit 6,928	H2	Orhaneli 3,335	C3
Kemah 3,038	H3	Orhangazi 12,181	C2
Kemaliye 3,014	H3	Orta 3,596	E2
Kemalpaşa 7,572	J2	Ortaca 8,604	C4
Kemerburgaz 7,234	D5	Ortakaraviran 3,856	E4
Kemirhisar 6,205	F4	Ortaköy, Çorum 2,657	F2
Kepsut 4,704	C3	Ortaköy, Niğde 6,371	F3
Keşan 27,088	B2	Osmancık 11,921	F2
Keşap 5,264	H2	Osmaneli 4,789	D2
Keskin 10,540	E3	Osmaniye 61,581	G4
Kiğı 5,598	J3	Ovacık, Tunceli 2,248	H3
Kilimli 26,649	D2	Özalp 4,188	K3
Kilis 54,055	G4	Palu 5,489	H3
Kınık 11,785	B3	Pasinler 14,267	J3
Kiraz 5,828	C3	Patnos 15,918	K3
Kirikhan 38,118	G4	Pazar, Rize 8,856	J2
Kırıkkale 137,874	E3	Pazar, Tokat 4,337	G2
Kırkağaç 15,078	B3	Pazarcık 15,943	G4
Kırşehir 41,415	F3	Pazaryeri 5,633	C3
Kızılcahamam 7,050	E2	Pera (Beyoğlu) 230,532	D6
Kızılhisar 11,119	C4	Perşembe 6,701	G2
Kızıltepe 21,531	J4	Pertek 4,176	H3
Kızılviran 3,260	E3	Pervari 4,126	K4
Kocaeli (İzmit) 165,483	D2	Pınarbaşı 9,503	G3
Koçarlı 5,182	B4	Pınarhisar 10,523	B2
Konya 246,727	E4	Polatlı 35,267	E3
Korkuteli 10,334	C4	Posof 2,209	J2
Köyceğiz 4,612	C4	Pozantı 5,408	F4
Koyulhisar 3,861	G2	Pülümür 3,442	H3
Kozaklı 6,200	F3	Pütürge 4,878	H3
Kozan 32,045	F4	Reşadiye 9,022	G2
Kozlu 27,322	D2	Refahiye 6,570	H3
Kozluk 6,197	J3	Reyhanlı 25,749	G4
Küçükköy 56,411	C6	Rize 36,044	J2
Kula 10,807	C3	Sabanözü 3,442	E2
Kulp 4,474	J3	Safranbolu 14,793	E2
Kulu 11,707	E3	Saimbeyli 3,622	G4
Kumkale 1,752	B6	Sakarya (Adapazarı) 114,130	D2
Kumluca 7,704	C4	Salihli 45,514	C3
Küre 2,378	E2	Samandağı 22,540	F4
Kurşunlu 6,562	E2	Samsat 2,083	H4
Kurtalan 7,001	J3	Samsun 168,478	F2
Kuşadası 10,269	B4	Sandıklı 13,181	D3
Kütahya 82,442	C3	Sapanca 9,040	D2
Kuyucak 6,039	C4	Şaphane 3,919	C3
Ladik 6,785	F2	Sarayköy 10,513	C4
Lapseki 3,727	C6	Sarayönü 8,946	E3
Lice 8,625	J3	Sarıgöl 6,979	C3
Lüleburgaz 32,401	B2	Sarıkamış 21,262	J2
Maden 15,151	H3	Sarıkaya 5,160	F3
Mağara 4,314	G3	Sariköy 4,695	B2
Mahmudiye 5,240	D3	Sarıoğlan 3,245	G3
Malatya 154,505	H3	Sarıyer 79,329	D5
Malazgirt 13,094	K3	Sarız 3,591	G3
Malkara 14,399	B2	Şarkikaraağaç 4,772	D3
Maltepe 66,343	D6	Şarkışla 12,763	G3
Manavgat 10,804	D4	Şarköy 5,396	B2
Manisa 78,114	B3	Sason 3,211	J3
Manyas 4,410	C2	Savaştepe 7,179	B3
Maraş (Kahramanmaraş) 135,782	G4	Şavşat 3,078	K2
Mardin 36,629	H4	Savur 4,983	J4
Marmaris 5,596	C4	Seben 2,471	D2
Mazgirt 3,141	H3	Şebinkarahisar 10,214	H2
Mazıdağı 4,842	J4	Şefaatli 6,769	F3
Mecitözü 6,066	F2	Seferihisar 6,484	B3
Menemen 18,464	B3	Selçuk 12,251	B3
Mengen 2,459	D2	Selendi 4,457	C3
Meriç 3,922	B2	Selim 3,569	K2
Mersin 152,236	F4	Selimiye 2,989	B4
Merzifon 30,801	F2	Senirkent 8,247	D3
Mesudiye 4,294	G2	Şenkaya 3,190	K2
Midyat 16,905	J4	Şereflikoçhisar 20,523	E3
Midye 2,003	C2	Serik 14,161	D4
Mihaliçcik 4,004	D3	Seydişehir 25,651	D4
Milâs 17,929	B4	Seyitgazi 2,819	D3
Mucur 9,398	F3	Siirt 35,654	J4
Mudanya 8,399	C2	Şile 4,062	D2
Mudurnu 3,905	D2	Silifke 19,257	E4
		Silivri 8,525	C2
		Silopi 4,460	K4

Silvan 29,599	J3	Yeşilyurt 7,451	H3
Simav 11,601	C3	Yıldızeli 7,043	G3
Sincanlı 3,847	D3	Yozgat 32,501	F3
Sındırgı 7,818	C3	Yüksekova 7,329	L4
Sinop 16,098	F2	Yumurtalık 2,442	F4
Şiran 5,048	H2	Yunak 6,187	D3
Şırnak 10,587	K4	Yusufeli 3,050	J2
Sivas 149,201	G3	Zara 10,376	G3
Sivaslı 4,394	C3	Zeytinburnu 123,548	D6
Siverek 40,990	H4	Zeytindağ 3,517	B3
Sivrihisar 8,713	D3	Zile 32,157	G2
Smyrna (İzmir) 636,834	B3	Zivarık 2,703	E3
Söğüt 5,329	D3	Zonguldak 90,221	D2
Solhan 7,014	J3		
Soma 23,713	B3	**OTHER FEATURES**	
Sorgun 14,081	F3		
Söke 35,407	B4	Abydos (ruins)	B6
Sultandağı 4,017	D3	Acı (lake)	C4
Suhut 8,154	D3	Adalar (isl.)	D6
Sulakyurt 4,311	E2	Aegean (sea)	A3
Sultanhanı 5,112	E3	Ağrı, Büyük (Ararat) (mt.)	L3
Suluova 21,278	F2	Akdağ (mt.)	C4
Sungurlu 21,641	F2	Aladağ (mt.)	F4
Sürmene 8,096	J2	Alexandretta (gulf)	F4
Sürüç 20,395	H4	Amanos (mts.)	G4
Suşehri 10,863	H2	Anamur (cape)	E5
Susurluk 14,000	C3	Anatolia (reg.)	D3
Susuz 5,006	K2	Ankara (riv.)	D3
Sütçüler 2,721	D4	Antalya (gulf)	D4
Tarsus 102,186	F4	Anti-Taurus (mts.)	G3
Taşkent 7,098	E4	Araks (riv.)	K2
Taşköprü 8,146	F2	Ararat (mt.)	L3
Taşlıçay 3,684	K3	Arpa (riv.)	K2
Taşova 6,516	G2	Baba (cape)	A3
Tatvan 29,271	J3	Bati Firat (riv.)	H3
Tavas 9,728	C4	Beyşehir (lake)	D4
Tavşanlı 19,575	C3	Black (sea)	E1
Tefenni 4,280	C4	Bosporus (str.)	C2
Tekirdağ 41,257	B2	Borcaadağ (isl.)	A3
Tercan 6,068	J3	Burgaz (isl.)	D6
Terme 15,660	G2	Büyük Ağrı (Ararat) (mt.)	L3
Tire 30,694	B3	Çanakkale Boğazı (Dardanelles) (str.)	B3
Tirebolu 7,385	H2	Çandarlı (gulf)	B3
Tokat 48,588	G2	Canik (mts.)	G2
Tomarza 4,948	F3	Ceyhan (riv.)	F4
Tömük 7,660	F4	Cilo Dağı (mt.)	K4
Tonya 10,544	H2	Çoruh (riv.)	J2
Torbalı 17,237	B3	Dardanelles (str.)	B6
Tortum 4,110	J2	Dicle (riv.)	J4
Torul 5,117	H2	Eastern Taurus (mts.)	J3
Tosya 17,515	F2	Ephesus (ruins)	B3
Trabzon 97,210	H2	Erciyas Dağı (mt.)	F3
Trebizond (Trabzon) 97,210	H2	Ergene (riv.)	B2
Tunceli (Kalan) 11,637	H3	Euphrates (Fırat) (riv.)	G4
Turgutlu 47,009	B3	Fırat (riv.)	G4
Turhal 39,170	G2	Gediz (riv.)	C3
Türkeli 2,194	F1	Gelidonya (cape)	D4
Türkoğlu 9,207	G4	Gökçeada (isl.)	A2
Tutak 4,325	K3	Göksu (riv.)	E4
Tuzluca 5,209	K2	Helles (cape)	B6
Tuzlukçu 4,613	D3	Heybeli (isl.)	D6
Ula 5,117	C4	Ilium (ruins)	B6
Ulaş 2,469	G3	İmroz (Gökçeada) (isl.)	A2
Ulubey 4,214	C3	İnce (cape)	F1
Uluborlu 10,016	D3	İstranca (mts.)	B2
Uludere 4,050	K4	Kaçkar Dağı (mt.)	J2
Ulukışla 6,336	F4	Karadeniz Boğazı (Bosporus) (str.)	C2
Umurbey 2,754	C2	Karasu-Aras (mts.)	J3
Ürgüp 9,758	F3	Kelkit (riv.)	G2
Urla 13,903	B3	Keşiş Tepesi (mt.)	H3
Uşak 58,578	C3	Kızılırmak (riv.)	F2
Üsküdar 202,957	D6	Koca (riv.)	C3
Uzunköprü 27,005	B2	Köroğlu (mts.)	E2
Uzunisa 5,740	G2	Küre (mts.)	E2
Vakfıkebir 12,556	H2	Mandalya (gulf)	B4
Van 63,663	K3	Marmara (sea)	C2
Varto 5,572	J3	Menderes, Büyük (riv.)	B4
Vezirköprü 17,735	F2	Meriç (riv.)	B2
Viranşehir 26,244	H4	Murat (riv.)	H3
Vize 8,203	B2	Pontic (mts.)	H2
Yahyalı 13,738	F4	Porsuk (riv.)	D3
Yalova, Istanbul 27,289	C2	Prinkipo (Adalar) (isl.)	D6
Yalvaç 18,305	D3	Sakarya (riv.)	D2
Yaprakli 3,020	E2	Saros (gulf)	B2
Yatağan 4,903	C4	Seyhan (riv.)	F4
Yayladağı 4,471	F5	Simav (riv.)	C3
Yenice, Çanakkale 4,004	C3	Sinop (cape)	F1
Yenice, Zonguldak 5,791	D2	Süphan Dağı (mt.)	K3
Yeniceoba 5,740	E3	Taurus (mts.)	D4
Yeniköy	D6	Tigris (Dicle)	J4
Yenimahalle 198,643	C3	Troy (Ilium) (ruins)	B6
Yenişehir 15,188	C2	Van (lake)	K3
Yerkesik 2,381	C4	Yeşilırmak (riv.)	G2
Yerköy 19,927	F3		
Yeşilhisar 10,409	F4		

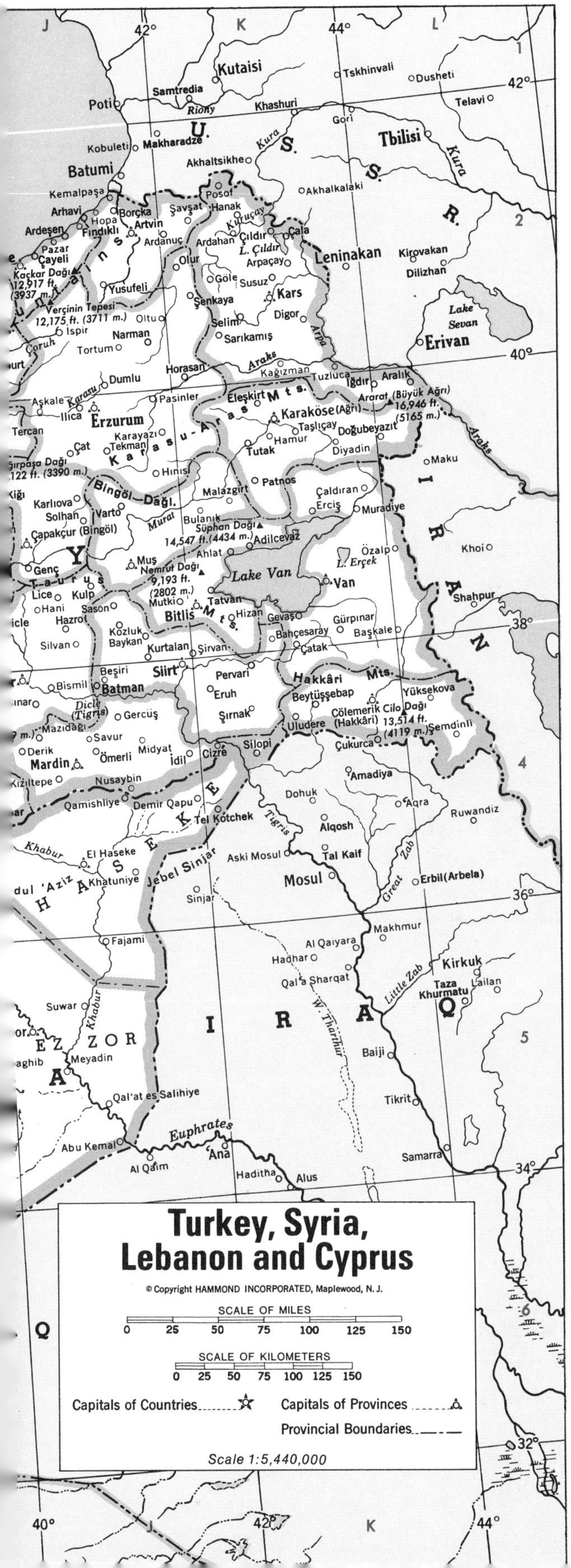

Turkey, Syria, Lebanon and Cyprus

SCALE OF MILES
0 25 50 75 100 125 150

SCALE OF KILOMETERS
0 25 50 75 100 125 150

Capitals of Countries .... ★   Capitals of Provinces .... △
Provincial Boundaries ....

Scale 1:5,440,000

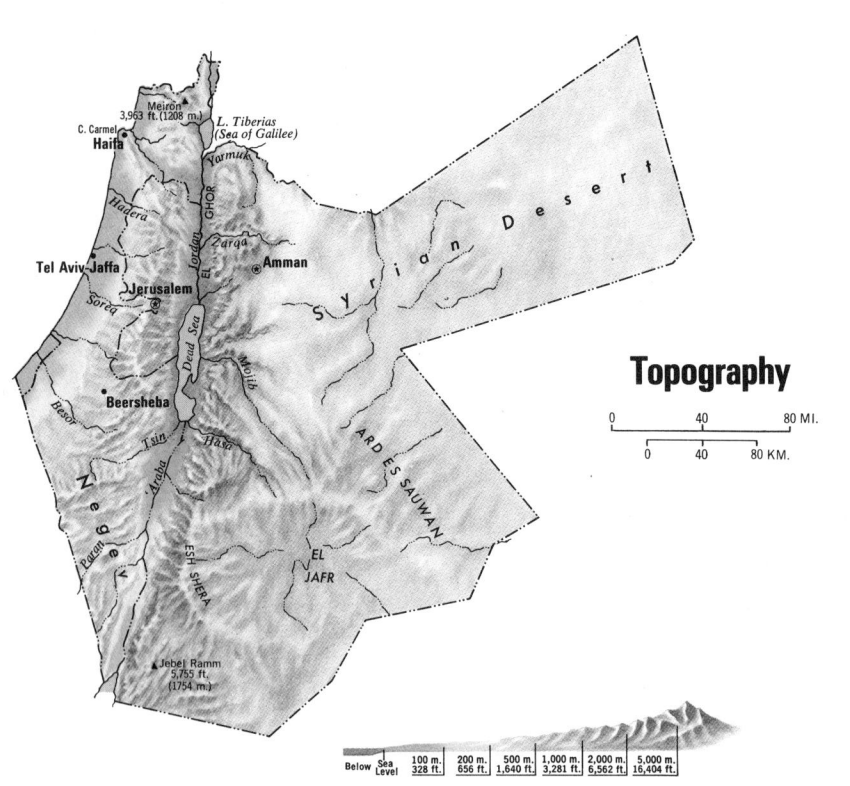

Topography

0   40   80 MI.

0   40   80 KM.

Below Sea Level	100 m. 328 ft.	200 m. 656 ft.	500 m. 1,640 ft.	1,000 m. 3,281 ft.	2,000 m. 6,562 ft.	5,000 m. 16,404 ft.

ISRAEL

DISTRICTS

Central 572,300 ....B3
Haifa 480,800 ....C2
Jerusalem 338,600 ....B4
Northern 473,700 ....C2
Southern 351,300 ....B5
Tel Aviv 905,100 ....B3

CITIES and TOWNS

Acre 34,400 ....C2
Afiqim 1,243 ....D2
'Atula 17,400 ....C2
Ahuzzam 407 ....B4
Akko (Acre) 34,400 ....C2
Arad 5,400 ....C5
'Arrabe 6,000 ....C2
Ashdod 40,500 ....B4
Ashdot Yaa'qov 1,197 ....D2
Ashqelon 43,100 ....A4
Atlit 1,516 ....C2
Avihayil 579 ....B3
Bat Shelomo 218 ....B2
Bat Yam 124,100 ....B3
Be'eri 390 ....A5
Be'er Menuha D5
Beersheba (Be'er
   Sheva) 101,000 ....B5
Be'er Tuveya 602 ....B4
Beit Guvrin B4
Bene Beraq 74,100 ....B3
Bet Qama 228 ....B5
Bet She'an 11,300 ....C2
Bet Shemesh 10,100 ....B4
Binyamina 2,701 ....B2
Carmel C2
Dafna 577 ....D1
Dalyat al-Karmel 6,200 ....C2
Dan 498 ....D1
Dimona 23,700 ....D4
Dor 195 ....B2
E'in Gedi C5
E'in Harod 1,372 ....C2
Elat D6
Elath (Elat) 12,800 ....D5
El 'Auja D5
Elyakim 568 ....C2
Elyashiv 435 ....B3
Even Yehuda 3,464 ....B3
Gal'on 356 ....B4
Gat 430 ....B4
Gedera 5,400 ....B4
Gesher 360 ....D5
Gesher Haziv 238 ....C1
Gevara'm 283 ....B4
Gilat 561 ....B5
Ginnosar 473 ....C2
Giv'atayim 48,500 ....B3
Giva't Brenner 1,505 ....B4
Giv'at Hayyim 1,360 ....B2
Habonim 189 ....B2
Hadera 31,900 ....B2
Haifa 227,800 ....B2
Haifa* 367,400 ....B2
Hatseva D5
Hazerim 127 ....B5

Hazor Hagelilit D2
Helez 466 ....B4
Herzeliyya 41,200 ....B3
Hod Hasharon 13,500 ....B3
Hodiyya 400 ....B4
Holon 121,200 ....B3
Iksal 2,156 ....C2
Jerusalem (cap.) 376,000 ....C4
Jish 1,498 ....C1
Kafar Kanna 5,200 ....C2
Kafar Yasif 2,975 ....C2
Karkur-Pardes Hanna 13,600 ..C3
Kefar Blum 565 ....D1
Kefar Gila'di 701 ....C1
Kefar Ruppin 306 ....D3
Kefar Sava 26,500 ....B3
Kefar Vitkin 808 ....B3
Kefar Zekhariya 420 ....B4
Kinneret 909 ....D2
Lod (Lydda) 30,500 ....B4
Lydda 30,500 ....B4
Magen 149 ....A5
Maa'lot-Tarshiha C1
Malkiya D1
Mash 'Abbe Sade 238 ....B6
Mavqii'm 177 ....A5
Megiddo C2
Metula 261 ....D1
Migdal 688 ....C2
Migdal Ha E'meq C2
Mikhmoret 608 ....B3
Mishmar Hanegev 336 ....B5
Mishmar Hayarden D1
Mivtahim 398 ....A5
Mizpe Ramon 331 ....D5
Moza Illit 219 ....C4
Mughar 4,010 ....C2
Muqeible 459 ....C2
Nahariyya 24,000 ....C1
Nazareth 33,300 ....C2
Nazerat I'lit C2
Negba 453 ....B4
Nes Ziyyona 11,700 ....B4
Netanya 70,700 ....B3
Netivot B5
Nevatim 436 ....B5
Newe Yam 211 ....B2
Newe Zohar C5
Nir Yitzhaq 209 ....A5
Nizzanim 479 ....B4
Ofaqim B5
O'mer B5
Oron C6
Or Yehuda B4
Pardes Hanna-Karkur 13,600 ..B2
Peduyim 361 ....B5
Petah Tiqwa 112,000 ....B3
Qadima 2,937 ....B3
Qalansuwa B3
Qedma 157 ....B4
Qiryat Atta C2
Qiryat Bialik 18,000 ....C2
Qiryat Gat 19,200 ....B4
Qiryat Mal'akhi B4
Qiryat Motzkin 17,600 ....C2
Qiryat Shemona 15,200 ....C1
Qiryat Tivo'n 9,800 ....C2
Qiryat Yam 19,800 ....C2
Raa'nana 14,900 ....B3
Ramat Gan 120,900 ....B3

Ramat Hasharon 20,100 ....B3
Rame 2,986 ....C2
Ramla 34,100 ....B4
Rehovot 39,200 ....B4
Rei'm 155 ....B5
Revadim 175 ....B4
Revivim 258 ....D5
Rishon Le Ziyyon 51,900 ....B4
Rosh Ha 'Ayin B3
Rosh Pinna 700 ....D2
Ruhama 497 ....B4
Saa'd 418 ....B5
Safad (Zefat) 13,600 ....C2
Sakhnin 8,400 ....C2
Sede Boqer D5
Sedom C5
Sedot Yam 511 ....B3
Shave Ziyyon 269 ....B3
Shefar'am 11,800 ....C2
Shefayim 614 ....B3
Shoval 393 ....B5
Tayibe 11,700 ....C3
Tel Aviv-Jaffa 343,300 ....B3
Tel Aviv-Jaffa* 1,219,900 ....B3
Tiberias 23,800 ....D2
Tirat Hakarmel 14,400 ....B2
Tirat Zevi 353 ....D3
Tur'an 2,304 ....C2
Umm el Fahm 13,300 ....C2
Urim 203 ....B5
Uzza 487 ....B4
Yad Mordekhai 416 ....A4
Yagur 1,266 ....C2
Yahav D5
Yavne 10,100 ....B4
Yavne'el 1,580 ....C2
Yehud 8,900 ....B3
Yeroham 5,800 ....C5
Yesodot 293 ....B4
Yesud Hamaa'la 428 ....D1
Yiftah D1
Yirka 2,715 ....C2
Yotvata D5
Zavdi'el 396 ....B4
Ze'elim 148 ....B5
Zefat 13,600 ....C2
Zikhron Yaa'qov 6,500 ....B2
Zippori 241 ....C2

OTHER FEATURES

Aqaba (gulf) D6
'Araba, Wadi (valley) D5
Beer Sheva (dry riv.) B5
Besor (riv.) B5
Carmel (cape) B2
Carmel (mt.) C2
Dead (sea) C4
Galilee, Sea of (Tiberias)
   (lake) D2
Galilee (reg.) C2
Gerar (dry riv.) B5
Hadera (dry riv.) B3
Haniqra, Rosh (cape) C1
Jordan (riv.) D3
Judaea (reg.) B5
Lakhish (dry riv.) B4
Meiron (mt.) C1
Negev (reg.) D5

Archaeological Sites in Palestine

■ Major Excavations

Miles
0   10   20   30

© Copyright HAMMOND INCORPORATED

Agriculture, Industry and Resources

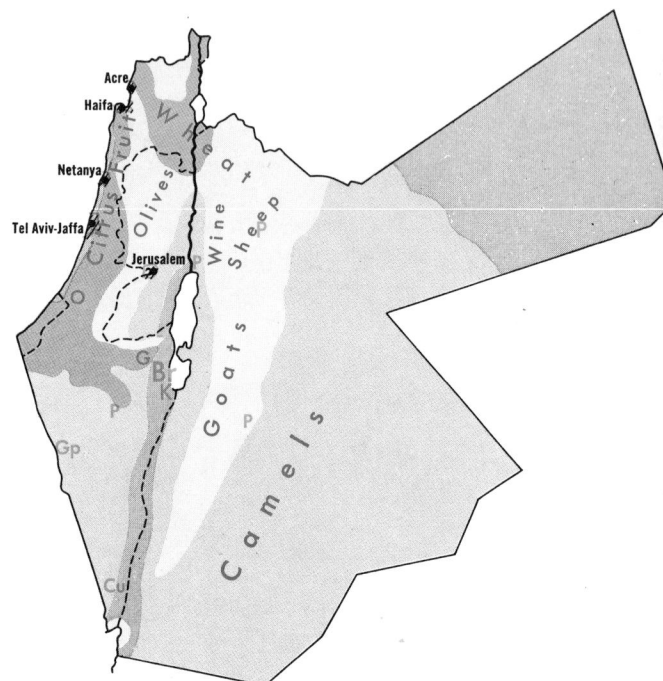

DOMINANT LAND USE

Cereals, Livestock

Cash Crops, Horticulture

Nomadic Livestock Herding

Nonagricultural Land

MAJOR MINERAL OCCURRENCES

Br Bromine
Cu Copper
G Natural Gas
Gp Gypsum

K Potash
O Petroleum
P Phosphates

▨ Major Industrial Areas

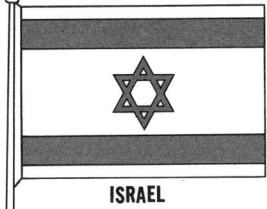

ISRAEL

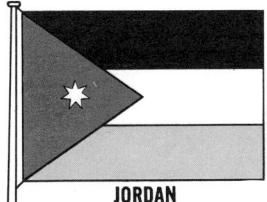

JORDAN

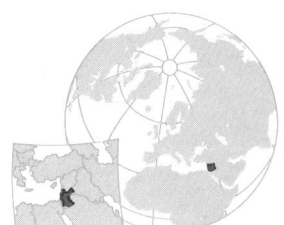

ISRAEL

AREA 7,847 sq. mi. (20,324 sq. km.)
POPULATION 3,878,000
CAPITAL Jerusalem
LARGEST CITY Tel Aviv-Jaffa
HIGHEST POINT Meiran 3,963 ft.
(1,208 m.)
MONETARY UNIT shekel
MAJOR LANGUAGES Hebrew, Arabic
MAJOR RELIGIONS Judaism, Islam,
Christianity

JORDAN

AREA (East Bank) 35,000 sq. mi.
(90,650 sq. km.)
POPULATION 2,152,273
CAPITAL Amman
LARGEST CITY Amman
HIGHEST POINT Jeb. Ramm 5,755 ft.
(1,754 m.)
MONETARY UNIT Jordanian dinar
MAJOR LANGUAGE Arabic
MAJOR RELIGION Islam

Israel and Jordan
CYLINDRICAL PROJECTION
© Copyright HAMMOND INCORPORATED, Maplewood, N.J.

SCALE OF MILES
0   5   10   15   20   25   30

SCALE OF KILOMETERS
0   5   10   15   20   25   30

Capitals of Countries .... ☆
Internal Capitals .... ⊙
International Boundaries .... — · —
Internal Boundaries .... — · · —

Scale 1:1,325,000

MEDITERRANEAN SEA

DEAD SEA

IRAN

INTERNAL DIVISIONS

Azerbaijan, East (prov.) 3,194,543 .... E1
Azerbaijan, West (prov.) 1,404,875 .... D1
Bakhtiari (governorate) 394,300 .... F4
Boyer Ahmediyeh and Kohkiluyeh (governor 244,750 .... G5
Bushehr (prov.) 345,427 .... G6
Central (Markazi) (prov.) 6,921,283 .... G3
Esfahan (Isfahan) (prov.) 1,974,938 .... H4
Fars (prov.) 2,020,947 .... H6
Gilan (prov.) 1,577,800 .... F2
Hamadan (governorate) 1,086,512 .... F3
Hormozgan (prov.) 463,419 .... J7
Ilam (governorate) 244,222 .... E4
Isfahan (Isfahan) (prov.) 1,974,938 .... H4
Kerman (prov.) 1,088,045 .... K6
Kermanshahan (prov.) 1,016,199 .... E3
Khorasan (prov.) 3,266,650 .... K3
Khuzestan (prov.) 2,176,612 .... F5
Kordestan (Kurdistan) (prov.) 781,889 .... E3
Lorestan (Luristan) (governorate) 924,848 .... F4
Mazandaran (prov.) 2,384,226 .... H2
Semnan (governorate) 485,875 .... J3
Sistan and Baluchestan (prov.) 659,297 .... M6
Yazd (governorate) 356,218 .... J5
Zanjan (governorate) 579,000 .... F2

CITIES and TOWNS

Abadan 296,081 .... F5
Abadeh 16,000 .... H5
Abarqu 8,000 .... H5
Abhar 24,000 .... F2
Agha Jari 24,195 .... F5
Ahvaz (Ahwaz) 329,006 .... F5
Amol 68,782 .... H2
Anarak 2,038 .... H4
Andimeshk 16,000 .... F4
Arak 14,507 .... H3
Ardabil 147,404 .... F1
Ardestan 5,868 .... H4
Asadabad 7,000 .... F3
Astarabad (Gorgan) 88,348 .... J2
Babol 67,790 .... H2
Babol Sar 7,237 .... H2
Bafq 5,000 .... J5
Baft 6,000 .... K6
Bahramabad (Rafsanjan) 21,000 .... K5
Bajgiran 1,151 .... L2
Bam 22,000 .... L6
Bampur 1,585 .... M7
Bandar 'Abbas 89,103 .... J7
Bandar-e Deylam 3,691 .... G5
Bandar-e Lengeh 4,920 .... J7
Bandar-e Mas hur 17,000 .... F5
Bandar-e Pahlavi (Enzeli) 55,978 .... F2
Bandar-e Rig 1,889 .... G6
Bandar-e Torkaman 13,000 .... H2
Bandar Khomeini 6,000 .... F5
Bandar Shahpur 6,000 .... F5
Bastak 2,473 .... J7
Bastam 3,296 .... J2

Behbehan 39,874 .... G5
Behshahr 26,032 .... H2
Bejestan 3,823 .... K3
Bijar 12,000 .... E3
Birjand 25,854 .... L4
Bojnurd 31,248 .... K2
Borazjan 20,000 .... G6
Borujerd 100,103 .... F4
Bostan 4,619 .... F5
Bowkan 9,000 .... E2
Bushehr (Bushire) 57,681 .... G6
Chah Bahar 1,800 .... M8
Chalus 15,000 .... G2
Damavand 5,319 .... H2
Damghan 13,000 .... J2
Darab 13,000 .... J6
Daran 4,609 .... G4
Darreh Gaz 11,000 .... L2
Deheq 4,115 .... G4
Dehkhvareqan 6,000 .... D1
Delijan 6,000 .... G4
Dizful (Dezful) 110,287 .... F4
Duzdab (Zahedan) 92,628 .... M6
Enzeli 55,978 .... F2
Esfahan (Isfahan) 671,820 .... G4
Evaz 6,064 .... J7
Ezna 5,000 .... F4
Fahrej (Iranshahr) 5,000 .... M7
Fariman 8,000 .... L3
Farrashband 3,532 .... H6
Fasa 19,000 .... H6
Ferdows 11,000 .... K3
Firuzabad 8,718 .... H6
Firuzkuh 4,684 .... H3
Fowman 9,000 .... F2
Gach Saran G5
Ganaveh 9,000 .... G6

Garmsar 4,723 .... H3
Gavater M8
Golpayegan 20,515 .... G4
Golshan (Tabas) 10,000 .... K4
Gomishan 6,000 .... H2
Gonbad 8,000 .... J3
Gonbad-e Kavus 59,868 .... J2
Gorgan (Gorgan) 88,348 .... J2
Haft Gel 10,000 .... F5
Hamadan 155,846 .... F3
Hashtgar 5,000 .... G2
Herowabad 5,422 .... F2
Hormoz 2,569 .... J7
Hoveyzeh 4,722 .... F5
Ilam 15,000 .... E4
Iranshahr 5,000 .... M7
Isfahan 671,825 .... G4
Izeh 1,983 .... F5
Jahrom 38,236 .... H6
Jajarm 3,641 .... J3
Jask 1,078 .... K8
Kakhk 4,043 .... L3
Kangan 2,682 .... G6
Kangavar 9,414 .... F3
Karaj 138,774 .... G3
Kashan 84,545 .... G3
Kashmar 17,000 .... L3
Kazvin (Qazvin) 138,527 .... F3
Kerman 140,309 .... K5
Kermanshah 290,861 .... E3
Khaf 5,000 .... M6
Khiyav 9,000 .... F1
Khomein 20,000 .... G4
Khorramabad 104,928 .... F4
Khorramshahr 146,709 .... F5
Khvaf 5,000 .... L3

Khvonsar 10,947 .... F4
Khvor 2,912 .... J4
Khvoy (Khoi) 70,040 .... D1
Kord Kuy 9,855 .... J2
Lahijan 25,725 .... F2
Lar 22,000 .... J7
Mahabad 28,610 .... E2
Mahallat 12,000 .... G4
Maku 7,000 .... D1
Malamir (Izeh) 1,983 .... F5
Malayer 28,434 .... F3
Maragheh 60,820 .... E2
Marand 24,000 .... D1
Marv Dasht 25,498 .... H6
Mashhad (Meshed) 670,180 .... L2
Masjed Soleyman 77,161 .... F4
Mehran 664 .... E4
Meshed 670,180 .... L2
Meybod 15,000 .... J4
Meshed-i-Sar (Babol) H2
Mianab 19,000 .... F5
Mianeh 28,447 .... E2
Minab 4,229 .... K7
Mirjaveh 11,000 .... M6
Naft-e Shah 3,043 .... D4
Nahavand 24,000 .... F4
Nain 5,925 .... H4
Najafabad 76,236 .... G4
Naraq 2,735 .... G4
Nasratabad (Zabol) 20,000 .... M5
Natanz 4,370 .... H4
Neyriz 16,114 .... J6
Semnan 31,058 .... J6
Nishapur (Neyshabur) 59,101 .... L2
Nosratabad 20,000 .... L3
Now Shahr 8,000 .... G2
Now Zovmiri 5,000 .... D2

Pahlevi (Enzeli) 55,978 .... F2
Pazanan 81 .... G5
Qasr-e-Shirin 15,094 .... E3
Qayen 6,000 .... L4
Qazvin 138,527 .... F3
Qom 246,831 .... G3
Qorveh 2,929 .... E3
Quchan 29,133 .... L2
Qum (Qom) 246,831 .... G3
Rafsanjan 21,000 .... K5
Ramhormoz 9,000 .... F5
Ramsar 12,000 .... G2
Rasht (Rashti) 187,203 .... F2
Ravar 5,074 .... K5
Resht (Rasht) 187,203 .... F2
Rey 102,825 .... G3
Rezaiyeh (Urmia) 163,991 .... D1
Rigan 8,255 .... L6
Rud Sar 7,460 .... G2
Sabzevar 69,174 .... K2
Sabzvaran 7,000 .... K6
Sai dabad 20,000 .... J6
Sanandaj 95,834 .... E3
Sang-e Sar 9,000 .... H3
Saqqez 17,000 .... E2
Sarab 16,000 .... E2
Sarakhs 3,461 .... M2
Saravan 4,012 .... N7
Sar Dasht 6,000 .... D2
Sar Eskand Khan 3,153 .... E2
Saveh 17,565 .... G3
Semnan 31,058 .... H3
Shadegan 4,000 .... F5
Shahabad 12,000 .... E3
Shahdad 2,777 .... K5
Shahi 63,289 .... H2
Shahin Dezh 4,195 .... E2

Shahistan (Saravan) 4,012 .... N7
Shahreza 34,220 .... H4
Shahr Kord 24,000 .... G4
Shahrud 30,767 .... J2
Shahsavar 12,000 .... G2
Sharafkhaneh 1,260 .... D1
Shiraz 416,408 .... H6
Shirvan 11,000 .... L2
Shush 1,433 .... F4
Shushtar 24,000 .... F4
Sinneh (Sanandaj) 95,834 .... E3
Sirjan (Sai'dabad) 20,000 .... J6
Sivand 1,811 .... H6
Songor 10,433 .... F3
Sufian 2,914 .... D1
Sultanabad (Kashmar) 17,000 .... L3
Susangerd 21,000 .... F5
Tabas 10,000 .... K4
Tabriz 598,576 .... E1
Taft 7,000 .... J5
Tajrish 157,486 .... G3
Takestan 13,485 .... F2
Tehran (cap.) 4,496,159 .... G3
Torbat-e-Heydariyeh 30,106 .... L3
Torbat-e Jam 13,000 .... M3
Tun (Ferdows) 11,000 .... K3
Turbat-i-Shaikh Jam 13,000 .... M3
Urmia 163,991 .... D1
Varamin 11,183 .... G3
Yazd (Yezd) 135,978 .... J5
Yazd-e Khvast 3,544 .... H5
Zabol 20,000 .... M5
Zahedan 92,628 .... M6
Zarand 5,000 .... K6
Zarqam 7,000 .... H6
Zenjan (Zanjan) 99,967 .... F2

Iran and Iraq

CONIC PROJECTION

SCALE OF MILES
0 25 50 100 150 200

SCALE OF KILOMETERS
0 25 50 100 150 200

Capitals of Countries .... ★
Capitals of Provinces .... △
Capitals of Governorates .... ◉
International Boundaries ....
Provincial Boundaries ....
Governorate Boundaries ....

Scale 1:8,160,000

© Copyright HAMMOND INCORPORATED, Maplewood, N.J.

Iran consists of fifteen provinces called ostans. Attached to seven of these provinces are eight governorates.

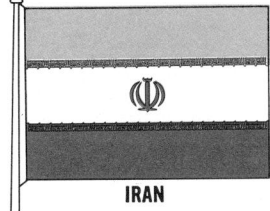

IRAN

IRAQ

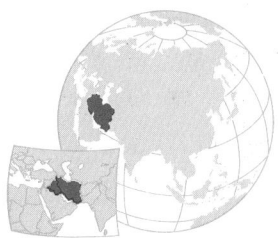

AREA 636,293 sq. mi. (1,648,000 sq. km.)
POPULATION 37,447,000
CAPITAL Tehran
LARGEST CITY Tehran
HIGHEST POINT Damavand 18,376 ft. (5,601 m.)
MONETARY UNIT Iranian rial
MAJOR LANGUAGES Persian, Azerbaijani, Kurdish
MAJOR RELIGION Islam

AREA 172,476 sq. mi. (446,713 sq. km.)
POPULATION 12,767,000
CAPITAL Baghdad
LARGEST CITY Baghdad
HIGHEST POINT Haji Ibrahim 11,811 ft. (3,600 m.)
MONETARY UNIT Iraqi dinar
MAJOR LANGUAGES Arabic, Kurdish
MAJOR RELIGION Islam

Topography

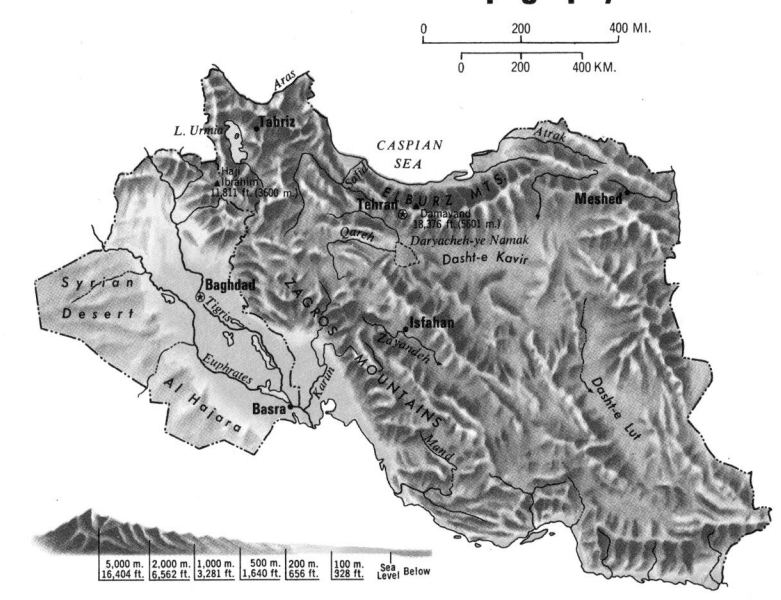

Agriculture, Industry and Resources

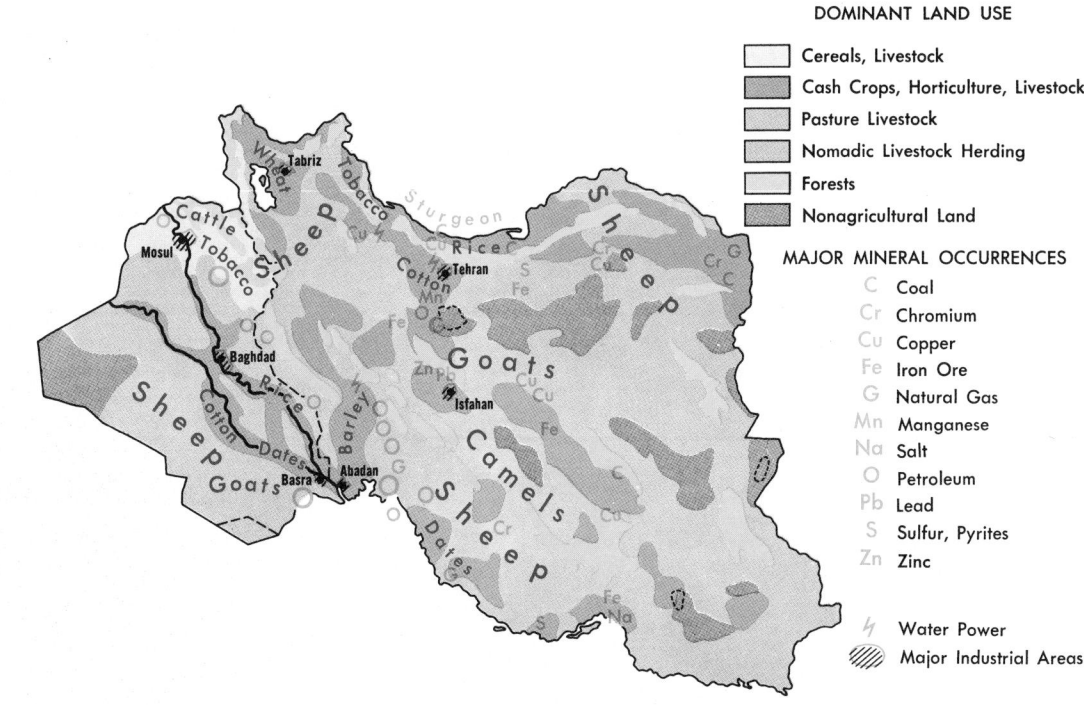

DOMINANT LAND USE

- Cereals, Livestock
- Cash Crops, Horticulture, Livestock
- Pasture Livestock
- Nomadic Livestock Herding
- Forests
- Nonagricultural Land

MAJOR MINERAL OCCURRENCES

- C Coal
- Cr Chromium
- Cu Copper
- Fe Iron Ore
- G Natural Gas
- Mn Manganese
- Na Salt
- O Petroleum
- Pb Lead
- S Sulfur, Pyrites
- Zn Zinc

⚡ Water Power
▨ Major Industrial Areas

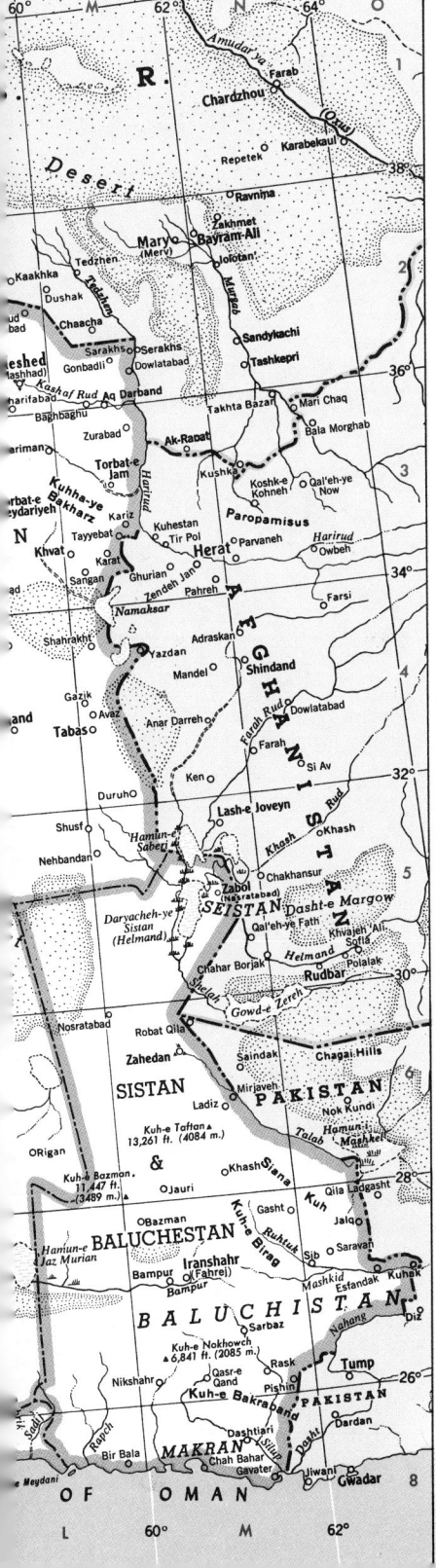

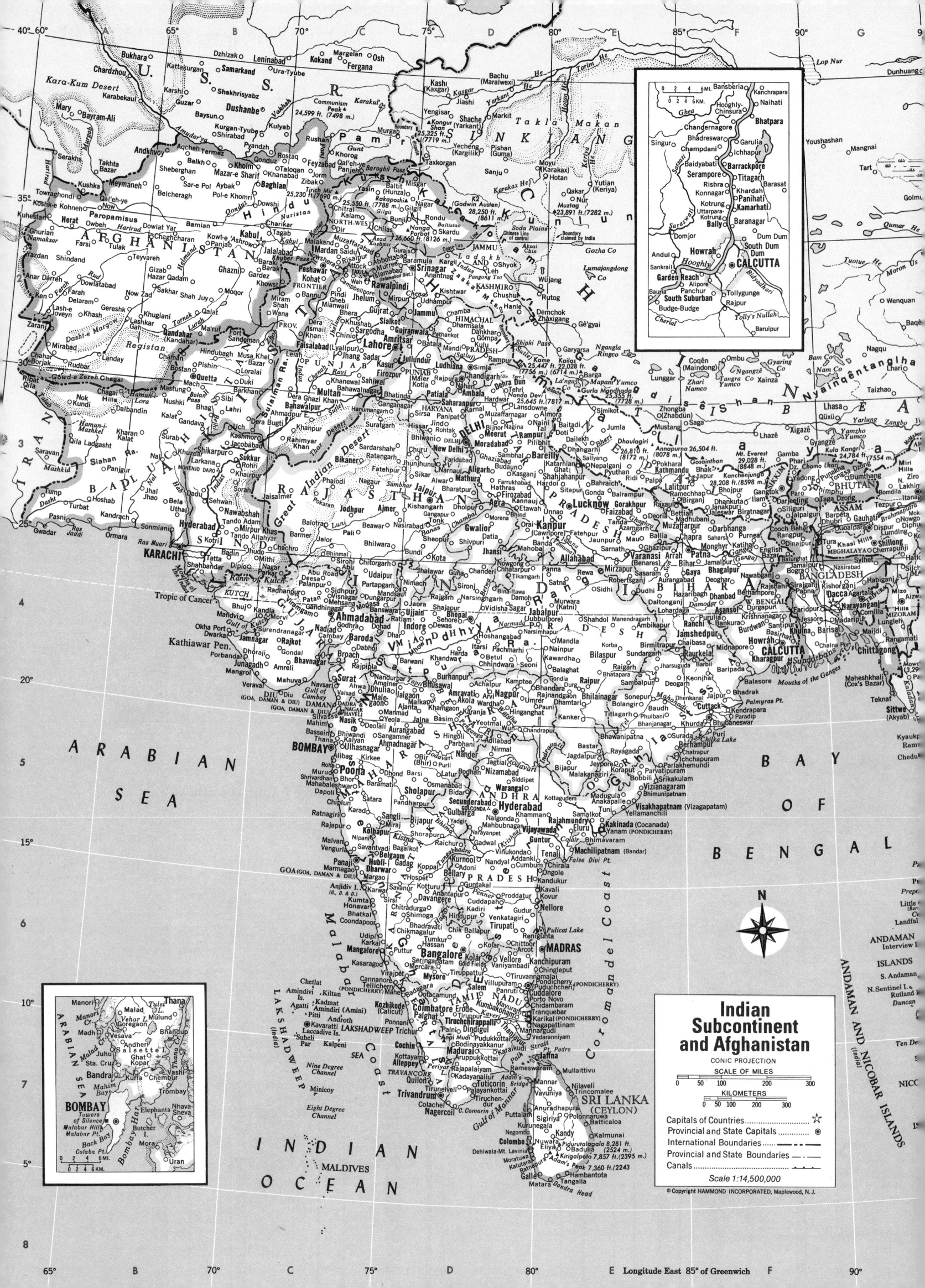

Indian Subcontinent and Afghanistan

CONIC PROJECTION

SCALE OF MILES

KILOMETERS

Capitals of Countries .... ☆
Provincial and State Capitals .... ◉
International Boundaries ...... -------
Provincial and State Boundaries ...-..-..-
Canals ....

Scale 1:14,500,000

© Copyright HAMMOND INCORPORATED, Maplewood, N.J.

BOMBAY

CALCUTTA

Longitude East 85° of Greenwich

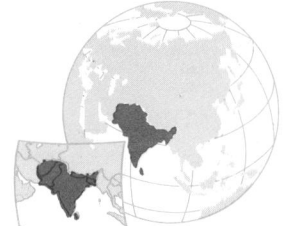

INDIA

AREA 1,269,339 sq. mi. (3,287,588 sq. km.)
POPULATION 683,810,051
CAPITAL New Delhi
LARGEST CITY Calcutta (greater)
HIGHEST POINT Nanda Devi 25,645 ft. (7,817 m.)
MONETARY UNIT Indian rupee
MAJOR LANGUAGES Hindi, English, Bihari, Telugu,
Marathi, Bengali, Tamil, Gujarati, Rajasthani,
Kanarese, Malayalam, Oriya, Punjabi, Assamese,
Kashmiri, Urdu
MAJOR RELIGIONS Hinduism, Islam, Christianity,
Sikhism, Buddhism, Jainism, Zoroastrianism, Animism

PAKISTAN

AREA 310,403 sq. mi. (803,944 sq. km.)
POPULATION 83,782,000
CAPITAL Islamabad
LARGEST CITY Karachi
HIGHEST POINT K2 (Godwin Austen)
28,250 ft. (8,611 m.)
MONETARY UNIT Pakistani rupee
MAJOR LANGUAGES Urdu, English, Punjabi,
Pushtu, Sindhi, Baluchi, Brahui
MAJOR RELIGIONS Islam, Hinduism, Sikhism,
Christianity, Buddhism

SRI LANKA (CEYLON)

AREA 25,332 sq. mi.
(65,610 sq. km.)
POPULATION 14,850,001
CAPITAL Colombo
LARGEST CITY Colombo
HIGHEST POINT Pidurutalagala
8,281 ft. (2,524 m.)
MONETARY UNIT Sri Lanka rupee
MAJOR LANGUAGES Sinhala, Tamil,
English
MAJOR RELIGIONS Buddhism,
Hinduism, Christianity, Islam

AFGHANISTAN

AREA 250,775 sq. mi.
(649,507 sq. km.)
POPULATION 15,540,000
CAPITAL Kabul
LARGEST CITY Kabul
HIGHEST POINT Nowshak
24,557 ft. (7,485 m.)
MONETARY UNIT afghani
MAJOR LANGUAGES Pushtu, Dari,
Uzbek
MAJOR RELIGION Islam

NEPAL

AREA 54,663 sq. mi.
(141,577 sq. km.)
POPULATION 14,179,301
CAPITAL Kathmandu
LARGEST CITY Kathmandu
HIGHEST POINT Mt. Everest
29,028 ft. (8,848 m.)
MONETARY UNIT Nepalese rupee
MAJOR LANGUAGES Nepali,
Maithili, Tamang, Newari, Tharu
MAJOR RELIGIONS Hinduism,
Buddhism

MALDIVES

AREA 115 sq. mi. (298 sq. km.)
POPULATION 143,046
CAPITAL Male
LARGEST CITY Male
HIGHEST POINT 20 ft. (6 m.)
MONETARY UNIT Maldivian rupee
MAJOR LANGUAGE Divehi
MAJOR RELIGION Islam

BHUTAN

AREA 18,147 sq. mi.
(47,000 sq. km.)
POPULATION 1,298,000
CAPITAL Thimphu
LARGEST CITY Thimphu
HIGHEST POINT Kula Kangri
24,784 ft. (7,554 m.)
MONETARY UNIT ngultrum
MAJOR LANGUAGES Dzongka,
Nepali
MAJOR RELIGIONS Buddhism,
Hinduism

BANGLADESH

AREA 55,126 sq. mi.
(142,776 sq. km.)
POPULATION 87,052,024
CAPITAL Dacca
LARGEST CITY Dacca
HIGHEST POINT Keokradong
4,034 ft. (1,230 m.)
MONETARY UNIT taka
MAJOR LANGUAGES Bengali,
English
MAJOR RELIGIONS Islam,
Hinduism, Christianity

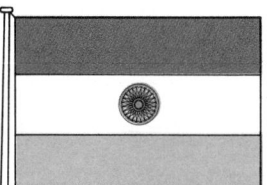
INDIA

PAKISTAN

SRI LANKA (CEYLON)

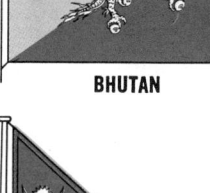
BHUTAN

AFGHANISTAN

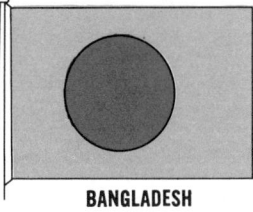
MALDIVES

BANGLADESH

NEPAL

AFGHANISTAN

CITIES and TOWNS

Andkhvoy A1
Aqcheh B1
Aybak 33,016 .... B1
Baghlan 75,130 .... B1
Balkh B1
Bamian 7,355 .... B2
Belcheragh B1
Chaghcharan 2,974 .... B2
Chahar Borjak A2
Charikar 25,093 .... B1
Delaram A2
Dowlatabad A1
Dowlat Yar B2
Dowshi B1
Farah 18,797 .... A2
Farsi A2
Feyzabad 10,142 .... C1
Gardez 11,415 .... B2
Gereshk A2
Ghazni 30,425 .... B2
Ghurian A2
Gizab B2
Hazar Qadam B2
Herat 163,960 .... A2
Jalalabad 56,384 .... B2
Jorm C1
Kabul (cap.) 905,108 .... B2
Kalat (Qalat) 5,946 .... B2
Kandahar (Qandahar) 178,409 .... B2
Ken A2
Khanabad B1
Khash A2
Kholm B1
Khowst B2
Khugiani B2
Koshke-e Kohneh A2
Kowt-e 'Ashrow B2
Kuhestan A2
Landay A2
Lash-e Joveyn A2
Lashkar Gah 26,646 .... A2
Mar'uf B2
Mazar-e Sharif 122,567 .... B1
Meymaneh 54,954 .... A1
Mirabad A2
Moqor B2
Now Zad A2
Oruzgan (Hazar Qadam) B2
Owbeh A2
Panjab B2
Pol-e Khomri B1
Qalat 5,946 .... B2
Qale'h-ye Now 5,340 .... A1
Qale'h-ye Panjeh C1
Qandahar 178,409 .... B2
Qonduz 107,191 .... B1
Rostaq B1
Rudbar A2
Sakhar B2
Sar-e Pol B1
Shay Juy B2
Sheberghan 54,870 .... B1
Shindand A2
Spin Buldak B2
Tagab B1
Taloqan 46,202 .... B1
Teyvareh A2
Towraghondi A1
Tulak A2
Zaranj 6,477 .... A2
Zibak C1

OTHER FEATURES

Farah Rud (riv.) A2

Hanrud (riv.) A1
Helmand (riv.) B2
Hindu Kush (mts.) B1
Kabul (riv.) C1
Konar (riv.) C1
Lurah (riv.) B2
Margow, Dasht-e (des.) A2
Namaksar (salt lake) A2
Paropamisus (range) A2
Tarnak (riv.) B2

BANGLADESH

CITIES and TOWNS

Barisal 98,127 .... G4
Bogra 47,154 .... F4
Chalna Port 14,590 .... G4
Chittagong 889,760 .... G4
Comilla 86,446 .... G4
Cox's Bazar
(Maheshkhali) 15,720 .... G4
Dacca (cap.) 1,679,572 .... G4
Dinajpur 61,866 .... F3
Faridpur 46,232 .... F4
Habiganj 16,281 .... G4
Jamalpur 60,261 .... F4
Jessore 76,168 .... F4
Khulna 437,304 .... F4
Kishorganj 35,605 .... G4
Madaripur 32,488 .... G4
Maheshkhali 15,720 .... G4
Mymensingh (Nasirabad) 182,153 .... G4
Narayanganj 270,680 .... G4
Nasirabad 182,153 .... G4
Nawabganj 46,059 .... F4
Noakhali 32,490 .... G4
Pabna 62,254 .... F4
Rajshahi 132,909 .... F4
Rangamati 20,473 .... G4
Rangpur 72,829 .... F3
Sirajganj 74,457 .... F4
Sylhet 59,546 .... G4
Teknaf G4

OTHER FEATURES

Bengal, Bay of (sea) F5
Brahmaputra (riv.) F3
Ganges (riv.) F3
Sundarbans F4

BHUTAN

CITIES and TOWNS

Bumthang 10,000 .... G3
Paro 35,000 .... G3
Punakha 12,000 .... G3
Taga Dzong 18,000 .... G3
Thimphu (cap.) 50,000 .... G3
Tongsa Dzong 2,500 .... G3

OTHER FEATURES

Chomo Lhari (mt.) F3
Himalaya (mts.) E2
Kula Kangri (mt.) G3

INDIA

INTERNAL DIVISIONS

Andaman and Nicobar Isls.
(terr.) 188,254 .... G6
Andhra Pradesh
(state) 53,403,619 .... D5
Arunachal Pradesh
(terr.) 628,050 .... G3

(continued on following page)

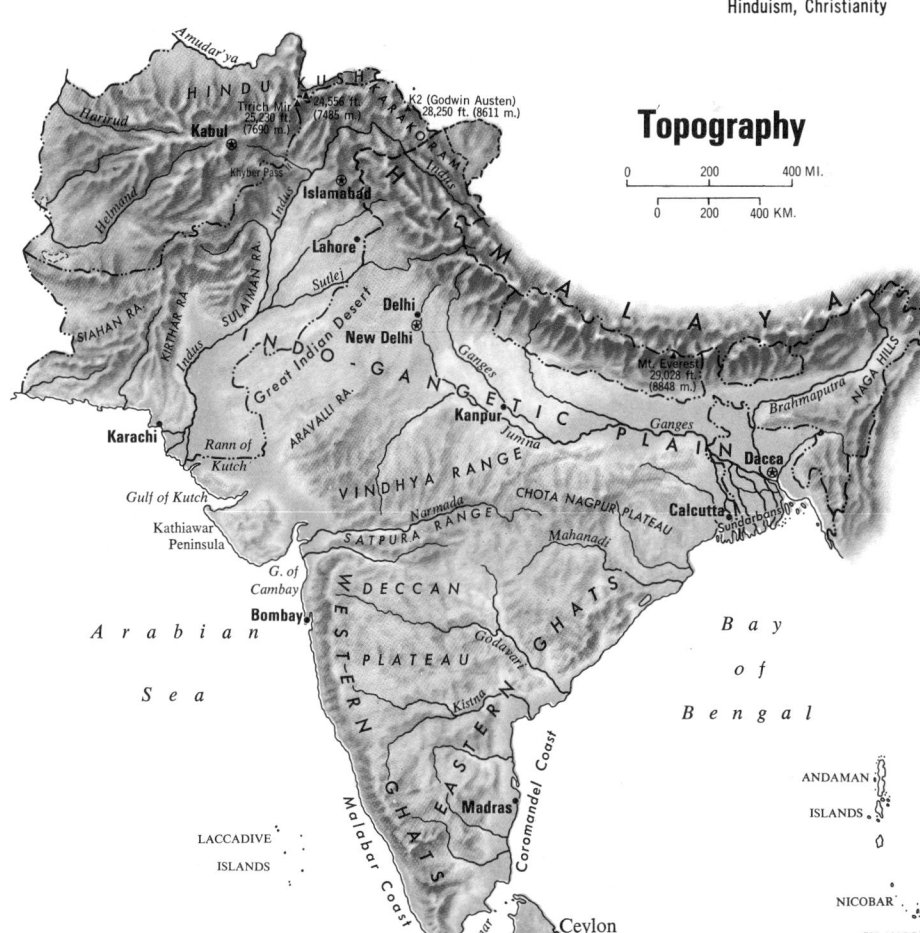

Topography

0   200   400 MI.

0   200   400 KM.

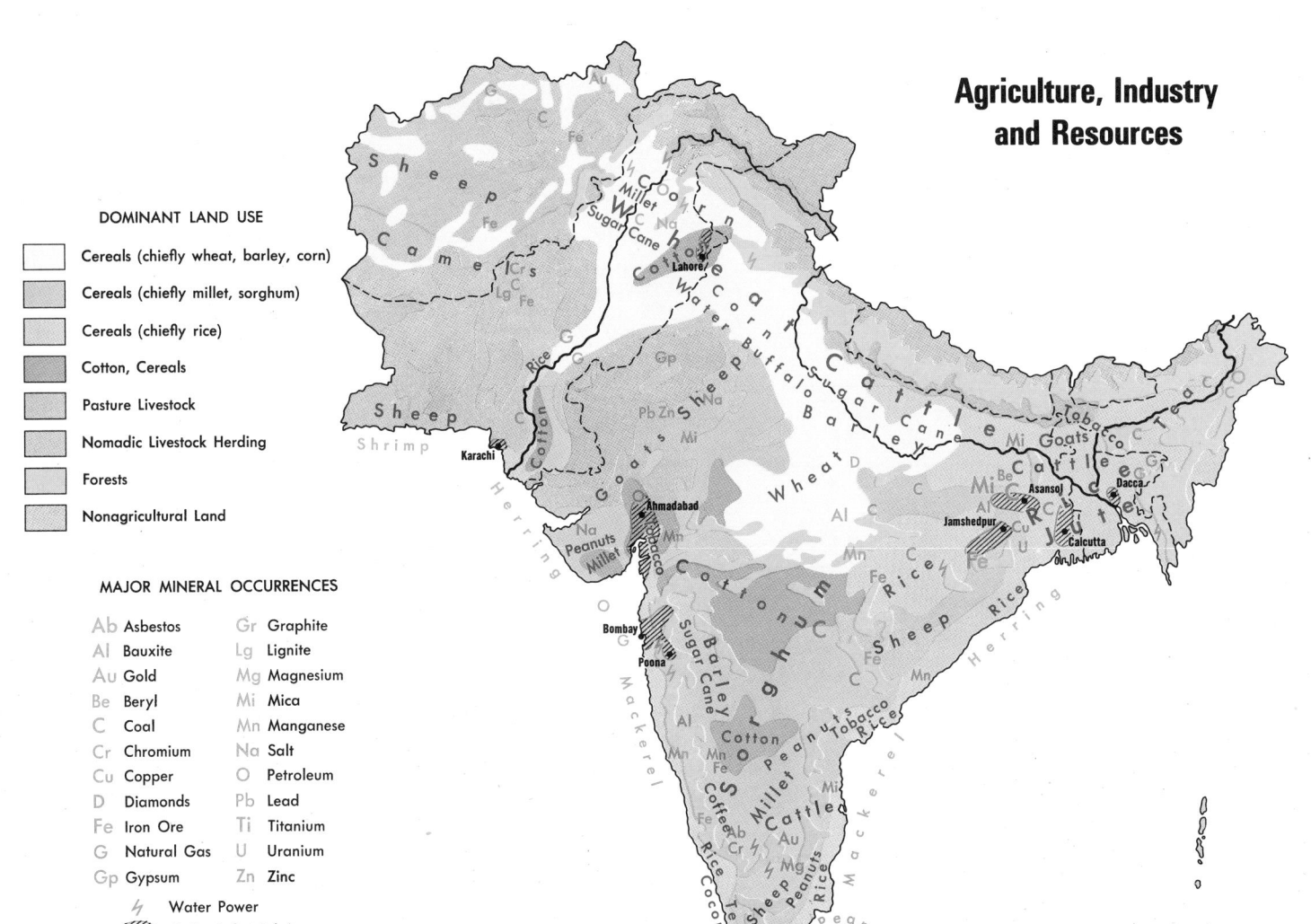

Agriculture, Industry and Resources

DOMINANT LAND USE

- Cereals (chiefly wheat, barley, corn)
- Cereals (chiefly millet, sorghum)
- Cereals (chiefly rice)
- Cotton, Cereals
- Pasture Livestock
- Nomadic Livestock Herding
- Forests
- Nonagricultural Land

MAJOR MINERAL OCCURRENCES

Ab	Asbestos	Gr	Graphite
Al	Bauxite	Lg	Lignite
Au	Gold	Mg	Magnesium
Be	Beryl	Mi	Mica
C	Coal	Mn	Manganese
Cr	Chromium	Na	Salt
Cu	Copper	O	Petroleum
D	Diamonds	Pb	Lead
Fe	Iron Ore	Ti	Titanium
G	Natural Gas	U	Uranium
Gp	Gypsum	Zn	Zinc

⚡ Water Power

▨ Major Industrial Areas

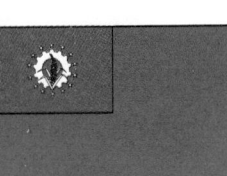

BURMA

THAILAND

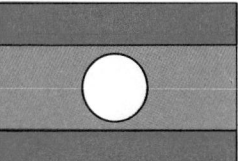

LAOS

CAMBODIA

VIETNAM

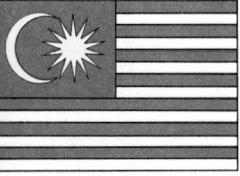

MALAYSIA

SINGAPORE

BURMA

AREA 261,789 sq. mi. (678,034 sq. km.)
POPULATION 32,913,000
CAPITAL Rangoon
LARGEST CITY Rangoon
HIGHEST POINT Hkakabo Razi 19,296 ft. (5,881 m.)
MONETARY UNIT kyat
MAJOR LANGUAGES Burmese, Karen, Shan, Kachin, Chin, Kayah, English
MAJOR RELIGIONS Buddhism, tribal religions

THAILAND

AREA 198,455 sq. mi. (513,998 sq. km.)
POPULATION 46,455,000
CAPITAL Bangkok
LARGEST CITY Bangkok
HIGHEST POINT Doi Inthanon 8,452 ft. (2,576 m.)
MONETARY UNIT baht
MAJOR LANGUAGES Thai, Lao, Chinese, Khmer, Malay
MAJOR RELIGIONS Buddhism, tribal religions

LAOS

AREA 91,428 sq. mi. (236,800 sq. km.)
POPULATION 3,721,000
CAPITAL Vientiane
LARGEST CITY Vientiane
HIGHEST POINT Phou Bia 9,252 ft. (2,820 m.)
MONETARY UNIT kip
MAJOR LANGUAGE Lao
MAJOR RELIGIONS Buddhism, tribal religions

CAMBODIA

AREA 69,898 sq. mi. (181,036 sq. km.)
POPULATION 5,200,000
CAPITAL Phnom Penh
LARGEST CITY Phnom Penh
HIGHEST POINT 5,948 ft. (1,813 m.)
MONETARY UNIT riel
MAJOR LANGUAGE Khmer (Cambodian)
MAJOR RELIGION Buddhism

VIETNAM

AREA 128,405 sq. mi. (332,569 sq. km.)
POPULATION 52,741,766
CAPITAL Hanoi
LARGEST CITY Ho Chi Minh City (Saigon)
HIGHEST POINT Fan Si Pan 10,308 ft. (3,142 m.)
MONETARY UNIT dong
MAJOR LANGUAGES Vietnamese, Thai, Muong, Meo, Yao, Khmer, French, Chinese, Cham
MAJOR RELIGIONS Buddhism, Taoism, Confucianism, Roman Catholicism, Cao-Dai

MALAYSIA

AREA 128,308 sq. mi. (332,318 sq. km.)
POPULATION 13,435,588
CAPITAL Kuala Lumpur
LARGEST CITY Kuala Lumpur
HIGHEST POINT Mt. Kinabalu 13,455 ft. (4,101 m.)
MONETARY UNIT ringgit
MAJOR LANGUAGES Malay, Chinese, English, Tamil, Dayak, Kadazan
MAJOR RELIGIONS Islam, Confucianism, Buddhism, tribal religions, Hinduism, Taoism, Christianity, Sikhism

SINGAPORE

AREA 226 sq. mi. (585 sq. km.)
POPULATION 2,413,945
CAPITAL Singapore
LARGEST CITY Singapore
HIGHEST POINT Bukit Timah 581 ft. (177 m.)
MONETARY UNIT Singapore dollar
MAJOR LANGUAGES Chinese, Malay, Tamil, English, Hindi
MAJOR RELIGIONS Confucianism, Buddhism, Taoism, Hinduism, Islam, Christianity

Topography

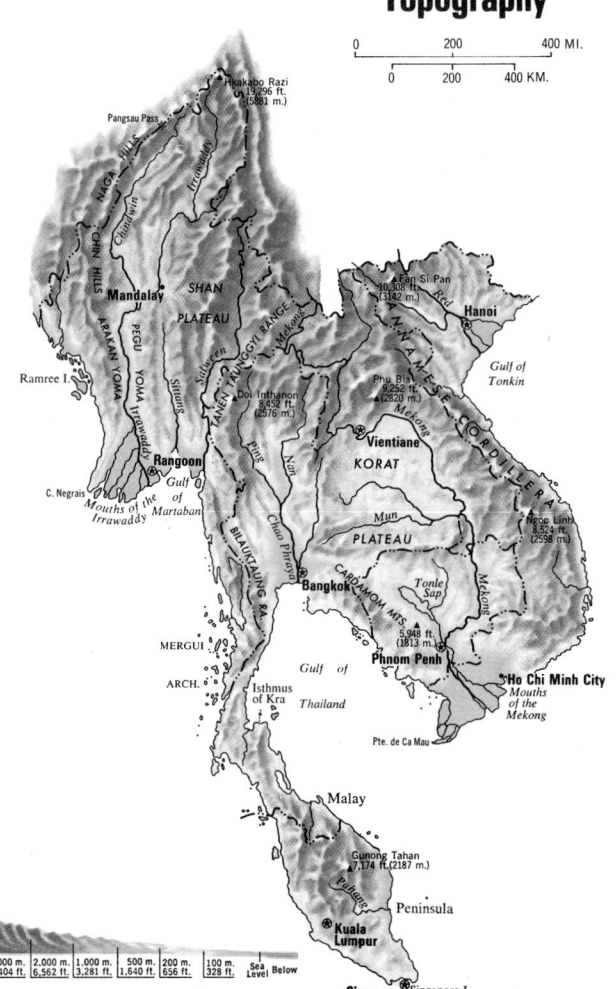

BURMA	
INTERNAL DIVISIONS	
Arakan (state) 1,710,913	B3
Chin (state) 323,094	B2
Irrawaddy (div.) 4,152,521	B3
Kachin (state) 735,144	C1
Karen (state) 865,218	C3
Kayah (state) 126,492	C3
Magwe (div.) 2,632,144	B2
Mandalay (div.) 3,662,312	B2
Mon (state) 1,313,111	C3
Pegu (div.) 3,174,109	C3
Rangoon (div.) 3,186,886	C3
Sagaing (div.) 3,115,502	B1
Shan (state) 3,178,214	C2
Tenasserim (div.) 717,607	C4
CITIES and TOWNS	
Akyab (Sittwe) 42,329	B2
Allanmyo 15,580	B3
Amarapura 11,268	B2
Amherst 6,000	C3
An	B3
Anin	C4
Bassein 126,045	B3
Bhamo 9,821	C1
Chauk 24,466	B2
Danubyu	B3
Falam	C2
Fort Hertz (Putao)	C1
Gawai	C1
Gokteik	C2
Gwa	B3
Gyobingauk 9,922	C3
Haka	B2
Henzada 61,972	B3
Hmawbi 23,032	C3
Homalin	B1
Hsenwi	C2
Hsipaw	C2
Htawgaw	C1
Insein 143,625	C3
Kamaing	C1
Karathuri	C5
Katha 7,648	C1
Kawludo	C5
Kawthaung 1,520	C5
Keng Hkam	C2
Keng Tung	C2
Koma	C4
Kunlong	C2
Kyaikto 13,154	C3
Kya-in Seikkyi	C3
Kyangin 6,073	B3
Kyaukme	C2
Kyaukpadaung 5,480	B2
Kyaukpyu 7,335	B3
Kyaukse 8,659	C2
Labutta 12,982	B3
Lai-hka	C2
Lamu	B3
Lashio	C2
Lenya	C5
Letpadan 15,896	C3
Lewe	C3
Loi-kaw	C3
Lonton	B1
Magwe 13,270	B2
Maingkwan	C1
Maliwun	C5
Mandalay 418,008	C2
Man Hpang	C2
Martaban 5,661	C3
Ma-ubin 23,362	B3
Maungdaw 3,772	B2
Mawkmai	C2
Mawlaik 2,993	B2
Mawlu	C1
Maymyo 22,287	C2
Meiktila 19,474	B2
Mergui 33,697	C4
Minbu 9,096	B2
Minhla 6,470	B3
Mogaung 2,920	C1
Mogok 8,334	C1
Mohnyin	C1
Möng Hsat	C2
Möng Maü	C3
Möng Mit	C2
Möng Pan	C2
Möng Si	C2
Möng Ton	C2
Möng Tung	C2
Monywa 26,279	B2
Moulmein 171,977	C3
Mudon 20,136	C3
Myanaung 11,155	B3
Myaungmya 24,532	B3
Myingyan 36,439	B2
Myitkyina 12,382	C1
Myohaung 6,534	B3
Naba	B1
Namhkam	C2
Namlan	C2
Namtu	C2
Natmauk	B2
Okkan 14,443	B3
Okpo 12,155	C3
Pakokku 30,943	B2
Palaw 5,596	C4
Paletwa	B2
Pantha	B2
Papun	C3
Pasawng	C3
Paungde 17,286	B3
Pegu 47,378	C3
Prome (Pye) 36,997	B3
Putao	C1
Pyapon 19,174	B3
Pye 36,997	B3
Pyinmana 22,025	C3
Pyu 10,443	C3
Rangoon (cap.) 1,586,422	C3
Rangoon* 2,055,365	C3
Rathedaung 2,969	B2
Sadon	C1
Sagaing 15,382	B2
Samka	C2
Sandoway 5,172	B3
Shingbwiyang	B1
Shwebo 17,827	B2
Shwenyaung	C2
Singkaling Hkamti	B1
Singu 4,027	C2
Sinlumkaba	C1
Sittwe 42,329	B2
Sumprabum	C1
Syriam 15,296	C3
Taungdwingyi 16,233	C2
Taunggyi	C2
Tavoy 40,312	C4
Tharrawaddy 8,977	B3
Thaton 38,047	C3
Thaungdut	B1
Thayetmyo 11,649	B3
Thazi 7,531	C2
Thongwa 10,829	C3
Toungoo 31,589	C3
Wakema 20,716	B3
Yamethin 11,167	C2
Yandoon 15,245	B3
Ye 12,852	C4
Yenangyaung 24,416	B2
Yesagyo 7,880	B2
Ye-u 5,307	B2
Ywathit	C3
Zadi	C4
Zalun 899	B3
OTHER FEATURES	
Amya (pass)	C4
Andaman (sea)	B4
Arakan Yoma (mts.)	B3
Ataran (riv.)	C4
Bengal, Bay of (sea)	B3
Bentinck (isl.)	C5

(continued on following page)

Agriculture, Industry and Resources

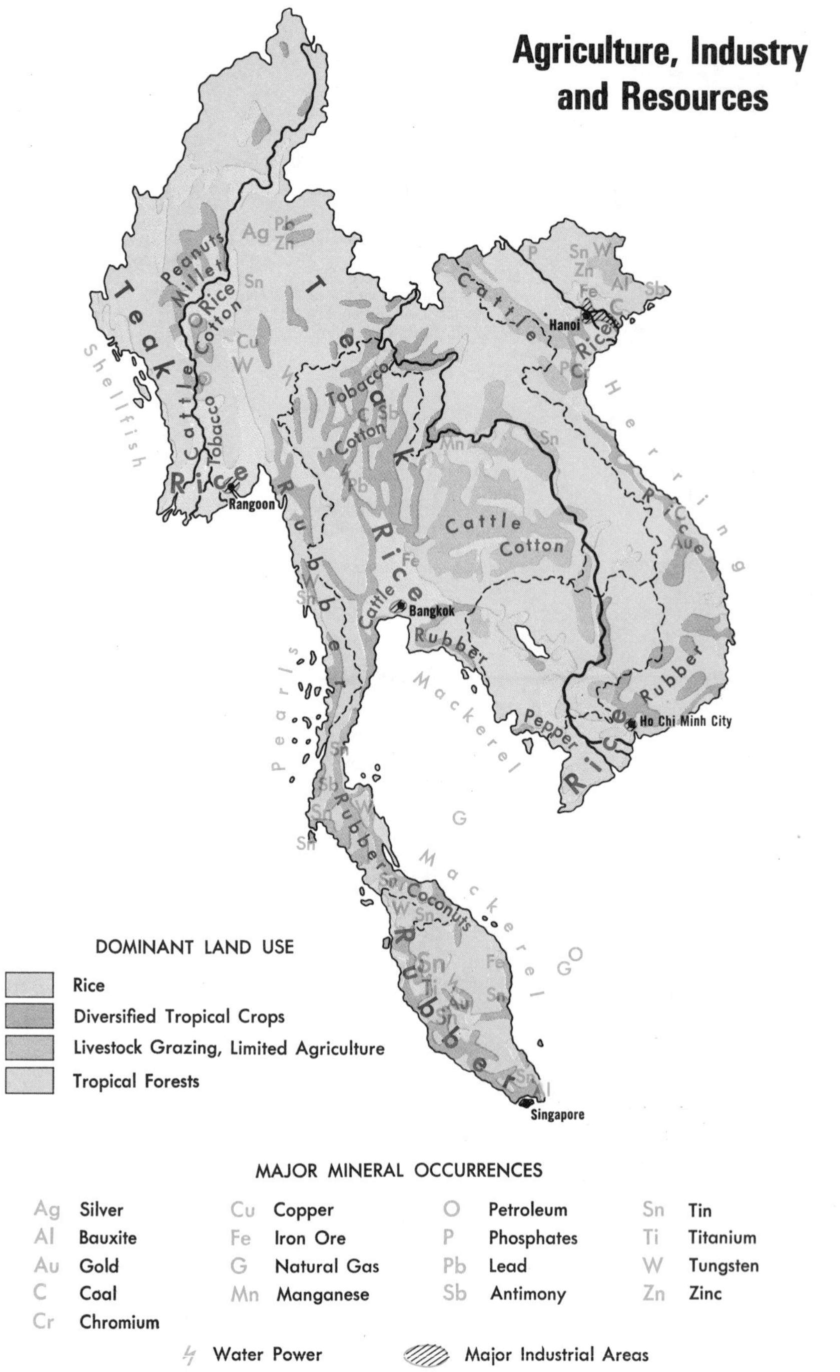
Teak
Peanuts
Millet
Rice
Cotton
Cattle
Tobacco
Shellfish
Rangoon
Rubber
Teak
Tobacco
Cotton
Rice
Cattle
Cotton
Cattle
Bangkok
Rubber
Pearls
Mackerel
Pepper
Rubber
Ho Chi Minh City
Rice
Cattle
Hanoi
Rice
Herring
Rice
Rubber
Coconuts
Mackerel
Singapore
Ag
Pb
Zn
Sn
Cu
W
Mn
Fe
P
Al
C
Sb
G
O
DOMINANT LAND USE
Rice
Diversified Tropical Crops
Livestock Grazing, Limited Agriculture
Tropical Forests
MAJOR MINERAL OCCURRENCES
Ag Silver
Al Bauxite
Au Gold
C Coal
Cr Chromium
Cu Copper
Fe Iron Ore
G Natural Gas
Mn Manganese
O Petroleum
P Phosphates
Pb Lead
Sb Antimony
Sn Tin
Ti Titanium
W Tungsten
Zn Zinc
Water Power
Major Industrial Areas

Bilauktaung (range) C4
Chaukan (pass) C1
Cheduba (isl.) B3
Chin (hills) B2
Chindwin (riv.) B2
Coco (chan.) B4
Combermere (bay) B3
Daung Kyun (isl.) C4
Dawna (range) C3
Great Coco (isl.) B4
Great Tenasserim (riv.) C4
Heinze Chaung (bay) C4
Heywood (chan.) B3
Hka, Nam (riv.) C2
Hkakabo Razi (mt.) C1
Indawgyi (lake) C1
Inle (lake) C2
Irrawaddy (riv.) B3
Irrawaddy, Mouths of the (delta) B4
Kadan Kyun (isl.) C4
Kaladan (riv.) B2
Kalegauk (isl.) C4
Khao Luang (mt.) C5
Lanbi Kyun (isl.) C5
Launglon Bok (isls.) C4
Loi Leng (mt.) C2
Manipur (riv.) B2
Martaban (gulf) C4
Mekong (riv.) D2
Mergui (arch.) C5
Mon (riv.) B2
Mu (riv.) B2
Negrais (cape) B3
Pakchan (riv.) C5
Pangsau (pass) C1
Pawn, Nam (riv.) C2
Pegu Yoma (mts.) B3
Preparis (isl.) B4
Ramree (isl.) B3
Salween (riv.) C3
Shan (plat.) C2
Sittang (riv.) C3
Taungthonton (mt.) B1
Tavoy (pt.) C4
Tenasserim (isl.) C4
Teng, Nam (riv.) C2
Three Pagodas (pass) C4
Victoria (mt.) B2

CAMBODIA (KAMPUCHEA)

CITIES and TOWNS

Batdambang (Battambang) D4
Choam Khsant E4
Kampong Cham E4
Kampong Chhnang D4
Kampong Khleang E4
Kampong Saom D5
Kampong Spoe E5
Kampong Thum E4
Kampong Trabek E5
Kampot E5
Kaoh Nhek E4
Kracheh E4
Krong Kaoh Kong D4
Krong Keb E5
Kulen E4
Lumphat E4
Moung Roessei D4
Pailin D4
Paoy Pet D4
Phnom Penh (cap.) c. 300,000 E5
Phnum Tbeng Meanchey E4
Phsar Ream D5
Phumi Banam E5
Phumi Phsar E4
Phumi Prek Kak E4
Phumi Samraong D4
Pouthisat D4
Prek Pouthi E5
Prey Veng E5
Pursat (Pouthisat) D4
Rovieng Tbong E4
Sambor E4
Senmonoron E4
Siempang E4
Siemreab D4
Sisophon D4
Sre Ambel D5
Sre Khtum E4
Stoeng Treng E4
Suong E5
Svay Rieng E5
Takev E5
Virochey E4

OTHER FEATURES

Angkor Wat (ruins) E4
Dangrek (mts.) D4
Drang, Ia (riv.) E4
Joncs (plain) E5
Khong, Se (riv.) E4
Kong, Kaoh (isl.) D5
Mekong (riv.) E4
Rung, Kaoh (isl.) D5
San, Se (riv.) E4
Sen, Stoeng (riv.) E4
Srepok (riv.) E4
Tang, Kaoh (isl.) D5
Thailand (gulf) D5
Tonle Sap (lake) D4
Wai, Poulo (isls.) D5

LAOS

CITIES and TOWNS

Attapu 2,750 E4
Ban Khon E4
Ban Lahanam E3
Borikan D3
Champasak 3,500 E4
Dônghén E3
Khamkeut⊙ 31,206 E3
Louang Namtha 1,459 D2
Louangphrabang 7,596 D3
Muang Hinboun 1,750 E3
Muang Kènthao D3
Muang Khammoun 5,500 E3
Muang Không 1,750 E4
Muang Khôngxédôn 2,000 E4
Muang Khoua D2
Muang May E4
Muang Ou Tai D2
Muang Paktha D2
Muang Phin E3
Muang Tahoi E3
Muang Vapi E4
Muang Xaignabouri (Sayaboury) 2,500 D3
Mounlapamôk E4
Napè E3
Nong Het E3
Pakxé 8,000 E4
Phiafai⊙ 17,216 E4
Phôngsali 2,500 D2
San Nua (Sam Neua) 3,000 E2
Saravan 2,350 E4
Savannakhét 8,500 E3
Sayaboury (Muang Xaignabouri) 2,500 D3
Thakhek (Muang Khammouan) 5,500 E3
Tourakom D3
Viangchan (Vientiane) 132,253 D3
Vientiane (cap.) 132,253 D3
Xiangkhoang 3,500 D3

OTHER FEATURES

Bolovens (plat.) E4
Hou, Nam (riv.) D2
Jars (plain) D3
Mekong (riv.) D3
Ou, Nam (riv.) D2
Phou Bia (mt.) D3
Phou Cô Pi (mt.) E3
Phou Loi (mt.) D2
Rao Co (mt.) E3
Se Khong (riv.) E4
Tha, Nam (riv.) D2
Xianghoang (plat.) D3

MALAYA, MALAYSIA★

STATES

Federal Territory 937,875 D7
Johor (Johore) 1,601,504 D7
Kedah 1,102,200 D6
Kelantan 877,575 D6
Melaka 453,153 D7
Negeri Sembilan 563,955 D7
Pahang 770,644 D7
Perak 1,762,288 D6
Perlis 147,726 D6
Pinang (Penang) 911,586 D6
Selangor 1,467,441 D7
Terengganu 542,280 D6

CITIES and TOWNS

Alor Gajah 2,222 D7
Alor Setar 66,260 D6
Bandar Maharani (Muar) 61,218 D7
Bandar Penggaram (Batu Pahat) 53,291 D7
Batu Gajah 10,692 D6
Batu Pahat 53,291 D7
Bentong 22,683 D7
Butterworth 61,187 D6
Chukai 12,514 D6
Gemas 5,214 D7
George Town (Pinang) 269,603 C6
Ipoh 247,953 D6
Johor Baharu (Johore Bharu) 136,234 F5
Kampar 26,591 D6
Kangar 8,758 D6
Kelang 113,611 D7
Keluang 43,272 D7
Kota Baharu 55,124 D6
Kota Tinggi 8,725 F5
Kuala Dungun 17,560 D6
Kuala Lipis 9,270 D6
Kuala Lumpur (cap.) 451,977 D7
Kuala Lumpur* 937,875 D7
Kuala Pilah 12,508 D7
Kuala Rompin 1,384 D7
Kuala Selangor 3,132 D7
Kuala Terengganu 53,320 D6
Kuantan 43,358 D7
Kulai 11,841 F5
Lumut 3,255 D6
Malacca (Melaka) 87,160 D7
Mawai F5
Melaka 87,160 D7
Mersing 18,246 E7
Muar 61,218 D7
Pekan 4,682 D7
Pekan Nanas 9,003 E5
Pinang (George Town) 269,603 C6
Pontian Kechil 8,349 E5
Port Dickson 10,300 D7
Port Kelang D7
Port Weld 3,233 D6
Raub 18,433 D7
Segamat 17,796 D7
Seremban 80,921 D7
Sungai Petani 35,959 C6
Taiping 54,645 D6
Tanah Merah 7,012 D6
Telok Anson 44,524 D6
Tumpat 10,673 D6

OTHER FEATURES

Aur, Pulau (isl.) E7
Belumut, Gunong (mt.) D7
Gelang, Tanjong (pt.) D6
Johor, Sungai (riv.) F5
Johore (str.) E6
Kelantan, Sungai (riv.) D6
Langkawi, Pulau (isl.) C6
Ledang, Gunong (mt.) D7
Lima, Pulau (isl.) F6
Malacca (str.) D7
Malay (pen.) D6
Pahang, Sungai (riv.) D7
Pangkor, Pulau (isl.) D6
Perak, Gunong (mt.) D6
Perhentian, Kepulauan (isls.) D6
Pulai, Sungai (riv.) E5
Ramunia, Tanjong (pt.) F6
Redang, Pulau (isl.) D6
Sedili Kechil, Tanjong (pt.) F5
Tahan, Gunong (mt.) D6
Temiang, Bukit (mt.) D6
Tenggol, Pulau (isl.) D6
Tinggi, Pulau (isl.) E7

SINGAPORE

CITIES and TOWNS

Jurong 50,974 E6
Nee Soon 37,641 F6
Serangoon 89,558 F6
Singapore (cap.) 2,413,945 F6

OTHER FEATURES

Keppel (harb.) F6
Main (str.) F6
Singapore (str.) F6
Tekong Besar, Pulau (isl.) F6

THAILAND (SIAM)

CITIES and TOWNS

Ang Thong 7,267 C4
Ayutthaya (Phra Nakhon Si Ayutthaya) 37,213 D4
Ban Aranyaprathet 12,276 D4
Bangkok (cap.) 1,867,297 D4
Bangkok* 2,495,312 D4
Bang Lamung D4
Bang Saphan C5
Ban Kantang 9,247 C6
Ban Kapong C5
Ban Khlong Yai D5
Ban Kui Nua D4
Ban Ngon D3
Ban Pak Phanang 13,590 D5
Banphot Phisai C3
Ban Pua D3
Ban Sattahip D4
Ban Tha Uthen D3
Bua Chum D4
Buriram 16,431 D4
Chachoengsao 22,106 D4
Chai Badan D4
Chai Buri D3
Chainat 9,944 D4
Chaiya C5
Chaiyaphum 12,540 D4
Chang Khoeng C3
Chanthaburi 15,479 D4
Chiang Dao C3
Chiang Khan D3
Chiang Mai 83,729 C3
Chiang Rai 13,927 C3
Chiang Saen C2
Chon Buri 39,367 D4
Chumphon 11,643 C5
Den Chai C3
Hat Yai 47,953 C6
Hot C3
Hua Hin 21,426 D4
Kalasin 14,960 D3
Kamphaeng Phet 12,378 C3
Kanchanaburi 16,397 C4
Khanu C3
Khemmarat E4
Khon Kaen 29,431 D3
Khorat (Nakhon Ratchasima) 66,071 D4
Krabi 8,764 C5
Krung Thep (Bangkok) (cap.) 1,867,297 D4
Kumphawapi D3
Lae D3
Lampang 40,100 C3
Lamphun 11,309 C3
Lang Suan 4,020 C5
Loei 10,137 D3
Lom Sak 10,597 D3
Lop Buri 23,112 D4
Mae Hong Son 3,981 C3
Maha Sarakham 19,707 D3
Mukdahan E3
Nakhon Nayok 8,185 D4
Nakhon Pathom 34,300 C4
Nakhon Phanom 20,385 D3
Nakhon Ratchasima 66,071 D4
Nakhon Sawan 46,853 D4
Nakhon Si Thammarat 40,671 D5
Nan 17,738 D3
Nang Rong D4
Narathiwat 21,256 D6
Ngao D3
Nong Khai 21,150 D3
Pattani 21,938 D6
Phanat Nikhom 10,514 D4
Phangnga 5,738 C5
Phatthalung 13,336 D6
Phayao 20,346 C3
Phet Buri 27,755 C4
Phetchabun 6,240 D3
Phichai D3
Phichit 10,814 D3
Phitsanulok 33,883 D3
Phon Phisai D3
Phrae 17,555 D3
Phra Nakhon Si Ayutthaya 37,213 D4
Phuket 34,362 C6
Phutthaisong D4
Prachin Buri 14,167 D4
Prachuap Khiri Khan 9,075 D5
Pran Buri D4
Rahaeng (Tak) 16,317 C3
Ranong 10,301 C5
Rat Buri 32,271 C4
Rayong 14,846 D4
Roi Et 20,242 D4
Rong Kwang D3
Sakon Nakhon 18,943 E3
Samut Prakan 46,632 D4
Samut Sakhon 33,619 D4
Samut Songkhram 23,574 C4
Sara Buri 25,025 D4
Satun 7,315 C6
Sawankhalok 8,387 C3
Selaphum E3
Sing Buri 9,050 D4
Singora (Songkhla) 41,193 D6
Sisaket 13,662 E4
Songkhla 41,193 D6
Sukhothai 15,488 D3
Suphan Buri 18,768 C4
Surat Thani 24,923 C5
Surin 16,342 D4
Suwannaphum D4
Tak 16,317 C3
Takua Pa 7,825 C5
Thoen C3
Thon Buri 628,015 D4
To Mo D6
Trang 32,985 C6
Trat 7,917 D4
Ubon 40,650 E4
Udon Thani 56,218 D3
Uthai Thani 10,525 C4
Uttaradit 12,022 D3
Warin Chamrap 21,520 E4
Yala 30,051 D6
Yasothon 12,079 D4

OTHER FEATURES

Amya (pass) C4
Bilauktaung (range) C4
Chang, Ko (isl.) D4
Chao Phraya, Mae Nam (riv.) D4
Chi, Mae Nam (riv.) D3
Dangrek (Dong Rak) (mts.) D4
Doi Inthanon (mt.) C3
Doi Pha Hom Pok (mt.) C2
Doi Pia Fai (mt.) D4
Kao Prawa (mt.) C3
Khao Luang (mt.) C5
Khwae Noi, Mae Nam (riv.) C4
Kra (isth.) C5
Kut, Ko (isl.) D5
Laem Pho (cape) D6
Laem Talumphuk (cape) D5
Lanta, Ko (isl.) C6
Luang (mt.) C5
Mae Klong, Mae Nam (riv.) C4
Mekong (riv.) E3
Mun, Mae Nam (riv.) D4
Nan, Mae Nam (riv.) D3
Nong Lahan (lake) D3
Pakchan (riv.) C5
Pa Sak, Mae Nam (riv.) D4
Phangan, Ko (isl.) D5
Phuket, Ko (isl.) C5
Ping, Mae Nam (riv.) C3
Samui (str.) D5
Samui, Ko (isl.) D5
Siam (Thailand) (gulf) D5
Tao, Ko (isl.) C5
Tapi, Mae Nam (riv.) C5
Terutao, Ko (isl.) C6
Tha Chin, Mae Nam (riv.) C4
Thale Luang (lag.) D6
Thalu, Ko (isls.) C5
Three Pagodas (pass) C4
Wang, Mae Nam (riv.) C3

VIETNAM

CITIES and TOWNS

An Loc (Binh Long) 15,276 E5
An Nhon F4
An Tuc (An Khe) F4
Ap Long Ha F5
Ap Vinh Hao F5
Bac Can E2
Bac Giang E2
Bac Lieu 53,841 E5
Bac Ninh 22,560 E2
Ba Don E3
Bai Thuong E3
Ban Me Thuot 68,771 F4
Bao Ha D2
Bao Lac E2
Bien Hoa 87,135 E5
Binh Long (An Loc) 15,276 E5
Binh Son F4
Bo Duc E4
Bong Son (Hoai Nhon) F4
Cam Ranh 118,111 F5
Can Tho 182,424 E5
Cao Bang E2
Cao Lanh 16,482 E5
Chau Phu 37,175 E5
Chu Lai F4
Con Cuong E3
Cua Rao E3
Da Lat 105,072 F5
Dam Doi E5
Da Nang 492,194 E3
Dien Bien Phu D2
Dong Hoi E3
Duong Dong D5
Gia Dinh E5
Go Cong 33,191 E5
Ha Giang E2
Haiphong* 1,279,067 E2
Hanoi (cap.)* 2,570,905 E2
Ha Tien E5
Ha Tinh E3
Hau Bon E4
Hoa Binh E2
Hoa Da F5
Hoai Nhon F4
Ho Chi Minh City (Saigon)* 3,419,678 E5
Hoi An 45,059 F4
Hoi Xuan E2
Hon Chong E5
Hon Gai 100,000 E2
Hue 209,043 E3
Huong Khe E3
Ke Bao E2
Khanh Hoa F4
Khanh Hung 59,015 E5
Khe Sanh E3
Kien Hung E5
Kontum 33,554 E4
Lac Giao (Ban Me Thuot) 68,771 E4
Lai Chau D2
Lang Son 15,071 E2
Lao Cai E2
Loc Ninh E5
Long Xuyen 72,658 E5
Mo Duc F4
Mong Cai E2
Muong Khuong E2
My Tho 119,892 E5
Nam Dinh E2
Nghia Lo D2
Nha Trang 216,227 F4
Ninh Binh E3
Phan Rang 33,377 F5
Phan Thiet 80,122 F5
Phu Cuong 28,267 E5
Phu Lang Thuong (Bac Giang) E2
Phuc Loi E3
Phu Dien E3
Phu Ly E2
Phu My F4
Phu Qui E3
Phu Rieng E5
Phu Tho 10,888 E2
Phu Vinh 48,485 E5
Pleiku 23,720 E4
Quang Nam E4
Quang Ngai 14,119 F4
Quang Tri 15,874 E3
Quang Yen E2
Quan Long 59,331 E5
Qui Nhon 213,757 F4
Rach Gia 104,161 E5
Ron E3
Sa Dec 51,867 E5
Saigon (Ho Chi Minh City)* 3,419,678 E5
Song Cau F4
Son Ha F4
Son La D2
Son Tay 19,213 E2
Tam Ky 38,532 F4
Tam Quan F4
Tan An 38,082 E5
Tay Ninh 22,957 E5
Thai Binh 14,739 E2
Thai Nguyen E2
Thanh Hoa 31,211 E3
Thanh Tri E5
That Khe E2
Tien Yen E2
Tra Vinh (Phu Vinh) 48,485 E5
Truc Giang 68,629 E5
Trung Khanh Phu E2
Tuyen Quang E2
Tuy Hoa 63,552 F4
Van Hoa E2
Van Ninh F4
Van Yen E2
Vinh 43,954 E3
Vinh Long 30,667 E5
Vinh Yen E2
Vu Liet E3
Vung Tau 108,436 E5
Xuan Loc E5
Yen Bai E2

OTHER FEATURES

Bach Long Vi, Dao (isl.) F2
Ba Den, Nui (mt.) E5
Bai Bung, Mui (Ca Mau) (pt.) E5
Black (riv.) D2
Ca Mau (Mui Bai Bung) (pt.) E5
Cam Ranh, Vinh (bay) F5
Cat Ba, Dao (isl.) E2
Chon May, Vung (bay) F3
Cu Lao, Hon (isls.) F5
Deux Frères, Les (isls.) E5
Dinh, Mui (cape) F5
Fan Si Pan (mt.) D2
Ia Drang (riv.) E4
Joncs (plain) E5
Kontum (plat.) E4
Khoai, Hon (isl.) E5
Lang Bian, Nui (mts.) E4
Lay, Mui (cape) E3
Mekong, Mouths of the (delta) E5
Nam Tram, Mui (cape) F4
Nightingale (Bach Long Vi) (isl.) F2
Panjang, Hon (Hon Tho Chau) (isl.) D5
Phu Quoc, Dao (isl.) D5
Rao Co (mt.) E3
Red (riv.) E2
Se San (riv.) E4
Sip Song Chau Thai (mts.) D2
Song Ba (riv.) F4
Song Ca (riv.) E3
Song Cai (riv.) E4
South China (sea) F4
Tonkin (gulf) E3
Varella, Mui (cape) F4
Wai, Poulo (isls.) E4
Yang Sin, Chu (mt.) F4

★See Southeast Asia, p. 85 for other part of Malaysia.

*City and suburbs.
⊙Population of district.

CHINA (MAINLAND)

AREA 3,691,000 sq. mi. (9,559,690 sq. km.)
POPULATION 958,090,000
CAPITAL Peking (Beijing)
LARGEST CITY Shanghai
HIGHEST POINT Mt. Everest 29,028 ft. (8,848 m.)
MONETARY UNIT yuan
MAJOR LANGUAGES Chinese, Chuang, Uigur, Yi, Tibetan, Miao, Mongol, Kazakh
MAJOR RELIGIONS Confucianism, Buddhism, Taoism, Islam

CHINA (TAIWAN)

AREA 13,971 sq. mi. (36,185 sq. km.)
POPULATION 16,609,961
CAPITAL Taipei
LARGEST CITY Taipei
HIGHEST POINT Yü Shan 13,113 ft. (3,997 m.)
MONETARY UNIT new Taiwan yüan (dollar)
MAJOR LANGUAGES Chinese, Formosan
MAJOR RELIGIONS Confucianism, Buddhism, Taoism, Christianity, tribal religions

MONGOLIA

AREA 606,163 sq. mi. (1,569,962 sq. km.)
POPULATION 1,594,800
CAPITAL Ulaanbaatar
LARGEST CITY Ulaanbaatar
HIGHEST POINT Tabun Bogdo 14,288 ft. (4,355 m.)
MONETARY UNIT tughrik
MAJOR LANGUAGES Khalkha Mongolian, Kazakh (Turkic)
MAJOR RELIGION Buddhism

HONG KONG

AREA 403 sq. mi. (1,044 sq. km.)
POPULATION 5,022,000
CAPITAL Victoria
MONETARY UNIT Hong Kong dollar
MAJOR LANGUAGES Chinese, English
MAJOR RELIGIONS Confucianism, Buddhism, Christianity

MACAU

AREA 6 sq. mi. (16 sq. km.)
POPULATION 271,000
CAPITAL Macau
MONETARY UNIT pataca
MAJOR LANGUAGES Chinese, Portuguese
MAJOR RELIGIONS Confucianism, Buddhism, Taoism, Christianity

CHINA (MAINLAND)

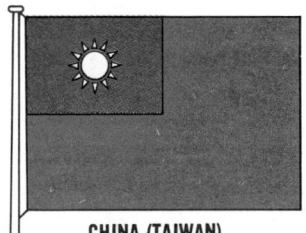

CHINA (TAIWAN)

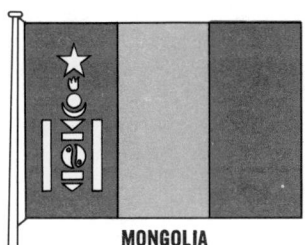

MONGOLIA

CHINA

PROVINCES

Anhui (Anhwei) 47,130,000	J5
Chekiang (Zhejiang) 37,510,000	K6
Fujian (Fukien) 24,500,000	J6
Gansu (Kansu) 18,730,000	E3
Guangdong (Kwangtung) 55,930,000	H7
Guangxi Zhuangzu (Kwangsi Chuang Aut. Reg.) 34,020,000	G7
Guizhou (Kweichow) 26,860,000	G6
Heilongjiang (Heilungkiang) 33,760,000	K2
Hebei (Hopei) 50,570,000	J4
Henan (Honan) 70,660,000	H5
Hubei (Hupei) 45,750,000	H5
Hunan 51,660,000	H6
Inner Mongolian Aut. Reg. (Nei Monggol) 8,900,000	H3
Jiangxi (Kiangsi) 31,830,000	J6
Jiangsu (Kiangsu) 58,340,000	K5
Jilin (Kirin) 24,740,000	L3
Kansu (Gansu) 18,730,000	E3
Kiangsi (Jiangxi) 31,830,000	J6
Kiangsu (Jiangsu) 58,340,000	K5
Kirin (Jilin) 24,740,000	L3
Kwangsi Chuang Aut. Reg. (Guangxi Zhuang) 34,020,000	G7
Kwangtung (Guangdong) 55,930,000	H7
Kweichow (Guizhou) 26,860,000	G6
Liaoning 37,430,000	K3
Nei Monggol (Inner Mongolian Aut. Reg.) 8,900,000	H3
Ningxia Huizu (Ningsia Hui Aut. Reg.) 3,660,000	F3
Qinghai (Tsinghai) 3,650,000	E4
Shaanxi (Shensi) 27,790,000	G5
Shanxi (Shansi) 24,340,000	H4
Shandong (Shantung) 71,600,000	J4
Sichuan (Szechwan) 97,070,000	F5
Sinkiang-Uigur Aut. Reg. (Xinjiang Uygur) 12,330,000	B3
Taiwan 16,609,961	K7
Tibet Aut. Reg. (Xizang) 1,790,000	B5

Tsinghai (Qinghai) 3,650,000	E4
Xinjiang Uygur (Sinkiang-Uigur Aut. Reg.) 12,330,000	B3
Xizang (Tibet Aut. Reg.) 1,790,000	B5
Yunnan 30,920,000	F7
Zhejiang (Chekiang) 37,510,000	K6

CITIES AND TOWNS†

Aba	F5
Abagnar (Silinhot)	J3
Aihui (Aigun) (Heihe)	L1
Aksu (Aqsu)	B3
Altay	C2
Alxa Youqi	F4
Alxa Zuoqi	F4
Amoy (Xiamen) 400,000	J7
Anda (Anta)	L2
Ankang	G5
Anqing (Anking) 160,000	J5
Anshan 1,500,000	K3
Anshun	G6
Antu	L3
Anxi	E3
Anyang 225,000	H4
Aqsu (Aksu)	B3
Aratürük (Yiwu)	D3
Ar Horqin	K3
Arixang (Wenquan)	B3
Artux (Atushi)	A4
Bachu (Maralwexi)	A4
Baicheng, Jilin	K2
Baicheng (Bay), Xinjiang Uygur	B3
Bairin Zuoqi	J3
Baoding (Paoting) 350,000	J4
Baoji (Paoki) 275,000	G5
Baoshan	E7
Baoshan	G8
Baotou (Paotow) 800,000	G3
Bargrax (Bohu)	C3
Batang	E5
Bay (Baicheng)	B3
Bayan Obo	G3
Ba Xian	J4
Bei'an (Pehan) 130,000	L2
Beihai (Pakhoi) 175,000	G7
Beijing (Peking) (cap.)● 8,500,000	J3
Bengbu (Pengpu) 400,000	J5
Benxi (Penki) 750,000	K3
Bohu (Bagrax)	C3
Bole	B3
Bortala (Bole)	B3
Boshan	J4
Bo Xian (Pohsien)	J5
Butha	K2
Cangzhou (Tsangchow)	J4
Canton (Guangzhou) 2,300,000	H7
Chamdo (Qamdo)	E5
Changchih (Changzhi)	H4
Changchow (Changzhou) 400,000	J5
Changchow (Zhangzhou)	J7
Changchun 1,500,000	K3
Changde (Changteh) 225,000	H6
Changhua 137,236	K7
Changji	C3
Changjiang	G8
Changsha 850,000	H6
Changteh (Changde) 225,000	H6
Changyeh (Zhangye)	F4
Changzhi (Changchih)	H4
Changzhou (Changchow) 400,000	K5
Changjiang (Zhanjiang) 220,000	H7
Chao'an (Chaochow)	J7
Chaotung (Zhaotong)	F6
Chaoyang, Liaoning	K3
Chaoyang, Guangdong	J7
Charkhlia (Ruoqiang)	C4
Chefoo (Yantai) 180,000	K4
Chengchow (Zhengzhou) 1,500,000	H5
Chengde (Chengteh) 200,000	J3
Chengdu (Chengtu) 2,000,000	F5
Chen Xian	H6
Chenchen (Qiemo)	C4
Chiai 238,713	K7
Chifeng	J3
Chinchow (Jinzhou) 750,000	K3
Chindu	E5
Chinkiang (Zhenjiang) 250,000	J5
Chinsi (Jinxi)	K3
Chinwangtao (Qinhuangdao) 400,000	K4
Chishui	G6
Chongqing (Chungking) 3,500,000	G6
Chüanchow (Quanzhou) 130,000	J7
Chuchow (Zhuzhou) 350,000	H6
Chuguchak (Tacheng)	B2
Chumatien (Zhumadian)	H5
Chungking (Chongqing) 3,500,000	G6
Chungshan (Zhongshan) 135,000	H7
Da'an (Taan)	K2
Danba	F5
Dandong (Tantung) 450,000	K3
Dali	E6
Dan Xian	G8
Da Qaidam	E4
Datong (Tatung), Shanxi 300,000	H3
Datong, Qinghai	F4
Da Xian	G5
Dazhai	H4
Dengkou	G3
Deyang	F5
Dezhou (Tehchow)	J4
Dingxing	H4
Dongchuan	F6
Dongfang	G8
Dongsheng	H4
Dongtai	K5
Dorbiljin (Emin)	B2
Dukou	F6
Dulan	E4
Dunhua (Tunhwa)	L3
Duolun	J3
Dushan	G6
Duyun (Tuyün)	G6
Ejin	F3
Emin (Dorbiljin)	B2
Erenhot	H3
Ergun Youqi	K1
Ergun Zuoqi	K1
Ertai	C2
Fatshan (Foshan)	H7

(continued on following page)

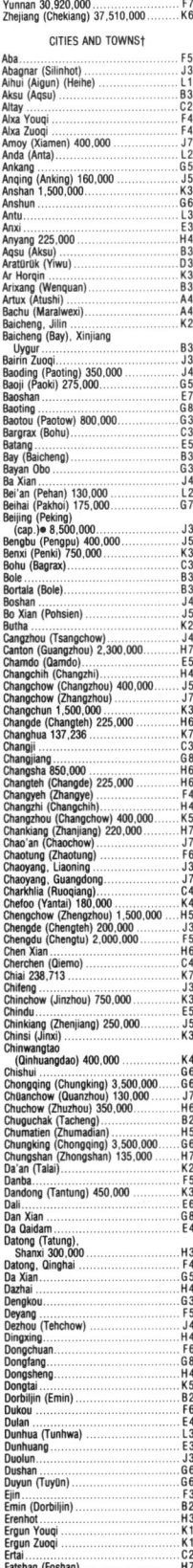

China and Mongolia
Transportation

Railroads	——————
Under Construction	- - - - -
Connecting Roads	——————
Navigable Rivers	
Canals	
Major Seaports	‡

© Copyright HAMMOND INCORPORATED, Maplewood, N.J.

Foochow (Fuzhou) 900,000 .... J6
Foshan (Fatshan) H7
Fowyang (Fuyang) J5
Fushun 1,700,000 .... K3
Fusingchen (Simao) F7
Fu Xian, Liaoning K4
Fu Xian, Shaanxi G4
Fuxin (Fusin) 350,000 .... K3
Fuyang (Fowyang) J5
Fuyu, Jilin K2
Fuyu, Heilongjiang L2
Fuyuan, Heilongjiang M2
Fuyuan, Yunnan F6
Fuyun C1
Fuzhou (Foochow),
  Fujian 900,000 .... J6
Fuzhou, Jiangxi J6
Ganzhou (Kanchow) 135,000 .... H6
Garyarsa (Gartok) B5
Gejiu (Kokiu) 250,000 .... F7
Golmud (Golmo) D4
Gonghe F4
Guangyuan G5
Guan Xian F5
Guangzhou (Canton) 2,300,000 .... H7
Guilin (Kweilin) 225,000 .... G6
Guiyang (Kweiyang),
  Guizhou 1,500,000 .... G6
Guiyang, Hunan H6
Gulja (Yining) 160,000 .... B3
Guma (Pishan) A4
Guyang G3
Guyuan G4
Gyaca D6
Gyangzê C6
Habahe C2
Haikou (Hoihow) 500,000 .... H7
Hailar J2
Hami (Kumul) D3
Hancheng H4
Hanchung (Hanzhong) 120,000 .... G5
Handan (Hantan) 500,000 .... H4
Hangzhou (Hangchow) 1,100,000 .... J5
Hantan (Handan) 500,000 .... H4
Hanzhong (Hanchung) 120,000 .... G5
Harbin 2,750,000 .... L2
Hebi H4
Hechuan (Hochwan) G5
Hefei (Hofei) 400,000 .... J5
Hegang (Hokang) 350,000 .... L2
Heihe (Aihui) (Aigun) L1
Hekou F7
Hengchun K7
Hengshan G4
Hengyang 310,000 .... H6
Hepu (Hoppo) G7
Hexigten J3
Hezuo F5
Hochwan (Hechuan) G5
Hofei (Hefei) 400,000 .... J5
Hohhot (Huhehot) 700,000 .... H3
Hoihow (Haikou) 500,000 .... H7
Hokang (Hegang) 350,000 .... L2
Hoppo (Hepu) G7
Horqin Youyi Qianqi
  (Ulanhot) 100,000 .... K2
Hotan B4
Houma H4
Hsuchang (Xuchang) H5

Huadian L3
Huaibei J5
Huaide (Hwaiteh) K3
Huainan 350,000 .... J5
Hualien K7
Huangling G4
Huangshi 200,000 .... J5
Huangzhong F4
Huizhou H7
Hulin M2
Hunchun M3
Hunjiang L3
Hwainan (Huainan) 350,000 .... J5
Hwaiteh (Huaide) K3
Hwangshih (Huangshi) 200,000 .... J5
Ichang (Yichang) 150,000 .... H5
Ichun (Yichun) 200,000 .... L2
Ilan K7
Ipin (Yibin) 275,000 .... F6
Jeminay C2
Jiamusi (Kiamusze) 275,000 .... M2
Ji'an (Kian) 100,000 .... J6
Jiangmen (Kongmoon) 150,000 .... H7
Jian'ou J6
Jiaozuo (Tsiaotso) 300,000 .... H4
Jiaxing (Kashing) K5
Jiayuguan E4
Jieyang J7
Jilin (Kirin) 1,200,000 .... L3
Jinan (Tsinan) 1,500,000 .... J4
Jingdezhen
  (Kingtehchen) 300,000 .... J6
Jinghong F7
Jing Xian, Anhui J5
Jing Xian, Hunan H6
Jingyuan F4
Jinhua (Kinhwa) J6
Jining (Tsining), Nei
  Monggol 160,000 .... H3
Jining (Tsining), Shandong J4
Jinshi (Tsingshih) 100,000 .... H6
Jinxi (Chinsi) K3
Jinzhou (Chinchow) 750,000 .... K3
Jiujiang (Kiukiang) 120,000 .... J6
Jiuquan (Kiuchüan) E4
Jixi (Kisi) 350,000 .... M2
Juichin (Ruijin) J6
Jun Xian H5
Kaba (Habahe) C2
Kaifeng 330,000 .... H5
Kailu K3
Kaiyuan, Liaoning K3
Kaiyuan, Yunnan F7
Kalgan (Zhangjiakou) 1,000,000 .... J3
Kanchow (Ganzhou) 135,000 .... H6
Kangding F5
Kaohsiung 1,028,334 .... J7
Karakax (Kara Kashi) (Moyu) A4
Karamay B2
Karghalik (Yecheng) A4
Kashgar (Kashi) 175,000 .... A4
Kashing (Jiaxing) K5
Kaxgar (Kashi) 175,000 .... A4
Keelung 342,604 .... K6
Kenli J4
Keriya (Yutian) B4
Khotan (Hotan) B4

Kiamusze (Jiamusi) 275,000 .... M2
Kian (Ji'an) 100,000 .... J6
Kienyang (Qianyang) H6
Kingtehchen
  (Jingdezhen) 300,000 .... J6
Kinhwa (Jinhua) J6
Kirin (Jilin) 1,200,000 .... L3
Kisi (Jixi) 350,000 .... M2
Kiukiang (Jiujiang) 120,000 .... J6
Kiuchüan (Jiuquan) E4
Kokiu (Gejiu) 250,000 .... F7
Kongmoon (Jiangmen) 150,000 .... H7
Korla C3
Kuldja (Yining) 160,000 .... B3
Kumul (Hami) D3
Kunming 1,700,000 .... F6
Kuqa C3
Kuytun C3
Kwangchow (Canton) 2,300,000 .... H7
Kweilin (Guilin) 225,000 .... G6
Kweisui (Hohhot) 700,000 .... H3
Lanzhou (Lanchow) 1,500,000 .... F4
Lenghu D4
Lengshuijiang H6
Leshan (Loshan) 250,000 .... F6
Lhasa 175,000 .... D6
Lhazê (Lhatse) C6
Lianyungang
  (Lienyünkang) 300,000 .... J5
Liaoyang 250,000 .... K3
Liaoyuan 300,000 .... K3
Lijiang F6
Linfen H4
Linhe G3
Linhe H6
Linqing (Lintsing) J4
Linxi J3
Linxia (Linsia) F4
Liuzhou (Liuchow) 250,000 .... G7
Loho (Luohe) H5
Lopnur (Yuli) C3
Loshan (Leshan) 250,000 .... F6
Loyang (Luoyang) 750,000 .... H5
Lu'an J5
Luchow (Luzhou) 225,000 .... G6
Luohe H5
Luoyang (Loyang) 750,000 .... H5
Lüda (Lüta) 4,000,000 .... K4
Lüshun K4
Lüta (Lüda) 4,000,000 .... K4
Luxi F7
Luzhou (Luchow) 225,000 .... G6
Ma'anshan J5
Manas C3
Manzhouli (Manchouli) J2
Manchouli (Manzhouli) J2
Maoming (Mowming) H7
Maralwexi (Bachu) A4
Mengcheng J5
Mengzi F7
Mianyang, Hubei H5
Mianyang, Sichuan G5
Minfeng (Niya) B4
Minle F4
Mowming (Maoming) H7
Moyu (Karakax) A4

Mudanjiang
  (Mutankiang) 400,000 .... M3
Mukden (Shenyang) 3,750,000 .... K3
Muli F6
Nagqu D5
Nanchang 900,000 .... J6
Nanchong (Nanchung) 275,000 .... G5
Nanjing (Nanking) 2,000,000 .... J5
Nanping 375,000 .... J6
Nantong 300,000 .... K5
Nanping J6
Napo G7
Neijiang (Neikiang) 240,000 .... G6
Neijiang L2
Ningbo (Ningpo) 350,000 .... K6
Ningbo (Ningpo) 350,000 .... K6
Ningsia (Yinchuan) F4
  Yinchuan 175,000 .... G4
Nyingri (Minfeng) B4
Ongniud J3
Oroqen K1
Paicheng (Baicheng) K2
Pakhoi (Beihai) 175,000 .... G7
Paoki (Baoji) 275,000 .... G5
Paoting (Baoding) 350,000 .... J4
Paotow (Baotou) 800,000 .... G3
Pehan (Bei'an) 130,000 .... L2
Peking (Beijing)
  (cap.) ● 8,500,000 .... J3
Pengpu (Bengbu) 400,000 .... J5
Penki (Benxi) 750,000 .... K3
Pingdingshan H5
Pinglang G4
Pingtung 165,360 .... K7
Pingxiang, Guangxi Zhuangzu G7
Pingxiang, Jiangxi H6
Piqan (Shanshan) D3
Pishan (Guma) A4
Pohsien (Bo Xian) J5
Qamdo E5
Qarklik (Ruoqiang) C4
Qianwang (Kienyang) H6
Qiemo (Qarqan) C4
Qingdao (Tsingtao) 1,900,000 .... K4
Qingjiang, Jiangxi J6
Qingjiang, Anhui 110,000 .... J5
Qinhuangdao
  (Chinwangtao) 400,000 .... K4
Qionghai H8
Qiqihar (Tsitsihar) 1,500,000 .... K2
Qitai C3
Qog G4
Qoqek (Tacheng) B2
Quanzhou (Chüanchow) 130,000 .... J7
Qu Xian, Sichuan G5
Qu Xian, Zhejiang J6
Qüxü D6
Ruijin (Juichin) J6
Ruoqiang (Qarklik) C4
Rutog A5
Sanmenxia H5
Sanming J6
Sêrxu E5
Shache (Yarkand) A4
Shandan F4
Shangdu H3
Shanghai ● 10,980,000 .... K5
Shangqiu (Shangkiu) 250,000 .... J5

Shangrao (Shangjao) 100,000 .... J6
Shangshui (Shiangshui) J5
Shanshan (Piqan) D3
Shantou (Swatow) 400,000 .... J7
Shaoguan (Shiukwan) 125,000 .... H7
Shaoxing (Shaohing) 225,000 .... K5
Shaoyang 275,000 .... H6
Shashi 125,000 .... H5
Shenyang (Mukden) 3,750,000 .... K3
Shigatse (Xigazê) C6
Shihezi (Shihhotzu) C3
Shijiazhuang
  (Shihkiachwang) 1,500,000 .... J4
Shiquanhe A5
Shiukwan (Shaoguan) 125,000 .... H7
Shiyan H5
Shizuishan (Shihsuishan) G4
Shuangcheng L2
Shuangyashan 150,000 .... M2
Shuo Xian H3
Siakwan (Xiaguan) E6
Sian (Xi'an) 1,900,000 .... G4
Siangtan (Xiangtan) 150,000 .... H6
Siangtan (Xiangtan) 300,000 .... H6
Sienyang (Xianyang) 125,000 .... G5
Silinhot (Abnagar) J3
Simao (Fusingchen) F7
Sinchu 208,038 .... K7
Singtai (Xingtai) H4
Sining (Xining) 250,000 .... F4

Sinsiang (Xinxiang) 300,000 .... H4
Sinyang (Xinyang) 125,000 .... H5
Siping (Szeping) 180,000 .... K3
Soche (Shache) A4
Soochow (Suzhou) 1,300,000 .... K5
Suao K7
Süchow (Xuzhou) 1,500,000 .... J5
Suifenhe M3
Suihua L2
Suining G5
Suzhou (Soochow) 1,300,000 .... K5
Swatow (Shantou) 400,000 .... J7
Szeping (Siping) 180,000 .... K3
Tacheng (Qoqek) B2
Taibus J4
Taichow (Taizhou) 275,000 .... K5
Taichung 565,255 .... K7
Taigu H4
Tainan 541,390 .... K7
Taipei 2,108,193 .... K7
Taitung K7
Taiyuan 2,725,000 .... H4
Taizhou (Taichow) 275,000 .... K5
Talai (Da'an, Dalai) K2
Tali (Dali) E6
Tangshan 1,200,000 .... J4
Tantung (Dandong) 450,000 .... K3
Tao'an K2
Taoyuan 105,841 .... K6

Tart D4
Tatung (Datong) 500,000 .... H3
Taxkorgan A4
Tehchow (Dezhou) J4
Tengchong E6
Tianjin (Tientsin) ● 7,210,000 .... J4
Tianjin J4
Tianshui 100,000 .... G5
Tienshan (Tianshan) D3
Tientsin (Tianjin) ● 7,210,000 .... J4
Tingri C6
Togtoh H3
Toksu (Xinhe) C3
Tongchuan (Cangzhou) J4
Tonghua (Tunghwa) 275,000 .... L3
Tongjiang (Tungkiang) M2
Tongliao K3
Tongren G6
Tongxin G4
Tsangchow (Cangzhou) J4
Tsiaotso (Jiaozuo) 300,000 .... H4
Tsinan (Jinan) 1,500,000 .... J4
Tsingkiang (Jinshi) 110,000 .... H6
Tsingshih (Jinshi) 100,000 .... H6
Tsingtao (Qingdao) 1,900,000 .... K4
Tsining (Jining), Nei
  Monggol 160,000 .... H3

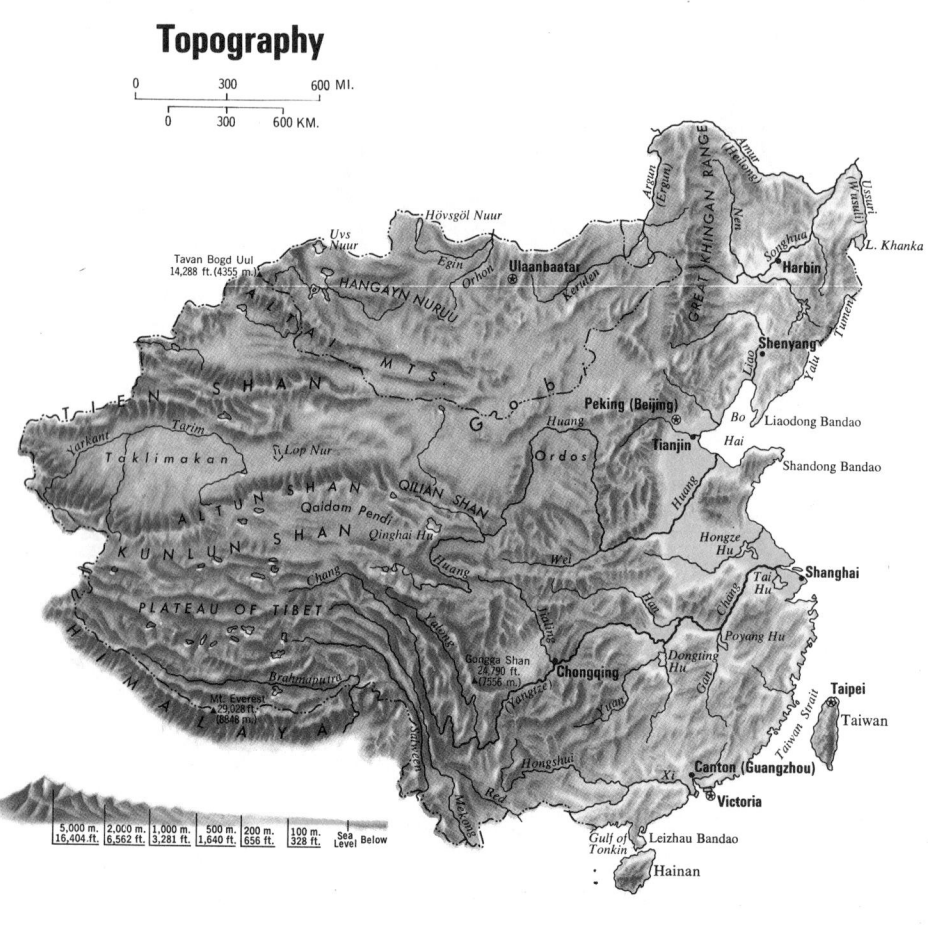

Topography

0   300   600 MI.

0   300   600 KM.

5,000 m.	2,000 m.	1,000 m.	500 m.	200 m.	100 m.	Sea
16,404 ft.	6,562 ft.	3,281 ft.	1,640 ft.	656 ft.	328 ft.	Level Below

On this map Chinese place-names have been rendered according to the Pinyin spelling system within the area controlled by the People's Republic of China. Alphabetically listed below are selected Chinese place-names spelled in the traditional manner, followed by the equivalent Pinyin form.

Amoy (Hsiamen)	Xiamen	Kirin	Jilin	Sian	Xi'an
Anhwei	Anhui	Kiukiang	Jiujiang	Siangtan	Xiangtan
Canton		Kwangsi		Sining	Xining
(Kwangchow)	Guangzhou	Chuang	Guangxi	Sinkiang-	
Chefoo (Yentai)	Yantai		Zhuangzu	Uighur	Xinjiang Uygur
Chekiang	Zhejiang	Kwangtung	Guangdong	Soochow	Suzhou
Chengchow	Zhengzhou	Kweichow	Guizhou	Süchow	Xuzhou
Chengtu	Chengdu	Kweilin	Guilin	Swatow	Shantou
Chinchow	Jinzhou	Kweiyang	Guiyang	Szechuan	Sichuan
Chungking	Chongqing	Lanchow	Lanzhou	Tachai	Dazhai
Foochow	Fuzhou	Liuchow	Liuzhou	Tatung	Datong
Fukien	Fujian	Loyang	Luoyang	Tibet	Xizang
Hangchow	Hangzhou	Lüta	Lüda	Tientsin	Tianjin
Heilungkiang	Heilongjiang	Mutankiang	Mudanjiang	Tsinan	Jinan
Hofei	Hefei	Nanking	Nanjing	Tsinghai	Qinghai
Honan	Henan	Ningpo	Ningbo	Tsingtao	Qingdao
Hopei	Hebei	Ningsia Hui	Ningxia Huizu	Tsining	Jining
Huhehot	Hohhot	Paoting	Baoding	Tsitsihar	Qiqihar
Hupeh	Hubei	Paotow	Baotou	Tsunyi	Zunyi
Inner Mongolia	Nei Monggol	Peking	Beijing	Tungchwan	Tongchuan
Kansu	Gansu	Pengpu	Bengbu	Tzepo	Zibo
Kiangsi	Jiangxi	Penki	Benxi	Urumchi	Ürümqi
Kiangsu	Jiangsu	Shansi	Shanxi	Wusih	Wuxi
Kingtehchen	Jingdezhen	Shantung	Shandong	Yenan	Yan'an
		Shensi	Shaanxi	Yinchwan	Yinchuan
		Shihkiachwang	Shijiazhuang		

Tsining (Jining), Shandong J4
Tsitsihar (Qiqihar) 1,500,000 ...... K2
Tsunyi (Zunyi) 275,000 ...... G6
Tumen M3
Tungchwan (Tongchuan) G5
Tunghwa (Tonghua) 275,000 ...... M2
Tungkiang (Tongjiang) K3
Tungliao (Tongliao) L3
Tunhwa (Dunhua) J3
Tunxi (Tunki) J5
Turpan (Turfan) C3
Tuyün (Duyun) G6
Tzekung (Zigong) 350,000 ...... F6
Tzepo (Zibo) 1,750,000 ...... J4
Ulanhot (Horquin Youyi
　Qianqi) 100,000 ...... K2
Uluqchat (Wuqia) A4
Ürümqi (Urumchi) 500,000 ...... C3
Usu B3
Wanning H8
Wanxian (Wanhsien) 175,000 ...... G5
Weichang J3
Weihai 260,000 ...... J4
Weihai (Weihaiwei) K4
Weixi E6
Weixin F6
Wenchow (Wenzhou) 250,000 ...... J6
Wenquan, Qinghai D5
Wenquan, Xinjiang Uygur B3

Wenzhou 250,000 ...... J6
Wuchang L3
Wuchuan, Guizhou G6
Wuchuan, Nei Monggol H3
Wuchuan (Wuzhong) F4
Wuda G4
Wuhai 4,250,000 ...... G4
Wuhing (Wuxing) 160,000 ...... K5
Wuhu 300,000 ...... J5
Wuqi G4
Wushan A3
Wushi A3
Wusih (Wuxi) 900,000 ...... J5
Wutai H4
Wuwei E4
Wuxi (Wusih) 900,000 ...... J5
Wuxing (Wuhing) 160,000 ...... K5
Wuyuan G3
Wuzhong (Wuchuan) F4
Wuzhou (Wuchow) 150,000 ...... H7
Xiaguan (Siakwan) E6
Xiamen (Amoy) 400,000 ...... J7
Xi'an (Sian) 1,900,000 ...... G5
Xiangfan (Siangfan) 150,000 ...... H5
Xiangtan (Siangtan) 300,000 ...... H6
Xianyang (Sienyang) 125,000 ...... G5
Xiapu (Siapu) K6
Xichang (Sichang) F6

Xigazê (Shigatse) C6
Ximiao F3
Xin Barag Zuoqi J2
Xingtai (Singtai) H4
Xinhe (Toksu) B3
Xining (Sining) 250,000 ...... F4
Xinxiang (Sinsiang) 300,000 ...... H4
Xinyang (Sinyang) 125,000 ...... H5
Xinyuan (Künes) B3
Xuchang (Hsüchang) H5
Xuguit J2
Xuzhou (Süchow) 1,500,000 ...... J5
Ya'an 100,000 ...... F5
Yadong C6
Yan'an (Yenan) G4
Yancheng K5
Yangchow (Yangzhou) 210,000 ...... J5
Yangchüan (Yangquan) 350,000 ...... H4
Yangjiang H7
Yanji (Yenki) 130,000 ...... M3
Yangquan (Yangchüan) 350,000 ...... H4
Yangzhou (Yangchow) 210,000 ...... J5
Yantai (Chefoo) 180,000 ...... K4
Yarkand (Shache) A4
Ya Xian G8
Yecheng A4
Yenan (Yan'an) G4
Yenki (Yanji) 130,000 ...... L3
Yibin (Ipin) 275,000 ...... F6

Yichang (Ichang) 150,000 ...... H5
Yichun, Jiangxi H6
Yichun, Heilongjiang 200,000 ...... L2
Yidu, Hubei H5
Yidu, Shandong J4
Yining (Ining) 250,000 ...... B3
Yingkou 215,000 ...... K3
Yining 160,000 ...... H5
Yiwu (Aratürük) D3
Yiyang H6
Yongxin H6
Yueyang H6
Yuci (Yütze) H4
Yuli (Lopnur) C3
Yulin, Guangxi Zhuangzu G7
Yulin, Shanxi G4
Yumen 325,000 ...... E4
Yuncheng G5
Yungkia (Wenzhou) 250,000 ...... J6
Yushu, Jilin L3
Yushu, Qinghai E5
Yutian, Xinjiang Uygur B4
Yütze (Yuci) H4
Zaozhuang J5
Zayü E6
Zêtang D6
Zhanghei J3
Zhangjiakou (Kalgan) 1,000,000 ...... J3
Zhangye (Changyeh) F4

Zhangzhou (Changchow) J7
Zhanjiang (Chankiang) 220,000 ...... H7
Zhaodong K2
Zhaoqing H7
Zhaojue E5
Zhaotong (Chaotung) F6
Zhengzhou (Chengchow) 1,500,000 ...... H5
Zhenjiang (Chinkiang) 250,000 ...... J5
Zhenyuan G6
Zhongba B6
Zhongshan (Chungshan) 135,000 ...... H7
Zhongwei F4
Zhoumadian (Chumatien) H5
Zhushan G5
Zhuzhou (Chuchow) 350,000 ...... H6
Zibo (Tzepo) 1,750,000 ...... J4
Zigong (Tzekung) 350,000 ...... F6
Zinhui H7
Zunhua J3
Zunyi (Tsunyi) 275,000 ...... G6

OTHER FEATURES

Altun Shan (range) C4
Alxa Shamo (des.) F4
Amur (Heilong Jiang) (riv.) L2
A'nyêmaqên Shan (mts.) E5
Aqqikkol Hu (lake) C4
Argun' (Ergun He) (riv.) K1

Bagrax (Bosten Hu) (lake) C3
Bangong Co (lake) A5
Bashi (chan.) K7
Bayan Har Shan (range) E5
Bo Hai (gulf) J4
Bosten (Bagrax) Hu (lake) C3
Chang Jiang (Yangtze) (riv.) K5
Da Hingan Ling (range) K3
Dian Chi (lake) F7
Dongsha (isl.) J7
Dongting Hu (riv.) H6
East China (sea) K5
Ebinur Hu (lake) B2
Ergun He (Argun') (riv.) K1
Er Hai (lake) F6
Fen He (riv.) G4
Formosa (Taiwan) (isl.) J7
Formosa (Taiwan) (str.) J7
Gangdisê Shan (range) K7
Gaoyou Hu (lake) J5
Ghenghis Khan Wall (ruin) B2
Gobi (des.) F3
Gongga Shan (mt.) F6
Grand (canal) J4
Great Wall (ruins) G4,J
Gurla Mandhata (mt.) B5
Hailar He (riv.) K2
Hainan (isl.) H8

Hangzhou Wan (bay) K5
Han Shui (riv.) H5
Heilong Jiang (Amur) (riv.) L2
Himalaya (mts.) C6
Hongshui He (riv.) G7
Hongze Hu (lake) J5
Hotan; He (riv.) B4
Huang He (Yellow) (riv.) J4
Hulun Nur (lake) J2
Hungtow (isl.) K7
Inner Mongolia (reg.) H3
Jinmen (Quemoy) (isl.) J7
Jinsha Jiang (Yangtze) (riv.) E6
Junggar Pendi (desert basin) C2
Kanganbao Feng (mt.) B5
Karakhoto (ruins) F3
Karamiran Shankou (pass) C4
Keriya Shankou (pass) B4
Khanka (lake) M3
Kongur Shan (mt.) A4
Künes He (riv.) B3
Kunlun Shan (range) B4
Lancang Jiang (riv.) F6
Leizhou Bandao (pen.) G7
Liaodong Bandao (pen.) K4
Lop Nor (Lop Nur) (lake) D3
Manas He (riv.) C3
Manas Hu (lake) C3

(continued on following page)

China and Mongolia

SCALE OF MILES
0   100   200   300   400   500

SCALE OF KILOMETERS
0   100   200   300   400   500

Capitals of Countries ......   International Boundaries _ . . _
Provincial Capitals ......   Provincial Boundaries _ . . _
Canals ......   Walls ......

Scale 1:19,100,000

Copyright HAMMOND INCORPORATED, Maplewood, N.J.

† Populations of mainland cities, excluding Peking (Beijing), Shanghai and Tianjin (Tientsin), courtesy of Kingsley Davis, Office of Int'l Pop. and Research, Inst. of Int'l Studies Univ. of California.

● Population of municipality.
* City and suburbs.

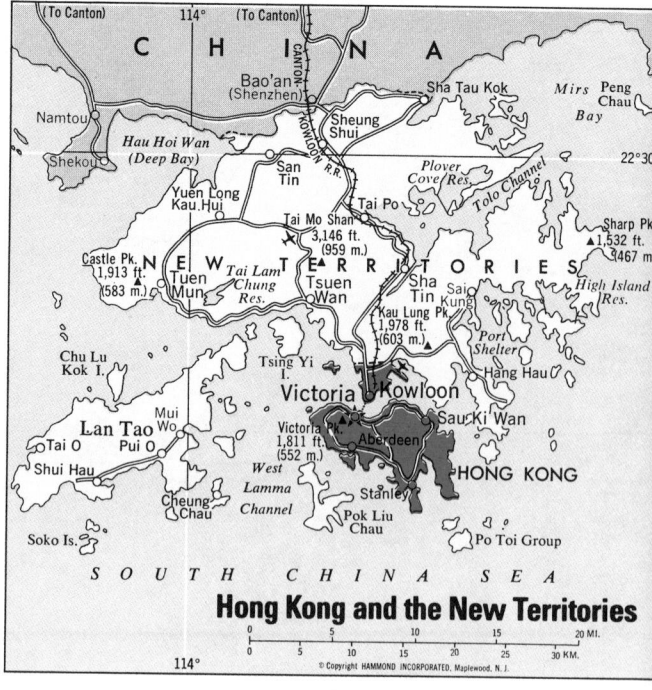

Hong Kong and the New Territories

© Copyright HAMMOND INCORPORATED, Maplewood, N.J.

Agriculture, Industry and Resources

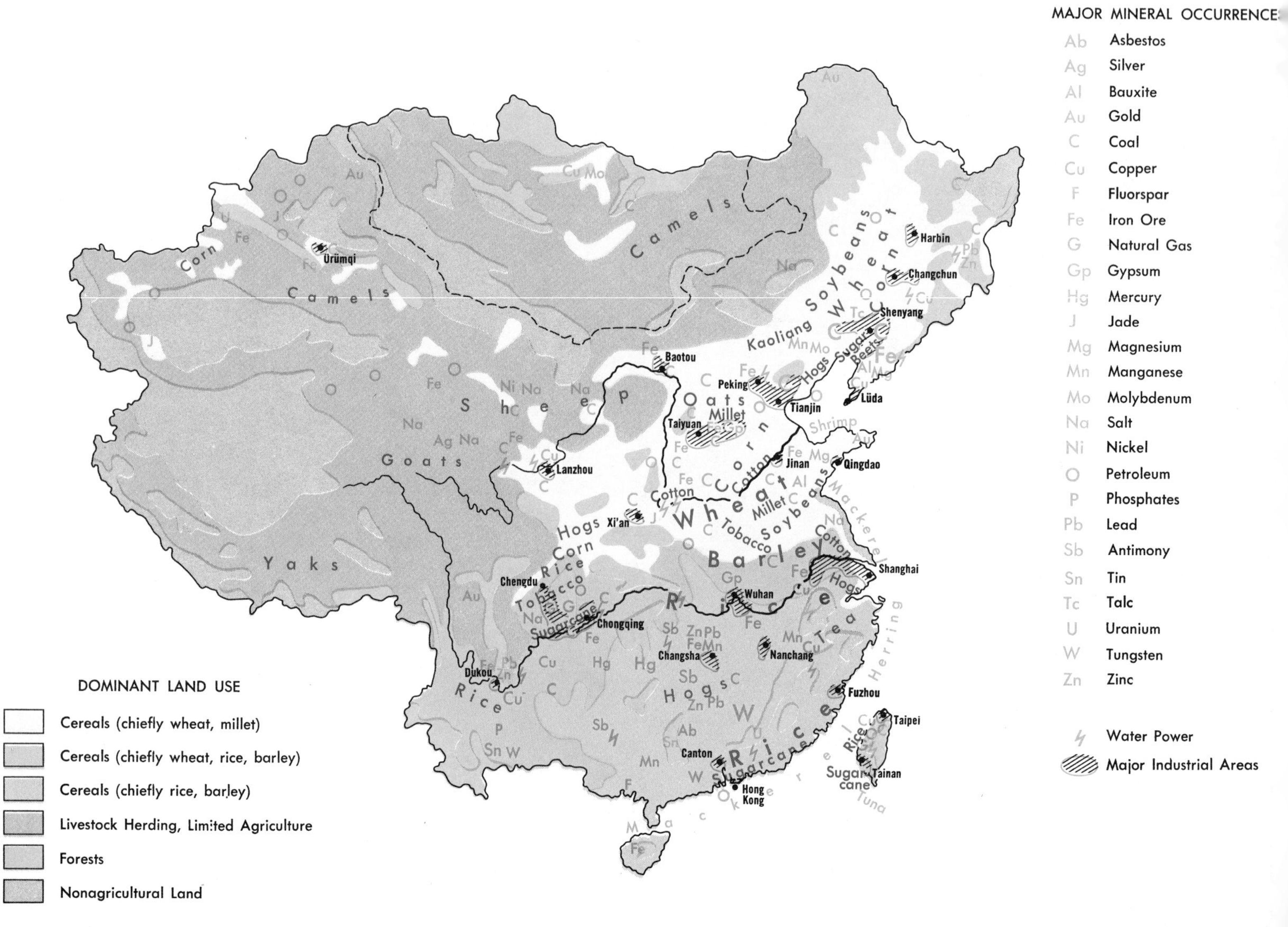

DOMINANT LAND USE

Cereals (chiefly wheat, millet)

Cereals (chiefly wheat, rice, barley)

Cereals (chiefly rice, barley)

Livestock Herding, Limited Agriculture

Forests

Nonagricultural Land

MAJOR MINERAL OCCURRENCE

Ab	Asbestos
Ag	Silver
Al	Bauxite
Au	Gold
C	Coal
Cu	Copper
F	Fluorspar
Fe	Iron Ore
G	Natural Gas
Gp	Gypsum
Hg	Mercury
J	Jade
Mg	Magnesium
Mn	Manganese
Mo	Molybdenum
Na	Salt
Ni	Nickel
O	Petroleum
P	Phosphates
Pb	Lead
Sb	Antimony
Sn	Tin
Tc	Talc
U	Uranium
W	Tungsten
Zn	Zinc

Water Power

Major Industrial Areas

AREA 145,730 sq. mi. (377,441 sq. km.)
POPULATION 117,057,485
CAPITAL Tokyo
LARGEST CITY Tokyo
HIGHEST POINT Fuji 12,389 ft. (3,776 m.)
MONETARY UNIT yen
MAJOR LANGUAGE Japanese
MAJOR RELIGIONS Buddhism, Shintoism

AREA 46,540 sq. mi. (120,539 sq. km.)
POPULATION 17,914,000
CAPITAL P'yŏngyang
LARGEST CITY P'yŏngyang
HIGHEST POINT Paektu 9,003 ft. (2,744 m.)
MONETARY UNIT won
MAJOR LANGUAGE Korean
MAJOR RELIGIONS Confucianism, Buddhism, Ch'ondogyo

AREA 38,175 sq. mi. (98,873 sq. km.)
POPULATION 37,448,836
CAPITAL Seoul
LARGEST CITY Seoul
HIGHEST POINT Halla 6,398 ft. (1,950 m.)
MONETARY UNIT won
MAJOR LANGUAGE Korean
MAJOR RELIGIONS Confucianism, Buddhism, Ch'ondogyo, Christianity

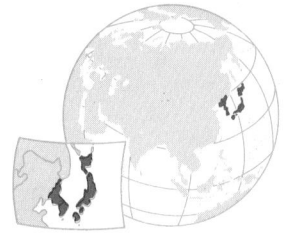

JAPAN

North Korea flag

NORTH KOREA

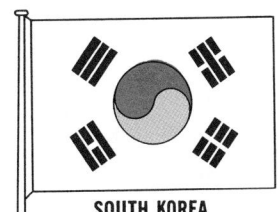

SOUTH KOREA

JAPAN

PREFECTURES

ichi 5,923,569	H6
kita 1,232,481	J4
omori 1,468,646	K3
hiba 4,149,147	P2
ukui 773,599	G5
ukuoka 4,292,963	D7
ukushima 1,970,616	K5
ifu 1,867,978	J5
umma 1,756,480	O2
iroshima 2,646,324	E6
okkaido 5,338,206	K2
yogo 4,992,140	H7
baraki 2,342,198	K5
shikawa 1,069,872	H5
wate 1,385,563	K4
Kagawa 961,292	G6
Kagoshima 1,723,902	E8
Kanagawa 6,397,748	O2
Kochi 808,397	F7
umamoto 1,715,273	E7
Kyoto 2,424,856	J7
Mie 1,626,002	H6
Miyagi 1,955,267	K4
Miyazaki 1,085,055	E8
Nagano 2,017,564	J5
Nagasaki 1,571,912	D7
Nara 1,077,491	J7
Niigata 2,391,938	J5
Oita 1,190,314	E7
Okayama 1,814,305	F6
Okinawa 1,042,572	N6
Osaka 8,278,925	J8
Saga 837,674	E7

Saitama 4,821,340	O2
Shiga 985,621	J7
Shimane 768,886	F6
Shizuoka 3,308,799	K5
Tochigi 1,698,003	O2
Tokushima 805,166	G7
Tokyo 11,673,554	O2
Tottori 581,311	G6
Toyama 1,070,791	H5
Wakayama 1,072,118	H6
Yamagata 1,220,302	K4
Yamaguchi 1,555,218	E6
Yamanashi 783,050	J6

CITIES and TOWNS

Abashiri 43,825	M1
Ageo 146,358	O2
Aikawa 13,546	H4
Aizuwakamatsu 108,650	J5
Ajigasawa 18,086	J3
Akashi 234,905	F7
Aki 24,480	J4
Akita 261,246	J4
Akkeshi 16,778	M2
Akune 30,295	D7
Amagasaki 545,783	H8
Amagi 42,725	E7
Anan 60,439	G7
Aomori 264,222	K6
Asahi 34,028	D7
Asahikawa 320,526	L2
Ashibetsu 36,520	L2
Ashikaga 162,359	J5
Ashiya 76,211	J6
Atami 51,437	J6
Atsugi 108,955	O2
Awaji 9,623	H8

Ayabe 43,490	G6
Beppu 133,894	E7
Bibai 38,416	L2
Biratori 9,331	L2
Chiba 659,356	P2
Chichibu 61,798	J5
Chigasaki 152,023	O3
Chitose 61,031	K2
Chofu 175,924	O2
Choshi 90,374	K6
Daito 110,829	J8
Ebetsu 77,624	K2
Eniwa 39,884	K2
Esashi, Hokkaido 10,172	L1
Esashi, Hokkaido 14,409	J3
Esashi, Iwate 36,336	K4
Fuchu, Hiroshima 50,217	F6
Fuchu, Tokyo 182,474	O2
Fuji 199,195	J6
Fujieda 90,358	J6
Fujisawa 265,975	O3
Fukagawa 36,000	L2
Fukuchiyama 60,003	G6
Fukue 32,018	D7
Fukui 231,364	G5
Fukuoka 1,002,201	D7
Fukushima 246,531	K5
Fukuyama 329,714	F6
Funabashi 423,101	P2
Furukawa 54,356	K4
Gifu 408,707	H6
Gobo 30,272	G7
Gose 37,554	J8
Gosen 39,376	J5
Goshogawara 49,040	K3
Gotsu 27,992	F6
Habikino 94,160	O2
Haboro 13,624	K1

Hachinohe 224,366	K3
Hachioji 322,580	O2
Hadano 103,663	O3
Hagi 52,724	E6
Hakodate 307,453	K3
Hakui 28,726	H5
Hamada 50,316	E6
Hamamatsu 468,884	H6
Hanamaki 65,826	K4
Hanno 55,926	O2
Haramachi 43,483	K5
Hayama 24,026	O3
Higashiosaka 524,750	J8
Hikone 85,066	H6
Himeji 436,086	G6
Himi 61,789	H5
Hino 126,847	J7
Hirakata 297,618	J7
Hirara 29,301	L7
Hirata 30,942	F6
Hiratsuka 195,635	O3
Hiroo 11,399	L2
Hirosaki 164,911	K3
Hiroshima 852,611	E6
Hitachi 202,383	K5
Hitachiota 35,322	K5
Hitoyoshi 41,118	E7
Hofu 105,540	E6
Hondo 40,432	E7
Honjo 40,488	J4
Hyuga 53,446	E7
Ibaraki 210,286	J7
Ibusuki 32,339	E8
Ichihara 194,068	P3
Ichikawa 319,291	P2
Ichinohe 21,433	K3
Ichinomiya 238,463	H6
Ichinoseki 59,122	K4

Ide 9,112	J7
Iida 77,112	H6
Iizuka 75,417	E7
Ikeda, Hokkaido 12,306	L2
Ikeda, Osaka 100,268	H7
Ikoma 44,848	J8
Ikuno 6,658	G6
Imabari 119,726	F6
Imari 60,913	D7
Imazu 11,519	G6
Ina 54,468	H6
Isahaya 73,341	D7
Ise 104,957	H6
Ishigaki 34,657	L7
Ishige 19,220	P2
Ishinomaki 115,085	K4
Ishioka 43,679	K5
Ito 68,072	J6
Itoigawa 36,946	H5
Ittoman 39,363	N6
Iwaizumi 20,219	K4
Iwaki 330,213	K5
Iwakuni 111,069	E6
Iwami 16,063	K4
Iwamizawa 72,305	L2
Iwanai 25,823	K2
Iwasaki 4,437	J3
Iwata 67,665	H6
Iwatsuki 83,825	O2
Iyo 27,805	F7
Izuhara 18,460	D6
Izumi 118,237	J8
Izumiotsu 66,250	J8
Izumisano 86,139	G6
Izumo 71,568	F6
Joetsu 123,418	H5
Joyo 58,923	J7

Kadoma 143,238	J7
Kaga 71,420	H5
Kagoshima 456,827	E8
Kaizuka 79,506	J8
Kakogawa 169,293	G6
Kamaishi 68,981	K4
Kamakura 165,552	O3
Kameoka 58,184	J7
Kamiiso 27,229	K3
Kaminoyama 37,858	J4
Kamiyaku 8,668	E8
Kamo 8,953	J7
Kanazawa 395,263	H5
Kanonji 44,131	F6
Kanoya 67,951	E8
Kanuma 81,799	O7
Karatsu 75,224	D7
Kaseda 24,969	D8
Kashihara 95,701	J8
Kashiwa 203,065	P2
Kashiwara 63,586	J8
Kashiwazaki 80,351	J5
Kasugai 213,857	H6
Kasukabe 121,639	O2
Katsuta 79,996	K5
Katsuura 26,755	K6
Kawachinagano 66,936	J8
Kawagoe 225,465	O2
Kawaguchi 345,538	J6
Kawanishi 115,773	H7
Kawasaki 1,014,951	O2
Kesennuma 66,616	K4
Kikonai 10,034	K3
Kimitsu 76,016	O3
Kiryu 134,239	J5
Kisarazu 96,840	P3
Kishiwada 174,952	J8
Kitaibaraki 44,332	K5

Kitakami 48,759	K4
Kitakata 37,471	J5
Kitakyushu 1,058,058	E6
Kitami 91,519	L2
Kizu 11,890	J7
Kobayashi 38,325	E8
Kobe 1,360,605	H7
Kochi 280,962	F7
Kodaira 156,181	O2
Kofu 193,879	J6
Koga 55,973	J5
Koganei 102,714	O2
Kokubu 31,660	E8
Komagane 30,318	H6
Komatsu 100,273	H5
Koriyama 264,628	K5
Koshigaya 195,917	P2
Koyama 38,122	E8
Kubohama 17,817	F7
Kuji 38,122	K3
Kuki 45,797	O2
Kumamoto 488,166	E7
Kumano 27,026	G7
Kumiyama 11,540	J7
Kurashiki 392,755	F6
Kurayoshi 50,785	F6
Kure 242,655	F6
Kuroiso 42,349	K5
Kurume 204,474	E7
Kushima 30,038	E8
Kushimoto 18,997	G7
Kushiro 206,840	M2
Kyonan 13,067	O3
Kyoto 1,461,059	J7
Machida 255,305	O2
Maebashi 250,241	J5
Maihara 12,845	G6
Maizuru 97,780	G6
Makubetsu 18,444	L2
Makurazaki 29,685	O3
Mashike 9,312	K2
Masuda 50,734	E6
Matsubara 132,662	H8
Matsue 127,440	F6
Matsumae 18,307	J3
Matsumoto 185,595	H5
Matsusaka 108,893	H6
Matsuto 36,170	H5
Matsuyama 367,323	F7
Mihara 83,679	F6
Miki 53,731	H7
Mikuni 21,602	G5
Minamata 36,782	E7
Minobu 10,345	J6
Minoo 79,621	J7
Misawa 37,437	K3
Mitaka 164,950	O2
Mito 197,953	K5
Mitsukaido 38,820	P2
Miura 47,888	O3
Miyako 61,912	L4
Miyakonojo 118,289	E8
Miyazaki 234,347	E8
Miyazu 30,194	G6
Miyoshi 37,193	F6
Mizusawa 52,266	K4
Mobara 64,942	K6
Mombetsu 32,825	L1
Monbetsu 15,029	L2
Mooka 47,345	K5
Mori 17,030	K2
Moriguchi 178,383	J7
Morioka 216,223	K4
Motobu 17,823	N6
Muko 45,886	J7
Murakami 32,939	J4
Muroran 158,715	K2
Muroto 26,660	G7
Musashino 139,508	O2
Mutsu 44,646	K3
Nachikatsuura 23,596	H7
Nagahama, Ehime 13,144	F7
Nagahama, Shiga 54,064	H6
Nagano 306,637	J5
Nagaoka, Kyoto 65,557	J7
Nagaoka, Niigata 171,742	J5
Nagaokakyo 65,557	J7
Nagasaki 450,194	D7
Nagato 27,327	E6
Nago 45,210	N6
Nagoya 2,079,740	H6
Naha 295,006	N6
Nakaminato 33,147	K5
Nakamura 34,437	F7
Nakasato 14,248	K3
Nakatsu 59,111	E7
Nanao 49,493	H5
Nara 257,538	J8
Narashino 117,852	P2
Nayoro 35,145	L1
Naze 46,359	O5
Nemuro 45,817	M2
Neyagawa 254,311	J7
Nichinan 52,171	E8
Niigata 423,188	J5
Niihama 131,712	F6
Niimi 30,014	F6
Niitsu 58,970	J5
Nishinomiya 400,622	H8

(continued on following page)

Agriculture, Industry and Resources

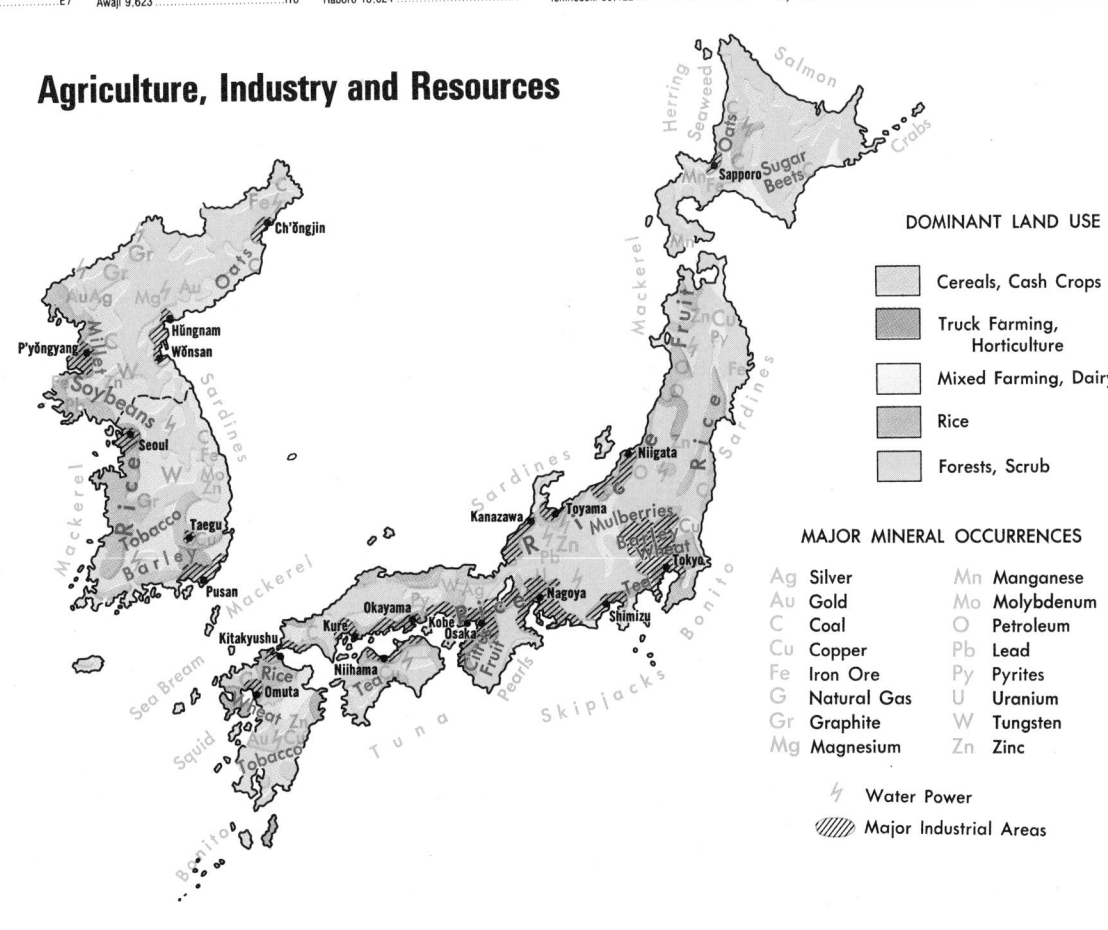

DOMINANT LAND USE

- Cereals, Cash Crops
- Truck Farming, Horticulture
- Mixed Farming, Dairy
- Rice
- Forests, Scrub

MAJOR MINERAL OCCURRENCES

Ag	Silver	Mn	Manganese
Au	Gold	Mo	Molybdenum
C	Coal	O	Petroleum
Cu	Copper	Pb	Lead
Fe	Iron Ore	Py	Pyrites
G	Natural Gas	U	Uranium
Gr	Graphite	W	Tungsten
Mg	Magnesium	Zn	Zinc

⚡ Water Power

▨ Major Industrial Areas

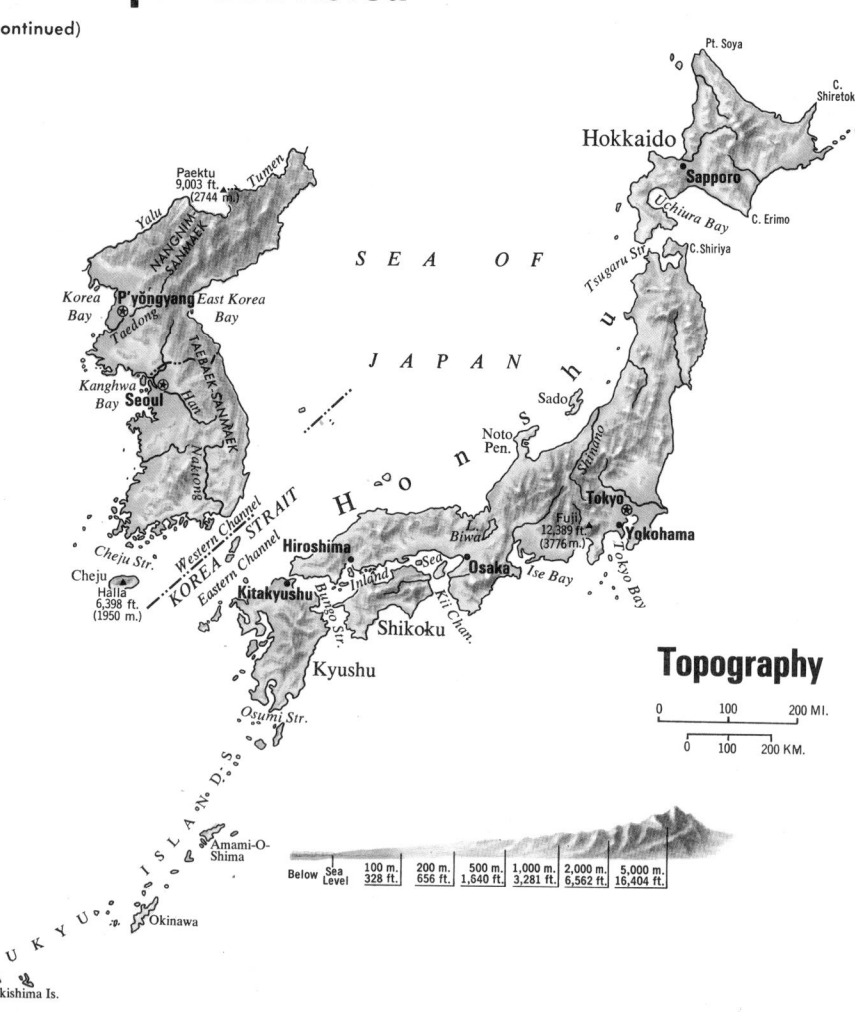

Hokkaido

Sapporo

S E A   O F

J A P A N

Tokyo

Yokohama

Hiroshima

Osaka

Shikoku

Kyushu

Topography

Below Sea Level	100 m. 328 ft.	200 m. 656 ft.	500 m. 1,640 ft.	1,000 m. 3,281 ft.	2,000 m. 6,562 ft.	5,000 m. 16,404 ft.

Amami-O-Shima

Okinawa

Sakishima Is.

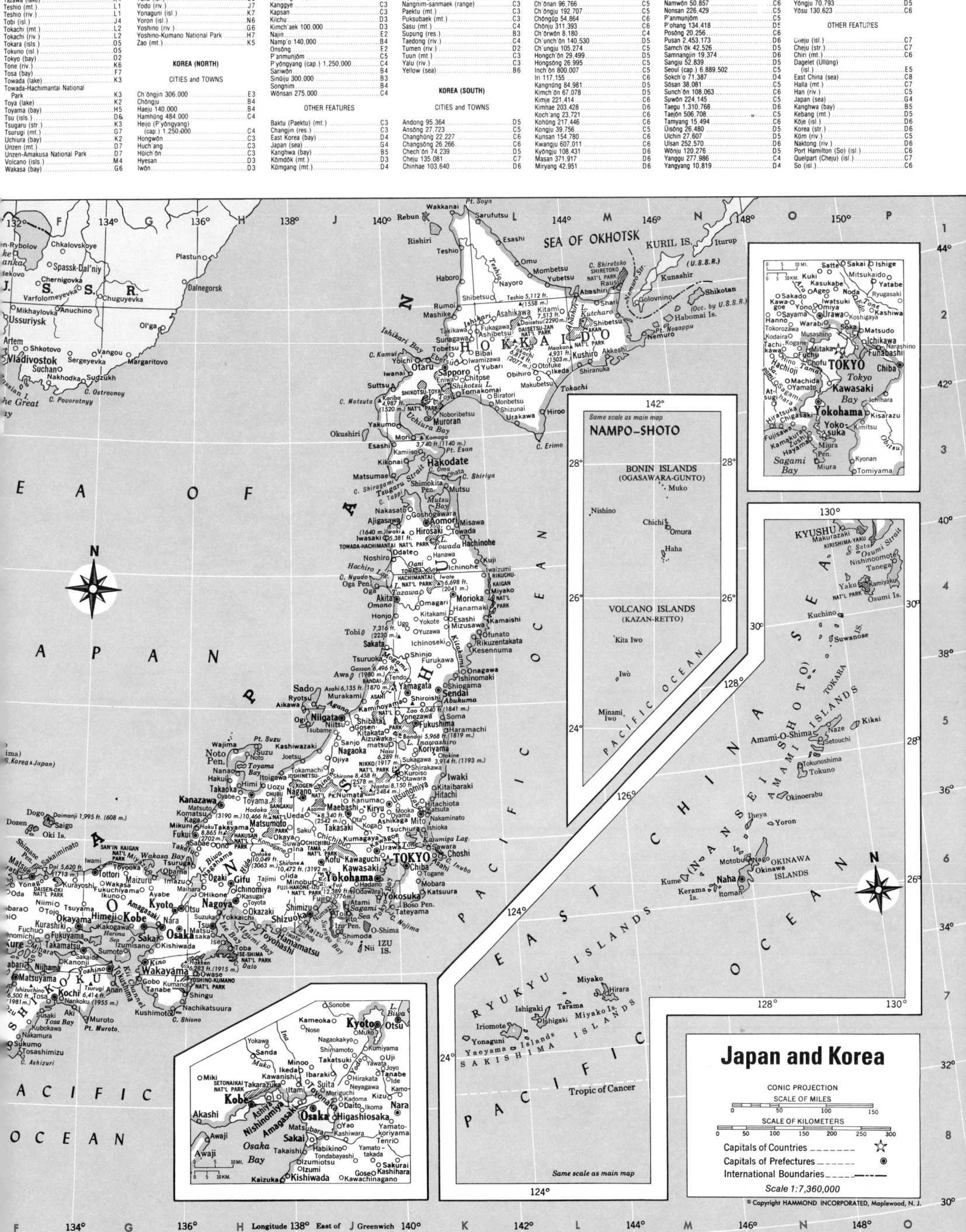

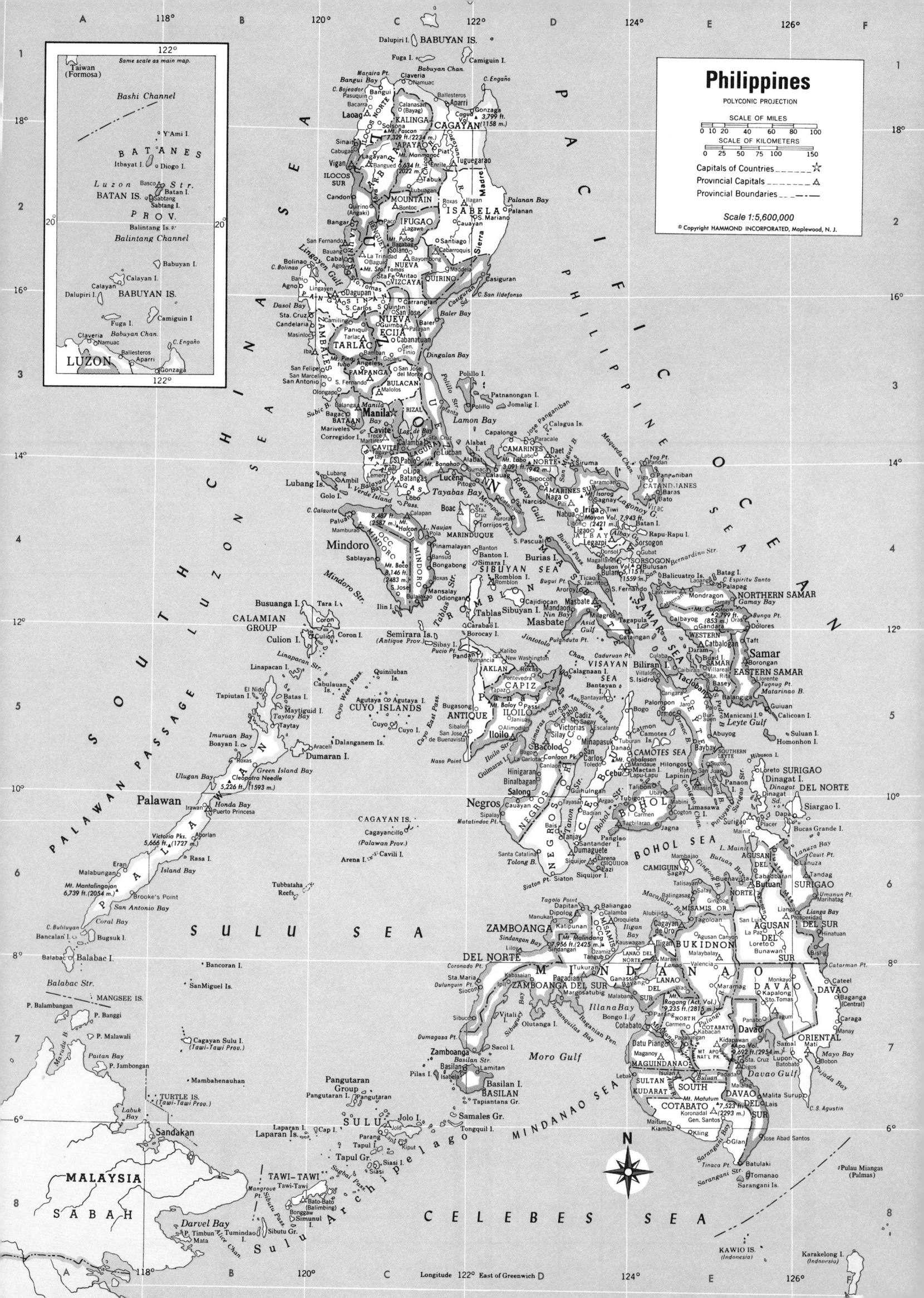

Philippines

POLYCONIC PROJECTION

SCALE OF MILES

0 10 20 40 60 80 100

SCALE OF KILOMETERS

0 25 50 75 100 150

Capitals of Countries _ _ _ _ _ _ _ ☆

Provincial Capitals _ _ _ _ _ _ _ △

Provincial Boundaries _ _ _ · _ · _

Scale 1:5,600,000

© Copyright HAMMOND INCORPORATED, Maplewood, N. J.

PROVINCES

- Abra 168,196 C2
- Agusan del Norte 366,721 E6
- Agusan del Sur 260,576 E6
- Aklan 325,491 D5
- Albay 803,274 D4
- Antique 344,905 D5
- Basilan 199,029 D7
- Bataan 321,860 C3
- Batanes 12,111 A2
- Batangas 1,173,767 C4
- Benguet 355,577 C2
- Bohol 805,924 E6
- Bukidnon 630,128 E6
- Bulacan 1,095,963 C3
- Cagayan 712,029 C1
- Camarines Norte 307,995 D3
- Camarines Sur 1,100,044 D4
- Camiguin 57,128 E6
- Capiz 492,766 D5
- Catanduanes 175,657 E4
- Cavite 771,796 C3
- Cebu 2,090,317 D5
- Davao del Norte 692,654 E7
- Davao del Sur 1,134,436 E7
- Davao Oriental 341,586 F7
- Eastern Samar 321,477 E5
- Ifugao 111,403 C2
- Ilocos Norte 393,485 C1
- Ilocos Sur 443,591 C2
- Iloilo 1,432,000 D5
- Isabela 870,389 C2
- Kalinga-Apayao 190,118 C1
- Laguna 972,730 C3
- Lanao del Norte 429,260 E6
- Lanao del Sur 405,627 E7
- La Union 453,211 C2
- Leyte 1,302,377 E5
- Maguindanao 542,104 E7
- Manila 5,924,563 C3
- Marinduque 178,725 C4
- Masbate 550,444 D4
- Misamis Occidental 391,013 D6
- Misamis Oriental 694,423 E6
- Mountain 103,052 C2
- National Capital Region (Manila) 5,924,563 C3
- Negros Occidental 1,936,770 D6
- Negros Oriental 822,923 D6
- North Cotabato 549,521 E7
- Northern Samar 383,245 E4
- Nueva Ecija 1,069,406 C3
- Nueva Vizcaya 240,962 C2
- Occidental Mindoro 222,025 C4
- Oriental Mindoro 446,857 C4
- Palawan 370,991 B6
- Pampanga 1,175,314 C3
- Pangasinan 1,636,520 C3
- Quezon 1,129,138 C3
- Quirino 83,232 C2
- Rizal 552,312 C3
- Romblon 193,190 D4
- Siquijor 70,161 D6
- Sorsogon 499,614 E4
- South Cotabato 768,321 E7
- Southern Leyte 256,581 E5
- Sultan Kudarat 285,459 E7
- Sulu 317,876 C7
- Surigao del Norte 346,491 F5
- Surigao del Sur 373,705 F6
- Tarlac 687,980 C3
- Tawi-Tawi 187,403 B8
- Western Samar 509,073 E5
- Zambales 443,859 C3
- Zamboanga del Norte 583,550 D6
- Zamboanga del Sur 1,178,700 D7

CITIES and TOWNS

- Angeles 185,995 C3
- Aparri 14,597 C1
- Bacolod 266,604 D5
- Bago 103,166 D5
- Baguio 118,611 C2
- Bais 49,301 D6
- Balanga 1,298 C3
- Baler• 14,632 C3
- Balimbing (Bato-Bato) 3,880 C8
- Bangued 10,482 C2
- Bantayan 11,771 D5
- Basco• 3,757 A2
- Basilan 171,266 C7
- Batangas 143,554 C4
- Bato-Bato 3,880 C8
- Baybay 11,989 E5
- Bayombong 11,697 C2
- Binalbagan 17,456 D5
- Bislig 26,625 F6
- Boac 3,497 C4
- Bogo 11,069 E5
- Bontoc 3,336 C2
- Bulan 19,716 D4
- Burauen 12,172 E5
- Butuan 172,404 E6
- Cabanatuan 138,297 C3
- Cabarroquis C2
- Cadiz 128,839 D5
- Cagayan de Oro 228,409 E6
- Calamba, Laguna 22,750 C3
- Calapan 11,376 C4
- Calbayog 110,938 E4
- Camiling 12,996 C3
- Canlaon 28,785 D5
- Carigara 11,824 E5
- Catarman 13,018 E4
- Catbalogan 18,413 E5
- Catmon• 14,837 E5
- Cavite 87,813 C3
- Cebu 489,208 D5
- Cotabato 88,486 D7
- Daet 23,739 D3
- Dagupan 98,362 C2
- Danao 56,957 D5
- Dapitan 54,698 D6
- Davao 611,311 E7
- Digos 17,334 E7
- Dipolog 61,928 D6
- Dumaguete 63,411 D6
- Escalante 16,324 D5
- Ganassi• 13,227 D7
- Gapan 11,958 C3
- General Santos 146,556 E7
- Gingoog 81,098 E6
- Gubat 11,369 E4
- Guimba 10,077 C3
- Gumaca 9,459 D4
- Hinigaran 10,864 D5
- Iba 4,486 B3
- Ilagan 11,494 C2
- Iligan 165,742 E6
- Iloilo 244,211 D5
- Iriga 66,117 D4
- Isabela 12,879 C7
- Isulan 10,075 E7
- Jolo 46,586 C8
- Jose Panganiban 9,970 D3
- Kalibo 10,564 D5
- Kauswagan• 12,316 E6
- Kidapawan 11,344 E7
- Koronadal 14,003 E7
- La Carlota 42,651 D5
- Lagawe 3,038 C2
- Lais 15,209 E7
- Laoag 69,648 C1
- Lapu-Lapu 98,860 E5
- La Trinidad• 18,551 C2
- Lazi• 14,875 D6
- Legazpi 100,488 D4
- Lianga 12,689 E6
- Lingayen 15,333 C2
- Lipa 121,162 C4
- Loreto, Agusan del Sur• 13,057 E6
- Lucban 18,466 C3
- Lucena 107,872 C4
- Maasin 12,661 E5
- Maganoy 1,648 E7
- Mainit 3,559 E6
- Malabang 9,244 D7
- Malaybalay 10,193 E6
- Malita 9,705 E7
- Malolos 73,996 C3
- Mandaue 110,665 E5
- Manila (cap.) 1,626,249 C3
- Marawi 53,198 E6
- Mariveles 4,502 C3
- Masbate 17,749 D4
- Mati 16,186 F7
- Mondragon• 14,974 E4
- Naga 90,712 D4
- Olongapo 156,312 C3
- Ormoc 104,912 E5
- Oroquieta 47,176 D6
- Ozamiz 78,036 D6
- Padada• 14,402 E7
- Pagadian 80,519 D7
- Palayan 14,959 C3
- Paniqui 11,789 C3
- Parang, Sulu• 21,115 C8
- Prosperidad 3,043 F6
- Puerto Princesa 59,347 B6
- Romblon 4,241 D4
- Roxas, Capiz 81,183 D5
- Roxas, Isabela 9,849 C2
- Sabiayan• 18,256 C4
- Sagay, Negros Occ. 36,855 D5
- Sagnay• 16,968 D4
- Salong 35,137 D5
- San Antonio 13,270 B3
- San Carlos, Negros Occ. 93,268 D5
- San Carlos, Pangasinan 101,254 C3
- San Fernando, La Union 11,084 C2
- San Fernando, Pampanga 84,362 C3
- San Isidro• 23,569 E5
- San Jose, Nueva Ecija 64,250 C3
- San Jose, Occ. Mindoro 10,388 C4
- San Mariano• 20,227 D2
- San Pablo, Laguna 131,686 C3
- Santa Cruz, Davao del Sur 9,787 E7
- Santa Cruz, Laguna 47,114 C3
- Santa Rita• 20,713 E5
- Santiago• 49,688 C2
- Siasi 9,930 C8
- Silay 104,018 D5
- Sindangan 10,965 D6
- Sipalay• 34,771 D6
- Sipocot• 38,153 D4
- Siquijor 766 D6
- Solano 14,274 C2
- Solsona• 12,803 C1
- Sorsogon 19,008 E4
- Surigao 78,235 E6
- Tacloban 102,609 E5
- Tagaytay 16,312 C3
- Tagbilaran 42,275 E6
- Tagum 17,161 E7
- Tangub 44,903 D6
- Tanjay 12,676 D6
- Tarlac 23,547 C3
- Toledo 91,618 D5
- Tuguegarao 14,116 C2
- Tukuran• 19,274 D7
- Victorias 13,416 D5
- Vigan 30,252 C2
- Virac 10,314 E4
- Zamboanga 344,275 C7

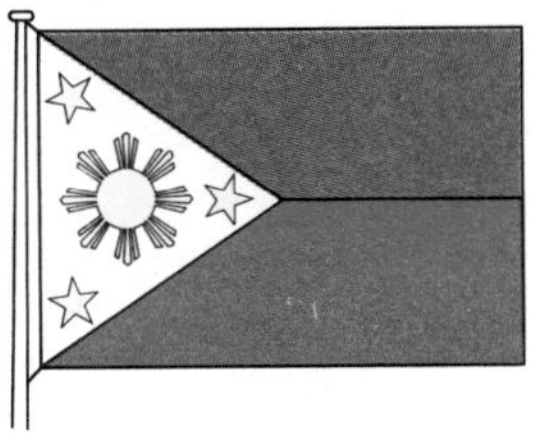

AREA 115,707 sq. mi. (299,681 sq. km.)
POPULATION 47,914,017
CAPITAL Manila
LARGEST CITY Manila
HIGHEST POINT Apo 9,692 ft. (2,954 m.)
MONETARY UNIT piso
MAJOR LANGUAGES Pilipino (Tagalog), English, Spanish, Bisayan, Ilocano, Bikol
MAJOR RELIGIONS Roman Catholicism, Islam, Protestantism, tribal religions

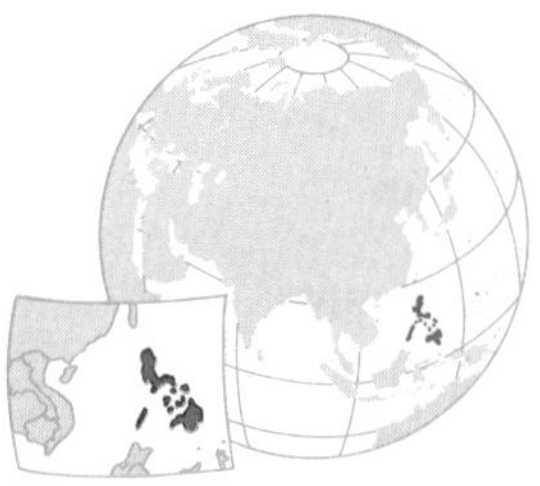

Topography

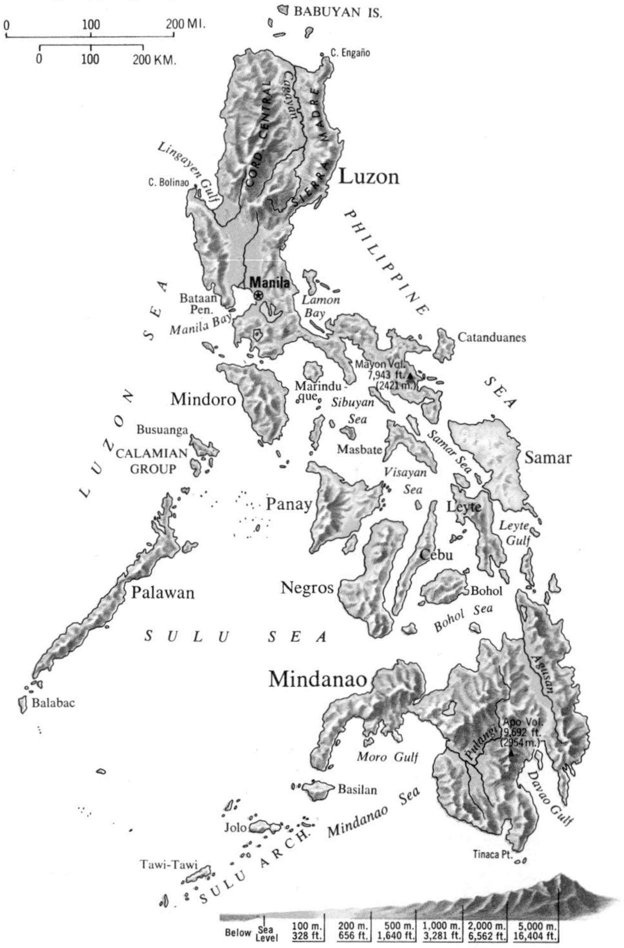

Agriculture, Industry and Resources

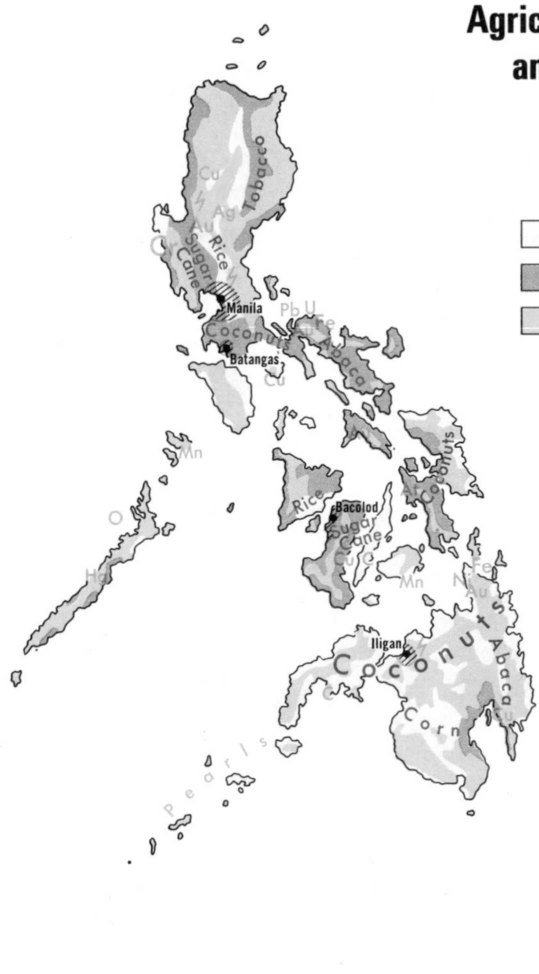

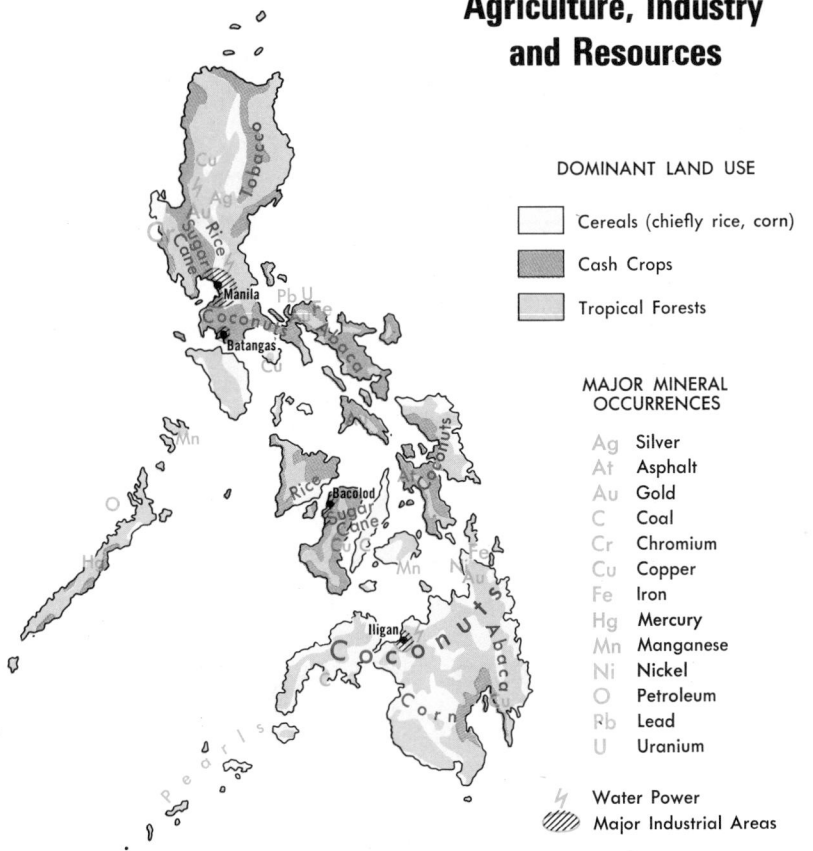

DOMINANT LAND USE

- Cereals (chiefly rice, corn)
- Cash Crops
- Tropical Forests

MAJOR MINERAL OCCURRENCES

- Ag Silver
- At Asphalt
- Au Gold
- C Coal
- Cr Chromium
- Cu Copper
- Fe Iron
- Hg Mercury
- Mn Manganese
- Ni Nickel
- O Petroleum
- Pb Lead
- U Uranium

- Water Power
- Major Industrial Areas

OTHER FEATURES

- Abra (riv.) C2
- Agusan (riv.) E6
- Agutaya (isl.) C5
- Alabat (isl.) D3
- Ambil (isl.) C4
- Apo (vol.) E7
- Asid (gulf) D4
- Babuyan (isl.) B2
- Baganian (pen.) D7
- Balabac (isl.) A7
- Balayan (bay) C4
- Balicuatro (isls.) E4
- Balintang (chan.) A2
- Baloy (mt.) D5
- Bancalan (isl.) A6
- Bantayan (isl.) D5
- Banton (isl.) D4
- Bashi (chan.) A1
- Basilan (isl.) D7
- Batag (isl.) E4
- Batan, Albay (isl.) E4
- Batan, Batanes (isl.) B2
- Batan (isls.) A2
- Batas (isl.) B5
- Bay, Laguna de (lake) C3
- Biliran (isl.) E5
- Bohol (isl.) E6
- Bojeador (cape) C1
- Bongo (isl.) D7
- Borocay (isl.) D5
- Buad (isl.) E5
- Bucas Grande (isl.) F6
- Bugsuk (isl.) A6
- Buliluyan (cape) A6
- Bunga (pt.) E4
- Burias (isl.) D4
- Busuanga (isl.) B4
- Cabalasan (mt.) E5
- Cabulauan (isls.) C5
- Cagayan (isls.) C6
- Cagayan (riv.) C2
- Cagayan Sulu (isl.) B7
- Cagua (vol.) D1
- Calagnaan (isl.) D5
- Calagua (isls.) D3
- Calamian Group (isls.) B4
- Calayan (isl.) A2
- Calicoan (isl.) E5
- Camiguin, Cagayan (isl.) B3
- Camiguin, Camiguin (isl.) E6
- Camotes (isls.) E5
- Camotes (sea) E5
- Canigao (chan.) E5
- Canlaon (peak) D5
- Capotoan (mt.) E4
- Carabao (isl.) D4
- Catanduanes (isl.) E4
- Cebu (isl.) D5
- Celebes (sea) D8
- Cleopatra Needle (mt.) B5
- Coron (isl.) C5
- Culion (isl.) B5
- Cuyo (isl.) C5
- Cuyo (isls.) C5
- Dalanganem (isls.) C5
- Daram (isl.) E5
- Davao (gulf) E7
- Dinagat (isl.) E5
- Diuata (mts.) E6
- Dumanquilas (bay) D7
- Dumaran (isl.) C5
- Engaño (cape) D1
- Espiritu Santo (cape) E4
- Fuga (isl.) A3
- Golo (isl.) C4
- Guimaras (isl.) D5
- Halcon (mt.) C4
- Hibuson (isl.) E5
- Homonhon (isl.) E5
- Honda (bay) B6
- Iligan (bay) E6
- Ilin (isl.) C4
- Illana (bay) D7
- Imuruan (bay) B5
- Island (bay) B6
- Itbayat (isl.) A2
- Jintotolo (chan.) D5
- Jolo (isl.) C7
- Jomalig (isl.) D3
- Lagonoy (gulf) E4
- Lamon (bay) C3
- Lanao (lake) E7
- Laparan (isls.) B8
- Lapinin (isl.) E5
- Leyte (gulf) E5
- Leyte (isl.) E5
- Limasawa (isl.) E6
- Linapacan (isl.) B5
- Lingayen (gulf) C2
- Lubang (isls.) B4
- Luzon (isl.) C3
- Luzon (str.) A2
- Macajalar (bay) E6
- Mactan (isl.) E5
- Malindang (mt.) D6
- Mangsee (isls.) A7
- Manicani (isl.) E5
- Manila (bay) C3
- Mantalingajan (mt.) A6
- Maqueda (chan.) D3
- Maraira (pt.) C1
- Marinduque (isl.) C4
- Masbate (isl.) D4
- Mayon (vol.) D4
- Maytiguid (isl.) B5
- Mindanao (isl.) D7
- Mindanao (riv.) E7
- Mindoro (isl.) C4
- Mindoro (str.) C4
- Mompog (passage) D4
- Moro (gulf) D7
- Mount Apo National Park E7
- Naso (pt.) C5
- Negros (isl.) D6
- Olutanga (isl.) D7
- Pacsan (mt.) C2
- Palawan (isl.) B6
- Palawan (passage) A6
- Panaon (isl.) E5
- Panay (isl.) D5
- Panglao (isl.) D6
- Pangutaran (isl.) C7
- Pangutaran Group (isls.) C7
- Patnanongan (isl.) D3
- Philippine (sea) D3
- Pilas (isl.) C7
- Pinatubo (mt.) C3
- Polillo (isl.) C3
- Pujada (bay) F7
- Pulangi (riv.) E7
- Quiniluban (isls.) C5
- Ragang (vol.) E7
- Ragay (gulf) D4
- Rapu-Rapu (isl.) E4
- Romblon (isl.) D4
- Sabtang (isl.) B2
- Sacol (isl.) D7
- Samal (isl.) E7
- Samales Group (isls.) D7
- Samar (isl.) E5
- Samar (sea) E4
- San Agustin (cape) F7
- San Bernardino (str.) E4
- San Miguel (bay) D3
- San Pedro (bay) E5
- Santo Tomas (mt.) C2
- Sarangani (isls.) E8
- Semirara (isls.) C5
- Siargao (isl.) F6
- Siasi (isl.) C8
- Sibay (isl.) C5
- Sibuguey (bay) D7
- Sibutu Group (isls.) B8
- Sibuyan (isl.) D4
- Sibuyan (sea) D4
- Sierra Madre (mts.) D2
- Simara (isl.) D4
- Simunul (isl.) B8
- Siquijor (isl.) D6
- South China (sea) B3
- Subic (bay) C3
- Sulu (arch.) B8
- Sulu (sea) B6
- Suluan (isl.) F5
- Taal (lake) C4
- Tablas (isl.) D4
- Tablas (str.) C4
- Tagapula (isl.) E4
- Tagolo (pt.) D6
- Tanon (str.) D6
- Tapiantana Group (isls.) D7
- Tapul (isl.) C8
- Tapul Group (isls.) C8
- Tara (isl.) C4
- Tawi-Tawi (isl.) B8
- Tayabas (bay) C4
- Ticao (isl.) D4
- Tinaca (pt.) E8
- Tongquil (isl.) D8
- Tumindao (isl.) B8
- Turtle (isls.) B7
- Verde Island (passage) C4
- Victoria (peaks) B6
- Visayan (sea) D5
- Vitali (isl.) D7

•Population of municipality.

BRUNEI

CITIES and TOWNS

Bandar Seri Begawan 36,987 ....E 4

INDONESIA

CITIES and TOWNS

Topography

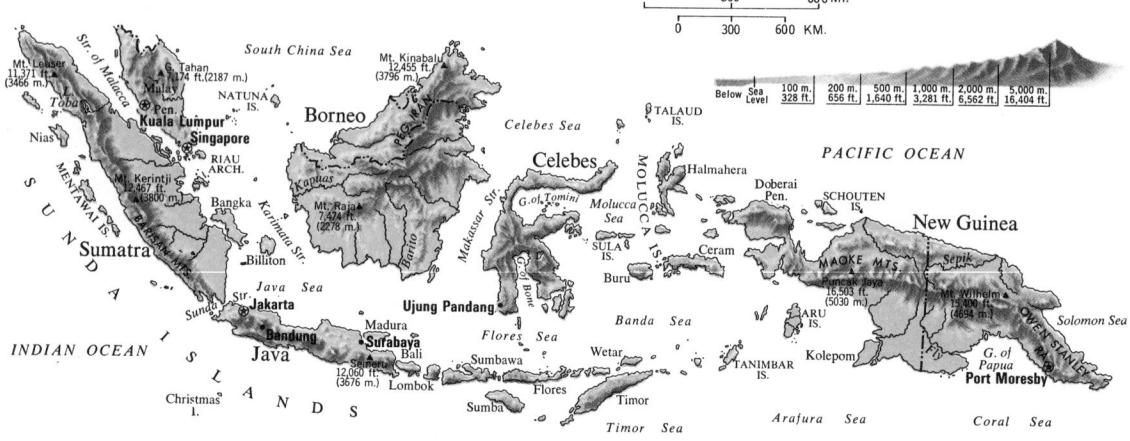

Agriculture, Industry and Resources

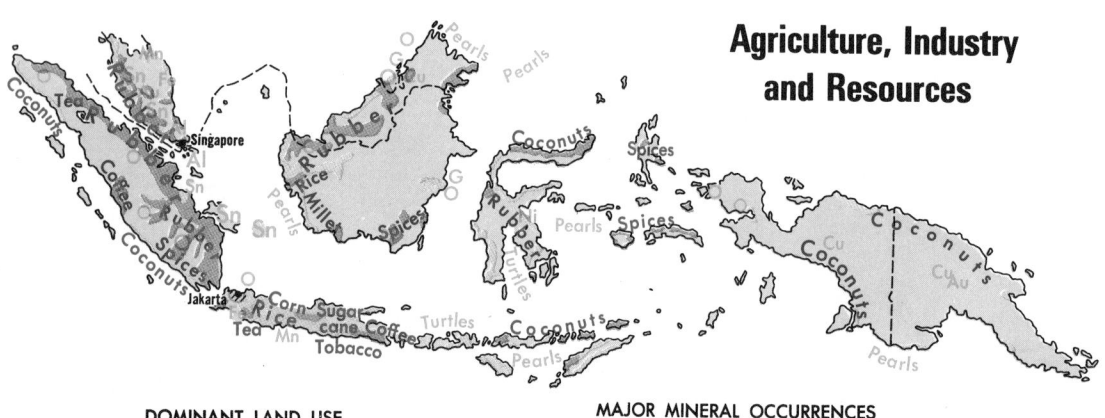

DOMINANT LAND USE

- Cereals (chiefly rice, corn)
- Diversified Tropical Crops
- Forests

MAJOR MINERAL OCCURRENCES

Al Bauxite	Cu Copper	Mn Manganese	O Petroleum
Au Gold	Fe Iron Ore	Ni Nickel	Sn Tin
C Coal	G Natural Gas		

////// Major Industrial Areas

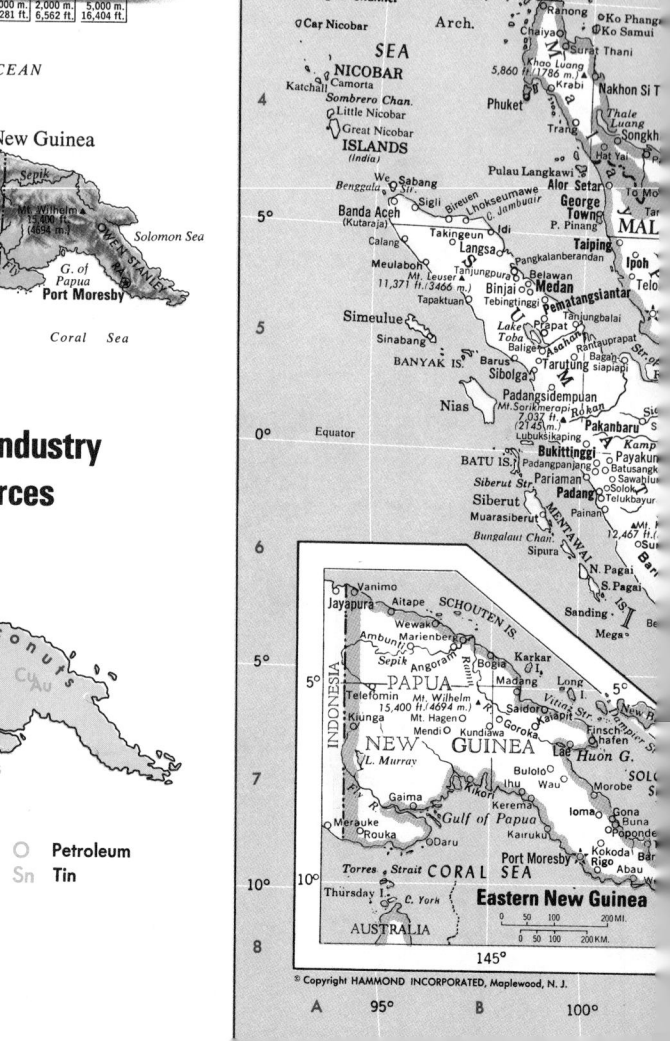

Eastern New Guinea

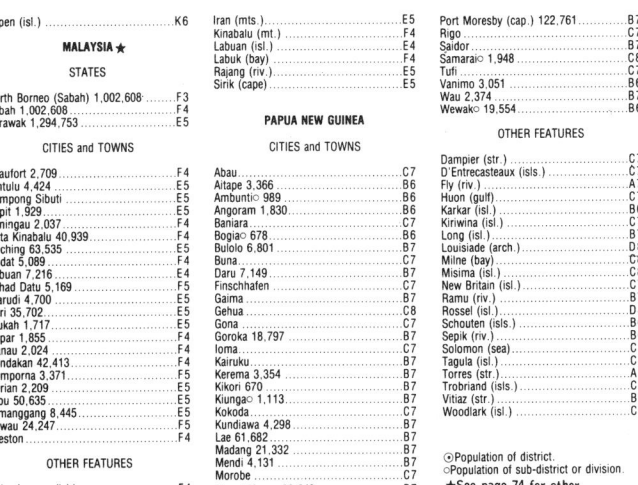

Yapen (isl.) K6

MALAYSIA ★

STATES

North Borneo (Sabah) 1,002,608 ...F3
Sabah 1,002,608 ....F4
Sarawak 1,294,753 ....E5

CITIES and TOWNS

Beaufort 2,709 ....F4
Bintulu 4,424 ....E5
Kampong Sibuti E5
Kapit 1,929 ....E5
Keningau 2,037 ....F4
Kota Kinabalu 40,939 ....E5
Kuching 63,535 ....E5
Kudat 5,089 ....E4
Labuan 7,216 ....F4
Lahad Datu 5,169 ....F4
Marudi 4,700 ....E5
Miri 35,702 ....E5
Mukah 1,717 ....E5
Ranau 2,024 ....F4
Sandakan 42,413 ....F4
Semporna 3,371 ....F4
Serian 2,209 ....E5
Sibu 50,635 ....E5
Simanggang 8,445 ....F5
Tawau 24,247 ....F5
Weston E5

OTHER FEATURES

Balambangan (isl.) F4
Banggi (isl.) F4

PAPUA NEW GUINEA

CITIES and TOWNS

Abau C7
Aitape 3,366 ....B6
Ambunto 989 ....B6
Angoram 1,830 ....B6
Baniara C7
Bogia 678 ....B6
Bulolo 6,801 ....B7
Buna C7
Daru 7,149 ....C7
Finschhafen B7
Gaima C7
Gehua C8
Gona C7
Goroka 18,797 ....B7
Ioma B7
Kairuku B7
Kerema 3,354 ....B7
Kikori 670 ....B7
Kiunga 1,113 ....B7
Kokoda C7
Kundiawa 4,298 ....B7
Lae 61,682 ....B7
Madang 21,332 ....B7
Mendi 4,131 ....B7
Morobe B7
Mount Hagen 13,642 ....B7
Popondetta 6,343 ....C7

Port Moresby (cap.) 122,761 ...B7
Rigo C7
Saidor B7
Samarai 1,948 ....C8
Tufi C7
Vanimo 3,051 ....B6
Wau 2,374 ....B7
Wewak 19,554 ....B6

OTHER FEATURES

Dampier (str.) C7
D'Entrecasteaux (isls.) C7
Fly (riv.) A7
Huon (gulf) C7
Karkar (isl.) B6
Kiriwina (isl.) C7
Long (isl.) B7
Louisiade (arch.) D8
Milne (bay) C8
Misima (isl.) D8
New Britain (isl.) C7
Ramu (riv.) B7
Rossel (isl.) D8
Schouten (isls.) B6
Sepik (riv.) B6
Solomon (sea) C7
Tagula (isl.) D8
Torres (str.) A7
Trobriand (isls.) C7
Vitiaz (str.) B7
Woodlark (isl.) C7

⊙ Population of district.
⊙ Population of sub-district or division.
★See page 74 for other Malaysian entries.

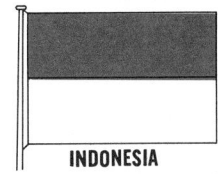

INDONESIA

PAPUA NEW GUINEA

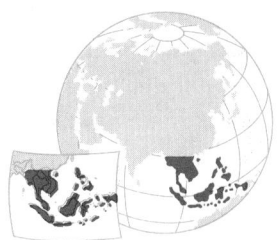

AREA 788,430 sq. mi. (2,042,034 sq. km.)
POPULATION 147,383,075
CAPITAL Jakarta
LARGEST CITY Jakarta
HIGHEST POINT Puncak Jaya 16,503 ft. (5,030 m.)
MONETARY UNIT rupiah
MAJOR LANGUAGES Bahasa Indonesia, Indonesian and Papuan languages, English
MAJOR RELIGIONS Islam, tribal religions, Christianity, Hinduism

AREA 183,540 sq. mi. (475,369 sq. km.)
POPULATION 3,006,799
CAPITAL Port Moresby
LARGEST CITY Port Moresby
HIGHEST POINT Mt. Wilhelm 15,400 ft. (4,694 m.)
MONETARY UNIT kina
MAJOR LANGUAGES pidgin English, Hiri Motu, English
MAJOR RELIGIONS Tribal religions, Christianity

BRUNEI
AREA 2,226 sq. mi. (5,765 sq. km.)
POPULATION 212,840
CAPITAL Bandar Seri Begawan

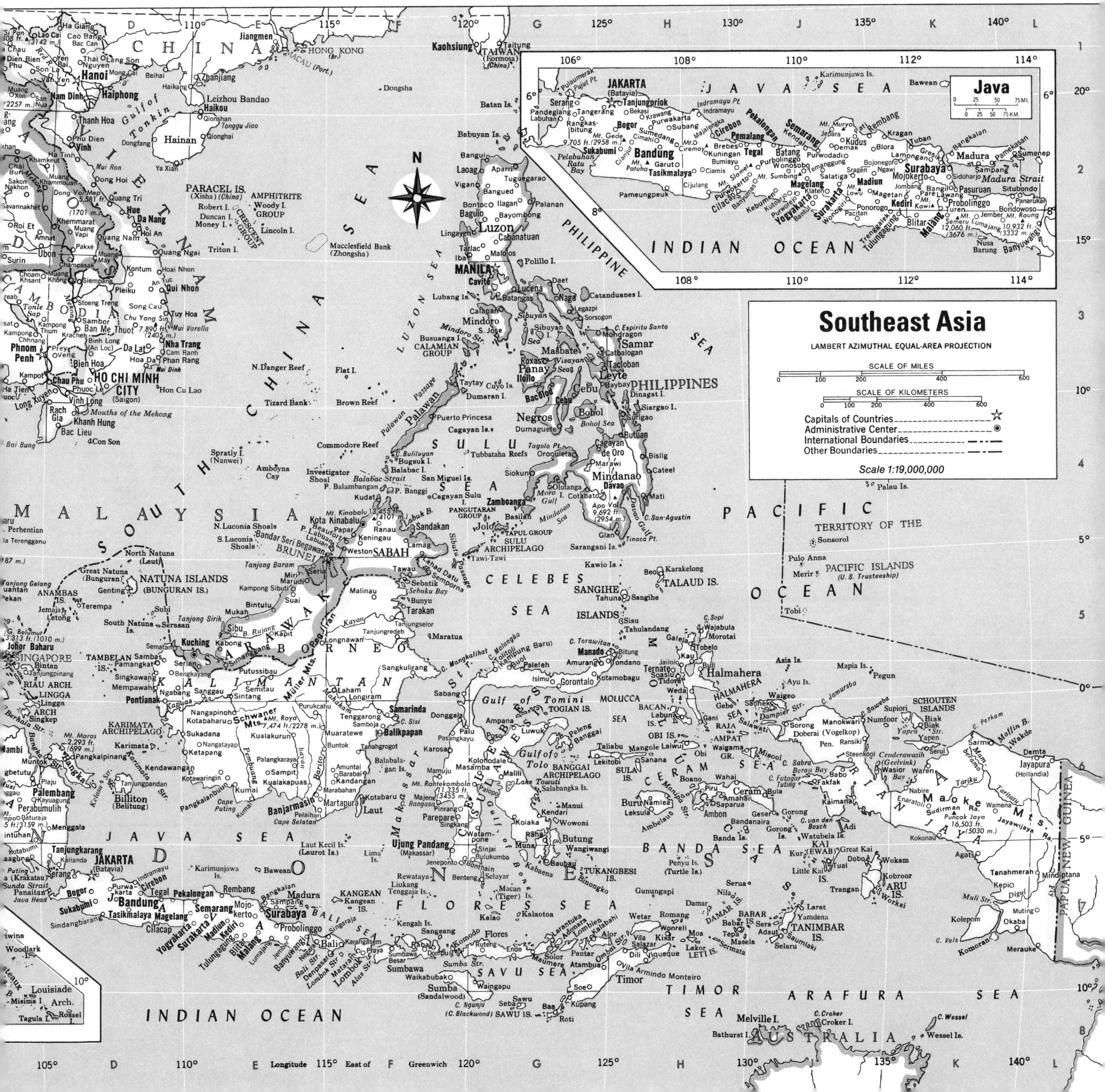

Southeast Asia

LAMBERT AZIMUTHAL EQUAL-AREA PROJECTION

SCALE OF MILES
0   100   200   300   400   500   600

SCALE OF KILOMETERS
0   100   200   300   400   500   600

Capitals of Countries _____ ☆
Administrative Center _____ ◉
International Boundaries _____ — ∙ —
Other Boundaries _____ — — —

Scale 1:19,000,000

FIJI

AREA 7,055 sq. mi. (18,272 sq. km.)
POPULATION 588,068
CAPITAL Suva
LARGEST CITY Suva
HIGHEST POINT Tomaniivi 4,341 ft.
(1,323 m.)
MONETARY UNIT Fijian dollar
MAJOR LANGUAGES Fijian, Hindi, English
MAJOR RELIGIONS Protestantism, Hinduism

KIRIBATI

AREA 291 sq. mi. (754 sq. km.)
POPULATION 56,213
CAPITAL Bairiki (Tarawa)
HIGHEST POINT (on Banaba I.) 285 ft. (87 m.)
MONETARY UNIT Australian dollar
MAJOR LANGUAGES I-Kiribati, English
MAJOR RELIGIONS Protestantism, Roman
Catholicism

NAURU

AREA 7.7 sq. mi. (20 sq. km.)
POPULATION 7,254
CAPITAL Yaren (district)
MONETARY UNIT Australian dollar
MAJOR LANGUAGES Nauruan, English
MAJOR RELIGION Protestantism

SOLOMON ISLANDS

AREA 11,500 sq. mi. (29,785 sq. km.)
POPULATION 221,000
CAPITAL Honiara
HIGHEST POINT Mount Popomanatseu
7,647 ft. (2,331 m.)
MONETARY UNIT Solomon Islands dollar
MAJOR LANGUAGES English, pidgin English,
Melanesian dialects
MAJOR RELIGIONS Tribal religions,
Protestantism, Roman Catholicism

TONGA

AREA 270 sq. mi. (699 sq. km.)
POPULATION 90,128
CAPITAL Nuku'alofa
LARGEST CITY Nuku'alofa
HIGHEST POINT 3,389 ft. (1,033 m.)
MONETARY UNIT pa'anga
MAJOR LANGUAGES Tongan, English
MAJOR RELIGION Protestantism

TUVALU

AREA 9.78 sq. mi. (25.33 sq. km.)
POPULATION 7,349
CAPITAL Fongafale (Funafuti)
HIGHEST POINT 15 ft. (4.6 m.)
MONETARY UNIT Australian dollar
MAJOR LANGUAGES English, Tuvaluan
MAJOR RELIGION Protestantism

Abaiang (atoll) 3,296	H5
Abemama (atoll) 2,300	H5
Adamstown (cap.), Pitcairn Is. 61	N8
Admiralty (isls.)	E6
Agaña (cap.), Guam 881	E4
Agrihan (isl.)	E4
Ahau 1,117	H7
Ailinglapalap (atoll)	G5
Ailuk (atoll)	H4
Aitutaki (atoll) 2,423	K7
Alamagan (isl.)	E4
Alofi (cap.), Niue 957	K7
Alotau 4,310	E7
Amanu (atoll)	N7
Ambrym (isl.) 6,324	G7
American Samoa 32,395	J7
Anaa (atoll) 444	M7
Anatahan (isl.)	E4
Aneityum (Anatom) (isl.) 464	H8
Angaur (isl.)	D5
Apataki (atoll)	M7
Apia (cap.), W. Samoa 32,099	J7
Arafura (sea)	D6
Arno (atoll)	H5
Arorae (atoll) 1,626	H6
Asuncion (isl.)	E4
Atafu (atoll) 577	J6
Atiu (isl.) 1,312	L8
Auki 1,926	G6
Austral (isls.) 5,208	L8
Australia 13,548,448	C8
Babelthuap (isl.)	D5
Bairiki (cap.), Kiribati 1,777	H5
Baker (isl.)	J5
Banaba (isl.) 2,314	G6
Banks (isls.) 3,158	G7
Bass (isls.)	M8
Belau (Palau) 12,177	D5
Belep (isls.) 624	G7
Bellona (reefs)	G7
Beru (atoll) 2,318	H6
Bikar (atoll)	H4
Bikini (atoll)	G4
Bismarck (arch.) 314,308	E6
Bonin (isls.) 1,507	E3
Bora-Bora (isl.) 2,572	L7
Bougainville (isl.) 128,890	F6
Bounty (isls.)	H10
Bourail 3,149	G8
Buka 1,517	F6
Butaritari (atoll) 2,971	H5
Canberra (cap.), Australia 197,622	F9
Canton (isl.)	J6
Capitol Hill (cap.), No. Marianas 1,245	E4
Caroline (isl.)	M7
Caroline (isls.)	E5
Chesterfield (isls.)	F7
Chichi (isl.) 1,507	E3
Choiseul (isl.) 10,349	F6
Christmas (isl.) 674	L5
Cook (isls.) 18,128	K7
Coral (sea)	F7
Danger (Pukapuka) (atoll) 785	K7
Daru 7,149	E6
D'Entrecasteaux (isls.)	F6
Disappointment (isls.) 373	N7
Ducie (isl.)	P8
Duke of Gloucester (isls.)	M8
Easter (isl.) 1,598	Q8
Eauripik (atoll)	E5
Ebon (atoll)	G5
Efate (isl.) 18,038	G7
Eiao (isl.)	M6
Elato (atoll)	E5
Enderbury (isl.)	J6
Enewetak (Eniwetok) (atoll)	G4
Erromanga (isl.) 945	H7
Espiritu Santo (isl.) 16,220	G7
Fais (isl.)	E5
Fakaofo (atoll) 654	J6
Fakarava (atoll)	M7
Fanning (isl.) 340	L5
Farallon de Pajaros (isl.)	E3
Faraulep (atoll)	E5
Fatuhiva (isl.) 386	N7
Fiji 588,068	H8
Flint (isl.)	L7
Fly (riv.)	E6
Fongafale (cap.), Tuvalu	H6
French Polynesia 137,382	M7
Funafuti (atoll) 2,120	H6
Futuna (Hoorn) (isls.) 3,173	J7
Gaferut (isl.)	E5
Gambier (isls.) 556	N8
Gardner (isl.)	J6
Gilbert (isls.) 47,711	H6
Greenwich (Kapingamarangi) (atoll)	F5
Guadalcanal (isl.) 46,619	F7
Guam (isl.) 105,821	E4
Ha'apai Group (isls.) 10,812	J8
Haha (isl.)	E3
Hall (isls.)	F5
Hao (atoll)	N7
Hawaiian (isls.) 769,913	J3
Henderson (isl.)	O8
Hikueru (atoll)	M7
Hivaoa (isl.) 1,159	N6
Honiara (cap.), Solomon Is. 14,942	F6
Hoorn (isls.) 3,173	J7
Howland (isl.)	J5
Huahine (isl.) 3,140	L7
Hull (isl.)	J6
Huon (gulf)	E6
Huon (isls.)	G7
Ifalik (atoll)	E5
Iwo (isl.)	E3
Jaluit (atoll)	G5
Jarvis (isl.)	K6
Johnston (atoll) 339	K4
Kadavu (Kandavu) (isl.) 8,699	H7
Kanton (Canton) (isl.)	J6
Kapingamarangi (atoll)	F5
Kavieng 4,566	E6
Kermadec (isls.) 11	J9
Kieta 3,445	F6
Kili (isl.)	G5
Kimbe 4,680	F6
Kingman (reef)	K5
Kiribati 57,500	J6
Kita Iwo (isl.)	D3

Kingman (reef)	K5
Kiribati 57,500	J6
Kita Iwo (isl.)	D3
Maiden (isl.)	L6
Nadi 6,938	H7
Malakula (isl.) 15,931	G7
Maloelap (atoll)	H5
Mangaia (isl.) 1,530	L8
Mangareva (isl.) 556	N8
Manihiki (atoll) 266	K7
Manra (Sydney) (isl.)	K6
Manua (isls.) 1,740	K7
Manue (atoll)	K7
Manus (isl.) 25,844	E6
Marcus (isl.)	F3
Maré (isl.) 4,156	G8
Maria (isl.)	L8
Marianas, Northern 16,862	E4
Mariana Trench	E4
Marquesas (isls.) 5,419	N6
Marshall Islands 31,042	G4
Marutea (atoll)	N8
Mata Utu (cap.), Wallis and Futuna 558	J7
Mauke (isl.) 711	L8
Mehetia (isl.)	M7
Melanesia (reg.)	E5
Merir (isl.)	D5
Micronesia (reg.) 2,572	E4
Micronesia, Federated States of 73,755	F5
Midway (isls.) 526	J3
Mili (atoll)	H5
Minami Iwo (isl.)	D3
Minerva (reefs)	H8
Moen (isl.)	F5
Mokil (atoll)	G5
Moorea (isl.) 5,788	L7
Morane (isl.)	N8
Mururoa (isl.)	M8
Nadi 6,938	H7
Namonuito (atoll)	E5
Namorik (atoll)	G5
Nanumea (atoll) 844	H5
Napier☐ 50,164	H9
Nassau (isl.) 123	K7
Nauru 7,254	G6
Ndeni (isl.) 4,854	G7
Nelalu 3,307	J7
New Britain (isl.) 222,759	E6
New Caledonia (isl.) 118,715	G8
New Caledonia 133,233	G8
New Georgia (isl.) 16,472	F6
New Guinea (isl.)	B6
New Hanover (Lavongai)	E6
New Hebrides (Vanuatu) 112,596	G7
New Ireland (isl.) 65,705	F6
New Zealand 3,167,357	G9
Ngatik (atoll)	F5
Ngulu (atoll)	D5
Nikumaroro (Gardner) (isl.)	J6
Ninigo Group (isls.)	E6
Niuafo'ou (isl.) 678	J7
Niuatoputapu (isl.) 1,650	J7
Niue (isl.) 3,843	K7
Niutao (atoll) 866	H6
Nomoi (isls.)	F5
Nonouti (atoll) 2,223	H6
Norfolk Island (terr.) 2,180	G8
Northern Marianas 168,621	E4
North Pacific (ocean)	F4
Nouméa (cap.), New Caled. 56,078	G8

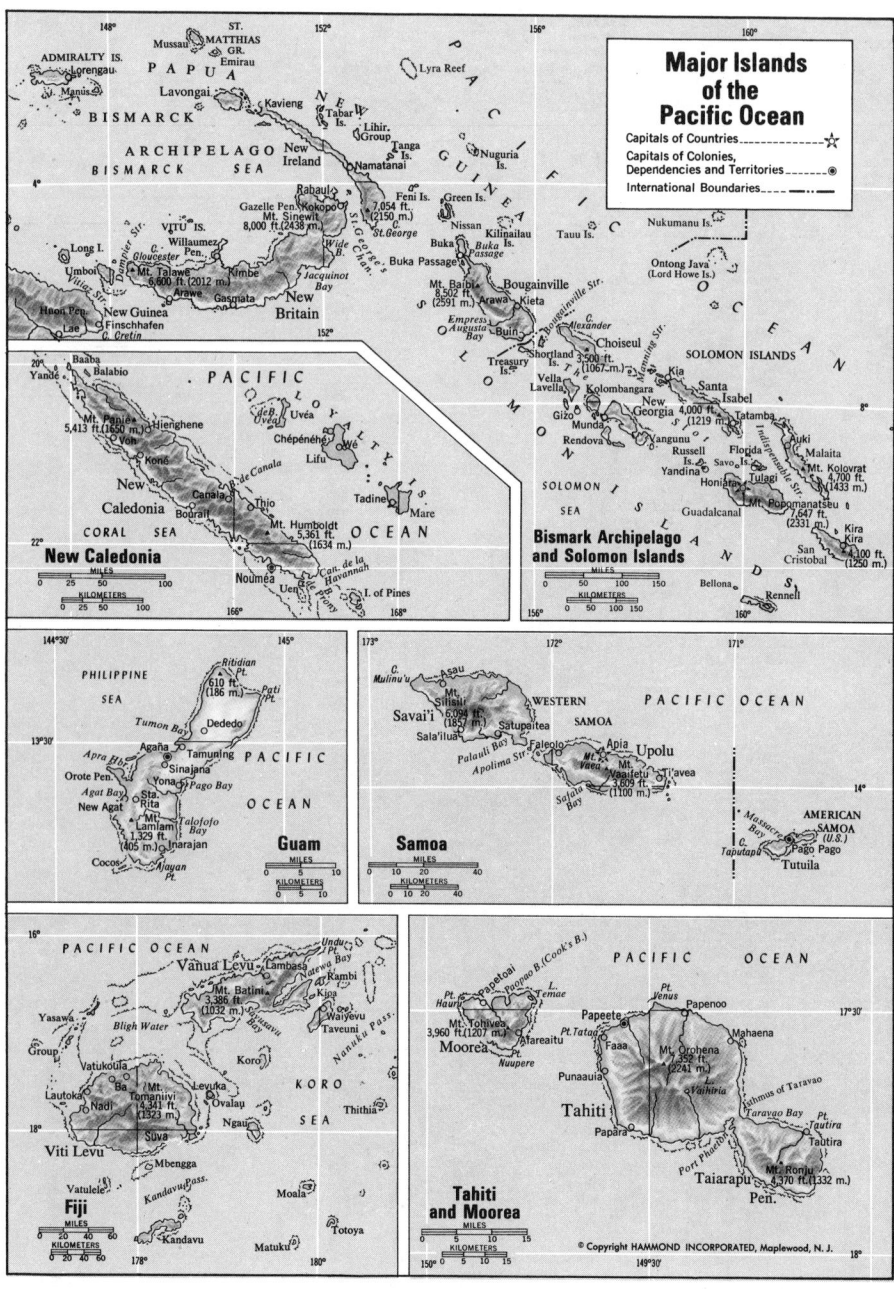

Major Islands of the Pacific Ocean

Capitals of Countries .... ☆
Capitals of Colonies, Dependencies and Territories .... ◉
International Boundaries .... ____

New Caledonia

Bismark Archipelago and Solomon Islands

Guam

Samoa

Fiji

Tahiti and Moorea

© Copyright HAMMOND INCORPORATED, Maplewood, N.J.

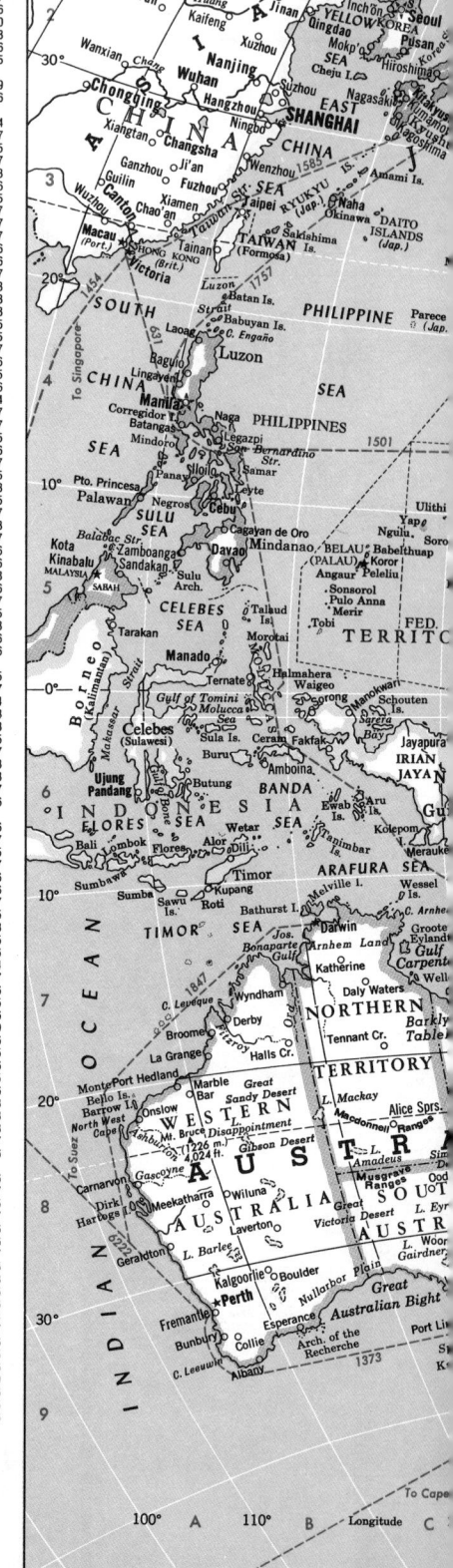

VANUATU

AREA 5,700 sq. mi. (14,763 sq. km.)
POPULATION 112,596
CAPITAL Vila
HIGHEST POINT Mt. Tabwemasana
6,165 ft. (1,879 m.)
MONETARY UNIT vatu
MAJOR LANGUAGES Bislama, English,
French
MAJOR RELIGIONS Christian, animist

WESTERN SAMOA

AREA 1,133 sq. mi. (2,934 sq. km.)
POPULATION 151,983
CAPITAL Apia
LARGEST CITY Apia
HIGHEST POINT Mt. Silisili 6,094 ft.
(1,857 m.)
MONETARY UNIT tala
MAJOR LANGUAGES Samoan, English
MAJOR RELIGIONS Protestantism,
Roman Catholicism

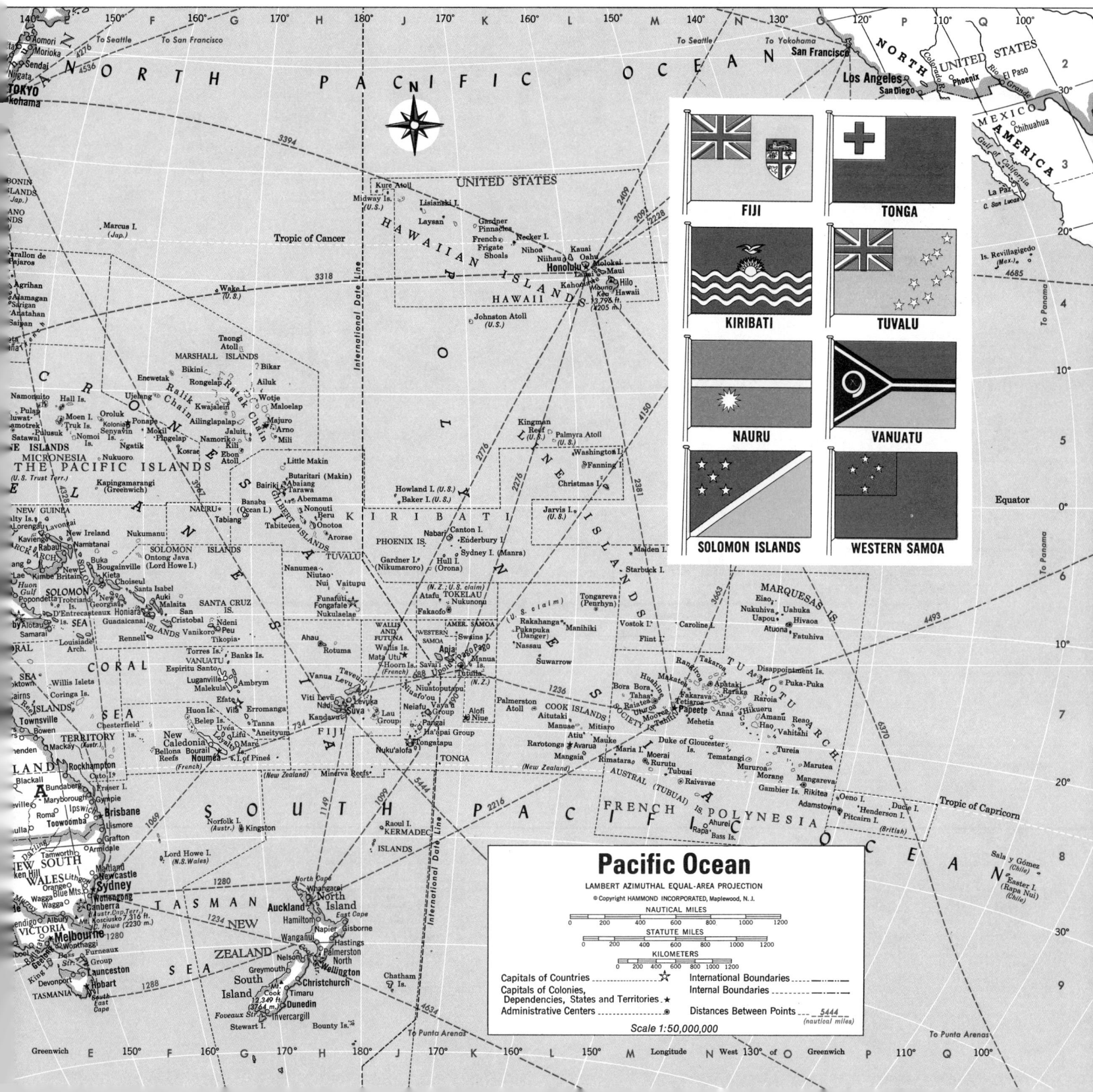

Pacific Ocean

LAMBERT AZIMUTHAL EQUAL-AREA PROJECTION

© Copyright HAMMOND INCORPORATED, Maplewood, N.J.

NAUTICAL MILES
STATUTE MILES
KILOMETERS

Capitals of Countries
Capitals of Colonies,
Dependencies, States and Territories
Administrative Centers

International Boundaries
Internal Boundaries

Distances Between Points 5444
(nautical miles)

Scale 1:50,000,000

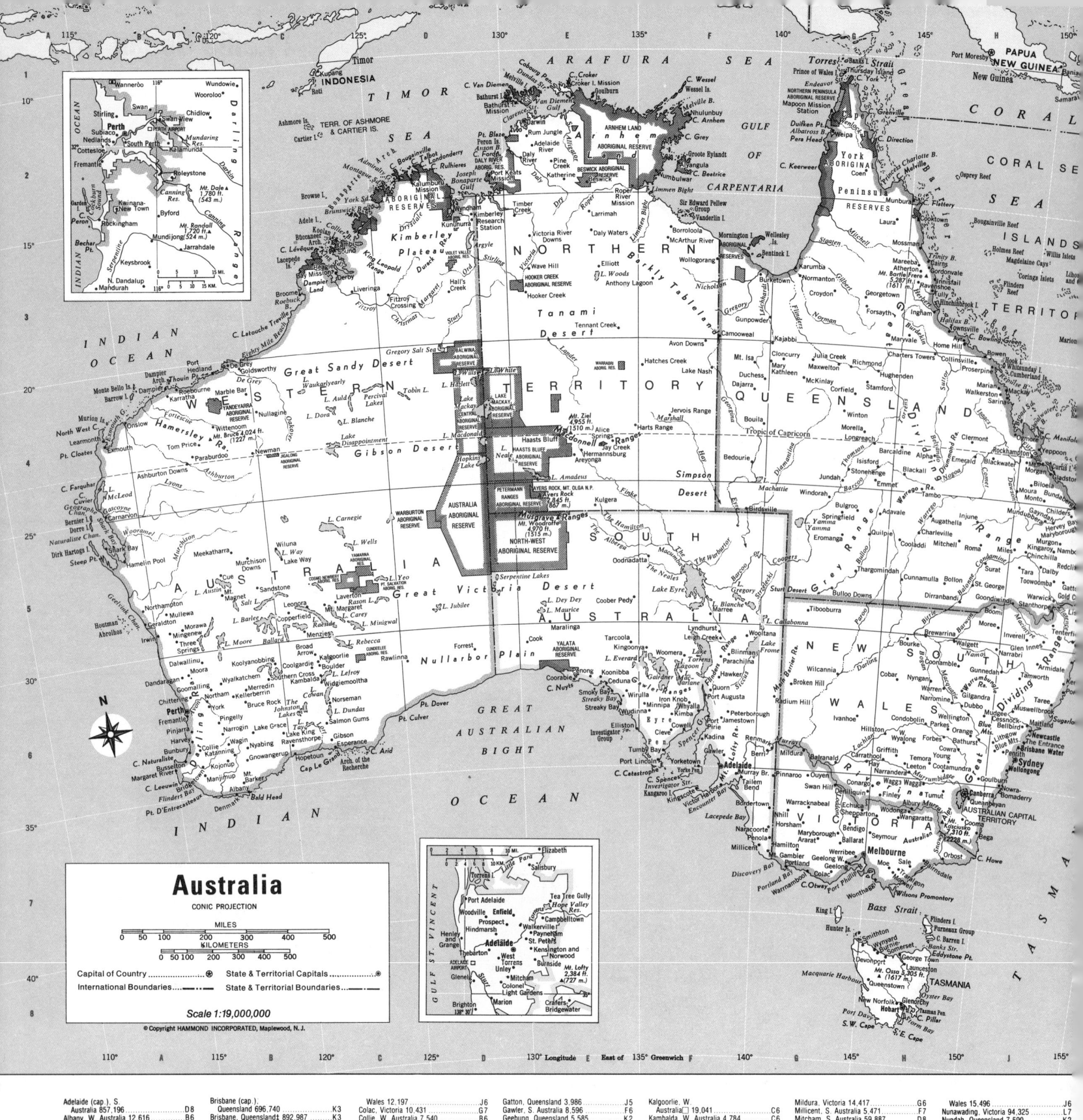

Australia

CONIC PROJECTION

MILES
0 50 100   200   300   400   500

KILOMETERS
0 50 100   200   300   400   500

Capital of Country .... ⊛
International Boundaries .... ─··─··─
State & Territorial Capitals .... ⊛
State & Territorial Boundaries .... ─·─·─

Scale 1:19,000,000

© Copyright HAMMOND INCORPORATED, Maplewood, N.J.

Adelaide (cap.), S.
  Australia 857,196 .... D8
Albany, W. Australia 12,616 .... B6
Albury, N. S. Wales 31,954 ..... H7
Alice Springs, North.
  Terr. 14,149 .... E4
Altona, Victoria 30,272 .... K7
Ararat, Victoria 8,288 .... G7
Armidale, N. S. Wales 19,711 ... J6
Ascot, Queensland 4,606 .... K2
Ashfield, N. S. Wales 42,322 ... K4
Ashgrove, Queensland 11,423 .... K2
Ashmore and Cartier Is., Terr.
  of C2
Aspley, Queensland 10,406 ...... K2
Auburn, N. S. Wales 47,556 ..... K4
Australian Capital
  Territory 203,300 .... H7
Bairnsdale, Victoria 9,130 ..... H7
Ballarat, Victoria 37,863 ...... G7
Ballarat, Victoria‡ 60,737 ..... G7
Bankstown, N. S. Wales 155,843 . K4
Banyo, Queensland 5,146 .... K2
Bathurst, N. S. Wales 18,589 ... H6
Beenleigh, Queensland 4,216 .... J5
Bega, N. S. Wales 4,253 .... H7
Bendigo, Victoria 32,573 .... G7
Bendigo, Victoria‡ 50,169 ...... G7
Biloela, Queensland 4,575 ...... J4
Blacktown, N. S. Wales 159,734 . K4
Blackwater, Queensland 4,638 ... H4
Blue Mountains, N. S.
  Wales 45,798 .... J6
Botany, N. S. Wales 35,739 ..... L4
Boulder, W. Australia 19,041 ... C6
Bowen, Queensland 6,707 .... H3
Box Hill, Victoria 50,280 ...... L7
Brighton, S. Australia 21,407 .. D8
Brighton, Victoria 35,783 ...... L7

Brisbane (cap.),
  Queensland 696,740 .... K3
Brisbane, Queensland‡ 892,987 .. K3
Brisbane Water, N. S.
  Wales 54,819 .... J6
Broadmeadows, Victoria 108,744 . L6
Broken Hill, N. S.
  Wales 27,647 .... G6
Brunswick, Victoria 46,192 ..... K7
Bunbury, W. Australia 19,513 ... B6
Bundaberg, Queensland 31,189 ... J4
Burnie-Somerset,
  Tasmania 19,465 .... H8
Burnside, S. Australia 38,461 .. E8
Burwood, N. S. Wales 29,045 .... K4
Busselton, W. Australia 5,550 .. A6
Cairns, Queensland 39,305 ...... H3
Caloundra, Queensland 10,602 ... J5
Camberwell, Victoria 89,865 .... L7
Campbelltown, S.
  Australia 41,252 .... E8
Camp Hill, Queensland 9,961 .... K3
Canberra (cap.), A. C.
  T.‡ 197,622 .... H7
Canterbury, N. S.
  Wales 128,710 .... K4
Carina, Queensland 7,563 .... K3
Carnarvon, W. Australia 5,341 .. A4
Casino, N. S. Wales 9,456 ...... J5
Caulfield, Victoria 73,630 ..... L7
Cessnock-Bellbird, N. S.
  Wales 16,256 .... J6
Cessnock-Bellbird, N. S.
  Wales* 36,199 .... J6
Charters Towers,
  Queensland 7,914 .... H4
Chelsea, Victoria 26,357 .... L8
Chermside, Queensland 7,666 .... K2
Coburg, Victoria 58,379 .... K7
Coffs Harbour, N. S.

Wales 12,197 .... J6
Colac, Victoria 10,431 .... G7
Collie, W. Australia 7,540 ..... B6
Collingwood, Victoria 16,645 ... L7
Concord, N. S. Wales 24,598 .... K4
Cooma, N. S. Wales 7,353 .... H7
Coopers Plains,
  Queensland 5,017 .... K3
Cootamundra, N. S. Wales 6,384 . H6
Corinda, Queensland 4,132 ...... J4
Cowra, N. S. Wales 7,734 .... H6
Cranbourne, Victoria 5,162 ..... M8
Croydon, Victoria 5,162 .... M7
Dalby, Queensland 8,997 .... J5
Dandenong, Victoria 48,444 ..... M7
Darwin (cap.), North.
  Terr. 39,193 .... E2
Deniliquin, N. S. Wales 6,865 .. G7
Devonport, Tasmania 19,399 ..... H8
Doncaster and Templestowe,
  Victoria 82,090 .... L7
Drummoyne, N. S. Wales 31,516 .. K4
Dubbo, N. S. Wales 20,149 ...... H6
East Brisbane,
  Queensland 5,506 .... K3
Echuca, Victoria 7,873 .... G7
Elizabeth, S. Australia 33,721 . D7
Eltham, Victoria 28,631 .... L6
Enfield, S. Australia 73,505 ... D7
Enoggera, Queensland 6,668 ..... K2
Esperance, W. Australia 5,262 .. C6
Essendon, Victoria 51,133 ...... K7
Fairfield, N. S. Wales 114,603 . H4
Fitzroy, Victoria 20,451 .... L7
Footscray, Victoria 51,774 ..... K7
Forbes, N. S. Wales 7,754 ...... H6
Fremantle, W. Australia 23,497 . B6

Gatton, Queensland 3,986 .... J5
Gawler, S. Australia 8,596 ..... F6
Geebung, Queensland 5,585 ...... K2
Geelong, Victoria 15,727 .... L7
Geelong West, Victoria 15,978 . G7
Geelong, Victoria‡ 122,080 ..... L7
George Town, Tasmania 5,296 .... H8
Geraldton, W. Australia 18,773 . A5
Gladstone, Queensland 18,591 ... J4
Glen Innes, N. S. Wales 5,953 .. J5
Glenorchy, Tasmania 42,437 ..... H8
Gold Coast, Queensland 87,510 . J5
Goulburn, N. S. Wales 21,735 ... J6
Graceville, Queensland 3,929 ... K3
Grafton, N. S. Wales 16,516 .... J5
Greenslopes, Queensland 7,345 .. K3
Griffith, N. S. 11,930 .... H6
Gunnedah, N. S. Wales 8,689 .... H6
Gympie, Queensland 11,205 ...... J5
Hamilton, Victoria 9,504 .... G7
Hawthorne, Victoria 32,505 ..... L7
Heidelberg, Victoria 66,108 .... L7
Hervey Bay, Queensland 9,150 ... J5
Hindmarsh, S. Australia 8,691 .. D8
Holroyd, N. S. Wales 79,867 .... K4
Hornsby, N. S. Wales 104,110 ... K4
Horsham, Victoria 11,647 .... G7
Hunters Hill, N. S.
  Wales 13,017 .... K4
Hurstville, N. S. Wales 66,450 . K4
Inala, Queensland 20,037 .... K3
Indooroopilly,
  Queensland 8,534 .... K3
Ingham, Queensland 5,868 .... H3
Innisfail, Queensland 7,933 .... H3
Inverell, N. S. Wales 9,432 .... J5
Ipswich, Queensland 69,242 ..... J3
Kalgoorlie, W. Australia 9,067 . C6

Kalgoorlie, W.
  Australia☐ 19,041 .... C6
Kambalda, W. Australia 4,784 ... C6
Karratha, W. Australia 4,243 ... B4
Katanning, W. Australia 4,162 .. B6
Keilor, Victoria 20,597 .... L7
Kempsey, N. S. Wales 8,881 ..... J6
Kenmore, Queensland 8,630 ...... J3
Kensington and Norwood, S.
  Australia 13,476 .... E8
Kew, Victoria 29,683 .... L7
Kingaroy, Queensland 5,088 ..... J5
Knox, Victoria 74,456 .... M7
Kogarah, N. S. Wales 46,721 .... L4
Kwinana-Newtown, W.
  Australia 10,981 .... B2
Lane Cove, N. S. Wales 29,341 .. L4
Launceston, Tasmania 32,953 .... H8
Launceston, Tasmania‡ 63,386 .. H8
Leeton, N. S. Wales 6,631 ...... H6
Leichhardt, N. S. Wales 62,520 . L4
Lismore, N. S. Wales 22,082 .... J5
Lithgow, N. S. Wales 12,703 .... J6
Liverpool, N. S. Wales 89,682 .. K4
Mackay, Queensland 31,522 ...... H4
Maitland, N. S. Wales 36,030 ... J6
Malvern, Victoria 45,566 .... L7
Mandurah, W. Australia 7,050 ... B3
Manly, N. S. Wales 36,709 ...... L4
Mareeba, Queensland 5,776 ...... G3
Marion, S. Australia 67,283 .... D8
Maroochydore-Mooloolaba,
  Queensland 10,283 .... J5
Marrickville, N. S.
  Wales 87,821 .... L4
Maryborough, Victoria 7,569 .... G7
Maryborough, Queensland 21,521 . J5
Melbourne (cap.),
  Victoria 64,970 .... H7
Melbourne, Victoria‡ 2,479,225 . H7
Nowra-Bomaderry, N. S.

Mildura, Victoria 14,417 .... G6
Millicent, S. Australia 94,325 . F7
Mitcham, S. Australia 59,887 ... D8
Mitchelton, Queensland 6,115 .. J2
Moe, Victoria 15,345 .... H7
Moorabbin, Victoria 103,059 .... L7
Moorooka, Queensland 9,639 ..... K3
Mordialloc, Victoria 28,615 .... L7
Moree, N. S. Wales 9,359 .... H5
Morningside, Queensland 7,495 .. K2
Morwell, Victoria 16,094 .... H7
Mosman, N. S. Wales 26,811 ..... L4
Mount Gambier, S.
  Australia 17,858 .... G7
Mount Isa, Queensland 25,377 ... F4
Mudgee, N. S. Wales 5,724 ...... J6
Murray Bridge, S.
  Australia 7,476 .... F7
Murwillumbah, N. S.
  Wales 7,294 .... J5
Muswellbrook, N. S.
  Wales 7,805 .... J6
Nambucca, S. Australia 4,571 ... J5
Naracoorte, S. Australia 4,511 . F7
Narrabri, N. S. Wales 6,951 .... H6
Narrandera, N. S. Wales 4,984 .. H6
Narrogin, W. Australia 4,812 ... B6
Nedlands, W. Australia 20,974 .. B2
Newcastle, N. S. Wales 138,718 . J6
Newcastle, N. S. Wales* 251,132 J6
Newman, W. Australia 5,779 ..... C4
Newmarket, Queensland 3,935 .... K2
New Norfolk, Tasmania 6,679 .... H8
New South Wales 4,914,300 ...... H6
Norfolk Island 2,180 .... L5
Northam, W. Australia 6,866 .... B6
Northcote, Victoria 54,881 ..... L7
Northern Territory 97,090 ...... E3
North Sydney, N. S.
  Wales 48,536 .... L4
Nowra-Bomaderry, N. S.

Wales 15,496 .... J6
Nunawading, Victoria 94,325 .... L7
Nundah, Queensland 7,590 .... K2
Oakleigh, Victoria 54,532 ...... L7
Orange, N. S. Wales 26,254 ..... H6
Parkes, N. S. Wales 8,905 ...... H6
Parramatta, N. S.
  Wales 131,659 .... K4
Payneham, S. Australia 17,545 .. E8
Penrith, N. S. Wales 79,043 .... J6
Perth (cap.), W.
  Australia 87,598 .... B2
Perth, W. Australia‡ 731,275 ... B2
Port Adelaide, S.
  Australia 36,024 .... D7
Port Augusta, S.
  Australia 13,092 .... F6
Port Hedland, W.
  Australia 11,144 .... B3
Portland, Victoria 6,368 .... G7
Port Lincoln, S.
  Australia 9,809 .... E6
Port Melbourne, Victoria 9,356 . K7
Port Macquarie, N. S.
  Wales 13,362 .... J6
Port Pirie, S.
  Australia 15,005 .... F6
Prahran, Victoria 48,462 .... L7
Preston, Victoria 88,384 .... L7
Prospect, S. Australia 19,485 .. D8
Queanbeyan, N. S. Wales 18,923 . H7
Queensland 2,111,700 .... G4
Queenstown, Tasmania 4,520 ..... H8
Randwick, N. S. Wales 119,500 .. L4
Red Cliffe, Queensland 39,073 .. J3
Renmark, S. Australia 6,247 .... G6
Richmond, Victoria 26,179 ...... L7
Ringwood, Victoria 37,085 ...... M7
Rockdale, N. S. Wales 83,797 ... L4
Rockhampton, Queensland 50,132 . J4

AREA 2,966,136 sq. mi. (7,682,300 sq. km.)
POPULATION 13,548,448
CAPITAL Canberra
LARGEST CITY Sydney
HIGHEST POINT Mt. Kosciusko 7,310 ft. (2,228 m.)
LOWEST POINT Lake Eyre -39 ft. (-12 m.)
MONETARY UNIT Australian dollar
MAJOR LANGUAGE English
MAJOR RELIGIONS Protestantism, Roman Catholicism

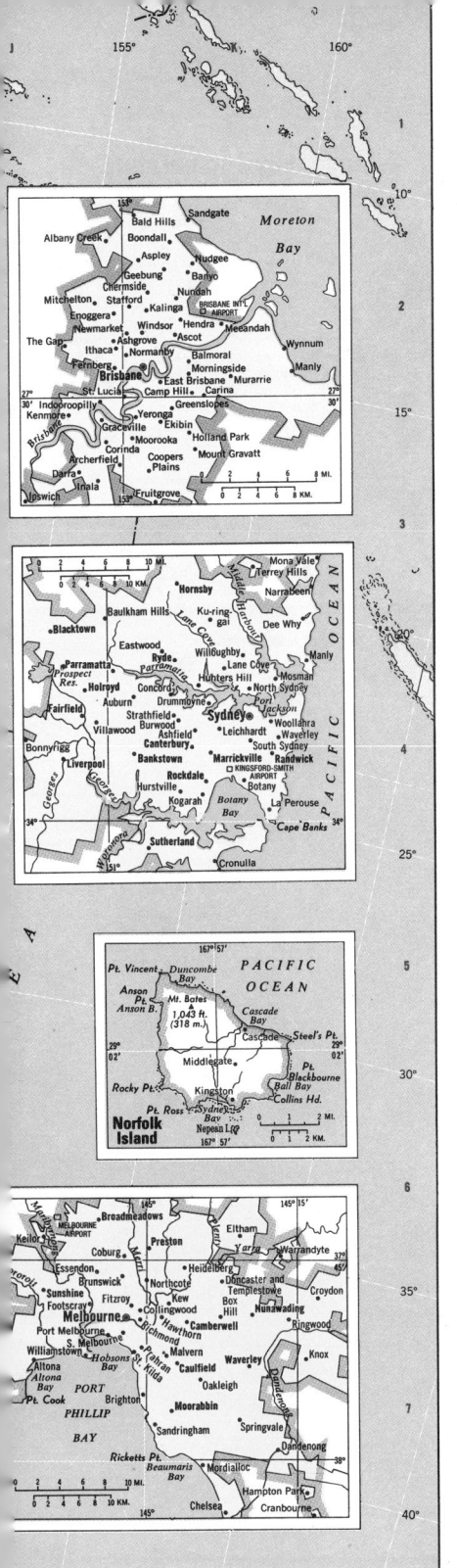

Population Distribution

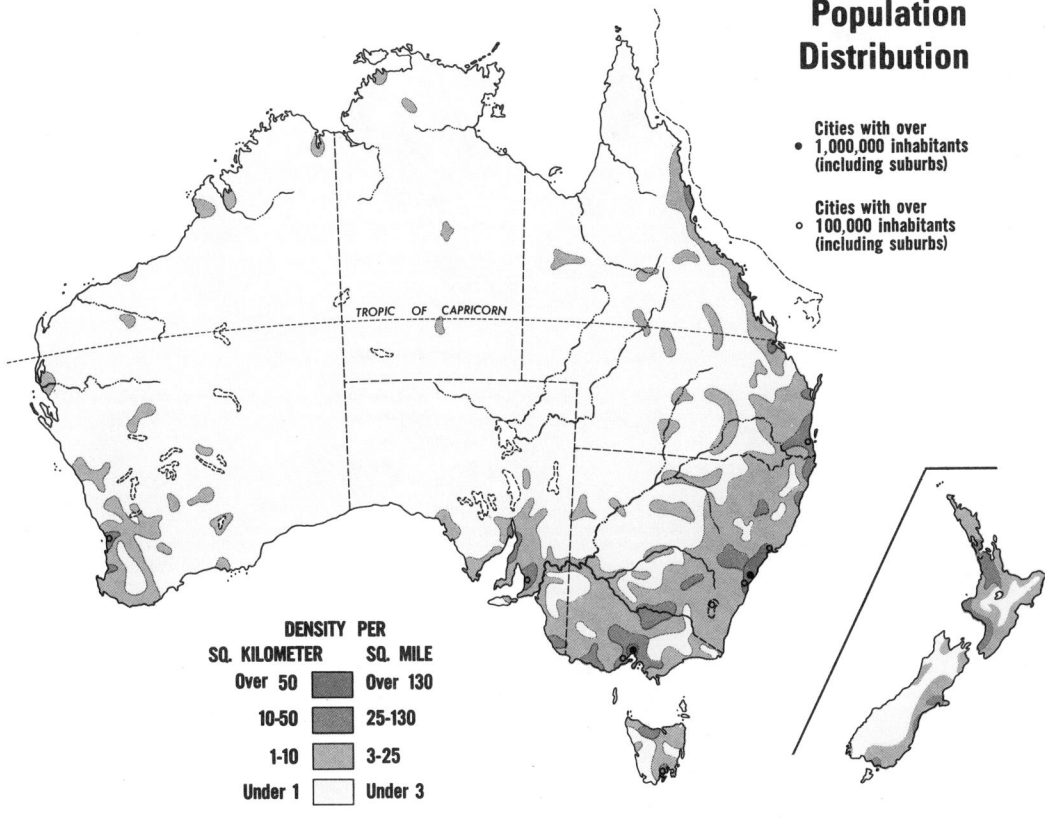

- Cities with over **1,000,000 inhabitants** (including suburbs)

○ Cities with over **100,000 inhabitants** (including suburbs)

DENSITY PER

SQ. KILOMETER	SQ. MILE
Over 50	Over 130
10-50	25-130
1-10	3-25
Under 1	Under 3

Vegetation

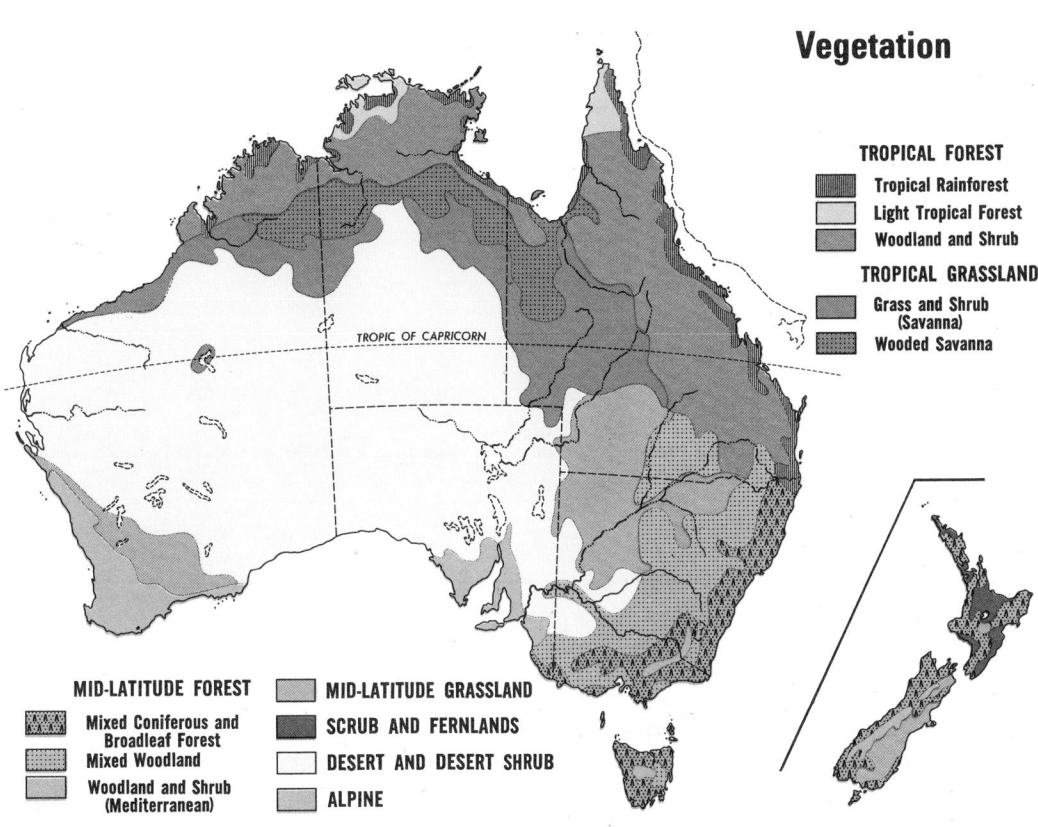

TROPICAL FOREST
- Tropical Rainforest
- Light Tropical Forest
- Woodland and Shrub

TROPICAL GRASSLAND
- Grass and Shrub (Savanna)
- Wooded Savanna

MID-LATITUDE FOREST
- Mixed Coniferous and Broadleaf Forest
- Mixed Woodland
- Woodland and Shrub (Mediterranean)

MID-LATITUDE GRASSLAND

SCRUB AND FERNLANDS

DESERT AND DESERT SHRUB

ALPINE

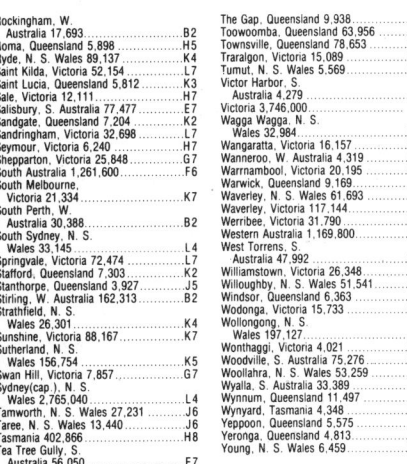

*City and suburbs.
‡Population of metropolitan area.
□Population of urban area.

Average January Temperature

Darwin 83°
Derby 88°
Onslow 85°
Alice Springs 82°
Cairns 81°
Brisbane 77°
Perth 74°
Kalgoorlie 78°
Broken Hill 79°
Adelaide 72°
Sydney 70°
Albany 63°
Melbourne 67°
Hobart 62°
Auckland 66°
Dunedin 60°

FAHRENHEIT	CELSIUS
Over 86°	Over 30°
68° to 86°	20° to 30°
50° to 68°	10° to 20°
32° to 50°	0° to 10°
Under 32°	Under 0°

Tropic of Capricorn

• Sydney 70° Average January temperature in degrees Fahrenheit at selected stations

Average July Temperature

Darwin 76°
Derby 72°
Onslow 63°
Alice Springs 52°
Cairns 70°
Brisbane 59°
Perth 55°
Kalgoorlie 52°
Broken Hill 51°
Adelaide 52°
Sydney 54°
Albany 53°
Melbourne 49°
Hobart 46°
Auckland 52°
Dunedin 43°

FAHRENHEIT	CELSIUS
Over 68°	20° to 30°
50° to 68°	10° to 20°
32° to 50°	0° to 10°
Under 32°	Under 0°

Tropic of Capricorn

• Sydney 54° Average July temperature in degrees Fahrenheit at selected stations

Rainfall

Darwin 60
Thursday Island 66
Derby 23
Tennant Creek 15
Cloncurry 19
Cairns 86
Mackay 63
Onslow 12
Alice Springs 12
William Creek 5
Brisbane 45
Geraldton 19
Kalgoorlie 9
Broken Hill 9
Perth 36
Adelaide 20
Albury 28
Sydney 47
Albany 37
Melbourne 26
Hobart 25
Auckland 48
Hokitika 116
Wellington 48
Dunedin 36

Tropic of Capricorn

AVERAGE ANNUAL RAINFALL	
INCHES	CENTIMETERS
Over 80	Over 200
60 to 80	150 to 200
40 to 60	100 to 150
20 to 40	50 to 100
10 to 20	25 to 50
Under 10	Under 25

• Sydney 47 Average annual rainfall in inches at selected stations

DOMINANT LAND USE

- Cereals (chiefly wheat), Livestock
- Dairy, Truck Farming
- Cash Crops, Horticulture, Fruit
- Pasture Livestock
- Range Livestock
- Forests
- Nonagricultural Land

MAJOR MINERAL OCCURRENCES

Ab	Asbestos	Na	Salt
Ag	Silver	Ni	Nickel
Al	Bauxite	O	Petroleum
Au	Gold	Op	Opals
C	Coal	P	Phosphates
Cu	Copper	Pb	Lead
D	Diamonds	S	Sulfur, Pyrites
Fe	Iron Ore	Sb	Antimony
G	Natural Gas	Sn	Tin
Gp	Gypsum	Ti	Titanium
Lg	Lignite	U	Uranium
Ls	Limestone	W	Tungsten
Mg	Magnesium	Zn	Zinc
Mi	Mica	Zr	Zirconium
Mn	Manganese		

⚡ Water Power

▨ Major Industrial Areas

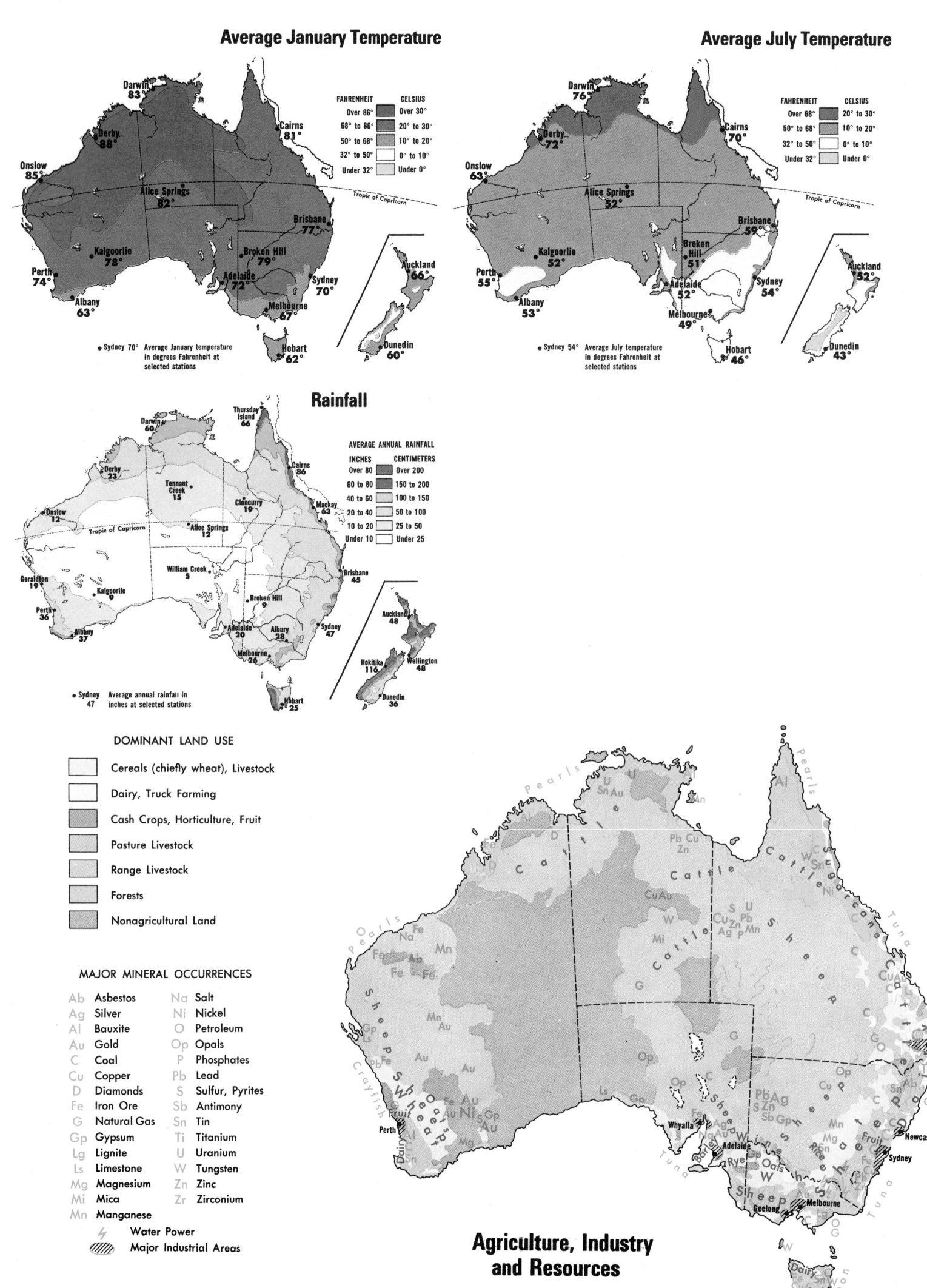

Agriculture, Industry and Resources

INDONESIA
Sumba
Timor

ARAFURA SEA

New Guinea
PAPUA
NEW
GUINEA
Port Moresby

TIMOR SEA

Ashmore Is. TERR. OF ASHMORE
Cartier I. & CARTIER IS.

Melville I.
Cobourg Pen.
C. Wessel

Torres Strait
C. York

Gulf of

INDIAN

10°

Darwin

Arnhem Land

Groote Eylandt

Cape York Peninsula

Great

CORAL

Daly

Carpentaria

Mitchell

Kimberley Plateau

Derby

Fitzroy

Ord

Victoria

Barkly Tableland

NORTHERN

Flinders

Mt. Bartle Frere
5,287 ft.
(1611 m.)
Cairns

Barrier

15°

OCEAN

Tanami Desert

Townsville

Reef

Great

Port Hedland

Great Sandy Desert

TERRITORY

Mt. Isa

QUEENSLAND

20°

North West C.

Fortescue

Hamersley Ra.
Mt. Bruce
4,024 ft.
(1227 m.)

WESTERN

Lake Mackay

Lake Disappointment

Tropic of Capricorn

Macdonnell Ranges

Alice Springs

Georgina

Dividing

Mackay

Rockhampton

Gibson Desert

Finke

Simpson

Diamantina

Barcoo

Range

Bundaberg

25°

Lake Carnegie

AUSTRALIA

Ayers Rock
2,845 ft. (867 m.)

SOUTH

Desert

Grey Range

Warrego

Toowoomba

Brisbane
Gold Coast

Musgrave Ranges

Geraldton

Great Victoria Desert

Lake Eyre

Barcoo

Sturt Desert

AUSTRALIA

Darling

NEW SOUTH

Tamworth

30°

Lake Barlee

Nullarbor Plain

Lake Torrens

Flinders Range

Lake Frome

Broken Hill

Darling

Kalgoorlie-Boulder

Lake Gairdner

Newcastle

Perth
Fremantle

Darling Ra.

Great

Whyalla

WALES

Sydney

Bunbury

Australian Bight

Eyre Pen.

Wagga Wagga

Wollongong

C. Leeuwin

Albany

INDIAN

Kangaroo I.

Adelaide

Mt. Lofty Ra.

Spencer Gulf

Murray

Albury

Lachlan

Canberra
AUSTRALIAN CAPITAL TERRITORY

Mt. Kosciusko
7,316 ft.
(2230 m.)

35°

OCEAN

Mt. Gambier

Bendigo

VICTORIA

Great

Ballarat

Geelong

Melbourne

C. Howe

King I.

Bass Strait

TASMAN

40°

Furneaux Group

SEA

Launceston

TASMANIA

Hobart

South Cape

© Copyright HAMMOND INCORPORATED, Maplewood, N. J.

110°   115°   120°   125°   130°   135°   Longitude 140° East of Greenwich 145°   150°   155°

Vegetation/Relief

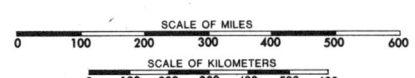

SCALE OF MILES
0 100 200 300 400 500 600

SCALE OF KILOMETERS
0 100 200 300 400 500 600

Capital of Country..................................⊛
State and Territorial Capitals....................⊙
International Boundaries............................——
State and Territorial Boundaries...............— —

Depths in Fathoms

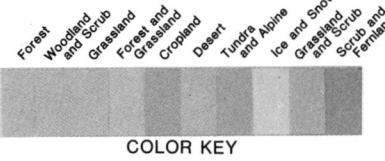

Forest
Woodland and Scrub
Grassland
Forest and Grassland
Cropland
Desert
Tundra and Alpine
Ice and Snow
Grassland and Scrub
Scrub and Fernlands

COLOR KEY

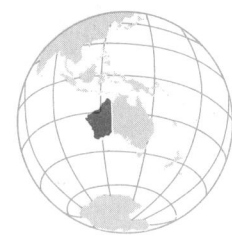

AREA 975,096 sq. mi.
(2,525,500 sq. km.)
POPULATION 1,169,800
CAPITAL Perth
LARGEST CITY Perth
HIGHEST POINT Mt. Bruce 4,024 ft.
(1,227 m.)

Topography

CITIES and TOWNS

Albany 13,696	B6	
Australind 832	A2	
Beverley 755	B1	
Boulder-Kalgoorlie 19,041	C5	
Bridgetown 1,316	B6	
Broome 2,920	C2	
Brunswick Junction 893	A2	
Bunbury 19,513	A2	
Busselton 5,550	A6	
Canning 43,337	A1	
Capel 669	A2	
Carnarvon 5,341	A4	
Collie 6,771	B2	
Coolgardie 643	C5	
Corrigin 853	B6	
Cuballing⊙ 624	B2	
Cunderdin 756	B5	
Dalwallinu 683	B5	
Dampier 2,727	B3	
Dandaragan⊙ 1,725	A5	
Denmark 786	B6	
Derby 2,411	C2	
Donnybrook 1,008	A2	
Esperance 5,262	C6	
Exmouth 2,336	A3	
Fremantle 23,497	A1	
Geraldton 18,773	A5	
Gnowangerup 892	B6	
Goldsworthy 989	B3	
Goomalling 644	B1	
Halls Creek 767	D2	
Harvey 2,418	A2	
Kalbarri 695	A4	
Kalgoorlie 9,067	C5	
Kalgoorlie-Boulder 19,041	C5	
Kambalda 4,784	C5	
Karratha 4,243	B3	
Katanning 4,162	B6	
Kellerberrin 1,198	B5	
Kojonup 944	B6	
Kununurra 1,540	E2	
Kwinana New Town 10,981	A1	
Lake Grace 616	B6	
Laverton 848	C5	
Learmonth	A3	
Mandurah 7,050	A2	
Manjimup 3,734	A6	
Margaret River 701	A6	
Meekatharra 829	B4	
Melville 54,384	A1	
Merredin 3,661	B5	
Moora 1,545	B5	
Morawa 814	B5	
Mount Barker 1,562	B6	
Mullewa 933	A5	
Narrogin 4,812	B6	
Nedlands 20,974	A1	
Newman 4,672	B3	
Norseman 929	C5	
Northam 6,866	B1	
Northampton 703	A5	
Onslow 220	A3	
Paraburdoo 2,402	B3	
Pardoo	B3	
Pemberton 777	A6	
Perth (cap.) 87,598	A1	
Perth‡ 731,275	A1	
Pingelly 978	B2	
Pinjarra 1,196	A2	
Port Hedland 11,144	B3	
Quairading 808	B1	
Rockingham 17,693	A2	
Roebourne 1,368	B3	
Shay Gap 856	C3	
Southern Cross 880	B5	
South Perth 30,388	A1	
Stirling 162,313	A1	
Three Springs 605	A5	
Tom Price 3,193	B3	
Wagin 1,658	B2	
Wanneroo 4,319	A1	
Waroona 1,160	A2	
Wickham 2,312	B3	
Wiluna⊙ 879	C4	
Wittenoom 962	B3	
Wongan Hills 888	B5	
Wundowie 969	B1	
Wyndham 1,383	E1	
Yampi Sound	C2	
York 1,108	B1	

OTHER FEATURES

Adele (isl.)	C1	Kimberley (plat.)	D2
Admiralty (gulf)	D1	King (sound)	C2
Aloysius (mt.)	E4	King Leopold (range)	D2
Amherst (mt.)	D2	Koolan (isl.)	C2
Argyle (lake)	E2	Lacepede (isls.)	C2
Arid (cape)	C6	Latouche Treville (cape)	C2
Arthur (riv.)	B2	Leeuwin (cape)	A6
Ashburton (riv.)	A3	Lefroy (lake)	C5
Augustus (isl.)	D1	Le Grand (cape)	C6
Augustus (mt.)	B4	Lévêque (cape)	C2
Austin (lake)	B4	Londonderry (cape)	D1
Australia Aboriginal Res.	E4	Long (reef)	C2
Avon (riv.)	A1	Lyons (riv.)	A4
Bald (head)	B6	Macdonald (lake)	E3
Balwina Aboriginal Res.	E3	Mackay (lake)	E3
Barlee (lake)	B5	Madley (mt.)	D3
Barrow (isl.)	A3	McLeod (lake)	A4
Beaglebay Aboriginal Res.	C2	Minigwal (lake)	C5
Bernier (isl.)	A4	Montague (sound)	D1
Bigge (isl.)	D1	Monte Bello (isls.)	A3
Bluff Knoll (mt.)	B6	Moore (lake)	B5
Bonaparte (arch.)	D1	Muiron (isls.)	A3
Bougainville (cape)	D1	Murchison (mt.)	B5
Bouvard (cape)	A2	Murchison (riv.)	A4
Brassey (range)	C4	Murray (riv.)	A2
Browse (isl.)	C1	Naturaliste (cape)	A6
Bruce (mt.)	B3	Naturaliste (chan.)	A4
Brunswick (bay)	D1	North West (cape)	A3
Buccaneer (arch.)	C2	North-West Aboriginal Res.	E4
Carey (lake)	C5	Nullarbor (plain)	D5
Carnegie (lake)	C4	Oakover (riv.)	C3
Central Aboriginal Res.	E3	Ord (mt.)	D2
Cheyne (bay)	B6	Ord (riv.)	D1
Churchman (mt.)	B5	Peel (inlet)	A2
Cloates (pt.)	A3	Percival (lakes)	C3
Collier (bay)	C1	Peron (pen.)	A4
Cosmo Newbery Aboriginal Res.	C5	Petermann (range)	E4
Cowan (lake)	C5	Point Salvation Aboriginal Res.	D5
Culver (pt.)	D6	Raeside (lake)	C5
Cundeelee Aboriginal Res.	C5	Rason (lake)	D5
Cuvier (cape)	A4	Rebecca (lake)	C5
Dale (riv.)	B1	Recherche (arch.)	C6
Dampier (arch.)	B3	Robinson (ranges)	B4
Dampier Land (reg.)	C2	Roebuck (bay)	C2
Darling (range)	A1	Rottnest (isl.)	A1
De Grey (riv.)	B3	Rowley (shoals)	B2
D'Entrecasteaux (pt.)	A6	Ruhliere (cape)	D1
Dirk Hartogs (isl.)	A4	Saint George (ranges)	D2
Disappointment (lake)	C3	Salt (lake)	C5
Dora (lake)	C3	Shark (bay)	A4
Dorre (isl.)	A4	Southesk Tablelands	D2
Dover (pt.)	D6	Steep (pt.)	A4
Drysdale (riv.)	D1	Sturt (creek)	D2
Dundas (lake)	C6	Swan (riv.)	A1
Egerton (mt.)	B4	Talbot (cape)	D1
Eighty Mile (beach)	C2	Thouin (pt.)	A3
Enid (mt.)	B3	Timor (sea)	D1
Esperance (bay)	C6	Tomkinson (ranges)	E4
Exmouth (gulf)	A3	Wanna (lkes)	E5
Farquhar (cape)	A3	Warburton Aboriginal Res.	D4
Fitzroy (riv.)	D2	Way (lake)	C4
Flinders (bay)	A6	Weld (range)	B4
Forrest River Aboriginal Res.	D1	Wells (lake)	C4
Fortescue (riv.)	B3	Whaleback (mt.)	B3
Garden (isl.)	A1	Wooramel (riv.)	A4
Gascoyne (riv.)	B4	Yamarna Aboriginal Res.	D5
Geelvink (chan.)	A5	Yeo (lake)	D5
Geographe (bay)	A6	York (sound)	C2
Geographe (chan.)	A4	Yule (riv.)	B3
Gibson (des.)	D3	
Great Australian (bight)	E6	
Great Sandy (des.)	C3	
Great Victoria (des.)	D5	
Gregory (lake)	C4	
Hale (mt.)	B4	
Hamersley (range)	B3	
Hann (mt.)	D1	
Hopkins (lake)	E4	
Houtman Abrolhos (isls.)	A5	
Indian Ocean	A5	
Johnston, The (lkes)	C6	
Joseph Bonaparte (gulf)	E1	
Keats (mt.)	A2	

⊙ Population of district.
‡ Population of met. area.

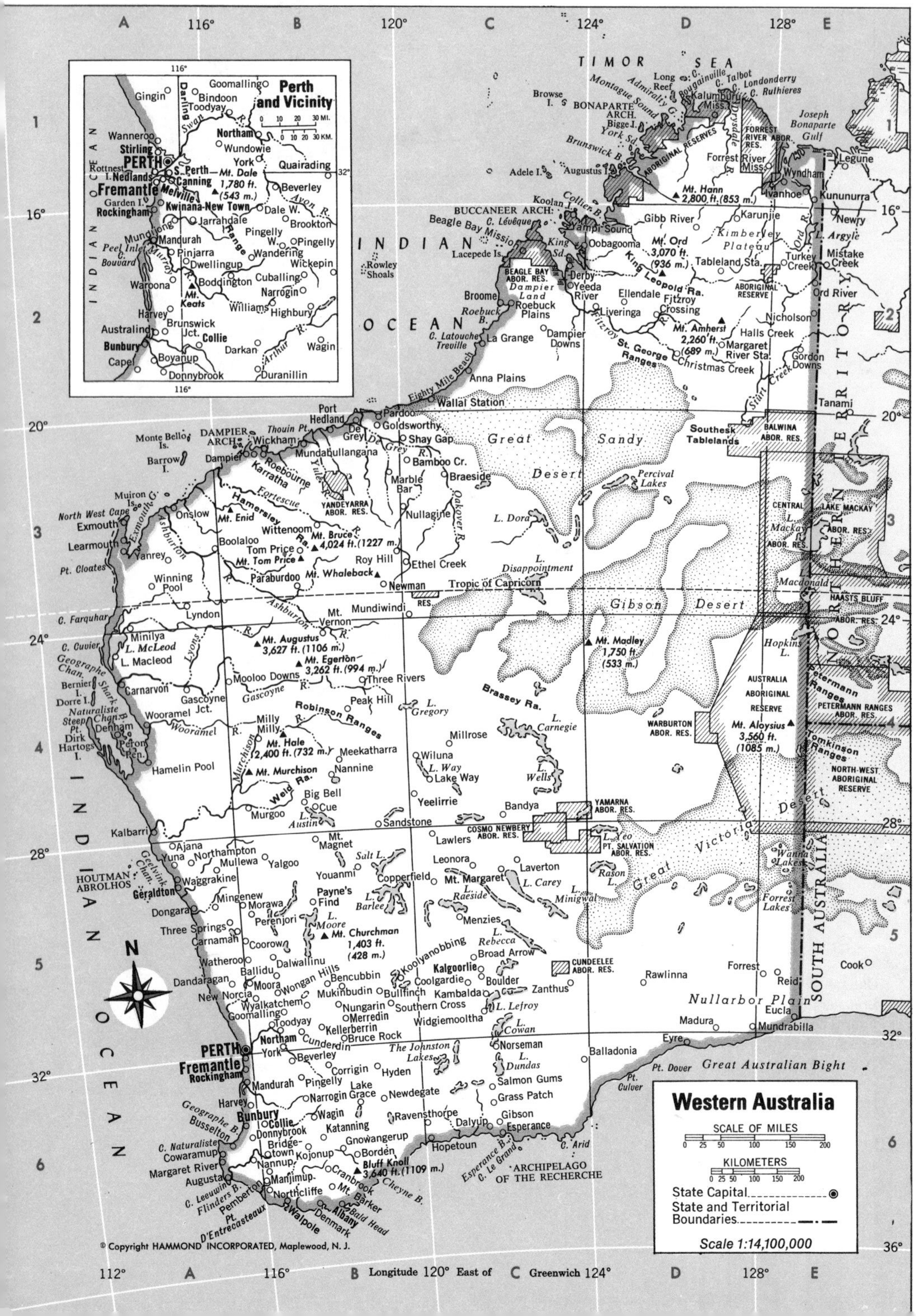

Perth and Vicinity

Western Australia

SCALE OF MILES

KILOMETERS

State Capital ◉
State and Territorial Boundaries
Scale 1:14,100,000

© Copyright HAMMOND INCORPORATED, Maplewood, N.J.

AREA 519,768 sq. mi.
(1,346,200 sq. km.)
POPULATION 97,090
CAPITAL Darwin
LARGEST CITY Darwin
HIGHEST POINT Mt. Ziel 4,955 ft.
(1,510 m.)

CITIES and TOWNS

Adelaide River	B2
Alexandria	E5
Alice Springs 14,149	D7
Alyangula 988	E2
Angas Downs	C8
Angurugu 700	E3
Anthony Lagoon	D4
Areyonga 291	C8
Argadargada	E6
Arltunga	D7
Avon Downs	E5
Bamyili-Beswick 675	C3
Banka Banka	C5
Barrow Creek	D6
Batchelor	B2
Bathurst Island 895	B1
Birdum	C3
Birrimbah	C3
Birrindudu	A5
Borroloola 370	E4
Bundooma	D8
Burramurra	E6
Charlotte Waters	D8
Coniston	C7
Coolibah	B3
Creswell Downs	E4
Crocker Island Mission 244	C1
Daly River 430	B2
Daly Waters	C3
Darwin (cap.) 39,193	B2
Docker River 275	A8
Epenarra	D6
Erldunda	C8
Eva Downs	D5
Ewaninga	D7
Goulburn Island 243	C1
Gove (Nhulunbuy) 3,553	E2
Harts Range	D7
Hatches Creek	D6
Helen Srings	C5
Hermannsburg 694	C7
Hooker Creek 616	B5
Humpty Doo	B2
Juno	B2
Katherine 3,127	B3
Kildurk	A4
Koolpinyah	B2
Kulgera	C8
Kurundi	D6
Larrimah	C3
Legune	A3
Limbunya	B4
Lucy Creek	E7
Mainoru	C3
Maningrida 660	C2
Mataranka	C3
Milingimbi 677	D2
Mistake Creek	A4
Montejinnie	C4
Mount Cavenagh	C8
Mount Doreen	B7
Murray Downs	D6
Napperby	C7
Newcastle Waters	C4
Nhulunbuy 3,553	E2
Numbulwar 378	D3
Oenpelli 508	C2
O. T. Downs	D4
Papunya 455	B7
Plenty River Mine	D7
Port Keats 882	A3
Powell Creek	C5
Rankine Store	E5
Robinson River	E4
Rockhampton Downs	D5
Rodinga	D8
Roper River 357	D3
Rum Jungle	B2
Santa Teresa 579	D8
Soudan	E6
Stirling Station	C6
Tarlton Downs	E7
Tea Tree Well	C7
Tempe Downs	C8
Tennant Creek 2,236	C5
The Granites	B6
Ucharonidge	D4
Umbakumba 371	E3
Umbeara	C8
Urapunga	D3
Utopia	D7
Victoria River Downs	B4
Warrego	C5
Wave Hill	B4
White Quartz Hill	D7
Willeroo	B3
Willowra	C6
Wollogorang	F4
Yambah	C7
Yirrkala 647	E2
Yuendumu 460	B7

OTHER FEATURES

Amadeus (lake)	B8
Arafura (sea)	D1
Arnhem Land (reg.)	D2
Arnhem Land Aboriginal Res.	C2
Arnold (riv.)	D3
Ayers Rock Nat'l Park	B8
Barkly Tableland	D4
Bathurst (isl.)	A1
Beagle (gulf)	A2
Beatrice (cape)	E3
Bennett (lake)	B7
Beswick Aboriginal Res.	C3
Bickerton (isl.)	E2
Blaze (pt.)	A2
Boucaut (bay)	D1
Carpentaria (gulf)	E3
Central Wedge (mt.)	C7
Clarence (str.)	B2
Cobourg (pen.)	C1
Conner (mt.)	B8
Croker (cape)	C1
Daly (riv.)	B2
Daly River Aboriginal Res.	A2
Davenport (mt.)	B7
Dobbie (mt.)	A8
Drummond (mt.)	E5
Dry (riv.)	C3
Dundas (str.)	C1
East Alligator (riv.)	C2
Ehrenberg (range)	B7
Elcho (isl.)	D1
Ewing (mt.)	E7
Fitzmaurice (riv.)	B3
Flora (riv.)	B3
Ford (cape)	A2
Georgina (riv.)	E6
Goulburn (isls.)	C1
Grey (cape)	E2
Groote Eylandt (isl.)	E3
Haasts Bluff Aboriginal Res.	B7
Hale (riv.)	D8
Hanson (riv.)	C6
Hay (cape)	A3
Hay (dry riv.)	E7
Hogarth (mt.)	E6
Hopkins (lake)	A8
Joseph Bonaparte (gulf)	A3
Katherine (riv.)	C3
Lake MacKay Aboriginal Res.	A6
Lander (riv.)	C6
Leisler (mt.)	A7
Limmen (bight)	D3
Limmen Bight (riv.)	D4
Macdonald (lake)	B7
Macdonnell (ranges)	C7
MacKay (lake)	A7
Mann (riv.)	D2
Marshall (riv.)	D7
Melville (bay)	E2
Melville (isl.)	B1
Mount Olga Nat'l Park	B8
Murchison (range)	D6
Napier (mt.)	A4
Neale (lake)	A8
Newcastle (creek)	C4
Nicholson (riv.)	E5
Old Marsh Bed	B6
Olga (mt.)	B8
Peron (isls.)	A2
Petermann (ranges)	A8
Petermann Ranges Aboriginal Res.	A8
Port Darwin (inlet)	B2
Ranken (riv.)	E6
Robinson (riv.)	E4
Roper (riv.)	C3
Rose (riv.)	D2
Sandover (riv.)	D6
Simpson (des.)	E8
Singleton (mt.)	B7
Sir Edward Pellew Group (isls.)	E3
South Alligator (riv.)	C2
Stanley (mt.)	B7
Stewart (cape)	D1
Stirling (creek)	A4
Sturt (plain)	C4
Sylvester (lake)	D5
Tanami (des.)	C5
Timor (sea)	A2
Todd (riv.)	D8
Vanderlin (isl.)	E3
Van Diemen (cape)	A1
Van Diemen (gulf)	B1
Victoria (riv.)	B3
Wagait Aboriginal Res.	A3
Warwick (chan.)	E3
Wessel (isls.)	E1
West Baines (riv.)	A4
White (lake)	A6
Winnecke (creek)	B5
Woods (lake)	C4
Ziel (mt.)	C7

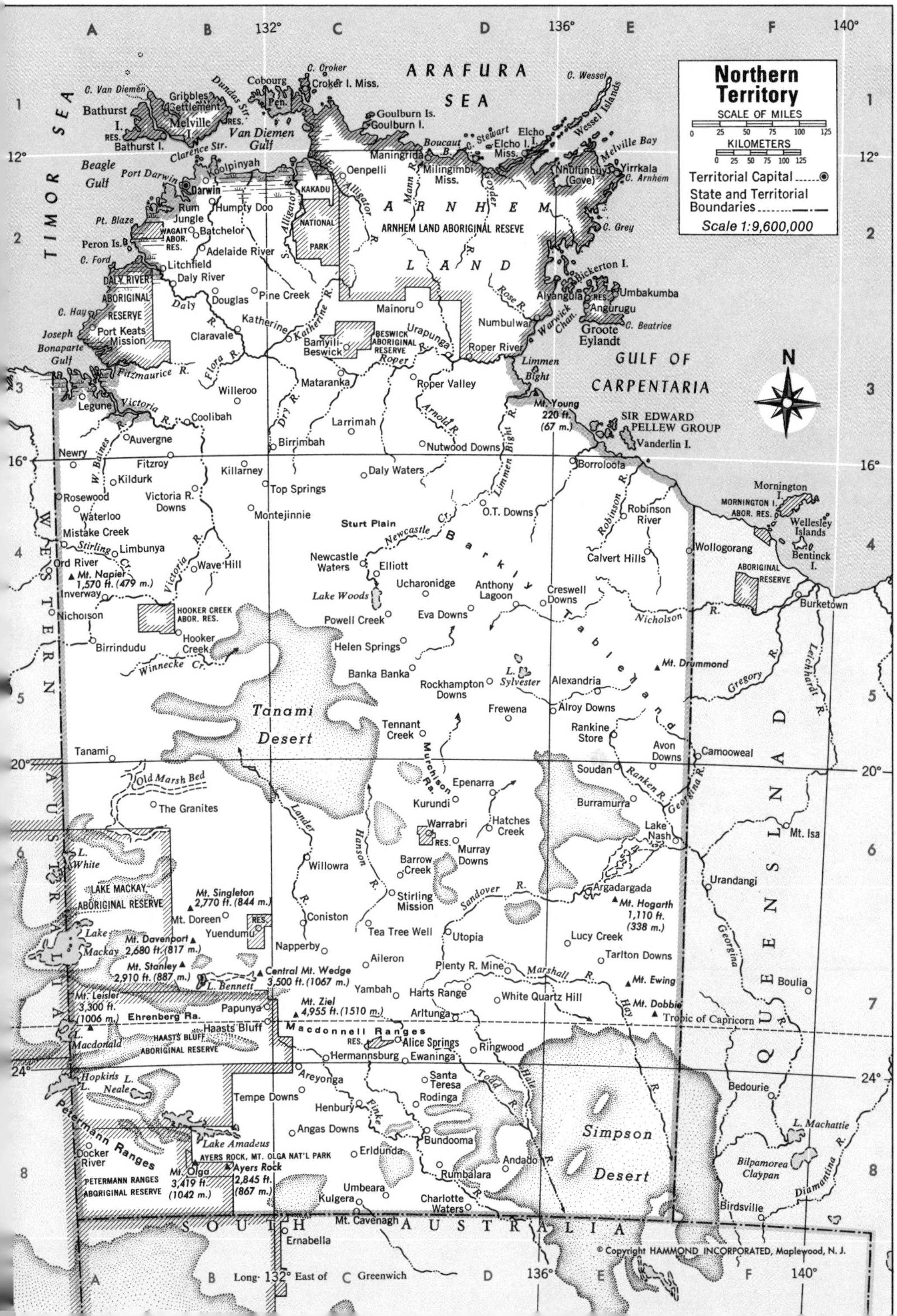

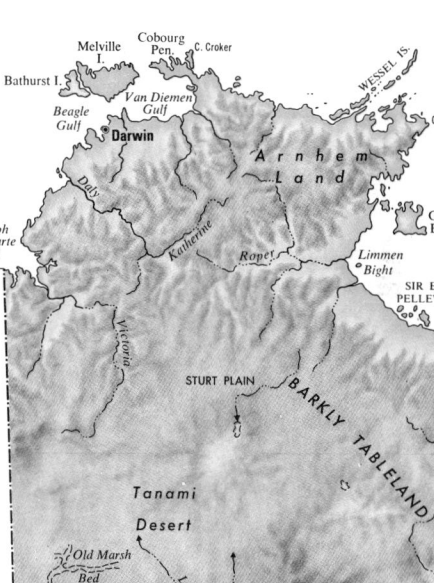

Topography

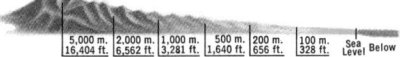

5,000 m. 16,404 ft.	2,000 m. 6,562 ft.	1,000 m. 3,281 ft.	500 m. 1,640 ft.	200 m. 656 ft.	100 m. 328 ft.	Sea Level	Below

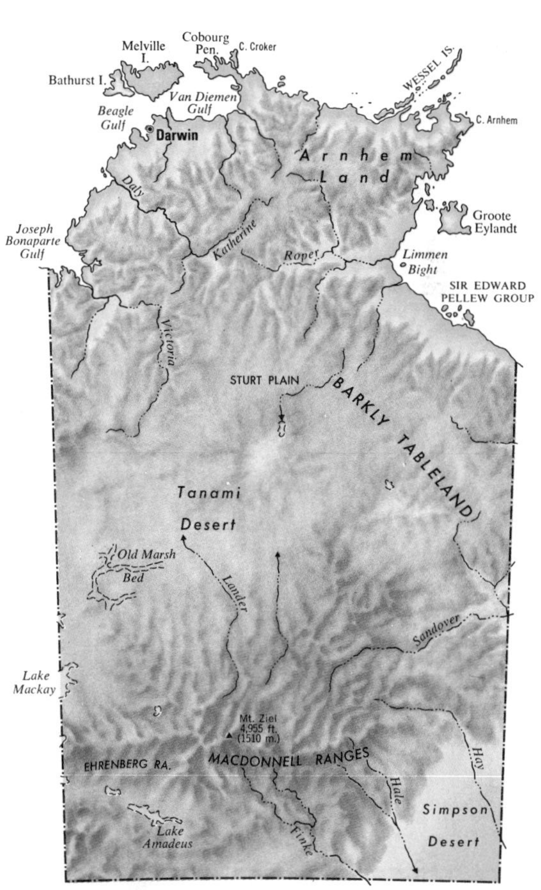

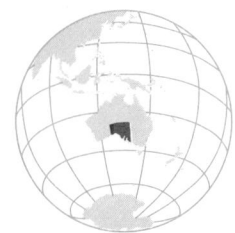

AREA 379,922 sq. mi. (984,000 sq. km.)
POPULATION 1,261,600
CAPITAL Adelaide
LARGEST CITY Adelaide
HIGHEST POINT Mt. Woodroffe 4,970 ft.
(1,515 m.)

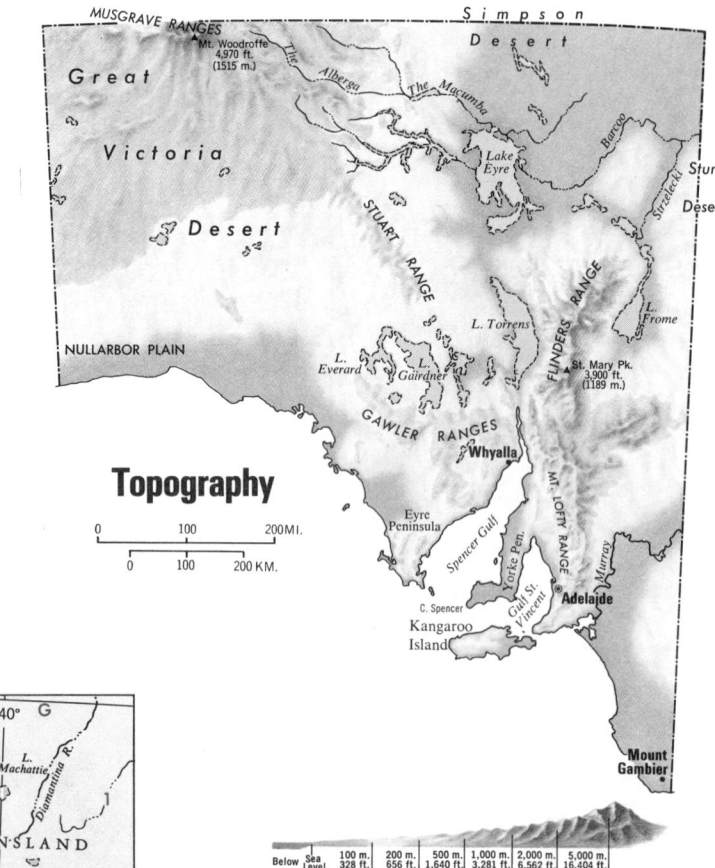

Topography

Below Sea Level	100 m. 328 ft.	200 m. 656 ft.	500 m. 1,640 ft.	1,000 m. 3,281 ft.	2,000 m. 6,562 ft.	5,000 m. 16,404 ft.

CITIES and TOWNS

Adelaide (cap.)‡ 857,196 ....B6
Andamooka 420 ....E4
Angaston 1,734 ....F6
Balaklava 1,237 ....F6
Barmera 1,946 ....G6
Berri 2,890 ....G6
Bordertown 1,983 ....G7
Brighton 21,407 ....A8
Burnside 38,461 ....B8
Burra 1,201 ....F5
Campbelltown 41,252 ....B7
Ceduna 2,327 ....D5
Clare 2,260 ....F5
Cleve 804 ....E5
Coober Pedy 1,903 ....D3
Cowell 627 ....E5
Crafters-Bridgewater 6,600...B8
Crystal Brook 1,410 ....E5
Cummins 761 ....D6
Elizabeth 33,721 ....B7
Elliston⊙ 1,268 ....D5
Enfield 73,505 ....B7
Gawler 8,596 ....B6
Gladstone 802 ....F5
Glenelg 14,413 ....A8
Hahndorf 937 ....C8
Hindmarsh 8,691 ....A7
Iron Knob 691 ....E5
Jamestown 1,215 ....F5
Kadina 2,849 ....F5
Kapunda 1,362 ....F6
Keith 1,191 ....G7
Kensington and Norwood
9,651 ....B8
Kimba 819 ....E5
Kingscote 1,121 ....E6
Kingston 1,250 ....G7
Laura 472 ....F5
Leigh Creek 999 ....F4
Lobethal 1,422 ....C7
Loxton 2,786 ....G6
Maitland 1,017 ....E6
Mannum 2,137 ....F6
Marion 67,283 ....A8
Meningie 736 ....F6
Millicent 5,471 ....F7
Minlaton 822 ....E6
Mitcham 59,887 ....B8
Moonta 1,379 ....E5
Mount Barker 3,204 ....C8
Mount Gambier 17,858 ....G7
Murray Bridge 7,476 ....F6
Nairne 594 ....C8
Nangwarry 863 ....G7
Naracoorte 4,571 ....G7
Nuriootpa 2,808 ....F6
Orroroo 631 ....F5
Payneham 17,545 ....B7
Penola 1,254 ....G7
Peterborough 2,760 ....F5
Pinnaroo 758 ....G6
Port Adelaide 36,024 ......A7
Port Augusta 13,092 ....E5

Port Broughton 654 ....F5
Port Lincoln 9,809 ....E6
Port Pirie 15,005 ....E5
Prospect 19,485 ....B7
Quorn 1,048 ....F5
Radium Hill G5
Renmark 6,247 ....G5
Robe 490 ....F7
Salisbury 77,477 ....B7
Snowtown 511 ....E5
Stirling North 1,028 ....E5
Strathalbyn 1,701 ....F6
Streaky Bay 1,008 ....D5
Tailem Bend 1,999 ....F6
Tanunda 2,254 ....C6
Tea Tree Gully 56,050 .....B7
Thebarton 10,315 ....A7
Tumby Bay 900 ....E6
Unley 37,016 ....B8
Victor Harbor 4,279 ....F6
Waikerie 1,611 ....F6
Wallaroo 1,969 ....E5
West Torrens 47,992 ....A8
Whyalla 33,389 ....E5
Williamstown 475 ....C7
Willunga 537 ....F6
Woodside 724 ....C8
Woodville 75,276 ....A7
Womera 2,958 ....B3
Wudinna 507 ....D5
Yorketown 679 ....E6

OTHER FEATURES

Acraman (lake).................D5
Alberga The, (riv.)............D2
Alexandrina (lake)............F6
Anxious (bay)..................D5
Arckaringa (creek)...........D2
Barcoo (creek).................F3
Barossa (res.)..................C6
Birksgate (range).............A2
Blanche (lake)..................F3
Brady (mt.).......................D3
Cadibarrawirracanna (lake) D3
Callabonna (lake).............F3
Catastrophe (cape)...........D6
Coffin (bay)......................D6
Coffin Bay (pen.)..............D6
Coopers (Barcoo) (creek)...F3
Coorong, The (lag.)..........F6
Dey Dey (lake).................B3
Encounter (bay)...............F6
Everard (lake)..................D4
Everard (ranges)..............C2
Eyre (pen.).......................D5
Eyre North (lake)..............E3
Eyre South (lake)..............E3
Finke (riv.).......................C1
Flinders (range)................F4
Frome (lake).....................G4
Gairdner (lake).................D4
Gawler (ranges)...............D5
Gawler (riv.).....................B6
Gilles (lake).....................E5
Goyders (lag.)..................F2
Great Australian (bight).....A5
Great Victoria (des.)..........B3
Gregory (lake)..................F3

Hack (mt.).........................F4
Hamilton, The (riv.)...........D2
Harris (lake).....................D4
Head of Bight (bay)...........B4
Indian Ocean....................E7
Investigator (str.)..............E6
Investigator Group (isls.)...D5
Island (lag.).....................E4
Jaffa (cape).....................F7
Kangaroo (isl.)..................E7
Lacepede (bay).................F7
Little Para (riv.).................B7
Lofty (mt.)........................B8
Macfarlane (lake)..............E5
Macumba The, (riv.)..........E2
Maurice (lake)..................B3
Meramangye (lake)...........C2
Morris (mt.)......................B2
Mount Bold (res.).............B8
Murray (riv.).....................F6
Musgrave (ranges)...........B2
Neales, The (riv.)..............E3
Neptune (isls.).................D6
Northumberland (cape).....G7
Nukey Bluff (mt.)..............D5
Nullarbor (plain)...............A4
Nurrari (lakes)..................B3
Nuyts (arch.)....................C5
Nuyts (cape)....................C5
Onkaparinga (riv.).............C8
Peera Peera Poolanna (lake) F2
Saint Mary (peak)............E4
Saint Vincent (gulf)...........E6
Serpentine (lkes.)............A2
Simpson (des.).................E1
Sir Joseph Banks Group
(isls.)...........................E6
South Para (riv.)...............C7
Spencer (cape).................E6
Spencer (gulf)..................E6
Stevenson, The (riv.).........D2
Streaky (bay)....................D5
Strzelecki (creek)..............G3
Stuart (range)...................D3
Sturt (des.).......................G2
Sturt (riv.)........................B8
The Alberga (riv.)..............D2
The Coorong (lag.)...........F6
The Hamilton (riv.)............D2
The Macumba (riv.)...........E2
The Neales (riv.)...............E3
The Stevenson (riv.).........D2
The Warburton (riv.)..........E2
Thistle (isl.)......................E6
Torrens (lake)...................E4
Torrens (riv.).....................B8
Warburton The, (riv.).........E2
Warren (res.)....................C7
Whidbey (isls.).................D6
Wilkinson (lkes.)...............B3
Wilson Bluff (prom.)..........A5
Woodroffe (mt.)................C2
Wright (lake)....................B3
Yalata Aboriginal Res.........C4
Yarle (lkes.)......................B3
Yorke (pen.).....................E6

⊙ Population of district.
‡ Population of met. area.

South Australia

SCALE OF MILES
0   25   50   75   100   125   150

KILOMETERS
0   25   50   75   100   125   150

State Capital ⊙
State and Territorial
Boundaries
Scale 1:9,790,000

Adelaide and Vicinity

© Copyright HAMMOND INCORPORATED, Maplewood, N.J.

CITIES and TOWNS

Ascot 4,606...................E2
Atherton 3,611................C3
Ayr 8,606.....................D3
Beaudesert 4,029..............E6
Biloela 4,586.................D5
Blackwater 4,638..............D4
Bowen 6,707...................D3
Brisbane (cap.) 696,740.......E2
Brisbane‡ 892,987.............D2
Bundaberg 31,189..............D5
Cairns 39,305.................C3
Caloundra 10,602..............E5
Camp Hill 9,961...............E3
Charleville 3,802.............C5
Charters Towers 7,914.........C4
Chermside 7,666...............D2
Coopers Plains 5,017..........E3
Corinda 4,132.................D3
Dalby 8,997...................D5
East Brisbane 5,506...........E3
Emerald 3,161.................D4
Gatton 3,986..................E5
Geebung 5,585.................E2
Gladstone 18,591..............D4
Gold Coast 87,510.............E6
Goondiwindi 3,741.............D6
Greenslopes 7,349.............E3
Gympie 11,205.................E5
Hervey Bay 9,150..............E5
Holland Park 7,708............E3
Home Hill 3,330...............C3
Inala 20,037..................D3
Indooroopilly 8,534...........D3
Ingham 5,868..................C3
Innisfail 7,933...............C3
Ipswich 69,242................E5
Kingaroy 5,088................D5
Longreach 3,354...............B4
Mackay 31,522.................D4
Mareeba 5,776.................C3
Maroochydore-Mooloolaba
10,283........................E5
Maryborough 21,527............E5
Mary Kathleen 811.............B4
Mitchelton 6,115..............D2
Moorooka 9,639................D3
Moranbah 4,053................C9
Mount Isa 25,377..............A4
Mount Morgan 3,246............D4
Nambour 7,435.................E5
Newmarket 3,955...............D2
Nundah 7,590..................E2
Redcliffe 39,073..............D2
Rockhampton 50,132............D4
Roma 5,898....................D5
Sandgate 7,204................D2

Stafford 7,303................D2
Stanthorpe 3,927..............D6
Tewantin-Noosa 5,834..........E5
Toowoomba 63,956..............D5
Townsville 78,653.............C3
Warwick 9,169.................D6
Weipa 2,876...................B2
Windsor 6,363.................D2
Wynnum 11,497.................E5
Yeppoon 5,575.................D4
Yeronga 4,813.................D3

OTHER FEATURES

Albatross (bay)...............B2
Alice (riv.)..................C4
Archer (riv.).................B2
Balonne (riv.)................D6
Banks (isl.)..................B1
Barcoo (creek)................B5
Barkly Tableland..............A4
Bartle Frere (mt.)............C3
Beal (range)..................B5
Belyando (riv.)...............C4
Bentinck (isl.)...............A3
Bigge (range).................D5
Bowling Green (cape)..........C3
Bramble (bay).................D2
Brisbane (riv.)...............D2
Brisbane Airport..............E2
Broad (sound).................D4
Bulimba (creek)...............E3
Bulloo (lake).................B6
Bulloo (riv.).................B6
Bunker Group (isls.)..........E4
Burdekin (riv.)...............C3
Cabbage Tree (creek)..........D2
Cape York (pen.)..............B2
Capricorn (chan.).............D4
Capricorn Group (isls.).......E4
Carnarvon (range).............D5
Carpentaria (gulf)............A2
Caryapundy (swamp)............B6
Clarke (range)................C4
Cloncurry (riv.)..............B4
Coleman (riv.)................B2
Comet (riv.)..................D5
Condamine (riv.)..............D5
Coopers (Barcoo) (creek)......B5
Coral (sea)...................C1
Culgoa (riv.).................C6
Cumberland (isls.)............D4
Curtis (isl.).................D4
Darling Downs.................D5
Dawson (riv.).................D5
Diamantina (riv.).............B5
Direction (cape)..............B2
Downfall (creek)..............D2

Drummond (range)..............C5
Duifken (pt.).................B2
Endeavour (str.)..............B1
Enoggera (creek)..............D2
Fitzroy (riv.)................D4
Flattery (cape)...............C2
Flinders (riv.)...............B3
Fraser (isl.).................E5
Galilee (lake)................C4
Georgina (riv.)...............A4
Gilbert (riv.)................B3
Great Dividing (range)........C4
Great Sandy (Fraser) (isl.)...E5

Gregory (range)...............B3
Gregory (riv.)................A3
Grenville (cape)..............B1
Grey (range)..................B5
Halifax (bay).................C3
Hamilton (riv.)...............B4
Hervey (bay)..................E5
Hinchinbrook (isl.)...........C3
Holroyd (riv.)................B2
Hook (isl.)...................D4
Isaacs (riv.).................D4
Kedron (brook)................D2
Keerweer (cape)...............B2

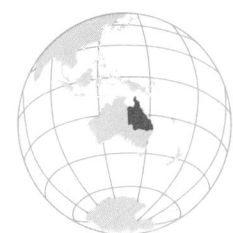

AREA 666,872 sq. mi. (1,727,200 sq. km.)
POPULATION 2,111,700
CAPITAL Brisbane
LARGEST CITY Brisbane
HIGHEST POINT Mt. Bartle Frere 5,287 ft.
(1,611 m.)

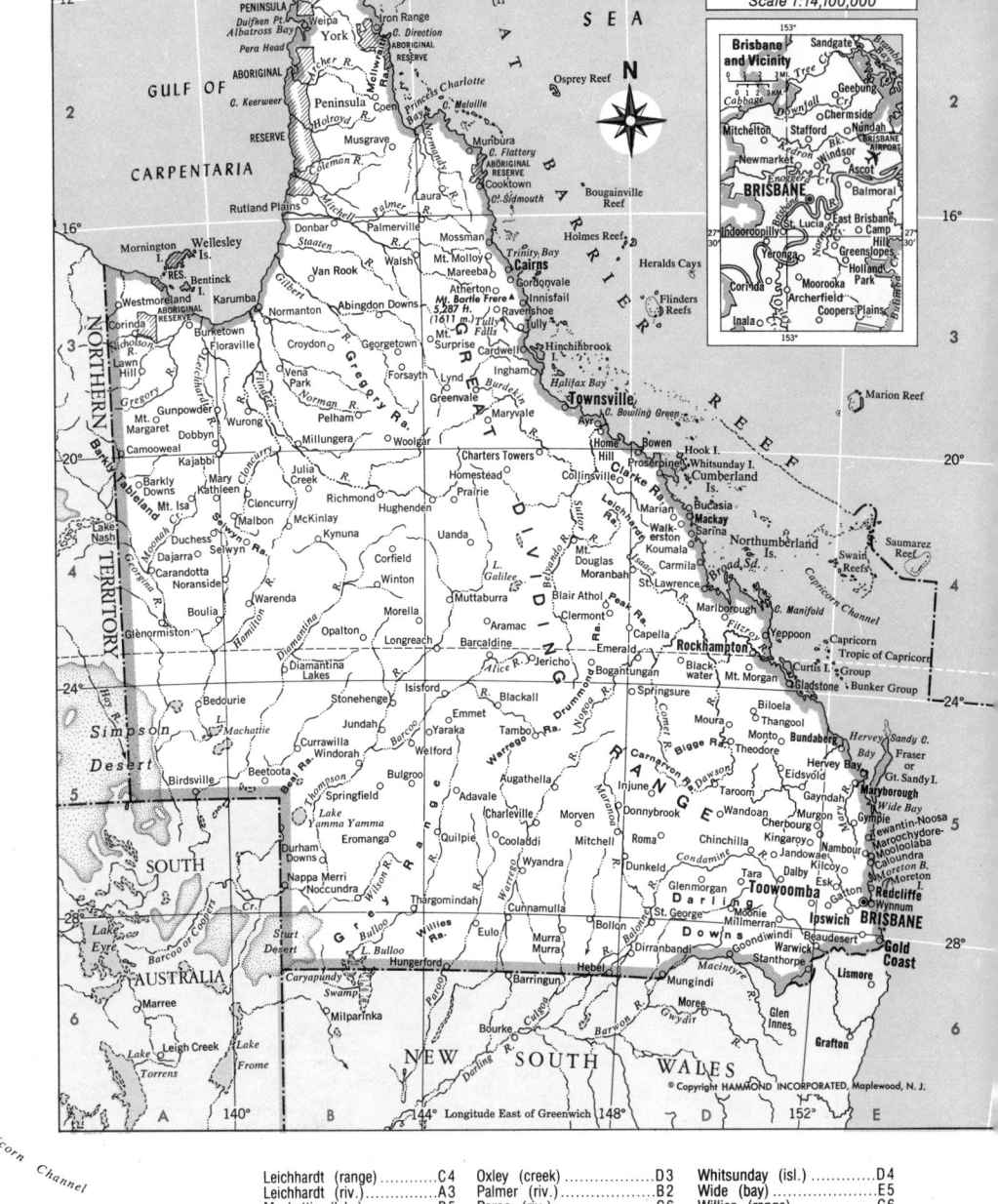

Topography

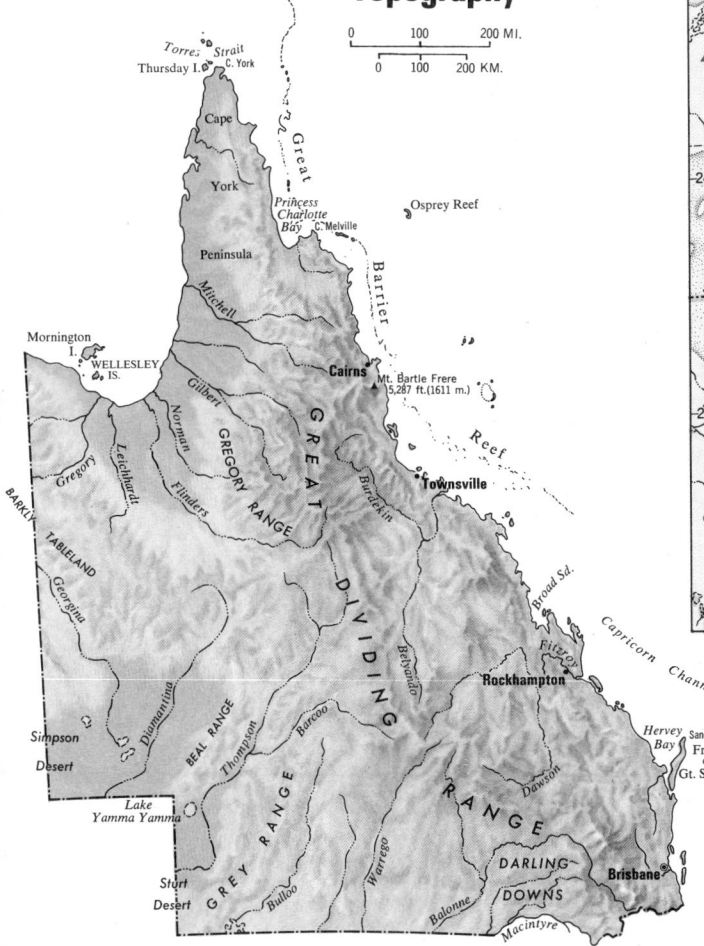

Leichhardt (range)............C4
Leichhardt (riv.).............A3
Machattie (lake)..............B5
Macintyre (riv.)..............D6
Manifold (cape)...............D4
Maranoa (riv.)................C5
Mary (riv.)...................E5
McIlwraith (range)............B2
Melville (cape)...............C2
Mitchell (riv.)...............B2
Moonah (creek)................A4
Moreton (bay).................E5
Moreton (isl.)................E5
Mornington (isl.).............A3
Nicholson (riv.)..............A3
Nogoa (riv.)..................C5
Norman (creek)................D3
Norman (riv.).................B3
Normandy (riv.)...............C2
Northern Peninsula Aboriginal
Res...........................B1
Northumberland (isls.)........D4

Oxley (creek).................D3
Palmer (riv.).................B2
Paroo (riv.)..................C6
Peak (range)..................C4
Pera (head)...................B2
Prince of Wales (isl.)........B1
Princess Charlotte (bay)......C2
Sandy (cape)..................E5
Selwyn (range)................B4
Sidmouth (cape)...............C2
Simpson (des.)................A5
Staaten (riv.)................B3
Sturt (des.)..................B5
Suttor (riv.).................C4
Swain (reefs).................E4
Thompson (riv.)...............B5
Torres (str.).................B1
Trinity (bay).................C3
Tully (falls).................C3
Warrego (range)...............C5
Warrego (riv.)................C5
Wellesley (isls.).............A3

Whitsunday (isl.).............D4
Wide (bay)....................E5
Willies (range)...............C6
Wilson (riv.).................B5
Yamma Yamma (lake)............B5
York (cape)...................B1

CORAL SEA ISLANDS TERR.

PHYSICAL FEATURES

Bougainville (reef)...........C2
Flinders (reefs)..............D3
Great Barrier (reef)..........C2
Heralds (cays)................D3
Holmes (reef).................C3
Marion (reef).................E3
Osprey (reef).................C2
Saumarez (reef)...............E4

‡Population of met. area.

AUSTRALIAN CAPITAL TERRITORY

CITIES and TOWNS

Canberra (cap.), Australia 196,538 ....E4
Canberra‡ 197,622 ....E4
Jervis Bay F4

OTHER FEATURES

St. Georges (Head) F4

NEW SOUTH WALES
CITIES and TOWNS

Aberdeen 1,133 ....F3
Adelong 766 ....D4
Albert D3
Albury 31,954 ....D5
Alstonville 1,457 ....G1
Ardlethan 675 ....D4
Armidale 19,711 ....F2
Ashfield 42,322 ....J3
Ashford 692 ....F1
Ashley E1
Auburn 47,556 ....J3
Avondale 1,929 ....F3

Baan Baa E2
Ballina 7,323 ....G1
Balpunga A3
Balranald 1,396 ....B4
Bangalow 568 ....G1
Bankstown 155,843 ....J3
Baradine 754 ....E2
Bargo 669 ....F4
Barham 1,108 ....B4
Barraba 1,947 ....F2
Barringun C1
Baryulgil G1
Batemans Bay 3,463 ....F4
Bathurst 18,589 ....E4
Batlow 1,374 ....E4

Baulkham Hills 21,182 ....H3
Bega 4,253 ....E5
Bellata E1
Bellbird-Cessnock 16,256 ....F3
Bellingen 1,398 ....G2
Belmore J3
Bemboka E5
Benanee B4
Bendemeer F2
Berrigan 952 ....C4
Berry 1,132 ....E5
Bibbenluke⊙ 1,808 ....E5
Bigga E4
Binda E4
Bingara 1,295 ....F1

Binnaway 612 ....E2
Birriwa E3
Blacktown 159,734 ....H3
Blayney 2,535 ....E3
Blue Mountains 45,798 ....F3
Bobadah D3
Bogan Gate D3
Boggabri 973 ....F2
Bomaderry-Nowra 15,496 ....F4
Bombala 1,474 ....E5
Bonnyrigg H3
Booligal C3
Boomi⊙ 2,301 ....E1
Boorooban C4
Boorowa 1,192 ....E4

Botany 35,739 ....J4
Bourke 3,534 ....D2
Bowral 6,283 ....F4
Bowraville 801 ....G2
Braidwood 989 ....E4
Branxton-Greta 2,485 ....F3
Bredbo E4
Brewarrina 1,386 ....D1
Bribbaree D3
Brisbane Water 54,819 ....F3
Broken Hill 27,647 ....A3
Browning E4
Brunswick Heads 1,402 ....G1
Budgewoi Lake 15,748 ....F3
Bugaldie E2

Bulahdelah 986 ....G3
Bundanoon 843 ....F4
Bungendore 601 ....E4
Burcher D3
Burns C4
Burraboi C4
Burta A3
Burwood 29,045 ....J3
Byrock D2
Byron Bay 2,525 ....G1
Camden 7,644 ....F4
Camden Haven 2,168 ....G2
Campbelltown 52,299 ....F4
Canbelego D2
Canowindra 1,743 ....E4

Canterbury 128,710 J3
Caragabal D3
Carinda D2
Carrathool⊙ 3,311 C4
Carroll F2
Casino 9,456 G1
Cassilis E3
Cessnock-Bellbird 16,256 F3
Clare B3
Cobar 3,339 C2
Cobbadah F2
Coffs Harbour 12,197 G2
Collarenebri 599 E1
Collie E2
Comboyne G2
Come-by-Chance E2
Conargo⊙ 1,943 C4
Concord 24,598 J3
Condobolin 3,273 D3
Coogee K3
Coolah 851 E2
Coolamon 1,084 D4
Cooma 7,353 E5
Coonabarabran 3,068 E2
Coonamble 3,054 E2
Cootamundra 6,384 D4
Copmanhurst⊙ 2,326 G1
Coraki 912 G1
Corowa 3,013 D4
Cowra 7,734 E3
Crescent Head 798 G2
Cronulla J4
Crookwell 2,147 E4
Cullburra-Orient Point 1,416 F4
Culcairn 933 D4
Dareton 601 B4
Darlington Point 658 C4
Dee Why K3
Deniliquin 6,865 C4
Denman 808 F3
Dorrigo 1,152 G2
Drummoyne 31,516 J3
Dubbo 20,149 E3
Dunedoo 797 E3
Dungalear Station D1

NEW SOUTH WALES

AREA 309,498 sq. mi. (801,600 sq. km.)
POPULATION 4,914,300
CAPITAL Sydney
LARGEST CITY Sydney
HIGHEST POINT Mt. Kosciusko 7,310 ft. (2,228 m.)

VICTORIA

AREA 87,876 sq. mi. (227,600 sq. km.)
POPULATION 3,746,000
CAPITAL Melbourne
LARGEST CITY Melbourne
HIGHEST POINT Mt. Bogong 6,508 ft. (1,984 m.)

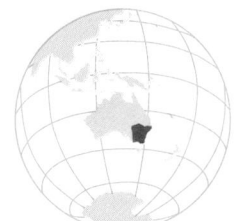

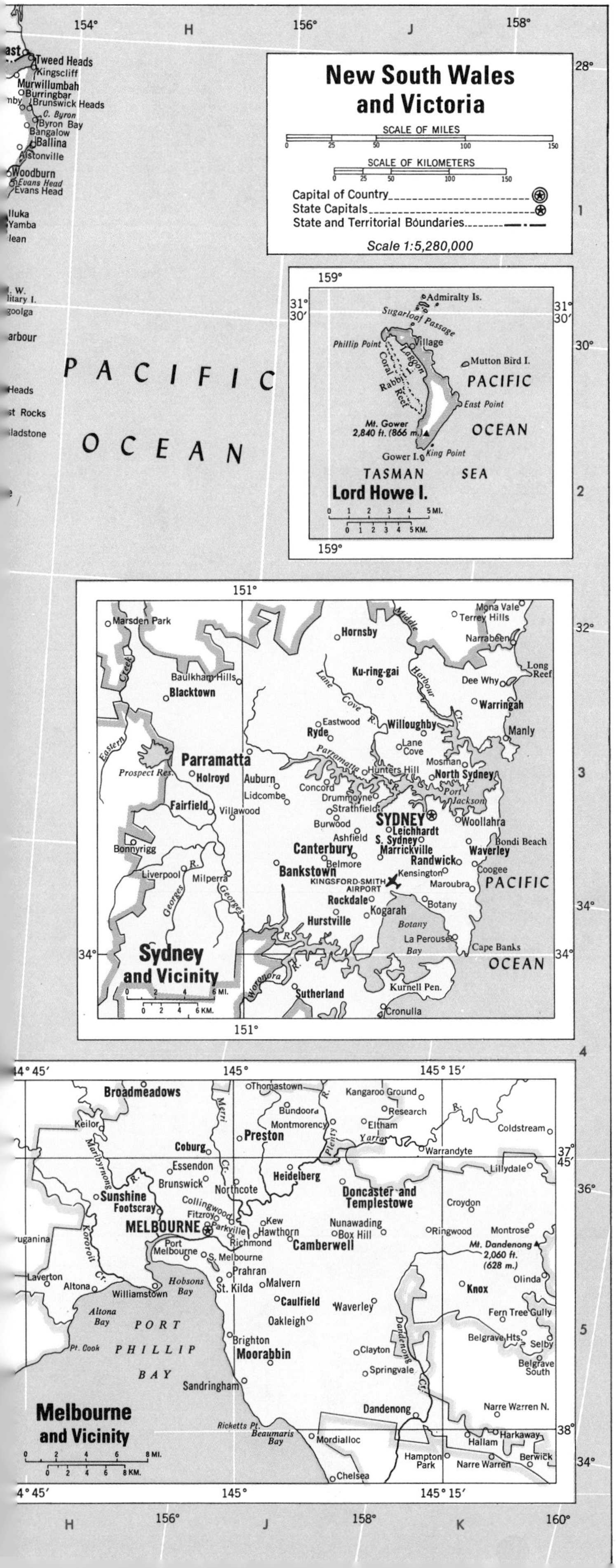

Topography

Dungog 2,175 F3
Eden 2,978 E5
Ermeran Station D3
Eugowra 651 E3
Evans Head 1,591 G1
Fairfield 114,603 H3
Finley 2,072 C4
Forbes 7,754 E3
Forest Hill 1,591 D4
Forster-Tuncurry 6,195 G3
Frederickton 611 G2
Ganmain 656 D4
Gerringong 1,240 F4
Gilgandra 2,494 E2
Gilgunnia C3
Glen Innes 5,953 F1
Gloucester 2,313 F2
Goombalie C1
Goulburn 21,735 E4
Grafton 16,516 G1
Grenfell 2,156 E3
Greta-Branxton 2,485 F3
Griffith 11,930 C4
Gulgong 1,618 E3
Gundagai 2,074 D4
Gunnedah 8,689 F2
Guyra 1,933 F2
Harrington 896 G2
Hatfield B3
Hay 2,872 C4
Helensburgh 2,663 F4
Henty 832 D4
Hillston 889 C3
Holbrook 1,157 D4
Holroyd 79,867 H3
Hornsby 104,110 J3
Howlong 666 D4
Hunters Hill 13,017 J3
Hurstville 66,450 J4
Huskisson 1,502 F4
Illabo⊙ 1,780 D4
Illuka 789 G1
Inverell 9,432 F1
Jerilderie 1,001 C4
Jindabyne 950 E5
Junee 4,005 D4
Kandos 1,792 F3
Karpakora B3
Katoomba-Wentworth Falls 12,301 F3
Keewong C3
Kempsey 8,881 G2
Kiama 6,133 F4
Kinalung B3
Kogarah 46,721 J4
Kurri Kurri-Weston 12,143 F3
Kyogle 2,959 G1
Lake Cargelligo 1,171 D3
Lane Cove 29,341 J3
Leeton 6,631 D4
Leichhardt 62,550 J3
Lette B4
Lidcombe J3
Lightning Ridge 825 E1
Lismore 22,082 G1
Lithgow 12,703 F3
Liverpool 89,682 H4
Lockhart 913 D4
Macksville 2,277 G2
Maclean 2,488 G1
Maitland 36,030 F3
Manilla 1,849 F2
Manly 36,709 K3
Maroubra K3
Marrickville 87,821 J3
Marsden D3
Melrose D3
Merimbula 1,006 F5
Merriwa 925 F3
Millthorpe 640 E5
Milpa B2
Milperra H4
Milton 729 F4
Mittagong 3,865 F4
Moama C5
Mogil Mogil E1
Molong 1,504 E3
Mona Vale K2
Moree 9,359 E1
Morisset 1,595 F3
Moruya 1,869 F4
Mosman 26,811 J3
Moss Vale 3,638 F4
Mossgiel C4
Mount Arrowsmith A2
Mount Drysdale C2
Mudgee 5,724 E3
Mullumbimby 2,028 G1
Mungindi 606 E1
Murrumburrah 2,112 E4
Murrurundi 930 F2
Murwillumbah 7,294 G1
Muswellbrook 7,805 F3
Nambucca Heads 3,217 G2
Narellan 1,253 F3
Narooma 2,038 F5
Narrabeen K3
Narrabri 6,951 E2
Narrandera 4,984 D4
Narromine 2,802 E3
New Angledool E1
Newcastle 138,718 F3
Newcastle* 251,132 F3
North Sydney 48,536 J3
Nowra-Bomaderry 15,496 F4
Nymboida⊙ 1,547 G1
Nyngan 2,359 D2
Oberon 1,892 E3
Old Bar 666 G2
Orange 26,254 E3
Para Station B3
Parkes 8,905 E3
Parramatta 131,659 H3
Peak Hill 994 E3
Penrith 79,043 F3
Picton 1,715 F4
Popiltah A3
Portland 1,883 E3
Port Macquarie 13,362 G2
Queanbeyan 18,923 E4
Quirindi 2,955 F2
Randwick 119,500 J3
Raymond Terrace 6,989 F3
Richmond-Windsor 13,440 F3
Rockdale 83,797 J4
Ryde 89,137 J3
Rylstone 691 E3
Salisbury Downs B1
Sawtell 3,711 G2
Scone 3,424 F3
Shellharbour 37,316 F4
Singleton 7,917 F3
Smithtown-Gladstone 977 G2
South Sydney 33,145 J3
South West Rocks 1,176 G2
Stephen's Creek A2
Strathfield 26,301 J3
Sussex Inlet 933 F4
Sutherland 156,754 J4
Sydney (cap.)‡ 2,765,040 J3
Tamworth 27,273 F2
Taree 13,440 G2
Tathra 847 F5
Temora 4,324 D4
Tenterfield 3,563 G1
Terrey Hills 2,513 J3

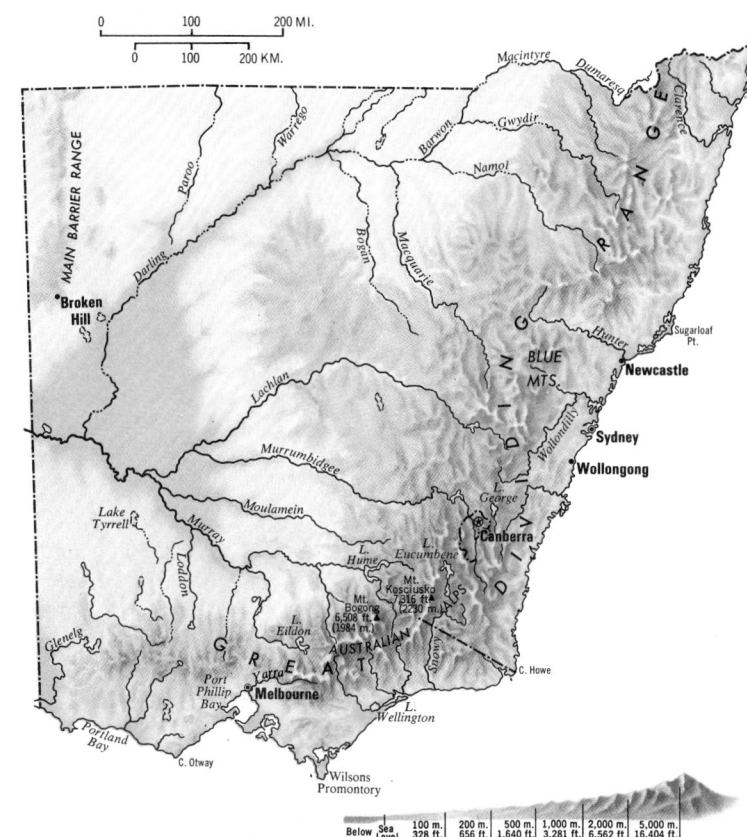

(continued on following page)

*City and suburbs.
⊙Population of district.
‡Population of met. area.
□Population of urban area.

Irrigation Areas and Artesian Basins in Australia

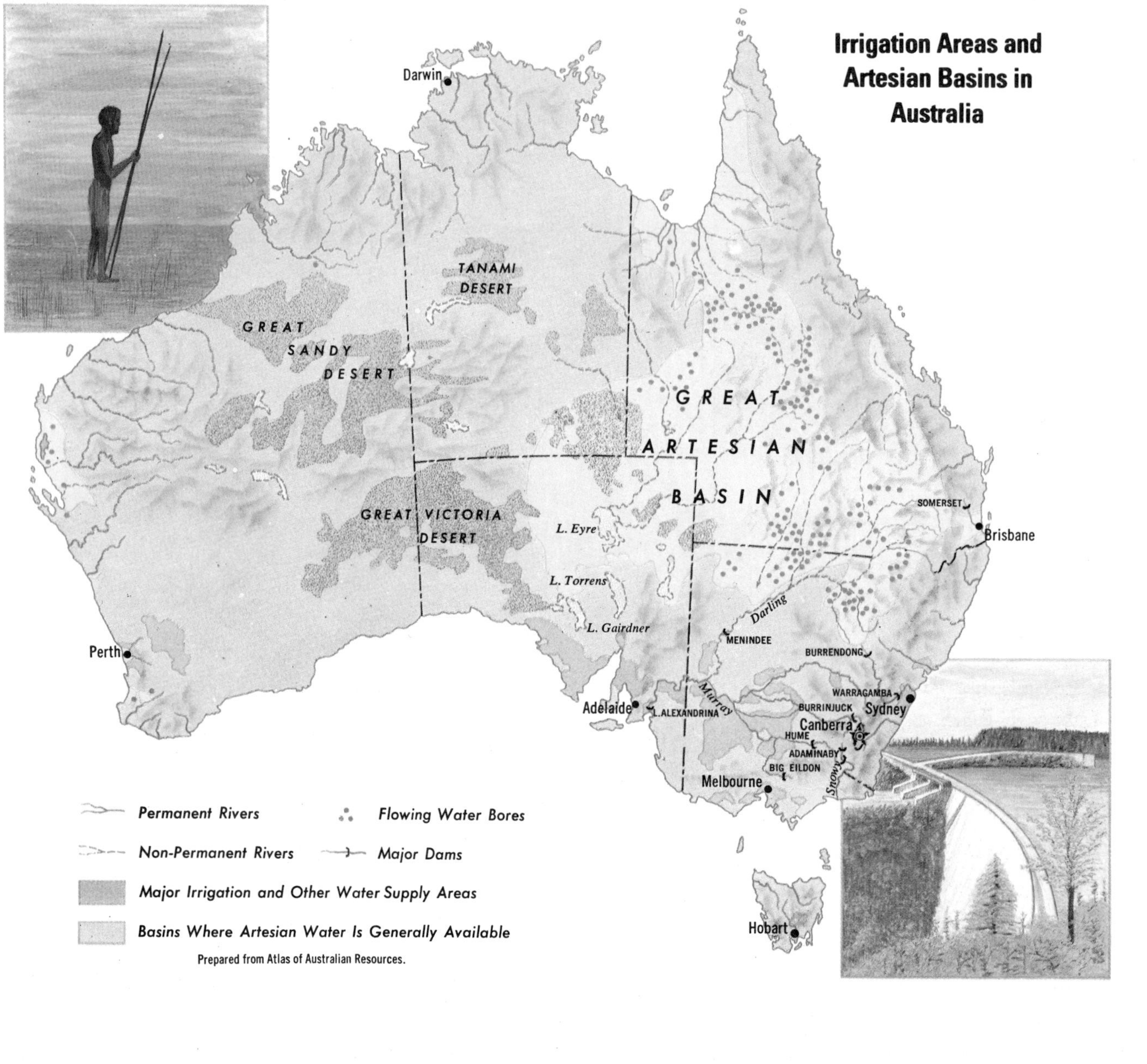
Darwin
TANAMI DESERT
GREAT SANDY DESERT
GREAT ARTESIAN BASIN
GREAT VICTORIA DESERT
L. Eyre
L. Torrens
L. Gairdner
SOMERSET
Brisbane
Darling
MENINDEE
BURRENDONG
Perth
Adelaide
L. ALEXANDRINA
Murray
WARRAGAMBA
BURRINJUCK
Sydney
Canberra
HUME
ADAMINABY
BIG EILDON
Snowy
Melbourne
Hobart
Permanent Rivers
Flowing Water Bores
Non-Permanent Rivers
Major Dams
Major Irrigation and Other Water Supply Areas
Basins Where Artesian Water Is Generally Available

Prepared from Atlas of Australian Resources.

Topography

0   30   60 MI.
0   30   60 KM.

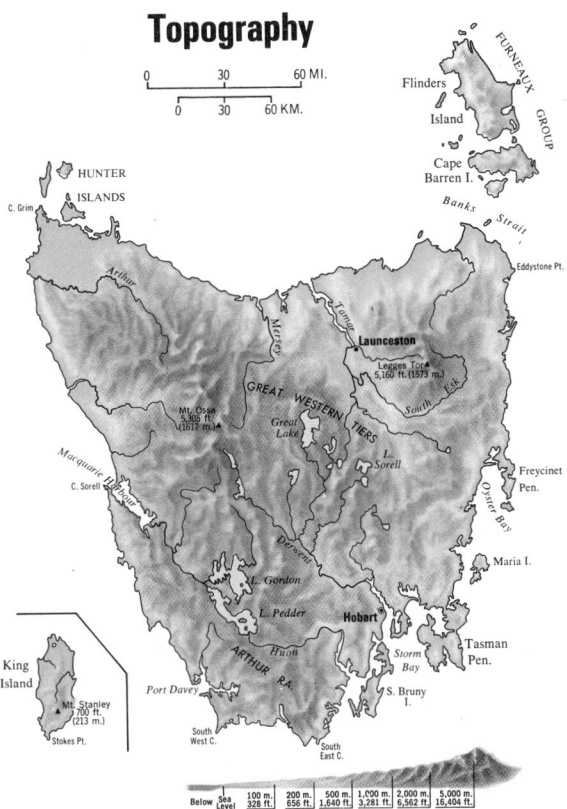

FURNEAUX GROUP
Flinders Island
Cape Barren I.
Banks Strait
Eddystone Pt.
HUNTER ISLANDS
C. Grim
Arthur
Mersey
Tamar
LAUNCESTON
Legges Tor 5,160 ft. (1573 m.)
GREAT WESTERN TIERS
Mt. Ossa 5,300 ft. (1617 m.)
Great Lake
L. Sorell
South Esk
Freycinet Pen.
Oyster Bay
Macquarie
C. Sorell
Macquarie Harbour
Derwent
L. Gordon
Maria I.
L. Pedder
Huon
Hobart
ARTHUR RA.
Storm Bay
Tasman Pen.
Port Davey
South West C.
S. Bruny I.
South East C.

King Island
Mt. Stanley 700 ft. (213 m.)
Stokes Pt.

Below Sea Level | 100 m. 328 ft. | 200 m. 656 ft. | 500 m. 1,640 ft. | 1,000 m. 3,281 ft. | 2,000 m. 6,562 ft. | 5,000 m. 16,404 ft.

AREA 26,178 sq. mi. (67,800 sq. km.)
POPULATION 402,866
CAPITAL Hobart
LARGEST CITY Hobart
HIGHEST POINT Mt. Ossa 5,305 ft. (1,617 m.)

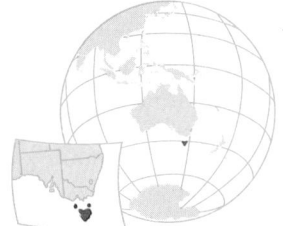

Great (lake)	C3
Great Western Tiers (mts.)	C3
Grim (cape)	A2
Hartz (mt.)	C5
Hibbs (pt.)	B4
High Rocky (pt.)	B4
Hogan Group (isls.)	D1
Hummock (mt.)	D2
Hunter (isl.)	A2
Hunter (isls.)	B2
Huon (riv.)	C5
Indian Ocean	A4
Kent Group (isls.)	D1
King (isl.)	A1
King (riv.)	B4
King William (lake)	C4
Lake (riv.)	D3
Legges Tor (mt.)	D3
Leven (riv.)	B3
Lodi (cape)	E3
Lofty (range)	B3
Long (pt.)	E3
Low Rocky (pt.)	B4
Lyell (mt.)	B4
Maatsuyker (isls.)	C5
Macquarie (harb.)	B4
Macquarie (riv.)	D3
Maria (isl.)	E4
Marion (bay)	E4
Mersey (riv.)	C3
Munro (mt.)	E2
Naturaliste (cape)	E2
Nive (riv.)	C4
Norfolk (bay)	D4
North (pt.)	E1
North Bruny (isl.)	D5
North Esk (riv.)	D3
Ossa (mt.)	C3
Ouse (riv.)	C4
Oyster (bay)	E4
Pedder (lake)	B4
Peron (cape)	E4
Phoques (bay)	A1
Picton (mt.)	C5
Pieman (riv.)	B3
Pillar (cape)	E5
Port Davey (inlet)	B5
Portland (cape)	D2
Ramsey (mt.)	B3
Raoul (cape)	D5
Reid (rocks)	B1
Ringarooma (bay)	D2
Robbins (isl.)	B2
Rocky (cape)	B2
Saint Clair (lake)	C4
Saint Helens (pt.)	E3
Saint Vincent (cape)	B5
Sandy (cape)	A3
Savage (riv.)	B3
Schouten (isl.)	E4
Sorell (cape)	B4
Sorell (lake)	D4
South (cape)	C5
South Bruny (isl.)	D5
South East (cape)	C5
South Esk (riv.)	D3
South West (cape)	B5
Stanley (mt.)	A1
Stokes (pt.)	A1
Stony (head)	C2
Storm (bay)	D5
Strzelecki (mt.)	D2
Swan (isl.)	E2
Tamar (riv.)	D3
Tasman (head)	D5
Tasman (pen.)	E5
Tasman (sea)	E4
Three Hummock (isl.)	B2
Tooms (lake)	D4
Vansittart (isl.)	E2
Walker (isl.)	B2
Waterhouse (isl.)	D2
West (pt.)	A2
West Sister (isl.)	D1
Wickham (cape)	A1

‡Population of met. area.

CITIES and TOWNS

Adventure Bay	D5
Bagdad	D4
Barrington	C3
Beaconsfield 936	C3
Beauty Point 1,012	C3
Bell Bay	C3
Boat Harbour	B2
Bridgewater 2,750	D4
Bridport 725	D3
Brighton 4,927	D4
Burnie 19,465	B3
Bushy Park	C4
Cambridge	D4
Campbell Town 936	D3
Chudleigh	C3
Colebrook	D4
Conara Junction	D3
Cornwall	E3
Cranbrook	D4
Cressy 621	C3
Currie 861	A1
Cygnet 720	C5
Deloraine 1,843	C3
Derwent Bridge	C4
Devonport 19,399	C3
Egg Lagoon	A1
Ellendale	C4
Elliott	B3
Emita	D2
Evandale 529	D3
Flowerdale	B2
Franklin 530	C5
Geeveston 900	C5
George Town 5,296	C3
Glenorchy 42,437	D4
Grassy 718	B1
Gravelly Beach 522	C3
Hadspen 619	D3
Hobart (cap.) 50,384	D4
Hobart‡ 131,524	D4
Huonville-Ranelagh 1,340	C5
Kingston 6,259	D4
Latrobe 2,375	C3
Lauderdale 1,881	D4
Launceston 32,953	C3
Launceston‡ 63,386	C3
Longford 1,785	C3
Maydena 537	C4
New Norfolk 6,679	C4
Oatlands 553	D3
Penguin 2,502	C3
Perth 1,141	D3
Port Sorell 772	C3
Queenstown 4,520	B4
Railton 926	C3
Rosebery 2,534	B3
Saint Helens 817	E3
Saint Marys 677	E3
Savage River 1,186	B3
Scottsdale 1,815	D3
Sheffield 833	C3
Smithton 3,235	A2
Snug 668	D5
Sorell-Midway Point 2,183	D4
Stanley 650	B2
Strathgordon 912	C4
Temma	A3
Triabunna 881	D4
Ulverstone 8,793	C3
Westbury 1,006	C3
Wynyard 4,348	B3
Zeehan 1,754	B3

OTHER FEATURES

Anderson (bay)	D2
Anne (mt.)	C4
Anser Group (isls.)	C1
Arthur (lake)	D4
Arthur (range)	C5
Arthur (riv.)	B3
Babel (isl.)	E1
Banks (str.)	D2
Barn Bluff (mt.)	B3
Barren (cape)	E2
Bass (str.)	C1
Bathurst (harb.)	C5
Cape Barren (isl.)	E2
Chappell (isls.)	D2
Circular (head)	B2
Clarke (isl.)	E2
Clyde (riv.)	D4
Cox (bight)	B5
Cradle (mt.)	B3
Cradle Mt. Lake St. Clair Nat'l Park	B3
Crescent (lake)	D4
Curtis Group (isls.)	C1
D'Aguilar (range)	B4
Davey (riv.)	B4
Deal (isl.)	D1
Dee (riv.)	C4
Denison (range)	C4
D'Entrecasteaux (chan.)	D5
Derwent (riv.)	C4
East Sister (isl.)	E1
Echo (lake)	C4
Eddystone (pt.)	E2
Elliott (bay)	B5
Fires (bay)	E3
Flinders (isl.)	D1
Florence (riv.)	C4
Forestier (cape)	E4
Forestier (pen.)	E4
Forth (riv.)	C3
Frankland (cape)	D1
Frankland (range)	B4
Franklin (riv.)	B4
Frenchmans Cap (mt.)	B4
Freycinet (pen.)	E4
Furneaux Group (isls.)	E1
Gordon (lake)	C4
Gordon (riv.)	B4

Main Map

KING I. Same Scale as Main Map.
Phoques B. • C. Wickham
Egg Lagoon
Currie • Narracoopa • Pegarah
Mt. Stanley 700 ft. (213 m.) • Grassy
Stokes Pt. • Reid Rocks

BASS STRAIT
VICTORIA
Wilsons Promontory
Glennie Gr.
Anser Gr.
Hogan Gr.
Curtis Gr.
Kent Group • Deal I.
W. Sister I. • E. Sister I.
North Point
FURNEAUX GROUP
C. Frankland • Flinders
Emita • Island
Hummock I. • Whitemark
Mt. Strzelecki 2,481 ft. (756 m.) • Lady Barron
Chappell Is. • Cape Barren I. • C. Barren
Clarke I.
Banks Strait
Waterhouse I. • C. Portland • Swan I.

HUNTER ISLANDS
Three Hummock I.
Hunter Island
Walker I.
Robbins I.
Cape Grim • Stanley
West Point • Port Latta • Rocky Cape
Marrawah • Smithton • Boat Harbour
Redpa • Irishtown • Flowerdale
Lileah • Mawbanna
Trowutta
Anderson B. • Gladstone
Stony Hd. • Ringarooma • C. Naturaliste
Eddystone Pt.
Bay of Fires
St. Helens Pt.
St. Helens
Bridport • Winnaleah • Herrick
George Town • Scottsdale • Derby • Branxholm
Beauty Pt. • Legerwood • Ringarooma • Pyengana
Beaconsfield • Lilydale
Burnie • Somerset • Penguin • Ulverstone • Devonport • Wesley Vale
Heybridge • Sulphur Creek • Pt. Sorell • Latrobe • Gravelly Beach • Legana
Elliott • Yolla • Ridgley • Stowport • Riana • Spreyton • N. Motton • Railton • Launceston
Temma • Sassafras • Barrington • Sheffield • Deloraine • Hagley • Hadspen • N. Esk R. • Evandale • Legges Tor 5,160 ft. (1573 m.) • Mathinna
Lofty Ra. • Guildford Jct. • Wilmot • Gowrie Park • Mole Creek • Chudleigh • Meander • Bracknell • Cressy • Poatina • Storeys Creek • Cornwall
Arthur R. • Luina • Waratah • Great Western Tiers • Rossarden • St. Marys • Fingal
Sandy Cape • Savage River • Cradle Mtn. • Mt. Ramsey 3,806 ft. (1160 m.) • Barn Bluff 5,114 ft. (1559 m.) • Mt. Ossa 5,305 ft. (1617 m.) • Great Lake • Arthurs Lake • Avoca • Bicheno
Tullah • Roseberry • Conara Jct. • C. Lodi
Zeehan • Williamsford • CRADLE MT.-LAKE ST. CLAIR NAT'L PARK • Campbell Town • Long Point
Mt. Lyell 4,013 ft. • Queenstown • Mt. King William • St. Clair • Derwent Bridge • Ross • Cranbrook • Swansea
Strahan • Gormanston • L. St. Clair • Waddamana • L. Sorell • Freycinet Pen.
Cape Sorell • L. King William • L. Echo • Oatlands • C. Forestier
Macquarie Harbour • Tarraleah • Bothwell • Parattah • Schouten I.
Frenchmans Cap 4,379 ft. (1444 m.) • Wayatinah • Ouse • Kempton • Tunnack • Triabunna
D'Aguilar Ra. • Hamilton • Colebrook • Orford
Gordon R. • Ellendale • Gretna • Bagdad • Maria I.
High Rocky Pt. • Bushy Park • Brighton • Richmond • C. Peron
Maydena • New Norfolk • Bridgewater • Sorell-Midway • Marion Bay
L. Pedder • Strathgordon • Glenorchy • HOBART • Dunalley • Forestier Pen.
Frankland Ra. • Huonville-Ranelagh • Lauderdale • Tasman Pen.
Mt. Anne 4,675 ft. (1425 m.) • Margate • Kingston • Norfolk • Taranna • C. Raoul
Pt. Hibbs • Geeveston • Snug • Kettering • Storm Bay • Nubeena • C. Pillar
Huon R. • Franklin • Cygnet • Woodbridge • N. Bruny • Tasman Hd.
Elliott Bay • Mt. Picton 4,353 ft. (1327 m.) • Hartz Mt. 4,113 ft. (1254 m.) • Dover • Gordon • Adventure Bay • S. Bruny I.
C. St. Vincent • Port Davey • Hythe
Bathurst Harbour • South West Cape • Maatsuyker Islands • Cox Bight • South Cape • South East Cape

INDIAN OCEAN
TASMAN SEA

Tasmania
MILES 0 10 20 30
KILOMETERS 0 10 20 30
State Capital .... ◉
State Boundaries ....
Scale 1:3,000,000

© Copyright HAMMOND INCORPORATED, Maplewood, N.J.

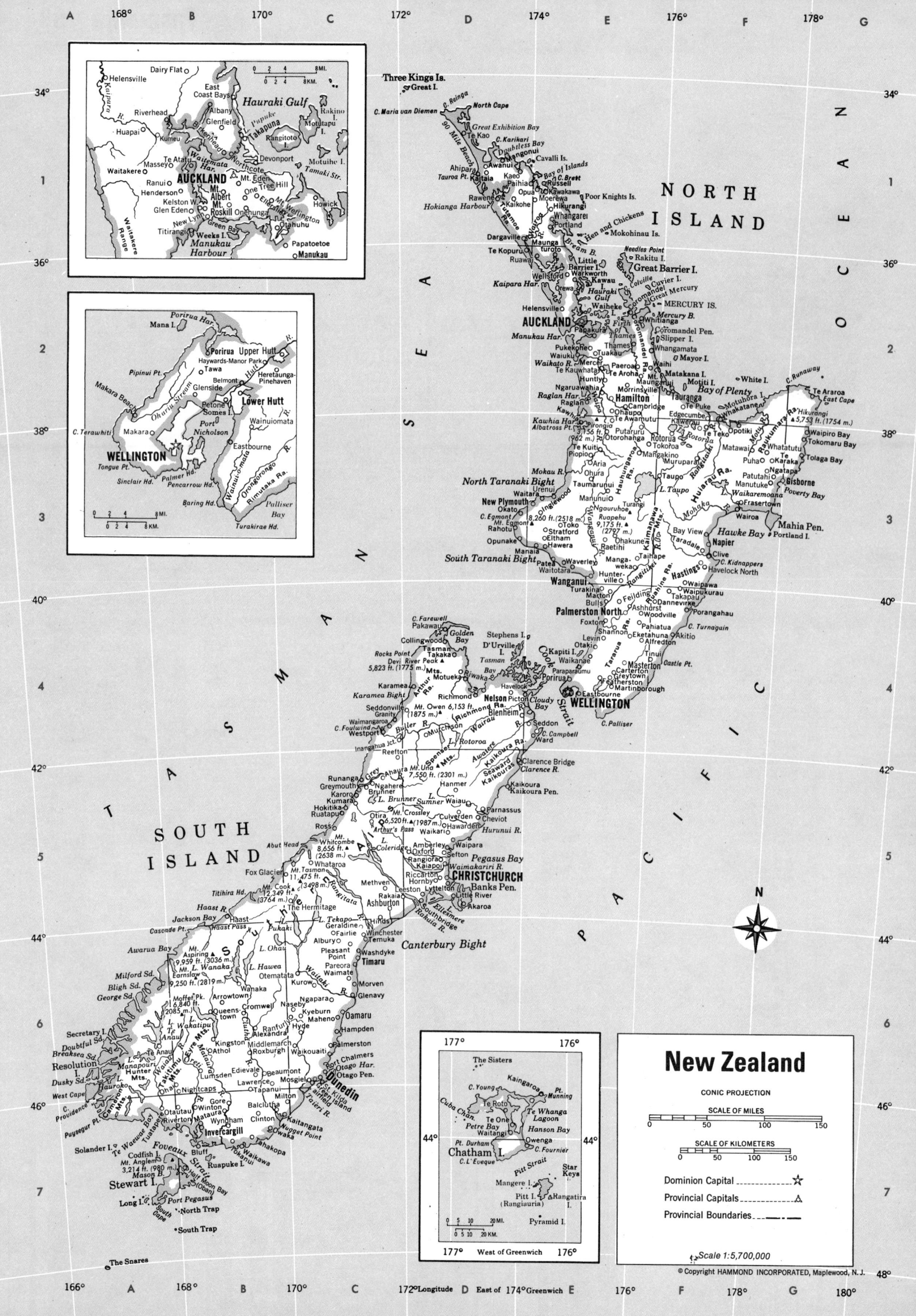

New Zealand

CONIC PROJECTION

SCALE OF MILES

SCALE OF KILOMETERS

Dominion Capital ------------ ☆

Provincial Capitals ------------ △

Provincial Boundaries ---------

Scale 1:5,700,000

© Copyright HAMMOND INCORPORATED, Maplewood, N.J.

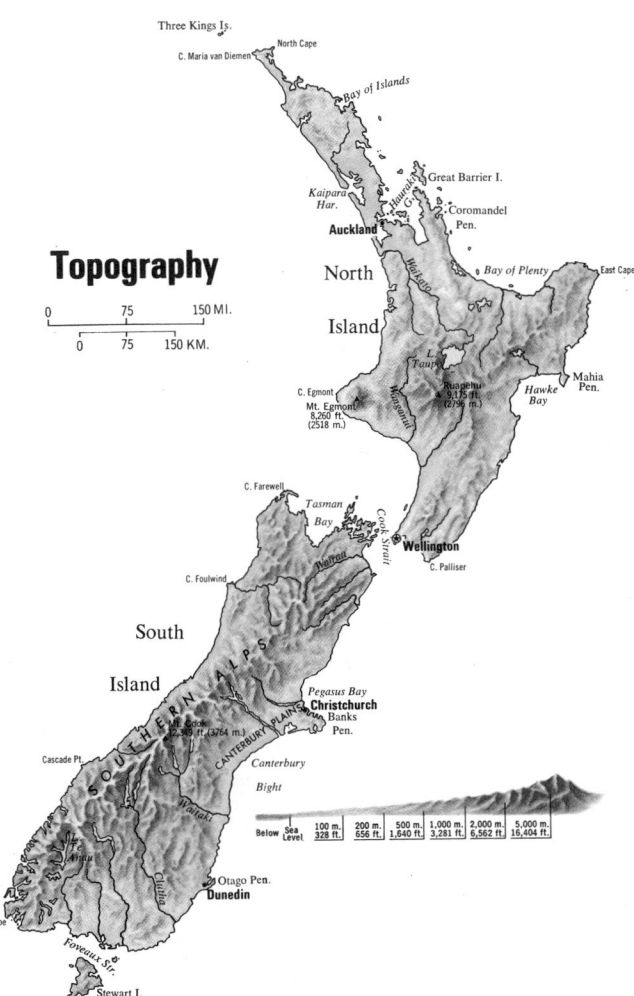

Topography

North Island

South Island

AREA 103,736 sq. mi. (268,676 sq. km.)
POPULATION 3,167,357
CAPITAL Wellington
LARGEST CITY Auckland
HIGHEST POINT Mt. Cook 12,349 ft.
   (3,764 m.)
MONETARY UNIT New Zealand dollar
MAJOR LANGUAGES English, Maori
MAJOR RELIGIONS Protestantism,
   Roman Catholicism

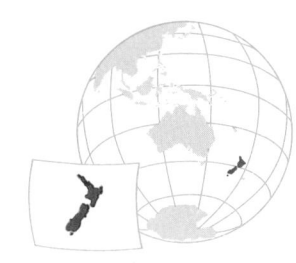

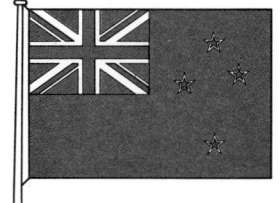

Kaikoura (pen.)	E5
Kaimanawa (range)	E3
Kaipara (harb.)	D2
Kaipara (riv.)	A1
Kapiti (isl.)	E4
Karamea (bight)	C4
Karikari (cape)	D1
Kawau (isl.)	E2
Kawhia (harb.)	D2
Kidnappers (cape)	F3
L'Eveque (cape)	D7
Little Barrier (isl.)	E2
Long (isl.)	A7
Mahia (pen.)	G3
Mana (isl.)	B2
Manapouri (lake)	A6
Mangere (isl.)	E7
Manukau (harb.)	B1
Maria van Diemen (cape)	D1
Mason (bay)	A7
Matakana (isl.)	F2
Mataura (riv.)	B6
Mavora (mt.)	B6
Mayor (isl.)	F2
Mercury (bay)	F2
Mercury (isls.)	F2
Milford (sound)	A6
Moffet (peak)	B6
Mohaka (riv.)	F3
Mokau (riv.)	E3
Mokohinau (isl.)	E1
Motiti (isl.)	F2
Motu (riv.)	F3
Motuhora (isl.)	F2
Motuihe (isl.)	C1
Motutapu (isl.)	C1
Munning (pt.)	E7
Needles (pt.)	C1
Ngauruhoe (mt.)	E3
Nicholson Port, (inlet)	B3
Ninety Mile (beach)	D1
North (cape)	D1
North (isl.)	F1
North Taranaki, (bight)	D3
North Trap (isl.)	B7
Nugget (pt.)	B7
Ohariu (stream)	B2
Ohau (lake)	B6
Oreti (riv.)	B6
Orongorongo (riv.)	B3
Otago (harb.)	C6
Otago (pen.)	C6
Owen (mt.)	D4
Palliser (bay)	D3
Palliser (cape)	E4
Palmer (head)	B3
Pegasus (bay)	D5
Pegasus Port (inlet)	B7
Pencarrow (head)	B3
Petre (bay)	D7
Pipinui (pt.)	B2
Pirongia (mt.)	E3
Pitt (isl.)	E7
Pitt (str.)	E7
Plenty (bay)	F2
Poor Knights (isls.)	E1
Porirua (harb.)	B2
Portland (isl.)	G3
Port Nicholson (inlet)	B3
Port Pegasus (inlet)	B7
Poverty (bay)	G3
Providence (cape)	A7
Pukaki (lake)	B6
Pupuke (lake)	B1
Puysegur (pt.)	A7
Pyramid (pt.)	E7
Raglan (harb.)	D2
Rakaia (riv.)	C5
Rakino (isl.)	C1
Rakitu (isl.)	E2
Rangatira (isl.)	E7
Rangitaiki (riv.)	F3
Rangitata (riv.)	C5
Rangitikei (riv.)	E3
Rangitoto (isl.)	C1
Raukumara (range)	F3
Reinga (cape)	D1
Resolution (isl.)	A6
Richmond (range)	D4
Rimutaka (range)	B3
Rocks (pt.)	C4
Rotoroa (lake)	D4
Rotorua (lake)	F3
Ruahine (range)	F4
Ruapehu (mt.)	E3
Ruapuke (isl.)	B7
Runaway (cape)	G2
Seaward Kaikouras (range)	D5
Secretary (isl.)	A6
Sinclair (head)	A3
Sisters The, (isls.)	D6
Slipper (isl.)	F2
Snares, The (isls.)	A7
Solander (isl.)	A7
Somes (isl.)	C3
South (cape)	A7
South (isl.)	B5
Southern Alps (range)	C5
South Taranaki (bight)	D3
South Trap (isl.)	B7
Spenser (mts.)	D5
Star Keys (isl.)	E7
Stephens (isl.)	D3
Stewart (isl.)	A7
Sumner (lake)	D5
Taieri (riv.)	C7
Takitimu (mts.)	A6
Tamaki (riv.)	C1
Tararua (range)	E4
Tasman (bay)	D4
Tasman (mt.)	C5
Tasman (mts.)	D4
Tasman (sea)	B4
Taupo (lake)	E3
Tauroa (pt.)	D1
Te Anau (lake)	A6
Tekapo (lake)	C5
Terawhiti (cape)	A3
Te Waewae (bay)	A7
Te Whanga (mts.)	A7
Thames (firth)	E2
Three Kings (isls.)	D1
Titihira, (head)	B5

Tongue (pt.)	A3
Turakirae (head)	B3
Turnagain (cape)	F4
Tutamoe (range)	D1
Una (mt.)	D5
Waiau (riv.)	A6
Waiheke (isl.)	E2
Waikaremoana (lake)	F3
Waikato (riv.)	E2
Waimakariri (riv.)	D5
Waipa (riv.)	E2
Wairau (riv.)	D4
Wairoa (riv.)	E1
Waitakere (range)	A1
Waitaki (riv.)	C6
Waitemata (harb.)	B1
Wakatipu (lake)	B6
Wanaka (lake)	B6
Wanganui (riv.)	E3
Weeks (isl.)	B1
West (cape)	A6
Whitcombe (mt.)	C5
White (isl.)	F2
Young (cape)	D7

☐ Population of urban area.

Agriculture, Industry and Resources

CITIES and TOWNS

Alexandra 4,137	B6
Ashburton 14,225	C5
Balclutha 150,708	B1
Auckland☐ 742,786	B1
Balclutha 4,740	B7
Birkenhead 19,683	B1
Blenheim 17,156	D4
Bluff 3,016	B7
Cambridge 7,841	E2
Carterton 3,985	E4
Christchurch 171,987	D5
Christchurch☐ 295,296	D5
Clive 4,216	F3
Dannevirke 5,638	F4
Dargaville 4,559	D1
Devonport 11,003	C1
Dunedin 82,546	C6
Dunedin☐ 113,222	C6
Eastbourne 4,779	B3
East Coast Bays 23,490	C1
Ellerslie 5,574	C1
Feilding 10,893	E4
Gisborne 29,698	G3
Gisborne☐ 31,790	G3
Glen Eden 8,370	B1
Glenfield 17,746	B1
Gore 9,179	B7
Green Bay	B1
Green Island 6,979	C7
Greymouth 8,282	C5
Hamilton 87,968	E2
Hamilton☐ 94,777	E2
Hastings 33,960	F3
Hastings☐ 50,814	F3
Havelock North 8,348	F3
Hawera 8,506	E3
Henderson 7,076	B1
Heretaunga-Pinehaven 5,849	C2
Hokitika 3,530	C5
Hornby 8,679	D5
Howick 13,949	C1
Huntly 5,559	E2
Hutt (Upper and Lower)☐ 115,604	B2
Invercargill 49,738	B7
Invercargill☐ 53,762	B7
Kaiapoi 4,746	D5
Kaikohe 3,567	D1
Kaitaia 4,243	D1
Kawerau 7,743	F3
Kelston West	B1
Kumeu 3,125	B1
Levin 14,759	E4
Lower Hutt 64,553	B2
Lyttelton 3,327	D5
Mangonui 459	D1
Manukau 139,059	C1
Marton 4,910	E3
Massey 8,318	B1
Masterton 19,460	E4
Morrinsville 4,783	E2
Mosgiel 9,289	C6
Motueka 4,384	D4
Mount Albert 28,131	B1
Mount Eden 19,815	B1
Mount Maunganui 10,103	F2
Mount Roskill 34,645	B1
Mount Wellington 20,533	C1
Napier 46,994	F3
Napier☐ 50,164	F3
Nelson 32,793	D4
New Lynn 10,466	B1
New Plymouth 37,711	D3
New Plymouth☐ 43,914	D3

Ngaruawahia 4,385	E2
Northcote 9,921	B1
Oamaru 13,480	C6
Oban (Half Moon Bay) 333	B7
Onehunga 16,655	B1
One Tree Hill 11,711	B1
Orewa 4,328	E2
Otahuhu 10,558	C1
Otaki 4,202	E4
Paeroa 3,796	E2
Palmerston North 57,931	E4
Palmerston North☐ 63,873	E4
Papakura 21,452	C1
Papatoetoe 22,864	C1
Petone 8,883	B2
Picton 3,276	D4
Pinehaven (Heretaunga-Pinehaven) 5,849	C2
Porirua 42,833	B2
Port Chalmers 3,123	C6
Pukekohe 8,770	E2
Putaruru 4,442	E3
Queenstown 3,133	B6
Rangiora 5,991	D5
Riccarton 7,280	D5
Richmond 6,587	D4
Rotorua 37,229	F3
Rotorua☐ 46,650	F3
Saint Kilda 6,542	C7
Stratford 5,444	E3
Takapuna 62,220	B1
Taradale 4,747	F3
Taumarunui 6,479	E3
Taupo 12,898	F3
Tauranga 33,672	F2
Tauranga☐ 48,153	F2
Tawa 12,297	B2
Te Aroha 3,202	E2
Te Atatu 16,393	B1
Te Awamutu 7,619	E3
Te Kuiti 4,840	E3
Te Puke 3,810	F2
Temuka 3,711	C6
Thames 6,769	E2
The Hermitage	C5
Timaru 29,267	C6
Timaru☐ 29,958	C6
Titirangi 8,227	B1
Tokoroa 18,635	F3
Turangi 5,496	E3
Upper Hutt 30,616	B2
Waihi 3,415	E2
Waikanae 4,184	E4
Waimate 3,378	C6
Wainuiomata 19,318	B3
Waipara 292	D5
Waipukurau 3,632	F4
Wairoa 5,466	F3
Waitangi 251	D7
Waitara 6,036	E3
Waiuku 3,494	E2
Wanaka 1,178	B6
Wanganui 37,307	E3
Wanganui☐ 39,679	E3
Wellington (cap.) 139,566	A3
Wellington☐ 327,414	A3
Westport 4,988	C4
Whakatane 11,542	F2
Whangarei 34,981	E1
Whangarei☐ 39,069	E1

OTHER FEATURES

Abut (head)	B5
Albatross (pt.)	E3
Anglem (mt.)	A7

Arthur (range)	D4
Arthur's (pass)	C5
Aspiring (mt.)	B6
Awarua (bay)	A6
Awatere (riv.)	D5
Banks (pen.)	D5
Baring (head)	B3
Bligh (sound)	A6
Bonpland (mt.)	A6
Breaksea (sound)	A6
Bream (bay)	E1
Brett (cape)	E1
Brunner (lake)	C5
Buller (riv.)	D4
Cameron (mts.)	A7
Campbell (cape)	E4
Canterbury (bight)	D6
Cascade (pt.)	B6
Castle, (pt.)	F4
Cavalli (isls.)	E1
Chatham (isl.)	D7
Chatham (isls.)	D7
Clarence (riv.)	E5
Cloudy (bay)	E4
Clutha (riv.)	B6
Codfish (isl.)	A7
Coleridge (lake)	C5
Colville (cape)	E2
Cook (mt.)	C5
Cook (str.)	E4
Coromandel (pen.)	F2
Coromandel (range)	E2
Crossley (mt.)	D5
Cuba (chan.)	D7
Cuvier (isl.)	F2
Devil River (peak)	D4
Doubtful (sound)	A6
Doubtless (bay)	D1
Durham (pt.)	D7
D'Urville (isl.)	D4
Dusky (sound)	A6
Earnslaw (mt.)	B6
East (cape)	G2
Egmont (cape)	D3
Egmont (mt.)	D3
Ellesmere (lake)	D5
Eyre (mts.)	B6
Farewell (cape)	D4
Foulwind (cape)	C4
Fournier (cape)	E7
Foveaux (str.)	A7
George (sound)	A6
Golden (bay)	D4
Great (isl.)	D1
Great Barrier (isl.)	E2
Great Exhibition (bay)	D1
Great Mercury (isl.)	F2
Grey (riv.)	C5
Haast (pass)	B6
Haast (riv.)	B5
Hanson (bay)	E7
Hauhungaroa (range)	E3
Hauraki (gulf)	C1
Hauroko (lake)	A6
Hawea (lake)	B6
Hawke (bay)	F3
Hen and Chickens (isls.)	E1
Hikurangi (mt.)	G2
Hokianga (harb.)	D1
Huiarau (range)	F3
Hunter (mts.)	A6
Hurunui (riv.)	D5
Hutt (riv.)	C2
Islands (bay)	E1
Jackson (bay)	B5
Kaikoura (range)	D5

DOMINANT LAND USE

- Mixed Farming, Livestock
- Dairy
- Truck Farming, Horticulture
- Pasture Livestock (chiefly sheep)
- Livestock Herding
- Forests
- Nonagricultural Land

MAJOR MINERAL OCCURRENCES

C	Coal	Lg	Lignite
G	Natural Gas	O	Petroleum
J	Jade	U	Uranium
Ka	Kaolin		

- ⚡ Water Power
- ▨ Major Industrial Areas

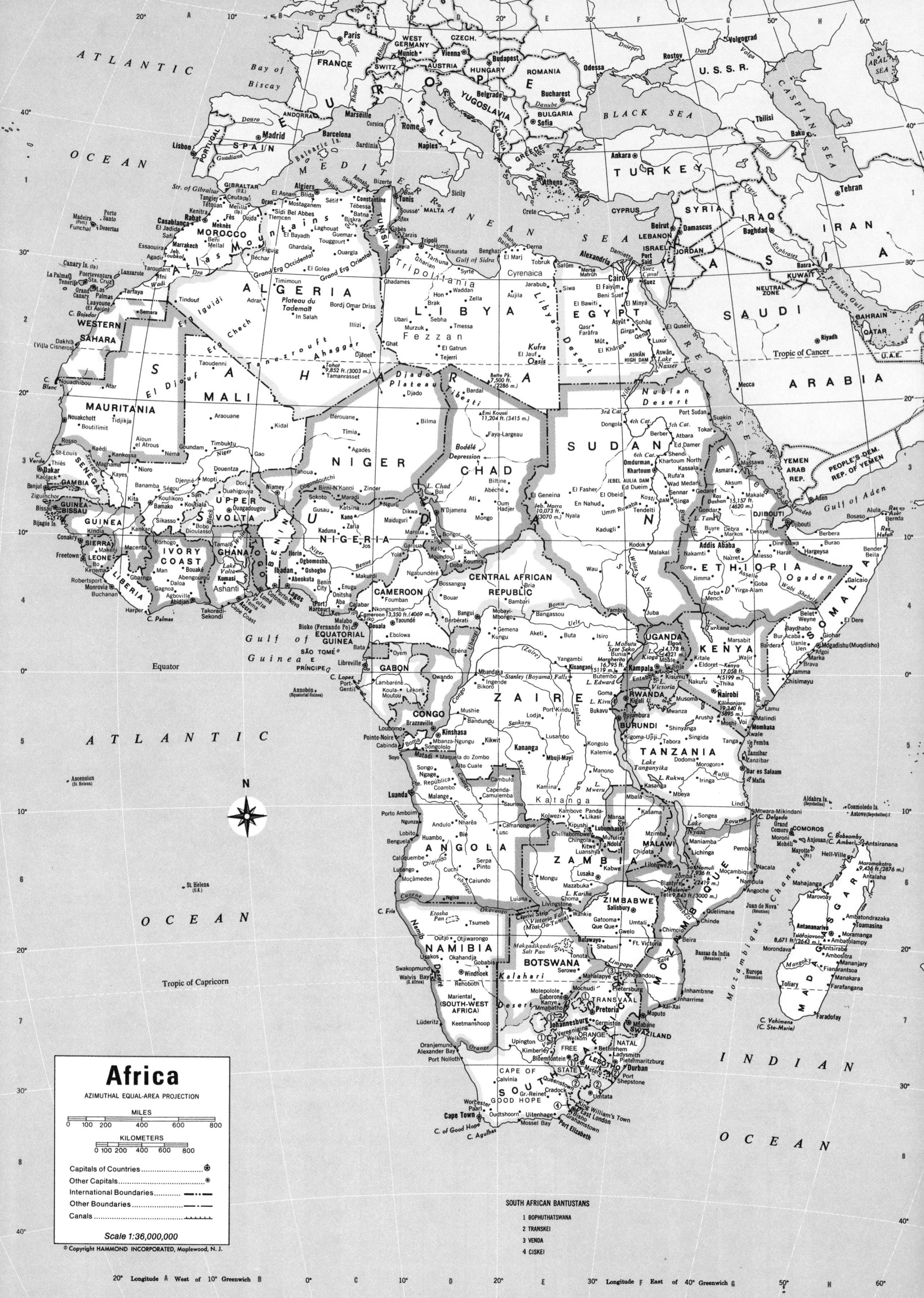

Africa

AZIMUTHAL EQUAL-AREA PROJECTION

MILES
0 100 200 400 600 800

KILOMETERS
0 100 200 400 600 800

Capitals of Countries .... ⊛
Other Capitals .... ⊛
International Boundaries .... ▬ ▪ ▬ ▪ ▬
Other Boundaries .... ▬ ▬ ▬ ▬
Canals ....

Scale 1:36,000,000

© Copyright HAMMOND INCORPORATED, Maplewood, N.J.

SOUTH AFRICAN BANTUSTANS

1 BOPHUTHATSWANA
2 TRANSKEI
3 VENDA
4 CISKEI

Population Distribution

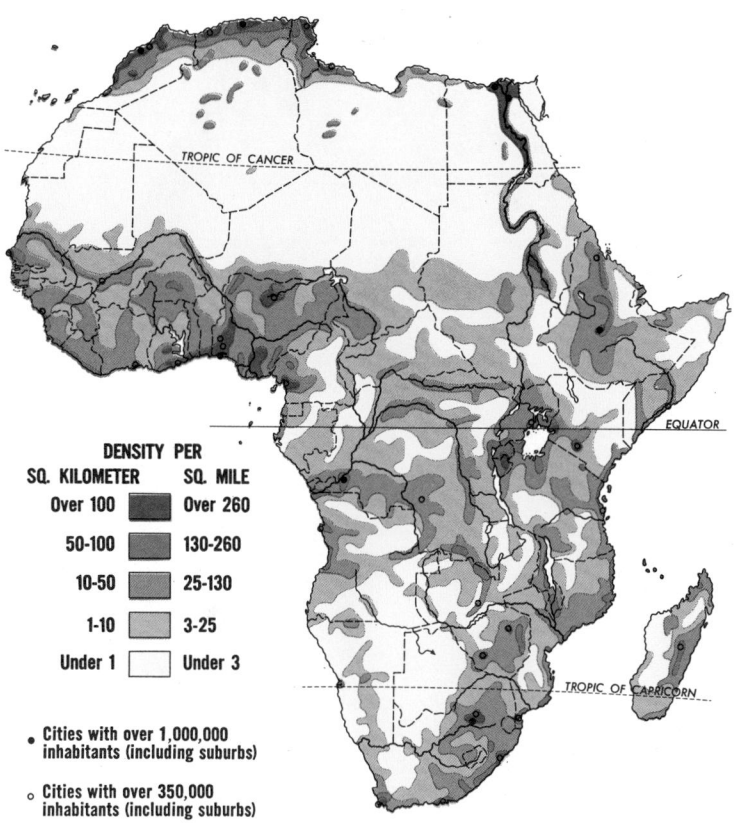

AFRICA
AREA 11,707,000 sq. mi. (30,321,130 sq. km.)
POPULATION 469,000,000
LARGEST CITY Cairo
HIGHEST POINT Kilimanjaro 19,340 ft.
(5,895 m.)
LOWEST POINT Lake Assal, Djibouti -512 ft.
(-156 m.)

DENSITY PER

SQ. KILOMETER	SQ. MILE
Over 100	Over 260
50-100	130-260
10-50	25-130
1-10	3-25
Under 1	Under 3

● Cities with over 1,000,000
inhabitants (including suburbs)

○ Cities with over 350,000
inhabitants (including suburbs)

Vegetation

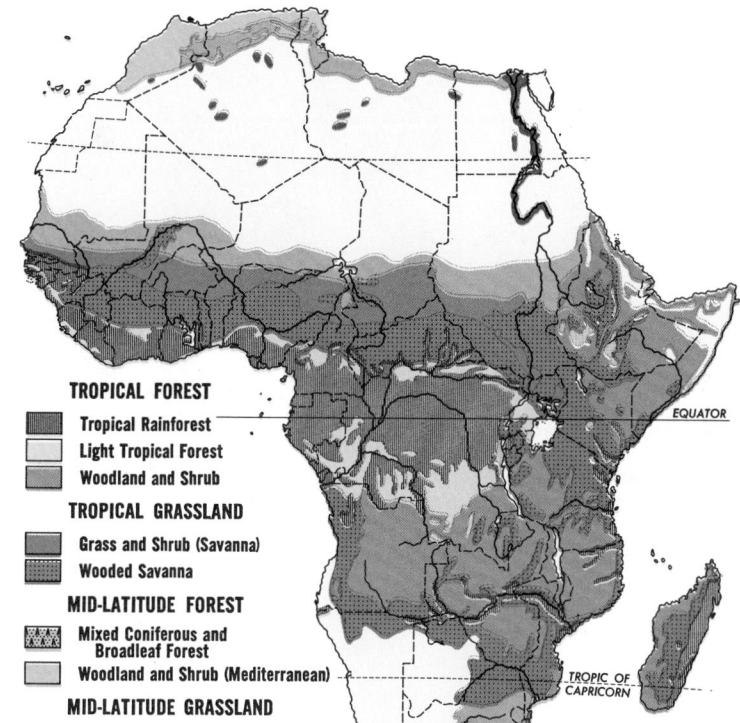

TROPICAL FOREST
Tropical Rainforest
Light Tropical Forest
Woodland and Shrub

TROPICAL GRASSLAND
Grass and Shrub (Savanna)
Wooded Savanna

MID-LATITUDE FOREST
Mixed Coniferous and
Broadleaf Forest
Woodland and Shrub (Mediterranean)

MID-LATITUDE GRASSLAND
Short Grass (Steppe)

RIVER VALLEY AND OASIS

DESERT AND DESERT SHRUB

UNCLASSIFIED HIGHLANDS

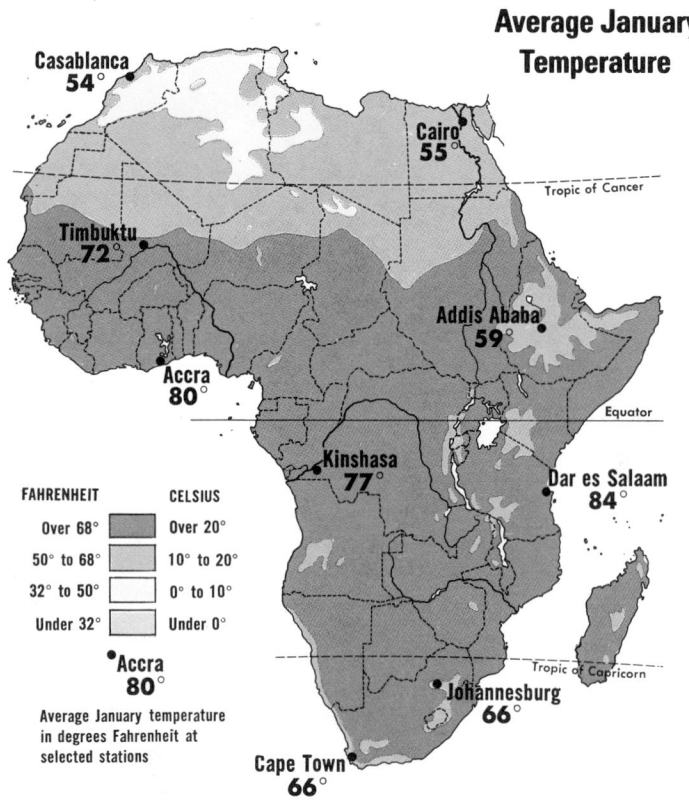

Average January Temperature

Casablanca 54°

Cairo 55°

Timbuktu 72°

Addis Ababa 59°

Accra 80°

Tropic of Cancer

Equator

Kinshasa 77°

Dar es Salaam 84°

FAHRENHEIT | CELSIUS
Over 68° | Over 20°
50° to 68° | 10° to 20°
32° to 50° | 0° to 10°
Under 32° | Under 0°

•Accra 80°

Average January temperature in degrees Fahrenheit at selected stations

Johannesburg 66°

Cape Town 66°

Tropic of Capricorn

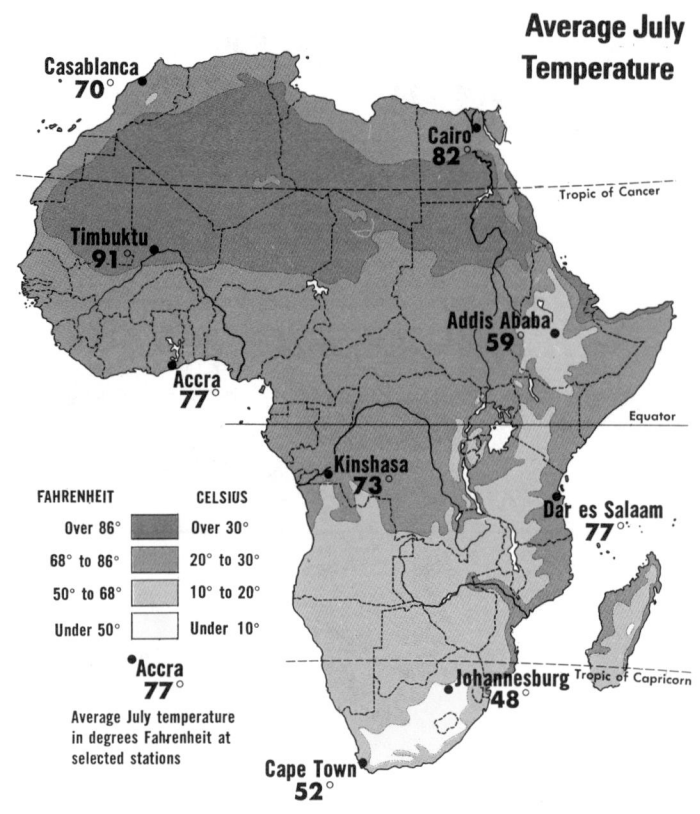

Average July Temperature

Casablanca 70°

Cairo 82°

Timbuktu 91°

Addis Ababa 59°

Accra 77°

Tropic of Cancer

Equator

Kinshasa 73°

Dar es Salaam 77°

FAHRENHEIT | CELSIUS
Over 86° | Over 30°
68° to 86° | 20° to 30°
50° to 68° | 10° to 20°
Under 50° | Under 10°

•Accra 77°

Average July temperature in degrees Fahrenheit at selected stations

Johannesburg 48°

Cape Town 52°

Tropic of Capricorn

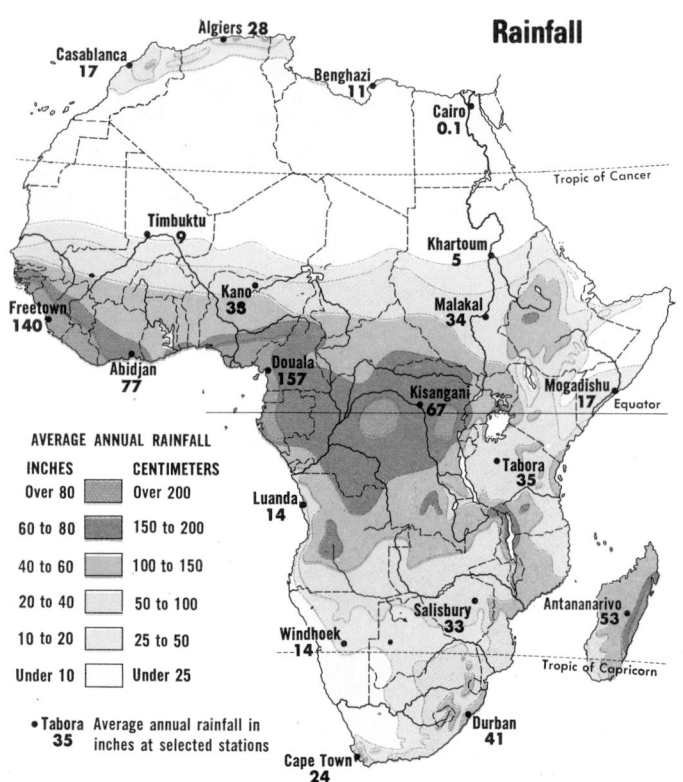

Rainfall

Algiers 28

Casablanca 17

Benghazi 11

Cairo 0.1

Tropic of Cancer

Timbuktu 9

Khartoum 5

Kano 35

Malakal 34

Freetown 140

Abidjan 77

Douala 157

Kisangani 67

Mogadishu 17

Equator

Tabora 35

Luanda 14

AVERAGE ANNUAL RAINFALL

INCHES | CENTIMETERS
Over 80 | Over 200
60 to 80 | 150 to 200
40 to 60 | 100 to 150
20 to 40 | 50 to 100
10 to 20 | 25 to 50
Under 10 | Under 25

•Tabora 35 | Average annual rainfall in inches at selected stations

Salisbury 33

Antananarivo 53

Windhoek 14

Tropic of Capricorn

Durban 41

Cape Town 24

Vegetation/Relief

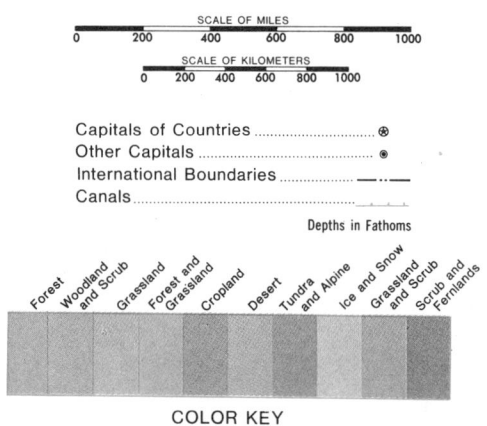

SCALE OF MILES
0 200 400 600 800 1000

SCALE OF KILOMETERS
0 200 400 600 800 1000

Capitals of Countries .... ⊛
Other Capitals .... ⊛
International Boundaries .... — ·· —
Canals ....

Depths in Fathoms

Forest
Woodland and Scrub
Grassland
Forest and Grassland
Cropland
Desert
Tundra and Alpine
Ice and Snow
Grassland and Scrub
Scrub and Fernlands

COLOR KEY

© Copyright HAMMOND INCORPORATED, Maplewood, N.J.

Longitude 10° West of Greenwich   Longitude 10° East of Greenwich

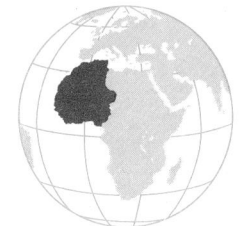

ALGERIA

AREA 919,591 sq. mi. (2,381,740 sq. km.)
POPULATION 17,422,000
CAPITAL Algiers
LARGEST CITY Algiers
HIGHEST POINT Tahat 9,852 ft. (3,003 m.)
MONETARY UNIT Algerian dinar
MAJOR LANGUAGES Arabic, Berber, French
MAJOR RELIGION Islam

BENIN

AREA 43,483 sq. mi. (112,620 sq. km.)
POPULATION 3,338,240
CAPITAL Porto-Novo
LARGEST CITY Cotonou
HIGHEST POINT Atakora Mts. 2,083 ft. (635 m.)
MONETARY UNIT CFA franc
MAJOR LANGUAGES Fon, Somba, Yoruba, Bariba, French, Mina, Dendi
MAJOR RELIGIONS Tribal religions, Islam, Roman Catholicism

CAPE VERDE

AREA 1,557 sq. mi. (4,033 sq. km.)
POPULATION 324,000
CAPITAL Praia
LARGEST CITY Praia
HIGHEST POINT 9,281 ft. (2,829 m.)
MONETARY UNIT Cape Verde escudo
MAJOR LANGUAGE Portuguese
MAJOR RELIGION Roman Catholicism

GAMBIA

AREA 4,127 sq. mi. (10,689 sq. km.)
POPULATION 601,000
CAPITAL Banjul
LARGEST CITY Banjul
HIGHEST POINT 100 ft. (30 m.)
MONETARY UNIT dalasi
MAJOR LANGUAGES Mandingo, Fulani, Wolof, English, Malinke
MAJOR RELIGIONS Islam, tribal religions, Christianity

GHANA

AREA 92,099 sq. mi. (238,536 sq. km.)
POPULATION 11,450,000
CAPITAL Accra
LARGEST CITY Accra
HIGHEST POINT Togo Hills 2,900 ft. (884 m.)
MONETARY UNIT cedi
MAJOR LANGUAGES Twi, Fante, Dagbani, Ewe, Ga, English, Hausa, Akan
MAJOR RELIGIONS Tribal religions, Christianity, Islam

GUINEA

AREA 94,925 sq. mi. (245,856 sq. km.)
POPULATION 5,143,284
CAPITAL Conakry
LARGEST CITY Conakry
HIGHEST POINT Nimba Mts. 6,070 ft. (1,850 m.)
MONETARY UNIT syli
MAJOR LANGUAGES Fulani, Mandingo, Susu, French
MAJOR RELIGIONS Islam, tribal religions

GUINEA-BISSAU

AREA 13,948 sq. mi. (36,125 sq. km.)
POPULATION 777,214
CAPITAL Bissau
LARGEST CITY Bissau
HIGHEST POINT 689 ft. (210 m.)
MONETARY UNIT Guinea-Bissau escudo
MAJOR LANGUAGES Balante, Fulani, Crioulo, Mandingo, Portuguese
MAJOR RELIGIONS Islam, tribal religions, Roman Catholicism

IVORY COAST

AREA 124,504 sq. mi. (322,465 sq. km.)
POPULATION 7,920,000
CAPITAL Abidjan
LARGEST CITY Abidjan
HIGHEST POINT 5,745 ft. (1,751 m.)
MONETARY UNIT CFA franc
MAJOR LANGUAGES Bale, Bete, Senufu, French, Dioula
MAJOR RELIGIONS Tribal religions, Islam

LIBERIA

AREA 43,000 sq. mi. (111,370 sq. km.)
POPULATION 1,873,000
CAPITAL Monrovia
LARGEST CITY Monrovia
HIGHEST POINT Wutivi 5,584 ft. (1,702 m.)
MONETARY UNIT Liberian dollar
MAJOR LANGUAGES Kru, Kpelle, Bassa, Vai, English
MAJOR RELIGIONS Christianity, tribal religions, Islam

MALI

AREA 464,873 sq. mi. (1,204,021 sq. km.)
POPULATION 6,906,000
CAPITAL Bamako
LARGEST CITY Bamako
HIGHEST POINT Hombori Mts. 3,789 ft. (1,155 m.)
MONETARY UNIT Mali franc
MAJOR LANGUAGES Bambara, Senufu, Fulani, Soninke, French
MAJOR RELIGIONS Islam, tribal religions

MAURITANIA

AREA 419,229 sq. mi. (1,085,803 sq. km.)
POPULATION 1,634,000
CAPITAL Nouakchott
LARGEST CITY Nouakchott
HIGHEST POINT 2,972 ft. (906 m.)
MONETARY UNIT ouguiya
MAJOR LANGUAGES Arabic, Wolof, Tukolor, French
MAJOR RELIGION Islam

MOROCCO

AREA 172,414 sq. mi. (446,550 sq. km.)
POPULATION 20,242,000
CAPITAL Rabat
LARGEST CITY Casablanca
HIGHEST POINT Jeb. Toubkal 13,665 ft. (4,165 m.)
MONETARY UNIT dirham
MAJOR LANGUAGES Arabic, Berber, French
MAJOR RELIGIONS Islam, Judaism, Christianity

NIGER

AREA 489,189 sq. mi. (1,267,000 sq. km.)
POPULATION 5,098,427
CAPITAL Niamey
LARGEST CITY Niamey
HIGHEST POINT Banguezane 6,234 ft. (1,900 m.)
MONETARY UNIT CFA franc
MAJOR LANGUAGES Hausa, Songhai, Fulani, French, Tamashek, Djerma
MAJOR RELIGIONS Islam, tribal religions

NIGERIA

AREA 357,000 sq. mi. (924,630 sq. km.)
POPULATION 82,643,000
CAPITAL Lagos
LARGEST CITY Lagos
HIGHEST POINT Dimlang 6,700 ft. (2,042 m.)
MONETARY UNIT naira
MAJOR LANGUAGES Hausa, Yoruba, Ibo, Ijaw, Fulani, Tiv, Kanuri, Ibibio, English, Edo
MAJOR RELIGIONS Islam, Christianity, tribal religions

SÃO TOMÉ E PRÍNCIPE

AREA 372 sq. mi. (963 sq. km.)
POPULATION 85,000
CAPITAL São Tomé
LARGEST CITY São Tomé
HIGHEST POINT Pico 6,640 ft. (2,024 m.)
MONETARY UNIT dobra
MAJOR LANGUAGES Bantu languages, Portuguese
MAJOR RELIGIONS Tribal religions, Roman Catholicism

SENEGAL

AREA 75,954 sq. mi. (196,720 sq. km.)
POPULATION 5,508,000
CAPITAL Dakar
LARGEST CITY Dakar
HIGHEST POINT Futa Jallon 1,640 ft. (500 m.)
MONETARY UNIT CFA franc
MAJOR LANGUAGES Wolof, Peul (Fulani), French, Mende, Mandingo, Dida
MAJOR RELIGIONS Islam, tribal religions, Roman Catholicism

SIERRA LEONE

AREA 27,925 sq. mi. (72,325 sq. km.)
POPULATION 3,470,000
CAPITAL Freetown
LARGEST CITY Freetown
HIGHEST POINT Loma Mts. 6,390 ft. (1,947 m.)
MONETARY UNIT leone
MAJOR LANGUAGES Mende, Temne, Vai, English, Krio (pidgin)
MAJOR RELIGIONS Tribal religions, Islam, Christianity

TOGO

AREA 21,622 sq. mi. (56,000 sq. km.)
POPULATION 2,472,000
CAPITAL Lomé
LARGEST CITY Lomé
HIGHEST POINT Agou 3,445 ft. (1,050 m.)
MONETARY UNIT CFA franc
MAJOR LANGUAGES Ewe, French, Twi, Hausa
MAJOR RELIGIONS Tribal religions, Roman Catholicism, Islam

TUNISIA

AREA 63,378 sq. mi. (164,149 sq. km.)
POPULATION 6,367,000
CAPITAL Tunis
LARGEST CITY Tunis
HIGHEST POINT Jeb. Chambi 5,066 ft. (1,544 m.)
MONETARY UNIT Tunisian dinar
MAJOR LANGUAGES Arabic, French
MAJOR RELIGION Islam

UPPER VOLTA

AREA 105,869 sq. mi. (274,200 sq. km.)
POPULATION 6,908,000
CAPITAL Ouagadougou
LARGEST CITY Ouagadougou
HIGHEST POINT 2,352 ft. (717 m.)
MONETARY UNIT CFA franc
MAJOR LANGUAGES Mossi, Lobi, French, Samo, Gourounsi
MAJOR RELIGIONS Islam, tribal religions, Roman Catholicism

WESTERN SAHARA

AREA 102,703 sq. mi. (266,000 sq. km.)
POPULATION 76,425
HIGHEST POINT 2,700 ft. (823 m.)
MAJOR LANGUAGE Arabic
MAJOR RELIGION Islam

Topography

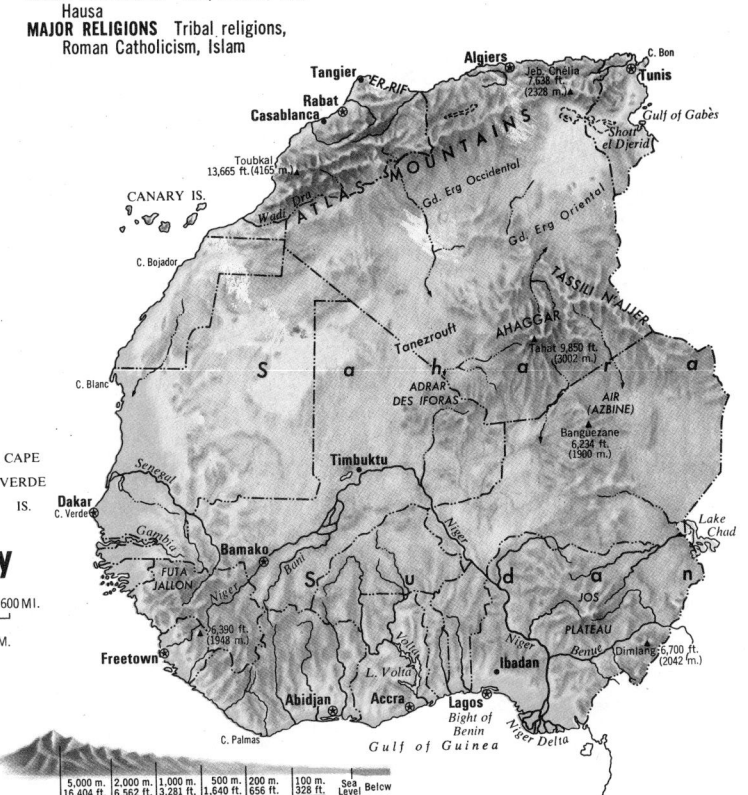

ALGERIA

CITIES and TOWNS

Abadla 12,200 D2
Adrar 22,800 D3
Aîn Beîda 26,976 F1
Aîn Sefra 22,400 D2
Aîn Temouchent 42,000 D1
Algiers (cap.) 1,365,400 E1
Amguid F3
Annaba 255,900 F1
Aoulef 17,200 E3
Arak E3
Batna 112,100 F1
Béchar 72,800 D2
Bejaîa 89,500 F1
Beni Abbès 5,000 D2
Beni Ounif 7,500 D2
Beni Saf 30,700 D1
Berga E3
Bidon 5 (Poste Maurice Cordier) E4
Biskra 90,500 F2
Blida 160,900 E1
Bône (Annaba) 255,900 F1
Bordj Bou Arreridj 65,000 E1
Bordj Fly Sainte Marie D3
Bordj Omar Driss 1,900 F3
Boufarik 50,000 E1
Bougie (Béjaîa) 89,500 F1
Bou Saâda 50,000 E1
Brezina 10,000 E2
Charouine D3
Chenachane D3
Cherchell 36,800 E1
Constantine 335,100 F1
Deldoul E3
Dellys 29,700 E1
Djanet 5,300 F4
Djelfa 51,000 E2
Djemaa 34,600 F2
Edjeleh F3
El Abiod Sidi Cheikh 15,300 E2
El Asnam 106,100 E1
El Bayadh 38,500 E2
El Djezair (Algiers) (cap.) 1,365,400 E1
El Goléa 24,400 E2
El Oued 72,100 F2
Fort Lallemand F2
Fort MacMahon E3
Fort Miribel E3
Fort Tarat F3
Ghardaîa 70,500 E2
Ghazaouet 25,900 D2
Guelma 60,100 F1
Guemar F2
Guerara 22,300 E2
Guerzim D3
Hassi Messaoud F2
Hassi R'Mel E2
Idelès F4
Igli 3,400 D2
Illizi 4,600 F3
In Amenas 4,200 F3
In Amguel E4
In Eker F4
In Guezzam F5
In Rhar E3
In Salah 18,800 E3
Jijel 49,800 F1
Kenadsa 7,600 D2
Kerzaz 2,900 D3
Khemis Miliana 57,800 E1
Ksar el Boukhari 41,200 E1
Laghouat 59,200 E2
Mascara 62,300 D1
Mecheria 22,600 D2
Médéa 72,300 E1
Metlili Chaamba 21,300 E2
Miliana 36,400 E1
Mohammadia 53,700 D1
Mostaganem 101,600 D1
M'Sila 49,100 E1
Oran 491,900 D1
Orléansville (El Asnam) 106,100 E1
Ouallene E4
Ouargla 77,400 F2
Ouled Djellal 22,700 F2
Philippeville (Skikda) 107,700 F1
Poste Maurice Cortier E4
Poste Weygand D4
Reggane 11,300 D3
Relizane 60,000 E1
Saîda 62,100 E2
Sbaa D3
Sétif 144,200 F1
Sidi Bel-Abbes 116,000 D1
Silet E4
Skikda 107,700 F1
Souk Ahras 60,200 F1
Tabelbala 3,100 D3
Taghit 3,500 D2
Tamanrasset 23,200 F4
Tamentit D3
Taourirt E3
Tébessa 67,200 F1
Temacine F2
Ténès 30,100 E1
Tiaret 62,900 E1
Tiguentourine F3
Timgad 9,800 F1
Timimoun 20,500 E3
Tindouf 6,500 C3
Tinjoub C3
Tin-Zaouatene E5
Tizi Ouzou 73,100 E1
Tlemcen 109,400 D2
Touggourt 75,600 F2
Zaouiet Kounta 13,800 D3

OTHER FEATURES

Adrar des Iforas (plat.) E5
Ahaggar (range) F4
Anaî (well) G4
Aouinet Bel Egrâ (well) C3
Atlas (mts.) E2
Aurès (lag.) F1
Azzel Mati, Sebkha (lake) E3
Bougaroun (cape) F1
Chech, Erg (des.) D3
Chelia (mt.) F1
Chelif (riv.) E1
Chergui, Chott Ech (salt lake) E2
Gourara (oasis) E3
Grand Erg Occidental (des.) E2
Grand Erg Oriental (des.) F2
Guir Hamada (des.) D2
High Plateaus (ranges) D2
Iguidi, Erg (des.) C3
In Ezzane (well) G4
Irharhar, Wadi (dry riv.) F3
Issaouane Erg (des.) F3
Kabylia (reg.) E1
Mediterranean (sea) E1
Medjerda (riv.) F1
Melrhir, Chott (salt lake) F2
Mouydir (mts.) E3
Mya, Wadi (dry riv.) E2
M'zab (oasis) E2
Raoui, Erg er (des.) D3
Rhir, Wadi (dry riv.) F2
Sahara (des.) E4
Saharan Atlas (ranges) E2
Saoura, Wadi (dry riv.) D3
Souf (oasis) F2
Tademaît, Plateau du (plat.) E3
Tafassasset, Wadi (dry riv.) F4
Tahat (mt.) F4
Tamanrasset, Wadi (dry riv.) E4
Tanezrouft (des.) E4
Tassili N'Ahagger (plat.) E4
Tassili N'Ajjer (plat.) F3
Tidikelt (oasis) E3
Timmissao (well) E4
Tindouf, Sebkha de (salt lake) C3
Tinrhert, Hamada de (des.) F3
Tni Haîa (well) D4
Touat (oasis) E3
Touila (well) C3

BENIN

CITIES and TOWNS

Abomey 38,000 E7
Cotonou 178,000 E7
Djougou E7
Grand-Popo E7
Kandi E6
Lokossa 6,000 E7
Malanville E6
Natitingou 49,000 E6
Nikki E7
Ouidah E7
Parakou 21,000 E7
Porto-Novo (cap.) 104,000 E7
Savalou E7
Savé E7

OTHER FEATURES

Atakora (mts.) E6
Benin (bight) E8
Guinea (gulf) E8
Mono (riv.) E7
Niger (riv.) E6
Ouémé (riv.) E7
Slave Coast (reg.) E7
Sudan (reg.) E6

CAPE VERDE

CITIES and TOWNS

Mindelo 28,797 A7
Praia (cap.) 21,494 B8
Ribeira Grande 1,892 B7
Sal Rei 1,296 B8
Santa Maria 956 B8

OTHER FEATURES

Boa Vista (isl.) B8
Brava (isl.) B8
Fogo (isl.) B8
Maio (isl.) B8
Sal (isl.) B7
Santa Luzia (isl.) B8
Santo Antão (isl.) A7
São Nicolau (isl.) B8
São Tiago (isl.) B8
São Vicente (isl.) B7

GAMBIA

CITIES and TOWNS

Basse Santa Su 2,899 B6
Bathurst (cap.) 39,476 A6
Brikama 9,483 A6
Georgetown 2,510 A6

OTHER FEATURES

Gambia (riv.) B6

GHANA

CITIES and TOWNS

Accra (cap.) 564,194 D7
Accra* 738,498 D7
Ada 4,285 E7
Akuse 3,791 E7
Attebubu 6,630 D7
Awaso 5,449 D7
Axim 8,107 D8
Bawku 20,567 D6
Bekwai 11,287 D7
Berekum 14,296 D7
Bole 4,772 D7
Bolgatanga 18,896 D6
Cape Coast 51,653 D7
Daboya 1,872 D7
Damongo 7,760 D7
Dunkwa 15,437 D7
Elmina 11,401 D8
Enchi 4,382 D7
Gambaga 3,730 D6
Gyasikan 6,403 D7
Half Assini 5,429 D8
Ho 24,199 E7
Keta 14,446 E7
Kete Krachi 5,097 E7
Kintampo 7,149 D7
Koforidua 46,235 D7
Kpandu 12,842 D7
Kumasi 260,286 D7
Kumasi* 345,117 D7
Lawra 2,709 D6
Mampong 13,895 D7
Mpraeso 5,908 D7
Navrongo D6
Nsawam 25,518 D7
Nsuta 3,854 D7
Obuasi 31,005 D7
Oda 20,957 D7
Prestea 15,143 D7
Salaga 6,413 D7
Sekondi 33,713 D8
Sekondi-Takoradi* 160,868 D8
Sunyani 23,780 D7
Takoradi 58,161 D8
Tamale 83,653 D7
Tarkwa 14,702 D7
Tema 60,767 E7
Tumu 4,366 D6
Wa 21,374 D6
Wenchi 13,836 D7
Wiawso 5,558 D7
Winneba 30,778 D7
Yapei 1,203 D7
Yendi 22,072 D7

OTHER FEATURES

Ashanti (reg.) D7
Benin (bight) E8
Black Volta (riv.) D6
Gold Coast (reg.) D8
Guinea (gulf) E8
Oti (riv.) E7
Red Volta (riv.) D6
Saint Paul (cape) E7
Three Points (cape) D8
Volta (lake) D7
Volta (riv.) E7
White Volta (riv.) D6

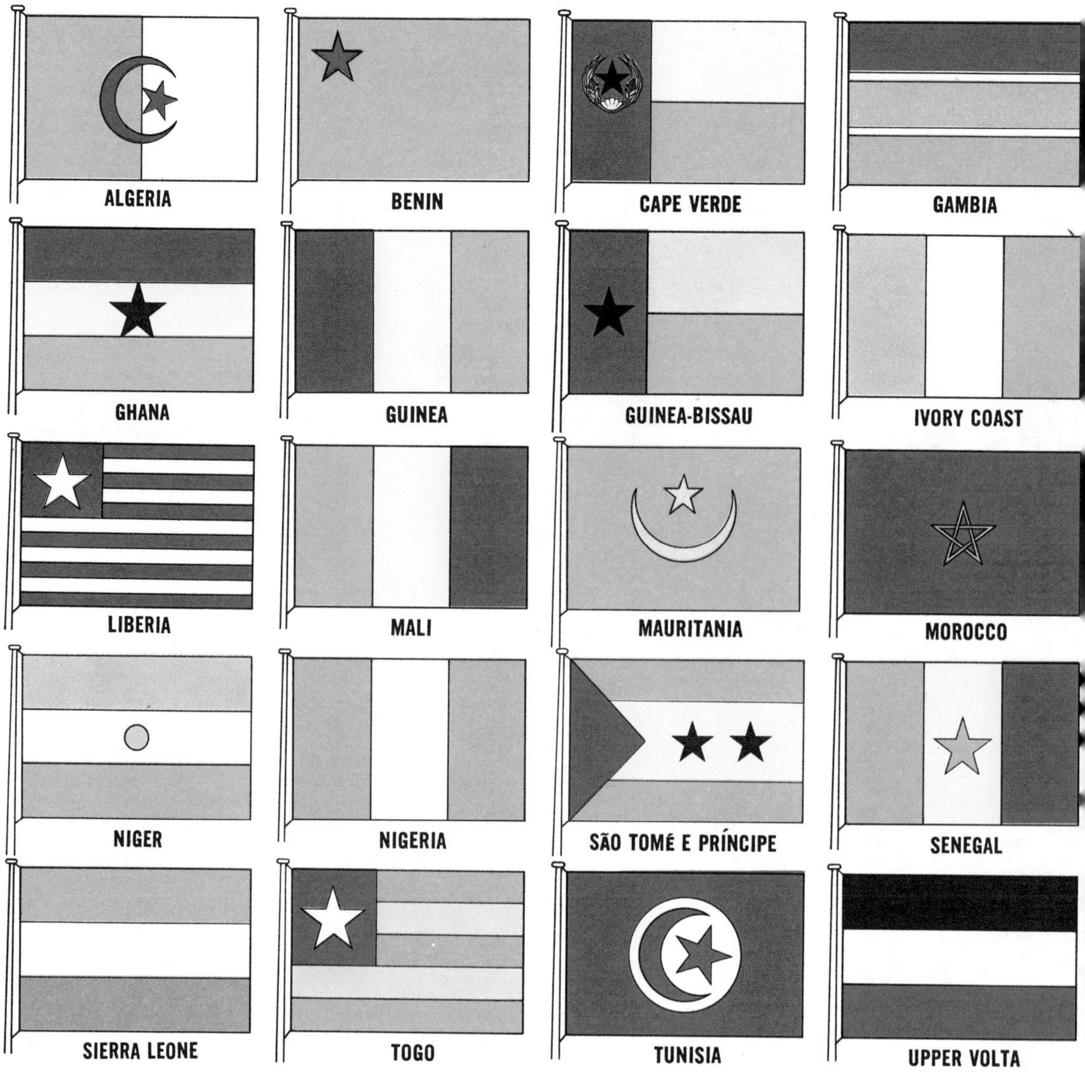

GUINEA

CITIES and TOWNS

Beyla C7
Boffa B6
Boké B6
Conakry (cap.)* 525,671 B7
Dabola B6
Dalaba B6
Dinguiraye B6
Dubréka B7
Faranah B6
Forécariah B7
Fria B6
Gaoual B6
Guéckédou B7
Kamsar B6
Kankan 85,310 C6
Kérouané C7
Kindia 79,861 B6
Kissidougou B7
Koundara 6,000 B6
Kouroussa C6
Labé 79,670 B6
Macenta C7
Mali B6
Mamou B6
N'Zérékoré 23,000 C7
Sangaredyi B6
Siguiri C6
Télimélé 12,000 B6
Tougué B6
Victoria B6

OTHER FEATURES

Bafing (riv.) B6
Bakoy (riv.) B6
Futa Jallon (lag.) B6
Los (isls.) B7
Milo (riv.) C7
Moa (riv.) B7
Niger (riv.) C6
Nimba (lag.) C7
Verga (cape) B6

GUINEA-BISSAU

CITIES and TOWNS

Bissau (cap.) 109,486 A6
Bolama○ 9,133 A6
Bubao○ 6,706 B6
Bubaque○ 8,441 A6
Cacheu○ 15,194 A6

OTHER FEATURES

Bijagós (isls.) A6

IVORY COAST

CITIES and TOWNS

Abengourou 31,239 D7
Abidjan (cap.) 685,828 D7
Aboisso 14,272 D7
Agboville 27,192 D7
Bingerville 18,218 D7
Bondoukou 19,111 D7
Bouaflé 15,917 C7
Bouaké 173,248 D7
Bouna 5,787 D7
Boundiali 9,869 C7
Dabakala 3,272 D7
Dabou 23,870 D7
Daloa 60,958 C7
Danané 19,872 C7
Dimbokro 30,986 D7
Divo 37,896 C7
Ferkessédougou 25,307 D7
Fresco 1,865 C7
Gagnoa 42,362 C7
Grand-Bassam 25,808 D7
Grand-Lahou 4,070 C8
Guiglo 10,441 C7
Issia 11,143 C7
Katiola 21,559 C7
Kong 2,551 D7
Korhogo 47,657 C7
Man 50,315 C7
Mankono 6,570 C7
Odienné 13,864 C7
Port-Bouet 72,616 D7
San Pedro 27,616 C8
Sassandra 9,404 C8
Séguéla 12,587 C7
Sinfra 16,399 C7
Tabou 7,255 C8
Touba 5,256 C7
Toumodi 12,983 D7

OTHER FEATURES

Aby (lag.) D8
Bagoé (riv.) C6
Bandama (riv.) C7
Baoulé (riv.) C6
Black Volta (riv.) D6
Cavally (riv.) C7
Comoé (riv.) D7
Ebrié (lag.) D8
Guinea (gulf) E8
Ivory Coast (reg.) C8
Kossou, Lac de (lake) C7
Nimba (lag.) C7
Sassandra (riv.) C7

LIBERIA

CITIES and TOWNS

Buchanan 23,999 B7
Gbarnga 6,896 C7
Grand Cess C8
Greenville 8,462 C8
Harbel 11,445 B7
Harper 10,627 C8
Kolahun C7
Marshall B7
Monrovia (cap.) 166,507 B7
Plahn C7
River Cess 2,041 C7
Robertsport 2,562 B7
Sasstown C8
Tapeta 3,927 C7
Tchien 6,094 C7
Tubmanburg 14,089 B7

OTHER FEATURES

Bong (range) B7
Cavalla (riv.) C7
Cestos (riv.) C7
Grain Coast (reg.) B8
Kru Coast (reg.) C8
Mano (riv.) B7
Mount (cape) B7
Nimba (lag.) C7
Palmas (cape) C8
Roberts Field Int'l Airport C7

MALI

CITIES and TOWNS

Anéfis E5
Ansongo 3,485 E5
Araouane D5
Bafoulabé 2,163 B6
Bamako (cap.) 404,022 C6
Bamba D5
Banamba 6,776 C6
Bandiagara 8,920 D6
Bankass 3,229 D6
Bou Djebeha D5
Bougouni 17,246 C6
Bourem 4,538 E5
Dioila 4,953 C6
Dire 8,941 D5
Djenné 10,251 D6
Douentza 6,746 D6
Gao 30,714 E5
Goundam 10,262 D5
Gourma-Rharous 4,671 D5
Hombori D5
Kadiolo 3,991 C6
Kangaba 3,184 C6
Kati 24,991 C6
Kayes 44,736 B6
Ké-Macina 5,426 C6
Kéniéba 4,510 B6
Kerchoual E5
Kidal 3,308 E5
Kita 17,538 C6
Kolokani 8,923 C6
Kolondiéba 5,882 C6
Koulikoro 16,376 C6
Kourouba B6
Koutiala 27,497 C6
Mabrouk D5
Ménaka 3,693 E5
Mopti 53,885 D6
Nampala C5
Nara 6,091 C5
Niafunké 6,399 D5
Niono 12,290 C6
Nioro 11,617 C5
San 22,962 D6
Satadougou B6
Ségou 64,890 C6
Sikasso 47,030 C6
Sokolo C6
Taoudenni D4
Ténenkou 4,708 C6
Tessalit E4
Timbuktu (Tombouctou) 20,483 D5
Toukoto C6
Yanfolila 3,809 C6
Yelimané 1,481 B5
Yorosso 2,390 C6

OTHER FEATURES

Achourat (well) D4
Adrar des Iforas (plat.) E5
Asselar (well) D5
Azaouad (reg.) D5
Azaouak (dry riv.) E5
Bafing (riv.) B6
Bagoé (riv.) C6
Bakoy (riv.) B6
Bani (riv.) C6
Baoulé (dry riv.) C6
Baoulé (riv.) C6
Bir Ounane (well) D4
Chech, Erg (des.) D4
Debo (lake) D5
El Mraiti (well) D5
Faguibine (lake) D5
Falémé (riv.) B6
Haricha Hamada (des.) D4
Hombori (mts.) D5
In Dagouber (well) D4
Macina (depr.) D6
Niger (riv.) D5
Oum el Asel (well) D4
Sahara (des.) D4
Sekkane, Erg (des.) D4
Senegal (riv.) B5
Sudan (reg.) D6
Tadjnout Hagguerete (well) D4
Terhazza (ruins) C4
Tilemsi (valley) E5
Toufourine (well) C4

MAURITANIA

CITIES and TOWNS

Aîoun el Atrous C5
Akjoujt 8,044 B5
Akreîjit C5
Aleg 6,415 B5
Atar 16,326 B4
Bassikounou C5
Bir Mogreîn B3
Boutilimit 7,261 B5
Bogué 8,056 B5
Chinguetti B4
Fderik (Fort-Gouraud) 2,160 B4
Kaédi 20,848 B5
Kankossa B5
Kiffa 10,629 B5
Maghama B5
M'Bout B5
Méderdra A5
Néma 8,232 C5
Nouakchott (cap.) 134,986 A5
Nouadhibou 21,961 A4
Ouadane B4
Oualata C5
Oujaf C5
Oujeft B4
Rosso 16,466 A5
Sélibaby 5,994 B5
Tamchakett B5
Tamsagout C4
Tazadit B4
Tichitt C5
Tidjikja 7,870 B5
Timbédra 5,317 C5
Zouîrât 17,474 B4

OTHER FEATURES

Adafer (reg.) B5
Adrar (reg.) B4
Affolé (reg.) B5
Agueraktem (well) C4
Aîn ben Tili (well) C3
Arguin (bay) A4
Assaba (reg.) B5
Atoui, Wadi (dry riv.) B4
Ben Guerdane (well) B3
Bir el Khzaim (well) C4
Blanc (cape) A4
Brakna (reg.) B5
Chegga (well) C3
Djouf, El (des.) C4
El Mrayer (well) C4
El Mreîti (well) C4
Gorgol (reg.) B5
Hodh (reg.) C5
Iguidi, Erg (des.) C3
Inchiri (reg.) A5
Koumbi Saleh (ruins) C5
Lévrier (bay) A4
Makteîr (des.) B4
Meraia (reg.) C5
Mirik (Timiris) (cape) A5
Ouarane (reg.) B4
Sahara (des.) C4
Senegal (riv.) B5
Tagant (reg.) B5
Tidra (isl.) A5
Timiris (cape) A5
Touila (well) C3
Trarza (reg.) A5

MOROCCO

CITIES and TOWNS

Agadir 61,192 C2
Al Hoceima 18,686 D1
Asilah 14,074 C1
Azemmour 17,182 C2
Azrou 20,756 C2
Beni Mellal 53,826 C2
Berguent 3,356 D2
Bou Arfa D2
Bou Izakarn 2,342 C3
Boujad 18,838 C2
Casablanca 1,506,373 C2
Chechaouene 15,362 D1
Dar-el-Beida (Casablanca) 1,506,373 C2
El Jadida 55,501 C2
El Kelaa des Srarhna 17,163 C2
Erfoud 5,400 D2
Essaouira 30,061 B2
Fédala (Mohammedia) 70,392 C2
Fès (Fez) 325,327 D2
Figuig 13,660 D2
Goulmima 4,056 C2
Inezgane 11,495 C2
Ifni 13,650 B3

Agriculture, Industry and Resources

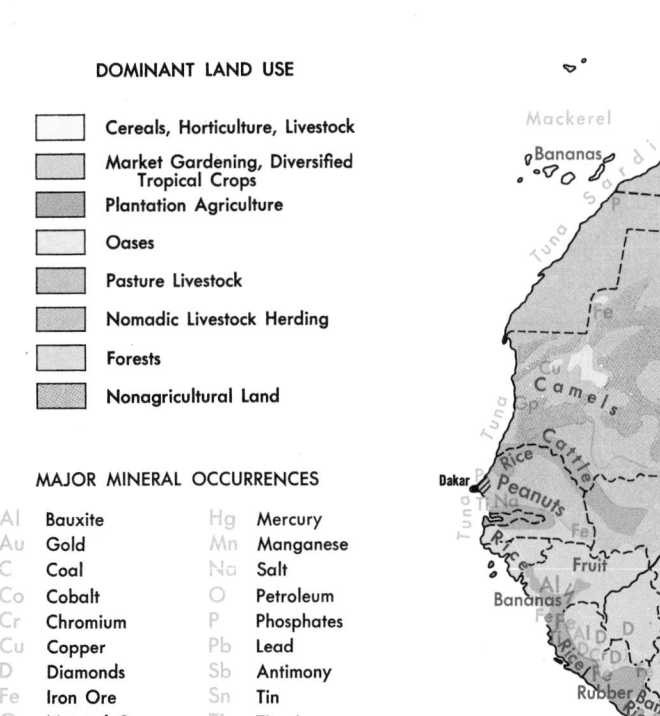

DOMINANT LAND USE

- Cereals, Horticulture, Livestock
- Market Gardening, Diversified Tropical Crops
- Plantation Agriculture
- Oases
- Pasture Livestock
- Nomadic Livestock Herding
- Forests
- Nonagricultural Land

MAJOR MINERAL OCCURRENCES

Al	Bauxite	Hg	Mercury
Au	Gold	Mn	Manganese
C	Coal	Na	Salt
Co	Cobalt	O	Petroleum
Cr	Chromium	P	Phosphates
Cu	Copper	Pb	Lead
D	Diamonds	Sb	Antimony
Fe	Iron Ore	Sn	Tin
G	Natural Gas	Ti	Titanium
Gn	Granite	U	Uranium
Gp	Gypsum	Zn	Zinc

⚡ Water Power

▨ Major Industrial Areas

LIBYA   **EGYPT**   **CHAD**   **SUDAN**   **ETHIOPIA**

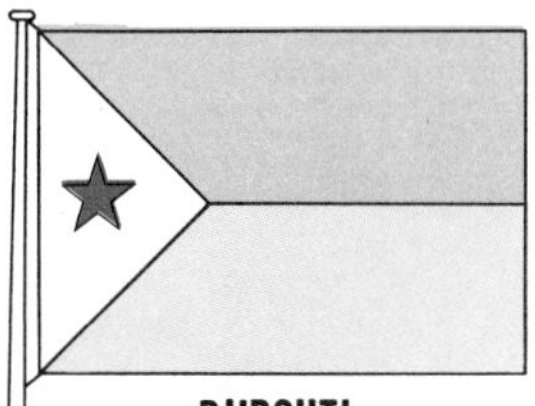

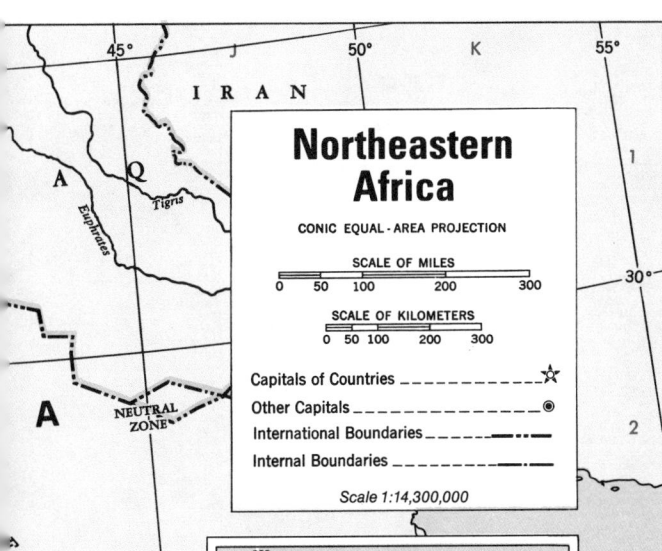

LIBYA

AREA 679,358 sq. mi. (1,759,537 sq. km.)
POPULATION 2,856,000
CAPITAL Tripoli
LARGEST CITY Tripoli
HIGHEST POINT Bette Pk. 7,500 ft. (2,286 m.)
MONETARY UNIT Libyan dinar
MAJOR LANGUAGES Arabic, Berber
MAJOR RELIGION Islam

DJIBOUTI

EGYPT

AREA 386,659 sq. mi. (1,001,447 sq. km.)
POPULATION 41,572,000
CAPITAL Cairo
LARGEST CITY Cairo
HIGHEST POINT Jeb. Katherina 8,651 ft. (2,637 m.)
MONETARY UNIT Egyptian pound
MAJOR LANGUAGE Arabic
MAJOR RELIGIONS Islam, Coptic Christianity

CHAD

AREA 495,752 sq. mi. (1,283,998 sq. km.)
POPULATION 4,309,000
CAPITAL N'Djamena
LARGEST CITY N'Djamena
HIGHEST POINT Emi Koussi 11,204 ft. (3,415 m.)
MONETARY UNIT CFA franc
MAJOR LANGUAGES Arabic,-Bagirmi, French, Sara, Massa, Moudang
MAJOR RELIGIONS Islam, tribal religions

SUDAN

AREA 967,494 sq. mi. (2,505,809 sq. km.)
POPULATION 18,691,000
CAPITAL Khartoum
LARGEST CITY Khartoum
HIGHEST POINT Jeb. Marra 10,073 ft. (3,070 m.)
MONETARY UNIT Sudanese pound
MAJOR LANGUAGES Arabic, Dinka, Nubian, Beja, Nuer
MAJOR RELIGIONS Islam, tribal religions

ETHIOPIA

AREA 471,776 sq. mi. (1,221,900 sq. km.)
POPULATION 31,065,000
CAPITAL Addis Ababa
LARGEST CITY Addis Ababa
HIGHEST POINT Ras Dashan 15,157 ft. (4,620 m.)
MONETARY UNIT birr
MAJOR LANGUAGES Amharic, Gallinya, Tigrinya, Somali, Sidamo, Arabic, Ge'ez
MAJOR RELIGIONS Coptic Christianity, Islam

DJIBOUTI

AREA 8,880 sq. mi. (23,000 sq. km.)
POPULATION 386,000
CAPITAL Djibouti
LARGEST CITY Djibouti
HIGHEST POINT Moussa Ali 6,768 ft. (2,063 m.)
MONETARY UNIT Djibouti franc
MAJOR LANGUAGES Arabic, Somali, Afar, French
MAJOR RELIGIONS Islam, Roman Catholicism

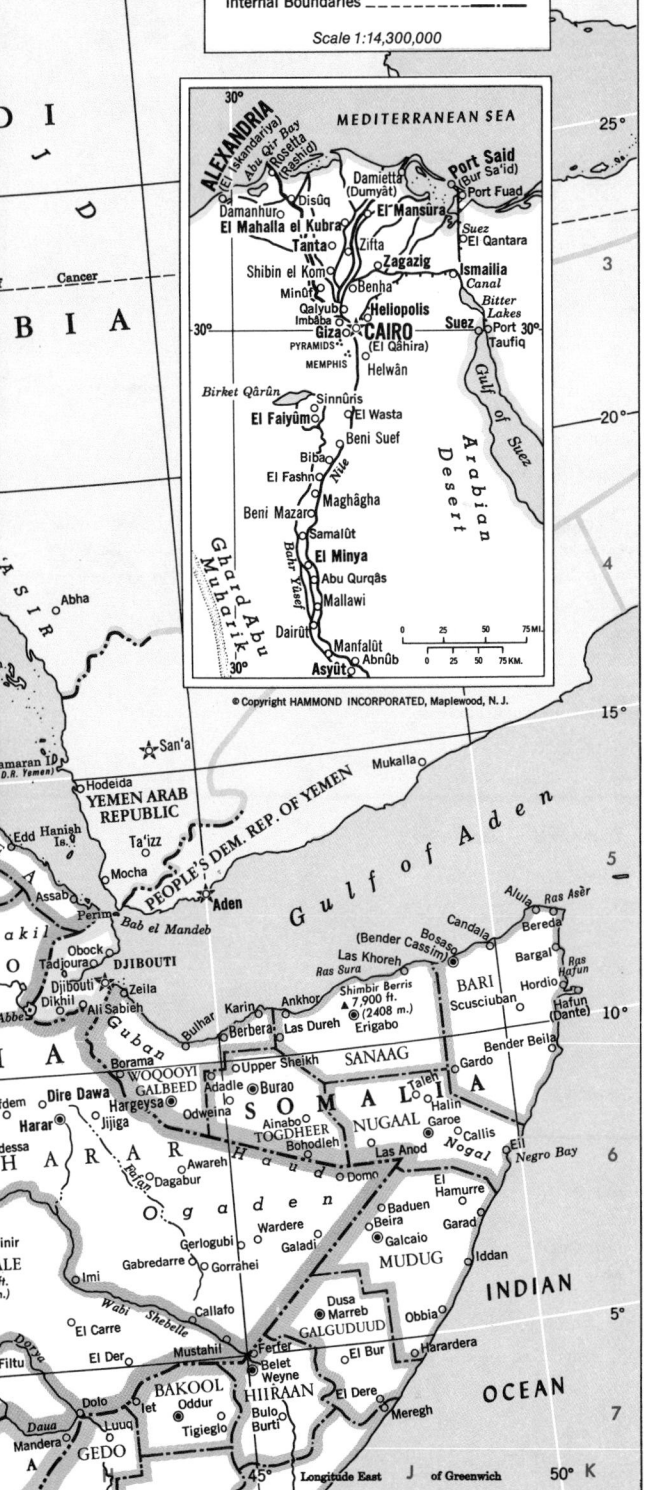

Northeastern Africa

CONIC EQUAL - AREA PROJECTION

SCALE OF MILES
0 50 100 200 300

SCALE OF KILOMETERS
0 50 100 200 300

Capitals of Countries _____ ☆
Other Capitals _____ ◉
International Boundaries _____
Internal Boundaries _____

Scale 1:14,300,000

© Copyright HAMMOND INCORPORATED, Maplewood, N.J.

CHAD

CITIES and TOWNS

Abéché 28,100	D5
Abou Dela	D5
Adré	D5
Ain-Galakka	C4
Am-Dam	D5
Am-Timan 4,200	D5
Arada	D5
Ati 7,500	C5
Baibokoum 5,500	C6
Bardai	C3
Biltine 3,900	D5
Bitkine 5,000	C5
Bokoro 6,500	C5
Bol 2,500	B5
Bongor 14,300	C6
Bousso 4,500	C6
Doba 13,300	C6
Fada	D4
Faya-Largeau 6,800	C4
Fianga 10,000	C6
Goré	C6
Gouro	C4
Goz Belda	D5
Guéréda	D5
Ham	C5

Haraz	C5
Iriba	D4
Kélo 16,800	C6
Koro Toro	C4
Koumra 17,000	C6
Kouno	C6
Kyabé 5,000	C6
Lal 10,400	C6
Léré	B6
Madadi	D4
Mangueigne	C5
Mao 4,900	C5
Massakory	C5
Massénya	C5
Melfi	C5
Mogororo	C5
Moïssala 5,100	C6
Mongo 8,300	C5
Moundou 39,600	C6
Moussoro 7,700	C5
N'Djamena (cap.) 179,000	C6
Nokou	B5
Oum Chalouba	D4
Oum Hadjer 5,600	D5
Ounianga-Kébir	C3
Pala 13,200	B6
Rig Rig	B5
Sarh 43,700	C6
Wour	C3
Yarda	C4

Yebbi-Bou	C3
Ziguei	C5
Zouar	C3

OTHER FEATURES

Azoum, Bahr	D5
Baguirmi (reg.)	C5
Bahr el Ghazal (dry riv.)	C5
Batha (riv.)	C5
Bodélé (depr.)	C4
Borku 72	C4
Chad (lake)	B5
Domar (dry riv.)	C4
Emi Koussi (mt.)	C4
Ennedi (plat.)	D4
Fittri (lake)	C5
Haouach, Wadi (dry riv.)	C4
Jef Jel es Seghin (plat.)	D3
Kanem (reg.)	C5
Logone (riv.)	C5
Maro (dry riv.)	C5
Mbéré (riv.)	C6
Mourdi (depr.)	D4
Ouham (riv.)	C6
Pendé (riv.)	C6
Sahara (des.)	C3
Salamat, Bahr (riv.)	C6
Sara (riv.)	C5
Shari (riv.)	C5

Sudan (reg.)	C5
Tibesti (mts.)	C3
Wadai (reg.)	D5

DJIBOUTI

CITIES and TOWNS

Ali Sabieh	H5
Dikhil	H5
Djibouti (cap.) 96,000	H5
Obock	H5
Tadjoura	H5

OTHER FEATURES

Abbe (lake)	H5
Aden (gulf)	J5
Bab el Mandeb (str.)	H5

EGYPT

CITIES and TOWNS

Abnûb 39,343	J4
Abu Qurqâs	J4
Akhmim 53,234	F2
Alexandria 2,318,655	J2

(continued on following page)

EGYPT (inset map)

ALEXANDRIA (El Iskandarîya)
MEDITERRANEAN SEA
Abu Qîr Bay
Rosetta (Rashîd)
Damanhur
Disûq
Damietta (Dumyât)
Port Said (Bûr Sa'îd)
Port Fuad
El Mansûra
El Mahalla el Kubra
Tanta
Zifta
Zagazig
Ismailia
Suez (El Qantara)
Shibin el Kom
Minûf
Benha
Heliopolis
Suez Canal
Qalyûb
Imbâba
Giza
CAIRO (El Qâhira)
PYRAMIDS
MEMPHIS
Helwân
Bitter Lakes
Port Taufiq
Suez
Gulf of Suez
Birket Qârûn
Sinnûris
El Faiyûm
El Wasta
Beni Suef
Biba
El Fashn
Maghâgha
Samalût
El Minya
Abu Qurqâs
Mallawi
Dairût
Manfalût
Abnûb
Asyût
Arabian Desert
Ghard Abu Muharik
Nile
Bahr Yûsef

Main map labels

IRAN, Tigris, Euphrates, NEUTRAL ZONE, of Cancer, ASIR, Abha

San'a, Kamaran I. (P.D.R. Yemen), Hodeida, YEMEN ARAB REPUBLIC, Ta'izz, Mukalla

Edd, Hanish Is., Mocha, Assab, Perim, Bab el Mandeb, PEOPLE'S DEM. REP. OF YEMEN, Aden, Gulf of Aden, Alula, Ras Asèr, Candala, Bereda, Bargal, (Bender Cassim), Bosaso, Ras Hafun, Las Khoreh, Ras Sura, Hordio, Hafun (Dante), Shimbir Berris 7,900 ft. (2,408 m.), BARI, Scusciuban, Bender Beila

Obock, DJIBOUTI, Zeila, Dikhil, Ali Sabieh, Ankhor, Karin, Bulhar, Berbera, Las Dureh, Erigabo, Garad, Gardo, Callis, Eil, Negro Bay

Borama, WOQOOYI GALBEED, Hargeysa, Adadle, Burao, Upper Sheikh, SANAAG, Talch, Halin, SOMALIA, Garoe, NUGAAL

Afdem, Dire Dawa, Jijiga, Odweina, TOGDHEER, Bohodleh, Las Anod, Nogal

Harar, HARAR, edessa, Dagabur, Awareh, El Hamurre, Domo, El Hamurre

Ginir, Imi, Wardere, Galadi, Gerlogubi, Garad, Gabredarre, Gorrahei, Iddan, MUDUG, Dusa, Marreb, Obbia, GALGUDUUD

Filtu, El Carre, El Der, Callafo, Wabi Shebelle, Mustahil, Ferfer, El Bur, Hararadere

Daua, Mandera, Dolo, let, Luuq, Oddur, Tigieglo, BAKOOL, Belet Weyne, HIIRAAN, Bulo Burti, El Dere, Mereghh, OCEAN, INDIAN, GEDO

O'gaden, nakil, Guban, SOMALIA

Topography

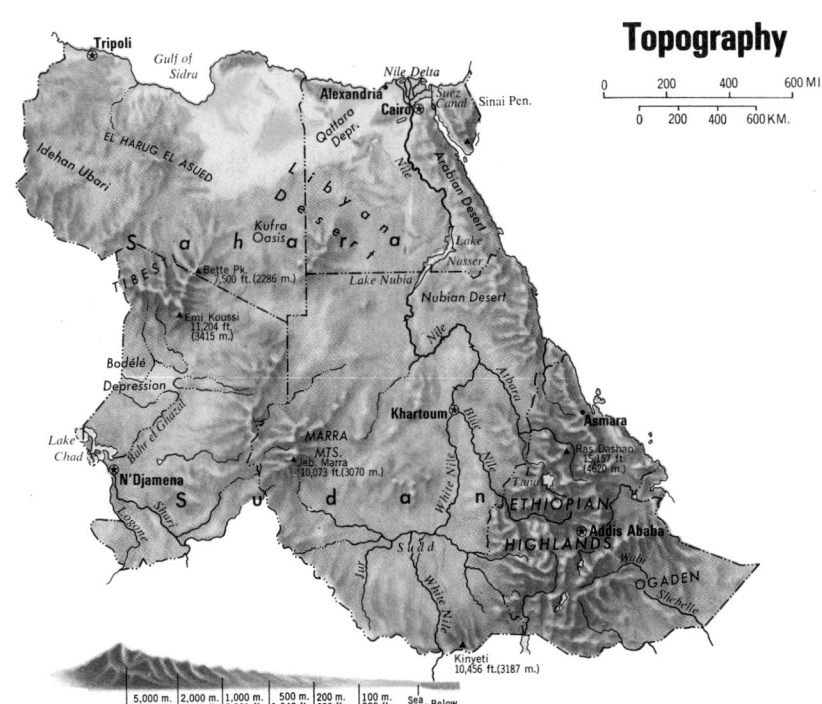

Topography

0 200 400 600 MI.
0 200 400 600 KM.

Tripoli, Gulf of Sidra, Nile Delta, Alexandria, Cairo, Suez Canal, Sinai Pen., Qattara Depr., Libyan Desert, Arabian Desert, Nile, Lake Nasser, Lake Nubia, Nubian Desert, Idehan Ubari, EL HARUG EL ASUED, Kufra Oasis, Sahara, TIBESTI, Bette Pk. 7,500 ft. (2286 m.), Emi Koussi 11,204 ft. (3415 m.), Bodélé Depression, Lake Chad, N'Djamena, Bahr el Ghazal, Shari, Logone, Sudan, Sudd, White Nile, Blue Nile, Atbara, Khartoum, MARRA MTS. Jeb. Marra 10,073 ft. (3070 m.), Asmara, ETHIOPIAN HIGHLANDS, Addis Ababa, Wabi, OGADEN, Shebelle, Kinyeti 10,456 ft. (3187 m.)

| 5,000 m. 16,404 ft. | 2,000 m. 6,562 ft. | 1,000 m. 3,281 ft. | 500 m. 1,640 ft. | 200 m. 656 ft. | 100 m. 328 ft. | Sea Level | Below |

112 Northeastern Africa

(continued)

Aswân 144,377 .... F3
Asyût 213,983 .... J4
Bâris F3
Benha 88,992 .... J3
Beni Mazar 39,373 .... J4
Beni Suef 118,148 .... J3
Biba 33,074 .... J4
Bûlaq F2
Bur Sai'd (Port Said) 262,620 .... K2
Cairo (cap.) 5,084,463 .... J3
Dahab F2
Dairût 31,624 .... J4
Damanhur 188,927 .... J3
Damietta 93,546 .... J3
Disûq 58,650 .... J3
Dumyât (Damietta) 93,546 .... J3
Dûsh F3
El A'lamein E1
El A'rish F1
El Bawiti E2
El Faiyûm 167,081 .... J3
El Fashn 33,506 .... J4
El Hammam 6,588 .... E1
El Iskandariya (Alexandria) 2,318,655 .... J2
El Karnak F2
El Khârga 26,375 .... F2
El Mahalla el Kubra 292,853 .... J3
El Mansûra 257,866 .... K3
El Minya 146,423 .... J4
El Qâhira (Cairo) (cap.) 5,084,463 .... J3
El Qantara 919 .... K3
El Qasr E2
El Quseir 12,297 .... F2
El Tûr F2
El Wasta 17,659 .... J3
Gemsa F2
Girga 51,110 .... F2
Giza 1,246,713 .... J3
Heliopolis J3
Helwân J3
Hurghada F2
Idfu 34,858 .... F3
Imbâba J3
Ismailia 145,978 .... K3
Isna 34,186 .... F2
Karnak (El Karnak) F2
Kôm Ombo 44,531 .... F3
Luxor 92,748 .... F2
Maghâgha 40,802 .... J4
Mallawi 74,256 .... J4
Manfalût 41,126 .... J4
Mersâ Matrûh 27,857 .... E1
Minûf 55,131 .... J3
Mût 8,032 .... E2
Nuweiba F2
Port Fuad K3
Port Safâga F2
Port Said 262,620 .... K2
Port Taufiq K3
Qalyub 62,739 .... J3
Qasr Farâfra E2
Qena 94,013 .... F2
Ras Ghârib F2
Rashid (Rosetta) 42,962 .... J2
Rudeis F2
Salûm 4,161 .... E1
Samalût 48,146 .... J4
Shibin el Kom 102,844 .... J3
Sidi Barrani 1,574 .... E1
Sinnûris 42,022 .... J3
Siwa 4,999 .... E2
Sohâg 101,758 .... F2
Suez 194,001 .... K3
Tahta 45,242 .... F2
Tanta 284,636 .... J3
Zagazig 202,637 .... K3
Zifta 50,410 .... J3

OTHER FEATURES

Abu Qir (bay) J2
Abydos (ruins) F2
A'llaqi, Wadi (dry riv.) F3
A'qaba (gulf) G2
Arabian (des.) F2
Aswân (dam) F3
Aswân High (dam) F3
Bahariya (oasis) E2
Bahr Yusef (stream) J4
Bânâs, Ras (cape) G3
Berenice (ruins) F3
Birket Qârûn (lake) J3
Bir Taba (well) F2
Bitter (lkes) K3
Dakhla (oasis) E2
Eastern (Arabian) (des.) F2
El Sollum (gulf) E1
Farâfra (oasis) E2
Foul (bay) G3
Ghard Abu Muharik (des.) J4
Gilf Kebir (plat.) E3
Great Sand Sea (des.) D2
Katherina, Jebel (mt.) F2
Khârga (oasis) F2
Libyan (des.) E2
Libyan (plat.) E1
Mediterranean (sea) E1
Memphis (ruins) J3
Muhammad, Ras (cape) F2
Nasser (lake) F3
Nile (riv.) F2
Pyramids (ruins) J3
Qattara (depr.) E2
Red (sea) G3
Sahara (des.) E3
Sinai (mt.) F2
Sinai (pen.) F2
Siwa (oasis) E2
Suez (canal) K3
Suez (gulf) F2
Tiran (str.) F2
U'weinat, Jebel (mt.) E3

ETHIOPIA

PROVINCES

Arusi 852,900 .... G6
Bale 707,800 .... H6
Begemdir 1,355,800 .... G5
Eritrea 1,947,600 .... G4
Gamu-Gofa 698,800 .... G6
Gojjam 1,750,100 .... G5
Harar 3,359,200 .... H6
Ilubabor 688,800 .... F6
Kaffa 1,693,000 .... G6
Shoa 5,369,500 .... G6
Sidamo 2,479,800 .... G7
Tigre 1,828,900 .... H5
Wallaga 1,269,100 .... G6
Wallo 2,459,900 .... H5

CITIES and TOWNS

Addis Ababa (cap.) 1,196,300 .... G6
Addis Alam 5,500 .... G6
Adigrat 9,400 .... G5
Adi Ugri 12,800 .... G5
Adwa 16,400 .... G5
Afdem H6
Agordat G4
Aksum 12,800 .... G5
Ankober H6
Arba Mench 7,660 .... G6
Asmara 393,800 .... G4
Asosa F5
Assab 16,000 .... H5
Asselle 19,390 .... G6
Awareh H6
Awash H6
Axum (Aksum) 12,800 .... G5
Bahir Dar 25,100 .... G5
Burei G6
Burye G5
Callafo H6
Chilga G5
Dagabur H6
Dallol G5
Dangila G5
Debra Birhan 16,700 .... G6
Debra Markos 30,260 .... G5
Debra Tabor 8,700 .... G5
Dembidollo 7,600 .... F6
Dessye 49,750 .... G5
Dilla 13,800 .... G6
Dire Dawa 63,700 .... H6
Dolo H7
Domo J6
Edd H5
El Carre H6
El Der H6
Filtu H6
Gabredarre H6
Galadi J6
Gambela F6
Gardula 5,800 .... G6
Gedo G6
Gerlogubi H6
Ghimbi 8,300 .... G6
Ginir H6
Goba 13,500 .... H6
Gondar 38,600 .... G5
Gore 8,500 .... G6
Gorrahei H6
Harar 48,440 .... H6
Harkiko G4
Hosseina 8,500 .... G6
Imi H6
Jijiga 8,000 .... H6
Jimma 47,360 .... G6
Jiran G6
Karkabat G4
Keren G4
Kibre Mengist 8,300 .... G6
Lalibela G5
Magdala G5
Maji G6
Makale 30,780 .... G5
Massawa 19,800 .... G4
Mega G7
Mendi G6
Mersa Fatma H5
Metamma G5
Miesso H6
Mizan Teferi G6
Moyale G7
Murle G6
Mustahil H6
Nakamti 18,310 .... G6
Nakfa G4
Nazret 42,900 .... G6
Negelli 8,800 .... G6
Nejo G6
Saio (Dembidollo) 7,600 .... F6
Soddu 11,900 .... G6
Sokota G5
Tessenei G4
Thio H5
Tori F6
Umm Hajar G5
Waka G6
Waldia 9,600 .... G5
Wardere J6
Wolta G6
Yaballo G6
Yirga Alam 14,500 .... G6
Zula G4

OTHER FEATURES

Abay (riv.) G5
Abaya (lake) G6
Akobo (riv.) F6
Assale (lake) H5
Atbara (riv.) G4
Awash (riv.) H5
Bale (mt.) G6
Baraka (riv.) G4
Baro (riv.) G6
Billate (riv.) G6
Blue Nile (Abay) (riv.) G5
Buri (pen.) H4
Chamo (lake) G6
Dahlak (arch.) H4
Dahlak (isl.) H4
Danakil (reg.) H5
Dawa (riv.) G7
Fafan (riv.) H6
Ganale Dorya (riv.) H6
Gash Mareb (riv.) G5
Gughe (mt.) G6
Haud (reg.) J6
Kasar, Ras (cape) G4
Ogaden (reg.) H6
Omo (riv.) G6
Ras Dashan (mt.) G5
Red (sea) H4
Rudolf (Turkana) (lake) G7
Simen (mts.) G5
Stefanie (lake) G7
Takkaze (riv.) G5
Tana (lake) G5
Tisisat (fall) G5
Turkana (lake) G7
Wabi (riv.) H6
Wabi Shebelle (riv.) H6
Zwai (lake) G6

LIBYA

CITIES and TOWNS

Ajedabia○ 53,170 .... D1
Aujila○ 6,695 .... D2
Baida○ 59,765 .... D1
Barce (El Marj)○ 55,444 .... D1
Benghazi (cap.)○ 286,943 .... C1
Beni Ulid○ 19,113 .... B1
Berken B2
Brak○ 12,507 .... B2
Bu Ngem C1
Cyrene (Shahat)○ 17,157 .... D1
Derj○ 2,152 .... B1
Derna○ 44,145 .... D1
Edri B2
El Abiar○ 17,685 .... D1
El Agheila C1
El Azizia○ 34,077 .... B1
El Bardi○ 4,330 .... D1
El Barkat○ 2,139 .... B3
El Fogaha C2
El Gatrun B3
El Gezira D2
El Jauf○ 6,481 .... D3
El Marj○ 55,444 .... D1
El' Uweinat B2
Es Sidr○ 706 .... C1
Ez Zuetina○ 7,256 .... D1
Ghadames○ 6,172 .... A2
Gharîan○ 65,224 .... B1
Ghat○ 6,924 .... B3
Ghemines○ 4,313 .... C1
Homs○ 66,890 .... B1
Hon○ 2,766 .... C2
Jaghbub (Jarabub)○ 1,436 .... D2
Jalo D2
Jarabub○ 1,436 .... D2
Marada○ 3,201 .... C2
Marsa el Brega○ 2,618 .... D1
Marsa el Hariga○ 5,043 .... D1
Mekili D1
Misurata○ 102,439 .... C1
Mizda○ 11,472 .... B1
Murzuk○ 22,185 .... B2
Nalut○ 23,535 .... B1
Ras Lanuf○ 1,990 .... C1
Sabrathaa○ 30,836 .... B1
Sebha○ 35,879 .... B2
Shahat○ 17,157 .... D1
Sinawen○ 1,549 .... B1
Sokna○ 3,757 .... C2
Soluk○ 6,501 .... D1
Susa D1
Syrte○ 22,797 .... C1
Tarhuna○ 52,657 .... B1
Tejerri B3
Tesawa B2
Tmessa C2
Tobruk○ 58,384 .... D1
Tokra○ 10,714 .... D1
Traghen B2
Tripoli (cap.)○ 550,438 .... B1
Ubari○ 19,132 .... B2
Umm el Abid C2
Waddan○ 5,347 .... C2
Wau el Kebir C2
Zawia○ 72,092 .... B1
Zella○ 4,835 .... C2
Zliten○ 58,981 .... C1
Zuila C2
Zwara○ 15,078 .... B1

OTHER FEATURES

Ain Zueiya (well) D3
Akhdar, Jebel (mts.) D1
A'mir, Ras (cape) D1
Barqa (Cyrenaica) (reg.) D1
Ben Ghnema, Jebel (mts.) C2
Bette (peak) C3
Bey el Kebir, Wadi (dry riv.) B1
Bir Hakeim (ruins) D1
Bishiara (well) D3
Bomba (gulf) D1
Buzeima (well) D3
Calansho Sand Sea (des.) D2
Calansho, Serir (des.) D2
Cyrenaica (reg.) D1
Fezzan (reg.) B2
Great Sand Sea (des.) D2
Harug el Asued, El (mts.) C2
Homra, Hamada el (des.) B2
Hosenofu (well) D3
Idehan Ubari (des.) B2
Idehan Murzuk (des.) B2
Jalo (oasis) D2
Jefara (reg.) B1
Jef Jef es Seghin (plat.) D3
Jofra (oasis) C2
Kufra (oasis) D3
Leptis Magna (ruins) B1
Libyan (des.) D2
Libyan (plat.) D1
Mediterranean (sea) C1
Nefusa, Jebel (mts.) B1
Rebiana○ (oasis) D3
Rebiana Sand Sea (des.) D3
Sahara (des.) C3
Sarra (well) D3
Shati, Wadi esh (dry riv.) B2
Sidra (gulf) C1
Soda, Jebel es (mts.) C2
Tazerbo○ (oasis) D2
Tibesti, Serir (des.) C3
Tinghert Hamada (Tinrhert) (des.) B2
Tripolitania (reg.) B1
U'weinat, Jebel (mt.) E3
Zelten, Jebel (mts.) D2

SUDAN

PROVINCES

Bahr El Ghazal 813,000 .... E6
Blue Nile 216,000 .... F5
Darfur, Northern 1,013,000 .... D5
Darfur, Southern 1,160,000 .... E5
El Buheyrat 574,000 .... E6
El Gezira 1,775,000 .... F5
Equatoria, Eastern 507,000 .... F6
Equatoria, Western 251,000 .... E6
Junglei 202,000 .... F6
Kassala 1,113,000 .... F4
Khartoum 1,160,000 .... F4
Kordofan, Northern 1,266,000 .... E5
Kordofan, Southern 951,000 .... E5
Nile 552,000 .... F4
Northern 416,000 .... E3
Red Sea 446,000 .... G4
Upper Nile 621,000 .... F6
White Nile 1,122,000 .... F5

CITIES and TOWNS

A'bri F3
Abu Hamed F4
Abu Matariq E5
Abu Zabad E5
Abwong F6
Abyei E6
Adarama G4
Adok F6
Akasha F3
Akobo F6
Amadi F6
A'qiq G4
Argo F4
Aroma G4
Atbara 66,000 .... F4
Aweil E6
Ayod F6
Babanusa E5
Bara F5
Bentiu E6
Berber F4
Bor F6
Bo River Post E6
Buram E5
Damazin (Ed Damazin) 12,000 .... F5
Deim Zubeir E6
Delgo F3
Derudeb G4
Dilling E5
Dongola 6,000 .... F4
Dungunab G3
Ed Dae'in E5
Ed Damer 17,000 .... F4
Ed Damazin 12,000 .... F5
Ed Debba F4
Ed Dueim 27,000 .... F5
El Abbasiya F5
El Fasher 52,000 .... E5
El Fifi D5
El Geneina 33,000 .... D5
El Geteina F5
El Hilla E5
El Khandaq E4
El Manaqil F5
El Obeid 90,000 .... E5
El Odaiya E5
En Nahud 23,000 .... E5
Er Rahad F5
Er Roseires F5
Famaka F5
Fangak F6
Fashoda (Kodok) F6
Gabras E5
Gallabat G5
Gebeit Mine G3
Gedaref 92,000 .... G5
Gogrial E6
Goz Regeb G4
Haiya Junction G4
Halaib G3
Heiban F5
Jonglei F6
Juba 57,000 .... F7
Kadugli 18,000 .... E5
Kafia Kingi D6
Kajok E6
Kaka F5
Kapoeta F7
Karima F4
Karora G4
Kassala 99,000 .... G4
Kerma F4
Khartoum (cap.) 334,000 .... F4
Khartoum North 151,000 .... F4
Khashm el Girba G5
Kodok F6
Kongor F6
Korti F4
Kosti 57,000 .... F5
Kubbum D5
Kurmuk F5
Kutum D5
Lado F6
Loka F7
Malakal 35,000 .... F6
Maridi E7
Marsa Oseif G3
Melut F5
Merowe F4
Meshra er Req E6
Mongalla F6
Muglad E5
Muhammad Qol G3
Musmar G4
Nagishot F7
Nasir F6
Nimule F7
Nyala 60,000 .... E5
Nyamlell E6
Nyerol F6
Omdurman 299,000 .... F4
Opari F7
Pibor Post F6
Port Sudan 133,000 .... G4
Qalae'n Nahl F5
Raga E6
Rashad F5
Rejaf F7
Renk F5
Rufaa' F5
Rumbek 17,000 .... E6
Sennar F5
Shambe F6
Shendi F4
Shereik F4
Showak G5
Singa F5
Sinkat G4
Sodiri E5
Suakin G4
Suki F5
Tali Post F6
Talodi F5
Tambura E6
Tendelti F5
Tokar G4
Tombe F6
Tonga F6
Tonj E6
Torit F7
Towot F6
Trinkitat G4
Umm Keddada E5
Umm Ruwaba F5
Wadi Halfa F3
Wad Medani 107,000 .... F5
Wankai E6
Wau 53,000 .... E6
Yambio 7,000 .... E7
Yei F7
Yirol F6
Zalingei D5

OTHER FEATURES

Abu Dara, Ras (cape) G3
Abu Habl, Wadi (dry riv.) F5
Abu Shagara, Ras (cape) G3
Abu Tabari (well) E4
Adda (riv.) D6
Akobo (riv.) F6
A'mur, Wadi (dry riv.) G4
Asoteriba, Jebel (mt.) G3
Atbara (riv.) G4
Bahr Azoum (riv.) D5
Bahr el A'rab (riv.) E6
Bahr ez Zeraf (riv.) F6
Baraka (riv.) G4
Blue Nile (riv.) F5
Dar Hamid (reg.) F5
Dar Masalit (reg.) D5
Dinder (riv.) F5
El A'trun (oasis) E4
Fifth Cataract F4
Fourth Cataract F4
Gabgaba, Wadi (dry riv.) F3
Gezira, El (reg.) F5
Ghalla, Wadi el (dry riv.) E5
Hadarba, Ras (cape) G3
Howar, Wadi (dry riv.) E4
Ibra, Wadi (dry riv.) D5
Jebel Abyad (plat.) E4
Jebel Aulia (dam) F4
Jur (riv.) E6
Kasar, Ras (cape) G4
Kinyeti (mt.) F7
Laqiya U'mran (well) E3
Libyan (des.) E3
Lol (dry riv.) E6
Lotagipi Swamp (plain) F6
Marra, Jebel (mt.) D5
Meroe (ruins) F4
Milk, Wadi el (dry riv.) E4
Muqaddam, Wadi (dry riv.) F4
Napata (ruins) F4
Naqa (ruins) F4
Nile (riv.) F4
Nuba (mts.) E5
Nubia (lake) F3
Nubian (des.) F3
Nukheila (oasis) E4
Nuri (ruins) F4
Oda, Jebel (mt.) G3
Pibor (riv.) F6
Red (sea) G3
Sahara (des.) E3
Second Cataract F3
Selima (oasis) E3
Sennar (dam) F5
Setit (riv.) G5
Sixth Cataract F4
Sobat (riv.) F6
Suakin (arch.) G4
Sudan (reg.) E5
Sudd (swamp) F6
Sue (riv.) E6
Third Cataract E4
U'weinat, Jebel (mt.) E3
White Nile (riv.) F5

○Population of sub-district or division.

Agriculture, Industry and Resources

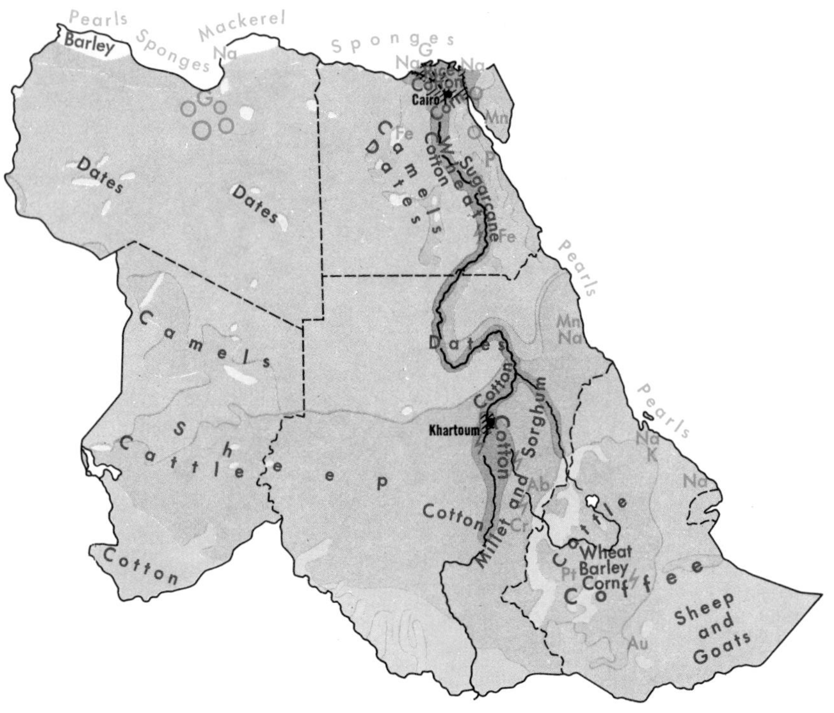

DOMINANT LAND USE

- Cereals, Horticulture, Livestock
- Cash Crops, Mixed Cereals
- Cotton, Cereals
- Market Gardening, Diversified Tropical Crops
- Plantation Agriculture
- Oases
- Pasture Livestock
- Nomadic Livestock Herding
- Forests
- Nonagricultural Land

MAJOR MINERAL OCCURRENCES

Ab	Asbestos	Mn	Manganese
Au	Gold	Na	Salt
Cr	Chromium	O	Petroleum
Fe	Iron Ore	P	Phosphates
G	Natural Gas	Pt	Platinum
K	Potash		

Water Power

Major Industrial Areas

ANGOLA

AREA 481,351 sq. mi. (1,246,700 sq. km.)
POPULATION 7,078,000
CAPITAL Luanda
LARGEST CITY Luanda
HIGHEST POINT Mt. Moco 8,593 ft. (2,620 m.)
MONETARY UNIT kwanza
MAJOR LANGUAGES Mbundu, Kongo, Lunda, Portuguese
MAJOR RELIGIONS Tribal religions, Roman Catholicism

BURUNDI

AREA 10,747 sq. mi. (27,835 sq. km.)
POPULATION 4,021,910
CAPITAL Bujumbura
LARGEST CITY Bujumbura
HIGHEST POINT 8,858 ft. (2,700 m.)
MONETARY UNIT Burundi franc
MAJOR LANGUAGES Kirundi, French, Swahili
MAJOR RELIGIONS Tribal religions, Roman Catholicism, Islam

CAMEROON

AREA 183,568 sq. mi. (475,441 sq. km.)
POPULATION 8,503,000
CAPITAL Yaoundé
LARGEST CITY Douala
HIGHEST POINT Cameroon 13,350 ft. (4,069 m.)
MAJOR LANGUAGES Fang, Bamileke, Fulani, Duala, French, English
MAJOR RELIGIONS Tribal religions, Christianity, Islam

CENTRAL AFRICAN REP.

AREA 242,000 sq. mi. (626,780 sq. km.)
POPULATION 2,284,000
CAPITAL Bangui
LARGEST CITY Bangui
HIGHEST POINT Gao 4,659 ft. (1,420 m.)
MONETARY UNIT CFA franc
MAJOR LANGUAGES Banda, Gbaya, Sangho, French
MAJOR RELIGIONS Tribal religions, Christianity, Islam

CONGO

AREA 132,046 sq. mi. (342,000 sq. km.)
POPULATION 1,537,000
CAPITAL Brazzaville
LARGEST CITY Brazzaville
HIGHEST POINT Leketi Mts. 3,412 ft. (1,040 m.)
MONETARY UNIT CFA franc
MAJOR LANGUAGES Kikongo, Bateke, Lingala, French
MAJOR RELIGIONS Christianity, tribal religions, Islam

EQUATORIAL GUINEA

AREA 10,831 sq. mi. (28,052 sq. km.)
POPULATION 244,000
CAPITAL Malabo
LARGEST CITY Malabo
HIGHEST POINT 9,868 ft. (3,008 m.)
MONETARY UNIT ekuele
MAJOR LANGUAGES Fang, Bubi, Spanish
MAJOR RELIGIONS Tribal religions, Christianity

GABON

AREA 103,346 sq. mi. (267,666 sq. km.)
POPULATION 551,000
CAPITAL Libreville
LARGEST CITY Libreville
HIGHEST POINT Ibounzi 5,165 ft. (1,574 m.)
MONETARY UNIT CFA franc
MAJOR LANGUAGES Fang and other Bantu languages, French
MAJOR RELIGIONS Tribal religions, Christianity, Islam

KENYA

AREA 224,960 sq. mi. (582,646 sq. km.)
POPULATION 15,327,061
CAPITAL Nairobi
LARGEST CITY Nairobi
HIGHEST POINT Kenya 17,058 ft. (5,199 m.)
MONETARY UNIT Kenya shilling
MAJOR LANGUAGES Kikuyu, Luo, Kavirondo, Kamba, Swahili, English
MAJOR RELIGIONS Tribal religions, Christianity, Hinduism, Islam

MALAWI

AREA 45,747 sq. mi. (118,485 sq. km.)
POPULATION 5,968,000
CAPITAL Lilongwe
LARGEST CITY Blantyre
HIGHEST POINT Mulanje 9,843 ft. (3,000 m.)
MONETARY UNIT Malawi kwacha
MAJOR LANGUAGES Chichewa, Yao, English, Nyanja, Tumbuka, Tonga, Ngoni
MAJOR RELIGIONS Tribal religions, Islam, Christianity

RWANDA

AREA 10,169 sq. mi. (26,337 sq. km.)
POPULATION 4,819,317
CAPITAL Kigali
LARGEST CITY Kigali
HIGHEST POINT Karisimbi 14,780 ft. (4,505 m.)
MONETARY UNIT Rwanda franc
MAJOR LANGUAGES Kinyarwanda, French, Swahili
MAJOR RELIGIONS Tribal religions, Roman Catholicism, Islam

SOMALIA

AREA 246,200 sq. mi. (637,658 sq. km.)
POPULATION 3,645,000
CAPITAL Mogadishu
LARGEST CITY Mogadishu
HIGHEST POINT Surud Ad 7,900 ft. (2,408 m.)
MONETARY UNIT Somali shilling
MAJOR LANGUAGES Somali, Arabic, Italian, English
MAJOR RELIGION Islam

TANZANIA

AREA 363,708 sq. mi. (942,003 sq. km.)
POPULATION 17,527,560
CAPITAL Dar es Salaam
LARGEST CITY Dar es Salaam
HIGHEST POINT Kilimanjaro 19,340 ft. (5,895 m.)
MONETARY UNIT Tanzanian shilling
MAJOR LANGUAGES Nyamwezi-Sukuma, Swahili, English
MAJOR RELIGIONS Tribal religions, Christianity, Islam

UGANDA

AREA 91,076 sq. mi. (235,887 sq. km.)
POPULATION 12,630,076
CAPITAL Kampala
LARGEST CITY Kampala
HIGHEST POINT Margherita 16,795 ft. (5,119 m.)
MONETARY UNIT Ugandan shilling
MAJOR LANGUAGES Luganda, Acholi, Teso, Nyoro, Soga, Nkole, English, Swahili
MAJOR RELIGIONS Tribal religions, Christianity, Islam

ZAIRE

AREA 905,063 sq. mi. (2,344,113 sq. km.)
POPULATION 28,291,000
CAPITAL Kinshasa
LARGEST CITY Kinshasa
HIGHEST POINT Margherita 16,795 ft. (5,119 m.)
MONETARY UNIT zaire
MAJOR LANGUAGES Tshiluba, Mongo, Kikongo, Kingwana, Zande, Lingala, Swahili, French
MAJOR RELIGIONS Tribal religions, Christianity

ZAMBIA

AREA 290,586 sq. mi. (752,618 sq. km.)
POPULATION 5,679,808
CAPITAL Lusaka
LARGEST CITY Lusaka
HIGHEST POINT Sunzu 6,782 ft. (2,067 m.)
MONETARY UNIT Zambian kwacha
MAJOR LANGUAGES Bemba, Tonga, Lozi, Luvale, Nyanja, English
MAJOR RELIGIONS Tribal religions

ANGOLA

BURUNDI

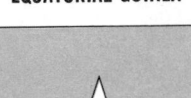

CAMEROON

CENTRAL AFRICAN REP.

CONGO

EQUATORIAL GUINEA

GABON

KENYA

MALAWI

RWANDA

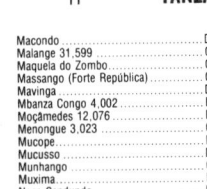

SOMALIA

TANZANIA

UGANDA

ZAIRE

ZAMBIA

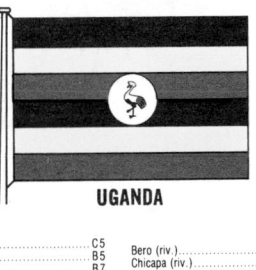
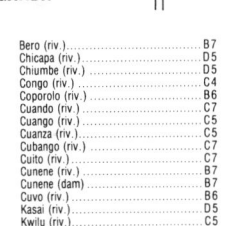
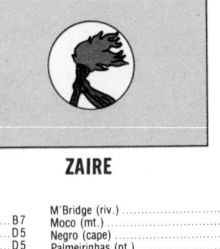

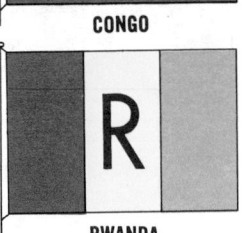
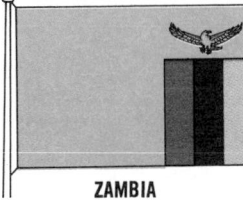

(continued on following page)

Kounde		B2
Mbalki 12,346		C3
Mbres 2,622		C3
Mobaye 4,220		D3
Mouka		D3
Ndele 5,858		C2
Ngourou		D2
Nola 6,703		C3
Obo 3,978		D2
Ouada 3,009		C2
Paoua 7,052		C2
Possel		C3
Sibut 13,341		C2
Zako		D2
Zemio 3,259		D2

Zemongo	E2

OTHER FEATURES

Bamingui (riv.)	C2
Bomu (riv.)	D3
Dar Rounga (reg.)	D2
Kadei (riv.)	C3
Kotto (riv.)	D2
Lobaye (riv.)	C3
Mbéré (riv.)	B2
Ouham (riv.)	C2
Pendé (riv.)	C2
Sanga (riv.)	C3
Sara (riv.)	C2
Shari (riv.)	C2
Shinko (riv.)	D2
Ubangi (riv.)	C3

CONGO
CITIES and TOWNS

Abala	B4
Boko	B4
Brazzaville (cap.) 298,967	C4
Boundji	C4
Djambala	B4
Dongou	C3
Enyellé	C3
Epéna	C3
Etoumbi	B4
Ewo	B4
Gamboma	C4
Ikelemba	C3
Impfondo	C3
Kellé	B4
Kinkala	C4
Komono	B4
Loubomou 29,600	B4
Loudima	B4
Madingo-Kayes	B4
Madingou	B4
Makoua	C4
Mbinda	B4
Mindouli	B4
Mossaka	C4
Mossendjo	B4
M'Pouya	C4
Nkayi 30,600	B4
Okoyo	C4
Ouesso	C3
Owando	C4
Oyo	C4
Pangala	C4
Pointe-Noire 141,700	B4
Sembé	B3
Sibiti	B4
Souanké	B3
Zanaga	B4
Tchibanga 14,001	B4

OTHER FEATURES

Crystal (mts.)	B4
Ibounzi (mt.)	B4
Ivindo (riv.)	B3
Lopez (cape)	A4
N'Dogo (lag.)	A4
N'Gounie (riv.)	A4
N'Komi (lag.)	A4
Ogooué (riv.)	A4
Onangué (lake)	A4
Pongara (pt.)	A3

EQUATORIAL GUINEA
TERRITORIES

Bioko 78,000	A3
Rio Muni 203,000	B3

CITIES and TOWNS

Bata 27,024	B3
Luba 19,933	A3
Malabo (cap.) 37,237	A3
Mbini 14,503	A3

OTHER FEATURES

Biafra (bight)	A3
Bioko (isl.)	A3
Corisco (isl.)	A3
Elobey (isls.)	A3
Fernando Po (Bioko) (isl.)	A3

GABON
CITIES and TOWNS

Banda	B4
Bitam 5,936	B3
Booué	A4
Chinchoua	B3
Cocobeach	B3
Fougamou	A4
Franceville 9,345	B4
Iguéla	A4
Kango	B3
Kemboma	B3
Koula-Moutou 8,032	B4
Lalara	B3
Lambaréné 17,770	A4
Lastoursville	B4
Lekoni	B4
Libreville (cap.) 105,080	A3
Makokou 5,005	B3
Mayumba	A4
M'Bigou	B4
Médouneu	B3
Mekambo	B3
Minvoul	B3
Mitzic	B3
Moanda 10,709	B4
Mouila 15,016	B4
Mounana 4,000	B4
N'Dendé	B4
N'Djolé	A4
Nyanga	B4
Okondja	B4
Omboué	A3
Oyem 12,455	B3
Port-Gentil 48,190	A4
Sette-Cama	A4

OTHER FEATURES

Alima	B4
Congo (riv.)	C4
Crystal (mts.)	B4
Dja (riv.)	B4
Ivindo (riv.)	B3
Kadei (riv.)	C3
'Kouilou (riv.)	B4
N'Gounié (riv.)	B4
Niari (riv.)	B4
Ogooué (riv.)	A4
Sangha (riv.)	C3
Ubangi (riv.)	C3

KENYA
PROVINCES

Central 1,675,647	G4
Coast 944,082	G4
Eastern 1,907,301	G4
Nairobi 509,286	G4
North-Eastern 245,757	G4
Nyanza 2,122,045	G3
Rift Valley 2,210,289	G4
Western 1,328,298	G3

CITIES and TOWNS

Buna	G3
Bunyala	G4
Bura	H4
Eldoret 18,196	G3
El Wak	H3
Embu 3,928	G4
Fort Hall 4,750	G4
Galole 3,609	G4
Garba Tula	G4
Garissa	G4
Garsen	G4
Gilgil 4,725	G4
Isiolo 8,201	G3
Kakamega 6,244	F3
Kaningo	G4
Kericho 10,144	G4
Kiambu 2,776	G4
Kilifi 2,662	G4
Kipini	H4
Kisii 6,080	G4
Kisumu 32,431	F3
Kitale 11,573	G3
Kitui 3,071	G4
Kolbio	H4
Konza	G4
Laisamis	G3
Lamu 7,403	H4
Lodwar	G3
Lokitaung 4,090	G3
Lolgorien	G4
Machakos 6,312	G4
Magadi	G4
Malindi 10,757	H4
Mambrui	H4
Maralal 3,876	G3
Marsabit 6,635	G3
Meru 4,475	G4
Moyale	G3
Mombasa 247,073	G4
Nairobi (cap.) 509,286	G4
Naivasha 6,920	G4
Nakuru 47,151	G4
Namanga	G4
Nanyuki 11,624	G3
Narok 2,608	G4
North Horr	G3
South Horr	G3
Taveta	G4
Thika 18,387	G4
Thomson's Falls 7,602	G3
Todenyang	G3
Tsavo	G4
Vanga	G4
Voi 5,313	G4
Wajir	H3
Wamba 2,650	G3

OTHER FEATURES

Daua (riv.)	H3
Elgon (mt.)	F3
Formosa (bay)	H4
Galana (riv.)	G4
Gedi (ruins)	H4
Kavirondo (gulf)	F4
Kenya (mt.)	G4
Lak Dera (dry riv.)	H3
Lorian (swamp)	G3
Natron (lake)	G3
Nzoia (riv.)	G3
Patta (isl.)	H4
Rudolf (Turkana) (lake)	G3
Tana (riv.)	G4
Tsavo Nat'l Park	G4
Turkana (lake)	G3
Victoria (lake)	F4
Winam (bay)	F4

MALAWI
CITIES and TOWNS

Bandawe	F6
Blantyre 222,153	F7
Chilumba	F6
Chipoka	F7
Chiromo	F7
Chitipa 3,079	F5
Dedza 5,448	F6
Karonga 11,873	F6
Kasungu	F6
Lilongwe (cap.) 102,924	F6
Livingstonia	F6
Mangochi 3,341	G6
Mzimba 4,962	F6
Nkhata Bay 4,024	F6
Nkhotakota 10,312	F6
Nsanje 6,091	G7
Rumphi 3,998	F6
Salima 4,646	F6
Thyolo 4,186	F7
Zomba 21,000	G7

OTHER FEATURES

Chilwa (lake)	G7
Malawi (Nyasa) (lake)	F6
Mulanje (mts.)	G7
Nyasa (lake)	F6
Shire (riv.)	G7

RWANDA
CITIES and TOWNS

Butare 21,691	E4
Cyangugu 7,042	E4
Gisenyi 12,436	E4
Kigali (cap.) 117,749	E4
Nyabisindu 8,587	E4

OTHER FEATURES

Kagera Nat'l Park	F4
Karisimbi (mt.)	E4
Kivu (lake)	E4
Ruzizi (riv.)	E4
Virunga (range)	E4

SOMALIA
PROVINCES

Bakool 100,000	H3
Bari 155,000	J1
Bay 302,000	H3
Galguduud 182,000	J2
Gedo 212,000	H3
Hiiraan 147,000	J3
Jubbada Hoose 246,000	H3
Mogadiscio 371,000	J3
Mudug 215,000	J2
Nugaal 85,000	J2
Sanaag 146,000	J1
Shabeellaha Dhexe 237,000	J3
Shabeellaha Hoose 398,000	J3
Togdheer 258,000	J2
Woqooyi Galbeed 440,000	H1

CITIES and TOWNS

Adale	H2
Afgoi	J3
Afmadu 2,580	H3
Alula	K1
Ankhor	J1
Audegle	J3
Baduen	J2
Barawa (Brava)	H3
Bardera	H3
Bargal	K1
Baydhabo 14,962	H3
Belet Weyne 11,426	J3
Bender Beila	K2
Bender Cassim (Bosaso)	J1
Berbera 12,219	H1
Bereda	H1
Bircao	H4
Bohodleh	J2
Borama 3,244	H1

(continued on following page)

Topography

SCALE
0 200 400 600 MI.
0 200 400 600 KM.

Below Sea Level	100 m. 328 ft.	200 m. 656 ft.	500 m. 1,640 ft.	1,000 m. 3,281 ft.	2,000 m. 6,562 ft.	5,000 m. 16,404 ft.

Central Africa

CYLINDRICAL EQUAL-AREA PROJECTION

SCALE OF MILES
0 50 100 200 300

SCALE OF KILOMETERS
0 50 100 200 300

Capitals of Countries ☆
Other Capitals
International Boundaries
Internal Boundaries

Scale 1:13,800,000

Bosaso	J1
Brava 6,167	H3
Bulhar	H1
Bulo Burti 5,247	J3
Bur Acaba	H3
Burao 12,617	J2
Callis	J2
Candala	J1
Chisimayu 17,872	H4
Chiambone	H4
Coriole 4,341	H3
Dante (Hafun)	K1
Dif	H3
Dinsor	H3
Dusa Marreb	J2
Eil	J2
El Athale (Itala)	J3
El Bur	J3
El Dere	J3
El Hamurre	J2
Erigabo 4,279	J1
Ferfer	J2
Galcaio	J2
Garad	J2
Garbahaarrey	H3
Gardo	J2
Garoe	J2
Giohar 13,156	J3
Gobwen	H4
Hafun	K1
Halin	J2
Harardera	J3
Hargeysa 40,254	H2
Hordio	K1
Iddan	J2
Iet	H3
Itala	J3
Jamama 5,408	H3
Jilib 3,232	H3
Karin	J1
Kismayu (Chisimayu) 17,872	H4
Las Dureh	J1
Luuq	H3
Margherita (Jamama)	H3
Marka (Merka) 17,708	H3
Mogadishu (cap.) 371,000	J3
Muqdisho (Mogadishu) (cap.) 371,000	J3
Obbia	J2
Oddur	H3
Taleh	J2
Uanle Uen	H3
Upper Sheikh	J2
Villabruzzi (Johar)	J3
Zeila 1,226	H1

OTHER FEATURES

Aden (gulf)	J1
Asèr, Ras (cape)	K1
Giuba (riv.)	H3
Guban (reg.)	H1
Hafun, Ras (cape)	K1
Haud (plat.)	J2
Lak Dera (dry riv.)	H3
Negro (bay)	J2
Nogal (reg.)	J2
Shimbir Berris (mt.)	J1
Sura, Ras (cape)	J1
Surud Ad (mt.)	J1
Webi Shabelle (riv.)	H3

TANZANIA

REGIONS

Arusha 928,478	G4
Dodoma 971,921	G5
Iringa 922,801	G5
Kigoma 648,950	F4
Kilimanjaro 902,394	G4
Lindi 527,902	G5
Mara 723,295	F4
Mbeya 1,080,241	F5
Morogoro 939,190	G5
Mtwara 771,726	G5
Mwanza 1,443,418	F4
Pemba 205,870	H5
Pwani (Coast) 516,949	G5
Rukwa 451,897	F5
Ruvuma 564,113	G6
Shinyanga 1,323,482	F4
Singida 614,030	F5
Tabora 818,049	F5
Tanga 1,088,592	G5
Zanzibar Mjini 143,616	G5
Zanzibar Shambani North 77,424	G5
Zanzibar Shambani South 52,325	G5
Ziwa Magharibi (West Lake) 1,009,379	F4

CITIES and TOWNS

Arusha 55,281	G4
Babati	G4
Bagamoyo 5,112	G5
Bukoba 20,430	F4
Chake Chake 4,862	H5
Dar es Salaam (cap.) 757,346	G5
Dodoma 45,703	G5
Geita 3,066	F4
Handeni	G5
Ifakara	G5
Iringa 57,182	G5
Itigi	F5
Kahama 3,211	F4
Kaliua	F5
Kanga	G5
Karema	F5
Kasanga	F5
Kasulu	F4
Kibara	F4
Kibaya	G5
Kibondo	F4
Kigoma-Ujiji 50,044	E4
Kilosa 4,458	G5
Kilwa Kivinje 2,790	G5
Kilwa Masoko	G5
Kinyangiri	G4
Kipili	F5
Kisiju	G5
Kitunda	F5
Kizimkazi	G5
Kondoa 4,514	G4
Kongwa	G5
Korogwe 6,675	G5
Lindi 27,308	G5
Liuli	F6
Liwale	G5
Longido	G4
Mahenge	G5
Makumbako	G5
Manda	F6
Manyoni	G5
Masasi	G6
Mbamba Bay	G6
Mbeya 76,606	F5
Mbulu	G4
Mchinga	H5
Mohoro	G5
Mombo	G4
Morogoro 61,890	G5
Moshi 52,223	G4
Mpanda	F5
Mtakuja	F5
Mtwara-Mikindani 48,510	H6
Murongo	F4
Musoma 32,658	F4
Muwale	F5
Mwadui 7,383	F4
Mwanza 110,611	F4
Mwaya	F5
Mwesi	F5
Nachingwea 3,751	G6
Newala	G6
Ngara	F4
Njombe	F5
Pangani 2,955	G5
Rungwa	F5
Sadani	G5
Same	G4
Sekenke	F4
Shinyanga 21,703	F4
Singida 29,252	F4
Songea 17,954	G6
Sumbawanga 28,586	F5
Tabora 67,392	F5
Tanga 103,409	G4
Tukuyu 4,089	F5
Tunduru	G6
Urambo	F4
Utete	G5
Uvinza	F5
Wete 8,469	G4
Zanzibar 110,669	G5

OTHER FEATURES

Eyasi (lake)	F4
Great Ruaha (riv.)	G5
Juani (isl.)	G5
Kalambo (falls)	F5
Kanzi (cape)	G5
Kilimanjaro (mt.)	G4
Kilombero (riv.)	G5
Mafia (isl.)	H5
Manyara (lake)	G4
Masai (steppe)	G4
Mbarangandu (riv.)	G5
Mbemkuru (riv.)	G5
Meru (mt.)	G4
Mikumi Nat'l Park	G5
Natron (lake)	G4
Ngorongoro (crater)	F4
Njombe (riv.)	F5
Nyasa (lake)	F6
Olduvai Gorge (canyon)	G4
Pangani (riv.)	G4
Pemba (isl.)	H5
Rovuma (riv.)	G6
Rufiji (riv.)	G5
Ruaha Nat'l Park	F5
Rukwa (lake)	F5
Rungwa (riv.)	F5
Rungwe (mt.)	F5
Serengeti Nat'l Park	F4
Tanganyika (lake)	E5
Tarangire Nat'l Park	G4
Victoria (lake)	F4
Wami (riv.)	G5
Wembere (riv.)	F4
Zanzibar (isl.)	G5

UGANDA

CITIES and TOWNS

Arua 10,837	F3
Atura	F3
Butiaba 261	F3
Entebbe 21,096	F4
Fort Portal 7,947	F3
Gulu 18,170	F3
Hoima 2,339	F3
Jinja 52,509	F3
Kabale 8,234	E4
Kampala (cap.) 478,895	F3
Kasese 7,213	F3
Kilembe	F3
Kitgum 3,242	F3
Lira 7,340	F3
Masaka 12,987	F4
Masindi 2,100	F3
Mbale 23,544	F3
Mbarara 16,078	F4
Moroto 5,488	F3
Moyo 2,656	F3
Mubende 6,004	F3
Rhino Camp 198	F3
Soroti 8,130	F3
Tororo 15,977	F3

OTHER FEATURES

Albert (Mobuto Sese Seko) (lake)	F3
Edward (lake)	E4
Elgon (mt.)	F3
George (lake)	F4
Kabarega Nat'l Park	F3
Kidepo Nat'l Park	F3
Kioga (lake)	F3
Margherita (mt.)	E3
Mobuto Sese Seko (lake)	F3
Murchison (falls)	F3
Owen Falls (dam)	F3
Ruwenzori (range)	E3
Sese (isls.)	F4
Victoria (lake)	F4
Virunga Nat'l Park	F4
Virunga (range)	E4

ZAIRE

PROVINCES

Bandundu 2,600,556	C4
Bas-Zaïre 1,504,361	B4
Equateur 2,431,812	D3
Haut-Zaïre 3,356,419	E3
Kasai-Occidental 2,433,861	D4
Kasai-Oriental 1,872,231	D5
Kinshasa 1,323,039	C4
Kivu 3,361,883	E4
Shaba 2,753,714	E5

CITIES and TOWNS

Aba 7,600	F3
Abumombazi	D3
Aketi 17,200	D3
Andoma	E3
Ango	E3
Ankoro	E5
Bagata	C4
Balangala	D3
Bambesa	E3
Bambili	E3
Banalia	E3
Banana	B5
Bandundu 74,467	C4
Baraka	E4
Basankusu	C3
Basoko 9,100	D3
Basongo	D4
Befale	D3
Bena-Dibele	D4
Beni 22,800	E3
Bikoro	C4
Boende 12,800	D4
Bokote	D4
Bokungu	D4
Bolobo 10,300	C4
Bolomba 7,200	C3
Boma 61,100	B5
Bomboma	C3
Bomongo	C3
Bondo 10,000	D3
Bongandanga 12,900	D3
Bosobolo 11,100	D3
Budjala	C3
Bukama	E5
Bukavu 134,861	E4
Bulungu 16,300	C4
Bumba 34,700	D3
Bunia 28,800	E3
Bunkeya 5,100	E6
Businga 11,000	D3
Busu-Djanoa	D3
Buta 19,800	D3
Butembo 27,800	E3
Dekese	D4
Demba 22,000	D5
Dibaya 11,400	D5
Dibaya-Lubue 7,900	C4
Dilolo 14,000	D6
Dimbelenge	D5
Djolu	D3
Djugu	F3
Dongo	C3
Doruma	E3
Dungu 9,100	E3
Etoile	E6
Faradje 10,400	E3
Feshi	C5
Fizi	E4
Gandajika 60,100	D5
Gemena 37,300	D3
Goma 48,600	E4
Gungu	C5
Idiofa	C4
Ikela	D4
Ilebo 32,200	D4
Imese	C3
Ingende	C4
Inongo 14,800	C4
Irumu 9,300	E3
Isangi	D3
Isiro 49,300	E3
Kabalo 22,600	E5
Kabambare	E4
Kabare 12,600	E4
Kabinda 60,500	D5
Kabongo 6,500	E5
Kahemba	C5
Kalehe	E4
Kalemie 62,300	E5
Kalima 27,500	E4
Kama 17,700	E4
Kambove 18,900	E6
Kamina 56,300	D5
Kampene 14,600	E4
Kananga 428,960	D5
Kanda-Kanda	D5
Kaniama	D5
Kapanga	D5
Kasaji	D6
Kasangulu 11,900	C4
Kasenga	E6
Kasenyi	E3
Kasese	E4
Kasongo 37,800	E4
Kasongo-Lunda	C5
Katako-Kombe	D4
Katenga	E5
Kazumba	D5
Kenge 17,500	C4
Kiambi	E5
Kibombo	E4
Kikwit 111,960	C5
Kilembe	C5
Kilwa	E5
Kilo	E3
Kinda	D5
Kiniama	E6
Kinshasa (cap.) 1,323,039	C4
Kipushi 32,900	E6
Kiri	C4
Kirundu	E4
Kisangani 229,596	E3
Kole, Kasai-Oriental	D4
Kole, Haut-Zaïre	E3
Kolwezi 81,600	E6
Komba	D3
Kongolo 14,800	E5
Kungu	C3
Kutu 10,000	C4
Kwamouth	C4
Libenge 12,500	C3
Likasi, Panda- 146,394	E6
Likati	D3
Lisala	D3
Lodja 20,300	D4
Lokolama	D4
Lomela	D4
Loto	D4
Luashi	D6
Lubefu	D4
Lubero	E4
Lubudi 6,000	E5
Lubumbashi 318,000	E6
Lubutu	E4
Luebo 21,800	D5
Luishia	E6
Luiza	D5
Lukolela, Equateur	C4
Lukolela, Kasai-Oriental	D5
Lukula 9,400	B5
Luozi 7,000	B5
Lusambo 13,100	D4
Makanza	C3
Malemba-Nkulu	E5
Mambasa 7,400	E3
Mangai 15,200	C4
Manono 44,500	E5
Masi-Manimba 6,300	C4
Masisi	E4
Matadi 110,436	B5
Mbandaka 107,910	C3
Mbanza-Ngungu 55,800	C5
Mbuji-Mayi 256,154	D5
Mitwaba	E5
Moanda 6,400	B5
Mobayi-Mbongo	D3
Moliro	E5
Monga	D3
Monkoto	D4
Mulongo	E5
Mungbere	E3
Mushie 13,700	C4
Mutshatsha	D6
Muyumba	E5
Mwadingusha	E6
Mwanza	E5
Mweka 24,900	D4
Mwene-Ditu 71,200	D5
Mwenga	E4
Niangara 9,200	E3
Niemba	E5
Nyunzu 11,300	E5
Opala	D4
Oshwe	C4
Panda-Likasi 146,394	E6
Pangi	E4
Penge	D5
Poko	E3
Popokabaka	C5
Port Kindu 42,800	E4
Punia	E4
Pweto	E5
Rutshuru	E4
Sakania	E6
Sampwe	E5
Sandoa	D5
Seke-Banza	B5
Sentery 24,300	E5
Shabunda 6,900	E4
Songololo 4,600	B5
Tenke	E6
Titule	E3
Tshela 10,700	B4
Tshikapa 38,900	D5
Tshofa	D5
Ubundu 6,300	E4
Uvira 15,900	E4
Virunga 21,900	E5
Waka	D3
Walikale	E4
Wamba 11,500	E3
Watsa 21,300	E3
Yahuma	D3
Yakoma	D3
Yangambi 22,600	D3
Zongo	C3

OTHER FEATURES

Albert (Mobuto Sese Seko) (lake)	F3
Aruwimi (riv.)	E3
Bomu (riv.)	D3
Boyama (Stanley) (falls)	D3
Chicapa (riv.)	D5
Congo (riv.)	C4
Edward (lake)	E4
Elila (riv.)	E4
Fimi (riv.)	C4
Garamba Nat'l Park	E3
Giri (riv.)	C3
Itimbiri (riv.)	D3
Ituri (for.)	E3
Karisimbi (mt.)	E4
Kasai (riv.)	C4
Kivu (lake)	E4
Kwa (riv.)	C4
Kwango (riv.)	C5
Kwilu (riv.)	C5
Lindi (riv.)	E3
Livingstone (falls)	B5
Loange (riv.)	C5
Lokoro (riv.)	C4
Lomami (riv.)	D4
Lomela (riv.)	D4
Lowa (riv.)	E4
Lua (riv.)	C3
Lualaba (riv.)	E4
Luapula (riv.)	E6
Lubilash (riv.)	D5
Lufira (riv.)	E5
Luilaka (riv.)	C4
Lukenie (riv.)	D4
Lukuga (riv.)	E5
Lulua (riv.)	D5
Luvua (riv.)	E5
Mai-Ndombe (lake)	C4
Malebo (Stanley Pool) (lake)	C4
Margherita (mt.)	E3
Marungu (mts.)	E5
Mobuto Sese Seko (lake)	F3
Mweru (lake)	E5
Ruwenzori (range)	E3
Ruzizi (riv.)	E4
Salonga Nat'l Park	D4
Sankuru (riv.)	D4
Stanley (falls)	D3
Stanley Pool (lake)	C4
Tanganyika (lake)	E5
Tshuapa (riv.)	D4
Tumba (lake)	C4
Ubangi (riv.)	C3
Uele (riv.)	E3
Ulindi (riv.)	E4
Upemba (lake)	E5
Upemba Nat'l Park	E5
Virunga (range)	E4
Virunga Nat'l Park	E4
Zaire (Congo) (riv.)	C4

ZAMBIA

CITIES and TOWNS

Abercorn (Mbala) 11,179	F5
Bancroft (Chililabombwe) 61,928	E6
Broken Hill (Kabwe) 143,635	E6
Chibwe	E6
Chilanga 12,503	E7
Chililabombwe 61,928	E6
Chingola 145,869	E6
Chinsali 4,211	F6
Chipata 32,291	F6
Choma 17,943	E7
Fort Rosebery (Mansa) 34,801	E6
Isoka 6,832	F6
Kabompo 5,357	D6
Kabwe 143,635	E6
Kafue 29,794	E7
Kalabo 7,398	D6
Kalomo 5,878	E7
Kaoma 6,731	D6
Kapiri Mposhi 13,677	E6
Kasama 38,093	F6
Kasempa 3,063	E6
Kataba	D7
Kawambwa 7,235	E5
Kitwe 314,794	E6
Lealui	D6
Livingstone 71,987	E7
Luanshya 132,164	E6
Lundazi 4,083	F6
Lusaka (cap.) 538,469	E7
Luwingu 3,763	E6
Mansa 34,801	E6
Mazabuka 29,602	E7
Mbala 11,179	F5
Mkushi 4,104	E6
Mongu 24,919	D7
Monze 13,141	E7
Mpika 25,880	F6
Mporokoso 6,008	F5
Mpulungu 6,354	F5
Mufulira 149,778	E6
Mulobezi 2,589	E7
Mumbwa 7,570	E6
Mwinilunga 3,169	D6
Nakonde 4,599	F5
Namwala 3,008	E7
Ndola 282,439	E6
Petauke 7,531	F6
Senanga 7,204	D7
Serenje 6,008	F6
Sesheke 3,500	D7
Solwezi 15,032	E
Zambezi 8,166	D

OTHER FEATURES

Bangweulu (lake)	F
Barotseland (reg.)	D7
Chambeshi (riv.)	F
Cuando (riv.)	D7
Dongwe (riv.)	D
Kabompo (riv.)	D
Kafue (riv.)	E
Kafue Nat'l Park	E
Kalambo (falls)	F5
Kariba (dam)	E7
Kariba (lake)	E7
Luangwa (riv.)	F
Luapula (riv.)	E
Lungwebungu (riv.)	D
Mosi-Oa-Tunya (Victoria) (falls)	E7
Mulungushi (dam)	E6
Mweru (lake)	E5
Sunzu (mt.)	F5
Tanganyika (lake)	E5
Victoria (falls)	E7
Zambezi (riv.)	D7

Agriculture, Industry and Resources

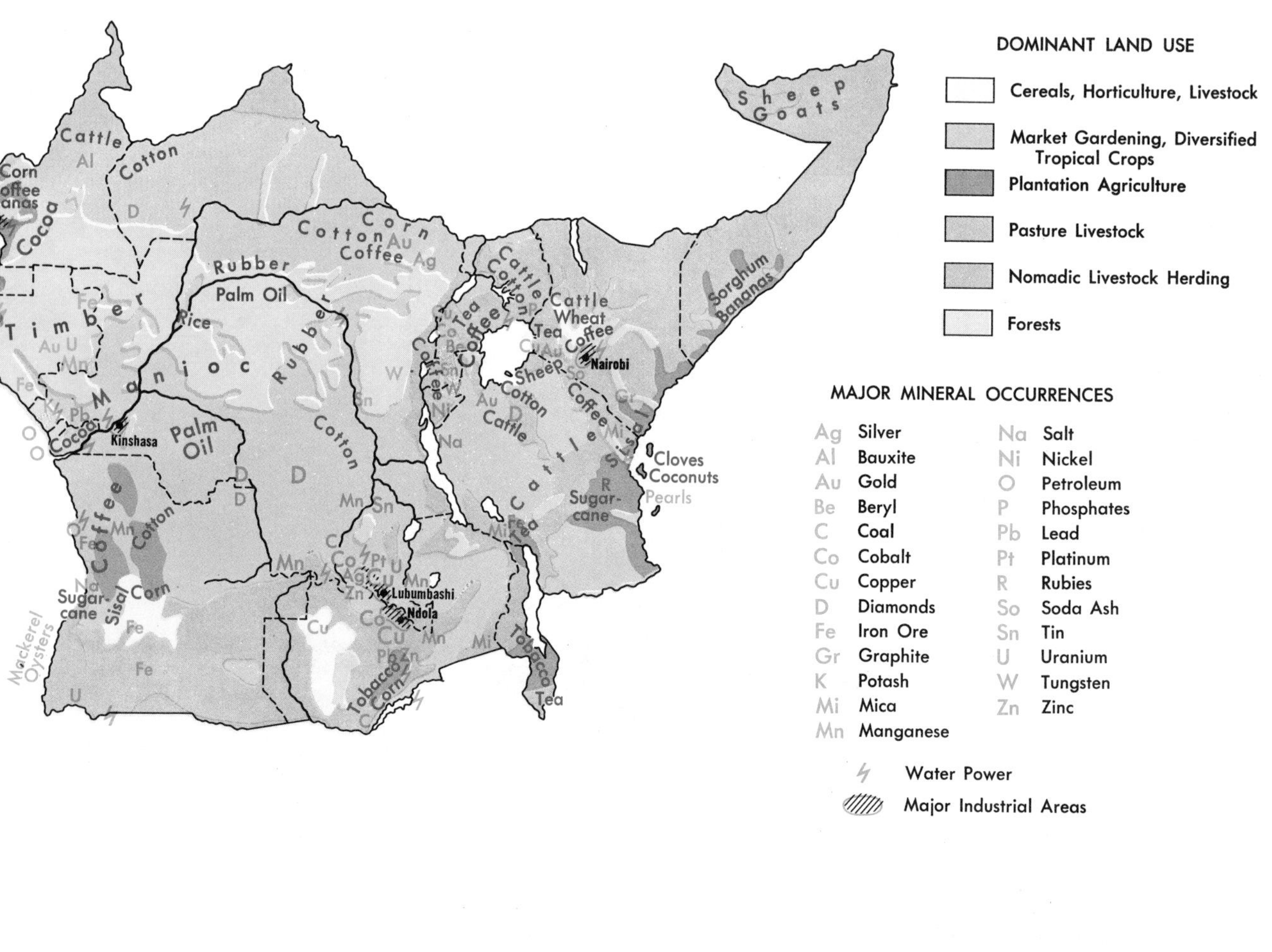
Cattle
Cotton
Corn
Coffee
Bananas
Douala
Cocoa
Rubber
Palm Oil
Rice
Timber
Manioc
Kinshasa
Sugar-cane
Sisal
Mackerel Oysters
Lubumbashi
Ndola
Tobacco
Tea
Sheep Goats
Sorghum Bananas
Wheat
Nairobi
Sheep
Cloves
Coconuts
Pearls
DOMINANT LAND USE
Cereals, Horticulture, Livestock
Market Gardening, Diversified Tropical Crops
Plantation Agriculture
Pasture Livestock
Nomadic Livestock Herding
Forests
MAJOR MINERAL OCCURRENCES
Ag Silver
Al Bauxite
Au Gold
Be Beryl
C Coal
Co Cobalt
Cu Copper
D Diamonds
Fe Iron Ore
Gr Graphite
K Potash
Mi Mica
Mn Manganese
Na Salt
Ni Nickel
O Petroleum
P Phosphates
Pb Lead
Pt Platinum
R Rubies
So Soda Ash
Sn Tin
U Uranium
W Tungsten
Zn Zinc
Water Power
Major Industrial Areas

NAMIBIA (SOUTH-WEST AFRICA)

AREA 317,827 sq. mi. (823,172 sq. km.)
POPULATION 1,200,000
CAPITAL Windhoek
LARGEST CITY Windhoek
HIGHEST POINT Brandberg 8,550 ft. (2,606 m.)
MONETARY UNIT rand
MAJOR LANGUAGES Ovambo, Hottentot, Herero, Afrikaans, English
MAJOR RELIGIONS Tribal religions, Protestantism

SOUTH AFRICA

AREA 455,318 sq. mi. (1,179,274 sq. km.)
POPULATION 23,771,970
CAPITALS Cape Town, Pretoria
LARGEST CITY Johannesburg
HIGHEST POINT Injasuti 11,182 ft. (3,408 m.)
MONETARY UNIT rand
MAJOR LANGUAGES Afrikaans, English, Xhosa, Zulu, Sesotho
MAJOR RELIGIONS Protestantism, Roman Catholicism, Islam, Hinduism, tribal religions

LESOTHO

AREA 11,720 sq. mi. (30,355 sq. km.)
POPULATION 1,339,000
CAPITAL Maseru
LARGEST CITY Maseru
HIGHEST POINT 11,425 ft. (3,482 m.)
MONETARY UNIT loti
MAJOR LANGUAGES Sesotho, English
MAJOR RELIGIONS Tribal religions, Christianity

BOTSWANA

AREA 224,764 sq. mi. (582,139 sq. km.)
POPULATION 819,000
CAPITAL Gaborone
LARGEST CITY Francistown
HIGHEST POINT Tsodilo Hill 5,922 ft. (1,805 m.)
MONETARY UNIT pula
MAJOR LANGUAGES Setswana, Shona, Bushman, English, Afrikaans
MAJOR RELIGIONS Tribal religions, Protestantism

MOZAMBIQUE

AREA 303,769 sq. mi. (786,762 sq. km.)
POPULATION 12,130,000
CAPITAL Maputo
LARGEST CITY Maputo
HIGHEST POINT Mt. Binga 7,992 ft. (2,436 m.)
MONETARY UNIT metical
MAJOR LANGUAGES Makua, Thonga, Shona, Portuguese
MAJOR RELIGIONS Tribal religions, Roman Catholicism, Islam

SWAZILAND

AREA 6,705 sq. mi. (17,366 sq. km.)
POPULATION 547,000
CAPITAL Mbabane
LARGEST CITY Manzini
HIGHEST POINT Emlembe 6,109 ft. (1,862 m.)
MONETARY UNIT lilangeni
MAJOR LANGUAGES siSwati, English
MAJOR RELIGIONS Tribal religions, Christianity

ZIMBABWE

AREA 150,803 sq. mi. (390,580 sq. km.)
POPULATION 7,360,000
CAPITAL Salisbury
LARGEST CITY Salisbury
HIGHEST POINT Mt. Inyangani 8,517 ft. (2,596 m.)
MONETARY UNIT Zimbabwe dollar
MAJOR LANGUAGES English, Shona, Ndebele
MAJOR RELIGIONS Tribal religions, Protestantism

MADAGASCAR

AREA 226,657 sq. mi. (587,041 sq. km.)
POPULATION 8,742,000
CAPITAL Antananarivo
LARGEST CITY Antananarivo
HIGHEST POINT Maromokotro 9,436 ft. (2,876 m.)
MONETARY UNIT Madagascar franc
MAJOR LANGUAGES Malagasy, French
MAJOR RELIGIONS Tribal religions, Roman Catholicism, Protestantism

COMOROS

AREA 719 sq. mi. (1,862 sq. km.)
POPULATION 290,000
CAPITAL Moroni
LARGEST CITY Moroni
HIGHEST POINT Karthala 7,746 ft. (2,361 m.)
MONETARY UNIT CFA franc
MAJOR LANGUAGES Arabic, French, Swahili
MAJOR RELIGION Islam

MAURITIUS

AREA 790 sq. mi. (2,046 sq. km.)
POPULATION 959,000
CAPITAL Port Louis
LARGEST CITY Port Louis
HIGHEST POINT 2,711 ft. (826 m.)
MONETARY UNIT Mauritian rupee
MAJOR LANGUAGES English, French, French Creole, Hindi, Urdu
MAJOR RELIGIONS Hinduism, Christianity, Islam

SEYCHELLES

AREA 145 sq. mi. (375 sq. km.)
POPULATION 63,000
CAPITAL Victoria
LARGEST CITY Victoria
HIGHEST POINT Morne Seychellois 2,993 ft. (912 m.)
MONETARY UNIT Seychellois rupee
MAJOR LANGUAGES English, French, Creole
MAJOR RELIGION Roman Catholicism

REUNION

AREA 969 sq. mi. (2,510 sq. km.)
POPULATION 491,000
CAPITAL St-Denis

MAYOTTE

AREA 144 sq. mi. (373 sq. km.)
POPULATION 47,300
CAPITAL Dzaoudzi

ZIMBABWE · **BOTSWANA** · **SOUTH AFRICA** · **LESOTHO** · **SWAZILAND**

MOZAMBIQUE · **COMOROS** · **MADAGASCAR** · **MAURITIUS** · **SEYCHELLES**

Agriculture, Industry and Resources

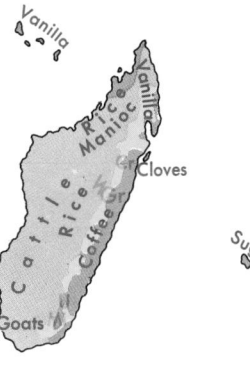

DOMINANT LAND USE

	Cereals, Horticulture, Livestock
	Market Gardening, Diversified Tropical Crops
	Plantation Agriculture
	Pasture Livestock
	Nomadic Livestock Herding
	Forests
	Nonagricultural Land

 Water Power
/////// Major Industrial Areas

MAJOR MINERAL OCCURRENCES

Ab	Asbestos	Cu	Copper	Pb	Manganese	Sb	Antimony
Ag	Silver	D	Diamonds	Pt	Salt	Sn	Tin
Al	Bauxite	Fe	Iron Ore	Mn	Nickel	U	Uranium
Au	Gold	Gr	Graphite	Na	Phosphates	V	Vanadium
Be	Beryl	Lt	Lithium	Ni	Lead	W	Tungsten
C	Coal	Mg	Magnesium	P	Platinum	Zn	Zinc
Cr	Chromium	Mi	Mica				

(continued on following page)

Topography

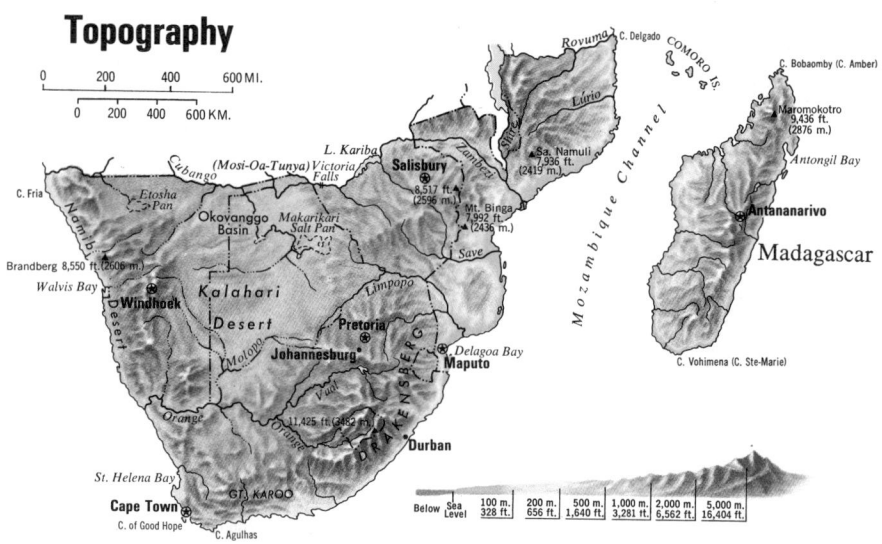

Hawston 2,501	G7	Kuilsrivier 8,132	F6	Newcastle 14,407	E5
Heidelberg 12,521	J7	Kuruman 5,758	C5	Nigel 41,179	J7
Heilbron 8,258	D5	Ladybrand 8,757	D5	Noupoort 7,403	C6
Hermanus 4,956	G7	Ladysmith 28,920	D5	Nyanga 15,655	C6
Hopetown 3,273	C5	Lambert's Bay 3,247	B6	Nylstroom 5,906	D4
Houtbaai 5,691	E6	Lombardy 3,395	H6	Odendaalsrus 15,603	D5
Howick 12,429	E5	Louis Trichardt 8,906	E4	Okiep 4,983	B5
Humansdorp 4,215	C6	Lydenburg 7,427	E4	Oudtshoorn 26,907	C6
Ingwavuma 718	F5			Paarl 49,244	F6
Jagersfontein 4,142	D5	Macassar 882	F6	Parow 60,768	F6
Jameson Park 2,280	J7	Maclear 3,279	D6	Parys 17,447	D5
Johannesburg 654,232	H6	Mafikeng (Mafeking) 6,515	C5	Phalaborwa 7,543	F4
Johannesburg□ 1,417,818	H6	Malmesbury 9,314	F6	Pietermaritzburg 114,822	E5
Keimoes 4,534	C5	Margate 4,410	E6	Pietermaritzburg□ 174,179	E5
Kempton Park 37,205	J6	Matatiele 3,853	D6	Pietersburg 27,174	E4
Kenhardt 3,230	C5	Melkbosstrand 453	E6	Piet Retief 10,056	E5
Kimberley 105,258	C5	Messina 12,121	D4	Piketberg 3,638	B6
Kimberley□ 108,609	C5	Meyerton 8,654	H7	Pinelands 11,769	F6
King William's Town 15,798	D6	Middelburg, C. of Good		Pinetown 22,721	E6
Kirkwood 5,151	D6	Hope 11,121	C6	Pniel 1,596	F6
Kleinmond 1,115	F7	Middelburg, Transvaal 26,942	E5	Port Alfred 8,640	D6
Klerksdorp 63,558	D5	Milnerton 10,893	F6	Port Elizabeth 392,231	D6
Koffiefontein 3,672	D5	Modderfontein 8,538	H6	Port Elizabeth□ 413,961	D6
Kokstad 10,227	D6	Molteno 5,425	D6	Port Nolloth 2,893	B5
Kraaifontein 10,286	F6	Montagu 5,504	C6	Port Saint Johns	
Kroonstad 51,988	D5	Moorreesburg 4,945	B6	(Umzimvubu) 1,817	D6
Krugersdorp 92,725	H6	Mossel Bay 17,574	C6	Port Shepstone 5,581	E6
		Nababeep 8,293	B5	Postmasburg 9,020	C5
		Nelspruit 25,092	E5		

Miandrivazo 2,371	G3	Côbué 770	F2	**NAMIBIA (SOUTH-WEST AFRICA)**		La Digue (isl.)	J5
Midongy Atsimo 1,068	H4	Cuamba 1,416	F2			Mahé (isl.)	H5
Mitsinjo 3,118	H3	Dona Ana (Mutarara) 686	F3	**CITIES and TOWNS**		North (isl.)	H5
Moramanga 10,806	H3	Dondo 2,112	F3			Praslin (isl.)	H5
Morombe 6,967	G4	Errego 418	F3	Aroab 783	B5	Silhouette (isl.)	H5
Morondava 19,061	G4	Espungabera 405	E4	Aus 767	B5	
Nosy-Varika 1,252	H4	Fingoè 1,137	E2	Berseba	B5	
Port-Bergé 4,734	H3	Funhalouro 42,366	E4	Bethanie 1,207	B5	**SOUTH AFRICA**
Sambava 6,215	J2	Guija 530	E5	Gibeon	B4	
Soanierana-Ivongo 2,876	H3	Homoine 1,122	F4	Gobabis 4,428	B4	**PROVINCES**
Sosumav 10,946	H3	Ibo 1,015	G2	Grootfontein 4,627	B3	
Tamatave (Toamasina) 77,395	H3	Inhambane 4,975	F4	Kalkfeld 587	B4	Cape of Good Hope 5,543,506	C6
Tambohorano 1,383	G3	Inhaminga 1,607	F3	Kamanjab 713	A3	Natal 5,722,215	E5
Tananarive (Antananarivo)		Inharrime 856	F4	Karasburg 2,693	B5	Orange Free State 1,833,216	D5
(cap.) 451,808	H3	Karibib 1,653	B4	Katima Mulilo	C3	Transvaal 10,673,033	D4
Tanganiony 6,952	H4	Lichinga 3,011	F2	Keetmanshoop 10,297	B5	
Toamasina 77,395	H3	Lumbo 11,080	G3	Khorixas 1,299	A4	**REPUBLICS**
Toliary (Tuléar) 45,676	G4	Lúrio 13,417	G2	Koes 514	B5	
Tsihombe 1,008	H5	Mabalaneo 13,158	F4	Lüderitz 6,642	A5	Bophuthatswana 1,200,000	D5
Tsiroanomandidy 11,444	H3	Maboteo 28,970	E4	Maltahöhe 1,313	B4	Transkei 2,000,000	D6
Tsivory 1,036	H4	Machangao 15,754	E4	Mariental 4,629	B4	Venda 450,000	E4
Vangaindrano 3,249	H4	Machazeo 42,255	E4	Ohopoho	A3	
Vatomandry 4,202	H3	Macia 1,203	E5	Okahandja 1,688	B4	**CITIES and TOWNS**
Vohibinany 1,741	H3	Macomia 730	G2	Omaruru 2,783	B4	
Vohimarina (Vohémar) 4,289	J2	Magude 1,502	E5	Ondangua	B3	Aberdeen 4,968	C6
Vohipeno 2,736	H4	Malema 430	F2	Ongwediva	B3	Adelaide 7,227	D6
		Mandièo 24,382	E3	Oranjemund 2,594	B5	Alberton 33,988	H6
OTHER FEATURES		Mandimbao 7,634	F2	Otavi 1,814	B3	Alexandra 57,040	H6
		Manhiça 1,680	E5	Otjiwarongo 8,018	B4	Alexander Bay 2,675	B5
Alaotra (lake)	H3	Maniamba 2,045	F2	Outjo 2,545	B4	Aliwal North 12,311	D6
Amber (Bobaomby) (cape)	H2	Manica 1,529	E3	Rehoboth 5,363	B4	Barberton 12,382	E5
Antongil (bay)	J3	Manjacaze 641	E5	Runtu 521	B3	Barkly East 4,023	D6
Betsiboka (riv.)	H3	Maputo (cap.) 755,300	E5	Stampriet 271	B4	Beaufort West 17,862	C6
Bobaomby (Amber) (cape)	H2	Marracuene 1,342	E5	Swakopmund 5,681	A4	Bellville 49,026	F6
Mangoky (riv.)	G4	Marromeu 1,330	F3	Tsumeb 12,338	B3	Benoni 151,294	J6
Mangoro (riv.)	H3	Marrupa 824	F2	Usakos 2,334	B4	Benoni□ 164,543	J6
Maromokotro (mt.)	H2	Massangenao 3,301	F4	Warmbad 810	B5	Bethal 29,918	D5
Masoala (pen.)	J3	Massinga 517	F4	Windhoek (cap.) 61,369	B4	Bethlehem 29,918	D5
Mozambique (chan.)	H3	Maxixe 902	F4	Witvlei 303	B4	Bethulie 4,918	D6
Nosy Be (isl.)	H2	Meconta 1,051	G2			Bloemfontein 149,836	D5
Nosy Boraha (isl.)	J3	Memba 379	G2	**OTHER FEATURES**		Bloemfontein□ 182,329	C5
Onilahy (riv.)	G4	Metangula 1,502	F2			Bloubergstrand 378	E6
Saint-André (cape)	G3	Milanje 1,048	F3	Brandberg (mt.)	A4	Boksburg 106,126	J6
Sainte-Marie (Vohimena)		Moamba 643	E5	Caprivi Strip (reg.)	C3	Botrivier 743	F7
(cape)	G5	Moçambique 1,730	G3	Chobe (riv.)	C3	Brakpan 73,210	J6
Sainte-Marie (Nosy Boraha)		Mocímboa da Praia 935	G2	Cubango (riv.)	B3	Brandvlei 1,337	B6
(isl.)	J3	Mocuba 2,293	F3	Damaraland (reg.)	B4	Bredasdorp 5,264	B6
Tsiafajavona (mt.)	H3	Moma 433	F3	Diamond Coast (reg.)	A5	Brentwood Park 5,296	J6
Tsiribihina (riv.)	H3	Morapo 902	G2	Elephant (riv.)	B6	Brits 12,182	D5
Vohimena (cape)	G5	Montepez 2,837	F2	Etosha Pan (salt pan)	B3	Britstown 3,039	C6
		Morrumbala 415	F3	Fish (riv.)	B5	Burgersdorp 8,340	D6
MAURITIUS		Morrumbene 1,121	F4	Great Namaland (reg.)	B4	Butterworth (Gcuwa) 2,769	D6
		Mualamao 34,992	G2	Hottentot (bay)	A5	Caledon 5,406	G7
CITIES and TOWNS		Mucojo 15,867	G2	Kalahari (des.)	C4	Calvinia 6,386	B6
		Mueda 1,583	G2	Kaokoveld (reg.)	A3	Cape Town (cap.) 697,514	E6
Curepipe 52,709	G5	Murrupula 444	F2	Kaukauveld (mts.)	C3	Cape Town□ 833,731	E6
Mahébourg 15,463	G5	Mutarara (Dona Ana) 686	F3	Namib (des.)	A3	Carltonville 40,641	G7
Port Louis (cap.) 141,022	G5	Nacala 4,601	G2	Nossob (riv.)	B4	Carnarvon 5,199	C6
Poudre d'Or 1,799	G5	Namacurra 399	F3	Okovango (riv.)	C3	Ceres 9,230	B6
Quatre Bornes 51,638	G5	Namapa 440	G2	Ovamboland (reg.)	B3	Christiana 6,882	D5
Souillac 3,361	G5	Nametil 453	F2	Skeleton Coast (reg.)	A3	Clanwilliam 2,724	B6
		Nampula 23,072	F2	Swakop (riv.)	B4	Clayville 3,994	H6
OTHER FEATURES		Negomaneo 656	F3	Zambezi (riv.)	C3	Colesberg 7,088	C6
		Nova Lusitânia 1,363	F3			Constantia 7,220	F6
Mascarene (isls.)	F5	Nova Mambone 883	F4			Cradock 20,822	D6
		Nova Sofala 274	F4			De Aar 18,057	C6
MAYOTTE		Pafúrio 2,599	E4			Delmas 6,424	H6
		Pemba 3,629	G2	**RÉUNION**		Dibeng 945	C5
CITIES and TOWNS		Quelimane 10,522	F3			Douglas 4,335	C5
		Quionga□ 3,181	G2	**CITIES and TOWNS**		Dundee 17,162	E5
Dzaoudzi (cap.) 196	H2	Quissico 2,615	F4			Dunnottar 3,089	J6
		Ribaué 437	F2	Le Port 21,564	F5	Durban 736,852	E5
MOZAMBIQUE		Songo 1,350	E3	Saint-André 6,584	G5	Durban□ 975,494	E5
		Tete 4,549	E3	Saint-Benoît 7,778	G5	Durbanville 7,438	F6
PROVINCES		Ulongue 451	E2	Saint-Denis (cap.) 80,075	F5	East London 119,727	D6
		Vila de Senao 21,074	E3	Saint-Denis* 104,603	F5	East London□ 126,671	D6
Cabo Delgado 940,000	F2	Vila Fontes 1,363	F3	Saint-Joseph 8,928	G6	Edenburg 3,710	D5
Gaza 999,900	E4	Vilanculos 887	F4	Saint-Louis 10,252	F5	Edendale 41,194	E5
Inhambane 977,000	E4	Vila Paiva de Andrada 435	F3	Saint-Pierre 21,817	F6	Edenvale 25,126	H6
Manica 541,200	E3	Xai-Xai 5,234	E5			Eersterivier 1,459	F6
Maputo 491,800	E5			**OTHER FEATURES**		Elliot 3,739	D6
Maputo (city) 755,300	E5					Eloff 1,134	H6
Nampula 2,402,700	F2	**OTHER FEATURES**		Bassas da India (isl.)	F4	Elsburg 3,501	H6
Niassa 514,100	F2			Europa (isl.)	G4	Elsiesrivier 63,706	F6
Sofala 1,055,200	E3	Angoche (isl.)	G3	Glorioso (isls.)	H2	Empangeni 7,532	E5
Tete 831,000	E3	Bazaruto, Ilha do (isl.)	F4	Juan de Nova (isl.)	G3	Ermelo 19,036	E5
Zambézia 2,500,000	F3	Binga (mt.)	E3	Piton des Neiges (mt.)	G5	Estcourt 10,922	E5
		Changane (riv.)	E4			Ficksburg 9,504	D5
CITIES and TOWNS		Chilwa (lake)	F3			Firgrove 2,535	F6
		Delagoa (bay)	E5	**SEYCHELLES**		Fort Beaufort 11,640	D6
Alto Molócuè 415	F3	Delgado (cape)	G2			Franschhoek 1,216	F6
Angoche 1,714	G3	Ligonha (riv.)	F3	**CITIES and TOWNS**		Garies 1,339	B6
Bartolomeu Diaso 6,102	F4	Limpopo (riv.)	E4			Gcuwa 2,769	D6
Beira 46,293	F3	Lugenda (riv.)	F2	Anse Boileau 3,420	H5	George 24,625	C6
Beira* 130,398	F3	Lúrio (riv.)	F2	Anse Royale† 3,182	H5	Germiston 221,972	H6
Bela Vista 851	E5	Mazoe (riv.)	E3	Cascade† 2,600	H5	Germiston□ 293,257	H6
Benga 1,398	E3	Mozambique (chan.)	F3	Victoria (cap.) 15,559	H5	Glencoe 10,513	E5
Catandica 663	E3	Namuli, Serra (mt.)	F3	Victoria* 23,012	H5	Goodwood 31,592	F6
Chemba 588	E3	Nyasa (lake)	F2			Gordon's Bay 1,112	F7
Chibuto 23,763	E4	Olifants (riv.)	D4	**OTHER FEATURES**		Graaff-Reinet 22,392	C6
Chicualacuala 2,050	E4	Rovuma (riv.)	F2			Grabouw 4,286	D6
Chimoio 4,507	E3	São Sebastião (pt.)	F4	Aldabra (isl.)	H1	Grahamstown 41,302	D6
Chinde 742	F3	Save (riv.)	E4	Assumption (isl.)	H1	Grassy Park 32,709	F6
		Shire (riv.)	F3	Astove (isl.)	H2	Greytown 9,028	E5
		Zambezi (riv.)	F3	Cosmoledo (isls.)	H1	Griquatown 2,996	C5
				Frigate (isl.)	J5	Halfway House 3,639	H6
						Harrismith 16,082	D5

*Population of met. area.
†Population of district.
□Population of met. area.

Potchefstroom 57,443 .... D5
Potgietersrus 6,667 .... D4
Pretoria (cap.) 573,282 .... D5
Pretoria□ 545,450 .... D5
Prieska 8,521 .... C5
Prince Albert 3,346 .... C6
Queenstown 39,304 .... C6
Randburg 43,257 .... H6
Randfontein 50,481 .... G5
Reitz 5,650 .... D5
Rensburg 2,042 .... J7
Richards Bay 598 .... E5
Richmond 3,185 .... C6
Robertson 10,237 .... C6
Robertson 10,237 .... C6
Rustenburg 22,303 .... D5
Senekal 9,124 .... D5
Sesfontein 2,731 .... A3
Simonstown 12,137 .... C7
Sishen 2,692 .... C5
Somerset East 10,383 .... D6
Somerset West 11,828 .... F6
Soweto 602,043 .... H6
Springbok 4,357 .... B5
Springs 142,812 .... J6
Springs□ 146,831 .... J6

Standerton 21,038 .... D5
Stanger 11,064 .... F5
Stellenbosch 29,955 .... C6
Strand 24,503 .... F7
Stutterheim 12,077 .... D6
Sundra 2,088 .... J6
Swellendam 6,423 .... C6
Taung 1,316 .... C5
Tembisa 81,821 .... H6
Thabazimbi 6,711 .... D4
Thohoyandou E4
Tzaneen 4,331 .... E4
Ubombo□ 3,697 .... E5
Uitenhage 70,517 .... D6
Ulundi E5
Umtata 25,216 .... D6
Umzimvubu 1,817 .... D6
Umzinto 5,272 .... E6
Upington 28,632 .... C5
Vaalplas 5,699 .... C5
Vanderbijl Park 78,754 .... D5
Vanrhynsdorp 2,279 .... B6
Veldrif 3,361 .... B6
Venterspos G6
Vereeniging 172,549 .... D5
Vereeniging□ 200,078 .... D5
Victoria West 3,949 .... C6
Villiersdorp 2,349 .... G6

Vishoek 6,721 .... H6
Volksrust 11,064 .... D5
Vrede 6,309 .... H6
Vredenburg 6,094 .... B6
Vredendal 5,377 .... B6
Vryburg 16,916 .... C5
Vryheid 16,992 .... E5
Walvis Bay 21,725 .... A4
Warmbad 8,343 .... D5
Warrenton 9,614 .... C5
Waterval-Bo 6,951 .... E5
Welkom 67,472 .... D5
Wellington 17,092 .... B6
Westonaria 36,253 .... H7
Willowmore 3,740 .... C6
Winburg 6,761 .... D5
Witbank 37,456 .... D5
Wolmaransstad 7,219 .... D5
Worcester 41,198 .... B6
Zastron 4,483 .... D6
Zeerust 6,972 .... D5
Zwelitsha 22,131 .... D6

OTHER FEATURES

Addo Nat'l Park D6
Agulhas (cape) B6
Bot (riv.) G7

Bredasdorp Nat'l Park C6
Cape (pen.) E7
Crocodile (riv.) H6
Drakensberg (range) D6
False (bay) F7
Good Hope (cape) E7
Great Fish (riv.) D6
Great Karoo (reg.) C6
Great Kei (riv.) D6
Griqualand West (reg.) C5
Groote (riv.) C6
Hartbees (riv.) C5
Kalahari Gemsbok Nat'l Park C5
King George's (falls) B5
Klip (riv.) H6
Kruger Nat'l Park E4
Limpopo (riv.) D4
Molopo (riv.) C5
Mountain Zebra Nat'l Park D6
Olifants (riv.) D4
Orange (riv.) B5
Palmiet (riv.) F7
Plettenberg (bay) C6
Pondoland (reg.) D6
Robben (isl.) E6
Royal Natal Nat'l Park D5
Saint Helena (bay) B6
Saint Lucia (lake) E5

Sak (riv.) C6
Sand (riv.) C6
Slangkop (pt.) E7
Sneeuwkop (mt.) D6
Table (bay) E6
Table (mt.) E6
Vaal (riv.) C5
Walvis (bay) A4
Witwatersberg (range) G5
Witwatersrand (reg.) H7
Zonderend (riv.) C6
Zululand (reg.) E5

SWAZILAND

CITIES and TOWNS

Manzini 28,837 .... E5
Mbabane (cap.) 23,109 .... E5
Siteki 1,362 .... E5

ZIMBABWE

CITIES and TOWNS

Beitbridge 1,986 .... E4
Bindura 17,000 .... E3

Bulawayo 359,000 .... D3
Chipinga 2,350 .... E4
Dett 2,473 .... D3
Enkeldoorn 1,669 .... E4
Fort Victoria 22,000 .... E4
Gatooma 32,000 .... D4
Gwaaii 2,710 .... D3
Gwanda 2,049 .... D4
Gwelo 68,000 .... D3
Hartley 12,000 .... E3
Inyanga 733 .... E3
Kariba 3,943 .... D3
Marandellas 23,000 .... E3
Matopos 11,330 .... D4
Melsetter 667 .... E4
Mount Darwin 904 .... E3
Nuanetsi 7,830 .... E4
Plumtree 2,041 .... D4
Que Que 54,000 .... D3
Rusape 5,286 .... E3
Salisbury (cap.) 601,000 .... E3
Selukwe 8,387 .... E4
Shabani 20,000 .... E4
Shamva 785 .... E3
Sinoia 25,000 .... D3
Tuli 340 .... D4

Wankie 33,000 .... D3
West Nicholson 1,929 .... D4

OTHER FEATURES

Kariba (lake) D3
Lundi (riv.) E4
Mashonaland (reg.) E3
Matabeleland (reg.) D3
Mazoe (riv.) E3
Mushandike Nat'l Park D4
Rhodes Inyanga Nat'l Park E3
Sabi (riv.) E3
Shangani (riv.) D3
Shashe (riv.) D3
Umvukwe (range) E3
Victoria (falls) C3
Zambezi (riv.) D3
Zimbabwe Nat'l Park E4

*City and suburbs.
†Population of parish.
○Population of subdivision.
□Population of urban area.

Umtali 61,000 .... E3
Umvuma 1,525 .... D3

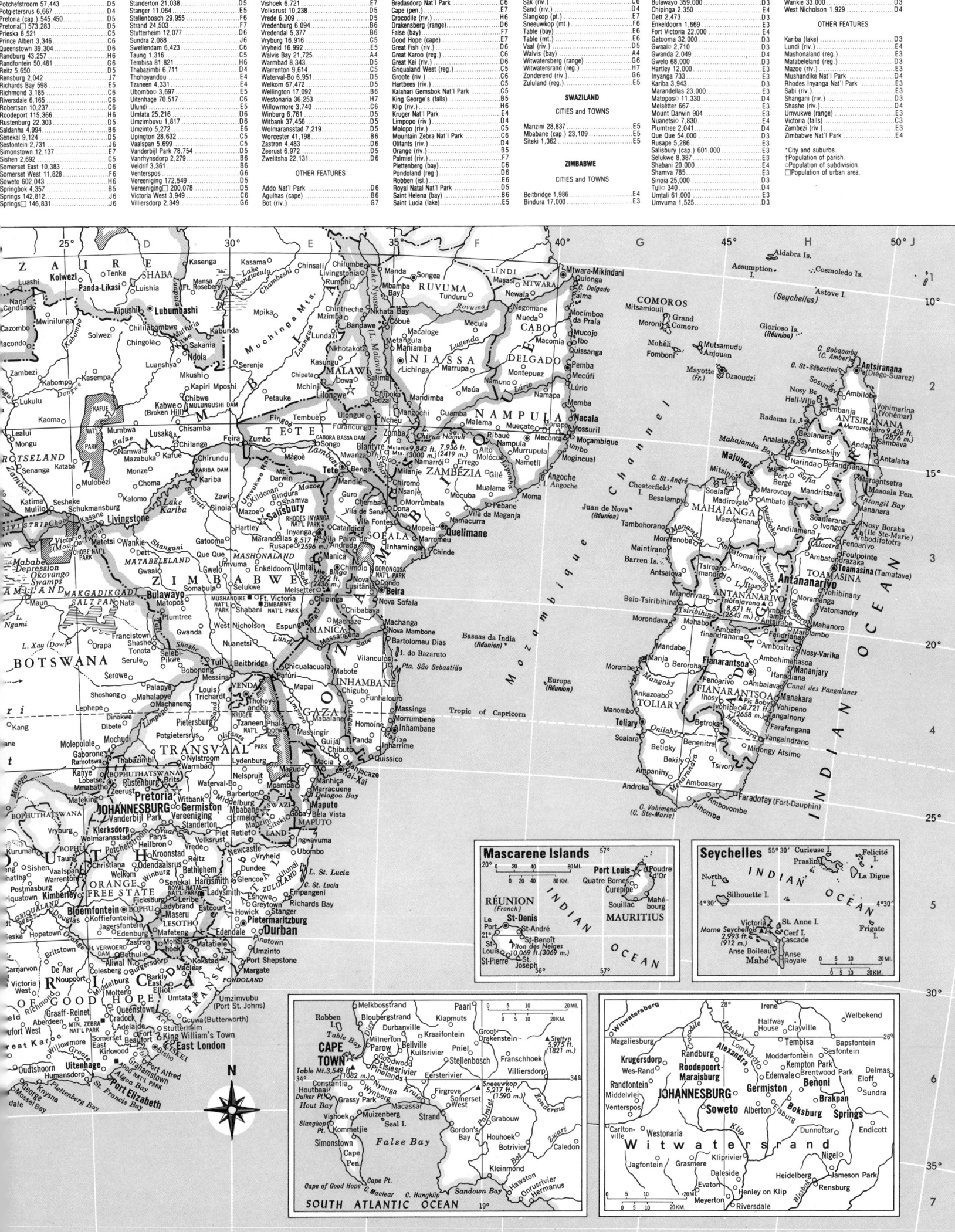

Population Distribution

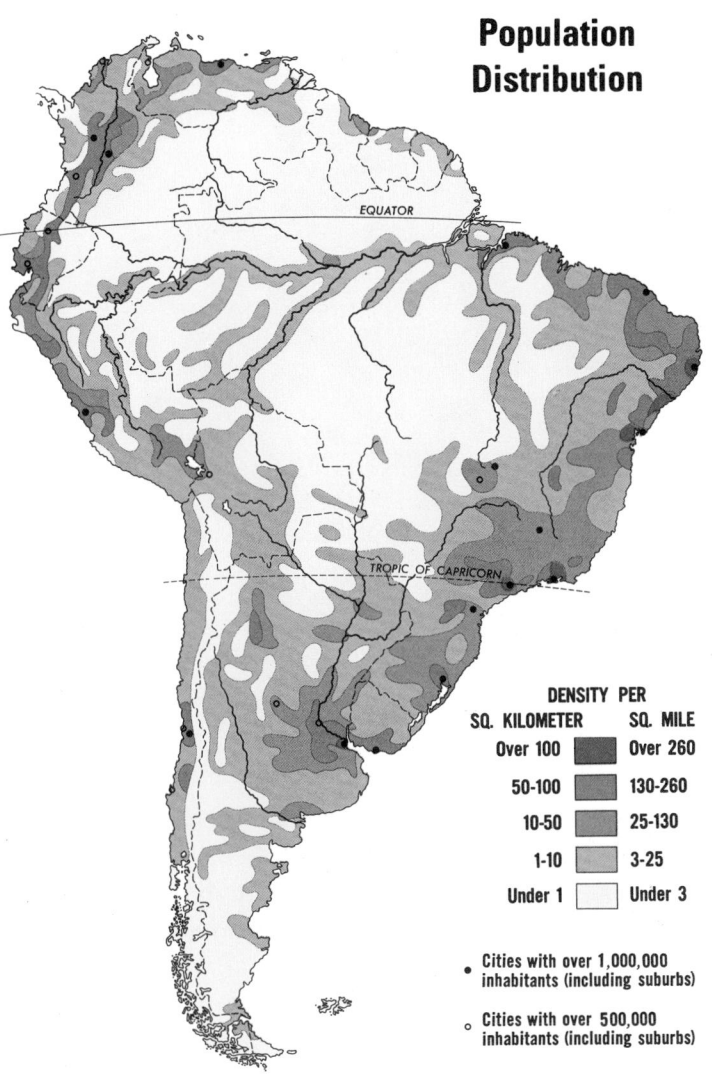

AREA 6,875,000 sq. mi. (17,806,250 sq. km.)
POPULATION 245,000,000
LARGEST CITY São Paulo
HIGHEST POINT Cerro Aconcagua 22,831 ft. (6,959 m.)
LOWEST POINT Salina Grande -131 ft. (-40 m.)

Vegetation

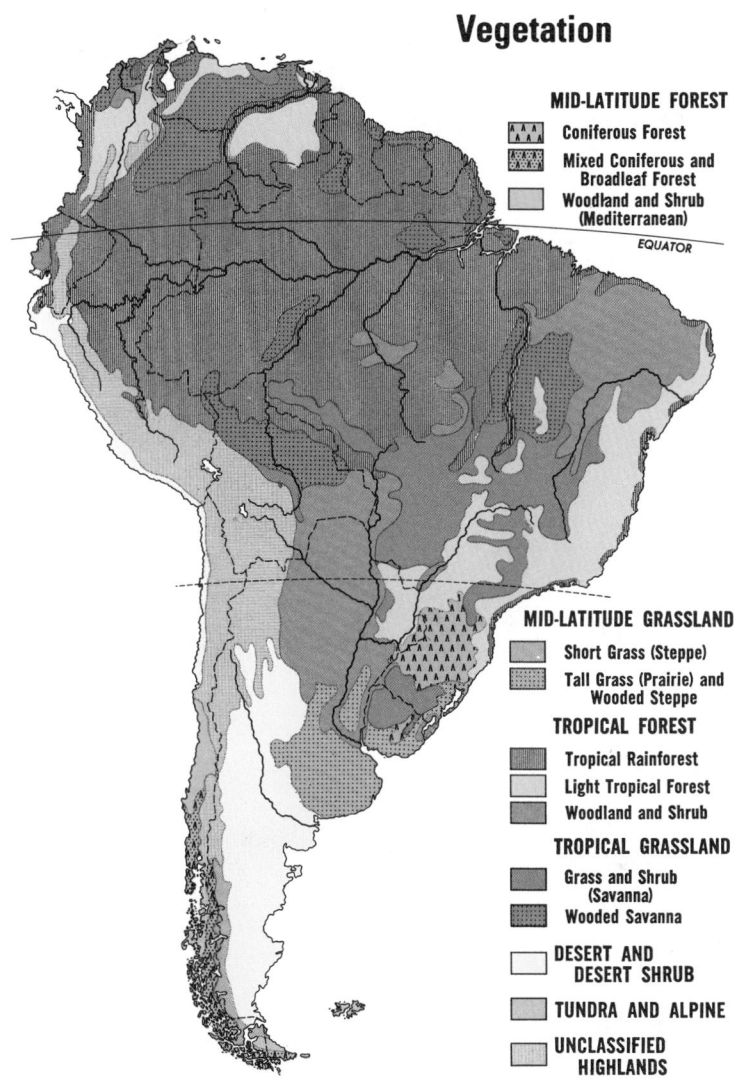

DENSITY PER

SQ. KILOMETER	SQ. MILE
Over 100	Over 260
50-100	130-260
10-50	25-130
1-10	3-25
Under 1	Under 3

● Cities with over 1,000,000 inhabitants (including suburbs)

○ Cities with over 500,000 inhabitants (including suburbs)

MID-LATITUDE FOREST
- Coniferous Forest
- Mixed Coniferous and Broadleaf Forest
- Woodland and Shrub (Mediterranean)

MID-LATITUDE GRASSLAND
- Short Grass (Steppe)
- Tall Grass (Prairie) and Wooded Steppe

TROPICAL FOREST
- Tropical Rainforest
- Light Tropical Forest
- Woodland and Shrub

TROPICAL GRASSLAND
- Grass and Shrub (Savanna)
- Wooded Savanna

DESERT AND DESERT SHRUB

TUNDRA AND ALPINE

UNCLASSIFIED HIGHLANDS

Average January Temperature

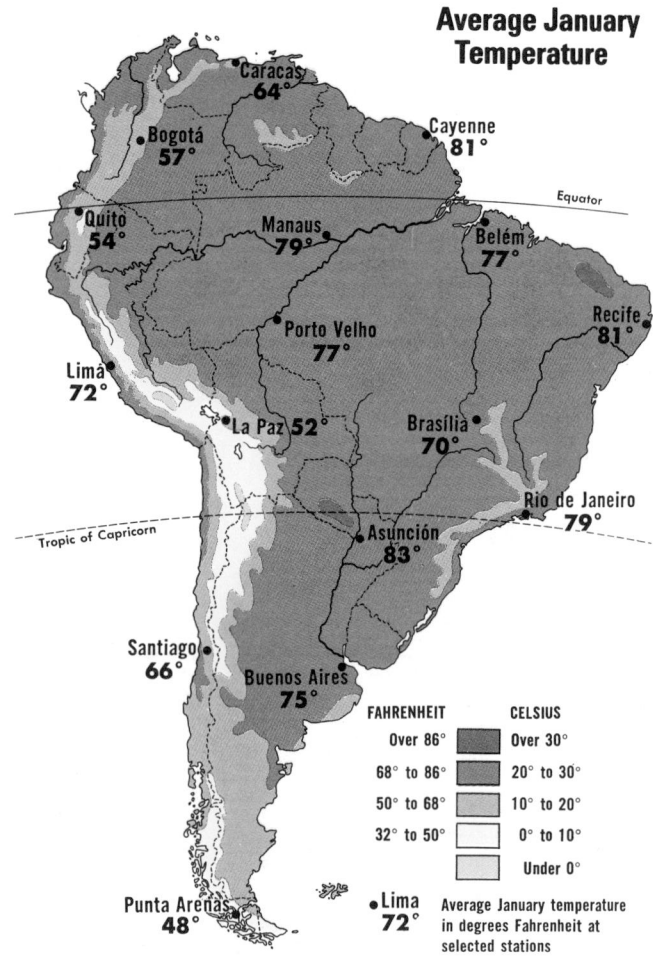

Caracas 64°
Bogotá 57°
Cayenne 81°
Equator
Quito 54°
Manaus 79°
Belém 77°
Porto Velho 77°
Recife 81°
Lima 72°
La Paz 52°
Brasília 70°
Tropic of Capricorn
Rio de Janeiro 79°
Asunción 83°
Santiago 66°
Buenos Aires 75°
Punta Arenas 48°

FAHRENHEIT	CELSIUS
Over 86°	Over 30°
68° to 86°	20° to 30°
50° to 68°	10° to 20°
32° to 50°	0° to 10°
	Under 0°

• Lima 72° Average January temperature in degrees Fahrenheit at selected stations

Average July Temperature

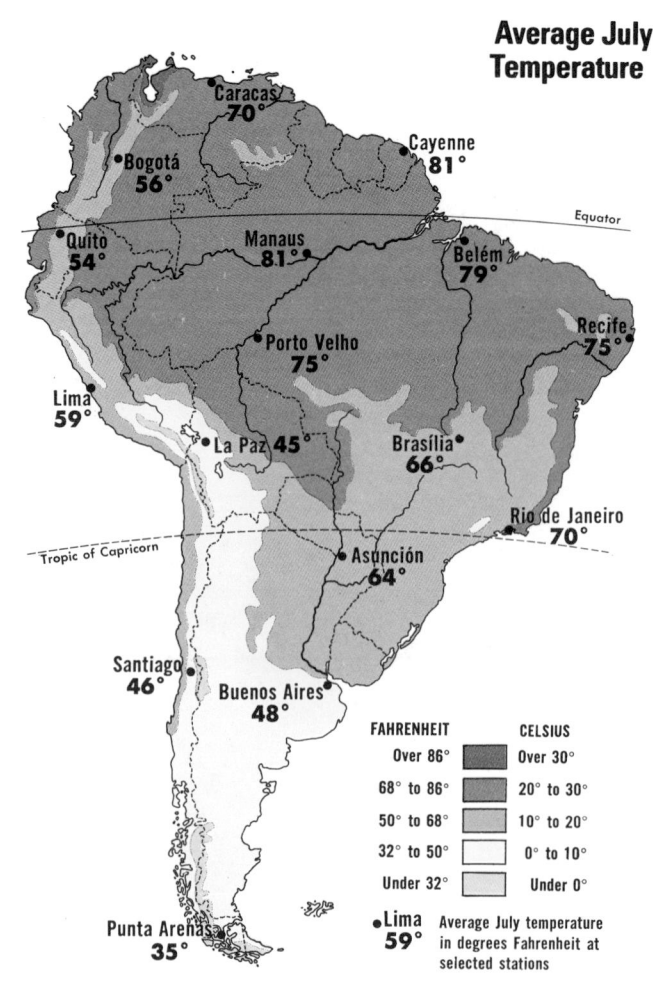

Caracas 70°
Bogotá 56°
Cayenne 81°
Equator
Quito 54°
Manaus 81°
Belém 79°
Porto Velho 75°
Recife 75°
Lima 59°
La Paz 45°
Brasília 66°
Tropic of Capricorn
Rio de Janeiro 70°
Asunción 64°
Santiago 46°
Buenos Aires 48°
Punta Arenas 35°

FAHRENHEIT	CELSIUS
Over 86°	Over 30°
68° to 86°	20° to 30°
50° to 68°	10° to 20°
32° to 50°	0° to 10°
Under 32°	Under 0°

• Lima 59° Average July temperature in degrees Fahrenheit at selected stations

Rainfall

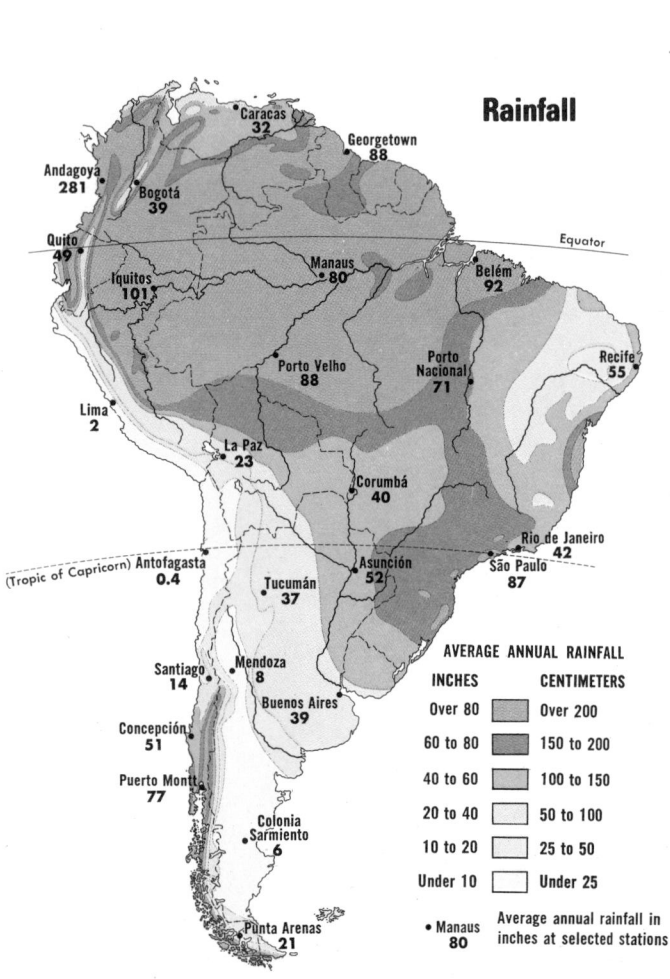

Caracas 32
Georgetown 88
Andagoya 281
Bogotá 39
Quito 49
Equator
Iquitos 101
Manaus 80
Belém 92
Porto Velho 88
Porto Nacional 71
Recife 55
Lima 2
La Paz 23
Corumbá 40
(Tropic of Capricorn) Antofagasta 0.4
Tucumán 37
Asunción 52
Rio de Janeiro 42
São Paulo 87
Santiago 14
Mendoza 8
Buenos Aires 39
Concepción 51
Puerto Montt 77
Colonia Sarmiento 6
Punta Arenas 21

AVERAGE ANNUAL RAINFALL

INCHES	CENTIMETERS
Over 80	Over 200
60 to 80	150 to 200
40 to 60	100 to 150
20 to 40	50 to 100
10 to 20	25 to 50
Under 10	Under 25

• Manaus 80 Average annual rainfall in inches at selected stations

Vegetation/Relief

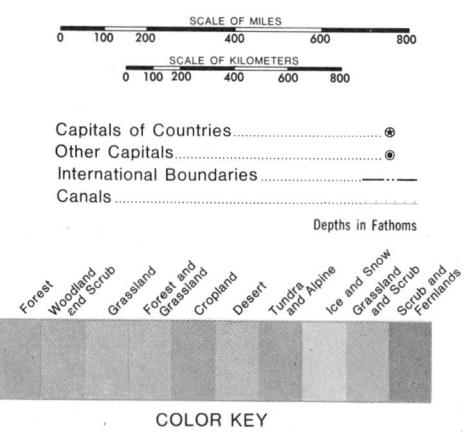

SCALE OF MILES
0 100 200 400 600 800

SCALE OF KILOMETERS
0 100 200 400 600 800

Capitals of Countries .... ⊛
Other Capitals .... ⊙
International Boundaries ....
Canals ....

Depths in Fathoms

Forest | Woodland and Scrub | Grassland | Forest and Grassland | Cropland | Desert | Tundra and Alpine | Ice and Snow | Grassland and Scrub | Scrub and Fernlands

COLOR KEY

STATES

Amazonas (terr.) 21,696 .....E5
Anzoátegui 506,297 .....F3
Apure 164,705 .....D4
Aragua 543,170 .....E3
Barinas 231,046 .....D3
Bolívar 391,665 .....F7
Carabobo 659,339 .....D2
Cojedes 94,351 .....D3
Delta Amacuro (terr.) 48,139 .....H3
Dependencias federales (terr.) 463 .....E2
Distrito Federal 1,860,637 .....E2
Falcón 407,957 .....D2
Guárico 318,905 .....E3
Lara 671,410 .....C2
Mérida 347,095 .....C3
Miranda 856,272 .....E2
Monagas 298,239 .....G3
Nueva Esparta 118,830 .....G2
Portuguesa 297,047 .....D3
Sucre 469,004 .....G2
Táchira 511,346 .....C4
Trujillo 381,334 .....C3
Yaracuy 223,545 .....D2
Zulia 1,299,030 .....B2

CITIES and TOWNS

Acarigua 56,743 .....D3
Achaguas 4,633 .....D4

Adícora 707 .....D2
Aguada Grande 2,901 .....D2
Agua Fría D2
Agua Linda E5
Aguasay 1,752 .....G3
Altagracia 11,116 .....C2
Altagracia de Orituco 18,717 .....E3
Amuay C2
Anaco 29,487 .....F3
Apartaderos G5
Apurito 740 .....D4
Arabopó H5
Aragua de Barcelona 9,107 .....F3
Aragua de Maturín 4,051 .....G3
Araure 22,466 .....D3
Aricagua 231 .....C3
Arichuna 1,204 .....E4
Aripao 296 .....F4
Arismendi 1,257 .....D3
Aroa 5,418 .....D2
Atapirire 337 .....F3
Bachaquero C2
Baragua 659 .....D2
Barbacoas 2,513 .....E3
Barcelona 78,201 .....F2
Barinas 56,329 .....C3
Barinitas 9,644 .....C3
Barquisimeto 330,815 .....D2
Barrancas, Barinas 4,489 .....C3
Barrancas, Monagas 5,738 .....G3
Betijoque 5,851 .....C3
Biruaca 2,266 .....E4

Biscucuy 6,114 .....D3
Bobare 1,204 .....D2
Bobures 2,468 .....C3
Boca de Arca 2,756 .....C3
Boca del Mangle D2
Boca del Pao 403 .....F3
Bocono 15,915 .....C3
Borbón C2
Borojó 423 .....D2
Bruzual 941 .....D3
Buena Vista, Anzoátegui F3
Buena Vista, Apure D4
Buena Vista, Falcón 944 .....D2
Cabimas 118,037 .....C2
Cabruta 1,927 .....E4
Cabudare 14,593 .....D2
Cabure 1,673 .....D2
Cachipo G3
Cacuri F5
Cagua 29,601 .....E2
Caicara 6,092 .....C3
Caicara de Orinoco 6,867 .....E4
Calabozo 37,282 .....E3
Calderas 1,195 .....C3
Camaguán 4,143 .....E3
Camatagua 3,335 .....E3
Campo Claro 1,832 .....G2
Candelaria F4
Cantaura 15,839 .....F3
Capatárida 1,375 .....C2
Capibara E6
Carabobo, Bolívar H4

Carabobo, Carabobo D3
Caracas (cap.) 1,035,499 .....D2
Caracas* 2,183,935 .....E2
Carache 3,966 .....C3
Carapa 119 .....G3
Cariaco 6,549 .....G2
Caribén E4
Caripe 4,729 .....G3
Caripito 19,053 .....G3
Carirubana 15,701 .....C2
Carmelo 2,556 .....C2
Carora 36,115 .....C2
Carrasquero 2,193 .....B2
Carúpano 50,935 .....G2
Casanay 4,985 .....G2
Casigua, Falcón 460 .....C2
Casigua, Zulia 3,665 .....B3
Caucagua 6,218 .....E2
Cazorla 700 .....E3
Chaguaramas 2,748 .....E3
Chichiriviche 3,236 .....D2
Chivacoa 19,210 .....D2
Chivacoro 534 .....C2
Churuguara 6,636 .....D2
Ciudad Bolívar 103,728 .....F3
Ciudad Bolivia 4,864 .....C3
Ciudad de Nutrias 769 .....D3
Ciudad Ojeda 83,083 .....C2
Ciudad Piar 3,965 .....G4
Clarines 2,099 .....F2
Cojoro C2

Colón E6
Comunidad E6
Coporito H3
Coro 68,701 .....D2
Corozo Pando E3
Cúa 9,953 .....E2
Cubiro 1,988 .....D2
Cuchivero F4
Cumaná 119,751 .....G2
Cumanacoa 9,179 .....G2
Cunaviche 795 .....E4
Curiapo H3
Dabajuro 4,516 .....C2
Delicias 1,616 .....B4
Democracia E6
Dolores 1,454 .....C3
Duaca 7,519 .....D2
Ejido 11,170 .....C3
El Almacén G4
El Amparo de Apure 2,015 .....C4
El Baúl 1,715 .....D3
El Callao 4,270 .....H4
El Calvario 384 .....E3
El Chaparro 3,768 .....F3
El Cristo G4
El Dorado 1,888 .....H4
El Empedrado 1,788 .....C3
El Guapo 1,231 .....F2
El Manteco 1,962 .....H4
El Miamo 335 .....H4
Elorza 3,184 .....C4
El Oso H5

El Palmar 2,758 .....G4
El Pao, Anzoátegui 761 .....F3
El Pao, Bolívar 1,259 .....G3
El Pao, Cojedes 1,715 .....D3
El Perú 3,278 .....H4
El Pilar 3,278 .....G2
El Rastro 903 .....E3
El Roque E2
El Samán de Apure 1,399 .....D4
El Socorro F3
El Sombrero 8,373 .....E3
El Tigre 49,801 .....F3
El Tocuyo 19,351 .....C3
El Toro H3
El Vigía 20,970 .....C3
El Vínculo D1
Encontrados 5,607 .....B3
Esperanza E6
Espino 559 .....F3
Garcitas C3
Guaca 35,111 .....G2
Guachara 577 .....C3
Guadarrama 334 .....D3
Guaina G5
Guana G5
Guanare 34,148 .....D3
Guanarito 3,150 .....D3
Guanoco G2
Guanta 9,017 .....F2
Guardatinaja 1,206 .....E3
Guarero B2

Guarico 3,259 .....D3
Guariquén 619 .....G2
Guasdualito 7,793 .....C4
Guasimal 582 .....C3
Guasipati 4,807 .....H4
Guayabal, Amazonas E5
Guayabal, Guárico 1,403 .....E3
Güiria 13,905 .....G2
Guri G4
Guzmán Blanco E6
Higuerote 5,008 .....F2
Icabarú G5
Independencia 4,897 .....D3
Irapa 4,470 .....G2
Juangriego 6,062 .....G2
Judibana C2
Juguín E5
Kavanayén G4
La Aduana C3
La Asunción 6,381 .....G2
La Canoa G4
La Ceiba, Apure D4
La Ceiba, Trujillo 212 .....C3
La Concepción C2
La Concepción 13,885 .....B2
La Esmeralda F5
La Esperanza D3
La Fría 8,134 .....B3
La Grita 9,954 .....C3
La Guaira 20,344 .....E2
Lagunetas C2
Lagunillas C3

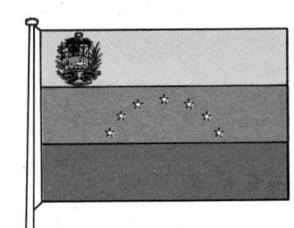

AREA 352,143 sq. mi. (912,050 sq. km.)
POPULATION 13,913,000
CAPITAL Caracas
LARGEST CITY Caracas
HIGHEST POINT Pico Bolívar 16,427 ft.
(5,007 m.)
MONETARY UNIT Bolívar
MAJOR LANGUAGE Spanish
MAJOR RELIGION Roman Catholicism

Topography

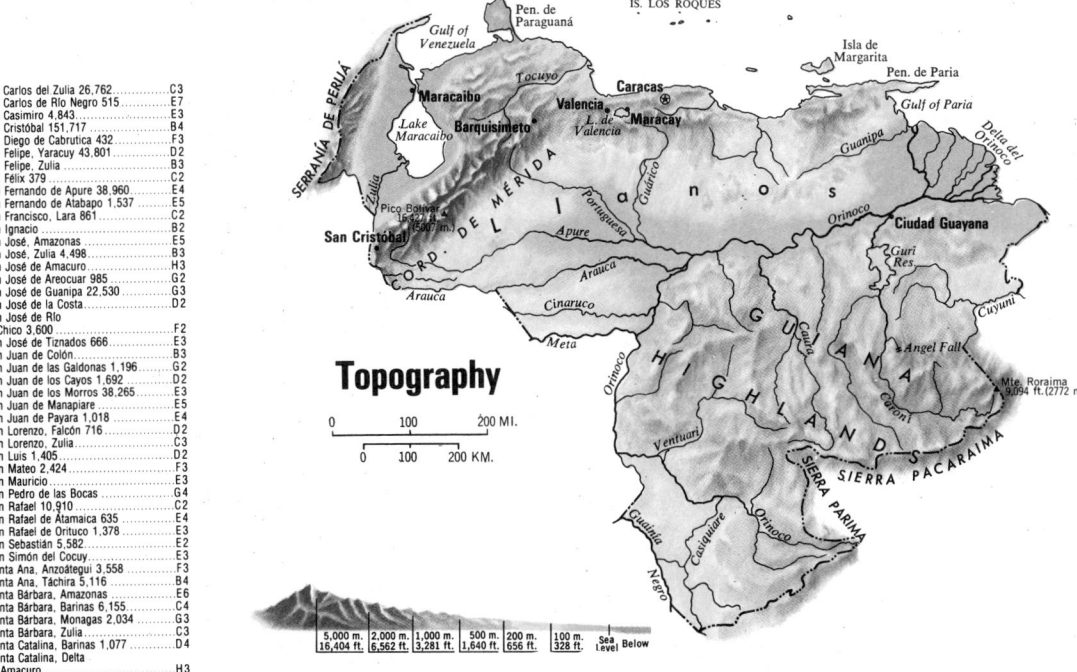

5,000 m. 16,404 ft.	2,000 m. 6,562 ft.	1,000 m. 3,281 ft.	500 m. 1,640 ft.	200 m. 656 ft.	100 m. 328 ft.	Sea Level / Below

Agriculture, Industry and Resources

MAJOR MINERAL OCCURRENCES

- Al   Bauxite
- Au   Gold
- C   Coal
- D   Diamonds
- Fe   Iron Ore
- G   Natural Gas
- Mn   Manganese
- Na   Salt
- O   Petroleum

- ⚡   Water Power
- ▨   Major Industrial Areas

DOMINANT LAND USE

- Diversified Tropical Crops (chiefly plantation agriculture)
- Upland Cultivated Areas
- Upland Livestock Grazing, Limited Agriculture
- Extensive Livestock Ranching
- Forests

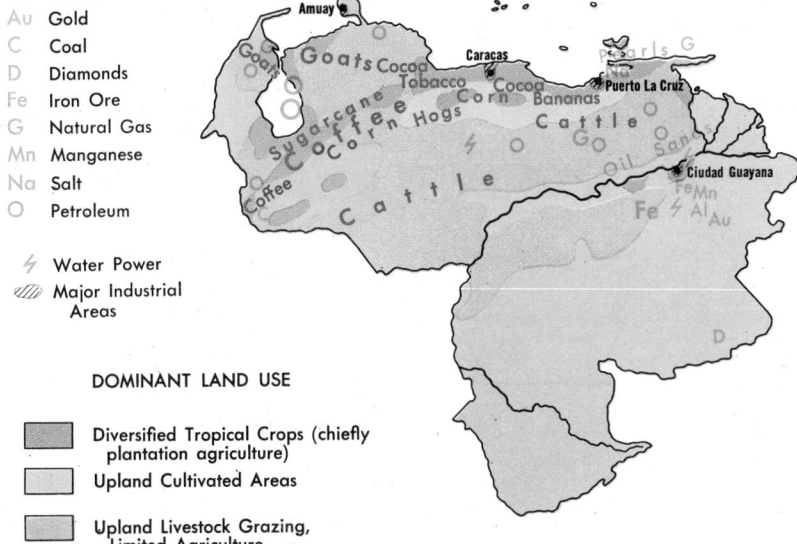

Colombia

MERCATOR PROJECTION

SCALE OF MILES

0 25 50 75 100 125 150

SCALE OF KILOMETERS

0 25 50 75 100 125 150

Capitals of Countries............ ☆
Other Capitals.................... ●
International Boundaries.........
Other Boundaries................
Canals...........................

Scale 1:6,800,000

INTENDENCIA DE
SAN ANDRÉS Y PROVIDENCIA
Same scale as main map

© Copyright HAMMOND INCORPORATED, Maplewood, N.J.

INTERNAL DIVISIONS

Amazonas (comm.) 6,825	D8
Antioquia (dept.) 2,976,153	B4
Arauca (inten.) 19,884	E4
Atlántico (dept.) 958,560	C2
Bolívar (dept.) 802,407	C3
Boyacá (dept.) 1,084,766	D5
Caldas (dept.) 700,954	C5
Caquetá (inten.) 57,103	C7
Casanare (inten.)	B3
Cauca (dept.) 603,894	B6
César (dept.) 339,843	D3
Chocó (dept.) 201,915	B4
Córdoba (dept.) 645,478	C3
Cundinamarca (dept.) 1,106,626	C5
Distrito Especial 2,855,065	C5
Guainía (comm.) 1,792	F6
Guajira, La (dept.) 180,520	D2
Huila (dept.) 469,834	C6
La Guajira (dept.) 180,520	D2
Magdalena (dept.) 536,122	C3
Meta (dept.) 245,176	D6
Nariño (dept.) 807,112	B7
Norte de Santander (dept.) 693,298	D3
Putumayo (inten.) 22,916	C7
Quindío (dept.) 321,677	C5
Risaralda (dept.) 452,626	B5
San Andrés y Providencia (inten.) 22,719	B10
Santander (dept.) 1,130,977	D4
Sucre (dept.) 354,412	C3
Tolima (dept.) 903,520	C5
Valle del Cauca (dept.) 2,204,722	B6
Vaupés (comm.) 6,923	E7
Vichada (comm.) 2,172	F5

CITIES and TOWNS

Acacías 9,238	D6
Acandí 2,358	B3
Agrado 2,771	C6
Aguachica 16,771	D3
Aguadas 9,995	C5
Agua de Dios 9,689	C5
Agustín Codazzi 21,932	D3
Aipe 3,794	C6
Algeciras 5,022	C6
Almaguer 1,518	B7
Amalfi 6,494	C4
Andes 14,957	C5
Anserma 15,559	B5
Antioquia 6,841	B4
Anzá 647	C4
Aracataca 7,511	D2
Arauca 7,613	E4
Arauquita 1,096	E4
Arjona 20,571	C2
Armenia 135,615	B5
Armero 19,567	C5
Ayapel 7,475	C3
Bagadó 1,575	B5
Baranoa 18,397	C2
Baraya 2,581	C6
Barbacoas 4,653	A7
Barbosa 7,960	D5
Barichara 2,548	D4
Barrancabermeja 87,191	C4
Barrancas 2,979	D2
Barranco de Loba 2,215	C3
Barranquilla 661,009	C2
Belén de los Andaquíes 2,190	C7
Bello 115,119	C4
Bogotá (cap.) 2,696,270	D5
Bogotá* 2,855,065	D5
Bolívar, Antioquia 13,259	C5
Bucaramanga 291,661	D4
Buenaventura 115,770	B6
Buesaco 2,763	B7
Buga 71,016	B6
Cáceres 7,154	C4
Caicedonia 23,567	C5
Calamar, Bolívar 5,867	C2
Calarcá 29,349	C5
Cali 898,253	B6
Campoalegre 11,799	C6
Campo de la Cruz 13,137	C2
Cañasgordas 3,900	B4
Cartagena 292,512	C2
Cartago 69,154	B5
Caucasia 19,348	C4
Cereté 18,788	C3
Cerro de San Antonio 3,394	C2
Chaparral 14,546	C6
Chimichaqua 6,382	D3
Chinácota 4,478	D4
Chinchiná 24,891	C5
Chinú 10,023	C3
Chiquinquirá 21,727	C5
Chiriguaná 6,611	D3
Ciénaga 42,546	C2
Ciénaga de Oro 10,607	C3
Cisneros 7,226	C4
Colombia 2,903	C6
Colón 1,306	B7
Condoto 4,798	B5
Contratación 3,057	D4
Convención 7,545	D3
Corinto 6,933	B6
Corozal 17,419	C3
Cravo Norte 771	F4
Cúcuta 219,772	D4
Cumbal 2,891	B7
Dabeiba 7,600	B4
Dagua 5,392	B6
Duitama 36,551	D5
El Banco 20,756	D3
El Carmen, Chocó 1,879	B5
El Carmen, Norte de Santander 2,362	D3
El Carmen de Bolívar 23,392	C3
El Cerrito 17,357	B6
El Cocuy 2,740	D4
El Tambo 2,179	B6
Envigado 63,584	C4
Espinal 32,475	C5
Facatativá 27,892	C5
Florencia 31,817	C7
Fonseca 9,988	D2
Fresno 8,141	C5
Fundación 17,497	C2
Fusagasugá 25,456	C5
Gachalá 1,364	D5
Gamarra 5,071	D3
Garzón 13,783	C6
Gigante 4,880	C6
Girardot 59,165	C5
Gramalote 2,880	D4
Guamal, Magdalena 4,986	C3
Guamal, Meta 2,854	D6
Guapí 5,005	B6
Guateque 6,032	D5
Honda 21,506	C5
Ibagué 176,223	C5
Inírida 1,792	F6
Ipiales 30,871	B7
Iscuandé 561	A6
Istmina 5,575	B5
Itagüí 96,972	C4
Ituango 5,561	C4
Juradó 935	B4
La Cruz 4,353	B7
La Dorada 30,962	C5
La Gloria 2,632	D3
La Palma 5,430	C5
La Plata 8,047	C6
La Unión 5,392	B7
Leticia 6,285	F10
Líbano 19,132	C5
Lorica 18,251	C3
Los Andes 1,414	B7
Magangué 34,396	C3
Maicao 21,645	D2
Majagual 2,329	C3
Málaga 10,645	D4
Maní 951	D5
Manizales 199,904	C5
Matanza 1,211	D4
Medellín 1,070,924	C4
Medina 1,436	D5
Mercaderes 3,877	B7
Miraflores, Boyacá 3,584	D5
Miraflores, Vaupés 536	D7
Miranda 6,439	B6
Mitú 1,637	E7
Mocoa 6,221	B7
Mompós 14,076	C3
Moniquirá 5,711	D5
Montería 89,583	B3
Morichal	E6
Mosquera 594	A6
Murindó 485	B4
Muzo 1,823	D5
Natagaima 7,772	C6
Neiva 105,476	C6
Nóvita 802	B5
Nunchía 437	D5
Nuquí 1,115	B5
Ocaña 38,352	D3
Orocué 1,011	E5
Ortega 5,150	C6
Pacho 6,786	C5
Páez 2,098	C6
Paipa 4,260	D5
Palmira 140,481	B6
Pamplona 31,817	D4
Pasto 119,339	B7
Patía 5,306	B6
Paz de Ariporo 2,584	E5
Paz de Río 3,464	D4
Pedraza 1,872	C2
Pereira 174,128	C5
Piedecuesta 17,308	D4
Piendamó 5,046	B6
Pitalito 15,049	B7
Pivijay 10,172	C2
Planeta Rica 12,932	C3
Plato 18,589	C3
Popayán 77,669	B6
Pore 389	D5
Pradera 15,732	B6
Puente Nacional 4,317	D5
Puerto Asís 6,364	B7
Puerto Berrío 19,579	C4
Puerto Carreño 2,172	G4
Puerto Colombia 9,255	C2
Puerto Escondido 1,368	B3
Puerto Leguízamo 3,179	C8
Puerto López, Meta 4,948	D5
Puerto Murillo	G4
Puerto Mutis	B4
Puerto Nare	D7
Puerto Paulina	D7
Puerto Rico, Caquetá 4,853	C7
Puerto Rondón 1,010	E4
Puerto Salgar 6,396	C5
Puerto Tejada 18,315	B6
Puerto Wilches 5,282	D4
Pupiales 2,723	B7
Purificación 8,164	C6
Quibdó 28,040	B5
Remedios 4,681	C4
Remolino 3,408	C2
Restrepo 2,704	D5
Ricaurte 1,205	A7
Río de Oro 2,985	D3
Riohacha 19,604	D2
Rionegro, Antioquia 22,654	C4
Rionegro, Santander 3,491	D4
Riosucio, Caldas 11,619	C5
Riosucio, Chocó 2,184	B4
Roberto Payán 445	A7
Robles 5,422	D2
Rovira 5,105	C5
Sabanalarga 26,542	C2
Sácama 69	D4
Sahagún 18,717	C3
Salamina 12,136	C5
Salazar 2,791	D4
Samaniego 4,790	B7
San Agustín 4,532	B7
San Andrés, Antioquia 2,003	C4
San Andrés, San Andrés y Providencia 14,428	A9
San Antero 7,129	C3
Sandoná 7,222	B7
San Francisco 1,654	B7
San Gil 21,679	D4
San Jacinto 13,459	C3
San José del Guaviare 4,138	D6
San Juan del César 9,468	D2
San Marcos 10,415	C3
San Martín 8,281	D6
San Onofre 7,899	C3
San Pablo 3,662	B7
San Roque 4,972	C4
Santa Bárbara 11,848	C5
Santa Marta 102,484	D2
Santander 13,625	B6
Santa Rosa de Cabal 28,368	C5
Santa Rosa de Osos 8,593	C4
San Vicente del Caguán 3,182	C6
Sardinata 3,726	D3
Segovia 10,000	C4
Sevilla 31,143	C5
Sibundoy 2,853	B7
Silvia 3,045	B6
Simití 3,062	C4
Sincé 11,909	C3
Sincelejo 68,797	C3
Sipí 153	B5
Sitionuevo 5,919	C2
Soatá 4,294	D4
Socorro 15,596	D4
Sogamoso 48,891	D5
Soledad 64,469	C2
Sonsón 15,990	C5
Sopetrán 5,223	C4
Tadó 3,102	B5
Támara 947	D5
Tame 4,811	E4
Tibaná 1,100	D5
Tierralta 7,950	C3
Timaná 4,262	C7
Timbío 4,755	B6
Timbiquí 1,048	B6
Toledo 2,942	D4
Tolú 9,118	C3
Trinidad 729	E5
Tuluá 86,736	B5
Tumaco 38,742	A7
Tunja 51,620	D5
Túquerres 12,058	B7
Turbaco 19,360	C2
Turbo 16,070	B3
Ubaté 7,716	D5
Uribia 2,193	D2
Urrao 8,577	B4
Valdivia 4,318	C4
Valledupar 87,425	D2
Vélez 8,241	D4
Venadillo 8,383	C5
Villanueva 9,836	D2
Villa Rosario 8,668	D4
Villavicencio 82,869	D5
Villeta 6,507	C5
Yarumal 21,333	C4
Yopal 5,851	D5
Yumbo 28,011	B6
Zapatoca 6,258	D4
Zaragoza 9,660	C4
Zarzal 21,370	B5
Zipaquirá 25,413	D5

OTHER FEATURES

Abibe, Serranía de, (mts.)	B3
Aguarico, (riv.)	B7
Aguja, La, (cape)	C2
Albuquerque, (cays)	A10
Alicia, (bank)	B8
Alto Ritacuva, (mt.)	D4
Amazon, (riv.)	E9
Ancón de Sardinas, (bay)	A7
Angostura, (falls)	E6
Apaporis, (riv.)	F8
Araracuara, Cerros de, (mts.)	E7
Arauca, (riv.)	E4
Ariari, (riv.)	D6
Ariguaní, (riv.)	D3
Ariporo, (riv.)	E4
Atabapo, (riv.)	G6
Atrato, (riv.)	B4
Augusta, (cape)	C2
Ayapel, Serranía de, (mts.)	C4
Bajo Nuevo, (shoal)	C8
Barú, (isl.)	C2
Baudó, Serranía de, (mts.)	B5
Baudó, (riv.)	B5
Bita, (riv.)	F5
Buenaventura, (bay)	B6
Caguán, (riv.)	C7
Cahuinari, (riv.)	E8
Caquetá, (riv.)	E8
Caraparaná, (riv.)	D8
Casanare, (riv.)	E4
Catatumbo, (riv.)	D3
Cauca, (riv.)	C4
Cazueleja, Cerro, (mt.)	C6
Central, Cordillera, (range)	C5
César, (riv.)	D2
Chaira, Laguna, (lake)	C7
Chamusa, Sierra, (mts.)	C6
Charambirá, (pt.)	B5
Chicamocha, (riv.)	D4
Chiribiquete, Sierra de, (mts.)	D7
Cinaruco, (riv.)	F4
Chocó, (bay)	B6
Cocuy, Sierra Nevada del, (mts.)	D4
Coredó (Humboldt), (bay)	B4
Corrientes, (cape)	B5
Courtown (Este Sudeste), (cays)	A10
Cravo Norte, (riv.)	E4
Cravo Sur, (riv.)	E5
Cristóbal Colón, Pico, (peak)	D2
Cuemaní, (riv.)	D7
Cupica, (gulf)	B4
Cuquiari, (riv.)	E7
Cusachón, (isl.)	D1
Cusiana, (riv.)	D5
Espada, (pt.)	E1
Este Sudeste, (cays)	A10
Fuerte, (isl.)	B3
Gallinas, (pt.)	E1
Gorgona, (isl.)	A6
Grande, (isl.)	B4
Grande, Salto, (falls)	D8
Guainía, (riv.)	F6
Guajira, (pen.)	E1
Guapi, (bay)	A6
Guaviare, (riv.)	F6
Guayabero, (riv.)	D6
Huila, Nevado del, (mt.)	C6
Humboldt, (bay)	B4
Igara-Paraná, (riv.)	D8
Inírida, (riv.)	F6
Isana, (riv.)	F7
La Aguja, (cape)	C2
La Macarena, Serranía de, (mts.)	D6
La Vela, (cape)	D1
Lebrija, (riv.)	D4
Llanos, (plains)	D5
Losada, (riv.)	C6
Macarena, Serranía de La, (mts.)	D6
Magdalena, (riv.)	C3
Manacacías, (riv.)	D6
Mapiripán, Laguna, (lake)	E6
Marzo, (pt.)	B4
Mesai, (riv.)	D7
Meta, (riv.)	E5
Metica, (riv.)	D6
Mira, (riv.)	A7
Miritiparaná, (riv.)	E8
Morrosquillo, (gulf)	C3
Muco, (riv.)	E5
Naipo, (isl.)	F6
Nechí, (riv.)	C4
Negro, (riv.)	G7
Occidental, Cordillera, (range)	B5
Oriental, Cordillera, (range)	D5
Orinoco, (riv.)	G5
Orteguaza, (riv.)	C7
Papunáua, (riv.)	E6
Papurí, (riv.)	F7
Patía, (riv.)	B6
Pauto, (riv.)	E5
Perijá, Serranía de, (mts.)	D2
Providencia, (isl.)	B9
Puracé, (vol.)	B6
Putumayo, (riv.)	E9
Quitasueño, (bank)	A8
Roca que Vela, (cay)	B8
Roncador, (cays)	B9
Saldaña, (riv.)	C6
Salto Grande, (falls)	D8
San Andrés, (isl.)	A10
San Bernardo, (isls.)	C3
San Jorge, (riv.)	C3
San Juan, (riv.)	B5
San Miguel, (riv.)	B7
Santa Catalina, (isl.)	A9
Santa Marta, Sierra Nevada de, (range)	D2
Serrana, (bank)	B9
Serranilla, (bank)	B8
Sinú, (riv.)	B3
Sogamoso, (riv.)	D4
Solano, (pt.)	B4
Suárez, (riv.)	D4
Sucio, (riv.)	B4
Taraíra, (riv.)	F8
Tequendama, (falls)	C5
Tibugá, (gulf)	B5
Tolima, Nevado del, (mt.)	C5
Tomo, (riv.)	F5
Tortugas, (gulf)	B6
Tota, Laguna de, (lake)	D5
Truandó, (riv.)	B4
Tumaco, Rada de, (bay)	A6
Tunahí, Sierra, (mts.)	E7
Upía, (riv.)	D5
Urabá, (gulf)	B3
Uva, Laguna, (lake)	E6
Uva, (riv.)	E6
Vaupés, (riv.)	E7
Vela, La, (cape)	D1
Vela, Roca que, (cay)	B8
Vichada, (riv.)	F5
Vigía, (cay)	A10
Yarí, (riv.)	D8
Zapatosa, Ciénaga de, (swamp)	D3

*City and suburbs.

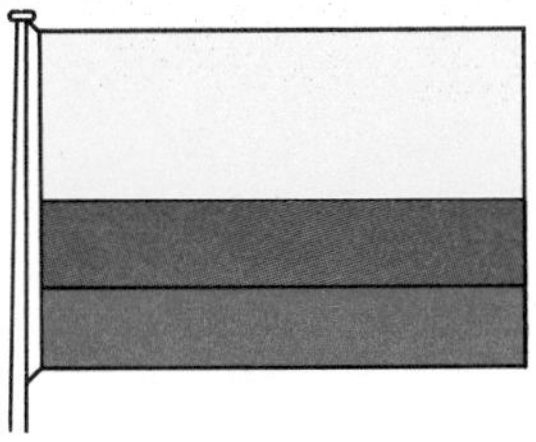

AREA 439,513 sq. mi. (1,138,339 sq. km.)
POPULATION 27,520,000
CAPITAL Bogotá
LARGEST CITY Bogotá
HIGHEST POINT Pico Cristóbal Colón 19,029 ft. (5,800 m.)
MONETARY UNIT Colombian peso
MAJOR LANGUAGE Spanish
MAJOR RELIGION Roman Catholicism

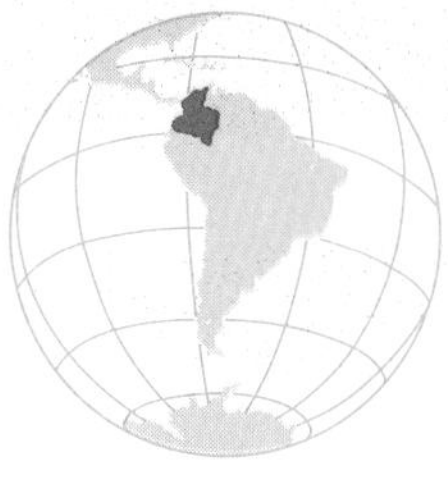

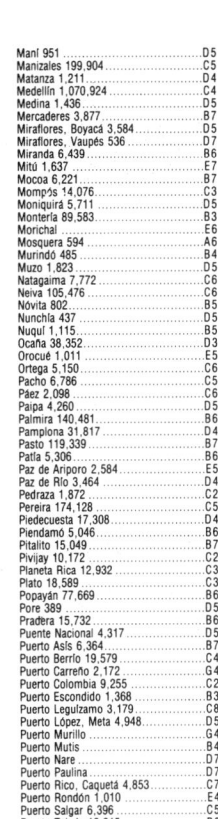

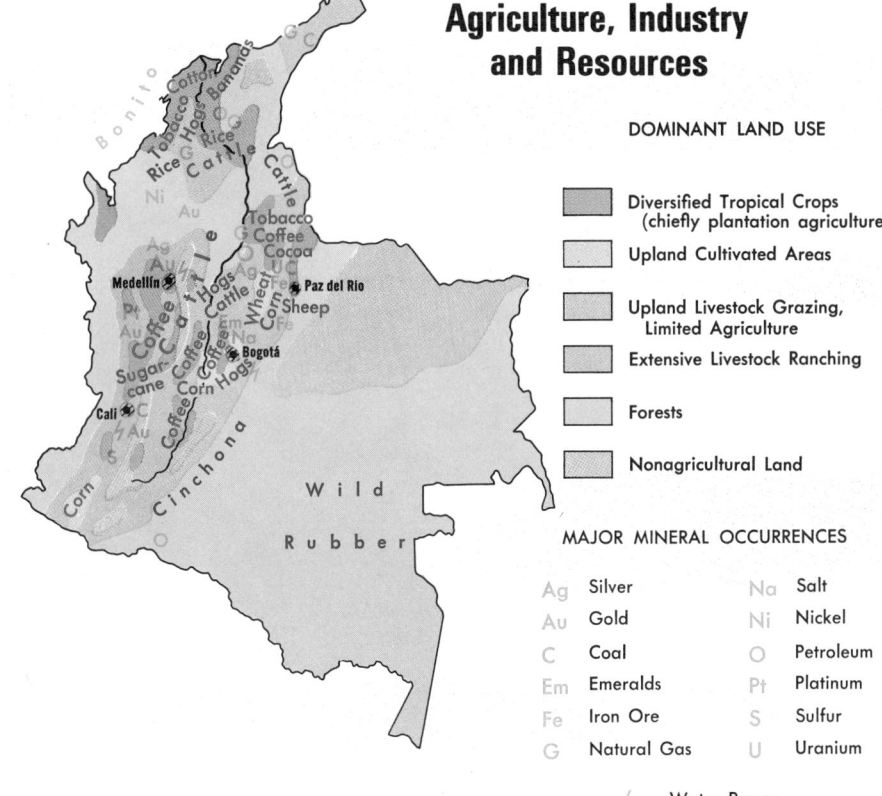

Agriculture, Industry and Resources

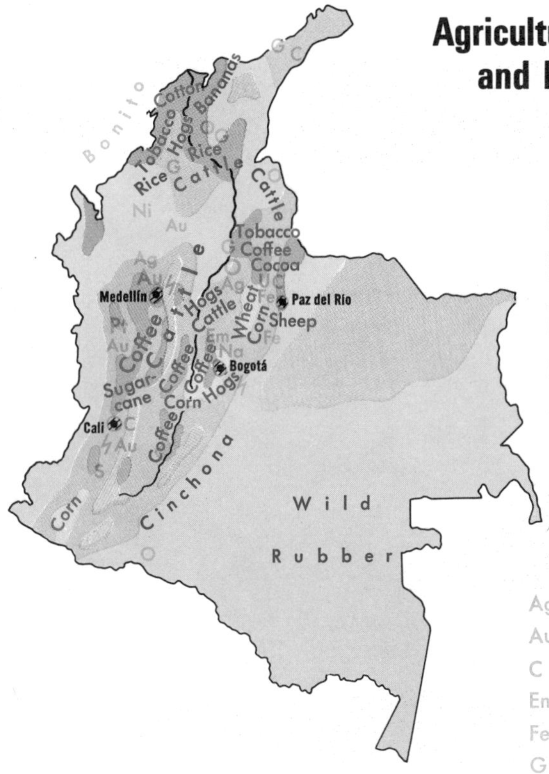
Bonito
Tobacco
Cotton
Hogs
Bananas
Rice
Cattle
Ni
Au
Ag
Medellín
Coffee
Cocoa
Paz del Rio
Wheat
Corn
Sheep
Em
Bogotá
Sugar-cane
Cali
Cinchona
Wild
Rubber

DOMINANT LAND USE

- Diversified Tropical Crops (chiefly plantation agriculture)
- Upland Cultivated Areas
- Upland Livestock Grazing, Limited Agriculture
- Extensive Livestock Ranching
- Forests
- Nonagricultural Land

MAJOR MINERAL OCCURRENCES

Ag	Silver	Na	Salt
Au	Gold	Ni	Nickel
C	Coal	O	Petroleum
Em	Emeralds	Pt	Platinum
Fe	Iron Ore	S	Sulfur
G	Natural Gas	U	Uranium

Water Power

Major Industrial Areas

Topography

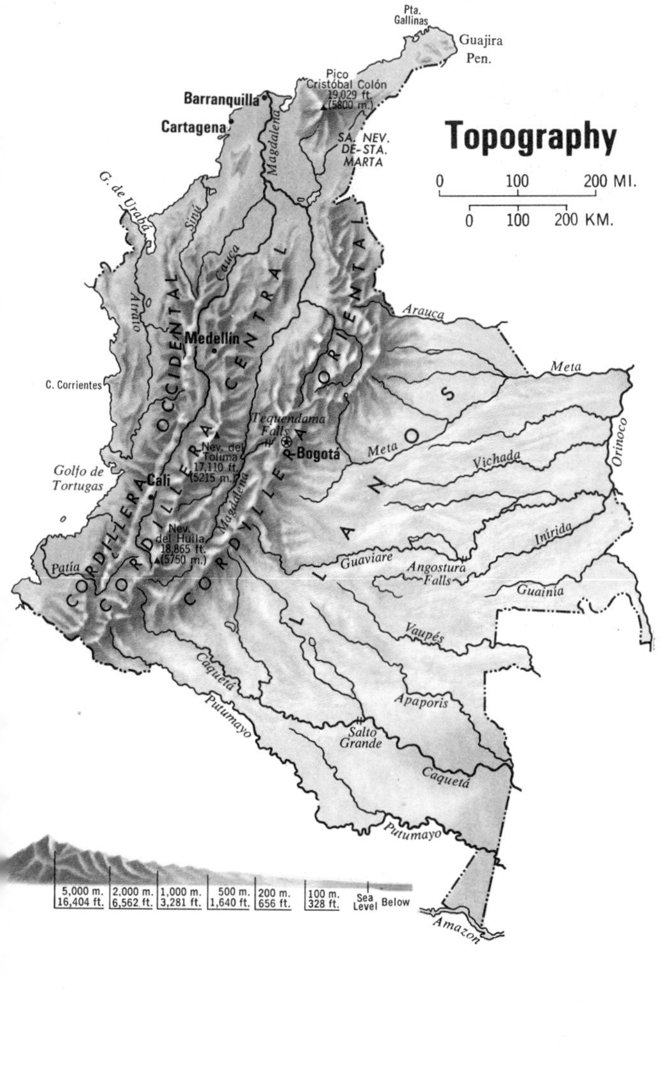
Pta. Gallinas
Guajira Pen.
Pico Cristóbal Colón 19,029 ft. (5800 m.)
Barranquilla
Cartagena
SA. NEV. DE STA. MARTA
Magdalena
G. de Urabá
Sinú
Cauca
Atrato
Arauca
Medellín
C. Corrientes
CORDILLERA OCCIDENTAL
CORDILLERA CENTRAL
CORDILLERA ORIENTAL
Meta
Tequendama Falls
Bogotá
Nev. del Tolima 17,110 ft. (5215 m.)
Cali
Golfo de Tortugas
Nev. del Huila 18,865 ft. (5750 m.)
Patía
LLANOS
Vichada
Orinoco
Guaviare
Inírida
Angostura Falls
Guainía
Vaupés
Caquetá
Apaporis
Putumayo
Salto Grande
Amazon
0 100 200 MI.
0 100 200 KM.
5,000 m. 16,404 ft.
2,000 m. 6,562 ft.
1,000 m. 3,281 ft.
500 m. 1,640 ft.
200 m. 656 ft.
100 m. 328 ft.
Sea Level
Below

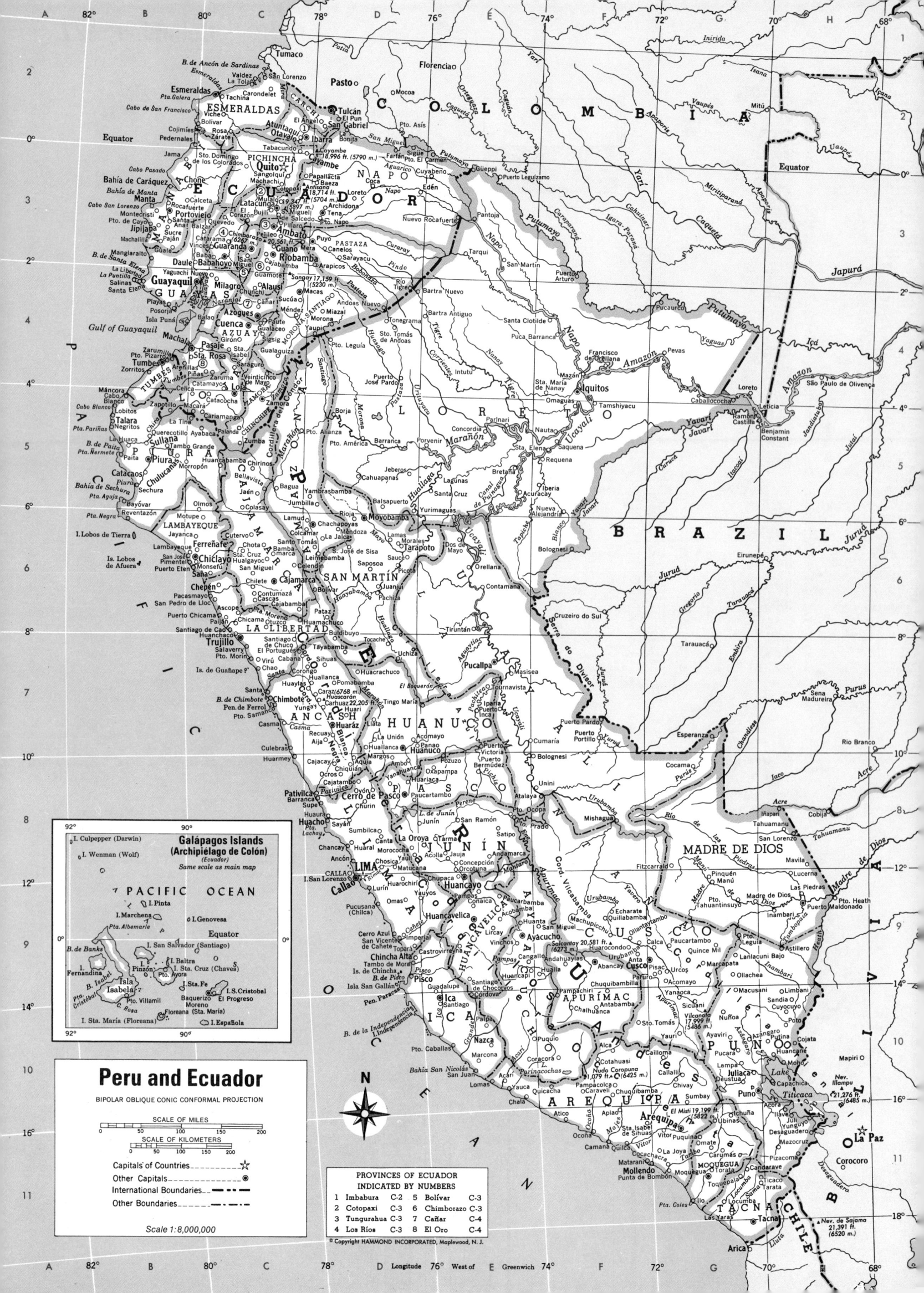

Peru and Ecuador

BIPOLAR OBLIQUE CONIC CONFORMAL PROJECTION

SCALE OF MILES
0   50   100   150   200

SCALE OF KILOMETERS
0   50   100   150   200

Capitals of Countries .... ☆
Other Capitals .... ⊛
International Boundaries .... — ∙∙ —
Other Boundaries .... — — —

Scale 1:8,000,000

Galápagos Islands
(Archipiélago de Colón)
(Ecuador)
Same scale as main map

PACIFIC OCEAN

I. Culpepper (Darwin)
I. Wenman (Wolf)
I. Pinta
I. Marchena
Pta. Albemarle
I. Genovesa
Equator
I. San Salvador (Santiago)
B. de Banks
I. Fernandina
Pinzón
I. Baltra
I. Sta. Cruz (Chaves)
Pta. Cristóbal
Isla Isabela
B. de Isabel
I. Sta. María (Floreana)
Pto. Ayora
Pto. Villamil
Sta. Fe
I.S. Cristóbal
Baquerizo Moreno
El Progreso
Floreana (Sta. María)
I. Española

PROVINCES OF ECUADOR
INDICATED BY NUMBERS
1 Imbabura   C-2   5 Bolívar   C-3
2 Cotopaxi   C-3   6 Chimborazo   C-3
3 Tungurahua   C-3   7 Cañar   C-3
4 Los Ríos   C-3   8 El Oro   C-4

© Copyright HAMMOND INCORPORATED, Maplewood, N.J.

Longitude 76° West of Greenwich 74°

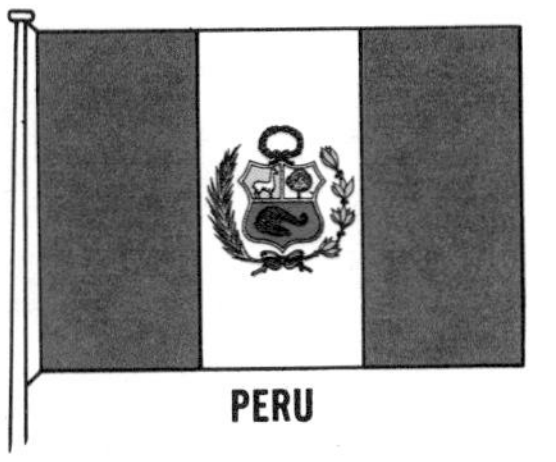
PERU

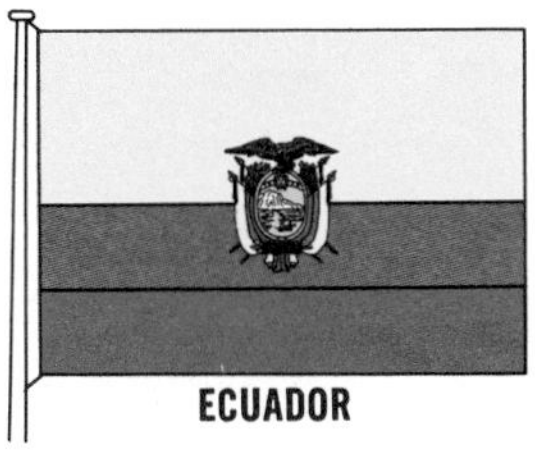
ECUADOR

PERU

AREA 496,222 sq. mi. (1,285,215 sq. km.)
POPULATION 17,031,221
CAPITAL Lima
LARGEST CITY Lima
HIGHEST POINT Huascarán 22,205 ft. (6,768 m.)
MONETARY UNIT sol
MAJOR LANGUAGES Spanish, Quechua, Aymara
MAJOR RELIGION Roman Catholicism

ECUADOR

AREA 109,483 sq. mi. (283,561 sq. km.)
POPULATION 8,354,000
CAPITAL Quito
LARGEST CITY Guayaquil
HIGHEST POINT Chimborazo 20,561 ft. (6,267 m.)
MONETARY UNIT sucre
MAJOR LANGUAGES Spanish, Quechua
MAJOR RELIGION Roman Catholicism

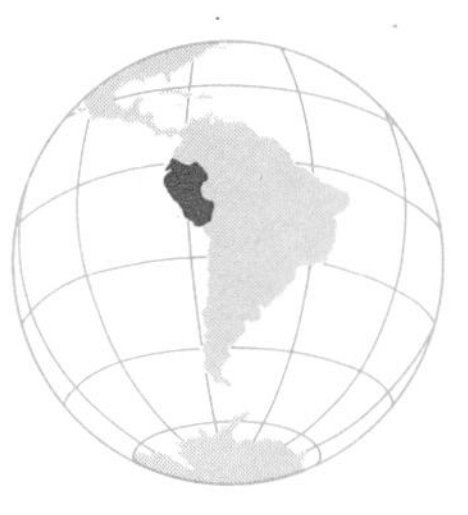

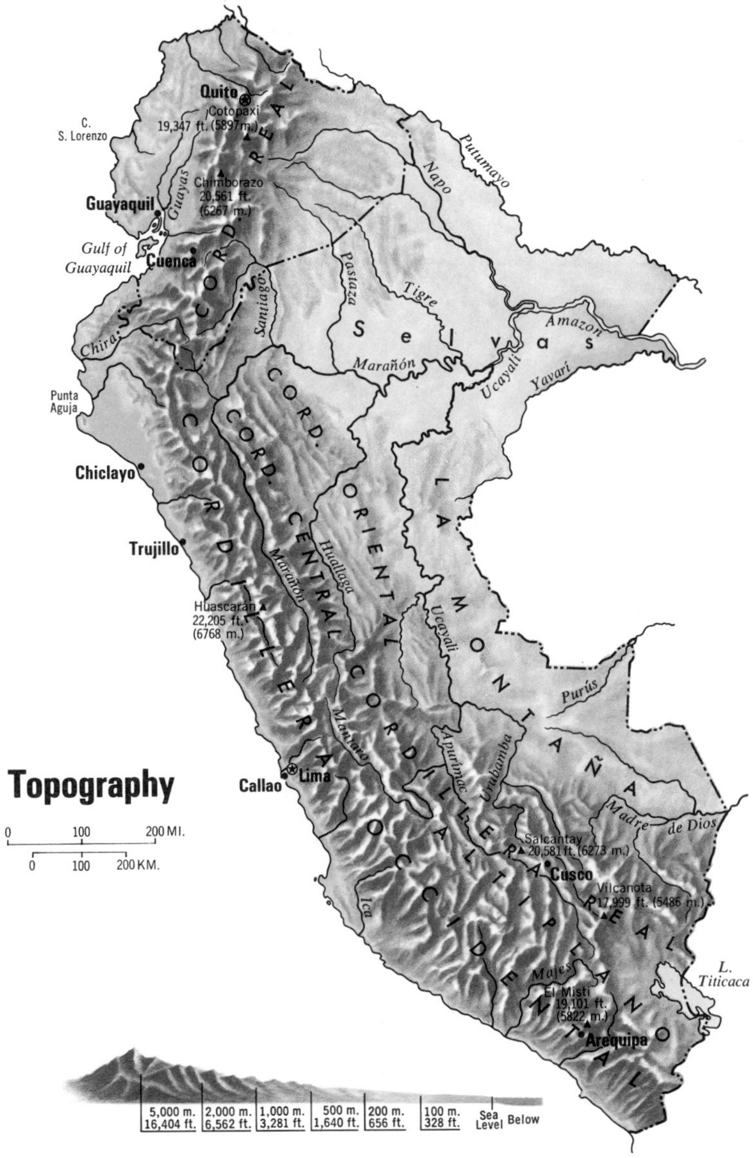
Topography
0 100 200 MI.
0 100 200 KM.
Quito
Cotopaxi 19,347 ft. (5897 m.)
C. S. Lorenzo
Chimborazo 20,561 ft. (6267 m.)
Guayaquil
Gulf of Guayaquil
Cuenca
Guayas
Putumayo
Napo
Pastaza
Santiago
Tigre
Amazon
S e l v a s
Marañón
Ucayali
Yavari
Chira
Punta Aguja
Chiclayo
Trujillo
Huascarán 22,205 ft. (6768 m.)
Huallaga
Marañón
Ucayali
Purús
Callao
Lima
Apurímac
Urubamba
Madre de Dios
Salcantay 20,581 ft. (6273 m.)
Cusco
Vilcanota 17,999 ft. (5486 m.)
L. Titicaca
El Misti 19,101 ft. (5822 m.)
Arequipa
Majes
Ica
CORD. OCCIDENTAL
CORD. CENTRAL
CORD. ORIENTAL
LA MONTAÑA
ALTIPLANO
5,000 m. 16,404 ft.
2,000 m. 6,562 ft.
1,000 m. 3,281 ft.
500 m. 1,640 ft.
200 m. 656 ft.
100 m. 328 ft.
Sea Level
Below

PERU

DEPARTMENTS

Amazonas 196,469 C5
Ancash 726,665 D7
Apurímac 307,805 F10
Arequipa 530,528 F10
Ayacucho 459,747 E9
Cajamarca 916,331 C6
Callao (prov.) 315,605 D9
Cuzco 712,918 F9
Huancavelica 331,155 E9
Huánuco 420,764 D7
Ica 357,973 E10
Junín 691,130 E8
La Libertad 806,368 C6
Lambayeque 515,363 B6
Lima 3,485,411 D8
Loreto 339,298 E5
Madre de Dios 21,968 G8
Moquegua 74,573 G11
Pasco 176,750 E8
Piura 854,668 B5
Puno 779,594 G10
San Martín 224,310 D6
Tacna 95,263 G11
Tumbes 75,399 B4
Ucayali 155,637 E6

CITIES and TOWNS

Abancay 12,172 F9
Acarí 4,364 E10
Acobamba 2,069 E9
Acolla 5,061 E8
Acomayo, Cuzco 1,795 G9
Acomayo, Huánuco 734 E7
Acora 1,510 H11
Acuracay 1,025 F5
Aija 2,027 D7
Alca 698 F10
Ambo 2,006 D8
Ancón 5,761 D8
Andahuaylas 4,912 F9
Andamarca 243 E8
Anta 2,797 F9
Antabamba 1,962 F10
Aplao 1,561 F11
Aquia 1,014 D8
Arequipa 304,653 G11
Arequipa⊙ 72
Ascope 9,438 C6
Astillero H9
Atalaya 2,132 E8
Atico 3,053 F11
Ayabaca 4,292 C5
Ayacucho 43,304 F9
Ayaviri 9,719 G10
Azángaro 6,565 H10
Bagua 4,907 C5
Balsapuerto 121 D5
Bambamarca 5,045 C6
Barranca, Lima 23,399 C8
Barranca, Loreto 222 D5
Bartra Antiguo E4
Bartra Nuevo E4
Bayóvar B5
Bellavista 23,666 C5
Bolívar 1,083 D6
Bolognesi F6
Bolognesi 553 F8
Borja 220 D5
Bretaña 757 E5
Buldibuyo 509 D7
Caballococha 1,827 G4
Cabana 1,981 C7
Cabo Blanco B5
Cahuapanas 194 D5
Cailloma 1,905 G10
Cajabamba 5,851 C6
Cajacay 667 D8
Cajamarca 37,608 C6
Cajatambo 3,811 D8
Calca 4,457 G9
Callalli 465 G10
Callao 296,220 D9
Camaná 10,121 F11
Candarave 1,009 G11
Cangallo 1,536 E9
Canta 2,439 D8
Capachica 271 H10
Carás 5,214 D7
Caravelí 2,002 F10
Carhuás 2,386 D7
Carumás 3,138 G11
Cascas 2,511 C6
Casma 9,037 C7
Castrovirreyna 1,501 E9
Catacaos 19,155 B5
Celendín 7,957 D6
Cerro Azul 2,022 D9
Cerro de Pasco 47,178 D8
Chachapoyas 10,418 D6
Chala 1,335 E10
Chalhuanca 3,544 F10
Chancay 20,034 D8
Chao C7
Chepén 23,562 C6
Chicama 10,087 C6
Chiclayo 189,685 C6
Chilca (Pucusana) 2,397 D9
Chilete 1,297 C6
Chimbote 159,045 C7
Chincha Alta 28,785 D9
Chiquián 3,841 D8
Chirinos 863 C5
Chivay 2,448 G10
Chosica D8
Chota 6,430 C6
Chulucanas 26,278 B5
Chupaca 2,875 E9
Chuquibamba 3,044 F10
Chuquibambilla 1,733 F9
Churín 1,303 D8
Cocachacra 2,682 G11
Cocama G8
Cojata 658 H10
Colasay 747 C5
Colcamar 1,578 D6
Conaica 2,058 E9
Concepción 5,864 E8
Concordia 304 E5
Contamana 5,088 E6
Contumazá 2,632 C6
Coracora 4,508 F10
Córdova 567 E10
Corongo 1,619 D7
Cotahuasi 2,308 F10
Culebras C7
Cumaría F7
Cutervo 5,856 C6
Cuyocuyo 896 H10
Cuzco 120,881 F9
Desaguadero 1,467 H11
Deustua 392 G10
Dos de Mayo 1,948 E6
Echarate 229 F9
El Portugués C7
Esperanza 240 G7
Ferreñafe 16,251 C6
Fitzcarrald G8
Francisco de Orellana 511 F4
Guadalupe 5,484 E9
Güeppi E3
Huacho 36,697 D8
Huacrachuco 1,604 D7
Hualgayoc 1,018 C6
Hualla 4,027 F9
Huallanca, Ancash 953 D7
Huallanca, Huánuco D7
Huamachuco 7,368 D6
Huancabamba 4,427 C5
Huancané 5,187 H10
Huancapi 2,646 E9
Huancavelica 15,916 E9
Huancayo 115,693 E9
Huanchaco 2,641 C7
Huanta 7,729 E9
Huánuco 41,123 E7
Huaral 20,331 D8
Huaráz 29,719 D7
Huari 2,461 D7
Huariaca 3,427 E8
Huarmey 11,818 C8
Huarochirí⊙ 2,446 D9
Huarocondo 2,790 F9
Huaura⊙ 11,209 D8
Huaylas 1,066 C7
Iberia 518 F5
Ica 73,883 E10
Ichuña 180 G11
Ilave 6,832 H11
Ilo 21,551 G11
Imperial⊙ 14,571 D9
Inambari 190 H9
Iñapari 86 H8
Intutu 743 E4
Iparia 284 E7
Iquitos 111,327 F4
Jaén 13,912 C5
Jauja 13,936 E8
Jayanca 5,694 B6
Jeberos 1,626 D5
Juanjuí 6,386 D6
Juli 5,398 H11
Juliaca 38,475 G10
Jumbilla 1,146 C5
Junín 8,282 E8
Lagunas 4,584 E5
La Huaca 2,006 B5
La Jalca 1,944 D6
La Joya 2,412 G11
Lamas 6,553 D6
Lambayeque 18,167 B6
Lampa 3,852 G10
Lamud 2,897 C6
Lanlacuni Bajo 77 G9
La Oroya 25,908 D8
Las Piedras H9
Las Yaras 289 G11
La Tina B5
La Unión 2,524 D7
Leimebamba 1,327 D6
Lima 354,292 D8
Lima* 2,386,374 D8
Limbani 389 H10
Lircay 2,268 E9
Llata 2,266 D7
Lobitos 2,488 B5
Locumba 260 G11
Lomas 240 E10
Lucerna H9
Lurín⊙ 12,789 D9
Machupicchu 235 F9
Macusani 2,790 G10
Madre de Dios G9
Máncora 3,896 B5
Manú G9
Marcapata 380 G9
Marcona 8,218 E10
Margos 1,235 D8
Masisea 1,791 E7
Matarani F11
Matucana 2,643 D8
Mavila H8
Mazán 947 F4
Mazocruz 2,369 H11
Mendoza 1,272 D6
Mishagua F8
Moho 2,028 H10
Mollendo 15,573 F11
Monsefú 14,255 C6
Moquegua 16,959 G11
Morales 3,274 D6
Morococha 6,145 D8
Morropón 5,643 C5
Motupe 6,753 C6
Moyobamba 10,004 D6
Nauta 3,768 F5
Nazca 21,025 E10
Negritos 18,024 B5
Nueva Alejandría 56 F5
Nuñoa 3,001 G10
Ocoña 3,039 F11
Ocros 1,061 D8
Ollachea 1,000 G9
Ollantaytambo 1,240 F9
Olmos 4,066 C5
Omaguas F5
Omas 277 D9
Omate 887 G11
Orcotuna 3,286 E8
Orellana 1,550 E6
Otuzco 8,410 C6
Oxapampa 4,338 E8
Oyón 5,798 D8
Pacasmayo 15,381 C6
Pachiza 683 D6
Paiján 10,321 C6
Paita 14,875 B5
Palpa 2,935 E10
Pampachiri 452 F10
Pampacolca 2,046 F10
Pampas 2,123 E9
Panao 1,455 E7
Pantoja 204 E3
Paramonga C8
Parinari 138 E5
Paruro 1,746 F9
Pataz 450 D6
Paucarbamba 636 E9
Paucartambo, Cuzco 2,055 G9
Paucartambo, Pasco 2,172 E8
Pevas 1,347 G4
Picota 2,265 D6
Pimentel 7,742 B6
Pinquén G9
Pisac 1,182 G9
Pisco 41,429 D9
Piura 126,702 B5
Pizacoma 220 H11
Pomabamba 2,802 D7
Porvenir E5
Poto 161 H10
Pozuzo 260 E8
Puca Barranca E4
Pucallpa 57,525 E7
Pucará 1,252 G10
Pucaurco 632 G4
Pucusana 2,397 D9
Puerto Alianza D5
Puerto América 144 D5
Puerto Bermúdez 366 E8
Puerto Chicama 4,741 C6
Puerto Eten 8,932 B6
Puerto Leguía, Loreto D4
Puerto Leguía, Puno G9
Puerto Maldonado 6,419 H9
Puerto Morín C7
Puerto Ocopa 1,492 E8
Puerto Pardo F7
Puerto Pizarro B4
Puerto Portillo F7
Puerto Prado 265 E8
Puerto Samanco 1,795 C7
Puerto Tahuantinsuyo G9
Puerto Victoria E7
Puno 41,166 G10
Punta de Bombón 3,907 F11
Punta Moreno C6
Puquina 1,087 G11
Puquio 8,691 F10
Putina 4,581 H10
Querecotillo 8,008 B5
Quicacha 615 F10
Quilca 199 F11
Quillabamba 10,857 F9
Quince Mil G9
Ramón Castilla 1,327 G5
Recuay 2,169 D7
Requena 7,300 F5
Reventazón B6
Rioja 6,066 D6
Salaverry 5,316 C7
Saña 26,933 C6
Sandia 1,752 H10
San José 3,480 B6
San José de Sisa 4,147 D6
San Juan E10
San Lorenzo 120 H8
San Martín E3
San Miguel, Ayacucho 1,084 F9
San Miguel, Cajamarca 3,800 C6
San Pedro de Lloc 9,326 C6
San Ramón 4,646 E8
Santa 13,956 C7
Santa Clotilde 863 E4
Santa Cruz, Cajamarca 2,846 C6
Santa Cruz, Loreto 602 E5
Santa Elena 400 F5
Santa Isabel de Sihuas 116 F11
Santa María de Nanay 251 F4
Santiago 3,624 E10
Santiago de Cao 18,635 C6
Santiago de Chocorvos 407 E9
Santiago de Chuco C7
Santo Tomás, Amazonas 1,039 C6
Santo Tomás, Cuzco 2,095 G10
Santo Tomás de Andoas 122 D4
San Vicente de Cañete 8,751 D9
Saposoa 4,339 D6
Saquena 2,281 F5
Satipo 5,944 E8
Sauce 1,726 D6
Sayán 4,052 D8
Sechura 6,174 B5
Sicuani 12,956 G10
Sihuas 1,509 D7
Sullana 60,112 B5
Sumbilca 1,724 D8
Supe 15,623 D8
Tacna 55,752 G11
Tahuamanu 120 H8
Talara 29,884 B5
Tambo de Mora 2,717 D9
Tambo Grande 7,184 B5
Tamshiyacu 2,220 F5
Tarapoto 21,260 D6
Tarata 2,808 H11
Tarma 28,100 E8
Tarqui E3
Tayabamba 1,786 D7
Ticaco 963 H11
Tingo María 20,320 D7
Tiruntán 743 E6
Tocache 3,503 D7
Tonegrama D4
Topará D9
Toquepala G11
Torata 1,732 G11
Tournavista E7
Trujillo 241,882 C7
Tumbes 32,972 B4
Ubinas 384 G11
Uchiza 1,999 D7
Unini F8
Urcos 3,180 G9
Urubamba 3,504 F9
Vinchos 768 E9
Virú 3,205 C7
Vitor 200 G11
Yambrasbamba 360 D5
Yanahuanca 6,278 D8
Yanaoca 1,090 G10
Yauca 2,043 E10
Yauli 1,962 D8
Yauri 4,066 G10
Yauyos 1,845 E9
Yunguyo 4,360 H11
Yurimaguas 17,414 E5
Zarumilla 5,083 B4
Zorritos 3,796 B4

OTHER FEATURES

Acarí (riv.) E10
Aguaytía (riv.) E7
Aguja (pt.) B5
Amazon (riv.) F4
Andes, Cordillera de los (mts.) F10
Apurímac (riv.) F9
Azángaro (riv.) G10
Azul, Cordillera (mts.) E7
Blanca, Cordillera (mts.) D7
Blanco (cape) B5
Blanco (riv.) F6
Boquerón, El (pass) E7
Cañete (riv.) D9
Casma (riv.) C7
Chimbote (bay) C7
Chincha (isls.) D9
Coles (pt.) G11
Cóndor, Cordillera del (range) C5
Coropuna, Nudo (mt.) F10
Corrientes (riv.) E4
El Boquerón (pass) E7
El Misti (mt.) G11
Ene (riv.) E8
Ferrol (pen.) C7
Grande (riv.) E10
Guañape (isls.) C7
Heath (riv.) H9
Huallaga (riv.) D5
Huasaga (riv.) D4
Huascarán (mt.) D7
Huayabamba (riv.) D6
Ica (riv.) E10
Inambari (riv.) H9
Independencia (bay) D10
Independencia (isl.) D10
Junín (lake) E8
Juruá (riv.) F7
Lachay (pt.) D8
Lobos de Afuera (isls.) B6
Lobos de Tierra (isl.) B6
Locumba (riv.) G11
Madre de Dios (riv.) G9
Majes (riv.) F11
Mantaro (riv.) E8
Manú (riv.) G8
Marañón (riv.) E5
Mayo (riv.) D6
Misti, El (mt.) G11
Montaña, La (reg.) F8
Morona (riv.) D5
Nanay (riv.) E4
Napo (riv.) F4
Negra, Cordillera (mts.) D7
Negra (pt.) B6
Ñermete (pt.) B5
Occidental, Cordillera (range) F10
Ocoña (riv.) F11
Oriental, Cordillera (range) H10
Pachitea (riv.) E7
Paita (bay) B5
Pampas (riv.) E9
Paracas (pen.) D9
Parinacochas (lake) F10
Pariñas (pt.) B5
Pastaza (riv.) D5
Pativilca (riv.) D8
Perené (riv.) E8
Pichis (riv.) E8
Piedras, Las (riv.) G8
Pisco (bay) D9
Pisco (riv.) D9
Piura (riv.) B5
Puinagua, Canal de (riv.) E5
Purús (riv.) G8
Putumayo (riv.) G4
Rímac (riv.) D9
Salcantay (mt.) F9
Sama (riv.) G11
San Gallán (isl.) D9
San Lorenzo (isl.) D9
San Nicolás (bay) E10
Santa (riv.) C7
Santiago (riv.) D4
Sechura (bay) B5
Tahuamanu (riv.) H8
Tambo (riv.) G11
Tambopata (riv.) H9
Tapiche (riv.) E6
Tigre (riv.) E4
Titicaca (lake) H10
Tumbes (riv.) B4
Ucayali (riv.) F5

(continued on following page)

(continued)

Urituyacu (riv.) D5
Urubamba (riv.) F8
Vilcabamba, Cordillera (mts.) F9
Vilcanota (mt.) G10
Vitor (riv.) F11
Yaguas (riv.) G4
Yavarí (riv.) G5
Yavero (riv.) F9
Yuruá (riv.) F7

ECUADOR

PROVINCES

Azuay 367,324 C4
Bolívar 144,593 C3
Cañar 146,570 C4
Carchi 120,857 C2
Chimborazo 304,316 C3
Colón, Archipiélago de (terr.) 4,037 C8
Cotopaxi 236,313 C3
El Oro 262,564 C4
Esmeraldas 203,151 C2
Guayas 1,512,333 B4
Imbabura 216,027 C2
Loja 342,339 C4
Los Ríos 383,432 C3
Manabí 817,966 B3
Morona-Santiago 53,325 C4
Napo 62,186 D3
Pastaza 23,465 D3
Pichincha 988,306 C3
Tungurahua 279,920 C3
Zamora-Chinchipe 34,493 C5

CITIES and TOWNS

Alausí 7,137 C4
Ambato 77,955 C3
Andoas Nuevo D4
Arapicos D3
Archidona D3
Arenillas 5,862 B4
Atuntaqui 9,907 C2
Azogues 10,953 C4
Baba 953 C3
Babahoyo 28,914 C3
Baeza 253 D3
Bahía de Caráquez 11,258 B3
Balao C4
Balzar 10,924 C3
Baquerizo Moreno 1,311 C9
Bolívar 410 C2
Cajabamba 2,318 C3
Calceta 7,152 C3
Cañar 6,727 C4
Cariamanga 6,682 C5
Catacocha C5
Catamayo C4
Catarama 2,868 C3
Cayambe 11,199 D3
Celica 3,081 B4
Chone 23,627 B3
Chunchi 2,802 C4
Coca 1,211 D3
Cojimíes B2
Cuenca 104,470 C4
Cuyabeno E3
Daule 13,170 B3
Edén E3
El Ángel 3,660 C2
El Corazón 1,073 C3
El Progreso C9
El Pun D2
Esmeraldas 60,364 B2
Farfán D2
Floreana (Sta María) B10
Girón 2,361 C4
Gualaceo 4,575 C4
Gualaquiza 1,679 C4
Guale B3
Guamote 2,438 C4
Guano 5,389 C3
Guaranda 11,364 C3
Guayaquil 823,219 B4
Ibarra 41,335 D2
Jama B3
Jipijapa 19,996 B3
La Bonita 184 D2
La Libertad 26,078 B4
Latacunga 21,921 C3
La Tola C2
Loja 47,697 C4
Loreto D3
Macará 8,063 C5
Macas 1,934 D4
Machachi 4,745 C3
Machala 69,170 B4
Machalilla B3
Manglaralto B3
Manta 64,519 B3
Méndez 1,043 C4
Mera 631 C3
Miazal D4
Milagro 53,106 C4
Montecristi 6,386 B3
Morona D4
Mulaló C3
Nuevo Rocafuerte 198 E3
Otavalo 13,605 C2
Paján 2,610 B3
Palanda C5
Papallacta D3
Pasaje 20,790 C4
Paute 1,998 C4
Pedernales B2
Pelileo 3,754 C3
Píllaro 4,052 C3
Piñas 5,770 C4
Playas B4
Portoviejo 59,550 B3
Posorja B4
Puerto Ayora 900 B9
Puerto de Cayo B3
Puerto El Carmen 308 E3
Puerto Napo D3
Pujilí 2,510 C3
Putumayo E3
Puyo 4,730 D3
Quevedo 43,101 C3
Quito (cap.) 599,828 C3
Riobamba 58,087 C3
Río Tigre D4
Rocafuerte 5,519 B3
Rosa Zárate 4,847 C2
Salinas 12,409 B4
San Gabriel 10,036 D2
Sangolquí 10,554 C3
San Lorenzo C2
San Miguel 2,743 C3
San Miguel de Salcedo 4,159 C3
Santa Ana 5,004 B3
Santa Elena 7,687 B4
Santa Isabel 2,068 C4
Santa Rosa 19,696 C4
Santo Domingo de los Colorados 30,523 C3
Saraguro 1,739 C4
Sarayacu D3
Sigsig 2,021 C4
Sigüe D2
Sucre 2,929 B3
Sucúa 9,694 C4
Tabacundo 1,942 C2
Tachina C2
Tena D3
Tulcán 24,398 D2
Valdez 3,837 C2
Veinticinco de Mayo 266 C4
Viche C2
Villamil B9
Vinces 10,126 C3
Yaguachi 3,816 C4
Yaupi D4
Zamora 2,667 C5
Zapotillo B5
Zaruma C4
Zumba 905 C5

OTHER FEATURES

Aguarico (riv.) D3
Albemarle (pt.) B9
Ancón de Sardinas (bay) C2
Antisana (mt.) D3
Baltra (isl.) B9
Banks (bay) B9
Bobonaza (riv.) D3
Cayambe (mt.) D2
Chaves (Santa Cruz) (isl.) C9
Chimborazo (mt.) C3
Chira (riv.) B5
Cóndor, Cordillera del (range) C5
Cotopaxi (mt.) C3
Cristóbal (pt.) B9
Culpepper (isl.) B8
Curaray (riv.) D3
Darwin (Culpepper) (isl.) B8
Esmeraldas (riv.) C2
Española (isl.) C10
Fernandina (isl.) B9
Floreana (Santa María) (isl.) B10
Galápagos (isls.) C8
Galera (pt.) B2
Genovesa (isl.) C9
Guayaquil (gulf) B4
Guayas (riv.) C4
Isabel (bay) B9
Isabela (isl.) B9
La Puntilla (cape) B4
Manta (bay) B3
Marchena (isl.) B9
Mira (riv.) C2
Napo (riv.) D3
Naranjal (riv.) C4
Pasado (cape) B3
Pastaza (riv.) D4
Pindo (riv.) D3
Pinta (isl.) B9
Pinzón (isl.) B9
Puná (isl.) B4
Putumayo (riv.) E2
Rosa (cape) B10
San Cristóbal (isl.) C9
San Francisco (cape) B2
Sangay (mt.) C4
San Lorenzo (cape) B3
San Miguel (riv.) D2
San Salvador (isl.) B9
Santa Cruz (isl.) C9
Santa Elena (bay) B3
Santa Fe (isl.) C9
Santa María (isl.) B10
Santiago (San Salvador) (isl.) B9
Tumbes (riv.) B4
Wenman (isl.) B8
Wolf (Wenman) (isl.) B8
Zamora (riv.) B4

* City and suburbs
○Population of district.

FRENCH GUIANA

DISTRICTS

Cayenne 45,987 E3
Saint-Laurent du Maroni 9,270 E4

CITIES and TOWNS

Aouara E3
Bienvenue E4
Camopi 18 E4
Cayenne (cap.) 28,888 E3
Clément E4
Counamama E3
Délices E3
Dépôt Lézard E3
Edmondt E3
Grand Santi 81 D3
Guisanbourg F3
Inini E4
Iracoubo 715 E3
Kaw E3
Kourou 4,140 E3
Macouria 93 E3
Malmanoury E3
Mana 659 E3
Maripa E4
Maripasoula 364 D4
Matoury 309 E3
Montsinéry 139 E3
Organabo E3
Oscar E4
Ouanary 65 F3
Ouaqui D4
Paul Isnard D3
Régina 208 E3
Rémire 867 E3
Roura 114 E3
Saint-Élie 81 E3
Saint-Georges 668 F4
Saint-Jean D3
Saint-Laurent du Maroni 2,754 E3
Saint-Nazaire E3
Saül 84 E4
Saut-Tigre E3
Sinnamary 1,769 E3
Sophie E4
Tonate 93 E3

OTHER FEATURES

Approuague (riv.) E4
Araoua (mts.) E4
Béhague (pt.) F3
Camopi (riv.) E4
Comté (riv.) E3
Connétable (isls.) F3
Devil's (isl.) E3
Granitique, Chaîne (range) E4
Inini (riv.) E4
Lawa (riv.) D4
Litani (riv.) D4
Mana (riv.) E3
Maroni (riv.) D3
Marouini (riv.) D4
Oyapock (riv.) E4
Rémire (isls.) F3
Saint-Marcel (mt.) E4
Salut (isls.) F3
Sinnamary (riv.) E3
Tampoc (riv.) E4
Tumuc-Humac (mts.) D3

GUYANA

DISTRICTS

East Berbice-Corantyne C3
East Demerara-West Coast Berbice C2
Mazaruni-Potaro A2
North West A2
Rupununi B4
West Demerara-Essequibo Coast B2

CITIES and TOWNS

Adventure○ 645 B2
Annai○ 569 B4
Anna Regina 1,124 B2
Apoteri○ 74 B3
Aurora○ 210 B2
Baramanni○ 231 B2
Baramita A2
Bartica○ 4,087 B2
Biloku○ 290 B5
Charity○ 1,175 B2
Corriverton 10,502 C3
Dadanawa B4
Danielstown 861 B2
Enmore C2
Enterprise B2
Epira○ 230 C3
Five Stars A2
Fort Wellington C2
Georgetown (cap.) 63,184 C2
Georgetown○* 164,039 C2
Imbaimadai○ 270 A3
Isherton B4
Issano○ 207 B3
Issineru○ 124 A2
Ituni B3
Kamakusa○ 211 A3
Kamarang○ 308 A3
Kangaruma B3
Kumaka B4
Kurupukari○ 284 B3
Kwakwani C3
Lethem○ 645 B4
Linden 23,956 L2
Mabaruma○ 391 B1
Mahaica○ 6,967 C2
Mahaicony○ 4,665 C2
Mahaicony Village○ 4,665 C2
Mahdia○ 147 B3
Mara○ 203 C3
Matthews Ridge B2
Morawhanna○ 292 B1
Mount Everard○ 369 B2
New Amsterdam 17,782 B2
Orealla○ 674 C3
Paradise C3
Parika○ 1,101 B2
Pickersgill○ 508 B2
Port Kaituma A2
Queenstown○ 1,211 B2
Rockstone○ 728 B2
Rosignol○ 2,001 C2
Suddie○ 705 B2
Takama C3
Towakaima B2
Tumatumari○ 353 B3
Tumereng○ 238 B2
Vreed-en-Hoop○ 3,054 B2
Wichabai○ 216 B4

OTHER FEATURES

Acarai (mts.) B5
Amakura (riv.) A2
Amuku (mts.) B4
Atkinson Field B2
Barama (riv.) A2
Barima (riv.) B2
Berbice (riv.) B3
Burro-Burro (riv.) B3
Caburai (mt.) A3
Canje (riv.) C2

Agriculture, Industry and Resources

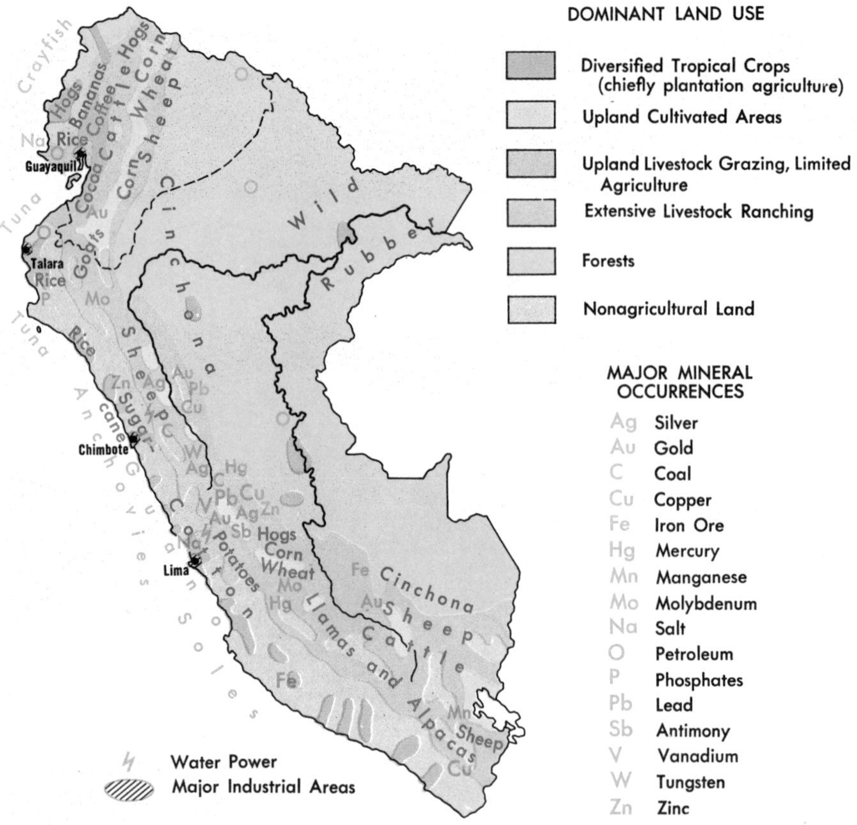

DOMINANT LAND USE
Diversified Tropical Crops (chiefly plantation agriculture)
Upland Cultivated Areas
Upland Livestock Grazing, Limited Agriculture
Extensive Livestock Ranching
Forests
Nonagricultural Land
MAJOR MINERAL OCCURRENCES
Ag Silver
Au Gold
C Coal
Cu Copper
Fe Iron Ore
Hg Mercury
Mn Manganese
Mo Molybdenum
Na Salt
O Petroleum
P Phosphates
Pb Lead
Sb Antimony
V Vanadium
W Tungsten
Zn Zinc
Water Power
Major Industrial Areas
Guayaquil
Talara
Chimbote
Lima
Crayfish
Tuna
Anchovies
Soles
Rice
Bananas
Coffee
Cacao
Cattle
Corn
Wheat
Sheep
Hogs
Goats
Sugar cane
Potatoes
Cotton
Cinchona
Wild Rubber
Llamas and Alpacas

Agriculture, Industry and Resources

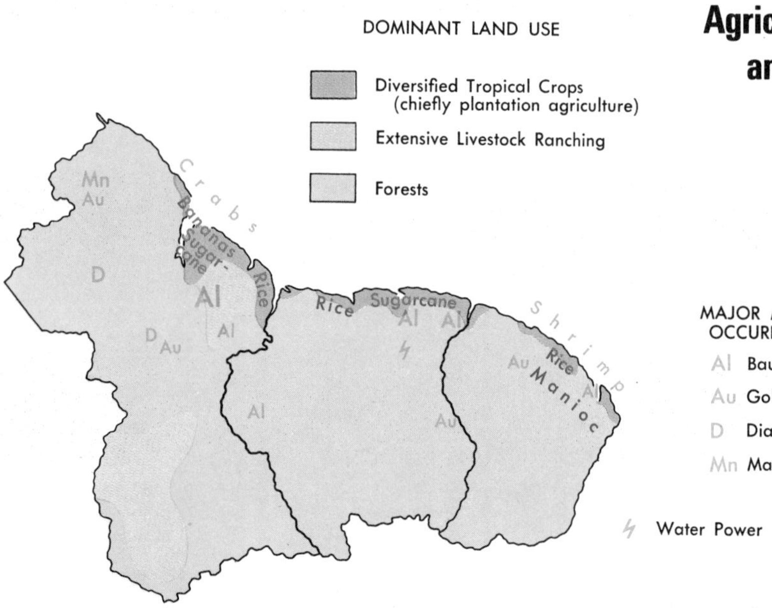

DOMINANT LAND USE
Diversified Tropical Crops (chiefly plantation agriculture)
Extensive Livestock Ranching
Forests
MAJOR MINERAL OCCURRENCES
Al Bauxite
Au Gold
D Diamonds
Mn Manganese
Water Power
Crabs
Shrimp
Bananas
Sugar cane
Rice
Sugarcane
Manioc

GUYANA

AREA 83,000 sq. mi. (214,970 sq. km.)
POPULATION 820,000
CAPITAL Georgetown
LARGEST CITY Georgetown
HIGHEST POINT Mt. Roraima 9,094 ft. (2,772 m.)
MONETARY UNIT Guyana dollar
MAJOR LANGUAGES English, Hindi
MAJOR RELIGIONS Christianity, Hinduism, Islam

SURINAME

AREA 55,144 sq. mi. (142,823 sq. km.)
POPULATION 352,041
CAPITAL Paramaribo
LARGEST CITY Paramaribo
HIGHEST POINT Julianatop 4,200 ft. (1,280 m.)
MONETARY UNIT Suriname guilder
MAJOR LANGUAGES Dutch, Hindi, Indonesian
MAJOR RELIGIONS Christianity, Islam, Hinduism

FRENCH GUIANA

AREA 35,135 sq. mi. (91,000 sq. km.)
POPULATION 64,000
CAPITAL Cayenne
LARGEST CITY Cayenne
HIGHEST POINT 2,723 ft. (830 m.)
MONETARY UNIT French franc
MAJOR LANGUAGE French
MAJOR RELIGIONS Roman Catholicism, Protestantism

Courantyne (riv.)	C3
Cuyuni (riv.)	B2
Demerara (riv.)	B3
Enwarak (mt.)	B3
Essequibo (riv.)	B3
Great (fall)	B3
Ireng (riv.)	B3
Kaieteur (fall)	B3
Kamaria (falls)	B2
Kuyuwini (riv.)	B4
Kwitaro (riv.)	B4
Leguan (isl.)	B2
Marudi (isl.)	B5
Mazaruni (riv.)	A2
Moruka (riv.)	B2
New (riv.)	C4
Pakaraima (mts.)	A3
Playa (pt.)	B1
Pomeroon (riv.)	B2
Potaro (riv.)	B2
Puruni (riv.)	B2
Roraima (mt.)	A3
Rupununi (riv.)	B4
Sororieng (mt.)	B2
Surwakwima (fall)	A2
Takutu (riv.)	B4
Venamo (mt.)	A3
Waini (riv.)	B2
Wenamu (riv.)	A2

SURINAME

DISTRICTS

Brokopondo 17,763	D4
Commewijne 18,740	D3
Coronie 3,251	C3
Marowijne 25,911	D4
Nickerie 35,178	C3
Para 16,635	D3
Paramaribo 102,297	D2
Saramacca 13,554	C3
Suriname 151,585	D3

CITIES and TOWNS

Ajoewa	C4
Alalapadu	C4

Albina 1,000	D3
Asidonhoppo	D4
Berg en Dal	D3
Bitagron	D3
Brokopondo	D3
Burnside	C2
Calcutta 1,100	C3
Cottica	D4
Domburg 1,200	D3
Groningen 600	D2
Huwelijkszorg	C2
Kwakoegron	C3
Lelydorp 300	D3
Majoli	D4
Mariënburg 3,500	D2
Moengo 2,100	D3
Nieuw-Amsterdam 1,400	D2
Nieuw-Nickerie 7,400	C2
Onverwacht	D3
Paramaribo (cap.) 102,297	D2
Paranam	D3
Totness 1,300	C3
Wageningen 800	C3
Zanderij	D3

OTHER FEATURES

Bakhuys (mts.)	C3
Coeroeni (riv.)	C4
Commewijne (riv.)	D3
Coppename (riv.)	C3
Corantijn (riv.)	C3
Cottica (riv.)	D3
Eilerts de Haan (mts.)	C4
Frederik Willem IV (falls)	C4
Julianatop (mt.)	C4
Kayser (mts.)	C4
Lely (mts.)	D3
Litani (riv.)	D4
Marowijne (riv.)	D3
Nickerie (riv.)	C3
Orange (mts.) j.	D4
Saramacca (riv.)	D3
Sipaliwini (riv.)	D4
Suriname (riv.)	D3
Tapanahoni (riv.)	D4
Toekomstig (res.)	C3
Van Blommestein (lake)	D3
Wilhelmina (mts.)	C4

Topography

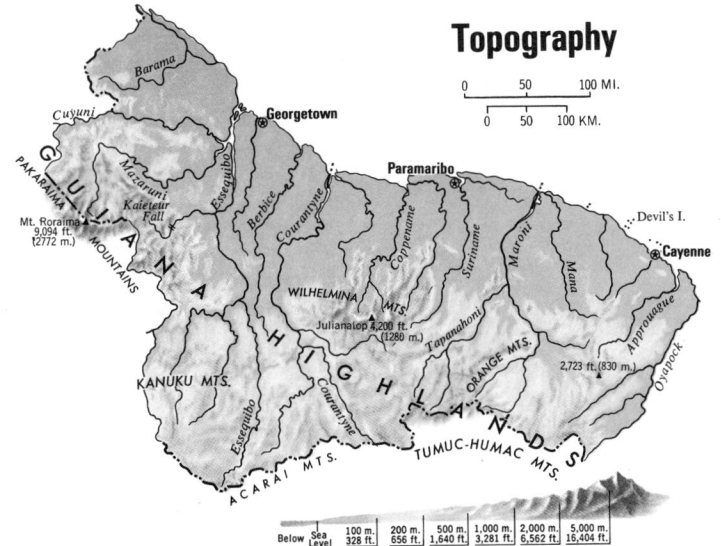

Below Sea Level	100 m. 328 ft.	200 m. 656 ft.	500 m. 1,640 ft.	1,000 m. 3,281 ft.	2,000 m. 6,562 ft.	5,000 m. 16,404 ft.

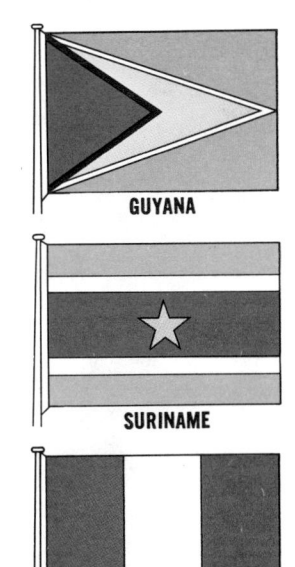

GUYANA

SURINAME

FRENCH GUIANA

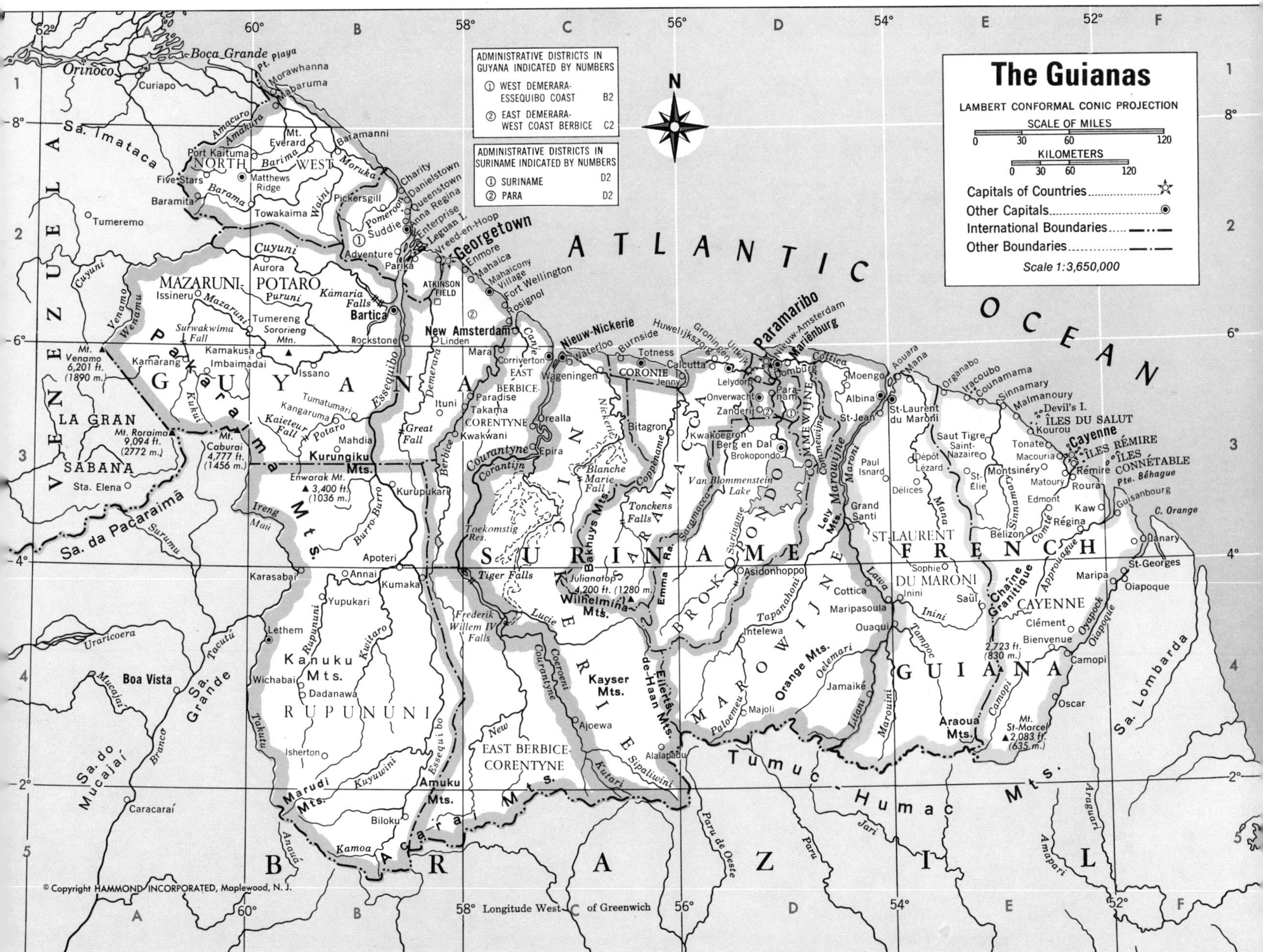

The Guianas

LAMBERT CONFORMAL CONIC PROJECTION

SCALE OF MILES

KILOMETERS

Capitals of Countries .... ☆
Other Capitals .... ◉
International Boundaries .... —··—
Other Boundaries .... —·—

Scale 1:3,650,000

ADMINISTRATIVE DISTRICTS IN GUYANA INDICATED BY NUMBERS
① WEST DEMERARA-ESSEQUIBO COAST — B2
② EAST DEMERARA-WEST COAST BERBICE — C2

ADMINISTRATIVE DISTRICTS IN SURINAME INDICATED BY NUMBERS
① SURINAME — D2
② PARA — D2

© Copyright HAMMOND INCORPORATED, Maplewood, N.J.

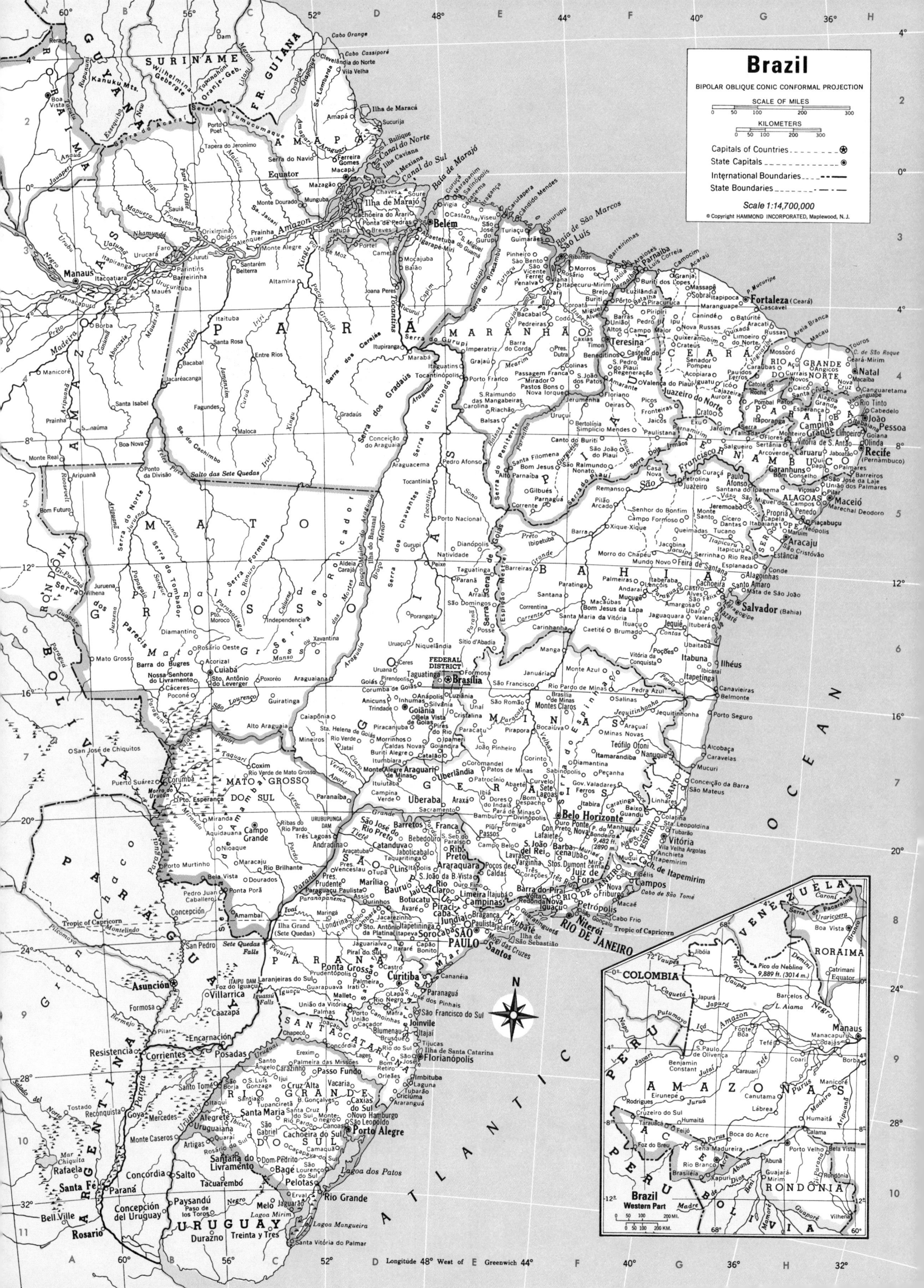

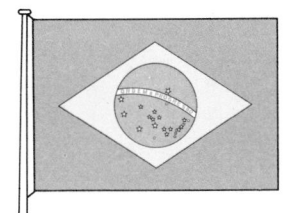

AREA 3,284,426 sq. mi. (8,506,663 sq. km.)
POPULATION 119,024,600
CAPITAL Brasília
LARGEST CITY São Paulo (greater)
HIGHEST POINT Pico da Neblina 9,889 ft. (3,014 m.)
MONETARY UNIT cruzeiro
MAJOR LANGUAGE Portuguese
MAJOR RELIGION Roman Catholicism

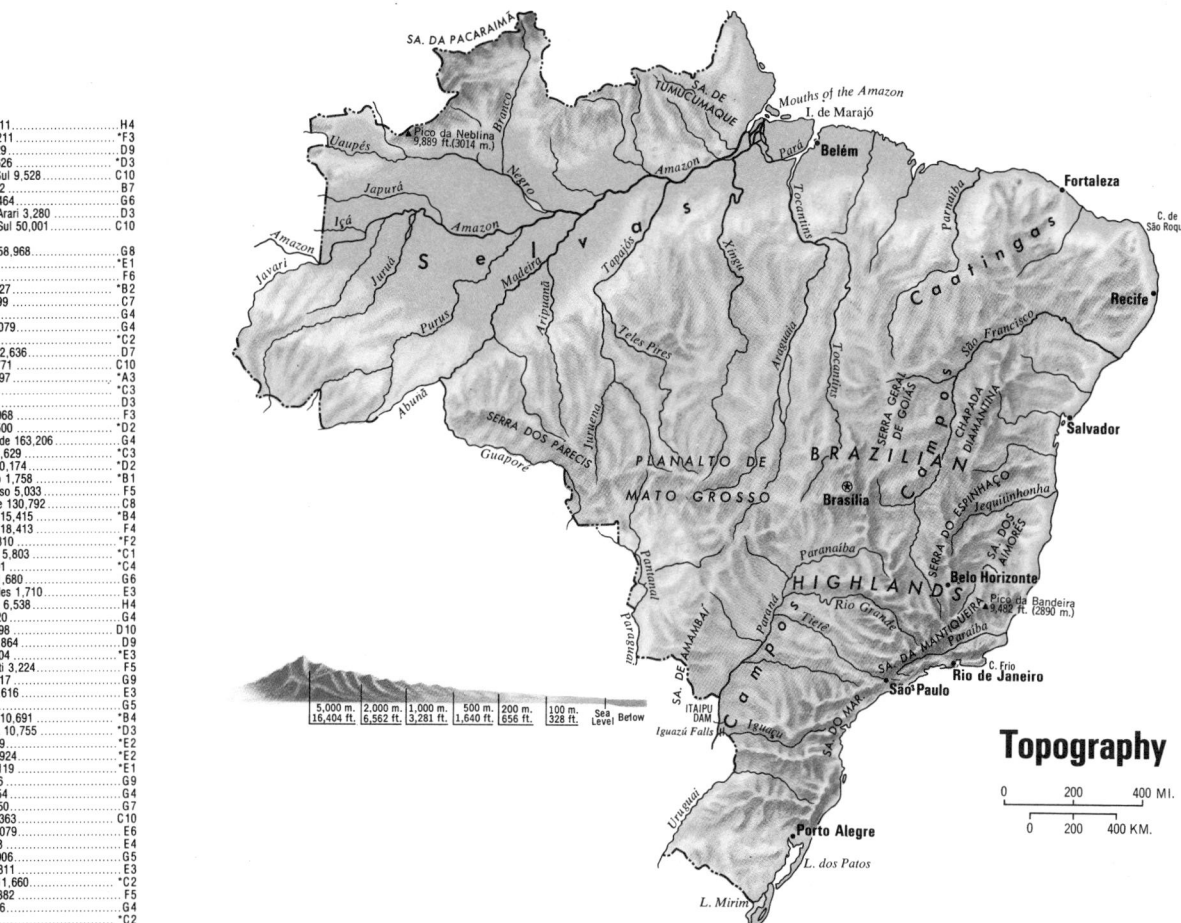

Topography

5,000 m.	2,000 m.	1,000 m.	500 m.	200 m.	100 m.	Sea	Below
16,404 ft.	6,562 ft.	3,281 ft.	1,640 ft.	656 ft.	328 ft.	Level	

0   200   400 MI.

0   200   400 KM.

(continued on following page)

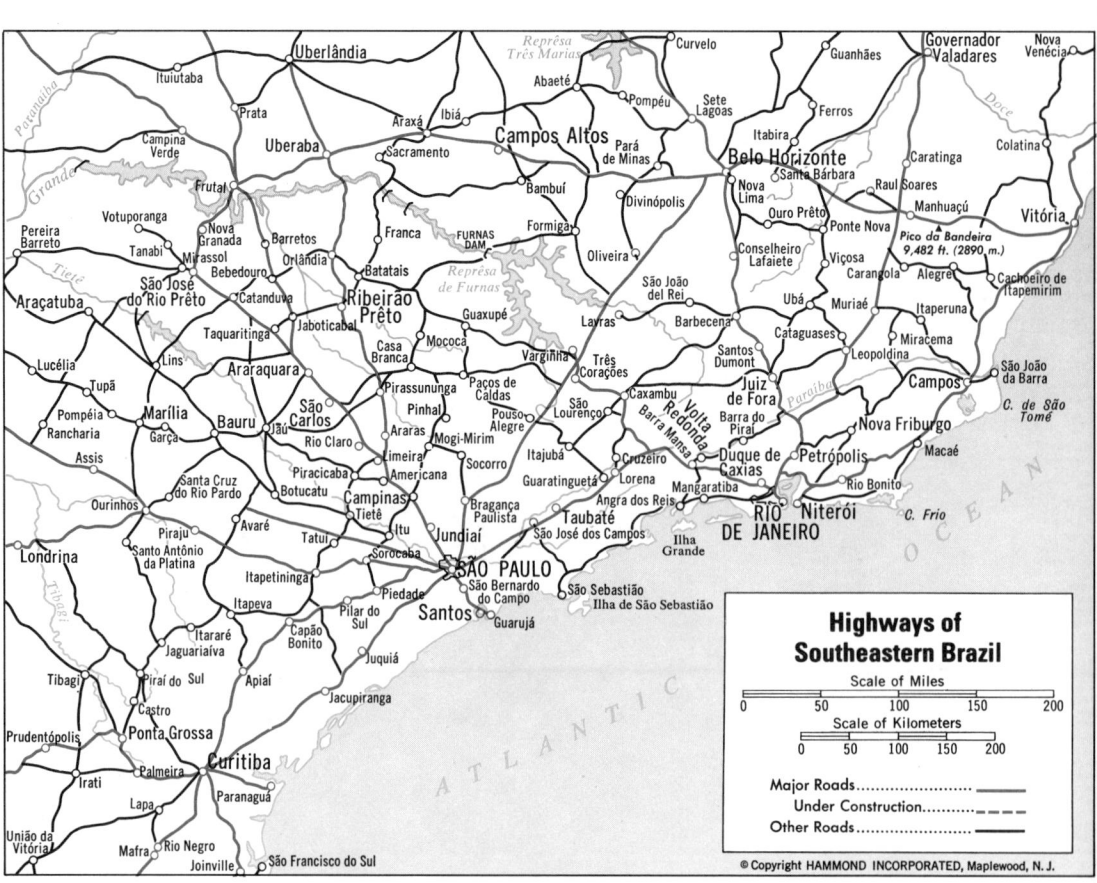

Highwayss of Southeastern Brazil

Scale of Miles
0   50   100   150   200

Scale of Kilometers
0   50   100   150   200

Major Roads ....
Under Construction ....
Other Roads ....

© Copyright HAMMOND INCORPORATED, Maplewood, N.J.

Agriculture, Industry and Resources

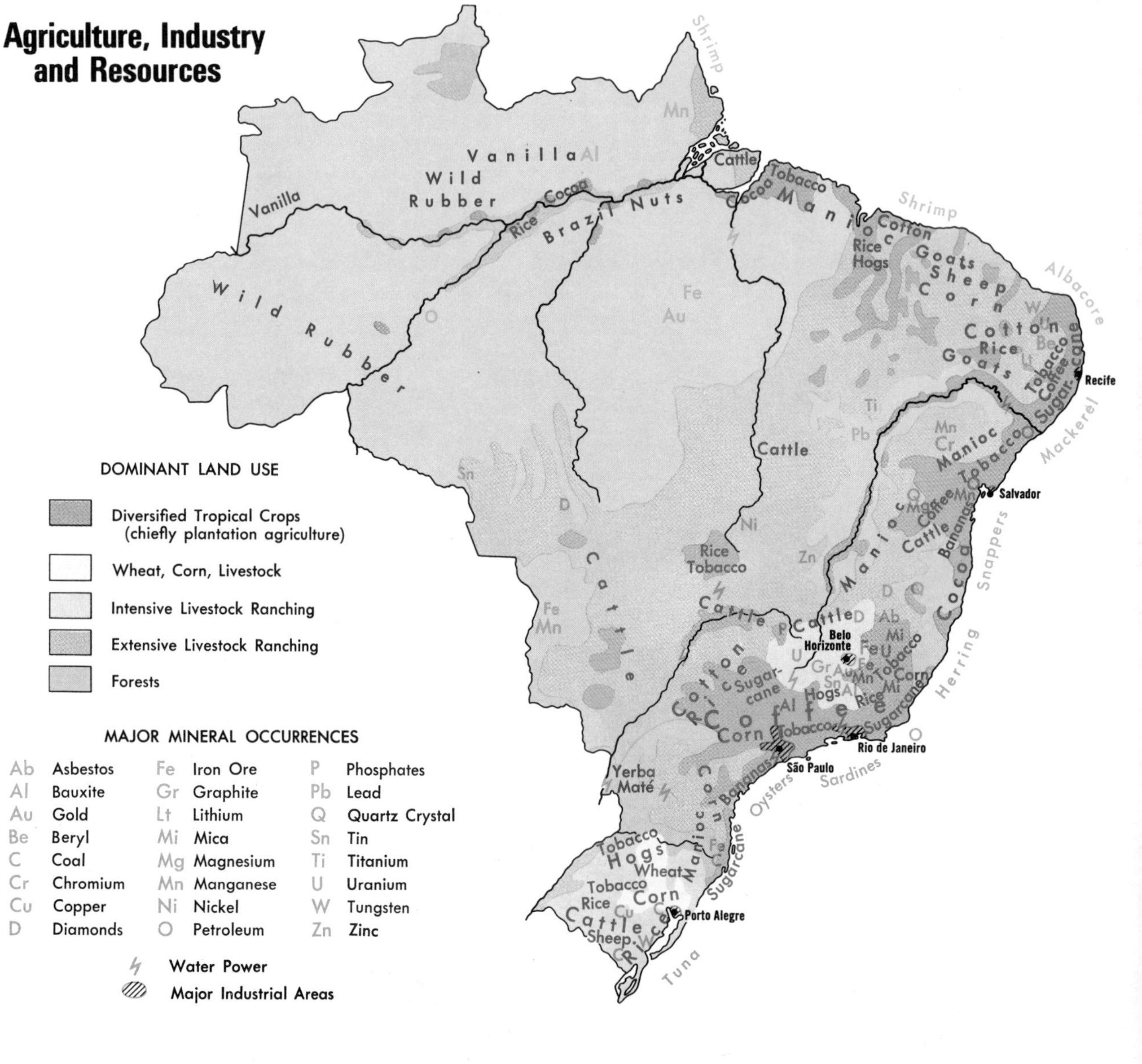

DOMINANT LAND USE

Diversified Tropical Crops
(chiefly plantation agriculture)

Wheat, Corn, Livestock

Intensive Livestock Ranching

Extensive Livestock Ranching

Forests

MAJOR MINERAL OCCURRENCES

Ab	Asbestos	Fe	Iron Ore	P	Phosphates
Al	Bauxite	Gr	Graphite	Pb	Lead
Au	Gold	Lt	Lithium	Q	Quartz Crystal
Be	Beryl	Mi	Mica	Sn	Tin
C	Coal	Mg	Magnesium	Ti	Titanium
Cr	Chromium	Mn	Manganese	U	Uranium
Cu	Copper	Ni	Nickel	W	Tungsten
D	Diamonds	O	Petroleum	Zn	Zinc

⚡ Water Power

▨ Major Industrial Areas

Piauí 2,887	F4	União da Vitória 18,426	D9	Cassiporé (cape) ... D2

Piaui 2,887 ...F4
São Raimundo das Mangabeiras 3,220 ...E4
São Raimundo Nonato 5,264 ...F5
São Romão 1,558 ...E7
São Roque 16,474 ...*C3
São Sebastião 6,847 ...*D3
São Sebastião do Paraíso 19,037 ...*C2
São Simão 7,705 ...*C4
São Vicente 116,075 ...*C4
São Vicente Ferrer 1,038 ...E3
Saúl ...B3
Senador Pompeu 9,057 ...F4
Sena Madureira 3,293 ...G10
Senhor do Bonfim 21,414 ...F5
Serra do Navio ...D3
Serrinha 15,971 ...G5
Sertânia 8,793 ...G5
Sete Lagoas 61,063 ...E7
Sertãozinho 3,595 ...D7
Simplício Mendes 2,998 ...F4
Sítio d'Abadia 309 ...E6
Sobral 51,864 ...E4
Socorro 8,262 ...*C3
Sorocaba 165,990 ...*C3
Soure 8,958 ...D3
Taguatinga, Fed. Dist. 106,320 ...D6
Taguatinga, Goiás 1,388 ...E6
Tapera do Jeronimo ...D3
Taquaritinga 17,830 ...*B2
Tarauacá 3,810 ...G10
Tatuí 30,895 ...*C3
Tefé 7,076 ...G9
Teofilo Otoni 64,568 ...F7
Teresina 181,071 ...F4
Teresópolis 53,462 ...*E3
Tibagi 2,073 ...*A4
Tijucas 6,474 ...D9
Timon 16,038 ...F4
Tocantínia 1,437 ...D5
Tocantinópolis 4,321 ...D5
Touros 1,951 ...H4
Três Corações 25,707 ...*D2
Três Lagoas 40,157 ...C8
Três Pontas 14,289 ...*D2
Três Rios 31,733 ...*E3
Trindade 13,786 ...D7
Tubarão 51,121 ...D10
Tucano 5,525 ...G5
Tucuruí 5,549 ...D3
Tupã 34,753 ...*A2
Tupancireta 10,172 ...C10
Turiaçu 2,496 ...E3
Utóia 4,263 ...F3
Úba 29,025 ...*E2
Ubaíra 3,068 ...G6
Ubaitaba 4,947 ...G6
Ubatuba 8,804 ...*D3
Uberaba 108,576 ...*C1
Uberlândia 110,463 ...E7
Una 12,750 ...E7
União 6,348 ...F4

União da Vitória 18,426 ...D9
União dos Palmares 15,751 ...H5
Uraricoera ...H8
Uruaçu 8,930 ...D6
Uruana 5,194 ...D6
Urucará 2,122 ...B3
Uruçuí 2,870 ...E4
Urucurituba 509 ...B3
Uruguaiana 60,667 ...B10
Vacaria 25,162 ...D10
Valença 24,186 ...*E3
Valença do Piauí 5,366 ...F4
Viana 5,986 ...E3
Varginha 36,447 ...*D2
Vera Cruz 5,771 ...*B3
Viçosa 8,625 ...G5
Viçosa 15,552 ...*E2
Vigia 10,231 ...E3
Vila Velha Argolas 43,177 ...F8
Viscondé do Rio ...
Vitória 13,737 ...*E2
Viseu 2,416 ...E3
Vitória 121,978 ...G8
Vitória da Conquista 82,477 ...F6
Vitória de Santo Antão 41,130 ...G4
Volta Redonda 120,645 ...*D3
Votuporanga 29,128 ...*B2
Xapuri 1,865 ...G10
Xique-Xique 9,998 ...F5

OTHER FEATURES

Abacaxis (riv.) ...B4
Abunã (riv.) ...G10
Acaraí, Serra do (range) ...B2
Acre (riv.) ...G10
Aiama (lake) ...H9
Amambaí, Serra de (range) ...C7
Amapari (riv.) ...C2
Amazon (riv.) ...C3
Anauá (riv.) ...B2
Apore (riv.) ...D4
Aragua (riv.) ...D2
Araguari (riv.) ...D2
Ararauama (lake) ...*E3
Arinos (riv.) ...B5
Araraé (riv.) ...A4
Bailique (isl.) ...D2
Balsas (riv.) ...E5
Bananal (isl.) ...D5
Bandeira, Pico da (mt.) ...*E2
Braço Maior do Araguaia ...D5
Braço Menor do Araguaia ...D6
Branco (riv.) ...H8
Buzios (cape) ...*F3
Canumã (riv.) ...B4
Capim (riv.) ...D3
Carajás, Serra dos (range) ...D4
Cardoso (isl.) ...*C4

Cassiporé (cape) ...D2
Caviana (isl.) ...D2
Chavantes, Serra dos (range) ...D5
Claro (riv.) ...D7
Cochimbo, Serra do (mts.) ...D5
Comprida (isl.) ...*C4
Contas (riv.) ...F6
Corrente (riv.) ...E6
Cuiabá (riv.) ...B7
Culuene (riv.) ...C6
Curuá (riv.) ...C4
Demini (riv.) ...H8
Dois Irmãos, Serra (range) ...F5
Espigão Mestre (Geral de Goiás) (range) ...E6
Espinhaço, Serra do (range) ...F7
Estrondo, Serra do (range) ...D5
Feia (lake) ...*F3
Feio (riv.) ...*B2
Formosa, Serra (range) ...C5
Frio (cape) ...*F3
Furnas (dam) ...*C2
Geral de Goiás, Serra ...E6
Gi-Paraná (riv.) ...H10
Gradaús, Serra dos (range) ...D4
Grajaú (riv.) ...E4
Grande (isl.) ...*D3
Grande (riv.) ...*B2,
Guanabara (bay) ...*E3
Guaporé (riv.) ...H10
Gurguéia (riv.) ...E5
Gurupi, Serra do (range) ...*E2
Gurupi (riv.) ...D3
Ibicuí (riv.) ...C10
Içá (riv.) ...G9
Iguaçu (riv.) ...C9
Iguaçu (falls) ...*B3
Ilha Grande (bay) ...*D3
Iriri (riv.) ...C4
Itaipu (dam) ...B9
Itapecuru (riv.) ...F4
Itapi (riv.) ...G5
Itapicuru (riv.) ...G5
Itararé (riv.) ...*B3
Ival (riv.) ...C8
Jaculpe (riv.) ...E5
Jaguaribe (riv.) ...G4
Jamanxim (riv.) ...C4
Japurá (riv.) ...F9
Jari (riv.) ...C3
Jauaperi (riv.) ...A2
Jauari, Serra (mts.) ...A3
Javari (riv.) ...F9
Jequitinhonha (riv.) ...F7
Juruá (riv.) ...G10
Juruena (riv.) ...B5
Jutaí (riv.) ...G9
Lombarda, Serra (mts.) ...D2
Madeira (riv.) ...A4

Maicuru (riv.) ...C2
Mangueira (lag.) ...D11
Manso (riv.) ...B7
Mantiqueira, Serra da (range) ...*D3
Mapuera (riv.) ...B3
Mar, Serra do (range) ...*C4,
Maracá (isl.) ...D2
Marajó (bay) ...E2
Marajó (isl.) ...D3
Mato Grosso, Planalto de (plat.) ...B6
Maués-Açu (riv.) ...B4
Mearim (riv.) ...E4
Mexiana (isl.) ...D2
Miranda (riv.) ...B8
Mirim (lake) ...C11
Mogi Guaçu (riv.) ...*C2
Mortes (Manso) (riv.) ...D6
Mucuripe (pt.) ...G3
Negro (riv.) ...H9
Negro (riv.) ...H9
Nhamundá (riv.) ...B3
Norte (riv.) ...D2
Norte, Serra do (range) ...B5
Oiapoque (Oyapock) (riv.) ...C2
Orange (cape) ...D1
Órgãos (range) ...*E3
Oyapock (riv.) ...C2
Pacaja (riv.) ...D4
Pacaraíma, Serra da (mts.) ...H8
Papagaio (riv.) ...B6
Pará (riv.) ...D3
Paracatu (riv.) ...E7
Paraguaçu (riv.) ...F6
Paraguai (riv.) ...B8
Paraíba (riv.) ...C8
Paraná (riv.) ...E7
Paraná (riv.) ...C9
Paranapanema (riv.) ...*B3,
Paranaíba (riv.) ...*B4
Paranatinga (riv.) ...C6
Pardo (riv.) ...*B2,
Pardo (riv.) ...D7
Pardo (riv.) ...F6
Parecis, Serra dos (range) ...B6
Parnaíba (riv.) ...F3
Paru (riv.) ...C3
Paru de Oeste (riv.) ...B3
Patos (lag.) ...D10

(isl.) ...E9
Piauí, Serra do (range) ...F5
Piauí (riv.) ...F5
Piquiri (riv.) ...C7
Piquiri (riv.) ...C9
Preto (riv.) ...A4
Preto (riv.) ...E5
Purus (riv.) ...H9
Ribeira (riv.) ...F9
Roncador, Serra do (range) ...D5
Ronuro (riv.) ...C6
Roosevelt (riv.) ...A5
Sangue (riv.) ...B6
Santa Catarina (isl.) ...D2
São Lourenço (riv.) ...C7
São Marcos (bay) ...F3
São Roque (cape) ...H4
São Francisco (riv.) ...*D2,
São Simão (isl.) ...*D3,
São Tomé (cape) ...*F8
Sapucaí (riv.) ...*D2
Sepetiba (bay) ...*D3
Sete Quedas (isl.) ...C9
Sete Quedas (falls) ...C9
(isl.) ...C8
Sono (riv.) ...E5

Turiaçu (riv.) ...*E3
Turvo (riv.) ...*B2
Uatumã (riv.) ...B3
Uaupés (riv.) ...G9
Uraricoera (riv.) ...H8
Urubu (riv.) ...A3
Urubupungá (dam) ...C8
Urucún, Morro do (mt.) ...B7
Uruçuí (riv.) ...C9
Vasa Barris (riv.) ...G5
Velhas (riv.) ...E7
Verde (riv.) ...D7
Verdinho (riv.) ...D7
Xingu (riv.) ...C3
Tacutu (riv.) ...B2
Tapajós (riv.) ...B4
Taquari (riv.) ...H4
Tefé (riv.) ...G9
Teles Pires (riv.) ...B5
Tibagi (riv.) ...*A4
Tietê (riv.) ...*B2,
Tiracambu, Serra ...E3
Tocantins (riv.) ...D4
Tombador, Serra do (range) ...B6
Trombetas (riv.) ...B3
Tumucumaque, Serra de (range) ...C2

†Population of metropolitan area.
*Preceding reference indicates that the name will be found on S.E. Brazil Map, page 135.

Brasília

0   5 MI.
0   5 KM.

© Copyright HAMMOND INCORPORATED, Maplewood, N.J.

Southeastern Brazil

POLYCONIC PROJECTION

SCALE OF MILES
0   25   50   100   150

SCALE OF KILOMETERS
0   25 50   100   150

State Capitals .... ⊙
State Boundaries ....

Scale 1:4,480,000

© Copyright HAMMOND INCORPORATED, Maplewood, N.J.

DEPARTMENTS

Beni, El 168,367 ....C3
Chuquisaca 358,516 ....C6
Cochabamba 720,952 ....C5
El Beni 168,367 ....C3
La Paz 1,465,078 ....A4
Oruro 310,409 ....A6
Pando 34,493 ....B2
Potosí 657,743 ....B7
Santa Cruz 710,724 ....E5
Tarija 187,204 ....D7

CITIES and TOWNS

Abapó 466 ....D6
Acchila 208 ....C7
Achacachi 3,621 ....A5
Aiquile 3,465 ....C6
Alcalá 236 ....C6
Alejandrí‡ 198 ....C3
Alto Seco‡ 3,414 ....D6
Amarete 992 ....A4
Ananea 302 ....A4
Ancoraimes 769 ....A4
Andamarca‡ 5,187 ....B6
Añimbo 443 ....C7
Anzaldo 1,056 ....C5

Apolo 1,043 ....A4
Aracaţ 3,537 ....B5
Arampampa 829 ....B5
Arani 2,200 ....B5
Arcopongo‡ 2,223 ....B5
Aromaţ 873 ....A5
Arque 1,254 ....B5
Arroyo Grande A4
Ascensión (Añez) D4
Asunta 45 ....B5
Atén 199 ....A4
Atochaţ 3,964 ....A4
Ayacucho 729 ....D5
Ayata 479 ....A4

Azurduy 1,234 ....C6
Barrera B3
Baures 592 ....D3
Bella Flor A2
Bella Vista E3
Berenguela 2,412 ....A5
Betanzos 1,097 ....C6
Bolívar A5
Bolpebra A2
Boyuibe 537 ....D7
Buena Vista, Santa Cruz D5
Cabezas 298 ....D6
Cachuela Esperanza 1,073 ....C2
Caiza 838 ....C7
Cajuata 447 ....B5

Calacoto 415 ....A5
Calamarca 802 ....A5
Callapa 636 ....A5
Camacho‡ 875 ....C7
Camargo 1,609 ....C7
Camatindi‡ 297 ....D7
Camiri 4,969 ....D7
Candelaria‡ 468 ....F5
Capinota 1,734 ....B5
Capinota 148 ....A7
Capirenda D7
Caquiaviri 760 ....A5
Carabuco 626 ....A4
Caracollo 909 ....B5
Caranaviţ 525 ....B4

Carandaiti 1,403 ....D7
Caraparí 351 ....D7
Carmenţ 845 ....B2
Cataricahua 3,240 ....B6
Cavari 249 ....B5
Cavinas 1,011 ....B3
Chachacomani 159 ....A6
Chacoma‡ 330 ....A6
Chaguaya 643 ....C7
Challacollo 284 ....B6
Challana‡ 1,206 ....A4
Challapata 2,529 ....B6
Chapacura‡ 152 ....A2
Chaquí 291 ....C6
Charagua 1,185 ....D6

Charaña 794 ....A5
Chayanta 1,272 ....B6
Chiguana 154 ....A7
Chiflijo 27 ....A4
Chivet 336 ....B7
Chocaya 444 ....B7
Choqueコ‡ 1,976 ....A6
Chulumani 2,362 ....B5
Chuma 931 ....A4
Chuquichambi‡ 1,094 ....C6
Chuquichuqui‡ 1,892 ....C6
Cliza 3,121 ....C5
Cobija 3,650 ....A2
Cocaniᵼ 658 ....A4
Cocapata‡ 2,855 ....B5

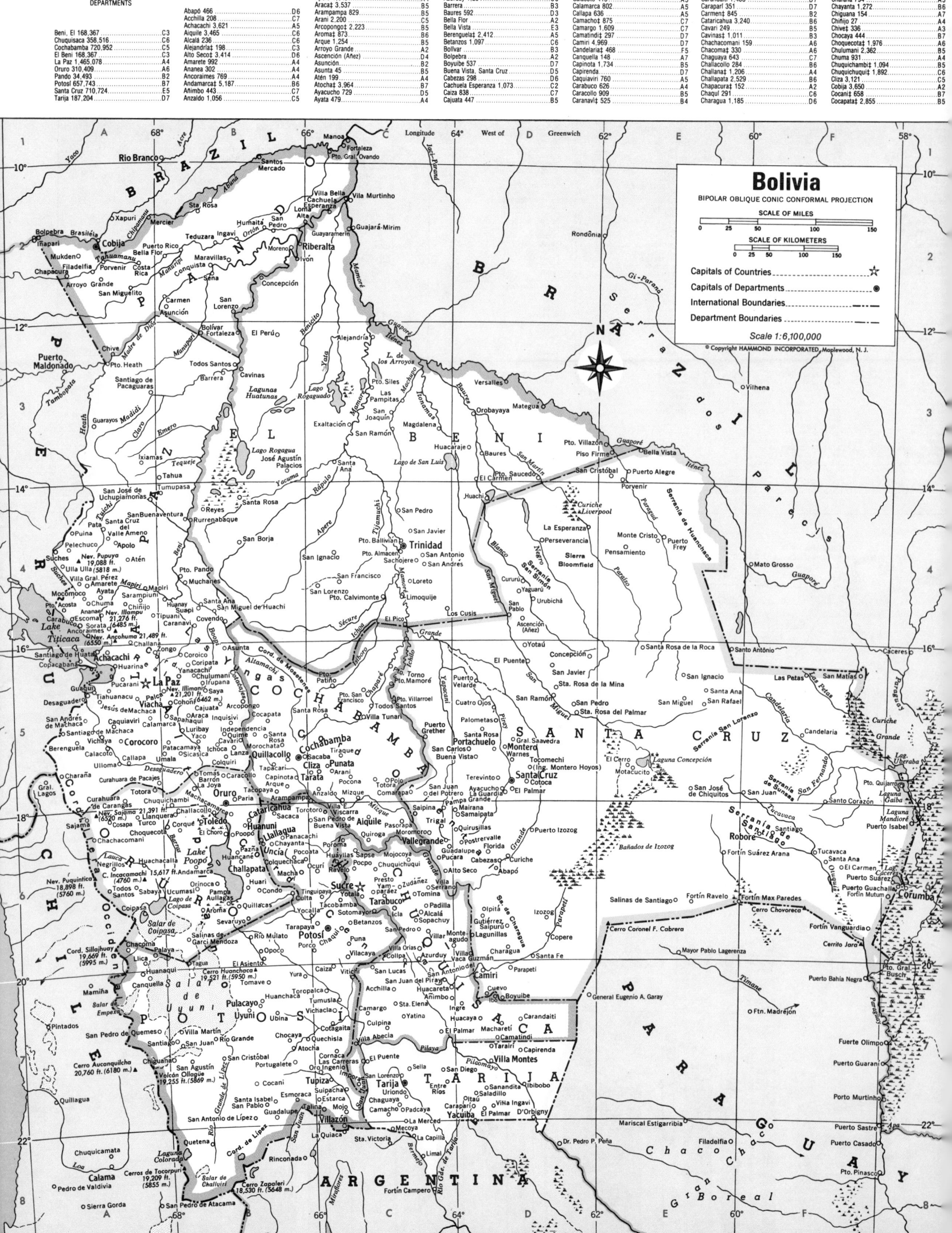

Cochabamba 204,684 .... C5
Cohoni 890 .... B5
Coipasa‡ 202 .... A6
Collpa 481 .... C6
Colquechaca 1,070 .... B6
Colquiri 806 .... B5
Comarapa 1,096 .... C5
Concepción, El Beni‡ 61 .... B2
Concepción, Santa Cruz 1,056 .... D5
Condo‡ 5,525 .... B6
Conquista‡ 1,162 .... B2
Copacabana 1,981 .... A5
Copere D6
Coripata 1,647 .... B5
Cornaca 264 .... C7
Corocoro 4,431 .... A5
Coroico 2,235 .... B5
Corque 423 .... B6
Cosapa 297 .... A6
Costa Rica‡ 43 .... A2
Cotagaita 1,353 .... C7
Cotoca 915 .... D5
Covendo 71 .... B4
Cuatro Ojos‡ 465 .... D5
Cuevo 902 .... D7
Culpina 981 .... C7
Culta‡ 4,412 .... B6
Curahuara de Carangas 235 .... A5
Curahuara de Pacajes 510 .... A5
Curiche 257 .... D6
Cururú D4
Desaguadero 201 .... A5
D'Orbigny‡ 214 .... D7
El Asiento B6
El Carmen, El Beni 232 .... D3
El Carmen, Santa Cruz F6
El Cerro 117 .... E5
El Choro 224 .... B6
El Palmar, Chuquisaca‡ 772 .... D7
El Palmar, Santa Cruz 437 .... D5
El Palmar, Tarija 832 .... D7
El Perú B3
El Pico C4
El Puente, Santa Cruz‡ 1,185 .... D5
El Puente, Tarija‡ 1,310 .... C7
Entre Ríos 1,011 .... C7
Escoma 220 .... A4
Esmoraca‡ 1,137 .... B7
Estarca‡ 2,331 .... C7
Exaltación, El Beni 405 .... C3
Filadelfia‡ 942 .... A2
Florida, Santa Cruz 128 .... D6
Fortaleza‡ 765 .... B3
Fortaleza C1
Fortín Campero‡ 87 .... C8
Fortín Max Paredes F6
Fortín Mutum F6
Fortín Ravelo E6
Fortín Suárez Arana F6
Fortín Vanguardia F6
General Saavedra 1,006 .... D5
Guadalupe, Potosí 71 .... B7
Guadalupe, Santa Cruz 2,355 .... C6
Guaqui 2,266 .... A5
Guayaramerín 1,470 .... C2
Huacaraje 673 .... D3
Huacareta 239 .... C7
Huacaya 229 .... D7
Huachacalla 801 .... A6
Huachi D4
Huanaqui 359 .... A7
Huanay 574 .... B4
Huancané 148 .... B6
Huanchaca B7
Huanuni 5,696 .... B6
Huari 1,070 .... B6
Huarina 1,151 .... A5
Huayllas 206 .... C6
Humaitá‡ 429 .... B2
Ibibobo D7
Ibo D7
Ichoca 591 .... B5
Icla 196 .... C6
Impora 274 .... C7
Independencia 1,742 .... B5
Ingavi‡ 111 .... B2
Ingeniero Montero Hoyos
(Tocomechi) 575 .... D5
Ingre 162 .... D7
Inquisivi 530 .... B5
Irupana 1,937 .... B5
Itaú 102 .... D7
Ivón‡ 772 .... C2
Ixiamas 292 .... A3
Izozog‡ 2,759 .... D6
Jesús de Machaca 529 .... A5
José Agustín
Palacios‡ 2,273 .... B3
La Capilla‡ 1,870 .... C8
La Esmeralda D8
La Esperanza D4
La Guardia 470 .... D5
Lagunillas 840 .... D6
La Joya 401 .... B5
La Merced‡ 688 .... C8
Lanza 526 .... B5
La Paz (cap.) 635,283 .... B5
Las Carreras 155 .... C7
Las Pampitas‡ 71 .... C3
Las Petas‡ 383 .... F5
Limal‡ 524 .... C8
Limoquije C4
Llallagua 6,719 .... B6
Llanquera 613 .... A6
Llica 560 .... A6
Loma Alta B2
Loreto 589 .... C4
Los Cusis D4
Luribay 392 .... B5
Macha 1,050 .... B6
Machacamarca 1,746 .... B5
Macharetí‡ 1,164 .... D7
Magdalena 1,724 .... C3
Mairana 508 .... D6
Manoa C1
Mapiri 289 .... B4
Maravillas B2
Mateguá 38 .... D3
Mecoya‡ 585 .... C8
Mercier‡ 272 .... B2
Mizque 870 .... C5
Mocomoco 977 .... A4
Mojo 469 .... C7
Mojocoya 498 .... C6
Monteagudo 971 .... D6
Monte Cristo E4
Montero 2,713 .... D5
Moreno B2
Morochata 461 .... B5
Moromoro 556 .... C6
Motacucito‡ 585 .... E5
Muchanes B4
Mukden‡ 84 .... A2
Negrillos 85 .... A6
Ocurí 1,531 .... C6
Opoco B6
Orinoca‡ 2,380 .... B6
Orobayaya‡ 1,132 .... D3
Oro Ingenio‡ 945 .... C7
Oruro 124,213 .... B5
Padcaya 324 .... C7
Padilla 2,462 .... C6
Palaya 300 .... A6
Palca 887 .... A5
Palometas‡ 3,453 .... D5
Pampa Aullagas‡ 1,834 .... B6
Pampa Grande 727 .... D5
Panacachi 952 .... B6
Paria 335 .... B5
Pasorapa 1,016 .... C6
Pata 122 .... A4
Patacamaya 1,278 .... B5
Pazña 671 .... B6
Pelechuco 873 .... A4
Pensamiento E4
Perseverancia D4
Piso Firme D3
Pocoata 859 .... B6
Pocona 518 .... C5
Pocpo‡ 2,791 .... C6
Pojo 1,047 .... C5
Poopó 736 .... B6
Porco 817 .... B6
Poroma 171 .... C6
Portachuelo 2,456 .... D5
Portugalete‡ 1,590 .... B7
Porvenir, Pando‡ 846 .... A2
Porvenir, Santa Cruz E4
Postrervalle 750 .... D6
Potosí 77,397 .... C6
Presto 725 .... C6
Pucara 762 .... C6
Pucarani 1,041 .... A5
Puerto Acosta 1,302 .... A4
Puerto Alegre E3
Puerto Almacen 358 .... C4
Puerto Ballivián C4
Puerto Calvimonte C4
Puerto Frey E4
Puerto General Ovando 50
Puerto Grether C5
Puerto Guachalla F6
Puerto Heath‡ 570 .... A3
Puerto Isabel F6
Puerto Izozog D6
Puerto Mamoré C5
Puerto Pando B4
Puerto Patiño C5
Puerto Quijarro G5
Puerto Rico‡ 539 .... B2
Puerto San Francisco C5
Puerto Saucedo D3
Puerto Siles 357 .... C3
Puerto Suárez 1,159 .... F6
Puerto Torno C5
Puerto Velarde D5
Puerto Villarroel C5
Puerto Villazón D3

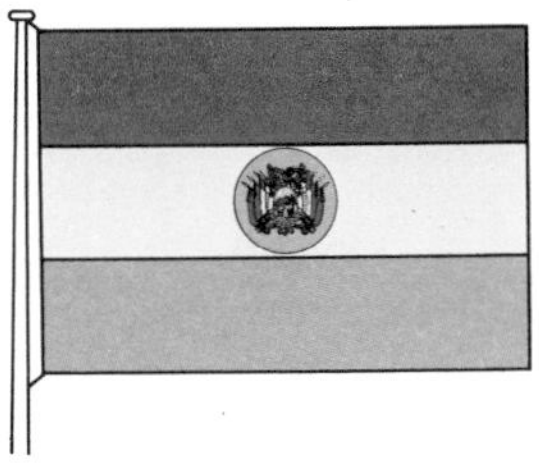

AREA 424,163 sq. mi. (1,098,582 sq. km.)
POPULATION 5,600,000
CAPITALS La Paz, Sucre
LARGEST CITY La Paz
HIGHEST POINT Nevada Ancohuma 21,489 ft. (6,550 m.)
MONETARY UNIT Bolivian peso
MAJOR LANGUAGES Spanish, Quechua, Aymara
MAJOR RELIGION Roman Catholicism

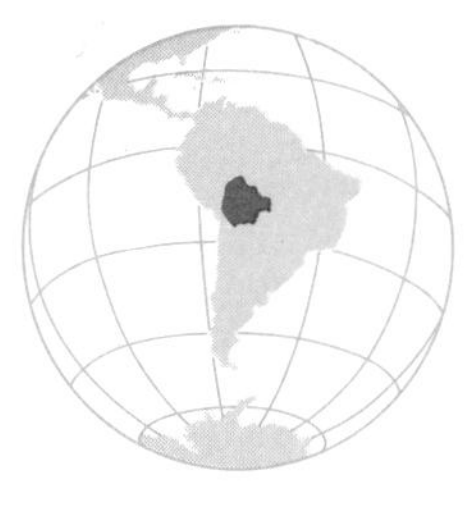

Topography

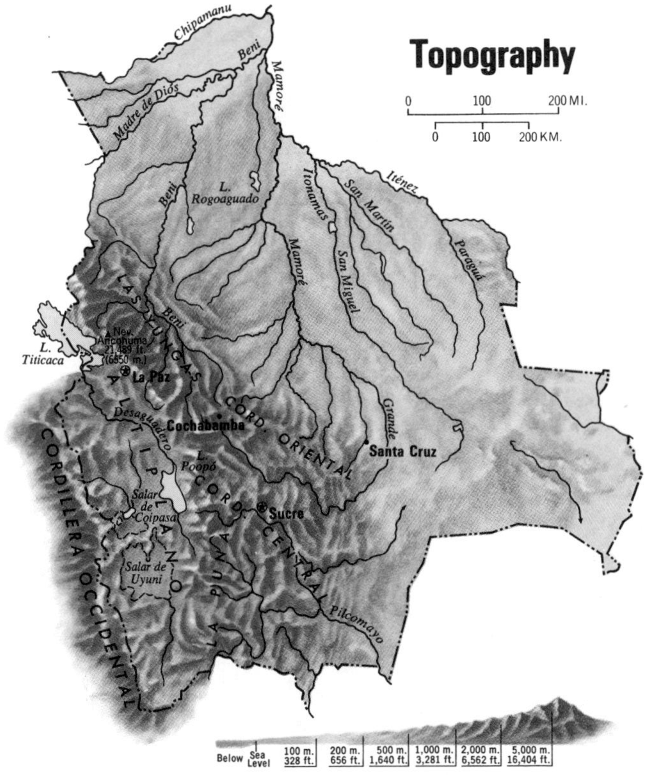
0 100 200 MI.
0 100 200 KM.
Chipamanu
Beni
Mamoré
Madre de Diós
Iténez
San Martín
Itonamas
L. Rogoaguado
Paraguá
San Miguel
L. Titicaca
Nev. Ancohuma 21,489 ft. (6550 m.)
La Paz
Cochabamba
Santa Cruz
Sucre
Desaguadero
L. Poopó
Salar de Coipasa
Salar de Uyuni
Grande
Pilcomayo
CORD. ORIENTAL
CORD. CENTRAL
CORDILLERA OCCIDENTAL
Below Sea Level
100 m. 328 ft.
200 m. 656 ft.
500 m. 1,640 ft.
1,000 m. 3,281 ft.
2,000 m. 6,562 ft.
5,000 m. 16,404 ft.

Puina A4
Pulacayo 7,984 .... B7
Puna 852 .... C6
Punata 5,014 .... C5
Quechisla 171 .... C7
Queteña 183 .... B8
Quillacas 1,170 .... B6
Quillacollo 9,123 .... B5
Quime 1,256 .... B5
Quiroga‡ 3,467 .... C6
Quirusillas 433 .... D6
Ravelo 907 .... C6
Reyes 1,404 .... B4
Riberalta 6,549 .... C2
Río Grande 281 .... B7
Río Mulato 381 .... B6
Roboré 3,715 .... F6
Rurrenabaque 1,225 .... B4
Sabaya 649 .... A6
Sacaba 2,752 .... C5
Sacaca 1,778 .... B6
Sachojere 401 .... C4
Saipina 573 .... C6
Sajama 231 .... A6
Saladillo‡ 1,315 .... D7
Salinas de Garci Mendoza 335 .... B6
Salinas de Santiago E6
Samaipata 1,656 .... D6
San Agustín‡ 810 .... B7
Sanandita 379 .... D7
San Andrés 399 .... C4
San Andrés de Machaca 101 .... A5
San Antonio, El Beni 436 .... C4
San Antonio de Lípez‡ 177 .... B7
San Antonio del
Parapetí 497 .... D7
San Borja 708 .... B4
San Buenaventura 307 .... A4
San Carlos 570 .... D5
San Cristóbal,
Potosí‡ 1,200 .... B7
San Cristóbal, Santa Cruz E3
San Diego‡ 773 .... D7
San Francisco, El Beni 185 .... C4
San Ignacio, El Beni 1,757 .... C4
San Ignacio, Santa Cruz 1,819 .... E5
San Javier, El Beni 233 .... C4
San Javier, Santa Cruz 564 .... D5
San Joaquín 1,959 .... C3
San José de Chiquitos 1,933 .... E5
San José de
Uchupiamonas 277 .... A4
San Juan, Potosí 131 .... B7
San Juan, Santa Cruz‡ 1,482 .... F5
San Juan del Piray 541 .... C7
San Juan del Potrero 263 .... C5
San Lorenzo, El Beni 496 .... C4
San Lorenzo, Pando‡ 317 .... B2
San Lorenzo, Tarija 785 .... C7
San Lucas 925 .... C7
San Matías 887 .... F5
San Miguel 502 .... E5
San Miguel de Huachi 25 .... B4
San Miguelito A2
San Pablo, Potosí 11 .... B7
San Pablo, Santa Cruz D4
San Pedro, Chuquisaca 182 .... C6
San Pedro, El Beni 262 .... C4
San Pedro, Pando‡ 312 .... B2
San Pedro, Santa Cruz 80 .... D5
San Pedro de Buena Vista 1,094 .... C6
San Pedro de Quemes‡ 290 .... A7
San Rafael‡ 1,282 .... E5
San Ramón, El Beni 1,161 .... C3
San Ramón, Santa Cruz 379 .... D5
Santa Ana, El Beni 2,225 .... C3
Santa Ana, La Paz 171 .... B4
Santa Ana, Santa Cruz 275 .... E5
Santa Ana, Santa Cruz 663 .... F6
Santa Cruz, Santa Cruz 254,682 .... D5
Santa Cruz del Valle
Ameno 442 .... A4
Santa Elena‡ 4,474 .... C7
Santa Fe D6
Santa Isabel‡ 323 .... B7
Santa Rosa, Cochabamba‡ 942 .... B5
Santa Rosa, Cochabamba‡ 276 .... C5
Santa Rosa, El Beni 765 .... B4
Santa Rosa, Pando‡ 105 .... B2
Santa Rosa, Santa Cruz 995 .... D5
Santa Rosa de la Mina 99 .... D5
Santa Rosa de la Roca 101 .... E5
Santa Rosa del Palmar 441 .... E5
Santiago, Potosí 172 .... A7
Santiago, Santa Cruz 765 .... F6
Santiago de Huata 948 .... A5
Santiago de Machaca 218 .... A5
Santiago de Pacaguaras A3
Santo Corazón‡ 963 .... F5
Santos Mercado B1
Sapahaqui 55 .... B5
Sapse‡ 89 .... C6
Sarampiuni 138 .... A4
Saya 339 .... B5
Sella C7
Sena‡ 660 .... B2
Sevaruyo 475 .... B6
Sicasica 1,486 .... B5
Sopachuy 713 .... C6
Sorata 2,087 .... A4
Sotomayor 510 .... C6
Suapi‡ 1,750 .... B4
Suches‡ 231 .... A4
Sucre (cap.) 63,625 .... C6
Suipacha‡ 2,701 .... C7
Tacobamba‡ 6,933 .... C6
Tacopaya 795 .... B5
Tagua B6
Tahua B3
Talina 122 .... B7
Tapacarí 980 .... B5
Tarabuco 2,833 .... C6
Tarairí‡ 394 .... D7
Tarapaya 357 .... B6
Tarata 3,016 .... C5
Tarija 38,916 .... C7
Teduzara‡ 271 .... B2
Terevinto‡ 3,790 .... D5
Tiahuanacu 1,227 .... A5
Tinguipaya 766 .... C6
Tipuani‡ 1,216 .... B4
Tiraque 1,390 .... C5
Tocomechi 575 .... D5
Todos Santos, Cochabamba 408 .... C5
Todos Santos, La Paz B3
Todos Santos, Oruro 68 .... A6
Toledo 3,273 .... B6
Tomás Barrón 1,852 .... B5
Tomave 201 .... B7
Tomina 708 .... C6
Toropalca‡ 199 .... B7
Torotoro 1,233 .... C6
Totora, Cochabamba C5
Totora, Oruro A5
Trigal 749 .... C6
Trinidad, El Beni 27,487 .... C4
Trinidad, Pando‡ 332 .... B2
Tucavaca F6
Tumupasa 349 .... B4
Tumusla‡ 526 .... C7
Tupiza 8,248 .... C7
Turco 131 .... A6
Ubina‡ 462 .... B7
Ucumasi‡ 1,040 .... B6
Ulla Ulla 52 .... A4
Ulloma 116 .... A5
Umala 481 .... B5
Uncía 4,507 .... B6
Uriondo 860 .... C7
Urubichá 1,369 .... D4
Uyuni 6,968 .... B7
Vallegrande 5,094 .... C6
Versalles 83 .... D3
Viacha 6,607 .... A5
Vichacla 317 .... C7
Vichaya 422 .... A5
Vilacaya 200 .... C6
Villa Abecia 539 .... C7
Villa Bella 88 .... C2
Villa E. Viscarra 658 .... C6
Villa General Pérez 802 .... A4
Villa Ingavi 122 .... D7
Villa Martín 543 .... B7
Villa Montes 3,105 .... D7
Villa Orías 404 .... C6
Villar 322 .... C6
Villa Serrano 1,570 .... C6
Villa Tunari 510 .... C5
Villa Vaca Guzmán 699 .... D6
Villazón 6,261 .... C7
Vitichi 1,515 .... C7
Warnes 1,571 .... D5
Yaco 835 .... B5
Yacuiba 5,027 .... D7
Yaguarú D4
Yamparaéz 725 .... C6
Yanacachi‡ 1,964 .... B5
Yatina‡ 1,850 .... C7
Yocalla‡ 1,814 .... B6
Yotala 1,554 .... C6
Yotaú D5
Yura 136 .... B7
Zongo 141 .... B5
Zudáñez 1,868 .... C6

OTHER FEATURES

Abuná (riv.) B2
Altamachi (riv.) B5
Ancohuma, Nevada (mt.) A4
Apere (riv.) C4
Arroyas, Los (lake) C3
Barras (riv.) B6
Baures (riv.) D3
Beni (riv.) B2
Benicito (riv.) C3
Bermejo (riv.) C8
Blanco (riv.) D4
Bloomfield, Sierra (mts.) D4
Boopi (riv.) B4
Cáceres (lag.) G6
Candelaria (riv.) F5
Capitán Ustarés, Cerro
(mt.) E6
Central, Cordillera (range) C6
Challviri (salt dep.) B8
Chaparé (riv.) C5
Charagua, Sierra de (mts.) D6
Chipamanu (riv.) A2
Chovoreca, Cerro (mt.) F6
Claro (riv.) A3
Coipasa (lake) B6
Coipasa (salt dep.) A6
Colorada (lag.) A8
Concepción (lag.) E5
Coronel F. Gabrera E6
Cotacajes (riv.) B5
Desaguadero (riv.) B5
Emero (riv.) B3
Empexa (salt dep.) A7
Gaiba (lag.) F5
Grande (marsh) F5
Grande (riv.) C4
Grande (riv.) C6
Grande de Lípez (riv.) B7
Guaporé (riv.) C3
Heath (riv.) A3
Huanchaca, Cerro (mt.) B7
Huanchaca, Serranía de
(mts.) E4
Huatunas (lag.) B3
Ichilo (riv.) C5
Ichoa (riv.) C4
Illampu, Nevada (mt.) A4
Illimani, Nevada (mt.) B5
Incacamachi, Cerro (mt.) A6
Isiboro (riv.) C5
Iténez (Guaporé) (riv.) C3
Itonamas (riv.) C3
Izozog (swamp) E6
Jara, Cerrito (mt.) F6
Las Yungas (reg.) B5
Lauca (riv.) A6
Lípez, Cordillera de
(range) B8
Liverpool (swamp) D4
Machupo (riv.) C3
Madidi (riv.) A3
Madre de Diós (riv.) A3
Mamoré (riv.) C2
Mandioré (lag.) F6
Manuripi (riv.) B2
Mizque (riv.) C6
Mosetenes, Cordillera de
(range) B5
Negro (riv.) D4
Occidental, Cordillera
(range) A6
Ollagüe (vol.) B7
Oriental, Cordillera (range) C5
Ortón (riv.) B2
Otuquis (riv.) F6
Paraguá (riv.) E4
Paraguay (riv.) F7
Parapetí (riv.) D6
Petas, Las (riv.) F5
Pilaya (riv.) C7
Pilcomayo (riv.) D7
Piray (riv.) D5
Poopó (lake) B6
Pupuya, Nevada (mt.) A4
Puquintica, Nevado (mt.) A6
Rápulo (riv.) C4
Real, Cordillera (range) A5
Rogagua (lake) B3
Rogaguado (lake) C3
Sajama, Nevada (mt.) A6
San Fernando (riv.) F5
San Juan (riv.) C7
San Lorenzo, Serranía
(mts.) E5
San Luis (lake) C3
San Martín (riv.) D3
San Miguel (riv.) D4
San Simón, Serranía
(mts.) D4
Santiago, Serranía de
(mts.) F6
Sécure (riv.) C4
Sillajhuay, Cordillera (mt.) A6
Suches (riv.) A4
Sunsas, Serranía de (mts.) F5
Tahuamanu (riv.) A2
Tarija, Rio Grande de (riv.) C8
Tequeje (riv.) B3
Tijamuchi (riv.) C4
Titicaca (lake) A4
Tocorpuri, Cerros de (mt.) A8
Tucavaca (riv.) F6
Tuichi (riv.) A4
Uberaba (lag.) G5
Uyuni (salt dep.) B7
Yacuma (riv.) B3
Yapacani (riv.) C5
Yata (riv.) C3
Yungas, Las (reg.) B5
Zapaleri, Cerro (mt.) B8

‡Population of canton.

Agriculture, Industry and Resources

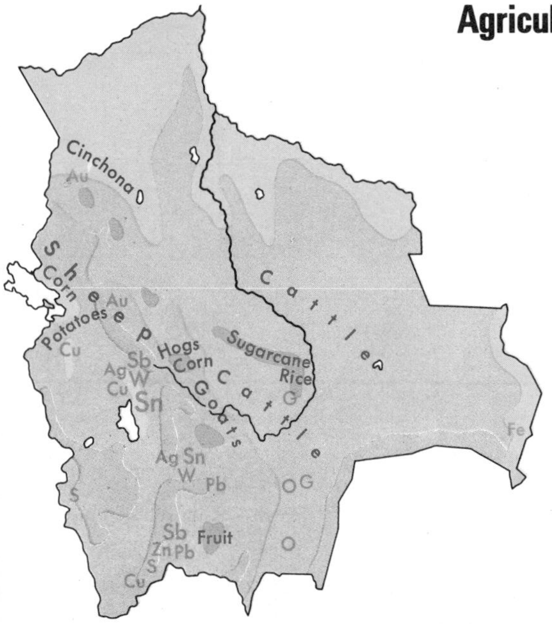
Cinchona
Sheep
Corn
Potatoes
Cattle
Hogs
Corn
Sugarcane
Rice
Goats
Cattle
Fruit
Au
Ag
Cu
Sb
W
Sn
Pb
O
G
Fe
S
Zn

DOMINANT LAND USE

- Diversified Tropical Crops (chiefly plantation agriculture)
- Upland Cultivated Areas
- Upland Livestock Grazing, Limited Agriculture
- Extensive Livestock Ranching
- Forests
- Nonagricultural Land

MAJOR MINERAL OCCURRENCES

Ag	Silver	G	Natural Gas	Sb	Antimony
Au	Gold	O	Petroleum	Sn	Tin
Cu	Copper	Pb	Lead	W	Tungsten
Fe	Iron Ore	S	Sulfur	Zn	Zinc

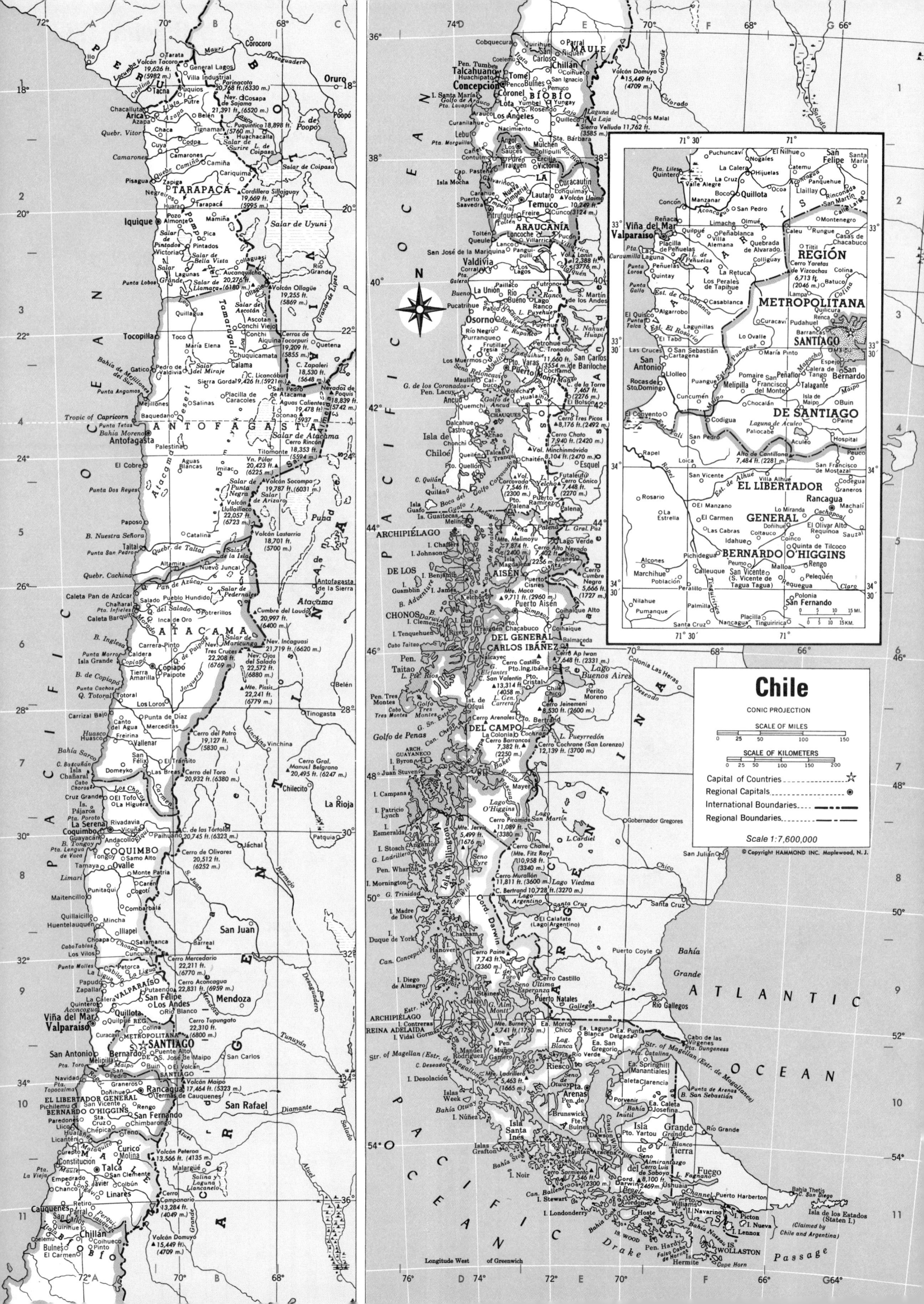

Chile

CONIC PROJECTION

SCALE OF MILES
0 25 50 100 150

SCALE OF KILOMETERS
0 25 50 100 150 200

Capital of Countries .... ☆
Regional Capitals .... ◉
International Boundaries ....
Regional Boundaries ....

Scale 1:7,600,000

© Copyright HAMMOND INC. Maplewood, N.J.

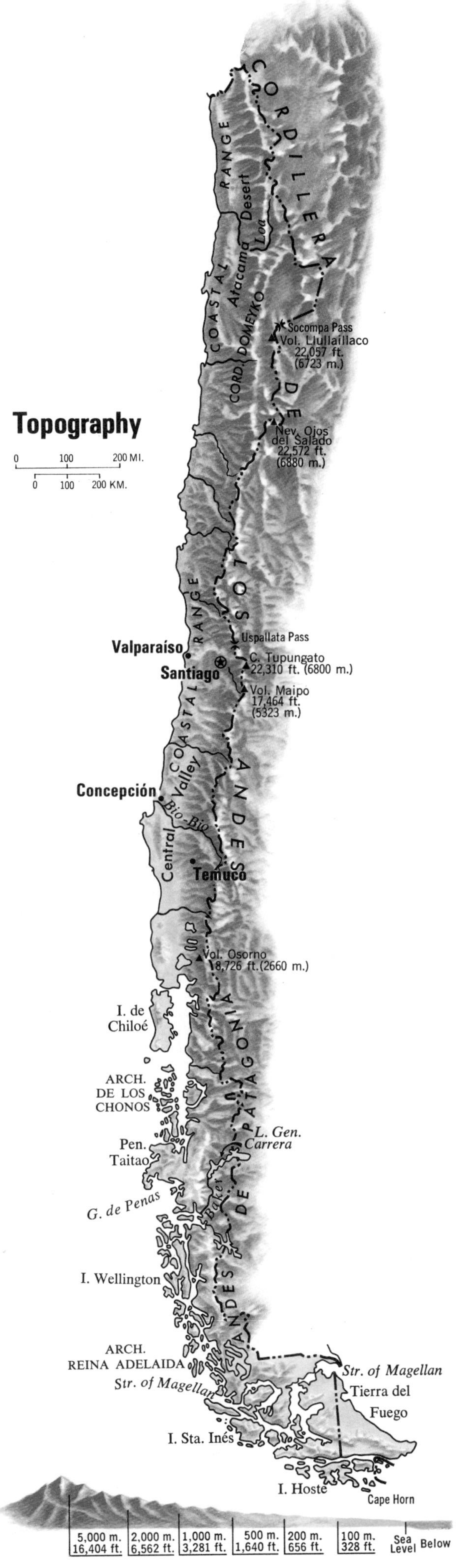

Topography
0 100 200 MI.
0 100 200 KM.
CORDILLERA DE LOS ANDES
COASTAL RANGE
Atacama Desert
Loa
CORD. DOMEYKO
Socompa Pass
Vol. Llullaillaco 22,057 ft. (6723 m.)
Nev. Ojos del Salado 22,572 ft. (6880 m.)
Valparaíso
Santiago
Uspallata Pass
C. Tupungato 22,310 ft. (6800 m.)
Vol. Maipo 17,464 ft. (5323 m.)
Central Valley
Concepción
Bío-Bío
Temuco
Vol. Osorno 8,726 ft. (2660 m.)
I. de Chiloé
ARCH. DE LOS CHONOS
Pen. Taitao
L. Gen. Carrera
G. de Penas
Baker
ANDES DE PATAGONIA
I. Wellington
ARCH. REINA ADELAIDA
Str. of Magellan
Tierra del Fuego
I. Sta. Inés
I. Hoste
Cape Horn
5,000 m. 16,404 ft.
2,000 m. 6,562 ft.
1,000 m. 3,281 ft.
500 m. 1,640 ft.
200 m. 656 ft.
100 m. 328 ft.
Sea Level
Below

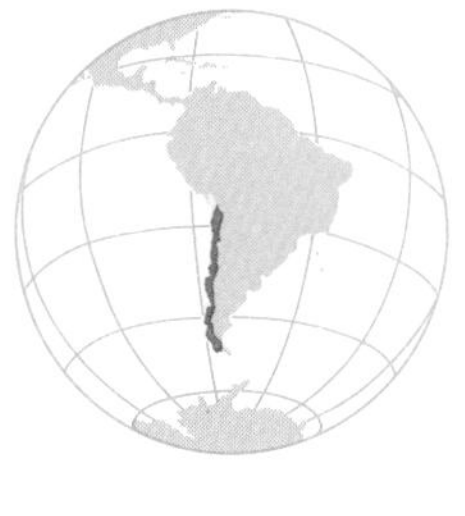

AREA 292,257 sq. mi. (756,946 sq. km.)
POPULATION 11,198,789
CAPITAL Santiago
LARGEST CITY Santiago
HIGHEST POINT Ojos del Salado 22,572 ft. (6,880 m.)
MONETARY UNIT Chilean escudo
MAJOR LANGUAGE Spanish
MAJOR RELIGION Roman Catholicism

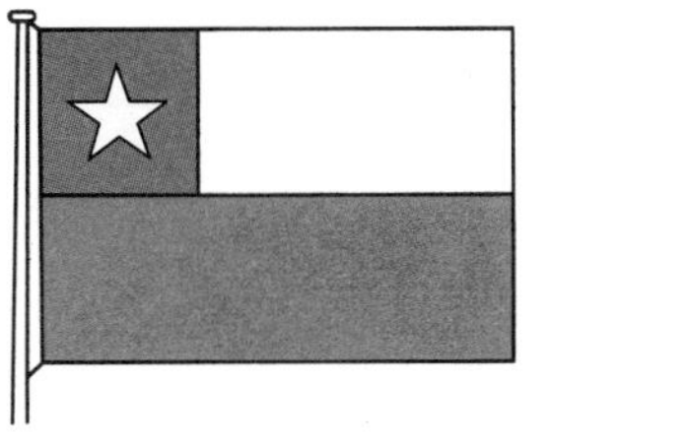

REGIONS

Aconcagua A9
Aisén del General Carlos Ibáñez del Campo E6
Antofagasta B4
Atacama B6
Bíobío E1
Coquimbo A8
El Libertador General Bernardo O'Higgins A10
La Araucanía E2
Los Lagos D3
Magallanes E10
Maule A11
Santiago, Región Metropolitana de (Santiago Metropolitan Region) A9
Tarapacá B2
Valparaíso A9

CITIES and TOWNS

Achao† 11,501 D4
Aguas Blancas† 203 B4
Algarrobo† 3,941 F3
Ancud 11,900 D4
Andacollo 6,000 A8
Angol 23,500 D1
Antofagasta 125,100 A4
Arauco 5,400 D1
Arica 87,700 A1
Ascotán B3
Baquedano A4
Barrancas† 184,241 G3
Batuco G3
Belén† 925 B1
Boco F2
Buin 11,800 G4
Bulnes 6,900 E1
Cabildo 5,800 A9
Calama 45,900 B3
Calbuco† 21,673 D4
Caldera† 3,268 A6
Calera de Tango† 6,198 G4
Caleta Barquito A6
Caleta Clarencia E10
Caleta Pan de Azúcar A5
Caleu G2
Calle Larga† 7,172 G2
Calleuque F5
Camarones B2
Camiña B2
Cañete 7,900 D2
Canto del Agua A7
Capitán Pastene D2
Carahue† 12,733 D2
Carén A8
Cariquima B2
Carrera Pinto B6
Carrizal Bajo A7
Cartagena† 7,124 F3
Casablanca 5,500 F3
Castro 11,200 D4
Catalina† 1,637 B5
Catemu† 8,728 G2
Cauquenes 20,200 A11
Cerro Castillo† 537 E9
Cerro Manantiales F10
Chaca B1
Chacabuco G2
Chacalluta A1
Chaitén† 4,067 E4
Chañaral† 36,949 A6
Chanco† 12,433 A11
Chépica† 11,199 A10
Chile Chico E6
Chillán 87,600 A11
Chimbarongo 5,300 A10
Choapa A9
Chocalán F4
Chonchi† 8,911 D4
Chuquicamata 22,100 B3
Cobquecura† 6,298 D1
Cochamó† 5,042 E3
Codegua† 6,757 G4
Codigua F4
Codpa† 950 B1
Coelemu 5,400 D1
Cogotí A8
Coihaique 16,100 E6
Coihaique Alto E6
Coihueco† 17,276 A11
Coinco† 4,942 G5
Colbún† 12,924 A11
Colina 7,400 G3
Collaguasi B3
Colliguay F3
Collipulli 7,200 E2
Coltauco† 11,857 F5
Combarbalá† 17,332 A8
Concepción 178,200 D1
Conchi B3
Conchi Viejo B3
Concón F2
Constitución 11,500 A11
Contulmo† 13,987 D2
Copiapó 45,200 B6
Coquimbo 52,700 A8
Coronel 37,300 D1
Corral† 5,533 D3
Cruz Grande A7
Cunco† 18,836 E2
Cuncumén, Coquimbo A9
Cuncumén, Santiago F4
Curacautín 9,800 E2
Curacaví 5,800 G3
Curanilahue 13,200 D1
Curepto† 13,020 A10
Curicó 41,300 A10
Cuya B2
Dalcahue† 7,084 D4
Domeiko A7
Doñihue† 8,837 G5
El Carmen, Ñuble† 13,226 A11
El Carmen, O'Higgins F5
El Cobre A4
El Convento F4
El Manzano F5
El Monte 7,000 G4
El Ñilhue G2
El Quisco† 2,152 E3
El Tabo† 2,180 F3
El Tofo A7
El Tránsito B7
El Volcán B10
Empedrado† 7,887 A11
Ercilla† 8,061 E2
Espejo G3
Estancia Caleta Josefina† 1,042 F10
Estancia Laguna Blanca E9
Estancia Morro Chico† 785 E9
Estancia Punta Delgada E9
Estancia San Gregorio† 1,156 E9
Estancia Springhill (Cerro Manantiales) F10
Freire† 23,313 E2
Freirina† 5,523 A7
Fresia† 15,359 D3
Frutillar† 12,721 D3
Fuerte Bulnes E10
Futaleufú† 2,366 E4
Futrono† 7,109 E3
Galvarino† 9,495 D2
Gatico A4
General Lagos† 810 B1
Graneros 8,900 G5
Guayacán A8
Hijuelas† 7,128 F2
Hospital G4
Huachipato D1
Hualaihué E4
Hualañé† 6,912 A10
Huara† 1,934 B2
Huasco† 4,971 A7
Huentelauquén A8
Illapel 12,200 A8
Imilac B4
Inca de Oro 1,406 B6
Iquique 64,500 A2
Isla de Maipo† 12,903 G4
La Calera 24,600 F2
La Cruz† 8,907 F2
La Estrella† 3,707 F5
Lago Ranco† 12,767 E3
Lago Verde E5
Lagunas† 5,653 B3
Lagunillas F3
La Higuera† 6,991 A7
La Laguna F2
La Ligua 7,500 A9
Lampa† 10,220 G3
Lanco 5,200 D2
La Retuca F3
Las Breas B7
Las Cabras† 12,119 F5
Las Cruces F3
La Serena 61,900 A8
La Unión 15,200 D3
Lautaro 11,900 E2
Lebu 12,500 D1
Licantén† 6,354 A10
Limache 15,200 F2
Linares 37,900 A11
Llay-Llay 9,700 G2
Llico A10
Llolleo F4
Loica F4
Lo Miranda G5
Loncoche† 17,539 D2
Longaví† 15,909 A11
Lonquimay† 9,524 E2
Lo Ovalle F3
Los Andes 23,500 B9
Los Ángeles 49,500 D1
Los Lagos† 14,934 D3
Los Loros B6
Los Muermos† 9,296 D3
Los Perales de Tapihue F3
Los Sauces† 7,613 D2
Los Vilos† 10,453 A9
Lota 48,100 D1
Machalí 5,800 G5
Maipú† 117,872 G3
Maitencillo A8
Malloa† 9,742 G5
Mamiña B2
Manzanar F2
Marchigüe† 4,451 F5
María Elena 5,900 B3
María Pinto† 5,980 G3
Maullín† 14,544 D4
Mayer E7
Mejillones† 3,333 A4
Melinca D5
Melipilla 23,900 F4
Merceditas B7
Mincha† 11,329 A8
Molina 9,400 A10
Montenegro G2
Monte Patria† 18,927 A8
Mulchén 13,700 E1
Nacimiento† 17,651 D1
Nancagua† 11,076 F6
Navidad† 6,618 A10
Negreiros† 1,144 B2
Nilahue E6
Ñiquén† 13,640 E1
Nogales† 18,529 F2
Nueva Imperial 8,000 D2
Nuevo Juncal B5
Ocoa G2
Olivar Alto† 5,414 G5
Olmué† 8,804 F2
Osorno 68,800 D3
Ollagüe B3
Ovalle 31,700 A8
Paihuano† 6,048 B8
Paillaco 5,200 D3
Paine† 21,876 G4
Paipote B6
Palena† 2,508 E5
Palestina B4
Paliocabe (Payocabe) F4
Palmilla† 7,965 F6
Panguipulli 5,700 E2
Panquehue† 4,230 G2
Paposo A5
Papudo† 2,594 A9
Paredones† 7,404 A10
Parral 17,000 A11
Pedro de Valdivia 6,200 B4
Pelequén G5
Pemuco† 7,577 E1
Peñablanca F2
Peñaflor 15,500 G4
Penco† 33,962 D1
Peñuelas F3
Petorca† 8,343 A9
Petrohué E3
Peuco G4
Peumo† 11,308 F5
Pica† 1,487 B2
Pichidegua† 13,550 F5
Pichilemu† 8,042 A10
Pintados B2
Pinto† 8,687 A11
Pisagua† 1,880 A2
Pitrufquén 7,800 D2
Placilla† 6,441 F6
Placilla de Caracoles B4
Placilla de Peñuelas F2
Población F5
Polonia G6
Pomaire F4
Porvenir† 3,600 E10
Potrerillos 5,800 B6
Pozo Almonte† 1,798 B2
Puangue F4
Pucatrihue D3
Puchuncaví† 7,542 F2
Pucón† 16,872 E2
Pudahuel G3
Pueblo Hundido 6,200 B6
Puente Alto 65,100 B10
Puerto Aisén 7,100 E6
Puerto Bertrand E7
Puerto Chacabuco D6
Puerto Cisnes† 2,800 E5
Puerto Ingeniero Ibáñez† 1,900 E6
Puerto Montt 62,700 E4
Puerto Natales 11,500 E9
Puerto Palena D5
Puerto Quellón† 7,734 D4
Puerto Varas 10,900 E3
Puerto Williams† 949 F11
Pumanque† 3,137 F6
Punitaqui† 16,167 A8
Punta Arenas 61,800 E10
Punta de Díaz B7
Puquios B1
Purén† 11,604 D2
Purranque 5,900 D3
Putaendo† 12,806 A9
Putre† 855 B1
Puyehue E3
Quebrada de Alvarado F2
Queilén† 6,055 D4
Quemchi† 6,707 D4
Queule D2
Quilicura 8,100 G3
Quillagua B3
Quillaicillo A8
Quilleco† 16,043 E1
Quillota 36,500 F2
Quilpué 40,600 F2
Quinta de Tilcoco† 6,513 G5
Quintay F3
Quintero 9,900 F2
Quirihue† 11,178 E1
Rancagua 86,500 G5
Rapel F4
Reñaca F2
Renca† 67,168 G3
Rengo 12,400 G5
Requegua G5
Requínoa† 10,730 G5
Retiro† 15,146 A11
Rinconada San Martín† 4,118 G2
Río Blanco B9
Río Bueno 9,600 D3
Río Cisnes E5
Río Negro 5,100 D3
Río Verde† 554 E10
Rivadavia A7
Rocas de Santo Domingo† 4,114 F4
Rolecha D4
Rosario† 3,383 F5
Rungue G2
Salado A6
Salamanca† 18,741 A9
Salinas B4
Samo Alto† 5,689 A8
San Antonio 46,700 F3
San Bernardo† 117,766 G4
San Carlos 17,000 E1
San Clemente† 23,273 A11
San Felipe 26,100 G2
San Félix A7
San Fernando 23,600 G6
San Francisco de Mostazal† 11,439 G4
San Ignacio† 13,523 E1
San Javier 10,800 A11
San José de la Mariquina D2
San José de Maipo† 9,601 B10
San Pablo† 7,978 D3
San Pedro, Santiago† 8,255 F4
San Pedro, Valparaíso F2
San Pedro de Atacama C4
San Rosendo† 14,337 E1
Santa Bárbara† 14,345 E1
Santa Cruz 8,600 F6
Santa María† 8,162 G2
Santiago (cap.) 2,728,600 G3
Santiago* 3,691,548 G3
San Vicente F4
San Vicente (San Vicente de Tagua)† 28,333 F5
Sauzal G5
Sierra Gorda† 8,805 B4
Talagante 16,500 G4
Talca 94,400 A11
Talcahuano 148,300 D1
Taltal 6,400 A5
Tamaya A8
Tarapacá B2
Temuco 110,300 E2
Teno† 17,675 A10
Termas de Cauquenes B10
Tierra Amarilla† 7,899 A6
Tignamar B1
Tilomonte B4
Tiltil† 9,198 G2
Tinguiririca G6
Toco† 8,734 B3
Toconao C4
Tocopilla 22,000 A3
Toltén† 16,265 D2
Tomé 29,600 D1
Tongoy A8
Totoral A6
Traiguén 11,400 D2
Valdivia 82,300 D3
Valle Alegre F2
Vallenar 26,800 A7
Valparaíso 250,400 E2
Victoria, Malleco 16,500 D2
Victoria, Tarapacá A3
Vicuña 5,100 A8
Villa Alemana 29,600 F2
Villa Alhué† 5,078 G4
Villa Industrial B1
Villarrica 13,000 E2
Viña del Mar 182,000 F2
Yumbel† 21,858 E1
Yungay† 10,725 E1
Zapallar† 2,894 A9
Zapiga B2

OTHER FEATURES

Aconcagua (riv.) F2
Aculeo (lag.) G4
Adventure (bay) D5
Aguas Calientes, Cerro (mt.) C4
Alhué, Estero de (riv.) F4
Almeida, Sierra (mts.) C4
Almirantazgo (bay) F11
Almirante Montt (gulf) D9
Alto de Cantillana (mt.) G4
Alto Nevado, Cerro (mt.) E5
Ancud (gulf) D4
Andes, Cordillera de los (mts.) C5,E
Angamos (isl.) D8
Angamos (pt.) A4
Ap Iwan, Cerro (mt.) E6
Arauco (gulf) D1
Arenales, Cerro (mt.) D7
Ascotán, Salar de (salt dep.) B3
Atacama (des.) B4
Atacama, Salar de (salt dep.) C4
Aucanquilcha, Cerro (mt.) B3
Azapa, Quebrada (riv.) B1
Baker (riv.) D7
Ballenero (chan.) E11
Barrancos, Cerro (mt.) D7
Bascuñán (cape) A7
Beagle (chan.) E11
Bella Vista, Salar de (salt dep.) B3
Benjamín (isl.) D5
Bertrand, Cerro (mt.) D8
Bío-Bío (riv.) E2
Blanca (lag.) E10
Blanco (lake) F10
Bravo (riv.) D7
Brunswick (pen.) E10
Bueno (riv.) D3
Buenos Aires (lake) E6
Burney (mt.) D9
Byron (isl.) D7
Cachapoal (riv.) G5
Cachina, Quebrada (riv.) A5
Cachos (pt.) A6
Calafquén (lake) E3
Camarones (riv.) A2
Camiña, Quebrada (riv.) B2
Campana (isl.) D7
Campanario, Cerro (mt.) A10
Cantillana, Alto de (mt.) G4
Capitán Aracena (isl.) E10
Carmen (riv.) B7
Casablanca, Estero de (riv.) F3
Castillo, Cerro (mt.) E6
Catalina (pt.) F10
Chaffers (isl.) D5
Chaltel, Cerro (mt.) E8
Chañaral (isl.) A7
Chatham (isl.) D9
Chato, Cerro (mt.) E4
Chauques (isls.) D4
Cheap (chan.) D7
Chiloé (isl.) D4
Choapa (riv.) A9
Chonos (arch.) D6

(continued on following page)

Agriculture, Industry and Resources

DOMINANT LAND USE

- Cereals, Livestock
- Mediterranean Agriculture (cereals, fruit, livestock)
- Pasture Livestock
- Extensive Livestock Ranching
- Limited Seasonal Grazing
- Forests
- Nonagricultural Land

MAJOR MINERAL OCCURRENCES

Ag	Silver	Hg	Mercury
Au	Gold	Id	Iodine
C	Coal	Mn	Manganese
Cu	Copper	Mo	Molybdenum
Fe	Iron Ore	N	Nitrates
G	Natural Gas	Na	Salt
Gp	Gypsum	O	Petroleum
		S	Sulfur

⚡ Water Power   ▨ Major Industrial Areas

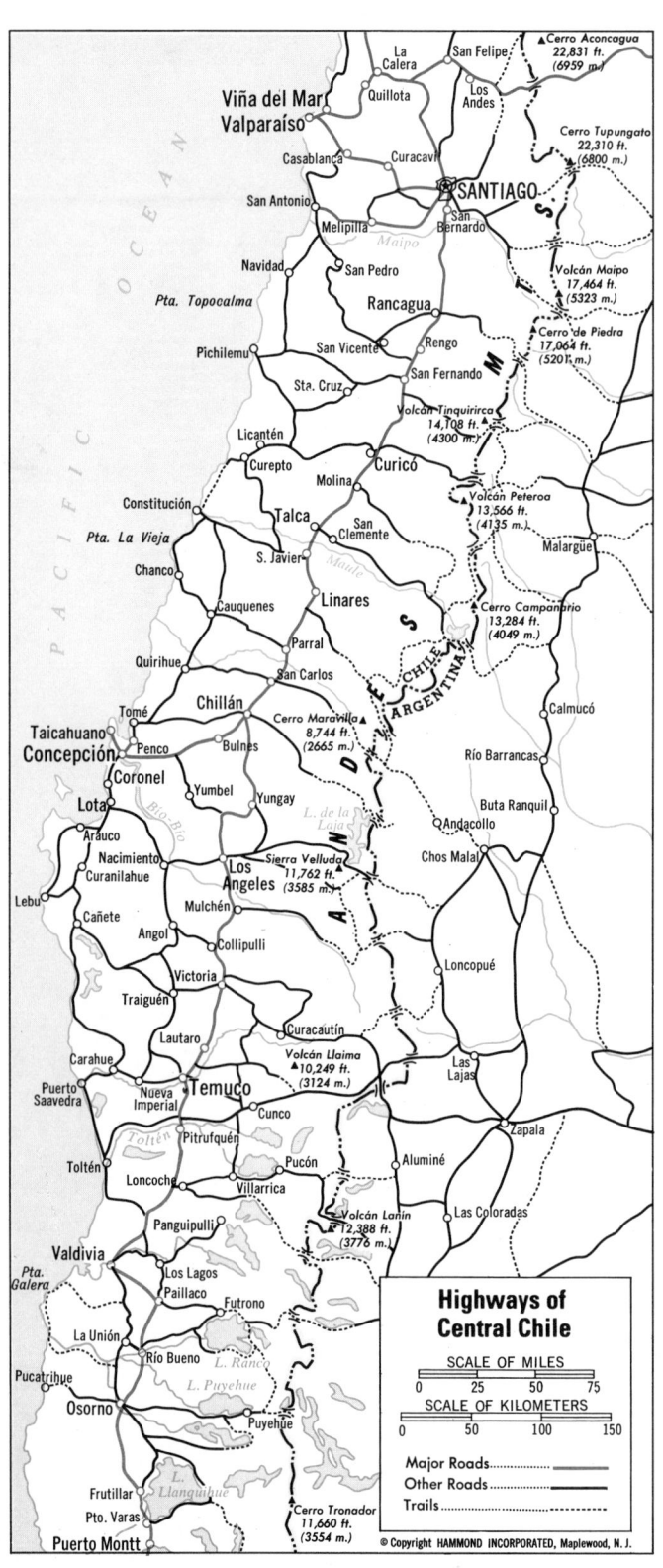

Highways of Central Chile

SCALE OF MILES

0   25   50   75

SCALE OF KILOMETERS

0   50   100   150

Major Roads ————
Other Roads ————
Trails ‑ ‑ ‑ ‑ ‑

© Copyright HAMMOND INCORPORATED, Maplewood, N.J.

PROVINCES

Buenos Aires 10,796,036	D4
Catamarca 206,204	D2
Chaco 692,410	D2
Chubut 262,196	C5
Córdoba 2,407,135	D3
Corrientes 657,716	E2
Distrito Federal 2,908,001	H7
Entre Ríos 902,241	E3
Formosa 292,479	D1
Jujuy 408,514	C1
La Pampa 207,132	C4
La Rioja 163,342	C2
Mendoza 1,187,305	C3
Misiones 579,579	F2
Neuquén 241,904	C4
Río Negro 383,896	C5
Salta 662,369	D1
San Juan 469,973	C3
San Luis 212,837	C3
Santa Cruz 114,479	C6
Santa Fe 2,457,188	D3
Santiago del Estero 652,318	D2
Tierra del Fuego, Antártida, e Islas d 29,066	C7
Tucumán 968,066	C2

CITIES and TOWNS

Abra Pampa 2,091	C1
Acevedo 1,263	F6
Acuña	G5
Adolfo Alsina 6,323	D4
Aguaray 5,069	D1
Aguilares 11,924	C2
Aimogasta 4,134	C2
Alberti 5,792	G7
Alcaraz 1,518	G5
Alcorta 4,996	F6
Alejandra 1,381	F5
Algarrobo del guila	C4
Allen 9,380	C4
Alpachiri 1,374	D4
Alta Gracia 24,371	D3
Aluminé 1,098	B4
Alvear 2,258	F2
Ameghino 3,195	D3
Añatuya 11,918	D2
Andacollo	B4
Andalgalá 5,687	C2
Antofagasta de la Sierra	C2
Apóstoles 8,111	E2
Arrecifes 13,503	F7
Arribeños 2,286	F6
Arroyo Seco 11,969	F6
Ascensión 2,888	F7
Avellaneda 337,538	G7
Ayacucho 12,046	E4
Azul 36,023	E4
Bahía Blanca 182,158	D4
Bahía Bustamante	C6
Bahía Thetis	C7
Baigorrita 1,426	F7
Balcarce 26,461	E4
Balnearia 4,502	E3
Bandera 1,920	D2
Barrancas 29,107	F6
Barranqueras	D2
Barreal	C3
Basavilbaso 7,338	G6
Belén 6,152	C2
Bella Vista, Corrientes 10,554	E2
Bella Vista, Tucumán 7,013	D2
Bell Ville 22,528	D3
Bernardo de Irigoyen 1,206	F2
Bernasconi 1,563	D4
Bolívar 18,643	D4
Bovril 2,988	G5
Bragado 23,366	F7
Buena Esperanza 1,192	C3
Buenos Aires (cap.) 2,908,001	H7
Buenos Aires* 9,749,000	H7
Bustinza	F6
Buta-Ranquil	C4
Cabo Vírgenes	C7
Cachi 1,018	C2
Cafayate 3,365	C2
Calafate	B7
Calchaquí 4,362	F5
Caleta Olivia 13,366	C6
Caleufú 1,081	C4
Camarones	C5
Campana 33,919	G6
Cañada de Gómez 20,611	F6
Canals 6,331	D3
Captain Bermúdez	F6
Cañuelas 10,390	G7
Carabelas 1,029	F7
Carcarañá 8,201	F6
Carlos Casares 10,775	D4
Carlos Tejedor 3,555	D4
Carmen de Areco 6,556	F7
Carmen de Patagones 10,587	D5
Casilda 19,240	F6
Castelli, Buenos Aires 3,658	H7
Castelli, Chaco	D2
Catamarca 64,410	C2
Catriló 1,697	D4
Caucete 10,719	C3
Cayasta 1,554	F5
Cayastacito	F5
Ceres 9,108	D2
Chabás 3,812	F6
Chacabuco 23,660	F7
Chajarí 10,720	G5
Chamical 4,634	C3
Charadai	D2
Charata 7,975	D2
Chascomús 17,103	H7
Chepes 4,108	C3
Chicoana 1,274	C2
Chilecito 11,234	C2
Chivilcoy 37,190	F7
Choele-Choel 3,510	C4
Chos-Malal 2,545	C4
Chumbicha 2,118	C2
Cinco Saltos 11,122	C4
Cipolletti 23,768	C4
Clorinda 16,125	E2
Colón, Buenos Aires 12,530	F6
Colón, Entre Ríos 10,122	G6
Colonia Elisa 1,047	D2
Colonia Josefa	D4
Colonia Las Heras 2,151	C6
Comandante Fontana 2,752	D2
Comandante Luis Piedrabuena 2,586	C6
Comodoro Rivadavia 72,906	C6
Concepción, Corrientes 2,679	E2
Concepción, Tucumán 20,694	C2
Concepción de la Sierra 2,457	E2

AREA 1,072,070 sq. mi. (2,776,661 sq. km.)
POPULATION 27,862,771
CAPITAL Buenos Aires
LARGEST CITY Buenos Aires
HIGHEST POINT Cerro Aconcagua 22,831 ft. (6,959 m.)
MONETARY UNIT Argentine peso
MAJOR LANGUAGE Spanish
MAJOR RELIGION Roman Catholicism

Agriculture, Industry and Resources

DOMINANT LAND USE

- Wheat, Livestock
- Wheat, Corn, Livestock
- Diversified Tropical Crops (chiefly plantation agriculture)
- Truck Farming, Horticulture, Special Crops
- Intensive Livestock Ranching
- Upland Livestock Grazing, Limited Agriculture
- Extensive Livestock Ranching
- Forests
- Nonagricultural Land

MAJOR MINERAL OCCURRENCES

Ag	Silver	O	Petroleum
Be	Beryl	Pb	Lead
C	Coal	S	Sulfur
Cu	Copper	Sn	Tin
Fe	Iron Ore	U	Uranium
G	Natural Gas	W	Tungsten
Mn	Manganese	Zn	Zinc
Na	Salt		

⚡ Water Power
▨ Major Industrial Areas

Concepción del Uruguay 38,967	G6
Concordia 72,136	G5
Constanza	C2
Copacabana	C2
Córdoba 790,508	D3
Coronda 9,100	F6
Coronel Bogado 1,432	F6
Coronel Brandsen 7,688	H7
Coronel Dorrego 10,448	D4
Coronel Moldes 1,617	C2
Coronel Pringles 16,228	D4
Coronel Suárez 14,570	D4
Coronel Vidal 3,746	E4
Corral de Bustos 7,296	D3
Corrientes 136,924	E2
Cosquín 11,436	D3
Coto	D2
Crespo 7,615	F6
Cruz del Eje 23,401	C3
Cuadro Nacional 1,690	C3
Cuchillo-Có	D4
Curuzú Cuatiá 20,636	G5
Cutral-Có 19,404	C4
Daireaux 6,614	D4
Deán Funes 15,592	D3
Del Valle	D3
Diamante 12,686	F6
Díaz 1,311	F6
Doblas 1,231	D4
Dolavon 1,281	C5
Dolores 17,414	E4
Domínguez	G6
Dudignac 2,377	F7
Eduardo Castex 3,739	D4
El Bolsón 2,678	B5
El Chorro	D1
El Cuy	C4
El Huecú	B4
Elisa	F5
El Maitén	B5
El Milagro 1,824	C3
Elortondo 4,026	F6
El Pintado	D1
El Piquete	D1
El Quebrachal	D2
Embarcación 7,207	D1
Emilio Ayarza 1,050	F7
Empedrado 4,269	E2
Enrique Carbó	G6
Ensenada 31,586	H7
Escobar 36,278	G7
Esperanza 17,636	F5
Espinillo 1,249	E2
Esquel 13,771	B5
Esquina 6,931	G5
Facundo	C6
Famatina 1,204	C2
Federación 4,876	G5
Felipe Yofre	G4
Fernández 4,800	D2
Fiambalá 1,119	C2
Firmat 11,127	F6
Formosa 61,071	E2
Fortín Olmos	F4
French 1,109	F7
Frías 12,421	D2
Gaiman 1,702	C5
Gálvez 12,195	F6
Gan Gan	C5
Gastre	C5
General Acha 6,270	C4
General Alvear, Buenos Aires 4,875	F7
General Alvear, Mendoza 17,277	C3
General Arenales 2,855	F7
General Belgrano 9,213	G7
General Campos 1,475	G5
General Conesa 3,117	C5
General Galarza	C6
General Güemes 11,159	D1
General Guido 1,073	E4
General José de San Martín 9,588	E2
General Juan Madariaga 10,280	E4
General La Madrid 5,523	D4
General Las Heras 4,972	G7
General Lavalle 1,103	E4
General O'Brien 1,771	F7
General Paz 4,327	H7
General Pico 21,897	D4
General Ramírez 4,439	F6
General Roca 29,320	C4
General San Martín 1,883	D4
General San Martín	G4
General Viamonte 8,896	F7
General Villegas 8,884	D4
Gobernador Crespo 2,527	F5
Gobernador Gregores 1,129	C6
Gobernador Mansilla 1,050	G6
Godoy Cruz 112,481	C3
Gorchs	G7
Goya 39,367	G5
Gualeguay 20,401	G6
Gualeguaychú 40,661	G6
Guandacol 1,073	C2

Guardia Mitre	D5
Hale	F7
Hasenkamp 1,950	F5
Helvecia 2,948	F5
Hernandarias 2,735	F5
Hernández 1,035	F6
Hernando 7,370	D3
Herradura	E2
Herrera	D2
Huanqueros	F5
Huinca Renancó 6,181	D3
Humahuaca 2,918	C1
Humberto 3,903	F5
Ibarreta 2,578	D2
Ibicuy 3,073	G6
Icaño, Catamarca	C2
Icaño, Santiago del Estero 1,528	D2
Ingeniero Huergo 2,226	C4
Ingeniero Jacobacci 3,233	C5
Ingeniero Luiggi 2,113	D4
Intendente Alvear 2,534	D4
Itatí 2,327	E2
Ituzaingó 2,429	E2
Jáchal 6,815	C3
Jesús María 14,163	D3
Joaquín V. González 4,351	D2
José de San Martín 1,313	B5
José M. Micheo	G7
Juárez 11,329	D4
Jujuy 82,637	C1
Juncal	F6
Junín 59,020	F7
Junín de los Andes 3,870	B4
La Banda 33,032	D2
Laboulaye 13,537	D3
La Carlota	D3
La Clarita	G5
La Cruz 3,069	E2
La Cumbre 4,790	C3
La Esperanza	B7
La Falda 10,551	D3
La Gallareta 2,261	F5
Lago Blanco	B6
Laguna Paiva 11,196	F5
La Merced 2,087	C2
Lanús 449,824	H7
La Paz, Entre Ríos 12,299	G5
La Paz, Mendoza 3,533	C3
La Pelada	F5
La Plata 478,666	H7
Laprida 6,802	D4
La Quiaca 6,034	C1
La Rioja 46,090	C2
Larroque 2,138	F5
Las Flores 15,655	E4
Las Lajas 1,300	B4
Las Lomitas 3,490	D1
Las Palmas 2,805	E2
Las Parejas 4,880	F6
Las Plumas	C5
Las Rosas 8,708	F6
Las Termas	D2
Las Varillas 8,608	D3
La Toma 3,113	C3
Lavalle	G4
Leleque	B5
Lezama 3,118	H7
Lincoln 17,391	F7
Lobería 9,923	E4
Lobos 13,677	G7
Lomas de Zamora 410,806	H7
Loncopué 1,078	B4
Lucas González 3,085	G6
Luján 38,393	G7
Lules 6,044	C2
Macachín 1,701	D4
Maciel 3,849	F6
Magdalena 5,398	H7
Maipú 6,997	E4
Makallé 1,286	E2
Malabrigo 2,791	F4
Malargüe 5,462	C4
Maquinchao 1,495	C5
Marcos Juárez 16,533	D3
Mar del Plata 302,282	E4
Margarita 1,740	F5
Mariano I. Loza 1,186	G4
Máximo Paz 2,653	F6
Mburucuyá 2,533	E2
Médanos, Buenos Aires 4,112	D4
Médanos, Entre Ríos	G6
Media Agua 1,870	C3
Melincué 2,130	F6
Mendoza 470,896	C3
Mercedes, Buenos Aires 39,760	G7
Mercedes, Corrientes 18,476	G4
Mercedes, San Luis 40,052	C3
Merlo 184,843	G7
Metán 14,615	D2
Miguel Riglos 1,344	D4
Miramar 10,512	E4
Moisés Ville 2,959	E5
Monte Caseros 14,306	G5
Monte Común 2,350	C4
Monte Quemado 4,046	D2
Monteros 11,872	C2

(continued on following page)

Morón 485,983 ...G7
Morteros 9,669 ...D3
Navarro 5,973 ...G7
Necochea 39,868 ...E4
Nelson 2,032 ...F5
Neuquén 43,070 ...C4
Nogoyá 128,777 ...F5
Norberto de la Riestra 2,089 ...F7
Norquinco ...B5
Norumbega ...F7
Nueve de Julio 19,762 ...F7
Oberá 16,994 ...F2
Olavarría 52,453 ...D4
Oliva 7,799 ...D3
Olta 1,241 ...C3
Ordoqui ...F7
Palo Santo 1,984 ...E2
Pampa de las Salinas ...C3
Pampa del Infierno 1,293 ...D2
Paraná 127,635 ...F5
Paso de Indios ...C5
Paso de Los Libres 17,341 ...E2
Paso Flores ...C5
Patoula ...C5
Pedernal ...C3
Pedro Díaz Colodrero ...E2
Pedro Luro 2,641 ...D4
Pehuajó 21,078 ...D4
Pellegrini 2,974 ...D4
Pergamino 56,078 ...F6
Perito Moreno 1,793 ...B6
Peugoorfla 1,133 ...E4
Peyrano 2,005 ...F5
Pico Truncado 6,021 ...C6
Pigüé 8,703 ...D4
Pila 1,054 ...H7
Pilar 3,520 ...F5
Pipinas 1,226 ...H7
Pirané 4,210 ...E2
Plaza Huincul 4,714 ...B4
Pomán 1,156 ...C2
Posadas 97,514 ...F2
Pozo Hondo ...D2
Presidencia de la Plaza 3,834 ...D2
Presidencia Roque Sáenz
  Peña 38,620 ...D2
Puán 3,406 ...D4
Puelches ...C4
Puelén ...C4
Puente del Inca ...B3
Puerto Coig ...C7
Puerto Deseado 3,735 ...D6
Puerto Harberton ...C7
Puerto Iguazú 3,001 ...F2
Puerto Madryn 6,115 ...C5
Puerto Rico ...D1
Punta Alta 36,805 ...D4
Punta Medanosa ...D2
Quebracho Coto ...D2
Quemú-Quemú 2,423 ...E4
Quequén 9,299 ...E4
Quimili 4,076 ...D2
Quines 2,853 ...C3
Quitilipi 1,839 ...F7
Quitilipi 7,232 ...D2
Rafaela 43,695 ...F5
Ralces ...G6
Ramallo 6,704 ...F6
Rauch 8,689 ...E4
Rawson, Buenos Aires 1,987 ...F7
Rawson, Chubut 7,229 ...D5

Reconquista 25,333 ...F4
Recreo 2,806 ...C2
Resistencia 142,848 ...D2
Rinconada ...C1
Río Colorado, La Pampa ...D4
Río Colorado, Río
  Negro 5,670 ...D4
Río Cuarto 88,852 ...D3
Río Gallegos 27,833 ...C7
Río Grande ...C7
Río Segundo 9,587 ...D3
Río Tercero 21,907 ...D3
Rivadavia, Mendoza 13,072 ...C3
Rivadavia, Salta ...D1
Rivadavia, San Juan 22,683 ...C3
Rojas 10,074 ...F7
Roldán 6,126 ...F6
Romang 3,134 ...F4
Roque Pérez 4,377 ...G7
Rosario 806,942 ...F6
Rosario de la Frontera 9,075 ...D2
Rosario de Lerma 6,268 ...C1
Rosario del Tala 8,005 ...G6
Rufino 14,138 ...E3
Saladas 5,468 ...E2
Saladillo 13,617 ...G7
Salliqueló 4,566 ...D4
Salta 176,216 ...C1
Salto 14,551 ...F7
San Antonio de Areco 10,788 ...G7
San Antonio de los
  Cobres 1,947 ...C1
San Antonio Oeste 6,566 ...C5
San Carlos, Mendoza 1,463 ...C3
San Carlos, Santa Fe 5,973 ...F6
San Carlos de Bariloche 26,799 ...B5
San Cayetano 6,025 ...E4
San Cristóbal 11,825 ...F5
San Fernando 113,249 ...G7
San Francisco,
  Córdoba 48,896 ...D3
San Francisco, San Luis 1,952 ...C3
San Genaro 2,230 ...F6
San Ignacio 2,332 ...C2
San Isidro ...C2
Saime de la frontera 2,517 ...G5
San Javier, Río Negro ...D5
San Javier, Santa Fe 5,585 ...B5
San José de Feliciano 3,884 ...G5
San Juan 217,514 ...C3
San Julián 3,589 ...C6
San Justo 11,085 ...F5
San Lorenzo 56,487 ...F6
San Luis 50,771 ...C3
San Martín de los
  Andes 5,960 ...C5
San Miguel 1,540 ...B5
San Miguel del Monte 5,768 ...G7
San Miguel de
  Tucumán 366,392 ...D2
San Nicolás 64,730 ...F6
San Pedro, Buenos Aires 23,365 ...F6
San Pedro, Jujuy 25,265 ...D1
San Rafael 58,237 ...C3
San Ramón de la Nva.
  Orán 20,212 ...D1
San Salvador 4,529 ...G5
San Sebastián ...C7
Santa Cruz 1,448 ...C7
Santa Elena 11,525 ...F5

Santa Fe 244,655 ...F5
Santa Lucía, Buenos
  Aires 1,817 ...F6
Santa Lucía,
  Corrientes 3,738 ...E2
Santa María 3,736 ...C2
Santa Rosa, Córdoba 3,488 ...D3
Santa Rosa, La Pampa 33,649 ...C4
Santa Rosa, San Luis 2,609 ...C3
Santa Victoria ...D1
Santiago del Estero 105,127 ...D2
Santo Tomé,
  Corrientes 11,058 ...E2
Santo Tomé, Santa Fe 23,572 ...F5
San Urbano ...F6
Sarmiento 5,555 ...B6
Sauce 4,134 ...E2
Sauce de Luna 1,161 ...G5
Segui 2,232 ...F6
Selva 1,575 ...D2
Sierra Colorada ...C5
Sierra Grande ...C5
Soledad ...F5
Stroeder 2,206 ...D5
Suipacha 4,002 ...G7
Sumampa 2,334 ...D2
Sunchales 10,393 ...F5
Suncho Corral 3,597 ...D2
Susques ...C1
Tafí Viejo 21,602 ...C2
Tamberías ...C3
Tandil 65,876 ...E4
Tapalqués 4,769 ...E4
Tartagal 23,696 ...D1
Tecka ...B5
Telsen ...C5
Tigre 146,451 ...G7
Tilcara 2,082 ...C1
Tinogasta 5,478 ...C2
Tintina 2,215 ...D2
Toay 2,191 ...D4
Tornquist 3,054 ...D4
Tostado 7,921 ...D2
Trelew 24,214 ...C5
Trenel 1,644 ...D4
Trenque Lauquen 18,169 ...D4
Tres Arroyos 37,991 ...D4
Trevelin 1,214 ...B5
Tunuyán 10,813 ...C3
Urdinarraín 4,577 ...G6
Ushuaia 5,373 ...C7
Valchetá 1,776 ...C5
Valdés ...C3
Vedia 5,139 ...F7
Veinticinco de Mayo 16,678 ...F7
Veintiocho de Noviembre 5,168 ...B7
Venado Tuerto 35,677 ...D3
Vera 10,644 ...F5
Vergara ...H7
Verónica 4,938 ...H7
Viale 4,411 ...F5
Vicente López 285,178 ...G7
Victoria 17,046 ...F6
Victorica 3,184 ...C4
Vicuña Mackenna 4,594 ...D3
Viedma 12,888 ...D5
Vieytes ...H7
Villa Ana 1,208 ...E2
Villa Ángela 17,091 ...D2
Villa Atamisqui ...D2
Villa Atuel 2,783 ...C3

Villa Cañas 6,206 ...F6
Villa Clara 1,736 ...G5
Villa Constitución 25,148 ...F6
Villa Diego ...D3
Villa de María 1,343 ...D2
Villa Dolores 19,010 ...C3
Villa Elisa 3,227 ...G6
Villa Federal 6,977 ...G5
Villa General Ramírez 4,439 ...F6
Villa General Roca ...D3
Villaguay 15,591 ...G5
Villa Guillermina 2,237 ...D2
Villa Huidobro 3,280 ...D3
Villa Krause ...C3
Villa Mantero ...G6
Villa María 56,087 ...D3
Villa María Grande 3,431 ...F5
Villa Nueva 10,975 ...C4
Villa Ocampo 8,104 ...D2
Villa Regina 10,975 ...C4
Villa San Agustín 1,795 ...C3
Villa San José 4,046 ...G6
Villa San Martín 4,013 ...D2
Villa Unión 1,789 ...C2
Vinchina 1,491 ...C2
Winifreda 1,314 ...D4
Zapala 11,385 ...B4
Zárate 54,772 ...G6
Zavala 2,887 ...F6

OTHER FEATURES

Aconcagua, Cerro (mt.) ...C3
Andes, Cordillera de los
  (mts.) ...C2
Argentino (lake) ...B7
Arizaro, Salar de (salt dep.) ...C1
Arrecifes (riv.) ...G6
Atacama, Puna de (reg.) ...C1
Atuel (riv.) ...C4
Barrancas (riv.) ...C4
Bermejo (riv.) ...E2
Blanca (bay) ...D4
Brazo Sur, Pilcomayo (riv.) ...E1
Buenos Aires (lake) ...B6
Campanario, Cerro (mt.) ...C4
Chaco Austral (reg.) ...D2
Chaco Central (reg.) ...D1
Chato, Cerro (mt.) ...C5
Chico (riv.) ...C5
Chico (riv.) ...C6
Chubut (riv.) ...C5
Colhué Huapi (lake) ...C6
Colorado (riv.) ...D4
Cónico, Cerro (mt.) ...B5
Corrientes (riv.) ...E2
Coyle (riv.) ...B7
Delgada (pt.) ...D5
Desaguadero (riv.) ...C3
Deseado (riv.) ...C6
Diamante (riv.) ...C3
Domuyo (vol.) ...B4
Dos Bahías (cape) ...D5
Dulce (riv.) ...C2
Dungeness (pt.) ...C7
El Chocón (riv.) ...C4
Estados, Los (isl.) ...D7
Fagnano (lake) ...C7
Famatina, Sierra de (mts.) ...C2
Feliciano (riv.) ...G5

Topography

C. Aconcagua
22,831 ft (6959 m.)
Uspallata Pass
Socompa Pass

0 150 300 MI.
0 150 300 KM.

| 5,000 m. 16,404 ft. | 2,000 m. 6,562 ft. | 1,000 m. 3,281 ft. | 500 m. 1,640 ft. | 200 m. 656 ft. | 100 m. 328 ft. | Sea Level | Below |

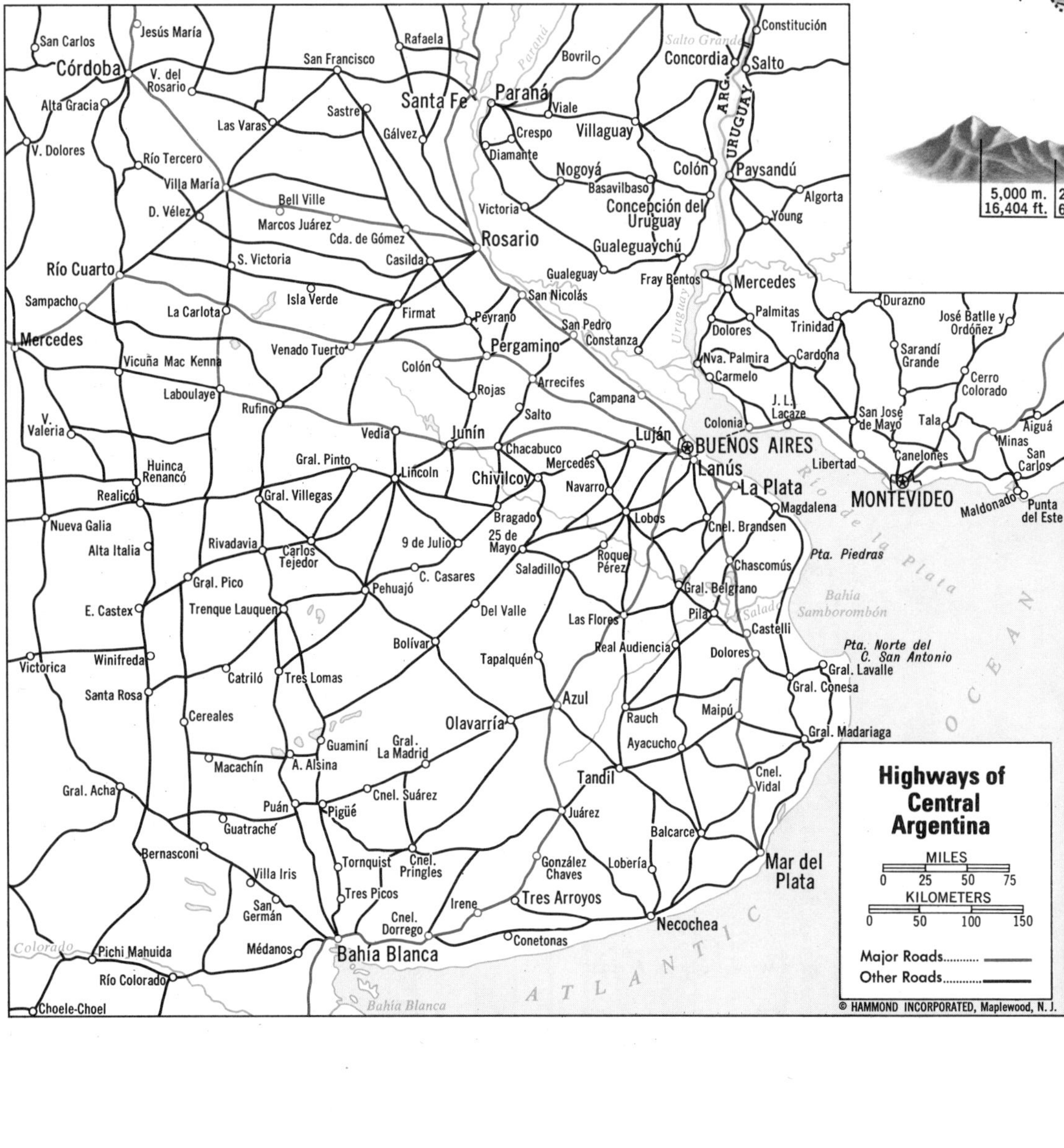

Highways of Central Argentina

MILES
0 25 50 75
KILOMETERS
0 50 100 150

Major Roads
Other Roads

© HAMMOND INCORPORATED, Maplewood, N.J.

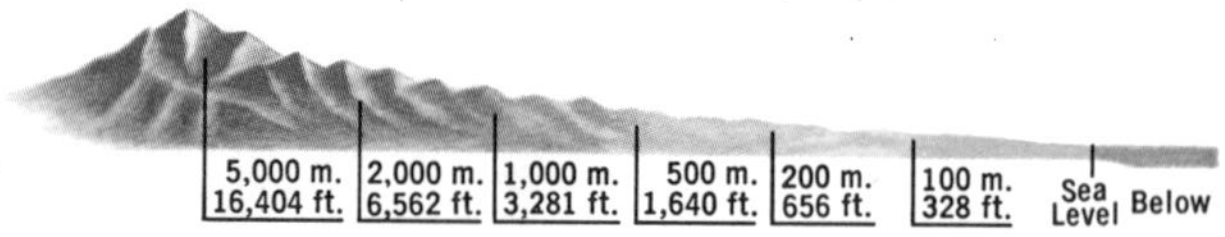

Flores, Las (riv.) ...G7
Gallegos (riv.) ...B7
General Manuel Belgrano, Cerro
  (mt.) ...C2
Gran Chaco (reg.) ...D1
Grande (bay) ...C7
Grande (falls) ...E3
Grande (riv.) ...C4
Grande de Tierra del Fuego
  (isl.) ...C7
Gualeguay (riv.) ...G5
Guayaquiaró (riv.) ...G5
Iguazú (falls) ...F2
Iguazú Nat'l Park ...F2
Incahuasi, Cerro de (mt.) ...C2
Lanín (vol.) ...B4
Lanín Nat'l Park ...B4
Lechiguanas (isls.) ...G6
Lennox (isl.) ...C7
Limay (riv.) ...C4
Llancanelo (lag.) ...C4
Llullaillaco (vol.) ...C1
Magallanes (Magellan) (str.) ...C7
Maipo (vol.) ...C3
Mar Chiquita (lake) ...D3
Martín García (isl.) ...H6
Mendoza (riv.) ...C3
Mercedario, Cerro (mt.) ...C3
Mogotes (pt.) ...E4
Montemayor (plat.) ...C5
Muralión, Cerro (mt.) ...B6
Nahuel Huapi (lake) ...B5
Nahuel Huapi Nat'l Park ...B5
Negro (riv.) ...C4
Neuquén (riv.) ...C4
Ninfas (pt.) ...D5
Norte del Cabo San Antonio
  (pt.) ...E4
Nuevo (gulf) ...D5
Ojos del Salado, Cerro (mt.) ...C2
Olivares, Cerro de (mt.) ...C3
Pampa de la Tres Hermanas
  (plain) ...C6
Pampas (plain) ...D4
Paraná (riv.) ...E2
Patagonia (reg.) ...C5
Peteroa (vol.) ...B4
Pilcomayo (riv.) ...E1
Pissis (mt.) ...C2
Plata, Río de la (est.) ...E4
Pueyrredón (lake) ...B6
Puna de Atacama (reg.) ...C2
Quinto (riv.) ...D3
Rincón, Cerro (mt.) ...C1
Saladillo (riv.) ...D3
Salado (riv.) ...C4
Salado (riv.) ...H7

Salado del Norte (riv.) ...D2
Sali (riv.) ...C2
Salto (riv.) ...F7
Samborombón (bay) ...H7
San Antonio (cape) ...C5
San Diego (cape) ...D7
San Jorge (gulf) ...C6
San Juan (riv.) ...C3
San Lorenzo, Cerro (mt.) ...B6
San Martín (lake) ...B6
San Matías (gulf) ...D5
Santa Cruz (riv.) ...C6
Senguerr (riv.) ...C6
Staten (Los Estados) (isl.) ...D7
Sur del Cabo San Antonio
  (pt.) ...E4
Tarija (riv.) ...D1
Tercero (riv.) ...D3
Teuco (riv.) ...D1
Tierra del Fuego, Grande de
  (isl.) ...C7
Toro, Cerro del (mt.) ...C2
Tres Puntas (cape) ...C6
Trinidad (isl.) ...C7
Tronador (mt.) ...B5
Tunuyán (riv.) ...C3
Tupungato, Cerro (mt.) ...C3
Uruguay (riv.) ...F3
Valdés (pen.) ...D5
Vallimanca (riv.) ...D4
Viedma (lake) ...B6
Zapaleri, Cerro (mt.) ...C1

*City and suburbs

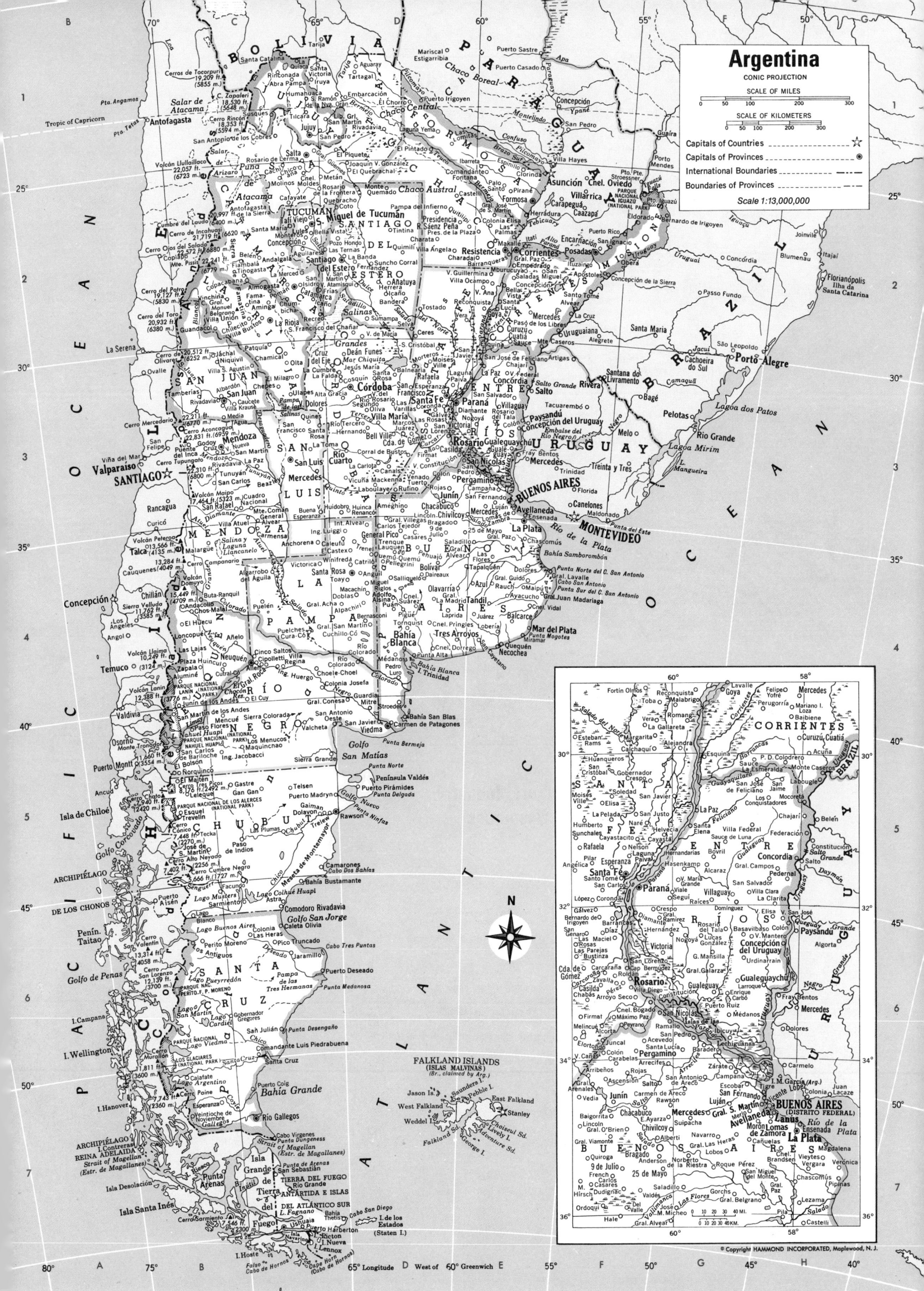

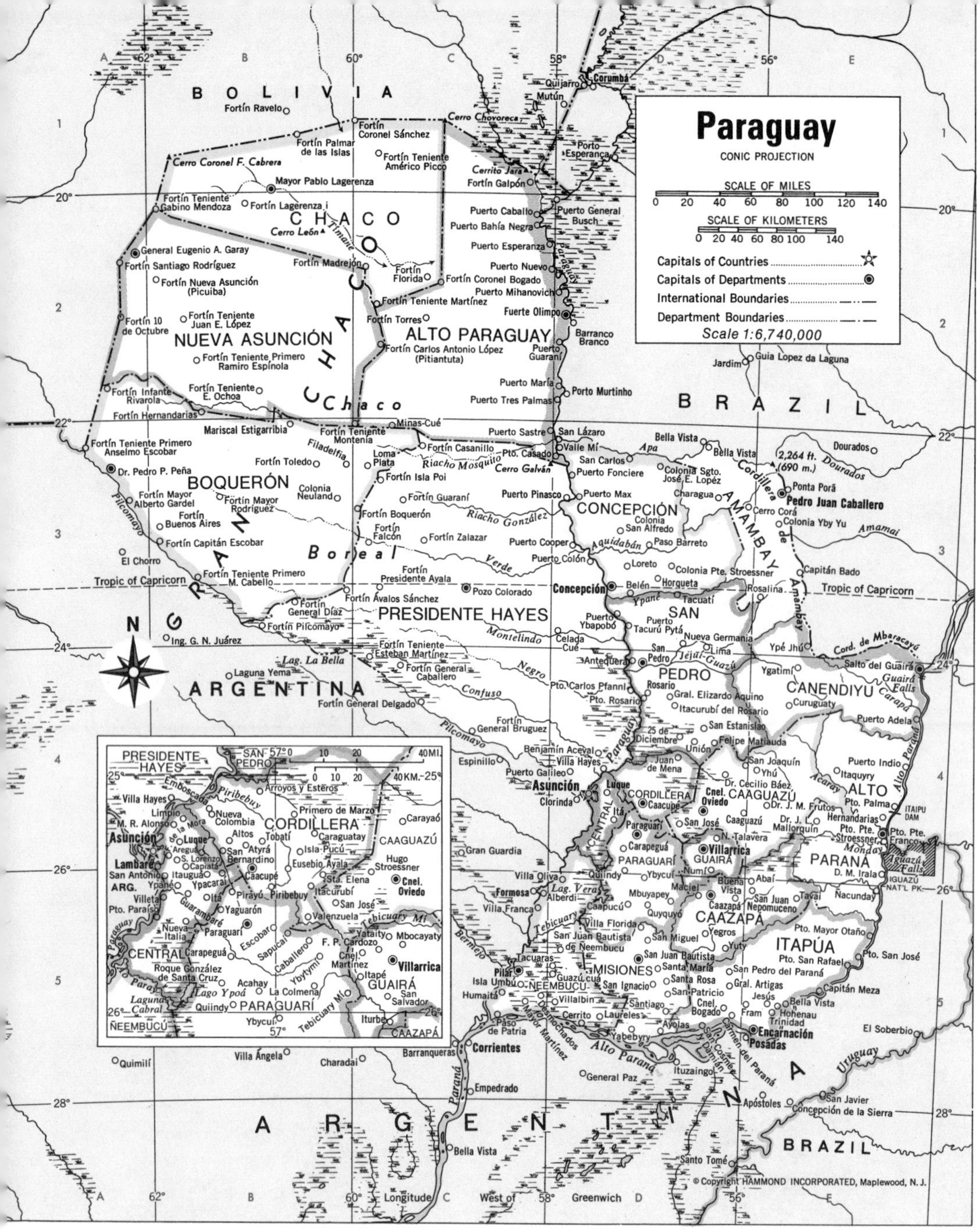

Paraguay

CONIC PROJECTION

SCALE OF MILES
0 20 40 60 80 100 120 140

SCALE OF KILOMETERS
0 20 40 60 80 100 140

Capitals of Countries ★
Capitals of Departments ◉
International Boundaries — — —
Department Boundaries — · —

Scale 1:6,740,000

(Main reference map of Paraguay showing countries BOLIVIA, BRAZIL, ARGENTINA and departments including CHACO, GRAN CHACO, NUEVA ASUNCIÓN, ALTO PARAGUAY, BOQUERÓN, PRESIDENTE HAYES, CONCEPCIÓN, SAN PEDRO, AMAMBAY, CANENDIYÚ, ALTO PARANÁ, CORDILLERA, CAAGUAZÚ, GUAIRÁ, PARAGUARÍ, CAAZAPÁ, MISIONES, ÑEEMBUCÚ, ITAPÚA, CENTRAL, with an inset map of the Asunción region.)

© Copyright HAMMOND INCORPORATED, Maplewood, N.J.

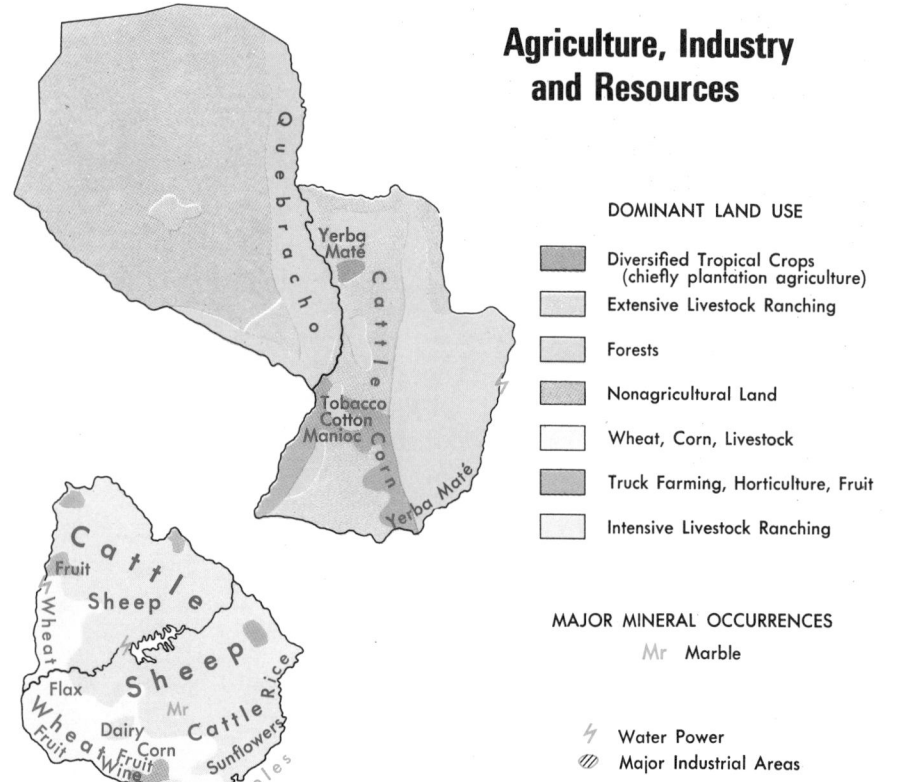

Agriculture, Industry and Resources

DOMINANT LAND USE

- Diversified Tropical Crops (chiefly plantation agriculture)
- Extensive Livestock Ranching
- Forests
- Nonagricultural Land
- Wheat, Corn, Livestock
- Truck Farming, Horticulture, Fruit
- Intensive Livestock Ranching

MAJOR MINERAL OCCURRENCES

Mr Marble

Water Power
Major Industrial Areas

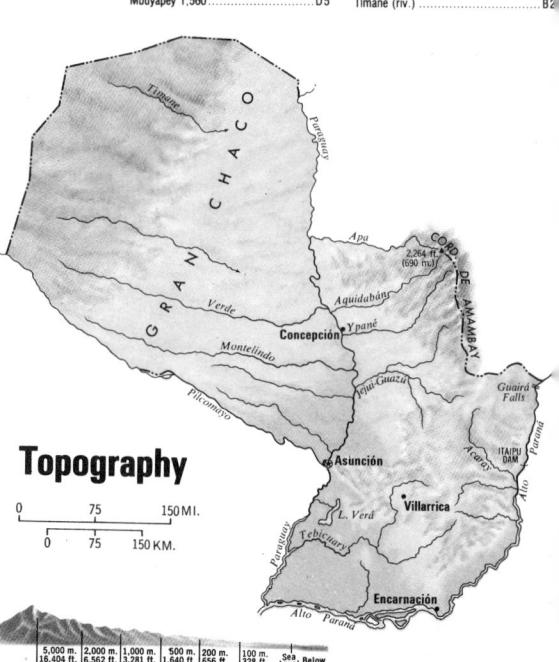

Topography

0 75 150 MI.
0 75 150 KM.

5,000 m. 16,404 ft. / 2,000 m. 6,562 ft. / 1,000 m. 3,281 ft. / 500 m. 1,640 ft. / 200 m. 656 ft. / 100 m. 328 ft. / Sea Level / Below

URUGUAY

DEPARTMENTS

PARAGUAY

AREA 157,047 sq. mi. (406,752 sq. km.)
POPULATION 2,973,000
CAPITAL Asunción
LARGEST CITY Asunción
HIGHEST POINT Amambay Range
2,264 ft. (690 m.)
MONETARY UNIT guaraní
MAJOR LANGUAGES Spanish, Guaraní
MAJOR RELIGION Roman Catholicism

URUGUAY

AREA 72,172 sq. mi. (186,925 sq. km.)
POPULATION 2,899,000
CAPITAL Montevideo
LARGEST CITY Montevideo
HIGHEST POINT Mirador Nacional 1,644 ft.
(501 m.)
MONETARY UNIT Uruguayan peso
MAJOR LANGUAGE Spanish
MAJOR RELIGION Roman Catholicism

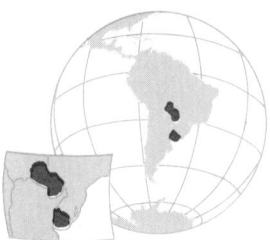

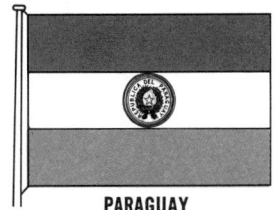

PARAGUAY

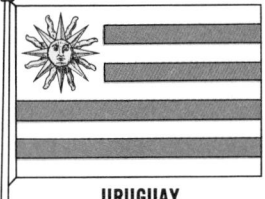

URUGUAY

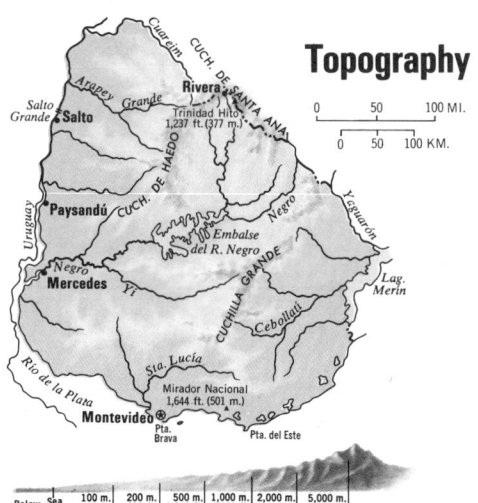

Topography

Below Sea Level | 100 m. 328 ft. | 200 m. 656 ft. | 500 m. 1,640 ft. | 1,000 m. 3,281 ft. | 2,000 m. 6,562 ft. | 5,000 m. 16,404 ft.

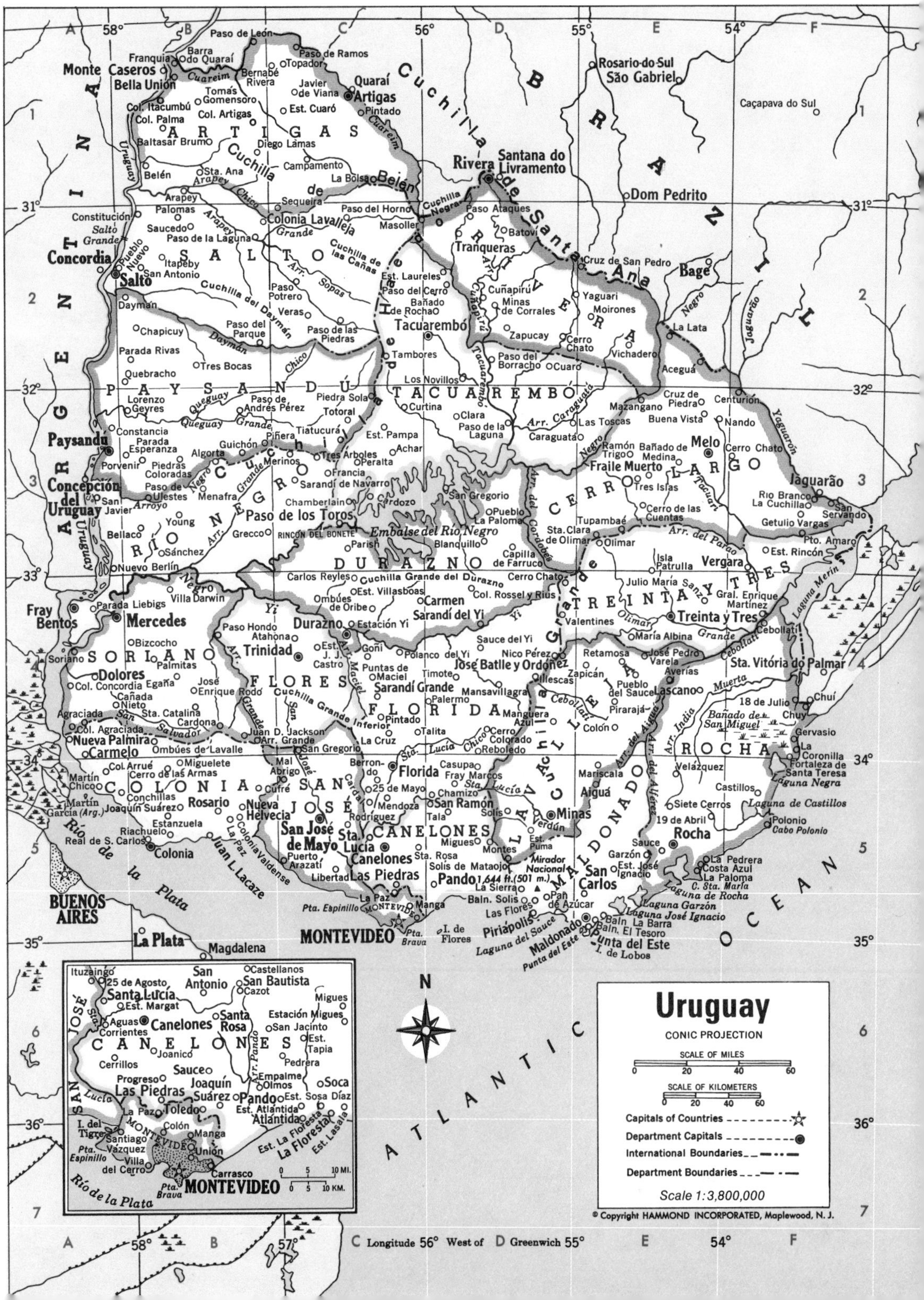

Uruguay

CONIC PROJECTION

SCALE OF MILES
0 20 40 60

SCALE OF KILOMETERS
0 20 40 60

Capitals of Countries ......☆
Department Capitals ....◉
International Boundaries ....
Department Boundaries .....

Scale 1:3,800,000

© Copyright HAMMOND INCORPORATED, Maplewood, N.J.

North America

LAMBERT AZIMUTHAL EQUAL-AREA PROJECTION

MILES
0 100 200 400 600 800

KILOMETERS
0 100 200 400 600 800

Capitals of Countries .... ⊛
Other Capitals .... ⊛
International Boundaries .... —··—
Other Boundaries .... —·—

Scale 1:36,600,000

Population Distribution

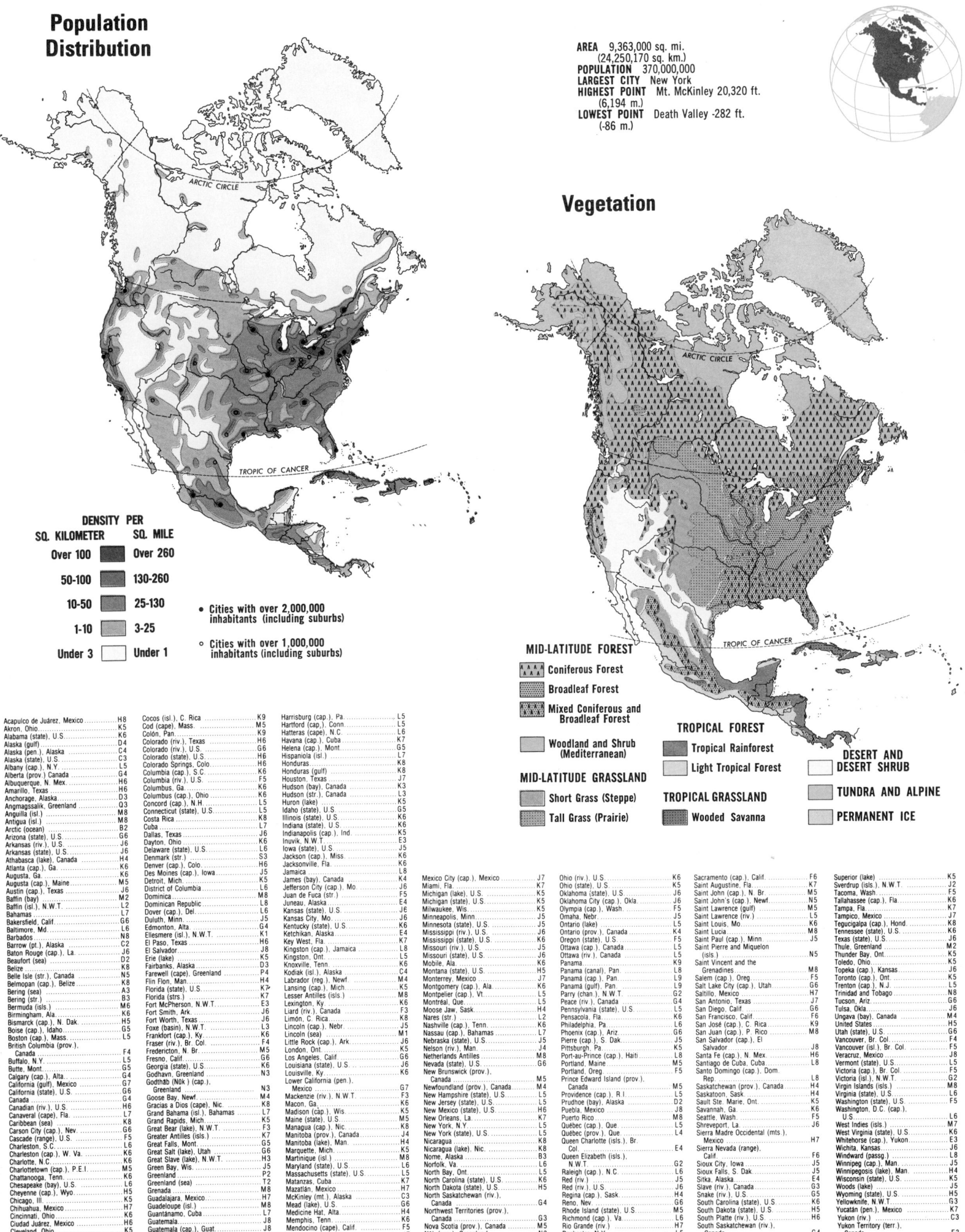

AREA 9,363,000 sq. mi.
(24,250,170 sq. km.)
POPULATION 370,000,000
LARGEST CITY New York
HIGHEST POINT Mt. McKinley 20,320 ft.
(6,194 m.)
LOWEST POINT Death Valley -282 ft.
(-86 m.)

Vegetation

DENSITY PER

SQ. KILOMETER	SQ. MILE
Over 100	Over 260
50-100	130-260
10-50	25-130
1-10	3-25
Under 3	Under 1

- Cities with over 2,000,000 inhabitants (including suburbs)
- Cities with over 1,000,000 inhabitants (including suburbs)

MID-LATITUDE FOREST
- Coniferous Forest
- Broadleaf Forest
- Mixed Coniferous and Broadleaf Forest
- Woodland and Shrub (Mediterranean)

MID-LATITUDE GRASSLAND
- Short Grass (Steppe)
- Tall Grass (Prairie)

TROPICAL FOREST
- Tropical Rainforest
- Light Tropical Forest

TROPICAL GRASSLAND
- Wooded Savanna

DESERT AND DESERT SHRUB

- TUNDRA AND ALPINE
- PERMANENT ICE

Average January Temperature

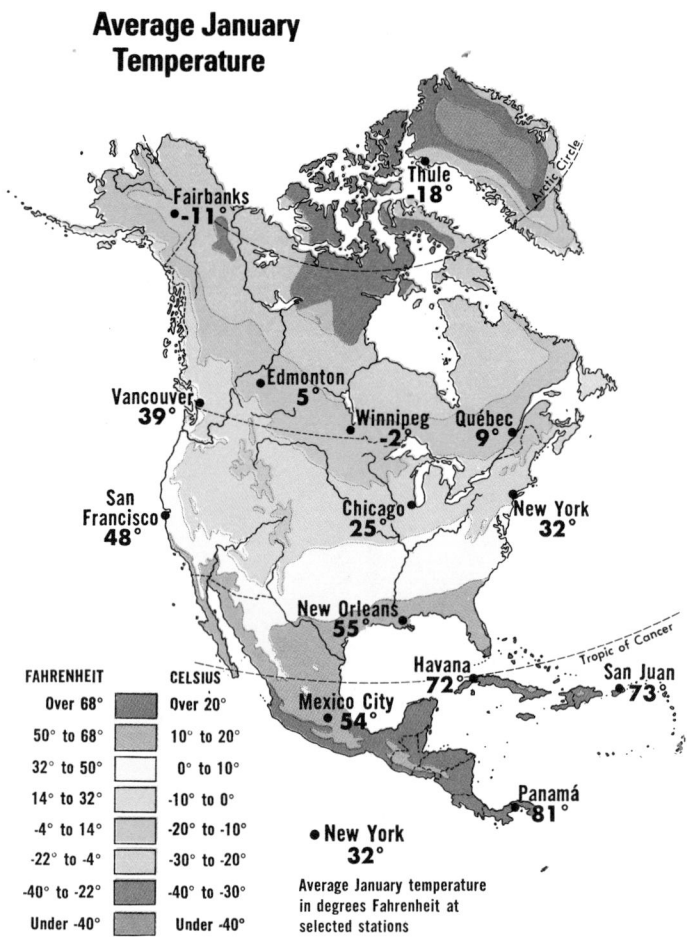

FAHRENHEIT	CELSIUS
Over 68°	Over 20°
50° to 68°	10° to 20°
32° to 50°	0° to 10°
14° to 32°	-10° to 0°
-4° to 14°	-20° to -10°
-22° to -4°	-30° to -20°
-40° to -22°	-40° to -30°
Under -40°	Under -40°

● New York
32°

Average January temperature in degrees Fahrenheit at selected stations

Average July Temperature

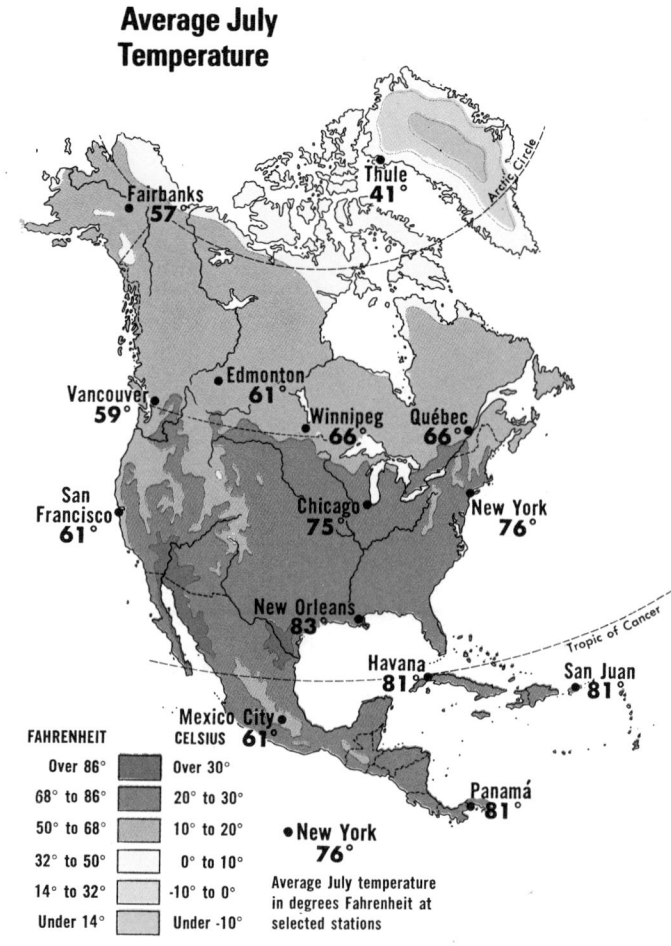

FAHRENHEIT	CELSIUS
Over 86°	Over 30°
68° to 86°	20° to 30°
50° to 68°	10° to 20°
32° to 50°	0° to 10°
14° to 32°	-10° to 0°
Under 14°	Under -10°

● New York
76°

Average July temperature in degrees Fahrenheit at selected stations

Rainfall

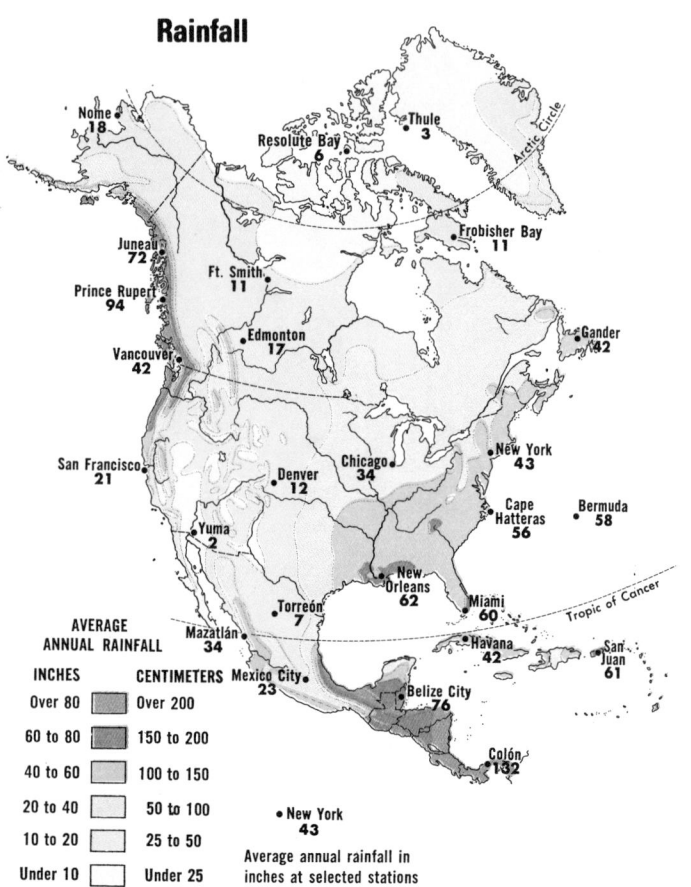

AVERAGE ANNUAL RAINFALL	
INCHES	CENTIMETERS
Over 80	Over 200
60 to 80	150 to 200
40 to 60	100 to 150
20 to 40	50 to 100
10 to 20	25 to 50
Under 10	Under 25

● New York
43

Average annual rainfall in inches at selected stations

Vegetation/Relief

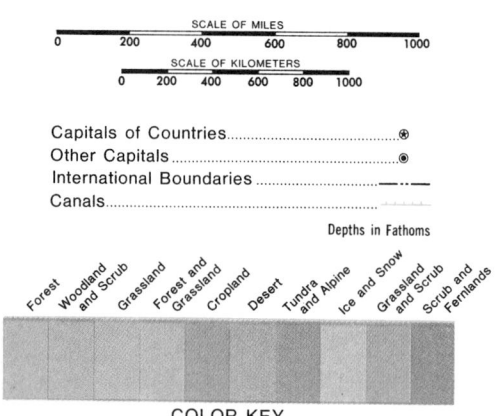

SCALE OF MILES
0 200 400 600 800 1000

SCALE OF KILOMETERS
0 200 400 600 800 1000

Capitals of Countries............................ ⊛
Other Capitals .... ◉
International Boundaries .... —
Canals... —

Depths in Fathoms

Forest | Woodland and Scrub | Grassland | Forest and Grassland | Cropland | Desert | Tundra and Alpine | Ice and Snow | Grassland and Scrub | Scrub and Fernlands

COLOR KEY

ASIA
U.S.S.R.

EAST SIBERIAN SEA

North Pole

A B C D E F G H J K L M N O P Q R

GREENLAND
(Den.)

ICELAND
⊛ Reykjavik

BERING SEA

St. Lawrence I.
Seward Pen.
Nome
Pt. Barrow

Queen
Elizabeth
Islands

Arctic Circle

C. Farewell

Kodiak I.
Alaska Pen.

Brooks Range
Alaska
Yukon
Mt. McKinley
20,320 ft.
(6194 m.)
Alaska Range
Fairbanks
Anchorage

Inuvik

Great Bear
L.

Victoria I.

Melville I.

Banks
I.

Devon I.

Baffin
I.

Davis Strait

LABRADOR SEA

Juneau
Alexander
Arch.
Prince Rupert
Queen
Charlotte
Is.

Whitehorse
Yukon

Coast Mountains

Rocky
Mountains

Yellowknife

Great
Slave L.

L. Athabasca

C. Chidley

Ungava
Peninsula

Labrador

C A N A D A

Smallwood
Res.
Churchill

Newfoundland

Gander

St. John's
C. Race
Cape Breton
I.

Vancouver I.
Victoria
Vancouver

Peace
Athabasca
Fraser
Columbia

North Saskatchewan
Edmonton
Calgary
South Saskatchewan
Regina

Saskatoon

L. Winnipeg
Albany

Churchill
Nelson

Hudson
Bay

James Bay

Eastmain

Laurentian Plateau

Gulf of St. Lawrence

C. Mendocino
San Francisco

Seattle
Mt. Rainier
14,410 ft.
(4392 m.)
Portland

Cascade Ranges

Sierra Nevada

Mt. Whitney
14,494 ft.
(4418 m.)

Great
Salt Lake
Salt Lake City

Snake
Great Basin

Missouri

North Platte

South Platte

Denver
Pikes Peak
14,110 ft. (4301 m.)

Winnipeg
Red
Thunder Bay
Duluth

Minneapolis

Omaha
Missouri

L. Superior

Sudbury

L. Michigan

Milwaukee
Chicago

Montréal
Ottawa ⊛
Toronto
L. Ontario
L. Erie

Québec
St. Lawrence

St. John
Halifax

Boston
C. Cod

Buffalo
Cleveland
Detroit
Pittsburgh
Columbus

New York
Philadelphia
Washington ⊛

Appalachian Mts.

UNITED STATES

Colorado

Las Vegas

Los Angeles

San Diego

Phoenix
Tucson

Albuquerque

Arkansas

Kansas City
St. Louis
Wichita

Ozark
Plateau

Tulsa
Oklahoma City

Red

Mississippi

Memphis
Tennessee

Indianapolis
Cincinnati
Ohio

Nashville

Birmingham

Norfolk
C. Hatteras

Mt. Mitchell
6,684 ft. (2037 m.)
Charlotte

Atlanta

Bermuda
(U.K.)

El Paso
Ciudad
Juárez
Rio Grande

Fort Worth
Dallas

Jacksonville

Jackson

San Antonio

Houston

New Orleans
C. Canaveral

Tampa

Lower California

C. San Lucas

Sierra Madre Occidental
Chihuahua

Culiacán

Monterrey

Corpus Christi

Gulf
of
Mexico

Tropic of Cancer

BAHAMAS

Miami
Nassau

Turks and
Caicos Is.
(U.K.)

West
Indies

M E X I C O

Sierra Madre Oriental

Tampico

Mexico
Bay of
Campeche

Havana
CUBA
Santiago
de Cuba

Greater

Antilles

HAITI
Port-au-Prince

DOMINICAN REPUBLIC
Santo
Domingo

San Juan
PUERTO
RICO

Guadalajara
Popocatépetl
17,887 ft.
(5452 m.)
Mexico City
Acapulco

Veracruz
Mérida
Yucatán
Pen.

BELIZE

JAMAICA
Kingston

CARIBBEAN SEA

NETHERLANDS
ANTILLES
Aruba Curaçao
Bonaire
Willemstad

GUATEMALA
Guatemala
San Salvador
EL SALVADOR

HONDURAS
Tegucigalpa
NICARAGUA
Managua

COSTA
RICA
San José
PANAMA
Panamá

Barranquilla

Caracas
VENEZUELA

SOUTH

Bogotá
COLOMBIA

AMERICA

120°   110°   100°   Longitude 90° West of Greenwich   80°   70°

© Copyright HAMMOND INCORPORATED, Maplewood, N.J.

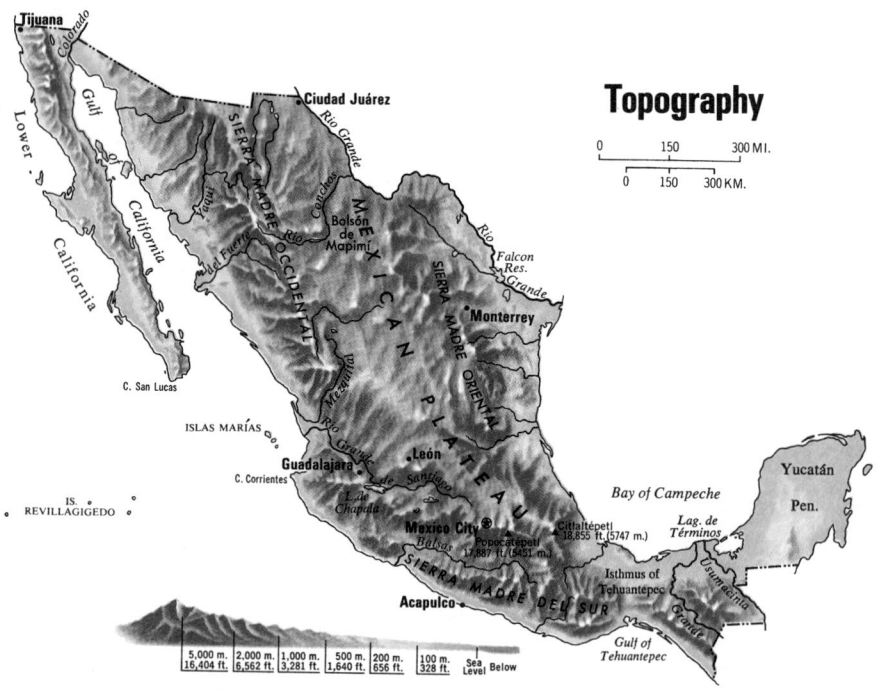

Topography

0   150   300 MI.

0   150   300 KM.

| 5,000 m. | 2,000 m. | 1,000 m. | 500 m. | 200 m. | 100 m. | Sea | Below |
| 16,404 ft. | 6,562 ft. | 3,281 ft. | 1,640 ft. | 656 ft. | 328 ft. | Level | |

STATES

Aguascalientes 504,300 ....H6
Baja California 1,227,400 ....B1
Baja California Sur 221,000 ....C3
Campeche 371,800 ....O7
Chiapas 2,097,500 ....N8
Chihuahua 1,935,100 ....F2
Coahuila 1,561,000 ....H3
Colima 339,400 ....G7
Distrito Federal 9,377,300 ....L1
Durango 1,160,300 ....G4
Guanajuato 3,045,600 ....J6
Guerrero 2,174,200 ....J8
Hidalgo 1,518,200 ....K6
Jalisco 4,296,500 ....H6
México 7,542,300 ....K7
Michoacán 3,049,400 ....H7
Morelos 931,400 ....K7
Nayarit 729,500 ....G6
Nuevo León 2,463,500 ....K4
Oaxaca 2,517,500 ....L8
Puebla 3,285,300 ....L7
Querétaro 730,900 ....J6
Quintana Roo 209,900 ....P7
San Luis Potosí 1,669,900 ....J5
Sinaloa 1,882,200 ....F4
Sonora 1,923,400 ....D2
Tabasco 1,150,000 ....N7
Tamaulipas 1,924,900 ....K4
Tlaxcala 548,500 ....N1
Veracruz 5,263,800 ....L7
Yucatán 1,034,300 ....P6
Zacatecas 1,144,700 ....H5

CITIES and TOWNS

Acala 11,483 ....N8
Acámbaro 32,257 ....J7
Acaponeta 11,844 ....G5
Acapulco de Juárez 309,254 ....K8
Acatlán de Osorio 7,624 ....K7
Acatzingo de Hidalgo 6,905 ....N2
Acayucan 21,173 ....M8
Aconchi 1,596 ....D2
Actopan, Hidalgo 11,037 ....K6
Actopan, Veracruz 2,265 ....N1
Agua Dulce 21,060 ....M7
Agualeguas 2,502 ....J3
Agua Prieta 20,754 ....E1
Aguascalientes 181,277 ....H6
Aguililla 5,715 ....H7
Ahome 4,182 ....E4
Ahuacatitlán 6,436 ....K7
Ahuacatlán 5,350 ....G6
Ahumada 6,466 ....F2
Ajalpan 8,238 ....L7
Alamo 9,954 ....L6
Alamos 4,269 ....E3
Aldama, Chihuahua 6,047 ....G2
Aldama, Tamaulipas 3,033 ....L5
Aljojuca 3,204 ....O1
Allende, Coahuila 11,076 ....J2
Allende, Nuevo León 9,914 ....J4
Atmolaya del Río 3,714 ....K1
Altamira 6,053 ....L5
Altar 2,519 ....D1
Altepexi 6,661 ....L7
Alto Lucero 3,698 ....P1
Altotonga 6,754 ....P1
Alvarado 15,592 ....M7
Amatlán de los Reyes 3,664 ....P2
Amealco 2,960 ....K6
Ameca 21,018 ....H6
Amecameca de Juárez 16,276 ....L1
Amozoc de Mota 9,203 ....N2
Anáhuac, Chihuahua 10,886 ....F2
Anáhuac, Nuevo León 8,168 ....J3
Angostura 2,663 ....E4
Antiguo Morelos 1,569 ....K5
Apan 13,705 ....M1
Apatzingán de la
  Constitución 44,849 ....H7
Apizaco 21,189 ....N1
Aquiles Serdán 2,565 ....G2
Aramberri 1,786 ....J5
Arandas 18,934 ....H6
Arcelia 10,024 ....J7
Ario de Rosales 8,774 ....H7
Arizpe 1,736 ....D1
Armería 10,616 ....G7
Arriaga 13,193 ....N8
Arteaga 5,324 ....H7
Ascensión 4,104 ....E1
Asunción Nochixtlán 3,235 ....L7
Atlixco 41,967 ....M2
Atotonilco el Alto 16,271 ....H6
Atoyac de Álvarez 8,874 ....J8
Autlán de Navarro 20,398 ....G7
Axochiapan 8,283 ....L7
Ayutla de los Libres 3,618 ....K8
Azcapotzalco 534,554 ....L1
Azoyú 1,736 ....K8
Bacadéhuachi 1,514 ....E2

Bacalar 2,121 ....P7
Bachíniva 1,809 ....F2
Bácum 2,668 ....D3
Bahía Tortugas 1,457 ....B3
Balancán de
  Domínguez 3,669 ....O8
Bamoa 5,866 ....E4
Banderilla 3,488 ....P1
Bavícora 2,049 ....P2
Benjamín Hill 5,366 ....D1
Bernardino de Sahagún 12,327 ....M1
Boca del Río 2,354 ....Q2
Bolonchén de Rejón 2,342 ....O7
Buenaventura 3,924 ....F2
Burgos 673 ....K4
Cabo San Lucas 1,534 ....E5
Cacahoatán 5,079 ....N9
Cadereyta Jiménez 13,586 ....K4
Calkiní 6,870 ....O6
Calnali 3,318 ....K6
Calpulalpan 8,659 ....M1
Calvillo 6,453 ....H6
Campeche 69,506 ....O7
Cananea 17,518 ....D1
Canatlán 5,983 ....G4
Cancún 326 ....G6
Candela 1,689 ....J3
Candelaria 1,982 ....O7
Cañitas de Felipe
  Pescador 4,885 ....H5
Capulhuac de Mirafuentes 8,289 ....L1
Cárdenas, San Luis
  Potosí 12,020 ....J6
Cárdenas, Tabasco 15,643 ....N8
Carichic 1,520 ....F3
Castaños 8,996 ....J3
Catemaco 11,786 ....M7
Cedillos 2,937 ....H1
Cedral 4,057 ....J5
Celaya 79,977 ....J6
Celestún 1,490 ....O6
Cerritos 10,421 ....J5
Cerro Azul 20,259 ....L6
Chahuites 5,218 ....N8
Chalchihuites 1,894 ....G5
Chalco de Díaz
  Covarrubias 12,172 ....L1
Champotón 6,606 ....O7
Chapantongo 3,805 ....J5
Charcas 10,491 ....J5
Chetumal 23,685 ....Q7
Chiapa de Corzo 8,571 ....N8
Chiautempan 12,327 ....N1
Chietla 4,602 ....L7
Chignahuapan 3,805 ....N1
Chihuahua 327,313 ....G2
Chilapa de Álvarez 9,204 ....K8
Chilpancingo de los
  Bravos 36,193 ....K8
China, Nuevo León 4,958 ....K4
Chocomán 5,114 ....P2
Choix 2,503 ....E3
Cholula de Rivadavia 15,399 ....M1
Chumatlán 9,451 ....G7
Cintalapa de Figueroa 12,036 ....M8
Ciudad Acuña (Villa
  Acuña) 30,276 ....J2
Ciudad Altamirano 8,694 ....J7
Ciudad Camargo,
  Chihuahua 24,030 ....G3
Ciudad Camargo,
  Tamaulipas 5,953 ....K3
Ciudad del Carmen 34,656 ....N7
Ciudad Delicias 52,446 ....G2
Ciudad del Maíz 5,241 ....K5
Ciudad de Río Grande 11,651 ....H5
Ciudad Guerrero 3,110 ....F2
Ciudad Guzmán 59,581 ....G7
Ciudad Hidalgo, Chiapas 4,105 ....N9
Ciudad Hidalgo,
  Michoacán 24,692 ....J7
Ciudad Juárez 424,135 ....F1
Ciudad Lerdo 19,803 ....H4
Ciudad Madero 115,302 ....L5
Ciudad Mante 51,247 ....K5
Ciudad Mendoza 18,696 ....O2
Ciudad Miguel Alemán 11,259 ....K3
Ciudad Obregón 144,795 ....E3
Ciudad Río Bravo 39,018 ....K4
Ciudad Satélite 35,083 ....L1
Ciudad Serdán 9,581 ....O2
Ciudad Valles 47,587 ....K5
Ciudad Victoria 83,897 ....K5
Coalcomán de Matamoros 4,875 ....H7
Coatepec 21,542 ....P1
Coatetelco 5,268 ....L7
Coatzacoalcos 69,753 ....M7
Coatzingo 3,038 ....M2
Cocorit 4,478 ....E3
Colima 58,450 ....H7
Colón 3,346 ....K6
Colotlán 6,135 ....H5
Comala 5,592 ....H7
Comalcalco 14,963 ....N7

Comitán de
  Domínguez 21,249 ....O8
Compostela 9,801 ....G6
Concepción del Oro 8,144 ....J4
Concordia 3,947 ....G5
Contla 7,517 ....N1
Copala 3,783 ....K8
Coquimatlán 6,212 ....G7
Córdoba 78,495 ....P2
Coscá 2,279 ....H4
Cosamaloapan de Carpio 19,766 ....M7
Cosautlán de Carvajal 2,039 ....P1
Coscomatepec de Bravo 6,023 ....P2
Coslo 2,680 ....H5
Costa Rica 11,795 ....F4
Cotija de la Paz 9,178 ....H7
Coyoacán 339,446 ....L1
Coyotepec 8,888 ....L1
Coyuca de Benítez 6,328 ....J8
Coyuca de Catalán 2,926 ....J7
Coyutla 3,726 ....L6
Cozumel 5,858 ....Q6
Creel 2,449 ....F3
Cuatrociénagas de
  Carranza 5,523 ....H3
Cuauhtémoc 20,598 ....F2
Cuautepec de Hinojosa 5,501 ....K6
Cuautitlán de Romero
  Rubio 11,439 ....L1
Cuautla Morelos 13,946 ....L1
Cuencamé de Ceniceros 3,774 ....H4
Cuernavaca 239,813 ....L2
Cuicatlán 2,733 ....L8
Cuitláhuac 4,813 ....P2
Culiacán 228,001 ....F4
Cumpas 2,395 ....E1
Cunduacán 4,397 ....N7
Dimas 2,194 ....F5
Doctor Arroyo 4,290 ....K5
Dolores Hidalgo de la Independencia
  Naci 16,849 ....J6
Dzidzantún 1,917 ....P7
Dzibalchén 1,917 ....P7
Dzidzantún 7,064 ....P6
Dzitbalché 4,393 ....O6
Ebano 17,489 ....K5
Ecatepec de Morelos 11,899 ....L1
Ejutla de Crespo 5,263 ....L8
Eldorado 8,115 ....E4
El Fuerte 7,179 ....E3
El Porvenir 3,030 ....G1
El Potosí 2,032 ....J4
El Salto 7,818 ....G5
El Zacatón 2,686 ....J5
Empalme 24,927 ....D2
Encarnación de Díaz 10,474 ....H6
Ensenada 77,687 ....A1
Escárcega 7,248 ....O7
Escuinapa de Hidalgo 16,442 ....G5
Escuintla 4,111 ....N9
Esperanza, Puebla 4,813 ....O2
Esperanza, Sonora 11,762 ....E3
Espita 5,394 ....P6
Esqueda 1,458 ....E1
Etchojoa 4,185 ....E3
Ezequiel Montes 3,139 ....K6
Fortín de las Flores 9,358 ....P2
Francisco I. Madero 12,613 ....H4
Fresnillo de González
  Echeverría 44,475 ....H5
Frontera 10,066 ....N7
Galeana, Nuevo León 3,429 ....J4
General Bravo 2,894 ....K4
General Cepeda 3,486 ....J4
General Terán 5,354 ....K4
Gómez Farías 3,030 ....F2
Gómez Palacio 79,650 ....H4
González 6,440 ....K5
Guadalajara 1,478,383 ....H6
Guadalajara* 2,343,034 ....H6
Guadalupe, Nuevo León 51,899 ....K4
Guadalupe, Zacatecas 13,246 ....H5
Guadalupe Bravo 3,333 ....F1
Guadalupe Victoria,
  Durango 7,931 ....H4
Guadalupe Victoria,
  Puebla 3,946 ....O1
Guamúchil 17,151 ....E4
Guanajuato 36,809 ....J6
Guasave 26,080 ....E4
Guaymas 57,492 ....D2
Gustavo Díaz Ordaz 10,154 ....K3
Gutiérrez Zamora 9,099 ....L6
Halachó 4,804 ....O6
Hecelchakán 4,279 ....O6
Hermosillo 232,691 ....D2
Heroica Caborca 20,771 ....C1
Heroica Nogales 52,108 ....D1
Hidalgo, Tamaulipas 2,450 ....K4
Hidalgo del Parral
  (Parral) 57,619 ....G3
Hopelchén 3,699 ....P7
Huajuapan de León 13,822 ....L8

Huamantla 15,565 ....N1
Huaquechula 2,294 ....M2
Huatabampo 18,506 ....D3
Huatusco de Chicuellar 9,501 ....P2
Huauchinango 16,826 ....L6
Huautla de Jiménez 6,132 ....L7
Huehuetlán el Chico 2,667 ....M2
Huejotzingo 8,552 ....M1
Huejutla 6,854 ....K6
Huetamo 9,333 ....J7
Hueyotlipan de Hidalgo 2,353 ....M1
Huimanguillo 7,075 ....N8
Huitzilán 3,573 ....O1
Huitzuco de los Figueroa 9,406 ....K7
Huixcolotla 4,039 ....N2
Huixtepec 5,927 ....L8
Huixtla 15,737 ....N9
Hunucmá 8,020 ....O6
Ignacio de la Llave 3,962 ....Q2
Iguala de la
  Independencia 45,355 ....K7
Imuris 1,958 ....D1
Irapuato 135,596 ....J6
Isla Mujeres 2,663 ....Q6
Isla, Veracruz 8,075 ....M7
Ixmiquilpan 6,048 ....K6
Ixtapa J8
Ixtapalapa 522,095 ....L1
Ixtenco 5,035 ....N1
Ixtepec 14,025 ....M8
Ixtlán del Río 10,986 ....G6
Izamal 9,749 ....P6
Ízucar de Matamoros 21,164 ....M2
Jala 4,535 ....G6
Jalacingo 3,427 ....P1
Jalapa Enríquez 161,352 ....P1
Jalpa 9,904 ....H6
Jalpa de Méndez 4,785 ....N7
Jalpan 1,878 ....K6
Jáltipan de Morelos 15,170 ....M8
Jantetelco 2,015 ....L2
Jaumave 3,072 ....K5
Jerez de García
  Salinas 20,325 ....H5
Jico 7,269 ....P1
Jilotepec de Abasolo 4,252 ....K7
Jiménez, Chihuahua 18,095 ....G3
Joachín 3,918 ....Q2
Jojutla de Juárez 14,438 ....L2
Jonacatepec 3,868 ....M2
Jonuta 2,746 ....N7
José Cardel 5,396 ....Q1
Juan Aldama 9,667 ....H4
Juchipila 6,328 ....H6
Juchitán de Zaragoza 30,218 ....M8
Kantunilkin 1,970 ....Q6
La Barca 18,055 ....H6
La Barra de Navidad 1,829 ....G7
La Concordia 3,559 ....N9
La Cruz, Sinaloa 4,218 ....F4
La Huerta 4,328 ....G7
La Paz, Baja California
  Sur 46,011 ....D5
La Paz, San Luis
  Potosí 3,735 ....J5
La Piedad Cavadas 34,963 ....H6
Las Choapas 20,166 ....M7
Las Hadas G7
Las Nieves 2,262 ....G3
Las Rosas 7,658 ....N8
León 468,887 ....J6
Lerdo de Tejada 11,628 ....M8
Lerma 4,158 ....O7
Libres 4,830 ....O1
Linares 24,456 ....K4
Liera de Canales 3,564 ....K5
Loma Bonita 15,804 ....M7
Loreto, Baja California 2,570 ....D4
Loreto, Zacatecas 7,132 ....J5
Los Mochis 67,953 ....E4
Los Reyes de Salgado 19,452 ....H7
Macuspana 12,293 ....N8
Madera 9,759 ....F2
Magdalena de Kino 10,281 ....D1
Maltrata 5,457 ....O2
Manzanillo 20,777 ....G7
Mapastepec 5,907 ....N9
Mapimí 2,737 ....G4
Martínez de la Torre 17,203 ....L6
Mascota 5,674 ....G6
Matamoros, Coahuila 15,125 ....H4
Matamoros, Tamaulipas 165,124 ....L4
Matehuala 28,799 ....J5
Matías Romero 13,200 ....M8
Maxcanú 6,055 ....O6
Mazatlán 147,010 ....F5
Melchor Múzquiz 18,868 ....H3
Melchor Ocampo del
  Balsas 4,766 ....H8
Meoqui 12,308 ....G2
Mérida 233,912 ....P6
Metepec 4,625 ....M2
Metlatonoc 1,870 ....K8

Mexicali 317,228 ....B1
Mexico City (cap.) 9,377,300 ....L1
Mexico City* 13,993,866 ....L1
Miacatlán 3,980 ....K2
Mier 5,636 ....K3
Miguel Auza 9,303 ....H4
Minatitlán 68,397 ....M8
Mineral del Monte 8,887 ....K6
Miquihuana 1,971 ....J5
Misantla 8,799 ....P1
Miahuatlán de Porfirio
  Díaz 5,714 ....L8
Mocorito 3,993 ....F4
Moctezuma, San Luis
  Potosí 1,734 ....J5
Moctezuma, Sonora 2,700 ....E2
Monclova 78,134 ....J3
Montemorelos 18,642 ....K4
Monterrey 1,006,221 ....J4
Monterrey* 1,923,402 ....J4
Morelia 199,099 ....J7
Morelos 6,356 ....O8
Morelos, Coahuila 2,288 ....J2
Moroleón 25,620 ....J6
Motozintla de Mendoza 4,682 ....N9

Motul de Felipe Carillo
  Puerto 12,949 ....P6
Muna 5,491 ....P6
Nacajuca 3,580 ....D1
Nacozari 2,976 ....E1
Nadadores 2,461 ....H3
Naica 7,190 ....M8
Namiquipa 4,875 ....F2
Nanacamilpa 6,356 ....M1
Naolinco de Victoria 4,365 ....P1
Naranjos 14,732 ....L6
Naucalpan de Juárez 9,425 ....L1
Nautla 1,935 ....L6
Nava 4,097 ....J2
Navojoa 43,817 ....E3
Navolato 12,799 ....F4
Nazas 2,881 ....G4
Netzahualcóyotl 580,436 ....L1
Nieves 3,966 ....H5
Nochistlán 8,780 ....H6
Nogales 14,254 ....P2

Nueva Italia de Ruiz 14,718 ....J7
Nueva Rosita 34,706 ....J2
Nuevo Ideal 5,252 ....G4
Nuevo Laredo 184,622 ....J3
Oaxaca de Juárez 114,948 ....L8
Ocampo, Coahuila 1,613 ....H3
Ocampo, Tamaulipas 4,801 ....K5
Ocosingo 2,946 ....O8
Ocotlán 35,361 ....H6
Ocotlán de Morelos 5,882 ....L8
Ojinaga 12,757 ....G2
Ojocaliente 7,582 ....H5
Ometepec 7,342 ....K8
Oriental 6,009 ....O1
Orizaba 105,150 ....P2
Otumba de Gómez
  Farías 3,198 ....M1
Oxkutzcab 8,182 ....P6
Ozuluama 2,851 ....L6
Ozumba de Alzate 6,876 ....M1
Pachuca de Soto 83,892 ....K6
Padilla 4,581 ....K5
Palenque 2,746 ....O8
Palizada 2,332 ....O7
Palomas 2,129 ....E1

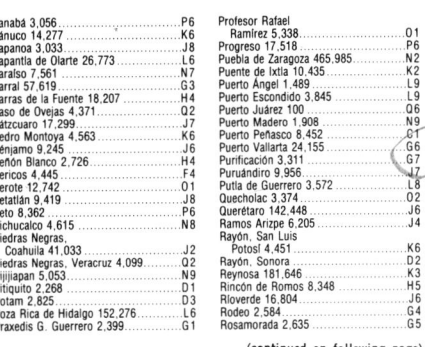

AREA 761,601 sq. mi. (1,972,546 sq. km.)
POPULATION 67,395,826
CAPITAL Mexico City
LARGEST CITY Mexico City
HIGHEST POINT Citlaltépetl 18,855 ft. (5,747 m.)
MONETARY UNIT Mexican peso
MAJOR LANGUAGE Spanish
MAJOR RELIGION Roman Catholicism

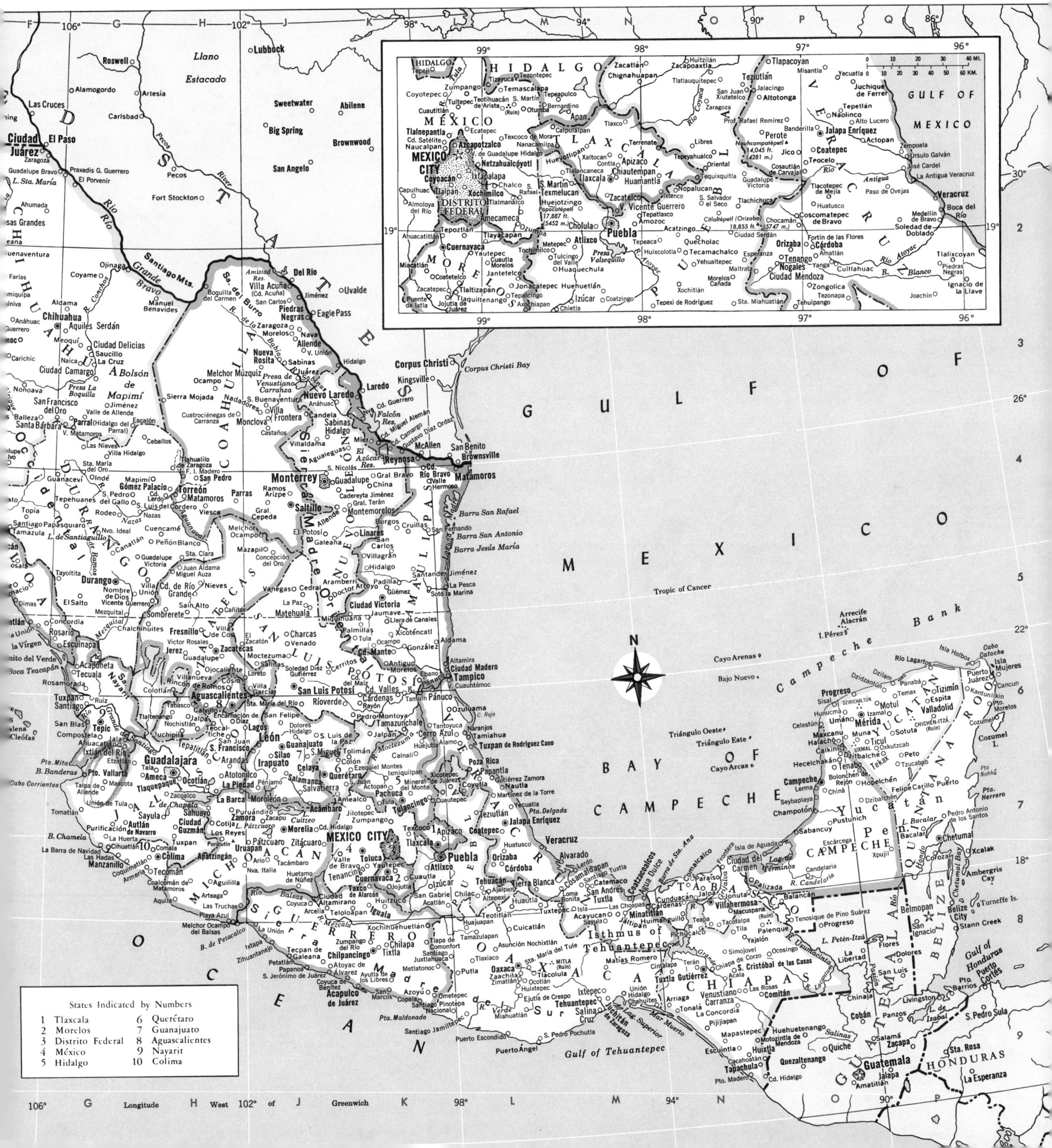

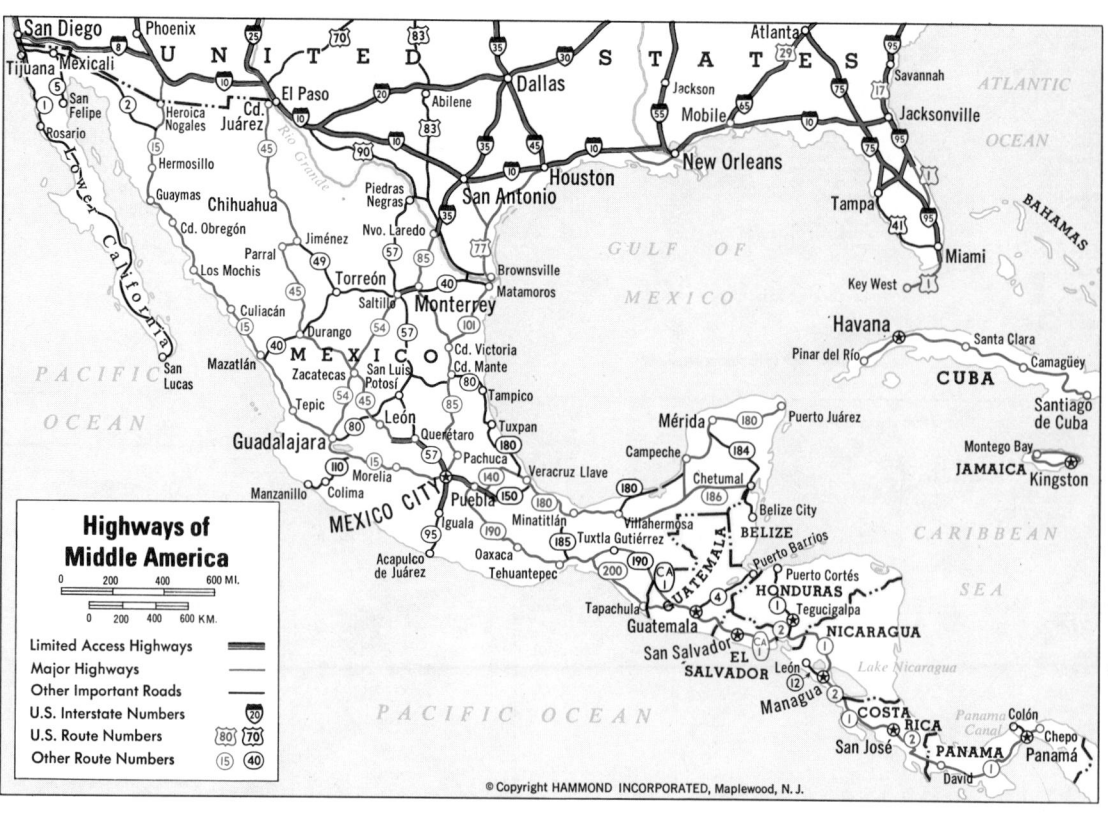

Highways of Middle America

0 200 400 600 MI.

0 200 400 600 KM.

Limited Access Highways
Major Highways
Other Important Roads
U.S. Interstate Numbers
U.S. Route Numbers
Other Route Numbers

© Copyright HAMMOND INCORPORATED, Maplewood, N.J.

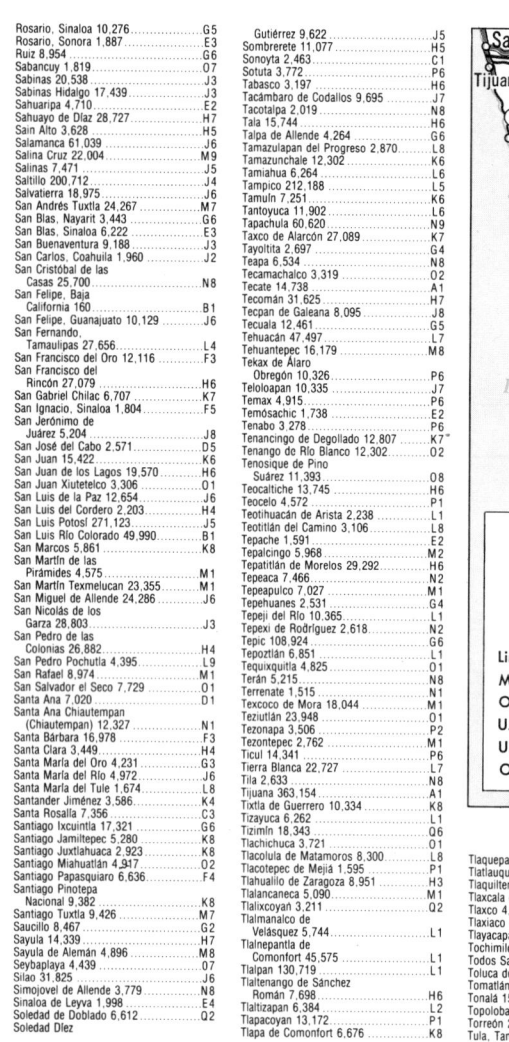

Agriculture, Industry and Resources

DOMINANT LAND USE

- Wheat, Livestock
- Cereals (chiefly corn), Livestock
- Diversified Tropical Cash Crops
- Cotton, Mixed Cereals
- Livestock, Limited Agriculture
- Range Livestock
- Forests
- Nonagricultural Land

⚡ Water Power
Major Industrial Areas

MAJOR MINERAL OCCURRENCES

Ag	Silver	G	Natural Gas	O	Petroleum
Au	Gold	Gr	Graphite	Pb	Lead
C	Coal	Hg	Mercury	S	Sulfur
Cu	Copper	Mn	Manganese	Sb	Antimony
F	Fluorspar	Mo	Molybdenum	Sn	Tin
Fe	Iron Ore	Na	Salt	W	Tungsten
				Zn	Zinc

GUATEMALA

AREA 42,042 sq. mi. (108,889 sq. km.)
POPULATION 7,262,419
CAPITAL Guatemala
LARGEST CITY Guatemala
HIGHEST POINT Tajumulco 13,845 ft. (4,220 m.)
MONETARY UNIT quetzal
MAJOR LANGUAGES Spanish, Quiché
MAJOR RELIGION Roman Catholicism

BELIZE

AREA 8,867 sq. mi. (22,966 sq. km.)
POPULATION 144,857
CAPITAL Belmopan
LARGEST CITY Belize City
HIGHEST POINT Victoria Peak 3,681 ft. (1,122 m.)
MONETARY UNIT Belize dollar
MAJOR LANGUAGES English, Spanish, Mayan
MAJOR RELIGIONS Roman Catholicism, Protestantism

EL SALVADOR

AREA 8,260 sq. mi. (21,393 sq. km.)
POPULATION 4,813,000
CAPITAL San Salvador
LARGEST CITY San Salvador
HIGHEST POINT Santa Ana 7,825 ft. (2,385 m.)
MONETARY UNIT colón
MAJOR LANGUAGE Spanish
MAJOR RELIGION Roman Catholicism

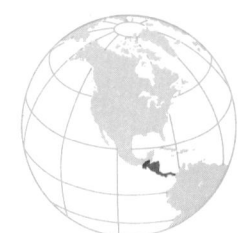

HONDURAS

AREA 43,277 sq. mi. (112,087 sq. km.)
POPULATION 3,691,000
CAPITAL Tegucigalpa
LARGEST CITY Tegucigalpa
HIGHEST POINT Las Minas 9,347 ft. (2,849 m.)
MONETARY UNIT lempira
MAJOR LANGUAGE Spanish
MAJOR RELIGION Roman Catholicism

NICARAGUA

AREA 45,698 sq. mi. (118,358 sq. km.)
POPULATION 2,703,000
CAPITAL Managua
LARGEST CITY Managua
HIGHEST POINT Cerro Mocotón 6,913 ft. (2,107 m.)
MONETARY UNIT córdoba
MAJOR LANGUAGE Spanish
MAJOR RELIGION Roman Catholicism

COSTA RICA

AREA 19,575 sq. mi. (50,700 sq. km.)
POPULATION 2,245,000
CAPITAL San José
LARGEST CITY San José
HIGHEST POINT Chirripó Grande 12,530 ft. (3,819 m.)
MONETARY UNIT colón
MAJOR LANGUAGE Spanish
MAJOR RELIGION Roman Catholicism

PANAMA

AREA 29,761 sq. mi. (77,082 sq. km.)
POPULATION 1,830,175
CAPITAL Panamá
LARGEST CITY Panamá
HIGHEST POINT Vol. Baru 11,401 ft. (3,475 m.)
MONETARY UNIT balboa
MAJOR LANGUAGE Spanish
MAJOR RELIGION Roman Catholicism

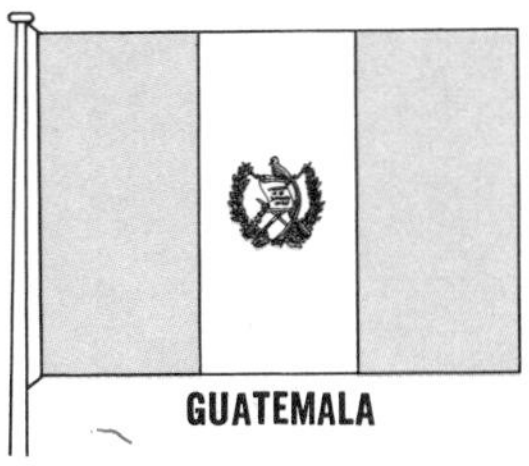

GUATEMALA

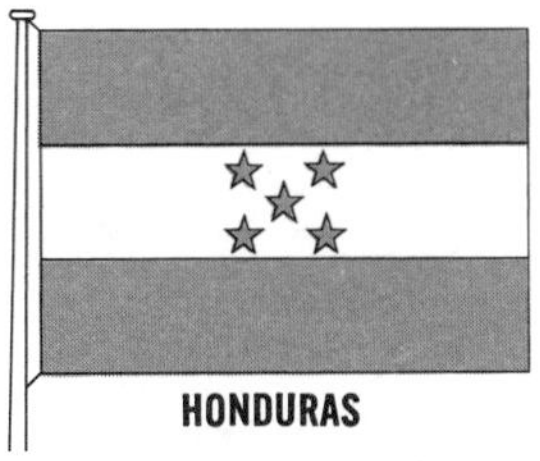

HONDURAS

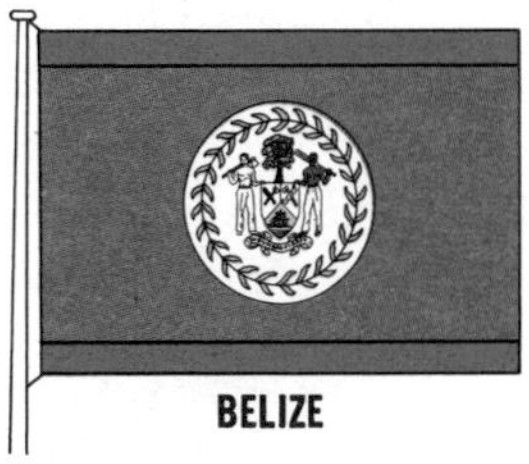

BELIZE

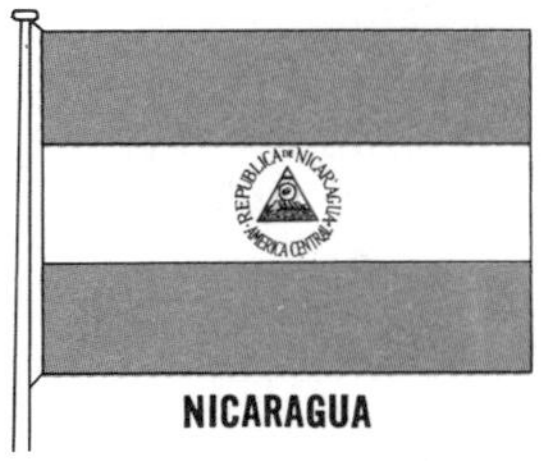

NICARAGUA

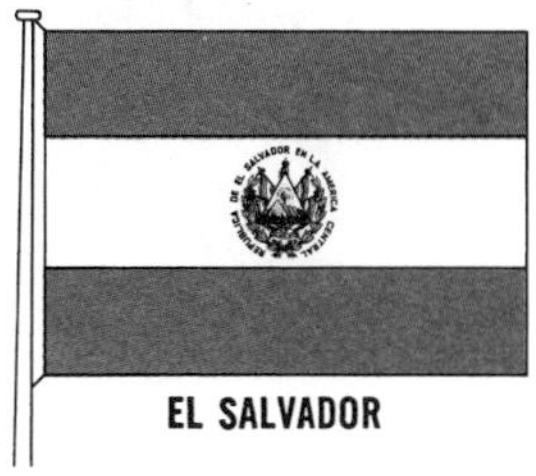

EL SALVADOR

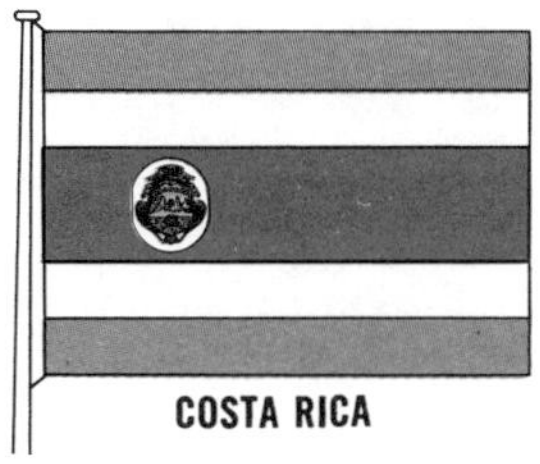

COSTA RICA

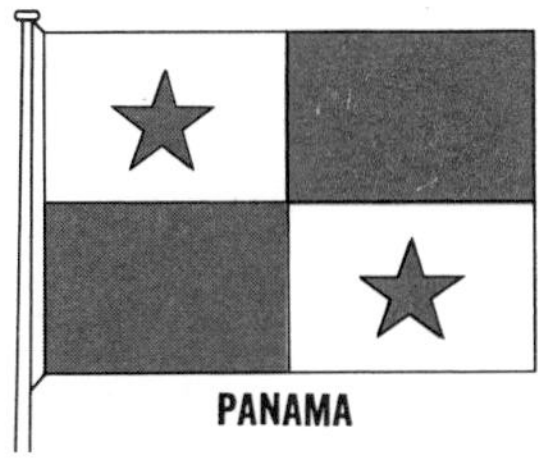

PANAMA

Agriculture, Industry and Resources

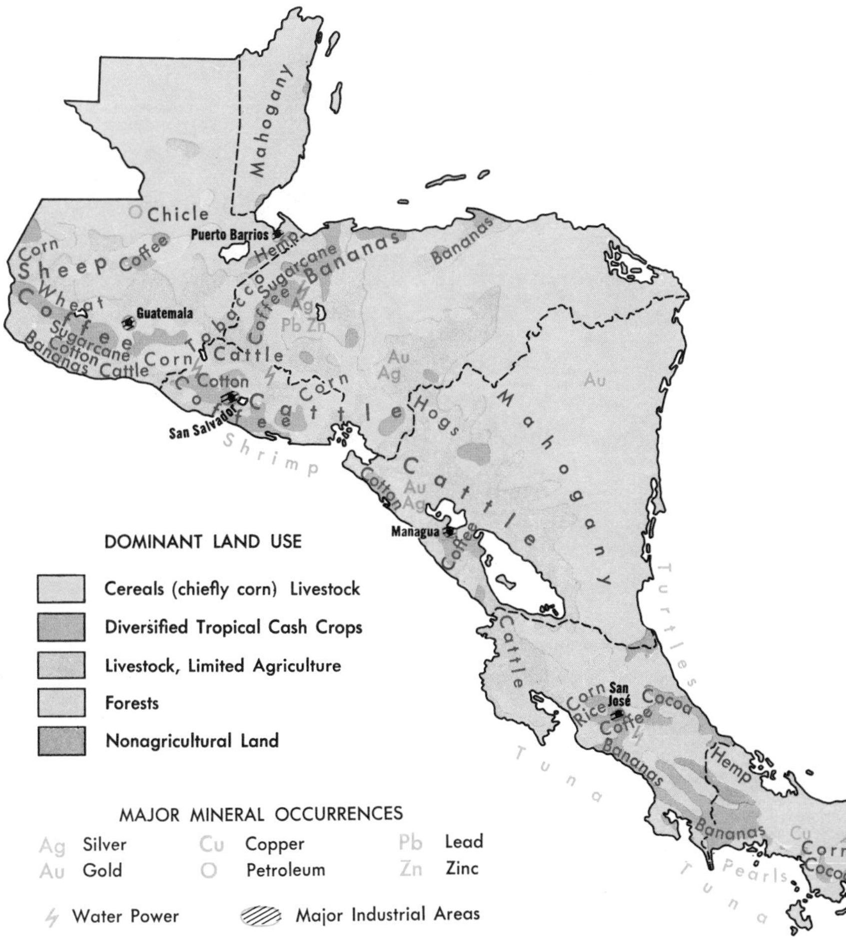
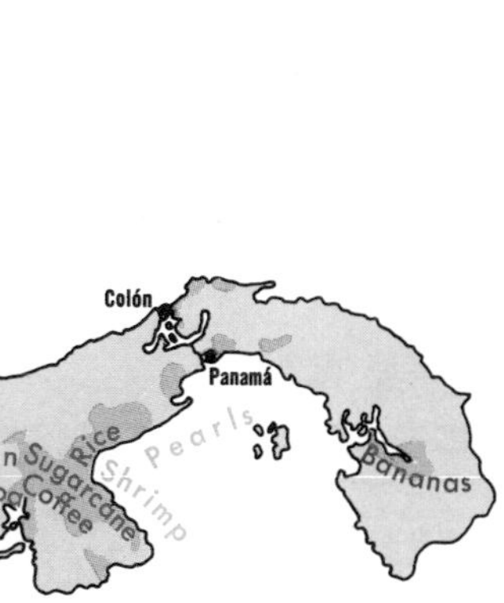
Mahogany
Chicle
Puerto Barrios
Corn
Sheep
Coffee
Wheat
Guatemala
Sugarcane
Cotton
Bananas
Cattle
Hemp
Tobacco
Ag
Pb Zn
Au
Hogs
San Salvador
Shrimp
Managua
Turtles
San José
Cocoa
Rice
Tuna
Colón
Panamá
Cu
Pearls
DOMINANT LAND USE
Cereals (chiefly corn) Livestock
Diversified Tropical Cash Crops
Livestock, Limited Agriculture
Forests
Nonagricultural Land
MAJOR MINERAL OCCURRENCES
Ag Silver
Au Gold
Cu Copper
O Petroleum
Pb Lead
Zn Zinc
Water Power
Major Industrial Areas

(continued on following page)

OTHER FEATURES		
Blanca (pt.)	F5
Blanco (cape)	E6
Blanco (peak)	F6
Burica (pt.)	F6
Cahuita (pt.)	F6
Caño (isl.)	F6
Carreta (pt.)	F6
Chirripó Grande (mt.)	F6
Coronada (gulf)	F6
Cuilapa Miravalles (vol.)	E5
Dulce (gulf)	F6
Góngora (mt.)	E5
Guionos (pt.)	E6
Irazú (mt.)	F6
Judas (pt.)	F6
Llorena (pt.)	F6
Matapalo (cape)	E6
Nicoya (gulf)	E6
Nicoya (pen.)	E6
Papagayo (gulf)	E5
Salinas (bay)	D5
San Juan (riv.)	E5
Santa Elena (cape)	D5

Talamanca (range)	F6
Velas (cape)	D5

EL SALVADOR

CITIES and TOWNS

Acajutla 8,598	B4
Ahuachapán 17,242	C4
Atiquizaya 7,035	C3
Chalatenango 7,633	C3
Chinameca 6,303	D4
Cojutepeque 20,615	C4
Estanzuelas 2,548	C4
Ilobasco 6,572	C4
Intipucá 3,469	D4
Jucuarán 1,443	D4
La Libertad	C4
La Palma 1,998	C3
La Unión 17,207	D4
Metapán 7,704	C3
Nueva San Salvador 35,106	C4
Puerto de la Concordia	C4
San Francisco Gotera 4,725	C4

San Miguel 59,304	D4
San Salvador (cap.) 337,171	C4
Santa Ana 96,306	C4
Santa Rosa de Lima 5,707	D4
San Vicente 18,872	C4
Sensuntepeque 7,226	C4
Sonsonate 33,562	C4
Suchitoto 5,540	C4
Texistepeque 1,722	C3
Usulután 19,616	D4
Zacatecoluca 15,718	C4

OTHER FEATURES

Fonseca (gulf)	D4
Güija (lake)	C3
Lempa (riv.)	D4
Remedios (pt.)	B4
Santa Ana	C4

GUATEMALA

CITIES and TOWNS

Amatitlán 15,251	B3

Antigua 17,994	B3
Asunción Mita 7,477	C3
Cabañón 1,344	B3
Chajul 4,329	B3
Champerico 5,722	A3
Chichicastenango 2,635	B3
Chimaltenango 12,860	B3
Chiquimula 16,126	C3
Coatepeque 15,979	A3
Cobán 11,418	B3
Comalapa 10,980	B3
Cubulco 2,021	B3
Cuilapa 4,287	B3
Cuilco 862	B3
Dolores 973	C2
El Estor 2,324	C2
El Progreso 4,009	B3
Escuintla 33,205	B3
Flores 1,477	C2
Gualán 5,169	C3
Guatemala (cap.) 700,538	B3
Huehuetenango 12,570	B3
Ipala 3,386	C3
Iztapa 1,237	B4

Jacaltenango 4,517	B3
Jalapa 13,788	B3
Jutiapa 8,210	B3
La Gomera 2,394	B3
La Libertad 908	B2
Livingston 2,898	C3
Los Amates 1,383	C3
Masagua 1,178	B3
Mazatenango 23,285	B3
Momostenango 5,210	B3
Morales 2,113	C3
Ocós 741	A3
Panzós 1,643	C3
Puerto Barrios 22,598	C3
Quezaltenango 53,021	B3
Quezaltepeque 2,222	C3
Rabinal 4,625	B3
Retalhuleu 19,060	B3
Río Hondo 1,416	C3
Sacapulas 1,439	B3
Salamá 5,529	B3
San Andrés 1,066	B2
San Felipe 3,903	B3
San José 9,402	B4
San Luis 1,136	C2

San Luis Jilotepeque 6,055	C3
San Marcos 5,700	A3
San Martín Jilotepeque 3,770	B3
San Mateo Ixtatán 1,834	B3
San Pedro Carchá 4,465	B3
Santa Cruz del Quiché 7,651	B3
Santa Rosa de Lima 1,161	B3
Sololá 3,960	B3
Tacaná 1,280	A3
Tejutla 1,205	B3
Tikal	B2
Totonicapán 8,568	B3
Zacapa 12,688	C3

OTHER FEATURES

Atitlán (lake)	B3
Atitlán (vol.)	B3
Azul (riv.)	C2
Chixoy (riv.)	B3
Güija (lake)	C3
Honduras (gulf)	D2
Izabal (lake)	C3
Minas (mts.)	C3
Motagua (riv.)	C3

Pasión (riv.)	B2
Petén-Itzá (lake)	B2
San Pedro (riv.)	B2
Sarstún (riv.)	A3
Tacaná (vol.)	A3
Tajumulco (vol.)	A3
Tres Puntas (cape)	C3
Usumacinta (riv.)	B2

HONDURAS

CITIES and TOWNS

Amapala 2,274	D4
Brus Laguna 933	E3
Catacamas 9,134	E3
Cedros 917	D3
Choloma 961	D2
Choluteca 26,152	D4
Comayagua 15,941	D3
Copán 3,902	C3
Danlí 10,825	D3
El Dulce Nombre 1,297	C3

Central America

CONIC PROJECTION

SCALE OF MILES

0   25   50   100   150

SCALE OF KILOMETERS

0   25 50   100   150

Capitals of Countries .... ☆
International Boundaries ....
Canals ....

Scale 1:5,780,000

© Copyright HAMMOND INCORPORATED, Maplewood, N.J.

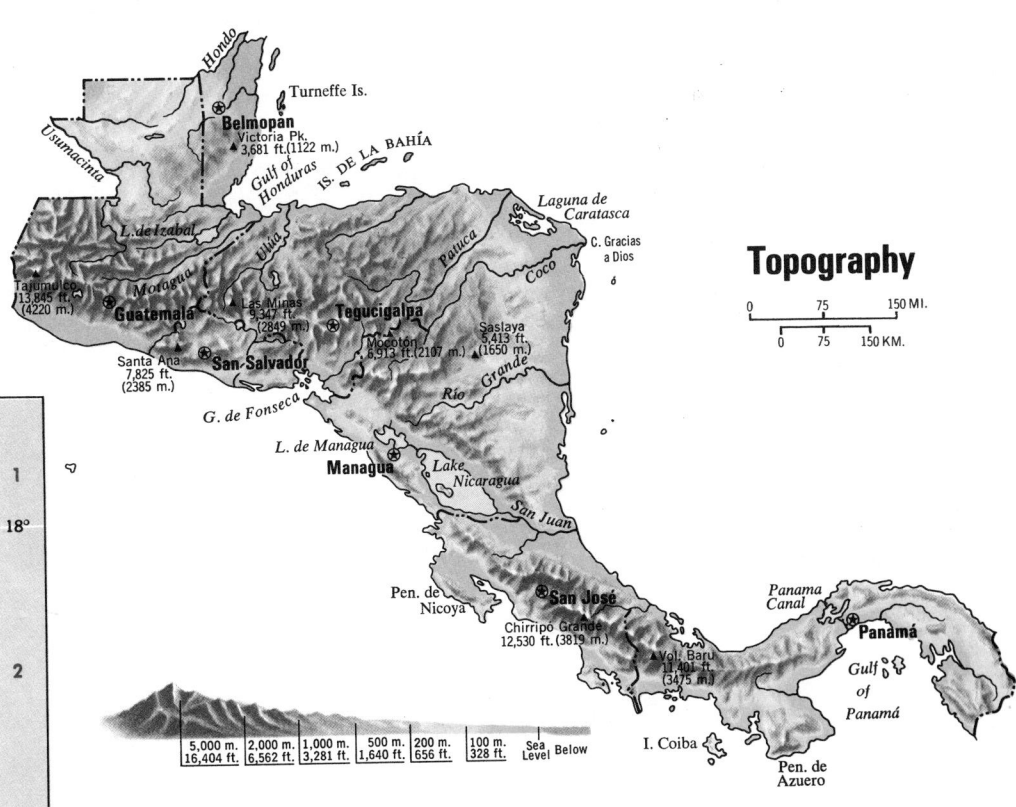

Topography

0   75   150 MI.
0   75   150 KM.

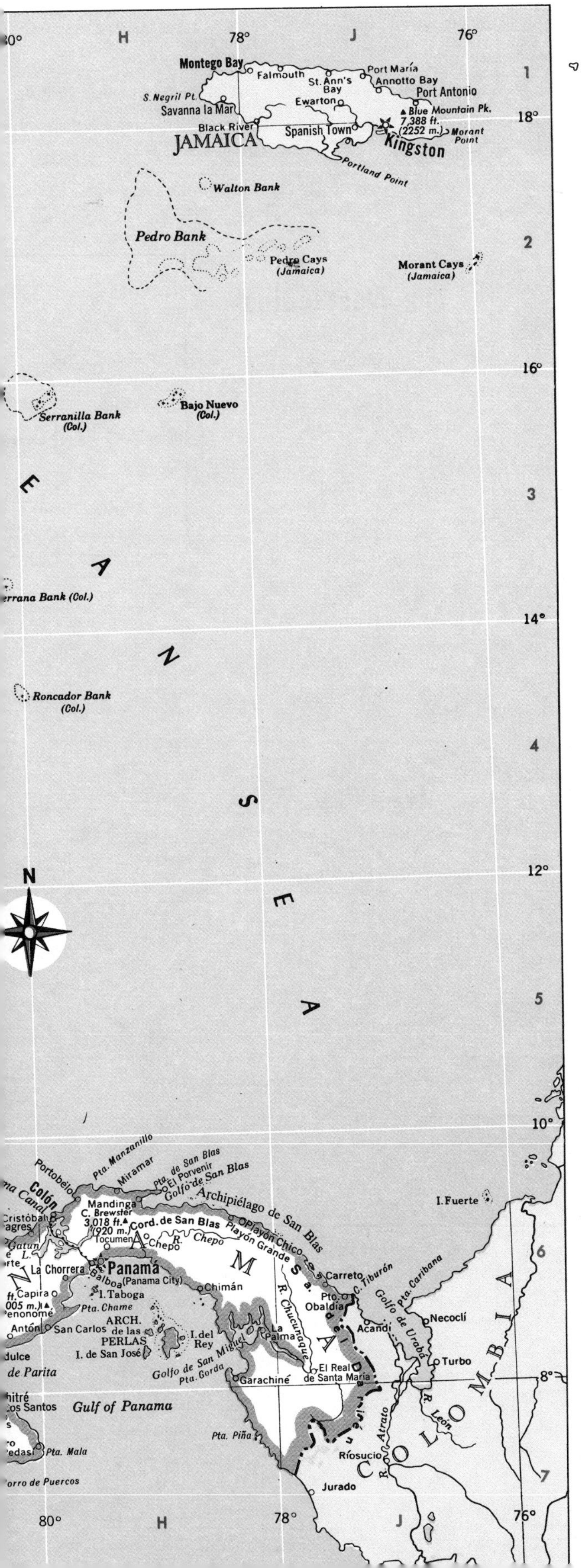

| 5,000 m. 16,404 ft. | 2,000 m. 6,562 ft. | 1,000 m. 3,281 ft. | 500 m. 1,640 ft. | 200 m. 656 ft. | 100 m. 328 ft. | Sea Level | Below |

Flags (top two rows)

CUBA HAITI DOMINICAN REPUBLIC JAMAICA TRINIDAD AND TOBAGO BARBADOS

GRENADA BAHAMAS DOMINICA ST. LUCIA ST. VINC. & GRENS. ANTIGUA AND BARBUD

CUBA
AREA 44,206 sq. mi. (114,494 sq. km.)
POPULATION 9,706,369
CAPITAL Havana
LARGEST CITY Havana
HIGHEST POINT Pico Turquino
6,561 ft. (2,000 m.)
MONETARY UNIT Cuban peso
MAJOR LANGUAGE Spanish
MAJOR RELIGION Roman Catholicism

HAITI
AREA 10,694 sq. mi. (27,697 sq. km.)
POPULATION 5,009,000
CAPITAL Port-au-Prince
LARGEST CITY Port-au-Prince
HIGHEST POINT Pic La Selle 8,793 ft.
(2,680 m.)
MONETARY UNIT gourde
MAJOR LANGUAGES Creole French, French
MAJOR RELIGION Roman Catholicism

DOMINICAN REPUBLIC
AREA 18,704 sq. mi. (48,443 sq. km.)
POPULATION 5,431,000
CAPITAL Santo Domingo
LARGEST CITY Santo Domingo
HIGHEST POINT Pico Duarte
10,417 ft. (3,175 m.)
MONETARY UNIT Dominican peso
MAJOR LANGUAGE Spanish
MAJOR RELIGION Roman Catholicism

JAMAICA
AREA 4,411 sq. mi. (11,424 sq. km.)
POPULATION 2,161,000
CAPITAL Kingston
LARGEST CITY Kingston
HIGHEST POINT Blue Mountain Peak
7,402 ft. (2,256 m.)
MONETARY UNIT Jamaican dollar
MAJOR LANGUAGE English
MAJOR RELIGIONS Protestantism,
Roman Catholicism

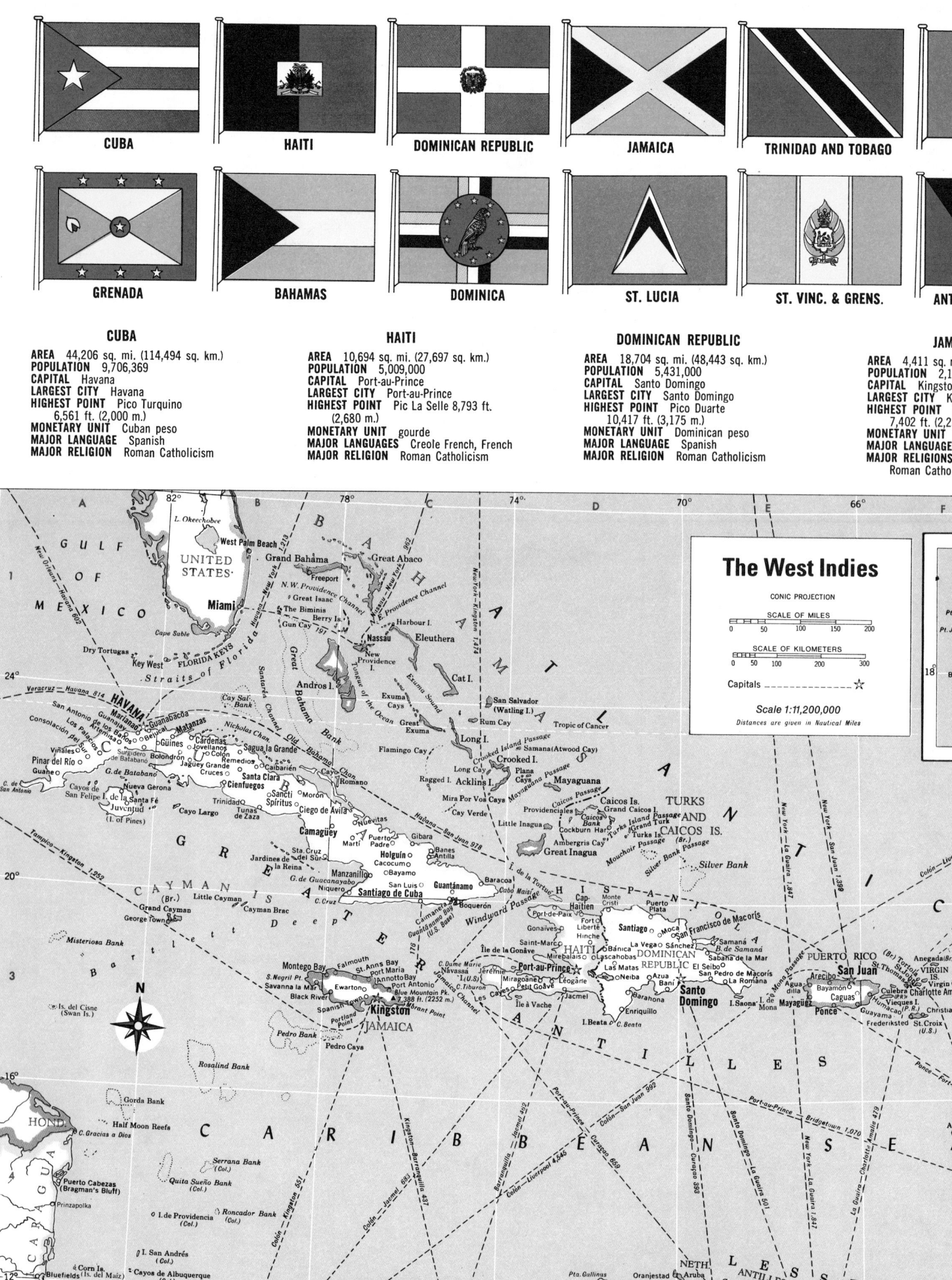

The West Indies

CONIC PROJECTION

SCALE OF MILES
0 50 100 150 200

SCALE OF KILOMETERS
0 50 100 200 300

Capitals --------- ☆

Scale 1:11,200,000
Distances are given in Nautical Miles

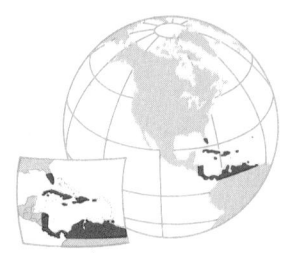

TRINIDAD AND TOBAGO

AREA 1,980 sq. mi. (5,128 sq. km.)
POPULATION 1,067,108
CAPITAL Port of Spain
LARGEST CITY Port of Spain
HIGHEST POINT Mt. Aripo 3,084 ft. (940 m.)
MONETARY UNIT Trinidad and Tobago dollar
MAJOR LANGUAGES English, Hindi
MAJOR RELIGIONS Roman Catholicism,
  Protestantism, Hinduism, Islam

BARBADOS

AREA 166 sq. mi. (430 sq. km.)
POPULATION 249,000
CAPITAL Bridgetown
LARGEST CITY Bridgetown
HIGHEST POINT Mt. Hillaby 1,104 ft.
  (336 m.)
MONETARY UNIT Barbadian dollar
MAJOR LANGUAGE English
MAJOR RELIGION Protestantism

GRENADA

AREA 133 sq. mi. (344 sq. km.)
POPULATION 110,000
CAPITAL St. George's
LARGEST CITY St. George's
HIGHEST POINT Mt. St. Catherine
  2,757 ft. (840 m.)
MONETARY UNIT East Caribbean dollar
MAJOR LANGUAGES English, French patois
MAJOR RELIGIONS Roman Catholicism,
  Protestantism

BAHAMAS

AREA 5,382 sq. mi. (13,939 sq. km.)
POPULATION 223,455
CAPITAL Nassau
LARGEST CITY Nassau
HIGHEST POINT Mt. Alvernia 206 ft. (63 m.)
MONETARY UNIT Bahamian dollar
MAJOR LANGUAGE English
MAJOR RELIGIONS Roman Catholicism,
  Protestantism

DOMINICA

AREA 290 sq. mi. (751 sq. km.)
POPULATION 74,089
CAPITAL Roseau
HIGHEST POINT Morne Diablotin
  4,747 ft. (1,447 m.)
MONETARY UNIT Dominican dollar
MAJOR LANGUAGES English, French patois
MAJOR RELIGIONS Roman Catholicism,
  Protestantism

SAINT LUCIA

AREA 238 sq. mi. (616 sq. km.)
POPULATION 115,783
CAPITAL Castries
HIGHEST POINT Mt. Gimie 3,117 ft. (950 m.)
MONETARY UNIT East Caribbean dollar
MAJOR LANGUAGES English, French patois
MAJOR RELIGIONS Roman Catholicism,
  Protestantism

SAINT VINCENT AND THE GRENADINES

AREA 150 sq. mi. (388 sq. km.)
POPULATION 124,000
CAPITAL Kingstown
HIGHEST POINT Soufrière 4,000 ft. (1,219 m.)
MONETARY UNIT East Caribbean dollar
MAJOR LANGUAGE English
MAJOR RELIGIONS Protestantism,
  Roman Catholicism

BERMUDA

AREA 21 sq. mi. (54 sq. km.)
POPULATION 67,761
CAPITAL Hamilton
MONETARY UNIT Bermuda dollar
MAJOR LANGUAGE English
MAJOR RELIGION Protestantism

PUERTO RICO

AREA 3,515 sq. mi. (9,104 sq. km.)
POPULATION 3,186,076
CAPITAL San Juan
MONETARY UNIT U.S. dollar
MAJOR LANGUAGES Spanish, English
MAJOR RELIGION Roman Catholicism

NETHERLANDS ANTILLES

AREA 390 sq. mi. (1,010 sq. km.)
POPULATION 246,000
CAPITAL Willemstad
MONETARY UNIT Antilles guilder
MAJOR LANGUAGES Dutch, Papiamento, English
MAJOR RELIGIONS Roman Catholicism,
  Protestantism

ANTIGUA AND BARBUDA

AREA 171 sq. mi. (443 sq. km.)
POPULATION 72,000
CAPITAL St. John's
HIGHEST POINT Boggy Peak 1,319 ft. (402 m.)
MONETARY UNIT East Caribbean dollar
MAJOR LANGUAGE English
MAJOR RELIGION Protestantism

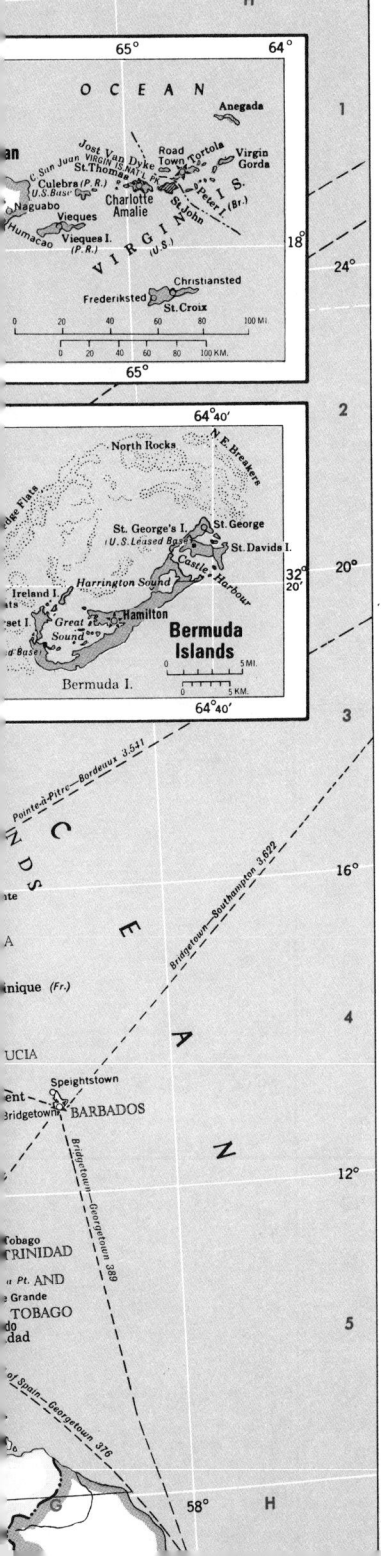

ANGUILLA

Anguilla 6,519 .... F3

ANTIGUA AND BARBUDA

Antigua (isl.)	G3
Barbuda (isl.)	G3
Caribbean (sea)	B4
Codrington 1,071	G3
Falmouth 1,134	F3
Redonda (isl.)	F3

BAHAMAS

Acklins (isl.)	C2
Andros (isl.)	B1
Atwood (Samana) (cay)	D2
Berry (isls.)	B1
Biminis, The (isls.)	B1
Caicos (passage)	D2
Cat (isl.)	C1
Cay Sal (bank)	B2
Crooked (isl.)	D2
Crooked Island (passage)	C2
Eleuthera (isl.)	C1
Exuma (cays)	C1
Exuma (sound)	C1
Flamingo (cay)	C2
Freeport 15,546	B1
Grand Bahama (isl.)	B1
Great Abaco (isl.)	C1
Great Bahama (bank)	B1
Great Exuma (isl.)	C2
Great Inagua (isl.)	D2
Great Isaac (isl.)	B1
Gun (cay)	B1
Harbour (isl.)	C1
Little Inagua (isl.)	D2
Long (cay)	C2
Long (isl.)	C2
Mayaguana (isl.)	D2
Mayaguana (passage)	D2
Mira Por Vos (cays)	C2

Nassau (cap.) 105,352	C1
New Providence (isl.)	C1
North East Providence (chan.)	C1
North West Providence (chan.)	B1
Old Bahama (chan.)	B2
Plana (cays)	D2
Ragged (isl.)	C2
Rum (cay)	C2
Samana (chan.)	D2
San Salvador (isl.)	D1
Santarén (chan.)	B1
Tongue of the Ocean (chan.)	C1
Verde (cay)	C2
Watling (San Salvador)
(isl.)	C1

BARBADOS

Bridgetown (cap.) 8,868	G4
Speightstown	G4

BERMUDA

Bermuda (isl.)	H3
Castle (harb.)	H2
Great (sound)	G3
Hamilton (cap.) 2,060	G3
Harrington (sound)	H2
Ireland (isl.)	G3
North (rocks)	H2
Saint Davids (isl.)	H2
Saint George 1,604	H2
Saint George's (isl.)	H2
Somerset (isl.)	G3

CAYMAN ISLANDS

Bartlett Deep	B3
Cayman Brac (isl.)	B3
George Town (cap.) 7,617	B3
Grand Cayman (isl.)	B3
Little Cayman (isl.)	B3
Misteriosa (bank)	A3

CUBA

Bayamo 81,000	C2
Camagüey 216,000	B2
Cienfuegos 88,000	B2
Florida (isl.)	B1
Guanabacoa 69,706	B2
Guantánamo 145,000	C2
Havana (cap.) 1,966,435	A2
Holguín 148,000	C2
Jagüey Grande 8,721	B2
Juventud (Pines) (isl.)	A2
Manzanillo 82,000	C2
Marianao• 368,747	A2
Matanzas 94,000	B2
Pinar del Río 83,000	A2
Sancti Spíritus 83,000	B2
San Felipe (cays)	A2
Santa Clara 143,000	B2
Santiago de Cuba 310,000	C3
Viñales 2,049	A2
Windward (passage)	C3

DOMINICA

Portsmouth 2,329	G4
Roseau (cap.) 9,968	G4

DOMINICAN REPUBLIC

Santiago 155,000	D3
Santo Domingo (cap.) 673,470	E3

GRENADA

Carriacou (isl.)	G4
Gouyave 2,498	F4
Grenadines (isls.)	G4
Saint George's (cap.) 6,313	F5

GUADELOUPE

Basse-Terre (cap.) 15,206	F4
Saint-Barthélemy (isl.)	F3
Saint Martin (isl.)	F3

HAITI

Jacmel 11,391	D3
Léogâne 4,603	D3
Port-au-Prince (cap.) 306,053	D3
Gonâve (isl.)	D3
Jamaica (chan.)	C3
Tortuga (isl.)	D2

JAMAICA

Blue Mountain (peak)	C3
Jamaica (isl.)	C3
Kingston (cap.) 106,791	C3
Pedro (cays)	C3
Port Antonio 10,538	C3
Savanna-la-Mar 11,759	B3

MARTINIQUE

Fort-de-France (cap.) 96,815	G4
Saint-Pierre 5,358	G4
Pelée (vol.)	G4

MONTSERRAT

Plymouth (cap.) 1,623	F3

NETHERLANDS ANTILLES

Aruba (isl.)	E4
Bonaire (isl.)	E4
Curaçao (isl.)	E4
Oranjestad 10,100	D4
Saba (isl.)	F3
Saint Eustatius (isl.)	F3
Saint Martin (Sint Maarten)
(isl.)	F3
Willemstad 95,000	E4

PUERTO RICO

Bayamón 184,854	G1
Caguas 87,218	G1
Culebra (isl.)	G1
Mayagüez 82,703	F1
Mona (passage)	E3
Ponce 161,260	F1
San Juan (cap.) 422,701	G1
Vieques (isl.)	H1

SAINT CHRISTOPHER-NEVIS

Basseterre (cap.) 14,725	F3
Charlestown (cap.)	
Nevis 1,326	F3

SAINT LUCIA

Vieux Fort⊙ 10,675	G4

SAINT VINCENT and THE GRENADINES

Bequia (isl.)	G4
Canouan (isl.)	G4
Georgetown 1,100	G4
Grenadines (isls.)	G4
Union (isl.)	G4

TRINIDAD and TOBAGO

Scarborough	G5
Tobago (isl.)	G5
Trinidad (isl.)	G5

TURKS and CAICOS ISLANDS

Caicos (isls.)	D2
Cockburn Harbour	D2
Grand Caicos (isl.)	D2
Grand Turk (isl.)	D2
Providenciales (isl.)	D2
Turks (isls.)	D2

VIRGIN ISLANDS (British)

Anegada (isl.)	H1
Jost Van Dyke (isl.)	G1
Road Town (cap.) 2,183	H1
Tortola (isl.)	H1
Virgin Gorda (isl.)	H1

VIRGIN ISLANDS (U.S.)

Charlotte Amalie (cap.) 11,670	H1
Christiansted 2,846	H2
Frederiksted 1,032	G2
Saint Croix (isl.)	H2
Saint John (isl.)	H1
Saint Thomas (isl.)	G1

WEST INDIES

Antilles, Greater (isls.)	B2
Antilles, Lesser (isls.)	E4
Aves (Bird) (isl.)	F4
Hispaniola (isl.)	D2
Leeward (isls.)	C3
Navassa (isl.)	C3
Windward (isls.)	G4

⊙Population of district.
•Population of municipality.

Topography

CUBA

PROVINCES

Camagüey 620,529	G2
Ciego de 'vila 301,348	F2
Cienfuegos 318,638	E2
Granma 725,519	H4
Guantánamo 459,690	K4
Habana 1,966,435	C1
Habana, La (Havana) 577,933	C1
Holguín 881,114	J3
Juventud (municipio especial) 48,432	C2
Las Tunas 423,619	H3
Matanzas 546,717	D1
Pinar del Río 616,978	A2
Sancti Spíritus 393,508	F2
Santiago de Cuba 897,090	H4
Villa Clara 760,417	E1

CITIES and TOWNS

Artemisa 31,234	B1
Banes 27,090	J3
Baracoa 20,926	K4
Bauta 21,147	C1
Bayamo 81,000	H4
Bejucal 15,446	C1
Buey Arriba 4,649	H4
Cabaiguán 21,657	F2
Cabañas 4,897	B1
Cabezas 5,262	D1
Cacocum 3,240	H3
Caibarién 27,030	F2
Caimanera 5,470	K4
Calabazar de Sagua 9,023	E1
Calicito	
Calimete 4,108	D1
Camagüey 216,000	G3
Camajuaní 15,945	E2
Campechuela 9,733	H4
Cananova	K3
Cañas	B1
Canasí 1,637	C1
Candelaria 7,911	B1
Caonao	
Cárdenas 55,209	D1
Cartagena 2,166	E2
Cascajal 3,530	E1
Cascorro	H3
Casilda	
Cauto del Embarcadero 949	H4
Cauto el Cristo 813	J3
Central Amancio Rodríguez 12,264	G3
Central América	J4
Central Bolivia 2,893	G2
Central Brasil 4,904	G2
Central Cándido	
Central Colombia 11,001	K3
Central Frank Pals 6,305	K3
Central Guatemala 5,584	J3
Central Haití 3,609	J3
Central Loynaz Echevarría 3,245	J3
Central Los Reynaldos 3,997	J4
Central Manuel Tames 5,964	K4
Central Niágara	
Céspedes 6,634	G2
Chambas 4,984	F2
Chaparra 8,428	H3
Cidra 3,567	D1
Ciego de 'vila 60,910	F2
Cienfuegos 88,000	E2
Colón 25,986	D1
Condado 33,115	E2
Consolación del Norte 4,681	B1
Consolación del Sur 15,126	B2
Contramaestre 22,943	J4
Corralillo 3,956	D1
Cortés	A2
Cruces 19,057	E2
Cuatro Compañeros	G3
Cueto 9,565	J3
Cumanayagua 10,695	E2
Daiquirí	J4
Delicias 10,562	H3
Dimas	A2
Dos Caminos 3,772	J4
Dos Ríos 1,786	J4
El Caney 3,921	J4
El Cobre 3,952	J4
El Pilar	
El Santo 2,473	E1
Encrucijada 6,690	E1
Esmeralda 7,888	G1
Esperanza 9,241	E2
Falla	F2
Florencia de San Pedro	F3
Florida 3,190	D1
Florida 32,679	G2
Fomento 12,923	F2
Fray Benito	J3
Gaspar 2,822	F2
Gibara 12,088	J3
Guacanamar	G3
Guáimaro 5,477	G3
Guamo	H3
Guanabacoa 69,706	C1
Guanajay 18,823	B1
Guane 8,343	A2
Guantánamo 145,000	K4
Guaro 3,086	J3
Guasimal 3,057	F2
Guayabal 3,703	G3
Guayos 6,753	F2
Güines 41,409	C1
Güira de Melena 19,851	C1
Guisa 8,980	H4
Hatuey	
Havana 1,966,435	C1
Herradura 3,762	B1
Holguín 148,000	J3
Ignacio Agramonte 1,487	G3
Imías 974	K4
Isabela de Sagua 3,721	D1
Jagua	E2
Jagüey Grande 8,721	D2
Jamaica 5,128	K4
Jaruco 9,988	C1
Jatibonico 9,807	F2
Jauco	K4
Jíbaro 1,263	F2
Jiguaní 10,752	H4
Jobabo 6,196	H3
Jovellanos 16,548	D1
Júcaro	F2
La Coloma 3,462	B2
La Gloria	G2
La Maya 8,494	J4
Lancret	D1
La Puerto	H3
La Rioja	H3
Limonar 4,365	D1
Los Arabos 4,506	E1
Los Arroyos	A2
Los Indios	B2
Los Negros	B2
Los Palacios 10,243	B1
Lugareño 4,396	G2
Mabay 6,176	H4
Maceo 2,652	J4
Magarabomba	G2
Maisí	K4
Majagua 4,178	F2
Manacas 5,914	E1
Manatí 7,814	H3
Manguito 2,739	D1
Manicaragua 10,671	E2
Mantua 4,131	A2
Mapos (Amazonas) 1,066	F2
Manzanillo 82,000	H4
Marianao 368,747	C1
Mariel 11,897	B1
Martí, Matanzas 7,572	D1
Matanzas 94,000	C1
Matún	D2
Máximo Gómez, Ciego de Ávila 5,116	F2
Máximo Gómez, Matanzas 4,970	D1
Mayajigua 4,425	F2
Mayarí 17,621	J3
Mayarí Arriba 2,302	J4
McKinley	B2
Media Luna 8,902	G4
Mendoza 2,914	E2
Meneses 4,768	F2
Minas 10,074	G2
Minas de Matahambre 9,902	A1
Moa 14,965	K3
Morón 28,981	F2
Nicaro 9,506	J3
Niquero 11,344	G4
Nueva Gerona 17,175	C2
Nuevitas 20,734	G2
Orozco 4,256	B1
Palma Soriano 41,188	J4
Palmira 10,877	E2
Palo Alto	F3
Pedro Betancourt 10,953	D1
Perico 10,548	D1
Pilón 7,296	H4
Pilotos	B1
Pinar del Río 83,000	B2
Placetas 32,261	E2
Presidio Modelo	C2
Primero Enero 8,658	F2
Puerto Esperanza 3,499	A1
Puerto Padre 16,539	H3
Puerto Tarafa	H3
Quiebra Hacha	B1
Ramón de las Yaguas	J4
Rancho Veloz 3,966	D1
Ranchuelo 12,992	E2
Regla 35,966	C1
Remates	A2
Remedios 13,121	E1
República Dominicana 2,540	F2
Río Cauto 8,788	H4
Río Seco	A2
Rodas 7,770	E2
Sábalo	A2
Sabana	K4
Sagua de Tánamo 9,552	K3
Sagua la Grande 35,809	E1
San Andrés 2,127	
San Antonio de los Baños 25,339	C1
San Cristóbal 15,674	B1
Sancti Spíritus 83,000	F2
San Diego de los Baños 1,430	B1
San Germán 12,362	J3
San José de las Lajas 24,927	C1
San José de los Ramos 1,726	D1
San Juan y Martínez 11,121	B2
San Luis, Pinar del Río	B2
San Luis, Santiago de Cuba 17,300	J4
San Miguel	H3
San Nicolás 10,957	C1
San Pedro	B2
San Ramón 2,774	H4
Santa Bárbara	B2
Santa Clara 143,000	E2
Santa Cruz del Norte 7,839	C1
Santa Cruz del Sur 10,783	G3
Santa Fe 3,925	B2
Santa Isabel de las Lajas 7,279	E2
Santa Lucía, Camagüey	H3
Santa Lucía, Holguín 3,734	J3
Santa Rita 6,358	H4
Santiago de las Vegas 29,325	C1
Santo Domingo 10,247	E1
Siboney	
Sola 2,436	G2
Sumidero 980	A2
Surgidero de Batabanó 11,533	C1
Tacajó 4,469	K3
Tánamo	
Torriente 1,759	
Trinidad 31,474	F2
Tunas de Zaza	
Unión de Reyes 7,044	D1
Varadero 9,072	
Vázquez 3,851	E2
Velasco, Ciego de vila	
Velasco, Holguín 5,618	
Venezuela 6,743	
Vertientes 13,953	
Victoria de las Tunas 60,000	H3
Viñales 2,049	B2
Vista Hermosa	
Yaguajay 7,091	
Yara 7,140	
Zaza del Medio 7,495	
Zulueta 5,425	

OTHER FEATURES

Abalos	B2
Ana María (gulf)	
Ancitas (cay)	
Barcos (cay)	
Batabanó (gulf)	
Birama (pt.)	
Broa (inlet)	
Buenavista (bay)	H3
Caballones (chan.)	
Camagüey (arch.)	
Cañada, La (mt.)	
Canarreos, Los (arch.)	
Cantiles (cay)	
Cárdenas (bay)	
Carraguao (pt.)	
Casilda (pt.)	

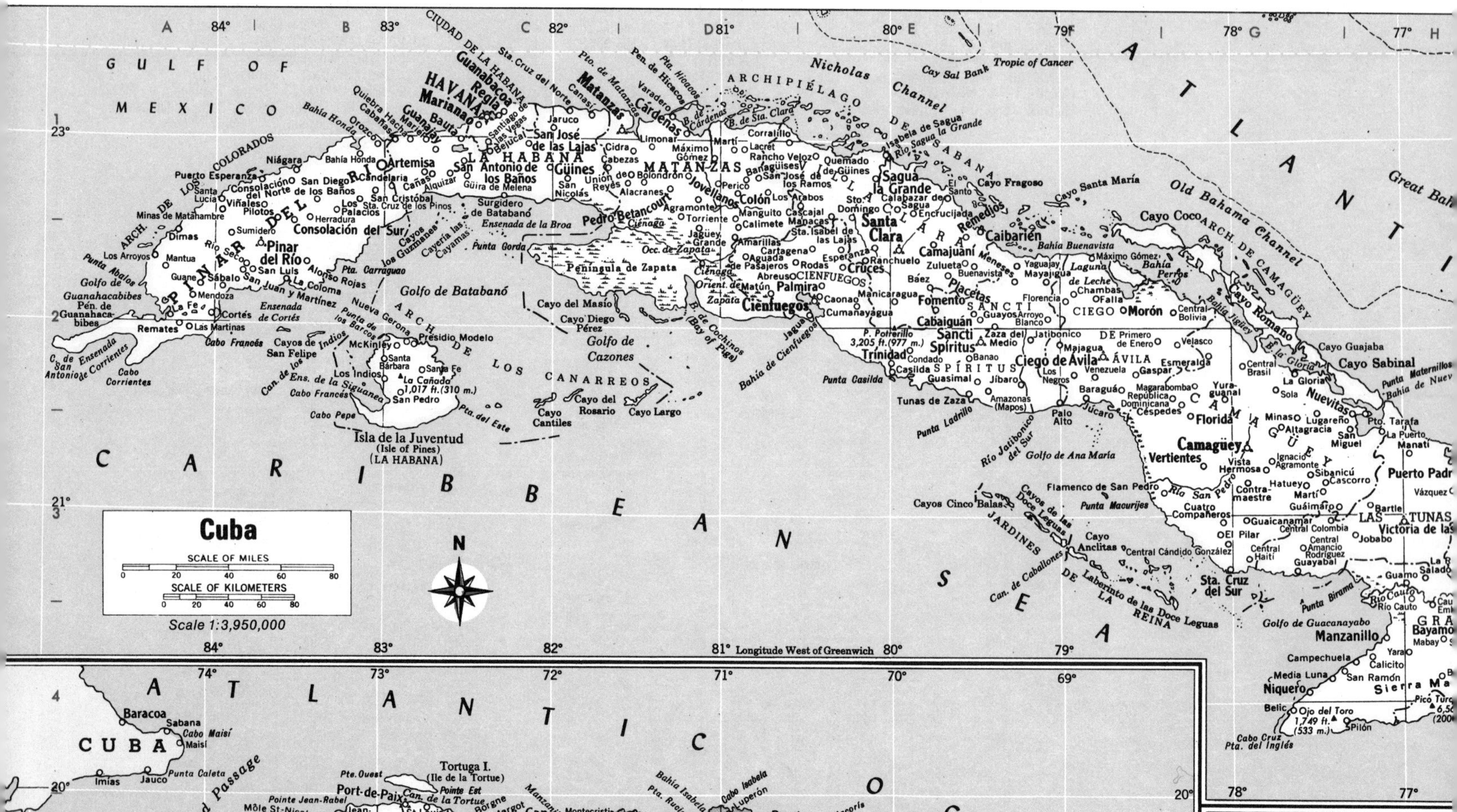

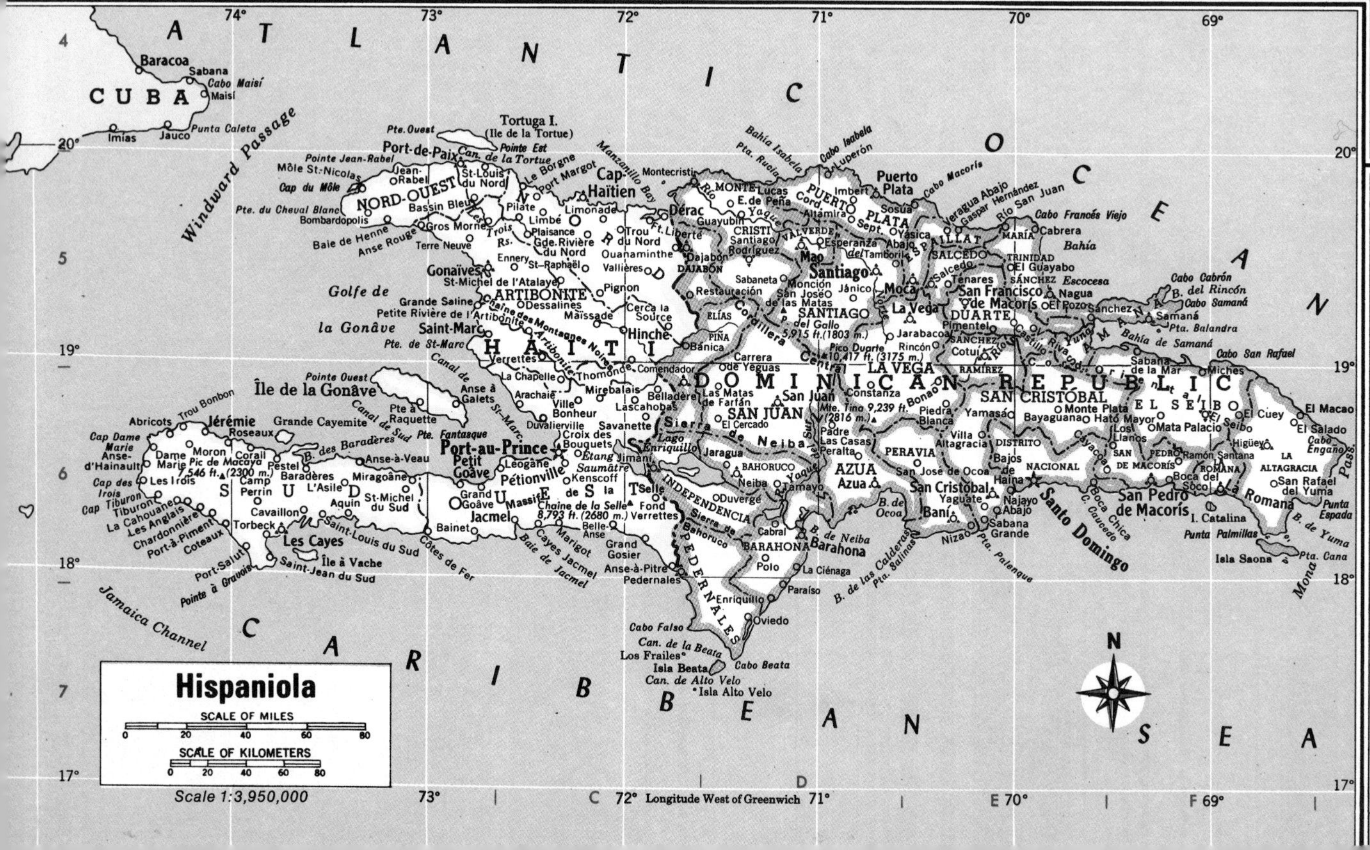

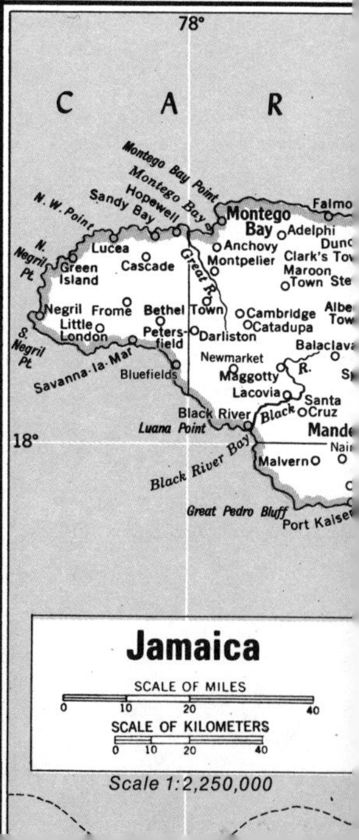

Cuba
SCALE OF MILES
0 20 40 60 80
SCALE OF KILOMETERS
0 20 40 60 80
Scale 1:3,950,000

Hispaniola
SCALE OF MILES
0 20 40
SCALE OF KILOMETERS
0 20 40
Scale 1:3,950,000

Jamaica
SCALE OF MILES
0 10 20 30
SCALE OF KILOMETERS
0 10 20 30
Scale 1:2,250,000

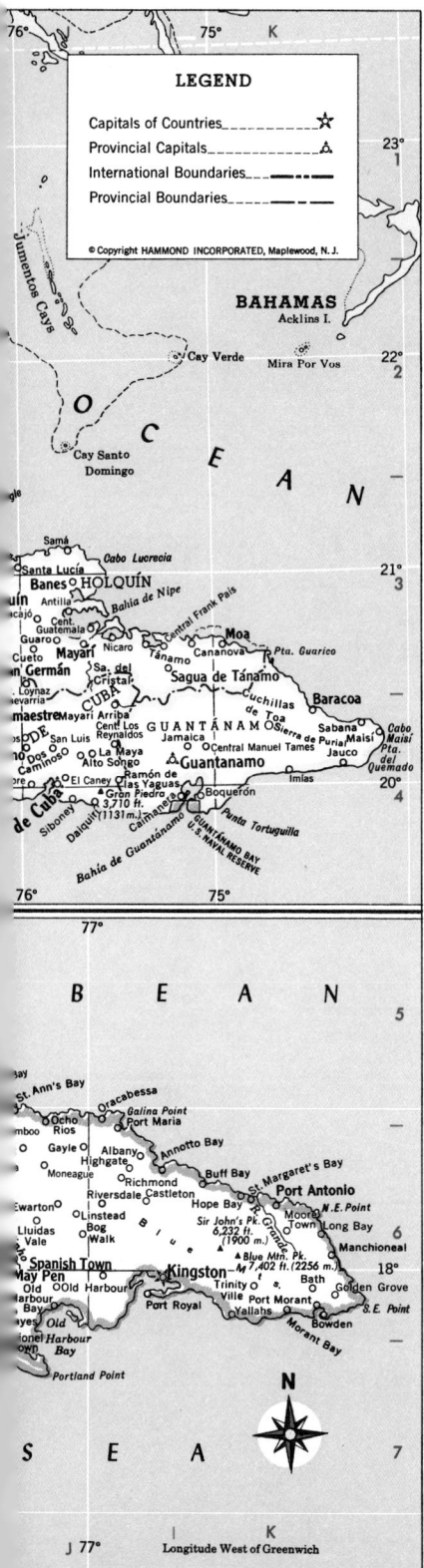

Cauto (riv.)	H3
Cayamas (cays)	C2
Cazones (gulf)	C2
Cienfuegos (bay)	D2
Cinco Balas (cays)	F3
Cochinos (bay)	D2
Coco (cay)	G1
Colorados, Los (arch.)	A1
Corrientes (cape)	A2
Corrientes (inlet)	A2
Cortés (inlet)	B2
Cristal, Sierra del (mts.)	G4
Cruz (cape)	G4
Diego Pérez (cay)	C2
Doce Leguas (cays)	F3
Este (pt.)	F1
Fragoso (cay)	F1
Francés (cape)	A2
Francés (cape)	B2
Gorda (pt.)	J3
Gorda (mt.)	J4
Gran Piedra (mt.)	J4
Guacanayabo (gulf)	G2
Guajaba (cay)	G2
Guanahacabibes (gulf)	A2
Guanahacabibes (pen.)	A2
Guantánamo (pt.)	J4
Guantánamo Bay U.S. Nav. Reserve	K4
Quemado (pt.)	K3
Guzmanes (cays)	B2
Icacos (pen.)	D1
Icacos (pt.)	D1
Jagua (bay)	B1
Jardines (chan.)	B2
Ingles (pt.)	B2
Jardines de la Reina (arch.)	F3
Jatibonico del Sur (riv.)	F2
Júguey (bay)	G2
Juventud, (Isla de la) (Pines) 30,103	B3
Laberinto de las Doce Leguas (cays)	F3
Ladrillo (pt.)	E3
Largo (pt.)	D2
Leche (lag.)	F2
Los Barcos (pt.)	B2
Los Canarreos (arch.)	C2
Los Colorados (arch.)	A1
Lucrecia (cape)	J3
Macurijes (pt.)	F3
Maestra, Sierra (mts.)	H4
Maisí (cape)	K4
Malagueta (bay)	H3
Mangle (pt.)	J3
Maslo (cape)	C2
Matanzas (bay)	D1
Maternillos (pt.)	H2
Mexico (gulf)	A1
Nicholas (chan.)	E1
Nipe (bay)	J3
Nuevitas (bay)	H2
Ojo del Toro (mt.)	G4
Old Bahama (chan.)	G1
Pepe (cape)	B3
Perros (bay)	G2
Pigs (Cochinos) (bay)	D2
Pines (Isla de la Juventud) (isl.)	B3
Potrerillo (peak)	E2
Purial, Sierra de (mts.)	J4
Quemado (pt.)	K4
Romano (cay)	K3
Rosario (cay)	C2
Sabana (arch.)	E1
Sabinal (pt.)	H2
Sagua la Grande (riv.)	E1
San Antonio (cape)	A2
San Felipe (cays)	B2
San Pedro (riv.)	G3
Santa Clara (bay)	D1
Santa María (pt.)	F1
Siguanea (bay)	B2
Tabacal (pt.)	H4
Toa, Cuchillas de (mts.)	K4
Tortuguilla (pt.)	K4

Turquino (peak)	H4
Zapata (pen.)	C2
Zapata Occidental (swamp)	D2
Zapata Oriental (swamp)	D2

DOMINICAN REPUBLIC

PROVINCES

Azua 86,850	D6
Bahoruco 67,025	D6
Barahona 111,115	D6
Dajabón 52,695	D5
Distrito Nacional 817,645	E6
Duarte 201,795	E5
El Seibo 132,480	F6
Espaillat 138,265	E5
Independencia 32,525	D6
La Altagracia 86,070	F6
La Estrelleta 54,495	C5
La Romana 56,980	F6
La Vega 293,730	D6
María Trinidad Sánchez 95,635	E5
Montecristi 69,605	D5
Pedernales 12,625	D7
Peravia 129,335	E6
Puerto Plata 189,490	D5
Salcedo 88,415	E5
Samaná 53,015	F5
Sánchez Ramírez 106,775	E5
San Cristóbal 323,535	E6
San Juan 190,905	D6
San Pedro de Macorís 105,405	F6
Santiago 387,255	D5
Santiago Rodríguez 47,490	D5
Valverde 75,250	D5

CITIES and TOWNS

Altamira 1,907	D5
Azua 13,880	D6
Bajos de Haina 11,180	E6
Baní 23,530	E6
Bánica 1,294	D5
Barahona 37,260	D6
Bayaguana 2,975	E6
Boca Chica	E6
Boca del Soco	F6
Bonao 22,020	E6
Cabral 5,549	D6
Cabrera 1,920	E5
Carrera de Yeguas	D6
Castillo 3,220	E5
Cayacoa	E5
Comendador 4,296	C6
Constanza 5,128	D6
Cotuí 7,653	E5
Dajabón 6,030	D5
Duvergé 7,793	D6
El Cercado 3,348	C6
El Cuey	F6
El Macao	F6
El Pozo	E6
El Salado	F6
El Seibo 9,101	F6
Enriquillo 4,071	D7
Esperanza 10,530	D5
Gaspar Hernández 2,182	E5
Guayubín 1,407	D5
Hato Mayor 10,135	F6
Higüey 17,995	F6
Imbert 4,440	D5
Jánico 1,110	D5
Jarabacoa 6,317	D5
Jaragua 4,904	D6
Jimaní 2,248	C6
La Ciénaga	D6
La Romana 36,720	F6
Las Matas de Farfán 8,001	C6
La Vega 31,060	E5
Los Llanos 1,840	F6
Lucas E. de Peña	D5
Luperón 2,046	D5
Mao 25,660	D5
Mata Palacio	E6
Miches 4,498	F6
Moca 24,195	D5
Monción 2,007	D5
Montecristi 8,312	D5
Monte Plata 3,672	E6

Nagua 13,740	E5
Najayo Abajo	E6
Neiba 9,785	D6
Nizao 3,007	E6
Oviedo 2,139	D7
Padre Las Casas 4,776	D6
Paraíso 3,660	D7
Pedernales 5,539	C7
Piedra Blanca	E6
Pimentel 5,823	E5
Polo	D6
Puerto Plata 32,105	D5
Ramón Santana 965	F6
Restauración 1,969	D5
Rincón	E5
Río San Juan 2,755	E5
Sabana de la Mar 6,849	F5
Sabana Grande 1,965	E6
Sabaneta 6,619	D5
Salcedo 8,919	E5
Samaná 4,541	F5
Sánchez 16,193	F5
San Cristóbal 26,930	E6
San Francisco de Macorís 43,620	E5
San José de las Matas 2,691	D5
San José de Ocoa 10,243	E6
San Juan 32,965	D6
San Pedro de Macorís 43,010	F6
San Rafael del Yuma 1,835	F6
Santiago 155,000	D5
Santo Domingo (cap.) 673,470	E6
Sosúa 3,521	E5
Tamayo 3,840	D6
Tamboril 4,299	D5
Tenares	E5
Valverde	D5
Veragua Abajo	E5
Villa Altagracia 11,900	E6
Villa Riva 2,162	E5
Yaguate 1,872	E6
Yamasá 2,701	E6
Yásica Abajo	E5

OTHER FEATURES

Alto Velo (chan.)	C7
Alto Velo (isl.)	D7
Bahoruco, Sierra de (mts.)	D6
Balandra (pt.)	F5
Beata (cape)	D7
Beata (chan.)	C7
Beata (isl.)	D7
Cabrón (cape)	F5
Calderas (bay)	D6
Cana (pt.)	F6
Catalina (isl.)	F6
Caucedo (cape)	E6
Central, Cordillera (range)	D5
Duarte (peak)	D5
Engaño (cape)	F6
Enriquillo (lake)	C6
Escocesa (bay)	E5
Española (pt.)	F6
Falso (cape)	C7
Frailes, Los (isl.)	C7
Francés Viejo (cape)	E5
Gallo (pt.)	D5
Isabela (bay)	D5
Isabela (pt.)	D5
Los Frailes (isl.)	C7
Macorís (cape)	E5
Manzanillo (bay)	C5
Mona (passage)	F6
Neiba (bay)	D6
Neiba, Sierra de (mts.)	D6
Noires (mts.)	C5
Ocoa (bay)	E6
Oriental, Cordillera (range)	F6
Palenque (pt.)	E6
Palmillas (pt.)	E6
Rincón (bay)	F5
Rucía (pt.)	D5
Salinas (pt.)	E6
Samaná (bay)	F5
San Rafael (cape)	F6
Saona (isl.)	F6
Septentrional, Cordillera (range)	D5
Tina (mt.)	D6

Yaque del Norte (riv.)	D5
Yaque del Sur (riv.)	D6
Yuma (bay)	F6
Yuna (riv.)	E5

HAITI

DEPARTMENTS

Artibonite 755,760	C5
Nord 699,886	C5
Nord-Ouest 216,504	B5
Ouest 1,669,691	C6
Sud 972,787	A6

CITIES and TOWNS

Abricots 1,226	A6
Anse à Galets	B6
Anse-à-Pitre 696	C6
Anse-à-Veau 1,253	B6
Anse-d'Hainault 3,680	A6
Anse Rouge 1,230	B5
Aquin 2,173	B6
Arcahaie 2,498	B5
Bainet 1,509	B6
Baradères 1,083	B6
Bassin Bleu 616	B5
Belladère 2,207	C6
Belle-Anse 1,985	C6
Bombardopolis 940	A5
Camp Perrin 1,091	A6
Cap-Haïtien 46,217	C5
Cavaillon 988	A6
Cayes Jacmel 712	C6
Cerca la Source 1,262	C6
Chardonnière 2,156	A6
Corail 1,733	A6
Coteaux 1,426	A6
Côtes de Fer 1,023	B6
Croix des Bouquets 3,958	C6
Dame Marie 4,038	A6
Dérac 761	C5
Dessalines 3,842	C5
Duvalierville 1,378	C5
Ennery 974	C5
Fort Liberté 2,982	C5
Gonaïves 29,261	B5
Grand Goâve 2,287	B6
Grand Gosier 359	C6
Grande Rivière du Nord 5,285	C5
Grande Saline 1,020	C5
Gros Morne 3,257	B5
Hinche 8,462	C5
Jacmel 11,391	C6
Jean-Rabel 2,019	B5
Jérémie 17,624	A6
La Cahouane 519	A6
La Chapelle 793	C5
Lascahobas 3,132	C6
L'Asile 585	B6
Le Borgne 2,273	C5
Léogâne 4,603	C6
Les Anglais 1,808	A6
Les Cayes 22,065	B6
Les Irois 2,024	A6
Limbé 6,502	C5
Limonade 1,793	C5
Maïssade 2,280	C5
Marigot 1,814	C6
Miragoâne 3,570	B6
Môle Saint Nicolas 771	B5
Moron 2,367	A6
Ouanaminthe 5,320	C5
Pestel 802	A6
Pétionville 35,257	C6
Petit-Goâve 8,779	B6
Petite Rivière de l'Artibonite 8,462	B5
Pignon 3,069	C5
Pilate 2,155	C5
Plaisance 1,859	C5
Pointe à Raquette	B6
Port-à-Piment 3,280	A6
Port-au-Prince (cap.) 306,053	C6
Port-de-Paix 13,913	B5
Port Margot 2,673	C5
Port-Salut 1,034	A6

Roseaux 689	A6
Saint-Jean du Sud 401	B6
Saint-Louis du Nord 5,642	B5
Saint-Louis du Sud 1,039	B6
Saint-Marc 17,263	B5
Saint-Michel de l'Atalaye 4,636	C5
Saint-Michel du Sud 621	A6
Saint-Raphaël 2,691	C5
Savanette 834	C6
Terre Neuve 776	B5
Thomonde 1,911	C5
Tiburon 1,494	A6
Torbeck 797	A6
Trou Bonbon 658	A6
Trou du Nord 5,367	C5
Vallières 400	C5
Verrettes 2,448	C5
Ville Bonheur 1,866	C6

OTHER FEATURES

Artibonite (riv.)	C5
Baradères (bay)	B6
Cheval Blanc (pt.)	A6
Dame Marie (cape)	A6
Est (pt.)	C4
Fantasque (pt.)	B6
Gonâve (gulf)	B5
Gonâve (isl.)	B6
Grande Cayemite (isl.)	B6
Gravois (pt.)	A7
Irois (cape)	A6
Jean-Rabel (pt.)	B5
Macaya (mt.)	A6
Manzanillo (bay)	C5
Môle (cape)	B5
Noires (mts.)	C5
Ouest (pt.)	B4
Ouest (pt.)	A6
Saint-Marc (bay)	C5
Saint-Marc (chan.)	B6
Saumâtre (lake)	C6
Selle (peak)	C6
Sud (chan.)	A6
Tiburon (cape)	A6
Tortue (isl.)	C5
Tortue (Tortuga) (isl.)	C4
Tortuga (isl.)	C4
Trois-Rivières (riv.)	B5
Vache (isl.)	B6
Windward (passage)	A5

JAMAICA

CITIES and TOWNS

Adelphi 1,649	H5
Albany	J6
Albert Town	H6
Alexandria 1,213	J6
Alley	J7
Alligator Pond	H6
Anchovy 2,558	H5
Annotto Bay	J6
Balaclava 1,553	H6
Bamboo 2,971	J6
Bath	K6
Bethel Town	H6
Black River 2,701	G6
Bluefields	G6
Bog Walk	J6
Bowden	K6
Browns Town 5,479	J6
Buff Bay	K6
Bull Savanna-Junction 5,110	H6
Cambridge 2,449	H6
Cascade	H6
Castleton	J6
Catadupa	H6
Chapelton	J6
Christiana	H6
Claremont 2,212	J6
Clark's Town	H6
Darliston	H6
Devon	J6
Discovery Bay 1,814	J5
Duncans	J6
Ewarton	J6
Falmouth 3,937	H5

Four Paths	J6
Frankfield	H6
Frome	G6
Gayle	J6
Golden Grove	K6
Green Island	G6
Hayes	J6
Highgate	J6
Hope Bay	K6
Hopewell	G5
Kingston (cap.) 106,791	K6
Kingston* 516,865	J7
Lacovia 2,478	H6
Linstead	J6
Lionel Town	J6
Little London	G6
Long Bay	K6
Lucea 5,819	G5
Maggotty 1,753	H6
Malvern 1,316	H6
Manchioneal	K6
Mandeville 14,421	H6
Maroon Town 2,717	H6
May Pen 26,074	J6
Moneague 1,963	J6
Montego Bay 43,521	H5
Montpelier	H5
Moore Town	K6
Morant Bay 7,465	K7
Nain 1,830	H6
Negril	G6
Newmarket 1,793	G6
Ocho Rios 5,851	J6
Old England	H6
Old Harbour	J6
Old Harbour Bay	J6
Oracabessa	J5
Petersfield	G6
Port Antonio 10,538	K6
Port Kaiser	H7
Port Maria 5,259	J6
Port Morant	K6
Port Rhoades	H5
Port Royal	J6
Porus	H6
Richmond	J6
Rio Bueno	J6
Riversdale	J6
Runaway Bay 1,116	J5
Saint Ann's Bay 7,101	J5
Saint Margaret's Bay	K6
Sandy Bay	G5
Santa Cruz 2,050	H6
Savanna-la-Mar 11,759	G6
Spaldings	H6
Spanish Town 40,731	J6
Spur Tree	H6
Stewart Town	H6
Trinity Ville	K6
Trout Hall	J6
Ulster Spring	H6
Williamsfield	H6
Yallahs	K6

OTHER FEATURES

Black (riv.)	H6
Black River (bay)	G6
Blue (mts.)	J6
Blue Mountain (peak)	K6
Galina (pt.)	J5
Grande (riv.)	K6
Great (riv.)	H5
Great Pedro Bluff (prom.)	H6
Long (bay)	H7
Luana (pt.)	G6
Minho (riv.)	J6
Montego (pt.)	G5
Montego Bay (bay)	G5
North East (pt.)	K6
North Negril (pt.)	G6
North West (pt.)	G5
Old Harbour (bay)	J6
Portland (pt.)	J7
Sir John's (peak)	K6
South East (pt.)	K6
South Negril (pt.)	G6

*City and suburbs.
●Population of municipality.
*City and suburbs.

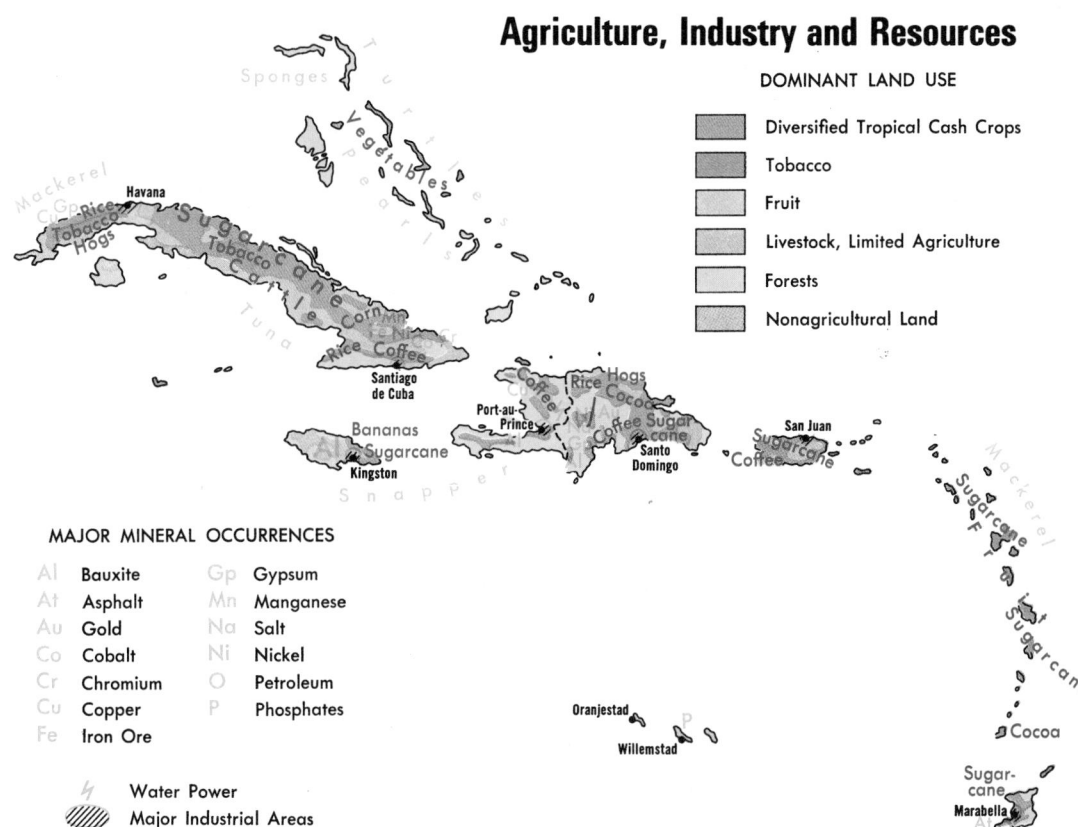

Agriculture, Industry and Resources

DOMINANT LAND USE

- Diversified Tropical Cash Crops
- Tobacco
- Fruit
- Livestock, Limited Agriculture
- Forests
- Nonagricultural Land

MAJOR MINERAL OCCURRENCES

Al	Bauxite	Gp	Gypsum
At	Asphalt	Mn	Manganese
Au	Gold	Na	Salt
Co	Cobalt	Ni	Nickel
Cr	Chromium	O	Petroleum
Cu	Copper	P	Phosphates
Fe	Iron Ore		

⚡ Water Power
▨ Major Industrial Areas

LEGEND

Capitals of Countries	☆
Provincial Capitals	△
International Boundaries	— · —
Provincial Boundaries	— · · —

© Copyright HAMMOND INCORPORATED, Maplewood, N.J.

PUERTO RICO

DISTRICTS

Aguadilla ... A1
Arecibo ... C1
Bayamón ... D1
Guayama ... D2
Humacao ... E2
Mayagüez ... B2
Ponce ... C2
San Juan ... D1

CITIES and TOWNS

Adjuntas 5,184 ... B2
Aguada 5,028 ... A1
Aguadilla 20,879 ... A1
Aguas Buenas 3,769 ... E2
Aibonito 9,369 ... D2
Añasco 5,340 ... A1
Ángeles• 2,802 ... B2
Arecibo 48,586 ... B1
Arroyo 8,486 ... E3
Arus ... C3
Bahomamey ... A1
Bajadero ... C1
Barceloneta 4,498 ... C1
Barranquitas 3,613 ... D2
Bayamón 184,854 ... D1
Boquerón• 1,427 ... A3
Cabo Rojo 10,254 ... A2
Caguas 87,218 ... E2
Caguas‡ 173,929 ... E2
Camuy 3,832 ... B1
Carolina 147,100 ... E1
Cataño 26,318 ... D1
Cayey 23,315 ... D2
Ceiba 4,964 ... F2
Central Aguirre ... D3
Ciales 3,590 ... C1
Cidra 6,065 ... D2
Coamo 12,834 ... D2
Comerío 5,751 ... D2
Coquí ... D3
Corozal 5,891 ... D1
Corral Viejo ... C2
Coto Laurel• 5,084 ... C2
Culebra 937 ... G1
Dewey (Culebra) 937 ... G1
Dorado 10,204 ... D1
Ensenada ... B3
Esperanza ... G2
Fajardo 26,845 ... F1
Guánica 9,627 ... B3
Guayama 21,044 ... E3
Guayanilla 6,191 ... B3
Guaynabo 65,091 ... D1
Gurabo 7,646 ... E2
Hatillo 5,039 ... B1
Hato Rey ... E1
Hormigüeros 11,991 ... A2
Humacao 19,135 ... E2
Isabela 12,097 ... A1
Isabel Segunda 2,322 ... G2
Jayuya 3,577 ... C2
Jobos ... D3
Juana Díaz 10,496 ... C2
Juncos 7,898 ... E2
Lajas 4,267 ... A2
Lares 5,178 ... B2
Las Marías 801 ... B2
Las Piedras 4,878 ... E2
Levittown ... D1
Loíza 3,942 ... E1
Loíza Aldea ... E1
Luquillo 4,536 ... F1
Manatí 17,254 ... C1
Maricao 1,403 ... B2
Maunabo 2,992 ... E3
Mayagüez 82,703 ... A2
Mayagüez‡ 132,814 ... A2
Moca 3,890 ... A1
Morovis 2,636 ... D1
Naguabo 4,140 ... F2
Naranjito 2,845 ... D1
Orocovis 1,257 ... C2
Palmer ... F1
Palo Seco ... D1
Parguera ... A3
Patillas 3,148 ... E2
Peñuelas 3,471 ... B2
Playa de Fajardo ... F1
Playa de Humacao ... F2
Ponce 161,260 ... C3
Ponce‡ 8,252,420 ... C3
Puerto Nuevo ... D1
Puerto Real (Playa de Fajardo) ... F1
Punta Santiago (Playa de Humacao)• 1,912 ... F2
Quebradillas 3,787 ... B1
Rincón 1,702 ... A1
Río Blanco ... F2
Río Grande 12,068 ... E1
Río Piedras ... E1
Rosario ... A2
Sabana Grande 7,368 ... B2
Sabana Seca ... D1
Salinas 6,240 ... D3
San Antonio ... A1
San Germán 13,093 ... A2
San Juan (cap.) 422,701 ... E1
San Juan‡ 1,083,664 ... E1
San Lorenzo 8,886 ... E2
San Sebastián 10,792 ... B1
Santa Isabel 6,965 ... C3
Santurce ... E1
Tallaboa ... B3
Toa Alta 4,419 ... D1
Toa Baja 1,979 ... D1
Trujillo Alto 41,097 ... E1
Utuado 11,049 ... B2
Vega Alta 10,554 ... D1
Vega Baja 18,020 ... D1
Vieques (Isabel Segunda) 2,322 ... G2
Villalba 3,468 ... C2
Yabucoa 6,782 ... E2
Yauco 14,598 ... B2

OTHER FEATURES

Aguadilla (bay) ... A1
Algarrobo (pt.) ... A2
Añasco (bay) ... A1
Arenas (pt.) ... F2
Bauta (riv.) ... C2
Bayamón (riv.) ... D1
Boquerón (bay) ... A3
Borinquen (pt.) ... A1
Cabullones (pt.) ... C3
Caja de Muertos (isl.) ... C3
Camuy (riv.) ... B1
Candelero (pt.) ... F2
Canóvanas (riv.) ... E1
Caonillas (lake) ... C2
Carite (lake) ... E2
Carraízo (lake) ... E1
Cayey, Sierra de (mts.) ... D2
Central, Cordillera (range) ... C2
Cerro Gordo (pt.) ... D1
Coamo (res.) ... D3
Coamo (riv.) ... D3
Culebra (isl.) ... G1
Culebrinas (riv.) ... A1
Culebrita (isl.) ... G2
El Toro (mt.) ... F2
El Yunque (mt.) ... F1
Este (pt.) ... G2
Fajardo (riv.) ... F1
Figuras (pt.) ... E3
Fosforescente (bay) ... A3
Grande de Añasco (riv.) ... B2
Grande de Arecibo (riv.) ... C1
Grande de Loíza (riv.) ... E1
Grande de Manatí (riv.) ... C1
Guajataca (lake) ... B1
Guanajibo (pt.) ... A2
Guanajibo (riv.) ... A2
Guánica (lake) ... B3
Guaniquilla (pt.) ... A2
Guayabal (lake) ... C2
Guayanés (pt.) ... F2
Guayanés (riv.) ... E2
Guayanilla (bay) ... B3
Guayo (lake) ... B2
Guilarte (mt.) ... B2
Honda (bay) ... F2
Humacao (riv.) ... E2
Jacaguas (riv.) ... C2
Jaicoa, Cordillera (mts.) ... B1
Jiguero (pt.) ... A1
Jobos (bay) ... D3
La Bandera (pt.) ... F1
Lima (pt.) ... F2
Lobo (cay) ... G1
Luquillo, Sierra de (mts.) ... E2
Manglillo (pt.) ... B3
Mayagüez (bay) ... A2
Miquillo (pt.) ... F1
Molinos (pt.) ... G1
Mona (passage) ... A2
Negra (pt.) ... G2
Nigua (riv.) ... D2
Ola Grande (pt.) ... D3
Palmas Altas (pt.) ... C1
Patillas (lake) ... E2
Peñón (pt.) ... B1
Petrona (pt.) ... D3
Pirata (mt.) ... F2
Plata (riv.) ... D2
Puerca (pt.) ... F2
Puerto Medio Mundo (bay) ... F2
Puerto Nuevo (pt.) ... C1
Punta, Cerro de (mt.) ... C2
Ramey A.F.B. ... A1
Rincón (bay) ... D3
Rojo (cape) ... A3
Roosevelt Road Naval Res. ... F2
Salinas (pt.) ... D1
San José (lag.) ... E1
San Juan, Cabezas de (prom.) ... F1
San Juan Nat'l Hist. Site ... D1
Sardina (pt.) ... A1
Soldado (pt.) ... G2
Sucia (bay) ... A3
Tanamá (riv.) ... B1
Toro, El (mt.) ... F2
Torrecilla (lag.) ... E1
Tortuguero (lag.) ... D1
Tuna (pt.) ... E3
Vacía Talega (pt.) ... E1
Viento (pt.) ... E3
Vieques (isl.) ... G2
Vieques (passage) ... F2
Vieques (sound) ... G2
Yagüez (riv.) ... A2
Yauco (lake) ... B2
Yeguas (pt.) ... F3

ANTIGUA

Total Population, 72,000

CITIES and TOWNS

All Saints 1,796 ... E11
Cedar Grove 1,460 ... E11
Falmouth 1,134 ... E11
Freetown 1,250 ... E11
Jennings 1,370 ... D11
Johnsons Point 725 ... D11
Liberta 2,394 ... E11
Old Road 1,244 ... D11
Parham 1,570 ... E11
Saint John's (cap.) 21,814 ... E11

OTHER FEATURES

Antigua (isl.) ... E11
Boggy (peak) ... D11
Boon (pt.) ... E11
Green (isl.) ... E11
Guiana (isl.) ... E11
Long (isl.) ... E11
Saint John's (harb.) ... C11
Standfast (pt.) ... E11
Willoughby (bay) ... E11

BARBADOS

CITIES and TOWNS

Bathsheba ... B8
Belleplaine ... B8
Bridgetown (cap.) 8,868 ... B9
Carlton ... B8
Cave Hill ... B9
Checker Hall ... B8
Codrington ... B8
Crab Hill ... B8
Crane ... C9
Drax Hall ... B8
Ellerton ... B9
Greenland ... B8
Holetown ... B8
Kendal ... B8
Lodge Hill ... B8
Marchfield ... B9
Mount Standfast ... B8
Oistins ... B9
Portland ... B8
Rose Hill ... B8
Rouen ... B9
Saint Lawrence ... B9
Saint Martins ... C9
Scarboro ... B9
Seawell ... B9
Six Mens ... B8
Speightstown ... B8
Spring Hall ... B8
Welchman Hall ... B8

OTHER FEATURES

Carlisle (bay) ... B9
Hillaby (mt.) ... B8
Long (bay) ... B9
North (pt.) ... B8
Oistins (bay) ... B9
Pelican (isl.) ... B9
Ragged (pt.) ... C8
Sam Lord's Castle ... C9
South (pt.) ... B9

DOMINICA

CITIES and TOWNS

Barroui 1,480 ... E6
Castle Bruce 1,975 ... F6
Coulihaut 1,735 ... E6
Delice ... F7
Grand Bay 3,152 ... F7
Laudat 366 ... E6
Mahout 2,095 ... E6
Marigot 3,183 ... F6
Petit Soufrière ... F6
Portsmouth 2,329 ... E5
Rosalie ... F6
Roseau (cap.) 9,968 ... E7
Roseau* 16,035 ... E7
Saint Joseph 2,643 ... E6
Salybia ... F6
Soufrière ... E7
Vieille Case ... E5
Wesley 2,002 ... F5

OTHER FEATURES

Capuchin (cape) ... E5
Carib Reserve ... F6
Clyde (riv.) ... F6
Crumpton (pt.) ... F5
Diablotin, Morne (mt.) ... E6
Dominica (passage) ... E5
Douglas (bay) ... E5
Grand (bay) ... F7
Jaquet (pt.) ... E5
Layou (riv.) ... E6
Martinique (passage) ... E7
Micotrin (mt.) ... F6
Pagoua (bay) ... F6
Prince Rupert (bay) ... E5
Roseau (riv.) ... E7
Scotts (head) ... E7
Soufrière (bay) ... E7
Trois Pitons, Morne (mt.) ... E6

GRENADA

CITIES and TOWNS

Crochu ... D8
Gouyave 2,498 ... C8
Grand Anse ... C9
Grand Roy ... C8
Grenville 1,723 ... D8
Hermitage ... D8
La Taste ... D8
Marquis ... D8
Mount Tivoli ... D8
Providence ... D9
Saint George's (cap.) 6,313 ... C9
Saint George's* 29,860 ... C9
Sauteurs 6,055 ... D8
Union ... D8
Victoria 1,673 ... D8
Woburn ... C9
Woodford ... C8

OTHER FEATURES

Bedford (pt.) ... D8
David (pt.) ... D8
Great Bacolet (pt.) ... D8
Green (isl.) ... D8
Grenville (bay) ... D8
Gros (pt.) ... C8
Halifax (harb.) ... C8
Irvin's (bay) ... D8
Les Tantes (isls.) ... D7
Molinière (pt.) ... C8
Prickly (pt.) ... C9
Ronde (isl.) ... D7
Saint Catherine (mt.) ... D8
Saline (pt.) ... C9
Sinai (mt.) ... D8
Telescope (pt.) ... D8

GUADELOUPE

Total Population, 319,000

CITIES and TOWNS

Anse-Bertrand 2,236 ... A5
Baie-Mahault 2,576 ... A6
Baillif 2,214 ... A7
Bananier ... A7
Basse-Terre (cap.) 15,206 ... A7
Bouillante 1,882 ... A6
Bourg-des-Saintes 1,039 ... A7
Capesterre 6,857 ... A7
Capesterre, Marie-Galante 931 ... B7
Deshaies 736 ... A6
Ferry ... A6
Gosier 5,111 ... B6
Gourbeyre 2,822 ... A7
Goyave 1,301 ... A6
Grand-Bourg 3,332 ... B7
Grippon ... B6
Lamentin 1,849 ... A6
Les Abymes 10,202 ... B6
Morne-à-l'Eau 9,384 ... A6
Moule 8,636 ... B6
Petit-Bourg 3,631 ... A6
Petit-Canal 1,874 ... A6
Pigeon ... A6
Pointe-à-Pitre 23,750 ... B6
Pointe-Noire 2,128 ... A6
Port-Louis 5,069 ... B5
Saint-Claude 3,858 ... A7
Sainte-Anne 3,660 ... B6
Sainte-Marguerite ... B6
Sainte-Marie ... A6
Sainte-Rose 3,312 ... A6
Saint-François 3,151 ... B6
Saint-Louis 1,378 ... B7
Trois-Rivières 1,669 ... A7
Vieux-Fort 1,120 ... B7
Vieux-Habitants 1,927 ... A7

OTHER FEATURES

Allègre (pt.) ... A6
Antigues (pt.) ... A5
Basse-Terre (isl.) ... A6
Châteaux (pt.) ... B6
Constant, Morne (hill) ... B7
Désirade, La (isl.) ... B6
Fajou (isl.) ... A6
Grand Cul-de-Sac Marin (bay) ... A6
Grande-Terre ... B6
Grande Vigie ... B5
Grand-Îlet (isl.) ... A7
Guadeloupe (isl.) ... B6
Guadeloupe (passage) ... A5
Guadeloupe Nat'l Park ... A6
Kahouanne (isl.) ... A6
Marie-Galante (isl.) ... B7
Nord (pt.) ... B7
Nord-Est (bay) ... B6
Petit Cul-de-Sac Marin (bay) ... A6
Petite-Terre (isls.) ... B6
Saintes (chan.) ... A7
Saintes (isls.) ... A7
Salée (riv.) ... A6
Sans Toucher (mt.) ... A6
Soufrière (mt.) ... A7
Terre-de-Bas (isl.) ... A7
Terre-de-Haut (isl.) ... A7
Vieux-Fort (pt.) ... A7

MARTINIQUE

Total Population, 308,000

CITIES and TOWNS

Ajoupa-Bouillon 1,515 ... C5
Basse-Pointe 2,329 ... C5
Bellefontaine 1,240 ... C6
Case-Pilote 1,609 ... C6
Ducos 1,809 ... D6
Fond-Lahaye ... C6
Fond-Saint-Denis 931 ... C6
Fort-de-France (cap.) 96,815 ... C6
Fort-Desaix ... D6
Grande' Rivière 1,219 ... C5
Gros-Morne 1,326 ... D6
La Trinité 4,230 ... D6
Le Carbet 2,446 ... C6
Le Diamant 598 ... D7
Le François 3,288 ... D6
Le Lamentin 7,198 ... D6
Le Lorrain 1,808 ... D6
Le Marin 2,725 ... D7
Le Morne-Rouge 3,036 ... C5
Le Morne-Vert 413 ... C6
Le Prêcheur 1,710 ... C5
Le Robert 2,377 ... D6
Le Saint-Esprit 2,842 ... D6
Les Anse-d' Arlets 794 ... C7
Les Trois-Îlets 1,302 ... D6
Le Vauclin 3,534 ... D6
Macouba 1,113 ... C5
Marigot 1,816 ... D5
Rivière-Pilote 1,653 ... D7
Rivière-Salée 1,837 ... D7
Sainte-Anne 957 ... D7
Sainte-Luce 1,299 ... D7
Sainte-Marie 3,751 ... D5
Saint-Joseph 2,040 ... D6
Saint-Pierre 5,358 ... C6
Schoelcher 13,792 ... C6
Vert-Pré ... D6

OTHER FEATURES

Cabet, Pitons du (mt.) ... C6
Cabrits (isl.) ... D7
Caravelle (pen.) ... D6
Cul-de-Sac du Marin (bay) ... D7
Diable (pt.) ... D5
Diamant, Rocher du (isl.) ... C7
Ferré (cape) ... E7
Fort-de-France (bay) ... C6
Galion (bay) ... D6
Lézarde (riv.) ... D6
Long (isl.) ... D6
Lorrain (riv.) ... D5
Martinique (passage) ... C5
Pelée (vol.) ... C5
Pilote (riv.) ... D7
Ramièrs (isl.) ... C6
Ramville (isl.) ... D6
Robert (harb.) ... D6
Rose (pt.) ... D6
Saint-Martin (cape) ... C5
Saint-Pierre (bay) ... C6
Salines (pt.) ... D7
Salomon (pt.) ... C7
Vauclin (mt.) ... D6

NETHERLANDS ANTILLES

CITIES and TOWNS

Aresji ... D9
Ascension ... F8
Bacuna ... E8
Balashi ... E10
Boven Bolivia ... E8
Bubali ... D10
Bushiribana ... E10
Dokterstuin ... F8
Druif ... D10
Emmastad ... F9
Entrejo ... E8
Fontein ... E8
Fuik ... G9
Groot Sint Joris ... G9
Hato ... G8
Kralendijk (cap.), Bonaire 2,500 ... E8
Lago ... E10
Lagoen ... F8
Montanja di Reij ... G9
New Port ... G9
Noord di Salinja ... E8
Onima ... E8
Oranjestad (cap.), Aruba 10,100 ... D10
Otrabanda ... F9
Patrick ... F8
Rincon ... E8
Rooi⊙ 1,989 ... E8
Santa Barbara ... G9
Santa Catharina ... G9
Savaneta ... E10
Savonet ... F8
Sint Anna ... D10
Sint Jan ... D8
Sint Kruis ... F8
Sint Martha ... F8
Sint Michiel ... F9
Sint Nicolaas ... E10
Sint Willebrordus ... F8
Terra Corra ... E8
Westpunt, Aruba ... D10
Westpunt, Curaçao ... F8
Willemstad (cap.) 95,000 ... F9
Willemstad* 130,000 ... F9

OTHER FEATURES

Aruba (isl.) ... E9
Basora (pt.) ... E10
Bonaire (isl.) ... E9
Bullen (bay) ... F8
Caracas (bay) ... G9
Curaçao (isl.) ... G7
Goto (lake) ... D8
Jamanota (mt.) ... E10
Kanon (pt.) ... G9
Klein Bonaire (isl.) ... E8
Kudarebe (pt.) ... D9
Lac (bay) ... D9
Lacre (pt.) ... E9
Malmok (mt.) ... E8
Noord (pt.) ... D8
Noord (pt.) ... F8
Paarden (bay) ... D10
Palm (beach) ... D10
Pekelmeer (lake) ... E9
Piscadera (bay) ... F9
Schottegat (bay) ... G9
Sint Anna (bay) ... F9
Sint Christoffel (mt.) ... F8
Sint Joris (bay) ... G9
Slag (bay) ... D8
Vierkant (pt.) ... E8

SAINT CHRISTOPHER, and NEVIS

Total Population, 44,404

CITIES and TOWNS

Basseterre (cap.) 14,725 ... C10
Cayon ... C10
Charlestown 1,326 ... C11
Cotton Ground 471 ... C11
Dieppe Bay ... C10
Frigate ... C10
Gingerland ... D11
Golden Rock ... C10
Newcastle ... D11
Old Road Town ... C10
Sadlers Village ... C10
Sandy Point 862 ... C10
Tabernacle ... C10

OTHER FEATURES

Brimstone (hill) ... C10
Dogwood (pt.) ... D11
Fort (pt.) ... C11
Great Salt (pond) ... D10
Heldens (pt.) ... C10
Horse Shoe (pt.) ... C11
Misery (mt.) ... C10
Monkey (hill) ... C10
Muddy (pt.) ... C10
Narrows, The (str.) ... D11
Nevis (isl.) ... D11
Nevis (peak) ... D11
North Friars (bay) ... D10
Palmetto (pt.) ... C10
Pinney's (beach) ... D11
Saint Christopher (isl.) ... D10
Saint Kitts (Saint Christopher) (isl.) ... D10
South Friars (bay) ... C10

SAINT LUCIA

CITIES and TOWNS

Anse la Raye⊙ 5,007 ... F6
Canaries⊙ 2,075 ... G6
Castries (cap.)⊙ 42,770 ... G6
Choc ... G5
Choiseul⊙ 6,382 ... F7
Dauphin ... G5
Dennery⊙ 9,654 ... G6
Gros Islet⊙ 10,329 ... G5
Laborie⊙ 6,944 ... G7
Marigot ... G6
Marquis ... G6
Micoud⊙ 12,264 ... G6
Praslin ... G6
Soufrière⊙ 7,456 ... F6
Vieux Fort⊙ 10,675 ... G7

OTHER FEATURES

Beaumont (pt.) ... F6
Canaries, Piton (mt.) ... G6
Cannelles (pt.) ... G7
Cannelles (riv.) ... G6
Cap (pt.) ... G5
Choc (bay) ... G5
Fond d'Or (bay) ... G6
Gimie (mt.) ... G6
Grand Caille (pt.) ... F6
Grand Cul de Sac (riv.) ... G6
Gros Islet (bay) ... G5
Gros Piton (mt.) ... G6
La Sorcière (mt.) ... G6
Maria (isls.) ... G7
Ministre (pt.) ... G7
Moule à Chique (cape) ... G7
Petit Piton (mt.) ... G6
Pigeon (isl.) ... G5
Port Castries (harb.) ... G6
Port Praslin (bay) ... G6
Roseau (riv.) ... G6
Saint Lucia (chan.) ... G5
Saint Vincent (chan.) ... G7
Savannes (bay) ... G7
Sorcière, La (mt.) ... G6
Soufrière (bay) ... F6
Vierge (pt.) ... G6
Vieux Fort (riv.) ... G6

SAINT VINCENT & THE GRENADINES

CITIES and TOWNS

Barrouallie 1,298 ... A9
Calliaqua 627 ... A9
Camden Park ... A9
Chateaubelair 237 ... A8
Colonarie ... A9
Georgetown 1,100 ... A8
Kingstown (cap.) 17,117 ... A9
Kingstown* 23,330 ... A9
Layou 1,147 ... A9
Orange Hill ... A8
Wallibu ... A8

OTHER FEATURES

Colonarie (pt.) ... A9
Cumberland (bay) ... A8
Dark (head) ... A8
De Volet (pt.) ... A8
Espagnol (pt.) ... A8
Greathead (bay) ... A9
Kingstown (bay) ... A9
Owia (bay) ... A8
Porter (pt.) ... A8
Richmond (peak) ... A8
Saint Andrew (mt.) ... A9
Saint Vincent (passage) ... A8
Soufrière (mt.) ... A8
Yambou (head) ... A9

TRINIDAD and TOBAGO

CITIES and TOWNS

Arima 11,636 ... B10
Arouca ... B10
Basse Terre ... B11
Biche ... B10
Blanchisseuse ... B10
California ... A11
Carapichaima ... B10
Caroni ... B10
Cedros ... A11
Chaguanas ... B10
Chaguaramas ... A10
Couva ... B10
Cunapo ... B10
Débé ... B11
Ecclesville ... B11
Flanagin Town ... B10
Fullarton ... A11
Fyzabad ... A11
Gran Couva ... B11
Grande Rivière ... B10
Guaico ... B10
Guayaguayare ... B11
La Brea ... A11
La Lune ... B11
Marabella ... A11
Matelot ... B10
Matura ... B10
Mayaro ... B11
Moruga ... B11
Mucurapo ... A10
Nestor ... B10
Palo Seco ... A11
Peñal ... B11
Piarco ... B10
Point Fortin ... A11
Port-of-Spain (cap.) 62,680 ... A10
Princes Town ... B11
Redhead ... B10
Rio Claro ... B11
Sadhoowa ... B11
Saint Joseph ... B10
Saint Joseph ... B11
San Fernando 36,870 ... A11
San Francique ... A11
Sangre Grande 8,286 ... B10
San Juan ... A10
Sans Souci ... B10
Siparia 6,154 ... B11
Tabaquite ... B11
Tableland ... B11
Tacarigua ... B10
Talparo ... B10
Toco ... B10
Tunapuna ... B10
Upper Manzanilla ... B10
Valencia ... B10
Waterloo ... A10

OTHER FEATURES

Aripo, El Cerro del (mt.) ... B10
Boca Grande (passage) ... A10
Casa Cruz (cape) ... B11
Chacachacare (isl.) ... A10
Chupara (pt.) ... B10
Cocos (bay) ... B10
Dragons Mouth (str.) ... A10
El Tucuche (mt.) ... B10
Erin (bay) ... A11
Erin (pt.) ... A11
Galeota (pt.) ... B11
Galera (pt.) ... C10
Guapo (bay) ... A11
Guatuaro (pt.) ... B11
Icacos (pt.) ... A11
Maracas (bay) ...
Matura (bay) ... B10
Mayaro (bay) ... B11
Monos (isl.) ... A10
Nariva (swamp) ... B10
Oropuche (riv.) ... B10
Ortoire (riv.) ... B11
Paria (gulf) ... A11
Pitch (lake) ... A11
Serpents Mouth (passage) ... A11
Tamana (mt.) ... B10
Trinidad (isl.) ... A9

VIRGIN ISLANDS (Br.)

CITIES and TOWNS

Road Town (cap.) 2,183 ... D
West End ... C

OTHER FEATURES

Flanagan (passage) ... D
Frenchman (cay) ... C
Great Thatch (isl.) ... C
Great Tobago (isl.) ... B
Jost Van Dyke (isl.) ... C
Little Tobago (isl.) ... B
Narrows, The (str.) ... C
Norman (isl.) ... D4
Peter (isl.) ... D
Road (bay) ... D
Sage (mt.) ... D
Sir Francis Drake (chan.) ... D
Tortola (isl.) ... D

VIRGIN ISLANDS (U.S.)

CITIES and TOWNS

Bethlehem ... E
Canebay ... E
Charlotte Amalie (cap.) 11,670 ... B
Christiansted 2,846 ... F
Cruz Bay 1,930 ... C
Diamond ... F
Eastend ... D
Emmaus ... C
Fredensdal ... F
Frederiksted 1,032 ... E
Grove Place ... E
Kingshill ... F
Longford ... F
Negro Bay ... E

OTHER FEATURES

Altona (lag.) ... F
Annaly (bay) ... E
Baron Bluff (prom.) ... E
Bordeaux (mt.) ... C
Brass (isls.) ... A
Buck (isl.) ... G
Buck Island (chan.) ... F
Buck Island Reef Nat'l Mon. ... G
Butler (bay) ... E
Caneel (bay) ... E
Capella (isls.) ... E
Christiansted Nat'l Hist. Site ... F
Coral (bay) ... C
Crown (mt.) ... A
Dutch Cap (cay) ... A
Eagle (mt.) ... E
East (pt.) ... G
Flanagan (passage) ... D
Flat (cays) ... A
Grass (pt.) ... G
Great (pond) ...
Great Pond (bay) ...
Green (cay) ...
Hams Bluff (prom.) ... E
Hans Lollik (isls.) ... E
Hassel (isl.) ... E
Jersey (bay) ... E
Krause (chan.) ...
Leeward (passage) ... E
Long (pt.) ... E
Long (pt.) ...
Lovango (cay) ... C
Magens (bay) ... E
Maho (bay) ... C
Narrows, The (str.) ... C
Nulliberg (mt.) ... E
Perseverance (bay) ... A
Picara (pt.) ... E
Pillsbury (sound) ...
Privateer (pt.) ... D
Pull (pt.) ...
Ram (head) ... C
Red (pt.) ...
Reef (bay) ...
Saba (isl.) ...
Saint Croix (isl.) ... C
Saint James (isls.) ... E
Saint John (isl.) ... C
Saint Thomas (harb.) ... E
Saint Thomas (isl.) ... A
Salt (cay) ...
Salt (riv.) ...
Salt River (bay) ...
Sandy (pt.) ...
Savana (isl.) ...
Southwest (cape) ...
Tague (bay) ...
Thatch (cay) ...
Turner Hole (bay) ... C
U.S. Nav. Air Sta. ...
Vagthus (pt.) ...
Virgin (str.) ...
Virgin Isls. Nat'l Park ...
Water (isl.) ...
Westend Saltpond (lag.) ...

⊙Population of district.
• Population of municipality.
*City and suburbs.
‡ Population of metropolitan area.

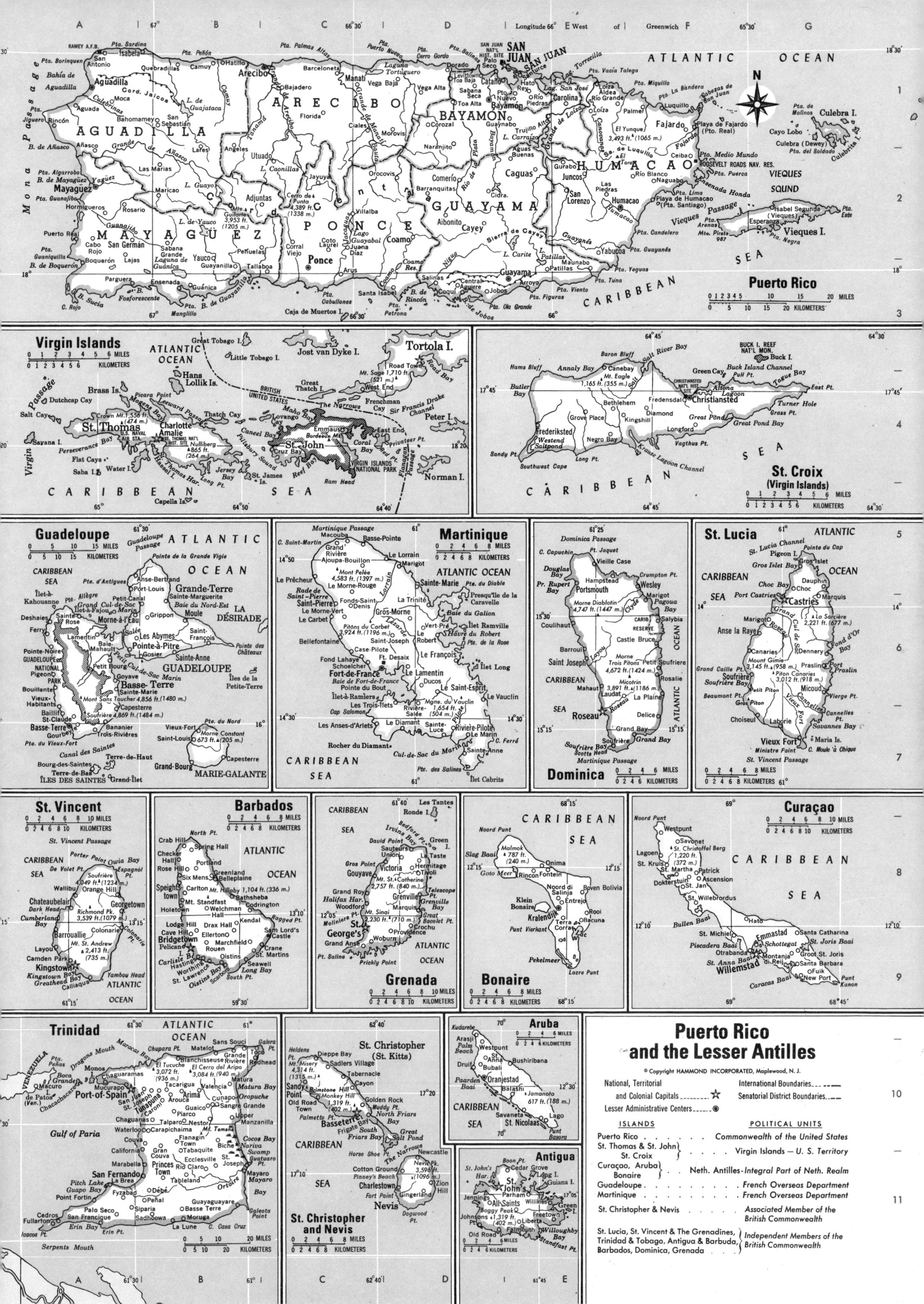

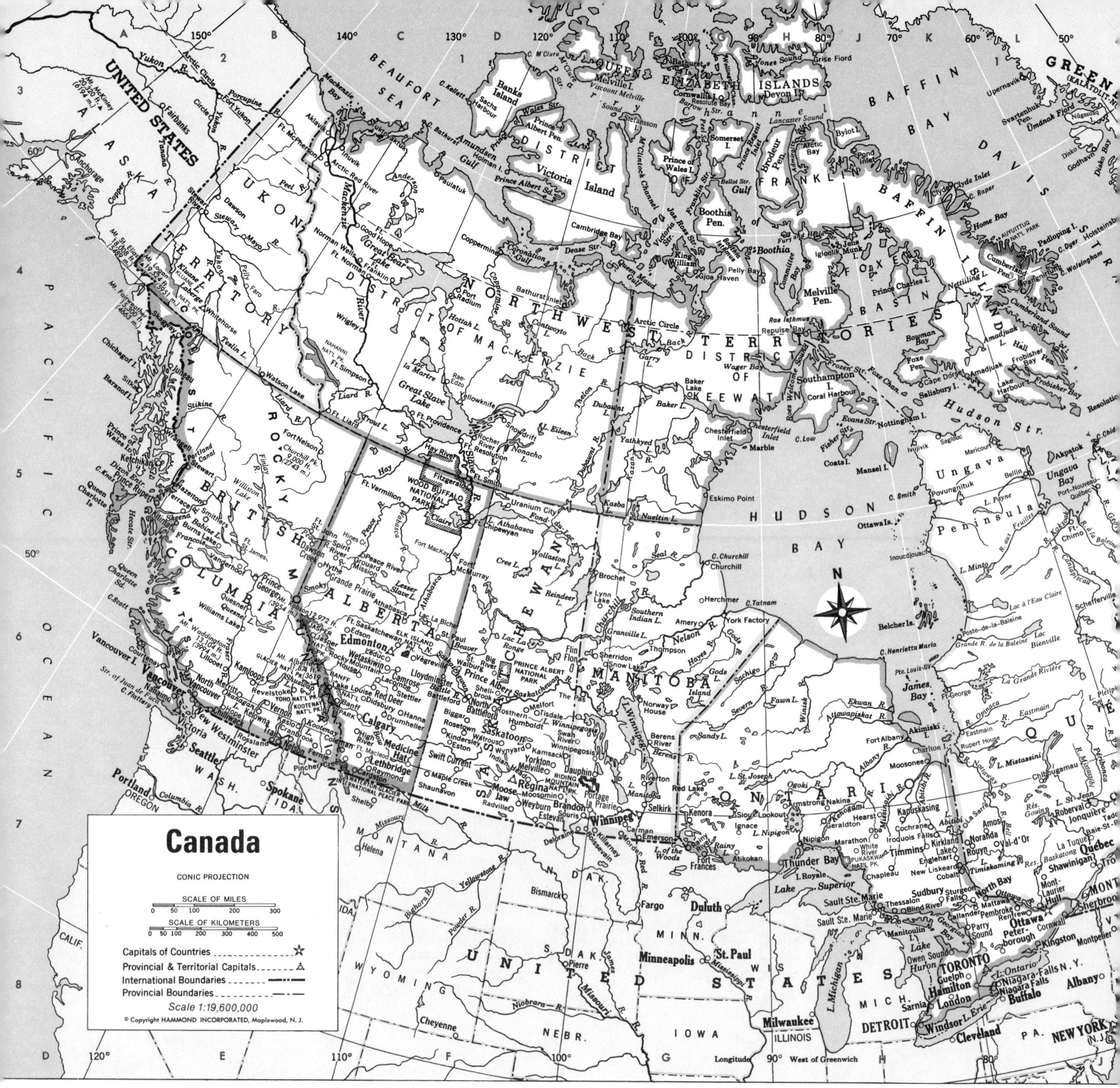

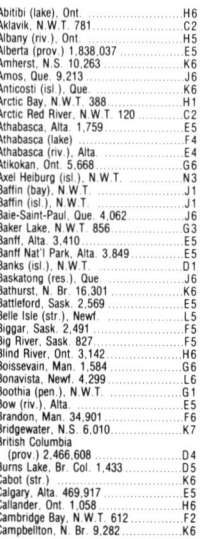

Canada
CONIC PROJECTION
SCALE OF MILES
0 50 100 200 300
SCALE OF KILOMETERS
0 50 100 200 300 400 500
Capitals of Countries
Provincial & Territorial Capitals
International Boundaries
Provincial Boundaries
Scale 1:19,600,000
© Copyright HAMMOND INCORPORATED, Maplewood, N. J.

Abitibi (lake), Ont. H6
Aklavik, N.W.T. 781 C2
Albany (riv.), Ont. H5
Alberta (prov.) 1,838,037 E5
Amherst, N.S. 10,263 K6
Amos, Que. 9,213 J6
Anticosti (isl.), Que. K6
Arctic Bay, N.W.T. 388 H1
Arctic Red River, N.W.T. 120 C2
Athabasca, Alta. 1,759 E5
Athabasca (lake) F4
Athabasca (riv.), Alta. E4
Atikokan, Ont. 5,668 G6
Axel Heiburg (isl.), N.W.T. N3
Baffin (bay), N.W.T. J1
Baffin (isl.), N.W.T. J1
Baie-Saint-Paul, Que. 4,062 J6
Baker Lake, N.W.T. 856 G3
Banff, Alta. 3,410 E5
Banff Nat'l Park, Alta. 3,849 E5
Banks (isl.), N.W.T. D1
Baskatong (res.), Que. J6
Bathurst, N. Br. 16,301 K6
Battleford, Sask. 2,569 E5
Belle Isle (str.), Newf. L5
Biggar, Sask. 2,491 F5
Big River, Sask. 827 F5
Blind River, Ont. 3,142 H6
Boissevain, Man. 1,584 G6
Bonavista, Newf. 4,299 L6
Boothia (pen.), N.W.T. G1
Bow (riv.), Alta. E5
Brandon, Man. 34,901 F6
Bridgewater, N.S. 6,010 K7
British Columbia (prov.) 2,466,608 D4
Burns Lake, Br. Col. 1,433 D5
Cabot (str.) K6
Calgary, Alta. 469,917 E5
Callander, Ont. 1,058 H6
Cambridge Bay, N.W.T. 612 F2
Campbellton, N. Br. 9,282 K6
Camrose, Alta. 10,104 E5
Cap-Chat, Que. 3,617 K6
Cape Breton (isl.), N.S. K6
Cardston, Alta. 3,043 E6
Carman, Man. 2,272 G6
Cartwright, Newf. 675 L5
Chandler, Que. 4,011 K6
Channel-Port aux Basques, Newf. 6,187 L6
Chapleau, Ont. 3,253 H6
Charlottetown (cap.), P.E.I. 17,063 K6
Chatham, N. Br. 7,601 K6
Chesterfield Inlet, N.W.T. 241 G3
Chibougamu, Que. 10,536 J6
Chicoutimi, Que. 57,737 J6
Chidley (cape), Newf. K3
Chilliwack, Br. Col. 8,634 D6
Churchill, Man. 1,699 G4
Clyde, N.W.T. 348 J1
Coast (mts.) C4
Cobalt, Ont. 2,056 H6
Cochrane, Ont. 4,974 H6
Coleman, Alta. 1,543 E6
Coppermine, N.W.T. 755 E2
Corner Brook, Newf. 25,198 K6
Cornwall, Ont. 46,121 J7
Courtenay, Br. Col. 7,733 D6
Cranbrook, Br. Col. 13,510 E6
Cree (lake), Sask. F4
Dartmouth, N.S. 65,341 K7
Dauphin, Man. 9,109 F5
Davis (str.), N.W.T. K1
Dawson, Yukon 838 C3
Devon (isl.), N.W.T. M3
Didsbury, Alta. 2,153 E5
Drumheller, Alta. 6,154 E5
Edmonton (cap.), Alta. 461,361 E5
Edmundston, N. Br. 12,710 K6
Edson, Alta. 4,038 E5
Ellesmere (isl.), N.W.T. N3
Emerson, Man. 756 G6
Englehart, Ont. 1,767 H6
Eskimo Point, N.W.T. 835 G3
Estevan, Sak. 8,847 F6
Eston, Sask. 1,354 F5
Fernie, Br. Col. 4,608 E6
Finlay (riv.), Br. Col. D4
Flin Flon, Man.-Sask. 9,560 F4
Fogo (isl.), Newf. 1,103 L6
Fort-Chimo, Que. 867 K4
Fort Frances, Ont. 9,325 G6
Fort Franklin, N.W.T. 422 D3
Fort-George, Que. 1,074 J5
Fort Good Hope, N.W.T. 440 D2
Fort Liard, N.W.T. 296 D3
Fort Macleod, Alta. 3,067 E6
Fort McMurray, Alta. 15,424 E4
Fort McPherson, N.W.T. 704 C2
Fort Nelson, Br. Col. 2,916 D4
Fort Norman, N.W.T. 230 D3
Fort Providence, N.W.T. 598 E3
Fort Resolution, N.W.T. 497 E3
Fort Saskatchewan, Alta. 8,304 E5
Fort Simpson, N.W.T. 1,136 D3
Fort Smith, N.W.T. 2,288 E3
Foxe (basin), N.W.T. J2
Franklin (dist.), N.W.T. H1
Fraser (riv.), Br. Col. D5
Fredericton, N. Br. 45,248 K6
Frobisher Bay, N.W.T. 2,320 K3
Fundy (bay) K7
Gagnon, Que. 3,423 K5
Gander, Newf. 9,301 L6
Gaspé, Que. 16,842 K6
Georgian (bay), Ont. H6
Geraldton, Ont. 3,127 H6
Gjoa Haven, N.W.T. 416 G2
Glace Bay, N.S. 21,836 L6
Goose Bay, Newf. 8,075 K5
Gouin (res.), Que. J6
Grand Falls, Newf. 8,729 L6
Grande Prairie, Alta. 17,626 E4
Great Bear (lake), N.W.T. D2
Great Slave (lake), N.W.T. E3
Guelph, Ont. 67,538 H7
Halifax (cap.), N.S. 117,882 K7
Hamilton, Ont. 312,003 H7
Hanna, Alta. 2,627 E5
Harbour Grace, Newf. 2,937 L6
Havre-St-Pierre, Que. 3,208 K5
Hay River, N.W.T. 3,268 E3
Hearst, Ont. 5,195 H6
Hecate (str.), Br. Col. C5
High River, Alta. 3,598 E5
Hope, Br. Col. 2,963 D6
Hopedale, Newf. 447 L4
Hull, Que. 61,039 J6
Humboldt, Sask. 4,265 F5
Indian Head, Sask. 1,720 F5
Inuvik, N.W.T. 3,116 C2
Inverness, N.S. 1,980 K6
Iroquois Falls, Ont. 6,887 H6
Jasper, Alta. 3,404 E5
Jasper Nat'l Park, Alta. E5
Jonquière, Que. J6
Juan de Fuca (str.), Br. Col. D6
Kamloops, Br. Col. 58,311 D5
Kamsack, Sask. 2,726 F5
Kane (basin), N.W.T. N3
Kapuskasing, Ont. 12,676 H6
Keewatin (dist.), N.W.T. 3,978 G3
Kelowna, Br. Col. 51,955 E6
Kenora, Ont. 10,565 G5
Killarney, Man. 2,348 G6
Kindersley, Sask. 3,523 F5
Kingston, Ont. 56,032 J7
Kirkland Lake, Ont. 13,567 H6
Kitimat, Br. Col. 11,791 D5
Kluane (lake), Yukon C3
Kootenay (lake), Br. Col. E5
Labrador (reg.), Newf. K4
Labrador (sea) L4
Lac La Biche, Alta. 1,954 E5
Lacombe, Alta. 3,888 E5
Lake Harbour, N.W.T. 233 J3
Lake Louise, Alta. 140 E5
Lancaster (sound), N.W.T. H1
La Sarre, Que. 4,978 J6
La Tuque, Que. 12,067 J6
Leduc, Alta. 8,576 E5
Lesser Slave (lake), Alta. E4
Lethbridge, Alta. 46,752 E6
Liard (riv.) D3
Lillooet, Br. Col. 2,218 D5
Lloydminster, Alta.-Sask. 10,311 E5
Logan (mt.), Yukon B3
London, Ont. 240,392 H7
Lunenburg, N.S. 3,024 K7
Lynn Lake, Man. 2,568 G4
Mackenzie (dist.), N.W.T. E3
Mackenzie (riv.), N.W.T. C2
Magdalen (isls.), Que. K6
Manicouagan (riv.), Que. K5
Manitoba (lake), Man. G5
Manitoba (prov.) G5
Manitoulin (isl.), Ont. H6
Maple Creek, Sask. 2,330 F6
Marathon, Ont. 2,250 H6
Mattawa, Ont. 2,849 J6
Mayo, Yukon 448 C3
M'Clintock (chan.), N.W.T. F1
Medicine Hat, Alta. 32,811 E5
Melfort, Sask. 5,141 F5
Melville, Sask. 5,149 F5
Melville (isl.), N.W.T. E1
Merritt, Br. Col. 5,680 D5
Minto (lake), Que. J4
Mistassibi (riv.), Que. J5
Mistassini (lake), Que. J5
Moncton, N. Br. 55,934 K6
Mont-Joli, Que. 6,508 K6
Mont-Laurier, Que. 8,565 J6
Montréal, Que. 1,080,546 J7
Moose Jaw, Sask. 32,581 F6
Moosomin, Sask. 2,449 F5
Moosonee, Ont. 1,349 H5
Morden, Man. 3,886 G6
Nain, Newf. 812 K4
Nanaimo, Br. Col. 40,336 D6
Nares (str.), N.W.T. N3
Nelson, Br. Col. 9,235 E6
Nelson (riv.), Man. G4
New Brunswick (prov.) 677,250 K6
Newcastle, N. Br. 6,423 K6
Newfoundland (isl.) L6
Newfoundland (prov.) 557,725 L5
New Liskeard, Ont. 5,601 H6
New Westminster, Br. Col. D6
Noranda, Que. 9,809 J6
Norman Wells, N.W.T. 364 D2
North Battleford, Sask. 13,158 F5
North Bay, Ont. 51,639 J6
North Vancouver, Br. Col. 63,471 D6
Northwest Territories 21,836 E2
Nottaway (riv.), Que. J5
Nova Scotia (prov.) 828,571 K7
Okanagan (lake), Br. Col. D6
Ontario (prov.) 8,264,465 H5
Ottawa (cap.), Canada 304,462 J6
Ottawa (riv.) J6
Owen Sound, Ont. 19,525 H7
Pangnirtung, N.W.T. 807 K2
Parry (chan.), N.W.T. E-H1
Parry Sound, Ont. 5,501 J6
Peace (riv.), Alta. E4
Peace River, Alta. 4,840 E4
Peel (riv.) C2
Pelly (riv.), Yukon C3
Pembroke, Ont. 14,927 J6
Péribonca (riv.), Que. 59,683 J5
Peterborough, Ont. 59,683 J7
Pincher Creek, Br. Col. 3,448 E6
Pond Inlet, N.W.T. 500 J1
Portage la Prairie, Man. 12,555
Port-Cartier, Que. 8,139
Port Radium, N.W.T. 51
Poste-de-la-Baleine, Que. 718
Povungnituk, Que.
Prince Albert, Sask. 28,631
Prince Albert Nat'l Park, Sask.
Prince Edward Island (prov.) 118,229
Prince George, Br. Col. 59,929
Prince Patrick (isl.), N.W.T.
Prince Rupert, Br. Col. 14,754
Québec (cap.), Que. 177,082
Québec (prov.) 6,234,445
Queen Charlotte (isls.), Br. Col.
Queen Elizabeth (isls.), N.W.T.
Quesnel, Br. Col. 7,637
Race (cape), Newf.
Radville, Sask. 1,008
Rae-Edzo, N.W.T. 1,158
Rainy (lake), Ont.
Rainy River, Ont. 1,092
Ray (cape), Newf.
Raymond, Alta. 2,290
Red Deer, Alta. 32,184
Regina (cap.), Sask. 149,593
Reindeer (lake)
Renfrew, Ont. 8,617
Revelstoke, Br. Col. 4,615
Riding Mountain Nat'l Park, Man.
Rigolet, Newf. 238
Rimouski, Que. 27,897
Rivière-du-Loup, Que. 13,103
Roberval, Que. 8,543
Robson (mt.), Br. Col.
Rocky (mts.)
Rocky Mountain House,

AREA 3,851,787 sq. mi. (9,976,139 sq. km.)
POPULATION 24,105,163
CAPITAL Ottawa
LARGEST CITY Montréal
HIGHEST POINT Mt. Logan 19,524 ft. (5,951 m.)
MONETARY UNIT Canadian dollar
MAJOR LANGUAGES English, French
MAJOR RELIGIONS Protestantism, Roman Catholicism

Population Distribution

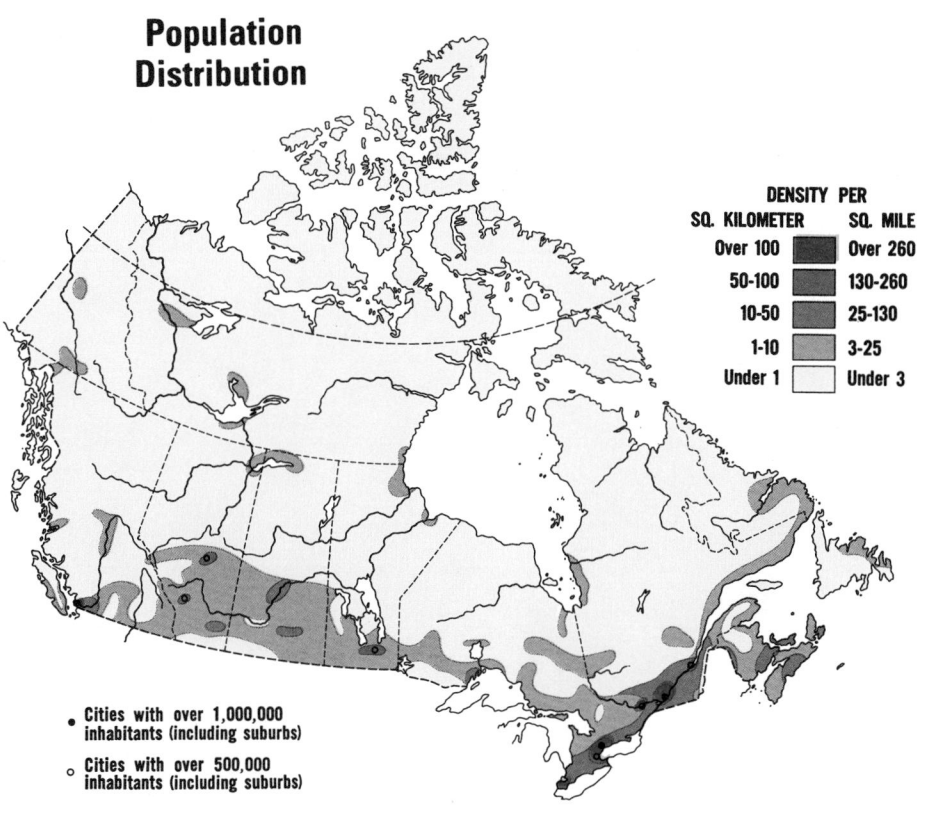

DENSITY PER	
SQ. KILOMETER	SQ. MILE
Over 100	Over 260
50-100	130-260
10-50	25-130
1-10	3-25
Under 1	Under 3

• Cities with over 1,000,000 inhabitants (including suburbs)

○ Cities with over 500,000 inhabitants (including suburbs)

Vegetation

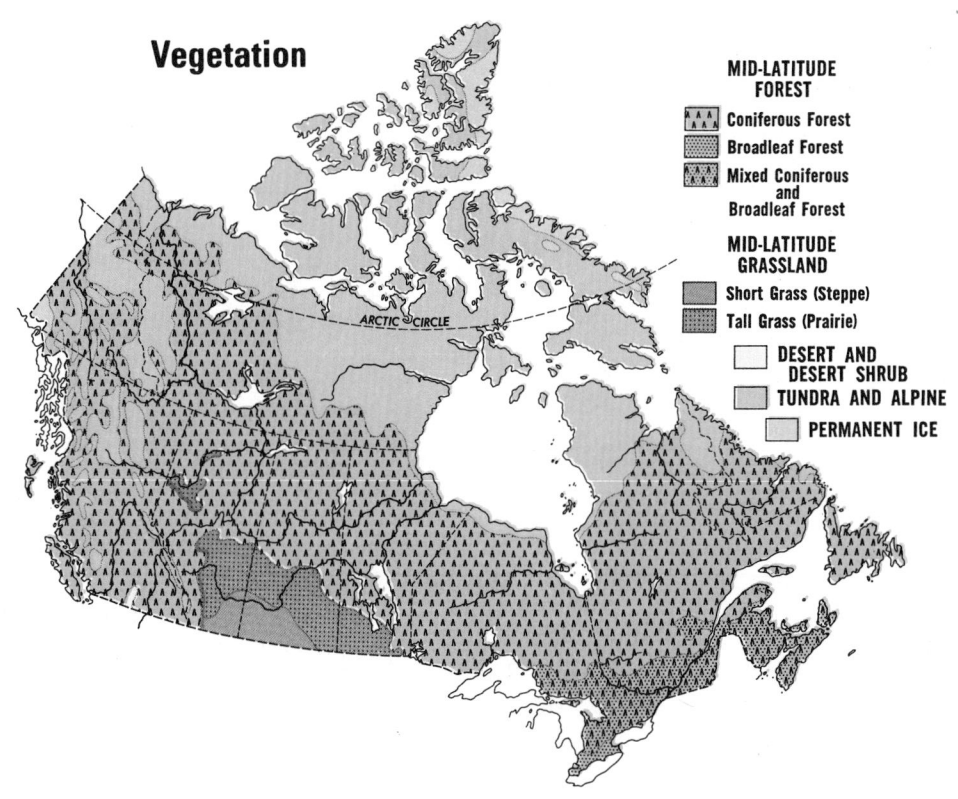

MID-LATITUDE FOREST
- Coniferous Forest
- Broadleaf Forest
- Mixed Coniferous and Broadleaf Forest

MID-LATITUDE GRASSLAND
- Short Grass (Steppe)
- Tall Grass (Prairie)

- DESERT AND DESERT SHRUB
- TUNDRA AND ALPINE
- PERMANENT ICE

Average January Temperature

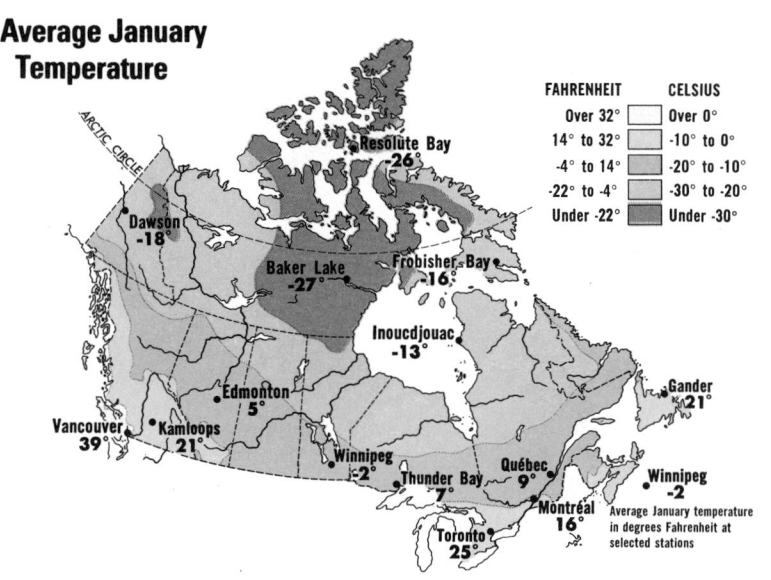

FAHRENHEIT CELSIUS
Over 32° Over 0°
14° to 32° -10° to 0°
-4° to 14° -20° to -10°
-22° to -4° -30° to -20°
Under -22° Under -30°
ARCTIC CIRCLE
Resolute Bay -26
Dawson -18°
Baker Lake -27°
Frobisher Bay -16
Inoucdjouac -13°
Edmonton 5°
Vancouver 39°
Kamloops 21°
Gander 21°
Winnipeg -2°
Thunder Bay 7°
Québec 9°
Montréal 16°
Toronto 25°
Winnipeg -2
Average January temperature in degrees Fahrenheit at selected stations

Average July Temperature

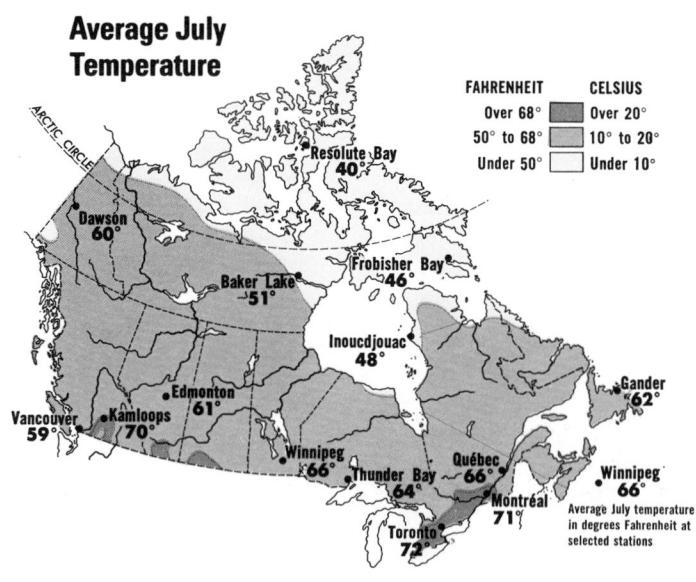

FAHRENHEIT CELSIUS
Over 68° Over 20°
50° to 68° 10° to 20°
Under 50° Under 10°
ARCTIC CIRCLE
Resolute Bay 40°
Dawson 60°
Baker Lake 51°
Frobisher Bay 46°
Inoucdjouac 48°
Edmonton 61°
Vancouver 59°
Kamloops 70°
Gander 62°
Winnipeg 66°
Thunder Bay 64°
Québec 66°
Montréal 71°
Toronto 72°
Winnipeg 66°
Average July temperature in degrees Fahrenheit at selected stations

Agriculture, Industry and Resources

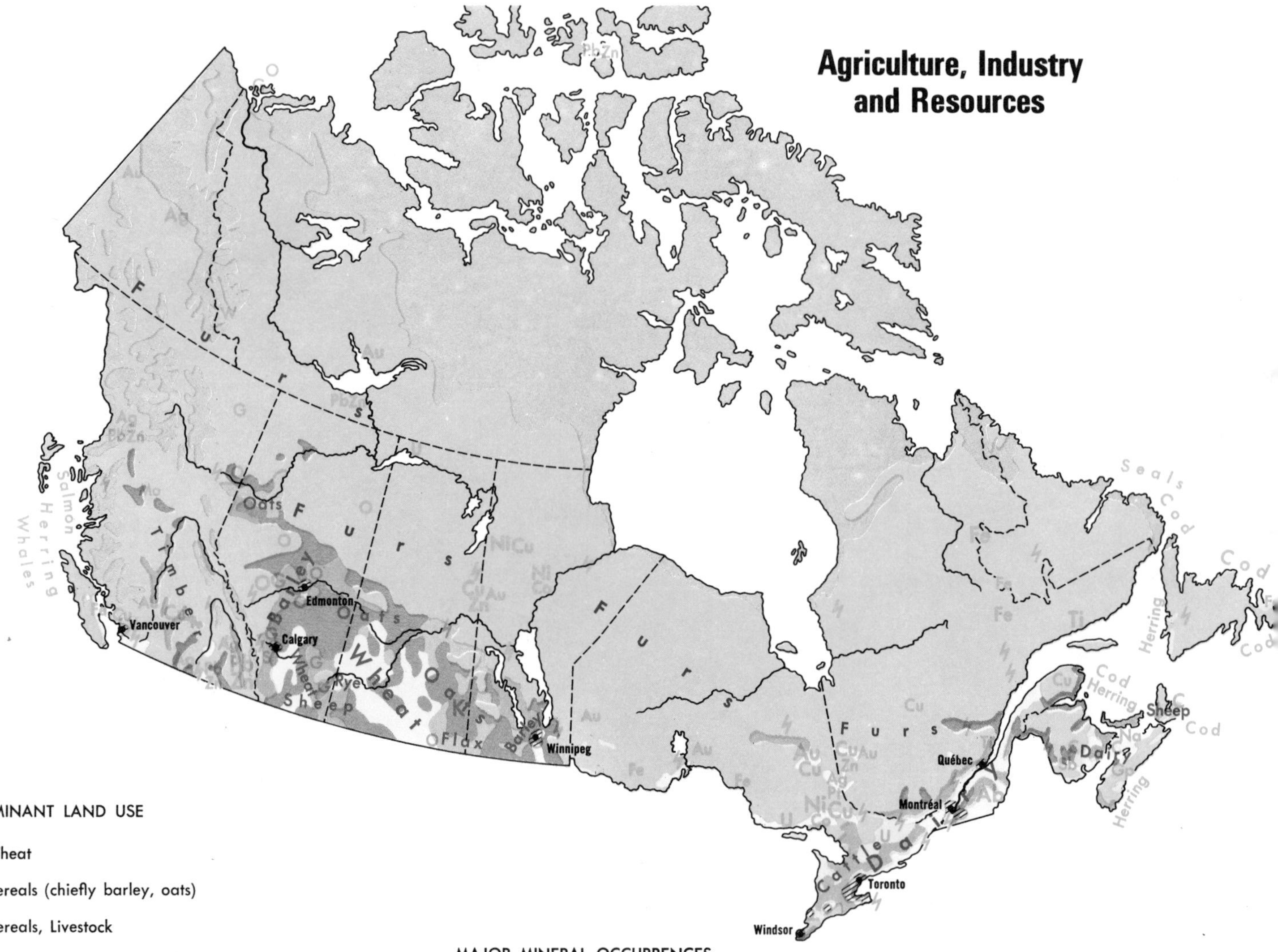

Furs
Timber
Salmon
Herring
Whales
Oats
Barley
Wheat
Sheep
Rye
Flax
Edmonton
Calgary
Vancouver
Winnipeg
Québec
Montréal
Toronto
Windsor
Seals
Cod
Herring
Sheep
Dairy

DOMINANT LAND USE

- Wheat
- Cereals (chiefly barley, oats)
- Cereals, Livestock
- General Farming, Livestock
- Dairy
- Fruit, Vegetables
- Pasture Livestock
- Range Livestock
- Forests
- Nonagricultural Land

MAJOR MINERAL OCCURRENCES

Ab	Asbestos	Fe	Iron Ore	Ni	Nickel	Sb	Antimony
Ag	Silver	G	Natural Gas	O	Petroleum	Ti	Titanium
Au	Gold	Gp	Gypsum	Pb	Lead	U	Uranium
C	Coal	K	Potash	Pt	Platinum	W	Tungsten
Co	Cobalt	Mo	Molybdenum	S	Sulfur	Zn	Zinc
Cu	Copper	Na	Salt				

- Water Power
- Major Industrial Areas

Rainfall

AVERAGE ANNUAL RAINFALL

INCHES	CENTIMETERS
Over 80	Over 200
60 to 80	150 to 200
40 to 60	100 to 150
20 to 40	50 to 100
10 to 20	25 to 50
Under 10	Under 25

Toronto
•31
Average annual rainfall
in inches at selected
stations

Resolute Bay
6

Dawson
13

ARCTIC CIRCLE

Frobisher Bay
11

Baker Lake
8

Ft. Smith
11

Prince Rupert
94

Inoucdjouac
15

Gander
42

Edmonton
17

Sept-Îles
42

Vancouver
42

Winnipeg
20

Thunder Bay
29

Montréal
38

Halifax
54

Toronto
31

Topography

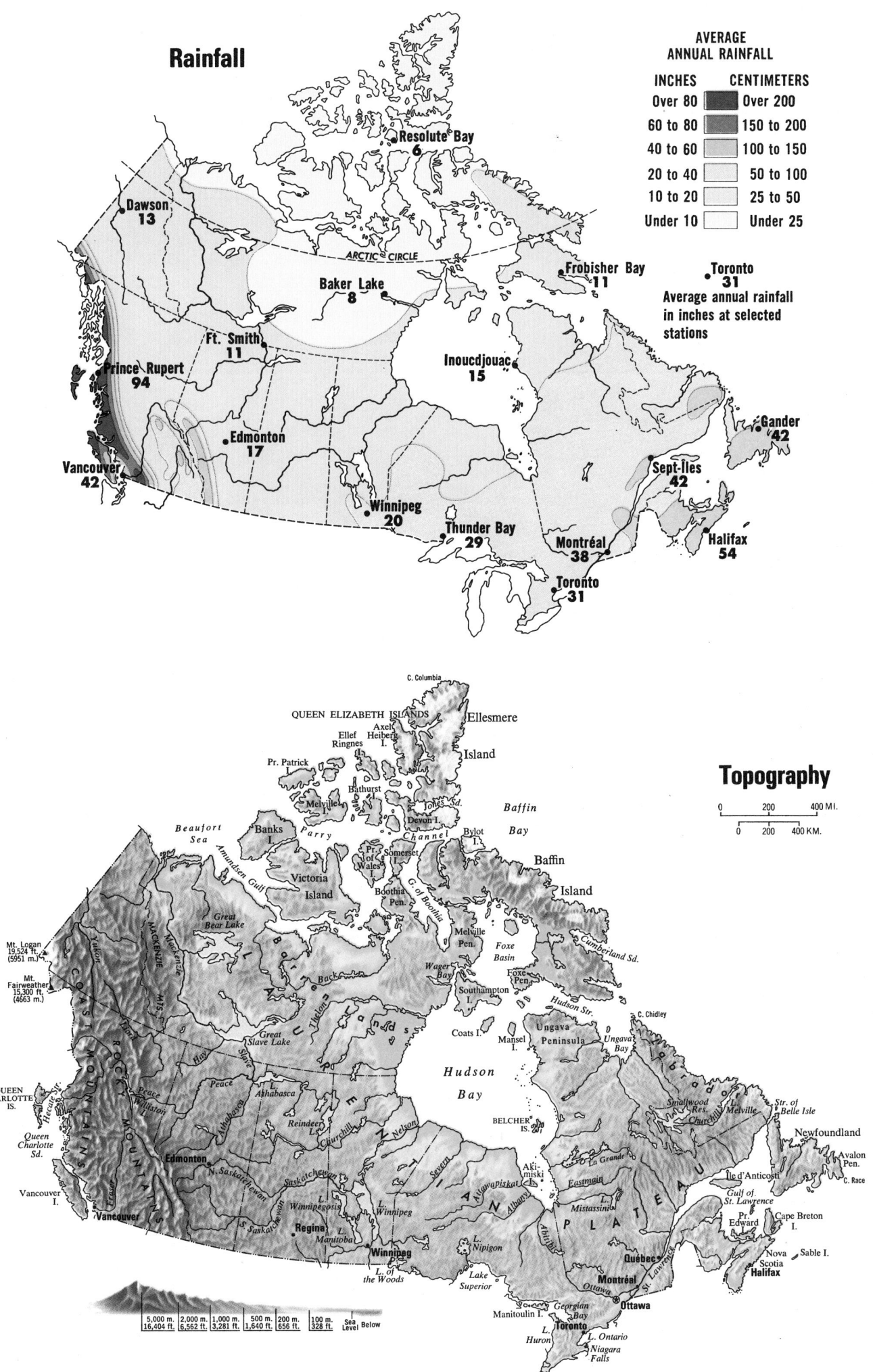

C. Columbia

QUEEN ELIZABETH ISLANDS — Ellesmere

Axel Heiberg I.
Ellef Ringnes

Pr. Patrick I.

Bathurst

Island

Melville

Baffin

Beaufort Sea

Banks I.

Parry

Jones Sd.
Devon I.

Bylot I.

Baffin Bay

Amundsen Gulf

Victoria Island

Pr. of Wales I.

Somerset

G. of Boothia

Boothia Pen.

Baffin Island

Mt. Logan
19,524 ft.
(5951 m.)

Great Bear Lake

Melville Pen.

Foxe Basin

Cumberland Sd.

Mt. Fairweather
15,300 ft.
(4663 m.)

Back

Wager Bay

Foxe Pen.

C. Chidley

Great Slave Lake

Southampton

Hudson Str.

QUEEN CHARLOTTE IS.

Peace

Athabasca

Hay

Slave

Coats I.

Mansel I.

Ungava Peninsula

Ungava Bay

Hudson Bay

Queen Charlotte Sd.

Liard

Peace

L. Athabasca

Reindeer L.

Churchill

Nelson

BELCHER IS.

Smallwood Res.

L. Melville

Str. of Belle Isle

Vancouver I.

Edmonton

N. Saskatchewan

Saskatchewan

Churchill

Seven

Aki-miski

La Grande

Churchill

Newfoundland

Avalon Pen.

C. Race

Vancouver

S. Saskatchewan

Winnipegosis

Winnipeg

Attawapiskat

Albany

Eastmain

Île d'Anticosti

Regina

L. Manitoba

Winnipeg

L. Nipigon

Abitibi

Mistassini

Gulf of St. Lawrence

Pr. Edward I.

Cape Breton I.

Sable I.

L. of the Woods

Lake Superior

Québec

PLATEAU

Nova Scotia
Halifax

Montréal

St. Lawrence

Ottawa

Manitoulin I.

Georgian Bay

Toronto

L. Ontario

Niagara Falls

L. Huron

Topography scale:
0   200   400 MI.
0   200   400 KM.

| 5,000 m. | 2,000 m. | 1,000 m. | 500 m. | 200 m. | 100 m. | Sea Level | Below |
| 16,404 ft. | 6,562 ft. | 3,281 ft. | 1,640 ft. | 656 ft. | 328 ft. | | |

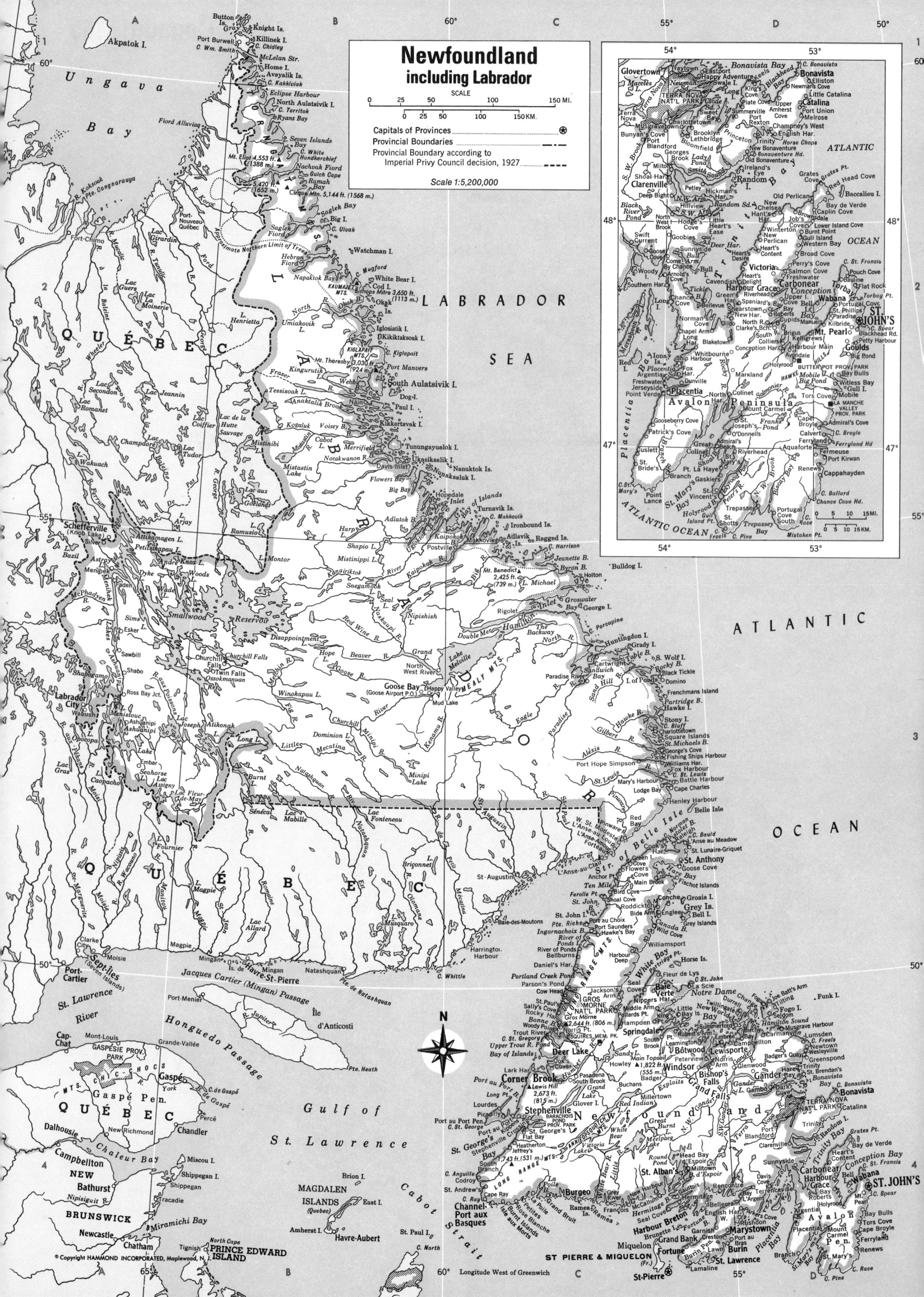

Newfoundland
including Labrador

SCALE

0 25 50   100   150 MI.

0 25 50   100   150 KM.

Capitals of Provinces .... ⊛
Provincial Boundaries .... — · —
Provincial Boundary according to
Imperial Privy Council decision, 1927 .... – – –

Scale 1:5,200,000

© Copyright HAMMOND INCORPORATED, Maplewood, N.J.

Longitude West of Greenwich

NEWFOUNDLAND

CITIES and TOWNS

Argentia 68 ..... C2
Arnold's Cove 1,160 ..... C2
Avondale 937 ..... D2
Badger 1,160 ..... C4
Badger's Quay 649 ..... D4
Baie Verte 2,528 ..... C4
Battle Harbour C3
Bay Bulls 1,104 ..... D2
Bay de Verde 749 ..... D2
Bay Roberts 4,072 ..... D2
Bishop's Falls 4,504 ..... C4
Birchy Bay 646 ..... D4
Blackhead Road 1,840 ..... D2
Blaketown 537 ..... D2
Bloomfield 677 ..... D2
Bonavista 4,299 ..... D2
Botwood 4,554 ..... C4
Brigus 912 ..... D2
Burgeo 2,474 ..... C4
Burin 2,892 ..... C4
Burnt Islands 914 ..... C4
Campbellton 757 ..... D4
Cape Broyle 711 ..... D2
Carbonear 5,026 ..... D2
Carmanville 911 ..... D4
Cartwright 675 ..... C3
Catalina 1,129 ..... D2
Channel-Port aux Basques 6,187 ..... C4
Chapel Arm 712 ..... D2
Churchill Falls 930 ..... B3
Clarenville 2,807 ..... C2
Clarke's Beach 997 ..... D2
Colliers 840 ..... D2
Conception Harbour 910 ..... D2
Corner Brook 25,198 ..... C4
Cow Head 650 ..... C4
Cox's Cove 1,004 ..... C4
Creston 768 ..... C4
Cupids 750 ..... D2
Daniel's Harbour 579 ..... C3
Dark Cove 1,418 ..... D4
Deer Lake 4,546 ..... C4
Dildo 858 ..... D2
Dunville 1,909 ..... D2
Durrell 1,137 ..... D4
Eastport 567 ..... D1
Elliston 540 ..... D2
Embree 855 ..... C4
Englee 989 ..... C3
Ferryland 656 ..... D2
Flat Rock 743 ..... D2
Fleur de Lys 694 ..... C3
Fogo 1,103 ..... D4
Fortune 2,406 ..... C4
Fox Harbour 627 ..... D2
Gander 9,301 ..... D4
Garnish 678 ..... C4
Gaultois 588 ..... C4
Glenwood 1,128 ..... D4
Glovertown 2,176 ..... C1
Goose Bay-Happy Valley 8,075 ..... B3
Goulds 3,317 ..... D2
Grand Bank 3,802 ..... C4
Grand Falls 8,729 ..... C4
Green's Harbour 705 ..... D2
Hampden 780 ..... C4
Happy Valley-Goose Bay 8,075 ..... B3
Harbour Breton 2,317 ..... C4
Harbour Grace 2,937 ..... D2
Harbour Main 992 ..... D2
Hare Bay 1,598 ..... D4
Head of Bay d'Espoir 560 ..... C4
Heart's Content 634 ..... D2
Heart's Delight 590 ..... D2
Hermitage 675 ..... C4
Holyrood 1,610 ..... D2
Hopedale 447 ..... B2
Isle aux Morts 1,270 ..... C4
Jerseyside 1,024 ..... B3
Joe Batt's Arm 821 ..... D4
King's Point 770 ..... C4
Kippens 1,267 ..... C4
Labrador City 12,012 ..... A3
Lamaline 543 ..... C4
Lark Harbour 771 ..... C4
La Scie 1,256 ..... C4
Lawn 1,025 ..... C4
Lethbridge 736 ..... D2
Lewisporte 3,782 ..... C4
Little Catalina 736 ..... D2
Lourdes 987 ..... C4
Lumsden 597 ..... D4
Main Brook 551 ..... C3
Marystown 5,915 ..... D4
Middle Arm 555 ..... C4
Milltown 748 ..... C4
Mount Pearl 10,193 ..... D2
Musgrave Harbour 1,530 ..... D4
Musgravetown 641 ..... C2
Nain 812 ..... B2
New Harbour 779 ..... D2
Norman's Cove 842 ..... D2
Norris Arm 1,342 ..... C4
Norris Point 1,065 ..... C4
North West River 1,022 ..... B3
Old Perlican 626 ..... D2
Paradise 2,131 ..... D2
Parson's Pond 544 ..... C3
Pasadena 1,850 ..... C4
Peterview 1,099 ..... C4
Petty Harbour 824 ..... D2
Placentia 2,209 ..... C2
Point Leamington 882 ..... C4
Port au Choix 1,141 ..... C3
Port au Port 660 ..... C4
Port Blandford 815 ..... C2
Port Hope Simpson 548 ..... C3
Port Saunders 691 ..... C3
Portugal Cove 1,527 ..... D2
Port Union 678 ..... D2
Pouch Cove 1,543 ..... D2
Ramea 1,226 ..... C4
Rigolet 238 ..... C3
Robert's Arm 1,064 ..... C4
Rocky Harbour 1,267 ..... C4
Roddickton 1,234 ..... C3
Rose Blanche 766 ..... C4
Saint Alban's 2,040 ..... C4
Saint Anthony 2,987 ..... C3
Saint Bride's 578 ..... C2
Saint George's 1,976 ..... C4
Saint John's (cap.) 86,576 ..... D2
Saint Lawrence 2,258 ..... C4
Saint Lunaire-Griquet 921 ..... C3
Saint Phillips 807 ..... D2
Saint Vincent's 604 ..... D2
Salmon Cove 733 ..... D2
Seal Cove 774 ..... C3
Shoal Harbour 1,009 ..... C2
South Brook, Green Bay dist. 828 ..... C4
Southern Harbour 759 ..... C2
South River 598 ..... D2
Spaniard's Bay 1,568 ..... D2
Springdale 3,513 ..... C4
Stephenville 10,284 ..... C4
Stephenville Crossing 2,207 ..... C4
Summerford 1,099 ..... C4
Sunnyside 726 ..... D2
Terrenceville 764 ..... D4
Torbay 2,908 ..... D2
Trepassey 1,427 ..... D2
Trinity 559 ..... D2
Trout River 784 ..... C4
Twillingate 1,404 ..... C4
Upper Island Cove 1,851 ..... D2
Victoria 1,767 ..... D2
Wabana 4,824 ..... D2
Wabush 3,769 ..... A3
Wesleyville 1,167 ..... D4
Whitbourne 1,268 ..... D2
Windsor 6,349 ..... C4
Winterton 796 ..... D2
Witless Bay 888 ..... D2

OTHER FEATURES

Adlatok, (bay) B2
Adlavik, (isls.) C2
Aguanus, (riv.) B3
Alexis, (riv.) C3
Anaktalik Brook, (riv.) B2
Andre, (lake) A3
Anguille, (cape) C4
Annieopscotch, (mts.) C4
Ashuanipi, (lake) A3
Ashuanipi, (riv.) A3
Assigny, (lake) A3
Astray, (lake) A3
Atikonak, (lake) B3
Attikamagen, (lake) A3
Avalon, (pen.) D2
Avayalik, (isls.) B1
Baccalieu, (isl.) D2
Backway, The, (inlet) C3
Ballard, (cape) D2
Barachois Pond Prov. Park C4
Bauld, (cape) C3
Beaver, (riv.) B3
Bell, (isl.) C3
Bell, (isl.) D2
Belle Isle, (isl.) C3
Belle Isle, (str.) C3
Benedict, (mt.) C3
Big, (bay) B2
Big, (isl.) C3
Big, (riv.) C3
Biscay Bay, (riv.) D2
Bishops Mitre, (mt.) B2
Blackhead, (bay) D2
Black River, (pond) C2
Bluff, (cape) C3
Bonaventure, (cape) D2
Bonavista, (bay) D1
Bonavista, (cape) D1
Bonne, (bay) C4
Branch, (riv.) C2
Broyle, (cape) D2
Brunette, (isl.) C4
Bull, (isl.) C3
Bull Arm, (inlet) D2
Bulldog, (isl.) C3
Burin, (pen.) C4
Burnt, (lake) B3
Butter Pot Prov. Park D2
Byron, (bay) C3
Cabot, (lake) B2
Cabot, (str.) B4
Canada, (bay) C3
Chance Cove, (cape) D2
Chidley, (cape) B1
Churchill, (falls) B3
Churchill, (riv.) B3
Cirque, (mt.) B2
Clode, (sound) D2
Cod, (isl.) B2
Conception, (bay) D2
Deep, (inlet) B2
Deer, (harb.) D2
Disappointment, (lake) B3
Dog, (isl.) B2
Dominion, (lake) B3
Double Mer, (lake) C3
Dyke, (lake) A3
Eagle, (riv.) C3
Eclipse, (harb.) B2
Eliot, (mt.) B2
Espoir, (bay) C4
Exploits, (riv.) C4
Ferolle, (pt.) C3
Ferryland, (cape) D2
Fig, (riv.) B3
Fleur-de-May, (lake) B3
Flowers, (bay) B2
Fogo, (isl.) D4
Fonteneau, (lake) B3
Fortune, (bay) C4
Four, (peaks) B2
Franks, (pond) D2
Fraser, (riv.) B2
Freels, (cape) D3
Funk, (isl.) D4
Gander, (lake) D4
Gander, (riv.) D4
George, (isl.) C3
Gilbert, (riv.) C3
Glover, (isl.) C4
Goose, (riv.) B3
Grady, (isl.) C3
Grand, (lake) B3
Grand, (lake) C4
Grates, (pt.) D2
Great Burnt, (lake) C4
Great Colinet, (isl.) D2
Grey, (isls.) C3
Groais, (isl.) C3
Gros Morne, (mt.) C4
Gros Morne Nat'l Park C4
Groswater, (bay) C3
Gulch, (cape) B2
Gull, (isl.) D2
Gull Island, (pt.) D2
Hamilton, (inlet) C3
Hamilton, (sound) D4
Hare, (bay) C3
Harp, (lake) B2
Harrison, (cape) C3
Hawke, (isl.) C3
Hawke, (hills) D2
Hawke, (riv.) C3
Hebron, (fjord) B2
Hermitage, (bay) C4
Holyrood, (bay) D2
Holyrood, (pond) D2
Home, (isl.) B1
Hope, (lake) B3
Horse, (isls.) C3
Horse Chops, (head) D2
Humber, (riv.) C4
Huntingdon, (isl.) C3
Iglosiatik, (isl.) B2
Ingornachoix, (bay) C3
Iona, (isls.) C2
Ireland's Eye, (isl.) D2
Ironbound, (isls.) C2
Islands, (bay) C2
Islands, (bay) C4
Jeanette, (bay) C3
Joseph, (lake) B3
Kaipokok, (bay) B2
Kaipokok, (riv.) B3
Kakkiviak, (cape) B1
Kanairiktok, (riv.) B3
Kaumajet, (mts.) B2
Kenamu, (riv.) B3
Kiglapait, (cape) B2
Kiglapait, (mts.) B2
Kikiktaksoak, (isl.) B2
Kikkertavak, (isl.) B2
Kingurutik, (mesa) B2
Knox, (lake) A3
Kogaluk, (riv.) B2
Labrador, (reg.) B2
Labrador, (sea) C2
Lady, (pond) D2
La Manche Valley Prov. Park D2
La Poile, (bay) C4
Lewis Hill, (mt.) C4
Little Mecatina, (riv.) B3
Little Trout River, (pond) C4
Long, (isl.) C2
Long, (isl.) D2
Long, (lake) B3
Long, (lake) A3
Long, (pt.) C4
Long Range, (mts.) C4
Lozeau, (lake) B3
Mabille, (lake) B3
Maccles, (lake) C1
Main Topsail, (mt.) C4
Makkovik, (cape) C2
McLelan, (str.) B1
McPhadyen, (riv.) A3
Mealy, (lake) C3
Meelpaeg, (lake) C4
Melville, (lake) C3
Menihek, (lkes) A3
Menistouc, (lake) A3
Merasheen, (isl.) C2
Merrifield, (bay) B2
Metchin, (riv.) B3
Michael, (lake) C3
Minipi, (lake) B3
Minipi, (riv.) B3
Mistaken, (pt.) D2
Mistastin, (lake) B2
Mistastin, (riv.) B2
Mistinippi, (lake) B3
Mobile Big, (pond) D2
Mugford, (cape) B2
Nachvak, (fjord) B2
Nanuktok, (isls.) C2
Napaktok, (bay) B2
Naskaupi, (riv.) B3
Natashquan, (riv.) B3
Natashquan-Est, (riv.) B3
Newfoundland, (isl.) C4
Newman, (sound) D2
New World, (isl.) C4
Nipishish, (lake) B3
Norman, (cape) C3
North, (riv.) B2
North, (riv.) C3
North Aulatsivik, (isl.) B2
North West Arm, (inlet) D2
North West Brook, (riv.) D2
North West Gander, (riv.) C4
Notakwanon, (riv.) B2
Notre Dame, (bay) C4
Nunaksaluk, (isl.) B2
Okak, (bay) B2
Okak, (isls.) B2
Ossokmanuan, (res.) B3
Paradise, (riv.) C3
Partridge, (bay) C3
Partridge, (pt.) C3
Paul, (isl.) B2
Peter's, (riv.) D2
Petitsikapau, (lake) A3
Pine, (cape) D2
Pinware, (riv.) C3
Pistolet, (bay) C3
Placentia, (bay) C2
Placentia, (sound) C2
Poissons, (riv.) A3
Ponds, (isl.) C3
Porcupine, (cape) C3
Port au Port, (bay) C4
Port au Port, (pen.) C4
Portland Creek, (pond) C3
Port Manvers, (harb.) B2
Race, (cape) D2
Ragged, (isls.) C2
Ramah, (bay) B2
Ramea, (isls.) C4
Random, (isl.) D2
Random, (sound) D2
Ray, (cape) C4
Red, (isl.) C4
Red Indian, (lake) C4
Red Wine, (riv.) B3
Riche, (pt.) C3
River of Ponds, (lake) C3
Rocky, (bay) D2
Rocky, (riv.) D2
Romaine, (riv.) B3
Round, (pond) C4
Ryans, (bay) B2
Saglek, (bay) B2
Saglek, (fjord) B2
Saint Augustin, (riv.) C3
Saint Francis, (cape) D2
Saint George, (cape) C4
Saint George's, (bay) C4
Saint Gregory, (cape) C4
Saint John, (bay) C3
Saint John, (cape) C3
Saint John, (isl.) C3
Saint Lawrence, (gulf) B4
Saint Lewis, (cape) C3
Saint Lewis, (riv.) C3
Saint Mary's, (bay) C2
Saint Mary's, (cape) C2
Saint Michaels, (bay) C3
Saint Paul, (riv.) C3
Salmonier, (riv.) D2
Sand Hill, (riv.) C3
Sandwich, (bay) C3
Sandy, (lake) C4
Seahorse, (lake) A3
Seal, (lake) B3
Senécal, (lake) B3
Seven Islands, (bay) B2
Shabogamo, (lake) A3
Shapio, (lake) B3
Shoal, (bay) D2
Sims, (lake) A3
Smallwood, (res.) B3
Smith, (sound) D2
Snegamook, (lake) B3
South Aulatsivik, (isl.) B2
South West, (brook) C2
South West Arm, (inlet) D2
South West Gander, (riv.) C4
South Wolf, (isl.) C3
Spear, (cape) D2
Squires Mem. Park C4
Stony, (isl.) C3
Swale, (isl.) D1
Table, (bay) C3
Tasisuak, (lake) B2
Ten Mile, (lake) C3
Terra Nova, (riv.) C2
Terra Nova Nat'l Park D2
Territok, (cape) B2
Thoresby, (mt.) B2
Tickle, (bay) D2
Torbay, (pt.) D2
Torngat, (mts.) B2
Trespassey, (bay) D2
Trinity, (bay) D2
Tunungayualok, (isl.) B2
Turnavik, (isls.) C2
Ugjoktok, (bay) B2
Uivak, (cape) B2
Ukasiksalik, (isl.) B2
Umiakovik, (lake) B2
Victoria, (lake) C4
Voisey, (bay) B2
Wade, (lake) A3
Watchman, (isl.) B2
Webb, (bay) B2
White, (bay) C3
White Bear, (isl.) B2
White Bear, (lake) C4
White Bear, (riv.) C4
White Handkerchief, (cape) B2
Winokapau, (lake) B3
Woods, (lake) B3

SAINT PIERRE AND MIQUELON

CITIES and TOWNS

Saint-Pierre (cap.) 5,232 ..... C4

OTHER FEATURES

Miquelon, (isl.) C4
Saint Pierre, (isl.) C4

AREA 156,184 sq. mi. (404,517 sq. km.)
POPULATION 561,996
CAPITAL St. John's
LARGEST CITY St. John's
HIGHEST POINT in Torngat Mountains 5,420 ft. (1,652 m.)
SETTLED IN 1610
ADMITTED TO CONFEDERATION 1949
PROVINCIAL FLOWER Pitcher Plant

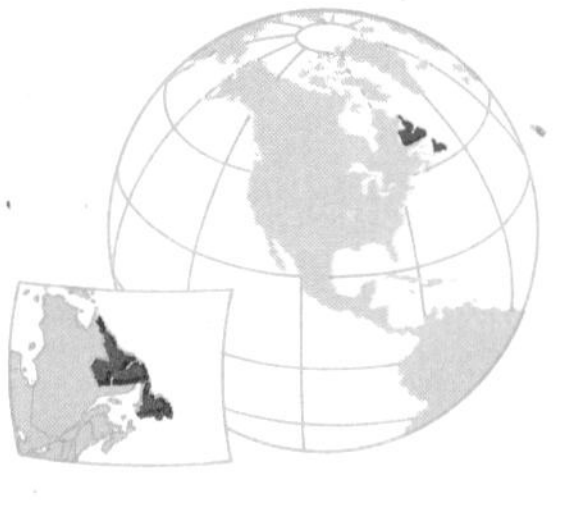

Agriculture, Industry and Resources

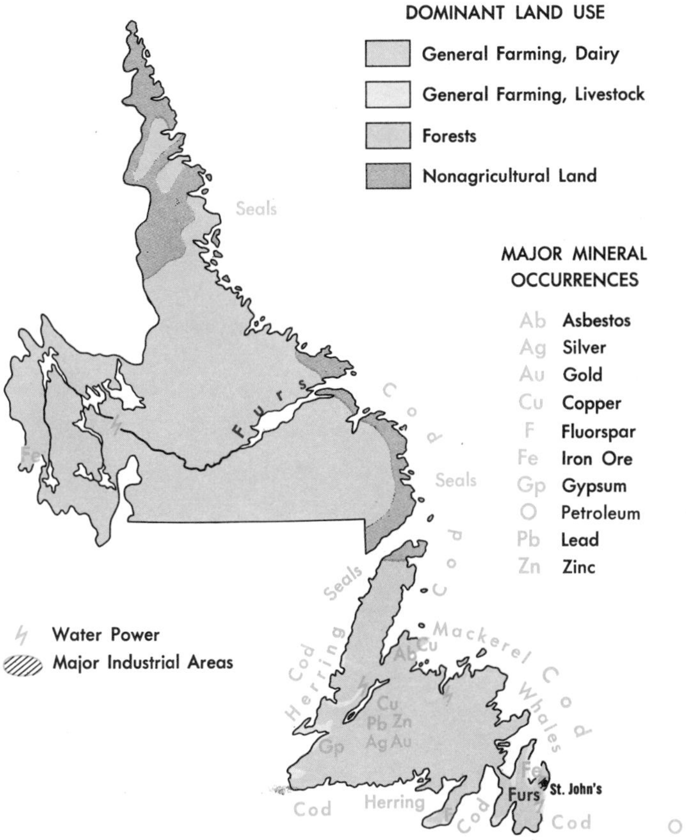

DOMINANT LAND USE
General Farming, Dairy
General Farming, Livestock
Forests
Nonagricultural Land
MAJOR MINERAL OCCURRENCES
Ab Asbestos
Ag Silver
Au Gold
Cu Copper
F Fluorspar
Fe Iron Ore
Gp Gypsum
O Petroleum
Pb Lead
Zn Zinc
Water Power
Major Industrial Areas
Seals
Furs
Cod
Mackerel
Herring
Whales
St. John's

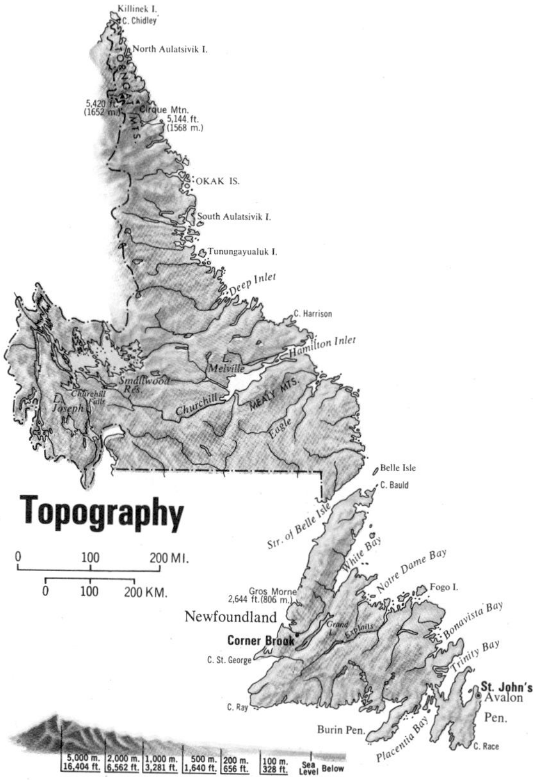

Killinek I.
C. Chidley
North Aulatsivik I.
5,420 ft. (1652 m.)
Cirque Mtn. 5,144 ft. (1568 m.)
OKAK IS.
South Aulatsivik I.
Tunungayualuk I.
Deep Inlet
C. Harrison
Hamilton Inlet
Melville
Smallwood Res.
Churchill
MEALY MTS.
Eagle
Belle Isle
C. Bauld
Topography
0 100 200 MI.
0 100 200 KM.
Str. of Belle Isle
White Bay
Notre Dame Bay
Fogo I.
Gros Morne 2,644 ft. (806 m.)
Newfoundland
Corner Brook
C. St. George
Bonavista Bay
Trinity Bay
St. John's
Avalon Pen.
C. Ray
Burin Pen.
Placentia Bay
C. Race
5,000 m. 16,404 ft.
2,000 m. 6,562 ft.
1,000 m. 3,281 ft.
500 m. 1,640 ft.
200 m. 656 ft.
100 m. 328 ft.
Sea Level
Below

NOVA SCOTIA

COUNTIES

Annapolis 23,208 ....C4
Antigonish 17,573 ....F3
Cape Breton 128,229 ....H3
Colchester 41,771 ....E3
Cumberland 35,914 ....D3
Digby 20,932 ....C4
Guysborough 12,825 ....F4
Halifax 278,531 ....E4
Hants 32,383 ....D4
Inverness 21,773 ....G2
Kings 42,388 ....D4
Lunenburg 42,388 ....D4
Pictou 49,076 ....F3
Queens 12,947 ....D5
Richmond 12,447 ....H3
Shelburne 16,970 ....C5
Victoria 8,417 ....H2
Yarmouth 25,210 ....C5

CITIES and TOWNS

Alder Point H2
Aldershot D3
Amherst⊙ 10,263 ....D3
Annapolis Royal⊙ 738 .....C4
Arichat⊙ 893 ....H3
Baddeck⊙ 943 ....H2
Bear River 716 ....C4
Beaverbank 1,294 ....E4
Berwick 1,701 ....D4
Bible Hill 4,266 ....E3
Bridgetown 1,077 ....C4
Bridgewater 6,010 ....D4
Brookfield 892 ....E3
Brooklyn 1,179 ....D4
Cambridge Station 922 .....D3
Canso 1,173 ....G3
Cape North 136 ....H2
Centreville, Kings 736 ......D4
Chester 1,121 ....D4
Chéticamp 1,027 ....G2

Church Point 377 ....B4
Clark's Harbour 1,077 ......C5
Dartmouth 65,341 ....E4
Digby⊙ 2,542 ....C4
Dominion 2,938 ....J2
Donkin 1,087 ....J2
Echo Lake 1,048 ....H3
Elmsdale 944 ....E4
Elmsvale 132 ....E4
Enfield 1,234 ....E4
Fall River 1,060 ....E4
Falmouth 1,017 ....D3
Florence 2,111 ....H2
Glace Bay 21,836 ....J2
Guysborough⊙ 514 ....G3
Halifax (cap.)⊙ 117,882 ....E4
Hantsport 1,423 ....D3
Harrietsfield 949 ....E4
Herring Cove 1,363 ....E4
Hilden 1,076 ....E3
Ingonish 407 ....H2
Inverness 1,980 ....G2
Judique 770 ....G3

Kentville⊙ 5,056 ....D3
Kingston 1,562 ....D4
Lakeside 1,831 ....E4
Lantz 769 ....E4
Liverpool⊙ 3,336 ....D4
Lockeport 1,030 ....C5
Louisbourg 1,519 ....J3
Louisdale 1,026 ....G3
Lower West Pubnico 778 ...C5
Lunenburg⊙ 3,024 ....D4
Mahone Bay 1,236 ....D4
Meteghan 761 ....B4
Middleton 1,823 ....C4
Milton 1,918 ....D4
Mira Road 1,496 ....H2
Mulgrave 1,206 ....G3
New Germany 910 ....D4
New Glasgow 10,672 ....F3
New Minas 2,873 ....D3
New Road 1,151 ....E4
New Victoria 1,345 ....H2
New Waterford 9,223 ....J2
North Sydney 8,319 ....H2

Oxford 1,498 ....E3
Parrsboro 1,857 ....D3
Petit-de-Grat 762 ....H3
Pictou⊙ 4,588 ....F3
Porters Lake 991 ....E4
Port Hastings 719 ....G2
Port Hawkesbury 4,008 ....G3
Port Hood⊙ 769 ....G2
Port Morien 763 ....J2
Port Williams 993 ....D3
Pugwash 746 ....E3
Reserve Mines 2,394 ....H2
River Hébert 861 ....D3
Sackville 14,590 ....E4
Saint Peters 705 ....H3
Salmon River, Colchester
  1,889 ....E3
Scotchtown 2,086 ....J2
Sheet Harbour 762 ....F4
Shelburne⊙ 2,511 ....C5
Springhill 5,220 ....E3
Stellarton 5,366 ....F3
Stewiacke 1,174 ....E3

Sydney⊙ 30,645 ....H2
Sydney Mines 8,965 ....H2
Sydney River 2,468 ....H2
Terence Bay 1,087 ....E4
Thorburn 965 ....F3
Three Mile Plains 950 ....D4
Timberlea 1,657 ....E4
Trenton 3,224 ....F3
Truro⊙ 12,840 ....E3
Waterville 1,215 ....D4
Waverley 1,142 ....E4
Wedgeport 797 ....C5
Western Shore 1,242 ....D4
Westmount 2,080 ....H2
Westville 4,251 ....F3
Wileville 890 ....D4
Windsor⊙ 3,702 ....D4
Wolfville 3,073 ....D3
Yarmouth⊙ 7,801 ....B5

OTHER FEATURES

Advocate, (bay) D3

Ainslie, (lake) ....G
Amet, (sound) ....E
Andrew, (isl.) ....H
Annapolis, (basin) C
Annapolis, (riv.) ....D
Antigonish, (harb.) ....F
Argos, (cape) ....H
Aspy, (bay) ....H
Avon, (riv.) ....D
Baccaro, (cape) C
Baddeck, (riv.) ....H
Barachois, (pt.) ....H
Barren, (isl.) ....D
Barrington, (bay) C
Bedford, (basin) ....E
Berry, (head) ....D
Boularderie, (isl.) ....H
Bras d'Or, (lake) ....H
Breton, (cape) ....J
Brier, (isl.) ....B
Canso, (cape) ....G
Canso, (str.) ....G
Cap d'Or, (cape) ....D

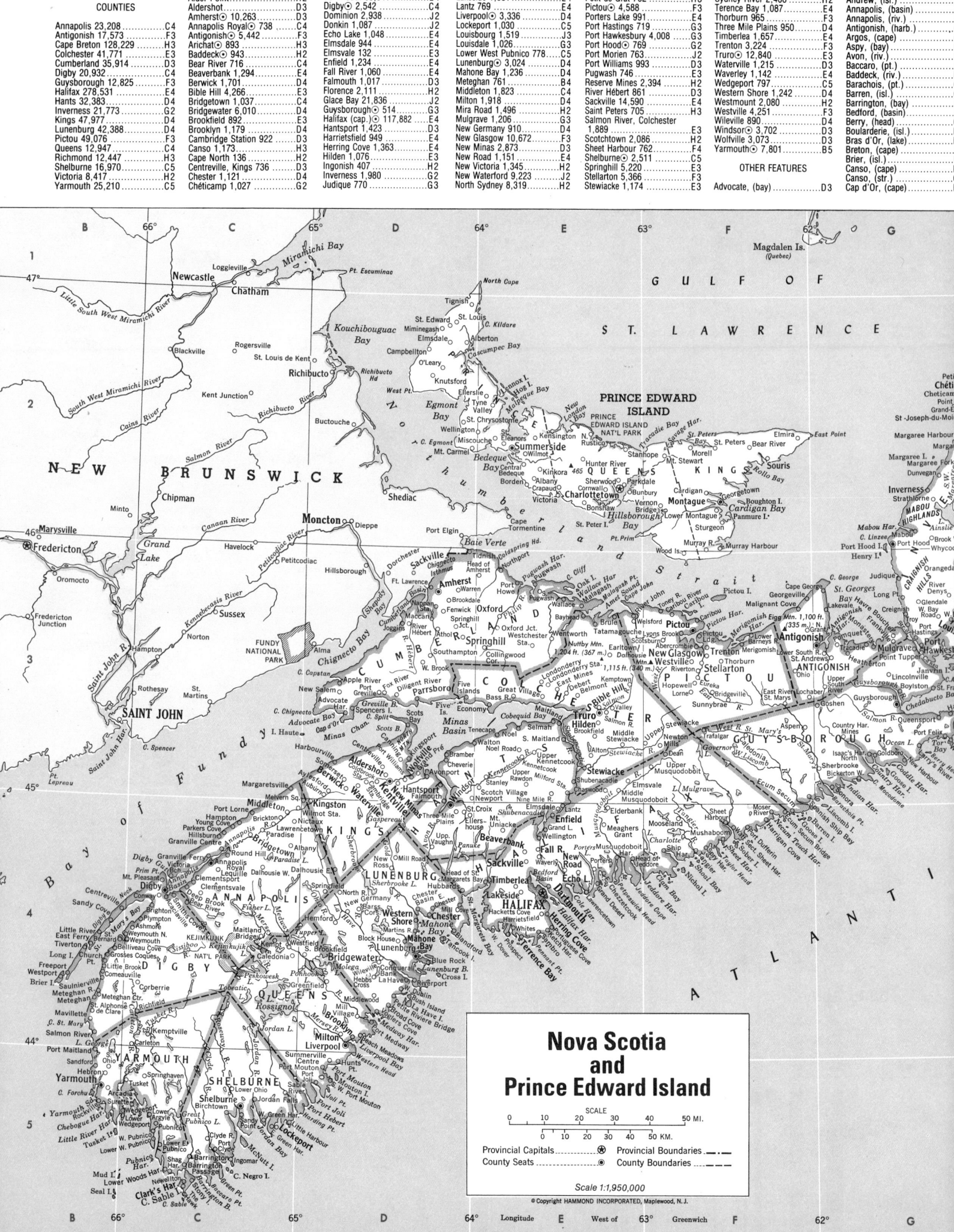

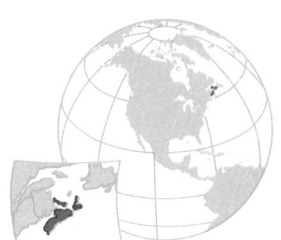

PRINCE EDWARD ISLAND

AREA 2,184 sq. mi. (5,657 sq. km.)
POPULATION 121,328
CAPITAL Charlottetown
LARGEST CITY Charlottetown
HIGHEST POINT 465 ft. (142 m.)
SETTLED IN 1720
ADMITTED TO CONFEDERATION 1873
PROVINCIAL FLOWER Lady's Slipper

NOVA SCOTIA

AREA 21,425 sq. mi. (55,491 sq. km.)
POPULATION 837,789
CAPITAL Halifax
LARGEST CITY Halifax
HIGHEST POINT Cape Breton Highlands
  1,747 ft. (532 m.)
SETTLED IN 1605
ADMITTED TO CONFEDERATION 1867
PROVINCIAL FLOWER Trailing Arbutus or
  Mayflower

Topography

0   30   60 MI.

0   30   60 KM.

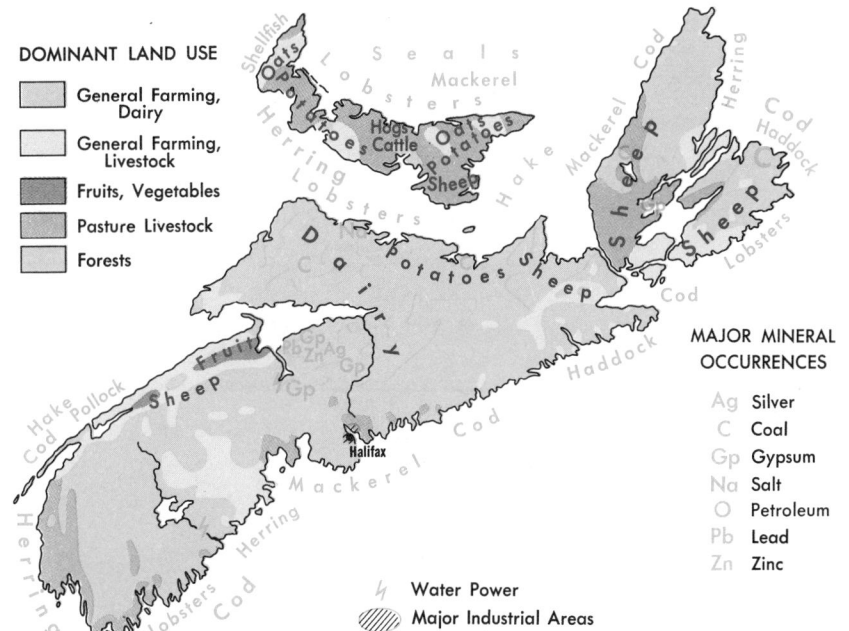

Below 100 m. 200 m. 500 m. 1,000 m. 2,000 m. 5,000 m.
Sea   328 ft. 656 ft. 1,640 ft. 3,281 ft. 6,562 ft. 16,404 ft.
Level

Agriculture, Industry and Resources

DOMINANT LAND USE

General Farming, Dairy

General Farming, Livestock

Fruits, Vegetables

Pasture Livestock

Forests

MAJOR MINERAL OCCURRENCES

Ag Silver
C   Coal
Gp Gypsum
Na Salt
O   Petroleum
Pb Lead
Zn Zinc

Water Power
Major Industrial Areas

New Brunswick

SCALE

Provincial Capitals ⊕
County Seats ⊙
International Boundaries
Provincial Boundaries
County Boundaries

Scale 1:1,900,000

© Copyright Hammond Incorporated, Maplewood, N.J.

Harvey, Albert 75 ....F3
Harvey, York 376............D3
Hatfield Point 179............E3
Havelock 351 ....E3
Hayesville 130..................D2
Hazeldean 130..................C2
Head of Millstream 79 ....E3
Heath Steele D1
Hillman 80 ....C2
Hillsborough 1,153 ....F3
Holmesville 136 ....C2
Holtville 229 ....D2
Honeydale 72 ....C3
Hopewell Cape⊙ 129 ....F3
Hopewell Hill 178 ....F3
Howard 152........................E2
Howland Ridge 67 ....C2
Hoyt D3
Inkerman 324.....................F1
Irishtown 232 ....F2
Island View 260..................D3
Jacksonville 328 ....C2
Jacquet River 735 ....E1
Janeville 192......................E1
Jeanne Mance 97 ....E1
Jemseg 188 ....D3
Jolicure 87 ....F3
Juniper 572........................C2
Kedgwick 1,271 ....C1
Kedgwick Ouest 21 ....C1
Kedgwick River 15...............C1
Keenan Siding 91 ....E2
Kent Junction 104 ....E2
Kent Lake E2
Keswick 288.......................D3
Kilburn 111 ....C2
Killam 65 ....E2
Kingsclear 178 ....D3
Kingsley 129 ....D2
King's Landing C3
Kirkland 63 ....C3
Knowlesville 64 ....C2
Kouchibouguac 97 ....F2
Lac Baker 325.....................B1
Lagacéville 220...................E1
Lake George 172.................C3
Laketon 109 ....E2
Lakeville 530 ....C2
Lambertville 153 ....C3
Lamèque 973 ....F1
Landry 94 ....E1
Laplante 222.......................E1
Lavillette 580 ....E1
Lawrence Station 187 ....C3
Leech 574...........................E1
Léger Brook 423 ....F2
Légerville 183......................F2
Le Goulet 1,059 ....F1
Leonardville 138 ....C4
Lepreau 183 ....D3
Levesque 76 ....C1
Little Cape 550 ....F2
Little Shippegan 111...........F1
Loggieville 784 ....E1
Lorne 987..........................D1
Lower Cloverdale 576 ....F2
Lower Derby 209 ....E2
Lower Durham 55 ....D2
Lower Hainesville 99 ....C2
Lower Kars 32....................E3
Lower Millstream 176 ....E3
Lower Sapin 201 ....F2
Lower Southampton 88 ....C2
Ludlow 97 ....D2
Maces Bay 117 ....D3
Madran 255........................E1
Magaguadavic 98 ....C3
Maisonnette 714 ....E1
Malden 80 ....G2
Manners Sutton 187 ....D3
Manuels 330.......................F1
Mapleview 110 ....C2
Marcelville 51.....................E2
Martin 105.........................C1
Maugerville 266..................D3
Maxwell 47 ....C3
McAdam 1,985...................C3
McGivney 175....................D2
McGraw Brook D2
McKendrick 547 ....D1
McNamee 154.....................D2
Meductic 170......................C3
Melrose 97.........................F2
Memramcook 262................F2
Menneval 111 ....C1
Midgic Station 170..............F3
Mill Cove 50......................D3
Millerton 144 ....D2
Millville 308.......................C2
Minto 3,714 ....D2
Miscou Centre 519..............F1
Miscou Harbour 97 ....F1
Mispec 152 ....E3
Moncton 55,934 ....F2
Moores Mills 106 ....C3
Morrisdale 188...................D3
Moulin-Morneault 433 ....B1
Murray Corner 162 ....G2
Nackawic 1,341 ....C2
Napadogan 103 ....D2
Nash Creek 183..................D1
Nashwaak Bridge 161.........D2
Nashwaak Village 275.........D2
Nauwigewauk 201 ....E3
Neguac 1,733 ....E1
Nelson-Miramichi 1,543 ......E2
Newcastle⊙ 6,423 ....E2
Newcastle Creek 235..........D2
New Denmark 100..............C1
New Jersey 176 ....E1
New Market 110 ....D3
New Maryland 481 ....D3
New River Beach 43 ....D3
Newtown 108......................E3
New Zion 152 ....D2
Nicholas Denys 174 ....D1
Nictau 29...........................C1
Nigadoo 799 ....E1
Noinville E2
Nordin 350.........................E1
North Head 647..................D4
Norton 1,285 ....E3
Notre-Dame 282..................F2
Oak Bay 254 ....C3
Oak Point 106 ....D3
Odell River 28 ....C2
Oromocto 10,276................D3
Paquetville 601 ....E1
Peel 98 ....C2
Pelletier Mills 85.................B1
Pennfield 305 ....D3
Penniac 176 ....D2
Penobsquis 275 ....E3
Perth-Andover⊙ 1,973 ....C2
Petitcodiac 1,472 ....E3
Petite-Rivière-de-l'Île 539 ....F1
Petit Rocher 1,790 ....E1
Petit Rocher Sud 310 ....E1
Pigeon Hill 527 ....F1
Plaster Rock 1,368..............C2
Pocologan 65 ....D3
Point de Bute 147................F3
Pointe-du-Chêne 468 ....F2
Pointe-Verte 617 ....E1
Pointe-Sapin 326.................F2
Pollett River 57...................E3
Pontgrave 215 ....F1
Pont-Lafrance 806 ....E1
Pont-Landry 322 ....F1
Port Elgin 492 ....F2
Prime 87 ....B1
Prince of Wales..................D3
Prince William 242 ....C3
Quarryville 213 ....E2
Queenstown 98 ....D3
Quispamsis 4,968 ....E3
Red Bank 161 ....E2
Renforth 1,572...................E3
Renous 161........................E2
Rexton 872.........................F2
Richardsville 819 ....D1
Richibucto⊙ 1,909 ....E2
Richibucto Village 432 ....F2
Richmond Corner 79 ....C2
Riley Brook 111 ....C1
Ripples 192.........................D3
River de Chute 42 ....C2
River Glade 264 ....E3
Rivière-du-Portage 672.........F1
Riverside-Albert 467 ....F3
Riverview 14,177 ....F2
Rivière Verte 1,009.............B1
Robertville 628 ....E1
Robichaud 392 ....F2
Robinsonville 211................C1
Rogersville 1,138 ....E2
Rollingdam 81....................C3
Rosaireville 73...................E2
Rothesay 1,283 ....E3
Rowena 78.........................C2
Roy 147 ....F2
Royal Road 65 ....D2
Rusagonis 195 ....D3
Sackville 5,755 ....F3
Saint Almo 26.....................C2
Saint-André 310..................C1
Saint Andrews⊙ 1,711 ....C3
Saint-Antoine 1,062 ....F2
Saint Arthur 391 ....D1
Saint Basile 3,072 ....B1
Saint-Charles 310 ....F2
Saint Croix C3
Sainte-Anne 321 ....E1
Sainte-Anne-de-Kent 142 .....F2
Sainte-Anne-de-Madawaska 1,341 ....B1
Saint-Édouard-de-Kent 163...F2
Sainte-Marie-de-Kent 250.....F2
Sainte-Marie-sur-Mer 563 ....F1
Sainte-Rose-Gloucester 412 F1
Saint François de Madawaska 650.............B1
Saint George 1,148 ....D3
Saint Hilaire 168 ....B1
Saint-Ignace.......................F2
Saint-Isidore 286.................E1
Saint-Jacques 1,374 ....B1
Saint-Jean-Baptiste-de-Restigouche 227 ....C1
Saint John⊙ 85,956 ....E3
Saint-Joseph 741 ....F3
Saint-Joseph-de-Madawaska 188...................................B1
Saint-Léolin 770..................E1
Saint Leonard 1,593 ....C1
Saint-Louis-de-Kent 1,278....F2
Saint Margarets 77 ....E2
Saint Martin de Restigouche 158 ....C1
Saint Martins 544 ....E3
Saint-Paul 341....................E2
Saint Quentin 2,246 ....C1
Saint-Raphaël-sur-Mer 373...F1
Saint Sauveur 299 ....E1
Saint Stephen 5,264 ....C3
Saint Wilfred 360 ....E1
Salisbury 1,410 ....E2
Salmon Beach 275...............E1
Salmon Creek 39.................E2
Saumarez 238 ....E1
Scoudouc 171 ....F2
Seal Cove 526.....................D4
Shannon 30.........................E3
Shediac 4,216 ....F2
Shediac Bridge 424 ....F2
Sheffield 109.......................D3
Sheila 753..........................F1
Shemogue 197 ....F2
Shepody 72 ....F3
Shippegan 2,344 ....F1
Siegas 227...........................C1
Sillikers 313 ....E2
Simonds 201 ....C2
Sisson Ridge 134.................C2
Six Roads 118......................F1
Smiths Creek 141 ....E3
Somerville 326 ....C2
South Branch 111.................F2
Springfield, King's 138 ....E3
Springfield, York 138 ....C2
Stanley 435.........................D2
Stickney 223 ....C2
Storeytown 144 ....D2
Sunny Corner 369 ....E2
Sunnyside 98.......................D1
Sussex 3,938.......................E3
Sussex Corner 864 ....E3
Tabusintac 304 ....E1
Taxis River 103 ....D2

AREA 28,354 sq. mi. (73,437 sq. km.)
POPULATION 688,926
CAPITAL Fredericton
LARGEST CITY Saint John
HIGHEST POINT Mt. Carleton 2,690 ft. (820 m.)
SETTLED IN 1611
ADMITTED TO CONFEDERATION 1867
PROVINCIAL FLOWER Purple Violet

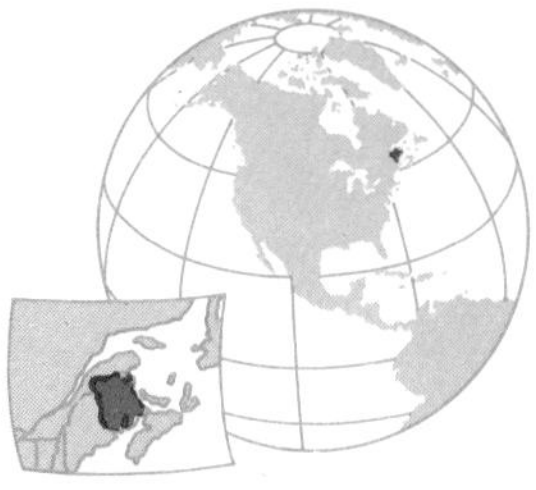

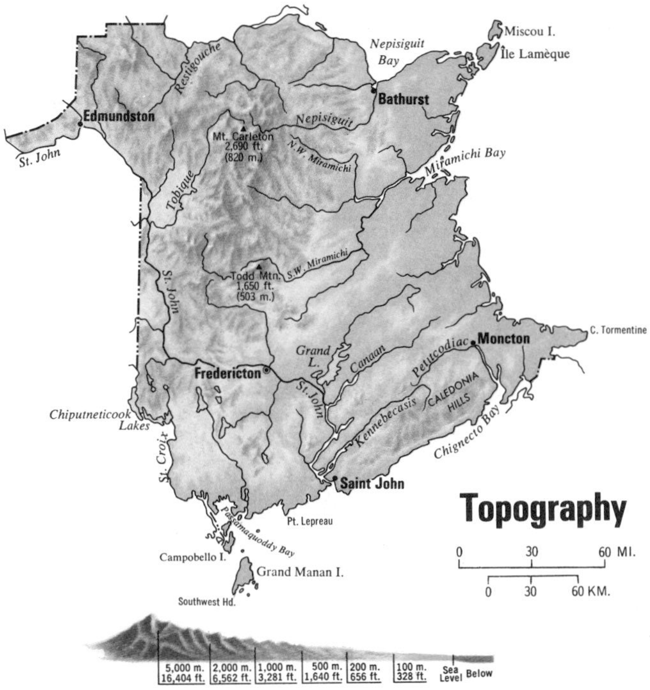

Miscou I.
Île Lamèque
Nepisiguit Bay
Bathurst
Restigouche
Edmundston
St. John
Nepisiguit
Mt. Carleton 2,690 ft. (820 m.)
N.W. Miramichi
Miramichi Bay
Tobique
S.W. Miramichi
Todd Mtn. 1,650 ft. (503 m.)
St. John
C. Tormentine
Grand L.
Canaan
Petitcodiac
Moncton
Fredericton
St. John
Caledonia Hills
Chiputneticook Lakes
Kennebecasis
Chignecto Bay
St. Croix
Saint John
Pt. Lepreau
Passamaquoddy Bay
Campobello I.
Grand Manan I.
Southwest Hd.
0 30 60 MI.
0 30 60 KM.
5,000 m. 16,404 ft.
2,000 m. 6,562 ft.
1,000 m. 3,281 ft.
500 m. 1,640 ft.
200 m. 656 ft.
100 m. 328 ft.
Sea Level
Below

Topography

Tay Creek 161..................D2
Taymouth 287..................D2
Temperance Vale 331 ....C2
The Range 53 ....E2
Thibault 286......................C1
Tide Head 897 ....D1
Tilley 177 ....C2
Tobique Narrows 129 ....C2
Tracadie 2,591 ....F1
Tracy 662 ....D3
Turtle Creek 127 ....F3
Tweedside 75.....................C3
Upham 94..........................E3
Upper Blackville 193 ....E2
Upper Buctouche 138 ....F2
Upper Gagetown 200 ....D3
Upper Hainesville 185.........C2
Upper Kent 190 ....C2
Upper Maugerville 554........D3
Upper Mills 138..................C3
Upper Rockport 18 ....F3
Upper Sheila 764 ....E1
Upper Woodstock 291 ....C2
Upsalquitch 173 ....D1
Val-Comeau 489..................F1
Val d'Amour 489 ....D1
Val Doucet 521...................E1
Verret 244 ....B1
Village-Saint-Laurent 210.....E1
Violette Brook C1
Waasis 273.........................D3
Wapske 206 ....C2
Waterford 95 ....E3
Waterville 155 ....C2
Waweig 113 ....C3
Wayerton 153 ....E1
Weaver E2
Weldon 215........................F3
Welsford 231......................D3
Welshpool 200....................D4
Westfield 1;048 ....D3
West Quaco 29....................E3
White Head 183..................D4
White Rapids 212................E2
Whitney 234 ....E2
Wickham 65 ....D3
Wicklow 104.......................C2
Williamsburg 261................D2
Williamstown 160................C2
Willow Grove 402................E3
Wilmot 66..........................C3
Wilson Point 49 ....F1
Wilsons Beach 915..............D4
Windsor 59 ....C2
Wirral 95............................D3
Woodstock⊙ 4,869 ....C2
Woodwards Cove 120 ....D4
Youngs Cove 76 ....E3
Zealand 466 ....D2

OTHER FEATURES

Bald (mt.).........................C1
Baritbog (riv.) E1
Bay du Vin (riv.) E2
Big Tracadie (riv.) E1
Buctouche (harb.)...............F2
Buctouche (riv.) F2
Campobello (isl.) D4
Canaan (riv.).....................E2
Carleton (mt.) D1
Chaleur (bay) E1
Chignecto (bay) F3
Chiputneticook (lkes)..........C3
Cocagne (isl.) F2
Cumberland (basin)............F3
Deer (isl.)..........................D4
Digdeguash (riv.) C3
Escuminac (bay) D1
Escuminac (pt.) F1
Fundy (bay).......................E3
Fundy Nat'l Park E3
Gaspereau (riv.) D2
Grand (bay).......................D3
Grand (lake) C3
Grand (lake) D3
Grande (riv.).....................C1
Grand Manan (chan.) C4
Grand Manan (isl.) D4
Green (riv.) B1
Hammond (riv.) E3
Harvey (lake) C3
Heron (isl.) D1
Kedgwick (riv.)..................C1
Kennebecasis (riv.) E3
Keswick (riv.) C2
Kouchibouguac (bay) F2
Kouchibouguacis (riv.)........E2
Kouchobouguac Nat'l Park F2
Lamèque (isl.) F1
Lepreau (riv.) D3
Little (riv.) D2
Long (isl.) D3
Long Reach (inlet).............D3
Maces (bay) D3
Mactaquac (lake)...............C3
Madawaska (riv.) B1
Magaguadavic (lake) C3
Magaguadavic (riv.) C3
Miramichi (bay) E1
Miscou (isl.) F1
Miscou (pt.) F1
Mount Carleton Prov. Park D1
Musquash (harb.) D3
Nashwaak (riv.) D2
Nepisiguit (bay) E1
Nepisiguit (riv.) D1
Nerepis (riv.) D3
Northern (head)...............D4
North Sevogle (riv.)..........D1
Northumberland (str.).........F2
Northwest Miramichi (riv.)...D1
Oromocto (lake)................C3
Oromocto (riv.) D3
Passamaquoddy (bay) C3
Patapédia (riv.).................C1
Petitcodiac (riv.) F3
Pokemouche (riv.).............E1
Pokesudie (isl.).................F1
Pollett (riv.).....................E3
Quaco (head) E3
Renous (riv.)....................D2
Restigouche (riv.) C1
Richibucto (harb.) F2
Richibucto (riv.)................E2
Roosevelt Campobello Int'l Park D4
Saint Croix (riv.)...............C3
Saint Francis (riv.)............A1
Saint John (harb.) E3
Saint John (riv.) C2
Saint Lawrence (gulf).........F1
Salisbury (bay) F3
Salmon (riv.) C1
Salmon (riv.) E2
Shediac (isl.)....................F2
Shepody (bay) F3
Shippegan (bay) E1
Shippegan (gully) F1
South Sevogle (riv.)...........D1
Southwest (head)...............D4
Southwest Miramichi (riv.)...D2
Spear (cape)......................G2
Spednik (lake)...................C3
Spencer (cape) E3
Tabusintac (gully) F1
Tabusintac (riv.) E1
Tetagouche (riv.) D1
Tobique (riv.)....................C2
Upsalquitch (riv.)...............D1
Utopia (lake).....................D3
Verte (bay)........................G2
Washademoak (lake) E3
West (isls.)........................D4
White Head (isl.) D4

⊙ County seat.

Agriculture, Industry and Resources

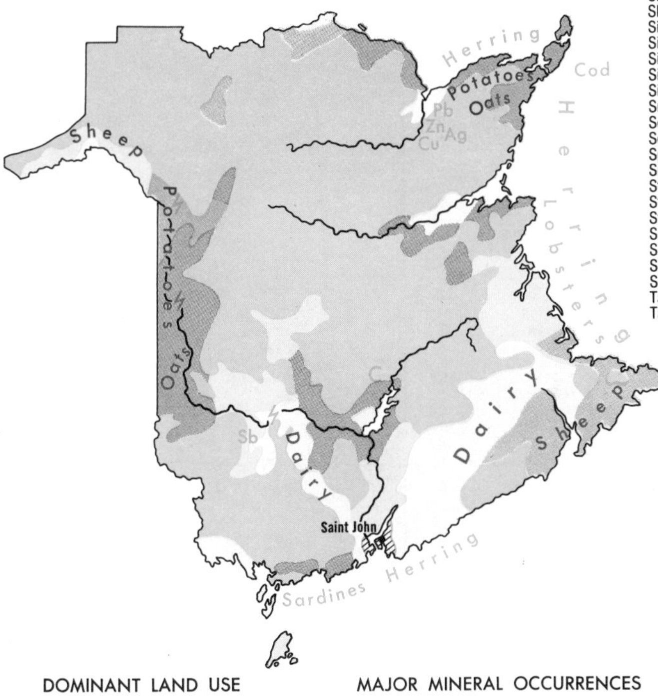

Herring
Potatoes
Oats
Cod
Pb
Zn
Ag
Cu
Sheep
Potatoes
Oats
Herring
Lobsters
C
Sb
Dairy
Dairy
Sheep
Saint John
Herring
Sardines

DOMINANT LAND USE

- Cereals, Livestock
- Dairy
- Potatoes
- General Farming, Livestock
- Pasture Livestock
- Forests

MAJOR MINERAL OCCURRENCES

- Ag Silver
- Pb Lead
- C Coal
- Sb Antimony
- Cu Copper
- Zn Zinc
- Water Power
- Major Industrial Areas

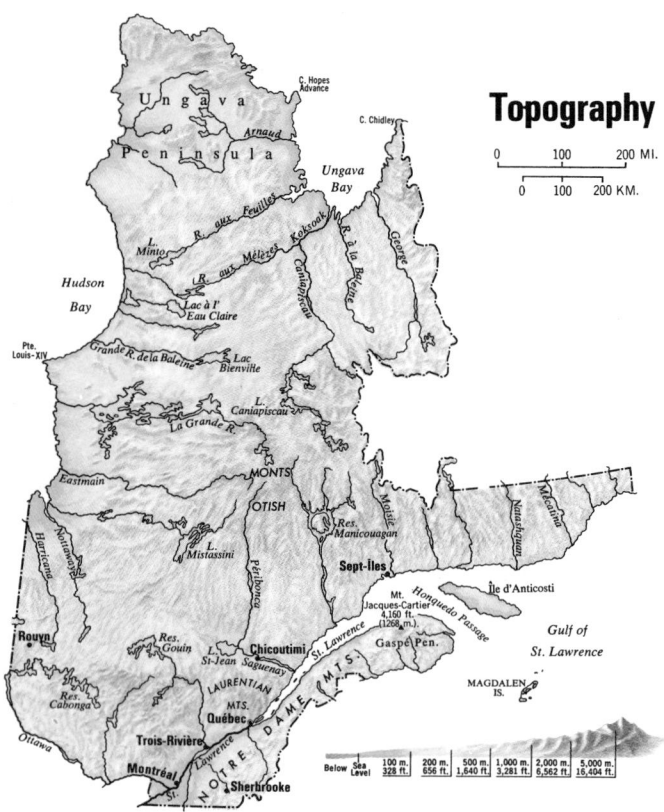

Topography

0 100 200 MI.

0 100 200 KM.

Below Sea Level | 100 m. 328 ft. | 200 m. 656 ft. | 500 m. 1,640 ft. | 1,000 m. 3,281 ft. | 2,000 m. 6,562 ft. | 5,000 m. 16,404 ft.

COUNTIES

Argenteuil 31,654	C4	
Arthabaska 54,176	F3	
Bagot 24,791	E4	
Beauce 67,083	G3	
Beauharnois 53,026	D4	
Bellechasse 22,908	G3	
Berthier 28,465	C3	
Bonaventure 40,724	C2	
Brome 16,410	E4	
Chambly 286,130	J4	
Champlain 114,078	E2	
Charlevoix-Est 17,085	G2	
Charlevoix-Ouest 13,601	G2	
Châteauguay 57,252	D4	
Chicoutimi 165,859	G1	
Compton 20,512	F4	
Deux-Montagnes 58,568	C4	
Dorchester 32,396	G3	
Drummond 66,122	E4	
Frontenac 26,203	G4	

Gaspé-Est 40,720	D1	
Gaspé-Ouest 19,238	C1	
Gatineau 52,193	B3	
Hull 134,518	B4	
Huntingdon 16,653	C4	
Iberville 21,296	D4	
Île-de-Montréal 1,869,641	H4	
Île-Jésus 246,243	H4	
Joliette 55,524	C3	
Kamouraska 27,740	H2	
Labelle 31,065	B3	
Lac-Saint-Jean-Est 45,558	F1	
Lac-Saint-Jean-Ouest 57,556	E1	
Laprairie 84,217	H4	
L'Assomption 84,967	D4	
Lévis 75,916	J3	
L'Islet 22,223	G2	
Lotbinière 27,780	F3	
Maskinongé 20,879	D3	
Matane 28,954	B1	
Matapédia 24,063	B2	
Mégantic 56,566	F3	

Missisquoi 34,853	D4	
Montcalm 23,534	C3	
Montmagny 26,622	G3	
Montmorency No. 1 20,712	F2	
Montmorency No. 2 5,869	G3	
Napierville 12,595	D4	
Nicolet 31,102	E3	
Papineau 36,275	B4	
Pontiac 20,559	A3	
Portneuf 51,643	E3	
Québec 449,633	F2	
Richelieu 49,944	D4	
Richmond 39,895	E4	
Rimouski 64,768	J1	
Rivière-du-Loup 39,339	H2	
Rouville 36,672	D4	
Saguenay 115,736	H1	
Saint-Hyacinthe 52,417	D4	
Saint-Jean 50,587	D4	
Saint-Maurice 106,023	D3	
Shefford 65,528	E4	
Sherbrooke 109,589	E4	

Soulanges 13,254	C4	
Stanstead 36,737	F4	
Témiscouata 52,871	J2	
Terrebonne 164,502	H4	
Vaudreuil 44,257	C4	
Verchères 49,298	J4	
Wolfe 15,254	F4	
Yamaska 14,490	E3	

CITIES and TOWNS

Acton Vale 4,326	E4	
Albanel 889	E1	
Alma⊙ 25,638	F1	
Amqui⊙ 3,949	B2	
Ancienne-Lorette 11,694	A1	
Angers	B4	
Anjou 36,596	H4	
Annaville 586	E3	
Armagh 966	G3	
Arthabaska⊙ 5,907	F3	
Arvida	F1	
Asbestos 9,075	F4	
Ascot Corner 895	F4	
Audet 674	G4	
Ayer's Cliff 873	E4	
Aylmer 25,714	B4	
Baie-Comeau 11,911	A1	
Baie-des-Sables 588	A1	
Baie-d'Urfé 3,955	G4	
Baie-Saint-Paul⊙ 4,062	G2	
Baie-Trinité 802	B1	
Beaconsfield 20,417	H4	
Beauceville 4,276	G3	
Beaumont 635	F3	
Beauport 55,539	J3	
Beaupré 2,821	G2	
Bécancour⊙ 9,043	E3	
Bedford⊙ 3,010	E4	
Beebe Plain 1,155	E4	
Bélair 10,716	H3	
Beloeil 15,913	D4	
Bernierville 2,182	F3	
Berthier-en-Bas 576	G3	
Berthierville⊙ 4,249	D3	
Bic 2,670	J1	
Biencourt 818	J2	
Black Lake 4,051	F3	
Blainville 12,517	H4	
Boischatel 2,279	J3	
Bois-des-Filion 4,346	H4	
Bolduc 1,593	G4	
Bonaventure 1,195	C2	
Boucherville 25,530	J4	
Boulanger 953	E1	
Bromont 2,505	E4	
Bromptonville 2,992	F4	
Brossard 37,641	H4	
Brownsburg 3,114	C4	
Buckingham 14,328	B4	
Cabano 3,193	J2	
Cacouna 1,083	H2	
Calumet 708	C4	
Candiac 7,166	J4	
Cap-à-l'Aigle 712	G2	
Cap-Chat 3,617	B1	
Cap-de-la-Madeleine 32,126	E3	
Cap-des-Rosiers 691	D1	
Cap-Saint-Ignace 1,312	G2	
Cap-Santé⊙ 1,312	F3	
Carignan 3,585	J4	
Carleton 2,538	C2	
Caughnawaga 3,708	H4	

Causapscal 2,743	B2	
Chambly 11,815	J4	
Chambord 1,058	E1	
Champlain 548	E3	
Chandler 4,011	D2	
Charette 538	D3	
Charlemagne 4,025	H4	
Charlesbourg 63,147	J3	
Charny 6,416	J3	
Châteauguay 36,329	H4	
Châteauguay-Centre	H4	
Château-Richer⊙ 3,075	F3	
Chénéville 699	B4	
Chicoutimi⊙ 57,737	G1	
Chicoutimi-Nord	F1	
Chute-aux-Outardes 2,103	A1	
Clermont 3,518	G2	
Cloridorme 553	D1	
Coaticook 6,392	F4	
Coleraine 1,485	F4	
Compton 584	F4	
Contrecoeur 1,195	D4	
Cookshire⊙ 1,453	F4	
Coteau-du-Lac 1,248	C4	
Coteau-Landing⊙ 1,106	C4	
Côte-Saint-Luc 25,721	H4	
Courcelles 677	G4	
Courville	J3	
Cowansville 11,902	E4	
Crabtree 1,942	D4	
Danville 2,367	E4	
Daveluyville 1,321	E3	
Dégelis 3,304	J2	
Delisle 1,249	F1	
Delson 4,241	H4	
Desbiens 1,673	E1	
Deschambault 1,018	E3	
Deschênes	B4	
Deux-Montagnes 8,957	H4	
Didyme 759	E1	
Disraëli 3,306	F4	
Dixville 534	F4	
Dolbeau 8,451	E1	
Dollard-des-Ormeaux 36,837	H4	
Donnacona 5,800	F3	
Dorion 5,843	C4	
Dorval 19,131	H4	
Douville	D4	
Drummondville⊙ 29,286	E4	
Drummondville-Nord 2,298	E4	
Drummondville-Sud 9,420	E4	
Dunham 2,505	E4	
Durham-Sud 1,040	E4	
East Angus 4,417	F4	
East Broughton 1,371	F3	
East Broughton Station 1,191	F3	
Eastman 557	E4	
Escoumins 2,324	H1	
Farnham 6,476	E4	
Ferme-Neuve 2,113	B3	
Forestville 1,819	H1	
Frampton 759	G3	
Francoeur 1,389	F3	
Gaspé 16,842	D1	
Gatineau 73,479	B4	
Giffard	J3	
Girardville 1,035	E1	
Godbout 593	B1	
Gracefield 927	A3	
Granby 37,132	E4	
Grande-Rivière 4,390	D2	
Grandes-Bergeronnes 779	H1	
Grande-Vallée 881	D1	
Grand'Mère 15,999	E3	
Greenfield Park 18,430	J4	
Grenville 1,517	C4	
Gros-Morne 584	C1	
Hampstead 7,562	H4	
Ham-Sud⊙ 67	F4	
Hauterive 14,724	A1	
Hébertville 1,520	F1	
Hébertville-Station 1,362	F1	
Hemmingford 763	D4	
Henryville 590	D4	
Howick 660	D4	
Huberdeau 679	C4	
Hudson 4,480	C4	
Huntingdon⊙ 3,098	C4	
Iberville⊙ 8,897	D4	
Île-Bizard 2,985	H4	
Île-Perrot 5,272	G4	
Inverness⊙ 365	F3	
Joliette⊙ 18,118	D3	
Jonquière 60,691	F1	
Kingsey Falls 601	E4	
Kirkland 7,476	H4	
La Baie 20,116	G1	
La Baie-de-Shawinigan 632	E3	
Labelle 2,007	C3	
Lac-Alouette 738	D4	
Lac-au-Saumon 1,309	B2	
Lac-aux-Sables 818	E3	
Lac-Beauport	F3	
Lac-Bouchette 1,685	E1	
Lac-Carré 687	C3	
Lac-des-Aigles 787	J2	
Lac-des-Écorces 638	B3	
Lac-Drolet 1,015	G4	
Lac-Etchemin 2,746	G3	
Lachenaie 7,118	D4	
Lachine 41,503	H4	
Lachute⊙ 11,928	C4	
Lac-Mégantic⊙ 6,457	G4	
Lacolle 1,193	D4	
Lac-Saint-Charles 3,285	H3	
La Durantaye 763	G3	
Lafontaine 4,442	C4	
La Guadeloupe 1,804	F4	
La Malbaie⊙ 4,069	G2	
Lambton 777	F4	
Lamartine 675	G2	
L'Ange-Gardien 1,838	F3	
Langlais 1,197	F1	
L'Annonciation 2,186	C3	

Lanoraie 1,362	D4	
La Pérade 1,032	E3	
La Pêche 4,662	B4	
La Pocatière 4,319	H2	
La Prairie⊙ 9,173	J4	
La Providence	E4	
La Rédemption 808	B2	
Larouche 549	F1	
La Salle 76,713	H4	
L'Ascension, Lac-St-Jean E. 1,090	F1	
L'Assomption⊙ 4,832	D4	
La Station-du-Coteau 869	C4	
La Trinité-des-Monts 592	J1	
La Tuque 12,067	E2	
Laurentides 1,804	D4	
Laurier-Station 1,260	F3	
Laurierville 867	F3	
Lauzon 12,663	J3	
Laval 246,243	H4	
Lavaltrie 1,473	D4	
Lawrenceville 528	E4	
Le Moyne 7,202	J4	
Lennoxville 3,682	F4	
L'Épiphanie 2,912	D4	
Léry 6,842	H4	
Les Becquets 577	E3	
Les Éboulements 1,190	G2	
Les Méchins 1,049	B1	
Lévis 17,819	J3	
Linière 1,176	G3	
L'Islet 1,113	G2	
L'Islet-sur-Mer 817	G2	

L'Isle-Verte 1,201	G1	
Longueuil⊙ 122,429	J4	
Loretteville⊙ 14,767	H3	
Lorraine 5,388	H4	
Louiseville⊙ 3,993	E3	
Lucerne 8,000	B4	
Luceville 1,513	J1	
Lyster 811	F3	
Magog 13,290	E4	
Maniwaki⊙ 5,969	B3	
Manseau 656	E3	
Mansonville 590	E4	
Maple Grove 1,857	H4	
bmarbleton 551	F4	
Maria 1,016	C2	
Marieville⊙ 4,853	D4	
Marsoui 541	B1	
Mascouche 14,266	H4	
Maskinongé 1,001	E3	
Masson	B4	
Massueville	E4	
Matane⊙ 12,726	B1	
Matapédia 581	B2	
Melocheville 1,660	C4	
Mercier 4,957	H4	
Metabetchouan 3,016	F1	
Mirabel⊙ 13,486	H4	
Mistassini 5,473	E1	
Montauban 903	E3	
Mont-Carmel 852	H2	
Montcerf 587	A3	
Montebello 1,276	B4	
Mont-Joli 6,508	J1	
Mont-Laurier⊙ 8,565	B3	

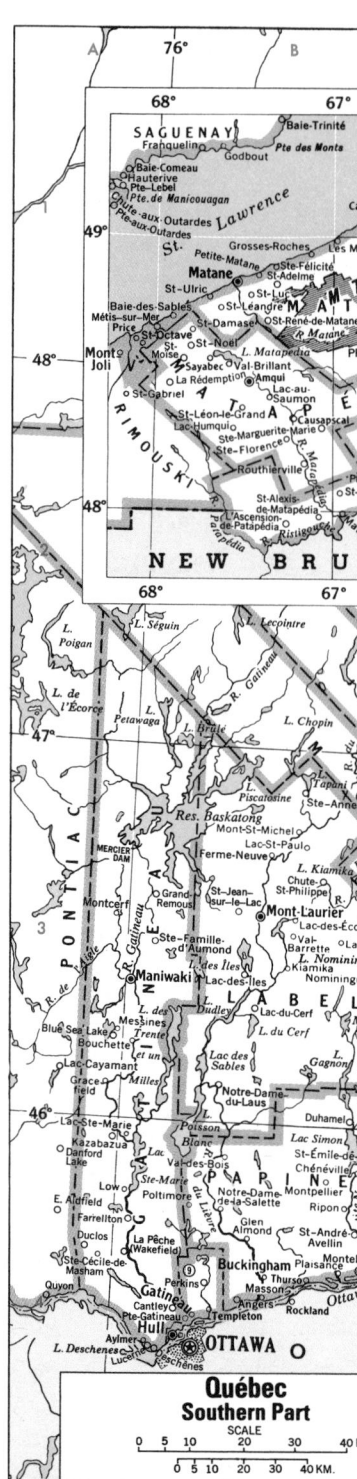

Québec
Southern Part
SCALE
0 5 10 20 30 40 MI.
0 5 10 20 30 40 KM.

National Capital ⊛
Provincial Capital ⊛
County Seats ⊙
International Boundaries

Provincial & State Boundaries
County Boundaries

Scale 1:2,250,000

Agriculture, Industry and Resources

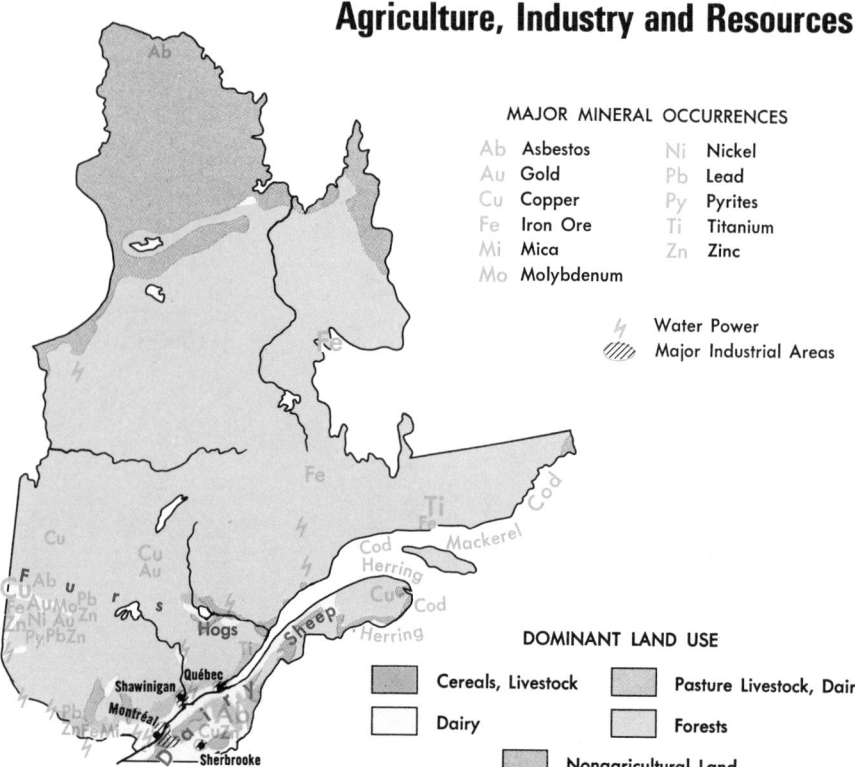

MAJOR MINERAL OCCURRENCES

Ab	Asbestos		Ni	Nickel
Au	Gold		Pb	Lead
Cu	Copper		Py	Pyrites
Fe	Iron Ore		Ti	Titanium
Mi	Mica		Zn	Zinc
Mo	Molybdenum			

Water Power

Major Industrial Areas

DOMINANT LAND USE

Cereals, Livestock

Dairy

Nonagricultural Land

Pasture Livestock, Dairy

Forests

Montmagny⊙ 12,326 ....G3	Pabos-Mills 1,512 ....D2	Richelieu 1,755 ....D4
Montréal⊙ 1,080,546 ....H4	Packington 700 ....J2	Richmond⊙ 4,021 ....E4
Montréal-Est 4,372 ....J4	Papineauville⊙ 1,509 ....C4	Rigaud 2,203 ....C4
Montréal-Nord 97,250 ....H4	Paspébiac 1,807 ....D2	Rimouski 27,897 ....J1
Mont-Rolland 1,591 ....C4	Percé 5,198 ....D1	Rimouski-Est 2,328 ....J1
Mont-Royal 20,514 ....H4	Petit Cap 1,028 ....D1	Rivière-à-Pierre 604 ....E3
Mont-Saint-Hilaire 7,688 ....D4	Perkins 3,551 ....B4	Rivière-au-Renard 1,772 ....D1
Murdochville 3,704 ....C1	Petite-Matane 920 ....B1	Rivière-du-Loup⊙ 13,103 ....H2
Napierville 2,166 ....D4	Petit-Saguenay (Saint-François	Rivière-du-Moulin 1,088 ....G1
Neuville 918 ....F3	-d'Assis 680 ....G1	Rivière-Éternité 709 ....G1
New Carlisle⊙ 1,403 ....D2	Pierrefonds 35,402 ....H4	Rivière-Portneuf 959 ....H1
Newport 558 ....D2	Pierreville 1,311 ....E3	Robertsonville 1,666 ....F3
New Richmond 4,295 ....C2	Pincourt 7,892 ....H4	Roberval⊙ 8,543 ....E1
Nicolet 4,818 ....E3	Plaisance 634 ....B4	Rock Forest 652 ....F4
Nominingue 757 ....B3	Plessisville 7,238 ....F3	Rock Island 1,230 ....E4
Normandin 1,874 ....E1	Pohénégamooke 3,627 ....H2	Rougemont 933 ....D4
North Hatley 788 ....F4	Pointe-à-la-Croix 1,515 ....C2	Roxboro 7,106 ....H4
Notre-Dame-de-la-Doré	Pointe-aux-Outardes 968 ....A1	Roxton Falls 1,215 ....E4
1,119 ....E1	Pointe-aux-Trembles 35,618 ....J4	Saint-Adelme 738 ....B1
Notre-Dame-des-Anges 903 ....E3	Pointe-Claire 25,917 ....H4	Saint-Adelphe 1,220 ....E3
Notre-Dame-des-Laurentides H3	Pointe-du-Lac 2,737 ....E3	Saint-Adolphe-d'Howard
Notre-Dame-des-Prairies	Pointe-Gatineau B4	1,315 ....C4
5,744 ....D3	Pointe-Lebel 1,302 ....A1	Saint-Agapitville 1,672 ....F3
Notre-Dame-du-Bon-Conseil	Pont-Rouge 3,342 ....F3	Saint-Aimé-des-Lacs 805 ....G2
1,023 ....E4	Port-Alfred G1	Saint-Alban 726 ....E3
Notre-Dame-du-Lac⊙ 2,153 ....J2	Portneuf 1,320 ....F3	Saint-Alexandre-de-Kamouraska
Nouvelle 682 ....C2	Price 2,461 ....A1	966 ....H2
Oka 1,483 ....C4	Princeville 3,852 ....F3	Saint-Alexis-des-Monts
Omerville 1,308 ....E4	Proulxville 608 ....E3	1,815 ....D3
Ormstown 1,503 ....D4	Québec (cap.) 177,082 ....H3	Saint-Amable 1,557 ....J4
Orsainville H3	Quyon 690 ....A4	Saint-Ambroise 3,169 ....F1
Otterburn Park 4,159 ....D4	Rawdon 2,808 ....D3	Saint-Anaclet 1,009 ....J1
Outremont 27,089 ....H4	Repentigny 26,698 ....J4	Saint-André-Avellin 1,088 ....B4
Pabos 1,018 ....D2		

Saint-André-Est 1,206 ....C4			
Saint-Anselme 1,735 ....F3			
Saint-Antoine 6,872 ....H4			
Saint-Aubert 881 ....G2			
Saint-Augustin-de-Québec			
3,904 ....E3			
Saint-Basile-le-Grand 5,843 ....J4			
Saint-Basile-Sud 1,649 ....F3			
Saint-Benjamin 1,072 ....G3			
Saint-Bernard 562 ....F3			
Saint-Boniface-de-Shawinigan			
2,680 ....D3			
Saint-Bruno 2,259 ....F1			
Saint-Bruno-de-Montarville			
21,272 ....J4			
Saint-Camille-de-Bellechasse			
1,235 ....G3	Saint-Denis 888 ....D4	Sainte-Aurélie 1,103 ....G3	Sainte-Julie-de-Verchères
Saint-Casimir 1,184 ....E3	Saint-Dominique 1,772 ....E4	Sainte-Blandine 1,008 ....J1	8,666 ....J4
Saint-Césaire 2,701 ....D4	Saint-Donat-de-Montcal	Sainte-Catherine 901 ....F3	Sainte-Julienne⊙ 809 ....D4
Saint-Charles,	1,460 ....C3	Sainte-Claire 1,528 ....G3	Sainte-Justine 1,116 ....G3
Bellechasse 1,027 ....G3	Sainte-Adèle 4,186 ....C4	Sainte-Croix 1,719 ....F3	Saint-Éleuthère 1,033 ....H2
Saint-Charles-de-Mandeville	Sainte-Agathe 727 ....F3	Sainte-Émélie-de-l'Énergie	Saint-Élie 601 ....E3
847 ....D3	Sainte-Agathe-des-Monts	558 ....D3	Sainte-Louise 851 ....G2
Saint-Charles-Garnier 558 ....J1	5,435 ....C3	Sainte-Félicité 762 ....B1	Saint-Elzéar 643 ....F3
Saint-Chrysostome 1,065 ....D4	Sainte-Agnes-de-Charlevoix	Sainte-Foy 71,237 ....H3	Saint-Elzéar-de-Bonaventure
Saint-Côme 839 ....D3	551 ....G2	Sainte-Françoise 647 ....H1	617 ....C2
Saint-Constant 7,659 ....H4	Sainte-Anne-de-Beaupré	Sainte-Geneviève 2,869 ....H4	Sainte-Marie, Beauce 4,462 ....G3
Saint-Cyprien 791 ....J2	3,284 ....F2	Sainte-Geneviève-de-Batiscan	Sainte-Martine⊙ 1,957 ....D4
Saint-Cyrille 1,059 ....E4	Sainte-Anne-de-Bellevue	412 ....E3	Sainte-Émile 4,205 ....H3
Saint-Damien-de-Buckland	3,738 ....H4	Sainte-Hedwidge-de-Roberval	Sainte-Monique,
1,676 ....G3	Sainte-Anne-des-Monts⊙	966 ....E1	Lac-St-Jean-E. 596 ....F1
Saint-David 4,386 ....E3	5,945 ....C1	Sainte-Hélène-de-Kamouraska	Sainte-Perpétue-de-L'Islet
Saint-David-de-Falardeau	Sainte-Anne-des-Plaines	658 ....H2	1,269 ....H2
1,692 ....F1	2,329 ....H4	Sainte-Hénédine⊙ 561 ....F3	Saint-Éphrem-de-Tring 880 ..G3

AREA 594,857 sq. mi. (1,540,680 sq. km.)
POPULATION 6,377,518
CAPITAL Québec
LARGEST CITY Montréal
HIGHEST POINT Mont D'Iberville 5,420 ft. (1,652 m.)
SETTLED IN 1608
ADMITTED TO CONFEDERATION 1867
PROVINCIAL FLOWER White Garden Lily

Internal divisions represent Municipal Counties

© Copyright HAMMOND INCORPORATED, Maplewood, N.J.

Counties indicated by numbers:
1 Iberville D4
2 Napierville D4
3 Rouville D4
4 St-Hyacinthe E4
5 Île-de-Montréal H4
6 Deux-Montagnes C4
7 Soulanges C4
8 Laprairie D4
9 Hull B4
10 Île-Jésus H4
11 Richelieu D4
12 Vaudreuil C4

Sainte-Pudentienne 802 ..... E4
Saint-Esprit 948 .... D4
Sainte-Thècle 1,761 .... E3
Sainte-Thérèse 17,479 .... H4
Saint-Étienne-de-Grès 728 .... E3
Saint-Eustache 21,248 .... H4
Saint-Évariste-de-Forsyth 787 .... F4
Saint-Fabien 1,458 .... J1
Saint-Félicien 4,985 .... E1
Saint-Félix-de-Valois 1,495 .. D3
Saint-Flavien 693 .... F3
Saint-François-d'Assise 680 .. G1
Saint-François-de-Sales 803 .. E1
Saint-François-du-Lac⊙ 971 .. D3
Saint-Fulgence 966 .... G1
Saint-Gabriel 3,271 .... D3
Saint-Gédéon, Frontenac 1,292 .... G4
Saint-Gédéon, Lac-St-Jean-E. 697 .... F1
Saint-Georges, Beauce 8,605 G3
Saint-Georges, Champlain 2,707 .... E3
Saint-Georges-Ouest 6,478 .. G3
Saint-Germain-de-Grantham 1,289 .... E4
Saint-Gervais 780 .... G3
Saint-Gilles 905 .... F3
Saint-Grégoire-de-Greenlay 622 .... E4
Saint-Henri J3
Saint-Honoré, Beauce 1,115 G4
Saint-Honoré, Chicoutimi 1,546 .... F1
Saint-Honoré-de-Témiscouata 539 .... H2
Saint-Hubert 49,706 .... J4
Saint-Hubert-de-Témiscouata 539 .... J2
Saint-Hyacinthe⊙ 37,500 .... D4
Saint-Isidore 768 .... D4
Saint-Isidore-de-Laprairie 846 .... D4
Saint-Jacques 2,095 .... D4
Saint-Jacques-le-Mineur 1,086 .... H4
Saint-Jean⊙ 34,363 .... D4
Saint-Jean-Chrysostome 3,606 .... J3
Saint-Jean-de-Dieu 1,261 ... J1
Saint-Jean-de-Matha 947 ... D3
Saint-Jean-Port-Joli⊙ 1,844 G3
Saint-Jérôme, Terrebonne⊙ 25,175 ..... H4
Saint-Joachim 943 .... G2

Saint-Joseph-de-Beauce⊙ 3,213 .... G3
Saint-Joseph-de-Sorel 2,811 D3
Saint-Jovite 3,595 .... C3
Saint-Lambert 20,318 .... J4
Saint-Laurent 64,404 .... H4
Saint-Lazare 558 .... G3
Saint-Léonard 78,452 .... H4
Saint-Léonard-d'Aston 1,049 E3
Saint-Léonard-de-Portneuf 555 .... F3
Saint-Léon-de-Standon 855 . G3
Saint-Léon-le-Grand 1,325 .. B2
Saint-Liboire⊙ 648 .... E4
Saint-Louis-de-Terrebonne 8,479 .... H4
Saint-Louis-du-Ha Ha 672 .. H2
Saint-Luc 7,103 .... D4
Saint-Luc-de-Matane 609 ... B1
Saint-Marc-des-Carrières 2,625 .... E3
Saint-Méthode-de-Frontenac 898 .... F3
Saint-Michel-de-Bellechasse 960 .... G3
Saint-Michel-des-Saints 1,966 .... D3
Saint-Nazaire-de-Chicoutimi 938 .... F1
Saint-Nérée 907 .... G3
Saint-Noël 777 .... B1
Saint-Odilon 697 .... G3
Saint-Omer 569 .... C2
Saint-Ours 742 .... D4
Saint-Pacôme 1,167 .... G2
Saint-Pamphile 3,450 .... H3
Saint-Pascal 2,552 .... H2
Saint-Paul 544 .... D4
Saint-Paul-de-Montminy 691 G3
Saint-Paulin 734 .... D3
Saint-Paul-l'Ermite 6,107 .. H4
Saint-Petronille 801 .... J3
Saint-Philippe-de-Néri 732 . H2
Saint-Pie 1,720 .... E4
Saint-Pierre, Île-de-Mont. 6,039 .... H4
Saint-Pierre, Joliette 679 . D3
Saint-Pierre-d'Orléans 619 . G3
Saint-Polycarpe 540 .... C4
Saint-Prime 2,266 .... E1
Saint-Prosper-de-Dorchester 1,878 .... G3
Saint-Raphaël 1,328 .... G3
Saint-Raymond 3,742 .... F3
Saint-Rédempteur 3,031 ...... J3
Saint-Régis C4

Saint-Rémi 4,866 .... D4
Saint-Roch-de-l'Achigan 1,052 .... D4
Saint-Roch-de-Richelieu 614 D4
Saint-Romuald-d'Etchemin⊙ 9,160 .... J3
Saint-Sauveur-des-Monts 1,999 .... C4
Saint-Siméon 1,163 .... G2
Saint-Siméon-de-Bonaventure 650 .... C2
Saint-Simon 675 .... H1
Saint-Thomas-de-Joliette 577 D3
Saint-Timothée 1,927 .... C4
Saint-Tite 3,128 .... E3
Saint-Tite-des-Caps 609 .... G2
Saint-Ubald B1
Saint-Ulric 804 .... B1
Saint-Urbain-de-Charlevoix 650 .... G2
Saint-Victor 1,044 .... G3
Saint-Zacharie 1,300 .... G3
Saint-Zotique 1,519 .... C4
Sault-au-Mouton 914 .... H1
Sawyerville 878 .... F4
Sayabec 1,818 .... B2
Scotstown 827 .... F4
Scott-Jonction 571 .... F3
Senneville 1,333 .... H4
Shawbridge 831 .... C4
Shawinigan 24,921 .... E3
Shawinigan-Sud 11,155 ...... E3
Shawville 1,724 .... A4
Sherbrooke⊙ 76,804 .... F4
Sillery 13,580 .... J3
Sorel⊙ 19,666 .... D4
Squatec 920 .... J2
Stanstead Plain 1,163 ...... F4
Sully 833 .... H2
Sutton 1,655 .... E4
Tadoussac⊙ 998 .... H1
Terrebonne 11,204 .... H4
Thetford Mines 20,874 ...... F3
Thurso 3,066 .... B4
Tourville 669 .... H2
Tracy 12,284 .... D3
Tring-Jonction 1,248 .... G3
Trois-Pistoles 4,554 .... H1
Trois-Rivières 52,518 ...... E3
Trois-Rivières-Ouest 10,564 E3
Upton 822 .... E4
Val-Brillant 677 .... B1
Valcourt 2,566 .... E4
Val-David 2,073 .... C3
Vallée-Jonction 1,288 ...... G3
Valleyfield 29,716 .... C4

Vanier 10,683 .... J3
Varennes 6,469 .... J4
Vaudreuil⊙ 5,630 .... C4
Verchères 3,586 .... J4
Verdun 68,013 .... H4
Victoriaville 21,825 .... F3
Villeneuve J3
Warwick 2,865 .... F4
Waterloo⊙ 4,746 .... E4
Waterville 1,458 .... F4
Weedon-Centre 1,264 .... F4
Westmount 22,153 .... H4
Windsor 5,637 .... F4
Woburn 542 .... G4
Wottonville 700 .... F4
Yamachiche⊙ 1,202 .... E3

OTHER FEATURES

Alma (isl.) F1
Aylmer (lake) F4
Baskatong (res.) B3
Batiscan (riv.) E2
Bécancour (riv.) F3
Bonaventure (isl.) D1
Bonaventure (riv.) C1
Brome (lake) E4
Brompton (lake) E4
Cascapédia (riv.) C1
Chaleur (bay) C2
Champlain (lake) C4
Chaudière (riv.) G4
Chic-Chocs (mts.) B1
Chicoutimi (riv.) F2
Coudres (isl.) G2
Deschênes (lake) A4
Deux Montagnes (lake) C4
Ditton (riv.) F4
Forillon Nat'l Park D1
Fort Chambly Nat'l Hist. Park J4
Gaspé (bay) D1
Gaspé (cape) D1
Gaspé (pen.) C1
Gaspésie Prov. Park C1
Gatineau (riv.) B3
Îles (lake) B3
Jacques-Cartier (mt.) C1
Jacques-Cartier (riv.) F2
Kénogami (lake) F1
Kiamika (lake) B3
La Maurice Nat'l Park D3
Laurentides Prov. Park F2
Lièvre (riv.) B4
Lièvres (isl.) H2
Maskinongé (riv.) C3

Matane (riv.) B1
Matane Prov. Park B1
Matapédia (riv.) B2
Mégantic (lake) G4
Memphremagog (lake) E4
Mercier (riv.) A1
Métabetchouane (riv.) F1
Mille Îles (riv.) H4
Montmorency (riv.) F2
Mont-Tremblant Prov. Park . C3
Nicolet (riv.) E3
Nominingue (lake) B3
Nord (riv.) C4
Orléans (isl.) F3
Ottawa (riv.) B4
Ouareau (riv.) C3
Patapédia (riv.) B2
Péribonca (riv.) F1
Petite Nation (riv.) B4
Prairies (riv.) H4
Rimouski (riv.) J1
Ristigouche (riv.) B2
Saguenay (riv.) G1
Sainte-Anne (riv.) F3
Sainte-Anne (riv.) G2
Saint-François (lake) E4
Saint-François (riv.) E4
Saint-Jean (lake) E1
Saint Lawrence (gulf) D2
Saint Lawrence (riv.) H1
Saint-Louis (lake) H4
Saint-Maurice (riv.) E2
Saint-Pierre (lake) E3
Shawinigan (riv.) E3
Shipshaw (riv.) F1
Soeurs (isl.) H4
Témiscouata (lake) H2
Tremblant (lake) C3
Trente et un Milles (lake) . B3
Verte (isl.) H1
Yamaska (riv.) E4
York (riv.) D1

QUÉBEC, NORTHERN

INTERNAL DIVISIONS

Abitibi (county) 88,229 ..... B2
Abitibi (terr.) B3
Berthier (county) 28,465 .... B3
Bonaventure (county) 40,724 D3
Champlain (county) 114,078 . C3
Charlevoix-Est (county) 17,065 .... C3

Charlevoix-Ouest (county) 13,601 .... C3
Chicoutimi (county) 165,859 C3
Gaspé-Est (county) 40,720 .. E3
Gaspé-Ouest (county) 19,238 D3
Gatineau (county) 52,193 ... B3
Joliette (county) 55,524 ... C3
Lac-Saint-Jean-Est (county) 45,558 .... C3
Lac-Saint-Jean-Ouest (county) 57,556 .... C2
Maskinongé (county) 20,879 C3
Matane (county) 28,954 ..... D3
Matapédia (county) 24,063 . D3
Montcalm (county) 23,534 .. B3
Montmorency No. I 20,712 ... C3
Nouveau-Québec (terr.) 38,982 .... E1
Pontiac (county) 20,559 .... B3
Portneuf (county) 51,643 ... C3
Québec (county) 449,633 ... C3
Rimouski (county) 64,768 .. D3
Saguenay (county) 115,736 D2
Saint-Maurice (county) 106,023 .... C3
Témiscamingue (county) 52,871 .... B3

CITIES and TOWNS

Alma 25,638 .... C3
Amos⊙ 9,213 .... B3
Baie-Comeau 11,911 .... D3
Baie-du-Poste C2
Chibougamau 10,536 .... C3
Chicoutimi⊙ 57,737 .... C3
Gaspé 16,842 .... E3
Hauterive 14,724 .... D3
Jonquière 60,691 .... C3
La Tuque 12,067 .... C3
Lévis 17,819 .... C3
Manicouagan D3
Matane⊙ 12,726 .... D3
Mistassini (Baie-du-Poste) . C2
Montmagny⊙ 12,326 .... C3
New Carlisle⊙ 1,403 ...... E3
Noranda 9,809 .... B3
Nouveau-Comptoir B2
Percé⊙ E3
Port-Cartier-Ouest 1,171 .. D3
Port-Menier⊙ 438 .... D3
Povungnituk E1
Québec (cap.)⊙ 177,082 .. C3
Rimouski⊙ 27,897 .... D3

Rivière-au-Tonnerre D2
Rivière-du-Loup⊙ 13,103 .. D3
Rouyn 17,678 .... B3
Sept-Îles 30,617 .... D2
Seven Islands (Sept-Îles) 30,617 .... D2
Shawinigan 24,921 .... C3
Tadoussac⊙ 998 .... C3
Val d'Or 19,915 .... B3
Ville-Marie⊙ 2,274 ...... B3

OTHER FEATURES

Allard (lake) E2
Anticosti (isl.) E3
Baleine, Grand Rivière de la (riv.) B1
Bell (riv.) B3
Betsiamites (riv.) C2
Bienville (lake) C2
Broadback (riv.) B3
Cabonga (res.) B3
Caniapiscau (riv.) D1
Eastmain (riv.) B2
Eau Claire (lake) C1
Feuilles (riv.) C1
Gaspésie Prov. Park D3
George (riv.) D1
Gouin (res.) B3
Grande Rivière, La (riv.) B2
Honguedo (passage) E3
Hudson (bay) A1
Hudson (str.) F1
Jacques-Cartier (passage) A2
James (bay) A2
Koksoak (riv.) D1
Laurentides Prov. Park ... C3
Louis-XIV (pt.) B2
Manicouagan (res.) D2
Minto (lake) C1
Mistassibi (riv.) C2
Mistassini (lake) C2
Mistassini (riv.) C2
Moisie (riv.) D2
Mont-Tremblant Prov. Park C3
Natashquan (riv.) E2
Nottaway (riv.) A3
Nouveau-Québec (crater) .. F1
Otish (mts.) C2
Ottawa (riv.) B3
Péribonca (riv.) C2
Plétipi (lake) C2
Saguenay (riv.) C3
Saint-Jean (lake) C3
Saint Lawrence (gulf) E3
Saint Lawrence (riv.) C3
Ungava (pen.) E1

© Copyright HAMMOND INCORPORATED, Maplewood, N.J.

Northern Québec

SCALE
0 — 50 — 100 — 150 — 200 MI.
0 — 50 — 100 — 150 — 200 KM.

Provincial Capital .... ⊛ Provincial Boundaries _____
County Seats .... ⊙ County Boundaries _ _ _ _
International Boundaries ....   Territorial Boundaries ......

Scale 1:8,400,000

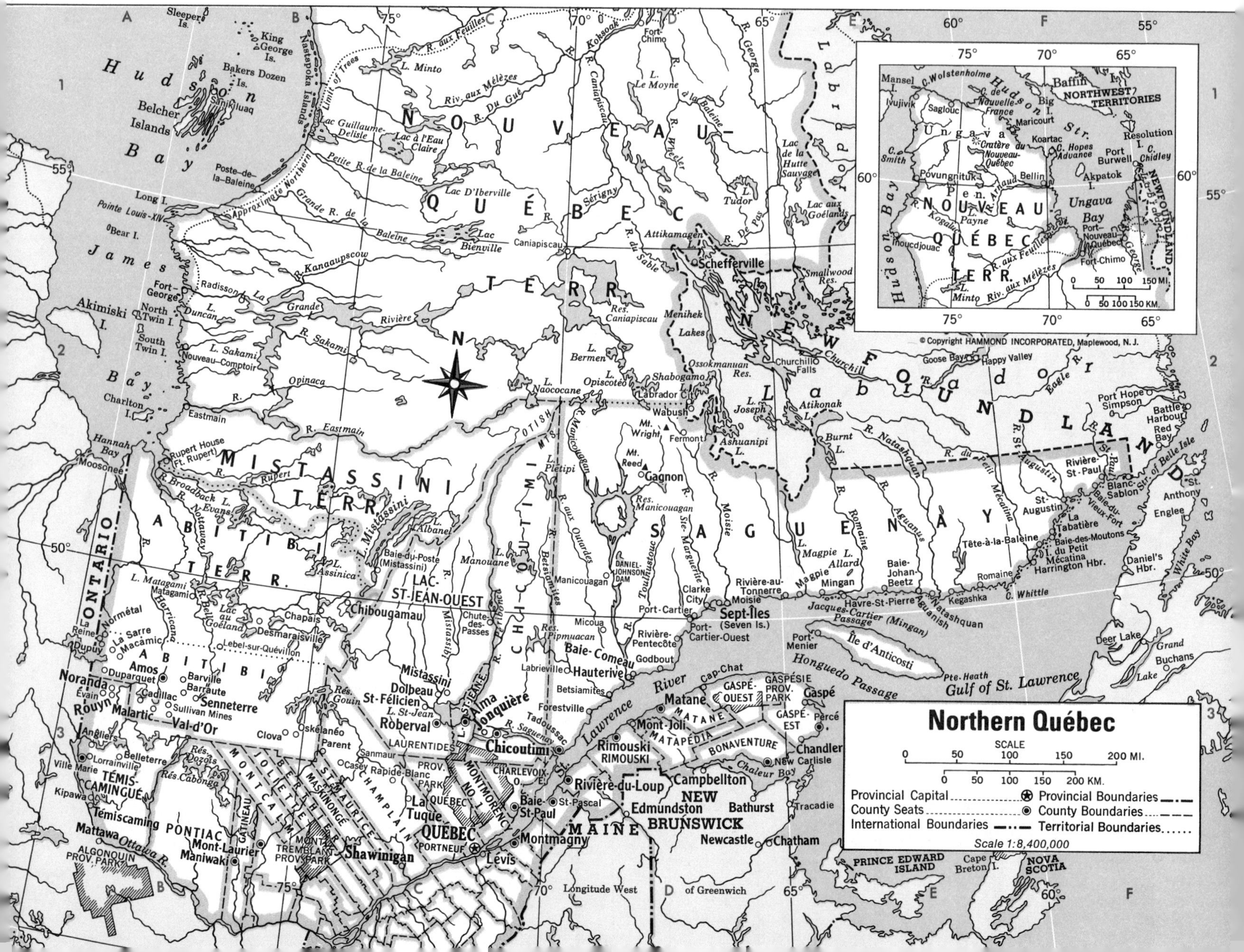

AREA 412,580 sq. mi. (1,068,582 sq. km.)
POPULATION 8,551,733
CAPITAL Toronto
LARGEST CITY Toronto
HIGHEST POINT in Timiskaming Dist. 2,275 ft. (693 m.)
SETTLED IN 1749
ADMITTED TO CONFEDERATION 1867
PROVINCIAL FLOWER White Trillium

ONTARIO, NORTHERN

INTERNAL DIVISIONS

Algoma (terr. dist.) 122,883 D3
Cochrane (terr. dist.) 96,825 D2
Kenora (terr. dist.) 57,980 .. C2
Manitoulin (terr. dist.) 10,893 .... D3
Nipissing (terr. dist.) 81,739 E3
Parry Sound (terr. dist.) 32,654 .... E3
Rainy River (terr. dist.) 24,768 .... B3
Renfrew (county) 89,099 .... E3
Sudbury (reg. munic.) 167,705 .... D3
Sudbury (terr. dist.) 27,287 . D3
Thunder Bay (terr. dist.) 150,647 .... C3
Timiskaming (terr. dist.) 43,760 .... D3

CITIES and TOWNS

Chalk River 1,095 .... E3
Fort Albany D2
Huntsville 11,123 .... E3
Kapuskasing 12,676 .... D3
Kenora⊙ 10,565 .... B3
Kirkland Lake 13,567 .... D3
Moose Factory 554 .... D2
Moosonee 1,349 .... D2
Nickel Centre 13,157 .... D3
North Bay⊙ 51,639 .... E3
Pembroke⊙ 14,927 .... E3
Sault Sainte Marie⊙ 81,048 D3
Sudbury 97,604 .... D3
Thunder Bay⊙ 111,476 ...... C3
Timmins 44,747 .... D3
Valley East 19,591 .... D3
Walden 10,453 .... D3

OTHER FEATURES

Abitibi (lake) E3
Abitibi (riv.) D2
Albany (riv.) C2
Algonquin Prov. Park E3
Asheweig (riv.) C2
Attawapiskat (lake) C2
Attawapiskat (riv.) C2
Basswood (lake) B3
Berens (riv.) A2
Big Trout (lake) B2
Black Duck (riv.) C1
Bloodvein (riv.) A2
Caribou (isl.) C3
Cobham (riv.) A2
Eabamet (lake) C2
Ekwan (riv.) C2
English (riv.) B2
Fawn (riv.) C2
Finger (lake) B2
Georgian (bay) D3
Hannah (bay) D2
Henrietta Maria (cape) D1
Hudson (bay) D1
Huron (lake) D3
James (bay) D2
Kapiskau (riv.) D2
Kapuskasing (riv.) D3
Kenogami (riv.) C2
Kesagami (lake) E2
Lake of the Woods (lake) B3
Lake Superior Prov. Park ... D3
Little Current (riv.) C2
Long (lake) C3
Manitoulin (isl.) D3
Mattagami (riv.) D3
Michipicoten (isl.) C3
Mille Lacs (lake) B3
Missinaibi (lake) D3
Missinaibi (riv.) D2
Missisa (lake) D2
Nipigon (lake) C3
Nipissing (lake) E3
North (chan.) D3
North Caribou (lake) B2
Nungesser (lake) B2
Ogidaki (mt.) D3
Ogoki (riv.) C2
Opazatika (riv.) D3
Opinnagau (riv.) D2
Otoskwin (riv.) B2
Ottawa (riv.) E3
Pipestone (riv.) B2
Polar Bear Prov. Park D2
Pukaskwa Prov. Park C3
Quetico Prov. Park B3
Rainy (lake) B3
Red (lake) B2
Sachigo (riv.) B2
Saganaga (lake) B3
Saint Ignace (isl.) C3
Saint Joseph (lake) B2
Sandy (lake) B2
Savant (lake) B2
Seine (riv.) B3
Seul (lake) B2
Severn (lake) B2
Severn (riv.) B2
Shamattawa (riv.) C2
Shibogama (lake) C2
Sibley Prov. Park C3
Slate (isls.) C3
Stout (lake) B2
Superior (lake) C3
Sutton (lake) D2
Sutton (riv.) D2
Timagami (lake) D3
Timiskaming (lake) E3
Trout (lake) B2
Wabuk (pt.) D1
Winisk (lake) C2
Winisk (riv.) C2
Winnipeg (riv.) A2
Woods (lake) B3

ONTARIO

INTERNAL DIVISIONS

Algoma (terr. dist.) 122,883 J5
Brant (county) 99,950 .... D4
Bruce (county) 57,472 .... C3
Cochrane (terr. dist.) 96,825 J4
Dufferin (county) 28,528 ..... D3
Dundas (county) 18,507 ...... J2
Durham (reg. munic.) 247,473 .... F3
Elgin (county) 69,092 .... C5
Essex (county) 310,362 ...... B5
Frontenac (county) 108,052 H3
Glengarry (county) 19,270 ... K2
Grenville (county) 26,025 ..... J3
Grey (county) 72,176 .... D3
Haldimand-Norfolk (reg. munic.) 89,252 .... E5
Haliburton (county) 10,795 ... F2
Halton (reg. munic.) 128,497 E4
Hamilton-Wentworth (reg. munic.) 409,490 .... D4
Hastings (county) 105,837 ... G3
Huron (county) 56,007 .... C4
Kenora (terr. dist.) 57,980 ... G5
Kent (county) 106,130 .... B5
Lambton (county) 120,576 ... B5
Lanark (county) 44,197 .... H3
Leeds (county) 52,579 .... H3
Lennox and Addington (county) 32,633 .... G3
Manitoulin (terr. dist.) 10,893 .... B2
Middlesex (county) 303,745 C4
Muskoka (dist. munic.) 36,691 .... E3
Niagara (reg. munic.) 365,438 E4
Nipissing (terr. dist.) 81,739 F2
Northumberland (county) 64,441 .... G3
Ottawa-Carleton (reg. munic.) 520,533 .... J2
Oxford (county) 85,337 ...... D4
Parry Sound (terr. dist.) 32,654 .... D2
Peel (reg. munic.) 375,910 . E4
Perth (county) 66,279 .... C4
Peterborough (county) 99,930 .... F3
Prescott (county) 29,100 .... K2
Prince Edward (county) 22,559 .... G3
Rainy River (terr. dist.) 24,768 .... G5
Renfrew (county) 89,099 .... G2
Russell (county) 19,735 ..... J2
Simcoe (county) 210,691 .... E3
Stormont (county) 61,173 ... K2
Sudbury (reg. munic.) 167,705 .... K6
Sudbury (terr. dist.) 27,287 . J5
Thunder Bay (terr. dist.) 150,647 .... H5
Timiskaming (terr. dist.) 43,760 .... K5
Toronto (metro. munic.) 2,124,291 .... K4
Victoria (county) 43,543 ..... F3
Waterloo (reg. munic.) 289,129 .... D4
Wellington (county) 123,736 D4
York (reg. munic.) 203,915 . E4

CITIES and TOWNS

Ailsa Craig 701 .... C4
Ajax 20,774 .... E4
Alban 351 .... D1
Alcona Beach 861 .... E3
Alexandria 3,498 .... K2
Alfred 1,105 .... K2
Alliston 4,155 .... E3
Alma 271 .... D4
Almonte 3,693 .... H2
Alvinston 672 .... B5
Amherstburg 5,566 .... A5
Amherst View 5,295 .... H3
Ancaster 14,255 .... D4
Angus 3,494 .... E3
Apple Hill 271 .... K2
Apsley 281 .... F3
Arkona 458 .... C4
Armstrong 323 .... H4
Arnprior 6,111 .... H2
Arthur 1,660 .... D4
Astorville 373 .... E1
Athens 1,054 .... J3
Atherley 367 .... E3
Atikokan 5,668 .... G5
Atwood 720 .... D4
Aurora 14,249 .... J3
Avonmore 300 .... K2
Aylmer 5,125 .... C5
Ayr 1,331 .... D4
Ayton 450 .... D3
Baden 824 .... D4
Bala 536 .... E2
Bancroft 2,332 .... G2
Barrie⊙ 34,389 .... E3
Barry's Bay 1,256 .... G2
Batawa 484 .... G3
Bath 762 .... H3
Bayfield 549 .... C4
Bayside 3,356 .... G3
Beachburg 649 .... H2
Beachville 988 .... D4
Beardmore 656 .... H5
Beaverton 1,737 .... E3
Beeton 1,604 .... E3
Belle River 3,254 .... B5
Belleville⊙ 35,311 .... G3
Belmont 739 .... C5
Bethany 314 .... F3
Bewdley 475 .... F3
Binbrook 465 .... E4
Blackstock 767 .... F3
Blenheim 3,804 .... C5
Blind River 3,142 .... J5
Bloomfield 756 .... G4
Blyth 866 .... C4
Bobcaygeon 1,562 .... F3
Bonfield 722 .... E1
Bothwell 899 .... C5
Bourget 949 .... J2
Bracebridge⊙ 8,428 .... E2
Bradford 5,080 .... E3
Braeside 538 .... H2
Brampton⊙ 103,459 .... J4
Brantford⊙ 66,950 .... D4
Bridgenorth 1,368 .... F3
Brigden 548 .... B5
Brighton 3,199 .... G3
Brights Grove 1,113 .... B4
Britt 468 .... D2
Brockville⊙ 19,903 .... J3
Bruce Mines 517 .... J5
Brussels 1,043 .... C4
Burford 1,051 .... D4
Burgessville 289 .... D4
Burk's Falls 871 .... E2
Burlington 104,314 .... E4
Cache Bay 691 .... D1
Caesarea 547 .... F3
Calabogie 289 .... H2
Caledon 22,434 .... E4
Callander 1,058 .... E1
Cambridge 72,383 .... D4
Campbellford 3,487 .... G3
Cannington 1,419 .... E3
Capreol 4,089 .... K5
Caramat 382 .... H5
Cardinal 1,867 .... J3
Carleton Place 5,256 .... H2
Carlisle 565 .... D4
Carlsbad Springs 478 .... J2
Carp 681 .... H2
Cartier 673 .... J5
Casselman 1,422 .... J2
Castleton 326 .... F3
Cedar Springs 281 .... B5
Chalk River 1,095 .... G1
Chapleau 3,253 .... J5
Charing Cross 441 .... B5
Chatham⊙ 38,685 .... B5
Chatsworth 394 .... D3
Cherry Valley 273 .... G4
Chesley 1,839 .... C3
Chesterville 1,324 .... J2
Chute-à-Blondeau 350 .... K2
City View J2
Clarence Creek 395 .... J2
Clarksburg 481 .... D3
Clifford 641 .... D4
Clinton 3,151 .... C4
Cobalt 2,056 .... K5
Cobden 1,025 .... H2
Coboconk 377 .... F3
Cobourg⊙ 11,421 .... F4
Cochrane⊙ 4,974 .... K5
Codes Corner 407 .... H3
Colborne 1,724 .... G4
Colchester 990 .... B6
Coldwater 803 .... E3
Collingwood 11,114 .... D3
Collins Bay 6,897 .... H3
Comber 649 .... B5
Consecon 363 .... G3
Cookstown 874 .... E3
Cornwall⊙ 46,121 .... K2
Corunna 3,723 .... B5
Cottam 514 .... B5
Courtland 602 .... D5
Coverdale 1,573 .... F4
Crediton 439 .... C4
Creemore 1,089 .... D3
Crysler 490 .... J2
Cumberland 550 .... J2
Cumberland Beach 686 .... E3
Dashwood 434 .... C4
Deep River 5,565 .... G1
Delaware 346 .... C5
Delhi 3,929 .... D5
Delta 310 .... H3
Denbigh 294 .... G2
Deseronto 1,893 .... G3
Dorchester 2,756 .... C5
Douglas 291 .... H2
Drayton 801 .... D4
Dresden 2,484 .... B5
Drumbo 397 .... D4
Dryden 6,799 .... G4
Dublin 282 .... C4
Dubreuilville 818 .... J5
Dundalk 1,165 .... D3
Dundas 19,179 .... D4
Dunnville 11,642 .... E5
Durham 2,501 .... D3
Dutton 1,036 .... C5
Earlton 1,008 .... K5
East York 106,950 .... J4
Echo Bay 745 .... J5
Eden Mills 332 .... D4
Eganville 1,328 .... G2
Egmondville 429 .... C4
Elgin 292 .... H3
Elk Lake 564 .... K5
Elliot Lake 8,849 .... B1
Elmira 7,034 .... D4
Elmvale 1,176 .... E3
Elmwood 423 .... C3
Elora 2,589 .... D4
Embro 800 .... C4
Embrun 1,763 .... J2
Emeryville B5
Emo 792 .... F5
Englehart 1,767 .... K5
Enterprise 295 .... H3
Erieau 453 .... C5
Erin 2,007 .... D4
Espanola 5,926 .... J5
Essex 5,577 .... B5
Etobicoke 297,109 .... J4
Everett 438 .... E3
Exeter 3,494 .... C4
Fauquier 620 .... J5
Fenelon Falls 1,637 .... F3
Fergus 6,001 .... D4
Field 568 .... E1
Finch 407 .... J2
Fingal 345 .... C5
Fitzroy Harbour 431 .... H2
Flesherton 568 .... D3
Foleyet 538 .... J5
Fordwich 412 .... C4
Forest 2,557 .... C4
Formosa 395 .... C3
Fort Erie 24,031 .... E5
Fort Frances⊙ 9,325 .... F5
Foxboro 560 .... G3
Frankford 1,851 .... G3
Fraserdale 385 .... J5
Freelton 310 .... D4
Gananoque 5,103 .... H3
Garden Village 265 .... E1
Geraldton 3,127 .... H5
Glencoe 1,818 .... C5
Glen Miller 605 .... G3
Glen Robertson 312 .... K2
Glen Walter 662 .... K2
Goderich⊙ 7,385 .... C4
Gogama 702 .... J5

(continued on following page)

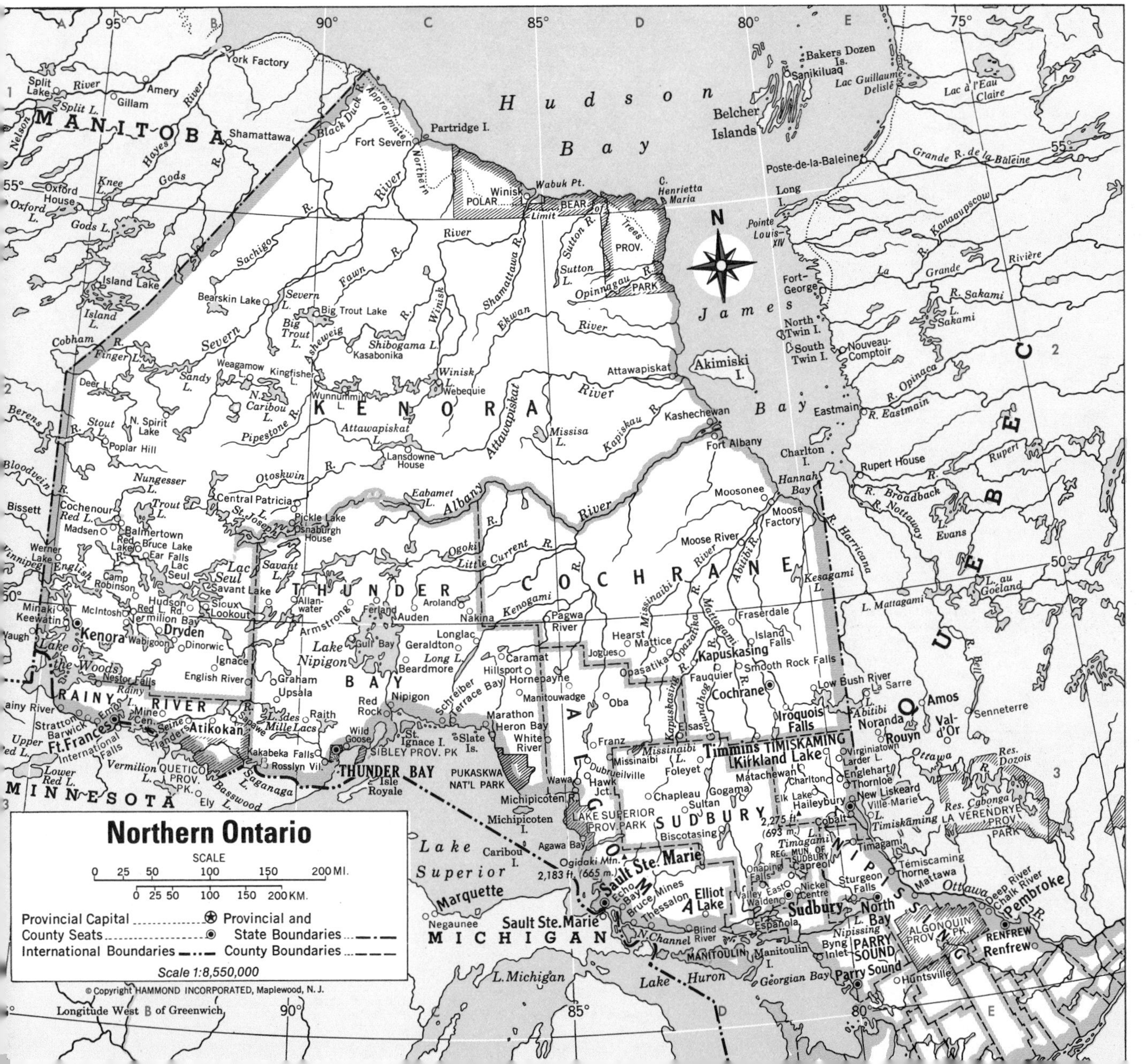
Northern Ontario
SCALE
0 25 50 100 150 200 MI.
0 25 50 100 150 200 KM.
Provincial Capital ⊛ Provincial and State Boundaries
County Seats ⊙ County Boundaries
International Boundaries
Scale 1:8,550,000
© Copyright HAMMOND INCORPORATED, Maplewood, N. J.
Longitude West B of Greenwich
Hudson Bay
James Bay
MANITOBA
KENORA
THUNDER BAY
COCHRANE
SUDBURY
TIMISKAMING
RAINY RIVER
ALGOMA
NIPISSING
QUEBEC
MINNESOTA
MICHIGAN
Lake Superior
Lake Huron
L. Michigan
Thunder Bay
Sault Ste. Marie
Timmins
Kirkland Lake
Sudbury
North Bay
Kenora
Pembroke
Parry Sound
Renfrew
Cochrane
Kapuskasing
Moosonee
Moose Factory
Fort Albany
Attawapiskat
Fort Severn

Gore Bay⊙ 767 ....B2	Hudson 565 ....G4	Lambeth 2,876 ....C5	Manotick 1,410 ....J2	Moose Creek 382 ....K2	Oakville 68,950 ....E4	Plattsville 498 ....D
Gorrie 424 ....C4	Huntsville 11,123 ....E2	Lanark 803 ....H2	Marathon 2,250 ....H5	Morpeth 305 ....C5	Oakwood 382 ....F3	Point Edward 2,524 ....D
Grafton 402 ....G4	Huron Park 1,341 ....C4	Lancaster 540 ....K2	Markdale 1,361 ....D3	Morrisburg 2,188 ....J3	Odessa 877 ....H3	Pontypool 497 ....F3
Grand Bend 750 ....C4	Ignace 515 ....G5	Langton 421 ....D5	Markham 56,206 ....K4	Mount Albert 909 ....E3	Oil Springs 618 ....B5	Port Burwell 726 ....D
Grand Valley 1,096 ....D4	Ilderton 330 ....C4	Lansdowne 542 ....H3	Markstay 521 ....D1	Mount Brydges 1,573 ....C5	Omemee 790 ....F3	Port Carling 628 ....E
Granton 313 ....C4	Ingersoll 8,198 ....C4	Larder Lake 1,238 ....K5	Marmora 1,326 ....G3	Mount Elgin 289 ....D5	Onaping Falls 6,776 ....J5	Port Colborne 20,536 ....E
Gravenhurst 7,986 ....E3	Ingleside 1,106 ....J2	Latchford 457 ....K5	Martintown 366 ....K2	Mount Forest 3,376 ....D4	Opasatika 798 ....J5	Port Elgin 5,069 C
Greely 509 ....J2	Innerkip 655 ....D4	Leamington 11,169 ....B5	Massey 1,345 ....C1	Mount Hope 687 ....E4	Orangeville⊙ 12,021 ....D4	Port Hope 9,788 ....F
Green Valley 478 ....K2	Inverhuron 275 ....C3	Lefroy 534 ....E3	Matachewan 619 ....J5	Mount Pleasant 545 ....D4	Orillia 24,412 ....E3	Port Lambton 716 ....B
Grimsby 15,567 ....E4	Iron Bridge 790 ....A1	Limoges 616 ....J2	Matheson 703 ....K5	Munster 1,119 ....J2	Orleans 4,316 ....J2	Portland 282 ....J
Guelph⊙ 67,538 ....D4	Iroquois 1,278 ....J3	Lincoln 14,460 ....E4	Mattawa 2,849 ....F1	Nairn 457 ....C1	Osgoode 984 ....J2	Port McNicoll 1,522 ....E
Haileybury⊙ 4,939 ....K5	Iroquois Falls 6,887 ....J5	Linden Beach 484 ....B6	Mattice 816 ....J5	Nakina 602 ....H4	Oshawa 107,023 ....F4	Port Perry 3,917 ....F
Haldimand 16,375 ....E5	Jasper 374 ....H3	Lindsay⊙ 13,062 ....F3	Maxville 852 ....K2	Nanticoke 19,489 ....E5	Ottawa (cap.), Canada⊙	Port Rowan 960 ....D
Halton Hills 34,477 ....E4	Johnstown 560 ....J3	Linwood 455 ....D4	Maynooth 281 ....G2	Napanee⊙ 4,844 ....H3	304,462 ....J2	Port Stanley 1,707 C
Hamilton⊙ 312,003 ....E4	Kakabeka Falls 367 ....G5	Lion's Head 500 ....C2	McGregor 810 ....B5	Neustadt 543 ....D3	Otterville 785 ....D5	Pottageville 298 ....E
Hanover 5,691 ....C3	Kaladar 262 ....H3	Listowel 5,126 ....D4	McKerrow 323 ....C1	Newburgh 628 ....H3	Owen Sound⊙ 19,525 ....D3	Powassan 1,238 ....F
Harriston 1,872 ....D4	Kanata 6,304 ....J2	Little Britain 359 ....F3	Meaford 4,319 ....D3	Newbury 388 ....C5	Paincourt 43 ....B5	Prescott⊙ 4,975 ....J
Harrow 1,936 ....B5	Kapuskasing 12,676 ....J5	Little Current 1,476 ....B2	Melbourne 339 ....C5	Newcastle 31,928 ....F4	Painswick 785 ....E3	Princeton 435 ....D
Harrowsmith 533 ....H3	Kars 409 ....J2	London 240,392 ....C5	Merlin 722 ....B5	New Hamburg 3,628 ....D4	Paisley 1,033 ....C3	Rainy River 1,092 ....F
Harwood 262 ....F3	Kearney 285 ....E2	Longlac 1,923 ....H5	Merrickville 932 ....J3	Newington 278 ....K2	Pakenham 1,322 ....H2	Ramore 335 ....J
Hastings 990 ....G3	Keene 275 ....F3	Long Sault 1,096 ....K2	Metcalfe 681 ....J2	New Liskeard 5,601 ....K5	Palmerston 1,961 ....D4	Rayside-Balfour 16,035 ....J
Havelock 1,280 ....G3	Keewatin 1,954 ....F5	L'Orignal⊙ 1,380 ....K2	Midhurst 626 ....E3	Newmarket⊙ 24,795 ....E3	Paris 6,173 ....D4	Red Rock 1,244 ....H
Hawkesbury 9,789 ....K2	Kemptville 2,544 ....J2	Lucan 1,377 ....C4	Midland 11,568 ....D3	Niagara Falls 69,423 ....E4	Parkhill 1,300 ....C4	Renfrew 8,617 ....H
Hawkestone 309 ....E3	Kenora⊙ 10,565 ....F4	Lucknow 1,127 ....C4	Mildmay 990 ....C3	Niagara-on-the-Lake 12,485 ....E4	Parry Sound⊙ 5,501 ....E2	Richards Landing 313 ....A
Hawk Junction 363 ....J5	Keswick 1,217 ....E3	Lyn 562 ....J3	Milford Bay 320 ....E2	Nickel Centre 13,157 ....D1	Pefferlaw 750 ....E3	Richmond 2,667 ....J
Hearst 5,195 ....J5	Killaloe Station 699 ....G2	Lynden 457 ....D4	Millbank 383 ....D4	Nipigon 2,724 ....H5	Pelham 10,071 ....E4	Richmond Hill 34,716 ....E
Hensall 993 ....C4	Killarney 445 ....C2	Lynhurst 429 ....C5	Millbrook 898 ....F3	Nobel 291 ....E2	Penetanguishene 6,221 ....D3	Ridgetown 3,100 C
Hepworth 377 ....C3	Kincardine 4,182 ....C3	Macdiarmid 445 ....H5	Milton⊙ 20,756 ....E4	Nobleton 1,537 ....J3	Perkinsfield 342 ....D3	Ripley 577 C
Heyden 316 ....J5	King City 2,182 ....J3	MacGregor's Bay 885 ....G2	Milverton 1,393 ....D4	Noelville 665 ....D1	Perth⊙ 5,675 ....H3	Rockcliffe Park 2,117 ....J
Highgate 418 ....C5	Kingston⊙ 56,032 ....H3	MacTier 690 ....E2	Mindemoya 407 ....B2	North Bay⊙ 51,639 ....E1	Petawawa 5,815 ....G2	Rockland 3,930 ....J
Hillsburgh 819 ....D4	Kingsville 4,692 ....B6	Madawaska 288 ....F2	Minden⊙ 990 ....F3	North Brook 409 ....G3	Peterborough⊙ 59,683 ....F3	Rockwood 959 ....D
Hillsdale 274 ....E3	Kinmount 270 ....F3	Madoc 1,363 ....G3	Mississauga 250,017 ....J4	North Gower 625 ....J2	Petrolia 4,393 ....B5	Rodney 983 C
Holland Landing 1,782 ....E3	Kirkland Lake 13,567 ....K5	Maitland 584 ....J3	Mitchell 2,742 ....C4	North York 558,398 ....J4	Pickering 27,879 ....K4	Rolphton 260 ....F
Honey Harbour 289 ....E3	Kitchener⊙ 131,870 ....D4	Mallorytown 290 ....J3	Monkton 550 ....D4	Norwich 1,891 ....D5	Picton⊙ 4,649 ....G3	Rosseau 260 ....E
Hornepayne 1,694 ....J5	Komoka 812 ....C5	Manitouwadge 3,551 ....H5	Moonbeam 925 ....J5	Norwood 1,243 ....F3	Plantagenet 919 ....K2	Rosslyn Village 320 ....H
	Lakefield 2,240 ....F3	Manitowaning 373 ....C2	Moorefield 530 ....D4	Nottawa 326 ....D3		Russell 857 ....J

Ruthven 384 ....⊙....B6
Saint Catharines⊙ 123,351 ..E4
Saint Charles 347 ....D1
Saint Clair Beach 1,953....B5
Saint Clements 954 ....D4
Saint-Eugène 493 ....K2
Saint George 930 ....D4
Saint Isidore de Prescott 689K2
Saint Jacobs 852 ....D4
Saint Mary's 4,843 ....C4
Saint Thomas⊙ 27,206 .....C5
Saint Williams 458 ....D5
Salem 743 ....D4
Sarnia⊙ 55,576 ....B5
Sauble Beach 769 ....C3
Sault Sainte Marie⊙ 81,048 J5
Scarborough 387,149 ....K4
Schomberg 782 ....J3
Schreiber 1,982 ....H5
Scotland 687 ....D4
Seaforth 2,084 ....C4
Searchmont 390 ....J5
Sebringville 534 ....C4
Seeleys Bay 452 ....H3
Shakespeare 606 ....C4
Shallow Lake 411 ....C3
Shannonville 299 ....G3
Shanty Bay 333 ....E3
Sharbot Lake 296 ....H3
Shedden 346 ....C5
Shelburne 2,928 ....D3
Simcoe⊙ 14,189 ....D5
Sioux Lookout 3,108 ....G4
Smithfield 357 ....H3
Smiths Falls 9,279 ....H3
Smithville 1,737 ....E4

Smooth Rock Falls 2,446....J5
Sombra 439 ....B5
Southampton 2,734 ....C3
South River 1,094 ....E2
Spanish 1,082 ....J5
Spencerville 434 ....J3
Springfield 558 ....C5
Springford 279 ....D5
Stayner 2,454 ....E3
Stirling 1,571 ....G3
Stittsville 2,703 ....J2
Stoney Creek 30,294 ....E4
Stoney Point 1,041 ....B5
Strafford 759 ....D5
Stratford⊙ 25,657 ....C4
Strathroy 7,769 ....C5
Stroud 892 ....E3
Sturgeon Falls 6,400 ....E1
Sudbury⊙ 97,604 ....K5
Sultan 274 ....J5
Sunderland 769 ....D3
Sundridge 692 ....E2
Sutton 3,655 ....E3
Sydenham 528 ....H3
Tamworth 350 ....H3
Tara 717 ....C3
Tavistock 1,783 ....D4
Tecumseh 5,326 ....B5
Teeswater 988 ....C3
Terrace Bay 2,088 ....J5
Thamesford 1,872 ....C4
Thamesville 1,003 ....C5
Thedford 715 ....C4
Thessalon 1,824 ....J5
Thornbury 1,326 ....D3
Thorndale 476 ....C4

Thornton 421 ....E3
Thorold 14,944 ....E4
Thunder Bay⊙ 111,476...H5
Tilbury 4,248 ....B5
Tillsonburg 9,404 ....D5
Timagami 518 ....K5
Timmins 44,747 ....J5
Tiverton 825 ....C3
Tobermory 317 ....C2
Toronto (cap.)⊙ 633,318..K4
Tottenham 2,747 ....E3
Trenton 15,465 ....G3
Trout Creek 623 ....E2
Turkey Point 369 ....D5
Tweed 1,654 ....G3
Udora 310 ....E3
Union 462 ....C5
Uxbridge 4,354 ....E3
Valley East 19,591 ....J5
Vanier 19,812 ....J2
Vankleek Hill 1,568 ....K2
Vars 564 ....J2
Vaughan 17,782 ....J4
Vermilion Bay 570 ....G4
Verner 1,055 ....D1
Vernon 305 ....J2
Verona 991 ....H3
Victoria Harbour 1,310.....E3
Vienna 398 ....D5
Virginiatown 1,189 ....K5
Vittoria 425 ....D5
Wabigoon 362 ....G5
Walden 10,453 ....J5
Walkerton⊙ 4,626 ....C3
Wallaceburg 11,132 ....B5
Wallacetown 266 ....C5
Wardsville 448 ....C5
Warkworth 552 ....G3
Warren 612 ....D1
Wasaga Beach 4,985 ......D3
Washago 442 ....E3
Waterdown 2,737 ....D4
Waterloo 46,623 ....D4
Watford 1,365 ....C5
Waubaushene 820 ....E3
Wawa 4,272 ....J5
Webbwood 464 ....C1
Welland 45,047 ....E5
Wellesley 842 ....D4
Wellington 1,057 ....G4
Wendover 362 ....J2
West Lorne 1,171 ....C5
Westmeath 275 ....H2
Westport 644 ....H3
Wheatley 1,637 ....B5
Whitby 28,173 ....F4
Whitchurch-Stouffville 12,884J3
White River 754 ....J5
Whitney 767 ....F2
Wiarton 2,144 ....C3
Wikwemikong 941 ....C2
Wilberforce 266 ....F3
Williamston 407 ....J3
Williamsford 264 ....D3
Williamstown 336 ....K2
Winchester 1,745 ....J3
Windsor⊙ 196,526 ....B5
Wingham 2,871 ....C4
Wolfe Island 331 ....H3
Woodstock⊙ 26,779 ......D4
Woodville 573 ....F3

Wroxeter 287 ....C4
Wyoming 1,646 ....B5
Yarker 365 ....H3
Wheatley 1,637 ....B5
York 141,367 ....J4
Zurich 753 ....C4

OTHER FEATURES

Abitibi (riv.) J5
Algonquin Prov. Park F2
Amherst (isl.) H3
Balsam (lake) F3
Barrie (isl.) B1
Bays (pt.) F2
Big Rideau (lake) H3
Black (riv.) E3
Bruce (pen.) C2
Buckhorn (lake) F3
Cabot (head) C2

Charleston (lake) J3
Christian (isl.) D3
Clear (lake) F3
Cockburn (isl.) A2
Couchiching (lake) E3
Croker (cape) D3
Don (riv.) J4
Doré (lake) G2
Douglas (pt.) C3
Erie (lake) E5
Flowerpot (isl.) C2
French (riv.) D1
Georgian (bay) D2
Georgina (isl.) E3
Grand (riv.) D4
Humber (riv.) J3
Hurd (cape) C2
Huron (lake) B3
Ipperwash Prov. Park C4

Joseph (lake) E2
Killarney Prov. Park C1
Killbear Point Prov. Park ..D2
Lake of the Woods F5
Lake Superior Prov. Park .J5
Lonely (isl.) C2
Long (pt.) D5
Long Point (bay) D5
Madawaska (riv.) G2
Magnetawan (riv.) D2
Main (chan.) C2
Manitou (lake) C2
Manitoulin (isl.) B2
Mattagami (riv.) J5
Michipicoten (isl.) H5
Missinaibi (riv.) J5
Mississagi (riv.) A1
Mississippi (lake) H2
Muskoka (lake) E2
Niagara (riv.) E4
Nipigon (lake) H5
Nipissing (lake) E1
North (chan.) A1
Nottawasaga (bay) D3
Ogidaki (mt.) J5
Ontario (lake) G4
Opeongo (lake) F2
Ottawa (riv.) H2
Owen (sound) D3
Panache (lake) C1
Parry (isl.) D2
Parry (sound) D2
Pelee (pt.) B6
Petre (pt.) G4
Point Pelee Nat'l Park B5
Presqu'ile Prov. Park G4

Pukaskwa Prov. Park H5
Quetico Prov. Park G5
Rainy (lake) G5
Rice (lake) F3
Rideau (lake) H3
Rondeau Prov. Park C5
Rosseau (lake) E2
Saint Clair (lake) B5
Saint Clair (riv.) B5
Saint Lawrence (lake) K3
Saint Lawrence (riv.) J3
Saint Lawrence Is. Nat'l
  Park J3
Saugeen (riv.) C3
Scugog (lake) F3
Seul (lake) G4
Severn (riv.) E3
Sibley Prov. Park H5
Simcoe (lake) E3
South (bay) C2
Spanish (riv.) C1
Stony (lake) G3
Superior (lake) H5
Sydenham (riv.) B5
Thames (riv.) B5
Theano (pt.) J5
Thousand (isls.) H3
Timagami (lake) K5
Trout (lake) E1
Vernen (lake) E2
Walpole (isl.) B5
Welland (canal) E5
Woods (lake) F5

⊙County seat.

Ontario
Southern Part

SCALE
0 10 20 30 40 50MI.
0 10 20 30 40 50KM.

⊛ National Capital   ⊛ Provincial & State
⊛ Provincial Capital   Boundaries
⊙ County Seats   County Boundaries-----
  International   Canals
  Boundaries

Scale 1:2,620,000

Topography

0   100   200 MI.
0   100   200 KM.

C. Henrietta Maria

Sandy L.
Severn
Winisk
Attawapiskat
L. St. Joseph
Lac Seul
Albany
Albany
Kenogami
Missinaibi
Abitibi
English
Lake Nipigon
2,275 ft. (693 m.)
Lake of the Woods
Rainy Lake
Thunder Bay
Ogidaki Mtn. 2,183 ft. (665 m.)
Sudbury
Ottawa
Sault Ste. Marie
L. Nipissing
Manitoulin I.
C. Hurd
Georgian Bay
L. Simcoe
St. Lawrence
Ottawa
London
Toronto
Thames
Niagara Falls
Long Pt.
Windsor
Pt. Pelee

Below Sea Level	100 m. 328 ft.	200 m. 656 ft.	500 m. 1,640 ft.	1,000 m. 3,281 ft.	2,000 m. 6,562 ft.	5,000 m. 16,404 ft.

Agriculture, Industry and Resources

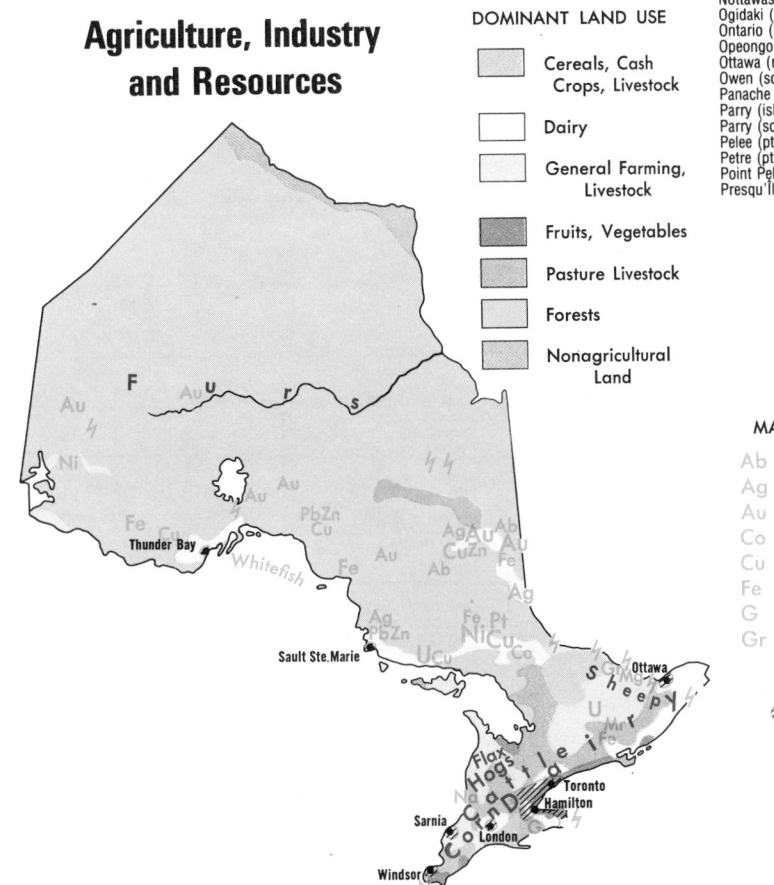

DOMINANT LAND USE

Cereals, Cash Crops, Livestock
Dairy
General Farming, Livestock
Fruits, Vegetables
Pasture Livestock
Forests
Nonagricultural Land

MAJOR MINERAL OCCURRENCES

Ab Asbestos   Mg Magnesium
Ag Silver   Mr Marble
Au Gold   Na Salt
Co Cobalt   Ni Nickel
Cu Copper   Pb Lead
Fe Iron Ore   Pt Platinum
G   Natural Gas   U   Uranium
Gr Graphite   Zn Zinc

⚡ Water Power
▨ Major Industrial Areas

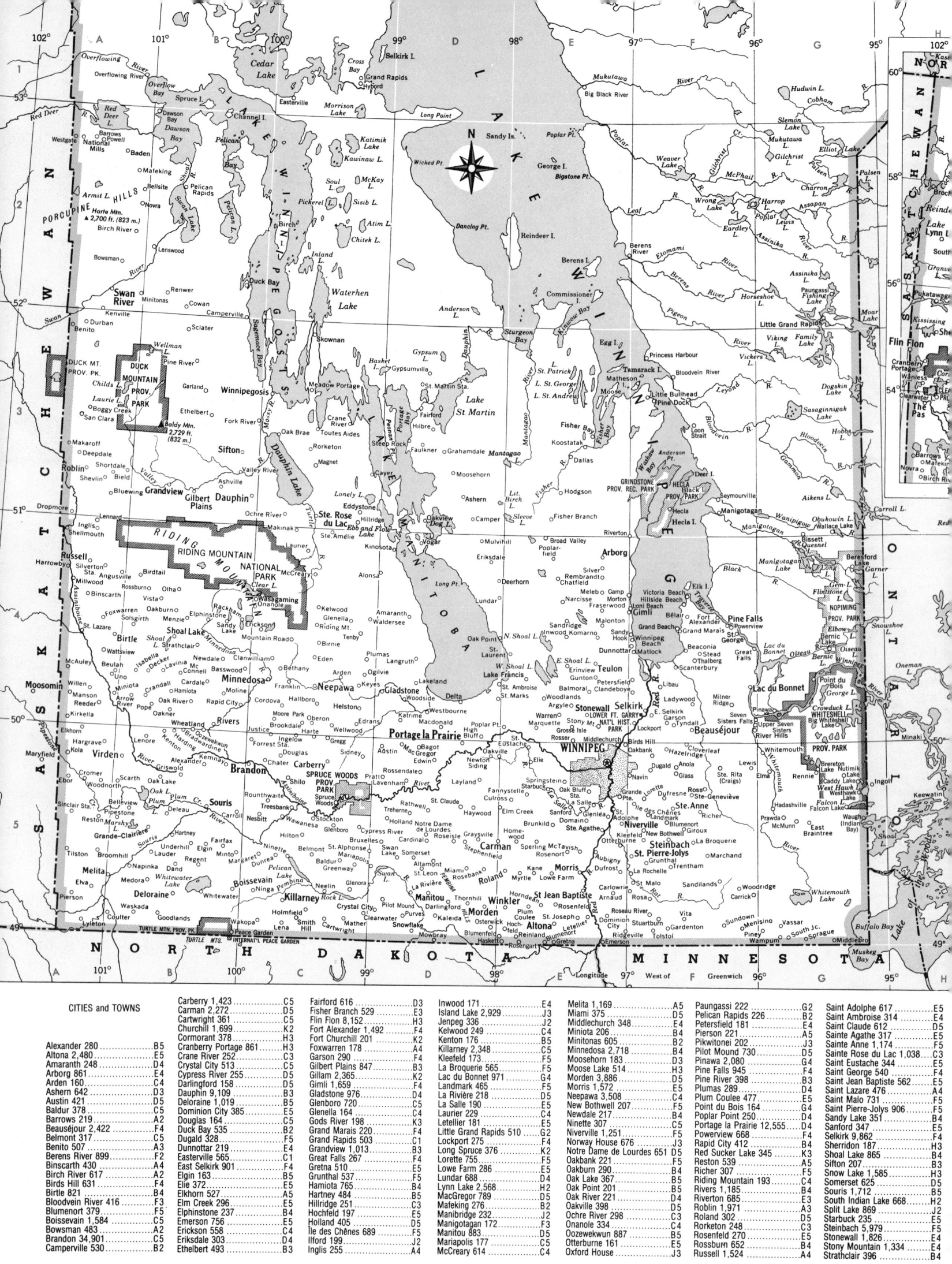

Manitoba
Northern Part

0   40   80   120 MI.

0 40 80 120 KM.

ST TERRS *Tha-anne R.*
Thlewiaza R.

Baralzon L.
Nejanilini L.

Duck Lake Post

60°

1

53°

Hubbart Pt.

HUDSON

BAY

C. Churchill
Churchill

Chesnaye

Seal
North Knife L.
South Knife Lake
N. Knife L.

C. Tatnam

58°

2

Windigo Lake

Missi Falls

Northern Indian L.

Churchill R.
S. Knife R.
Owl R.
M'Clintock
Herchmer

Etawney L.

York Factory

Weir River

Churchill R.

Amery

56°

52°

Moak L.
Split L.
Ilford
Wivenhoe
Fox
Long Spruce
Nelson House
Split L.

Shamattawa

Nelson R.
Grass R.

Thompson
Pikwitonei

Thicket Portage

Burntwood R.

Sipiwesk L.
Wabowden
Oxford House
Gods River

Knee L.
Oxford L.
Gods L.

Bigstone R.
Hayes R.

O N T A R I O

54°

3

Cross L.
Cross Lake

Red Sucker Lake

Mystery Lake

Beaverhill L.
Island Lake

Sachigot L.

Big Trout L.

Saint L.
Norway House
Gunisao L.
Stevenson
Molson L.
Bigstone
Cobham R.

Theresa Pt.
Island L.

N. Caribou L.

Winnipeg
Negginan

Sandy L.

Favourable O
L.

Windigo L.

Severn R.

Sachigot R.

Fry Lake

51°

4

98° 96° 94° 92° 90°

Manitoba
Southern Part

SCALE

0 5 10   20   40   60 MI.

0 5 10   20   40   60 KM.

Provincial Capital ⊛
International Boundaries — —
Provincial Boundaries — · —

Scale 1:2,340,000

© Copyright HAMMOND INCORPORATED, Maplewood, N.J.

94°   93°   92°

Balmertown
Red Lake

AREA 250,999 sq. mi. (650,087 sq. km.)
POPULATION 1,017,323
CAPITAL Winnipeg
LARGEST CITY Winnipeg
HIGHEST POINT Baldy Mtn. 2,729 ft.
(832 m.)
SETTLED IN 1812
ADMITTED TO CONFEDERATION 1870
PROVINCIAL FLOWER Prairie Crocus

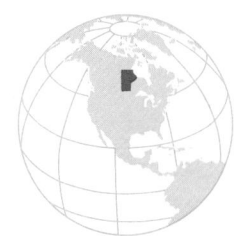

Swan Lake 338 ....D5
Swan River 3,443 ....A2
Teulon 873 ....E4
The Pas 6,602 ....H3
Thicket Portage 255 ....H3
Thompson 17,291 ....J2
Treherne 706 ....D5
Tyndall 411 ....F4
Virden 2,936 ....A5
Vita 213 ....F5
Wabowden 847 ....J3
Wanless 252 ....H3
Warren 302 ....E4
Waskada 257 ....B5
Wawanesa 487 ....C5
Whitemouth 314 ....G5
Whitewater 885 ....B5
Winkler 3,749 ....E5
Winnipeg (cap.) 560,874 ...E5
Winnipeg Beach 582 ....F4
Winnipegosis 893 ....B3
Woodridge 175 ....G5
York Landing 198 ....J2

OTHER FEATURES

Aikens (lake) G3
Anderson (lake) D2
Anderson (pt.) F3
Armit (lake) A2
Assapan (riv.) G2
Assiniboine (riv.) C5
Assinika (lake) G2
Assinika (riv.) G2
Atim (lake) C2
Baldy (mt.) B3
Baralzon (lake) J1
Basket (lake) C3
Beaverhill (lake) J3
Berens (isl.) E2
Berens (riv.) F2
Bernic (lake) G4
Big Sand (lake) H2
Bigstone (lake) J3
Bigstone (pt.) E2
Bigstone (riv.) J3
Birch (lake) B1
Black (isl.) F3
Black (lake) F4
Bloodvein (riv.) F3
Bonnet (lake) G4
Buffalo (bay) G5
Burntwood (riv.) J2
Caribou (riv.) J1
Carroll (lake) G3
Cedar (lake) B1
Channel (isl.) B2
Charron (lake) G2
Childs (lake) A3
Chitek (lake) C2
Churchill (cape) K2
Churchill (riv.) J2
Clear (lake) C4
Clearwater Lake Prov. Park H3
Cobham (riv.) G1
Cochrane (riv.) H2
Commissioner (isl.) E2
Cormorant (lake) H3
Cross (bay) C1
Cross (lake) J3
Crowduck (lake) G4
Dancing (pt.) D2
Dauphin (lake) C3
Dauphin (riv.) D3
Dawson (bay) B2
Dog (lake) D3
Dogskin (lake) G3
Duck Mountain Prov. Park ...B3

Eardley (lake) F2
East Shoal (lake) E4
Ebb and Flow (lake) C3
Egg (isl.) E3
Elbow (lake) G4
Elk (isl.) F4
Elliot (lake) G2
Etawney (lake) J2
Etomami (riv.) F2
Falcon (lake) G5
Fisher (bay) E3
Fisher (riv.) E3
Fishing (lake) G2
Flintstone (lake) G4
Fox (riv.) K2
Gammon (riv.) G3
Garner (lake) G4
Gem (lake) G4
George (isl.) E2
George (lake) G4
Gilchrist (creek) F2
Gilchrist (riv.) G2
Gods (lake) K3
Gods (riv.) K3
Granville (lake) H2
Grass (riv.) J3
Grass River Prov. Park H3
Grindstone Prov. Rec. Park F3
Gunisao (lake) J3
Gypsum (lake) D3
Harrop (lake) G2
Harte (mt.) A2
Hayes (riv.) K3
Hecla (isl.) F3
Hecla Prov. Park F3
Hobbs (lake) G3
Horseshoe (lake) G2
Hubbart (pt.) K2
Hudson (bay) K2
Hudwin (lake) G1
Inland (lake) G2
International Peace Garden..B5
Island (lake) K3
Katimik (lake) C2
Kawinaw (lake) C2
Kinwow (bay) E2
Kississing (lake) H2
Knee, (lake) J3
Lake of the Woods (lake)...H5
La Salle (riv.) E5
Laurie (lake) A3
Leaf (riv.) F2
Lewis (lake) G2
Leyond (riv.) F3
Little Birch (lake) E3
Lonely (lake) C3
Long (lake) G4
Long (pt.) D1
Long (pt.) D4

Manigotagan (lake) G4
Manigotagan (riv.) G3
Manitoba (lake) D4
Mantagao (lake) E3
Mantagao (riv.) E3
Marshy (lake) B5
McKay (lake) C2
McPhail (riv.) F2
Minnedosa (riv.) B4
Moar (lake) G2
Molson (lake) J3
Moose (isl.) B3
Morrison (lake) C1
Mossy (riv.) C3
Mukutawa (riv.) E1
Muskeg (bay) G6
Nejanilini (lake) J1
Nelson (riv.) J2
Nopiming Prov. Park G4
Northern Indian (lake) J2
North Knife (lake) J2
North Seal (riv.) H2
North Shoal (lake) E4
Nueltin (lake) H1
Oak (lake) B5
Obukowin (lake) G3
Oiseau (lake) G4
Oiseau (riv.) G4
Overflow (bay) A1
Overflowing (riv.) A1
Owl (riv.) K2
Oxford (lake) J3
Paint (lake) J2
Palsen (riv.) G2
Pelican (bay) B2
Pelican (lake) B2
Pelican (lake) C5
Pembina (hills) D5
Pembina (riv.) C5
Peonan (pt.) D3
Pickerel (lake) C2
Pigeon (riv.) F2
Pipestone (creek) A5
Plum (creek) B5
Plum (lake) B5
Poplar (pt.) E2
Poplar (riv.) E2
Porcupine (hills) A2
Portage (bay) D3
Punk (isl.) F3
Quesnel (lake) G4
Rat (riv.) F5
Red (riv.) F4
Red Deer (lake) A2
Red Deer (riv.) A2
Reindeer (isl.) E2
Reindeer (lake) H2
Riding (mt.) B4
Riding Mountain Nat'l Park.B4
Rock (lake) C5

Ross (isl.) J3
Sagemace (bay) B3
Saint Andrew (lake) E3
Saint George (lake) E3
Saint Martin (lake) D3
Saint Patrick (lake) E3
Sale (riv.) E5
Sandy (isls.) D2
Sasaginnigak (lake) G3
Seal (riv.) J2
Selkirk (isl.) C1
Setting (lake) H3
Shoal (lake) B4
Shoal (lake) G5
Shoal (riv.) B2
Sipiwesk (lake) J3
Sisib (lake) C2
Sieeve (lake) E3
Slemon (lake) G1
Snowshoe (lake) G4
Soul (lake) C2
Souris (riv.) B5
Southern Indian (lake) H2
South Knife (riv.) J2
South Seal (riv.) J2
Split (lake) J2
Spruce (isl.) B1
Spruce Woods Prov. Park..C5
Stevenson (lake) J3
Sturgeon (bay) E3
Swan (lake) B2
Swan (lake) D5
Swan (riv.) A3
Tadoule (lake) J2
Tamarack (isl.) F3
Tatnam (cape) K2
Traverse (bay) F4
Turtle (mts.) B5
Turtle (riv.) C3
Turtle Mountain Prov. Park B5
Valley (riv.) B3
Vickers (lake) F3
Viking (lake) G3
Wanipigow (riv.) G3
Washow (bay) F3
Waterhen (lake) C2
Weaver (lake) F2
Wellman (lake) B3
West Hawk (lake) G5
West Shoal (lake) E4
Whitemouth (lake) G5
Whitemouth (riv.) G5
Whiteshell Prov. Park G4
Whitewater (lake) B5
Wicked (pt.) D2
Winnipeg (lake) E2
Winnipeg (riv.) G4
Winnipegosis (lake) C2
Woods (lake) H5
Wrong (lake) F2

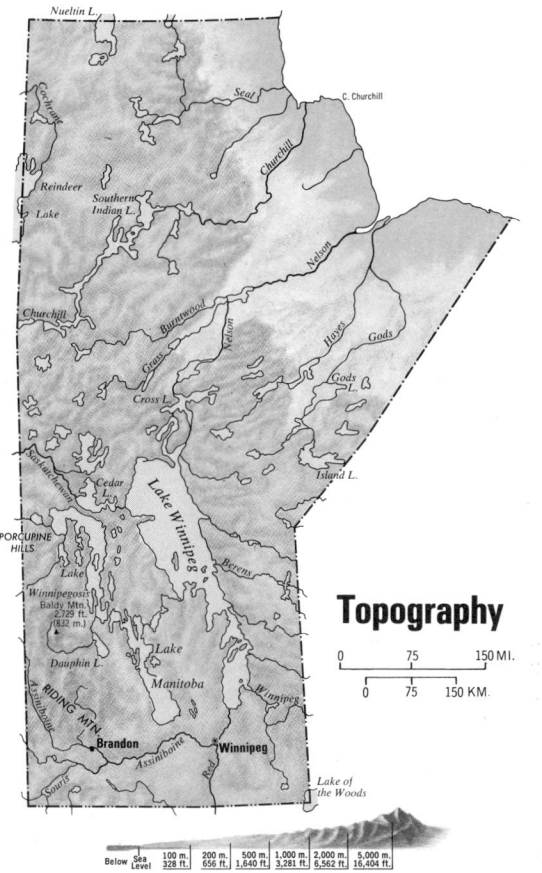

Topography

0   75   150 MI.

0   75   150 KM.

Below Sea Level | 100 m. 328 ft. | 200 m. 656 ft. | 500 m. 1,640 ft. | 1,000 m. 3,281 ft. | 2,000 m. 6,562 ft. | 5,000 m. 16,404 ft.

Agriculture, Industry and Resources

DOMINANT LAND USE

Cereals (chiefly barley, oats)

Cereals, Livestock

Dairy

Livestock

Forests

Nonagricultural Land

MAJOR MINERAL OCCURRENCES

Au Gold
Co Cobalt
Cu Copper
Na Salt
Ni Nickel
O Petroleum
Pb Lead
Pt Platinum
Zn Zinc

⚡ Water Power
▨ Major Industrial Areas

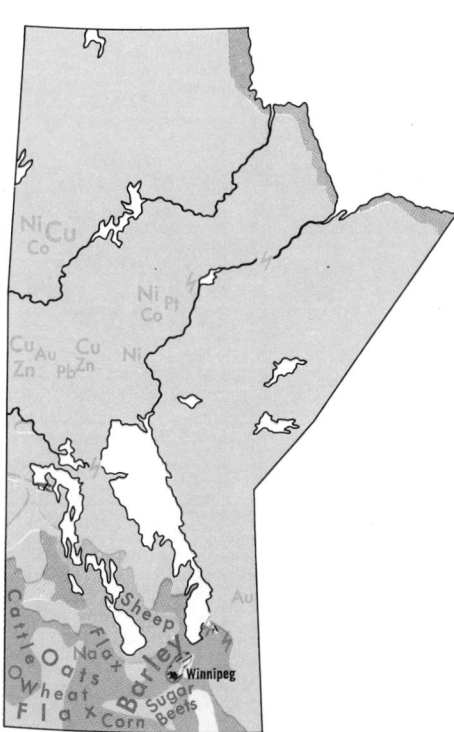

Topography

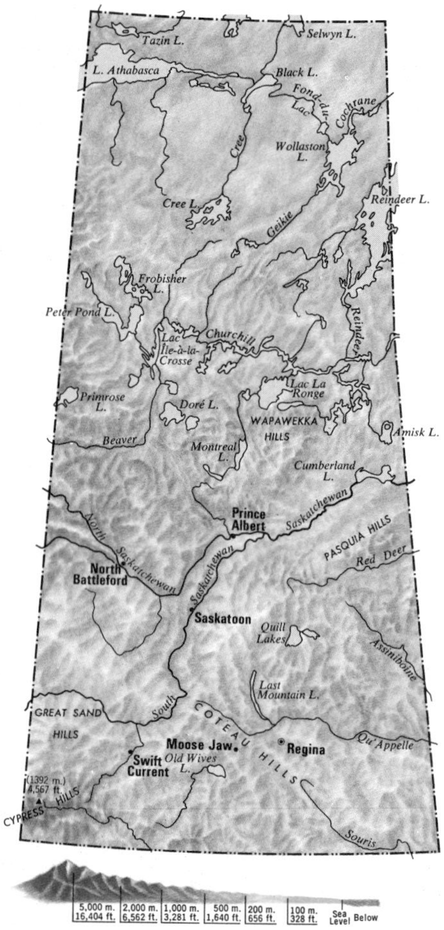
0 60 120 MI.
0 60 120 KM.
Tazin L.
Selwyn L.
L. Athabasca
Black L.
Fond du Lac
Cochrane
Wollaston L.
Cree
Cree L.
Geikie
Reindeer L.
Frobisher L.
Peter Pond L.
Churchill
Lac Île-à-la-Crosse
Reindeer
Primrose L.
Doré L.
Lac La Ronge
WAPAWEKKA HILLS
Amisk L.
Beaver
Montreal L.
Cumberland L.
Prince Albert
Saskatchewan
PASQUIA HILLS
North Battleford
Red Deer
Saskatoon
Quill Lakes
Assiniboine
Last Mountain L.
GREAT SAND HILLS
Moose Jaw
Regina
Qu'Appelle
Swift Current
Old Wives L.
(1392 m.) 4,567 ft.
CYPRESS HILLS
COTEAU HILLS
Souris
5,000 m. 16,404 ft.
2,000 m. 6,562 ft.
1,000 m. 3,281 ft.
500 m. 1,640 ft.
200 m. 656 ft.
100 m. 328 ft.
Sea Level
Below

CITIES and TOWNS

Abbey 259 C5
Aberdeen 373 E3
Abernethy 299 H5
Air Ronge 348 M3
Alameda 319 J6
Alida 163 K6
Allan 720 E4
Alsask 734 B4
Aneroid 153 D6
Annaheim 187 G3
Antelope 150 C5
Arborfield 400 H2
Archerwill 272 H3
Arcola 547 J6
Asquith 416 D3
Assiniboia 2,738 E6
Avonlea 415 G5
Aylsham 153 H2
Balcarres 729 H5
Balgonie 715 G5
Batoche E3
Battleford 2,569 C3
Beauval 518 L3
Beechy 344 D5
Bellevue 145 F3
Bengough 603 F6
Bethune 317 F5
Bienfait 807 J6
Biggar 2,491 C3
Big River 827 D2
Birch Hills 752 F3
Bjorkdale 248 H3
Blaine Lake 631 D3
Borden 195 D3
Bredenbury 441 K5
Broadview 861 J5
Brock 183 C4
Broderick 135 E4
Bruno 762 F3
Buchanan 434 J4
Buffalo Narrows 837 L3
Burstall 548 B5
Cabri 631 C5
Cadillac 203 D6
Calder 158 K4
Cando 144 C3
Canoe Lake 155 L3
Canora 2,689 J4
Carievale 245 K6
Carlyle 1,057 J6
Carnduff 1,071 K6
Carrot River 1,020 H2
Central Butte 518 E5
Ceylon 259 G6
Chaplin 382 E5
Chitek Lake 172 D2
Choiceland 535 G2
Christopher Lake 193 F2
Churchbridge 928 J5
Climax 277 C6
Cochin 221 C2
Codette 214 H2
Coleville 398 B4
Colonsay 542 F4
Connaught Heights 162 G3
Conquest 265 D4
Consul 160 B6
Coronach 386 F6
Craik 543 F4
Craven 185 G5
Creelman 178 H6
Creighton 1,746 N4
Crooked River 155 H3
Cudworth 907 F3
Cumberland House 796 J2
Cupar 611 G5
Cut Knife 530 B3
Dalmeny 602 E3
Davidson 1,092 E4
Debden 381 E2
Delisle 783 D4
Delmas 153 C3
Denare Beach 308 M4
Denzil 230 B3
Deschambault Lake 372 M3
Dinsmore 398 D4
Dodsland 312 C4
Domremy 188 F3
Dorintosh 159 L4
Drake 251 G4
Dubuc 142 J5
Duck Lake 683 E3
Dundurn 409 E4
Dysart 236 H5
Earl Grey 242 G5
Eastend 771 C6
Eatonia 553 B4
Ebenezer 155 J4
Edam 348 C2
Edenwold 134 G5
Elbow 286 E4
Elfros 213 H4
Elrose 614 D4
Elstow 146 E4
Endeavour 220 J3
Englefeld 258 G3
Esterhazy 2,894 K5
Estevan 8,847 J6
Eston 1,354 C4
Eyebrow 198 E5
Fillmore 350 H6
Fleming 164 K5
Flin Flon 408 N4
Foam Lake 1,387 H4
Fond du Lac 449 L2
Fort Qu'Appelle 1,764 H5
Fox Valley 429 B5
Francis 150 H6
Frobisher 187 J6
Frontier 385 C6
Gainsborough 311 K6
Gerald 139 K5
Glaslyn 383 C2
Glenavon 295 J5
Glen Ewen 143 K6
Goodeve 134 H4
Goodsoil 217 L4
Govan 323 G4
Gravelbourg 1,326 E6
Grayson 260 J5
Green Acres 165 F2
Green Lake 616 L4
Grenfell 1,363 J5
Guernsey 222 F4
Gull Lake 1,053 C5
Hafford 515 D3
Hague 530 E3
Hanley 446 E4
Harris 233 D4
Hawarden 133 E4
Hepburn 352 E3
Herbert 986 D5
Hodgeville 332 E5
Holdfast 312 F5
Hudson Bay 2,280 J3
Humboldt 4,265 F3
Hyas 190 J4
Île-à-la-Crosse 821 L3
Imperial 456 F4
Indian Head 1,720 H5
Invermay 397 J4
Ituna 910 H4
Jansen 209 G4
Kamsack 2,726 K4
Kelliher 411 H4
Kelvington 1,053 H3
Kenaston 352 E4
Kennedy 241 J5
Kenosee Park 135 J6
Kerrobert 1,100 C4
Killaly 137 J5
Kincaid 245 D6
Kindersley 3,523 B4
Kinistino 763 F3
Kipling 949 J5
Kisbey 252 J6
Kuroki 145 H4
Kyle 499 C5
Lafleche 639 E6
Laird 201 E3
Lake Lenore 385 G3
La Loche 1,651 L3
Lampman 720 J6
Lancer 171 C5
Landis 285 C3
Lang 189 G6
Langenburg 1,197 K5
Langham 729 E3
Lanigan 1,646 F4
La Ronge 1,714 L3
Lashburn 517 B2
Leader 1,160 B5
Leask 446 E2
Lebret 268 H5
Lemberg 417 H5
Leoville 404 D2
Leroy 436 G4
Lestock 414 G4
Limerick 166 E6
Lintlaw 225 H3
Lipton 353 H5
Lloydminster 4,493 A2
Loon Lake 365 B1
Loreburn 224 E4
Lucky Lake 340 D5
Lumsden 1,116 G5
Luseland 682 B3
Macdowall 146 E2
Macklin 873 A3
MacNutt 141 K4
Macoun 163 H6
Maidstone 747 B2
Major 150 B4
Manitou Beach 136 F4
Mankota 406 D6
Manor 348 K6
Maple Creek 2,330 B6
Marcelin 273 E3
Margo 178 H4
Marsden 211 B3
Marshall 326 B2
Martensville 960 E3
Maryfield 408 K6
Maymont 172 D3
McLean 184 G5
Meacham 184 F3
Meadow Lake 3,662 C1
Meath Park 298 F2
Medstead 197 C2
Melfort 5,141 G3
Melville 5,149 J5
Meota 248 C2
Mervin 174 C2
Midale 572 H6
Middle Lake 270 F3
Milden 234 D4
Milestone 511 G5
Minton 159 G6
Mistatim 139 H3
Molanosa 248 M4
Montmartre 534 H5
Montreal Lake 306 F1
Moose Jaw 32,581 F5
Moosomin 2,449 K5
Morse 435 D5
Mortlach 278 E5
Mossbank 444 E6
Muenster 333 F3
Naicam 739 G3
Neilburg 369 B3
Neudorf 394 J5
Neuhorst 146 E3
Nipawin 4,317 H2
Nokomis 535 F4
Norquay 520 J4
North Battleford 13,158 C3
North Portal 157 J6
Odessa 203 H5
Ogema 432 G6
Ormiston 144 F6
Osler 225 E3
Outlook 1,687 E4
Oxbow 1,221 J6
Paddockwood 179 F2
Pangman 208 G6
Paradise Hill 395 B2
Patuanak 136 L3
Paynton 186 B2
Pelican Narrows 212 N3
Pelly 354 K4
Pennant 216 C5
Pense 356 G5
Perdue 393 D3
Pierceland 358 K4
Pilot Butte 585 G5
Pine House 528 M3
Plenty 193 C4
Plunkett 139 F4
Ponteix 760 D6
Porcupine Plain 935 H3
Preeceville 1,170 J4
Prelate 337 B5
Prince Albert 28,631 F2
Prud'homme 239 F3
Punnichy 400 G4
Qu'Appelle 551 H5
Quill Lake 534 G3
Quinton 189 G4
Rabbit Lake 166 D2
Radisson 432 D3
Radville 1,008 G6
Rama 163 H4
Raymore 562 G4
Redvers 843 K6
Regina (cap.) 149,593 G5
Regina Beach 488 F5
Reserve 187 J3
Rhein 284 J4
Richmound 174 B5
Ridgedale 147 H2
Riverhurst 182 E5
Rocanville 872 K5
Rockglen 508 F6
Rosetown 2,551 D4
Rose Valley 534 H3
Rosthern 1,604 E3
Rouleau 380 G5
Saint Benedict 164 F3
Saint Brieux 362 G3
Saint Gregor 144 G3
Saint Louis 394 F3
Saint Philips 636 K4
Saint Walburg 718 B2
Saltcoats 488 J4
Sandy Bay 555 N3
Saskatoon 133,750 E3
Sceptre 204 B5
Scott 209 C3
Sedley 289 H5
Semans 343 G4
Shaunavon 2,183 C6
Sheho 311 H4
Shellbrook 1,098 E2
Shell Lake 217 D2
Simmie 174 C6
Simpson 223 F4
Sintaluta 213 H5
Smeaton 275 G2
Southey 604 G5
Spalding 375 G3
Speers 135 D3
Spiritwood 841 D2
Springside 474 J4
Spy Hill 351 K5
Squaw Rapids 1,024 H2
Star City 539 G3
Stenen 182 J4
Stockholm 329 J5
Stony Rapids 526 M2
Storthoaks 152 K6
Stoughton 705 J6
Strasbourg 812 G4
Sturgis 705 J4
Swift Current 14,264 D5
Tantallon 186 K5
Theodore 463 J4
Tisdale 3,026 H3
Togo 197 K4
Tompkins 274 C5
Torquay 344 H6
Tramping Lake 200 B3
Tugaske 179 E5
Turnor Lake 190 L3
Turtleford 442 B2
Unity 2,244 B3
Uranium City 1,765 L2
Val Marie 253 D6
Vanguard 286 D6
Vanscoy 276 D4
Veregin 140 K4
Vibank 305 H5
Viscount 424 F4
Vonda 311 F3
Wadena 1,377 H4
Wakaw 1,031 F3
Waldeck 196 D5
Waldheim 647 E3
Wapella 453 K5
Warman 1,117 E3
Waskesiu Lake 176 E2
Watrous 1,520 F4
Watson 940 G3
Wawota 619 J6
Weekes 166 J3
Weirdale 160 F2
Weldon 272 F2
Welwyn 180 K5
Weyburn 8,892 H6
White City 340 G5
White Fox 380 H2
Whitewood 1,072 J5
Wilcox 175 G5
Wilkie 1,604 C3
Willow Bunch 417 F6
Windthorst 215 J5
Wiseton 201 D4
Wishart 238 H4
Wollaston Lake 263 N2
Wolseley 883 H5
Wymark 148 D5
Wynyard 2,045 G4
Yarbo 139 K5
Yellow Creek 166 F3
Yellow Grass 461 H6
Yorkton 14,119 J4
Young 495 F4
Zealandia 150 D4
Zenon Park 313 H2

OTHER FEATURES

Allan (hills) E4
Amisk (lake) M4
Antelope (lake) C5
Antler (riv.) K6
Arm (riv.) F5
Assiniboine (riv.) J3
Athabasca (lake) L2
Bad (lake) C4
Bad (hills) C4
Basin (lake) F3
Batoche Nat'l Hist. Site E3
Battle (creek) B6
Battle (riv.) B3
Bear (hills) C4
Beaver (hills) H4
Beaver (riv.) L4
Beaverlodge (lake) L2
Big Muddy (lake) G6
Bigstick (lake) B5
Birch (lake) C2
Bitter (lake) B5
Black (lake) M2

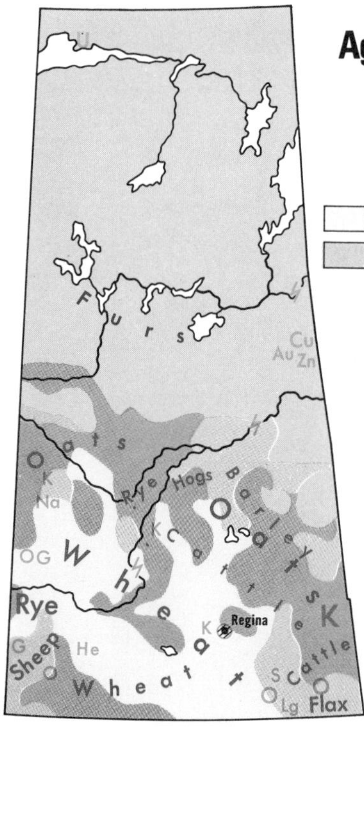

Agriculture, Industry and Resources

DOMINANT LAND USE

Wheat
Cereals (chiefly barley, oats)
Cereals, Livestock
Livestock
Forests

MAJOR MINERAL OCCURRENCES

Au Gold
Cu Copper
G Natural Gas
He Helium
K Potash
Lg Lignite
Na Salt
O Petroleum
S Sulfur
U Uranium
Zn Zinc

Water Power
Major Industrial Areas

Meadow Lake
Lloydminster
Battleford
Unity
Wilkie
Kerrobert
Kindersley
Leader
Maple Creek
Gull Lake
Shaunavon
GREAT SAND HILLS
CYPRESS HILLS
BOUNDARY PLATEAU
110°
109°
54°
53°
52°
51°
50°
49°

AREA 251,699 sq. mi. (651,900 sq. km.)
POPULATION 957,025
CAPITAL Regina
LARGEST CITY Regina
HIGHEST POINT Cypress Hills 4,567 ft. (1,392 m.)
SETTLED IN 1774
ADMITTED TO CONFEDERATION 1905
PROVINCIAL FLOWER Prairie Lily

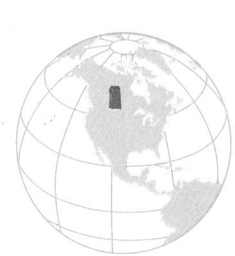

undary (plat.)	B6
ightsand (lake)	B2
ronson (lake)	B2
uffalo Pound Prov. Park	F5
actus (hills)	F5
andle (lake)	B4
annington Manon Hist. Park	J6
anoe (lake)	L3
arrot (riv.)	J2
haplin (lake)	E5
hipman (riv.)	M2
hitek (lake)	D2
hurchill (riv.)	M3
earwater (riv.)	L3
ochrane (riv.)	N2
oteau (hills)	D4
wan (lake)	D2
rane (lake)	B5
ree (lake)	E1
ree (lake)	L3
ree (riv.)	M2
umberland (lake)	J1
ypress (hills)	B6
ypress (lake)	B6
ypress Hills Prov. Park	B6
anielson Prov. Park	E4
elaronde (lake)	E1
oré (lake)	L3
ouglas Prov. Park	E4
uck Lake Hist. Park	E3

Duck Mountain Prov. Park	K4
Eagle (hills)	C3
Eaglehill (creek)	D4
Ear (lake)	B3
Echo Valley Prov. Park	G5
Etomami (riv.)	J3
Eyebrow (lake)	E5
Eyehill (creek)	B3
Fife (lake)	E6
File (lake)	H5
Fir (riv.)	J2
Fond du Lac (riv.)	M2
Forrest (lake)	L3
Fort Battleford Nat'l Hist. Park	C3
Fort Carlton Hist. Park	E3
Fort Pitt Hist. Park	B2
Fort Walsh Nat'l Hist. Park	A6
Foster (riv.)	M3
Frenchman (riv.)	C6
Frobisher (lake)	L3
Gap (creek)	B6
Gardiner (dam)	D4
Geikie (riv.)	M3
Good Spirit (lake)	J4
Goodspirit Lake Prov. Park	J4
Great Sand (hills)	B5
Green (lake)	D1
Greenwater Lake Prov. Park	H3
Haultain (riv.)	L3
Île-à-la-Crosse (lake)	L3
Ironspring (creek)	G3

Jackfish (lake)	C2
Katepwa Prov. Park	H5
Kingsmere (lake)	E1
Kiyiu (lake)	C4
Lac La Ronge Prov. Park	M3
Lanigan (creek)	F4
Last Mountain (lake)	F4
Leaf (lake)	J2
Leech (lake)	J4
Lenore (lake)	G3
Little Manitou (lake)	F4
Lodge (creek)	B6
Long (creek)	H6
Loon (creek)	G4
Makwa (lake)	B1
Makwa (lake)	B1
Manito (lake)	B3
Maple (creek)	B5
McFarlane (riv.)	L2
Meadow (lake)	C1
Meadow Lake Prov. Park	K4
Meeting (lake)	D2
Midnight (lake)	C2
Ministikwan (lake)	B1
Missouri Coteau (riv.)	F5
Montreal (lake)	F1
Mocse (mt.)	J6
Moose Jaw (riv.)	G5
Moose Mountain (creek)	J6
Moose Mountain Prov. Park	J6
Mossy (riv.)	H1
Muddy (lake)	B3

Mudjatik (riv.)	L3
Nipawin Prov. Park	G1
North Saskatchewan (riv.)	D3
Notukeu (creek)	D6
Oldman (riv.)	L2
Old Wives (lake)	E5
Opuntia (lake)	C4
Overflowing (riv.)	K2
Pasqua (lake)	J2
Pasquia (hills)	K2
Pelican (lake)	E5
Peter Pond (lake)	L3
Pheasant (hills)	J5
Pine Lake Prov. Park	E4
Pinto (creek)	D6
Pipestone (creek)	K6
Pipestone (lake)	L2
Ponass (hills)	H3
Poplar (riv.)	E6
Porcupine (hills)	K3
Primrose (lake)	K4
Primrose Lake Air Weapons Range	L3
Prince Albert Nat'l Park	E1
Qu'Appelle (riv.)	J5
Quill (lkes)	G4
Red Deer (lake)	A5
Red Deer (riv.)	K3
Reindeer (lake)	N3
Reindeer (riv.)	M3
Riou (lake)	M2
Rivers (lake)	F6

Ronge, La (lake)	M3
Rowans Ravine Prov. Park	F4
St. Victor Petroglyths Hist. Park	E6
Saskatchewan (riv.)	H2
Saskatchewan Landing Prov. Park	C5
Saskeram (riv.)	K2
Scott (lake)	M2
Selwyn (lake)	M2
Souris (riv.)	H6
South Saskatchewan (riv.)	C5
Steele Narrows Hist. Park	B2
Stripe (lake)	C4
Sturgeon (riv.)	E2

Swan (riv.)	J3
Swift Current (creek)	D5
Tazin (lake)	L2
The Battlefords Prov. Park	D2
Thickwood (hills)	L4
Thunder (hills)	L4
Tobin (lake)	F6
Torch (riv.)	F2
Touchwood (hills)	G4
Tramping (lake)	C3
Trout (riv.)	F6
Turtle (lake)	C2
Twelvemile (lake)	E6
Vermilion (hills)	E5
Wapawekka (hills)	M4

Waskana (creek)	G5
Waskesiu (lake)	E2
Wathaman (riv.)	M3
Weed (hills)	J5
White Fox (riv.)	G2
White Gull (creek)	G2
Whiteshore (lake)	C3
Whiteswan (lkes)	F1
William (riv.)	F6
Willow Bunch (lake)	F6
Witchekan (lake)	D2
Wollaston (lake)	N2
Wood (mt.)	E6
Wood (riv.)	E6
Wood Mountain Hist. Park	E6

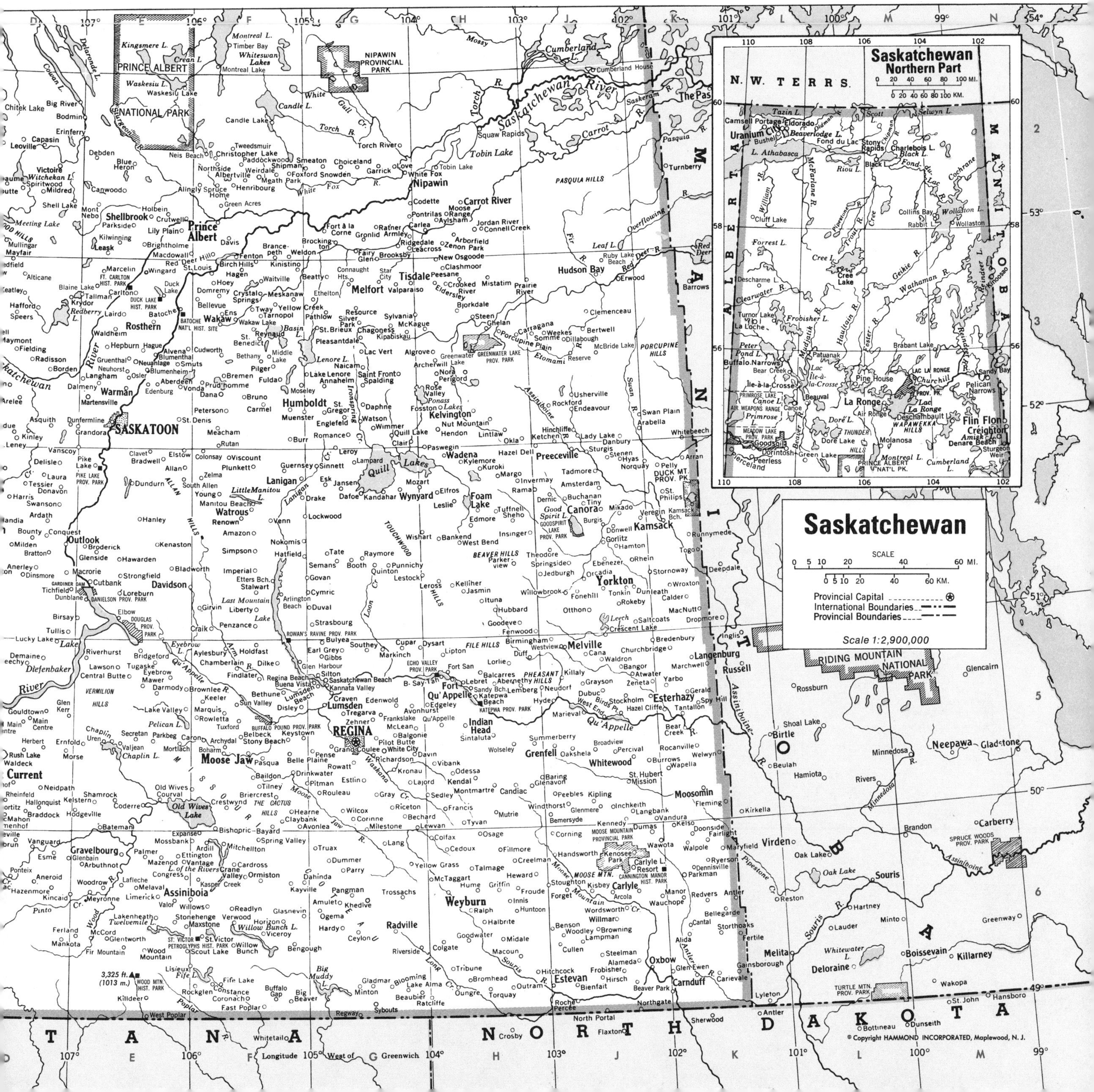

Saskatchewan Northern Part

Saskatchewan

SCALE

Provincial Capital
International Boundaries
Provincial Boundaries

Scale 1:2,900,000

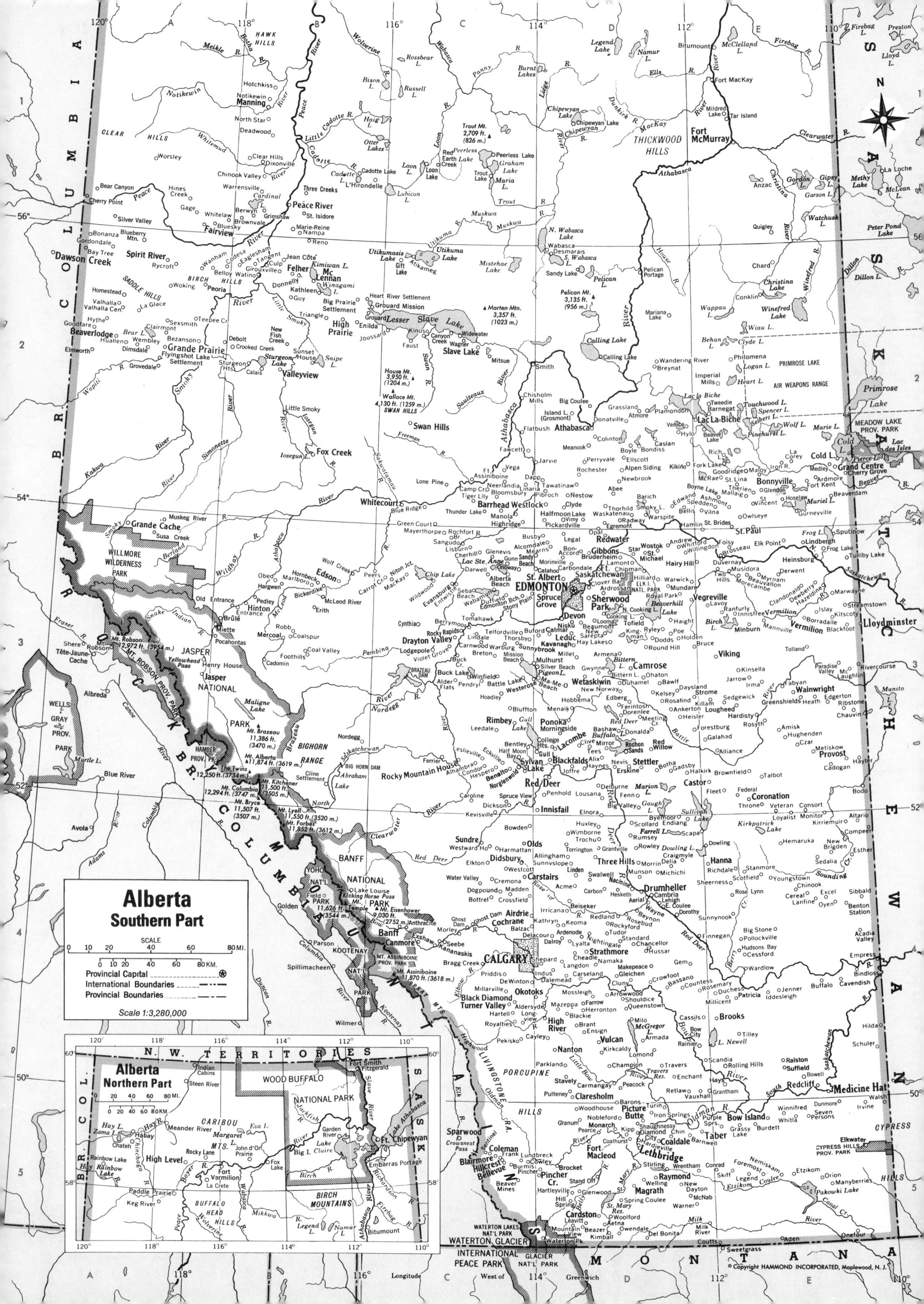

Alberta
Southern Part

SCALE
0 10 20 40 60 80 MI.
0 10 20 40 60 80 KM.
Provincial Capital ⊛
International Boundaries
Provincial Boundaries

Scale 1:3,280,000

Alberta
Northern Part
20 40 60 80 MI.
0 20 40 60 80KM.

© Copyright HAMMOND INCORPORATED, Maplewood, N.J.

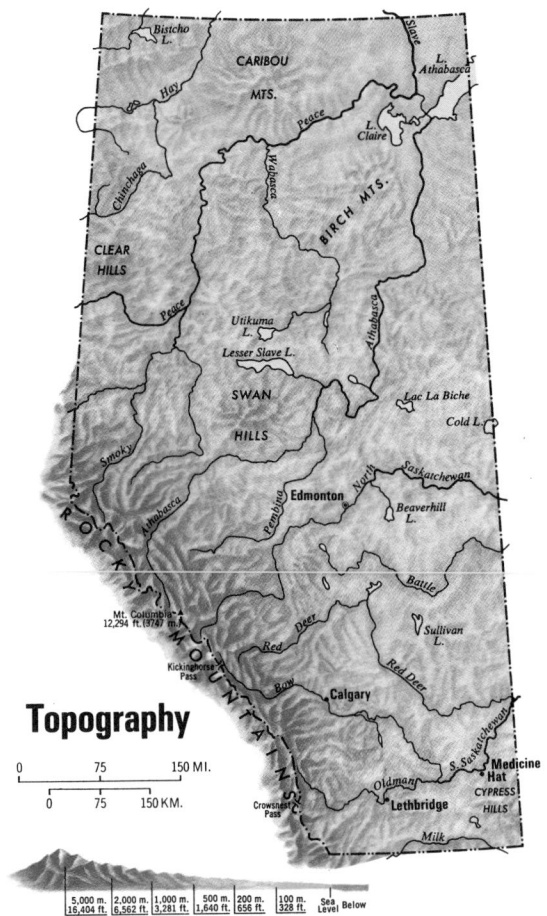

Topography

0	75	150 MI.
0	75	150 KM.

5,000 m. 16,404 ft.   2,000 m. 6,562 ft.   1,000 m. 3,281 ft.   500 m. 1,640 ft.   200 m. 656 ft.   100 m. 328 ft.   Sea Level   Below

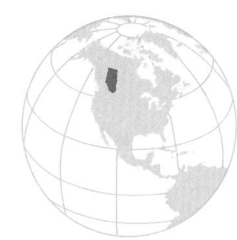

Rycroft 533 ....A2
Ryley 432 ....D3
Saint Albert 24,129 ....D3
Saint Paul 4,337 ....E3
Sangudo 409 ....C3
Sedgewick 825 ....E3
Sexsmith 770 ....A2
Shaughnessy 299 ....D5
Sherwood Park 26,534 ....D3
Slave Lake 3,561 ....C2
Smith 353 ....D2
Smoky Lake 925 ....D2
Spirit River 1,020 ....A2
Spruce Grove 6,907 ....D3
Standard 305 ....D4
Stavely 432 ....D4
Stettler 4,182 ....D3
Stirling 543 ....D5
Stony Plain 2,717 ....C3
Strathmore 1,561 ....D4
Strome 227 ....E3
Sundre 1,099 ....C4
Swan Hills 2,012 ....C2
Sylvan Lake 1,837 ....C3
Taber 5,296 ....E5
Thorhild 533 ....D2
Thorsby 657 ....C3
Three Hills 1,564 ....D4
Tilley 329 ....E4
Tofield 1,120 ....D3
Trochu 752 ....D4
Turner Valley 1,132 ....C4
Two Hills 943 ....E3
Valleyview 1,716 ....B2
Vauxhall 954 ....D4
Vegreville 4,158 ....E3
Vermilion 3,182 ....E3
Veteran 279 ....E3
Viking 1,217 ....E3
Vilna 348 ....E2
Vulcan 1,442 ....D4
Wabamun 581 ....C3
Wabasca 528 ....D2
Wainwright 3,890 ....E3
Wanham 225 ....A2
Warburg 408 ....C3
Warner 434 ....D5
Waskatenau 271 ....D2
Wayne 255 ....D4
Wembley 507 ....A2
Westlock 3,721 ....C2
Wetaskiwin 6,754 ....D3
Whitecourt 3,878 ....C2
Wildwood 360 ....C3
Willingdon 308 ....E3
Youngstown 272 ....E4

OTHER FEATURES

AREA 255,285 sq. mi. (661,185 sq. km.)
POPULATION 2,207,856
CAPITAL Edmonton
LARGEST CITY Edmonton
HIGHEST POINT Mt. Columbia 12,294 ft. (3,747 m.)
SETTLED IN 1861
ADMITTED TO CONFEDERATION 1905
PROVINCIAL FLOWER Wild Rose

Birch (hills) A2
Birch (lake) E3
Birch (mts.) B5
Birch (riv.) B5
Bison (lake) B1
Bittern (lake) D3
Botha (riv.) B1
Bow (riv.) D4
Boyer (riv.) A5
Brazeau (dam) C3
Brazeau (mt.) B3
Brazeau (riv.) B3
Buffalo (lake) D3
Buffalo Head (hills) B5
Burnt (lkes) C1
Cadotte (lake) B1
Cadotte (riv.) B1
Calling (lake) D2
Canal (creek) E5
Cardinal (lake) B1
Caribou (mts.) B5
Chinchaga (riv.) A5
Chip (lake) C3
Chipewyan (lake) D1
Chipewyan (riv.) D1
Christina (lake) E2
Christina (riv.) E1
Claire (lake) B5
Clear (hills) A1
Clearwater (riv.) C4
Clearwater (riv.) E1
Clyde (lake) E1
Cold (lake) E2
Columbia (mt.) B3
Crowsnest (pass) C5
Cypress (hills) E5
Cypress Hills Prov. Park E5
Dillon (riv.) E2
Dowling (lake) D4
Dunkirk (riv.) D1
Eisenhower (mt.) C4
Elbow (riv.) C4
Elk Island Nat'l Park 33 ....D3
Ells (riv.) D1
Etzikom Coulee (riv.) E5
Eva (lake) B5
Farrell (lake) D4
Firebag (riv.) E1
Forbes (mt.) B4
Freeman (riv.) C2
Frog (lake) E3
Garson (lake) E1
Gipsy (lake) E1
Gordon (lake) E1
Gough (lake) D3
Graham (lake) C1
Gull (lake) C3
Haig (lake) B1
Hawk (hills) B1
Hay (lake) A5
Hay (riv.) A5

Heart (lake) E2
Highwood (riv.) C4
House (mt.) C2
House (riv.) D2
Iosegun (lake) B2
Iosegun (riv.) B2
Jackfish (riv.) B5
Jasper Nat'l Park 3,602 ....A3
Kakwa (riv.) A2
Kickinghorse (pass) B4
Kimiwan (lake) B2
Kirkpatrick (lake) E4
Kitchener (mt.) B3
Legend (lake) D1
Lesser Slave (lake) C2
Liége (riv.) D1
Little Bow (riv.) D4
Little Cadotte (riv.) B1
Little Smoky (riv.) B2
Livingstone (range) C4
Logan (lake) E2
Loon (lake) C1
Loon (riv.) C1
Lubicon (lake) C1
Lyell (mt.) B4
MacKay (riv.) D1
Maligne (lake) B3
Margaret (lake) B5
Marie (lake) E2
Marion (lake) D3
Marten (lake) C2
McClelland (lake) E1
McGregor (lake) D4
McLeod (riv.) B3
Meikle (riv.) A1
Mikkwa (riv.) B5
Milk (riv.) D5
Mistehae (lake) B2
Muriel (lake) E2
Muskwa (lake) C1
Muskwa (riv.) C1
Namur (lake) D1
Newell (lake) E4
Nordegg (riv.) C3
North Saskatchewan (riv.) C3
North Wabasca (lake) D1
Notikewin (riv.) B1
Oldman (riv.) D5
Otter (lkes) B1
Pakowki (lake) E5
Panny (riv.) C1
Peace (riv.) B1
Peerless (lake) C1
Pelican (lake) C1
Pelican (mt.) D2
Pelican (mts.) D2
Pembina (riv.) C3
Pigeon (lake) C3
Pinehurst (lake) E2
Porcupine (hills) C4
Primrose (lake) E2

Rainbow (lake) A5
Red Deer (lake) C4
Red Deer (riv.) D4
Richardson (riv.) C5
Rocky (mts.) C4
Rosebud (riv.) D4
Rossbear (lake) C1
Russell (lake) C1
Saddle (hills) A2
Sainte Anne (lake) C3
Saint Mary (res.) D5
Saint Mary (riv.) D5
Sakwatamau (riv.) C2
Saulteaux (riv.) C2
Seibert (lake) E2
Simonette (riv.) A2
Slave (riv.) C5
Smoky (riv.) A2
Snake Indian (riv.) A3
Snipe (lake) B2
Sounding (creek) E4
South Saskatchewan (riv.) E4
South Wabasca (lake) D2
Spencer (lake) E2
Spray (mts.) B4
Sturgeon (lake) B2
Sullivan (lake) D3
Swan (hills) C2
Swan (riv.) C2
Temple (mt.) B4
The Twins (mts.) B3
Thickwood (hills) D1
Touchwood (lake) E2
Travers (res.) D4
Trout (mt.) C1
Trout (riv.) C1
Utikuma (lake) C2
Utikuma (riv.) C2
Utikumasis (lake) C2
Vermilion (riv.) E3
Wabasca (riv.) C1
Wallace (mt.) C3
Wapiti (riv.) A2
Wappau (lake) E2
Watchusk (lake) E1
Waterton-Glacier Int'l Peace Park 194 ....C5
Waterton Lakes Nat'l Park 194 ....C5
Whitemud (riv.) A1
Wiau (lake) E2
Wildhay (riv.) B3
Willmore Wilderness Prov. Park A3
Winagami (lake) B2
Winefred (lake) E2
Winefred (riv.) E2
Wolf (lake) E2
Wolverine (riv.) B1
Wood Buffalo Nat'l Park 199 ....B5
Yellowhead (pass) A3
Zama (lake) A5

CITIES and TOWNS

Acme 351 ....D4
Airdrie 1,408 ....C4
Alberta Beach 432 ....C3
Alix 669 ....D3
Alliance 228 ....E3
Andrew 486 ....D3
Ardmore 238 ....E2
Athabasca 1,759 ....D2
Banff 3,410 ....C4
Barons 283 ....D4
Barrhead 2,944 ....C2
Bashaw 773 ....D3
Bassano 999 ....D4
Beaumont 851 ....D3
Beaverlodge 1,332 ....A2
Beiseker 486 ....D4
Bellevue 1,186 ....C5
Bentley 730 ....C3
Berwyn 433 ....B1
Big Valley 344 ....D3
Black Diamond 1,242 ....C4
Blackfalds 1,024 ....D3
Blackie 223 ....D4
Blairmore 2,321 ....C5
Bon Accord 882 ....D3
Bonnyville 2,885 ....E2
Bowden 661 ....C4
Bow Island 1,296 ....E5
Boyle 576 ....D2
Bragg Creek 384 ....C4
Breton 424 ....C3
Brocket 405 ....D5
Brooks 6,339 ....E4
Bruce 93 ....E3
Bruderheim 484 ....D3
Burdett 214 ....E5
Calgary 469,917 ....C4
Calmar 872 ....D3
Camrose 10,104 ....D3
Canmore 1,927 ....C4
Carbon 435 ....D4
Cardston 3,043 ....D5
Carmangay 263 ....D4
Caroline 385 ....C3
Carstairs 1,059 ....D4
Castor 1,207 ....E3
Cereal 231 ....E4
Champion 300 ....D4
Chateh 400 ....A5
Chauvin 296 ....E3
Chipman 296 ....D3
Clairmont 599 ....A2
Claresholm 3,276 ....D4
Clive 254 ....D3
Clyde 312 ....D2
Coaldale 3,654 ....D5
Coalhurst 473 ....D5
Cochrane 1,493 ....C4
Cold Lake 1,317 ....E2
Coleman 1,543 ....C5
College Heights 332 ....D3
Consort 609 ....E3

Cooking Lake 237 ....D3
Coronation 1,198 ....E3
Coutts 387 ....D5
Cowley 284 ....D5
Cremona 227 ....C4
Crossfield 777 ....C4
Daysland 615 ....D3
Delburne 417 ....D3
Delia 232 ....D4
Devon 2,786 ....D3
Didsbury 2,153 ....C4
Donnelly 278 ....B2
Drayton Valley 4,303 ....C3
Drumheller 6,154 ....D4
Duchess 343 ....E4
Eaglesham 229 ....B2
East Coulée 261 ....D4
Eckville 774 ....C3
Edgerton 324 ....E3
Edmonton (cap.) 461,361 ....D3
Edmonton Beach 243 ....D3
Edson 4,038 ....B3
Elk Point 807 ....E3
Elkton 226 ....C4
Elnora 211 ....D3
Empress 238 ....E4
Entwistle 380 ....C3
Erskine 234 ....D3
Evansburg 671 ....C3
Exshaw 389 ....C4
Fairview 2,248 ....A1
Falher 1,120 ....B2
Faust 298 ....C2
Foremost 534 ....E5
Forestburg 808 ....E3
Fort Assiniboine 185 ....C2
Fort Chipewyan 1,179 ....E1
Fort Macleod 3,067 ....D5
Fort McMurray 15,424 ....E1
Fort Saskatchewan 8,304 ....D3
Fort Vermilion 729 ....B5
Fox Creek 1,625 ....B2
Fox Lake 482 ....B5
Gibbons 1,093 ....D3
Gift Lake 432 ....C2
Girouxville 303 ....B2
Gleichen 339 ....D4
Glendon 370 ....E2
Grand Centre 2,780 ....E2
Grande Cache 4,116 ....A3
Grande Prairie 17,626 ....A2
Granum 413 ....D4
Grimshaw 1,665 ....B1
Grouard Mission 213 ....C2
Gunn 223 ....C3
Hanna 2,627 ....E4
Hardieville 546 ....D5
Hardisty 534 ....E3
Hay Lakes 236 ....D3
High Level 1,562 ....A5
High Prairie 2,813 ....B2
High River 3,598 ....D4
Hillcrest 653 ....C5
Hines Creek 503 ....A1
Hinton 6,731 ....B3
Holden 393 ....D3
Hughenden 236 ....E3

Hythe 460 ....A2
Innisfail 2,897 ....D3
Innisfree 265 ....E3
Irma 428 ....E3
Irricana 264 ....D4
Irvine 221 ....E5
Jasper 3,404 ....B3
John d'Or Prairie 326 ....B5
Joussard 270 ....C2
Killam 887 ....E3
Kinuso 305 ....C2
Kitscoty 391 ....E3
Lac La Biche 1,954 ....E2
Lacombe 3,888 ....D3
La Crete 349 ....B5
Lake Louise 140 ....B4
Lamont 997 ....D3
Leduc 8,576 ....D3
Legal 874 ....D3
Lethbridge 46,752 ....D5
Linden 264 ....D4
Lloydminster 5,818 ....E3
Lougheed 213 ....E3
Magrath 1,315 ....D5
Mallaig 339 ....E2
Manning 1,050 ....B1
Mannville 681 ....E3
Marwayne 376 ....E3
Mayerthorpe 1,018 ....C3
McLennan 1,133 ....B2
Medicine Hat 32,811 ....E4
Midlandvale 449 ....D4
Milk River 814 ....D5
Millet 762 ....D3
Mirror 335 ....D3
Morinville 2,097 ....D3
Morrin 230 ....D4
Mundare 555 ....D3
Myrnam 396 ....E3
Nacmine 330 ....D4
Nampa 268 ....B1
Nanton 1,152 ....D4
New Norway 276 ....D3
New Sarepta 237 ....D3
Nobleford 573 ....D5
Okotoks 1,795 ....C4
Olds 3,658 ....D4
Onoway 444 ....C3
Oyen 962 ....E4
Peace River 4,840 ....B1
Penhold 773 ....D3
Picture Butte 1,164 ....D5
Pincher Creek 3,448 ....D5
Plamondon 228 ....D2
Pollockville 29 ....E4
Ponoka 4,636 ....D3
Provost 1,532 ....E3
Rainbow Lake 434 ....A5
Ralston 465 ....E4
Raymond 2,290 ....D5
Redcliff 3,006 ....E4
Red Deer 32,184 ....D3
Redwater 1,493 ....D3
Rimbey 1,452 ....C3
Rockyford 276 ....D4
Rocky Mountain House 3,432 ....C3
Rosemary 273 ....E4

Agriculture, Industry and Resources

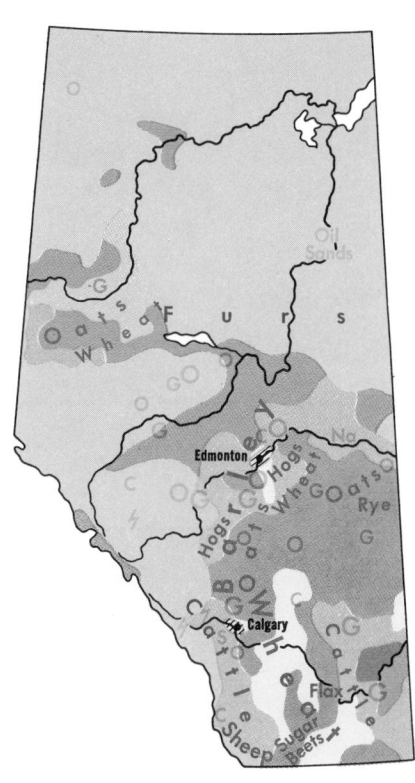

DOMINANT LAND USE

- Wheat
- Cereals (chiefly barley, oats)
- Cereals, Livestock
- Dairy
- Pasture Livestock
- Range Livestock
- Forests
- Nonagricultural Land

MAJOR MINERAL OCCURRENCES

C	Coal	O	Petroleum
G	Natural Gas	S	Sulfur
Na	Salt		

Water Power
Major Industrial Areas

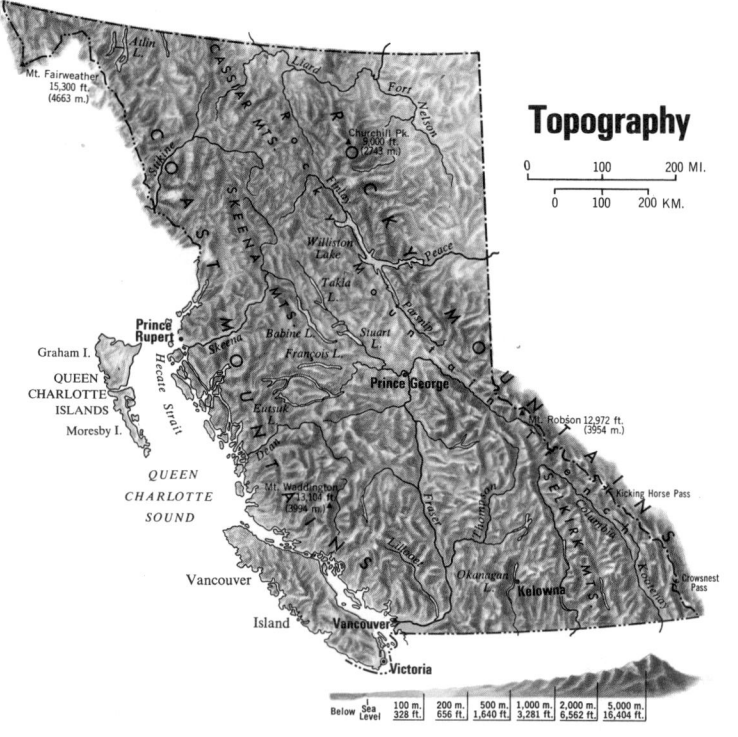

Topography

0   100   200 MI.

0   100   200 KM.

Below Sea Level | 100 m. 328 ft. | 200 m. 656 ft. | 500 m. 1,640 ft. | 1,000 m. 3,281 ft. | 2,000 m. 6,562 ft. | 5,000 m. 16,404 ft.

CITIES and TOWNS

Abbotsford 9,507 ....L3
Alert Bay 605 ....D5
Armstrong 2,260 ....H5
Ashcroft 2,032 ....G5
Barrière 835 ....H4
Bear Lake 431 ....F3
Big Eddy 833 ....H4
Blueberry Creek 660 ....J5
Blue River 425 ....H4
Boston Bar 602 ....G5
Brackendale 1,410 ....F5
Britannia Beach 431 ....K2
Burnaby● 131,599 ....K3
Burns Lake 1,433 ....D3
Cache Creek 1,050 ....G5
Campbell River 11,781 ....E5
Canal Flats 832 ....K5
Cassiar 801 ....K2
Castlegar 6,255 ....J5

Central Saanich● 7,413 ....K3
Chase 1,425 ....H5
Chemainus 2,129 ....J3
Cherry Creek 496 ....G5
Chetwynd 1,487 ....G2
Chilliwack 8,634 ....M3
Clearbrook 4,849 ....L3
Clearwater 766 ....G4
Clinton 808 ....G4
Coldstream 4,995 ....H5
Comox 5,359 ....H2
Coquitlam● 55,464 ....K3
Courtenay 7,733 ....E5
Cranbrook 13,510 ....K5
Creston 3,552 ....J5
Crofton 1,143 ....J3
Cultus Lake 470 ....M3
Cumberland 1,697 ....H3
Dawson Creek 10,528 ....G2
Delta● 64,492 ....K3
Duncan 4,106 ....J3
East Kelowna 607 ....H5
Edgewater 424 ....J5
Elkford 1,873 ....K5

Enderby 1,482 ....H5
Erickson 1,008 ....J5
Errington 466 ....J3
Esquimalt● 15,053 ....K4
Falkland 456 ....H5
Fernie 4,608 ....K5
Fort Fraser 443 ....E3
Fort Langley 2,072 ....L3
Fort Nelson 2,916 ....M2
Fort Saint James 2,110 ......E2
Fort Saint John 8,947 ....G2
Fraser Lake 1,430 ....E3
Fraser Mills● 663 ....J5
Fruitvale 1,481 ....J5
Gabriola 1,169 ....K3
Galiano 480 ....K3
Ganges 444 ....J3
Gibsons 2,074 ....K3
Gillies Bay 560 ....H2
Golden 3,282 ....J4
Gold River 1,942 ....D5
Grand Forks 3,096 ....H5
Granisle 1,210 ....D3
Greenwood 931 ....H5

Haney 2,441 ....L3
Harrison Hot Springs 572 ...M3
Hatzic 1,140 ....L3
Hedley 480 ....G5
Holberg 421 ....C5
Honeymoon Bay 501 ....J3
Hope 2,963 ....M3
Hornby Island 411 ....H2
Houston 1,266 ....D3
Hudson Hope 981 ....F2
Invermere 1,194 ....J5
Kaleden 789 ....H5
Kamloops 58,311 ....G5
Kaslo 756 ....J5
Kelowna 51,955 ....H5
Kent● 2,924 ....M3
Keremeos 702 ....G5
Kimberley 7,111 ....K5
Kitimat 11,791 ....C3
Ladysmith 4,004 ....J3
Lake Cowichan 2,369 ....J3
Langley 10,123 ....L3
Lantzville 813 ....J3
Lillooet 2,218 ....G5
Lion's Bay 785 ....K3
Logan Lake 1,388 ....G5
Lumby 1,081 ....H5
Lytton 468 ....G5
Mackenzie● 5,338 ....F2
Mackenzie 5,266 ....F2
Maple Bay 578 ....K3
Maple Ridge● 29,462 ....L3
Masset 1,563 ....B3
Matsqui 31,178 ....L3
Mayne 480 ....K3
McBride 619 ....G3
Merritt 5,680 ....G5
Metchosin 517 ....K4
Mica Creek 738 ....H4
Midway 589 ....H6
Mill Bay 566 ....K3
Mission● 14,997 ....L3
Mission City 8,278 ....L3
Montrose 1,197 ....J5
Nakusp 1,416 ....J5
Nanaimo 40,336 ....J3
Naramata 741 ....H5
Nelson 9,235 ....J5
New Denver 668 ....J5
New Hazelton 462 ....D2
New Westminster 33,393 ...K3
Nootka D5
North Cowichan● 15,956 ...J3
North Pender Island 709 ...K3
North Saanich● 4,697 .....K3
North Vancouver● 63,471 ...K3
North Vancouver 31,934 ...K3
Oak Bay● 17,658 ....K4
Ocean Falls 985 ....D4
Okanagan Falls 874 ....H5
Okanagan Landing 825 .....H5
Old Barkerville 9 ....G3
Oliver 1,641 ....H5
One Hundred Mile House
  1,584 ....G4
Osoyoos 2,100 ....H5
Oyama 460 ....H5
Parksville 3,187 ....J3
Peachland 2,286 ....H5
Penticton 21,344 ....H5
Pitt Meadows● 4,689 .....L3
Port Alberni 19,585 .....H3

Port Alice 1,497 ....D5
Port Clements 409 ....B3
Port Coquitlam 23,926 .....L3
Port Edward 1,189 ....B3
Port Hammond 1,353 ....L3
Port Hardy● 3,653 ....D5
Port McNeill 1,480 ....D5
Port Moody 11,649 ....L3
Pouce-Coupé 776 ....G2
Powell River● 13,694 .....E5
Prince George 59,929 .....F3
Prince Rupert 14,754 .....B3
Princeton 3,132 ....G5
Qualicum Beach 1,724 .....J3
Queen Charlotte 727 ......A3
Quesnel 7,637 ....F4
Revelstoke 4,615 ....J5
Richmond● 80,034 ....K3
Roberts Creek 711 ....J3
Robson 1,044 ....J5
Rossland 3,716 ....H6
Royston 635 ....H2
Rutland 1,283 ....H5
Saanich● 73,383 ....K3
Salmo 1,089 ....J5
Salmon Arm● 9,391 ......H5
Salmon Arm 1,876 ....H5
Saltair 1,339 ....J3
Sandspit 598 ....B3
Sardis 1,430 ....M3
Saseenos 772 ....J3
Savona 609 ....G5
Sechelt 822 ....J2
Shoreacres 426 ....J5
Sicamous 809 ....H5
Sidney 6,732 ....K3
Slocan Park 446 ......J5
Smithers 3,783 ....D3
Sointula 546 ....D5
Sooke 650 ....J4
South Hazelton 578 ...D2
South Wellington 606 ..J3
Spallumcheen 3,378 ....H5
Sparwood 3,081 ....K5
Sproat Lake 408 ......H3
Squamish 1,611 ....F5
Stewart 1,382 ....C2
Summerland● 6,724 ....G5
Surrey● 116,497 ......K3
Tahsis 1,663 ....D5
Taylor 649 ....G2
Telkwa 691 ....D3
Terrace● 10,251 .....C3
Terrace 7,576 ....C3
Thornhill 3,938 .....C3
Tofino 612 ....E5
Trail 9,976 ....J6
Ucluelet 1,180 ......E6
Union Bay 513 ....H2
Valemount 878 ......H4
Vananda 407 ....E5
Vancouver 410,188 ...K3
Vancouver (Greater)●
  1,085,242 ....K3
Vanderhoof 1,990 ...E3
Vavenby 845 ....H4
Vernon 17,546 ......H5
Victoria (cap.) 62,551 ...K4
Victoria‡ 230,592 ....K4
Warfield 1,957 .....J5
Wasa 403 ....K5
Westbank 1,067 ....H5
West Vancouver● 37,144 ..K3
Westwold 451 ......G5
Whistler 531 ....F5
White Rock 12,497 ...K3
Williams Lake 6,199 ...F4
Wilson Creek 417 ...J2
Windermere 635 ....K5
Winfield 1,033 .....H5
Winlaw 444 ....J5
Woss Lake 408 .....D5
Wynndel 528 ....J5
Yarrow 1,070 ......M3
Youbou 1,064 ......J3

OTHER FEATURES

Adams (lake) H4
Adams (riv.) H4
Alberni (inlet) H3
Alsek (riv.) H1
Aristazabal (isl.) C4
Assiniboine (mt.) K5
Atlin (lake) J1
Azure (lake) G4
Babine (lake) E3
Babine (riv.) D2
Banks (isl.) B3
Barkley (sound) E6
Beale (cape) E6
Bear (lake) D2
Beatton (riv.) G1
Bella Coola (riv.) D4
Bell-Irving (riv.) C3
Bennett, W.A.C. (dam) F2
Birkenhead Lake Prov. Park F5
Bowron Lake Prov. Park ...G3
Bowser (lake) C2
Brooks (pen.) C5
Browning Entrance (str.) .B3
Bryce (mt.) H4
Bugaboo Glacier Prov. Park J5
Bulkley (riv.) D2
Burke (chan.) D4
Burnaby (isl.) B4
Bute (inlet) E5
Caamaño (sound) C4
Calvert (isl.) C4
Canim (lake) G4
Canoe (riv.) H4
Cariboo (mts.) G3
Carpenter (lake) F5
Carp Lake Prov. Park ...F3
Cassiar (mts.) K2
Castle (mt.) A2
Cathedral Prov. Park ...H5

Charlotte (lake) E4
Chatham (sound) B3
Chehalis (lake) L3
Chilcotin (riv.) E4
Chilko (lake) F4
Chilko (riv.) E4
Chilkoot (pass) J1
Chuchi (lake) E2
Churchill (peak) L2
Clayoquot (sound) D5
Clearwater (lake) G4
Clearwater (riv.) G4
Coast (mts.) D3
Columbia (lake) K5
Columbia (mt.) J4
Columbia (riv.) H4
Cook (cape) C5
Cowichan (lake) J3
Crowsnest (pass) K5
Cypress Prov. Park K3
Dean (chan.) D4
Dean (riv.) D4
Dease (lake) K2
Dease (riv.) K2
Devils Thumb (mt.) A1
Dixon Entrance (chan.) A3
Douglas (chan.) C3
Duncan (riv.) J5
Dundas (isl.) B3
Elk (riv.) K5
Elk Lakes Prov. Park K5
Eutsuk (lake) D3
Fairweather (mt.) H1

Finlay (riv.) E1
Fitzhugh (sound) D4
Flathead (riv.) K6
Flores (isl.) D5
Fontas (riv.) J2
Forbes (mt.) J4
Fort Nelson (riv.) J2
François (lake) D3
Fraser (lake) E3
Fraser (riv.) K3
Fraser Reach (chan.) C3
Galiano (isl.) K3
Gardner (canal) C3
Garibaldi Prov. Park F5
Georgia (str.) J3
Germansen (lake) E2
Gil (isl.) C3
Golden Ears Prov. Park L3
Gordon (riv.) H3
Graham (isl.) B3
Graham Reach (chan.) C3
Grenville (chan.) C3
Halfway (riv.) F2
Hamber Prov. Park H4
Harrison (lake) M2
Hawkesbury (isl.) C3
Hazelton (mts.) C2
Hecate (str.) B3
Hobson (lake) H4
Homathko (riv.) E4
Horsefly (lake) G4
Howe (sound) K2

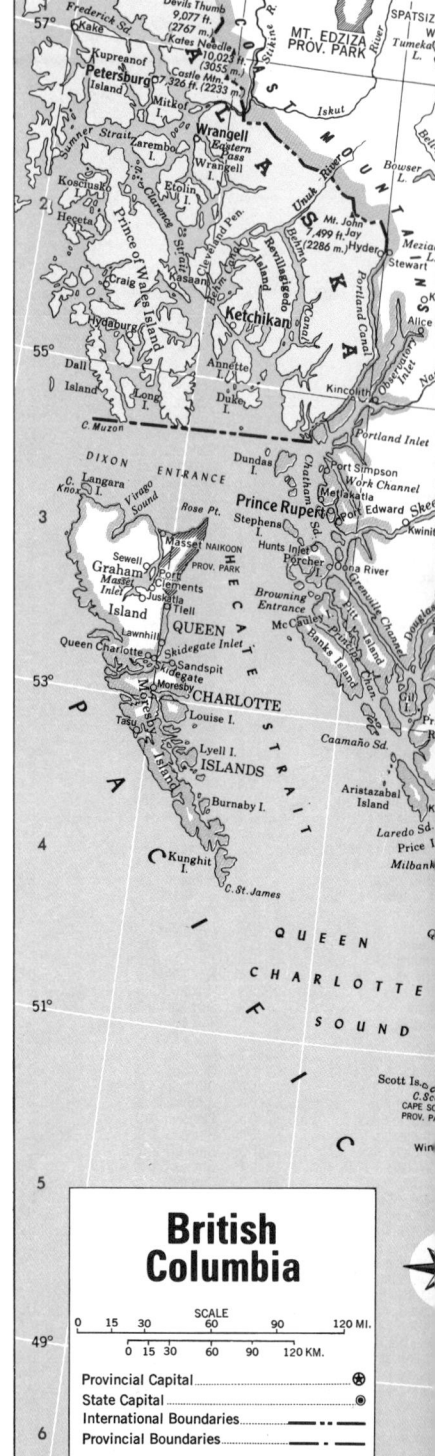

Agriculture, Industry and Resources

DOMINANT LAND USE

Cereals, Livestock
Dairy
Fruits, Vegetables
Pasture Livestock
Forests
Nonagricultural Land

MAJOR MINERAL OCCURRENCES

Ab Asbestos
Ag Silver
Au Gold
C   Coal
Cu Copper
Fe Iron Ore
G   Natural Gas
Gp Gypsum
Mo Molybdenum
Ni Nickel
O   Petroleum
Pb Lead
S   Sulfur
Sn Tin
Zn Zinc

⚡ Water Power
▨ Major Industrial Areas

British Columbia

SCALE

0   15   30   60   90   120 MI.

0   15   30   60   90   120 KM.

Provincial Capital ....⊛
State Capital ....◉
International Boundaries ....▬ ▬
Provincial Boundaries ....▬ ▬

Scale 1:5,200,000

AREA 366,253 sq. mi. (948,596 sq. km.)
POPULATION 2,716,301
CAPITAL Victoria
LARGEST CITY Vancouver
HIGHEST POINT Mt. Fairweather 15,300 ft.
(4,663 m.)
SETTLED IN 1806
ADMITTED TO CONFEDERATION 1871
PROVINCIAL FLOWER Dogwood

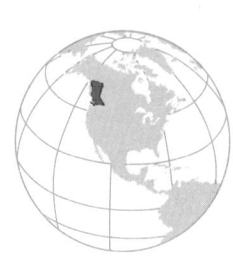

Topography

0   200   400 MI.

0   200   400 KM.

| 5,000 m. | 2,000 m. | 1,000 m. | 500 m. | 200 m. | 100 m. | Sea | Below |
| 16,404 ft. | 6,562 ft. | 3,281 ft. | 1,640 ft. | 656 ft. | 328 ft. | Level | |

Agriculture, Industry and Resources

DOMINANT LAND USE

Forests

Nonagricultural Land

MAJOR MINERAL OCCURRENCES

Ab	Asbestos	G	Natural Gas
Ag	Silver	O	Petroleum
Au	Gold	Pb	Lead
C	Coal	W	Tungsten
Cu	Copper	Zn	Zinc
Fe	Iron Ore		

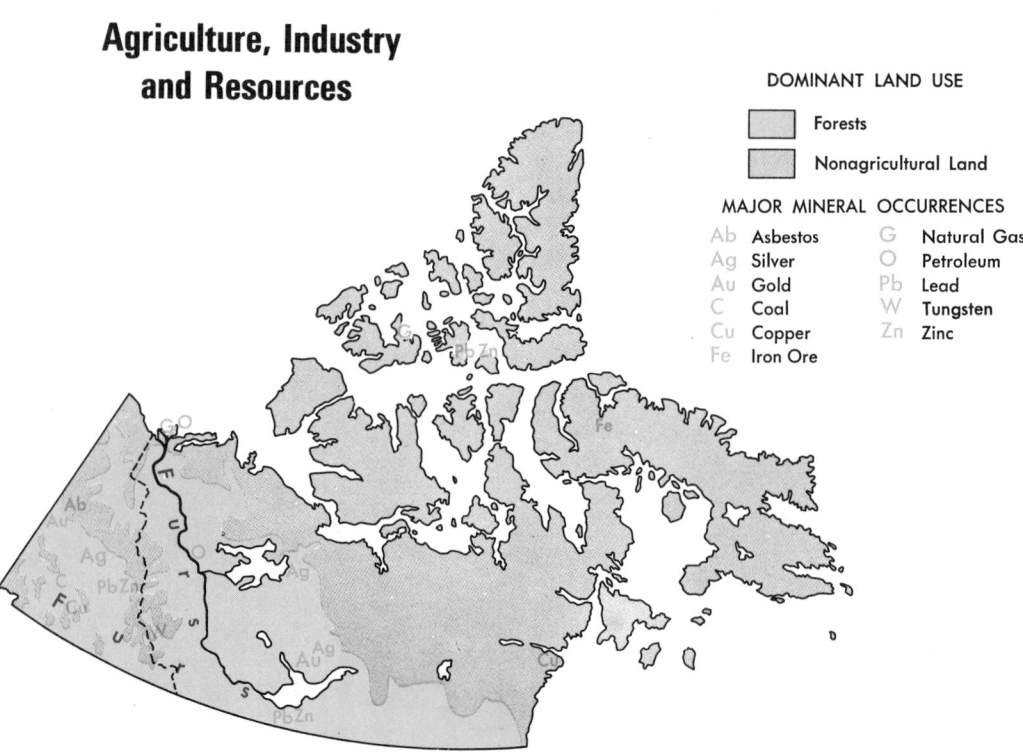

YUKON TERRITORY
AREA 207,075 sq. mi.
(536,324 sq. km.)
POPULATION 22,684
CAPITAL Whitehorse
LARGEST CITY Whitehorse
HIGHEST POINT Mt. Logan 19,524 ft.
(5,951 m.)
SETTLED IN 1897
ADMITTED TO CONFEDERATION 1898
PROVINCIAL FLOWER Fireweed

NORTHWEST TERRITORIES
AREA 1,304,896 sq. mi. (3,379,683 sq. km.)
POPULATION 44,684
CAPITAL Yellowknife
LARGEST CITY Yellowknife
HIGHEST POINT Mt. Sir James MacBrien
9,062 ft. (2,762 m.)
SETTLED IN 1800
ADMITTED TO CONFEDERATION 1870
PROVINCIAL FLOWER Mountain Avens

Yukon and Northwest Territories

SCALE
0   50 100   200   300 MI.
0 50 100   200   300 KM.

Territorial Capitals .... ⊛
International Boundaries .... ▬ ▪ ▬
Provincial & Territorial Boundaries ...... ▬ ▪▪ ▬
District Boundaries .... ▬ ▪▪ ▬

Scale 1:14,000,000

All islands in Hudson and James Bays lie within the District of Keewatin.

© Copyright HAMMOND INCORPORATED, Maplewood, N.J.

United States

POLYCONIC PROJECTION

SCALE OF MILES

SCALE OF KILOMETERS

Capitals of Countries .... ☆
State Capitals .... △
International Boundaries .... ———

Scale 1:17,400,000

© Copyright HAMMOND INCORPORATED, Maplewood, N.J.

AREA 3,623,420 sq. mi.
(9,384,658 sq. km.)
POPULATION 226,504,825
CAPITAL Washington
LARGEST CITY New York
HIGHEST POINT Mt. McKinley 20,320 ft.
(6,194 m.)
MONETARY UNIT U.S. dollar
MAJOR LANGUAGE English
MAJOR RELIGIONS Protestantism,
Roman Catholicism, Judaism

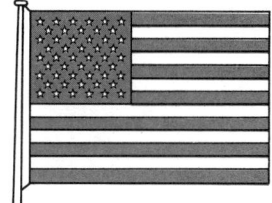

Population Distribution

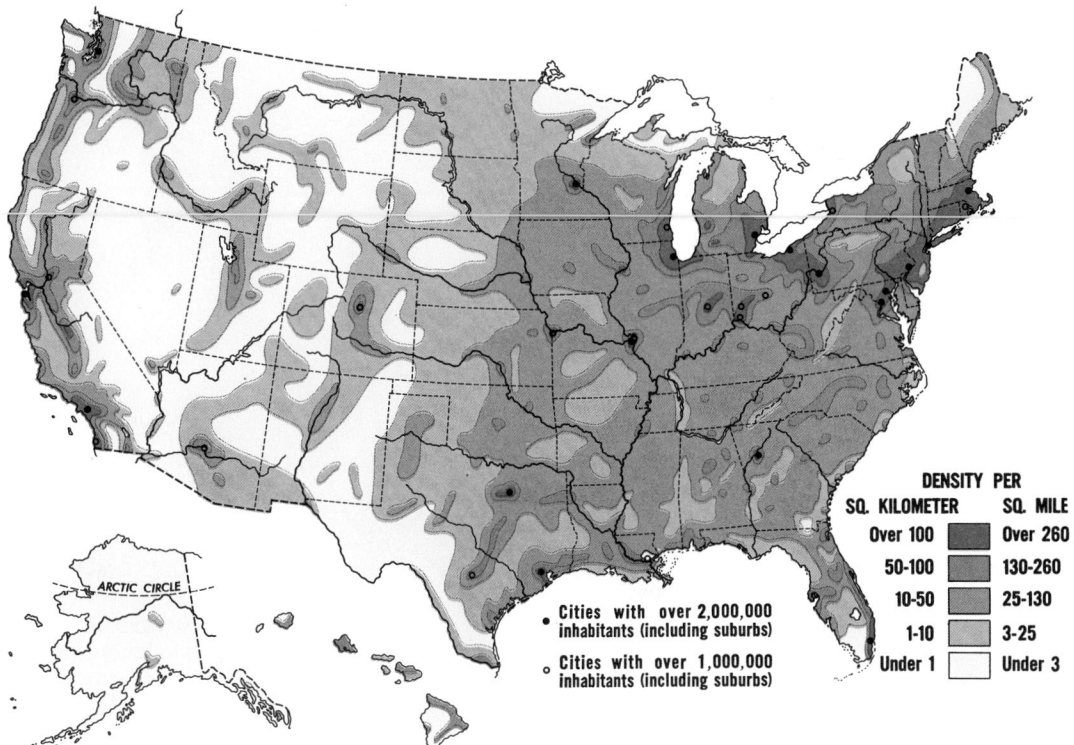

DENSITY PER	
SQ. KILOMETER	SQ. MILE
Over 100	Over 260
50-100	130-260
10-50	25-130
1-10	3-25
Under 1	Under 3

• Cities with over 2,000,000 inhabitants (including suburbs)
○ Cities with over 1,000,000 inhabitants (including suburbs)

ARCTIC CIRCLE

Vegetation

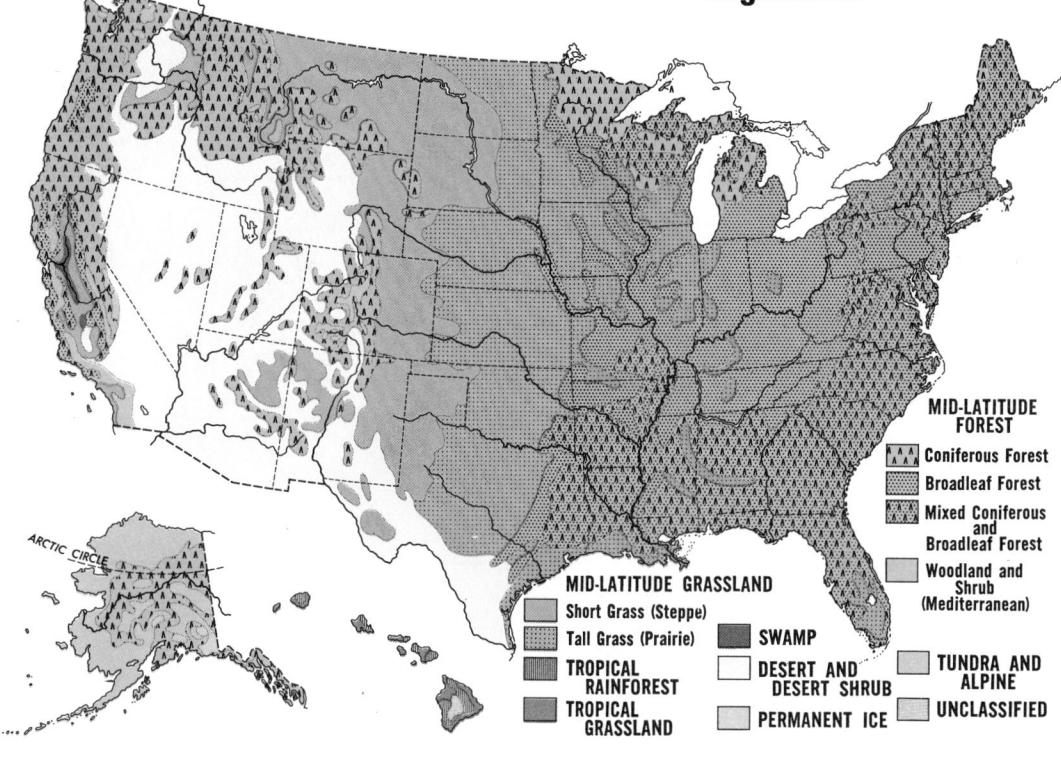

ARCTIC CIRCLE

MID-LATITUDE FOREST
🌲 Coniferous Forest
Broadleaf Forest
Mixed Coniferous and Broadleaf Forest
Woodland and Shrub (Mediterranean)

MID-LATITUDE GRASSLAND
Short Grass (Steppe)
Tall Grass (Prairie)

SWAMP
DESERT AND DESERT SHRUB
PERMANENT ICE

TROPICAL RAINFOREST
TROPICAL GRASSLAND

TUNDRA AND ALPINE
UNCLASSIFIED

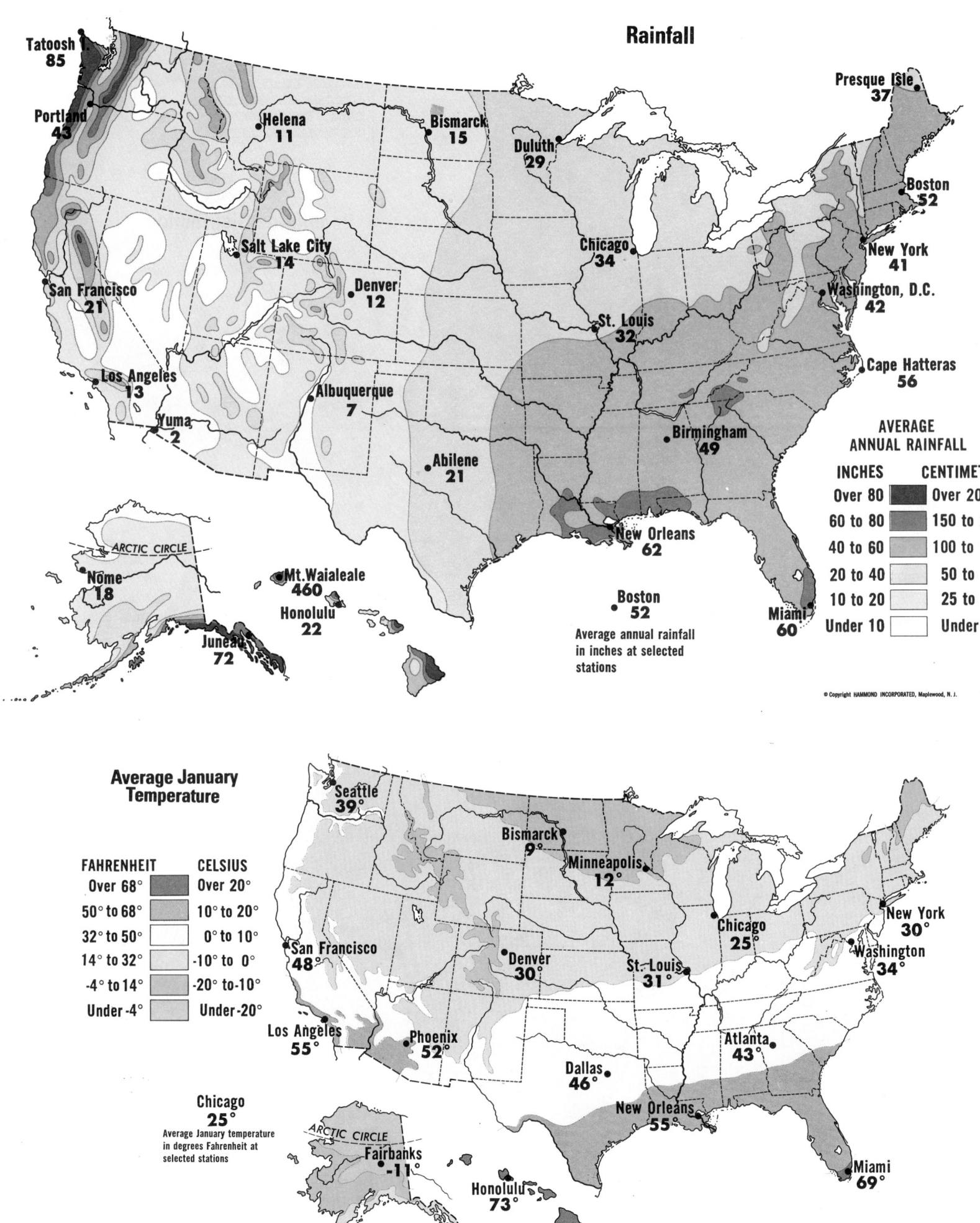

Rainfall

Tatoosh I.
85

Portland
43

Helena
11

Bismarck
15

Duluth
29

Presque Isle
37

Boston
52

Salt Lake City
14

Denver
12

Chicago
34

New York
41

San Francisco
21

St. Louis
32

Washington, D.C.
42

Los Angeles
13

Albuquerque
7

Cape Hatteras
56

Yuma
2

Abilene
21

Birmingham
49

ARCTIC CIRCLE

Nome
18

Mt. Waialeale
460

New Orleans
62

Boston
52

Average annual rainfall
in inches at selected
stations

Miami
60

Honolulu
22

Juneau
72

AVERAGE
ANNUAL RAINFALL

INCHES		CENTIMET
Over 80		Over 200
60 to 80		150 to 2
40 to 60		100 to 1
20 to 40		50 to 1
10 to 20		25 to 5
Under 10		Under 2

© Copyright HAMMOND INCORPORATED, Maplewood, N. J.

Average January Temperature

Seattle
39°

Bismarck
9°

Minneapolis
12°

New York
30°

FAHRENHEIT		CELSIUS
Over 68°		Over 20°
50° to 68°		10° to 20°
32° to 50°		0° to 10°
14° to 32°		-10° to 0°
-4° to 14°		-20° to -10°
Under -4°		Under -20°

San Francisco
48°

Denver
30°

St. Louis
31°

Chicago
25°

Washington
34°

Los Angeles
55°

Phoenix
52°

Dallas
46°

Atlanta
43°

Chicago
25°

Average January temperature
in degrees Fahrenheit at
selected stations

ARCTIC CIRCLE

New Orleans
55°

Fairbanks
-11°

Honolulu
73°

Miami
69°

© Copyright HAMMOND INCORPORATED, Maplewood, N. J.

Topography

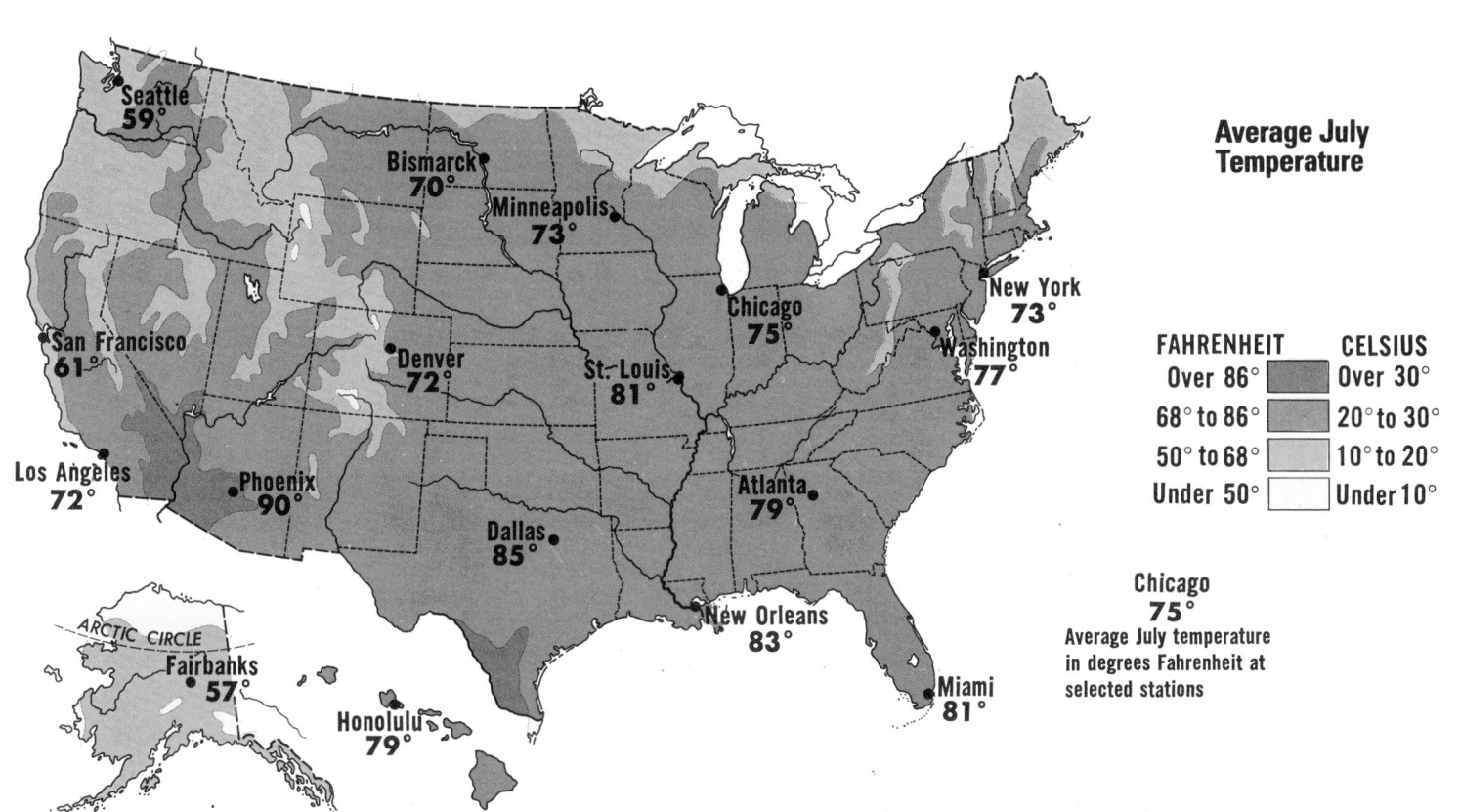

Average July Temperature

FAHRENHEIT — **CELSIUS**
- Over 86° — Over 30°
- 68° to 86° — 20° to 30°
- 50° to 68° — 10° to 20°
- Under 50° — Under 10°

Chicago 75°
Average July temperature in degrees Fahrenheit at selected stations

United States Standard Time Zones

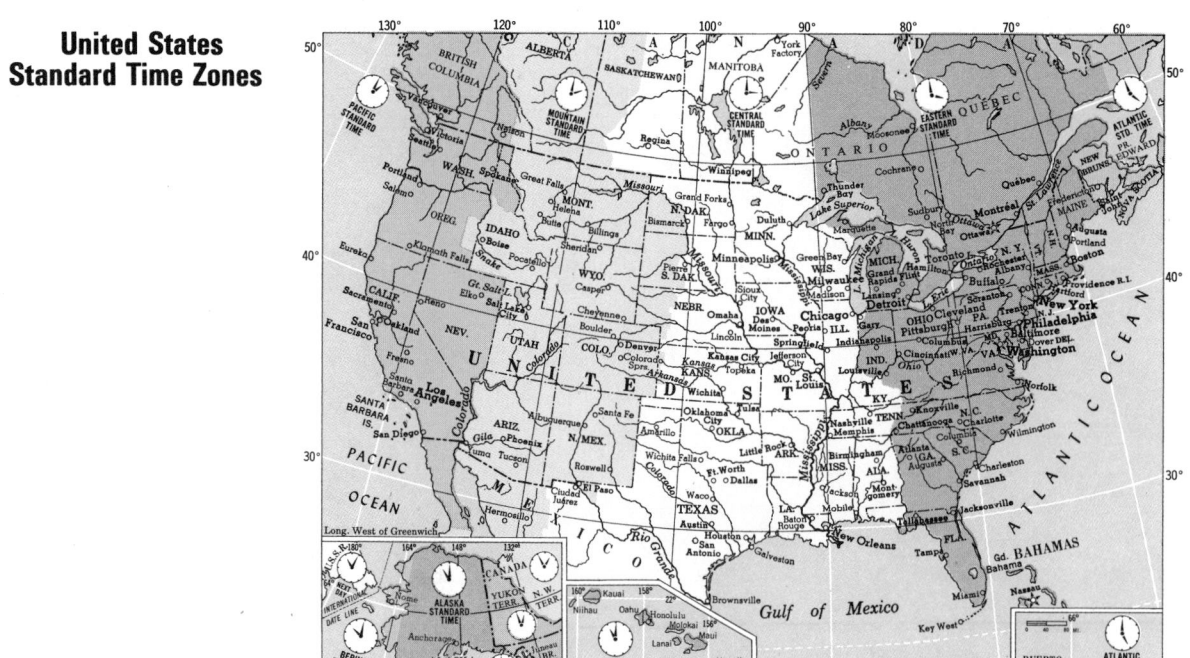

Agriculture, Industry and Resources

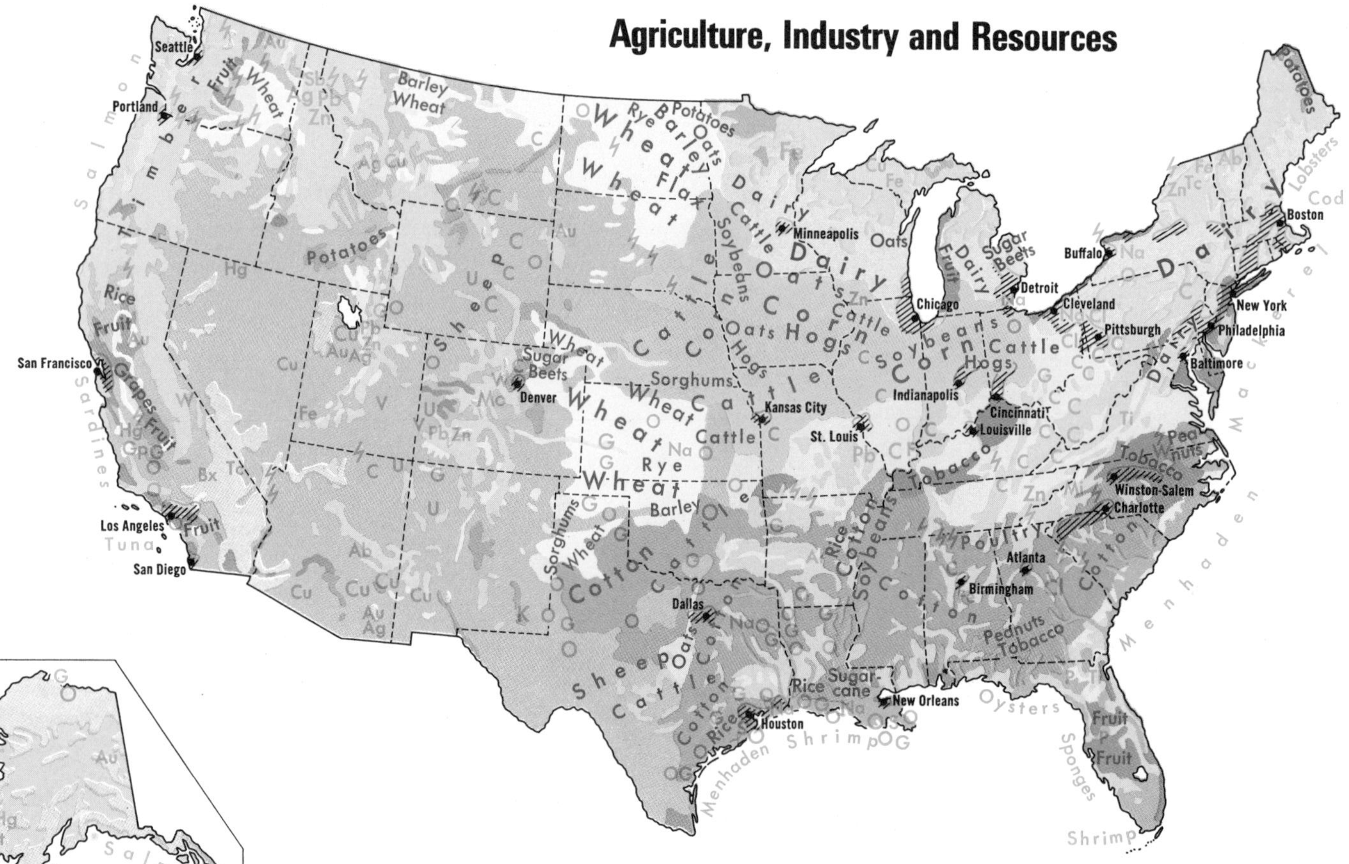

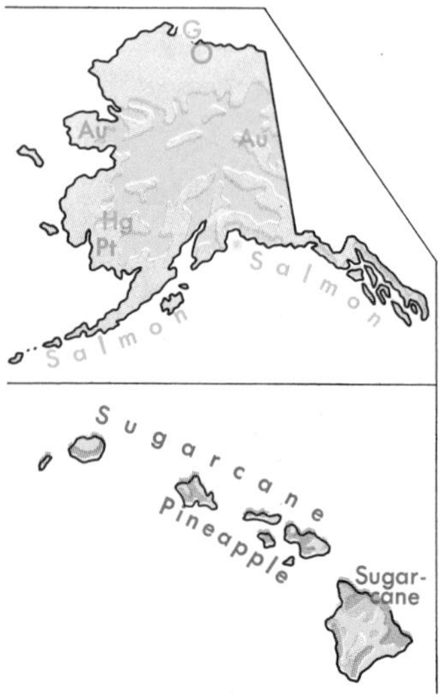

DOMINANT LAND USE

- Wheat and Small Grains
- Feed Grains and Livestock
- Dairy
- General Farming
- Cotton
- Fruit, Truck and Mixed Farming
- Tobacco and General Farming
- Special Crops and General Farming
- Range Livestock
- Forests
- Swampland
- Nonagricultural Land

MAJOR MINERAL OCCURRENCES

Ab	Asbestos	Gp	Gypsum	Sb	Antimony
Ag	Silver	Hg	Mercury	Tc	Talc
Al	Bauxite	K	Potash	Ti	Titanium
Au	Gold	Mi	Mica	U	Uranium
Bx	Borax	Mo	Molybdenum	V	Vanadium
C	Coal	Na	Salt	W	Tungsten
Cl	Clay	O	Petroleum	Zn	Zinc
Cu	Copper	P	Phosphates		
F	Fluorspar	Pb	Lead	⚡	Water Power
Fe	Iron Ore	Pt	Platinum	▨	Major Industrial Areas
G	Natural Gas	S	Sulfur		

Established by the Uniform Time Act

AREA 51,705 sq. mi. (133,916 sq. km.)
POPULATION 3,893,888
CAPITAL Montgomery
LARGEST CITY Birmingham
HIGHEST POINT Cheaha Mtn. 2,407 ft. (734 m.)
SETTLED IN 1702
ADMITTED TO UNION December 14, 1819
POPULAR NAME Heart of Dixie; Cotton State; Yellowhammer State
STATE FLOWER Camellia
STATE BIRD Yellowhammer

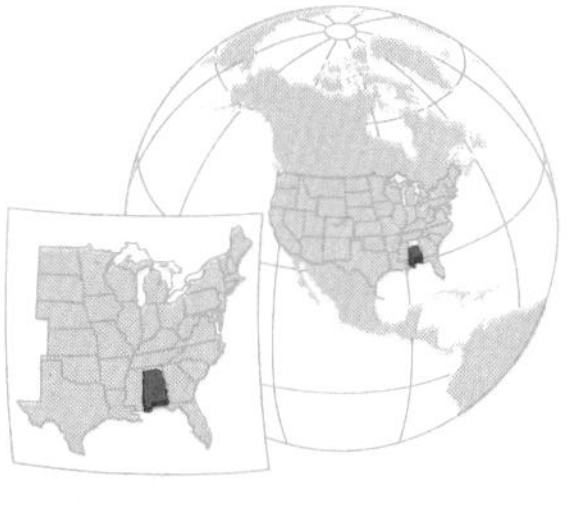

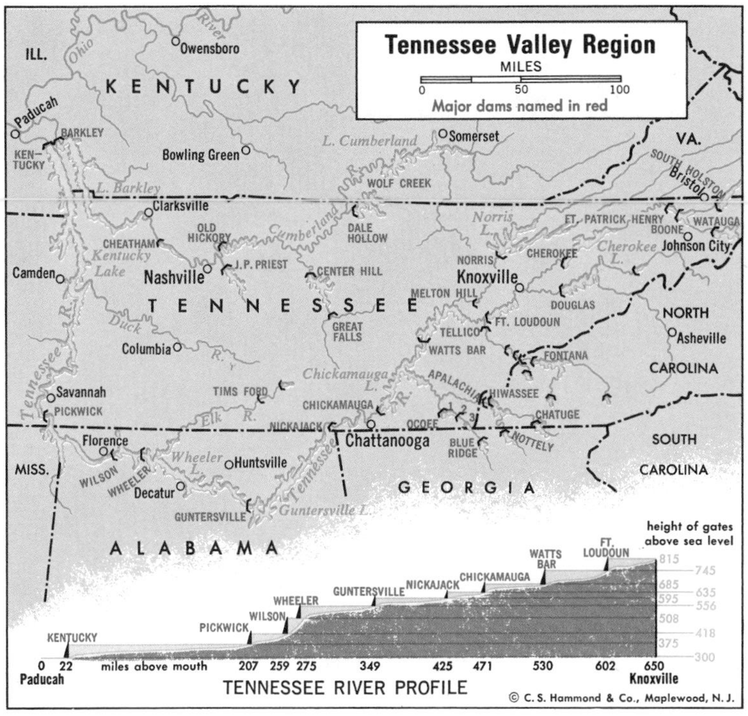

COUNTIES

Autauga 32,259 E5
Baldwin 78,556 C9
Barbour 24,756 H7
Bibb 15,723 D5
Blount 36,459 E2
Bullock 10,596 G6
Butler 21,680 E7
Calhoun 119,761 G3
Chambers 39,191 H5
Cherokee 18,760 G2
Chilton 30,612 E5
Choctaw 16,839 B6
Clarke 27,702 C7
Clay 13,703 G4
Cleburne 12,595 G3
Coffee 38,533 G8
Colbert 54,519 C1
Conecuh 15,884 E8
Coosa 11,377 F5
Covington 36,850 F8
Crenshaw 14,110 F7
Cullman 61,642 E2
Dale 47,821 G8
Dallas 53,981 D6
De Kalb 53,658 G2
Elmore 43,390 F5
Escambia 38,440 D8
Etowah 103,057 F2
Fayette 18,809 C3
Franklin 28,350 C2
Geneva 24,253 G8
Greene 11,021 C5
Hale 15,604 C5
Henry 15,302 H7
Houston 74,632 H8
Jackson 51,407 F1
Jefferson 671,324 E3
Lamar 16,453 B3
Lauderdale 80,546 C1
Lawrence 30,170 D1
Lee 76,283 H5
Limestone 46,005 E1
Lowndes 13,253 E6
Macon 26,829 G6
Madison 196,966 E1
Marengo 25,047 C6
Marion 30,041 C2
Marshall 65,622 F2
Mobile 364,980 B9
Monroe 22,651 D7
Montgomery 197,038 F6
Morgan 90,231 E2
Perry 15,012 D5
Pickens 21,481 B4
Pike 28,050 G7
Randolph 20,075 H4
Russell 47,356 H6
Saint Clair 41,205 F3
Shelby 66,298 E4
Sumter 16,908 B5
Talladega 73,826 F4
Tallapoosa 38,676 G5
Tuscaloosa 137,541 C4
Walker 68,660 D3
Washington 16,821 B8
Wilcox 14,755 D7
Winston 21,953 D2

CITIES and TOWNS

Zip Name/Pop. Key

36310 Abbeville⊙ 3,155 H7
35440 Abernant 405 D4
35005 Adamsville 2,498 D3
35540 Addison 746 D2
35006 Adger 400 D4
35441 Akron 604 C5
35007 Alabaster 7,079 E4
35950 Albertville 12,039 F2
†35115 Aldrich 500 E4
35010 Alexander City 13,807 G5
36250 Alexandria 600 G3
35442 Aliceville 3,207 B4
35013 Allgood 387 F3
36501 Alma 500 C8
35952 Altoona 928 F2
36420 Andalusia⊙ 10,415 E8
35610 Anderson 405 D1
36201 Anniston⊙ 29,523 G3
Anniston‡ 116,936 G3
35016 Arab 5,967 E2
35805 Ardmore 1,096 E1
†35173 Argo 600 E3
36311 Ariton 844 G7
35033 Arkadelphia 150 E3
35541 Arley 276 D2
†35035 Ashby 500 E4
36312 Ashford 2,165 H8
36251 Ashland⊙ 2,052 G4
35953 Ashville⊙ 1,489 F3
35611 Athens⊙ 14,558 E1
36503 Atmore 8,789 C8
35954 Attalla 7,737 F2
36830 Auburn 28,471 H5
36003 Autaugaville 843 E6
†36312 Avon 433 H8
36505 Axis 500 B9
†36420 Babbie 553 F8
35019 Baileyton 396 E2
36005 Banks 160 G7
†36532 Barnwell 700 C10
36507 Bay Minette⊙ 7,455 C9
36509 Bayou La Batre 2,005 B10
35543 Bear Creek 353 C2
36425 Beatrice 558 D7
35544 Beaverton 360 B3
†35653 Belgreen 500 C2
35545 Belk 308 C3
36901 Bellamy 700 B6
35615 Belle Mina 675 E1
36313 Bellwood 400 G8
36785 Benton 74 E6
35546 Berry 916 C3
35020 Bessemer 31,729 D4
†36872 Beulah 500 H5
36006 Billingsley 106 E5
*35201 Birmingham⊙ 284,413 D3
Birmingham‡ 847,360 D3
36314 Black 156 G8
35031 Blountsville 1,509 E2
36201 Blue Mountain 284 G3
†36017 Blue Springs 112 G7
35957 Boaz 7,151 F2
35443 Boligee 164 C5
35032 Bon Air 118 F4
36511 Bon Secour 850 C10
†35120 Branchville 365 F3
36009 Brantley 1,151 F7
35034 Brent 2,862 D5
36426 Brewton⊙ 6,680 D8
35740 Bridgeport 2,974 G1
35020 Brighton 5,308 D4
35548 Brilliant 871 C2
35036 Brookside 1,409 E3
35444 Brookwood 492 D4
36010 Brundidge 3,213 G7
36725 Burkville 250 E6
36431 Burnt Corn 60 D7
36904 Butler⊙ 1,882 B6
†36767 Cahaba 75 D6
35040 Calera 2,035 E4
†36047 Calhoun 950 F6
36513 Calvert 600 B8
36726 Camden⊙ 2,406 D7
36850 Camp Hill 1,628 G5
†36502 Canoe 560 D8
†36726 Canton Bend 300 D6
35549 Carbon Hill 2,452 D3
35041 Cardiff 140 E3
†36420 Carolina 203 E8
35447 Carrollton⊙ 1,104 B4
†36023 Carrville 820 G5
†36548 Carson 400 C8
36432 Castleberry 847 D8
35959 Cedar Bluff 1,129 G2
35960 Centre⊙ 2,351 G2
35042 Centreville⊙ 2,504 D5
36518 Chatom⊙ 1,122 B8
35043 Chelsea 600 E4
35616 Cherokee 1,589 C1
36611 Chickasaw 7,402 B9
35044 Childersburg 5,084 F4
36254 Choccolocco 500 G3
36905 Choctaw 600 B6
†36550 Chrysler 400 C8
36521 Chunchula 700 B9
36522 Citronelle 2,841 B8
35045 Clanton⊙ 5,832 E5
†36322 Clayhatchee 560 G8
36015 Clayton⊙ 1,589 G7
35049 Cleveland 487 E3
36017 Clio 1,224 G7
35449 Coaling 400 D4
36523 Coden 600 B10
36318 Coffee Springs 339 G8
36524 Coffeeville 448 B7
35452 Coker 800 C4
35961 Collinsville 1,383 G2
36319 Columbia 881 H8
35051 Columbiana⊙ 2,655 E4
36020 Coosada 980 F5
35550 Cordova 3,123 D3
35453 Cottondale 500 D4
36320 Cottonwood 1,352 H8
†35172 County Line 199 E3
†36467 County Line 124 F8
35618 Courtland 456 D1
36321 Cowarts 418 H8
36435 Coy 950 D7
36525 Creola 1,652 B9
36906 Cromwell 650 B6
35962 Crossville 1,222 G2
36907 Cuba 486 B6
35055 Cullman⊙ 13,084 E2
36852 Cusseta 650 H5
36853 Dadeville⊙ 3,263 G5
36322 Daleville 4,250 G8
36526 Daphne 3,406 C9
36528 Dauphin Island 950 B10
36256 Daviston 334 G4
36731 Dayton 113 C6
*35601 Decatur⊙ 42,002 D1
36257 De Armanville 350 G3
36732 Demopolis 7,678 C6
35552 Detroit 326 B2
35062 Dora 2,327 D3
*36303 Dothan⊙ 48,750 H8
35553 Double Springs⊙ 1,057 D2
35964 Douglas 116 F2
36028 Dozier 494 F7
35744 Dutton 276 G1
36426 East Brewton 3,012 E8
36024 Eclectic 1,124 F5
36261 Edwardsville 207 H3
36323 Elba⊙ 4,355 F8
36530 Elberta 491 C10
35554 Eldridge 230 C3
35620 Elkmont 429 E1
36025 Elmore 600 F5
35458 Elrod 746 C4
35063 Empire 600 D3
36330 Enterprise 18,033 G8
35460 Epes 399 B5
35461 Ethelsville 95 B4
36027 Eufaula 12,097 H7
†36340 Eunola 169 G8
35462 Eutaw⊙ 2,444 C5
35621 Eva 185 E2
36401 Evergreen⊙ 4,171 E8
36439 Excel 385 D8
35746 Fackler 250 G1
36854 Fairfax 3,776 H5
35064 Fairfield 13,242 E4
36532 Fairhope 7,286 C10
35208 Fairview 450 E2
35622 Falkville 1,310 E2
36738 Faunsdale 174 C6
35555 Fayette⊙ 5,287 C3
36855 Five Points 197 H4
35966 Flat Rock 750 G1
†35601 Flint City 673 D1
36441 Flomaton 1,882 D8
36442 Florala 2,165 F8
*35630 Florence⊙ 37,029 C1
Florence‡ 135,023 C1
36535 Foley 4,003 C10
35214 Forestdale 10,814 E3
36740 Forkland 429 C5
36031 Fort Davis 500 G6
36032 Fort Deposit 1,519 E7
36856 Fort Mitchell 900 H6
35967 Fort Payne⊙ 11,485 G2
35463 Fosters 400 C4
36444 Franklin 133 G6
36445 Frisco City 1,424 D8
36539 Fruitdale 500 B8
36262 Fruithurst 239 G3
36446 Fulton 606 C7
35068 Fultondale 6,217 E3
35971 Fyffe 1,305 G2
*35901 Gadsden⊙ 47,565 G2
Gadsden‡ 103,057 G2
35464 Gainesville 207 B5
35972 Gallant 475 F2
36038 Gantt 314 E8
35070 Garden City 655 E2
35071 Gardendale 7,928 E3
35973 Gaylesville 192 G2
†35459 Geiger 200 B5
36340 Geneva⊙ 4,866 G8
36033 Georgiana 1,993 E7
35974 Geraldine 911 G2
36908 Gilbertown 218 B7
35559 Glen Allen 312 C3
35905 Glencoe 4,648 G3
36034 Glenwood 341 F7
†35010 Goldville 89 G4
†36024 Good Hope 1,442 F2
35072 Goodwater 1,895 F4
35466 Gordo 2,112 C4
36343 Gordon 362 H8
†35580 Gorgas 500 D3
36035 Goshen 365 F7
†36482 Gosport 500 C7
36541 Grand Bay 3,185 B10
35747 Grant 632 F1
35073 Graysville 2,642 D3
35074 Green Pond 750 D4
36744 Greensboro⊙ 3,248 C5
36037 Greenville⊙ 7,807 E7
†36350 Grimes 298 H8
36451 Grove Hill⊙ 1,912 C7
35563 Guin 2,418 C3
36542 Gulf Shores 1,349 C10
35976 Guntersville⊙ 7,041 F2
35748 Gurley 735 F1
†35563 Gu-Win 266 C3
35564 Hackleburg 883 C2
†36319 Haleburg 106 H8
35565 Haleyville 5,306 C2
35570 Hamilton⊙ 5,093 C2
†35989 Hammondville 369 G1
35077 Hanceville 2,220 E2
36039 Hardaway 600 G6
35078 Harpersville 934 F4
36344 Hartford 2,647 G8
35640 Hartselle 8,858 E2
36858 Hatchechubbee 840 H6
†35672 Hatton 950 D1
35079 Hayden 268 E3
36040 Hayneville⊙ 592 E6
35750 Hazel Green 1,503 E1
36345 Headland 3,327 H8
†36558 Healing Springs 100 B7
†36420 Heath 354 F8
36264 Heflin⊙ 3,014 G3
35080 Helena 2,130 E4
35978 Henagar 1,188 G1
35979 Higdon 925 G1
†35013 Highland Lake 210 F3
35643 Hillsboro 278 D1
†36201 Hobson City 1,268 G3
35571 Hodges 250 C2
35903 Hokes Bluff 3,216 G3
35082 Hollins 500 F4
35083 Holly Pond 493 E2
35752 Hollywood 1,110 G1
35209 Homewood 21,412 E4
†35216 Hoover 19,792 E4
36043 Hope Hull 975 F6
†36467 Horn Hill 186 F8
35020 Hueytown 13,478 D4
*35801 Huntsville⊙ 142,513 E1
Huntsville‡ 308,593 E1
36860 Hurtsboro 752 H6
35981 Ider 698 G1
35210 Irondale 6,510 E3
36545 Jackson 6,073 C8
36861 Jacksons Gap 800 G5
36265 Jacksonville 9,735 G3
35501 Jasper⊙ 11,894 D3
35085 Jemison 1,828 E5
35573 Kansas 267 C3
35574 Kennedy 604 B3
35645 Killen 747 D1
35091 Kimberly 1,043 E3
†36301 Kinsey 1,239 H8
36453 Kinston 604 F8
36862 Lafayette⊙ 3,647 H5
†35986 Lakeview 441 G2
36863 Lanett 6,897 H5
36864 Langdale 2,034 H5
†35768 Larkinsville 425 F1
36911 Lavaca 500 B6
35094 Leeds 8,638 E3
35983 Leesburg 116 G2
35646 Leighton 1,218 D1
36548 Leroy 699 B8
35647 Lester 117 D1
†36322 Level Plains 867 G8
35648 Lexington 884 D1
†36420 Libertyville 141 F8
35096 Lincoln 2,081 F3
36748 Linden⊙ 2,773 C6
36266 Lineville 2,257 G4
35020 Lipscomb 3,741 E4
36912 Lisman 638 B6
†36876 Little Shawmut 2,793 H5
†35653 Littleville 1,262 C1
35470 Livingston⊙ 3,187 B5
36865 Loachapoka 335 G5
36455 Lockhart 547 F8
35097 Locust Fork 488 E3
†35137 Longview 475 E4
36048 Louisville 791 G7
36751 Lower Peach Tree 926 C7
36752 Lowndesboro 207 E6
36551 Loxley 804 C9
36049 Luverne⊙ 2,639 F7
35575 Lynn 554 C2
35758 Madison 4,057 E1
36348 Madrid 172 H8
36555 Magnolia Springs 800 C10
36349 Malvern 558 G8
36750 Maplesville 754 E5
35112 Margaret 757 F3
36756 Marion⊙ 4,467 D5
35114 Maylene 500 E4
35111 McCalla 657 E4
36552 McCullough 500 D8
36553 McIntosh 319 B8
36456 McKenzie 605 E7
†35442 Memphis 95 B4
35984 Mentone 476 G1
35759 Meridianville 1,403 F1
35228 Midfield 6,203 E4
36350 Midland City 1,903 H8
36053 Midway 593 H6
†35150 Mignon 2,054 F4
36054 Millbrook 3,101 F6
35576 Millport 1,287 B3
36558 Millry 956 B7
36761 Minter 450 D6
*36601 Mobile⊙ 200,452 B9
Mobile‡ 442,819 B9
36460 Monroeville⊙ 5,674 D7
†35804 Monrovia 500 E1
35115 Montevallo 3,965 E4
*36101 Montgomery
(cap.)⊙ 178,857 F6
Montgomery‡ 272,687 F3
36559 Montrose 750 C9
†35125 Moody 1,840 F3
35649 Mooresville 58 E1
35116 Morris 623 E3
35650 Moulton⊙ 3,197 D2
35474 Moundville 1,310 C5
†35957 Mountainboro 266 F2
35223 Mountain Brook 19,718 E4
36560 Mount Vernon 1,038 B8
36268 Munford 700 F3
35660 Muscle Shoals 8,911 C1
36763 Myrtlewood 252 C6
36764 Nanafalia 500 B6
36303 Napier Field 493 H8
35578 Nauvoo 259 D3
†35049 Nectar 367 E3
36765 Newbern 307 C5
36351 New Brockton 1,392 G8
35760 New Hope 1,546 F1
35761 New Market 680 F1
†35010 New Site 340 G4
36352 Newton 1,540 G8
36353 Newville 814 H8
35086 North Johns 243 D4
35476 Northport 14,291 C4
36866 Notasulga 876 G5
35006 Oak Grove 638 F4
36766 Oak Hill 63 D7
35579 Oakman 770 D3
35120 Odenville 724 F3
36271 Ohatchee 860 G3
35121 Oneonta⊙ 4,824 E3
†36467 Onycha 147 F8
36801 Opelika⊙ 21,896 H5
36467 Opp 7,204 F8
36561 Orange Beach 600 C10
36767 Orrville 349 D6
35763 Owens Cross Roads 804 E1
36203 Oxford 8,939 G3
36360 Ozark⊙ 13,188 G8
35764 Paint Rock 221 F1
35580 Parrish 1,583 D3
35124 Pelham 6,759 E4
35125 Pell City⊙ 6,616 F3
36916 Pennington 355 B6
36562 Perdido 500 C8
36471 Peterman 600 D7
36062 Petrey 93 F7
36867 Phenix City⊙ 26,928 H6
35581 Phil Campbell 1,549 C2
†35447 Pickensville 132 B4
36272 Piedmont 5,544 G3
36371 Pinckard 771 G8
36768 Pine Apple 298 E7
36769 Pine Hill 510 C7
35765 Pisgah 699 G1
36758 Plantersville 650 E5
35127 Pleasant Grove 7,102 D4
36564 Point Clear 1,812 C10
†36441 Pollard 144 D8

(continued on following page)

Agriculture, Industry and Resources

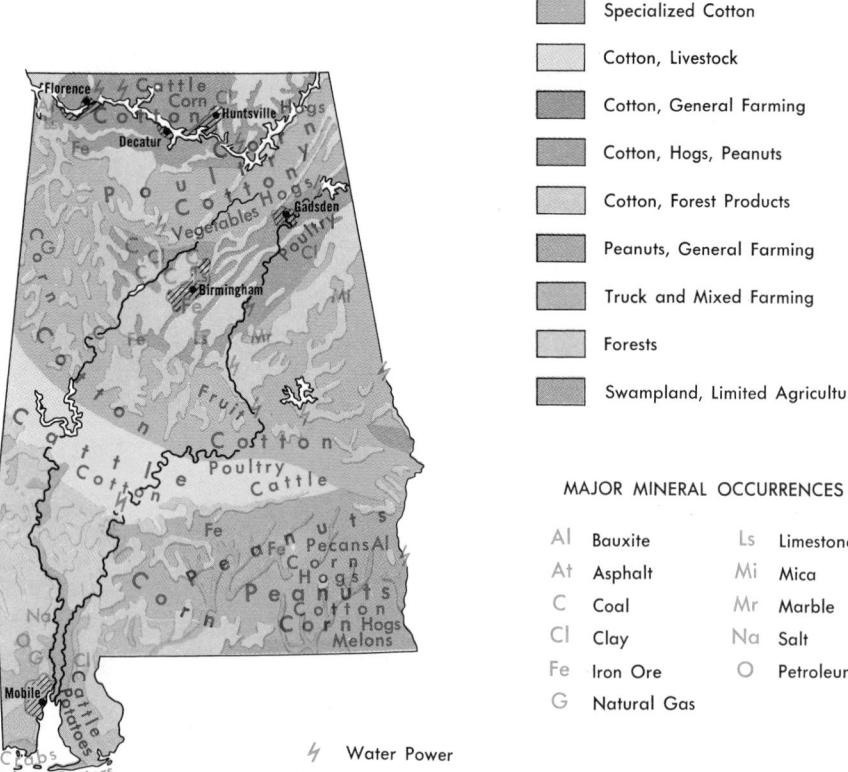

DOMINANT LAND USE

- Specialized Cotton
- Cotton, Livestock
- Cotton, General Farming
- Cotton, Hogs, Peanuts
- Cotton, Forest Products
- Peanuts, General Farming
- Truck and Mixed Farming
- Forests
- Swampland, Limited Agriculture

MAJOR MINERAL OCCURRENCES

Al	Bauxite	Ls	Limestone
At	Asphalt	Mi	Mica
C	Coal	Mr	Marble
Cl	Clay	Na	Salt
Fe	Iron Ore	O	Petroleum
G	Natural Gas		

- ⚡ Water Power
- ◌ Major Industrial Areas

Topography

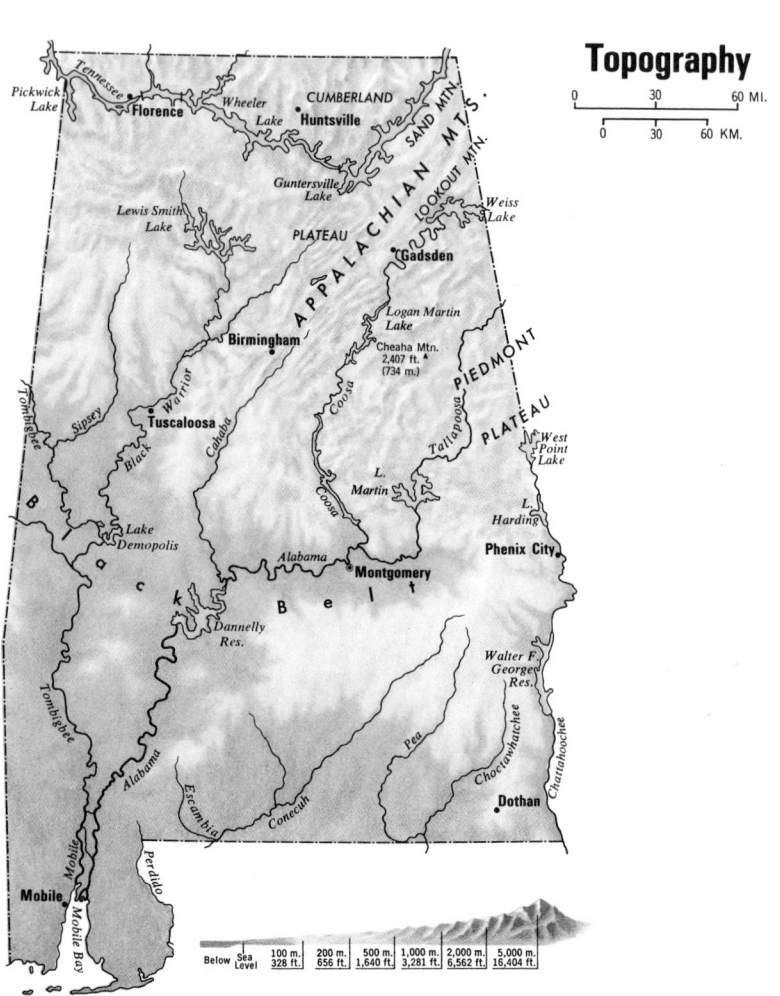

0   30   60 MI.

0   30   60 KM.

Below Sea Level | 100 m. 328 ft. | 200 m. 656 ft. | 500 m. 1,640 ft. | 1,000 m. 3,281 ft. | 2,000 m. 6,562 ft. | 5,000 m. 16,404 ft.

Alabama

SCALE
0 5 10   20   30   40 MI.

0 5 10 20   30   40 KM.

State Capitals .... ⊛
County Seats .... ⊙
Major Limited Access Hwys. ⎯⎯⎯

Scale 1:1,930,000

© Copyright HAMMOND INCORPORATED, Maplewood, N.J.

SENATORIAL DISTRICTS

Central H2
Northwestern E2
South Central G3
Southeastern L3

CITIES and TOWNS

Zip	Name/Pop.	Key
†99609	Akolmiut (Kasigluk) 641..	F2
99554	Alakanuk 522	E2
*99501	Anchorage⊙ 174,431 ...	B1
	Anchorage‡ 174,431	B1
†99760	Anderson 517..................	H2
99723	Barrow 2,207	G1
99559	Bethel 3,576	F2
99704	Clear 504	J2
99701	College 4,043	J1
99574	Cordova 1,879................	D1
99921	Craig 527	M2
99737	Delta Junction 945	J2
99576	Dillingham 1,563.............	G3
†99685	Dutch Harbor 250	E4
99581	Emanguk (Emmonak) 567	E2
99701	Fairbanks⊙ 22,645	J2
99740	Fort Yukon 619	J1
99741	Galena 765	G2
99588	Glennallen 511................	D1
99827	Haines 993	M1
99603	Homer 2,209....................	B2
99829	Hoonah 680	M1
99604	Hooper Bay 627	E2
99801	Juneau (cap.)⊙ 19,528...	N1
99830	Kake 555	M1
99609	Kasigluk 641	F2
99611	Kenai 4,324	B1
99901	Ketchikan 7,198	N2
99615	Kodiak 4,756...................	H3
99752	Kotzebue 2,054	F1
99926	Metlakatla 1,056.............	N2
†99901	Mountain Point 396.......	N2
99632	Mountain Village 583	E2
99762	Nome⊙ 2,301..................	E2
99763	Noorvik 492	F1
99645	Palmer 2,141	C1
99833	Petersburg 2,821............	N2
99660	Saint Paul Island 551......	D3
99661	Sand Point 625	G3
99664	Seward 1,843	C1
99835	Sitka 7,803	M1
99840	Skagway 768	M1
99669	Soldotna 2,320	B1
99503	Spenard	C1
99672	Sterling 919	B1
99780	Tok 589	K2
99684	Unalakleet 623................	G2
99685	Unalaska 1,322	E4
99686	Valdez 3,079...................	D1
99929	Wrangell 2,184	N2
99689	Yakutat 449	L3

OTHER FEATURES

Adak (isl.)...........................	L4
Admiralty (isl.)...................	M1
Afognak (isl.)......................	H3
Agattu (isl.)	J3
Akutan (isl.).......................	E4
Alaska (gulf).......................	K3
Alaska (range)	H2
Aleutian (isls.)	J4
Aleutian (range)	G3
Alexander (arch.)	L1
Amchitka (isl.)	K4
†Amlia (passage)................	L4
Amukta (isl.)	D4
Andreanof (isls.)................	L4
Atka (isl.)	L4
Attu (isl.)...........................	J3
Baird (mts.)........................	F1
Baranof (isl.)......................	M1
Barrow (pt.)........................	G1
Bear (mt.)..........................	K2
Beaufort (sea)....................	K1
Becharof (lake)	G3
Bering (glac.)......................	K2
Bering (sea).......................	D2
Bering (str.)	E1
Blackburn (mt.)..................	K2
Bona (mt.)	K2
Bristol (bay).......................	F3
British (mts.)......................	K1
Brooks (range)	G1
Chandalar (riv.)	J1
Chatham (str.)....................	M1
Chichagof (isl.)...................	M1
Chignik (bay)......................	G3
Chilkoot (pass)	M1
Chirikof (isl.)......................	G3
Chitina (riv.)	K2
Christian (sound)...............	M2
Chugach (mts.)...................	C1
Chukchi (sea).....................	E1
Clarence (str.)....................	N2
Clark (lake)........................	H2
Coast (mts.)	N1
Columbia (glac.).................	C1
Colville (riv.)......................	G1
Constantine (cape).............	G3
Cook (inlet)........................	B1
Cook (mt.)..........................	K2
Copper (riv.).......................	J2
Cordova (bay).....................	M2
Coronation (isl.)	M2
Cross (sound).....................	L1
Dease (inlet)	H1
Decision (cape)...................	M2
Denali Nat'l Park	H2
Devils Paw (mt.).................	N1
Dixon Entrance (chan.)	M2
Douglas (mt.)	H3
Dry (bay)	L3
Eielson A.F.B. 5,232	J2
Elmendorf A.F.B.	B1
Endicott (mts.)...................	H1
Etolin (isl.)	N2
Fairweather (cape).............	L1
Fairweather (mt.)...............	L1
Firth (riv.)	K1
Foraker (mt.)	H2
Fort Davis	E2
Fort Greely 1,635..............	J2
Fort Richardson	C1
Fort Wainwright	J1
Four Mountains (isls.)........	E4
Fox (isls.)	E4
Frederick (sound)..............	N1
Gates of the Arctic Nat'l	
Park	H1
Glacier (bay)......................	M1
Glacier Bay Nat'l Park	M1
Goodhope (bay)	F1
Great Sitkin (isl.)	L4
Guyot (glac.)	K2
Hagemeister (isl.)	F3
Halkett (cape)	H1
Hall (isl.)...........................	D2
Harding Icefield	C2
Harrison (bay)....................	H1
Hayes (mt.)........................	J2
Hazen (bay)	E2
Hinchinbrook (isl.)	C1
Hoonah (sound)	M1
Hope (pt.)	E1
Howard (pass)....................	G1
Icy (bay)	K3
Icy (cape)..........................	F1
Icy (pt.)..............................	L1
Icy (str.)............................	L1
Iliamna (lake)	G3
Iliamna (vol.).....................	H2
Innoko (riv.)	G2
Kachemak (bay)	B2
Kanaga (isl.)	L4
Kates Needle (mt.)	N1
Katmai (vol.)......................	H3
Katmai Nat'l Park	H3
Kayak (isl.)	K3
Kenai (lake)	C1
Kenai (mt.).........................	C2
Kenai (pen.).......................	C2
Kenai Fjords Nat'l Park	C2
Kennedy Entrance (str.)	H3
King (isl.)	E1
Kiska (isl.)..........................	J4
Kiska (vol.).........................	J4
Klondike Gold Rush Nat'l Hist.	
Park	N1
Knight (isl.)........................	D1
Knik Arm (inlet).................	B1
Kobuk (riv.)	G1
Kobuk Valley Nat'l Park	G1
Kodiak (isl.)	H3
Kotzebue (sound)	F1
Koyukuk (riv.).....................	G2
Krusenstern (cape)	F1
Kuiu (isl.)	M2
Kuskokwim (bay)................	F3
Kuskokwim (mts.)	G2
Kuskokwim (riv.)	G2
Kvichak (bay)	G3
Lake Clark Nat'l Park	H2
Lisburne (cape)..................	E1
Little Diomede (isl.)	E1
Little Sitkin (isl.)	K4
Lynn Canal (inlet)	M1
Makushin (vol.)...................	E4
Malaspina (glac.)	K3
Marcus Baker (mt.)	C1
Marmot (isl.)	H3
Matanuska (riv.).................	C1

Agriculture, Industry and Resources

DOMINANT LAND USE

- General Farming, Dairy, Vegetables
- General Farming, Livestock, Dairy
- Forests
- Nonagricultural Land

⚡ Water Power

MAJOR MINERAL OCCURRENCES

Au	Gold	G	Natural Gas
Be	Beryl	Hg	Mercury
C	Coal	O	Petroleum
Fe	Iron Ore	Pt	Platinum
U	Uranium		

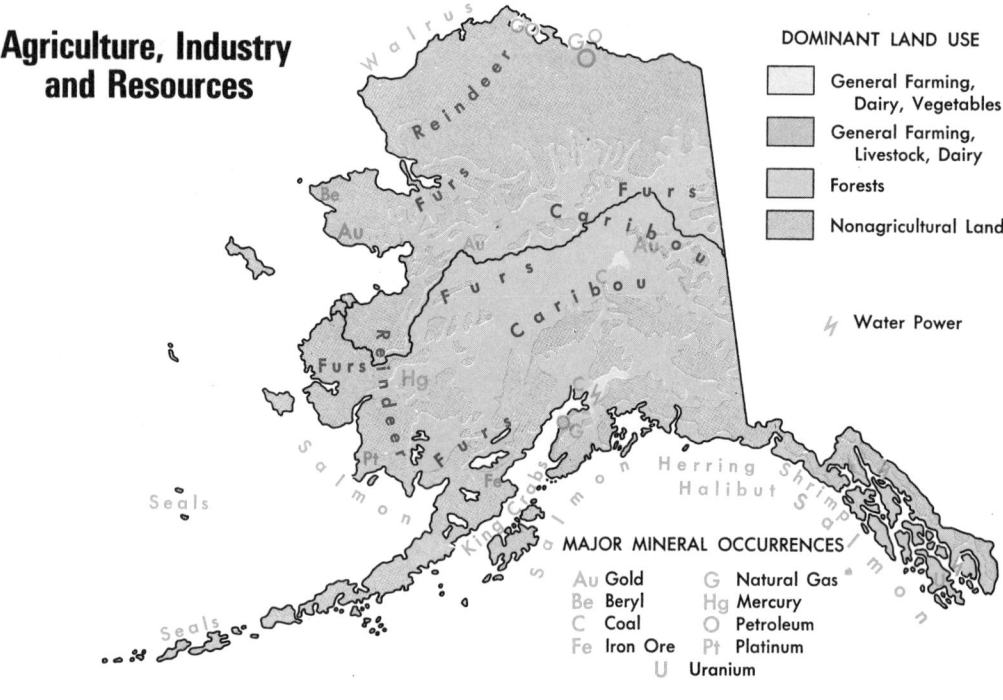

Topography

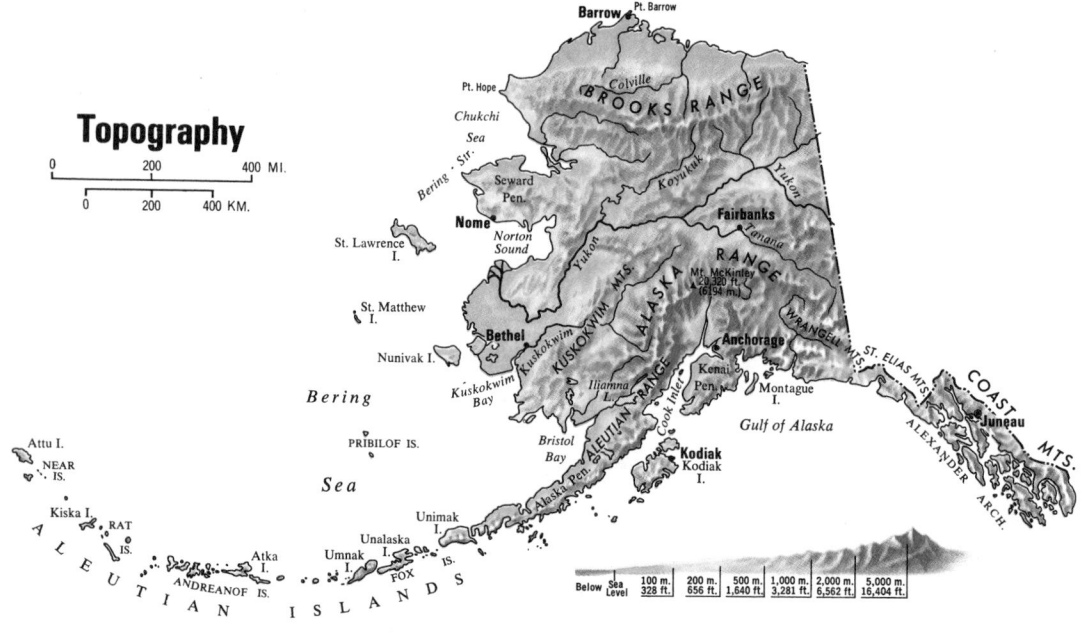

Alaska

POLYCONIC PROJECTION

SCALE

State and Territorial Capitals ...... ⊛
Court Houses .... ⊙
International Boundaries .... ___
Senatorial District Boundaries ...... _ _ _
Major Highways

Scale 1:10,500,000

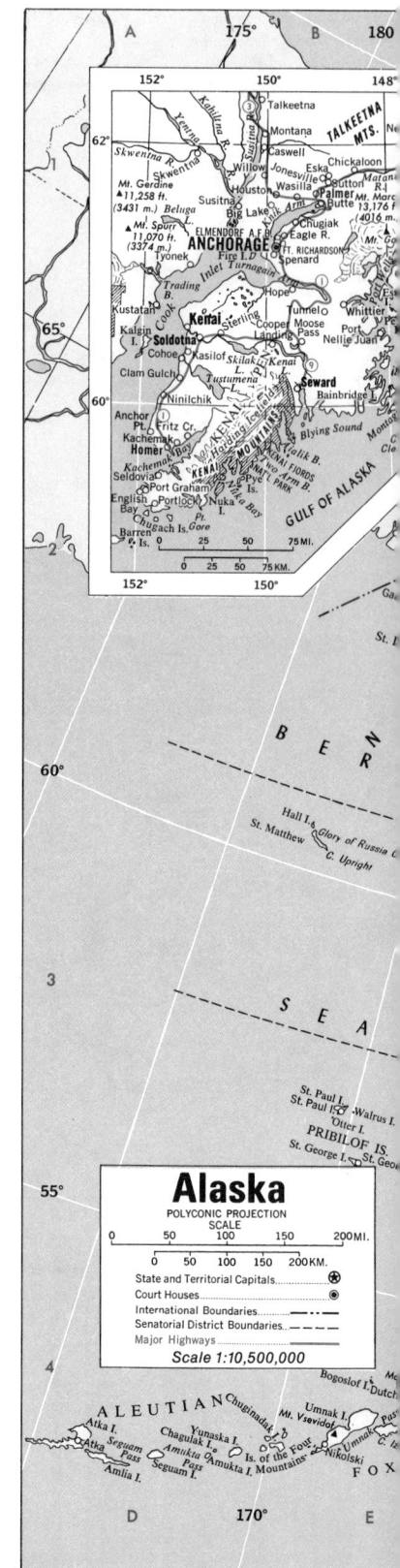

McKinley (mt.) H2
Meade (riv.) G1
Mendenhall (cape) E3
Mentasta (pass) K2
Merrill (pass) H2
Michelson (mt.) K1
Middleton (isl.) J3
Misty Fjords Nat'l Mon. N2
Mitkof (isl.) N2
Montague (isl.) D1
Muir (glac.) M1
Mulchatna (riv.) G2
Muzon (cape) M2
Naknek (lake) G3
Near (isls.) H3
Nelson (isl.) E2
Newenham (cape) F3
Noatak (riv.) F1
Norton (bay) F2
Norton (sound) E2
Nowitna (riv.) H2
Nuka (bay) C2
Nunivak (isl.) E3
Nushagak (riv.) G2
Nuyakuk (lake) F3
Ommaney (cape) M2
Otter (isl.) D3
Pastol (bay) F2
Pavlof (bay) F3
Pavlof (vol.) F3
Philip Smith (mts.) J1
Porcupine (riv.) K1
Port Clarence (inlet) E1
Port Heiden (inlet) G3
Portland Canal (inlet) N2
Port Moller (inlet) F3
Port Wells (inlet) C1
Pribilof (isls.) D3
Prince of Wales (cape) E1
Prince of Wales (isl.) N2
Prince William (sound) D1
Prudhoe (bay) J1
Rat (isls.) K4
Redoubt (vol.) H2
Revillagigedo (chan.) N2
Revillagigedo (isl.) N2
Romanzof (cape) E2
Sagavanirktok (riv.) J1
Saint Elias (cape) K3
Saint Elias (mts.) L2
Saint George (isl.) D3
Saint Lawrence (isl.) D2
Saint Matthew (isl.) D2
Saint Paul (isl.) D3
Salisbury (sound) M1
Sanak (isl.) F4
Sanford (mt.) K2
Schwatka (mts.) G1
Seguam (isl.) D4
Selawik (lake) F1
Semichi (isls.) J3
Semidi (isls.) G3
Semisopochnoi (isl.) K4
Seward (pen.) E1
Seymour (canal) N1
Sheenjek (riv.) K1
Shelikof (str.) H3
Shemya (isl.) J3
Shishaldin (vol.) E4
Shumagin (isls.) G4
Shuyak (isl.) H3
Sitka (sound) M1
Sitka Nat'l Hist. Park M1
Sitkinak (str.) H3
Skilak (lake) C1
Skwentna (riv.) A1
Smith (bay) H1
Spencer (cape) L1
Stephens (passage) N1
Stevenson Entrance (str.) H3
Stikine (riv.) N2
Stikine (str.) N2
Stony (riv.) G2
Stuart (isl.) F2
Suemez (isl.) M2
Sumner (str.) M2
Susitna (riv.) B1
Sutwik (isl.) G3
Taku (glac.) N1
Taku (riv.) N1
Talkeetna (mts.) J2
Tanaga (isl.) K4
Tanaga (vol.) K4
Tanana (riv.) J2
Taylor (mts.) G2
Tazlina (lake) D1
Tazlina (riv.) D1
Teshekpuk (lake) H1
Tigalda (isl.) F4
Tikchik (lkes) G2
Togiak (bay) F3
Tugidak (isl.) G3
Turnagain Arm (inlet) B1
Tustumena (lake) C1
Two Arm (bay) C2
Ugashik (lkes) G3
Umnak (isl.) E4
Umnak (passage) E4
Unalaska (isl.) E4
Unga (isl.) F3
Unimak (isl.) E4
Unimak (passage) F4
Utukok (riv.) F1
Valley of Ten Thousand Smokes G3
Vancouver (mt.) L2
Veniaminof (crater) F3
Vsevidof (mt.) E4
Walrus (isl.) E3
Walrus (isls.) F3
Waring (mts.) G1
West Point (mt.) K2
White (pass) N1
White (riv.) K2
White Mountains Nat'l Rec. Area J1
Witherspoon (mt.) C1
Wrangell (cape) H3
Wrangell (isl.) N2
Wrangell (mts.) K2
Wrangell-St. Elias Nat'l Park K2
Yakobi (isl.) M1
Yakutat (bay) K3
Yentna (riv.) A1
Yukon (riv.) F2

⊙Court House
‡Population of metropolitan area.
† Zip of nearest p.o.
* Multiple zips.

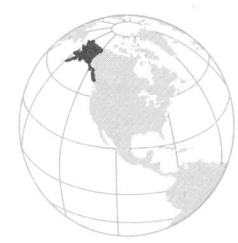

AREA 591,004 sq. mi. (1,530,700 sq. km.)
POPULATION 401,851
CAPITAL Juneau
LARGEST CITY Anchorage
HIGHEST POINT Mt. McKinley 20,320 ft. (6194 m.)
SETTLED IN 1801
ADMITTED TO UNION January 3, 1959
POPULAR NAME Great Land; Last Frontier
STATE FLOWER Forget-me-not
STATE BIRD Willow Ptarmigan

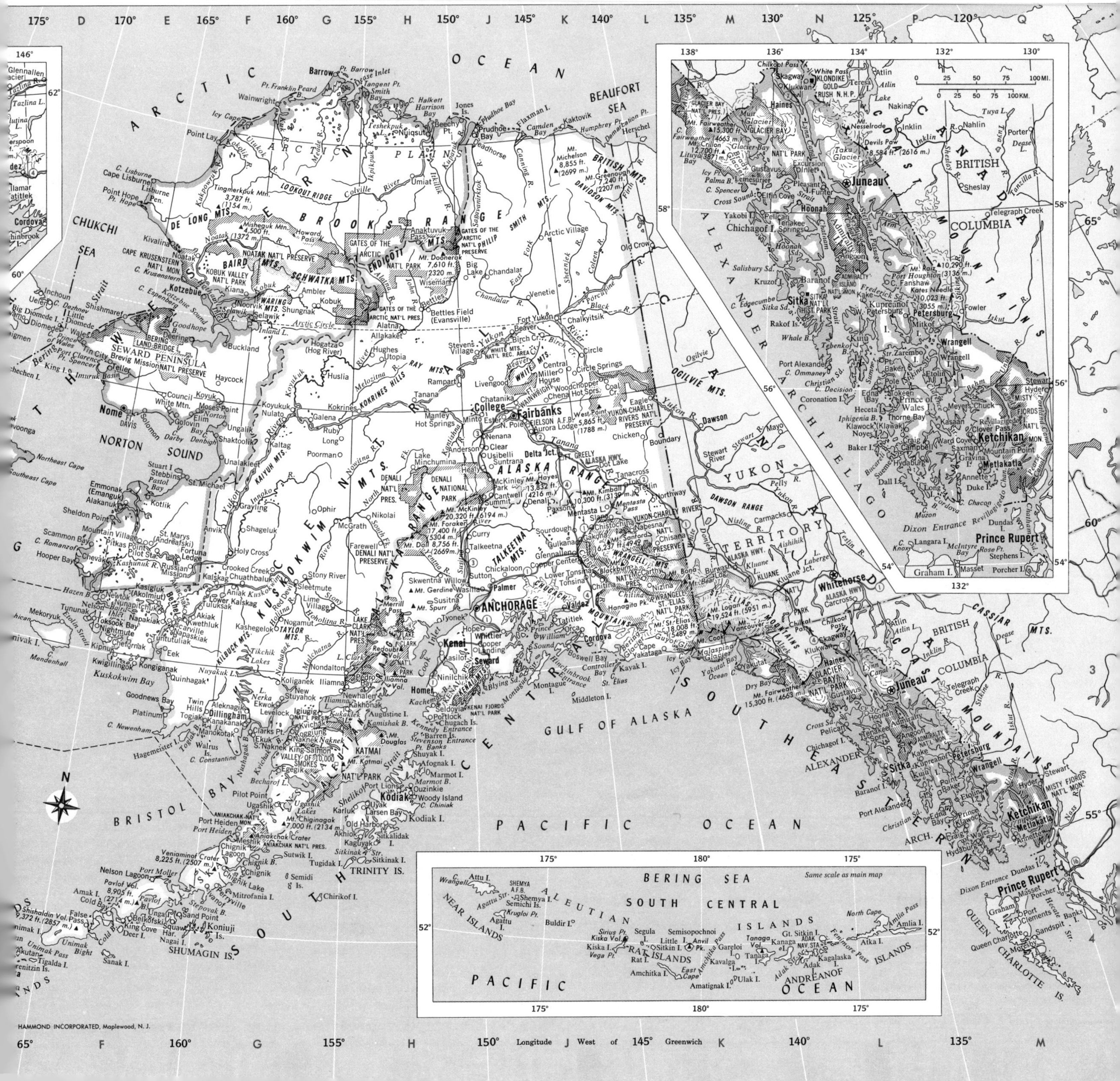

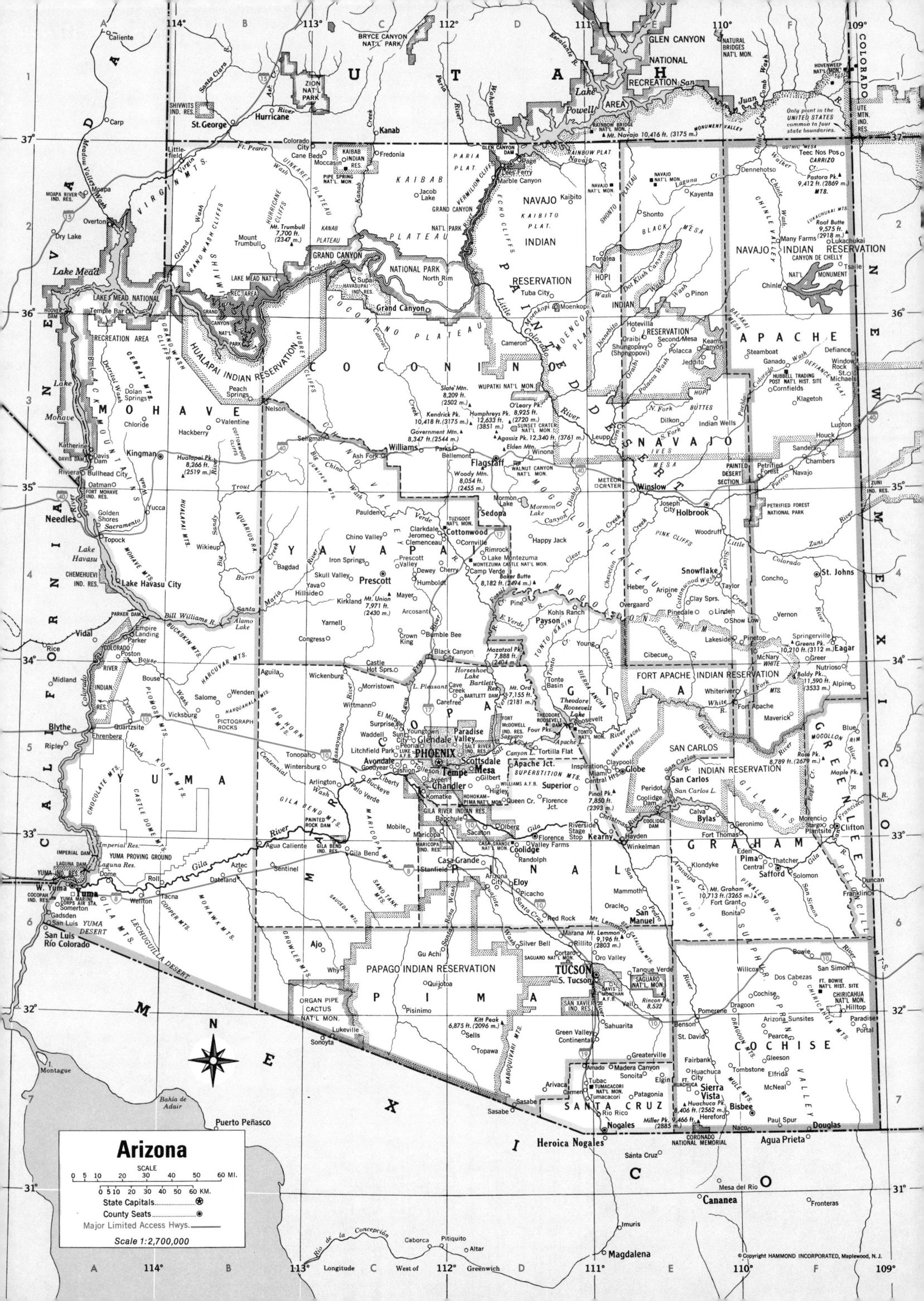

AREA 114,000 sq. mi. (295,260 sq. km.)
POPULATION 2,718,425
CAPITAL Phoenix
LARGEST CITY Phoenix
HIGHEST POINT Humphreys Pk. 12,633 ft. (3851 m.)
SETTLED IN 1752
ADMITTED TO UNION February 14, 1912
POPULAR NAME Grand Canyon State
STATE FLOWER Saguaro Cactus Blossom
STATE BIRD Cactus Wren

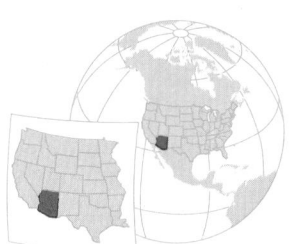

Agriculture, Industry and Resources

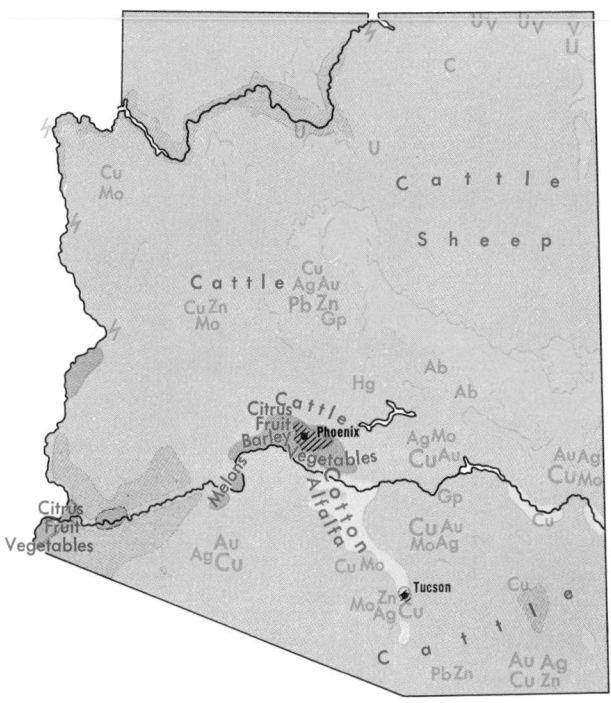

MAJOR MINERAL OCCURRENCES

Ab Asbestos	Cu Copper	Pb Lead
Ag Silver	Gp Gypsum	U Uranium
Au Gold	Hg Mercury	V Vanadium
C Coal	Mo Molybdenum	Zn Zinc

DOMINANT LAND USE

- Fruit, Truck and Mixed Farming
- Cotton and Alfalfa
- General Farming, Livestock, Special Crops
- Range Livestock
- Forests
- Nonagricultural Land

⚡ Water Power
▨ Major Industrial Areas

COUNTIES

Apache 52,108 .... F3
Cochise 85,686 .... F7
Coconino 75,008 .... C3
Gila 37,080 .... E5
Graham 22,862 .... E6
Greenlee 11,406 .... F5
Maricopa 1,509,052 .... C5
Mohave 55,865 .... A3
Navajo 67,629 .... E3
Pima 531,443 .... D6
Pinal 90,918 .... D6
Santa Cruz 20,459 .... E7
Yavapai 68,145 .... C4
Yuma 90,554 .... A5

CITIES and TOWNS

Zip	Name/Pop.	Key
†85333	Agua Caliente 60	B6
85320	Aguila 900	B5
85321	Ajo 5,189	C6
85920	Alpine 450	F5
85640	Amado 75	D7
85220	Apache Junction 9,935	D5
†85901	Aripine 25	E4
85601	Arivaca 400	D7
85223	Arizona City 825	D6
85625	Arizona Sunsites 825	F7
85322	Arlington 950	C5
86320	Ash Fork 800	C3

85323 Avondale 8,168 ....C5
†85333 Aztec 20 ....B6
86321 Bagdad 2,331 ....B4
85221 Bapchule 400 ....D5
86015 Bellemont 210 ....D3
85602 Benson 4,190 ....E7
85603 Bisbee⊙ 7,154 ....F7
85324 Black Canyon City 600 .....C4
85922 Blue 50 ....F5
†85643 Bonita 20 ....E6
85325 Bouse 500 ....A5
85605 Bowie 600 ....F6
85326 Buckeye 3,434 ....C5
86430 Bullhead
        City-Riviera 10,364 ....A3
†86301 Bumble Bee 15 ....C4
85530 Bylas 1,175 ....E5
†85530 Calva 10 ....E5
86020 Cameron 600 ....D3
86322 Camp Verde 1,125 ....D4
†86022 Cane Beds 30 ....B2
85331 Carefree 986 ....C5
†85640 Carmen 200 ....D7
85222 Casa Grande 14,971 .....D6
85329 Cashion 3,014 ....C5
†85342 Castle Hot Springs 50 ...C5
85331 Cave Creek 1,589 ....D5
85531 Central 300 ....F6
†85501 Central Heights-Midland
        City 2,791 ....E5
86502 Chambers 500 ....F3
85224 Chandler 29,673 ....D5
†86327 Cherry 20 ....C4
86503 Chinle 2,815 ....F2

86323 Chino Valley 2,858 ....C4
86431 Chloride 225 ....A3
†85292 Christmas 201 ....E5
85911 Cibecue 100 ....E4
86324 Clarkdale 1,512 ....C4
85532 Claypool 2,362 ....E5
†85934 Clay Springs 500 ....E4
†86326 Clemenceau 300 ....C4
85533 Clifton⊙ 4,245 ....F5
85606 Cochise 150 ....F6
86021 Colorado City 350 ....B2
85924 Concho 100 ....F4
85332 Congress 800 ....C4
85228 Coolidge 6,851 ....D6
†85542 Coolidge Dam 42 ....E5
†86505 Cornfields 200 ....F3
86325 Cornville 425 ....D4
85230 Cortaro 375 ....D6
86326 Cottonwood 4,550 ....D4
86333 Crown King 100 ....C4
85333 Dateland 100 ....B6
†86430 Davis Dam 125 ....A3
86327 Dewey 100 ....C4
86047 Dilkon 90 ....E3
86441 Dolan Springs 870 ....A3
†85364 Dome 48 ....A6
†85643 Dos Cabezas 30 ....F6
85607 Douglas 13,058 ....F7
85609 Dragoon 150 ....F6
85534 Duncan 603 ....F6
85925 Eagar 2,791 ....F4
85535 Eden 89 ....F6
85334 Ehrenburg 93 ....A5

(continued on following page)

Topography

0 — 50 — 100 MI.
0 — 50 — 100 KM.

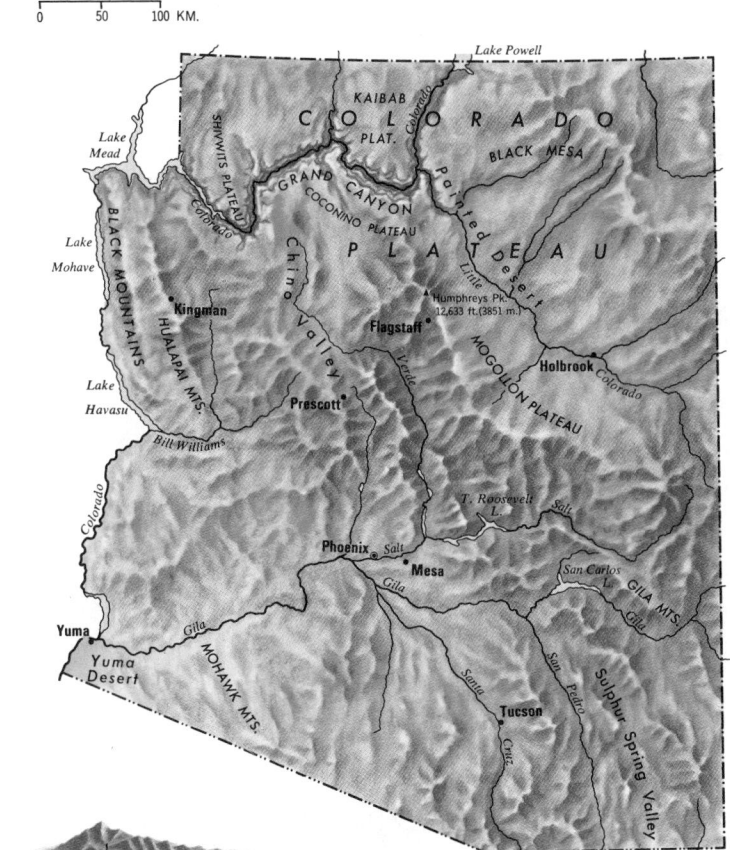

5,000 m. / 2,000 m. / 1,000 m. / 500 m. / 200 m. / 100 m. / Sea Level / Below
16,404 ft. / 6,562 ft. / 3,281 ft. / 1,640 ft. / 656 ft. / 328 ft.

200 Arizona
(continued)

†85617 Elfrida 700 F7
†85637 Elgin 525 E7
85335 El Mirage 4,307 C5
85231 Eloy 6,240 D6
85612 Fairbank 100 E7
86001 Flagstaff⊙ 34,743 D3
85232 Florence⊙ 3,391 D5
†85220 Florence Junction 35 D5
85926 Fort Apache 500 F5
86504 Fort Defiance 3,431 F3
85643 Fort Grant 240 E6
85536 Fort Thomas 450 E5
85534 Franklin 300 F6
86022 Fredonia 1,040 C2
85336 Gadsden 250 A6
86505 Ganado 816 F3
†85536 Geronimo 25 F5
85337 Gila Bend 1,585 C6
85234 Gilbert 5,717 D5
†85617 Gleeson 15 F7
*85301 Glendale 97,172 C5
85501 Globe⊙ 6,886 E5
85323 Goodyear 2,747 C5
86023 Grand Canyon 1,348 C2
†85637 Greaterville 15 E7
85614 Green Valley 7,999 D7
85927 Greer 385 F4
†85634 Gu Achi 339 C6
86411 Hackberry 250 B3
86024 Happy Jack 50 D4
85235 Hayden 1,205 E5
85928 Heber 750 E4
85615 Hereford 10 E7
85236 Higley 500 D5
†86301 Hillside 100 B4
†85632 Hilltop 9 F6
86025 Holbrook⊙ 5,785 E4
86030 Hotevilla 3,009 E3
86506 Houck 900 F3
85616 Huachuca City 1,661 E7
86329 Humboldt 787 C4
86031 Indian Wells 150 E3
85537 Inspiration 500 D5
86330 Iron Springs 175 C4
86051 Jacob Lake 16 C2
†86025 Jeddito 20 E3
86331 Jerome 420 C4
86032 Joseph City 650 E4
86053 Kaibito 275 D2
†86430 Katherine 102 A3
86033 Kayenta 3,343 E2
86034 Keams Canyon 400 E3
85237 Kearny 2,646 E5
86401 Kingman⊙ 9,257 A3
86332 Kirkland 100 C4
†86505 Klagetoh 200 F3
85643 Klondyke 86 E6
85538 Kohls Ranch 100 D4
†85339 Komatke 300 C5
86403 Lake Havasu City 15,909 A4
86342 Lake Montezuma 900 D4
85929 Lakeside 1,333 E4
85339 Laveen 800 C5
†86036 Lees Ferry 10 D2
86035 Leupp 150 E3
†85326 Liberty 150 C5
†85901 Linden 50 E4
85340 Litchfield Park 3,657 C5
86432 Littlefield 40 B2
86507 Lukachukai 1,049 F2
85341 Lukeville 50 C7
86508 Lupton 250 F3
†85637 Madera Canyon 75 E7
85618 Mammoth 1,906 E6
86538 Many Farms 1,364 F2
85238 Marana 1,674 D6
86036 Marble Canyon 6 D2
85239 Maricopa 750 C5

†85920 Maverick 50 F5
86333 Mayer 810 C4
85930 McNary 1,320 F4
85617 McNeal 100 F7
*85201 Mesa 152,453 D5
85539 Miami 2,716 E5
†85239 Mobile 100 C5
†86022 Moccasin 150 C2
†86045 Moenkopi D2
85540 Morenci 2,736 F5
86038 Mormon Lake 20 D4
85342 Morristown 400 C5
85619 Mount Lemmon 400 E6
†84770 Mount Trumbull 14 B2
85620 Naco 750 E7
86509 Navajo 100 F3
†86434 Nelson 39 B3
85621 Nogales⊙ 15,683 E7
86052 North Rim 50 C2
85932 Nutrioso 500 F5
86433 Oatman 175 A3
†85247 Olberg 65 D5
85623 Oracle 2,484 E6
86039 Oraibi 600 E3
†85704 Oro Valley 1,489 E6
85933 Overgaard 750 E4
86040 Page 4,907 D2
85343 Palo Verde 500 C5
†85632 Paradise 15 F7
85253 Paradise Valley 11,085 D5
85344 Parker 2,542 A4
86018 Parks 175 C3
85624 Patagonia 980 E7
86334 Paulden 350 C4
†85607 Paul Spur 34 F7
85541 Payson 5,068 D4
86434 Peach Springs 900 B3
85625 Pearce 700 F7
85345 Peoria 12,307 C5
85542 Peridot 950 E5
86028 Petrified Forest 80 F3
*85001 Phoenix (cap.)⊙ 789,704 C5
Phoenix‡ 1,508,030 C5
85241 Picacho 850 D6
85543 Pima 1,599 F6
85544 Pine 800 D4
85934 Pinedale 400 E4
85935 Pinetop 1,527 F4
86510 Pinon 100 E2
85634 Pisinimo 187 C6
†85540 Plantsite F5
86042 Polacca 500 E3
85627 Pomerene 365 E6
85632 Portal 72 F7
85371 Poston 500 A4
86301 Prescott⊙ 20,055 C4
†86301 Prescott Valley 2,284 C4
85346 Quartzsite 255 A5
85242 Queen Creek 600 D5
†85634 Quijotoa 200 C6
85243 Randolph 350 D6
85245 Red Rock 250 D6
85246 Rillito 400 D6
86335 Rimrock 217 D4
85237 Riverside Stage Stop 418 D5
86440 Riviera-Bullhead City 10,364 A3
85347 Roll 700 A6
85545 Roosevelt 125 D5
85247 Sacaton 1,951 D5
85546 Safford⊙ 7,010 F6
85629 Sahuarita 200 E7
85630 Saint David 800 E7
85936 Saint Johns⊙ 3,368 F4
86511 Saint Michaels 250 F3
85348 Salome 800 B5
85550 San Carlos 2,668 E5
86512 Sanders 900 F3

85349 San Luis 1,946 A6
85631 San Manuel 5,443 E6
85632 San Simon 400 F6
85633 Sasabe 50 D7
*85251 Scottsdale 88,622 D5
86043 Second Mesa 450 E3
86336 Sedona 5,368 D4
86337 Seligman 510 B3
85634 Sells 1,864 D7
†85333 Sentinel 40 B6
86054 Shonto 700 E2
85901 Show Low 4,298 F4
†86043 Shungopavy (Shongopovi) 570 E3
85635 Sierra Vista 24,937 E7
85270 Silver Bell 900 D6
86338 Skull Valley 250 C4
85937 Snowflake 3,510 E4
85551 Solomon 700 F6
85350 Somerton 5,761 A6
85637 Sonoita 220 E7
85713 South Tucson 6,554 D6
85938 Springerville 1,452 F4
85272 Stanfield 150 C6
†85540 Stargo 1,038 F5
†86505 Steamboat 100 F3
*85351 Sun City 40,505 C5
86435 Supai 350 C2
85273 Superior 4,600 D5
85345 Surprise 3,723 C5
85352 Tacna 950 B6
†85701 Tanque Verde 850 E6
85939 Taylor 1,915 E4
86514 Teec Nos Pos 550 F2
*85282 Tempe 106,743 D5
86443 Temple Bar 84 A2
85552 Thatcher 3,374 F6
85353 Tolleson 4,433 C5
85638 Tombstone 1,632 F7
86044 Tonalea 125 E2
85354 Tonopah 54 B5
85553 Tonto Basin 250 D5
85639 Topawa 500 D7
86436 Topock 325 A4
85290 Tortilla Flat 37 D5
85640 Tubac 140 E7
86045 Tuba City 5,045 D2
*85701 Tucson⊙ 330,537 D6
Tucson‡ 531,263 D6
85640 Tumacacori 100 D7
85641 Vail 175 E6
86437 Valentine 120 B3
85291 Valley Farms 240 D6
85940 Vernon 75 F4
†85348 Vicksburg 16 B5
85355 Waddell 100 C5
85356 Wellton 911 A6
85357 Wenden 400 B5
85941 Whiteriver 2,256 E5
85321 Why 65 C6
85358 Wickenburg 3,535 C5
85360 Wikieup 150 B4
85643 Willcox 3,243 F6
86046 Williams 2,266 C3
86515 Window Rock 2,230 F3
85292 Winkelman 1,060 E6
†86001 Winona 25 D3
86047 Winslow 7,921 E3
†85322 Wintersburg 400 B5
85361 Wittmann 600 C5
85942 Woodruff 280 E4
85362 Yarnell 800 C4
†86301 Yava 40 C4
85554 Young 500 D4
85363 Youngtown 2,254 C5
86438 Yucca 250 A4
85364 Yuma⊙ 42,481 A6

OTHER FEATURES

Agassiz (peak) D3
Agua Fria (riv.) C5
Alamo (lake) B4
Apache (lake) D5
Aquarius (range) B4
Aravaipa (creek) E6
Aubrey (cliffs) B3
Baboquivari (mts.) D7
Baker Butte (mt.) D4
Balakai (mesa) F3
Baldy (peak) F5
Bartlett (dam) D5
Bartlett (res.) D5
Big Chino Wash (dry riv.) C3
Big Horn (mts.) B5
Big Sandy (riv.) B4
Bill Williams (riv.) B4
Black (mesa) E2
Black (mts.) A3
Black (riv.) E5
Blue (riv.) F5
Bouse Wash (dry riv.) A4
Buckskin (mts.) B4
Burro (creek) B4
Canyon (lake) D5
Canyon de Chelly Nat'l Mon. F2
Carrizo (creek) E4
Carrizo (mts.) G2
Casa Grande Ruins Nat'l Mon. D6
Castle Dome (mts.) A5
Cataract (creek) C3
Centennial Wash (dry riv.) B5
Cerbat (mts.) A3
Cherry (creek) E4
Chevelon (creek) E4
Chinle (creek) F2
Chinle (valley) F2
Chinle Wash (dry riv.) F2
Chino (valley) C3
Chiricahua (mts.) F6
Chiricahua Nat'l Mon. F6
Chocolate (mts.) A5
Clear (creek) D4
Coconino (plat.) C3
Cocopah Ind. Res. 355 A6
Colorado (riv.) A5
Colorado River Ind. Res. 6,640 A5
Coolidge (dam) E5
Copper (mts.) B6
Corn (creek) E3
Coronado Nat'l Memorial E7
Cottonwood (cliffs) B3
Cottonwood Wash (dry riv.) E4
Davis (dam) A3
Davis-Monthan A.F.B. 6,279 E6
Defiance (plat.) F3
Detrital Wash (dry riv.) A3
Diablo (canyon) D4
Dinnebito Wash (dry riv.) E3
Dot Klish (canyon) E2
Dragoon (mts.) F7
Eagle (creek) F5
East Verde (riv.) D4
Echo (cliffs) D2
Elden (mt.) D3
Fort Apache Ind. Res. 7,774 E5
Fort Bowie Nat'l Hist. Site F6
Fort Huachuca E7
Fort McDowell Ind. Res. 349 D5
Fort Mohave Ind. Res. 183 A4
Fort Pearce Wash (dry riv.) B2
Fossil (creek) D4
Four Peaks (mt.) D5
Galiuro (mts.) E6
Gila (mts.) A6
Gila (mts.) F5

Gila (riv.) B6
Gila Bend (mts.) B5
Gila Bend Ind. Res. 353 C6
Gila River Ind. Res. 7,445 C5
Glen Canyon (dam) D2
Glen Canyon Nat'l Rec. Area D1
Gothic (mesa) F2
Government (mt.) C3
Graham (mt.) F6
Grand Canyon Nat'l Park C2
Grand Wash (butte) B2
Grand Wash (riv.) B2
Greens (peak) F4
Growler (mts.) B6
Harcuvar (mts.) B5
Harquahala (mts.) B5
Hassayampa (riv.) C5
Havasu (lake) A4
Havasupai Ind. Res. 282 C2
Hohokam Pima Nat'l Mon. D5
Hoover (dam) A2
Hopi (buttes) E3
Hopi Ind. Res. 6,896 E2
Horseshoe (lake) D5
Huachuca (peak) E7
Hualapai (mts.) B4
Hualapai (peak) B3
Hualapai Ind. Res. 849 B3
Hubbell Trading Post Nat'l Hist. Site F3
Humphreys (peak) D3
Hurricane (cliffs) B2
Imperial (res.) A6
Ives (mesa) E3
Juniper (mts.) C3
Kaibab (plat.) C2
Kaibab Ind. Res. 173 C2
Kaibito (plat.) D2
Kanab (creek) C2
Kanab (plat.) C2
Kellogg (mt.) E6
Kendrick (peak) D3
Kitt (peak) D7
Kofa (mts.) B5
Laguna (creek) E2
Laguna (res.) A6
Lake Mead Nat'l Rec. Area A2
Lechuguilla (des.) A6
Lemmon (mt.) E6
Little Colorado (riv.) D3
Lukachukai (mts.) F2
Luke A.F.B. 3,515 C5
Maple (peak) F5
Marble Canyon Nat'l Mon. D2
Maricopa (mts.) C5
Maricopa Ind. Res. 397 C6
Mazatzal (peak) D4
Mead (lake) A2
Meteor (crater) E3
Miller (peak) E7
Moencopi (plat.) D3
Moenkopi Wash (dry riv.) D2
Mogollon (plat.) D4
Mogollon Rim (cliffs) D4
Mohave (lake) A3
Mohave (mts.) A4
Mohawk (mts.) B6
Montezuma Castle Nat'l Mon. D4
Mormon (lake) D4
Mule (mts.) E7
Navajo (creek) D2
Navajo Ind. Res. 76,173 D2
Navajo Nat'l Mon. E2
Navajo Ord. Depot D3
O'Leary (peak) D3
Oraibi Wash (dry riv.) E3
Ord (mt.) D5
Organ Pipe Cactus Nat'l Mon. C6

Painted (des.)
Painted Desert Section (Petrified Forest
Painted Rock (dam)
Papago Ind. Res. 7,171
Paria (plat.)
Paria (riv.)
Parker (dam)
Pastora (peak)
Peloncillo (mts.)
Petrified Forest Nat'l Park
Pictograph (rocks)
Pinal (peak)
Pinaleno (mts.)
Pink (cliffs)
Pipe Spring Nat'l Mon.
Pleasant (lake)
Plomosa (mts.)
Polacca Wash (dry riv.)
Powell (lake)
Pueblo Colorado Wash (dry riv.)
Puerco (riv.)
Quajote Wash (dry riv.)
Rainbow (plat.)
Rincon (peak)
Roof Butte (mt.)
Rose (peak)
Sacramento Wash (dry riv.)
Saguaro (lake)
Saguaro Nat'l Mon.
Salt (riv.)
Salt River Ind. Res. 4,089
San Carlos (lake)
San Carlos (riv.)
San Carlos Ind. Res. 6,104
Sand Tank (mt.)
San Francisco (riv.)
San Pedro (riv.)
San Simon (riv.)
Santa Catalina (mts.)
Santa Cruz (riv.)
Santa Maria (riv.)
Santa Rosa Wash (dry riv.)
San Xavier Ind. Res. 875
Sauceda (mts.)
Shivwits (plat.)
Shonto (plat.)
Sierra Ancha (mts.)
Sierra Apache (mts.)
Silver (creek)
Slate (mt.)
Sulphur Spring (valley)
Sunset Crater Nat'l Mon.
Superstition (mts.)
Theodore Roosevelt (lake)
Tonto (creek)
Tonto Nat'l Mon.
Trout (creek)
Trumbull (mt.)
Tumacacori Nat'l Mon.
Tuzigoot Nat'l Mon.
Tyson Wash (dry riv.)
Uinkaret (plat.)
Union (mt.)
Verde (riv.)
Vermilion (cliffs)
Virgin (mts.)
Walker (creek)
Walnut Canyon Nat'l Mon.
White (riv.)
Williams A.F.B. 3,435
Woody (mt.)
Wupatki Nat'l Mon.
Yuma (des.)
Yuma Proving Ground 1,098
Zuni (riv.)

⊙County seat.
‡Population of metropolitan area.
† Zip of nearest p.o. * Multiple zip

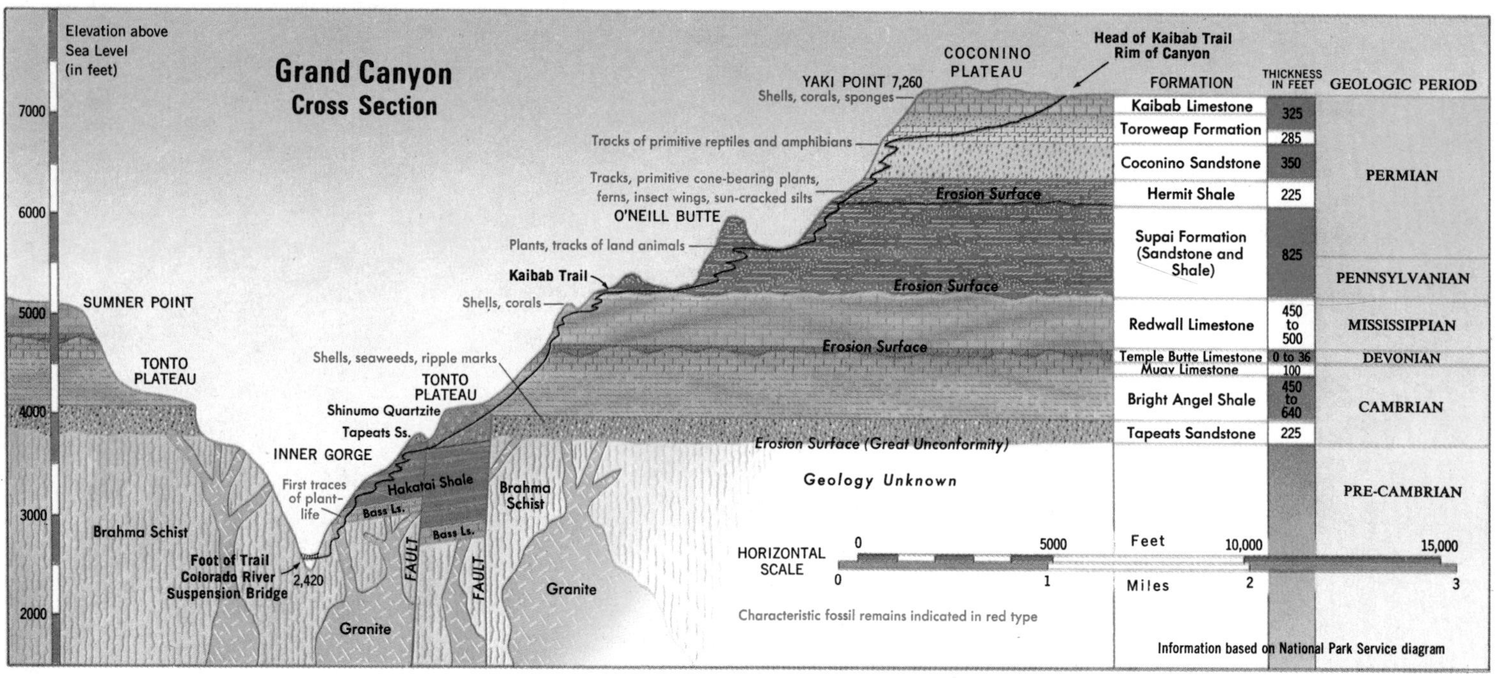
Elevation above Sea Level (in feet)
Grand Canyon Cross Section
7000
6000
5000
4000
3000
2000
SUMNER POINT
TONTO PLATEAU
Brahma Schist
INNER GORGE
Foot of Trail Colorado River Suspension Bridge
2,420
Granite
FAULT
Brahma Schist
Hakatai Shale
Bass Ls.
First traces of plant-life
Shinumo Quartzite
Tapeats Ss.
TONTO PLATEAU
Shells, seaweeds, ripple marks
Shells, corals
Kaibab Trail
Plants, tracks of land animals
O'NEILL BUTTE
Tracks, primitive cone-bearing plants, ferns, insect wings, sun-cracked silts
Tracks of primitive reptiles and amphibians
YAKI POINT 7,260
Shells, corals, sponges
COCONINO PLATEAU
Head of Kaibab Trail Rim of Canyon
Erosion Surface
Erosion Surface (Great Unconformity)
Geology Unknown
FORMATION
THICKNESS IN FEET
GEOLOGIC PERIOD
Kaibab Limestone 325
Toroweap Formation 285
Coconino Sandstone 350
Hermit Shale 225
PERMIAN
Supai Formation (Sandstone and Shale) 825
PENNSYLVANIAN
Redwall Limestone 450 to 500
MISSISSIPPIAN
Temple Butte Limestone 0 to 36
DEVONIAN
Muav Limestone 100
Bright Angel Shale 450 to 640
CAMBRIAN
Tapeats Sandstone 225
PRE-CAMBRIAN
HORIZONTAL SCALE
0 5000 Feet 10,000 15,000
0 1 Miles 2 3
Characteristic fossil remains indicated in red type
Information based on National Park Service diagram

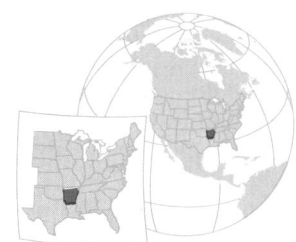

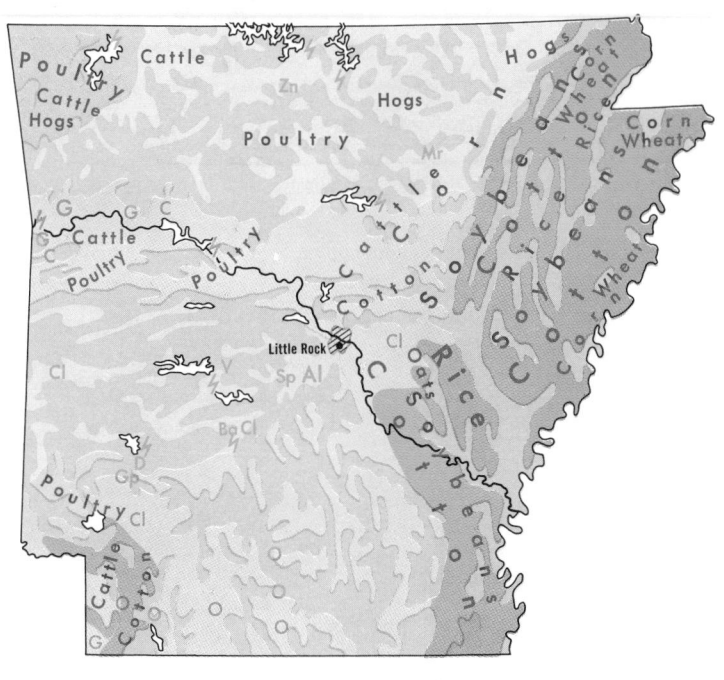

AREA 53,187 sq. mi. (137,754 sq. km.)
POPULATION 2,286,435
CAPITAL Little Rock
LARGEST CITY Little Rock
HIGHEST POINT Magazine Mtn. 2,753 ft. (839 m.)
SETTLED IN 1685
ADMITTED TO UNION June 15, 1836
POPULAR NAME Land of Opportunity
STATE FLOWER Apple Blossom
STATE BIRD Mockingbird

Agriculture, Industry and Resources

COUNTIES

Arkansas 24,175 ....H5
Ashley 26,538 ....G7
Baxter 27,409 ....F1
Benton 78,115 ....B1
Boone 26,067 ....D1
Bradley 13,803 ....F7
Calhoun 6,079 ....E6
Carroll 16,203 ....C1
Chicot 17,793 ....H7
Clark 23,326 ....D5
Clay 20,616 ....K1
Cleburne 16,909 ....F2
Cleveland 7,868 ....F6
Columbia 26,644 ....D7
Conway 19,505 ....E3
Craighead 63,239 ....J2
Crawford 36,892 ....B2
Crittenden 49,499 ....K3
Cross 20,434 ....J3
Dallas 10,515 ....E6
Desha 19,760 ....H6
Drew 17,910 ....G6
Faulkner 46,192 ....F3
Franklin 14,705 ....C2
Fulton 9,975 ....G1
Garland 70,531 ....D4
Grant 13,008 ....F5
Greene 30,744 ....J1
Hempstead 23,635 ....D6
Hot Spring 26,819 ....E5
Howard 13,459 ....C5
Independence 30,147 ....G2
Izard 10,768 ....G1
Jackson 21,646 ....H2
Jefferson 90,718 ....G5
Johnson 17,423 ....C2
Lafayette 10,213 ....C7
Lawrence 18,447 ....H1
Lee 15,539 ....J4
Lincoln 13,369 ....G6
Little River 13,952 ....B6
Logan 20,144 ....C3
Lonoke 34,518 ....G4
Madison 11,373 ....C1
Marion 11,334 ....E1
Miller 37,766 ....C7
Mississippi 59,517 ....K2
Monroe 14,052 ....H4
Montgomery 7,771 ....C4
Nevada 11,097 ....D6
Newton 7,756 ....D2
Ouachita 30,541 ....E6
Perry 7,266 ....E4
Phillips 34,772 ....J5
Pike 10,373 ....C5
Poinsett 27,032 ....J2
Polk 17,007 ....B5
Pope 39,021 ....D3
Prairie 10,140 ....G4
Pulaski 340,613 ....F4
Randolph 16,834 ....H1
Saint Francis 30,858 ....J3
Saline 53,161 ....E4
Scott 9,685 ....B4
Searcy 8,847 ....E2
Sebastian 95,172 ....B3
Sevier 14,060 ....B6
Sharp 14,607 ....G1
Stone 9,022 ....F2
Union 48,573 ....E7
Van Buren 13,357 ....E2
Washington 100,494 ....B2
White 50,835 ....G3
Woodruff 11,222 ....H3
Yell 17,026 ....D3

CITIES and TOWNS

Zip   *Name/Pop.*   *Key*

72001 Adona 230 ....E3
72002 Alexander 223 ....F4
72410 Alicia 246 ....H2
72820 Alix 225 ....C3
†72046 Allport 295 ....G4
72921 Alma 2,755 ....B3
72003 Almyra 294 ....H5
72611 Alpena 344 ....D1
72004 Altheimer 1,231 ....G5
72821 Altus 441 ....C3
72005 Amagon 126 ....H2
71921 Amity 859 ....D5
71922 Antoine 194 ....D5
71923 Arkadelphia⊙ 10,005 ...D5
71630 Arkansas City⊙ 668 ....H6
72310 Armorel 500 ....L2
71822 Ashdown⊙ 4,218 ......B6
72513 Ash Flat⊙ 524 ....G1
72823 Atkins 3,002 ....E3
72311 Aubrey 267 ....J4
72006 Augusta⊙ 3,496 ....H3
72007 Austin 269 ....G4
72711 Avoca 256 ....B1
72010 Bald Knob 2,756 ....G3
71631 Banks 216 ....F6
72922 Barber 35 ....B3
72923 Barling 3,761 ....B3
72313 Bassett 243 ....K2
72924 Bates B4
72501 Batesville⊙ 8,263 ....G2
72411 Bay 1,605 ....J2
72613 Beaver C1
72012 Beebe 3,599 ....G3
72014 Beedeville 183 ....H3
†72712 Bella Vista 2,589 ......B1
†72601 Bellefonte 393 ....D1
72824 Belleville 571 ....D3
71823 Ben Lomond 155 ......B6
72015 Benton⊙ 17,717 ....E4
72712 Bentonville⊙ 8,756 .....B1
72616 Bergman 320 ....E1
72616 Berryville⊙ 2,966 ......C1
†72764 Bethel Heights 296 ....B1
72016 Bigelow 373 ....E3
72617 Big Flat 150 ....F1
72413 Biggers 363 ....J1
72017 Biscoe 486 ....H4
72414 Black Oak 309 ....K2
72415 Black Rock 848 ....H1
†71960 Black Springs 92 ......C5
71825 Blevins 314 ....C6
65611 Blue Eye 43 ....D1
72826 Blue Mountain 112 ....C3
71722 Bluff City 292 ....D6
72315 Blytheville⊙ 23,844 ....L2
†71858 Bodcaw 197 ....D6
†72901 Bonanza 553 ....B3
72416 Bono 967 ....J2
72927 Booneville⊙ 3,718 .....C3
72020 Bradford 950 ....G3
71826 Bradley 790 ....C7
72928 Branch 353 ....C3
72021 Brinkley 4,909 ....H4
72417 Brookland 840 ....J2
72022 Bryant 2,682 ....F4
72519 Bull Shoals 1,312 ......E1
72321 Burdette 328 ....L2
72023 Cabot 4,806 ....F4
72322 Caldwell 283 ....J3
71828 Cale 110 ....D6
72519 Calico Rock 1,046 .....F1
71724 Calion 638 ....E7
71701 Camden⊙ 15,356 .....E6
†72201 Cammack Village 920 ..E4
72419 Caraway 1,165 ....K2
72024 Carlisle 2,567 ....G4
71725 Carthage 568 ....E5
72025 Casa 179 ....D3
72421 Cash 285 ....J2
72026 Casscoe 297 ....H4
†72951 Caulksville 234 ....C3
72521 Cave City 1,634 ....G2
72718 Cave Springs 429 ......B1
72932 Cedarville 375 ....B2
72719 Centerton 425 ....B1
72829 Centerville 300 ....D3
†72923 Central City 339 ....B3
72933 Charleston⊙ 1,748 ....B3
†72525 Cherokee Village-Hidden
     Valley 4,058 ....G1
72324 Cherry Valley 729 ......J3
72934 Chester 139 ....B2
71726 Chidester 342 ....D6
72029 Clarendon⊙ 2,361 .....H4
72325 Clarkedale 300 ....K3
72830 Clarksville⊙ 5,237 ....D3
72031 Clinton⊙ 1,284 ....F2
72832 Coal Hill 859 ....C3
72326 Colt 378 ....J3
71831 Columbus 265 ....C6
72523 Concord 234 ....G2
72032 Conway⊙ 20,375 ......F3
72524 Cord 250 ....H2
72422 Corning⊙ 3,650 ....J1
72626 Cotter 920 ....E1
72036 Cotton Plant 1,323 ....H3
71937 Cove 391 ....B5
72037 Coy 183 ....G4
72327 Crawfordsville 685 .....K3
71635 Crossett 6,706 ....G7
71728 Curtis 300 ....D6
72526 Cushman 556 ....G2
†71950 Daisy 177 ....C5
72039 Damascus 307 ....F3
72833 Danville⊙ 1,698 ....D3
72834 Dardanelle⊙ 3,621 ....D3
72424 Datto 112 ....J1
72722 Decatur 1,013 ....A1
72425 Delaplaine 161 ....J1
71940 Delight 431 ....C5
72426 Dell 310 ....K2
†72821 Denning 238 ....C3
71832 De Queen⊙ 4,594 ....B5
71638 Dermott 4,731 ....H7
72040 Des Arc⊙ 2,001 ......G4
72041 De Valls Bluff⊙ 738 ...H4
72042 De Witt⊙ 3,928 ....H5
72922 Barber 35

72644 Diamond City 650 ....E1
72043 Diaz 1,192 ....H2
71833 Dierks 1,249 ....B5
71941 Donaldson 300 ....E5
72837 Dover 948 ....D3
71639 Dumas 6,091 ....H6
72935 Dyer 608 ....B3
72330 Dyess 446 ....K2
72331 Earle 3,517 ....K3
71701 East Camden 632 .....E6
72332 Edmondson 344 ....K3
72333 Elaine 991 ....J5
71730 El Dorado⊙ 25,270 ...E7
72727 Elkins 579 ....C1
72728 Elm Springs 781 ....B1
71740 Emerson 444 ....D7
71835 Emmet 475 ....D6
72046 England 3,081 ....G4
72047 Enola 186 ....F3
71640 Eudora 3,840 ....H7
72632 Eureka Springs⊙ 1,989 ..C1
72532 Evening Shade 397 ....G1
72633 Everton 134 ....E1
72730 Farmington 1,283 .....B1
72701 Fayetteville⊙ 36,608 ...B1
     Fayetteville-Springdale
     07 ....B1
†71747 Felsenthal 220 ....F7
72429 Fisher 302 ....J2
72634 Flippin 1,072 ....E1
71742 Fordyce⊙ 5,175 ....F6
71836 Foreman 1,377 ....B6
72335 Forrest City⊙ 13,803 ...J3
*72901 Fort Smith⊙ 71,626 ...B3
     Fort Smith‡ 203,269 ....B3
71837 Fouke 614 ....C7
71642 Fountain Hill 352 ......G7
†72016 Fourche 51 ....E4
72536 Franklin 253 ....G1
72017 Fredonia (Biscoe) 486 ..H4
71942 Friendship 163 ....E5
71838 Fulton 326 ....C6
72732 Garfield 187 ....C1
71839 Garland 660 ....C7
72052 Garner 216 ....G3
72635 Gassville 859 ....F1
72733 Gateway 75 ....B1
71840 Genoa 350 ....C7
72734 Gentry 1,468 ....A1
72636 Gilbert 43 ....E2
72055 Gillett 927 ....H5
71841 Gillham 252 ....B5
72339 Gilmore 503 ....K3
71943 Glenwood 1,402 ......C5
72340 Goodwin 225 ....J4
†72315 Gosnell 3,215 ....K2
71643 Gould 1,671 ....G6
71644 Grady 488 ....G5
71944 Grannis 349 ....B5
72838 Gravelly 300 ....C4
72736 Gravette 1,218 ....B1
72058 Greenbrier 1,423 ......F3
72638 Green Forest 1,609 ....D1
72737 Greenland 622 ....B1
72430 Greenway 317 ....K1
72936 Greenwood⊙ 3,317 ...B3
†72067 Greers Ferry 558 ......F2
72060 Griffithville 254 ....G3
72431 Grubbs 546 ....H2
72540 Guion 177 ....G2
†71923 Gum Springs 255 ......D5
71743 Gurdon 2,707 ....D6
72061 Guy 209 ....F3
72937 Hackett 505 ....B3
†71638 Halley H6
71646 Hamburg⊙ 3,394 .....G7
71744 Hampton⊙ 1,627 .....F6
72542 Hardy 643 ....H1
72745 Harrell 302 ....F7
72432 Harrisburg⊙ 1,921 ....J2
72601 Harrison⊙ 9,567 ......D1
72938 Hartford 613 ....B3
72840 Hartman 517 ....C3
†72015 Haskell 1,074 ....E4
71945 Hatfield 410 ....B5
72842 Havana 352 ....D3
72341 Haynes 359 ....J4
72064 Hazen 1,636 ....G4
72543 Heber Springs⊙ 4,589 ..G2
72843 Hector 449 ....E3
72342 Helena⊙ 9,598 ....J4
72065 Hensley 500 ....F4
71647 Hermitage 378 ....F7
72347 Hickory Ridge 478 ....F2
72067 Higden 45 ....F2
72068 Higginson 333 ....G3
†72734 Highfill 92 ....B1
72738 Hindsville C1
72069 Holly Grove 754 ....H4
†72958 Hon 250 ....B4
71801 Hope⊙ 10,290 ....C6
71842 Horatio 989 ....B3
72512 Horseshoe Bend 1,909 ..G1
71901 Hot Springs National
     Park⊙ 35,781 ....D4
72070 Houston 183 ....E3

(continued on following page)

DOMINANT LAND USE

- Fruit and Mixed Farming
- Specialized Cotton
- Cotton, General Farming
- Rice, General Farming
- General Farming, Livestock, Truck Farming, Cotton
- Forests
- Swampland, Limited Agriculture

MAJOR MINERAL OCCURRENCES

Al	Bauxite	Gp	Gypsum
Ba	Barite	Mr	Marble
C	Coal	O	Petroleum
Cl	Clay	Sp	Soapstone
D	Diamonds	V	Vanadium
G	Natural Gas	Zn	Zinc

⚡ Water Power   ▨ Major Industrial Areas

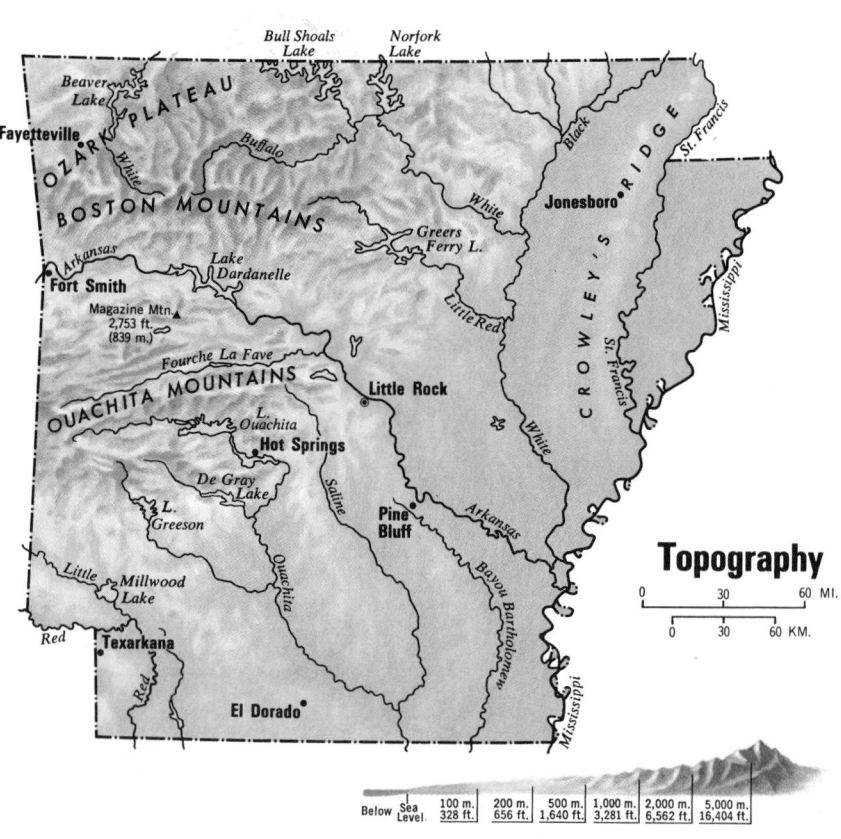

Topography

0   30   60 MI.

0   30   60 KM.

| Below Sea Level | Sea Level | 100 m. 328 ft. | 200 m. 656 ft. | 500 m. 1,640 ft. | 1,000 m. 3,281 ft. | 2,000 m. 6,562 ft. | 5,000 m. 16,404 ft. |

72433 Hoxie 2,961 .... H1
72348 Hughes 1,919 .... J4
72072 Humnoke 442 .... G4
72073 Humphrey 872 .... G5
72074 Hunter 170 .... H3
72940 Huntington 662 .... B3
72740 Huntsville⊙ 1,394 ..... C1
71747 Huttig 976 .... F7
72434 Imboden 661 .... H1
72075 Jacksonport 288 .... H2
72076 Jacksonville 27,589 .. F4
†72501 Jamestown G2
72641 Jasper⊙ 519 .... D1
72079 Jefferson 250 .... F5
71650 Jerome 54 .... G7
72080 Jerusalem 300 .... E3
71949 Jessieville 350 .... D4
72741 Johnson 519 .... B1
72350 Joiner 725 .... K3
72401 Jonesboro⊙ 31,530 .. J2
72081 Judsonia 2,025 .... G3
71749 Junction City 813 .... E7
72351 Keiser 962 .... K2
72082 Kensett 1,751 .... G3
72083 Keo 208 .... G4
†72956 Kibler 798 .... B3
71652 Kingsland 320 .... F6
71950 Kirby 800 .... C5
72435 Knobel 503 .... J1
72845 Knoxville 264 .... D3
72436 Lafe 215 .... J1
72437 Lake City⊙ 1,842 .... K2
72642 Lakeview 512 .... E1
†72389 Lake View 609 ...... J5
71653 Lake Village⊙ 3,088 . H7
72846 Lamar 708 .... D3
72941 Lavaca 1,092 .... B3
71750 Lawson 250 .... F7
72438 Leachville 1,882 ..... K2
72644 Lead Hill 247 .... D1
72084 Leola 481 .... E5
72354 Lepanto 1,964 .... K2
72645 Leslie 501 .... E2
72085 Letona 231 .... G3
71845 Lewisville⊙ 1,476 ... C7
72355 Lexa 500 .... J4
72744 Lincoln 1,422 .... B2
†72712 Little Flock 663 .... B1
*72201 Little Rock
(cap.)⊙ 158,461 .... F4
Little Rock-North Little
Rock‡ 393,494 ..... F4
71846 Lockesburg 616 ..... B6
72847 London 859 .... D3
72086 Lonoke⊙ 4,128 ...... G4
72087 Lonsdale 117 .... E4
71751 Louann 282 .... E7
72745 Lowell 1,078 .... B1
*72856 Lurton 38 .... D2
72358 Luxora 1,739 .... K2
72440 Lynn 345 .... H2
72359 Madison 1,238 ..... J4
72943 Magazine 799 ...... C3
72553 Magness 196 .... H2
71753 Magnolia⊙ 11,909 .. D7
72104 Malvern⊙ 10,163 ... E5
72554 Mammoth Spring 1,158 . G1
72442 Manila 2,553 .... K2
72944 Mansfield 1,000 ... B3
72360 Marianna⊙ 6,220 ... J4
†72395 Marie 287 .... K2
72364 Marion⊙ 2,996 ..... K3

72365 Marked Tree 3,201 ...... K2
72443 Marmaduke 1,168 ...... K1
72650 Marshall⊙ 1,595 ...... E2
72366 Marvell 1,724 .... J4
72106 Mayflower 1,381 ...... F4
72444 Maynard 381 .... J1
71847 McCaskill 87 .... C6
72101 McCrory 1,942 .... H3
72441 McDougal 239 .... K1
71654 McGehee 5,671 ...... H6
71752 McNeil 725 .... D7
72102 McRae 641 .... G3
72556 Melbourne⊙ 1,619 ... G1
72367 Mellwood 250 .... H5
71953 Mena⊙ 5,154 .... B4
72107 Menifee 368 .... E3
72945 Midland 286 .... B3
71851 Mineral Springs 936 .. C6
72445 Minturn 169 .... H2
†71639 Mitchellville 618 .... H6
72447 Monette 1,165 ...... K2
72108 Monroe 250 .... H4
71655 Monticello⊙ 8,259 .. G6
71658 Montrose 641 .... H7
†72501 Moorefield 129 ..... G2
72368 Moro 327 .... H4
72110 Morrilton⊙ 7,355 ... E3
71659 Moscow 325 .... G5
72946 Mountainburg 595 .. B2
72653 Mountain Home⊙ 8,066 .. F1
71956 Mountain Pine 1,068 .. D4
72560 Mountain View⊙ 2,147 . F2
71758 Mount Holly 250 .... E7
71957 Mount Ida⊙ 1,023 .. C4
72561 Mount Pleasant 438 . G2
72111 Mount Vernon 157 .. F3
72947 Mulberry 1,444 ..... B2
71958 Murfreesboro⊙ 1,883 . C5
71852 Nashville⊙ 4,554 ... C6
72562 Newark 1,128 ...... H2
72851 New Blaine 200 .... D3
71959 Newhope 300 ...... C5
72112 Newport⊙ 8,339 ... H2
72461 Nimmons 112 ...... K1
†71601 Noble Lake 250 .... G5
72658 Norfork 399 .... F1
71960 Norman 539 .... C5
71759 Norphlet 756 ...... E7
†72801 Norristown 625 .... D3
71635 North Crossett 3,513 . G7
*72114 North Little Rock 64,288 . F4
72660 Oak Grove 265 .... C1
†71801 Oakhaven 72 .... C6
71961 Oden 186 .... C4
71853 Ogden 334 .... B6
72564 Oil Trough 280 ..... G2
72449 O'Kean 291 .... J1
71962 Okolona 200 .... D5
72853 Ola 1,121 .... D3
72662 Omaha 191 .... D1
†72110 Oppelo 486 .... E3
72370 Osceola⊙ 8,881 ... K2
72565 Oxford 520 .... G1
71855 Ozan 111 .... C6
72949 Ozark⊙ 3,597 ..... C3
72372 Paiestine 976 ...... J4
72121 Pangburn 673 ..... G3
72450 Paragould⊙ 15,248 . J1
72855 Paris⊙ 3,991 ...... C3
71661 Parkdale 471 ...... H7
72373 Parkin 2,035 ...... J3
72950 Parks 600 .... B4

†71801 Patmos 88 .... C7
72123 Patterson 567 .... H3
72453 Peach Orchard 243 .... J1
71964 Pearcy 400 .... D5
72751 Pea Ridge 1,488 ...... B1
†72104 Perla 149 .... E5
72125 Perry 254 .... E3
71801 Perrytown 282 .... C6
72126 Perryville⊙ 1,058 .... E3
72454 Piggott⊙ 3,762 ...... K1
*71601 Pine Bluff⊙ 56,636 ... F5
Pine Bluff‡ 90,718 .... F5
†72847 Piney 2,283 .... D3
72857 Plainview 752 .... D4
72568 Pleasant Plains 267 .. G2
72127 Plumerville 785 ...... E3
72455 Pocahontas⊙ 5,995 .. H1
72456 Pollard 298 .... K1
72374 Poplar Grove 300 ... J4
72457 Portia 480 .... H1
71663 Portland 701 .... H7
72858 Pottsville 564 .... D3
72458 Powhatan 49 .... H1
72128 Poyen 329 .... E5
72753 Prairie Grove 1,708 . B2
72129 Prattsville 317 ..... F5
71857 Prescott⊙ 4,103 ... D6
72672 Pyatt 217 .... E1
72131 Quitman 556 .... F3
72951 Ratcliff 197 .... C3
†72333 Ratio 250 .... J5
72459 Ravenden 338 ..... H1
72460 Ravenden Springs 230 . H1
71726 Reader 127 .... D6
72461 Rector 2,336 ...... K1
72132 Redfield 745 .... F5
71670 Reed 395 .... H6
72462 Reyno 521 .... J1
71665 Rison⊙ 1,325 ..... F6
†72104 Rockport 231 ...... E5
72134 Roe 136 .... H4
72756 Rogers 17,429 .... B1
†72355 Rondo 330 .... J4
72137 Rose Bud 202 .... F3
71858 Rosston 274 ...... D6
72952 Rudy 79 .... B2
72139 Russell 232 ...... G3
72801 Russellville⊙ 14,031 . D3
72140 Saint Charles 199 . H5
72464 Saint Francis 266 . K1
72760 Saint Paul 198 .... C2
72576 Salem⊙ 1,424 .... G1
†72658 Salesville 406 .... F1
72863 Scranton 244 ..... C3
72143 Searcy⊙ 13,612 .. G3
72465 Sedgwick 205 .... J2
†72103 Shannon Hills 1,656 . F4
72150 Sheridan⊙ 3,042 . F5
72152 Sherrill 161 ...... F5
72116 Sherwood 10,406 . F4
72153 Shirley 354 ...... F2
72577 Sidney 270 ...... G1
72761 Siloam Springs 7,940 . B1
71762 Smackover 2,453 . E7
72466 Smithville 113 ... H1
†71658 Snyder 700 ...... G7
71763 Sparkman 622 ... E6
72764 Springdale 23,458 . B1
Springdale-Fayetteville‡
177,850 ...... B1
71860 Stamps 2,859 ... D7
71667 Star City⊙ 2,066 . G6

71764 Stephens 1,366 .... E7
72159 Steprock 600 .... G3
72469 Strawberry 280 .... H2
71765 Strong 785 .... F7
72160 Stuttgart⊙ 10,941 .... H4
72865 Subiaco 744 .... C3
72470 Success 223 .... J1
72579 Sulphur Rock 316 ... H2
72768 Sulphur Springs 496 . B1
72677 Summit 506 .... E1
72471 Swifton 859 .... H2
71861 Taylor 657 .... D7
75502 Texarkana⊙ 21,459 . C7
Texarkana‡ 127,019 . C7
71766 Thornton 711 ...... F6
72166 Tichnor 350 .... H5
71670 Tillar 280 .... H6
71767 Tinsman 112 ...... F6
71851 Tollette 407 ...... C6

72770 Tontitown 615 .... B
72167 Traskwood 459 .... E
72472 Trumann 6,405 ...... J
72168 Tucker 375 .... G
72473 Tuckerman 2,078 .... H
†72015 Tull 281 .... E
72169 Tupelo 248 .... K
72384 Turrell 1,041 ...... K
72386 Tyronza 777 .... J
72170 Ulm 201 .... K
72955 Uniontown 600 ..... B2
71768 Urbana 500 .... E
72682 Valley Springs 190 . D1
72956 Van Buren⊙ 12,020 . B3
71972 Vandervoort 98 .... B
72370 Victoria 175 .... K
72173 Vilonia 736 .... G
†72002 Vimy Ridge 600 ... F
72583 Viola 362 .... G1

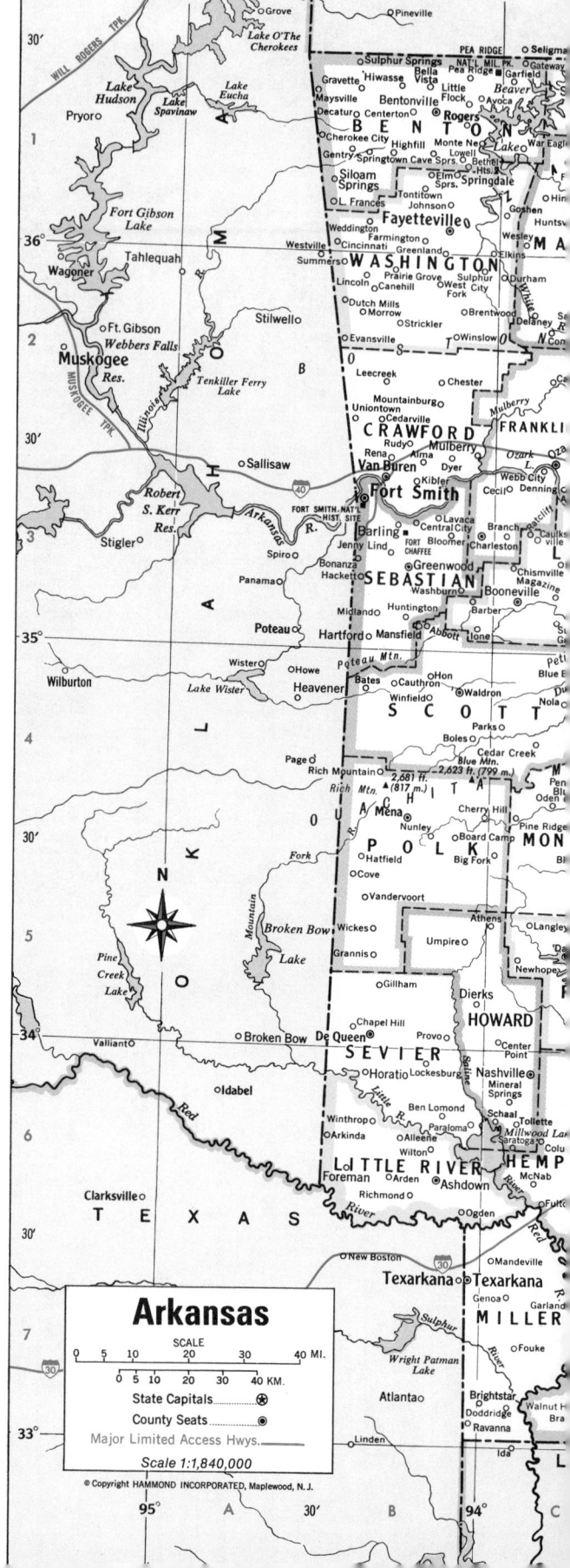

Arkansas

SCALE
0 5 10   20   30   40 MI.

0 5 10   20   30   40 KM.

State Capitals .... ⊛

County Seats .... ⊙

Major Limited Access Hwys. _____

Scale 1:1,840,000

© Copyright HAMMOND INCORPORATED, Maplewood, N.J.

California

SCALE

0 10 20 40 60 80 MI.

0 10 20 40 60 80 KM.

State Capitals..............⊛

County Seats...............◎

Canals

Major Limited Access Hwys.

Scale 1:4,400,000

San Francisco
and Vicinity

0 5 10 15 20MI.

0 5 10 15 20KM.

Sacramento
and Vicinity

0 5 10 15 20MI.

0 5 10 15 20KM.

Los Angeles
and Vicinity

0 5 10 15 20KM.

© Copyright HAMMOND INCORPORATED, Maplewood, N.J.

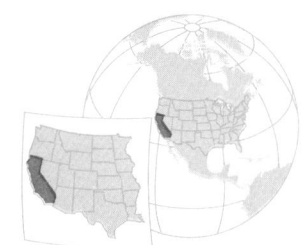

COUNTIES

Alameda 1,105,379 ....D6
Alpine 1,097 ....F5
Amador 19,314 ....E5
Butte 143,851 ....D4
Calaveras 20,710 ....E5
Colusa 12,791 ....C4
Contra Costa 656,380 ....D6
Del Norte 18,217 ....B2
El Dorado 85,812 ....E5
Fresno 514,229 ....E7
Glenn 21,350 ....C4
Humboldt 108,514 ....B3
Imperial 92,110 ....K10
Inyo 17,895 ....H7
Kern 403,089 ....G8
Kings 73,738 ....G8
Lake 36,366 ....C4
Lassen 21,661 ....E3
Los Angeles 7,477,503 ....G9
Madera 63,116 ....F6
Marin 222,592 ....C5
Mariposa 11,108 ....E6
Mendocino 66,738 ....B4
Merced 134,558 ....E6
Modoc 8,610 ....E2
Mono 8,577 ....F5
Monterey 290,444 ....D7
Napa 99,199 ....C5
Nevada 51,645 ....E4
Orange 1,932,709 ....H10
Placer 117,247 ....E4
Plumas 17,340 ....E4
Riverside 663,199 ....J10
Sacramento 783,381 ....D5
San Benito 25,005 ....D7
San Bernardino 895,016 ......J9
San Diego 1,861,846 ....J10
San Francisco (city county)
   678,974 ....J2
San Joaquin 347,342 ....D6
San Luis Obispo 155,435 .....E8
San Mateo 587,329 ....C3
Santa Barbara 298,694 ....E9
Santa Clara 1,295,071 ....D6
Santa Cruz 188,141 ....C6
Shasta 115,715 ....C3
Sierra 3,073 ....E4
Siskiyou 39,732 ....C2
Solano 235,203 ....D5
Sonoma 299,681 ....C5
Stanislaus 265,900 ....D6
Sutter 52,246 ....D4
Tehama 38,888 ....C3
Trinity 11,858 ....B3
Tulare 245,738 ....G7
Tuolumne 33,928 ....F5
Ventura 529,174 ....F9
Yolo 113,374 ....D5

Yuba 49,733 ....D4

CITIES and TOWNS

Zip	Name/Pop.	Key

94501 Alameda 63,852 ....J2
94507 Alamo 8,505 ....K2
94706 Albany 15,130 ....J2
*91801 Alhambra 64,615 ....C10
92001 Alpine 5,368 ....J11
91001 Altadena 40,983 ....C10
96101 Alturas⊙ 3,025 ....E2
†95116 Alum Rock 16,890 ....L3
*92801 Anaheim 219,494 ....D11
   Anaheim-Santa Ana-Garden
   Grove‡ 1,931,570 ....D11
96007 Anderson 7,381 ....C3
95222 Angels Camp 2,302 ....E5
94508 Angwin 3,526 ....C5
94509 Antioch 42,683 ....L1
92307 Apple Valley 14,305 ....H9
95003 Aptos 7,039 ....K4
91006 Arcadia 45,994 ....C10
95521 Arcata 12,850 ....A3
95825 Arden-Arcade 87,570 ....B8
94701 Artesia 14,301 ....C11
93203 Arvin 6,863 ....G8
†94577 Ashland 13,983 ....K2
95413 Asti 75 ....C5
93422 Atascadero 16,232 ....E8
94025 Atherton 7,797 ....K3
95301 Atwater 17,530 ....E6
95603 Auburn⊙ 7,540 ....C8
90704 Avalon 2,022 ....G10
93204 Avenal 4,137 ....E8
92315 Big Bear Lake J9
91702 Azusa 29,380 ....D10
91706 Baldwin Park 50,554 ....D10
92220 Banning 14,020 ....J10
92311 Barstow 17,690 ....H9
†93402 Baywood Park-Los
   Osos 10,933 ....E8
92223 Beaumont 6,818 ....J10
90201 Bell 25,450 ....C11
90706 Bellflower 53,441 ....C11
90201 Bell Gardens 34,117 ......C11
94002 Belmont 24,505 ....J3
94510 Benicia 15,376 ....K1
95005 Ben Lomond 7,238 ....K4
*94701 Berkeley 103,328 ....J2
*90210 Beverly Hills 32,367 ......B10
92315 Big Bear Lake J9
93920 Big Sur 500 ....D7
95514 Bishop 3,333 ....G6
92316 Bloomington 18,888 ....E10
92225 Blythe 6,805 ....L10

94923 Bodega Bay 800 ....B5
93516 Boron 2,040 ....H8
92004 Borrego Springs 1,405 ....J10
95006 Boulder Creek 5,662 ....J4
92227 Brawley 14,946 ....K11
92621 Brea 27,913 ....D11
94513 Brentwood 4,434 ....L2
93517 Bridgeport⊙ 525 ....F5
94005 Brisbane 2,969 ....J2
95605 Broderick-Bryte 10,194 ...B8
*90622 Buena Park 64,165 ....D11
*91501 Burbank 84,625 ....C10
94010 Burlingame 26,173 ....J2
96013 Burney 3,187 ....D3
92231 Calexico 14,412 ....K11
93505 California City 2,743 ....H8
94515 Calistoga 3,879 ....C5
93745 Calwa 6,640 ....F7
93010 Camarillo 37,797 ....F9
95008 Campbell 26,910 ....K3
*91303 Canoga Park B10
92624 Capistrano Beach 6,168 ..H10
95010 Capitola 9,095 ....K4
92007 Cardiff-by-the-Sea 10,054 H10
92008 Carlsbad 35,490 ....H10
93923 Carmel 4,707 ....D7
93924 Carmel Valley 4,013 ....D7
95608 Carmichael 43,108 ....C8
93013 Carpinteria 10,835 ....F9
90745 Carson 81,221 ....C11
94546 Castro Valley 44,011 ....K2
95012 Castroville 4,396 ....D7
92234 Cathedral City 4,130 ......J10
96019 Central Valley 3,424 ....C3
95307 Ceres 13,281 ....D6
†90701 Cerritos 53,020 ....C11
†94541 Cherryland 9,425 ....K2
95926 Chico 26,603 ....D4
   Chico‡ 143,851 ....D4
†93555 China Lake 4,275 ....H8
95309 Chinese Camp 150 ....E6
91710 Chino 40,165 ....D10
93610 Chowchilla 5,122 ....E6
*92010 Chula Vista 83,927 ....J11
95610 Citrus Heights 85,911 ......C8
91711 Claremont 30,950 ....D10
95425 Cloverdale 3,989 ....K5
93612 Clovis 33,021 ....F7
92236 Coachella 9,129 ....J10
93210 Coalinga 6,593 ....E7
95713 Colfax 981 ....E4
92324 Colton 15,201 ....E10
95932 Colusa⊙ 4,075 ....C4
90040 Commerce 10,509 ....C10
*90220 Compton 81,286 ....C11
94520 Concord 103,255 ....K1
93212 Corcoran 6,454 ....F7
94021 Corning 4,745 ....C4
91720 Corona 37,791 ....E11
92118 Coronado 16,859 ....J11
94925 Corte Madera 8,074 ....J2
*92626 Costa Mesa 82,562 ....D11
94928 Cotati 3,346 ....C5
*91722 Covina 33,751 ....D10
95531 Crescent City⊙ 3,075 ......A2
92325 Crestline 6,715 ....H9
90201 Cudahy 17,984 ....C11
90230 Culver City 38,139 ....B10
95014 Cupertino 34,265 ....K3
*92640 Garden Grove 123,307 ...D11
95020 Gilroy 21,641 ....D6
93615 Cutler 3,149 ....F7
90630 Cypress 40,391 ....D11
*94014 Daly City 78,519 ....H2
92629 Dana Point 10,602 ....H10
94526 Danville 26,446 ....K2
95616 Davis 36,640 ....B8
93215 Delano 16,491 ....F8
95315 Delhi 2,832 ....E6
92014 Del Mar 5,017 ....H11
92240 Desert Hot Springs 5,941 ..J9
93618 Dinuba 9,907 ....F7
95620 Dixon 7,541 ....B9
93620 Dos Palos 3,121 ....E6
*90240 Downey 82,602 ....C11
95936 Downieville⊙ 500 ....E4

91010 Duarte 16,766 ....D10
94566 Dublin 13,496 ....K2
93219 Earlimart 4,578 ....F8
90022 East Los Angeles 100,017 C10
*92020 El Cajon 73,892 ....J11
92243 El Centro⊙ 23,996 ....K11
94530 El Cerrito 22,731 ....J2
95630 El Dorado Hills 3,453 ......C8
94018 El Granada 3,582 ....H3
95624 Elk Grove 10,959 ....B9
90245 El Segundo 13,752 ....B11
92630 El Toro 38,153 ....E11
94608 Emeryville 3,714 ....J2
92024 Encinitas 10,796 ....H10
91316 Encino B10
95320 Escalon 3,127 ....E6
*92025 Escondido 64,355 ....J10
93221 Exeter 5,606 ....F7
94533 Fairfield 58,099 ....K1
95628 Fair Oaks 22,602 ....C8
92028 Fallbrook 14,041 ....H10
93223 Farmersville 5,544 ....F7
95018 Felton 4,564 ....K4
93015 Fillmore 9,602 ....G9
93622 Firebaugh 3,740 ....E7
95828 Florin 16,523 ....B8
95630 Folsom 11,003 ....C8
92335 Fontana 37,107 ....E10
†93268 Ford City 3,392 ....F8
94538 Fremont 131,945 ....K3
*93706 Fresno⊙ 217,289 ....F7
   Fresno‡ 515,013 ....F7
*92631 Fullerton 102,034 ....D11
95632 Galt 5,514 ....C9
*90747 Gardena 45,165 ....C11
*92640 Garden Grove 123,307 ...D11
95020 Gilroy 21,641 ....D6
92509 Glen Avon Heights 8,444 ..E10
*91201 Glendale 139,060 ....C10
91740 Glendora 38,500 ....D10
93926 Gonzales 2,891 ....D7
91344 Granada Hills B10
92324 Grand Terrace 8,498 ......E10
95945 Grass Valley 6,697 ....D4
93308 Greenacres 5,381 ....F8
93927 Greenfield 4,181 ....D7
95948 Gridley 3,982 ....D4
93433 Grover City 8,827 ....E8
93434 Guadalupe 3,629 ....E9
95322 Gustine 3,142 ....D6
94019 Half Moon Bay 7,282 ....H3
93230 Hanford⊙ 20,958 ....F7
90250 Hawthorne 56,447 ....C11
*94541 Hayward 94,342 ....K2
95448 Healdsburg 7,217 ....B5
92343 Hemet 22,454 ....H10
94547 Hercules 5,963 ....J1
90254 Hermosa Beach 18,070 ..B11
92345 Hesperia 13,540 ....H9
92346 Highland 10,908 ....H9
94010 Hillsborough 10,372 ....J2
95023 Hollister⊙ 11,488 ....D7

90028 Hollywood C10
92250 Holtville 4,399 ....K11
†91720 Home Gardens 5,783 ....E11
95326 Hughson 2,943 ....E6
*92646 Huntington Beach 170,505 C11
90255 Huntington Park 46,223 ..C11
92251 Imperial 3,451 ....K11
92032 Imperial Beach 22,689 ....H11
93526 Independence⊙ 748 ....H7
92201 Indio 21,611 ....J10
*90301 Inglewood 94,245 ....B11
92713 Irvine 62,134 ....D11
95642 Jackson⊙ 2,331 ....C9
*94701 Kensington 5,342 ....J2
93600 Kerman 4,002 ....E7
93930 King City 5,495 ....D7
93631 Kingsburg 5,115 ....F7
91011 La Canada 20,153 ....C10
91214 La Crescenta-
   Montrose 16,531 ....C10
95651 Lafayette 20,879 ....K2
*92651 Laguna Beach 17,901 ...G10
92653 Laguna Hills 13,600 ....D11
92677 Laguna Niguel 12,237 ....H10
90631 La Habra 45,232 ....D11
92037 La Jolla H11
92352 Lake Arrowhead 6,272 ....H9
92330 Lake Elsinore 5,982 ....F11
93240 Lake Isabella 3,428 ....G8
95453 Lakeport⊙ 3,675 ....C4
*90712 Lakewood 74,654 ....C11
92041 La Mesa 50,308 ....H11
90638 La Mirada 40,986 ....D11
93241 Lamont 9,616 ....G8
93534 Lancaster 48,027 ....G9
*91744 La Puente 30,882 ....D10
94939 Larkspur 11,064 ....H1
95330 Lathrop 3,717 ....D6
91750 La Verne 23,508 ....D10
90260 Lawndale 23,460 ....B11
92045 Lemon Grove 20,780 ....J11
93245 Lemoore 8,832 ....F7
†92311 Leucadia⊙ 2,974 ....H9
92024 Leucadia 9,478 ....H10
95648 Lincoln 4,132 ....B8
†95901 Linda 10,225 ....D4
93247 Lindsay 6,924 ....F7
95953 Live Oak 3,103 ....D4
†95073 Live Oak 11,482 ....K4
94550 Livermore 48,349 ....L2
95334 Livingston 5,326 ....E6
95240 Lodi 35,221 ....C9
92354 Loma Linda 10,694 ....F10
90717 Lomita 18,807 ....C11
93436 Lompoc 26,267 ....E9
*90801 Long Beach 361,334 ....C11
90720 Los Alamitos 11,529 ......D11
94022 Los Altos 25,769 ....K3
94022 Los Altos Hills 7,421 ....J3
*90001 Los Angeles⊙ 2,966,850 C10
   Los Angeles-Long Beach‡
   7,477,657 ....C10
93635 Los Banos 10,341 ....E6
95030 Los Gatos 26,906 ....K4
†93402 Los Osos-Baywood
   Park 10,933 ....E8
90262 Lynwood 48,548 ....C11
93637 Madera⊙ 21,732 ....F7
90265 Malibu B10
93546 Mammoth Lakes 3,929 ....G6
90266 Manhattan Beach 31,542 ..B11
95336 Manteca 24,925 ....D6
93933 Marina 20,647 ....D7
95338 Mariposa⊙ 1,150 ....F6
94553 Martinez⊙ 22,582 ....K1
95901 Marysville⊙ 9,898 ....D4
90201 Maywood 21,810 ....C10
93250 McFarland 5,151 ....F8
93023 Meiners Oaks-Mira
   Monte 9,512 ....F9
93640 Mendota 5,038 ....E7
94025 Menlo Park 26,369 ....J3
95340 Merced⊙ 36,499 ....E6
94030 Millbrae 20,058 ....J2
94941 Mill Valley 12,967 ....H2
95035 Milpitas 37,820 ....L3
91752 Mira Loma 8,707 ....E10
92691 Mission Viejo 50,666 ......D11
*95350 Modesto⊙ 106,602 ....D6
   Modesto‡ 265,902 ....D6
93501 Mojave 2,886 ....H8
91016 Monrovia 30,531 ....D10
91763 Montclair 22,628 ....D10
90640 Montebello 52,929 ....C10
93940 Monterey 27,558 ....D7
91754 Monterey Park 54,338 ....C10
95030 Mont Sereno 3,434 ....K4
91214 Montrose-La
   Crescenta 16,531 ....C10
93021 Moorpark 4,030 ....G9
94556 Moraga 15,014 ....K2
95037 Morgan Hill 17,060 ....L4
93442 Morro Bay 9,064 ....D8
*94042 Mountain View 58,655 ....K3

96067 Mount Shasta 2,837 ....C5
92405 Muscoy 6,188 ....E10
94558 Napa⊙ 50,879 ....C5
92050 National City 48,772 ....J11
92363 Needles 4,120 ....L9
95959 Nevada City⊙ 2,431 ....D4
94560 Newark 32,126 ....K3
91321 Newhall 12,029 ....G9
95360 Newman 2,785 ....D6
*92660 Newport Beach 62,556 ...D11
93444 Nipomo 5,247 ....E8
91760 Norco 21,126 ....E11
95660 North Highlands 37,825 ...B8
*91601 North Hollywood B10
90650 Norwalk 85,286 ....C11
94947 Novato 43,916 ....H1
95361 Oakdale 8,474 ....E6
*94601 Oakland⊙ 339,337 ....J2
93022 Oak View 4,671 ....F9
93445 Oceano 4,478 ....E8
92054 Oceanside 76,698 ....H10
93308 Oildale 23,382 ....F8
93023 Ojai 6,816 ....F9
*91761 Ontario 88,820 ....D10
†95060 Opal Cliffs 5,101 ....K4
*92666 Orange 91,450 ....D11
93646 Orange Cove 4,026 ....D7
94563 Orinda 16,825 ....J2
95963 Orland 4,031 ....C4
93647 Orosi 4,076 ....F7
95965 Oroville⊙ 8,683 ....D4
93030 Oxnard 108,195 ....F9
   Oxnard-Simi Valley-
   Ventura‡ 529,899 ....F9
94553 Pacheco-Vine Hill 6,129 ..K1
94044 Pacifica 36,866 ....H2
93550 Palmdale 12,277 ....G9
92260 Palm Desert 11,801 ....J10
92262 Palm Springs 32,366 ....J10
*94301 Palo Alto 55,225 ....K3
90274 Palos Verdes
   Estates 14,376 ....B11
95969 Paradise 22,571 ....D4
90723 Paramount 36,407 ....C11
93648 Parlier 2,902 ....F7
*91101 Pasadena 118,072 ....C10
93446 Paso Robles 9,163 ....E8
95363 Patterson 3,908 ....D6
93953 Pebble Beach C7
92370 Perris 6,827 ....F11
94952 Petaluma 33,834 ....H1
90660 Pico Rivera 53,387 ....C10
94611 Piedmont 10,498 ....J2
94564 Pinole 14,253 ....J1
93449 Pismo Beach 5,364 ....E8
94565 Pittsburg 33,034 ....L1
92670 Placentia 35,041 ....D11
95667 Placerville⊙ 6,739 ....C8
94523 Pleasant Hill 25,124 ....K2
94566 Pleasanton 35,160 ....L2
*91766 Pomona 92,742 ....D10
93257 Porterville 19,707 ....G7
93041 Port Hueneme 17,803 ......F9
94025 Portola Valley 3,939 ....J3
92064 Poway 32,263 ....J11
93534 Quartz Hill 7,421 ....G9
95971 Quincy⊙ 4,451 ....E4
92065 Ramona 8,173 ....J10
95670 Rancho Cordova 42,881 ..C8
91730 Rancho Cucamonga
   55,250 ....E10
92270 Rancho Mirage 6,281 ......J10
90274 Rancho Palos
   Verdes 36,577 ....B11
92067 Rancho Santa Fe 4,014 ...H10
96080 Red Bluff⊙ 9,490 ....C3
96001 Redding⊙ 41,995 ....C3
   Redding‡ 80
92373 Redlands 43,619 ....H9
*90277 Redondo Beach 57,102 ...B11
*94061 Redwood City⊙ 54,951 ...J3
93654 Reedley 11,071 ....F7
91335 Reseda B10
92501 Rialto 37,474 ....E10
*94801 Richmond 74,676 ....J1
93555 Ridgecrest 15,929 ....H8
95562 Rio Dell 2,687 ....A3
95670 Rio Linda 7,359 ....B8
94571 Rio Vista 3,142 ....L1
95366 Ripon 3,509 ....D6
95367 Riverbank 5,695 ....E6
*92501 Riverside⊙ 170,591 ....E11
   Riverside-San Bernardino-
   Ontario‡ 1,557,080 ....E11
95677 Rocklin 7,344 ....B8
94572 Rodeo 8,286 ....J1
94928 Rohnert Park 22,965 ....C5
90274 Rolling Hills 2,049 ....B11
90274 Rolling Hills
   Estates 7,701 ....B11
91770 Rosemead 42,604 ....C10
95678 Roseville 24,347 ....B8
94957 Ross 2,801 ....H1
92509 Rubidoux 17,048 ....E10

(continued on following page)

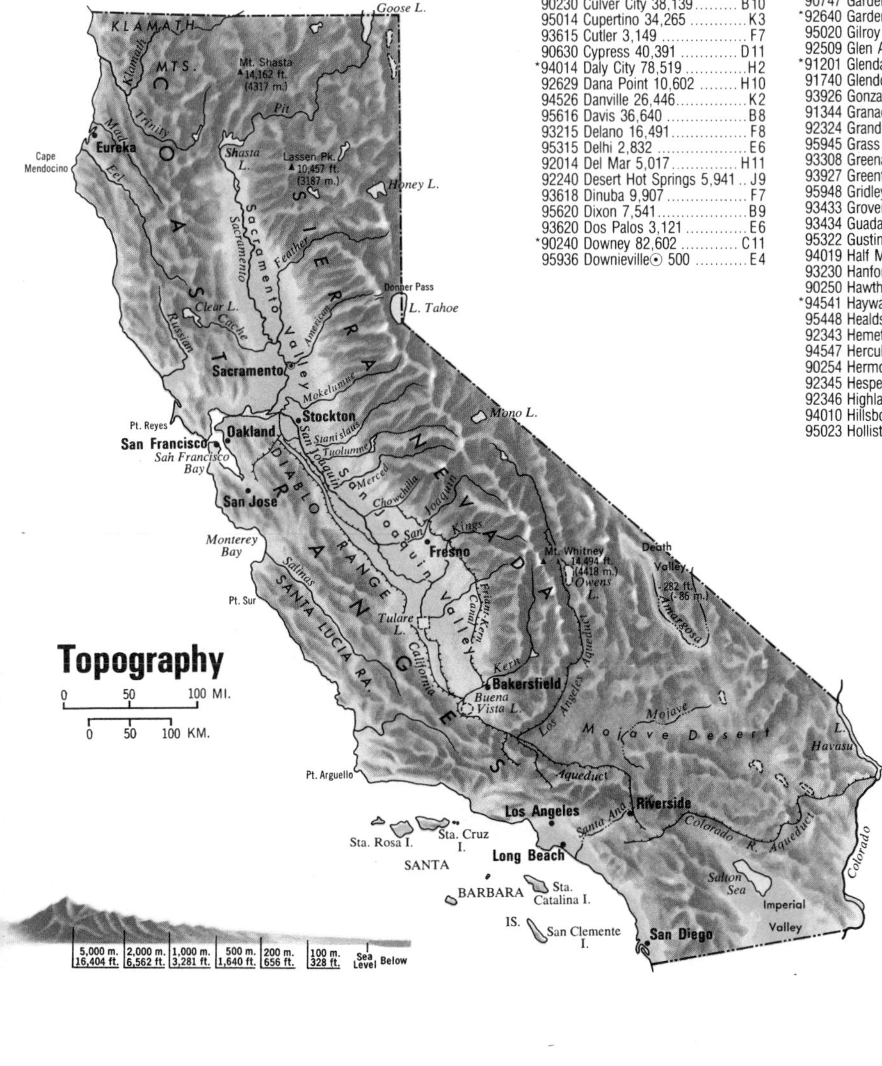

AREA / POPULATION

AREA 158,706 sq. mi. (411,049 sq. km.)
POPULATION 23,667,565
CAPITAL Sacramento
LARGEST CITY Los Angeles
HIGHEST POINT Mt. Whitney 14,494 ft.
   (4418 m.)
SETTLED IN 1769
ADMITTED TO UNION September 9, 1850
POPULAR NAME Golden State
STATE FLOWER Golden Poppy
STATE BIRD California Valley Quail

Topography

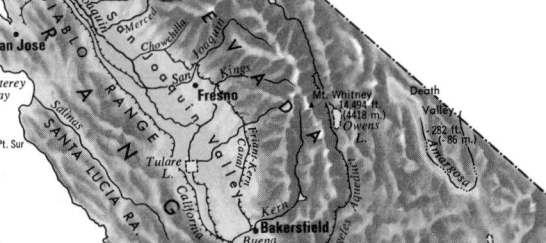

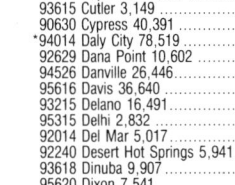
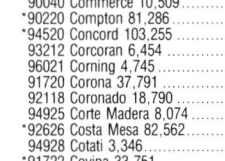

0   50   100 MI.

0   50   100 KM.

5,000 m.	2,000 m.	1,000 m.	500 m.	200 m.	100 m.	Sea	Below
16,404 ft.	6,562 ft.	3,281 ft.	1,640 ft.	656 ft.	328 ft.	Level	

*95801 Sacramento (cap.)⊙ 275,741 ... B8
Sacramento‡ 1,014,002 ... B8
94574 Saint Helena 4,898 ... C5
93901 Salinas⊙ 80,479 ... D7
Salinas-Seaside-Monterey‡ 290,444 ... D7
95249 San Andreas⊙ 1,912 ... E5
94960 San Anselmo 12,067 ... H1
*92401 San Bernardino⊙ 118,794 ... E10
94066 San Bruno 35,417 ... J2
94070 San Carlos 24,710 ... J3
92672 San Clemente 27,325 ... H10
*92101 San Diego⊙ 875,538 ... H11
San Diego‡ 1,861,846 ... H11
91773 San Dimas 24,014 ... D10
*91340 San Fernando 17,731 ... C10
*94101 San Francisco⊙ 678,974 ... H2
San Francisco-Oakland‡ 3,252,721 ... H2
*91775 San Gabriel 30,072 ... C10
93657 Sanger 12,542 ... F7
92383 San Jacinto 7,098 ... H10
*95101 San Jose⊙ 629,546 ... L3
San Jose‡ 1,295,071 ... L3
†92691 San Juan Capistrano 18,959 ... H10
*94577 San Leandro 63,952 ... J2
94580 San Lorenzo 20,545 ... K2
93401 San Luis Obispo⊙ 34,252 ... E8
92069 San Marcos 17,479 ... H10
91108 San Marino 13,307 ... D10
*94401 San Mateo 77,640 ... J3
94806 San Pablo 19,750 ... J1
94964 San Quentin 450 ... H1
*94901 San Rafael⊙ 44,700 ... J1
94583 San Ramon 22,356 ... K2
93452 San Simeon 350 ... D8
*92701 Santa Ana⊙ 204,023 ... D11
*93101 Santa Barbara⊙ 74,414 ... F9
Santa Barbara-Santa Maria-Lompoc‡ 298,660 ... F9
*95050 Santa Clara 87,700 ... K3
*95060 Santa Cruz⊙ 41,483 ... K4
Santa Cruz‡ 188,141 ... K4
90670 Santa Fe Springs 14,520 ... C11
93454 Santa Maria 39,685 ... E9
*90401 Santa Monica 88,314 ... B10
93060 Santa Paula 20,552 ... F9
*95401 Santa Rosa⊙ 83,320 ... C5
Santa Rosa‡ 299,827 ... C5
92071 Santee 47,080 ... J11
95070 Saratoga 29,261 ... K4
94965 Sausalito 7,338 ... H2
95060 Scotts Valley 6,891 ... K4
90740 Seal Beach 25,975 ... C11
93955 Seaside 36,567 ... D7
95472 Sebastopol 5,595 ... C5
93662 Selma 10,942 ... F7
93263 Shafter 7,010 ... F8
96125 Sierra City 500 ... E4
91024 Sierra Madre 10,837 ... D10
†90806 Signal Hill 5,734 ... C11
*93065 Simi Valley 77,500 ... G9
92075 Solana Beach 13,047 ... H11
93960 Soledad 5,928 ... D7
93463 Solvang 3,091 ... E9
95476 Sonoma 6,054 ... C5
95370 Sonora⊙ 3,247 ... E6
95073 Soquel 6,212 ... K4
91733 South El Monte 16,623 ... C10
90280 South Gate 66,784 ... C11
95705 South Lake Tahoe 20,681 ... F5
†95965 South Oroville 7,246 ... D4
91030 South Pasadena 22,681 ... C10
94080 South San Francisco 49,393 ... J2
94305 Stanford 11,045 ... J3
90680 Stanton 23,723 ... D11
*95201 Stockton⊙ 149,779 ... D6
Stockton‡ 347,342 ... D6
94585 Suisun City 11,087 ... K1
92381 Sun City 8,460 ... F11
92388 Sunnymead 11,554 ... F11
*94086 Sunnyvale 106,618 ... K3
96130 Susanville⊙ 6,520 ... E3
95685 Sutter Creek 1,705 ... C9
93268 Taft 5,316 ... F8
95730 Tahoe City ... E4
93561 Tehachapi 4,126 ... G8
91780 Temple City 28,972 ... D10
†95965 Thermalito 4,961 ... D4
*91360 Thousand Oaks 77,072 ... G9
92276 Thousand Palms 1,718 ... J10
94920 Tiburon 6,685 ... J2
90290 Topanga ... B10
*90501 Torrance 129,881 ... C11
95376 Tracy 18,428 ... D6
93274 Tulare 22,526 ... F7
95380 Turlock 26,287 ... E6
92680 Tustin 32,317 ... D11
92277 Twentynine Palms 7,465 ... K9
†95060 Twin Lakes 4,502 ... K4
95482 Ukiah⊙ 12,035 ... B4
94587 Union City 39,406 ... K2
91786 Upland 47,647 ... E10
95688 Vacaville 43,367 ... D5
91355 Valencia 12,163 ... G9
94590 Vallejo 80,303 ... J1
Vallejo-Fairfield-Napa‡ 334,402 ... J1
*91401 Van Nuys ... B10
90291 Venice ... B11
*93001 Ventura⊙ 74,393 ... F9
92392 Victorville 14,220 ... H9
92667 Villa Park 7,137 ... D11
93277 Visalia⊙ 49,729 ... F7
Visalia-Tulare-Porterville‡ 245,738 ... F7
92083 Vista 35,834 ... H10
91789 Walnut 12,478 ... D10
*94595 Walnut Creek 53,643 ... K2
93280 Wasco 9,613 ... F8
95386 Waterford 2,683 ... E6
95076 Watsonville 23,663 ... D7
96093 Weaverville⊙ 2,787 ... B3
96094 Weed 2,879 ... C2
*91790 West Covina 80,291 ... D10
†90069 West Hollywood 35,703 ... B10
90025 West Los Angeles ... B10
92683 Westminster 71,133 ... D11
†90047 Westmont 27,916 ... C11
†94565 West Pittsburg 8,773 ... K1
95691 West Sacramento 10,875 ... B8
*90601 Whittier 69,717 ... D11
95490 Willits 4,008 ... B4
95988 Willows⊙ 4,777 ... C4
*90744 Wilmington ... C11
95388 Winton 4,995 ... E6
93286 Woodlake 4,343 ... G7
95695 Woodland⊙ 30,235 ... B8
*91364 Woodland Hills ... B10
94062 Woodside 5,291 ... J3
95697 Yolo 600 ... B8
92686 Yorba Linda 28,254 ... D11
94599 Yountville 2,893 ... C5
96097 Yreka⊙ 5,916 ... C2
95991 Yuba City⊙ 18,736 ... D4
Yuba City‡ 101,979 ... D4
92399 Yucaipa 23,345 ... J9
92284 Yucca Valley 8,294 ... J9

OTHER FEATURES

Agua Caliente Ind. Res. ... J10
Alameda (creek) ... K3
Alamo (riv.) ... K10
Alcatraz (isl.) ... J2
Alkali (lkes) ... E2
All American (canal) ... K11
Almanor (lake) ... D3
Amargosa (range) ... J7
Amargosa (riv.) ... J7
American (riv.) ... C8
Anacapa (isl.) ... F10
Angel (isl.) ... J2
Ano Nuevo (pt.) ... J4
Arena (pt.) ... B5
Arguello (pt.) ... E9
Argus (range) ... H7
Arroyo del Valle (dry riv.) ... L3
Arroyo Hondo (dry riv.) ... L3
Arroyo Mocho (dry riv.) ... L2
Arroyo Seco (dry riv.) ... K10
Beale A.F.B. ... D4
Berryessa (lake) ... D5
Bethany (res.) ... L2
Big Sage (res.) ... E2
Black Butte (lake) ... C4
Bodega (bay) ... B5
Bonita (pt.) ... H2
Bristol (lake) ... K9
Buchon (pt.) ... D8
Buena Vista (lake) ... F8
Cabrillo Nat'l Mon. ... H11
Cachuma (lake) ... F9
Cadiz (lake) ... K9
Cahuilla Ind. Res. ... J10
Calaveras (res.) ... L3
California Aqueduct ... E7
Camanche (res.) ... C9
Camp Pendleton 10,017 ... H10
Campo Ind. Res. ... J11
Capitan Grande Ind. Res. ... J11
Cascade (range) ... D1
Castle A.F.B. ... E6
Channel Islands Nat'l Park ... E11
China Lake Naval Weapons Center ... H8
Chemehuevi Valley Ind. Res. ... L9
Chocolate (mts.) ... K10
Clair Engle (lake) ... C3
Clear (lake) ... C4
Clear Lake (res.) ... D2
Coachella (canal) ... K10
Coast (ranges) ... D7
Colorado (riv.) ... L8
Colorado River Aqueduct ... K10
Colorado River Ind. Res. ... L10
Conception (pt.) ... E9
Cooper (pt.) ... D7
Copco (lake) ... C2
Cosumnes (riv.) ... C9
Cottonwood (creek) ... C3
Coyote (res.) ... L4
Crowley (lake) ... G6
Crystal Springs (res.) ... J3
Cuyama (riv.) ... E8
Cuyapaipe Ind. Res. ... J11
Danby (lake) ... K9
Death (valley) ... H7
Death Valley Nat'l Mon. ... H7
Delgada (pt.) ... A3
Del Valle (lake) ... L3
Devils Postpile Nat'l Mon. ... F6
Donner (pass) ... E4
Dume (pt.) ... G10
Duxbury (pt.) ... H2
Eagle (lake) ... E3
Eagle (peak) ... E2
Eagle Crags (mt.) ... J8
Edison (lake) ... F6
Edwards A.F.B. 8,554 ... H9
Eel (riv.) ... B4
Elsinore (lake) ... E11
El Toro Marine Air Sta. 7,632 ... D11
Estero (bay) ... D8
Estero (pt.) ... D8
Estrella (riv.) ... E8
Eugene O'Neill Nat'l Hist. Site ... K2
Farallon (isls.) ... B6
Farallons, The (gulf) ... H2
Feather (riv.) ... D4
Florence (lake) ... G6
Folsom (lake) ... C8
Fort Bidwell Ind. Res. ... E2
Fort Hunter Liggett ... D8
Fort Independence Ind. Res. ... G7
Fort MacArthur ... C11
Fort Mohave Ind. Res. ... L9
Fort Ord ... D7
Fort Point Nat'l Hist. Site ... J2
Freel (peak) ... F5
Fremont (peak) ... H8
Fresno (riv.) ... E7
Friant-Kern (canal) ... F8
General Grant Grove Section (King's Canyon) ... G7
George A.F.B. 7,061 ... H9
Golden Gate (chan.) ... H2
Golden Gate Nat'l Rec. Area ... H2
Goose (lake) ... E1
Grapevine (mts.) ... H7
Grizzly (bay) ... K1
Guadalupe (riv.) ... K3
Haiwee ... H7
Hamilton (mt.) ... L3
Hat (peak) ... E2
Havasu (lake) ... L9
Hetch Hetchy (res.) ... F6
Hoffman (mt.) ... D2
Honey (lake) ... E3
Hoopa Valley Ind. Res. ... A2
Humboldt (bay) ... A3
Imperial (res.) ... L10
Imperial (valley) ... K10
Ingalls (mt.) ... E3
Inyo (mts.) ... G6
Iron Gate (res.) ... C2
Isabella (lake) ... G8
John Muir Nat'l Hist. Site ... K1
Joshua Tree Nat'l Mon. ... J10
Kern (riv.) ... G8
Kings (riv.) ... F7
Kings Canyon Nat'l Park ... G7
Klamath (riv.) ... B2
Laguna (res.) ... L11
La Jolla Ind. Res. ... J10
Lassen (peak) ... D3
Lassen Volcanic Nat'l Park ... D3
Lava Beds Nat'l Mon. ... D2
Lemoore N.A.S. 5,888 ... F7
Leroy Anderson (res.) ... L4
Lopez (pt.) ... D7
Los Angeles Aqueduct ... G8
Los Coyotes Ind. Res. ... J10
Lost (riv.) ... D1
Lower Alkali (lake) ... E2
Lower Klamath (lake) ... D2
Mad (riv.) ... B3
Manzanita Ind. Res. ... J11
March A.F.B. 3,607 ... E11
Mare Island Navy Yard ... J1
Mather A.F.B. 5,245 ... C8
Mathews (lake) ... E11
McClellan A.F.B. ... B8
McClure (lake) ... E6
Mendocino (cape) ... A3
Merced (riv.) ... E6
Middle Alkali (lake) ... E2
Mill (creek) ... D3
Millerton (lake) ... F6
Moffett Nav. Air Sta. ... K3
Mojave (des.) ... H9
Mojave (riv.) ... J9
Mokelumne (riv.) ... C9
Mono (lake) ... G5
Monterey (bay) ... K4
Moon (lake) ... E2
Morongo Ind. Res. ... J10
Mountain Meadows (res.) ... E3
Muir Woods Nat'l Mon. ... H2
Nacimiento (riv.) ... D8
Navarro (riv.) ... B4
Nevada, Sierra (mts.) ... E4
New (riv.) ... K11
Norton A.F.B. ... F10
Noyo (riv.) ... B4
Oakland Army Base ... J2
Old (riv.) ... L1
Oroville (lake) ... D4
Owens (lake) ... H7
Owens (peak) ... H8
Owens (riv.) ... G6
Oxnard A.F.B. ... F9
Paiute Ind. Res. ... G6
Pala Ind. Res. ... H10
Palomar (mt.) ... J10
Panamint (range) ... H7
Panamint (valley) ... H7
Pescadero (pt.) ... J3
Piedras Blancas (pt.) ... D8
Pillar (pt.) ... H3
Pillsbury (lake) ... C4
Pine (creek) ... D3
Pine Flat (lake) ... F7
Pinnacles Nat'l Mon. ... D7
Pit (riv.) ... D2
Point Mugu Pacific Missile Test Center ... F9
Point Reyes Nat'l Seashore ... H1
Presidio ... J2
Providence (mts.) ... K8
Punta Gorda (pt.) ... A3
Quartz (peak) ... L11
Railroad Canyon (res.) ... E11
Redwood Nat'l Park ... A2
Reyes (pt.) ... B6
Rogers (lake) ... H9
Rosamond (lake) ... G9
Round Valley Ind. Res. ... B4
Russian (riv.) ... B4
Sacramento (riv.) ... D5
Sacramento Army Depot ... B8
Saint George (pt.) ... A2
Salinas (riv.) ... D7
Salmon (riv.) ... B2
Salton Sea (lake) ... K10
San Andreas (lake) ... H2
San Antonio (lake) ... E8
San Benito (riv.) ... D7
San Bernardino (mts.) ... J10
San Clemente (isl.) ... G11
San Diego (bay) ... H11
San Francisco (bay) ... J2
San Gabriel (res.) ... D10
San Joaquin (riv.) ... E6
San Joaquin (valley) ... D6
San Lorenzo (riv.) ... K4
San Luis (res.) ... E7
San Martin (cape) ... D8
San Miguel (isl.) ... E9
San Nicolas (isl.) ... F10
San Pablo (bay) ... J1
San Pedro (bay) ... C11
Santa Ana (riv.) ... E11
Santa Barbara (chan.) ... E9
Santa Barbara (isl.) ... G10
Santa Barbara (isls.) ... F10
Santa Catalina (gulf) ... G11
Santa Catalina (isl.) ... G10
Santa Cruz (chan.) ... F10
Santa Cruz (isl.) ... F10
Santa Maria (riv.) ... E9
Santa Monica (bay) ... B11
Santa Rosa (isl.) ... E10
Santa Rosa Ind. Res. ... J10
Santa Ynez (riv.) ... E9
Santa Ysabel Ind. Res. ... J10
Searles (lake) ... H8
Sequoia Nat'l Park ... G7
Sharpe Army Depot ... D6
Shasta (lake) ... C3
Shasta (mt.) ... C2
Shasta (riv.) ... C2
Sierra Army Depot ... E3
Sierra Nevada (mts.) ... E4
Siskiyou (mts.) ... C2
Smith (riv.) ... A2
Soda (lake) ... K8
South Bay Aqueduct ... L2
South Cow (creek) ... C3
Stony Gorge (res.) ... C4
Suisun (bay) ... K1
Sur (pt.) ... D7
Tahoe (lake) ... F4
Tamalpais (mt.) ... H1
Tehachapi (mts.) ... G9
Telescope (peak) ... H7
Tomales (pt.) ... B5
Torres Martinez Ind. Res. ... J10
Travis A.F.B. ... L1
Trinidad (head) ... A2
Trinity (riv.) ... B3
Truckee (riv.) ... F4
Tulare (lake) ... F7
Tule (lake) ... D2
Tule River Ind. Res. ... G7
Twentynine Palms Marine Base 7,079 ... J9
Twitchell (res.) ... E9
Upper Alkali (lake) ... E2
Vandenberg A.F.B. 8,136 ... E9
Vizcaino (cape) ... B4
Walnut (creek) ... K1
Wheeler (peak) ... F5
Whipple (mts.) ... L9
Whiskeytown-Shasta-Trinity Nat'l Rec. Area ... C3
Whitney (mt.) ... G7
Willow (creek) ... E3
Wilson (mt.) ... D10
Yosemite Nat'l Park ... F6
Yuba (riv.) ... D4
Yuma Ind. Res. ... L11

⊙County seat.
‡Population of metropolitan area.
† Zip of nearest p.o. * Multiple zips.

Agriculture, Industry and Resources

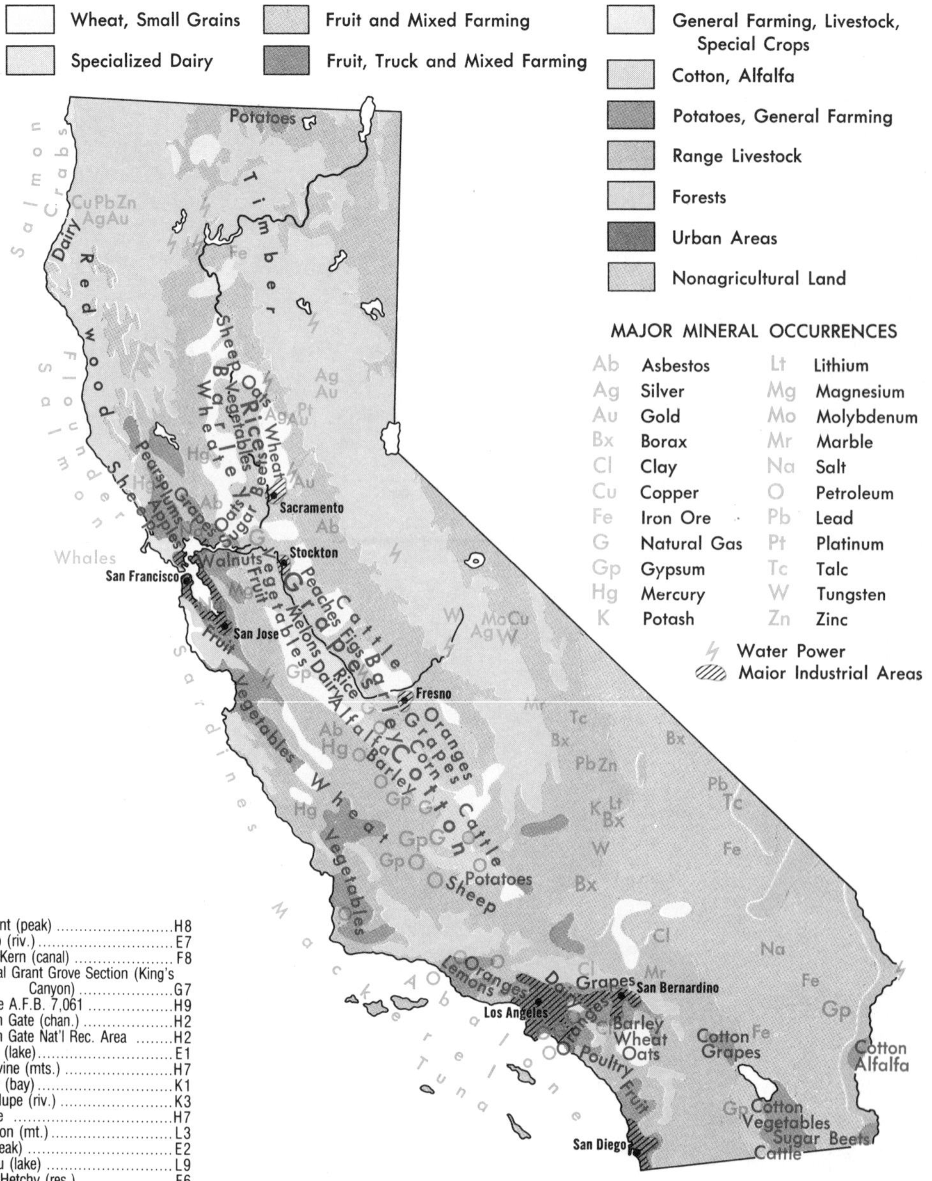
DOMINANT LAND USE
Wheat, Small Grains
Specialized Dairy
Fruit and Mixed Farming
Fruit, Truck and Mixed Farming
General Farming, Livestock, Special Crops
Cotton, Alfalfa
Potatoes, General Farming
Range Livestock
Forests
Urban Areas
Nonagricultural Land
MAJOR MINERAL OCCURRENCES
Ab Asbestos
Ag Silver
Au Gold
Bx Borax
Cl Clay
Cu Copper
Fe Iron Ore
G Natural Gas
Gp Gypsum
Hg Mercury
K Potash
Lt Lithium
Mg Magnesium
Mo Molybdenum
Mr Marble
Na Salt
O Petroleum
Pb Lead
Pt Platinum
Tc Talc
W Tungsten
Zn Zinc
Water Power
Major Industrial Areas
Sacramento
Stockton
San Francisco
San Jose
Fresno
Los Angeles
San Bernardino
San Diego
Salmon
Crabs
Dairy
Redwood
Timber
Whales
Sardines
Mackerel
Albacore
Tuna
Potatoes
Cattle
Sheep
Grapes
Cotton
Barley
Wheat
Oats
Vegetables
Sugar Beets
Alfalfa

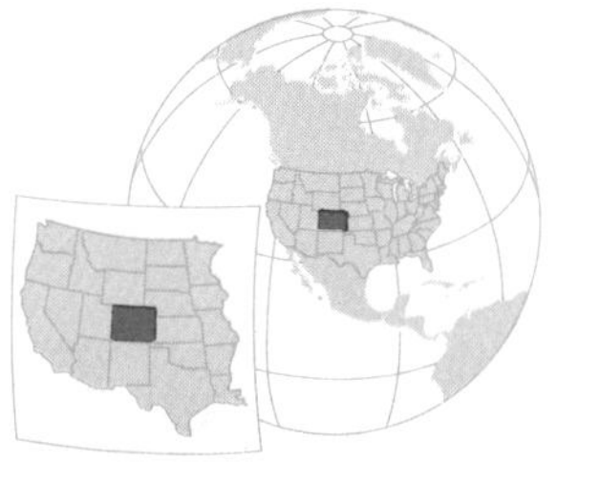

AREA 104,091 sq. mi. (269,596 sq. km.)
POPULATION 2,889,735
CAPITAL Denver
LARGEST CITY Denver
HIGHEST POINT Mt. Elbert 14,433 ft. (4399 m.)
SETTLED IN 1858
ADMITTED TO UNION August 1, 1876
POPULAR NAME Centennial State
STATE FLOWER Rocky Mountain Columbine
STATE BIRD Lark Bunting

COUNTIES

Adams 245,944 .... L3
Alamosa 11,799 .... H7
Arapahoe 293,621 .... L3
Archuleta 3,664 .... E8
Baca 5,419 .... O8
Bent 5,945 .... N7
Boulder 189,625 .... J2
Chaffee 13,227 .... G5
Cheyenne 2,153 .... O5
Clear Creek 7,308 .... H3
Conejos 7,794 .... G8
Costilla 3,071 .... J8
Crowley 2,988 .... M6
Custer 1,528 .... J6
Delta 21,225 .... D5
Denver 492,365 .... K3
Dolores 1,658 .... C7
Douglas 25,153 .... K4
Eagle 13,320 .... F3
Elbert 6,850 .... L4
El Paso 309,424 .... K5
Fremont 28,676 .... J5
Garfield 22,514 .... C3
Gilpin 2,441 .... H3
Grand 7,475 .... G2
Gunnison 10,689 .... E5
Hinsdale 408 .... E7
Huerfano 6,440 .... K7
Jackson 1,863 .... G1
Jefferson 371,741 .... J3
Kiowa 1,936 .... O6
Kit Carson 7,599 .... O4
Lake 8,830 .... G4
La Plata 27,195 .... D8
Larimer 149,184 .... H1
Las Animas 14,897 .... L8
Lincoln 4,663 .... M5
Logan 19,800 .... N1
Mesa 81,530 .... B5
Mineral 804 .... F7
Moffat 13,133 .... C1
Montezuma 16,510 .... B8
Montrose 24,352 .... C6
Morgan 22,513 .... M2
Otero 22,567 .... M7
Ouray 1,925 .... D6
Park 5,333 .... H4
Phillips 4,542 .... P1
Pitkin 10,338 .... F4
Prowers 13,070 .... P7
Pueblo 125,972 .... K6
Rio Blanco 6,255 .... C3
Rio Grande 10,511 .... G7
Routt 13,404 .... E1
Saguache 3,935 .... G6
San Juan 833 .... D7
San Miguel 3,192 .... C6
Sedgwick 3,266 .... P1
Summit 8,848 .... G3
Teller 8,034 .... J5
Washington 5,304 .... N3
Weld 123,438 .... L1

Washington 5,304 .... N3
Weld 123,438 .... L1
Yuma 9,682 .... P2

CITIES and TOWNS

Zip *Name/Pop.* *Key*

80101 Agate 90 .... M4
81020 Aguilar 624 .... K8
80720 Akron⊙ 1,716 .... N2
81101 Alamosa⊙ 6,830 .... H8
80510 Allenspark 200 .... J2
80420 Alma 132 .... G4
81210 Almont 135 .... F5
80721 Amherst 85 .... P1
80801 Anton 55 .... N3
81120 Antonito 1,103 .... H8
80802 Arapahoe 300 .... P5
81021 Arlington 37 .... N6
80804 Arriba 236 .... N4
†81323 Arriola 56 .... B8
*80001 Arvada 84,576 .... J3
81611 Aspen⊙ 3,678 .... F4
80722 Atwood 100 .... N1
80610 Ault 1,056 .... K1
*80010 Aurora 158,588 .... K3
81410 Austin D5
81620 Avon 640 .... F3
81022 Avondale 750 .... L6
80421 Bailey 150 .... H4
†80624 Barnesville 20 .... L2
81621 Basalt 529 .... E4
81122 Bayfield 724 .... D8
81411 Bedrock 45 .... B6
†80758 Beecher Island 5 .... P3
80512 Bellvue 250 .... J1
80102 Bennett 942 .... L3
80513 Berthoud 2,362 .... J2
†80438 Berthoud Pass 40 .... H3
80805 Bethune 149 .... P4
81023 Beulah 650 .... K6
80908 Black Forest 3,372 .... K4
80422 Black Hawk 232 .... J3
81123 Blanca 252 .... H8
†80424 Blue River 230 .... G4
†81155 Bonanza 8 .... G6
81024 Boncarbo 200 .... K8
80423 Bond 65 .... F3
81025 Boone 431 .... L6
*80301 Boulder⊙ 76,685 .... J2
†81428 Bowie 18 .... D5
80821 Boyero 12 .... N5
81026 Brandon 30 .... P6
81027 Branson 73 .... M8
80424 Breckenridge⊙ 818 .... G4
80611 Briggsdale 85 .... L1
80601 Brighton⊙ 12,773 .... K3
81028 Bristol 200 .... P6
†81212 Brookside 178 .... J6
80020 Broomfield 20,730 .... J3
80723 Brush 4,082 .... M2
†80742 Buckingham 5 .... L1
81211 Buena Vista 2,075 .... G5
80425 Buffalo Creek 150 .... J4
80807 Burlington⊙ 3,107 .... P4
80426 Burns 100 .... F3
80103 Byers 490 .... L3
81320 Cahone 200 .... B7
80808 Calhan 541 .... L4
81029 Campo 185 .... O8
81212 Canon City⊙ 13,037 .... J6
81124 Capulin 600 .... G8
81623 Carbondale 2,084 .... E4
80612 Carr 49 .... K1
80909 Cascade 950 .... K5
80104 Castle Rock⊙ 3,921 .... K4
81413 Cedaredge 1,184 .... D5
81125 Center 1,630 .... G7
80427 Central City⊙ 329 .... J3
81126 Chama 239 .... J8
81030 Cheraw 233 .... N6
80810 Cheyenne Wells⊙ 950 .... P5
81127 Chimney Rock 76 .... E8
81031 Chivington 20 .... O6
81128 Chromo 115 .... F8
81220 Cimarron 50 .... D6
80428 Clark 20 .... F1
81520 Clifton 5,223 .... C4
80429 Climax 975 .... G4
81221 Coal Creek 190 .... J6
81222 Coaldale 153 .... H6
80430 Coalmont 50 .... F1
81032 Cokedale 90 .... K8
81624 Collbran 344 .... C4
†81401 Colona 54 .... D6
81019 Colorado City 411 .... K6
*80901 Colorado Springs⊙ 214,821 .... K5
Colorado Springs‡ 317,458 .... K5
†80428 Columbine 12 .... E1
80022 Commerce City 16,234 .... K3
80432 Como 30 .... H4
81129 Conejos⊙ 200 .... G8
80812 Cope 110 .... O3
†80611 Cornish 15 .... L2
81321 Cortez⊙ 7,095 .... B8
81223 Cotopaxi 250 .... H6
80434 Cowdrey 80 .... G1
81625 Craig⊙ 8,133 .... D2
81415 Crawford 268 .... D5
81130 Creede⊙ 610 .... E7
81224 Crested Butte 959 .... E5
81131 Crestone 54 .... H7
80813 Cripple Creek⊙ 655 .... J5
80726 Crook 177 .... O1
81033 Crowley 192 .... M6
81055 Cuchara 43 .... J8
80514 Dacono 2,321 .... K2
†80728 Dailey 20 .... O1
81630 De Beque 279 .... C4
†80135 Deckers 4 .... J4
80105 Deer Trail 463 .... M3
†81059 Delhi 10 .... M7
81132 Del Norte⊙ 1,709 .... G7
81416 Delta⊙ 3,931 .... D5
*80201 Denver (cap.)⊙ 492,365 .... K3
Denver‡ 1,619,921 .... K3
†81054 Deora 2 .... O7
80435 Dillon 337 .... H3
81610 Dinosaur 313 .... B2
80814 Divide 700 .... J5
81323 Dolores 802 .... C8
81324 Dove Creek⊙ 826 .... A7
†81239 Doyleville 75 .... F6
80515 Drake 300 .... J2
81301 Durango⊙ 11,649 .... D8
81036 Eads⊙ 878 .... O6
81631 Eagle⊙ 950 .... F3
80615 Eaton 1,932 .... K1
80727 Eckley 262 .... P2
80214 Edgewater 4,766 .... J3
81632 Edwards 250 .... F3
81325 Egnar 50 .... B7
80106 Elbert 200 .... L4
†80466 Eldora 100 .... H3
80107 Elizabeth 789 .... K4
81633 Elk Springs 18 .... C2
80438 Empire 423 .... H3
†80110 Englewood 30,021 .... K3
80516 Erie 1,254 .... K2
80517 Estes Park 2,703 .... J2
†81433 Eureka 25 .... D7
80620 Evans 5,063 .... K2
80439 Evergreen 6,376 .... J3
80440 Fairplay⊙ 421 .... H4
81037 Farisita 116 .... J7
†80221 Federal Heights 7,846 .... J3
80520 Firestone 1,204 .... K2
†80810 Firstview 6 .... O5
80815 Flagler 550 .... N4
80728 Fleming 388 .... O1
81226 Florence 2,987 .... J6
80816 Florissant 130 .... J5
80521 Fort Collins⊙ 65,092 .... J1
Fort Collins‡ 149,184 .... J1
81133 Fort Garland 700 .... J8
80621 Fort Lupton 4,251 .... K2
81038 Fort Lyon 500 .... N6
80701 Fort Morgan⊙ 8,768 .... M2
80817 Fountain 8,324 .... K5
81039 Fowler 1,227 .... L6
80441 Foxton 12 .... J4
80116 Franktown 200 .... K4
80442 Fraser 470 .... H3
80530 Frederick 855 .... K2
80820 Freshwater (Guffey) 24 .... H5
80443 Frisco 1,221 .... G3
81521 Fruita 2,810 .... B4
80622 Galeton 200 .... K1
81134 Garcia 75 .... J8
81040 Gardner 100 .... J7
81227 Garfield 30 .... G5
81522 Gateway 350 .... B5
80818 Genoa 165 .... N4
80444 Georgetown⊙ 830 .... H3
80623 Gilcrest 1,025 .... K2
80624 Gill 250 .... L2
81634 Gilman 160 .... G3
81523 Glade Park 100 .... B5
†80485 Glendevey 50 .... H1
80532 Glen Haven 110 .... H2
81601 Glenwood Springs⊙ 4,637 .... E4
80401 Golden⊙ 12,237 .... J3
†80653 Goodrich 85 .... M2
†80480 Gould 12 .... G2
81041 Granada 557 .... P6
80446 Granby 963 .... H2
81501 Grand Junction⊙ 27,956 .... B4
80447 Grand Lake 382 .... H2
81228 Granite 47 .... G4
80448 Grant 50 .... H4
80631 Greeley⊙ 53,006 .... K2
Greeley‡ 123,438 .... K2
†80118 Greenland 21 .... K4
80819 Green Mountain Falls 607 .... K5
†81640 Greystone 2 .... B1
80729 Grover 158 .... L1
80820 Guffey 24 .... H5
81042 Gulnare 6 .... K8
81230 Gunnison⊙ 5,785 .... E5
81637 Gypsum 743 .... F3
80730 Hale 4 .... P3
81638 Hamilton 100 .... D2
81043 Hartman 122 .... P6
80449 Hartsel 69 .... H4
81044 Hasty 150 .... O6
81045 Haswell 126 .... N6
80731 Haxtun 1,014 .... O1
81639 Hayden 1,720 .... E2
80732 Hereford 50 .... L1
81326 Hesperus 250 .... C8
80733 Hillrose 213 .... N2
81232 Hillside 79 .... H6
81046 Hoehne 400 .... L8
81047 Holly 969 .... P6
80734 Holyoke⊙ 2,092 .... P1
81136 Hooper 71 .... H7
81419 Hotchkiss 849 .... D5
80451 Hot Sulphur Springs⊙ 405 .... H2
81233 Howard 200 .... H6
80641 Hoyt 60 .... L2
80642 Hudson 698 .... K2
80821 Hugo⊙ 776 .... N4
80533 Hygiene 450 .... J2
80452 Idaho Springs 2,077 .... H3
80735 Idalia 125 .... P3
81137 Ignacio 667 .... D8
80736 Iliff 218 .... N1
80455 Jamestown 223 .... J2
†81082 Jansen 267 .... K8
81138 Jaroso 50 .... H8
80456 Jefferson 50 .... H4
80822 Joes 100 .... O3
80534 Johnstown 1,535 .... K2
80737 Julesburg⊙ 1,528 .... P1
80823 Karval 51 .... N5
80643 Keenesburg 541 .... L2
†80729 Keota 4 .... L1
80644 Kersey 913 .... L2
81049 Kim 100 .... N8
80117 Kiowa⊙ 206 .... L4
80824 Kirk 30 .... P3
80825 Kit Carson 278 .... O5
80459 Kremmling 1,296 .... G2
†80832 Kutch 2 .... M5
80026 Lafayette 8,935 .... K3
†81132 La Garita 10 .... G7
80739 Laird 105 .... P2
81140 La Jara 858 .... H8
81050 La Junta⊙ 8,388 .... M7
81235 Lake City⊙ 206 .... E6
80827 Lake George 500 .... J5
80215 Lakewood 113,808 .... J3
81052 Lamar⊙ 7,713 .... O6
80535 Laporte 950 .... J1
80118 Larkspur 141 .... K4
80645 La Salle 1,929 .... K2
81054 Las Animas⊙ 2,818 .... N6
†81151 Lasauces 150 .... H8
†81153 Lavalley 237 .... J8
81055 La Veta 611 .... J8
†80452 Lawson 108 .... H3
†81625 Lay 40 .... D2
81420 Lazear 60 .... D5
80461 Leadville⊙ 3,879 .... G4
†81323 Lebanon 50 .... B8
81327 Lewis 150 .... B8
80828 Limon 1,805 .... M4
†81212 Lincoln Park 2,984 .... J6
80740 Lindon 60 .... N3
*80120 Littleton⊙ 28,631 .... K3
80536 Livermore 150 .... J1
†80601 Lochbuie 895 .... K2
†80701 Log Lane Village 709 .... M2
81524 Loma 265 .... B4
80501 Longmont 42,942 .... J2
†80135 Longview 10 .... J4
80027 Louisville 5,593 .... J3
80131 Louviers 300 .... K4
80537 Loveland 30,244 .... J2
80646 Lucerne 135 .... K2
†81054 Lycan 4 .... P7
80540 Lyons 1,137 .... J2
81525 Mack 380 .... B4
81421 Maher 75 .... D5
†80461 Malta 200 .... G4
81141 Manassa 945 .... H8
81328 Mancos 870 .... C8
80829 Manitou Springs 4,475 .... J5
81058 Manzanola 459 .... M6
†81623 Marble 30 .... E4
81329 Marvel 176 .... C8
80541 Masonville 200 .... J2
†80649 Masters 50 .... L2
80830 Matheson 120 .... M4
81640 Maybell 130 .... C2
81057 McClave 125 .... O6
80463 McCoy 62 .... F3
80542 Mead 356 .... K2
81641 Meeker⊙ 2,356 .... D2
81642 Meredith 47 .... F4
80741 Merino 255 .... N2
81005 Mesa 120 .... C4
81330 Mesa Verde National Park 45 .... C8
81142 Mesita 70 .... H8
80543 Milliken 1,506 .... K2
80477 Milner 196 .... F2
81645 Minturn 1,060 .... G3

(continued on following page)

Agriculture, Industry and Resources

DOMINANT LAND USE

- Specialized Wheat
- Wheat, Range Livestock
- Wheat, Grain Sorghums, Range Livestock
- Dry Beans, General Farming
- Sugar Beets, Dry Beans, Livestock, General Farming
- Fruit, Mixed Farming
- General Farming, Livestock, Special Crops
- Range Livestock
- Forests
- Urban Areas
- Nonagricultural Land

MAJOR MINERAL OCCURRENCES

Ag	Silver	Mi	Mica
Au	Gold	Mo	Molybdenum
Be	Beryl	Mr	Marble
C	Coal	O	Petroleum
Cl	Clay	Pb	Lead
Cu	Copper	U	Uranium
F	Fluorspar	V	Vanadium
Fe	Iron Ore	W	Tungsten
G	Natural Gas	Zn	Zinc

Water Power
Major Industrial Areas

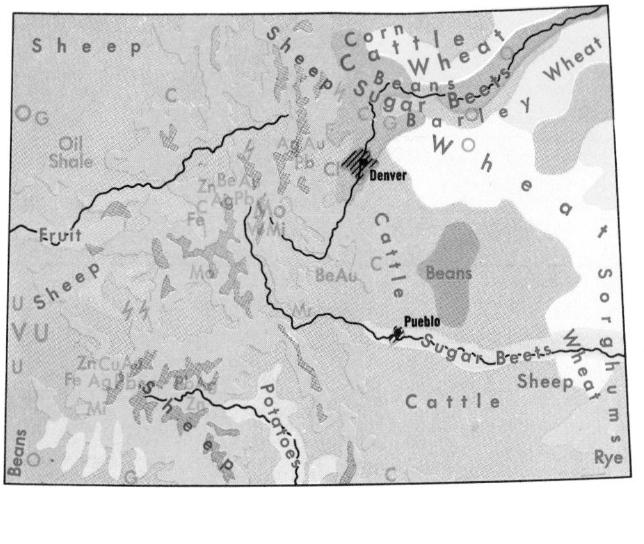

Topography

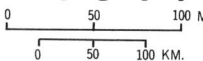

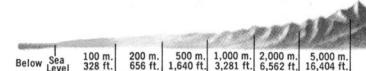

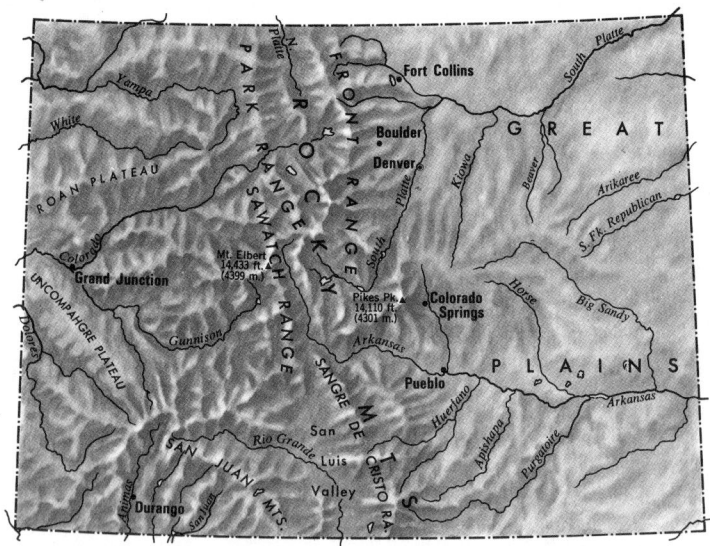

81646 Molina 200 .... D4
81144 Monte Vista 3,902 ...... G7
†80435 Montezuma 6 .... H3
81401 Montrose⊙ 8,722 .... D6
80132 Monument 690 .... K4
80465 Morrison 478 .... J3
81146 Mosca 100 .... H7
81236 Nathrop 150 .... H5
81422 Naturita 819 .... B6
80466 Nederland 1,212 .... H3
81647 New Castle 563 .... E3
80742 New Raymer 80 .... M1
†81054 Niniaview 2 .... N7
80544 Niwot 500 .... J2
†81022 North Avondale 110 ... L6
80233 Northglenn 29,847 ..... K3
†81050 North La Junta 1,076 . N7
81423 Norwood 478 .... C6
80648 Nunn 295 .... K1
80467 Oak Creek 929 .... F2
81237 Ohio 100 .... F5
81425 Olathe 1,262 .... D5
81062 Olney Springs 253 ..... M6
81426 Ophir 38 .... D7
80649 Orchard 79 .... L2
†81501 Orchard Mesa 4,876 ... C4
81063 Ordway⊙ 1,135 .... M6
†81120 Ortiz 163 .... D7
80743 Otis 534 .... O2
81427 Ouray⊙ 684 .... D6
80744 Ovid 439 .... P1
80745 Padroni 100 .... N1
†81147 Pagosa Junction 15 .. E8
81147 Pagosa Springs⊙ 1,331 E8
81526 Palisade 1,551 .... C4
80133 Palmer Lake 1,130 .... J4
80746 Paoli 81 .... P1
81428 Paonia 1,425 .... D5
81635 Parachute 338 .... C4
81429 Paradox 250 .... B6
†81212 Parkdale 21 .... H6
80134 Parker 200 .... K4
81239 Parlin 100 .... F6
80468 Parshall 80 .... G2
80747 Peetz 220 .... N1
81240 Penrose 500 .... K6
80831 Peyton 250 .... K4
80469 Phippsburg 300 ..... F2
80650 Pierce 878 .... K1
80470 Pine 100 .... J4
80471 Pinecliffe 375 .... J3
†81001 Pinon 50 .... K6
81241 Pitkin 59 .... F5
81430 Placerville 50 ... D6
81237 Plateau City 35 .. C4
†80743 Platner 30 .... N2
80651 Platteville 1,662 K2
81331 Pleasant View 300 B7
81242 Poncha Springs 321 G6
†81226 Portland 17 ...... K6
†81427 Portland D6
81243 Powderhorn 100 ... E6
81064 Pritchett 183 .... O8
†80736 Proctor 25 ...... N1
81065 Pryor 50 .... K8
*81001 Pueblo⊙ 101,686 .. K6
       Pueblo‡ 125,972 .. K6
80472 Radium 22 .... G3
80832 Ramah 119 .... L4
80473 Rand 50 .... G2
81648 Rangely 2,113 ... B2

80473 Rand 50 .... G2
81648 Rangely 2,113 .... B2
80742 Raymer (New Raymer) 80 M1
81649 Red Cliff 409 .... G4
80545 Red Feather Lakes 150 H1
†81326 Red Mesa 100 .... C8
81623 Redstone 115 .... E4
81431 Redvale 300 .... B6
81066 Red Wing 200 .... J7
81332 Rico 76 .... C7
81432 Ridgway 369 .... D6
81650 Rifle 3,215 .... D3
†81650 Rio Blanco 4 .... C3
81244 Rockvale 338 .... J6
81067 Rocky Ford 4,804 .... M6
80652 Roggen 100 .... L2
81148 Romeo 308 .... G8
80833 Rush 40 .... L5
81069 Rye 232 .... K7
†81149 Saguache⊙ 656 ..... G6
81236 Saint Elmo 75 ..... G5
81201 Salida⊙ 44,870 ... H6
81150 San Acacio 50 .... J8
81151 Sanford 687 ...... H8
81069 San Isabel 8 ..... K7
81152 San Luis⊙ 842 ... J8
81153 San Pablo 150 ... J8
81248 Sargents 31 ..... F6
80911 Sawpit 41 .... D7
†80135 Sedalia 200 .... K4
80749 Sedgwick 258 ... O1
81070 Segundo 200 .... K8
80834 Seibert 180 .... O4
80546 Severance 102 .. K1
80475 Shawnee 100 ... H4
†80110 Sheridan 5,377 J3
81071 Sheridan Lake 87 P6
81652 Silt 923 .... D4
81249 Silver Cliff 280 J6
80476 Silver Plume 140 H3
80498 Silverthorne 989 G3
81433 Silverton⊙ 794 . D7
80835 Simla 494 ...... M4
81653 Slater 10 ...... E1
81654 Snowmass 999 ... E4
80750 Snyder 200 ..... M2
81434 Somerset 200 ... E5
81154 South Fork 500 . F7
81073 Springfield⊙ 1,657 O8
81074 Starkville 127 . L8
80477 Steamboat Springs⊙ 5,098 F2
80751 Sterling⊙ 11,385 N1
80754 Stoneham 35 .... M1
81075 Stonington 27 .. P8
80136 Strasburg 1,005 L3
80836 Stratton 705 ... O4
81076 Sugar City 306 . M6
†81640 Sunbeam 19 .... C1
†80027 Superior 208 .. J3
81077 Swink 668 ..... M7
80478 Tabernash 250 . H3
81435 Telluride⊙ 1,047 D7
†80461 Tennessee Pass 5 G4
81250 Texas Creek 100 H6
†81082 Thatcher 50 ... L7
80229 Thornton 40,343 K3
81137 Tiffany 24 .... D8
81034 Timpas 25 ..... M7
†81210 Tincup 8 ...... F5
80479 Toponas 55 .... F2

81334 Towaoc 300 .... B8
81080 Towner 61 .... P6
81081 Trinchera 30 .... M8
81082 Trinidad⊙ 9,663 ...... L8
†80864 Truckton 10 .... L5
81251 Twin Lakes 40 .... G4
81084 Two Buttes 84 .... P7
†81059 Tyrone 9 .... L8
81436 Uravan 500 .... B6
81064 Utleyville 2 .... O8
81657 Vail 2,261 .... G3
†81082 Valdez 12 .... K8
80755 Vernon 50 .... P3
80860 Victor 265 .... J5
81087 Vilas 118 .... P8
81155 Villa Grove 37 .. G6
81088 Villegreen 6 .... M8
81001 Vineland 100 .... K6
80548 Virginia Dale 2 . J1
80861 Vona 94 .... O4
†81130 Wagon Wheel Gap 20 F7
80480 Walden⊙ 947 .... G1
81089 Walsenburg⊙ 3,945 K7
81090 Walsh 884 ...... P8
80481 Ward 129 .... H2
80653 Weldona 200 .... M2
80549 Wellington 1,215 K1
81252 Westcliffe⊙ 324 H6
†80135 Westcreek 2 .... J4
80030 Westminster 50,211 J3
81091 Weston 150 ..... K8
81253 Wetmore 150 .... J6
80033 Wheat Ridge 30,293 J3
81527 Whitewater 300 . C5
80654 Wiggins 531 .... L2
80862 Wild Horse 13 .. N5
81092 Wiley 425 ...... O6
†81226 Williamsburg 72 J6
80550 Windsor 4,277 .. J2
80482 Winter Park 480 H3
81655 Wolcott 30 ..... F3
80863 Woodland Park 2,634 J4
80757 Woodrow 24 ..... M3
81656 Woody Creek 400 F4
80758 Wray⊙ 2,131 .... P2
81335 Yellow Jacket 115 B7
80864 Yoder 25 .... L5
80759 Yuma 2,824 ..... O2

OTHER FEATURES

Adams (mt.) H6
Adobe Creek (res.) N6
Air Force Academy 8,655 ..... K5
Alamosa (creek) G8
Alva B. Adams (tunnel) H2
Animas (riv.) D8
Antero (mt.) G5
Antero (res.) H5
Antora (peak) G6
Apishapa (riv.) K8
Arapaho Nat'l Rec. Area G2
Arapahoe (peak) H2
Arikaree (riv.) O3
Arkansas (riv.) P6
Arkansas Divide (mts.) L4
Baker (mt.) H2
Bald (mt.) H4
Bear (creek) P8
Beaver (creek) M3
Bennett (peak) G7

Bent's Old Fort Nat'l Hist.
   Site M6
Big Grizzly (creek) G1
Big Sandy (creek) N4
Big Thompson (riv.) H2
Bijou (creek) L3
Black Canyon of the Gunnison Nat'l
   Mon. D5
Black Squirrel (creek) L5
Blanca (peak) H7
Blue (mt.) B2
Blue (riv.) G3
Blue Mesa (res.) E5
Bonny (res.) P3
Box Elder (creek) K4
Cache la Poudre (riv.) H1
Cameron (peak) H1
Camp Hale G4
Carbon (peak) E5
Castle (peak) F5
Cebolla (creek) E6
Chacuaco (creek) M8
Cheesman (lake) J4
Clay (creek) O7

Cochetopa (creek) F6
Colorado (riv.) A5
Colorado Nat'l Mon. B4
Conejos (peak) G8
Conejos (riv.) G8
Crestone (peak) H7
Crow (creek) L1
Culebra (creek) J8
Culebra (peak) J8
Curecanti Nat'l Rec. Area ... F6
Del Norte (peak) F7
De Weese (plat.) J6
Dinosaur Nat'l Mon. B2
Disappointment (creek) B7
Dolores (riv.) B5
Douglas (creek) B3
Eagle (riv.) F3
El Diente (peak) C7
Eleven Mile Canyon (res.) ... H5
Elk (riv.) F1
Empire (res.) L2
Ent A.F.B. K5
Ethel (mt.) F1

Evans (mt.) H3
Florissant Fossil Beds Nat'l
   Mon. J5
Fort Carson 19,399 .... K5
Fountain (creek) K5
Frenchman (creek) P1
Frenchman, North Fork (creek) O1
Frenchman, South Fork (creek) O1
Front (range) H1
Gore (range) G3
Graham (peak) E8
Granby (lake) H3
Great Sand Dunes Nat'l Mon. . H7
Green (riv.) A2
Green Mountain (res.) G3
Gunnison (riv.) C5
Gunnison (tunnel) D6
Gunnison, North Fork (riv.) . D5
Hale, Camp G4
Handies (peak) E7
Harvard (mt.) G5
Hermosa (peak) D7
Hesperus (mt.) C8
Holy Cross (mt.) G4

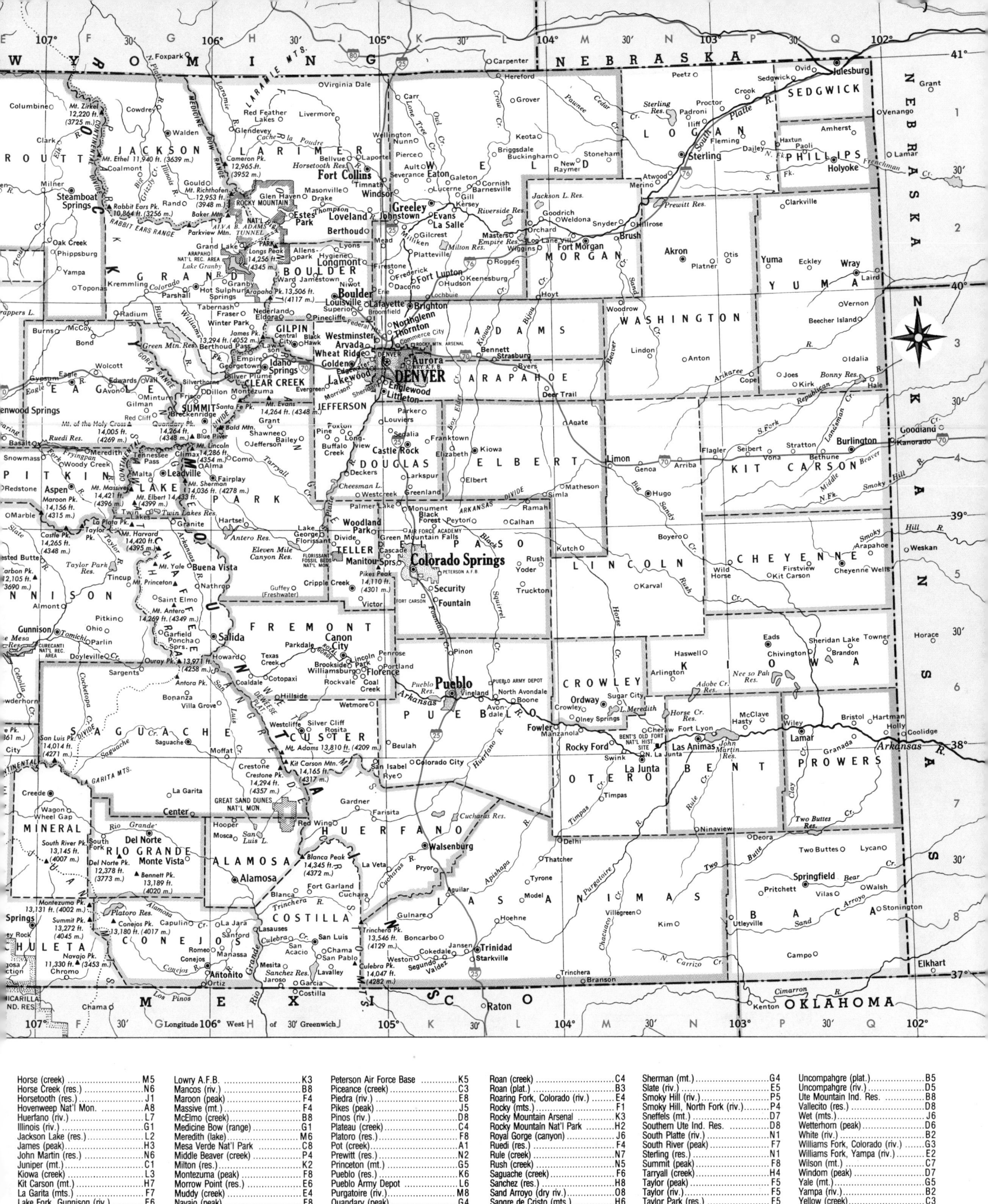

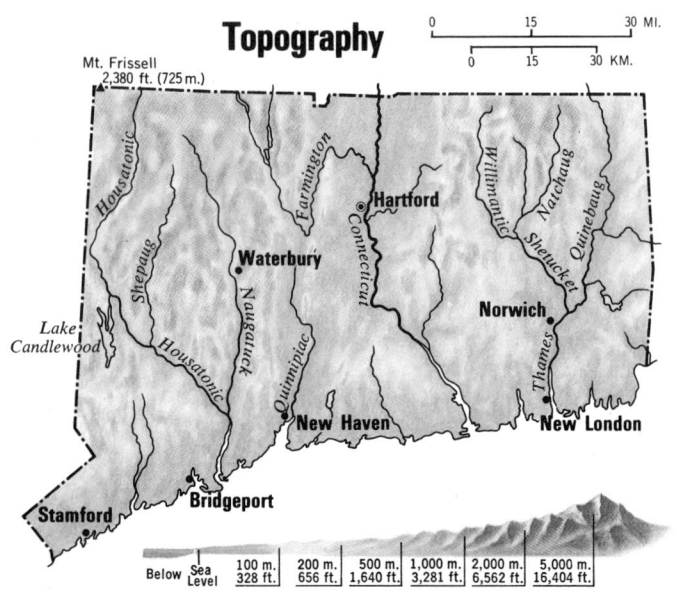

Topography

Mt. Frissell
2,380 ft. (725 m.)

Below Sea Level	100 m. 328 ft.	200 m. 656 ft.	500 m. 1,640 ft.	1,000 m. 3,281 ft.	2,000 m. 6,562 ft.	5,000 m. 16,404 ft.

Connecticut

SCALE

0   5   10   15 MI.

0   5   10   15 KM.

State Capitals .... ⊛
Major Limited Access Hwys. ———
Scale 1:610,000

COUNTIES

Fairfield 807,143	....	B3
Hartford 807,766	....	D1
Litchfield 156,769	....	B1
Middlesex 129,017	....	E3
New Haven 761,337	....	D3
New London 238,409	....	G2
Tolland 114,823	....	F1
Windham 92,312	....	H1

CITIES and TOWNS

Zip	Name/Pop.	Key
06230	Abington 600	G1
06231	Amston 900	F2
06232	Andover 2,144	F2
06401	Ansonia 19,039	C3
06278	Ashford 3,221	G1
06278	Ashford P.O.	
	(Warrenville) 500	G1
†06241	Attawaugan 400	H1
†06001	Avon 11,201	D1
06001	Avon 1,434	D1
06233	Ballouville 800	H1
06330	Baltic	G2
06750	Bantam 860	B2
†06063	Barkhamsted 2,935	D1
†06423	Bashan 90	F2
06037	Beacon Falls 3,995	C3
06037	Berlin 15,121	E2
†06501	Bethany 4,330	C3
06801	Bethel 16,004	B3
06801	Bethel 8,755	B3
06751	Bethlehem 2,573	C2
06751	Bethlehem 1,762	C2
06002	Bloomfield 18,608	E1
06040	Blue Hills	E1
06040	Bolton 3,951	F1
06404	Botsford 400	C3
†06829	Branchville 600	B3
06405	Branford 23,363	D3
06405	Branford 5,438	D3
*06601	Bridgeport 142,546	C4
	Bridgeport‡ 395,455	C4
06752	Bridgewater 1,563	B2
06010	Bristol 57,370	D2
	Bristol‡ 73,762	D2
06016	Broad Brook	E1
06804	Brookfield 12,872	B3
06234	Brooklyn○ 5,691	H1
06013	Burlington 5,660	D1
06830	Byram	A4
06018	Canaan 1,002	B1
06018	Canaan 1,160	B1
†06897	Cannondale 400	B4
06331	Canterbury○ 3,426	H2
06019	Canton○ 7,635	D1
06019	Canton 1,680	D1
06409	Centerbrook 800	F3
06332	Central Village 950	H2
06235	Chaplin 1,793	G1
06410	Cheshire 21,788	D2
06410	Cheshire 5,722	D2
06412	Chester○ 3,068	F3
06412	Chester 1,388	F3
06413	Clinton 11,195	E3
06413	Clinton 3,168	E3
06414	Cobalt 700	E2
06415	Colchester○ 7,761	F2
06415	Colchester 3,190	F2
06021	Colebrook○ 1,221	C1
06022	Collinsville 2,555	D1
06237	Columbia○ 3,386	F2
06753	Cornwall○ 1,288	B1
06807	Cos Cob	A4
06238	Coventry○ 8,895	F1
06416	Cromwell○ 10,265	E2
06810	Danbury 60,470	B3
	Danbury‡ 146,405	B3
06239	Danielson 4,553	H1
06820	Darien○ 18,892	B4
06241	Dayville	H1
06417	Deep River 3,994	F3
06417	Deep River 2,495	F3
06418	Derby 12,346	C3
06422	Durham○ 5,143	E3
06422	Durham 2,641	E3
06023	East Berlin 950	E2
†06239	East Brooklyn 1,251	H1
06024	East Canaan 800	B1
06242	Eastford○ 1,028	G1
06025	East Glastonbury 300	E2
06026	East Granby○ 4,102	E1
06423	East Haddam○ 5,621	F3
06424	East Hampton 8,572	E2

AREA 5,018 sq. mi. (12,997 sq. km.)
POPULATION 3,107,576
CAPITAL Hartford
LARGEST CITY Bridgeport
HIGHEST POINT Mt. Frissell (S. Slope) 2,380 ft. (725 m.)
SETTLED IN 1635
ADMITTED TO UNION January 9, 1788
POPULAR NAME Constitution State; Nutmeg State
STATE FLOWER Mountain Laurel
STATE BIRD Robin

© Copyright HAMMOND INCORPORATED, Maplewood, N.J.

06351 Lisbon○ 3,279	G2
06759 Litchfield○ 7,605	C2
06759 Litchfield 1,489	C2
†06378 Lords Point 500	H3
06443 Madison○ 14,031	E3
06443 Madison 2,069	E3
06040 Manchester○ 49,761	E1
06040 Manchester 31,058	E1
†06250 Mansfield 20,634	F1
06250 Mansfield Center 1,043	G1
06777 Marble Dale 300	B2
06444 Marion 900	D2
06447 Marlborough○ 4,746	F2
06447 Marlborough 1,039	F2
†06382 Massapeag 350	G2
06252 Mechanicsville 425	H1
06450 Meriden 57,118	D2
Meriden‡ 57,118	D2
06762 Middlebury○ 5,995	C2
06455 Middlefield○ 3,796	D2
06456 Middle Haddam 325	E2
06457 Middletown 39,040	E2
06460 Milford 49,101	C4
06467 Milldale 975	D2
†06759 Milton 600	C1
06468 Monroe○ 14,010	C3
06468 Monroe P.O. (Stepney)	B3
06353 Montville○ 16,455	G3
06353 Montville 1,711	G3
06469 Moodus 1,179	F2
06354 Moosup 3,308	H2
06763 Morris 1,899	C2
06355 Mystic 2,333	H3
06770 Naugatuck 26,456	C2
*06050 New Britain 73,840	E2
New Britain‡ 142,241	E2
06840 New Canaan○ 17,931	B4
06810 New Fairfield○ 11,260	B3
06057 New Hartford○ 4,884	C1
06057 New Hartford 1,310	C1
*06501 New Haven 126,109	D3
New Haven-West Haven‡ 417,592	D3
06111 Newington○ 28,841	E2
06320 New London 28,842	G3
New London-Norwich‡ 248,554	G3
06776 New Milford○ 19,420	B2
06776 New Milford 5,186	B2
06777 New Preston 1,209	B2
06470 Newtown○ 19,107	B3
06470 Newtown 2,022	B3
06357 Niantic 3,151	G3
06340 Noank 1,406	G3
06058 Norfolk○ 2,156	C1
06471 North Branford 11,554	E3
06778 Northfield 600	C2
06254 North Franklin 500	G2
06060 North Granby 450	D1
06255 North Grosvenor Dale 1,856	H1
†06437 North Guilford 500	E3
06473 North Haven 22,080	D3
06359 North Stonington○ 4,219	H3
06256 North Windham 200	G1
*06850 Norwalk 77,767	B4
06360 Norwich 38,074	G2
06370 Oakdale 608	G3
06779 Oakville 8,737	C2
06371 Old Lyme○ 6,159	F3

06372 Old Mystic 600	H3
06475 Old Saybrook○ 9,287	F3
06475 Old Saybrook 1,857	F3
06373 Oneco 550	H2
06477 Orange○ 13,237	C3
06483 Oxford○ 6,634	C3
06379 Pawcatuck 5,216	H3
06781 Pequabuck 642	C2
06061 Pine Meadow 400	D1
†06405 Pine Orchard 300	D3
06374 Plainfield○ 12,774	H2
06374 Plainfield 2,799	H2
06062 Plainville○ 16,401	D2
06063 Pleasant Valley 300	C1
†06385 Pleasure Beach 1,356	G3
06782 Plymouth○ 10,732	C2
06258 Pomfret○ 2,775	H1
†06340 Poquonock Bridge 2,549	G3
06480 Portland○ 8,383	E2
06480 Portland 5,914	E2
06712 Prospect○ 6,807	D2
06260 Putnam○ 8,580	H1
06260 Putnam 6,855	H1
06375 Quaker Hill 2,052	G3
06262 Quinebaug 1,088	H1
06875 Redding○ 7,272	B3
06876 Redding Ridge 550	B3
06877 Ridgefield○ 20,120	B3
06877 Ridgefield 6,066	B3
06065 Riverton 250	D1
06481 Rockfall 900	E2
†06066 Rockville	F1
06067 Rocky Hill 14,559	E2
06263 Rogers 650	H1
06783 Roxbury○ 1,468	B2
†06415 Salem○ 2,335	F3
06068 Salisbury○ 3,896	B1
06264 Scotland○ 1,072	G2
06483 Seymour○ 13,434	C3
06069 Sharon○ 2,623	B1
06484 Shelton 31,314	C3
06784 Sherman○ 2,281	B2
06070 Simsbury○ 21,161	D1
06070 Simsbury 5,488	D1
06071 Somers○ 8,473	F1
06071 Somers 1,643	F1
06072 Somersville 750	F1
06487 South Britain 390	B3
06488 Southbury○ 14,156	C3
†06238 South Coventry (Coventry) 3,769	F1
06073 South Glastonbury 1,800	E2
06489 Southington○ 36,879	D2
06785 South Kent 450	B2
06265 South Willington 450	F1
06266 South Windham 1,399	G2
06074 South Windsor○ 17,198	E1
06267 South Woodstock 1,319	G1
06075 Stafford○ 9,268	F1
06076 Stafford Springs 3,392	F1
06077 Staffordville 500	F1
*06901 Stamford 102,453	A4
Stamford‡ 198,854	A4
†06468 Stepney	B3
06377 Sterling○ 1,791	H2
06491 Stevenson 300	C3
06378 Stonington○ 16,220	H3
06378 Stonington 1,228	H3
06268 Storrs 11,394	F1
06497 Stratford○ 50,541	C4

06078 Suffield○ 9,294	E1
06078 Suffield 1,122	E1
06079 Taconic 400	B1
06380 Taftville	G2
06081 Tariffville 1,324	D1
06786 Terryville 5,234	C2
06787 Thomaston○ 6,276	C2
06277 Thompson○ 8,141	H1
†06082 Thompsonville	E1
06084 Tolland○ 9,694	F1
06790 Torrington 30,987	C1
06611 Trumbull○ 32,989	C4
06382 Uncasville 1,597	G3
†06076 Union○ 546	G1
06066 Vernon○ 27,974	F1
06383 Versailles 540	G2
06384 Voluntown○ 1,637	H2
06492 Wallingford○ 37,274	D3
06492 Wallingford 17,821	D3
06754 Warren○ 1,027	B2
†06278 Warrenville 500	G1
06793 Washington○ 3,657	B2
06794 Washington Depot 900	B2
*06701 Waterbury 103,266	C2
Waterbury‡ 228,178	C2
06385 Waterford○ 17,843	G3
06385 Waterford 2,736	G3
06795 Watertown○ 19,489	C2
06089 Weatogue 2,249	D1
06498 Westbrook○ 5,216	E3
06498 Westbrook 2,035	E3
06796 West Cornwall 425	B1
06090 West Granby 567	D1
06107 West Hartford○ 61,301	D1
06516 West Haven 53,184	D3
06388 West Mystic 3,364	H3
06883 Weston○ 8,284	B4
06880 Westport○ 25,290	B4
06896 West Redding 500	B3
06092 West Simsbury 2,140	D1
06109 Wethersfield 26,013	E2
06517 Whitneyville	D3
06226 Willimantic 14,652	G2
†06279 Willington○ 4,694	F1
06897 Wilton○ 15,351	B4
06094 Winchester○ 10,841	C1
06094 Winchester Center 350	C1
06280 Windham○ 21,062	G2
06095 Windsor○ 25,204	E1
06095 Windsor 17,517	E1
06096 Windsor Locks○ 12,190	E1
06097 Windsorville 450	E1
06098 Winsted 8,092	C1
†06417 Winthrop 750	E3
06716 Wolcott○ 13,008	D2
06515 Woodbridge○ 7,761	D3
06798 Woodbury○ 6,942	C2
06798 Woodbury 1,240	C2
†06460 Woodmont 1,797	D4
06281 Woodstock○ 5,117	H1

OTHER FEATURES

Aspetuck (res.)	B4
Bantam (lake)	C2
Barkhamsted (res.)	D1
Bear (mt.)	B1
Byram (riv.)	A4
Candlewood (lake)	A2
Coast Guard Academy	G3
Colebrook River (lake)	C1
Congamond (lkes.)	E1
Connecticut (riv.)	E2
Dennis (hill)	C1
Easton (res.)	B3
Eight Mile (riv.)	F3
Farmington (riv.)	D1
French (riv.)	H1
Frissell (mt.)	B1
Gaillard (lake)	D3
Gardner (lake)	G2
Hammonasset (pt.)	E3
Hammonasset (res.)	E3
Haystack (mt.)	C1
Highland (lake)	C1
Hockanum (riv.)	F1
Hop (riv.)	F1
Housatonic (riv.)	C3
Lillinonah (lake)	B3
Little (riv.)	G2
Long Island (sound)	C4
Mad (riv.)	C1
Mashapaug (lake)	G1
Mason (isl.)	H3
Mattabesset (riv.)	E2
Mianus (riv.)	A4
Mohawk (mt.)	B1
Moosup (riv.)	H2
Mount Hope (riv.)	G1
Mudge (pond)	B1
Mystic (riv.)	H3
Natchaug (riv.)	G1
Naugatuck (riv.)	C3
Nepaug (res.)	D1
Niantic (riv.)	G3
Norwalk (riv.)	B4
Pachaug (pond)	H2
Pawcatuck (riv.)	H3
Pequabuck (riv.)	D2
Pequonnock (riv.)	C3
Pocotopaug (lake)	E2
Quaddick (res.)	H1
Quinebaug (riv.)	G2
Quinnipiac (riv.)	D3
Rippowam (riv.)	A4
Sachem (head)	E4
Salmon (brook)	D1
Salmon (riv.)	F2
Saugatuck (res.)	B3
Scantic (riv.)	E1
Shenipsit (lake)	F1
Shepaug (riv.)	B2
Shetucket (riv.)	G2
Silvermine (riv.)	B4
Spectacle (lkes.)	B2
Still (riv.)	B3
Still (riv.)	C1
Talcott (range)	D1
Thames (riv.)	G3
Thomaston (res.)	C2
Titicus (riv.)	A3
Trap Falls (res.)	C3
Twin (lkes.)	B1
Wamgumbaug (lake)	F1
Waramaug (lake)	B2
West Rock Ridge (hills)	D3
Willimantic (riv.)	F1
Wononskopomuc (lake)	B1
Yantic (riv.)	G2

‡Population of metropolitan area.
○Population of town or township.
† Zip of nearest p.o.
* Multiple zips.

06424 East Hampton 2,152	E2
06108 East Hartford 52,563	E1
06027 East Hartland 900	D1
06512 East Haven 25,028	D3
06243 East Killingly 900	H1
06333 East Lyme○ 13,870	G3
†06763 East Morris 800	C2
06612 Easton○ 5,962	B4
†06088 East Windsor○ 8,925	E1
06028 East Windsor Hill 500	E1
06244 East Woodstock 400	H1
06029 Ellington○ 9,711	F1
06082 Enfield 42,695	E1
06082 Enfield 8,151	E1
06426 Essex○ 5,078	F3
06426 Essex 2,501	F3
06245 Fabyan 600	H1
06430 Fairfield 54,849	B4
06031 Falls Village 600	B1
06032 Farmington○ 16,407	D2
06334 Fitchville 400	G2
†06254 Franklin○ 1,592	G2
06335 Gales Ferry 1,191	G3
06755 Gaylordsville 960	A2
06829 Georgetown 1,834	B4
06336 Gilman 350	G2
06337 Glasgo 450	H2
06033 Glastonbury○ 24,327	E2
06033 Glastonbury 7,049	E2
06756 Goshen○ 1,706	C1
06035 Granby○ 7,956	D1
06035 Granby 1,912	D1

06830 Greenwich○ 59,578	A4
06246 Grosvenor Dale 700	H1
06340 Groton○ 41,062	G3
06340 Groton 10,086	G3
06437 Guilford○ 17,375	E3
06437 Guilford 2,555	E3
06438 Haddam○ 6,383	E2
06439 Hadlyme 450	F3
06514 Hamden○ 51,071	D3
06247 Hampton○ 1,322	G1
06350 Hanover 500	G2
*06101 Hartford (cap.) 136,392	E1
Hartford‡ 726,114	E1
†06091 Hartland○ 1,416	D1
06791 Harwinton○ 4,889	C1
06791 Harwinton 3,293	C1
06440 Hawleyville 600	B3
06082 Hazardville 5,436	E1
06248 Hebron○ 5,453	F2
06441 Higganum 1,660	E2
†06040 Highland Park 500	E1
06351 Jewett City 3,294	H2
06037 Kensington 7,502	D2
06757 Kent○ 2,505	B2
†06241 Killingly○ 14,519	H1
†06413 Killingworth○ 3,976	E3
†06424 Lake Pocotopaug 2,137	F2
06758 Lakeside 350	B2
06249 Lebanon○ 4,762	G2
06339 Ledyard○ 13,735	G3
†06437 Leetes Island 500	E3
†06039 Lime Rock 350	B1

Agriculture, Industry and Resources

DOMINANT LAND USE

- Specialized Dairy
- Dairy, Poultry, Mixed Farming
- Forests
- Urban Areas

MAJOR MINERAL OCCURRENCES

- Cl Clay
- Mi Mica
- Major Industrial Areas

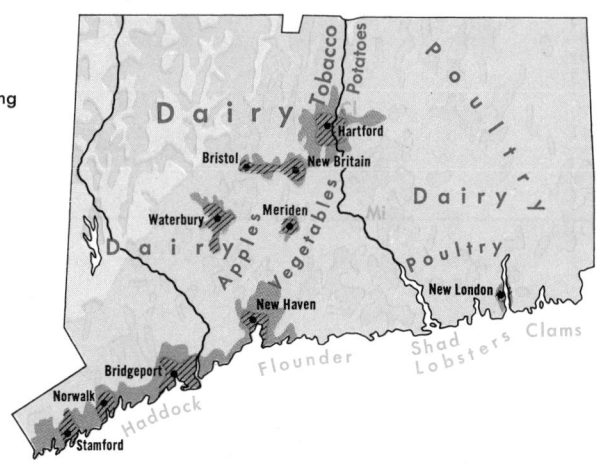

AREA 58,664 sq. mi. (151,940 sq. km.)
POPULATION 9,746,342
CAPITAL Tallahassee
LARGEST CITY Jacksonville
HIGHEST POINT (Walton County) 345 ft. (105 m.)
SETTLED IN 1565
ADMITTED TO UNION March 3, 1845
POPULAR NAME Sunshine State; Peninsula State
STATE FLOWER Orange Blossom
STATE BIRD Mockingbird

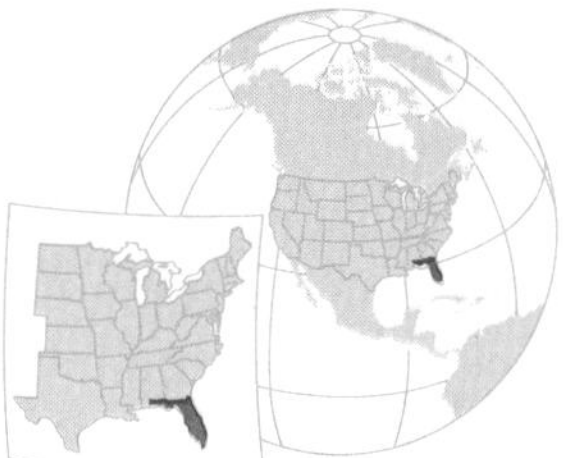

Topography

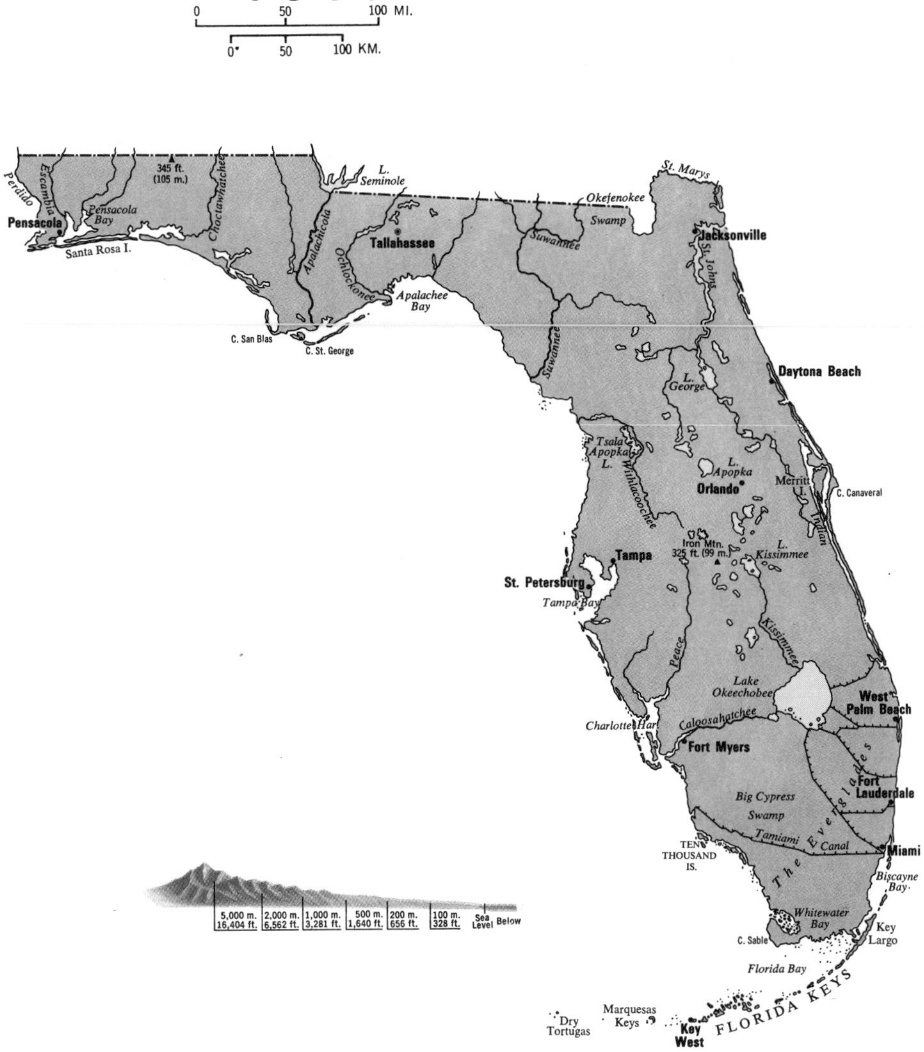

COUNTIES

Alachua 151,348 D2
Baker 15,289 D1
Bay 97,740 C6
Bradford 20,023 D2
Brevard 272,959 F3
Broward 101,820 F5
Calhoun 9,294 D6
Charlotte 58,460 E5
Citrus 54,703 D3
Clay 67,052 E2
Collier 85,791 E5
Columbia 35,399 D1
Dade 1,625,781 F6
De Soto 19,039 E4
Dixie 7,751 C2
Duval 571,003 E1
Escambia 233,794 B6
Flagler 10,913 E2
Franklin 7,661 B2
Gadsden 41,565 B1
Gilchrist 5,767 D2
Glades 5,992 E5
Gulf 10,658 D7
Hamilton 8,761 D1
Hardee 19,379 E4
Hendry 18,599 E5
Hernando 44,469 3
Highlands 47,526 E4
Hillsborough 646,960 D4
Holmes 14,723 C5
Indian River 59,896 F4
Jackson 39,154 D5
Jefferson 10,703 C1
Lafayette 4,035 C2
Lake 104,870 E3
Lee 205,266 E5
Leon 148,655 B1
Levy 19,870 D2
Liberty 4,260 B1
Madison 14,894 C1
Manatee 148,442 D4
Marion 122,488 D2
Martin 64,014 F4
Monroe 63,188 E7
Nassau 32,894 E1
Okaloosa 109,920 C6
Okeechobee 20,264 F4
Orange 471,016 E3
Osceola 49,287 E3
Palm Beach 576,863 F5
Pasco 193,643 D3
Pinellas 728,531 D4
Polk 321,652 E4
Putnam 50,549 E2
Saint Johns 51,303 E2
Saint Lucie 87,182 F4
Santa Rosa 55,988 B6
Sarasota 202,251 D4
Seminole 179,752 E3
Sumter 24,272 D3
Suwannee 22,287 C1
Taylor 16,532 C1
Union 10,166 D1
Volusia 258,762 E2
Wakulla 10,887 B1
Walton 21,300 C6
Washington 14,509 C6

CITIES and TOWNS

Zip	Name/Pop.	Key
32615	Alachua 3,561	D2
32420	Alford 548	D6
32701	Altamonte Springs 22,028	E3
32421	Altha 478	A1
33820	Alturas 900	E4
33501	Anna Maria 1,537	D4
32320	Apalachicola⊙ 2,565	A2
33570	Apollo Beach 4,014	C3
32703	Apopka 6,019	E3
33821	Arcadia⊙ 6,002	E4
32618	Archer 1,230	D2
33502	Aripeka 450	D3
32705	Astatula 755	E3
32233	Atlantic Beach 7,847	E1
33823	Auburndale 6,501	E3
33825	Avon Park 8,026	E4
32807	Azalea Park 8,301	E3
32530	Bagdad 1,479	B6
32234	Baldwin 1,526	E1
†33101	Bal Harbour 2,973	C4
33830	Bartow⊙ 14,780	E4
32423	Bascom 134	A1
†33101	Bay Harbor Islands 4,869	B4
†32786	Bay Lake 74	E3
33504	Bay Pines 5,757	B3
33507	Bayshore Gardens 14,945	D4
†33578	Bee Ridge 3,313	D4
32619	Bell 227	D2
33540	Belleair 3,673	B2
†33540	Belleair Beach 1,643	B2
33540	Belleair Bluffs 2,522	B3
†33540	Belleair Shores 80	B3
33430	Belle Glade 16,535	F5
†33430	Belle Glade Camp 1,645	F5
†32801	Belle Isle 2,848	E3
32620	Belleview 1,913	D2
†32036	Beverly Beach 217	E2
33152	Biscayne Park 3,088	B4
†32801	Bithlo 3,143	E3
32424	Blountstown⊙ 2,632	A1
33921	Boca Grande 900	D5
*33432	Boca Raton 49,505	F5
32425	Bonifay⊙ 2,534	C5
33923	Bonita Springs 5,435	E5
33834	Bowling Green 2,310	E4
*33435	Boynton Beach 35,624	F5
*33506	Bradenton⊙ 30,170	D4
	Bradenton‡ 148,442	D4
33510	Bradenton Beach 1,595	D4
33835	Bradley 1,108	D4
33511	Brandon 41,826	D4
32008	Branford 622	D2
†33435	Briny Breezes 387	G5
32321	Bristol⊙ 1,044	B1
†33314	Broadview Park 6,022	B4
32621	Bronson⊙ 853	D2
32622	Brooker 429	D2
33512	Brooksville⊙ 5,582	D3
†33311	Browardale 7,409	B4
32010	Bunnell⊙ 1,816	E2
33513	Bushnell⊙ 983	D3
32011	Callahan 869	E1
32401	Calloway 7,154	D6
32426	Campbellton 336	D5
32624	Candler 275	E2
32920	Cape Canaveral 5,733	F3
33904	Cape Coral 32,103	E5
33055	Carol City 47,349	B4
	Carrabelle 1,304	B2
32427	Caryville 633	C6
32707	Casselberry 15,247	E3
†32401	Cedar Grove 1,104	D6
32625	Cedar Key 700	C2
33514	Center Hill 751	D3
32535	Century 495	B5
†33950	Charlotte Harbor 2,084	E5
32324	Chattahoochee 5,332	B1
32626	Chiefland 1,986	D2
32428	Chipley⊙ 3,330	D6
†32548	Cinco Bayou 202	B6
*33515	Clearwater⊙ 85,528	B2
32711	Clermont 5,461	E3
†33950	Cleveland 2,417	E5
33440	Clewiston 5,219	E5
32922	Cocoa 16,096	F3
32931	Cocoa Beach 10,926	F3
†33060	Coconut Creek 6,288	F5
33521	Coleman 1,022	D3
33328	Cooper City 10,140	B4
†33559	Coral Cove 2,042	D4
33134	Coral Gables 43,241	B5
33060	Coral Springs 37,349	F5
33522	Cortez 3,821	D4
32431	Cottondale 1,056	D6
32327	Crawfordville⊙ 1,110	B1
32012	Crescent City 1,722	E2
32536	Crestview⊙ 7,617	C6
32628	Cross City⊙ 2,154	C2
32629	Crystal River 2,778	D3
33157	Cutler Ridge 20,886	F6
33880	Cypress Gardens 8,043	E3
†33472	Cypress Quarters 1,479	F4
33525	Dade City⊙ 4,923	D3
33004	Dania 11,811	B4
33837	Davenport 1,509	E3
33314	Davie 20,877	B4
*32014	Daytona Beach 54,176	F2
	Daytona Beach‡ 258,762	F2
32016	Daytona Beach Shores 1,324	F2
32713	De Bary 4,980	E3
33441	Deerfield Beach 39,193	F5
32433	De Funiak Springs⊙ 5,563	C6
32720	De Land⊙ 15,354	E2
32028	De Leon Springs 1,669	E2
*33444	Delray Beach 34,325	F5
32725	Deltona 15,710	E3
32541	Destin 3,672	C6
33527	Dover 2,354	D4
33838	Dundee 2,227	E3
33528	Dunedin 30,203	B2
32630	Dunnellon 1,427	D2
33839	Eagle Lake 1,678	E4
†33601	East Lake-Orient Park 5,612	C2
†33940	East Naples 12,127	E5
32031	East Palatka 1,613	E2
32328	Eastpoint 1,246	B2
32751	Eatonville 2,185	E3
32437	Ebro 233	C6
32032	Edgewater 6,726	F3
†32801	Edgewood 1,034	E3
†33614	Egypt Lake 11,932	C2
33531	Elfers 11,396	D3
†33101	El Portal 1,819	B4
33533	Englewood 9,633	D5
32504	Ensley 14,422	B6
32425	Esto 304	C5
32726	Eustis 9,453	E3
33929	Everglades City 524	E6
32634	Fairfield 450	D2
†32693	Fanning Springs (Suwannee Riv.) 314	D2
32948	Fellsmere 1,161	F4
32034	Fernandina Beach⊙ 7,224	E1
32922	Five Points 1,691	D1
32036	Flagler Beach 2,208	E2
32636	Floral City 1,181	D3
33034	Florida City 6,174	F6
†32960	Florida Ridge 4,988	F4
†33472	Fort Drum 70	F4
*33301	Fort Lauderdale⊙ 153,279	C4
	Fort Lauderdale-Hollywood‡ 1,014,043	C4
33841	Fort Meade 5,546	E4
*33901	Fort Myers⊙ 36,638	E5
	Fort Myers-Cape Coral‡ 205,266	E5
33931	Fort Myers Beach 5,753	E5
33842	Fort Ogden 900	E4
*33450	Fort Pierce⊙ 33,802	F4
32548	Fort Walton Beach 20,829	C6
	Fort Walton Beach‡ 109,920	C6
32038	Fort White 386	D2
32438	Fountain 900	D6
32439	Freeport 669	C6
33843	Frostproof 2,995	E4
32731	Fruitland Park 2,259	D3
33578	Fruitville 3,070	D4
*32601	Gainesville⊙ 81,371	D2
	Gainesville‡ 151,348	D2
32732	Geneva 1,120	E3
33534	Gibsonton 7,219	C3
32960	Gifford 6,240	F4
32040	Glen Saint Mary 462	D1
†33160	Golden Beach 612	C4
33999	Golden Gate 4,327	E5
†33444	Golf 110	F5
32560	Gonzalez 6,084	B6
33933	Goodland 600	E6
†32502	Goulding 5,352	B6
33170	Goulds 7,078	F6
32440	Graceville 2,918	D5
32442	Grand Ridge 591	A1
33463	Greenacres City 8,843	F5
32043	Green Cove Springs⊙ 4,154	E2
32330	Greensboro 562	B1
32331	Greenville 1,096	C1
32443	Greenwood 577	A1
32332	Gretna 1,448	B1
33533	Grove City 1,932	D5
32736	Groveland 1,992	E3
32561	Gulf Breeze 5,478	B6
33737	Gulfport 11,180	B3
†33444	Gulf Stream 475	F5
†33301	Hacienda Village 126	B4
33844	Haines City 10,799	E3
33009	Hallandale 36,517	B4
32044	Hampton 466	D2
33440	Harlem 2,669	F5
32045	Hastings 636	E2
32333	Havana 2,782	B1
32640	Hawthorne 1,303	D2
32642	Hernando 1,653	D3
*33010	Hialeah 145,254	B4
†33010	Hialeah Gardens 2,700	B4
33431	Highland Beach 2,030	F5
33846	Highland City 1,555	E4
32401	Highland Park 184	E4
32643	High Springs 2,491	D2
32405	Hiland Park 4,763	C6
†33827	Hillcrest Heights 177	E4
32046	Hilliard 1,869	E1
†33060	Hillsboro Beach 1,554	F5
33455	Hobe Sound 6,822	F4
32047	Hollister 980	E2
32017	Holly Hill 9,953	E2
*33020	Hollywood 121,323	B4
33509	Holmes Beach 4,023	D4
*33030	Homestead 20,668	F6
32646	Homosassa 1,426	D3
32648	Horseshoe Beach 304	C2
32334	Hosford 750	B1
32737	Howey In The Hills 626	E3
33568	Hudson 5,799	D3
†33460	Hypoluxo 573	F5
33934	Immokalee 11,038	E5
32903	Indialantic 2,883	F3
†33139	Indian Creek 103	B4
†32901	Indian Harbour Beach 5,967	F3
32960	Indian River Shores 1,254	F4
33535	Indian Rocks Beach 3,717	B3
†33535	Indian Shores 984	B3
33456	Indiantown 3,383	F4
32649	Inglis 1,173	D2
32048	Interlachen 848	E2
32650	Inverness⊙ 4,095	D3
33036	Islamorada 1,441	F7
†33101	Islandia 12	F6
*32201	Jacksonville⊙ 540,920	E1
	Jacksonville‡ 737,519	E1
32250	Jacksonville Beach 15,462	E1
†33568	Jasmine Estates 11,995	D3
32052	Jasper⊙ 2,093	D1
32565	Jay 633	B5
32053	Jennings 749	C1
33457	Jensen Beach 6,639	F4
†32901	June Park 4,051	F3
†33404	Juno Beach 1,142	F5
33458	Jupiter 9,868	F5
†33455	Jupiter Island 364	F4
33849	Kathleen 1,866	D3
33156	Kendall 73,758	B5
33709	Kenneth City 4,344	B3
33149	Key Biscayne 6,313	B5
33051	Key Colony Beach 977	F7
33037	Key Largo 7,447	F6
32656	Keystone Heights 1,056	E2
33040	Key West⊙ 24,382	E7
32741	Kissimmee⊙ 15,487	E3
33935	La Belle⊙ 2,287	E5
33537	Lacoochee 1,720	D3
32658	La Crosse 170	D2
32659	Lady Lake 1,193	E3
33850	Lake Alfred 3,134	E3
†32830	Lake Buena Vista 98	E3
32054	Lake Butler⊙ 1,830	D1
†33601	Lake Carroll 13,012	C2
32055	Lake City⊙ 9,257	D1
32744	Lake Helen 2,047	E3
*33801	Lakeland 47,406	D3
	Lakeland-Winter Haven‡ 321,652	D3
†33612	Lake Magdalene 13,331	D3
32746	Lake Mary 2,853	E3
33403	Lake Park 6,909	F5
33852	Lake Placid 963	E4
33853	Lake Wales 8,466	E4
*33460	Lake Worth 27,048	G5
33539	Land O'Lakes 4,515	D3
33462	Lantana 8,048	F5
*33540	Largo 58,977	B3
33308	Lauderdale-by-the-Sea 2,639	C3
†33313	Lauderdale Lakes 25,426	B3
33313	Lauderhill 37,271	B3
33545	Laurel 6,368	D4
32567	Laurel Hill 610	C5
32058	Lawtey 692	D1
†33050	Layton 88	F7
†33301	Lazy Lake 31	B3
32059	Lee 297	C1
32748	Leesburg 13,191	E3
33936	Lehigh Acres 9,604	E5
33033	Leisure City 17,905	F6
†33614	Leto 9,003	C2
33064	Lighthouse Point 11,488	F5
32060	Live Oak⊙ 6,732	D1
32662	Lochloosa 450	E2
33548	Longboat Key 4,843	D4
32750	Longwood 10,029	E3
33549	Lutz 5,555	D3
32444	Lynn Haven 6,239	C6
32063	Macclenny⊙ 3,851	D1

(continued on following page)

(continued)

33738 Madeira Beach 4,520 ... B3
32340 Madison⊙ 3,487 ... C1
32751 Maitland 8,763 ... E3
32950 Malabar 1,118 ... F3
32445 Malone 897 ... A1
33550 Mango 6,493 ... D4
33050 Marathon 7,568 ... E7
33937 Marco (Marco Island) 4,679 ... E6
33063 Margate 35,900 ... F5
32446 Marianna⊙ 7,006 ... A1
†32084 Marineland 31 ... E2
32569 Mary Esther 3,530 ... B6
32753 Mascotte 1,112 ... E3
32066 Mayo⊙ 891 ... C1
32664 McIntosh 404 ... D2
†33101 Medley 537 ... B4
*32901 Melbourne 46,536 ... F3
Melbourne-Titusville-Cocoa‡ 272,959 ... F3
32951 Melbourne Beach 2,713 ... F3
†33301 Melrose Park 5,672 ... B4
†33561 Memphis 5,501 ... D4
32952 Merritt Island 30,708 ... F3
32410 Mexico Beach 632 ... D6
*33101 Miami⊙ 346,931 ... B5
Miami‡ 1,625,979 ... B5
33139 Miami Beach 96,298 ... C5
†33101 Miami Lakes 9,809 ... B4
33153 Miami Shores 9,244 ... B4
33166 Miami Springs 12,350 ... B5
32667 Micanopy 737 ... D2
†32960 Micco 3,585 ... F4
32343 Midway 950 ... B1
32570 Milton⊙ 7,206 ... B6
32754 Mims 7,583 ... F3
32755 Minneola 851 ... E3
33023 Miramar 32,813 ... B4
32577 Molino 1,456 ... B6
32344 Monticello⊙ 2,994 ... C1
32756 Montverde 397 ... E3
33471 Moore Haven⊙ 1,250 ... E5
32757 Mount Dora 5,883 ... E3
33860 Mulberry 2,932 ... E4
33938 Murdock 272 ... D4
32506 Myrtle Grove 14,238 ... B6
*33940 Naples⊙ 17,581 ... E5
†33940 Naples Park 5,438 ... E5
33032 Naranja 10,381 ... F6
32233 Neptune Beach 5,248 ... E1
32669 Newberry 1,826 ... D2
*33552 New Port Richey 11,196 ... D3
32069 New Smyrna Beach 13,557 F2
32578 Niceville 8,543 ... C6
33555 Nokomis 3,108 ... D4
32452 Noma 113 ... C5
†33169 Norland 19,471 ... B4
33141 North Bay Village 4,920 ... B4
33903 North Fort Myers 22,808 ... E5
†33063 North Lauderdale 18,653 ... B3
33161 North Miami 42,566 ... B4
33161 North Miami Beach 36,481 C4
33940 North Naples 7,950 ... E5
33403 North Palm Beach 11,344 .. F5
33595 North Port 6,205 ... D4
†33708 North Redington Beach 1,156 ... B3
32759 Oak Hill 938 ... F3
32760 Oakland 658 ... E3
33334 Oakland Park 23,035 ... B3
*32670 Ocala⊙ 37,170 ... D2
Ocala‡ 122,488 ... D2
†33457 Ocean Breeze Park 469 ... F4
33444 Ocean Ridge 1,355 ... F5
32761 Ocoee 7,803 ... E3
33163 Ojus 17,344 ... B4
32762 Okahumpka 900 ... D3
33472 Okeechobee⊙ 4,225 ... F4
32557 Oldsmar 2,608 ... B2
33558 Oneco 6,417 ... D4
33054 Opa Locka 14,460 ... B4
32763 Orange City 2,795 ... E3
32073 Orange Park 8,766 ... E1
†32970 Orchid 42 ... F4
*32801 Orlando⊙ 128,291 ... E3
Orlando‡ 700,699 ... E3
32074 Ormond Beach 21,378 ... E2
32074 Ormond-by-the-Sea 7,665 . E2
33559 Osprey 1,660 ... D4
32683 Otter Creek 167 ... D2
32765 Oviedo 3,074 ... E3
32570 Pace 5,006 ... B6
33476 Pahokee 6,346 ... F5
†32036 Painters Hill 40 ... E2
32077 Palatka⊙ 10,175 ... E2
32905 Palm Bay 18,560 ... F3
32084 Palm Beach 9,729 ... G4
†33403 Palm Beach Gardens 14,407 ... F5
†33404 Palm Beach Shores 1,232 . G5
33490 Palm City 2,177 ... F4
32037 Palm Coast 2,837 ... E2
33561 Palmetto 8,637 ... D4
33563 Palm Harbor 5,215 ... D3
33619 Palm River-Clair Mel 14,447 ... C3
†32901 Palm Shores 77 ... F3
33460 Palm Springs 8,166 ... F5
*32401 Panama City⊙ 33,346 ... C6
Panama City‡ 97,740 ... C6
32407 Panama City Beach 2,148 .. C6
32401 Parker 4,298 ... C6
†33441 Parkland 545 ... F5
32538 Paxton 659 ... C5
†33023 Pembroke Park 4,783 ... B4
33024 Pembroke Pines 35,776 ... B4
32079 Penney Farms 630 ... E2
†33010 Pennsuco 15 ... B4
*32501 Pensacola⊙ 57,619 ... B6
Pensacola‡ 289,782 ... B6
33157 Perrine 16,129 ... F6
32347 Perry⊙ 8,254 ... C1
32080 Pierson 1,085 ... E2
32808 Pine Hills 35,771 ... E3
33565 Pinellas Park 32,811 ... B3
33317 Plantation 48,653 ... B4
33566 Plant City 17,064 ... D3
33868 Polk City 576 ... E3
32081 Pomona Park 791 ... E2
*33060 Pompano Beach 52,618 ... F5
32455 Ponce de Leon 454 ... C6
†32019 Ponce Inlet 1,003 ... F2
33952 Port Charlotte 25,770 ... D5
32019 Port Orange 18,756 ... F2
33568 Port Richey 2,165 ... D3
32456 Port Saint Joe 4,027 ... D6
33452 Port Saint Lucie 14,690 ... F4
33492 Port Salerno 4,511 ... F4
33032 Princeton 10,381 ... F6
*33950 Punta Gorda⊙ 6,797 ... E5
32351 Quincy⊙ 8,591 ... B1
32083 Raiford 259 ... D1
32686 Reddick 657 ... D2
33708 Redington Beach 1,708 ... B3
†33708 Redington Shores 2,142 ... B3
†33158 Richmond Heights 8,577 ... F6
†33301 Riverland 5,919 ... B4
33404 Riviera Beach 26,489 ... G5
32955 Rockledge 11,877 ... F3
32957 Roseland 1,607 ... F4
33570 Ruskin 5,117 ... C3
33572 Safety Harbor 6,461 ... B2
32084 Saint Augustine⊙ 11,985 .. E2
32084 Saint Augustine Beach 1,289 ... E2
32769 Saint Cloud 7,840 ... E3
33956 Saint James City 1,298 ... D5
33574 Saint Leo 917 ... D3
33452 Saint Lucie 593 ... F4
32355 Saint Marks 286 ... B1
*33701 Saint Petersburg 238,647 .. B3
33736 Saint Petersburg Beach 9,354 ... B3
†33508 Samoset 5,747 ... D4
†32069 Samsula 1,971 ... E2
33576 San Antonio 529 ... D3
32771 Sanford⊙ 23,176 ... E3
33957 Sanibel 3,363 ... D5
*33577 Sarasota⊙ 48,868 ... D4
Sarasota‡ 202,251 ... D4
†33577 Sarasota Springs 13,860 ... D4
32935 Satellite Beach 9,163 ... F3
32775 Scottsmoor 900 ... F3
†33301 Sea Ranch Lakes 584 ... C3
32958 Sebastian 2,831 ... F4
33870 Sebring⊙ 8,736 ... E4
33584 Seffner 6,493 ... D4
33542 Seminole 4,586 ... B3
†33457 Sewalls Point 1,187 ... F4
32579 Shalimar 390 ... C6
32959 Sharpes 4,149 ... F3
32688 Silver Springs 1,082 ... D2
32460 Sneads 1,690 ... B1
32358 Sopchoppy 444 ... B1
33493 South Bay 3,886 ... F5
32021 South Daytona 11,252 ... F2
33143 South Miami 10,944 ... B5
†33157 South Miami Heights 23,559 ... F6
33707 South Pasadena 4,188 ... B3
†32901 South Patrick Shores 9,816 ... F3
†32401 Southport 1,992 ... C6
33452 South Port Saint Lucie (Port Saint Lucie 14,690 ... F4
33595 South Venice 8,075 ... D4
32690 Sparr 902 ... D2
32401 Springfield 7,220 ... D6
32091 Starke⊙ 5,306 ... D2
33494 Stuart⊙ 9,467 ... F4
33586 Sun City ... D4
†33570 Sun City Center 5,605 ... C3
†33450 Sunland Gardens ... F4
33160 Sunny Isles 12,564 ... C4
33313 Sunrise 39,681 ... B4
33154 Surfside 3,763 ... B4
32692 Suwannee (Fanning Sprs.) 314 ... C2
†33144 Sweetwater 8,251 ... B5
†32043 Switzerland 3,906 ... E1
32809 Taft 900 ... E3
*32301 Tallahassee (cap.)⊙ 81,548 ... B1
Tallahassee‡ 159,542 ... B1
†33321 Tamarac 29,376 ... B3
*33601 Tampa⊙ 271,523 ... C2
Tampa-Saint Petersburg‡ 1,569,492 .. C2
*33589 Tarpon Springs 13,251 ... D3
32778 Tavares⊙ 4,103 ... E3
33070 Tavernier 1,834 ... F6
33617 Temple Terrace 11,097 ... C2
33458 Tequesta 3,685 ... F5
33905 Tice 6,645 ... E5
32780 Titusville⊙ 31,910 ... F3
33740 Treasure Island 6,316 ... B3
32693 Trenton⊙ 1,131 ... D2
32784 Umatilla 1,872 ... E3
33620 University 24,514 ... C2
32580 Valparaiso 6,142 ... C6
*33595 Venice 12,153 ... D4
32462 Vernon 885 ... C6
32960 Vero Beach⊙ 16,176 ... F4
†33166 Virginia Gardens 2,098 ... B5
32970 Wabasso 2,157 ... F4
†32327 Wakulla 225 ... B1
32694 Waldo 993 ... D2
†32456 Ward Ridge 104 ... D6
32507 Warrington 15,792 ... B6
†32055 Watertown 3,804 ... D1
33873 Wauchula⊙ 2,986 ... E4
32463 Wausau 347 ... D6
33877 Waverly 1,208 ... E4
33597 Webster 856 ... D3
†33512 Weeki Wachee 8 ... D3
32093 Welaka 492 ... E2
32935 West Eau Gallie 2,591 ... F3
†32901 West Melbourne 5,078 ... F3
†33101 West Miami 6,076 ... B5
*33401 West Palm Beach⊙ 63,305 F5
West Palm Beach-Boca Raton‡ 573,125 ... F5
†32502 West Pensacola 24,371 ... B6
32464 Westville 343 ... C6
†33165 Westwood Lakes 11,478 ... B5
32465 Wewahitchka⊙ 1,742 ... D6
†32465 White City 4,110 ... F4
32096 White Springs 781 ... D1
32785 Wildwood 2,665 ... D3
32696 Williston 2,240 ... D2
33334 Wilton Manors 12,742 ... B3
33598 Wimauma 1,477 ... D4
32786 Windermere 1,302 ... E3
33880 Winter Haven 21,119 ... E3
*32789 Winter Park 22,339 ... E3
†32801 Winter Springs 10,475 ... E3
32362 Woodville 1,768 ... B1
32697 Worthington Springs 220 .. D2
32698 Yankeetown 600 ... D2
32097 Yulee 3,168 ... E1
32798 Zellwood 1,760 ... E3
33599 Zephyrhills 5,742 ... D3
33890 Zolfo Springs 1,495 ... E4

OTHER FEATURES

Alapaha (riv.) ... C1
Alligator (lake) ... E3
Amelia (isl.) ... E1
Anastasia (isl.) ... E2
Anclote (keys) ... D3
Apalachee (bay) ... B2
Apalachicola (bay) ... B2
Apalachicola (riv.) ... A1
Apopka (lake) ... E3
Arbuckle (lake) ... E4
Aucilla (riv.) ... C1
Banana (riv.) ... F3
Beresford (lake) ... E3
Big Cypress (swamp) ... E5
Big Cypress Nat'l Preserve ... E5
Biscayne (bay) ... F6
Biscayne (key) ... B5
Biscayne Nat'l Park ... F6
Blackwater (riv.) ... B6
Blue Cypress (lake) ... F4
Boca Chica (key) ... E7
Boca Ciega (bay) ... B3
Boca Grande (key) ... D7
Bryant (lake) ... E2
Caloosahatchee (riv.) ... E5
Captiva (isl.) ... D5
Casey (key) ... D4
Castillo de San Marcos Nat'l Mon. ... E2
Cecil Field Naval Air Sta. ... E1
Charlotte (harb.) ... D5
Chattahoochee (riv.) ... B1
Chipola (riv.) ... D6
Choctawhatchee (riv.) ... C6
Crescent (lake) ... E2
Cumberland Island Nat'l Seashore ... E1
Cypress (lake) ... E3
De Soto Nat'l Mem. ... D4
Dead (lake) ... D6
Dexter (lake) ... E2
Dog (isl.) ... B2
Dorr (lake) ... E2
Dry Tortugas (keys) ... D7
Dumfoundling (bay) ... C4
East (pt.) ... E6
Eglin A.F.B. 7,574 ... C6
Egmont (key) ... D4
Elliott (key) ... F6
Escambia (riv.) ... B6
Estero (isl.) ... E5
Eureka (res.) ... E2
Everglades, The (swamp) ... F6
Everglades Nat'l Park ... F6
Fenholloway (riv.) ... C1
Florida (bay) ... F6
Florida (cape) ... F6
Florida (keys) ... E7
Florida (strs) ... F7
Fort Caroline Nat'l Mem. ... E1
Fort Jefferson Nat'l Mon. ... C7
Fort Matanzas Nat'l Mon. ... E2
Gasparilla (isl.) ... D5
George (lake) ... E2
Grassy (key) ... F7
Gulf Island Nat'l Seashore ... B6
Harney (lake) ... F3
Hart (lake) ... E3
Hillsborough (bay) ... C3
Hillsborough (canal) ... F5
Hillsborough (riv.) ... C2
Homosassa (isls.) ... D3
Homestead A.F.B. 7,594 ... F6
Iamonia (lake) ... B1
Indian (riv.) ... F3
Iron (mt.) ... E4
Istokpoga (lake) ... E4
Jackson (lake) ... B1
Jackson (lake) ... E4
Jacksonville Naval Air Sta. ... E1
John F. Kennedy Space Center ... F3
June in Winter (lake) ... E4
Kennedy (Canaveral) (cape) ... F3
Kerr (lake) ... E2
Key Largo (key) ... F6
Key Vaca (key) ... E7
Key West Naval Air Sta. ... E7
Kissimmee (lake) ... E4
Kissimmee (riv.) ... E4
Largo (key) ... F6
Levy (lake) ... D2
Lochloosa (lake) ... D2
Long (key) ... B3
Long (key) ... F7
Longboat (key) ... D4
Lower Matecumbe (key) ... F7
Lowery (lake) ... E3
MacDill A.F.B. ... C3
Manatee (riv.) ... D4
Marco (isl.) ... E6
Marian (lake) ... E4
Marquesas (keys) ... D7
Matanzas (inlet) ... E2
Mayport Naval Air Sta. ... E1
McCoy A.F.B. ... E3
Merritt (isl.) ... F3
Mexico (gulf) ... C4
Miami (canal) ... F5
Miami (riv.) ... B5
Miccosukee (lake) ... B1
Monroe (lake) ... E3
Mosquito (lag.) ... F3
Mullet (key) ... D4
Myakka (riv.) ... D4
Nassau (riv.) ... E1
Nassau (sound) ... E1
New (riv.) ... B1
New (riv.) ... D1
Newnans (lake) ... D2
North Merritt (isl.) ... F3
North New River (canal) ... F5
Ochlockonee (riv.) ... B1
Okaloacoochee Slough (swamp) ... E5
Okeechobee (lake) ... F5
Okefenokee (swamp) ... D1
Oklawaha (riv.) ... E2
Old Rhodes (key) ... F6
Old Tampa (bay) ... B3
Olustee (riv.) ... D1
Orange (lake) ... D2
Patrick A.F.B. 2,843 ... F3
Peace (riv.) ... E4
Pensacola (bay) ... B6
Pensacola Naval Air Sta. ... B6
Perdido (riv.) ... B6
Pine (isl.) ... D5
Pine Island (sound) ... D5
Pine Log (creek) ... C6
Pinellas (pt.) ... C3
Piney (isl.) ... B1
Piney (pt.) ... C2
Placid (lake) ... E4
Plantation (key) ... F7
Poinsett (lake) ... F3
Ponce de Leon (bay) ... E6
Port Everglades (harb.) ... C4
Port Tampa (harb.) ... B3
Reedy (lake) ... E4
Romano (cape) ... E6
Sable (cape) ... E6
Saint Andrew (pt.) ... D6
Saint George (cape) ... A2
Saint George (isl.) ... B2
Saint George (sound) ... B2
Saint Johns (riv.) ... E2
Saint Joseph (bay) ... D6
Saint Joseph (pt.) ... D6
Saint Lucie (canal) ... F4
Saint Lucie (inlet) ... F4
Saint Marys (riv.) ... D1
Saint Marys Entrance (inlet) ... E1
Saint Vincent (isl.) ... D7
San Blas (cape) ... D7
Sand (key) ... B3
Sands (key) ... F6
Sanibel (isl.) ... D5
Santa Fe (lake) ... D2
Santa Fe (riv.) ... D2
Santa Rosa (isl.) ... B6
Santa Rosa (sound) ... B6
Sarasota (pt.) ... D4
Seminole (lake) ... B1
Seminole Ind. Res. ... E4
Seminole Ind. Res. ... F5
Shark (pt.) ... E6
Shoal (riv.) ... C6
Snake Creek (canal) ... B4
South New River (canal) ... F5
Stafford (lake) ... D2
Sugarloaf (key) ... E7
Suwannee (riv.) ... C2
Suwannee (sound) ... C2
Talbot (isl.) ... E1
Talquin (lake) ... B1
Tamiami (canal) ... E6
Tampa (bay) ... D4
Ten Thousand (isls.) ... E
Torch (key) ... E
Treasure (isl.) ... B
Tsala Apopka (lake) ... D
Tyndall A.F.B. 4,542 ... C
Upper Matecumbe (key) ... F
Vaca (key) ... E
Virginia (key) ... B
Waccasassa (bay) ... D
Waccasassa (riv.) ... D
Washington (lake) ... F
Weir (lake) ... E
Weohyakapka (lake) ... E
West Palm Beach (canal) ... F
Whitewater (bay) ... F
Whiting Field Naval Air Sta. ... B
Wimico (lake) ... A
Winder (lake) ... F
Withlacoochee (riv.) ... C
Withlacoochee (riv.) ... D
Yale (lake) ... E
Yellow (riv.) ... B

⊙County seat.
‡Population of metropolitan area.
† Zip of nearest p.o. * Multiple zips

Agriculture, Industry and Resources

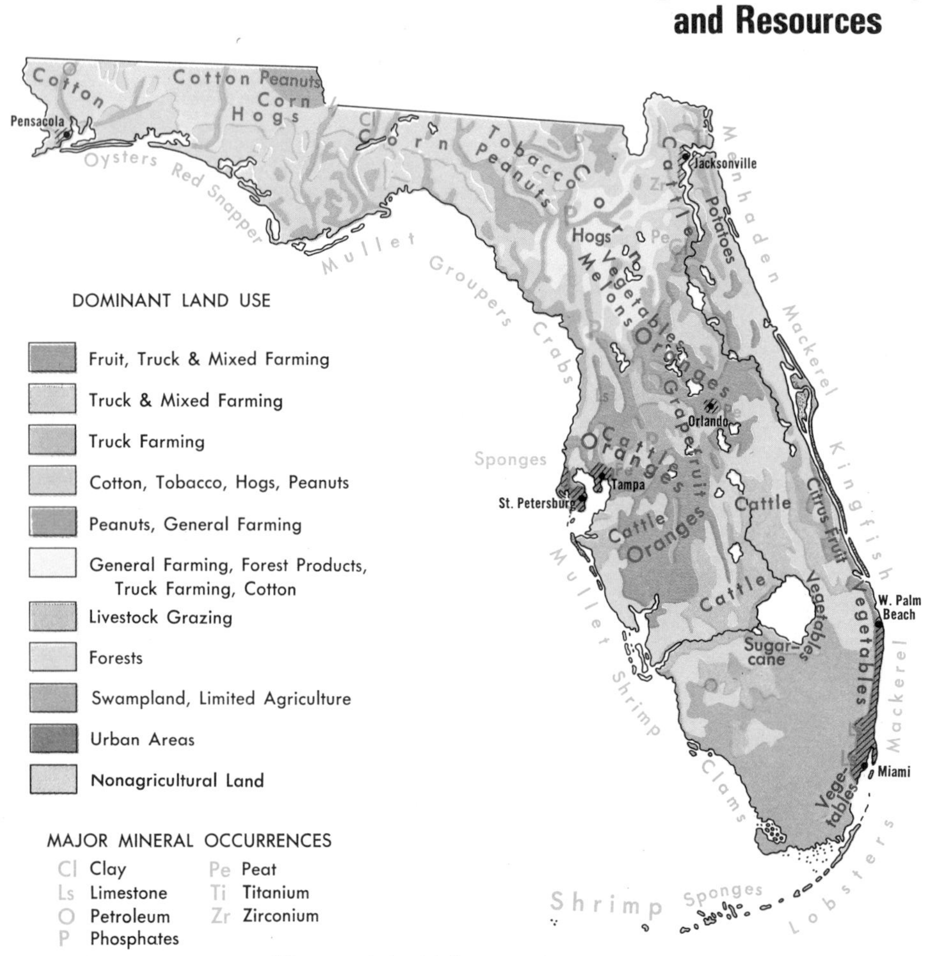

Cotton
Cotton Peanuts
Corn
Hogs
Pensacola
Oysters
Red Snapper
Mullet
Groupers
Tobacco
Peanuts
Corn
Cattle
Jacksonville
Potatoes
Menhaden
Hogs
Corn
Vegetables
Melons
Oranges
Crabs
Mackerel
Grapefruit
Orlando
Sponges
Tampa
St. Petersburg
Cattle
Oranges
Cattle
Kingfish
Citrus Fruit
Mullet
Cattle
Vegetables
W. Palm Beach
Sugar-cane
Shrimp
Clams
Vegetables
Mackerel
Miami
Vegetables
Lobsters
Shrimp
Sponges
DOMINANT LAND USE
Fruit, Truck & Mixed Farming
Truck & Mixed Farming
Truck Farming
Cotton, Tobacco, Hogs, Peanuts
Peanuts, General Farming
General Farming, Forest Products, Truck Farming, Cotton
Livestock Grazing
Forests
Swampland, Limited Agriculture
Urban Areas
Nonagricultural Land
MAJOR MINERAL OCCURRENCES
Cl Clay
Pe Peat
Ls Limestone
Ti Titanium
O Petroleum
Zr Zirconium
P Phosphates
Water Power
Major Industrial Areas

AREA 58,910 sq. mi. (152,577 sq. km.)
POPULATION 5,463,105
CAPITAL Atlanta
LARGEST CITY Atlanta
HIGHEST POINT Brasstown Bald 4,784 ft.
(1458 m.)
SETTLED IN 1733
ADMITTED TO UNION January 2, 1788
POPULAR NAME Empire State of the South;
Peach State
STATE FLOWER Cherokee Rose
STATE BIRD Brown Thrasher

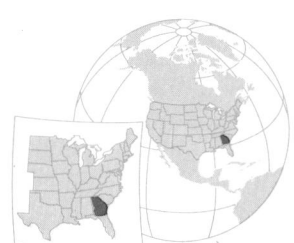

COUNTIES

Appling 15,565 ....H7
Atkinson 6,141 ....G8
Bacon 9,379 ....G7
Baker 3,808 ....D8
Baldwin 34,686 ....F4
Banks 8,702 ....E2
Barrow 21,293 ....E2
Bartow 40,760 ....C2
Ben Hill 16,000 ....F7
Berrien 13,525 ....F8
Bibb 151,085 ....E5
Bleckley 10,767 ....F6
Brantley 8,701 ....J8
Brooks 15,255 ....E9
Bryan 10,175 ....K6
Bulloch 35,785 ....J6
Burke 19,349 ....J4
Butts 13,665 ....E4
Calhoun 5,717 ....C7
Camden 13,371 ....J9
Candler 7,518 ....H6
Carroll 56,346 ....B3
Catoosa 36,991 ....B1
Charlton 7,343 ....H9
Chatham 202,226 ....K6
Chattahoochee 21,732 ...C6
Chattooga 21,856 ....B1
Cherokee 51,699 ....D2
Clarke 74,498 ....F3
Clay 3,553 ....B7
Clayton 150,357 ....D3
Clinch 6,660 ....G9

Cobb 297,694 ....C3
Coffee 26,894 ....G8
Colquitt 35,376 ....E8
Columbia 40,118 ....H3
Cook 13,490 ....F8
Coweta 39,268 ....C4
Crawford 7,684 ....E5
Crisp 19,489 ....E7
Dade 12,318 ....A1
Dawson 4,774 ....D2
Decatur 25,495 ....C9
De Kalb 483,024 ....D3
Dodge 16,955 ....F6
Dooly 10,826 ....E6
Dougherty 100,978 ....D7
Douglas 54,573 ....C3
Early 13,158 ....C8
Echols 2,297 ....G9
Effingham 18,327 ....K6
Elbert 18,758 ....G2
Emanuel 20,795 ....H5
Evans 8,428 ....J6
Fannin 14,748 ....D1
Fayette 29,043 ....C4
Floyd 79,800 ....B2
Forsyth 27,958 ....D2
Franklin 15,185 ....F2
Fulton 589,904 ....D3
Gilmer 11,110 ....D1
Glascock 2,382 ....G4
Glynn 54,981 ....J8
Gordon 30,070 ....C2
Grady 19,845 ....D9
Greene 11,391 ....F3

Gwinnett 166,903 ....D2
Habersham 25,020 ....E1
Hall 75,649 ....E2
Hancock 9,466 ....G4
Haralson 18,422 ....B3
Harris 15,464 ....C5
Hart 18,585 ....G2
Heard 6,520 ....B4
Henry 36,309 ....D3
Houston 77,605 ....E6
Irwin 8,988 ....F7
Jackson 25,343 ....E2
Jasper 7,553 ....E4
Jeff Davis 11,473 ....G7
Jefferson 18,403 ....H4
Jenkins 8,841 ....J5
Johnson 8,660 ....G5
Jones 16,579 ....E5
Lamar 12,215 ....D4
Lanier 5,654 ....F8
Laurens 36,990 ....G6
Lee 11,684 ....D7
Liberty 37,583 ....J7
Lincoln 6,949 ....H3
Long 4,524 ....J7
Lowndes 67,972 ....F9
Lumpkin 10,762 ....D1
Macon 14,003 ....D6
Madison 17,747 ....F2
Marion 5,297 ....C6
McDuffie 18,546 ....H4
McIntosh 8,046 ....K7
Meriwether 21,229 ....C4
Miller 7,038 ....C8

Mitchell 21,114 ....D8
Monroe 14,610 ....E4
Montgomery 7,011 ....G6
Morgan 11,572 ....F3
Murray 19,685 ....C1
Muscogee 170,108 ....C6
Newton 34,489 ....E3
Oconee 12,427 ....F3
Oglethorpe 8,929 ....F3
Paulding 26,042 ....C3
Peach 19,151 ....E5
Pickens 11,652 ....D2
Pierce 11,897 ....H8
Pike 8,937 ....D4
Polk 32,386 ....B3
Pulaski 8,950 ....E6
Putnam 10,295 ....F4
Quitman 2,357 ....B7
Rabun 10,466 ....F1
Randolph 9,599 ....C7
Richmond 181,629 ....H4
Rockdale 36,747 ....D3
Schley 3,433 ....D6
Screven 14,043 ....J5
Seminole 9,057 ....C9
Spalding 47,899 ....D4
Stephens 21,763 ....F1
Stewart 5,896 ....C6
Sumter 29,360 ....D6
Talbot 6,536 ....C5
Taliaferro 2,032 ....G3
Tattnall 18,134 ....J6
Taylor 7,902 ....D5
Telfair 11,445 ....G7

Terrell 12,017 ....D7
Thomas 38,098 ....E9
Tift 32,862 ....E7
Toombs 22,592 ....H6
Towns 5,638 ....E1
Treutlen 6,087 ....G6
Troup 50,003 ....B4
Turner 9,510 ....E7
Twiggs 9,354 ....F5
Union 9,390 ....E1
Upson 25,998 ....D5
Walker 56,470 ....B1
Walton 31,211 ....E3
Ware 37,180 ....H8
Warren 6,583 ....G4
Washington 18,842 ....G4
Wayne 20,750 ....J7
Webster 2,341 ....C6
Wheeler 5,155 ....G6
White 10,120 ....E1
Whitfield 65,780 ....B1
Wilcox 7,682 ....F7
Wilkes 10,951 ....G3
Wilkinson 10,368 ....F5
Worth 18,064 ....E8

CITIES and TOWNS

Zip   Name/Pop.   Key

31001 Abbeville⊙ 985 ....F7
30101 Acworth 3,648 ....C2
30103 Adairsville 1,739 ....C2
31620 Adel⊙ 5,592 ....F8
31002 Adrian 756 ....G5
30410 Ailey 579 ....G6
30411 Alamo⊙ 993 ....G6
31622 Alapaha 771 ....F8
*31701 Albany‡ 74,550 ......D7
     Albany‡ 112,456 ......D7
†30204 Aldora 139 ....D4
31301 Allenhurst 606 ....J7
31003 Allentown 321 ....F5
31510 Alma⊙ 3,819 ....G7
30201 Alpharetta 3,128 ......D2
30412 Alston 111 ....H6
30510 Alto 618 ....E2
†30161 Alto Park B2
31512 Ambrose 360 ....G7
31709 Americus⊙ 16,120 ...D6
31711 Andersonville 267 ....D6
30802 Appling⊙ 150 ....H3
31712 Arabi 376 ....E7
30104 Aragon 855 ....B2
†30549 Arcade 223 ....E2
†31520 Arco J8
31623 Argyle 206 ....G8
31713 Arlington 1,572 ....C8
30619 Arnoldsville 187 ......F3
31714 Ashburn⊙ 4,766 ......E7
*30601 Athens⊙ 42,549 .....F3
     Athens‡ 130,015 ......F3
*30301 Atlanta (cap.)⊙ 425,022 ...K1
     Atlanta‡ 2,029,618 ....K1
31715 Attapulgus 623 ....D9
30203 Auburn 692 ....E2
*30901 Augusta⊙ 47,532 ....J4
     Augusta‡ 327,372 .....J4
30001 Austell 3,939 ....J1
†30557 Avalon 200 ....F1
30803 Avera 248 ....G4
30002 Avondale Estates 1,313 ...L1
31716 Baconton 763 ....D8
31717 Bainbridge⊙ 10,553 ..C9
30511 Baldwin 1,080 ....E2
30107 Ball Ground 640 ......D2
30204 Barnesville⊙ 4,887 ...D4
31625 Barney 146 ....E8
30413 Bartow 357 ....G5
31720 Barwick 413 ....E9
31513 Baxley⊙ 3,586 ....H7
*31554 Beach G8
30414 Bellville 173 ....H6
31721 Benevolence 138 ....C7
†30166 Berkeley Lake 503 ...D3
31722 Berlin 538 ....E8
30620 Bethlehem 281 ....E3
†31901 Bibb City 667 ....B5
30621 Bishop 172 ....F3
31516 Blackshear⊙ 3,222 ..H8
30512 Blairsville⊙ 530 ....E1
31723 Blakely⊙ 5,880 ....C8
30513 Blue Ridge⊙ 1,376 ...D1
31302 Bloomingdale 1,855 ..K6
31724 Bluffton 132 ....C7
30805 Blythe 367 ....H4
30622 Bogart 819 ....E3
31626 Boston 1,424 ....E9
30623 Bostwick 357 ....F3
30108 Bowdon 1,743 ....B3
30516 Bowersville 318 ......G2
30624 Bowman 890 ....G2
30517 Braselton 308 ....E2
†30153 Braswell 282 ....C3
30110 Bremen 3,966 ....B3
31725 Brinson 274 ....C9
31726 Bronwood 524 ....D7

30415 Brooklet 1,035 ....J6
30205 Brooks 199 ....D4
31519 Broxton 1,117 ....G7
31520 Brunswick⊙ 17,605 ..K8
30113 Buchanan⊙ 1,019 ....B3
30625 Buckhead 219 ....F3
31803 Buena Vista⊙ 1,544 ..C6
30518 Buford 6,578 ....D2
31006 Butler⊙ 1,959 ....D5
31007 Byromville 567 ....E6
31008 Byron 1,661 ....E5
31009 Cadwell 353 ....G6
31728 Cairo⊙ 8,777 ....D9
30701 Calhoun⊙ 5,335 ......C1
30807 Camak 283 ....G4
31730 Camilla⊙ 5,414 ....D8
30520 Canon 704 ....F2
30114 Canton⊙ 3,601 ....C2
32003 Carl 239 ....E3
30627 Carlton 291 ....F2
30521 Carnesville⊙ 465 .....F2
30117 Carrollton⊙ 14,078 ...C3
30120 Cartersville⊙ 9,247 ..C2
30124 Cave Spring 883 ......B2
31627 Cecil 280 ....F8
†30125 Cedartown⊙ 8,619 ...B2
†30601 Center 330 ....F2
31028 Centerville 2,622 .....E5
30217 Centralhatchee 240 ..B4
†31816 Chalybeate Springs 265 ...C5
30341 Chamblee 7,137 ......K1
30705 Chatsworth⊙ 2,493 ..C1
31011 Chauncey 350 ....F6
31012 Chester 409 ....F6
30707 Chickamauga 2,232 ..B1
30523 Clarkesville⊙ 1,348 ..F1
30021 Clarkston 4,539 ......L1
30417 Claxton⊙ 2,694 ......J6
30525 Clayton⊙ 1,838 ......F1
30527 Clermont 300 ....E2
30528 Cleveland⊙ 1,578 ....E1
31734 Climax 407 ....D9
31735 Cobb E7
30420 Cobbtown 494 ....H6
31014 Cochran⊙ 5,121 ......F6
30710 Cohutta 407 ....C1
30628 Colbert 498 ....F2
31736 Coleman 164 ....C7
30337 College Park 24,632 ..K2
30421 Collins 639 ....H6
31737 Colquitt⊙ 2,065 ......C8
*31901 Columbus⊙ 169,441 ..C6
     Columbus‡ 239,196 ...C6
30629 Comer 930 ....F2
30529 Commerce 4,092 .....E2
30206 Concord 317 ....D4
*30207 Conyers⊙ 6,567 .....D3
31738 Coolidge 736 ....E8
31015 Cordele⊙ 11,184 .....E7
30531 Cornelia 3,203 ....E1
31739 Cotton 122 ....D8
30209 Covington⊙ 10,586 ..E3
30711 Crandall C1
30630 Crawford 498 ....F3
30631 Crawfordville⊙ 594 ..G3
†31771 Crosland E8
31016 Culloden 281 ....D5
30130 Cumming⊙ 2,094 ....D2
31805 Cusseta⊙ 1,218 ......C6
31740 Cuthbert⊙ 4,340 .....C7
30211 Dacula 1,577 ....E3
30533 Dahlonega⊙ 2,844 ...D1
30423 Daisy 174 ....J6
30132 Dallas⊙ 2,440 ....C3
30720 Dalton⊙ 20,743 ......C1
31741 Damascus 403 ....C8
30633 Danielsville⊙ 354 ....F2
31017 Danville 529 ....F5
31305 Darien⊙ 1,731 ....K8
31601 Dasher 659 ....F9
31018 Davisboro 433 ....G5
31742 Dawson⊙ 5,699 ......D7
30534 Dawsonville⊙ 342 ....D2
30808 Dearing 539 ....H4
*30030 Decatur⊙ 18,404 ....K1
†31501 Deenwood H8
31082 Deepstep 120 ....G4
30535 Demorest 1,130 ......F1
31532 Denton 286 ....G7
31743 De Soto 248 ....D7
31019 Dexter 527 ....G6
30537 Dillard 238 ....F1
31629 Dixie 259 ....E9
†31520 Dock Junction (Arco) ...J8
31744 Doerun 1,062 ....E8
31745 Donalsonville⊙ 3,320 ..C8
30340 Doraville 7,414 ....K1
31533 Douglas⊙ 10,980 ....G7
*30133 Douglasville⊙ 7,641 ..C3
31021 Dublin⊙ 16,083 ......G5
31022 Dudley 425 ....F5
30136 Duluth 2,956 ....D2
31630 Du Pont 267 ....G9
31021 East Dublin 2,916 ....G5
30539 East Ellijay 469 ....C1

(continued on following page)

Agriculture, Industry and Resources

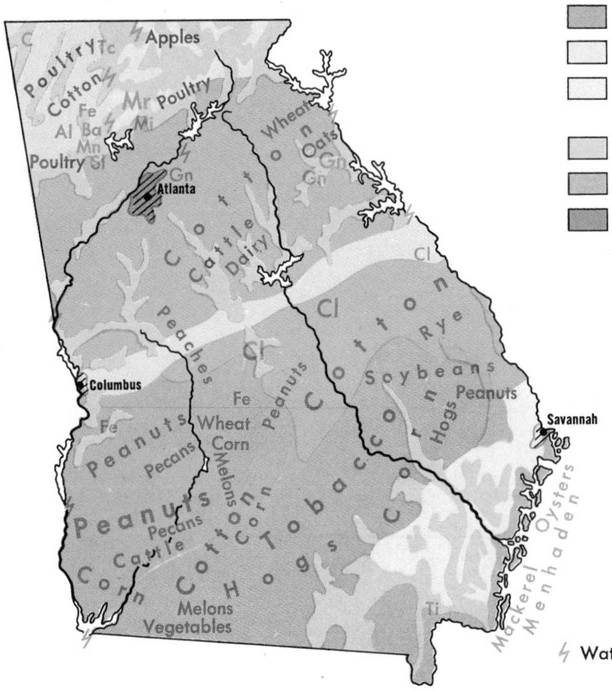

DOMINANT LAND USE

- Specialized Cotton
- Cotton, General Farming
- Cotton, Tobacco, Hogs, Peanuts
- Peanuts, General Farming
- General Farming, Livestock, Fruit, Tobacco
- General Farming, Forest Products, Cotton, Truck Farming
- Forests
- Swampland, Limited Agriculture
- Urban Areas

MAJOR MINERAL OCCURRENCES

Al   Bauxite
Ba   Barite
C   Coal
Cl   Clay
Fe   Iron Ore
Gn   Granite
Mi   Mica
Mn   Manganese
Mr   Marble
Sl   Slate
Tc   Talc
Ti   Titanium

⚡ Water Power

◿ Major Industrial Areas

(continued)

†31046 East Juliette E4
31023 Eastman⊙ 5,330 .... F6
†30263 East Newnan C4
30344 East Point 37,486 .... K2
†30677 Eastville E3
31024 Eatonton⊙ 4,833 .... F4
31307 Eden 990 .... K6
31746 Edison 1,128 .... C7
30635 Elberton⊙ 5,686 .... G2
31806 Ellaville⊙ 1,684 .... D6
31747 Ellenton 277 .... E8
31807 Ellerslie 700 .... C5
30540 Ellijay⊙ 1,507 .... C1
30137 Emerson 1,110 .... C2
31749 Enigma 574 .... F8
†30217 Ephesus 184 .... B4
30724 Eton 301 .... C1
†30120 Euharlee 477 .... C2
30809 Evans H3
30212 Experiment D4
30213 Fairburn 3,466 .... J2
30139 Fairmount 842 .... C2
30214 Fayetteville⊙ 2,715 .... C4
†31071 Finleyson 101 .... F6
31750 Fitzgerald⊙ 10,187 .... F7
†31313 Flemington 440 .... K7
30216 Flovilla 458 .... E4
30542 Flowery Branch 755 .... E2
31537 Folkston⊙ 2,243 .... H9
30050 Forest Park 18,782 .... K2
31029 Forsyth⊙ 4,624 .... E4
31751 Fort Gaines⊙ 1,260 .... C7
30742 Fort Oglethorpe 5,443 .... B1
31030 Fort Valley⊙ 9,000 .... E5
30217 Franklin⊙ 711 .... B4
30639 Franklin Springs 797 .... F2
31753 Funston 337 .... E8
30501 Gainesville⊙ 15,280 .... E2
31408 Garden City 6,895 .... K6
30425 Garfield 222 .... H5
30218 Gay 175 .... C4
31810 Geneva 232 .... C5
31754 Georgetown⊙ 935 .... B7
30810 Gibson⊙ 730 .... G4
30426 Girard 225 .... J4
30427 Glennville 4,144 .... J7
30428 Glenwood 824 .... L1
30641 Good Hope 200 .... E3
31031 Gordon 2,768 .... F5
30220 Grantville 1,110 .... C4
31032 Gray⊙ 2,145 .... F4
30221 Grayson 464 .... E3
30726 Graysville 193 .... B1
30642 Greensboro⊙ 2,985 .... F3
30222 Greenville⊙ 1,213 .... C4
30223 Griffin⊙ 20,728 .... D4
30813 Grovetown 3,491 .... H4
31312 Guyton 749 .... K6
31033 Haddock 800 .... F4
30429 Hagan 880 .... J6
31632 Hahira 1,534 .... F9
31811 Hamilton⊙ 506 .... C5
30228 Hampton 2,059 .... D4
30354 Hapeville 6,166 .... K2
30229 Haralson 123 .... C4
31034 Hardwick F4
30814 Harlem 1,485 .... H4
31035 Harrison 456 .... G5
30643 Hartwell⊙ 4,855 .... G2
31036 Hawkinsville⊙ 4,372 .... E6
31539 Hazlehurst⊙ 4,249 .... G7
30545 Helen 265 .... E1
31037 Helena 1,390 .... G6
30815 Hephzibah 1,452 .... H4
30546 Hiawassee⊙ 491 .... E1
†30410 Higgston 152 .... G6
30467 Hilltonia 515 .... J5
31313 Hinesville⊙ 11,309 .... J7
30141 Hiram 711 .... C3
31542 Hoboken 514 .... H8
30230 Hogansville 3,362 .... C4
30142 Holly Springs 687 .... D2
†31537 Homeland 683 .... H9
30547 Homer⊙ 734 .... F2
31634 Homerville⊙ 3,112 .... G8
30548 Hoschton 490 .... E2
30646 Hull 188 .... F2
31041 Ideal 619 .... D6
30647 Ila 287 .... F2
†30705 Industrial City 1,054 .... C1
31759 Iron City 367 .... C8
31042 Irwinton⊙ 841 .... F5
†31031 Ivey 455 .... F5
30233 Jackson⊙ 4,133 .... E4
31544 Jacksonville 206 .... G7
31761 Jakin 194 .... C8
30143 Jasper⊙ 1,556 .... D2
30549 Jefferson⊙ 1,820 .... F2
31044 Jeffersonville⊙ 1,473 .... F5
30234 Jenkinsburg 360 .... E4
30235 Jersey 201 .... E3
31545 Jesup⊙ 9,418 .... J7
30236 Jonesboro⊙ 4,132 .... D4
31812 Junction City 254 .... C5
30144 Kennesaw 5,095 .... C2
31548 Kingsland 2,008 .... J9
30145 Kingston 733 .... C2
31049 Kite 328 .... G5
31050 Knoxville⊙ 75 .... E5
30728 La Fayette⊙ 6,517 .... B1
30240 La Grange⊙ 24,204 .... B4
30252 Lake 2,963 .... D3
31635 Lakeland⊙ 2,647 .... F8
31636 Lake Park 448 .... F9
30553 Lavonia 2,024 .... F2
30245 Lawrenceville⊙ 8,928 .... D3
31762 Leary 783 .... C8
30146 Lebanon 800 .... D2
31763 Leesburg⊙ 1,301 .... D7
31637 Lenox 965 .... F8
31764 Leslie 470 .... D7
30648 Lexington⊙ 278 .... F3
30247 Lilburn 3,765 .... D3
31051 Lilly 202 .... E6
†30286 Lincoln Park D5
30817 Lincolnton⊙ 1,406 .... G3
30147 Lindale B2
†30728 Linwood 417 .... B1
30058 Lithonia 2,637 .... D3
30248 Locust Grove 1,479 .... D4
30249 Loganville 1,841 .... E3
30433 Lollie G6
†30230 Lone Oak 119 .... C4
†30741 Lookout Mountain 1,505 .... B1
30434 Louisville⊙ 2,823 .... H4
30250 Lovejoy 205 .... D4
31316 Ludowici⊙ 1,286 .... J7
30554 Lula 857 .... E2
31549 Lumber City 1,426 .... G7
31815 Lumpkin⊙ 1,335 .... C6
30251 Luthersville 597 .... C4
30730 Lyerly 482 .... B2
30436 Lyons⊙ 4,203 .... H6
30059 Mableton J1
*31201 Macon⊙ 116,860 .... E5
Macon‡ 254,623 .... E5
30650 Madison⊙ 2,954 .... F3
30438 Manassas 116 .... H6
31816 Manchester 4,796 .... C5
30255 Mansfield 435 .... E4
*30060 Marietta⊙ 30,805 .... J1
31057 Marshallville 1,540 .... D6
30557 Martin 305 .... F2
30671 Maxeys 205 .... F3
30558 Maysville 619 .... E2
30555 McCaysville 1,219 .... D1
30253 McDonough⊙ 2,778 .... D4
31054 McIntyre 386 .... F5
31055 McRae⊙ 3,409 .... G6
30256 Meansville 303 .... D4
30040 Mechanicsville L1
31765 Meigs 1,231 .... D8
30731 Menlo 611 .... B2
†31792 Metcalf E9
30439 Metter⊙ 3,531 .... H6
30441 Midville 670 .... H5
31320 Midway 457 .... K7
31060 Milan 1,115 .... G6
31061 Milledgeville⊙ 12,176 .... F4
30442 Millen⊙ 3,988 .... J5
30257 Milner 320 .... D4
30207 Milstead D3
30559 Mineral Bluff 130 .... D1
30820 Mitchell 214 .... G4
30258 Molena 379 .... D4
30655 Monroe⊙ 8,854 .... E3
31063 Montezuma 4,830 .... E6
31064 Monticello⊙ 2,382 .... E4
31065 Montrose 170 .... F5
30259 Moreland 358 .... C4
31766 Morgan⊙ 364 .... C7
30560 Morganton 263 .... D1
30260 Morrow 3,791 .... K2
31638 Morven 471 .... E9
31768 Moultrie⊙ 15,708 .... E8
30562 Mountain City 701 .... F1
†30075 Mountain Park 378 .... D2
30563 Mount Airy 670 .... F1
30149 Mount Berry B2
30445 Mount Vernon⊙ 1,737 .... G6
30261 Mountville 168 .... C4
30150 Mount Zion 445 .... B3
31553 Nahunta⊙ 951 .... H8
31639 Nashville⊙ 4,831 .... F8
31641 Naylor 228 .... F9
30151 Nelson 562 .... D2
30262 Newborn 391 .... E3
30446 Newington 402 .... J5
30263 Newnan⊙ 11,449 .... C4
31770 Newton⊙ 711 .... D8
31554 Nicholls 1,114 .... G7
30565 Nicholson 491 .... F2
*30071 Norcross 3,317 .... D3
31771 Norman Park 757 .... E8
†30645 North High Shoals 256 .... F3
30821 Norwood 306 .... G4
30448 Nunez 168 .... H5
31772 Oakfield 113 .... E7
30732 Oakman 150 .... C1
31903 Oak Park 256 .... H6
30566 Oakwood 723 .... E2
31773 Ochlocknee 627 .... E9
31774 Ocilla⊙ 3,436 .... F7
31067 Oconee 306 .... G5
†30222 Odessadale 142 .... C5
31555 Odum 401 .... H7
31406 Oglethorpe⊙ 1,305 .... D6
30449 Oliver 239 .... J5
31821 Omaha 169 .... C6
31775 Omega 996 .... E8
30266 Orchard Hill 162 .... D4
30267 Oxford 1,750 .... E3
30268 Palmetto 2,086 .... C3
31777 Parrott 222 .... D7
31557 Patterson 763 .... H8
31778 Pavo 830 .... E9
†31201 Payne 196 .... E5
30269 Peachtree City 6,429 .... C4
31642 Pearson⊙ 1,827 .... G8
31779 Pelham 4,306 .... D8
31321 Pembroke⊙ 1,400 .... J6
30567 Pendergrass 302 .... E2
31069 Perry⊙ 9,453 .... E6
†31794 Phillipsburg E8
31070 Pinehurst 431 .... E6
30072 Pine Lake 901 .... D3
31822 Pine Mountain 984 .... C5
†31312 Pineora 387 .... K6
†31728 Pine Park D9
31071 Pineview 564 .... F6
31072 Pitts 384 .... E7
31073 Plainfield 128 .... F6
31780 Plains 651 .... D6
30733 Plainville 281 .... C2
31322 Pooler 2,543 .... K6
30450 Portal 694 .... J5
30270 Porterdale 1,451 .... E3
31407 Port Wentworth 3,947 .... K6
31781 Poulan 818 .... E8
30073 Powder Springs 3,381 .... C3
31824 Preston⊙ 429 .... C6
30451 Pulaski 257 .... J6
31643 Quitman⊙ 5,188 .... E9
30734 Ranger 171 .... C2
31645 Ray City 658 .... F8
30660 Rayle 177 .... G3
31783 Rebecca 272 .... E7
30453 Reidsville⊙ 2,296 .... H6
31601 Remerton 443 .... F9
31075 Rentz 337 .... G6
†30518 Rest Haven 231 .... E2
31076 Reynolds 1,298 .... D5
31077 Rhine 590 .... F7
31323 Riceboro 216 .... K7
31825 Richland 1,802 .... C6
31324 Richmond Hill 1,177 .... K7
†31018 Riddleville 154 .... G5
31326 Rincon 1,988 .... K6
30736 Ringgold⊙ 1,821 .... B1
*30274 Riverdale 7,121 .... K2
†31768 Riverside 99 .... E8
†30759 Riverside B2
31078 Roberta 859 .... D5
31079 Rochelle 1,626 .... F7
30153 Rockmart 3,645 .... B2
30455 Rocky Ford 223 .... J5
30161 Rome⊙ 29,654 .... B2
30170 Roopville 229 .... B4
30741 Rossville 3,851 .... B1
*30075 Roswell 23,337 .... D2
30662 Royston 2,404 .... F2
†30680 Russell 378 .... E3
30663 Rutledge 694 .... E3
31558 Saint Marys 3,596 .... J9
31522 Saint Simons Island K8
31784 Sale City 336 .... D8
31082 Sandersville⊙ 6,137 .... G5
†20436 Santa Claus 167 .... H6
30456 Sardis 1,180 .... J5
30275 Sargent 800 .... C4
31785 Sasser 407 .... D7
*31401 Savannah⊙ 141,634 .... L6
Savannah‡ 230,728 .... L6
31083 Scotland 222 .... G6
31095 Scott 139 .... G5
31560 Screven 872 .... H7
30276 Senoia 900 .... C4
31084 Seville 209 .... E7
31085 Shady Dale 155 .... E4
30172 Shannon B2
30664 Sharon 140 .... G3
30277 Sharpsburg 194 .... C4
31786 Shellman 1,254 .... C7
31826 Shiloh 392 .... C5
30665 Siloam 446 .... F3
31787 Smithville 867 .... D7
30080 Smyrna 20,312 .... K1
30278 Snellville 8,514 .... D3
30279 Social Circle 2,591 .... E3
30457 Soperton⊙ 2,981 .... G6
31647 Sparks 1,353 .... F8
31087 Sparta⊙ 1,754 .... F4
31329 Springfield⊙ 1,075 .... K6
†30705 Spring Place 246 .... C1
30823 Stapleton 388 .... H4
31648 Statenville⊙ 700 .... G9
30458 Statesboro⊙ 14,866 .... J6
30666 Statham 1,101 .... E3
30464 Stillmore 527 .... H6
30281 Stockbridge 2,103 .... D3
*30083 Stone Mountain 4,867 .... D3
†30518 Sugar Hill 2,473 .... E2
30746 Sugar Valley C1
30466 Summertown 215 .... H5
30747 Summerville⊙ 4,878 .... B2
31789 Sumner 213 .... E7
30284 Sunny Side 338 .... D4
31563 Surrency 368 .... H7
30174 Suwanee 1,026 .... D2
30401 Swainsboro⊙ 7,602 .... H5
31790 Sycamore 474 .... E7
30467 Sylvania⊙ 3,352 .... J5
31791 Sylvester⊙ 5,860 .... E7
31827 Talbotton⊙ 1,140 .... C5
30176 Tallapoosa 2,647 .... B3
30573 Tallulah Falls 162 .... F1
30575 Talmo E2
30470 Tarrytown 145 .... H6
30178 Taylorsville 266 .... C2
30179 Temple 1,520 .... B3
31089 Tennille 1,709 .... G5
30285 The Rock 78 .... D5
30286 Thomaston⊙ 9,682 .... D5
31792 Thomasville⊙ 18,463 .... E9
30824 Thomson⊙ 7,001 .... H4
†31404 Thunderbolt 2,165 .... K6
31794 Tifton⊙ 13,749 .... F8
30576 Tiger 299 .... F1
30668 Tignall 733 .... G3
30577 Toccoa⊙ 9,104 .... F1
31090 Toomsboro 673 .... F5
30752 Trenton⊙ 1,636 .... A1
30753 Trion 1,732 .... B1
30755 Tunnel Hill 867 .... C1
30289 Turin 260 .... C4
30471 Twin City 1,402 .... H5
31328 Tybee Island 2,240 .... L6
30290 Tyrone 1,038 .... C4
31795 Ty Ty 618 .... E8
31091 Unadilla 1,566 .... E6
30291 Union City 4,780 .... J2
30669 Union Point 1,750 .... F3
†31794 Unionville F8
30473 Uvalda 646 .... H6
31601 Valdosta⊙ 37,596 .... F9
30672 Vanna F2
†30153 Van Wert 303 .... B3
30756 Varnell 288 .... C1
†31401 Vernonburg 178 .... K7
30474 Vidalia 10,393 .... H6
†30830 Vidette H4
31092 Vienna⊙ 2,886 .... E6
30180 Villa Rica 3,420 .... C3
30182 Waco 471 .... B3
30477 Wadley 2,438 .... H5
30183 Waleska 450 .... D2
†30209 Walnut Grove 387 .... E3
31333 Walthourville 905 .... J7
31830 Warm Springs 425 .... C5
31093 Warner Robins 39,893 .... E5
30828 Warrenton⊙ 2,172 .... G4
31796 Warwick 488 .... E7
30673 Washington⊙ 4,662 .... G3
30677 Watkinsville⊙ 1,240 .... E3
31831 Waverly Hall 913 .... C5
31501 Waycross⊙ 19,371 .... H8
30830 Waynesboro⊙ 5,760 .... J4
31832 Weston 109 .... C7
31833 West Point 4,294 .... B5
31797 Whigham 507 .... D9
30184 White 501 .... C2
31568 White Oak 450 .... J8
30678 White Plains 231 .... F4
30185 Whitesburg 775 .... B4
31650 Willacoochee 1,166 .... G8
30292 Williamson 250 .... D4
31410 Wilmington Island L7
30680 Winder⊙ 6,705 .... E3
31406 Windsor Forest K7
30683 Winterville 621 .... F3
31569 Woodbine⊙ 910 .... J9
30293 Woodbury 1,738 .... C5
31836 Woodland 664 .... D5
30188 Woodstock 2,699 .... D2
30670 Woodville 455 .... F3
30833 Wrens 2,415 .... H4
31096 Wrightsville⊙ 2,526 .... G5
31097 Yatesville 390 .... D5
30582 Young Harris 687 .... E1
30295 Zebulon⊙ 995 .... D4

OTHER FEATURES

Alapaha (riv.) F7
Allatoona (lake) C2
Altamaha (riv.) H7
Andersonville Nat'l Hist. Site D6
Atlanta Nav. Air Sta. J1
Banks (lake) F9
Bartletts Ferry (dam) B5
Blackshear (lake) E7
Blue Ridge (mts.) D1
Brasstown Bald (mt.) E1
Burton (lake) E1
Carters (lake) C1
Chattahoochee (riv.) B8
Chattahoochee River Nat'l Rec. Area K1
Chattooga (riv.) A2
Chattooga (riv.) F1
Chatuge (lake) E1
Chickamauga and Chattanooga Nat'l Mil. Park B1
Clark Hill (lake) H3
Coosa (riv.) A2
Coosawattee (riv.) C1
Cumberland (isl.) K9
Cumberland Island Nat'l Seashore K9
Dobbins A.F.B. J1
Doboy (sound) K8
Etowah (riv.) C2
Eufaula (Walter F. George Res.) (lake) B7
Flint (riv.) D8
Fort Benning B6
Fort Frederica Nat'l Mon. K8
Fort Gordon H4
Fort McPherson K1
Fort Pulaski Nat'l Mon. L6
Fort Stewart J7
Goat Rock (lake) B5
Harding (lake) B5
Hartwell (lake) G2
Jekyll (isl.) K8
Kennesaw Mtn. Nat'l Battlefield Park J1
Lawson A.A.F. B6
Martin Luther King, Jr., Nat'l Hist. Site K1
Moody A.F.B. F9
Nottely (lake) D1
Ochlockonee (riv.) C10
Ocmulgee (riv.) E5
Ocmulgee Nat'l Mon. F5
Oconee (riv.) F5
Ogeechee (riv.) J5
Okefenokee (swamp) H9
Oliver (lake) B5
Oostanaula (riv.) B2
Ossabaw (sound) K7
Rabun (lake) E1
Robins A.F.B. F5
Saint Andrew (sound) K9
Saint Catherines (isl.) K7
Saint Marys (riv.) J9
Saint Simons K8
Sapelo (isl.) K8
Satilla (riv.) G8
Savannah (riv.) K5
Sea (isls.) K9
Seminole (lake) B9
Sidney Lanier (lake) D2
Sinclair (lake) F4
Skidaway (isl.) L7
Springer (mt.) D1
Suwannee (riv.) G10
Tugaloo (riv.) F1
Walter F. George (res.) B7
Wassaw (sound) L7
Weiss (lake) A2
West Point (lake) B4

⊙County seat.
‡Population of metropolitan area.
† Zip of nearest p.o. * Multiple zips.

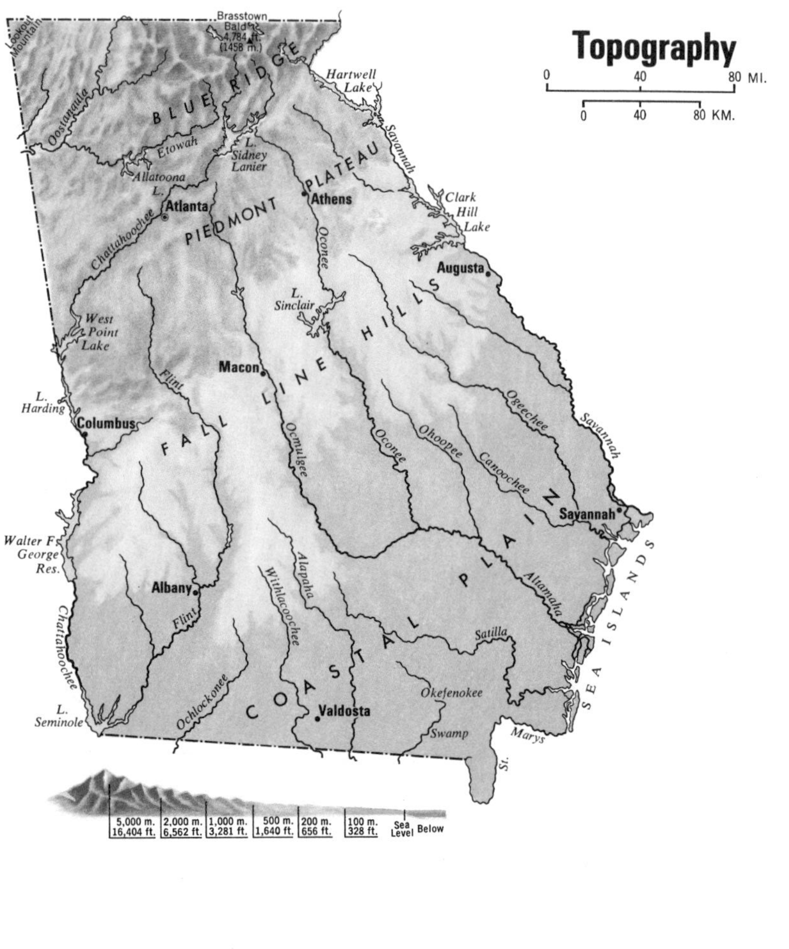

Topography
0 40 80 MI.
0 40 80 KM.
Brasstown Bald 4,784 ft. (1458 m)
BLUE RIDGE
PIEDMONT
PLATEAU
FALL LINE HILLS
COASTAL PLAIN
SEA ISLANDS
Hartwell Lake
Clark Hill Lake
L. Sidney Lanier
Allatoona L.
L. Sinclair
West Point Lake
L. Harding
Walter F. George Res.
L. Seminole
Okefenokee Swamp
Atlanta
Athens
Augusta
Macon
Columbus
Albany
Valdosta
Savannah
Oostanaula
Etowah
Chattahoochee
Oconee
Savannah
Flint
Ocmulgee
Ogeechee
Ohoopee
Canoochee
Altamaha
Alapaha
Withlacoochee
Ochlockonee
Satilla
St. Marys
5,000 m. 16,404 ft.
2,000 m. 6,562 ft.
1,000 m. 3,281 ft.
500 m. 1,640 ft.
200 m. 656 ft.
100 m. 328 ft.
Sea Level
Below

Georgia

COUNTIES

Hawaii 92,053 ....K7
Honolulu 762,565 ....D3
Kalawao 144 ....G1
Kauai 39,082 ....A1
Maui 70,847 ....J1

CITIES and TOWNS

Zip	Name/Pop.	Key

96701 Aiea 32,879 ....B3
96821 Aina Haina F2
Ala Moana 96,820 ....C4
96703 Anahola 915 ....C1
†96706 Barbers Point 1,373 ......E2
96704 Captain Cook 2,008 ......G5
96705 Eleele 580 ....C2
96706 Ewa 2,637 ....A4
96706 Ewa Beach 14,369 ......A4
†96701 Foster Village B3
†96714 Haena 200 ....C1
96708 Haiku 619 ....J2
96710 Hakalau J4
96711 Halawa, Hawaii 50 ......G3
†96748 Halawa, Molokai 15 ......H1
†96701 Halawa Heights B3
96712 Haleiwa 2,412 ....E1
†96718 Halfway House 150 ......H6
96787 Haliimaile 741 ....J2

†96713 Hamoa 35 ....K2
96713 Hana 643 ....K2
96714 Hanalei 483 ....C1
96715 Hanamaulu 3,227 ......C1
96716 Hanapepe 1,417 ......C2
96717 Hauula 2,997 ....E1
96825 Hawaii Kai F2
96718 Hawaii Nat'l Park 250 ....J6
96719 Hawi 795 ....G3
96824 Hickam Housing 4,425 ...B4
96720 Hilo⊙ 35,269 ....J5
96725 Holualoa 1,243 ....G5
96726 Honaunau 950 ....G6
96727 Honokaa 1,936 ....H4
†96761 Honokahua 309 ....H1
*96801 Honolulu (cap.)⊙ 365,048 .C4
Honolulu‡ 762,874 ....C4
96728 Honomu 559 ....J4
96729 Hoolehua G1
†96706 Iroquois Point 3,915 ......A4
96730 Kaaawa 959 ....F1
†96761 Kaanapali 541 ....H2
†96793 Kahakuloa 75 ....J1
96801 Kahala D5
†96744 Kahaluu 2,925 ....E2
96731 Kahuku 935 ....E1
96732 Kahului 12,978 ....J2
96740 Kailua (Kailua Kona),
Hawaii 4,751 ....F5
96734 Kailua, Oahu 35,812 ...F2

96740 Kailua Kona 4,751 ....F5
96741 Kainaliu 512 ....G5
96750 Kalaheo 2,500 ....C2
†96742 Kalaupapa⊙ 170 ....G1
†96754 Kalihiwai 40 ....C1
†96748 Kalmaelo 60 ....H1
96743 Kamuela 1,179 ....G3
96744 Kaneohe 29,919 ....F2
96746 Kapaa 4,467 ....D1
96755 Kapaau 612 ....G3
96817 Kapalama C4
96747 Kaumakani 888 ....C2
96748 Kaunakakai 2,231 ......G1
†96708 Kaupakulua 600 ....K2
96713 Kaupo 65 ....K2
96743 Kawaihae 50 ....G4
†96712 Kawailoa 200 ....E1
96749 Keaau 775 ....J5
96750 Kealakekua 1,033 ......G5
96751 Kealia, Kauai 300 ....D1
†96708 Keanae 280 ....K2
96752 Kekaha 3,260 ....C2
96753 Kihei 5,644 ....J2
96754 Kilauea 895 ....C1
96713 Kipahulu 75 ....K2
96713 Koali 60 ....K2
96755 Kohala (Kapaau) 612 ......G3
†96708 Kokomo 500 ....K2
96756 Koloa 1,457 ....C2

†96756 Koloa Landing C2
96757 Kualapuu 502 ....G1
†96775 Kukaiau 75 ....H4
96727 Kukuihaele 332 ....H3
96790 Kula 800 ....J2
96759 Kunia 550 ....E2
96760 Kurtistown 900 ....J5
96761 Lahaina 6,095 ....H2
96762 Laie 4,643 ....E1
96763 Lanai City 2,092 ....H2
96764 Laupahoehoe 500 ....J4
96765 Lawai 950 ....G1
96766 Lihue⊙ 4,000 ....C2
†96779 Lower Paia 1,500 ....J1
†96719 Mahukona 2. ....G3
96792 Maili 5,026 ....D2
96792 Makaha 6,582 ....D2
96706 Makakilo 7,691 ....E2
96768 Makawao 2,900 ....K2
96769 Makaweli 500 ....B2
96790 Makena 100 ....J2
96822 Makiki C4
96770 Maunaloa 633 ....G1
96744 Maunawili 5,239 ....F2
96789 Mililani Town 21,365 ......E2
96828 Moiliili C4
96734 Mokapu 11,615 ....F2
96771 Mountainview 540 ....J5
96772 Naalehu 1,168 ....H7
†96713 Nahiku 50 ....K2

96792 Nanakuli 8,185 ....D2
†96761 Napili-Honokowai 2,446 ...H1
96773 Ninole 75 ....J4
96775 Nole 75 ....H4
96731 Onomea 10. ....J4
96774 Ookala 401 ....J4
96775 Paauhau 350 ....H4
96776 Paauilo 755 ....H4
96777 Pahala 1,619 ....H6
96778 Pahoa 923 ....J5
96779 Paia J2
96780 Papaaloa J4
96781 Papaikou 1,567 ....J5
†96781 Paukaa 544 ....J5
96708 Pauwela 468 ....K2
†96708 Peahi 308 ....K2
96782 Pearl City 42,575 ....B3
96783 Pepeekeo J4
†96756 Poipu 685 ....C2
96714 Princeville 500 ....C1
96766 Puhi 991 ....C2
†96781 Pukalani 3,950 ....J2
96748 Pukoo 50 ....H1
96713 Puuiki 75 ....K2
96784 Puunene 572 ....J2
†96801 Puunui C4
96786 Schofield Barracks 18,851 .E2
†96779 Spreckelsville 350 ....J1
†96776 Umikoa 25 ....H4
96822 Ulumalu 201 ....K2
96785 Volcano 400 ....J6

96786 Wahiawa 16,911 ....
†96788 Waiakoa ....
96816 Waialae ....
96731 Waialee 50 ....
†96748 Waialua, Molokai 30 ......
96791 Waialua, Oahu 4,051 ......
96792 Waianae 7,941 ....
†96793 Waikapu 698 ....
96815 Waikiki ....
†96748 Wailau 20 ....
†96710 Wailea, Hawaii 150 ......
96790 Wailea, Maui 1,124 ......
96746 Wailua 1,587 ....
96793 Wailuku⊙ 10,260 ....
96795 Waimanalo 3,562 ....
96795 Waimanalo Bch. 4,161 ......
†96743 Waimea (Kamuela),
Hawaii 1,179 ....
96796 Waimea, Kauai 1,569 ......
†96720 Wainaku 1,045 ....
96714 Wainiha 175 ....
96797 Waipahu 29,139 ....
†96786 Waipio Acres 4,091 ......
†96786 Whitmore Village 2,318 ......

OTHER FEATURES

Alalakeiki (chan.) ....
Alenuihaha (chan.) ....

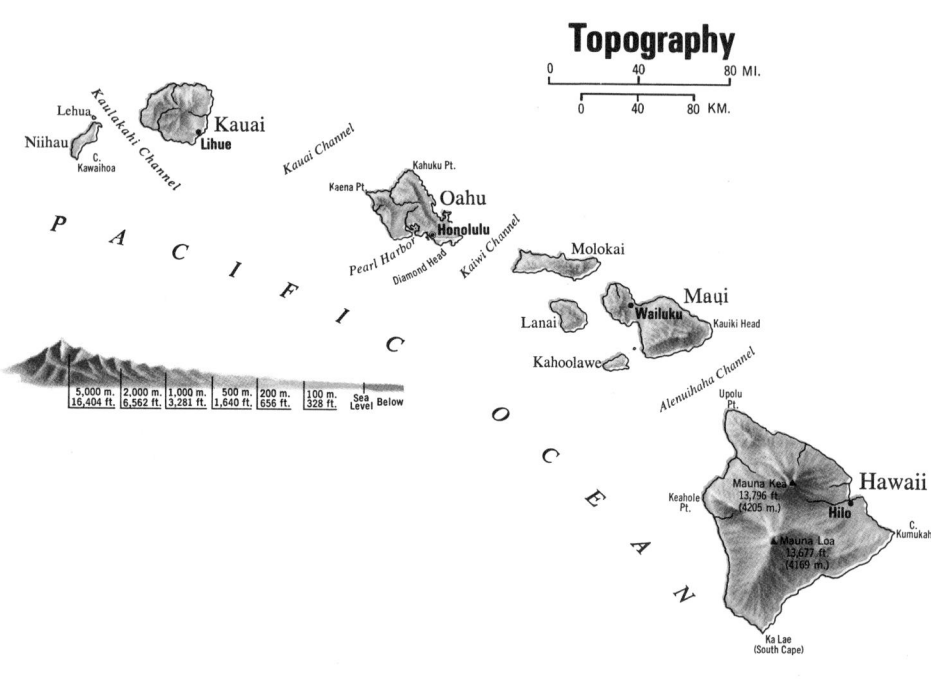

Topography

0	40	80 MI.	
0	40	80 KM.	

5,000 m. 16,404 ft.	2,000 m. 6,562 ft.	1,000 m. 3,281 ft.	500 m. 1,640 ft.	200 m. 656 ft.	100 m. 328 ft.	Sea Level	Below

Agriculture, Industry and Resources

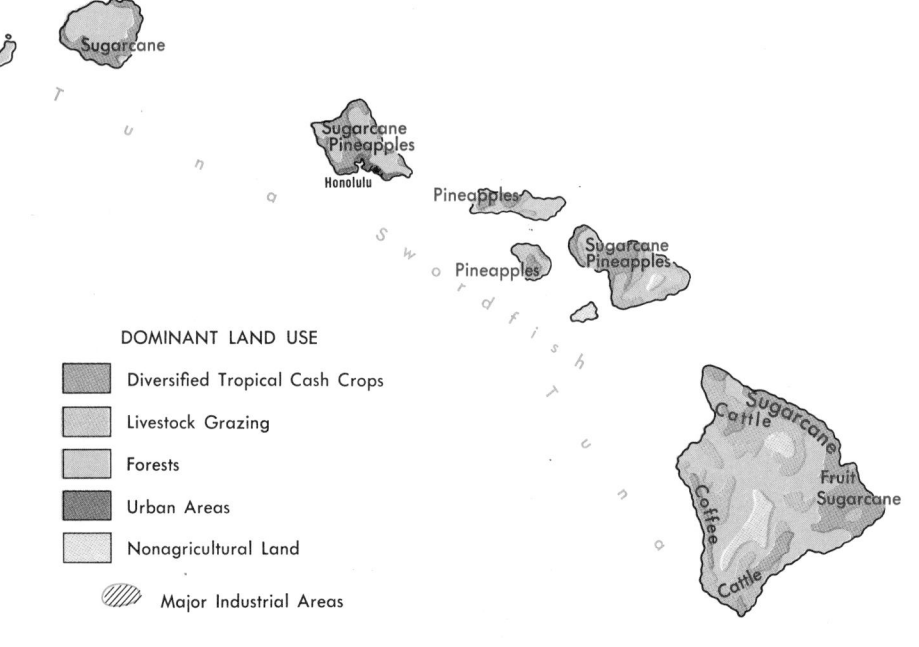

DOMINANT LAND USE

- Diversified Tropical Cash Crops
- Livestock Grazing
- Forests
- Urban Areas
- Nonagricultural Land

///// Major Industrial Areas

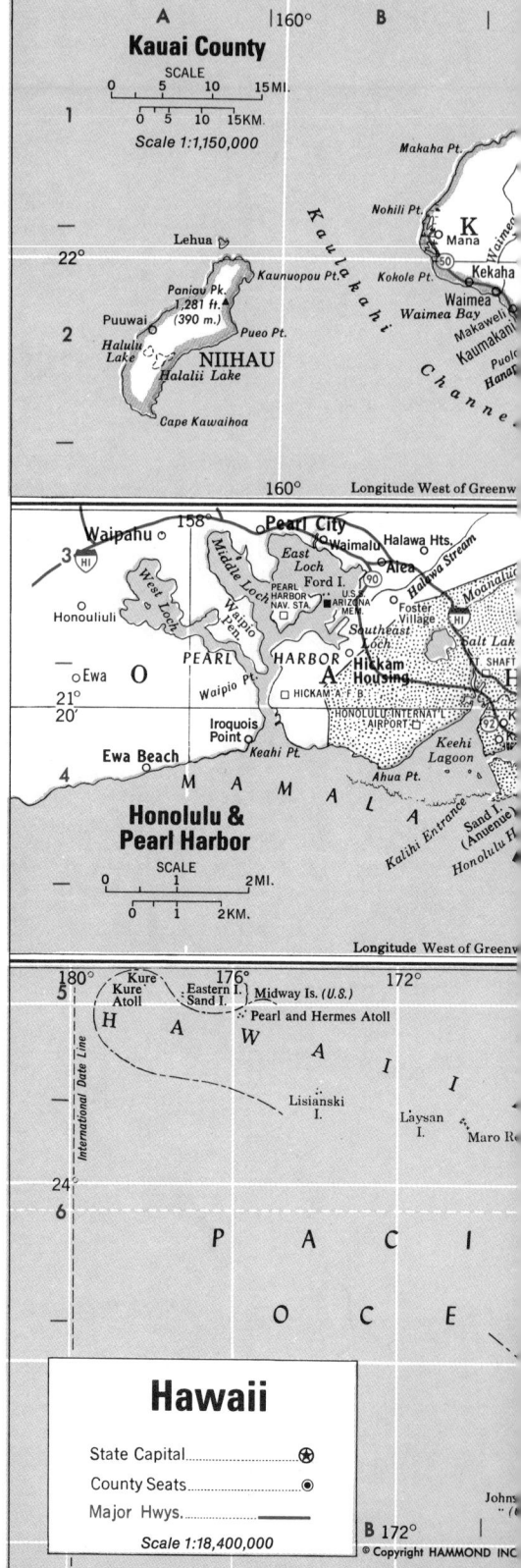

Kauai County

SCALE
0   5   10   15 MI.
0 5 10 15 KM.
Scale 1:1,150,000

Longitude West of Greenw

Honolulu & Pearl Harbor

SCALE
0   1   2 MI.
0   1   2 KM.

Longitude West of Greenw

Hawaii

State Capital..............⊛
County Seats..............⊙
Major Hwys.............. ——
Scale 1:18,400,000

© Copyright HAMMOND INC.

Anuenue (Sand) (isl.)	C4	Kanapou (bay)	J3
Auau (chan.)	H2	Kaneohe Bay U.S.M.C. Air	
Barbers Point Nav. Air Sta.	E2	Station	F2
Diamond (head)	C5	Kau (des.)	J6
East Loch (inlet)	B3	Kauai (chan.)	E6
Ford (isl.)	B3	Kauai (isl.)	C1
Fort Shafter	C3	Kauiki (head)	K2
French Frigate (shoals)	C6	Kaula (isl.)	D6
Gardner Pinnacles (isls.)	C6	Kaulakahi (chan.)	B2
Halalii (lake)	A2	Kawaihae (bay)	G4
Halawa (bay)	H1	Kawaihoa (pt.)	A2
Haleakala (crater)	K2	Kawaikini (peak)	C1
Haleakala Nat'l Park	K2	Keahi (pt.)	A4
Hawaii (isl.)	H5	Kealaikahiki (chan.)	H3
Hawaii Volcanoes Nat'l Park	H6	Kealakekua (bay)	F6
Hickam A.F.B.	B4	Keanapapa (pt.)	G2
Hilo (bay)	J5	Keehi (lag.)	B4
Honolulu Int'l Airport	B4	Kiholo (bay)	F4
Honolulu (harb.)	C4	Kilauea (crater)	H6
Ilio (pt.)	G1	Kohala (mts.)	G4
Kaala (mt.)	D1	Koko (head)	F2
Kahala (pt.)	D1	Konahuanui (peaks)	C3
Kahala (bay)	F1	Koolau (range)	E2
Kaiwi (chan.)	E6	Kumukahi (cape)	K5
Ka Lae (cape)	G7	Kure (atoll)	A5
Kalaupapa Nat'l Hist. Park	H1	Kure (chan.)	A5
Kalohi (chan.)	G1	Laau (pt.)	G1
Koloko-Honokohau Nat'l Hist.		Lanai (isl.)	H2
Park	F6	Lanaihale (mt.)	H2
Kamakou (peak)	H1	Laysan (isl.)	B5

Lisianski (isl.)	B5	Puolo (pt.)	C2
Lua Makika (mt.)	J3	Puuhonua O Honaunau Nat'l Hist.	
Maalaea (bay)	J2	Park	F6
Makaha (pt.)	B1	Puu Keahiakahoe (mt.)	D3
Makahuena (pt.)	C2	Puukohola Heiau Nat'l Hist.	
Makapuu (pt.)	F2	Site	G4
Mamala (bay)	B4	Puu Kukui (mt.)	J2
Manana (isl.)	F2	Red Hill (mt.)	K2
Maro (reef)	C6	Roundtop (mt.)	C4
Maui (isl.)	J2	Salt (lake)	B3
Mauna Kea (mt.)	H4	Sand (isl.)	B4
Mauna Loa (mt.)	G6	South (Ka Lae) (cape)	G7
Middle Loch (inlet)	A3	Southeast Loch (inlet)	B3
Moanalua (stream)	B3	Sugarloaf (hill)	C4
Mokapu (pen.)	F2	Tantalus (mt.)	D4
Mokuaweoweo (crater)	H6	Upolu (pt.)	G3
Molokai (isl.)	G1	U.S.S. Arizona Memorial	B3
Molokini (isl.)	J2	Waialeale (mt.)	C1
Nawiliwili (bay)	D2	Waikiki (beach)	C4
Necker (isl.)	D6	Wailuku (riv.)	J5
Nihoa (isl.)	D6	Waimea (bay)	B2
Niihau (isl.)	A2	Waimea (riv.)	C1
Oahu (isl.)	E2	Wainiha (riv.)	C1
Pailolo (chan.)	H1	Waipio (bay)	H3
Palolo (stream)	D4	Waipio (pen.)	A3
Paniau (peak)	A2	Waipio (pt.)	A4
Pearl (harb.)	A3	West Loch (inlet)	A3
Pearl and Hermes (atoll)	B5	Wheeler A.F.B.	E1
Pearl Harbor Naval Sta.	B3	
Punchbowl (hill)	C4	

⊙County seat.
‡Population of metropolitan area.
† Zip of nearest p.o   * Multiple zips.

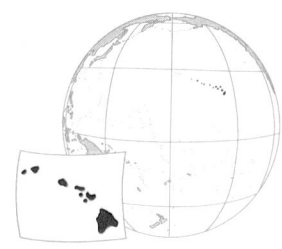

AREA 6,471 sq. mi. (16,760 sq. km.)
POPULATION 964,691
CAPITAL Honolulu
LARGEST CITY Honolulu
HIGHEST POINT Mauna Kea 13,796 ft. (4205 m.)
SETTLED IN —
ADMITTED TO UNION August 21, 1959
POPULAR NAME Aloha State
STATE FLOWER Hibiscus
STATE BIRD Nene (Hawaiian Goose)

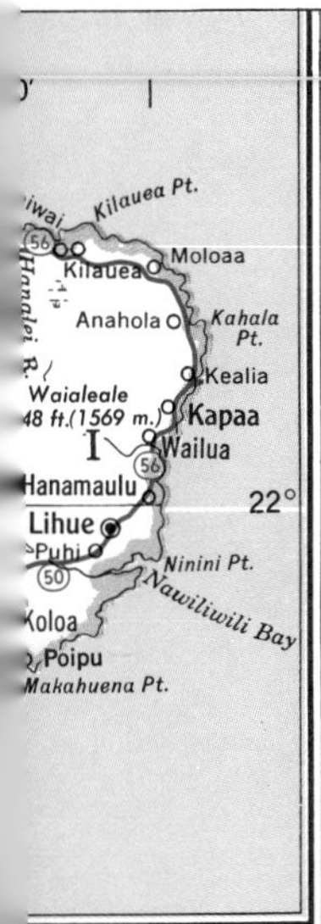

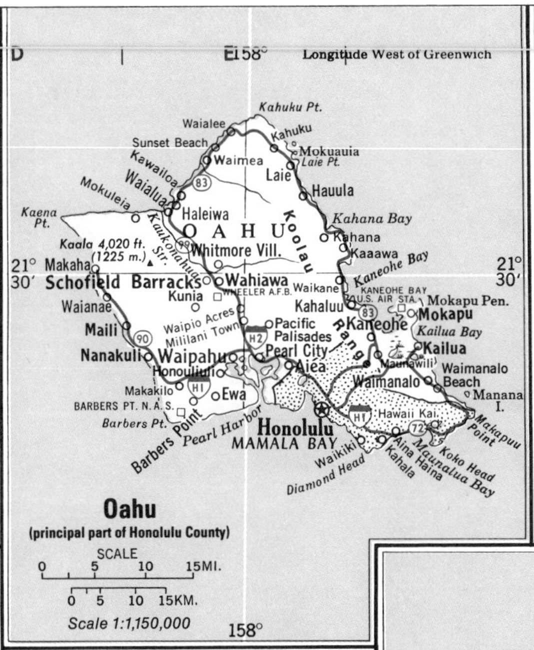

Oahu
(principal part of Honolulu County)
SCALE
0   5   10   15MI.
0   5   10   15KM.
Scale 1:1,150,000

Maui & Kalawao Counties
SCALE
0   5   10   15MI.
0   5   10   15KM.
Scale 1:1,150,000

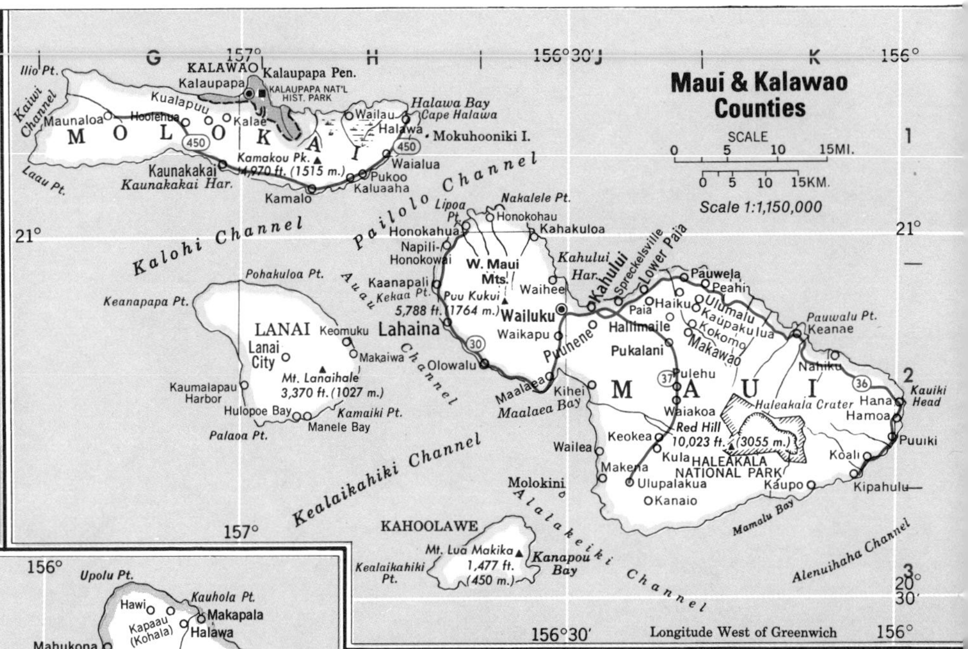

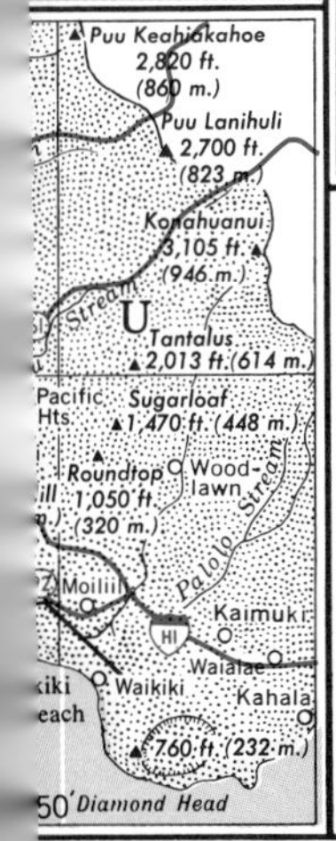

Map below shows relative position of the islands comprising the State of Hawaii. The other maps show the more important island counties in detail.

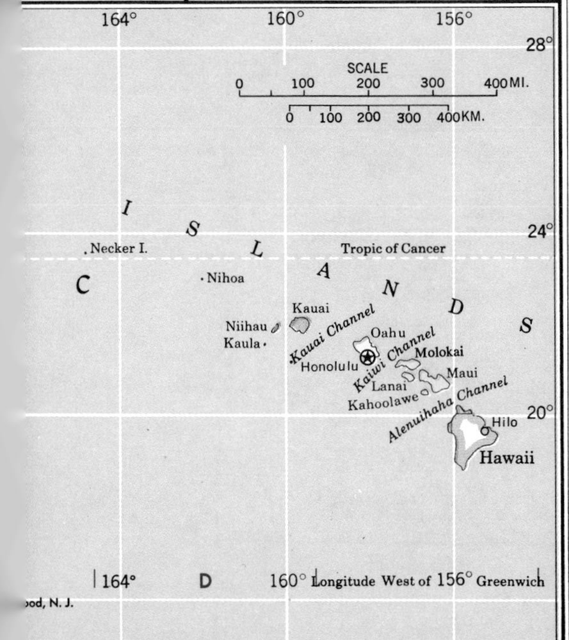

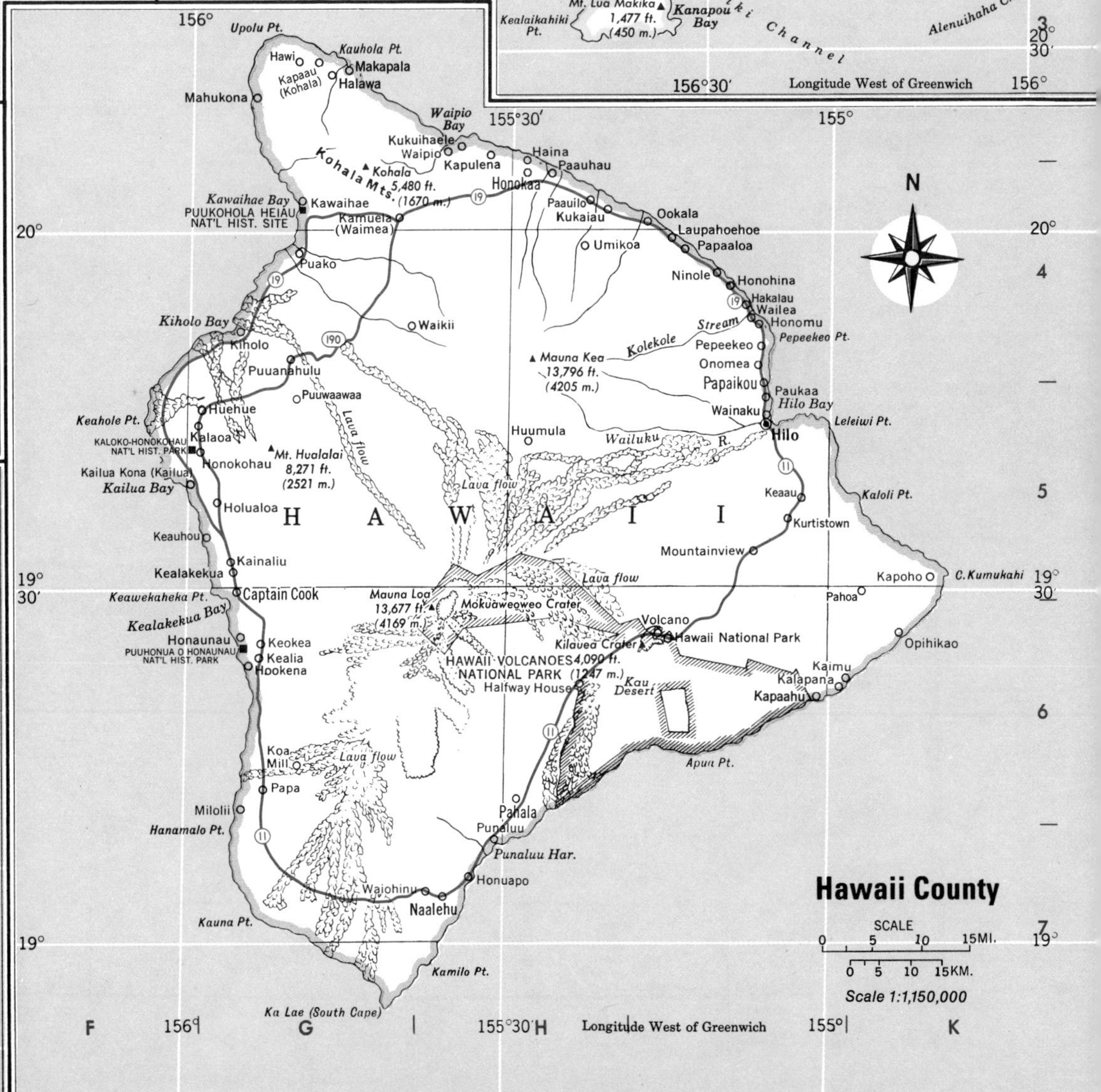

SCALE
0   100   200   300   400MI.
0   100   200   300   400KM.

Hawaii County
SCALE
0   5   10   15MI.
0   5   10   15KM.
Scale 1:1,150,000

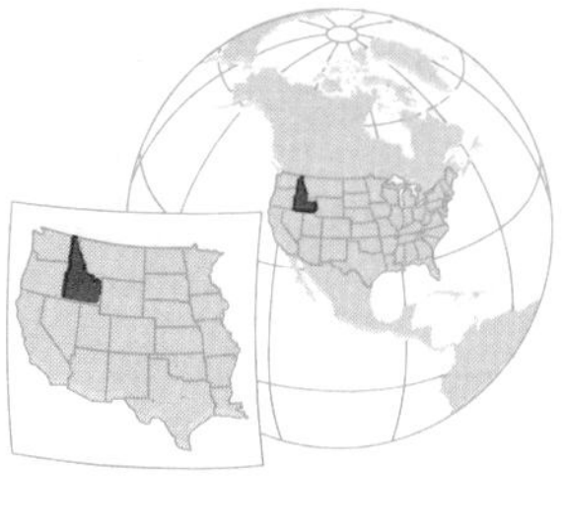

AREA 83,564 sq. mi. (216,431 sq. km.)
POPULATION 944,038
CAPITAL Boise
LARGEST CITY Boise
HIGHEST POINT Borah Pk. 12,662 ft. (3859 m.)
SETTLED IN 1842
ADMITTED TO UNION July 3, 1890
POPULAR NAME Gem State
STATE FLOWER Syringa
STATE BIRD Mountain Bluebird

COUNTIES

Ada 173,036 B6
Adams 3,347 B5
Bannock 65,421 F7
Bear Lake 6,931 G7
Benewah 8,292 B2
Bingham 36,489 F6
Blaine 9,841 D6
Boise 2,999 C6
Bonner 24,163 B1
Bonneville 65,980 G6
Boundary 7,289 B1
Butte 3,342 E6
Camas 818 D6
Canyon 83,756 B6
Caribou 8,695 G7
Cassia 19,427 E7
Clark 798 F5
Clearwater 10,390 C3
Custer 3,385 D5
Elmore 21,565 C6
Franklin 8,895 G7
Fremont 10,813 G5
Gem 11,972 B6
Gooding 11,874 D6
Idaho 14,769 C4
Jefferson 15,304 F6
Jerome 14,840 D7
Kootenai 59,770 B2
Latah 28,749 B3
Lemhi 7,460 D4
Lewis 4,118 B3
Lincoln 3,436 D6
Madison 19,480 G6
Minidoka 19,718 E7
Nez Perce 33,220 B3
Oneida 3,258 F7
Owyhee 8,272 B7
Payette 15,825 B5
Power 6,844 F7
Shoshone 19,226 B2
Teton 2,897 G6
Twin Falls 52,927 D7
Valley 5,604 C5
Washington 8,803 B5

CITIES and TOWNS

Zip Name/Pop. Key

83210 Aberdeen 1,528 F7
83350 Acequia 100 E7
83311 Albion 286 E7
83211 American Falls⊙ 3,626 E7
†83401 Ammon 4,669 G6
83213 Arco⊙ 1,241 E6
83214 Arimo 338 F7
83420 Ashton 1,219 G5
83801 Athol 312 B2
83217 Bancroft 505 G7
83218 Basalt 414 F6
83313 Bellevue 1,016 D6
83221 Blackfoot⊙ 10,065 F6
83314 Bliss 208 D7
83223 Bloomington 212 G7
*83701 Boise (cap.)⊙ 102,160 B6
Boise‡ 173,036 B6
83805 Bonners Ferry⊙ 1,906 B1
83806 Bovill 289 B3
83316 Buhl 3,629 D7
83318 Burley⊙ 8,761 E7
83213 Butte City 93 E6
83605 Caldwell⊙ 17,699 B6
83610 Cambridge 428 B5
83611 Cascade⊙ 945 C5
83321 Castleford 191 C7
83226 Challis⊙ 758 D5
†83851 Chatcolet 181 B2
83202 Chubbuck 7,052 F7
83811 Clark Fork 449 B1
83227 Clayton 43 D5
83228 Clifton 208 F7
83814 Coeur d'Alene⊙ 20,054 B2
83522 Cottonwood 941 B3
83612 Council⊙ 917 B5
83523 Craigmont 617 B3
†83622 Crouch 69 B5
83524 Culdesac 261 B3
†83814 Dalton Gardens 1,795 B2
83232 Dayton 368 F7
83823 Deary 539 B3
83323 Declo 276 E7
83324 Dietrich 101 D7
83615 Donnelly 139 B5
83234 Downey 645 F7
83422 Driggs⊙ 727 G6
83423 Dubois⊙ 413 F5
83616 Eagle 2,620 B6
†83836 East Hope 258 B1
83325 Eden 355 D7
83827 Elk River 265 B3
83617 Emmett⊙ 4,605 B6
83327 Fairfield⊙ 404 D6
83526 Ferdinand 144 B3
†83814 Fernan Lake 178 B2
83328 Filer 1,645 D7
83236 Firth 460 F6
83203 Fort Hall 750 F6
83237 Franklin 423 G7
83619 Fruitland 2,456 B6
†83704 Garden City 4,571 B6
83832 Genesee 791 B3
83239 Georgetown 544 G7
83623 Glenns Ferry 1,374 C7
83330 Gooding⊙ 2,949 D7
83241 Grace 1,216 G7
83624 Grand View 366 B7
83530 Grangeville⊙ 3,666 B4
83626 Greenleaf 663 B6
83332 Hagerman 602 D7
83333 Hailey⊙ 2,109 D6
83425 Hamer 93 F6
83334 Hansen 1,078 D7
83833 Harrison 260 B2
†83854 Hauser 305 A2
†83835 Hayden 2,586 B2
83835 Hayden Lake 273 B2
83335 Hazelton 496 E7
83336 Heyburn 2,889 E7
†83301 Hollister 167 D7
83628 Homedale 2,078 A6
83836 Hope 106 B1
83629 Horseshoe Bend 700 B6
†83854 Huetter 65 B2
83631 Idaho City⊙ 300 C6
*83401 Idaho Falls⊙ 39,590 F6
83245 Inkom 830 F7
83427 Iona 1,072 G6
83428 Irwin 113 G6
83429 Island Park 154 G5
83338 Jerome⊙ 6,891 D7
83535 Juliaetta 522 B3
83536 Kamiah 1,478 B3
83837 Kellogg 3,417 B2
83537 Kendrick 395 B3
83340 Ketchum 2,200 D6
83341 Kimberly 2,307 D7
83539 Kooskia 784 C3
83840 Kootenai 280 B1
83634 Kuna 1,767 B6
83540 Lapwai 1,043 B3
83246 Lava Hot Springs 467 F7
83464 Leadore 114 E5
83501 Lewiston⊙ 27,986 A3
83431 Lewisville 502 F6
83251 Mackay 541 E6
83252 Malad City⊙ 1,915 F7
83342 Malta 196 E7
83639 Marsing 786 B6
83638 McCall 2,188 C5
83250 McCammon 770 F7
83641 Melba 276 B6
83434 Menan 605 F6
83642 Meridian 6,658 B6
83644 Middleton 1,901 B6
83645 Midvale 205 B5
83343 Minidoka 101 E7
83254 Montpelier 3,107 G7
83255 Moore 210 E6
83843 Moscow⊙ 16,513 B3
83647 Mountain Home⊙ 7,540 C6
83845 Moyie Springs 386 B1
†83450 Mud Lake 243 F6
83846 Mullan 1,269 C2
83650 Murphy⊙ 200 B6
83344 Murtaugh 114 D7
83651 Nampa 25,112 B6
83436 Newdale 329 G6
83654 New Meadows 576 B4
83655 New Plymouth 1,186 B6
83543 Nezperce⊙ 517 B3
83656 Notus 437 B6
83346 Oakley 663 D7
†99156 Oldtown 257 A1
†83855 Onaway 254 B3
83544 Orofino⊙ 3,711 B3
83849 Osburn 2,220 B2
†83263 Oxford 66 F7
83261 Paris⊙ 707 G7
83438 Parker 262 G6
83660 Parma 1,820 B6
83347 Paul 940 E7
83661 Payette⊙ 5,448 B5
83545 Peck 209 B3
83546 Pierce 1,060 C3
83850 Pinehurst 2,183 B2
83851 Plummer 634 B2
*83201 Pocatello⊙ 46,340 F7
83852 Ponderay 399 B1
83854 Post Falls 5,736 A2
83855 Potlatch 819 A3
83263 Preston⊙ 3,759 G7
83856 Priest River 1,639 A1
83858 Rathdrum 1,369 A2
83548 Reubens 87 B3
83440 Rexburg⊙ 11,559 G6
83349 Richfield 357 D6
83442 Rigby⊙ 2,624 F6
83549 Riggins 527 B4
83443 Ririe 555 G6
83444 Roberts 466 F6
83271 Rockland 283 F7
83350 Rupert⊙ 5,476 E7
83445 Saint Anthony⊙ 3,212 G6
83272 Saint Charles 211 G7
83861 Saint Maries⊙ 2,794 B2
83467 Salmon⊙ 3,308 D4
83864 Sandpoint⊙ 4,460 B1
83274 Shelley 3,300 F6
83352 Shoshone⊙ 1,242 D7
†83650 Silver City 1 B6
83868 Smelterville 776 B2
83276 Soda Springs⊙ 4,051 G7
83869 Spirit Lake 834 A2
83278 Stanley 99 D5
83552 Stites 253 C3
83448 Sugar City 1,022 G6
83353 Sun Valley 545 D6
83449 Swan Valley 135 G6
83870 Tensed 113 B2
83451 Teton 559 G6
83452 Tetonia 191 G6
83871 Troy 820 B3
83301 Twin Falls⊙ 26,209 D7
83454 Ucon 833 F6
83455 Victor 323 G6
83873 Wallace⊙ 1,736 C2
†83837 Wardner 423 B2
83553 Weippe 828 C3
83672 Weiser⊙ 4,771 B5
83355 Wendell 1,974 D7
83286 Weston 310 F7
83554 White Bird 154 B4
83676 Wilder 1,260 A6
83555 Winchester 343 B3
83876 Worley 206 B2

OTHER FEATURES

Albeni Falls (dam) B1
Albion (mts.) E7
Allan (mt.) D4
American Falls (res.) F6
Anderson Ranch (res.) C6
Antelope (creek) E6
Arrowrock (res.) C6
Auger (falls) D7
Badger (peak) E7
Bald (mt.) D5
Bannock (creek) F7
Bannock (peak) F7
Bannock (range) F7
Bargamin (creek) C4
Battle (creek) B7
Bear (lake) G7
Bear (riv.) G7
Beaver (creek) F5
Beaverhead (mts.) E4
Big (creek) C4
Big Boulder (creek) B7
Big Elk (peak) G6
Big Hole (mts.) G6
Big Lost (riv.) E6
Big Southern (butte) E6
Big Wood (riv.) D6
Birch (creek) F5
Birch Creek (valley) E5
Bitterroot (range) D3
Blackfoot (res.) G7
Black Pine (mts.) E7
Blue Nose (mt.) D4
Boise (mts.) B6
Boise (riv.) B6
Borah (peak) E5
Boulder (mts.) D6
Brownlee (dam) B5
Bruneau (riv.) C7
Camas (creek) D5
Camas (creek) D7
Camas (creek) F5
Canyon (creek) C6
Cape Horn (mt.) C5
Caribou (mt.) G6
Caribou (range) G6
Cascade (res.) C5
Castle (creek) B7
Castle (peak) D5
Cedar Creek (peak) E7
Cedar Creek (res.) D7
Centennial (mts.) F5
Clearwater (mts.) C3
Clearwater (riv.) B3
Coeur d'Alene (lake) B2
Coeur d'Alene (mts.) C2
Coeur d'Alene (riv.) B2
Cottonwood (butte) C4
Craig (mts.) B4
Crane Creek (res.) B5
Craters of the Moon Nat'l Mon. E6
Deadwood (res.) C5
Deep (creek) B7
Deep (creek) F7
Deep Creek (mts.) F7
Diamond (peak) E5
Dworshak (res.) C3
East Sister (peak) C2
Eighteen Mile (peak) E5
Fish Creek (res.) E6
Fort Hall Ind. Res. F6
Goldstone (mt.) E4
Goose (creek) E7
Goose Creek (mts.) E7
Grand Canyon of the Snake River (canyon) B4
Grays (lake) G6
Grays Lake Outlet (creek) G6
Greylock (mt.) C6
Hayden (lake) B2
Hells (canyon) B4
Hells Canyon Nat'l Rec. Area B4
Henrys (lake) G5
Henrys Fork, Snake (riv.) G5
Hunter (peak) D3
Hyndman (peak) D6
Indian (creek) C5
Island Park (res.) G5
Jarbidge (riv.) C7
Johnson (creek) C5
Jordan (creek) A7
Kootenai (riv.) C1
Lemhi (pass) E5
Lemhi (range) E5
Lemhi (riv.) E5
Little Lost (riv.) E5
Little Owyhee (riv.) B7
Little Salmon (riv.) B4
Little Weiser (riv.) B5
Little Wood (riv.) D6
Lochsa (riv.) C3
Lolo (creek) C3
Lolo (pass) D3
Lone Pine (peak) D5
Lookout (mt.) D5
Lookout (mt.) F5
Lost River (range) E5
Lost Trail (pass) E4
Lowell (lake) B6
Lower Goose Creek (res.) D7
Lower Granite (lake) A3
Lucky Peak (lake) B6
Mackay (res.) E6
Magic (res.) D6
Malad (riv.) F7
Marsh (creek) F7
McGuire (mt.) D4
Meade (peak) G7
Meadow (creek) C4
Medicine Lodge (creek) F5
Middle Fork (peak) D5
Monument (peak) B4
Moose (creek) D3
Mores (creek) C6
Mormon (mt.) D4
Mountain Home (res.) C6
Mountain Home A.F.B. 6,403 C6
Moyie (riv.) B1
Mud (lake) F6
National Reactor Testing Sta. (U.S.A.E.C.) F6
Nez Perce Nat'l Hist. Park B-C3
North Fork (riv.) B7
Norton (peak) D6
Orofino (creek) C3
Owyhee (mts.) B6
Owyhee, East Fork (riv.) B7
Oxbow (dam) B5
Pack (riv.) B1
Pahsimeroi (riv.) E5
Palisades (res.) G6
Palouse (riv.) B3
Panther (creek) D4
Payette (lake) C4
Payette (mts.) B5
Payette (riv.) B6
Peale (mts.) G7
Pend Oreille (lake) B1
Pend Oreille (mt.) B1
Pend Oreille (riv.) A1
Pilot (peak) C4
Pilot (peak) C6
Pilot Knob (mt.) C4
Pinyon (peak) C5
Pioneer (mts.) D6
Portneuf (res.) F7
Pot (mt.) C3
Potlatch (riv.) B3
Priest (lake) B1
Priest (riv.) B1
Purcell (mts.) B1
Pyramid (peak) E4
Raft (riv.) E7
Rainbow (mt.) C4
Ranger (peak) D3
Rays (lake) F6
Red (riv.) C4
Redfish (lake) D5
Reynolds (creek) B6
Rhodes (peak) D3
Rocky (mts.) D1
Rocky Ridge (mt.) C3
Ryan (peak) D6
Saddle (mt.) D3
Saddle (mt.) F6
Sailor (creek) C7
Saint Joe (riv.) B2
Saint Maries (riv.) B2
Salmon (falls) C7
Salmon (riv.) B4
Salmon Falls (creek) D7
Salmon Falls Creek (res.) D7
Salmon River (mts.) C5
Sawtooth (range) C6
Sawtooth Nat'l Rec. Area D5
Secesh (riv.) C4
Selkirk (mts.) B1
Selway (riv.) C3
Seven Devils (mts.) B4
Shoshone (falls) D7
Sleeping Deer (mt.) D5
Smith (creek) B1
Smoky (mts.) D6
Snake (riv.) A3
Snake River (plain) D7
Snake River (range) G6
Spirit (lake) B2
Squaw (creek) B5
Squaw (peak) D4
Steamboat (mt.) C4
Steel (mt.) C6
Strike, C.J. (res.) C7
Sublett (mts.) E7
Sunset (peak) E6
Taylor (mt.) D5
Teton (riv.) G6
Thompson (peak) C5
Trinity (mt.) C6
Trout (creek) B1
Twin (falls) D7
Twin Peaks (mt.) D5
Walcott (lake) E7
Wasatch (range) G7
Waugh (mt.) D4
Weiser (riv.) B5
Western Shoshone Ind. Res. B7
White Knob (mts.) E6
Wickahoney (creek) C7
Willow (creek) G6
Wilson Lake (res.) D7
Yankee Fork, Salmon (riv.) D5
Yellowstone Nat'l Park G5

⊙County seat.
‡Population of metropolitan area.
† Zip of nearest p.o.
* Multiple zips.

Agriculture, Industry and Resources

DOMINANT LAND USE

Wheat, General Farming
Wheat, Peas
Specialized Dairy
Potatoes, Beans, Sugar Beets, Livestock, General Farming
General Farming, Dairy, Hay, Sugar Beets
General Farming, Livestock, Special Crops
General Farming, Dairy, Range Livestock
Range Livestock
Forests

MAJOR MINERAL OCCURRENCES

Ag Silver
Au Gold
Co Cobalt
Cu Copper
Fe Iron Ore
Hg Mercury
Mo Molybdenum
P Phosphates
Pb Lead
Sb Antimony
Th Thorium
Ti Titanium
V Vanadium
W Tungsten
Zn Zinc

Water Power

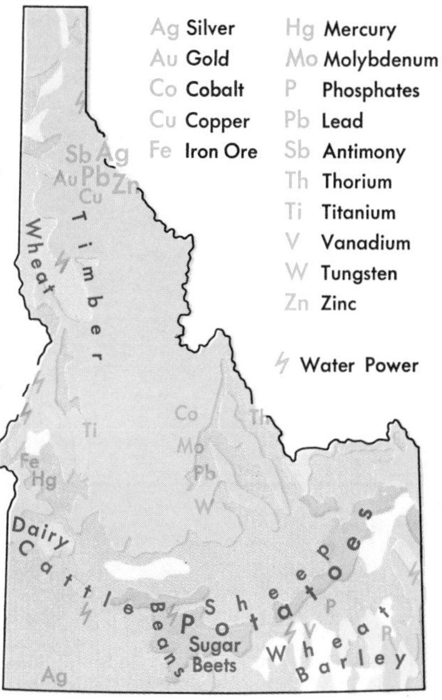

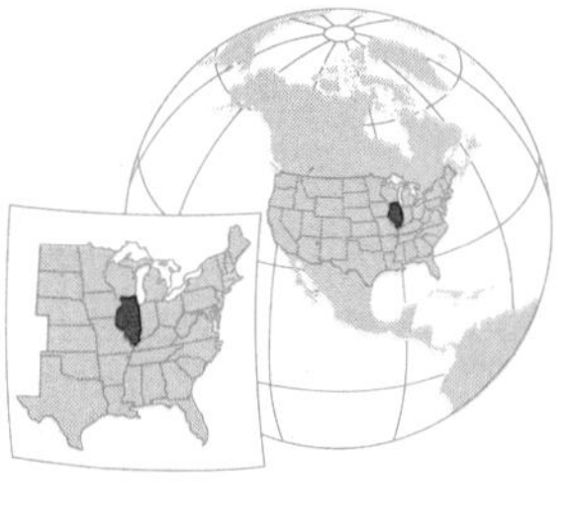

AREA 56,345 sq. mi. (145,934 sq. km.)
POPULATION 11,426,596
CAPITAL Springfield
LARGEST CITY Chicago
HIGHEST POINT Charles Mound 1,235 ft. (376 m.)
SETTLED IN 1720
ADMITTED TO UNION December 3, 1818
POPULAR NAME Prairie State; Land of Lincoln
STATE FLOWER Native Violet
STATE BIRD Cardinal

COUNTIES

Name/Pop.	Key
dams 71,622	B4
lexander 12,264	D6
ond 16,224	D5
oone 28,630	E1
rown 5,411	C4
ureau 39,114	D2
alhoun 5,867	C4
arroll 18,779	D1
ass 15,084	C4
hampaign 168,392	E3
hristian 36,446	D4
lark 16,913	F4
lay 15,283	E5
linton 32,617	D5
oles 52,260	E4
ook 5,253,655	F2
rawford 20,818	F4
umberland 11,062	E4
e Kalb 74,624	E2
e Witt 18,108	E3
ouglas 19,774	E4
u Page 658,835	E2
dgar 21,725	F4
dwards 7,961	E5
ffingham 30,944	E4
ayette 22,167	D4
ord 15,265	E3
ranklin 43,201	E5
ulton 43,687	C3
allatin 7,590	E6
reene 16,661	C4
rundy 30,582	E2
amilton 9,172	E5
ancock 23,877	B3
ardin 5,383	E6
enderson 9,114	C3
enry 57,968	C2
oquois 32,976	F3
Jackson 61,522	D6
Jasper 11,318	E4
Jefferson 36,354	E5
Jersey 20,538	C4
Jo Daviess 23,520	C1
Johnson 9,624	E6
Kane 278,405	E2
Kankakee 102,926	F2
Kendall 37,202	E2
Knox 61,607	C3
Lake 440,372	E1
La Salle 112,033	E2
Lawrence 17,807	F5
Lee 36,328	D2
Livingston 41,381	E3
Logan 31,802	D3
Macon 131,375	E4
Macoupin 49,384	D4
Madison 247,691	D5
Marion 43,523	E5
Marshall 14,479	D2
Mason 19,492	D3
Massac 14,990	E6
McDonough 37,467	C3
McHenry 147,897	E1
McLean 119,149	E3
Menard 11,700	D3
Mercer 19,286	C2
Monroe 20,117	C5
Montgomery 31,686	D4
Morgan 37,502	C4
Moultrie 14,546	E4
Ogle 46,338	D1
Peoria 200,466	D3
Perry 21,714	D5
Piatt 16,581	E4
Pike 18,896	C4
Pope 4,404	E6
Pulaski 8,840	D6
Putnam 6,085	D2
Randolph 35,652	D5
Richland 17,587	E5
Rock Island 165,968	C2
Saint Clair 267,531	D5
Saline 28,448	E6
Sangamon 176,089	D4
Schuyler 8,365	C3
Scott 6,142	C4
Shelby 23,923	E4
Stark 7,389	D2
Stephenson 49,536	D1
Tazewell 132,078	D3
Union 17,765	D6
Vermilion 95,222	F3
Wabash 13,713	F5
Warren 21,943	C3
Washington 15,472	D5
Wayne 18,059	E5
White 17,864	E5
Whiteside 65,970	D2
Will 324,460	F2
Williamson 56,538	E6
Winnebago 250,884	D1
Woodford 33,320	D3

CITIES and TOWNS

Zip	Name/Pop.	Key
61410	Abingdon 4,210	C3
60101	Addison 29,826	B5
61230	Albany 1,014	C2
62806	Albion⊙ 2,285	E5
61231	Aledo⊙ 3,881	C2
61412	Alexis 1,076	C2
60102	Algonquin 5,834	E1
62207	Alorton 2,237	B2
61413	Alpha 815	C2
†60658	Alsip 17,134	B6
62411	Altamont 2,389	E4
62002	Alton 34,171	A2
61310	Amboy 2,377	D2
61232	Andalusia 1,238	C2
62906	Anna 5,408	D6
61234	Annawan 908	C2
60002	Antioch 4,419	E1
61910	Arcola 2,714	E4
62501	Argenta 994	E4
*60004	Arlington Heights 66,116	B5
61911	Arthur 2,122	E4
60911	Ashkum 735	E3
62612	Ashland 1,351	C4
62808	Ashley 658	D5
61912	Ashmore 883	F4
61006	Ashton 1,140	D2
62510	Assumption 1,283	E4
61501	Astoria 1,370	C3
62613	Athens 1,371	D4
61235	Atkinson 1,138	C2
61723	Atlanta 1,807	D3
61913	Atwood 1,464	E4
62615	Auburn 3,616	D4
62311	Augusta 764	C3
*60504	Aurora 81,293	E2
62907	Ava 811	D6
62216	Aviston 846	D5
61415	Avon 1,019	C3
†60015	Bannockburn 1,316	B5
60010	Barrington 9,029	A5
†60010	Barrington Hills 3,631	A5
62312	Barry 1,487	B4
60103	Bartlett 13,254	A5
61607	Bartonville 6,137	D3
60510	Batavia 12,574	E2
62618	Beardstown 6,338	C3
62219	Beckemeyer 1,119	D5
60401	Beecher 2,024	F2
*62220	Belleville⊙ 41,580	B3
60104	Bellwood 19,811	B5
61008	Belvidere⊙ 15,176	E1
61813	Bement 1,770	E4
62009	Benld 1,638	D4
60106	Bensenville 16,124	B5
62812	Benton⊙ 7,778	E6
60162	Berkeley 5,467	B5
60402	Berwyn 46,849	B6
62010	Bethalto 8,630	B2
61914	Bethany 1,550	E4
61420	Blandinsville 886	C3
60108	Bloomingdale 12,659	A5
61701	Bloomington⊙ 44,189	D3
	Bloomington-Normal‡ 119,149	D3
60406	Blue Island 21,855	B6
62513	Blue Mound 1,338	D4
62621	Bluffs 821	C4
60439	Bolingbrook 37,261	A6
60914	Bourbonnais 13,280	F2
60407	Braceville 721	E2
61421	Bradford 924	D2
60915	Bradley 11,008	F2
60408	Braidwood 3,429	E2
62230	Breese 3,516	D5
62417	Bridgeport 2,281	F5
60455	Bridgeview 14,155	B6
62012	Brighton 2,364	C4
61517	Brimfield 890	D3
60153	Broadview 8,618	B6
60513	Brookfield 19,395	B6
†62059	Brooklyn (Lovejoy) 1,233	A2
62910	Brookport 1,128	E6
61314	Buda 668	D2
†60090	Buffalo Grove 22,230	B5
62014	Bunker Hill 1,700	D4
60459	Burbank 28,462	B6
†60601	Burnham 4,030	C6
†60558	Burr Ridge 3,833	B6
61422	Bushnell 3,811	C3
61010	Byron 2,035	D1
62206	Cahokia 18,904	A3
62914	Cairo⊙ 5,931	D6
60409	Calumet City 39,697	C6
†60643	Calumet Park 8,788	C6
62915	Cambria 1,090	D6
61238	Cambridge⊙ 2,217	C2
62320	Camp Point 1,285	B3
61520	Canton 14,626	C3
61239	Carbon Cliff 1,578	C2
62901	Carbondale 26,414	D6
62626	Carlinville⊙ 5,439	D4
62231	Carlyle⊙ 3,388	D5
62821	Carmi⊙ 6,264	E5
†60187	Carol Stream 15,472	A5
60110	Carpentersville 23,272	E1
62917	Carrier Mills 2,268	E6
62016	Carrollton⊙ 2,816	C4
62918	Carterville 3,445	D6
62321	Carthage⊙ 2,978	B3
60013	Cary 6,640	E1
62420	Casey 3,026	F4
62232	Caseyville 4,308	B2
61817	Catlin 2,226	F3
61013	Cedarville 766	D1
†62801	Central City 1,505	D5
62801	Centralia 15,126	D5
62206	Centreville 9,747	B3
61818	Cerro Gordo 1,553	E4
61820	Champaign 58,133	E3
	Champaign-Urbana-Rantoul‡ 168,392	E3
62627	Chandlerville 842	C3
60410	Channahon 3,734	E2
61920	Charleston⊙ 19,355	E4
62629	Chatham 5,597	D4
60921	Chatsworth 1,187	E3
60922	Chebanse 1,191	F3
61726	Chenoa 1,847	E3
61016	Cherry Valley 946	D1
62233	Chester⊙ 8,401	D6
*60601	Chicago⊙ 3,005,072	C5
	Chicago‡ 7,102,328	C5
60411	Chicago Heights 37,026	C6
60415	Chicago Ridge 13,473	B6
61523	Chillicothe 6,176	D3
61924	Chrisman 1,413	F4
62822	Christopher 3,086	D6
60650	Cicero 61,232	B5
60924	Cissna Park 825	F3
60514	Clarendon Hills 6,870	B6
62824	Clay City 1,038	E5
62324	Clayton 889	B3
60927	Clifton 1,390	F3
61727	Clinton⊙ 8,014	E3
60416	Coal City 3,028	E2
61240	Coal Valley 3,800	C2
62920	Cobden 1,210	D6
62017	Coffeen 842	D4
62326	Colchester 1,729	C3
61728	Colfax 920	E3
62234	Collinsville 19,613	B2
61241	Colona 2,172	C2
62236	Columbia 4,269	C5
60112	Cortland 1,019	E2
62018	Cottage Hills	B2
62237	Coulterville 1,118	D5
†60525	Countryside 6,538	B6
62922	Creal Springs 845	E6
60431	Crest Hill 9,252	E2
†60445	Crestwood 10,852	B6
60417	Crete 5,417	F2
61611	Creve Coeur 6,851	D3
62827	Crossville 944	F5
60014	Crystal Lake 18,590	E1
61427	Cuba 1,648	C3
62330	Dallas City 1,408	B3
61320	Dalzell 824	D2
61732	Danvers 921	D3
61832	Danville⊙ 38,985	F3
†60559	Darien 14,536	B6
*62521	Decatur⊙ 94,081	E4
	Decatur‡ 131,375	E4
60015	Deerfield 17,430	B5
†60010	Deer Park 1,368	A5
60115	De Kalb 33,099	E2
61734	Delavan 1,973	D3
61322	Depue 1,873	D2
62924	De Soto 1,589	D6
*60016	Des Plaines 53,568	B5
62530	Divernon 1,081	D4
†60469	Dixmoor 4,175	C6
61021	Dixon⊙ 15,701	D2
60419	Dolton 24,766	C6
62926	Dongola 886	D6
60515	Downers Grove 42,572	A6
60118	Dundee (East and West Dundee) 6,169	E1
61525	Dunlap 824	D3
62239	Dupo 3,039	A3
62832	Du Quoin 6,594	D5
61024	Durand 1,073	D1
60420	Dwight 4,146	E2
60518	Earlville 1,382	E2
62024	East Alton 7,096	A2
†60411	East Chicago Heights 5,347	C6
61025	East Dubuque 2,194	C1
†60118	East Dundee (Dundee) 2,618	E1
61430	East Galesburg 928	C3
†60429	East Hazelcrest 1,362	C6
61244	East Moline 20,907	C2
61611	East Peoria 22,385	D3
*62201	East Saint Louis 55,200	A2
62531	Edinburg 1,231	D4
62025	Edwardsville⊙ 12,480	B2
62401	Effingham⊙ 11,270	E4
60119	Elburn 1,224	E2
62930	Eldorado 5,198	E6
60120	Elgin 63,981	E1
61028	Elizabeth 772	C1
62931	Elizabethtown⊙ 478	E6
60007	Elk Grove Village 28,907	B5
62932	Elkville 973	D6
60126	Elmhurst 44,276	B5
61529	Elmwood 2,117	D3
60635	Elmwood Park 24,016	B5
61738	El Paso 2,676	D3
62028	Elsah 990	C5
60421	Elwood 814	E2
62933	Energy 1,138	E6
62835	Enfield 890	E5
62934	Equality 831	E6
61250	Erie 1,725	C2
61530	Eureka⊙ 4,306	D3
*60201	Evanston 73,706	B5
62242	Evansville 863	D5
60642	Evergreen Park 22,260	B6
61739	Fairbury 3,544	E3
62837	Fairfield⊙ 5,954	E5
†62201	Fairmont City 2,313	B2
61841	Fairmount 851	F3
62208	Fairview Heights 12,414	B3
61842	Farmer City 2,252	E3
61531	Farmington 3,118	C3
62534	Findlay 868	E4
61843	Fisher 1,572	E3
61740	Flanagan 978	E3
62839	Flora 5,379	E5
60422	Flossmoor 8,423	B6
60130	Forest Park 15,177	B5
†60402	Forest View 764	B6
61741	Forrest 1,246	E3
61030	Forreston 1,384	D1
60020	Fox Lake 6,831	A4
60021	Fox River Grove 2,515	A5
60423	Frankfort 4,357	B6
61031	Franklin Grove 965	D2
60131	Franklin Park 17,507	B5
62243	Freeburg 2,989	D5
61032	Freeport⊙ 26,266	D1
61252	Fulton 3,936	C2
62935	Galatia 1,042	E6
61036	Galena⊙ 3,876	C1
61401	Galesburg⊙ 35,305	C3
61434	Galva 3,185	D2
60424	Gardner 1,322	E2
61254	Geneseo 6,373	C2
60134	Geneva⊙ 9,881	E2
60135	Genoa 3,276	E1
61846	Georgetown 4,220	F4
62245	Germantown 1,191	D5
60936	Gibson City 3,498	E3
61847	Gifford 848	E3
62033	Gillespie 3,740	D4
60938	Gilman 1,913	E3
62640	Girard 2,246	D4
61533	Glasford 1,201	D3
62034	Glen Carbon 5,197	B2
60022	Glencoe 9,200	B5
†60108	Glendale Heights 23,163	A5
60137	Glen Ellyn 23,717	A5
60025	Glenview 32,060	B5
60425	Glenwood 10,538	C6
62035	Godfrey	A2
62938	Golconda⊙ 960	E6
62939	Goreville 978	E6
62037	Grafton 1,024	C5
62942	Grand Tower 748	D6
†62701	Grandview 1,794	D4
62040	Granite City 36,815	A2
60940	Grant Park 1,038	F2
61326	Granville 1,537	D2
60030	Grayslake 5,260	B4
62844	Grayville 2,313	B4
62044	Greenfield 1,090	C4
†60048	Green Oaks 1,415	B4
†61241	Green Rock 3,324	C2
62428	Greenup 1,655	E4
61534	Green Valley 768	D3
62642	Greenview 830	D3
62246	Greenville⊙ 5,271	D5
61744	Gridley 1,246	E3
62340	Griggsville 1,301	C4
60031	Gurnee 7,179	B4
62341	Hamilton 3,509	B3
60140	Hampshire 1,735	E1
61256	Hampton 1,873	C2
61536	Hanna City 1,361	D3
61041	Hanover 1,069	C1
60103	Hanover Park 28,719	A5
62047	Hardin⊙ 1,107	C4
62946	Harrisburg⊙ 10,410	E6
62537	Harristown 1,456	D4
62048	Hartford 1,887	A2
60033	Harvard 5,126	E1
60426	Harvey 35,810	B6
60656	Harwood Heights 8,228	B5
62644	Havana⊙ 4,277	D3
†60047	Hawthorn Woods 1,658	B5
60429	Hazel Crest 13,973	B6
60034	Hebron 786	E1
†61832	Hegeler 1,853	F3
61327	Hennepin⊙ 716	D2
61537	Henry 2,740	D2
62948	Herrin 10,708	E6
60941	Herscher 1,214	E2
61745	Heyworth 1,598	E3
60457	Hickory Hills 13,778	B6
62249	Highland 7,122	D5
60035	Highland Park 30,611	B5
60040	Highwood 5,452	B5
62049	Hillsboro⊙ 4,408	D4
60162	Hillside 8,279	B5
60520	Hinckley 1,447	E2
60521	Hinsdale 16,726	B6
60525	Hodgkins 2,005	B6
60195	Hoffman Estates 37,272	A5
61849	Homer 1,279	F3
60456	Hometown 5,324	B6
60430	Homewood 19,724	B6
60942	Hoopeston 6,411	F3
61747	Hohedale 913	D3
61748	Hudson 929	E3

(continued on following page)

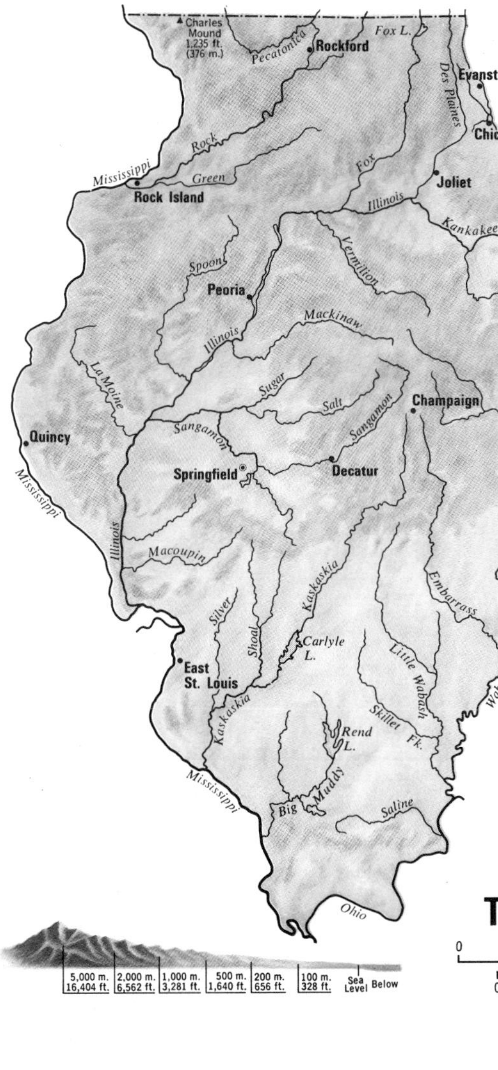
Charles Mound 1,235 ft. (376 m.)
Fox L.
Pecatonica
Rockford
Evanston
Des Plaines
Chicago
Rock
Mississippi
Green
Rock Island
Fox
Joliet
Illinois
Kankakee
Vermilion
Spoon
Peoria
Mackinaw
Illinois
La Moine
Sugar
Salt
Sangamon
Champaign
Quincy
Sangamon
Springfield
Decatur
Mississippi
Illinois
Macoupin
Kaskaskia
Embarrass
Silver
Shoal
Carlyle L.
Little Wabash
East St. Louis
Wabash
Kaskaskia
Skillet Fk.
Rend L.
Mississippi
Big Muddy
Saline
Ohio
5,000 m. 16,404 ft.
2,000 m. 6,562 ft.
1,000 m. 3,281 ft.
500 m. 1,640 ft.
200 m. 656 ft.
100 m. 328 ft.
Sea Level
Below

Topography

0 40 80 MI.
0 40 80 KM.

Agriculture, Industry and Resources

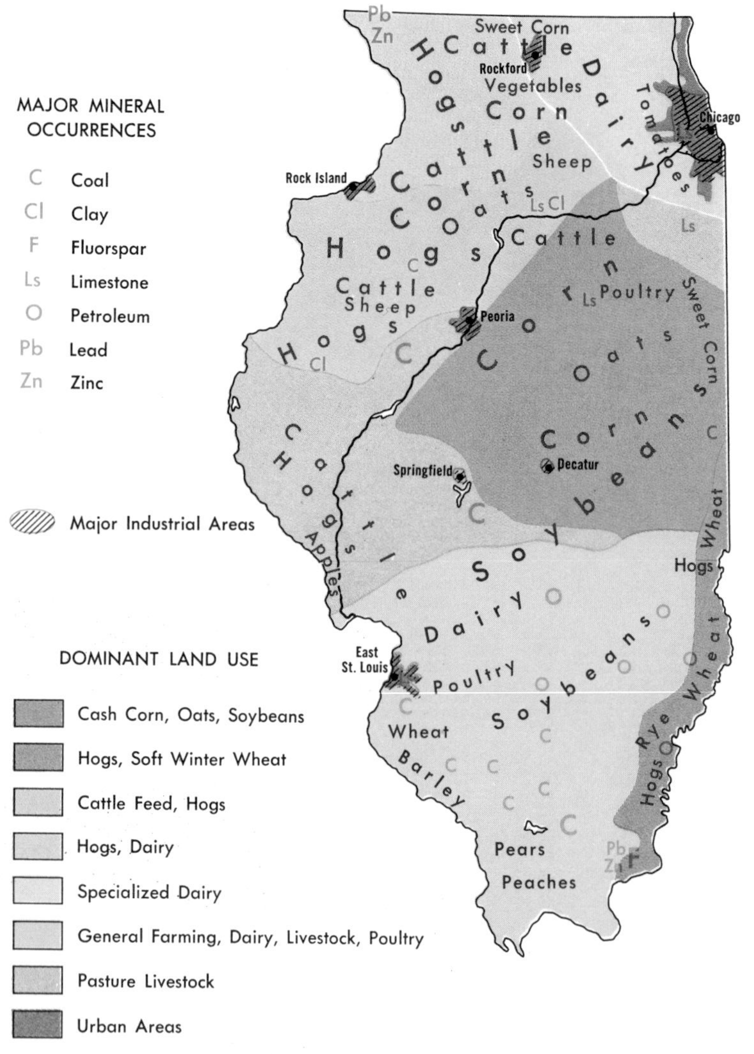
MAJOR MINERAL OCCURRENCES
C Coal
Cl Clay
F Fluorspar
Ls Limestone
O Petroleum
Pb Lead
Zn Zinc
Major Industrial Areas
DOMINANT LAND USE
Cash Corn, Oats, Soybeans
Hogs, Soft Winter Wheat
Cattle Feed, Hogs
Hogs, Dairy
Specialized Dairy
General Farming, Dairy, Livestock, Poultry
Pasture Livestock
Urban Areas
Sweet Corn
Cattle
Rockford
Vegetables
Dairy
Corn
Hogs
Tomatoes
Chicago
Sheep
Rock Island
Oats
Poultry
Peoria
Sweet Corn
Springfield
Decatur
Soybeans
Wheat
Apples
East St. Louis
Barley
Rye
Pears
Peaches

60142 Huntley 1,646 .... E1
62949 Hurst 938 .... D6
62539 Illiopolis 1,118................ D4
†60067 Inverness 4,046.............. A5
62848 Irvington 789 .... D5
60042 Island Lake 2,293............ A4
60143 Itasca 7,129 .... B5
62650 Jacksonville⊙ 20,284....... C4
†62701 Jerome 1,374................. D4
62052 Jerseyville⊙ 7,506 .... C4
62436 Jewett 230 .... E4
62951 Johnston City 3,873......... E6
*60431 Joliet⊙ 77,956.............. E2
62952 Jonesboro⊙ 1,842.......... D6
†60458 Justice 10,552............... B6
60901 Kankakee⊙ 30,141.......... F2
Kankakee‡ 102,926 .... F2
61933 Kansas 791 .... F4
†63673 Kaskaskia 33.................. C6
61442 Keithsburg 936 .... B2
60043 Kenilworth 2,708............. B5
61443 Kewanee 14,508 .... C2
†60069 Kildeer 1,609 .... A5
62540 Kincaid 1,591................. D4
62854 Kinmundy 945................. E5
60146 Kirkland 1,155................ E1
61447 Kirkwood 1,008 .... C3
61448 Knoxville 3,432............... C3
61540 Lacon⊙ 2,135 .... D2
61329 Ladd 1,337..................... D2
60525 La Grange 15,445 .... B6
60525 La Grange Park 13,359..... B5
61450 La Harpe 1,471 .... C3
†60010 Lake Barrington 2,320 ...... A5
60044 Lake Bluff 4,434 .... B4
†60002 Lake Catherine 1,335........ E1
60045 Lake Forest 15,245.......... B4
†60102 Lake in the Hills 5,651...... E1
60046 Lake Villa 1,462.............. A4
62438 Lakewood 1,254 .... E4
60047 Lake Zurich 8,225 .... A5
61330 La Moille 734.................. D2
61046 Lanark 1,483 .... D1
60438 Lansing 29,039 .... C6
61301 La Salle 10,347 .... E2
62439 Lawrenceville⊙ 5,652 ...... F5
62254 Lebanon 3,245 .... D5
60531 Leland 775 .... E2

60439 Lemont 5,640 .... B6
61048 Lena 2,295...................... D1
61752 Le Roy 2,870................... E3
61542 Lewistown⊙ 2,758.......... C3
61753 Lexington 1,806.............. E3
60048 Libertyville 16,520 .... B4
62656 Lincoln⊙ 16,327 .... D3
†60015 Lincolnshire 4,151 .... B5
†60645 Lincolnwood 11,921......... B5
†60046 Lindenhurst 6,220 .... B4
60532 Lisle 13,625 .... A6
62056 Litchfield 7,204............... D4
62058 Livingston 949................ D5
62661 Loami 770...................... D4
60441 Lockport 9,170................ B6
60148 Lombard 36,897 .... B5
60047 Long Grove 2,013 .... B5
62858 Louisville⊙ 1,166 .... E5
62059 Lovejoy 1,233 .... A2
61111 Loves Park 13,192 .... E1
61937 Lovington 1,313 .... E4
61261 Lyndon 777 .... D2
†60411 Lynwood 4,195 .... C6
60534 Lyons 9,925 .... B6
61755 Mackinaw 1,354 .... D3
61455 Macomb⊙ 19,863 .... C3
62544 Macon 1,300 .... E4
62060 Madison 5,915................. A2
61853 Mahomet 1,986 .... E3
60150 Malta 995 .... E2
60442 Manhattan 1,944.............. F2
61546 Manito 1,869 .... D3
61854 Mansfield 921 .... E3
60950 Manteno 3,155................. F2
60152 Marengo 4,361................. E1
62061 Marine 957...................... D5
62959 Marion⊙ 14,031.............. E6
62257 Marissa 2,568.................. D5
60426 Markham 15,172 .... B6
61756 Maroa 1,760.................... E3
†61554 Marquette Heights 3,386 ... D3
61341 Marseilles 4,766 .... E2
62441 Marshall⊙ 3,655 .... F4
62442 Martinsville 1,298............ F4
62062 Maryville 1,937................ B2
62258 Mascoutah 4,962 .... D5
62664 Mason City 2,719............. D3
61263 Matherville 793................ C2

60443 Matteson 10,223............. B6
61938 Mattoon 19,055.............. E4
60153 Maywood 27,998 .... B5
60444 Mazon 828 .... E2
60050 McHenry 10,908 .... E1
†60050 McHenry Shores 1,041 ..... E1
61754 McLean 836 .... D3
62859 McLeansboro⊙ 2,960...... E5
†62010 Meadowbrook 1,082 .... B2
*60160 Melrose Park 20,735........ B5
62351 Mendon 979 .... B3
61342 Mendota 7,134 .... D2
62665 Meredosia 1,272............. C4
†60601 Merrionette Park 2,054 ..... B6
61548 Metamora 2,482 .... D3
62960 Metropolis⊙ 7,171 .... E6
60445 Midlothian 14,274 .... B6
61264 Milan 6,264.................... C2
60953 Milford 1,716.................. F3
61051 Milledgeville 1,209.......... D1
62260 Millstadt 2,736 .... B3
61759 Minier 1,261 .... D3
61760 Minonk 2,039 .... D3
60447 Minooka 1,565 .... E2
60448 Mokena 4,578................. B6
61265 Moline 46,278................. C2
60954 Momence 3,297 .... F2
60449 Monee 993..................... F2
61462 Monmouth⊙ 10,706........ C3
60538 Montgomery 3,369.......... E2
61856 Monticello⊙ 4,753 .... E3
60450 Morris⊙ 8,833................ E2
61270 Morrison⊙ 4,605............ C2
62546 Morrisonville 1,208.......... D4
61550 Morton 14,178 .... D3
60053 Morton Grove 23,747....... B5
62963 Mound City⊙ 1,102 .... D6
62964 Mounds 1,669................ D6
62863 Mount Carmel⊙ 8,908 ..... F5
61053 Mount Carroll⊙ 1,936...... D1
61054 Mount Morris 2,989......... D1
62069 Mount Olive 2,357........... D4
60056 Mount Prospect 52,634 .... B5
62548 Mount Pulaski 1,783........ D3
62353 Mount Sterling⊙ 2,186 .... C4
62864 Mount Vernon⊙ 17,193 ... E5
62549 Mount Zion 4,563 .... E4
62550 Moweaqua 1,922 .... E4

60060 Mundelein 17,053 .... A4
62966 Murphysboro⊙ 9,866 ...... D6
60540 Naperville 42,601 .... A6
62263 Nashville⊙ 3,186............ D5
62354 Nauvoo 1,133 .... B3
62447 Neoga 1,736................... E4
60541 Newark 798.................... E2
62264 New Athens 1,937........... D5
62265 New Baden 2,476............ D5
62670 New Berlin 834............... D4
61272 New Boston 731 .... B2
60451 New Lenox 5,792............ B6
61942 Newman 1,079............... B6
62448 Newton⊙ 3,186 .... E5
61465 New Windsor 863 .... C2
62551 Niantic 761..................... D4
60648 Niles 30,363 .... B5
62868 Noble 832 .... E5
62075 Nokomis 2,656............... D4
61761 Normal 35,672 .... E3
†60656 Norridge 16,483.............. B5
62869 Norris City 1,515 .... E6
60542 North Aurora 5,205 .... E2
†60010 North Barrington 1,475 ..... A5
60062 Northbrook 30,778 .... B5
60064 North Chicago 38,774 ...... B4
60093 Northfield 5,807.............. B5
60164 Northlake 12,166 .... B5
†61111 North Park 15,806........... D1
†61554 North Pekin 1,824 .... D3
60546 North Riverside 6,764 ...... B5
†61373 North Utica (Utica) 1,067 .. E2
60521 Oak Brook 6,641............. B6
†60181 Oakbrook Terrace 2,285.... B5
60452 Oak Forest 26,096........... B6
61943 Oakland 1,035................ F4
*60453 Oak Lawn 60,590............ B6
*60303 Oak Park 54,887............. B5
61858 Oakwood 1,627 .... F3
62449 Oblong 1,840.................. F5
60460 Odell 1,083 .... E2
62870 Odin 1,285..................... D5
62269 O'Fallon 12,241 .... B2
61859 Ogden 818 .... F3
61348 Oglesby 3,979................ D2
62271 Okawville 1,337 .... D5
62450 Olney⊙ 9,026................ E5
60461 Olympia Fields 4,146........ B6
60955 Onarga 1,269................. F3
61467 Oneida 765..................... C2
61469 Oquawka⊙ 1,533............ C3
62554 Oreana 999.................... E4
61061 Oregon⊙ 3,559.............. D1
61273 Orion 2,013.................... C2
60462 Orland Park 23,045 .... B6
60543 Oswego 3,021................ E2
61350 Ottawa⊙ 18,166............. E2
60067 Palatine 32,166............... B5
62451 Palestine 1,718............... F4
62674 Palmyra 864 .... C4
60463 Palos Heights 11,096 .... B6
60465 Palos Hills 16,654 .... B6
60464 Palos Park 3,150 .... B6
62557 Pana 6,040..................... D4
61944 Paris⊙ 9,885.................. F4
†60085 Park City 3,673............... B4
60466 Park Forest 26,222 .... B6
60466 Park Forest South 6,245 ... F2
60068 Park Ridge 38,704 .... B5
62558 Pawnee 2,577 .... D4
61353 Pawpaw 839................... E2
60957 Paxton⊙ 4,258 .... E3
62360 Payson 1,065................. B4
61063 Pecatonica 1,732 .... D1
61554 Pekin⊙ 33,967 .... D3
*61601 Peoria⊙ 124,160 .... D3
Peoria‡ 365,864 .... D3
61614 Peoria Heights 7,453........ D3
60468 Peotone 2,832................ F2
62272 Percy 1,053................... D5
61354 Peru 10,886 .... D2
62675 Petersburg⊙ 2,419 .... D4
61864 Philo 973 .... E3
†60426 Phoenix 2,850................ C6
62274 Pinckneyville⊙ 3,319 .... D5
60959 Piper City 905 .... E3
62363 Pittsfield⊙ 4,170 .... C4
60544 Plainfield 3,767............... A6
60545 Plano 4,875................... E2
62366 Pleasant Hill 1,112 .... C4
62275 Pocahontas 866.............. D5
61074 Polo 2,643 .... D1
61764 Pontiac⊙ 11,227 .... E3
†62040 Pontoon Beach 3,336 .... A2
61065 Poplar Grove 818 .... E1
61275 Port Byron 1,289 .... C2
60469 Posen 4,642................... B6
61865 Potomac 874 .... F3
61470 Prairie City 580............... C3
61356 Princeton⊙ 7,342 .... D2
61559 Princeville 1,712 .... D3
61277 Prophetstown 2,141......... D2
60070 Prospect Heights 11,808 ... B5
62301 Quincy⊙ 42,554............. B4
62080 Ramsey 1,058................ D4
60960 Rankin 727.................... F3
61866 Rantoul 20,161............... E3
61278 Rapids City 1,058............ C2
62560 Raymond 957 .... D4
62278 Red Bud 2,850................ D5
60071 Richmond 1,068 .... E1
60471 Richton Park 9,403.......... B6
61870 Ridge Farm 1,096 .... F4
62979 Ridgway 1,245 .... E6
60627 Riverdale 13,233............. C6
60305 River Forest 12,392 .... B5
60171 River Grove 10,368 .... B5
60546 Riverside 9,236 .... B6
62561 Riverton 2,783 .... D4
†60015 Riverwoods 2,804 .... B5
61561 Roanoke 2,001................ D3
60472 Robbins 8,853 .... B6
62454 Robinson⊙ 7,285 .... F5
61068 Rochelle 8,982................ D2
62563 Rochester 2,488 .... D4
60436 Rockdale 1,913 .... E2
61071 Rock Falls 10,633 .... D2

*61101 Rockford⊙ 139,712......... D1
Rockford‡ 279,514.......... D1
61201 Rock Island⊙ 46,928....... C2
Rock Island-Moline-
Davenport‡ 383,958..... C2
61072 Rockton 2,313 .... E1
60008 Rolling Meadows 20,167... A5
61562 Rome 2,744 .... D3
60441 Romeoville 15,519........... B6
62082 Roodhouse 2,364............ C4
61073 Roscoe 1,388 .... D1
60172 Roselle 16,948 .... A5
60018 Rosemont 4,137 .... B5
61473 Roseville 1,254............... C3
†62024 Rosewood Heights 5,085 .. B2
62982 Rosiclare 1,441 .... E6
60963 Rossville 1,363............... F3
60673 Round Lake 2,644........... A4
†60673 Round Lake Beach 12,921 . A4
†60673 Round Lake Heights 1,192. E1
†60673 Round Lake Park 4,032 .... A4
62084 Roxana 1,587 .... B2
62983 Royalton 1,320............... D6
62681 Rushville⊙ 3,348............ C3
60964 Saint Anne 1,421 .... F2
60174 Saint Charles 17,492........ E2
61563 Saint David 786 .... C3
62458 Saint Elmo 1,611 .... E4
62460 Saint Francisville 1,040 ..... F5
62281 Saint Jacob 792.............. D5
61873 Saint Joseph 1,900.......... E3
62881 Salem⊙ 7,813 .... E5
62882 Sandoval 1,734 .... D5
60548 Sandwich 5,244.............. E2
62682 San Jose 784................. D3
60411 Sauk Village 10,906 .... C6
61074 Savanna 4,529 .... C1
61874 Savoy 2,126 .... E3
61770 Saybrook 882................. E3
60194 Schaumburg 53,305 .... A5
60176 Schiller Park 11,458......... B5
61360 Seneca 2,098................. E2
62884 Sesser 2,238 .... D5
60550 Shabbona 851 .... E2
61078 Shannon 938 .... D1
62984 Shawneetown⊙ 1,841...... E6
61361 Sheffield 1,130 .... D2
62565 Shelbyville⊙ 5,259.......... E4
60966 Sheldon 1,215................ F3
62684 Sherman 1,501............... D4
61281 Sherrard 811.................. C2
†62220 Shiloh 1,045 .... B3
60435 Shorewood 4,714............. E2
61877 Sidney 886 .... E3
61282 Silvis 7,130 .... C2
*60076 Skokie 60,278 .... B5
†60118 Sleepy Hollow 2,000 .... E1
62285 Smithton 1,447 .... C5
60552 Somonauk 1,344 .... E2
†60010 South Barrington 1,168..... A5
61080 South Beloit 4,088........... E1
60411 South Chicago
Heights 3,932 .... C6
60177 South Elgin 5,970 .... E2
60473 South Holland 24,977....... C6
†62650 South Jacksonville 3,382... C4
61564 South Pekin 1,243........... D3
62087 South Roxana 2,286 .... B2
60474 South Wilmington 747...... E2
62286 Sparta 4,957.................. D5
*62701 Springfield (cap.)⊙
100,054.................. D4
Springfield‡ 187,789........ D4
61362 Spring Valley 5,822 .... D2
61774 Stanford 720.................. D3
62088 Staunton 4,744............... D5
62288 Steeleville 2,240............. D6
60475 Steger 9,269.................. F2
61081 Sterling 16,281............... D2
62463 Stewardson 745.............. E4
60402 Stickney 5,893 .... B6
61084 Stillman Valley 961 .... D1
61085 Stockton 1,872................ C1
†60160 Stone Park 4,273 .... B5
62567 Stonington 1,184 .... D4
60103 Streamwood 23,456......... A5
61364 Streator 14,795 .... E2
61480 Stronghurst 865.............. C3
60554 Sugar Grove 1,366 .... E2
61951 Sullivan⊙ 4,526 .... E4
60501 Summit-Argo 10,110........ B6
62466 Sumner 1,238 .... F5
†60050 Sunnyside 1,432.............. A4
62221 Swansea 5,347............... B3
60178 Sycamore⊙ 9,219........... E2
62888 Tamaroa 885 .... D5
62988 Tamms 826.................... D6
61283 Tampico 966.................. D2
62568 Taylorville⊙ 11,386 .... D4
62467 Teutopolis 1,414 .... E4
62689 Thayer 759.................... D4
61878 Thomasboro 1,242 .... E3
61285 Thomson 911.................. C2
60476 Thornton 3,024 .... C6
62292 Tilden 1,025 .... D5
†61832 Tilton 2,405................... F3
60477 Tinley Park 26,171 .... B6
61368 Tiskilwa 990 .... D2
62468 Toledo⊙ 1,284 .... E4
61880 Tolono 2,434 .... E3
61369 Toluca 1,471.................. D2
61483 Toulon⊙ 1,390 .... D2
†60010 Tower Lakes 1,177 .... A4
61568 Tremont 2,096 .... D3
62293 Trenton 2,504 .... D5
62294 Troy 3,772..................... B2
61953 Tuscola⊙ 3,839 .... E4
61801 Urbana⊙ 35,978 .... E3
61373 Utica 1,067 .... E2
62891 Valier 729 .... D5
†60120 Valley View 2,112............ E2
62295 Valmeyer 898................. C5
62471 Vandalia⊙ 5,338 .... D5
62090 Venice 3,480.................. A2
61484 Vermont 885.................. C3
60061 Vernon Hills 9,827........... B4
62995 Vienna⊙ 1,420 .... E6

61956 Villa Grove 2,707 .... E4
60181 Villa Park 23,185 .... B5
61486 Viola 1,144.................... C2
62690 Virden 3,899.................. D4
62691 Virginia⊙ 1,825.............. C4
60083 Wadsworth 1,104............ B4
61376 Walnut 1,513 .... D2
†62801 Wamac 1,665 .... D5
61777 Wapella 768................... E3
61087 Warren 1,595................. C1
62573 Warrensburg 1,372.......... D4
60555 Warrenville 7,519 .... A6
62379 Warsaw 1,842................. B3
61570 Washburn 1,206 .... D3
61571 Washington 10,364 .... D3
62204 Washington Park 8,223 .... B2
61488 Wataga 996 .... C2
62298 Waterloo⊙ 4,646............ C5
60556 Waterman 943................ E2
60970 Watseka⊙ 5,543 .... F3
60084 Wauconda 5,688............. A4
60085 Waukegan⊙ 67,653 .... B4
62692 Waverly 1,537................. D4
60184 Wayne 940..................... E2
62895 Wayne City 1,132............ E5
61377 Wenona 1,025................ E2
60153 Westchester 17,730 .... B5
60185 West Chicago 12,550 .... A5
†60118 West Dundee
(Dundee) 3,551............ E1
60558 Western Springs 12,876 ... B6
62474 Westfield 733................. F4
62896 West Frankfort 9,437 .... E6
†60462 Westhaven 2,784 .... B6
60559 Westmont 16,718 .... B6
62476 West Salem 1,145............ F5
61883 Westville 3,573............... F3
60187 Wheaton⊙ 43,043 .... A5
60090 Wheeling 23,266............. B5
62092 White Hall 2,935.............. C4
62693 Williamsville 996 .... D4
†60521 Willowbrook 4,953 .... B6
60480 Willow Springs 4,147 .... B6
60091 Wilmette 28,229 .... B5
60481 Wilmington 4,424............. E2
62694 Winchester⊙ 1,716 .... C4
61957 Windsor 1,228 .... E4
†61465 Windsor (New
Windsor) 863 .... C2
60190 Winfield 4,422................. A5
61088 Winnebago 1,644............. D
60093 Winnetka 12,772............. B5
60096 Winthrop Harbor 5,431 ..... F
62094 Witt 1,205...................... D4
60191 Wood Dale 11,251 .... B5
61490 Woodhull 901 C
†60517 Woodridge 22,561............ B6
62095 Wood River 12,446 .... B2
60098 Woodstock⊙ 11,725 .... E
62097 Worden 953 .... B
60482 Worth 11,592 .... B6
61379 Wyanet 1,069 .... D
61491 Wyoming 1,614............... D
61572 Yates City 860................ C
60560 Yorkville⊙ 3,422 .... E
62999 Zeigler 1,858 .... D
60099 Zion 17,861.................... F

OTHER FEATURES

Apple (creek)............................ C
Apple (riv.) C
Argonne Nat'l Laboratory .... B
Big Bureau (riv.)........................ D
Big Muddy (riv.)......................... D
Bonpas (creek)........................... F
Cache (riv.)............................... D
Calumet (lake) C
Carlyle (lake) .... D
Chanute A.F.B. .... E
Charles Mound (hill).................. C
Chicago Portage Nat'l Hist. Site .... B
Crab Orchard (lake)................... E
Des Plaines (riv.)....................... A
Du Page (riv.)............................ E
Edwards (riv.)............................ C
Embarras (riv.) .... E
Fort Sheridan .... B
Fox (lake) .... A
Fox (riv.).................................. E
Fox (riv.).................................. E
Glenview Nav. Air. Sta. .... B
Granite City Army Depot .... A
Great Lakes Nav. Trng. Ctr. .... B
Green (riv.)............................... D
Henderson (riv.)......................... C
Illinois (riv.) C
Illinois - Mississippi (canal) C
Iroquois (riv.) .... F
Kankakee (riv.).......................... F
Kaskaskia (riv.) .... E
La Moine (riv.)........................... C
Little Wabash (riv.) .... E
Mackinaw (riv.).......................... E
Macoupin (riv.) C
Michigan (lake) .... F
Mississippi (riv.)......................... C
O'Hare Field-Chicago International
Airport .... B
Ohio (riv.) .... E
Plum (riv.)................................. C
Pope (creek) C
Rend (lake) .... E
Rock (creek) .... D
Rock (riv.)................................. C
Rock Island Arsenal C
Saline (riv.)............................... E
Salt (creek) .... D
Sangamon (riv.) C
Savanna Army Depot C
Scott A.F.B. 8,648...................... B
Shelbyville (lake)........................ E
Spoon (riv.) C
Wabash (riv.) .... F

⊙County seat.
‡Population of metropolitan area.
† Zip of nearest p.o. * Multiple zip

AREA 36,185 sq. mi. (93,719 sq. km.)
POPULATION 5,490,260
CAPITAL Indianapolis
LARGEST CITY Indianapolis
HIGHEST POINT 1,257 ft. (383 m.) (Wayne County)
SETTLED IN 1730
ADMITTED TO UNION December 11, 1816
POPULAR NAME Hoosier State
STATE FLOWER Peony
STATE BIRD Cardinal

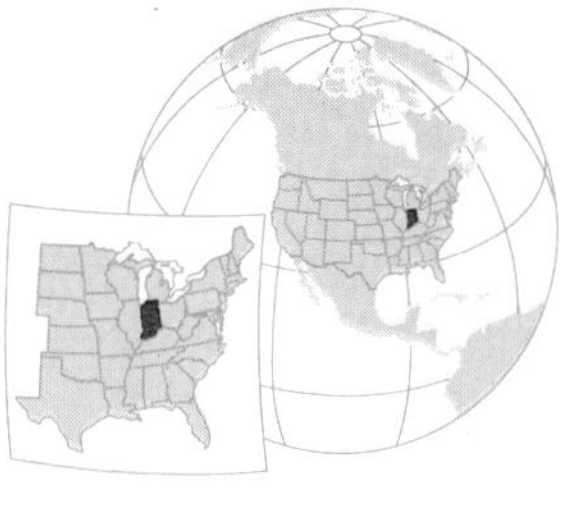

COUNTIES

Adams 29,619 H3
Allen 294,335 G2
Bartholomew 65,088 F6
Benton 10,218 C3
Blackford 15,570 G4
Boone 36,446 E4
Brown 12,377 E6
Carroll 19,722 D3
Cass 40,936 E3
Clark 88,838 F8
Clay 24,862 C6
Clinton 31,545 E4
Crawford 9,820 E8
Daviess 27,836 C7
Dearborn 34,291 H6
Decatur 23,841 G6
De Kalb 33,606 H2
Delaware 128,587 G4
Dubois 34,238 D8
Elkhart 137,330 F1
Fayette 28,272 G5
Floyd 61,169 F8
Fountain 19,033 C4
Franklin 19,612 G6
Fulton 19,335 E2
Gibson 33,156 B8
Grant 80,934 F3
Greene 30,416 D6
Hamilton 82,027 E4
Hancock 43,939 F5
Harrison 27,276 E8
Hendricks 69,804 D5
Henry 53,336 G5
Howard 86,896 E4
Huntington 35,596 G3
Jackson 36,523 E7
Jasper 26,138 C2
Jay 23,239 G4
Jefferson 30,419 G7
Jennings 22,854 F7
Johnson 77,240 E6
Knox 41,838 C7
Kosciusko 59,555 F2
Lagrange 25,550 G1
Lake 522,965 C2
LaPorte 108,632 D1
Lawrence 42,472 E7
Madison 139,336 F4
Marion 765,233 E5
Marshall 39,155 E2
Martin 11,001 D7
Miami 39,820 E3
Monroe 98,785 D6
Montgomery 35,501 D4
Morgan 51,999 E6
Newton 14,844 C3
Noble 35,443 G2
Ohio 5,114 H7
Orange 18,677 E7
Owen 15,841 D6
Parke 16,372 C5
Perry 19,346 D8
Pike 13,465 C8
Porter 119,816 C2
Posey 26,414 B8
Pulaski 13,258 D2
Putnam 29,163 D5
Randolph 29,997 G4
Ripley 24,398 G6
Rush 19,604 G5
Saint Joseph 241,617 E1
Scott 20,422 F7
Shelby 39,887 F5
Spencer 19,361 C9
Starke 21,997 D2
Steuben 24,694 G1
Sullivan 21,107 C6
Switzerland 7,153 G7
Tippecanoe 121,702 D4
Tipton 16,819 E4
Union 6,860 H5
Vanderburgh 167,515 B8
Vermillion 18,229 C5
Vigo 112,385 C6
Wabash 36,640 F3
Warren 8,976 C4
Warrick 41,474 C8
Washington 21,932 E7
Wayne 76,058 G5
Wells 25,401 G3
White 23,867 D3
Whitley 26,215 F2

CITIES and TOWNS

Zip *Name/Pop.* *Key*

47240 Adams 250 F6
†46947 Adamsboro 325 E3
46102 Advance 559 D5
46910 Akron 1,045 E2
47320 Albany 2,625 G4
46701 Albion⊙ 1,637 G2
†47283 Alert 102 F6
46001 Alexandria 6,028 F4
†46738 Altona 263 G2
47917 Ambia 274 C4
46911 Amboy 450 F3
†46131 Amity 200 E6
46103 Amo 444 D5
*46011 Anderson⊙ 64,695 F4
Anderson‡ 139,336 F4
†47024 Andersonville 225 G5
46702 Andrews 1,243 F3
46703 Angola⊙ 5,486 G1
46030 Arcadia 1,801 E4
46704 Arcola 300 G2
†46624 Ardmore 800 E1
46501 Argos 1,547 E2
46104 Arlington 500 F5
46705 Ashley 841 G1
46031 Atlanta 657 E4
47918 Attica 3,841 C4
46502 Atwood 300 F2
46706 Auburn⊙ 8,122 G2
47001 Aurora 3,816 H6
47102 Austin 4,857 F7
46710 Avilla 1,272 G2
47420 Avoca 400 D7
46105 Bainbridge 644 D5
46106 Bargersville 1,647 E5
47006 Batesville 4,152 G6
47920 Battle Ground 812 D3
47421 Bedford⊙ 14,410 E7
46107 Beech Grove 13,196 E5
†46526 Benton 220 F2
46711 Berne 3,300 H3
†46111 Bethany 127 E5
46301 Beverly Shores 864 C1
47512 Bicknell 4,713 C7
46713 Bippus 300 F3
47513 Birdseye 533 D8
†46406 Black Oak C1
47831 Blanford 500 B5
47138 Blocher 400 F7
47424 Bloomfield⊙ 2,705 D6
47832 Bloomingdale 409 C5
47401 Bloomington⊙ 52,044 D6
Bloomington‡ 98,387 D6
†47360 Blountsville 213 G4
†46176 Blue Ridge 219 F5
46714 Bluffton⊙ 8,705 G3
46110 Boggstown 200 F5
46302 Boone Grove 220 C2
47601 Boonville⊙ 6,300 C8
47106 Borden 384 F8
47324 Boston 189 H5
47921 Boswell 810 C3
46504 Bourbon 1,522 E2
47833 Bowling Green 200 D6
47107 Bradford 350 E8
47834 Brazil⊙ 7,852 C5
46506 Bremen 3,565 E2
47836 Bridgeton 250 C5
†45030 Bright 450 H6
46720 Brimfield 292 G2
46913 Bringhurst 275 E3
46507 Bristol 1,203 F1
47922 Brook 926 C3
46111 Brooklyn 889 E5
†47250 Brooksburg 132 G7
47923 Brookston 1,701 D3
47012 Brookville⊙ 2,874 G6
46112 Brownsburg 6,242 E5
47220 Brownstown⊙ 2,704 F7
47325 Brownsville 250 H5
47516 Bruceville 646 C7
47326 Bryant 277 G3
47924 Buck Creek 225 D4
47647 Buckskin 200 C8
47925 Buffalo 500 D3
46914 Bunker Hill 984 E3
46508 Burket 260 F2
46915 Burlington 680 E4
47926 Burnettsville 496 D3
47222 Burney 300 F6
†46401 Burns Harbor 920 C1
46916 Burrows 250 E3
46721 Butler 2,509 H2
47223 Butlerville 300 F6
†46371 Byron 200 C5
†47362 Cadiz 180 G5
47327 Cambridge City 2,407 G5
46917 Camden 618 D3
47108 Campbellsburg 695 E7
47224 Canaan 90 G7
47519 Cannelburg 152 C7
47520 Cannelton⊙ 2,373 D9
47837 Carbon 307 C5
47838 Carlisle 717 C7
46032 Carmel 18,272 E5
46114 Cartersburg 300 E5
46115 Carthage 886 F5
47927 Cates 125 C4
47928 Cayuga 1,258 C5
47016 Cedar Grove 217 H6
46303 Cedar Lake 8,754 C2
47521 Celestine 150 D8
†47842 Centenary 150 B5
†46901 Center 310 E4
47840 Centerpoint 242 C6
46116 Centerton 250 E5
47330 Centerville 2,284 H5
47929 Chalmers 554 D3
47610 Chandler 3,043 C8
47111 Charlestown 5,596 F8
46117 Charlottesville 300 F5
†47138 Chelsea 200 F7
46017 Chesterfield 2,701 F4
46304 Chesterton 8,531 D1
47611 Chrisney 537 C8
46723 Churubusco 1,638 G2
46034 Cicero 2,557 E4
47225 Clarksburg 300 G6
47930 Clarks Hill 653 D4
47130 Clarksville 15,164 F8
47841 Clay City 883 C6
46510 Claypool 464 F2
46118 Clayton 703 D5
47426 Clear Creek 200 E6
†46737 Clear Lake 301 H1
47226 Clifford 310 F6
47842 Clinton 5,267 C5
46120 Cloverdale 1,357 D5
†47834 Cloverland 175 C6
47427 Coal City 225 D6
47845 Coalmont 450 C6
46121 Coatesville 474 D5
47931 Colburn 300 D3
46035 Colfax 823 D4
47978 Collegeville 1,059 C3
46725 Columbia City⊙ 5,091 G2
47201 Columbus⊙ 30,614 E6
47331 Connersville⊙ 17,023 G5
46919 Converse 1,279 F3
47228 Cortland 175 F7
46730 Corunna 304 G2
47112 Corydon⊙ 2,724 E8
47932 Covington⊙ 2,883 C4
†47302 Cowan 428 G4
47114 Crandall 176 E8
47522 Crane D7
47933 Crawfordsville⊙ 13,325 D4
46732 Cromwell 458 F2
47229 Crothersville 1,747 F7
46307 Crown Point⊙ 16,455 C2
46511 Culver 1,601 E2
46229 Cumberland 3,375 E5
47612 Cynthiana 874 B8
47523 Dale 1,693 D8
47334 Daleville F4
47847 Dana 803 C5
46122 Danville⊙ 4,220 D5
47940 Darlington 811 D4
47618 Darmstadt 1,280 B8
47941 Dayton 781 D4
46733 Decatur⊙ 8,649 H3
47524 Decker 256 B7
†46917 Deer Creek 250 E3
46923 Delphi⊙ 3,042 D3
46310 Demotte 2,559 C2
46926 Denver 589 E3
47230 Deputy 200 F7
47302 Desoto 385 G4
47018 Dillsboro 1,038 G6
46513 Donaldson 320 E2
†47118 Doolittle Mills 200 D8
47335 Dublin 979 G5
47525 Dubois 550 D8
47848 Dugger 1,118 C6
†46304 Dune Acres 291 C1
47336 Dunkirk 3,180 G4
†46514 Dunlap 5,397 F1
47337 Dunreith 184 F5
47231 Dupont 392 G7
46311 Dyer 9,555 C1
†46074 Eagletown 306 E4
47942 Earl Park 469 C3
46312 East Chicago 39,786 C1
47019 East Enterprise 250 H7
†47370 East Germantown (Pershing) 438 G5
47338 Eaton 1,804 G4
47116 Eckerty 108 D8
47339 Economy 237 G5
†46011 Edgewood 2,215 F4
46124 Edinburgh 4,856 E6
47528 Edwardsport 459 C7
†47150 Edwardsville 700 F8
47613 Elberfeld 640 C8
47117 Elizabeth 178 F8
47232 Elizabethtown 603 F6
46514 Elkhart 41,305 F1
Elkhart‡ 137,330 F1
47429 Ellettsville 3,328 D6
47529 Elnora 756 C7
†47018 Elrod 200 G6
†47901 Elston 500 D4
46036 Elwood 10,867 F4
46125 Eminence 200 D5
47118 English⊙ 633 E8
46524 Etna Green 522 E2
†47928 Eugene 400 B5
*47701 Evansville⊙ 130,496 C9
Evansville‡ 309,408 C9
†47331 Everton 500 G5
46126 Fairland 950 F5
46928 Fairmount 3,286 F4
†47842 Fairview Park 1,545 C5
47850 Farmersburg 1,240 C6
47340 Farmland 1,560 G4
†47421 Fayetteville 180 D7
47532 Ferdinand 2,192 D8
46128 Fillmore 550 D5
46129 Finly 400 F5
46038 Fishers 2,008 E5
47234 Flat Rock 323 F6
46929 Flora 2,303 E3
47119 Floyds Knobs 500 F8
47851 Fontanet 325 C5
46039 Forest 400 E4
47648 Fort Branch 2,504 B8
46040 Fortville 2,787 F5
*46801 Fort Wayne⊙ 172,028 G2
Fort Wayne‡ 382,961 G2
47341 Fountain City 839 H5
46130 Fountaintown 225 F5
47944 Fowler⊙ 2,319 C3
46930 Fowlerton 300 F4
47946 Francesville 944 D3
47649 Francisco 612 B8
46041 Frankfort⊙ 15,168 E4
46131 Franklin⊙ 11,563 E6
46044 Frankton 2,080 F4
47120 Fredericksburg 233 E8
47431 Freedom 100 D6
47535 Freelandville 600 C7
47235 Freetown 600 E7
46737 Fremont 1,180 H1
47432 French Lick 2,265 D7
46931 Fulton 393 E3
†47119 Galena 1,186 F8
46932 Galveston 1,822 E3
46738 Garrett 4,751 G2
*46401 Gary 151,953 C1
Gary-Hammond-East Chicago‡ 642,781 C1
46933 Gas City 6,370 F4
47342 Gaston 1,150 G4
46740 Geneva 1,430 H3
47537 Gentryville 299 C8
47122 Georgetown 1,494 F8
46133 Glenwood 370 G5
†47567 Glezen 300 C8
46045 Goldsmith 235 E4

(continued on following page)

Agriculture, Industry and Resources

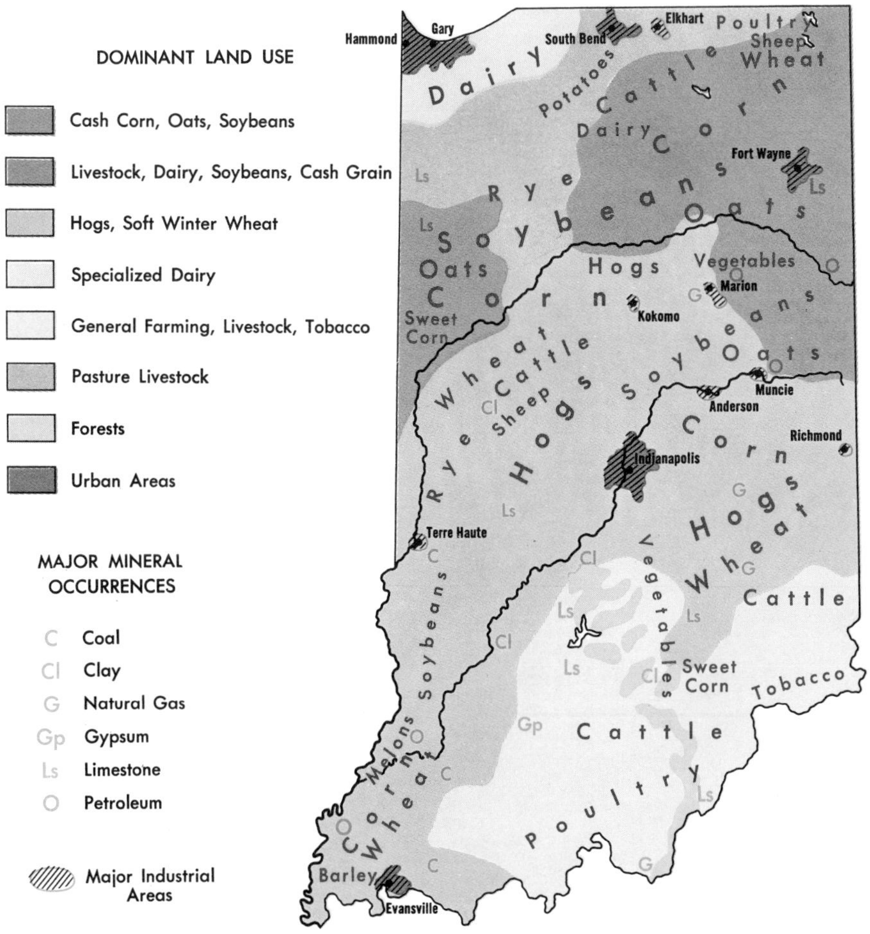
DOMINANT LAND USE
Cash Corn, Oats, Soybeans
Livestock, Dairy, Soybeans, Cash Grain
Hogs, Soft Winter Wheat
Specialized Dairy
General Farming, Livestock, Tobacco
Pasture Livestock
Forests
Urban Areas
MAJOR MINERAL OCCURRENCES
C Coal
Cl Clay
G Natural Gas
Gp Gypsum
Ls Limestone
O Petroleum
Major Industrial Areas
Hammond
Gary
South Bend
Elkhart
Fort Wayne
Marion
Kokomo
Muncie
Anderson
Richmond
Indianapolis
Terre Haute
Evansville
Dairy
Potatoes
Cattle
Corn
Poultry
Sheep
Wheat
Rye
Soybeans
Oats
Hogs
Vegetables
Sweet Corn
Melons
Barley
Tobacco

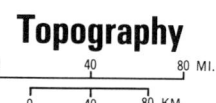

Topography

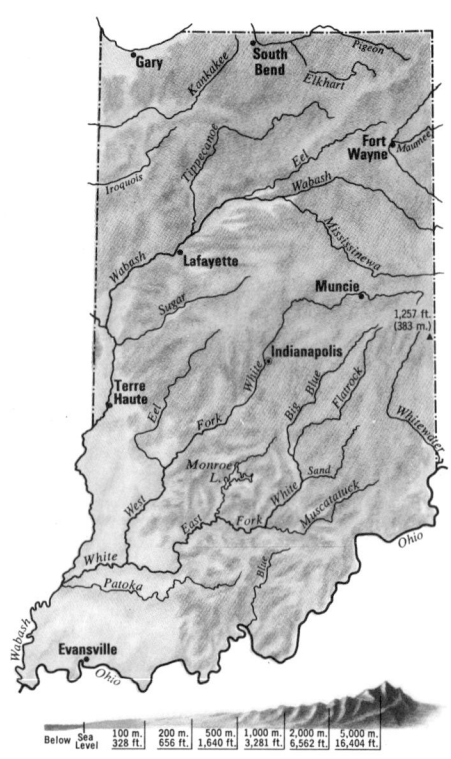

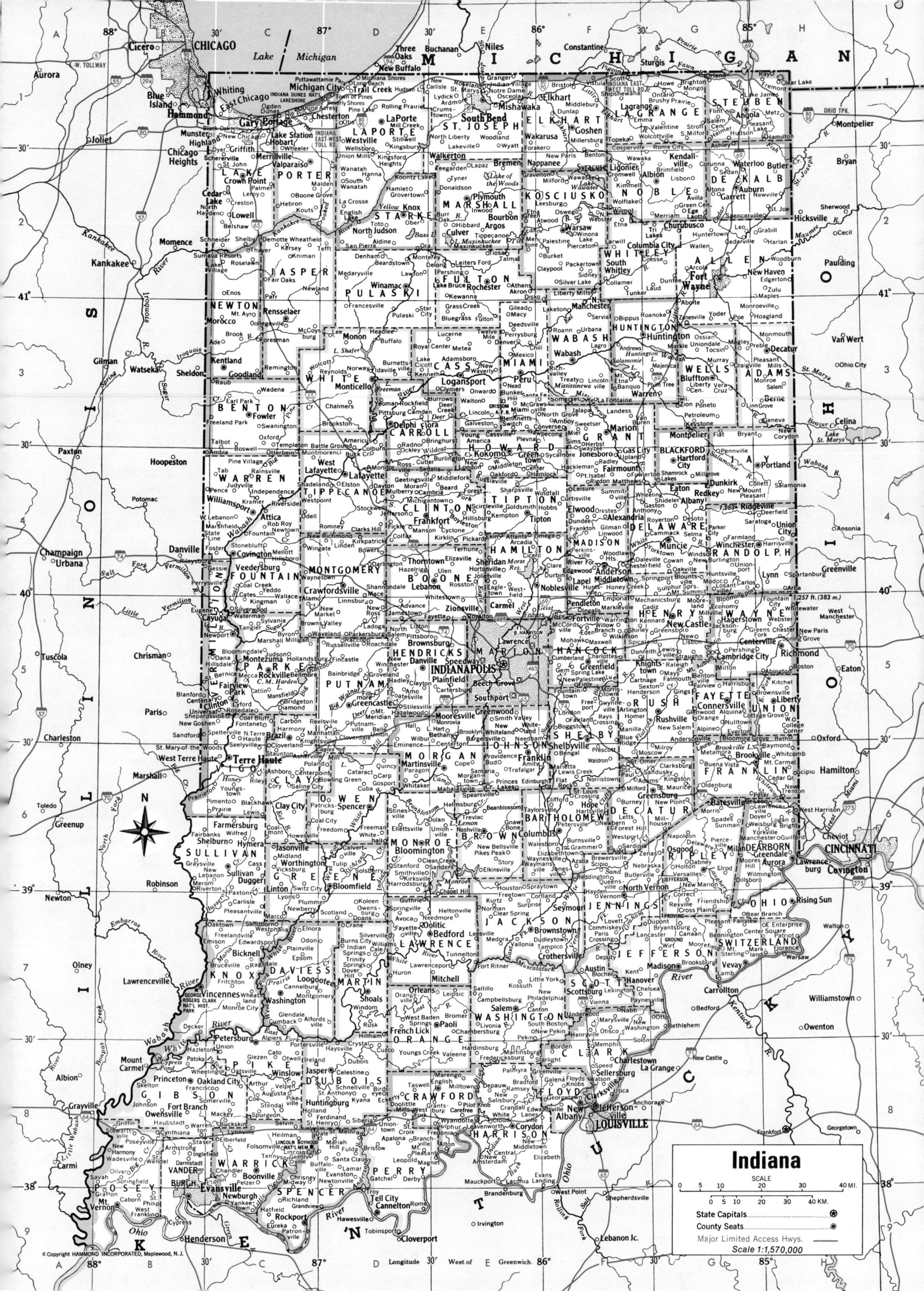

Indiana

SCALE
0 5 10   20   30   40 MI.
0 5 10   20   30   40 KM.

State Capitals .... ⊛
County Seats .... ◉
Major Limited Access Hwys. ——

Scale 1:1,570,000

© Copyright HAMMOND INCORPORATED, Maplewood, N.J.

COUNTIES

County	Key
Adair 9,509	E6
Adams 5,731	D6
Allamakee 15,108	L2
Appanoose 15,511	H7
Audubon 8,559	D5
Benton 23,649	J4
Black Hawk 137,961	J4
Boone 26,184	F5
Bremer 24,820	J3
Buchanan 22,900	K4
Buena Vista 20,774	C3
Butler 17,668	H3
Calhoun 13,542	D4
Carroll 22,951	D4
Cass 16,932	D6
Cedar 18,635	L5
Cerro Gordo 48,458	G2
Cherokee 16,238	B3
Chickasaw 15,437	J2
Clarke 8,612	F6
Clay 19,576	C2
Clayton 21,098	L3
Clinton 57,122	M5
Crawford 18,935	C4
Dallas 29,513	E5
Davis 9,104	J7
Decatur 9,794	F7
Delaware 18,933	L4
Des Moines 46,203	L7
Dickinson 15,629	C2
Dubuque 93,745	M4
Emmet 13,336	D2
Fayette 25,488	K3
Floyd 19,597	H2
Franklin 13,036	G3
Fremont 9,401	B7
Greene 12,119	E5
Grundy 14,366	H4
Guthrie 11,983	D5
Hamilton 17,862	F4
Hancock 13,833	F2
Hardin 21,776	G4
Harrison 16,348	B5
Henry 18,890	K6
Howard 11,114	J2
Humboldt 12,246	E3
Ida 8,908	C4
Iowa 15,429	J5
Jackson 22,503	M4
Jasper 36,425	G5
Jefferson 16,316	K6
Johnson 81,717	K5
Jones 20,401	L4
Keokuk 12,921	J6
Kossuth 21,891	E2
Lee 43,106	L7
Linn 169,775	K4
Louisa 12,055	L6
Lucas 10,313	G6
Lyon 12,896	A2
Madison 12,597	E6
Mahaska 22,867	H6
Marion 29,669	G6
Marshall 41,652	G4
Mills 13,406	B6
Mitchell 12,329	H2
Monona 11,692	B4
Monroe 9,209	H7
Montgomery 13,413	C6
Muscatine 40,436	L5
O'Brien 16,972	B2
Osceola 8,371	B2
Page 19,063	C7
Palo Alto 12,721	D2
Plymouth 24,743	A3
Pocahontas 11,369	D3
Polk 303,170	F5
Pottawattamie 86,561	B6
Poweshiek 19,306	H5
Ringgold 6,112	E7
Sac 14,118	C4
Scott 160,022	M5
Shelby 15,043	C5
Sioux 30,813	A2
Story 72,326	G4
Tama 19,533	H4
Taylor 8,353	D7
Union 13,858	E7
Van Buren 8,626	K7
Wapello 40,241	J6
Warren 34,878	F6
Washington 20,141	K6
Wayne 8,199	G7
Webster 45,953	E4
Winnebago 13,010	F2
Winneshiek 21,876	K2
Woodbury 100,884	B4
Worth 9,075	G2
Wright 16,319	F3

CITIES and TOWNS

Zip	Name/Pop.	Key
50601	Ackley 1,900	H3
50002	Adair 883	D6
50003	Adel ⊙ 2,846	E5
50830	Afton 985	E6
52530	Agency 657	J7
52201	Ainsworth 547	K6
51001	Akron 1,517	A3
50510	Albert City 818	C3
52531	Albia ⊙ 4,184	H6
50005	Albion 739	H4
50511	Algona ⊙ 6,289	E2
50007	Alleman 307	F5
50008	Allerton 670	G7
50602	Allison ⊙ 1,132	H3
51002	Alta 1,720	C3
50603	Alta Vista 314	J2
51003	Alton 986	A3
50009	Altoona 5,764	G5
51230	Alvord 246	A2
52203	Amana 300	K5
50010	Ames 45,775	G4
52205	Anamosa ⊙ 4,958	L4
52030	Andrew 349	M4
50020	Anita 1,153	D6
50021	Ankeny 15,429	F5
51004	Anthon 687	B4
50604	Aplington 1,027	H3
52201	Arcadia 454	D4
50606	Arlington 498	K3
51430	Arcadia 454	D4
50514	Armstrong 1,153	D2
51431	Arthur 288	C4
50022	Atlantic ⊙ 7,789	D6
50020	Ashton 441	B2
52720	Atalissa 360	L5
52206	Atkins 678	K4
51232	Ashton 441	B2
52001	Asbury 2,017	M4
52202	Alburnett 411	K4
51331	Arnolds Park 1,051	C2

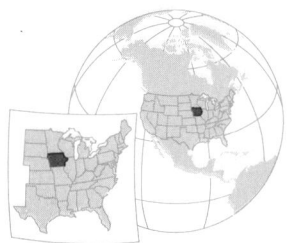

51433 Auburn 320 ......D4
50025 Audubon⊙ 2,841 ......D5
51005 Aurelia 1,143 ......C3
50607 Aurora 248 ......K3
51521 Avoca 1,650 ......C6
50515 Ayrshire 243 ......D2
50516 Badger 653 ......E3
50026 Bagley 370 ......E5
50517 Bancroft 1,082 ......E2
50027 Barnes City 266 ......H6
52533 Batavia 525 ......J7
51006 Battle Creek 919 ......B4
50028 Baxter 951 ......G5
50029 Bayard 637 ......D5
52534 Beacon 530 ......H6
50833 Bedford⊙ 1,692 ......D7
52208 Belle Plaine 2,903 ......J5
52031 Bellevue 2,450 ......M4
50421 Belmond 2,505 ......F3
52721 Bennett 458 ......L5
50032 Berwick 600 ......G5
52722 Bettendorf 27,381 ......N5
52535 Birmingham 410 ......K7
50034 Blairsburg 288 ......F4

52209 Blairstown 695 ......J5
52536 Blakesburg 404 ......H7
51523 Blencoe 247 ......A5
50836 Blockton 280 ......D7
52537 Bloomfield⊙ 2,849 ......J7
52726 Blue Grass 1,377 ......M5
50519 Bode 406 ......E3
52620 Bonaparte 489 ......K7
50036 Boone⊙ 12,602 ......F4
50040 Boxholm 267 ......E4
51234 Boyden 708 ......B2
52210 Brandon 337 ......K4
51436 Breda 502 ......C4
50837 Bridgewater 233 ......D6
52540 Brighton 804 ......K6
50611 Bristow 252 ......H3
50423 Britt 2,185 ......F2
51007 Bronson 289 ......A4
52211 Brooklyn 1,509 ......J5
52728 Buffalo 1,569 ......M6
50424 Buffalo Center 1,233 ......F2
52601 Burlington⊙ 29,529 ......L7
50522 Burt 689 ......E2

AREA 56,275 sq. mi. (145,752 sq. km.)
POPULATION 2,913,808
CAPITAL Des Moines
LARGEST CITY Des Moines
HIGHEST POINT (Osceola Co.) 1670 ft. (509 m.)
SETTLED IN 1788
ADMITTED TO UNION December 28, 1846
POPULAR NAME Hawkeye State
STATE FLOWER Wild Rose
STATE BIRD Eastern Goldfinch

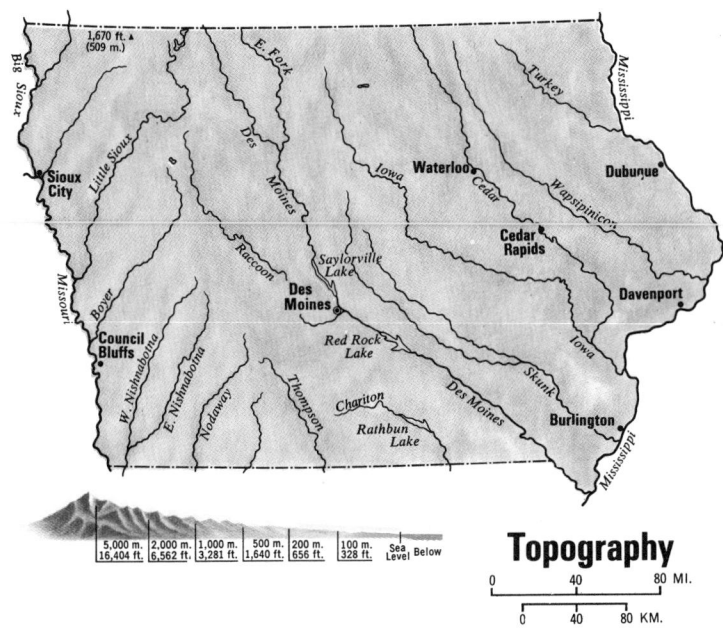

Topography

50044 Bussey 579 ......H6
52729 Calamus 452 ......M5
50523 Callender 446 ......E4
52132 Calmar 1,053 ......K2
52730 Camanche 4,725 ......N5
50046 Cambridge 732 ......G5
52542 Cantril 299 ......J7
50047 Carlisle 3,073 ......G6
51401 Carroll⊙ 9,705 ......D4
51525 Carson 716 ......C6
†68101 Carter Lake 3,438 ......B6
52033 Cascade 1,912 ......L4
50048 Casey 473 ......D5
50613 Cedar Falls 36,322 ......H3
*52401 Cedar Rapids⊙ 110,243 ......K5
   Cedar Rapids‡ 169,775 ......K5
52213 Center Point 1,591 ......K4
52544 Centerville⊙ 6,558 ......H7
52214 Central City 1,067 ......K4
50049 Chariton⊙ 4,987 ......G6
50616 Charles City⊙ 8,778 ......H2
52731 Charlotte 442 ......M5
51439 Charter Oak 615 ......C4
52215 Chelsea 376 ......J5
51012 Cherokee⊙ 7,004 ......B3
50050 Churdan 540 ......D4
52549 Cincinnati 598 ......G7
52216 Clarence 1,001 ......M5
51632 Clarinda⊙ 5,458 ......C7
50525 Clarion⊙ 3,060 ......F3
50619 Clarksville 1,424 ......H3
50840 Clearfield 433 ......D7
50428 Clear Lake 7,458 ......G2
51014 Cleghorn 275 ......B3
52135 Clermont 621 ......K3
52732 Clinton⊙ 32,828 ......N5
50318 Clive 6,064 ......F5
52217 Clutier 249 ......J4
52218 Coggon 639 ......L4
51636 Coin 316 ......C7
52035 Colesburg 463 ......L3
50054 Colfax 2,234 ......G5
51637 College Springs 307 ......C7
50055 Collins 451 ......G5
50056 Colo 808 ......G4
52737 Columbus City 367 ......L6
52738 Columbus Junction 1,429 ......L6
52739 Conesville 301 ......L6
50631 Conrad 1,133 ......H4
52220 Conroy 250 ......J5
50058 Coon Rapids 1,448 ......D5
52241 Coralville 7,687 ......K5
50841 Corning⊙ 1,939 ......D7
51016 Correctionville 935 ......B4
50430 Corwith 480 ......F3
50060 Corydon⊙ 1,818 ......G7
50431 Coulter 264 ......G3
51501 Council Bluffs⊙ 56,449 ......B6
52621 Crawfordsville 290 ......K6
52136 Cresco⊙ 3,860 ......J2
50801 Creston⊙ 8,429 ......E6
50432 Crystal Lake 314 ......F2
50843 Cumberland 351 ......D6

51018 Cushing 270 ......B4
50529 Dakota City⊙ 1,072 ......E3
50062 Dallas 451 ......G6
50063 Dallas Center 1,360 ......E5
51019 Danbury 492 ......B4
52623 Danville 994 ......L7
*52801 Davenport⊙ 103,264 ......M5
   Davenport-Rock Island-Moline‡ 383,958 ......M5
50065 Davis City 327 ......F7
50530 Dayton 941 ......E4
52101 Decorah⊙ 7,991 ......K2
51440 Dedham 321 ......D5
52222 Deep River 323 ......J5
51527 Defiance 383 ......C5
52223 Delhi 511 ......L4
52037 Delmar 633 ......M4
51441 Deloit 345 ......C4
52550 Delta 482 ......J6
51442 Denison⊙ 6,675 ......C4
52624 Denmark 480 ......L7
50622 Denver 1,647 ......J3
*50301 Des Moines (cap.)⊙ 191,003 ......G5
   Des Moines‡ 338,048 ......G5
50069 De Soto 1,035 ......E5
50623 Dewar 230 ......J3
52742 De Witt 4,512 ......N5
50070 Dexter 678 ......E5
50845 Diagonal 362 ......E7
50624 Dike 987 ......H4
52745 Dixon 312 ......M5
52746 Donahue 289 ......M5
52625 Donnellson 972 ......K7
51235 Doon 537 ......A2
52551 Douds 425 ......J7
51528 Dow City 616 ......B5
50071 Dows 771 ......F3
52001 Dubuque⊙ 62,321 ......M3
   Dubuque‡ 93,745 ......M3
50625 Dumont 815 ......H3
50532 Duncombe 504 ......E4
50626 Dunkerton 718 ......J3
51529 Dunlap 1,374 ......B5
52747 Durant 1,583 ......M5
52040 Dyersville 3,825 ......L3
52224 Dysart 1,355 ......J4
50533 Eagle Grove 4,324 ......F3
50072 Earlham 1,140 ......E6
51530 Earling 520 ......C5
52041 Earlville 844 ......L4
50535 Early 670 ......C4
52553 Eddyville 1,116 ......H6
52042 Edgewood 900 ......K3
52554 Eldon 1,255 ......J7
50627 Eldora⊙ 3,063 ......G4
52748 Eldridge 3,279 ......M5
52141 Elgin 702 ......K3
52043 Elkader⊙ 1,688 ......L3
50073 Elkhart 256 ......F5
51531 Elk Horn 746 ......C5
†50700 Elk Run Heights 1,186 ......J4
51532 Elliott 493 ......C6

50075 Ellsworth 480 ......F4
50628 Elma 714 ......J2
52227 Ely 425 ......K5
51533 Emerson 502 ......C6
50536 Emmetsburg⊙ 4,621 ......D2
52045 Epworth 1,380 ......M4
51638 Essex 1,001 ......C7
51334 Estherville⊙ 7,518 ......D2
51338 Everly 796 ......C2
50076 Exira 978 ......D5
50629 Fairbank 980 ......K3
52228 Fairfax 683 ......K5
52556 Fairfield⊙ 9,428 ......J6
52046 Farley 1,287 ......L4
52047 Farmersburg 276 ......L3
52626 Farmington 869 ......K7
50538 Farnhamville 461 ......D4
51639 Farragut 603 ......C7
52142 Fayette 1,515 ......K3
50539 Fenton 394 ......E2
50434 Fertile 372 ......G2
50435 Floyd 408 ......H2
50540 Fonda 863 ......D3
50846 Fontanelle 805 ......E6
50436 Forest City⊙ 4,270 ......F2
52144 Fort Atkinson 374 ......J2
50501 Fort Dodge⊙ 29,423 ......E3
52627 Fort Madison⊙ 13,520 ......L7
51340 Fostoria 261 ......C2
50630 Fredericksburg 1,075 ......J3
50631 Frederika 223 ......J3
52561 Fremont 730 ......H6
52749 Fruitland 461 ......L6
51020 Galva 420 ......C3
50103 Garden Grove 297 ......F7
52049 Garnavillo 723 ......L3
50438 Garner⊙ 2,908 ......F2
52229 Garrison 411 ......J4
50632 Garwin 626 ......H4
51237 George 1,241 ......B2
50105 Gilbert 805 ......F4
50634 Gilbertville 740 ......J4
50106 Gilman 642 ......H5
50541 Gilmore City 626 ......D3
50635 Gladbrook 970 ......H4
51534 Glenwood⊙ 5,280 ......B6
51443 Glidden 1,076 ......D4
50542 Goldfield 789 ......F3
52750 Goose Lake 274 ......N5
50543 Gowrie 1,089 ......E4
51342 Graettinger 923 ......D2
50440 Grafton 255 ......G2
50107 Grand Junction 970 ......E4
52751 Grand Mound 674 ......M5
52752 Grandview 473 ......L6
50109 Granger 619 ......F5
51022 Granville 336 ......B3
50848 Gravity 245 ......D7
52050 Greeley 313 ......L3
50636 Greene 1,332 ......H3
50849 Greenfield⊙ 2,243 ......D6
50111 Grimes 1,973 ......F5
50112 Grinnell 8,868 ......H5

(continued on following page)

Agriculture, Industry and Resources

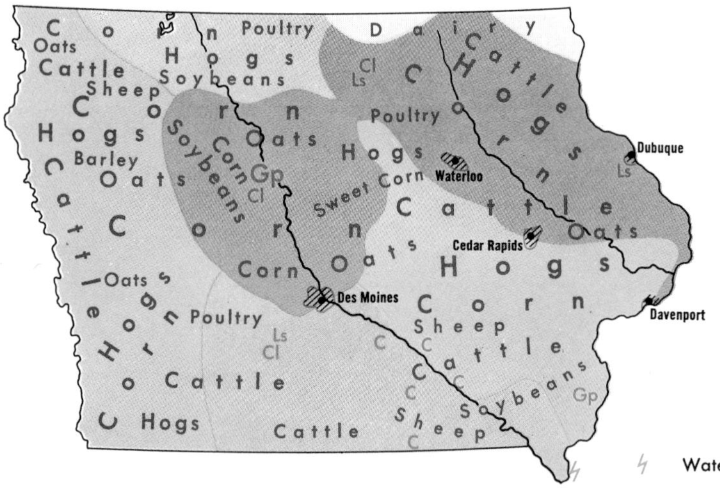

DOMINANT LAND USE

- Cattle Feed, Hogs
- Cash Corn, Oats, Soybeans
- Hogs, Dairy
- Livestock, Cash Grain
- Dairy, Livestock
- Pasture Livestock

MAJOR MINERAL OCCURRENCES

- C Coal
- Cl Clay
- Gp Gypsum
- Ls Limestone

Water Power

Major Industrial Areas

51535	Griswold 1,176	C6
50638	Grundy Center⊙ 2,880	H4
50115	Guthrie Center⊙ 1,713	D5
52052	Guttenberg 2,428	L3
51640	Hamburg 1,597	B7
50441	Hampton⊙ 4,630	G3
51536	Hancock 254	C6
50544	Harcourt 347	E4
51537	Harlan⊙ 5,357	C5
52146	Harpers Ferry 258	L2
50118	Hartford 761	G6
51346	Hartley 1,700	C2
50119	Harvey 275	H6
50546	Havelock 279	D3
51023	Hawarden 2,722	A2
52147	Hawkeye 512	J3
50641	Hazleton 877	K3
52563	Hedrick 847	J6
51541	Henderson 236	B6
52233	Hiawatha 4,825	K4
52235	Hills 547	K5
52630	Hillsboro 208	K7
51024	Hinton 659	A3
50642	Holland 278	H4
51025	Holstein 1,477	B4
52053	Holy Cross 310	L3
52237	Hopkinton 774	L4
51026	Hornick 239	A4
51238	Hospers 655	B2
50122	Hubbard 852	G4
50643	Hudson 2,267	H4
51239	Hull 1,714	A2
50548	Humboldt 4,794	E3
50123	Humeston 671	G7
50124	Huxley 1,884	F5
51445	Ida Grove⊙ 2,285	B4
50644	Independence⊙ 6,392	K4
50125	Indianola⊙ 10,843	F6
51240	Inwood 755	A2
50645	Ionia 350	J2
52240	Iowa City⊙ 50,508	L5
	Iowa City○‡ 81,717	L5
50126	Iowa Falls 6,174	G3
51027	Ireton 588	A3
51446	Irwin 427	C5
50128	Jamaica 275	E5
50647	Janesville 840	J3
50129	Jefferson⊙ 4,854	E4
50648	Jesup 2,343	J4
50130	Jewell 1,145	F4
50131	Johnston 2,617	F5
52247	Kalona 1,862	K6
50447	Kanawha 756	F3
50133	Kellerton 278	E7
50134	Kelley 237	F5
50135	Kellogg 654	H5
50448	Kensett 360	G2
52632	Keokuk⊙ 13,536	L8
52565	Keosauqua⊙ 1,003	J7
52248	Keota 1,034	K6
50136	Keswick 300	J6
52249	Keystone 618	J5
51543	Kimballton 362	D5
51028	Kingsley 1,209	A3
51448	Kiron 317	C4
50449	Klemme 620	F3
50138	Knoxville⊙ 8,143	G6
50139	Lacona 376	G6
52251	Ladora 289	J5
51449	Lake City 2,006	D4
50450	Lake Mills 2,281	F2
51347	Lake Park 1,123	C2
50588	Lakeside 589	C3
51450	Lake View 1,291	C4
50451	Lakota 330	E2
50140	Lamoni 2,705	E7
50650	Lamont 554	K3
52054	La Motte 322	M4
52151	Lansing 1,181	L2
50651	La Porte City 2,324	J4
51241	Larchwood 701	A2
50452	Latimer 441	G3
50141	Laurel 278	H5
50554	Laurens 1,606	D3
52154	Lawler 534	J2
51030	Lawton 447	A4
52753	Le Claire 2,899	N5
50142	Le Grand 921	H5
50557	Lehigh 654	E4
50453	Leland 274	F2
51031	Le Mars⊙ 8,276	A3
50851	Lenox 1,338	D7
50144	Leon⊙ 2,094	F7
51242	Lester 274	A2
52754	Letts 473	L6
51544	Lewis 497	C6
52567	Libertyville 281	K7
52155	Lime Springs 476	J2
50146	Linden 264	E5
50147	Lineville 319	G7
52253	Lisbon 1,458	L5
50148	Liscomb 296	H4
51243	Little Rock 490	B2
51545	Little Sioux 251	B5
50558	Livermore 490	E3
52635	Lockridge 271	K7
51546	Logan⊙ 1,540	B5
51453	Lohrville 521	D4
52755	Lone Tree 1,014	L6
52756	Long Grove 596	M5
50149	Lorimor 405	E6
52254	Lost Nation 524	M5
50150	Lovilia 637	H6
52255	Lowden 717	L5
52757	Low Moor 346	N5
52156	Luana 246	K2
50151	Lucas 292	G6
50560	Lu Verne 418	E3
52056	Luxemburg 271	L3
50153	Lynnville 406	H5
50561	Lytton 377	D4
51549	Macedonia 279	C6
50156	Madrid 2,281	F5
50157	Malcom 418	H5
50562	Mallard 407	D3
51551	Malvern 1,244	B7
52057	Manchester⊙ 4,942	L3
51454	Manilla 1,020	C5
50456	Manly 1,496	G2
51455	Manning 1,609	C5
50563	Manson 1,924	D3
51034	Mapleton 1,495	B4
52060	Maquoketa⊙ 6,313	M4
50565	Marathon 442	C3
50653	Marble Rock 419	H3
51035	Marcus 1,206	B3
52301	Marengo⊙ 2,308	J5
52302	Marion 19,474	K4
52158	Marquette 528	L2
50158	Marshalltown⊙ 26,938	G4
52305	Martelle 316	L4
50160	Martensdale 438	F6
50401	Mason City⊙ 30,144	G2
50853	Massena 518	D6
51036	Maurice 288	A3
50161	Maxwell 783	G5
50655	Maynard 561	K3
50154	McCallsburg 304	G4
52758	McCausland 381	M5
52157	McGregor 945	L2
52306	Mechanicsville 1,166	L5
52637	Mediapolis 1,685	L6
50162	Melbourne 732	G5
50163	Melcher 953	G6
51350	Melvin 277	B2
50164	Menlo 410	E5
51037	Meriden 233	B3
51038	Merrill 737	A3
50457	Meservey 324	G3
52307	Middle 335	K5
52638	Middletown 487	L7
52064	Miles 398	N4
51351	Milford 2,076	C2
50166	Milo 778	G6
52570	Milton 567	J7
50167	Minburn 390	E5
51553	Minden 419	C6
50168	Mingo 303	G5
51555	Missouri Valley 3,107	B5
50169	Mitchellville 1,530	G5
51556	Modale 373	B5
51557	Mondamin 423	B5
52159	Monona 1,530	L2
50170	Monroe 1,875	G5
50171	Montezuma⊙ 1,485	H5
52310	Monticello 3,641	L4
50173	Montour 387	H5
52759	Montpelier 250	M6
52639	Montrose 1,038	L7
51558	Moorhead 264	B5
50566	Moorland 257	E4
52571	Moravia 706	H7
52640	Morning Sun 959	L6
52760	Moscow 350	L5
52572	Moulton 762	H7
50854	Mount Ayr⊙ 1,938	E7
52641	Mount Pleasant⊙ 7,322	L7
52314	Mount Vernon 3,325	K5
51039	Moville 1,273	A4
50174	Murray 703	F6
52761	Muscatine⊙ 23,467	L6
52574	Mystic 665	H7
50658	Nashua 1,846	J3
51559	Neola 839	B6
50201	Nevada⊙ 5,912	G5
52160	New Albin 609	L2
50568	Newell 913	D3
52315	Newhall 899	K5
50660	New Hartford 764	H3
52645	New London 2,043	L7
51646	New Market 554	D7
50206	New Providence 249	G4
50207	New Sharon 1,225	H6
50208	Newton⊙ 15,292	H5
52065	New Vienna 430	L3
50210	New Virginia 512	F6
52766	Nichols 375	L6
50458	Nora Springs 1,572	H2
52316	North English 990	J5
52317	North Liberty 2,046	K5
50459	Northwood⊙ 2,193	G2
50211	Norwalk 2,676	F6
52318	Norway 633	K5
52319	Oakdale 300	K5
51560	Oakland 1,552	C6
52646	Oakville 470	L6
51354	Ocheyedan 599	B2
51458	Odebolt 1,299	C4
50662	Oelwein 7,564	K3
50212	Ogden 1,953	E4
51355	Okoboji 559	C2
52320	Olin 735	L5
52576	Ollie 232	J6
51040	Onawa⊙ 3,283	A4
51041	Orange City⊙ 4,588	A2
50858	Orient 416	E6
†51360	Orleans 546	C2
50461	Osage⊙ 3,718	H2
50213	Osceola⊙ 3,750	F6
52577	Oskaloosa⊙ 10,984	H6
52161	Ossian 829	K2
50569	Otho 692	E4
52501	Ottumwa⊙ 27,381	J6
52322	Oxford 676	K5
52323	Oxford Junction 600	M4
51561	Pacific Junction 511	B6
50571	Palmer 288	D3
52324	Palo 529	K4
51562	Panama 229	B5
50216	Panora 1,211	E5
50665	Parkersburg 1,968	H3
52325	Parnell 234	J5
50217	Paton 291	E4
51046	Paullina 1,224	B3
50219	Pella 8,349	H6
50220	Perry 7,053	E5
50221	Pershing 325	G6
51563	Persia 355	B5
51047	Peterson 470	C3
51048	Pierson 408	B3
51564	Pisgah 307	B5
50666	Plainfield 469	J3
50225	Pleasantville 1,531	G6
50464	Plymouth 463	G2
50574	Pocahontas⊙ 2,352	D3
50226	Polk City 1,658	F5
50575	Pomeroy 895	D3
51565	Portsmouth 240	C5
52162	Postville 1,475	K2
50228	Prairie City 1,278	G5
50859	Prescott 349	D6
52069	Preston 1,120	N4
	Primghar⊙ 1,050	B2
52768	Princeton 965	N5
52163	Protivin 368	J2
52584	Pulaski 267	J7
52326	Quasqueton 599	K4
51049	Quimby 424	B3
50230	Radcliffe 593	G4
50465	Rake 283	F2
50667	Raymond 655	J4
50668	Readlyn 858	J3
50232	Reasnor 277	G5
50233	Redfield 959	E5
51566	Red Oak⊙ 6,810	C6
50669	Reinbeck 1,808	H4
50576	Rembrandt 291	C3
51050	Remsen 1,592	B3
50577	Renwick 410	E3
50234	Rhodes 367	G5
50466	Riceville 919	H2
52585	Richland 600	K6
52165	Ridgeway 308	K2
50578	Ringsted 557	D2
50235	Rippey 304	E5
†52722	Riverdale 462	N5
52327	Riverside 826	K6
51650	Riverton 342	B7
52328	Robins 726	K4
50468	Rockford 1,012	H2
51246	Rock Rapids⊙ 2,693	A2
51247	Rock Valley 2,706	A2
50469	Rockwell 1,039	G3
50579	Rockwell City⊙ 2,276	D4
50236	Roland 1,005	F4
50581	Rolfe 796	D3
50470	Rowan 259	F3
52329	Rowley 275	K4
51357	Royal 522	C2
50471	Rudd 460	H2
50237	Runnells 377	G5
50238	Russell 593	G7
51358	Ruthven 769	D2
52330	Ryan 390	K4
52070	Sabula 824	N4
50583	Sac City⊙ 3,000	C4
†52001	Sageville 291	M3
50472	Saint Ansgar 1,100	H2
50240	Saint Charles 507	F6
52649	Salem 463	K7
51052	Salix 429	A4
51248	Sanborn 1,398	B2
51053	Schaller 832	C4
51461	Schleswig 868	B4
51462	Scranton 748	D4
51054	Sergeant Bluff 2,416	A4
52590	Seymour 1,036	G7
50475	Sheffield 1,224	G3
51570	Shelby 665	C5
50243	Sheldahl 315	F5
51201	Sheldon 5,003	B2
50670	Shell Rock 1,478	H3
52332	Shellsburg 771	K4
51601	Shenandoah 6,274	C7
†52401	Shueyville 287	K5
51249	Sibley⊙ 3,051	B2
51652	Sidney⊙ 1,308	B7
52591	Sigourney⊙ 2,330	J6
51571	Silver City 291	B6
51250	Sioux Center 4,588	A2
*51101	Sioux City⊙ 82,003	A3
	Sioux City‡ 117,457	A3
50585	Sioux Rapids 897	C3
50244	Slater 1,312	F5
51055	Sloan 978	A4
51056	Smithland 282	B4
51572	Soldier 257	B5
52333	Solon 969	L5
51301	Spencer⊙ 11,726	C2
52168	Spillville 415	J2
51360	Spirit Lake⊙ 3,976	C2
52336	Springville 1,165	L4
50476	Stacyville 538	H2
50246	Stanhope 492	F4
51573	Stanton 747	C7
52337	Stanwood 705	L5
50247	State Center 1,292	G5
50672	Steamboat Rock 387	G4
52651	Stockport 272	K7
52769	Stockton 240	M5
50588	Storm Lake⊙ 8,814	C3
50248	Story City 2,762	F4
50249	Stratford 806	F4
52076	Strawberry Point 1,463	K3
50250	Stuart 1,650	E6
50251	Sully 828	H5
50674	Sumner 2,335	J3
51058	Sutherland 897	B3
50590	Swea City 813	E2
52338	Swisher 654	K5
51653	Tabor 1,088	B7
52339	Tama 2,968	H5
51463	Templeton 319	D5
51364	Terril 420	C2
50478	Thompson 668	F2
50479	Thornton 442	G3
52340	Tiffin 413	K5
52772	Tipton⊙ 3,055	L5
50480	Titonka 607	E2
52342	Toledo⊙ 2,445	H4
50675	Traer 1,703	J4
51575	Treynor 981	B6
50676	Tripoli 1,280	J3
50257	Truro 407	F6
51576	Underwood 448	B6
50258	Union 515	G4
†52240	University Heights 1,069	K5
52595	University Park 645	H6
52345	Urbana 574	K4
50322	Urbandale 17,869	F5
51060	Ute 479	B4
51465	Vail 490	C4
52346	Van Horne 682	J4
50261	Van Meter 747	E5
50262	Van Wert 245	F7
50482	Ventura 614	F2
52347	Victor 1,046	J5
50864	Villisca 1,434	C7
52349	Vinton⊙ 5,040	J4
52077	Volga 310	L3
52169	Wadena 230	K3
†51360	Wahpeton 372	C2
52773	Walcott 1,425	M5
52351	Walford 285	K5
52352	Walker 733	K4
51365	Wallingford 256	D2
51466	Wall Lake 892	C4
51577	Walnut 897	C6
52653	Wapello⊙ 2,011	L6
52353	Washington⊙ 6,584	K6
51061	Washta 320	B3
*50701	Waterloo⊙ 75,985	J4
	Waterloo-Cedar Falls‡ 137,961	J4
52171	Waucoma 308	J2
50263	Waukee 2,227	F5
52172	Waukon⊙ 3,983	L2
50677	Waverly⊙ 8,444	J3
52654	Wayland 720	K6
52356	Wellman 1,125	K6
50680	Wellsburg 761	H4
50483	Wesley 598	E2
50597	West Bend 941	D3
52358	West Branch 1,867	L5
52655	West Burlington 3,371	L7
50318	West Des Moines 21,894	F5
50681	Westgate 263	K3
52776	West Liberty 2,723	L5
†51351	West Okoboji 435	C2
52656	West Point 1,133	K7
51467	Westside 387	C4
52175	West Union⊙ 2,783	K3
50268	What Cheer 803	J6
52777	Wheatland 840	M5
51063	Whiting 734	A4
50598	Whittemore 647	E2
50271	Williams 410	F3
52361	Williamsburg 2,033	J5
52778	Wilton 2,502	M5
50311	Windsor Heights 5,474	F5
52659	Winfield 1,042	L6
50273	Winterset⊙ 4,021	E6
50682	Winthrop 767	K4
50484	Woden 287	F2
51579	Woodbine 1,463	B5
50276	Woodward 1,212	E5
50599	Woolstock 235	F3
52078	Worthington 432	L4
52362	Wyoming 702	L4
50277	Yale 299	E5
50278	Zearing 630	G4

OTHER FEATURES

Big Sioux (riv.)	A3
Boyer (riv.)	B5
Cedar (riv.)	K4
Chariton (riv.)	G7
Clear (lake)	G2
Eagle (lake)	F2
East Nishnabotna (riv.)	C6
Effigy Mounds Nat'l Mon.	L2
Five Island (lake)	D2
Floyd (riv.)	A3
Herbert Hoover Nat'l Hist. Site	L5
Iowa (riv.)	H4
Little Sioux (riv.)	B3
Lost Island (lake)	D2
Mississippi (riv.)	L7
Missouri (riv.)	A4
Nodaway (riv.)	D7
Palo Alto (lake)	D2
Platte (riv.)	D8
Raccoon (riv.)	D4
Rathbun (lake)	G7
Red Rock (lake)	G6
Rock (riv.)	A2
Sac and Fox Ind. Res.	H5
Saylorville (lake)	F5
Skunk (riv.)	K6
Spirit (lake)	C2
Storm (lake)	C3
Thompson (riv.)	E7
Trumbull (lake)	C2
Turkey (riv.)	K2
Upper Iowa (riv.)	K2
Wapsipinicon (riv.)	J3
West Nishnabotna (riv.)	C6

⊙County seat.
‡Population of metropolitan area.
† Zip of nearest p.o. * Multiple zips.

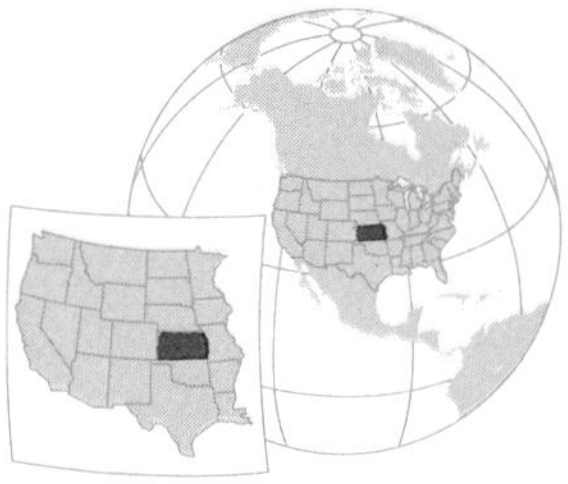

AREA 82,277 sq. mi. (213,097 sq. km.)
POPULATION 2,364,236
CAPITAL Topeka
LARGEST CITY Wichita
HIGHEST POINT Mt. Sunflower 4,039 ft. (1231 m.)
SETTLED IN 1831
ADMITTED TO UNION January 29, 1861
POPULAR NAME Sunflower State
STATE FLOWER Sunflower
STATE BIRD Western Meadowlark

Agriculture, Industry and Resources

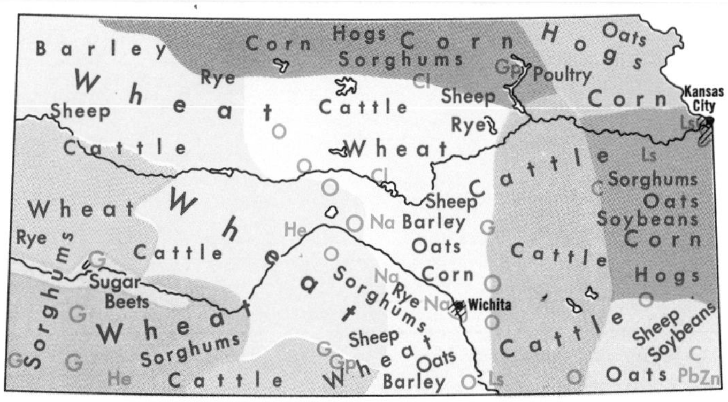

DOMINANT LAND USE

- Specialized Wheat
- Wheat, General Farming
- Wheat, Range Livestock
- Wheat, Grain Sorghums, Range Livestock
- Cattle Feed, Hogs
- Livestock, Cash Grain
- Livestock, Cash Grain, Dairy
- General Farming, Livestock, Cash Grain
- General Farming, Livestock, Special Crops
- Range Livestock

MAJOR MINERAL OCCURRENCES

C	Coal	Ls	Limestone
Cl	Clay	Na	Salt
G	Natural Gas	O	Petroleum
Gp	Gypsum	Pb	Lead
He	Helium	Zn	Zinc

Major Industrial Areas

COUNTIES

County	Key
Allen 15,654	G4
Anderson 8,749	G3
Atchison 18,397	G2
Barber 6,548	D4
Barton 31,343	D3
Bourbon 15,969	H4
Brown 11,955	G2
Butler 44,782	F4
Chase 3,309	F3
Chautauqua 5,016	F4
Cherokee 22,304	H4
Cheyenne 3,678	A2
Clark 2,599	C4
Clay 9,802	E2
Cloud 12,494	E2
Coffey 9,370	G3
Comanche 2,554	C4
Cowley 36,824	F4
Crawford 37,916	H4
Decatur 4,509	B2
Dickinson 20,175	E3
Doniphan 9,268	G2
Douglas 67,640	G3
Edwards 4,271	C4
Elk 3,918	F4
Ellis 26,098	C3
Ellsworth 6,640	D3
Finney 23,825	B3
Ford 24,315	C4
Franklin 22,062	G3
Geary 29,852	F3
Gove 3,726	B3
Graham 3,995	C2
Grant 6,977	A4
Gray 5,138	B4
Greeley 1,845	A3
Greenwood 8,764	F4
Hamilton 2,514	A3
Harper 7,778	D4
Harvey 30,531	E3
Haskell 3,814	B4
Hodgeman 2,269	C3
Jackson 11,644	G2
Jefferson 15,207	G2
Jewell 5,241	D2
Johnson 270,269	H3
Kearny 3,435	A3
Kingman 8,960	D4
Kiowa 4,046	C4
Labette 25,682	G4
Lane 2,472	B3
Leavenworth 54,809	G2
Lincoln 4,145	D2
Linn 8,234	H3
Logan 3,478	A3
Lyon 35,108	F3
Marion 13,522	E3
Marshall 12,787	F2
McPherson 26,855	E3
Meade 4,788	B4
Miami 21,618	H3
Mitchell 8,117	D2
Montgomery 42,281	G4
Morris 6,419	F3
Morton 3,454	A4
Nemaha 11,211	F2
Neosho 18,967	G4
Ness 4,498	C3
Norton 6,689	C2
Osage 15,319	G3
Osborne 5,959	D2
Ottawa 5,971	E2
Pawnee 8,065	C3
Phillips 7,406	C2
Pottawatomie 14,782	F2
Pratt 10,275	D4
Rawlins 4,105	A2
Reno 64,983	D4
Republic 7,569	E2
Rice 11,900	D3
Riley 63,505	F2
Rooks 7,006	C2
Rush 4,516	C3
Russell 8,868	D3
Saline 48,905	E3
Scott 5,782	B3
Sedgwick 367,088	E4
Seward 17,071	B4
Shawnee 154,916	G2
Sheridan 3,544	B2
Sherman 7,759	A2
Smith 5,947	D2
Stafford 5,694	D3
Stanton 2,339	A4
Stevens 4,736	A4
Sumner 24,928	E4
Thomas 8,451	A2
Trego 4,165	C3
Wabaunsee 6,867	F3
Wallace 2,045	A3
Washington 8,543	E2
Wichita 3,041	A3
Wilson 12,128	G4
Woodson 4,600	G4
Wyandotte 172,335	H2

CITIES and TOWNS

Zip	Name/Pop.	Key
67510	Abbyville 123	D4
67410	Abilene⊙ 6,572	E3
66830	Admire 158	F3
66930	Agenda 106	E2
67621	Agra 321	C2
67511	Albert 236	C3
67512	Alden 214	D3
67513	Alexander 116	C3
66833	Allen 205	F3
66401	Alma⊙ 925	F2
67622	Almena 517	C2
67330	Altamont 1,054	G4
66834	Alta Vista 430	F3
67623	Alton 135	D2
66710	Altoona 564	G4
66835	Americus 915	F3
67001	Andale 538	E4
67002	Andover 2,801	E4
67003	Anthony⊙ 2,661	D4
66711	Arcadia 460	H4
67004	Argonia 587	E4
67005	Arkansas City 13,201	E4
67514	Arlington 631	D4
66712	Arma 1,676	H4
67831	Ashland⊙ 1,096	C4
67416	Assaria 414	E3
66002	Atchison⊙ 11,407	G2
66932	Athol 90	D2
67008	Atlanta 256	F4
67009	Attica 730	D4
67730	Atwood⊙ 1,665	B2
66402	Auburn 890	G3
67010	Augusta 6,968	F4
67417	Aurora 130	E2
66403	Axtell 470	F2
66404	Baileyville 130	F2
66006	Baldwin City 2,829	G3
67418	Barnard 163	D2
66933	Barnes 257	F2
67332	Bartlett 163	G4
66007	Basehor 1,483	G2
†66749	Bassett 31	G4
66713	Baxter Springs 4,730	H4
67516	Bazine 385	C3
66406	Beattie 316	F2
67013	Belle Plaine 1,706	E4
66935	Belleville⊙ 2,805	E2
67420	Beloit⊙ 4,367	D2
67519	Belpre 154	C4
66407	Belvue 212	F2
66714	Benedict 111	G4
67422	Bennington 579	E2
67016	Bentley 311	E4
67017	Benton 609	E4
66408	Bern 220	F2
67423	Beverly 171	E2
67731	Bird City 546	A2
67520	Bison 279	C3
66010	Blue Mound 319	H3
66411	Blue Rapids 1,280	F2
67018	Bluff City 95	E4
67625	Bogue 197	C2
66012	Bonner Springs 6,266	H2
67732	Brewster 327	A2
66716	Bronson 414	H4
67425	Brookville 259	E3
67521	Brownell 92	C3
67834	Bucklin 786	C4
66717	Buffalo 386	G4
67522	Buhler 1,188	E3
67626	Bunker Hill 124	D3
67019	Burden 518	F4
67523	Burdett 275	C3
66413	Burlingame 1,239	G3
66839	Burlington⊙ 2,901	G3
66840	Burns 224	F3
66936	Burr Oak 366	D2
67020	Burrton 976	E3
66841	Bushong 62	F3
67427	Bushton 388	D3
67021	Byers 47	D4
67022	Caldwell 1,401	E4
67023	Cambridge 113	F4
67333	Caney 2,284	G4
67428	Canton 926	E3
66414	Carbondale 1,518	G3
67429	Carlton 49	E3
66842	Cassoday 122	F3
67430	Cawker City 640	D2
67628	Cedar 53	D2
66843	Cedar Point 66	F3
67024	Cedar Vale 848	F4
66415	Centralia 486	F2
66720	Chanute 10,506	G4
67431	Chapman 1,255	E3
67524	Chase 753	D3
67334	Chautauqua 156	F4
67025	Cheney 1,404	E4
66724	Cherokee 775	H4
67335	Cherryvale 2,769	G4
67336	Chetopa 1,751	G4
67835	Cimarron⊙ 1,491	B4
66416	Circleville 164	G2
67525	Claflin 764	D3
67432	Clay Center⊙ 4,948	E2
67629	Clayton 102	B2
67026	Clearwater 1,684	E4
66937	Clifton 695	E2
67027	Climax 81	F4
66938	Clyde 909	E2
67028	Coats 153	D4
67337	Coffeyville 15,185	G4
67701	Colby⊙ 5,544	A2
67029	Coldwater⊙ 989	C4
67631	Collyer 151	B2
66015	Colony 474	G3
66725	Columbus⊙ 3,426	H4
67030	Colwich 935	E4
66901	Concordia⊙ 6,847	E2
67031	Conway Springs 1,313	E4
67836	Coolidge 82	A3
67837	Copeland 323	B4
66417	Corning 158	F2
66845	Cottonwood Falls⊙ 954	F3
66846	Council Grove⊙ 2,381	F3
66939	Courtland 377	E2
66727	Coyville 98	G4
66940	Cuba 286	E2
†67124	Cullison 154	D4
67435	Culver 167	E3
67035	Cunningham 540	D4
67632	Damar 204	C2
67036	Danville 71	E4
67340	Dearing 470	G4
67838	Deerfield 538	A4
66418	Delia 181	G2
67436	Delphos 570	E2
66419	Denison 231	G2
66017	Denton 156	G2
67037	Derby 9,786	E4
66018	De Soto 2,061	H3
67038	Dexter 366	F4
67839	Dighton⊙ 1,390	B3
67801	Dodge City⊙ 18,001	B4
67634	Dorrance 220	D3
67039	Douglass 1,450	F4
67437	Downs 1,324	D2
67635	Dresden 84	B2
66848	Dunlap 82	F3
67438	Durham 130	E3
66849	Dwight 320	F3
†66720	Earlton 79	G4
†67201	Eastborough 854	E4
66020	Easton 460	G2
66021	Edgerton 1,214	H3
67636	Edmond 56	C2
67342	Edna 537	G4
66113	Edwardsville 3,364	H2
66023	Effingham 634	G2
67041	Elbing 175	E3
67042	El Dorado⊙ 10,510	F4
†67361	Elgin 139	F4
67344	Elk City 404	G4
67345	Elk Falls 151	F4
67950	Elkhart⊙ 2,243	A4
67526	Ellinwood 2,508	D3
67637	Ellis 2,062	C3
67439	Ellsworth⊙ 2,465	D3
66850	Elmdale 109	F3
66732	Elsmore 104	G4
66024	Elwood 1,275	H2
66422	Emmett 223	F2
66801	Emporia⊙ 25,287	F3
67840	Englewood 111	C4
67841	Ensign 209	B4
67441	Enterprise 839	E3
66733	Erie⊙ 1,415	G4
66941	Esbon 234	D2
66423	Eskridge 603	F3
66025	Eudora 2,934	G3
67045	Eureka⊙ 3,425	F4
66424	Everest 331	G2
66425	Fairview 258	G2
†66101	Fairway 4,619	H2
67047	Fall River 173	G4
66851	Florence 729	E3
66026	Fontana 173	H3
67842	Ford 272	C4
66942	Formoso 166	D2
67843	Fort Dodge 400	C4
66027	Fort Leavenworth	H2
66701	Fort Scott⊙ 8,893	H4
67844	Fowler 592	B4
66427	Frankfort 1,038	F2
66735	Franklin 400	H4
66736	Fredonia⊙ 3,047	G4
67049	Freeport 12	E4
66762	Frontenac 2,586	H4
66738	Fulton 194	H4
66739	Galena 3,587	H4
66740	Galesburg 181	G4
67443	Galva 651	E3
67846	Garden City⊙ 18,256	B4
67050	Garden Plain 775	E4
66030	Gardner 2,392	H3
67529	Garfield 277	C3
66032	Garnett⊙ 3,310	G3
66742	Gas 543	G4
67638	Gaylord 203	D2
67734	Gem 101	B2
67444	Geneseo 496	D3
67051	Geuda Springs 217	E4
66743	Girard⊙ 2,888	H4
67639	Glade 131	C2
67445	Glasco 710	E2
67446	Glen Elder 491	D2
67052	Goddard 1,427	E4
67053	Goessel 421	E3
66428	Goff 196	G2
67735	Goodland⊙ 5,708	A2
67640	Gorham 355	D3
67736	Gove⊙ 148	B3
67737	Grainfield 417	B2
†66441	Grandview Plaza 1,189	F2
66429	Grantville 220	G2
67530	Great Bend⊙ 16,608	D3
66033	Greeley 405	G3
67447	Green 155	E2
66943	Greenleaf 462	E2
67054	Greensburg⊙ 1,885	C4
67346	Grenola 335	F4
66852	Gridley 404	G3
67738	Grinnell 410	B2
67448	Gypsum 423	E3
66944	Haddam 239	E2
67056	Halstead 1,994	E4
66853	Hamilton 363	F4
66945	Hanover 802	F2
67849	Hanston 257	C3
67057	Hardtner 336	D4
67058	Harper 1,823	D4
66854	Hartford 551	F3
66431	Harveyville 280	F3
67347	Havana 169	G4
67543	Haven 1,125	E4
66432	Havensville 183	F2
67059	Haviland 770	C4

(continued on following page)

67601 Hays⊙ 16,301 ....C3	67545 Hudson 157 ....D3	66039 Kincaid 192 ....G3	67073 Lehigh 189 ....E3	66053 Louisburg 1,744 ....H3	67745 McDonald 239 .....A2
67060 Haysville 8,006 ......E4	67951 Hugoton⊙ 3,165 ....A4	67068 Kingman⊙ 3,563 ....D4	66215 Lenexa 18,639 .....H2	66450 Louisville 207 ......F2	66501 McFarland 242 .....F2
67850 Healy 275 ....B3	66748 Humboldt 2,230 ....G4	67547 Kinsley⊙ 2,074 .....C4	67645 Lenora 444 ....C2	67648 Lucas 524 ....D2	66054 McLouth 700 ......G2
67061 Hazelton 143 ....D4	67061 Hunter 135 ....D2	67070 Kiowa 1,409 ....D4	67074 Leon 667 ....F4	67649 Luray 295 ....D2	67460 McPherson⊙ 11,753 .E3
66746 Hepler 165 ....H4	66038 Huron 107 ....G2	67644 Kirwin 249 ....C2	66448 Leona 73 ....G2	66451 Lyndon⊙ 1,132 .....G3	67864 Meade⊙ 1,777 .....B4
67449 Herington 2,930 .....E3	67501 Hutchinson⊙ 40,284 ..D4	67859 Kismet 368 ....B4	66449 Leonardville 437 ...F2	67554 Lyons⊙ 4,134 ......D3	67104 Medicine Lodge⊙ 2,384 .D4
67739 Herndon 220 ....B2	67301 Independence⊙ 10,598 .G4	67350 Labette 123 ....G4	67861 Leoti⊙ 1,869 ......A3	67557 Macksville 546 .....D4	66510 Melvern 481 ....G3
67062 Hesston 3,013 ....E3	67853 Ingalls 274 ....B4	67548 La Crosse⊙ 1,618 ...C3	66857 Le Roy 701 ....G3	66860 Madison 1,099 .....F3	67746 Menlo 42 ....B2
66434 Hiawatha 3,702 ......G2	67546 Inman 947 ....E3	66040 La Cygne 1,025 .....H3	67552 Lewis 551 ....C4	66955 Mahaska 119 ....E2	66512 Meriden 707 ......G2
†67880 Hickock 68 ....A4	66749 Iola⊙ 6,938 ....G4	66751 La Harpe 687 ......G4	67901 Liberal⊙ 14,911 ....B4	67101 Maize 1,294 ....E4	66203 Merriam 10,794 ....H3
66035 Highland 954 ....G2	67065 Isabel 137 ....D4	67860 Lakin⊙ 1,823 ......A4	67351 Liberty 174 ....G4	67463 Manchester 98 .....E3	67105 Milan 135 ....E4
67642 Hill City⊙ 2,028 .....C2	67066 Iuka 235 ....D4	66041 Lancaster 274 ......G2	67553 Liebenthal 163 .....C3	66502 Manhattan⊙ 32,644 .F2	66055 Mildred 64 ....G3
67063 Hillsboro 2,717 ......E3	66948 Jamestown 440 .....E2	66042 Lane 249 ....G3	67455 Lincoln⊙ 1,599 ....D2	66956 Mankato⊙ 1,205 ...D2	66514 Milford 465 ....E2
67544 Hoisington 3,678 ....D3	67643 Jennings 194 ......B2	67549 Langdon 84 ....D4	66858 Lincolnville 235 ....F3	67862 Manter 205 ....A4	67466 Miltonvale 588 .....E2
67851 Holcomb 816 ....B3	66949 Jewell 589 ....D2	66043 Lansing 5,307 .....H2	67456 Lindsborg 3,155 ....E3	66507 Maple Hill 381 .....F2	67467 Minneapolis⊙ 2,075 .E2
66946 Hollenberg 57 ....F2	66441 Junction City⊙ 19,305 .E2	67550 Larned⊙ 4,811 .....C3	66953 Linn 483 ....E2	66754 Mapleton 121 ......H3	67865 Minneola 712 .....B4
66436 Holton⊙ 3,132 ......G2	67454 Kanopolis 729 ......D3	67072 Latham 148 ....F4	66052 Linwood 343 ......G2	66861 Marion⊙ 1,951 .....F3	66205 Mission 8,643 ......H3
67450 Holyrood 567 ....D3	67741 Kanorado 217 ......A2	66044 Lawrence⊙ 52,738 ..H2	67457 Little River 529 ....E3	67464 Marquette 639 .....E3	67353 Moline 553 ....F4
67451 Hope 468 ....E3	*66101 Kansas City⊙ 161,148 .H2	Lawrence‡ 67,640 ..H2	67646 Logan 720 ....C2	66508 Marysville⊙ 3,670 ..F2	67867 Montezuma 730 ....B4
†67879 Horace 137 ....A3	Kansas City‡ 1,327,020 .H2	66048 Leavenworth⊙ 33,656 .H2	67458 Longford 109 ......E2	66862 Matfield Green 71 ..F3	66755 Moran 643 ....G4
66439 Horton 2,130 ....G2	67067 Kechi 288 ....E4	66206 Leawood 13,360 ....H3	67647 Long Island 187 ....C2	66509 Mayetta 287 ....G2	67468 Morganville 261 ...E2
67349 Howard⊙ 965 ....F4	66951 Kensington 681 .....C2	66952 Lebanon 440 ....D2	67352 Longton 396 ....F4	67103 Mayfield 128 ....E4	67650 Morland 223 ......B2
67740 Hoxie⊙ 1,462 ....B2		66856 Lebo 966 ....G3	67459 Lorraine 157 ......D3	67556 McCracken 292 ....C3	66515 Morrill 336 ....G2
66440 Hoyt 536 ....G2		66050 Lecompton 576 ....G2	67556 Lost Springs 94 ....E3	66753 McCune 528 ....G4	66958 Morrowville 180 ...E2

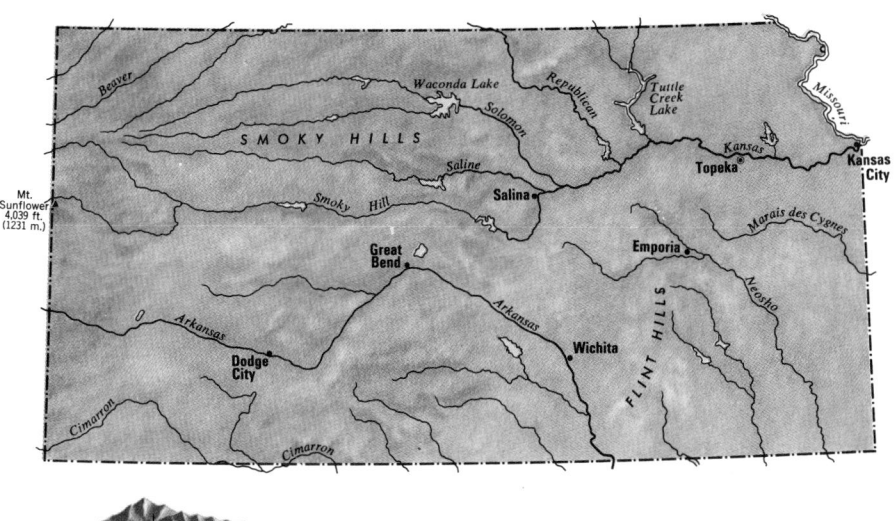

Topography

| | 5,000 m. / 16,404 ft. | 2,000 m. / 6,562 ft. | 1,000 m. / 3,281 ft. | 500 m. / 1,640 ft. | 200 m. / 656 ft. | 100 m. / 328 ft. | Sea Level | Below |

0   50   100 MI.

0   50   100 KM.

KENTUCKY

COUNTIES

Adair 15,233 ... L6
Allen 14,128 ... J7
Anderson 12,567 ... M5
Ballard 8,798 ... C6
Barren 34,009 ... K7
Bath 10,025 ... O4
Bell 34,330 ... O7
Boone 45,842 ... M3
Bourbon 19,405 ... N4
Boyd 55,513 ... R4
Boyle 25,066 ... M5
Bracken 7,738 ... N3
Breathitt 17,004 ... P5
Breckinridge 16,861 ... H5
Bullitt 43,346 ... K5
Butler 11,064 ... H6
Caldwell 13,473 ... F6
Calloway 30,031 ... E7
Campbell 83,317 ... N3
Carlisle 5,487 ... C7
Carroll 9,270 ... L3
Carter 25,060 ... P4
Casey 14,818 ... M6
Christian 66,878 ... F7
Clark 28,322 ... N4
Clay 22,752 ... O6
Clinton 9,321 ... L7
Crittenden 9,207 ... E6
Cumberland 7,289 ... L7
Daviess 85,949 ... G5
Edmonson 9,962 ... J6
Elliott 6,908 ... P4
Estill 14,495 ... O5
Fayette 204,165 ... N4
Fleming 12,323 ... O4
Floyd 48,764 ... R5
Franklin 41,830 ... M4
Fulton 8,971 ... C7
Gallatin 4,842 ... M3
Garrard 10,853 ... M5
Grant 13,308 ... M3
Graves 34,049 ... D7
Grayson 20,854 ... J5
Green 11,043 ... K6
Greenup 39,132 ... R3
Hancock 7,742 ... H5
Hardin 88,917 ... K5
Harlan 41,889 ... P7
Harrison 15,166 ... N4
Hart 15,402 ... K6
Henderson 40,849 ... F5
Henry 12,740 ... L4
Hickman 6,065 ... C7
Hopkins 46,174 ... F6
Jackson 11,996 ... N6
Jefferson 684,565 ... K4
Jessamine 26,065 ... M5
Johnson 24,432 ... R5
Kenton 137,058 ... M3
Knott 17,940 ... R6
Knox 30,239 ... O7
Larue 11,922 ... K5
Laurel 38,982 ... N6
Lawrence 14,121 ... R4
Lee 7,754 ... O5
Leslie 14,882 ... P6
Letcher 30,687 ... R6
Lewis 14,545 ... P3
Lincoln 19,053 ... M6
Livingston 9,219 ... E6
Logan 24,138 ... H7
Lyon 6,490 ... E6
Madison 53,352 ... N5
Magoffin 13,515 ... P5
Marion 17,910 ... L5
Marshall 25,637 ... E7
Martin 13,925 ... R5
Mason 17,765 ... O3
McCracken 61,310 ... D6
McCreary 15,634 ... N7
McLean 10,090 ... G5
Meade 22,854 ... J5
Menifee 5,117 ... O5
Mercer 19,011 ... M5
Metcalfe 9,484 ... K7
Monroe 12,353 ... K7
Montgomery 20,046 ... O4
Morgan 12,103 ... P5
Muhlenberg 32,238 ... G6
Nelson 27,584 ... K5
Nicholas 7,157 ... N4
Ohio 21,765 ... H6
Oldham 27,795 ... L4
Owen 8,924 ... M3
Owsley 5,709 ... O6
Pendleton 10,989 ... N3
Perry 33,763 ... P6
Pike 81,123 ... S6
Powell 11,101 ... O5
Pulaski 45,803 ... M6
Robertson 2,265 ... N3
Rockcastle 13,973 ... N6
Rowan 19,049 ... P4
Russell 13,708 ... L7
Scott 21,813 ... M4
Shelby 23,328 ... L4
Simpson 14,673 ... H7
Spencer 5,929 ... L4
Taylor 21,178 ... L6
Todd 11,874 ... G7
Trigg 9,384 ... F7
Trimble 6,253 ... L3
Union 17,821 ... F5
Warren 71,828 ... H6
Washington 10,764 ... L5
Wayne 17,022 ... M7
Webster 14,832 ... F5
Whitley 33,396 ... N7
Wolfe 6,698 ... O5
Woodford 17,778 ... M4

CITIES and TOWNS

Zip *Name/Pop.* *Key*

42202 Adairville 1,105 ... H7
42602 Albany⊙ 2,083 ... L7
41001 Alexandria⊙ 4,735 ... N3
41601 Allen 338 ... R5
42204 Allensville 170 ... G7
40223 Anchorage 1,726 ... L2
41101 Ashland 27,064 ... R4
Ashland-Huntington‡ 311,350 ... R4
42206 Auburn 1,467 ... H7
†40201 Audubon Park 1,571 ... J2
41002 Augusta 1,455 ... N3
41602 Auxier 900 ... R5
†40222 Bancroft 725 ... K1
41603 Banner 950 ... R5
†40201 Barbourmeade 1,038 ... K1
40906 Barbourville⊙ 3,333 ... O7
40004 Bardstown⊙ 6,155 ... L5
42023 Bardwell⊙ 988 ... D7
42024 Barlow 746 ... D6
41311 Beattyville⊙ 1,068 ... O5
42320 Beaver Dam 3,185 ... H6
40006 Bedford⊙ 835 ... L3
40359 Beechwood Village 1,462 ... K2
†40201 Bellemeade 918 ... L2
41073 Bellevue 7,678 ... S1
40807 Benham 936 ... R7
42025 Benton⊙ 3,700 ... E7
40403 Berea 8,226 ... N5
41003 Berry 287 ... N3
41605 Betsy Layne 975 ... R5
41124 Blaine 358 ... R4
40008 Bloomfield 954 ... L5
†40201 Blue Ridge Manor 465 ... L2
42713 Bonnieville 372 ... K6
†40403 Boone 300 ... N5
41314 Booneville⊙ 191 ... O6
42101 Bowling Green⊙ 40,450 ... H7
40009 Bradfordsville 331 ... L6
40108 Brandenburg⊙ 1,831 ... J4
†42025 Briensburg ... E7
†40201 Broadfields 311 ... K2
40409 Brodhead 686 ... N6
†41016 Bromley 844 ... S2
40109 Brooks 1,344 ... K4
41004 Brooksville⊙ 680 ... N3
†40201 Brownsboro Farm 790 ... L1
42210 Brownsville⊙ 674 ... J6
40218 Buechel 6,709 ... K2
40310 Burgin 1,008 ... M5
42717 Burkesville⊙ 2,051 ... L7
41005 Burlington⊙ 500 ... R2
42519 Burnside 775 ... M6
41006 Butler 663 ... N3
42211 Cadiz⊙ 1,661 ... F7
42327 Calhoun⊙ 1,080 ... G5
41007 California 135 ... N3
42029 Calvert City 2,388 ... E6
†40337 Camargo 1,301 ... K4
40011 Campbellsburg 714 ... L3
42718 Campbellsville⊙ 8,715 ... L6
41301 Campton⊙ 486 ... O5
42721 Caneyville 642 ... J6
40311 Carlisle⊙ 1,757 ... N4
41008 Carrollton⊙ 3,967 ... L3
42030 Carrsville 99 ... E6
†42459 Caseyville 43 ... E5
41129 Catlettsburg⊙ 3,005 ... R4
42127 Cave City 2,098 ... K6
†41522 Cedarville 81 ... S6
42328 Centertown 462 ... G6
42330 Central City 5,214 ... G6
42726 Clarkson 666 ... J6
42404 Clay 1,356 ... F6
40312 Clay City 1,276 ... O5
40313 Clearfield 1,250 ... P4
42031 Clinton⊙ 1,720 ... D7
40111 Cloverport 1,585 ... H5
†41501 Coal Run 348 ... R5
41076 Cold Spring 2,117 ... T2
42728 Columbia⊙ 3,710 ... L6
42032 Columbus 296 ... C7
41729 Combs 900 ... P6
41131 Concord 67 ... P3
40701 Corbin 8,075 ... N7
41010 Corinth 258 ... M3
42406 Corydon 874 ... F5
*41011 Covington 49,563 ... S2
40419 Crab Orchard 843 ... M6
†41016 Crescent Springs 1,951 ... R2
†41076 Crestview 528 ... S2
†41017 Crestview Hills 1,408 ... R2
40014 Crestwood 531 ... L4
41030 Crittenden 597 ... M3
42217 Crofton 823 ... G6
40823 Cumberland 3,712 ... R6
41031 Cynthiana⊙ 5,881 ... N4
40422 Danville⊙ 12,942 ... M5
42408 Dawson Springs 3,275 ... F6
41074 Dayton 6,979 ... T1
†40201 Devondale 1,164 ... K2
42036 Dexter ... E7
42409 Dixon⊙ 533 ... F5
†40243 Douglass Hills 4,384 ... L2
41034 Dover 305 ... O3
42337 Drakesboro 798 ... H6
41035 Dry Ridge 1,250 ... M3
42037 Dycusburg 64 ... E6
42410 Earlington 2,011 ... F6
42038 Eddyville⊙ 1,949 ... E6
†41017 Edgewood 7,230 ... S2
42129 Edmonton⊙ 1,401 ... K7
40117 Ekron 239 ... J5
42701 Elizabethtown⊙ 15,380 ... K5
41522 Elkhorn City 1,446 ... S6
42220 Elkton⊙ 1,815 ... G7
†41018 Elsmere 7,203 ... R2
40019 Eminence 2,260 ... L4
40826 Eolia 875 ... R6
41018 Erlanger 14,433 ... R2
40827 Essie 650 ... P6
42567 Eubank 207 ... M6
40828 Evarts 1,234 ... P7
41039 Ewing 144 ... O4
40118 Fairdale 7,315 ... K4
40020 Fairfield 169 ... L5
†41101 Fairview 198 ... S2
41040 Falmouth⊙ 2,482 ... N3
41524 Fedscreek 950 ... S6
42533 Ferguson 1,009 ... M6
†40222 Fincastle 804 ... L1
41139 Flatwoods 8,354 ... R4
41816 Fleming-Neon 1,195 ... R6
41041 Flemingsburg⊙ 2,835 ... O4
41042 Florence 15,586 ... R2
42343 Fordsville 561 ... H5
41527 Forest Hills 502 ... L2
40121 Fort Knox 31,055 ... K5
41017 Fort Mitchell 7,297 ... S2
41075 Fort Thomas 16,012 ... S2
†41011 Fort Wright 4,481 ... S2
41043 Foster 80 ... N3
42133 Fountain Run 340 ... K7
40601 Frankfort (cap.)⊙ 25,973 ... M4
42134 Franklin⊙ 7,738 ... J7
42411 Fredonia 535 ... E6
40322 Frenchburg⊙ 550 ... O5
†41175 Fullerton 950 ... P3
42041 Fulton 3,137 ... D7
42140 Gamaliel 456 ... K7
40324 Georgetown⊙ 10,972 ... M4
41044 Germantown 347 ... O3
41045 Ghent 439 ... L3
42044 Gilbertsville ... E7
42141 Glasgow⊙ 12,958 ... J7
41046 Glencoe 354 ... M3
†40222 Glenview 212 ... K1
†40222 Goose Creek 394 ... L1
42045 Grand Rivers 428 ... E7
†41005 Grant 150 ... M3
40327 Gratz 124 ... M4
†40201 Graymoor 1,167 ... K1
41143 Grayson⊙ 3,423 ... R4
42743 Greensburg⊙ 2,377 ... K6
41144 Greenup⊙ 1,386 ... R3
42345 Greenville⊙ 4,631 ... G6
42234 Guthrie 1,361 ... G7
42413 Hanson 485 ... G6
42048 Hardin 545 ... E7
40143 Hardinsburg⊙ 2,211 ... H5
41531 Hardy 900 ... S5
40831 Harlan⊙ 3,024 ... P7
40330 Harrodsburg⊙ 7,265 ... M5
42347 Hartford⊙ 2,512 ... H6
42348 Hawesville⊙ 1,036 ... H5
41701 Hazard⊙ 5,371 ... P6
42049 Hazel 465 ... E7
40949 Heidrick 400 ... O7
42420 Henderson⊙ 24,834 ... F5
42050 Hickman⊙ 2,894 ... C7
42051 Hickory ... D7
41076 Highland Heights 4,435 ... T2
41822 Hindman⊙ 876 ... R6
42152 Hiseville 349 ... K6
42748 Hodgenville⊙ 2,531 ... K5
†40228 Hollow Creek 1,023 ... K4
†41018 Hopeful Heights ... R2
42240 Hopkinsville⊙ 27,318 ... F7
42749 Horse Cave 2,045 ... K6
†40201 Houston Acres 608 ... K2
40437 Hustonville 339 ... M6
41749 Hyden⊙ 488 ... P6
41051 Independence⊙ 7,998 ... M3
†40201 Indian Hills 787 ... K1
41224 Inez⊙ 413 ... S5
40336 Irvine⊙ 2,889 ... O5
40146 Irvington 1,409 ... J5
42350 Island 532 ... G6
41642 Ivel 850 ... R5
41339 Jackson⊙ 2,651 ... P5
42629 Jamestown⊙ 1,441 ... L7
40299 Jeffersontown 15,795 ... L2
40337 Jeffersonville 1,528 ... O5
41537 Jenkins 3,271 ... R6
40440 Junction City 2,045 ... M5
40737 Keavy 900 ... N6
†41011 Kenton Vale 145 ... S2
42053 Kevil 382 ... D6
†40201 Kingsley 464 ... K2
42055 Kuttawa 560 ... E6
42056 La Center 1,044 ... C6
41643 Lackey ... R6
42254 La Fayette 160 ... F7
40031 La Grange⊙ 2,971 ... L4
†41017 Lakeside Park 3,038 ... R2
40444 Lancaster⊙ 3,365 ... M5
40342 Lawrenceburg⊙ 5,167 ... M4
40033 Lebanon⊙ 6,590 ... L5
40150 Lebanon Junction 1,581 ... K5
42754 Leitchfield⊙ 4,533 ... J6
42256 Lewisburg 972 ... G6
42351 Lewisport 1,832 ... H5
*40501 Lexington⊙ 204,165 ... N4
Lexington‡ 318,136 ... N4
42539 Liberty⊙ 2,206 ... M6
42352 Livermore 1,672 ... G5
40445 Livingston 334 ... N6
40036 Lockport 84 ... M4
40741 London⊙ 4,002 ... N6
42001 Lone Oak 443 ... D6
40037 Loretto 954 ... L5
41230 Louisa⊙ 1,832 ... R4
*40201 Louisville⊙ 298,840 ... J2
Louisville‡ 906,240 ... J2
40854 Loyall 1,210 ... P7
41016 Ludlow 4,959 ... S2
40855 Lynch 1,614 ... R7
†40201 Lynnview 1,157 ... K4
40040 Mackville 229 ... L5
42431 Madisonville⊙ 16,979 ... F6
40962 Manchester⊙ 1,838 ... O6
42064 Marion⊙ 3,392 ... E6
41649 Martin 827 ... R5
42066 Mayfield⊙ 10,705 ... D7
41056 Maysville⊙ 7,983 ... O3
41543 McAndrews 975 ... S5
42354 McHenry 582 ... H6
40447 McKee⊙ 759 ... O6
41835 McRoberts 1,106 ... R6
†40201 Meadow Vale 1,008 ... L1
41059 Melbourne 628 ... T2
†41060 Mentor 169 ... N3
40965 Middlesboro 12,251 ... O7
40243 Middletown 414 ... L2
40347 Midway 1,445 ... M4
40348 Millersburg 987 ... N4
40045 Milton 718 ... L3
†40201 Minor Lane Heights 1,882 ... K4
†40359 Monterey 186 ... M4
42633 Monticello⊙ 5,677 ... M7
†40223 Moorland 513 ... L2
40351 Morehead⊙ 7,789 ... P4
42437 Morganfield⊙ 3,781 ... E5
42261 Morgantown⊙ 2,000 ... H6
42440 Mortons Gap 1,201 ... F6
41064 Mount Olivet⊙ 346 ... N3
†40437 Mount Salem 50 ... M6
40353 Mount Sterling⊙ 5,820 ... N4
40456 Mount Vernon⊙ 2,334 ... N6
40047 Mount Washington 3,997 ... K4
41548 Mouthcard 900 ... S6
40155 Muldraugh 1,752 ... J5
42765 Munfordville⊙ 1,783 ... J6
42071 Murray⊙ 14,248 ... E7
42441 Nebo 269 ... F6
41840 Neon-Fleming 1,195 ... R6
40050 New Castle⊙ 832 ... L4
40051 New Haven 926 ... K5
*41071 Newport 21,587 ... S2
40356 Nicholasville⊙ 10,319 ... N5
†40201 Northfield 906 ... K1
40357 North Middletown 637 ... N4
42442 Nortonville 1,336 ... G6
42262 Oak Grove 2,088 ... G7
42159 Oakland 264 ... J6
41238 Oil Springs 900 ... P5
40219 Okolona 20,039 ... K4
41164 Olive Hill 2,539 ... P4
42301 Owensboro⊙ 54,450 ... G5
Owensboro‡ 85,949 ... G5
40359 Owenton⊙ 1,341 ... M3
40360 Owingsville⊙ 1,419 ... O4
42001 Paducah⊙ 29,315 ... D6
41240 Paintsville⊙ 3,815 ... R5
40361 Paris⊙ 7,935 ... N4
42160 Park City 614 ... J6
†41011 Park Hills 3,500 ... S2
†40201 Parkway Village 754 ... J2
42266 Pembroke 636 ... G7
40468 Perryville 841 ... M5
40056 Pewee Valley 982 ... L4
41553 Phelps 1,126 ... S6
41501 Pikeville⊙ 4,756 ... S6
42635 Pine Knot 1,389 ... M7
40977 Pineville⊙ 2,599 ... O7
†40201 Plantation 969 ... K1
40258 Pleasure Ridge Park 27,332 ... J4
40057 Pleasureville 837 ... L4
†42101 Plum Springs 393 ... J7
42367 Powderly 848 ... G6
41653 Prestonsburg⊙ 4,011 ... R5
†41008 Prestonville 205 ... L3
42445 Princeton⊙ 7,073 ... F6
40059 Prospect 1,981 ... K4
42450 Providence 4,434 ... F6
41169 Raceland 1,970 ... R3
40160 Radcliff 14,519 ... K5
40472 Ravenna 793 ... O5
40475 Richmond⊙ 21,705 ... N5
†40222 Riverwood 435 ... K1
42273 Rochester 289 ... H6

Agriculture, Industry and Resources

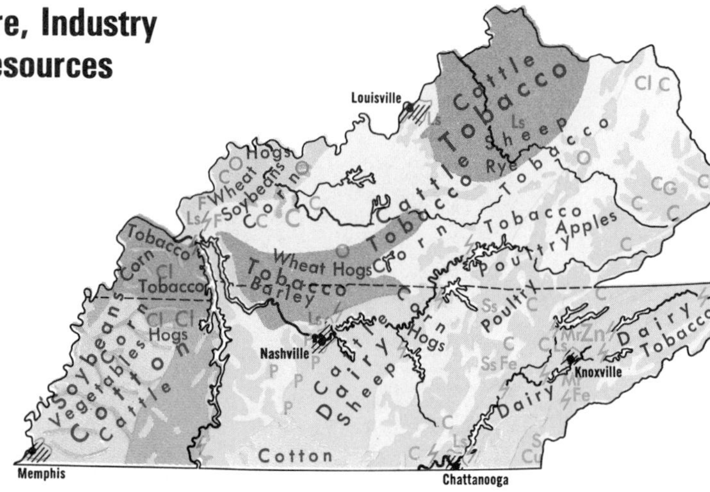

DOMINANT LAND USE

- Hogs, Soft Winter Wheat
- Tobacco, General Farming
- General Farming, Livestock, Tobacco
- General Farming, Livestock, Dairy
- General Farming, Livestock, Fruit, Tobacco
- Specialized Cotton
- Cotton, General Farming
- Cotton, Livestock
- Forests
- Swampland, Limited Agriculture

MAJOR MINERAL OCCURRENCES

C Coal
Cl Clay
Cu Copper
F Fluorspar
Fe Iron Ore
G Natural Gas
Ls Limestone
Mr Marble
O Petroleum
P Phosphates
S Pyrites
Ss Sandstone
Zn Zinc

Water Power
Major Industrial Areas

KENTUCKY

AREA 40,409 sq. mi. (104,659 sq. km.)
POPULATION 3,660,257
CAPITAL Frankfort
LARGEST CITY Louisville
HIGHEST POINT Black Mtn. 4,145 ft. (1263 m.)
SETTLED IN 1774
ADMITTED TO UNION June 1, 1792
POPULAR NAME Bluegrass State
STATE FLOWER Goldenrod
STATE BIRD Cardinal

TENNESSEE

AREA 42,144 sq. mi. (109,153 sq. km.)
POPULATION 4,591,120
CAPITAL Nashville
LARGEST CITY Memphis
HIGHEST POINT Clingmans Dome 6,643 ft. (2025 m.)
SETTLED IN 1757
ADMITTED TO UNION June 1, 1796
POPULAR NAME Volunteer State
STATE FLOWER Iris
STATE BIRD Mockingbird

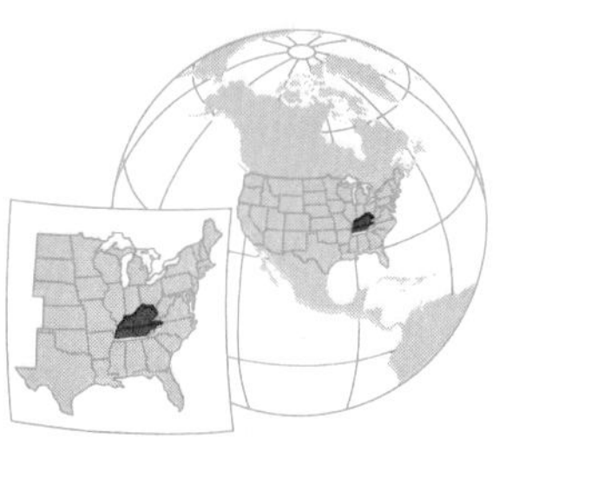

42369 Rockport 511 .... H6
†40201 Rolling Fields 731 .... K2
†40201 Rolling Hills 1,122 .... L1
41169 Russell 3,824 .... R3
42642 Russell Springs 1,831 .... L6
42276 Russellville⊙ 7,520 .... H7
†41015 Ryland Heights 252 .... M3
42372 Sacramento 538 .... G6
40370 Sadieville 253 .... M4
42453 Saint Charles 405 .... F6
40207 Saint Matthews 13,519 .... K2
†40201 Saint Regis Park 1,735 .... K2
42078 Salem 833 .... E6
40371 Salt Lick 347 .... O4
41465 Salyersville⊙ 1,352 .... P5
41083 Sanders 332 .... M3
41171 Sandy Hook⊙ 627 .... P4
41056 Sardis 198 .... O3
42553 Science Hill 655 .... M6
42164 Scottsville⊙ 4,278 .... J7
42455 Sebree 1,516 .... F5
†40201 Seneca Gardens 748 .... K2
40983 Sextons Creek 975 .... O6
40374 Sharpsburg 339 .... O4
40065 Shelbyville⊙ 5,329 .... L4
40165 Shepherdsville⊙ 4,454 .... K4
40216 Shively 16,819 .... K4
41085 Silver Grove 1,260 .... T2
40067 Simpsonville 642 .... L4
42456 Slaughters 269 .... F6
41764 Smilax 987 .... P6
40068 Smithfield 137 .... L4
42081 Smithland⊙ 512 .... E6
42171 Smiths Grove 767 .... J6
42501 Somerset⊙ 10,649 .... M6
42776 Sonora 416 .... K5
42374 South Carrollton 262 .... G6
41071 Southgate 2,833 .... T2
41174 South Portsmouth 900 .... P3
41175 South Shore 1,525 .... R3
25661 South Williamson 1,016 .... S5
41086 Sparta 192 .... M3
42458 Spottsville 914 .... G5
40069 Springfield⊙ 3,179 .... L5
†40201 Springlee 498 .... K2
40379 Stamping Ground 562 .... M4
40484 Stanford⊙ 2,764 .... M5
40380 Stanton⊙ 2,691 .... O5
42647 Stearns 1,557 .... N7
41567 Stone 900 .... S5
†40201 Strathmoor Village 466 .... J2
42459 Sturgis 2,293 .... F5
†41011 Taylor Mill 4,509 .... S2
40071 Taylorsville⊙ 801 .... L4
†40222 Thornhill 233 .... K1
41189 Tollesboro 808 .... O3
42167 Tompkinsville⊙ 4,366 .... K7
42286 Trenton 465 .... G7
41091 Union 601 .... M3
42461 Uniontown 1,169 .... F5
42784 Upton 731 .... K6
40272 Valley Station 24,474 .... K4
41179 Vanceburg⊙ 1,939 .... P3
41265 Van Lear 2,035 .... R5
†40828 Verda 1,133 .... P7
40383 Versailles⊙ 6,427 .... M4
41773 Vicco 456 .... P6
†41017 Villa Hills 4,402 .... R2
40175 Vine Grove 3,583 .... K5
†41063 Visalia 198 .... N3
40873 Wallins Creek 459 .... O7
41094 Walton 1,651 .... M3
41095 Warsaw⊙ 1,328 .... M3
41096 Washington 624 .... O3
42085 Water Valley 395 .... D7
42462 Waverly 434 .... F5
41666 Wayland 601 .... R6
41667 Weeksbury 850 .... R6
†40201 Wellington 653 .... K2
†40218 West Buechel 1,205 .... K2
41472 West Liberty⊙ 1,381 .... P5
40177 West Point 1,339 .... J4
†42501 West Somerset 850 .... M6
41101 Westwood 5,973 .... R4
†40207 Westwood 826 .... L1
42463 Wheatcroft 325 .... F5
41669 Wheelwright 865 .... R6
41390 Whick 280 .... P6
42464 White Plains 859 .... G6
41858 Whitesburg⊙ 1,525 .... R6
42378 Whitesville 788 .... H5
42653 Whitley City⊙ 1,683 .... N7
42087 Wickliffe⊙ 1,034 .... C7
†41071 Wilders 633 .... S2
40769 Williamsburg⊙ 5,560 .... N7
41097 Williamstown⊙ 2,502 .... M3
40078 Willisburg 235 .... L5
40390 Wilmore 3,787 .... M5
40391 Winchester⊙ 15,216 .... N5
†40201 Windy Hills 2,214 .... K1
42088 Wingo 606 .... D7
40771 Woodbine 900 .... N7
42170 Woodburn 330 .... J7
†40201 Woodland Hills 839 .... L2
†42001 Woodlawn-Oakdale 4,722 .... D6
†41071 Woodlawn 331 .... T2
†40201 Woodlawn Park 1,052 .... K2
41183 Worthington 1,948 .... R3
41098 Worthville 272 .... L3
41144 Wurtland 1,301 .... R3

OTHER FEATURES

Abraham Lincoln Birthplace Nat'l Hist. Site K5
Barkley (dam) E6
Barkley (lake) F7
Barren (riv.) H6
Barren River (lake) J7
Beech Fork (riv.) L5
Big Sandy (riv.) R4
Black (mt.) R7
Buckhorn (lake) O6
Chaplin (riv.) L5
Clarks, East Fork (riv.) E7
Cove Run (lake) O4
Cumberland (lake) M7
Cumberland (mt.) P7
Cumberland (riv.) K8
Cumberland Gap Nat'l Hist. Park P7
Dale Hollow (lake) L7
Dewey (lake) R5
Dix (riv.) M5
Drakes (creek) J7
Dry (creek) R3
Eagle (creek) M3
Fishtrap (lake) S6
Fort Campbell G7
Grayson (lake) P4
Green (riv.) G6
Green River (lake) L6
Herrington (lake) M5
Hinkston (creek) N4
Kentucky (dam) E7
Kentucky (lake) E8
Kentucky (riv.) M3
Land Between The Lakes Rec. Area E7
Laurel River (lake) N6
Lexington Blue Grass Army Depot N5
Licking (riv.) N3
Mammoth Cave Nat'l Park J6
Mayfield (creek) C7
Mississippi (riv.) A10
Mud (riv.) H7
Nolin (lake) K6
Nolin (riv.) J6
Obion (creek) C7
Ohio (riv.) F5
Paint Lick (riv.) M5
Panther (creek) G5
Pine (mt.) O7
Pond (riv.) G6
Red (riv.) O5
Red (riv.) G7
Rockcastle (riv.) N6
Rolling Fork (riv.) L5
Rough (riv.) H5
Rough River (lake) J5
Salt (riv.) K5
Tennessee (riv.) D6
Tradewater (riv.) F6
Tug Fork (riv.) S5

TENNESSEE

COUNTIES

Anderson 67,346 .... N8
Bedford 27,916 .... J9
Benton 14,901 .... E8
Bledsoe 9,478 .... L9
Blount 77,770 .... O9
Bradley 67,547 .... M10
Campbell 34,923 .... N8
Cannon 10,234 .... J9
Carroll 28,285 .... E9
Carter 50,205 .... S8
Cheatham 21,616 .... G8
Chester 12,727 .... D10
Claiborne 24,595 .... O8
Clay 7,676 .... K7
Cocke 28,792 .... P9
Coffee 38,311 .... J9
Crockett 14,941 .... C9
Cumberland 28,676 .... L9
Davidson 477,811 .... H8
Decatur 10,857 .... E9
De Kalb 13,589 .... K9
Dickson 30,037 .... G8
Dyer 34,663 .... C8
Fayette 25,305 .... C10
Fentress 14,826 .... M8
Franklin 31,983 .... J10
Gibson 49,467 .... D9
Giles 24,625 .... G10
Grainger 16,751 .... O8
Greene 54,422 .... R8
Grundy 13,787 .... K10
Hamblen 49,300 .... P8
Hamilton 287,740 .... L10
Hancock 6,887 .... P7
Hardeman 23,873 .... C10
Hardin 22,280 .... E10
Hawkins 43,751 .... P8
Haywood 20,318 .... C9
Henderson 21,390 .... E9
Henry 28,656 .... E8
Hickman 15,151 .... G9
Houston 6,871 .... F8
Humphreys 15,957 .... F8
Jackson 9,398 .... K8
Jefferson 31,284 .... P8
Johnson 13,745 .... T7
Knox 319,694 .... O9
Lake 7,455 .... B8
Lauderdale 24,555 .... B9
Lawrence 34,110 .... G10
Lewis 9,700 .... F9
Lincoln 26,483 .... H10
Loudon 28,553 .... N9
Macon 15,700 .... J7
Madison 74,546 .... D9
Marion 24,416 .... K10
Marshall 19,698 .... H10
Maury 51,095 .... G9
McMinn 41,878 .... M10
McNairy 22,525 .... D10
Meigs 7,431 .... M9
Monroe 28,700 .... N10
Montgomery 83,342 .... G8
Moore 4,510 .... J10
Morgan 16,604 .... M8
Obion 32,781 .... C8
Overton 17,575 .... L8
Perry 6,111 .... F9
Pickett 4,358 .... M7
Polk 13,602 .... N10
Putnam 47,690 .... K8
Rhea 24,235 .... M9
Roane 48,425 .... M9
Robertson 37,021 .... H7
Rutherford 84,058 .... J9
Scott 19,259 .... M8
Sequatchie 8,605 .... L10
Sevier 41,418 .... O9
Shelby 777,113 .... B10
Smith 14,935 .... J8
Stewart 8,665 .... F7
Sullivan 143,968 .... S7
Sumner 85,790 .... J8
Tipton 32,930 .... B9
Trousdale 6,137 .... J8
Unicoi 16,362 .... S8
Union 11,707 .... O8
Van Buren 4,728 .... L9
Warren 32,653 .... K9
Washington 88,755 .... R8
Wayne 13,946 .... F10
Weakley 32,896 .... D8
White 19,567 .... L9
Williamson 58,108 .... H9
Wilson 56,064 .... J8

CITIES and TOWNS

Zip *Name/Pop.* *Key*

†38301 Adair 70 .... D9
37010 Adams 600 .... G7
38310 Adamsville 1,453 .... E10
38001 Alamo⊙ 2,615 .... C9
37701 Alcoa 6,870 .... N9
37012 Alexandria 689 .... J8
38501 Algood 2,406 .... K8
38504 Allardt 654 .... M8
37301 Altamont⊙ 679 .... K10
38449 Ardmore 835 .... H10
38002 Arlington 1,778 .... B10
37015 Ashland City⊙ 2,329 .... G8
37303 Athens⊙ 12,080 .... M10
38004 Atoka 691 .... B10
38220 Atwood 1,143 .... D9
37016 Auburntown 204 .... J9
37743 Baileyton 333 .... R8
†37650 Banner Hill 2,913 .... R8
38134 Bartlett 17,170 .... B10
38544 Baxter 1,411 .... K8
37305 Beersheba Springs 643 .... K10
37020 Bell Buckle 450 .... J9
37205 Belle Meade 3,182 .... H8
38006 Bells 1,571 .... C9
37307 Benton⊙ 1,115 .... M10
†37201 Berry Hill 1,113 .... H8
†37027 Berry's Chapel 2,703 .... H9
38315 Bethel Springs 873 .... D10
38221 Big Sandy 650 .... E8
37709 Blaine 1,147 .... O8
37660 Bloomingdale 12,088 .... R7
37617 Blountville⊙ 2,554 .... S7
37618 Bluff City 1,121 .... S8
38008 Bolivar⊙ 6,597 .... C10
38010 Braden 293 .... B10
38316 Bradford 1,146 .... D8
37027 Brentwood 9,431 .... H8
37710 Briceville 850 .... N8
38011 Brighton 976 .... B10
37620 Bristol 23,986 .... S7
38012 Brownsville⊙ 9,307 .... C9
38317 Bruceton 1,579 .... E8
37711 Bulls Gap 821 .... P8
38015 Burlison 386 .... B9
37029 Burns 777 .... G8
38549 Byrdstown⊙ 884 .... L7
37309 Calhoun 590 .... M10
38320 Camden⊙ 3,279 .... E8
37030 Carthage⊙ 2,672 .... K8
37714 Caryville 2,039 .... N8
37032 Cedar Hill 420 .... H7
38551 Celina⊙ 1,580 .... K7
†37110 Centertown 300 .... K9
37033 Centerville⊙ 2,824 .... G9
37034 Chapel Hill 861 .... H9
37310 Charleston 756 .... M10
37036 Charlotte⊙ 788 .... G8
*37401 Chattanooga⊙ 169,558 .... K10
Chattanooga‡ 426,540 .... K10
37642 Church Hill 4,110 .... R7
38324 Clarksburg 400 .... E9
37040 Clarksville⊙ 54,777 .... G7
Clarksville‡ 150,220 .... G7
37311 Cleveland⊙ 26,415 .... M10
38425 Clifton 773 .... F10
37716 Clinton⊙ 5,245 .... N8
37313 Coalmont 625 .... K10
37315 Collegedale 4,607 .... M10
38017 Collierville 7,839 .... B10
38450 Collinwood 1,064 .... F10
37663 Colonial Heights 6,744 .... R8
38401 Columbia⊙ 26,571 .... G9
37720 Concord 8,569 .... N9
38501 Cookeville⊙ 20,535 .... L8
37317 Copperhill 418 .... N10
37047 Cornersville 722 .... H10
38224 Cottage Grove 117 .... E8
38326 Counce 975 .... E10
38019 Covington⊙ 6,065 .... B9
37318 Cowan 1,790 .... K10
37723 Crab Orchard 1,065 .... M9
37049 Cross Plains 655 .... H7
38555 Crossville⊙ 6,394 .... L9
37050 Cumberland City 276 .... F8
37724 Cumberland Gap 263 .... O8
37725 Dandridge⊙ 1,383 .... O8
37321 Dayton⊙ 5,913 .... L9
37322 Decatur⊙ 1,069 .... M9
38329 Decaturville⊙ 1,004 .... E9
37324 Decherd 2,233 .... J10
38391 Denmark 51 .... D9
37055 Dickson 7,040 .... G8
37058 Dover⊙ 1,197 .... F8
37059 Dowelltown 341 .... K8
38559 Doyle 344 .... K9
38225 Dresden⊙ 2,256 .... D8
37326 Ducktown 583 .... N10
37327 Dunlap⊙ 3,681 .... L10
38330 Dyer 2,419 .... D8
38024 Dyersburg⊙ 15,856 .... C8
†37801 Eagleton Village 5,331 .... O9
37060 Eagleville 444 .... H9
37412 East Ridge 21,236 .... L11
†38367 Eastview 552 .... D10
37643 Elizabethton⊙ 12,431 .... S8
38455 Elkton 540 .... H10
38029 Ellendale 850 .... B10
37329 Englewood 1,840 .... M10
38332 Enville 287 .... E10
37061 Erin⊙ 1,614 .... F8
37650 Erwin⊙ 4,739 .... S8
37330 Estill Springs 1,324 .... J10
38456 Ethridge 548 .... G10
37331 Etowah 3,758 .... M10
37062 Fairview 3,648 .... G9
37656 Fall Branch 1,340 .... R8
37334 Fayetteville⊙ 7,559 .... H10
38334 Finger 245 .... D10
38030 Finley 1,014 .... B8
†37201 Forest Hills 4,516 .... H8
37064 Franklin⊙ 12,407 .... H9
38034 Friendship 763 .... C9
37737 Friendsville 694 .... N9
38337 Gadsden 683 .... D9
38562 Gainesboro⊙ 1,119 .... K8
37066 Gallatin⊙ 17,191 .... H8
38036 Gallaway 804 .... B10
†38019 Garland 301 .... B9
38037 Gates 729 .... C9
37738 Gatlinburg 3,210 .... O9
38138 Germantown 21,482 .... B10
38338 Gibson 458 .... D9
†38015 Gilt Edge 142 .... B9
38229 Gleason 1,335 .... D8
37072 Goodlettsville 8,327 .... H8
38563 Gordonsville 893 .... K8
38039 Grand Junction 360 .... C10
37338 Graysville 1,380 .... L10
37742 Greenback 546 .... N9
37073 Greenbrier 3,180 .... H8
37743 Greeneville⊙ 14,097 .... R8
38230 Greenfield 2,109 .... D8
37339 Gruetli 910 .... K10
38040 Halls 2,444 .... C9
37658 Hampton 2,236 .... S8
37748 Harriman 8,303 .... M9
37341 Harrison 6,206 .... L10
37752 Harrogate-Shawanee 2,530 .... O8
37074 Hartsville⊙ 2,674 .... J8
38340 Henderson⊙ 4,449 .... D10
37075 Hendersonville 26,561 .... H8
38041 Henning 638 .... B9
38231 Henry 295 .... E8
38042 Hickory Valley 252 .... C10
38462 Hohenwald⊙ 3,922 .... F9
38342 Hollow Rock 955 .... E8
38232 Hornbeak 452 .... C8
38044 Hornsby 401 .... D10
38343 Humboldt 10,209 .... D9
38344 Huntingdon⊙ 3,962 .... E8
37345 Huntland 983 .... J10
37756 Huntsville⊙ 519 .... N8
37078 Hurricane Mills 850 .... F9
38463 Iron City 482 .... F10
37757 Jacksboro⊙ 1,722 .... N8
38301 Jackson⊙ 49,131 .... D9
38556 Jamestown⊙ 2,364 .... M8
37347 Jasper⊙ 2,633 .... K10
37760 Jefferson City 5,612 .... P8
37762 Jellico 2,798 .... N7
37601 Johnson City 39,753 .... S8
Johnson City-Kingspoint-Bristol‡ 433,638 .... S8
37659 Jonesboro⊙ 2,829 .... R8
37921 Karns 1,173 .... N9
38233 Kenton 1,551 .... C8
†37347 Kimball 1,220 .... K10
*37660 Kingsport 32,027 .... R7
37763 Kingston⊙ 4,441 .... N9
37082 Kingston Springs 1,017 .... G8
*37901 Knoxville⊙ 175,045 .... O9
Knoxville‡ 476,517 .... O9
37083 Lafayette⊙ 3,808 .... J7
37766 La Follette 8,198 .... N8
38046 La Grange 185 .... C10
37769 Lake City 2,335 .... N8
†38134 Lakeland 612 .... B10
†37379 Lakesite 651 .... L10
†37138 Lakewood 2,325 .... H8
37086 La Vergne 5,495 .... H9
38464 Lawrenceburg⊙ 10,184 .... G10
37087 Lebanon⊙ 11,872 .... J8
37771 Lenoir City 5,446 .... N9
37091 Lewisburg⊙ 8,760 .... H10
38351 Lexington⊙ 5,934 .... E9
37095 Liberty 365 .... K8
37096 Linden⊙ 1,087 .... F9
38570 Livingston⊙ 3,372 .... L8
37097 Lobelville 993 .... F9
37350 Lookout Mountain 1,886 .... L11
38469 Loretto 1,612 .... G10
37774 Loudon⊙ 3,943 .... N9
37779 Luttrell 962 .... O8
37352 Lynchburg⊙ 668 .... J10
38472 Lynnville 383 .... G10
37354 Madisonville⊙ 2,884 .... N9
37355 Manchester⊙ 7,250 .... J10
38237 Martin 8,898 .... D8
37801 Maryville⊙ 17,480 .... O9
37806 Mascot 2,203 .... O8
38049 Mason 471 .... B10
38050 Maury City 989 .... C9
37807 Maynardville⊙ 924 .... O8
37101 McEwen 1,352 .... F8
38201 McKenzie 5,405 .... E8
38235 McLemoresville 311 .... D9
37110 McMinnville⊙ 10,683 .... K9
38355 Medina 687 .... D9
38356 Medon 169 .... D10
*38101 Memphis⊙ 646,174 .... B10
Memphis‡ 912,887 .... B10
38357 Michie 530 .... E10
38052 Middleton 596 .... D10
38358 Milan 8,083 .... D9
38359 Milledgeville 392 .... E10
38053 Millington 20,236 .... B10
38473 Minor Hill 564 .... G10
37119 Mitchellville 209 .... J7
37356 Monteagle 1,126 .... K10
38574 Monterey 2,610 .... L8
37357 Morrison 587 .... K9
†37660 Morrison City 2,032 .... R7
37814 Morristown⊙ 19,683 .... P8
38057 Moscow 499 .... C10
37818 Mosheim 1,539 .... R8
37683 Mountain City⊙ 2,125 .... T8
37642 Mount Carmel 3,764 .... R8
37122 Mount Juliet 2,879 .... H8
38474 Mount Pleasant 3,375 .... G9
38058 Munford 2,336 .... B10
37130 Murfreesboro⊙ 32,845 .... J9
*37201 Nashville (cap.)⊙ 455,651 .... H8
Nashville-Davidson‡ 850,505 .... H8
38059 Newbern 2,794 .... C8
†37380 New Hope 681 .... K11
37134 New Johnsonville 1,824 .... E8
37820 New Market 1,216 .... O8
37821 Newport⊙ 7,580 .... P9
37825 New Tazewell 1,677 .... O8
37826 Niota 765 .... M9
37360 Normandy 118 .... J10
37828 Norris 1,374 .... N8
37829 Oakdale 323 .... M9
†37201 Oak Hill 4,609 .... H8
38060 Oakland 472 .... B10
37830 Oak Ridge 27,662 .... N8
38240 Obion 1,282 .... C8
37840 Oliver Springs 3,659 .... N8
37841 Oneida 3,717 .... N7
37363 Ooltewah 950 .... M10
†37660 Orebank 1,284 .... R7
37141 Orlinda 382 .... H7
35740 Orme 181 .... K10
37365 Palmer 1,027 .... K10
38242 Paris⊙ 10,728 .... E8
37843 Parrottsville 118 .... P8
38363 Parsons 2,422 .... E9
37143 Pegram 1,081 .... H8
37144 Petersburg 681 .... H10
37845 Petros 1,286 .... M8
37846 Philadelphia 507 .... M9
37863 Pigeon Forge 1,822 .... O9
37367 Pikeville⊙ 2,085 .... L9
†38017 Piperton 746 .... B10
†37738 Pittman Center 488 .... P9
38578 Pleasant Hill 371 .... L9
37148 Portland 4,030 .... H7
37849 Powell 7,220 .... N8
†37397 Powells Crossroads 918 .... L10
38478 Pulaski⊙ 7,184 .... G10
38251 Puryear 624 .... E8
38367 Ramer 429 .... D10
37415 Red Bank 13,299 .... L10
37150 Red Boiling Springs 1,173 .... K7
†37641 Rheatown R8
†37380 Richard City 87 .... K11
38080 Ridgely 1,932 .... B8
†37401 Ridgeside 417 .... L10
37152 Ridgetop 1,225 .... H8
38063 Ripley⊙ 6,366 .... B9
38253 Rives 386 .... C8
37687 Roan Mountain 1,108 .... S8
37853 Rockford 567 .... O9
37854 Rockwood 5,767 .... M9
37857 Rogersville⊙ 4,368 .... P8
38053 Rosemark 950 .... B10
38066 Rossville 379 .... B10
37860 Russellville 1,069 .... P8
38369 Rutherford 1,378 .... C8
37861 Rutledge⊙ 1,058 .... P8
38481 Saint Joseph 897 .... G10
37373 Sale Creek 900 .... L10
38370 Saltillo 434 .... E10
38254 Samburg 465 .... C8
38371 Sardis 301 .... E10
38067 Saulsbury 156 .... C10
38372 Savannah⊙ 6,992 .... E10
38374 Scotts Hill 668 .... E10
38375 Selmer⊙ 3,979 .... D10
37862 Sevierville⊙ 4,556 .... P9
37375 Sewanee 2,298 .... K10
38255 Sharon 1,134 .... D8
37160 Shelbyville⊙ 13,530 .... H10
37376 Sherwood 900 .... K10
37377 Signal Mountain 5,818 .... L10
38377 Silerton 100 .... D10
37165 Slayden 69 .... G8
37166 Smithville⊙ 3,839 .... K9
37167 Smyrna 8,839 .... H9
37869 Sneedville⊙ 1,110 .... P7
37319 Soddy-Daisy 8,388 .... L10
38068 Somerville⊙ 2,264 .... C10
†37030 South Carthage 1,004 .... K8
†37311 South Cleveland 4,360 .... M10
†37716 South Clinton 1,671 .... N8
†42041 South Fulton 2,735 .... D8
37380 South Pittsburg 3,636 .... K10
37171 Southside 800 .... G8
38583 Sparta⊙ 4,864 .... K9
38585 Spencer⊙ 1,126 .... L9
37381 Spring City 1,951 .... M9
37172 Springfield⊙ 10,814 .... H8
37174 Spring Hill 989 .... H9
38069 Stanton 540 .... C10
38379 Stantonville 271 .... E10
†37660 Sullivan Gardens 2,513 .... R8
38483 Summertown 850 .... G10
37873 Surgoinsville 1,536 .... R8
37874 Sweetwater 4,725 .... N9
37877 Talbott 975 .... P8
37879 Tazewell⊙ 2,090 .... O8
37385 Tellico Plains 698 .... N10
37178 Tennessee Ridge 1,325 .... F8
38079 Tiptonville⊙ 2,438 .... B8
38381 Toone 355 .... D10
37882 Townsend 351 .... O9
37387 Tracy City 1,356 .... K10
38382 Trenton⊙ 4,601 .... D9
38258 Trezevant 921 .... D8
38259 Trimble 722 .... C8
38260 Troy 1,093 .... C8
37388 Tullahoma 15,800 .... J10
37743 Tusculum 1,242 .... R8
38261 Union City⊙ 10,436 .... C8
37181 Vanleer 401 .... G8
†37397 Victoria 800 .... K10
37394 Viola 149 .... K9

(continued on following page)

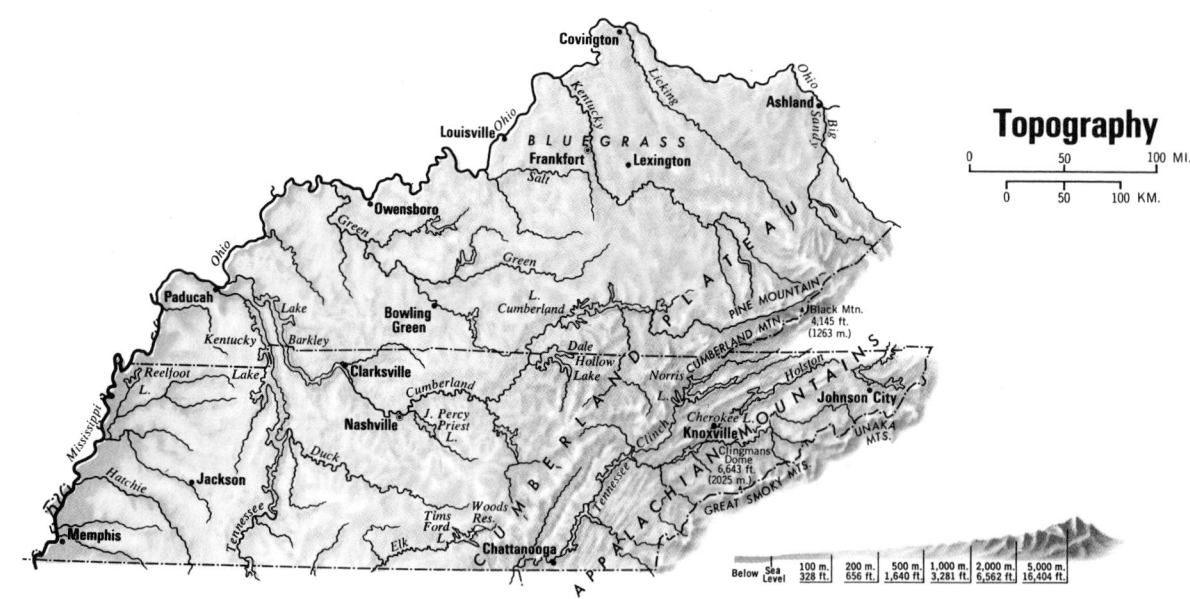

Topography

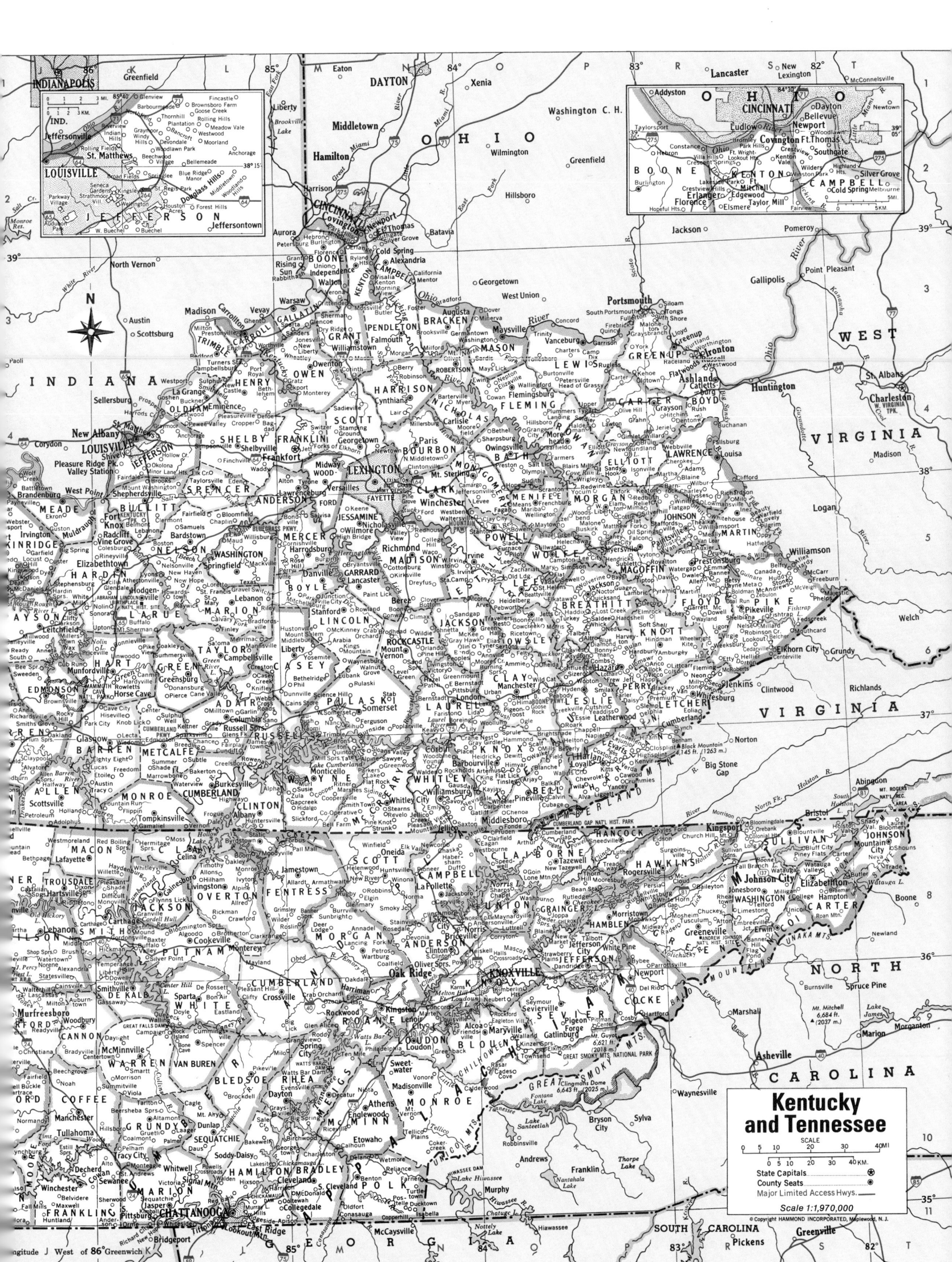

Kentucky
and Tennessee

SCALE
0 5 10   20   30   40 MI.
0 5 10   20   30   40 KM.
State Capitals............................⊛
County Seats.............................⊙
Major Limited Access Hwys._____

Scale 1:1,970,000

© Copyright HAMMOND INCORPORATED, Maplewood, N.J.

238 Louisiana

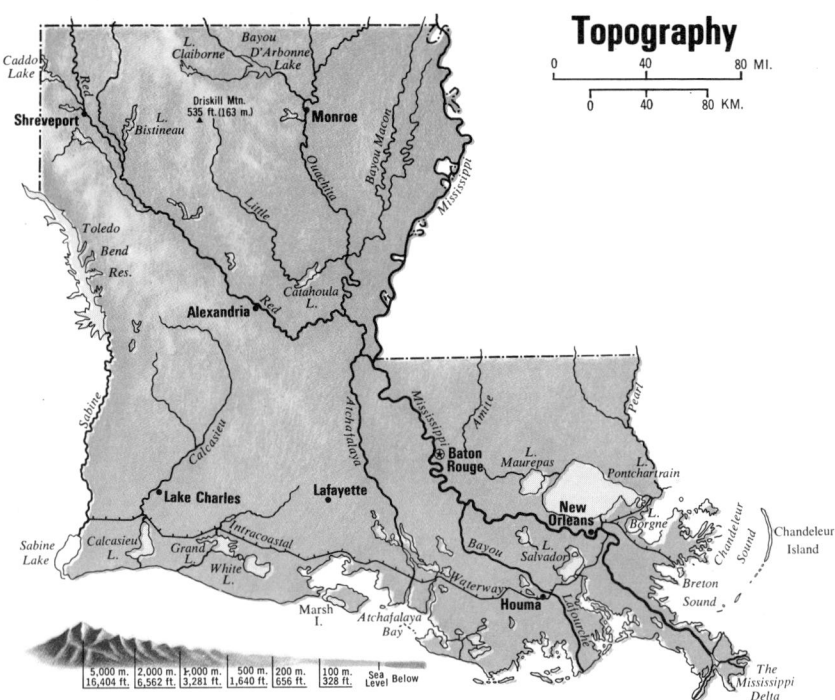

Topography

0 40 80 MI.

0 40 80 KM.

5,000 m.	2,000 m.	1,000 m.	500 m.	200 m.	100 m.	Sea
16,404 ft.	6,562 ft.	3,281 ft.	1,640 ft.	656 ft.	328 ft.	Level	Below

PARISHES

Acadia 56,427 .... F6
Allen 21,390 .... E5
Ascension 50,068 .... J6
Assumption 22,084 .... H7
Avoyelles 41,393 .... G4
Beauregard 29,692 .... D5
Bienville 16,387 .... D2
Bossier 80,721 .... C1
Caddo 252,358 .... C1
Calcasieu 167,223 .... D6
Caldwell 10,761 .... F2
Cameron 9,336 .... D7
Catahoula 12,287 .... G3
Claiborne 17,095 .... D1
Concordia 22,981 .... G4
De Soto 25,727 .... C2
East Baton Rouge 366,191 ... K1
East Carroll 11,772 .... H1
East Feliciana 19,015 .... H5
Evangeline 33,343 .... F5
Franklin 24,141 .... G2
Grant 16,703 .... E3
Iberia 63,752 .... G7
Iberville 32,159 .... H6
Jackson 17,321 .... E2
Jefferson 454,592 .... K7
Jefferson Davis 32,168 ...... E6
Lafayette 150,017 .... F6
Lafourche 82,483 .... K7
La Salle 17,004 .... F3
Lincoln 39,763 .... E1
Livingston 58,806 .... L2
Madison 15,975 .... H2
Morehouse 34,803 .... G1
Natchitoches 39,863 .... D3
Orleans 557,515 .... L6
Ouachita 139,241 .... F2
Plaquemines 26,049 .... L8
Pointe Coupee 24,045 ...... G5
Rapides 135,282 .... E4
Red River 10,433 .... D2
Richland 22,187 .... G2
Sabine 25,280 .... C3
Saint Bernard 64,097 .... L7
Saint Charles 37,259 .... K7
Saint Helena 9,827 .... J5
Saint James 21,495 .... L3
Saint John the Baptist 31,924 .. M3
Saint Landry 84,128 .... F5
Saint Martin 40,214 .... G6
Saint Mary 64,253 .... H7
Saint Tammany 110,869 .... L6
Tangipahoa 80,698 .... K5
Tensas 8,525 .... H2
Terrebonne 94,393 .... J8
Union 21,167 .... F1
Vermilion 48,458 .... F7
Vernon 53,475 .... D4
Washington 44,207 .... K5
Webster 43,631 .... D1
West Baton Rouge 19,086 ... H6
West Carroll 12,922 .... H1
West Feliciana 12,186 ...... H5
Winn 17,253 .... E3

CITIES and TOWNS

Zip	Name/Pop.	Key
70510	Abbeville⊙ 12,391	F7
70420	Abita Springs 1,072	L6
71316	Acme 235	G4
70710	Addis 1,320	J2
71401	Aimwell 55	G3
70421	Akers 150	N2

70711	Albany 857	M1
71301	Alexandria⊙ 51,565	E4
	Alexandria‡ 151,985	E4
†70458	Alton 500	L6
70340	Amelia 3,617	H7
70422	Amite⊙ 4,301	K5
71403	Anacoco 820	D4
70426	Angie 311	L5
70712	Angola 600	G5
70032	Arabi 10,248	P4
71001	Arcadia⊙ 3,403	E1
71218	Archibald 425	G2
70512	Arnaudville 1,679	G6
71002	Ashland 307	D2
71003	Athens 419	E1
71404	Atlanta 127	E3
70513	Avery Island 500	G7
70714	Baker 12,865	K1
70514	Baldwin 2,644	H7
71405	Ball 3,405	F4
70401	Baptist 150	M1
70036	Baratara 1,123	K7
70515	Basile 2,635	E5
71219	Baskin 286	G2
71220	Bastrop⊙ 15,527	G1
70715	Batchelor 500	G5
*70801	Baton Rouge (cap.)⊙ 219,419	K2
	Baton Rouge‡ 493,973	K2
†70360	Bayou Cane 15,723	J7
†70380	Bayou Vista 5,805	H7
71004	Belcher 436	C1
70630	Bell City 400	D6
70037	Belle Chasse 5,412	O4
71406	Belmont 350	C3
71407	Bentley 120	E3
71006	Benton⊙ 1,864	C1
†70558	Bermuda 50	D3
71222	Bernice 1,956	E1
70342	Berwick 4,466	H7
71007	Bethany 300	B2
71008	Bienville 249	D2
71009	Blanchard 1,128	C1
70427	Bogalusa 16,976	L5
†71064	Bolinger 200	C1
71223	Bonita 503	G1
71320	Bordelonville 350	G4
70343	Bourg 2,073	J7
71409	Boyce 1,198	E4
70040	Braithwaite 350	P4
70516	Branch 200	F6
70517	Breaux Bridge 5,922	G6
70718	Brittany 475	L3
70518	Broussard 2,923	F6
70719	Brusly 1,762	J2
71014	Bryceland 94	E2
71321	Buckeye 280	F4
71322	Bunkie 5,364	F5
70041	Buras-Triumph 4,137	L8
70519	Cade 175	G6
71225	Calhoun 352	F2
71410	Calvin 263	E3
70631	Cameron⊙ 1,736	D7
71411	Campti 1,069	D3
†70584	Cankton 303	F6
70520	Carencro 3,712	G6
70042	Carlisle 975	L7
70721	Carville 1,037	K3
71015	Caspiana 50	C2
71016	Castor 195	D2
70522	Centerville 600	H7
70043	Chalmette⊙ 33,847	P4
†70767	Chamberlin 20	J1
71324	Chase 200	G2
70524	Chataignier 431	F5

71226	Chatham 714	F2
70344	Chauvin 3,338	J8
71325	Cheneyville 865	F4
71412	Chopin 175	E4
71227	Choudrant 809	F1
70525	Church Point 4,599	F6
71414	Clarence 612	E3
71415	Clarks 931	F2
71326	Clayton 1,204	H3
70722	Clinton⊙ 1,919	J5
71416	Cloutierville 100	E3
71417	Colfax⊙ 1,680	E3
71229	Collinston 439	G1
71418	Columbia⊙ 687	F2
70723	Convent⊙ 400	L3
71419	Converse 449	C3
†71107	Cooper Road	C1
71327	Cottonport 1,911	F5
71018	Cotton Valley 1,445	D1
71019	Coushatta⊙ 2,084	D2
70433	Covington⊙ 7,892	K5
†70510	Cow Island 200	F7
71656	Cravens 200	E5
71020	Creston 135	E3
70526	Crowley⊙ 16,036	F6
71230	Crowville 400	G2
71021	Cullen 1,869	D1
70345	Cut Off 5,049	K7
71420	Cypress 55	D3
70046	Davant 600	L7
70528	Delcambre 2,216	G7
71232	Delhi 3,290	H2
71233	Delta 295	J2
70726	Denham Springs 8,563	L2
70633	De Quincy 3,966	D6
70634	De Ridder⊙ 11,057	D5
71421	Derry 75	E3
70030	Des Allemands 2,920	N4
70047	Destrehan 2,382	N4
†71055	Dixie Inn 453	D1
71422	Dodson 469	E2
70346	Donaldsonville⊙ 7,901	K3
70352	Donner 500	J7
71234	Downsville 213	F1
71023	Doyline 801	D1
70637	Dry Creek 300	D5
71423	Dry Prong 526	E3
71235	Dubach 1,161	E1
71024	Dubberly 421	D1
70353	Dulac 675	J8
71236	Dunn 245	G2
70728	Duplessis 500	K2
70529	Duson 1,253	F6
†71247	East Hodge 439	E2
71025	East Point 100	D2
71330	Echo 525	F4
70049	Edgard⊙ 400	M3
†71019	Edgefield 312	D2
71331	Effie 300	F4
70638	Elizabeth 454	E5
71424	Elmer 200	E4
71051	Elm Grove 100	C2
70532	Elton 1,450	E6
71425	Enterprise 375	G3
71332	Eola 47	F5
71237	Epps 672	G1
70533	Erath 2,133	F7
71238	Eros 158	F2
70534	Estherwood 691	F6
70730	Ethel 250	H5
70535	Eunice 12,479	F6
70639	Evans 500	D5
71333	Evergreen 272	F5
71240	Fairbanks 300	F1
71241	Farmerville⊙ 3,768	F1
70640	Fenton 491	E6

(continued)

Louisiana

SCALE

0 5 10 20 30 40 MI.

0 5 10 20 30 40 KM.

State Capitals .... ⊛
Parish Seats .... ⊙
Canals ....
Major Limited Access Hwys. ━━━

Scale 1:2,000,000

AREA 47,752 sq. mi. (123,678 sq. km.)
POPULATION 4,206,312
CAPITAL Baton Rouge
LARGEST CITY New Orleans
HIGHEST POINT Driskill Mtn. 535 ft. (163 m.)
SETTLED IN 1699
ADMITTED TO UNION April 30, 1812
POPULAR NAME Pelican State
STATE FLOWER Magnolia
STATE BIRD Eastern Brown Pelican

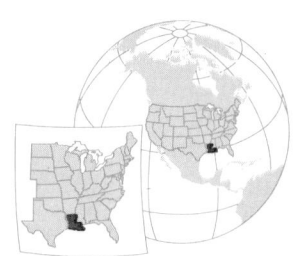

New Orleans, Baton Rouge and Vicinity

Longitude 91° West of Greenwich

© Copyright HAMMOND INCORPORATED, Maplewood, N.J.

(continued)

71334 Ferriday 4,472 G3
71426 Fisher 325 D4
71427 Flatwoods 360 E4
71428 Flora 300 D3
71429 Florien 964 D4
70436 Fluker 400 K5
70437 Folsom 319 K5
70732 Fordoche 676 G5
71242 Forest 299 H1
71430 Forest Hill 494 E4
70538 Franklin⊙ 9,584 G7
70438 Franklinton⊙ 4,119 K5
70733 French Settlement 761 L2
†71447 Galbraith 30 E4
70354 Galliano 5,159 K8
70540 Garden City 225 H7
70051 Garyville 2,856 M3
71432 Georgetown 381 F3
70355 Gheens 350 K7
71028 Gibsland 1,354 E1
71336 Gilbert 800 G2
71029 Gilliam 244 C1
71244 Girard 150 G2
71433 Glenmora 1,479 E5
71030 Gloster 780 C2
70736 Glynn 700 H5
70357 Golden Meadow 2,282 K8
71031 Goldonna 526 D2
70737 Gonzales 7,287 L2
†70079 Good Hope 500 N3
†71342 Good Pine-Trout 1,033 F3
71434 Gorum 150 E4
71338 Goudeau 25 G5
71245 Grambling 4,226 E1
70052 Gramercy 3,211 M3
71032 Grand Cane 252 C2
70541 Grand Coteau 1,165 G6
70358 Grand Isle 1,982 L8
70644 Grant 225 E5
71435 Grayson 564 F2
70441 Greensburg⊙ 662 J5
70739 Greenwell Springs 350 K1
71033 Greenwood 1,043 B2
70053 Gretna⊙ 20,615 O4
70740 Grosse Tete 749 G6
70542 Gueydan 1,695 E6
70057 Hahnville⊙ 2,947 N4
71034 Hall Summit 276 D2
70401 Hammond 15,043 N1
71035 Hanna 138 D3
70123 Harahan 11,384 O4
71340 Harrisonburg⊙ 610 G3
70058 Harvey 22,709 O4
71037 Haughton 1,510 C1
†71446 Hawthorn 400 D4
70646 Hayes 600 E6
71038 Haynesville 3,454 D1
71039 Heflin 279 D2
†70517 Henderson 1,560 G6
71341 Hessmer 743 F4
70743 Hester 250 L3
71437 Hicks 379 E4
71438 Hineston 400 E4
71247 Hodge 708 E2
70744 Holden 600 M1
71248 Holly Ridge 100 G2
71040 Homer⊙ 4,307 D1
71439 Hornbeck 470 D4
71043 Hosston 480 C1
70360 Houma⊙ 32,602 J7
70746 Iberville 367 K2
71044 Ida 306 C1
70443 Independence 1,684 M1
70747 Innis 200 G5
70543 Iota 1,326 E6
70647 Iowa 2,437 D6
†70427 Isabel 550 K5
70748 Jackson 3,133 H5
71045 Jamestown 131 D2
70544 Jeanerette 6,511 G7
†70067 Jean Lafitte 936 K7
70121 Jefferson 15,550 O4
71342 Jena⊙ 4,375 F3
70546 Jennings⊙ 12,401 E6
71249 Jigger 300 G2
71250 Jones 350 G1
71251 Jonesboro⊙ 5,061 E2
71343 Jonesville 2,828 G3
71749 Junction City 727 E1
70548 Kaplan 5,016 F6
71046 Keatchie 342 C2
71441 Kelly 325 F3
70062 Kenner 66,382 N4
70444 Kentwood 2,667 J5
71253 Kilbourne 286 H1
†70462 Killian 611 M2
70066 Killona 950 M3
70648 Kinder 2,603 E6
70371 Kraemer 350 M4
70750 Krotz Springs 1,374 G5
71443 Kurthwood 65 D4
70372 Labadieville 2,138 K4
71444 Lacamp 150 E4
70650 Lacassine 400 E6
70445 Lacombe 5,146 L6
*70501 Lafayette⊙ 81,961 F6
Lafayette‡ 150,017 F6
70067 Lafitte 1,312 K7
70549 Lake Arthur 3,615 E6
*70601 Lake Charles⊙ 75,226 D6
Lake Charles‡ 167,048 D6
70752 Lakeland 800 H5
71254 Lake Providence⊙ 6,361 H1
70068 La Place 16,112 N3
70373 Larose 5,234 K7
71344 Larto 500 G4
70550 Lawtell 1,014 F5
71445 Leander 145 E4
71345 Lebeau 200 F5
70651 Le Blanc 400 E5
71346 Lecompte 1,661 F4
71446 Leesville⊙ 9,054 D4
71447 Lena 300 E4
70551 Leonville 1,143 G6
†71008 Liberty Hill 50 E2
71348 Libuse 500 F4
71256 Lillie 172 E1

Agriculture, Industry and Resources

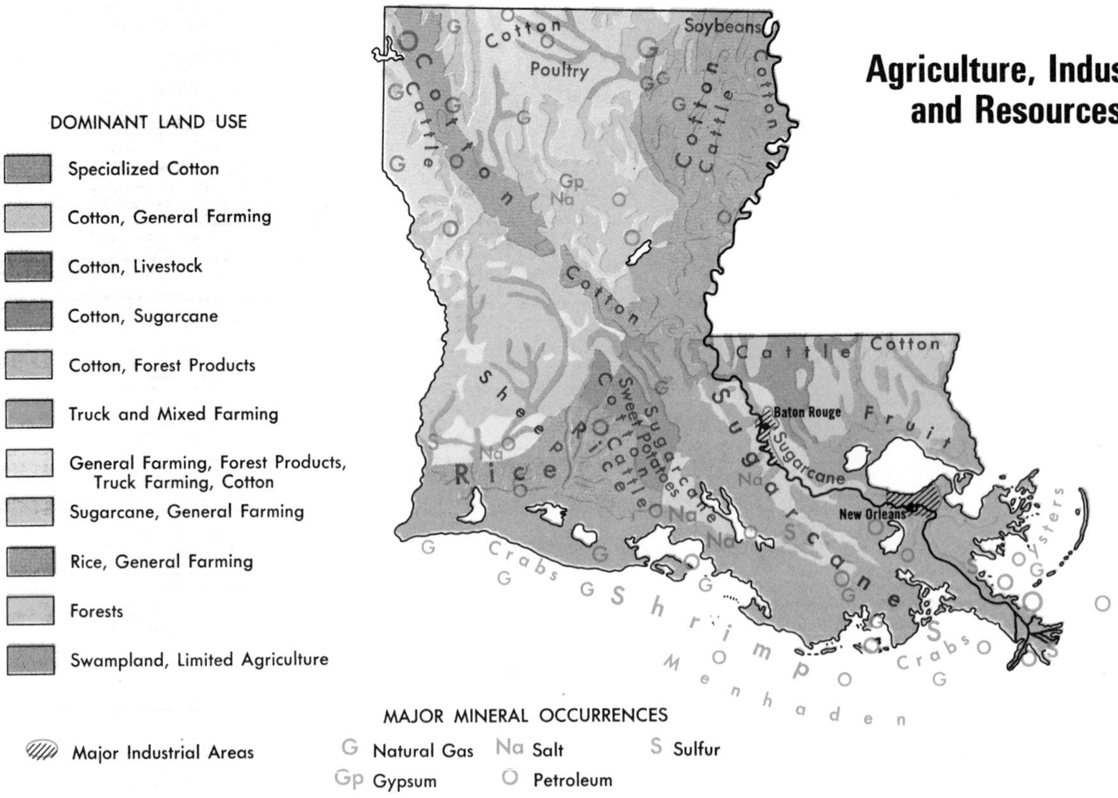

DOMINANT LAND USE
Specialized Cotton
Cotton, General Farming
Cotton, Livestock
Cotton, Sugarcane
Cotton, Forest Products
Truck and Mixed Farming
General Farming, Forest Products, Truck Farming, Cotton
Sugarcane, General Farming
Rice, General Farming
Forests
Swampland, Limited Agriculture
Major Industrial Areas
MAJOR MINERAL OCCURRENCES
G Natural Gas
Gp Gypsum
Na Salt
O Petroleum
S Sulfur
Soybeans
Cotton
Poultry
Cattle
Baton Rouge
New Orleans
Fruit
Sugarcane
Sweet Potatoes
Sheep
Rice
Crabs
Shrimp
Menhaden
Oysters

71257 Linville 150 F1
71048 Lisbon 138 E1
70754 Livingston⊙ 1,260 L1
70755 Livonia 980 G5
†70767 Lobdell 200 J1
70374 Lockport 2,424 K7
71049 Logansport 1,565 C3
71448 Longleaf 80 E4
71050 Longstreet 281 B2
70652 Longville 300 D5
70446 Loranger 250 N1
70552 Loreauville 860 G6
70756 Lottie 400 G5
†71008 Lucky 370 E2
70070 Luling 4,006 N4
70071 Lutcher 4,730 L3
70447 Madisonville 799 K6
70554 Mamou 3,194 F5
70448 Mandeville 6,076 L6
71259 Mangham 867 G2
71052 Mansfield⊙ 6,485 C2
71350 Mansura 2,074 G4
71449 Many⊙ 3,988 C3
70757 Maringouin 1,291 G6
71260 Marion 989 F1
71351 Marksville⊙ 5,113 G4
70072 Marrero 36,548 O4
†71019 Martin 584 D2
70555 Maurice 478 F6
†71433 McNary 240 E5
71346 Meeker 50 F4
71451 Melder 150 E4
71452 Melrose 500 E3
71353 Melville 1,764 G5
70556 Mermentau 771 E6
71261 Mer Rouge 802 G1
70653 Merryville 1,286 D5
*70001 Metairie 164,160 O4
70557 Midland 560 F6
70558 Milton 450 F6
†70070 Mimosa Park 3,737 N4
71055 Minden⊙ 15,074 D1
71059 Mira 354 C1
71453 Mitchell 155 C3
70376 Modeste 225 K3
*71201 Monroe⊙ 57,597 F1
Monroe‡ 139,241 F1
71454 Montgomery 843 E3
†70422 Montpelier 219 M1
71060 Mooringsport 911 B1
71455 Mora 427 E4
71355 Moreauville 853 G4
70380 Morgan City 16,114 H7
70759 Morganza 846 G5
71356 Morrow 600 F5
70559 Morse 835 F6
71262 Mound 40 H2
70450 Mount Hermon 170 K5
†71028 Mount Lebanon 105 D2
70390 Napoleonville⊙ 829 K4
70451 Natalbany 900 N1
71456 Natchez 527 D3
71457 Natchitoches⊙ 16,664 D3
71460 Negreet 400 C4
71357 Newellton 1,726 H2
70560 New Iberia⊙ 32,766 G6
71461 Newllano 2,213 D4
*70101 New Orleans⊙ 557,927 O4
New Orleans‡ 1,186,725 O4
70760 New Roads⊙ 3,924 G5

70078 New Sarpy 2,249 N4
71462 Noble 194 C3
70079 Norco 4,416 N3
†71247 North Hodge 573 E2
70761 Norwood 421 H5
71463 Oakdale 7,155 E5
71263 Oak Grove⊙ 2,214 H1
71264 Oak Ridge 257 G1
70655 Oberlin⊙ 1,764 E5
71061 Oil City 1,323 C1
71465 Olla 1,603 F3
70570 Opelousas⊙ 18,903 G5
70762 Oscar 650 H5
71466 Otis 400 E4
70391 Paincourtville 2,004 K3
71358 Palmetto 327 G5
70582 Parks 545 G6
70392 Patterson 4,693 H7
70452 Pearl River 1,693 L6
71063 Pelican 250 C3
70575 Perry 230 F7
70081 Pilottown 175 M8
70453 Pine Grove 570 J5
70576 Pine Prairie 734 E5
71360 Pineville 12,034 F4
71266 Pioneer 221 H1
70656 Pitkin 600 E5
71064 Plain Dealing 1,213 C1
70764 Plaquemine⊙ 7,521 J2
70393 Plattenville 205 K4
71362 Plaucheville 196 G5
71065 Pleasant Hill 776 C3
70082 Pointe a la Hache⊙ 750 L7
71467 Pollock 399 F3
70454 Ponchatoula 5,469 N2
70767 Port Allen⊙ 6,114 J2
70577 Port Barre 2,625 G5
70083 Port Sulphur 3,318 L8
†70726 Port Vincent 450 L2
71066 Powhatan 279 D3
71468 Provencal 695 D3
71268 Quitman 231 E2
70394 Raceland 6,302 J7
70578 Rayne 9,066 F6
71269 Rayville⊙ 4,610 G2
70580 Reddell 500 F5
70658 Reeves 199 D5
70084 Reserve 7,288 M3
†71282 Richmond 505 H2
†71201 Richwood 1,223 F2
†71334 Ridgecrest 895 G3
71068 Ringgold 1,655 D2
†70427 Rio 400 L5
70581 Roanoke 800 E6
71469 Robeline 238 D3
71069 Rodessa 337 B1
71364 Rosa 300 G5
70772 Rosedale 658 G6
70456 Roseland 1,346 J5
70659 Rosepine 953 D5
71365 Ruby 400 F4
71270 Ruston⊙ 20,585 E1
70457 Saint Benedict 190 K5
70775 Saint
Francisville⊙ 1,471 H5
71366 Saint Joseph⊙ 1,687 H3
71367 Saint Landry 550 F5
70582 Saint Martinville⊙ 7,965 G6
71471 Saint Maurice 560 E3
71070 Saline 293 E2

71071 Sarepta 831 D1
70807 Scotlandville 15,113 J1
70583 Scott 2,239 F6
†70764 Seymourville 2,891 J2
71072 Shongaloo 163 D1
*71101 Shreveport⊙ 205,820 C2
Shreveport‡ 376,646 C2
71073 Sibley 1,211 D1
71368 Sicily Island 691 G3
71472 Sieper 226 E4
71473 Sikes 226 F2
71369 Simmesport 2,293 G5
71474 Simpson 534 D4
71275 Simsboro 553 E1
70660 Singer 250 D5
71475 Slagle 650 D4
70777 Slaughter 729 H5
70458 Slidell 26,718 L6
71276 Sondheimer 225 H1
70778 Sorrento 1,197 L3
†71052 South Mansfield 1,463 C3
71277 Spearsville 181 E1
71278 Spencer 50 F1
70462 Springfield 424 M2
71075 Springhill 6,516 D1
†71049 Stanley 151 C3
71280 Sterlington 1,400 F1
71078 Stonewall 1,175 C2
70662 Sugartown 375 D5
70663 Sulphur 19,709 D6
70463 Sun 404 L5
70584 Sunset 2,300 F6
70464 Talisheek 315 L5
71282 Tallulah⊙ 11,634 H2
70465 Tangipahoa 493 J5
71080 Taylor 500 D1
71476 Temple 250 E4
71285 Terry 50 H1
†70053 Terry Town 23,548 O4
70397 Theriot 450 J8
70301 Thibodaux⊙ 15,810 J7
70466 Tickfaw 571 M1
71286 Transylvania 400 H1
71081 Trees 327 B1
†70041 Triumph-Buras 4,137 L8
71371 Trout-Good Pine 1,033 F3
71479 Tullos 776 F3
70782 Tunica 500 G5
70585 Turkey Creek 366 F5
71480 Urania 849 F3
70090 Vacherie 2,169 L3
70467 Varnado 249 L5
71481 Verda 100 E3
71373 Vidalia⊙ 5,936 G3
†71270 Vienna 519 E1
70586 Ville Platte⊙ 9,201 F5
70668 Vinton 3,631 C6
70092 Violet 11,678 P4
71082 Vivian 4,146 B1
†71418 Vixen 40 F2
70784 Wakefield 400 H5
†70433 Waldheim 25 L5
70785 Walker 2,957 L1
71289 Warden 130 H1
70589 Washington 1,266 G5
71375 Waterproof 1,339 H3
70786 Watson 800 L1
70591 Welsh 3,515 E6
70669 Westlake 5,246 D6
71291 West Monroe 14,993 F1

70094 Westwego 12,663 O4
70787 Weyanoke 500 H5
70788 White Castle 2,160 J3
†71371 White Sulphur Springs 50 F3
71376 Whiteville 150 F5
71377 Wildsville 800 G3
†70040 Wills Point 150 L7
70789 Wilson 656 H5
71483 Winnfield⊙ 7,311 E3
71295 Winnsboro⊙ 5,921 G2
71378 Wisner 1,424 G3
71485 Woodworth 412 E4
70592 Youngsville 1,053 G6
70791 Zachary 7,297 K1
†71371 Zenoria 76 F3
†71409 Zimmerman 20 E4
71486 Zwolle 2,602 C3

OTHER FEATURES

Allemands (lake) M4
Alligator (pt.) L6
Amite (riv.) L2
Anacoco (lake) D4
Atchafalaya (bay) H8
Atchafalaya (riv.) G6
Barataria (bay) L8
Barataria (passage) L8
Barksdale A.F.B. C2
Bayou D'Arbonne (lake) F1
Bird (isl.) M8
Bistineau (lake) D2
Black (lake) D3
Black Lake (bayou) D1
Boeuf (lake) J7
Boeuf (riv.) G1
Bonnet Carré Spillway and Floodway N3
Borgne (lake) L7
Boudreau (bay) M7
Boudreaux (lake) J8
Breton (isls.) M8
Breton (sound) M7
Bundick (lake) D5
Caddo (lake) B1
Caillou (bay) J8
Calcasieu (lake) D7
Calcasieu (passage) D7
Calcasieu (riv.) E5
Catahoula (lake) F4
Cataouatche (lake) N4
Cat Island (chan.) M6
Cat Island (passage) J8
Chandeleur (isls.) N7
Chandeleur (sound) M7
Chenier (lake) F2
Chicot (pt.) M7
Claiborne (lake) E1
Clear (lake) D3
Cocodrie (lake) E5
Cotile (lake) E4
Cross (lake) C2
Curlew (isls.) M7
Dernieres (isls.) J8
Door (pt.) M6
Driskill (mt.) E2
Drum (bay) M7
East (bay) M8
East Cote Blanche (bay) G7
Edwards (lake) C2
Eloi (bay) M7
England A.F.B. E4
Fields (lake) J7
Fort Polk 14,142 D4
Free Mason (isls.) M7
Garden Island (bay) M8
Grand (lake) E7
Grand (lake) H8
Grand Terre (isls.) L8
Iatt (lake) E3
Jean Lafitte Nat'l Hist. Park P4
Lafourche (bayou) K8
Little (riv.) F3
Louisiana (pt.) C7
Macon (bayou) H1
Main (passage) M8
Manchac (passage) N2
Marsh (isl.) G7
Maurepas (lake) M2
Mermentau (riv.) E7
Mexico (gulf) F8
Mississippi (delta) M8
Mississippi (riv.) H3
Mississippi (sound) M6
Mississippi River Gulf Outlet (canal) L7
Mozambique (pt.) M7
Mud (lake) D7
Naval Air Sta. O4
North (isls.) M7
North (pass) N8
North (pt.) M7
Northeast (pass) M8
Ouachita (riv.) F1
Palourde (lake) H7
Pearl (riv.) L5
Point au Fer (isl.) H8
Point au Fer (pt.) H8
Pontchartrain (lake) O3
Pontchartrain Causeway O3
Raccoon (pt.) H8
Red (riv.) G4
Sabine (lake) C7
Sabine (passage) C7
Sabine (riv.) C5
Saline (lake) E3
Salvador (lake) K7
Smithport (lake) C2
South (pass) M8
South (pt.) G8
Southeast (pass) M8
Southwest (pass) L8
Tangipahoa (riv.) N1
Tensas (riv.) G3
Terrebonne (bay) J8
Tickfaw (riv.) M1
Timbalier (bay) K8
Timbalier (isl.) K8
Toledo Bend (res.) C3
Turkey Creek (lake) G3
Vermilion (bay) F7
Vernon (lake) D4
Verret (lake) H7
Wallace (lake) C2
West (bay) M8
West Cote Blanche (bay) G7
White (lake) E7

⊙Parish seat.
‡Population of metropolitan area.
† Zip of nearest p.o. * Multiple zips.

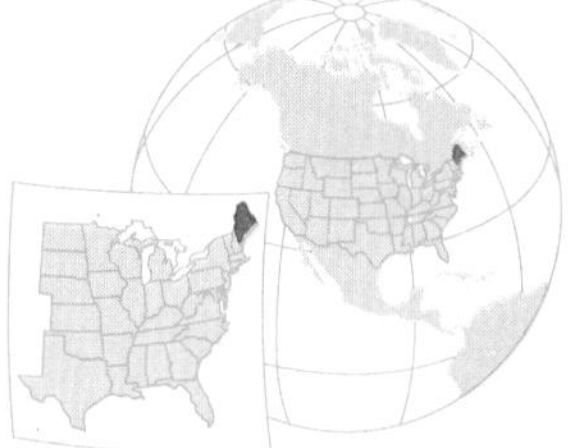

AREA 33,265 sq. mi. (86,156 sq. km.)
POPULATION 1,125,027
CAPITAL Augusta
LARGEST POINT Portland
HIGHEST POINT Katahdin 5,268 ft. (1606 m.)
SETTLED IN 1624
ADMITTED TO UNION March 15, 1820
POPULAR NAME Pine Tree State
STATE FLOWER White Pine Cone & Tassel
STATE BIRD Chickadee

COUNTIES

County	Key
Androscoggin 99,657	C7
Aroostook 91,331	F2
Cumberland 215,789	C8
Franklin 27,098	B5
Hancock 41,781	G6
Kennebec 109,889	D7
Knox 32,941	E7
Lincoln 25,691	D7
Oxford 48,968	B7
Penobscot 137,015	F5
Piscataquis 17,634	E4
Sagadahoc 28,795	D7
Somerset 45,028	C4
Waldo 28,414	E6
Washington 34,963	H6
York 139,666	B9

CITIES and TOWNS

Zip	Name/Pop.	Key
04406	Abbot Village○ 576	D5
04001	Acton○ 1,228	B8
04606	Addison○ 1,061	H6
04910	Albion○ 1,551	E6
†04610	Alexander○ 385	H5
04002	Alfred○ 1,890	B9
†04774	Allagash○ 448	F1
†04938	Allens Mills 100	C6
04535	Alna○ 425	D7
†04468	Alton○ 468	F5
†04408	Amherst○ 203	G6
04216	Andover○ 850	B6
04911	Anson○ 2,226	D6
†04862	Appleton○ 818	E7
†04468	Argyle 225	F5
04732	Ashland○ 1,865	G2
04607	Ashville 36	G7
04912	Athens○ 802	D6
†04426	Atkinson○ 306	E5
04608	Atlantic 120	G7
04210	Auburn⊙ 23,128	C7
04330	Augusta (cap.)⊙ 21,819	D7
04408	Aurora○ 110	G6
04003	Bailey Island 500	D8
†04497	Bancroft○ 61	H4
04401	Bangor⊙ 31,643	F6
	Bangor‡ 83,919	F6
04609	Bar Harbor○ 4,124	G7
04609	Bar Harbor 2,685	G7
†04619	Baring○ 308	J5
04004	Bar Mills 800	C8
04653	Bass Harbor 450	G7
04530	Bath⊙ 10,246	D8
†04915	Bayside	F7
04611	Beals○ 695	H7
†04622	Beddington○ 36	H6
04915	Belfast⊙ 6,243	F7
04917	Belgrade○ 2,043	D7
†04915	Belmont○ 520	E7
04733	Benedicta○ 225	G4
†04937	Benton○ 2,188	D6
03901	Berwick○ 4,149	B9
03901	Berwick 2,378	B9
04217	Bethel○ 2,340	B7
04005	Biddeford 19,638	B9
04920	Bingham○ 1,184	D5
04920	Bingham 1,074	D5
04613	Birch Harbor 300	H7
04734	Blaine○ 922	H2
04734	Blaine-Mars Hill 1,921	H2
04614	Blue Hill○ 1,644	F7
04615	Blue Hill Falls 135	F7
04537	Boothbay○ 2,308	D8
04538	Boothbay Harbor 2,207	D8
04008	Bowdoinham○ 1,828	D7
†04481	Bowerbank○ 27	E5
04410	Bradford○ 888	F5
†04410	Bradford Center 105	F5
04411	Bradley○ 1,149	F6
04412	Brewer 9,017	F6
04735	Bridgewater○ 742	H3
04009	Bridgton○ 3,528	B7
04009	Bridgton 1,639	B7
†04990	Brighton○ 74	D5
04539	Bristol○ 2,095	D8
04616	Brooklin○ 619	F7
04921	Brooks○ 804	E6
04617	Brooksville○ 753	F7
04413	Brookton 175	H4
04010	Brownfield○ 767	B8
04414	Brownville○ 1,545	E5
04011	Brunswick○ 17,366	C8
04011	Brunswick 10,990	C8
04219	Bryant Pond 600	B7
†04232	Buckfield○ 1,333	C7
04618	Bucks Harbor 300	J6
04416	Bucksport○ 4,345	F6
04416	Bucksport 2,853	F6
04540	Burkettville 120	E7
04417	Burlington○ 322	G5
04922	Burnham○ 951	E6
†04093	Buxton○ 5,775	C8
†04275	Byron○ 114	B6
04619	Calais 4,262	J5
04923	Cambridge○ 445	E5
04843	Camden○ 4,584	F7
04843	Camden 3,743	F7
04924	Canaan○ 1,189	D6
04221	Canton○ 831	C7
03902	Cape Neddick 850	B9
04014	Cape Porpoise 500	C9
04736	Caribou 9,916	G2
04419	Carmel○ 1,695	E6
†04947	Carrabassett Valley○ 107	C5
†04487	Carroll○ 175	G5
†04224	Carthage○ 438	C6
†04465	Cary○ 229	H4
04015	Casco○ 2,243	B7
04421	Castine○ 1,304	F7
†04941	Center Montville 16	E7
†04623	Centerville○ 28	H6
†04757	Chapman○ 406	G2
04422	Charleston○ 1,037	F5
†04666	Charlotte○ 300	J5
04017	Chebeague Island 900	C8
†04345	Chelsea○ 2,522	D7
04622	Cherryfield○ 983	H6
†04458	Chester○ 434	F5
†04938	Chesterville○ 869	C6
†04478	Chesuncook 6	D3
04926	China○ 2,918	E7
†04239	Chisholm 1,796	C7
†04428	Clifton○ 462	G6
04927	Clinton○ 2,696	D6
04927	Clinton 1,305	D6
†04623	Columbia○ 275	H6
04623	Columbia Falls○ 517	H6
†04638	Cooper○ 105	H6
04624	Corea 375	H7
04928	Corinna○ 1,887	E6
04020	Cornish○ 1,047	B8
†04976	Cornville○ 838	D6
04625	Cranberry Isles○ 198	G7
†04610	Crawford○ 86	H5
†04015	Crescent Lake 325	C7
†04851	Criehaven 5	F8
04738	Crouseville 450	G2
†04747	Crystal○ 349	G4
04021	Cumberland Center○ 5,284	C8
04021	Cumberland Center 2,015	C8
04563	Cushing○ 795	E7
04626	Cutler○ 726	J6
04543	Damariscotta○ 1,493	E7
04543	Damariscotta-Newcastle 1,411	E7
04424	Danforth○ 826	H4
†04622	Deblois○ 44	H6
†04429	Dedham○ 841	F6
04627	Deer Isle○ 1,492	F7
04022	Denmark○ 672	B8
04628	Dennysville○ 296	J6
04929	Detroit○ 744	E6
04930	Dexter○ 4,286	E5
04930	Dexter 3,118	E5
04224	Dixfield○ 2,389	C6
04224	Dixfield 1,725	C6
04932	Dixmont○ 812	E6
04426	Dover-Foxcroft○ 4,323	E5
04426	Dover-Foxcroft⊙ 2,974	E5
†04426	Dover South Mills 54	E5
04342	Dresden○ 998	D7
†04747	Dyer Brook○ 275	G3
04739	Eagle Lake○ 1,019	F1
04226	East Andover 250	B6
04544	East Boothbay 800	D8
04427	East Corinth 525	F5
04227	East Dixfield 250	C6
04429	East Holden 600	F6
04027	East Lebanon 950	B9
04228	East Livermore 500	C7
04630	East Machias○ 1,233	J6
04430	East Millinocket○ 2,372	F4
04430	East Millinocket 2,361	F4
04740	Easton○ 1,305	H2
04028	East Parsonfield 400	B8
04229	East Peru 200	C7
†04210	East Poland 200	C7
04631	Eastport 1,982	K6
04231	East Stoneham 300	B7
†04607	East Sullivan 496	G6
†04220	East Sumner 120	C7
†04862	East Union 75	E7
†04428	Eddington○ 1,769	F6
†04556	Edgecomb○ 841	D8
03903	Eliot○ 4,948	B9
04605	Ellsworth⊙ 5,179	F6
04031	Emery Mills 100	B8
04433	Enfield○ 1,397	F5
04434	Etna○ 758	E6
04936	Eustis○ 582	B5
04435	Exeter○ 823	E6
†04938	Fairbanks 400	C6
04937	Fairfield○ 6,113	D6
04937	Fairfield 3,169	D6
04105	Falmouth○ 6,853	C8
04105	Falmouth 1,655	C8
†04345	Farmingdale○ 2,535	D7
†04345	Farmingdale 2,014	D7
04938	Farmington○ 6,730	C6
04938	Farmington⊙ 3,583	C6
04940	Farmington Falls 500	C6
†04349	Fayette○ 812	C7
04546	Five Islands 225	D8
04742	Fort Fairfield○ 4,376	H2
04742	Fort Fairfield 2,282	H2
04743	Fort Kent○ 4,826	F1
04743	Fort Kent 2,375	F1
04744	Fort Kent Mills 200	F1
04438	Frankfort○ 783	F6
04634	Franklin○ 979	G6
04941	Freedom○ 458	E7
04032	Freeport○ 5,863	C8
04032	Freeport 1,906	C8
04635	Frenchboro○ 43	G7
04745	Frenchville○ 1,450	G1
04547	Friendship○ 1,000	E7
04037	Fryeburg○ 2,715	A7
04037	Fryeburg 1,644	A7
04345	Gardiner 6,485	D7
04939	Garland○ 718	E5
04548	Georgetown○ 735	D8
†04217	Gilead○ 191	B7
†04401	Glenburn○ 2,319	F6
04846	Glen Cove 250	E7
04038	Gorham○ 10,101	C8
04038	Gorham 4,052	C8
†04607	Gouldsboro○ 1,574	H7
04746	Grand Isle○ 719	G1
04637	Grand Lake Stream○ 198	H5
04039	Gray○ 4,344	C8
†04408	Great Pond○ 45	G6
04236	Greene○ 3,037	C7
04441	Greenville○ 1,839	D5
04441	Greenville 1,640	D5
04442	Greenville Junction 650	D5
04443	Guilford○ 1,793	E5
04443	Guilford 1,235	E5
04347	Hallowell 2,502	D7
†04785	Hamlin○ 340	H1
04444	Hampden○ 5,250	F6
04444	Hampden 3,538	F6
04445	Hampden Highlands 950	F6
04640	Hancock○ 1,409	G6
04237	Hanover○ 256	B7
04942	Harmony○ 755	D6
†04011	Harpswell○ 3,796	D8
04643	Harrington○ 859	H6
04040	Harrison○ 1,667	B7
†04221	Hartford○ 480	C7
04943	Hartland○ 1,669	D6
04943	Hartland 1,041	D6
04446	Haynesville○ 169	G4
04238	Hebron○ 665	C7
†04401	Hermon○ 3,170	F6
04944	Hinckley 140	D6
04041	Hiram○ 1,067	B8
†04730	Hodgdon○ 1,084	H3
04042	Hollis Center○ 2,892	B8
04847	Hope○ 730	E7
04730	Houlton○ 6,766	H3
04730	Houlton⊙ 5,730	H3
04448	Howland○ 1,602	F5
04448	Howland 1,502	F5
04449	Hudson○ 797	F5
04644	Hulls Cove 200	G7
04747	Island Falls○ 981	G3
04645	Isle Au Haut○ 57	F7
04848	Islesboro○ 521	F7
04945	Jackman○ 1,003	C4
†04630	Jacksonville 200	J6
04239	Jay○ 5,080	C7
04348	Jefferson○ 1,616	D7
04648	Jonesboro○ 553	J6
04649	Jonesport○ 1,512	H6
04649	Jonesport 1,050	H6
04450	Kenduskeag○ 1,210	E6
04043	Kennebunk○ 6,621	B9
04043	Kennebunk 3,294	B9
†04043	Kennebunk Beach 200	C9
04046	Kennebunkport○ 2,952	C9
04046	Kennebunkport 1,685	C9
04349	Kents Hill 300	D7
04947	Kingfield○ 1,083	C6
04451	Kingman 281	G4
†04990	Kingsbury○ 4	D5
03904	Kittery○ 9,314	B9
03904	Kittery 5,465	B9
03905	Kittery Point 1,260	B9
†04986	Knox○ 558	E6
04453	La Grange○ 509	F5
†04463	Lake View○ 20	F5
†04605	Lamoine○ 953	G7
04455	Lee○ 688	G5
†04263	Leeds○ 1,463	C7
04456	Levant○ 1,117	F6
04240	Lewiston 40,481	C7
	Lewiston-Auburn‡ 72,378	C7
04949	Liberty○ 694	E7
04749	Lille 300	G1
04048	Limerick○ 1,356	B8
04750	Limestone○ 8,719	H2
04750	Limestone 1,334	H2
04049	Limington○ 2,203	B8
04457	Lincoln○ 5,066	G5
04457	Lincoln 3,524	G5
04849	Lincolnville○ 1,414	E7
04850	Lincolnville Center 200	E7
†04730	Linneus○ 752	H3
04250	Lisbon○ 8,769	C7
04250	Lisbon-Lisbon Center 1,865	C7
04252	Lisbon Falls 4,370	D7
04350	Litchfield○ 1,954	D7
†04627	Little Deer Isle 475	F7
04082	Little Falls-South Windham 1,366	C8
†04760	Littleton○ 1,009	H3
04253	Livermore○ 1,826	C7
04254	Livermore Falls○ 3,572	C7
04254	Livermore Falls 2,441	C7
04255	Locke Mills 600	B7
04051	Lovell○ 767	B7
†04433	Lowell○ 194	F5
04652	Lubec○ 2,045	K6
†04730	Ludlow○ 403	G3
04654	Machias○ 2,458	J6
04654	Machias⊙ 1,277	J6
04655	Machiasport○ 1,108	H6
†04451	Macwahoc○ 126	G4
04756	Madawaska○ 5,282	G1
04756	Madawaska 4,165	G1
04950	Madison○ 4,367	D6
04950	Madison 2,788	D6
†04966	Madrid○ 178	B6
†04942	Mainstream 100	D6
04351	Manchester○ 1,949	D7
04757	Mapleton○ 1,895	G2
04758	Mars Hill○ 1,892	H2
04758	Mars Hill-Blaine 1,921	H2
04759	Masardis○ 328	G3
04851	Matinicus 66	F8
04459	Mattawamkeag○ 1,000	G5
04256	Mechanic Falls○ 2,616	C7
04256	Mechanic Falls 2,198	C7
04657	Meddybemps○ 110	J5
†04453	Medford○ 163	F5
†04453	Medford Center 100	F5
04460	Medway○ 1,871	G4
04957	Mercer○ 448	D6
04257	Mexico○ 3,698	B6
04257	Mexico 3,207	B6
†04216	Middledam 10	B6
04658	Milbridge○ 1,306	H6
04461	Milford○ 2,160	F6
04461	Milford 1,688	F6
04462	Millinocket○ 7,567	F4

(continued on following page)

Agriculture, Industry and Resources

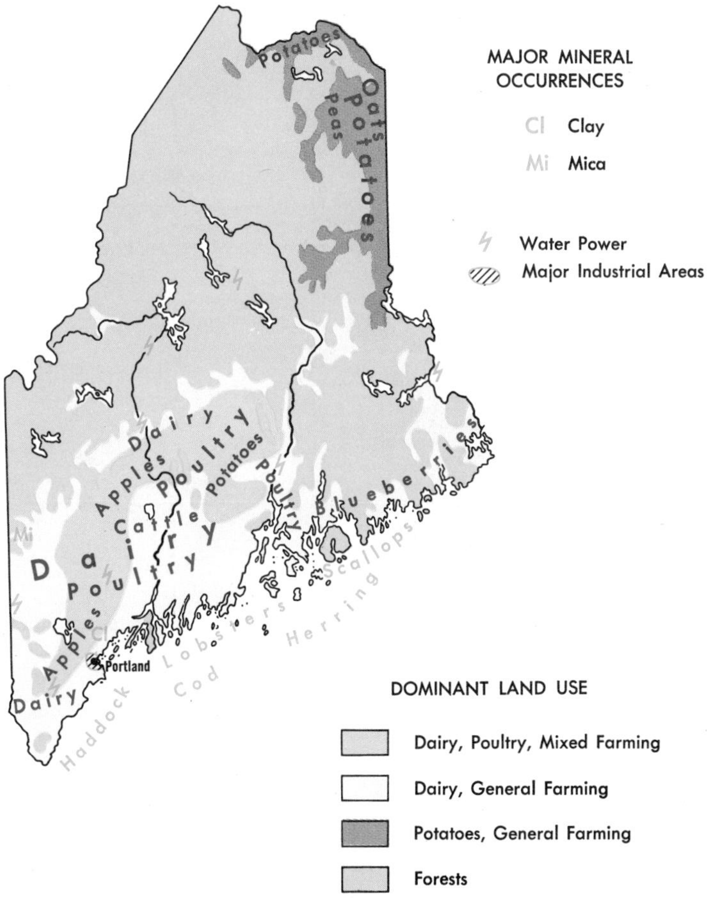
Potatoes
Oats
Peas
Potatoes
Dairy
Poultry
Potatoes
Apples
Cattle
Poultry
Blueberries
Dairy
Poultry
Apples
Dairy
Portland
Lobsters
Scallops
Herring
Cod
Haddock
MAJOR MINERAL OCCURRENCES
Cl Clay
Mi Mica
Water Power
Major Industrial Areas
DOMINANT LAND USE
Dairy, Poultry, Mixed Farming
Dairy, General Farming
Potatoes, General Farming
Forests

(continued)

04463 Milo○ 2,624 .... F5
04463 Milo 2,255 .... F5
04258 Minot○ 1,631 .... C7
04659 Minturn 150 .... G7
†04776 Monarda 100 .... G4
04852 Monhegan○ 109 .... E8
04259 Monmouth○ 2,888 .... D7
04951 Monroe○ 657 .... E6
04464 Monson○ 804 .... E5
04760 Monticello○ 950 .... H3
†04941 Montville○ 631 .... E7
04054 Moody 500 .... B9
†04478 Moosehead 6 .... D4
†04945 Moose River○ 252 .... C4
04952 Morrill○ 506 .... E7
04660 Mount Desert○ 2,063 .... G7
04352 Mount Vernon○ 1,021 .... D7
04055 Naples○ 1,833 .... B8
04552 Newagen 100 .... D8
†04445 Newburgh○ 1,228 .... F6
04553 Newcastle○ 1,227 .... D7
04553 Newcastle-Damariscotta 1,411 .... E7
04056 Newfield○ 644 .... B8
04260 New Gloucester○ 3,180 .... C8
04554 New Harbor 850 .... E8
04761 New Limerick○ 513 .... G3
04953 Newport○ 2,755 .... E6
04953 Newport 1,748 .... E6
04954 New Portland○ 651 .... C6
04261 Newry○ 235 .... B6
04955 New Sharon○ 969 .... C6
04762 New Sweden○ 737 .... G2
04956 New Vineyard○ 607 .... C6
04555 Nobleboro○ 1,154 .... D7
†04462 Norcross 13 .... F4
04957 Norridgewock○ 2,552 .... D6
04957 Norridgewock 1,318 .... D6
04958 North Anson 950 .... D6
03906 North Berwick○ 2,878 .... B9
03906 North Berwick 1,436 .... B9
04057 North Bridgton 300 .... B7
†04938 North Chesterville 50 .... C6
†04441 North East Carry 2 .... D4
04662 Northeast Harbor 800 .... G7
†04654 Northfield○ 88 .... H6
04853 North Haven○ 373 .... F7
04262 North Jay 800 .... C6
†04254 North Livermore 250 .... C7
04961 North New Portland 500 .... C6
†04476 North Penobscot 246 .... F7
†04849 Northport○ 958 .... E7
†04274 North Raymond 225 .... C8
04266 North Turner 350 .... C7
04962 North Vassalboro 950 .... D7
04267 North Waterford 390 .... B7
04062 North Windham 5,492 .... C8
†04219 North Woodstock 75 .... B7
†04096 North Yarmouth○ 1,919 .... C8
04268 Norway○ 4,042 .... B7
04268 Norway 2,653 .... B7
†04268 Norway Lake 75 .... B7
04763 Oakfield○ 847 .... G3
04963 Oakland○ 5,162 .... D6
04963 Oakland 3,387 .... D6
04063 Ocean Park 200 .... C9
03907 Ogunquit 1,492 .... B9
04064 Old Orchard Beach○ 6,291 .... C9
04064 Old Orchard Beach 6,023 .... C9
04468 Old Town 8,422 .... F6
04964 Oquossoc 150 .... B6
04471 Orient○ 97 .... H4
04472 Orland○ 1,645 .... F6
04473 Orono○ 10,578 .... F6
04473 Orono 9,891 .... F6
04474 Orrington○ 3,244 .... F6
04066 Orrs Island 600 .... D8
†04270 Otisfield○ 897 .... B7
04665 Otter Creek 260 .... G7
04854 Owls Head○ 1,633 .... F7
04764 Oxbow○ 84 .... G3
04270 Oxford○ 3,143 .... B7
04354 Palermo○ 760 .... E7
04965 Palmyra○ 1,485 .... E6
04271 Paris○ 4,168 .... B7
†04443 Parkman○ 621 .... D5
04475 Passadumkeag○ 430 .... F5
04765 Patten○ 1,368 .... F4
04765 Patten 1,057 .... F4
04558 Pemaquid 200 .... E8
04666 Pembroke○ 920 .... J6
04476 Penobscot○ 1,104 .... F7
04766 Perham○ 437 .... G2
04667 Perry○ 737 .... J6
04272 Peru○ 1,564 .... C6
04966 Phillips○ 1,092 .... C6
04562 Phippsburg○ 1,527 .... D8
04967 Pittsfield○ 4,125 .... E6
04967 Pittsfield 3,117 .... E6
†04345 Pittston○ 2,267 .... D7
04767 Plaisted 125 .... F1
†04925 Pleasant Pond 18 .... D5
04969 Plymouth○ 811 .... E6
04273 Poland○ 3,578 .... C7
04562 Popham Beach 40 .... D8
04768 Portage○ 562 .... G2
04855 Port Clyde 400 .... E8
04068 Porter○ 1,222 .... B8
*04101 Portland⊙ 61,572 .... C8
Portland‡ 183,625 .... C8
04069 Pownal○ 1,189 .... C8
†04487 Prentiss○ 205 .... G5
04769 Presque Isle 11,172 .... H2
04668 Princeton○ 994 .... H5
†04981 Prospect○ 511 .... F6
04669 Prospect Harbor 445 .... H7
04770 Quimby 50 .... F2
†04345 Randolph○ 1,834 .... D7
04970 Rangeley○ 1,023 .... B6
04071 Raymond○ 2,251 .... B8
04355 Readfield○ 1,943 .... D7
04357 Richmond○ 2,627 .... D7
04357 Richmond 1,578 .... D7
†04262 Riley 50 .... C6
†04930 Ripley○ 439 .... E5
04671 Robbinston○ 492 .... J5
†04734 Robinsons 160 .... H3

04841 Rockland⊙ 7,919 .... E7
04856 Rockport○ 2,749 .... F7
04478 Rockwood 265 .... D4
†04957 Rome○ 627 .... D6
†04654 Roque Bluffs○ 244 .... H6
04564 Round Pond 400 .... E8
04275 Roxbury○ 373 .... B6
04276 Rumford○ 8,240 .... B6
04276 Rumford 6,256 .... B6
04279 Rumford Point 320 .... B6
04280 Sabattus○ 3,081 .... C7
04280 Sabattus 1,234 .... C7
04072 Saco 12,921 .... C8
04772 Saint Agatha○ 1,035 .... G1
04971 Saint Albans○ 1,400 .... E6
04773 Saint David 915 .... G1
04774 Saint Francis○ 839 .... E1
04857 Saint George○ 1,948 .... E7
†04743 Saint John○ 322 .... F1
†04983 Salem 125 .... C6
†04009 Sandy Creek 132 .... B7
04972 Sandy Point 350 .... F7
04073 Sanford○ 18,020 .... B9
04073 Sanford 10,268 .... B9
04479 Sangerville○ 1,219 .... E5
†04417 Saponac 8 .... G5
04074 Scarborough○ 11,347 .... C8
04074 Scarborough 2,280 .... C8
04674 Seal Cove 215 .... G7
04675 Seal Harbor 500 .... G7
04973 Searsmont○ 782 .... E7
04974 Searsport○ 2,309 .... F7
04974 Searsport 1,348 .... F7
04075 Sebago Lake 800 .... B8
04481 Sebec○ 469 .... E5
04484 Seboeis○ 53 .... F5
†04478 Seboomook 3 .... D4
04676 Sedgwick○ 795 .... F7
04076 Shapleigh○ 1,370 .... B8
04975 Shawmut 500 .... D6
04775 Sheridan 300 .... F2
†04777 Sherman○ 1,021 .... G4
04777 Sherman Station 650 .... F4
04485 Shirley Mills○ 242 .... D5
†04330 Sidney○ 2,052 .... D7
04779 Sinclair 264 .... G1
04976 Skowhegan○ 8,098 .... D6
04976 Skowhegan⊙ 6,517 .... D6
04567 Small Point 22 .... D8
04978 Smithfield○ 748 .... D6
04780 Smyrna Mills○ 354 .... G3
04979 Solon○ 827 .... D6
†04341 Somerville○ 377 .... D7
†04660 Somesville (Mount Desert) 150 .... G7
04677 Sorrento○ 276 .... G7
03908 South Berwick○ 4,046 .... B9
†04009 South Bridgton 373 .... B8
04568 South Bristol○ 800 .... D8
04077 South Casco 750 .... B8
†03903 South Eliot 1,681 .... B9
†04928 South Exeter 100 .... E6
04080 South Hiram 350 .... B8
†04862 South Hope 200 .... E7
†04453 South La Grange 150 .... F5
†04259 South Monmouth 400 .... D7
04281 South Paris⊙ 2,128 .... C7
†04538 Southport○ 598 .... D8
04106 South Portland 22,712 .... C8
04858 South Thomaston○ 1,064 .... E7
†04864 South Union 50 .... E7
04081 South Waterford 300 .... B7
04679 Southwest Harbor○ 1,855 .... G7
04679 Southwest Harbor 1,052 .... G7
04082 South Windham (Little Falls-South Windham 1,366 .... C8
04487 Springfield○ 443 .... G5
04083 Springvale 2,940 .... B9
04782 Stacyville○ 554 .... F4
04084 Standish○ 5,946 .... B8
†04980 Starks○ 440 .... D6
04488 Stetson○ 618 .... E6
04680 Steuben○ 970 .... H6
04489 Stillwater 700 .... F6
04783 Stockholm○ 319 .... G1
04981 Stockton Springs○ 1,230 .... F7
04681 Stonington○ 1,273 .... F7
†04058 Stow○ 186 .... A7
04982 Stratton 600 .... B5
04983 Strong○ 1,506 .... C6
†04689 Sullivan○ 967 .... G6
†04292 Sumner○ 613 .... C7
04232 Sumner-East Sumner C7
04683 Sunset 165 .... F7
†04627 Sunshine 100 .... G7
04684 Surry○ 894 .... F7
04685 Swans Island○ 337 .... G7
†04915 Swanville○ 873 .... E6
†04040 Sweden○ 163 .... B7
04984 Temple○ 518 .... C6
04860 Tenants Harbor 900 .... E8
04861 Thomaston○ 2,900 .... E7
04861 Thomaston 2,348 .... E7
04986 Thorndike○ 603 .... E6
04490 Topsfield○ 240 .... H5
04086 Topsham○ 6,431 .... D8
04086 Topsham 4,657 .... D8
†04653 Tremont○ 1,222 .... G7
†04605 Trenton○ 718 .... G7
04571 Trevett 400 .... D8
04987 Troy○ 701 .... E6
04282 Turner○ 3,539 .... C7
04862 Union○ 1,569 .... E7
04988 Unity○ 1,431 .... E6
†04293 Upper Dam 2 .... B6
04784 Upper Frenchville 405 .... G1
04261 Upton○ 65 .... B6
04785 Van Buren○ 3,557 .... G1
04785 Van Buren 3,282 .... G1
04491 Vanceboro○ 256 .... J4
04989 Vassalboro○ 3,410 .... D7
04401 Veazie○ 1,610 .... F6
04360 Vienna○ 454 .... D6
04863 Vinalhaven○ 1,211 .... F7
04492 Waite○ 130 .... H5
†04915 Waldo○ 495 .... E7
04572 Waldoboro○ 3,985 .... E7

04572 Waldoboro 1,195 .... E7
†04605 Waltham○ 186 .... G6
04864 Warren○ 2,566 .... E7
04786 Washburn○ 2,028 .... G2
04786 Washburn 1,221 .... G2
04574 Washington○ 954 .... E7
04087 Waterboro○ 2,943 .... B8
04088 Waterford○ 951 .... B7
04901 Waterville 17,779 .... D6
04284 Wayne○ 680 .... D7
04285 Weld○ 435 .... C6
04990 Wellington○ 287 .... D5
04090 Wells○ 8,211 .... B9
04686 Wesley○ 140 .... H6
†04530 West Bath○ 1,309 .... D8
04092 Westbrook 14,976 .... C8
04493 West Enfield 609 .... F5
04787 Westfield○ 647 .... G2
04985 West Forks○ 72 .... D5
†04649 West Jonesport 400 .... H6
04094 West Kennebunk 750 .... B9
†04938 West Mills 75 .... C6
04288 West Minot 400 .... C7
04095 West Newfield 300 .... B8
04424 Weston○ 155 .... H4
04289 West Paris○ 1,390 .... B7
04290 West Peru 700 .... C7
04291 West Poland 250 .... C7
04074 West Scarborough 500 .... C8
04690 West Tremont 250 .... G7
04362 Whitefield○ 1,606 .... D7
04691 Whiting○ 335 .... J6
04692 Whitneyville○ 264 .... H6
†04443 Willimantic○ 164 .... E5
04293 Wilsons Mills 50 .... B6
04294 Wilton○ 4,382 .... C6
04294 Wilton 2,262 .... C6
04363 Windsor○ 1,702 .... D7
04495 Winn○ 503 .... G5
†04901 Winslow○ 8,057 .... D6
†04901 Winslow 5,903 .... D6
04693 Winter Harbor○ 1,120 .... G7
04496 Winterport○ 2,675 .... F6
04496 Winterport 1,126 .... F6
04788 Winterville○ 235 .... F2
04364 Winthrop○ 5,889 .... C7
04364 Winthrop 3,264 .... C7
04578 Wiscasset○ 2,832 .... D7
04694 Woodland○ 1,363 .... H5
04579 Woolwich○ 2,156 .... D8
04497 Wytopitlock 130 .... G4
04096 Yarmouth○ 6,585 .... C8
04096 Yarmouth 2,981 .... C8
03909 York○ 8,465 .... B9
03909 York 4,530 .... B9
03910 York Beach 900 .... B9
03911 York Harbor 950 .... B9

OTHER FEATURES

Abraham (mt.) C5
Acadia Nat'l Park G7
Allagash (lake) D3
Allagash (riv.) E2
Androscoggin (riv.) C7
Aroostook (riv.) G2
Atteam (pond) C4
Baker (lake) D3
Baskahegan (lake) H5
Bear (riv.) B6
Big (brook) E2
Big (lake) H5
Big Black (riv.) D2
Bigelow (bight) C9
Big Spencer (mt.) E4
Black (pond) D3
Blue (mt.) C6
Blue Hill (bay) G7
Bog (lake) H6
Brassua (lake) D4
Casco (bay) C8
Cathance (lake) J6
Caucomgomoc (lake) D3
Center (pond) E5
Chamberlain (lake) E3
Chemquasabamticook (lake) D3
Chesuncook (lake) E3
Chiputneticook (lakes) H4
Clayton (lake) D2
Clifford (lake) H5
Cold Stream (pond) G5
Crawford (lake) H5
Cross (isl.) J6
Cross (lake) G1
Cupsuptic (riv.) B5
Dead (riv.) C5
Deer (isl.) F7
Duck (isls.) G7
Eagle (lake) E3
Eagle (lake) F1
East Machias (riv.) H6
East Musquash (lake) H5
Elizabeth (cape) C8
Ellis (pond) B6
Ellis (riv.) B6
Embden (pond) D6
Endless (lake) F5
Englishman (bay) J6
Eskutassis (pond) G5
Fifth (lake) H5
Fish (riv.) F2
Fish River (lake) F2
Flagstaff (lake) C5
Fourth (lake) H5
Frenchman (bay) G7
Gardner (lake) J6
Georges (isls.) E8
Graham (lake) G6
Grand (lake) H4
Grand Falls (lake) H5
Grand Lake Seboeis (lake) F3
Grand Manan (chan.) K6
Great Moose (lake) D6
Great Wass (isl.) J7
Green (isl.) F8
Harrington (lake) E4
Haut (isl.) G7
Indian Pond (lake) D4
Islesboro (isl.) F7
Jo-Mary (lakes) E4
Katahdin (mt.) F4
Kennebec (riv.) D7
Kezar (lake) B7
Kezar (pond) B7
Kingsbury (pond) D5
Little Black (riv.) E1
Little Madawaska (riv.) G2
Lobster (lake) E4
Long (lake) B7
Long (lake) E2
Long (lake) G1
Long (pond) C4
Long (pond) D6
Long (pond) E5
Long Falls (dam) C5
Longfellow (mts.) B6
Loon (lake) D3
Loring A.F.B. 6,572 .... H2
Lower Roach (pond) E4
Lower Sysladobsis (lake) G5
Machias (bay) J6
Machias (riv.) F2
Machias (riv.) H6
Machias Seal (isl.) J7
Madagascal (pond) G5
Marshall (isl.) G7
Matinicus Rock (isl.) F8
Mattamiscontis (lake) F4
Mattawamkeag (lake) G4
Mattawamkeag (riv.) G4
Meddybemps (lake) J5
Metinic (isl.) E8
Millinocket (lake) F4
Millinocket (lake) F3
Molunkus (lake) G4
Monhegan (isl.) E8
Moose (pond) B7
Moose (riv.) D4
Moosehead (lake) D4
Mooseleuk (stream) F2
Mooselookmeguntic (lake) B6
Mopang (lake) H6
Mount Desert (isl.) G7
Mount Desert Rock (isl.) G8
Moxie (lake) D5
Munsungan (lake) E3
Muscongus (bay) E8
Musquacook (lakes) E2
Nahmakanta (lake) E4
Nicatous (lake) G5
Nollesemic (lake) F4
Old (stream) H6
Onawa (lake) E5
Parlin (pond) C4
Parmachenee (lake) B5
Passamaquoddy (bay) J5
Passamaquoddy Ind. Res. J6
Pemadumcook (lake) E4
Penobscot (bay) F7
Penobscot (lake) C4
Penobscot (riv.) F5
Penobscot Ind. Res. F6
Pierce (pond) C5
Piscataqua (riv.) B9
Piscataquis (riv.) E5
Pleasant (lake) E3
Pleasant (lake) G3
Pleasant (lake) H5
Pleasant (riv.) H6
Pocomoonshine (lake) H5
Portage (lake) F2
Presque Isle A.F.B. G2
Priestly (lake) E2
Pushaw (lake) F6
Ragged (isl.) F8
Ragged (lake) E4
Rainbow (lake) E4
Rangeley (lake) B6
Richardson (lakes) B6
Rocky (lake) J6
Round (pond) E2
Rowe (lake) F2
Saco (riv.) B8
Saint Croix (riv.) J5
Saint Croix Isl. Nat'l Mon. J5
Saint Francis (riv.) E1
Saint Froid (lake) F2
Saint John (pond) D3
Saint John (riv.) G1
Salmon Falls (riv.) B9
Sandy (riv.) C6
Schoodic (lake) F5
Scraggly (lake) F3
Scraggly (lake) H5
Seal (isl.) F8
Sebago (lake) B8
Sebasticook (lake) E6
Seboeis (lake) F5
Seboeis (riv.) F3
Seboomook (lake) D4
Shallow (lake) E3
Small (cape) D8
Sourdnahunk (lake) F3
Spencer (pond) D4
Spencer (stream) C5
Spider (lake) E3
Squa Pan (lake) G2
Square (lake) G1
Sunday (riv.) B6
Swift (riv.) B6
Sysladobsis, Lower (lake) G5
Third (lake) H5
Twin (lakes) F4
Umbagog (lake) A6
Umcalcus (lake) G3
Umsaskis (lake) E2
Union, West Branch (riv.) G6
Vinalhaven (isl.) F7
Wassataquoik (stream) F4
Webb (lake) C6
Webster (brook) E3
West Grand (lake) H5
West Musquash (lake) H5
West Quoddy (head) K6
Wilson E5
Winnecook (lake) E6
Wooden Ball (isl.) F8
Wyman (lake) C5
Wytopitlock (lake) G4

⊙County seat.
‡Population of metropolitan area.
○Population of town or township.
† Zip of nearest p.o.
* Multiple zips.

Topography

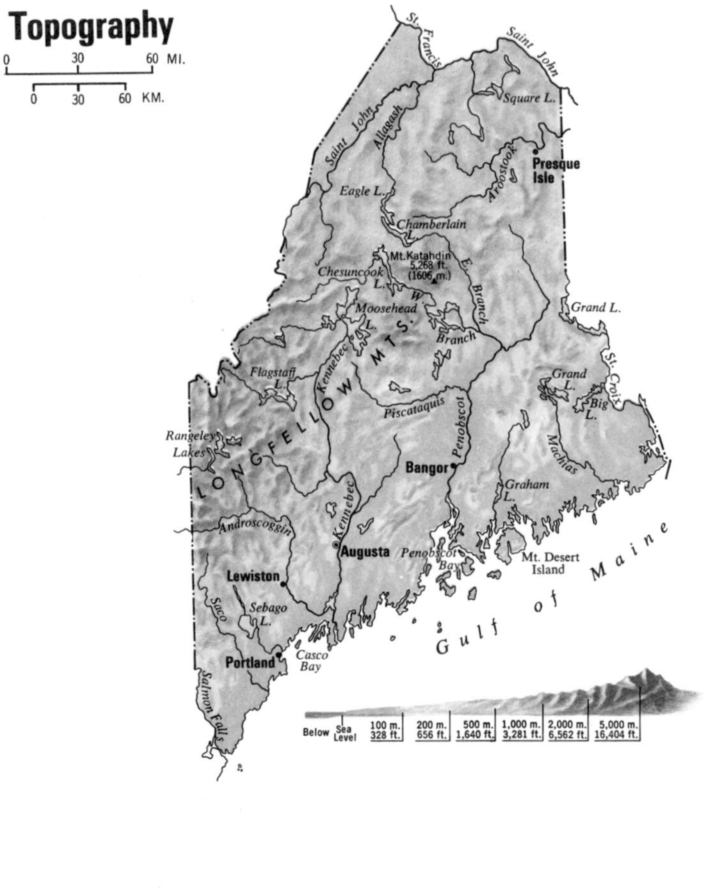

0
30
60 MI.
0
30
60 KM.
St. Francis
Saint John
Square L.
Saint John
Allagash
Presque Isle
Eagle L.
Aroostook
Chamberlain
Mt. Katahdin 5,268 ft. (1606 m.)
Chesuncook L.
Moosehead L.
W. Branch
E. Branch
Grand L.
Flagstaff L.
Kennebec
LONGFELLOW MTS.
Piscataquis
Penobscot
Grand L.
Big L.
St. Croix
Machias
Rangeley Lakes
Bangor
Graham L.
Androscoggin
Kennebec
Augusta
Penobscot Bay
Mt. Desert Island
Gulf of Maine
Lewiston
Sebago L.
Saco
Portland
Casco Bay
Salmon Falls
Below Sea Level
100 m. 328 ft.
200 m. 656 ft.
500 m. 1,640 ft.
1,000 m. 3,281 ft.
2,000 m. 6,562 ft.
5,000 m. 16,404 ft.

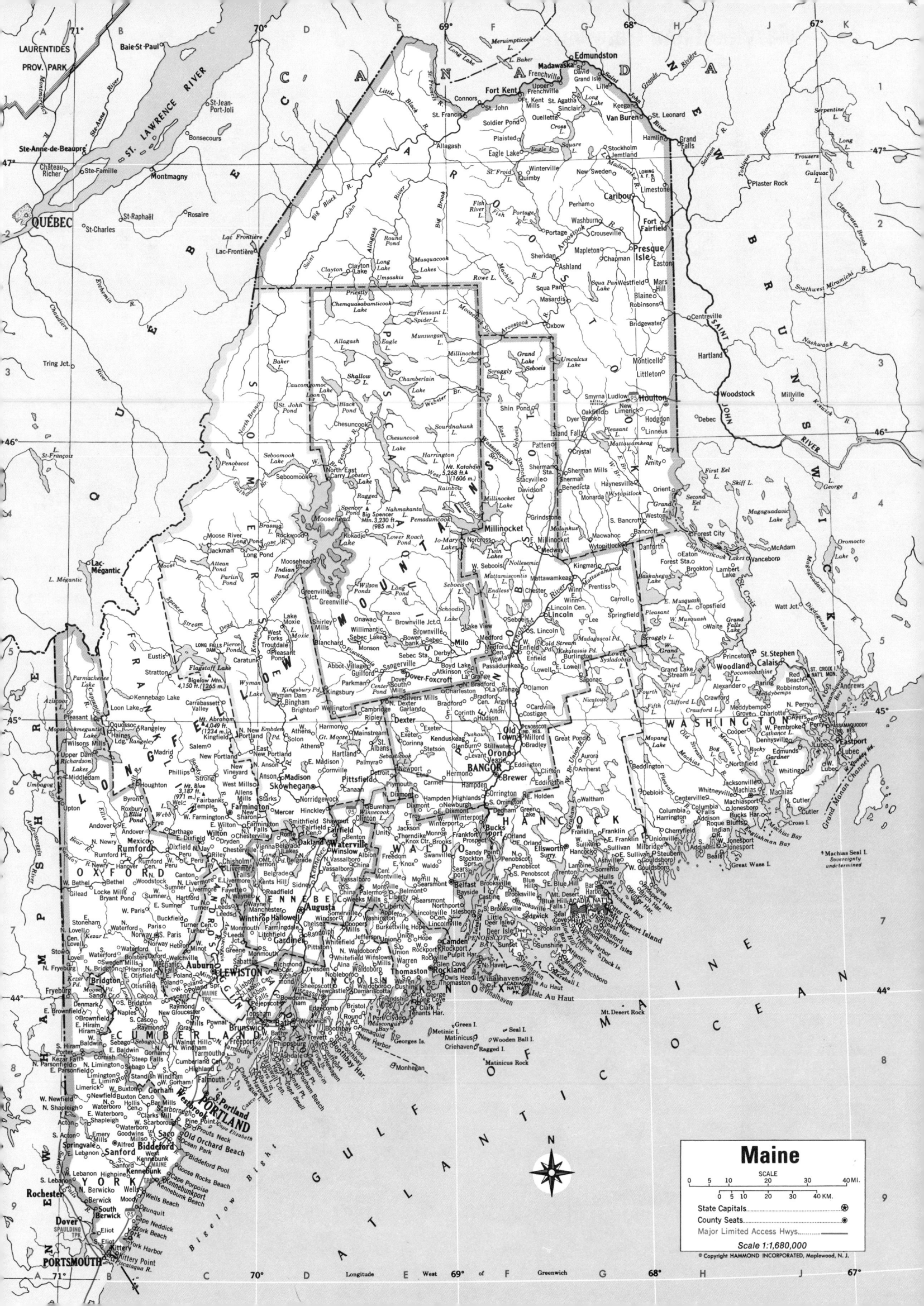

Maine

SCALE

0 5 10 20 30 40 MI.

0 5 10 20 30 40 KM.

State Capitals..⊛

County Seats...◉

Major Limited Access Hwys.........................

Scale 1:1,680,000

© Copyright HAMMOND INCORPORATED, Maplewood, N.J.

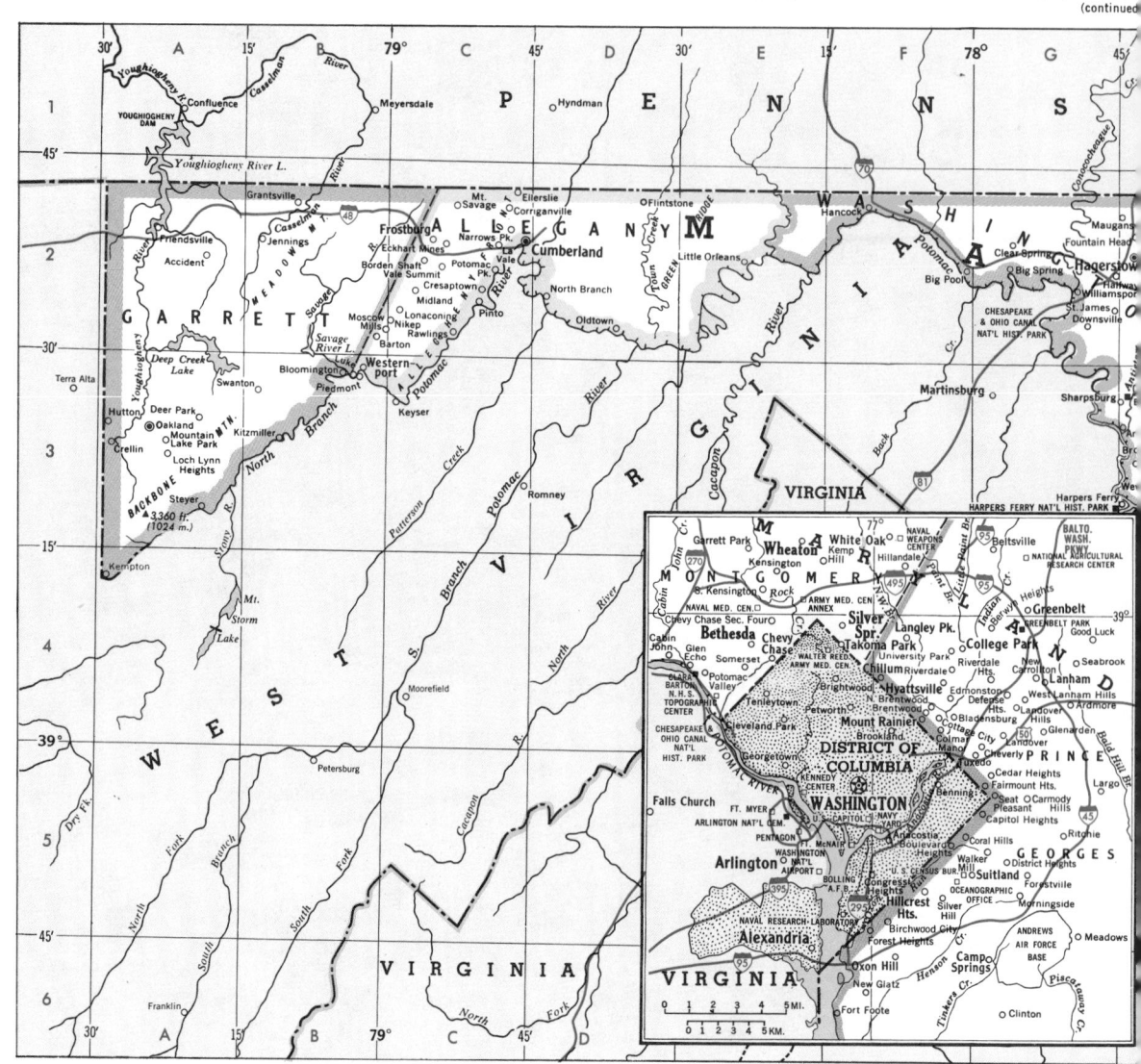

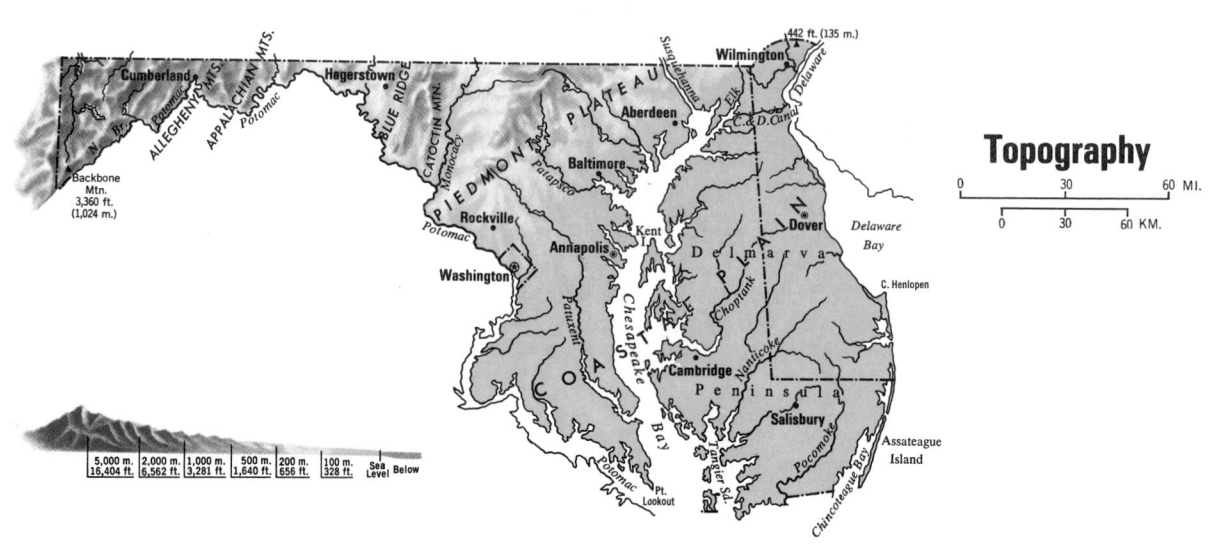

Topography

0   30   60 MI.

0   30   60 KM.

5,000 m. 2,000 m. 1,000 m. 500 m. 200 m. 100 m. Sea Level Below
16,404 ft. 6,562 ft. 3,281 ft. 1,640 ft. 656 ft. 328 ft.

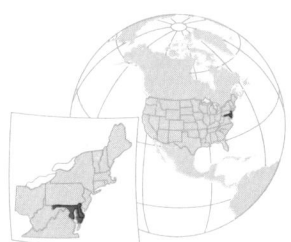

MARYLAND

AREA 10,460 sq. mi. (27,091 sq. km.)
POPULATION 4,216,975
CAPITAL Annapolis
LARGEST CITY Baltimore
HIGHEST POINT Backbone Mtn. 3,360 ft. (1024 m.)
SETTLED IN 1634
ADMITTED TO UNION April 28, 1788
POPULAR NAME Old Line State; Free State
STATE FLOWER Black-eyed Susan
STATE BIRD Baltimore Oriole

DELAWARE

AREA 2,044 sq. mi. (5,294 sq. km.)
POPULATION 594,317
CAPITAL Dover
LARGEST CITY Wilmington
HIGHEST POINT Ebright Road 442 ft. (135 m.)
SETTLED IN 1627
ADMITTED TO UNION December 7, 1787
POPULAR NAME First State; Diamond State
STATE FLOWER Peach Blossom
STATE BIRD Blue Hen Chicken

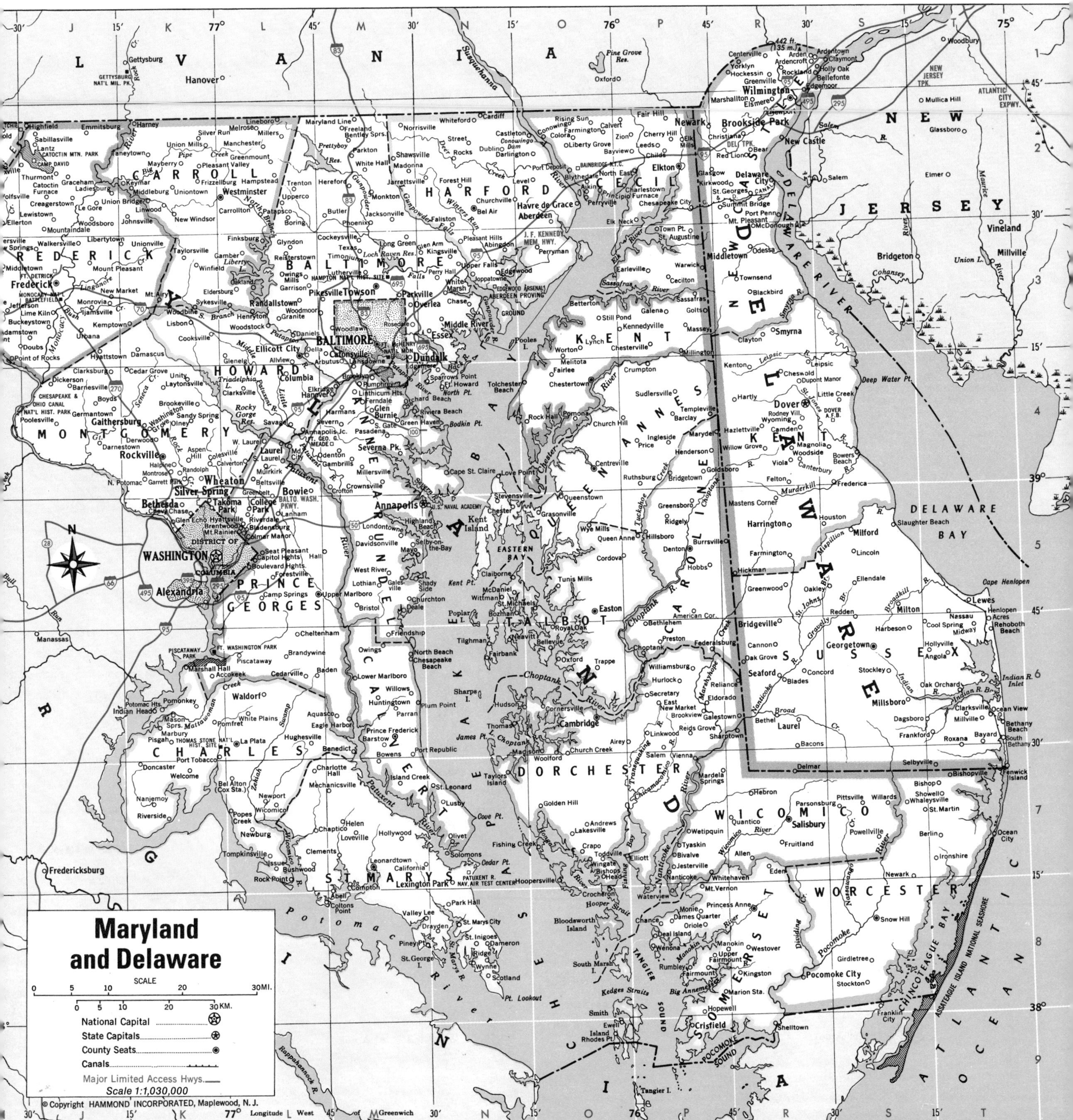

Maryland and Delaware

SCALE

| 0 | 5 | 10 | 20 | 30 MI. |

| 0 | 5 | 10 | 20 | 30 KM. |

National Capital .... ⊛
State Capitals .... ⊛
County Seats .... ◉
Canals ....
Major Limited Access Hwys. ____

Scale 1:1,030,000

© Copyright HAMMOND INCORPORATED, Maplewood, N.J.

(continued)

21701 Lewistown 600 J2
20653 Lexington Park 10,361 M7
21762 Libertytown 400 J3
21090 Linthicum Heights 7,457 M4
21766 Little Orleans 600 E2
†21550 Loch Lynn Heights 503 A3
21539 Lonaconing 1,420 C2
†21035 Londontowne 6,052 M4
21092 Long Green 1,626 M3
20656 Loveville 600 M7
21540 Luke 329 B3
21093 Lutherville-Timonium 16,871 M3
21648 Madison 350 O6
21102 Manchester 1,830 L2
20658 Marbury 1,189 K6
21837 Mardela Springs 320 P7
21838 Marion Station 400 R8
†20616 Marshall Hall 325 K6
21649 Marydel 152 P4
†21113 Maryland City 6,949 L4
21767 Maugansville 1,707 H2
21106 Mayo 2,795 M5
20659 Mechanicsville 784 M7
21220 Middle River 26,756 N3
21769 Middletown 1,748 J3
21542 Midland 601 C2
21108 Millersville 380 M4
21651 Millington 546 P3
†20028 Morningside 1,395 G5
†21701 Mountaindale 400 J2
21550 Mountain Lake Park 1,597 A3
21771 Mount Airy 2,450 K3
†21701 Mount Pleasant 400 J3
20822 Mount Rainier 7,361 F4
21545 Mount Savage 1,640 C2
†21853 Mount Vernon 900 P8
†20705 Muirkirk 950 L4
21773 Myersville 432 H3
21840 Nanticoke 450 P7
†21502 Narrows Park-La Vale 5,523 C2
21841 Newark 900 S7
20664 Newburg 550 L7
20784 New Carrollton 12,632 G4
21774 New Market 306 J3
21776 New Windsor 799 K2
20831 North Beach 1,504 N6
†20722 North Brentwood 580 F4
21901 North East 1,469 P2
†20854 North Potomac K4
21550 Oakland⊙ 1,994 A3
†21784 Oakland 2,242 L3
21842 Ocean City 4,946 T7
21113 Odenton 13,270 M4
†21228 Oella 600 L3
20832 Olney 13,026 K4
21206 Overlea 12,965 N3
20836 Owings 700 M6
21117 Owings Mills 9,526 L3
21654 Oxford 754 O6
20745 Oxon Hill 36,267 F6
20667 Park Hall 775 N8
21234 Parkville 35,159 M3

21122 Pasadena 7,439 M4
21128 Perry Hall 13,455 N3
21130 Perryman 1,819 O3
21903 Perryville 2,018 O2
21208 Pikesville 22,555 M3
20674 Piney Point 950 M8
†20735 Piscataway 500 L6
20640 Pisgah 650 K6
21850 Pittsville 519 S7
†21087 Pleasant Hills 2,790 N3
21851 Pocomoke City 3,558 R8
20675 Pomfret 600 L6
†20640 Pomonkey 410 K6
20837 Poolesville 3,428 J4
21904 Port Deposit 664 O2
20677 Port Tobacco 40 K6
20640 Potomac Heights 2,456 K6
†21502 Potomac Park-Bowling Green 2,275 C2
21852 Powellville 400 S7
21655 Preston 498 P6
20678 Prince Frederick⊙ 1,805 M6
21853 Princess Anne⊙ 1,499 P8
†21090 Pumphrey 5,666 M4
21657 Queen Anne 259 O5
21658 Queenstown 491 O5
21133 Randallstown 25,927 L3
21557 Rawlings 500 C2
21136 Reisterstown 19,385 L3
20680 Ridge 550 N8
21660 Ridgely 933 P5
21911 Rising Sun 1,160 O2
†20027 Ritchie 950 G5
†20840 Riverdale Heights G4
†21061 Riviera Beach 8,812 N4
21661 Rock Hall 1,511 O4
†21084 Rocks 450 N2
*20850 Rockville⊙ 43,811 K4
21779 Rohrersville 525 H3
21237 Rosedale 19,956 M3
†21758 Rosemont 305 H3
21662 Royal Oak 600 O6
21780 Sabillasville 450 J2
20684 Saint Inigoes 750 N8
21663 Saint Michaels 1,301 N5
21801 Salisbury⊙ 16,429 R7
20860 Sandy Spring-Ashton 2,659 K4
20863 Savage-Guilford 2,928 L4
20687 Scotland 475 N8
20801 Seabrook-Lanham 15,814 G4
20027 Seat Pleasant 5,217 G5
21664 Secretary 487 P6
†21037 Selby-on-the-Bay 3,125 N5
21144 Severn 20,147 M4
21146 Severna Park 21,253 M4
20867 Shady Side 2,877 M5
21782 Sharpsburg 721 G3
21861 Sharptown 654 R6
20023 Silver Hill-Suitland 32,164 F5
†21157 Silver Run 350 K2
*20901 Silver Spring 72,893 F4
21783 Smithsburg 833 H2
21863 Snow Hill⊙ 2,192 S8

†20015 Somerset 1,101 E4
†21113 South Gate 24,185 M4
†20795 South Kensington 9,344 E4
†20810 South Laurel 18,034 L4
21219 Sparrows Point N4
21666 Stevensville 500 N5
21667 Still Pond 350 O3
21864 Stockton 400 S8
21668 Sudlersville 443 P4
†20746 Suitland-Silver Hill 32,164 F5
21784 Sykesville 1,712 K3
20912 Takoma Park 16,231 F4
21787 Taneytown 2,618 K2
21669 Taylors Island 400 N7
21670 Templeville 96 P4
21788 Thurmont 2,934 J2
21671 Tilghman 979 N6
21093 Timonium-Lutherville 16,871 M3
21672 Toddville 500 O7
21204 Towson⊙ 51,083 M3
21673 Trappe 739 O6
†20780 Tuxedo 500 G5
21791 Union Bridge 927 K2
†20740 University Park 2,536 F4
21155 Upperco 500 L2
21867 Upper Fairmount 500 P8
21156 Upper Falls 550 N3
20870 Upper Marlboro⊙ 828 M5
20692 Valley Lee 600 M8
21869 Vienna 300 P7
20601 Waldorf 9,782 L6
†20023 Walker Mill 10,651 F5
21793 Walkersville 2,212 J3
21912 Warwick 550 P3
20880 Washington Grove 527 K4
20693 Welcome 438 K7
21562 Westernport 2,706 B3
†20784 West Lanham Hills 350 G4
21157 Westminster⊙ 8,808 L2
21871 Westover 450 R8
20902 Wheaton-Glenmont 48,598 E3
21160 Whiteford 500 N2
21161 White Hall 360 M2
21162 White Marsh 500 N3
†20901 White Oak 13,700 F3
20695 White Plains 5,167 L6
21874 Willards 540 S7
21795 Williamsport 2,153 G2
21676 Wittman 544 N5
21797 Woodbine 872 K3
21798 Woodsboro 506 J2
21163 Woodstock 700 L3
21677 Woolford 330 O7
21679 Wye Mills 315 O5
†20680 Wynne 450 N8
†21701 Yellow Springs 940 H3

OTHER FEATURES

Aberdeen Proving Ground 5,722 N3
Allegheny Front (mts.) C2
Andrews A.F.B. 10,064 G5
Antietam (creek) H2
Antietam Nat'l Battlefield H3
Army Chemical Center O3
Back (riv.) N4
Backbone (mt.) A3
Bainbridge N.T.C. O2
Bald Hill Branch (riv.) G4
Big Annemessex (riv.) P8
Big Pipe (creek) K2
Bloodsworth (isl.) O8
Blue Ridge (mts.) H3
Bodkin (pt.) N4
Bush (creek) J3
Cabin John (creek) E4
Camp David J2
Casselman (riv.) B2
Catoctin (creek) H3
Catoctin Mt. Park J2
Cedar (pt.) N7
Census Bureau F5
Chesapeake (bay) N7
Chesapeake and Delaware (canal) R2
Chesapeake and Ohio Canal Nat'l Hist. Park J4
Chester (riv.) O4
Chicamacomico (riv.) P7
Chincoteague (bay) S8
Choptank (riv.) O6
Clara Barton Nat'l Hist. Site E4
Conococheague (creek) G1
Conowingo (dam) O2
Cove (pt.) N7
Deep Creek (lake) A3
Deer (creek) N2
Dividing (creek) R8
Eastern (bay) N5
Elk (riv.) P3
Fishing (bay) O7
Fort Detrick J3
Fort George G. Meade 14,083 L4
Fort McHenry Nat'l Mon. M3
Fort Ritchie 1,754 H2
Fort Washington Park L6
Great Seneca (creek) J4
Greenbelt Park G4
Green Ridge (mts.) E2
Gunpowder (riv.) N3
Gunpowder Falls (creek) M2
Hampton Nat'l Hist. Site M3
Harpers Ferry Nat'l Hist. Park G3
Henson (creek) F6
Honga (riv.) O7
Hooper (str.) O8
Indian (creek) G4
James (pt.) N6
Kedges (strs) O8
Kent (isl.) N5
Kent (pt.) N5
Liberty (lake) L3
Linganore (creek) J3
Little Choptank (riv.) N6
Little Gunpowder Falls (creek) M2

Little Paint Branch (riv.) F4
Little Patuxent (riv.) L4
Loch Raven (res.) M3
Lookout (pt.) N8
Manokin (riv.) P8
Marshyhope (creek) P6
Mattawoman (creek) K6
Meadow (mt.) B2
Middle Patuxent (riv.) L3
Monocacy (riv.) J3
Monocacy Nat'l Battlefield J3
Nanticoke (riv.) P7
Nassawango (creek) S8
National Agricultural Research Center G3
Naval Academy, U.S. 5,367 N5
Naval Medical Center E4
Naval Weapons Center F3
North (pt.) N4
Oceanographic Office F5
Oxon Run (riv.) F5
Paint Branch (riv.) F4
Patapsco (riv.) M4
Patuxent (riv.) M7
Patuxent River Nav. Air Test Ctr. N7
Piscataway (creek) G6
Piscataway Park K6
Pocomoke (riv.) S8
Pocomoke (sound) P9
Pooles (isl.) O3
Poplar (isl.) N5
Potomac (riv.) M8
Prettyboy (res.) M2
Rock (creek) K4
Rocky Gorge (res.) L4
Saint George (isl.) M8
Saint Marys (riv.) N8
Sassafras (riv.) P3
Savage (riv.) B2
Savage River (lake) B2
Severn (riv.) N4
Sharps (isl.) N6
Smith (isl.) O8
South Marsh (isl.) O8
Susquehanna (riv.) N1
Tangier (sound) P8
Thomas Stone Nat'l Hist. Site K6
Tinkers (creek) F6
Topographic Center E4
Town (creek) E2
Transquaking (riv.) P7
Triadelphia (lake) L4
Tuckahoe (creek) P5
Walter Reed Army Med. Ctr. Annex E4
Wicomico (riv.) L7
Wicomico (riv.) R7
Winters Run (creek) N2
Youghiogheny (riv.) A3
Youghiogheny River (lake) A2
Zekiah Swamp (riv.) L7

DELAWARE

COUNTIES

Kent 98,219 R4
New Castle 398,115 R2
Sussex 97,983 S6

CITIES and TOWNS

Zip Name/Pop. Key

†19801 Arden 516 R1
†19810 Ardencroft 267 R1
†19810 Ardentown 307 S1
19809 Bellefonte 1,279 S1
19930 Bethany Beach 330 T6
19931 Bethel 197 R6
†19973 Blades 664 R6
†19962 Bowers Beach 198 S4
19993 Bridgeville 1,238 R6
19711 Brookside 15,255 R2
19934 Camden 1,757 R4
†19801 Centerville 800 R1
19936 Cheswold 269 R4
†19711 Christiana 500 R2
19937 Clarksville 350 T6
19703 Claymont 10,022 S1
19938 Clayton 1,216 R3
19930 Dagsboro 344 S6
19706 Delaware City 1,858 R2
19940 Delmar 948 R7
19901 Dover (cap.)⊙ 23,507 R4
†19901 Dupont Manor 1,059 R4
†19801 Edgemoor 7,397 S1
19941 Ellendale 361 S5
†19801 Elsmere 6,493 R2
19942 Farmington 141 R5
19943 Felton 547 R4
19944 Fenwick Island 114 T7
19945 Frankford 828 S6
19946 Frederica 864 S4
19947 Georgetown⊙ 1,710 S6
†19711 Glasgow 350 R2
19950 Greenwood 578 R5
19952 Harrington 2,405 R5
†19971 Henlopen Acres 176 T6
19707 Hockessin 950 R1
†19801 Holly Oak S1
19954 Houston 357 S5
19955 Kenton 243 R4
19708 Kirkwood 350 R2
19956 Laurel 3,052 R6
†19901 Leipsic 228 S4
19958 Lewes 2,197 T5
19960 Lincoln 757 S5
19961 Little Creek 230 S4
19962 Magnolia 197 R4
19709 Middletown 2,946 R3
19963 Milford 5,366 S5
19966 Millsboro 1,233 S6
19967 Millville 178 T6
19968 Milton 1,359 S5
19711 Newark 25,247 P2
19720 New Castle 4,907 R2
19804 Newport 1,167 R2
†19966 Oak Orchard 350 T6
19970 Ocean View 495 T6
19730 Odessa 384 R3
19971 Rehoboth Beach 1,730 T6
19901 Rodney Village 1,753 R4
19733 Saint Georges 450 R2
19973 Seaford 5,256 R6
19975 Selbyville 1,251 S7
†19963 Slaughter Beach 121 S5
19977 Smyrna 4,750 R3
†19930 South Bethany 115 T6
19734 Townsend 386 R3
19979 Viola 167 R4
*19801 Wilmington⊙ 70,195 R2
Wilmington‡ 524,108 R2
19980 Woodside 248 R4
19934 Wyoming 960 R4
19736 Yorklyn 600 R1

OTHER FEATURES

Broad (creek) R6
Broadkill (riv.) S5
Chesapeake and Delaware (canal) R2
Choptank (riv.) P5
Deep Water (pt.) S4
Delaware (bay) T5
Delaware (riv.) R3
Dover A.F.B. 4,391 S4
Henlopen (cape) T5
Indian (riv.) S6
Indian River (bay) T6
Indian River (inlet) T6
Leipsic (riv.) R4
Mispillion (riv.) S5
Murderkill (riv.) R5
Nanticoke (riv.) R6
Saint Jones (riv.) R4
Smyrna (res.) R3

DISTRICT OF COLUMBIA

CITIES and TOWNS

Zip Name/Pop. Key

20007 Georgetown E5
*20001 Washington, D.C. (cap.), U.S. 638,432 F5
Washington‡ 3,060,240 F5

OTHER FEATURES

Anacostia (riv.) F5
Bolling A.F.B. E5
Fort Lesley J. McNair E5
Kennedy Center A5
Naval Yard F5
U.S. Capitol F5
Walter Reed Army Med. Ctr. E4

⊙County seat.
‡Population of metropolitan area.
† Zip of nearest p.o.
* Multiple zips.

Agriculture, Industry and Resources

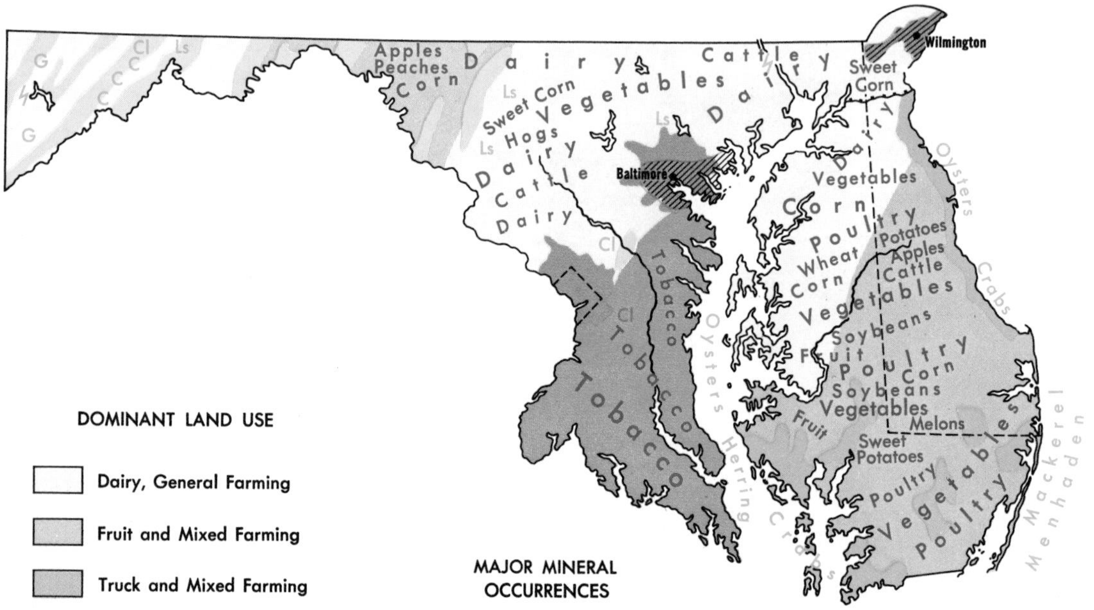

DOMINANT LAND USE

- Dairy, General Farming
- Fruit and Mixed Farming
- Truck and Mixed Farming
- Tobacco, General Farming
- Forests
- Swampland, Limited Agriculture
- Urban Areas

MAJOR MINERAL OCCURRENCES

- C Coal
- Cl Clay
- G Natural Gas
- Ls Limestone

Water Power

Major Industrial Areas

MASSACHUSETTS

AREA 8,284 sq. mi. (21,456 sq. km.)
POPULATION 5,737,037
CAPITAL Boston
LARGEST CITY Boston
HIGHEST POINT Mt. Greylock 3,491 ft. (1064 m.)
SETTLED IN 1620
ADMITTED TO UNION February 6, 1788
POPULAR NAME Bay State; Old Colony
STATE FLOWER Mayflower
STATE BIRD Chickadee

RHODE ISLAND

AREA 1,212 sq. mi. (3,139 sq. km.)
POPULATION 947,154
CAPITAL Providence
LARGEST CITY Providence
HIGHEST POINT Jerimoth Hill 812 ft. (247 m.)
SETTLED IN 1636
ADMITTED TO UNION May 29, 1790
POPULAR NAME Little Rhody; Ocean State
STATE FLOWER Violet
STATE BIRD Rhode Island Red

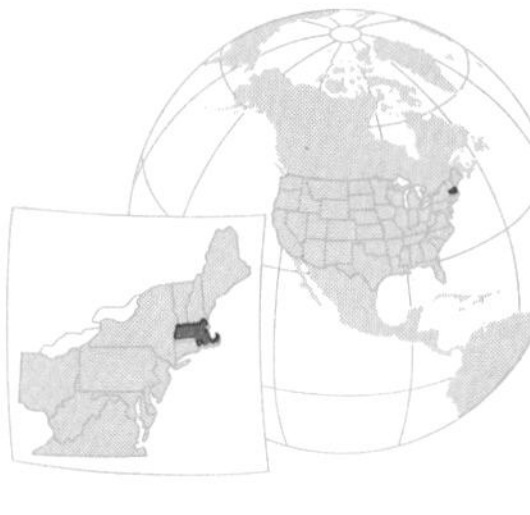

Agriculture, Industry and Resources

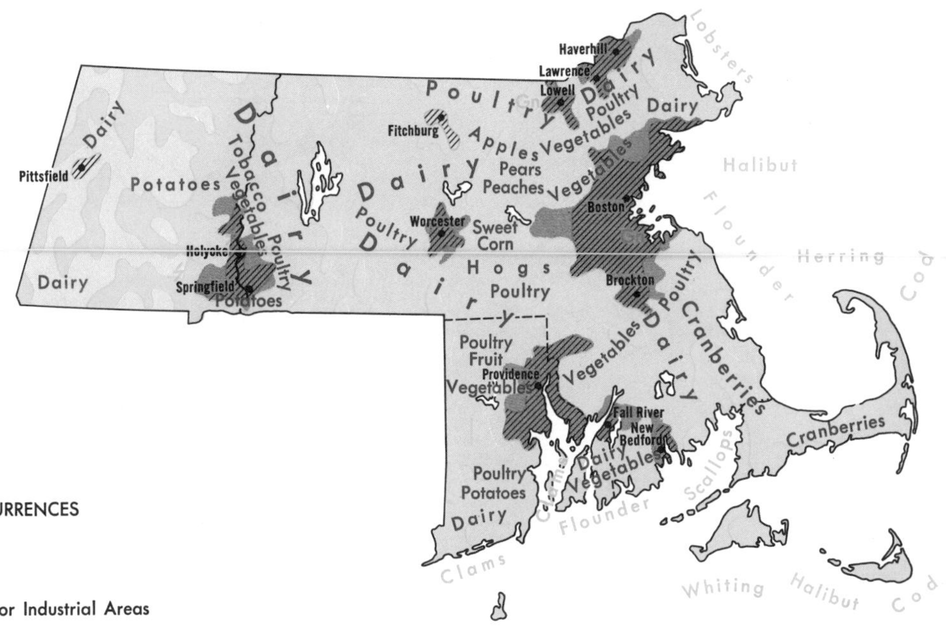

DOMINANT LAND USE

Specialized Dairy

Dairy, Poultry, Mixed Farming

Forests

Urban Areas

MAJOR MINERAL OCCURRENCES

Gn Granite

Water Power

Major Industrial Areas

MASSACHUSETTS

COUNTIES

Barnstable 147,925 ... N6
Berkshire 145,110 ... B3
Bristol 474,641 ... K5
Dukes 8,942 ... M7
Essex 633,632 ... L2
Franklin 64,317 ... D2
Hampden 443,018 ... D4
Hampshire 138,813 ... D3
Middlesex 1,367,034 ... J3
Nantucket 5,087 ... O7
Norfolk 606,587 ... K4
Plymouth 405,437 ... L5
Suffolk 650,142 ... K3
Worcester 646,352 ... G3

CITIES and TOWNS

Zip *Name/Pop.* *Key*

02351 Abington○ 13,517 ... L4
01720 Acton○ 17,544 ... J3
02743 Acushnet○ 8,704 ... L6
01220 Adams○ 10,381 ... B2
01220 Adams 6,857 ... B2
01001 Agawam○ 26,271 ... D4
†01261 Alford○ 394 ... A4
01913 Amesbury○ 13,971 ... L1
01913 Amesbury 12,236 ... L1
01002 Amherst○ 33,229 ... E3
01002 Amherst 17,773 ... E3
01810 Andover○ 26,370 ... K2
01810 Andover 8,445 ... K2
02174 Arlington○ 48,219 ... C6
01430 Ashburnham○ 4,075 ... G2
01430 Ashburnham 900 ... G2
01431 Ashby○ 2,311 ... G2
01330 Ashfield○ 1,458 ... C2
01721 Ashland○ 9,165 ... J3
01331 Athol○ 10,634 ... F2
01331 Athol 8,708 ... F2
02703 Attleboro 34,196 ... J5
01501 Auburn○ 14,845 ... G4
02322 Avon○ 5,026 ... K4
*01432 Ayer○ 6,993 ... H2
*01432 Ayer 3,165 ... H2
01436 Baldwinville 1,709 ... F2
02630 Barnstable○ 30,898 ... N6
02630 Barnstable⊙ 2,033 ... N6
01005 Barre○ 4,102 ... F3
01005 Barre 1,136 ... F3
01223 Becket○ 1,339 ... B3
01730 Bedford○ 13,067 ... B6
01007 Belchertown○ 8,339 ... E3
01007 Belchertown 2,531 ... E3
02019 Bellingham○ 14,300 ... J4
02019 Bellingham 4,454 ... J4
02178 Belmont○ 26,100 ... C6
†02780 Berkley○ 2,731 ... K5
01503 Berlin○ 2,215 ... H3
01337 Bernardston○ 1,750 ... D2
01915 Beverly 37,655 ... E5
01821 Billerica○ 36,727 ... J2
01504 Blackstone○ 6,570 ... H4
01008 Blandford○ 1,038 ... C4
01740 Bolton○ 2,530 ... H3
01009 Bondsville 1,906 ... E4
*02101 Boston (cap.)⊙ 562,994 ... D7
Boston‡ 2,763,357 ... D7
02532 Bourne○ 13,874 ... M6
02532 Bourne 2,678 ... M6
01719 Boxborough○ 3,126 ... H3
01921 Boxford○ 5,374 ... L2
01921 Boxford 1,841 ... L2
01505 Boylston○ 3,470 ... H3
02184 Braintree○ 36,337 ... D8
02020 Brant Rock-Ocean Bluff 4,055 ... M4
02631 Brewster○ 5,226 ... O5
02631 Brewster 1,744 ... O5
02324 Bridgewater○ 17,202 ... K5
02324 Bridgewater 6,781 ... K5
01010 Brimfield○ 2,318 ... F4
*C2401 Brockton 95,172 ... K4
Brockton‡ 169,374 ... K4
01506 Brookfield○ 2,397 ... F4
01506 Brookfield 1,037 ... F4
02146 Brookline○ 55,062 ... C7
01338 Buckland○ 1,864 ... C2
01803 Burlington○ 23,486 ... C5
02532 Buzzards Bay 3,375 ... M5
02138 Cambridge⊙ 95,322 ... C7
02021 Canton○ 18,182 ... C8
01741 Carlisle○ 3,306 ... J2
02330 Carver○ 6,988 ... M5
02632 Centerville 3,640 ... N6
01339 Charlemont○ 1,149 ... C2
01507 Charlton○ 6,719 ... F4
02633 Chatham○ 6,071 ... P6
02633 Chatham 1,922 ... P6
01824 Chelmsford○ 31,174 ... J2
02150 Chelsea 25,431 ... D6
01225 Cheshire○ 3,124 ... B2
01011 Chester○ 1,123 ... C3
01012 Chesterfield○ 1,000 ... C3
*01013 Chicopee 55,112 ... D4
02535 Chilmark○ 489 ... M7
†02054 Clicquot-Millis 3,777 ... A8
01510 Clinton○ 12,771 ... H3
01778 Cochituate 6,126 ... A7
02025 Cohasset○ 7,174 ... F7
01340 Colrain○ 1,552 ... D2
01742 Concord○ 16,293 ... B6
01341 Conway○ 1,213 ... D2
†01772 Cordaville 1,384 ... H3
01026 Cummington○ 657 ... C3
01226 Dalton○ 6,797 ... B3
01923 Danvers○ 24,100 ... D5
02714 Dartmouth○ 23,966 ... K6
02026 Dedham⊙○ 25,298 ... C7
01342 Deerfield○ 4,517 ... D2
02638 Dennis○ 12,360 ... O5
02639 Dennis Port 2,570 ... O6
02715 Dighton○ 5,352 ... K5
†02122 Dorchester ... D7
†01516 Douglas○ 3,730 ... H4
02030 Dover○ 4,703 ... B7
02030 Dover 2,051 ... B7
01826 Dracut○ 21,249 ... J2
01570 Dudley○ 8,717 ... G4
01827 Dunstable○ 1,671 ... J2
02332 Duxbury○ 11,807 ... M4
02332 Duxbury 1,685 ... M4
02333 East Bridgewater○ 9,945 ... L4
01515 East Brookfield○ 1,955 ... G4
01515 East Brookfield 1,443 ... G4
01516 East Douglas 1,683 ... G4
02536 East Falmouth (Teaticket) 5,181 ... M6
02642 Eastham○ 3,472 ... O5
01027 Easthampton○ 15,580 ... D3
01028 East Longmeadow○ 12,905 ... E4
02334 Easton○ 16,623 ... K4
01437 East Pepperell 2,212 ... H2
02539 Edgartown○ 2,204 ... M7
02539 Edgartown⊙ 1,138 ... M7
01344 Erving○ 1,326 ... E2
01929 Essex○ 2,998 ... L2
01929 Essex 1,490 ... L2
02149 Everett 37,195 ... D6
02719 Fairhaven○ 15,759 ... L6
*02720 Fall River 92,574 ... K6
Fall River‡ 176,831 ... K6
*02540 Falmouth○ 23,640 ... M6
*02540 Falmouth 5,720 ... M6
01518 Fiskdale 1,859 ... F4
01420 Fitchburg⊙ 39,580 ... G2
Fitchburg-Leominster‡ 99,957 ... G2
†01247 Florida○ 730 ... B2
02035 Foxboro○ 14,148 ... J4
02035 Foxboro 5,697 ... J4
01701 Framingham○ 65,113 ... A7
02038 Franklin○ 18,217 ... J4
02038 Franklin 9,296 ... J4
01440 Gardner 17,900 ... G2
†02535 Gay Head○ 220 ... L7
01833 Georgetown○ 5,687 ... L2
01031 Gilbertville 1,029 ... F3
†01376 Gill○ 1,259 ... D2
01930 Gloucester 27,768 ... M2
01032 Goshen○ 651 ... C3
01519 Grafton○ 11,238 ... H4
01033 Granby○ 5,380 ... E3
01033 Granby 1,302 ... E3
01034 Granville○ 1,204 ... C4
01230 Great Barrington○ 7,405 ... A4
01230 Great Barrington 3,150 ... A4
01301 Greenfield○ 18,436 ... D2
01301 Greenfield⊙ 14,198 ... D2
02041 Green Harbor 2,002 ... M4
01450 Groton○ 6,154 ... H2
01450 Groton 1,264 ... H2
01830 Groveland○ 5,040 ... L1
01035 Hadley○ 4,125 ... D3
02338 Halifax○ 5,513 ... L5
01936 Hamilton○ 6,960 ... L2
01036 Hampden○ 4,745 ... E4
01237 Hancock○ 643 ... A2
02339 Hanover○ 11,358 ... L4
02341 Hanson○ 8,617 ... L4
02341 Hanson 2,120 ... L4
01037 Hardwick○ 2,272 ... F3
01451 Harvard○ 12,170 ... H2
02645 Harwich○ 8,971 ... O6
02645 Harwich 4,399 ... O6
01038 Hatfield○ 3,045 ... D3
01038 Hatfield 1,251 ... D3
01830 Haverhill 46,865 ... K1
01346 Heath○ 482 ... C2
02043 Hingham○ 20,339 ... E8
02043 Hingham 5,742 ... E8
01235 Hinsdale○ 1,707 ... B3
02343 Holbrook○ 11,140 ... D8
01520 Holden○ 13,336 ... G3
†01550 Holland○ 1,589 ... F4
01746 Holliston○ 12,622 ... A8
01040 Holyoke 44,678 ... D4
01747 Hopedale○ 3,905 ... H4
01747 Hopedale 2,810 ... H4
01748 Hopkinton○ 7,114 ... J4
01748 Hopkinton 2,542 ... J4
01236 Housatonic 1,314 ... A3
01452 Hubbardston○ 1,797 ... F3
01749 Hudson○ 16,408 ... H3
01749 Hudson 14,156 ... H3
02045 Hull○ 9,714 ... E7
01050 Huntington○ 1,804 ... C4
02601 Hyannis 9,118 ... N6
01938 Ipswich○ 11,158 ... L2
01938 Ipswich 4,548 ... L2
02364 Kingston○ 7,362 ... M5
02364 Kingston 4,405 ... M5
02346 Lakeville○ 5,931 ... L5
02346 Lakeville 1,948 ... L5
01523 Lancaster○ 6,334 ... H3
01237 Lanesboro○ 3,131 ... A2
*01840 Lawrence⊙ 63,175 ... K2
Lawrence-Haverhill‡ 281,981 ... K2
01238 Lee○ 6,247 ... B3
01238 Lee 2,140 ... B3
01524 Leicester○ 9,446 ... G4
01240 Lenox○ 6,523 ... A3
01240 Lenox 2,668 ... A3
01453 Leominster 34,508 ... G2
01054 Leverett○ 1,471 ... E3
02173 Lexington○ 29,479 ... B6
†01301 Leyden○ 498 ... D2
01773 Lincoln○ 7,098 ... B6
01460 Littleton○ 6,970 ... H2
†01460 Littleton Common 3,109 ... J2
01106 Longmeadow○ 16,301 ... D4
*01850 Lowell⊙ 92,418 ... J2
Lowell‡ 233,410 ... J2
01056 Ludlow○ 18,150 ... E4
01462 Lunenburg○ 8,405 ... H2
01462 Lunenburg 1,789 ... H2
*01901 Lynn 78,471 ... D6
01940 Lynnfield○ 11,267 ... D5
02148 Malden 53,386 ... D6
01944 Manchester○ 5,424 ... F5
02048 Mansfield○ 13,453 ... J4
02048 Mansfield 6,786 ... J4
01945 Marblehead○ 20,126 ... E7
02738 Marion○ 3,932 ... L6
02738 Marion 1,438 ... L6
01752 Marlborough 30,617 ... H3
02050 Marshfield○ 20,916 ... M4
02050 Marshfield 4,421 ... M4
02051 Marshfield Hills 2,308 ... M4
02649 Mashpee○ 3,700 ... M6
02739 Mattapoisett○ 5,597 ... L6
02739 Mattapoisett 3,159 ... L6
01754 Maynard○ 9,590 ... J3
02052 Medfield○ 10,220 ... B8
02052 Medfield 6,108 ... B8
02155 Medford 58,076 ... C6
02053 Medway○ 8,447 ... J4
02176 Melrose 30,055 ... D6
01756 Mendon○ 3,108 ... H4
01860 Merrimac○ 4,451 ... L1
01844 Methuen○ 36,701 ... K2
02346 Middleboro○ 16,404 ... L5
02346 Middleboro 7,012 ... L5
01243 Middlefield○ 385 ... B3
01949 Middleton○ 4,135 ... K2
01757 Milford○ 23,390 ... H4
01757 Milford 21,730 ... H4
01527 Millbury○ 11,808 ... H4
01349 Millers Falls 1,101 ... E2
02054 Millis○ 6,908 ... A8
02054 Millis-Clicquot 3,777 ... A8
01529 Millville○ 1,693 ... H4
02186 Milton○ 25,860 ... D7
01057 Monson○ 7,315 ... E4
01057 Monson 2,167 ... E4
01351 Montague○ 8,011 ... E2
01245 Monterey○ 818 ... B4
†12517 Mount Washington○ 93 ... A4
01908 Nahant○ 3,947 ... E6
02554 Nantucket○ 5,087 ... O7
02554 Nantucket⊙ 3,229 ... O7
01760 Natick○ 29,461 ... A7
02192 Needham○ 27,901 ... B7
*02740 New Bedford⊙ 98,478 ... K6
New Bedford‡ 169,425 ... K6
01531 New Braintree○ 671 ... F3
01950 Newbury○ 4,529 ... L1
01950 Newburyport⊙ 15,900 ... L1
†01230 New Marlborough○ 1,160 ... B4
01355 New Salem○ 688 ... E2
†02158 Newton 83,622 ... C7
02056 Norfolk○ 6,363 ... J4
01247 North Adams 18,063 ... B2
01059 North Amherst 5,616 ... E3
01060 Northampton⊙ 29,286 ... D3
01845 North Andover○ 20,129 ... K2
*02760 North Attleboro○ 21,095 ... J5
01532 Northborough○ 10,568 ... H3
01532 Northborough 5,670 ... H3
01534 Northbridge○ 12,246 ... H4
01535 North Brookfield○ 4,150 ... F3
01535 North Brookfield 2,543 ... F3
02764 North Dighton 1,174 ... K5
02651 North Eastham 1,318 ... O5
01360 Northfield○ 2,386 ... E2
01360 Northfield 1,182 ... E2
02358 North Pembroke 2,215 ... M4
02360 North Plymouth 3,250 ... L5
01864 North Reading○ 11,455 ... C5
02060 North Scituate 5,221 ... F8
02766 Norton○ 12,690 ... K5
02766 Norton 2,035 ... K5
02061 Norwell○ 9,182 ... F8
02062 Norwood○ 29,711 ... B8
02557 Oak Bluffs○ 1,984 ... M7
02557 Oak Bluffs 1,124 ... M7
01068 Oakham○ 994 ... F3
02065 Ocean Bluff-Brant Rock 4,055 ... M4
†01566 Old Sturbridge Village 500 ... F4
02558 Onset 1,493 ... M6
01364 Orange○ 6,844 ... E2
01364 Orange 3,942 ... E2
02653 Orleans○ 5,306 ... O5
02653 Orleans 1,811 ... O5
02655 Osterville 1,799 ... N6
01253 Otis○ 963 ... B4
01540 Oxford○ 11,680 ... G4
01540 Oxford 6,369 ... G4
01069 Palmer○ 11,389 ... E4
01069 Palmer 3,854 ... E4
01612 Paxton○ 3,762 ... G3
01960 Peabody 45,976 ... E5
†01002 Pelham○ 1,112 ... E3
02359 Pembroke○ 13,487 ... L4
01463 Pepperell○ 8,061 ... H2
01463 Pepperell 2,076 ... H2
01366 Petersham○ 1,024 ... F3
†01331 Phillipston○ 953 ... F2
01866 Pinehurst 6,588 ... B5
01201 Pittsfield⊙ 51,974 ... A3
Pittsfield‡ 90,505 ... A3
01070 Plainfield○ 425 ... C2
02762 Plainville○ 5,857 ... J4
02360 Plymouth○ 35,913 ... M5
02360 Plymouth⊙ 7,232 ... M5
02367 Plympton○ 1,974 ... L5
01541 Princeton○ 2,425 ... G3
02657 Provincetown○ 3,536 ... O4
02657 Provincetown 3,372 ... O4
02169 Quincy 84,743 ... D7
02368 Randolph○ 28,218 ... D8
02767 Raynham○ 9,085 ... K5
02768 Raynham Center 3,776 ... K5
01867 Reading○ 22,678 ... C5
02769 Rehoboth○ 7,570 ... K5
02151 Revere 42,423 ... D6

(continued on following page)

01266 West Stockbridge○ 1,280 ..A3	02152 Winthrop○ 19,294 ....D6
02575 West Tisbury○ 1,010....... M7	02135 Woburn 36,626 ....C6
01587 West Upton-Upton 2,184....H4	02543 Woods Hole 1,080 ....M6
02576 West Wareham 1,837......L5	*01601 Worcester⊙ 161,799 ....H3
02090 Westwood○ 13,212 ......B8	Worcester‡ 372,940 ......H3
02673 West Yarmouth 3,852 ....N6	01098 Worthington○ 932 ....C3
02188 Weymouth 55,601 ......D8	02093 Wrentham○ 7,580 ....J4
01093 Whately○ 1,341 ....D3	Yarmouth○ 18,449 .....O6
01588 Whitinsville 5,379......H4	02675 Yarmouth Port 2,490 ....N6
02382 Whitman○ 13,534 ......L4	
01095 Wilbraham 12,053 ....E4	OTHER FEATURES
01095 Wilbraham 3,379 ....E4	
01096 Williamsburg○ 2,237 ....C3	Adams Nat'l Hist. Site D7
01267 Williamstown○ 8,741 ....B2	Agawam (riv.) M5
01267 Williamstown 4,798 ....B2	Allerton (pt.) E7
01887 Wilmington 17,471 ....C5	Ann (cape) M2
01475 Winchendon○ 7,019 ....F2	Ashmere (lake) B3
01475 Winchendon 4,030 ....F2	Assabet (riv.) H3
01890 Winchester 20,701 ....C6	Assawompset (pond) L5
01270 Windsor○ 598 ....B2	Bachelor (brook) D3

Berkshire (hills) B4	Cod (cape) O4	Otis A.F.B. M6	02822 Exeter○ 4,453 ....H6
Big (pond) B4	Concord (riv.) J2	Pasque (isl.) L7	02825 Foster○ 3,370 ....H5
Bigelow (bight) M1	Congamond (lkes.) D4	Plum (isl.) L2	02828 Greenville 7,516 ....H5
Blackstone (riv.) G3	Connecticut (riv.) D2	Plymouth (bay) M5	02830 Harrisville 1,224 ....H5
Blue (hills) C8	Cuttyhunk (isl.) L7	Poge (cape) N7	02832 Hope Valley 1,414 ....H6
Boston (bay) E6	Deer (isl.) E7	Pontoosuc (lake) A3	02833 Hopkinton○ 6,406 ....H7
Boston (harb.) D7	Deerfield (riv.) C2	Quabbin (res.) E3	02835 Jamestown○ 4,040 ......J6
Boston Nat'l Hist. Park D6	East (pt.) E6	Quaboag (riv.) F4	02835 Jamestown 2,156........J6
Brewster (isls.) E7	East Chop (pt.) M7	Quincy (bay) D7	02881 Kingston 5,479 ....J7
Buel (lake) A4	Eastern (pt.) M2	Quinebaug (riv.) F4	02837 Little Compton 3,085 ....K6
Buzzards (bay) L7	Elizabeth (isls.) L7	Race (pt.) N4	02840 Middletown 17,216 ......J6
Cambridge (res.) B6	Everett (mt.) A4	Salem Maritime Nat'l Hist.	02882 Narragansett○ 12,088 ...J7
Cape Cod (bay) N5	Falls (riv.) D2	Site E5	02882 Narragansett 3,342 .....J7
Cape Cod (canal) M5	Fort Devens H2	Saugus Iron Works Nat'l Hist.	02840 Newport○ 29,259 ....J7
Cape Cod Nat'l Seashore P5	Fort Rodman L6	Site D6	†02807 New Shoreham (Block
Chappaquiddick (isl.) N7	Fresh (pond) C6	Shawsheen (riv.) K2	Island)○ 620 ....H8
Charles (riv.) C7	Gammon (pt.) N6	Silver (lake) L4	02852 North Kingstown○
Chicopee (riv.) D4	Gay Head (prom.) L7	South (riv.) D2	21,938 ....J6
Cobble Mountain (res.) C4	Grace (mt.) E2	Springfield Armory Nat'l Hist.	02908 North Providence○
Cochituate (lake) A7	Great (pt.) O7	Site D4	29,188...............J5
	Green (riv.) B2	Squibnocket (pt.) M7	02859 Pascoag 3,807 ....H5
	Greylock (mt.) B2	Stillwater (riv.) G3	*02860 Pawtucket 71,204.......J5
	Gurnet (pt.) M4	Sudbury (res.) H3	02883 Peace
	Hingham (bay) E7	Sudbury (riv.) A6	Dale-Wakefield 6,474 ....J7
	Holyoke (range) D3	Swift (riv.) E4	02871 Portsmouth○ 14,257 .....J6
	Hoosac (mts.) B2	Taconic (mts.) A2	*02901 Providence
	Hoosic (riv.) A1	Taunton (riv.) K5	(cap.)⊙ 156,804 ......H5
	Housatonic (riv.) A4	Thompson (isl.) D7	Providence-Warwick-
	Ipswich (riv.) L2	Toby (mt.) E3	Pawtucket‡ 919,216 ...H5
	John F. Kennedy Nat'l Hist.	Tom (mt.) D4	02878 Tiverton○ 13,526 ....K6
	Site C7	Tuckernuck (isl.) N7	02878 Tiverton 7,653 ....K6
	Knightville (res.) C3	Vineyard (sound) L7	†02864 Valley Falls 10,892 ......J5
	Laurence G. Hanscom Field ...B6	Wachusett (mt.) G3	*02879 Wakefield-Peace
	Little (riv.) C4	Wachusett (res.) G3	Dale 6,474 ....J7
	Logan Internat'l Airport D7	Walden (pond) A6	02885 Warren○ 10,640 ....J6
	Long (isl.) E7	Ware (riv.) F3	*02886 Warwick 87,123 ....J6
	Long (isl.) O4	Watuppa (pond) K6	02891 Westerly○ 18,580 ....G7
	Long (pond) L5	Webster (lake) G4	02891 Westerly⊙ 14,093 ....G7
	Lowell Nat'l Hist. Park J2	Wellfleet (harb.) O5	02893 West Warwick 27,026 ....H6
	Maine (gulf) M2	West (riv.) H4	02895 Woonsocket⊙ 45,914 ....J4
	Manhan (riv.) D4	West Branch, Farmington	
	Manomet (pt.) N5	(riv.) B4	OTHER FEATURES
	Marblehead (neck) F6	West Chop (pt.) M7	
	Martha's Vineyard (isl.) M7	Westfield (riv.) C3	Black Rock (pt.) H8
	Massachusetts (bay) M4	Westover A.F.B. D4	Block (isl.) H8
	Merrimack (riv.) K1	Weweantic (riv.) L5	Block Island (sound) H8
	Mill (riv.) C3	Whitman (riv.) G2	Brenton (pt.) J7
	Mill (riv.) D3	Winter I. Coast Guard Air Sta. ..E5	Conanicut (isl.) J6
	Millers (riv.) E2		Dickens (pt.) H8
	Minute Man Nat'l Hist. Park ...B6	RHODE ISLAND	Durfee (hill) G5
	Mishaum (pt.) L6		Grace (pt.) H8
	Monomonac (lake) G2	COUNTIES	Jerimoth (hill) G5
	Monomoy (isl.) O6		Judith (pt.) J7
	Monomoy (pt.) O6	Bristol 46,942 ....J6	Mount Hope (bay) K6
	Mount Hope (bay) K6	Kent 154,163 ....H6	Narragansett (bay) J6
	Muskeget (chan.) N7	Newport 81,383 ....K6	Noyes (pt.) H7
	Muskeget (isl.) N7	Providence 571,349 ....H5	Pawcatuck (riv.) G7
	Mystic (lake) C6	Washington 93,317 ....H7	Prudence (isl.) J6
	Mystic (riv.) C6		Rhode Island (isl.) J6
	Nahant (bay) E6	CITIES and TOWNS	Rhode Island (sound) J7
	Nantucket (isl.) O8	Zip Name/Pop. Key	Roger Williams Nat'l Mem. J5
	Nantucket (sound) N6		Sakonnet (pt.) K7
	Nashawena (isl.) L7	02804 Ashaway 1,747 ....G7	Sakonnet (riv.) K7
	Nashua (riv.) H3	02806 Barrington○ 16,174.....J6	Sandy (pt.) H8
	Naushon (isl.) L7	02807 Block Island 620 ....H8	Scituate (res.) H5
	Neponset (riv.) C8	02808 Bradford 1,354 ....H7	Stillwater (res.) C2
	Nomans Land (isl.) L7	02809 Bristol⊙ 20,128 ....J6	Touro Synagogue Nat'l Hist.
	Nonamesset (isl.) M6	02863 Central Falls 16,995 ....J5	Site J7
	North (riv.) D2	02816 Coventry○ 27,065.......H6	Watch Hill (pt.) G7
	North (riv.) L4	02910 Cranston 71,992 ....J5	⊙County seat (Shire town)
	Onota (lake) A3	02818 East Greenwich○⊙ 10,211 H6	‡Population of metropolitan area.
	Otis (res.) B4	02914 East Providence 50,980 ...J5	○Population of town or township.
			† Zip of nearest p.o. * Multiple zips.

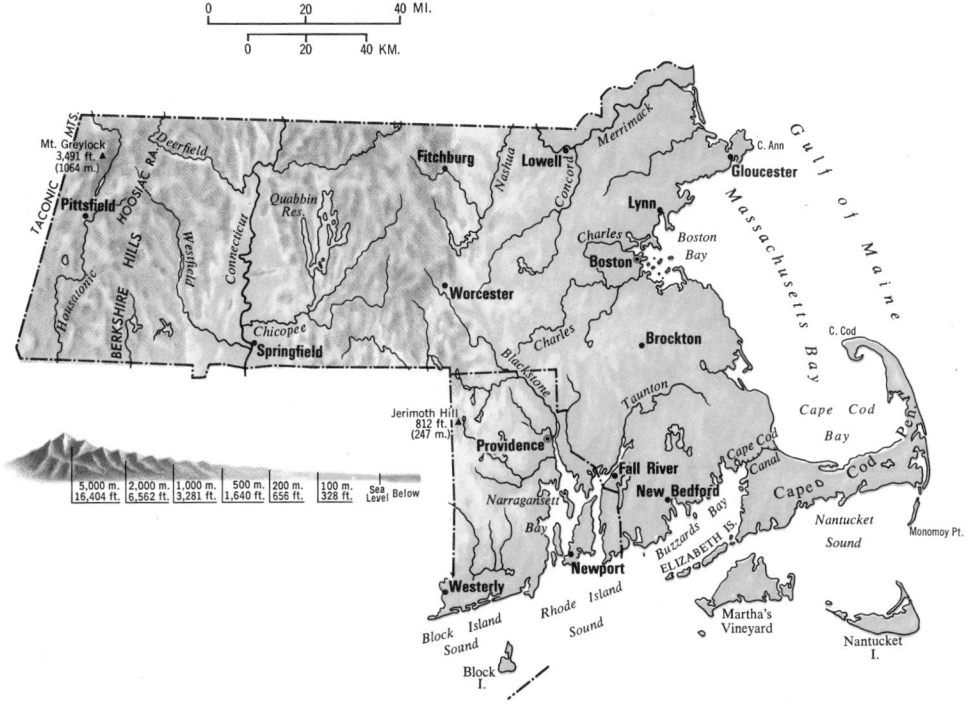

Topography

Michigan

SCALE

0 5 10   20   30   40   50 MI.

0 5 10 20 30 40 50 KM.

State Capitals............⊛
County Seats.............◉
Canals...................

Major Limited Access Hwys. ▬▬▬

Scale 1:2,360,000

© Copyright HAMMOND INCORPORATED, Maplewood, N.J.

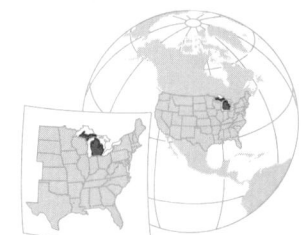

AREA 58,527 sq. mi. (151,585 sq. km.)
POPULATION 9,262,078
CAPITAL Lansing
LARGEST CITY Detroit
HIGHEST POINT Mt. Curwood 1,980 ft. (604 m.)
SETTLED IN 1650
ADMITTED TO UNION January 26, 1837
POPULAR NAME Wolverine State
STATE FLOWER Apple Blossom
STATE BIRD Robin

Topography

0   50   100 MI.

0   50   100 KM.

COUNTIES

Alcona 9,740	F4
Alger 9,225	C2
Allegan 81,555	D6
Alpena 32,315	F4
Antrim 16,194	D3
Arenac 14,706	F4
Baraga 8,484	A2
Barry 45,781	D6
Bay 119,881	E5
Benzie 11,205	C4
Berrien 171,276	C7
Branch 40,188	D7
Calhoun 141,557	D6
Cass 49,499	C7
Charlevoix 19,907	D3
Cheboygan 20,649	E3
Chippewa 29,029	E2
Clare 23,822	E5
Clinton 55,893	E6
Crawford 9,465	E4
Delta 38,947	C2
Dickinson 25,341	B2
Eaton 88,337	E6
Emmet 22,992	E3
Genesee 450,449	F5
Gladwin 19,957	E4
Gogebic 19,686	F2
Grand Traverse 54,899	D4
Gratiot 40,448	E5
Hillsdale 42,071	E7
Houghton 37,872	G1
Huron 36,459	F5
Ingham 275,520	E6
Ionia 51,815	D6
Iosco 28,349	F4
Iron 13,635	G2
Isabella 54,110	E5
Jackson 151,495	E6
Kalamazoo 212,378	D6
Kalkaska 10,952	D4
Kent 444,506	D5
Keweenaw 1,963	A1
Lake 7,711	D5
Lapeer 70,038	F5
Leelanau 14,007	D4
Lenawee 89,948	E7
Livingston 100,289	F6
Luce 6,659	D2
Mackinac 10,178	D2
Macomb 694,600	G6
Manistee 23,019	C4
Marquette 74,101	B2
Mason 26,365	C4
Mecosta 36,961	D5
Menominee 26,201	B3
Midland 73,578	E5
Missaukee 10,009	D4
Monroe 134,659	F7
Montcalm 47,555	D5
Montmorency 7,492	E3
Muskegon 157,589	C5
Newaygo 34,917	C5
Oakland 1,011,793	F6
Oceana 22,002	C5
Ogemaw 16,436	E4
Ontonagon 9,861	F1
Osceola 18,928	D5
Oscoda 6,858	E4
Otsego 14,993	E3
Ottawa 157,174	C6
Presque Isle 14,267	F3
Roscommon 16,374	E4
Saginaw 228,059	E5
Saint Clair 138,802	G6
Saint Joseph 56,083	D7
Sanilac 40,789	G5
Schoolcraft 8,575	C2
Shiawassee 71,140	E6
Tuscola 56,961	F5
Van Buren 66,814	C6
Washtenaw 264,748	F6
Wayne 2,337,891	F6
Wexford 25,102	D4

CITIES and TOWNS

Zip	Name/Pop.	Key
49220	Addison 655	E7
49221	Adrian⊙ 21,186	F7
48701	Akron 538	F5
†48763	Alabaster 46	F4
49224	Albion 11,059	E6
49001	Algonac 4,412	G6
49010	Allegan⊙ 4,576	D6
48101	Allen Park 34,196	B7
48801	Alma 9,652	E5
48003	Almont 1,857	F6
49707	Alpena⊙ 12,214	F3
*48103	Ann Arbor⊙ 107,966	F6
	Ann Arbor‡ 264,748	F6
48005	Armada 1,392	G6
48806	Ashley 570	E5
49011	Athens 960	D6
49709	Atlanta⊙ 475	E3
48611	Auburn 1,921	F5
48703	Au Gres 768	F4
49012	Augusta 913	D6
†48750	Au Sable 1,240	F4
48413	Bad Axe⊙ 3,184	G5
49304	Baldwin⊙ 674	D5
48414	Bancroft 618	E6
49013	Bangor 2,001	C6
49908	Baraga 1,055	G1
49101	Baroda 627	C7
*49014	Battle Creek 35,724	D6
	Battle Creek‡ 187,338	D6
48706	Bay City⊙ 41,593	F5
	Bay City‡ 119,881	F5
48612	Beaverton 1,025	E5
48809	Belding 5,634	D5
49615	Bellaire⊙ 1,063	D4
48111	Belleville 3,366	F6
49021	Bellevue 1,289	E6
49022	Benton Harbor 14,707	C6
	Benton Harbor‡ 171,276	C6
†49022	Benton Heights 6,787	C6
48072	Berkley 18,637	B6
49103	Berrien Springs 2,042	C7
49911	Bessemer⊙ 2,553	F2
49617	Beulah⊙ 454	C4
†48010	Beverly Hills 11,598	B6
49307	Big Rapids⊙ 14,361	D5
48415	Birch Run 1,196	F5
*48008	Birmingham 21,689	B6
49228	Blissfield 3,107	F7
48013	Bloomfield Hills 3,985	B6
49026	Bloomingdale 537	C6
49712	Boyne City 3,348	E3
48615	Breckenridge 1,495	E5
49106	Bridgman 2,235	C7
48116	Brighton 4,268	F6
49229	Britton 693	F6
49028	Bronson 2,271	D7
49230	Brooklyn 1,110	E6
48416	Brown City 1,163	G5
49107	Buchanan 5,142	C7
49030	Burr Oak 853	D7
48507	Burton 29,976	F6
48418	Byron 689	E6
49601	Cadillac⊙ 10,199	D4
49316	Caledonia 722	D6
49913	Calumet 1,013	A1
48014	Capac 1,377	G5
48117	Carleton 2,786	F6
48723	Caro⊙ 4,317	F5
48724	Carrollton 7,482	E5
48811	Carson City 1,229	E5
48419	Carsonville 622	G5
48725	Caseville 851	F5
49915	Caspian 1,038	G2
48726	Cass City 2,258	F5
49319	Cedar Springs 2,615	D5
49233	Cement City 539	E6
48015	Center Line 9,293	B6
49622	Central Lake 895	D3
49032	Centreville⊙ 1,202	D7
49720	Charlevoix⊙ 3,296	D3
48813	Charlotte⊙ 8,251	E6
48428	Dryden 650	F6
48131	Dundee 2,575	F7
48429	Durand 4,241	E6
49924	Eagle River⊙ 20	A1
48021	East Detroit 38,280	B6
†49506	East Grand Rapids 10,914	D6
49727	East Jordan 2,185	D3
†49801	East Kingsford	A3
48823	East Lansing 51,392	E6
48730	East Tawas 2,584	F4
48827	Eaton Rapids 4,510	E6
49111	Eau Claire 573	C6
48229	Ecorse 14,447	B7
48829	Edmore 1,176	E5
49112	Edwardsburg 1,135	C7
49628	Elberta 556	C4
49629	Elk Rapids 1,504	D4
48731	Elkton 953	F5
48831	Elsie 1,022	E5
48929	Escanaba⊙ 14,355	C3
48732	Essexville 4,378	F5
49631	Evart 1,945	D5
48733	Fairgrove 691	F5
49027	Fair Plain 8,289	C6
*48024	Farmington 11,022	F6
48024	Farmington Hills 58,056	F6
48622	Farwell 804	E5
49408	Fennville 934	C6
48430	Fenton 8,098	F6
48220	Ferndale 26,227	B6
49409	Ferrysburg 2,440	C5
48134	Flat Rock 6,853	F6
*48501	Flint⊙ 159,611	F5
	Flint‡ 521,589	F5
48433	Flushing 8,624	F5
48835	Fowler 1,021	E5
48836	Fowlerville 2,289	F6

48734	Frankenmuth 3,753	F5
49635	Frankfort 1,603	C4
48025	Franklin 2,864	B6
48026	Fraser 14,560	B6
48623	Freeland 1,364	E5
49412	Fremont 3,672	D5
49415	Fruitport 1,143	C5
49053	Galesburg 1,822	D6
49113	Galien 692	C7
48135	Garden City 35,640	F6
49735	Gaylord⊙ 3,011	E3
48173	Gibraltar 4,458	F6
49837	Gladstone 4,533	C3
48624	Gladwin⊙ 2,479	E5
49055	Gobles 816	D6
48438	Goodrich 795	F6
48439	Grand Blanc 6,848	F6
49417	Grand Haven⊙ 11,763	C5
48837	Grand Ledge 6,920	E6
*49501	Grand Rapids⊙ 181,843	D5
	Grand Rapids‡ 601,680	D5
49418	Grandville 12,412	D6
49327	Grant 683	D5
49240	Grass Lake 962	E6
49738	Grayling⊙ 1,792	E4
48838	Greenville 8,019	D5
48138	Grosse Ile 9,320	B7
48236	Grosse Pointe 5,901	B7
†48236	Grosse Pointe Farms 10,551	B6
†48236	Grosse Pointe Park 13,639	B7
†48236	Grosse Pointe Shores 3,122	B6
†48236	Grosse Pointe Woods 18,886	B6
49841	Gwinn 1,408	B2
48212	Hamtramck 21,300	B6
49930	Hancock 5,122	G1

48441	Harbor Beach 2,000	G5
49740	Harbor Springs 1,567	D3
48225	Harper Woods 16,361	B6
48625	Harrison⊙ 1,700	E4
48740	Harrisville⊙ 559	F4
49420	Hart⊙ 1,888	C5
49057	Hartford 2,493	C6
48840	Haslett 7,025	E6
49058	Hastings⊙ 6,418	D6
48030	Hazel Park 20,914	B6
48626	Hemlock 1,362	E5
49421	Hesperia 875	D5
48203	Highland Park 27,909	B6
49242	Hillsdale⊙ 7,432	E7
49423	Holland 26,281	C6
48842	Holt 10,097	E6
49245	Homer 1,791	E6
49931	Houghton⊙ 7,512	G1
48629	Houghton Lake 2,449	E4
48630	Houghton Lake Heights	E4
49329	Howard City 1,118	D5
48843	Howell⊙ 6,976	E6
49934	Hubbell 1,278	A1
49247	Hudson 2,545	E7
49426	Hudsonville 4,844	D6
48444	Imlay City 2,495	F5
48141	Inkster 35,190	B7
49643	Interlochen 600	D4
48846	Ionia⊙ 5,920	D6
49801	Iron Mountain⊙ 8,341	B3
49935	Iron River 2,426	G2
49938	Ironwood 7,741	F2
49849	Ishpeming 7,538	B2
48847	Ithaca⊙ 2,950	E5
*49201	Jackson⊙ 39,739	E6
	Jackson‡ 151,495	E6
49428	Jenison 16,330	D6
49250	Jonesville 2,172	E6

*49001	Kalamazoo⊙ 79,722	D6
	Kalamazoo-Portage‡ 279,192	D6
49646	Kalkaska⊙ 1,654	D4
48030	Keego Harbor 3,083	F6
49330	Kent City 860	D5
49508	Kentwood 30,438	D6
48445	Kinde 600	G5
49801	Kingsford 5,290	A3
49649	Kingsley 664	D4
48848	Laingsburg 1,145	E6
49651	Lake City⊙ 843	D4
49945	Lake Linden 1,181	A1
†49039	Lake Michigan Beach 2,001	C6
48849	Lake Odessa 2,171	D6
48035	Lake Orion 2,907	F6
48850	Lakeview 1,139	D5
†49440	Lakewood Club 695	C5
48144	Lambertville 6,341	F7
49946	L'Anse⊙ 2,500	G1
*48901	Lansing (cap.) 130,414	E6
	Lansing-East Lansing‡ 468,482	E6
48446	Lapeer⊙ 6,198	F5
49913	Laurium 2,678	A1
49064	Lawrence 903	C6
49065	Lawton 1,558	C6
49654	Leland⊙ 776	D3
48449	Lennon 600	E5
49251	Leslie 2,110	E6
48742	Lincoln 361	F4
48146	Lincoln Park 45,105	B7
48451	Linden 2,174	F6
49252	Litchfield 1,353	E6
*48150	Livonia 104,814	F6
49331	Lowell 3,707	D6
49431	Ludington⊙ 8,937	C5

(continued on following page)

48157 Luna Pier 1,443 .... F7
48851 Lyons 708 .... E6
49757 Mackinac Island 479 .... E3
49701 Mackinaw City 820 .... E3
48071 Madison Heights 35,375 .... B6
49659 Mancelona 1,432 .... E4
48158 Manchester 1,686 .... E6
49660 Manistee⊙ 7,566 .... C4
49854 Manistique⊙ 3,962 .... C3
49663 Manton 1,212 .... D4
48853 Maple Rapids 683 .... E5
49067 Marcellus 1,134 .... D6
48039 Marine City 4,414 .... G6
49665 Marion 816 .... D4
48453 Marlette 1,761 .... G5
49855 Marquette⊙ 23,288 .... B2
49068 Marshall⊙ 7,201 .... E6
49070 Martin 447 .... D6
48040 Marysville 7,345 .... G6
48854 Mason⊙ 6,019 .... E6
49071 Mattawan 2,143 .... D6
48744 Mayville 958 .... F5
49657 McBain 519 .... D4
48122 Melvindale 12,322 .... B7
48041 Memphis 1,171 .... G6
49072 Mendon 951 .... D7
49858 Menominee⊙ 10,099 .... B3
48637 Merrill 851 .... E5
48455 Metamora 552 .... F6
49254 Michigan Center 5,244 .... E6
49333 Middleville 1,797 .... D6
48640 Midland⊙ 37,250 .... E5
48160 Milan 4,182 .... F6
48042 Milford 5,041 .... F6
48746 Millington 1,237 .... F5
48647 Mio⊙ 975 .... E4
48161 Monroe⊙ 23,531 .... F7
49437 Montague 2,332 .... C5
48457 Montrose 1,706 .... F5
49256 Morenci 2,110 .... E7
49336 Morley 507 .... D5
48857 Morrice 733 .... E6
48043 Mount Clemens⊙ 18,806 .... G6
48458 Mount Morris 3,246 .... F5
48858 Mount Pleasant⊙ 23,746 .... E5
48860 Muir 698 .... D5
48861 Mulliken 550 .... E6
49862 Munising⊙ 3,083 .... C2
*49440 Muskegon⊙ 40,823 .... C5
Muskegon-Norton Shores-Muskegon Heights‡ 179,591 .... C5
49444 Muskegon Heights 14,611 .... C5
49261 Napoleon 1,400 .... E6
49073 Nashville 1,628 .... D6
49866 Negaunee 5,189 .... B2
49337 Newaygo 1,271 .... D5
48047 New Baltimore 5,439 .... G6
49868 Newberry⊙ 2,120 .... D2
48164 New Boston 1,200 .... F6
49117 New Buffalo 2,821 .... C7
48048 New Haven 1,871 .... G6
48460 New Lothrop 646 .... F5

49120 Niles 13,115 .... C7
49262 North Adams 565 .... E7
48461 North Branch 896 .... F5
49445 North Muskegon 4,024 .... C5
49670 Northport 611 .... D3
48167 Northville 5,698 .... F6
†49441 Norton Shores 22,025 .... C5
49870 Norway 2,919 .... B3
48050 Novi 22,525 .... F6
48237 Oak Park 31,537 .... B6
48864 Okemos 8,882 .... E6
49076 Olivet 1,604 .... E6
49765 Onaway 1,084 .... E3
49675 Onekama 582 .... C4
49265 Onsted 670 .... E6
49953 Ontonagon⊙ 2,182 .... F1
48033 Orchard Lake 1,798 .... F6
48462 Ortonville 1,190 .... F6
48750 Oscoda 2,431 .... F4
48463 Otisville 682 .... F5
49078 Otsego 3,802 .... D6
48866 Ovid 1,712 .... E5
48867 Owosso 16,455 .... E5
48051 Oxford 2,746 .... F6
49004 Parchment 1,817 .... D6
49269 Parma 873 .... E6
49079 Paw Paw⊙ 3,211 .... D6
†49038 Paw Paw Lake 4,193 .... C6
48052 Pearl Beach 3,430 .... G6
48466 Peck 606 .... G5
49769 Pellston 565 .... E3
49449 Pentwater 1,165 .... C5
48872 Perry 2,051 .... E6
49270 Petersburg 1,222 .... F7
49770 Petoskey⊙ 6,097 .... E3
48755 Pigeon 1,247 .... F5
48169 Pinckney 1,390 .... F6
48650 Pinconning 1,430 .... F5
49080 Plainwell 3,751 .... D6
48069 Pleasant Ridge 3,217 .... B6
*48170 Plymouth 9,986 .... F6
*48053 Pontiac⊙ 76,715 .... F6
49081 Portage 38,157 .... D6
48467 Port Austin 839 .... F4
48060 Port Huron⊙ 33,981 .... G6
48875 Portland 3,963 .... E6
48469 Port Sanilac 598 .... G5
49776 Posen 270 .... F3
48876 Potterville 1,502 .... E6
49082 Quincy 1,569 .... E7
49959 Ramsay F2
49451 Ravenna 951 .... D5
49274 Reading 1,203 .... E7
49677 Reed City⊙ 2,221 .... D5
48757 Reese 1,645 .... F5
48062 Richmond 3,536 .... G6
48218 River Rouge 12,912 .... B7
48192 Riverview 14,569 .... B7
48063 Rochester 7,203 .... F6
49341 Rockford 3,324 .... D5
48173 Rockwood 3,346 .... F6
49779 Rogers City⊙ 3,923 .... F3
48065 Romeo 3,509 .... F6

48174 Romulus 24,857 .... F6
49444 Roosevelt Park 4,015 .... C5
48653 Roscommon⊙ 834 .... E4
48654 Rose City 661 .... E4
48066 Roseville 54,311 .... B6
49452 Rothbury 522 .... C5
*48067 Royal Oak 70,893 .... B6
*48601 Saginaw⊙ 77,508 .... F5
Saginaw‡ 228,059 .... F5
48655 Saint Charles 2,276 .... E5
48079 Saint Clair 4,780 .... G6
*48080 Saint Clair Shores 76,210 .... B6
49781 Saint Ignace⊙ 2,632 .... E3
48879 Saint Johns⊙ 7,376 .... E6
49085 Saint Joseph⊙ 9,622 .... C6
48880 Saint Louis 4,107 .... E5
48176 Saline 6,483 .... F6
48471 Sandusky⊙ 2,216 .... G5
48657 Sanford 864 .... E5
48881 Saranac 1,421 .... D6
49453 Saugatuck 1,079 .... C6
49783 Sault Sainte Marie⊙ 14,448 .... E2
49087 Schoolcraft 1,359 .... D6
49454 Scottville 1,241 .... C5
48759 Sebewaing 2,046 .... F5
49455 Shelby 1,624 .... C5
48883 Shepherd 1,534 .... E5
48884 Sheridan 664 .... D5
†49085 Shoreham 742 .... C6
†49125 Shorewood 1,735 .... C7
*48034 Southfield 75,568 .... F6
48195 Southgate 32,058 .... F6
49090 South Haven 5,943 .... C6
48178 South Lyon 5,214 .... F6
†48161 South Monroe 4,232 .... F7
49963 South Range 861 .... G1
48179 South Rockwood 1,353 .... F7
†48060 Sparlingville 1,718 .... G6
49345 Sparta 3,373 .... D5
49283 Spring Arbor 2,101 .... E6
49015 Springfield 5,917 .... D6
49456 Spring Lake 2,731 .... C5
49284 Springport 675 .... E6
49964 Stambaugh 1,442 .... G2
48658 Standish⊙ 1,264 .... F5
48888 Stanton⊙ 1,315 .... D5
49887 Stephenson 967 .... B3
48659 Sterling 457 .... E4
48077 Sterling Heights 108,999 .... B6
49127 Stevensville 1,268 .... C6
49285 Stockbridge 1,213 .... E6
49091 Sturgis 9,468 .... D7
48890 Sunfield 591 .... D6
49682 Suttons Bay 504 .... D3
48473 Swartz Creek 5,013 .... F6
†48053 Sylvan Lake 1,949 .... F6
48763 Tawas City⊙ 1,967 .... F4
48180 Taylor 77,568 .... B7
49286 Tecumseh 7,320 .... E7
49092 Tekonsha 755 .... E6
49128 Three Oaks 1,774 .... C7
49093 Three Rivers 7,015 .... D7

49684 Traverse City⊙ 15,516 .... D4
48183 Trenton 22,762 .... B7
*48084 Troy 67,102 .... B6
48475 Ubly 862 .... G5
49094 Union City 1,667 .... D6
49129 Union Pier 1,039 .... C7
48767 Unionville 578 .... F5
*48087 Utica 5,282 .... F6
49095 Vandalia 447 .... D7
49795 Vanderbilt 525 .... E3
48768 Vassar 2,727 .... F5
49096 Vermontville 832 .... E6
48476 Vernon 1,008 .... F6
49097 Vicksburg 2,224 .... D6
49968 Wakefield 2,591 .... F2
49288 Waldron 570 .... E7
49504 Walker 15,088 .... D6
48088 Walled Lake 4,748 .... F6
*48089 Warren 161,134 .... B6
49098 Watervliet 1,867 .... C6
49348 Wayland 2,023 .... D6
48184 Wayne 21,159 .... F6
48892 Webberville 1,535 .... E6
49894 Wells B3
48661 West Branch⊙ 1,785 .... E4
48185 Westland 84,603 .... F6
48894 Westphalia 896 .... E6
49349 White Cloud⊙ 1,101 .... D5
49461 Whitehall 2,856 .... C5
49099 White Pigeon 1,478 .... D7
49971 White Pine 1,142 .... F1
48189 Whitmore Lake 2,920 .... F6
48770 Whittemore 438 .... F4
48895 Williamston 2,981 .... E6
48096 Wixom 6,705 .... F6
†49440 Wolf Lake 3,876 .... D5
49799 Wolverine 364 .... E3
†48183 Woodhaven 10,902 .... F6
48897 Woodland 431 .... D6
48192 Wyandotte 34,006 .... B7
49509 Wyoming 59,616 .... D6
48097 Yale 1,814 .... G5
48197 Ypsilanti 24,031 .... F6
49464 Zeeland 4,764 .... D6
†48601 Zilwaukee 2,201 .... F5

OTHER FEATURES

Abbaye (pt.) B2
Au Sable (pt.) C2
Au Sable (pt.) F4
Au Sable (riv.) E4
Au Train (bay) C2
Bad (riv.) E5
Barques (pt.) C3
Beaver (isl.) D3
Beaver (lake) F4
Belle (riv.) G6
Bete Grise (bay) B1
Betsy (riv.) D2
Big Bay (pt.) B2
Big Bay de Noc (bay) C3
Big Iron (riv.) F1
Big Sable (pt.) C4
Big Sable (riv.) C4
Big Star (lake) C5
Black (lake) E3
Black (riv.) E3
Black (riv.) G5
Blake (pt.) E1
Boardman (riv.) D4
Bois Blanc (isl.) E3
Bond Falls (res.) G2
Brevoort (lake) D3
Brule (riv.) A3
Burt (lake) E3
Cass (riv.) F5
Cedar (lake) F4
Charlevoix (lake) D3
Chippewa (riv.) E5
Crisp (pt.) D2
Crystal (lake) C4
Curwood (mt.) A2
Dead (riv.) B2
Deer (riv.) A2
De Tour (passage) E3
Detour (pt.) C3
Detroit (riv.) B7
Drummond (isl.) F2
Duck (lake) F4
Elk (lake) D4
Erie (lake) G7
Escanaba (riv.) B2
False Detour (chan.) F3
Fawn (riv.) D7
Fence (riv.) A2
Firesteel (riv.) G1
Fletcher (pond) F4
Flint (riv.) F5
Ford (riv.) B2
Forty Mile (pt.) F3
Fourteen Mile (pt.) F1
Garden (isl.) D3
Garden (pen.) C3
Glen (lake) C4
Gogebic (lake) F2
Good Harbor (bay) D3
Government (peak) F1
Grand (isl.) C2
Grand (lake) F3
Grand (riv.) D6
Grand Traverse (bay) D3
Granite (pt.) B2
Green (bay) B4
Gun (lake) D6
Hamlin (lake) C4
Higgins (lake) E4
High (isl.) D3
Hog (isl.) D3
Houghton (lake) E4
Hubbard (lake) F4
Huron (bay) A2
Huron (lake) G4
Huron (riv.) F6
Huron River (pt.) B2
Independence (lake) B2

Indian (lake) C2
Isle Royale Nat'l Park E1
Kalamazoo (riv.) C6
Keweenaw (bay) A1
Keweenaw (pt.) B1
K.I. Sawyer A.F.B. 7,345 .... B2
L'Anse Ind. Res. A2
Laughing Fish (pt.) B2
Leelanau (lake) D4
Light House (pt.) D3
Little Bay de Noc (bay) B3
Little Girl (pt.) E1
Little Sable (pt.) C5
Little Summer (isl.) C3
Little Traverse (bay) D3
Long (lake) F3
Lookingglass (riv.) E6
Mackinac (isl.) E3
Mackinac (str.) E3
Manistee (riv.) C4
Manistique (lake) D2
Manistique (riv.) C2
Manitou (isl.) B1
Maple (riv.) E5
Margrethe (lake) E4
Marquette (isl.) E3
Maumee (bay) F7
Menominee (riv.) B3
Michigamme (lake) A2
Michigamme (res.) B2
Michigamme (riv.) A2
Michigan (lake) B5
Mill (creek) G5
Millecoquins (lake) D2
Misery (bay) G1
Misery (riv.) G1
Montreal (riv.) F1
Mullett (lake) E3
Munuscong (lake) E2
Muskegon (riv.) C5
Neebish (isl.) E2
Net (riv.) G2
Ninemile (pt.) E3
North (chan.) F2
North (pt.) F3
North Fox (isl.) D3
North Manitou (isl.) C3
Oak (pt.) F5
Ontonagon (riv.) G1
Ontonagon Ind. Res. F1
Otsego (lake) E4
Paint (riv.) A2
Paradise (lake) E3
Passage (isl.) E1
Patterson (pt.) D3
Paw Paw (riv.) C6
Peninsula (pt.) C3
Perch (lake) G2
Perch (riv.) G2
Pere Marquette (riv.) D5
Pictured Rocks (cliff) C2
Pictured Rocks Nat'l Lakeshore C2
Pigeon (riv.) D7
Pigeon (riv.) E3
Pine (lake) F4
Pine (riv.) D4
Pine (riv.) E5
Platte (lake) C4
Porcupine (mts.) F1
Potagannissing (bay) F2
Poverty (isl.) C3
Prairie (riv.) D7
Presque Isle (riv.) F1
Rabbit (riv.) D6
Raisin (riv.) F7
Rapid (riv.) B2
Reedsburg (res.) E4
Rifle (riv.) E4
Royale (isl.) E1
Saginaw (bay) F5
Saginaw (riv.) F5
Saint Clair (lake) G6
Saint Clair (riv.) G6
Saint Joseph (riv.) C7
Saint Martin (bay) E3
Saint Martin (isl.) C3
Saint Marys (riv.) E2
Salt (pt.) E2
Sand (pt.) F5
Seul Choix (pt.) D3
Shiawassee (riv.) E5
Siskiwit (bay) E1
Sleeping Bear Dunes Nat'l Lakeshore C4
South (bay) C2
South (chan.) E3
South (pt.) F4
South Fox (isl.) D3
South Manitou (isl.) C3
Sturgeon (riv.) C2
Sugar (isl.) E2
Summer (isl.) C3
Superior (lake) C2
Tahquamenon (falls) D2
Tahquamenon (riv.) D2
Tawas (lake) F4
Tawas (pt.) F4
Thunder (bay) F4
Thunder Bay (riv.) F3
Tittabawassee (riv.) E5
Torch (lake) D3
Traverse (isl.) A1
Traverse (pt.) A1
Turtle (lake) F4
Two Hearted (riv.) D2
Vieux Desert (lake) G2
Walloon (lake) E3
White (riv.) C5
Whitefish (bay) E2
Whitefish (pt.) E2
Whitefish (riv.) C2
Wood (isl.) C2
Wurtsmith A.F.B. 5,166 .... F4
Yellow Dog (riv.) B2

⊙County seat.
‡Population of metropolitan area.
○Population of township.
† Zip of nearest p.o.
* Multiple zips.

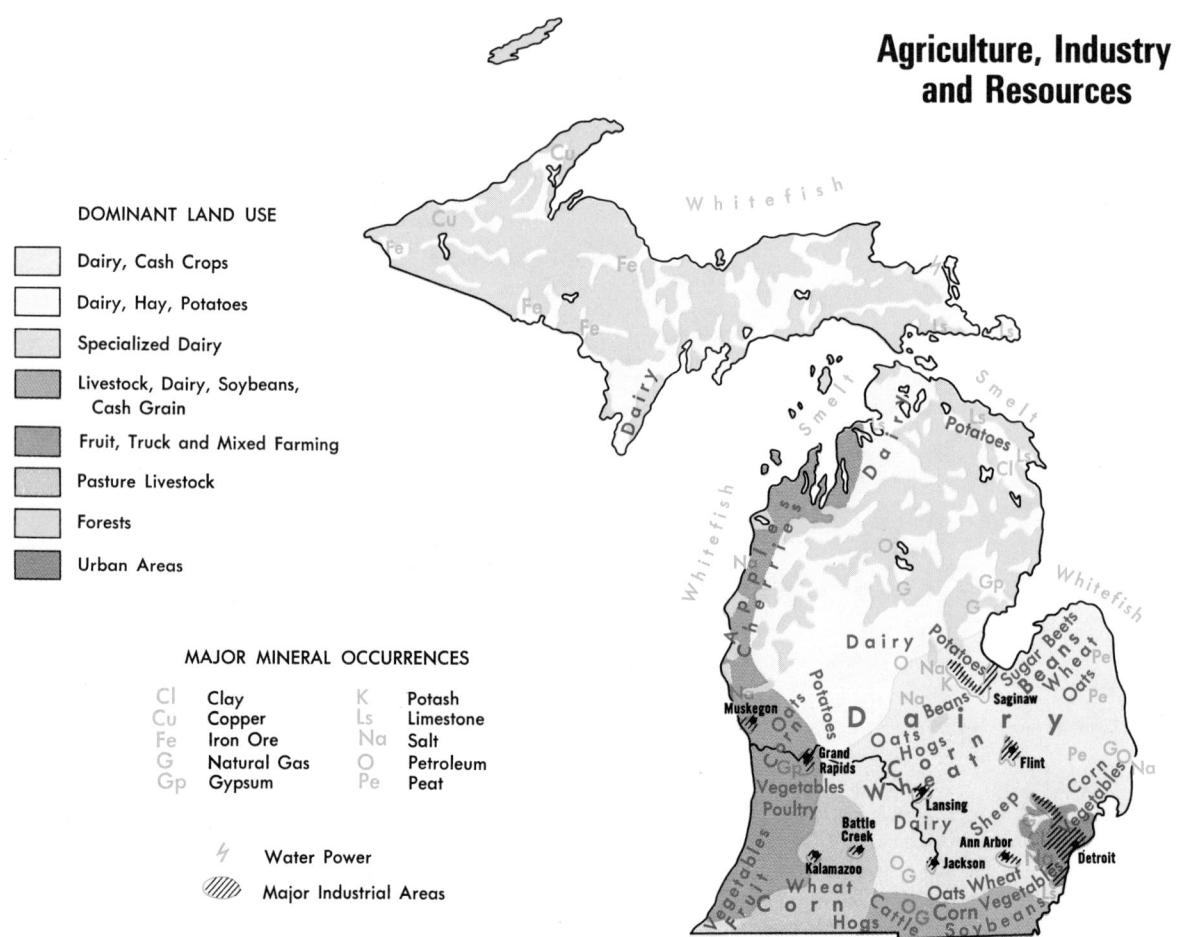

Agriculture, Industry and Resources

DOMINANT LAND USE

- Dairy, Cash Crops
- Dairy, Hay, Potatoes
- Specialized Dairy
- Livestock, Dairy, Soybeans, Cash Grain
- Fruit, Truck and Mixed Farming
- Pasture Livestock
- Forests
- Urban Areas

MAJOR MINERAL OCCURRENCES

Cl Clay
Cu Copper
Fe Iron Ore
G Natural Gas
Gp Gypsum
K Potash
Ls Limestone
Na Salt
O Petroleum
Pe Peat

Water Power
Major Industrial Areas

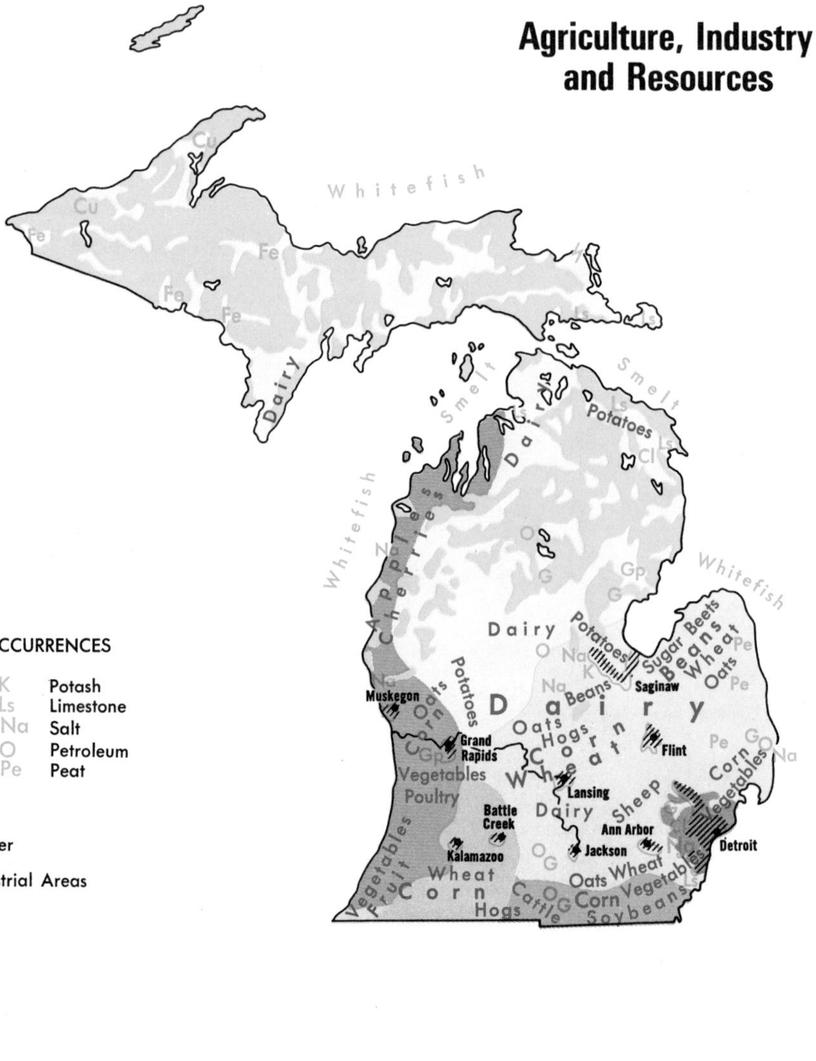

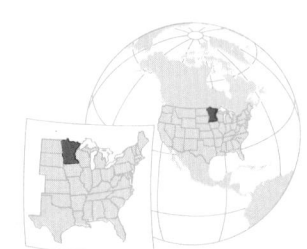

AREA 84,402 sq. mi. (218,601 sq. km.)
POPULATION 4,075,970
CAPITAL St. Paul
LARGEST CITY Minneapolis
HIGHEST POINT Eagle Mtn. 2,301 ft. (701 m.)
SETTLED IN 1805
ADMITTED TO UNION May 11, 1858
POPULAR NAME North Star State; Gopher State
STATE FLOWER Pink & White Lady's-Slipper
STATE BIRD Common Loon

COUNTIES

Aitkin 13,404	E4
Anoka 195,998	E5
Becker 29,336	C4
Beltrami 30,982	C2
Benton 25,187	D5
Big Stone 7,716	B5
Blue Earth 52,314	D6
Brown 28,645	D6
Carlton 29,936	F4
Carver 37,046	E6
Cass 21,050	D4
Chippewa 14,941	C5
Chisago 25,717	F5
Clay 49,327	B4
Clearwater 8,761	C3
Cook 4,092	H3
Cottonwood 14,854	C6
Crow Wing 41,722	D4
Dakota 194,279	E6
Dodge 14,773	F7
Douglas 27,839	C5
Faribault 19,714	D7
Fillmore 21,930	F7
Freeborn 36,329	E7
Goodhue 38,749	F6
Grant 7,171	B5
Hennepin 941,411	E5
Houston 18,382	G7
Hubbard 14,098	D3
Isanti 23,600	E5
Itasca 43,069	E3
Jackson 13,690	C7
Kanabec 12,161	E5
Kandiyohi 36,763	C5
Kittson 6,672	B2
Koochiching 17,571	E2
Lac qui Parle 10,592	B6
Lake 13,043	G3
Lake of the Woods 3,764	D2
Le Sueur 23,434	E6
Lincoln 8,207	B6
Lyon 25,207	C6
Mahnomen 5,535	C3
Marshall 13,027	B2
Martin 24,687	D7
McLeod 29,657	D6
Meeker 20,594	D5
Mille Lacs 18,430	E5
Morrison 29,311	D4
Mower 40,390	F7
Murray 11,507	C6
Nicollet 26,929	D6
Nobles 21,840	C7
Norman 9,379	B3
Olmsted 92,006	F7
Otter Tail 51,937	C4
Pennington 15,258	B2
Pine 19,871	F4
Pipestone 11,690	B6
Polk 34,844	B3
Pope 11,657	C5
Ramsey 459,784	E5
Red Lake 5,471	B3
Redwood 19,341	C6
Renville 20,401	C6
Rice 46,087	E6
Rock 10,703	B7
Roseau 12,574	C2
Saint Louis 222,229	F3
Scott 43,784	E6
Sherburne 29,908	E5
Sibley 15,448	D6
Stearns 108,161	D5
Steele 30,328	E7
Stevens 11,322	B5
Swift 12,920	C5
Todd 24,991	D4
Traverse 5,542	B5
Wabasha 19,335	F6
Wadena 14,192	D4
Waseca 18,448	E6
Washington 113,571	F5
Watonwan 12,361	D7
Wilkin 8,454	B4
Winona 46,256	G6
Wright 58,681	D5
Yellow Medicine 13,653	B6

CITIES and TOWNS

Zip	Name/Pop.	Key
56510	Ada⊙ 1,971	B3
55909	Adams 797	F7
56110	Adrian 1,336	C7
55001	Afton 2,550	F6
56430	Ah-Gwah-Ching 400	D3
56431	Aitkin⊙ 1,770	E4
56433	Akeley 486	D3
56307	Albany 1,569	D5
56207	Alberta 145	B5
56007	Albert Lea⊙ 19,200	E7
55301	Albertville 564	E5
56009	Alden 687	E7
56308	Alexandria⊙ 7,608	C5
56111	Alpha 180	D7
55910	Altura 354	G6
56710	Alvarado 385	B2
56010	Amboy 606	D7
†55303	Andover 9,387	E5
55302	Annandale 1,568	D5
55303	Anoka⊙ 15,634	E5
56208	Appleton 1,842	C5
†55124	Apple Valley 21,818	G6
56713	Argyle 741	B2
55307	Arlington 1,779	D6
56309	Ashby 486	C4
55704	Askov 350	F4
56209	Atwater 1,128	D5
56511	Audubon 383	C4
55705	Aurora 2,670	F3
55912	Austin⊙ 23,020	E7
56114	Avoca 201	C7
56310	Avon 804	D5
55706	Babbitt 2,435	G3
56435	Backus 255	D4
56714	Badger 320	B2
56621	Bagley⊙ 1,321	C3
56115	Balaton 752	C6
56514	Barnesville 2,207	B4
55707	Barnum 464	F4
56311	Barrett 388	B5
55615	Battle Lake 708	C4
56623	Baudette⊙ 1,170	D1
†56401	Baxter 2,625	D4
55003	Bayport 2,932	F5
56211	Beardsley 344	B5
55601	Beaver Bay 283	G3
56116	Beaver Creek 260	B7
55308	Becker 601	E5
56312	Belgrade 805	C5
†55027	Bellechester 220	F6
56011	Belle Plaine 2,754	E6
56212	Bellingham 290	B5
56214	Belview 438	C6
56601	Bemidji⊙ 10,949	D3
56626	Bena 153	D3
56215	Benson⊙ 3,656	C5
56437	Bertha 510	C4
55005	Bethel 272	E5
56117	Bigelow 249	C7
56627	Big Falls 490	E2
56628	Bigfork 457	E3
55309	Big Lake 2,210	E5
56118	Bingham Lake 222	C7
55310	Bird Island 1,372	D6
55708	Biwabik 1,428	F3
56630	Blackduck 653	D3
55321	Cokato 2,056	D5
56320	Cold Spring 2,294	D5
55722	Coleraine 1,116	E3
55322	Cologne 545	E6
55421	Columbia Heights 20,029	G5
56019	Comfrey 548	D6
56020	Conger 183	E7
55723	Cook 800	F3
55433	Coon Rapids 35,826	G5
†55340	Corcoran 4,252	F5
56228	Cosmos 571	C6
55016	Cottage Grove 18,994	F6
56229	Cottonwood 924	C6
56021	Courtland 399	D6
55726	Cromwell 229	F4
56716	Crookston⊙ 8,628	B3
56441	Crosby 2,218	D4
56442	Crosslake 1,064	E4
†55428	Crystal 25,543	G5
55323	Crystal Bay (Orono) 6,845	F5
56123	Currie 359	C6
56323	Cyrus 334	C5
55925	Dakota 350	G7
56324	Dalton 248	C4
56230	Danube 590	C6
56231	Danvers 152	C5
56022	Darfur 139	D6
55324	Darwin 282	D5
55325	Dassel 1,066	D5
56232	Dawson 1,901	B6
55327	Dayton 4,070	E5
55391	Deephaven 3,716	G5
56527	Deer Creek 392	C4
56636	Deer River 907	E3
56444	Deerwood 580	E4
56233	De Graff 179	C5
55328	Delano 2,480	E5
56023	Delavan 262	D7
†55110	Dellwood 751	F5
56528	Dent 167	C4
56501	Detroit Lakes⊙ 7,106	C4
55926	Dexter 279	F7
55927	Dilworth 2,585	B4
55927	Dodge Center 1,816	F6
56235	Donnelly 317	B5
55929	Dover 312	F7
*55801	Duluth⊙ 92,811	F4
	Duluth-Superior‡ 266,650	F4
56236	Dumont 173	B5
55019	Dundas 422	E6
56127	Dunnell 216	D7
55111	Eagan 20,700	G6
56446	Eagle Bend 593	C4
56024	Eagle Lake 1,470	E6
†55005	East Bethel 6,626	E5
56721	East Grand Forks 8,537	B3
†56401	East Gull Lake 586	D4
56025	Easton 283	E7
56237	Echo 334	C6
55344	Eden Prairie 16,263	G6
55329	Eden Valley 763	D5
56128	Edgerton 1,123	B7
55424	Edina 46,073	G5
55931	Eitzen 226	G7
†55910	Elba 198	F6
56531	Elbow Lake⊙ 1,358	B5
55932	Elgin 667	F6
56533	Elizabeth 195	B4
55020	Elko 274	E6
55330	Elk River⊙ 6,785	E5
56026	Ellendale 555	E7
56129	Ellsworth 629	C7
56027	Elmore 882	D7
56325	Elrosa 214	C5

55922	Canton 386	F7
56319	Carlos 364	C5
55718	Carlton⊙ 862	F4
55315	Carver 642	E6
56633	Cass Lake 1,001	D3
55012	Center City⊙ 458	F5
†55038	Centerville 734	G5
56121	Ceylon 543	D7
55316	Champlin 9,006	G5
56122	Chandler 344	C7
55317	Chanhassen 6,359	F6
55318	Chaska⊙ 8,346	F6
55923	Chatfield 2,055	F7
55013	Chisago City 1,634	F5
55719	Chisholm 5,930	F3
56221	Chokio 559	B5
55014	Circle Pines 3,321	G5
56222	Clara City 1,574	C6
55924	Claremont 591	E6
56440	Clarissa 663	C4
56223	Clarkfield 1,171	C6
56016	Clarks Grove 620	E7
56634	Clearbrook 579	C3
55319	Clear Lake 266	E5
55320	Clearwater 379	D5
56224	Clements 227	D6
56017	Cleveland 699	E6
56523	Climax 273	B3
56225	Clinton 622	B5
56226	Clontarf 196	C5
55720	Cloquet 11,142	F4
†55068	Coates 207	E6

55731	Ely 4,820	G3
56028	Elysian 454	E6
56447	Emily 588	E4
56029	Emmons 465	E7
56534	Erhard 194	B4
56535	Erskine 585	B3
56326	Evansville 571	C4
55734	Eveleth 5,042	F3
55331	Excelsior 2,523	E6
55934	Eyota 1,244	F7
55332	Fairfax 1,405	D6
56031	Fairmont⊙ 11,506	D7
55113	Falcon Heights 5,291	G5
55021	Faribault⊙ 16,241	E6
55024	Farmington 4,370	E6
56641	Federal Dam 192	D3
56536	Felton 264	B3
56537	Fergus Falls⊙ 12,519	B4
56540	Fertile 869	B3
56448	Fifty Lakes 263	D4
55735	Finlayson 202	F4
56723	Fisher 453	B3
56328	Flensburg 256	D5
55736	Floodwood 648	E4
56329	Foley⊙ 1,606	D5
†56308	Forada 191	C5
55025	Forest Lake 4,596	F5
56330	Foreston 283	E5
56542	Fosston 1,599	C3
55935	Fountain 327	F7
56543	Foxhome 161	B4
55333	Franklin 512	D6
56544	Frazee 1,284	C4
56032	Freeborn 323	E7
56331	Freeport 563	D5
55432	Fridley 30,228	G5
56033	Frost 293	D7
56131	Fulda 1,308	C7
56332	Garfield 284	C5
56450	Garrison 174	E4
56132	Garvin 172	C6
56545	Gary 241	B3
55334	Gaylord⊙ 1,933	D6
56035	Geneva 417	E7
56239	Ghent 356	C6
55335	Gibbon 787	D6
55741	Gilbert 2,721	F3
56333	Gilman 156	E5
55336	Glencoe⊙ 4,396	D6
56036	Glenville 851	E7
56334	Glenwood⊙ 2,523	C5
56547	Glyndon 882	B4
55427	Golden Valley 22,775	G5
56644	Gonvick 362	C3
55027	Goodhue 657	F6
56725	Goodridge 191	C2
56037	Good Thunder 560	D6
55027	Goodview 2,567	G6
56240	Graceville 780	B5
56039	Granada 377	D7
55604	Grand Marais⊙ 1,289	G2
55936	Grand Meadow 965	F7
55744	Grand Rapids⊙ 7,934	E3
56241	Granite Falls⊙ 3,451	C6
55030	Grasston 123	E5
56726	Greenbush 817	B2
†55373	Greenfield 1,391	F5
55338	Green Isle 357	E6
56335	Greenwald 259	D5
56336	Grey Eagle 338	D5
56243	Grove City 596	D5
56727	Grygla 216	C2
56452	Hackensack 285	D4
56728	Hallock⊙ 1,405	A2
56548	Halstad 690	B3
55339	Hamburg 475	D6
55340	Hamel 2,623	F5
55304	Ham Lake 7,832	E5
55938	Hammond 178	F6
55031	Hampton 299	E6
56244	Hancock 877	C5
56245	Hanley Falls 265	C6
55341	Hanover 647	E5
56041	Hanska 429	D6
56134	Hardwick 279	B7
55939	Harmony 1,133	F7
55032	Harris 678	F5
56042	Hartland 322	E7
55033	Hastings⊙ 12,827	F6
56549	Hawley 1,634	B4
55940	Hayfield 1,243	F7
56043	Hayward 294	E7
55342	Hector 1,252	D6
56044	Henderson 739	E6
56136	Hendricks 737	B6
56550	Hendrum 336	B3
56551	Henning 832	C4
56248	Herman 600	B5
†55811	Hermantown 6,759	F4
56137	Heron Lake 783	C7
56453	Hewitt 299	C4
55746	Hibbing 21,193	F3
55748	Hill City 533	E4
56138	Hills 598	B7
55037	Hinckley 963	E4
56552	Hitterdal 253	B4

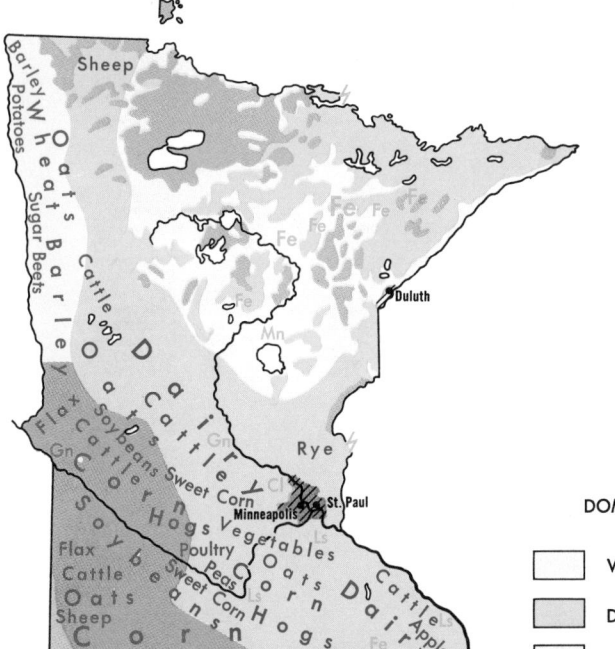

Agriculture, Industry and Resources

DOMINANT LAND USE

- ☐ Wheat, General Farming
- ☐ Dairy, Livestock
- ☐ Dairy, Hay, Potatoes
- ☐ Cattle Feed, Hogs
- ☐ Livestock, Cash Grain
- ☐ Forests
- ☐ Swampland, Limited Agriculture
- ☐ Urban Areas

MAJOR MINERAL OCCURRENCES

Cl	Clay	Gn	Granite
Fe	Iron Ore	Ls	Limestone
		Mn	Manganese

- ⚡ Water Power
- ▨ Major Industrial Areas

(continued on following page)

56339 Hoffman 631 .... C5
55941 Hokah 686 .... G7
56340 Holdingford 635 .... D5
56139 Holland 234 .... B6
56045 Hollandale 290 .... E7
56249 Holloway 142 .... C5
55343 Hopkins 15,336 .... G5
55943 Houston 1,057 .... G7
55349 Howard Lake 1,240 .... D5
55750 Hoyt Lakes 3,186 .... F3
55038 Hugo 3,771 .... E5
55350 Hutchinson 9,244 .... D6
†55359 Independence 2,640 .... F5
56649 International Falls⊙ 5,611 .... E2
55075 Inver Grove Heights 17,171 .... E6
56141 Iona 248 .... C7
56455 Ironton 537 .... D4
55040 Isanti 858 .... E5
56342 Isle 573 .... E4
56142 Ivanhoe⊙ 761 .... B6
56143 Jackson⊙ 3,797 .... C7
56048 Janesville 1,897 .... E6
56144 Jasper 731 .... B7
56145 Jeffers 437 .... C6
56456 Jenkins 219 .... D4
55352 Jordan 2,663 .... E6
56251 Kandiyohi 447 .... D5
56732 Karlstad 934 .... B2
56050 Kasota 739 .... D6
55944 Kasson 2,827 .... F6
55753 Keewatin 1,443 .... E3
56650 Kelliher 324 .... D3
55945 Kellogg 440 .... G6
55754 Kelly Lake 900 .... F3
56733 Kennedy 405 .... B2
56343 Kensington 331 .... C5
55946 Kenyon 1,529 .... E6
56252 Kerkhoven 761 .... C5
56051 Kiester 670 .... E7
56052 Kilkenny 177 .... E6
55353 Kimball 651 .... D5
55758 Kinney 447 .... F3
55947 La Crescent 3,674 .... G7
56054 Lafayette 507 .... D6
56149 Lake Benton 869 .... B6
56734 Lake Bronson 298 .... B2
55041 Lake City 4,505 .... F6
56055 Lake Crystal 2,078 .... D6
55042 Lake Elmo 5,296 .... F6
56150 Lakefield 1,845 .... C7
†55398 Lake Fremont (Zimmerman) 1,074 .... E5
55043 Lakeland 1,812 .... F6
56253 Lake Lillian 329 .... C6
56554 Lake Park 716 .... B4
†55043 Lake Saint Croix Beach 1,176 .... F6
†56401 Lake Shore 583 .... D4
55044 Lakeville 14,790 .... E6
56151 Lake Wilson 380 .... B7
56152 Lamberton 1,032 .... C6
56735 Lancaster 368 .... B2
55949 Lanesboro 923 .... G7
56461 Laporte 160 .... D3
†55744 La Prairie 536 .... E3
56344 Lastrup 150 .... D4
†55101 Lauderdale 1,985 .... G5
56057 Le Center⊙ 1,967 .... E6
55951 Le Roy 930 .... F7
55354 Lester Prairie 1,229 .... D6
56058 Le Sueur 3,763 .... E6
55952 Lewiston 1,226 .... G7
56060 Lewisville 273 .... D7
†55014 Lexington 2,150 .... G5
†55050 Lilydale 417 .... G5
55045 Lindstrom 1,972 .... F5
†55038 Lino Lakes 4,966 .... G5
56155 Lismore 276 .... B7
55355 Litchfield⊙ 5,904 .... D5
56345 Little Falls⊙ 7,250 .... D5
56653 Littlefork 918 .... E2
†56334 Long Beach 263 .... C5
55356 Long Lake 1,747 .... F5
56347 Long Prairie⊙ 2,859 .... D5
56655 Longville 191 .... D4
55046 Lonsdale 1,160 .... E6
55357 Loretto 297 .... F5
56349 Lowry 283 .... C5
56255 Lucan 262 .... C6
56156 Luverne⊙ 4,568 .... B7
55953 Lyle 576 .... F7
56157 Lynd 304 .... C6
55954 Mabel 861 .... G7
56062 Madelia 2,130 .... D6
56256 Madison⊙ 2,212 .... B5
56063 Madison Lake 592 .... E6
56158 Magnolia 234 .... B7
56557 Mahnomen⊙ 1,283 .... C3
55115 Mahtomedi 3,851 .... F5
56001 Mankato⊙ 28,651 .... E6
55955 Mantorville⊙ 705 .... F6
†55369 Maple Grove 20,525 .... G5
55358 Maple Lake 1,132 .... D5
55359 Maple Plain 1,421 .... F5
56065 Mapleton 1,516 .... E7
†55912 Mapleview 253 .... E7
55109 Maplewood 26,990 .... G5
55764 Marble 757 .... E3
56257 Marietta 279 .... B5
55047 Marine on Saint Croix 543 .... F5
56258 Marshall⊙ 11,161 .... C6
55360 Mayer 388 .... E6
56260 Maynard 428 .... C6
55956 Mazeppa 680 .... F6
55760 McGregor 447 .... E4
56556 McIntosh 681 .... C3
55761 McKinley 230 .... F3
55049 Medford 775 .... E6
55441 Medicine Lake 419 .... G5
†55340 Medina (Hamel) 2,623 .... F5
†56352 Meire Grove 174 .... C5
56352 Melrose 2,409 .... D5
56464 Menahga 980 .... C4
55050 Mendota 219 .... G5
†55050 Mendota Heights 7,288 .... G6
56736 Mentor 219 .... B3
56737 Middle River 349 .... B2
†55033 Miesville 179 .... F6
56262 Milan 417 .... C5
55957 Millville 186 .... F6
56263 Milroy 242 .... C6
56354 Miltona 187 .... C4
*55401 Minneapolis⊙ 370,951 .... G5
Minneapolis-Saint Paul‡ 2,114,256 .... G5
56264 Minneota 1,470 .... C6
55959 Minnesota City 265 .... G6
56068 Minnesota Lake 744 .... E7
55343 Minnetonka 38,683 .... G5
†55364 Minnetrista 3,236 .... F5
56265 Montevideo⊙ 5,845 .... C6
56069 Montgomery 2,349 .... E6
55362 Monticello 2,830 .... E5
55363 Montrose 762 .... E5
56560 Moorhead⊙ 29,998 .... B4
Moorhead-Fargo‡ 137,574 B4
55767 Moose Lake 1,408 .... F4
55051 Mora⊙ 2,890 .... E5
56266 Morgan 975 .... D6
56267 Morris⊙ 5,367 .... C5
55052 Morristown 639 .... E6
56270 Morton 549 .... C6
56466 Motley 444 .... D4
55364 Mound 9,280 .... E6
†55112 Mounds View 12,593 .... G5
55768 Mountain Iron 4,134 .... F3
56159 Mountain Lake 2,277 .... D7
56271 Murdock 343 .... C5
55769 Nashwauk 1,419 .... E3
56355 Nelson 209 .... C5
55053 Nerstrand 255 .... E6
56467 Nevis 332 .... D4
55366 New Auburn 331 .... D6
55112 New Brighton 23,269 .... G5
56738 Newfolden 384 .... B2
55367 New Germany 347 .... E6
†55428 New Hope 23,087 .... G5
56273 New London 812 .... C5
55054 New Market 286 .... E6
56356 New Munich 302 .... D5
55055 Newport 3,323 .... F6
56071 New Prague 2,952 .... E6
56072 New Richland 1,263 .... E7
56073 New Ulm⊙ 13,755 .... D6
56567 New York Mills 972 .... C4
56074 Nicollet 709 .... D6
56568 Nielsville 145 .... B3
56468 Nisswa 1,407 .... D4
55056 North Branch 1,597 .... F5
55057 Northfield 12,562 .... E6
56001 North Mankato 9,145 .... D6
†55101 North Oaks 2,846 .... G5
56661 Northome 312 .... D3
56275 North Redwood 206 .... D6
56075 Northrop 269 .... D7
55109 North Saint Paul 11,921 .... G5
55368 Norwood 1,219 .... E6
†55109 Oakdale 12,123 .... E5
56276 Odessa 177 .... B5
56160 Odin 134 .... D7
56569 Ogema 215 .... C3
56358 Ogilvie 423 .... E5
56161 Okabena 263 .... C7
56742 Oklee 536 .... C3
56277 Olivia⊙ 2,802 .... C6
56359 Onamia 691 .... E4
56162 Ormsby 181 .... D7
†55323 Orono 6,845 .... F5
55960 Oronoco 574 .... F6
55771 Orr 294 .... F2
56278 Ortonville⊙ 2,550 .... B5
56360 Osakis 1,355 .... C5
56744 Oslo 379 .... A2
55369 Osseo 2,974 .... G5
55961 Ostrander 293 .... F7
56571 Ottertail 239 .... C4
55060 Owatonna⊙ 18,632 .... E6
56469 Palisade 155 .... E4
56361 Parkers Prairie 917 .... C4
56470 Park Rapids⊙ 2,976 .... D4
56362 Paynesville 2,140 .... D5
56363 Pease 174 .... E5
†56472 Pelican Lakes (Breezy Point) 384 .... D4
56572 Pelican Rapids 1,867 .... B4
56078 Pemberton 208 .... E7
56279 Pennock 410 .... C5
56472 Pequot Lakes 681 .... D4
56573 Perham 2,086 .... C4
55962 Peterson 291 .... G7
†56364 Pierz 1,018 .... D5
56473 Pillager 341 .... D4
55063 Pine City⊙ 2,489 .... F5
55963 Pine Island 1,986 .... F6
56474 Pine River 881 .... D4
56164 Pipestone⊙ 4,887 .... B7
55964 Plainview 2,416 .... F6
55370 Plato 390 .... D6
56748 Plummer 353 .... B3
†55441 Plymouth 31,615 .... G5
56280 Porter 211 .... B6
55965 Preston⊙ 1,478 .... F7
55371 Princeton 3,146 .... E5
56281 Prinsburg 557 .... C6
55372 Prior Lake 7,284 .... E6
55810 Proctor 3,180 .... F4
55967 Racine 285 .... F7
56475 Randall 527 .... D4
55065 Randolph 351 .... E6
56668 Ranier 237 .... E2
56282 Raymond 723 .... C5
56750 Red Lake Falls⊙ 1,732 .... B3
55066 Red Wing⊙ 13,736 .... F6
56283 Redwood Falls⊙ 5,210 .... C6
56672 Remer 396 .... E3
56284 Renville 1,493 .... C6
56166 Revere 158 .... C6
56367 Rice 499 .... D5
55423 Richfield 37,851 .... G6
56368 Richmond 867 .... D5
55422 Robbinsdale 14,422 .... G5
55901 Rochester⊙ 57,890 .... F6
Rochester‡ 91,971 .... F6
55067 Rock Creek 890 .... F5
55373 Rockford 2,408 .... F5
56369 Rockville 597 .... D5
55374 Rogers 652 .... E5
55969 Rollingstone 528 .... G6
56371 Roscoe 154 .... D5
56751 Roseau⊙ 2,272 .... C2
55970 Rose Creek 371 .... F7
55068 Rosemount 5,083 .... E6
55113 Roseville 35,820 .... G5
56579 Rothsay 476 .... B4
56167 Round Lake 480 .... C7
56373 Royalton 660 .... D5
55069 Rush City 1,198 .... F5
55971 Rushford 1,478 .... G7
56168 Rushmore 387 .... C7
56169 Russell 412 .... C6
56170 Ruthton 328 .... B6
55778 Rutledge 185 .... F4
56580 Sabin 446 .... B4
56285 Sacred Heart 666 .... C6
55414 Saint Anthony 7,981 .... G5
55375 Saint Bonifacius 857 .... F5
55972 Saint Charles 2,184 .... F7
56080 Saint Clair 655 .... E6
56301 Saint Cloud⊙ 42,566 .... D5
Saint Cloud‡ 163,256 .... D5
55070 Saint Francis 1,184 .... E5
56554 Saint Hilaire 388 .... B2
56081 Saint James⊙ 4,346 .... D7
56374 Saint Joseph 2,994 .... D5
55426 Saint Louis Park 42,931 .... G5
56376 Saint Martin 220 .... D5
55376 Saint Michael 1,519 .... E5
*55101 Saint Paul (cap.)⊙ 270,230 .... G6
Saint Paul-Minneapolis‡ 2,114,256 .... G5
55071 Saint Paul Park 4,864 .... G6
56082 Saint Peter⊙ 9,056 .... E6
56375 Saint Stephen 453 .... D5
56755 Saint Vincent 141 .... A2
56083 Sanborn 518 .... C6
55072 Sandstone 1,594 .... F4
56377 Sartell 3,427 .... D5
56378 Sauk Centre 3,709 .... C5
56379 Sauk Rapids 5,793 .... D5
55337 Savage 3,954 .... G6
†55720 Scanlon 1,050 .... F4
56477 Sebeka 774 .... C4
55074 Shafer 180 .... F5
55379 Shakopee⊙ 9,941 .... F6
56581 Shelly 276 .... B3
56171 Sherburn 1,275 .... D7
56676 Shevlin 193 .... C3
†55112 Shoreview 17,300 .... G5
†55331 Shorewood 4,646 .... F5
55614 Silver Bay 2,917 .... G3
55381 Silver Lake 698 .... D6
†56001 Skyline 399 .... D6
56172 Slayton⊙ 2,420 .... C7
56085 Sleepy Eye 3,581 .... D6
†56345 Sobieski 219 .... D5
55382 South Haven 205 .... D5
56679 South International Falls 2,806 .... E2
55075 South Saint Paul 21,235 .... G6
56288 Spicer 909 .... C5
56087 Springfield 2,303 .... C6
55974 Spring Grove 1,275 .... G7
†55432 Spring Lake Park 6,477 .... E5
55384 Spring Park 1,465 .... F5
55975 Spring Valley 2,616 .... F7
56681 Squaw Lake 162 .... D3
55079 Stacy 996 .... E5
56479 Staples 2,887 .... D4
56381 Starbuck 1,224 .... C5
56173 Steen 153 .... B7
56757 Stephen 898 .... A2
55385 Stewart 616 .... D6
55976 Stewartville 3,925 .... F7
55082 Stillwater⊙ 12,290 .... F5
55988 Stockton 517 .... G6
56174 Storden 341 .... C6
56758 Strandquist 136 .... B2
55783 Sturgeon Lake 222 .... F4
†55075 Sunfish Lake 344 .... E6
56382 Swanville 295 .... D5
55786 Taconite 331 .... E3
56291 Taunton 177 .... B6
55084 Taylors Falls 623 .... F5
56683 Tenstrike 159 .... D3
56701 Thief River Falls⊙ 9,105 .... B2
†56319 Thomson 152 .... F4
†55331 Tonka Bay 1,354 .... F5
55790 Tower 640 .... F3
56175 Tracy 2,478 .... C6
56176 Trimont 805 .... D7
56088 Truman 1,392 .... D7
56089 Twin Lakes 210 .... E7
56584 Twin Valley 907 .... B3
55616 Two Harbors⊙ 4,039 .... G3
56178 Tyler 1,353 .... B6
56585 Ulen 514 .... B3
56586 Underwood 332 .... C4
56384 Upsala 400 .... D5
55979 Utica 249 .... G7
†55101 Vadnais Heights 5,111 .... G5
56587 Vergas 287 .... C4
55085 Vermillion 438 .... F6
56481 Verndale 504 .... C4
56090 Vernon Center 365 .... D7
56292 Vesta 360 .... C6
55386 Victoria 1,425 .... F6
56385 Villard 275 .... C5
55792 Virginia 11,056 .... F3
55981 Wabasha⊙ 2,372 .... G6
56293 Wabasso 745 .... C6
55387 Waconia 2,638 .... E6
56482 Wadena⊙ 4,699 .... C4
56386 Wahkon 271 .... E4
56387 Waite Park 3,496 .... D5
56091 Waldorf 249 .... E7
56484 Walker⊙ 970 .... D3
56180 Walnut Grove 753 .... C6
55982 Waltham 176 .... F7
55983 Wanamingo 717 .... F6
55743 Warba 150 .... E3
56762 Warren⊙ 2,105 .... B2
56763 Warroad 1,216 .... C2
56093 Waseca⊙ 8,219 .... E6
55388 Watertown 1,818 .... E6
56096 Waterville 1,717 .... E6
55389 Watkins 757 .... D5
56295 Watson 238 .... C5
56589 Waubun 390 .... C3
55390 Waverly 470 .... E5
55391 Wayzata 3,621 .... G5
56181 Welcome 855 .... D7
56097 Wells 2,777 .... E7
56590 Wendell 216 .... B4
56183 Westbrook 978 .... C6
55985 West Concord 762 .... F6
55118 West Saint Paul 18,527 .... G5
56296 Wheaton⊙ 1,969 .... B5
55110 White Bear Lake 22,538 .... G5
55090 Willernie 654 .... G5
56686 Williams 217 .... D2
56201 Willmar⊙ 15,895 .... C5
55795 Willow River 303 .... F4
56185 Wilmont 380 .... C7
56687 Wilton 176 .... C3
56101 Windom⊙ 4,666 .... C7
56592 Winger 200 .... B3
56098 Winnebago 1,869 .... D7
55987 Winona⊙ 25,075 .... G6
55395 Winsted 1,522 .... D6
55396 Winthrop 1,376 .... D6
55796 Winton 276 .... G3
56594 Wolverton 177 .... B4
†55798 Woodbury 10,297 .... F6
56297 Wood Lake 420 .... C6
56186 Woodstock 180 .... B7
56187 Worthington⊙ 10,243 .... C7
55797 Wrenshall 333 .... F4
55798 Wright 162 .... E4
55990 Wykoff 482 .... F7
55092 Wyoming 1,559 .... F5
55397 Young America 1,237 .... E6
55398 Zimmerman 1,074 .... E5
55991 Zumbro Falls 208 .... F6
55992 Zumbrota 2,129 .... F6

OTHER FEATURES

Ash (riv.) F2
Bald Eagle (lake) G3
Basswood (lake) G2
Battle (riv.) D3
Baudette (riv.) D2
Bear (riv.) E3
Bemidji (lake) D3
Benton (lake) B6
Big Fork (riv.) E2
Big Sandy (lake) E4
Big Stone (lake) B5
Birch (lake) G3
Black (riv.) D2
Blue Earth (riv.) D7
Bois de Sioux (riv.) B4
Bowstring (lake) E3
Buffalo (riv.) B4
Burntside (lake) F3
Cass (lake) D3
Cedar (riv.) F7
Chippewa (riv.) C5
Christina (lake) C4
Clearwater (riv.) C3
Cloquet (riv.) F4
Cobb (riv.) E7
Cottonwood (riv.) C6
Crooked (creek) F4
Crooked (lake) G2
Crow (riv.) F5
Crow Wing (riv.) D4
Cuyuna (range) D4
Dead (lake) C4
Deer (lake) E3
Des Moines (riv.) C7
Eagle (mt.) G2
East Swan (riv.) F3
Elbow (lake) C3
Emily (lake) C5
Fond du Lac Ind. Res. F4
Grand Portage Ind. Res. G2
Grand Portage Nat'l Mon. G2
Green (lake) D5
Greenwood (lake) G3
Gull (lake) D4
Heron (lake) C7
Hill (riv.) C3
Independence (lake) F5
Isabella (lake) G3
Itasca (lake) C3
Kabetogama (lake) E2
Kanaranzi (creek) C7
Kettle (riv.) F4
Knife (lake) G2
La Croix (lake) F2
Lac qui Parle (lake) C5
Lac qui Parle (riv.) B6
Lake of the Woods (lake) D1
Leaf (riv.) C4
Leech (lake) D3
Leech Lake Ind. Res. D3
Lida (lake) C4
Little Fork (riv.) E2
Little Rock (creek) C7
Long (lake) D4
Long (lake) F3
Long Prairie (riv.) D4
Lost (riv.) C3
Lower Red (lake) C3
Maple (lake) B3
Maple (riv.) E7
Marsh (lake) B5
Mary (lake) C5
Mesabi (range) E3
Middle (riv.) B2
Mille Lac Ind. Res. E4
Mille Lacs (lake) E4
Miltona (lake) C4
Minneapolis-Saint Paul Airport G5
Minnesota (riv.) E6
Minnetonka (lake) F5
Minnewaska (lake) C5
Misquah (hills) F2
Mississippi (riv.) D4
Moose (riv.) C2
Mud (lake) C2
Mud (riv.) C2
Muskeg (bay) C2
Mustinka (riv.) B5
Nemadji (riv.) F4
Nett (lake) E2
Nett Lake Ind. Res. E2
North (lake) F1
Otter Tail (lake) C4
Otter Tail (riv.) B4
Partridge (riv.) G3
Pelican (lake) C4
Pelican (lake) D4
Pelican (lake) F2
Pelican (riv.) B4
Pelican (riv.) F2
Pepin (lake) F6
Pigeon (riv.) G2
Pike (riv.) F3
Pipestone Nat'l Mon. B6
Pokegama (lake) E3
Pomme de Terre (riv.) C5
Poplar (riv.) C3
Prairie (riv.) E3
Rainy (lake) E2
Rainy (riv.) D2
Rapid (riv.) D2
Redeye (riv.) D4
Red Lake (riv.) B2
Red Lake Ind. Res. C2
Red River of the North (riv.) A2
Redwood (riv.) C6
Reno (lake) C5
Rice (lake) E4
Rock (riv.) B7
Root (riv.) G7
Roseau (riv.) B2
Rum (riv.) E5
Saganaga (lake) H2
Saint Croix (riv.) F5
Saint Louis (riv.) F4
Sand (creek) F5
Sand Hill (riv.) B3
Sarah (lake) F5
Schoolcraft (riv.) C3
Shakopee (creek) C5
Shell (riv.) C4
Shetek (lake) C6
Sleepy Eye (creek) C6
Snake (riv.) A2
Snake (riv.) E4
South Fowl (lake) G1
Star (lake) C4
Sturgeon (riv.) F3
Superior (lake) G3
Swan (lake) D6
Tamarac (riv.) A2
Tamarack (riv.) D2
Thief (lake) C2
Thief (riv.) B2
Traverse (lake) B5
Trout (lake) F2
Two Rivers (riv.) A1
Upper Red (lake) D2
Vermilion (lake) F3
Vermilion (range) F3
Vermilion (riv.) F2
Voyageurs Nat'l Park F2
Wabatawangang (lake) D3
West Swan (riv.) F3
White Earth Ind. Res. C3
Whiteface (riv.) F3
Whitefish (lake) D4
White Iron (lake) G3
Wild Rice (lake) F4
Wild Rice (riv.) B3
Willow (riv.) E4
Winnibigoshish (lake) D3
Woods (lake) D1
Zumbro (riv.) F6

⊙County seat.
‡Population of metropolitan area.
† Zip of nearest p.o. * Multiple zips.

Topography

0 50 100 MI.
0 50 100 KM.
Lake of the Woods
Rainy
Rainy Lake
Upper Red Lake
Red Lake
Lower Red Lake
Vermilion
Little Fork
VERMILION RA.
Eagle Mtn. 2,301 ft. (701 m.)
MISQUAH HILLS
Lake Superior
Hibbing
MESABI
RANGE
Louis
Wild Rice
L. Itasca
Leech Lake
Red River of the North
Moorhead
Crow Wing
Mississippi
Duluth
CUYUNA RANGE
Otter Tail
Lake Traverse
Big Stone Lake
Chippewa
Mille Lacs Lake
Rum
St. Cloud
Mississippi
St. Croix
Minneapolis
St. Paul
Lake Pepin
Minnesota
Zumbro
Mississippi
Mankato
Rochester
Root
Des Moines
Below Sea Level
100 m. 328 ft.
200 m. 656 ft.
500 m. 1,640 ft.
1,000 m. 3,281 ft.
2,000 m. 6,562 ft.
5,000 m. 16,404 ft.

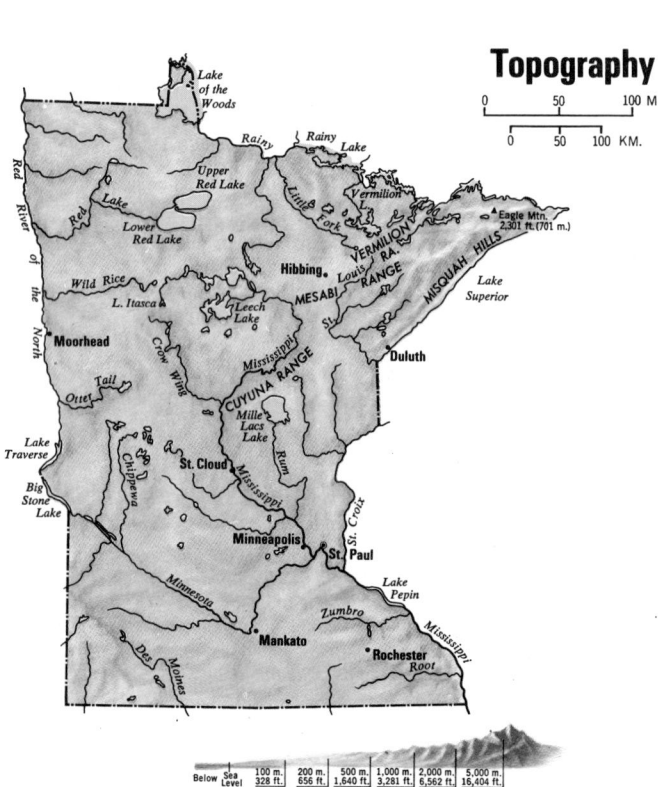

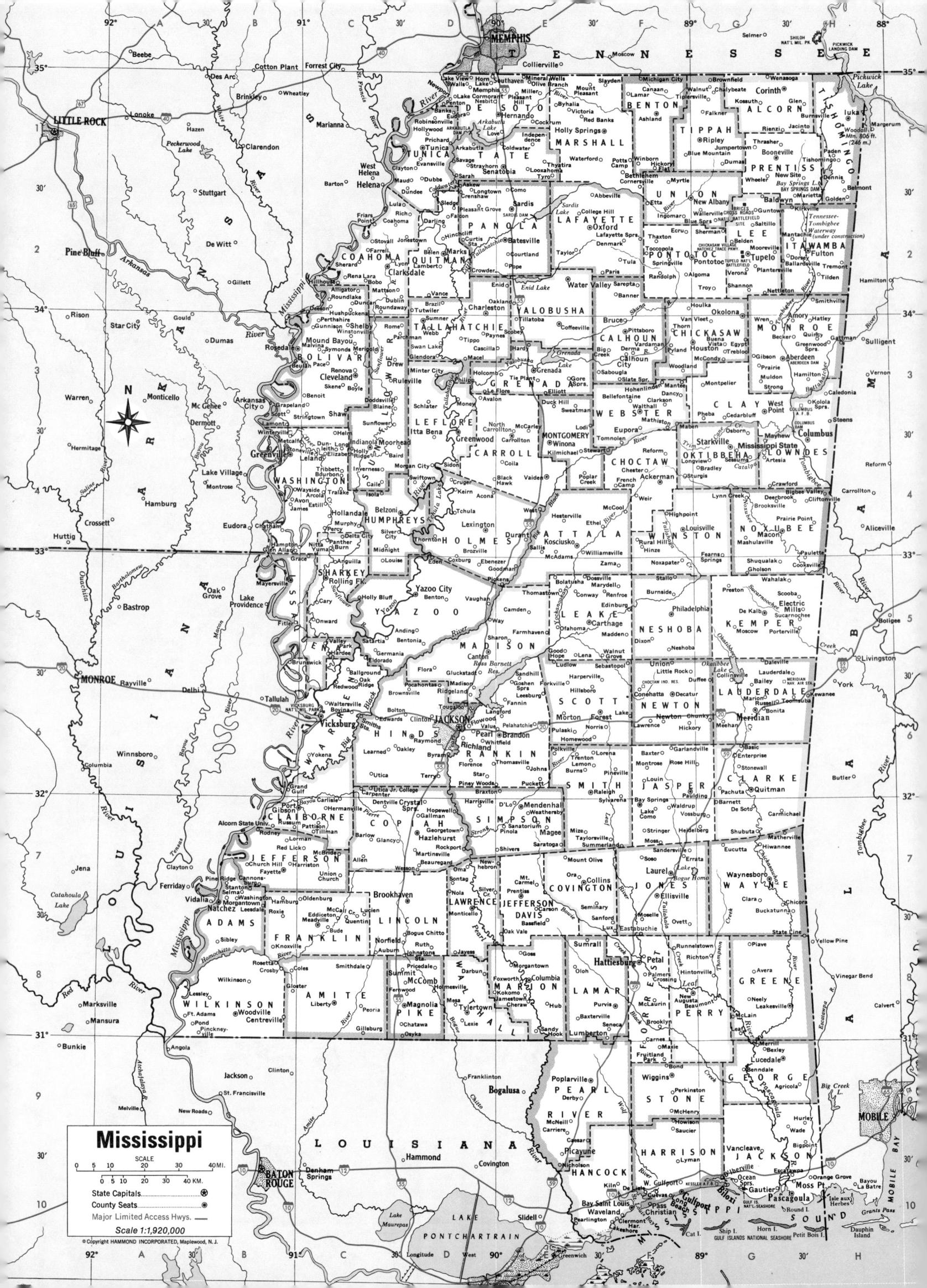

Mississippi

SCALE

0 5 10 20 30 40 MI.

0 10 20 30 40 KM.

State Capitals............................ ⊛

County Seats............................ ◉

Major Limited Access Hwys. ——

Scale 1:1,920,000

© Copyright HAMMOND INCORPORATED, Maplewood, N.J.

AREA 47,689 sq. mi. (123,515 sq. km.)
POPULATION 2,520,638
CAPITAL Jackson
LARGEST CITY Jackson
HIGHEST POINT Woodall Mtn. 806 ft. (246 m.)
SETTLED IN 1716
ADMITTED TO UNION December 10, 1817
POPULAR NAME Magnolia State
STATE FLOWER Magnolia
STATE BIRD Mockingbird

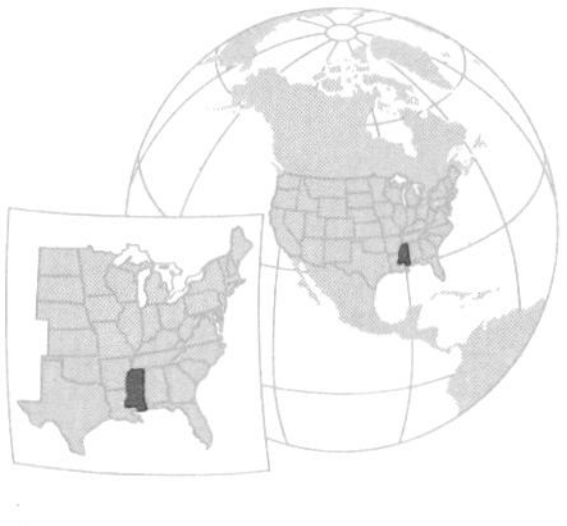

Topography

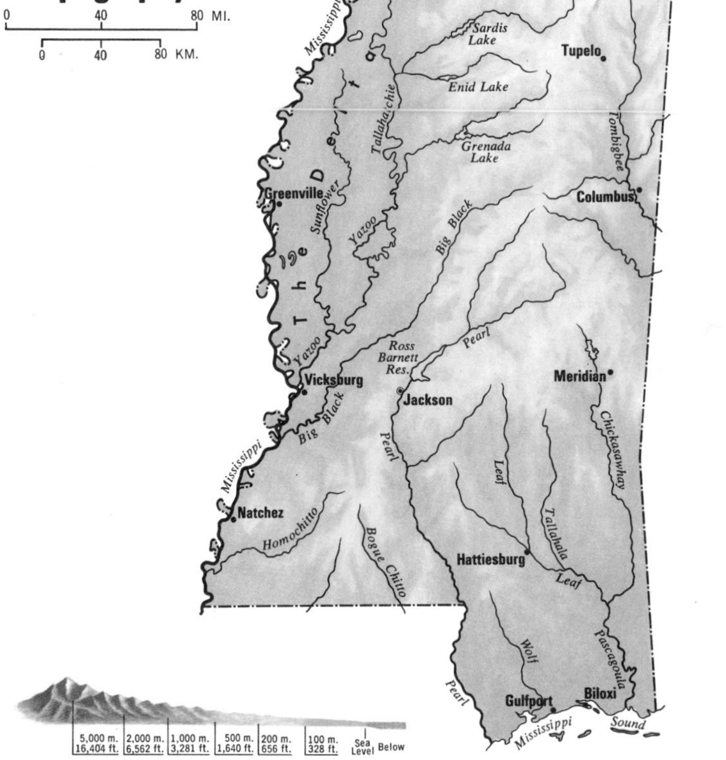

0 40 80 MI.
0 40 80 KM.
Arkabutla Lake
Pickwick Lake
Woodall Mtn. 806 ft. (246 m.)
Mississippi
Sardis Lake
Tupelo
Enid Lake
Tallahatchie
Grenada Lake
Tombigbee
Greenville
Columbus
Sunflower
Yazoo
Big Black
The Delta
Ross Barnett Res.
Pearl
Vicksburg
Jackson
Meridian
Chickasawhay
Natchez
Homochitto
Bogue Chitto
Leaf
Tallahala
Hattiesburg
Wolf
Pascagoula
Gulfport
Biloxi
Mississippi Sound
5,000 m. 16,404 ft.
2,000 m. 6,562 ft.
1,000 m. 3,281 ft.
500 m. 1,640 ft.
200 m. 656 ft.
100 m. 328 ft.
Sea Level
Below

COUNTIES

Adams 38,035 B8
Alcorn 33,036 G1
Amite 13,369 C8
Attala 19,865 E4
Benton 8,153 F1
Bolivar 45,965 C3
Calhoun 15,664 F3
Carroll 9,776 E4
Chickasaw 17,853 G3
Choctaw 8,996 F4
Claiborne 12,279 C7
Clarke 16,945 G6
Clay 21,082 G3
Coahoma 36,918 C2
Copiah 26,503 D7
Covington 15,927 E7
De Soto 53,930 E1
Forrest 66,018 F8
Franklin 8,208 C8
George 15,297 G9
Greene 9,827 G8
Grenada 21,043 E3
Hancock 24,537 E10
Harrison 157,665 F10
Hinds 250,998 D6
Holmes 22,970 D4
Humphreys 13,931 C4
Issaquena 2,513 B5
Itawamba 20,518 H2
Jackson 118,015 G9
Jasper 17,265 F6
Jefferson 9,181 B7
Jefferson Davis 13,846 E7
Jones 61,912 F7
Kemper 10,148 G5
Lafayette 31,030 E2
Lamar 23,821 E8
Lauderdale 77,285 G6
Lawrence 12,518 D7
Leake 18,790 E5
Lee 57,061 G2
Leflore 41,525 D3
Lincoln 30,174 D8
Lowndes 57,304 H4
Madison 41,613 D5
Marion 25,708 E8
Marshall 29,296 E1
Monroe 36,404 H3
Montgomery 13,366 E4
Neshoba 23,789 F5
Newton 19,944 F6
Noxubee 13,212 G4
Oktibbeha 36,018 G4
Panola 28,164 E2
Pearl River 33,795 E9
Perry 9,864 G8
Pike 36,173 D8
Pontotoc 20,918 F2
Prentiss 24,025 G1
Quitman 12,636 D2
Rankin 69,427 E6
Scott 24,556 E6
Sharkey 7,964 C5
Simpson 23,441 E7
Smith 15,077 E6
Stone 9,716 F9
Sunflower 34,844 C3
Tallahatchie 17,157 D3
Tate 20,119 E1
Tippah 18,739 G1
Tishomingo 18,434 H1
Tunica 9,652 D1
Union 21,741 F2
Walthall 13,761 D8
Warren 51,627 C6
Washington 72,344 C4
Wayne 19,135 G7
Webster 10,300 F3
Wilkinson 10,021 B8
Winston 19,474 F4
Yalobusha 13,139 E2
Yazoo 27,349 D5

CITIES and TOWNS

Zip Name/Pop. Key

38601 Abbeville 448 F2
39730 Aberdeen⊙ 7,184 H3
39735 Ackerman⊙ 1,567 F4
39096 Alcorn State University B7
38820 Algoma 175 G2
†39083 Allen 15 C7
38720 Alligator 256 C2
38821 Amory 7,307 H3
38721 Anguilla 950 C5
38722 Arcola 588 C4
38602 Arkabutla 400 D1
39736 Artesia 526 G4
38603 Ashland⊙ 532 F1
38604 Askew 300 D1
†39664 Auburn 500 C8
38912 Avalon 100 D3
38723 Avon 400 B4
39320 Bailey 320 G6
38724 Baird 150 C4
38824 Baldwyn 3,427 G2
†39156 Ballground 30 C5
38913 Banner 120 F2
†39083 Barlow 20 C7
†39330 Basic 60 G6
39421 Bassfield 325 E8
38606 Batesville⊙ 4,692 E2
†39343 Baxter 75 F6
†39455 Baxterville 100 E8
39520 Bay Saint Louis⊙ 7,891 F10
39422 Bay Springs⊙ 1,884 F7
39423 Beaumont 1,112 G8
†39191 Beauregard 185 D7
38825 Becker 350 G3
38826 Belden 241 G2
38609 Belen 400 D2
39737 Bellefontaine 400 F3
38827 Belmont 1,420 H1
39038 Belzoni⊙ 2,982 C4
†39450 Benndale 500 G9
38725 Benoit 499 C3
39039 Benton 350 D5
39040 Bentonia 518 D5
†38659 Bethlehem 210 F1
38726 Beulah 431 B3
39738 Bigbee Valley 370 H4
38914 Big Creek 146 F3
†39567 Bigpoint 350 H9
*39530 Biloxi 49,311 G10
Biloxi-Gulfport‡ 191,918 G10
†38917 Black Hawk 41 E4
38727 Blaine 75 C3
38610 Blue Mountain 867 G1
38828 Blue Springs 131 G2
†38614 Bobo 200 C2
39629 Bogue Chitto 575 D8
39041 Bolton 664 D6
39550 Bond 350 F9
†39301 Bonita 300 G6
38829 Booneville⊙ 6,199 G1
†38756 Bourbon 200 C4
†39180 Bovina 50 C6
38730 Boyle 888 C3
39042 Brandon⊙ 9,626 E6
39044 Braxton 172 D6
38963 Brazil 229 D2
39601 Brookhaven⊙ 10,800 C7
39425 Brooklyn 450 F8
39739 Brooksville 1,038 G4
†38683 Brownfield 125 G1
38915 Bruce 2,208 F3
39322 Buckatunna 500 G7
39630 Bude 1,092 C8
38833 Burnsville 889 H1
38611 Byhalia 757 E1
†39205 Byram 250 D6
†38754 Caile 30 C4
39740 Caledonia 497 H3
38916 Calhoun City 2,033 F3
39045 Camden 150 E5
38612 Canaan 200 F1
39046 Canton⊙ 11,116 D5
39049 Carlisle 425 C7
†39360 Carmichael 75 G7
39050 Carpenter 200 C6
39426 Carriere 900 E9
38917 Carrollton⊙ 338 E4
39427 Carson 400 E7
39051 Carthage⊙ 3,453 E5
39054 Cary 470 C5
38920 Cascilla 230 D3
39741 Cedarbluff 175 G3
39631 Centreville 1,844 B8
38684 Chalybeate 350 G1
38921 Charleston⊙ 2,878 D2
39632 Chatawa 300 D8
38731 Chatham 150 B4
39323 Chunky 277 G6
39055 Church Hill 350 B7
39324 Clara 275 G7
38614 Clarksdale⊙ 21,137 D2
39551 Clermont Harbor 550 F10
38732 Cleveland⊙ 14,524 C3
39056 Clinton 14,660 D6
38617 Coahoma 350 C2
†38632 Cockrum 150 E1
38922 Coffeeville⊙ 1,129 E3
38923 Coila 75 E4
38618 Coldwater 1,505 E1
†39638 Coles 150 C8
†38655 College Hill 150 E2
39428 Collins⊙ 2,131 E7
39325 Collinsville 700 G6
39429 Columbia⊙ 7,733 E8
39701 Columbus⊙ 27,383 H3
38619 Como 1,378 E1
39057 Conehatta 200 F6
†39051 Conway 25 E5
38834 Corinth⊙ 13,839 G1
†38659 Cornersville 65 F1
38620 Courtland 381 E2
†39095 Coxburg 300 D5
39743 Crawford 495 G4
38621 Crenshaw 1,019 D2
39633 Crosby 349 B8
38622 Crowder 789 D2
38924 Cruger 540 D4
39059 Crystal Springs 4,902 D7
†38606 Curtis Station 350 D2
39326 Daleville 210 G5
†39643 Darbun 100 D8
38623 Darling 275 D2
39327 Decatur⊙ 1,148 F6
†39739 Deerbrook 30 G4
39328 De Kalb⊙ 1,159 G5
†39571 De Lisle 450 F10
39061 Delta City 310 C4
†38655 Denmark 40 F2
38838 Dennis 150 H1
†39059 Dentville 175 C7
†39470 Derby 298 E9
38839 Derma 793 F3
†39532 D'Iberville 13,369 G10
39062 D'Lo 463 E7
38736 Doddsville 232 C3
38737 Drew 2,528 C3
38739 Dublin 100 C2
38925 Duck Hill 706 E3
†39337 Duffee 175 G6
38625 Dumas 312 G1
38740 Duncan 501 C2
38626 Dundee 600 D1
39063 Durant 2,889 E4
39436 Eastabuchie 200 F8
39064 Ebenezer 200 D5
38841 Ecru 687 F2
39634 Eddiceton 65 C8
39065 Eden 150 D5
39066 Edwards 1,515 C6
†39156 Eldorado 20 C5
39329 Electric Mills 100 G5
38742 Elizabeth 500 C4
38926 Elliott 200 E3
39437 Ellisville⊙ 4,652 F7
38927 Enid E2
39330 Enterprise 607 G6
†39440 Errata 85 F7
39552 Escatawpa 5,367 G10
39067 Ethel 486 F4
38627 Etta 75 F2
39744 Eupora 2,048 F3
†38676 Evansville 60 D1
38628 Falcon 260 D2
38629 Falkner 251 G1
38630 Farrell 300 C2
39069 Fayette⊙ 2,033 B7
39635 Fernwood 500 D8
39070 Fitler 175 B5
39071 Flora 1,507 D5
39073 Florence 1,111 D6
†39201 Flowood 943 D6
39074 Forest⊙ 5,229 F6
39076 Forkville 185 E6
39636 Fort Adams 75 B8
39483 Foxworth 800 E8
39745 French Camp 306 F4
38631 Friars Point 1,400 C2
39577 Fruitland Park 75 F9
38843 Fulton⊙ 3,238 H2
39077 Gallman D7
38844 Gattman 151 H3
39553 Gautier 8,917 G10
39078 Georgetown 343 D7
†39354 Gholson 50 G5
†39083 Glancy 25 C7
38846 Glen 100 H1
38744 Glen Allan 650 B4
38928 Glendora 220 D3
39638 Gloster 1,726 B8
†39110 Gluckstadt 150 D5
38847 Golden 292 H2
39079 Goodman 1,285 E5
38929 Gore Springs 125 E3
38745 Grace 325 C5
†38725 Grapeland 200 B3
38701 Greenville⊙ 40,613 B4
38930 Greenwood⊙ 20,115 D4
38848 Greenwood Springs 170 H3
38901 Grenada⊙ 12,641 E3
*39501 Gulfport⊙ 39,676 F10
38746 Gunnison 708 C3
38849 Guntown 359 G2
†39661 Hamburg 150 B7
39746 Hamilton 500 H3
†38901 Hardy 45 E3
39080 Harperville 200 E6
39081 Harriston 500 C7
39082 Harrisville 500 D7
†38821 Hatley 497 H3
39401 Hattiesburg⊙ 40,829 F8
39083 Hazlehurst⊙ 4,437 D7
39439 Heidelberg 1,098 F7
39086 Hermanville 750 C7
38632 Hernando⊙ 2,969 E1
†39192 Hesterville 25 E4
39332 Hickory 670 F6
38633 Hickory Flat 458 F1
39087 Hillsboro 800 E6
†38646 Hinchcliff 60 D2
†39462 Hintonville 300 F8
†39108 Hinze 30 F4
†39751 Hohenlinden 96 F3
38940 Holcomb 50 D3
38748 Hollandale 4,336 C4
39088 Holly Bluff 700 C5
38749 Holly Ridge 350 C4
38635 Holly Springs⊙ 7,285 E1
†38676 Hollywood 80 D1
†39648 Holmesville 50 D8
38637 Horn Lake 4,326 D1
38850 Houlka 710 G2
38851 Houston⊙ 3,747 G3
†39574 Howison 300 F9
†39429 Hub 80 E8
39555 Hurley 500 H9
†38774 Hushpuckena 60 C2
38638 Independence 150 E1
38751 Indianola⊙ 8,221 C4
†38652 Ingomar 150 F2
38753 Inverness 1,034 C4
38754 Isola 834 C4
38941 Itta Bena 2,904 D4
38852 Iuka⊙ 2,846 H1
†38865 Jacinto 65 H1
*39201 Jackson (cap.)⊙ 202,895 D6
Jackson‡ 320,425 D6
39641 Jayess 200 D8
38639 Jonestown 1,231 D2
†38829 Jumpertown 472 G1
†38924 Keim 3 D4
†39364 Kewanee 250 H6
39747 Kilmichael 906 E4
39556 Kiln 800 F10
†39661 Knoxville 65 B8
39643 Kokomo 250 E8
†39740 Kolola Springs 100 H3
39090 Kosciusko⊙ 7,415 E4
38834 Kossuth 190 G1
38640 Lafayette Springs 80 F2
†39092 Lake 524 F6
38641 Lake Cormorant 300 D1
39558 Lakeshore 550 F10
38642 Lamar 200 F1
38643 Lambert 1,624 D2
38755 Lamont 400 B3
39335 Lauderdale 600 G5
39440 Laurel⊙ 21,897 F7
39336 Lawrence 250 F6
39450 Leaf 250 G8
39451 Leakesville⊙ 1,120 G8
39093 Learned 113 C6
38756 Leland 6,667 C4
39094 Lena 231 E5
†39667 Lexie 40 D8
39095 Lexington⊙ 2,628 D4
39645 Liberty⊙ 669 C8
39337 Little Rock 70 F5
39560 Long Beach 7,967 F10
†39759 Longview 800 G4
39096 Lorman 350 B7
39338 Louin 338 F6
39097 Louise 400 C5
39339 Louisville⊙ 7,323 G4
†38632 Love 50 D1
39452 Lucedale⊙ 2,429 G9
39646 Lucien 75 C7
39098 Ludlow 350 E5
38644 Lula 394 C2
39455 Lumberton 2,217 E8
†39501 Lyman 500 F10
†39739 Lynn Creek 20 G4
38645 Lyon 531 D2
39750 Maben 855 F3
39341 Macon⊙ 2,396 G4
39109 Madden 450 F5
39110 Madison 2,241 D6
39111 Magee 3,497 E7
39652 Magnolia⊙ 2,461 D8
†38769 Malvina 100 C3
38855 Mantachie 732 H2
39751 Mantee 158 F3
38856 Marietta 298 H2
39342 Marion 771 G6
38646 Marks⊙ 2,260 D2
†39083 Martinsville 30 D7
†39051 Marydell 99 F5
39752 Mathiston 632 F3
38758 Mattson 200 C2
†39458 Maxie 233 F9
39113 Mayersville⊙ 378 B5
39753 Mayhew 150 G4
39107 McAdams 350 E4
†39144 McBride 2 C7
39647 McCall Creek 250 C7
38943 McCarley 250 E3
39648 McComb 12,331 D8
38854 McCondy 150 G3
39108 McCool 203 F4
39561 McHenry 660 F9
39456 McLain 688 G8
39457 McNeill 800 E9
39653 Meadville⊙ 575 C8
39114 Mendenhall⊙ 2,533 E7
39301 Meridian⊙ 46,577 G6
38759 Merigold 574 C3
†39667 Mesa 30 D8
38760 Metcalfe 952 B4
38647 Michigan City 350 F1
39115 Midnight 500 C4
38648 Mineral Wells 250 E1
38944 Minter City 150 D3
39762 Mississippi State G4
39116 Mize 363 E7
38945 Money 350 D3
39654 Monticello⊙ 1,834 D7
39754 Montpelier 175 G3
†39338 Montrose 120 F6
38857 Mooreville 200 G2
38761 Moorhead 2,358 C4
38946 Morgan City 319 D4
39484 Morgantown 325 E8
†39120 Morgantown 3,445 B7
39117 Morton 3,303 E6
†39328 Moscow 30 G5
39459 Moselle 525 F8
39460 Moss 65 F7
39563 Moss Point 18,998 G10
38762 Mound Bayou 2,917 C3
†39474 Mount Carmel 30 E7
39119 Mount Olive 993 E7
38649 Mount Pleasant 250 E1
38650 Myrtle 402 F1
39120 Natchez⊙ 22,015 B7
39461 Neely 270 G8
38651 Nesbit 366 D1
39365 Neshoba 250 F5
38858 Nettleton 1,911 G2
38652 New Albany⊙ 7,072 G2
39462 New Augusta⊙ 589 F8
39140 Newhebron 470 D7
38850 New Houlka (Houlka) 710 G2
38859 New Site 100 H1
39345 Newton 3,708 F6
39463 Nicholson 400 E10
38763 Nitta Yuma 150 C4
†39629 Norfield 75 C8
38947 North Carrollton 859 E3
39346 Noxapater 516 F5
38948 Oakland 540 E2
†39154 Oakley 133 D6
39656 Oak Vale E8
39564 Ocean Springs 14,504 G10
39141 Ofahoma 350 E5
38860 Okolona⊙ 3,409 G2
38654 Olive Branch 2,067 E1
†39482 Oloh 93 E8
†39654 Oma 200 D7
†39501 Orange Grove 13,476 H10
39657 Osyka 581 D8
39464 Ovett 600 F8
38655 Oxford⊙ 9,882 F2
38764 Pace 519 C3
39347 Pachuta 256 G6
38861 Paden 119 H1
†39401 Palmers Crossing 2,765 F8
38765 Panther Burn 300 C4
38738 Parchman 200 D3
38949 Paris 253 F2
39567 Pascagoula⊙ 29,318 G10
Pascagoula-Moss Point‡ 118,015 G10
39571 Pass Christian 5,014 F10
39144 Pattison 540 C7
39348 Paulding⊙ 630 F6
39349 Paulette 230 H4
†38920 Paynes 100 D3
39028 Pearl 18,580 D6
39572 Pearlington 500 E10
39145 Pelahatchie 1,445 E6
39573 Perkinston 950 F9
†38746 Perthshire 25 C3
39465 Petal 8,476 F8
39755 Pheba 280 G3
39350 Philadelphia⊙ 6,434 F5
38950 Philipp 975 D3
†39476 Piave 150 G8
39466 Picayune 10,361 E9
39146 Pickens 1,386 E5
39148 Piney Woods 450 D6
39149 Pinola E7

(continued on following page)

**Mississippi-
Missouri
River System**

MILES
0   100   200   300

Navigable Waterways
over 9 feet deep............
Major River Ports................⊙

©Copyright HAMMOND INCORPORATED.

Agriculture, Industry and Resources

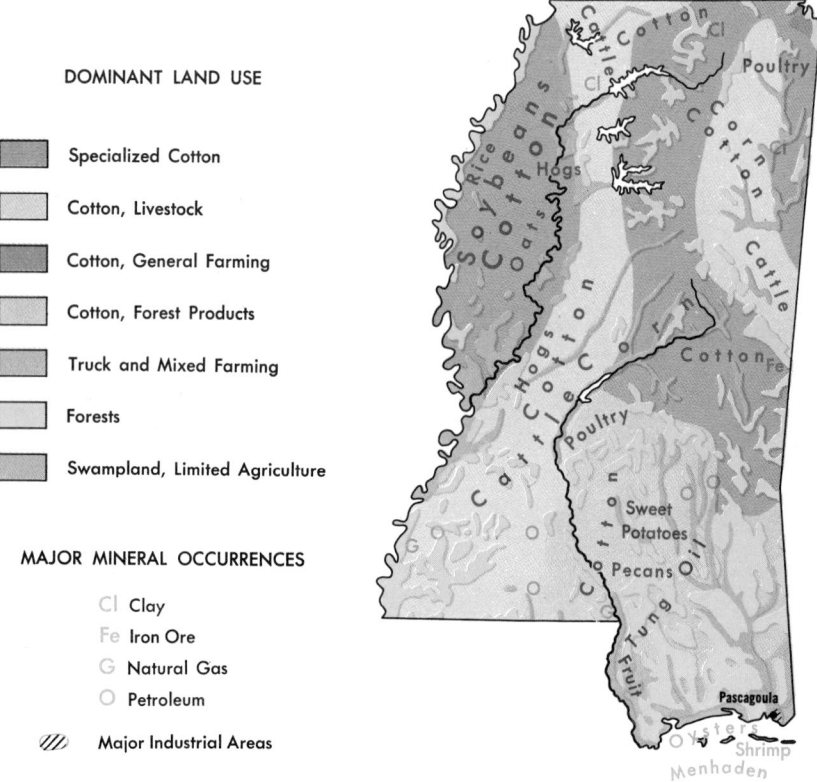

DOMINANT LAND USE

Specialized Cotton

Cotton, Livestock

Cotton, General Farming

Cotton, Forest Products

Truck and Mixed Farming

Forests

Swampland, Limited Agriculture

MAJOR MINERAL OCCURRENCES

Cl Clay

Fe Iron Ore

G Natural Gas

O Petroleum

/// Major Industrial Areas

AREA 69,697 sq. mi. (180,515 sq. km.)
POPULATION 4,916,759
CAPITAL Jefferson City
LARGEST CITY St. Louis
HIGHEST POINT Taum Sauk Mtn. 1,772 ft. (540 m.)
SETTLED IN 1764
ADMITTED TO UNION August 10, 1821
POPULAR NAME Show Me State
STATE FLOWER Hawthorn
STATE BIRD Bluebird

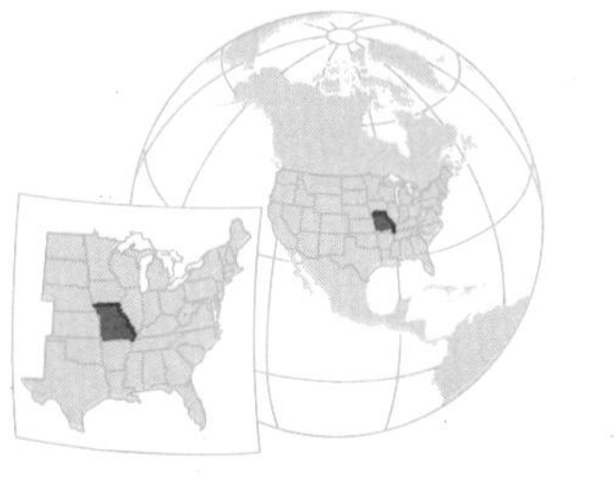

COUNTIES

Adair 24,870 .... G2
Andrew 13,980 .... C3
Atchison 8,605 .... B2
Audrain 26,458 .... J4
Barry 24,408 .... E9
Barton 11,292 .... D7
Bates 15,873 .... D6
Benton 12,183 .... F6
Bollinger 10,301 .... M8
Boone 100,376 .... H4
Buchanan 87,888 .... C3
Butler 37,693 .... M9
Caldwell 8,660 .... E3
Callaway 32,252 .... J5
Camden 20,017 .... G6
Cape Girardeau 58,837 .... N8
Carroll 12,131 .... F4
Carter 5,428 .... L9
Cass 51,029 .... D5
Cedar 11,894 .... E7
Chariton 10,489 .... F3
Christian 22,402 .... F9
Clark 8,493 .... J2
Clay 136,488 .... D4
Clinton 15,916 .... D3
Cole 56,663 .... H6
Cooper 14,643 .... G5
Crawford 18,300 .... K7
Dade 7,383 .... E8
Dallas 12,096 .... F7
Daviess 8,905 .... E3
De Kalb 8,222 .... D3
Dent 14,517 .... J7
Douglas 11,594 .... G9
Dunklin 36,324 .... M10
Franklin 71,233 .... K6
Gasconade 13,181 .... J6
Gentry 7,887 .... D2
Greene 185,302 .... F8
Grundy 11,959 .... E2
Harrison 9,890 .... E2
Henry 19,672 .... E6
Hickory 6,367 .... F7
Holt 6,882 .... B2
Howard 10,008 .... G4
Howell 28,807 .... J9
Iron 11,084 .... L7
Jackson 629,266 .... R5
Jasper 86,958 .... D8
Jefferson 146,183 .... L6
Johnson 39,059 .... E5
Knox 5,508 .... H2
Laclede 24,323 .... G7
Lafayette 29,925 .... E4
Lawrence 28,973 .... E8
Lewis 10,901 .... J2
Lincoln 22,193 .... L4
Linn 15,495 .... F3
Livingston 15,739 .... E3
Macon 16,313 .... G3
Madison 10,725 .... M8
Maries 7,551 .... J6
Marion 28,638 .... J3
McDonald 14,917 .... D9
Mercer 4,685 .... E2
Miller 18,532 .... H6
Mississippi 15,726 .... O9
Moniteau 12,068 .... G5
Monroe 9,716 .... H3
Montgomery 11,537 .... K5
Morgan 13,807 .... G6
New Madrid 22,945 .... N9
Newton 40,555 .... D9
Nodaway 21,996 .... C2
Oregon 10,238 .... K9
Osage 12,014 .... J6
Ozark 7,961 .... H9
Pemiscot 24,987 .... N10
Perry 16,784 .... N7
Pettis 36,378 .... F5
Phelps 33,633 .... J7
Pike 17,568 .... K4
Platte 46,341 .... C4
Polk 18,822 .... F7
Pulaski 42,011 .... H7
Putnam 6,092 .... F2
Ralls 8,984 .... J3
Randolph 25,460 .... G3
Ray 21,378 .... E4
Reynolds 7,230 .... L8
Ripley 12,458 .... L9
Saint Charles 144,107 .... M2
Saint Clair 8,622 .... E6
Sainte Genevieve 15,180 .... M7
Saint Francois 42,600 .... M7
Saint Louis 973,896 .... O3
Saint Louis (city county) 453,085 ... P3
Saline 24,919 .... F4
Schuyler 4,979 .... G2
Scotland 5,415 .... H2
Scott 39,647 .... N8
Shannon 7,885 .... K8
Shelby 7,826 .... H3
Stoddard 29,009 .... N9
Stone 15,587 .... F9
Sullivan 7,434 .... F2
Taney 20,467 .... F9
Texas 21,070 .... J8
Vernon 19,806 .... D7
Warren 14,900 .... K5
Washington 17,983 .... L7
Wayne 11,277 .... L8
Webster 20,414 .... G8
Worth 3,008 .... D2
Wright 16,188 .... H8

CITIES and TOWNS

Zip Name/Pop. Key

64720 Adrian 1,484 .... D6
63730 Advance 1,054 .... N8
63123 Affton 23,181 .... P4
64401 Agency 419 .... C3
64830 Alba 474 .... D8
64402 Albany⊙ 2,152 .... D2
63430 Alexandria 417 .... K2
64001 Alma 445 .... E4
65606 Alton⊙ 721 .... K9
64421 Amazonia 314 .... C3
64723 Amsterdam 231 .... D6
64831 Anderson 1,237 .... D9
63620 Annapolis 370 .... L8
63820 Anniston 320 .... O9
64724 Appleton City 1,257 .... D6
63821 Arbyrd 704 .... M10
63621 Arcadia 683 .... L7
64725 Archie 753 .... D5
65230 Armstrong 360 .... G4
63010 Arnold 19,141 .... M6
65604 Ash Grove 1,157 .... E8
65010 Ashland 1,021 .... H5
63530 Atlanta 441 .... H3
63332 Augusta 308 .... L5
65605 Aurora 6,437 .... E9
65231 Auxvasse 858 .... J4
65608 Ava⊙ 2,761 .... G9
64010 Avondale 612 .... P5
63011 Ballwin 12,656 .... N3
64011 Bates City 199 .... E5
†65619 Battlefield 1,227 .... F8
†63101 Bella Villa 758 .... R4
63735 Bell City 539 .... N8
65013 Belle 1,233 .... J6
†63137 Bellefontaine Neighbors 12,082 .... R2
63333 Bellflower 403 .... K4
†63101 Bel-Nor 2,047 .... P2
†63101 Bel-Ridge 3,682 .... P2
64012 Belton 12,708 .... C5
63736 Benton⊙ 674 .... O8
63134 Berkeley 15,922 .... P2
63822 Bernie 1,975 .... M9
63823 Bertrand 688 .... O9
64424 Bethany⊙ 3,095 .... E2
63532 Bevier 733 .... G3
65610 Billings 911 .... F8
65438 Birch Tree 622 .... K9
63624 Bismarck 1,625 .... L7
65321 Blackburn 314 .... F4
†63031 Black Jack 5,293 .... R1
65014 Bland 662 .... J6
63825 Bloomfield⊙ 1,795 .... M9
63627 Bloomsdale 397 .... M6
64015 Blue Springs 25,927 .... R6
†64101 Blue Summit R5
65613 Bolivar⊙ 5,919 .... F7
63628 Bonne Terre 3,797 .... L7
65233 Boonville⊙ 6,959 .... G5
64723 Bosworth 394 .... F4
65441 Bourbon 1,259 .... K6
63334 Bowling Green⊙ 3,022 .... K4
65616 Branson 2,550 .... F9
63533 Brashear 332 .... H2
64624 Braymer 986 .... E3
64625 Breckenridge 523 .... E3
†63114 Breckenridge Hills 5,666 .... O2
63144 Brentwood 8,209 .... P3
63044 Bridgeton 18,445 .... O2
†63044 Bridgeton Terrace 334 .... O2
64628 Brookfield 5,555 .... F3
64630 Browning 368 .... F2
65236 Brunswick 1,272 .... F4
64631 Bucklin 713 .... G3
64016 Buckner 2,848 .... R5
65622 Buffalo⊙ 2,217 .... F7
65237 Bunceton 419 .... G5
63629 Bunker 673 .... K8
64428 Burlington Junction 657 .... B2
64730 Butler⊙ 4,107 .... D6
65689 Cabool 2,090 .... H8
64632 Cainsville 496 .... E2
65239 Cairo 315 .... H4
65323 Calhoun 427 .... E6
65018 California⊙ 3,381 .... H5
63534 Callao 326 .... G3
†63101 Calverton Park 1,717 .... P2
65020 Camdenton⊙ 2,303 .... G6
64429 Cameron 4,519 .... D3
63933 Campbell 2,134 .... M9
63828 Canalou 369 .... N9
63435 Canton 2,435 .... J2
63701 Cape Girardeau 34,361 .... O8
63829 Cardwell 831 .... M10
64834 Carl Junction 3,937 .... C8
64633 Carrollton⊙ 4,700 .... E4
64835 Carterville 1,973 .... D8
64836 Carthage⊙ 11,104 .... D8
63830 Caruthersville⊙ 7,958 .... N10
65625 Cassville⊙ 2,091 .... E9
65022 Cedar City 427 .... H5
63436 Center 669 .... J3
65023 Centertown 304 .... H5
63633 Centerville⊙ 241 .... L8
65240 Centralia 3,537 .... H4
63740 Chaffee 3,241 .... N8
65024 Chamois 546 .... J5
†63101 Charlack 1,537 .... P2
63834 Charleston⊙ 5,230 .... O9
64733 Chilhowee 349 .... E5
64601 Chillicothe⊙ 9,089 .... E3
63437 Clarence 1,147 .... H3
65243 Clark 304 .... H4
65025 Clarksburg 352 .... G5
64430 Clarksdale 278 .... D3
†63017 Clarkson Valley 1,435 .... N3
63336 Clarksville 585 .... K4
63837 Clarkton 1,228 .... M10
†64119 Claycomo 1,671 .... P5
63105 Clayton⊙ 14,273 .... P3
64734 Cleveland 485 .... C5
65631 Clever 551 .... F8
64735 Clinton⊙ 8,366 .... E6
65325 Cole Camp 1,022 .... F6
65201 Columbia⊙ 62,061 .... H5
Columbia‡ 100,376 .... H5
†63128 Concord 20,896 .... P4
64020 Concordia 2,129 .... E5
65632 Conway 601 .... G7
†63101 Cool Valley 2,084 .... P2
63839 Cooter 479 .... N10
64021 Corder 483 .... E4
†64501 Country Club Village 1,234 .... C3
64437 Craig 379 .... B2
65633 Crane 1,185 .... E9
64739 Creighton 301 .... D6
†63126 Crestwood 12,815 .... O3
63141 Creve Coeur 11,757 .... O2
65452 Crocker 979 .... H7
63019 Crystal City 3,618 .... M6
†63101 Crystal Lake Park 496 .... O3
65453 Cuba 2,120 .... K6
63339 Curryville 323 .... K4
64439 Dearborn 547 .... C3
64740 Deepwater 475 .... E6
64440 De Kalb 245 .... C3
†63135 Dellwood 6,200 .... R2
63744 Delta 524 .... N8
63636 Des Arc 237 .... L8
63601 Desloge 3,481 .... M7
63020 De Soto 5,993 .... L6
63131 Des Peres 8,254 .... O3
63841 Dexter 7,043 .... N9
64840 Diamond 766 .... D9
65459 Dixon 1,402 .... H6
63935 Doniphan⊙ 1,921 .... L9
†65550 Doolittle 701 .... J7
63536 Downing 462 .... H2
64742 Drexel 908 .... C6
64841 Duenweg 703 .... D8
†64801 Duquesne 1,252 .... D8
64442 Eagleville 364 .... D2
64443 Easton 313 .... C3
63845 East Prairie 3,713 .... O9
64444 Edgerton 584 .... C3
63537 Edina⊙ 1,520 .... H2
†63101 Edmundson 1,374 .... O2
65026 Eldon 4,342 .... G6
64744 El Dorado Springs 3,868 .... E7
63638 Ellington 1,215 .... L8
†63011 Ellisville 6,233 .... M3
63937 Ellsinore 362 .... L9
63343 Elsberry 1,272 .... L4
63639 Elvins 1,548 .... L7
65466 Eminence⊙ 614 .... K8
63344 Eolia 401 .... L4
63846 Essex 545 .... N9
†63601 Esther 1,038 .... M7
63025 Eureka 3,862 .... M4
65646 Everton 317 .... E8
63440 Ewing 400 .... J2
64024 Excelsior Springs 10,424 .... R4
65647 Exeter 588 .... D9
64446 Fairfax 835 .... B2
65648 Fair Grove 863 .... F8
65649 Fair Play 384 .... E7
63345 Farber 503 .... J4
63640 Farmington⊙ 8,270 .... M7
65248 Fayette⊙ 2,983 .... G4
63026 Fenton 2,417 .... O4
63135 Ferguson 24,740 .... P2
64163 Ferrelview 447 .... O4
63028 Festus 7,574 .... M6
64449 Fillmore 265 .... C2
63940 Fisk 450 .... M9
63601 Flat River 4,443 .... M7
*63031 Florissant 55,372 .... P1
65652 Fordland 569 .... G8
64451 Forest City 387 .... B3
65653 Forsyth⊙ 1,010 .... F9
63441 Frankford 443 .... K4
63645 Fredericktown⊙ 4,036 .... M7
65035 Freeburg 554 .... J6
64746 Freeman 485 .... C5
†63101 Frontenac 3,654 .... O3
65251 Fulton⊙ 11,046 .... J5
65655 Gainesville⊙ 707 .... G9
65656 Galena⊙ 423 .... F9
64640 Gallatin⊙ 2,063 .... E3
64641 Galt 323 .... F2
64747 Garden City 1,021 .... D5
63037 Gerald 921 .... K6
63848 Gideon 1,240 .... N10
64642 Gilman City 414 .... D2
64118 Gladstone 24,990 .... P5
65254 Glasgow 1,336 .... G4
†64068 Glenaire 541 .... R5
63122 Glendale 6,035 .... P3
64748 Golden City 900 .... D8
63843 Goodman 1,030 .... C9
63543 Gorin H2
64454 Gower 1,276 .... C3
64029 Grain Valley 1,327 .... S6
64844 Granby 1,908 .... D9
64030 Grandview 24,502 .... P6
64456 Grant City⊙ 1,068 .... D2
†63155 Grantwood Village 1,002 .... O4
65037 Gravois Mills G6
63545 Green City 719 .... F2
65661 Greenfield⊙ 1,394 .... E8
65332 Green Ridge 488 .... F5
63546 Greentop 538 .... H2
63944 Greenville⊙ 393 .... M8
64034 Greenwood 1,315 .... R6
64643 Hale 529 .... F3
65255 Hallsville 624 .... H4
64644 Hamilton 1,582 .... E3
†63101 Hanley Hills 2,439 .... P2
63401 Hannibal 18,811 .... K3
64035 Hardin 688 .... E4
64701 Harrisonville⊙ 6,372 .... D5
65667 Hartville⊙ 576 .... G8
63945 Harviell M9
63349 Hawk Point 386 .... K5
63851 Hayti 3,964 .... N10
†63851 Hayti Heights 1,023 .... N10
†63736 Haywood City 425 .... N9
*63042 Hazelwood 12,935 .... P2
64036 Henrietta 424 .... E4
63048 Herculaneum 2,293 .... M6
65041 Hermann⊙ 2,695 .... K5
65668 Hermitage⊙ 384 .... F7
65257 Higbee 817 .... H4
64037 Higginsville 4,595 .... E4
63350 High Hill 254 .... K5
63050 Hillsboro⊙ 1,508 .... L6
†63101 Hillsdale 2,247 .... R2
63852 Holcomb 632 .... N10
64040 Holden 2,195 .... E5
63853 Holland 295 .... N10
65672 Hollister 1,439 .... F9
64048 Holt 276 .... D4
65043 Holts Summit 2,540 .... H5
†63879 Homestown 306 .... N10
64461 Hopkins 634 .... C1
63855 Hornersville 704 .... M10
65483 Houston⊙ 2,157 .... J8
65333 Houstonia 327 .... F5
†64152 Houston Lake 280 .... O5
†63869 Howardville 536 .... N9
65674 Humansville 907 .... E7
64752 Hume 315 .... C6
63443 Hunnewell 235 .... J3
†63101 Huntleigh 428 .... O3
65259 Huntsville⊙ 1,657 .... H4
63547 Hurdland 227 .... H2
65486 Iberia 852 .... H6
63754 Illmo 1.368 .... O8

(continued on following page)

Agriculture, Industry and Resources

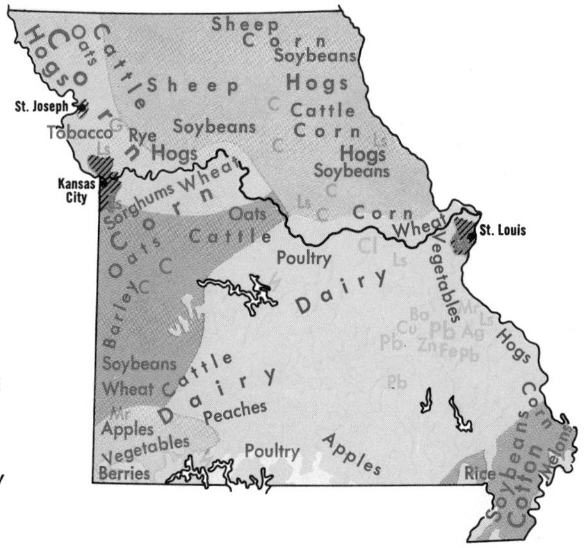

DOMINANT LAND USE

- Cattle Feed, Hogs
- Livestock, Cash Grain, Dairy
- Pasture Livestock
- Specialized Cotton
- General Farming, Dairy, Livestock, Poultry
- General Farming, Livestock, Truck Farming, Cotton
- Fruit and Mixed Farming
- Forests
- Urban Areas

MAJOR MINERAL OCCURRENCES

Ag	Silver	G	Natural Gas
Ba	Barite	Ls	Limestone
C	Coal	Mr	Marble
Cl	Clay	Pb	Lead
Cu	Copper	Zn	Zinc
Fe	Iron Ore		

Water Power · Major Industrial Areas

*64050 Independence⊙ 111,806 ... R5
†64648 Irondale 349 ... L7
†64801 Iron Gates 314 ... C8
63650 Ironton⊙ 1,743 ... L7
63755 Jackson⊙ 7,827 ... N8
64648 Jamesport 651 ... E3
65046 Jamestown 317 ... G5
64755 Jasper 1,012 ... D8
65101 Jefferson City (cap.) ⊙
33,619 ... H5
63136 Jennings 17,026 ... R2
63351 Jonesburg 614 ... K5
64801 Joplin 39,023 ... C8
Joplin‡ 127,513 ... C8
†63645 Junction City 238 ... M7
63445 Kahoka⊙ 2,101 ... J2
*64101 Kansas City 448,159 ... P5
Kansas City‡ 1,327,020 ... P5
64060 Kearney 1,433 ... D4
63758 Kelso 455 ... O8
63857 Kennett⊙ 10,145 ... M10
65261 Keytesville⊙ 689 ... G4
64649 Kidder 265 ... D3
65686 Kimberling City 1,285 ... F9
64463 King City 1,063 ... D2
64650 Kingston⊙ 280 ... E3
64061 Kingsville 365 ... D5
63140 Kinloch 4,455 ... P2
63501 Kirksville⊙ 17,167 ... H2
63122 Kirkwood 27,987 ... O3
65336 Knob Noster 2,040 ... F5
63446 Knox City 281 ... H2
63447 La Belle 845 ... J2
64651 Laclede 445 ... F3
63352 Laddonia 726 ... J4
†63124 Ladue 9,376 ... P3
63448 La Grange 1,217 ... K2
64063 Lake Lotawana 1,875 ... R6
65049 Lake Ozark 427 ... G6
†63336 Lake Saint Louis 3,843 ... N2
63101 Lakeshire 1,593 ... P4
†64015 Lake Tapawingo 925 ... R6
†64152 Lake Waukomis 1,050 ... P5
64034 Lake Winnebago 681 ... R6
64759 Lamar⊙ 4,053 ... D8
65337 La Monte 1,054 ... F5
64847 Lanagan 440 ... C9
63548 Lancaster⊙ 855 ... H1
63549 La Plata 1,423 ... H2
64652 Laredo 340 ... E2
64760 Latour 84 ... D5
64062 Lawson 1,688 ... D4
†63640 Leadington 238 ... M7
63353 Leadwood 1,371 ... L7
65535 Leasburg 304 ... K6
65536 Leasburg⊙ 9,507 ... G7
64063 Lee's Summit 28,741 ... R6
64761 Leeton 604 ... E5
63125 Lemay 35,424 ... R4
64066 Levasy 235 ... S5
63452 Lewistown 502 ... J2
64067 Lexington⊙ 5,063 ... E4
64762 Liberal 701 ... D7
64068 Liberty⊙ 16,251 ... R5
65542 Licking 1,272 ... J8
63862 Lilbourn 1,463 ... N9
65338 Lincoln 819 ... F5
65051 Linn⊙ 1,211 ... J5
65052 Linn Creek 286 ... G6
64653 Linneus⊙ 421 ... F3
65682 Lockwood 971 ... E8
64070 Lone Jack 420 ... S6
63353 Louisiana 4,261 ... K4
64763 Lowry City 676 ... E6

63762 Lutesville 865 ... M8
63552 Macon⊙ 5,680 ... H3
65263 Madison 656 ... H4
64466 Maitland 415 ... B2
63863 Malden 6,096 ... M9
65339 Malta Bend 292 ... F4
63011 Manchester 6,191 ... O3
63143 Maplewood 10,960 ... P3
63764 Marble Hill⊙ 601 ... N8
64658 Marceline 2,938 ... F3
65705 Marionville 1,920 ... E8
†63101 Marlborough 2,012 ... P3
63655 Marquand 397 ... M8
65340 Marshall⊙ 12,781 ... F4
65706 Marshfield⊙ 3,871 ... G8
63866 Marston 742 ... N9
63357 Marthasville 543 ... L5
65264 Martinsburg 309 ... J4
63043 Maryland Heights 5,676 ... O2
64468 Maryville⊙ 9,558 ... C2
63857 Matthews 547 ... N9
64469 Maysville⊙ 1,187 ... D3
64071 Mayview 291 ... E4
64659 Meadville 416 ... F3
63555 Memphis⊙ 2,105 ... H2
64660 Mendon 252 ... F3
64661 Mercer 442 ... F2
65058 Meta 336 ... H6
65265 Mexico⊙ 12,276 ... J4
63359 Middletown 268 ... J4
63556 Milan⊙ 1,947 ... F2
65707 Miller 795 ... E8
63952 Mill Spring 257 ... L8
64769 Mindenmines 318 ... C8
†63801 Miner 1,182 ... N9
63660 Mineral Point 358 ... L7
64072 Missouri City 343 ... R5
65270 Moberly 13,418 ... G4
65059 Mokane 293 ... J5
†63101 Moline Acres 2,774 ... R2
65708 Monett 6,148 ... E9
63456 Monroe City 2,557 ... J3
63361 Montgomery City⊙ 2,101 ... K5
63457 Monticello⊙ 134 ... J2
64770 Montrose 498 ... E6
63868 Mooreshouse 1,220 ... N9
63767 Morley 745 ... N8
65710 Morrisville 331 ... F4
64073 Mosby 284 ... R4
63362 Moscow Mills 484 ... L5
64470 Mound City 1,447 ... B2
65711 Mountain Grove 3,974 ... H8
65548 Mountain View 1,664 ... J8
64665 Mount Moriah 162 ... E2
65712 Mount Vernon⊙ 3,341 ... E8
63088 Murphy 8,121 ... O4
64074 Napoleon 271 ... E4
63953 Naylor 602 ... L9
63954 Neelyville 474 ... M9
65347 Nelson 248 ... F4
64850 Neosho⊙ 9,493 ... D9
64772 Newburg 1,180 ... J7
65063 New Bloomfield 519 ... J5
65550 Newburg 841 ... J7
63558 New Cambria 246 ... G3
63363 New Florence 731 ... K5
65274 New Franklin 1,228 ... G4
†63740 New Hamburg ... O8
64471 New Hampton 358 ... D2
63068 New Haven 1,581 ... K5
63459 New London⊙ 1,161 ... K3
63869 New Madrid⊙ 3,204 ... O9
65713 Niangua 376 ... G8

65714 Nixa 2,662 ... F8
64854 Noel 1,161 ... D9
64668 Norborne 931 ... E4
63121 Normandy 5,174 ... R2
64116 North Kansas City 4,507 ... P5
†64152 Northmoor 506 ... P5
65717 Norwood 364 ... H8
63559 Novinger 626 ... G2
64075 Oak Grove 4,067 ... S6
†63080 Oak Grove 386 ... K6
63101 Oakland 1,728 ... P3
63769 Oak Ridge 252 ... N7
64116 Oakview 497 ... P5
64076 Oakwood 227 ... R5
65348 Odessa 3,088 ... E5
65066 Owensville 2,241 ... K6
63366 O'Fallon 8,677 ... L5
63369 Old Monroe 272 ... L5
63124 Olivette 7,985 ... O2
63050 Olympian Village 774 ... M6
63771 Oran 1,266 ... N8
64473 Oregon⊙ 901 ... B2
64855 Oronogo 525 ... D8
64077 Orrick 922 ... E4
65065 Osage Beach 1,992 ... G6
64474 Osborn 381 ... D3
64776 Osceola⊙ 841 ... E6
65066 Owensville 2,241 ... K6
65721 Ozark⊙ 2,980 ... F8
63069 Pacific 4,410 ... L5
†63101 Pagedale 4,542 ... P2
63461 Palmyra⊙ 3,469 ... J3
65275 Paris⊙ 1,598 ... J4
64152 Parkville 1,997 ... O5
64130 Parkway 254 ... L6
63870 Parma 1,081 ... N9
64670 Pattonsburg 502 ... D2
64078 Peculiar 1,571 ... D5
63462 Perry 836 ... J4
64476 Perryville⊙ 7,343 ... N7
63070 Pevely 2,732 ... M6
64476 Pickering 215 ... C2
63957 Piedmont 2,359 ... L8
65723 Pierce City 1,391 ... E9
65276 Pilot Grove 745 ... G5
63663 Pilot Knob 722 ... L7
†63120 Pine Lawn 6,662 ... R2
64856 Pineville⊙ 504 ... D9
64079 Platte City⊙ 2,114 ... C4
†64152 Platte Woods 467 ... O5
64477 Plattsburg⊙ 2,095 ... D3
64080 Pleasant Hill 3,301 ... D5
65725 Pleasant Hope 354 ... F8
†64836 Pleasant Valley 1,545 ... R5
64671 Polo 583 ... D3
63901 Poplar Bluff⊙ 17,139 ... L9
63373 Portage Des Sioux 488 ... M5
63873 Portageville 3,470 ... N10
63664 Potosi⊙ 2,528 ... L7
65068 Prairie Home 279 ... G5
64673 Princeton⊙ 1,264 ... E2
64857 Purcell 322 ... D8
64674 Purdin 243 ... F3
65734 Purdy 928 ... E9
63960 Puxico 833 ... M9
63561 Queen City 783 ... H2
63961 Qulin 545 ... M9
64101 Randolph 91 ... P5
64479 Ravenwood 436 ... C2
65555 Raymondville 388 ... J8
64083 Raymore 3,154 ... D5
64133 Raytown 31,759 ... P6
65737 Reeds Spring 461 ... F9

65738 Republic 4,485 ... E8
64779 Rich Hill 1,471 ... D6
65556 Richland 1,922 ... H7
63121 Richmond⊙ 5,499 ... E4
63117 Richmond Heights 11,516 ... P3
64481 Ridgeway 516 ... D2
63874 Risco 446 ... N9
†63601 Rivermines 414 ... L7
64168 Riverside 3,206 ... O5
†63101 Riverview 3,367 ... R2
65279 Rocheport 272 ... H5
65740 Rockaway Beach 292 ... F9
63119 Rock Hill 5,702 ... P3
64482 Rock Port⊙ 1,511 ... B2
64780 Rockville 281 ... D6
65742 Rogersville 741 ... G8
65401 Rolla⊙ 13,303 ... J7
63091 Rosebud 326 ... K6
64483 Rosendale 223 ... C2
64484 Rushville 271 ... B3
65074 Russellville 667 ... H6
64864 Saginaw 293 ... C8

63074 Saint Ann 15,523 ... O2
63301 Saint Charles⊙ 37,379 ... N1
63077 Saint Clair 3,485 ... K6
63870 Sainte Genevieve⊙ 4,481 ... M6
65075 Saint Elizabeth 312 ... H6
†63101 Saint George 1,545 ... P4
63114 Saint John 7,854 ... P2
*64501 Saint Joseph⊙ 76,691 ... C3
Saint Joseph‡ 101,868 ... C3
*63101 Saint Louis‡ 453,085 ... R3
Saint Louis‡ 2,355,276 ... R3
†65101 Saint Martins 739 ... H5
63673 Saint Marys 565 ... M7
63366 Saint Paul 607 ... L5
63376 Saint Peters 15,700 ... M1
65583 Saint Robert 1,735 ... H7
65560 Salem⊙ 4,454 ... J7
65281 Salisbury 1,975 ... G4
63126 Sappington 11,388 ... O4
64862 Sarcoxie 1,381 ... D8
64485 Savannah⊙ 4,184 ... C3

64783 Schell City 327 ... D6
63780 Scott City 3,262 ... O8
65301 Sedalia⊙ 20,927 ... F5
65745 Seligman 508 ... D9
63876 Senath 1,728 ... M10
64865 Seneca 1,853 ... C9
65746 Seymour 1,535 ... G8
63468 Shelbina 2,169 ... G4
63469 Shelbyville⊙ 645 ... H3
64784 Sheldon 491 ... D7
†63101 Shrewsbury 5,077 ... P3
64088 Sibley 382 ... S5
63801 Sikeston 17,431 ... N9
63377 Silex 287 ... L5
64487 Skidmore 437 ... B2
65349 Slater 2,492 ... F4
65350 Smithton 559 ... F5
64089 Smithville 1,873 ... D4
64863 South West City 516 ... D9
†63138 Spanish Lake 20,632 ... R1
65753 Sparta 743 ... F9
64679 Spickard 389 ... F2

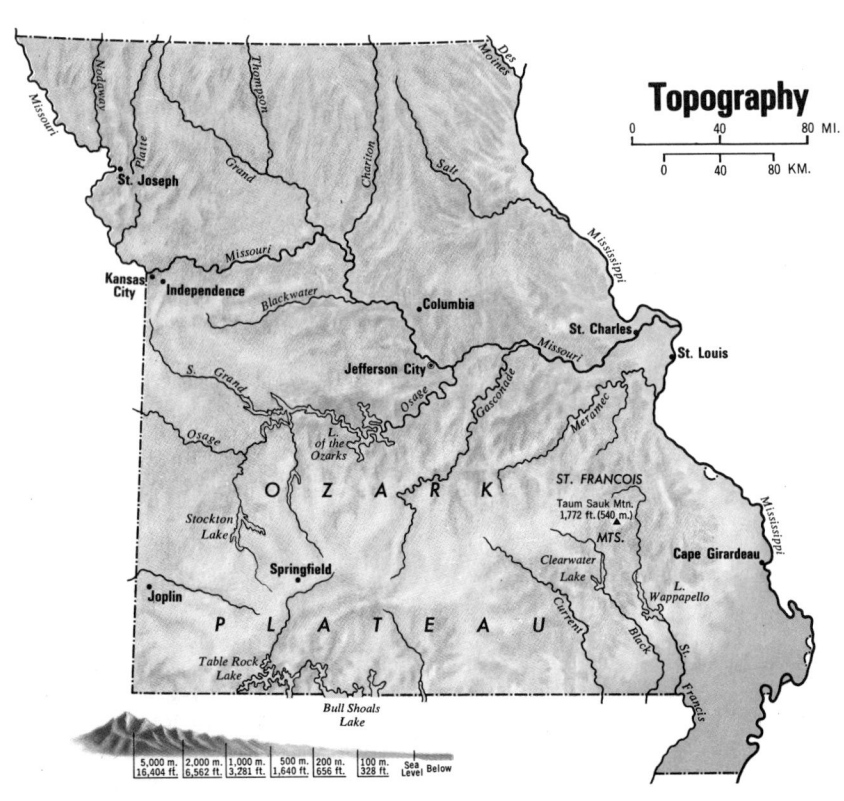

Topography

Taum Sauk Mtn.
1,772 ft. (540 m.)

| 5,000 m. | 2,000 m. | 1,000 m. | 500 m. | 200 m. | 100 m. | Sea Level | Below |
| 16,404 ft. | 6,562 ft. | 3,281 ft. | 1,640 ft. | 656 ft. | 328 ft. | | |

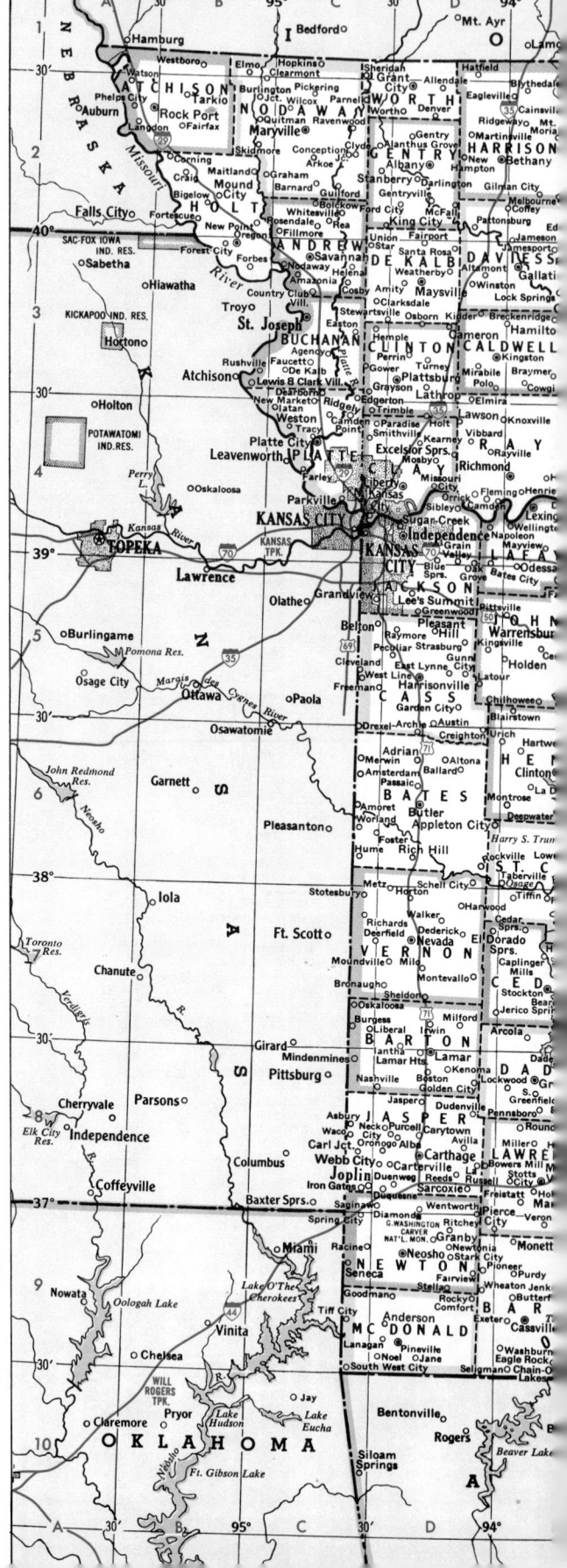

*65801 Springfield⊙ 133,116......F8
  Springfield‡ 207,704......F8
64489 Stanberry 1,387......C2
63877 Steele 2,419......N10
65565 Steelville† 1,470......K7
64490 Stewartsville 832......C3
65785 Stockton⊙ 1,432......E7
65567 Stoutland 286......G7
65078 Stover 1,041......G6
65757 Strafford 1,121......F8
65284 Sturgeon 901......H4
64054 Sugar Creek 4,305......R5
63080 Sullivan 5,461......K6
65571 Summersville 551......J8
†63101 Sunset Hills 4,363......O4
65351 Sweet Springs 1,694......F5
65759 Taneyville 300......F9
†65101 Taos 759......H5
64491 Tarkio 2,375......B2
†64063 Tarsney Lakes 329......R5
65791 Thayer 2,211......J9
†63025 Times Beach 2,041......N4

65081 Tipton 2,155......G5
†63101 Town and Country 3,187......O3
64079 Tracy 310......C4
64683 Trenton⊙ 6,811......E2
63379 Troy⊙ 2,624......L5
65082 Tuscumbia⊙ 241......H6
†63088 Twin Oaks 426......N3
63084 Union⊙ 5,506......L6
64494 Union Star 423......C2
63565 Unionville⊙ 2,178......G2
63130 University City 42,738......P3
65767 Urbana 329......F7
64788 Urich 509......E6
63088 Valley Park 3,232......O3
63965 Van Buren⊙ 850......L8
63382 Vandalia 3,170......J4
63784 Vanduser 320......N9
†63101 Velda 1,988......P2
65769 Verona 592......E9
65084 Versailles⊙ 2,406......G6
65566 Viburnum 836......K7
†63020 Victoria 375......M6

65582 Vienna⊙ 514......H6
†63101 Vinita Park 2,283......P2
64790 Walker 325......D7
65770 Walnut Grove 504......F8
65101 Wardsville 535......H6
64093 Warrensburg⊙ 13,807......E5
63383 Warrenton⊙ 3,219......K5
65355 Warsaw⊙ 1,494......F6
†63101 Warson Woods 2,127......O3
63090 Washington 9,251......K5
64096 Waverly 941......E4
65583 Waynesville⊙ 2,879......H7
†64152 Weatherby Lake 1,446......O5
65774 Weaubleau 464......F7
64870 Weeks City 7,309......C8
63119 Webster Groves 23,097......P3
64097 Wellington 780......E4
63112 Wellston 4,495......P3
63384 Wellsville 1,546......K4
63385 Wentzville 3,193......L5
64498 Westboro 188......B1

64098 Weston 1,440......C4
65775 West Plains⊙
  7,741......J9
†63101 Westwood 319......O3
65779 Wheatland 364......F7
64874 Wheaton 548......E9
64688 Wheeling 379......F3
†63101 Wilbur Park 564......P3
65781 Willard 1,799......F8
63977 Williamsville 418......L9
65793 Willow Springs 2,215......H9
63834 Wilson City 309......N9
63389 Winfield 592......L5
65360 Windsor 3,058......F6
64689 Winston 246......D3
64024 Woods Heights 747......S4
†63101 Woodson Terrace 4,788......P2
63390 Wright City 1,179......K5
63474 Wyaconda 359......J2
63882 Wyatt 441......O9

OTHER FEATURES

Bagnell (dam)......G6
Big (riv.)......L6
Black (riv.)......L10
Bull Shoals (lake)......G10
Chariton (riv.)......G1
Clearwater (lake)......L8
Cuivre (riv.)......N2
Current (riv.)......K8
Des Moines (riv.)......J1
Fort Leonard Wood 21,262......H7
Gasconade (riv.)......H7
George Washington Carver Nat'l
  Mon.......D9
Grand (riv.)......F3
Jefferson Nat'l Expansion Mem. Nat'l
  His.......R3
Lake City Arsenal......R5
Meramec (riv.)......N3
Mississippi (riv.)......L4
Missouri (riv.)......H5

Norfork (lake)......H10
Osage (riv.)......E6
Ozark (plat.)......F9
Ozark Nat'l Scenic Riverways......K8
Ozarks, Lake of the (lake)......F6
Platte (riv.)......C3
Pomme de Terre (riv.)......E7
Richards Gebaur A.F.B. 4,305......P6
Sac (riv.)......E7
Saint Francis (riv.)......M9
Salt (riv.)......J3
Stockton (lake)......E7
Table Rock (res.)......E9
Taum Sauk (mt.)......L7
Taneycomo (lake)......F9
Wappapello (lake)......L9
White (riv.)......G10
Whiteman A.F.B.......E5
Wilson's Creek Nat'l Battlefield......F8

⊙County seat.
‡Population of metropolitan area.
† Zip of nearest p.o.   * Multiple zips.

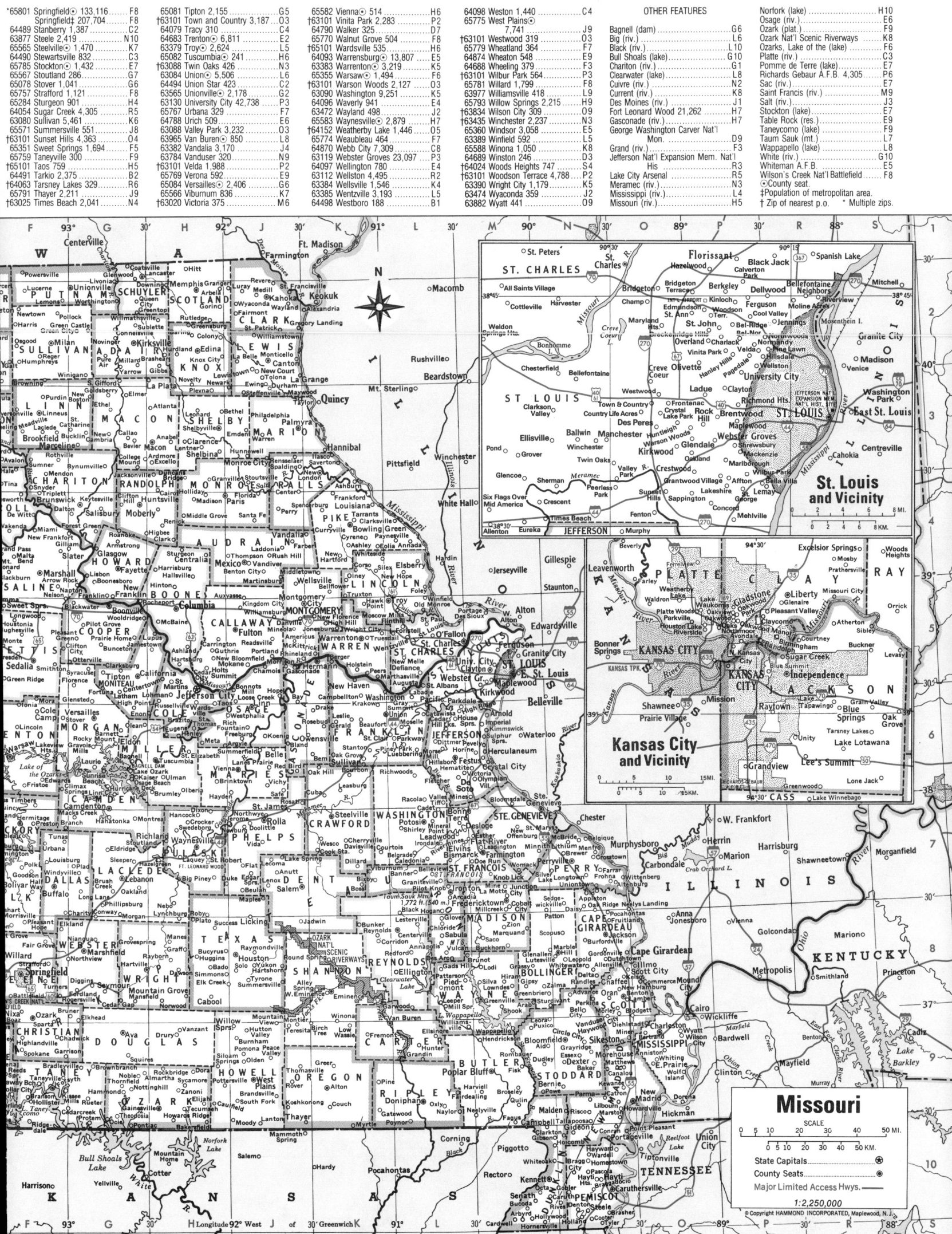

Missouri

SCALE

0 5 10   20   30   40   50 MI.

0 5 10   20   30   40   50 KM.

State Capitals......⊛
County Seats......⊙
Major Limited Access Hwys.——

1:2,250,000

© Copyright HAMMOND INCORPORATED, Maplewood, N.J.

Agriculture, Industry and Resources

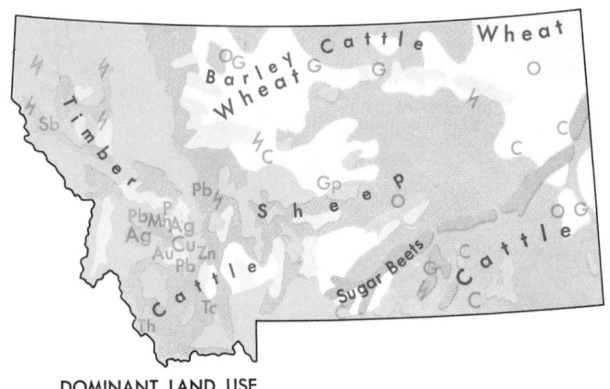

DOMINANT LAND USE

- ☐ Specialized Wheat
- ☐ Wheat, Range Livestock
- ☐ General Farming, Dairy, Range Livestock
- ☐ General Farming, Livestock, Special Crops
- ☐ Range Livestock
- ☐ Sugar Beets, Beans, Livestock, General Farming
- ☐ Forests

MAJOR MINERAL OCCURRENCES

Ag	Silver	O	Petroleum
Au	Gold	P	Phosphates
C	Coal	Pb	Lead
Cu	Copper	Sb	Antimony
G	Natural Gas	Tc	Talc
Gp	Gypsum	Th	Thorium
Mn	Manganese	Zn	Zinc

⚡ Water Power

COUNTIES

Beaverhead 8,186 ....C5
Big Horn 11,096 ....J5
Blaine 6,999 ....G2
Broadwater 3,267 ....E4
Carbon 8,099 ....G5
Carter 1,799 ....M5
Cascade 80,696 ....E3
Chouteau 6,092 ....F3
Custer 13,109 ....L4
Daniels 2,835 ....L2
Dawson 11,805 ....M3
Deer Lodge 12,518 ....C5
Fallon 3,763 ....M4
Fergus 13,076 ....G3
Flathead 51,966 ....B2
Gallatin 42,865 ....E5
Garfield 1,656 ....J3
Glacier 10,628 ....C2
Golden Valley 1,026 ....G4
Granite 2,700 ....C4
Hill 17,985 ....F2
Jefferson 7,029 ....D4
Judith Basin 2,646 ....F4
Lake 19,056 ....B3
Lewis and Clark 43,039 ....D3
Liberty 2,329 ....E2
Lincoln 17,752 ....A2
Madison 5,448 ....D5
McCone 2,702 ....L3
Meagher 2,154 ....F4
Mineral 3,675 ....B3
Missoula 76,016 ....C3
Musselshell 4,428 ....H4
Park 12,869 ....F5
Petroleum 655 ....H3
Phillips 5,367 ....J2
Pondera 6,731 ....D2
Powder River 2,520 ....L5
Powell 6,958 ....D4
Prairie 1,836 ....L4
Ravalli 22,493 ....B4
Richland 12,243 ....M3
Roosevelt 10,467 ....L2
Rosebud 9,899 ....K4
Sanders 8,675 ....A3
Sheridan 5,414 ....M2

Silver Bow 38,092 ....D5
Stillwater 5,598 ....G5
Sweet Grass 3,216 ....G5
Teton 6,491 ....D3
Toole 5,559 ....E2
Treasure 981 ....J4
Valley 10,250 ....K2
Wheatland 2,359 ....G4
Wibaux 1,476 ....M4
Yellowstone 108,035 ....H4
Yellowstone Nat'l Park 275 ....F6

CITIES and TOWNS

Zip	Name/Pop.	Key
59001	Absarokee 830	G5
59820	Alberton 368	B3
59710	Alder 120	D5
†59741	Amsterdam 130	E5
59711	Anaconda-Deer Lodge County⊙ 12,518	C4
59312	Angela 50	K4
59211	Antelope 83	M2
59821	Arlee 200	B3
59003	Ashland 600	K5
59410	Augusta 497	D3
59713	Avon 125	D4
59411	Babb 150	C2
59212	Bainville 245	M2
59313	Baker⊙ 2,354	M4
59006	Ballantine 380	J5
†59725	Bannack 2	C5
59613	Basin 350	D4
59007	Bearcreek 61	G5
59008	Belfry 80	H5
59714	Belgrade 2,336	E5
59412	Belt 825.	E3
59314	Biddle 28	L5
59910	Big Arm 250	B3
59911	Bigfork 1,080	C2
59520	Big Sandy 835	G2
59011	Big Timber 1,690	G5
*59101	Billings⊙ 66,842	H5
	Billings‡ 108,035	H5
59012	Birney 100	K5
59414	Black Eagle 1,500	E3

Zip	Name/Pop.	Key
59415	Blackfoot 100	D2
59823	Bonner-West Riverside 1,742	C4
59632	Boulder⊙ 1,441	E4
59521	Box Elder 300	F2
59715	Bozeman⊙ 21,645	E5
59416	Brady 450	E2
59014	Bridger 724	H5
59317	Broadus⊙ 712	L5
59015	Broadview 120	H4
59213	Brockton 374	M2
59417	Browning 1,226	C2
59016	Busby 700	J5
59701	Butte-Silver Bow County⊙ 37,205	D4
59720	Cameron 150	D5
59633	Canyon Creek 100	D4
†59347	Cartersville 115	K4
59421	Cascade 773	E3
59824	Charlo 250	B3
59522	Chester⊙ 963	E2
59523	Chinook⊙ 1,660	G2
59422	Choteau⊙ 1,798	D3
59215	Circle⊙ 931	L3
59634	Clancy 550	E4
59018	Clyde Park 283	F5
†59351	Coalwood 2	L5
59922	Cohagen 12	K3
59323	Colstrip 1,476	K5
59912	Columbia Falls 3,112	B2
59019	Columbus⊙ 1,439	G5
59826	Condon 300	C3
59827	Conner 420	B4
59425	Conrad⊙ 3,074	D2
59020	Cooke City 120	F6
59913	Coram 450	C2
59828	Corvallis 500	C4
59217	Crane 163	M3
59022	Crow Agency 975	J5
59218	Culbertson 887	M2
59024	Custer 300	J4
59427	Cut Bank⊙ 3,688	C2
59829	Darby 581	B4
59914	Dayton 140	B3
59830	De Borgia 300	A3
59025	Decker 150	K5
59722	Deer Lodge⊙ 4,023	D4
59430	Denton 356	F3

Montana

SCALE
0 5 10   20   40   60 MI.
0 5 10   20   40   60 KM.

State Capitals ....⊛
County Seats ....⊙
Major Limited Access Hwys. _____

Scale 1:3,450,000

© Copyright HAMMOND INCORPORATED, Maplewood, N.J.

Topography

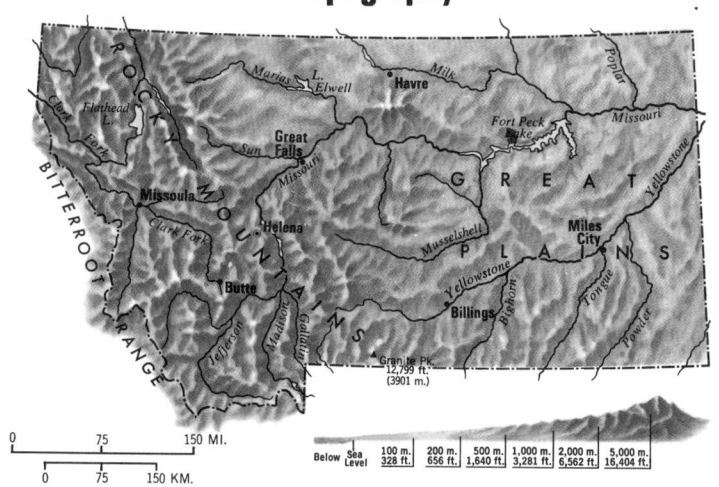

0 75 150 MI.

0 75 150 KM.

Below Sea Level | 100 m. 328 ft. | 200 m. 656 ft. | 500 m. 1,640 ft. | 1,000 m. 3,281 ft. | 2,000 m. 6,562 ft. | 5,000 m. 16,404 ft.

AREA 147,046 sq. mi. (380,849 sq. km.)
POPULATION 786,690
CAPITAL Helena
LARGEST CITY Billings
HIGHEST POINT Granite Pk. 12,799 ft. (3901 m.)
SETTLED IN 1809
ADMITTED TO UNION November 8, 1889
POPULAR NAME Treasure State; Big Sky Country
STATE FLOWER Bitterroot
STATE BIRD Western Meadowlark

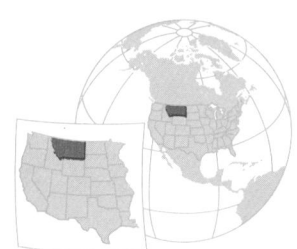

59725 Dillon⊙ 3,976	D5
59727 Divide 275	D5
59831 Dixon 550	B3
59524 Dodson 158	H2
59832 Drummond 414	D4
59432 Dupuyer 105	D2
59433 Dutton 359	E3
59434 East Glacier Park 475	C2
59635 East Helena 1,647	E4
59026 Edgar 220	H5
59324 Ekalaka⊙ 620	M5
59728 Elliston 250	D4
59915 Elmo 250	B3
59918 Fortine 250	A2
59729 Ennis 660	E5
59917 Eureka 1,119	B2
59436 Fairfield 650	D3
59221 Fairview 1,366	M3
59326 Fallon 225	L4
59222 Flaxville 142	L2
59833 Florence 700	B4
59026 Edgar 220	H5
59441 Forestgrove 100	H3
59327 Forsyth⊙ 2,553	K4
†59526 Fort Belknap 185	H2
59442 Fort Benton⊙ 1,693	F3
59223 Fort Peck 456	K2
59443 Fort Shaw 200	E3
†59075 Fort Smith 300	J5
59225 Frazer 200	K2
59834 Frenchtown 300	B3
59226 Froid 323	M2
59029 Fromberg 469	H5
59444 Galata 100	E2
59730 Gallatin Gateway 600	E5
59030 Gardiner 600	F5
59731 Garrison 300	D4
59031 Garryowen 200	J5
59446 Geraldine 305	F3
59447 Geyser 125	F3
59525 Gildford 250	F2
59230 Glasgow⊙ 4,455	K2
59330 Glendive⊙ 5,978	M3
59733 Goldcreek 100	D4
59835 Grantsdale 500	B4
59032 Grass Range 139	H3
59401 Great Falls⊙ 56,725	E3
Great Falls‡ 80,696	E3
59836 Greenough 120	C4
59837 Hall 130	C4
59840 Hamilton⊙ 2,661	B4
59034 Hardin⊙ 3,300	J5
59526 Harlem 1,023	H2
59036 Harlowton⊙ 1,181	F4
59735 Harrison 94	E5
59842 Haugan 90	A3
59501 Havre⊙ 10,891	G2
59527 Hays 400	H2
59448 Heart Butte 300	C2
59601 Helena (cap.)⊙ 23,938	E4
59843 Helmville 250	C4
59450 Highwood 150	F3
59528 Hingham 186	F2
59241 Hinsdale 260	K2
59452 Hobson 261	G4
59845 Hot Springs 601	B3
59919 Hungry Horse 700	C2
59037 Huntley 250	H5
59846 Huson 97	B3
59038 Hysham⊙ 449	J4
59530 Inverness 150	F2
59336 Ismay 31	M4
59736 Jackson 210	C5
59638 Jefferson City 162	E4
59041 Joliet 580	G5
59531 Joplin 300	F2
59337 Jordan⊙ 485	J3
59453 Judith Gap 213	G4
59901 Kalispell⊙ 10,648	B2
59454 Kevin 208	D2
59920 Kila 350	B2
59338 Kinsey 100	L4
†59072 Klein 250	H4
59532 Kremlin 304	F2
59922 Lakeside 663	B2
59243 Lambert 203	M3
59043 Lame Deer 460	K5
59044 Laurel 5,481	H5
59046 Lavina 164	H4
59457 Lewistown⊙ 7,104	G3
59923 Libby⊙ 2,748	A2
59739 Lima 272	D6
59639 Lincoln 473	D4
59047 Livingston⊙ 6,994	F5
59050 Lodge Grass 771	J5
†59524 Lodge Pole 292	H2
59847 Lolo 2,418	B4
†59847 Lolo Hot Springs 25	B4
59460 Loma 200	F3
59225 Lustre 25	K2
59538 Malta⊙ 2,367	J2
59741 Manhattan 988	E5
59925 Marion 450	B2
59052 McLeod 150	G5
59247 Medicine Lake 408	M2
59743 Melrose 350	D5
59054 Melstone 238	H4
59055 Melville 100	F4
59301 Miles City⊙ 9,602	L4
59851 Milltown 300	C4
*59801 Missoula⊙ 33,388	C4
59463 Monarch 120	F3
59464 Moore 229	G4
59059 Musselshell 117	H4
59248 Nashua 495	K2
59465 Neihart 91	F4
59853 Noxon 800	A3
59927 Olney 200	B2
59250 Opheim 210	K2
59252 Outlook 122	M2
59854 Ovando 300	C3
59855 Pablo 500	B3
59856 Paradise 400	B3
59063 Park City 800	H5
59253 Peerless 110	L2
59467 Pendroy 100	D2
59858 Philipsburg⊙ 1,138	C4
59859 Plains 1,116	B3
59254 Plentywood⊙ 2,476	M2
59344 Plevna 191	M4
59860 Polson⊙ 2,798	B3
59064 Pompeys Pillar 300	J5
59747 Pony 130	E5
59255 Poplar 995	L2
59468 Power 159	E3
59929 Proctor 150	B3
59066 Pryor 146	H5
59641 Radersburg 104	E4
59863 Ravalli 150	B3
59068 Red Lodge⊙ 1,896	G5
59069 Reedpoint 160	G5
59258 Reserve 80	M2
59930 Rexford 130	A2
59259 Richey 417	L3
59642 Ringling 102	F4
59070 Roberts 312	G5
59931 Rollins 200	B3
59864 Ronan 1,530	C3
59347 Rosebud 259	K4
59072 Roundup⊙ 2,119	H4
59471 Roy 200	H3
59074 Ryegate⊙ 273	G4
59261 Saco 252	J2
59865 Saint Ignatius 877	C3
59866 Saint Regis 500	A3
59075 Saint Xavier 200	J5
59867 Saltese 90	A3
59472 Sand Coulee 600	E3
59473 Santa Rita 120	D2
59262 Savage 300	M3
59263 Scobey⊙ 1,382	L2
59868 Seeley Lake 900	C3
59474 Shelby⊙ 3,142	E2
59079 Shepherd 200	H5
59749 Sheridan 646	D5
59270 Sidney⊙ 5,726	M3
59751 Silver Star 125	D5
59477 Simms 200	E3
59932 Somers 700	B2
59479 Stanford⊙ 595	F3
59870 Stevensville 1,207	C4
59480 Stockett 500	E3
59933 Stryker 96	B2
59871 Sula 200	B5
59482 Sunburst 476	E2
59483 Sun River 300	E3
59872 Superior⊙ 1,054	B3
59911 Swan Lake 100	C3
59484 Sweetgrass 250	E2
59349 Terry⊙ 929	L4
59873 Thompson Falls⊙ 1,478	A3
59752 Three Forks 1,247	E5
59644 Townsend⊙ 1,587	E4
59874 Trout Creek 300	A3
59935 Troy 1,088	A2
59542 Turner 150	H2
59754 Twin Bridges 437	D5
59085 Twodot 285	F4
59485 Ulm 450	E3
59486 Vaughn 2,270	E3
59875 Victor 700	B4
59755 Virginia City⊙ 192	E5
59351 Volborg 125	L5
59701 Walkerville 887	D4
59756 Warmsprings 500	D4
59275 Westby 291	M2
59936 West Glacier 150	C2
59758 West Yellowstone 735	E6
59937 Whitefish 3,703	B2
59759 Whitehall 1,030	D5
59645 White Sulphur Springs⊙ 1,302	E4
59276 Whitetail 150	L2
59544 Whitewater 100	J2
59353 Wibaux⊙ 782	M3
59760 Willow Creek 150	E5
59086 Wilsall 250	F5
59489 Winifred 155	G3
59087 Winnett⊙ 207	H4
59647 Winston 120	E4
59761 Wisdom 140	C5
59762 Wise River 150	C5
59648 Wolf Creek 500	D3
59201 Wolf Point⊙ 3,074	L2
59088 Worden 600	H5
59089 Wyola 350	J5

OTHER FEATURES

Absaroka (range)	F5
Allen (mt.)	C2
Arrow (creek)	F3
Ashley (lake)	B2
Battle (creek)	G1
Bearhat (mt.)	C2
Bearpaw (mts.)	G2
Beartooth (mts.)	G5
Beaver (creek)	J2
Beaverhead (riv.)	D5
Benton (lake)	E3
Big (lake)	G5
Big Belt (mts.)	E4
Big Dry (creek)	K3
Big Hole (riv.)	C5
Big Hole Nat'l Battlefield	C5
Bighorn (lake)	H5
Bighorn (riv.)	J5
Big Muddy (riv.)	M2
Big Porcupine (creek)	J4
Birch (creek)	D2
Birch Creek (res.)	D2
Bitterroot (range)	B4
Bitterroot (riv.)	B4
Blackfeet Ind. Res.	D2
Blackfoot (riv.)	C4
Blackmore (mt.)	F5
Bowdoin (lake)	J2
Boxelder (creek)	H3
Boxelder (creek)	M5
Bynum (res.)	D2
Cabinet (mts.)	A2
Canyon Ferry (lake)	E4
Clark Canyon (res.)	D6
Clark Fork (riv.)	A3
Clarks Fork, Yellowstone (riv.)	G6
Cottonwood (creek)	E2
Cow (creek)	G2
Crazy (peak)	F4
Crow Ind. Res.	H5
Custer Battlefield Nat'l Mon.	J5
Cut Bank (creek)	D2
Douglas (mt.)	F5
Earthquake (lake)	E6
Electric (peak)	F6
Elwell (lake)	E2
Emigrant (peak)	F5
Ennis (lake)	E5
Flathead (lake)	C3
Flathead (riv.)	B2
Flathead, North Fork (riv.)	C2
Flathead, South Fork (riv.)	C3
Flathead Ind. Res.	B3
Flatwillow (creek)	H4
Fort Belknap Ind. Res.	H2
Fort Peck (lake)	K3
Fort Union Trading Post Nat'l Hist. Site	N2
Frances (lake)	D2
Freezeout (lake)	D3
Frenchman (riv.)	J1
Fresno (res.)	F2
Gallatin (peak)	E5
Gallatin (riv.)	E5
Georgetown (lake)	C4
Gibson (res.)	D3
Glacier Nat'l Park	C2
Granite (peak)	F5
Grant-Kohrs Ranch Nat'l Hist. Site	D4
Hauser (lake)	E4
Haystack (peak)	A3
Hebgen (lake)	E6
Helena (lake)	E4
Holter (lake)	E3
Hungry Horse (res.)	C2
Hurricane (mt.)	D2
Hyalite (peak)	E5
Jackson (mt.)	C2
Jefferson (riv.)	D5
Judith (riv.)	G3
Koocanusa (lake)	A2
Kootenai (riv.)	A2
Lemhi (pass)	C6
Lewis (range)	C2
Lima (res.)	D6
Little Bighorn (riv.)	J5
Little Bitterroot (lake)	B2
Little Dry (creek)	K3
Little Missouri (riv.)	M5
Lockhart (mt.)	D3
Lodge (creek)	G1
Lolo (pass)	B4
Lone (mt.)	E5
Lost Trail (pass)	B5
Lower Red Rock (lake)	E6
Lower Saint Mary (lake)	C2
Madison (riv.)	E5
Malmstrom A.F.B. 6,675	E3
Marias (riv.)	D2
Martinsdale (res.)	F4
Mary Ronan (lake)	B3
McDonald (lake)	B2
McGloughlin (peak)	C4
McGregor (lake)	B3
Medicine (lake)	M2
Milk (riv.)	J2
Mission (range)	C3
Missouri (riv.)	L3
Musselshell (riv.)	J3
Nelson (res.)	J2
Ninepipe (res.)	C3
Northern Cheyenne Indian Reservation	K5
O'Fallon (creek)	L4
Pishkun (res.)	D3
Poplar (riv.)	L2
Porcupine (creek)	K2
Powder (riv.)	L4
Purcell (mts.)	A2
Railley (mt.)	C3
Red Rock (lkes)	E6
Red Rock (riv.)	D6
Redwater (riv.)	L3
Rock (creek)	C4
Rocky (mts.)	D4
Rocky Boy's Ind. Res.	G2
Rosebud (creek)	K4
Ruby (riv.)	D5
Ruby River (res.)	D5
Sage (creek)	E2
Saint Mary (lake)	C2
Saint Mary (riv.)	C1
Sandy (creek)	C2
Sheep (mt.)	C2
Shields (riv.)	F4
Siyeh (mt.)	C2
Smith (riv.)	E3
Sphinx (mt.)	E5
Stillwater (riv.)	G5
Stimson (mt.)	C2
Sun (riv.)	D3
Swan (lake)	C3
Teton (riv.)	E3
Tongue (riv.)	K5
Upper Red Rock (lake)	E6
Ward (creek)	A3
Waterton-Glacier Int'l Peace Park	C2
Whitefish (lake)	B2
Willow (creek)	E2
Willow Creek (res.)	D3
Yellowstone (riv.)	M3
Yellowstone National Park	F6

⊙County seat.
‡Population of metropolitan area.
† Zip or nearest p.o.   * Multiple zips.

COUNTIES

Adams 30,656 F4
Antelope 8,675 F2
Arthur 513 C3
Banner 918 A3
Blaine 867 E3
Boone 7,391 F3
Box Butte 13,696 A2
Boyd 3,331 F2
Brown 4,377 E2
Buffalo 34,797 E4
Burt 8,813 H3
Butler 9,330 G3
Cass 20,297 H4
Cedar 11,375 G2
Chase 4,758 C4
Cherry 6,758 C2
Cheyenne 10,057 A3
Clay 8,106 F4
Colfax 9,890 G3
Cuming 11,664 H3
Custer 13,877 E3
Dakota 16,573 H2
Dawes 9,609 A2
Dawson 22,304 E4
Deuel 2,462 B3
Dixon 7,137 H2
Dodge 35,847 H3
Douglas 397,038 H3
Dundy 2,861 C4
Fillmore 7,920 G4
Franklin 4,377 F4
Frontier 3,647 D4
Furnas 6,486 E4
Gage 24,456 H4
Garden 2,802 B3
Garfield 2,363 F3
Gosper 2,140 E4
Grant 877 C3
Greeley 3,462 F3
Hall 47,690 F4
Hamilton 9,301 F4
Harlan 4,292 E4
Hayes 1,356 C4
Hitchcock 4,079 C4
Holt 13,552 F2
Hooker 990 C3
Howard 6,773 F3
Jefferson 9,817 G4
Johnson 5,285 H4
Kearney 7,053 F4
Keith 9,364 C3
Keya Paha 1,301 E2
Kimball 4,882 A3
Knox 11,457 G2
Lancaster 192,884 H4
Lincoln 36,455 D4
Logan 983 D3
Loup 859 E3
Madison 31,382 G3
McPherson 593 C3
Merrick 8,945 F3
Morrill 6,085 A3
Nance 4,740 F3
Nemaha 8,367 J4
Nuckolls 6,726 F4
Otoe 15,183 H4
Pawnee 3,937 H4
Perkins 3,637 C4
Phelps 9,769 E4
Pierce 8,481 G2
Platte 28,852 G3
Polk 6,320 G3
Red Willow 12,615 D4
Richardson 11,315 J4
Rock 2,383 E2
Saline 13,131 G4
Sarpy 86,015 H3
Saunders 18,716 H3
Scotts Bluff 38,344 A3
Seward 15,789 G4
Sheridan 7,544 B2
Sherman 4,226 F3
Sioux 1,845 A2
Stanton 6,549 G3
Thayer 7,582 G4
Thomas 973 D3
Thurston 7,186 H2
Valley 5,633 E3
Washington 15,508 H3
Wayne 9,858 G2
Webster 4,858 F4
Wheeler 1,060 F3
York 14,798 G4

CITIES and TOWNS

Zip *Name/Pop.* *Key*

68301 Adams 395 H4
69210 Ainsworth⊙ 2,256 D2
68620 Albion⊙ 1,997 F3
68810 Alda 601 F4
68710 Allen 390 H2
69301 Alliance⊙ 9,920 A2
68920 Alma⊙ 1,369 E4
68304 Alvo 144 H4
68812 Amherst 269 E4
68814 Ansley 644 E3
68922 Arapahoe 1,107 E4
68815 Arcadia 412 F3
68002 Arlington 1,117 H3
69120 Arnold 813 D3
69121 Arthur⊙ 124 C3
68003 Ashland 2,274 H3
68713 Atkinson 1,521 E2
68305 Auburn⊙ 3,482 J4
68818 Aurora⊙ 3,717 F4
68924 Axtell 602 E4
68004 Bancroft 552 H2
68622 Bartlett⊙ 144 F3
69020 Bartley 342 D4
68714 Bassett⊙ 1,009 E2
68715 Battle Creek 948 G3
69334 Bayard 1,435 A3
68310 Beatrice⊙ 12,891 H4
68926 Beaver City⊙ 775 E4
68313 Beaver Crossing 458 G4
68716 Beemer 853 H3
68005 Bellevue 21,813 J3
68624 Bellwood 407 G3
69021 Benkelman⊙ 1,235 C4
68317 Bennet 523 H4
68007 Bennington 631 H3
68927 Bertrand 775 E4
69122 Big Springs 505 B3
68928 Bladen 298 F4
68008 Blair⊙ 6,418 H3
68718 Bloomfield 1,393 G2
68930 Blue Hill 883 F4
68318 Blue Springs 521 H4
68010 Boys Town 622 H3
68319 Bradshaw 373 G4
69123 Brady 377 D3
68821 Brewster⊙ 46 D3
69336 Bridgeport⊙ 1,668 A3
68822 Broken Bow⊙ 3,979 E3
69127 Brule 438 C3
68322 Bruning 330 G4
68823 Burwell⊙ 1,383 E3
68722 Butte⊙ 529 F2
68824 Cairo 737 F3
68825 Callaway 579 D3
69022 Cambridge 1,206 D4
68932 Campbell 441 F4
68015 Cedar Bluffs 632 H3
68016 Cedar Creek 311 H3
68627 Cedar Rapids 447 F3
68724 Center⊙ 123 G2
68826 Central City⊙ 3,083 F3
68017 Ceresco 836 H3
69337 Chadron⊙ 5,933 B2
68725 Chambers 390 F2
68827 Chapman 349 F3
69129 Chappell⊙ 1,095 B3
68327 Chester 435 G4
68628 Clarks 445 G3
68629 Clarkson 817 G3
68328 Clatonia 273 H4
68933 Clay Center⊙ 962 F4
68726 Clearwater 409 F2
†69343 Clinton 80 B2
68727 Coleridge 673 G2
68601 Columbus⊙ 17,328 G3
68329 Cook 341 H4
68331 Cortland 403 H4
69130 Cozad 4,453 E4
69339 Crawford 1,315 A2
68729 Creighton 1,341 G2
68333 Crete 4,872 G4
68730 Crofton 948 G2
69024 Culbertson 767 C4
69025 Curtis 1,014 D4
68731 Dakota City⊙ 1,440 H2
69131 Dalton 345 B3
68831 Dannebrog 356 F3
68335 Davenport 445 G4
68632 David City⊙ 2,514 G3
68020 Decatur 723 H2
68340 Deshler 997 G4
68341 De Witt 642 G4
68342 Diller 311 H4
69133 Dix 275 A3
68633 Dodge 815 H3
68832 Doniphan 696 F4
68343 Dorchester 611 G4
68634 Duncan 410 G3
68347 Eagle 832 H4
68935 Edgar 705 F4
68636 Elgin 807 F3
68022 Elkhorn 1,344 H3
68836 Elm Creek 862 E4
68349 Elmwood 598 H4
68937 Elwood⊙ 716 E4
68733 Emerson 874 H2
68350 Endicott 198 G4
69028 Eustis 460 D4
68735 Ewing 520 F2
68351 Exeter 807 G4
68352 Fairbury⊙ 4,885 G4
68938 Fairfield 543 G4
68354 Fairmont 767 G4
68355 Falls City⊙ 5,374 J4
69029 Farnam 268 D4
68358 Firth 384 H4
68023 Fort Calhoun 641 J3
68939 Franklin⊙ 1,167 E4
68025 Fremont⊙ 23,979 H3
68359 Friend 1,079 G4
68638 Fullerton⊙ 1,506 F3
68361 Geneva⊙ 2,400 G4
68640 Genoa 1,090 G3
69341 Gering⊙ 7,760 A3
68840 Gibbon 1,531 F4
68841 Giltner 400 F4
68941 Glenvil 363 F4
69343 Gordon 2,167 B2
69138 Gothenburg 3,479 D4
68801 Grand Island⊙ 33,180 F4
69140 Grant⊙ 1,270 C4
68842 Greeley⊙ 597 F3
68366 Greenwood 587 H3
68367 Gresham 320 G3
68028 Gretna 1,609 H3
68942 Guide Rock 344 F4
68738 Hadar 286 G2
68368 Hallam 290 H4
68843 Hampton 419 G4
69346 Harrison⊙ 361 A2
68739 Hartington⊙ 1,730 G2
68944 Harvard 1,217 F4
68901 Hastings⊙ 23,045 F4
69032 Hayes Center⊙ 231 C4
69347 Hay Springs 794 B2
68370 Hebron⊙ 1,906 G4
69348 Hemingford 1,023 A2
68371 Henderson 1,072 G4
68029 Herman 340 H3
69143 Hershey 633 D3
68372 Hickman 687 H4
68947 Hildreth 394 E4
68948 Holbrook 297 D4
68949 Holdrege⊙ 5,624 E4
68030 Homer 564 H2
68031 Hooper 932 H3
68740 Hoskins 306 G2
68641 Howells 677 H3
68376 Humboldt 1,176 J4
68642 Humphrey 799 G3
69350 Hyannis⊙ 336 C3
69033 Imperial⊙ 1,941 C4
69034 Indianola 856 D4
68743 Jackson 287 H2
68378 Johnson 341 J4
68955 Juniata 703 F4
68847 Kearney⊙ 21,158 E4
68956 Kenesaw 854 F4
68034 Kennard 372 H3
69145 Kimball⊙ 3,120 A3
69035 Lamar 60 C4
68745 Laurel 1,031 G2
†68046 La Vista 9,588 J3
68957 Lawrence 350 F4
68643 Leigh 509 G3
69147 Lewellen 368 B3
68850 Lexington⊙ 7,040 E4
*68501 Lincoln (cap.)⊙ 171,932 H4
Lincoln‡ 192,884 H4
68644 Lindsay 383 G3
69149 Lodgepole 413 B3
69217 Long Pine 521 E2
68958 Loomis 447 E4
68037 Louisville 1,022 H3
68853 Loup City⊙ 1,368 E3
69352 Lyman 551 A3
68746 Lynch 357 F2
68038 Lyons 1,214 H3
68748 Madison⊙ 1,950 G3
69150 Madrid 284 C4
68402 Malcolm 355 H4
68854 Marquette 303 G4
69151 Maxwell 410 D3
69038 Maywood 332 D4
69001 McCook⊙ 8,404 D4
68401 McCool Junction 404 G4
68041 Mead 506 H3
68752 Meadow Grove 400 G2
68856 Merna 389 E3
68405 Milford 2,108 H4
68406 Milligan 332 G4
69356 Minatare 969 A3
68959 Minden⊙ 2,939 F4
69357 Mitchell 1,956 A3
68647 Monroe 294 G3
69358 Morrill 1,097 A3
69152 Mullen⊙ 720 C2
68409 Murray 465 J4
68410 Nebraska City⊙ 7,127 J4
68413 Nehawka 270 H4
68756 Neligh⊙ 1,893 G2
68961 Nelson⊙ 733 F4
68757 Newcastle 348 H2
68758 Newman Grove 930 G3
68760 Niobrara 419 G2
68962 Nora 24 G4
68701 Norfolk 19,449 G2
68649 North Bend 1,368 H3
68859 North Loup 405 F3
69101 North Platte⊙ 24,509 D3
68761 Oakdale 410 F2
68045 Oakland 1,393 H3
68415 Odell 322 H4
69153 Ogallala⊙ 5,638 C3
*68101 Omaha⊙ 313,911 J3
Omaha‡ 570,399 J3
68763 O'Neill⊙ 4,049 F2
68764 Orchard 482 F2
68862 Ord⊙ 2,658 F3
68966 Orleans 527 E4
68651 Osceola⊙ 975 G3
69154 Oshkosh⊙ 1,057 B3
68765 Osmond 871 G2
68863 Overton 633 E4
68967 Oxford 1,109 E4
69040 Palisade 401 C4
68864 Palmer 487 F3
68418 Palmyra 512 H4
68046 Papillion⊙ 6,399 J3
68420 Pawnee City⊙ 1,156 H4
69155 Paxton 568 C3
68047 Pender⊙ 1,318 H2
68421 Peru 998 J4
68652 Petersburg 381 G3
68865 Phillips 405 F4
68767 Pierce⊙ 1,535 G2
.68768 Pilger 400 G2
68769 Plainview 1,483 G2
68653 Platte Center 367 G3
68048 Plattsmouth⊙ 6,295 J3
68866 Pleasanton 349 E4
68424 Plymouth 506 G4
68654 Polk 440 G3
68770 Ponca⊙ 1,057 H2
68867 Poole F4
69156 Potter 369 A3
68050 Prague 285 H3
68127 Ralston 5,143 J3
68771 Randolph 1,106 G2
68869 Ravenna 1,296 F4
68970 Red Cloud⊙ 1,300 F4
68658 Rising City 392 G3
69360 Rushville⊙ 1,217 B2
68660 Saint Edward 891 G3
68873 Saint Paul⊙ 2,094 F3
†68760 Santee 388 G2
68874 Sargent 828 E3
68661 Schuyler⊙ 4,151 G3
68875 Scotia 349 F3
69361 Scottsbluff 14,156 A3
68057 Scribner 1,011 H3
68434 Seward⊙ 5,713 H4
68662 Shelby 724 G3
68876 Shelton 1,046 F4
68436 Shickley 413 G4
69162 Sidney⊙ 6,010 B3
68663 Silver Creek 496 G3
68664 Snyder 387 H3
68776 South Sioux City 9,339 H2
68665 Spalding 645 F3
68777 Spencer 596 F2
68059 Springfield 782 H3
68778 Springview⊙ 326 E2
68779 Stanton⊙ 1,603 G3
68439 Staplehurst 306 G4
69163 Stapleton⊙ 340 D3
68442 Stella 289 J4
68443 Sterling 526 H4
69042 Stockville⊙ 45 D4
69043 Stratton 499 C4
68666 Stromsburg 1,290 G3
68780 Stuart 641 E2
68978 Superior 2,502 F4
69165 Sutherland 1,238 C3
68979 Sutton 1,416 G4
68446 Syracuse 1,638 H4
68447 Table Rock 393 H4

Agriculture, Industry and Resources

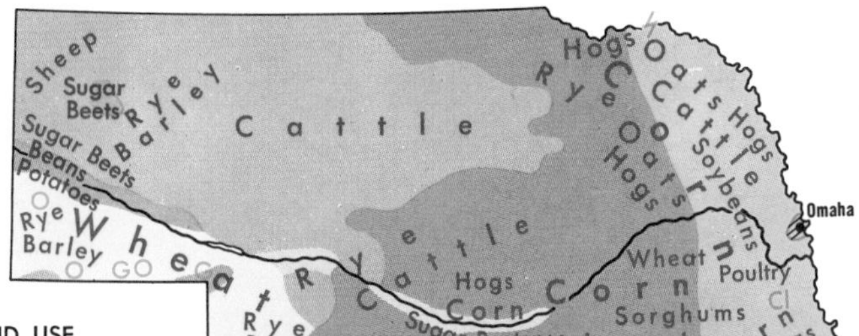

Sheep
Sugar Beets
Rye
Barley
Cattle
Sugar Beets
Beans
Potatoes
Rye
Barley
Wheat
Hogs
Rye
Oats
Corn
Cattle
Hogs
Soybeans
Omaha
Cattle
Wheat
Hogs
Corn
Poultry
Sorghums
Sugar Beets
Wheat
Corn
Hogs
Cattle

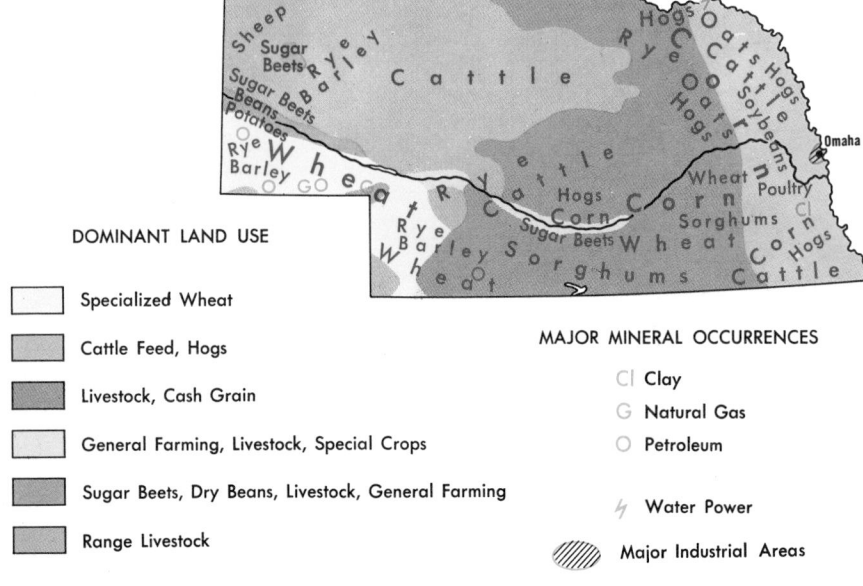

DOMINANT LAND USE

Specialized Wheat
Cattle Feed, Hogs
Livestock, Cash Grain
General Farming, Livestock, Special Crops
Sugar Beets, Dry Beans, Livestock, General Farming
Range Livestock

MAJOR MINERAL OCCURRENCES

Cl Clay
G Natural Gas
O Petroleum

Water Power

Major Industrial Areas

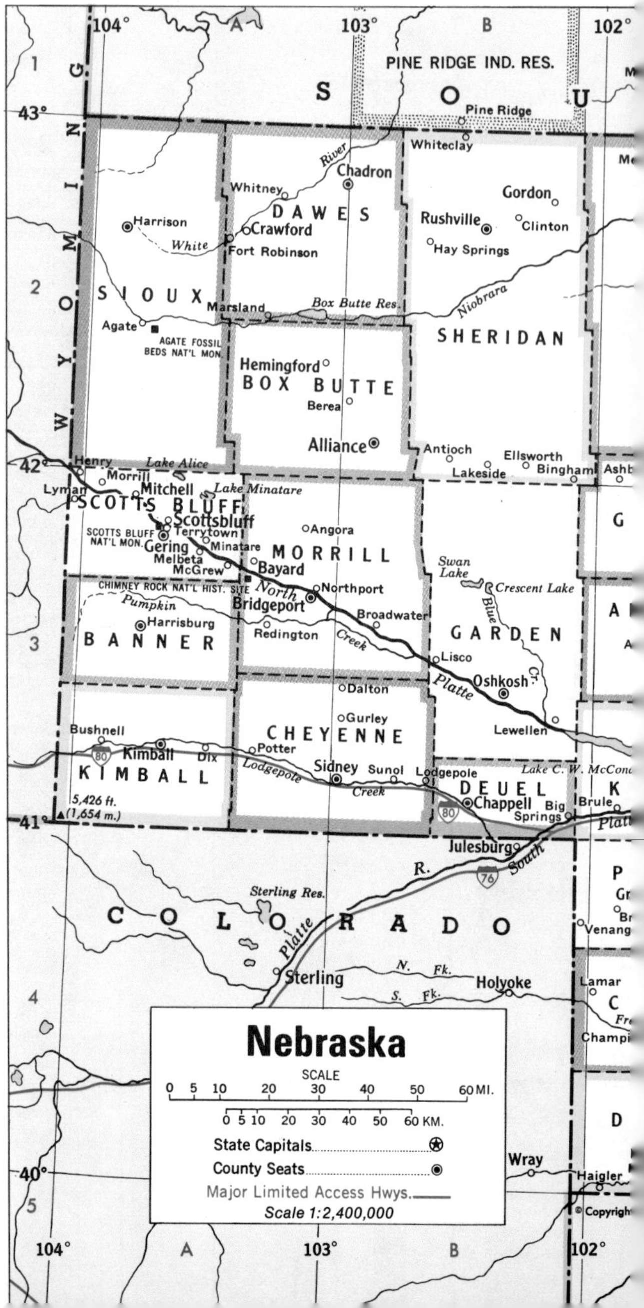

104°
103°
102°
PINE RIDGE IND. RES.
S O U
Pine Ridge
Whiteclay
Chadron
Whitney
DAWES
Crawford
Fort Robinson
Harrison
Rushville
Gordon
Clinton
Hay Springs
SIOUX
Marsland
Box Butte Res.
Agate
AGATE FOSSIL BEDS NAT'L MON.
SHERIDAN
Hemingford
BOX BUTTE
Berea
Alliance
Antioch
Lakeside
Ellsworth
Bingham
Henry
Lake Alice
Morrill
Lyman
Mitchell
Lake Minatare
SCOTTS BLUFF
Scottsbluff
Terrytown
SCOTTS BLUFF NAT'L MON.
Gering
Melbeta
McGrew
Minatare
Angora
MORRILL
Bayard
CHIMNEY ROCK NAT'L HIST. SITE
North Platte
Northport
Pumpkin Creek
Bridgeport
Broadwater
Harrisburg
Redington
BANNER
Swan Lake
Crescent Lake
GARDEN
Lisco
Oshkosh
Dalton
Gurley
CHEYENNE
Lewellen
Bushnell
Kimball
Dix
Potter
Sidney
Sunol
Lodgepole
KIMBALL
DEUEL
Chappell
Big Springs
Brule
Lake C. W. McConaughy
5,426 ft. (1,654 m.)
Julesburg
Sterling Res.
COLORADO
Sterling
Holyoke
Lamar
Venango
Champion
Wray
Haigler
43°
42°
41°
40°
Nebraska
SCALE
0 5 10 20 30 40 50 60 MI.
0 5 10 20 30 40 50 60 KM.
State Capitals
County Seats
Major Limited Access Hwys.
Scale 1:2,400,000

AREA 77,355 sq. mi. (200,349 sq. km.)
POPULATION 1,569,825
CAPITAL Lincoln
LARGEST CITY Omaha
HIGHEST POINT (Kimball Co.) 5,246 ft. (1654 m.)
SETTLED IN 1847
ADMITTED TO UNION March 1, 1867
POPULAR NAME Cornhusker State
STATE FLOWER Goldenrod
STATE BIRD Western Meadowlark

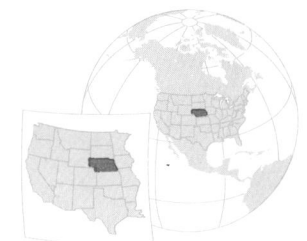

Topography

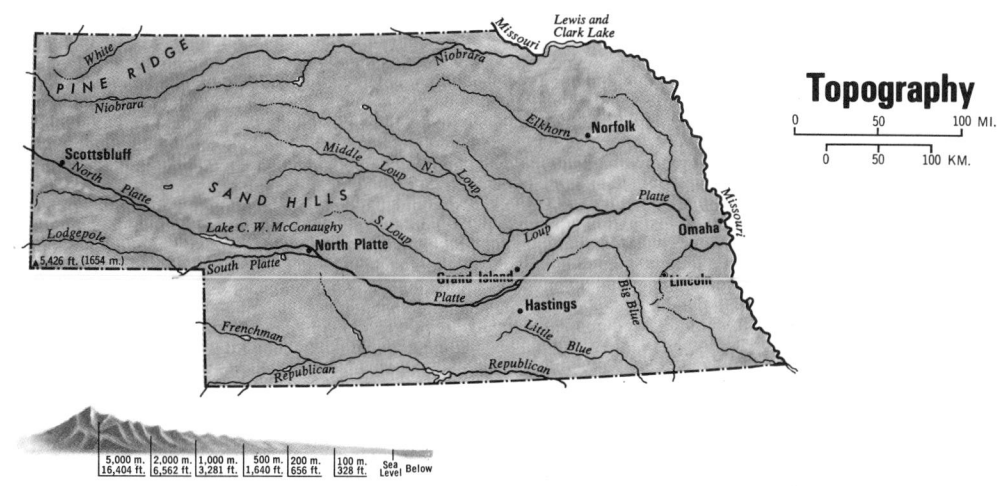

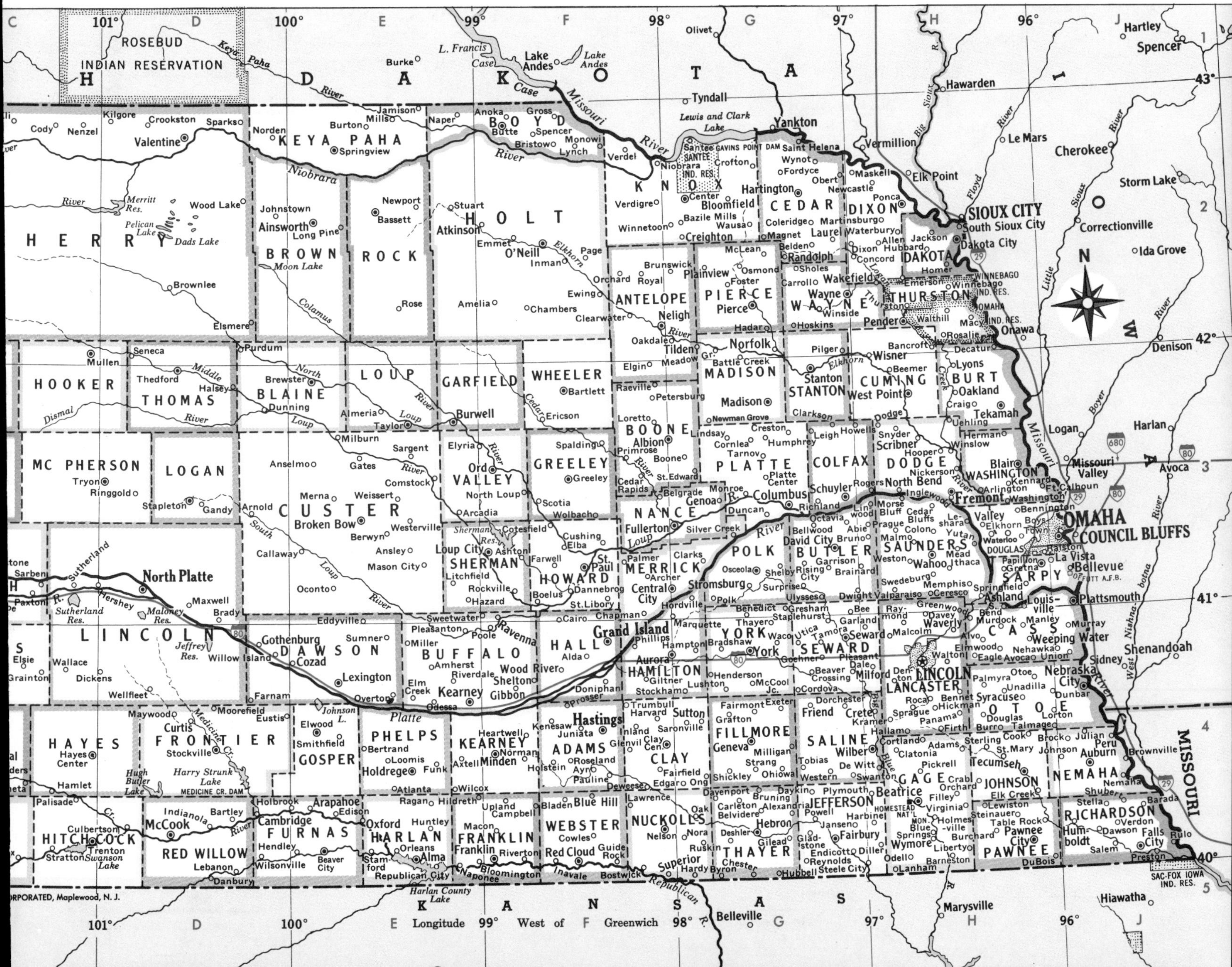

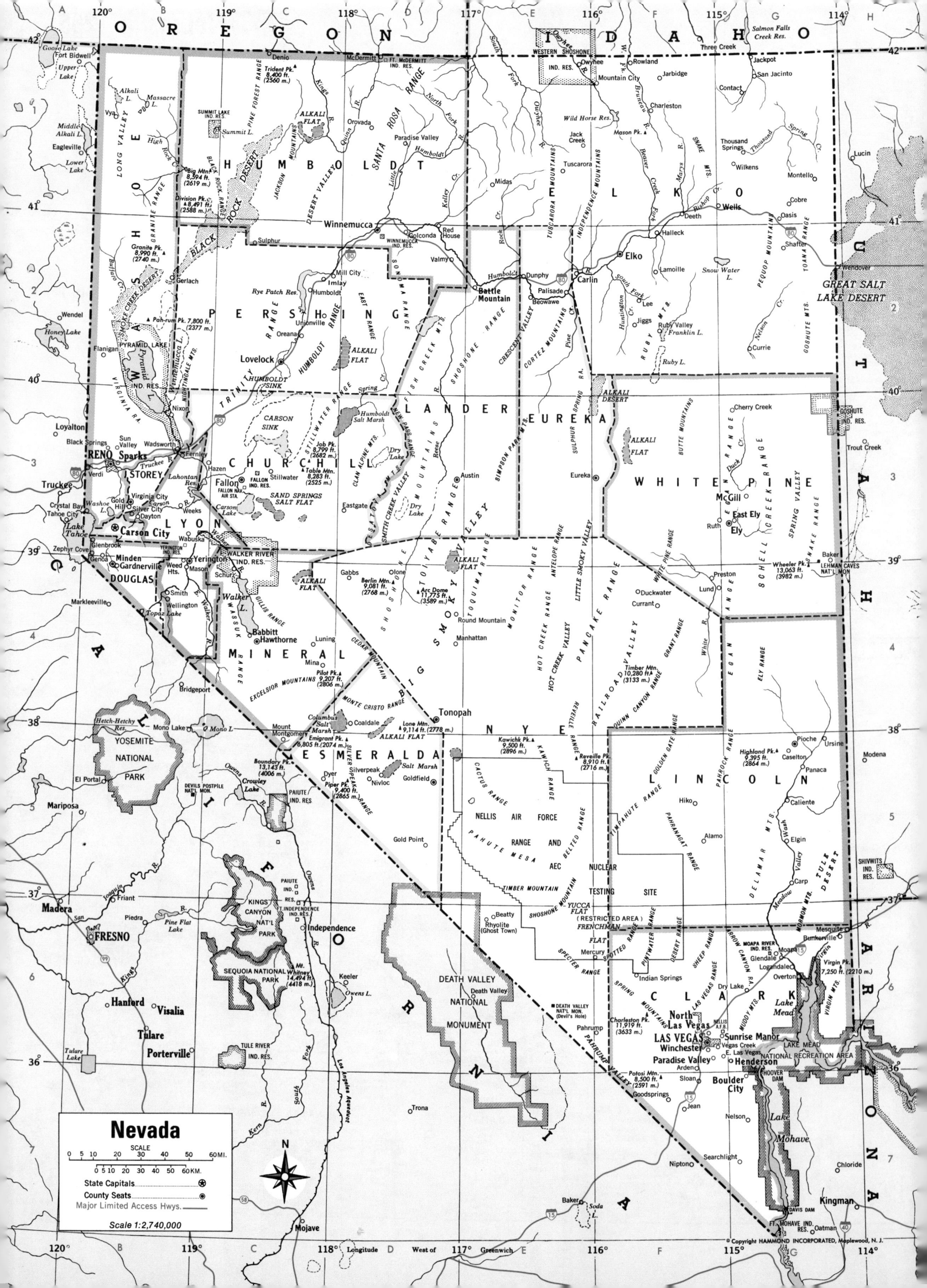

Agriculture, Industry and Resources

AREA 110,561 sq. mi. (286,353 sq. km.)
POPULATION 800,493
CAPITAL Carson City
LARGEST CITY Las Vegas
HIGHEST POINT Boundary Pk. 13,143 ft.
 (4006 m.)
SETTLED IN 1850
ADMITTED TO UNION October 31, 1864
POPULAR NAME Silver State; Sagebrush
 State
STATE FLOWER Sagebrush
STATE BIRD Mountain Bluebird

MAJOR MINERAL OCCURRENCES

- Ag Silver
- Au Gold
- Ba Barite
- Cu Copper
- Gp Gypsum
- Hg Mercury
- Lt Lithium
- Mg Magnesium
- Mo Molybdenum
- Na Salt
- O Petroleum
- Pb Lead
- S Sulfur
- W Tungsten
- Zn Zinc
- ⚡ Water Power

DOMINANT LAND USE

- General Farming, Dairy, Livestock
- General Farming, Livestock, Special Crops
- Range Livestock
- Forests
- Nonagricultural Land

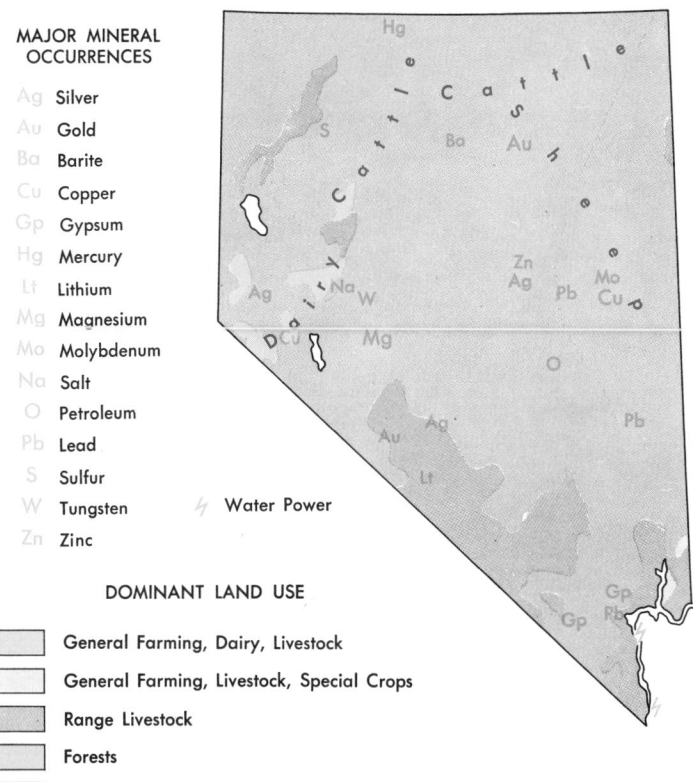

Topography

0   60   120 MI.
0   60   120 KM.

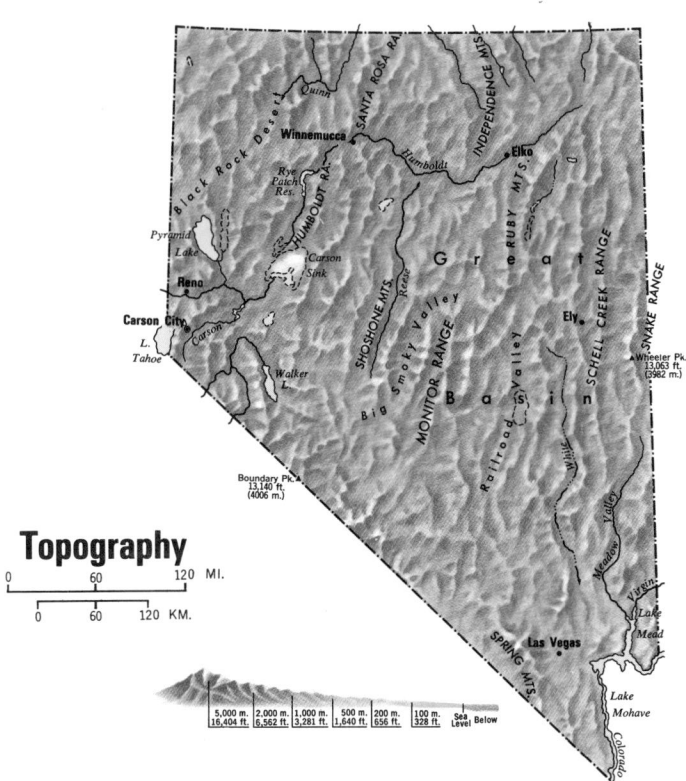

5,000 m. 2,000 m. 1,000 m. 500 m. 200 m. 100 m. Sea
16,404 ft. 6,562 ft. 3,281 ft. 1,640 ft. 656 ft. 328 ft. Level Below

COUNTIES

Carson City (city) 32,022	B3
Churchill 13,917	C3
Clark 463,087	F6
Douglas 19,421	B4
Elko 17,269	F1
Esmeralda 777	D5
Eureka 1,198	E3
Humboldt 9,434	C1
Lander 4,076	D3
Lincoln 3,732	F5
Lyon 13,594	B3
Mineral 6,217	C4
Nye 9,048	E4
Pershing 3,408	C2
Storey 1,503	B3
Washoe 193,623	B2
White Pine 8,167	F3

CITIES and TOWNS

Zip	Name/Pop.	Key
89001	Alamo 300	F5
89310	Austin⊙ 300	E3
89416	Babbitt	C4
89311	Baker 140	G3
89820	Battle Mountain 2,749	E2
89003	Beatty 600	E6
89821	Beowawe 77	E2
†89508	Black Springs 180	B3
89005	Boulder City 9,590	G7
89007	Bunkerville 300	G6
89008	Caliente 982	G5
89822	Carlin 1,232	E2
†89008	Carp 30	G5
89701	Carson City (cap.) 32,022	B3
†89043	Caselton	G5
†89301	Cherry Creek 80	G3
89402	Crystal Bay 6,225	A3
89403	Dayton 350	B3
89823	Deeth 125	F1
89404	Denio 35	C1
89314	Duckwater 80	F4
89010	Dyer 56	C5
89315	East Ely	G3
89112	East Las Vegas 6,449	F6
89801	Elko⊙ 8,758	F2
89301	Ely⊙ 4,882	G3
89316	Eureka⊙ 300	E3
89406	Fallon⊙ 4,262	C3
89408	Fernley 750	B3
89409	Gabbs 811	D4
89410	Gardnerville 1,610	B4
89411	Genoa 254	B4
89412	Gerlach 400	B2
89413	Glenbrook 800	B3
89414	Golconda 275	D2
89013	Goldfield⊙ 500	D5
89019	Goodsprings 80	F7
89824	Halleck 68	F2
89415	Hawthorne⊙ 3,741	C4
89417	Hazen 76	C3
89015	Henderson 24,363	G6
89017	Hiko 210	F5
†89418	Humboldt 14	C2
89418	Imlay 250	C2
89018	Indian Springs 500	F6
†89310	Ione 20	D4
†89834	Jack Creek	E1
89825	Jackpot 400	G1
89826	Jarbidge 11	F1
89019	Jean 125	F7
89828	Lamoille 100	F2
*89101	Las Vegas⊙ 164,674	F6
	Las Vegas‡ 461,816	F6
89829	Lee 125	F2
89021	Logandale 410	G6
89419	Lovelock⊙ 1,680	C2
89317	Lund 380	F4
89420	Luning 90	C4
89022	Manhattan 93	E4
89421	McDermitt 240	D1
89318	McGill 1,419	G3
89023	Mercury 900	E6
89024	Mesquite 500	G6
89422	Mina 450	C4
89423	Minden⊙ 1,029	B4
89025	Moapa 500	G6
89830	Montello 100	G1
89831	Mountain City 100	F1
†89046	Nelson 75	G7
89424	Nixon 400	B3
89030	North Las Vegas 42,739	F6
89425	Orovada 200	D1
89040	Overton 1,111	G6
89041	Pahrump 400	E6
89042	Panaca 650	G5
89119	Paradise Valley 84,818	F6
89426	Paradise Valley 115	D1
89043	Pioche⊙ 850	G5
*89501	Reno⊙ 100,756	B3
	Reno‡ 193,623	B3
†89003	Rhyolite (Ghost Town) 8	E6
89045	Round Mountain 400	E4
89833	Ruby Valley 150	F2
89319	Ruth 455	F3
89427	Schurz 800	C4
89046	Searchlight 500	F7
89428	Silver City 150	B3
89047	Silverpeak 100	D5
89430	Smith 200	B4
89431	Sparks 40,780	B3
†89406	Stillwater 150	C3
†89445	Sulphur	C2
†89110	Sunrise Manor 44,155	F6
89431	Sun Valley 8,822	B3
†89835	Thousand Springs	G1
89049	Tonopah⊙ 1,952	D4
89834	Tuscarora 24	E1
89438	Valmy 200	D2
89121	Vegas Creek	G6
89440	Virginia City⊙ 750	B3
89442	Wadsworth 400	B3
89443	Weed Heights 8	B4
89444	Wellington 505	B4
89835	Wells 1,218	G1
†89109	Winchester 19,728	F6
89445	Winnemucca⊙ 4,140	D2
89447	Yerington⊙ 2,021	B4
89448	Zephyr Cove 1,316	A3

OTHER FEATURES

Alkali (lake)	B1
Antelope (range)	E3
Arc Dome (mt.)	D4
Arrow Canyon (range)	G6
Beaver Creek Fork, Humboldt (riv.)	F1
Belted (range)	E5
Berlin (mt.)	D4
Big (mt.)	B1
Big Smoky (valley)	D4
Bishop (creek)	F1
Black Rock (des.)	B2
Black Rock (range)	B1
Boundary (peak)	C5
Buffalo (creek)	B2
Butte (mts.)	F3
Cactus (range)	E5
Carson (lake)	C3
Carson (riv.)	B3
Carson (sink)	C3
Cedar (mt.)	D4
Charleston (peak)	F6
Clan Alpine (mts.)	D3
Columbus Salt (marsh)	C4
Cortez (mts.)	E2
Crescent (valley)	E2
Davis (dam)	G7
Death Valley Nat'l Mon.	E6
Delamar (mts.)	G5
Desatoya (mts.)	D3
Desert (range)	F6
Desert (valley)	C1
Devil's Hole (Death Valley Nat'l Mon.)	E6
Division (peak)	B1
Duck (creek)	G3
East (range)	D2
East Walker (riv.)	B4
Egan (range)	G4
Ely (range)	G4
Emigrant (peak)	C5
Excelsior (mts.)	C4
Fallon Ind. Res.	C3
Fallon Nav. Air Sta.	C3
Fish Creek (mts.)	D2
Fort McDermitt Ind. Res.	D1
Fort Mohave Ind. Res.	G7
Franklin (lake)	F2
Frenchman Flat (basin)	F6
Gillis (range)	C4
Golden Gate (range)	F5
Goshute (mts.)	G2
Goshute Ind. Res.	G3
Granite (peak)	B2
Granite (range)	B2
Grant (range)	F4
Great Salt Lake (des.)	H2
High Rock (creek)	B1
Highland (peak)	G5
Hoover (dam)	G7
Hot Creek (range)	E4
Hot Creek (valley)	E4
Humboldt (range)	C2
Humboldt (riv.)	E2
Humboldt (sink)	C2
Humboldt Salt (marsh)	D3
Huntington (creek)	F2
Independence (mts.)	E1
Jackson (mts.)	C1
Job (peak)	C3
Kawich (peak)	E5
Kawich (range)	E5
Kelley (creek)	D1
Kings (riv.)	C1
Lahontan (lake)	B3
Lake Mead Nat'l Rec. Area	G6
Las Vegas (range)	F6
Lehman Caves Nat'l Mon.	G4
Little Humboldt (riv.)	D1
Little Smoky (valley)	E4
Lone (mt.)	D4
Long (valley)	B1
Marys (riv.)	F1
Mason (peak)	F1
Massacre (lake)	B1
Mead (lake)	G6
Meadow Valley Wash (riv.)	G5
Moapa River Ind. Res.	G6
Mohave (lake)	G7
Monitor (range)	E4
Monte Cristo (range)	D4
Mormon (mts.)	G5
Muddy (mts.)	G6
Nellis A.F.B. 7,476	F6
Nellis Air Force Range and AEC Nuclear Testing Site	E5
Nelson (creek)	G2
New Pass (range)	D3
Nightingale (mts.)	B2
Owyhee (riv.)	E1
Pahranagat (range)	F5
Pahrock (range)	F5
Pah-rum (peak)	B2
Pahrump (valley)	F6
Pahute (mesa)	E5
Pancake (range)	F4
Pequop (mts.)	G2
Pilot (peak)	C4
Pine (creek)	E2
Pine Forest (range)	C1
Pintwater (range)	F6
Piper (peak)	D5
Potosi (mt.)	F7
Pyramid (lake)	B2
Pyramid Lake Ind. Res.	B2
Quinn (riv.)	D1
Quinn Canyon (range)	F4
Railroad (valley)	F4
Reese (riv.)	D3
Reveille (range)	E5
Reveille (range)	E4
Ruby (lake)	F2
Ruby (mts.)	F2
Rye Patch (res.)	C2
Sand Springs (salt flat)	C3
Santa Rosa (range)	D1
Schell Creek (range)	G3
Sheep (range)	F6
Shoshone (mt.)	E6
Shoshone (mts.)	D3
Shoshone (range)	E2
Silver Peak (range)	D5
Simpson Park (mts.)	E3
Smith Creek (valley)	D3
Smoke Creek (des.)	B2
Snake (mts.)	F1
Snake (range)	G3
Snow Water (lake)	G2
Sonoma (range)	D2
Specter (range)	E6
Spotted (range)	F6
Spring (creek)	D2
Spring (mts.)	F6
Spring (valley)	G3
Stillwater (range)	C3
Sulphur Spring (range)	E3
Summit (lake)	C1
Summit Lake Ind. Res.	B1
Table (mt.)	C3
Tahoe (lake)	B3
Thousand Spring (creek)	G1
Timber (mt.)	F4
Timber (mt.)	E5
Timpahute (range)	F5
Toana (range)	G2
Toiyabe (range)	D3
Topaz (lake)	B4
Toquima (range)	E4
Trident (peak)	C1
Trinity (range)	C2
Truckee (riv.)	B3
Tule (des.)	G5
Tuscarora (mts.)	E1
Virgin (mts.)	G6
Virgin (peak)	G6
Virgin (riv.)	G6
Virginia (range)	B3
Walker (lake)	C4
Walker (riv.)	C3
Walker River Ind. Res.	C3
Washoe (lake)	B3
Wassuk (range)	C4
Western Shoshone Ind. Res.	E1
Wheeler (peak)	G4
White (riv.)	F4
White Pine (range)	F3
Wild Horse (res.)	E1
Winnemucca (lake)	B2
Winnemucca Ind. Res.	D2
Yerington Ind. Res.	B3
Yucca Flat (basin)	E6

⊙County seat.
‡Population of metropolitan area.
† Zip of nearest p.o.
* Multiple zips.

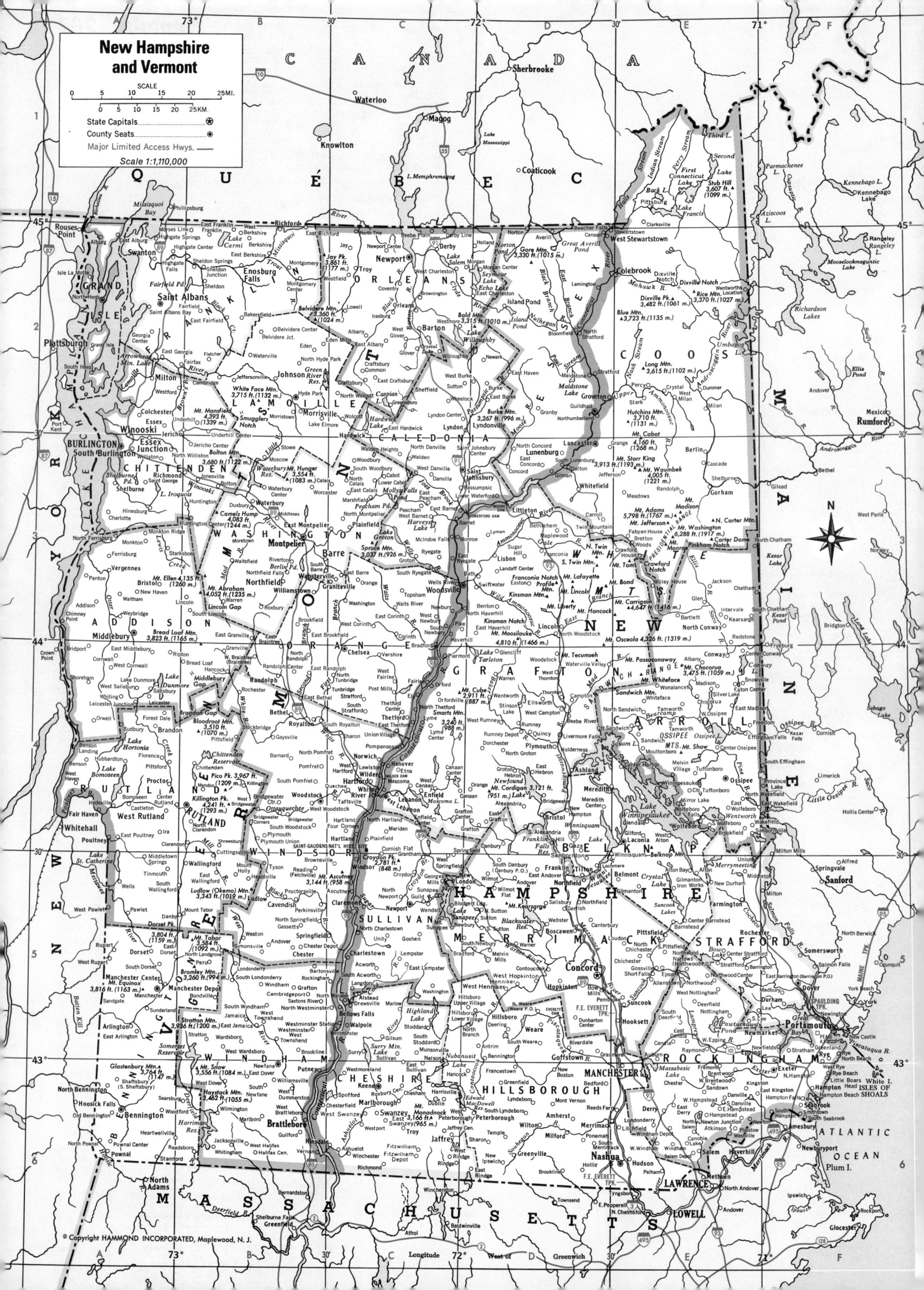

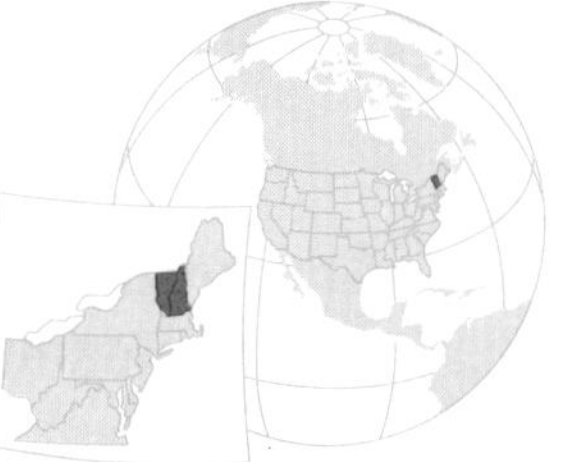

NEW HAMPSHIRE
AREA 9,279 sq. mi. (24,033 sq. km.)
POPULATION 920,610
CAPITAL Concord
LARGEST CITY Manchester
HIGHEST POINT Mt. Washington 6,288 ft. (1917 m.)
SETTLED IN 1623
ADMITTED TO UNION June 21, 1788
POPULAR NAME Granite State
STATE FLOWER Purple Lilac
STATE BIRD Purple Finch

VERMONT
AREA 9,614 sq. mi. (24,900 sq. km.)
POPULATION 511,456
CAPITAL Montpelier
LARGEST CITY Burlington
HIGHEST POINT Mt. Mansfield 4,393 ft. (1339 m.)
SETTLED IN 1764
ADMITTED TO UNION March 4, 1791
POPULAR NAME Green Mountain State
STATE FLOWER Red Clover
STATE BIRD Hermit Thrush

Topography

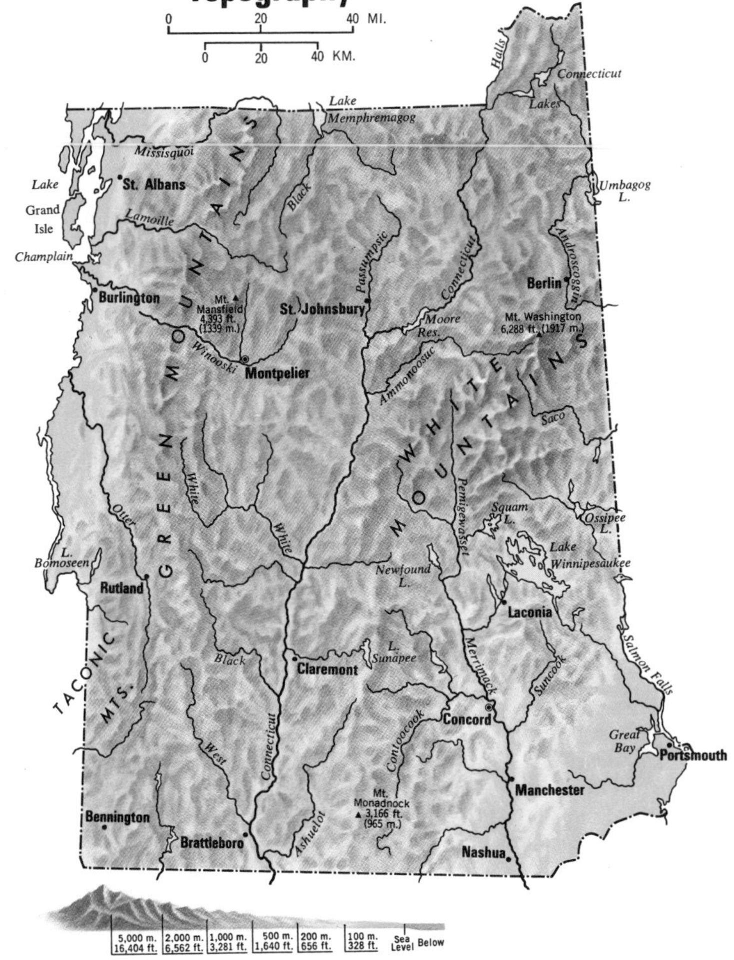
0 20 40 MI.
0 20 40 KM.
Connecticut
Lakes
Halls
Lake
Memphremagog
Missisquoi
Lake
Grand
Isle
Champlain
St. Albans
Lamoille
Black
Umbagog
L.
Androscoggin
Berlin
Passumpsic
Connecticut
Burlington
Mt. Mansfield 4,393 ft. (1339 m.)
St. Johnsbury
Moore
Res.
Mt. Washington 6,288 ft. (1917 m.)
Winooski
Montpelier
Ammonoosuc
GREEN MOUNTAINS
WHITE MOUNTAINS
Saco
White
Otter
Pemigewasset
Squam
L.
Ossipee
L.
White
L.
Bomoseen
Lake
Winnipesaukee
Newfound
L.
Rutland
Laconia
Salmon Falls
Black
L.
Sunapee
Claremont
Merrimack
Suncook
TACONIC MTS.
Concord
Contoocook
Great
Bay
Portsmouth
West
Connecticut
Mt.
Monadnock
3,166 ft.
(965 m.)
Manchester
Bennington
Ashuelot
Brattleboro
Nashua
5,000 m. 16,404 ft.
2,000 m. 6,562 ft.
1,000 m. 3,281 ft.
500 m. 1,640 ft.
200 m. 656 ft.
100 m. 328 ft.
Sea Level
Below

NEW HAMPSHIRE

COUNTIES

Belknap 42,884 ..... D4
Carroll 27,931 ..... E4
Cheshire 62,116 ..... C6
Coos 35,147 ..... E2
Grafton 65,806 ..... D4
Hillsborough 276,608 ..... D6
Merrimack 98,302 ..... D5
Rockingham 190,345 ..... E5
Strafford 85,408 ..... E5
Sullivan 36,063 ..... C5

CITIES and TOWNS

Zip *Name/Pop.* *Key*

03601 Acworth○ 590 ..... C5
†03864 Albany○ 383 ..... E4
†03222 Alexandria○ 706 ..... D4
†03275 Allenstown○ 4,398 ..... E5
03602 Alstead○ 1,461 ..... C5
03809 Alton○ 2,440 ..... E5
03810 Alton Bay 500 ..... E5
03031 Amherst○ 8,243 ..... D6
03216 Andover○ 1,587 ..... D5
03440 Antrim○ 2,208 ..... D5
03440 Antrim 1,142 ..... D5
03217 Ashland○ 1,807 ..... D4
03217 Ashland 1,479 ..... D4
03441 Ashuelot 810 ..... C6
03811 Atkinson○ 4,397 ..... E6
03032 Auburn○ 2,883 ..... E5
03218 Barnstead○ 2,292 ..... E5
†03825 Barrington○ 4,404 ..... F5
03812 Bartlett○ 1,566 ..... E3
03740 Bath○ 761 ..... D3
03102 Bedford○ 9,481 ..... D6
03220 Belmont○ 4,026 ..... E5
03442 Bennington○ 890 ..... D5
†03785 Benton○ 333 ..... D3
03570 Berlin 13,084 ..... E3
03574 Bethlehem○ 1,784 ..... D3
03301 Boscawen○ 3,435 ..... D5
03221 Bradford○ 1,115 ..... D5
†03833 Brentwood○ 2,004 ..... E6
†03222 Bridgewater○ 606 ..... D4
03222 Bristol○ 2,198 ..... D4
03222 Bristol 1,258 ..... D4
†03872 Brookfield○ 385 ..... E4
03033 Brookline○ 1,766 ..... D6
03223 Campton○ 1,694 ..... D4
03741 Canaan○ 2,456 ..... C4
03034 Candia○ 2,989 ..... E5
03224 Canterbury○ 1,410 ..... D5
†03595 Carroll○ 647 ..... D3
03813 Center Conway 558 ..... E4
03226 Center Harbor○ 808 ..... E4
03814 Center Ossipee 800 ..... E4
03603 Charlestown○ 4,417 ..... C5
03603 Charlestown 1,294 ..... C5
†04037 Chatham○ 189 ..... E3
03036 Chester○ 2,006 ..... E6
03443 Chesterfield○ 2,561 ..... C6
†03258 Chichester○ 1,492 ..... E5
03817 Chocorua 575 ..... E4
03743 Claremont 14,557 ..... C5
†05902 Clarksville○ 262 ..... E1
03576 Colebrook○ 2,459 ..... E2
03576 Colebrook 1,131 ..... E2
03301 Concord (cap.)⊙ 30,400 ..... D5
03229 Contoocook 1,499 ..... D5
03818 Conway○ 7,158 ..... E4
03818 Conway 1,781 ..... E4
03746 Cornish Flat 450 ..... C4
†03753 Croydon○ 457 ..... C5
†03598 Dalton○ 672 ..... D3
03230 Danbury○ 680 ..... D4
03819 Danville○ 1,318 ..... E6
03037 Deerfield○ 1,979 ..... E5
†03244 Deering○ 1,041 ..... D5
03038 Derry○ 18,875 ..... E6
03038 Derry 12,248 ..... E6
†03266 Dorchester○ 244 ..... D4
03820 Dover⊙ 22,377 ..... F5
03444 Dublin○ 1,303 ..... C6
†03588 Dummer○ 390 ..... E2
†03301 Dunbarton○ 1,174 ..... D5
03824 Durham○ 10,652 ..... F5
03824 Durham 8,448 ..... F5
03231 East Andover 500 ..... D5
03826 East Hampstead 900 ..... E6
03827 East Kingston○ 1,135 ..... F6
†03580 Easton○ 124 ..... D3
03446 East Swanzey 500 ..... C6
03832 Eaton (Eaton Center)○ 256 ..... E4
†03264 Ellsworth○ 53 ..... D4
03748 Enfield○ 3,175 ..... C4
03748 Enfield 1,581 ..... C4
03042 Epping○ 3,460 ..... E5
03042 Epping 1,384 ..... E5
03234 Epsom○ 2,743 ..... E5
03579 Errol○ 313 ..... E2
03750 Etna 550 ..... C4
03833 Exeter○ 11,024 ..... F6
03833 Exeter⊙ 8,947 ..... F6
03835 Farmington○ 4,630 ..... E5
03835 Farmington 3,284 ..... E5
03447 Fitzwilliam○ 1,795 ..... C6
03043 Francestown○ 830 ..... D6
03580 Franconia○ 743 ..... D3
03235 Franklin 7,901 ..... D5
03836 Freedom○ 720 ..... E4
03044 Fremont○ 1,333 ..... E6
†03246 Gilford○ 4,841 ..... E4
03237 Gilmanton○ 1,941 ..... E5
03448 Gilsum○ 652 ..... C5
03838 Glen 600 ..... E3
03045 Goffstown○ 11,315 ..... D5
03581 Gorham○ 3,322 ..... E3
03581 Gorham 2,180 ..... E3
03752 Goshen○ 549 ..... C5
03240 Grafton○ 739 ..... D4
03753 Grantham○ 704 ..... C5
03047 Greenfield○ 972 ..... D6
03840 Greenland○ 2,129 ..... F5
03048 Greenville○ 1,988 ..... D6
03048 Greenville 1,447 ..... D6
†03241 Groton○ 255 ..... D4
03582 Groveton 1,389 ..... D2
03754 Guild 500 ..... C5
03841 Hampstead○ 3,785 ..... E6
03842 Hampton○ 10,493 ..... F6
03842 Hampton 6,779 ..... F6
03844 Hampton Falls○ 1,372 ..... F6
03449 Hancock○ 1,193 ..... C6
03755 Hanover○ 9,119 ..... C4
03755 Hanover 6,861 ..... C4
03450 Harrisville○ 860 ..... C6
03765 Haverhill○ 3,445 ..... C3
03241 Hebron○ 349 ..... D4
03242 Henniker○ 3,246 ..... D5
03242 Henniker 1,538 ..... D5
03243 Hill○ 736 ..... D4
03244 Hillsboro○ 3,437 ..... D5
03244 Hillsboro 1,797 ..... D5
03451 Hinsdale○ 3,631 ..... C6
03451 Hinsdale 1,546 ..... C6
03245 Holderness○ 1,586 ..... D4
03049 Hollis○ 4,679 ..... D6
03106 Hooksett○ 7,303 ..... E5
03106 Hooksett 1,868 ..... E5
03301 Hopkinton○ 3,861 ..... D5
03051 Hudson○ 14,022 ..... E6
03051 Hudson 6,248 ..... E6
03845 Intervale 725 ..... E3
03846 Jackson○ 642 ..... E3
03452 Jaffrey○ 4,349 ..... C6
03452 Jaffrey 2,684 ..... C6
03583 Jefferson○ 803 ..... D3
03431 Keene⊙ 21,449 ..... C6
03848 Kingston○ 4,111 ..... E6
03246 Laconia⊙ 15,575 ..... E4
03584 Lancaster○ 3,401 ..... D3
03584 Lancaster⊙ 2,134 ..... D3
†03585 Landaff○ 266 ..... D3
†03602 Langdon○ 437 ..... C5
03766 Lebanon 11,134 ..... C4
†03857 Lee○ 2,111 ..... F5
03606 Lempster○ 637 ..... C5
03251 Lincoln○ 1,313 ..... D3
03585 Lisbon○ 1,517 ..... D3
03585 Lisbon 1,151 ..... D3
†03051 Litchfield○ 4,150 ..... E6
03561 Littleton○ 5,558 ..... D3
03561 Littleton 4,480 ..... D3
03053 Londonderry○ 13,598 ..... E6
03301 Loudon○ 2,454 ..... E5
†03585 Lyman○ 281 ..... D3
03768 Lyme○ 1,289 ..... C4
†03082 Lyndeborough○ 1,070 ..... D6
†03820 Madbury○ 987 ..... F5
03849 Madison○ 1,051 ..... E4
*03101 Manchester 90,936 ..... E6
Manchester‡ 160,767 ..... E6
03455 Marlborough○ 1,846 ..... C6
03455 Marlborough 1,184 ..... C6
03456 Marlow○ 542 ..... C5
03850 Melvin Village 450 ..... E4
03253 Meredith○ 4,646 ..... D4
03253 Meredith 1,202 ..... D4
03770 Meriden 800 ..... C4
03054 Merrimack○ 15,406 ..... D6
†03887 Middleton○ 734 ..... E5
03588 Milan○ 1,013 ..... E2
03055 Milford○ 8,685 ..... D6
03055 Milford 6,269 ..... D6
03851 Milton○ 2,438 ..... F5
03852 Milton Mills 450 ..... F4
03771 Monroe○ 619 ..... C3
03057 Mont Vernon○ 1,444 ..... D6
03254 Moultonboro○ 2,206 ..... E4
03060 Nashua⊙ 67,865 ..... D6
Nashua‡ 114,221 ..... D6
†03457 Nelson○ 442 ..... C5
03070 New Boston○ 1,928 ..... D6
03255 Newbury○ 961 ..... C5
03854 New Castle○ 936 ..... F5
03855 New Durham○ 1,183 ..... E5
03856 Newfields○ 817 ..... F5
03256 New Hampton○ 1,249 ..... D4
†03801 Newington○ 716 ..... F5
03071 New Ipswich○ 2,433 ..... D6
03257 New London○ 2,935 ..... D5
03257 New London 1,335 ..... D5
03857 Newmarket○ 4,290 ..... F5
03857 Newmarket 3,749 ..... F5
03773 Newport○ 6,229 ..... C5
03773 Newport⊙ 4,388 ..... C5
03858 Newton○ 3,068 ..... E6
03859 Newton Junction 450 ..... E6
03860 North Conway 2,104 ..... E3
†03276 Northfield○ 3,051 ..... D5
†03276 Northfield-Tilton 2,574 ..... D5
03862 North Hampton○ 3,425 ..... F6
03590 North Stratford 600 ..... D2
†03582 Northumberland○ 2,520 ..... D2
03261 Northwood○ 2,175 ..... E5
03262 North Woodstock 750 ..... D3
03290 Nottingham○ 1,952 ..... E5
†03741 Orange○ 197 ..... D4
03777 Orford○ 928 ..... C4
03864 Ossipee 2,465 ..... E4
03076 Pelham○ 8,090 ..... E6
†03275 Pembroke○ 4,861 ..... E5
03458 Peterborough○ 4,895 ..... D6
03458 Peterborough 2,568 ..... D6
03779 Piermont○ 507 ..... C4
03592 Pittsburg○ 780 ..... E1
03263 Pittsfield○ 2,889 ..... E5
03263 Pittsfield 1,584 ..... E5
03781 Plainfield○ 1,749 ..... C4
03865 Plaistow○ 5,609 ..... E6
03264 Plymouth○ 5,094 ..... D4
03264 Plymouth 3,628 ..... D4
03801 Portsmouth 26,254 ..... F5
Portsmouth-Dover-Rochester‡ 163,880 ..... F5
03593 Randolph○ 274 ..... E3
03077 Raymond○ 5,453 ..... E5
03077 Raymond 1,192 ..... E5
†03470 Richmond○ 518 ..... C6
03461 Rindge○ 3,375 ..... C6
03867 Rochester 21,560 ..... E5
†03431 Roxbury○ 190 ..... C6
03266 Rumney○ 1,212 ..... D4
03870 Rye○ 4,508 ..... F5
03871 Rye Beach 600 ..... F6
03079 Salem○ 24,124 ..... E6
03268 Salisbury○ 781 ..... D5
03269 Sanbornton○ 1,679 ..... D5
03872 Sanbornville 750 ..... F4
03873 Sandown○ 2,057 ..... E6
03270 Sandwich○ 905 ..... E4
03874 Seabrook○ 5,917 ..... F6
†03458 Sharon○ 184 ..... D6
†03581 Shelburne○ 318 ..... E3
03878 Somersworth 10,350 ..... F5
†01913 South Hampton○ 660 ..... F6
03462 Spofford 750 ..... C6
†03284 Springfield○ 532 ..... C4
†03582 Stark○ 470 ..... E2
†03576 Stewartstown○ 943 ..... E2
03464 Stoddard○ 482 ..... C5
03884 Strafford○ 1,663 ..... E5
†03590 Stratford○ 989 ..... D2
03885 Stratham○ 2,507 ..... F5
03585 Sugar Hill○ 397 ..... D3
†03445 Sullivan○ 585 ..... C5
03782 Sunapee○ 2,312 ..... C5
03275 Suncook 4,698 ..... D5
03431 Surry○ 656 ..... C5
†03260 Sutton○ 1,091 ..... D5
†03431 Swanzey○ 5,183 ..... C6
03886 Tamworth○ 1,672 ..... E4
03084 Temple○ 692 ..... D6
†03285 Thornton○ 952 ..... D4
03276 Tilton○ 3,387 ..... D5
03276 Tilton-Northfield 2,574 ..... D5
03465 Troy○ 2,131 ..... C6
03465 Troy 1,318 ..... C6
†03816 Tuftonboro○ 1,500 ..... E4
03595 Twin Mountain 500 ..... D3
†03743 Unity○ 1,092 ..... C5
†03872 Wakefield○ 2,237 ..... F4
03608 Walpole○ 3,188 ..... C5
03278 Warner○ 1,963 ..... D5
03279 Warren○ 650 ..... D4
03280 Washington○ 411 ..... C5
03223 Waterville Valley○ 180 ..... D4
03281 Weare○ 3,232 ..... D5
†03301 Webster○ 1,095 ..... D5
03282 Wentworth○ 527 ..... D4
†03579 Wentworths Location○ 49 ..... E2
†03242 West Henniker 500 ..... D5
03784 West Lebanon C4
03467 Westmoreland○ 1,452 ..... C6
03597 West Stewartstown 700 ..... E2
03469 West Swanzey 1,022 ..... C6
03865 Westville 750 ..... E6
03598 Whitefield○ 1,681 ..... D3
03598 Whitefield 1,005 ..... D3
†03287 Wilmot○ 725 ..... D5
03287 Wilmot Flat 450 ..... D5
03086 Wilton○ 2,669 ..... D6
03086 Wilton 1,310 ..... D6
03470 Winchester○ 3,465 ..... C6
03470 Winchester 1,732 ..... C6
03087 Windham○ 5,664 ..... E6
03289 Winnisquam 500 ..... E5
03894 Wolfeboro○ 3,968 ..... E4
03894 Wolfeboro 2,271 ..... E4
03896 Wolfeboro Falls 600 ..... E4
03293 Woodstock○ 1,008 ..... D4
03785 Woodsville⊙ 1,195 ..... C3

OTHER FEATURES

Adams (mt.) E3
Ammonoosuc (riv.) D3
Androscoggin (riv.) E2
Ashuelot (riv.) C6
Back (lake) E1
Baker (riv.) D4
Bearcamp (riv.) E4
Beaver (brook) E6
Belknap (mt.) E5
Blackwater (res.) D5
Blue (mt.) E2
Bond (mt.) E3
Bow (lake) E5
Cabot (mt.) E2
Cannon (mt.) D3
Cardigan (mt.) D4
Carrigain (mt.) E3
Carter Dome (mt.) E3
Chocorua (mt.) E4
Cocheco (riv.) E5
Cold (riv.) C5
Comerford (dam) D3
Connecticut (riv.) B6
Contoocook (riv.) D6
Conway (lake) E4
Crawford Notch (pass) E3
Croydon (peak) C5
Croydon Branch, Sugar (riv.) C5
Crystal (lake) E5
Cube (mt.) D4
Dixville (peak) E2
Dixville Notch (pass) E2
Edward MacDowell (res.) D6
Ellis (riv.) E3
Everett (dam) D5
Exeter (riv.) E6
First Connecticut (lake) E1
Francis (lake) E1
Franconia Notch (pass) D3
Franklin Falls (res.) D4
Gale (riv.) D3
Great (bay) F5
Halls (stream) E1
Hancock (mt.) D3
Highland (lake) C5
Hutchins (mt.) E2
Indian (stream) E1
Jefferson (mt.) E3
Kearsarge (mt.) D5
Kinsman (mt.) D3
Kinsman Notch (pass) D3
Lafayette (mt.) D3
Lamprey (riv.) E5
Liberty (mt.) D3
Lincoln (mt.) D3
Long (mt.) E2
Mad (riv.) D4
Madison (mt.) E3
Mascoma (lake) C4
Massabesic (lake) E6
Merrimack (riv.) D5
Merrymeeting (lake) E5
Mohawk (riv.) E2
Monadnock (mt.) C6
Monroe (mt.) E3
Moore (dam) D3
Moore (res.) D3
Moosilauke (mt.) D3
Nash (stream) E2
Newfound (lake) D4
North Carter (mt.) E3
North Twin (mt.) D3
Nubanusit (lake) C5
Osceola (mt.) E3
Ossipee (lake) E4
Ossipee (mts.) E4
Ossipee (riv.) F4
Passaconaway (mt.) E4
Pawtuckaway (pond) E5
Pease A.F.B. F5
Pemigewasset (riv.) D4
Perry (stream) E1
Pine (riv.) E4
Pinkham Notch (pass) E3
Piscataqua (riv.) F5
Piscataquog (riv.) D5
Presidential (range) E3
Rice (mt.) E2
Saco (riv.) E3
Saint-Gaudens Nat'l Hist. Site B4
Salmon Falls (riv.) F5

(continued on following page)

Agriculture, Industry and Resources

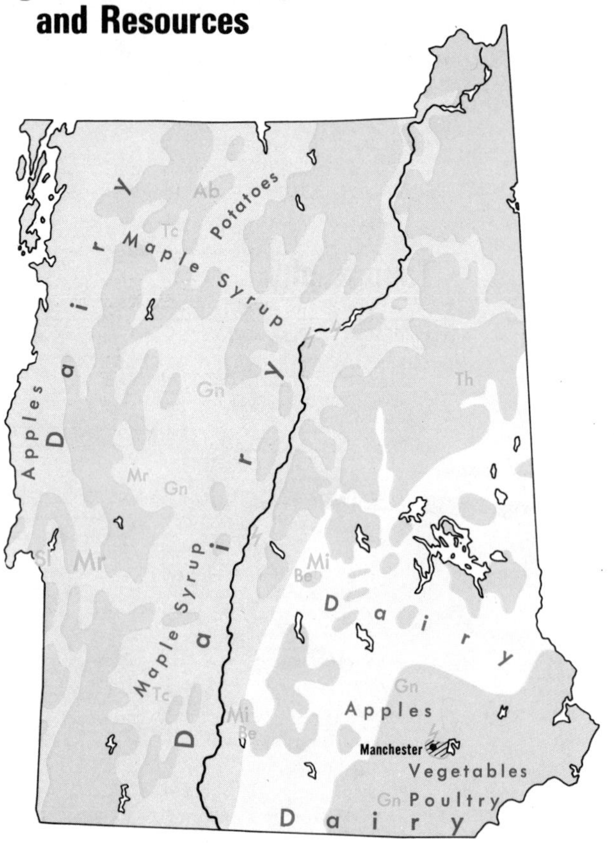

DOMINANT LAND USE

Specialized Dairy
Dairy, General Farming
Dairy, Poultry, Mixed Farming
Forests

Water Power
Major Industrial Areas

MAJOR MINERAL OCCURRENCES

Ab Asbestos
Be Beryl
Gn Granite
Mi Mica
Mr Marble
Sl Slate
Tc Talc
Th Thorium

Sandwich (mt.) E4
Sandwich (range) E4
Second (lake) E1
Shaw (mt.) E4
Shoals (isls.) F6
Smarts (mt.) C4
Souhegan (riv.) D6
South Twin (mt.) D3
Squam (lake) E4
Starr King (mt.) E3
Stub Hill (mt.) E1
Sugar (riv.) C5
Sunapee (lake) C5
Suncook (lkes) E5
Suncook (riv.) E5
Surry Mountain (lake) C5
Tarleton (lake) D4
Tecumseh (mt.) D4
Third (lake) E1
Tom (mt.) E3
Umbagog (lake) E2
Upper Ammonoosuc (riv.) E2
Warner (riv.) D5
Washington (mt.) E3
Waumbek (mt.) E3
Wentworth (lake) E4
White (isl.) F6
White (mts.) E3
Whiteface (mt.) E4
Wild Ammonoosuc (riv.) D3
Wilder (dam) C4
Winnipesaukee (lake) E4
Winnipesaukee (riv.) D5
Winnisquam (lake) D4

VERMONT

COUNTIES

Addison 29,406 .... A3
Bennington 33,345 .... A6
Caledonia 25,808 .... C2
Chittenden 115,534 .... A3
Essex 6,313 .... D2
Franklin 34,788 .... B2
Grand Isle 4,613 .... A2
Lamoille 16,767 .... B2
Orange 22,739 .... C3
Orleans 23,440 .... C2
Rutland 58,347 .... A4
Washington 52,393 .... B3
Windham 36,933 .... B5
Windsor 51,030 .... B4

CITIES and TOWNS

Zip *Name/Pop.* *Key*

05820 Albany○ 705 .... C2
05440 Alburg○ 1,352 .... A2
05440 Alburg 496 .... A2
†05143 Andover○ 350 .... B5
05250 Arlington○ 2,184 .... A5
05250 Arlington 1,309 .... A5
05441 Bakersfield○ 852 .... B2
05031 Barnard○ 790 .... B4
05821 Barnet○ 1,338 .... C3
05641 Barre 9,824 .... C3
05641 Barre○ 7,090 .... C3
05822 Barton○ 2,990 .... C2
05822 Barton 1,062 .... C2
05823 Beebe Plain 500 .... C2
05902 Beecher Falls 950 .... D2
05101 Bellows Falls 3,456 .... C5
05442 Belvidere○ 218 .... B2
05201 Bennington○ 15,815 .... A6
05201 Bennington⊙ 9,349 .... A6
05731 Benson○ 739 .... A4
†05476 Berkshire○ 1,116 .... B2
05032 Bethel○ 1,715 .... B4
05032 Bethel 1,016 .... B4
†03590 Bloomfield○ 188 .... D2
†05466 Bolton○ 715 .... B3
05732 Bomoseen 700 .... A4
05340 Bondville 500 .... B5
05033 Bradford○ 2,191 .... C3
05033 Bradford 831 .... C3
†05669 Braintree○ 1,065 .... B4
05733 Brandon○ 4,194 .... A4
05733 Brandon 1,925 .... A4
05301 Brattleboro○ 11,886 .... B6
05301 Brattleboro 8,596 .... B6
05034 Bridgewater○ 867 .... B4
05734 Bridport○ 997 .... A4
05443 Bristol○ 3,293 .... A3
05443 Bristol 1,793 .... A3
05036 Brookfield○ 959 .... B3
†05345 Brookline○ 310 .... B5
†05860 Brownington○ 708 .... C2
†05871 Burke○ 1,385 .... D2
05401 Burlington⊙ 37,712 .... A3
Burlington‡ 114,070 .... A3
05647 Cabot○ 958 .... C3
05647 Cabot 259 .... C3
05648 Calais○ 1,207 .... B3
05444 Cambridge○ 2,019 .... B2
05444 Cambridge 217 .... B2
05903 Canaan○ 1,196 .... D2
05735 Castleton○ 3,637 .... A4
05142 Cavendish○ 1,355 .... B5
05736 Center Rutland 465 .... A4
05445 Charlotte○ 2,561 .... A3
05038 Chelsea 1,091 .... C4
05143 Chester○ 2,791 .... B5
05143 Chester-Chester Depot 1,267 .... B5
05737 Chittenden○ 927 .... B4
†05759 Clarendon○ 2,372 .... A4
05446 Colchester○ 12,629 .... A2
05824 Concord○ 1,125 .... D3
05039 Corinth○ 904 .... C3
†05753 Cornwall○ 993 .... A4
05825 Coventry○ 674 .... C2
05826 Craftsbury○ 844 .... C2
05739 Danby○ 992 .... A5
05828 Danville○ 1,705 .... C3
05829 Derby○ 4,222 .... C2
05829 Derby (Derby Center) 598 .... C2
05830 Derby Line 874 .... C2
05251 Dorset○ 1,648 .... A5
†05676 Duxbury○ 877 .... B3
05252 East Arlington 600 .... A5
05649 East Barre-Graniteville 2,172 .... C3
05253 East Dorset 550 .... A5
05837 East Haven○ 280 .... D2
05740 East Middlebury 550 .... A4
05651 East Montpelier○ 2,205 .... B3
05741 East Poultney 450 .... A4
05742 East Wallingford 500 .... B5
05652 Eden○ 612 .... B2
05450 Enosburg Falls 1,207 .... B2
05451 Essex○ 14,392 .... A2
05452 Essex Junction 7,033 .... A3
05454 Fairfax○ 1,805 .... B2
05455 Fairfield○ 1,493 .... B2
05743 Fair Haven○ 2,819 .... A4
05743 Fair Haven 2,363 .... A4
05045 Fairlee○ 770 .... C4
05456 Ferrisburg○ 2,117 .... A3
†05444 Fletcher○ 626 .... B2
05745 Forest Dale 500 .... A4
05457 Franklin○ 1,006 .... B2
†05478 Georgia○ 2,818 .... A2
05904 Gilman 600 .... D3
05839 Glover○ 843 .... C2
05146 Grafton○ 604 .... B5
05840 Granby○ 70 .... D2
05458 Grand Isle○ 1,238 .... A2
05654 Graniteville-East Barre 2,172 .... C3
05747 Granville○ 288 .... B4
05841 Greensboro○ 677 .... C2
05046 Groton○ 667 .... C3
05905 Guildhall 202 .... D2
†05301 Guilford○ 1,532 .... B6
†05358 Halifax○ 488 .... B6
05748 Hancock○ 334 .... B4
05843 Hardwick○ 2,613 .... C2
05843 Hardwick 1,476 .... C2
05047 Hartford○ 7,963 .... C4
05048 Hartland○ 2,396 .... C4
†05459 Highgate○ 2,493 .... B2
05461 Hinesburg○ 2,690 .... A3
†05830 Holland○ 473 .... D2
05749 Hubbardton○ 490 .... A4
05462 Huntington○ 1,161 .... B3
05655 Hyde Park○ 2,021 .... B2
05655 Hyde Park⊙ 475 .... B2
05750 Hydeville 500 .... A4
†05777 Ira○ 354 .... A4
05845 Irasburg○ 870 .... C2
05846 Island Pond 1,216 .... D2
05463 Isle La Motte○ 393 .... A2
05342 Jacksonville 252 .... B6
05343 Jamaica○ 681 .... B5
†05859 Jay○ 302 .... C2
05464 Jeffersonville 491 .... B2
05465 Jericho○ 3,575 .... A2
05465 Jericho 1,340 .... A2
05656 Johnson○ 2,581 .... B2
05656 Johnson 1,393 .... B2
05751 Killington 700 .... B4
†05752 Leicester○ 803 .... A4
†03576 Lemington○ 108 .... D2
†05443 Lincoln○ 870 .... B3
05148 Londonderry○ 1,510 .... B5
05847 Lowell○ 573 .... C2
05149 Ludlow○ 2,414 .... B5
05149 Ludlow 1,352 .... B5
05906 Lunenburg○ 1,138 .... D3
05849 Lyndon○ 4,924 .... C2
05850 Lyndon Center C2
05851 Lyndonville 1,401 .... D2
†05905 Maidstone○ 100 .... D2
05254 Manchester○ 3,261 .... A5
05254 Manchester⊙ 563 .... A5
05255 Manchester Center 1,719 .... A5
05344 Marlboro○ 695 .... B6
05658 Marshfield○ 1,267 .... C3
05658 Marshfield 301 .... C3
†05701 Mendon○ 1,056 .... B4
05753 Middlebury○ 7,574 .... A3
05753 Middlebury⊙ 5,591 .... A3
†05602 Middlesex○ 1,235 .... B3
05757 Middletown Springs○ 603 .... A5
05468 Milton○ 6,829 .... A2
05468 Milton 1,411 .... A2
05469 Monkton○ 1,201 .... A3
05470 Montgomery○ 681 .... B2
05471 Montgomery Center 400 .... B2
05602 Montpelier (cap.)⊙ 8,241 .... B3
05660 Moretown○ 1,221 .... B3
05853 Morgan○ 460 .... D2
†05661 Morristown○ 4,448 .... B2
05661 Morrisville 2,074 .... B2
05758 Mount Holly○ 938 .... B5
†05739 Mount Tabor○ 211 .... B5
†05871 Newark○ 280 .... D2
05051 Newbury○ 1,699 .... C3
05051 Newbury 425 .... C3
05345 Newfane○ 1,129 .... B6
05345 Newfane⊙ 119 .... B6
05472 New Haven○ 1,217 .... A3
05855 Newport○ 1,319 .... C2
05855 Newport⊙ 4,756 .... C2
05257 North Bennington 1,685 .... A6
05663 Northfield○ 5,435 .... B3
05663 Northfield 2,033 .... B3
05664 Northfield Falls 600 .... B3
05052 North Hartland 500 .... C4
05474 North Hero 442 .... A2
05665 North Hyde Park 450 .... B2
05053 North Pomfret 400 .... B4
05260 North Pownal 700 .... A6
05150 North Springfield B5
05859 North Troy 717 .... C2
†05101 North Westminster 310 .... B5
05907 Norton○ 184 .... D2
05055 Norwich○ 2,398 .... C4
†05201 Old Bennington 353 .... A6
†05649 Orange○ 752 .... C3
05860 Orleans 983 .... C2
05760 Orwell○ 901 .... A4
†05491 Panton○ 537 .... A3
05761 Pawlet○ 1,244 .... A5
05862 Peacham○ 531 .... C3
05151 Perkinsville 187 .... B5
05152 Peru○ 312 .... B5
05762 Pittsfield○ 396 .... B4
05763 Pittsford○ 2,590 .... A4
05763 Pittsford 666 .... A4
05667 Plainfield○ 1,249 .... C3
05667 Plainfield 599 .... C3
05056 Plymouth○ 405 .... B4
†05067 Pomfret○ 856 .... B4
05058 Post Mills 500 .... C4
05764 Poultney○ 3,196 .... A4
05764 Poultney 1,554 .... A4
05261 Pownal○ 3,269 .... A6
05765 Proctor○ 1,998 .... A4
05153 Proctorsville 481 .... B5
05346 Putney○ 1,850 .... B6
05059 Quechee 900 .... C4
05060 Randolph○ 4,689 .... B4
05060 Randolph 2,217 .... B4
05062 Reading○ 647 .... B5
05350 Readsboro○ 638 .... B6
05350 Readsboro 402 .... B6
05476 Richford○ 2,206 .... B2
05476 Richford 1,471 .... B2
05477 Richmond○ 3,159 .... A3
05477 Richmond 865 .... A3
05766 Ripton○ 327 .... A4
05767 Rochester○ 1,054 .... B4
†05101 Rockingham○ 5,538 .... B5
05669 Roxbury○ 452 .... B3
†05068 Royalton○ 2,100 .... B4
05768 Rupert○ 605 .... A5
05701 Rutland○ 3,300 .... B4
05701 Rutland⊙ 18,436 .... B4
05042 Ryegate○ 1,000 .... C3
05478 Saint Albans○ 3,555 .... A2
05478 Saint Albans⊙ 7,308 .... A2
†05401 Saint George○ 677 .... A2
05819 Saint Johnsbury○ 7,938 .... D3
05819 Saint Johnsbury⊙ 7,150 .... D3
05863 Saint Johnsbury Center 400 .... D3
05769 Salisbury○ 881 .... A4
†05250 Sandgate○ 234 .... A5
05154 Saxtons River 593 .... B5
†05363 Searsburg○ 72 .... A6
05262 Shaftsbury○ 3,001 .... A6
05065 Sharon○ 828 .... C4
05866 Sheffield○ 435 .... C2
05482 Shelburne○ 5,000 .... A3
05483 Sheldon○ 1,618 .... B2
05770 Shoreham○ 972 .... A4
†05738 Shrewsbury○ 866 .... B4
05670 South Barre 1,301 .... B3
05401 South Burlington 10,679 .... A3
05486 South Hero○ 1,188 .... A2
05155 South Londonderry 500 .... B5
05068 South Royalton 700 .... C4
05069 South Ryegate 400 .... C3
05156 Springfield○ 10,190 .... B5
05156 Springfield 5,603 .... B5
05352 Stamford○ 773 .... A6
05487 Starksboro○ 1,336 .... A3
05772 Stockbridge○ 508 .... B4
05672 Stowe○ 2,991 .... B3
05672 Stowe 531 .... B3
05072 Strafford○ 731 .... C4
†05360 Stratton○ 122 .... B5
†05733 Sudbury○ 380 .... A4
†05250 Sunderland○ 768 .... A5
05867 Sutton○ 667 .... C2
05488 Swanton○ 5,141 .... A2
05488 Swanton 2,520 .... A2
05074 Thetford○ 2,188 .... C4
†05773 Tinmouth○ 406 .... A5
05076 Topsham○ 767 .... C3
05353 Townshend○ 849 .... B5
05868 Troy○ 1,498 .... C2
05077 Tunbridge○ 925 .... C4
05489 Underhill○ 2,172 .... B2
05490 Underhill Center 575 .... B2
05491 Vergennes 2,273 .... A3
05354 Vernon○ 1,175 .... B6
05079 Vershire○ 442 .... C4
05673 Waitsfield○ 1,300 .... B3
†05873 Walden○ 575 .... C3
05773 Wallingford○ 1,893 .... B5
05773 Wallingford 1,141 .... B5
†05491 Waltham○ 394 .... A3
05355 Wardsboro○ 505 .... B5
05674 Warren○ 956 .... B3
05675 Washington○ 855 .... C3
05676 Waterbury○ 4,465 .... B3
05676 Waterbury 1,892 .... B3
05492 Waterville○ 470 .... B2
05678 Websterville 700 .... B3
05774 Wells○ 815 .... A5
05081 Wells River 396 .... C3
05301 West Brattleboro 2,795 .... B6
05871 West Burke 338 .... C2
05356 West Dover 550 .... B6
05083 West Fairlee○ 427 .... C4
05874 Westfield○ 418 .... C2
05494 Westford○ 1,413 .... A2
05875 West Glover C2
†05743 West Haven○ 253 .... A4
05158 Westminster○ 2,493 .... C5
05158 Westminster 319 .... C5
†05860 Westmore○ 257 .... C2
05161 Weston○ 627 .... B5
05777 West Rutland○ 2,351 .... A4
05777 West Rutland 2,169 .... A4
05359 West Townshend 500 .... B5
†05753 Weybridge○ 667 .... A3
†05851 Wheelock○ 444 .... C2
05001 White River Junction 2,582 .... C4
05778 Whiting○ 379 .... A4
05361 Whitingham○ 1,043 .... B6
05088 Wilder 1,461 .... C4
05679 Williamstown○ 2,284 .... B3
05495 Williston○ 3,843 .... A3
05363 Wilmington○ 1,808 .... B6
†05359 Windham○ 223 .... B5
05089 Windsor○ 4,084 .... C5
05089 Windsor 3,478 .... C5
05404 Winooski 6,318 .... A2
05680 Wolcott○ 986 .... C2
05681 Woodbury○ 573 .... C3
†05201 Woodford○ 314 .... A6
05091 Woodstock○ 3,214 .... B4
05091 Woodstock⊙ 1,178 .... B4
05682 Worcester○ 727 .... B3

OTHER FEATURES

Abraham (mt.) B3
Arrowhead Mountain (lake) A2
Ascutney (mt.) C5
Bald (mt.) D2
Barton (riv.) C2
Batten Kill (riv.) A5
Belvidere (mt.) B2
Black (riv.) B5
Black (riv.) C2
Bloodroot (mt.) B4
Bolton (mt.) B3
Bomoseen (lake) A4
Brandon Gap (pass) B4
Bread Loaf (mt.) A3
Bromley (mt.) B5
Brown's (riv.) A2
Burke (mt.) D2
Camels Hump (mt.) B3
Carmi (lake) B2
Caspian (lake) C2
Champlain (lake) A2
Chittenden (res.) B4
Clyde (riv.) C2
Comerford (dam) D3
Connecticut (riv.) C4
Crystal (lake) C2
Dorset (peak) A5
Dunmore (lake) A4
Echo (lake) D2
Ellen (mt.) B3
Equinox (mt.) A5
Fairfield (pond) A2
Glastenbury (mt.) A6
Gore (mt.) D2
Green (mts.) B4
Green River (res.) B2
Groton (lake) C3
Hardwick (lake) C2
Harriman (res.) B6
Harveys (lake) C3
Haystack (mt.) B6
Hoosic (riv.) A6
Hortonia (lake) A4
Hunger (mt.) B3
Iroquois (lake) A3
Island (pond) D2
Jay (peak) B2
Joes (brook) C3
Killington (peak) B4
Lamoille (riv.) A2
Lewis (creek) A3
Lincoln Gap (pass) B3
Little (riv.) B3
Mad (riv.) B3
Maidstone (lake) D2
Mansfield (mt.) B2
Memphremagog (lake) C1
Mettawee (riv.) A5
Middlebury Gap (pass) B4
Mill (riv.) B4
Missisquoi (riv.) B2
Mollys Falls (pond) C3
Moore (dam) D3
Moore (res.) D3
Moose (riv.) D2
Norton (pond) D2
Nulhegan (riv.) D2
Ottauquechee (riv.) B4
Otter (creek) A3
Passumpsic (riv.) D2
Pico (peak) B4
Poultney (riv.) A4
Saint Catherine (lake) A5
Salem (lake) C2
Seymour (lake) D2
Shelburne (pond) A3
Smugglers Notch (pass) B2
Snow (mt.) B6
Somerset (res.) A5
Spruce (mt.) C3
Stratton (mt.) B5
Tabor (mt.) B5
Trout (riv.) B2
Waits (riv.) C3
Waterbury (res.) B3
Wells (riv.) C3
West (riv.) B5
White (riv.) C4
White Face (mt.) B2
Wilder (dam) C4
Willoughby (lake) D2
Winooski (riv.) B3

⊙County seat.
‡Population of metropolitan area.
○Population of town or township.
† Zip of nearest p.o. * Multiple zips.

AREA 7,787 sq. mi. (20,168 sq. km.)
POPULATION 7,364,823
CAPITAL Trenton
LARGEST CITY Newark
HIGHEST POINT High Point 1,803 ft. (550 m.)
SETTLED IN 1617
ADMITTED TO UNION December 18, 1787
POPULAR NAME Garden State
STATE FLOWER Purple Violet
STATE BIRD Eastern Goldfinch

Agriculture, Industry and Resources

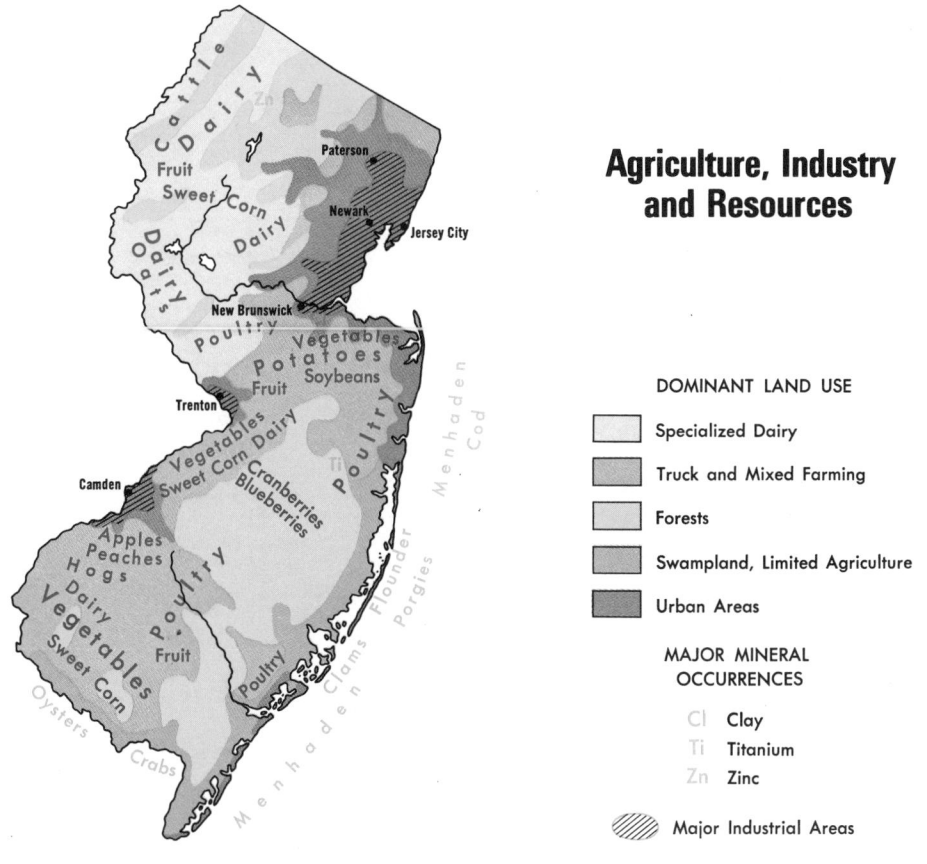

DOMINANT LAND USE

Specialized Dairy

Truck and Mixed Farming

Forests

Swampland, Limited Agriculture

Urban Areas

MAJOR MINERAL OCCURRENCES

Cl   Clay

Ti   Titanium

Zn   Zinc

Major Industrial Areas

The Urban Northeast

- Urbanized Areas
- • Places with more than 10,000 inhabitants
- • Places with 5,000-10,000 inhabitants
- · Places with 2,500-5,000 inhabitants

© Copyright HAMMOND INCORPORATED, Maplewood, N. J.

COUNTIES

County	Pop.	Key
Atlantic	194,119	D5
Bergen	845,385	E2
Burlington	362,542	D4
Camden	471,650	D4
Cape May	82,266	D5
Cumberland	132,866	C5
Essex	851,116	E2
Gloucester	199,917	C4
Hudson	556,972	E2
Hunterdon	87,361	D2
Mercer	307,863	D3
Middlesex	595,893	E3
Monmouth	503,173	E3
Morris	407,630	D2
Ocean	346,038	E4
Passaic	447,585	E1
Salem	64,676	C4
Somerset	203,129	D2
Sussex	116,119	D1
Union	504,094	E2
Warren	84,429	C2

CITIES and TOWNS

Zip	Name/Pop.	Key
08201	Absecon 6,859	D5
07820	Allamuchy 600	D2
07401	Allendale 5,901	B1
07711	Allenhurst 912	F3
08501	Allentown 1,962	D3
08720	Allenwood	E3
08001	Alloway 1,370	C4
08865	Alpha 2,644	C2
07620	Alpine 1,549	C1
07821	Andover 892	D2
08801	Annandale 1,040	D2
07712	Asbury Park 17,015	F3
	Asbury Park-Long Branch‡ 503,173	F3
†08033	Ashland	B3
08004	Atco	D4
*08401	Atlantic City 40,199	E5
	Atlantic City‡ 194,119	E5
07716	Atlantic Highlands 4,950	F3
08106	Audubon 9,533	B3
†08106	Audubon Park 1,274	B3
08202	Avalon 2,162	D5
07001	Avenel	E2
07717	Avon By The Sea 2,337	E3
08005	Barnegat 1,012	E4
08006	Barnegat Light 619	E4
08007	Barrington 7,418	B3
07920	Basking Ridge	D2
08742	Bay Head 1,340	E3
07002	Bayonne 65,047	B2
08008	Beach Haven 1,714	E4
08722	Beachwood 7,687	E4
07921	Bedminster○ 2,469	D2
08502	Belle Mead	D3
07109	Belleville 35,367	B2
08031	Bellmawr 13,721	B3
07719	Belmar 6,771	E3
07823	Belvidere⊙ 2,475	C2
07621	Bergenfield 25,568	C1
07922	Berkeley Heights○ 12,549	E2
08009	Berlin 5,786	D4
07924	Bernardsville 6,715	D2
08010	Beverly 2,919	D3
08012	Blackwood 5,219	C4
07825	Blairstown○ 4,360	C2
07003	Bloomfield 47,792	B2
07403	Bloomingdale 7,867	E1
08804	Bloomsbury 864	C2
07603	Bogota 8,344	B2
07005	Boonton 8,620	E2
08505	Bordentown 4,441	D3
08805	Bound Brook 9,710	D2
07720	Bradley Beach 4,772	F3
07826	Branchville 870	D1
08723	Breton Woods	E3
08723	Brick○ 53,629	E3
08014	Bridgeport 750	C4
08302	Bridgeton⊙ 18,795	C5
08807	Bridgewater○ 29,175	D2
08730	Brielle 4,068	E3
08203	Brigantine 8,318	E5
08030	Brooklawn 2,133	B3
08015	Browns Mills 10,568	D4
08310	Buena 3,642	D4
08016	Burlington 10,246	D3
07405	Butler 7,616	E2
07006	Caldwell 7,624	B2
07830	Califon 1,023	D2
*08101	Camden⊙ 84,910	B3
†08701	Candlewood 6,750	E3
08204	Cape May 4,853	D6
08210	Cape May Court House⊙ 3,597	D5
07072	Carlstadt 6,166	B2
08069	Carneys Point 7,574	C4
07008	Carteret 20,598	E2
07009	Cedar Grove○ 12,600	B2
†08723	Cedarwood Park	E3
07928	Chatham 8,537	E2
08019	Chatsworth 700	D4
08879	Cheesequake	E3
*08034	Cherry Hill○ 68,785	B3
†08089	Chesilhurst 1,590	D4
07930	Chester 1,433	D2
†08505	Chesterfield○ 3,867	D3
†08077	Cinnaminson○ 16,072	B3
07066	Clark○ 16,699	A3
08020	Clarksboro	C4
08510	Clarksburg 800	E3
08021	Clayton 6,013	C4
08021	Clementon 5,764	D4
07010	Cliffside Park 21,464	C2
07721	Cliffwood	E3
*07011	Clifton 74,388	B2
08809	Clinton 1,910	D2
07624	Closter 8,164	C1
08108	Collingswood 15,838	B3
08213	Cologne 800	D4
07722	Colts Neck 950	E3
07832	Columbia 600	C2
08022	Columbus 800	D3
07961	Convent Station	E2
†08270	Corbin City 254	D5
†07821	Cranberry Lake 500	D2
08512	Cranbury 1,255	E3
07016	Cranford○ 24,573	E2
07626	Cresskill 7,609	C1
08515	Crosswicks 265	D3
07723	Deal 1,952	F3
08023	Deepwater 800	C4
08110	Delair	B3
08075	Delanco○ 3,730	D3
08075	Delran○ 14,811	B3
07627	Demarest 4,963	C1
08214	Dennisville 890	D5
07834	Denville○ 14,380	E2
08096	Deptford○ 23,473	B4
08317	Dorothy 900	D5
07801	Dover 14,681	D2
07628	Dumont 18,334	C1
08812	Dunellen 6,593	D2
08816	East Brunswick○ 37,711	E3
07936	East Hanover○ 9,319	E2
07734	East Keansburg	E3
08873	East Millstone 950	D3
†07100	East Newark 1,923	B2
*07017	East Orange 77,690	B2
07073	East Rutherford 7,849	B2
07724	Eatontown 12,703	E3
07020	Edgewater 4,628	C2
†08010	Edgewater Park○ 9,273	D3
*08817	Edison○ 70,193	E2
08215	Egg Harbor City 4,618	D4
07740	Elberon	F3
*07201	Elizabeth⊙ 106,201	B2
08318	Elmer 1,569	C4
†07407	Elmwood Park 18,377	B2
08217	Elwood 1,538	D4
07630	Emerson 7,793	B1
*07631	Englewood 23,701	C2
07632	Englewood Cliffs 5,698	C2
07726	Englishtown 976	E3
07021	Essex Fells 2,363	B2
08319	Estell Manor 848	D5
08025	Ewan 610	C4
07006	Fairfield○ 7,987	A2
07701	Fair Haven 5,679	E3
07410	Fair Lawn 32,229	B1
08320	Fairton 1,107	C5
07022	Fairview 10,519	C2
07023	Fanwood 7,767	E2
07931	Far Hills 677	D2
07727	Farmingdale 1,348	E3
†08505	Fieldsboro 597	D3
07836	Flanders	D2
08822	Flemington⊙ 4,132	D2
08518	Florence-Roebling 7,677	D3
07932	Florham Park 9,359	E2
†08037	Folsom 1,892	D4
08863	Fords	E2
08731	Forked River 900	E4
07024	Fort Lee 32,449	C2
07416	Franklin 4,486	D1
07417	Franklin Lakes 8,769	B1
†08823	Franklin Park○ 31,358	D3
08322	Franklinville	C4
07728	Freehold⊙ 10,020	E3
08825	Frenchtown 1,573	C2
07026	Garfield 26,803	B2
07027	Garwood 4,752	E2
08026	Gibbsboro 2,510	B4
08027	Gibbstown	C4
†08753	Gilford Park 6,528	E4
07933	Gillette	E2
08028	Glassboro 14,574	C4
08029	Glendora 5,632	B4
08826	Glen Gardner 834	D2
07028	Glen Ridge 7,855	B2
07452	Glen Rock 11,497	B1
08030	Gloucester City 13,121	B3
07435	Green Pond 800	E1
07935	Green Village 800	D2
08323	Greenwich○ 973	C5
08032	Grenloch 700	C4

(continued on following page)

07093 Guttenberg 7,340 .... C2
*07601 Hackensack⊙ 36,039 .... B2
07840 Hackettstown 8,850 .... D2
08033 Haddonfield 12,337 .... B3
08035 Haddon Heights 8,361 ...... B3
08036 Hainesport○ 3,236 .... D4
07508 Haledon 6,607 .... B1
07419 Hamburg 1.832 .... D1
08690 Hamilton Square-
Mercerville 25,446 .... D3
08037 Hammonton 12,298 .... D4
08827 Hampton 1,614 .... D2
07640 Harrington Park 4,532 ...... C1
07029 Harrison 12,242 .... B2
†08057 Hartford 650 .... D4
08008 Harvey Cedars 363 .... E4
07604 Hasbrouck Heights 12,166 . B2
07641 Haworth 3,509 .... C1
07507 Hawthorne 18,200 .... B2
07730 Hazlet 23,013 .... E3
08828 Helmetta 955 .... E3
07421 Hewitt 950 .... E1
08829 High Bridge 3,435 .... D2
07422 Highland Lakes 2,888 .... E1
08904 Highland Park 13,396 .... D2
07732 Highlands 5,187 .... F3
08520 Hightstown 4,581 .... D3
07642 Hillsdale 10,495 .... B1
07205 Hillside○ 21,440 .... B2
†08083 Hi-Nella 1,250 .... B4
07030 Hoboken 42,460 .... C2
07423 Ho Ho Kus 4,129 .... B1
07733 Holmdel○ 8,447 .... E3
07843 Hopatcong 15,531 .... D2
07844 Hope 310 .... D2
08525 Hopewell 2,001 .... D3
07731 Howell○ 25,065 .... E3
†07712 Interlaken 1,037 .... E3
07845 Ironia D2
07111 Irvington 61,493 .... B2
08830 Iselin E2
08732 Island Heights 1,575 .... E4
08527 Jackson○ 25,644 .... E3
08831 Jamesburg 4,114 .... E3
*07301 Jersey City⊙ 223,532 ...... B2
Jersey City‡ 556,972 .... B2
07734 Keansburg 10,613 .... E3
07032 Kearny 35,735 .... B2
08824 Kendall Park 7,419 .... D3
07033 Kenilworth 8,221 .... E2
07735 Keyport 7,413 .... E3
08528 Kingston D3
07405 Kinnelon 7,770 .... E2
07848 Lafayette 900 .... D1
07034 Lake Hiawatha E2
07849 Lake Hopatcong D2
08733 Lakehurst 2,908 .... E3
†07871 Lake Mohawk 8,498 .... D1
08701 Lakewood 22,863 .... E3
08530 Lambertville 4,044 .... D3
07850 Landing D2
08734 Lanoka Harbor E4
08021 Laurel Springs 2,249 .... B4
08879 Laurence Harbor 6,737 ..... E3
08735 Lavallette 2,072 .... E4
08045 Lawnside 3,042 .... B3
08648 Lawrenceville 19,724 .... D3
08833 Lebanon 820 .... D2
07852 Ledgewood D2
08327 Leesburg 700 .... D5
07737 Leonardo E3
07605 Leonia 8,027 .... C2
07938 Liberty Corner D2
07035 Lincoln Park 8,806 .... A1
07738 Lincroft E3
07036 Linden 37,836 .... A3
08021 Lindenwold 18,196 .... B4
08221 Linwood 6,144 .... D5
07424 Little Falls○ 11,496 .... B2
07643 Little Ferry 9,399 .... B2
07739 Little Silver 5,548 .... F3
07039 Livingston○ 28,040 .... E2
07644 Lodi 23,956 .... B2
07740 Long Branch 29,819 .... F3
Long Branch-Asbury Park‡
503,173 .... F3
08403 Longport 1,249 .... D5
07853 Long Valley 1,682 .... D2
08048 Lumberton 600 .... D4
07071 Lyndhurst○ 20,326 .... B2
07939 Lyons D2
07940 Madison 15,357 .... E2
08049 Magnolia 4,881 .... B3
07430 Mahwah○ 12,127 .... E1
08328 Malaga 950 .... C4
08050 Manahawkin 1,469 .... E4
08736 Manasquan 5,354 .... E3
08738 Mantoloking 433 .... E3
08051 Mantua○ 9,193 .... C4
08835 Manville 11,278 .... D2
08052 Maple Shade○ 20,525 ...... B3
07040 Maplewood○ 22,950 .... E2
08402 Margate City 9,179 .... E5
07746 Marlboro○ 17,560 .... E3
08053 Marlton 9,411 .... D4
08223 Marmora 650 .... D5
08836 Martinsville D2
07747 Matawan 8,837 .... E3
08330 Mays Landing⊙ 2,054 ..... D5
07607 Maywood 9,895 .... B2
07428 McAfee 800 .... D1
†08232 McKee City 950 .... D5
08055 Medford D4
08055 Medford Lakes 4,958 .... D4
07945 Mendham 4,899 .... D2
08837 Menlo Park E2
08619 Mercerville-Hamilton
Square 25,446 .... D3
08109 Merchantville 3,972 .... B3
08840 Metuchen 13,762 .... E2
08846 Middlesex 13,480 .... E2
07748 Middletown○ 62,574 .... E3
07432 Midland Park 7,381 .... B1
08848 Milford 1,368 .... C2
07041 Millburn○ 19,543 .... E2
07946 Millington 975 .... D2
†08876 Millstone 530 .... D2
08850 Milltown 7,136 .... E3
08332 Millville 24,815 .... C5
†07801 Mine Hill○ 3,325 .... D2
08342 Mizpah 900 .... D5
07750 Monmouth Beach 3,318 .... F3
08852 Monmouth Junction 2,579 . D3
07434 Monroe○ 15,858 .... E3
*07042 Montclair 38,321 .... B2
07645 Montvale 7,318 .... B1
07045 Montville○ 14,290 .... E2
†07070 Moonachie 2,706 .... B2
08057 Moorestown 13,695 .... B3
07950 Morris Plains 5,305 .... D2
07960 Morristown⊙ 16,614 .... D2
07046 Mountain Lakes 4,153 ...... E2
07092 Mountainside 7,118 .... E2
07856 Mount Arlington 4,251 ...... D2
08059 Mount Ephraim 4,863 ...... B3
07970 Mount Freedom D2
08060 Mount Holly 10,818 .... D4
†08054 Mount Laurel○ 17,614 ...... D4
†07828 Mount Olive○ 18,748 .... D2
08061 Mount Royal 900 .... C4
08062 Mullica Hill 1,050 .... C4
08087 Mystic Islands 4,929 .... E4
08063 National Park 3,552 .... B3
07752 Navesink E3
07753 Neptune○ 28,366 .... E3
07753 Neptune City 5,276 .... E3
07857 Netcong 3,557 .... D2
*07101 Newark⊙ 329,248 .... B2
Newark‡ 1,965,304 .... B2
*08901 New Brunswick⊙ 41,442 .. E3
New Brunswick-Perth
Amboy-Sayreville‡
595,893 .... E3
08533 New Egypt 2,111 .... E3
08344 Newfield 1,563 .... D4
07435 Newfoundland 900 .... D1
08224 New Gretna 800 .... E4
07646 New Milford 16,876 .... B1
07974 New Providence 12,426 .... E2
07860 Newton⊙ 7,748 .... D1
08346 Newtonville 950 .... D4
07976 New Vernon D2
07032 North Arlington 16,587 ..... B2
07047 North Bergen○ 47,019 ...... B2
08876 North Branch 610 .... D2
08902 North Brunswick○ 22,220 .. D3
†07006 North Caldwell 5,832 .... B2
08204 North Cape May 4,029 ..... C6
08225 Northfield 7,795 .... D5
07508 North Haledon 8,177 .... B1
07060 North Plainfield 19,108 ..... E2
07647 Northvale 5,046 .... F1
08260 North Wildwood 4,714 ..... D6
07648 Norwood 4,413 .... C1
07110 Nutley 28,998 .... B2
07755 Oakhurst E3
07436 Oakland 13,443 .... B1
08107 Oaklyn 4,223 .... B3
08226 Ocean City 13,949 .... D5
08740 Ocean Gate 1,385 .... E4
07756 Ocean Grove F3
07757 Oceanport 5,888 .... F3
07439 Ogdensburg 2,737 .... D1
08857 Old Bridge 21,815 .... E3
07675 Old Tappan 4,168 .... C1
07649 Oradell 8,658 .... B1
*07050 Orange 31,136 .... B2
08723 Osbornsville E3
07863 Oxford 1,587 .... C2
07470 Packanack Lake B1
07650 Palisades Park 13,732 ...... C2
08065 Palmyra 7,085 .... B3
07652 Paramus 26,474 .... B1
07656 Park Ridge 8,515 .... B1
07054 Parsippany-Troy
Hills○ 49,868 .... E2
07055 Passaic 52,463 .... E2
*07501 Paterson⊙ 137,970 .... B2
Paterson-Clifton-Passaic‡
447.585 .... B2
08066 Paulsboro 6,944 .... C4
07977 Peapack-Gladstone 2,038 .. D2
08067 Pedricktown C4
08068 Pemberton 1,198 .... D4
08534 Pennington 2,109 .... D3
08110 Pennsauken○ 33,775 .... B3
08069 Penns Grove 5,760 .... C4
08070 Pennsville 12,467 .... C4
07440 Pequannock○ 13,776 .... B1
*08861 Perth Amboy 38,951 .... E2
08865 Phillipsburg 16,647 .... C2
08741 Pine Beach 1,796 .... E4
07058 Pine Brook E2
08021 Pine Hill 8,684 .... D4
08854 Piscataway○ 42,223 .... D2
08071 Pitman 9,744 .... C4
*07060 Plainfield 45,555 .... E2
08536 Plainsboro D3
08232 Pleasantville 13,435 .... D5
08742 Point Pleasant 17.747 ...... E3
08742 Point Pleasant Beach
5,415 .... E3
08240 Pomona 2,358 .... D5
07442 Pompton Lakes 10,660 ..... A1
07444 Pompton Plains B1
07758 Port Monmouth E3
†07850 Port Morris 616 .... D2
07865 Port Murray 250 .... D2
08349 Port Norris 1,730 .... C5
08241 Port Republic 837 .... D4
08540 Princeton 12,035 .... D3
08550 Princeton Junction 2,419 ... D3
†07885 Prospect Park 5,142 .... B1
08072 Quinton 750 .... C4
*07065 Rahway 26,723 .... E2
†08054 Ramblewood 6,475 .... D4
07446 Ramsey 12,899 .... B1
†07801 Randolph○ 17,828 .... D2
08869 Raritan 6,128 .... D2
07701 Red Bank 12,031 .... E3
07657 Ridgefield 10,294 .... B2
07660 Ridgefield Park 12,738 ..... B2
*07450 Ridgewood 25,208 .... B1
08551 Ringoes 682 .... D3
07456 Ringwood 12,625 .... E1
08242 Rio Grande 2,016 .... D5
07457 Riverdale 2,530 .... A1
07661 River Edge 11,111 .... B1
08075 Riverside○ 7,941 .... B3
08077 Riverton 3,068 .... B3
07675 River Vale○ 9,489 .... B1
07662 Rochelle Park○ 5,603 .... B2
07866 Rockaway 6,852 .... D2
07647 Rockleigh 192 .... C1
08553 Rocky Hill 717 .... D3
08554 Roebling-Florence 7,677 .... D3
08555 Roosevelt 835 .... E3
07068 Roseland 5,330 .... A2
07203 Roselle 20,641 .... B2
07204 Roselle Park 13,377 .... A2
08352 Rosenhayn 950 .... C5
†07876 Roxbury○ 18,878 .... D2
07760 Rumson 7,623 .... F3
08078 Runnemede 9,461 .... B3
*07070 Rutherford 19,068 .... B2
07662 Saddle Brook○ 14,084 ...... B1
07458 Saddle River 2,763 .... B1
08079 Salem⊙ 6,959 .... C4
08872 Sayreville 29,969 .... E3
07076 Scotch Plains○ 20,774 ...... E2
07760 Sea Bright 1,812 .... F3
08302 Seabrook 1,411 .... C5
08750 Sea Girt 2,650 .... E3
08243 Sea Isle City 2,644 .... D5
08751 Seaside Heights 1,802 ...... E4
08752 Seaside Park 1,795 .... E4
07094 Secaucus 13,719 .... B2
07077 Sewaren E2
08080 Sewell C4
08353 Shiloh 604 .... C5
08008 Ship Bottom 1,427 .... E4
07078 Short Hills E2
07701 Shrewsbury 2,962 .... E3
08081 Sicklerville D4
08558 Skillman D3
08201 Smithville 70 .... E5
08083 Somerdale 5,900 .... B4
08244 Somers Point 10,330 .... D5
08876 Somerville⊙ 11,973 .... D2
08879 South Amboy 8,322 .... E3
†07719 South Belmar 1,566 .... E3
08880 South Bound Brook 4,331 . E2
†08852 South Brunswick○ 17,127 . E3
07079 South Orange○ 15,864 ..... A2
07080 South Plainfield 20,521 ..... E2
08882 South River 14,361 .... E3
08753 South Toms River 3,954 ... E4
07871 Sparta○ 13,333 .... D1
08884 Spotswood 7,840 .... E3
07081 Springfield○ 13,955 .... E2
07762 Spring Lake 4,215 .... F3
†07762 Spring Lake Heights 5,424 . E3
07874 Stanhope 3,638 .... D2
08886 Stewartsville 950 .... C2
07980 Stirling E2
07460 Stockholm D1
08559 Stockton 643 .... D3
08247 Stone Harbor 1,187 .... D5
08084 Stratford 8,005 .... B4
†07747 Strathmore E3
07876 Succasunna 10,931 .... D2
07901 Summit 21,071 .... E2
08008 Surf City 1,571 .... E4
07461 Sussex 2,418 .... D1
08085 Swedesboro 2,031 .... C4
07878 Tabor E2
07666 Teaneck○ 39,007 .... B2
07670 Tenafly 13,552 .... C1
07608 Teterboro 19 .... B2
08086 Thorofare B4
08887 Three Bridges 750 .... D2
07724 Tinton Falls 7,740 .... E3
08753 Toms River⊙ 7,465 .... E4
07512 Totowa 11,448 .... B1
07082 Towaco E2
*08601 Trenton (cap.)⊙ 92,124 ... D3
Trenton‡ 307,863 .... D3
08087 Tuckerton 2,472 .... E4
07083 Union○ 50,184 .... A2
07735 Union Beach 6,354 .... E3
07087 Union City 55,593 .... C2
†07421 Upper Greenwood
Lake 2,734 .... E1
†07458 Upper Saddle River 7,958 .. B1
08406 Ventnor City 11,704 .... E5
07462 Vernon 800 .... E1
07044 Verona 14,166 .... B2
08251 Villas 5,909 .... D5
08088 Vincentown 900 .... D4
08360 Vineland 53,753 .... C5
Vineland-Millville-Bridgeton‡
132,866 .... C5
†08043 Voorhees○ 12,919 .... B3
07463 Waldwick 10,802 .... B1
07719 Wall○ 18,952 .... E3
07057 Wallington 10,741 .... B2
†07712 Wanamassa E3
07465 Wanaque 10,025 .... B1
08758 Waretown 1,175 .... E4
†07060 Warren○ 9,805 .... D2
07882 Washington 6,429 .... D2
07060 Watchung 5,290 .... E2
07470 Wayne○ 46,474 .... A1
07087 Weehawken○ 13,168 .... C2
08090 Wenonah 2,303 .... C4
07006 West Caldwell 11,407 .... A2
†08204 West Cape May 1,091 ...... D6
08092 West Creek 827 .... E4
†08086 West Deptford○ 18,002 ..... B3
*07090 Westfield 30,447 .... E2
07764 West Long Branch 7,380 ... F3
07480 West Milford 950 .... E1
08108 Westmont 15,875 .... B3
07093 West New York 39,194 ..... C2
07052 West Orange 39,510 .... A2
07424 West Paterson 11,293 ...... B2
08628 West Trenton D3
08093 Westville 4,786 .... B3
†08260 West Wildwood 360 .... D6
07675 Westwood 10,714 .... B1
07885 Wharton 5,485 .... D2

Topography

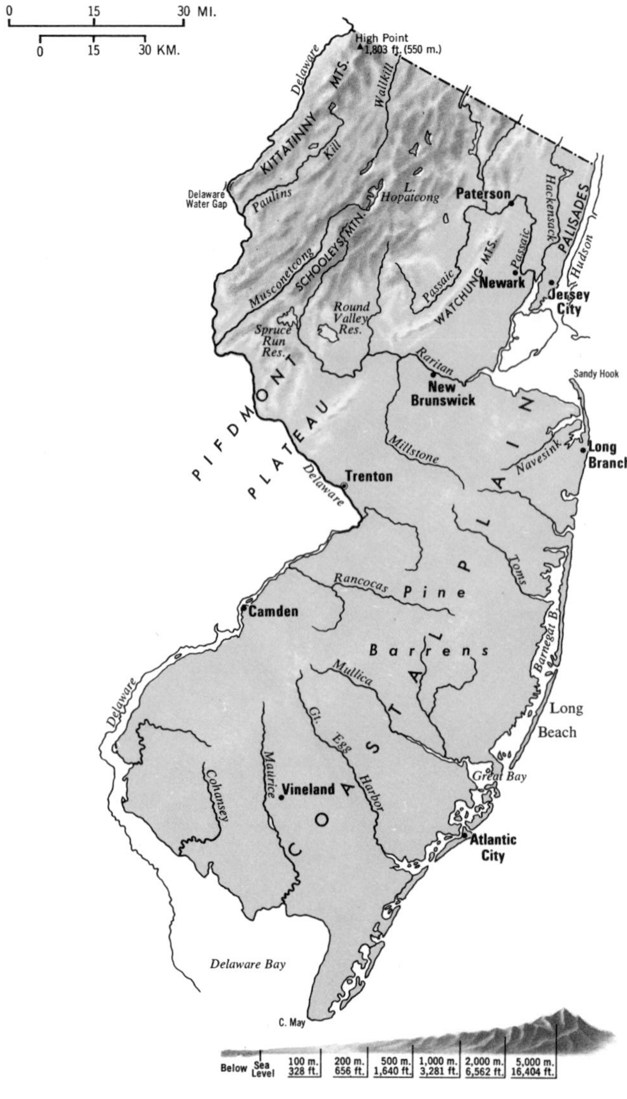

07981 Whippany E2
08889 White House Station D2
†07866 White Meadow Lake 8,429 D2
08252 Whitesboro 1,583 .... D5
07765 Wickatunk 950 .... E3
08260 Wildwood 4,913 .... D6
08260 Wildwood Crest 4,149 ...... D6
08094 Williamstown 5,768 .... D4
08046 Willingboro○ 39,912 .... D3
†07036 Winfield○ 1,785 .... B2
08270 Woodbine 2,809 .... D5
07095 Woodbridge○ 90,074 .... E2
08096 Woodbury⊙ 10,353 .... B4
08097 Woodbury Heights 3,460 ... B4
07675 Woodcliff Lake 5,644 .... B1
†08107 Wood-Lynne 2,578 .... B3
†07885 Woodport D2
07075 Wood-Ridge 7,929 .... B2
08098 Woodstown 3,250 .... C4
08562 Wrightstown 3,031 .... D3
07481 Wyckoff○ 15,500 .... B1
08620 Yardville 9,414 .... D3

OTHER FEATURES

Absecon (inlet) E5
Alloways (creek) C4
Arthur Kill (str.) B3
Atlantic Highlands (ridge) E3
Barnegat (bay) E4
Batsto (riv.) D4
Bayonne Military Ocean Terminal .. B2
Beach Haven (inlet) E4
Beaver (brook) C2
Ben Davis (pt.) C5
Big Flat (brook) D1
Big Timber (creek) C4
Boonton (res.) E2
Brigantine (inlet) E5
Budd (lake) D2
Canistear (res.) E1
Cedar (creek) E4
Clinton (res.) E1
Cohansey (riv.) C5
Cold Spring (inlet) D6
Cooper (riv.) B3
Corson (inlet) D5
Crosswicks (creek) D3
Culvers (lake) D1
Delaware (bay) C5
Delaware (riv.) D3
Delaware Water Gap Nat'l Rec.
Area C1
Earle Naval Weapons Sta. E3
Echo (lake) E1
Edison Nat'l Hist. Site A2
Egg Island (pt.) C5
Fort Dix 14,297 .... D3
Fort Hancock F3
Fort Monmouth E3
Gateway Nat'l Rec. Area E2
Great (bay) E4
Great Egg Harbor (inlet) E5
Greenwood (lake) E1
Hackensack (riv.) C1
Hereford (inlet) D5
High Point (mt.) D1
Hopatcong (lake) D2
Hudson (riv.) C1
Island (beach) E4
Kill Van Kull (str.) B2
Kittatinny (mts.) D1
Lakehurst Naval Air Engineering
Center E3
Lamington (riv.) D2
Landing (creek) D4
Little Egg (harb.) E4
Lockatong (creek) C3
Long (beach) E4
Long Beach (isl.) E4
Lower New York (bay) E2
Manasquan (riv.) E3
Manumuskin (riv.) D5
Maurice (riv.) C4
May (cape) C6
McGuire A.F.B. 7,853 .... D3
Metedeconk (riv.) E3
Mill (creek) E4
Millstone (riv.) D3
Mohawk (lake) D1
Morristown Nat'l Hist. Park D2
Mullica (riv.) D4
Musconetcong (riv.) C2
Navesink (riv.) E3
Newark (bay) B2
Oak Ridge (res.) D1
Oldmans (creek) C4
Oradell (res.) B1
Oswego (riv.) E4
Owassa (lake) D1
Palisades C1
Passaic (riv.) E2
Paulins Kill (riv.) D1
Pennsauken (creek) B3
Pequest (riv.) D2
Picatinny Arsenal D2
Pohatcong (creek) C2
Pompton (lake) B1
Raccoon (creek) C4
Ramapo (riv.) E1
Rancocas (creek) D3
Raritan (bay) E3
Raritan (riv.) D2
Ridgeway Branch, Toms (riv.) E3
Round Valley (res.) D2
Saddle (riv.) B1
Salem (riv.) C4
Sandy Hook (spit) F3
Shoal Branch, Wading (riv.) D4
Spruce Run (res.) D2
Statue of Liberty Nat'l Mon. B2
Stony (brook) D3
Stow (creek) C5
Swartswood (lake) D1
Tappan (lake) C1
The Narrows (str.) E2
Toms (riv.) E3
Townsend (inlet) D5
Tuckahoe (riv.) D5
Union (lake) C5
Upper New York (bay) B2
Wading (riv.) D4
Wallkill (riv.) D1
Wanaque (res.) E1
Wawayanda (lake) E1

⊙County seat.
‡Population of metropolitan area.
○Population of town or township.
† Zip of nearest p.o. * Multiple zips.

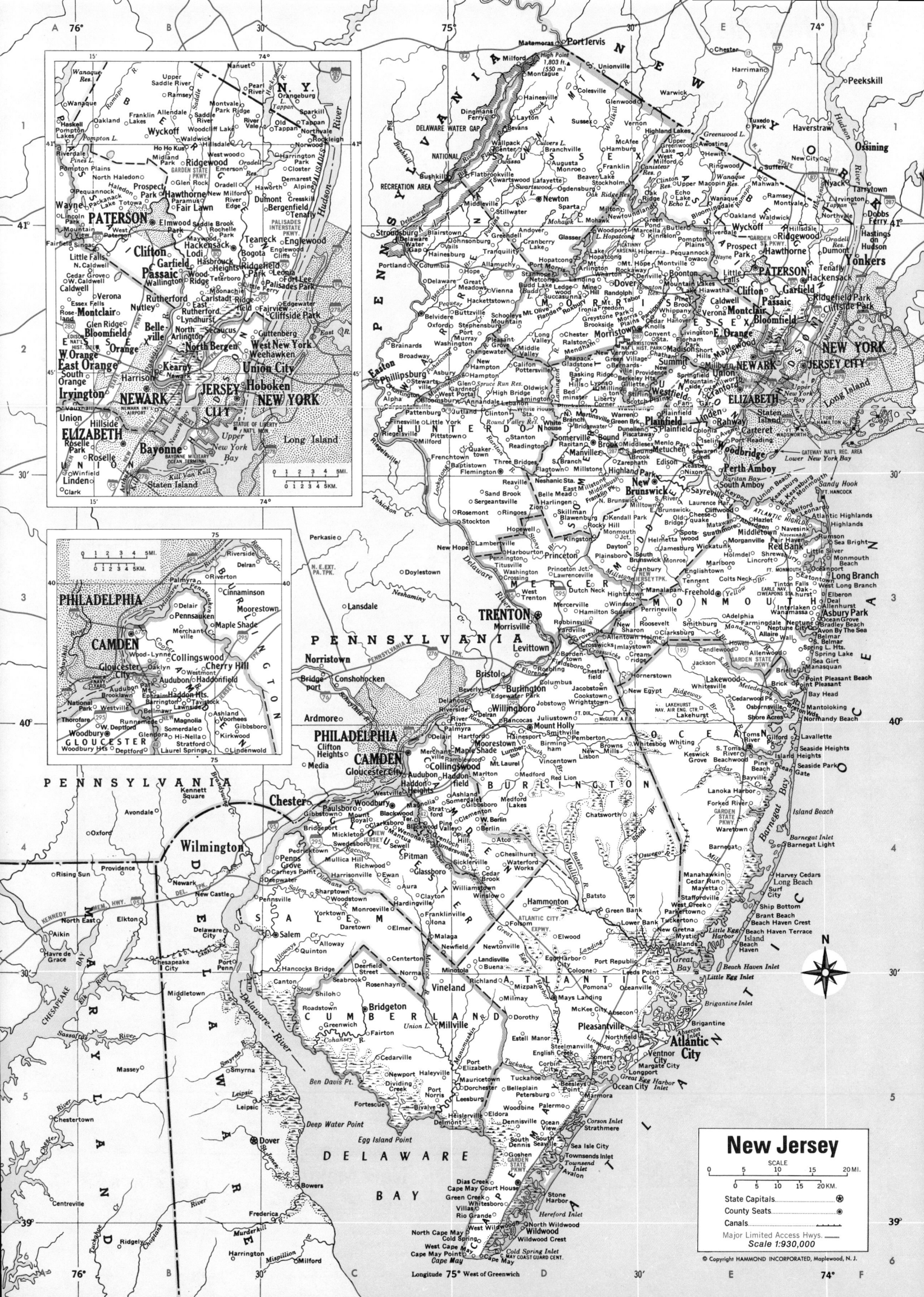

New Jersey

SCALE

0   5   10   15   20 MI.

0   5   10   15   20 KM.

State Capitals .... ⊛

County Seats .... ◉

Canals ....

Major Limited Access Hwys. _____

Scale 1:930,000

© Copyright HAMMOND INCORPORATED, Maplewood, N.J.

Longitude 75° West of Greenwich

COUNTIES

County	Pop.	Key
Bernalillo	419,700	C4
Catron	2,720	A4
Chaves	51,103	E5
Cibola		B3
Colfax	13,667	E2
Curry	42,019	F4
De Baca	2,454	E4
Dona Ana	96,340	C6
Eddy	47,855	E6
Grant	26,204	A5
Guadalupe	4,496	E4
Harding	1,090	F3
Hidalgo	6,049	A7
Lea	55,993	F6
Lincoln	10,997	D5
Los Alamos	17,599	C3
Luna	15,585	B6
McKinley	56,449	A3
Mora	4,205	E3
Otero	44,665	D6
Quay	10,577	F3
Rio Arriba	29,282	B2
Roosevelt	15,695	F4
Sandoval	34,799	C3
San Juan	81,433	A2
San Miguel	22,751	D3
Santa Fe	75,360	C3
Sierra	8,454	B5
Socorro	12,566	C5
Taos	19,456	D2
Torrance	7,491	D4
Union	4,725	F2
Valencia	61,115	C4

CITIES and TOWNS

Zip	Name/Pop.	Key
87510	Abiquiu 500	C2
†87034	Acoma 150	B4
†87034	Acomita (Pueblo of Acoma) 975	B4
88310	Alamogordo⊙ 24,024	C6
*87101	Albuquerque⊙ 331,767	C3
	Albuquerque‡ 454,499	C3
87511	Alcalde 975	C2
87001	Algodones 195	C3
88312	Alto 285	D5
87512	Amalia 200	D2
88021	Anthony 3,285	C6
87711	Anton Chico 400	D3
87930	Arrey 367	B6
87513	Arroyo Hondo 400	D2
87514	Arroyo Seco 500	D2
88210	Artesia 10,385	E6
87410	Aztec⊙ 5,512	B2
88023	Bayard 3,036	A6
87002	Belen 5,617	C4
88314	Bent 294	D5
88024	Berino 600	C6
87004	Bernalillo⊙ 3,012	C3
87412	Blanco 200	B2
87413	Bloomfield 4,881	A2
87005	Bluewater 300	A3
87006	Bosque (Bosque Farms) 3,353	C4
87712	Buena Vista 178	D3
87515	Canjilon 380	C2
87516	Canones 300	C2
88316	Capitan 762	D5
88414	Capulin 100	F2
88220	Carlsbad⊙ 25,496	E6
88301	Carrizozo⊙ 1,222	D5
87007	Casa Blanca 560	B4
88113	Causey 81	F5
87518	Cebolla 100	C2
87008	Cedar Crest 600	C3
88314	Cedar Hill 145	B2
†87410	Cedar Hill 145	B2
88026	Central 1,968	A6
87010	Cerrillos 500	D3
87519	Cerro 400	D2
87713	Chacon 310	D2
87520	Chama 1,090	C2
88027	Chamberino 700	C6
87521	Chamisal 642	D2
87522	Chimayo 1,993	D3
87714	Cimarron 888	E2
88415	Clayton⊙ 2,968	F2
87715	Cleveland 450	D2
88028	Cliff 600	A6
88317	Cloudcroft 521	D6
88101	Clovis⊙ 31,194	F4
†87041	Cochiti 983	C3
88029	Columbus 414	B7
88416	Conchas Dam 240	E3
87523	Cordova 750	D2
88318	Corona 236	D4
87048	Corrales 2,791	C3
87524	Costilla 400	D2
87313	Crownpoint 1,134	A3
†86504	Crystal 200	A2
87013	Cuba 609	B3
87014	Cubero '300	B3
87821	Datil 150	A5
88030	Deming⊙ 9,964	B6
87933	Derry 175	B6
88418	Des Moines 178	F2
88230	Dexter 882	E5
87527	Dixon 800	D2
88032	Dona Ana 800	C6

New Mexico map. Scale 1:2,910,000. © Copyright HAMMOND INCORPORATED, Maplewood, N.J.

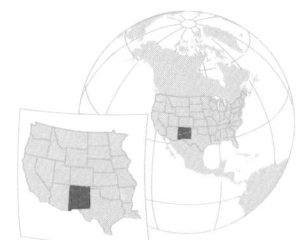

88115 Dora 168 ....F5	87031 Los Lunas⊙ 3,525 ....C4	†87001 San Felipe Pueblo 1,465.....C3
87528 Dulce 1,648 ....B2	†87101 Los Ranchos De	†87501 San Ildefonso 232 ....C3
87718 Eagle Nest 202 ....D2	Albuquerque 2,702......C3	88434 San Jon 341 ....F3
88116 Elida 202 ....F5	88256 Loving 1,355 ....E6	87565 San Jose 150 ....D3
87529 El Prado 200 ....D2	88260 Lovington⊙ 9,727 ....F6	87566 San Juan Pueblo 870 ......C2
87530 El Rito 475 ....C2	87547 Lumberton 175 ....C2	88041 San Lorenzo 200 ....B6
87531 Embudo 400 ....C2	87824 Luna 200 ....A5	87050 San Mateo 200 ....B3
88321 Encino 155 ....D4	87825 Magdalena 1,022 ....B4	88058 San Miguel 400 ....C6
87532 Espanola 6,803 ....C3	88263 Malaga 300 ....E6	88348 San Patricio 300 ....D5
87016 Estancia⊙ 830 ....D4	87728 Maxwell 316 ....E2	87051 San Rafael 300 ....A3
88231 Eunice 2,970 ....F6	88339 Mayhill 300 ....D6	87567 Santa Cruz 754 ....D2
88033 Fairacres 700 ....C6	87401 Farmington 31,222 ....A2	87319 Mentmore 315 ....A3	87501 Santa Fe (cap.)⊙ 48,953...C3
87401 Farmington 31,222 ....A2	88340 Mescalero 1,259 ....D5	†88041 Santa Rita 600 ....B6
†88041 Fierro 200 ....A6	88046 Mesilla 2,029 ....C6	88435 Santa Rosa⊙ 2,469 ....E4
87415 Flora Vista 500 ....A2	88047 Mesilla Park C6	87052 Santo Domingo
88118 Floyd 146 ....F4	88048 Mesquite 500 ....C6	Pueblo 2,082.............C3
88419 Folsom 73 ....F2	87320 Mexican Springs 150 ......A3	87053 San Ysidro 199 ....C3
88036 Fort Bayard 400 ....A6	87729 Miami 112 ....E2	87745 Sapello 600 ....D3
88323 Fort Stanton 80 ....D5	87021 Milan 3,747 ....B3	87055 Seboyeta 125 ....B3
88119 Fort Sumner⊙ 1,421 ....E4	88049 Mimbres 300 ....B6	87568 Sena 150 ....D3
87316 Fort Wingate 800 ....A3	87731 Montezuma 250 ....D3	87569 Serafina 225 ....D3
87416 Fruitland 800 ....A2	87939 Monticello 125 ....B5	87420 Shiprock 7,237 ....A2
†87540 Galisteo 125 ....D3	88265 Monument 300 ....F6	88061 Silver City⊙ 9,887 ....A6
87017 Gallina 420 ....C2	87732 Mora⊙ D3	87801 Socorro⊙ 7,173 ....C4
87301 Gallup⊙ 18,167 ....A3	87035 Moriarty 1,276 ....D4	†87565 Soham 104................D3
87317 Gamerco 800 ....A3	87733 Mosquero⊙ 197 ....F3	87747 Springer 1,657 ....E2
87936 Garfield 600 ....B6	87036 Mountainair 1,170 ....C4	87057 Tajique 145 ....C4
88038 Gila 350 ....A6	†87501 Nambe 1,017 ....D3	87571 Taos⊙ 3,369 ....D2
88324 Glencoe 125 ....D5	88430 Nara Visa 250 ....F3	†87571 Taos Pueblo 900 ....D2
88039 Glenwood 220 ....A5	87328 Navajo 920 ....A3	88267 Tatum 896 ....F5
87535 Glorieta 300 ....D3	†87325 Newcomb 500 ....A2	87574 Tesuque 1,014 ....D3
88120 Grady 122 ....F4	87038 New Laguna 250 ....B4	88135 Texico 958 ....F4
87020 Grants 11,439 ....B3	88266 Oil Center 236 ....F6	87323 Thoreau 1,099 ....A3
88424 Grenville 39 ....F2	87549 Ojo Caliente 600 ....D2	87575 Tierra Amarilla⊙ 850 .....D2
87722 Guadalupita 300 ....D2	88735 Ojo Feliz 133 ....E2	87059 Tijeras 311 ....C3
88232 Hagerman 936 ....E5	88550 Ojo Sarco 380 ....D2	87324 Toadlena 200 ....A2
88041 Hanover 300 ....A6	88052 Organ 300 ....C6	87325 Tohatchi 1,011 ....A3
87937 Hatch 1,028 ....B6	88040 Paguate 500 ....B3	87060 Tome 500 ....C4
87537 Hernandez 500 ....C2	87552 Pecos 885 ....D3	87577 Tres Piedras 200 ....D2
88325 High Rolls-Mountain	87041 Pena Blanca 700 ....C3	87578 Truchas 275 ....D2
Park 555 ....D5	87553 Penasco 860 ....D2	†87701 Trujillo 148 ....E3
88042 Hillsboro 175 ....B6	87042 Peralta 400 ....C4	87901 Truth or
88240 Hobbs 29,153 ....F6	88343 Picacho 100 ....D5	Consequences⊙ 5,219..B5
87723 Holman 400 ....D2	88053 Pinos Altos 250 ....A6	88401 Tucumcari⊙ 6,765 ....F3
88336 Hondo 425 ....D5	87044 Ponderosa 300 ....C3	88352 Tularosa 2,536 ....C5
88250 Hope 111 ....E6	88130 Portales⊙ 9,940 ....F4	88003 University Park 4,353 .....C6
87901 Hot Springs (Truth or	87045 Prewitt 300 ....A3	87579 Vadito 400 ....D2
Consequences)⊙ 5,219.B5	88432 Puerto de Luna 175 ....E4	88072 Vado 325 ....C6
88121 House 117 ....F4	87829 Quemado 450 ....A4	87580 Valdez 300 ....D2
88043 Hurley 1,616 ....A6	87556 Questa 1,202 ....D2	†87031 Valencia 500 ....C4
87022 Isleta 1,246 ....C4	88054 Radium Springs 150 ....B6	87581 Vallecitos 450 ....C2
87252 Jal 2,675 ....F6	87736 Rainsville 350 ....D3	88073 Vanadium 150 ....A6
87023 Jarales 700 ....C4	87321 Ramah 574 ....A3	88353 Vaughn 737 ....D4
87024 Jemez Pueblo 1,503 ....C3	87557 Ranches of Taos 1,411.....D2	87582 Velarde 950 ....D2
87025 Jemez Springs 316 ....C3	87740 Raton⊙ 8,225 ....E2	87583 Villanueva 500 ....D3
87417 Kirtland 2,358 ....A2	87558 Red River 332 ....D2	†88055 Virden 246 ....A6
87026 Laguna 900 ....B3	87322 Rehoboth 200 ....A3	87752 Wagon Mound 416 ....E2
87027 La Jara 210 ....B2	87830 Reserve⊙ 439 ....A5	87421 Waterflow 475 ....A2
88253 Lake Arthur 327 ....E5	87560 Ribera 84 ....D3	87753 Watrous 175 ....D3
88337 La Luz 1,194 ....C6	87940 Rincon 300 ....C6	87544 White Rock 6,560 ....C3
87539 La Madera 200 ....C2	87124 Rio Rancho 9,985 ....C3	88002 White Sands Missile
88044 La Mesa 900 ....C6	87561 Rodarte 650 ....D2	Range 3,120 ....C6
87418 La Plata 150 ....A2	88201 Roswell⊙ 39,676 ....E5	87063 Willard 166 ....D4
88001 Las Cruces⊙ 45,086 ....C6	87562 Rowe 290 ....D3	87942 Williamsburg 433 ....B5
Las Cruces‡ 96,340 ......C6	87743 Roy 381 ....E3	88136 Yeso 200 ....E4
87701 Las Vegas⊙ 14,322 ....D3	88345 Ruidoso 4,260 ....D5	87064 Youngsville 125 ....C2
87725 Ledoux 300 ....D3	88346 Ruidoso Downs 949 ....D5	†87053 Zia Pueblo 500 ....C3
87823 Lemitar 800 ....B4	87941 Salem 400 ....B6	87327 Zuni 5,551 ....A3
88338 Lincoln 100 ....D5	87831 San Acacia 286 ....B4	
87543 Llano 325 ....D2	87832 San Antonio 359 ....B5	OTHER FEATURES
88255 Loco Hills 375 ....F6	87564 San Cristobal 350 ....D2	
88426 Logan 735 ....F3	87047 Sandia Park 450 ....C3	Abiquiu (res.) C2
88045 Lordsburg⊙ 3,195 ....A6		Alamosa (riv.) B5
87544 Los Alamos⊙ 11,039.......C3		Animas (riv.) B1

Avalon (res.) E6	Gila Cliff Dwellings Nat'l Mon. A5	Puerco (riv.)...................A3
Aztec Ruins Nat'l Mon. A2	Grouse (mts.) A5	Red Bluff (lake) E7
Baldy (peak) D3	Guadalupe (mts.) D6	Revuelto (creek) F3
Bandelier Nat'l Mon. C3	Hatchet (mts.) A7	Rio Brazos (riv.) C2
Big Burro (mts.) A6	Holloman A.F.B. 7,245 ....C6	Rio Chama (riv.) C2
Black (mt.) A6	Hueco (mts.) D6	Rio Felix (riv.) E5
Black (range) B5	Jemez (riv.) C3	Rio Grande (riv.) C5
Blanco (creek) F4	Jemez Canyon (res.) C3	Rio Hondo (riv.) E5
Bluewater (creek) B4	Jicarilla Ind. Res. B2	Rio Penasco (riv.) E6
Bluewater (creek) D6	Jornada del Muerto (valley) C5	Rio Puerco (riv.) C4
Bluewater (lake) B3	Kirtland A.F.B. C3	Rio Salado (riv.) B4
Boulder (lake) C2	Ladron (mts.) B4	Rocky (mts.) C1
Brazos (peak) C2	La Plata (riv.) A1	Sacramento (mts.) D6
Burford (lake) C2	Largo, Cañon (creek) B2	Salinas Nat'l Mon. C4
Caballo (res.) B6	Las Animas (creek) B5	Salt (creek) E5
Canadian (riv.) F3	Llano Estacado (Staked) (plain)..F5	Salt (lake) F4
Cannon A.F.B. 3,798.............F4	Lucero (lake) C6	San Agustin (plains) B5
Canyon Blanco (creek) D4	Macho, Arroyo del (creek) D5	San Andres (mts.) C6
Capitan (mts.) D5	Magdalena (mts.) B4	San Antonio (peak) C2
Capitan (peak) D5	Manzano (mts.) C4	Sandia (peak) C3
Capulin Mountain Nat'l Mon. E2	Manzano (peak) C4	San Francisco (riv.) A5
Carlsbad Caverns Nat'l Park E6	McMillan (lake) E6	Sangre de Cristo (mts.) D3
Carrizo (creek) F2	Mescalero (ridge) F6	San Jose (riv.) B3
Chaco (mesa) B3	Mescalero (mts.) F5	San Juan (riv.) B2
Chaco (riv.) A2	Mescalero Apache Ind. Res. D5	San Mateo (mts.) B5
Chaco Culture Nat'l Hist. Park ..B2	Mimbres (mts.) B6	Seven Rivers (riv.) E6
Chico Arroyo (creek) B3	Mimbres (riv.) A6	Ship Rock (peak) A2
Chivato (mesa) B3	Mogollon (mts.) A5	Sierra Blanca (peak) C5
Chupadera (mesa) C5	Mogollon Baldy (peak) A5	Staked (Llano Estacado) (plain)..F5
Chuska (mts.) A2	Montosa (mesa) E3	Sumner (lake) E4
Cimarron (riv.) E2	Mora (riv.) E3	Taylor (mt.) B3
Colorado, Arroyo (riv.) B4	Nacimiento (mts.) C3	Tecolote (creek) D3
Compañero, Arroyo (creek) B2	Nacimiento (peak) C2	Tequesquite (creek) E2
Conchas (lake) E3	Navajo (res.) B2	Thompson (peak) D3
Conchas (riv.) E3	Navajo Ind. Res. A2	Tierra Blanca (creek) B6
Cookes (range) B6	North Truchas (peak) D3	Tramperos (creek) F2
Corrumpa (creek) E2	Ocate (creek) E2	Tularosa (valley) C6
Costilla (peak) D2	O'Keeffe Nat'l Hist. Site C2	Ute (creek) F3
Cuchillo Negro (creek) B5	Oscura (mts.) C5	Ute (peak) D2
Cuervo (creek) E3	Osha (peak) C4	Ute (res.) F3
Dark Canyon (creek) E6	Padilla (creek) D5	Ute Mountain Ind. Res. A1
Datil (mts.) B4	Pajarito (creek) A2	Vermejo (riv.) E2
Dry Cimarron (riv.) F2	Pecos (riv.) E5	Wheeler (peak) D2
Eagle Nest (lake) D2	Pecos Nat'l Mon. D3	White Sands (des.) C5
Elephant Butte (res.) B5	Peloncillo (mts.) A6	White Sands Missile Range C5
El Morro Nat'l Mon. A3	Perro (mts.) D4	White Sands Nat'l Mon. C6
El Rito (riv.) C2	Pinos, Rio de los (riv.) B2	Whitewater Baldy (mt.) A5
Fifteenmile Arroyo (creek) D4	Pintada Arroyo (creek) E4	Wingate Army Depot A3
Florida (mts.) B7	Playas (lake) A7	Yeso (creek) E4
Fort Bliss Mil. Res. C6	Potrillo (mts.) B7	Zuni (mts.) A3
Fort Union Nat'l Mon. E3	Pueblo Ind. Res. B4	Zuni (riv.) A3
Gallinas (mts.) B4	Pueblo Ind. Res. D3	Zuni Ind. Res. A3
Gallinas (riv.) E3	Pueblo Ind. Res. C4	⊙County seat.
Gila (riv.) A6	Pueblo Ind. Res. D2	‡Population of metropolitan area.
		† Zip of nearest p.o. * Multiple zips.

AREA 121,593 sq. mi. (314,926 sq. km.)
POPULATION 1,302,981
CAPITAL Santa Fe
LARGEST CITY Albuquerque
HIGHEST POINT Wheeler Pk. 13,161 ft.
(4011 m.)
SETTLED IN 1605
ADMITTED TO UNION January 6, 1912
POPULAR NAME Land of Enchantment
STATE FLOWER Yucca
STATE BIRD Road Runner

Topography

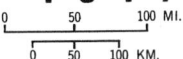

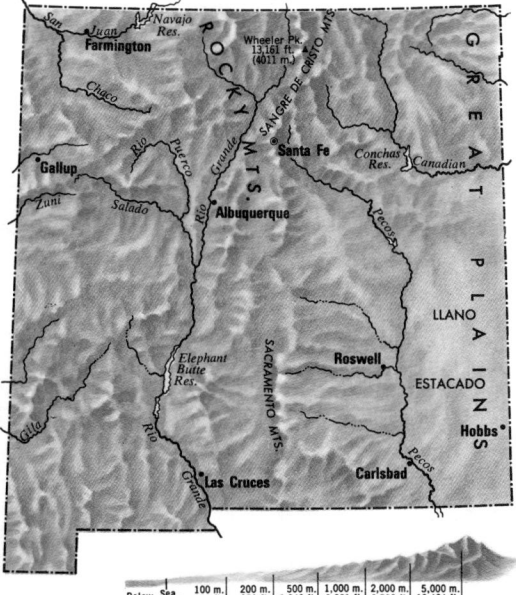

Below Sea Level | 100 m. 328 ft. | 200 m. 656 ft. | 500 m. 1,640 ft. | 1,000 m. 3,281 ft. | 2,000 m. 6,562 ft. | 5,000 m. 16,404 ft.

Agriculture, Industry and Resources

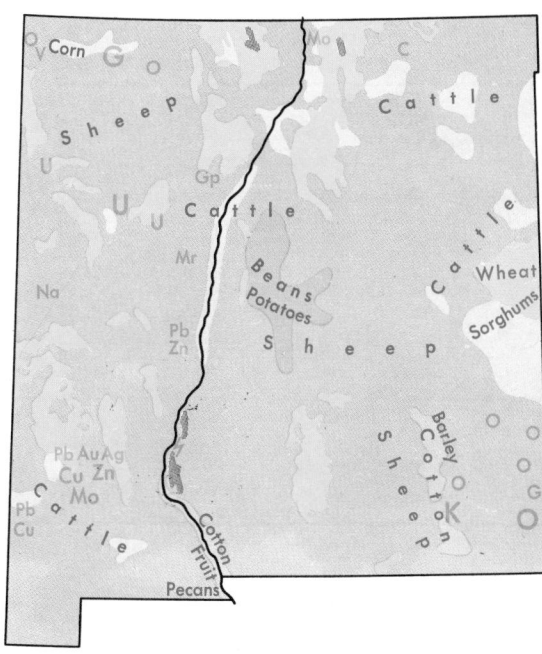

DOMINANT LAND USE

- Wheat, Grain Sorghums, Range Livestock
- General Farming, Livestock, Special Crops
- General Farming, Livestock, Cash Grain
- Dry Beans, General Farming
- Cotton, Forest Products
- Range Livestock
- Forests
- Nonagricultural Land

MAJOR MINERAL OCCURRENCES

Ag	Silver	Gp	Gypsum			
Au	Gold	K	Potash			
C	Coal	Mo	Molybdenum	O	Petroleum	U Uranium
Cu	Copper	Mr	Marble			V Vanadium
G	Natural Gas	Na	Salt	Pb	Lead	Zn Zinc

U Uranium
V Vanadium
⚡ Water Power

New York

SCALE
0 5 10 20 30 40 MI.
0 5 10 20 30 40 KM.
State Capitals............⊛
County Seats.............◉
Canals...................
Major Limited Access Hwys. ____
Scale 1:1,920,000

COUNTIES

Albany 285,909	M5	
Allegany 51,742	D6	
Bronx 1,168,972	N9	
Broome 213,648	J6	
Cattaraugus 85,697	C6	
Cayuga 79,894	G4	
Chautauqua 146,925	B6	
Chemung 97,656	G6	
Chenango 49,344	J6	
Clinton 80,750	N1	
Columbia 59,487	N6	
Cortland 48,820	H5	
Delaware 46,824	K6	
Dutchess 245,055	N7	
Erie 1,015,472	C5	
Essex 36,176	N2	
Franklin 44,929	M1	
Fulton 55,153	M4	
Genesee 59,400	D4	
Greene 40,861	M6	
Hamilton 5,034	L3	
Herkimer 66,714	L4	
Jefferson 88,151	J2	
Kings 2,230,936	N9	
Lewis 25,035	K3	
Livingston 57,006	E5	
Madison 65,150	J5	
Monroe 702,238	E4	
Montgomery 53,439	M5	
Nassau 1,321,582	N9	
New York 1,428,285	M9	
Niagara 227,354	C4	
Oneida 253,466	K4	
Onondaga 463,920	H5	
Ontario 88,909	F5	

Orange 259,603	M8	
Orleans 38,496	D4	
Oswego 113,901	H4	
Otsego 59,075	K5	
Putnam 77,193	N8	
Queens 1,891,325	N9	
Rensselaer 151,966	O5	
Richmond 352,121	M9	
Rockland 259,530	M8	
Saint Lawrence 114,254	K2	
Saratoga 153,759	N4	
Schenectady 149,946	M5	
Schoharie 29,710	M5	
Schuyler 17,686	G6	
Seneca 33,733	G5	
Steuben 99,217	F6	
Suffolk 1,284,231	P9	
Sullivan 65,155	L7	
Tioga 49,812	H6	
Tompkins 87,085	H6	
Ulster 158,158	M7	
Warren 54,854	N3	
Washington 54,795	O4	
Wayne 84,581	F4	
Westchester 866,599	N8	
Wyoming 39,895	D5	
Yates 21,459	F5	

CITIES and TOWNS

Zip	Name/Pop.	Key
13605	Adams 1,701	J3
14801	Addison 2,028	F6
14001	Akron 2,971	C4
*12201	Albany (cap.) ⊛ 101,727	N5
	Albany-Schenectady-Troy‡	
	795,019	N5
14411	Albion ◉ 4,897	D4
14004	Alden 2,488	C5
13607	Alexandria Bay 1,265	J2
14802	Alfred 4,967	E6
14706	Allegany 2,078	C6
12009	Altamont 1,292	M5
11930	Amagansett 2,188	R9
11701	Amityville 9,076	O9
12010	Amsterdam 21,872	M5
14006	Angola 2,292	C5
14009	Arcade 2,052	D5
10502	Ardsley 4,183	O6
12603	Arlington 11,305	N7
12015	Athens 1,738	N6
11509	Atlantic Beach 1,775	P7
14011	Attica 2,659	D5
13021	Auburn ◉ 32,548	G5
13026	Aurora 926	G5
12018	Averill Park 1,337	O5
14516	Avon 3,006	E5
*11702	Babylon 12,388	O9
13733	Bainbridge 1,603	J6
11510	Baldwin 31,630	R7
13027	Baldwinsville 6,446	H4
12020	Ballston Spa ◉ 4,711	N5
12550	Balmville 2,919	M7
14020	Batavia ◉ 16,703	D5
14810	Bath ◉ 6,042	F6
11705	Bayport 9,282	O9
11706	Bay Shore 10,784	O9
11709	Bayville 7,034	R6
12508	Beacon 12,937	N7
11710	Bellmore 18,106	R7
11713	Bethpage 2,809	P9
14813	Belmont ◉ 1,024	E6
11714	Bethpage 16,840	R7
14814	Big Flats 2,892	G6
*13901	Binghamton ◉ 55,860	J6
	Binghamton‡ 301,336	J6

13612	Black River 1,384	J3
14219	Blasdell 3,288	C5
14715	Bolivar 1,345	D6
13309	Boonville 2,344	K4
13613	Brasher	
	Falls-Winthrop 1,454	L1
11717	Brentwood 44,321	O9
13029	Brewerton 2,472	H4
10509	Brewster 1,650	N8
11932	Bridgehampton 1,941	R9
†12524	Brinckerhoff 3,030	N7
12025	Broadalbin 1,415	M4
14420	Brockport 9,776	D4
14716	Brocton 1,416	B6
*10401	Bronx	
	(borough) 1,168,972	N9
10708	Bronxville 6,267	O7
*11201	Brooklyn	
	(borough) 2,230,936	N9
†11545	Brookville 3,290	R6
10511	Buchanan 2,041	N8
*14201	Buffalo ◉ 357,870	B5
	Buffalo‡ 1,242,573	B5
12413	Cairo 1,281	M6
14423	Caledonia 2,188	E5
12816	Cambridge 1,820	O4
13316	Camden 2,667	J4
13031	Camillus 1,298	H4
13317	Canajoharie 2,412	L5
14424	Canandaigua ◉ 10,419	F5
13032	Canastota 4,773	J4
14823	Canisteo 2,679	E6
13617	Canton ◉ 7,055	K1
10512	Carmel ◉ 27,948	N8
13619	Carthage 3,643	J3
12033	Castleton-on-Hudson 1,627	N5
12414	Catskill ◉ 4,718	N6
†14850	Cayuga Heights 3,170	H6

13035	Cazenovia 2,599	J5
11516	Cedarhurst 6,162	P7
14720	Celoron 1,405	B6
11720	Centereach 30,136	O9
11934	Center Moriches 5,703	P9
11722	Central Islip 19,734	O9
13036	Central Square 1,418	H4
10917	Central Valley 1,705	M8
12919	Champlain 1,410	N1
12037	Chatham 2,001	N6
14225	Cheektowaga 92,145	C5
10918	Chester 1,910	M8
13037	Chittenango 4,290	J4
14428	Churchville 1,399	E4
14031	Clarence 18,146	C5
13624	Clayton 1,816	H2
†12118	Clifton Park 23,989	N5
14432	Clifton Springs 2,039	F4
13323	Clinton 2,107	K4
14433	Clyde 2,491	G4
12043	Cobleskill 5,272	L5
12047	Cohoes 18,144	N5
10516	Cold Spring 2,161	N8
11724	Cold Spring Harbor 5,336	R6
*12201	Colonie 8,869	N5
11725	Commack 34,719	O9
13326	Cooperstown ◉ 2,342	L5
11726	Copiague 20,132	O9
12822	Corinth 2,702	N4
14830	Corning 12,953	F6
12518	Cornwall On Hudson 3,164	M8
13045	Cortland ◉ 20,138	H5
12051	Coxsackie 2,786	N6
10520	Croton-on-Hudson 6,889	N8
14727	Cuba 1,739	D6
11935	Cutchogue-New	
	Suffolk 2,788	P8
12929	Dannemora 3,770	N1

AREA 49,108 sq. mi. (127,190 sq. km.)
POPULATION 17,558,072
CAPITAL Albany
LARGEST CITY New York
HIGHEST POINT Mt. Marcy 5,344 ft. (1629 m.)
SETTLED IN 1614
ADMITTED TO UNION July 26, 1788
POPULAR NAME Empire State
STATE FLOWER Rose
STATE BIRD Bluebird

Topography

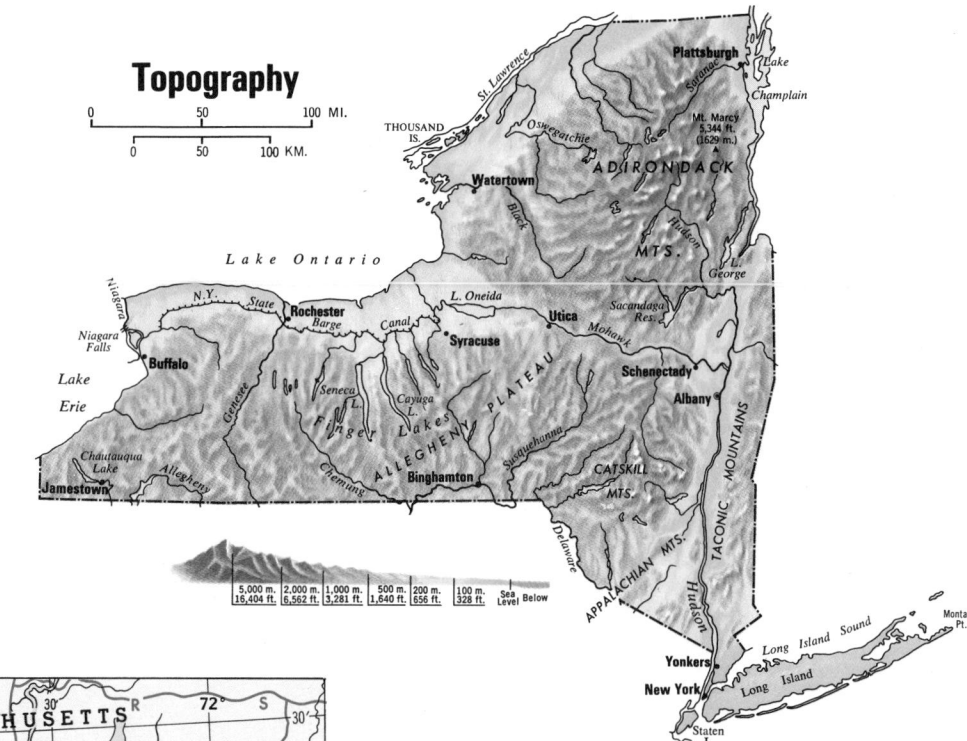

14437 Dansville 4,979	E5
11729 Deer Park 30,394	O9
13753 Delhi⊙ 3,374	L6
12054 Delmar 8,423	N5
14043 Depew 19,819	C5
13754 Deposit 1,897	K6
13214 DeWitt 9,024	H4
11746 Dix Hills 26,693	O9
10522 Dobbs Ferry 10,053	O6
13329 Dolgeville 2,602	L4
12522 Dover Plains 1,753	O7
14837 Dundee 1,556	F5
14048 Dunkirk 15,310	B5
14052 East Aurora 6,803	C5
10709 Eastchester 20,305	P6
11937 East Hampton 1,886	R9
11554 East Meadow 39,317	R7
11731 East Northport 20,187	O9
14445 East Rochester 7,596	F4
11518 East Rockaway 10,917	R7
13057 East Syracuse 3,412	H4
14057 Eden 3,000	C5
14058 Elba 750	D4
12932 Elizabethtown⊙ 659	N2
12428 Ellenville 4,405	M7
14059 Elma 2,459	C5
*14901 Elmira⊙ 35,327	G6
Elmira‡ 97,656	G6
14903 Elmira Heights 4,279	G6
11003 Elmont 27,592	P7
10523 Elmsford 3,361	O6
11731 Elwood 11,847	O9
13760 Endicott 14,457	H6
13760 Endwell 13,745	H6
14450 Fairport 5,970	F4
†12601 Fairview 5,852	N7
14733 Falconer 2,778	B6
11735 Farmingdale 7,946	R7
13066 Fayetteville 4,709	J4
†12801 Fernwood 3,640	N4
12524 Fishkill 1,555	N7
†11901 Flanders-Riverside 5,400	P9
*11001 Floral Park 16,805	P7
10921 Florida 1,947	M8
12068 Fonda⊙ 1,006	M5
12937 Fort Covington 1,804	M1
12828 Fort Edward 3,561	O4
13339 Fort Plain 2,555	L5
13340 Frankfort 2,995	K4
11010 Franklin Square 29,051	R7
14737 Franklinville 1,887	D6
14063 Fredonia 11,126	B6
11520 Freeport 38,272	R7
14738 Frewsburg 1,908	B6
14739 Friendship 1,461	D6
13069 Fulton 13,312	H4
11530 Garden City 22,927	R7
14067 Gasport 1,339	C4
14454 Geneseo⊙ 6,746	E5
14456 Geneva 15,133	G5
11542 Glen Cove 24,618	R6
12801 Glens Falls 15,897	N4
Glens Falls‡ 109,649	N4
12078 Gloversville 17,836	M4
10526 Golden's Bridge 1,367	N8
10924 Goshen⊙ 4,874	M8
13642 Gouverneur 4,285	K2
14070 Gowanda 2,713	B6
12832 Granville 2,696	O4
*11020 Great Neck 9,168	P6
14616 Greece 16,177	E4
13778 Greene 1,747	J6
12183 Green Island 2,696	N5
11944 Greenport 2,273	P8
12834 Greenwich 1,955	O4
10925 Greenwood Lake 2,809	M8
13073 Groton 2,313	H5
12835 Hadley-Lake Luzerne 1,988	N4
12086 Hagaman 1,331	M5
14075 Hamburg 10,582	C5
13346 Hamilton 3,725	J5
11946 Hampton Bays 7,256	R9
13783 Hancock 1,526	K7
10528 Harrison 23,046	P6
10530 Hartsdale 10,216	P6
10706 Hastings On Hudson 8,573	O6
11787 Hauppauge 20,960	O9
10927 Haverstraw 8,800	M8
10532 Hawthorne 5,010	O6
*11550 Hempstead 40,404	R7
13350 Herkimer⊙ 8,383	L4
11557 Hewlett 6,986	P7
†11557 Hewlett Harbor 1,331	P7
*11801 Hicksville 43,245	R7
12528 Highland 3,967	M7
10928 Highland Falls 4,187	M8
10931 Hillburn 926	M8
10977 Hillcrest 5,733	K8
14468 Hilton 4,151	E4
14080 Holland 1,347	C5
14470 Holley 1,882	D4
13077 Homer 3,635	H5
14472 Honeoye Falls 2,410	F5
12090 Hoosick Falls 3,609	O5
12533 Hopewell Junction 1,754	N7
14843 Hornell 10,234	E6
14845 Horseheads 7,348	G6
14744 Houghton 1,604	D6
12534 Hudson⊙ 7,986	N6
12839 Hudson Falls⊙ 7,419	O4
11743 Huntington 21,727	R6
11746 Huntington Station 28,769	R6
12443 Hurley 4,892	M7
12538 Hyde Park 2,550	N6
13357 Ilion 9,450	K5
11696 Inwood 8,228	P7
14617 Irondequoit 57,648	E4
10533 Irvington 5,774	O6
11558 Island Park 4,847	R7

(continued on following page)

© Copyright HAMMOND INCORPORATED, Maplewood, N.J.

11751 Islip 13,438 .... O9
14850 Ithaca⊙ 28,732 .... G6
*11401 Jamaica⊙ N9
14701 Jamestown 35,775 .... B6
11753 Jericho 12,739 .... R6
13790 Johnson City 17,126 .... J6
12095 Johnstown⊙ 9,360 .... M4
13080 Jordan 1,371 .... H4
12944 Keeseville 2,025 .... O2
14271 Kenmore 18,474 .... C5
12446 Kerhonkson 1,646 .... M7
12106 Kinderhook 1,377 .... N6
11754 Kings Park 16,131 .... O9
11024 Kings Point 5,234 .... P6
12401 Kingston⊙ 24,481 .... M7
14218 Lackawanna 22,701 .... B5
10512 Lake Carmel 7,295 .... N8
†14006 Lake Erie Beach 4,625 .... B5
12845 Lake George⊙ 1,047 .... N4
12449 Lake Katrine 2,011 .... M7
12846 Lake Luzerne-Hadley 1,988 N4
12946 Lake Placid 2,490 .... N2
12108 Lake Pleasant⊙ 700 .... M4
11040 Lake Success 2,396 .... P7
14750 Lakewood 3,941 .... B6
14086 Lancaster 13,056 .... C5
14882 Lansing 3,039 .... H5
10538 Larchmont 6,308 .... P7
12110 Latham 11,182 .... N5
†11560 Lattingtown 1,749 .... R6
11559 Lawrence 6,175 .... P7
14482 Le Roy 4,900 .... E5
11756 Levittown 57,045 .... R7
14092 Lewiston 3,326 .... B4
12754 Liberty 4,293 .... L7
14485 Lima 2,025 .... E5
11757 Lindenhurst 26,919 .... O9
13365 Little Falls 6,156 .... L4
14755 Little Valley⊙ 1,203 .... C6
13088 Liverpool 2,849 .... H4
12758 Livingston Manor 1,436 .... L7
†11743 Lloyd Harbor 3,405 .... R6
14094 Lockport⊙ 24,844 .... C4
†11791 Locust Grove 9,670 .... R6
11561 Long Beach 34,073 .... R7
13367 Lowville⊙ 3,364 .... J3
11563 Lynbrook 20,424 .... P7
14489 Lyons⊙ 4,160 .... F4
14502 Macedon 1,400 .... F4
10541 Mahopac 7,681 .... N8
12953 Malone⊙ 7,668 .... M1
11565 Malverne 9,262 .... R7
10543 Mamaroneck 17,616 .... P7
14504 Manchester 1,698 .... F5
11030 Manhasset 8,485 .... P7
*10001 Manhattan
(borough) 1,428,285 ... M9
13404 Manlius 5,241 .... J5
13108 Marcellus 1,870 .... H5
12542 Marlboro 2,275 .... M7
11758 Massapequa 24,454 .... R7
11762 Massapequa Park 19,779 .. R7
13662 Massena 12,851 .... L1
11950 Mastic Beach 8,318 .... P9
11952 Mattituck 3,923 .... P9
12543 Maybrook 2,007 .... M8
14757 Mayville⊙ 1,626 .... A6
12118 Mechanicville 5,500 .... N5
14103 Medina 6,392 .... D4
†13021 Melrose Park 2,171 .... G5
11746 Melville 8,139 .... O9
†12201 Menands 4,012 .... N5
11566 Merrick 24,478 .... R7
13114 Mexico 1,621 .... H4
12122 Middleburgh 1,358 .... M5
12550 Middle Hope 3,229 .... M7
14105 Middleport 1,995 .... C4
10940 Middletown 21,454 .... L8
†12020 Milton 2,063 .... N4
11501 Mineola⊙ 20,757 .... R7
13115 Minetto 1,629 .... H4
12956 Mineville-Witherbee 1,925 .. O2
13116 Minoa 3,640 .... H4
13407 Mohawk 2,956 .... L4
10950 Monroe 5,996 .... M8
10952 Monsey 12,380 .... J8
12549 Montgomery 2,316 .... M7
12701 Monticello⊙ 6,306 .... L7
14865 Montour Falls 1,791 .... G6
13118 Moravia 1,582 .... H5
12962 Morrisonville 1,721 .... N1
13408 Morrisville 2,707 .... J5
10549 Mount Kisco 8,025 .... N8
14510 Mount Morris 3,039 .... E5
*10550 Mount Vernon 66,713 .... O7
10954 Nanuet 12,578 .... K8
12123 Nassau 1,285 .... N5
Nassau-Suffolk‡ 2,605,813 R7
14513 Newark 10,017 .... G4
13411 New Berlin 1,392 .... K5
12550 Newburgh 23,438 .... M7
Newburgh-Middletown‡
259,603 .... M7
10956 New City⊙ 35,859 .... K8
14108 Newfane 3,120 .... C4
13413 New Hartford 2,313 .... K4
11040 New Hyde Park 9,801 .... P7
12561 New Paltz 4,938 .... M7
*10801 New Rochelle 70,794 .... P7
†10901 New Square 1,750 .... K8
12550 New Windsor 7,812 .... N8
*10001 New York⊙ 7,071,639 .... M9
New York‡ 9,119,737 .... M9
13417 New York Mills 3,549 .... K4
*14301 Niagara Falls 71,384 .... C4
†12301 Niskayuna 5,223 .... N5
13667 Norfolk 1,599 .... K1
14110 North Boston 2,743 .... C5
14111 North Collins 1,496 .... C5
11768 Northport 7,651 .... O9
13212 North Syracuse 7,970 .... H4
10591 North Tarrytown 7,994 .... O6
14120 North Tonawanda 35,760 .. C4
12134 Northville 1,304 .... M4
13815 Norwich⊙ 8,082 .... J5
13668 Norwood 1,902 .... L1
10960 Nyack 6,428 .... K8

14125 Oakfield 1,791 .... D4
11572 Oceanside 33,639 .... R7
13669 Ogdensburg 12,375 .... K1
14126 Olcott 1,571 .... C4
14760 Olean 18,207 .... D6
13421 Oneida 10,810 .... J4
13820 Oneonta 14,933 .... K6
14127 Orchard Park 3,671 .... C5
13424 Oriskany 1,680 .... K4
10562 Ossining 20,196 .... N8
13126 Oswego⊙ 19,793 .... G4
14521 Ovid⊙ 666 .... G5
13827 Owego⊙ 4,364 .... H6
13830 Oxford 1,765 .... J6
11771 Oyster Bay 6,497 .... R6
14870 Painted Post 2,196 .... F6
14522 Palmyra 3,729 .... F4
11772 Patchogue 11,291 .... P9
12564 Pawling 1,996 .... N7
10965 Pearl River 15,893 .... K8
10566 Peekskill 18,236 .... N8
10803 Pelham 6,848 .... O7
†10803 Pelham Manor 6,130 .... O7
14527 Penn Yan⊙ 5,242 .... F5
14530 Perry 4,198 .... D5
12972 Peru 1,716 .... N1
14532 Phelps 2,004 .... F5
12565 Philmont 1,539 .... N6
13135 Phoenix 2,357 .... H4
10968 Piermont 2,269 .... K8
12567 Pine Plains 1,303 .... N7
14534 Pittsford 1,568 .... E4
11803 Plainview 28,037 .... R7
12901 Plattsburgh⊙ 21,057 .... O1
10570 Pleasantville 6,749 .... N8
13140 Port Byron 1,400 .... G4
10573 Port Chester 23,565 .... P7
†13901 Port Dickinson 1,974 .... J6
12466 Port Ewen 2,813 .... N7
12974 Port Henry 1,450 .... O2
11777 Port Jefferson 6,731 .... P9
12771 Port Jervis 8,699 .... L8
11050 Port Washington 14,521 ... R6
13676 Potsdam 10,635 .... K1
*12601 Poughkeepsie⊙ 29,757 .... N7
Poughkeepsie‡ 245,055 .... N7
14873 Prattsburg○ 1,657 .... F5
13142 Pulaski 2,415 .... H3
10579 Putnam Valley○ 8,994 .... N8
*11101 Queens (borough)
1,891,325 .... N9
14772 Randolph 1,398 .... C6
14131 Ransomville 1,401 .... C4
12143 Ravena 3,091 .... N6
12571 Red Hook 1,692 .... N7
†12601 Red Oaks Mill 5,236 .... N7
12144 Rensselaer 9,047 .... N5
12572 Rhinebeck 2,542 .... N7
13439 Richfield Springs 1,561 ..... K5
*10301 Richmond (Staten Island)
(borough) 352,121 ..... M9
11901 Riverhead⊙ 6,339 .... P9
*14601 Rochester⊙ 241,741 .... E4
Rochester‡ 971,879 .... E4
*11570 Rockville Centre 25,412 .... R7
13440 Rome 43,826 .... J4
11575 Roosevelt 14,109 .... R7
11576 Roslyn 2,134 .... R6
12979 Rouses Point 2,266 .... O1
10580 Rye 15,083 .... P6
11963 Sag Harbor 2,581 .... R8
11780 Saint James 12,122 .... O9
13452 Saint Johnsville 1,974 .... L5
14779 Salamanca 6,890 .... C6
†13132 Sand Ridge 1,293 .... H4
†11050 Sands Point 2,742 .... P6
12983 Saranac Lake 5,578 .... M2
12866 Saratoga Springs 23,906 ... N4
12477 Saugerties 3,882 .... M6
13146 Savannah○ 1,905 .... G4
11782 Sayville 12,013 .... O9
10583 Scarsdale 17,650 .... P6
*12301 Schenectady⊙ 67,972 .... M5
12157 Schoharie⊙ 1,016 .... M5
12871 Schuylerville 1,256 .... N4
12302 Scotia 7,280 .... N5
14546 Scottsville 1,789 .... E4
11579 Sea Cliff 5,364 .... R6
11783 Seaford 16,117 .... R7
13148 Seneca Falls 7,466 .... G5
13460 Sherburne 1,561 .... K5
13461 Sherrill 2,830 .... J4
14548 Shortsville 1,669 .... F5
13838 Sidney 4,861 .... K6
14136 Silver Creek 3,088 .... B5
13152 Skaneateles 2,789 .... H5
†14201 Sloan 4,529 .... C5
10974 Sloatsburg 3,154 .... M8
11787 Smithtown 30,906 .... O9
14551 Sodus 1,790 .... G4
14555 Sodus Point 1,334 .... G4
13209 Solvay 7,140 .... H4
11968 Southampton 4,000 .... R9
12779 South Fallsburg 2,196 .... L7
†12801 South Glens Falls 3,714 .... N4
†10960 South Nyack 3,602 .... K8
11971 Southold 4,770 .... P8
†14901 Southport 8,329 .... G6
14559 Spencerport 3,424 .... E4
10977 Spring Valley 20,537 .... K8
14141 Springville 4,285 .... C5
*10301 Staten Island
(borough) 352,121 ..... M9
12170 Stillwater 1,572 .... N5
11790 Stony Brook 16,155 .... O9
10980 Stony Point 8,686 .... M8
12172 Stottville 1,387 .... N6
10901 Suffern 10,794 .... J8
11791 Syosset 9,818 .... R6
*13201 Syracuse⊙ 170,105 .... H4
Syracuse‡ 642,375 .... H4
10983 Tappan 8,267 .... K8
10591 Tarrytown 10,648 .... O6
†11020 Thomaston 2,684 .... P7
12883 Ticonderoga 2,938 .... N3
12486 Tillson 1,529 .... M7
14150 Tonawanda 18,693 .... B4

*12180 Troy⊙ 56,638 .... N5
14886 Trumansburg 1,722 .... G5
10707 Tuckahoe 6,076 .... O7
12986 Tupper Lake 4,478 .... M2
13849 Unadilla 1,367 .... K6
11553 Uniondale 20,016 .... R7
*13501 Utica⊙ 75,632 .... K4
Utica-Rome‡ 320,180 .... K4
12184 Valatie 1,492 .... N6
10989 Valley Cottage 8,214 .... K8
*11580 Valley Stream 35,769 .... P7
13850 Vestal○ 27,238 .... H6
14564 Victor 2,370 .... F5
†10901 Viola 5,340 .... J8
12186 Voorheesville 3,320 .... M5
12586 Walden 5,659 .... M7
12589 Wallkill 2,064 .... M7
13856 Walton 3,329 .... K6
13163 Wampsville⊙ 569 .... J4
11793 Wantagh 19,817 .... R7
12590 Wappingers Falls 5,110 ..... N7
12885 Warrensburg 2,834 .... N3
14569 Warsaw⊙ 3,619 .... D5
10990 Warwick 4,320 .... M8
10992 Washingtonville 2,380 ..... M8
12188 Waterford 2,405 .... N5
13165 Waterloo⊙ 5,303 .... G5
13601 Watertown⊙ 27,861 .... J3
13480 Waterville 1,672 .... K5
12189 Watervliet 11,354 .... N5
14891 Watkins Glen⊙ 2,440 .... G6
14892 Waverly 4,738 .... G7
14572 Wayland 1,846 .... E5
14580 Webster 5,499 .... F4
13166 Weedsport 1,952 .... G4
14895 Wellsville 5,769 .... E6
11590 Westbury 13,871 .... R7
†13619 West Carthage 1,824 .... J3
†14901 West Elmira 5,485 .... G6
14787 Westfield 3,446 .... A6
†12801 West Glens Falls 5,331 ..... N4
11977 Westhampton 2,774 .... P9
11978 Westhampton Beach 1,629 P9
12491 West Hurley 2,382 .... M6
10994 West Nyack 8,553 .... K8
14788 Westons Mills 1,837 .... D6
10996 West Point 8,105 .... M8
11796 West Sayville 8,185 .... O9
14224 West Seneca 51,210 .... C5
12887 Whitehall 3,241 .... O3
*10601 White Plains⊙ 46,999 .... P6
13492 Whitesboro 4,460 .... K4
14588 Willard 1,339 .... G5
14589 Williamson 1,768 .... F4
14221 Williamsville 6,017 .... C5
11596 Williston Park 8,216 .... R7
13865 Windsor 1,155 .... J6

13697 Winthrop-Brasher
Falls 1,454 .... L1
12998 Witherbee-Mineville 1,925 .. N2
14590 Wolcott 1,496 .... G4
11598 Woodmere 17,205 .... P7
12498 Woodstock 2,280 .... M6
12790 Wurtsboro 1,128 .... L7
11798 Wyandanch 13,215 .... N9
*10701 Yonkers 195,351 .... O6
10598 Yorktown Heights 7,696 .... N8
13495 Yorkville 3,115 .... K4
14174 Youngstown 2,191 .... C4

OTHER FEATURES

Adirondack (mts.) M3
Algonquin (peak) M2
Allegany Ind. Res. 1,243 .... C6
Allegheny (res.) C7
Allegheny (riv.) C6
Ashokan (res.) M7
Ausable (riv.) N2
Batten Kill (riv.) O4
Beaver (riv.) K3
Big Moose (lake) L3
Black (lake) J1
Black (riv.) K3
Block Island (sound) S8
Blue Mountain (lake) M3
Bonaparte (lake) K2
Brandreth (lake) L3
Brant (lake) N3
Brookhaven Nat'l Lab. P9
Butterfield (lake) J2
Canandaigua (lake) F5
Canisteo (riv.) F6
Cannonsville (res.) K6
Catskill (mts.) L6
Cattaraugus (creek) C6
Cattaraugus Ind. Res. 1,994 .... C5
Cayuga (lake) G5
Champlain (lake) O1
Chateaugay, Upper (lake) M1
Chautauqua (lake) A6
Chazy (lake) N1
Chenango (riv.) J6
Cohocton (riv.) F6
Conesus (lake) E5
Conewango (creek) B6
Cranberry (lake) L2
Deer (riv.) J3
Deer (riv.) L1
Delaware (riv.) K7
East (riv.) N9
Erie (lake) A5
Fire Island Nat'l Seashore P9
Fishers (isl.) S8
Forked (lake) L3
Fort Drum J2
Fort Niagara C4
Fort Stanwix Nat'l Mon. J4
Fulton Chain (lkes) K3
Galloo (isl.) H3
Gardiners (bay) R8
Gardiners (isl.) R8
Gateway Nat'l Rec. Area M9
Genesee (riv.) E5
George (lake) N4
Grand (isl.) B5
Grass (riv.) K1
Great Sacandaga (lake) M4
Great South (bay) O9
Great South (beach) O9
Greenwood (lake) M8
Grenadier (isl.) H2
Griffiss A.F.B. K4
Haystack (mt.) N2
Hemlock (lake) E5
Hinckley (res.) K4
Honeoye (lake) F5
Honnedaga (lake) L3
Hudson (riv.) N7
Hunter (mt.) M6
Indian (lake) M3
Jones (beach) R7
Keuka (lake) F5
Lila (lake) L2
Little Tupper (lake) L2
Long (isl.) P9
Long (lake) M2
Long Island (sound) P9
Manhattan (isl.) M9
Marcy (mt.) N2
Martin Van Buren Nat'l Hist.
Site N6
Meacham (lake) M1
Mohawk (riv.) L5
Montauk (pt.) S8
Moose (riv.) K3
Neversink (res.) L7
New York State Barge (canal) C4
Niagara (riv.) B4
Oil Spring Ind. Res. 6 .... D6
Oneida (lake) J4
Onondaga Ind. Res. 596 .... H5
Ontario (lake) F3
Orient (pt.) R8
Oswegatchie (riv.) K2
Oswego (riv.) H4
Otisco (lake) H5
Otsego (lake) L5
Otselic (riv.) J5
Owasco (lake) G5
Peconic (bay) R9
Peninsula (pt.) H3
Pepacton (res.) L6
Piseco (lake) M4
Placid (lake) N2
Plattsburgh A.F.B. 5,905 .... N1
Pleasant (lake) M4
Plum (isl.) R8
Poosepatuck Ind. Res. 203 .... P9
Raquette (lake) L3
Rondout (res.) M7
Round (lake) L2
Sacandaga (lake) L3
Sackets (harb.) H3
Sagamore Hill Nat'l Hist. Site R6
Saint Lawrence (lake) K1
Saint Lawrence (riv.) J2
Saint Regis (riv.) L1
Saint Regis Ind. Res. 1,802 .... M1
Salmon (res.) J3
Salmon (riv.) H3
Salmon (riv.) M1
Saranac (lkes) M2
Saranac (riv.) N1
Saratoga (lake) N4
Saratoga Nat'l Hist. Park N4
Schoharie (res.) M6
Schroon (lake) N3
Seneca (lake) G5
Seneca (riv.) G5
Shelter (isl.) R8
Shinnecock Ind. Res. 297 .... R9
Silver (lake) N1
Skaneateles (lake) H5
Skylight (mt.) M2
Slide (mt.) L6
Staten (isl.) M9
Statue of Liberty Nat'l Mon. M9
Stony (isl.) H3
Stony (pt.) H3
Susquehanna (riv.) H6
Thousand (isls.) H2
Tioughnioga (riv.) H6
Titus (lake) M1
Tomhannock (res.) O5
Tonawanda Ind. Res. 467 .... D4
Toronto (res.) L7
Tupper (lake) M2
Tuscarora Ind. Res. 921 .... B4
Unadilla (riv.) K5
Upper Chateaugay (lake) M1
Valcour (isl.) N1
Wallkill (riv.) L8
Whiteface (mt.) N2
Whitney Point (lake) J6
Woodhull (lake) L3

⊙County seat.
‡Population of metropolitan area.
○Population of town or township.
† Zip of nearest p.o. * Multiple zips.

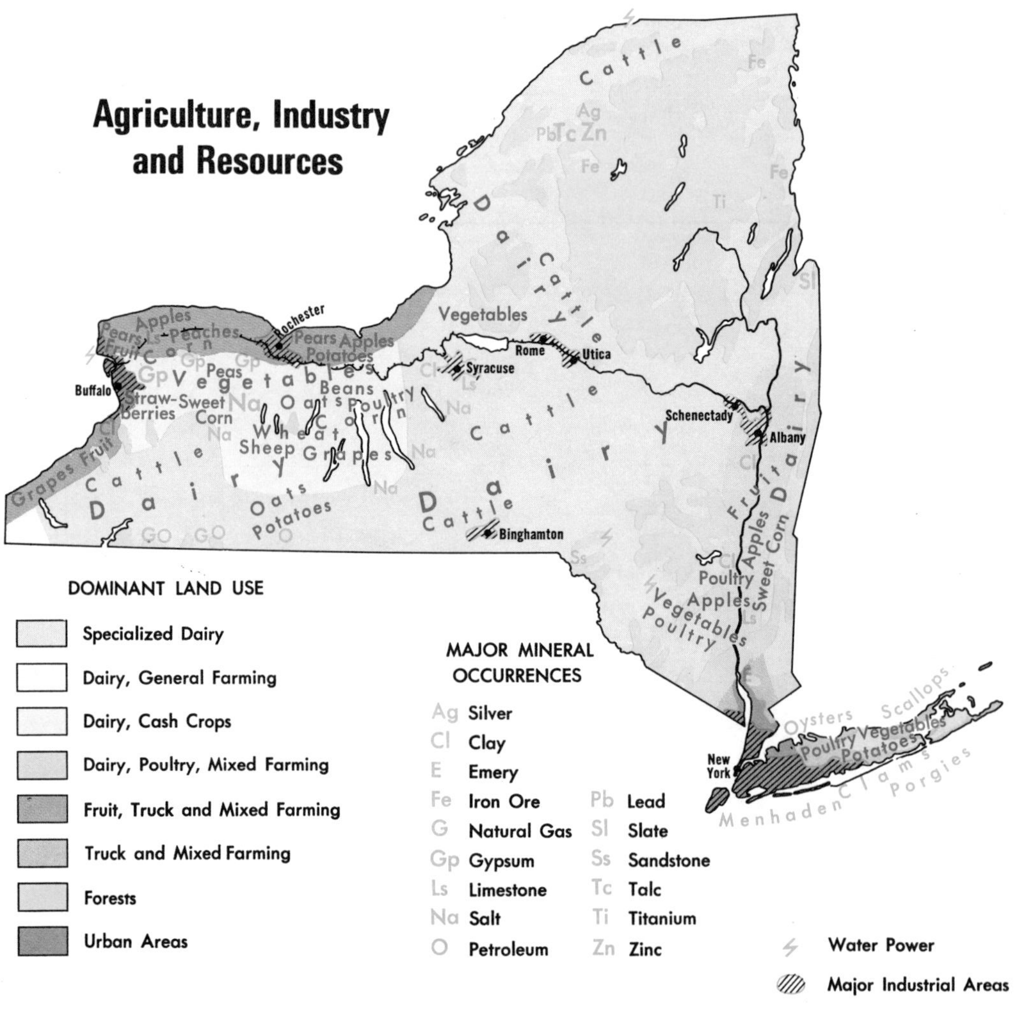
Agriculture, Industry and Resources
Cattle
Dairy
Vegetables
Apples
Pears
Peaches
Fruit
Corn
Rochester
Potatoes
Peas
Vegetables
Beans
Oats
Poultry
Syracuse
Rome
Utica
Buffalo
Straw-Sweet Berries Corn
Sheep
Wheat
Grapes
Schenectady
Albany
Grapes Fruit
Cattle
Dairy
Oats
Potatoes
Binghamton
Fruit
Apples
Sweet Corn
Poultry
Apples
Vegetables
Poultry
Oysters
Scallops
Poultry Vegetables
Potatoes
Clams
Porgies
Menhaden
New York
DOMINANT LAND USE
Specialized Dairy
Dairy, General Farming
Dairy, Cash Crops
Dairy, Poultry, Mixed Farming
Fruit, Truck and Mixed Farming
Truck and Mixed Farming
Forests
Urban Areas
MAJOR MINERAL OCCURRENCES
Ag Silver
Cl Clay
E Emery
Fe Iron Ore
G Natural Gas
Gp Gypsum
Ls Limestone
Na Salt
O Petroleum
Pb Lead
Sl Slate
Ss Sandstone
Tc Talc
Ti Titanium
Zn Zinc
Water Power
Major Industrial Areas

AREA 52,669 sq. mi. (136,413 sq. km.)
POPULATION 5,881,813
CAPITAL Raleigh
LARGEST CITY Charlotte
HIGHEST POINT Mt. Mitchell 6,684 ft. (2037 m.)
SETTLED IN 1650
ADMITTED TO UNION November 21, 1789
POPULAR NAME Tarheel State
STATE FLOWER Flowering Dogwood
STATE BIRD Cardinal

COUNTIES

Alamance 99,319...............L3
Alexander 24,999...............G3
Alleghany 9,587...............G1
Anson 25,649...............J4
Ashe 22,325...............F2
Avery 14,409...............F2
Beaufort 40,355...............R4
Bertie 21,024...............P2
Bladen 30,491...............M5
Brunswick 35,777...............N6
Buncombe 160,934...............D3
Burke 72,504...............F3
Cabarrus 85,895...............H4
Caldwell 67,746...............F3
Camden 5,904...............S2
Carteret 41,092...............R5
Caswell 20,705...............L2
Catawba 105,208...............G3
Chatham 33,415...............L3
Cherokee 18,933...............A4
Chowan 12,558...............R2
Clay 6,619...............B4
Cleveland 83,435...............F4
Columbus 51,037...............M6
Craven 71,043...............P4
Cumberland 247,160...............M4
Currituck 11,089...............S2
Dare 13,377...............T3
Davidson 113,162...............J3
Davie 24,599...............H3
Duplin 40,952...............O5
Durham 152,785...............M3
Edgecombe 55,988...............O3
Forsyth 243,683...............J2
Franklin 30,055...............N2
Gaston 162,568...............G4
Gates 8,875...............R2
Graham 7,217...............B4
Granville 34,043...............M2
Greene 16,117...............O3
Guilford 317,154...............K3
Halifax 55,286...............O2
Harnett 59,570...............M4
Haywood 46,495...............C3
Henderson 58,580...............D4
Hertford 23,368...............P2
Hoke 20,383...............L4
Hyde 5,873...............S3
Iredell 82,538...............H3
Jackson 25,811...............C4
Johnston 70,599...............N4
Jones 9,705...............P4
Lee 36,718...............L4
Lenoir 59,819...............O4
Lincoln 42,372...............G3
Macon 20,178...............B4
Madison 16,827...............D3
Martin 25,948...............P3
McDowell 35,135...............E3
Mecklenburg 404,270...............H4
Mitchell 14,428...............E2
Montgomery 22,469...............K4
Moore 50,505...............L4
Nash 67,153...............O2
New Hanover 103,471...............O6
Northampton 22,584...............P2
Onslow 112,784...............P5
Orange 77,055...............L2
Pamlico 10,398...............R4
Pasquotank 28,462...............S2
Pender 22,215...............O5
Perquimans 9,486...............S2
Person 29,164...............M2
Pitt 90,146...............P3
Polk 12,984...............E4
Randolph 91,728...............K3
Richmond 45,481...............K4
Robeson 101,610...............L5
Rockingham 83,426...............K2
Rowan 99,186...............H3
Rutherford 53,787...............E4
Sampson 49,687...............N4
Scotland 32,273...............L5
Stanly 48,517...............J4
Stokes 33,086...............J2
Surry 59,449...............H2
Swain 10,283...............B3
Transylvania 23,417...............D4
Tyrrell 3,975...............S3
Union 70,380...............H4
Vance 36,748...............N2
Wake 301,327...............M3
Warren 16,232...............N2
Washington 14,801...............R3
Watauga 31,666...............F2
Wayne 97,054...............N4
Wilkes 58,657...............G2
Wilson 63,132...............O3
Yadkin 28,439...............H2
Yancey 14,934...............E3

CITIES and TOWNS

Zip	Name/Pop.	Key
28315	Aberdeen 1,945	L4
27910	Ahoskie 4,887	P2

27201	Alamance 320	K2
28001	Albemarle⊙ 15,110	J4
†28043	Alexander Mills 643	F4
28509	Alliance 616	R4
28702	Almond 140	B4
28901	Andrews 1,621	B4
27501	Angier 1,709	M4
28007	Ansonville 794	J4
27502	Apex 2,847	M3
28510	Arapahoe 467	R4
27263	Archdale 5,326	K3
†28642	Arlington 872	H2
28420	Ash 150	N6
27203	Asheboro⊙ 15,252	K3
*28801	Asheville⊙ 53,583	D3
	Asheville‡ 177,761	D3
†27983	Askewville 227	R2
28421	Atkinson 298	N5
28512	Atlantic Beach 941	R5
27805	Aulander 1,214	P2
27806	Aurora 698	R4
28318	Autryville 228	M4

27915	Avon 500	U4
28513	Ayden 4,361	P4
27916	Aydlett 205	T2
28009	Badin 1,514	J4
27807	Bailey 685	N3
28705	Bakersville⊙ 373	E2
28706	Balfour 1,772	E4
28707	Balsam 200	C4
28604	Banner Elk 1,087	F2
†27030	Bannertown 1,028	H1
27008	Barber 155	H3
†28739	Barker Heights 1,267	D4
28710	Bat Cave 450	E4
27808	Bath 207	R4
27809	Battleboro 632	O2
28515	Bayboro⊙ 759	R4
†27892	Beargrass 82	P3
28516	Beaufort⊙ 3,826	R5
27810	Belhaven 2,430	R3
27811	Bellarthur 350	O3
28012	Belmont 4,607	H4
†28451	Belville 102	N6

†28090	Belwood 613	F4
27208	Bennett 254	K3
27504	Benson 2,792	N4
28016	Bessemer City 4,787	G4
27812	Bethel 1,825	P3
28518	Beulaville 1,060	O5
†28803	Biltmore Forest 1,499	E3
27209	Biscoe 1,334	K4
27813	Black Creek 523	O3
28711	Black Mountain 4,083	E3
28320	Bladenboro 1,428	M5
27212	Blanch 200	L2
28605	Blowing Rock 1,337	F2
28092	Boger City 2,252	G4
28461	Boiling Spring Lakes 998	N7
28017	Boiling Springs 2,381	F4
28422	Bolivia 252	N6
28423	Bolton 563	N6
27213	Bonlee 300	L3
28606	Boomer 250	G2
28607	Boone⊙ 10,191	F2
27011	Boonville 1,028	H2
28322	Bowdens 200	N4
28712	Brevard⊙ 5,323	D4
28519	Bridgeton 461	R4
27505	Broadway 908	L4
†28601	Brookford 467	G3
28424	Brunswick 223	M6
28713	Bryson City⊙ 1,556	C4
27506	Buies Creek 1,939	M4
27507	Bullock 525	M2
27508	Bunn 505	N3
28425	Burgaw⊙ 1,738	N5
27215	Burlington 37,266	K2
	Burlington‡ 99,136	F2
28714	Burnsville⊙ 1,452	E3
27509	Butner 4,240	M2
27312	Bynum 350	L3
†29566	Calabash 128	M7
28325	Calypso 689	N4
27921	Camden⊙ 300	S2
28326	Cameron 225	L4
27229	Candor 868	K4
28716	Canton 4,631	D3
†28584	Cape Carteret 944	P5
28428	Carolina Beach 2,000	O6
27510	Carrboro 7,336	L3
28327	Carthage⊙ 925	K4
27511	Cary 21,763	M3
28020	Casar 346	F3
28717	Cashiers 553	C4
27816	Castalia 358	O2
28429	Castle Hayne 1,087	O6
†28461	Caswell Beach 110	N7
28609	Catawba 509	G3
27230	Cedar Falls 400	K3
27231	Cedar Grove 250	L2
28520	Cedar Island 310	S5
†27549	Centerville 135	N2
28430	Cerro Gordo 295	M6
28431	Chadbourn 1,975	M6
†28445	Chadwick Acres 15	P6
27514	Chapel Hill 32,421	L3
*28201	Charlotte⊙ 314,447	H4
	Charlotte-Gastonia‡ 637,218	H4
28021	Cherryville 4,844	G4
28023	China Grove 2,081	H3
28521	Chinquapin 280	O5
27817	Chocowinity 644	P4
28610	Claremont 880	G3
28433	Clarkton 664	M6
27520	Clayton 4,091	N3
27012	Clemmons 7,401	J2

27013	Cleveland 595	H3
28328	Clinton⊙ 7,552	N5
28721	Clyde 1,008	D3
27521	Coats 1,385	M4
27922	Cofield 465	R2
27924	Colerain 284	R2
28925	Columbia⊙ 758	S3
28722	Columbus⊙ 727	E4
28522	Comfort 325	O5
27818	Como 89	P1
28025	Concord⊙ 16,942	H4
27819	Conetoe 215	O3
28613	Conover 4,245	G3
27820	Conway 678	P2
27014	Cooleemee 1,448	H3
28031	Cornelius 1,460	H4
27927	Corolla 158	T2
28523	Cove City 500	P4
28032	Cramerton 1,869	G4
27522	Creedmoor 1,641	M2
27928	Creswell 426	S3
27852	Crisp 435	O3
28616	Crossnore 297	F2
28331	Cumberland 400	M5
27237	Cumnock 200	L3
27929	Currituck⊙ 700	T2
28034	Dallas 3,340	G4
27016	Danbury⊙ 140	J2
28036	Davidson 3,241	H4
28524	Davis 612	R5
27239	Denton 949	J3
28725	Dillsboro 179	C4
27017	Dobson⊙ 1,222	H2
†28801	Dortches 885	O2
28526	Dover 600	P4
28619	Drexel 1,392	F3
28332	Dublin 477	M5
28334	Dunn 8,962	M4
*27701	Durham⊙ 100,538	M2
	Durham-Raleigh‡ 530,673	M2
27242	Eagle Springs 280	K4
28038	Earl 206	F4
†28434	East Arcadia 461	N6
27018	East Bend 602	H2
28726	East Flat Rock 3,365	E4
†28723	East Laport 150	C4
28352	East Laurinburg 536	L5
†28752	East Marion 1,851	F3
28039	East Spencer 2,150	J3
27288	Eden 15,672	K1
27932	Edenton⊙ 5,357	R2
27909	Elizabeth City⊙ 14,004	S2
28337	Elizabethtown⊙ 3,551	M5
28621	Elkin 2,858	H2
28622	Elk Park 535	E2
28040	Ellenboro 560	F4
28338	Ellerbe 1,415	K4
27822	Elm City 1,561	O3
27244	Elon College 2,873	L2
†28557	Emerald Isle 865	P5
27823	Enfield 2,995	O2
28728	Enka 5,567	D3
28339	Erwin 2,828	M4
27247	Ether 425	K4
27935	Eure 300	R2
27830	Eureka 303	O3
27825	Everetts 213	P3
28438	Evergreen 310	M6
28439	Fair Bluff 1,095	M6
27826	Fairfield 900	S3
28340	Fairmont 2,658	L6
28730	Fairview 1,122	D3
28341	Faison 636	N4
28041	Faith 552	J3

(continued on following page)

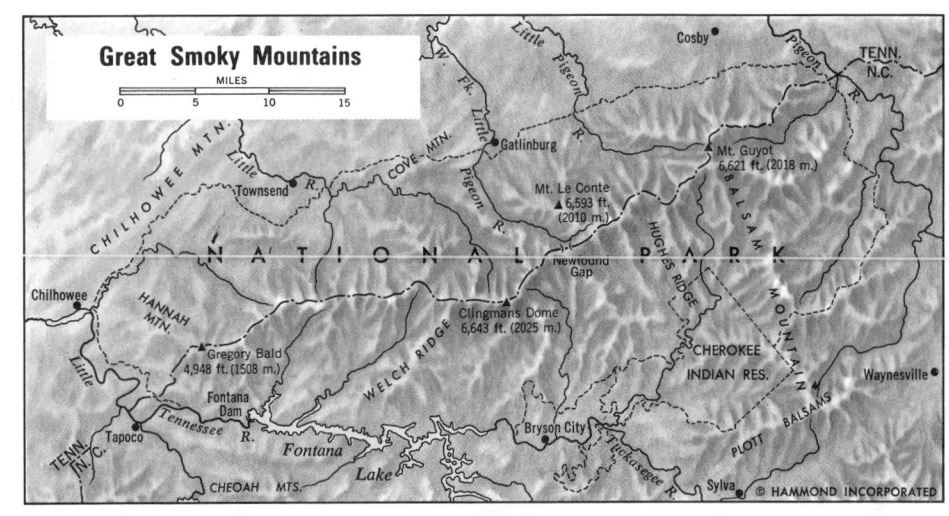

Great Smoky Mountains

Agriculture, Industry and Resources

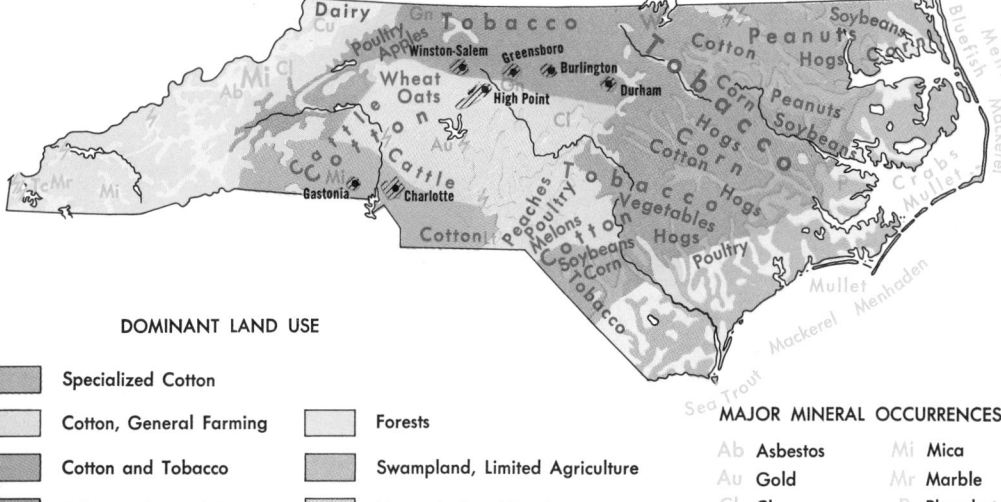

DOMINANT LAND USE

- Specialized Cotton
- Cotton, General Farming
- Cotton and Tobacco
- Tobacco, General Farming
- Peanuts, General Farming
- General Farming, Livestock, Fruit, Tobacco
- General Farming, Truck Farming, Tobacco, Livestock
- Forests
- Swampland, Limited Agriculture
- Nonagricultural Land

⚡ Water Power
▨ Major Industrial Areas

MAJOR MINERAL OCCURRENCES

Ab	Asbestos	Mi	Mica
Au	Gold	Mr	Marble
Cl	Clay	P	Phosphates
Cu	Copper	Tc	Talc
Gn	Granite	W	Tungsten
Li	Lithium		

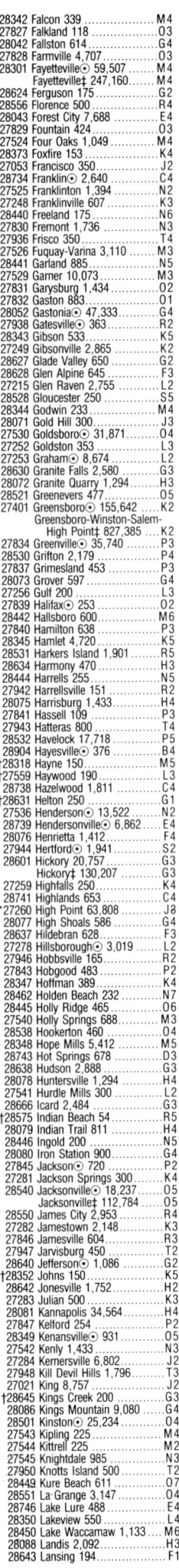

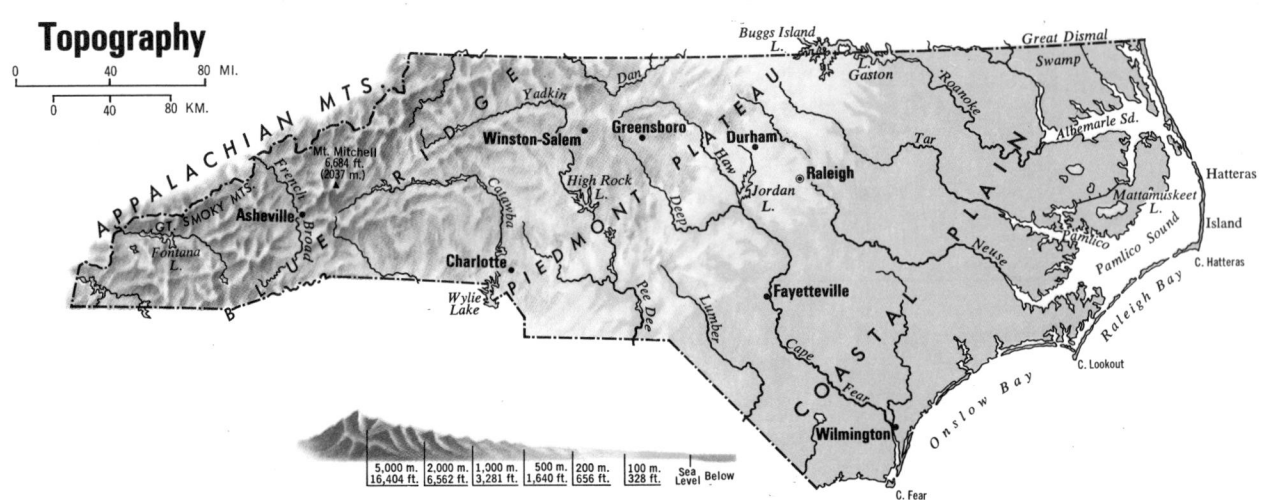

Topography

0　　40　　80 MI.

0　　40　　80 KM.

5,000 m. | 2,000 m. | 1,000 m. | 500 m. | 200 m. | 100 m. | Sea Level Below
16,404 ft. | 6,562 ft. | 3,281 ft. | 1,640 ft. | 656 ft. | 328 ft.

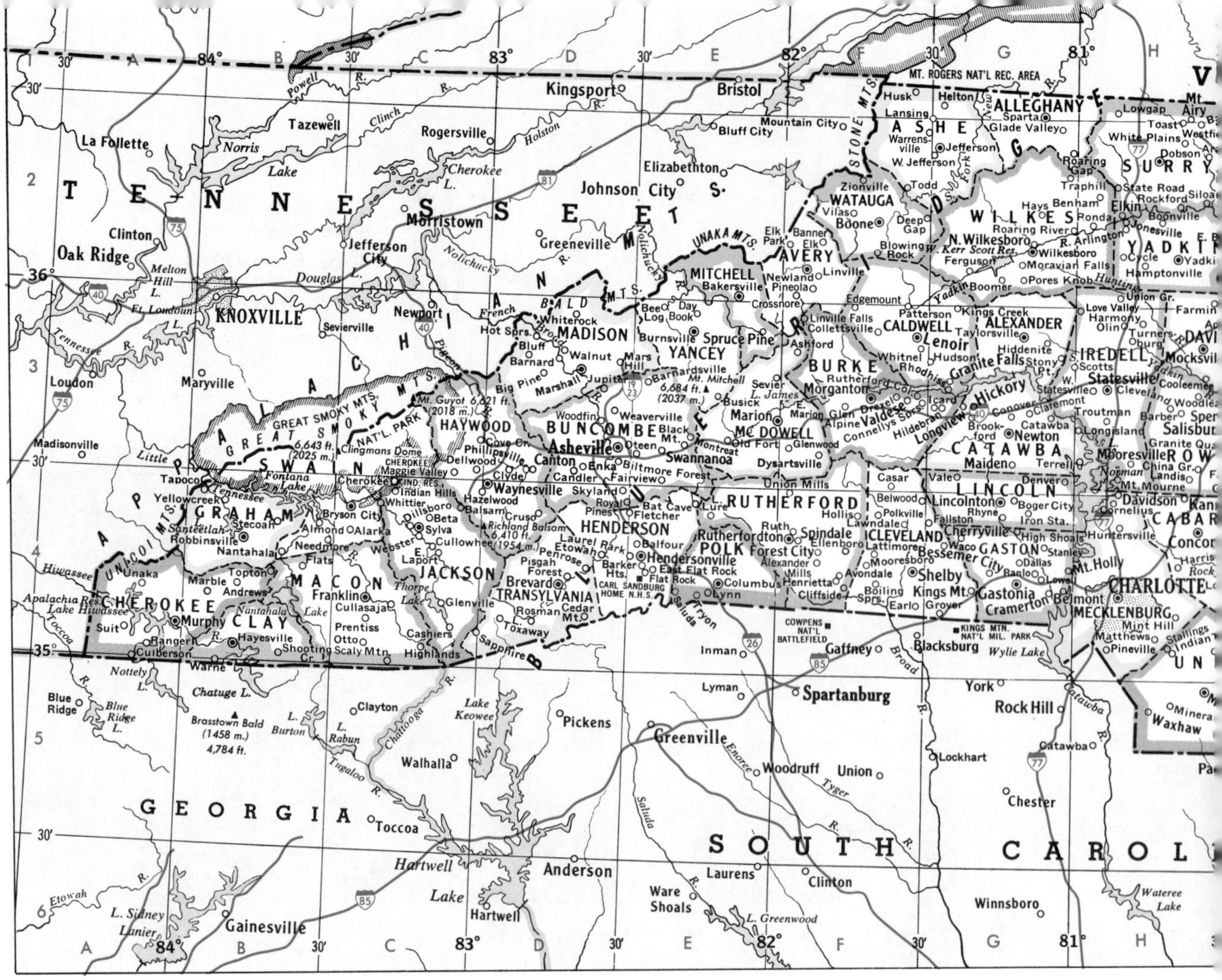

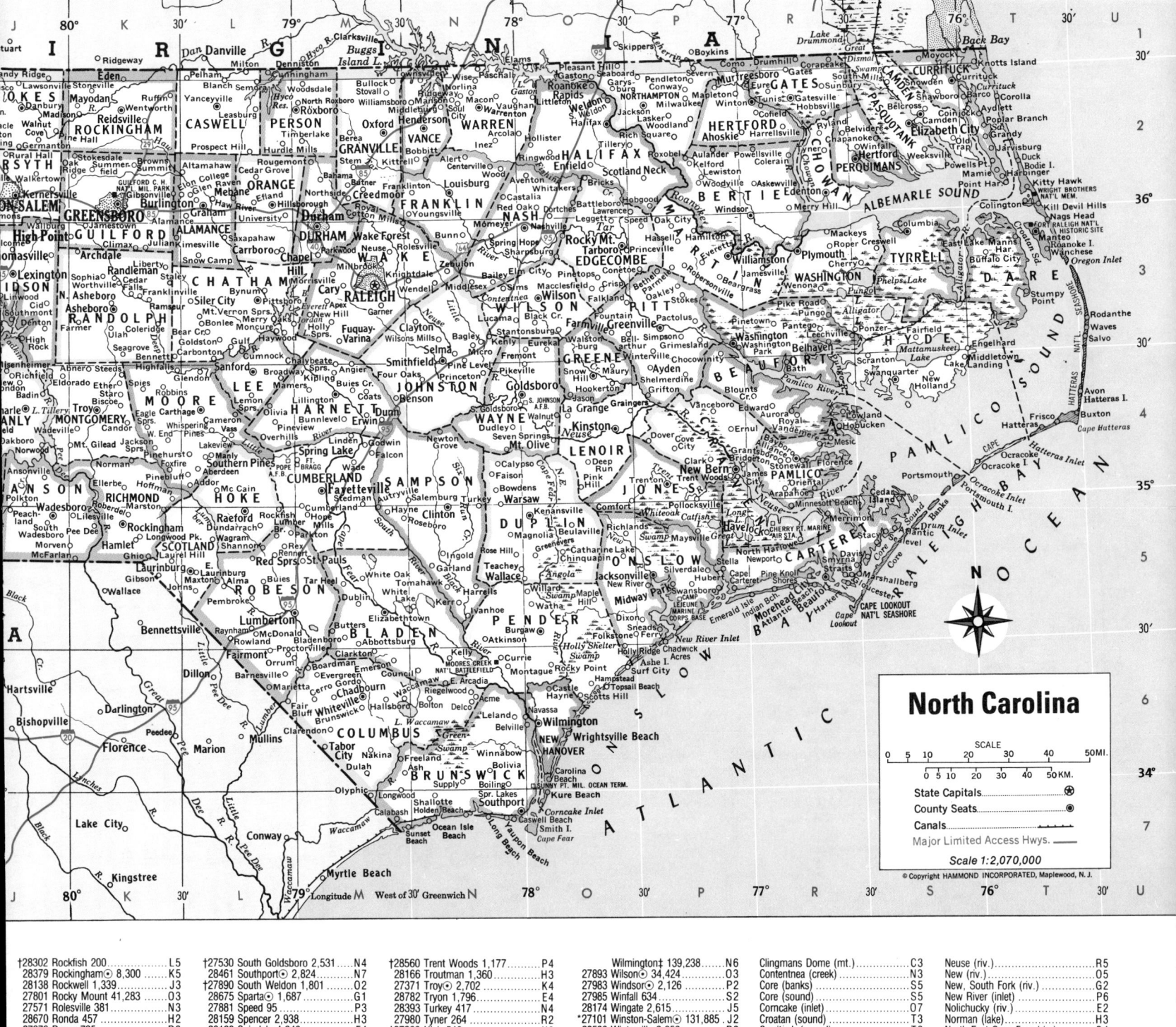

North Carolina

SCALE
0 5 10 20 30 40 50MI.
0 5 10 20 30 40 50 KM.
State Capitals..............⊛
County Seats..............⊙
Canals..............
Major Limited Access Hwys.
Scale 1:2,070,000
© Copyright HAMMOND INCORPORATED, Maplewood, N.J.

†28302 Rockfish 200	L5	†28560 Trent Woods 1,177	P4	Wilmington‡ 139,238	N6	Clingmans Dome (mt.)	C3	Neuse (riv.)	R5
28379 Rockingham⊙ 8,300	K5	28461 Southport⊙ 2,824	N7	27893 Wilson 34,424	O3	Contentnea (creek)	N3	New (riv.)	O5
28138 Rockwell 1,339	J3	†27890 South Weldon 1,801	O2	27983 Windsor⊙ 2,126	P2	Core (banks)	S5	New, South Fork (riv.)	G2
27801 Rocky Mount 41,283	O3	28675 Sparta⊙ 1,687	G1	27985 Winfall 634	S2	Core (sound)	S5	New River (inlet)	P6
27571 Rolesville 381	N3	27881 Speed 95	P3	28174 Wingate 2,615	J5	Corncake (inlet)	O7	Nolichucky (riv.)	E2
28670 Ronda 457	H2	28159 Spencer 2,938	H3	*27101 Winston-Salem⊙ 131,885	J2	Croatan (sound)	T3	Norman (lake)	H3
27970 Roper 795	R3	28160 Spindale 4,246	F4	28590 Winterville 2,052	P3	Currituck (sound)	T2	North East Cape Fear (riv.)	O4
28382 Roseboro 1,227	N5	27882 Spring Hope 1,254	N3	27986 Winton⊙ 825	P2	Dan (riv.)	L1	Ocracoke (inlet)	T5
28458 Rose Hill 1,508	N5	28390 Spring Lake 6,273	M4	27594 Wise 550	N2	Deep (riv.)	K3	Ocracoke (isl.)	T4
28772 Rosman 512	D4	28777 Spruce Pine 2,282	E3	†28804 Woodfin 3,260	D3	Dismal (Great) (swamp)	S1	Onslow (bay)	P6
28383 Rowland 1,841	L5	27355 Staley 204	K3	27897 Woodland 861	P2	Drum (inlet)	S5	Oregon (inlet)	U3
27573 Roxboro⊙ 7,532	M2	†28079 Stallings 1,826	H4	27054 Woodleaf 550	H3	Fear (cape)	O7	Pamlico (riv.)	R4
27872 Roxobel 278	P2	28163 Stanfield 463	J4	28394 Vass 828	L4	Fishing (creek)	O2	Pamlico (sound)	S4
27326 Ruffin 150	K2	28164 Stanley 2,341	G4	28169 Waco 322	G4	Fontana (lake)	B4	Pee Dee (riv.)	J4
27045 Rural Hall 1,336	J2	†27045 Stanleyville 5,039	J2	28395 Wade 474	M4	Fort Bragg 37,834	M4	Phelps (lake)	S3
†28139 Ruth 381	E4	27883 Stantonsburg 920	O3	28170 Wadesboro⊙ 4,206	J5	Fort Raleigh Nat'l Hist. Site	T3	Pigeon (riv.)	C3
28671 Rutherford College 1,108	F3	27356 Star 816	K4	28396 Wagram 617	L5	French Broad (riv.)	D3	Pope A.F.B.	L4
28139 Rutherfordton⊙ 3,434	E4	28677 Statesville⊙ 18,622	H3	27587 Wake Forest 3,780	N3	Gaston (res.)	O2	Portsmouth (isl.)	T5
28384 Saint Pauls 1,639	M5	28391 Stedman 723	M4	28466 Wallace 2,903	N5	Great (lake)	P5	Pungo (lake)	S3
28385 Salemburg 742	N4	28582 Stella 700	P5	27373 Wallburg 300	J3	Great Dismal (swamp)	S1	Pungo (riv.)	S3
28144 Salisbury⊙ 22,677	H3	27581 Stem 222	N3	27052 Walnut Cove 1,147	J2	Great Smoky (mts.)	B3	Raleigh (bay)	S5
Salisbury-Concord‡ 185,081	H3	27884 Stokes 450	P3	†27530 Walnut Creek 343	O4	Great Smoky Mts. Nat'l Park	B3	Richland Balsam (mt.)	D4
28773 Saluda 607	E4	27357 Stokesdale 1,070	K2	27888 Walstonburg 181	O3	Green (swamp)	N6	Roanoke (riv.)	T3
27972 Salvo 150	U3	27048 Stoneville 1,054	K2	28398 Wanchese 1,105	T3	Guyot (mt.)	C3	Roanoke (riv.)	P2
27330 Sanford⊙ 14,773	L4	28583 Stonewall 360	R4	27589 Warrenton⊙ 908	N2	Hatteras (cape)	U4	Rocky (riv.)	H4
28774 Sapphire 350	D4	28678 Stony Point 1,150	G3	28398 Warsaw 2,910	N4	Hatteras (inlet)	T4	Santeetlah (lake)	B4
27340 Saxapahaw 500	L3	27582 Stovall 417	M2	27591 Wendell 2,222	N3	Hatteras (isl.)	U4	Seymour Johnson A.F.B.	O4
28775 Scaly Mountain 250	C4	27978 Stumpy Point 250	T3	27375 Wentworth⊙ 150	K2	Haw (riv.)	K2	Six Run (creek)	N4
28699 Scotts 500	H3	27979 Sunbury 400	S2	27053 Westfield 450	H2	High Rock (lake)	J3	Smith (isl.)	O7
27875 Scranton 250	S4	28459 Sunset Beach 304	N7	28694 West Jefferson 822	F2	Hiwassee (lake)	A4	South (riv.)	M5
27876 Seaboard 687	O1	28445 Surf City 421	O6	†28389 Whispering Pines 1,160	L4	Hiwassee (riv.)	A4	South Yadkin (riv.)	H3
27341 Seagrove 294	K3	28778 Swannanoa 3,586	E3	27891 Whitakers 924	O3	Holly Shelter (swamp)	O6	Stone (mts.)	F2
27576 Selma 4,762	N3	28585 Swansboro 976	P5	28337 White Lake 968	M5	Hunting (isl.)	H2	Sunny Point Mil. Ocean Term.	O6
27343 Semora 500	L2	28779 Sylva⊙ 1,699	C3	27031 White Plains 200	H2	Hyco (lake)	L2	Tar (riv.)	O3
28578 Seven Springs 166	O4	28463 Tabor City 2,710	M6	28472 Whiteville⊙ 5,565	M6	James (lake)	E3	Thorpe (lake)	C4
28459 Shallotte 680	N7	27886 Tarboro⊙ 8,634	O3	28789 Whittier 200	C4	Jordan, B. Everett (lake)	M3	Tillery (lake)	J4
27878 Sharpsburg 997	O3	28392 Tar Heel 150	M5	28697 Wilkesboro⊙ 2,335	G2	Kerr, W. Scott (res.)	G2	Trent (riv.)	P4
27973 Shawboro 300	S2	28681 Taylorsville⊙ 1,103	G3	†27536 Williamsboro 59	M2	Lanes (creek)	J5	Unaka (mts.)	E2
28150 Shelby⊙ 15,310	G4	28464 Teachey 373	N5	27892 Williamston⊙ 6,159	R3	Little (creek)	N3	Unicoi (mts.)	A4
27344 Siler City 4,446	L3	27360 Thomasville 14,144	J3	28401 Wilmington⊙ 44,000	N6	Little (riv.)	L4	Waccamaw (lake)	N6
27879 Simpson 407	P3	27887 Tillery 400	O2			Little Pee Dee (riv.)	L6	Waccamaw (riv.)	M7
27880 Sims 192	N3	27583 Timberlake 500	M2			Little Tennessee (riv.)	B4	Whiteoak (swamp)	P5
27577 Smithfield⊙ 7,288	N3	28789 Whittier 200	C4			Long (lake)	P5	W. Scott Kerr (res.)	G2
28579 Smyrna 291	S5	28697 Wilkesboro⊙ 2,335	G2			Lookout (cape)	S5	Wright Brothers Nat'l Mem.	T2
28580 Snow Hill⊙ 1,374	O4					Lumber (riv.)	L6	Yadkin (riv.)	J3
27350 Sophia 350	K3	27049 Toast 2,339	H2			Mattamuskeet (lake)	S3	⊙County seat.	
28387 Southern Pines 8,620	L4	28685 Traphill 550	H2			Meherrin (riv.)	P1	‡Population of metropolitan area.	
		28585 Trenton⊙ 407	P4			Mitchell (mt.)	D3	† Zip of nearest p.o.	
						Moores Creek Nat'l Battlefield	N6	* Multiple zips.	
						Nantahala (lake)	B4		

OTHER FEATURES

Albemarle (sound) S2
Alligator (lake) S3
Alligator (riv.) S3
Angola (swamp) O5
Apalachia (res.) A4
Appalachian (mts.) D2
Ashe (isl.) P6
Bald (isl.) D3
Black (riv.) N5
Blue Ridge (mts.) E4
Bodie (isl.) T2
Broad (riv.) E4
Buggs Island (lake) M1
Camp Lejeune Marine Corps Base 30,764 ....P5
Cape Fear (riv.) M5
Cape Hatteras Nat'l Seashore T4
Carl Sandburg Home Nat'l Hist. Site D4
Catawba (lake) G4
Catawba (riv.) H5
Catfish (lake) P5
Chatuge (lake) B5
Cherokee Ind. Res. C3
Cherry Point Marine Air Sta. R5
Chowan (riv.) R2

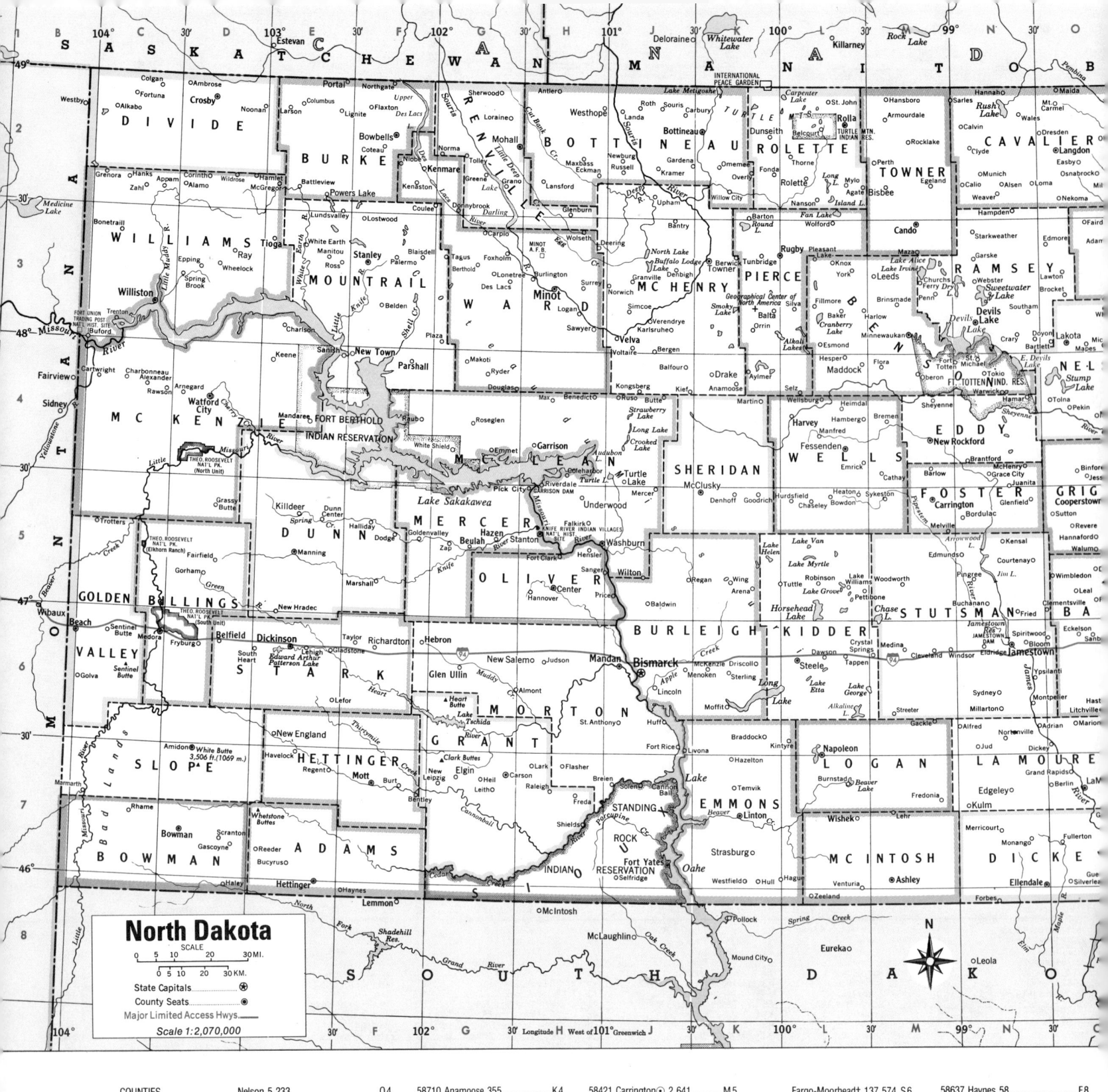

North Dakota

SCALE

0 5 10   20   30 MI.

0 5 10   20   30 KM.

State Capitals .... ⊛

County Seats .... ⊙

Major Limited Access Hwys.

Scale 1:2,070,000

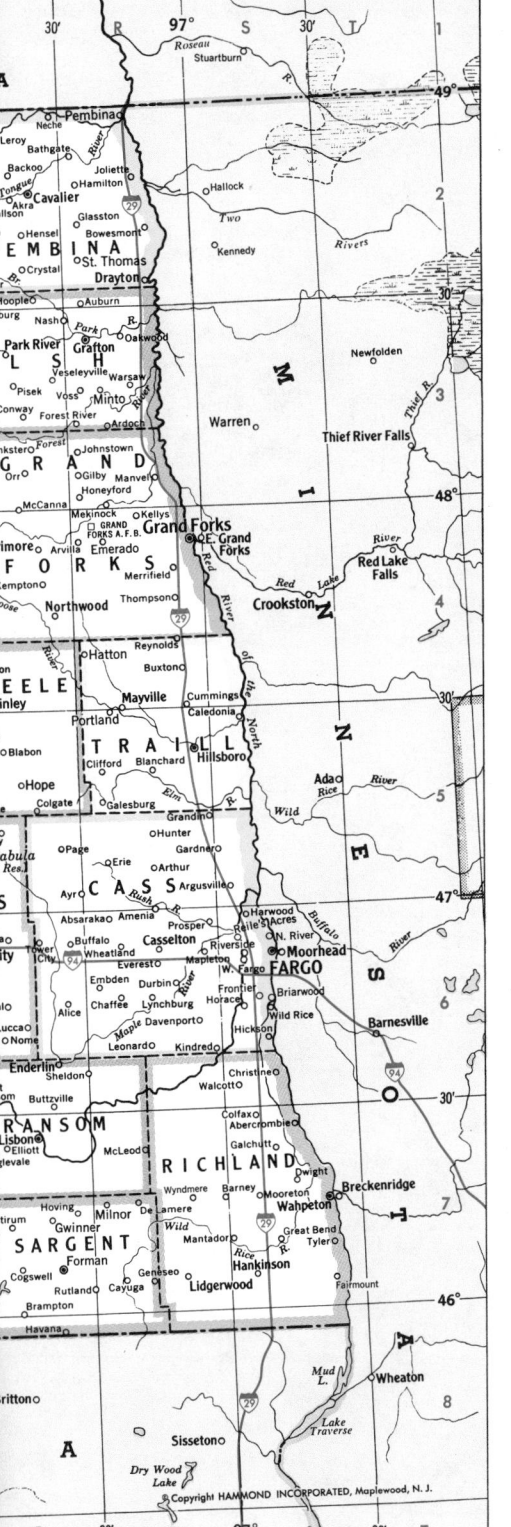

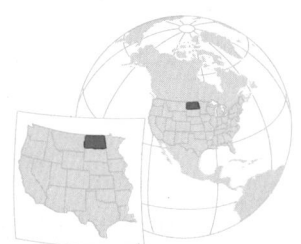

58276 Saint Thomas 528 ....R2
58780 Sanish........................E4
58781 Sawyer 417 ....H3
58653 Scranton 415 ....D7
58568 Selfridge 273 ....J7
58654 Sentinel Butte 86.............C6
58068 Sheldon 173 ....P6
58782 Sherwood 294 ....G2
58374 Sheyenne 307 ....M4
58655 South Heart 294 ....D6
58850 Spring Brook 52 ....D3
58784 Stanley⊙ 1,631 ....F3
58571 Stanton⊙ 623 ....H5
58482 Steele⊙ 796 ....L6
58573 Strasburg 623 ....K7
58483 Streeter 264 ....M6
58785 Surrey 999 ....H3
58487 Tappen 271 ....L6
58656 Taylor 239 ....F6
58278 Thompson 785 ....R4
58852 Tioga 1,597 ....E3
58380 Tolna 241 ....O4
58071 Tower City 293 ....P6
58788 Towner⊙ 867 ....K3
58575 Turtle Lake 802 ....J4
58576 Underwood 1,329 ....H5
58072 Valley City⊙ 7,774 ....P6
58790 Velva 1,101 ....J3
58792 Voltaire 65 ....J3
58075 Wahpeton⊙ 9,064 ....S7
58281 Wales 74 ....N2
58282 Walhalla 1,429 ....P2
58577 Washburn⊙ 1,767 ....J5
58854 Watford City⊙ 2,119 ....D4
58078 West Fargo 10,099 ....S6
58793 Westhope 741 ....H2
58794 White Earth 98 ....E3
58795 Wildrose 214 ....D2
58801 Williston⊙ 13,336 ....C3
58384 Willow City 329 ....K2
58579 Wilton 950 ....J5
58492 Wimbledon 330 ....O5
58495 Wishek 1,345 ....L7
58385 Wolford 76 ....L3
58081 Wyndmere 550 ....R7
58386 York 69 ....L3
58580 Zap 511 ....G5
58581 Zeeland 253 ....L8

OTHER FEATURES

Alkali (lkes) L3
Alkaline (lake) L6
Apple (creek) J6
Arrowwood (lake) N5
Ashtabula (lake) P5
Audubon (lake) H4
Bad Lands (reg.) C7
Baldhill (Ashtabula) (res.) P5
Bear (creek) O7
Beaver (creek) B5
Beaver (creek) K7
Beaver (creek) L7
Buffalo Lodge (lake) J3
Cannonball (riv.) G7
Carpenter (lake) L2
Cedar (creek) G7
Chase (lake) M5
Cherry (creek) D4
Clark (buttes) G7
Coteau du Missouri (plain) G3
Cranberry (lake) L3
Crooked (lake) J4
Cut Bank (creek) H2
Darling (lake) G2
Deep (riv.) J1
Des Lacs (riv.) G3
Devils (lake) N3
Dry (lake) M3
East Devils (lake) N4
Egg (creek) H3
Elm (riv.) N8
Elm (riv.) R5
Etta (lake) L6

Fan (lake) L2
Forest (riv.) P3
Fort Berthold Ind. Res. E4
Fort Totten Ind. Res. N4
Fort Union Trading Post Nat'l Hist.
   Site B3
Garrison (dam) H5
George (lake) L6
Goose (riv.) P4
Grand, North Fork (riv.) E8
Grand Forks A.F.B. 9,390 ....R4
Green (riv.) D5
Grove (lake) L5
Heart (butte) G6
Heart (riv.) F6
Helen (lake) K5
Horsehead (lake) L5
International Peace Garden K1
Irvine (lake) M3
Island (lake) L2
James (riv.) N6
Jamestown (res.) N6
Jim (riv.) N5
Knife (riv.) G5
Knife R. Indian Villages Nat'l Hist.
   Site H5
Little Deep (creek)...................G2
Little Knife (riv.) F3

Little Missouri (riv.)..................D4
Little Muddy (riv.).....................C3
Long (lake) J4
Long (lake) K6
Long (lake) L2
Maple (riv.) O8
Maple (riv.) R6
Metigoshe (lake) K2
Minot A.F.B. 9,880 ....H3
Missouri (riv.) H5
Muddy (creek) G6
Myrtle (lake) L5
North (lake) J3
Oahe (lake) J7
Oak (creek) J8
Park (riv.) R3
Patterson, Edward A. (lake) E6
Pembina (riv.) O1
Pipestem (riv.) M5
Porcupine (creek) J7
Red River of the North (riv.) S4
Round (lake) K3
Rush (lake) N2
Rush (riv.) R5
Sakakawea (lake) G5
Sentinel (butte) C6
Shell (creek) F3
Sheyenne (riv.) O6

Smoky (lake) K3
Souris (riv.) J2
Spring (creek) E5
Standing Rock Ind. Res. J7
Strawberry (lake) J4
Stump (lake) O4
Sweetwater (lake) N3
Theodore Roosevelt Nat'l Mem. Park
   ....C5, D4,D6
Thirty Mile (creek) F6
Tongue (riv.) P2
Tschida (lake) G6
Turtle (lake) H4
Turtle (mts.) K2
Turtle Mountain Ind. Res. L2
Upper Des Lacs (lake) F2
Van (lake) L5
Whetstone (buttes) E7
White (butte) D7
White Butte (mt.) D7
White Earth (riv.) E3
Wild Rice (riv.) R7
Yellowstone (riv.) B4

⊙County seat.
‡Population of metropolitan area.
† Zip of nearest p.o.
* Multiple zips.

AREA 70,702 sq. mi. (183,118 sq. km.)
POPULATION 652,717
CAPITAL Bismarck
LARGEST CITY Fargo
HIGHEST POINT White Butte 3,506 ft.
   (1069 m.)
SETTLED IN 1780
ADMITTED TO UNION November 2, 1889
POPULAR NAME Flickertail State; Sioux
   State
STATE FLOWER Wild Prairie Rose
STATE BIRD Western Meadowlark

Topography

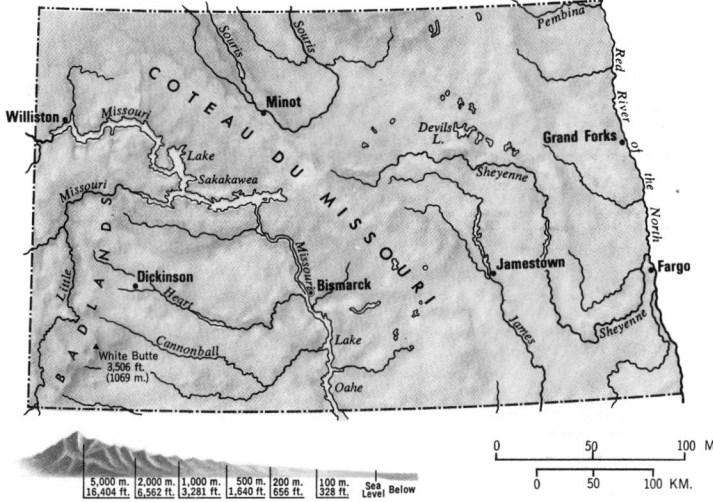

Agriculture, Industry and Resources

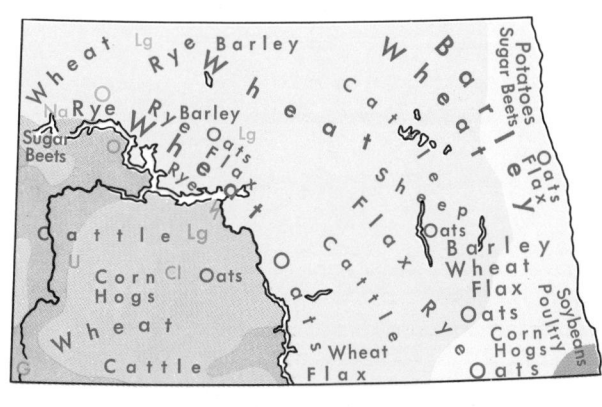

DOMINANT LAND USE

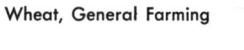 Specialized Wheat

 Sugar Beets, Dry Beans, Livestock, General Farming

 Wheat, General Farming

 Range Livestock

Wheat, Range Livestock

Livestock, Cash Grain

Water Power

MAJOR MINERAL OCCURRENCES

Cl Clay
G   Natural Gas
Lg Lignite
Na Salt
O   Petroleum
U   Uranium

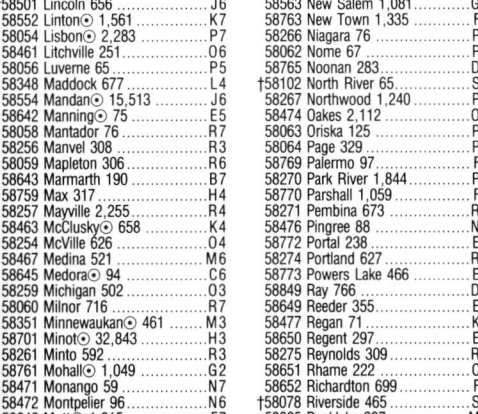

†58501 Lincoln 656 ....J6
58552 Linton⊙ 1,561 ....K7
58054 Lisbon⊙ 2,283 ....P7
58461 Litchville 251 ....O6
58056 Luverne 65 ....P5
58348 Maddock 677 ....L4
58554 Mandan⊙ 15,513 ....J6
58642 Manning⊙ 75 ....E5
58058 Mantador 76 ....R7
58256 Manvel 308 ....R3
58059 Mapleton 306 ....R6
58643 Marmarth 190 ....B7
58759 Max 317 ....H4
58257 Mayville 2,255 ....R4
58463 McClusky⊙ 658 ....K4
58254 McVille 626 ....O4
58467 Medina 521 ....M6
58645 Medora⊙ 94 ....C6
58259 Michigan 502 ....O3
58060 Milnor 716 ....R7
58351 Minnewaukan⊙ 461 ....M3
58701 Minot⊙ 32,843 ....H3
58261 Minto 592 ....R3
58761 Mohall⊙ 1,049 ....G2
58471 Monango 59 ....N7
58472 Montpelier 96 ....N6
58646 Mott⊙ 1,315 ....F7
58352 Munich 300 ....N2
58561 Napoleon⊙ 1,103 ....L6
58265 Neche 471 ....P2
58647 New England 825 ....E6
58562 New Leipzig 352 ....G7
58356 New Rockford⊙ 1,791 .....N4

58563 New Salem 1,081............G6
58763 New Town 1,335............F4
58266 Niagara 76 ....P4
58062 Nome 67 ....P6
58765 Noonan 283................D2
†58102 North River 65..............S6
58267 Northwood 1,240 ....P4
58474 Oakes 2,112 ....O7
58063 Oriska 125 ....P6
58064 Page 329 ....P5
58769 Palermo 97 ....F3
58270 Park River 1,844 ....P3
58770 Parshall 1,059 ....F4
58271 Pembina 673 ....R2
58476 Pingree 88 ....N5
58772 Portal 238 ....E2
58274 Portland 627 ....R5
58773 Powers Lake 466 ....E2
58849 Ray 766 ....D3
58649 Reeder 355 ....E7
58477 Regan 71 ....K5
58650 Regent 297 ....E7
58275 Reynolds 309 ....R4
58651 Rhame 222 ....C7
58652 Richardton 699 ....E6
†58078 Riverside 465 ....S6
58365 Rocklake 287 ....M2
58479 Rogers 68 ....O5
58366 Rolette 667 ....L2
58367 Rolla⊙ 1,538 ....L2
58368 Rugby⊙ 3,335 ....L3
58067 Rutland 250 ....P7
58369 Saint John 401 ....L2

Ohio

SCALE

State Capitals .... ⊛
County Seats .... ◉
Major Limited Access Hwys. ————

Scale 1:1,800,000

© Copyright HAMMOND INCORPORATED, Maplewood, N.J.

AREA 41,330 sq. mi. (107,045 sq. km.)
POPULATION 10,797,624
CAPITAL Columbus
LARGEST CITY Cleveland
HIGHEST POINT Campbell Hill 1,550 ft. (472 m.)
SETTLED IN 1788
ADMITTED TO UNION March 1, 1803
POPULAR NAME Buckeye State
STATE FLOWER Scarlet Carnation
STATE BIRD Cardinal

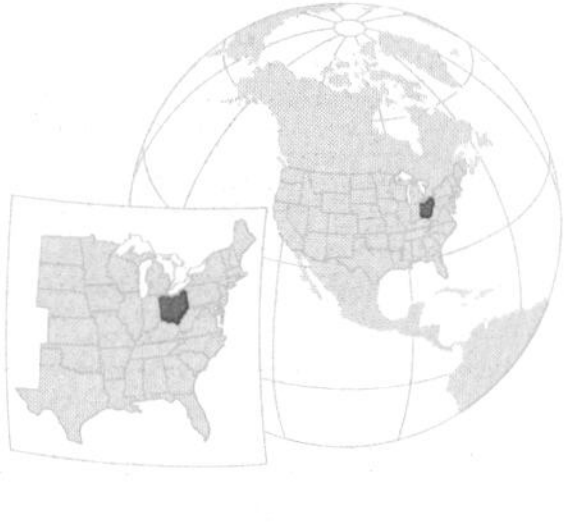

Topography

0 40 80 MI.
0 40 80 KM.

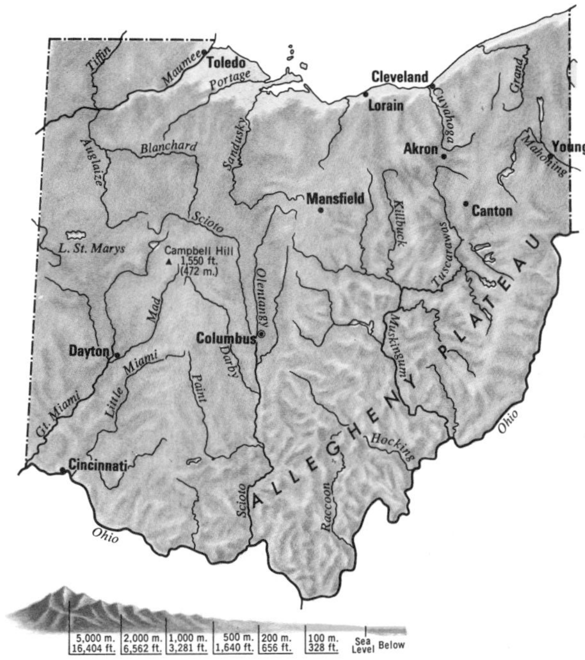

COUNTIES

Name/Pop.	Key
Adams 24,328	D8
Allen 112,241	B4
Ashland 46,178	F4
Ashtabula 104,215	J2
Athens 56,399	F7
Auglaize 42,554	B4
Belmont 82,569	J5
Brown 31,920	C8
Butler 258,787	A7
Carroll 25,598	H4
Champaign 33,649	C5
Clark 150,236	C6
Clermont 128,483	B7
Clinton 34,603	C7
Columbiana 113,572	J4
Coshocton 36,024	G5
Crawford 50,075	E4
Cuyahoga 1,498,400	G3
Darke 55,096	A5
Defiance 39,987	A3
Delaware 53,840	D5
Erie 79,655	E3
Fairfield 93,678	E6
Fayette 27,467	D6
Franklin 869,126	E5
Fulton 37,751	B2
Gallia 30,098	F8
Geauga 74,474	H3
Greene 129,769	C6
Guernsey 42,024	H5
Hamilton 873,224	A7
Hancock 64,581	C3
Hardin 32,719	C4
Harrison 18,152	H5
Henry 28,383	B3
Highland 33,477	C7
Hocking 24,304	F6
Holmes 29,416	G4
Huron 54,608	E3
Jackson 30,592	E7
Jefferson 91,564	J5
Knox 46,304	F5
Lake 212,801	H2
Lawrence 63,849	E8
Licking 120,981	F5
Logan 39,155	C5
Lorain 274,909	F3
Lucas 471,741	C2
Madison 33,004	D6
Mahoning 289,487	J4
Marion 67,974	D4
Medina 113,150	G3
Meigs 23,641	F7
Mercer 38,334	A4
Miami 90,381	B5
Monroe 17,382	H6
Montgomery 571,697	B6
Morgan 14,241	G6
Morrow 26,480	E4
Muskingum 83,340	G5
Noble 11,310	G6
Ottawa 40,076	D2
Paulding 21,302	A3
Perry 31,032	F6
Pickaway 43,662	D6
Pike 22,802	D7
Portage 135,856	H3
Preble 38,223	A6
Putnam 32,991	B3
Richland 131,205	E4
Ross 65,004	D7
Sandusky 63,267	D3
Scioto 84,545	D8
Seneca 61,901	D3
Shelby 43,089	B5
Stark 378,823	H4
Summit 524,472	G3
Trumbull 241,863	J3
Tuscarawas 84,614	H5
Union 29,536	D5
Van Wert 30,458	A4
Vinton 11,584	E7
Warren 99,276	B7
Washington 64,266	H7
Wayne 97,408	G4
Williams 36,369	A2
Wood 107,372	C3
Wyandot 22,651	D4

CITIES and TOWNS

Zip	Name/Pop.	Key
45101	Aberdeen 1,566	C8
45810	Ada 5,669	C4
45001	Addyston 1,195	B9
43101	Adelphi 472	E7
43901	Adena 1,062	J5
*44301	Akron⊙ 237,177	G3
	Akron‡ 660,328	G3
45710	Albany 905	F7
43001	Alexandria 489	E5
45812	Alger 992	C4
44601	Alliance 24,315	H4
43102	Amanda 720	E6
†45201	Amberley 3,442	C9
45102	Amelia 1,108	D10
44001	Amherst 10,638	F3
43903	Amsterdam 783	J5
44003	Andover 1,205	J2
45302	Anna 1,038	B5
45303	Ansonia 1,267	A5
45813	Antwerp 1,765	A3
44606	Apple Creek 741	G4
44804	Arcadia 580	D3
45304	Arcanum 2,002	A6
43502	Archbold 3,318	B2
45814	Arlington 1,187	C4
†45201	Arlington Heights 1,082	C9
44805	Ashland⊙ 20,326	F4
43003	Ashley 1,057	E5
44004	Ashtabula 23,449	J2
43103	Ashville 2,046	E6
45701	Athens⊙ 19,743	F7
44807	Attica 865	E3
44201	Atwater 975	H3
44202	Aurora 8,177	H3
44010	Austinburg 900	J2
44515	Austintown 33,636	J3
44011	Avon 7,241	F3
44012	Avon Lake 13,222	F2
†43512	Ayersville 950	B3
†44805	Bailey Lakes 397	F4
45612	Bainbridge 1,042	D7
43804	Baltic 563	G5
43105	Baltimore 2,689	E6
44203	Barberton 29,751	G4
43713	Barnesville 4,633	H6
43905	Barton 1,039	J5
45103	Batavia⊙ 1,896	B7
†44870	Bay View 804	E3
44140	Bay Village 17,846	G9
44608	Beach City 1,083	G4
44122	Beachwood 9,983	J9
43716	Beallsville 601	J6
45808	Beaverdam 492	C4
44146	Bedford 15,056	H9
†44146	Bedford Heights 13,214	J9
43906	Bellaire 8,241	J5
45305	Bellbrook 5,174	C6
43310	Belle Center 930	C4
43311	Bellefontaine⊙ 11,888	C5
44811	Bellevue 8,187	E3
44813	Bellville 1,714	E4
43718	Belmont 714	J5
44609	Beloit 1,093	J4
45714	Belpre 7,193	G7
44017	Berea 19,567	G10
43908	Bergholz 914	J4
44814	Berlin Heights 756	F3
45106	Bethel 2,231	B8
43719	Bethesda 1,429	H5
44815	Bettsville 752	D3
45715	Beverly 1,471	G6
43209	Bexley 13,405	E6
45107	Blanchester 3,202	B7
44817	Bloomdale 744	D3
43106	Bloomingburg 869	D6
44818	Bloomville 1,019	D3
†45242	Blue Ash 9,506	C9
45817	Bluffton 3,310	C4
44512	Boardman 39,161	J3
44612	Bolivar 989	G4
†44264	Boston Heights 781	J10
45306	Botkins 1,372	B5
44695	Bowerston 487	H5
43402	Bowling Green⊙ 25,728	C3
45308	Bradford 2,166	B5
43406	Bradner 1,175	C3
44211	Brady Lake 470	H3
†44101	Bratenahl 1,485	H9
44141	Brecksville 10,132	H10
43107	Bremen 1,432	F6
44613	Brewster 2,321	G4
43912	Bridgeport 2,642	J5
†45211	Bridgetown 11,460	B9
43913	Brilliant 1,751	J5
†44240	Brimfield 3,161	H3
44402	Bristolville 900	J3
†44141	Broadview Heights 10,920	H10
44403	Brookfield 1,527	J3
44144	Brooklyn 12,342	H9
†44131	Brooklyn Heights 1,653	H9
44142	Brook Park 26,195	G9
†43912	Brookside 887	J5
45309	Brookville 4,322	B6
44212	Brunswick 28,104	G3
43506	Bryan⊙ 7,879	A3
45716	Buchtel 585	F7
43008	Buckeye Lake	F6
44820	Bucyrus⊙ 13,433	E4
†45680	Burlington 900	F9
44021	Burton 1,401	H3
44822	Butler 991	F4
43723	Byesville 2,572	G6
43907	Cadiz⊙ 4,058	J5
45820	Cairo 596	B4
43920	Calcutta 1,121	J4
43724	Caldwell⊙ 1,935	G6
43314	Caledonia 759	D4
43725	Cambridge⊙ 13,573	G5
45311	Camden 1,971	A6
44405	Campbell 11,619	J3
45111	Camp Dennison 625	D9
44614	Canal Fulton 3,481	H4
43110	Canal Winchester 2,749	E6
44406	Canfield 5,535	J3
*44701	Canton⊙ 93,077	H4
	Canton‡ 404,421	H4
43315	Cardington 1,665	E5
43316	Carey 3,674	D4
45005	Carlisle 4,276	B6
43112	Carroll 641	E6
44615	Carrollton⊙ 3,065	J4
44824	Castalia 973	E3
45314	Cedarville 2,799	C6
45822	Celina⊙ 9,137	A4
43011	Centerburg 1,275	E5
45459	Centerville 18,886	B6
44022	Chagrin Falls 4,335	J9
†45631	Chambersburg	F8
44024	Chardon⊙ 4,434	H2
45719	Chauncey 1,050	F7
†45202	Cherry Grove 850	C10
45619	Chesapeake 1,370	E9
44026	Chesterland 2,301	H2
†45211	Cheviot 9,888	B9
45601	Chillicothe⊙ 23,420	E7
45389	Christiansburg 593	C5
*45201	Cincinnati⊙ 385,457	B9
	Cincinnati‡ 1,401,403	B9
43113	Circleville⊙ 11,700	D6
43915	Clarington 558	J6
43115	Clarksburg 483	D7
45113	Clarksville 525	C7
45315	Clayton 752	B6
*44101	Cleveland⊙ 573,822	H9
	Cleveland‡ 1,898,720	H9
44118	Cleveland Heights 56,438	H9
45002	Cleves 2,094	B9
44216	Clinton 1,277	G4
43410	Clyde 5,489	E3
†45638	Coal Grove 2,602	E9
45621	Coalton 639	E7
45828	Coldwater 4,220	A5
†44034	Colebrook 700	J2
44028	Columbia Station 518	G10
44408	Columbiana 4,987	J4
*43201	Columbus (cap.)⊙ 565,032	E6
	Columbus‡ 1,093,293	E6
45830	Columbus Grove 2,313	B4
43811	Conesville 451	G5
44030	Conneaut 13,835	J2
45831	Continental 1,179	B3
45832	Convoy 1,140	A4
45723	Coolville 649	G7
43730	Corning 789	F6
44410	Cortland 5,011	J3
43812	Coshocton⊙ 13,405	G5
†45238	Covedale 5,830	B10
45318	Covington 2,610	B5
†44429	Craig Beach 1,657	H3
44827	Crestline 5,406	E4
44217	Creston 1,828	G3
45806	Cridersville 1,843	B4
43731	Crooksville 2,766	F6
45623	Crown City 513	F8
†45341	Crystal Lakes 1,463	C6
*44221	Cuyahoga Falls 43,890	G3
†44101	Cuyahoga Heights 739	H9
43413	Cygnet 646	C3
44618	Dalton 1,357	G4
43014	Danville 1,127	F5
†43123	Darbydale 825	D6
*45401	Dayton⊙ 193,444	B6
	Dayton‡ 830,070	B6
44411	Deerfield 800	H3
45236	Deer Park 6,745	C9
43512	Defiance⊙ 16,810	B3
43318	Degraff 1,358	C5
43015	Delaware⊙ 18,780	E5
45833	Delphos 7,314	B4
43515	Delta 2,831	B2
44621	Dennison 3,398	H5
†45202	Dent 800	B9
43516	Deshler 1,870	C3
45750	Devola 2,708	H7
43917	Dillonvale 912	J5
44622	Dover 11,782	G4
44230	Doylestown 2,493	G4
43821	Dresden 1,646	G5
43017	Dublin 3,855	D5
43734	Duncan Falls 900	G6
45836	Dunkirk 954	C4
44730	East Canton 1,721	H4
44112	East Cleveland 36,957	H9
†44094	Eastlake 22,104	J8
43920	East Liverpool 16,687	J4
44413	East Palestine 5,306	J4
44626	East Sparta 868	H4
45320	Eaton⊙ 6,839	A6
†44035	Eaton Estates 1,806	G3
43517	Edgerton 1,813	A3
†44004	Edgewood 3,099	J2
43320	Edison 504	E4
43518	Edon 947	A2
45321	Eldorado 509	A6
45807	Elida 1,349	B4
43416	Elmore 1,271	D3
45216	Elmwood Place 2,840	B9
*44035	Elyria⊙ 57,538	F3
45322	Englewood 11,329	B6
45323	Enon 2,597	C6
44117	Euclid 59,999	J9
†45201	Evendale 1,954	C9
45042	Excello 900	B7
45324	Fairborn 29,702	B6
†45201	Fairfax 2,222	C9
45014	Fairfield 30,777	A7
44313	Fairlawn 6,100	G3
44077	Fairport Harbor 3,357	H2
44126	Fairview Park 19,311	G9
45325	Farmersville 950	A6
43521	Fayette 1,222	B2
45120	Felicity 929	B8
45840	Findlay⊙ 35,594	C3
45326	Fletcher 498	B5
43977	Flushing 1,266	J5
45843	Forest 1,633	C4
45405	Forest Park 18,675	B9
45230	Forestville 950	C10
45844	Fort Jennings 538	B4
45845	Fort Loramie 977	B5
†45426	Fort McKinley	B6
45846	Fort Recovery 1,370	A5
†45801	Fort Shawnee 4,541	B4
44830	Fostoria 15,743	D3
45628	Frankfort 1,008	D7
45005	Franklin 10,711	B6
45629	Franklin Furnace 1,093	E8
43822	Frazeysburg 1,025	F5
44627	Fredericksburg 511	G4
44019	Fredericktown 2,299	F5
43973	Freeport 525	H5
43420	Fremont⊙ 17,834	D3
45630	Friendship 900	D8
43230	Gahanna 18,001	E5
44833	Galion 12,391	E4
45631	Gallipolis⊙ 5,576	F8
43022	Gambier 2,056	F5
44125	Garfield Heights 34,938	J9
44231	Garrettsville 1,769	H3
44040	Gates Mills 2,236	J9
44041	Geneva 6,655	J2
44043	Geneva-on-the-Lake 1,634	H2
43430	Genoa 2,213	D2
45121	Georgetown⊙ 3,467	C8
45327	Germantown 5,015	B6
45328	Gettysburg 545	A5
43431	Gibsonburg 2,479	D3
44420	Girard 12,517	J3
45848	Glandorf 746	B3
45246	Glendale 2,368	C9
†44139	Glenwillow 492	J10
45732	Glouster 2,211	F6
44629	Gnadenhutten 1,320	G5
†45201	Golf Manor 4,317	C9
45122	Goshen	B7
44044	Grafton 2,231	F3
43522	Grand Rapids 962	C3
44045	Grand River 412	H2
†43212	Grandview Heights 7,420	D6
43023	Granville 3,851	E5
45330	Gratis 809	A6
43322	Green Camp 475	D4
45123	Greenfield 5,150	D7
45218	Greenhills 4,927	B9
44232	Greensburg 950	G4
44836	Green Springs 1,568	E3
44630	Greentown 300	H4
45331	Greenville⊙ 12,999	A5
44837	Greenwich 1,458	E3
43123	Grove City 16,816	D6
43125	Groveport 3,286	E6
45849	Grover Hill 486	B3
45634	Hamden 1,010	E7
45130	Hamersville 688	C8
*45011	Hamilton⊙ 63,189	A7
	Hamilton-Middletown‡ 258,787	A7
43524	Hamler 625	B3
43931	Hannibal 550	J6
†43055	Hanover 926	F5
43126	Harrisburg 363	D6
45030	Harrison 5,855	A9
45850	Harrod 506	C4
†44085	Hartsgrove 200	J2
44632	Hartville 1,772	H4
43525	Haskins 568	C3
43127	Haydenville 395	F7
44838	Hayesville 518	F4
43055	Heath 6,969	F5
43025	Hebron 2,035	E6
43526	Hicksville 3,929	A3
†44143	Highland Heights 5,739	J9
43026	Hilliard 8,008	D5
45133	Hillsboro⊙ 6,356	C7
44234	Hiram 1,360	H3
43527	Holgate 1,315	B3
43528	Holland 1,048	C2
45033	Hooven 550	A9
43976	Hopedale 857	J5
44425	Hubbard 9,245	J3
45424	Huber Heights 35,480	B6
44236	Hudson 4,615	H3
†44022	Hunting Valley 786	J9
44839	Huron 7,123	E3
44131	Independence 6,607	H9
†45201	Indian Hill 5,521	C9
43932	Irondale 535	J4
45638	Ironton⊙ 14,290	E8
45640	Jackson⊙ 6,675	E7
45334	Jackson Center 1,310	B5
45740	Jacksonville 651	F7
45335	Jamestown 1,702	C6
44047	Jefferson⊙ 2,952	J2
†43162	Jefferson (West Jefferson) 4,448	D6
43128	Jeffersonville 1,252	C6
44840	Jeromesville 582	F4
43437	Jerry City 512	C3
43986	Jewett 972	H5
43031	Johnstown 3,158	E5
43748	Junction City 754	F6
45853	Kalida 1,019	B4
44240	Kent 26,164	H3
43326	Kenton⊙ 8,605	C4
45429	Kettering 61,186	B6
44637	Killbuck 937	G5
45034	Kings Mills 500	B7
45644	Kingston 1,208	E7
44048	Kingsville	J2
44428	Kinsman 900	J3
43033	Kirkersville 626	E6
†44094	Kirtland 5,969	H2
43951	Lafferty 855	H5
44050	Lagrange 1,258	F3
44250	Lakemore 2,744	H3
43440	Lakeside 850	E2
43331	Lakeview 1,089	C4
44107	Lakewood 61,963	G9
43130	Lancaster⊙ 34,953	E6
43934	Lansing 950	J5
43332	La Rue 861	D4
43135	Laurelville 591	E7
†45501	Lawrenceville 307	C6
45036	Lebanon⊙ 9,636	B7
45135	Leesburg 1,019	D7
44431	Leetonia 2,121	J4
45856	Leipsic 2,171	C3
45338	Lewisburg 1,450	A6
44904	Lexington 3,823	E4
43532	Liberty Center 1,111	B3
*45801	Lima⊙ 47,381	B4
	Lima‡ 218,244	B4
†45201	Lincoln Heights 5,259	C9
43442	Lindsey 571	D3
44432	Lisbon⊙ 3,159	J4
44253	Litchfield 650	F3
43136	Lithopolis 652	E6
45742	Little Hocking 800	G7
45215	Lockland 4,292	C9
44254	Lodi 2,942	F3
43138	Logan⊙ 6,557	F6
43140	London⊙ 6,958	C6
*44052	Lorain 75,416	F3
	Lorain-Elyria‡ 274,909	F3
†44481	Lordstown 3,280	J3
44842	Loudonville 2,945	F4
44641	Louisville 7,996	H4
45140	Loveland 9,106	D9
45744	Lowell 729	H6
44436	Lowellville 1,558	J3
44843	Lucas 753	F4
45648	Lucasville 3,349	E8
43443	Luckey 895	D3
45142	Lynchburg 1,205	C7
44124	Lyndhurst 18,092	J9
43533	Lyons 596	B2
44056	Macedonia 6,571	J10
†45202	Mack	B9
45243	Madeira 9,341	C9
44057	Madison 2,291	H2
44643	Magnolia 986	H4
43758	Malta 956	G6
44644	Malvern 1,032	H4
45144	Manchester 2,313	C8
*44901	Mansfield⊙ 53,927	F4
	Mansfield‡ 131,205	F4
44255	Mantua 1,041	H3
44137	Maple Heights 29,735	H9
†43440	Marblehead 679	E2
45860	Maria Stein 950	A5

(continued on following page)

Agriculture, Industry and Resources

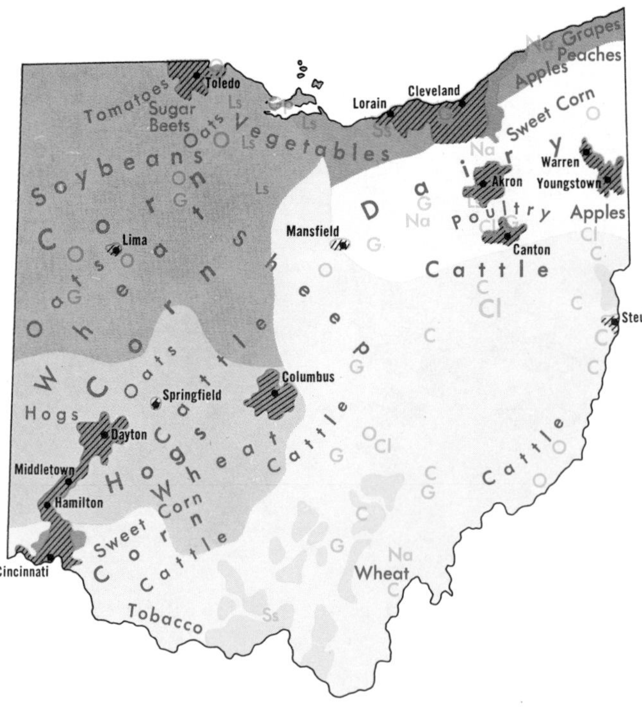

DOMINANT LAND USE

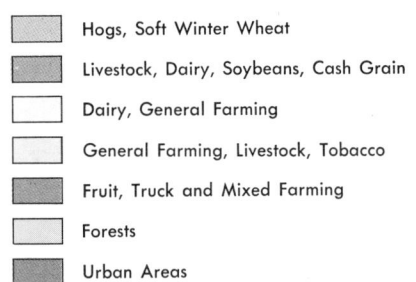

Hogs, Soft Winter Wheat
Livestock, Dairy, Soybeans, Cash Grain
Dairy, General Farming
General Farming, Livestock, Tobacco
Fruit, Truck and Mixed Farming
Forests
Urban Areas

MAJOR MINERAL OCCURRENCES

C Coal
Cl Clay
G Natural Gas
Gp Gypsum
Ls Limestone
Na Salt
O Petroleum
Ss Sandstone
Major Industrial Areas

45227 Mariemont 3,295 .... C9
45750 Marietta⊙ 16,467 .... G7
43302 Marion⊙ 37,040 .... D4
44645 Marshallville 788 .... G4
43935 Martins Ferry 9,331 .... J5
45146 Martinsville 539 .... C7
43040 Marysville⊙ 7,414 .... D5
45040 Mason 8,692 .... B7
44646 Massillon 30,557 .... H4
44438 Masury 1,836 .... J3
†45069 Maud 800 .... B7
43537 Maumee 15,747 .... C2
44124 Mayfield 3,577 .... J9
44124 Mayfield Heights 21,550 .... J9
45651 McArthur⊙ 1,912 .... F7
43534 McClure 694 .... C3
45858 McComb 1,608 .... C3
43756 McConnelsville⊙ 2,018 .... G6
44437 McDonald 3,744 .... J3
45859 McGuffey 646 .... C4
43044 Mechanicsburg 1,792 .... D5
44256 Medina⊙ 15,268 .... G3
45862 Mendon 749 .... A4
44060 Mentor 42,065 .... H2
44060 Mentor-on-the-Lake 7,919 .... G2
43540 Metamora 556 .... C2
45342 Miamisburg 15,304 .... B6
45041 Miamitown 800 .... A9
44652 Middlebranch 300 .... H4
†44017 Middleburg Heights 16,218 .... G10
44062 Middlefield 1,997 .... H3
45863 Middle Point 709 .... B4
45760 Middleport 2,971 .... F7
45042 Middletown 43,719 .... A6
44653 Midvale 654 .... H5
44846 Milan 1,569 .... E3
45150 Milford 5,232 .... D9
43045 Milford Center 764 .... D5
43447 Millbury 955 .... D2
44654 Millersburg⊙ 3,247 .... F4
43046 Millersport 844 .... E6
†45011 Millville 809 .... A7
44656 Mineral City 884 .... H4
44657 Minerva 4,549 .... H4
†43201 Minerva Park 1,618 .... E5
43938 Mingo Junction 4,834 .... J5
45865 Minster 2,557 .... B5
44260 Mogadore 4,190 .... H3
45050 Monroe 4,256 .... B7
44847 Monroeville 1,329 .... E3
45242 Montgomery 10,088 .... C9
43543 Montpelier 4,431 .... A2
†45439 Moraine 5,325 .... B6
†44022 Moreland Hills 3,083 .... J9
45152 Morrow 1,254 .... B7
43338 Mount Gilead⊙ 2,911 .... E4
45231 Mount Healthy 7,562 .... B9
45154 Mount Orab 1,573 .... C7
43939 Mount Pleasant 616 .... J5
43143 Mount Sterling 1,623 .... D6
43050 Mount Vernon⊙ 14,323 .... E5
43340 Mount Victory 667 .... D4
44262 Munroe Falls 4,731 .... H3
43144 Murray City 579 .... F6
43545 Napoleon⊙ 8,614 .... B3
44662 Navarre 1,343 .... H4
43940 Neffs 1,106 .... J5
44441 Negley 917 .... J4
45764 Nelsonville 4,567 .... F7
44849 Nevada 945 .... D4
43055 Newark⊙ 41,200 .... F5
Newark‡ 120,981 .... F5
45662 New Boston 3,188 .... E8
45869 New Bremen 2,393 .... B5
†44101 Newburgh Heights 2,678 .... H9
†45201 New Burlington 900 .... B9
45344 New Carlisle 6,498 .... C6
43832 Newcomerstown 3,986 .... G5
43762 New Concord 1,860 .... G6
43145 New Holland 783 .... D6
45871 New Knoxville 760 .... B5
45345 New Lebanon 4,501 .... B6
43764 New Lexington⊙ 5,179 .... F6
44851 New London 2,449 .... F3
45346 New Madison 1,008 .... A6
45767 New Matamoras J6
45011 New Miami 2,980 .... A7
44442 New Middletown 2,195 .... J4
45347 New Paris 1,709 .... A6
44663 New Philadelphia⊙ 16,883 .... G5
45768 Newport 975 .... H7
45157 New Richmond 2,769 .... B8
43766 New Straitsville 937 .... F6
44444 Newton Falls 4,960 .... J3
45244 Newtown 1,817 .... C10
45159 New Vienna 1,133 .... C7
44854 New Washington 1,213 .... E4
44445 New Waterford 1,314 .... J4
44446 Niles 23,088 .... J3
45872 North Baltimore 3,127 .... C3
45052 North Bend 546 .... B9
44450 North Bloomfield 650 .... J3
44720 North Canton 14,228 .... H4
45239 North College Hill 11,114 .... B9
44855 North Fairfield 525 .... E3
44067 Northfield 3,913 .... J10
44707 North Industry H4
44068 North Kingsville 2,939 .... J2
43060 North Lewisburg 1,072 .... C5
44452 North Lima 800 .... J4
†44057 North Madison 8,741 .... H2
44070 North Olmsted 36,486 .... G9
†44081 North Perry 897 .... H2
†44101 North Randall 1,054 .... H9
45414 Northridge 9,720 .... B6
44039 North Ridgeville 21,522 .... F3
44133 North Royalton 17,671 .... H10
†43619 Northwood 5,495 .... D2
†43701 North Zanesville 2,166 .... G6
44203 Norton 12,242 .... G3
44857 Norwalk⊙ 14,358 .... E3
45212 Norwood 26,342 .... C9
43449 Oak Harbor 2,678 .... D2
45656 Oak Hill 1,713 .... E8
†45419 Oakwood 9,372 .... B6
†44146 Oakwood 3,786 .... H9
45873 Oakwood 886 .... B3
44074 Oberlin 8,660 .... F3
†43201 Obetz 3,095 .... E6
45874 Ohio City 881 .... A4
44138 Olmsted Falls 5,868 .... G9
44862 Ontario 4,123 .... E4
†44101 Orange 2,376 .... J9
43616 Oregon 18,675 .... D2
44667 Orrville 7,511 .... G4
44076 Orwell 1,067 .... J2
45875 Ottawa⊙ 3,874 .... B3
†43601 Ottawa Hills 4,065 .... C2
45876 Ottoville 833 .... B4
45160 Owensville 858 .... B7
45056 Oxford 17,655 .... A6
44077 Painesville⊙ 16,391 .... H2
45877 Pandora 977 .... C4
44080 Parkman 600 .... H3
44129 Parma 92,548 .... H9
†44130 Parma Heights 23,112 .... G9
43062 Pataskala 2,284 .... E5
45879 Paulding⊙ 2,754 .... A3
45880 Payne 1,399 .... A3
45660 Peebles 1,790 .... D8
43450 Pemberville 1,321 .... C3
44264 Peninsula 604 .... G3
†44124 Pepper Pike 6,177 .... J9
44081 Perry 961 .... H2
43551 Perrysburg 10,215 .... C2
44864 Perrysville 836 .... F4
45354 Phillipsburg 705 .... B6
43771 Philo 799 .... G6
43147 Pickerington 3,917 .... E6
45661 Piketon 1,726 .... E7
43554 Pioneer 1,133 .... A2
45356 Piqua 20,480 .... B5
43064 Plain City 2,102 .... D5
43772 Pleasant City 481 .... G6
45359 Pleasant Hill 1,051 .... B5
43148 Pleasantville 780 .... F6
44865 Plymouth 1,939 .... E4
44514 Poland 3,084 .... J3
45769 Pomeroy⊙ 2,728 .... G7
43452 Port Clinton⊙ 7,223 .... E2
45770 Portland 150 .... G7
45662 Portsmouth⊙ 25,943 .... D8
43837 Port Washington 622 .... G5
43942 Powhatan Point 2,181 .... J6
45669 Proctorville 975 .... F9
43342 Prospect 1,159 .... D5
43456 Put-in-Bay 146 .... E2
43773 Quaker City 698 .... H6
43343 Quincy 633 .... C5
45771 Racine 908 .... G8
44265 Randolph 900 .... H3
44266 Ravenna⊙ 11,987 .... H3
43943 Rayland 566 .... J5
45215 Reading 12,843 .... C9
†44202 Reminderville 1,960 .... J10
†45202 Remington 600 .... C9
45773 Reno 576 .... H7
†43412 Reno Beach D2
44867 Republic 656 .... D3
43068 Reynoldsburg 20,661 .... E6
44286 Richfield 3,437 .... G3
43944 Richmond 624 .... J5
†44045 Richmond (Grand River) 412 .... H2
45673 Richmond Dale 950 .... E7
44143 Richmond Heights 10,095 .... H9
43344 Richwood 2,181 .... D5
45674 Rio Grande 864 .... F8
45167 Ripley 2,174 .... C8
43457 Risingsun 698 .... C3
44270 Rittman 6,063 .... G4
†43085 Riverlea 528 .... D5
44670 Robertsville 600 .... H4
44084 Rock Creek 652 .... J2
45882 Rockford 1,245 .... A4
44116 Rocky River 21,084 .... G9
44085 Rome 210 .... J2
44272 Rootstown 900 .... H3
†45662 Rosemount 1,747 .... D8
43777 Roseville 1,915 .... F6
45061 Ross 2,767 .... B9
43460 Rossford 5,978 .... C2
45236 Rossmoyne C9
†43943 Rush Run 560 .... J5
43347 Rushsylvania 610 .... C5
43348 Russells Point 1,156 .... C5
45775 Rutland 635 .... F7
45169 Sabina 2,799 .... C7
†44067 Sagamore Hills J10
45217 Saint Bernard 5,396 .... B9
43950 Saint Clairsville⊙ 5,452 .... J5
45883 Saint Henry 1,596 .... A5
45885 Saint Marys 8,414 .... B4
43072 Saint Paris 1,742 .... C5
44460 Salem 12,869 .... J4
43945 Salineville 1,629 .... J4
44870 Sandusky⊙ 31,360 .... E3
44671 Sandyville 500 .... H4
45171 Sardinia 826 .... C7
43946 Sardis 865 .... J6
43988 Scio 1,003 .... H5
†45662 Sciotodale 1,191 .... E8
45679 Seaman 1,039 .... C8
44672 Sebring 5,078 .... H4
†44131 Seven Hills 13,650 .... H9
45062 Seven Mile 841 .... A7
44273 Seville 1,568 .... G3
43947 Shadyside 4,315 .... J6
44120 Shaker Heights 32,487 .... H9
45241 Sharonville 10,108 .... C9
43782 Shawnee 924 .... F6
†44052 Sheffield 1,886 .... F3
44054 Sheffield Lake 10,484 .... F3
44875 Shelby 9,646 .... E4
43556 Sherwood 915 .... A3
44878 Shiloh 857 .... E4
44676 Shreve 1,608 .... F4
45365 Sidney⊙ 17,657 .... B5
†44221 Silver Lake 2,915 .... G3
†45201 Silverton 6,172 .... C9
43948 Smithfield 1,308 .... J5
44677 Smithville 1,467 .... G4
44139 Solon 14,341 .... J9
43783 Somerset 1,432 .... F6
†44001 South Amherst 1,848 .... F3
†43103 South Bloomfield 934 .... D6
45368 South Charleston 1,682 .... C6
44121 South Euclid 25,713 .... H9
45065 South Lebanon 2,700 .... B7
45680 South Point 3,918 .... E9
†44022 South Russell 2,784 .... H3
45369 South Vienna 464 .... C6
45682 South Webster 886 .... E8
43701 South Zanesville 1,739 .... F6
44275 Spencer 764 .... F3
45887 Spencerville 2,184 .... B4
45066 Springboro 4,962 .... B6
45246 Springdale 10,111 .... B9
*45501 Springfield⊙ 72,563 .... C6
Springfield‡ 183,885 .... C6
45370 Spring Valley 541 .... C6
44276 Sterling 600 .... G4
43952 Steubenville⊙ 26,400 .... J5
Steubenville-Weirton‡ 163,099 .... J5
43787 Stockport 558 .... G6
43154 Stoutsville 537 .... E6
44224 Stow 25,303 .... H3
44680 Strasburg 2,091 .... G4
44240 Streetsboro 9,055 .... H3
44136 Strongsville 28,577 .... G10
44471 Struthers 13,624 .... J3
43557 Stryker 1,423 .... B3
†44260 Suffield 650 .... H3
44681 Sugarcreek 1,966 .... G5
43074 Sunbury 2,101 .... E5
43558 Swanton 3,424 .... C2
44882 Sycamore 1,059 .... D4
43560 Sylvania 15,527 .... C2
45779 Syracuse 946 .... G7
44278 Tallmadge 15,269 .... H3
†43771 Taylorsville (Philo) 799 .... G6
45174 Terrace Park 2,044 .... D9
45780 The Plains 2,044 .... F7
43076 Thornville 838 .... F6
44883 Tiffin⊙ 19,549 .... D3
43963 Tiltonsville 1,750 .... J5
†44094 Timberlake 885 .... J8
45371 Tipp City 5,595 .... B6
†45245 Tobasco 950 .... C10
*43601 Toledo⊙ 354,635 .... D2
Toledo‡ 791,599 .... D2
43964 Toronto 6,934 .... J5
45067 Trenton 6,401 .... B7
45782 Trimble 579 .... F7
45426 Trotwood 7,802 .... B6
45373 Troy⊙ 19,086 .... B5
44682 Tuscarawas 917 .... H5
44087 Twinsburg 7,632 .... J10
44683 Uhrichsville 6,130 .... H5
45322 Union 5,219 .... B6
†47390 Union City 1,716 .... A5
44685 Uniontown 875 .... H4
44118 University Heights 15,401 .... H9
43221 Upper Arlington 35,648 .... D6
43351 Upper Sandusky⊙ 5,967 .... D4
43078 Urbana⊙ 10,762 .... C5
†43123 Urbancrest 880 .... D6
43080 Utica 2,238 .... F5
†43201 Valley View 730 .... D6
†44101 Valleyview 1,576 .... H9
45377 Vandalia 13,161 .... B6
45890 Vanlue 390 .... C4
45891 Van Wert⊙ 11,035 .... A4
44089 Vermilion 11,012 .... F3
45378 Verona 571 .... A6
45380 Versailles 2,384 .... A5
44473 Vienna 900 .... J3
44281 Wadsworth 15,166 .... G3
†44094 Waite Hill 529 .... H2
45687 Wakefield 300 .... E8
44889 Wakeman 906 .... F3
43465 Walbridge 2,900 .... C2
44687 Walnut Creek 550 .... G4
†44146 Walton Hills 2,199 .... J10
45895 Wapakoneta⊙ 8,402 .... B4
45785 Warner 250 .... H6
*44481 Warren⊙ 56,629 .... J3
44128 Warrensville Heights 16,565 .... H9
43844 Warsaw 765 .... G5
43160 Washington Court House⊙ 12,682 .... D6
44490 Washingtonville 865 .... J4
45786 Waterford 600 .... G6
43566 Waterville 3,884 .... C3
43567 Wauseon⊙ 6,173 .... B2
45690 Waverly⊙ 4,603 .... D7
43466 Wayne 894 .... C3
44688 Waynesburg 1,160 .... H4
45896 Waynesfield 826 .... C4
45068 Waynesville 1,796 .... B6
44090 Wellington 4,146 .... F3
45692 Wellston 6,016 .... F7
43968 Wellsville 5,095 .... J4
45381 West Alexandria 1,313 .... A6
45449 West Carrollton 13,148 .... B6
43081 Westerville 23,414 .... D5
44491 West Farmington 563 .... J3
44251 Westfield Center 791 .... G3
43162 West Jefferson 4,448 .... D6
43845 West Lafayette 2,225 .... G5
44145 Westlake 19,483 .... G9
43357 West Liberty 1,653 .... C5
43358 West Mansfield 716 .... C5
45383 West Milton 4,119 .... B6
43569 Weston 1,708 .... C3
†45662 West Portsmouth 4,095 .... D8
44287 West Salem 1,357 .... F4
45693 West Union⊙ 2,791 .... C8
43570 West Unity 1,639 .... B2
45694 Wheelersburg 4,796 .... E8
43213 Whitehall 21,299 .... E6
43571 Whitehouse 2,137 .... C2
44092 Wickliffe 16,790 .... J9
44890 Willard 5,720 .... E3
45176 Williamsburg 1,952 .... B7
44093 Williamsfield 950 .... J2
43164 Williamsport 792 .... D6
44094 Willoughby 19,329 .... J8
†44094 Willoughby Hills 8,612 .... J9
44094 Willowick 17,834 .... J8
45898 Willshire 564 .... A4
45177 Wilmington⊙ 10,431 .... C7
45697 Winchester 1,080 .... C8
44288 Windham 3,721 .... H3
43952 Wintersville 4,724 .... J5
45245 Withamsville 975 .... C10
†45201 Woodlawn 2,715 .... C9
†44101 Woodmere 877 .... J9
43793 Woodsfield⊙ 3,145 .... H6
43469 Woodville 2,050 .... D3
44691 Wooster⊙ 19,289 .... G4
43085 Worthington 15,016 .... E5
45215 Wyoming 8,282 .... C9
45385 Xenia⊙ 24,653 .... C6
45387 Yellow Springs 4,077 .... C6
43971 Yorkville 1,447 .... J5
*44501 Youngstown⊙ 115,436 .... J3
Youngstown-Warren‡ 531,350 .... J3
43701 Zanesville⊙ 28,655 .... G6
44697 Zoar 264 .... H4
44698 Zoarville 125 .... H4

OTHER FEATURES

Atwood (lake) H4
Auglaize (riv.) B4
Berlin (lake) H4
Big Walnut (creek) E5
Black (riv.) F3
Black Fork, Mohican (riv.) F4
Blanchard (riv.) C4
Blennerhassett (isl.) G7
Buckeye (lake) F6
Campbell (hill) C5
Captina (creek) J6
Cedar (pt.) D2
Chagrin (riv.) J8
Clear Fork (res.) E4
Clear Fork, Mohican (riv.) F4
Clendening (lake) H5
Cleveland-Hopkins Mun. Airport G9
Cuyahoga (riv.) H10
Darby (creek) D5
Deer (creek) D6
Delaware (lake) E5
Dillon (lake) F5
Dover (lake) H4
Duck (creek) H6
Erie (lake) H1
Eufaula (res.) L4
Grand (riv.) H2
Great Miami (riv.) A7
Hocking (riv.) F7
Hoover (res.) E5
Huron (riv.) E3
Indian (lake) C5
James A. Garfield Nat'l Hist. Site G2
Kelleys (isl.) E2
Keystone (res.) K2
Killbuck (creek) G4
Kokosing (riv.) E5
Leesville (lake) H5
Licking (riv.) F5
Little Beaver (creek) J4
Little Miami (riv.) B6
Little Miami, East Fork (riv.) C7
Little Muskingum (riv.) H6
Loramie (lake) B5
Mad (riv.) C6
Maumee (bay) D2
Maumee (riv.) A3
Middle Bass (isl.) E2
Mohican (riv.) F4
Mosquito Creek (lake) J3
Mound City Group Nat'l Mon. E7
Muskingum (riv.) G6
North Bass (isl.) E2
Ohio (riv.) B8
Ohio Brush (creek) D8
Olentangy (riv.) D4
Paint (creek) D7
Perry's Victory and Int'l Peace Mem. E2
Piedmont (lake) H5
Portage (riv.) D3
Pymatuning (res.) J2
Raccoon (creek) F8
Rattlesnake (creek) C7
Rickenbacker Air Force Base 1,763 .... E6
Rocky (riv.) G9
Rocky, West Branch (riv.) G10
Rocky Fork (lake) D7
Saint Joseph (riv.) A3
Saint Marys (lake) A4
Saint Marys (riv.) A4
Salt Fork (creek) H5
Sandusky (bay) E3
Sandusky (riv.) D3
Scioto (riv.) D8
Senecaville (lake) H6
Sevenmile (creek) A6
South Bass (isl.) E2
Stillwater (riv.) B5
Symmes (creek) F8
Tappan (lake) H5
Tiffin (riv.) B3
Tuscarawas (riv.) H5
Vermilion (riv.) F3
Wabash (riv.) A5
West Sister (isl.) D2
Whiteoak (creek) C7
William H. Taft Nat'l Hist. Site C10
Wills (creek) G5
Wills Creek (lake) G5
Wright-Patterson Air Force Base 9,155 .... B6
Yellow (creek) J4

⊙County seat.
‡Population of metropolitan area.
† Zip of nearest p.o. * Multiple zips

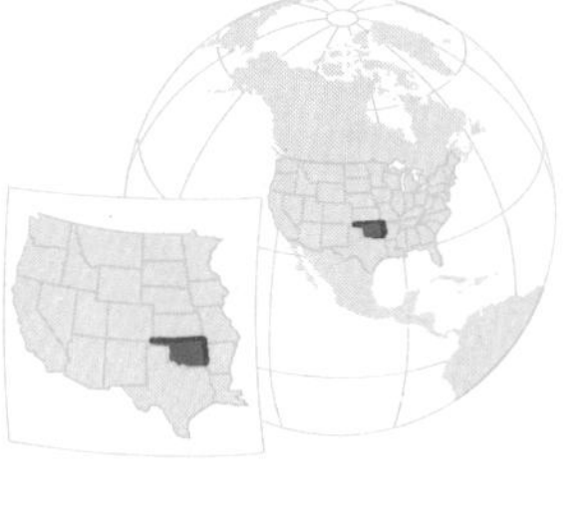

AREA 69,956 sq. mi. (181,186 sq. km.)
POPULATION 3,025,290
CAPITAL Oklahoma City
LARGEST CITY Oklahoma City
HIGHEST POINT Black Mesa 4,973 ft. (1516 m.)
SETTLED IN 1889
ADMITTED TO UNION November 16, 1907
POPULAR NAME Sooner State
STATE FLOWER Mistletoe
STATE BIRD Scissor-tailed Flycatcher

COUNTIES

Adair 18,575 S3
Alfalfa 7,077 K1
Atoka 12,748 O6
Beaver 6,806 E1
Beckham 19,243 G4
Blaine 13,443 K3
Bryan 30,535 O7
Caddo 30,905 K4
Canadian 56,452 K3
Carter 43,610 M6
Cherokee 30,684 R3
Choctaw 17,203 P6
Cimarron 3,648 A1
Cleveland 133,173 M4
Coal 6,041 O5
Comanche 112,456 K5
Cotton 7,338 K6
Craig 15,014 R1
Creek 59,016 O3
Custer 25,995 H3
Delaware 23,946 S2
Dewey 5,922 H2
Ellis 5,596 G2
Garfield 62,820 L2
Garvin 27,856 M5
Grady 39,490 L5
Grant 6,518 L1
Greer 7,028 G5
Harmon 4,519 G5
Harper 4,715 G1
Haskell 11,010 R4
Hughes 14,338 O4
Jackson 30,356 H5
Jefferson 8,183 L6
Johnston 10,356 N6
Kay 49,852 M1
Kingfisher 14,187 L3
Kiowa 12,711 J5
Latimer 9,840 R5
Le Flore 40,698 S5
Lincoln 26,601 N3
Logan 26,881 M3
Love 7,469 M7
Major 8,772 K2
Marshall 10,550 N6
Mayes 32,261 R2
McClain 20,291 L5
McCurtain 36,151 S6
McIntosh 15,562 P4
Murray 12,147 M6
Muskogee 66,939 R3
Noble 11,573 M2
Nowata 11,486 P1
Okfuskee 11,125 O3
Oklahoma 568,933 M3
Okmulgee 39,169 P3
Osage 39,327 O1
Ottawa 32,870 S1
Pawnee 15,310 N2
Payne 62,435 N2
Pittsburg 40,524 P5
Pontotoc 32,598 N5
Pottawatomie 55,239 N4
Pushmataha 11,773 R6
Roger Mills 4,799 G3
Rogers 46,436 P2
Seminole 27,473 N4
Sequoyah 30,749 S3
Stephens 43,419 L6
Texas 17,727 C1
Tillman 12,398 J6
Tulsa 470,593 P2
Wagoner 41,801 P3
Washington 48,113 P1
Washita 13,798 J4
Woods 10,923 J1
Woodward 21,172 H2

CITIES and TOWNS

Zip *Name/Pop.* *Key*

74720 Achille 480 O7
74820 Ada⊙ 15,902 N5
74330 Adair 508 R2
73901 Adams 150 D1
73520 Addington 141 L6
74331 Afton 1,174 S1
74824 Agra 354 N3
74721 Albany 65 O7
73001 Albert 100 K4
74521 Albion 165 R5
74522 Alderson 366 P5
73002 Alex 769 L5
73716 Aline 313 K1
74825 Allen 998 O5
73521 Altus⊙ 23,101 H5
73717 Alva⊙ 6,416 J1
73004 Amber 416 L4
73718 Ames 314 K2
73719 Amorita 66 K1
73005 Anadarko⊙ 6,378 K4
74523 Antlers⊙ 2,989 P6
73006 Apache 1,560 K5
73620 Arapaho⊙ 851 H3
73401 Ardmore⊙ 23,689 M6
74901 Arkoma 2,175 T4
73832 Arnett⊙ 714 G2
74826 Asher 659 N5
74524 Ashland 72 O5
74525 Atoka⊙ 3,409 O6
74827 Atwood 225 O5
74001 Avant 461 O2
†73860 Avard 51 J1
73930 Baker 70 D1
74002 Barnsdall 1,501 O1
†74965 Baron 300 S3
74003 Bartlesville⊙ 34,568 O1
74722 Battiest 250 S6
73932 Beaver⊙ 1,939 F1
74421 Beggs 1,428 P3
†74966 Bengal 300 R5
74723 Bennington 302 P7
74331 Bernice 318 S1
73622 Bessie 245 H4
73008 Bethany 22,130 L3
74724 Bethel 350 S6
†74801 Bethel Acres 2,314 M4
74332 Big Cabin 252 R1
74630 Billings 632 M1
73009 Binger 791 K4
73720 Bison 103 L2
74008 Bixby 6,969 P3
74058 Blackburn 114 N2
74631 Blackwell 8,400 M1
73526 Blair 1,092 H5
73010 Blanchard 1,688 L4
74528 Blanco 215 P5
74529 Blocker 135 P4
†74701 Blue 150 O7
74333 Bluejacket 247 R1
73933 Boise City⊙ 1,761 B1
74726 Bokchito 628 O6
74930 Bokoshe 556 S4
74829 Boley 423 O4
74727 Boswell 702 P6
74830 Bowlegs 522 N4
74009 Bowring 115 O1
74422 Boynton 518 P3
73011 Bradley 284 L5
74423 Braggs 351 R3
74632 Braman 355 M1
73012 Bray 591 L5
73721 Breckinridge 261 L2
†73047 Bridgeport 115 K3
74010 Bristow 4,702 O3
74012 Broken Arrow
35,761 P2
74728 Broken Bow 3,965 S7
74530 Bromide 180 N6
†74873 Brooksville 46 M4
†74437 Bryant 74 P4
73834 Buffalo⊙ 1,381 G1
74931 Bunch 64 S3
74633 Burbank 161 N1
73722 Burlington 206 K1
73430 Burneyville 150 M7
73624 Burns Flat 2,431 H4
73625 Butler 388 H3
74831 Byars 353 N5
†74820 Byng 833 N5
73723 Byron 67 K1
73527 Cache 1,661 J5
74729 Caddo 923 O6
74730 Calera 1,390 O7
73014 Calumet 469 K3
74531 Calvin 315 O5
73835 Camargo 264 H2
74932 Cameron 365 T4
74425 Canadian 279 P4
74533 Caney 147 O6
73724 Canton 854 J2
73626 Canute 676 H4
73725 Capron 54 J1
74335 Cardin 500 S1
73726 Carmen 516 J1
73015 Carnegie 2,016 J4
74832 Carney 622 N3
73727 Carrier 259 K2
73627 Carter 367 H4
74934 Cartersville 79 S4
73016 Cashion 547 L3
74833 Castle 130 O4
74015 Catoosa 1,561 P2
73017 Cement 884 K5
74534 Centrahoma 166 O5
74834 Chandler⊙ 2,926 N3
73528 Chattanooga 403 J6
74426 Checotah 3,454 R4
74016 Chelsea 1,754 P1
73728 Cherokee⊙ 2,105 K1
73838 Chester 104 J2
73628 Cheyenne⊙ 1,207 G3
73018 Chickasha⊙ 15,828 L4
74635 Chilocco 400 M1
73020 Choctaw 7,520 M3
74337 Chouteau 1,559 R2
†74965 Christie 375 S3
73111 Cimarron L3
74017 Claremore⊙ 12,085 R2
74535 Clarita 72 O6
74536 Clayton 833 R5
74835 Clearview 250 O4
73729 Cleo Springs 514 K2
74020 Cleveland 2,972 O2
73601 Clinton 8,796 H3
74538 Coalgate⊙ 2,001 O5
74733 Colbert 1,122 O7
74338 Colcord 530 S2
†73010 Cole 309 L5
73432 Coleman 200 O6
74021 Collinsville 3,556 P2
73021 Colony 185 J4
73529 Comanche 1,937 L6
74339 Commerce 2,556 R1
73022 Concho 300 L3
†73041 Cooperton 31 J5
74022 Copan 960 P1
73632 Cordell⊙ 3,301 H4
73024 Corn 542 J4
†73456 Cornish 115 L6
74428 Council Hill 141 P3
73025 Countyline 550 L6
73730 Covington 715 L2
74429 Coweta 4,554 P3
†74934 Cowlington 546 S4
73027 Coyle 345 M3
73638 Crawford 53 G3
73028 Crescent 1,651 L3
74837 Cromwell 337 N4
74430 Crowder 431 P4
†73446 Cumberland 100 N6
74023 Cushing 7,720 N3
73639 Custer City 530 J3
73029 Cyril 1,220 K5
73731 Dacoma 226 J1
74838 Dale 160 M4
74026 Davenport 974 N3
73530 Davidson 501 J6
73030 Davis 2,782 M5
74636 Deer Creek 174 L1
74027 Delaware 544 P1
73115 Del City 28,523 L4
74028 Depew 682 O3
73531 Devol 186 J6
74431 Dewar 1,048 P4
74029 Dewey 3,545 P1
73031 Dibble 348 L4
†73401 Dickson 996 M6
73641 Dill City 649 H4
74340 Disney 464 S2
73032 Dougherty 210 M6
73733 Douglas 89 L2
74341 Douthat 30 S1
73734 Dover 570 L3
73735 Drummond 482 L2
74030 Drumright 3,162 N3
73533 Duncan⊙ 22,517 L5
74701 Durant⊙ 11,972 O6
73642 Durham 30 G3
74839 Dustin 498 O4
74734 Eagletown 650 S6
73033 Eakly 452 K4
74840 Earlsboro 266 N4
†73532 East Duke 484 H5
73034 Edmond 34,637 M3
73537 Eldorado 688 G6
73538 Elgin 1,003 K5
73644 Elk City 9,579 G4
73539 Elmer 131 H6
73035 Elmore City 582 M5
73935 Elmwood 300 F1
73036 El Reno⊙ 15,486 K3
†73529 Empire City 13 L6
73701 Enid⊙ 50,363 L2
73645 Erick 1,375 G4
74342 Eucha 210 S2
74432 Eufaula⊙ 3,159 P4
74637 Fairfax 1,949 N1
74343 Fairland 1,073 S1
73736 Fairmont 419 L2
†74080 Fair Oaks 346 P2
73737 Fairview⊙ 3,370 J2
†74881 Fallis 22 M3
74935 Fanshawe 416 S5
73840 Fargo 409 G2
73540 Faxon 140 J6
73646 Fay 140 J3
73937 Felt 120 A1
74543 Finley 350 R6
74842 Fittstown 500 N5
74843 Fitzhugh 150 N5
†73569 Fleetwood 12 L7
73541 Fletcher 1,074 K5
74652 Foraker 34 O1
†73101 Forest Park 1,148 M3
73938 Forgan 611 E1
73038 Fort Cobb 760 K4
74434 Fort Gibson 2,477 R3
73841 Fort Supply 559 G1
74735 Fort Towson 789 R7
73647 Foss 188 H4
73039 Foster 100 M5
73435 Fox 400 M6
74031 Foyil 191 R2
74844 Francis 365 N5
73542 Frederick⊙ 6,153 H6
73842 Freedom 339 H1
73843 Gage 667 G2
74936 Gans 346 S4
73738 Garber 1,215 M2
74736 Garvin 162 S7
73844 Gate 146 F1
73040 Geary 1,700 K3
73436 Gene Autry 178 N6
73543 Geronimo 726 K6
†74531 Gerty 149 O5
74032 Glencoe 490 M2
74033 Glenpool 2,706 P3
74737 Golden 300 S6
†73093 Goldsby 603 L4
73739 Goltry 305 K1
†74740 Goodwater 240 S7
73939 Goodwell 1,186 C1
74435 Gore 445 R3
73041 Gotebo 457 J4
73544 Gould 318 G5
74545 Gowen 75 R5
73042 Gracemont 503 K4
73545 Grady 85 L6
73437 Graham 200 M6
†74652 Grainola 67 N1
73546 Grandfield 1,445 J6
†74349 Grand Lake Towne 36 S1
73547 Granite 1,617 H5
†74437 Grayson 150 P3
73043 Greenfield 233 K3
74344 Grove 3,378 S1
73044 Guthrie⊙ 10,312 M3
73942 Guymon⊙ 8,492 D1
74546 Haileyville 832 P5
74034 Hallett 186 N2
†73069 Hall Park 577 M4
73650 Hammon 866 H3
74845 Hanna 157 P4
74846 Harden City 250 N5
73944 Hardesty 243 D1
73832 Harmon 27 G2
73045 Harrah 2,897 M4
†74740 Harris 192 S7
74547 Hartshorne 2,380 R5
74436 Haskell 1,953 P3
73548 Hastings 246 K6
74740 Haworth 341 S7
73549 Headrick 223 H5
73438 Healdton 3,769 M6
74937 Heavener 2,776 S5
73741 Helena 710 K1
74741 Hendrix 106 O7
73046 Hennepin 300 M5
73742 Hennessey 2,287 L2
74437 Henryetta 6,432 O4
†73086 Hickory 95 N5
73743 Hillsdale 110 K1
73047 Hinton 1,432 K4
73744 Hitchcock 172 K3
74438 Hitchita 126 P3
73651 Hobart⊙ 4,735 J5
74439 Hoffman 407 P4
74848 Holdenville⊙ 5,469 O4
73550 Hollis⊙ 2,958 G5
73551 Hollister 82 J6
74035 Hominy 3,130 O2
74549 Honobia 80 R5
73945 Hooker 1,788 D1
†74366 Hoot Owl 3 R2
73746 Hopeton 42 J1
74940 Howe 562 S5
74440 Hoyt 160 R4
74743 Hugo⊙ 7,172 P7
74441 Hulbert 633 R3
74640 Hunter 276 L1
73048 Hydro 938 J3
74745 Idabel⊙ 7,622 S7
73552 Indiahoma 364 J5
74442 Indianola 254 P4
74036 Inola 1,550 P2
73747 Isabella 113 K2
74346 Jay⊙ 2,100 S2
†73759 Jefferson 92 L1
74037 Jenks 5,876 P2
74038 Jennings 395 N2
73749 Jet 352 K1
73049 Jones 2,270 M3
74347 Kansas 491 S2
74641 Kaw City 283 N1
74039 Kellyville 960 O3

(continued on following page)

Agriculture, Industry and Resources

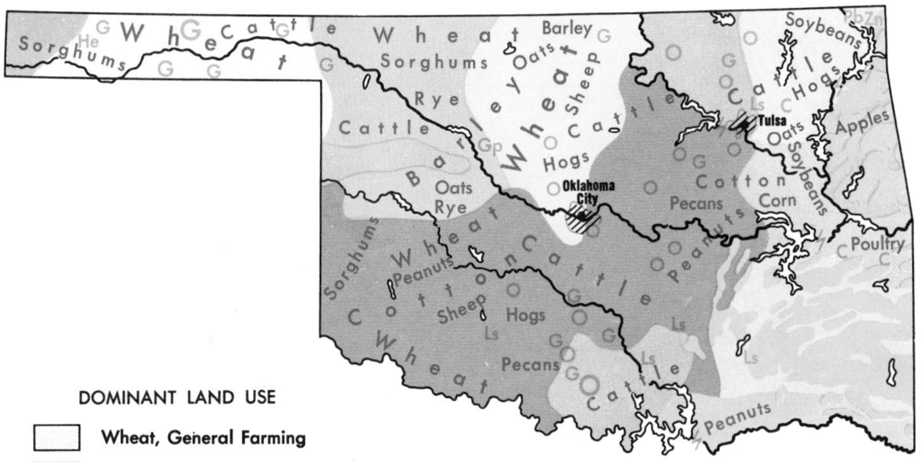

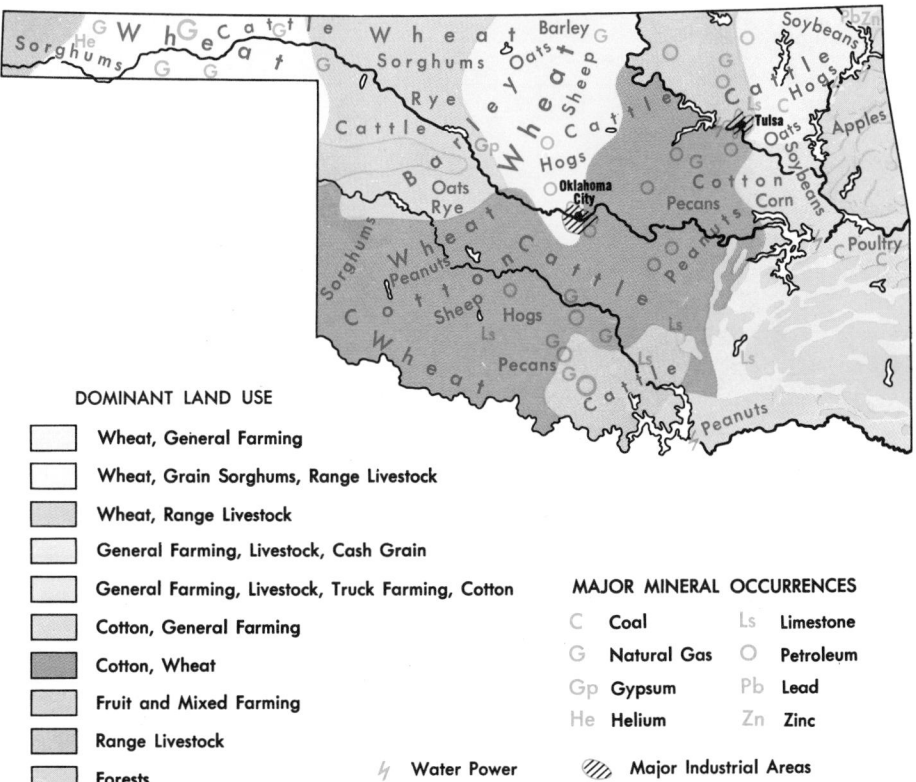

DOMINANT LAND USE

Wheat, General Farming
Wheat, Grain Sorghums, Range Livestock
Wheat, Range Livestock
General Farming, Livestock, Cash Grain
General Farming, Livestock, Truck Farming, Cotton
Cotton, General Farming
Cotton, Wheat
Fruit and Mixed Farming
Range Livestock
Forests

MAJOR MINERAL OCCURRENCES

C Coal
Ls Limestone
G Natural Gas
O Petroleum
Gp Gypsum
Pb Lead
He Helium
Zn Zinc

Water Power
Major Industrial Areas

74747 Kemp 178 ....O7
†74741 Kemp City (Hendrix) 106 ...O7
74040 Kendrick 132 ....N3
74748 Kenefic 140 ....O6
†74365 Kenwood 400 ....S2
74941 Keota 661 ....S4
74349 Ketchum 326 ....R1
73947 Keyes 557 ....B1
74041 Kiefer 912 ....O3
74601 Kildare 112 ....M1
73750 Kingfisher⊙ 4,245 ....L3
73439 Kingston 1,171 ....N7
74552 Kinta 303 ....R4
74553 Kiowa 866 ....P5
73847 Knowles 44 ....F1
74849 Konawa 1,711 ....N5
74554 Krebs 1,754 ....P5
73753 Kremlin 301 ....L1
73754 Lahoma 537 ....K2
74850 Lamar 121 ....O4
†73728 Lambert 20 ....J1
74643 Lamont 571 ....L1
74350 Langley 582 ....R2
73050 Langston 443 ....M3
73848 Laverne 1,563 ....G1
73501 Lawton⊙ 80,054 ....K5
     Lawton‡ 112,456 ....K5
74351 Leach 350 ....S2
74749 Lebanon 382 ....N7
73654 Leedey 499 ....H3
74942 Leflore 322 ....S5
74556 Lehigh 284 ....O6
74042 Lenapah 350 ....P1
73441 Leon 120 ....M7
74043 Leonard 400 ....P3
74943 Lequire 250 ....R4
73051 Lexington 1,731 ....M4
†74858 Lima (New Lima) 256 ...D4
73052 Lindsay 3,454 ....M5
73442 Loco 215 ....L6
74352 Locust Grove 1,179 ......R2
73849 Logan 18 ....F1
73443 Lone Grove 3,369 ....M6
73655 Lone Wolf 613 ....H5
73755 Longdale 405 ....K2
73053 Lookeba 221 ....K4
†73842 Lookout 3 ....H1
†74063 Lotsee 7 ....O2
73553 Loveland 21 ....J6
73756 Loyal 112 ....K3
73757 Lucien 350 ....M2
73054 Luther 1,159 ....M3
†74578 Lutie 100 ....R5
74852 Macomb 58 ....M4
73446 Madill⊙ 3,173 ....N6
73758 Manchester 146 ....L1
73554 Mangum⊙ 3,833 ....G5
73555 Manitou 322 ....J5
74044 Mannford 1,610 ....O2
73447 Mannsville 568 ....N6
74045 Maramec 101 ....N2
74945 Marble City 294 ....S3
73448 Marietta⊙ 2,494 ....M7
74644 Marland 340 ....M1
73055 Marlow 5,017 ....K5
73056 Marshall 372 ....L2
73556 Martha 219 ....H5
74854 Maud 1,444 ....N4
73851 May 89 ....G1
73656 Mayfield 17 ....G4
73057 Maysville 1,396 ....M5
74353 Mazie 118 ....R2
74501 McAlester⊙ 17,255 ....P5
†74441 McBride 91 ....N7
74944 McCurtain 549 ....R4
74851 McLoud 4,061 ....M6
73549 McMillan 50 ....M6
73449 Mead 143 ....O7
73759 Medford⊙ 1,419 ....L1
73557 Medicine Park 437 .....J5
74855 Meeker 1,032 ....N4
73760 Meno 171 ....K2
73058 Meridian 78 ....M3
74354 Miami⊙ 14,237 ....S1
73110 Midwest City 49,559 ...M4
73450 Milburn 376 ....O6
74046 Milfay 200 ....N3
74856 Mill Creek 431 ....N6
74750 Millerton 262 ....S7
73451 Milo 25 ....M6
73059 Minco 1,489 ....L4
74946 Moffett 269 ....S4

74947 Monroe 150 ....S4
74444 Moodys 250 ....S2
73160 Moore 35,063 ....M4
73852 Mooreland 1,383 ....H2
74445 Morris 1,288 ....P3
73061 Morrison 671 ....M2
74047 Mounds 1,086 ....O3
73559 Mountain Park 557 .....J5
73062 Mountain View 1,189 ...J4
74557 Moyers 312 ....P6
74948 Muldrow 2,538 ....S4
73063 Mulhall 301 ....M2
74949 Muse 350 ....S5
74401 Muskogee⊙ 40,011 ....R3
73064 Mustang 7,496 ....L4
73853 Mutual 135 ....H2
†74354 Narcissa 100 ....S1
74646 Nardin 98 ....M1
73761 Nash 301 ....K1
74558 Nashoba 50 ....R6
74049 New Alluwe 129 ....R1
†73632 New Cordell
     (Cordell)⊙ 3,301 ......H4
74647 Newkirk⊙ 2,413 ....N1
74884 New Lima 256 ....O4
†74060 New Prue (Prue) 554 ..O2
74080 New Tulsa 252 ....P2
†73116 Nichols Hills 4,171 ...L3
73066 Nicoma Park 2,588 ....M4
73068 Noble 3,497 ....M4
†73018 Norge 87 ....K4
*73069 Norman⊙ 68,020 .....M4
†73701 North Enid 992 ....L2

74358 North Miami 544 ....R1
74048 Nowata⊙ 4,270 ....P1
73452 Oakland 485 ....N6
74359 Oaks 591 ....S2
73658 Oakwood 140 ....J3
74051 Ochelata 480 ....P1
74958 Octavia 30 ....S5
74052 Oilton 1,244 ....N2
73762 Okarche 1,064 ....L3
74446 Okay 554 ....R3
73763 Okeene 1,601 ....K2
74859 Okemah⊙ 3,381 ......O4
*73101 Oklahoma City
    (cap.)⊙ 403,136 ......L4
    Oklahoma City‡ 834,088 ..L4
74447 Okmulgee⊙ 16,263 .....O3
†74538 Oktaha 376 ....R3
74538 Olney 125 ....O6
73560 Olustee 721 ....H5
73764 Omega 50 ....K3
74053 Oologah 798 ....P2
73948 Optima 133 ....D1
73765 Orienta 25 ....J2
73073 Orlando 218 ....M2
74054 Osage 243 ....O2
73561 Oscar 60 ....L7
73453 Overbrook 443 ......M6
74055 Owasso 6,149 ....P2
74860 Paden 448 ....N3
74951 Panama 1,425 ....S4
74559 Panola 75 ....R5
73074 Paoli 573 ....M5
†74435 Paradise Hill 154 ...R3
74451 Park Hill 200 ......R3

73075 Pauls Valley⊙ 5,664 ...M5
74056 Pawhuska⊙ 4,771 ......O1
74058 Pawnee⊙ 1,688 ....N2
74301 Pensacola 82 ....R2
†66713 Peoria 165 ....S1
73076 Pernell 110 ....M5
73077 Perry⊙ 5,796 ....M2
74862 Pharoah 100 ....O4
†74538 Phillips 178 ....O6
74360 Picher 2,180 ....S1
74752 Pickens 525 ....S6
73078 Piedmont 2,016 ....L3
†74873 Pink 911 ....M4
73079 Pocasset 220 ....L4
74902 Pocola 3,268 ....T4
74601 Ponca City 26,238 ....M1
74454 Porter 642 ....R3
74455 Porum 648 ....R4
74953 Poteau⊙ 7,089 ....S4
74864 Prague 2,208 ....N4
74456 Preston 350 ....P3
74060 Prue 554 ....O2
74361 Pryor⊙ 8,483 ....R2
73080 Purcell⊙ 4,638 ......M4
73659 Putnam 74 ....J3
74363 Quapaw 1,097 ....S1
74485 Quay 50 ....N2
†73852 Quinlan 64 ....J2
74561 Quinton 1,228 ......R4
74650 Ralston 495 ....N2
74061 Ramona 567 ....P1

†73160 Ranchwood Manor 296 ...L4
73562 Randlett 461 ....K6
73081 Ratliff City 350 ......M6
74562 Rattan 332 ....R6
73455 Ravia 487 ....N6
74458 Redbird 199 ....P3
74563 Red Oak 676 ....R5
74651 Red Rock 376 ....M2
73563 Reed 48 ....G5
73456 Ringling 1,561 ....L6
74754 Ringold 200 ....R6
73768 Ringwood 389 ....K2
74062 Ripley 451 ....N2
74932 Rock Island 160 .....T4
73661 Rocky 242 ....J4
74865 Roff 729 ....N5
74954 Roland 1,472 ....S4
73564 Roosevelt 396 ......J5
74364 Rose 100 ....R2
†74831 Rosedale 97 ....M5
73855 Rosston 66 ....G1
73457 Rubottom 35 ....M7
74755 Rufe 150 ....R6
73082 Rush Springs 1,451 ..L5
73565 Ryan 1,083 ....L6
74866 Saint Louis 109 .....N4
74365 Salina 1,115 ....R2
74955 Sallisaw⊙ 6,403 .....S4
†73449 Sand Point 179 ......N7
74063 Sand Springs 13,121 ..O2

74066 Sapulpa⊙ 15,853 .....O3
74867 Sasakwa 335 ....N5
74565 Savanna 828 ....P5
74756 Sawyer 200 ....R7
73662 Sayre⊙ 3,177 ....G4
74460 Schulter 600 ....P3
73663 Seiling 1,103 ....J2
73856 Selman 25 ....H1
74868 Seminole 8,590 ......N4
73664 Sentinel 1,016 ......H4
74956 Shady Point 235 .....S4
74068 Shamrock 218 ....O3
73857 Sharon 171 ....G2
73858 Shattuck 1,759 ......G2
74801 Shawnee⊙ 26,506 ....N4
74652 Shidler 708 ....N1
†74701 Silo 43 ....R7
74069 Skedee 117 ....N2
74070 Skiatook 3,596 .....O2
†73051 Slaughterville 1,953 ..M4
74071 Slick 187 ....N3
74957 Smithville 133 ......S6
74567 Snow 200 ....R6
73566 Snyder 1,848 ....J5
74759 Soper 465 ....P6
74072 South Coffeyville 873 ..P1
74869 Sparks 772 ....N3
74366 Spavinaw 623 ......R2
73084 Spencer 4,064 .....M3
74760 Spencerville 275 ...R6
74073 Sperry 1,276 ......P2
74959 Spiro 2,221 ....S4
73458 Springer 679 ......M6
73567 Sterling 702 ....K5

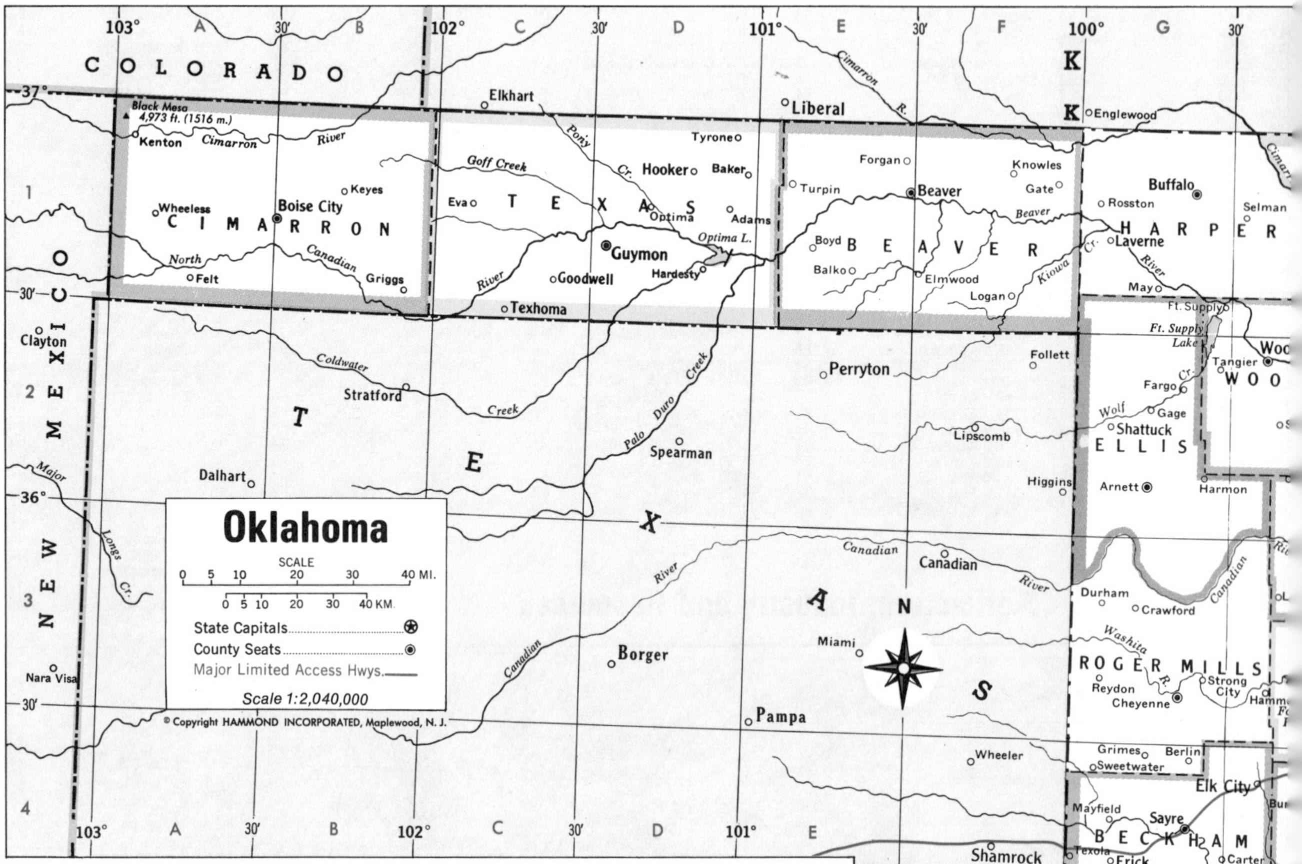

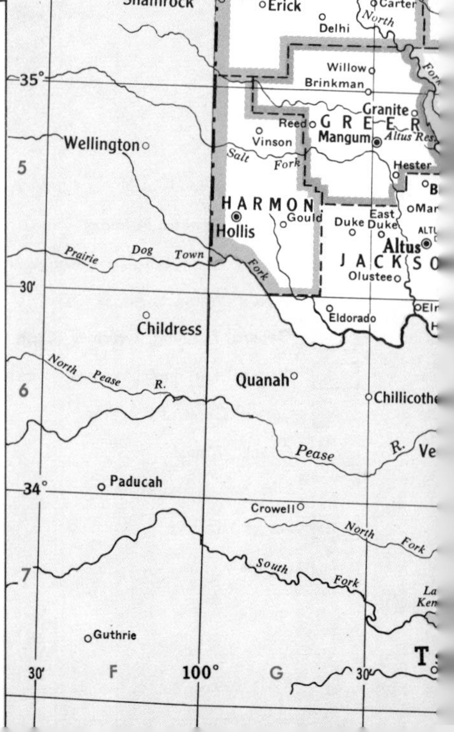

Oklahoma

SCALE

0 5 10   20   30   40 MI.

0 5 10   20   30   40 KM.

State Capitals .... ✵
County Seats .... ⊙
Major Limited Access Hwys. ____

Scale 1:2,040,000

© Copyright HAMMOND INCORPORATED, Maplewood, N. J.

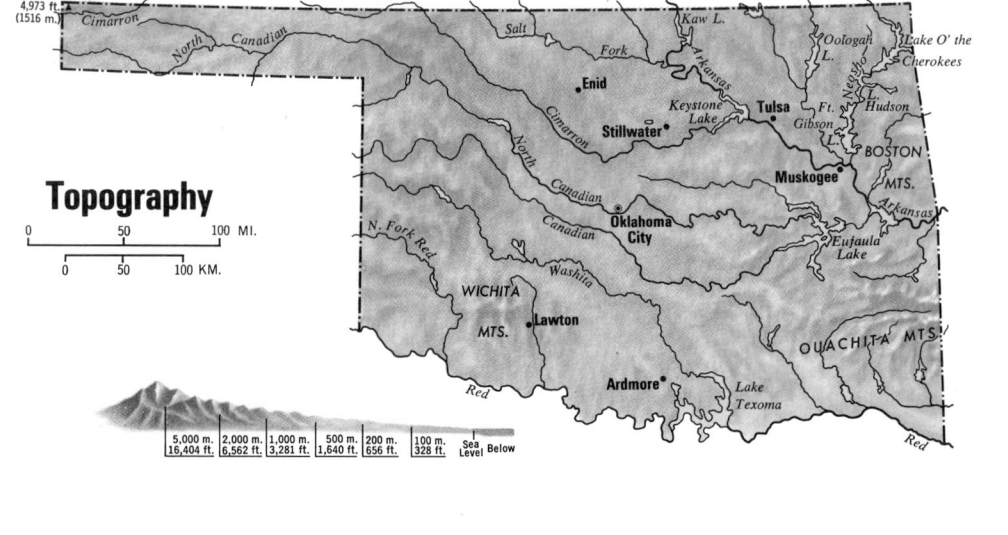

Topography

0   50   100 MI.

0   50   100 KM.

5,000 m. | 2,000 m. | 1,000 m. | 500 m. | 200 m. | 100 m. | Sea | Below
16,404 ft. | 6,562 ft. | 3,281 ft. | 1,640 ft. | 656 ft. | 328 ft. | Level |

Black Mesa
4,973 ft.
(1516 m.)

74461 Stidham 60	P4	74653 Tonkawa 3,524	M1	73461 Wapanucka 472	N6
74462 Stigler⊙ 2,630	R4	†74852 Tribbey 215	M4	74469 Warner 1,310	R4
74074 Stillwater⊙ 38,268	N2	†74856 Troy 92	N6	73132 Warr Acres 9,940	L3
74960 Stilwell⊙ 2,369	S3	74875 Tryon 435	N3	†74834 Warwick 167	M3
74871 Stonewall 672	O5	74466 Tullahassee 145	P3	73093 Washington 477	L4
74367 Strang 126	R2	*74101 Tulsa⊙ 360,919	O2	73094 Washita 180	K4
74872 Stratford 1,459	M5	Tulsa‡ 689,628	O2	73772 Watonga⊙ 4,139	K3
74569 Stringtown 1,047	P6	74572 Tupelo 542	O5	73773 Waukomis 1,551	K2
73665 Strong City 56	G3	73950 Turpin 450	E1	73573 Waurika⊙ 2,258	L6
74079 Stroud 3,148	N3	74573 Tushka 358	O6	73095 Wayne 621	M5
74570 Stuart 235	O5	74574 Tuskahoma 168	R5	73860 Waynoka 1,377	J1
†73565 Sugden 76	L6	73088 Tussy 150	L6	73096 Weatherford 9,640	J4
73086 Sulphur⊙ 5,516	N5	73089 Tuttle 3,051	L4	74654 Webb City 157	N1
74966 Summerfield 150	S5	73951 Tyrone 928	D1	74470 Webbers Falls 461	R3
73666 Sweetwater 85	G4	73090 Union City 558	L4	74369 Welch 697	R1
74463 Taft 489	R3	74763 Utica 38	O7	74880 Weleetka 1,195	O4
74464 Tahlequah⊙ 9,708	R3	†73101 Valley Brook 921	L3	74471 Welling 115	R3
74080 Talala 191	P1	74764 Valliant 927	R6	74881 Wellston 802	M3
74571 Talihina 1,387	S5	74820 Vanoss 130	N5	74882 Welty 80	O4
73667 Taloga⊙ 446	J2	73091 Velma 831	L6	†74020 Westport 265	O2
†74462 Tamaha 145	S4	74082 Vera 182	P2	†72761 West Siloam Springs 431	S2
73087 Tatums 235	M6	73092 Verden 825	K4	74965 Westville 1,049	S2
74873 Tecumseh 5,123	N4	†74017 Verdigris 150	P2	74884 Wetumka 1,725	O4
73568 Temple 1,339	K6	74877 Vernon 100	N5	74884 Wewoka⊙ 5,480	N4
74081 Terlton 155	O2	74962 Vian 1,521	S4	74472 Whitefield 240	R4
73569 Terral 604	L7	73859 Vici 845	H2	74577 Whitesboro 450	S5
73949 Texhoma 785	C1	74301 Vinita⊙ 6,740	R1	74578 Wilburton⊙ 2,996	R5
73668 Texola 106	G4	73571 Vinson 67	G5	74932 Williams 110	T4
73459 Thackerville 431	M7	74467 Wagoner⊙ 6,191	R3	73673 Willow 162	G4
73120 The Village 11,049	L3	74468 Wainwright 182	R3	73463 Wilson 1,585	M6
73669 Thomas 1,515	J3	73771 Wakita 526	L1	74966 Wister 982	S5
†74017 Tiawah 125	P2	73572 Walters⊙ 2,778	K6	†74868 Wolf 200	N4
73570 Tipton 1,475	H6	74878 Wanette 473	M5	73466 Woodville 94	N7
73460 Tishomingo⊙ 3,212	N6	74083 Wann 156	P1		

73801 Woodward⊙ 13,610	H2	Cimarron (riv.)	N2	North Canadian (riv.)	K3
74766 Wright City 1,168	R6	Clear Boggy (creek)	O6	North Carrizo (riv.)	A1
74370 Wyandotte 336	S1	Deep Fork, North Canadian (riv.)	N3	Oologah (lake)	P1
73098 Wynnewood 2,615	M5	Denison (dam)	O7	Optima (lake)	D1
74084 Wynona 780	O1	Elk (creek)	H4	Osage Ind. Res.	O1
74085 Yale 1,652	N2	Ellsworth (lake)	K5	Ouachita (mts.)	R5
†74574 Yanush 123	R5	Eucha (lake)	S2	Pine Creek (lake)	R6
†74848 Yeager 138	O4	Eufaula (lake)	P4	Platt Nat'l Park	N6
73099 Yukon 17,112	L3	Fort Cobb (res.)	J4	Poteau (riv.)	S5
		Fort Gibson (lake)	R2	Prairie Dog Town Fork, Red	
OTHER FEATURES		Fort Sill 15,924	K5	(riv.)	F5
		Fort Supply (lake)	G1	Red (riv.)	R7
Altus (res.)	H5	Foss (lake)	H3	Red, North Fork (riv.)	H4
Altus A.F.B.	H5	Great Salt Plains (lake)	K1	Salt Fork, Arkansas (riv.)	J1
Arbuckle Nat'l Rec. Area	N6	Heyburn (lake)	O3	Salt Fork, Red (riv.)	G5
Arbuckles, Lake of the (lake)	M6	Hudson (lake)	R2	Sans Bois (mts.)	R4
Arkansas (riv.)	S4	Hugo (lake)	R6	Scott (mt.)	K5
Atoka (res.)	P5	Hulah (lake)	O1	Spavinaw (lake)	S2
Beaver (creek)	K6	Illinois (riv.)	S3	Tenkiller Ferry (lake)	S3
Beaver (riv.)	F1	Jackfork (mt.)	P5	Texoma (lake)	N7
Bird (creek)	O1	Kaw (lake)	N1	Thunderbird (lake)	M4
Black Bear (creek)	M2	Kerr, Robert S. (res.)	S4	Tinker A.F.B.	M4
Black Mesa (mt.)	A1	Keystone (lake)	O2	Tom Steed (res.)	J5
Blue (riv.)	O6	Kiamichi (mts.)	R5	Vance A.F.B.	K2
Bluestem (lake)	O1	Kiamichi (riv.)	R6	Verdigris (riv.)	P2
Boston (mts.)	S3	Kiowa (lake)	F1	Washita (riv.)	M5
Broken Bow (lake)	S6	Lawtonka (lake)	K5	Waurika (lake)	K6
Cache (creek)	K6	Little (riv.)	R6	Webbers Falls (res.)	R3
Canadian (riv.)	O4	McAlester (lake)	P4	Wichita (riv.)	J5
Caney (riv.)	O1	Mountain Fork (riv.)	S6	Wildhorse (creek)	L5
Carl Blackwell (lake)	M2	Mud (creek)	L6	Wister (lake)	S5
Cherokees, Lake O'The (lake)	S1	Muddy Boggy (creek)	O5	Wolf (creek)	G2
Chickasha (lake)	K4	Murray (lake)	M6	⊙County seat.	
		Neosho (riv.)	R1	‡Population of metropolitan area.	
				† Zip of nearest p.o. * Multiple zips.	

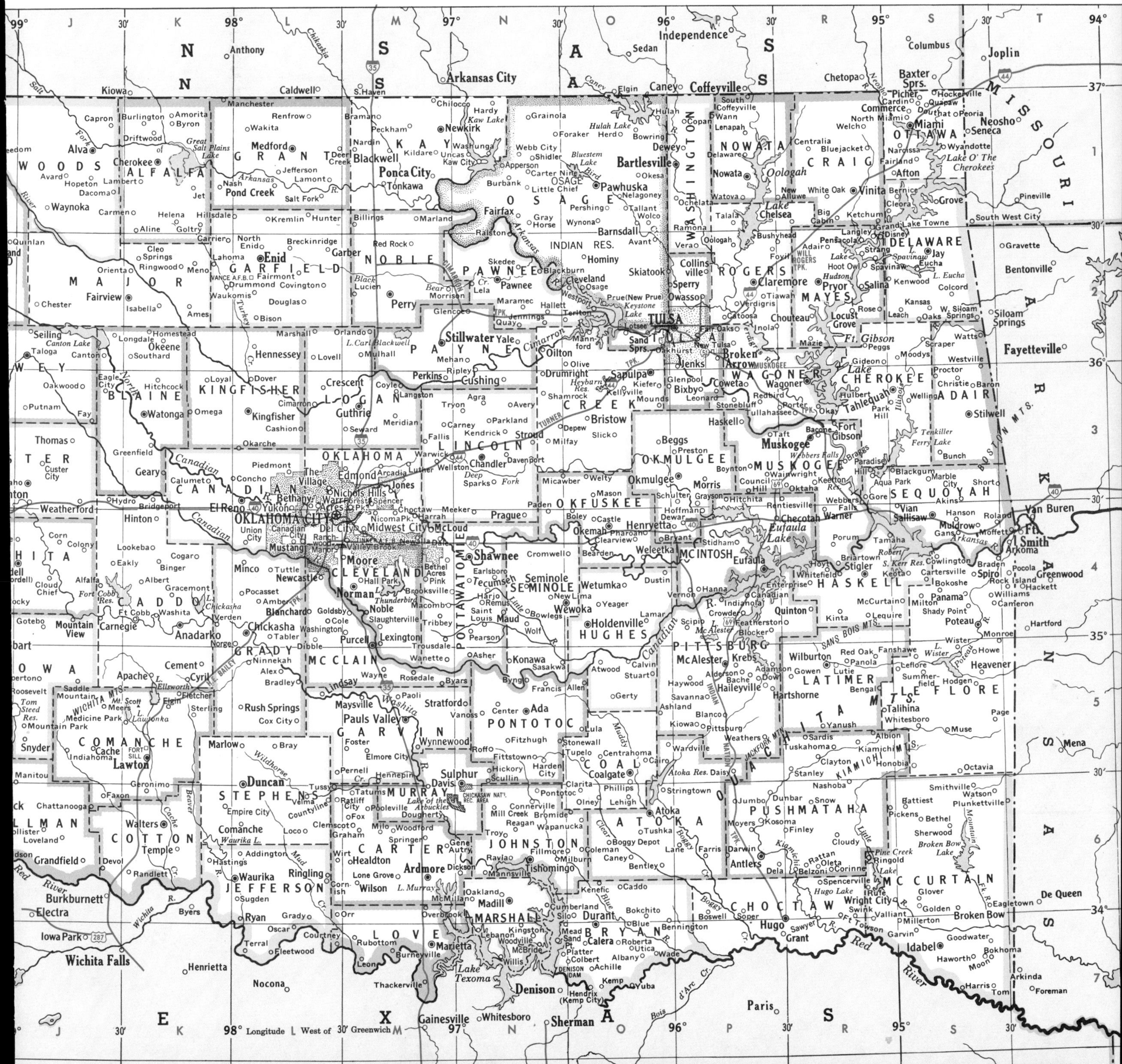

COUNTIES

Baker 16,134 .... K3
Benton 68,211 .... D3
Clackamas 241,911 .... E2
Clatsop 32,489 .... D1
Columbia 35,646 .... D2
Coos 64,047 .... C4
Crook 13,091 .... G3
Curry 16,992 .... C5
Deschutes 62,142 .... F4
Douglas 93,748 .... D4
Gilliam 2,057 .... G2
Grant 8,210 .... J3
Harney 8,314 .... H4
Hood River 15,835 .... F2
Jackson 132,456 .... E5
Jefferson 11,599 .... F3
Josephine 58,855 .... D5
Klamath 59,117 .... F5
Lake 7,532 .... G5
Lane 275,226 .... E4
Lincoln 35,264 .... D3
Linn 89,495 .... E3

Malheur 26,896 .... K4
Marion 204,692 .... E3
Morrow 7,519 .... H2
Multnomah 562,640 .... E2
Polk 45,203 .... D3
Sherman 2,172 .... G2
Tillamook 21,164 .... D2
Umatilla 58,861 .... J2
Union 23,921 .... J2
Wallowa 7,273 .... K2
Wasco 21,732 .... F2
Washington 245,860 ...... D2
Wheeler 1,513 .... G3
Yamhill 55,332 .... D2

CITIES and TOWNS

Zip   Name/Pop.   Key
†97330 Adair Village 589 ......D3
†97810 Adams 240 ....J2
97620 Adel 24 ....H5
97901 Adrian 162 ....K4

†97365 Agate Beach 975 ....C3
97406 Agness 150 ....C5
97321 Albany ⊙ 26,678 ....D3
97407 Allegany 300 ....D4
97005 Aloha 28,353 ....A2
97324 Alsea 125 ....D3
†97601 Altamont 19,805 ......F5
97409 Alvadore 800 ....D3
97101 Amity 1,092 ....D2
97001 Antelope 39 ....G3
97530 Applegate 150 ....D5
97458 Arago 200 ....C4
97812 Arlington 521 ....G2
97520 Ashland 14,943 ....E5
97103 Astoria ⊙ 9,998 ....D1
97813 Athena 965 ....J2
97325 Aumsville 1,432 ......E3
97002 Aurora 523 ....E2
97817 Austin 19 ....J3
97814 Baker ⊙ 9,471 ....K3
†97378 Ballston 120 ....D2
97411 Bandon 2,311 ....C4
97106 Banks 489 ....A1
†97013 Barlow 105 ....B2

†97009 Barton 100 ....B2
97136 Bar View 170 ....C2
†97420 Barview 1,462 ....C4
97817 Bates 56 ....J3
97107 Bay City 986 ....C2
97621 Beatty 350 ....F5
97108 Beaver 350 ....D2
97004 Beavercreek 708 ......B2
97005 Beaverton 30,582 .....A2
†97701 Bend ⊙ 17,263 ....F3
†97058 Biggs 50 ....G2
97412 Blachly 80 ....D3
97108 Blaine 38 ....D2
97326 Blodgett 250 ....D3
97413 Blue River 318 ......E3
97622 Bly 800 ....F5
97818 Boardman 1,261 ......H2
97623 Bonanza 270 ....F5
97008 Bonneville 80 ....F2
97009 Boring 150 ....E2
97010 Bridal Veil 20 ......E2
†97458 Bridge 200 ....D4
†97136 Brighton 150 ....C2
97001 Brightwood 200 ......E2

97414 Broadbent 400 ....C4
97903 Brogan 130 ....K3
97415 Brookings 3,384 .....C5
97305 Brooks 490 ....A3
†97524 Brownsboro 150 .....E5
97327 Brownsville 1,261 ...E3
†97351 Buena Vista 130 ....D3
†97420 Bunker Hill 1,555 ..C4
97720 Burns ⊙ 3,579 ....H4
97522 Butte Falls 428 ....E5
†97002 Butteville 20 ......A2
97109 Buxton 450 ....D2
97416 Camas Valley 750 ....D4
97730 Camp Sherman 350 ....F3
†97493 Canary 23 ....D4
97013 Canby 7,659 ....B2
97820 Canyon City ⊙ 639 ...J3
97417 Canyonville 1,288 ...D5
97111 Carlton 1,302 ....D2
97014 Cascade Locks 838 ...E2
97329 Cascadia 250 ....E3
97523 Cave Junction 1,023 .D5
97821 Cayuse 200 ....J2

97225 Cedar Hills 9,619 ...A2
†97005 Cedar Mill 900 .....A2
†97058 Celilo 50 ....G2
97502 Central Point 6,357 .D5
97420 Charleston 500 ......C4
97306 Chemawa 400 ....A3
97731 Chemult 800 ....F4
97058 Chenoweth 2,820 .....F2
†97119 Cherry Grove 350 ...D2
†97055 Cherryville 75 .....E2
97419 Cheshire 300 ....D3
97624 Chiloquin 778 ....F5
97015 Clackamas D1
97016 Clatskanie 1,648 ....D1
97112 Cloverdale 260 ......D2
97401 Coburg 699 ....E3
97017 Colton 305 ....E2
97018 Columbia City 678 ...D1
97823 Condon ⊙ 783 ....G2
97420 Coos Bay 14,424 .....C4
97423 Coquille ⊙ 4,481 ....C4
97113 Cornelius 4,462 .....A2
97330 Corvallis ⊙ 40,960 ..D3
97424 Cottage Grove 7,148 .D4

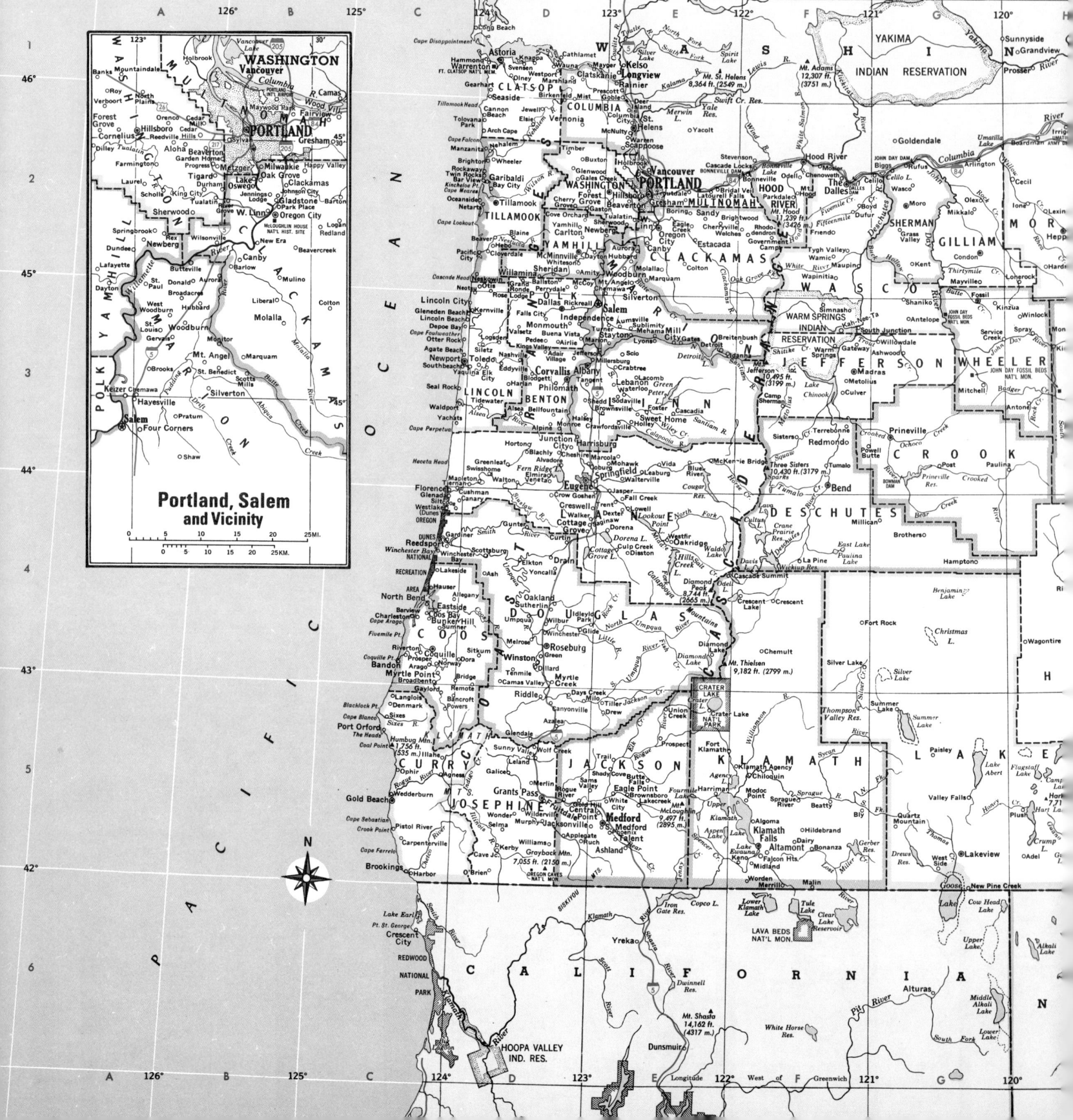

Portland, Salem and Vicinity

25 MI.

25 KM.

97824 Cove 451 ....K2
97335 Crabtree 200 ....E3
97732 Crane 84 ....J4
97336 Crawfordsville 350 .....E3
97733 Crescent 750 ....F4
97425 Crescent Lake 120 ....F4
97426 Creswell 1,770 ....D4
†97401 Crow 200 ....E4
97427 Culp Creek 600 ....E4
97734 Culver 514 ....F3
97524 Curtin 350 ....D4
†97439 Cushman 175 ....D4
97625 Dairy 80 ....F5
97338 Dallas⊙ 8,530 ....D3
97058 Dalles, The⊙ 10,820 ..F2
97429 Days Creek 550 ......D5
97114 Dayton 1,409 ....A3
97825 Dayville 199 ....H3
97054 Deer Island 225 .....E2
97341 Depoe Bay 723 ....C3
97342 Detroit 367 ....E3
97431 Dexter 500 ....E4
97432 Dillard 602 ....D4
†97116 Dilley 250...........A2

†97427 Disston 123 ....E4
97020 Donald 267 ....A3
97434 Dorena 200 ....E4
97435 Drain 1,148 ....D4
97021 Dufur 560 ....F2
97115 Dundee 1,223 ....A2
†97493 Dunes (Westlake) 1,124 ..C4
†97233 Durham 707 ....A2
97905 Durkee 158 ....K3
97022 Eagle Creek 250 .....E2
97524 Eagle Point 2,764 ...E5
97420 Eastside 1,601 ......C4
97826 Echo 624 ....H2
97343 Eddyville 564 ....D3
97827 Elgin 1,701 ....K2
97436 Elkton 155 ....D4
97437 Elmira 900 ....D4
97828 Enterprise⊙ 2,003 ...K2
97023 Estacada 1,419 ......E2
*97401 Eugene⊙ 105,624 .....D3
    Eugene-Springfield‡
    275,226 ....D3
97024 Fairview 1,749 ......B2
†97601 Falcon Heights F5

97344 Falls City 804 ......D3
97710 Fields 150 ....J5
97439 Florence 4,411 ......C4
97116 Forest Grove 11,499 ..A2
97626 Fort Klamath 200 ....E5
97735 Fort Rock 150 ....G4
97830 Fossil⊙ 535 ....G2
97345 Foster 850 ....E3
97301 Four Corners 11,331 ..A3
97831 Fox 30 ....H3
†97526 Fruitdale-Harbeck 4,733 ....D5
97117 Gales Creek 150 .....D2
97223 Garden Home-
    Whitford 6,926 ......A2
97441 Gardiner 750 ....C4
97118 Garibaldi 999 ....D2
97119 Gaston 471 ....D2
97346 Gates 455 ....E3
†97741 Gateway 108 ....F3
97458 Gaylord 80 ....C5
97138 Gearhart 967 ....C1
97026 Gervais 799 ....A3
†97810 Gibbon 100 ....J2
97027 Gladstone 9,500 .....B2

AREA 97,073 sq. mi. (251,419 sq. km.)
POPULATION 2,633,149
CAPITAL Salem
LARGEST CITY Portland
HIGHEST POINT Mt. Hood 11,239 ft.
    (3426 m.)
SETTLED IN 1810
ADMITTED TO UNION February 14, 1859
POPULAR NAME Beaver State
STATE FLOWER Oregon Grape
STATE BIRD Western Meadowlark

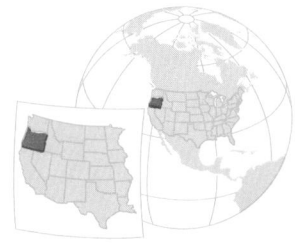

Topography

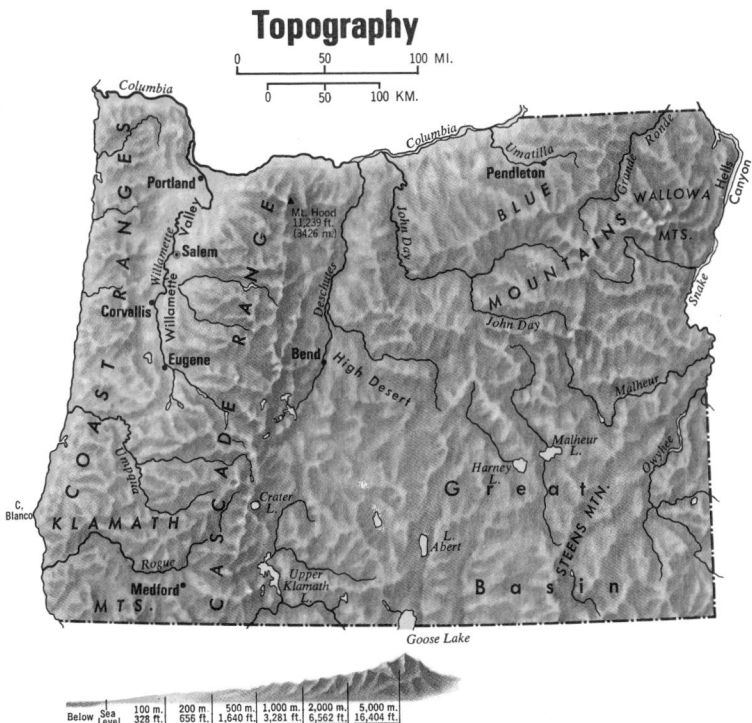

Goose Lake

Below Sea Level | 100 m. 328 ft. | 200 m. 656 ft. | 500 m. 1,640 ft. | 1,000 m. 3,281 ft. | 2,000 m. 6,562 ft. | 5,000 m. 16,404 ft.

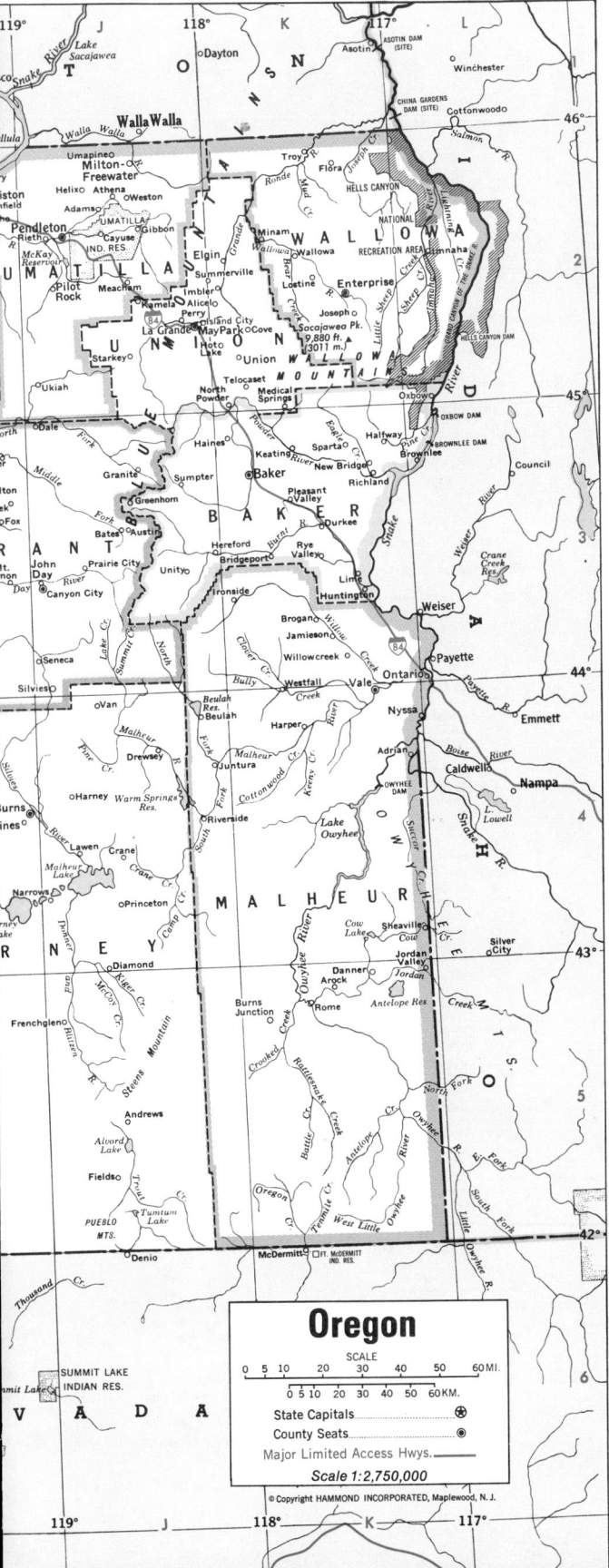

Oregon

SCALE
0 5 10 20 30 40 50 60 MI.
0 5 10 20 30 40 50 60KM.

⊛ State Capitals
⊙ County Seats
─── Major Limited Access Hwys.

Scale 1:2,750,000

© Copyright HAMMOND INCORPORATED, Maplewood, N.J.

†97439 Glenada 300 ....C4
97442 Glendale 712 ....D5
97388 Gleneden Beach 400 ...C3
97120 Glenwood 225 ....D2
97443 Glide 470 ....D4
97048 Goble 108 ....E1
97444 Gold Beach⊙ 1,515 ....C5
97525 Gold Hill 904 ....D5
97401 Goshen 200 ....D4
97028 Government Camp 230 ..F2
97347 Grand Ronde 289 .....D2
†97877 Granite 17 ....J3
97526 Grants Pass⊙ 15,032 ..D5
97029 Grass Valley 164 .....G2
†97470 Green 3,897 ....D4
97030 Gresham 33,005 ....B2
97833 Haines 341 ....J3
97834 Halfway 380 ....K3
97348 Halsey 693 ....D3
97121 Hammond 516 ....C1
†97222 Happy Valley 1,499 ...B2
97415 Harbor 2,856 ....C5
97906 Harper 400 ....K4
†97601 Harriman 250 ....E5
97446 Harrisburg 1,881 .....D3
†97459 Hauser 400 ....C4
97301 Hayesville 9,213 .....A3
97122 Hebo 400 ....D2
97835 Helix 155 ....J2
97836 Heppner⊙ 1,498 ....H2
97837 Hereford 128 ....K3
97838 Hermiston 9,408 ......H2
97123 Hillsboro⊙ 27,664 ....A2
97738 Hines 1,632 ....H4
†97208 Holbrook 494 ....A1
†97386 Holley 75 ....E3
97031 Hood River⊙ 4,329 ....F2
97448 Horton 175 ....D3
†97850 Hot Lake 4 ....K2
97032 Hubbard 1,640 ....A3
97907 Huntington 539 ....K3
97350 Idanha 319 ....E3
97447 Idleyld Park 300 .....D4
97841 Imbler 292 ....J2
97351 Independence 4,024 ...D3
97843 Ione 345 ....H2
97844 Irrigon 700 ....H2
97851 Island City 477 ......K2
97530 Jacksonville 2,030 ...D5
97909 Jamieson 120 ....K3
97401 Jasper 231 ....E3
97352 Jefferson 1,702 ......D3
†97201 Jennings Lodge B2
97845 John Day 2,012 ....J3
†97027 Johnson City 378 .....B2
97910 Jordan Valley 473 ....K5
97846 Joseph 999 ....K2
97448 Junction City 3,320 ..D3
97911 Juntura 500 ....K4
97303 Keizer 18,592 ....A3

97627 Keno 500 ....F5
97033 Kent 200 ....G2
97531 Kerby 650 ....D5
97223 King City 1,853 ......A2
†97361 Kings Valley 50 ......D3
97849 Kinzua 2 ....H3
97601 Klamath Falls⊙ 16,661 ..F5
†97103 Knappa 950 ....D1
97355 Lacomb 425 ....E3
97127 Lafayette 1,215 ......A2
97850 La Grande⊙ 11,354 ....J2
†97524 Lakecreek 160 ....E5
97034 Lake Oswego 22,527 ...B2
97449 Lakeside 1,453 ....C4
97630 Lakeview⊙ 2,770 ......G5
97450 Langlois 150 ....C5
97739 La Pine 850 ....F4
97401 Leaburg 150 ....E3
97355 Lebanon 10,413 ....E3
97839 Lexington 307 ....H2
†97042 Liberal 300 ....B3
†97341 Lincoln Beach 275 ....C3
97367 Lincoln City 5,469 ...C3
97405 Logan 450 ....B2
97823 Lonerock 26 ....H2
97856 Long Creek 252 ....H3
97857 Lostine 250 ....K2
97452 Lowell 661 ....E4
97358 Lyons 877 ....E3
97741 Madras⊙ 2,235 ....F3
97632 Malin 539 ....F5
97130 Manzanita 443 ....C2
97453 Mapleton 950 ....C3
97454 Marcola 900 ....E3
97359 Marion 300 ....D3
97037 Maupin 495 ....F2
†97850 May Park J2
97220 Maywood Park 1,083 ...B2
97401 McKenzie Bridge 500 ..E3
97128 McMinnville⊙ 14,080 ..D2
97858 McNary 330 ....H2
†97053 McNulty 1,805 ....E2
97859 Meacham 150 ....J2
97501 Medford⊙ 39,603 ......E5
    Medford‡ 132,456 ......E5
97384 Mehama 250 ....E3
97532 Merlin 500 ....D5
97633 Merrill 809 ....F5
†97741 Metolius 451 ....F3
†97223 Metzger 5,544 ....A2
97634 Midland 520 ....F5
97360 Mill City 1,565 ......E3
†97321 Millersburg 562 ......E3
†97417 Milo 600 ....E5
97862 Milton-Freewater 5,086 ..J2
97222 Milwaukie 17,931 .....B2
97750 Mitchell 183 ....G3
97038 Molalla 2,992 ....B3
97361 Monmouth 5,594 ....D3
97456 Monroe 412 ....D3

97864 Monument 192 ....H3
97039 Moro⊙ 336 ....G2
97040 Mosier 340 ....F2
97362 Mount Angel 2,876 ....B3
97041 Mount Hood 200 ....F2
97865 Mount Vernon 569 .....H3
97042 Mulino 720 ....B2
97533 Murphy 500 ....D5
97457 Myrtle Creek 3,365 ...D4
97458 Myrtle Point 2,859 ...C4
97131 Nehalem 258 ....D2
97364 Neotsu 300 ....C2
97149 Neskowin 250 ....D2
97143 Netarts 975 ....C2
97132 Newberg 10,394 ....A2
97635 New Pine Creek 400 ...G5
97365 Newport⊙ 7,519 ....C3
97459 North Bend 9,779 .....C4
97133 North Plains 715 .....A2
97867 North Powder 430 .....K2
97460 Norway 150 ....C4
97913 Nyssa 2,862 ....K4
97268 Oak Grove 11,640 .....B2
97462 Oakland 886 ....D4
97463 Oakridge 3,729 ....E4
97534 O'Brien 850 ....D5
97134 Oceanside 300 ....C2
97044 Odell 450 ....F2
97914 Ontario 8,814 ....K3
97464 Ophir 275 ....C5
97045 Oregon City⊙ 14,673 ..B2
†97123 Orenco 220 ....A2
97368 Otis 200 ....D2
97369 Otter Rock 450 ....C3
97840 Oxbow 100 ....L2
97135 Pacific City 500 .....C2
97636 Paisley 343 ....G5
97041 Parkdale 350 ....F2
†97045 Park Place 500 ....B2
97801 Pendleton⊙ 14,521 ....J2
†97101 Perrydale 200 ....D2
97370 Philomath 2,673 ......D3
97535 Phoenix 2,309 ....E5
97868 Pilot Rock 1,630 .....J2
*97201 Portland⊙ 366,383 ....B2
    Portland‡ 1,242,187 ...B2
97465 Port Orford 1,061 ....C5
97753 Powell Butte 350 .....G3
97466 Powers 819 ....D5
97869 Prairie City 1,106 ...J3
†97048 Prescott 73 ....D1
97721 Princeton 5 ....J4
97754 Prineville⊙ 5,276 ....G3
†97233 Progress 100 ....A2
97536 Prospect 200 ....E5
†97411 Prosper 110 ....C4
97048 Rainier 1,655 ....E1
†97045 Redland 700 ....B2
97756 Redmond 6,452 ....F3
97467 Reedsport 4,984 ......C4

(continued on following page)

Agriculture, Industry and Resources

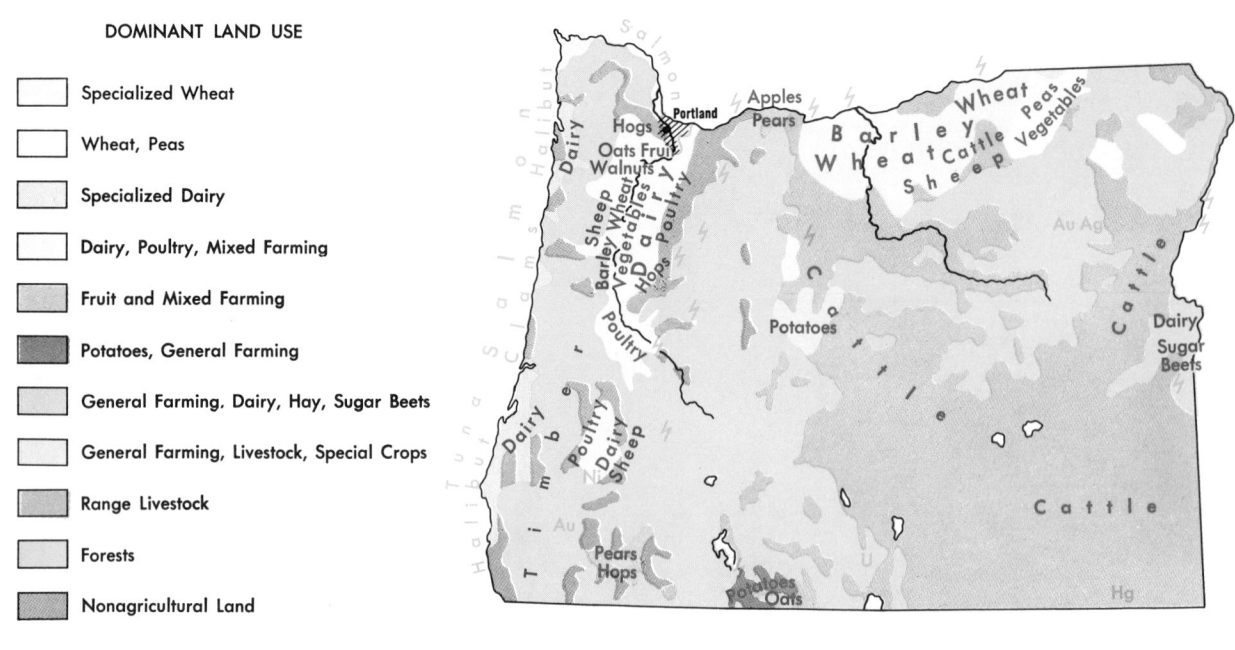

DOMINANT LAND USE

- ⬜ Specialized Wheat
- ⬜ Wheat, Peas
- ⬜ Specialized Dairy
- ⬜ Dairy, Poultry, Mixed Farming
- ⬜ Fruit and Mixed Farming
- ⬛ Potatoes, General Farming
- ⬜ General Farming, Dairy, Hay, Sugar Beets
- ⬜ General Farming, Livestock, Special Crops
- ⬜ Range Livestock
- ⬜ Forests
- ⬛ Nonagricultural Land

MAJOR MINERAL OCCURRENCES

Ag Silver	Hg Mercury	⚡	Water Power
Au Gold	Ni Nickel	▨	Major Industrial Areas
U Uranium			

DOMINANT LAND USE

- Specialized Dairy
- Dairy, General Farming
- Fruit and Mixed Farming
- Fruit, Truck and Mixed Farming
- General Farming, Livestock, Tobacco
- General Farming, Livestock, Fruit, Tobacco
- Forests
- Urban Areas

AREA 45,308 sq. mi. (117,348 sq. km.)
POPULATION 11,863,895
CAPITAL Harrisburg
LARGEST CITY Philadelphia
HIGHEST POINT Mt. Davis 3,213 ft. (979 m.)
SETTLED IN 1682
ADMITTED TO UNION December 12, 1787
POPULAR NAME Keystone State
STATE FLOWER Mountain Laurel
STATE BIRD Ruffed Grouse

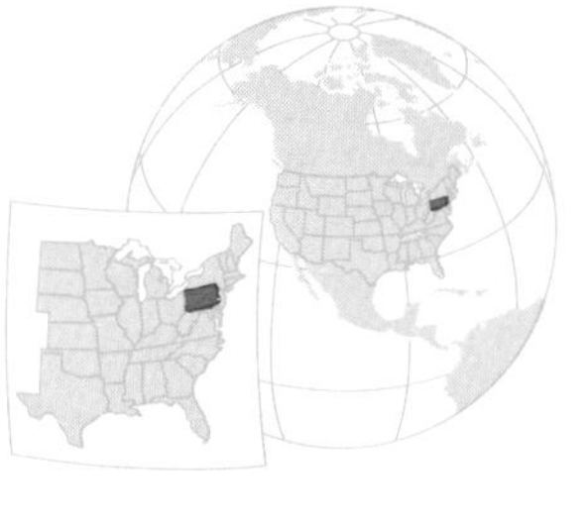

MAJOR MINERAL OCCURRENCES

- C Coal
- Cl Clay
- Co Cobalt
- Fe Iron Ore
- G Natural Gas
- Ls Limestone
- O Petroleum
- Sl Slate
- Ss Sandstone
- Zn Zinc

Water Power

Major Industrial Areas

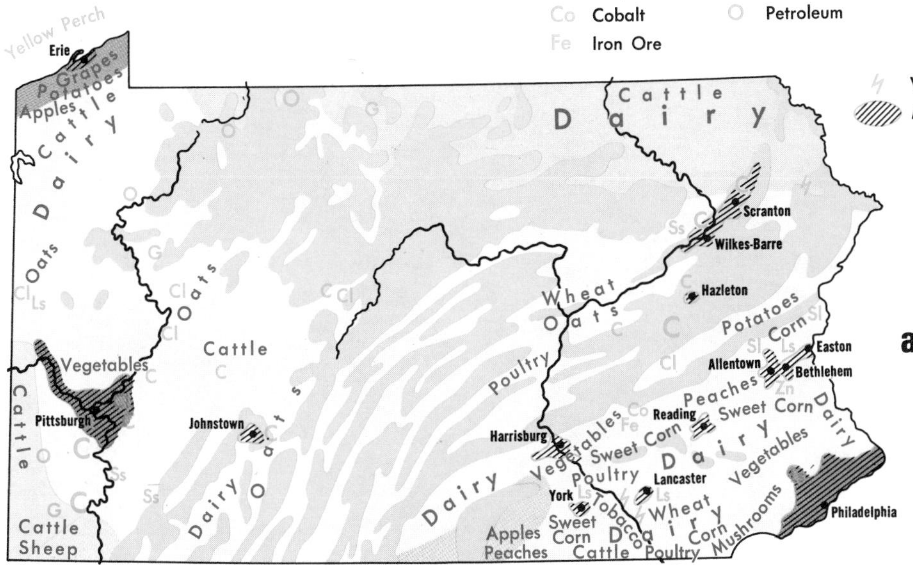

Agriculture, Industry and Resources

COUNTIES

Adams 68,292 .... H6
Allegheny 1,450,085 .... B5
Armstrong 77,768 .... D4
Beaver 204,441 .... B4
Bedford 46,784 .... E6
Berks 312,509 .... K5
Blair 136,621 .... F4
Bradford 62,919 .... J2
Bucks 479,211 .... M5
Butler 147,912 .... C4
Cambria 183,263 .... E4
Cameron 6,674 .... F3
Carbon 53,285 .... L4
Centre 112,760 .... G4
Chester 316,660 .... L6
Clarion 43,362 .... D3
Clearfield 83,578 .... F3
Clinton 38,971 .... G3
Columbia 61,967 .... K3
Crawford 88,869 .... B2
Cumberland 178,541 .... H5
Dauphin 232,317 .... J5
Delaware 555,007 .... M6
Elk 38,338 .... E3
Erie 279,780 .... B2
Fayette 159,417 .... C6
Forest 5,072 .... D2
Franklin 113,629 .... G6
Fulton 12,842 .... F6
Greene 40,476 .... B6
Huntingdon 42,253 .... F5
Indiana 92,281 .... D4
Jefferson 48,303 .... D3
Juniata 19,188 .... H4
Lackawanna 227,908 .... L3
Lancaster 362,346 .... K5
Lawrence 107,150 .... B4
Lebanon 108,582 .... K5
Lehigh 272,349 .... L4
Luzerne 343,079 .... L3
Lycoming 118,416 .... H3
McKean 50,635 .... E2
Mercer 128,299 .... B3
Mifflin 46,908 .... G4
Monroe 69,409 .... M3
Montgomery 643,621 .... M5
Montour 16,675 .... J3
Northampton 225,418 .... M4
Northumberland 100,381 .... J4
Perry 35,718 .... H5
Philadelphia (city county) 1,688,210 .... M6
Pike 18,271 .... M3
Potter 17,726 .... G2
Schuylkill 160,630 .... K4
Snyder 33,584 .... H4
Somerset 81,243 .... D6
Sullivan 6,349 .... J3
Susquehanna 37,876 .... L2
Tioga 40,973 .... H2
Union 32,870 .... H4
Venango 64,444 .... C3
Warren 47,449 .... D2
Washington 217,074 .... B5
Wayne 35,237 .... M2
Westmoreland 392,294 .... D5
Wyoming 26,433 .... K2
York 312,963 .... J6

CITIES and TOWNS

Zip *Name/Pop.* *Key*

19001 Abington○ 59,084 .... M5
19501 Adamstown 1,119 .... K5
17501 Akron 3,471 .... K5
16401 Albion 1,818 .... B2
18011 Alburtis 1,428 .... L5
†19018 Aldan 4,671 .... M7
15001 Aliquippa 17,094 .... B4
*18101 Allentown⊙ 103,758 .... L4
Allentown-Bethlehem-Easton‡ 636,714 .... L4
15101 Allison Park 10,000 .... C4
*16601 Altoona 57,078 .... F4
Altoona‡ 136,621 .... F4
19002 Ambler 6,628 .... M5
15003 Ambridge 9,575 .... B4
17003 Annville 4,493 .... J5
15613 Apollo 2,212 .... C4
18403 Archbald 6,295 .... F6
19003 Ardmore M6
15068 Arnold 6,853 .... C4
17921 Ashland 4,235 .... K4
18706 Ashley 3,512 .... E7
15215 Aspinwall 3,284 .... C6
18810 Athens 3,622 .... K2
17851 Atlas 1,162 .... K4
15202 Avalon 6,240 .... B6
15312 Avella 900 .... B5
17721 Avis 1,718 .... H3
18641 Avoca 3,536 .... F7
19311 Avondale 891 .... L6
15618 Avonmore 1,234 .... C4
15005 Baden 5,318 .... B4
19004 Bala-Cynwyd N6
†15208 Baldwin 24,598 .... B7
19503 Bally 1,051 .... L5
18013 Bangor 5,006 .... M4
15714 Barnesboro 2,741 .... E4
18014 Bath 1,953 .... M4
15009 Beaver⊙ 5,441 .... B4
15921 Beaverdale 1,187 .... E5
15010 Beaver Falls 12,525 .... B4
18216 Beaver Meadows 1,078 .... L4
15522 Bedford⊙ 3,326 .... F5
16823 Bellefonte⊙ 6,300 .... G4
15012 Belle Vernon 1,489 .... C5
17004 Belleville 1,689 .... G4
15202 Bellevue 10,128 .... B6
16617 Bellwood 2,114 .... F4
†15202 Ben Avon 2,314 .... B6
15314 Bentleyville 2,525 .... B5
15530 Berlin 1,999 .... E6
19506 Bernville 798 .... K5
18603 Berwick 11,850 .... K3
19312 Berwyn 5,246 .... L5
16112 Bessemer 1,293 .... B4
15102 Bethel Park 34,755 .... B7
*18015 Bethlehem 70,419 .... M4
19508 Birdsboro 3,481 .... L5
15716 Black Lick 1,313 .... D4
15717 Blairsville 4,166 .... D5
18447 Blakely 7,438 .... F6
15238 Blawnox 1,653 .... C6
17068 Bloomfield (New Bloomfield)⊙ 1,109 .... H5
17815 Bloomsburg⊙ 11,717 .... J3
16912 Blossburg 1,757 .... H2
16827 Boalsburg 2,295 .... G4
15315 Bobtown 1,008 .... B6
17007 Boiling Springs 2,223 .... H5
15923 Bolivar 706 .... D5
15531 Boswell 1,480 .... E5
18030 Bowmanstown 1,078 .... L4
19512 Boyertown 3,979 .... L5
15014 Brackenridge 4,297 .... C4
15104 Braddock 5,634 .... C7
16701 Bradford 11,211 .... E2
15227 Brentwood 11,907 .... B7
19405 Bridgeport 4,843 .... M5
15017 Bridgeville 6,154 .... B5
19007 Bristol 10,867 .... N5
19007 Bristol○ 58,733 .... N5
15824 Brockway 2,376 .... E3
19015 Brookhaven 7,912 .... M7
15825 Brookville⊙ 4,568 .... D3
19008 Broomall M6
15417 Brownsville 4,043 .... C5
19010 Bryn Mawr M5
15021 Burgettstown 1,867 .... A5
17009 Burnham 2,457 .... H4
16001 Butler⊙ 17,026 .... C4
15924 Cairnbrook 1,081 .... E5
15419 California 5,703 .... C5
16403 Cambridge Springs 2,102 .... C2
17011 Camp Hill 8,422 .... H5
15317 Canonsburg 10,459 .... B5
17724 Canton 1,959 .... J2
18407 Carbondale 11,255 .... L2
17013 Carlisle⊙ 18,314 .... H5
15106 Carnegie 10,099 .... B7
15722 Carrolltown 1,395 .... E4
15234 Castle Shannon 10,164 .... B7
18032 Catasauqua 6,711 .... M4
17820 Catawissa 1,568 .... K4
16404 Centerville 4,207 .... B6
15926 Central City 1,496 .... E5
17927 Centralia 1,017 .... K4
16828 Centre Hall 1,233 .... G4
18914 Chalfont 2,802 .... M5
17201 Chambersburg⊙ 16,174 .... G6
15022 Charleroi 5,717 .... C5
19012 Cheltenham○ 35,509 .... M5
*19013 Chester 45,794 .... L7
19017 Chester Heights 1,302 .... L7
†16866 Chester Hill 1,054 .... F4
15024 Cheswick 2,336 .... C6
16025 Chicora 1,192 .... C4
17509 Christiana 1,183 .... K6
†15235 Churchill 4,285 .... C7
15025 Clairton 12,188 .... C7
16214 Clarion⊙ 6,664 .... D3
†18411 Clarks Green 1,862 .... F6
18411 Clarks Summit 5,272 .... F6
16625 Claysburg 1,346 .... F5
15323 Claysville 1,029 .... B5
16830 Clearfield⊙ 7,580 .... F3
19018 Clifton Heights 7,320 .... M7
15728 Clymer 1,761 .... E4
18218 Coaldale 2,762 .... L4
19320 Coatesville 10,698 .... L5
16314 Cochranton 1,240 .... B2
19426 Collegeville 3,406 .... M5
19023 Collingdale 9,539 .... N7
17512 Columbia 10,466 .... K5
15927 Colver 1,165 .... E4
†19023 Colwyn 2,851 .... N7
15425 Connellsville 10,319 .... C5
19428 Conshohocken 8,475 .... M5
15027 Conway 2,747 .... B4
18219 Conyngham 2,242 .... K3
18036 Coopersburg 2,595 .... M5
18037 Coplay 3,130 .... L4
15108 Coraopolis 7,308 .... B4
17016 Cornwall 2,653 .... K5
16407 Corry 7,149 .... C2
16915 Coudersport⊙ 2,791 .... G2
15624 Crabtree 900 .... D5
15205 Crafton 7,623 .... B7
16630 Cresson 2,184 .... E5
17929 Cressona 1,810 .... K4
16833 Curwensville 3,116 .... E4
†15901 Dale 1,906 .... E5
18612 Dallas 2,679 .... E7
17313 Dallastown 3,949 .... J6
18414 Dalton 1,383 .... L2
17821 Danville⊙ 5,239 .... J4
19023 Darby 11,513 .... M7
18327 Delaware Water Gap 597 .... M4
15626 Delmont 2,159 .... D5
17517 Denver 2,018 .... K5
15627 Derry 3,072 .... D5
18519 Dickson City 6,699 .... F7
17019 Dillsburg 1,733 .... J5
15033 Donora 7,524 .... C5
15216 Dormont 11,275 .... B7
17315 Dover 1,910 .... J6
19335 Downingtown 7,650 .... L5
18901 Doylestown⊙ 8,717 .... M5
15034 Dravosburg 2,511 .... C7
19026 Drexel Hill M6
18221 Drifton 1,786 .... L3
18917 Dublin 1,565 .... M5
15801 DuBois 9,290 .... E3
†17701 Duboistown 1,218 .... H3
15431 Dunbar 1,369 .... C6
17020 Duncannon 1,645 .... H5
16635 Duncansville 1,355 .... F5
18512 Dunmore 16,781 .... F7
18641 Dupont 3,460 .... F7
15110 Duquesne 10,094 .... C7
18642 Duryea 5,415 .... F7
17316 East Berlin 1,054 .... J6
†18603 East Berwick 2,324 .... K3
16028 East Brady 1,153 .... C3
15909 East Conemaugh 2,128 .... E5
†17701 East Faxon 3,951 .... J3
18041 East Greenville 2,456 .... L5
†19050 East Lansdowne 2,806 .... M7
18042 Easton⊙ 26,027 .... M4
17520 East Petersburg 3,600 .... K5
18301 East Stroudsburg 8,039 .... M4
†15301 East Washington 2,241 .... B5
15931 Ebensburg⊙ 4,096 .... E5
†15005 Economy 9,538 .... B4
†19013 Eddystone 2,555 .... M7
†15218 Edgewood 4,382 .... B7
†15143 Edgeworth 1,738 .... B4
16412 Edinboro 6,324 .... B2
18704 Edwardsville 5,729 .... E7
16731 Eldred 965 .... F2
15037 Elizabeth 1,892 .... C5
17022 Elizabethtown 8,233 .... J5
17023 Elizabethville 1,531 .... J4
16920 Elkland 1,974 .... H1
15331 Ellsworth 1,228 .... B5
16117 Ellwood City 9,998 .... B4
17824 Elysburg 1,447 .... K4
17318 Emigsville 2,413 .... J5
16373 Emlenton 807 .... C3
18049 Emmaus 11,001 .... M4
15834 Emporium⊙ 2,837 .... F2
15202 Emsworth 3,074 .... B6
17025 Enola J5
17522 Ephrata 11,095 .... K5
*16501 Erie⊙ 119,123 .... B1
Erie‡ 279,780 .... B1
17815 Espy 1,571 .... K4
15223 Etna 4,534 .... B6
16033 Evans City 2,299 .... B4
15537 Everett 1,828 .... F5
15631 Everson 1,032 .... C5
15632 Export 1,143 .... C5
15436 Fairchance 2,106 .... C6
19030 Fairless Hills 16,000 .... N5
16415 Fairview 1,855 .... B1
15840 Falls Creek 1,208 .... E3
16121 Farrell 8,645 .... A3
17222 Fayetteville 3,202 .... G6
18921 Ferndale 2,204 .... E5
19522 Fleetwood 3,422 .... L5
†17745 Flemington 1,416 .... G3
19032 Folcroft 8,231 .... M7
16226 Ford City 3,923 .... D4
18421 Forest City 1,924 .... L2
†15221 Forest Hills 8,198 .... C7
18704 Forty Fort 5,590 .... F7
†18015 Fountain Hill 4,805 .... L4
†15238 Fox Chapel 5,049 .... C6
17931 Frackville 5,308 .... K4
16323 Franklin⊙ 8,146 .... C3
†16335 Fredericksburg 1,202 .... B2
15333 Fredericktown 1,052 .... C6
15042 Freedom 2,272 .... B4
18224 Freeland 4,285 .... L3
†18017 Freemansburg 1,879 .... M4
16229 Freeport 2,381 .... C4
16922 Galeton 1,462 .... G2
16641 Gallitzin 2,315 .... E4
†17701 Garden View 2,777 .... H3
15904 Geistown 3,304 .... E5
17325 Gettysburg⊙ 7,194 .... H6
17934 Gilberton 1,096 .... K4
16417 Girard 2,615 .... B2
17935 Girardville 2,268 .... K4
15045 Glassport 6,242 .... C7
18617 Glen Lyon 2,352 .... E7
19036 Glenolden 7,633 .... M7
17327 Glen Rock 1,662 .... J6
19038 Glenside M5
15634 Grapeville C5
18821 Great Bend 740 .... L2
17225 Greencastle 3,679 .... G6
15601 Greensburg⊙ 17,558 .... D5
15242 Greentree 5,722 .... B7
16125 Greenville 7,730 .... B3
16127 Grove City 8,162 .... B3
17032 Halifax 909 .... J5
17406 Hallam 1,428 .... J6
18822 Hallstead 1,280 .... L2
19526 Hamburg 4,011 .... L4
17331 Hanover 14,890 .... J6
16037 Harmony 1,334 .... B4
*17101 Harrisburg (cap.)⊙ 53,264 .... H5
Harrisburg‡ 446,072 .... H5
16038 Harrisville 1,033 .... B3
18618 Harveys Lake 2,318 .... E7
16646 Hastings 1,574 .... E4
19040 Hatboro 7,579 .... M5
19440 Hatfield 2,533 .... M5
19041 Haverford○ 52,349 .... M6
19083 Havertown M6
16840 Hawk Run 1,960 .... F4
18428 Hawley 1,181 .... M3
18201 Hazleton 27,318 .... L4
15106 Heidelberg 1,606 .... B7
17406 Hellam (Hallam) 1,428 .... J6
18055 Hellertown 6,025 .... M4
17033 Hershey 13,249 .... J5
†17044 Highland Park 1,879 .... H4
17034 Highspire 2,959 .... J5
16648 Hollidaysburg⊙ 5,892 .... F5
15748 Homer City 2,248 .... D4
15120 Homestead 5,092 .... B7
18431 Honesdale⊙ 5,128 .... M2
19344 Honey Brook 1,164 .... L5
15936 Hooversville 863 .... E5
15445 Hopwood 2,420 .... C6
15342 Houston 1,568 .... B5
16651 Houtzdale 1,222 .... F4
†18640 Hughestown 1,783 .... F7
17737 Hughesville 2,174 .... J3
17036 Hummelstown 4,267 .... J5
16652 Huntingdon⊙ 7,042 .... G5
16843 Hyde 1,791 .... F4
15545 Hyndman 1,106 .... E6
15126 Imperial 3,207 .... B5
15701 Indiana⊙ 16,051 .... D4
15052 Industry 2,417 .... B4
†15205 Ingram 4,346 .... B7
15642 Irwin 4,995 .... C5
17407 Jacobus 1,396 .... J6
15644 Jeannette 13,106 .... C5
†15025 Jefferson 8,643 .... B7
19046 Jenkintown 4,942 .... M5
18433 Jermyn 2,411 .... L2
15937 Jerome 1,196 .... D5
17740 Jersey Shore 4,631 .... H3
18434 Jessup 4,974 .... F6
18229 Jim Thorpe⊙ 5,263 .... L4
15845 Johnsonburg 3,938 .... E3
*15901 Johnstown 35,496 .... D5
Johnstown‡ 264,506 .... D5
16735 Kane 4,916 .... E2
†19607 Kenhorst 3,187 .... L5
19348 Kennett Square 4,715 .... L6
18704 Kingston 15,681 .... F7
16201 Kittanning⊙ 5,432 .... D4
16232 Knox 1,364 .... C3
16136 Koppel 1,146 .... B4
17834 Kulpmont 3,675 .... J4
19530 Kutztown 4,040 .... L4
16423 Lake City 2,384 .... B1
*17601 Lancaster⊙ 54,725 .... K5
Lancaster‡ 362,346 .... K5

(continued on following page)

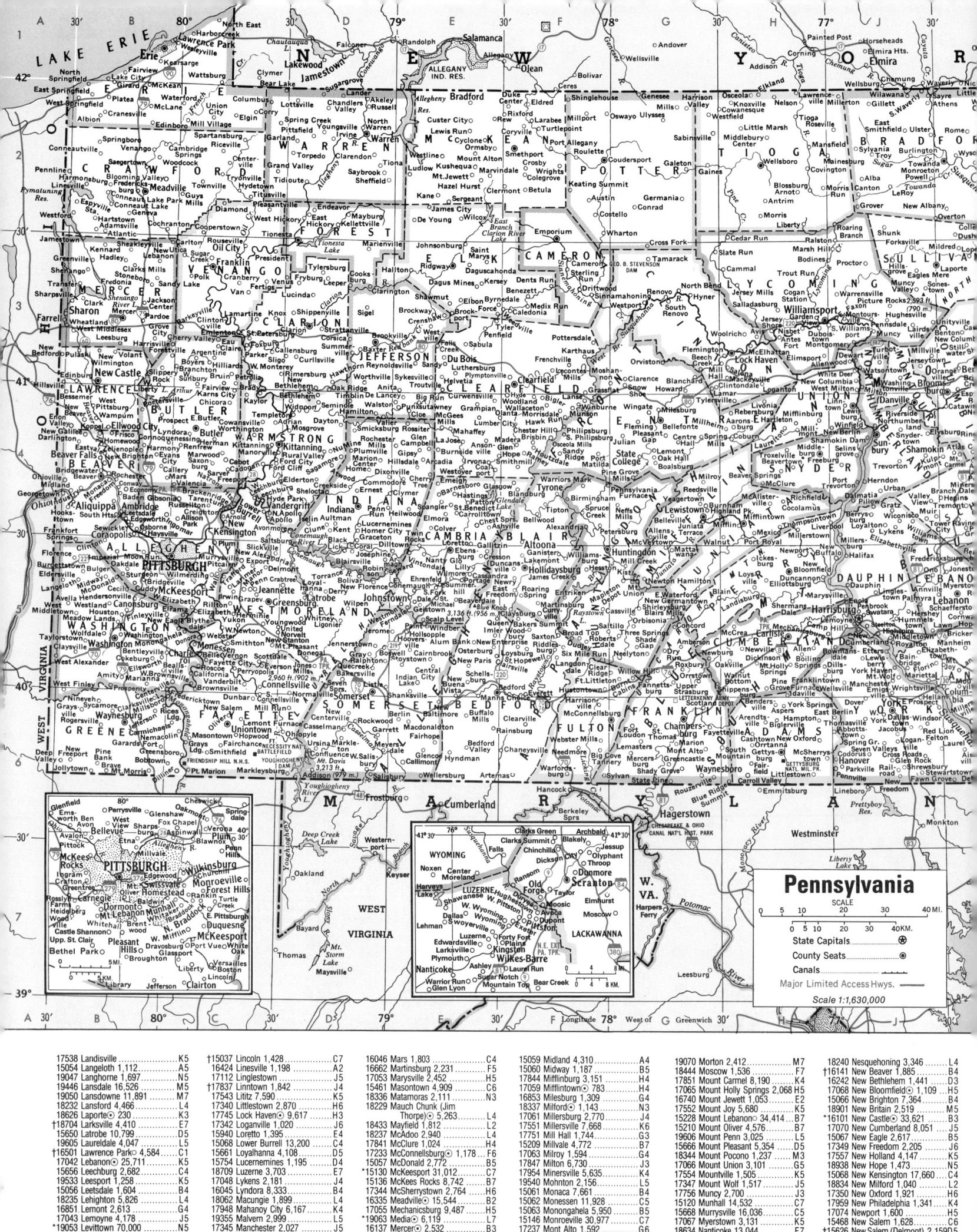

16823 Pleasant Gap 1,859 ....G4
15236 Pleasant Hills 9,676 ....B7
16341 Pleasantville 1,099 ....C2
15239 Plum 25,390 ....C5
18651 Plymouth 7,605 ....E7
15474 Point Marion 1,642 ......C6
16342 Polk 1,884 ....C3
15946 Portage 3,510 ....E5
16743 Port Allegany 2,593 ......F2
17965 Port Carbon 2,576 ....K4
†15133 Port Vue 5,316 ....C7
19464 Pottstown 22,729 ....L5
17901 Pottsville⊙ 18,195 ....K4
19076 Prospect Park 6,593 ......M7
18951 Quakertown 8,867 ....M5
17566 Quarryville 1,558 ....K6
†15104 Rankin 2,892 ....C7
*19601 Reading⊙ 78,686 ....L5
         Reading‡ 312,509.......L5
17567 Reamstown 1,308 ....K5
18076 Red Hill 1,727 ....L5
17356 Red Lion 5,824 ....J6
17084 Reedsville 1,023 ....G4
15851 Reynoldsville 3,016......D3
17764 Renovo 1,812 ....G3
17087 Richland 1,470 ....K5
18955 Richlandtown 1,180 ......M5
15853 Ridgway⊙ 5,604 ....E3
19078 Ridley Park 7,889 ......M7
18077 Riegelsville 993 ....M4
16248 Rimersburg 1,096 ....D3
17868 Riverside 2,266 ....J4
16673 Roaring Spring 2,962 .....F5
19551 Robesonia 1,748 ....K5
15074 Rochester 4,759 ....B4
†19101 Rockledge 2,538 ....M5
15557 Rockwood 1,058 ....D6
15477 Roscoe 1,123 ....C5
18013 Roseto 1,484 ....M4
*19065 Rose Valley 1,038 ......L7
17250 Rouzerville 1,371 ......G6
19468 Royersford 4,243 ....L5
16249 Rural Valley 1,033 ......D4
15076 Russellton 1,878 ....C4
17970 Saint Clair 4,037 ....K4
15857 Saint Marys 6,417 ......E3
15951 Saint Michael 1,445 .....E5
15681 Saltsburg 964 ....C4
†15801 Sandy 1,835 ....E3
16056 Saxonburg 1,336 ....C4
18840 Sayre 6,951 ....K2
†15963 Scalp Level 1,186.......E5
19473 Schwenksville 1,041....L5
15683 Scottdale 5,833 ....C5
*18501 Scranton⊙ 88,117 ....F7
         Scranton (Northeast
         Pa.)‡ 640,396 ......F7
17870 Selinsgrove 5,227 ......J4
18960 Sellersville 3,143 ......M5
15143 Sewickley 4,778 ....B4
17872 Shamokin 10,357 ....J4
17876 Shamokin Dam 1,622.....J4
16146 Sharon 19,057 ....B3
         Sharon‡ 128,299 ....B3
19079 Sharon Hill 6,221 ......N7
15215 Sharpsburg 4,351 ......B6
16150 Sharpsville 5,375 ......A3
16347 Sheffield 1,471 ....D2
17976 Shenandoah 7,589 ......K4
18655 Shickshinny 1,192 ......K3
19607 Shillington 5,601 ....K5
16748 Shinglehouse 1,310 .....F2
17257 Shippensburg 5,261 .....H5
19555 Shoemakersville 1,391...K4
17361 Shrewsbury 2,688 ......J6
19608 Sinking Spring 2,617 ....K5
18080 Slatington 4,277 ....L4
15684 Slickville 1,178 ....C5
16057 Slippery Rock 3,047 ......B3
16749 Smethport⊙ 1,797 ......F2
15478 Smithfield 1,084 ....C6
15501 Somerset⊙ 6,474 ....D6
18964 Souderton 6,657 ....M5
15425 South Connellsville 2,296.C6
15956 South Fork 1,401 ....E5
†18840 South Waverly 1,176.......J2

17701 South Williamsport 6,581..J3
15775 Spangler 2,399 ....E4
19475 Spring City 3,389 ......L5
15144 Springdale 4,418 ......C6
19064 Springfield⊙ 25,326 .....M7
17362 Spring Grove 1,832 ......J6
16801 State College 36,130 .....G4
         State College‡ 112,760....G4
17263 State Line 1,253 ....G6
17113 Steelton 6,484 ....J5
17363 Stewartstown 1,072 ......K6
16153 Stoneboro 1,177 ....B3
19464 Stowe 3,860 ....L5
17579 Strasburg 1,999 ....K6
18360 Stroudsburg⊙ 5,148......M4
15082 Sturgeon 1,312 ....B5
†16823 Sugar Creek 5,954......C3
18706 Sugar Notch 1,191 ......E7
18250 Summit Hill 3,418 ......L4
17801 Sunbury⊙ 12,292 ....J4
18847 Susquehanna 1,994 ......L2
19081 Swarthmore 5,950 ....M7
15218 Swissvale 11,345 ......C7
18704 Swoyersville 5,795 ......E7
15865 Sykesville 1,537 ....E3
18252 Tamaqua 8,843 ....L4
15084 Tarentum 6,419 ....C4
18517 Taylor 7,246 ....F7
18969 Telford 3,507 ....M5
15560 Temple 1,486 ....L5
17581 Terre Hill 1,217 ....L5
18512 Throop 4,166 ....F7
16351 Tidioute 844 ....D2
16353 Tionesta⊙ 659 ....C2
16684 Tipton 1,348 ....F4
16354 Titusville 6,884 ....C2
19562 Topton 1,818 ....L5
19374 Toughkenamon 1,111.....L6
18848 Towanda⊙ 3,526 ....J2
17980 Tower City 1,667 ....J4
17981 Tremont 1,796 ....K4
18254 Tresckow 1,128 ....K4
17881 Trevorton 2,192 ....J4
16947 Troy 1,381 ....J2
19007 Tullytown 2,277 ......N5
18657 Tunkhannock⊙ 2,144 .....L2
15145 Turtle Creek 6,959 ......C7
16686 Tyrone 6,346 ....F4
16438 Union City 3,623 ....C2
15401 Uniontown⊙ 14,510 ......C6
19013 Upland 3,458 ....L7
*19082 Upper Darby⊙ 84,054.....M6
15241 Upper Saint Claire 19,023 B7
19481 Valley Forge 400 ......L5
17983 Valley View 1,722 ....J4
15690 Vandergrift 6,823 ......D4
15147 Verona 3,179 ....C6
15132 Versailles 2,150 ....C7
19085 Villanova M6
18088 Walnutport 2,007 ....L4
16365 Warren⊙ 12,146 ....D2
15301 Washington⊙ 18,363 .....B5
16441 Waterford 1,568 ....B2
17777 Watsontown 2,366 ....J3
19087 Wayne M6
17268 Waynesboro 9,726 ......G6
15370 Waynesburg⊙ 4,482 ......B6
18255 Weatherly 2,891 ......L4
16901 Wellsboro⊙ 3,805 ......H2
19565 Wernersville 1,811 ......K5
16510 Wesleyville 3,998 ....C1
15417 West Brownsville 1,433 ...C5
19380 West Chester⊙ 17,435 ....L6
16950 Westfield 1,268 ....H2
19390 West Grove 1,820 ......L6
18201 West Hazleton 4,871 ......K4
†16201 West Kittanning 1,591 ....C4
15656 West Leechburg 1,395.....C4
16159 West Middlesex 860 ......B3
15122 West Mifflin 26,279 ......C7
†15905 Westmont 6,113 ....D5
15089 West Newton 3,387 ......C5
16160 West Pittsburg 1,133 .....B4
18643 West Pittston 5,980 ......F7
15229 West View 7,648 ....B6

18644 West Wyoming 3,288.......E7
†17401 West York 4,526 ....J6
15120 Whitaker 1,615 ....C7
†15234 Whitehall 15,206 ....B7
18661 White Haven 1,921 ......L3
15131 White Oak 9,480 ......C7
17097 Wiconisco 1,321 ....J4
*18701 Wilkes-Barre⊙ 51,551....F7
15221 Wilkinsburg 23,669 ......C7
16693 Williamsburg 1,400 ......F5
17701 Williamsport⊙ 33,401 ....H3
         Williamsport‡ 118,416 ...H3
17098 Williamstown 1,664 ......J4
19090 Willow Grove M5
15148 Wilmerding 2,421 ......C5
15025 Wilson 7,564 ....M4
15963 Windber 5,585 ....E5
18091 Windgap 2,651 ....M4
19567 Womelsdorf 1,827 ......K5
19094 Woodlyn M7
17368 Wrightsville 2,365 ......J5
18644 Wyoming 3,655 ....E7
19610 Wyomissing 6,551 ......K5
19067 Yardley 2,533 ....N5
19050 Yeadon 11,727 ....N7
17099 Yeagertown 1,305 ......G4
*17401 York⊙ 44,619 ....J6
         York‡ 381,255 ....J6
16371 Youngsville 2,006 ....D2
15697 Youngwood 3,749 ......D5
16063 Zelienople 3,502 ....B4

OTHER FEATURES

Allegheny (res.) E2
Allegheny (riv.) D2
Allegheny Front (mts.) E5
Appalachian (mts.) H4
Ararat (mt.) M2
Arthur (lake) C4
Beaver (riv.) B4
Blue (mt.) G5
Blue Knob (mt.) E5
Casselman (riv.) D6
Clarion (riv.) D3
Conemaugh (riv.) D5
Conemaugh River (lake) ...D4
Conewango (creek) D2
Davis (mt.) D6
Delaware (riv.) N3
Delaware Water Gap Nat'l Rec.
         Area N3
Erie (lake) B1
Fort Necessity Nat'l
         Battlefield C6
George B. Stevenson (dam)..G3
Gettysburg Nat'l Mil. Park ...H6
Glendale (lake) F4
Juniata (riv.) G5
Laurel Hill (mt.) D5
Lehigh (riv.) L3
Letterkenny Army Depot G6
Licking (creek) F6
Little Tinicum (isl.) M7
Lycoming (creek) H3
Monongahela (riv.) B5
North (mt.) K3
Ohio (riv.) A4
Oil (creek) C2
Pine (creek) H2
Pine Grove (res.) K6
Pocono (mts.) M3
Pymatuning (res.) A2
Redbank (creek) E3
Schuylkill (riv.) M5
Shenango River (lake) B3
Sinnemahoning (creek) F3
South (mt.) H6
Susquehanna (riv.) K6
Tioga (riv.) H1
Tionesta Creek (lake) D3
Towanda (creek) J2
Tuscarora (mt.) G5
Wallenpaupack (lake) M3
Youghiogheny River (lake)..D6

⊙County seat.
‡Population of metropolitan area.
○Population of town or township.
† Zip of nearest p.o.   * Multiple zips.

18067 Northampton 8,240 ....M4
15673 North Apollo 1,487 ....D4
15104 North Braddock 8,711....C7
†18032 North Catasauqua 2,554..L4
16428 North East 4,568 ....C1
17857 Northumberland 3,636 ....J4
19454 North Wales 3,391 ....M5
†16365 North Warren 1,232 ......D2
15674 Norvelt 2,541 ....D5
19074 Norwood 6,647 ....M7
15071 Oakdale 1,955 ....B5
15139 Oakmont 7,039 ....C6
†15059 Ohioville 4,217 ....B4
16301 Oil City 13,881 ....C3
18518 Old Forge 9,304 ....F7
15472 Oliver 3,777 ....C6
18447 Olyphant 5,204 ....F7
17961 Orwigsburg 2,700 ....K4
19301 Paoli 5,277 ....M5
†15963 Paint 1,177 ....E5
18071 Palmerton 5,455 ....L4
17078 Palmyra 7,228 ....J5

17562 Paradise 1,107 ....K5
19365 Parkesburg 2,578 ......L6
†19013 Parkside 2,464 ....M7
†17331 Parkville 5,009 ......J6
16668 Patton 2,441 ....E4
18072 Pen Argyl 3,388 ....M4
17103 Penbrook 3,006 ....J5
19047 Penndel 2,703 ....N5
18073 Pennsburg 2,339 ....M5
†17331 Pennville 1,398 ......J6
†19151 Penn Wynne M6
18944 Perkasie 5,241 ....M5
15473 Perryopolis 2,139 ......C5
*19101 Philadelphia⊙ 1,688,210..N6
         Philadelphia‡ 4,716,818...N6
16866 Philipsburg 3,533 ....F4
19460 Phoenixville 14,165 ......L5
17963 Pine Grove 2,244 ....K4
16868 Pine Grove Mills 1,030 ....G4
15140 Pitcairn 4,175 ....C5
*15201 Pittsburgh⊙ 423,938 .....B7
         Pittsburgh‡ 2,263,894.....B7
†18640 Pittston 9,930 ....F7
*18701 Plains 5,455 ....F7

Topography

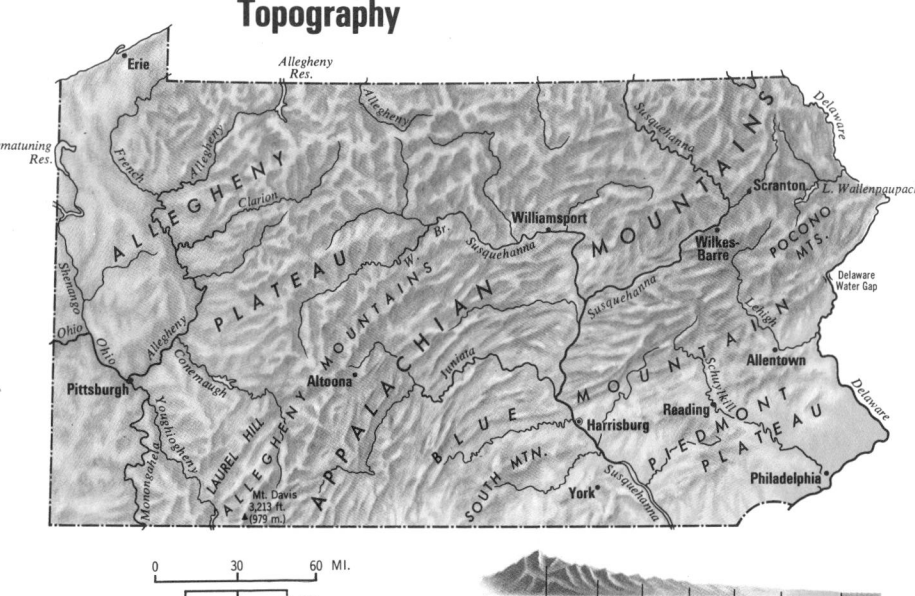

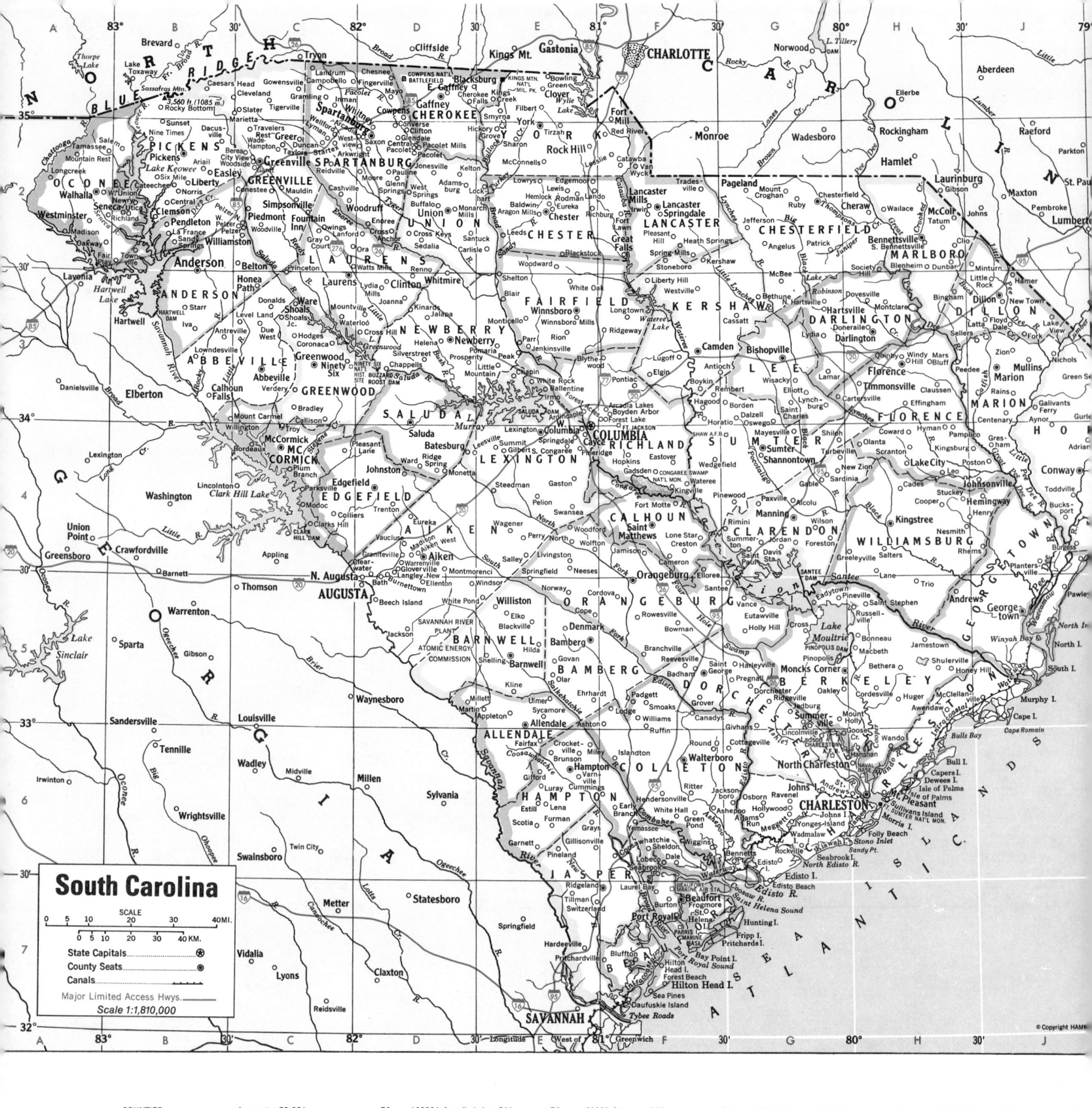

South Carolina

SCALE
0 5 10 20 30 40 MI.
0 5 10 20 30 40 KM.
State Capitals .... ⊛
County Seats .... ◉
Canals
Major Limited Access Hwys. ___
Scale 1:1,810,000

© Copyright HAMM

COUNTIES

Abbeville 22,627 .... B3
Aiken 105,625 .... D4
Allendale 10,700 .... E6
Anderson 133,235 .... B2
Bamberg 18,118 .... E5
Barnwell 19,868 .... E5
Beaufort 65,364 .... F7
Berkeley 94,727 .... G5
Calhoun 12,206 .... F4
Charleston 276,974 .... H6
Cherokee 40,983 .... D1
Chester 30,148 .... E2
Chesterfield 38,161 .... G2
Clarendon 27,464 .... G4
Colleton 31,776 .... F6
Darlington 62,717 .... H3
Dillon 31,083 .... J3
Dorchester 58,761 .... G5
Edgefield 17,528 .... D4
Fairfield 20,700 .... E3
Florence 110,163 .... H3
Georgetown 42,461 .... J5
Greenville 287,913 .... C2
Greenwood 57,847 .... C3
Hampton 18,159 .... E6
Horry 101,419 .... J4
Jasper 14,504 .... E6
Kershaw 39,015 .... F3
Lancaster 53,361 .... F2
Laurens 52,214 .... D2
Lee 18,929 .... G3
Lexington 140,353 .... E4
Marion 34,179 .... J3
Marlboro 31,634 .... H2
McCormick 7,797 .... C4
Newberry 31,242 .... D3
Oconee 48,611 .... A2
Orangeburg 82,276 .... F5
Pickens 79,292 .... B2
Richland 269,735 .... F4
Saluda 16,150 .... D3
Spartanburg 201,861 .... D2
Sumter 88,243 .... G4
Union 30,764 .... D2
Williamsburg 38,226 .... H4
York 106,720 .... E2

CITIES and TOWNS

Zip   Name/Pop.   Key

29620 Abbeville◉ 5,833 .... C3
29801 Aiken◉ 14,978 .... D4
†29801 Aiken West 3,083 .... D4
29810 Allendale◉ 4,400 .... E5
*29621 Anderson◉ 27,965 .... B2
       Anderson‡ 133,235 .... B2
29510 Andrews 3,129 .... H5
29320 Arcadia 2,088 .... C2
†29201 Arcadia Lakes 611 .... F3
†29640 Ariail 2,419 .... B2
†29301 Arkwright 2,623 .... C2
†29582 Atlantic Beach 289 ..... K4
29511 Aynor 643 .... J3
29003 Bamberg◉ 3,672 .... E5
29812 Barnwell◉ 5,572 .... E5
29006 Batesburg 4,023 .... D4
29816 Bath 2,242 .... D5
29902 Beaufort◉ 8,634 .... F7
29627 Belton 5,312 .... C2
29512 Bennettsville◉ 8,774 ..... H2
29611 Berea 13,164 .... C2
29009 Bethune 481 .... G3
29010 Bishopville◉ 3,429 .... G3
29702 Blacksburg 1,873 .... D1
29817 Blackville 2,840 .... E5
29516 Blenheim 202 .... H2
29910 Bluffton 541 .... F7
29016 Blythewood 92 .... E3
29431 Bonneau 401 .... H5
29018 Bowman 1,137 .... F5
29432 Branchville 1,769 .... F5
29911 Brunson 590 .... E6
29527 Bucksport 1,125 .... J4
29321 Buffalo 1,641 .... D2
29628 Calhoun Falls 2,491 .... B3
29020 Camden◉ 7,462 .... F3
29030 Cameron 536 .... F4
29322 Campobello 472 .... C1
29031 Carlisle 503 .... D2
29169 Cayce 11,701 .... E4
29519 Centenary 700 .... J3
29630 Central 1,914 .... B2
†29372 Central Pacolet 315 .... D1
29036 Chapin 311 .... E3
29037 Chappells 109 .... D3
*29401 Charleston◉ 69,510 .... G6
       Charleston-North
       Charleston‡ 430,301 ... G6
29520 Cheraw 5,654 .... H2
29323 Chesnee 1,069 .... C1
29706 Chester◉ 6,820 .... E2
29709 Chesterfield◉ 1,432 ... G2
29611 City View 1,662 .... C2
29822 Clearwater 3,967 ...... D4
29631 Clemson 8,118 .... B2
29635 Cleveland 800 .... C1
29324 Clifton 950 .... D2
29525 Clio 1,031 .... H2
29710 Clover 3,451 .... E1
29834 Columbia (cap.)◉ 100,385 F4
       Columbia‡ 408,176 ...... F4
29329 Converse 1,173 .... D2
29526 Conway◉ 10,240 .... J4
29902 Burton 3,619 .... F7
29628 Calhoun Falls 2,491 .... B3
29038 Cope 167 .... E5
29039 Cordova 202 .... F5
29206 Forest Acres 6,071 .... E3
29435 Cottageville 371 .... G6
29530 Coward 428 .... H4
29330 Cowpens 2,023 .... D1
29332 Cross Hill 604 .... D3
29532 Darlington◉ 7,989 ..... H3
29042 Denmark 4,434 .... E5
29536 Dillon◉ 7,060 .... J3
29638 Donalds 366 .... C3
†29532 Doneraile 1,276 .... H3
29639 Due West 1,366 .... C3
29334 Duncan 1,259 .... C2
29640 Easley◉ 14,264 .... B2
29044 Eastover 899 .... F4
29824 Edgefield◉ 2,713 ...... C4
29438 Edisto Beach 193 ...... G7
29438 Edisto Island 900 ..... G6
29081 Ehrhardt 353 .... E5
29045 Elgin 595 .... F3
29826 Elko 329 .... D4
29047 Elloree 909 .... F4
29335 Enoree 1,107 .... D2
29918 Estill 2,308 .... E6
†29706 Eureka 1,627 .... C4
29048 Eutawville 615 .... G5
29827 Fairfax 2,154 .... E6
29501 Florence◉ 29,176 ...... H3
       Harleyville 110,163 .... H3
29439 Folly Beach 1,478 ..... H6
29714 Fort Lawn 471 .... F2
29715 Fort Mill 4,162 .... F1
29050 Fort Motte 700 .... F4
29644 Fountain Inn 4,226 .... C2
29921 Furman 348 .... E6
29340 Gaffney◉ 13,453 .... C1
†29609 Gantt 13,719 .... C2
29053 Gaston 960 .... E4
29440 Georgetown◉ 10,144 ... J5
29923 Gifford 385 .... E6
29054 Gilbert 211 .... D4
29346 Glendale 1,049 .... D2
29828 Gloverville 2,619 ...... D4
29445 Goose Creek 17,811 .... H6
†29843 Govan 109 .... E5
29829 Graniteville 1,158 ..... D4
29645 Gray Court 988 .... C2
29055 Great Falls 2,601 ...... F2
29056 Greeleyville 593 .... H4
*29601 Greenville◉ 58,242 .... C2
       Greenville-Spartanburg‡
       568,758 .... C2
29646 Greenwood◉ 21,613 .... C3
29651 Greer 10,525 .... C2
29924 Hampton◉ 2,837 .... E6
29410 Hanahan 13,224 .... H6
29927 Hardeeville 1,250 ...... E7
29448 Gifford 385 .... G6
29550 Hartsville 7,631 ...... G3
29058 Heath Springs 979 .... F2

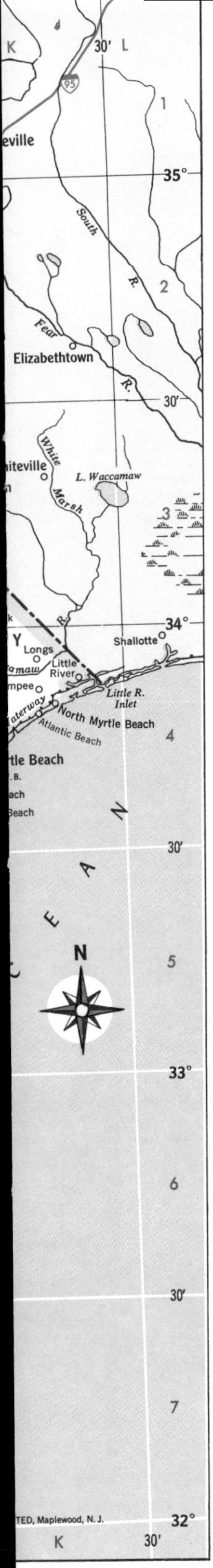

Elizabethtown
L. Waccamaw
Shallotte
Little River
Little R. Inlet
North Myrtle Beach
Atlantic Beach
N
35°
34°
33°
32°
TED, Maplewood, N. J.

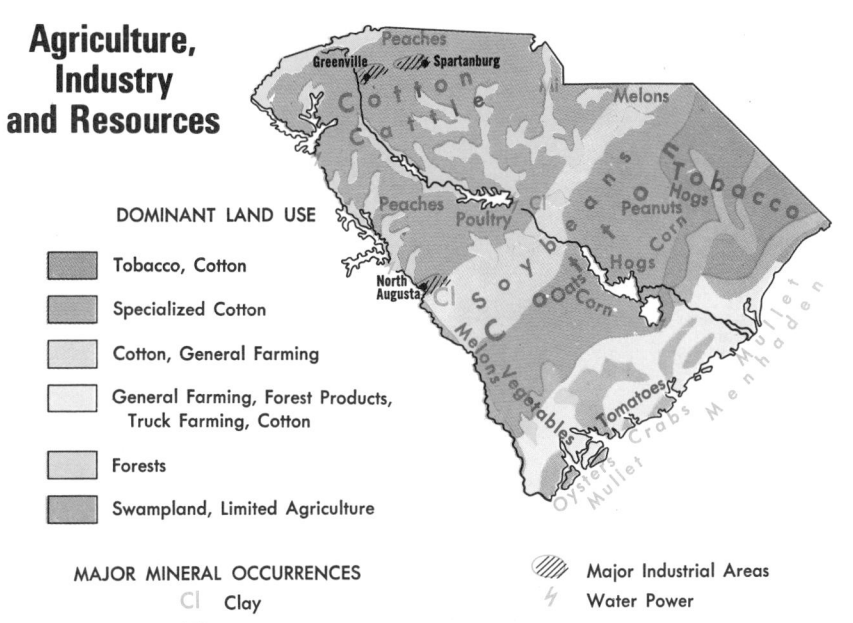

Agriculture, Industry and Resources

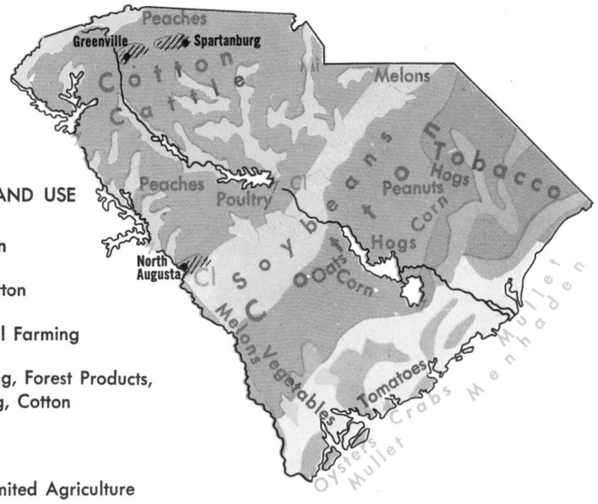

Peaches
Greenville
Spartanburg
Cotton
Cattle
Melons
Tobacco
Soybeans
Hogs
Peanuts
Corn
Peaches
Poultry
Cl
North Augusta
Oats
Vegetables
Tomatoes
Crabs
Menhaden
Mullet
Oysters

DOMINANT LAND USE

- Tobacco, Cotton
- Specialized Cotton
- Cotton, General Farming
- General Farming, Forest Products, Truck Farming, Cotton
- Forests
- Swampland, Limited Agriculture

MAJOR MINERAL OCCURRENCES

Cl Clay

Mi Mica

Major Industrial Areas

Water Power

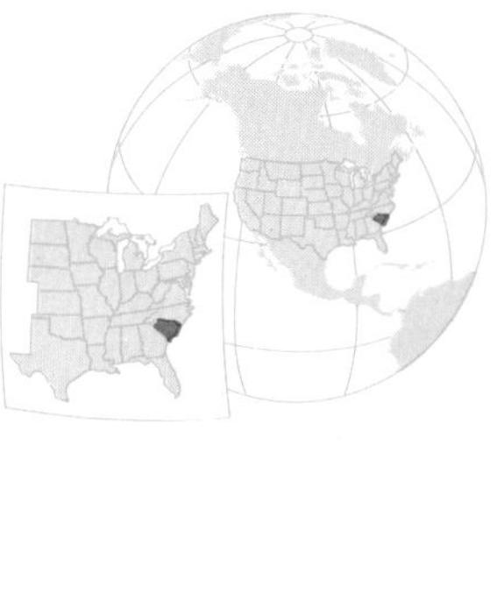

AREA 31,113 sq. mi. (80,583 sq. km.)
POPULATION 3,121,833
CAPITAL Columbia
LARGEST CITY Columbia
HIGHEST POINT Sassafras Mtn. 3,560 ft. (1085 m.)
SETTLED IN 1670
ADMITTED TO UNION May 23, 1788
POPULAR NAME Palmetto State
STATE FLOWER Carolina (Yellow) Jessamine
STATE BIRD Carolina Wren

29554 Hemingway 853 J4
†29706 Hemlock (Eureka) 1,627 E2
29717 Hickory Grove 344 E2
29813 Hilda 355 E5
29928 Hilton Head Island 11,344 F7
29653 Hodges 154 C3
29059 Holly Hill 1,785 G5
29449 Hollywood 729 G6
29654 Honea Path 4,114 C3
29349 Inman 1,554 C1
29063 Irmo 3,957 E3
†29720 Irwin 1,373 F2
29451 Isle of Palms 3,421 H6
29655 Iva 1,369 B3
29831 Jackson 1,771 D5
29453 Jamestown 193 H5
†29483 Jedburg 900 G5
29718 Jefferson 651 G2
29351 Joanna 1,839 D3
29555 Johnsonville 1,421 J4
29832 Johnston 2,624 D4
29353 Jonesville 1,201 D2
29067 Kershaw 1,993 G2
29556 Kingstree⊙ 4,147 H4
29814 Kline 315 E5
29456 Ladson 13,246 G6
29560 Lake City 6,731 H4
29563 Lake View 939 J3
29069 Lamar 1,333 G3
29720 Lancaster⊙ 9,703 F2
†29720 Lancaster Mills 2,096 F2
29356 Landrum 2,141 C1
29564 Lane 554 H5
29834 Langley 1,714 D4
29565 Latta 1,804 J3
29902 Laurel Bay 5,238 F7
29360 Laurens⊙ 10,587 C3
29070 Leesville 2,296 E4
†29730 Lesslie 1,102 E2
29072 Lexington⊙ 2,131 E4
29657 Liberty 3,167 B2
†29483 Lincolnville 808 G6
29075 Little Mountain 282 E3
29076 Livingston 166 E4
29364 Lockhart 85 E2
29082 Lodge 145 F5
29569 Loris 2,193 K3
29659 Lowndesville 197 B3
†29706 Lowrys 225 E2
29078 Lugoff 2,939 F3
29932 Luray 149 E6
29325 Lydia Mills 925 D3
29365 Lyman 1,067 C2
29080 Lynchburg 534 G3
†29829 Madison 1,150 D4
29102 Manning⊙ 4,746 G4
29661 Marietta-Slater 1,834 C1
29571 Marion⊙ 7,700 J3
29662 Mauldin 8,143 C2
29104 Mayesville 663 G4
29101 McBee 774 G3
29458 McClellanville 436 H5
29570 McColl 2,677 H2
29726 McConnells 171 E2
29835 McCormick⊙ 1,725 C4
29460 Meggett 249 G6
†29379 Monarch Mills 2,353 D2
29461 Moncks Corner⊙ 3,699 G5
29105 Monetta 167 D4
29840 Mount Carmel 182 C3
29727 Mount Croghan 146 G2
29464 Mount Pleasant 14,209 H6
29574 Mullins 6,068 J3
29576 Murrells Inlet 2,410 K4
29577 Myrtle Beach 18,446 K4
29107 Neeses 557 E4
29108 Newberry⊙ 9,866 D3
29809 New Ellenton 2,628 D5
†29536 New Town 950 J3
29581 Nichols 606 J3
29666 Ninety Six 2,249 C3
29667 Norris 903 B2
29112 North 1,304 E4
29841 North Augusta 13,593 C5
29406 North Charleston 62,534 G6
†29550 North Hartsville 2,650 G3
29582 North Myrtle Beach 3,960 K4
29113 Norway 518 E5
29114 Olanta 699 H4
29843 Olar 381 E5
29115 Orangeburg⊙ 14,933 F4
29372 Pacolet 1,556 D2
29373 Pacolet Mills 1,051 D2
29728 Pageland 2,720 G2
29583 Pamplico 1,213 H4
29844 Parksville 157 C4
29584 Patrick 375 G2
29102 Paxville 244 G4
29122 Peak 82 E3
29123 Pelion 213 E4
29669 Pelzer 130 B2
29670 Pendleton 3,154 B2
29124 Perry 273 E4
29671 Pickens⊙ 3,199 B2
29673 Piedmont 2,992 C2
29934 Pineland 800 E6
†29169 Pineridge 1,287 E4
29468 Pineville 900 H5
29125 Pinewood 689 G4
29469 Pinopolis 788 G5
29845 Plum Branch 73 C4
29126 Pomaria 271 E3
29935 Port Royal 2,977 F7
29127 Prosperity 803 D3
†29501 Quinby 952 H3
29470 Ravenel 1,655 G6
29471 Reevesville 241 F5
29729 Richburg 269 E2
29936 Ridgeland⊙ 1,143 E7
29129 Ridge Spring 969 D4
29472 Ridgeville 603 G5
29130 Ridgeway 343 F3
29730 Rock Hill 35,344 E2
Rock Hill‡ 106,720 E2
29133 Rowesville 388 F5
29741 Ruby 256 G2
29407 Saint Andrews 9,908 G6
29477 Saint George⊙ 2,134 F5
29135 Saint Matthews⊙ 2,496 F4
29479 Saint Stephen 1,850 H5
29676 Salem 194 A2
29137 Salley 584 E4
29138 Saluda⊙ 2,752 D4
29142 Santee 612 F5
†29301 Saxon 4,383 D2
29939 Scotia 72 E6
29591 Scranton 861 H4
29592 Sellers 388 H3
29678 Seneca 7,436 A2
29742 Sharon 323 E2
29145 Silverstreet 200 D3
29681 Simpsonville 9,037 C2
29682 Six Mile 470 B2
29683 Slater-Marietta 1,834 C1
29481 Smoaks 165 F5
29743 Smyrna 47 E1
†29812 Snelling 111 E5
29593 Society Hill 848 H2
†29512 South Bennettsville 1,065 H2
†29169 South Congaree 2,113 E4
*29301 Spartanburg⊙ 43,826 C1
29169 Springdale 2,985 E4
†29720 Springdale 2,570 F2
29146 Springfield 604 E4
†29067 Spring Mills 1,419 F2
29684 Starr 241 B3
29377 Startex 1,006 C2
29554 Stuckey 222 H4
29482 Sullivans Island 1,867 H6
29148 Summerton 1,173 G4
29483 Summerville 6,706 G5
†29054 Summit 172 E4
29150 Sumter⊙ 24,890 G4
29577 Surfside Beach 2,522 K4
29160 Swansea 888 E4
29846 Sycamore 261 E5
29594 Tatum 101 H2
29687 Taylors 15,801 C2
29688 Tigerville 975 C1
29161 Timmonsville 2,112 H3
29690 Travelers Rest 3,017 C2
29847 Trenton 404 D4
29848 Troy 705 C4
29162 Turbeville 549 G4
29849 Ulmer 91 E5
29379 Union⊙ 10,523 D2
†29678 Utica 1,501 B2
29163 Vance 89 G5
29944 Varnville 1,948 E6
†29607 Wade-Hampton 20,180 C2
29164 Wagener 903 E4
29691 Walhalla⊙ 3,977 A2
29488 Walterboro⊙ 6,209 F6
29166 Ward 98 D4
29692 Ware Shoals 2,370 C3
29851 Warrenville 1,029 D4
29384 Waterloo 200 C3
†29360 Watts Mills 1,324 D2
29385 Wellford 2,143 C2
29169 West Columbia 10,409 E4
29693 Westminster 3,114 A2
29669 West Pelzer 944 B2
29696 West Union 300 B2
†29301 Westview 1,999 C2
29178 Whitmire 2,038 D3
29303 Whitney 4,052 D1
29493 Williams 205 F5
29697 Williamston 4,310 B2
29853 Williston 3,173 E5
29856 Windsor 55 E5
†29501 Windy Hill 1,622 H3
29180 Winnsboro⊙ 2,919 E3
†29180 Winnsboro Mills 1,890 E3
†29112 Woodford 206 E4
29388 Woodruff 5,171 D2
29945 Yemassee 789 F6
29745 York⊙ 6,412 E1

OTHER FEATURES

Ashepoo (riv.) F6
Ashley (riv.) G6
Bay Point (isl.) F7
Beaufort Marine Air Sta. F7
Big Black (creek) G2
Black (riv.) H4
Blue Ridge (mts.) B1
Broad (riv.) E2
Broad (riv.) F7
Buck (creek) J3
Bull (isl.) H6
Bullock (creek) E2
Bulls (bay) H6
Bush (riv.) D3
Buzzard Roost (dam) D3
Cape (isl.) J5
Capers (isl.) H6
Catawba (riv.) F2
Catfish (creek) J3
Charleston A.F.B. G6
Chattooga (riv.) A2
Clark Hill (dam) C4
Clark Hill (lake) C4
Combahee (riv.) F6
Congaree (riv.) F4
Congaree Nat'l Mon. F4
Cooper (riv.) H6
Coosaw (riv.) G7
Coosawhatchie (riv.) E6
Cowpens Nat'l Battlefield D1
Crooked (creek) H2
Deep (creek) B2
Dewees (isl.) H6
Donaldson A.F.B. C2
Edisto (isl.) G6
Edisto (riv.) G7
Enoree (riv.) C2
Fort Jackson F4
Fort Sumter Nat'l Mon. H6
Four Hole Swamp (creek) F5
Fripp (isl.) G7
Great Pee Dee (riv.) J4
Greenwood (lake) D3
Hartwell (dam) B3
Hartwell (lake) A3
Hilton Head (isl.) F7
Hunting (isl.) G7
Intracoastal Waterway H5
James (isl.) H6
Johns (isl.) G6
Juniper (creek) H2
Keowee (lake) B2
Keowee (riv.) B2
Kiawah (isl.) G6
Kings Mountain Nat'l Mil. Park E1
Little (riv.) C3
Little (riv.) D3
Little Lynches (riv.) G3
Little Pee Dee (riv.) J4
Little River (inlet) L4
Lumber (riv.) J3
Lynches (riv.) H3
Marion (lake) G5
Morris (isl.) H6
Moultrie (lake) G5
Murphy (isl.) J5
Murray (lake) D4
Myrtle Beach A.F.B. K4
Naval Base H6
New (riv.) E6
Ninety Six Nat'l Hist. Site C3
North (inlet) J5
North (isl.) J5
North Edisto (riv.) G6
Pacolet (riv.) D1
Palms, Isle of (isl.) H6
Parris Island Marine Base F7
Pee Dee (riv.) H2
Pinopolis (dam) G5
Pocotaligo (riv.) G4
Port Royal (sound) F7
Pritchards (isl.) G7
Reedy (riv.) C2
Robinson (lake) G3
Romain (cape) J6
Saint Helena (isl.) F7
Saint Helena (sound) G7
Salkehatchie (riv.) E5
Saluda (riv.) D3
Sandy (pt.) H6
Sandy (riv.) E2
Santee (dam) G4
Santee (riv.) H5
Sassafras (mt.) B1
Savannah (riv.) E6
Savannah River Plant Atomic Energy Commission D5
Sea (isls.) G7
Seabrook (isl.) G6
Seneca (riv.) B2
Shaw A.F.B. 6,939 F4
South (isl.) J5
Stevens (creek) C4
Stono (inlet) H6
Thompsons (creek) G2
Tugaloo (riv.) A2
Turkey (creek) E2
Tybee Roads (chan.) F7
Tyger (riv.) D2
Waccamaw (riv.) J5
Wadmalaw (isl.) G6
Wando (riv.) H6
Wateree (lake) F3
Wateree (riv.) F3
Winyah (bay) J5
Wylie (lake) E1

⊙County seat.
‡Population of metropolitan area.
† Zip of nearest p.o. * Multiple zips.

Topography

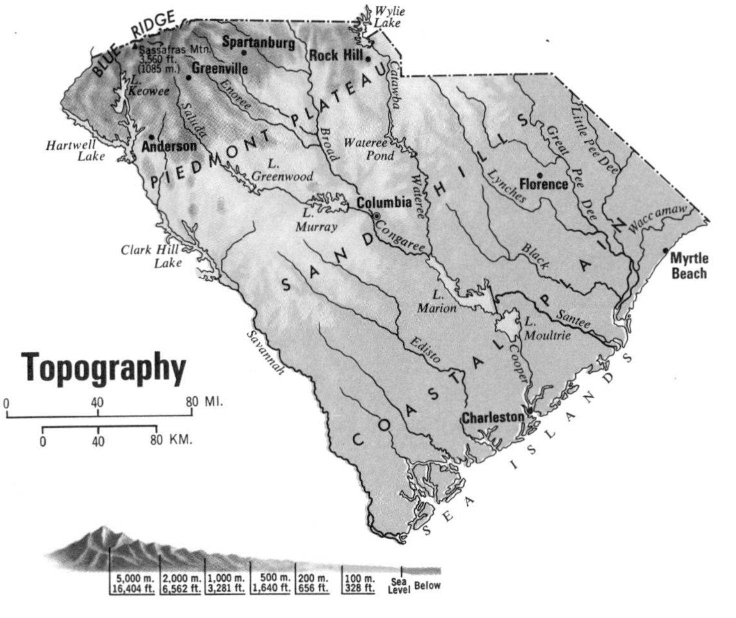

Blue Ridge
Sassafras Mtn. 3,560 ft. (1085 m.)
Spartanburg
Greenville
Rock Hill
Wylie Lake
L. Keowee
Anderson
Hartwell Lake
Piedmont Plateau
L. Greenwood
Wateree Pond
Columbia
L. Murray
Clark Hill Lake
Sand Hills
Florence
Myrtle Beach
L. Marion
L. Moultrie
Charleston
Coastal Plain
Sea Islands
0 40 80 MI.
0 40 80 KM.
5,000 m. 16,404 ft.
2,000 m. 6,562 ft.
1,000 m. 3,281 ft.
500 m. 1,640 ft.
200 m. 656 ft.
100 m. 328 ft.
Sea Level
Below

COUNTIES

Aurora 3,628	..................M6	
Beadle 19,195	..................N5	
Bennett 3,044	..................F7	
Bon Homme 8,059	..............O7	
Brookings 24,332	............R5	
Brown 36,962	..................N2	
Brule 5,245	..................L6	
Buffalo 1,795	..................L5	
Butte 8,372	..................B4	
Campbell 2,243	..................J2	
Charles Mix 9,680	..........M7	
Clark 4,894	..................O4	
Clay 13,689	..................P8	
Codington 20,885	............P4	
Corson 5,196	..................G2	
Custer 6,000	..................B6	
Davison 17,820	..................N6	
Day 8,133	..................O3	

Deuel 5,289	..................R4
Dewey 5,366	..................G3
Douglas 4,181	..................N7
Edmunds 5,159	..................L3
Fall River 8,439	............B7
Faulk 3,327	..................L3
Grant 9,013	..................R3
Gregory 6,015	..................L7
Haakon 2,794	..................F5
Hamlin 5,261	..................P4
Hand 4,948	..................L4
Hanson 3,415	..................O6
Harding 1,700	..................B2
Hughes 14,220	..................J5
Hutchinson 9,350	............O7
Hyde 2,069	..................K4
Jackson 3,437	..................F6
Jerauld 2,929	..................M5
Jones 1,463	..................H6
Kingsbury 6,679	............O5
Lake 10,724	..................P5
Lawrence 18,339	............B5
Lincoln 13,942	..................R7

Lyman 3,864	..................J6
Marshall 5,404	..................O2
McCook 6,444	..................P6
McPherson 4,027	............L2
Meade 20,717	..................D5
Mellette 2,249	..................H6
Miner 3,739	..................O5
Minnehaha 109,435	......R6
Moody 6,692	..................R5
Pennington 70,361	......C6
Perkins 4,700	..................D3
Potter 3,674	..................J3
Roberts 10,911	..................P2
Sanborn 3,213	..................N5
Shannon 11,323	..................D7
Spink 9,201	..................N4
Stanley 2,533	..................H5
Sully 1,990	..................J4
Todd 7,328	..................H7
Tripp 7,268	..................K7
Turner 9,255	..................P7
Union 10,938	..................R8
Walworth 7,011	..................J3

Yankton 18,952	..................P7
Ziebach 2,308	..................F4

CITIES and TOWNS

Zip	Name/Pop.	Key
57401	Aberdeen⊙ 25,851	M3
57310	Academy 10	M7
57520	Agar 139	J4
57420	Akaska 49	J3
57210	Albee 23	S3
57001	Alcester 885	R7
57311	Alexandria⊙ 588	O6
57714	Allen 300	F7
57312	Alpena 288	N5
57211	Altamont 58	R4
57421	Amherst 75	O2
57422	Andover 139	O3
57715	Ardmore 16	B7
57212	Arlington 991	P5
57313	Armour⊙ 819	N7
57423	Artas 43	K2
57314	Artesian 227	O6

Zip	Name/Pop.	Key
57424	Ashton 154	N3
57213	Astoria 154	S4
57425	Athol 38	M3
57002	Aurora 507	R5
57315	Avon 576	N8
57214	Badger 99	P5
57003	Baltic 679	R6
57316	Bancroft 41	O4
57426	Barnard 65	N2
57427	Bath 175	N3
57716	Batesland 163	E7
57717	Belle Fourche⊙ 4,692	B4
57521	Belvidere 80	G6
57215	Bemis 37	R4
57004	Beresford 1,865	R7
57216	Big Stone City 672	S3
†57310	Bijou Hills 12	L6
57620	Bison⊙ 457	E2
57718	Black Hawk 1,608	C5
57522	Blunt 424	J4
57317	Bonesteel 358	M7
57428	Bowdle 644	K3
57719	Box Elder 3,186	D5

Zip	Name/Pop.	Key
57217	Bradley 135	O3
57005	Brandon 2,589	R6
57218	Brandt 129	R4
57429	Brentford 91	N3
57319	Bridgewater 653	P6
57219	Bristol 445	O3
57430	Britton⊙ 1,590	O2
57006	Brookings⊙ 14,951	R5
57220	Bruce 254	R5
57221	Bryant 388	P4
57720	Buffalo⊙ 453	B2
57722	Buffalo Gap 186	C6
57621	Bullhead 400	G2
57010	Burbank 92	R8
57523	Burke⊙ 859	L7
†57276	Bushnell 76	R5
57222	Butler 22	P4
57724	Camp Crook 100	B2
57012	Canistota 626	P6
57321	Canova 194	O6
57013	Canton⊙ 2,886	R7
57725	Caputa 50	D5

South Dakota

SCALE

0 5 10   20   40   60 MI.

0 5 10   20   40   60 KM.

State Capitals ....⊛

County Seats ....⊙

Major Limited Access Hwys. _____

Scale 1:2,220,000

AREA 77,116 sq. mi. (199,730 sq. km.)
POPULATION 690,768
CAPITAL Pierre
LARGEST CITY Sioux Falls
HIGHEST POINT Harney Pk. 7,242 ft. (2207 m.)
SETTLED IN 1856
ADMITTED TO UNION November 2, 1889
POPULAR NAME Coyote State; Sunshine State
STATE FLOWER Pasqueflower
STATE BIRD Ring-necked Pheasant

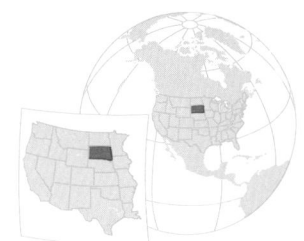

Topography

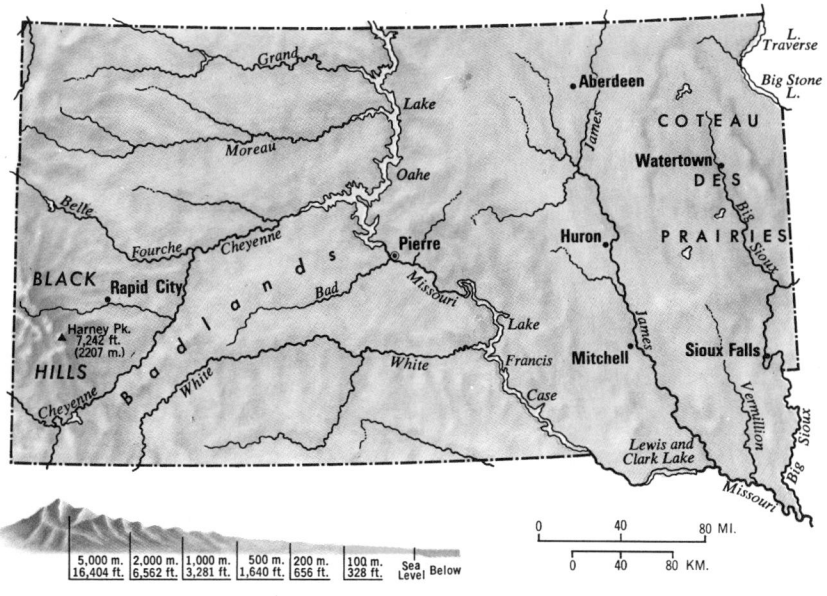

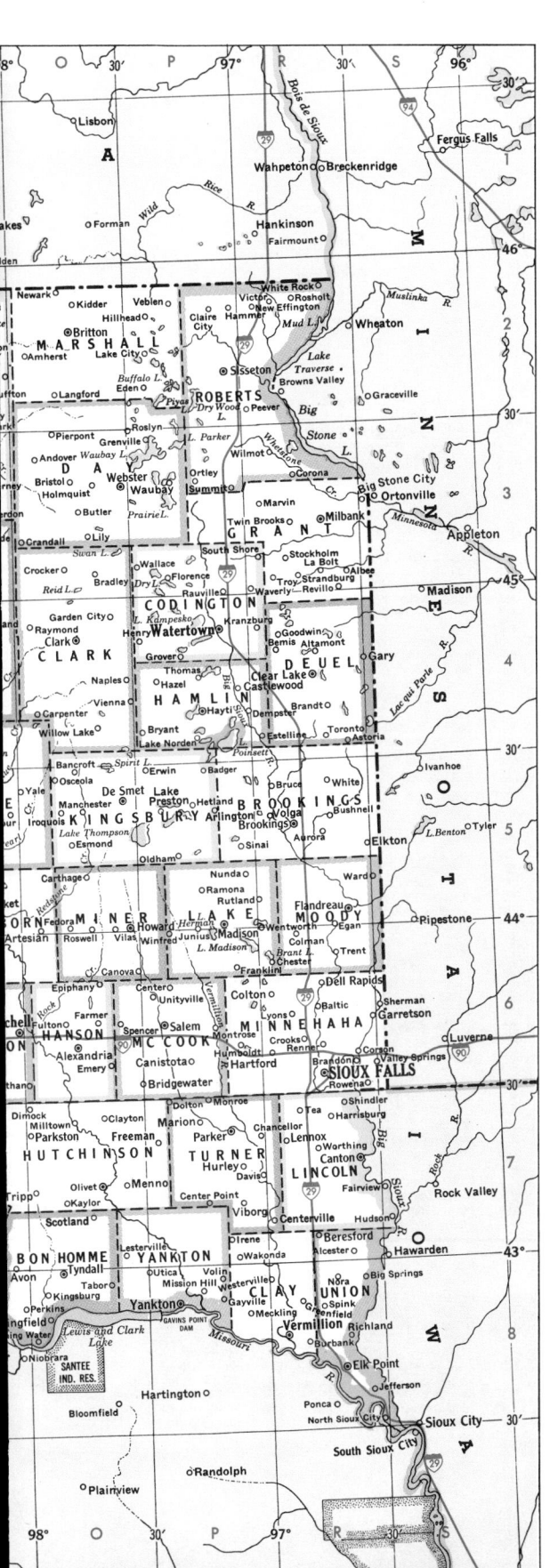

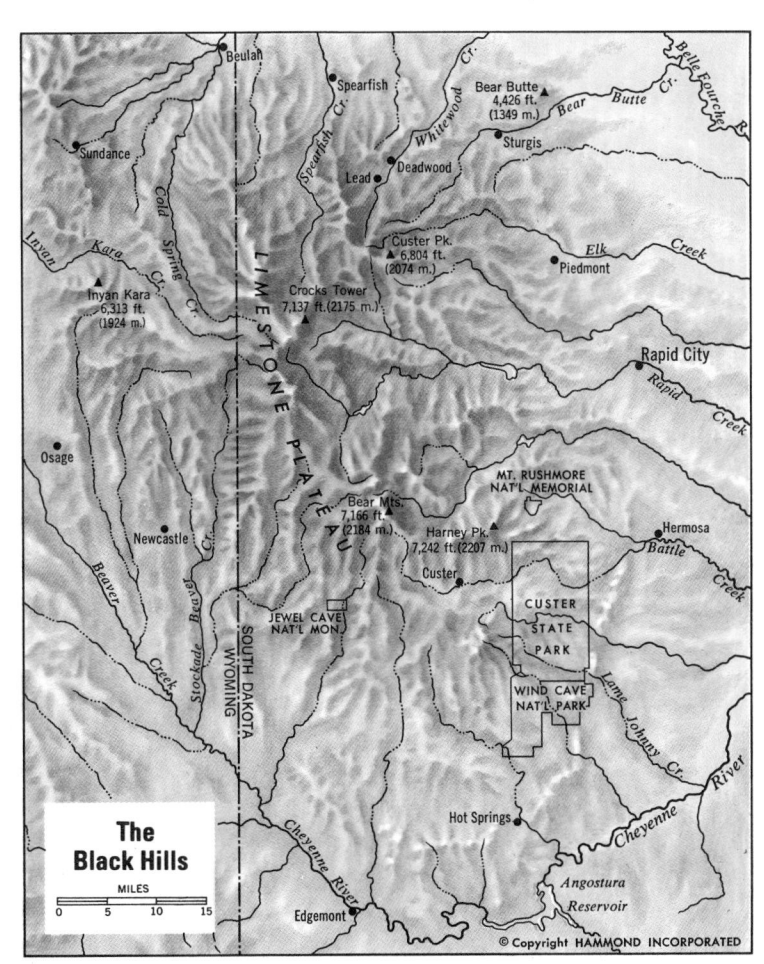

The Black Hills

© Copyright HAMMOND INCORPORATED

Agriculture, Industry and Resources

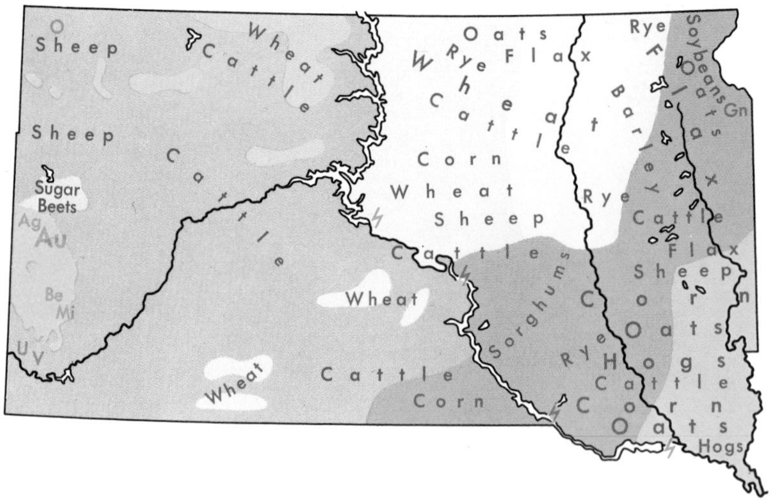

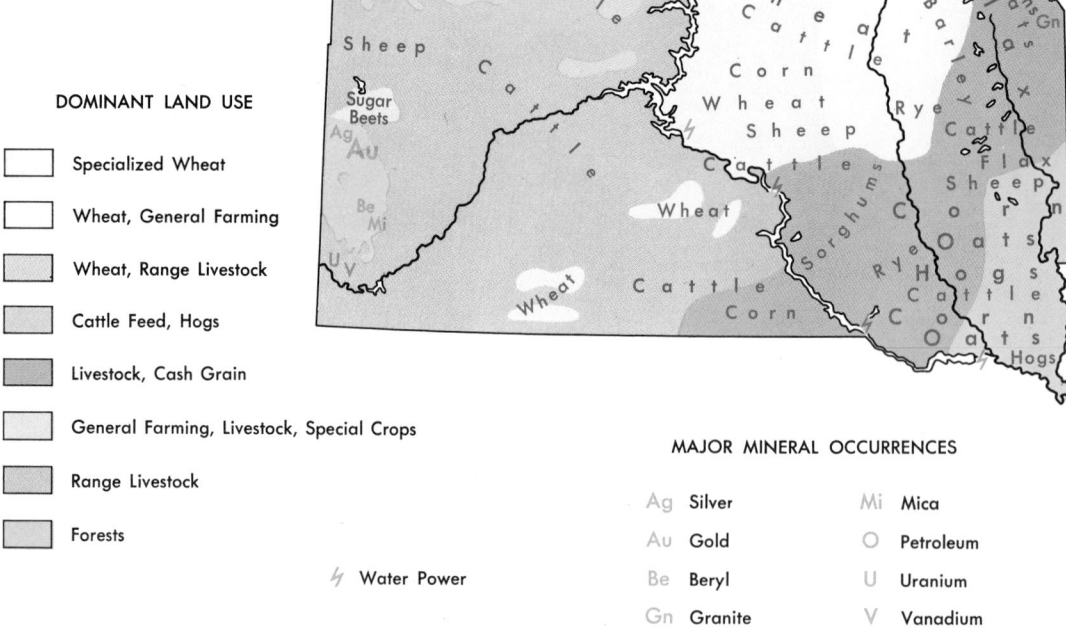

DOMINANT LAND USE

Specialized Wheat
Wheat, General Farming
Wheat, Range Livestock
Cattle Feed, Hogs
Livestock, Cash Grain
General Farming, Livestock, Special Crops
Range Livestock
Forests

Water Power

MAJOR MINERAL OCCURRENCES

Ag Silver
Au Gold
Be Beryl
Gn Granite
Mi Mica
O Petroleum
U Uranium
V Vanadium

57235 Florence 190 P3
57338 Forestburg 100 N5
57532 Fort Pierre⊙ 1,789 H5
57339 Fort Thompson 750 L5
57440 Frankfort 209 N4
57441 Frederick 307 N2
57029 Freeman 1,462 O7
57742 Fruitdale 88 B4
57340 Fulton 108 O6
57341 Gannvalley⊙ 70 L5
57236 Garden City 104 O4
57030 Garretson 963 S6
57237 Gary 354 S4
57031 Gayville 407 P8
57342 Geddes 303 M7
57442 Gettysburg⊙ 1,623 K3
57629 Glad Valley 75 F3
57630 Glencross 150 H3
57631 Glenham 169 J2
57238 Goodwin 139 R4
57533 Gregory 1,503 L7
57239 Grenville 119 O3
57445 Groton 1,230 N3
57534 Hamill 25 K6
57032 Harrisburg 558 R7
57344 Harrison 89 M7
57536 Harrold 196 K4
57033 Hartford 1,207 P6
57537 Hayes 25 H5
57241 Hayti⊙ 371 P4
57242 Hazel 94 P4
57446 Hecla 435 N2
57243 Henry 217 P4
57743 Hereford 50 D5
57744 Hermosa 251 C6
57632 Herreid 570 K2
57538 Herrick 115 L7
57244 Hetland 66 P5
57345 Highmore⊙ 1,055 L4
57745 Hill City 535 B6
†57437 Hillsview 9 L2
57348 Hitchcock 132 M4
57540 Holabird 30 K4
†57274 Holmquist 25 O3
57448 Hosmer 385 L2
57747 Hot Springs⊙ 4,742 C7
57449 Houghton 80 N2
57450 Hoven 615 K3
57349 Howard⊙ 1,169 P5
57748 Howes 4 E4
57034 Hudson 388 R7
57035 Humboldt 487 P6
57036 Hurley 419 P7
57350 Huron⊙ 13,000 N5
57541 Ideal 250 K6
57750 Interior 62 F6
57542 Iona 4 L6
57451 Ipswich⊙ 1,153 L3
57037 Irene 523 P7
57353 Iroquois 348 O5
57633 Isabel 332 G3
57452 Java 261 K3
57038 Jefferson 592 S8
57543 Kadoka⊙ 832 F6
57354 Kaylor 120 O7
57634 Keldron 17 F2
57544 Kennebec⊙ 334 K6
57545 Keyapaha 4 J7
57751 Keystone 295 C6
57355 Kimball 752 M6
57245 Kranzburg 136 R4
57752 Kyle 600 E7
57246 La Bolt 94 R3
57356 Lake Andes⊙ 1,029 M7
57247 Lake City 46 O2
57248 Lake Norden 417 P4
57249 Lake Preston 789 P5
57358 Lane 83 N5
57454 Langford 307 O2
57636 Lantry 200 G3
57754 Lead 4,330 B5
57455 Lebanon 129 K3
57638 Lemmon 1,871 E2
57039 Lennox 1,827 R7
57456 Leola⊙ 645 M2
57040 Lesterville 156 O7
57359 Letcher 221 N6
57250 Lily 38 O3
57639 Little Eagle 150 H2
57640 Lodgepole 20 D2
57457 Longlake 117 L2
57547 Longvalley 15 F7
57360 Loomis 55 N6
†57472 Lowry 22 K3
†57471 Loyalton 6 L3
57755 Ludlow 10 C2
57041 Lyons 100 R6
57042 Madison⊙ 6,210 P6
57643 Mahto 9 H2
57756 Manderson 450 D7
57460 Mansfield 120 N3
57757 Marcus 5 E4
57043 Marion 830 P7
57551 Martin⊙ 1,018 F7
57361 Marty 250 N8
57251 Marvin 52 R3
57641 McIntosh⊙ 418 G2
57642 McLaughlin 754 H2
57644 Meadow 21 E2
57044 Meckling 108 R8
57461 Mellette 192 N3
57045 Menno 793 P7
57552 Midland 277 G5
57252 Milbank⊙ 4,120 R3
57553 Milesville 6 F5
57554 Millboro 12 K7
57362 Miller⊙ 1,931 L4
57462 Mina 29 M3
57463 Miranda 30 M4
57555 Mission 748 H7
57046 Mission Hill 197 P8
57557 Mission Ridge 46 H4
57301 Mitchell⊙ 13,916 N6
57601 Mobridge 4,174 J2
57047 Monroe 170 P7
57048 Montrose 396 P6
57645 Morristown 127 F2
57558 Mosher 9 J7
57646 Mound City⊙ 111 K2
57363 Mount Vernon 402 N6
57758 Mud Butte 3 D4
57559 Murdo⊙ 723 H6
†57271 Naples 45 O4
57759 Nemo 42 B5
57255 New Effington 261 R2
57760 Newell 638 C4
57364 New Holland 125 M7
57761 New Underwood 517 D5
†57584 New Witten 134 K7
57762 Nisland 216 C4
57560 Norris 25 G7
†57625 North Eagle Butte 1,354 G3
57049 North Sioux City 1,992 R8
57465 Northville 138 M3
57050 Nunda 60 P5
57365 Oacoma 289 L6
57763 Oelrichs 124 C7
57764 Oglala 475 D7
57562 Okaton 30 H6
57563 Okreek 500 J7
57051 Oldham 222 P5
57052 Olivet⊙ 96 O7
57466 Onaka 70 L3
57564 Onida⊙ 851 K4
57765 Opal 5 D4
57766 Oral 60 C7
57467 Orient 87 L4
57256 Ortley 80 P3
57565 Ottumwa 3 G5
57767 Owanka 18 D5
57647 Parade 2 G3
57053 Parker⊙ 999 P7
57366 Parkston 1,545 O7
57566 Parmelee 600 G7
57257 Peever 232 R2
57567 Philip⊙ 1,088 F5
57367 Pickstown 225 M7
57769 Piedmont 500 C5
57468 Pierpont 184 O3
57501 Pierre (cap.)⊙ 11,973 J5
57770 Pine Ridge 3,059 E7
57771 Plainview 2 E4
57368 Plankinton⊙ 644 N6
57369 Platte 1,334 M7
57648 Pollock 355 J2
57772 Porcupine 260 E7
57649 Prairie City 50 D2
57568 Presho 760 J6
57773 Pringle 105 B6
57774 Provo 60 B7
57370 Pukwana 234 L6
57775 Quinn 80 E5
57650 Ralph 12 C2
57054 Ramona 241 P5
57701 Rapid City⊙ 46,492 C5
Rapid City‡ 90,850 C5
57357 Ravinia 88 N7
57258 Raymond 106 O4
57469 Redfield⊙ 3,027 N4
57776 Redig 50 C3
57777 Redowl 10 D4
57371 Ree Heights 88 L4
57569 Reliance 190 K6
57055 Renner 320 R6
57651 Reva 8 C2
57259 Revillo 158 R3
57652 Ridgeview 75 H3
†57701 Rockerville 28 C6
57470 Rockham 52 M4
57471 Roscoe 370 L3
57570 Rosebud 900 H7
57260 Rosholt 446 R2
57261 Roslyn 261 P2
57372 Roswell 19 O6
57056 Rowena 100 R6
57057 Rutland 30 P5
57571 Saint Charles 25 L7
57572 Saint Francis 766 H7
57373 Saint Lawrence 223 M4
57779 Saint Onge 250 B4
57058 Salem⊙ 1,486 P6
57780 Scenic 26 D6
57059 Scotland 1,022 O7
57472 Selby⊙ 884 J3
57473 Seneca 103 L3
57060 Sherman 100 S6
57781 Silver City 31 B5
57061 Sinai 129 P5
*57101 Sioux Falls⊙ 81,343 R6
Sioux Falls‡ 109,435 R6
57262 Sisseton⊙ 2,789 R2
57782 Smithwick 50 C7
57654 Sorum 2 D3
57263 South Shore 241 P3
57783 Spearfish 5,251 B5
57374 Spencer 380 O6
†57010 Spink 75 R8
57062 Springfield 1,377 N8
57346 Stephan 30 K5
57375 Stickney 409 M6
57264 Stockholm 95 R3
57784 Stoneville 20 D4
†57359 Storla 19 M6
57265 Strandburg 79 R3
57474 Stratford 82 N3
57785 Sturgis⊙ 5,184 B5
57266 Summit 290 P3
57063 Tabor 460 O8
†57433 Tacoma Park 20 N2
57064 Tea 729 R7
†57242 Thomas 12 P4
†57638 Thunder Hawk 26 F2
†57769 Tilford 75 C5
57656 Timber Lake⊙ 660 H3
57475 Tolstoy 97 K3
57268 Toronto 236 R4
57657 Trail City 68 H3
57065 Trent 197 R6
57376 Tripp 804 N7
†57754 Trojan 40 B5
†57265 Troy 18 R3
57476 Tulare 238 N4
57477 Turton 101 N3
57574 Tuthill 75 G7
57269 Twin Brooks 87 R3
57066 Tyndall⊙ 1,253 O8
57787 Union Center 63 D4
†57058 Unityville 20 P6
57067 Utica 100 P8
57788 Vale 160 C4
57068 Valley Springs 801 S6
†57381 Vayland 3 M5
57270 Veblen 368 P2
57478 Verdon 7 N3
57069 Vermillion⊙ 10,136 R8
57575 Vetal 19 G7
57070 Viborg 812 P7
†57260 Victor 9 R2
57271 Vienna 90 O4
†57349 Vilas 28 O6
†57701 Villa Ranchaero 1,666 C5
57379 Virgil 37 N5
57576 Vivian 95 J6
57071 Volga 1,221 R5
57072 Volin 156 P8
57380 Wagner 1,453 N7
57073 Wakonda 383 P7
57658 Wakpala 500 H2
57659 Walker 12 G2
57790 Wall 770 E6
57272 Wallace 90 P3
57577 Wanblee 550 F6
57074 Ward 43 R5
57479 Warner 322 M3
57791 Wasta 99 D5
57660 Watauga 50 F2
57201 Watertown⊙ 15,649 P4
57273 Waubay 675 P3
57202 Waverly 30 R3
57274 Webster⊙ 2,417 P3
57480 Wecota 30 L3
57075 Wentworth 193 R6
57381 Wessington 327 M5
57382 Wessington Springs⊙ 1,203 M5
†57069 Westerville 21 P8
57481 Westport 122 M2
57482 Wetonka 22 M2
57578 Wewela 6 K7
57276 White 474 R5
†57638 White Butte 21 E2
57661 Whitehorse 196 H3
57383 White Lake 414 M6
57792 White Owl 6 E4
57579 White River⊙ 561 H6
†57260 White Rock 10 R2
57793 Whitewood 821 B5
57278 Willow Lake 375 O4
57279 Wilmot 507 R3
57076 Winfred 81 P6
57580 Winner⊙ 3,472 K7
57584 Witten 134 J7
57384 Wolsey 437 N5
57585 Wood 134 J6
57385 Woonsocket⊙ 799 N5
57077 Worthing 388 R7
57794 Wounded Knee 376 D7
57386 Yale 136 O5
57078 Yankton⊙ 12,011 P8
57483 Zell 60 M4
57795 Zeona 2 D3

OTHER FEATURES

Aeber (creek) G4
Andes (lake) N7
Angostura (res.) B7
Antelope (creek) D3
Bad (riv.) G5
Badlands Nat'l Mon. E6
Battle (creek) C6
Bear in the Lodge (creek) F6
Beaver (creek) A6
Belle Fourche (res.) B4
Belle Fourche (riv.) C4
Big Bend (dam) K5
Big Sioux (riv.) S7
Big Stone (lake) R3
Black Hills (mts.) B5
Black Pine (creek) G6
Bois de Sioux (riv.) R1
Boxelder (creek) D5
Brant (lake) R6
Buffalo (creek) F6
Buffalo (lake) P2
Bull (creek) C2
Bull (creek) K6
Byron (lake) N4
Cain (creek) N5
Cherry (creek) F4
Cherry (creek) F5
Cheyenne (riv.) F4
Cheyenne River Ind. Res. F4
Choteau (creek) N7
Columbia Road (res.) N2
Cottonwood (creek) E5
Cottonwood (lake) M4
Crazy Horse Mon. B6
Crow (creek) A4
Crow Creek Ind. Res. L5
Dog Ear (creek) K6
Dry (creek) G4
Dry (lake) P3
Dry Wood (lake) P2
Elk (creek) C5
Ellsworth A.F.B. 4,766 C5
Elm (creek) D4
Elm (riv.) M2
Firesteel (creek) N6
Flint Rock (creek) E3
Fort Randall (dam) N7
Foster (creek) N4
Francis Case (lake) L7
French (creek) C6
Gavins Point (dam) P8
Geographical Center of U.S. B4
Grand (riv.) F2
Harney (peak) B6
Hat (creek) B7
Hell Canyon (creek) B6
Herman (lake) P5
Horsehead (creek) C7
Indian (creek) B4
James (riv.) N5
Jewel Cave Nat'l Mon. B6
Kampeska (lake) P4
Keya Paha (riv.) K7
Lame Johnny (creek) C6
Lewis and Clark (lake) O8
Little Missouri (riv.) B1
Little Moreau (riv.) G3
Little White (riv.) H7
Long (lake) L2
Lower Brule Ind. Res. K5
Madison (lake) P6
Maple (riv.) M1
Medicine (creek) J6
Medicine Knoll (creek) J5
Minnechaduza (creek) H7
Minnesota (riv.) S3
Missouri (riv.) P8
Mitchell (creek) G5
Moreau (riv.) G3
Mount Rushmore Nat'l Mem. B6
Mud (creek) N3
Mud (lake) R2
Mud Lake (res.) N2
Nasty (creek) C2
Oahe (dam) J5
Oahe (lake) J1
Oak (creek) H2
Oak (creek) J6
Okobojo (creek) J4
Old Lodge (creek) K6
Owl (creek) B4
Parker (lake) P3
Pearl (creek) N5
Pine Ridge Ind. Res. D7
Piyas (lake) P2
Platte (lake) M6
Pleasant Valley (creek) B6
Poinsett (lake) P4
Ponca (creek) L7
Prairie (lake) P3
Rabbit (creek) E3
Red (lake) L6
Red Owl (creek) E4
Red Scaffold (creek) F4
Redstone (creek) O5
Redwater (creek) A4
Reid (lake) O3
Rock (creek) O6
Rosebud Ind. Res. H7
Sand (creek) C2
Sand (creek) M5
Shadehill (res.) E2
Sharpe (lake) J5
Shue (creek) N5
Smith (creek) L6
Snake (creek) F4
Snake (creek) F5
Snake (creek) M3
Spirit (lake) O4
Spring (creek) C6
Spring (creek) J2
Squaw (creek) B3
Sulphur (creek) D4
Swan (creek) J3
Swan (lake) O3
Swan (lake) K3
Thompson (lake) O5
Thunder (creek) N4
Thunder Butte (creek) E3
Traverse (lake) R2
Turtle (creek) M4
Vermillion (riv.) P6
Virgin (creek) H3
Waubay (lake) O3
Whetstone (creek) R3
White (lake) M6
White (riv.) D7
Whitewood (creek) B4
Willow (creek) C4
Wind Cave Nat'l Park B6
Wolf (creek) L4
Wounded Knee (creek) E7

⊙County seat.
‡Population of metropolitan area.
† Zip of nearest p.o. * Multiple zips.

COUNTIES

Anderson 38,381 J6
Andrews 13,323 B5
Angelina 64,172 K6
Aransas 14,260 H10
Archer 7,266 F4
Armstrong 1,994 C3
Atascosa 25,055 F9
Austin 17,726 H8
Bailey 8,168 B3
Bandera 7,084 E8
Bastrop 24,726 G7
Baylor 4,919 E4
Bee 26,030 G9
Bell 157,820 G6
Bexar 988,798 F8
Blanco 4,681 F8
Borden 859 C5
Bosque 13,401 G6
Bowie 75,301 K4
Brazoria 169,587 J8
Brazos 93,588 H7
Brewster 7,573 A8
Briscoe 2,579 C3
Brooks 8,428 F11
Brown 33,057 F6
Burleson 12,313 H7
Burnet 17,803 F7
Caldwell 23,637 G8
Calhoun 19,574 H9
Callahan 10,992 E5
Cameron 209,727 G11
Camp 9,275 K5
Carson 6,672 C2
Cass 29,430 K4
Castro 10,556 B3
Chambers 18,538 K8
Cherokee 38,127 J6
Childress 6,950 D3
Clay 9,582 F4
Cochran 4,825 B4
Coke 3,196 D6
Coleman 10,439 E6
Collin 144,576 H4
Collingsworth 4,648 D3
Colorado 18,823 H8
Comal 36,446 F8
Comanche 12,617 F5
Concho 2,915 E6
Cooke 27,656 G4
Coryell 56,767 G6
Cottle 2,947 D3
Crane 4,600 B6
Crockett 4,608 C7
Crosby 8,859 C4
Culberson 3,315 C11
Dallam 6,531 B1
Dallas 1,556,390 H5
Dawson 16,184 C5
Deaf Smith 21,165 B3
Delta 4,839 J4
Denton 143,126 G4
De Witt 18,903 G9
Dickens 3,539 D4
Dimmit 11,367 E9
Donley 4,075 D2
Duval 12,517 F10
Eastland 19,480 F5
Ector 115,374 B6
Edwards 2,033 D7
Ellis 59,743 H5
El Paso 479,899 A10
Erath 22,560 F5
Falls 17,946 H6
Fannin 24,285 H4
Fayette 18,832 H8
Fisher 5,891 D5
Floyd 9,834 C3
Foard 2,158 E3
Fort Bend 130,846 J8
Franklin 6,893 J4
Freestone 14,830 H6
Frio 13,785 E9
Gaines 13,150 B5
Galveston 195,940 K8
Garza 5,336 C4
Gillespie 13,532 F7
Glasscock 1,304 C6
Goliad 5,193 G9
Gonzales 15,949 G8
Gray 26,386 D2
Grayson 89,796 H4
Gregg 99,495 K5
Grimes 13,580 J7
Guadalupe 46,708 G8
Hale 37,592 C3
Hall 5,594 D3
Hamilton 8,297 F6
Hansford 6,209 C1
Hardeman 6,368 E3
Hardin 40,721 K7
Harris 2,409,547 J8
Harrison 52,265 K5
Hartley 3,987 B2
Haskell 7,725 E4
Hays 40,594 F7
Hemphill 5,304 D2
Henderson 42,606 J5
Hidalgo 283,323 F11
Hill 25,024 G5
Hockley 23,230 B4
Hood 17,714 G5
Hopkins 25,247 J4
Houston 22,299 J6
Howard 33,142 C5
Hudspeth 2,728 B10
Hunt 55,248 H4
Hutchinson 26,304 C2
Irion 1,386 C6
Jack 7,408 F4
Jackson 13,352 H9
Jasper 30,781 K7
Jeff Davis 1,647 C11
Jefferson 250,938 K8
Jim Hogg 5,168 F11
Jim Wells 36,498 F10
Johnson 67,649 G5
Jones 17,268 E5
Karnes 13,593 G9
Kaufman 39,029 H5
Kendall 10,635 F8
Kenedy 543 G11
Kent 1,145 D4
Kerr 28,780 E7
Kimble 4,063 E7
King 425 D4
Kinney 2,279 D8
Kleberg 33,358 G10
Knox 5,329 E4
Lamar 42,156 J4
Lamb 18,669 B3
Lampasas 12,005 F6
La Salle 5,514 E9
Lavaca 19,004 H8
Lee 10,952 H7
Leon 9,594 J6
Liberty 47,088 K7
Limestone 20,224 H6
Lipscomb 3,766 D1
Live Oak 9,606 F9
Llano 10,144 F7
Loving 91 A6
Lubbock 211,651 C4
Lynn 8,605 C4
Madison 10,649 J6
Marion 10,360 K5
Martin 4,684 C5
Mason 3,683 E7
Matagorda 37,828 H9
Maverick 31,398 D9
McCulloch 8,735 E6
McLennan 170,755 G6
McMullen 789 F9
Medina 23,164 E8
Menard 2,346 E7
Midland 82,636 B6
Milam 22,732 H7
Mills 4,477 F6
Mitchell 9,088 D5
Montague 17,410 G4
Montgomery 128,487 J7
Moore 16,575 C2
Morris 14,629 K4

AREA 266,807 sq. mi. (691,030 sq. km.)
POPULATION 14,229,288
CAPITAL Austin
LARGEST CITY Houston
HIGHEST POINT Guadalupe Pk. 8,749 ft. (2667 m.)
SETTLED IN 1686
ADMITTED TO UNION December 29, 1845
POPULAR NAME Lone Star State
STATE FLOWER Bluebonnet
STATE BIRD Mockingbird

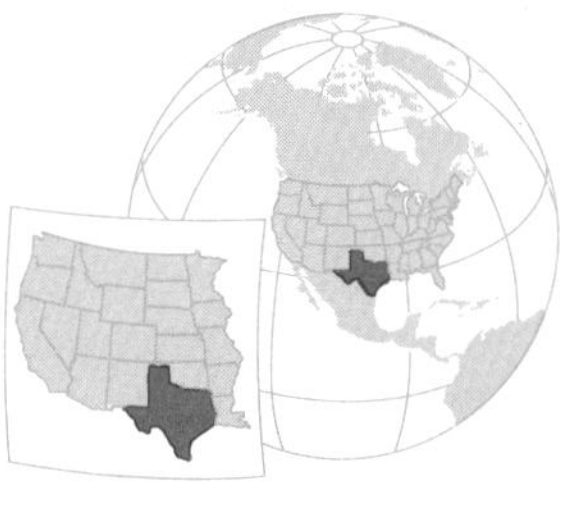

Motley 1,950 D3
Nacogdoches 46,786 K6
Navarro 35,323 H5
Newton 13,254 L7
Nolan 17,359 D5
Nueces 268,215 G10
Ochiltree 9,588 D1
Oldham 2,283 B2
Orange 83,838 L7
Palo Pinto 24,062 F5
Panola 20,724 K5
Parker 44,609 G5
Parmer 11,038 B3
Pecos 14,618 B7
Polk 24,407 K7
Potter 98,637 C2
Presidio 5,188 C12
Rains 4,839 J5
Randall 75,062 C2
Reagan 4,135 C6
Real 2,469 E8
Red River 16,101 J4
Reeves 15,801 D11
Refugio 9,289 G9
Roberts 1,187 D2
Robertson 14,653 H6
Rockwall 14,528 H5
Runnels 11,872 E6
Rusk 41,382 K5
Sabine 8,702 L6
San Augustine 8,785 K6
San Jacinto 11,434 J7
San Patricio 58,013 G10
San Saba 6,204 F6
Schleicher 2,820 D7
Scurry 18,192 D5
Shackelford 3,915 E5
Shelby 23,084 K6
Sherman 3,174 C1
Smith 128,366 J5
Somervell 4,154 G5
Starr 27,266 F11
Stephens 9,926 F5
Sterling 1,206 C6
Stonewall 2,406 D4
Sutton 5,130 D7
Swisher 9,723 C3
Tarrant 860,880 G5
Taylor 110,932 E5
Terrell 1,595 B7
Terry 14,581 B4
Throckmorton 2,053 E4
Titus 21,442 K4
Tom Green 84,784 D6
Travis 419,573 G7
Trinity 9,450 J6
Tyler 16,223 K7
Upshur 28,595 K5
Upton 4,619 B6
Uvalde 22,441 E8
Val Verde 35,910 C8
Van Zandt 31,426 J5
Victoria 68,807 H9
Walker 41,789 J7
Waller 19,798 J8
Ward 13,976 A6
Washington 21,998 H7
Webb 99,258 E10
Wharton 40,242 H8
Wheeler 7,137 D2
Wichita 121,082 F3
Wilbarger 15,931 E3
Willacy 17,495 G11
Williamson 76,507 G7
Wilson 16,756 F8
Winkler 9,944 A6
Wise 26,575 G4
Wood 24,697 J5
Yoakum 8,299 B4
Young 19,083 F4
Zapata 6,628 E11
Zavala 11,666 E9

CITIES and TOWNS

Zip	Name/Pop.	Key
*79601	Abilene⊙ 98,315	E5
	Abilene‡ 139,192	E5
78516	Alamo 5,831	F11
78209	Alamo Heights 6,252	K10
76430	Albany⊙ 2,450	E5
78332	Alice⊙ 20,961	F10
75002	Allen 8,314	H1
79830	Alpine⊙ 5,465	D12
77511	Alvin 16,515	J3
*79101	Amarillo⊙ 149,230	C2
	Amarillo‡ 173,699	C2
77514	Anahuac⊙ 1,840	K8
77830	Anderson⊙ 500	J7
79714	Andrews⊙ 11,061	B5
77515	Angleton⊙ 13,929	J8
79501	Anson⊙ 2,831	E5
78336	Aransas Pass 7,173	G10
76351	Archer City⊙ 1,862	F4
*76010	Arlington 160,123	F2
79502	Aspermont⊙ 1,357	D4
75751	Athens⊙ 10,197	J5
75551	Atlanta 6,272	K4
*78701	Austin (cap.)⊙ 345,496	G7
	Austin‡ 536,450	G7
76020	Azle 5,822	E2
77518	Bacliff 4,851	K2
79504	Baird⊙ 1,696	E5
75180	Balch Springs 13,746	H2
†78201	Balcones Heights 2,511	J10
76821	Ballinger⊙ 4,207	E6
78003	Bandera⊙ 947	F8
77532	Barrett 3,183	K1
78602	Bastrop⊙ 3,789	G7
77414	Bay City⊙ 17,837	H9
77520	Baytown 56,923	L2
*77701	Beaumont⊙ 118,102	K7
	Beaumont-Port Arthur-Orange‡ 375,497	K7
76021	Bedford 20,821	F2
78102	Beeville⊙ 14,574	G9
77401	Bellaire 14,950	J2
76704	Bellmead 7,569	H6
77418	Bellville⊙ 2,860	H8
76513	Belton⊙ 10,660	G7
76126	Benbrook 13,579	E2
79505	Benjamin⊙ 257	E4
76932	Big Lake⊙ 3,404	C6
79720	Big Spring⊙ 24,804	C5
78006	Boerne⊙ 3,229	J10
75418	Bonham⊙ 7,338	H4
79007	Borger 15,837	C2
75557	Boston⊙ 400	K4
76230	Bowie 5,610	G4
78832	Brackettville⊙ 1,676	D8
76825	Brady⊙ 5,969	E6
77422	Brazoria 3,025	J9
76024	Breckenridge⊙ 6,921	F5
77833	Brenham⊙ 10,966	H7
77611	Bridge City 7,667	L7
79316	Brownfield⊙ 10,387	B4
*78520	Brownsville⊙ 84,997	G12
	Brownsville-Harlingen-San Benito‡ 209,680	G12
76801	Brownwood⊙ 19,396	F6
77801	Bryan⊙ 44,337	H7
	Bryan-College Station‡ 93,588	H7
76354	Burkburnett 10,668	F3
76028	Burleson 11,734	F3
78611	Burnet⊙ 3,410	F7
77836	Caldwell⊙ 2,953	H7
76520	Cameron⊙ 5,721	H7
79014	Canadian⊙ 3,491	D2
75103	Canton⊙ 2,845	J5
79015	Canyon⊙ 10,724	C3
78834	Carrizo Springs⊙ 6,886	E9
*75006	Carrollton 40,595	G2
75633	Carthage⊙ 6,447	K5
†78213	Castle Hills 4,773	J10
75104	Cedar Hill 6,849	G3
75935	Center⊙ 5,827	K6
75833	Centerville⊙ 799	H6
77530	Channelview 17,471	K1
79018	Channing⊙ 304	B2
79201	Childress⊙ 5,817	D3
76437	Cisco 4,517	E5
79226	Clarendon⊙ 2,220	C3
75426	Clarksville⊙ 4,917	K4
79019	Claude⊙ 1,112	C2
†77565	Clear Lake Shores 755	K2
76031	Cleburne⊙ 19,218	G5
77327	Cleveland 5,977	K7
77531	Clute 9,577	J9
77331	Coldspring⊙ 569	J7
76834	Coleman⊙ 5,960	E6
77840	College Station 37,272	H7
76034	Colleyville 6,700	F2
79512	Colorado City⊙ 5,405	C5
78934	Columbus⊙ 3,923	H8
76442	Comanche⊙ 4,075	F6
75428	Commerce 8,136	J4
*77301	Conroe⊙ 18,034	J7
78109	Converse 5,150	K11
75432	Cooper⊙ 2,338	J4
76522	Copperas Cove 19,469	G6
*78401	Corpus Christi⊙ 231,999	G10
	Corpus Christi‡ 326,228	G10
75110	Corsicana⊙ 21,712	H5
78014	Cotulla⊙ 3,912	E9
79731	Crane⊙ 3,622	B6
75835	Crockett⊙ 7,405	J6
79322	Crosbyton⊙ 2,289	C4
79227	Crowell⊙ 1,509	E4
76036	Crowley 5,852	E3
78839	Crystal City⊙ 8,334	E9
77954	Cuero⊙ 7,124	G8
75638	Daingerfield⊙ 3,030	K4
79022	Dalhart⊙ 6,854	B1
*75201	Dallas⊙ 904,078	G2
	Dallas-Ft. Worth‡ 2,974,878	G2
77535	Dayton 4,908	J7
76234	Decatur⊙ 4,104	G4
77536	Deer Park 22,648	K2
76444	De Leon 2,478	F5
78840	Del Rio⊙ 30,034	D8
75020	Denison 23,884	H4
76201	Denton⊙ 48,063	G4

(continued on following page)

DOMINANT LAND USE

- Wheat, Grain Sorghums, Range Livestock
- Cotton, Wheat
- Specialized Cotton
- Cotton, General Farming
- Cotton, Forest Products
- Cotton, Range Livestock
- Rice, General Farming
- Peanuts, General Farming
- General Farming, Livestock, Cash Grain
- General Farming, Forest Products, Truck Farming, Cotton
- Fruit, Truck and Mixed Farming
- Range Livestock
- Forests
- Swampland, Limited Agriculture
- Nonagricultural Land
- Urban Areas

MAJOR MINERAL OCCURRENCES

At	Asphalt	He	Helium
Cl	Clay	Ls	Limestone
Fe	Iron Ore	Na	Salt
G	Natural Gas	O	Petroleum
Gn	Granite	S	Sulfur
Gp	Gypsum	Tc	Talc
Gr	Graphite	U	Uranium

Water Power
Major Industrial Areas

Agriculture, Industry and Resources

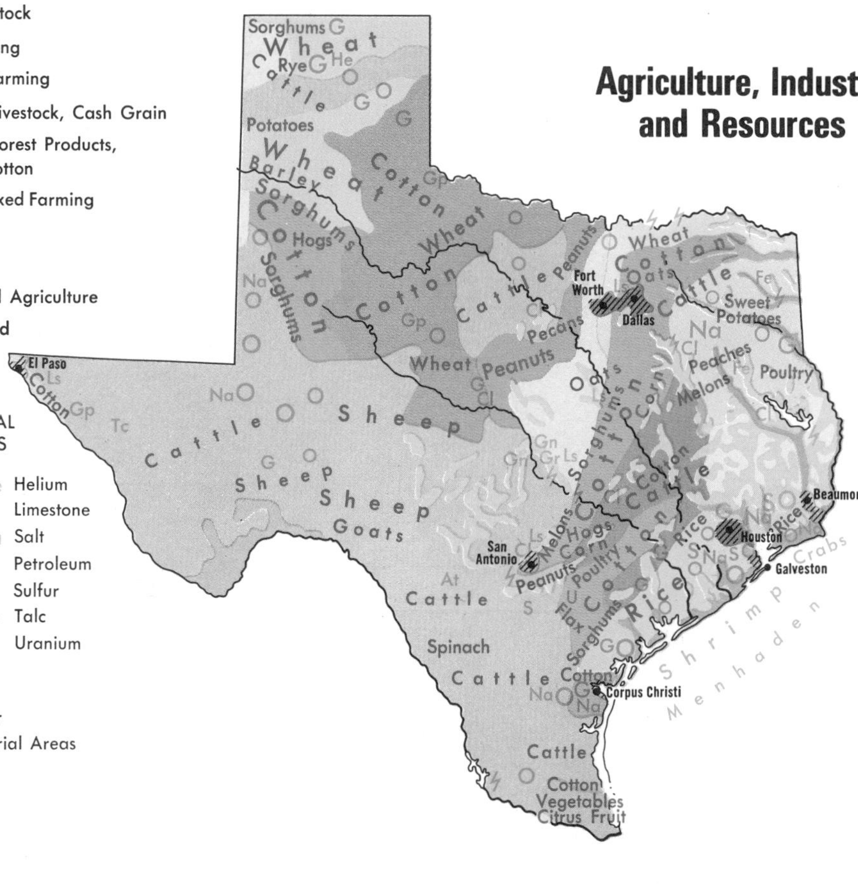

79323 Denver City 4,704 .... B4
75115 De Soto 15,538 .... G3
78016 Devine 3,756 .... E8
75941 Diboll 5,227 .... K6
79229 Dickens⊙ 409 .... D4
77539 Dickinson 7,505 .... K3
79027 Dimmitt⊙ 5,019 .... B3
78537 Donna 9,952 .... F11
79029 Dumas⊙ 12,194 .... C2
75116 Duncanville 27,781 .... G3
78852 Eagle Pass⊙ 21,407 .... D9
76448 Eastland⊙ 3,747 .... F5
78539 Edinburg⊙ 24,075 .... F11
77957 Edna⊙ 5,650 .... H9
77437 El Campo 10,462 .... H8
76936 Eldorado⊙ 2,061 .... D7
78621 Elgin 4,535 .... G7
*79901 El Paso⊙ 425,259 .... A10
El Paso‡ 479,899 .... A10
78543 Elsa 5,061 .... G11
75440 Emory⊙ 813 .... J5
75119 Ennis 12,110 .... H5
76039 Euless 24,002 .... F2
76140 Everman 5,387 .... F3
79838 Fabens 4,285 .... B10
75840 Fairfield⊙ 3,505 .... H6
78355 Falfurrias⊙ 6,103 .... F10
75234 Farmers Branch 24,863 .... G2
79325 Farwell⊙ 1,354 .... A3
78114 Floresville⊙ 4,381 .... K11
†75067 Flower Mound 4,402 .... F1
79235 Floydada⊙ 4,193 .... C3
†76119 Forest Hill 11,684 .... F2
79734 Fort Davis⊙ 900 .... D11
79735 Fort Stockton⊙ 8,688 ...... A7
*76101 Fort Worth⊙ 385,164 ...... F2
77856 Franklin⊙ 1,349 .... H7
78624 Fredericksburg⊙ 6,412 ..... E7
76842 Fredonia 50 .... E7
77541 Freeport 13,444 .... J9
77546 Friendswood 10,719 .... J2
79035 Friona 3,809 .... B3
75034 Frisco 3,499 .... H4
79738 Gail⊙ 171 .... C5
76240 Gainesville⊙ 14,081 .... G4
77547 Galena Park 9,879 .... J1
*77550 Galveston⊙ 61,902 .... L3
Galveston-Texas
City‡ 195,940 .... L3
79739 Garden City⊙ 350 .... C6
*75040 Garland 138,857 .... H2
76528 Gatesville⊙ 6,260 .... G6
78626 Georgetown⊙ 9,468 .... G7
78022 George West⊙ 2,627 .... F9
78942 Giddings⊙ 3,950 .... H7
75644 Gilmer⊙ 5,167 .... J5
75647 Gladewater 6,548 .... K5
76043 Glen Rose⊙ 2,075 .... G5
76844 Goldthwaite⊙ 1,783 .... F6
77963 Goliad⊙ 1,990 .... G9
78629 Gonzales⊙ 7,152 .... G8
76046 Graham⊙ 9,170 .... F4
76048 Granbury⊙ 3,332 .... G5
*75050 Grand Prairie 71,462 .... G2
76051 Grapevine 11,801 .... F2
75401 Greenville⊙ 22,161 .... H4
76642 Groesbeck⊙ 3,373 .... H6
77619 Groves 17,090 .... L8
75845 Groveton⊙ 1,262 .... J7
79236 Guthrie⊙ 170 .... D4
77964 Hallettsville⊙ 2,865 .... G8
76117 Haltom City 29,014 .... F2
76531 Hamilton⊙ 3,189 .... G6
78550 Harlingen 43,543 .... G11
79521 Haskell⊙ 3,782 .... E4
77859 Hearne 5,418 .... H7
78361 Hebbronville⊙ 4,684 .... F10
75948 Hemphill⊙ 1,353 .... L6
77445 Hempstead⊙ 3,456 .... J7
75652 Henderson⊙ 11,473 .... K5
76365 Henrietta⊙ 3,149 .... F4
79045 Hereford⊙ 15,853 .... B3
†75201 Highland Park 8,909 .... G2
77562 Highlands 6,467 .... K1
76645 Hillsboro⊙ 7,397 .... G5
77563 Hitchcock 6,655 .... K3
78861 Hondo⊙ 6,057 .... E8
*77001 Houston⊙ 1,595,138 .... J2
Houston‡ 2,905,350 .... J2
*77338 Humble 6,729 .... J7
†77001 Hunters Creek
Village 4,215 .... J1
77340 Huntsville⊙ 23,936 .... J7
76053 Hurst 31,420 .... F2
76367 Iowa Park 6,184 .... F4
*75061 Irving 109,943 .... G2
77029 Jacinto City 8,953 .... J1
76056 Jacksboro⊙ 4,000 .... F4
75766 Jacksonville 12,264 .... J5
75951 Jasper⊙ 6,959 .... L7
79528 Jayton⊙ 638 .... D4
75657 Jefferson⊙ 2,643 .... K5
†77001 Jersey Village 4,084 .... J1
78636 Johnson City⊙ 872 .... F7
78026 Jourdanton⊙ 2,743 .... F9
76849 Junction⊙ 2,593 .... E7
78118 Karnes City⊙ 3,296 .... G9
77450 Katy 5,660 .... J8
75142 Kaufman⊙ 4,658 .... H5
76248 Keller 4,156 .... F2
78119 Kenedy 4,356 .... G9
79745 Kermit⊙ 8,015 .... B6
78028 Kerrville⊙ 15,276 .... E7
75662 Kilgore 11,006 .... K5
76541 Killeen 46,296 .... G6
Killeen-Temple‡ 214,656 ... G6
78363 Kingsville⊙ 28,808 .... G10
†78109 Kirby 6,435 .... K11
77625 Kountze⊙ 2,716 .... K7
78945 La Grange⊙ 3,768 .... G8
77566 Lake Jackson 19,102 .... J8
76135 Lake Worth 4,394 .... E2
77568 La Marque 15,372 .... K3
79331 Lamesa⊙ 11,790 .... C5
76550 Lampasas⊙ 6,165 .... F6
*75146 Lancaster 14,807 .... G3
77571 La Porte 14,062 .... K2

*78040 Laredo⊙ 91,449 .... E10
Laredo‡ 99,258 .... E10
77573 League City 16,578 .... K2
78873 Leakey⊙ 468 .... E8
†78201 Leon Valley 9,088 .... J10
79336 Levelland⊙ 13,809 .... B4
*75067 Lewisville 24,273 .... G1
77575 Liberty⊙ 7,945 .... K7
75563 Linden⊙ 2,443 .... K4
79056 Lipscomb⊙ 52 .... D1
79339 Littlefield⊙ 7,409 .... B4
†78201 Live Oak 8,183 .... K10
77351 Livingston⊙ 4,928 .... K7
78643 Llano⊙ 3,071 .... F7
78644 Lockhart⊙ 7,953 .... G8
79241 Lockney 2,334 .... C3
*75601 Longview⊙ 62,762 .... K5
Longview-Marshall‡
151,752 .... K5
*79401 Lubbock⊙ 173,979 .... C4
Lubbock‡ 211,651 .... C4
75901 Lufkin⊙ 28,562 .... K6
78648 Luling 5,039 .... G8
77864 Madisonville⊙ 3,660 .... J7
76063 Mansfield 8,092 .... F3
77578 Manvel 3,549 .... J3
79843 Marfa⊙ 2,466 .... C12
76661 Marlin⊙ 7,099 .... H6
75670 Marshall⊙ 24,921 .... K5
76856 Mason⊙ 2,153 .... E7
79244 Matador⊙ 1,052 .... D3
78368 Mathis 5,667 .... G9
78501 McAllen 66,281 .... F11
McAllen-Pharr-Edinburg‡
283,229 .... F11
76657 McGregor 4,513 .... G6
75069 McKinney⊙ 16,256 .... H4
†77520 McNair K1
79245 Memphis⊙ 3,352 .... D3
76859 Menard⊙ 1,697 .... E7
79754 Mentone⊙ 50 .... D10
78570 Mercedes 11,851 .... F12
76665 Meridian⊙ 1,330 .... G6
76941 Mertzon⊙ 687 .... C6
*75149 Mesquite 67,053 .... H2
76667 Mexia 7,094 .... H6
79059 Miami⊙ 813 .... D2
*79701 Midland⊙ 70,525 .... C6
Midland‡ 82,636 .... C6
76065 Midlothian 3,219 .... G5
75773 Mineola 4,346 .... J5
76067 Mineral Wells 14,468 .... F5
78572 Mission 22,653 .... F11
77459 Missouri City 24,533 .... J2
79756 Monahans⊙ 8,397 .... B6
76251 Montague⊙ 1,253 .... G4
79346 Morton⊙ 2,674 .... B4
75455 Mount Pleasant⊙ 11,003 .. K4
75457 Mount Vernon⊙ 2,025 ...... J4
79347 Muleshoe⊙ 4,842 .... B3
75961 Nacogdoches⊙ 27,149 ..... J6
†77598 Nassau Bay 4,526 .... K2
77868 Navasota 5,971 .... J7
77627 Nederland 16,855 .... K8
75570 New Boston 4,628 .... K4
78130 New Braunfels⊙ 22,402 . K10
75966 Newton⊙ 1,620 .... L7
76118 North Richland
Hills 30,592 .... F2
79760 Odessa⊙ 90,027 .... B6
Odessa‡ 115,374 .... B6
76374 Olney 4,060 .... F4
77630 Orange⊙ 23,628 .... L7
76943 Ozona⊙ 3,766 .... C7
79248 Paducah⊙ 2,216 .... D4
76866 Paint Rock⊙ 256 .... E6
77465 Palacios 4,667 .... H9
75801 Palestine⊙ 15,948 .... J6
76072 Palo Pinto⊙ 350 .... F5
79065 Pampa⊙ 21,396 .... D2
79068 Panhandle⊙ 2,226 .... C2
75460 Paris⊙ 25,498 .... J4
*77501 Pasadena 112,560 .... J2
77581 Pearland 13,248 .... J2
78061 Pearsall⊙ 7,383 .... E9
79772 Pecos⊙ 12,855 .... D10
79070 Perryton⊙ 7,991 .... D1
78577 Pharr 21,381 .... F11
75686 Pittsburg⊙ 4,245 .... J4
79355 Plains⊙ 1,457 .... B4
79072 Plainview⊙ 22,187 .... C3
75074 Plano 72,331 .... G1
78064 Pleasanton 6,346 .... F9
77640 Port Arthur 61,251 .... K8
78578 Port Isabel 3,769 .... G11
78374 Portland 12,023 .... G10
77979 Port Lavaca⊙ 10,911 .... H9
77651 Port Neches 13,944 .... K7
79356 Post⊙ 3,961 .... C4
78065 Poteet 3,086 .... F8
77445 Prairie View 3,993 .... J7
79845 Presidio 1,723 .... C12
79252 Quanah⊙ 3,890 .... E3
76470 Ranger 3,142 .... F5
79778 Rankin⊙ 1,216 .... B6
78580 Raymondville⊙ 9,493 .... G11
78377 Refugio⊙ 3,898 .... G9
75080 Richardson 72,496 .... G2
76118 Richland Hills 7,977 .... F2
77469 Richmond⊙ 9,692 .... J8
78582 Rio Grande City⊙ 8,930 .. F11
77019 River Oaks 6,890 .... E2
76945 Robert Lee⊙ 1,202 .... D6
78380 Robstown 12,100 .... G10
79543 Roby⊙ 814 .... D5
76567 Rockdale 5,611 .... G7
78382 Rockport⊙ 3,686 .... H9
78880 Rocksprings⊙ 1,317 .... D8
75087 Rockwall⊙ 5,939 .... H5
78584 Roma-Los Saenz 3,384 .... E11
77471 Rosenberg 17,995 .... J8
78664 Round Rock 12,740 .... G7
75088 Rowlett 7,522 .... H2
75785 Rusk⊙ 4,681 .... J6
76179 Saginaw 5,736 .... E2
*76901 San Angelo⊙ 73,240 .... D6
San Angelo‡ 84,784 .... D6

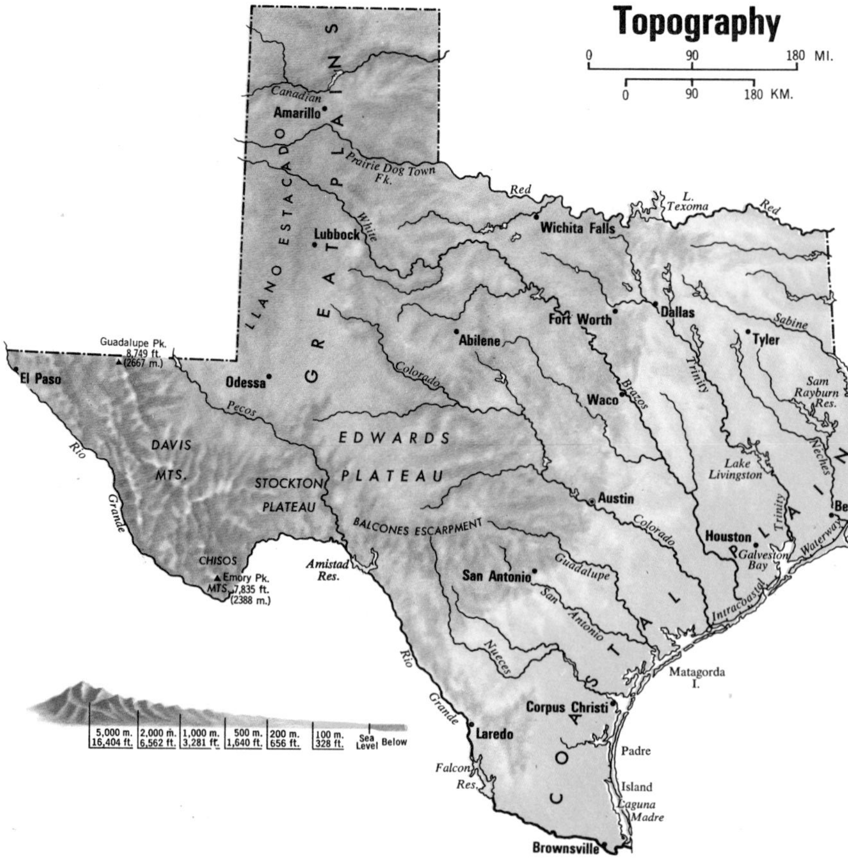
Topography
0 90 180 MI.
0 90 180 KM.
Amarillo
Canadian
Prairie Dog Town Fk.
Red
L. Texoma
Red
Lubbock
White
Wichita Falls
LLANO ESTACADO
GREAT PLAINS
Fort Worth
Dallas
Sabine
Tyler
Abilene
Guadalupe Pk. 8,749 ft. (2667 m.)
El Paso
Odessa
Colorado
Brazos
Trinity
Waco
Toledo Bend Res.
Sam Rayburn Res.
Pecos
DAVIS MTS.
EDWARDS PLATEAU
STOCKTON PLATEAU
Lake Livingston
Beaumont
Austin
BALCONES ESCARPMENT
Colorado
Houston
Galveston Bay
Intracoastal Waterway
Rio Grande
CHISOS MTS.
Emory Pk. 7,835 ft. (2388 m.)
Amistad Res.
San Antonio
Guadalupe
San Antonio
Nueces
COASTAL PLAIN
Matagorda I.
Corpus Christi
Laredo
Padre Island
Falcon Res.
Laguna Madre
Brownsville
5,000 m. 16,404 ft.
2,000 m. 6,562 ft.
1,000 m. 3,281 ft.
500 m. 1,640 ft.
200 m. 656 ft.
100 m. 328 ft.
Sea Level
Below

*78201 San Antonio⊙ 786,023 .... J11
San Antonio‡ 1,071,954 .. J11
75972 San Augustine⊙ 2,930 ..... K6
78586 San Benito 17,988 .... G12
79848 Sanderson⊙ 1,241 .... B7
78384 San Diego⊙ 5,225 .... F10
76266 Sanger 2,574 .... G4
78589 San Juan 7,608 .... F11
78666 San Marcos⊙ 23,420 ...... F8
76877 San Saba⊙ 2,847 .... F6
†76101 Sansom Park Village 3,921 E2
†77510 Santa Fe 6,172 .... K3
78385 Sarita⊙ 200 .... G10
78154 Schertz 7,262 .... K10
77586 Seabrook 4,670 .... K2
75159 Seagoville 7,304 .... H3
77474 Sealy 3,875 .... H8
78155 Seguin⊙ 17,854 .... G8
79360 Seminole⊙ 6,080 .... B5
†78357 Seven Sisters 2 .... F9
76380 Seymour⊙ 3,657 .... E4
75090 Sherman⊙ 30,413 .... H4
Sherman-Denison‡ 89,796 H4
79851 Sierra Blanca⊙ 800 .... B11
77656 Silsbee 7,684 .... K7
79257 Silverton⊙ 918 .... C3
78387 Sinton⊙ 6,044 .... G9
79364 Slaton 6,804 .... C4
78957 Smithville 3,470 .... G7
79549 Snyder⊙ 12,705 .... D5
76950 Sonora⊙ 3,856 .... D7
77587 South Houston 13,293 ..... J2
79081 Spearman⊙ 3,413 .... C1
*77373 Spring J7
†77001 Spring Valley 3,353 .... J1
77477 Stafford 4,755 .... J2
79553 Stamford 4,542 .... E5
79782 Stanton⊙ 2,314 .... C5
76401 Stephenville⊙ 11,881 .... F5
76951 Sterling City⊙ 915 .... D6
79083 Stinnett⊙ 2,222 .... C2
79084 Stratford⊙ 1,917 .... C1
77478 Sugar Land 8,826 .... J8
75482 Sulphur Springs⊙ 12,804 . J4
77480 Sweeny 3,538 .... J8
79556 Sweetwater⊙ 12,242 .... D5
78390 Taft 3,686 .... G9
79373 Tahoka⊙ 3,262 .... C4
76574 Taylor 10,619 .... G7
†77586 Taylor Lake Village 3,669 .. K2
75860 Teague 3,390 .... H6
76501 Temple 42,354 .... G6
79852 Terlingua 100 .... D12
75160 Terrell 13,269 .... H5
†78201 Terrell Hills 4,644 .... K11
*75501 Texarkana 31,271 .... L4
Texarkana, Tex.-Texarkana,
Ark.‡ 27,019 .... L4
77590 Texas City 41,403 .... K3
73949 Texhoma 358 .... C1
The Colony 11,586 .... G1
76083 Throckmorton⊙ 1,174 ..... F4
78072 Tilden⊙ 450 .... F9
77375 Tomball 3,996 .... J7
75862 Trinity 2,620 .... J7
79088 Tulia⊙ 5,033 .... C3
*75701 Tyler⊙ 70,508 .... J5
Tyler‡ 128,366 .... J5
78148 Universal City 10,720 ..... K10
†75205 University Park 22,254 ...... G2
78801 Uvalde⊙ 14,178 .... E8
75095 Van Alstyne 1,860 .... H4

79855 Van Horn⊙ 2,772 .... C11
79092 Vega⊙ 900 .... B2
76384 Vernon⊙ 12,695 .... E3
77901 Victoria⊙ 50,695 .... H9
Victoria‡ 68,807 .... H9
77662 Vidor 11,834 .... L7
*76701 Waco⊙ 101,261 .... G6
Waco‡ 170,755 .... G6
75501 Wake Village 3,865 .... K4
75165 Waxahachie⊙ 14,624 .... H5
76086 Weatherford⊙ 12,049 ...... G5
79095 Wellington⊙ 3,043 .... D3
78596 Weslaco 19,331 .... F11
77486 West Columbia 4,109 .... J8
77630 West Orange 4,610 .... L7
†77005 West University
Place 12,010 .... J2
†76101 Westworth 3,651 .... E2
77488 Wharton⊙ 9,033 .... J8
79096 Wheeler⊙ 1,584 .... D2
75693 White Oak 4,415 .... K5
76273 Whitesboro 3,197 .... H4
76108 White Settlement 13,508 ... E2
*76301 Wichita Falls⊙ 94,201 ...... F4
Wichita Falls‡ 130,664 ..... F4
†78201 Windcrest 5,332 .... K11
75494 Winnsboro 3,458 .... J5
79567 Winters 3,061 .... E6
75979 Woodville⊙ 2,821 .... K7
75098 Wylie 3,152 .... H1
78076 Zapata⊙ 3,831 .... E11

OTHER FEATURES

Amistad (res.) C8
Amistad Nat'l Rec. Area D8
Angelina (riv.) K6
Apache (mts.) C11
Aransas (passage) H10
Arlington (lake) F2
Baffin (bay) G10
Balcones Escarpment (plat.) E8
Beals (creek) C5
Benbrook (lake) E3
Bergstrom A.F.B. G7
Big Bend Nat'l Park A8
Bolivar (pen.) K8
Brazos (riv.) H7
Brownwood (lake) E6
Buchanan (lake) F7
Buck (creek) D3
Caddo (lake) L5
Canadian (riv.) D1
Carrizo (creek) A1
Carswell A.F.B. E2
Cathedral (mt.) D12
Cavallo (passage) H9
Cedar (lake) B5
Cerro Alto (mt.) B10
Chamizal Nat'l Mem. A10
Chase N.A.S. G9
Chinati (mts.) C12
Chinati (peak) C12
Chisos (mts.) A8
Cibolo (creek) K11
Clear Fork, Brazos (riv.) D5
Coldwater (creek) B1
Colorado (riv.) F7
Copano (bay) G9
Corpus Christi (lake) F9

Corpus Christi N.A.S. G10
Cottonwood Draw (dry riv.) C10
Davis (mts.) C11
Deep (creek) C5
Delaware (creek) C10
Delaware (mts.) C10
Denison (dam) H4
Devils (riv.) D7
Diablo, Sierra (mts.) C10
Double Mountain Fork, Brazos
(riv.) C4
Dyess A.F.B. D5
Eagle (peak) C11
Eagle Mountain (lake) E2
Edwards (plat.) C7
Elephant (mt.) D12
Ellington A.F.B. K2
Elm Fork, Trinity (riv.) G2
Emory (peak) A8
Falcon (res.) E11
Finlay (mts.) B10
Fort Bliss 12,687 .... A10
Fort Davis Nat'l Hist. Site D11
Fort Hood 31,250 .... G6
Frio (riv.) E8
Galveston (bay) L2
Galveston (isl.) K8
Glass (mts.) A7
Goodfellow A.F.B. D6
Grapevine (lake) F2
Guadalupe (mts.) C10
Guadalupe (peak) B10
Guadalupe (riv.) G8
Guadalupe Mts. Nat'l Park C10
Houston (lake) J8
Houston Ship (chan.) K2
Howard (creek) C7
Hubbard Creek (lake) F5
Hueco (mts.) B10
Intracoastal Waterway J9
Johnson Draw (dry riv.) C7
Kelly A.F.B. J11
Kemp (lake) E4
Kingsville N.A.S. G10
Kiowa (creek) D1
Lackland A.F.B. 14,459 .... J11
Lake Meredith Nat'l Rec. Area C2
Lampasas (riv.) G6
Laughlin A.F.B. 2,994 .... D8
Lavon (lake) H1
Leon (riv.) F6
Livermore (mt.) C11
Livingston (lake) K7
Llano (riv.) D7
Llano Estacado (plain) B4
Locke (mt.) D11
Los Olmos (creek) F10
Los Olmos (creek) F11
Lyndon B. Johnson Nat'l Hist.
Site F7
Lyndon B. Johnson Space Ctr. K2
Madre (lag.) G11
Maravillas (creek) A7
Matagorda (bay) H9
Matagorda (isl.) H9
Matagorda (pen.) J9
Matagorda Isl. Bombing and Gunnery
Range H9
Medina (lake) E8
Medina (riv.) J11
Mexico (gulf) K9
Middle Concho (riv.) C6

Mountain Creek (lake) G2
Mustang (creek) A1
Mustang (isl.) G10
Mustang Draw (dry riv.) B5
Navasota (riv.) H7
Navidad (riv.) H8
Neches (riv.) K6
North Concho (riv.) C6
North Pease (riv.) D3
Nueces (riv.) F9
Padre (isl.) G10
Padre Island Nat'l Seashore G11
Palo Duro (creek) B2
Palo Duro (creek) C1
Pease (riv.) D3
Pecos (riv.) C7
Pedernales (riv.) F7
Possum Kingdom (lake) F5
Prairie Dog Town Fork, Red (riv.) ... C3
Quitman (mts.) B11
Red (riv.) F3
Red Bluff (lake) A6
Reese A.F.B. 1,934 .... B4
Rio Grande (riv.) D9
Rita Blanca (creek) B2
Sabine (riv.) L7
Salt Fork, Red (riv.) D3
Sam Rayburn (res.) K6
San Antonio (bay) H9
San Antonio (mt.) B10
San Antonio Missions Nat'l Hist.
Park J11
San Francisco (creek) B8
San Luis (passage) K8
San Martine Draw (dry riv.) C11
San Saba (riv.) D7
Santa Isabel (creek) E10
Santiago (mts.) A8
Santiago (peak) D12
Sheppard A.F.B. F3
Sierra Diablo (mts.) C10
Sierra Vieja (mts.) C11
Staked (Llano Estacado) (plain) B4
Stamford (lake) E4
Stockton (plat.) B7
Sulphur (riv.) J4
Sulphur Draw (dry riv.) B4
Sulphur Springs (creek) B4
Tenmile (creek) G3
Terlingua (creek) D12
Texoma (lake) H3
Tierra Blanca (creek) B3
Toledo Bend (res.) L6
Toyah (creek) D11
Toyah (lake) A6
Travis (lake) G7
Trinity (bay) L2
Trinity (riv.) H5
Trinity, West Fork (riv.) G2
Trujillo (creek) A2
Vieja, Sierra (mts.) C11
Walnut (creek) F3
Washita (riv.) D2
West (bay) K3
White (riv.) C3
White River (lake) C4
White Rock (creek) G2
Wichita (riv.) F4
Wolf (creek) D1
Worth (lake) E2

⊙County seat.
‡Population of metropolitan area.
† Zip of nearest p.o. * Multiple zips

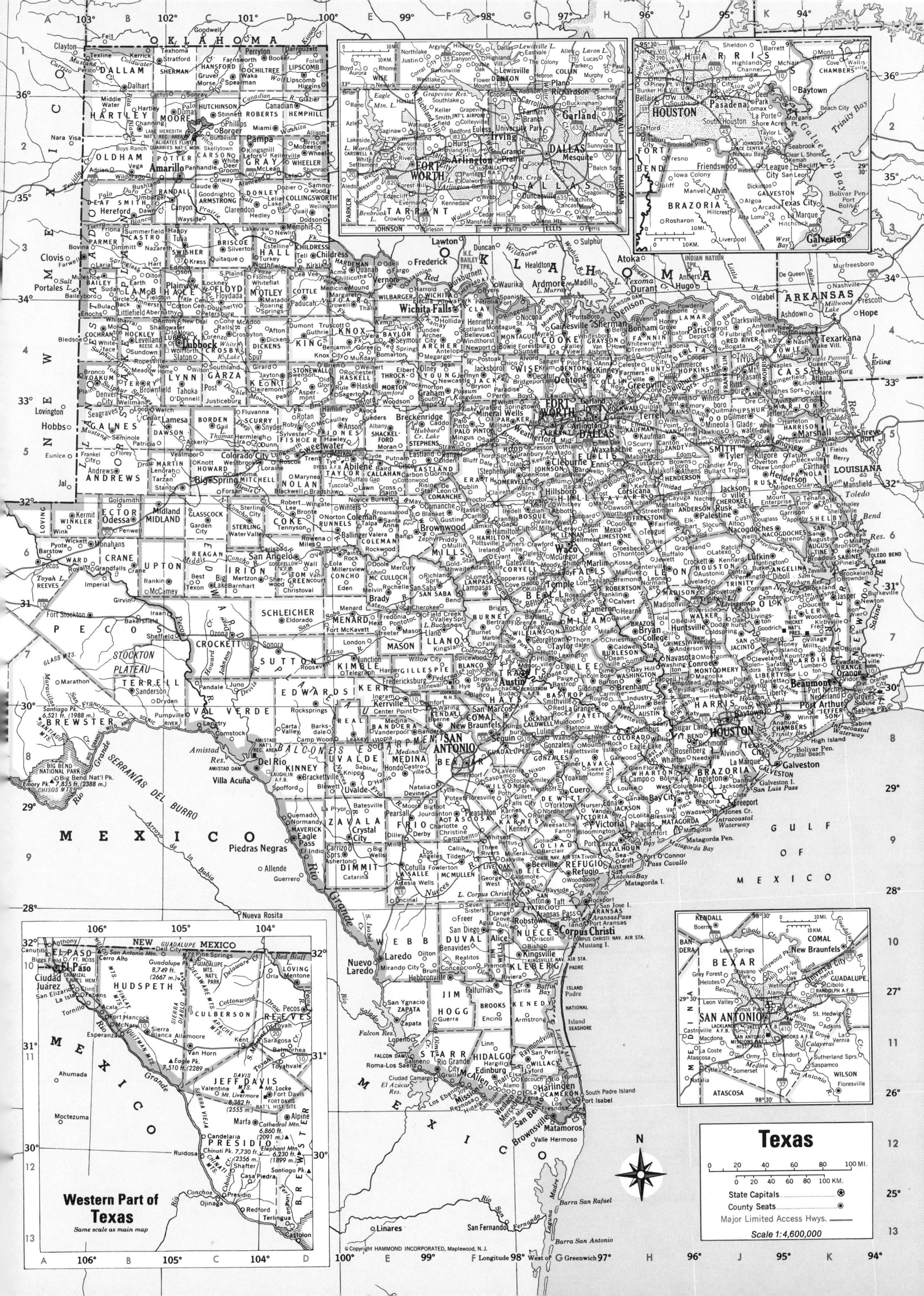

Texas

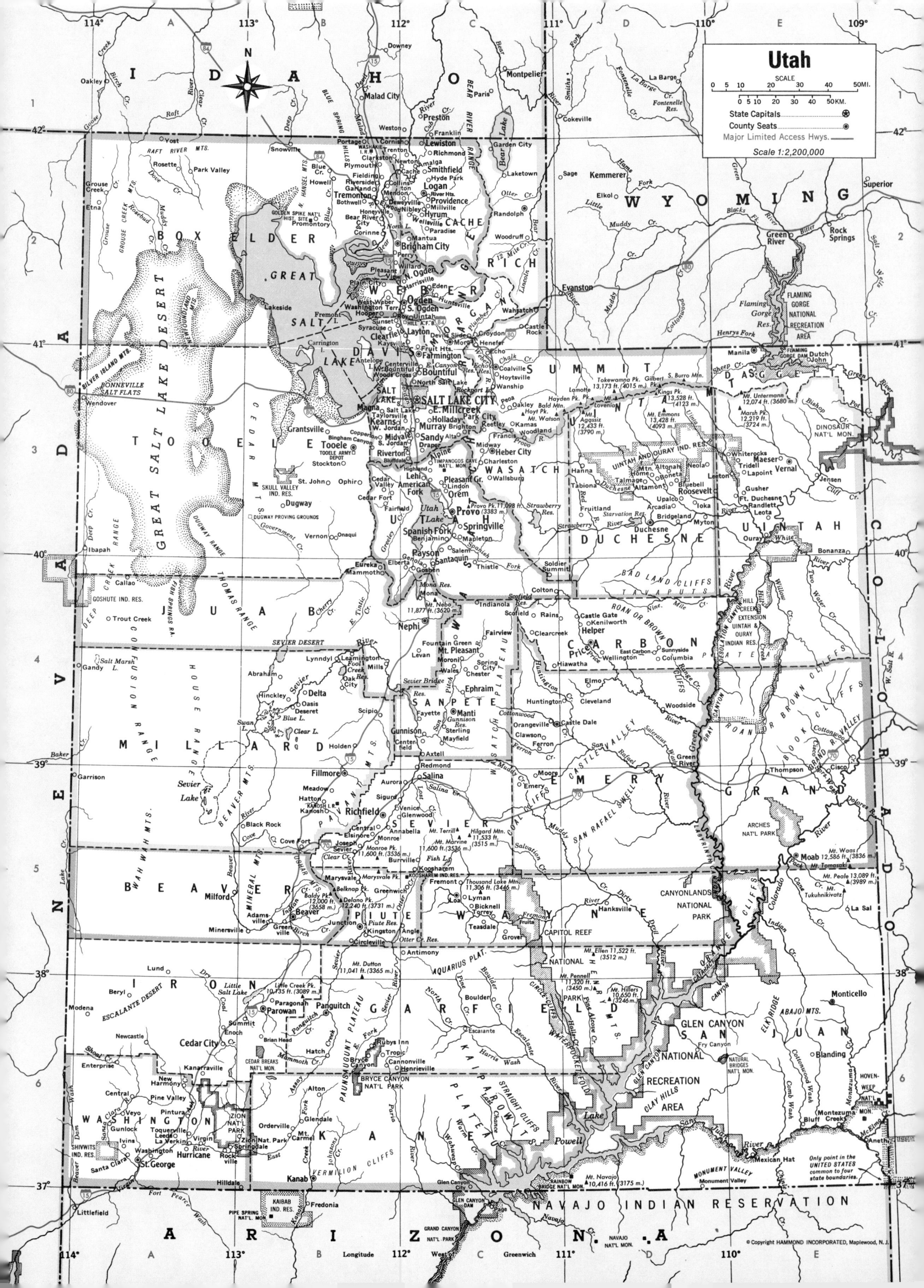

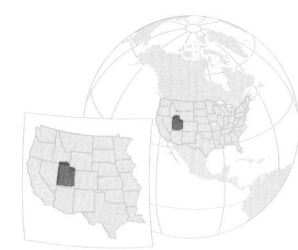

AREA 84,899 sq. mi. (219,888 sq. km.)
POPULATION 1,461,037
CAPITAL Salt Lake City
LARGEST CITY Salt Lake City
HIGHEST POINT Kings Pk. 13,528 ft. (4123 m.)
SETTLED IN 1847
ADMITTED TO UNION January 4, 1896
POPULAR NAME Beehive State
STATE FLOWER Sego Lily
STATE BIRD Sea Gull

COUNTIES

Beaver 4,378 ....A5
Box Elder 33,222 ....A2
Cache 57,176 ....C2
Carbon 22,179 ....D4
Daggett 769 ....E3
Davis 146,540 ....B3
Duchesne 12,565 ....D3
Emery 11,451 ....D4
Garfield 3,673 ....C6
Grand 8,241 ....E5
Iron 17,349 ....A6
Juab 5,530 ....A4
Kane 4,024 ....B6
Millard 8,970 ....A4
Morgan 4,917 ....C2
Piute 1,329 ....B5
Rich 2,100 ....C2
Salt Lake 619,066 ......B3
San Juan 12,253 ....E6
Sanpete 14,620 ....C4
Sevier 14,727 ....C5
Summit 10,198 ....D3
Tooele 26,033 ....A3
Uintah 20,506 ....E3
Utah 218,106 ....C3
Wasatch 8,523 ....C3
Washington 26,065 ......A6
Wayne 1,911 ....C5
Weber 144,616 ....B2

CITIES and TOWNS

Zip   Name/Pop.   Key

†84003 Alpine 2,649 ....C3
 84003 American Fork 12,693 ...C3
 84713 Beaver⊙ 1,792 ....B5
 84511 Blanding 3,118 ....E6
†84511 Bluffdale 1,300 ....B3
 84010 Bountiful 32,877 ......C3
 84302 Brigham City⊙ 15,596 ..C2
†84101 Brighton 150 ....C3
 84513 Castle Dale⊙ 1,910 ....D4
 84720 Cedar City 10,972 .....A6
 84014 Centerville 8,069 .....C3
 84015 Clearfield 17,982 .....B2
 84017 Coalville⊙ 1,031 ......C3
 84624 Delta 1,930 ....B4
 84020 Draper 5,521 ....C3
 84021 Duchesne⊙ 1,677 ....D3
 84022 Dugway 1,646 ....B3
 84520 East Carbon 1,942 .....D4
 84109 East Millcreek 24,150 .C3
 84627 Ephraim 2,810 ....C4

 84025 Farmington⊙ 4,691 .....C3
 84523 Ferron 1,718 ....C4
 84631 Fillmore⊙ 2,083 ....B5
†84037 Fruit Heights 2,728 ...C2
 84312 Garland 1,405 ....B2
 84029 Grantsville 4,419 .....B3
 84525 Green River 1,048 .....D4
 84634 Gunnison 1,255 ....C4
 84032 Heber City⊙ 4,362 .....C3
 84526 Helper 2,724 ....D4
†84043 Highland 2,435 ....C3
†84767 Hilldale 1,009 ....A6
 84117 Holladay 22,189 ....C3
 84528 Huntington 2,316 ......C4
 84737 Hurricane 2,361 ....A6
 84318 Hyde Park 1,495 ....C2
 84319 Hyrum 3,952 ....C2
 84740 Junction⊙ 151 ....B5
 84036 Kamas 1,064 ....C3
 84741 Kanab⊙ 2,148 ....B6
 84037 Kaysville 9,811 ....C2
 84118 Kearns 21,353 ....B3
 84745 La Verkin 1,174 ....A6
 84041 Layton 22,862 ....C2
 84043 Lehi 6,848 ....C3
 84320 Lewiston 1,438 ....C2
†84062 Lindon 2,796 ....C3
 84747 Loa⊙ 364 ....C5
 84321 Logan⊙ 26,844 ....C2
†84078 Maeser 2,216 ....E3
 84044 Magna 13,138 ....B3
 84046 Manila⊙ 272 ....E3
 84642 Manti⊙ 2,080 ....C4
†84663 Mapleton 2,726 ....C3
 84531 Mexican Hat 250 ....E6
 84047 Midvale 10,146 ....B3
 84049 Midway 1,194 ....C3
 84751 Milford 1,293 ....A5
 84532 Moab⊙ 5,333 ....E5
 84754 Monroe 1,476 ....B5
 84535 Monticello⊙ 1,929 .....E6
 84050 Morgan⊙ 1,896 ....C2
 84646 Moroni 1,086 ....C4
 84647 Mount Pleasant 2,049 ..C4
 84107 Murray 25,750 ....C3
 84648 Nephi⊙ 3,285 ....C4
†84321 Nibley 1,036 ....C2
†84404 North Ogden 9,309 .....C2
†84010 North Salt Lake 5,548 .C3
*84401 Ogden⊙ 64,407 ....C2
 Ogden-Salt Lake City‡
  936,255 ....C4
 84537 Orangeville 1,309 .....C4
 84057 Orem 52,399 ....C3
  Orem-Provo‡ 218,106 ....C3

 84759 Panguitch⊙ 1,343 ......B6
 84060 Park City 2,823 ....C3
 84761 Parowan⊙ 1,836 ....B6
 84651 Payson 8,246 ....C3
†84302 Perry 1,084 ....C2
†84401 Plain City 2,379 ......B2
 84062 Pleasant Grove 10,833 .C3
†84401 Pleasant View 3,983 ...B2
 84501 Price⊙ 9,086 ....D4
 84332 Providence 2,675 ......C2
 84601 Provo⊙ 74,108 ....C3
  Provo-Orem‡ 218,106 ....C3
 84064 Randolph⊙ 659 ....C2
 84701 Richfield⊙ 5,482 ......B5
 84333 Richmond 1,705 ....C2
†84321 River Heights 1,211 ...C2
 84065 Riverton 7,293 ....B3
 84066 Roosevelt 3,842 ....D3
 84067 Roy 19,694 ....C2
  Saint George⊙ 11,350 .....A6
 84653 Salem 2,233 ....C3
 84654 Salina 1,992 ....C5
*84101 Salt Lake City (cap)⊙
  163,697 ....C3
  Salt Lake City-Ogden‡
  936,255 ....C3
*84070 Sandy 52,210 ....C3
 84765 Santa Clara 1,091 .....A6
 84655 Santaquin 2,175 ....C4
 84335 Smithfield 4,993 ......C2
†84065 South Jordan 7,492 ....B3
†84403 South Ogden 11,366 ....C2
 84115 South Salt Lake 9,884 .C3
 84660 Spanish Fork 9,825 ....C3
 84663 Springville 12,101 ....C3
†84015 Sunset 5,733 ....B2
 84041 Syracuse 3,702 ....B2
†84101 Taylorsville 17,448 ...B3
 84074 Tooele⊙ 14,335 ....B3
 84337 Tremonton 3,464 ....C2
 84078 Vernal⊙ 6,600 ....E3
 84780 Washington 3,092 ......A6
†84403 Washington Terrace 8,212 .B2
 84542 Wellington 1,406 ......D4
 84339 Wellsville 1,952 ......C2
 84083 Wendover 1,099 ....A3
†84087 West Bountiful 3,556 ..C3
 84084 West Jordan 27,192 ....B3
 84340 Willard 1,241 ....B3
 84087 Woods Cross 4,263 .....B3

OTHER FEATURES

Abajo (mts.) E6
Agassiz (mt.) D3

Antelope (isl.) B3
Aquarius (plat.) C5
Arches Nat'l Park E5
Assay (creek) B6
Bad Land (cliffs) D4
Baldy (peak) B5
Bear (lake) C2
Bear (riv.) B2
Beaver (mts.) A5
Beaver (riv.) A5
Beaver Dam Wash (creek) ..A6
Birch (creek) B5
Blue (creek) B2
Bonneville (salt flats) ..A3
Book (cliffs) E4
Brown (Roan) (cliffs) E4
Bryce Canyon Nat'l Park ..B6
Canyonlands Nat'l Park ...D5
Capitol Reef Nat'l Park ..C5
Castle (valley) D4
Cedar (mts.) B3
Cedar Breaks Nat'l Mon. ..B6
Chalk (creek) C3
Chinle (creek) E6
Clear (lake) B4
Cliff (creek) E3
Coal (cliffs) C5
Colorado (riv.) E5
Confusion (range) A4
Cottonwood (creek) C4
Cub (creek) C1
Deep (creek) B1
Deep Creek (range) A4
Delano (peak) B5
Desolation (canyon) E4
Dinosaur Nat'l Mon. E3
Dirty Devil (riv.) D5
Dolores (riv.) E5
Dry Coal (creek) A6
Duchesne (riv.) D3
Dugway (range) A3
Dugway Proving Grounds ...B3
Dutton (mt.) B5
East Canyon (res.) C3
Echo (res.) C3
Elk (ridge) E6
Ellen (mt.) D5
Emmons (mt.) D3
Escalante (des.) A6
Escalante (riv.) C6
Fish (lake) C5
Fish Springs (range) A4
Flaming Gorge (res.) E3
Flaming Gorge Nat'l Rec. Area .E2
Fool Creek (res.) B4
Fremont (isl.) B2

Fremont (riv.) C5
Glen Canyon Nat'l Rec. Area .D6
Golden Spike Nat'l Hist. Site .B2
Goshute Ind. Res. A4
Government (creek) B3
Gray (canyon) D4
Great Salt (lake) B2
Great Salt Lake (des.) ...A3
Greeley (creek) B3
Green (riv.) D4
Grouse (creek) A2
Grouse Creek (mts.) A2
Gunnison (res.) C4
Henry (mts.) D6
Hilgard (mt.) C5
Hill (creek) E4
Hill A.F.B. C2
Hill Creek Ext., Uintah and Ouray Ind.
  Res. E4
Hillers (mt.) D6
House (range) A4
Hovenweep Nat'l Mon. E6
Huntington (creek) C4
Indian (creek) B5
Jordan (riv.) C3
Kaiparowits (plat.) C6
Kanab (creek) B7
Kanosh Ind. Res. B5
Kings (peak) D3
Koosharem Ind. Res. C5
Little Creek (peak) B6
Little Salt (lake) A6
Malad (riv.) B1
Marsh (peak) E3
Marvine (mt.) C5
Mineral (mts.) B5
Mona (res.) C4
Monroe (peak) B5
Montezuma (creek) E6
Monument (valley) D6
Muddy (creek) D4
Natural Bridges Nat'l Mon. .E6
Navajo (mt.) D6
Navajo Ind. Res. D7
Nebo (mt.) C4
Newfoundland (mts.) A2
Nine Mile (creek) D4
North (lake) B2
Orange (cliffs) D5
Otter (creek) C5
Otter Creek (res.) C5
Paria (riv.) B6
Paunsaugunt (plat.) B6
Pavant (mts.) B5
Peale (mt.) E5
Pennell (mt.) D6

Piute (res.) B5
Plumber (creek) C2
Powell (lake) D6
Price (riv.) D4
Provo (peak) C3
Provo (riv.) C3
Raft River (mts.) A2
Rainbow Bridge Nat'l Mon. .C6
Roan (cliffs) E4
Rockport (res.) C3
Salvation (creek) C5
San Juan (riv.) D6
San Rafael (riv.) D4
San Pitch (riv.) C4
San Rafael Swell (mts.) ..D5
Santa Clara (riv.) A6
Sevier (des.) A5
Sevier (lake) A5
Sevier (riv.) B4
Sevier Bridge (res.) C4
Shivwits Ind. Res. A6
Silver Island (mts.) A3
Skull Valley Ind. Res. ...B3
Spanish Fork (riv.) C3
Strait (cliffs) C6
Strawberry (res.) D3
Strawberry (riv.) D3
Swan (lake) D4
Tavaputs (plat.) D4
Thomas (range) B4
Thousand Lake (mt.) C5
Timpanogos Cave
  Nat'l Mon. C3
Tokewamna (peak) D3
Tooele Army Depot B3
Two Water (creek) E4
Uinta (mts.) D3
Uinta (riv.) D3
Uintah and Ouray Ind. Res. .D3
Utah (lake) C3
Virgin (riv.) A6
Waas (mt.) E5
Wah Wah (mts.) A5
Wahweap (creek) C6
Wasatch (range) C3
Washakie Ind. Res. C2
Waterpocket Fold (cliffs) .D6
Weber (riv.) C2
White (riv.) E3
Willow (creek) E4
Zion Nat'l Park A6

⊙County seat.
‡Population of metropolitan area.
† Zip of nearest p.o.
* Multiple zips.

Agriculture, Industry and Resources

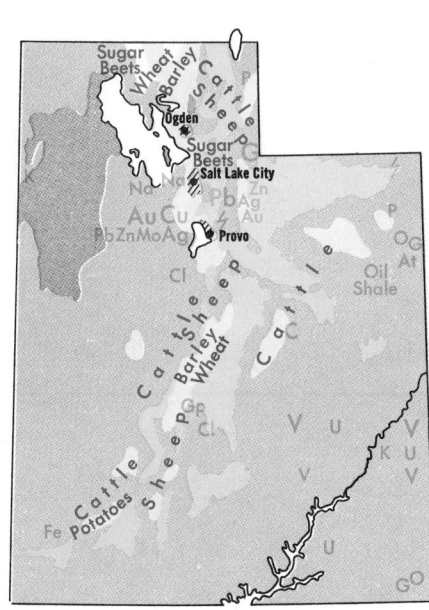

DOMINANT LAND USE

- Wheat, General Farming
- General Farming, Livestock, Special Crops
- Range Livestock
- Forests
- Nonagricultural Land

MAJOR MINERAL OCCURRENCES

Ag Silver
At Asphalt
Au Gold
C   Coal
Cl Clay
Cu Copper
Fe Iron Ore
G   Natural Gas
Gp Gypsum
K   Potash
Mo Molybdenum
Na Salt
O   Petroleum
P   Phosphates
Pb Lead
U   Uranium
V   Vanadium
Zn Zinc

⚡ Water Power
▨ Major Industrial Areas

Topography

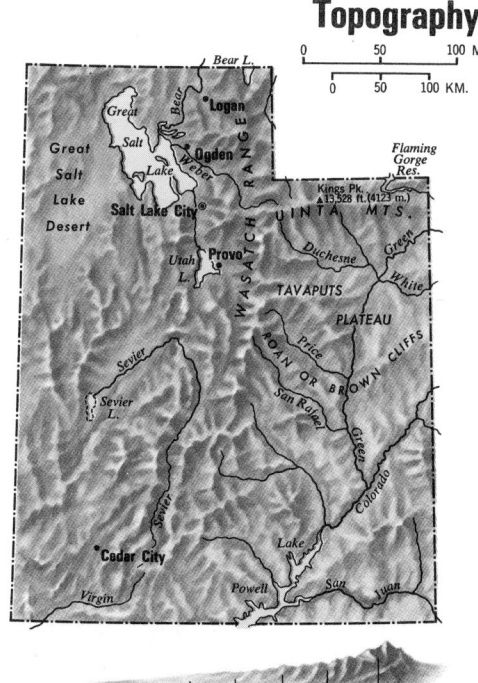

Topography

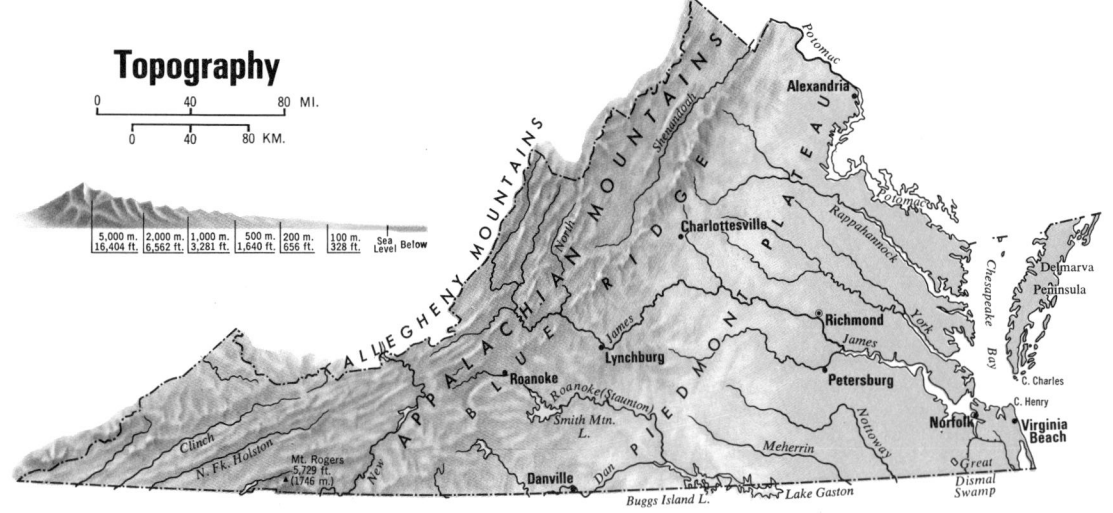

```
0    40    80 MI.
0    40    80 KM.
```

```
5,000 m.  2,000 m.  1,000 m.  500 m.  200 m.  100 m.   Sea
16,404 ft. 6,562 ft. 3,281 ft. 1,640 ft. 656 ft. 328 ft.  Level
                                                          Below
```

COUNTIES

Accomack 31,268 ....S5
Albemarle 55,783 ....L5
Alleghany 14,333 ....H5
Amelia 8,405 ....M6
Amherst 29,122 ....K5
Appomattox 11,971 ....L6
Arlington 152,599 ....S2
Augusta 53,732 ....K4
Bath 5,860 ....J4
Bedford 34,927 ....J6
Bland 6,349 ....F6
Botetourt 23,270 ....J5
Brunswick 15,632 ....N7
Buchanan 37,989 ....D6
Buckingham 11,751 ....L5
Campbell 45,424 ....K6
Caroline 17,904 ....O4
Carroll 27,270 ....G7
Charles City 6,692 ....O6
Charlotte 12,266 ....L6
Chesterfield 141,372 ....N6
Clarke 9,965 ....M2
Craig 3,948 ....H6
Culpeper 22,620 ....M3
Cumberland 7,881 ....M6
Dickenson 19,806 ....D6
Dinwiddie 22,602 ....N6
Essex 8,864 ....P5
Fairfax 596,901 ....O3
Fauquier 35,889 ....N3
Floyd 11,563 ....H7
Fluvanna 10,244 ....M5
Franklin 35,740 ....J6
Frederick 34,150 ....M2
Giles 17,810 ....G6
Gloucester 20,107 ....P6
Goochland 11,761 ....N5
Grayson 16,579 ....F7
Greene 7,625 ....M4
Greensville 10,903 ....N7
Halifax 30,599 ....L7
Hanover 50,398 ....N5
Henrico 180,735 ....O6
Henry 57,654 ....J7
Highland 2,937 ....J4
Isle of Wight 21,603 ....P7
James City 22,763 ....P6
King and Queen 5,968 ......P5
King George 10,543 ....O4
King William 9,334 ....O5
Lancaster 10,129 ....R5
Lee 25,956 ....B7
Loudoun 57,427 ....N2
Louisa 17,825 ....N5
Lunenburg 12,124 ....M7
Madison 10,232 ....M4
Mathews 7,995 ....R6
Mecklenburg 29,444 ....M7
Middlesex 7,719 ....R5
Montgomery 63,516 ....H6
Nelson 12,204 ....L5
New Kent 8,781 ....P5
Northampton 14,625 ....S6
Northumberland 9,828 ....R5
Nottoway 14,666 ....M6
Orange 18,063 ....M4
Page 19,401 ....M3
Patrick 17,647 ....H7
Pittsylvania 66,147 ....K7
Powhatan 13,062 ....N5
Prince Edward 16,456 ....M6
Prince George 25,733 ....O6
Prince William 144,703 ......O3
Pulaski 35,229 ....G6
Rappahannock 6,093 ....M3
Richmond 6,952 ....P5
Roanoke 72,945 ....H6
Rockbridge 17,911 ....K5
Rockingham 57,038 ....L4
Russell 31,761 ....D7
Scott 25,068 ....C7
Shenandoah 27,559 ....L3
Smyth 33,366 ....E7
Southampton 18,731 ....O7
Spotsylvania 34,435 ....N4
Stafford 40,470 ....O4
Surry 6,046 ....P6
Sussex 10,874 ....O7
Tazewell 50,511 ....E6
Warren 21,200 ....M3
Washington 46,487 ....D7
Westmoreland 14,041 ....P4
Wise 43,863 ....C6
Wythe 25,522 ....F7
York 35,463 ....P6

CITIES and TOWNS

Zip   Name/Pop.   Key

24210 Abingdon⊙ 4,318 ....D7
23301 Accomac⊙ 522 ....S5
23001 Achilles 525 ....R6
22920 Afton 350 ....L4
23821 Alberta 394 ....N7
*22301 Alexandria (I.C.)⊙ 103,217 ..S3
24310 Allisonia 325 ....G7
24517 Altavista 3,849 ....K6
24520 Alton 500 ....K7
23002 Amelia Court House⊙ 500 .N6
24521 Amherst⊙ 1,135 ....K5
24601 Amonate 350 ....E6
22003 Annandale 49,524 ......S3
24216 Appalachia 2,418 ......C7
24522 Appomattox⊙ 1,345 ...L6
24053 Ararat 500 ....G7
22922 Arrington 500 ....L5
23004 Arvonia 500 ....M5
22011 Ashburn 345 ....O2
23005 Ashland 4,640 ....N5
24311 Atkins 1,352 ....F7
24411 Augusta Springs 600 ...K4
24312 Austinville 750 ....F7
24054 Axton 540 ....J7
22041 Bailey's
          Crossroads 12,564 ...S3
24230 Banner 327 ....D7
22923 Barboursville 600 ....M4
24055 Bassett 2,034 ....J7
22924 Batesville 575 ....L5
23015 Beaverdam 500 ....N5
24523 Bedford (I.C.)⊙ 5,991 ...J6
23306 Belle Haven 589 ....S5
24218 Ben Hur 400 ....B7
22610 Bentonville 500 ....M3
22611 Berryville⊙ 1,752 ....M2
24526 Big Island 500 ....K5
24603 Big Rock 500 ....D6
24219 Big Stone Gap 4,748 ...C7
24220 Birchleaf 650 ....D6
23307 Birdsnest 736 ....S6
24604 Bishop 600 ....E6
24060 Blacksburg 30,638 .....H6
23824 Blackstone 3,624 ....N6
24527 Blairs 500 ....K7
24315 Bland⊙ 950 ....F6
23308 Bloxom 407 ....S5
24605 Bluefield 5,946 ....F6
24064 Blue Ridge 2,347 ....J6
24606 Boissevain 975 ....F6
23235 Bon Air 16,224 ....N5
24065 Boones Mill 344 ....J6
22713 Boston 400 ....M3
24067 Bowling Green⊙ 665 ...O4
22620 Boyce 401 ....M2
23917 Boydton⊙ 486 ....M7
23827 Boykins 791 ....O7
22714 Brandy Station 400 .....N4
22812 Bridgewater 3,289 ......K4
24201 Bristol (I.C.) 19,042 ....B7
24316 Broadford 500 ....E7
22815 Broadway 1,234 ....L3
23920 Brodnax 492 ....N7
24528 Brookneal 1,454 ....L6
24415 Brownsburg 300 ....K5
22613 Browntown 300 ....M3
22622 Brucetown 250 ....M2
24066 Buchanan 1,205 ....J5
23921 Buckingham⊙ 200 ....L5
24416 Buena Vista
          (I.C.) 6,717 ....K5
24529 Buffalo Junction 300 ...L7
22015 Burke 33,835 ....R3
24608 Burkes Garden 267 .....F6
23922 Burkeville 606 ....M6
22435 Callao 500 ....P5
24067 Callaway 350 ....H7
22016 Calverton 500 ....N3
23310 Cape Charles 1,512 ....R6
23313 Capeville 325 ....R6
23829 Capron 238 ....O7
23315 Carrsville 300 ....P7
23830 Carson 500 ....O6
22017 Casanova 370 ....N3
24069 Cascade 835 ....J7
24224 Castlewood 2,420 ....D7
24070 Catawba 350 ....J5
22019 Catlett 500 ....N3
24609 Cedar Bluff 1,550 ....E6
22437 Center Cross 360 ....P5
†22401 Chancellorsville 40 .....N4
22021 Chantilly 12,259 ....O3
23030 Charles City⊙ 5 ....O6
23923 Charlotte Court
          House⊙ 568 ....L6
*22901 Charlottesville
          (I.C.)⊙ 39,916 ....M4
          Charlottesville‡ 113,568 ..M4
23924 Chase City 2,749 ....M7
24531 Chatham⊙ 1,390 ....K7
23316 Cheriton 695 ....R6
*23320 Chesapeake (I.C.)
          114,486 ....R7
23831 Chester 11,728 ....O6
23832 Chesterfield⊙ 950 ....N6
22623 Chester Gap 400 ....M3
24319 Chilhowie 1,269 ....E7
23336 Chincoteague 1,607 ....T5
24073 Christiansburg⊙ 10,345 .H6
23032 Church View 200 ....P5
23899 Claremont 380 ....P6
23927 Clarksville 1,468 ....L7
†23061 Clay Bank 200 ....P6
†23139 Clayville 200 ....N6
22624 Clear Brook 300 ....M2
24225 Cleveland 360 ....D7
24422 Clifton Forge
          (I.C.) 5,046 ....J5
24321 Clinchburg 250 ....E7
24226 Clinchco 900 ....D6
24244 Clinchport 89 ....C7
24228 Clintwood⊙ 1,369 ......D6
24534 Clover 215 ....L7
24077 Cloverdale 850 ....J6
24535 Cluster Springs 350 ....L7
23035 Cobbs Creek 700 ....R6
24230 Coeburn 2,625 ....D7
24536 Coleman Falls 250 ......K6
†24450 Collierstown 300 ....J5
24078 Collinsville 7,017 ....J7
24443 Colonial Beach 2,474 ...P4
23834 Colonial Heights
          (I.C.) 16,509 ....O6
23038 Columbia 111 ....M5
24538 Concord 500 ....K6
23837 Courtland⊙ 976 ....O7
22931 Covesville 475 ....L5
24426 Covington (I.C.)⊙
          9,063 ....H5
24430 Craigsville 845 ....J4
23930 Crewe 2,325 ....M6
24431 Crimora 450 ....L4
24322 Cripple Creek 200 ......F7
24323 Crockett 200 ....F7
22932 Crozet 2,553 ....L4
23039 Crozier 300 ....N5
24539 Crystal Hill 475 ....L7
23934 Cullen 725 ....L6
22701 Culpeper⊙ 6,621 ....M4
23040 Cumberland⊙ 300 ......M6
22193 Dale City 33,127 ....O3
24083 Daleville 450 ....J6
24236 Damascus 1,330 ....E7
24237 Danville 1,083 ....D7
*24540 Danville (I.C.) 45,642 ..H5
          Danville‡ 111,789 ....H5

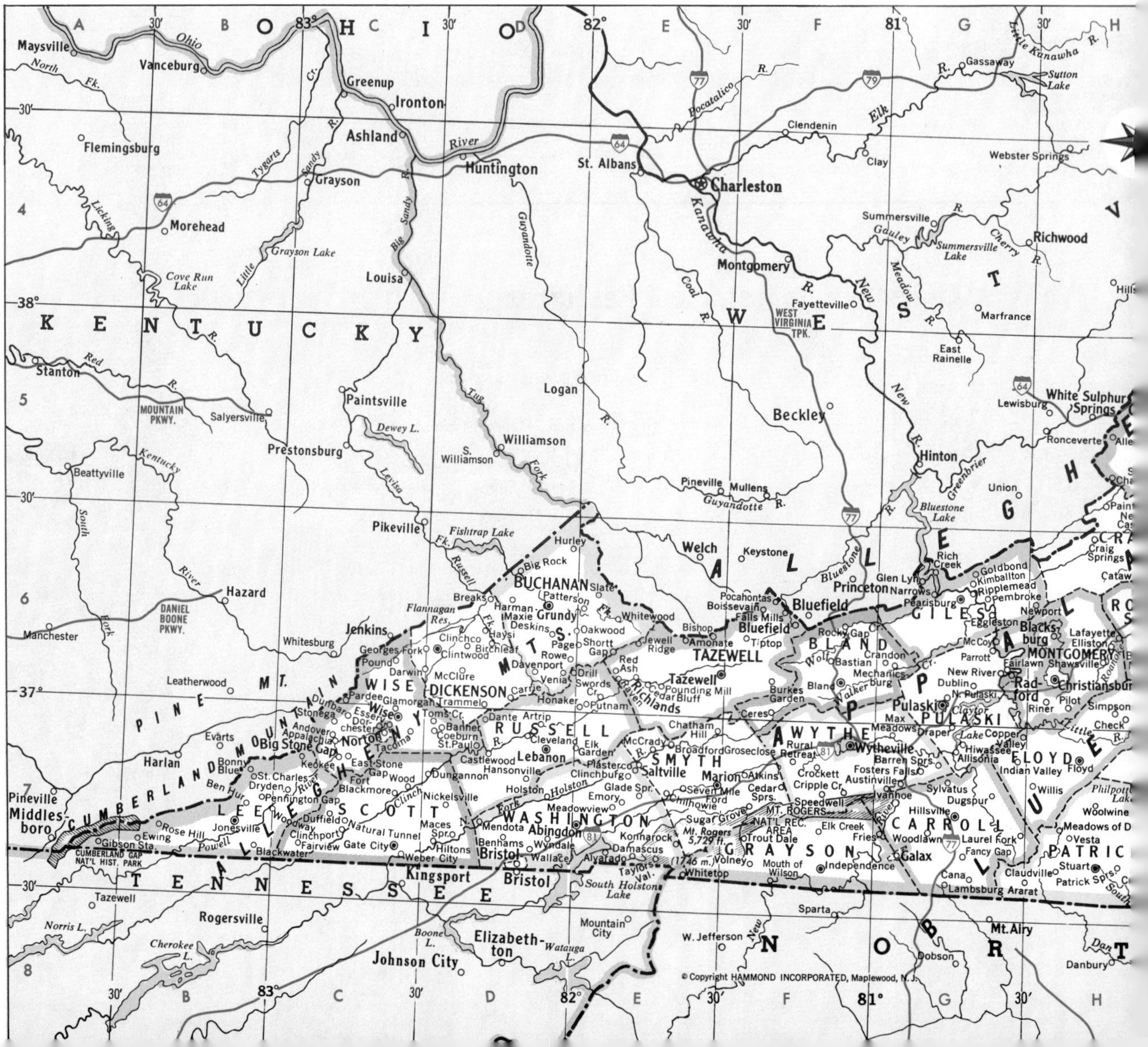

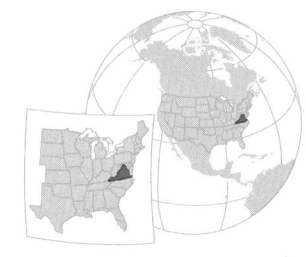

24239 Davenport 230............D6	22937 Esmont 950.................L5	22630 Front Royal⊙ 11,126.....M3	23066 Gwynn 205...............R5
22821 Dayton 1,017............L4	24274 Esserville 750............G2	22065 Gainesville 600...........N3	22469 Hague 425...............P4
24432 Deerfield 500............K4	23803 Ettrick 4,890.............O6	24333 Galax⊙ 6,524..........G7	24558 Halifax⊙ 772............L7
23043 Deltaville 1,082..........R5	23939 Evergreen 300............L6	22463 Garrisonville 200..........N4	23359 Hallwood 243............S5
23839 Dendron 307.............P6	24248 Ewing 800................B7	24251 Gate City⊙ 2,494......C7	22068 Hamilton 598............N2
23043 Deltaville 1,082..........R5	23350 Exmore 1,300............S5	24228 Georges Fork 200........C6	23943 Hampden-Sydney 1,011...L6
†24520 Denniston 200..........L7	22030 Fairfax (I.C.) 19,390.....R3	24340 Glade Spring 1,722......E7	*23601 Hampton (I.C.) 122,617..R6
23936 Dillwyn 637..............M5	22039 Fairfax Station...........R3	24554 Gladys 500..............K6	23069 Hanover⊙ 500...........O5
23841 Dinwiddie⊙ 500.........N6	24435 Fairfield 465.............K5	24555 Glasgow 1,259...........K5	23389 Harborton 200...........S5
23842 Disputanta 800..........O6	24141 Fairlawn 1,794...........C6	23060 Glen Allen 6,202.........N5	24101 Hardy 325...............J6
23937 Drakes Branch 617.......L7	22040 Falls Church (I.C.) 9,515..S2	24093 Glen Lyn 235.............G6	24618 Harman-Maxie 650.......D6
23844 Drewryville 200..........N7	24613 Falls Mills 800............F6	†24541 Glenwood 2,276........K7	22801 Harrisonburg
24243 Dryden 400..............B7	22401 Falmouth 3,271...........O4	23061 Gloucester⊙ 1,545.....P6	(I.C.) 19,671........K4
24549 Dry Fork 200............K7	24328 Fancy Gap 200...........G7	23062 Gloucester Point 5,841...R6	23071 Hartfield 700............R5
24084 Dublin 2,368............G6	23901 Farmville⊙ 6,067.......M6	24094 Goldbond 250...........G6	22069 Haymarket 230..........N3
24244 Duffield 148.............C7	24088 Ferrum 200...............H7	22720 Goldvein 500.............N4	22472 Haynesville 500..........P5
22026 Dumfries 3,214..........O3	24089 Fieldale 1,190............H7	23063 Goochland⊙ 800........N5	24256 Haysi 300...............J7
23938 Dundas 200.............M7	24090 Fincastle⊙ 282.........J6	24556 Goode 200..............K6	22473 Heathsville⊙ 300.......P5
24245 Dungannon 339..........D7	22939 Fishersville 975...........K4	22942 Gordonsville 1,421.......M4	24102 Henry 300...............J7
22027 Dunn Loring 6,077.......S2	24091 Floyd⊙ 411..............H7	22637 Gore 500................M2	*22070 Herndon 11,449........O3
22454 Dunnsville 800..........P5	24551 Forest 497...............K6	24439 Goshen 134.............K5	23075 Highland Springs 12,146..O5
24085 Eagle Rock 750..........J5	23055 Fork Union 350...........M5	23356 Greenbackville 300.......T5	24343 Hillsville⊙ 2,123.......G7
22936 Earlysville 210...........M4	24437 Fort Defiance 600........L4	23942 Green Bay 500...........M6	24258 Hiltons 300..............D7
24246 East Stone Gap 240.....C7	22578 Foxwells 400.............R5	23357 Greenbush 200..........S5	24347 Hiwassee 250...........G7
23347 Eastville⊙ 238.........R6	22310 Franconia 8,476..........S3	24440 Greenville 400...........K5	24020 Hollins College 12,295...H6
23845 Ebony 400..............N7	23851 Franklin (I.C.) 7,308......P7	22943 Greenwood 800..........L4	24260 Honaker 1,475..........D6
22824 Edinburg 752............M3	23354 Frankton 500.............S6	24557 Gretna 1,255............K7	23860 Hopewell (I.C.) 23,397...O6
24086 Eggleston 350...........G6	22401 Fredericksburg	24441 Grottoes 1,369..........L4	23395 Horntown 400...........T5
22827 Elkton 1,520............L4	(I.C.) 15,322........N4	†22306 Groveton 18,860......T3	24445 Hot Springs 300.........J4
24087 Elliston-Lafayette 1,172..H6	24330 Fries 758................F7	24614 Grundy⊙ 1,699.......D6	24104 Huddleston 300.........K6
24327 Emory-Meadowview 2,292..E7			
23847 Emporia (I.C.)⊙ 4,840..N7			(continued on following page)

(continued on following page)

AREA 40,767 sq. mi. (105,587 sq. km.)
POPULATION 5,346,818
CAPITAL Richmond
LARGEST CITY Norfolk
HIGHEST POINT Mt. Rogers 5,729 ft. (1746 m.)
SETTLED IN 1607
ADMITTED TO UNION June 26, 1788
POPULAR NAME Old Dominion
STATE FLOWER Dogwood
STATE BIRD Cardinal

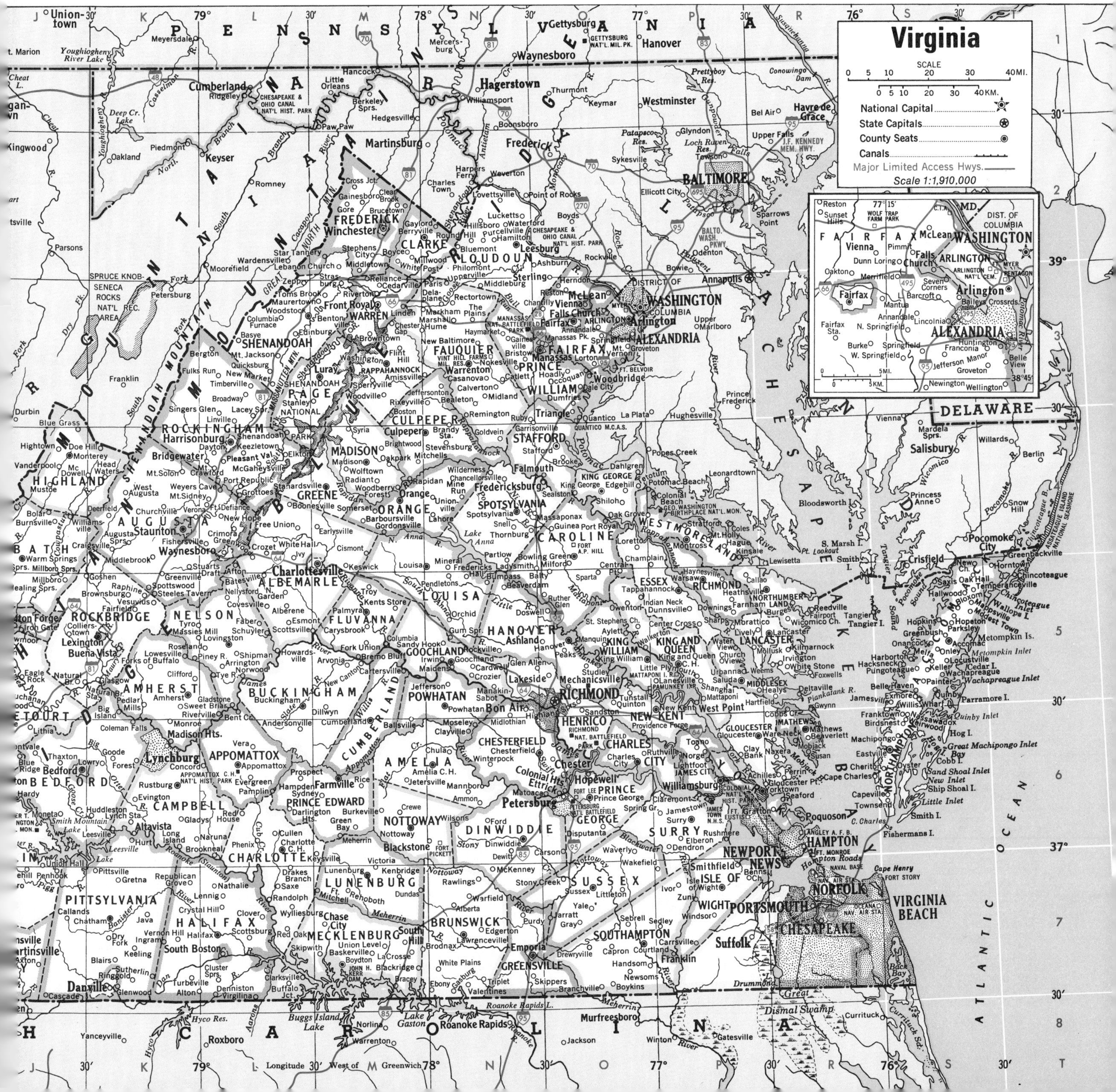

Agriculture, Industry and Resources

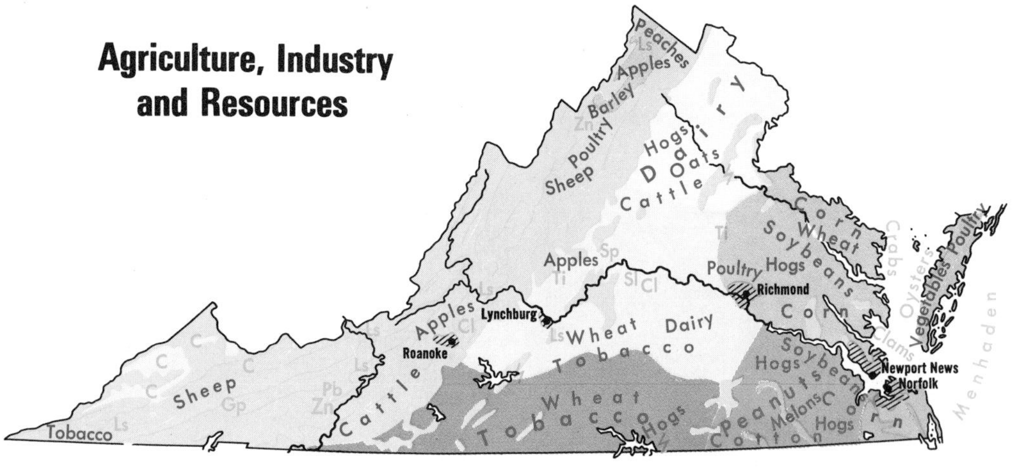

MAJOR MINERAL OCCURRENCES

C	Coal	Sl	Slate
Cl	Clay	Sp	Soapstone
Gp	Gypsum	Ti	Titanium
Ls	Limestone	Zn	Zinc
Pb	Lead		

Water Power
Major Industrial Areas

DOMINANT LAND USE

- Dairy, General Farming
- General Farming, Livestock, Dairy
- General Farming, Livestock, Tobacco
- General Farming, Livestock, Fruit, Tobacco
- General Farming, Truck Farming, Tobacco, Livestock
- Tobacco, General Farming
- Peanuts, General Farming
- Fruit and Mixed Farming
- Truck and Mixed Farming
- Forests
- Swampland, Limited Agriculture

22639 Hume 350 N3
†22301 Huntington 5,813 S3
24620 Hurley 850 D6
24563 Hurt 1,481 K6
24348 Independence⊙ 1,112 F7
24105 Indian Valley 300 G7
24448 Iron Gate 620 J5
22480 Irvington 567 R5
23397 Isle of Wight⊙ 185 P7
24350 Ivanhoe 900 G7
23866 Ivor 403 P7
22945 Ivy 900 L4
23081 Jamestown 12 P6
23398 Jamesville 500 S5
23867 Jarratt 614 O7
22303 Jefferson Manor S3
22724 Jeffersonton 300 N3
24622 Jewell Ridge 600 E6
24263 Jonesville⊙ 874 B7
24566 Keeling 680 K7
22832 Keezletown 975 L4
23401 Keller 236 S5
23944 Kenbridge 1,352 M7
24265 Keokee 300 C7
22947 Keswick 300 M4
23947 Keysville 704 M6
22482 Kilmarnock 945 R5
23085 King and Queen Court House⊙ 500 P5
22485 King George⊙ 575 O4
23086 King William⊙ 100 O5
22488 Kinsale 250 P4
23950 La Crosse 734 M7
22501 Ladysmith 360 N4
24108 Lafayette-Elliston 1,172 H6
†22041 Lake Barcroft 8,725 S3
23228 Lakeside 12,289 N5
24351 Lambsburg 800 G7
22503 Lancaster⊙ 110 P5
24352 Laurel Fork 300 G7
23868 Lawrenceville⊙ 1,484 N7
24266 Lebanon⊙ 3,206 D7
22641 Lebanon Church 300 L2
22075 Leesburg⊙ 8,357 N2
24450 Lexington (I.C.)⊙ 7,292 J5
†22313 Lincolnia 10,350 S3
22642 Linden 320 M3
22834 Linville 500 L3
22507 Lively 400 P5
22079 Lorton 5,813 O3
23093 Louisa⊙ 932 M4
22080 Lovettsville 613 N2
22949 Lovingston⊙ 600 L5
22951 Lowesville 500 K5
24457 Lowmoor 700 J5
†22075 Lucketts 500 N2
23952 Lunenburg⊙ 13 M7
22835 Luray⊙ 3,584 M3
*24501 Lynchburg (I.C.) 66,743 K6
Lynchburg‡ 153,260 K6
24571 Lynch Station 500 K6
23405 Machipongo 400 S6
22727 Madison⊙ 267 M4
24572 Madison Heights 14,146 K6
22110 Manassas (I.C.)⊙ 15,438 O3
22110 Manassas Park (I.C.) 6,524 O3
23106 Manquin 576 O5
†22030 Mantua 6,523 S3
23407 Mappsville 700 T5
24354 Marion⊙ 7,029 E7
22643 Markham 300 N3
22115 Marshall 800 N3
24112 Martinsville (I.C.)⊙ 18,149 J7
22954 Massies Mill 225 K5
23109 Mathews⊙ 500 R6
23803 Matoaca 1,967 N6
23110 Mattaponi 300 P5
24360 Max Meadows 782 G6
24269 McClure 300 D6
24111 McCoy 600 G6
22840 McGaheysville 600 L4
23872 McKenney 473 N7
*22101 McLean 35,664 S2
24361 Meadowview-Emory 2,292 D7
†24315 Mechanicsburg 350 G6
23111 Mechanicsville 9,269 O5
23954 Meherrin 400 M6
23410 Melfa 391 S5
24270 Mendota 375 D7
22116 Merrifield 7,525 S3
22117 Middleburg 619 N3
22645 Middletown 841 M2
22728 Midland 600 N3
23113 Midlothian 950 N6
22514 Milford 650 O4
24460 Millboro 400 J5
24460 Millboro Springs 200 J4
22646 Millwood 400 N2
23117 Mineral 399 N4
22568 Mine Run 450 N4
23118 Mobjack 210 R6
23412 Modest Town 225 T5
22517 Mollusk 800 P5
24121 Moneta 300 J6
24574 Monroe 500 K6
24465 Monterey⊙ 247 K4
22520 Montross⊙ 456 P4
24122 Montvale 900 J6
22523 Morattico 225 P5
23120 Moseley 210 N6
22841 Mount Crawford 315 L4
22524 Mount Holly 200 P4
22842 Mount Jackson 1,419 L3
24467 Mount Sidney 500 K4
22121 Mount Vernon 24,058 O3
24363 Mouth of Wilson 400 F7
24124 Narrows 2,516 G6
23413 Nassawadox 630 S6
24577 Nathalie 200 L7
24578 Natural Bridge 200 J5
24579 Natural Bridge Sta. 450 K5
23122 Naxera 300 R6
22958 Nellysford 290 L5
24127 New Castle⊙ 213 H5
23415 New Church 427 S5
24469 New Hope 200 L4
22122 Newington 8,313 S3
23124 New Kent⊙ 25 P5
22844 New Market 1,118 L3
24128 Newport 600 H6
*23601 Newport News (I.C.) 144,903 P6
Newport News-Hampton‡ 364,449 P6
24129 New River 500 G6
23874 Newsoms 368 O7
24271 Nickelsville 464 D7
22123 Nokesville 520 N3
22125 Nora 550 D6
*23501 Norfolk (I.C.) 266,979 R7
Norfolk-Virginia Beach-Portsmouth ‡ 806,691 R7
23127 Norge 750 P6
22959 North Garden 200 L5
†24301 North Pulaski 1,405 G6
22151 North Springfield 9,538 S3
24273 Norton (I.C.) 4,757 C7
23955 Nottoway⊙ 170 M6
23416 Oak Hall 221 S5
22124 Oakton 19,150 R3
24631 Oakwood 715 E6
22125 Occoquan 241 O3
23417 Onancock 1,461 S5
23418 Onley 526 S5
22960 Orange⊙ 2,631 M4
23419 Oyster 200 S6
24131 Paint Bank 235 H5
23420 Painter 321 S5
22963 Palmyra⊙ 250 M5
23958 Pamplin 273 L6
23421 Parksley 979 S5
24132 Parrott 750 G6
24133 Patrick Springs 800 H7
†23069 Peaks 500 O5
24134 Pearisburg⊙ 2,128 G6
24136 Pembroke 1,302 G6
24137 Penhook 500 J7
24277 Pennington Gap 1,716 C7
23803 Petersburg (I.C.) 41,055 N6
Petersburg-Colonial Heights-Hopewell‡ 129,296 N6
23959 Phenix 250 L6
22131 Philomont 265 N2
24138 Pilot 360 H6
22043 Pimmit 6,658 S2
22964 Piney River 778 L5
24139 Pittsville 600 K7
24635 Pocahontas 708 F6
23662 Poquoson (I.C.) 8,726 R6
22535 Port Royal 291 O4
*23701 Portsmouth (I.C.) 104,577 R7
24279 Pound 1,086 C6
24637 Pounding Mill 399 E6
23139 Powhatan⊙ 600 N5
23875 Prince George⊙ 150 O6
23960 Prospect 275 L6
23140 Providence Forge 500 P6
24301 Pulaski⊙ 10,106 G6
23422 Pungoteague 500 S5
22132 Purcellville 1,567 N2
†23847 Purdy 350 N7
22134 Quantico 621 O3
23423 Quinby 350 S5
24141 Radford (I.C.) 13,225 G6
22732 Radiant 250 M4
24472 Raphine 500 K5
24639 Raven 4,000 E6
23876 Rawlings 200 N7
22140 Rectortown 225 N3
24640 Red Ash 300 E6
23964 Red Oak 250 L7
22539 Reedville 400 R5
22734 Remington 425 N3
22090 Reston 36,407 R2
24147 Rich Creek 746 G6
24641 Richlands 5,796 E6
*23201 Richmond (cap.) (I.C.)⊙ 219,214 O5
Richmond‡ 632,015 O5
24148 Ridgeway 858 J7
24149 Riner 360 H6
24150 Ripplemead 600 G6
22651 Riverton 500 M3
*24001 Roanoke (I.C.) 100,220 H6
Roanoke‡ 224,341 H6
23146 Rockville 290 N5
24366 Rocky Gap 200 F6
24151 Rocky Mount⊙ 4,198 J7
24280 Rosedale 760 E7
24281 Rose Hill 700 B7
22967 Roseland 300 K5
22141 Round Hill 510 N2
24368 Rural Retreat 1,083 F7
†23430 Rushmere 1,070 P6
24588 Rustburg⊙ 650 K6
22546 Ruther Glen 200 O5
23147 Ruthville 300 P6
24282 Saint Charles 241 B7
24283 Saint Paul 973 D7
23148 St. Stephens Church 500 O5
24153 Salem (I.C.)⊙ 23,958 H6
24370 Saltville 2,376 E7
23149 Saluda⊙ 150 P5
23150 Sandston O5
23153 Sandy Hook 700 M5
23427 Saxis 415 S5
22969 Schuyler 250 L5
24589 Scottsburg 335 L7
24590 Scottsville 250 L5
23696 Seaford R6
22547 Sealston 200 O4
23878 Sedley 523 P7
24474 Selma 500 J5
22044 Seven Corners 6,058 S3
24373 Seven Mile Ford 425 E7
24162 Shawsville 950 H6
22849 Shenandoah 1,861 L4
22971 Shipman 350 L5
23430 Smithfield 3,718 P7
22553 Snell 300 N4
22972 Somerset 200 M4
24592 South Boston (I.C.) 7,093 L7
23970 South Hill 4,347 M7
22552 Sparta 485 O4
24374 Speedwell 650 F8
24165 Spencer 500 J7
22740 Sperryville 500 M3
22553 Spotsylvania⊙ 350 N4
*22150 Springfield 21,435 S3
22554 Stafford⊙ 750 O4
22973 Stanardsville⊙ 284 L4
22851 Stanley 1,204 L3
24168 Stanleytown 1,761 H7
22654 Star Tannery 500 L2
24401 Staunton (I.C.)⊙ 21,857 K4
24476 Steeles Tavern 200 K5
22655 Stephens City 1,179 M2
22170 Sterling 16,080 O2
24285 Stonega 275 C7
23882 Stony Creek 329 N7
22657 Strasburg 2,311 M3
24171 Stuart⊙ 1,131 H7
24477 Stuarts Draft 1,776 L4
23162 Studley 500 O5
*23432 Suffolk (I.C.) 47,621 P7
24375 Sugar Grove 1,027 E7
22090 Sunset Hills R2
23883 Surry⊙ 237 P6
23163 Susan 500 R6
23884 Sussex⊙ 75 O7
24595 Sweet Briar 900 K5
24649 Swords Creek 315 E6
†24343 Sylvatus 200 G7
23602 Tabb R6
23440 Tangier 771 R5
22560 Tappahannock⊙ 1,821 O5
24651 Tazewell⊙ 4,468 E6
23442 Temperanceville 400 T5
24174 Thaxton 450 K6
22171 The Plains 382 N3
22853 Timberville 1,510 L3
23168 Toano 950 P6
22660 Toms Brook 226 L3
23443 Townsend 525 R6
24289 Trammel 450 D6
22172 Triangle 4,770 O3
23886 Triplet 300 N7
24378 Trout Dale 248 F7
24175 Troutville 496 J6
22567 Unionville 500 N4
22176 Upperville 250 N2
23175 Urbanna 518 P5
23887 Valentines 400 N7
24656 Vansant 2,708 D6
24597 Vernon Hill 250 K7
24482 Verona 2,782 K4
24177 Vesta 350 H7
24483 Vesuvius 500 K5
23974 Victoria 2,004 M6
22180 Vienna 15,469 R2
24179 Vinton 8,027 J6
*23450 Virginia Beach (I.C.) 262,199 S7
23480 Wachapreague 404 S5
23888 Wakefield 1,355 O7
23177 Walkerton 985 O5
24484 Warm Springs⊙ 325 J4
22186 Warrenton⊙ 3,907 N3
22572 Warsaw⊙ 771 P5
22747 Washington⊙ 247 M3
22190 Waterford 350 N2
23180 Water View 265 P5
23890 Waverly 2,284 O6
22980 Waynesboro (I.C.) 15,329 K4
24251 Weber City 1,543 C7
22576 Weems 500 P5
23484 Weirwood 300 S6
24485 West Augusta 325 K4
23181 West Point 2,726 P5
22153 West Springfield 25,012 S3
24486 Weyers Cave 300 L4
22987 White Hall 250 L4
22578 White Stone 409 R5
24292 Whitetop 860 E7
24657 Whitewood 350 E6
22579 Wicomico Church 500 R5
†22553 Wilderness 200 N4
23185 Williamsburg (I.C.)⊙ 9,870 P6
23486 Willis Wharf 360 S5
22601 Winchester (I.C.)⊙ 20,217 M2
23487 Windsor 985 P7
24184 Wirtz 500 J6
24293 Wise⊙ 3,894 C7
22748 Wolftown 350 M4
22989 Woodberry Forest 450 M4
*22191 Woodbridge 24,004 O3
24381 Woodlawn 1,689 G7
22664 Woodstock⊙ 2,627 L3
†24277 Woodway 400 C7
23976 Wylliesburg 213 L7
24382 Wytheville⊙ 7,135 G7
23690 Yorktown⊙ 550 R6
23898 Zuni 300 P7

OTHER FEATURES

Aarons (creek) L7
Allegheny (mts.) H5
Anna (lake) N4
Appalachian (mts.) J5
Appomattox (riv.) M6
Appomattox Court House Nat'l Hist. Park K6
Arlington Nat'l Cemetery T3
Assateague Island Nat'l Seashore T4
Back (bay) S7
Back (creek) J4
Banister (riv.) K7
Big Otter (riv.) K6
Blackwater (riv.) J6
Blackwater (riv.) O6
Blue Ridge (mts.)
Bluestone (lake)
Booker T. Washington Nat'l Mon.
Buggs Island (lake)
Bull Run (creek)
Cedar (isl.)
Central Intelligence Agency (C.I.A.)
Charles (cape)
Chesapeake (bay)
Chesapeake and Ohio Canal Nat'l Mon.
Chincoteague (bay)
Chincoteague (inlet)
Claytor (lake)
Clinch (riv.)
Cobb (isl.)
Colonial Nat'l Hist. Park
Cowpasture (riv.)
Craig (creek)
Cub (creek)
Cumberland (mt.)
Cumberland Gap Nat'l Hist. Pk.
Dan (riv.)
Drummond (lake)
Fishermans (isl.)
Flannagan (res.)
Flat (creek)
Fort Belvoir 7,726
Fort Eustis
Fort A.P. Hill
Fort Lee 9,784
Fort Monroe
Fort Myer
Fort Pickett
Fort Story
Gaston (lake)
George Washington Birthplace Nat'l Mon.
Goose (creek)
Goose (creek)
Great Machipongo (inlet)
Great North (mt.)
Hampton Roads (est.)
Henry (cape)
Hog (isl.)
Hog Island (bay)
Holston, North Fork (riv.)
Hyco (riv.)
Jackson (riv.)
James (riv.)
Jamestown Nat'l Hist. Site
John H. Kerr (dam)
Langley A.F.B.
Leesville (lake)
Levisa Fork (riv.)
Little (inlet)
Little (riv.)
Little (riv.)
Manassas Nat'l Battlefield Pk.
Massanutten (mt.)
Mattaponi (riv.)
Mattaponi Ind. Res.
Maury (riv.)
Meherrin (riv.)
Metompkin (inlet)
Metompkin (isl.)
Mobjack (bay)
Mount Rogers Nat'l Rec. Area
Naval Air Station
New (inlet)
New (riv.)
Ni (riv.)
North Anna (riv.)
Nottoway (riv.)
Oceana N.A.S.
Pamunkey (riv.)
Pamunkey Ind. Res.
Parramore (isl.)
Pentagon
Petersburg Nat'l Battlefield
Philpott (lake)
Piankatank (riv.)
Pigg (riv.)
Po (riv.)
Pocomoke (sound)
Potomac (riv.)
Powell (riv.)
Quantico Marine Corps Air Sta. 7,121
Quinby (inlet)
Rapidan (riv.)
Rappahannock (riv.)
Richmond Nat'l Battlefield Pk.
Rivanna (riv.)
Roanoke (riv.)
Rogers (mt.)
Russell Fork (riv.)
Sand Shoal (inlet)
Shenandoah (mt.)
Shenandoah (riv.)
Shenandoah Nat'l Park
Ship Shoal (isl.)
Slate (riv.)
Smith (isl.)
Smith (riv.)
Smith Mountain (lake)
South Anna (riv.)
South Holston (lake)
South Mayo (riv.)
Staunton (Roanoke) (riv.)
Stony (creek)
Swift (creek)
Tangier (isl.)
Tangier (sound)
Tug Fork (riv.)
U.S. Naval Base
Vint Hill Farms Mil. Res.
Wachapreague (inlet)
Walker (creek)
Wallops (isl.)
Willis (riv.)
Wolf (creek)
Wolf Trap Farm Park
York (riv.)

I.C. Independent City.
⊙County seat.
‡Population of metropolitan area.
† Zip of nearest p.o * Multiple zi

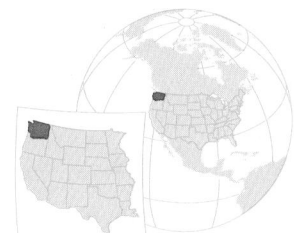

AREA 68,139 sq. mi. (176,480 sq. km.)
POPULATION 4,132,180
CAPITAL Olympia
LARGEST CITY Seattle
HIGHEST POINT Mt. Rainier 14,410 ft. (4392 m.)
SETTLED IN 1811
ADMITTED TO UNION November 11, 1889
POPULAR NAME Evergreen State
STATE FLOWER Western Rhododendron
STATE BIRD Willow Goldfinch

COUNTIES

Adams 13,267 ..... G3
Asotin 16,823 ..... H4
Benton 109,444 ..... F4
Chelan 45,061 ..... E3
Clallam 51,648 ..... B2
Clark 192,227 ..... C5
Columbia 4,057 ..... H4
Cowlitz 79,548 ..... C4
Douglas 22,144 ..... F3
Ferry 5,811 ..... G2
Franklin 35,025 ..... G4
Garfield 2,468 ..... H4
Grant 48,522 ..... F3
Grays Harbor 66,314 ..... B3
Island 44,048 ..... C2
Jefferson 15,965 ..... B3
King 1,269,749 ..... D3
Kitsap 147,152 ..... C3
Kittitas 24,877 ..... E3
Klickitat 15,822 ..... E5
Lewis 56,028 ..... C4
Lincoln 9,604 ..... G3
Mason 31,184 ..... B3
Okanogan 30,639 ..... F2
Pacific 17,237 ..... B4
Pend Oreille 8,580 ..... H2
Pierce 485,667 ..... C3
San Juan 7,838 ..... C2
Skagit 64,138 ..... D2
Skamania 7,919 ..... D5
Snohomish 337,720 ..... D2
Spokane 341,835 ..... H3
Stevens 28,979 ..... H2
Thurston 124,264 ..... C4
Wahkiakum 3,832 ..... B4
Walla Walla 47,435 ..... G4
Whatcom 106,701 ..... D2
Whitman 40,103 ..... H4
Yakima 172,508 ..... E4

CITIES and TOWNS

Zip	Name/Pop.	Key
98520	Aberdeen 18,739	B3
98220	Acme 500	C2
99001	Airway Heights 1,730	H3
99102	Albion 631	H4
†98328	Alder 300	C4
98002	Algona 1,467	C3
98524	Allyn 850	C3
99103	Almira 330	G3
98526	Amanda Park 495	A3
98601	Amboy 480	C5
98221	Anacortes 9,013	C2
98603	Ariel 386	C5
98223	Arlington 3,282	C2
98304	Ashford 300	C4
99402	Asotin⊙ 943	H4
98002	Auburn 26,417	C3
98110	Bainbridge Island-Winslow (Winslow) 2,196	A2
98604	Battle Ground 2,774	C5
†98004	Beaux Arts Village 328	B2
98305	Beaver 450	A2
98528	Belfair 500	C3
*98004	Bellevue 73,903	B2
98225	Bellingham⊙ 45,794	C2
	Bellingham‡ 106,701	C2
99320	Benton City 1,980	F4
98605	Bingen 644	D5
98010	Black Diamond 1,170	D3
98230	Blaine 2,363	C1
†98390	Bonney Lake 5,328	C3
98011	Bothell 7,943	B1
98310	Bremerton 36,208	A2
	Bremerton‡ 146,609	A2
98812	Brewster 1,337	F2
98813	Bridgeport 1,174	F2
†98036	Brier 2,915	C3
98320	Brinnon 500	B3
†98101	Bryn Mawr-Skyway 11,754	B2
98321	Buckley 3,143	C3
98530	Bucoda 519	C4
98921	Buena 590	E4
98166	Burien 23,189	A2
98233	Burlington 3,894	C2
98013	Burton 600	A2
98607	Camas 5,681	C5
98323	Carbonado 456	D3
98324	Carlsborg 500	B2
98814	Carlton 410	F2
98014	Carnation 913	D3
98610	Carson 500	D5
98815	Cashmere 2,240	E3
98611	Castle Rock 2,162	B4
98612	Cathlamet⊙ 635	B4
98531	Centralia 11,555	C4
98520	Central Park 2,709	B3
98532	Chehalis⊙ 6,100	C4
98816	Chelan 2,802	E3
99004	Cheney 7,630	H3
99109	Chewelah 1,888	H2
98614	Chinook 928	B4
98326	Clallam Bay 600	A2
99403	Clarkston 6,903	H4
98235	Clearlake 750	C2
98922	Cle Elum 1,773	E3
98236	Clinton 900	C3
†98004	Clyde Hill 3,229	B2
†98055	Coalfield 500	B2
99111	Colfax⊙ 2,780	H4
99324	College Place 5,771	G4
99113	Colton 307	H4
†98632	Columbia Heights 2,515	C4
99114	Colville⊙ 4,510	H2
98819	Conconully 157	F2
98237	Concrete 592	D2
99326	Connell 1,981	G4
98535	Copalis Beach 600	A3
98536	Copalis Crossing 500	A3
98537	Cosmopolis 1,575	B4
99115	Coulee City 510	F3
99116	Coulee Dam 1,412	G3
98239	Coupeville⊙ 1,006	C2
99117	Creston 309	G3
99119	Cusick 246	H2
98240	Custer 300	C2
98617	Dallesport 600	D5
98241	Darrington 1,064	D2
99122	Davenport⊙ 1,559	G3
99328	Dayton⊙ 2,565	H4
98243	Deer Harbor 400	B2
99006	Deer Park 2,140	H3
98188	Des Moines 7,378	B2
99213	Dishman 10,169	H3
99329	Dixie 210	G4
98821	Dryden 500	E3
†98382	Dungeness 675	B2
98327	Du Pont 559	C3
98019	Duvall 729	D3
98245	Eastsound 800	B2
98801	East Wenatchee 1,640	E3
98328	Eatonville 998	C4
98020	Edmonds 27,679	C3
99123	Electric City 927	F3
98926	Ellensburg⊙ 11,752	E3
98541	Elma 2,720	B4
99124	Elmer City 312	G2
99125	Endicott 290	H4
†98310	Enetai 2,638	A2
98822	Entiat 445	E3
98022	Enumclaw 5,427	D3
98823	Ephrata⊙ 5,359	F3
†98310	Erlands Point 1,254	A2
*98201	Everett⊙ 54,413	C3
98247	Everson 898	C2
99012	Fairfield 582	H3
†98901	Fairview-Sumach 2,788	E4
98024	Fall City 1,528	D3
99128	Farmington 176	H3
98248	Ferndale 3,855	C2
98424	Fife 1,823	C3
98466	Fircrest 5,477	C3
†98531	Fords Prairie 2,582	B4
98331	Forks 3,060	A3
99014	Four Lakes 500	H3
98250	Friday Harbor⊙ 1,200	B2
†98901	Fruitvale 3,967	E4
99130	Garfield 599	H3
†99362	Garrett 1,134	G4
98824	George 261	F3
98335	Gig Harbor 2,429	C3
98336	Glenoma 500	C4
98619	Glenwood 626	D4
98251	Gold Bar 794	D3
98620	Goldendale⊙ 3,575	E5
98337	Gorst 750	A2
99133	Grand Coulee 1,180	G3
98930	Grandview 5,615	F4
98932	Granger 1,812	E4
98252	Granite Falls 911	D2
98547	Grayland 750	A4
98621	Grays River 350	B4
98253	Greenbank 600	C2
98339	Hadlock-Irondale 1,752	C2
98255	Hamilton 268	D2
†98366	Harper 300	A2
98933	Harrah 343	E4
99134	Harrington 507	G3
99135	Hartline 165	F3
99332	Hatton 81	G4
98025	Hobart 500	D3
98548	Hoodsport 500	B3
98550	Hoquiam 9,719	A3
†98004	Hunts Point 480	B2
98624	Ilwaco 604	A4
98256	Index 147	D3
98342	Indianola 800	A1
99139	Ione 594	H2
98027	Issaquah 5,536	C3
98343	Joyce 375	B2
98033	Juanita 17,232	B1
99335	Kahlotus 203	G4
98625	Kalama 1,216	C4
98344	Kapowsin 500	C4
98626	Kelso⊙ 11,129	C4
98028	Kenmore 7,281	B1
99336	Kennewick 34,397	F4
98031	Kent 23,152	C3
99141	Kettle Falls 1,087	H2
98345	Keyport 900	A2
98346	Kingston 950	C3
98033	Kirkland 18,779	B2
98934	Kittitas 782	E4
98628	Klickitat 750	D5
†98632	Krupp (Marlin) 83	F3
98629	La Center 439	C5
98503	Lacey 13,940	C4
98257	La Conner 633	C2
99143	Lacrosse 373	H4
†98101	Lake Forest Park 2,485	B1
98258	Lake Stevens 1,660	D3
99017	Lamont 101	H3
98260	Langley 650	C2
98350	La Push 500	A3
98018	Latah 155	H3
98826	Leavenworth 1,522	E3
99019	Liberty Lake 1,599	J3
98555	Lilliwaup 75	B3
99341	Lind 567	G4
98556	Littlerock 850	B4
98631	Long Beach 1,199	A4
98351	Longbranch 640	C3
98632	Longview 31,052	B4
99148	Loon Lake 500	H2
98262	Lummi Island 675	C2
98635	Lyle 580	D5
98263	Lyman 285	D2
98264	Lynden 4,022	C2
98036	Lynnwood 22,641	C3
98935	Mabton 1,248	E4
99149	Malden 200	H3
98829	Malott 350	F2
98353	Manchester 400	A2
98830	Mansfield 315	F3
98266	Maple Falls 300	D2
98038	Maple Valley 900	C3
99151	Marcus 174	H2
98268	Marietta-Alderwood 2,324	C2
98832	Marlin 83	F3
98270	Marysville 5,080	C2
99344	Mattawa 299	F4
98557	McCleary 1,419	B3
99022	Medical Lake 3,600	H3
98039	Medina 3,220	B2
98040	Mercer Island (city) 21,522	B2
99343	Mesa 278	G4
99152	Metaline 190	H2
99153	Metaline Falls 296	H2
†99210	Millwood 1,717	H3
98354	Milton 3,162	C3
98355	Mineral 550	C4
98562	Moclips 500	A3
98836	Monitor 650	E3
98272	Monroe 2,869	D3
98563	Montesano⊙ 3,247	B4
98356	Morton 1,264	C4
98837	Moses Lake 10,629	F3
98564	Mossyrock 463	C4
98043	Mountlake Terrace 16,534	B1
98273	Mount Vernon⊙ 13,009	C2
98936	Moxee City 687	E4
98275	Mukilteo 1,426	C3
98937	Naches 644	E4
98565	Napavine 611	C4
98638	Naselle 500	B4
†98310	Navy Yard City 2,594	A2
98357	Neah Bay 800	A2
99155	Nespelem 284	G2
†98283	Newhalem 350	D2
99156	Newport⊙ 1,665	H2
†98501	Nisqually 500	C3
98276	Nooksack 429	C2
98358	Nordland 706	C2
†98100	Normandy Park 4,268	A2
98045	North Bend 1,701	D3
98639	North Bonneville 394	C5
99157	Northport 368	H2
99158	Oakesdale 444	H3
98277	Oak Harbor 12,271	C2
98568	Oakville 537	B4
98569	Ocean City 350	A3
98640	Ocean Park 918	A4
98551	Ocean Shores 1,692	A3
†98520	Ocosta 369	B4
99159	Odessa 1,009	G3
98840	Okanogan⊙ 2,302	F2
98359	Olalla 500	A2
*98501	Olympia (cap.)⊙ 27,447	C3
	Olympia‡ 124,264	C3
98841	Omak 4,007	F2
98570	Onalaska 600	C4
99214	Opportunity 21,241	H3
98662	Orchards 8,828	C5
98844	Oroville 1,483	F2
98360	Orting 1,787	C3
99344	Othello 4,454	F4
99027	Otis Orchards-East Farms 4,597	H3
98938	Outlook 300	E4
98047	Pacific 2,261	C3
98571	Pacific Beach 900	A3
98361	Packwood 800	D4
99161	Palouse 1,005	H4
98939	Parker 500	E4
98444	Parkland 23,355	C3
99301	Pasco⊙ 18,425	F4
98846	Pateros 555	E2
98572	Pe Ell 617	B4
98847	Peshastin 500	E3
98281	Point Roberts 500	B2
99347	Pomeroy⊙ 1,716	H4
98362	Port Angeles⊙ 17,311	B2
†98101	Port Blakely 600	A2
98366	Port Orchard⊙ 4,787	A2
98368	Port Townsend⊙ 6,067	C2
†98584	Potlach 100	B3
98370	Poulsbo 3,453	A1
99348	Prescott 341	G4
98050	Preston 500	D3
99350	Prosser⊙ 3,896	F4
99163	Pullman 23,579	H4
98371	Puyallup 18,251	C3
98376	Quilcene 900	B3
98575	Quinault 450	B3
98848	Quincy 3,525	F3
98576	Rainier 891	C4

(continued on following page)

Agriculture, Industry and Resources

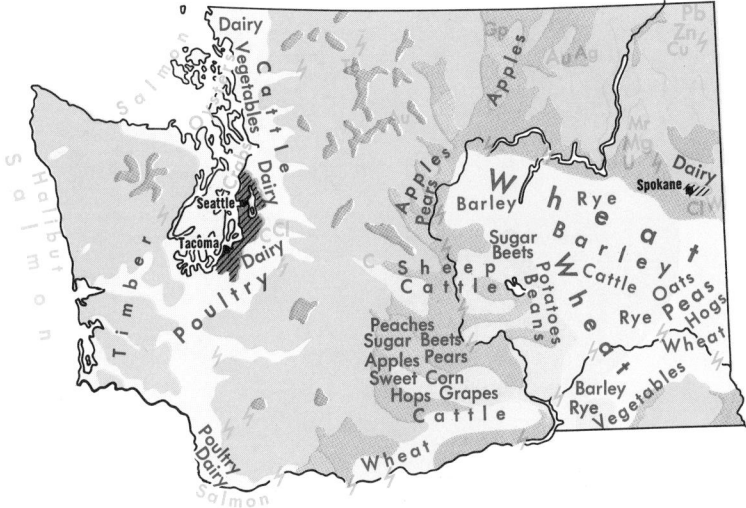

DOMINANT LAND USE

- Specialized Wheat
- Wheat, Peas
- Dairy, Poultry, Mixed Farming
- Fruit and Mixed Farming
- General Farming, Dairy, Range Livestock
- General Farming, Livestock, Special Crops
- Range Livestock
- Forests
- Urban Areas
- Nonagricultural Land

MAJOR MINERAL OCCURRENCES

Ag	Silver	Mr	Marble
Au	Gold	Pb	Lead
C	Coal	Tc	Talc
Cl	Clay	U	Uranium
Cu	Copper	W	Tungsten
Gp	Gypsum	Zn	Zinc
Mg	Magnesium		

⚡ Water Power
▨ Major Industrial Areas

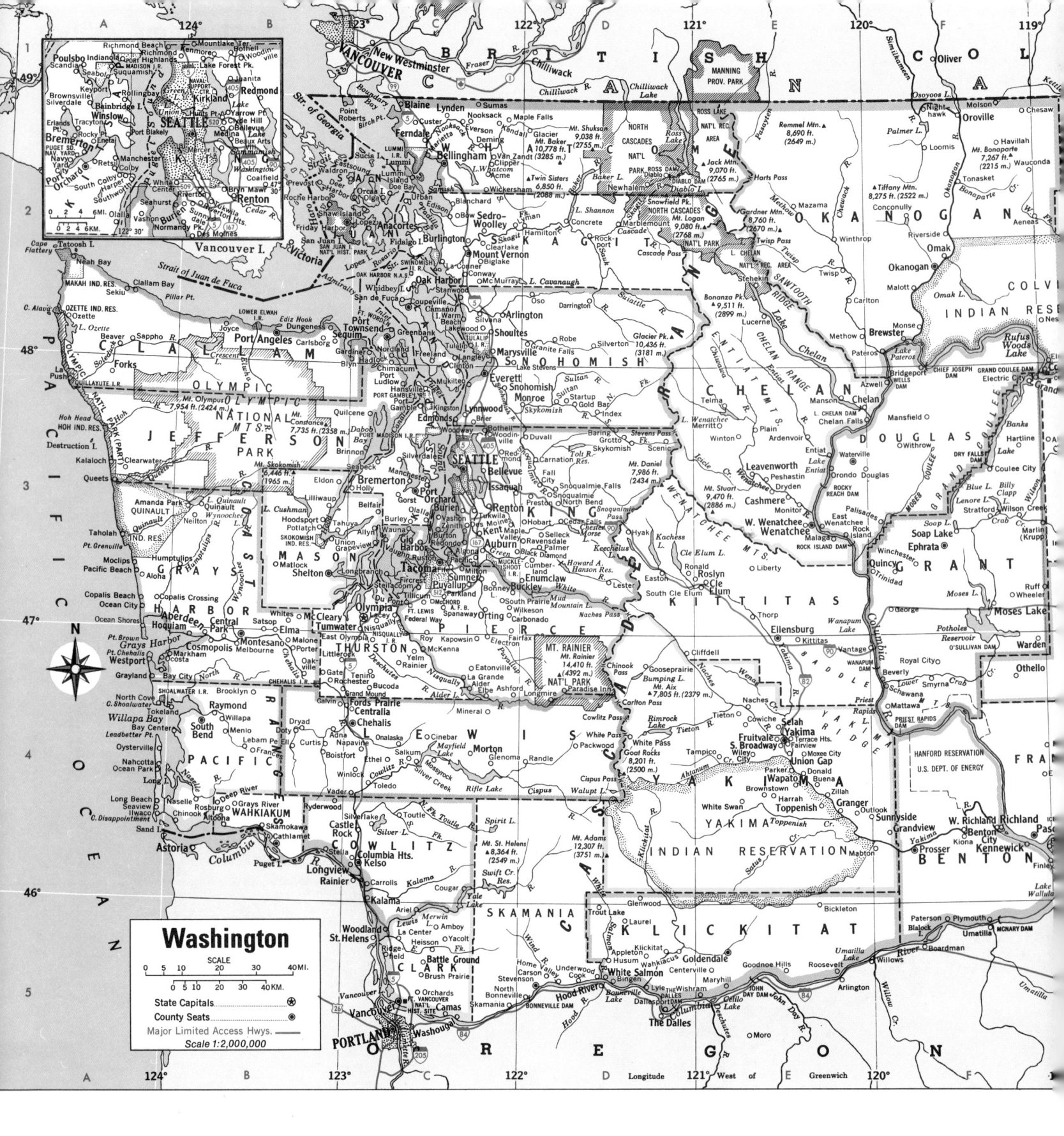

Washington

SCALE
0 5 10 20 30 40MI.
0 5 10 20 30 40KM.

⊗ State Capitals
⊙ County Seats
Major Limited Access Hwys.
Scale 1:2,000,000

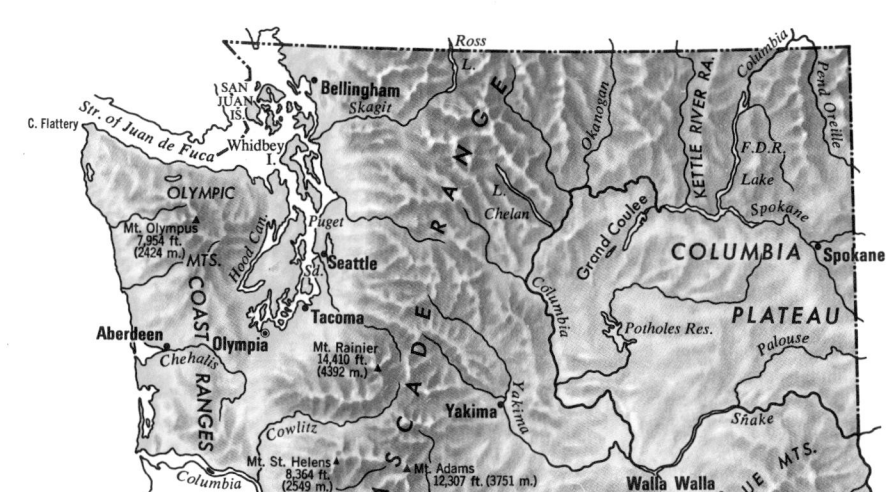

Topography

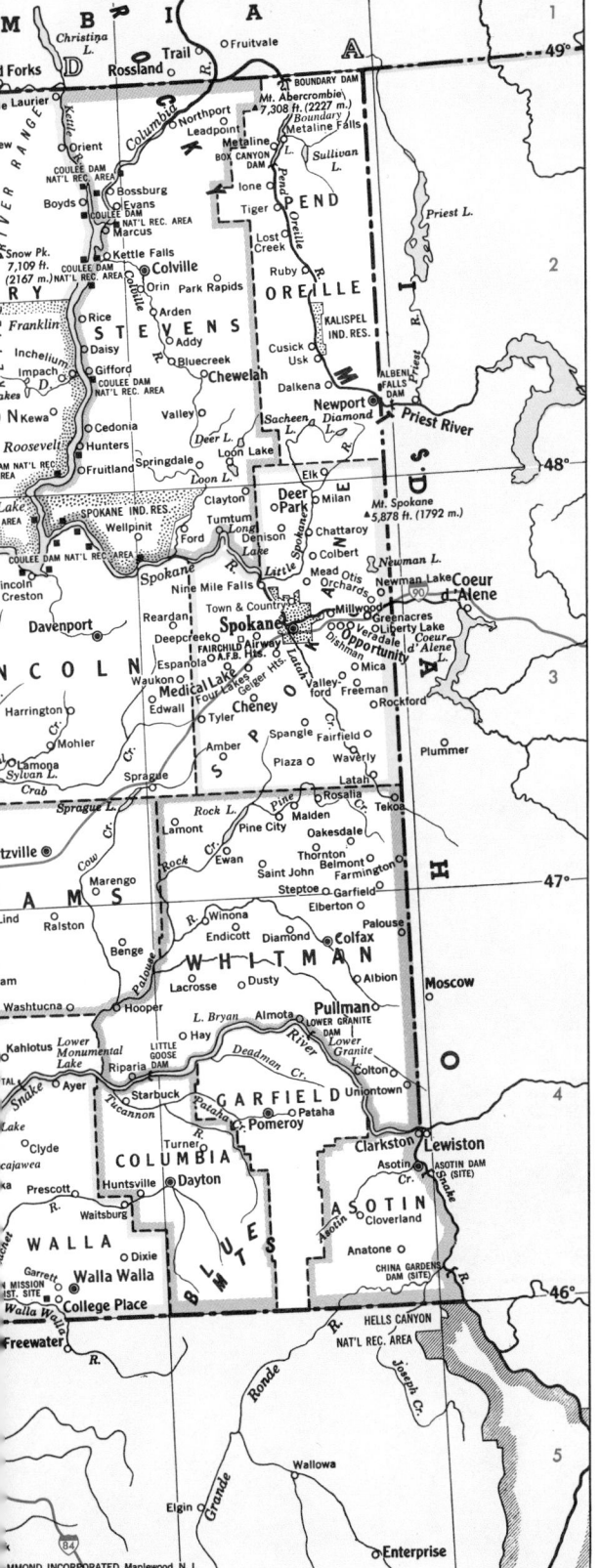

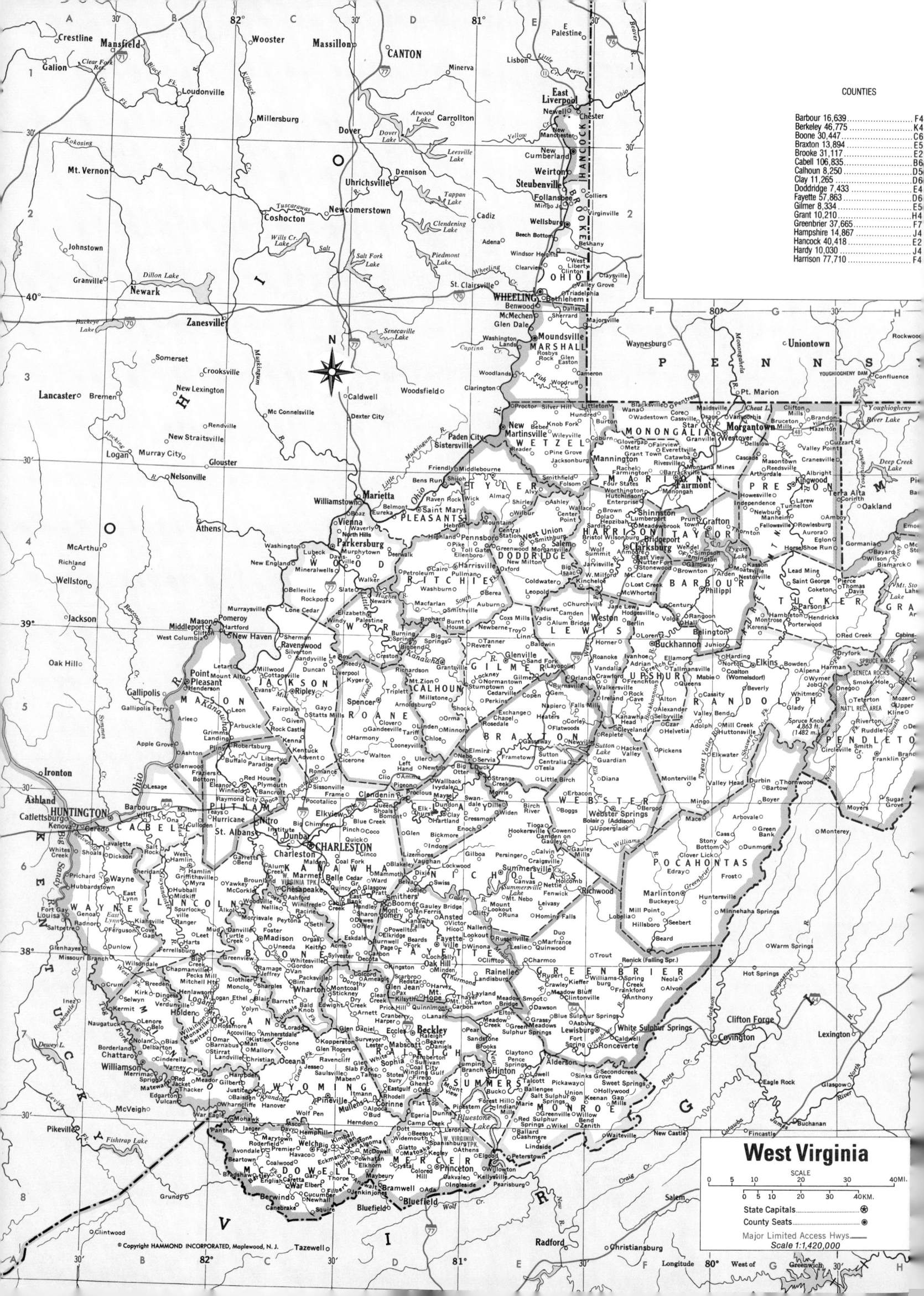

West Virginia

SCALE
0 5 10   20   30   40 MI.
0 5 10   20   30   40 KM.

State Capitals .... ⊛
County Seats .... ◉
Major Limited Access Hwys. ____
Scale 1:1,420,000

Jackson 25,794 .... C5
Jefferson 30,302 .... L4
Kanawha 231,414 .... C6
Lewis 18,813 .... E4
Lincoln 23,675 .... B6
Logan 50,679 .... C7
Marion 65,789 .... F4
Marshall 41,608 .... E3
Mason 27,045 .... B5
McDowell 49,899 .... C8
Mercer 73,942 .... D8
Mineral 27,234 .... J4
Mingo 37,336 .... B7
Monongalia 75,024 .... F3
Monroe 12,873 .... E7
Morgan 10,711 .... K3
Nicholas 28,126 .... E6
Ohio 61,389 .... E2
Pendleton 7,910 .... H5
Pleasants 8,236 .... D4
Pocahontas 9,919 .... F6
Preston 30,460 .... G4
Putnam 38,181 .... C6
Raleigh 86,821 .... D7
Randolph 28,734 .... G5
Ritchie 11,442 .... D4
Roane 15,952 .... D5
Summers 15,875 .... E7
Taylor 16,584 .... F4
Tucker 8,675 .... F4
Tyler 11,320 .... E4
Upshur 23,427 .... F5
Wayne 46,021 .... B6
Webster 12,245 .... F6
Wetzel 21,874 .... E3
Wirt 4,922 .... D4
Wood 93,648 .... D4
Wyoming 35,993 .... C7

CITIES and TOWNS

Zip Name/Pop. Key

25606 Accoville 975 .... C7
†26288 Addison (Webster Springs)⊙ 939 .... F6
26210 Adrian 510 .... F5
26519 Albright 357 .... G3
24910 Alderson 1,375 .... E7
24807 Algoma 200 .... D8
25501 Alkol 500 .... C6
26320 Alma 197 .... E4
24710 Alpoca 200 .... D7
26321 Alum Bridge 150 .... E4
25003 Alum Creek 900 .... C6
26322 Alvy 150 .... E4
25004 Ameagle 230 .... D7
25607 Amherstdale 1,075 .... C7
25005 Amma 200 .... D5
24808 Anawalt 652 .... D8

AREA 24,231 sq. mi. (62,758 sq. km.)
POPULATION 1,950,279
CAPITAL Charleston
LARGEST CITY Charleston
HIGHEST POINT Spruce Knob 4,863 ft. (1482 m.)
SETTLED IN 1774
ADMITTED TO UNION June 20, 1863
POPULAR NAME Mountain State
STATE FLOWER Big Rhododendron
STATE BIRD Cardinal

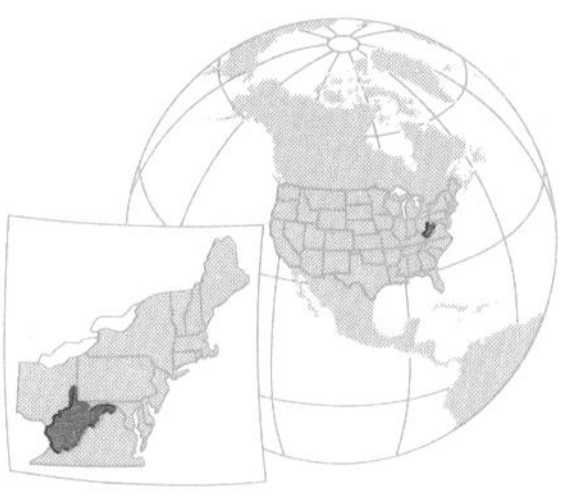

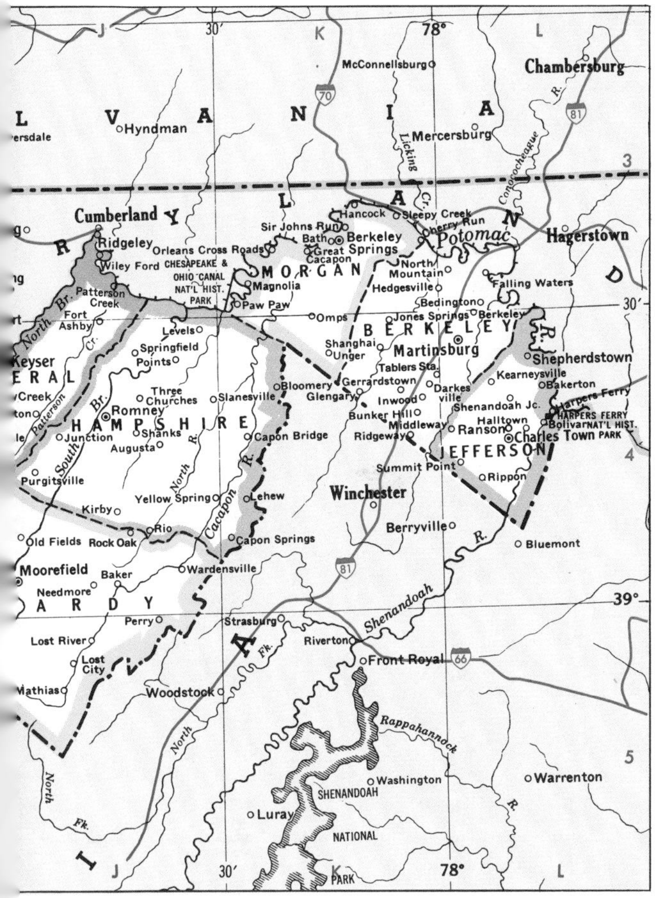

Chambersburg
McConnellsburg
Hyndman
Mercersburg
Cumberland
Hagerstown
Ridgeley
Orleans Cross Roads
Wiley Ford
Sir Johns Run
Bath
Berkeley Springs
Great Cacapon
MORGAN
Potomac
North Mountain
Hedgesville
Magnolia
Paw Paw
Patterson Creek
Falling Waters
Fort Ashby
Levels
Omps
Bedington
Jones Springs
Berkeley
BERKELEY
Martinsburg
Springfield
Points
Shanghai
Unger
Shepherdstown
Keyser
Tablers Sta.
Kearneysville
Three Churches
Slanesville
Bloomery
Gerrardstown
Glengary
Darkesville
Bakerton
Romney
Inwood
Harpers Ferry
Shenandoah Jc.
HAMPSHIRE
Bunker Hill
Halltown
Junction
Shanks
Capon Bridge
Middleway
Ranson
Charles Town
Augusta
Ridgeway
JEFFERSON
Summit Point
Purgitsville
Rippon
Lehew
Winchester
Kirby
Yellow Spring
Rio
Berryville
Old Fields
Rock Oak
Capon Springs
Bluemont
Moorefield
Baker
Wardensville
Needmore
HARDY
Perry
Strasburg
Lost River
Lost City
Riverton
Front Royal
Shenandoah
Mathias
Woodstock
Rappahannock
Washington
Warrenton
Luray
SHENANDOAH
NATIONAL
PARK

Topography

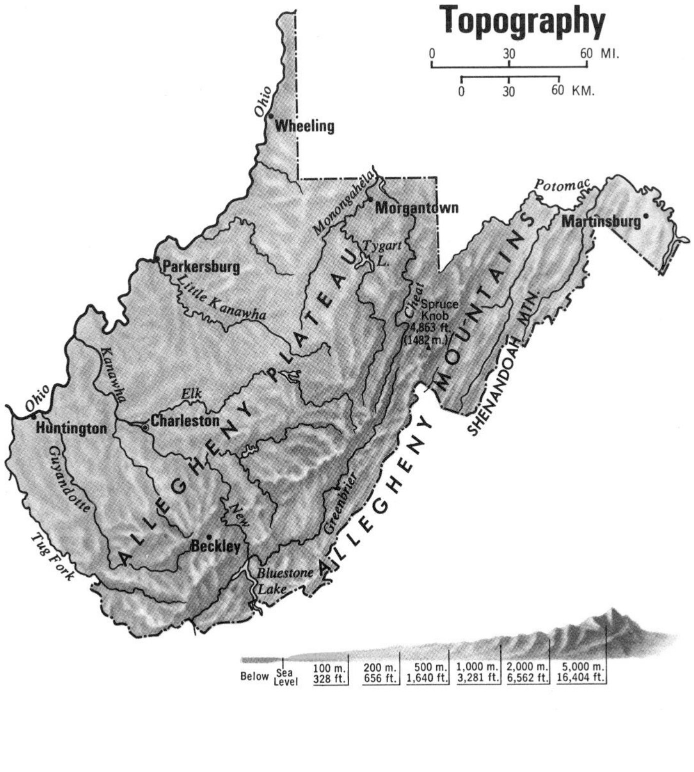

0 30 60 MI.
0 30 60 KM.
Wheeling
Ohio
Morgantown
Monongahela
Potomac
Martinsburg
Parkersburg
Tygart L.
Little Kanawha
Cheat
Spruce Knob 4,863 ft. (1482 m.)
ALLEGHENY PLATEAU
ALLEGHENY MOUNTAINS
SHENANDOAH MTN.
Kanawha
Elk
Huntington
Charleston
Guyandotte
New
Greenbrier
Beckley
Tug Fork
Bluestone Lake
ALLEGHENY
Below Sea Level 100 m. 328 ft. 200 m. 656 ft. 500 m. 1,640 ft. 1,000 m. 3,281 ft. 2,000 m. 6,562 ft. 5,000 m. 16,404 ft.

26323 Anmoore 865 .... F4
25812 Ansted 1,952 .... D6
25502 Apple Grove 900 .... B5
24915 Arbovale 610 .... G6
26816 Arthur 350 .... H4
26520 Arthurdale 1,063 .... G3
24916 Asbury 280 .... E7
24809 Asco 175 .... C8
25009 Ashford 400 .... C6
25503 Ashton 259 .... B5
24712 Athens 1,147 .... E8
26325 Auburn 116 .... E4
26704 Augusta 750 .... J4
26705 Aurora 250 .... G4
24811 Avondale 250 .... C8
25608 Baisden 500 .... C7
26801 Baker 200 .... J4
25410 Bakerton 125 .... L4
25010 Bald Knob 356 .... C7
26326 Baldwin 92 .... E5
25011 Bancroft 528 .... C5
25504 Barboursville 2,871 .... B6
25609 Barnabus 750 .... C7
26559 Barrackville 1,815 .... F3
25013 Barrett 950 .... C7
24813 Bartley 900 .... C8
24920 Bartow 500 .... G5
†25411 Bath (Berkeley Springs) 789 .... K3
26707 Bayard 540 .... H4
25014 Beards Fork 400 .... D6
25813 Beaver (Glen Hedrick) 1,122 .... D7
25801 Beckley⊙ 20,492 .... D7
26030 Beech Bottom 507 .... E2
24714 Beeson 300 .... D8
26250 Belington 2,038 .... F4
25015 Belle 1,621 .... C6
26133 Belleville 105 .... C4
26134 Belmont 887 .... D4
26656 Belva 275 .... D6
26135 Bens Run 85 .... D4
26031 Benwood 1,994 .... E2
26298 Bergoo 220 .... F6
25411 Berkeley Springs (Bath)⊙ 789 .... K3
24815 Berwind 615 .... C8
26032 Bethany 1,336 .... E2
†26003 Bethlehem 3,045 .... E2
26253 Beverly 475 .... G5
25019 Bickmore 300 .... D6
26136 Bigbend 120 .... D5
25302 Big Chimney 450 .... C6
25505 Big Creek 500 .... B7
26137 Big Springs 485 .... D5
25021 Bim 500 .... C7
26610 Birch River 650 .... E6
26521 Blacksville 248 .... F3
25022 Blair 800 .... C7
26817 Bloomery 200 .... K4
25026 Blue Creek 650 .... D6
24701 Bluefield 16,060 .... D8
26288 Bolair 450 .... F6
†25425 Bolivar 672 .... L4
25030 Bomont 170 .... D6
25031 Boomer 1,051 .... D6
24817 Bradshaw 1,002 .... C8
24715 Bramwell 989 .... D8
26523 Brandonville 92 .... G3
26802 Brandywine 300 .... H5
25666 Breeden 600 .... B7
26330 Bridgeport 6,604 .... F4
26138 Brohard 80 .... D4
25957 Brooks 196 .... E7
26334 Brownton 400 .... F4
26525 Bruceton Mills 296 .... G3
24924 Buckeye 125 .... F6
26201 Buckhannon⊙ 6,820 .... F5
24716 Bud 400 .... D7
25033 Buffalo 1,034 .... C5
25413 Bunker Hill 600 .... K4
26710 Burlington 300 .... J4
26335 Burnsville 531 .... E5
26336 Burnt House 175 .... D4
26562 Burton 200 .... F3
25035 Cabin Creek 900 .... C6
26337 Cairo 428 .... D4
24925 Caldwell 795 .... F7
26660 Calvin 400 .... E6
26208 Camden on Gauley 236 .... E6
26033 Cameron 1,474 .... E3
24819 Canebrake 300 .... C8
26662 Canvas 300 .... E6
26711 Capon Bridge 191 .... K4
26823 Capon Springs 580 .... K4
25037 Carbon 300 .... D6
24821 Caretta 650 .... C8
24927 Cass 148 .... G6
26527 Cassville 800 .... F3
25039 Cedar Grove 1,479 .... D6
26339 Center Point 250 .... E4
26612 Centralia 100 .... E5
26340 Central Station 200 .... E4
26214 Century 250 .... F4
25507 Ceredo 2,255 .... B6
25508 Chapmanville 1,164 .... B7
*25301 Charleston (cap.)⊙ 63,968 .... C6
Charleston‡ 269,595 .... C6
25414 Charles Town⊙ 2,857 .... L4
25958 Charmco 800 .... E6
25667 Chattaroy 1,383 .... B7
25418 Cherry Run 120 .... L3
†25301 Chesapeake 2,364 .... C6
26034 Chester 3,297 .... E1
26301 Clarksburg⊙ 22,371 .... F4
25043 Clay⊙ 940 .... D6
25044 Clear Creek 300 .... D7
†26003 Clearview 740 .... E2
25045 Clendenin 1,373 .... D5
26215 Cleveland 74 .... F5
25822 Clifftop 100 .... E6
25237 Clifton 325 .... B5
24928 Clintonville 250 .... E7
25046 Clio 300 .... D5
25047 Clothier 900 .... C7
25823 Coal City 2,324 .... D7
25306 Coal Fork 2,775 .... D6
26257 Coalton 306 .... G5
24824 Coalwood 650 .... C8
25048 Colcord 600 .... D7
26035 Colliers 864 .... E2
26615 Copen 50 .... E5
25826 Corinne 900 .... D7
25051 Costa 250 .... C6
25239 Cottageville 300 .... C5
25509 Cove Gap 650 .... B6
26206 Cowen 723 .... E6
26342 Coxs Mills 275 .... E4
26205 Craigsville 1,562 .... E6
25828 Cranberry 315 .... D7
24931 Crawley 395 .... E7
25669 Crum 500 .... B7
24826 Cucumber 274 .... C8
25510 Culloden 2,931 .... B6
24827 Cyclone 500 .... C7
26036 Dallas 450 .... E2
25832 Daniels 1,959 .... D7
25053 Danville 727 .... C6
†25428 Darkesville 150 .... L4
26260 Davis 979 .... H4
24828 Davy 882 .... C8
25054 Dawes 800 .... D6
24932 Dawson 300 .... E7
25670 Delbarton 981 .... B7
26531 Dellslow 300 .... G3
26217 Diana 300 .... F5
26617 Dille 300 .... E6
25671 Dingess 600 .... B7
25059 Dixie 985 .... D6
25060 Dorothy 400 .... D7
24721 Dott 100 .... D8
25062 Dry Creek 441 .... D7
26263 Dryfork 425 .... H5
25063 Duck 500 .... E5
25064 Dunbar 9,285 .... C6
24934 Dunmore 280 .... G6
26264 Durbin 379 .... G5
25067 East Bank 1,155 .... D6
25835 Eastgulf 300 .... D7
25512 East Lynn 150 .... B6
†26301 East View 1,222 .... F4
25836 Eccles 1,162 .... D7
24829 Eckman 750 .... C8
25672 Edgarton 415 .... B7
26716 Eglon 70 .... G4
24830 Elbert 400 .... C8
25070 Eleanor 1,282 .... C5
26143 Elizabeth⊙ 856 .... D4
26717 Elk Garden 291 .... H4
26241 Elkins⊙ 8,536 .... G5
25071 Elkview 1,161 .... C6
26267 Ellamore 250 .... F5
26346 Ellenboro 357 .... D4
25965 Elton 200 .... E7
24832 English 500 .... C8
26568 Enterprise 1,110 .... F4
25075 Eskdale 400 .... D6
25076 Ethel 450 .... C7
26144 Eureka 125 .... D4
25241 Evans 400 .... C5
26533 Everettville 175 .... F3
26554 Fairmont 23,863 .... F4
26570 Fairview 759 .... F3
†24966 Falling Spring (Renick) 240 .... F6
26571 Farmington 583 .... F3
25840 Fayetteville⊙ 2,366 .... D6
26202 Fenwick 500 .... E6
24835 Filbert 130 .... D8
26818 Fisher 500 .... H4
25841 Flat Top 550 .... D7
26621 Flatwoods 405 .... E5
26347 Flemington 452 .... F4
26037 Follansbee 3,994 .... E2
26348 Folsom 360 .... E4
24935 Forest Hill 314 .... E7
26719 Fort Ashby 1,205 .... J4
25514 Fort Gay 886 .... A6
26806 Fort Seybert 200 .... H5
24936 Fort Spring 250 .... E7
25081 Foster 500 .... C6
26572 Four States 500 .... F4
25071 Frame 76 .... C5
26623 Frametown 150 .... E5
26807 Franklin⊙ 780 .... H5
25082 Fraziers Bottom 250 .... B5
26219 Frenchton 102 .... F5
26146 Friendly 242 .... D3
25515 Gallipolis Ferry 325 .... B5
26349 Galloway 500 .... F4
25243 Gandeeville 150 .... D5
24941 Gap Mills 300 .... F7
24836 Gary 2,233 .... C8
26624 Gassaway 1,225 .... E5
25085 Gauley Bridge 1,177 .... D6
26240 Gauley Mills 165 .... E6
25244 Gay 300 .... C5
25420 Gerrardstown 240 .... K4
25843 Ghent 500 .... D7
25621 Gilbert 757 .... C7
26671 Gilboa 500 .... E6
26350 Gilmer 110 .... E5
26268 Glady 175 .... G5
25086 Glasgow 1,031 .... D6
25088 Glen 175 .... D6
26038 Glen Dale 1,875 .... E3
26039 Glen Easton 100 .... E3
25090 Glen Ferris 200 .... D6
25421 Glengary 250 .... K4
†25813 Glen Hedrick (Beaver) 1,122 .... D7
25846 Glen Jean D7
25848 Glen Rogers 500 .... D7
26351 Glenville⊙ 2,155 .... E5
25849 Glen White 300 .... D7
25520 Glenwood 400 .... B5
†26585 Glovergap 100 .... F3
25093 Gordon 300 .... C7
26720 Gormania 100 .... H4
26354 Grafton⊙ 6,845 .... G4
26147 Grantsville⊙ 788 .... D5
26574 Grant Town 987 .... F3
26534 Granville 992 .... F3
24943 Grassy Meadows 100 .... E7
25422 Great Cacapon 750 .... K3
24944 Green Bank 115 .... G6
25966 Green Sulphur Springs 225 .... E7
24945 Greenville 125 .... E7
26360 Greenwood 750 .... E4
25095 Grimms Landing 350 .... B5
26221 Guardian 175 .... F5
26222 Hacker Valley 440 .... F5
25423 Halltown 375 .... L4
26269 Hambleton 403 .... G4
25523 Hamlin⊙ 1,219 .... B6
25623 Hampden 300 .... C7
25424 Hancock 175 .... K3
25102 Handley 633 .... D6
†26250 Harding 100 .... G5
26270 Harman 181 .... G5
25246 Harmony 600 .... D5
25851 Harper 400 .... D7
25425 Harpers Ferry 361 .... L4
26362 Harrisville⊙ 1,673 .... E4
25247 Hartford 556 .... C4
25524 Harts 400 .... B6
25852 Harvey 300 .... D7
24841 Havaco 350 .... C8
26627 Heaters 440 .... E5
25427 Hedgesville 217 .... K3
26224 Helvetia 130 .... F5
24842 Hemphill 700 .... C8
25106 Henderson 604 .... B5
26271 Hendricks 390 .... G4
25624 Henlawson 900 .... B7
26369 Hepzibah 600 .... F4
24726 Herndon 500 .... D7
25854 Hico 750 .... D6
24946 Hillsboro 276 .... F6
25951 Hinton⊙ 4,622 .... E7
25625 Holden 2,036 .... B7
26372 Horner 125 .... F5
26769 Horse Shoe Run 500 .... G4
†25506 Hubball 145 .... B6
26575 Hundred 485 .... E3
*25701 Huntington⊙ 63,684 .... A6
Huntington-Ashland‡ 311,350 .... A6
25526 Hurricane 3,751 .... C6
26273 Huttonsville 242 .... G5
24844 Iaeger 833 .... C8
26374 Independence 200 .... G4
24949 Indian Mills 150 .... E7
25111 Indore 300 .... D6
25112 Institute C6
25428 Inwood 1,159 .... K4
24847 Itmann 600 .... D7
25113 Ivydale 800 .... D5
26377 Jacksonburg 400 .... E3
26378 Jane Lew 406 .... F4
25114 Jeffrey 900 .... C7
24848 Jenkinjones 750 .... D8
24849 Jesse 400 .... C7
26674 Jodie 440 .... D6
25969 Jumping Branch 700 .... E7
26824 Junction 75 .... J4

(continued on following page)

Agriculture, Industry and Resources

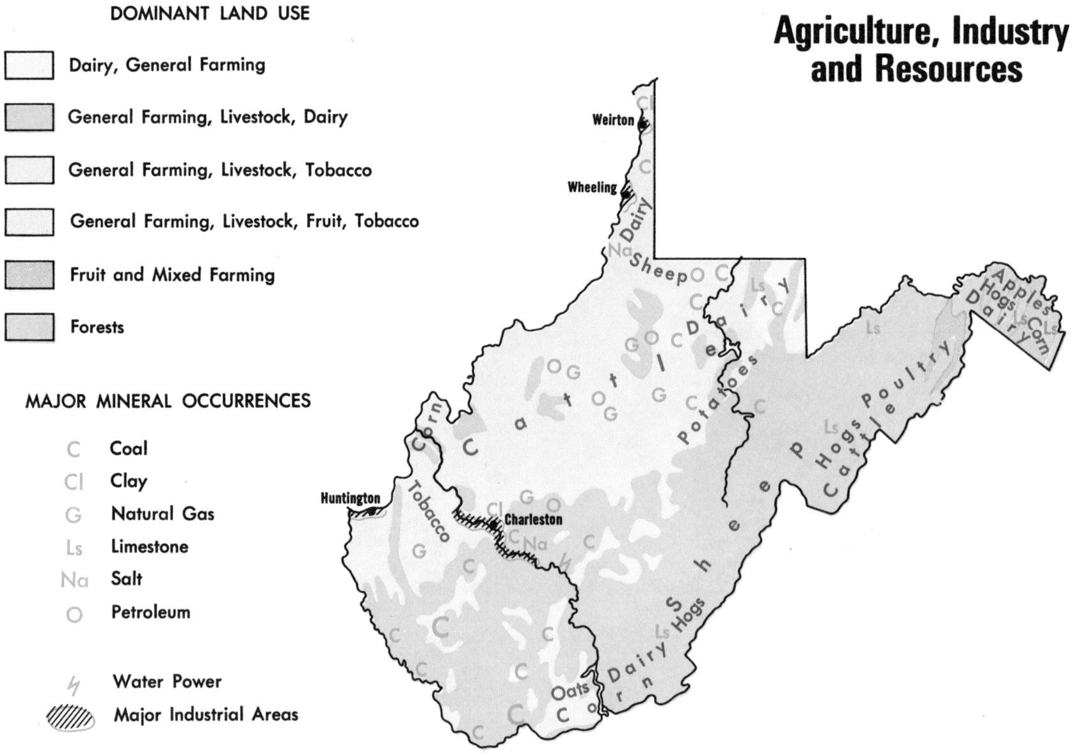

DOMINANT LAND USE
Dairy, General Farming
General Farming, Livestock, Dairy
General Farming, Livestock, Tobacco
General Farming, Livestock, Fruit, Tobacco
Fruit and Mixed Farming
Forests
MAJOR MINERAL OCCURRENCES
C Coal
Cl Clay
G Natural Gas
Ls Limestone
Na Salt
O Petroleum
Water Power
Major Industrial Areas
Weirton
Wheeling
Huntington
Charleston
Dairy
Sheep
Cattle
Potatoes
Corn
Tobacco
Hogs
Poultry
Apples
Oats

26275 Junior 591 .... G5
24851 Justice 600 .... C7
25115 Kanawha Falls 105 .... D6
25430 Kearneysville 250 .... L4
24731 Kegley 900 .... D8
24732 Kellysville 165 .... E8
25248 Kenna 150 .... C5
25530 Kenova 4,454 .... A6
25249 Kentuck 200 .... C5
25674 Kermit 705 .... B7
26726 Keyser⊙ 6,569 .... J4
24852 Keystone 902 .... D8
24950 Kieffer 135 .... E7
25859 Kilsyth 200 .... D7
24853 Kimball 871 .... C8
25120 Kingston 189 .... D7
26537 Kingwood⊙ 2,877 .... G4
26729 Kirby 110 .... J4
25628 Kistler 200 .... C7
26579 Knob Fork 106 .... E3
24854 Kopperston 700 .... C7
26731 Lahmansville 200 .... H4
25860 Lanark 559 .... D7
25629 Landville 400 .... C7
25535 Lavalette 600 .... B6
25863 Lawton 100 .... E7
25864 Layland 500 .... E7
†26430 Layopolis (Sand Fork) 280 .... E5
25251 Left Hand 700 .... D5
26676 Leivasy 200 .... E6
25676 Lenore 800 .... B7
25123 Leon 228 .... C5
25971 Lerona 550 .... D8
25537 Lesage 600 .... B5
25972 Leslie 350 .... E6
25865 Lester 626 .... D7
25253 Letart 350 .... C5
25431 Levels 180 .... J4
24901 Lewisburg⊙ 3,065 .... E7
26384 Linn 165 .... E4
26629 Little Birch 400 .... E5
26581 Littleton 335 .... F3
25125 Lizemores 400 .... D6
25866 Lochgelly 250 .... D6
25258 Lockney 190 .... E5
25601 Logan⊙ 3,029 .... B7
25630 Lorado 400 .... C7
†26201 Lorentz 200 .... F4
26810 Lost City 130 .... J5
26385 Lost Creek 604 .... F4
26811 Lost River 500 .... J5
†26101 Lubeck 1,356 .... C4
26386 Lumberport 939 .... F4
25631 Lundale 525 .... C7
25870 Maben 450 .... D7
26278 Mabie 550 .... F5
25871 Mabscott 1,668 .... D7
26148 Macfarlan 436 .... D4
25130 Madison⊙ 3,228 .... C6
26541 Maidsville 500 .... F3
25306 Malden 900 .... C6
25634 Mallory 1,330 .... C7
25132 Mammoth 563 .... D6
25635 Man 1,333 .... C7
26582 Mannington 3,036 .... F3
25975 Marfrance 225 .... E6
24954 Marlinton⊙ 1,352 .... F6
25315 Marmet 2,196 .... C6
25401 Martinsburg⊙ 13,063 .... K4
25260 Mason 1,432 .... B4
26542 Masontown 1,052 .... G3
25678 Matewan 822 .... B7
24736 Matoaka 613 .... D8
24861 Maybeury 300 .... D8
26833 Maysville 150 .... H4
24858 McDowell 500 .... D8
26040 McMechen 2,402 .... E3
26401 McWhorter 150 .... F4
24958 Meadow Bluff 250 .... E7
25976 Meadow Bridge 530 .... E7
26404 Meadowbrook 500 .... F4
25977 Meadow Creek 300 .... E7
26585 Metz 150 .... F3
26149 Middlebourne⊙ 941 .... E3
25540 Midkiff 650 .... B6
26280 Mill Creek 801 .... G5
24959 Mill Point 148 .... F6
25261 Millstone 850 .... D5
25262 Millwood 800 .... C5
25541 Milton 2,178 .... B6
25879 Minden 800 .... D7
26150 Mineralwells 325 .... C4
26281 Mingo 350 .... F5
25263 Minnora 500 .... D5
26405 Moatsville 150 .... G4
25636 Monaville 950 .... B7
26554 Monongah 1,132 .... F4
26586 Montana Mines 200 .... F3
25135 Montcoal 150 .... D7
26282 Monterville 250 .... F5
25136 Montgomery 3,104 .... D6
26283 Montrose 129 .... G4
26836 Moorefield⊙ 2,257 .... J4
26505 Morgantown⊙ 27,605 .... G3
25542 Morrisvale 450 .... C6
26041 Moundsville⊙ 12,419 .... E3
26407 Mountain 200 .... E4
25264 Mount Alto 200 .... C5
25139 Mount Carbon 450 .... D7
26408 Mount Clare 950 .... F4
25637 Mount Gay 4,366 .... C7
25880 Mount Hope 1,849 .... D7
26678 Mount Lookout 500 .... E6
26679 Mount Nebo 535 .... E6
26739 Mount Storm 500 .... H4
25882 Mullens 2,919 .... D7
26680 Nallen 250 .... E6
26631 Napier 158 .... E5
25685 Naugatuck 500 .... B7
25141 Nebo 200 .... D5
25142 Nellis 600 .... C6
24961 Neola 300 .... F7
26681 Nettie 500 .... E6
26410 Newburg 418 .... G4
26047 New Cumberland⊙ 1,752 .... E2
26050 Newell 2,032 .... E1
26154 New England 335 .... C4
24866 Newhall 400 .... C8
25265 New Haven 1,723 .... C5
26056 New Manchester 800 .... E1
26155 New Martinsville⊙ 7,109 .... E3
25266 Newton 390 .... D5
26632 Newville 160 .... E5
25143 Nitro 8,074 .... C6
25687 Nolan 250 .... B7
25267 Normantown 112 .... E5
24868 Northfork 1,105 .... D8
†26101 North Hills 940 .... D4
26285 Norton 400 .... G5
26301 Nutter Fort 2,078 .... F4
25901 Oak Hill 7,120 .... D6
24739 Oakvale 208 .... D8
24870 Oceana 2,143 .... C7
25902 Odd 500 .... D7
25147 Ohley 450 .... D6
25638 Omar 900 .... C7
26886 Onego 400 .... H5
25148 Orgas 500 .... C6
26412 Orlando 700 .... E5
25268 Orma D5
26543 Osage 285 .... F3
25151 Packsville 225 .... C7
26159 Paden City 3,671 .... D3
25152 Page 600 .... D6
26160 Palestine 110 .... D4
24872 Panther 450 .... C8
26101 Parkersburg⊙ 39,967 .... D4
Parkersburg-Marietta‡ 162,836 .... D4
26287 Parsons⊙ 1,937 .... G4
26746 Patterson Creek 157 .... J3
25434 Paw Paw 644 .... K3
25904 Pax 274 .... D7
†25955 Pear 100 .... E7
25547 Pecks Mill 350 .... B7
25905 Pemberton 300 .... D7
24962 Pence Springs 300 .... E7
26415 Pennsboro 1,652 .... E4
26544 Pentress 250 .... F3
26847 Petersburg⊙ 2,084 .... H5
24963 Peterstown 648 .... E8
25154 Peytona 175 .... C6
26416 Philippi⊙ 3,194 .... G4
24964 Pickaway 225 .... E7
26230 Pickens 240 .... F5
25689 Pie 250 .... B7
26750 Piedmont 1,491 .... H4
25156 Pinch 800 .... D6
26419 Pine Grove 767 .... E3
24874 Pineville⊙ 1,140 .... C7
25158 Pliny 900 .... B5
25159 Poca 1,142 .... C6
†25301 Pocotalico 2,420 .... C6
25550 Point Pleasant⊙ 5,682 .... B5
25437 Points 250 .... J4
25161 Powellton 1,339 .... D6
24877 Powhatan 400 .... D8
25162 Pratt 821 .... D6
24878 Premier 400 .... C8
†25880 Price Hill 175 .... D7
25555 Prichard 500 .... A6
24740 Princeton⊙ 7,493 .... D8
25164 Procious 600 .... D5
26055 Proctor 350 .... E3
26421 Pullman 196 .... D4
26852 Purgitsville 450 .... J4
25045 Quick 400 .... D6
†25015 Quincy 150 .... C6
25981 Quinwood 460 .... E6
26587 Rachel 550 .... F3
25165 Racine 725 .... C6
25556 Radnor 300 .... A6
25962 Rainelle 1,983 .... E7
25911 Raleigh 900 .... D7
25166 Ramage 350 .... C7
25557 Ranger 300 .... B6
25438 Ranson 2,471 .... L4
25913 Ravencliff 350 .... C7
26164 Ravenswood 4,126 .... C5
26167 Reader 950 .... E3
26289 Red Creek 125 .... H4
25168 Red House 600 .... C5
25692 Red Jacket 850 .... B7
26547 Reedsville 564 .... G3
25270 Reedy 338 .... D5
24966 Renick 240 .... F6
25915 Rhodell 472 .... D7
26261 Richwood 3,568 .... F6
26753 Ridgeley 994 .... J3
25440 Ridgeway 200 .... K4
26755 Rio 140 .... J4
25271 Ripley⊙ 3,464 .... C5
25441 Rippon 500 .... L4
26588 Rivesville 1,327 .... F3
26234 Rock Cave 400 .... F5
24881 Roderfield 900 .... C8
26757 Romney⊙ 2,094 .... J4
24970 Ronceverte 2,312 .... F7
26636 Rosedale 400 .... E5
25643 Rossmore 200 .... C7
26425 Rowlesburg 966 .... G4
26688 Runa 150 .... E6
25984 Rupert 1,276 .... E7
26689 Russellville 280 .... E6
25177 Saint Albans 12,402 .... C6
26290 Saint George 150 .... G4
26170 Saint Marys⊙ 2,219 .... D4
26426 Salem 2,706 .... E4
25559 Salt Rock 350 .... B6
26430 Sand Fork 280 .... E5
25985 Sandstone 300 .... E7
25275 Sandyville 500 .... C5
25876 Saulsville 250 .... C7
25917 Scarbro 800 .... D7
24975 Seebert 100 .... F6
25181 Seth 950 .... C6
26761 Shanks 500 .... J4
25182 Sharon 450 .... D6
25183 Sharples 250 .... C7
25443 Shepherdstown 1,791 .... L4
26173 Sherman 104 .... C5
26431 Shinnston 3,059 .... F4
26434 Shirley 275 .... E4
25562 Shoals 150 .... B6
26638 Shock 200 .... D5
†26164 Silverton 250 .... C5
26435 Simpson 250 .... F4
24976 Sinks Grove 156 .... F7
25320 Sissonville 450 .... C5
26175 Sistersville 2,367 .... D3
25920 Slab Fork 210 .... D7
25444 Slanesville 250 .... K4
26436 Smithburg 130 .... E4
25186 Smithers 1,482 .... D6
26437 Smithfield 278 .... E4
26178 Smithville 200 .... D4
24977 Smoot 300 .... E7
25921 Sophia 1,216 .... D7
25303 South Charleston 15,968 .... C6
25922 Spanishburg 550 .... D8
25276 Spencer⊙ 2,799 .... D5
25693 Sprigg 225 .... B7
26763 Springfield 250 .... J4
25565 Spurlockville 250 .... B6
24884 Squire 900 .... C8
26505 Star City 1,464 .... F3
25279 Statts Mills 400 .... C5
25188 Stickney 150 .... D7
25645 Stirrat 250 .... C7
26301 Stonewood 2,058 .... F4
24979 Stony Bottom 50 .... F6
25280 Stumptown 125 .... E5
26651 Summersville⊙ 2,972 .... E6
25446 Summit Point 455 .... K4
25932 Surveyor 300 .... D7
26601 Sutton⊙ 1,192 .... E5
26690 Swiss 500 .... D6
25647 Switzer 1,034 .... B7
25193 Sylvester 256 .... C6
24981 Talcott 800 .... E7
26237 Tallmansville 140 .... F5
26179 Tanner 375 .... E5
26764 Terra Alta 1,946 .... H4
26640 Tesla 300 .... E5
25694 Thacker 525 .... B7
26292 Thomas 747 .... H4
26440 Thornton 200 .... G4
24888 Thorpe 600 .... D8
26765 Three Churches 350 .... J4
25936 Thurmond 67 .... D7
26691 Tioga 825 .... E6
26059 Triadelphia 1,461 .... E2
26443 Troy 110 .... E4
26444 Tunnelton 510 .... G4
25203 Turtle Creek 566 .... C6
25205 Uneeda 700 .... C6
25447 Unger 300 .... K4
24983 Union⊙ 743 .... E7
26266 Upperglade 750 .... F6
26866 Upper Tract 155 .... H5
26445 Vadis 130 .... E4
26293 Valley Bend 950 .... F5
26060 Valley Grove 597 .... E2
26294 Valley Head 900 .... G5
25206 Van 800 .... C7
25696 Varney 750 .... B7
25649 Verdunville 950 .... B7
25938 Victor 500 .... D6
26105 Vienna 11,618 .... D4
24891 Vivian 500 .... D8
26238 Volga 125 .... F4
25697 Vulcan 130 .... B7
26589 Wadestown 300 .... F3
24984 Waiteville 230 .... F8
26180 Walker 100 .... D4
26448 Wallace 325 .... E4
25286 Walton 550 .... D5
26590 Wana 150 .... F3
24892 War 2,158 .... C8
26851 Wardensville 241 .... J4
26181 Washington 450 .... C4
26184 Waverly 500 .... D4
25570 Wayne⊙ 1,495 .... B6
26288 Webster Springs⊙ 939 .... F6
26062 Weirton 25,371 .... E2
Weirton-Steubenville‡ 163,099 .... E2
24801 Welch⊙ 3,885 .... C8
26070 Wellsburg⊙ 3,963 .... E2
25287 West Columbia 245 .... B5
25571 West Hamlin 643 .... B6
26074 West Liberty 744 .... E2
25601 West Logan 630 .... C7
26451 West Milford 510 .... F4
26452 Weston⊙ 6,250 .... F4
26505 Westover 4,884 .... G3
26456 West Union⊙ 1,090 .... E4
25651 Wharncliffe 900 .... C7
25208 Wharton 450 .... C7
26003 Wheeling⊙ 43,070 .... E2
Wheeling‡ 185,566 .... E2
24986 White Sulphur Springs 3,371 .... F7
25209 Whitesville 689 .... C6
26296 Whitmer 400 .... G5
25211 Widen 230 .... E6
26767 Wiley Ford 1,224 .... J3
26186 Wileyville 175 .... E3
25653 Wilkinson 975 .... B7
24991 Williamsburg 350 .... F7
25661 Williamson⊙ 5,219 .... B7
26187 Williamstown 3,095 .... C4
26461 Wilsonburg 350 .... F4
25699 Wilsondale 250 .... B7
26075 Windsor Heights 800 .... E2
25213 Winfield⊙ 329 .... C5
25214 Winifrede 750 .... C6
25942 Winona 250 .... E6
26462 Wolf Summit 750 .... F4
†26257 Womelsdorf (Coalton) 306 .... G5
25572 Woodville 300 .... C6
26591 Worthington 329 .... F4
25573 Yawkey 985 .... C6
26865 Yellow Spring 280 .... J4
25654 Yolyn 400 .... C7

OTHER FEATURES

Big Sandy (riv.) A6
Bluestone (lake) E7
Buckhannon (riv.) F5
Cacapon (riv.) J4
Cheat (riv.) G3
Cherry (riv.) E6
Chesapeake and Ohio Canal Nat'l Hist. Pa J3
Clear Fork, Guyandotte (riv.) C7
Coal (riv.) C6
Dry Fork (riv.) C8
Dry Fork (riv.) G5
East Lynn (lake) B6
Elk (riv.) D6
Fish (creek) E3
Gauley (riv.) D6
Greenbrier (riv.) F6
Guyandotte (riv.) B6
Harpers Ferry Nat'l Hist. Park L4
Hughes (riv.) D4
Kanawha (riv.) C5
Little Kanawha (riv.) D5
Meadow (riv.) E6
Mill (creek) C5
Monongahela (riv.) G3
Mount Storm (lake) H4
Mud (riv.) B6
New (riv.) E7
North (riv.) J4
Ohio (riv.) B5
Patterson (creek) J4
Pigeon (creek) B7
Pocatalico (riv.) C5
Pond Fork (riv.) C6
Potomac (riv.) L3
Potts (creek) F7
Reedy (creek) D5
Shavers Fork (riv.) G5
Shenandoah (riv.) K4
Spruce Knob (mt.) G5
Spruce Knob-Seneca Rocks Nat'l Rec. Area H5
Stony (riv.) H4
Summersville (lake) E6
Sutton (lake) F5
Tug Fork (riv.) B7
Twelvepole (creek) A6
Tygart (lake) G4
Tygart Valley (riv.) F5
West Fork (riv.) E5
Williams (riv.) F6

⊙County seat.
‡Population of metropolitan area.
† Zip of nearest p.o. * Multiple zips.

AREA 56,153 sq. mi. (145,436 sq. km.)
POPULATION 4,705,521
CAPITAL Madison
LARGEST CITY Milwaukee
HIGHEST POINT Timms Hill 1,951 ft. (595 m.)
SETTLED IN 1670
ADMITTED TO UNION May 29, 1848
POPULAR NAME Badger State
STATE FLOWER Wood Violet
STATE BIRD Robin

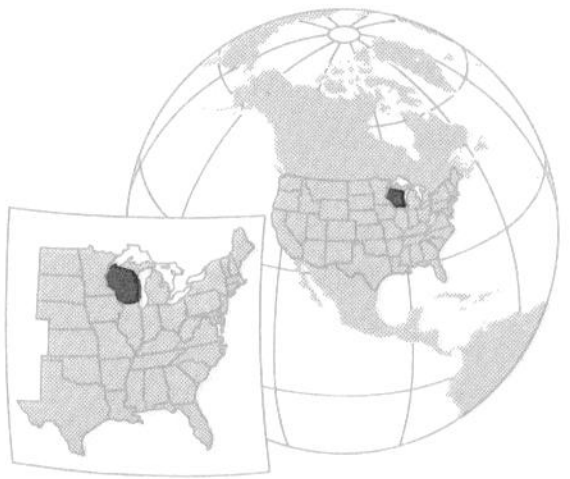

COUNTIES

County	Key
Adams 13,457	G7
Ashland 16,783	E3
Barron 38,730	C5
Bayfield 13,822	D3
Brown 175,280	L7
Buffalo 14,309	C7
Burnett 12,340	B4
Calumet 30,867	K7
Chippewa 52,127	D5
Clark 32,910	E6
Columbia 43,222	H9
Crawford 16,556	E9
Dane 323,545	H9
Dodge 75,064	J9
Door 25,029	M6
Douglas 44,421	C3
Dunn 34,314	C6
Eau Claire 78,805	D6
Florence 4,172	K4
Fond du Lac 88,964	K8
Forest 9,044	J4
Grant 51,736	E10
Green 30,012	G10
Green Lake 18,370	H8
Iowa 19,802	F9
Iron 6,730	F3
Jackson 16,831	E7
Jefferson 66,152	J9
Juneau 21,039	F8
Kenosha 123,137	K10
Kewaunee 19,539	L6
La Crosse 91,056	D8
Lafayette 17,412	F10
Langlade 19,978	H5
Lincoln 26,555	G5
Manitowoc 82,918	L7
Marathon 111,270	G6
Marinette 39,314	K5
Marquette 11,672	H8
Menominee 3,373	J5
Milwaukee 964,988	L9
Monroe 35,074	E8
Oconto 28,947	K6
Oneida 31,216	G4
Outagamie 128,799	K7
Ozaukee 66,981	L9
Pepin 7,477	C6
Pierce 31,149	B6
Polk 32,351	B5
Portage 57,420	G6
Price 15,788	F4
Racine 173,132	K10
Richland 17,476	F9
Rock 139,420	H10
Rusk 15,589	D5
Saint Croix 43,262	B5
Sauk 43,469	G9
Sawyer 12,843	D4
Shawano 35,928	J6
Sheboygan 100,935	L8
Taylor 18,817	E5
Trempealeau 26,158	D7
Vernon 25,642	E8
Vilas 16,535	G3
Walworth 71,507	J10
Washburn 13,174	C4
Washington 84,848	K9
Waukesha 280,080	K9
Waupaca 42,831	J6
Waushara 18,526	H7
Winnebago 131,722	J8
Wood 72,799	F7

CITIES and TOWNS

Zip	Name/Pop.	Key
54405	Abbotsford 1,901	F6
53910	Adams 1,744	G8
53001	Adell 545	L8
53501	Afton 225	H10
53502	Albany 1,051	G10
†53534	Albion 300	H10
54201	Algoma 3,656	M6
53002	Allenton 915	K9
†54301	Allouez 14,882	L7
54610	Alma⊙ 876	C7
54611	Alma Center 454	E7
54805	Almena 526	B5
54909	Almond 477	G7
54720	Altoona 4,393	C6
54102	Amberg 875	K5
54001	Amery 2,404	B5
54406	Amherst 701	H7
54407	Amherst Junction 225	H7
54408	Aniwa 273	H6
54409	Antigo⊙ 8,653	H5
54911	Appleton⊙ 58,913	J7
	Appleton-Oshkosh‡ 291,325	J7
†54568	Arbor Vitae 900	G4
54612	Arcadia 2,109	D7
53503	Arena 451	G9
54511	Argonne 600	J4
53504	Argyle 720	G10
54721	Arkansaw 400	B6
53911	Arlington 440	H9
54103	Armstrong Creek 615	K4
54410	Arpin 361	G6
53003	Ashippun 750	H1
54806	Ashland⊙ 9,115	E2
54304	Ashwaubenon 14,486	K7
54411	Athens 988	G5
54412	Auburndale 641	F6
54722	Augusta 1,560	D6
53506	Avoca 505	F9
†53520	Avon 120	H10
54413	Babcock 250	F7
53801	Bagley 317	D10
54202	Baileys Harbor 250	M5
54002	Baldwin 1,620	B6
54810	Balsam Lake⊙ 749	B5
54921	Bancroft 355	G7
54614	Bangor 1,012	E8
53913	Baraboo⊙ 8,081	G9
†54873	Barnes 225	D3
53507	Barneveld 579	F10
54812	Barron⊙ 2,595	C5
†53001	Batavia 125	K8
54723	Bay City 543	B6
54814	Bayfield 778	E2
†53201	Bayside 4,724	M1
54922	Bear Creek 454	J6
53916	Beaver Dam 14,149	J9
53802	Beetown 150	E10
53004	Belgium 892	L8
†54631	Bell Center 124	E9
53508	Belleville 1,302	G10
53510	Belmont 826	F10
53511	Beloit 35,207	H10
53803	Benton 983	F10
54923	Berlin 5,478	H8
†54410	Bethel 210	F6
†54440	Bevent 200	H6
53103	Big Bend 1,345	K2
54926	Big Falls 107	H6
54817	Birchwood 437	C4
54414	Birnamwood 688	H6
†54494	Biron 698	G7
54106	Black Creek 1,097	K7
53515	Black Earth 1,145	G9
54615	Black River Falls⊙ 3,434	E7
†54541	Blackwell 550	J4
54616	Blair 1,142	D7
53516	Blanchardville 803	G10
54617	Bloom City 167	E8
54724	Bloomer 3,342	D5
53804	Bloomington 743	E10
53517	Blue Mounds 387	G9
53518	Blue River 412	E9
†53581	Boaz 161	E9
†53105	Bohners Lake 1,507	K10
54107	Bonduel 1,160	K6
53805	Boscobel 2,662	E9
54512	Boulder Junction 780	G3
54416	Bowler 339	J6
54725	Boyceville 862	C5
54726	Boyd 660	E6
54203	Branch 300	L7
53919	Brandon 862	J8
54513	Brantwood 500	F4
53920	Briggsville 250	H8
54110	Brillion 2,907	L7
53520	Brodhead 3,153	G10
54417	Brokaw 298	G5
53005	Brookfield 34,035	K1
53521	Brooklyn 627	H10
53209	Brown Deer 12,921	L1
†53105	Brown's Lake 1,648	K3
53006	Brownsville 433	J8
53522	Browntown 284	G10
54819	Bruce 905	D5
54820	Brule 335	C2
54204	Brussels 500	L6
†54622	Buffalo 894	C7
53105	Burlington 8,385	K10
53922	Burnett 260	J9
53007	Butler 2,059	K1
54514	Butternut 438	E3
53009	Byron 40	K8
54821	Cable 227	D3
54727	Cadott 1,247	D6
53923	Cambria 680	H8
53523	Cambridge 844	H9
54822	Cameron 1,115	C5
†53019	Campbellsport 1,740	K8
54618	Camp Douglas 589	F8
53109	Camp Lake 2,060	K10
54823	Canton 100	C5
54928	Caroline 450	J6
53011	Cascade 615	K8
54205	Casco 484	L6
54619	Cashton 827	E8
53806	Cassville 1,270	E10
54620	Cataract 200	E7
54515	Catawba 205	E4
54206	Cato 85	L7
53924	Cazenovia 259	F8
54111	Cecil 445	K6
53012	Cedarburg 9,005	L9
53013	Cedar Grove 1,420	L8
54824	Centuria 711	A5
54621	Chaseburg 279	D8
54419	Chelsea 120	F5
†53029	Chenequa 532	J1
54728	Chetek 1,931	C5
54420	Chili 185	F6
53014	Chilton⊙ 2,965	K7
54729	Chippewa Falls⊙ 12,270	D6
54004	Clayton 425	B5
54005	Clear Lake 899	B5
53015	Cleveland 1,270	L8
53525	Clinton 1,751	J10
54929	Clintonville 4,567	J6
53016	Clyman 317	J9
53526	Cobb 409	F10
54622	Cochrane 512	C7
54421	Colby 1,496	F6
54112	Coleman 852	L5
54730	Colfax 1,149	C6
54930	Coloma 367	H7
53925	Columbus 4,049	H9
54113	Combined Locks 2,573	K7
†53147	Como 1,376	K10
54519	Conover 480	H3
54731	Conrath 86	E5
54623	Coon Valley 758	E8
54732	Cornell 1,583	D5
54827	Cornucopia 250	D2
54520	Crandon⊙ 1,969	H4
54114	Crivitz 1,041	L5
53528	Cross Plains 2,156	G9
53807	Cuba City 2,129	F10
53110	Cudahy 19,547	M2
54829	Cumberland 1,983	C4
54422	Curtiss 127	F6
54006	Cushing 150	A4
54931	Dale 410	J7
54733	Dallas 477	C5
53926	Dalton 300	H8
53529	Dane 518	G9
53114	Darien 1,152	J10
53530	Darlington⊙ 2,300	F10
53531	Deerfield 1,466	H9
54007	Deer Park 232	B5
53532	De Forest 3,367	H9
53018	Delafield 4,083	J1
53115	Delavan 5,684	J10
†53115	Delavan Lake 2,082	J10
†54856	Delta 35	D3
54208	Denmark 1,475	L7
54115	De Pere 14,892	K7
†54663	De Soto 318	D9
†54014	Diamond Bluff 100	A6
53808	Dickeyville 1,156	E10
54625	Dodge 185	D7
53533	Dodgeville⊙ 3,458	F10
54425	Dorchester 613	F5
53118	Dousman 1,153	J1
54734	Downing 242	B5
54735	Downsville 200	C6
53928	Doylestown 294	H9
54009	Dresser 670	A5
54832	Drummond 200	D3
54736	Durand⊙ 2,047	C6
53119	Eagle 1,008	H2
54521	Eagle River⊙ 1,326	H4
54626	Eastman 371	D9
53120	East Troy 2,385	J2
54701	Eau Claire⊙ 51,509	D6
	Eau Claire‡ 130,507	D6
53019	Eden 534	K8
54426	Edgar 1,194	G6
53534	Edgerton 4,335	H10
54209	Egg Harbor 238	M5
54427	Eland 230	H6
54428	Elcho 500	H5
54429	Elderon 191	H6
54932	Eldorado 200	J8
54738	Eleva 593	D6
53020	Elkhart Lake 1,054	L8
53121	Elkhorn⊙ 4,605	J10
54739	Elk Mound 737	C6
54210	Ellison Bay 112	M5
54011	Ellsworth⊙ 2,143	A6
53122	Elm Grove 6,735	K1
54740	Elmwood 885	B6
†53401	Elmwood Park 483	M3
53929	Elroy 1,504	F8
54430	Elton 150	J5
54933	Embarrass 496	J6
53930	Endeavor 335	G8
54211	Ephraim 319	M5
54627	Ettrick 462	D7
53536	Evansville 2,835	H10
54835	Exeland 219	D4
54741	Fairchild 577	D6
53931	Fair Water 310	J8
54742	Fall Creek 1,148	D6
53932	Fall River 850	H9
†54840	Falun 95	A4
54120	Fence 200	K4
53809	Fennimore 2,212	E9
54431	Fenwood 165	F6
54628	Ferryville 227	D9
54524	Fifield 310	F4
54212	Fish Creek 119	M5
54121	Florence⊙ 780	K4
54935	Fond du Lac⊙ 35,863	K8
53125	Fontana 1,764	J10
53537	Footville 794	H10
54123	Forest Junction 140	K7
54213	Forestville 455	L6
53538	Fort Atkinson 9,785	J10
54629	Fountain City 963	C7
54836	Foxboro 360	B2
53933	Fox Lake 1,373	J8
†53117	Fox Point 7,649	M1
54214	Francis Creek 589	L7
53132	Franklin 16,871	L2
54837	Frederic 1,039	B4
53021	Fredonia 1,437	L8
54940	Fremont 510	J7
53934	Friendship⊙ 744	G8
53935	Friesland 267	H8
54630	Galesville 1,239	D7
54631	Gays Mills 627	E9
53127	Genesee Depot 350	J2
54632	Genoa 283	D8
53128	Genoa City 1,202	K11
53022	Germantown 10,729	K1
54124	Gillett 1,356	K6
54433	Gilman 436	E5
54743	Gilmanton 300	C7
54435	Gleason 200	G5
53023	Glenbeulah 423	L8
†53209	Glendale 13,882	M1
54526	Glen Flora 83	E4
53810	Glen Haven 160	E10
54013	Glenwood City 950	B5
54527	Glidden 940	E3
54125	Goodman 875	K4
54838	Gordon 600	C3
53540	Gotham 250	F9
53024	Grafton 8,381	L9
53936	Grand Marsh 725	G8
54839	Grand View 447	D3
54436	Granton 399	E6
54840	Grantsburg⊙ 1,153	A4
53541	Gratiot 280	F10
*54301	Green Bay⊙ 87,899	K6
	Green Bay‡ 175,280	K6
53129	Greendale 16,928	L2
53220	Greenfield 31,467	L2
54941	Green Lake⊙ 1,208	H8
54126	Greenleaf 300	L7
54942	Greenville 900	J7
54437	Greenwood 1,124	E6
54128	Gresham 534	J6
54014	Hager City 110	A6
53130	Hales Corners 7,110	K2
54015	Hammond 991	A6
54943	Hancock 419	G7
54529	Harshaw 87	G4
53027	Hartford 7,046	K9
53029	Hartland 5,559	J1
54440	Hatley 300	H6
54841	Haugen 251	C4
54530	Hawkins 407	E4
54842	Hawthorne 200	C3
54843	Hayward⊙ 1,698	D3
53811	Hazel Green 1,282	F11
54531	Hazelhurst 630	G4
†53538	Hebron 450	J10
53137	Helenville 300	J10
54844	Herbster 100	D2
54441	Hewitt 470	F6
53543	Highland 860	F9
54129	Hilbert 1,176	K7
†54511	Hiles 350	J4

(continued on following page)

Agriculture, Industry and Resources

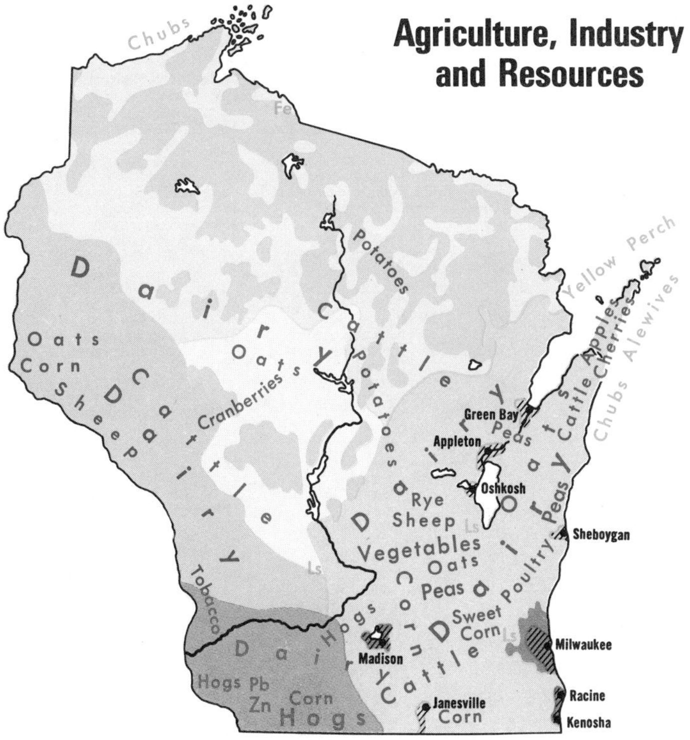

DOMINANT LAND USE

- Specialized Dairy
- Dairy, Hay, Potatoes
- Dairy, General Farming
- Hogs, Dairy
- Dairy, Livestock
- Forests
- Urban Areas

MAJOR MINERAL OCCURRENCES

- Fe Iron Ore
- Pb Lead
- Ls Limestone
- Zn Zinc

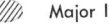

Major Industrial Areas

54634 Hillsboro 1,263 F8
53031 Hingham 250 K8
54635 Hixton 364 E7
54745 Holcombe 200 D5
53544 Hollandale 271 G10
54636 Holmen 2,411 D8
53138 Honey Creek 300 J3
53032 Horicon 3,584 J9
54944 Hortonville 2,016 J7
†55082 Houlton 915 A5
54303 Howard 8,240 K6
53081 Howards Grove-Millersville 1,838 L8
53033 Hubertus 600 K1
54016 Hudson⊙ 5,434 A6
54746 Humbird 190 E6
54534 Hurley⊙ 2,015 F3
53034 Hustisford 874 J9
54637 Hustler 170 F8
54747 Independence 1,180 D7
54945 Iola 957 H6
54536 Iron Belt 300 F3
53035 Iron Ridge 766 K9
54847 Iron River 878 D2
†53941 Ironton 206 F8
53036 Ixonia 525 H1
53037 Jackson 1,817 K9
†54235 Jacksonport 150 M6
53545 Janesville⊙ 51,071 H10
Janesville-Beloit‡ 139,420 H10
53549 Jefferson⊙ 5,647 J10
54748 Jim Falls 100 D5
53038 Johnson Creek 1,136 J9
53550 Juda 500 H10
54443 Junction City 523 G6
53039 Juneau⊙ 2,045 J9
53139 Kansasville 150 L3
54130 Kaukauna 11,310 K7
†53050 Kekoskee 224 J8
54215 Kellnersville 369 L7
54638 Kendall 486 F8
54537 Kennan 194 F5
*53140 Kenosha⊙ 77,685 M3
Kenosha‡ 123,137 M3
54135 Keshena⊙ 980 J6
53040 Kewaskum 2,381 K8
54216 Kewaunee⊙ 2,801 M7
53042 Kiel 3,083 L8
53812 Kieler 800 E10
54136 Kimberly 5,881 K7
53939 Kingston 328 H8
54749 Knapp 419 B6
†54455 Knowlton 127 G6
53044 Kohler 1,651 L8
53147 Krakow 345 K6
54538 Lac du Flambeau 500 G4
†53066 Lac La Belle 289 H1
54601 La Crosse⊙ 48,347 D8
La Crosse‡ 91,056 D8
54848 Ladysmith⊙ 3,826 D5
54639 La Farge 746 E8
53940 Lake Delton 1,158 G8
53147 Lake Geneva 5,612 K10
53551 Lake Mills 3,670 H9
54849 Lake Nebagamon 780 C3
54539 Lake Tomahawk 600 H4
†54494 Lake Wazeecha 2,176 G7
†54729 Lake Wissota 1,788 D6
54138 Lakewood 425 K5
53813 Lancaster⊙ 4,076 E10
54540 Land O'Lakes 786 H3
53046 Lannon 987 K1
53941 La Valle 412 F8
53047 Lebanon 250 H1
54139 Lena 585 K6
†54656 Leon 100 E8
54948 Leopolis 200 J6
54851 Lewis 200 B4
53942 Limeridge 191 F9
53553 Linden 395 F10
54140 Little Chute 7,907 K7
53554 Livingston 642 E10
53555 Lodi 1,959 G9
53943 Loganville 239 F9
†54970 Lohrville 336 H7
53048 Lomira 1,446 J8
53556 Lone Rock 577 F9
54542 Long Lake 150 J4
53557 Lowell 326 J9
54446 Loyal 1,252 E6
54447 Lublin 142 E5
54853 Luck 997 B4
54217 Luxemburg 1,040 L6
53944 Lyndon Station 375 F8
54640 Lynxville 174 D9
53148 Lyons 550 K10
*53701 Madison (cap.)⊙ 170,616 H9
Madison‡ 323,545 H9
54750 Maiden Rock 172 B6
54949 Manawa 1,205 J7
54220 Manitowoc⊙ 32,547 L7
54226 Maplewood 200 M6
54448 Marathon 1,552 G6
54855 Marengo 130 E3
54227 Maribel 363 L7
54143 Marinette⊙ 11,965 L5
54950 Marion 1,348 J6
53946 Markesan 1,446 J8
53947 Marquette 204 H8
53559 Marshall 2,363 H9
54449 Marshfield 18,290 F6
54856 Mason 102 D3
54450 Mattoon 382 J5
53948 Mauston⊙ 3,284 F8
53050 Mayville 4,333 K9
53560 Mazomanie 1,248 G9
53558 McFarland 3,783 H10
54543 McNaughton 450 H4
54451 Medford⊙ 4,035 F5
54546 Mellen 1,046 E3
54642 Melrose 507 E7
54619 Melvina 117 E8
54952 Menasha 14,728 J7
53051 Menomonee Falls 27,845 K1
54751 Menomonie⊙ 12,769 C6
53092 Mequon 16,193 L1
54452 Merrill⊙ 9,578 G5
54754 Merrillan 587 E7
53561 Merrimac 365 G9
53056 Merton 1,045 K1
53562 Middleton 11,848 G9
54857 Mikana 200 C4
54453 Milan 153 F6
†53038 Milford 35 J9
54454 Milladore 250 G6
54643 Millston 110 E7
54858 Milltown 732 B4
53563 Milton 4,092 J10
*53201 Milwaukee⊙ 636,236 M1
Milwaukee‡ 1,397,143 M1
54644 Mindoro 200 D7
53565 Mineral Point 2,259 F10
54548 Minocqua 950 G4
54859 Minong 557 C3
54228 Mishicot 1,503 L7
54755 Mondovi 2,545 C6
54549 Monico 250 H4
53716 Monona 8,809 H9
53566 Monroe⊙ 10,027 G10
53949 Montello⊙ 1,273 H8
53569 Montfort 616 E10
53570 Monticello 1,021 G10
54550 Montreal 887 F3
53571 Morrisonville 375 G9
54455 Mosinee 3,015 G6
54149 Mountain 250 K5
53057 Mount Calvary 585 K8
53816 Mount Hope 197 D10
53572 Mount Horeb 3,251 G10
54645 Mount Sterling 223 D9
†53572 Mount Vernon 138 G10
53149 Mukwonago 4,014 J2
53573 Muscoda 1,331 F9
53150 Muskego 15,277 K2
53058 Nashotah 513 J1
54646 Necedah 773 F7
54956 Neenah 22,432 J7
54456 Neillsville⊙ 2,780 E6
54457 Nekoosa 2,519 G7
54756 Nelson 389 C7
54458 Nelsonville 199 H7
54150 Neopit 1,065 J6
53059 Neosho 575 J9
54960 Neshkoro 386 H8
54551 Newald 375 J4
54757 New Auburn 466 D5
53151 New Berlin 30,529 K2
53060 Newburg 783 K9
†61075 New Diggings 65 F10
54229 New Franken 150 L6
53574 New Glarus 1,763 G10
53061 New Holstein 3,412 K8
53950 New Lisbon 1,390 F8
54961 New London 6,210 J7
54017 New Richmond 4,306 A5
54151 Niagara 2,079 K4
54152 Nichols 267 K6
†53401 North Bay 219 M3
†54935 North Fond du Lac 3,844 J8
53951 North Freedom 616 G9
†54016 North Hudson 2,218 A5
53064 North Lake 400 J1
53217 North Shore 14,930 M1
54648 Norwalk 517 E8
53154 Oak Creek 16,932 M2
54649 Oakdale 150 F8
53065 Oakfield 990 J8
53066 Oconomowoc 9,909 H1
†53066 Oconomowoc Lake 524 H1
54153 Oconto⊙ 4,505 L6
54154 Oconto Falls 2,500 K6
54962 Ogdensburg 214 J7
54459 Ogema 238 F5
53069 Okauchee 3,958 J1
†53555 Okee 250 H9
†54880 Oliver 253 B2
54963 Omro 2,763 J7
54650 Onalaska 9,249 D8
54155 Oneida 900 K7
54651 Ontario 398 E8
53070 Oostburg 1,647 L8
53575 Oregon 3,876 H10
53576 Orfordville 1,143 H10
54020 Osceola 1,581 A5
54901 Oshkosh⊙ 49,620 J8
54758 Osseo 1,474 D6
54460 Owen 998 F6
53952 Oxford 432 H8
53953 Packwaukee 271 G8
†53168 Paddock Lake 2,207 K10
53156 Palmyra 1,515 H2
53954 Pardeeville 1,594 H8
54552 Park Falls 3,192 F4
†54481 Park Ridge 643 H6
53817 Patch Grove 259 D10
53157 Pell Lake 1,826 K10
54553 Pence 234 F3
54759 Pepin 890 B7
54157 Peshtigo 2,807 L5
53072 Pewaukee 4,637 K1
54554 Phelps 950 H3
54555 Phillips⊙ 1,522 E4
54464 Phlox 150 J5
54465 Pickerel 107 J5
54760 Pigeon Falls 338 D7
54466 Pittsville 810 F7
53577 Plain 676 F9
54966 Plainfield 813 G7
†53017 Plat 120 K1
53818 Platteville 9,580 F10
53158 Pleasant Prairie 950 L10
54467 Plover 5,310 G7
54761 Plum City 505 B6
53073 Plymouth 6,027 L8
†54423 Polonia 200 H6
54864 Poplar 569 C2
53901 Portage⊙ 7,896 G8
54469 Port Edwards 2,077 G7
53074 Port Washington⊙ 8,612 L9
54865 Port Wing 290 D2
53820 Potosi 736 E10
54160 Potter 330 K7
54161 Pound 407 L5
53955 Poynette 1,447 G9
54967 Poy Sippi 425 J7
53821 Prairie du Chien⊙ 5,859 D9
53578 Prairie du Sac 2,145 G9
54762 Prairie Farm 387 C5
54556 Prentice 605 F4
54021 Prescott 2,654 A6
54968 Princeton 1,479 H8
54162 Pulaski 1,875 K6
54164 Pulcifer 35 K6
*53401 Racine⊙ 85,725 M3
Racine‡ 173,132 M3
54867 Radisson 280 D4
53956 Randolph 1,691 H8
53075 Random Lake 1,287 K8
†53126 Raymond 300 L2
54652 Readstown 396 E9
54970 Redgranite 976 J7
53959 Reedsburg 5,038 G8
54230 Reedsville 1,134 L7
53579 Reeseville 649 J9
53580 Rewey 233 F10
54501 Rhinelander⊙ 7,873 H4
54470 Rib Lake 945 F5
54868 Rice Lake 7,691 C5
53581 Richland Center⊙ 4,997 F9
54763 Ridgeland 300 B5
53582 Ridgeway 503 F10
53960 Rio 785 H9
54971 Ripon 7,111 J8
54022 River Falls 9,019 A6
†53201 River Hills 1,642 M1
54023 Roberts 833 A6
53167 Rochester 746 K3
†53523 Rockdale 200 J10
53077 Rockfield 200 L1
54653 Rockland 383 D8
53961 Rock Springs 426 F8
†53178 Rome 200 H1
54974 Rosendale 725 J8
54473 Rosholt 520 H6
54474 Rothschild 3,338 G6
†53583 Roxbury 260 G9
54475 Rudolph 392 G7
†54751 Rusk 40 C6
53079 Saint Cloud 560 K8
54024 Saint Croix Falls 1,497 A5
†53207 Saint Francis 10,042 M2
†54601 Saint Joseph Ridge 450 D8
54232 Saint Nazianz 738 L7
54765 Sand Creek 225 C5
53583 Sauk City 2,703 G9
53080 Saukville 3,494 L9
54559 Saxon 375 F3
54977 Scandinavia 292 H7
54476 Schofield 2,226 H6
†54843 Seeley 68 D3
54654 Seneca 235 E9
53584 Sextonville 225 F9
54165 Seymour 2,530 K6
53585 Sharon 1,280 J11
54166 Shawano⊙ 7,013 J6
53081 Sheboygan⊙ 48,085 L8
Sheboygan‡ 100,935 L8
53085 Sheboygan Falls 5,253 L8
54766 Sheldon 292 D5
54871 Shell Lake⊙ 1,135 C4
54169 Sherwood 372 K7
54170 Shiocton 805 K7
53211 Shorewood 14,327 M1
†53701 Shorewood Hills 1,837 G9
53586 Shullsburg 1,484 F10
53170 Silver Lake 1,598 K10
54872 Siren 896 B4
54234 Sister Bay 564 M5
53086 Slinger 1,612 K9
54655 Soldiers Grove 622 E9
54873 Solon Springs 590 C3
54025 Somerset 860 A5
53172 South Milwaukee 21,069 M2
53587 South Wayne 495 G10
54656 Sparta⊙ 6,934 E8
54479 Spencer 1,754 F6
54801 Spooner 2,365 B4
53588 Spring Green 1,265 G9
54767 Spring Valley 982 B6
54768 Stanley 2,095 E6
54026 Star Prairie 420 A5
54480 Stetsonville 487 F5
54657 Steuben 175 E9
54481 Stevens Point⊙ 22,970 G7
54172 Stiles 300 L6
53825 Stitzer 190 E10
53088 Stockbridge 567 K7
54769 Stockholm 104 B7
54658 Stoddard 762 D8
54876 Stone Lake 210 C4
53589 Stoughton 7,589 H10
54484 Stratford 1,385 F6
54770 Strum 944 D6
54235 Sturgeon Bay⊙ 8,847 M6
53177 Sturtevant 4,130 M3
54173 Suamico 900 K6
53178 Sullivan 434 H1
54485 Summit Lake 250 H5
53590 Sun Prairie 12,931 H9
54880 Superior⊙ 29,571 C2
Superior-Duluth‡ 266,650 C2
†54880 Superior Village 580 B2
54174 Suring 581 K5
53089 Sussex 3,482 K1
53090 Taycheedah 350 K8
54659 Taylor 411 E7
†53820 Tennyson 476 E10
53091 Theresa 766 K8
53092 Thiensville 3,341 L1
54771 Thorp 1,635 E6
54562 Three Lakes 950 H4
54486 Tigerton 865 H6
54240 Tisch Mills 315 L7
54660 Tomah 7,204 F8
54487 Tomahawk 3,527 G5
54563 Tony 146 E5
54888 Trego 280 C4
54661 Trempealeau 956 C8
54662 Tunnel City 200 E7
54889 Turtle Lake 762 B5
53181 Twin Lakes 3,474 K11

Topography

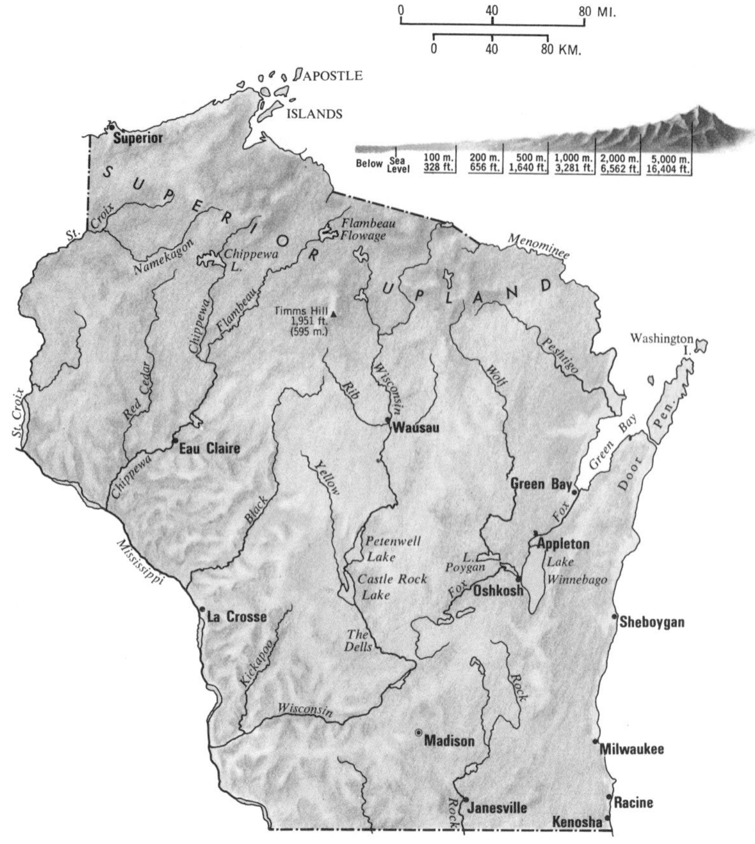

54241 Two Rivers 13,354 M7
53962 Union Center 216 F8
53182 Union Grove 3,517 L3
54488 Unity 418 F6
54245 Valders 984 L7
53593 Verona 3,336 G9
54489 Vesper 554 F7
54664 Viola 696 E8
54665 Viroqua⊙ 3,716 D8
54566 Wabeno 800 J5
53093 Waldo 416 L8
53183 Wales 1,992 J1
53184 Walworth 1,607 J10
54666 Warrens 300 E7
54890 Wascott 70 C3
54891 Washburn⊙ 2,080 D2
54246 Washington Island 550 M5
53185 Waterford 2,051 K3
53594 Waterloo 2,393 J9
53094 Watertown 18,113 J9
53021 Waubeka 450 L9
53186 Waukesha⊙ 50,365 K1
53597 Waunakee 3,866 G9
54981 Waupaca⊙ 4,472 H7
53963 Waupun 8,132 J8
54401 Wausau⊙ 32,426 G6
Wausau‡ 111,270 G6
54177 Wausaukee 648 K5
54982 Wautoma⊙ 1,629 H7
53226 Wauwatosa 51,308 L1
53826 Wauzeka 580 E9
†54126 Wayside 140 L7
54893 Webster 610 B4
53214 West Allis 63,982 L1
†53913 West Baraboo 846 G9
53095 West Bend⊙ 21,484 K9
54490 Westboro 750 F5
54667 Westby 1,797 E8
53964 Westfield 1,033 H8
†53201 West Milwaukee 3,535 L1
†54476 Weston 8,775 G6
54669 West Salem 3,276 D8
54983 Weyauwega 1,549 H7
54895 Weyerhaeuser 313 D5
54772 Wheeler 231 C5
54773 Whitehall⊙ 1,530 D7
54491 White Lake 309 J5
54247 Whitelaw 649 L7
53190 Whitewater 11,520 J10
†54481 Whiting 2,050 H7
54984 Wild Rose 741 H7
53191 Williams Bay 1,763 J10
54027 Wilson 155 B6
54670 Wilton 465 F8
54567 Winchester 300 G3
53185 Wind Lake 900 K2
†53401 Wind Point 1,695 M2
53598 Windsor 827 H9
54985 Winnebago 1,433 J8
54986 Winneconne 1,935 J7
54896 Winter 376 E4
53965 Wisconsin Dells 2,521 G8
54494 Wisconsin Rapids⊙ 17,995 G7
54498 Withee 509 E6
54499 Wittenberg 997 H6
53968 Wonewoc 842 F8
53827 Woodman 116 E9
54568 Woodruff 850 G4
54028 Woodville 725 B6
54180 Wrightstown 1,169 K7
54671 Wyeville 163 F7
53969 Wyocena 548 H9
54182 Zachow 135 K6

OTHER FEATURES

Apostle (isls.) F2
Apostle Islands Nat'l Lakeshore E1
Apple (riv.) A5
Bad River Ind. Res. E2
Bardon (lake) C3
Bear (isl.) E1
Beaver Dam (lake) J9
Beulah (lake) J2
Big Eau Pleine (res.) G6
Big Muskego (lake) K2
Big Rib (riv.) G5
Black (riv.) E7
Butternut (lake) J4
Castle Rock (lake) G8
Cat (isl.) E1
Chambers (isl.) M5
Chequamegon (bay) E2
Chetac (lake) D4
Chippewa (lake) D4
Chippewa (riv.) B7
Clam (lake) B4
Clam (riv.) A4
Dells, The (valley) G8
Denoon (lake) K2
Du Bay (lake) G6
Eagle (lake) H2
Eagle (lake) K3
Eau Claire (riv.) D6
Flambeau (riv.) E4
Flambeau Flowage (res.) F3
Fox (riv.) K2
Fox (riv.) K7
General Mitchell Field M2
Geneva (lake) K10
Golden (lake) H1
Green (bay) L6
Grindstone (lake) C4
Holcombe Flowage (res.) D5
Jump (riv.) E5
Kegonsa (lake) H10
Kickapoo (riv.) E9
Koshkonong (lake) H10
La Belle (lake) H1
Lac Court Oreilles Ind. Res. D4
Lac du Flambeau Ind. Res. G3
Long (lake) C4
Madeline (isl.) E2
Mendota (lake) H9
Menominee (riv.) L5
Metonga (lake) J4
Michigan (isl.) F2
Michigan (lake) M9
Mississippi (riv.) D10
Montreal (riv.) F2
Moose (lake) E3
Moose (lake) F3
Nagawicka (lake) J1
Namekagon (lake) D3
Namekagon (riv.) C3
North (lake) J1
Oak (isl.) E2
Oconomowoc (lake) H1
Oconto (riv.) K5
Okauchee (lake) J1
Outer (isl.) F1
Owen (lake) D3
Pecatonica (riv.) H11
Pelican (lake) H4
Pepin (lake) B7
Peshtigo (riv.) K5
Petenwell (lake) G7
Pewaukee (lake) K1
Phantom (lake) J2
Pine (lake) J1
Porte des Morts (str.) N5
Poygan (lake) J7
Puckaway (lake) H8
Red Cedar (riv.) C5
Red Cliff Ind. Res. E2
Rib (mt.) G6
Rock (riv.) J9
Round (lake) F4
Round (lake) D3
Saint Croix (lake) A6
Saint Croix (riv.) A4
Saint Croix Flowage (res.) C3
Saint Louis (riv.) A2
Sand (isl.) D2
Shawano (lake) K6
Shell (lake) C4
Spider (lake) D3
Stockbridge Ind. Res. J6
Stockton (isl.) F2
Sugar (riv.) H10
Sugarbush Hill (mt.) J4
Superior (lake) F1
Thunder (lake) H4
Tichigan (lake) K2
Timms Hill (mt.) F5
Trempealeau (riv.) C7
Trout (lake) G3
Vieux Desert (lake) J3
Washington (isl.) M5
Willow (res.) F4
Wind (lake) K2
Winnebago (lake) K7
Wisconsin (riv.) E9
Wolf (riv.) J5
Yellow (lake) B4
Yellow (riv.) F7

⊙County seat.
‡Population of metropolitan area.
† Zip of nearest p.o. * Multiple zips.

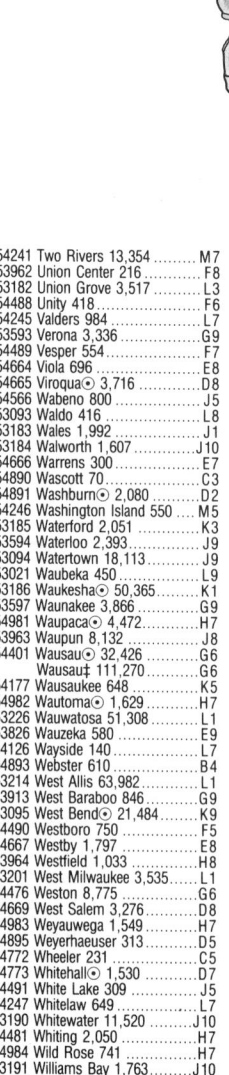

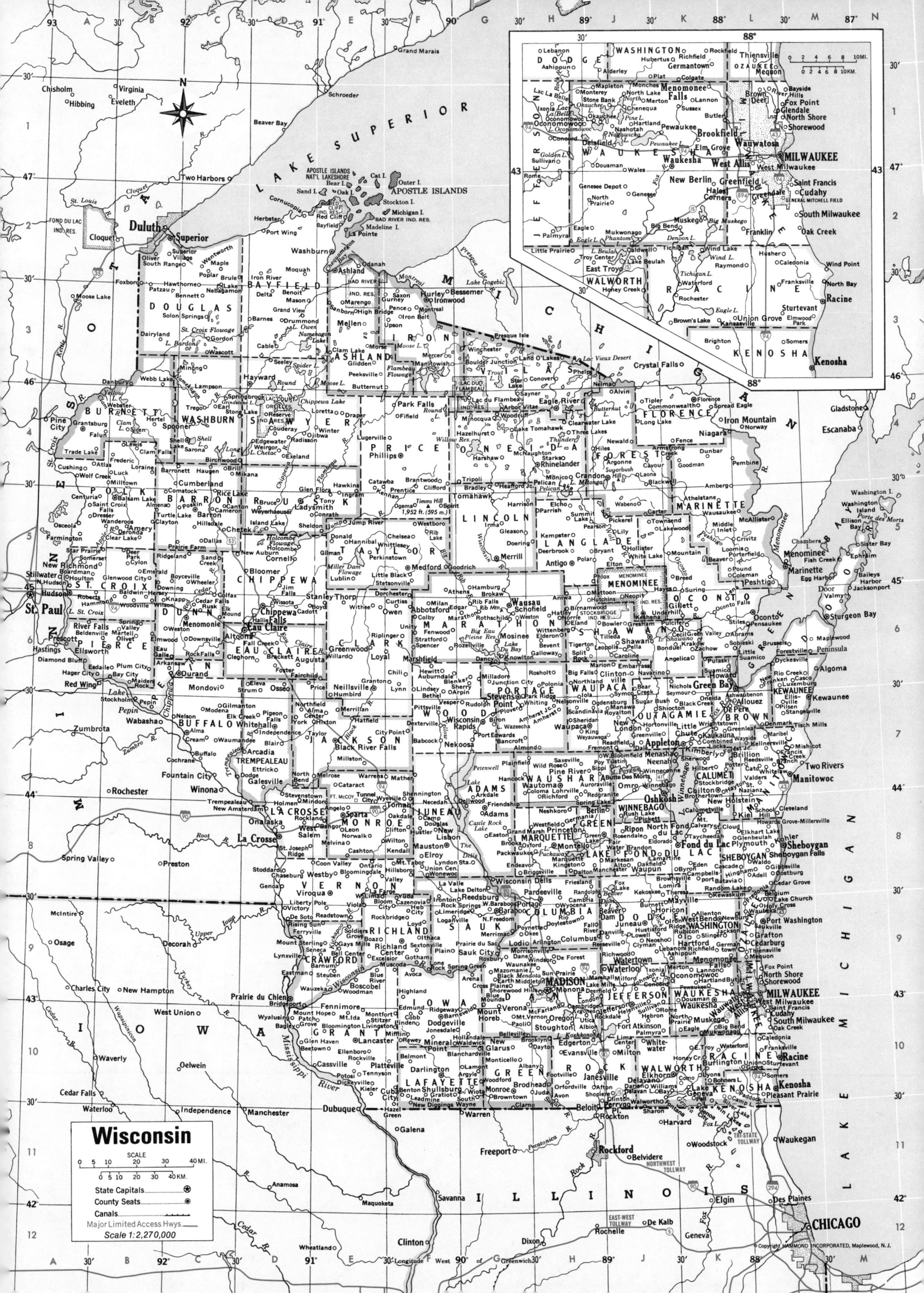

Wisconsin

SCALE
0 5 10   20   30   40 MI.
0 5 10   20   30   40 KM.

State Capitals .... ⊛
County Seats .... ⊙
Canals .... ╪╪╪╪
Major Limited Access Hwys. ═══

Scale 1:2,270,000

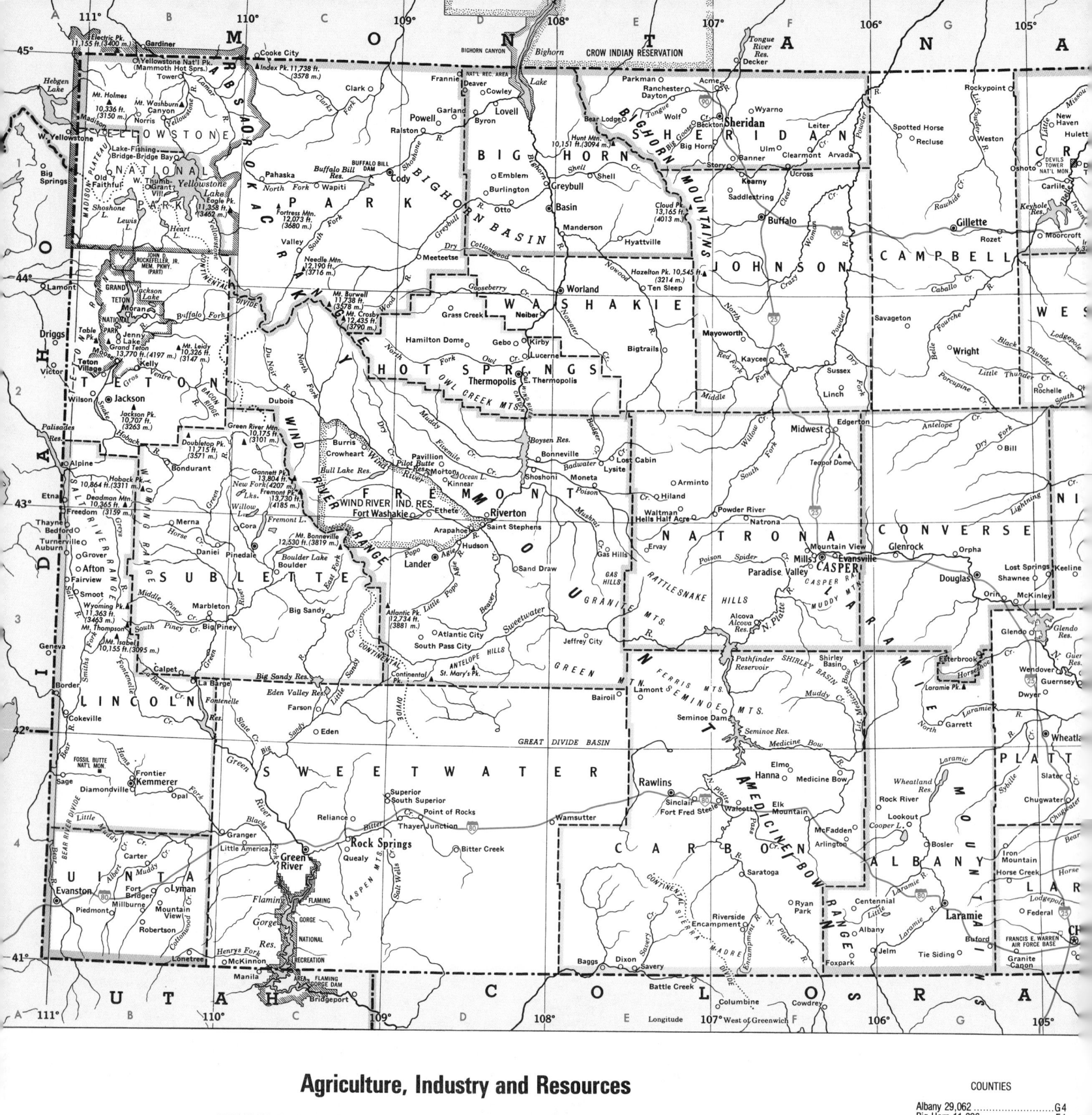

Agriculture, Industry and Resources

DOMINANT LAND USE

Specialized Wheat

Specialized Dairy

General Farming, Livestock, Special Crops

Sugar Beets, Dry Beans, Livestock, General Farming

Range Livestock

Forests

Nonagricultural Land

MAJOR MINERAL OCCURRENCES

C	Coal	G	Natural Gas	So	Soda Ash
Cl	Clay	O	Petroleum	U	Uranium
Fe	Iron Ore	P	Phosphates	V	Vanadium

⚡ Water Power

COUNTIES

Albany 29,062	G4
Big Horn 11,896	E1
Campbell 24,367	G1
Carbon 21,896	F4
Converse 14,069	G3
Crook 5,308	H1
Fremont 38,992	D2
Goshen 12,040	H4
Hot Springs 5,710	D2
Johnson 6,700	F1
Laramie 68,649	H4
Lincoln 12,177	B3
Natrona 71,856	F3
Niobrara 2,924	H2
Park 21,639	C1
Platte 11,975	H4
Sheridan 25,048	F1
Sublette 4,548	C3
Sweetwater 41,723	D4
Teton 9,355	B2
Uinta 13,021	B4
Washakie 9,496	E2
Weston 7,106	H2

CITIES and TOWNS

Zip	Name/Pop.	Key
83110	Afton 1,481	B3
82050	Albin 128	H4
82620	Alcova 275	F3

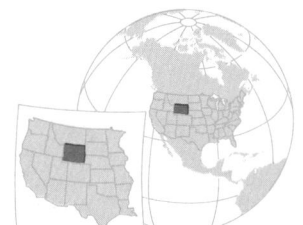

Wyoming

SCALE

0 5 10 20 30 40 MI.

0 5 10 20 30 40 KM.

State Capitals ⊛
County Seats ◉
Major Limited Access Hwys.

Scale 1:2,410,000

AREA 97,809 sq. mi. (253,325 sq. km.)
POPULATION 469,557
CAPITAL Cheyenne
LARGEST CITY Casper
HIGHEST POINT Gannett Pk. 13,804 ft. (4207 m.)
SETTLED IN 1834
ADMITTED TO UNION July 10, 1890
POPULAR NAME Equality State
STATE FLOWER Indian Paintbrush
STATE BIRD Meadowlark

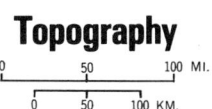

Topography

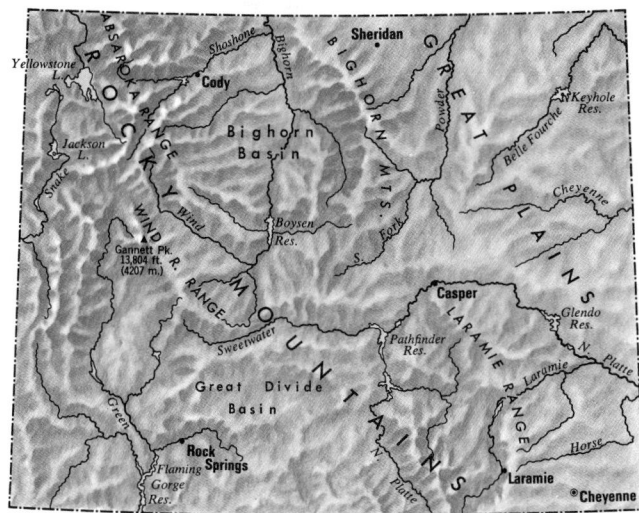

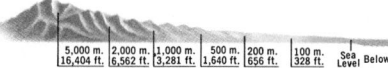

5,000 m. 16,404 ft.	2,000 m. 6,562 ft.	1,000 m. 3,281 ft.	500 m. 1,640 ft.	200 m. 656 ft.	100 m. 328 ft.	Sea Level Below

© Copyright HAMMOND INCORPORATED, Maplewood, N.J.

82510 Arapahoe 682 ....D3
83111 Auburn 360 ....A3
82321 Baggs 433 ....E4
82322 Bairoil 300 ....E3
82410 Basin⊙ 1,349 ....E1
82801 Beckton 110 ....E1
83112 Bedford 350 ....A3
82712 Beulah 184 ....H1
82833 Big Horn 350 ....E1
83113 Big Piney 530 ....B4
82051 Bosler 195 ....G4
82834 Buffalo⊙ 3,799 ....F1
82411 Burlington 300 ....D1
82053 Burns 268 ....H4
82412 Byron 633 ....D1
82601 Casper⊙ 51,016 ....F3
82055 Centennial 140 ....F4
†82001 Cheyenne (cap.)⊙ 47,283 ..H4
82210 Chugwater 282 ....H4
82835 Clearmont 191 ....F1
82414 Cody⊙ 6,790 ....D1
83114 Cokeville 515 ....B3
82420 Cowley 455 ....D1
82512 Crowheart 200 ....C2
83115 Daniel 75 ....B3
82836 Dayton 701 ....E1
82421 Deaver 178 ....D1
83116 Diamondville 1,000 ....B4
82323 Dixon 82 ....E4
82633 Douglas⊙ 6,030 ....G3
82513 Dubois 1,067 ....C2
82443 East Thermopolis 359 ..D2

82926 Eden 198 ....C3
82635 Edgerton 510 ....F2
82324 Elk Mountain 338 ......F4
82325 Encampment 611 ....F4
83118 Etna 200 ....A2
82930 Evanston⊙ 6,421 ......B4
82636 Evansville 2,335 .....F3
83119 Fairview 150 ....B3
82932 Farson 350 ....C3
82933 Fort Bridger 300 .....B4
82212 Fort Laramie 356 .....H3
82514 Fort Washakie 400 ....C2
†82001 Fox Farm 2,850 ......H4
82423 Frannie 138 ....D1
83120 Freedom 400 ....B3
83121 Frontier 150 ....B4
82501 Gas Hills 150 ....E3
82716 Gillette⊙ 12,134 .....G1
82213 Glendo 367 ....G3
82637 Glenrock 2,736 ....G3
82934 Granger 177 ....C4
82425 Grass Creek 152 ......D2
82935 Green River⊙ 12,807 ..C4
82426 Greybull 2,277 ....E1
83122 Grover 425 ....B3
82214 Guernsey 1,512 ....H3
82327 Hanna 2,288 ....F4
82215 Hartville 149 ....H3
82060 Hillsdale 160 ....H4
82061 Horse Creek 225 ......G4
82515 Hudson 514 ....D3
82720 Hulett 291 ....H1

83001 Jackson⊙ 4,511 ....B2
82310 Jeffrey City 1,882 ....E3
82639 Kaycee 271 ....F2
83011 Kelly 100 ....B2
82516 Kinnear 145 ....D2
82430 Kirby 129 ....D2
83123 La Barge 302 ....B3
82221 Lagrange 232 ....H4
82520 Lander⊙ 7,867 ....D3
82070 Laramie⊙ 24,410 ......G4
82640 Linch 187 ....F2
82223 Lingle 475 ....H3
82929 Little America 175 ...C4
†82642 Lost Cabin 25 ....E2
82224 Lost Springs 9 ....G3
82431 Lovell 2,447 ....D1
†82443 Lucerne 240 ....D2
82225 Lusk⊙ 1,650 ....H3
82937 Lyman 2,284 ....B4
82642 Lysite 175 ....E2
†82190 Mammoth Hot Springs
 (Yellowstone Nat'l Park 350 ..B1
82432 Manderson 174 ....E1
82227 Manville 94 ....H3
†83113 Marbleton 537 ....B3
82938 McKinnon 135 ....C4
82329 Medicine Bow 953 .....F4
82433 Meeteetse 512 ....D1
82643 Midwest 638 ....F2
82644 Mills 2,139 ....F3
82721 Moorcroft 1,014 ......H1
83012 Moose 150 ....B2
83013 Moran 200 ....B2
†82601 Mountain View F3
82939 Mountain View 628 ....B4
82701 Newcastle⊙ 3,596 .....H2
82190 Old Faithful 75 ......B1
†82001 Orchard Valley 3,327 .H4
82723 Osage 500 ....H2
†82601 Paradise Valley F3
82523 Pavillion 287 ....D2
82082 Pine Bluffs 1,077 ....H4
82941 Pinedale⊙ 1,066 ......C3
82942 Point of Rocks 425 ...D4
82435 Powell 5,310 ....D1
82839 Ranchester 655 ....E1
82301 Rawlins⊙ 11,547 ......E4
82523 Recluse 225 ....G1
†82325 Riverside 55 ....F4
82501 Riverton 9,247 ....D2
82944 Robertson 142 ....B4
82083 Rock River 415 ....G4
82901 Rock Springs 19,458 ..C4
82331 Saratoga 2,410 ....F4
82801 Sheridan⊙ 15,146 .....F1
82615 Shirley Basin 400 ....F3
82649 Shoshoni 879 ....D2
82334 Sinclair 586 ....E4
83126 Smoot 310 ....B3
†82945 South Superior 586 ...D4

82842 Story 637 ....F1
82729 Sundance⊙ 1,087 ......H1
82945 Superior 500 ....D4
82442 Ten Sleep 407 ....E1
83127 Thayne 256 ....A3
82443 Thermopolis⊙ 3,852 ...D2
82240 Torrington⊙ 5,441 ....H3
82730 Upton 1,193 ....H1
82242 Van Tassell 10 ....H3
82335 Walcott 200 ....F4
82336 Wamsutter 681 ....E4
82201 Wheatland⊙ 5,816 .....H3
83014 Wilson 480 ....B2
82401 Worland⊙ 6,391 ....E1
82732 Wright 1,117 ....G2
82190 Yellowstone Nat'l Pk. 350 ..B1
82244 Yoder 110 ....H4

OTHER FEATURES

Absaroka (range) C1
Antelope (creek) G2
Antelope (hills) D3
Aspen (mts.) C4
Atlantic (peak) D3
Badwater (creek) E2
Bear (creek) H4
Bear (riv.) B4
Bear Lodge (mts.) H1
Bear River Divide (mts.) B4
Beaver (creek) D3
Beaver (creek) H2
Belle Fourche (riv.) H1
Big Goose (creek) E1
Bighorn (basin) D1
Bighorn (lake) D1
Bighorn (mts.) E1
Bighorn (riv.) D1
Bighorn Canyon Nat'l Rec. Area .D1
Big Sandy (riv.) C3
Bitter (creek) C4
Blacks Fork, Green (riv.) C4
Black Thunder (creek) G2
Bonneville (mt.) C3
Boysen (res.) D2
Buffalo Bill (dam) D1
Buffalo Bill (res.) C1
Buffalo Fork, Snake (riv.) B2
Burwell (riv.) C2
Caballo (creek) G1
Casper (creek) F3
Cheyenne (riv.) H2
Chugwater (creek) G3
Clarks Fork (riv.) C1
Clear (creek) F1
Cloud (peak) E1
Cottonwood (creek) B4
Crazy Woman (creek) F1
Crosby (mt.) C2
Crow (mt.) H4
Deadman (mt.) B2
Devils Tower Nat'l Mon. H1

Doubletop (peak) B2
Dry (creek) C2
Dry Cottonwood (creek) D1
Eagle (peak) B1
Fivemile (creek) D2
Flaming Gorge (res.) C4
Flaming Gorge Nat'l Rec. Area ..C4
Fontenelle (creek) B3
Fontenelle (res.) B3
Fort Laramie Nat'l Hist. Site ..H3
Fortress (mt.) C1
Fossil Butte Nat'l Mon. B4
Francis E. Warren A.F.B. 3,627 .G4
Fremont (lake) C3
Fremont (peak) C2
Gannett (peak) C2
Gas (hills) E3
Glendo (res.) H3
Gooseberry (creek) D1
Grand (peak) B2
Grand Teton Nat'l Park B2
Granite (mts.) E3
Great Divide (basin) E3
Green (mt.) E3
Green (riv.) C4
Green, East Fork (riv.) C3
Green River (mt.) C2
Greybull (riv.) D1
Greys (riv.) B3
Gros Ventre (riv.) B2
Guernsey (res.) H3
Hams Fork (riv.) B4
Hazelton (peak) E1
Henrys Fork, Green (riv.) C4
Hoback (basin) B2
Hoback (riv.) B2
Holmes (mt.) B1
Horse (creek) H4
Horseshoe (creek) G3
Hunt (mt.) D1
Index (peak) C1
Inyan Kara, Green (riv.) H1
Inyan Kara (mt.) H1
Isabel (mt.) B3
Jackson (lake) B2
Jackson (peak) B2
John D. Rockefeller, Jr., Mem.
 Pkwy. B1
Keyhole (res.) H1
Lamar (riv.) B1
Lance (creek) H2
Laramie (mts.) G3
Laramie (peak) G3
Laramie (riv.) G4
Leidy (mt.) B2
Lewis (lake) B1
Lightning (creek) G2
Little Missouri (riv.) H1
Little Muddy (creek) B4
Little Powder (riv.) H1
Little Sandy (creek) C3
Little Thunder (creek) G2

Lodgepole (creek) H2
Lodgepole (creek) H4
Madison (plat.) B1
Medicine Bow (range) F4
Medicine Bow (riv.) F3
Middle Piney (creek) B3
Muddy (creek) D2
Muskrat (creek) E2
Needle (mt.) C1
Niobrara (riv.) J3
North Laramie (riv.) G3
North Platte (riv.) H3
Nowater (creek) E1
Nowood (riv.) E1
Owl, North Fork (creek) D2
Owl Creek (mts.) D2
Palisades (res.) A2
Pass (creek) F4
Pathfinder (res.) F3
Poison (creek) E2
Poison Spider (creek) F3
Popo Agie (riv.) D3
Powder (riv.) F2
Rattlesnake (range) E3
Rawhide (creek) G1
Rawhide (creek) H3
Rocky (mts.) C1
Salt (riv.) B3
Salt River (range) B3
Salt Wells (creek) D4
Seminoe (mts.) F3
Seminoe (res.) F3
Shell (creek) E1
Shirley (basin) F3
Shoshone (lake) B1
Shoshone (riv.) D1
Sierra Madre (mts.) E3
Slate (creek) C3
Smiths Fork (riv.) B3
Snake (riv.) B2
South Cheyenne (riv.) H2
South Piney (creek) B3
Sweetwater (riv.) D3
Sybille (creek) G3
Teapot Dome (mt.) F2
Teton (range) B2
Tongue (riv.) E1
Washburn (mt.) B1
Wheatland (res.) G4
Willow (creek) F2
Wind (riv.) D1
Wind River (canyon) D2
Wind River (range) C2
Wind River Ind. Res. C2
Wood (riv.) D1
Wyoming (peak) B3
Wyoming (range) B3
Yellowstone (lake) B1
Yellowstone (riv.) B1
Yellowstone Nat'l Park B1

⊙County seat.
† Zip of nearest p.o. * Multiple zips.

Acquisitions of Territory

OREGON COUNTRY 1846
OREGON Treaty with Great Britain
WASHINGTON
MONTANA
IDAHO
WYOMING
NEVADA
UTAH
CALIFORNIA
MEXICAN CESSION 1848
ARIZONA
NEW MEXICO
GADSDEN PURCHASE 1853
COLORADO
RED RIVER Title Established 1818
NORTH DAKOTA
SOUTH DAKOTA
NEBRASKA
IOWA
KANSAS
MISSOURI
OKLAHOMA
ARKANSAS
TEXAS Annexed in 1845
LOUISIANA Purchased from France 1803
MINNESOTA
WISCONSIN
MICHIGAN
ILLINOIS
INDIANA
OHIO
KENTUCKY
TENNESSEE
MISSISSIPPI
ALABAMA
GEORGIA
NORTH CAROLINA
SOUTH CAROLINA
WEST VIRGINIA
VIRGINIA
PENNSYLVANIA
NEW YORK
MAINE
VT.
N.H.
MASS.
CONN.
R.I.
NEW JERSEY
MD.
DEL.
UNITED STATES 1783
FLORIDA 1819 Treaty with Spain
ALASKA 1867 Purchased from Russia
HAWAII Annexed in 1898

The United States in 1783 comprised the thirteen original states and included lands acquired by conquest during the Revolution and by the Treaty of 1783.

Rank by Area

Rank by Population

YEAR OF ADMISSION TO THE UNION

DELAWARE ☆	1787
PENNSYLVANIA ☆	
NEW JERSEY ☆	
GEORGIA ☆	1788
CONNECTICUT ☆	
MASSACHUSETTS ☆	
MARYLAND ☆	
SOUTH CAROLINA ☆	
NEW HAMPSHIRE ☆	
VIRGINIA ☆	
NEW YORK ☆	
NORTH CAROLINA ☆	1789
RHODE ISLAND ☆	1790
VERMONT ☆	1791
KENTUCKY ☆	1792
TENNESSEE	1796
OHIO ☆	1803
LOUISIANA	1812
INDIANA	1816
MISSISSIPPI	1817
ILLINOIS	1818
ALABAMA ☆	1819
MAINE ☆	1820
MISSOURI	1821

1959 ☆ HAWAII ☆ ALASKA
1912 ☆ ARIZONA ☆ NEW MEXICO
1907 ☆ OKLAHOMA
1896 UTAH
1890 WYOMING ☆ ☆ WASHINGTON
1889 ☆ NORTH DAKOTA ☆ SOUTH DAKOTA ☆ MONTANA
IDAHO
1876 COLORADO ☆
1867 NEBRASKA ☆
1864 NEVADA ☆
1863 WEST VIRGINIA ☆
1861 KANSAS ☆
1859 OREGON ☆
1858 MINNESOTA ☆
1850 CALIFORNIA ☆
1848 WISCONSIN ☆
1846 IOWA ☆
1845 FLORIDA ☆ TEXAS ☆
1837 MICHIGAN
1836 ARKANSAS ☆

© Copyright
HAMMOND INCORPORATED

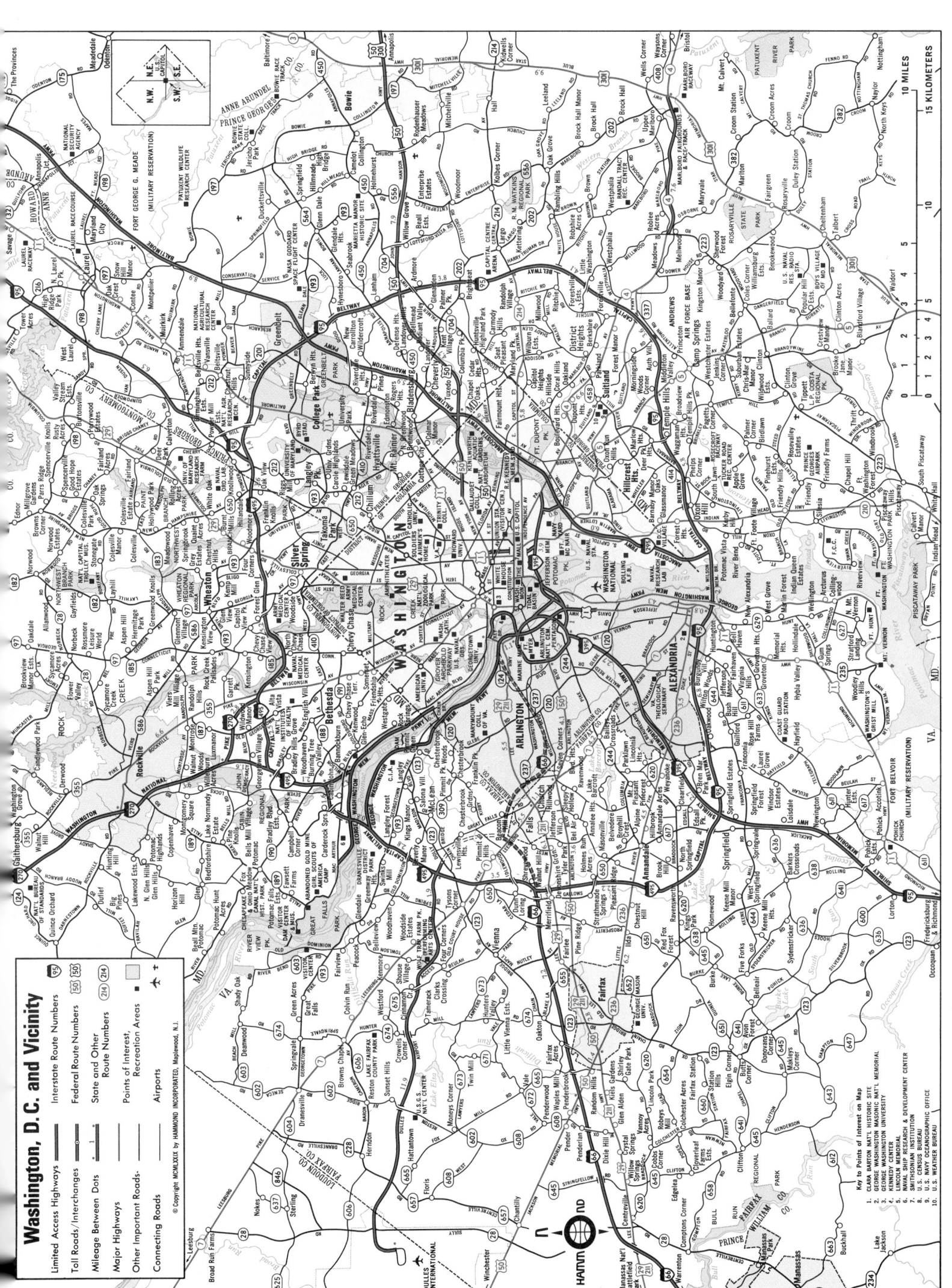

Washington, D.C. and Vicinity

Limited Access Highways
Toll Roads/Interchanges
Mileage Between Dots
Major Highways
Other Important Roads
Connecting Roads

Interstate Route Numbers
Federal Route Numbers
State and Other Route Numbers
Points of Interest, Recreation Areas
Airports

© Copyright MCMLXXIX by HAMMOND INCORPORATED, Maplewood, N.J.

Key to Points of Interest on Map
1. Clara Barton Nat'l Historic Site
2. Masonic Nat'l Memorial
3. George Washington University
4. Kennedy Center
5. Lincoln Memorial
6. Naval Ship Research & Development Center
7. Smithsonian Institution
8. U.S. Census Bureau
9. U.S. Navy Oceanographic Office
10. U.S. Weather Bureau

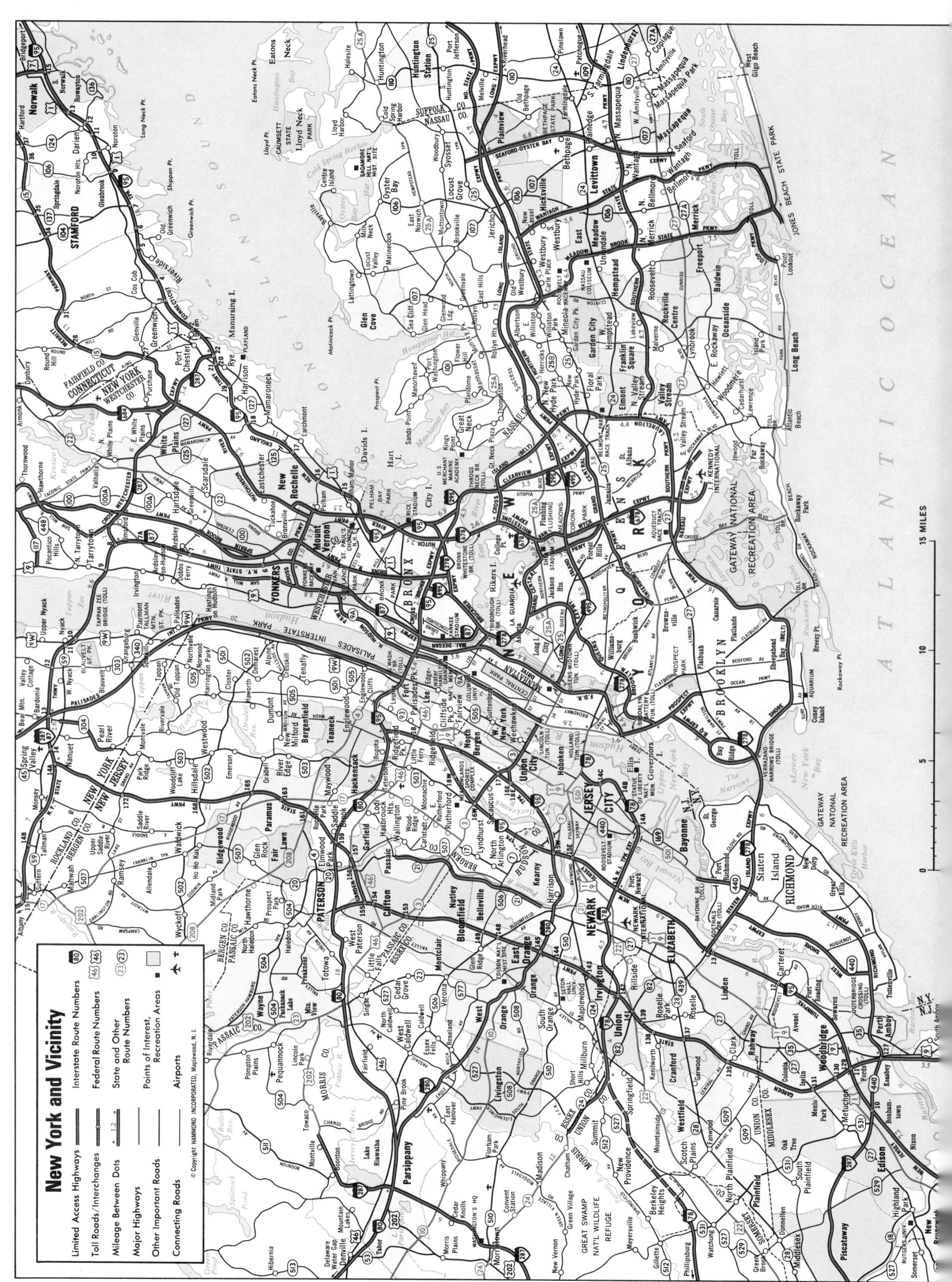

New York and Vicinity

Limited Access Highways	Interstate Route Numbers
Toll Roads/Interchanges	Federal Route Numbers
Mileage Between Dots	State and Other Route Numbers
Major Highways	Points of Interest, Recreation Areas
Other Important Roads	Airports
Connecting Roads	

© Copyright HAMMOND INCORPORATED, Maplewood, N.J.

15 MILES

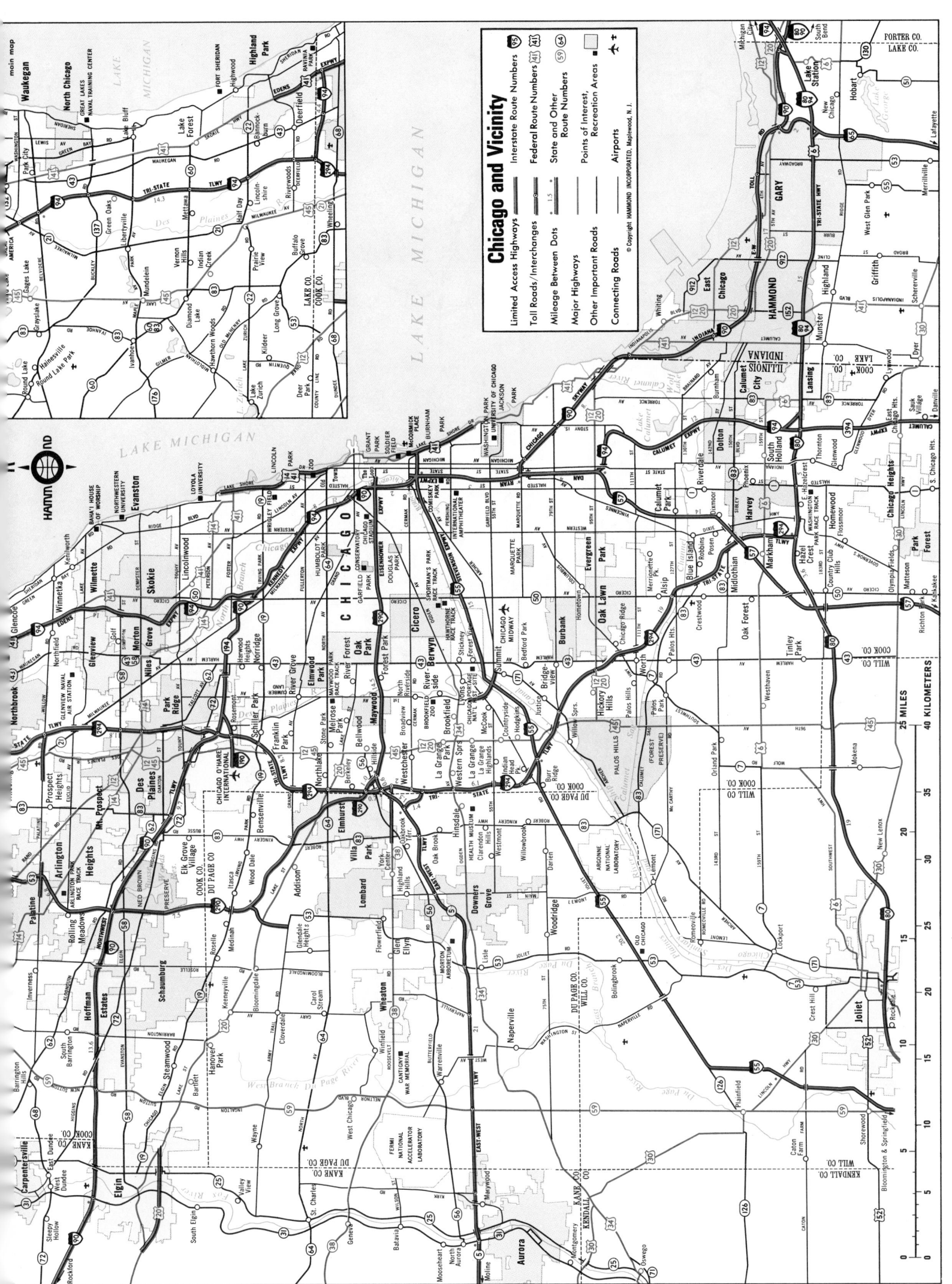

Chicago and Vicinity

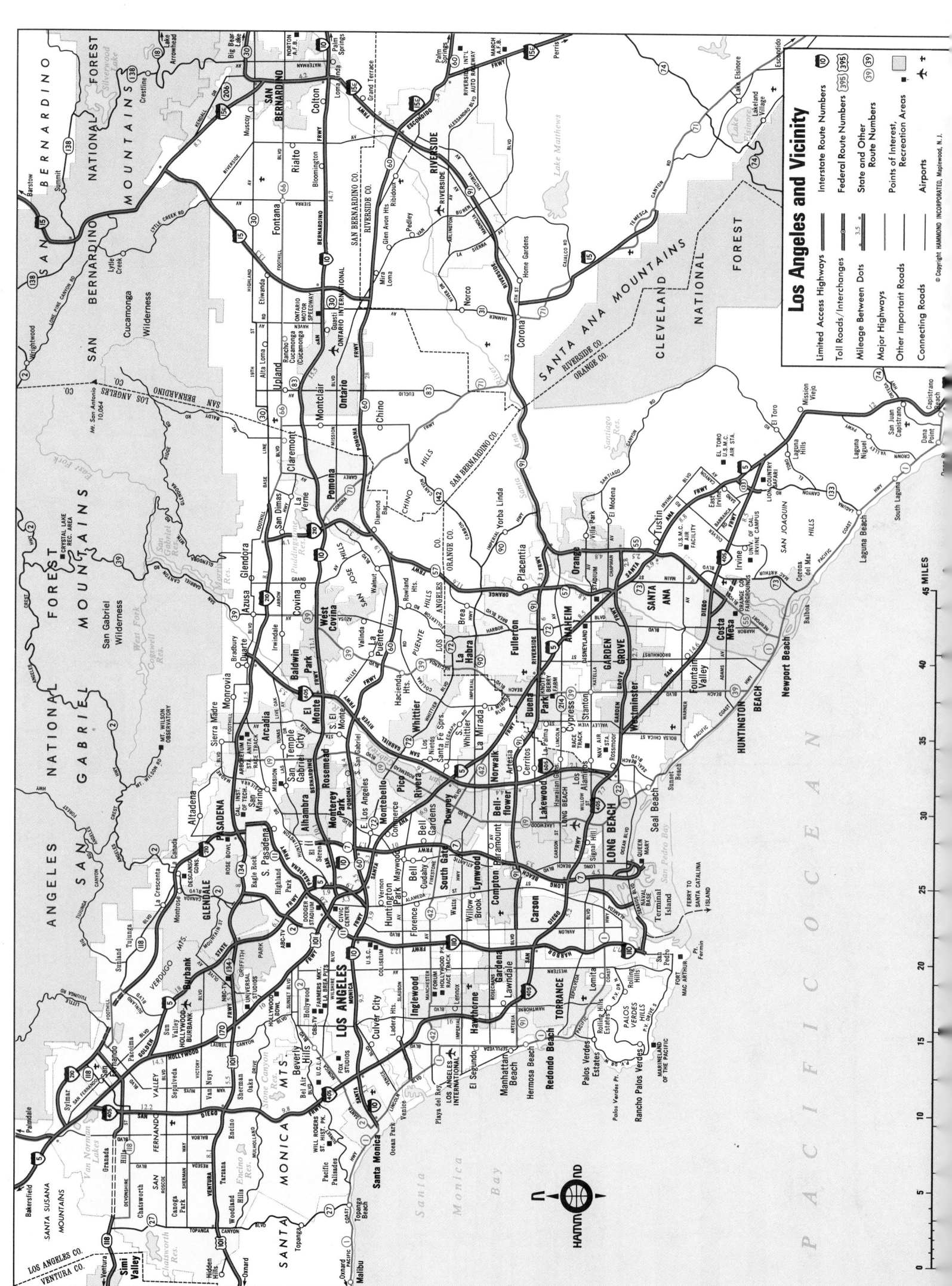

Los Angeles and Vicinity

INDEX OF THE WORLD

Introduction

This index contains a complete alphabetical listing of more than one hundred thousand names shown on all the maps included in this atlas. Names not found in the individual indexes accompanying the maps appear here. The user who is unfamiliar with the location of a country, town, or physical feature, or who is in doubt as to which country, state or province a place belongs will find the answers to his questions in this index. Entries are indexed to all maps or insets showing the place.

The name of the feature sought will be found in its proper alphabetical sequence, followed by the name of the political division in which it is located, the page number of the map on which it will be found, and the key reference necessary for finding its location on the map. After noting the key reference letter-number combination for the place name, turn to the page number indicated. The place name will be found within the square formed by the two lines of latitude and the two lines of longitude which enclose the coordinates—i.e., the marginal letters and numbers. An open circle (○) after the name signifies a township — better known as a town — in the northeastern U.S.

All index entries for cities and towns in the United States are followed by a five-digit postal ZIP code number applying to the community. This useful feature permits the reader to address his mail so that it will be routed and delivered more efficiently and quickly by the U.S. Postal Service. A dagger (†) designates those places that do not possess a post office. The ZIP code number listed in such cases refers to that of the nearest post office. An asterisk (*) marks those larger cities which are divided into multiple ZIP code areas. Using the single ZIP code number listed in such cases will direct your letter to the proper city with dispatch. However, if the precise ZIP code number of the address within the city is needed, it is suggested that the reader refer to the latest National ZIP Code Directory at his local post office. This detailed guide lists every street in a multiple ZIP code city with the proper ZIP code for the street.

Because of limitations of space on the map, place names do not always appear in their complete form on the map. The complete forms are, however, given in the index. Variant spellings of names and alternate names are also given in this index. The alternate form or spelling of the name appears first, followed in parentheses by the name as it appears on the map. Physical features are usually listed under their proper names and not according to their generic terms; that is to say, Rio Negro will be found under Negro and not under Rio Negro. Exceptions are familiar names such as Rio Grande.

The abbreviations for the political division names and geographical features are explained on page XVI of the atlas. In addition, reference can be made to the Gazetteer-Index appearing on pages IX through XIII in which area, population, capital, map reference and population source data may be found for all major political and physical divisions of the world. Population figures for most entries are also included in the comprehensive individual indexes accompanying each map.

326 Acree

Acree, Georgia (†31791) 217/D7
Acri, Italy 34/F5
Ács, Hungary 41/E3
Actinolite, Ontario 177/G3
Acton, Maine (04001) 243/B8
Acton○, Maine (04001) 243/B8
Acton○, Mass. (01720) 249/J3
Acton, Mont. (59002) 262/H5
Acton Vale, Québec 172/E4
Actopan, Hidalgo, Mexico 150/K6
Actopan, Veracruz, Mexico 150/Q1
Açu, Brazil 120/F3
Açu, Brazil 132/G4
Aculeo, Chile 138/G4
Aculeo (lag.), Chile 138/G4
Acuña, Argentina 143/G5
Acuracay, Peru 128/F5
Acushnet○, Mass. (02743) 249/L6
Acworth, Georgia (30101) 217/C2
Acworth○, N.H. (03601) 268/C5
Acy, La. (†70774) 238/L3
Ada, Ghana 106/E7
Ada (co.), Idaho 220/B6
Ada, Kansas (67414) 232/E2
Ada, Minn. (56510) 255/B3
Ada, Ohio (45810) 284/C4
Ada, Okla. 188/G4
Ada, Okla. (74820) 288/N5
Ada, W. Va. (†24701) 312/D8
Adadle, Somalia 115/H2
Adafer (reg.), Mauritania 106/B5
Adair, Ill. (61411) 222/C3
Adair (co.), Iowa 229/E6
Adair, Iowa (50002) 229/D6
Adair (co.), Ky. 237/L6
Adair (co.), Mo. 261/G2
Adair (cape), N.W. Terrs. 187/L2
Adair (co.), Okla. 288/S3
Adair, Okla. (74330) 288/R2
Adair, Tenn. (†38301) 237/D9
Adairsville, Georgia (30103) 217/C2
Adair Village, Oreg. (†97330) 291/D3
Adairville, Ky. (42202) 237/H7
Adaja (riv.), Spain 33/D2
Adak (isl.), Alaska 196/L4
Adak (str.), Alaska 196/K4
Adak Naval Air Station, Alaska 196/L4
Adalar (isl.), Turkey 63/D6
Adalia (Antalya), Turkey 63/D4
Adam, Oman 59/G5
Adamawa (reg.), Cameroon 115/B2
Adamawa (reg.), Nigeria 106/G7
Adaminaby, N.S. Wales 97/E5
Adams (lake), Br. Col. 184/H4
Adams (riv.), Br. Col. 184/H4
Adams (co.), Colo. 208/L3
Adams (mt.), Colo. 208/H6
Adams (co.), Idaho 220/B5
Adams (co.), Ill. 222/B4
Adams (co.), Ind. 227/H3
Adams, Ind. (47240) 227/F6
Adams (co.), Iowa 229/D6
Adams, Kansas (†67128) 232/E4
Adams, Ky. (41201) 237/R4
Adams, Mass. (01220) 249/B2
Adams○, Mass. (01220) 249/B2
Adams, Minn. (55909) 255/F7
Adams (co.), Miss. 256/B8
Adams (co.), Nebr. 264/F4
Adams, Nebr. (68301) 264/H4
Adams (mt.), N.H. 268/E3
Adams, N.Y. (13605) 276/J3
Adams (co.), N. Dak. 282/F7
Adams, N. Dak. (58210) 282/O3
Adams (co.), Ohio 284/D8
Adams, Okla. (73901) 288/D1
Adams, Oreg. (97810) 291/J2
Adams (co.), Pa. 294/H6
Adam's (peak), Sri Lanka 68/E7
Adams, Tenn. (37010) 237/G7
Adams (co.), Wash. 310/G3
Adams (mt.), Wash. 310/D4
Adams (co.), Wis. 317/G7
Adams, Wis. (53910) 317/G8
Adamsboro, Ind. (†46947) 227/E3
Adam's Bridge (sound), India 68/D7
Adam's Bridge (shoals), Sri Lanka 68/D7
Adamsburg, S.C. (29380) 296/D2
Adams Center, N.Y. (13606) 276/H3
Adams Lake, Br. Col. 184/G5
Adams Mills, Ohio (43801) 284/G5
Adams Nat'l Hist. Site, Mass. 249/D7
Adamson, Okla. (†74547) 288/P5
Adams Run, S.C. (29426) 296/G6
Adamstown, Md. (21710) 245/H3
Adamstown, Pa. (19501) 294/K5
Adamstown (cap.), Pitcairn Is. 87/N8
Adamsville, Ala. (35005) 195/D3
Adamsville, New Bruns. 170/E2
Adamsville, Ohio (43802) 284/G5
Adamsville, Pa. (16110) 294/B2
Adamsville, Québec 172/E4
Adamsville, R.I. (02801) 249/K6
Adamsville, Tenn. (38310) 237/E10
Adamsville, Texas (76510) 303/F6
Adamsville, Utah (†84713) 304/B5
Adana (prov.), Turkey 63/F4
Adana, Turkey 59/C2
Adana, Turkey 63/F4
Adana, Turkey 54/E6
Adanac, Sask. 181/B3
Adapazarı, Turkey 63/D2
Adapazarı, Turkey 59/B1
Adarama, Sudan 111/G4
Adarama, Sudan 59/C6
Adare (cape), Ant. 2/T10
Adare (cape) 5/B9
Adare, Ireland 17/D6
Adar Qaga, Jebel (mt.), Sudan 59/C5
Adaut, Indonesia 85/J7
Adavale, Queensland 88/G5
Adavale, Queensland 95/C5
Adaza, Iowa (†50050) 229/E4
Adda (riv.), Italy 34/B2
Adda (riv.), Sudan 111/D6
Addanki, India 68/D5
Addieville, Ill. (62214) 222/D5
Addington, Okla. (73520) 288/L6
Addis, La. (70710) 238/J2
Addis Ababa (cap.), Ethiopia 102/F4
Addis Ababa (cap.), Ethiopia 2/L5
Addis Ababa (cap.), Ethiopia 111/G6
Addis Alam, Ethiopia 111/G6
Addison, Ala. (35540) 195/D2
Addison, Conn. (†06033) 210/E2
Addison, Ill. (60101) 222/B5
Addison, Maine (04606) 243/H6
Addison○, Maine (04606) 243/H6
Addison, Mich. (49220) 250/E7
Addison, N.Y. (14801) 276/F6
Addison, Ohio (45610) 284/F8
Addison, Pa. (15411) 294/D6
Addison, Texas (75001) 303/G2
Addison (co.), Vt. 268/A3
Addison, Vt. (†05491) 268/A3
Addison (Webster Springs), W. Va. (†26288) 312/F6
Addi Ugri, Ethiopia 59/C7
Ad Diwaniya, Iraq 66/D5
Addo Nat'l Park, S. Africa 118/D6
Addor, N.C. (†28373) 281/L4
Addy, Wash. (99101) 310/H2
Addyston, Ohio (45001) 284/B9
Ade, Ind. (†47922) 227/C3
Adel, Georgia (31620) 217/F8
Adel, Iowa (50003) 229/E5
Adel, Oreg. (97620) 291/H5
Adelaide (isl.) 5/C15
Adelaide, Australia 87/D9
Adelaide, Australia 2/S7
Adelaide (pen.), N.W. Terrs. 187/J3
Adelaide, S. Africa 118/D6
Adelaide (cap.), S. Australia 88/D8
Adelaide Airport 88/D8
Adelaide River, North. Terr. 88/E2
Adelaide River, North. Terr. 93/B2
Adelanto, Calif. (92301) 204/H9
Adelboden, Switzerland 39/E3
Adele (isl.), W. Australia 88/C3
Adele (isl.), W. Australia 92/C1
Adélie Coast (reg.) 5/C7
Adeline, Ill. (†61047) 222/D1
Adeline, La. (†70544) 238/G7
Adell, Wis. (53001) 317/L8
Adelong, N.S. Wales 97/D4
Adelphi, Jamaica 158/H5
Adelphi, Ohio (43101) 284/E7
Adelphia, N.J. (07710) 273/E3
Aden (gulf) 54/F8
Aden (gulf) 2/M5
Aden (gulf) 102/G3
Aden, Alberta 182/E5
Aden (gulf), Djibouti 111/J5
Aden (cap.), P.D.R. Yemen 54/F8
Aden (cap.), P.D.R. Yemen 59/E7
Aden (gulf), Somalia 115/J1
Adena, Ohio (43901) 284/J5
Adenau, W. Germany 22/B3
Adger, Ala. (35006) 195/D4
Adhaim (riv.), Iraq 66/D3
Adi (isl.), Indonesia 85/J6
Adicora, Venezuela 124/D2
Adige (riv.), Italy 34/C2
Adigrat, Ethiopia 111/G5
Adilabad, India 68/D5
Adilcevaz, Turkey 63/K3
Adin, Calif. (96006) 204/E2
Adirondack, N.Y. (12808) 276/N3
Adirondack (mts.), N.Y. 276/M3
Adi Ugri, Ethiopia 111/G5
Adıyaman (prov.), Turkey 63/H4
Adıyaman, Turkey 63/H4
Adjuntas, P. Rico 161/B2
Adjuntas, P. Rico 156/F1
Adkins, Texas (78101) 303/K11
Adlatok (bay), Newf. 166/B2
Adlavik (isls.), Newf. 166/C2
Adliswil, Switzerland 39/F2
Admiral, Sask. 181/C6
Admiral's Beach, Newf. 166/D2
Admiral's Cove, Newf. 166/D2
Admiralty (inlet) 162/H1
Admiralty (isl.), Alaska 196/M1
Admiralty (isls.), N.S. Wales 97/J1
Admiralty (inlet), N.W. Terrs. 187/K2
Admiralty, Papua N.G. 86/A1
Admiralty (isls.), Papua N.G. 87/E6
Admiralty (inlet), Wash. 310/B2
Admiralty (gulf), W. Australia 88/D2
Admiralty (gulf), W. Australia 92/D1
Admiralty Island Nat'l Mon., Alaska 196/M1
Admire, Kansas (66830) 232/F3
Admont, Austria 41/C3
Adna, Wash. (98522) 310/B4
Ado, Nigeria 106/E7
Adobe Creek (res.), Colo. 208/N6
Adok, Sudan 111/F6
Adolfo Alsina, Argentina 143/D4
Adolph, Minn. (55701) 255/F4
Adolph, W. Va. (†26280) 312/F5
Adolphus, Ky. (42120) 237/J7
Adona, Ark. (72001) 202/E3
Adonara (isl.), Indonesia 85/G7
Adoni, India 68/D5
Adorf, E. Germany 22/E3
Adour (riv.), France 28/C6
Adra, Spain 33/E4
Adrano, Italy 34/E6
Adrar, Algeria 102/B2
Adrar, Algeria 106/xD3
Adrar (reg.), Mauritania 106/B4
Adrar des Iforas (plat.), Algeria 106/E5
Adrar des Iforas (plat.), Mali 106/E5
Adré, Chad 111/D5
Adria, Italy 34/D2
Adrian, Georgia (31002) 217/G5
Adrian, Ill. (62310) 222/B3
Adrian, Mich. (49221) 250/F7
Adrian, Minn. (56110) 255/C7
Adrian, Mo. (64720) 261/D6
Adrian, N. Dak. (58410) 282/O6
Adrian, Ohio (44801) 284/D3
Adrian, Oreg. (97901) 291/K4
Adrian, Pa. (16210) 294/D4
Adrian, S.C. (†29526) 296/J4
Adrian, Texas (79001) 303/B2
Adrian, W. Va. (26210) 312/F5
Adriatic (sea) 7/F4
Adriatic (sea), Albania 45/B4
Adriatic (sea), Italy 34/E3
Adriatic (sea), Yugoslavia 45/B4
Aduwa, Ethiopia 59/C7
Advance, Ind. (46102) 227/D5
Advance, Mich. (†49712) 250/D3
Advance, Mo. (63730) 261/N8
Advance, N.C. (27006) 281/J3
Advent, W. Va. (25231) 312/C5
Adventure (sound), 143/E7
Adventure (bay), Chile 138/D5
Adventure, Guyana 131/B2
Adventure Bay, Tasmania 99/D5
Advocate (bay), Nova Scotia 168/D3
Advocate Harbour, Nova Scotia 168/D3
Adwa, Ethiopia 111/G5
Adwick le Street, England 13/K2
Adygey Aut. Obl., U.S.S.R. 52/F6
Adygey Aut. Obl., U.S.S.R. 48/D5
Adzhar A.S.S.R., U.S.S.R. 52/F6
Adzhar A.S.S.R., U.S.S.R. 48/E5
Ae, Scotland 15/E5
Aeber (creek), S. Dak. 298/G4
Aegean (sea), Greece 7/G5
Aegean (sea), Greece 45/G6
Aegean (sea), Turkey 63/A3
Aegean Islands (reg.), Greece 45/G6
Aeneas, Wash. (†98855) 310/F2
Aerial, Alberta 182/D4
AErø (isl.), Denmark 21/D8
AErøskøbing, Denmark 21/D8
Aeschi bei Spiez, Switzerland 39/E3
Aetna, Alberta 182/D5
Aetna, Tenn. (†37033) 237/G9
'Afaq, Iraq 66/D4
Afareaitu, Fr. Poly. 86/S13
Afayan (pt.), Guam 86/K7
Afdem, Ethiopia 111/H6
Afféle (reg.), Mauritania 106/B5
Affoltern am Albis, Switzerland 39/F2
Affoltern im Emmental, Switzerland 39/E2
Affric, Loch (lake), Scotland 15/D3
Affton, Mo. (63123) 261/P4
Afghanistan 2/N4
Afghanistan 54/H6
AFGHANISTAN 68/A2
Afgoi, Somalia 102/G4
Afgoi, Somalia 115/J3
Afif, Saudi Arabia 59/D5
Afikpo, Nigeria 106/F7
Afiqim, Israel 65/D2
Åfjord, Norway 18/G5
Aflex, Ky. (41510) 237/S5
Afmadu, Somalia 115/H3
Afognak (isl.), Alaska 196/H3
Africa 2/K4
AFRICA 102
Afşin, Turkey 63/G3
Afton, Iowa (50830) 229/E6
Afton, La. (†71282) 238/H2
Afton, Mich. (49705) 250/E3
Afton, Minn. (55001) 255/F6
Afton, N.Y. (13730) 276/J6
Afton, Okla. (74331) 288/S1
Afton, Tenn. (37616) 237/R8
Afton, Texas (79220) 303/D4
Afton, Va. (22920) 307/L4
Afton, Wis. (53501) 317/H10
Afton, Wyo. (83110) 319/B3
Afuá, Brazil 132/D3
'Afula, Israel 65/C2
Afyonkarahisar (prov.), Turkey 63/D3
Afyonkarahisar, Turkey 63/D3
Afyonkarahisar, Turkey 59/A2
Agadem (well), Niger 106/G5
Agadès, Niger 106/F5
Agadès, Niger 102/C3
Agadir, Morocco 106/C2
Agadir, Morocco 102/A1
Agaña (cap.), Guam 87/E4
Agaña (cap.), Guam 86/K7
Agano (riv.), Japan 81/J4
Agar, S. Dak. (57520) 298/J4
Agartala, India 68/G4
Agassiz (peak), Ariz. 198/D3
Agassiz (mt.), Utah 304/D3
Agat (bay), Guam 86/K7
Agata, U.S.S.R. 48/K3
Agate, Colo. (80101) 208/M4
Agate, Nebr. (†69346) 264/A2
Agate, N. Dak. (58310) 282/L2
Agate Beach, Oreg. (†97365) 291/C3
Agate Fossil Beds Nat'l Mon., Nebr. 264/A2
Agats, Indonesia 85/K7
Agatti (isl.), India 68/C6
Agattu (isl.), Alaska 196/J3
Agattu (str.), Alaska 196/J3
Agawa Bay, Ontario 177/J5
Agawa Bay, Ontario 175/D3
Agawam○, Mass. (01001) 249/D4
Agawam (riv.), Mass. 249/M5
Agboville, Ivory Coast 102/B4
Agboville, Ivory Coast 106/D7
Agdam, U.S.S.R. 52/G6
Agde, France 28/E6
Agen, France 28/D5
Agency, Iowa (52530) 229/J7
Agency, Mo. (64401) 261/C3
Agency (lake), Oreg. 291/E5
Agenda, Kansas (66930) 232/E2
Ageo, Japan 81/O2
Agerbaek, Denmark 21/B6
Ägerisee (lake), Switzerland 39/G2
Ages, Ky. (40801) 237/P7
Aghada-Farsid-Rostellan, Ireland 17/E8
Aghadoe, Ireland 17/B7
Aghagower, Ireland 17/C4
Agha Jari, Iran 66/F5
Aginsk Buryat Aut. Okr., U.S.S.R. 48/M4
Aginskoye, U.S.S.R. 48/M4
Agiobampo (bay), Mexico 150/E3
Agira, Italy 34/E6
Ağlasun, Turkey 63/D4
Ağlı, Turkey 63/E2
Agness, Oreg. (97406) 291/C5
Agno, Philippines 82/B2
Agnone, Italy 34/E4
Agnos, Ark. (72510) 202/G1
Agoo, Philippines 82/C2
Agordat, Ethiopia 111/G4
Agordat, Ethiopia 59/C6
Agra, India 54/J7
Agra, India 68/D3
Agra, Kansas (67621) 232/C2
Agra, Okla. (74824) 288/N3
Agraciada, Uruguay 145/A4
Agrado, Colombia 126/C6
Agramonte, Cuba 158/D1
Ágreda, Spain 33/E2
Ağrı (prov.), Turkey 63/K3
Ağrı, Büyük (Ararat) (mt.), Turkey 63/L3
Ağrı (Karaköse), Turkey 63/K3
Agricola, Kansas (†66871) 232/G3
Agricola, Miss. (†39452) 256/G9
Agrigento (prov.), Italy 34/D6
Agrigento, Italy 34/D6
Agrihan (isl.), No. Marianas 87/E4
Agrínion, Greece 45/E6
Agropoli, Italy 34/E4
Agryz, U.S.S.R. 52/H3
Agua Caliente, Ariz. (†85333) 198/B6
Agua Caliente Ind. Res., Calif. 204/J10
Aguachica, Colombia 126/D3
Aguada, P. Rico 161/A1
Aguada de Pasajeros, Cuba 158/D2
Aguada Grande, Venezuela 124/D2
Aguadas, Colombia 126/C5
Agua de Dios, Colombia 126/C5
Aguadilla (dist.), P. Rico 161/A1
Aguadilla, P. Rico 156/F1
Aguadilla, P. Rico 161/A1
Aguadilla (bay), P. Rico 161/A1
Agua Dulce, Mexico 150/M7
Aguadulce, Panama 154/G6
Agua Dulce, Texas (78330) 303/F10
Agua Fria (riv.), Ariz. 198/C5
Agua Fría, Venezuela 124/D2
Agualeguas, Mexico 150/J3
Agua Linda, Venezuela 124/E5
Aguán (riv.), Honduras 154/D3
Aguanaval (riv.), Mexico 150/H4
Aguanish, Québec 174/E2
Aguanus (riv.), Newf. 166/B3
Aguanus (riv.), Québec 174/E2
Agua Prieta, Mexico 150/E1
Aguaray, Argentina 143/D1
Aguarico (riv.), Colombia 126/B7
Aguarico (riv.), Ecuador 128/D3
Aguasay, Venezuela 124/G3
Aguas Blancas, Chile 138/B4
Aguas Buenas, P. Rico 161/E2
Aguas Calientes, Cerro (mt.), Chile 138/C4
Aguascalientes (state), Mexico 150/H6
Aguascalientes, Mexico 150/H6
Aguascalientes, Mexico 146/H7
Aguas Corrientes, Uruguay 145/A6
Agua Vermelha (res.), Brazil 135/B1
Aguaytía (riv.), Peru 128/E7
Agudos, Brazil 135/B3
Águeda, Portugal 33/B2
Agueda (riv.), Spain 33/C2
Aguedaueda (riv.), Portugal 33/C2
Agueraktem (well), Mali 106/C4
Agueraktem (well), Mauritania 106/C4
Aguila, Ariz. (85320) 198/B5
Aguilar, Colo. (81020) 208/K8
Aguilar, Spain 33/D4
Aguilares, Argentina 143/C2
Aguilas, Spain 33/F4
Aguililla, Mexico 150/H7
Aguja, La (cape), Colombia 126/C2
Aguja (pt.), Peru 2/E6
Aguja (pt.), Peru 120/A3
Aguja (pt.), Peru 128/B5
Agulhas (cape), S. Africa 102/D8
Agulhas (cape), S. Africa 118/B6
Agusan (riv.), Philippines 82/E6
Agusan Canyon, Philippines 82/E6
Agusan del Norte (prov.), Philippines 82/E6
Agusan del Sur (prov.), Philippines 82/E6
Agustín Codazzi, Colombia 126/D3
Agutaya, Philippines 82/C5
Agutaya (isl.), Philippines 82/C5
Ahaggar (range), Algeria 102/C2
Ahaggar (range), Algeria 106/F4
Ahangaran, Afghanistan 59/J3
Ahar, Iran 66/E1
Ahascragh, Ireland 17/E5
Ahau, Fiji 87/H7
Ahaura, N. Zealand 100/C5
Ahaus, W. Germany 22/B2
Aherlow (riv.), Ireland 17/E7
Ah-Gwah-Ching, Minn. (56430) 255/D3
Ahipara, N. Zealand 100/D1
Ahlat, Turkey 63/K3
Ahlbeck, E. Germany 22/F2
Ahlen, W. Germany 22/B3
Ahmadabad, India 2/N4
Ahmadabad, India 68/C4
Ahmadabad, India 54/J7
Ahmadnagar, India 68/C5
Ahmadpur East, Pakistan 68/C3
Ahmeek, Mich. (49901) 250/A1
Ahmic (lake), Ontario 177/E2
Ahoghill, N. Ireland 17/J2
Ahome, Mexico 150/E4
Ahoskie, N.C. (27910) 281/P2
Ahousat, Br. Col. 184/D5
Ahrensburg, W. Germany 22/D2
Ahsahka, Idaho (83520) 220/B3
Ahtanum (creek), Wash. 310/D4
Ähtäri, Finland 18/N5
Ahua (pt.), Hawaii 218/B4
Ahuacatitlán, Mexico 150/L1
Ahuacatlán, Mexico 150/G6
Ahuachapán, El Salvador 154/B4
Ahuás, Honduras 154/E3
Ahumada, Mexico 150/F1
Ahurei, Fr. Poly. 87/M8
Åhus, Sweden 18/J9
Ahuzzam, Israel 65/B4
Ahvaz, Iran 54/F6
Ahvaz, Iran 59/E3
Ahvaz (Ahwaz), Iran 66/F5
Ahvenanmaa (prov.), Finland 18/L6
Ahwahnee, Calif. (93601) 204/F6
Ahwar, P.D.R. Yemen 59/E7
Ai-Ais, Namibia 118/B5
Aialik (bay), Alaska 196/C1
Aiama (lake), Brazil 132/H9
Aibonito, P. Rico 161/D2
Aichi (pref.), Japan 81/H6
Aid, Mo. (†63825) 261/M9
Aid, Ohio (†45645) 284/F8
Aiea, Hawaii (96701) 218/B3
Aigen im Mühlkreis, Austria 41/B2
Aigle (riv.), Québec 172/A3
Aigle, Switzerland 39/C4
Aiguá, Uruguay 145/E5
Aiguá (riv.), Uruguay 145/E4
Aigues-Mortes, France 28/F6
Aiguille d'Argentière (mt.), Switzerland 39/C5
Aihui (Aigun) (Heihe), China 77/L1
Aija, Peru 128/D7
Aikawa, Japan 81/H4
Aiken (co.), S.C. 296/D4
Aiken, S.C. (29801) 296/D4
Aikens (lake), Manitoba 179/G3
Aiken West, S.C. (†29801) 296/D4
Aikin, Md. (†21903) 245/O2
Aileron, North. Terr. 93/C7
Ailey, Georgia (30410) 217/G6
Ailinglapalap (atoll), Marshall Is. 87/G5
Aillon (lake), Québec 172/C2
Ailsa Craig, Ontario 177/C4
Ailsa Craig (isl.), Scotland 15/C5
Ailuk (atoll), Marshall Is. 87/H4
Aimogasta, Argentina 143/C2
Aimwell, La. (71401) 238/G3
Ain (dept.), France 28/F4
Ain (riv.), France 28/F4
Ainabo, Somalia 115/J2
Aina Haina, Hawaii (96821) 218/F2
'Ain al Mubarrak, Saudi Arabia 59/C5
Ainaži, U.S.S.R. 53/C2
Aïn Beïda, Algeria 106/F1
Aïn ben Tili (well), Mauritania 106/C3
'Ain el 'Arab, Syria 63/H4
Ain-Galakka, Chad 111/C4
Aïn Sefra, Algeria 106/D2
Ainslie (lake), Nova Scotia 168/G2
Ainsworth, Br. Col. 184/J5
Ainsworth, Iowa (52201) 229/K6
Ainsworth, Nebr. (69210) 264/D2
Aïn Temouchent, Algeria 106/D1
Ain Zueiya (well), Libya 111/D3
Aïoun el Atrous, Mauritania 106/C5
Aïoun el Atrous, Mauritania 102/B3
Aipe, Colombia 126/C6
Aiquile, Bolivia 136/C6
Aiquina, Chile 138/B3
Aïr (mts.), Niger 106/F5
Airdrie, Alberta 182/C4
Airdrie, Scotland 10/B1
Airdrie, Scotland 15/C2
Aire (riv.), England 10/F4
Aire (riv.), England 13/F4
Aire-sur-l'Adour, France 28/C6
Airey, Md. (†21613) 245/O6
Air Force (isl.), N.W. Terrs. 187/L3
Air Force Academy, Colo. 208/K5
Airlie, Oreg. (†97361) 291/D3
Airolo, Switzerland 39/G3
Air Ronge, Sask. 181/M3
Airville, Pa. (17302) 294/K6
Airway Heights, Wash. (99001) 310/H3
Aisén del General Carlos Ibáñez del Campo (reg.), Chile 138/E6
Aišiškes, U.S.S.R. 53/C3
Aisne (dept.), France 28/E3
Aisne (riv.), France 28/E3
Aitape, Papua N.G. 85/B6
Aith, Scotland 15/G2
Aitkin (co.), Minn. 255/E4
Aitkin, Minn. (56431) 255/E4
Aitutaki (atoll), Cook Is. 87/K7
Aiud, Romania 45/F2
Aix, France 7/E4
Aix (mt.), Wash. 310/D4
Aix-en-Provence, France 28/F6
Aix-les-Bains, France 28/G5
Aiyina, Greece 45/F7
Aiyion, Greece 45/F6
Aizpute, U.S.S.R. 53/A2
Aizuwakamatsu, Japan 81/J5
Aizwal, India 68/G4
Ajaccio, France 7/E4
Ajaccio, France 28/B7
Ajaccio (gulf), France 28/B7
Ajalpan, Mexico 150/L7
Ajana, W. Australia 92/A5
Ajanta, India 68/D4
Ajax, La. (†71450) 238/D3
Ajax, Ontario 177/E4
Ajedabia, Libya 111/D1
Aji Chai (riv.), Iran 66/E2
Ajigasawa, Japan 81/J3
'Ajja, West Bank 65/C3
Ajka, Hungary 41/D3
'Ajlun (dist.), Jordan 65/D3
'Ajlun, Jordan 65/D3
'Ajlun (range), Jordan 65/D3
'Ajman, U.A.E. 59/G4
Ajmer, India 68/C3
Ajmer, India 54/J7
Ajo, Ariz. (85321) 198/C6
Ajoewa, Suriname 131/C4
Ajoupa-Bouillon, Martinique 161/C5
Akan National Park, Japan 81/M2
Akaroa, N. Zealand 100/D5
Akasha, Sudan 111/F3
Akashi, Japan 81/H8
Akaska, S. Dak. (57420) 298/J3
Akbaba Tepesi (mt.), Turkey 63/H3
Akçaabat, Turkey 63/H2
Akçadağ, Turkey 63/G3
Akçakale, Turkey 63/H4
Akçakoca, Turkey 63/D2
Akçay, Turkey 63/C4
Akçay (riv.), Turkey 63/C4
Akdağ (mt.), Turkey 59/A2
Akdağ (mt.), Turkey 63/E4
Akdağ (mt.), Turkey 63/C4
Akdağmadeni, Turkey 63/F3
Akeley, Minn. (56433) 255/D3
Akeley, Pa. (†16345) 294/D2
Aken, E. Germany 22/D3
Akers, La. (70421) 238/N2
Akershus (co.), Norway 18/G6
Aketi, Zaire 102/E4
Aketi, Zaire 115/D3
Akhaltsikhe, U.S.S.R. 52/F6
Akhdar, Jebel (mts.), Libya 111/D1
Akhdar, Jebel (range), Oman 59/G5
Akhdar, Saudi Arabia 59/C4
Akhiok, Alaska (99615) 196/H3
Akhisar, Turkey 63/B3
Akhmim, Egypt 111/F2
Akhmim, Egypt 59/B4
Akhtopol, Bulgaria 45/H4
Akhtubinsk, U.S.S.R. 52/G5
Akhty, U.S.S.R. 52/G6
Akhtyrka, U.S.S.R. 52/E4
Aki, Japan 81/F7
Akiachak, Alaska (99551) 196/F2
Akiak, Alaska (99552) 196/F2
Akimiski (isl.), N.W.T. 162/H5
Akin, Ill. (62805) 222/E6
Akins, Okla. (†74955) 288/S3
Åkirkeby, Denmark 21/F9
Akita (pref.), Japan 81/J4
Akita, Japan 81/J4
Akita, Japan 54/P6
Akitio, N. Zealand 100/F4
Akjoujt, Mauritania 106/B5
Akkerman (Belgorod-Dnestrovskiy), U.S.S.R. 52/D5
Akkeshi, Japan 81/M2
Akko (Acre), Israel 65/C2
Akkrum, Netherlands 27/H2
Aklan (prov.), Philippines 82/D5
Aklavik, Canada 4/C16
Aklavik, N.W.T. 146/E3
Aklavik, N.W.T. 162/C2
Aklavik, N.W. Terrs. 187/E3
Akmolinsk (Tselinograd), U.S.S.R. 48/H4
Akobo (riv.), Ethiopia 111/F6
Akobo, Sudan 111/F6
Akobo (riv.), Sudan 111/F6
Akola, India 68/D4
Akolmiut (Kasigluk), Alaska (†99609) 196/F2
Akpatok (isl.), N.W.T. 162/K3
Akpatok (isl.), N.W. Terrs. 187/M3
Akpazar, Turkey 63/H3
Akpınar, Turkey 63/D5
Akqi, China 77/A3
Akra, N. Dak. (†58220) 282/P2
Akranes, Iceland 21/B1
Akreïjit, Mauritania 106/C5
Akrítas (cape), Greece 45/E7
Akron, Ala. (35441) 195/C5
Akron, Colo. (80720) 208/N2
Akron, Ind. (46910) 227/E2
Akron, Iowa (51001) 229/A3
Akron, Mich. (48701) 250/F5
Akron, N.Y. (14001) 276/C4
Akron, Ohio 188/K2
Akron, Ohio (*44301) 284/G3
Akron, Ohio 146/K5
Akron, Pa. (17501) 294/K5
Aksai Chin (reg.), Pakistan 68/D2
Aksaray, Turkey 63/F3
Aksay, China 77/D4
Aksay, U.S.S.R. 48/F4
Akşehir, Turkey 63/D3
Akşehir, Turkey 59/B2
Akşehir (lake), Turkey 63/D3
Akseki, Turkey 63/D4
Aksu (Aqsu), China 77/B3
Aksu, China 54/K5
Aksu (riv.), Turkey 63/D4
Aksum, Ethiopia 102/F3
Aksum, Ethiopia 111/G5
Aksum, Ethiopia 59/C7
Aktas, U.S.S.R. 48/G5
Aktash, U.S.S.R. 48/J4
Aktí (pen.), Greece 45/G5
Aktyubinsk, U.S.S.R. 54/G4
Aktyubinsk, U.S.S.R. 48/F4
Aku, Nigeria 106/F7
Akun (isl.), Alaska 196/E4
Akune, Japan 81/E7
Akure, Nigeria 106/F7
Akureyri, Ice. 4/C10
Akureyri, Iceland 21/C1
Akureyri, Iceland 7/C2
Akuse, Ghana 106/E7
Akutan, Alaska (99553) 196/E4
Akutan (isl.), Alaska 196/E4
Akutan (passage), Alaska 196/E4
Akviran, Turkey 63/E4
Akyab (Sittwe), Burma 72/B2
Akyazı, Turkey 63/D2
Ål, Norway 18/F6
Alabam, Ark. (†72740) 202/C1
Alabama 188/J4
ALABAMA 195
Alabama (riv.), Ala. 188/J4
Alabama (riv.), Ala. 195/C8
Alabama (state), U.S. 146/K6
Alabaster, Ala. (35007) 195/E4
Alabaster, Mich. (†48763) 250/F4
Alabat, Philippines 82/D3

Allgäu 327

Alabat (isl.), Philippines 82/D3
Alaca, Turkey 63/F2
Alacahan, Turkey 63/G3
Alaçam, Turkey 63/F2
Alachua (co.), Fla. 212/D2
Alachua, Fla. (32615) 212/D2
Alacrán (reef), Mexico 150/P5
Alacranes, Cuba 158/D1
Aladağ (mt.), Turkey 63/F4
Aladagh, Kuh-i- (mt.), Iran 59/G2
'Aladagh, Kuh-e (mts.), Iran 66/K2
Aladdin, Wyo. (82710) 319/H1
Alaejos, Spain 33/D2
Alagir, U.S.S.R. 52/F6
Alagoa Grande, Brazil 132/H4
Alagoas (state), Brazil 132/G5
Alagoinhas, Brazil 120/F4
Alagoinhas, Brazil 132/G6
Alagón, Spain 33/F2
Alagón (riv.), Spain 33/C2
Alah (riv.), Philippines 82/E7
Al Ahqaf (Bahr es Safi) (des.), Saudi Arabia 59/E6
Al 'Ain, Saudi Arabia 59/C4
Alajuela, C. Rica 154/E6
Alakanuk, Alaska (99554) 196/E2
Alakol' (lake), U.S.S.R. 48/J5
Al 'Ala, Saudi Arabia 59/C4
Alalakeiki (chan.), Hawaii 218/J3
Alalapadu, Suriname 131/C4
Alamagan (isl.), No. Marianas 87/E4
Alamance (co.), N.C. 281/L3
Alamance, N.C. (27201) 281/K2
Alameda (co.), Calif. 204/D6
Alameda, Calif. (94501) 204/J2
Alameda (creek), Calif. 204/K3
Alameda, N. Mex. (87114) 274/C3
Alameda, Sask. 181/J6
Alamikamba, Nicaragua 154/E4
Alamo (lake), Ariz. 198/B4
Alamo (riv.), Calif. 204/K11
Alamo, Georgia (30411) 217/G6
Alamo, Ind. (47916) 227/C5
Alamo, Mexico 150/L6
Alamo, Nev. (89001) 266/F5
Alamo, N. Dak. (58830) 282/D2
Alamo, Tenn. (38001) 237/C9
Alamo, Texas (78516) 303/F11
Ala Moana, Hawaii 218/C4
Alamo-Danville, Calif. (94507) 204/K2
Alamogordo, N. Mex. 188/E4
Alamogordo, N. Mex. (88310) 274/C6
Alamo Heights, Texas (78209) 303/K10
Álamos, Mexico 150/E3
Alamosa (co.), Colo. 208/H7
Alamosa, Colo. (81101) 208/H8
Alamosa (creek), Colo. 208/G8
Alamosa (riv.), N. Mex. 274/B5
Alamota, Kansas (67830) 232/B3
Åland (Ahvenanmaa) (prov.), Finland 18/L6
Åland (isls.), Finland 7/F2
Åland (isls.), Finland 18/L6
Alanje, Panama 154/F6
Alanreed, Texas (79002) 303/D2
Alanson, Mich. (49706) 250/E3
Alanthus Grove, Mo. (†64489) 261/D2
Alanya, Turkey 59/B2
Alanya, Turkey 63/D4
Alaotra (lake), Madagascar 118/H3
Alapaha (riv.), Fla. 212/C1
Alapaha, Georgia (31622) 217/F8
Alapaha (riv.), Georgia 217/F7
Alaqua (creek), Fla. 212/C6
Alarcón (res.), Spain 33/E3
Alarka, N.C. (†28713) 281/C4
Alas (str.), Indonesia 85/F7
Alaşehir, Turkey 63/C3
Alashtar, Iran 66/E4
Alaska (reg.) 4/C17
Alaska 188/C5
Alaska (gulf) 146/D4
ALASKA 196
Alaska (gulf), Alaska 188/D6
Alaska (pen.), Alaska 188/C6
Alaska (range), Alaska 188/C6
Alaska (range), Alaska 146/C3
Alaska (pen.), Alaska 146/C4
Alaska (gulf), Alaska 196/K3
Alaska (pen.), Alaska 196/G3
Alaska (range), Alaska 196/H2
Alaska, Mich. (†49316) 250/D6
Alaska (state), U.S. 2/B2
Alaska (state), U.S. 146/C3
Alaska (range), U.S. 4/C17
Alaska (pen.), U.S. 4/D18
Alaska (gulf), U.S. 4/D17
Alaska Highway, Yukon 187/E3
Alassio, Italy 34/A2
Alatna, Alaska (†99720) 196/H1
Alatna (riv.), Alaska 196/H1
Alatri, Italy 34/D4
Alatyr', U.S.S.R. 52/G4
Al 'Auda, Saudi Arabia 59/E4
Alausí, Ecuador 128/C4
Álava (prov.), Spain 33/E1
Alava (cape), Wash. 188/A1
Alava (cape), Wash. 310/A2
Alaverdi, U.S.S.R. 52/F6
Alavus, Finland 18/N5
Alayor, Spain 33/J3
Al 'Azair, Iraq 66/E5
Alazeya (riv.), U.S.S.R. 48/Q3
Al 'Aziziya, Iraq 59/E3
Al 'Aziziya, Iraq 66/D4
Alba, Italy 34/B2
Alba, Mich. (49611) 250/E4
Alba, Mo. (64830) 261/D8
Alba, Pa. (16910) 294/J2
Alba, Texas (75410) 303/J5
Albacete (prov.), Spain 33/E3
Albacete, Spain 7/D5
Albacete, Spain 33/F3
Alba de Tormes, Spain 33/D2
Albaida, Spain 33/F3
Alba Iulia, Romania 45/F2
Albalate del Arzobispo, Spain 33/F2
Alban, Ontario 177/D1
Albanel, Québec 172/E1
Albanel (lake), Québec 174/C2
Albania 2/K3
Albania 7/G4
ALBANIA 45/E5
Albano (lake), Italy 34/F7
Albano Laziale, Italy 34/F7
Albany, Australia 87/B9
Albany, Calif. (94706) 204/J2
Albany, Ga. 146/K6
Albany, Georgia (*31701) 217/D7
Albany, Ill. (61230) 222/C2
Albany, Ind. (47320) 227/G4
Albany, Jamaica 158/J6
Albany, Ky. (42602) 237/L7
Albany, La. (70711) 238/M1
Albany, Minn. (56307) 255/D5
Albany, Mo. (64402) 261/D2
Albany○, N.H. (†03864) 268/E4
Albany (cap.), N.Y. 188/M2
Albany (cap.), N.Y. 146/L5
Albany (co.), N.Y. 276/M5
Albany (cap.), N.Y. (*12201) 276/N5
Albany, N. Zealand 100/B1
Albany, Nova Scotia 168/C4
Albany, Ohio (45710) 284/F7
Albany, Okla. (74721) 288/O7
Albany (riv.), Ont. 146/K4
Albany (riv.), Ont. 162/H5
Albany (riv.), Ontario 175/C2
Albany, Oreg. 188/B2
Albany, Oreg. (97321) 291/D3
Albany, Pr. Edward I. 168/E2
Albany, Texas (76430) 303/E5
Albany, Vt. (05820) 268/C2
Albany○, Vt. (05820) 268/C2
Albany, W. Australia 88/B6
Albany, W. Australia 92/B6
Albany, Wis. (53502) 317/G10
Albany (co.), Wyo. 319/G4
Albany, Wyo. (†82055) 319/F4
Albany Creek, Queensland 88/J2
Albardon, Argentina 143/C3
Albarracín, Spain 33/F2
Albatross (pt.), N. Zealand 100/E3
Albatross (bay), Queensland 88/G2
Albatross (bay), Queensland 95/B2
Albay (prov.), Philippines 82/D4
Albay (gulf), Philippines 82/D4
Albee, S. Dak. (57210) 298/S3
Albemarle (pt.), Ecuador 128/B9
Albemarle (sound), N.C. 188/L3
Albemarle, N.C. (28001) 281/J4
Albemarle (sound), N.C. 281/S2
Albemarle (co.), Va. 307/L5
Albenga, Italy 34/B3
Albeni Falls (dam), Idaho 220/B1
Alberdi, Paraguay 144/D5
Alberene, Va. (†22959) 307/L5
Alberga, S. Australia 94/D2
Alberga, The (riv.), S. Australia 94/D2
Alberga, The (riv.), S. Australia 88/E5
Alberhill, Calif. (†92330) 204/E11
Alberni (inlet), Br. Col. 184/H3
Albers, Ill. (62215) 222/D5
Albert (canal), Belgium 27/F6
Albert, France 28/E2
Albert, Kansas (67511) 232/C3
Albert (co.), New Bruns. 170/F3
Albert, N. Mex. (87733) 274/F3
Albert, N.S. Wales 97/D3
Albert, Okla. (73001) 288/K4
Albert (lake), Québec 172/C3
Albert (Mobuto Sese Seko) (lake), Uganda 115/F3
Albert (creek), Wyo. 319/B4
Albert (Mobuto Sese Seko) (lake), Zaire 115/F3
Alberta (prov.) 162/E5
Alberta (prov.) Canada 146/G4
Alberta, Ala. (36720) 195/D6
ALBERTA 182
Alberta (mt.), Alberta 182/B3
Alberta (mt.), Alta. 162/E5
Alberta, La. (†71016) 238/D2
Alberta, Minn. (56207) 255/B5
Alberta, Va. (23821) 307/N7
Alberta Beach, Alberta 182/C3
Albert City, Iowa (50510) 229/C3
Albert Edward (bay), N.W. Terrs. 187/H3
Albert Head, Br. Col. 184/J4
Alberti, Argentina 143/G7
Albertirsa, Hungary 41/E3
Albert Lea, Minn. (56007) 255/E7
Albert Mines, New Bruns. 170/F3
Alberton, Mont. (59820) 262/B3
Alberton, Pr. Edward I. 168/E2
Alberton, S. Africa 118/H6
Albert Town, Jamaica 158/H6
Albertville, Ala. (35950) 195/F2
Albertville, France 28/G5
Albertville, Minn. (55301) 255/E5
Albertville, Sask. 181/F2
Albeuve, Switzerland 39/D3
Albi, France 28/E6
Albia, Iowa (52531) 229/H6
Albin, Wyo. (82050) 319/H4
Albina, Suriname 131/D3
Albino, Italy 34/B2
Albion, Calif. (95410) 204/B4
Albion, Idaho (83311) 220/E7
Albion (mts.), Idaho 220/E7
Albion, Ill. (62806) 222/E5
Albion, Ind. (46701) 227/G2
Albion, Iowa (50005) 229/H4
Albion○, Maine (04910) 243/E6
Albion, Mich. (49224) 250/E6
Albion, Nebr. (68620) 264/F3
Albion, N.Y. (14411) 276/D4
Albion, Okla. (74521) 288/R5
Albion, Pa. (16401) 294/B2
Albion, R.I. (02802) 249/H5
Albion, Wash. (99102) 310/H4
Albion, Wis. (†53534) 317/H10
Al Birk, Saudi Arabia 59/D6
Albocácer, Spain 33/F2
Alborán (isl.), Spain 7/D5
Alborán (isl.), Spain 33/E5
Ålborg, Denmark 7/F3
Ålborg, Denmark 18/G8
Ålborg (bay), Denmark 21/D4
Alborn, Minn. (55702) 255/F4
Albox, Spain 33/E4
Albreda, Br. Col. 184/H4
Albright, W. Va. (26519) 312/G3
Albrightsville, Pa. (18210) 294/L3
Albristhorn (mt.), Switzerland 39/D4
Albufeira, Portugal 33/B4
Albuñol, Spain 33/E4
Albuquerque (cays), Colombia 126/A10
Albuquerque, N. Mex. 146/H6
Albuquerque, N. Mex. 188/E3
Albuquerque, N. Mex. (*87101) 274/C3
Alburg, Vt. (05440) 268/A2
Alburg○, Vt. (05440) 268/A2
Alburnett, Iowa (52202) 229/K4
Alburquerque, Spain 33/C3
Alburtis, Pa. (18011) 294/L5
Albury, Australia 87/E9
Albury, N. S. Wales 88/H7
Albury, N.S. Wales 97/D5
Albury, N. Zealand 100/C6
Alca, Peru 128/F10
Alcácer do Sal, Portugal 33/B3
Alcalá, Bolivia 136/C6
Alcalá de Chivert, Spain 33/G2
Alcalá de Guadaira, Spain 33/D4
Alcalá de Henares, Spain 33/G4
Alcalá de los Gazules, Spain 33/D4
Alcalá la Real, Spain 33/E4
Alcalde, N. Mex. (87511) 274/C2
Alcamo, Italy 34/D6
Alcanar, Spain 33/G2
Alcañices, Spain 33/C2
Alcañiz, Spain 33/F2
Alcântara, Portugal 33/A1
Alcántara, Spain 33/C3
Alcántara (res.), Spain 33/C3
Alcântaratara (res.), Portugal 33/C3
Alcantarilla, Spain 33/F4
Alcaraz, Argentina 143/G5
Alcaraz, Spain 33/E3
Alcaraz, Sierra de (range), Spain 33/E3
Alcatraz (isl.), Calif. 204/J2
Alcaudete, Spain 33/E4
Alcázar de San Juan, Spain 33/E3
Alcester, S. Dak. (57001) 298/R7
Alcida, New Bruns. 170/E1
Alcira, Spain 33/F3
Alco, Ark. (72610) 202/F2
Alco, La. (71402) 238/D4
Alcoa, Tenn. (37701) 237/N9
Alcobaça, Brazil 132/G7
Alcobaça, Portugal 33/B3
Alcolu, S.C. (29001) 296/G4
Alcomdale, Alberta 182/C3
Alcona (co.), Mich. 250/F4
Alcona Beach, Ontario 177/E3
Alcones, Chile 138/F5
Alcony, Ohio (†45373) 284/B5
Alcora, Spain 33/F2
Alcorisa, Spain 33/F2
Alcorn, Ky. (†40447) 237/O5
Alcorn (co.), Miss. 256/G1
Alcorn State University, Miss. (39096) 256/B7
Alcorta, Argentina 143/F6
Alcoutim, Portugal 33/C4
Alcova, Wyo. (82620) 319/F3
Alcova (res.), Wyo. 319/F3
Alcoy, Spain 33/F3
Alcudia (bay), Spain 33/H3
Alda, Nebr. (68810) 264/F4
Aldabra (isls.), Seychelles 102/G5
Aldabra (isls.), Seychelles 118/H1
Aldama, Chihuahua, Mexico 150/G2
Aldama, Tamaulipas, Mexico 150/L5
Aldan, Pa. (†19018) 294/M7
Aldan, U.S.S.R. 54/O4
Aldan (riv.), U.S.S.R. 54/P3
Aldan, U.S.S.R. 48/N4
Aldan (plat.), U.S.S.R. 48/N4
Aldan (riv.), U.S.S.R. 48/O3
Aldeburgh, England 13/J5
Aldeburgh, England 10/G4
Aldeia Carajá, Brazil 132/D6
Aldeia Nova de São Bento, Portugal 33/C4
Alden, Ill. (60001) 222/E1
Alden, Iowa (50006) 229/G4
Alden, Kansas (67512) 232/D3
Alden, Mich. (49612) 250/D4
Alden, Minn. (56009) 255/E7
Alden, N.Y. (14004) 276/C5
Alden Bridge, La. (†71006) 238/C1
Aldenville, Pa. (18401) 294/M2
Alder, Mont. (59710) 262/D5
Alder, Wash. (†98328) 310/C4
Alder (lake), Wash. 310/C4
Alder Creek, N.Y. (13301) 276/K4
Alder Flats, Alberta 182/C3
Alderley, Wis. (†53066) 317/J1
Alderney (isl.), Chan. Is. 10/E6
Alderney (isl.), Chan. Is. 13/E8
Alderpoint, Calif. (95411) 204/B3
Alder Point, Nova Scotia 168/H2
Aldershot, England 10/F5
Aldershot, England 13/G8
Aldershot, Nova Scotia 168/D3
Alderson, Okla. (74522) 288/P5
Alderson, W. Va. (24910) 312/E7
Aldersyde, Alberta 182/C4
Aldine, Ind. (†46366) 227/D2
Aldora, Georgia (†30204) 217/D4
Aldouane, New Bruns. 170/E2
Aldrich, Ala. (†35115) 195/E4
Aldrich, Minn. (56434) 255/C4
Aldrich, Mo. (65601) 261/F7
Aldridge Brownhills, England 10/G3
Aldridge Brownhills, England 13/E5
Aledo, Ill. (61231) 222/C2
Aledo, Texas (76008) 303/E2
Aleg, Mauritania 106/B5
Alegre, Brazil 135/F2
Alegre, Brazil 132/F8
Alegrete, Brazil 132/B10
Alegrete, Brazil 120/D5
'Aleih, Lebanon 63/F6
Alejandra, Argentina 143/F5
Alejandría, Bolivia 136/C3
Alejandro Selkirk (isl.), Chile 120/A6
Aleknagik, Alaska (99555) 196/G3
Aleksandriya, U.S.S.R. 52/D5
Aleksandrov Gay, U.S.S.R. 52/G4
Aleksandrovsk, U.S.S.R. 52/J3
Aleksandrovsk-Sakhalinsky, U.S.S.R. 54/R4
Aleksandrovsk-Sakhalinskiy, U.S.S.R. 48/P5
Aleksandrów Kujawski, Poland 47/D2
Aleksandrów Łódzki, Poland 47/D3
Alekseyevka, U.S.S.R. 48/H4
Alekseyevka, U.S.S.R. 52/E4
Aleksin, U.S.S.R. 52/E4
Aleksinac, Yugoslavia 45/E4
Além Paraíba, Brazil 135/E2
Alençon, France 28/D3
Alenquer, Brazil 132/C3
Alenquer, Brazil 120/D3
Alenuihaha (chan.), Hawaii 218/E7
Aleppo (prov.), Syria 63/G4
Aleppo, Syria 54/E6
Aleppo, Syria 59/C2
Aleppo, Syria 63/G4
Aléria, France 28/B6
Alert, Canada 4/A12
Alert, Ind. (†47283) 227/F6
Alert, N.C. (†27589) 281/N2
Alert, N.W.T. 162/N3
Alert, N.W. Terrs. 187/M1
Alert (pt.), N.W. Terrs. 187/K1
Alert Bay, Br. Col. 184/D5
Alès, France 28/E5
Alessandria (prov.), Italy 34/B2
Alessandria, Italy 34/B2
Ålestrup, Denmark 21/C4
Ålesund, Norway 7/E2
Ålesund, Norway 18/D5
Aletschhorn (mt.), Switzerland 39/F4
Aleutian (isls.), Alaska 188/D6
Aleutian (isls.), Alaska 196/J4
Aleutian (range), Alaska 196/G3
Aleutian (isls.), U.S. 4/D18
Aleutian (isls.), U.S. 2/A3
Alex, Okla. (73002) 288/L5
Alexander (arch.), Alaska 146/E4
Alexander (arch.), Alaska 196/L1
Alexander (isl.) 5/B15
Alexander, Ark. (72002) 202/F4
Alexander (lake), Conn. 210/H1
Alexander, Georgia (30801) 217/J4
Alexander (co.), Ill. 222/D6
Alexander, Ill. (62601) 222/D4
Alexander, Iowa (50420) 229/G3
Alexander, Kansas (67553) 232/C3
Alexander○, Maine (†04610) 243/H5
Alexander, Manitoba 179/B5
Alexander, N.Y. (14005) 276/D5
Alexander (co.), N.C. 281/G3
Alexander, N. Dak. (58831) 282/C4
Alexander (cape), Solomon Is. 86/D2
Alexander (arch.), U.S. 4/D16
Alexander, W. Va. (26218) 312/F5
Alexander Bay, S. Africa 102/D7
Alexander Bay, S. Africa 118/B5
Alexander City, Ala. (35010) 195/G5
Alexander Mills, N.C. (†28043) 281/F4
Alexandra, N. Zealand 100/B6
Alexandra, S. Africa 118/H6
Alexandra, Victoria 97/C5
Alexandra Land (isl.), U.S.S.R. 4/A8
Alexandra Land (isl.), U.S.S.R. 48/E1
Alexandretta (Iskenderun), Turkey 63/G4
Alexandretta (gulf), Turkey 63/F4
Alexandria, Ala. (36250) 195/G3
Alexandria, Br. Col. 184/F4
Alexandria, Egypt 2/L4
Alexandria, Egypt 102/E1
Alexandria, Egypt 59/A3
Alexandria, Egypt 111/J2
Alexandria, Ind. (46001) 227/F4
Alexandria, Jamaica 158/J6
Alexandria, Ky. (41001) 237/N3
Alexandria, La. 146/J6
Alexandria, La. 188/H4
Alexandria, La. (71301) 238/E4
Alexandria, Minn. (56308) 255/C5
Alexandria, Mo. (63430) 261/K2
Alexandria, Nebr. (68303) 264/G4
Alexandria○, N.H. (†03222) 268/D4
Alexandria, North. Terr. 93/E5
Alexandria, Ohio (43001) 284/E5
Alexandria, Ontario 177/K2
Alexandria, Pa. (16611) 294/F4
Alexandria, Romania 45/G3
Alexandria, Scotland 15/A1
Alexandria, Scotland 10/A1
Alexandria, S. Dak. (57311) 298/O6
Alexandria, Tenn. (37012) 237/J8
Alexandria, Va. 188/L3
Alexandria (I.C.), Va. (*22301) 307/S3
Alexandria Bay, N.Y. (13607) 276/J2
Alexandrina (lake), S. Australia 94/F6
Alexandroúpolis, Greece 45/H5
Alexis, Ill. (61412) 222/C2
Alexis (riv.), Newf. 166/C3
Alexis Creek, Br. Col. 184/F4
Aleysk, U.S.S.R. 48/J4
Aleza Lake, Br. Col. 184/G3
Alfalfa (co.), Okla. 288/K1
Alfalfa, Okla. (†73015) 288/J4
Al Falluja, Iraq 59/D3
Al Falluja, Iraq 66/C4
Alfaro, Spain 33/F1
Alfatar, Bulgaria 45/H4
Al Fatha, Iraq 59/D2
Al Fatha, Iraq 66/C3
Alfeld, W. Germany 22/C2
Alfenas, Brazil 135/D2
Alférez (riv.), Uruguay 145/E5
Alford, England 13/H4
Alford, Fla. (32420) 212/D6
Alford○, Mass. (†01261) 249/A4
Alford, Scotland 15/F3
Alford, Scotland 10/E2
Alfordsville, Ind. (†47553) 227/C7
Alfred, Maine (04002) 243/B9
Alfred○, Maine (04002) 243/B9
Alfred, N.Y. (14802) 276/E6
Alfred, N. Dak. (58411) 282/N6
Alfred, Ontario 177/K2
Alfredton, N. Zealand 100/F4
Alfreton, England 13/F4
Alga, U.S.S.R. 48/F5
Ålgård, Norway 18/D7
Algarrobo, Chile 138/F3
Algarrobo (pt.), P. Rico 161/A2
Algarrobo del Aguila, Argentina 143/C4
Algeciras, Colombia 126/C6
Algeciras, Spain 33/D4
Algemesí, Spain 33/F3
Alger (co.), Mich. 250/C2
Alger, Mich. (48610) 250/E4
Alger, Ohio (45812) 284/C4
Algeria 2/J4
Algeria 102/C2
ALGERIA 106/D3
Algés, Portugal 33/A1
Algete, Spain 33/G4
Alghero, Italy 34/B4
Algiers (cap.), Algeria 102/C1
Algiers (cap.), Algeria 106/E1
Algiers (cap.), Algeria 2/K4
Algiers, Ind. (†47567) 227/C7
Algoa, Ark. (†72112) 202/H3
Algoa (bay), S. Africa 118/D6
Algoa, Texas (†77511) 303/K3
Algodones, N. Mex. (87001) 274/C3
Algoma, Miss. (38820) 256/G2
Algoma (terr. dist.), Ontario 177/J5
Algoma (terr. dist.), Ontario 175/D3
Algoma, Oreg. (†97601) 291/F5
Algoma, W. Va. (24807) 312/D8
Algoma, Wis. (54201) 317/M6
Algoma Mills, Ontario 177/B1
Algona, Iowa (50511) 229/E2
Algona, Wash. (98002) 310/C3
Algonac, Mich. (48001) 250/G6
Algonquin, Ill. (60102) 222/E1
Algonquin (peak), N.Y. 276/M2
Algonquin Park, Ontario 177/F2
Algonquin Prov. Park, Ontario 177/F2
Algonquin Prov. Park, Ontario 175/E3
Algood, Tenn. (38501) 237/K8
Algorta, Uruguay 145/B3
Algrove, Sask. 181/H3
Alhama de Granada, Spain 33/E4
Alhama de Murcia, Spain 33/F4
Alhambra, Alberta 182/C3
Alhambra, Calif. (*91801) 204/C10
Alhambra, Ill. (62001) 222/D5
Al Hawtah, P.D.R. Yemen 59/E6
Al Hilla, Saudi Arabia 59/E5
Al Hoceima, Morocco 106/D1
Alhos Vedros, Portugal 33/B3
Alhué, Estero de (riv.), Chile 138/F4
Alia, Spain 33/D3
'Aliabad, Kuh-e (mt.), Iran 59/F3
'Aliabad, Kuh-e (mt.), Iran 66/G3
Aliağa, Turkey 63/B3
Alibag, India 68/C5
Alibates Flint Quarries Nat'l Mon., Texas 303/C2
Ali-Bayramly, U.S.S.R. 52/G7
Alibeyköyü, Turkey 63/D6
Alicante (prov.), Spain 33/F3
Alicante, Spain 33/F3
Alicante, Spain 7/D5
Alice (lake), Nebr. 264/A2
Alice, N. Dak. (58003) 282/P6
Alice (lake), N. Dak. 282/M3
Alice, Ontario 177/G2
Alice (chan.), Philippines 82/B8
Alice (riv.), Queensland 95/C4
Alice, Texas (78332) 303/F10
Alice Arm, Br. Col. 184/C2
Alicel, Oreg. (†97824) 291/J2
Alice Springs, Australia 87/D8
Alice Springs, North. Terr. 88/E4
Alice Springs, North. Terr. 93/D7
Aliceville, Ala. (35442) 195/B4
Aliceville (dam), Ala. 195/B4
Alicia, Kansas (66832) 232/G3
Alicia, Ark. (72410) 202/H2
Alicia (bank), Colombia 126/B8
Alicudi (isl.), Italy 34/E5
Alida, Minn. (†56676) 255/C3
Alida, Sask. 181/K6
Aligarh, India 68/D3
'Ali Gharbi, Iraq 66/E4
Alijó, Portugal 33/C2
Alima (riv.), Congo 115/B4
Alimodian, Philippines 82/D5
Alindao, Cent. Afr. Rep. 115/D2
Aline, Georgia (†30420) 217/H6
Aline, Okla. (73716) 288/K1
Alingly, Sask. 181/E2
Alingsås, Sweden 18/H7
Alipore, India 68/F2
Aliquippa, Pa. (15001) 294/B4
Ali Sabieh, Djibouti 111/H5
'Ali Sharqi, Iraq 66/E4
Aliskerovo, U.S.S.R. 48/R3
Alivérion, Greece 45/G6
Aliwal North, S. Africa 118/D6
Alix, Alberta 182/D3
Alix, Ark. (72820) 202/C3
Aljezur, Portugal 33/B4
Aljojuca, Mexico 150/O1
Aljustrel, Portugal 33/B4
Alkabo, N. Dak. (58832) 282/C2
Alkali (lakes), Calif. 204/E2
Alkali (lake), Nev. 266/B1
Alkali (lakes), N. Dak. 282/L3
Alkali Lake, Br. Col. 184/F4
Alkaline (lake), N. Dak. 282/L6
Alken, Belgium 27/G7
Alkmaar, Netherlands 27/F3
Alkmaardermeer (lake), Netherlands 27/F3
Alkol, W. Va. (25501) 312/C6
Al Kufa, Iraq 66/D4
Al Kumait, Iraq 66/E4
Al Kuwait (cap.), Kuwait 59/E4
Al Kuwait (cap.), Kuwait 54/F7
Allagash○, Maine (†04774) 243/F1
Allagash (lake), Maine 243/D3
Allagash (riv.), Maine 243/E2
Allahabad, India 68/E3
Allahabad, India 54/K7
Allaine (riv.), Switzerland 39/D2
Allaire, N.J. (†07727) 273/E3
Allakaket, Alaska (99720) 196/H1
Allakh-Yun', U.S.S.R. 48/O3
Allamakee (co.), Iowa 229/L2
Allaman, Switzerland 39/B4
All American (canal), Calif. 204/K11
Allamoore, Texas (†79855) 303/C11
Allamuchy, N.J. (07820) 273/D2
Allan (mt.), Idaho 220/D4
Allan, Sask. 181/E4
Allan (hills), Sask. 181/E4
Allanmyo, Burma 72/B3
Allanwater, Ontario 175/C2
Allanwater, Ontario 177/G4
'Allaqi, Wadi (dry riv.), Egypt 111/F3
Allard (lake), Québec 174/E2
Allardt, Tenn. (38504) 237/M8
Allardville, New Bruns. 170/E1
Allariz, Spain 33/C1
Allatoona (lake), Georgia 217/C2
Alle, Switzerland 39/D2
Alleene, Ark. (71820) 202/B6
Allegan (co.), Mich. 250/D6
Allegan, Mich. (49010) 250/D6
Allegany (co.), Md. 245/C2
Allegany (co.), N.Y. 276/D6
Allegany, N.Y. (14706) 276/C6
Allegany, Oreg. (97407) 291/D4
Allegany Ind. Res., N.Y. 276/C6
Alleghany, Calif. (95910) 204/E4
Alleghany (co.), N.C. 281/G1
Alleghany (co.), Va. 307/H5
Alleghany, Va. (†24426) 307/H5
Allegheny (res.), N.Y. 276/C7
Allegheny (riv.), N.Y. 276/C6
Allegheny (co.), Pa. 294/B5
Allegheny (res.), Pa. 294/E2
Allegheny (riv.), Pa. 294/D2
Allegheny (mts.), Va. 307/H5
Allegheny Front (mts.), Md. 245/C2
Allegheny Front (mts.), Pa. 294/E5
Allègre (pt.), Guadeloupe 161/A6
Allegre, Ky. (42203) 237/G7
Alleman, Iowa (50007) 229/F5
Allemands (lake), La. 238/M4
Allen, Ala. (36419) 195/C7
Allen, Argentina 143/C4
Allen (co.), Ind. 227/G2
Allen, Lough (lake), Ireland 10/C3
Allen (lake), Ireland 17/E3
Allen, Bog of (marsh), Ireland 17/H5
Allen (co.), Kansas 232/G4
Allen, Kansas (66833) 232/F3
Allen (co.), Ky. 237/J7
Allen, Ky. (41601) 237/R5
Allen (par.), La. 238/E5
Allen, La. (†71469) 238/D3
Allen, Md. (21810) 245/R7
Allen, Mich. (49227) 250/E7
Allen, Miss. (†39083) 256/C7
Allen (mt.), Mont. 262/C2
Allen, Nebr. (68710) 264/H2
Allen (co.), Ohio 284/B4
Allen, Okla. (74825) 288/O5
Allen, Pa. (†17007) 294/H5
Allen, S. Dak. (57714) 298/F7
Allen, Texas (75002) 303/H1
Allendale, England 13/E3
Allendale, Ill. (62410) 222/F5
Allendale, Mo. (†64456) 261/D2
Allendale, N.J. (07401) 273/B1
Allendale (co.), S.C. 296/E6
Allendale, S.C. (29810) 296/E5
Allende, Coahuila, Mexico 150/J2
Allende, Nuevo León, Mexico 150/J4
Allendorf, Iowa (51330) 229/B2
Allenford, Ontario 177/C3
Allenhurst, Georgia (31301) 217/J7
Allenhurst, N.J. (07711) 273/F3
Allen Park, Mich. (48101) 250/B7
Allens Mills, Maine (†04938) 243/C6
Allenspark, Colo. (80510) 208/J2
Allen Springs, Ky. (†42122) 237/J7
Allenstein (Olsztyn), Poland 47/E2
Allenstown○, N.H. (†03275) 268/E5
Allensville, Ky. (42204) 237/G7
Allensville, Ohio (45611) 284/E7
Allensville, Pa. (17002) 294/G4
Allenton, Mo. (63001) 261/M4
Allenton, R.I. (†02852) 249/H6
Allenton, Wis. (53002) 317/K9
Allentown, Georgia (31003) 217/F5
Allentown, N.J. (08501) 273/D3
Allentown, N.Y. (14707) 276/E6
Allentown, Ohio (†45801) 284/B4
Allentown, Pa. 188/L2
Allentown, Pa. (*18101) 294/L4
Allentsteig, Austria 41/C2
Allenville, Ill. (†61951) 222/E4
Allenville, Mo. (†63740) 261/N8
Allenwood, N.J. (08720) 273/E3
Allenwood, Pa. (17810) 294/H3
Alleppey-Cochin, India 68/D7
Aller (riv.), W. Germany 22/C2
Allerton, Ill. (61810) 222/F4
Allerton, Iowa (50008) 229/G7
Allerton, Mass. (02045) 249/E7
Allerton (pt.), Mass. 249/E7
Alley, Jamaica 158/J7
Alley Spring, Mo. (†65466) 261/J8
Allgäu (reg.), W. Germany 22/D5

328 Allgäu

Allgäu Alps (mts.), Austria 41/A3
Allgood, Ala. (35013) 195/F3
Alliance, Alberta 182/E3
Alliance, Nebr. (69301) 264/A2
Alliance, N.C. (28509) 281/R4
Alliance, Ohio (44601) 284/H4
Al Lidam, Saudi Arabia 59/D5
Allier (dept.), France 28/E4
Allier (riv.), France 28/E5
Alligator (lake), Fla. 212/E3
Alligator (pt.), La. 238/L6
Alligator, Miss. (38720) 256/C2
Alligator (lake), N.C. 281/S3
Alligator (riv.), N.C. 281/S3
Alligator Pond, Jamaica 158/H6
Allingåbro, Denmark 21/D5
Allinge-Sandvig, Denmark 18/J9
Allinge-Sandvig, Denmark 21/F8
Allingham, Alberta 182/D4
Allingtown, Conn. (†06516) 210/D3
Allison, Iowa (50602) 229/H3
Allison, N. Mex. (†87301) 274/A3
Allison, Texas (79003) 303/D2
Allisona, Tenn. (†37046) 237/H9
Allisonia, Va. (24310) 307/G7
Allison Park, Pa. (15101) 294/C4
Alliston, Ontario 177/E3
Al Lith, Saudi Arabia 59/C5
Alloa, Scotland 10/B1
Alloa, Scotland 15/C1
Allock, Ky. (41710) 237/P6
Allons, Tenn. (38541) 237/L8
Allouez, Mich. (49805) 250/A1
Allouez, Wis. (†54301) 317/L7
Allow (riv.), Ireland 17/D7
Alloway, N.J. (08001) 273/C4
Alloways (creek), N.J. 273/C4
Allport, Ark. (†72046) 202/G4
Allred, Tenn. (38542) 237/L8
All Saints, Ant. & Bar. 161/E11
All Saints Village, Mo. (†63376) 261/M2
Allsboro, Ala. (†35616) 195/B1
Allsbrook, S.C. (†29569) 296/K3
Allschwil, Switzerland 39/D1
Allview, Md. (†21043) 245/L3
Allyn, Wash. (98524) 310/C3
Alma, Ala. (36501) 195/C8
Alma, Ark. (72921) 202/B3
Alma, Colo. (80420) 208/G4
Alma, Georgia (31510) 217/G7
Alma, Ill. (62807) 222/E5
Alma, Kansas (66401) 232/F2
Alma, Mich. (48801) 250/E5
Alma, Mo. (64001) 261/E4
Alma, Nebr. (68920) 264/E4
Alma, New Bruns. 170/F3
Alma, N. Mex. (†88039) 274/A5
Alma, N.C. (†28364) 281/35
Alma, Ontario 177/D4
Alma, Québec 174/C3
Alma, Québec 172/F1
Alma (isl.), Québec 172/F1
Alma, W. Va. (26320) 312/E4
Alma, Wis. (54610) 317/C7
Alma-Ata, U.S.S.R. 2/N3
Alma-Ata, U.S.S.R. 54/J5
Alma-Ata, U.S.S.R. 48/H5
Alma Center, Wis. (54611) 317/E7
Alma City, Minn. (†56048) 255/E6
Almada, Portugal 33/A1
Almadén, Spain 33/D3
Almagro, Spain 33/E3
Almaguer, Colombia 126/B7
Almanor (lake), Calif. 204/D3
Almansa, Spain 33/F3
Almanza, Spain 33/D1
Almanzor (mt.), Spain 33/D2
Almanzora (riv.), Spain 33/F4
Almartha, Mo. (†65773) 261/H9
Almazán, Spain 33/E2
Almaznyy, U.S.S.R. 48/M3
Almeida, Sierra (mts.), Chile 138/C4
Almeida, Portugal 33/C2
Almeirim, Portugal 33/B3
Almelo, Netherlands 27/K4
Almelund, Minn. (55002) 255/F5
Almena, Kansas (67622) 232/C2
Almena, Wis. (54805) 317/B5
Almenara, Brazil 120/E4
Almendra (res.), Spain 33/C2
Almendralejo, Spain 33/C3
Almere, Netherlands 27/G4
Almeria, Nebr. (68811) 264/E3
Almería (prov.), Spain 33/E4
Almería, Spain 7/D5
Almería, Spain 33/E4
Almería (gulf), Spain 33/E4
Al'met'yevsk, U.S.S.R. 52/H3
Älmhult, Sweden 18/H8
Almira, Wash. (99103) 310/G3
Almirantazgo (bay), Chile 138/F11
Almirante, Panama 154/F6
Almirante Montt (gulf), Chile 138/D9
Almirós, Greece 45/F6
Almo, Idaho (83312) 220/E7
Almo, Ky. (42020) 237/E7
Almodôvar, Portugal 33/B4
Almodóvar del Campo, Spain 33/D3
Almoharín, Spain 33/D3
Almoloya del Río, Mexico 150/K1
Almon, Georgia (†30209) 217/E3
Almond, N.Y. (14804) 276/E6
Almond, N.C. (28702) 281/B4
Almond (riv.), Scotland 15/E4
Almond, Wis. (54909) 317/G7
Almont, Colo. (81210) 208/of5
Almont, Mich. (48003) 250/F6
Almont, N. Dak. (58520) 282/H6
Almonte, Ontario 177/H2
Almonte, Spain 33/C4
Almora, India 68/D3
Almora, Minn. (†56551) 255/C4
Almorox, Spain 33/D2
Almota, Wash. (†99111) 310/H4
Al Muadhdham, Saudi Arabia 59/C4
Almudévar, Spain 33/F1
Almuñécar, Spain 33/E4
Almus, Turkey 63/G2
Al Musaiyib, Iraq 59/D3
Al Musaiyib, Iraq 66/D4
Almyra, Ark. (72003) 202/H5
Alna○, Maine (04535) 243/D7
Alness, Scotland 15/D3
Alness (riv.), Scotland 15/D3
Alnwick, England 10/F3
Alnwick, England 13/F2
Alofi (cap.), Niue 87/K7
Aloha, Oreg. (97005) 291/A2
Aloha, Wash. (98550) 310/A3
Alon, Burma 72/B2
Along, India 68/G3
Alonsa, Manitoba 179/C4
Alonso Rojas, Cuba 158/B2
Alor (isl.), Indonesia 85/G7
Álora, Spain 33/D4
Alor Gajah, Malaysia 72/D7
Alor Setar, Malaysia 72/D6
Alorton, Ill. (62207) 222/B2
Alost (Aalst), Belgium 27/D7
Alotau, Papua N.G. 87/E7
Aloysius (mt.), W. Australia 92/E4
Alpachiri, Argentina 143/D4
Alpaugh, Calif. (93201) 204/F8
Alpena, Ark. (72611) 202/D1
Alpena (co.), Mich. 250/F4
Alpena, Mich. (49707) 250/F3
Alpena, S. Dak. (57312) 298/N5
Alpena, W. Va. (†26254) 312/G5
Alpen Siding, Alberta 182/D2
Alpera, Spain 33/F3
Alpes-de-Haute-Provence (dept.), France 28/G5
Alpes-Maritimes (dept.), France 28/G6
Alpha, Ill. (61413) 222/C2
Alpha, Iowa (52130) 229/K3
Alpha, Ky. (42603) 237/L7
Alpha, Mich. (49902) 250/A2
Alpha, Minn. (56111) 255/D7
Alpha, N.J. (08865) 273/C2
Alpha, Queensland 88/H4
Alpharetta, Georgia (30201) 217/D2
Alphen aan de Rijn, Netherlands 27/F4
Alpiarça, Portugal 33/B3
Alpine, Ala. (35014) 195/F4
Alpine, Ariz. (85920) 198/F5
Alpine, Ark. (†71921) 202/D5
Alpine (co.), Calif. 204/F5
Alpine, Calif. (92001) 204/J11
Alpine, Ind. (†47331) 227/G5
Alpine, Ky. (42519) 237/M7
Alpine, N.J. (07620) 273/C1
Alpine, N.Y. (14805) 276/G6
Alpine, Oreg. (97456) 291/D3
Alpine, Tenn. (38543) 237/L8
Alpine, Texas (79830) 303/D12
Alpine, Utah (†84003) 304/C3
Alpine, Wyo. (83128) 319/B2
Alpirsbach, W. Germany 22/C4
Alpnach, Switzerland 39/F3
Alpoca, W. Va. (24710) 312/D7
Alportel, Portugal 33/C4
Alps (mts.) 7/E4
Alpu, Turkey 63/D3
Al Q'aim, Iraq 66/B3
Al Qaiyara, Iraq 66/C3
Al Qosh, Iraq 66/C2
Alquina, Ind. (†47331) 227/G5
Alquízar, Cuba 158/C1
Al Qurna, Iraq 66/E5
Al Qurna, Iraq 59/E3
Alroy Downs, North. Terr. 93/E5
Als (isl.), Denmark 21/C8
Alsace (trad. prov.), France, 29
Alsager, England 13/E4
Alsager, England 10/G2
Alsask, Sask. 181/B4
Alsatia, La. (†71276) 238/H1
Alsdorf, W. Germany 22/B3
Alsea, Oreg. (97324) 291/D3
Alsea (riv.), Oreg. 291/D3
Alsek (riv.), Alaska 196/L3
Alsek (riv.), Br. Col. 184/H1
Alsek (riv.), Yukon 187/E3
Alsen, N. Dak. (58311) 282/N2
Alsey, Ill. (62610) 222/C4
Alsfeld, W. Germany 22/C3
Alsip, Ill. (†60658) 222/B6
Alsózsolca, Hungary 41/F2
Alstead○, N.H. (03602) 268/C5
Alsten (isl.), Norway 18/H4
Alstfjorden (fjord), Norway 18/G3
Alston, England 13/E3
Alston, Georgia (30412) 217/H6
Alston, Mich. (†49958) 250/G1
Alstonville, N.S. Wales 97/G1
Alta, Iowa (51002) 229/C3
Alta, Norway 18/N2
Alta, Utah (84070) 304/C3
Altadena, Calif. (91001) 204/C10
Altaelv (riv.), Norway 18/N2
Alta Gracia, Argentina 143/D3
Altagracia, Cuba 158/G3
Altagracia, Venezuela 124/C2
Altagracia de Orituco, Venezuela 124/E3
Altai (mts.) 54/K5
Altai (mts.), Mongolia 77/C2
Alta Loma, Calif. (91701) 204/E10
Alta Loma, Texas (77510) 303/K3
Altamachi (riv.), Bolivia 136/B5
Altamaha (riv.), Ga. 188/K4
Altamaha (riv.), Georgia 217/H7
Altamaha (sound), Georgia 217/K8
Altamahaw, N.C. (27202) 281/L2
Altamira, Brazil 132/C3
Altamira, Chile 138/B5
Altamira, Dom. Rep. 158/D5
Altamira, Mexico 150/L5
Altamont, Ill. (62411) 222/E4
Altamont, Kansas (67330) 232/G4
Altamont, Manitoba 179/D5
Altamont, Mo. (64620) 261/D3
Altamont, N.Y. (12009) 276/M5
Altamont, Oreg. (†97601) 291/F5
Altamont, S. Dak. (57211) 298/R4
Altamont, Tenn. (37301) 237/K10
Altamont, Utah (84001) 304/D3
Altamonte Springs, Fla. (32701) 212/E3
Altamura, Italy 34/F4
Altar, Mexico 150/D1
Altario, Alberta 182/E4
Altata, Mexico 150/E4
Alt Aussee, Austria 41/B3
Alta Vista, Iowa (50603) 229/J2
Alta Vista, Kansas (66834) 232/F3
Altavista, Va. (24517) 307/K6
Altay, China 77/C2
Altay, Mongolia 77/E2
Altay (mts.), U.S.S.R. 48/J5
Altdorf, Switzerland 39/G3
Altea, Spain 33/G3
Altena, W. Germany 22/B3
Altenburg, E. Germany 22/E3
Altenburg, Mo. (63732) 261/O7
Altepexi, Mexico 150/L7
Alter do Chão, Portugal 33/C3
Altevatn (lake), Norway 18/L2
Altha, Fla. (32421) 212/A1
Altheim, Austria 41/B2
Altheimer, Ark. (72004) 202/G5
Althofen, Austria 41/C3
Alticane, Sask. 181/D3
Altındağ, Turkey 63/E2
Altınova, Turkey 63/B3
Altınözü, Turkey 63/G4
Altıntaş, Turkey 63/C3
Altiplano (plat.) 120/C4
Altkirch, France 28/G4
Altmar, N.Y. (13302) 276/J3
Altmark (reg.), E. Germany 22/D2
Altmühl (riv.), W. Germany 22/D4
Altnaharra, Scotland 15/D2
Alto, Georgia (30510) 217/E2
Alto, La. (71216) 238/G2
Alto, Mich. (49302) 250/D6
Alto, N. Mex. (88312) 274/D5
Alto, Tenn. (†37324) 237/K10
Alto, Texas (75925) 303/J6
Alto, Wis. (†53963) 317/J8
Alto Araguaia, Brazil 132/C7
Alto Chicapa, Angola 115/C6
Alto Cuale, Angola 115/C5
Alto Cuale, Angola 102/D5
Alto de Cantillana (mt.), Chile 138/G4
Alto Lucero, Mexico 150/P1
Alto Molócuè, Mozambique 118/F3
Alton, Ala. (†35210) 195/E3
Alton, Calif. (†95540) 204/A3
Alton, England 13/G6
Alton, England 10/F5
Alton, Ill. 188/J3
Alton, Ill. (62002) 222/A2
Alton, Ind. (†47137) 227/E8
Alton, Iowa (51003) 229/A3
Alton, Kansas (67623) 232/D2
Alton, Ky. (†40342) 237/M4
Alton, La. (†70458) 238/L6
Alton○, Maine (†04468) 243/F5
Alton, Mo. (65606) 261/K9
Alton○, N.H. (03809) 268/E5
Alton, N.Y. (14413) 276/G4
Alton, Nova Scotia 168/E3
Alton, R.I. (†02894) 249/G7
Alton, Utah (84710) 304/B6
Alton, Va. (24520) 307/K7
Alton, W. Va. (†26210) 312/F5
Altona, Ill. (61414) 222/C2
Altona, Ind. (†46738) 227/G2
Altona, Manitoba 179/E5
Altona, Mich. (†49336) 250/D5
Altona, Mo. (†64720) 261/D6
Altona, N.Y. (12910) 276/N1
Altona, Victoria 97/H5
Altona, Victoria 88/K7
Altona (bay), Victoria 97/H5
Altona (bay), Victoria 88/K7
Altona (lag.), Virgin Is. (U.S.) 161/F4
Altona, W. Germany 22/C2
Altonah, Utah (84002) 304/D3
Alton Bay, N.H. (03810) 268/E5
Alton Downs, S. Australia 94/F2
Alto Nevado, Cerro (mt.), Chile 138/E5
Altoona, Ala. (35952) 195/F2
Altoona, Fla. (32702) 212/E3
Altoona, Iowa (50009) 229/G5
Altoona, Kansas (66710) 232/G4
Altoona, Pa. 188/L2
Altoona, Pa. (*16601) 294/F4
Altoona, Wash. (†98643) 310/B4
Altoona, Wis. (54720) 317/C6
Alto Paraguay (dept.), Paraguay 144/C2
Alto Paraná (dept), Paraguay 144/E4
Alto Paraná (riv.), Paraguay 144/D5
Alto Park, Georgia (†30161) 217/B2
Alto Parnaíba, Brazil 132/E5
Alto Pass, Ill. (62905) 222/D6
Alto Ritacuva (mt.), Colombia 120/B2
Alto Ritacuva (mt.), Colombia 126/D4
Altos, Brazil 132/F4
Altos, Paraguay 144/B4
Alto Seco, Bolivia 136/D6
Alto Songo, Cuba 158/J4
Altotonga, Mexico 150/P1
Altötting, W. Germany 22/E4
Alto Velo (chan.), Dom. Rep. 158/C7
Alto Velo (isl.), Dom. Rep. 158/D7
Altrincham, England 13/H2
Altrincham, England 10/G2
Altro, Ky. (41306) 237/P6
Altstätten, Switzerland 39/J2
Altun Ha, Belize 154/C2
Altun Shan (range), China 54/K6
Altun Shan (range), China 77/C4
Altura, Minn. (55910) 255/G6
Alturas, Calif. (96101) 204/E2
Alturas, Fla. (33820) 212/E4
Altus, Ark. (72821) 202/C3
Altus, Okla. (73521) 288/H5
Altus (res.), Okla. 288/H5
Altus A.F.B., Okla. 288/H5
Alubijid, Philippines 82/E6
Alucra, Turkey 63/H2
Alūksne, U.S.S.R. 53/D2
Alula, Somalia 115/K1
Alula, Somalia 102/H3
Alum Bank, Pa. (15521) 294/E5
Alum Bridge, W. Va. (26321) 312/E4
Alum Creek, W. Va. (25003) 312/C6
Aluminé, Argentina 143/B4
Alum Rock, Calif. (†95116) 204/L3
Alus, Iraq 66/C3
Alushta, U.S.S.R. 52/D6
Alva, Fla. (33920) 212/E5
Alva, Ky. (†40977) 237/P7
Alva (lake), New Bruns. 170/D3
Alva, Okla. (73717) 288/J1
Alva, Scotland 10/B1
Alva, Scotland 15/C1
Alva, Wyo. (82711) 319/H1
Alva B. Adams (tunnel), Colo. 208/H2
Alvada, Ohio (44802) 284/D3
Alvadore, Oreg. (97409) 291/D3
Alvalade, Portugal 33/B4
Alvaneu, Switzerland 39/J3
Alvarado, Mexico 150/M7
Alvarado, Minn. (56710) 255/B2
Alvarado, Texas (76009) 303/G5
Álvaro S. Lima (res.), Brazil 135/B3
Alvaton, Georgia (30202) 217/C4
Alvaton, Ky. (42122) 237/J7
Alvdal, Norway 18/G5
Älvdalen, Sweden 18/J6
Alvear, Argentina 143/E2
Alvena, Sask. 181/E3
Alvesta, Sweden 18/J8
Alvin, Br. Col. 184/L2
Alvin, Ill. (61811) 222/F3
Alvin, Texas (77511) 303/J3
Alvin, Wis. (49936) 317/J4
Alvinston, Ontario 177/B5
Alvito, Portugal 33/B3
Älvkarleby, Sweden 18/K6
Alvo, Nebr. (68304) 264/H4
Alvon, W. Va. (†24986) 312/F7
Alvord, Iowa (51230) 229/A2
Alvord (lake), Oreg. 291/J5
Alvord, Texas (76225) 303/G4
Alvordton, Ohio (43501) 284/A2
Älvsborg (co.), Sweden 18/H7
Älvsbyn, Sweden 18/M4
Alvwood, Minn. (†56630) 255/D3
Alvy, W. Va. (26322) 312/E4
Alwar, India 68/D3
Alxa Shamo (des.), China 77/F4
Alxa Youqi, China 77/F4
Alxa Zuoqi, China 77/F4
Aly, Ark. (†72860) 202/D4
Alyangula, North. Terr. 88/F2
Alyangula, North. Terr. 93/E2
Alyth, Scotland 10/E2
Alyth, Scotland 15/E4
Alytus, U.S.S.R. 53/C3
Alz (riv.), W. Germany 22/E4
Alzada, Mont. (59311) 262/M5
Alzette (riv.), Luxembourg 27/J9
Alzey, W. Germany 22/C4
Amacuro (riv.), Venezuela 124/H4
Amadeus (lake), Australia 87/D8
Amadeus (lake), North. Terr. 88/E4
Amadeus (lake), North. Terr. 93/B8
Amadi, Sudan 111/F6
'Amadiya, Iraq 59/D2
'Amadiya, Iraq 66/C2
Amadjuak, N.W.T. 162/J3
Amadjuak (lake), N.W.T. 162/K3
Amadjuak, N.W. Terrs. 187/L3
Amadjuak (lake), N.W. Terrs. 187/L3
Amado, Ariz. (85640) 198/D7
Amador (co.), Calif. 204/E5
Amadora, Portugal 33/A1
Amador City, Calif. (95601) 204/C9
Amagansett, N.Y. (11930) 276/R9
Amagasaki, Japan 81/H8
Amager (isl.), Denmark 21/F6
Amagi, Japan 81/E7
Amagon, Ark. (72005) 202/H2
Amahai, Indonesia 85/H6
Amak (isl.), Alaska 196/F3
Amakura (riv.), Guyana 131/A2
Amakusa (isls.), Japan 81/D7
Åmål, Sweden 18/H7
Amalfi, Colombia 126/C4
Amalfi, Italy 34/E4
Amalga, Utah (†84335) 304/C2
Amalia, N. Mex. (87512) 274/D2
Amaliás, Greece 45/E7
Amalner, India 68/C4
Amambaí, Brazil 132/C8
Amambaí, Serra de (range), Brazil 132/C7
Amambay, Paraguay 144/D3
Amambay, Cordillera de (mts.), Paraguay 144/D-E3
Amami (isls.), Japan 54/P7
Amami (isls.), Japan 81/N5
Amami-O-Shima (isl.), Japan 81/N5
Amana, Iowa (52203) 229/K5
Amanavén, Colombia 126/G6
Amanda, Ohio (43102) 284/E6
Amanda Park, Wash. (98526) 310/A3
Amanos (mts.), Turkey 63/G4
Amantea, Italy 34/E5
Amanu (atoll), Fr. Poly. 87/N7
Amapá (terr.), Brazil 132/D2
Amapá, Brazil 120/D2
Amapá, Brazil 132/D2
Amapala, Honduras 154/D4
Amapari (riv.), Brazil 132/C2
'Amara, Iraq 66/E5
'Amara, Iraq 59/E3
Amarante, Brazil 132/F4
Amarante, Portugal 33/B2
Amaranth, Manitoba 179/D4
Amarapura, Burma 72/B2
Amareleja, Portugal 33/C3
Amarete, Bolivia 136/A4
Amargosa, Brazil 132/F6
Amargosa (range), Calif. 204/J7
Amargosa (riv.), Calif. 204/J7
Amarillas, Cuba 158/D2
Amarillo, Texas 188/F3
Amarillo, Texas 146/H6
Amarillo, Texas (*79101) 303/C2
Amasa, Mich. (49903) 250/G2
Amasra, Turkey 63/E2
Amasya (prov.), Turkey 63/F2
Amasya, Turkey 59/C1
Amasya, Turkey 63/G2
Amatignak (isl.), Alaska 196/K4
Amatitlán, Guatemala 154/B3
Amatlán de los Reyes, Mexico 150/P2
Amay, Belgium 27/G7
Amazon (riv.) 2/G6
Amazon (riv.), Brazil 120/D3
Amazon (riv.), Brazil 132/C3
Amazon (riv.), Colombia 126/E9
Amazon (riv.), Peru 128/F4
Amazon, Sask. 181/F4
Amazonas (state), Brazil 132/G9
Amazonas (comm.), Colombia 126/D8
Amazonas, Cuba 158/F2
Amazonas (dept.), Peru 128/C5
Amazonas (terr.), Venezuela 124/E5
Amazonia, Mo. (64421) 261/C3
Ambala, India 68/D2
Ambalavao, Madagascar 118/H4
Ambam, Cameroon 115/B3
Ambanja, Madagascar 118/H2
Ambarchik, U.S.S.R. 4/B1
Ambarchik, U.S.S.R. 48/R3
Ambato, Ecuador 120/B3
Ambato, Ecuador 128/C3
Ambato Boeny, Madagascar 118/H3
Ambatofinandrahana, Madagascar 118/H4
Ambatolampy, Madagascar 102/G6
Ambatolampy, Madagascar 118/H3
Ambatomainty, Madagascar 118/H3
Ambatondrazaka, Madagascar 118/H3
Ambatondrazaka, Madagascar 102/G6
Ambelau (isl.), Indonesia 85/H6
Amber, Iowa (†52205) 229/L4
Amber (Bobaomby) (cape), Madagascar 102/G6
Amber (Bobaomby) (cape), Madagascar 118/H2
Amber, Okla. (73004) 288/L4
Amber, Wash. (†99004) 310/H3
Amberg, W. Germany 22/D4
Amberg, Wis. (54102) 317/K5
Ambergris (cay), Belize 154/D1
Ambergris (cay), Turks & Caicos 156/D2
Ambérieu-en-Bugey, France 28/F5
Amberley, N. Zealand 100/D5
Amberley, Ohio (†45201) 284/C9
Amberson, Pa. (17210) 294/G5
Ambert, France 28/E5
Ambia, Ind. (47917) 227/C4
Ambikapur, India 68/E4
Ambil (isl.), Philippines 82/C4
Ambilobe, Madagascar 118/H2
Amble, England 13/F2
Amble, Mich. (†49329) 250/D5
Ambler, Alaska (99786) 196/G1
Ambler, Pa. (19002) 294/M5
Ambo, Peru 128/D8
Amboasary, Madagascar 118/H4
Ambodifototra, Madagascar 118/J3
Ambohimahasoa, Madagascar 118/H4
Amboise, France 28/D4
Ambon (Amboina), Indonesia 85/H6
Ambon, Indonesia 54/O10
Ambositra, Madagascar 102/G7
Ambositra, Madagascar 118/H4
Ambovombe, Madagascar 118/H5
Amboy, Calif. (92304) 204/K9
Amboy, Georgia (†31714) 217/E7
Amboy, Ill. (61310) 222/D2
Amboy, Ind. (46911) 227/F3
Amboy, Minn. (56010) 255/D7
Amboy, Wash. (98601) 310/C5
Amboy, W. Va. (26701) 312/G4
Amboyna (cay), Philippines 85/E4
Ambridge, Pa. (15003) 294/B4
Ambriz, Angola 115/B5
Ambrose, Georgia (31512) 217/G7
Ambrose, N. Dak. (58833) 282/D2
Ambrym (isl.), Vanuatu 87/G7
Ambunti, Papua N.G. 85/B6
Amburgey, Ky. (41801) 237/R6
Amchitka (isl.), Alaska 188/D6
Amchitka (isl.), Alaska 196/K4
Amchitka (passage), Alaska 196/K4
Am-Dam, Chad 111/D5
Amderma, U.S.S.R. 52/K1
Amderma, U.S.S.R. 48/F3
Amdo, China 77/D5
Ameagle, W. Va. (25004) 312/D7
Amealco, Mexico 150/K6
Ameca, Mexico 150/H6
Amecameca de Juárez, Mexico 150/L1
Ameghino, Argentina 143/D3
Amel, Belgium 27/J8
Ameland (isl.), Netherlands 27/H2
Amelia (isl.), Fla. 212/E1
Amelia, Italy 34/D3
Amelia, La. (70340) 238/H7
Amelia, Nebr. (68711) 264/F2
Amelia, Ohio (45102) 284/D10
Amelia (co.), Va. 307/M6
Amelia City, Fla. (†32034) 212/E1
Amelia Court House, Va. (23002) 307/N6
Amenia, N.Y. (12501) 276/N7
Amenia, N. Dak. (58004) 282/R6
America, Ill. (†62996) 222/D6
American (highlands), Ant. 2/N10
American (riv.), Calif. 204/C8
Americana, Brazil 135/C3
American Corner, Md. (†21632) 245/P5
American Falls, Idaho (83211) 220/E7
American Falls (res.), Idaho 188/D2
American Falls (res.), Idaho 220/F6
American Fork, Utah (84003) 304/C3
American Highland 5/B4
American Samoa 2/A6
AMERICAN SAMOA 86/N9
American Samoa 87/J7
Americus, Georgia (31709) 217/D6
Americus, Ind. (†47901) 227/D3
Americus, Kansas (66835) 232/F3
Americus, Mo. (†65069) 261/J5
Amersfoort, Netherlands 27/G4
Amersham, England 13/G7
Amery, Man. 162/G4
Amery, Manitoba 179/J2
Amery, Wis. (54001) 317/B5
Amery Ice Shelf, Ant. 2/N9
Amery Ice Shelf 5/C4
Ames, Iowa (50010) 229/F4
Ames, Kansas (66931) 232/E2
Ames, N.Y. (13317) 276/L5
Ames, Okla. (73718) 288/K2
Ames, Texas (†77575) 303/K7
Amesbury, England 13/F6
Amesbury, Mass. (01913) 249/L1
Amesbury○, Mass. (01913) 249/L1
Amesville, Conn. (†06031) 210/B1
Amesville, Ohio (45711) 284/F7
Amet (sound), Nova Scotia 168/E3
Amfilokhía, Greece 45/E6
Ámfissa, Greece 45/F6
Amga (riv.), U.S.S.R. 48/O3
Amguid, Algeria 106/F3
Amgun' (riv.), U.S.S.R. 48/O4
Amherst, Burma 72/C3
Amherst, Colo. (80721) 208/P1
Amherst○, Maine (†04408) 243/G6
Amherst, Mass. (01002) 249/E3
Amherst○, Mass. (01002) 249/E3
Amherst, Nebr. (68812) 264/E4
Amherst○, N.H. (03031) 268/D6
Amherst, N.Y. (†14226) 276/C4
Amherst, N.S. 162/K6
Amherst, Nova Scotia 168/D3
Amherst, Ohio (44001) 284/F3
Amherst (isl.), Ontario 177/H3
Amherst, S. Dak. (57421) 298/O2
Amherst, Texas (79312) 303/B4
Amherst (co.), Va. 307/K5
Amherst, Va. (24521) 307/K5
Amherst (mt.), W. Australia 92/D2
Amherst, Wis. (54406) 317/H7
Amherstburg, Ontario 177/A5
Amherstdale, W. Va. (25607) 312/C7
Amherst Junction, Wis. (54407) 317/H7
Amherst View, Ontario 177/H3
Amidon, N. Dak. (58620) 282/D7
Amiens, France 7/E4
Amiens, France 28/D3
Amindiri (isl.), India 68/C6
Amindivi (isls.), India 68/C6
Aminga, Argentina 143/C2
Amini (Amindiri) (isl.), India 68/C6
'Amir, Ras (cape), Libya 111/D1
Amiret, Minn. (56112) 255/C6
Amisk, Alberta 182/E3
Amisk (lake), Sask. 181/M4
Amissville, Va. (22002) 307/M3
Amistad (res.) 188/F5
Amistad (res.), Mexico 150/J2
Amistad, N. Mex. (88410) 274/F3
Amistad (dam), Texas 303/C8
Amistad (res.), Texas 303/C8
Amistad Nat'l Rec. Area, Texas 303/D8
Amite, La. (70422) 238/K5
Amite (riv.), La. 238/L2
Amite (co.), Miss. 256/C8
Amite (riv.), Miss. 256/C9
Amity, Ark. (71921) 202/D5
Amity, Georgia (†30817) 217/G3
Amity, Ind. (†46131) 227/E6
Amity, Mo. (†64469) 261/D3
Amity, Oreg. (97101) 291/D2
Amity, Pa. (15311) 294/B5
Amityville, N.Y. (11701) 276/O9
Åmli, Norway 18/F7
Amlia (isl.), Alaska 196/L4
Amlia (passage), Alaska 196/L4
Amlwch, Wales 10/D4
Amlwch, Wales 13/C4
Amma, W. Va. (25005) 312/D5
Amman (dist.), Jordan 65/D4
Amman (cap.), Jordan 54/E6
Amman (cap.), Jordan 65/D4
Amman (cap.), Jordan 59/C3
Ammanford, Wales 13/C6
Ammersee (lake), W. Germany 22/D4
Ammie, Ky. (†40933) 237/O6
Ammon, Idaho (†83401) 220/G6
Ammon, Va. (23822) 307/N6
Ammonoosuc (riv.), N.H. 268/D3
Amnat, Thailand 72/E4
Amo, Ind. (46103) 227/D5
Amol, Iran 59/F2
Amol, Iran 66/H2
Amonate, Va. (24601) 307/E6
Amor, Minn. (†56515) 255/C4
Amora, Portugal 33/A1
Amorbach, W. Germany 22/C4
Amoret, Mo. (64722) 261/C6
Amorgós (isl.), Greece 45/G7
Amorita, Okla. (73719) 288/K1
Amory, Miss. (38821) 256/H3
Amos, Que. 162/J6
Amos, Québec 174/B3
Åmotfors, Sweden 18/H7
Amoy (Xiamen), China 77/J7
Amozoc de Mota, Mexico 150/N2
Ampana, Indonesia 85/G6
Ampanihy, Madagascar 118/G4
Amparo, Brazil 135/C3
Amper (riv.), W. Germany 22/D4
Amphitrite (isls.), China 85/E2
Amposta, Spain 33/G2
Ampthill, England 13/G5
Amqui, Québec 172/B2
'Amran, Yemen Arab Rep. 59/D6
Amravati, India 68/D4
Amreli, India 68/C4
Amriswil, Switzerland 39/H1
'Amrit (ruins), Syria 63/F5
Amritsar, India 54/J6

Antsiranana 329

Amritsar, India 68/C2
Amrum (isl.), W. Germany 22/C1
Amsden, Ohio (44803) 284/D3
Amstelveen, Netherlands 27/B5
Amsterdam (isl.) 2/N7
Amsterdam, Georgia (31734) 217/D9
Amsterdam, Mo. (64723) 261/D6
Amsterdam, Mont. (†59741) 262/E5
Amsterdam (cap.), Netherlands 27/B4
Amsterdam (cap.), Netherlands 7/E3
Amsterdam, N.Y. (12010) 276/M5
Amsterdam, Ohio (43903) 284/J5
Amsterdam, Sask. 181/J4
Amstetten, Austria 41/C2
Amston, Conn. (06231) 210/F2
Am-Timan, Chad 111/D5
Amuay, Venezuela 124/C2
Amudar'ya (riv.) 2/N3
Amudar'ya (riv.), U.S.S.R. 54/H5
Amudar'ya (riv.), U.S.S.R. 48/G5
Amukta (isl.), Alaska 196/D4
Amukta (passage), Alaska 196/D4
Amuku (mts.), Guyana 131/B4
Amulet, Sask. 181/G6
Amund Ringnes (isl.), N.W.T. 162/M3
Amund Ringnes (isl.), N.W. Terrs. 187/J2
Amundsen (sea) 2/D10
Amundsen (bay) 5/C3
Amundsen (sea) 5/B13
Amundsen (gulf), Canada 4/B16
Amundsen (gulf), N.W.T. 162/D1
Amundsen (gulf), N.W.T. 146/F2
Amundsen (gulf), N.W. Terrs. 187/F2
Amundsen-Scott Station 5/A14
Amuntai, Indonesia 85/F6
Amur (riv.) 2/R3
Amur (riv.) 54/P5
Amur (Heilong Jiang) (riv.), China 77/L2
'Amur, Wadi (dry riv.), Sudan 111/G4
Amur (riv.), U.S.S.R. 48/O4
Amurang, Indonesia 85/G5
Amursk, U.S.S.R. 48/O4
Amy, Kansas (†67850) 232/B3
Amya (pass), Burma 72/C4
Amya (pass), Thailand 72/C4
Amyun, Lebanon 63/F5
An, Burma 72/B3
'Ana, Iraq 66/B3
'Ana, Iraq 59/D3
Anaa (atoll), Fr. Poly. 87/M7
Anabar (riv.), U.S.S.R. 48/M2
Anabel, Mo. (63431) 261/H3
Ana Branch, Darling (riv.), N.S. Wales 97/A3
'Anabta, West Bank 65/C3
Anacapa (isl.), Calif. 204/F10
Anaco, Venezuela 124/F3
Anacoco, La. (71403) 238/D4
Anacoco (lake), La. 238/D4
Anaconda, Mont. 188/D1
Anaconda-Deer Lodge County, Mont. (59711) 262/C4
Anacortes, Wash. (98221) 310/C2
Anacostia, D.C. (20020) 245/F5
Anacostia (riv.), D.C. 245/F5
Anadarko, Okla. (73005) 288/K4
Anadia, Portugal 33/B2
Anadolufeneri, Turkey 63/D5
Anadoluhisarı, Turkey 63/D6
Anadyr', U.S.S.R 2/T2
Anadyr', U.S.S.R. 4/C1
Anadyr' (gulf), U.S.S.R. 4/C18
Anadyr' (gulf), U.S.S.R. 54/V3
Anadyr' (riv.), U.S.S.R. 54/U3
Anadyr' (riv.), U.S.S.R. 4/C1
Anadyr', U.S.S.R. 48/S3
Anadyr' (gulf), U.S.S.R. 48/T3
Anadyr' (range), U.S.S.R. 48/S3
Anadyr' (riv.), U.S.S.R. 48/S3
Anadyr' U.S.S.R. 54/U3
Anáfi (isl.), Greece 45/G7
Anagance, New Bruns. 170/E3
Anaheim, Calif. 188/C4
Anaheim, Calif. (*92801) 204/D11
Anahim Lake, Br. Col. 184/E4
Anahola, Hawaii (96703) 218/C1
Anáhuac, Chihuahua, Mexico 150/F2
Anáhuac, Nuevo León, Mexico 150/J3
Anahuac, Texas (77514) 303/K8
Anaï (well), Algeria 106/G4
Anai Mudi (mt.), India 68/D6
'Anaiza, Saudi Arabia 59/D4
'Anaiza, Saudi Arabia 54/F7
Anak, N. Korea 81/B4
Anakapalle, India 68/E5
Anaktalik Brook (riv.), Newf. 166/B2
Anaktuvuk Pass, Alaska (99721) 196/H1
Analalava, Madagascar 118/H2
Ana Maria (gulf), Cuba 158/F3
Anambas (isls.), Indonesia 85/D5
Anambra (state), Nigeria 106/F7
Anamoose, N. Dak. (58710) 282/K4
Anamosa, Iowa (52205) 229/L4
Anamur, Turkey 63/E4
Anamur (cape), Turkey 59/B2
Anamur (cape), Turkey 63/E5
Anan, Japan 81/G7
Anandale, La. (†71301) 238/F4
Ananea, Bolivia 136/A4
Anantapur, India 68/D6
Anantnag, India 68/D2
Anapa, U.S.S.R. 52/E6
Anápolis, Brazil 132/D7
Anápolis, Brazil 120/E4
Anar, Iran 66/J5
Anar, Iran 59/G3
Anarak, Iran 66/H4
Anarak, Iran 59/F3
Anar Darreh, Afghanistan 59/H3
Anar Darreh, Afghanistan 68/A2
Añasco, P. Rico 161/A1
Añasco, P. Rico 156/F1
Añasco (bay), P. Rico 161/A1
Anastasia (isl.), Fla. 212/E2
Anatahan (isl.), No. Marianas 87/E4
Anatolia (reg.), Turkey 63/D3
Anatone, Wash. (99401) 310/H4
Añatuya, Argentina 143/D2
Anauá (riv.), Brazil 132/B2
Anawalt, W. Va. (24808) 312/D8
Anaye (well), Niger 106/G5
Anbar (gov.), Iraq 66/B4
Ancash (dept.), Peru 128/D7
Ancaster, Ontario 177/D4
Anceney, Mont. (†59741) 262/E5
Ancenis, France 28/C4
Anchieta, Brazil 132/F8
Ancho, N. Mex. (†88301) 274/D5
Anchor, Ill. (61720) 222/E3
Anchorage, Alaska 188/D6
Anchorage, Alaska 146/D3
Anchorage, Alaska (*99501) 196/B1
Anchorage, Ky. (40223) 237/L2
Anchorage, U.S. 2/B2
Anchorage, U.S. 4/D17
Anchorena, Argentina 143/C4
Anchor Point, Alaska (99556) 196/B2
Anchor Point, Newf. 166/C3
Anchorville, Mich. (48004) 250/G6
Anchovy, Jamaica 158/H5
Ancienne-Lorette, Québec 172/H3
Anclitas (cay), Cuba 158/F3
Anclote (keys), Fla. 212/D3
Anco, Ky. (41711) 237/P6
Ancohuma (mt.), Bolivia 120/C4
Ancohuma, Nevada (mt.), Bolivia 136/A4
Ancón, Peru 128/D8
Ancona, Ill. (61311) 222/E2
Ancona (prov.), Italy 34/D3
Ancona, Italy 34/D3
Ancona, Italy 7/F4
Ancón de Sardinas (bay), Colombia 126/A7
Ancón de Sardinas (bay), Ecuador 128/C2
Ancoraimes, Bolivia 136/A4
Ancram, N.Y. (12502) 276/N6
Ancroft, England 13/F2
Ancrum, Scotland 15/F5
Ancud, Chile 120/B7
Ancud, Chile 138/D4
Ancud (gulf), Chile 138/D4
Anda (Anta), China 77/L2
Andacollo, Argentina 143/B4
Andacollo, Chile 138/A8
Andado, North. Terr. 93/D8
Andahuaylas, Peru 128/F9
Andale, Kansas (67001) 232/E4
Andalgalá, Argentina 143/C2
Åndalsnes, Norway 18/F5
Andalusia, Ala. (36420) 195/E8
Andalusia, Ill. (61232) 222/C2
Andalusia, Pa. (†19020) 294/N5
Andalusia (reg.), Spain 33/C4
Andaman (sea) 54/L8
Andaman (sea), Burma 72/B4
Andaman (isls.), India 2/P5
Andaman (isls.), India 54/L8
Andaman (isls.), India 68/G6
Andaman (sea), India 68/G6
Andaman and Nicobar Isls. (terr.), India 68/G6
Andamarca, Bolivia 136/B6
Andamarca, Peru 128/E8
Andamooka, S. Australia 94/E4
Andapa, Madagascar 118/H2
Andaraí, Brazil 132/F6
Andau, Austria 41/D3
Andeer, Switzerland 39/H3
Andelfingen, Switzerland 39/G1
Andenne, Belgium 27/G8
Anderlecht, Belgium 27/B9
Anderlues, Belgium 27/E8
Andermatt, Switzerland 39/G3
Andernach, W. Germany 22/B3
Anderson, Ala. (35610) 195/D1
Anderson, Alaska (†99760) 196/H2
Anderson, Argentina 143/F7
Anderson, Calif. (96007) 204/C3
Anderson, Ind. 188/J2
Anderson, Ind. (*46011) 227/F4
Anderson (riv.), Ind. 227/D8
Anderson, Iowa (†51652) 229/B7
Anderson (co.), Kansas 232/G3
Anderson (co.), Ky. 237/M5
Anderson (lake), Manitoba 179/D2
Anderson (pt.), Manitoba 179/F3
Anderson, Mo. (64831) 261/D9
Anderson (riv.), N.W.T. 162/D2
Anderson (riv.), N.W. Terrs. 187/F3
Anderson, S.C. 188/K4
Anderson (co.), S.C. 296/B2
Anderson, S.C. (*29621) 296/B2
Anderson (bay), Tasmania 99/D2
Anderson (co.), Tenn. 237/N8
Anderson, Tenn. (†37376) 237/K10
Anderson (co.), Texas 303/J6
Anderson, Texas (77830) 303/J7
Anderson Ranch (res.), Idaho 220/C6
Andersonville, Georgia (31711) 217/D6
Andersonville, Ind. (†47024) 227/G5
Andersonville, Tenn. (37705) 237/O8
Andersonville, Va. (23911) 307/L6
Andersonville Nat'l Hist. Site, Georgia 217/D6
Andes (range), 120/B2-6
Andes, Cordillera de los (mts.), Argentina 143/C2
Andes, Cordillera de los (mts.), Chile 138/C5,E
Andes, Colombia 126/C5
Andes, Mont. (†59218) 262/M3
Andes, N.Y. (13731) 276/L6
Andes, Cordillera de los (mts.), Peru 128/F10
Andes (lake), S. Dak. 298/N7
Andheri, India 68/B7
Andhra Pradesh (state), India 68/D5
Andijk, Netherlands 27/G3
Andikíthira (isl.), Greece 45/F8
Andilamena, Madagascar 118/H3
Andimeshk, Iran 66/F4
Anding, Miss. (†39040) 256/D5
Andırın, Turkey 63/G4
Ándissa, Greece 45/H6
Andizhan, U.S.S.R. 54/J5
Andizhan, U.S.S.R. 48/H5
Andkhvoy, Afghanistan 68/A1
Andkhvoy, Afghanistan 59/H2
Andoas Nuevo, Ecuador 128/D4
Andoma, Zaire 115/E3
Andong, S. Korea 81/D5
Andorra 7/E4
ANDORRA 33/G1
Andorra, Spain 33/F2
Andorra la Vella (cap.), Andorra 33/G1
Andover○, Conn. (06232) 210/F2
Andover, England 10/F5
Andover, England 13/F6
Andover, Ill. (61233) 222/C2
Andover, Iowa (52701) 229/N5
Andover, Kansas (67002) 232/E4
Andover, Maine (04216) 243/B6
Andover○, Maine (04216) 243/B6
Andover, Mass. (01810) 249/K2
Andover○, Mass. (01810) 249/K2
Andover, Minn. (†55303) 255/E5
Andover○, N.H. (03216) 268/D5
Andover, N.J. (07821) 273/D2
Andover, N.Y. (14806) 276/E6
Andover, Ohio (44003) 284/J2
Andover, S. Dak. (57422) 298/O3
Andover○, Vt. (†05143) 268/B5
Andover, Va. (24215) 307/C7
Andøya (isl.), Norway 18/J2
Andradas, Brazil 135/C3
Andradina, Brazil 132/D8
Andraitx, Spain 33/H3
Andravídha, Greece 45/E6
Andre (lake), Newf. 166/A3
Andreafski (Saint Marys), Alaska (†99658) 196/F2
Andreanof (isls.), Alaska 196/L4
Andreas (cape), Cyprus 63/F5
Andrelândia, Brazil 135/D2
Andrés, Nicaragua 154/F3
Andrespol, Poland 47/D3
Andrew, Alberta 182/D3
Andrew, Iowa (52030) 229/M4
Andrew, La. (†70548) 238/F6
Andrew (co.), Mo. 261/C3
Andrew (isl.), Nova Scotia 168/H3
Andrew Johnson Nat'l Hist. Site, Tenn. 237/R8
Andrews, (†21626) 245/O7
Andrews, Ind. (46702) 227/F3
Andrews, N.C. (28901) 281/B4
Andrews, Oreg. (†97732) 291/J5
Andrews, S.C. (29510) 296/H5
Andrews (co.), Texas 303/B5
Andrews, Texas (79714) 303/B5
Andrews A.F.B., Md. 245/G5
Andreyevka, U.S.S.R. 52/H4
Andria, Italy 34/F4
Androka, Madagascar 118/G5
Andros (isl.), Bahamas 146/L7
Andros (isl.), Bahamas 156/B1
Ándros, Greece 45/G7
Ándros (isl.), Greece 45/G7
Androscoggin (co.), Maine 243/C7
Androscoggin (riv.), Maine 243/C7
Androscoggin (riv.), N.H. 268/E2
Androth (isl.), India 68/C6
Andrychów, Poland 47/D4
Andsfjorden (fjord), Norway 18/K2
Andújar, Spain 33/D3
Andul, India 68/F2
Andulo, Angola 102/D6
Andulo, Angola 115/C6
Anéfis, Mali 106/E5
Anegada (isl.), Virgin Is. (Br.) 156/H1
Anegada (passage), Virgin Is. (Br.) 156/F3
Aného (Anécho), Togo 106/E7
Aneityum (Anatom) (isl.), Vanuatu 87/H8
'Aneiza, Jebel (mt.), Iraq 66/A4
'Aneiza, Jebel (mt.), Iraq 59/C3
'Aneiza, Jebel (mt.), Jordan 59/C3
'Aneiza, Jebel (mt.), Saudi Arabia 59/C3
Añelo, Argentina 143/C4
Anerley, Sask. 181/D4
Aneroid, Sask. 181/D6
Aneta, N. Dak. (58212) 282/P4
Aneth, Utah (84510) 304/E6
Aneto (peak), Spain 33/G1
Angaki (Quirino), Philippines 82/C2
Angamos (isl.), Chile 138/D8
Angamos (pt.), Chile 138/A4
Angara (riv.), U.S.S.R. 54/L4
Angara (riv.), U.S.S.R. 48/K4
Angarsk, U.S.S.R. 54/M4
Angarsk, U.S.S.R. 48/L4
Angas Downs, North. Terr. 93/C8
Angaston, S. Australia 94/F6
Angaur (isl.), Belau 87/D5
Ånge, Sweden 18/J5
Ange-Gardien, Québec 172/E4
Angel (isl.), Calif. 204/J2
Angel (falls), Venezuela 120/C2
Angel (fall), Venezuela 124/G5
Angela, Mont. (59312) 262/K4
Ángel de la Guarda (isl.), Mexico 150/C2
Angeles, Philippines 82/C3
Ángeles, P. Rico 161/B2
Ängelholm, Sweden 18/H8
Angélica, Argentina 143/E5
Angelica, N.Y. (14709) 276/E6
Angelica, Wis. (†54162) 317/K6
Angelina (co.), Texas 303/K6
Angelina (riv.), Texas 303/K6
Angelo, Wis. (†54656) 317/E8
Angels Camp, Calif. (95222) 204/E5
Angelus, S.C. (†29718) 296/G2
Angerman (riv.), Sweden 7/F2
Ångermanälven (riv.), Sweden 18/K5
Angermünde, E. Germany 22/E2
Angers, France 7/D4
Angers, France 28/C4
Angers, Québec 172/B4
Angicos, Brazil 132/G4
Angie, La. (70426) 238/L5
Angier, N.C. (27501) 281/M4
Angijak (isl.), N.W. Terrs. 187/M3
Angikuni (lake), N.W. Terrs. 187/J3
Angkor Wat (ruins), Cambodia 72/E4
Angle, Utah (†84712) 304/C5
Angle Inlet, Minn. (56711) 255/C1
Anglem (mt.), N. Zealand 100/A7
Anglesey (isl.), Wales 13/C4
Anglesey (isl.), Wales 10/D4
Angleton, Texas (77515) 303/J8
Anglia, Sask. 181/C4
Angliers, Québec 174/B3
Angmagssalik, Greenl. 4/C11
Angmagssalik, Greenland 146/Q3
Ango, Zaire 115/E3
Angoche, Mozambique 118/G3
Angoche, Mozambique 102/G6
Angoche (isl.), Mozambique 118/G3
Angol, Chile 138/D1
Angola 2/K6
Angola 102/D6
ANGOLA 115/C6
Angola, Del. (†19966) 245/T6
Angola, Ind. (46703) 227/G1
Angola, Kansas (67331) 232/G4
Angola, La. (70712) 238/G5
Angola, N.Y. (14006) 276/C5
Angola (swamp), N.C. 281/O5
Angola on the Lake, N.Y. (†14006) 276/B5
Angoon, Alaska (99820) 196/M1
Angora, Minn. (55703) 255/F3
Angora, Nebr. (69331) 264/A3
Angoram, Papua N.G. 85/B6
Angostura (falls), Colombia 120/B2
Angostura (falls), Colombia 126/E6
Angostura, Mexico 150/E4
Angostura (res.), S. Dak. 298/B7
Angoulême, France 28/D5
Angoumois (trad. prov.), France, 29
Angra do Heroísmo (dist.), Portugal 33/C1
Angra do Heroísmo, Portugal 33/C1
Angra dos Reis, Brazil 135/D3
Angren, U.S.S.R. 48/H5
Ang Thong, Thailand 72/C4
Anguil, Argentina 143/D4
Anguilla (isl.) 146/M8
ANGUILLA 156
Anguilla, Anguilla 156/F3
Anguilla, Miss. (38721) 256/C5
Anguillara Sabazia, Italy 34/F6
Anguille (cape), Newf. 166/C4
Angurugu, North. Terr. 93/E3
Angus, Iowa (†50220) 229/E5
Angus, Minn. (56712) 255/B2
Angus, Ontario 177/E3
Angus (trad. prov.), Scotland, 15/B5
Angusville, Manitoba 179/A4
Angwin, Calif. (94508) 204/C5
Anhée, Belgium 27/F8
Anholt, Denmark 21/E4
Anholt (isl.), Denmark 21/E4
Anholt (isl.), Denmark 18/G8
Anhua, China 77/H6
Anhui (Anhwei), China 77/J5
Aniak, Alaska (99557) 196/G2
Aniakchak (vol.), Alaska 196/G3
Aniakchak Nat'l Mon., Alaska 196/G3
Aniakchak Nat'l Preserve, Alaska 196/G3
Anicuns, Brazil 132/D7
Aniene (riv.), Italy 34/F6
Animas (riv.), Colo. 208/D8
Animas, N. Mex. (88020) 274/A7
Animas (riv.), N. Mex. 274/B1
Añimbo, Bolivia 136/C7
Anin, Burma 72/C4
Anin, West Bank 65/C2
Anina, Romania 45/E3
Anita, Iowa (50020) 229/D6
Anita, Pa. (15711) 294/D3
Aniva (cape), U.S.S.R. 48/P5
Aniwa, Wis. (54408) 317/H6
'Anjara, Jordan 65/D3
Anjidiv (Angedeva) (isl.), India 68/C6
Anjou (trad. prov.), France, 29
Anjou, Québec 172/H4
Anjouan (isl.), Comoros 102/G6
Anjouan (isl.), Comoros 118/G2
Anju, N. Korea 81/B4
Anjum, Netherlands 27/J2
Ankang, China 77/G5
Ankara (prov.), Turkey 63/E3
Ankara (cap.), Turkey 63/E3
Ankara (cap.), Turkey 2/L4
Ankara (cap.), Turkey 54/E5
Ankara (cap.), Turkey 59/B2
Ankara (riv.), Turkey 63/D3
Ankazoabo, Madagascar 118/G4
Ankeny, Iowa (50021) 229/F5
Anker (riv.), England 10/G3
Ankerton, Alberta 182/D3
Ankhor, Somalia 115/J1
Anking (Anqing), China 77/J5
Anklam, E. Germany 22/E2
Ankober, Ethiopia 111/H6
Ankona, Fla. (†33450) 212/F4
Ankoro, Zaire 115/E5
An Loc (Binh Long), Vietnam 72/E5
Anlu, China 77/H5
Anmoore, W. Va. (26323) 312/F4
Ann (cape), Mass. 249/M2
Anna, Ill. (62906) 222/D6
Anna, Ky. (†42270) 237/J6
Anna, Ohio (45302) 284/B5
Anna, Texas (75003) 303/H4
Anna (lke), Va. 307/N4
Annaba, Algeria 102/C1
Annaba, Algeria 106/F1
Annabella, Utah (84711) 304/B5
Annaberg-Buchholz, E. Germany 22/E3
Anna Creek, S. Australia 94/D3
Annada, Mo. (63330) 261/L4
Annadel, Tenn. (†37770) 237/M8
Annagry, Ireland 17/E1
Annaheim, Sask. 181/G3
Annai, Guyana 131/B4
An Najaf (gov.), Iraq 66/C5
An Najaf, Iraq 59/D3
An Najaf, Iraq 66/D5
An Najaf, Iraq 54/F6
Annalee (riv.), Ireland 17/G3
Annalong, N. Ireland 17/K3
Annaly (bay), Virgin Is. (U.S.) 161/E3
Anna Maria, Fla. (33501) 212/D4
Annan, Scotland 15/E6
Annan, Scotland 10/E3
Annan (riv.), Scotland 15/E5
Annandale, Minn. (55302) 255/D5
Annandale, N.J. (08801) 273/D2
Annandale, Va. (22003) 307/S3
Annandale-on-Hudson, N.Y. (12504) 276/N6
Anna Plains, W. Australia 92/C2
Annapolis, Calif. (95412) 204/B5
Annapolis, Ill. (62413) 222/F4
Annapolis (cap.), Md. (*21401) 245/M5
Annapolis (cap.), Md. 188/L3
Annapolis, Mo. (63620) 261/L8
Annapolis (co.), Nova Scotia 168/C4
Annapolis (basin), Nova Scotia 168/C4
Annapolis (riv.), Nova Scotia 168/C4
Annapolis Junction, Md. (20701) 245/M4
Annapolis Royal, Nova Scotia 168/C4
Annapurna (mt.), Nepal 68/E3
Ann Arbor, Mich. 188/K2
Ann Arbor, Mich. (*48103) 250/F6
Anna Regina, Guyana 131/B2
Annascaul, Ireland 17/B7
An Nasiriya, Iraq 59/E3
An Nasiriya, Iraq 66/D5
Annat, Scotland 15/C3
Annaville, Québec 172/E3
Annawan, Ill. (61234) 222/C2
Annbank Station, Scotland 15/D5
Anne (mt.), Tasmania 99/C4
Anne Arundel (co.), Md. 245/M4
Annecy, France 28/G5
Annemanie, Ala. (36721) 195/D6
Anner (riv.), Ireland 17/F7
Anneta, Ky. (†42754) 237/J6
Annette, Alaska (99920) 196/N2
An Nhon, Vietnam 72/F4
Annieopscotch (mts.), Newf. 166/C4
Anniston, Ala. 188/J4
Anniston, Ala. (36201) 195/G3
Anniston, Mo. (63820) 261/O9
Anniston Army Depot, Ala. 195/F3
Annobon (isl.), Equat. Guinea 102/C5
Annona, Texas (75550) 303/K4
Annonay, France 28/F5
Annotto Bay, Jamaica 156/C3
Annotto Bay, Jamaica 158/K6
Annville, Ky. (40402) 237/O6
Annville, Pa. (17003) 294/J5
Annweiler am Trifels, W. Germany 22/B4
Anoka (co.), Minn. 255/E5
Anoka, Minn. (55303) 255/E5
Anoka, Nebr. (†68722) 264/F2
Anola, Manitoba 179/F5
Ano Nuevo (pt.), Calif. 204/J4
Áno Viánnos, Greece 45/G8
Anóyia, Greece 45/G8
Anqing (Anking), China 77/J5
Ans, Belgium 27/H7
Ansager, Denmark 21/B6
Ansai, China 77/G4
Ansbach, W. Germany 22/D4
Anse à Galets, Haiti 158/B6
Anse-à-Pitre, Haiti 158/C6
Anse-au-Griffon, Québec 172/D1
Anse-aux-Gascons, Québec 172/D2
Anse-à-Veau, Haiti 158/B6
Anse-Bertrand, Guadeloupe 161/A5
Anse-Bleue, New Bruns. 170/E1
Anse Boileau, Seychelles 118/H5
Anse-d'Hainault, Haiti 158/A6
Anse la Raye, St. Lucia 161/F6
Anselmo, Nebr. (68813) 264/E3
Anser Group (isls.), Tasmania 99/C1
Anserma, Colombia 126/B5
Anse Rouge, Haiti 158/B5
Anse Royale, Seychelles 118/H5
Anshan, China 77/K3
Anshan, China 54/O5
Anshun, China 77/G6
Ansley, Ala. (36001) 195/F7
Ansley, La. (†71228) 238/E2
Ansley, Nebr. (68814) 264/E3
Anson, Kansas (†67103) 232/E4
Anson, Maine (04911) 243/D6
Anson○, Maine (04911) 243/D6
Anson (pt.), Norfolk I. 88/K5
Anson (bay), Norfolk I. 88/K5
Anson (co.), N.C. 281/J4
Anson (bay), North. Terr. 88/D2
Anson, Texas (79501) 303/E5
Ansŏng, S. Korea 81/C5
Ansongo, Mali 106/E5
Ansonia, Conn. (06401) 210/C3
Ansonia, Ohio (45303) 284/A5
Ansonville, N.C. (28007) 281/K4
Ansonville, Pa. (†16656) 294/E4
Ansted, W. Va. (25812) 312/D6
Anta, Peru 128/F9
Antabamba, Peru 128/F10
Antakya, Turkey 59/C2
Antakya, Turkey 63/G4
Antalaha, Madagascar 118/J2
Antalaha, Madagascar 102/H6
Antalya (prov.), Turkey 63/D4
Antalya, Turkey 54/D6
Antalya, Turkey 63/D4
Antalya, Turkey 59/B2
Antalya (gulf), Turkey 63/D4
Antalya (gulf), Turkey 59/B2
Antananarivo (prov.), Madagascar 118/H3
Antananarivo (cap.), Madagascar 2/M6
Antananarivo (cap.), Madagascar 102/G6
Antananarivo (cap.), Madagascar 118/H3
Antarctic (pen.), Ant. 2/G9
Antarctic (pen.) 5/C15
Antarctica 2/E11
ANTARCTICA 5
Antarctic Circle 2/A9
An Teallach (mt.), Scotland 15/C3
Antelope (creek), Idaho 220/E6
Antelope, Kansas (66836) 232/F3
Antelope, Mont. (59211) 262/M2
Antelope (co.), Nebr. 264/F2
Antelope (range), Nev. 266/E3
Antelope, Oreg. (97001) 291/G3
Antelope (creek), Oreg. 291/K5
Antelope (res.), Oreg. 291/K5
Antelope, Sask. 181/C5
Antelope (lake), Sask. 181/C5
Antelope (creek), S. Dak. 298/D3
Antelope, Texas (76350) 303/F4
Antelope (isl.), Utah 304/B3
Antelope (creek), Wyo. 319/G2
Antelope (hills), Wyo. 319/D3
Antequera, Paraguay 144/D4
Antequera, Spain 33/D4
Antero (mt.), Colo. 208/G5
Antero (res.), Colo. 208/H5
Antes Fort, Pa. (17720) 294/H3
Anthon, Iowa (51004) 229/B4
Anthony, Fla. (32617) 212/D2
Anthony, Ind. (†47302) 227/G4
Anthony, Kansas (67003) 232/D4
Anthony, N. Mex. (88021) 274/C6
Anthony, R.I. (†02816) 249/H6
Anthony, Texas (88021) 303/A10
Anthony, W. Va. (24914) 312/F7
Anthony Lagoon, North. Terr. 88/E3
Anthony Lagoon, North. Terr. 93/D4
Anthracite, Alberta 182/C4
Anti-Atlas (ranges), Morocco 106/C3
Antibes, France 28/G6
Anticosti (isl.), Que. 146/M5
Anticosti (isl.), Que. 162/K6
Anticosti (isl.), Québec 174/E3
Antietam, Md. (†21782) 245/H3
Antietam (creek), Md. 245/H2
Antietam Nat'l Battlefield, Md. 245/H3
Antigo, Wis. (54409) 317/H5
Antigonish (co.), Nova Scotia 168/F3
Antigonish, Nova Scotia 168/F3
Antigonish (harb.), Nova Scotia 168/G3
Antigua (isl.) 146/M8
ANTIGUA & BARBUDA 156
ANTIGUA & BARBUDA 161
Antigua (isl.), Ant. & Bar. 161/E11
Antigua (isl.), Ant. & Bar. 156/G3
Antigua, Guatemala 154/B3
Antigua (riv.), Mexico 150/Q1
Antigua, Spain 33/B4
Antigues (pt.), Guadeloupe 161/A5
Antiguo Morelos, Mexico 150/K5
Antilla, Cuba 156/C2
Antilla, Cuba 158/J3
Antilles, Greater (isls.), W. Indies 156/B2
Antilles, Lesser (isls.), W. Indies 156/E4
Antimony, Utah (84712) 304/C5
Antioch, Calif. (94509) 204/L1
Antioch, Georgia (†30240) 217/B4
Antioch, Ill. (60002) 222/E1
Antioch, Nebr. (69340) 264/B2
Antioch, Ohio (43710) 284/H6
Antioch, S.C. (†29020) 296/F3
Antioch (Antakya), Turkey 63/G4
Antioch, W. Va. (†26743) 312/H4
Antioquia (dept.), Colombia 126/B4
Antioquia, Colombia 126/B4
Antique (prov.), Philippines 82/D5
Antiquity, Ohio (†45771) 284/G8
Antisana (mt.), Ecuador 128/D3
Anti-Taurus (mts.), Turkey 63/G3
Antler, N. Dak. (58711) 282/H2
Antler, Sask. 181/K6
Antler (riv.), Sask. 181/K6
Antler Lake, Alberta 182/D3
Antlers, Okla. (74523) 288/P6
Antofagasta (reg.), Chile 138/B4
Antofagasta, Chile 120/B5
Antofagasta, Chile 2/F7
Antofagasta, Chile 138/A4
Antofagasta de la Sierra, Argentina 143/C2
Antoine, Ark. (71922) 202/D5
Antoing, Belgium 27/C7
Anton, Colo. (80801) 208/N3
Antón, Panama 154/G6
Anton, Texas (79313) 303/B4
Anton Chico, N. Mex. (87711) 274/D3
Antone, Oreg. (†97750) 291/H3
Antongil (bay), Madagascar 118/J3
Antonina, Brazil 135/B4
Antonino, Kansas (67624) 232/C3
Antonito, Colo. (81120) 208/H8
Antony, France 28/B2
Antora (peak), Colo. 208/G6
Antreville, S.C. (†29620) 296/B3
Antrim (co.), Mich. 250/D3
Antrim, Mich. (†49659) 250/D4
Antrim, N.H. (03440) 268/D5
Antrim○, N.H. (03440) 268/D5
Antrim (dist.), N. Ireland 17/J2
Antrim, N. Ireland 10/C3
Antrim, N. Ireland 17/J2
Antrim, Ohio (†43973) 284/H5
Antrim, Pa. (†16901) 294/H2
Antsalova, Madagascar 118/G3
Antsirabe, Madagascar 102/G7
Antsirabe, Madagascar 118/H3
Antsiranana (prov.), Madagascar 118/H2
Antsiranana, Madagascar 118/H2
Antsiranana, Madagascar 102/G6

330 Antsia

Antsia, U.S.S.R. 53/D2
Antsohihy, Madagascar 118/H2
Antu, China 77/L3
An Tuc (An Khe), Vietnam 72/F4
Antwerp (prov.), Belgium 27/F6
Antwerp, Belgium 7/E3
Antwerp, Belgium 27/E6
Antwerp, N.Y. (13608) 276/J2
Antwerp, Ohio (45813) 284/A3
Antwerpen (Antwerp), Belgium 27/E6
An Uaimh, Ireland 10/C4
An Uaimh, Ireland 17/H4
Anuenue (Sand) (isl.), Hawaii 218/C4
Anuradhapura, Sri Lanka 68/E7
Anutt, Mo. (†65401) 261/J7
Anvik, Alaska (99558) 196/F2
Anvil (peak), Alaska 196/K4
Anxi, China 77/E3
Anxious (bay), S. Australia 94/D5
Anyang, China 77/H4
A'nyêmaqên Shan (mts.), China 77/E5
Anykščiai, U.S.S.R. 53/C3
Anzá, Colombia 126/C4
'Anza, West Bank 65/C3
Anzac, Alberta 182/E1
Anzaldo, Bolivia 136/C5
Anzhero-Sudzhensk, U.S.S.R. 54/K4
Anzhero-Sudzhensk, U.S.S.R. 48/J4
Anzio, Italy 34/D4
Anzoátegui (state), Venezuela 124/F3
Aoiz, Spain 33/F1
Aoji-ri, N. Korea 81/E2
Aomori (pref.), Japan 81/K3
Aomori, Japan 54/R5
Aomori, Japan 81/K3
Ao Paray (riv.), Paraguay 144/A5
Aosta (reg.), Italy 34/A2
Aosta (prov.), Italy 34/A2
Aosta, Italy 34/A2
Aouara, Fr. Guiana 131/E3
Aouinet Bel Egrâ (well), Algeria 106/C3
Aoulef, Algeria 106/E3
Aozou, Chad 111/C3
Apa (riv.), Paraguay 144/D3
Apache (co.), Ariz. 198/F3
Apache (lake), Ariz. 198/D5
Apache, Okla. (73006) 288/K5
Apache (mts.), Texas 303/C11
Apache Creek, N. Mex. (†87830) 274/A5
Apache Junction, Ariz. (85220) 198/D5
Apalachee (bay), Fla. 188/K5
Apalachee (bay), Fla. 212/B2
Apalachee, Georgia (†30650) 217/E3
Apalachia (res.), N.C. 281/A4
Apalachicola, Fla. (32320) 212/A2
Apalachicola (bay), Fla. 212/B2
Apalachicola (riv.), Fla. 212/A1
Apalachin, N.Y. (13732) 276/H6
Apalona, Ind. (†47576) 227/D8
Apan, Mexico 150/M1
Apaporis (riv.), Colombia 126/F8
Aparecida, Brazil 135/D3
Aparri, Philippines 82/C1
Aparri, Philippines 85/G2
Aparurén, Venezuela 124/G5
Apataki (atoll), Fr. Poly. 87/M7
Apatin, Yugoslavia 45/D3
Apatity, U.S.S.R. 52/D1
Apatzingán de la Constitución, Mexico 150/H7
Ape, U.S.S.R. 53/D2
Apeldoorn, Netherlands 27/H4
Apennines (mts.), Italy 7/F4
Apennines, Central (range), Italy 34/D3
Apennines, Northern (range), Italy 34/B2
Apennines, Southern (range), Italy 34/E4
Apere (riv.), Bolivia 136/C4
Apex, N.C. (27502) 281/M3
Apgar, Mont. (†59936) 262/B2
Apia (cap.), W. Samoa 2/A6
Apia (cap.), W. Samoa 87/J7
Apia (cap.), W. Samoa 86/M8
Apiaí, Brazil 135/B4
Apishapa (riv.), Colo. 208/L8
Apison, Tenn. (37302) 237/L10
Ap Iwan, Cerro (mt.), Chile 138/E6
Apizaco, Mexico 150/N1
Aplao, Peru 128/F11
Aplin, Ark. (†72126) 202/E4
Aplington, Iowa (50604) 229/H3
Ap Long Ha, Vietnam 72/F5
Apo (vol.), Philippines 82/E7
Apohaqui, New Bruns. 170/E3
Apolda, E. Germany 22/D3
Apolima (str.), W. Samoa 86/L8
Apollo, Georgia (†31024) 217/F4
Apollo, Pa. (15613) 294/C4
Apollo Bay, Victoria 97/B6
Apollo Beach, Fla. (33570) 212/C3
Apolo, Bolivia 136/A4
Aponguao (riv.), Venezuela 124/H5
Apopka, Fla. (32703) 212/E3
Apopka (lake), Fla. 212/E3
Aporé (riv.), Brazil 132/D7
Apostle (isls.), Wis. 317/F2
Apostle Islands Nat'l Lakeshore, Wis. 317/E1
Apóstoles, Argentina 143/E2
Apoteri, Guyana 131/B3
Appalachia, Va. (24216) 307/C7
Appalachian (mts.) 188/K3
Appalachian (mts.), N.C. 281/D2
Appalachian (mts.), Pa. 294/H4
Appalachian (mts.), Tenn. 237/M10
Appalachian (mts.), U.S. 146/K6
Appalachian (mts.), Va. 307/J5
Appam, N. Dak. (†58830) 282/C2
Appanoose (co.), Iowa 229/H7
Appelscha, Netherlands 27/J3
Appenzell, Ausser Rhoden (canton), 39/H2
Appenzell, Inner Rhoden (canton), Switzerland 39/H2
Appenzell, Switzerland 39/H2
Apperson, Okla. (†74633) 288/N1
Appin, Ontario 177/C5
Appin (dist.), Scotland 15/C4
Appingedam, Netherlands 27/K2
Apple (creek), Ill. 222/C4
Apple (riv.), Ill. 222/C1
Apple (creek), N. Dak. 282/J6
Apple (riv.), Wis. 317/A5
Appleby, England 13/E3
Appleby, England 10/E3
Appleby, Texas (75961) 303/K6
Apple Creek, Ohio (44606) 284/G4
Applecross, Scotland 15/C3
Appledale, Br. Col. 184/J5
Applegate, Calif. (95703) 204/E5
Applegate, Mich. (48401) 250/G5
Applegate, Oreg. (97530) 291/D5
Apple Grove, W. Va. (25502) 312/B5
Apple Hill, Ontario 177/K2
Apple River, Ill. (61001) 222/C1
Apple River, Nova Scotia 168/D3
Apples, Switzerland 39/B3
Appleton, Ark. (72822) 202/E3
Appleton, Maine (†04540) 243/E7
Appleton○, Maine (†04862) 243/E7
Appleton, Minn. (56208) 255/C5
Appleton (Old Appleton), Mo. (†63770) 261/N7
Appleton, N.Y. (14008) 276/C4
Appleton, Ontario 177/H2
Appleton, S.C. (†29836) 296/E5
Appleton, Wash. (98602) 310/D5
Appleton, Wis. 188/J2
Appleton, Wis. (54911) 317/J7
Appleton City, Mo. (64724) 261/D6
Apple Valley, Calif. (92307) 204/H9
Apple Valley, Minn. (†55124) 255/G6
Appling (co.), Georgia 217/H7
Appling, Georgia (30802) 217/H3
Appomattox (co.), Va. 307/L6
Appomattox, Va. (24522) 307/L6
Appomattox (riv.), Va. 307/M6
Appomattox Court House Nat'l Hist. Park, Va. 307/K6
Apponaug, R.I. (†02887) 249/J6
Approuague (riv.), Fr. Guiana 131/E4
Apra (harb.), Guam 86/K7
Aprilia, Italy 34/D4
Apsheron (pen.), U.S.S.R. 52/H6
Apsheronsk, U.S.S.R. 52/F6
Apsley, Ontario 177/F3
Apsley, Victoria 97/A5
Apt, France 28/F6
Aptos, Calif. (95003) 204/K4
Apua (pt.), Hawaii 218/J6
Apulia (Puglia) (reg.), Italy 34/F4
Apulia Station, N.Y. (13020) 276/H5
Apure (state), Venezuela 124/D4
Apure (riv.), Venezuela 124/E4
Apurímac (dept.), Peru 128/F10
Apurímac (riv.), Peru 120/B4
Apurímac (riv.), Peru 128/F9
Apurito, Venezuela 124/D4
Ap Vinh Hao, Vietnam 72/F5
Aqaba (gulf) 54/E7
'Aqaba (gulf), Egypt 111/G2
'Aqaba (gulf), Egypt 59/C4
'Aqaba (gulf), Israel 65/D6
'Aqaba, Jordan 65/D6
'Aqaba, Jordan 59/C4
Aqaba (gulf), Jordan 65/D6
'Aqaba (gulf), Saudi Arabia 59/C4
Aqcheh, Afghanistan 68/B1
Aqcheh, Afghanistan 59/J2
Aq Darband, Iran 66/M2
'Aqiq, Sudan 111/G4
'Aqqaba, West Bank 65/C3
Aqqikkol Hu (lake), China 77/C4
'Aqra, Iraq 66/D2
'Aqraba, West Bank 65/C3
Aqsu (Aksu), China 77/B3
Aquades Beach, Sask. 181/C2
Aquaforte, Newf. 166/D2
Aqua Park, Okla. (†74435) 288/R3
Aquarius (range), Ariz. 198/B4
Aquarius (plat.), Utah 304/C5
Aquasco, Md. (20608) 245/L6
Aquia, Peru 128/D8
Aquidabán (riv.), Paraguay 144/D3
Aquidauana, Brazil 120/D5
Aquidauana, Brazil 132/C8
Aquila, Mexico 150/H7
Aquila, Switzerland 39/G3
Aquiles Serdán, Mexico 150/G2
Aquilla, Ohio (†44024) 284/H2
Aquin, Haiti 158/B6
Ara (riv.), Japan 81/O2
Arab, Ala. (35016) 195/E2
'Arab, Shatt-al- (riv.), Iran 59/E4
'Arab, Shatt-al- (riv.), Iran 66/F5
'Arab, Shatt-al- (riv.), Iraq 59/E4
'Arab, Shatt-al- (riv.), Iraq 66/F5
Arab, Mo. (63733) 261/M8
'Araba, Wadi (valley), Israel 65/D5
'Araba, Wadi (valley), Jordan 65/D5
Arabela, N. Mex. (†88351) 274/D5
Arabella, Sask. 181/K3
Arabi, Georgia (31712) 217/E7
'Arabi (isl.), Iran 66/G7
Arabi, La. (70032) 238/P4
Arabia, Ky. (†40437) 237/M6
Arabia, Ohio (†45659) 284/F8
Arabian (sea) 54/H8
Arabian (sea) 2/N5
Arabian (des.), Egypt 111/F2
Arabian (des.), Egypt 59/B4
Arabian (sea), India 68/B5
Arabian (sea), Pakistan 68/B5
Arabian (sea), P.D.R. Yemen 59/H5
Arabopó, Venezuela 124/H5
Araç, Turkey 63/E2
Araca, Bolivia 136/B5
Aracaju, Brazil 120/F4
Aracaju, Brazil 132/G5
Aracataca, Colombia 126/D2
Aracati, Brazil 132/G4
Araçatuba, Brazil 132/D8
Araçatuba, Brazil 135/A2
Araceli, Philippines 82/C5
Aracena, Spain 33/C4
Araçuaí, Brazil 132/F7
Arad, Israel 65/C5
Arad, Romania 7/G4
Arad, Romania 45/E2
Arada, Chad 111/D4
'Aradah, U.A.E. 59/F5
Aradan, Iran 66/H3
Arafat, Jebel (mt.), Saudi Arabia 59/D5
Arafura (sea) 87/D6
Arafura (sea) 2/R6
Arafura (sea) 88/E2
Arafura (sea), Indonesia 85/J8
Arafura (sea), North. Terr. 93/D1
Arago, Minn. (†56470) 255/C3
Arago, Oreg. (97458) 291/C4
Arago (cape), Oreg. 291/C4
Aragon, Georgia (30104) 217/B2
Aragon, N. Mex. (87820) 274/A5
Aragón (reg.), Spain 33/F2
Aragón (riv.), Spain 33/F1
Aragona, Italy 34/D6
Aragua (state), Venezuela 124/E3
Araguacema, Brazil 132/D5
Aragua de Barcelona, Venezuela 124/F3
Aragua de Maturín, Venezuela 124/G3
Araguaia (riv.), Brazil 120/E3
Araguaia (riv.), Brazil 132/D4
Araguaiana, Brazil 132/C6
Araguaina, Brazil 120/E3
Araguari, Brazil 120/E4
Araguari, Brazil 132/D7
Araguari (riv.), Brazil 132/D2
Araioses, Brazil 132/F3
Arak, Algeria 106/E3
Arak, Iran 54/G6
Arak, Iran 59/E3
Arak, Iran 66/F3
Arakan (state), Burma 72/B3
Arakan Yoma (mts.), Burma 72/B3
Araks (riv.) 54/F6
Araks (riv.), Iran 59/E2
Araks (Aras) (riv.), Iran 66/E1
Araks (riv.), Turkey 63/K2
Araks (riv.), U.S.S.R. 7/J5
Araks (riv.), U.S.S.R. 52/G7
Aral (sea), U.S.S.R. 54/G5
Aral (sea), U.S.S.R. 48/F5
Aralık, Turkey 63/L3
Aral Sea (lake), U.S.S.R. 2/M3
Aral'sk, U.S.S.R. 54/H5
Aral'sk, U.S.S.R. 48/G5
Aramac, Queensland 95/C4
Aramberri, Mexico 150/J5
Arampampa, Bolivia 136/B5
Aran (isl.), Ireland 10/B3
Aran (isl.), Ireland 17/D2
Aran (isls.), Ireland 17/B5
Aran (isls.), Ireland 10/B4
Aranda de Duero, Spain 33/E2
Arandas, Mexico 150/H6
Aran Fawddwy (mt.), Wales 13/C5
Arani, Bolivia 136/C5
Aranjuez, Spain 33/E2
Aransas (co.), Texas 303/H10
Aransas (passage), Texas 303/H10
Aransas Pass, Texas (78336) 303/G10
Araoua (mts.), Fr. Guiana 131/E4
Araouane, Mali 106/D5
Araouane, Mali 102/B3
Arapaho, Okla. (73620) 288/H3
Arapahoe (co.), Colo. 208/L3
Arapahoe, Colo. (80802) 208/P5
Arapahoe (peak), Colo. 208/H2
Arapahoe, Nebr. (68922) 264/E4
Arapahoe, N.C. (28510) 281/R4
Arapahoe, Wyo. (82510) 319/D3
Arapaho Nat'l Rec. Area, Colo. 208/G2
Arapey, Uruguay 145/B1
Arapey Chico (riv.), Uruguay 145/B1
Arapey Grande (riv.), Uruguay 145/B2
Arapicos, Ecuador 128/D3
Arapiraca, Brazil 120/F3
Arapkir, Turkey 63/H3
Arapkir, Turkey 59/C2
'Ar'ar, Wadi (dry riv.), Iraq 66/B5
'Ar'ar, Wadi (dry riv.), Iraq 59/D3
'Ar'ar, Wadi (dry riv.), Saudi Arabia 59/D3
Araracuara, Colombia 126/E8
Araracuara, Cerros de (mts.), Colombia 126/E7
Araranguá, Brazil 132/D10
Araraquara, Brazil 132/E8
Araraquara, Brazil 135/B2
Araras, Brazil 135/C3
Ararat, Ala. (†36921) 195/B7
Ararat, N.C. (27007) 281/H2
Ararat (mt.), Pa. 294/M2
Ararat (mt.), Turkey 54/F6
Ararat (mt.), Turkey 63/L3
Ararat (mt.), Turkey 59/D2
Ararat, Victoria 88/G7
Ararat, Victoria 97/B5
Ararat, Va. (24053) 307/G7
Arari, Brazil 132/E3
Araruama (lake), Brazil 135/E3
Aras (Araks) (riv.), Iran 66/E1
Aras (Araks) (riv.), Iran 59/E2
Aratürük (Yiwu), China 77/D3
Arauca (riv.) 120/C2
Arauca (inten.), Colombia 126/E4
Arauca, Colombia 120/B2
Arauca, Colombia 126/E4
Arauca (riv.), Colombia 126/E4
Arauca (riv.), Venezuela 124/E4
Arauco, Chile 138/D1
Arauco (gulf), Chile 138/D1
Arauquita, Colombia 126/E4
Araure, Venezuela 124/D3
Aravaca, Spain 33/F4
Aravaipa (creek), Ariz. 198/E6
Arawa, Papua N.G. 86/C2
Arawe, Papua N.G. 86/B2
Arax (Araks)(riv), Asia 59/E2
Araxá, Brazil 132/E7
Araya, Venezuela 124/F2
Arba, Ind. (†47355) 227/H4
Arba Mench, Ethiopia 111/G6
Arba Mench, Ethiopia 102/F4
Arbeca, Spain 33/G2
Arbedo-Castione, Switzerland 39/G4
Arbela (Erbil), Iraq 59/D2
Arbela (Erbil), Iraq 66/D2
Arbela, Mo. (63432) 261/H2
Arboga, Sweden 18/J7
Arbois, France 28/F4
Arbon, Idaho (83212) 220/F7
Arbon, Switzerland 39/H1
Arborea, Italy 34/B5
Arborfield, Sask. 181/H2
Arborg, Manitoba 179/E4
Arbor Vitae, Wis. (†54568) 317/G4
Arbovale, W. Va. (24915) 312/G6
Arbrå, Sweden 18/K6
Arbroath, Scotland 15/F4
Arbroath, Scotland 10/E2
Arbroth, La. (†70736) 238/H5
Arbucias, Spain 33/H2
Arbuckle, Calif. (95912) 204/C4
Arbuckle (lake), Fla. 212/E4
Arbuckle, W. Va. (25006) 312/C5
Arbuckles, Lake of the (lake), Okla. 288/M6
Arbuthnot, Sask. 181/E6
Arbutus, Md. (†21227) 245/M4
Arbyrd, Mo. (63821) 261/M10
Arcachon, France 28/C5
Arcachon (bay), France 28/C5
Arcade, Georgia (†30549) 217/E2
Arcade, N.Y. (14009) 276/D5
Arcadia, Calif. (91006) 204/C10
Arcadia, Fla. (33821) 212/E4
Arcadia, Ind. (46030) 227/E4
Arcadia, Iowa (51430) 229/C4
Arcadia, Kansas (66711) 232/H4
Arcadia, La. (71001) 238/E1
Arcadia, Mich. (49613) 250/C4
Arcadia, Mo. (63621) 261/L7
Arcadia, Nebr. (68815) 264/F3
Arcadia, Nova Scotia 168/B5
Arcadia, Ohio (44804) 284/D3
Arcadia, Okla. (73007) 288/M3
Arcadia, Pa. (15712) 294/E4
Arcadia, R.I. (†02832) 249/H6
Arcadia, S.C. (29320) 296/C2
Arcadia, Texas (77517) 303/K3
Arcadia, Utah (†84012) 304/D3
Arcadia, Wis. (54612) 317/D7
Arcadia Lakes, S.C. (†29201) 296/F3
Arcahaie, Haiti 158/C6
Arcanum, Ohio (45304) 284/A6
Arcas (cay), Mexico 150/N6
Arcata, Calif. (95521) 204/A3
Arc Dome (mt.), Nev. 266/D4
Arcelia, Mexico 150/J7
Arch, N. Mex. (†88130) 274/F4
Archambault (lake), Québec 172/C3
Archangel, U.S.S.R. 4/C7
Archangel, U.S.S.R. 2/M2
Archangel, U.S.S.R. 7/J2
Archangel (Arkhangel'sk), U.S.S.R. 48/E3
Archangel (Arkhangel'sk), U.S.S.R. 52/F2
Archbald, Pa. (18403) 294/F6
Archbold, Ohio (43502) 284/B2
Arch Cape, Oreg. (97102) 291/D2
Archdale, N.C. (27263) 281/K3
Archena, Spain 33/F3
Archer, Fla. (32618) 212/D2
Archer, Iowa (51231) 229/B2
Archer, Nebr. (68816) 264/F3
Archer (fiord), N.W. Terrs. 187/M1
Archer (riv.), Queensland 95/B2
Archer (co.), Texas 303/F4
Archer City, Texas (76351) 303/F4
Archerfield, Queensland 88/K3
Archerfield, Queensland 95/D3
Archerwill, Sask. 181/H3
Arches Nat'l Park, Utah 304/E5
Archibald, La. (71218) 238/G2
Archidona, Ecuador 128/D3
Archidona, Spain 33/D4
Archie, La. (†71343) 238/G3
Archie, Mo. (64725) 261/D5
Archiestown, Scotland 15/E3
Archuleta (co.), Colo. 208/E8
Archydal, Sask. 181/F5
Arcis-sur-Aube, France 28/F3
Arckaringa (creek), S. Australia 94/D2
Arco, Georgia (†31520) 217/J8
Arco, Idaho (83213) 220/E6
Arco, Idaho 188/D2
Arco, Minn. (56113) 255/B6
Arcola, Ill. (61910) 222/E4
Arcola, Ind. (46704) 227/G2
Arcola, La. (†70456) 238/K5
Arcola, Miss. (38722) 256/C4
Arcola, Mo. (65603) 261/E7
Arcola, N.C. (27589) 281/N2
Arcola, Sask. 181/J6
Arcopongo, Bolivia 136/B5
Arcosanti, Ariz. (†86333) 198/C4
Arcos de Jalón, Spain 33/E2
Arcos de la Frontera, Spain 33/D4
Arcos de Valdevez, Portugal 33/B2
Arcot, India 68/D6
Arcoverde, Brazil 132/G5
Arctic (ocean) 54/C1
Arctic (ocean) 146/B2
Arctic (plain), Alaska 196/G1
Arctic, R.I. (†02893) 249/J6
Arctic Bay, Canada 4/B14
Arctic Bay, N.W.T. 162/H1
Arctic Bay, N.W. Terrs. 187/K2
Arctic Circle 2/J2
Arctic Ocean 2/B2
Arctic Ocean 4/A15
Arctic Ocean, U.S.S.R. 48/K1
Arctic Red (riv.), N.W. Terrs. 187/E3
Arctic Red River, N.W.T. 162/C2
Arctic Red River, N.W. Terrs. 187/E3
Arctic Village, Alaska (99722) 196/K1
Arda (riv.), Greece 45/G5
Ardabil, Iran 54/F6
Ardabil, Iran 59/E2
Ardabil, Iran 66/F1
Ardagh, Limerick, Ireland 17/C7
Ardagh, Longford, Ireland 17/F4
Ardahan, Turkey 59/D1
Ardahan, Turkey 63/K2
Ardal, Iran 66/G4
Årdal, Norway 18/F6
Årdalstangen, Norway 18/F6
Ardanuç, Turkey 63/K2
Ardara, Ireland 17/E2
Ardath, Sask. 181/D4
Ardavasar, Scotland 15/B3
Ardbeg, Ontario 177/D2
Ardèche (dept.), France 28/F5
Ardee, Ireland 17/H4
Ardee, Ireland 10/C4
Arden, Ark. (†71822) 202/B6
Arden, Del. (†19801) 245/R1
Arden, Denmark 21/C4
Arden, Manitoba 179/C4
Arden, Ontario 177/G3
Arden, Wash. (†99114) 310/H2
Arden, W. Va. (†26405) 312/G4
Arden-Arcade, Calif. (95825) 204/B8
Ardencroft, Del. (†19810) 245/R1
Ardennes (for.), Belgium 27/F9
Ardennes (dept.), France 28/F3
Ardenode, Alberta 182/D4
Ardentown, Del. (†19810) 245/S1
Ardenvoir, Wash. (98811) 310/E3
Ardersier, Scotland 15/E3
Ardeşen, Turkey 63/J2
Ardestan, Iran 59/F3
Ardestan, Iran 66/H4
Ardez, Switzerland 39/K3
Ardfert, Ireland 17/B7
Ardfinnan, Ireland 17/F7
Ardgay, Scotland 15/D3
Ardglass, N. Ireland 17/K3
Ardgour (dist.), Scotland 15/C4
Ardhéa, Greece 45/F5
Ardila (riv.), Spain 33/C3
Ardill, Sask. 181/F6
Ardino, Bulgaria 45/G5
Ardivachar (pt.), Scotland 15/A3
Ardle (riv.), Scotland 15/E4
Ardlethan, N.S. Wales 97/D4
Ardmore, Ala. (35805) 195/E1
Ardmore, Alberta 182/E2
Ardmore, Ind. (†46624) 227/E1
Ardmore, Ireland 17/F8
Ardmore, Md. (†20785) 245/G4
Ardmore, Mo. (†65247) 261/H3
Ardmore, Okla. 188/G4
Ardmore, Okla. (73401) 288/M6
Ardmore, Pa. (19003) 294/M6
Ardmore, S. Dak. (57715) 298/B7
Ardmore, Tenn. (38449) 237/H10
Ardnamurchan (pen.), Scotland 15/B4
Ardnamurchan (pt.), Scotland 15/B4
Ardoch, N. Dak. (58213) 282/R3
Ardon, Switzerland 39/D4
Ardooie, Belgium 27/C7
Ardrahan, Ireland 17/D5
Ardrishaig, Scotland 15/C4
Ardrossan, Alberta 182/D3
Ardrossan, Scotland 10/D3
Ardrossan, Scotland 15/D5
Ards (dist.), N. Ireland 17/K2
Ardsley, N.Y. (10502) 276/O6
Åre, Sweden 18/H5
Arecibo (dist.), P. Rico 161/C1
Arecibo, P. Rico 156/G1
Arecibo, P. Rico 161/B1
Aredale, Iowa (50605) 229/H3
Areguá, Paraguay 144/B4
Areia Branca, Brazil 132/G4
Arelee, Sask. 181/D3
Arena (pt.), Calif. 188/B3
Arena (pt.), Calif. 204/B5
Arena (pt.), Mexico 150/E5
Arena, N. Dak. (58412) 282/K5
Arena (isl.), Philippines 82/C6
Arena, Wis. (53503) 317/G9
Arenac (co.), Mich. 250/F4
Arenales, Cerro (mt.), Chile 138/D7
Arenas (pt.), Argentina 143/C7
Arenas (cay), Mexico 150/O5
Arenas (pt.), P. Rico 161/F2
Arenas de San Pedro, Spain 33/D2
Arendal, Norway 18/F7
Arendjelovac, Yugoslavia 45/E3
Arendonk, Belgium 27/G6
Arendtsville, Pa. (17303) 294/H6
Arenillas, Ecuador 128/B4
Arenys de Mar, Spain 33/H2
Arenzville, Ill. (62611) 222/C4
Areópolis, Greece 45/F7
Arequipa (dept.), Peru 128/F10
Arequipa, Peru 128/G11
Arequipa, Peru 120/B4
Arequipa, Peru 2/F6
Arequipa, Peru 128/72
Aresji, Neth. Ant. 161/D9
Areuse (riv.), Switzerland 39/C3
Arévalo, Spain 33/D2
Areyonga, North. Terr. 88/E4
Areyonga, North. Terr. 93/C8
Arezzo (prov.), Italy 34/C3
Arezzo, Italy 34/C3
Arfa Deh, Iran 66/H3
Arga (riv.), Spain 33/F1
Argadargada, North. Terr. 93/E6
Argalant, Mongolia 77/G3
Argalasti, Greece 45/F6
Argamasilla de Alba, Spain 33/E3
Arganda, Spain 33/G4
Argao, Philippines 82/D6
Argenta, Br. Col. 184/J5
Argenta, Ill. (62501) 222/E4
Argenta, Italy 34/D2
Argentan, France 28/D3
Argentat, France 28/D5
Argenteuil, France 28/A1
Argenteuil (co.), Québec 172/C4
Argentia, Newf. 166/C2
Argentina 2/F7
Argentina 120/C6
ARGENTINA 143
Argentine, Pa. (†16040) 294/C3
Argentino (lake), Argentina 143/B7
Argenton-sur-Creusot, France 28/D4
Argeş (riv.), Romania 45/G3
Argo, Ala. (†35173) 195/E3
Argo, Sudan 111/F4
Argo, Sudan 59/B6
Argolis (gulf), Greece 45/F7
Argonia, Kansas (67004) 232/E4
Argonne, Wis. (54511) 317/J4
Argonne Nat'l Laboratory, Ill. 222/B6
Árgos, Greece 45/F7
Argos, Ind. (46501) 227/E2
Argos (cape), Nova Scotia 168/G3
Argostólion, Greece 45/E6
Arguello (pt.), Calif. 204/E9
Arguin (bay), Mauritania 106/A4
Argun (riv.) 54/N4
Argun' (Ergun He) (riv.), China 77/K1
Argun' (riv.), U.S.S.R. 48/M4
Argungu, Nigeria 106/E6
Argus (range), Calif. 204/H7
Argusville, N. Dak. (58005) 282/R5
Arguvan, Turkey 63/H3
Argyle, Fla. (32422) 212/C6
Argyle, Georgia (31623) 217/G8
Argyle, Iowa (52619) 229/K7
Argyle, Maine (†04468) 243/F5
Argyle, Manitoba 179/E4
Argyle, Mich. (48410) 250/G5
Argyle, Minn. (56713) 255/B2
Argyle, Mo. (65001) 261/J6
Argyle, New Bruns. 170/C2
Argyle, N.Y. (12809) 276/O4
Argyle, Texas (76226) 303/F1
Argyle (lake), W. Australia 88/D3
Argyle (lake), W. Australia 92/E2
Argyle, Wis. (53504) 317/G10
Argyle Downs, W. Australia 92/E2
Argyll (dist.), Scotland 15/C4
Argyll (trad. co.), Scotland 15/B5
Arhangay, Mongolia 77/F2
Arhavi, Turkey 63/J2
Arhli (Arlit), Niger 106/F4
Ar Horqin, China 77/K3
Århus (co.), Denmark 21/D5
Århus, Denmark 7/E3
Århus, Denmark 21/D5
Århus, Denmark 18/F8
Aria, N. Zealand 100/E3
Ariah Park, N.S. Wales 97/D4
Ariail, S.C. (†29640) 296/B2
Ariano Irpino, Italy 34/E4
Ariari (riv.), Colombia 126/D6
Aribinda, Upper Volta 106/D6
Arica, Chile 120/B4
Arica, Chile 138/A1
Arica, Colombia 126/E9
Aricagua, Venezuela 124/C3
Ariccia, Italy 34/F7
Arichat, Nova Scotia 168/H3
Arichuna, Venezuela 124/E4
Arichuna (riv.), Venezuela 124/D4
Arid (cape), W. Australia 88/C6
Arid (cape), W. Australia 92/C6
Ariège (dept.), France 28/D6
Ariel, Wash. (98603) 310/C5
Ariguaní (riv.), Colombia 126/D3
Ariha (Jericho), West Bank 65/C4
Arikaree (riv.), Colo. 208/O3
Arima, Trin. & Tob. 156/G5
Arima, Trin. & Tob. 161/B10
Arimo, Idaho (83214) 220/F7
Arinagour, Scotland 15/B4
Aringa, Uganda 115/F3
Arinos (riv.), Brazil 132/B5
Ario de Rosales, Mexico 150/J7
Arion, Iowa (51520) 229/B5
Aripao, Venezuela 124/F4
Aripeka, Fla. (33502) 212/D3
Aripine, Ariz. (†85901) 198/E4
Aripo, El Cerro del (mt.), Trin. & Tob. 161/B10
Ariporo (riv.), Colombia 126/E4
Aripuanã, Brazil 120/C3
Aripuanã, Brazil 132/A5
Aripuanã (riv.), Brazil 120/D3
Aripuanã (riv.), Brazil 132/A4
Arisaig, Scotland 15/C4
Arisaig (sound), Scotland 15/C4
Arismendi, Venezuela 124/D3
Arispe, Iowa (50831) 229/E7
Aristazabal (isl.), Br. Col. 184/C4
Aritao, Philippines 82/C2
Ariton, Ala. (36311) 195/G7
Arivaca, Ariz. (85601) 198/D7
Arivonimamo, Madagascar 118/H3
Arixang (Wenquan), China 77/B3
Ariza, Spain 33/E2
Arizaro, Salar de (salt dep.), Argentina 143/C2
Arizona 188/D4
ARIZONA 198
Arizona (state), U.S. 146/G6
Arizona City, Ariz. (85223) 198/D6
Arizona Sunsites, Ariz. (85625) 198/F7
Arizpe, Mexico 150/D1
Årjäng, Sweden 18/H7
Arjay, Ky. (40902) 237/O7
Arjeplog, Sweden 18/L3
Arjona, Colombia 126/C2
Arkabutla, Miss. (38602) 256/D1
Arkabutla (dam), Miss. 256/D1
Arkabutla (lake), Miss. 256/D1
Arkadelphia, Ala. (35033) 195/E3
Arkadelphia, Ark. (71923) 202/D5
Arkaig, Loch (lake), Scotland 15/C4
Arkaig, Loch (lake), Scotland 10/D2
Arkalyk, U.S.S.R. 48/G4
Arkansas 188/H3
Arkansas (riv.) 188/H3
ARKANSAS 202
Arkansas (co.), Ark. 202/H5

Atchison 331

Arkansas (riv.), Ark. 202/G5
Arkansas (riv.), Colo. 208/P6
Arkansas (riv.), Kansas 232/D3
Arkansas (riv.), Okla. 288/S4
Arkansas (state), U.S. 146/J6
Arkansas (riv.), U.S. 2/E4
Arkansas (riv.), U.S. 146/J6
Arkansas City, Ark. (71630) 202/H6
Arkansas City, Kans. 188/G3
Arkansas City, Kansas (67005) 232/E4
Arkansas Divide (mts.), Colo. 208/L4
Arkansas Post Nat'l Mem., Ark. 202/H5
Arkansaw, Wis. (54721) 317/B6
Arkdale, Wis. (54613) 317/G7
Arkhángelos, Greece 45/J7
Arkhipo-Osipovka, U.S.S.R. 52/E6
Arkinda, Ark. (71821) 202/B6
Arklow, Ireland 10/C4
Arklow, Ireland 17/J6
Arklow (bank), Ireland 17/K6
Arkoe, Mo. (†64468) 261/C2
Arkoma, Okla. (74901) 288/T4
Arkona (cape), E. Germany 22/E1
Arkona, Ontario 177/C4
Arkport, N.Y. (14807) 276/E6
Arkticheskiy Institut (isls.), U.S.S.R. 48/H2
Arkville, N.Y. (12406) 276/L6
Arkwright, S.C. (†29301) 296/C2
Arlee, Mont. (59821) 262/B3
Arlee, W. Va. (†25106) 312/B5
Arles, France 28/F6
Arley, Ala. (35541) 195/D2
Arlington, Ala. (36722) 195/C6
Arlington, Ariz. (85322) 198/C5
Arlington, Colo. (81021) 208/N6
Arlington, Georgia (31713) 217/C8
Arlington, Ill. (61312) 222/D2
Arlington, Ind. (46104) 227/F5
Arlington, Iowa (50606) 229/K3
Arlington, Kansas (67514) 232/D4
Arlington, Ky. (42021) 237/D7
Arlington○, Mass. (02174) 249/C6
Arlington, Minn. (55307) 255/D6
Arlington, Nebr. (68002) 264/H3
Arlington, N.Y. (12603) 276/N7
Arlington, N.C. (†28642) 281/H2
Arlington, Ohio (45814) 284/C4
Arlington, Oreg. (97812) 291/G2
Arlington, S. Dak. (57212) 298/P5
Arlington, Tenn. (38002) 237/B10
Arlington, Tex. 188/G4
Arlington, Texas (*76010) 303/F2
Arlington (lake), Texas 303/F2
Arlington, Vt. (05250) 268/A5
Arlington○, Vt. (05250) 268/A5
Arlington (co.), Va. 307/S2
Arlington, Va. (*22201) 307/T3
Arlington, Wash. (98223) 310/C2
Arlington, Wis. (53911) 317/H9
Arlington, Wyo. (†82080) 319/F4
Arlington Beach, Sask. 181/F4
Arlington Heights, Ill. (*60004) 222/B5
Arlington Heights, Ohio (†45201) 284/C9
Arlington Nat'l Cemetery, Va. 307/T3
Arlit (Arhli), Niger 106/F4
Arló, Hungary 41/F2
Arlon, Belgium 27/H9
Arltunga, North. Terr. 93/D7
Arm (riv.), Sask. 181/F5
Arma, Kansas (66712) 232/H4
Arma (plat.), Saudi Arabia 59/E4
Armada, Alberta 182/D4
Armada, Mich. (48005) 250/G6
Armadale, Scotland 15/C2
Armadale, Scotland 10/B1
Armagh (dist.), N. Ireland 17/H3
Armagh, N. Ireland 10/C3
Armagh, N. Ireland 17/H3
Armagh, Pa. (15920) 294/E5
Armagh, Québec 172/G3
Armathwaite, Tenn. (38506) 237/M8
Armavir, U.S.S.R. 7/J4
Armavir, U.S.S.R. 48/E5
Armavir, U.S.S.R. 52/F5
Armena, Alberta 182/D3
Armenia, Colombia 120/B2
Armenia, Colombia 126/B5
Armenian S.S.R., U.S.S.R. 7/J4
Armenian S.S.R., U.S.S.R. 52/F6
Armenian S.S.R., U.S.S.R. 48/E6
Armentières, France 28/E2
Armeria, Mexico 150/G7
Armero, Colombia 126/C5
Armidale, Australia 87/F9
Armidale, N. S. Wales 88/J6
Armidale, N.S. Wales 97/F2
Armington, Ill. (61721) 222/D3
Armington, Mont. (†59412) 262/F3
Arminto, Wyo. (82630) 319/E2
Armistead, La. (†71019) 238/D3
Armit (lake), Manitoba 179/A2
Armley, Sask. 181/G2
Armona, Calif. (93202) 204/F7
Armorel, Ark. (72310) 202/L2
Armour, S. Dak. (57313) 298/N7
Armourdale, N. Dak. (†58365) 282/M2
Armoy, N. Ireland 17/J1
Armstrong, Br. Col. 184/H5
Armstrong, Ill. (61812) 222/F3
Armstrong, Ind. (†47708) 227/B8
Armstrong, Iowa (50514) 229/D2
Armstrong, Mo. (65230) 261/G4
Armstrong, Ont. 162/H5
Armstrong, Ontario 175/C2
Armstrong, Ontario 177/H4
Armstrong (co.), Pa. 294/D4
Armstrong (co.), Texas 303/C3
Armstrong, Texas (78338) 303/G11
Armstrong Brook, New Bruns. 170/E1
Armstrong Creek, Wis. (54103) 317/K4
Armstrongs Mills, Ohio (43904) 284/J6
Armuchee, Georgia (30105) 217/B2
Army Chemical Center, Md. 245/O3
Army Med. Ctr. Annex (Walter Reed), Md. 245/E4
Arnaia, Greece 45/F5
Arnaud, Manitoba 179/E5
Arnaud (riv.), Québec 174/F1
Arnaudville, La. (70512) 238/G6
Arnauti (cape), Cyprus 59/B2
Arnauti (cape), Cyprus 63/E5
Arnavutköy, Turkey 63/D6
Arnedo, Spain 33/E1
Arnegard, N. Dak. (58835) 282/D4
Årnes, Norway 18/G6
Arnett, Okla. (73832) 288/G2
Arnett, W. Va. (25007) 312/D7
Arney (riv.), N. Ireland 17/F3
Arnheim, Mich. (†49958) 250/G1
Arnhem (cape), Australia 87/D7
Arnhem, Netherlands 27/H4
Arnhem (cape), North. Terr. 88/F2
Arnhem (cape), North. Terr. 93/E2
Arnhem Land (reg.), Australia 87/D7
Arnhem Land (reg.), North. Terr. 88/E2
Arnhem Land (reg.), North. Terr. 93/D2
Arnhem Land Aboriginal Reserve, North. Terr. 88/E2
Arnhem Land Aboriginal Res., North. Terr. 93/C2
Arno (riv.), Italy 34/C3
Arno (atoll), Marshall Is. 87/H5
Arnold, Calif. (95223) 204/E5
Arnold, England 13/F4
Arnold, Kansas (67515) 232/B3
Arnold, Mich. (49819) 250/B2
Arnold, Minn. (†55801) 255/F4
Arnold, Mo. (63010) 261/M6
Arnold, Nebr. (69120) 264/D3
Arnold (riv.), North. Terr. 93/D3
Arnold, Pa. (15068) 294/C4
Arnold Mills, R.I. (†02864) 249/J5
Arnoldsburg, W. Va. (25234) 312/D5
Arnold's Cove, Newf. 166/C2
Arnolds Park, Iowa (51331) 229/C2
Arnoldstein, Austria 41/B3
Arnoldsville, Georgia (30619) 217/F3
Arnot, Pa. (16911) 294/H2
Arnøya (isl.), Norway 18/M1
Arnprior, Ontario 177/H2
Arnsberg, W. Germany 22/C3
Arnstadt, E. Germany 22/D3
Årø (isl.), Denmark 21/C7
Aro (riv.), Venezuela 124/F4
Aroa, Venezuela 124/D2
Aroab, Namibia 118/B5
Aroche, Spain 33/C4
Arock, Oreg. (97902) 291/K5
Aroland, Ontario 177/H4
Aroland, Ontario 175/C2
Arolla, Switzerland 39/E4
Arolsen, W. Germany 22/C3
Aroma, Bolivia 136/B6
Aroma, Sudan 111/G4
Aroma Park, Ill. (60910) 222/F2
Aromas, Calif. (95004) 204/D7
Aroostook (co.), Maine 243/F2
Aroostook (riv.), Maine 243/G2
Aroostook, New Bruns. 170/C2
Arorae (atoll), Kiribati 87/H6
Aroroy, Philippines 82/D4
Arosa, Ria de (est.), Spain 33/B1
Arosa, Switzerland 39/J3
Aroser Rothorn (mt.), Switzerland 39/J3
Årøsund, Denmark 21/C7
Arouca, Trin. & Tob. 161/B10
Arp, Georgia (†31783) 217/F7
Arp, Texas (75750) 303/J5
Arpa (riv.), Turkey 63/K2
Arpaçay, Turkey 63/K2
Arpin, Wis. (54410) 317/G6
Arque, Bolivia 136/B5
'Arraba, West Bank 65/C3
'Arrabe, Israel 65/C2
Arrah, India 68/E3
Ar Rahhaliya, Iraq 66/C4
Ar Rahhaliya, Iraq 59/D3
Arraias, Brazil 132/E6
Arran, Fla. (†32327) 212/B1
Arran, Sask. 181/K4
Arran (isl.), Scotland 15/C5
Arran (isl.), Scotland 10/D3
Arras, Br. Col. 184/G2
Arras, France 28/E2
Arrecifal, Colombia 126/F6
Arrecife, Spain 106/B3
Arrecife, Spain 33/C4
Arrecife de la Media Luna (reefs), Honduras 154/F3
Arrecifes, Argentina 143/F7
Arrecifes (riv.), Argentina 143/G6
Arrey, N. Mex. (87930) 274/B6
Arriaga, Mexico 150/N8
Arriba, Colo. (80804) 208/N4
Arribeños, Argentina 143/F7
Arrington, Kansas (†66436) 232/G2
Arrington, Tenn. (37014) 237/H9
Arrington, Va. (22922) 307/L5
Arriola, Colo. (†81323) 208/B8
Arrochar, Scotland 15/D4
Arronches, Portugal 33/C3
Arrow (lake), Ireland 17/E3
Arrow (creek), Mont. 262/F3
Arrow Canyon (range), Nev. 266/G6
Arrow Creek, Mont. (†59424) 262/F3
Arrowhead Mountain (lake), Vt. 268/A2
Arrow River, Manitoba 179/B4
Arrowrock (res.), Idaho 220/C6
Arrow Rock, Mo. (65320) 261/F4
Arrowsmith, Ill. (61722) 222/E3
Arrowtown, N. Zealand 100/B6
Arrowwood, Alberta 182/D4
Arrowwood (lake), N. Dak. 282/N5
Arroyas, Los (lake), Bolivia 136/C3
Arroyo, P. Rico 161/E3
Arroyo, P. Rico 156/G1
Arroyo Blanco, Cuba 158/F2
Arroyo de la Luz, Spain 33/C3
Arroyo del Valle (dry riv.), Calif. 204/L3
Arroyo Grande, Bolivia 136/A2
Arroyo Grande, Calif. (93420) 204/E8
Arroyo Hondo (dry riv.), Calif. 204/L3
Arroyo Hondo, N. Mex. (87513) 274/D2
Arroyo Mocho (dry riv.), Calif. 204/L2
Arroyo Seco, Argentina 143/F6
Arroyo Seco (dry riv.), Calif. 204/K10
Arroyo Seco, N. Mex. (87514) 274/D2
Arroyos y Esteros, Paraguay 144/B4
Ar Rumaila, Iraq 66/E5
Års, Denmark 21/C4
Ars-en-Ré, France 28/C4
Arsen'yev, U.S.S.R. 48/O5
Arsin, Turkey 63/H2
Arslanköy, Turkey 63/F4
Árta, Greece 45/E6
Artá, Spain 33/H3
Artas, S. Dak. (57423) 298/K2
Artawiya, Saudi Arabia 59/E4
Arteaga, Mexico 150/H7
Artem, U.S.S.R. 48/O5
Artemas, Pa. (17211) 294/E6
Artemisa, Cuba 158/B1
Artemisa, Cuba 156/A2
Artemovskiy, U.S.S.R. 48/M4
Artemus, Ky. (40903) 237/O7
Artena, Italy 34/F7
Artesia, Calif. (90701) 204/C11
Artesia, Miss. (39736) 256/G4
Artesia, N. Mex. 188/F4
Artesia, N. Mex. (88210) 274/E6
Artesian, S. Dak. (57314) 298/O6
Artesia Wells, Texas (78001) 303/E9
Arth, Switzerland 39/F2
Arthabaska (co.), Québec 172/E4
Arthabaska, Québec 172/F3
Arthur, Ill. (61911) 222/E4
Arthur, Ind. (†47598) 227/C8
Arthur, Iowa (51431) 229/C4
Arthur (co.), Nebr. 264/C3
Arthur, Nebr. (69121) 264/C3
Arthur (range), N. Zealand 100/D4
Arthur, N. Dak. (58006) 282/R5
Arthur, Ontario 177/D4
Arthur (lake), Pa. 294/C4
Arthur (lake), Tasmania 99/D4
Arthur (range), Tasmania 99/C5
Arthur (riv.), Tasmania 99/B3
Arthur, Tenn. (37707) 237/O7
Arthur (riv.), W. Australia 92/B2
Arthur, W. Va. (26816) 312/H4
Arthurdale, W. Va. (26520) 312/G3
Arthuret, England 13/E2
Arthurette, New Bruns. 170/C2
Arthur Kill (str.), N.J. 273/B3
Arthur's (pass), N. Zealand 100/C5
Arthurstown, Ireland 17/H7
Artibonite (dept.), Haiti 158/C5
Artibonite (riv.), Haiti 158/C5
Artigas (dept.), Uruguay 145/B1
Artigas, Uruguay 145/C1
Artillery (lake), N.W. Terrs. 187/H3
Artland, Sask. 181/B3
Artois, Calif. (95913) 204/C4
Artois (trad. prov.), France 29
Artova, Turkey 63/G2
Artux (Atushi), China 77/A4
Artvin (prov.), Turkey 63/J2
Artvin, Turkey 59/D1
Artvin, Turkey 63/J2
Aru (isls.), Indonesia 85/K7
Aru, Zaire 115/F3
Arua, Uganda 115/F3
Aruba (isl.), Neth. Ant. 161/E9
Aruba (isl.), Neth. Ant. 156/E4
Arucas, Spain 33/B5
Arunachal Pradesh (terr.), India 68/G3
Arundel, England 13/G7
Arundel, England 10/F5
Arundel, Québec 172/C4
Årup, Denmark 21/D7
Aruppukkottai, India 68/D7
'Arura, West Bank 65/C3
Arus, P. Rico 161/C3
Arusha (reg.), Tanzania 115/G4
Arusha, Tanzania 102/F5
Arusha, Tanzania 115/G4
Arusi (prov.), Ethiopia 111/G6
Aruwimi (riv.), Zaire 115/E3
Arva, Ireland 17/F4
Arva, Ontario 177/C4
Arvada, Colo. (*80001) 208/J3
Arvada, Wyo. (82831) 319/F1
Arvayheer, Mongolia 77/F2
Arvel, Ky. (†40447) 237/O5
Arvi, India 68/D4
Arvida, Québec 172/F1
Arvidsjaur, Sweden 18/L4
Arvika, Sweden 18/H7
Arvilla, N. Dak. (58214) 282/P4
Arvin, Calif. (93203) 204/G8
Arvonia, Va. (23004) 307/M5
Arwad (Ruad) (isl.), Syria 63/F5
Arxan, China 77/K2
Arys', U.S.S.R. 48/G5
Arzamas, U.S.S.R. 48/E4
Arzamas, U.S.S.R. 52/F3
Arzúa, Spain 33/B1
As, Belgium 27/H6
Aš, Czech. 41/B1
Aså, Denmark 21/D3
Asaba, Nigeria 106/F7
Asadabad, Iran 66/F3
Asahan (riv.), Indonesia 85/B5
Asahi, Japan 81/K6
Asahi (mt.), Japan 81/J4
Asahikawa, Japan 81/L2
Asahikawa, Japan 54/P5
Asama (mt.), Japan 81/J5
Asansol, India 68/F4
Åsarna, Sweden 18/J5
Asau, W. Samoa 86/L8
Asbest, U.S.S.R. 48/G4
Asbestos, Québec 172/F4
Asbury, Iowa (†52001) 229/M4
Asbury, Mo. (64832) 261/C8
Asbury, N.J. (08802) 273/D2
Asbury, W. Va. (24916) 312/E7
Asbury Park, N.J. (07712) 273/F3
As Busaiya, Iraq 66/E5
Ascención (Añez), Bolivia 136/D4
Ascensión, Argentina 143/F7
Ascension (par.), La. 238/J6
Ascensión, Mexico 150/E1
Ascension, Neth. Ant. 161/F8
Ascension (isl.), St. Helena 102/A5
Ascension (isl.), St. Helena 2/J6
Aschaffenburg, W. Germany 22/C4
Aschendorf, W. Germany 22/B2
Aschersleben, E. Germany 22/D3
Asco, W. Va. (24809) 312/C8
Ascog, Scotland 15/A2
Ascoli Piceno (prov.), Italy 34/D3
Ascoli Piceno, Italy 34/D3
Ascona, Switzerland 39/G4
Ascope, Peru 128/C6
Ascot, Queensland 88/K2
Ascot, Queensland 95/E2
Ascotán, Chile 138/B3
Ascotán, Salar de (salt dep.), Chile 138/B3
Ascot Corner, Québec 172/F4
Ascrib (isls.), Scotland 15/B3
Ascutney, Vt. (05030) 268/C5
Ascutney (mt.), Vt. 268/C5
Åseda, Sweden 18/J8
Åsele, Sweden 18/K4
Asenovgrad, Bulgaria 45/G5
Asèr, Ras (cape), Somalia 2/M5
Asèr, Ras (cape), Somalia 115/K1
Ash (riv.), Minn. 255/F2
Ash, N.C. (28420) 281/N6
Ash, Oreg. (†97473) 291/D4
Ash (creek), Utah 304/A6
'Ashaira, Saudi Arabia 59/D5
Ashanti (reg.), Ghana 102/B4
Ashanti (reg.), Ghana 106/D7
Ashaway, R.I. (02804) 249/G7
Ashboro, Ind. (†47840) 227/C6
Ashburn, Georgia (31714) 217/E7
Ashburn, Mo. (63433) 261/K3
Ashburn, Va. (22011) 307/O2
Ashburnham, Mass. (01430) 249/G2
Ashburnham○, Mass. (01430) 249/G2
Ashburton (riv.), Australia 87/B8
Ashburton, England 13/D7
Ashburton, N. Zealand 100/C5
Ashburton (riv.), W. Australia 88/B4
Ashburton (riv.), W. Australia 92/A3
Ashburton Downs, W. Australia 88/B4
Ashby, Ala. (†35035) 195/E4
Ashby○, Mass. (01431) 249/G2
Ashby, Minn. (56309) 255/C4
Ashby, Nebr. (69333) 264/C2
Ashbyburg, Ky. (†42456) 237/G5
Ash Creek, Minn. (†56173) 255/B7
Ashcroft, Br. Col. 184/G5
Ashdale, Maine (†04565) 243/D8
Ashdod, Israel 65/B4
Ashdot Ya'aqov, Israel 65/D2
Ashdown, Ark. (71822) 202/B6
Ashe (co.), N.C. 281/F2
Ashe (isl.), N.C. 281/P6
Asheboro, N.C. (27203) 281/K3
Ashepoo, S.C. (†29446) 296/G6
Ashepoo (riv.), S.C. 296/F6
Asher, Okla. (74826) 288/N5
Ashern, Manitoba 179/D3
Asherton, Texas (78827) 303/E9
Asherville, Ind. (†47834) 227/C6
Asherville, Kansas (67420) 232/D2
Asheville, N.C. 188/K3
Asheville, N.C. (*28801) 281/D3
Asheweig (riv.), Ontario 175/C2
Ashfield○, Mass. (01330) 249/C2
Ashfield, N. S. Wales 88/K4
Ashfield, N.S. Wales 97/J3
Ash Flat, Ark. (72513) 202/G1
Ashford, Ala. (36312) 195/H8
Ashford○, Conn. (06278) 210/G1
Ashford, England 10/G5
Ashford, England 13/H6
Ashford, Ireland 17/J5
Ashford, N.S. Wales 97/F1
Ashford, N.C. (†28752) 281/F3
Ashford, Wash. (98304) 310/C4
Ashford, W. Va. (25009) 312/C6
Ashford P.O. (Warrenville), Conn. (06278) 210/G1
Ash Fork, Ariz. (86320) 198/C3
Ash Grove, Kansas (†67455) 232/D2
Ash Grove, Mo. (65604) 261/E8
Ashgrove, Queensland 88/K2
Ashhurst, N. Zealand 100/E4
Ashibetsu, Japan 81/L2
Ashikaga, Japan 81/J5
Ashington, England 13/F2
Ashington, England 10/F3
Ashippun, Wis. (53003) 317/H1
Ashiya, Japan 81/H8
Ashizuri (cape), Japan 81/F7
Ashkhabad, U.S.S.R. 54/G6
Ashkhabad, U.S.S.R. 48/F6
Ashkum, Ill. (60911) 222/E3
Ash Lake, Minn. (†55771) 255/F2
Ashland, Ala. (36251) 195/G4
Ashland, Calif. (†94577) 204/K2
Ashland, Georgia (†30641) 217/F2
Ashland, Ill. (62612) 222/C4
Ashland, Kansas (67831) 232/C4
Ashland, Ky. (41101) 237/R4
Ashland, Ky. 188/K3
Ashland, La. (71002) 238/D2
Ashland, Maine (04732) 243/G2
Ashland○, Maine (04732) 243/G2
Ashland○, Mass. (01721) 249/J3
Ashland, Miss. (38603) 256/F1
Ashland, Mo. (65010) 261/H5
Ashland, Mont. (59003) 262/K5
Ashland, Nebr. (68003) 264/H3
Ashland, N.H. (03217) 268/D4
Ashland○, N.H. (03217) 268/D4
Ashland, N.J. (†08033) 273/B3
Ashland, N.Y. (12407) 276/M6
Ashland (co.), Ohio 284/F4
Ashland, Ohio (44805) 284/F4
Ashland, Okla. (74524) 288/O5
Ashland, Oreg. (97520) 291/E5
Ashland, Pa. (17921) 294/K4
Ashland, Va. (23005) 307/N5
Ashland (co.), Wis. 317/E3
Ashland, Wis. (54806) 317/E2
Ashland City, Tenn. (37015) 237/G8
Ashley (co.), Ark. 202/G7
Ashley, Ill. (62808) 222/D5
Ashley, Ind. (46705) 227/G1
Ashley, Mich. (48806) 250/E5
Ashley, Mo. (†63334) 261/K4
Ashley (lake), Mont. 262/B2
Ashley, N. S. Wales 97/E1
Ashley, N. Dak. (58413) 282/M7
Ashley, Ohio (43003) 284/E5
Ashley, Pa. (18706) 294/E7
Ashley (riv.), S.C. 296/G6
Ashley, W. Va. (†26339) 312/E4
Ashley Falls, Mass. (01222) 249/A4
Ashmere (lake), Mass. 249/B3
Ashmont, Alberta 182/E2
Ashmore, Ill. (61912) 222/F4
Ashmore, Nova Scotia 168/C4
Ashmore (isls.), Terr. of Ashmore and Cartier Is. 88/C2
Ashmore and Cartier Is., Terr. of, 88/C2
Ashokan, N.Y. (†12491) 276/M7
Ashokan (res.), N.Y. 276/M7
Ashport, Tenn. (†38063) 237/B9
Ashqelon, Israel 65/A4
Ash Shabicha, Iraq 66/C5
Ashtabula (lake), N. Dak. 282/P5
Ashtabula (co.), Ohio 284/J2
Ashtabula, Ohio (44004) 284/J2
Ashton, Idaho (83420) 220/G5
Ashton, Ill. (61006) 222/D2
Ashton, Iowa (51232) 229/B2
Ashton, Kansas (†67051) 232/E4
Ashton, Mich. (†49677) 250/D5
Ashton, Nebr. (68817) 264/F3
Ashton, R.I. (02864) 249/J5
Ashton, S.C. (†29082) 296/E5
Ashton, S. Dak. (57424) 298/N3
Ashton, W. Va. (25503) 312/B5
Ashton Creek, Br. Col. 184/H5
Ashton-under-Lyne, England 13/H2
Ashton-under-Lyne, England 10/G2
Ashuanipi (lake), Newf. 166/A3
Ashuanipi (riv.), Newf. 166/A3
Ashuanipi, Newf. 166/A3
Ashuelot, N.H. (03441) 268/C6
Ashuelot (riv.), N.H. 268/C6
Ash Valley, Kansas (†67550) 232/C3
Ashville, Ala. (35953) 195/F3
Ashville, Maine (04607) 243/G7
Ashville, Manitoba 179/B3
Ashville, Ohio (43103) 284/E6
Ashville, Pa. (16613) 294/F4
Ashwaubenon, Wis. (54304) 317/K7
Ashwood, Oreg. (97711) 291/G3
'Asi (Orontes) (riv.), Syria 63/G5
Asia 2/P3
Asia (isls.), Indonesia 85/J5
Asid (gulf), Philippines 82/D4
Asidonhoppo, Suriname 131/D4
Asilah, Morocco 106/C1
Asinara (gulf), Italy 34/B4
Asinara (isl.), Italy 34/B4
Asino, U.S.S.R. 48/J4
'Asir (reg.), Saudi Arabia 59/D6
Aşkale, Turkey 63/J3
Askeaton, Ireland 17/D6
Askew, Miss. (38604) 256/D1
Askewville, N.C. (†27983) 281/R2
Askim, Norway 18/E4
Askim, Sweden 18/G8
Aski Mosul, Iraq 66/C2
Askival (mt.), Scotland 15/B4
Askov, Denmark 21/C7
Askov, Minn. (55704) 255/F4
Askvoll, Norway 18/D6
Asmara, Ethiopia 111/G4
Asmara, Ethiopia 59/C6
Asmara, Ethiopia 102/F3
Asnaes, Denmark 21/E6
Åsnen (lake), Sweden 18/J8
Asnières-sur-Seine, France 28/A1
Aso (mt.), Japan 81/E7
Aso National Park, Japan 81/E7
Asosa, Ethiopia 111/F5
Asoteriba, Jebel (mt.), Sudan 111/G3
Asotin (co.), Wash. 310/H4
Asotin, Wash. (99402) 310/H4
Asotin (creek), Wash. 310/H4
Asotin (dam), Wash. 310/J4
Aspang Markt, Austria 41/D3
Aspatria, England 13/D3
Aspe, Spain 33/F3
Aspelund, Minn. (†55946) 255/F6
Aspen, Colo. (81611) 208/F4
Aspen, Nova Scotia 168/F3
Aspen (lake), Oreg. 291/E5
Aspen (mts.), Wyo. 319/C4
Aspen Grove, Br. Col. 184/G5
Aspen Hill, Md. 245/K4
Aspermont, Texas (79502) 303/D4
Aspers, Pa. (17304) 294/H6
Aspetuck, Conn. (†06880) 210/B4
Aspetuck (res.), Conn. 210/B4
Aspetuck (riv.), Conn. 210/B3
Aspinwall, Iowa (51432) 229/C5
Aspinwall, Pa. (15215) 294/C6
Aspiring (mt.), N. Zealand 100/B6
Aspley, Queensland 88/K2
Aspy (bay), Nova Scotia 168/H2
Asquith, Sask. 181/D3
Assab, Ethiopia 59/D7
Assab, Ethiopia 111/H5
Assaba (reg.), Mauritania 106/B5
Assabet (riv.), Mass. 249/H3
Assad, Bahrat (lake), Syria 63/H4
Assakarai (dry riv.), Niger 106/F5
Assale (lake), Ethiopia 111/H5
As Salman, Iraq 59/E3
As Salman, Iraq 66/D5
Assam (state), India 68/G3
Assapan (riv.), Manitoba 179/G2
Assaria, Kansas (67416) 232/E3
Assateague Island Nat'l Seashore, Va. 307/T4
Assawompset (pond), Mass. 249/L5
Assay (creek), Utah 304/B6
Asse, Belgium 27/E7
Asselar (well), Mali 106/D5
Asselle, Ethiopia 102/F4
Asselle, Ethiopia 111/G6
Assen, Netherlands 27/K3
Assenede, Belgium 27/D6
Assens, Århus, Denmark 21/D4
Assens, Fyn, Denmark 21/D7
Assesse, Belgium 27/G8
Assigny (lake), Newf. 166/A3
Assiniboia, Sask. 181/E6
Assiniboine (mt.), Alberta 182/C4
Assiniboine (mt.), Br. Col. 184/K5
Assiniboine (riv.), Manitoba 179/C5
Assiniboine (riv.), Sask. 181/J3
Assinica (lake), Québec 174/C3
Assinika (lake), Manitoba 179/G2
Assinika (riv.), Manitoba 179/G2
Assinippi, Mass. (02339) 249/E8
Assis, Brazil 132/D8
Assis, Brazil 135/A3
Assisi, Italy 34/D3
Assonet, Mass. (02702) 249/K5
Assumption, Ill. (62510) 222/E4
Assumption (par.), La. 238/H7
Assumption, Ohio (†43540) 284/B2
Assumption (isl.), Seychelles 118/H1
Assynt (dist.), Scotland 15/C2
Assynt, Loch (lake), Scotland 15/D2
Assyria, Mich. (†49021) 250/D6
Astara, U.S.S.R. 52/G7
Astatula, Fla. (32705) 212/E3
Asten, Netherlands 27/H6
Asterabad (Gorgan), Iran 59/F2
Asterabad (Gorgan), Iran 66/J2
Asti, Calif. (95413) 204/C5
Asti (prov.), Italy 34/B2
Asti, Italy 34/B2
Astillero, Peru 128/H9
Astipálaia, Greece 45/H7
Astipálaia (isl.), Greece 45/H7
Astle, New Bruns. 170/D2
Aston (bay), N.W. Terrs. 187/J2
Aston-Jonction, Québec 172/E3
Astor, Fla. (32002) 212/E2
Astorga, Spain 33/C1
Astoria, Ill. (61501) 222/C3
Astoria, Oreg. 188/B1
Astoria, Oreg. (97103) 291/D1
Astoria, S. Dak. (57213) 298/S4
Astorville, Ontario 177/E1
Astove (isl.), Seychelles 102/G6
Astove (isl.), Seychelles 118/H2
Astra, Argentina 143/C6
Astrakhan', U.S.S.R. 7/J4
Astrakhan', U.S.S.R. 52/G5
Astrakhan', U.S.S.R. 48/E5
Astray (lake), Newf. 166/A3
Astudillo, Spain 33/D1
Asturias (reg.), Spain 33/C1
Asunción, Bolivia 136/B2
Asuncion (isl.), No. Marianas 87/E4
Asunción, Paraguay 144/A4
Asunción (cap.), Paraguay 2/F7
Asunción (dept.), Paraguay 144/A4
Asunción (cap.), Paraguay 120/D5
Asuncion (passage), Philippines 82/D5
Asunción Mita, Guatemala 154/C3
Asunción Nochixtlán, Mexico 150/L8
Asunta, Bolivia 136/B5
Aswad, Ras al (cape), Saudi Arabia 59/C5
Aswân, Egypt 111/F3
Aswân, Egypt 59/B5
Aswân, Egypt 102/F2
Aswân (dam), Egypt 59/B5
Aswân (dam), Egypt 111/F3
Aswân High (dam), Egypt 102/F2
Aswân High (dam), Egypt 111/F3
Asyût, Egypt 111/J4
Asyût, Egypt 102/F2
Asyût, Egypt 59/B4
Aszód, Hungary 41/E3
Atabapo (riv.), Colombia 126/G6
Atabapo (riv.), Venezuela 124/E6
Atacama, Puna de (reg.), Argentina 143/C2
Atacama (reg.), Chile 138/B6
Atacama (des.), Chile 120/C5
Atacama (des.), Chile 138/B4
Atacama, Salar de (salt dep.), Chile 138/C4
Atafu (atoll), Tokelau Is. 87/J6
Atahona, Uruguay 145/B4
Atakora (mts.), Benin 106/E6
Atakpamé, Togo 106/E7
Atalándi, Greece 45/F6
Atalaya, Peru 128/E8
Atalissa, Iowa (52720) 229/L5
Atambua, Indonesia 85/G7
Atami, Japan 81/J6
Atapirire, Venezuela 124/F3
Atar, Mauritania 106/B4
Atar, Mauritania 102/A2
Ataran (riv.), Burma 72/C4
Atascadero, Calif. (93422) 204/E8
Atascosa (co.), Texas 303/F9
Atascosa, Texas (78002) 303/J11
Atbara (riv.), Ethiopia 111/G4
Atbara, Sudan 111/F4
Atbara, Sudan 59/B6
Atbara, Sudan 102/F3
Atbara (riv.), Sudan 59/C6
Atbara (riv.), Sudan 111/G4
Atbasar, U.S.S.R. 48/G4
Atchafalaya (bay), La. 238/H8
Atchafalaya (riv.), La. 238/G6
Atchison, Kans. 188/G3

332 Atchison

Atchison (co.), Kansas 232/G2
Atchison, Kansas (66002) 232/G2
Atchison (co.), Mo. 261/B2
Atco, N.J. (08004) 273/D4
Ateca, Spain 33/F2
Atén, Bolivia 136/A4
Atenas, C. Rica 154/E6
Atessa, Italy 34/E3
Atglen, Pa. (19310) 294/K6
Ath, Belgium 27/D7
Athabasca (lake) 162/F4
Athabasca, Alberta 182/D2
Athabasca (lake), Alberta 182/C5
Athabasca (riv.), Alberta 182/D1
Athabasca, Alta. 162/E5
Athabasca (riv.), Alta. 162/E4
Athabasca (riv.), Alta. 146/G4
Athabasca (lake), Canada 146/H4
Athabasca (lake), Sask. 181/L2
Athalia, Ohio (†45669) 284/F8
Athalmer, Br. Col. 184/K5
Athboy, Ireland 17/H4
Athea, Ireland 17/C7
Athelstan, Iowa (†50836) 229/D7
Athelstan, Québec 172/C4
Athelstane, Wis. (54104) 317/K5
Athena, Oreg. (97813) 291/J2
Athenry, Ireland 17/D5
Athens, Ala. (35611) 195/E1
Athens, Ark. (†71943) 202/C5
Athens, Ga. 188/K4
Athens, Georgia (*30601) 217/F3
Athens (cap.), Greece 7/G5
Athens (cap.), Greece 45/F7
Athens (cap.), Greece 2/K4
Athens, Greater, Greece 45/F7
Athens, Ill. (62613) 222/D4
Athens, Ind. (46912) 227/E2
Athens, La. (71003) 238/E1
Athens, Maine (04912) 243/D6
Athens○, Maine (04912) 243/D6
Athens, Mich. (49011) 250/D6
Athens, N.Y. (12015) 276/N6
Athens (co.), Ohio 284/F7
Athens, Ohio (45701) 284/F7
Athens, Ontario 177/J3
Athens, Pa. (18810) 294/K2
Athens, Tenn. (37303) 237/M10
Athens, Texas (75751) 303/J5
Athens, W. Va. (24712) 312/E8
Athens, Wis. (54411) 317/G5
Athensville, Ill. (†62082) 222/C4
Atherley, Ontario 177/E3
Atherton, Calif. (94025) 204/K3
Atherton, Mo. (†64050) 261/R5
Atherton, Queensland 95/C3
Atherton, Queensland 88/G3
Athertonville, Ky. (†42748) 237/K5
Athleague, Ireland 17/E4
Athlone, Ireland 10/C4
Athlone, Ireland 17/F5
Athok, Burma 72/B3
Athol, Idaho (83801) 220/B2
Athol, Kansas (66932) 232/D2
Athol, Mass. (01331) 249/F2
Athol○, Mass. (01331) 249/F2
Athol, N.Y. (12810) 276/N4
Athol, N. Zealand 100/B6
Athol, Nova Scotia 168/D3
Athol (dist.), Scotland 15/D4
Athol, S. Dak. (57425) 298/M3
Atholville, New Bruns. 170/D1
Áthos (mt.), Greece 45/G5
Athy, Ireland 17/H6
Athy, Ireland 10/C4
Ati, Chad 111/C5
Ati, Chad 102/D3
Atibaia, Brazil 135/C3
Atico, Peru 128/F11
Atienza, Spain 33/E2
Atikameg, Alberta 182/C2
Atikokan, Ont. 162/G6
Atikokan, Ontario 177/G5
Atikokan, Ontario 175/B3
Atikonak (lake), Newf. 166/B3
Atim (lake), Manitoba 179/C2
Atiquizaya, El Salvador 154/C3
Atitlán (lake), Guatemala 154/B3
Atitlán (vol.), Guatemala 154/B3
Atiu (isl.), Cook Is. 87/L8
Atka, Alaska (99502) 196/D4
Atka, Alaska 188/D6
Atka (isl.), Alaska 196/L4
Atka, U.S.S.R. 48/Q3
Atkarsk, U.S.S.R. 52/G4
Atkins, Ark. (72823) 202/E3
Atkins, Iowa (52206) 229/K4
Atkins, Va. (24311) 307/F7
Atkinson (co.), Georgia 217/G8
Atkinson, Georgia (†31543) 217/J8
Atkinson, Ill. (61235) 222/C2
Atkinson○, Maine (†04426) 243/E5
Atkinson, Minn. (†55718) 255/F4
Atkinson, Nebr. (68713) 264/E2
Atkinson○, N.H. (03811) 268/E6
Atkinson, N.C. (28421) 281/N5
Atkinson (pt.), N.W. Terrs. 187/E2
Atkinson Field, Guyana 131/B2
Atlanta, Ark. (†71740) 202/D7
Atlanta, C. Rica 154/F6
Atlanta (cap.), Ga. 188/K4
Atlanta (cap.), Ga. 146/K6
Atlanta (cap.), Georgia (*30301) 217/K1
Atlanta, Idaho (83601) 220/C6
Atlanta, Ill. (61723) 222/D3
Atlanta, Ind. (46031) 227/E4
Atlanta, Kansas (67008) 232/F4
Atlanta, La. (71404) 238/E3
Atlanta, Mich. (49709) 250/E3
Atlanta, Mo. (63530) 261/H3
Atlanta, Nebr. (68923) 264/E4
Atlanta, N.Y. (14808) 276/F5
Atlanta, Ohio (43104) 284/D6
Atlanta, Texas (75551) 303/K4
Atlanta, U.S. 2/E4
Atlanta Nav. Air Sta., Georgia 217/J1
Atlantic (ocean) 102/B5
Atlantic (ocean) 146/M6
Atlantic, Iowa (50022) 229/D6
Atlantic, Maine (04608) 243/G7
Atlantic (co.), N.J. 273/D5
Atlantic, N.C. (28511) 281/S5
Atlantic, Pa. (16111) 294/B3
Atlantic (peak), Wyo. 319/D3
Atlantic Beach, Fla. (32233) 212/E1
Atlantic Beach, N.Y. (11509) 276/P7
Atlantic Beach, N.C. (28512) 281/R5
Atlantic Beach, S.C. (†29582) 296/K4
Atlantic City, N.J. 188/M3
Atlantic City, N.J. (*08401) 273/E5
Atlantic City, Wyo. (†82520) 319/D3
Atlantic Highlands, N.J. (07716) 273/F3
Atlantic Highlands (ridge), N.J. 273/E3
Atlantic Mine, Mich. (49905) 250/G1
Atlántico (dept.), Colombia 126/C2
Atlantic Ocean 4/D11
Atlantic Ocean 7/C4
Atlantic Ocean, England 13/A7
Atlantic Ocean, Scotland 15/B2
Atlantic Ocean Ocean, Portugal 33/A3
Atlántida, Uruguay 145/B6
Atlas (mts.) 102/B1
Atlas (mts.), Algeria 106/E2
Atlas (mts.), Morocco 106/C2
Atlas, Pa. (17851) 294/K4
Atlas, Wis. (†54853) 317/A4
Atlin, Br. Col. 184/J1
Atlin (lake), Br. Col. 184/J1
Atlit, Israel 65/B2
Atlixco, Mexico 150/M2
Atmore, Ala. (36503) 195/C8
Atmore, Alberta 182/D2
Atnarko, Br. Col. 184/E4
Atocha, Bolivia 136/B7
Atoka (co.), Okla. 288/O6
Atoka, Okla. (74525) 288/O6
Atoka (res.), Okla. 288/P5
Atoka, Tenn. (38004) 237/B10
Atomic City, Idaho (83215) 220/F6
Atotonilco el Alto, Mexico 150/H6
Atoui, Wadi (dry riv.), Mauritania 106/B4
Atoui, Wadi (dry riv.), Western Sahara 106/B4
Atoyac (riv.), Mexico 150/N2
Atoyac (riv.), Mexico 150/Q2
Atoyac de Álvarez, Mexico 150/J8
Atrak (Atrek) (riv.), Iran 66/J2
Atrato (riv.), Colombia 126/B4
Atrek (riv.), Iran 59/G2
Atrek (Atrak) (riv.), Iran 66/J2
Atrek (riv.), U.S.S.R. 48/F6
Atri, Italy 34/D3
Atsugi, Japan 81/O2
Atsumi (bay), Japan 81/H6
Attachie, Br. Col. 184/G2
Attala (co.), Miss. 256/E4
Attalens, Switzerland 39/C3
Attalla, Ala. (35954) 195/F2
Attapu, Laos 72/E4
Attapulgus, Georgia (31715) 217/D9
Attawapiskat (riv.), Ont. 146/K4
Attawapiskat (riv.), Ont. 162/H5
Attawapiskat, Ontario 175/D2
Attawapiskat (lake), Ontario 175/C2
Attawapiskat (riv.), Ontario 175/C2
Attawaugan, Conn. (†06241) 210/H1
Attean (pond), Maine 243/C4
Attebubu, Ghana 106/D7
Atterberry, Ill. (†62675) 222/D3
Atter See (lake), Austria 41/B3
Attert, Belgium 27/H9
Attica, Ind. (47918) 227/C4
Attica, Iowa (†50138) 229/G6
Attica, Kansas (67009) 232/D4
Attica, Mich. (48412) 250/F5
Attica, N.Y. (14011) 276/D5
Attica, Ohio (44807) 284/E3
Attikamagen (lake), Newf. 166/A3
'Attil, West Bank 65/C3
Attleboro, Mass. (02703) 249/J5
Attleboro Falls, Mass. (02763) 249/J5
Attleborough, England 13/H5
Attnang-Puchheim, Austria 41/B2
Attock, Pakistan 68/C2
Attu (isl.), Alaska 188/D6
Attu (isl.), Alaska 196/J3
Attu (isl.), U.S. 4/D1
Attunga, N.S. Wales 97/F2
Atuel (riv.), Argentina 143/C4
Atuntaqui, Ecuador 128/C2
Atuona, Fr. Poly. 87/M7
Atura, Uganda 115/F3
Atushi (Artux), China 77/A4
Åtvidaberg, Sweden 18/K7
Atwater, Calif. (95301) 204/E6
Atwater, Minn. (56209) 255/D5
Atwater, Ohio (44201) 284/H3
Atwater, Sask. 181/J5
Atwood (Samana) (cay), Bahamas 156/D2
Atwood, Colo. (80722) 208/N1
Atwood, Ill. (61913) 222/E4
Atwood, Ind. (46502) 227/F2
Atwood, Kansas (67730) 232/B2
Atwood, Mich. (†49729) 250/D3
Atwood (lake), Ohio 284/H4
Atwood, Okla. (74827) 288/O5
Atwood, Ontario 177/D4
Atwood, Pa. (†16249) 294/D4
Atwood, Tenn. (38220) 237/D9
Atwoodville, Conn. (†06250) 210/G1
Atyrá, Paraguay 144/B4
Au, Switzerland 39/J2
Auasbila, Honduras 154/E3
Auau (chan.), Hawaii 218/H2
Aubagne, France 28/F6
Aubange, Belgium 27/H9
Aube (dept.), France 28/E3
Aube (riv.), France 28/F3
Aubenas, France 28/F5
Auberry, Calif. (93602) 204/F6
Aubervilliers, France 28/B1
Aubigny, Manitoba 179/E5
Aubonne, Switzerland 39/B4
Aubrey (cliffs), Ariz. 198/B3
Aubrey, Ark. (72311) 202/J4
Auburn, Ala. (36830) 195/H5
Auburn, Calif. (95603) 204/C8
Auburn, Georgia (30203) 217/E2
Auburn, Ill. (62615) 222/D4
Auburn, Ind. (46706) 227/G2
Auburn (mt.), Ind. 227/G5
Auburn, Iowa (51433) 229/D4
Auburn, Kansas (66402) 232/G3
Auburn, Ky. (42206) 237/H7
Auburn, Maine (04210) 243/C7
Auburn, Maine 188/M2
Auburn○, Mass. (01501) 249/G4
Auburn, Mich. (48611) 250/F5
Auburn, Miss. (†39664) 256/C8
Auburn, Nebr. (68305) 264/J4
Auburn○, N.H. (03032) 268/E5
Auburn, N. S. Wales 88/K4
Auburn, N.S. Wales 97/J3
Auburn, N.Y. 188/L2
Auburn, N.Y. (13021) 276/G5
Auburn, N. Dak. (†58237) 282/R2
Auburn, Nova Scotia 168/D3
Auburn, Ontario 177/C4
Auburn, Pa. (17922) 294/K4
Auburn, Wash. (98002) 310/C3
Auburn, W. Va. (26325) 312/E4
Auburn, Wyo. (83111) 319/A3
Auburndale, Fla. (33823) 212/E3
Auburndale, Mass. (†02166) 249/B7
Auburndale, Wis. (54412) 317/F6
Auburn Heights, Mich. (48057) 250/F6
Auburntown, Tenn. (37016) 237/J9
Aubusson, France 28/E4
Aucanquilcha, Cerro (mt.), Chile 138/B3
Auce, U.S.S.R. 53/B2
Auch, France 28/D6
Auchenblae, Scotland 15/F4
Auchencairn, Scotland 15/E6
Auchinleck, Scotland 15/D5
Auchterarder, Scotland 10/D2
Auchterarder, Scotland 15/E4
Auchtermuchty, Scotland 15/E4
Aucilla, Fla. (†32344) 212/C1
Aucilla (riv.), Fla. 212/C1
Auckland (isls.), N. Zealand 2/S8
Auckland, N.Zealand 2/T7
Auckland, N. Zealand 100/B1
Auckland, N. Zealand 87/B1
Auclair, Québec 172/J2
Aude (dept.), France 28/E6
Audegle, Somalia 115/J3
Auden, Ontario 177/H4
Auden, Ontario 175/C2
Audenarde (Oudenaarde), Belgium 27/D7
Auderghem, Belgium 27/C9
Audet, Québec 172/G4
Audincourt, France 28/G4
Audrain (co.), Mo. 261/J4
Audubon (co.), Iowa 229/D5
Audubon, Iowa (50025) 229/D5
Audubon, Minn. (56511) 255/C4
Audubon, N.J. (08106) 273/B3
Audubon (lake), N. Dak. 282/H4
Audubon Park, Ky. (†40201) 237/J2
Audubon Park, N.J. (†08106) 273/B3
Aue, E. Germany 22/E3
Auerbach, E. Germany 22/E3
Augathella, Queensland 95/C5
Augathella, Queensland 88/H5
Auger (falls), Idaho 220/D7
Augher, N. Ireland 17/G3
Aughnacloy, N. Ireland 17/H3
Aughrabies (King George's) (falls), S. Africa 118/B5
Aughrim, Ireland 17/J6
Auglaize (co.), Ohio 284/B4
Auglaize (riv.), Ohio 284/B4
Au Gres, Mich. (48703) 250/F4
Augsburg, W. Germany 7/E4
Augsburg, W. Germany 22/D4
Augusta, Ark. (72006) 202/H3
Augusta (cape), Colombia 126/C2
Augusta, Ga. 188/K4
Augusta, Ga. 146/K6
Augusta, Georgia (*30901) 217/J4
Augusta, Ill. (62311) 222/C3
Augusta, Ind. (†47598) 227/C8
Augusta, Iowa (†52658) 229/L7
Augusta, Italy 34/E6
Augusta, Kansas (67010) 232/F4
Augusta, Ky. (41002) 237/N3
Augusta (cap.), Maine 146/M5
Augusta (cap.), Maine (04330) 243/D7
Augusta (cap.), Maine 188/N2
Augusta, Mich. (49012) 250/D6
Augusta, Mo. (63332) 261/L5
Augusta, Mont. (59410) 262/D3
Augusta, N.J. (07822) 273/D1
Augusta, Ohio (44607) 284/J4
Augusta (co.), Va. 307/K4
Augusta, W. Australia 92/A6
Augusta, W. Va. (26704) 312/J4
Augusta, Wis. (54722) 317/D6
Augusta Springs, Va. (24411) 307/K4
Augustenborg, Denmark 21/D8
Augustine (isl.), Alaska 196/H3
Augustów, Poland 47/F2
Augustus (isl.), W. Australia 92/D1
Augustus (mt.), W. Australia 92/B4
Aujila, Libya 102/E2
Aujila, Libya 111/D2
Auki, Solomon Is. 86/E3
Auki, Solomon Is. 87/G6
Aulac, New Bruns. 170/F3
Aulander, N.C. (27805) 281/P2
Auld (lake), W. Australia 88/C4
Auldearn, Scotland 15/E3
Aulencia (riv.), Spain 33/F4
Aullville, Mo. (†64037) 261/E4
Aulnay-sous-Bois, France 28/B1
Ault, Colo. (80610) 208/K1
Ault (peak), Switzerland 39/H3
Aultbea, Scotland 15/C3
Aultman, Pa. (15713) 294/D4
Aumsville, Oreg. (97325) 291/E3
Auning, Denmark 21/D5
Aunis (trad. prov.), France 29
Aur, Pulau (isl.), Malaysia 72/E7
Aura, Mich. (49906) 250/A2
Aura, N.J. (†08028) 273/C4
Aurangabad, Bihar, India 68/E4
Aurangabad, Maharashtra, India 68/D5
Auraria, Georgia (†30534) 217/E1
Auray, France 28/B4
Aurelia, Iowa (51005) 229/C3
Aurès (lag.), Algeria 106/F1
Aurich, W. Germany 22/B2
Aurignac, France 28/D6
Aurillac, France 28/E5
Aurland, Norway 18/E6
Aurora, Ark. (†72740) 202/C2
Aurora, Brazil 132/G4
Aurora, Colo. 188/F3
Aurora, Colo. (*80010) 208/K3
Aurora, Guyana 131/B2
Aurora, Ill. (*60504) 222/E2
Aurora, Ind. (47001) 227/H6
Aurora, Iowa (50607) 229/K3
Aurora, Kansas (67417) 232/E2
Aurora○, Maine (04408) 243/G6
Aurora, Minn. (55705) 255/F3
Aurora, Mo. (65605) 261/E9
Aurora, Nebr. (68818) 264/F4
Aurora, N.Y. (13026) 276/G5
Aurora, N.C. (27806) 281/R4
Aurora, Ohio (44202) 284/H3
Aurora, Ontario 177/J3
Aurora, Oreg. (97002) 291/B2
Aurora, Philippines 82/E4
Aurora (co.), S. Dak. 298/M6
Aurora, S. Dak. (57002) 298/R5
Aurora, Texas (†76078) 303/E1
Aurora, Utah (84620) 304/B5
Aurora, W. Va. (26705) 312/G4
Aurora Lodge, Alaska (†99701) 196/J2
Auroraville, Wis. (†54923) 317/H7
Aus, Namibia 118/B5
Au Sable, Mich. (†48750) 250/F4
Au Sable (pt.), Mich. 250/F4
Au Sable (pt.), Mich. 250/C2
Au Sable (riv.), Mich. 250/E4
Ausable (riv.), N.Y. 276/N2
Au Sable Forks, N.Y. (12912) 276/N2
Auschwitz (Oświęcim), Poland 47/D3
Ausert (well), Western Sahara 106/B4
Auskerry (isl.), Scotland 15/F1
Aust-Agder (co.), Norway 18/E7
Austell, Georgia (30001) 217/J1
Austerlitz (Slavkov), Czech. 41/D2
Austin, Ark. (72007) 202/G4
Austin, Colo. (81410) 208/D5
Austin, Ind. (47102) 227/F7
Austin, Ky. (42123) 237/K7
Austin, Manitoba 179/D5
Austin, Minn. 188/H2
Austin, Minn. (55912) 255/E7
Austin, Mo. (†64725) 261/D5
Austin, Mont. (†59601) 262/D4
Austin, Nev. 188/C3
Austin, Nev. (89310) 266/E3
Austin, Oreg. (†97817) 291/J3
Austin, Pa. (16720) 294/F2
Austin (co.), Texas 303/H8
Austin (cap.), Texas 146/J6
Austin (cap.), Texas (*78701) 303/G7
Austin (cap.), Texas 188/G4
Austin (lake), W. Australia 88/B5
Austin (lake), W. Australia 92/B4
Austinburg, Ohio (44010) 284/J2
Austintown, Ohio (44515) 284/J3
Austinville, Iowa (50608) 229/H3
Austinville, Va. (24312) 307/F7
Austonio, Texas (†75835) 303/J6
Austral (isls.), Fr. Polynesia 2/B7
Austral (isls.), Fr. Poly. 87/L8
Australia 2/R7
Australia 87/C8
AUSTRALIA 88
Australia Aboriginal Reserve, W. Australia 88/D5
Australia Aboriginal Res., W. Australia 92/E4
Australian, Br. Col. 184/F4
Australian Alps (mts.), N.S. Wales 97/D5
Australian Alps (mts.), Victoria 97/D5
Australian Alps (mts.), Victoria 88/H7
Australian Capital Territory, /H7
Australian Capital Terr., Australia 87/F9
AUSTRALIAN CAPITAL TERRITORY 97/E4
Australind, W. Australia 92/A2
Austria 2/K3
Austria 7/F4
AUSTRIA 41
Austwell, Texas (77950) 303/H9
Autauga (co.), Ala. 195/E5
Autaugaville, Ala. (36003) 195/E6
Autlán de Navarro, Mexico 150/G7
Au Train, Mich. (49806) 250/C2
Au Train (bay), Mich. 250/C2
Autreyville, Georgia (†31768) 217/E8
Autryville, N.C. (28318) 281/M4
Autun, France 28/F4
Auvelais, Belgium 27/F8
Auvergne, Ark. (†72112) 202/H2
Auvergne (mts.), France 28/E5
Auvergne (trad. prov.) France 29
Auvergne, North. Terr. 93/B3
Auvergne, Québec 172/F3
Auxerre, France 28/E4
Auxier, Ky. (41602) 237/R5
Auxonne, France 28/F4
Auxvasse, Mo. (65231) 261/J4
Auyantepui (mt.), Venezuela 124/G5
Auyuittuq Nat'l Park, N.W. Terrs. /M3
Auyuittuq Nat'l Park, Que. 162/K2
Ava, Ill. (62907) 222/D6
Ava, Mo. (65608) 261/G9
Ava, N.Y. (13303) 276/K4
Ava, Ohio (43711) 284/G6
Avallon, France 28/E4
Avalon, Calif. (90704) 204/G10
Avalon, Georgia (†30557) 217/F1
Avalon, Miss. (38912) 256/D3
Avalon, Mo. (64621) 261/F3
Avalon (pen.), Newf. 166/D2
Avalon, N.J. (08202) 273/D5
Avalon (res.), N. Mex. 274/E6
Avalon, Pa. (15202) 294/B6
Avanos, Turkey 63/F3
Avans, Georgia (†30752) 217/A1
Avant, Okla. (74001) 288/O2
Avard, Okla. (†73860) 288/J1
Avaré, Brazil 132/D8
Avaré, Brazil 135/B3
Avarua (cap.), Cook Is. 87/L8
Avayalik (isls.), Newf. 166/B1
Avaz, Iran 66/M4
Aveiro (dist.), Portugal 33/B2
Aveiro, Portugal 33/B2
Avej, Iran 66/F3
Avella, Pa. (15312) 294/B5
Avellaneda, Argentina 143/G7
Avellino (prov.), Italy 34/E4
Avellino, Italy 34/E4
Avenal, Calif. (93204) 204/E8
Avenches, Switzerland 39/D3
Avenel, N.J. (07001) 273/E2
Aventon, N.C. (†27891) 281/O2
Avera, Georgia (30803) 217/G4
Avera, Miss. (†39456) 256/G8
Averías, Uruguay 145/E4
Averill, Mich. (†48640) 250/E5
Averill, Minn. (†56547) 255/B4
Averill○, Vt. (05901) 268/D2
Averill Park, N.Y. (12018) 276/O5
Aversa, Italy 34/E4
Avery, Idaho (83802) 220/C2
Avery, Iowa (†52531) 229/H6
Avery (co.), N.C. 281/F2
Avery, Ohio (†44846) 284/E3
Avery, Okla. (†74023) 288/N3
Avery, Texas (75554) 303/K4
Avery Island, La. (70513) 238/G7
Aves (Bird) (isl.), Venezuela 156/F4
Avesnes-sur-Helpe, France 28/F2
Avesta, Sweden 18/J6
Aveyron (dept.), France 28/E5
Avezzano, Italy 34/D3
Aviemore, Scotland 15/E3
Avigliano, Italy 34/E4
Avignon, France 28/F6
Avignon, France 7/E4
Avihayil, Israel 65/B3
Ávila (prov.), Spain 33/D2
Ávila de los Caballeros, Spain 33/D2
Avilés, Spain 33/C1
Avilla, Ind. (46710) 227/G2
Avilla, Mo. (64833) 261/D8
Avinger, Texas (75630) 303/K5
Avion, France 28/E2
Avis, Pa. (17721) 294/H3
Avis, Portugal 33/C3
Aviston, Ill. (62216) 222/D5
Avize, France 28/F3
Avlum, Denmark 21/B5
Avoca, Ark. (72711) 202/B1
Avoca, Ind. (47420) 227/D7
Avoca, Iowa (51521) 229/C6
Avoca, Ireland 17/J6
Avoca, Mich. (48006) 250/G5
Avoca, Minn. (56114) 255/C7
Avoca, Nebr. (68307) 264/H4
Avoca, N.Y. (14809) 276/F6
Avoca, Pa. (18641) 294/F7
Avoca, Tasmania 99/D3
Avoca, Texas (79503) 303/E5
Avoca, Victoria 97/B5
Avoca (riv.), Victoria 97/B5
Avoca, Wis. (53506) 317/F9
Avoch, Scotland 15/D3
Avola, Br. Col. 184/H4
Avola, Italy 34/E6
Avon, Ala. (†36312) 195/H8
Avon, Colo. (81620) 208/F3
Avon, Conn. (06001) 210/D1
Avon○, Conn. (06001) 210/D1
Avon (co.), England 13/E6
Avon (riv.), England 13/F7
Avon (riv.), England 13/F5
Avon (riv.), England 10/F4
Avon, Idaho (†83823) 220/B3
Avon, Ill. (61415) 222/C3
Avon○, Mass. (02322) 249/K4
Avon, Minn. (56310) 255/D5
Avon, Miss. (38723) 256/B4
Avon, Mont. (59713) 262/D4
Avon, N.Y. (14414) 276/E5
Avon, N.C. (27915) 281/U4
Avon (riv.), Nova Scotia 168/D4
Avon, Ohio (44011) 284/F3
Avon (riv.), Scotland 15/C1
Avon (riv.), Scotland 15/E3
Avon, S. Dak. (57315) 298/N8
Avon (riv.), W. Australia 88/B6
Avon (riv.), W. Australia 92/A1
Avon, Wis. (†53520) 317/H10
Avon By The Sea, N.J. (07717) 273/E3
Avondale, Ariz. (85323) 198/C5
Avondale, Colo. (81022) 208/L6
Avondale, Mich. (†49631) 250/D4
Avondale, Mo. (64010) 261/P5
Avondale, Newf. 166/D2
Avondale, N.S. Wales 97/F3
Avondale, N.C. (†28076) 281/F4
Avondale, Pa. (19311) 294/L6
Avondale, W. Va. (24811) 312/C8
Avondale Estates, Georgia (30002) 217/L1
Avon Downs, North. Terr. 88/F4
Avon Downs, North. Terr. 93/E5
Avonhurst, Sask. 181/G5
Avon Lake, Ohio (44012) 284/F2
Avonlea, Sask. 181/G5
Avonmore, Ontario 177/K2
Avonmore, Pa. (15618) 294/C4
Avon Park, Fla. (33825) 212/E4
Avonport, Nova Scotia 168/D3
Avon Water (riv.), Scotland 15/D5
Avoyelles (par.), La. 238/G4
Avranches, France 28/C3
Awa (isl.), Japan 81/J4
Awaji, Japan 81/H8
Awaji (isl.), Japan 81/H8
Awanui, N. Zealand 100/D1
Awareh, Ethiopia 111/H6
Awarua (bay), N. Zealand 100/A6
Awash, Ethiopia 111/H6
Awash (riv.), Ethiopia 111/H5
Awaso, Ghana 106/D7
Awat, China 77/A3
Awatere (riv.), N. Zealand 100/D5
Awbeg (riv.), Ireland 17/D7
Awe, Loch (lake), Scotland 10/D2
Awe, Loch (lake), Scotland 15/C4
Aweil, Sudan 111/E6
Awendaw, S.C. (29429) 296/H5
Awosting, N.J. (†07421) 273/E1
Axe Edge (mt.), England 13/H2
Axel, Netherlands 27/D6
Axel Heiberg (isl.), Canada 4/A14
Axel Heiberg (isl.), N.W.T. 146/J1
Axel Heiberg (isl.), N.W. Terrs. 187/J2
Axel Heiberg (isl.), N.W.T. 162/N3
Axim, Ghana 106/D8
Axis, Ala. (36505) 195/B9
Ax-les-Thermes, France 28/D6
Axminster, England 13/D7
Axminster, England 10/E5
Axochiapan, Mexico 150/M2
Axson, Georgia (31624) 217/G8
Axtell, Kansas (66403) 232/F2
Axtell, Nebr. (68924) 264/E4
Axtell, Utah (84621) 304/C4
Axton, Va. (24054) 307/J7
Axum (Aksum), Ethiopia 111/G5
Ayabaca, Peru 128/C5
Ayabe, Japan 81/G6
Ayacucho, Argentina 143/E4
Ayacucho, Bolivia 136/D5
Ayacucho (dept.), Peru 128/E9
Ayacucho, Peru 128/F9
Ayacucho, Peru 120/B4
Ayaguz, U.S.S.R. 54/K5
Ayaguz, U.S.S.R. 48/J5
Ayakkum Hu (lake), China 77/C4
Ayamonte, Spain 33/C4
Ayan, U.S.S.R. 54/P4
Ayan, U.S.S.R. 48/O4
Ayancık, Turkey 63/F1
Ayapel, Colombia 126/C3
Ayapel, Serranía de (mts.), Colombia 126/C4
Ayaş, Turkey 63/E2
Ayata, Bolivia 136/A4
Ayaviri, Peru 128/G10
Aybak, Afghanistan 68/B1
Aybak, Afghanistan 59/J2
Aybastı, Turkey 63/G2
Aycliffe, England 13/F3
Ayden, N.C. (28513) 281/P4
Aydın (prov.), Turkey 63/B4
Aydin, Turkey 59/A2
Aydın, Turkey 63/B4
Aydıncık, Turkey 63/E4
Aydlett, N.C. (27916) 281/T2
Aydyrlinskiy, U.S.S.R. 52/K4
Ayer, Mass. (*01432) 249/H2
Ayer○, Mass. (*01432) 249/H2
Ayer, Switzerland 39/E4
Ayer, Wash. (†99348) 310/G4
Ayers, Maine (†04666) 243/J6
Ayer's Cliff, Québec 172/E4
Ayers Rock, Mt. Olga Nat'l Park, North. Terr. 88/E5
Ayers Rock (mt.), North. Terr. 88/E5
Ayers Rock Nat'l Park, North. Terr. 93/B8
Ayersville, Ohio (†43512) 284/B3
Ayiá, Greece 45/F6
Áyion Óros (aut. dist.), Greece 45/G5
Áyios Evstrátios (isl.), Greece 45/G6
Áyios Kírikos, Greece 45/H7
Áyios Matthaíos, Greece 45/D6
Áyios Nikólaos, Greece 45/G8
Áyios Yeóryios (cape), Greece 45/G5
Aykhal, U.S.S.R. 48/M3
Aylen (lake), Ontario 177/G2
Aylesbury, England 13/G7
Aylesbury, England 10/F5
Aylesbury, Sask. 181/F5
Aylesford, England 13/J8
Aylesford, Nova Scotia 168/D3
Aylett, Va. (23009) 307/O5
Ayllón, Spain 33/E2
Aylmer, N. Dak. (†58710) 282/K4
Aylmer (lake), N.W. Terrs. 187/H3
Aylmer, Ontario 177/C5
Aylmer, Québec 172/B4
Aylmer (lake), Québec 172/F4
Aylsham, England 13/J5
Aylsham, Sask. 181/H2
Aynor, S.C. (29511) 296/J3
Ayod, Sudan 111/F6
Ayolas, Paraguay 144/D5
Ayon (isl.), U.S.S.R. 48/R2
Ayora, Spain 33/F3
Ayr, Nebr. (68925) 264/F4
Ayr, N. Dak. (58007) 282/P5
Ayr, Ontario 177/D4
Ayr, Queensland 95/C3
Ayr, Queensland 88/H3
Ayr, Scotland 15/D5
Ayr, Scotland 10/D3
Ayr, Heads of (cape), Scotland 15/D5
Ayr (trad. co.), Scotland 15/A5
Ayr (riv.), Scotland 15/D5
Ayrancı, Turkey 63/E4
Ayre (pt.), I. of Man 13/C3
Ayre (pt.), I. of Man 10/D3
Ayrshire, Iowa (50515) 229/D2
Ayton, Ontario 177/D3
Ayton, Scotland 15/F5

Aytos, Bulgaria 45/H4
Ayu (isls.), Indonesia 85/J5
Ayun, Saudi Arabia 59/D4
Ayutla de los Libres, Mexico 150/K8
Ayutthaya (Phra Nakhon Si Ayutthaya), Thailand 72/D4
Ayvacık, Turkey 63/B3
Ayvalık, Turkey 59/A2
Ayvalık, Turkey 63/B3
Aywaille, Belgium 27/H8
Azalea, Oreg. (97410) 291/D5
Azalea Park, Fla. (32807) 212/E3
Azalia, Ind. (†47232) 227/F6
Azalia, Mich. (48110) 250/F6
Azamgarh, India 68/E3
Azángaro, Peru 128/H10
Azángaro (riv.), Peru 128/G10
Azaoua (reg.), Niger 106/E5
Azaouad (reg.), Mali 106/D5
Azaouak (dry riv.), Mali 106/E5
Azapa, Chile 138/A1
Azapa, Quebrada (riv.), Chile 138/B1
Azare, Nigeria 106/G6
Azaz, Syria 63/G4
Azbine (Aïr) (mts.), Niger 106/F5
Azcapotzalco, Mexico 150/L1
Azdavay, Turkey 63/E2
Azemmour, Morocco 106/C2
Azerbaidzhan S.S.R., U.S.S.R. 7/J4
Azerbaidzhan S.S.R., U.S.S.R. 48/E5
Azerbaidzhan S.S.R., U.S.S.R. 52/G6
Azerbaijan, East (prov.), Iran 66/E1
Azerbaijan, West (prov.), Iran 66/D1
Azerbaijan (reg.), Iran 66/D1
Aziscoos (lake), Maine 243/A5
Azle, Texas (76020) 303/E2
Azogues, Ecuador 128/C4
AZORES 33
Azores (isls.), Portugal 2/H4
Azores (isls.), Portugal 33/A2
Azoum, Bahr, Chad 111/D5
Azov (sea), U.S.S.R. 7/H4
Azov, U.S.S.R. 52/E5
Azov (sea), U.S.S.R. 52/E5
Azov (sea), U.S.S.R. 48/D5
Azoyú, Mexico 150/K8
Azpeitia, Spain 33/E1
Azrou, Morocco 106/C2
Aztec, Ariz. (†85333) 198/B6
Aztec, N. Mex. (87410) 274/B2
Aztec Ruins Nat'l Mon., N. Mex. 274/A2
Azua (prov.), Dom. Rep. 158/D6
Azua, Dom. Rep. 156/D3
Azua, Dom. Rep. 158/D6
Azuaga, Spain 33/D3
Azuara, Spain 33/F2
Azuay (prov.), Ecuador 128/C4
Azuero (pen.), Panama 154/G7
Azul, Argentina 143/E4
Azul, Argentina 120/D6
Azul (riv.), Guatemala 154/C2
Azul, Cordillera (mts.), Peru 128/E7
Azurduy, Bolivia 136/C6
Azure (lake), Br. Col. 184/G4
Azusa, Calif. (91702) 204/D10
Azwell, Wash. (†98846) 310/F3
Azzel Mati, Sebkha (lake), Algeria 106/E3
Az Zubair, Iraq 66/E5

B

Ba, Fiji 86/P10
Baa, Indonesia 85/G8
Baaba (isl.), New Caled. 86/G4
Ba'albek, Lebanon 63/G5
Baan Baa, N.S. Wales 97/E2
Baar, Switzerland 39/F2
Baarle-Nassau, Netherlands 27/F6
Baarn, Netherlands 27/G4
Baatsagaan, Mongolia 77/E2
Baba, Ecuador 128/C3
Baba (cape), Turkey 63/D2
Baba (cape), Turkey 63/A3
Babadag, Romania 45/J3
Babadağ, Turkey 63/C4
Babaeski, Turkey 63/B2
Babahoyo, Ecuador 128/C3
Babanusa, Sudan 111/E5
Babar (isl.), Indonesia 85/H7
Babar (isls.), Indonesia 85/H7
Babati, Tanzania 115/G4
Babayevo, U.S.S.R. 52/E3
Babb, Mont. (59411) 262/C2
Babbie, Ala. (†36420) 195/F8
Babbitt, Minn. (55706) 255/G3
Babbitt, Nev. (89416) 266/C4
Babcock, Wis. (54413) 317/F7
Babel (isls.), Tasmania 99/E1
Bab el Mandeb (str.) 102/G3
Bab el Mandeb (str.), Djibouti 111/H5
Babelthuap (isl.), Belau 87/D5
Babia (riv.), Mexico 150/J2
Babil (heads), Iraq 66/D4
Babine (lake), Br. Col. 162/D5
Babine, Br. Col. 184/D2
Babine (lake), Br. Col. 184/E3
Babine (riv.), Br. Col. 184/D2
Babo, Indonesia 85/K7
Babol, Iran 54/G6
Babol, Iran 59/F2
Babol, Iran 66/H2
Babol Sar, Iran 66/H2
Baboquivari (mts.), Ariz. 198/D7
Baboua, Cent. Afr. Rep. 115/C2
Babson Park, Fla. (33827) 212/E4
Babuyan (isls.), Philippines 54/O8
Babuyan (chan.), Philippines 82/A3
Babuyan (isl.), Philippines 82/B2
Babuyan (isls.), Philippines 85/G2
Babuyan (isls.), Philippines 82/A2
Babylon (ruins), Iraq 66/D4
Babylon, N.Y. (*11702) 276/O9
Baca (co.), Colo. 208/O8
Bacabal, Brazil 120/E3
Bacabal, Maranhão, Brazil 132/E4
Bacabal, Pará, Brazil 132/B4
Bacadéhuachi, Mexico 150/E2
Bacalar, Mexico 150/P7
Bacalar (lake), Mexico 150/P7
Bacan (isls.), Indonesia 85/H6
Bacanora, Mexico 150/E2
Bacarra, Philippines 82/C1
Bacău, Romania 7/G4
Bacău, Romania 45/H2
Baccalieu (isl.), Newf. 166/D2
Bac Can, Vietnam 72/E2
Baccaro (pt.), Nova Scotia 168/C5
Bacchus Marsh, Victoria 97/C5
Bacerac, Mexico 150/E1
Bac Giang, Vietnam 72/E2
Bach, Mich. (†48759) 250/F5
Bachaquero, Venezuela 124/C3
Bache (pen.), N.W. Terrs. 187/L2
Bache, Okla. (74526) 288/P5
Bachelor (brook), Mass. 249/D3
Bachíniva, Mexico 150/F2
Bach Long Vi, Dao (isl.), Vietnam 72/F2
Bachu (Maralwexi), China 77/A4
Back (bay), India 68/B7
Back (riv.), Md. 245/N4
Back (lake), N.H. 268/E1
Back (riv.), N.W.T. 146/H3
Back (riv.), N.W.T. 162/G2
Back (riv.), N.W. Terrs. 187/J3
Back (bay), Va. 307/S7
Back (creek), Va. 307/J4
Bačka Topola, Yugoslavia 45/D3
Back Bay, New Bruns. 170/D3
Backbone (mt.), Md. 245/A3
Backnang, W. Germany 22/C4
Backoo, N. Dak. (58215) 282/P2
Backus, Minn. (56435) 255/D4
Backway, The (inlet), Newf. 166/C3
Bac Lieu, Vietnam 72/E5
Bacliff, Texas (77518) 303/K2
Bac Ninh, Vietnam 72/E2
Baco (mt.), Philippines 82/C4
Bacolod, Philippines 85/G3
Bacolod, Philippines 54/O8
Bacolod, Philippines 82/D5
Bacon (co.), Georgia 217/G7
Bacone, Okla. (†74401) 288/R3
Bacon Ridge (mts.), Wyo. 319/B2
Bacons, Del. (†19940) 245/R6
Baconton, Georgia (31716) 217/D8
Bácsalmás, Hungary 41/E3
Bács-Kiskun (co.), Hungary 41/E3
Bácum, Mexico 150/D3
Bacuna, Neth. Ant. 161/E8
Bacup, England 13/H1
Bacup, England 10/G1
Bad (riv.), Mich. 250/E5
Bad (hills), Sask. 181/C4
Bad (lake), Sask. 181/C4
Bad (riv.), S. Dak. 298/G5
Badacsonytomaj, Hungary 41/D3
Badagara, India 68/D6
Bad Aibling, W. Germany 22/D5
Badajoz (prov.), Spain 33/C3
Badajoz, Spain 33/C3
Badalona, Spain 33/H2
Bad Aussee, Austria 41/B3
Bad Axe, Mich. (48413) 250/G5
Bad Berleburg, W. Germany 22/C3
Bad Berneck, W. Germany 22/D3
Bad Bramstedt, W. Germany 22/C2
Bad Brückenau, W. Germany 22/C3
Baddeck, Nova Scotia 168/H2
Baddeck (riv.), Nova Scotia 168/H2
Bad Doberan, E. Germany 22/D1
Bad Driburg, W. Germany 22/C3
Bad Dürkheim, W. Germany 22/C4
Bad Dürrenberg, E. Germany 22/D3
Bad Ems, W. Germany 22/B3
Baden, Austria 41/D2
Baden, Manitoba 179/A2
Baden, Md. (†20613) 245/M6
Baden, Ontario 177/D4
Baden, Pa. (15005) 294/B4
Baden, Switzerland 39/F2
Ba Den, Nui (mt.), Vietnam 72/E5
Baden-Baden, W. Germany 22/C4
Badenoch (dist.), Scotland 15/D4
Badenweiler, W. Germany 22/B5
Baden-Württemberg (state), W. Germany 22/C4
Bad Freienwalde, E. Germany 22/F2
Bad Gandersheim, W. Germany 22/D3
Badgastein, Austria 41/B3
Badger (peak), Idaho 220/E7
Badger, Iowa (50516) 229/E3
Badger, Minn. (56714) 255/B2
Badger, Newf. 166/C4
Badger (creek), Oreg. 291/H3
Badger, S. Dak. (57214) 298/P5
Badger (creek), Wyo. 319/E2
Badger's Quay, Newf. 166/D4
Bad Goisern, Austria 41/B3
Badham, S.C. (†29471) 296/F5
Bad Harzburg, W. Germany 22/D3
Bad Hersfeld, W. Germany 22/C3
Badhoevedorp, Netherlands 27/B5
Bad Hofgastein, Austria 41/B3
Bad Homburg vor der Höhe, W. Germany 22/C3
Bad Honnef, W. Germany 22/B3
Badian, Philippines 82/D6
Badin, N.C. (28009) 281/J4
Badin, Pakistan 68/B4
Badiraguato, Mexico 150/F4
Bad Ischl, Austria 41/B3
Bad Kissingen, W. Germany 22/D3
Bad Kreuznach, W. Germany 22/B4
Bad Land (butte), Utah 304/D4
Bad Lands (reg.), N. Dak. 282/C7
Badlands Nat'l Park, S. Dak. 298/E6
Bad Langensalza, E. Germany 22/D3
Bad Lauterberg im Harz, W. Germany 22/D3
Bad Leonfelden, Austria 41/C2
Bad Liebenwerda, E. Germany 22/E3
Bad Lippspringe, W. Germany 22/C3
Bad Mergentheim, W. Germany 22/C4
Bad Münster-Ebernburg, W. Germany 22/B4
Bad Münstereifel, W. Germany 22/B3
Bad Muskau, E. Germany 22/F3
Bad Nauheim, W. Germany 22/C3
Bad Neuenahr-Ahrweiler, W. Germany 22/B3
Bad Neustadt an der Saale, W. Germany 22/D3
Bado, Mo. (†65447) 261/H8
Bad Oldesloe, W. Germany 22/D2
Ba Don, Vietnam 72/E3
Bad Orb, W. Germany 22/C3
Bad Pyrmont, W. Germany 22/C3
Badr, Saudi Arabia 59/C5
Badra, Iraq 66/D4
Bad Ragaz, Switzerland 39/H2
Bad Reichenhall, W. Germany 22/E5
Bad River Ind. Res., Wis. 317/E2
Bad Sachsa, W. Germany 22/D3
Bad Salzschlirf, W. Germany 22/C3
Bad Salzuflen, W. Germany 22/C2
Bad Salzungen, E. Germany 22/C3
Bad Sankt-Leonhard im Lavanttal, Austria 41/C3
Bad Schwartau, W. Germany 22/D2
Bad Segeberg, W. Germany 22/D2
Bad Tölz, W. Germany 22/D5
Baduen, Somalia 115/J2
Badulla, Sri Lanka 68/E7
Bad Vilbel, W. Germany 22/C3
Bad Waldsee, W. Germany 22/C5
Badwater (creek), Wyo. 319/E2
Bad Wildungen, W. Germany 22/C3
Bad Wimpfen, W. Germany 22/C4
Baelum, Denmark 21/D4
Baena, Spain 33/D4
Baerle-Hertog, Belgium 27/F6
Báez, Cuba 158/E2
Baeza, Ecuador 128/D3
Baeza, Spain 33/E4
Bafa (lake), Turkey 63/B4
Baffin (bay) 4/B13
Baffin (bay) 146/M2
Baffin (isl.), Canada 2/F2
Baffin (isl.), Canada 4/C13
Baffin (bay), Canada 2/F2
Baffin (isl.), N.W.T. 146/L2
Baffin (isl.), N.W.T. 162/J1
Baffin (bay), N.W.T. 162/J1
Baffin (dist.), N.W. Terrs. 187/K2
Baffin (bay), N.W. Terrs. 187/M2
Baffin (isl.), N.W. Terrs. 187/L2
Baffin (bay), Texas 303/G10
Bafia, Cameroon 115/B3
Bafing (riv.), Guinea 106/B6
Bafing (riv.), Mali 106/B6
Bafoulabé, Mali 106/B6
Bafoussam, Cameroon 115/B2
Bafq, Iran 59/G3
Bafq, Iran 66/J5
Bafra, Turkey 59/C1
Bafra, Turkey 63/F2
Bafra (cape), Turkey 59/C1
Bafra (cape), Turkey 63/G2
Baft, Iran 66/K6
Baft, Iran 59/G4
Baga, Nigeria 106/G6
Bagabag, Philippines 82/C2
Bagac, Philippines 82/C3
Bagaces, C. Rica 154/E5
Bagadó, Colombia 126/B5
Bagalkot, India 68/D5
Bagam (well), Niger 106/F5
Bagamoyo, Tanzania 115/G5
Baganga, Philippines 82/F7
Baganian (pen.), Philippines 82/D7
Bagansiapiapi, Indonesia 85/C5
Bagata, Zaire 115/C4
Bagdad, Ariz. (86321) 198/B4
Bagdad, Fla. (32530) 212/B6
Bagdad, Ky. (40003) 237/L4
Bagdad, Tasmania 99/D4
Bagdarin, U.S.S.R. 48/M4
Bagé, Brazil 120/D6
Bagé, Brazil 132/C10
Bagenalstown, Ireland 10/C4
Bagenalstown (Muinebeag), Ireland 17/H6
Bagenkop, Denmark 21/D8
Baggs, Wyo. (82321) 319/E4
Baghbaghu, Iran 66/M3
Baghdad (heads), Iraq 66/D4
Baghdad (cap.), Iraq 59/E3
Baghdad (cap.), Iraq 54/F6
Baghdad (cap.), Iraq 2/M4
Baghdad (cap.), Iraq 66/D4
Bagheria, Italy 34/D5
Baghlan, Afghanistan 54/H6
Baghlan, Afghanistan 59/J2
Baghlan, Afghanistan 68/B1
Baghu, Iran 66/K7
Bağırpaşa Dağı (mt.), Turkey 59/D2
Bağırpaşa Dağı (mt.), Turkey 63/J3
Bagley, Iowa (50026) 229/E5
Bagley, Minn. (56621) 255/C3
Bagley, N.C. (†27542) 281/N3
Bagley, Wis. (53801) 317/D10
Bagnell, Mo. (†65026) 261/G6
Bagnell (dam), Mo. 261/G6
Bagnères-de-Bigorre, France 28/D6
Bagnères-de-Luchon, France 28/D6
Bagnolet, France 28/B2
Bagnols-sur-Cèze, France 28/F5
Bågø (isl.), Denmark 21/C7
Bago, Philippines 82/D5
Bagoé (riv.), Ivory Coast 106/C6
Bagoé (riv.), Mali 106/C6
Bagot, Manitoba 179/D5
Bagot (co.), Québec 172/E4
Bagrax (Bosten Hu) (lake), China 77/C3
Bagua, Peru 128/C5
Báguanos, Cuba 158/J3
Baguio, Philippines 54/N8
Baguio, Philippines 85/G2
Baguio, Philippines 82/C2
Baguirmi (reg.), Chad 111/C5
Bagwell, Texas (75412) 303/J4
Bahama, N.C. (27503) 281/M2
Bahamas 2/F4
Bahamas 146/L7
BAHAMAS 156/C1
Bahariya (oasis), Egypt 111/E2
Bahariya (oasis), Egypt 59/A4
Bahawalnagar, Pakistan 68/C2
Bahawalpur, Pakistan 54/J7
Bahawalpur, Pakistan 68/C3
Bahawalpur, Pakistan 59/K4
Bahçe, Turkey 63/G4
Bahçesaray, Turkey 63/K3
Bahia (state), Brazil 132/F6
Bahia (Salvador), Brazil 132/G6
Bahia (isls.), Honduras 154/D2
Bahía Blanca, Argentina 2/F7
Bahía Blanca, Argentina 143/D4
Bahía Blanca, Argentina 120/C6
Bahía Bustamante, Argentina 143/C6
Bahía de Caráquez, Ecuador 128/B3
Bahía Honda, Cuba 158/B1
Bahía Kino, Mexico 150/C2
Bahía San Blas, Argentina 143/D5
Bahía Thetis, Argentina 143/C7
Bahía Tortugas, Mexico 150/B3
Bahir Dar, Ethiopia 111/G5
Bahomamey, P. Rico 161/A1
Bahoruco (prov.), Dom. Rep. 158/D6
Bahoruco, Sierra de (mts.), Dom. Rep. 158/D6
Bahraich, India 68/E3
Bahrain 54/G7
BAHRAIN 59/F4
Bahramabad (Rafsanjan), Iran 66/K5
Bahr Azoum (riv.), Sudan 111/D5
Bahr el 'Arab (riv.), Sudan 111/E6
Bahr el Ghazal (dry riv.), Chad 111/C5
Bahr El Ghazal (prov.), Sudan 111/E6
Bahr es Safi (des.), Saudi Arabia 59/E6
Bahr ez Zeraf (riv.), Sudan 111/F6
Bahr Yusef (stream), Egypt 111/J4
Baia de Aramă, Romania 45/F3
Baia dos Tigres, Angola 115/B7
Baia Farta, Angola 115/B6
Baia Mare, Romania 45/F2
Baião, Brazil 132/D3
Baibiene, Argentina 143/G4
Baibokoum, Chad 111/C6
Bai Bung, Mui (Ca Mau) (pt.), Vietnam 72/E5
Baicheng (Bay), Xinjiang Uygur, China 77/B3
Baicheng, Jilin, China 77/K2
Baida, Libya 102/E1
Baida, Libya 111/D1
Baidyabati, India 68/F1
Baie-Comeau, Québec 172/A1
Baie-Comeau, Québec 174/D3
Baie de Henne, Haiti 158/B5
Baie-des-Bacons, Québec 172/H1
Baie-des-Moutons, Québec 174/F2
Baie-des-Rochers, Québec 172/H2
Baie-des-Sables, Québec 172/A1
Baie-du-Poste, Québec 174/C2
Baie-d'Urfé, Québec 172/G4
Baie-du-Vieux-Fort, Québec 174/F2
Baie-Johan-Beetz, Québec 174/E2
Baie-Mahault, Guadeloupe 161/A6
Baiersbronn, W. Germany 22/C4
Baie-Sainte-Anne, New Bruns. 170/F1
Baie-Sainte-Catherine, Québec 172/H1
Baie-Saint-Paul, Que. 162/J6
Baie-Saint-Paul, Québec 174/C3
Baie-Saint-Paul, Québec 172/G2
Baie-Trinité, Québec 172/B1
Baie-Verte, New Bruns. 170/F2
Baie Verte, Newf. 166/C4
Baieville, Québec 172/E3
Baigorrita, Argentina 143/F7
Baiji, Iraq 66/C3
Baildon, Sask. 181/F5
Baile Átha Cliath (Dublin) (cap.), Ireland 17/K5
Baile Átha Cliath (Dublin) (cap.), Ireland 10/C4
Băile Herculane, Romania 45/F3
Bailén, Spain 33/E3
Băileşti, Romania 45/F3
Bailey, Colo. (80421) 208/H4
Bailey, Iowa (†50455) 229/H2
Bailey, Mich. (49303) 250/D5
Bailey, Miss. (39320) 256/G6
Bailey, N.C. (27807) 281/N3
Bailey (co.), Texas 303/B3
Baileyboro, Texas (†79371) 303/B3
Bailey Island, Maine (04003) 243/D8
Bailey Lakes, Ohio (†44805) 284/F4
Bailey's Crossroads, Va. (22041) 307/S3
Baileys Harbor, Wis. (54202) 317/M5
Baileyton, Ala. (35019) 195/E2
Baileyton, Tenn. (37743) 237/R8
Baileyville, Conn. (†06455) 210/E2
Baileyville, Ill. (61007) 222/D1
Baileyville, Kansas (66404) 232/F2
Bailieborough, Ireland 17/G4
Bailique (isl.), Brazil 132/D2
Baillivanish, Scotland 15/A3
Baillie (isls.), N.W. Terrs. 187/F2
Baillieston, Scotland 15/B2
Baillif, Guadeloupe 161/A7
Bailundo, Angola 115/C6
Baima, China 77/E5
Bainbridge (isl.), Alaska 196/C1
Bainbridge, Georgia (31717) 217/C9
Bainbridge, Ind. (46105) 227/D5
Bainbridge, N.Y. (13733) 276/J6
Bainbridge (dist.), N. Ireland 17/J3
Bainbridge, Ohio (45612) 284/D7
Bainbridge, Pa. (17502) 294/J5
Bainbridge (isl.), Wash. 310/A2
Bainbridge Island-Winslow (Winslow), Wash. (98110) 310/A2
Bainbridge N.T.C., Md. 245/O2
Bainet, Haiti 158/B6
Baingoin, China 77/D5
Bains, La. (70713) 238/H5
Bainville, Mont. (59212) 262/M2
Baird (inlet), Alaska 196/F2
Baird (mts.), Alaska 196/F1
Baird, Miss. (38724) 256/C4
Baird (pen.), N.W. Terrs. 187/L3
Baird, Texas (79504) 303/E5
Bairdstown, Ohio (†45872) 284/C3
Bairdsville, New Bruns. 170/C2
Baire, Cuba 158/H4
Bairiki (cap.), Kiribati 87/H5
Bairin Zuoqi, China 77/J3
Bairnsdale, Victoria 88/H7
Bairnsdale, Victoria 97/D5
Bairoil, Wyo. (82322) 319/E3
Bais, Philippines 82/D6
Baisden, W. Va. (25608) 312/C7
Baïse (riv.), France 28/D6
Baisha, China 77/G8
Baitadi, Nepal 68/E3
Bait al Faqih, Yemen Arab Rep. 59/D7
Bai Thuong, Vietnam 72/E3
Baixa da Banheira, Portugal 33/B3
Baixo (isl.), Portugal 33/B2
Baixo Guandu, Brazil 132/F7
Baja, Hungary 41/E3
Baja California (state), Mexico 150/B1
Baja California Sur (state), Mexico 150/C3
Bajadero, P. Rico 161/C1
Bajgiran, Iran 66/L2
Bajo Boquete, Panama 154/F6
Bajo Nuevo (shoal), Colombia 126/C8
Bajos de Haina, Dom. Rep. 158/E6
Bajram Curri, Albania 45/D4
Bakala, Cent. Afr. Rep. 115/D2
Bakar, Yugoslavia 45/B3
Bakel, Senegal 106/B6
Baker (isl.), Alaska 196/M2
Baker, Calif. (92309) 204/J8
Baker (riv.), Chile 138/D7
Baker (mt.), Colo. 208/H2
Baker (co.), Fla. 212/D1
Baker, Fla. (32531) 212/C5
Baker (co.), Georgia 217/D8
Baker, Idaho (†83467) 220/E4
Baker, La. (70714) 238/K1
Baker (lake), Maine 243/D3
Baker, Minn. (56513) 255/B4
Baker, Mo. (†63846) 261/N9
Baker, Mont. (59313) 262/M4
Baker, Nev. (89311) 266/G3
Baker (riv.), N.H. 268/D4
Baker, N. Dak. (†58386) 282/L3
Baker (lake), N.W. Terrs. 187/J3
Baker, Okla. (73930) 288/D1
Baker, Oreg. 188/C2
Baker (co.), Oreg. 291/K3
Baker, Oreg. (97814) 291/K3
Baker (isl.), Pacific 87/J5
Baker (creek), Utah 304/A4
Baker (lake), Wash. 310/D2
Baker (mt.), Wash. 310/D2
Baker (riv.), Wash. 310/D2
Baker, W. Va. (26801) 312/J4
Baker Brook, New Bruns. 170/B1
Baker Butte (mt.), Ariz. 198/D4
Baker Hill, Ala. (36004) 195/H7
Baker Lake, N.W.T. 162/G3
Baker Lake, N.W. Terrs. 187/J3
Bakers (isl.), Mass. 249/F5
Bakersfield, Calif. 146/G6
Bakersfield, Calif. 188/C3
Bakersfield, Calif. (*93301) 204/G8
Bakersfield, Mo. (65609) 261/H9
Bakersfield, Texas (†79752) 303/B7
Bakersfield○, Vt. (05441) 268/B2
Bakers Summit, Pa. (16614) 294/F5
Bakersville, Conn. (†06057) 210/C1
Bakersville, N.C. (28705) 281/E2
Bakersville, Ohio (43803) 284/G5
Bakersville, Pa. (†15501) 294/D5
Bakerton, Ky. (42711) 237/L7
Bakerton, W. Va. (25410) 312/L4
Bakerville, Tenn. (†37185) 237/F9
Bakewell, England 10/G2
Bakewell, England 13/J2
Bakewell, Tenn. (37304) 237/L10
Bakharz, Kuhha-ye (mt.), Iran 66/M3
Bakhchisaray, U.S.S.R. 52/D6
Bakhmach, U.S.S.R. 52/D4
Bakhtegan (lake), Iran 66/J6
Bakhtiari (gov.), Iran 66/F4
Bakhun, Kuh-e (mt.), Iran 66/K6
Bakhuys (mts.), Suriname 131/C3
Bakia, Cent. Afr. Rep. 115/E2
Bakırköy, Turkey 63/D6
Baklan, Turkey 63/C4
Bako, Ethiopia 111/G6
Bakony (mts.), Hungary 41/D3
Bakool (prov.), Somalia 115/H3
Bakouma, Cent. Afr. Rep. 115/D2
Bakoy (riv.), Guinea 106/B6
Bakoy (riv.), Mali 106/B6
Bakraband, Kuh-e (mts.), Iran 66/M7
Baktalórántháza, Hungary 41/G2
Baktu (Paektu) (mt.), N. Korea 81/C3
Baku, U.S.S.R. 2/M3
Baku, U.S.S.R. 7/J4
Baku, U.S.S.R. 48/F5
Baku, U.S.S.R. 52/H6
Bala, Kansas (†66531) 232/F2
Bala, Ontario 177/E2
Balâ, Turkey 63/E3
Bala, Wales 13/D5
Bala, Wales 10/E4
Balabac, Philippines 82/A7
Balabac (isl.), Philippines 85/F4
Balabac (isl.), Philippines 82/A7
Balabac (str.), Philippines 85/F4
Balabac (str.), Philippines 82/A7
Balabalagan (isls.), Indonesia 85/F6
Balabio (isl.), New Caled. 86/G4
Balaclava, Jamaica 158/H6
Bala-Cynwyd, Pa. (19004) 294/N6
Balad, Somalia 115/J3
Balaghat, India 68/E4
Balaguer, Spain 33/G2
Balaïtous (mt.), Spain 33/F1
Balakai (mesa), Ariz. 198/F3
Balakhna, U.S.S.R. 52/F3
Balaklava, S. Australia 94/F6
Balaklava, U.S.S.R. 52/D6
Balakovo, U.S.S.R. 7/J3
Balakovo, U.S.S.R. 48/E4
Balakovo, U.S.S.R. 52/G4
Balallan, Scotland 15/B2
Bal'ama, Jordan 65/E3
Balambangan (isl.), Malaysia 85/F4
Balancán de Domínguez, Mexico 150/O8
Balandra (pt.), Dom. Rep. 158/F5
Balanga, Philippines 82/C3
Balangala, Zaire 115/D3
Ba Lang An, Mui (cape), Vietnam 72/F4
Balangiga, Philippines 82/E5
Balao, Ecuador 128/C4
Balashi, Neth. Ant. 161/E10
Balashov, U.S.S.R. 7/J3
Balashov, U.S.S.R. 52/F4
Balashov, U.S.S.R. 48/E4
Balasore, India 68/F4
Balassagyarmat, Hungary 41/E2
Balaton (lake), Hungary 7/F4
Balaton (lake), Hungary 41/D3
Balaton, Minn. (56115) 255/C6
Balatonfüred, Hungary 41/D3
Balatonszentgyörgy, Hungary 41/D3
Balayan (bay), Philippines 82/C4
Balbi (mt.), Papua N.G. 86/C2
Balboa, Panama 154/H6
Balbriggan, Ireland 17/J4
Balbriggan, Ireland 10/C4
Balcarce, Argentina 143/E4
Balcarres, Sask. 181/H5
Balchik, Bulgaria 45/H4
Balch Springs, Texas (75180) 303/H2
Balclutha, N. Zealand 100/B7
Balcones Escarpment (plat.), Texas 303/E8
Balcones Heights, Texas (†78201) 303/J10
Bald (mt.), Colo. 208/H4
Bald (hill), Conn. 210/G1
Bald (mt.), Idaho 220/D5
Bald (mt.), New Bruns. 170/C1
Bald (mts.), N.C. 281/D3
Bald (mts.), Tenn. 237/R9
Bald (mt.), Utah 304/C3
Bald (mt.), Vt. 268/D2
Bald (head), W. Australia 88/B7
Bald (head), W. Australia 92/B6
Bald Eagle (lake), Minn. 255/G3
Baldeggersee (lake), Switzerland 39/F2
Baldhill (Ashtabula) (res.), N. Dak. 282/P5
Bald Hill Branch (riv.), Md. 245/G4
Bald Hills, Queensland 88/K2
Bald Knob, Ark. (72010) 202/G3
Bald Knob, W. Va. (25010) 312/C7
Baldonnel, Br. Col. 184/G2
Baldur, Manitoba 179/C5
Baldwin (co.), Ala. 195/C9
Baldwin, Fla. (32234) 212/E1
Baldwin (co.), Georgia 217/F4
Baldwin, Georgia (30511) 217/E2
Baldwin, Ill. (62217) 222/D5
Baldwin, Iowa (52207) 229/M4
Baldwin, La. (70514) 238/H7
Baldwin, Mich. (49304) 250/D5
Baldwin, N.Y. (11510) 276/R7
Baldwin, N. Dak. (58521) 282/J5
Baldwin, Pa. (†15208) 294/B7
Baldwin, W. Va. (26326) 312/E5
Baldwin, Wis. (54002) 317/B6
Baldwin-Aragon Mills, S.C. (†29706) 296/E2
Baldwin City, Kansas (66006) 232/G3
Baldwin Park, Calif. (91706) 204/D10
Baldwinsville, N.Y. (13027) 276/H4
Baldwinton, Sask. 181/B3
Baldwinville, Mass. (01436) 249/F2
Baldwyn, Miss. (38824) 256/G2
Baldy (peak), Ariz. 198/F5
Baldy (mt.), Manitoba 179/B3
Baldy (peak), N. Mex. 274/D3
Baldy (peak), Utah 304/B5
Bale (prov.), Ethiopia 111/H6
Bale (mt.), Ethiopia 111/G6
Baleares (prov.), Spain 33/H3
Balearic (isls.), Spain 7/E5
Balearic (Baleares) (isls.), Spain 33/H3
Baleine, Grande R. de la (riv.), Que. 162/J4
Baleine, Grand Rivière de la (riv.), Québec 174/B1
Baleine, Petite Rivière de la (riv.), Québec 174/B1
Baleine (riv.), Québec 174/D1
Baleine, R. à la (riv.), Que. 162/K4
Balen, Belgium 27/G6
Baler, Philippines 82/C3
Baler (bay), Philippines 82/C3
Balerna, Switzerland 39/G5
Balerno, Scotland 15/D2
Baleshare (isl.), Scotland 15/A3
Balestrand, Norway 18/E6
Baley, U.S.S.R. 48/M4
Balfate, Honduras 154/D3
Balfour, Br. Col. 184/J5
Balfour, N.C. (28706) 281/E4
Balfour, N. Dak. (58712) 282/J4
Balfron, Scotland 15/B1
Balgonie, Sask. 181/G5
Balhaf, P.D.R. Yemen 59/E7
Bal Harbour, Fla. (†33101) 212/C4
Bali, Cameroon 115/A2
Bali (isl.), Indonesia 54/N10
Bali (isl.), Indonesia 85/F7
Bali (sea), Indonesia 85/F7
Bali (str.), Indonesia 85/E7

Baxterville 335

Barham, N.S. Wales 97/C4
Bar Harbor, Maine (04609) 243/G7
Bar Harbor○, Maine (04609) 243/G7
Bari (prov.), Italy 34/F4
Bari, Italy 34/F4
Bari, Italy 7/F4
Bari (prov.), Somalia 115/J1
Baria (riv.), Venezuela 124/E7
Barich, Alberta 182/D2
Barichara, Colombia 126/D4
Barida, Ras (cape), Saudi Arabia 59/C5
Barima (riv.), Guyana 131/B2
Barinas (state), Venezuela 124/D3
Barinas, Venezuela 124/C3
Barinas, Venzuela 120/C2
Baring, Maine (†04619) 243/J5
Baring○, Maine (†04619) 243/J5
Baring, Mo. (63531) 261/H2
Baring (head), N. Zealand 100/B3
Baring (cape), N.W. Terrs. 187/G3
Baring, Sask. 181/J5
Baring, Wash. (98224) 310/D3
Barinitas, Venezuela 124/C3
Baripada, India 68/F4
Bariri, Brazil 135/B3
Bariri (res.), Brazil 135/B3
Bâris, Egypt 111/F3
Barisal, Bangladesh 68/G4
Barisan (mts.), Indonesia 85/C6
Baritbog (riv.), New Bruns. 170/E1
Barito (riv.), Indonesia 85/E6
Bark (lake), Ontario 177/G2
Barkam, China 77/F5
Barker, N.Y. (14012) 276/C4
Barker Heights, N.C. (†28739) 281/D4
Barkeyville, Pa. (†16038) 294/C3
Barkhamsted○, Conn. (†06063) 210/D1
Barkhamsted (res.), Conn. 210/D1
Barkhan, Pakistan 68/B3
Barkhan, Pakistan 59/J4
Barking, England 10/C5
Barking, England 13/H8
Barkley (sound), Br. Col. 184/E6
Barkley (dam), Ky. 237/E6
Barkley (lake), Ky. 237/F7
Barkley (lake), Tenn. 237/F7
Barkly Downs, Queensland 95/A4
Barkly East, S. Africa 118/D6
Barkly Tableland (plat.), Australia 87/D7
Barkly Tableland, North. Terr. 88/F3
Barkly Tableland, North. Terr. 93/D4
Barkly Tableland, Queensland 95/A4
Barkmere, Québec 172/C3
Barkol, China 77/D3
Bark River, Mich. (49807) 250/B3
Barksdale, Texas (78828) 303/D8
Barksdale A.F.B., La. 238/C2
Barlby, England 13/G4
Bar-le-Duc, France 28/F3
Barlee (lake), Australia 87/B8
Barlee (lake), W. Australia 88/B5
Barlee (lake), W. Australia 92/B5
Barletta, Italy 34/F4
Barlinek, Poland 47/B2
Barling, Ark. (72923) 202/B3
Barlow, Br. Col. 184/F3
Barlow, Ky. (42024) 237/D6
Barlow, Miss. (†39083) 256/C7
Barlow, N. Dak. (†58421) 282/M4
Barlow, Ohio (45612) 284/G7
Barlow, Oreg. (†97013) 291/B2
Barlow Bend, Ala. (†36545) 195/C8
Barmedman, N.S. Wales 97/D4
Barmer, India 68/C3
Barmera, S. Australia 94/G6
Bar Mills, Maine (04004) 243/C8
Barmouth, Wales 10/D4
Barmouth, Wales 13/C5
Barna, Ireland 17/C5
Barnabus, W. Va. (25609) 312/C7
Barnaby (riv.), New Bruns. 170/E2
Barnaby River, New Bruns. 170/E2
Barnard, Kansas (67418) 232/D2
Barnard, Mo. (64423) 261/C2
Barnard, N.C. (†28753) 281/D3
Barnard, S. Dak. (57426) 298/N2
Barnard○, Vt. (05031) 268/B4
Barnard Castle, England 13/E3
Barnardsville, N.C. (28709) 281/E3
Barnaul, U.S.S.R. 54/K4
Barnaul, U.S.S.R. 48/J4
Barn Bluff (mt.), Tasmania 99/B3
Barnegat, Alberta 182/E2
Barnegat, N.J. (08005) 273/E4
Barnegat (bay), N.J. 273/E4
Barnegat (inlet), N.J. 273/E4
Barnegat Light, N.J. (08006) 273/E4
Barnes (sound), Fla. 212/F6
Barnes, Kansas (66933) 232/F2
Barnes (co.), N. Dak. 282/O5
Barnes, Wis. (†54873) 317/D3
Barnesboro, Pa. (15714) 294/E4
Barnes City, Iowa (50027) 229/H6
Barnes Corners, N.Y. (13610) 276/J3
Barneston, Nebr. (68309) 264/H4
Barnesville, Colo. (†80624) 208/L2
Barnesville, Georgia (30204) 217/D4
Barnesville, Md. (20703) 245/J4
Barnesville, Minn. (56514) 255/B4
Barnesville, N.C. (28319) 281/L6
Barnesville, Ohio (43713) 284/H6
Barnet, England 13/H7
Barnet, England 10/B5
Barnet○, Vt. (05821) 268/C3
Barnett, Georgia (†30821) 217/G3
Barnett, Miss. (†39347) 256/G7
Barnett, Mo. (65011) 261/G6
Barnettville, New Bruns. 170/E2
Barneveld, Netherlands 27/H4
Barneveld, N.Y. (13304) 276/K4
Barneveld, Wis. (53507) 317/F10
Barneville-Carteret, France 28/C3
Barney, Georgia (31625) 217/E8
Barney, N. Dak. (58008) 282/S7
Barnhart, Texas (76930) 303/C6
Barnhill, Ohio (†44663) 284/H5
Barnoldswick, England 13/H1
Barnrock, Ky. (†41219) 237/R5
Barnsdall, Okla. (74002) 288/O1
Barnsley, England 13/J2
Barnsley, England 10/F4
Barnstable (co.), Mass. 249/N6
Barnstable, Mass. (02630) 249/N6
Barnstable○, Mass. (02630) 249/N6
Barnstaple, England 10/E5
Barnstaple, England 13/D6
Barnstaple (bay), England 10/D5
Barnstaple (bay), England 13/C6
Barnstead○, N.H. (03218) 268/E5
Barnum, Iowa (50518) 229/E3
Barnum, Minn. (55707) 255/F4
Barnum, W. Va. (†26726) 312/H4
Barnum, Wis. (†54631) 317/E9
Barnwell, Ala. (†36532) 195/C10
Barnwell, Alberta 182/D5
Barnwell (co.), S.C. 296/E5
Barnwell, S.C. (29812) 296/E5
Baro (riv.), Ethiopia 111/G6
Baro, Nigeria 106/F7
Baroda (Vadodara), India 68/C4
Baroda, India 54/J7
Baroda, Mich. (49101) 250/C7
Baroghil (pass), Afghanistan 68/C1
Baroghil (pass), Pakistan 68/C1
Baron, Okla. (†74965) 288/S3
Baron Bluff (prom.), Virgin Is. (U.S.) 161/E3
Barons, Alberta 182/D4
Barooga, N.S. Wales 97/C4
Barossa (res.), S. Australia 94/C6
Barotseland (reg.), Zambia 115/D7
Barpeta, India 68/G3
Barqa (Cyrenaica) (reg.), Libya 111/D1
Barques (pt.), Mich. 250/C3
Barquisimeto, Venezuela 124/D2
Barquisimeto, Venezuela 120/C2
Barr, Scotland 15/D5
Barr, Tenn. (†38040) 237/B9
Barra, Brazil 132/F5
Barra (head), Scotland 10/C2
Barra (head), Scotland 15/A4
Barra (isl.), Scotland 15/A4
Barra (isl.), Scotland 10/C2
Barra (isls.), Scotland 10/C2
Barra (sound), Scotland 15/A3
Barraba, N.S. Wales 97/F2
Barra Bonita (res.), Brazil 135/B3
Barrackpore, India 68/F1
Barrackville, W. Va. (26559) 312/F3
Barra de Río Grande, Nicaragua 154/F4
Barra do Bugres, Brazil 132/B6
Barra do Corda, Brazil 132/E4
Barra do Piraí, Brazil 132/E8
Barra do Piraí, Brazil 135/E3
Barra Isles (isls.), Scotland 15/A4
Barra Mansa, Brazil 135/D3
Barranca, Lima, Peru 128/C8
Barranca, Loreto, Peru 128/D5
Barrancabermeja, Colombia 126/C4
Barranca de Upía, Colombia 126/D5
Barrancas, Argentina 143/F6
Barrancas (riv.), Argentina 143/G5
Barrancas, Chile 138/G3
Barrancas, Colombia 126/D2
Barrancas, Barinas, Venezuela 124/C3
Barrancas, Monagas, Venezuela 124/G3
Barranco de Loba, Colombia 126/C3
Barrancos, Cerro (mt.), Chile 138/D7
Barrancos, Portugal 33/C3
Barranqueras, Argentina 143/E2
Barranquilla, Colombia 120/B1
Barranquilla, Colombia 126/C2
Barranquitas, P. Rico 161/D2
Barras (riv.), Bolivia 136/B6
Barras, Brazil 132/F4
Barras, Colombia 126/D8
Barraute, Québec 174/B3
Barre, Mass. (01005) 249/F3
Barre○, Mass. (01005) 249/F3
Barre, Québec 172/G3
Barre, Vt. (05641) 268/C3
Barre○, Vt. (05641) 268/C3
Barreal, Argentina 143/C3
Barreau (pt.), New Bruns. 170/F1
Barre Center, N.Y. (†14411) 276/D4
Barreiras, Brazil 120/E4
Barreiras, Brazil 132/E6
Barreirinha, Brazil 132/B3
Barreirinhas, Brazil 132/F3
Barreiro, Portugal 33/B1
Barreiros, Brazil 132/H5
Barren (isls.), Alaska 196/B2
Barren (isl.), India 68/G6
Barren (co.), Ky. 237/K7
Barren (riv.), Ky. 237/H6
Barren (isls.), Madagascar 118/G3
Barren (isl.), Nova Scotia 168/G4
Barren (cape), Tasmania 99/E2
Barren Plains, Tenn. (†37172) 237/H7
Barren River (lake), Ky. 237/J7
Barren Springs, Va. (24313) 307/G7
Barre Plains, Mass. (†01005) 249/F3
Barrera, Bolivia 136/B3
Barretos, Brazil 132/D8
Barretos, Brazil 135/B2
Barrett, Minn. (56311) 255/B5
Barrett, Texas (77532) 303/K1
Barrett, W. Va. (25013) 312/C7
Barretts, Georgia (†31601) 217/F8
Barrhead, Alberta 182/C2
Barrhead, Scotland 10/A1
Barrhead, Scotland 15/B2
Barrhill, Scotland 15/D5
Barrie, Ontario 177/E3
Barrie (isl.), Ontario 177/B1
Barrière, Br. Col. 184/H5
Barrineau Park, Fla. (†32533) 212/B6
Barrington, Ill. (60010) 222/A5
Barrington○, N.H. (†03825) 268/F5
Barrington, N.J. (08007) 273/B3
Barrington, Nova Scotia 168/C5
Barrington (bay), Nova Scotia 168/C5
Barrington○, R.I. (02806) 249/J6
Barrington, Tasmania 99/C3
Barrington Hills, Ill. (†60010) 222/A5
Barrington P.O. (East Barrington), N.H. (03825) 268/F5
Barrington Passage, Nova Scotia 168/C5
Barrington Tops (mt.), N.S. Wales 97/F2
Barringun, N.S. Wales 97/C1
Barron (co.), Wis. 317/C5
Barron, Wis. (54812) 317/C5
Barronett, Wis. (54813) 317/B4
Barrouallie, St. Vin. & Grens. 161/A9
Barroui, Dominica 161/E6
Barrow, Alaska (99723) 196/G1
Barrow, Alaska 188/C5
Barrow, Alaska 146/C2
Barrow (pt.), Alaska 146/C2
Barrow (pt.), Alaska 196/G1
Barrow (isl.), Australia 87/B8
Barrow (co.), Georgia 217/E2
Barrow (riv.), Ireland 17/H7
Barrow (riv.), Ireland 10/C4
Barrow (str.), N.W.T. 162/G1
Barrow (str.), N.W. Terrs. 187/J2
Barrow (bay), Ontario 177/C2
Barrow, U.S. 4/B17
Barrow (pt.), U.S. 2/B2
Barrow (pt.), U.S. 4/B18
Barrow (isl.), W. Australia 88/A4
Barrow (isl.), W. Australia 92/A3
Barrow Creek, North. Terr. 93/D6
Barrow-in-Furness, England 10/E3
Barrow-in-Furness, England 13/D3
Barrows, Manitoba 179/A2
Barrowsville, Mass. (†02766) 249/K5
Barr Smith (mt.) 5/C5
Barruelo de Santullán, Spain 33/D1
Barry, Ill. (62312) 222/B4
Barry (co.), Mich. 250/D6
Barry, Minn. (56210) 255/B5
Barry (co.), Mo. 261/E9
Barry (mts.), Victoria 97/D5
Barry, Wales 13/B7
Barry, Wales 10/E5
Barry's Bay, Ontario 177/G2
Barryton, Mich. (49305) 250/D5
Barryville, N.Y. (12719) 276/L8
Barsi, India 68/D5
Barsinghausen, W. Germany 22/C2
Barss Corners, Nova Scotia 168/D4
Barstow, Calif. (92311) 204/H9
Barstow, Md. (20610) 245/M6
Barstow, Texas (79719) 303/A6
Bar-sur-Aube, France 28/F3
Bar-sur-Seine, France 28/F3
Bartelso, Ill. (62218) 222/D5
Barterville, Ky. (†40311) 237/N4
Barth, E. Germany 22/E1
Barth, Fla. (†32533) 212/B6
Barthel, Sask. 181/B2
Bartholomew (bayou), Ark. 202/G6
Bartholomew (co.), Ind. 227/F6
Bartibog Bridge, New Bruns. 170/E1
Bartica, Guyana 120/D2
Bartica, Guyana 131/B2
Bartın, Turkey 63/E2
Bartle, Cuba 158/H3
Bartle Frere (mt.), Queensland 88/H3
Bartle Frere (mt.), Queensland 95/C3
Bartlesville, Okla. (74003) 288/O1
Bartlett (dam), Ariz. 198/D5
Bartlett (res.), Ariz. 198/D5
Bartlett, Ill. (60103) 222/A5
Bartlett, Iowa (51655) 229/B7
Bartlett, Kansas (67332) 232/G4
Bartlett, Nebr. (68622) 264/F3
Bartlett○, N.H. (03812) 268/E3
Bartlett, N. Dak. (†58344) 282/N3
Bartlett, Ohio (45713) 284/G7
Bartlett, Tenn. (38134) 237/B10
Bartlett, Texas (76511) 303/G7
Bartlett Deep, Cayman Is. 156/B3
Bartletts Ferry (dam), Ala. 195/H5
Bartletts Ferry (dam), Georgia 217/B5
Bartley, Nebr. (69020) 264/D4
Bartley, W. Va. (24813) 312/C8
Barto, Pa. (19504) 294/L5
Bartolomeu Dias, Mozambique 118/F4
Barton, Ala. (†35616) 195/C1
Barton, Ark. (72312) 202/J4
Barton (co.), Kansas 232/D3
Barton, Md. (21521) 245/B2
Barton (co.), Mo. 261/D7
Barton, N. Dak. (58315) 282/K2
Barton, Ohio (43905) 284/J5
Barton, Oreg. (†97009) 291/B2
Barton, Vt. (05822) 268/C2
Barton○, Vt. (05822) 268/C2
Barton (riv.), Vt. 268/C2
Barton City, Mich. (48705) 250/F4
Barton Hills, Mich. (48105) 250/F6
Bartonsville, Pa. (18321) 294/M4
Bartonsville, Vt. (†05143) 268/B5
Barton-upon-Humber, England 13/G4
Barton-upon-Humber, England 10/F4
Bartonville, Ill. (61607) 222/D3
Bartonville, Texas (†76226) 303/F1
Bartoszyce, Poland 47/E1
Bartow, Fla. (33830) 212/E4
Bartow (co.), Georgia 217/C2
Bartow, Georgia (30413) 217/G5
Bartow, W. Va. (24920) 312/G5
Bartra Antiguo, Peru 128/E4
Bartra Nuevo, Peru 128/E4
Barú (isl.), Colombia 126/C2
Barú (vol.), Panama 154/F6
Baruipur, India 68/F2
Barus, Indonesia 85/B5
Barut, Tanjong (cape), Malaysia 85/E5
Baruun-Urt, Mongolia 77/H2
Barvas, Scotland 10/C1
Barvas, Scotland 15/B2
Barview, Oreg. (†97420) 291/C4
Bar View, Oreg. (†97136) 291/C2
Barville, Québec 174/B3
Barwani, India 68/D4
Barwick, Georgia (31720) 217/E9
Barwick, Ontario 175/B3
Barwick, Ontario 177/F5
Barwon (riv.) 88/H5
Barwon (riv.), N.S. Wales 97/D2
Barysh, U.S.S.R. 52/G4
Baryulgil, N.S. Wales 97/G1
Basalt, Colo. (81621) 208/E4
Basalt, Idaho (83218) 220/F6
Basankusu, Zaire 115/C3
Basavilbaso, Argentina 143/G6
Bas-Caraquet, New Bruns. 170/F1
Bascharage, Luxembourg 27/H9
Basco, Ill. (62313) 222/B3
Basco, Philippines 82/A2
Bascom, Fla. (32423) 212/A1
Bascom, Ohio (44809) 284/D3
Bascuñán (cape), Chile 138/A7
Basehor, Kansas (66007) 232/G2
Basel, Switzerland 39/E1
Basel, Switzerland 7/E4
Baselland (canton), Switzerland 39/E2
Baselstadt (canton), Switzerland 39/E1
Basey, Philippines 82/E5
Bashan, Conn. (†06423) 210/F2
Bashan (lake), Conn. 210/F3
Bashaw, Alberta 182/D3
Bashi, Ala. (†36784) 195/C7
Bashi (chan.), China 77/K7
Bashi (chan.), Philippines 82/A1
Bashkir A.S.S.R., U.S.S.R. 48/F4
Bashkir A.S.S.R., U.S.S.R. 52/J4
Basht, Iran 66/G5
Basic, Miss. (†39330) 256/G6
Basilan (prov.), Philippines 82/D7
Basilan, Philippines 82/C7
Basilan (isl.), Philippines 85/G4
Basilan (isl.), Philippines 82/D7
Basilan (str.), Philippines 82/C7
Basildon, England 13/J8
Basildon, England 10/G5
Basile, La. (70515) 238/E5
Basilicata (reg.), Italy 34/F4
Basim, India 68/D4
Basin, Mont. (59613) 262/D4
Basin (lake), Sask. 181/F3
Basin, Wyo. (82410) 319/E1
Basinger, Fla. (†33472) 212/F4
Basingstoke, England 10/F5
Basingstoke, England 13/F6
Basirhat, India 68/F4
Basit (cape), Syria 63/F5
Baskahegan (lake), Maine 243/H5
Başkale, Turkey 63/K3
Baskatong (res.), Que. 162/J6
Baskatong (res.), Québec 172/B3
Baskerville, Va. (23915) 307/M7
Basket (lake), Manitoba 179/C3
Baskett, Ky. (42402) 237/F5
Baskil, Turkey 63/H3
Baskin, La. (71219) 238/G2
Basking Ridge, N.J. (07920) 273/D2
Başmakçı, Turkey 63/C4
Basodino (peak), Switzerland 39/G4
Basoko, Zaire 115/D3
Basom, N.Y. (14013) 276/D4
Basongo, Zaire 115/D4
Basora (pt.), Neth. Ant. 161/E10
Basra (gov.), Iraq 66/E5
Basra, Iraq 2/M4
Basra, Iraq 66/E5
Basra, Iraq 59/E3
Basra, Iraq 54/F6
Bas-Rhin (dept.), France 28/G3
Bass (str.) 88/H7
Bass (str.), Australia 87/E9
Bass (isls.), Fr. Poly. 87/M8
Bass (lake), Ind. 227/D2
Bass (str.), Tasmania 99/C1
Bassano, Alberta 182/D4
Bassano del Grappa, Italy 34/C2
Bassas da India (isl.), Réunion 102/F7
Bassas da India (isl.), Réunion 118/F4
Bassecourt, Switzerland 39/D2
Bassein, Burma 54/L8
Bassein, Burma 72/B3
Bassein, India 68/C5
Basse-Pointe, Martinique 161/C5
Basse-Sambre, Belgium 27/F8
Basse Santa Su, Gambia 106/B6
Basse-Terre (cap.), Guadeloupe 161/A7
Basse-Terre (cap.), Guadeloupe 156/F4
Basse-Terre (isl.), Guadeloupe 161/A6
Basseterre (cap.), St. Chris.-Nevis 161/C10
Basseterre (cap.), St. Chris.-Nevis 156/F3
Basse Terre, Trin. & Tob. 161/B11
Bassett, Ark. (72313) 202/K2
Bassett, Iowa (†50645) 229/J2
Bassett, Kansas (†66749) 232/G4
Bassett, Nebr. (68714) 264/E2
Bassett, Va. (24055) 307/J7
Bassfield, Miss. (39421) 256/E8
Bass Harbor, Maine (04653) 243/G7
Bassikounou, Mauritania 106/C5
Bassin Bleu, Haiti 158/B5
Bass River, New Bruns. 170/E2
Bass River, Nova Scotia 168/E3
Bassum, W. Germany 22/C2
Basswood, Manitoba 179/B4
Basswood (lake), Minn. 255/G2
Basswood (lake), Ontario 175/B3
Båstad, Sweden 18/H8
Bastak, Iran 66/J7
Bastam, Iran 66/J2
Bastar, India 68/E5
Bastelica, France 28/B6
Bastenaken (Bastogne), Belgium 27/H9
Bastia, France 7/E4
Bastia, France 28/B6
Bastian, Va. (24314) 307/F6
Bastimentos (isl.), Panama 154/G6
Bastogne, Belgium 27/H9
Bastrop, La. (71220) 238/G1
Bastrop (co.), Texas 303/G7
Bastrop, Texas (78602) 303/G7
Bastuträsk, Sweden 18/L4
Basye, Va. (22810) 307/L3
Bas-Zaïre (prov.), Zaire 115/B4
Bata, Equat. Guinea 102/C4
Bata, Equat. Guinea 115/B3
Bataan (prov.), Philippines 82/C3
Batabanó (gulf), Cuba 158/C2
Batabanó (gulf), Cuba 156/A2
Batag (isl.), Philippines 82/E4
Batagay, U.S.S.R. 48/O3
Batala, India 68/D2
Batalha, Brazil 132/F3
Batalha, Portugal 33/B3
Batan (isls.), Philippines 54/O7
Batan, Albay (isl.), Philippines 82/E4
Batan, Batanes (isl.), Philippines 82/B2
Batan (isls.), Philippines 85/G1
Batan (isls.), Philippines 82/A2
Batanes (prov.), Philippines 82/A2
Batang, China 77/E5
Batang, China 54/L6
Batang, Indonesia 85/J2
Batangafo, Cent. Afr. Rep. 115/C2
Batangas (prov.), Philippines 82/C4
Batangas, Philippines 82/B3
Batangas, Philippines 85/G3
Batas (isl.), Philippines 82/B5
Bátaszék, Hungary 41/E3
Batatais, Brazil 135/C2
Batavia, Ill. (60510) 222/E2
Batavia (Jakarta) (cap.), Indonesia 85/H1
Batavia, Iowa (52533) 229/J7
Batavia, Mich. (†49036) 250/D7
Batavia, N.Y. (14020) 276/D5
Batavia, Ohio (45103) 284/B7
Batavia, Wis. (†53001) 317/K8
Batawa, Ontario 177/G3
Bataysk, U.S.S.R. 52/E5
Bat Cave, N.C. (28710) 281/E4
Batchelor, La. (70715) 238/G5
Batchelor, North. Terr. 93/B2
Batchtown, Ill. (62006) 222/C4
Batchwana Bay, Ontario 177/J5
Batdambang, Cambodia 54/M8
Batdambang (Battambang), Cambodia 72/D4
Bateman, Sask. 181/E5
Batemans Bay, N.S. Wales 97/F4
Bates, Ark. (72924) 202/B4
Bates, Mich. (†49690) 250/D4
Bates (co.), Mo. 261/D6
Bates (mt.), Norfolk I. 88/L5
Bates, Oreg. (97817) 291/J3
Batesburg, S.C. (29006) 296/D4
Bates City, Mo. (64011) 261/E5
Batesland, S. Dak. (57716) 298/E7
Batesville, Ala. (†36018) 195/H6
Batesville, Ark. (72501) 202/G2
Batesville, Ind. (47006) 227/G6
Batesville, Miss. (38606) 256/E2
Batesville, Ohio (43715) 284/H6
Batesville, Texas (78829) 303/E9
Batesville, Va. (22924) 307/L5
Bath, England 13/E6
Bath, England 10/E5
Bath, Ill. (62617) 222/C3
Bath, Ind. (47010) 227/H5
Bath, Jamaica 158/K6
Bath (co.), Ky. 237/O4
Bath, Maine (04530) 243/D8
Bath, Mich. (48808) 250/E6
Bath, Netherlands 27/E6
Bath, New Bruns. 170/C2
Bath○, N.H. (03740) 268/D3
Bath, N.Y. (14810) 276/F6
Bath, N.C. (27808) 281/R4
Bath, Ontario 177/H3
Bath, Pa. (18014) 294/M4
Bath, S.C. (29816) 296/D5
Bath, S. Dak. (57427) 298/N3
Bath (co.), Va. 307/J4
Bath (Berkeley Springs), W. Va. (†25411) 312/K3
Batha (riv.), Chad 111/C5
Bathgate, N. Dak. (58216) 282/P2
Bathgate, Scotland 15/C2
Bathgate, Scotland 10/C1
Bathsheba, Barbados 161/B8
Bath Springs, Tenn. (38311) 237/E10
Bathurst (isl.), Australia 87/C7
Bathurst (isl.), Canada 4/B14
Bathurst (Banjul)(cap.), Gambia 106/A6
Bathurst, N. Br. 162/K6
Bathurst, New Bruns. 170/E1
Bathurst, N. S. Wales 88/H6
Bathurst, N.S. Wales 97/E3
Bathurst (isl.), North Terr. 88/D2
Bathurst (isl.), North Terr. 93/A1
Bathurst (isl.), N.W.T. 162/F1
Bathurst (isl.), N.W.T. 146/H2
Bathurst (cape), N.W.T. 162/D1
Bathurst (cape), N.W.Terrs. 187/F2
Bathurst (inlet), N.W. Terrs. 187/H3
Bathurst (isl.), N.W. Terrs. 187/H2
Bathurst (harb.), Tasmania 99/C5
Bathurst Inlet, N.W. Terrs. 187/H3
Bathurst Island, North. Terr. 93/B1
Bathurst Island Mission, North. Terr. 88/E2
Bathurst Mines, New Bruns. 170/E1
Batié, Upper Volta 106/D7
Batı Fırat (riv.), Turkey 63/H3
Batin, Wadi al (dry riv.), Iraq 59/E4
Batin, Wadi al (dry riv.), Iraq 66/E6
Batin, Wadi al (dry riv.), Saudi Arabia 59/E4
Batina (reg.), Oman 59/G5
Batini (mt.), Fiji 86/Q10
Batiscan, Québec 172/E3
Batiscan (lake), Québec 172/E2
Batiscan (riv.), Québec 172/E2
Batley, England 13/J1
Batlow, N.S. Wales 97/E4
Batman, Turkey 63/J4
Batna, Algeria 102/C1
Batna, Algeria 106/F1
Bato, Catanduanes, Philippines 82/E4
Bato, Leyte, Philippines 82/E5
Bato-Bato, Philippines 82/C8
Batobato, Philippines 82/E7
Batoche, Sask. 181/E3
Batoche Nat'l Hist. Site, Sask. 181/E3
Baton Rouge (cap.), La. 146/J6
Baton Rouge (cap.), La. 188/H4
Baton Rouge (cap.), La. (*70801) 238/K2
Batopilas, Mexico 150/F3
Batouri, Cameroon 115/B3
Batovi, Uruguay 145/D2
Batrun, Lebanon 63/F5
Bat Shelomo, Israel 65/B2
Batson, Texas (77519) 303/K7
Batsto, N.J. (08037) 273/D4
Batsto (riv.), N.J. 273/D4
Batten Kill (riv.), N.Y. 276/O4
Batten Kill (riv.), Vt. 268/A5
Batterbee (cape), Ant. 2/N9
Batterbee (cape) 5/C3
Bätterkinden, Switzerland 39/E2
Battersea, Ontario 177/H3
Batticaloa, Sri Lanka 68/E7
Battiest, Okla. (74722) 288/S6
Batti Malv (isl.), India 68/G7
Battle (riv.) 162/E5
Battle (riv.), Alberta 182/D3
Battle, England 13/H7
Battle, England 10/G5
Battle (creek), Idaho 220/B7
Battle (riv.), Minn. 255/D3
Battle (creek), Mont. 262/G1
Battle (creek), Oreg. 291/K5
Battle (creek), Sask. 181/B6
Battle (riv.), Sask. 181/B3
Battle (creek), S. Dak. 298/C6
Battleboro, N.C. (27809) 281/O2
Battle Creek, Iowa (51006) 229/B4
Battle Creek, Mich. 188/J2
Battle Creek, Mich. (*49014) 250/D6
Battle Creek, Nebr. (68715) 264/G3
Battlefield, Mo. (†65619) 261/F8
Battleford, Sask. 162/E5
Battleford, Sask. 181/C3
Battle Ground, Ind. (47920) 227/D3
Battle Ground, Wash. (98604) 310/C5
Battle Harbour, Newf. 166/C3
Battle Harbour, Newf. 162/L5
Battle Lake, Alberta 182/C3
Battle Lake, Minn. (56515) 255/C4
Battle Mountain, Nev. (89820) 266/E2
Battles Wharf, Ala. (†36532) 195/C10
Battletown, Ky. (40104) 237/J4
Battleview, N. Dak. (58714) 282/E2
Battock (mt.), Scotland 15/F4
Battonya, Hungary 41/F3
Battrum, Sask. 181/C5
Batu (isls.), Indonesia 85/B6
Batuco, Chile 138/G3
Batu Gajah, Malaysia 72/D6
Batulaki, Philippines 82/E8
Batumi, U.S.S.R. 48/E5
Batumi, U.S.S.R. 52/F6
Batu Pahat, Malaysia 72/D7
Baturaja, Indonesia 85/C6
Baturité, Brazil 132/G4
Batusangkar, Indonesia 85/C6
Bat Yam, Israel 65/B3
Bauang, Philippines 82/C2
Baubau, Indonesia 85/G7
Bauchi (state), Nigeria 106/F6
Bauchi, Nigeria 106/F6
Baudette, Minn. (56623) 255/D2
Baudette (riv.), Minn. 255/D2
Baudh, India 68/E4
Baudó, Serranía de (mts.), Colombia 126/B5
Baudó (riv.), Colombia 126/B5
Baugé, France 28/D4
Bauld (cape), Newf. 166/C3
Bauld (cape), Newf. 162/L5
Bauline, Newf. 166/D2
Baulkham Hills, N. S. Wales 88/K4
Baulkham Hills, N.S. Wales 97/H3
Baulmes, Switzerland 39/C3
Bauma, Switzerland 39/G2
Baumann (fjord), N.W. Terrs. 187/K2
Baume-les-Dames, France 28/G4
Baures, Bolivia 136/D3
Baures (riv.), Bolivia 136/D3
Bauria, India 68/E2
Baurtregaum (mt.), Ireland 17/A7
Bauru, Brazil 120/E5
Bauru, Brazil 135/B3
Bauru, Brazil 132/D8
Bauska, U.S.S.R. 53/B2
Bauta, Cuba 158/C1
Bauta (riv.), P. Rico 161/C2
Bautzen, E. Germany 22/F3
Bauxite, Ark. (72011) 202/F4
Bavaria, Kansas (67419) 232/E3
Bavaria (state), W. Germany 22/D4
Bavarian (for.), W. Germany 22/E4
Bavarian Alps (mts.), Austria 41/A3
Bavarian Alps (range), W. Germany 22/D5
Bavidcora, Mexico 150/E2
Bavispe, Mexico 150/E1
Bavispe, Río de (riv.), Mexico 150/E1
Bawean (isl.), Indonesia 85/K1
Bawku, Ghana 106/D6
Bawlf, Alberta 182/D3
Ba Xian, China 77/J4
Baxley, Georgia (31513) 217/H7
Baxoi, China 77/E5
Baxter (co.), Ark. 202/F1
Baxter, Iowa (50028) 229/G5
Baxter, Minn. (56425) 255/D4
Baxter, Miss. (†39343) 256/F6
Baxter, Pa. (†15829) 294/D3
Baxter, Tenn. (38544) 237/K8
Baxter Springs, Kansas (66713) 232/H4
Baxterville, Miss. (†39455) 256/E8

Bay, Ark. (72411) 202/J2
Bay (Baicheng), China 77/B3
Bay (co.), Fla. 212/C6
Bay (co.), Mich. 250/E5
Bay, Mo. (65041) 261/J5
Bay, Laguna de (lake), Philippines 82/C3
Bay (prov.), Somalia 115/H3
Bayag (Calanasan), Philippines 82/C1
Bayaguana, Dom. Rep. 158/E6
Bayamhongor, Mongolia 77/E2
Bayamo, Cuba 156/C2
Bayamo, Cuba 158/H4
Bayamón (dist.), P. Rico 161/D1
Bayamón, P. Rico 161/D1
Bayamón, P. Rico 156/G1
Bayamón (riv.), P. Rico 161/D1
Bayanbaraat, Mongolia 77/G2
Bayandalay, Mongolia 77/F3
Bayan Dobo Suma, Mongolia 77/G3
Bayang, Philippines 82/E7
Bayangovĭ, Mongolia 77/F3
Bayan Har Shan (range), China 77/E5
Bayanhongor, Mongolia 77/E2
Bayan Mod, China 77/F3
Bayan Obo, China 77/G3
Bayan-Ölgiy, Mongolia 77/C2
Bayan-Öndör, Mongolia 77/E3
Bayan-Uul, Mongolia 77/E2
Bayard, Del. (†19945) 245/T6
Bayard, Iowa (50029) 229/D5
Bayard, Nebr. (69334) 264/A3
Bayard, N. Mex. (88023) 274/A6
Bayard, Sask. 181/F5
Bayard, W. Va. (26707) 312/H4
Bayat, Turkey 63/F2
Baybay, Philippines 82/E5
Baybay, Philippines 85/H3
Bayble, Scotland 15/B2
Bayboro, N.C. (28515) 281/R4
Bay Bulls, Newf. 166/D2
Bayburt, Turkey 59/D1
Bayburt, Turkey 63/J2
Bay Center, Wash. (98527) 310/A4
Bay Chimo, N.W. Terrs. 187/H3
Bay City, Mich. 188/K2
Bay City, Mich. (48706) 250/F5
Bay City, Oreg. (97107) 291/D2
Bay City, Texas (77414) 303/H9
Bay City, Wash. (†98520) 310/B4
Bay City, Wis. (54723) 317/B6
Baydarata (bay), U.S.S.R. 52/L1
Bay de Verde, Newf. 166/D2
Baydhabo, Somalia 115/H3
Baydhabo, Somalia 102/G4
Baydrag, Mongolia 77/E2
Bay du Vin (riv.), New Bruns. 170/E2
Bayerischer Wald Nat'l Park, W. Germany 22/E4
Bayeux, France 28/C3
Bayfield, Colo. (81122) 208/D8
Bayfield, New Bruns. 170/G2
Bayfield, Ontario 177/C4
Bayfield (sound), Ontario 177/B2
Bayfield (co.), Wis. 317/D3
Bayfield, Wis. (54814) 317/E2
Bayham, Ontario 177/D5
Bay Harbor Islands, Fla. (†33101) 212/B4
Bay Head, N.J. (08742) 273/E3
Bayhead, Nova Scotia 168/E3
Bayındır, Turkey 63/B3
Bayırköy, Turkey 63/B6
Baykal (lake), U.S.S.R. 54/N4
Baykal (lake), U.S.S.R. 2/Q3
Baykal (lake), U.S.S.R. 48/L4
Baykal (mts.), U.S.S.R. 48/L4
Baykan, Turkey 63/J3
Baykit, U.S.S.R. 48/K3
Baykonyr, U.S.S.R. 48/G5
Bay Lake, Fla. (†32786) 212/E3
Bay Lake, Minn. (†56444) 255/E4
Bay L'Argent, Newf. 166/D4
Baylis, Ill. (62314) 222/C4
Baylor (co.), Texas 303/E4
Bay Minette, Ala. (36507) 195/C9
Bay Mission, W. Australia 88/C3
Baynes Lake, Br. Col. 184/K5
Bayombong, Philippines 82/C2
Bayombong, Philippines 85/G2
Bayonne, France 28/C6
Bayonne, N.J. (07002) 273/B2
Bayonne Military Ocean Terminal, N.J. 273/B2
Bayou, Ky. (†42081) 237/E6
Bayou Barbary, La. (†70754) 238/M2
Bayou Bodcau (res.), Ark. 202/C7
Bayou Cane, La. (†70360) 238/J7
Bayou Chicot, La. (†70586) 238/F5
Bayou Current, La. (†71353) 238/G5
Bayou D'Arbonne (lake), La. 238/F1
Bayou Des Arc (riv.), Ark. 202/G3
Bayou Goula, La. (70716) 238/J3
Bayou La Batre, Ala. (36509) 195/B10
Bayou Meto, Ark. (†72160) 202/H5
Bayou Vista, La. (†70380) 238/H7
Bayóvar, Peru 128/B5
Bay Pines, Fla. (33504) 212/B3
Bay Point, Maine (†04548) 243/D8
Bay Point (isl.), S.C. 296/F7
Bayport, Fla. (†33512) 212/D3
Bay Port, Mich. (48720) 250/F5
Bayport, Minn. (55003) 255/F5
Bayport, N.Y. (11705) 276/O9
Bayram-Ali, U.S.S.R. 48/G6
Bayramiç, Turkey 63/B3
Bayreuth, W. Germany 22/D4
Bayrischzell, W. Germany 22/E5
Bay Roberts, Newf. 166/D2
Bays, Ky. (41310) 237/P5
Bays (lake), Ontario 177/F2
Bay Saint Lawrence, Nova Scotia 168/H1
Bay Saint Louis, Miss. (39520) 256/F10
Bayshore, Fla. (†33902) 212/E5
Bayshore, Mich. (49711) 250/D3
Bay Shore, N.Y. (11706) 276/O9
Bayshore Gardens, Fla. (33507) 212/D4
Bayside, Calif. (95524) 204/B3
Bayside, Maine (†04915) 243/F7
Bayside, New Bruns. 170/C3
Bayside, Ontario 177/G3
Bayside, Texas (78340) 303/G9
Bayside, Wis. (†53201) 317/M1
Bay Springs, Fla. (†36502) 212/B6
Bay Springs, Miss. (39422) 256/F7
Bay Springs (dam), Miss. 256/H1
Bay Springs (lake), Miss. 256/H1
Bayston Hill, England 13/E5
Baysville, Ontario 177/E2
Baytown, Texas (77520) 303/L2
Bay Tree, Alberta 182/A2
Bayuca, Spain 33/B1
Bayview, Calif. (†95501) 204/A3
Bayview, Idaho (83803) 220/B2
Bayview, Md. (†21901) 245/P2
Bay View, Mich. (49770) 250/E3
Bay View, N. Zealand 100/F3
Bay View, Ohio (†44870) 284/E3
Bay Village, Ohio (44140) 284/G9
Bayville, N.J. (08721) 273/E4
Bayville, N.Y. (11709) 276/R6
Baywood, La. (†70739) 238/K1
Baywood Park-Los Osos, Calif. (†93402) 204/E8
Baza, Spain 33/E4
Bazaar, Kansas (†66845) 232/F3
Bazaruto, Ilha do (isl.), Mozambique 118/F4
Bazas, France 28/C5
Bazhong, China 77/G5
Bazile Mills, Nebr. (†68729) 264/G2
Bazine, Kansas (67516) 232/C3
Bazman, Iran 66/M7
Bazman, Kuh-e (mt.), Iran 66/H4
Bazman, Kuh-e (mt.), Iran 59/H4
Beach (pond), Conn. 210/H2
Beach, Georgia (†31554) 217/G8
Beach, N. Dak. (58621) 282/C6
Beachburg, Ontario 177/H2
Beach City, Ohio (44608) 284/G4
Beach City, Texas (†77520) 303/L2
Beach Haven, N.J. (08008) 273/E4
Beach Haven (inlet), N.J. 273/E4
Beach Haven Crest, N.J. (†08008) 273/E4
Beach Haven Terrace, N.J. (†08008) 273/E4
Beach Lake, Pa. (18405) 294/M2
Beach Meadows, Nova Scotia 168/D4
Beachport, S. Australia 94/F7
Beachton, Georgia (†31792) 217/D9
Beachville, Ontario 177/D4
Beachwood, N.J. (08722) 273/E4
Beachwood, Ohio (44122) 284/J9
Beachy (head), England 10/G5
Beachy (head), England 13/H7
Beacon, Iowa (52534) 229/H6
Beacon, N.Y. (12508) 276/N7
Beacon, Tenn. (†38363) 237/E9
Beacon Falls○, Conn. (06403) 210/C3
Beaconia, Manitoba 179/F4
Beaconsfield, England 13/G8
Beaconsfield, Iowa (50030) 229/E7
Beaconsfield, Québec 172/H4
Beaconsfield, Tasmania 99/C3
Beadle, Sask. 181/B4
Beadle (co.), S. Dak. 298/N5
Beagle (chan.), Chile 138/E11
Beagle, Kansas (†66064) 232/G3
Beagle (gulf), North. Terr. 93/A2
Beagle, W. Australia 88/C3
Beaglebay Aboriginal Res., W. Australia 92/C2
Beagle Bay Mission, W. Australia 92/C2
Beal (range), Queensland 95/B5
Bealanana, Madagascar 118/H2
Beal City, Mich. (†48858) 250/D5
Beale (cape), Br. Col. 184/E6
Beale A.F.B., Calif. 204/D4
Bealeton, Va. (22712) 307/N3
Beallsville, Ohio (43716) 284/J6
Beallsville, Pa. (15313) 294/C5
Beals, Ky. (†42451) 237/G5
Beals○, Maine (04611) 243/H7
Beals (creek), Texas 303/C5
Beaman, Iowa (50609) 229/H4
Beaminster, England 13/E7
Beanblossom, Ind. (†46160) 227/E6
Beanblossom (creek), Ind. 227/D6
Bean City, Fla. (†33459) 212/F5
Bean Station, Tenn. (37708) 237/P8
Bear (mt.), Alaska 196/K2
Bear (lake), Alberta 182/A2
Bear (lake), Br. Col. 184/D2
Bear (creek), Colo. 208/P8
Bear (hill), Conn. 210/B2
Bear (mt.), Conn. 210/B1
Bear, Del. (19701) 245/R2
Bear, Idaho (83612) 220/B4
Bear (lake), Idaho 220/G7
Bear (riv.), Idaho 220/G7
Bear (isl.), Ireland 17/B8
Bear (riv.), Maine 243/B6
Bear (riv.), Minn. 255/E3
Bear (creek), N. Dak. 282/O7
Bear (isl.), Norway 4/B9
Bear (creek), Oreg. 291/K2
Bear (creek), Oreg. 291/E5
Bear (creek), Oreg. 291/G4
Bear (hills), Sask. 181/C4
Bear (isls.), U.S.S.R. 4/B1
Bear (lake), Utah 304/C2
Bear (riv.), Utah 304/B2
Bear (isl.), Wis. 317/E1
Bear (creek), Wyo. 319/H4
Bear (riv.), Wyo. 319/B4
Bear Branch, Ind. (†47018) 227/G7
Bearcamp (riv.), N.H. 268/E4
Bear Canyon, Alberta 182/A1
Bear Creek, Ala. (35543) 195/C2
Bearcreek, Mo. (†65649) 261/E7
Bearcreek, Mont. (59007) 262/G5
Bear Creek, N.C. (27207) 281/L3
Bear Creek, Pa. (18602) 294/F7
Bear Creek, Sask. 181/K5
Bear Creek, Wis. (54922) 317/J6
Beard, Ind. (†46041) 227/E4
Beard, W. Va. (†24946) 312/F6
Bearden, Ark. (71720) 202/E6
Bearden, Okla. (74859) 288/O4
Beardmore (glac.) 5/A8
Beardmore, Ontario 177/H5
Beardmore, Ontario 175/C3
Beards Fork, W. Va. (25014) 312/D6
Beardsley, Kansas (†67745) 232/A2
Beardsley, Minn. (56211) 255/B5
Beardstown, Ill. (62618) 222/C3
Beardstown, Ind. (†46996) 227/D2
Beardstown, Tenn. (†37097) 237/F9
Beargrass, N.C. (†27892) 281/P3
Bearhat (mt.), Mont. 262/C2
Bear in the Lodge (creek), S. Dak. 298/F6
Bear Island, Ontario 177/K5
Bear Lake, Br. Col. 184/F3
Bear Lake (co.), Idaho 220/G7
Bear Lake, Mich. (49614) 250/C4
Bear Lake, Pa. (16402) 294/C1
Bear Lodge, Wyo. (†82836) 319/E1
Bear Lodge (mts.), Wyo. 319/H1
Bearmouth, Mont. (†59832) 262/C4
Béarn (trad. prov.), France 29
Bearpaw (mts.), Mont. 262/G2
Bear River, Minn. (†55723) 255/E3
Bear River, Nova Scotia 168/C4
Bear River, Pr. Edward I. 168/F2
Bear River (range), Utah 304/C1
Bear River City, Utah (84301) 304/B2
Bear River Divide (mts.), Wyo. 319/B4
Bearsden, Scotland 15/B2
Bearskin Lake, Ontario 175/B2
Bear Spring, Tenn. (†37058) 237/F8
Beartooth (mts.), Mont. 262/G5
Beartown, W. Va. (†24817) 312/C8
Beas de Segura, Spain 33/E3
Beason, Ill. (62512) 222/D3
Beata (cape), Dom. Rep. 158/D7
Beata (cape), Dom. Rep. 156/D3
Beata (chan.), Dom. Rep. 158/C7
Beata (isl.), Dom. Rep. 158/C7
Beata (isl.), Dom. Rep. 156/D3
Beatenberg, Switzerland 39/E3
Beaton, Br. Col. 184/J5
Beatrice, Ala. (36425) 195/D7
Beatrice, Nebr. 188/G2
Beatrice, Nebr. (68310) 264/H4
Beatrice (cape), North. Terr. 88/F2
Beatrice (cape), North. Terr. 93/E3
Beattie, Kansas (66406) 232/F2
Beattock, Scotland 15/E5
Beatton (riv.), Br. Col. 184/G1
Beatton River, Br. Col. 184/G1
Beatty, Nev. (89003) 266/E6
Beatty, Oreg. (97621) 291/F5
Beatty, Sask. 181/G3
Beattyville, Ky. (41311) 237/O5
Beau (lake), Québec 172/H2
Beaubier, Sask. 181/G6
Beaubois, New Bruns. 170/E1
Beaucaire, France 28/F6
Beauce (co.), Québec 172/G3
Beauceville, Québec 172/G3
Beaucoup, Ill. (†62263) 222/D5
Beaudesert, Queensland 95/E6
Beauford, Minn. (†56037) 255/D7
Beaufort (sea) 4/B16
Beaufort (sea) 146/D2
Beaufort (sea), Alaska 196/K1
Beaufort, Malaysia 85/F4
Beaufort, Mo. (65013) 261/K6
Beaufort (co.), N.C. 281/R4
Beaufort, N.C. (28516) 281/R5
Beaufort (sea), N.W.T. 162/C1
Beaufort (sea), N.W. Terrs. 187/D2
Beaufort (co.), S.C. 296/F7
Beaufort, S.C. (29902) 296/F7
Beaufort, Victoria 97/B5
Beaufort (sea), Yukon 187/E2
Beaufort Marine Air Sta., S.C. 296/F7
Beaufort West, S. Africa 118/C6
Beauharnois (co.), Québec 172/C4
Beauharnois, Québec 172/D4
Beaulac, Québec 172/F4
Beaulieu, Minn. (†56557) 255/C3
Beauly, Scotland 10/D2
Beauly, Scotland 15/D3
Beauly (riv.), Scotland 15/D3
Beaumaris (bay), Victoria 97/J6
Beaumaris (bay), Victoria 88/L8
Beaumaris, Wales 13/C4
Beaumaris, Wales 10/D4
Beaumont, Alberta 182/D3
Beaumont, Belgium 27/E8
Beaumont, Calif. (92223) 204/J10
Beaumont, Kansas (67012) 232/F4
Beaumont, Miss. (39423) 256/G8
Beaumont, N. Zealand 100/B6
Beaumont, Québec 172/F3
Beaumont (pt.), St. Lucia 161/F6
Beaumont, Texas 146/J6
Beaumont, Texas 188/H4
Beaumont, Texas (*77701) 303/K7
Beaune, France 28/F4
Beauport, Québec 172/J3
Beaupré, Québec 172/G2
Beauraing, Belgium 27/F8
Beauregard (par.), La. 238/D5
Beauregard, Miss. (†39191) 256/D7
Beauséjour, Manitoba 179/F4
Beauty, Ky. (41203) 237/S5
Beauty Point, Tasmania 99/C3
Beauvais, France 28/E3
Beauval, Sask. 181/L3
Beauvallon, Alberta 182/E3
Beaux Arts Village, Wash. (†98004) 310/B2
Beaver (riv.) 162/F5
Beaver, Alaska (99724) 196/J1
Beaver (creek), Alaska 196/J1
Beaver (riv.), Alberta 182/E2
Beaver, Ark. (72613) 202/C1
Beaver (lake), Ark. 202/C1
Beaver (creek), Colo. 208/M3
Beaver (creek), Idaho 220/F5
Beaver, Iowa (50031) 229/E4
Beaver, Kansas (67517) 232/D3
Beaver (creek), Kansas 232/A2
Beaver, La. (†71463) 238/E5
Beaver (isl.), Mich. 250/D3
Beaver (lake), Mich. 250/F4
Beaver (creek), Mont. 262/J2
Beaver (creek), Nebr. 264/D5
Beaver (riv.), Newf. 166/B3
Beaver (brook), N.H. 268/E6
Beaver (brook), N.J. 273/C2
Beaver (riv.), N.Y. 276/K3
Beaver (creek), N. Dak. 282/K7
Beaver (creek), N. Dak. 282/B5
Beaver (lake), N. Dak. 282/L7
Beaver, Ohio (45613) 284/E7
Beaver (co.), Okla. 288/E1
Beaver, Okla. (73932) 288/F1
Beaver (creek), Okla. 288/K6
Beaver (riv.), Okla. 288/F1
Beaver, Oreg. (97108) 291/D2
Beaver (co.), Pa. 294/B4
Beaver, Pa. (15009) 294/B4
Beaver (riv.), Pa. 294/B4
Beaver (hills), Sask. 181/H4
Beaver (riv.), Sask. 181/L4
Beaver (creek), S. Dak. 298/A6
Beaver (co.), Utah 304/A5
Beaver, Utah (84713) 304/B5
Beaver (mts.), Utah 304/A5
Beaver (riv.), Utah 304/A5
Beaver, Wash. (98305) 310/A2
Beaver (Glen Hedrick), W. Va. (25813) 312/D7
Beaver, Wis. (54105) 317/K5
Beaver (creek), Wyo. 319/H2
Beaver (creek), Wyo. 319/D3
Beaverbank, Nova Scotia 168/E4
Beaver Bay, Minn. (55601) 255/G3
Beaver Brook Station, New Bruns. 170/E1
Beaver City, Nebr. (68926) 264/E4
Beaver Cove, Br. Col. 184/D5
Beaver Creek, Md. (†21740) 245/H2
Beaver Creek, Minn. (56116) 255/B7
Beavercreek, Ohio (†45690) 284/C6
Beavercreek, Oreg. (97004) 291/B2
Beaver Creek, Yukon 187/D3
Beaver Creek Fork, Humboldt (riv.), Nev. 266/F1
Beaver Crossing, Nebr. (68313) 264/G4
Beaverdale, Pa. (15921) 294/E5
Beaverdam, Alberta 182/E2
Beaver Dam, Ky. (42320) 237/H6
Beaverdam, Ohio (45808) 284/C4
Beaverdam, Va. (23015) 307/N5
Beaver Dam, Wis. (53916) 317/J9
Beaver Dam (lake), Wis. 317/J9
Beaver Dams, N.Y. (14812) 276/F6
Beaver Dam Wash (creek), Utah 304/A6
Beaverdell, Br. Col. 184/H5
Beaver Falls, N.Y. (13305) 276/K3
Beaver Falls, Pa. (15010) 294/B4
Beaver Harbour, New Bruns. 170/D3
Beaverhead (mts.), Idaho 220/E4
Beaverhead (co.), Mont. 262/C5
Beaverhead (riv.), Mont. 262/D5
Beaverhill (lake), Alberta 182/D3
Beaverhill (lake), Manitoba 179/J3
Beaver Lake, Alberta 182/E2
Beaver Lake, N.J. (†07416) 273/D1
Beaverlett, Va. (23016) 307/R6
Beaverlodge, Alberta 182/A2
Beaverlodge (lake), Sask. 181/L2
Beaver Meadows, Pa. (18216) 294/L4
Beaver Mines, Alberta 182/C5
Beaver Park, Sask. 181/J6
Beaver River, N.Y. (13306) 276/L3
Beaver River Flow (lake), N.Y. 276/K3
Beaver Springs, Pa. (17812) 294/H4
Beaverton, Ala. (35544) 195/B3
Beaverton, Mich. (48612) 250/E5
Beaverton, Ontario 177/E3
Beaverton, Oreg. (97005) 291/A2
Beavertown, Pa. (17813) 294/H4
Beaverville, Ill. (60912) 222/F3
Beawar, India 68/C3
Beazer, Alberta 182/D5
Beazley, Argentina 143/C3
Bebedouro, Brazil 132/D8
Bebedouro, Brazil 135/B2
Bebee, W. Va. (†26155) 312/E3
Bebington, England 10/F2
Bebington, England 13/G2
Bebra, W. Germany 22/C3
Bécancour, Québec 172/E3
Bécancour (riv.), Québec 172/F3
Beccles, England 13/J5
Beccles, England 10/G4
Bečej, Yugoslavia 45/E3
Becerreá, Spain 33/C1
Béchar, Algeria 102/B1
Béchar, Algeria 106/D2
Bechar (pt.), W. Australia 88/A3
Bechard, Sask. 181/G5
Becharof (lake), Alaska 196/G3
Bechyn, Minn. (†56275) 255/C6
Bechyně, Czech. 41/C2
Becida, Minn. (56625) 255/C3
Beckemeyer, Ill. (62219) 222/D5
Becker (co.), Minn. 255/C4
Becker, Minn. (55308) 255/E5
Becker, Miss. (38825) 256/G3
Becket○, Mass. (01223) 249/B3
Becket, Mont. (†59941) 262/G4
Beckham (co.), Okla. 288/G4
Beckley, W. Va. (25801) 312/D7
Beckton, Wyo. (†82801) 319/E1
Beckville, Texas (75631) 303/K5
Beckwourth, Calif. (96129) 204/E4
Bečva (riv.), Czech. 41/E2
Bedale, England 13/F3
Bédarieux, France 28/E6
Beddington○, Maine (†04622) 243/H6
Beddouza, Ras (cape), Morocco 106/C2
Bedele, Ethiopia 111/G6
Bedeque (bay), Pr. Edward I. 168/E2
Bedessa, Ethiopia 111/H6
Bedford, England 10/F4
Bedford, England 13/G5
Bedford (pt.), Grenada 161/D8
Bedford, Ind. (47421) 227/E7
Bedford, Iowa (50833) 229/D7
Bedford, Ky. (40006) 237/L3
Bedford○, Mass. (01730) 249/B6
Bedford, Mich. (49020) 250/D6
Bedford, Mo. (†64643) 261/F3
Bedford○, N.H. (03102) 268/D6
Bedford (basin), Nova Scotia 168/E4
Bedford, Ohio (44146) 284/H9
Bedford (co.), Pa. 294/E6
Bedford, Pa. (15522) 294/F5
Bedford, Québec 172/E4
Bedford (co.), Tenn. 237/J9
Bedford, Texas (76021) 303/F2
Bedford (co.), Va. 307/J6
Bedford (I.C.), Va. (24523) 307/J6
Bedford, Wyo. (83112) 319/A3
Bedford Heights, Ohio (†44146) 284/J9
Bedford Hills, N.Y. (10507) 276/N8
Bedford Park, Ill. (†60601) 222/B6
Bedfordshire (co.), England 13/G5
Bedford Valley, Pa. (†15522) 294/E6
Bedias, Texas (77831) 303/J7
Bedington, W. Va. (†25401) 312/L3
Bedlington, England 13/F2
Bedlington, England 10/E3
Bedminster○, N.J. (07921) 273/D2
Bedminster, Pa. (18910) 294/M5
Bedouaram (well), Niger 106/G5
Bedourie, Queensland 95/A5
Bedourie, Queensland 88/F4
Bedretto, Switzerland 39/G4
Bedrock, Colo. (81411) 208/B6
Bedsted, Denmark 21/B4
Bedwas and Machen, Wales 13/B6
Bedwellty, Wales 13/B6
Bedworth, England 13/F5
Bedworth, England 10/F4
Będzin, Poland 47/B3
Bee, Nebr. (68314) 264/H3
Bee (co.), Texas 303/G9
Beebe, Ark. (72012) 202/G3
Beebe Plain, Québec 172/E4
Beebe Plain, Vt. (05823) 268/C2
Beebe River, N.H. (03219) 268/D4
Bee Branch, Ark. (72013) 202/F3
Beech Bluff, Tenn. (38313) 237/D9
Beech Bottom, W. Va. (26030) 312/E2
Beech Creek, Ky. (42321) 237/G6
Beech Creek, Pa. (16822) 294/G3
Beecher, Ill. (60401) 222/F2
Beecher City, Ill. (62414) 222/E4
Beecher Falls, Vt. (05902) 268/D2
Beecher Island, Colo. (†80758) 208/P3
Beech Fork (riv.), Ky. 237/L5
Beech Grove, Ind. (46107) 227/E5
Beech Grove, Ky. (42322) 237/G5
Beechgrove, Tenn. (37018) 237/J9
Beech Island, S.C. (29842) 296/D5
Beechwood, Mass. (02025) 249/F8
Beechwood, Mich. (†49423) 250/C6
Beechwood, New Bruns. 170/C2
Beechwood, N.S. Wales 97/G2
Beechwood Village, Ky. (40359) 237/K2
Beechworth, Victoria 97/D5
Beechy, Sask. 181/D5
Beechy Point, Alaska (†99723) 196/H1
Beedeville, Ark. (72014) 202/H3
Beekman, La. (†71220) 238/G1
Beeler, Kansas (67518) 232/B3
Bee Log, N.C. (†28714) 281/E3
Beemer, Nebr. (68716) 264/H3
Beenleigh, Queensland 88/J5
Beer Ef'e (well), Israel 65/C5
Be'eri, Israel 65/A5
Bee Ridge, Fla. (†33578) 212/D4
Be'er Menuha, Israel 65/D5
Beernem, Belgium 27/C6
Be'er Ora, Israel 65/D5
Beersheba (Be'er Sheva), Israel 65/B5
Beersheba Springs, Tenn. (37305) 237/K10
Beer Sheva' (dry riv.), Israel 65/B5
Beersville, New Bruns. 170/E2
Be'er Tuveya, Israel 65/B4
Beeskow, E. Germany 22/F2
Beesleys Point, N.J. (†08226) 273/D5
Beeson, W. Va. (24714) 312/D8
Bee Spring, Ky. (42207) 237/J6
Beeston and Stapleford, England 13/F5
Beeton, Ontario 177/E3
Beetown, Wis. (53802) 317/E10
Beeville, Texas (78102) 303/G9
Befale, Zaire 115/D3
Befandriana, Madagascar 118/H3
Beg (lake), N. Ireland 17/J2
Bega, N. S. Wales 88/J7
Bega, N.S. Wales 97/E5
Begemdir (prov.), Ethiopia 111/G5
Beger, Mongolia 77/E2
Beggs, Okla. (74421) 288/P3
Begnins, Switzerland 39/B4
Béhague (pt.), Fr. Guiana 131/F3
Behan (lake), Alberta 182/E2
Behbehan, Iran 66/G5
Behistun (ruins), Iran 66/E3
Behm Canal (inlet), Alaska 196/N2
Behshahr, Iran 66/H2
Bei'an (Pehan), China 77/L2
Beica, Ethiopia 111/F6
Beihai (Pakhoi), China 77/G7
Beijing (Peking) (cap.), Peoples Rep. of China 54/N5
Beijing (Peking) (cap.), Peoples Rep. of China 77/J3
Beilen, Netherlands 27/K3
Beinn a Ghlo (mt.), Scotland 15/E4
Beinn Bhan (mt.), Scotland 15/C3
Beinn Bheigeir (mt.), Scotland 15/B5
Beinn Dearg (mt.), Scotland 15/D3
Beinn Dearg (mt.), Scotland 15/E4
Beinn Dhorain (mt.), Scotland 15/E2
Beinn Dorain (mt.), Scotland 15/D4
Beinn Eighe (mt.), Scotland 15/C3
Beinwil am See, Switzerland 39/F2
Beira, Mozambique 118/F3
Beira, Mozambique 102/F7
Beira, Somalia 115/J2
Beirne, Ark. (71721) 202/D6
Beirut (cap.), Lebanon 54/E6
Beirut (cap.), Lebanon 59/C3
Beirut (cap.), Lebanon 63/F6
Beiseker, Alberta 182/D4
Beishan, China 77/E3
Beitbridge, Zimbabwe 118/E4
Beit Fajjar, West Bank 65/C4
Beit Guvrin, Israel 65/B4
Beith, Scotland 10/A1
Beith, Scotland 15/D5
Beit Hanina, West Bank 65/C4
Beit Hanun, Gaza Strip 65/A4
Beit Jala, West Bank 65/C4
Beit Lahm (Bethlehem), West Bank 65/C4
Beit Nuba, West Bank 65/C4
Beit Sahur, West Bank 65/C4
Beiuş, Romania 45/F2
Beja (dist.), Portugal 33/C3
Beja, Portugal 33/C3
Béja, Tunisia 106/F1
Bejaïa, Algeria 106/F1
Bejaïa, Algeria 102/C1
Béjar, Spain 33/D2
Bejestan, Iran 59/G3
Bejestan, Iran 66/K3
Bejhi (riv.), Pakistan 68/B3
Bejou, Minn. (56516) 255/B3
Bejucal, Cuba 158/C1
Bejucal, Cuba 156/A2
Bekasi, Indonesia 85/H2
Békés (co.), Hungary 41/F3
Békés, Hungary 41/F3
Békéscsaba, Hungary 41/F3
Bekily, Madagascar 118/G4
Bekwai, Ghana 106/D7
Bel, La. (†70658) 238/D6
Bela, Pakistan 68/B3
Bela, Pakistan 59/J4
Bélabo, Cameroon 115/B3
Bela Crkva, Yugoslavia 45/E3
Bélair, Manitoba 179/F4
Bel Air, Md. (21014) 245/N2
Bélair, Québec 172/H3
Bel Alton, Md. (20611) 245/L7
Belas, Portugal 33/A1
Belau (Palau) 87/D5
Bela Vista, Angola 115/C6
Bela Vista, Brazil 120/D5
Bela Vista, Mato Grosso, Brazil 132/C8
Bela Vista, Rondônia, Brazil 132/H10
Bela Vista, Mozambique 118/E5
Bela Vista de Goiás, Brazil 132/D7
Belawan, Indonesia 85/B5
Belaya (riv.), U.S.S.R. 7/K3
Belaya (riv.), U.S.S.R. 52/H3
Belaya Tserkov', U.S.S.R. 52/C5
Belbeck, Sask. 181/F5
Belbutte, Sask. 181/D2
Bełchatów, Poland 47/D3
Belcher, Ky. (41513) 237/S6
Belcher, La. (71004) 238/C1
Belcher (isls.), N.W.T. 146/K4
Belcher (isl.), N.W.T. 162/H4
Belcher (chan.), N.W. Terrs. 187/J2
Belcheragh, Afghanistan 68/B1
Belcheragh, Afghanistan 59/J2
Belchertown, Mass. (01007) 249/E3
Belchertown○, Mass. (01007) 249/E3
Belchite, Spain 33/F2
Belcourt, N. Dak. (58316) 282/L2
Belcross, N.C. (†27921) 281/S2
Belden, Calif. (95915) 204/D3
Belden, Miss. (38826) 256/G2
Belden, Nebr. 264/G2
Belden, N. Dak. (58715) 282/F3
Beldenville, Wis. (54003) 317/A6
Belding, Mich. (48809) 250/D5
Belebey, U.S.S.R. 52/H4
Belém, Brazil 2/G6
Belém, Brazil 120/E3
Belém, Brazil 132/E3
Belém, Portugal 33/A1
Belén, Argentina 143/C2
Belén, Chile 138/B1
Belén, Honduras 154/C3
Belen, Miss. (38609) 256/D2
Belen, N. Mex. (87002) 274/C4
Belén, Panama 154/G6
Belén, Paraguay 144/D3
Belén, Uruguay 145/B1
Belén (range), Uruguay 145/C1
Belén de los Andaquíes, Colombia 126/C7
Belep (isls.), New Caled. 87/G7
Belet Weyne, Somalia 115/J3
Belet Weyne, Somalia 102/G4
Belev, U.S.S.R. 52/E4
Belfair, Wash. (98528) 310/C3
Belfast, Maine (04915) 243/F7
Belfast, N.Y. (14711) 276/D6
Belfast (cap.), N. Ireland 7/D3
Belfast (dist.), N. Ireland 17/J2
Belfast (cap.), N. Ireland 10/D3
Belfast (cap.), N. Ireland 17/J2
Belfast (inlet), N. Ireland 17/K2
Belfast, Tenn. (37019) 237/H10
Belfast Lough (inlet), N. Ireland 10/D3
Belfaux, Switzerland 39/D3
Belfield, N. Dak. (58622) 282/D6
Belford, England 13/F2
Belford, N.J. (07718) 273/E3
Belfort (terr.), France 28/G4
Belfort, France 28/G4
Belfry, Ky. (41514) 237/S5
Belfry, Mont. (59008) 262/H5
Belgaum, India 68/C5
Belgique, Mo. (†63775) 261/N7
Belgium 2/K3
Belgium 7/E3

Bering 337

BELGIUM 27
Belgium, Ill. (†61883) 222/F3
Belgium, Wis. (53004) 317/L8
Belgorod, U.S.S.R. 7/H3
Belgorod, U.S.S.R. 52/E4
Belgorod, U.S.S.R. 48/D4
Belgorod-Dnestrovskiy, U.S.S.R. 52/D5
Belgrade, Maine (04917) 243/D7
Belgrade○, Maine (04917) 243/D7
Belgrade, Minn. (56312) 255/C5
Belgrade, Mo. (63622) 261/L7
Belgrade, Mont. (59714) 262/E5
Belgrade, Nebr. (68623) 264/G3
Belgrade (cap.), Yugoslavia 7/G4
Belgrade (cap.), Yugoslavia 2/K3
Belgrade (cap.), Yugoslavia 45/E3
Belgrade Lakes, Maine (04918) 243/D6
Belgrave, Ontario 177/C4
Belgrave Heights, Victoria 97/J5
Belgrave South, Victoria 97/K5
Belgreen, Ala. (†35653) 195/C2
Belhaven, N.C. (27810) 281/R3
Belic, Cuba 158/G4
Belice (riv.), Italy 34/D6
Beli Manastir, Yugoslavia 45/D3
Belington, W. Va. (26250) 312/F4
Belitung (Billiton) (isl.), Indonesia 85/D6
Belize 2/E5
Belize 146/K8
BELIZE 154/C2
Belize (riv.), Belize 154/C2
Belize City, Belize 154/C2
Bélizon, Fr. Guiana 131/E3
Belk, Ala. (35545) 195/C3
Belknap, Ill. (†62995) 222/E6
Belknap, Iowa (†52537) 229/J7
Belknap, Mont. (†59874) 262/A3
Belknap (co.), N.H. 268/D4
Belknap (mt.), N.H. 268/E5
Belknap (peak), Utah 304/B5
Belkofski, Alaska (†99612) 196/F3
Bell, Calif. (90201) 204/C11
Bell, Fla. (32619) 212/D2
Bell (co.), Ky. 237/O7
Bell (isl.), Newf. 166/D2
Bell (isl.), Newf. 166/C3
Bell (isl.), Newf. 162/L5
Bell (pen.), N.W. Terrs. 187/K3
Bell (riv.), Que. 162/J6
Bell (riv.), Québec 174/B3
Bell (co.), Texas 303/G6
Bella Bella, Br. Col. 184/D4
Bellac, France 28/D4
Bellaco, Uruguay 145/B3
Bella Coola, Br. Col. 184/D4
Bella Coola (riv.), Br. Col. 184/D4
Belladère, Haiti 158/C6
Bella Flor, Bolivia 136/A2
Bellaghy, N. Ireland 17/H2
Bellagio, Italy 34/B2
Bellaire, Kansas (66934) 232/D2
Bellaire, Mich. (49615) 250/D4
Bellaire, Ohio (43906) 284/J5
Bellaire, Texas (77401) 303/J2
Bellamy, Ala. (36901) 195/B6
Bellarmin, Québec 172/G4
Bellarthur, N.C. (27811) 281/O3
Bellary, India 68/D5
Bellata, N.S. Wales 97/E1
Bella Unión, Uruguay 145/B1
Bella Villa, Mo. (†63101) 261/R4
Bella Vista, Corrientes, Argentina 143/E2
Bella Vista, Tucumán, Argentina 143/D2
Bella Vista, Ark. (†72712) 202/B1
Bella Vista, Bolivia 136/E3
Bella Vista, Salar de (salt dep.), Chile 138/B3
Bella Vista, Paraguay 144/D3
Bella Vista, Paraguay 144/E5
Bellavista, Peru 128/C5
Bell Bay, Tasmania 99/C3
Bellbird-Cessnock, N.S. Wales 97/F3
Bellbrook, Ohio (45305) 284/C6
Bell Buckle, Tenn. (37020) 237/J9
Bellburns, Newf. 166/C3
Bell Center, Wis. (†54631) 317/E9
Bell City, La. (70630) 238/D6
Bell City, Mo. (63735) 261/N8
Belle (riv.), Mich. 250/G6
Belle, Mo. (65013) 261/J6
Belle, W. Va. (25015) 312/C6
Belleair, Fla. (33540) 212/B2
Belleair Beach, Fla. (†33540) 212/B2
Belleair Bluffs, Fla. (33540) 212/B3
Belleair Shores, Fla. (†33540) 212/B3
Belle-Anse, Haiti 158/C6
Belle Center, Ohio (43310) 284/C4
Belle Chasse, La. (70037) 238/O4
Bellechasse (co.), Québec 172/G3
Bellechester, Minn. (†55027) 255/F6
Belle Côte, Nova Scotia 168/G2
Belle D'Eau, La. (†71330) 238/F4
Belledune, New Bruns. 170/E1
Belleek, N. Ireland 17/E3
Bellefleur, New Bruns. 170/C1
Bellefond, New Bruns. 170/E1
Bellefont, Kansas (†67876) 232/C4
Bellefontaine, Martinique 161/C6
Bellefontaine, Miss. (39737) 256/F3
Bellefontaine, Mo. (†63017) 261/N2
Bellefontaine, Ohio (43311) 284/C5
Bellefontaine Neighbors, Mo. (†63137) 261/R2
Bellefonte, Ark. (†72601) 202/D1
Bellefonte, Del. (19809) 245/S1
Bellefonte, Pa. (16823) 294/G4
Belle Fourche (riv.) 188/F2
Belle Fourche, S. Dak. (57717) 298/B4
Belle Fourche (res.), S. Dak. 298/B4
Belle Fourche (riv.), S. Dak. 298/C4
Belle Fourche (riv.), Wyo. 319/H1
Bellegarde, Sask. 181/K6
Belle Glade, Fla. (33430) 212/F5
Belle Glade Camp, Fla. (†33430) 212/F5
Belle Haven, Va. (23306) 307/S5
Belle-Île (isl.), France 28/B4
Belle Isle (str.), Canada 146/N5
Belle Isle (str.), Canada 2/G3
Belle Isle, Fla. (†32801) 212/E3
Belleisle (bay), New Bruns. 170/E3
Belle Isle (isl.), Newf. 166/C3
Belle Isle (str.), Newf. 166/C3
Belle Isle (str.), Newf. 162/L5
Belleisle Creek, New Bruns. 170/E3
Belle-Marche, Nova Scotia 168/H2
Belle Mead, N.J. (08502) 273/D3
Bellemeade, Ky. (†40201) 237/K2
Belle Meade, Tenn. (37205) 237/H8
Belle Mina, Ala. (35615) 195/E1
Bellemont, Ariz. (86015) 198/D3
Belleoram, Newf. 166/C4
Belleplain, N.J. (†08270) 273/D5
Belleplaine, Barbados 161/B8
Belle Plaine, Iowa (52208) 229/J5
Belle Plaine, Kansas (67013) 232/E4
Belle Plaine, Minn. (56011) 255/E6
Belle Plaine, Sask. 181/F5
Belle Prairie City, Ill. (†62828) 222/E5
Belle Rive, Ill. (62810) 222/E5
Belle River, Minn. (†56319) 255/C5
Belle River, Ontario 177/B5
Belle Rose, La. (70341) 238/K3
Bellerose, N.Y. (11426) 276/P7
Belle Terre, N.Y. (†11777) 276/O9
Belleterre, Québec 174/B3
Belle Union, Ind. (†46121) 227/D5
Belle Valley, Ohio (43717) 284/G6
Belle Vernon, Pa. (15012) 294/C5
Belleview, Fla. (32620) 212/D2
Belleview, Manitoba 179/B5
Belleview, Mo. (63623) 261/L7
Belle View, Va. (22307) 307/T3
Belleville, Ark. (72824) 202/D3
Belleville, Fla. (†31636) 212/C1
Belleville, France 28/F4
Belleville, Ill. 188/J3
Belleville, Ill. (*62220) 222/B3
Belleville, Kansas (66935) 232/E2
Belleville, Mich. (48111) 250/F6
Belleville, N.J. (07109) 273/B2
Belleville, N.Y. (13611) 276/H3
Belleville, Ontario 177/G3
Belleville, Pa. (17004) 294/G4
Belleville, W. Va. (26133) 312/C4
Belleville, Wis. (53508) 317/G10
Bellevue, Alberta 182/C5
Bellevue, Idaho (83313) 220/D6
Bellevue, Iowa (52031) 229/M4
Bellevue, Ky. (41073) 237/S1
Bellevue, Md. (†21662) 245/O6
Bellevue, Mich. (49021) 250/E6
Bellevue, Nebr. (68005) 264/J3
Bellevue, Newf. 166/D2
Bellevue, Ohio (44811) 284/E3
Bellevue, Pa. (15202) 294/B6
Bellevue, Sask. 181/F3
Bellevue, Texas (76228) 303/F4
Bellevue, Wash. (*98004) 310/B2
Belley, France 28/F5
Bell Farm, Ky. (†42647) 237/M7
Bellflower, Calif. (90706) 204/C11
Bellflower, Ill. (61724) 222/E3
Bellflower, Mo. (63333) 261/K4
Bellfountain, Oreg. (†97456) 291/D3
Bell Gardens, Calif. (90201) 204/C11
Bellin, Que. 162/J3
Bellin, Québec 174/F1
Bellingen, N.S. Wales 97/G2
Bellingham, England 13/E2
Bellingham, Mass. (02019) 249/J4
Bellingham○, Mass. (02019) 249/J4
Bellingham, Minn. (56212) 255/B5
Bellingham, Wash. 188/B1
Bellingham, Wash. (98225) 310/C2
Bellingham, Wash. 310/80
Bellingshausen (sea), Ant. 2/E9
Bellingshausen (sea) 5/C14
Bellinzona, Switzerland 39/H4
Bell-Irving (riv.), Br. Col. 184/C2
Bellis, Alberta 182/D2
Belliveau Cove, Nova Scotia 168/B4
Bellmawr, N.J. (08031) 273/B3
Bellmead, Texas (76704) 303/H6
Bellmont, Ill. (62811) 222/F5
Bellmore, Ind. (47830) 227/C5
Bellmore, N.Y. (11710) 276/R7
Bello, Colombia 126/C4
Bello, Colombia 120/B2
Bellona (reefs), New Caled. 87/G8
Bellona (isl.), Solomon Is. 86/D3
Bellot (str.), N.W.T. 162/G1
Bellot (str.), N.W. Terrs. 187/J2
Bellows Falls, Vt. (05101) 268/C5
Belloy, Alberta 182/A2
Bellport, N.Y. (11713) 276/P9
Bell Rock, N.W. Terrs. 187/G3
Bell Rock (isl.), Scotland 15/F4
Bells, Tenn. (38006) 237/C9
Bells, Texas (75414) 303/H4
Bellsbank, Scotland 15/D5
Bellshill, Scotland 15/C2
Bellsite, Manitoba 179/B2
Bellsund, Norway 18/C2
Belluno (prov.), Italy 34/D1
Belluno, Italy 34/D1
Bellview, Ala. (†36452) 195/D7
Bellview, N. Mex. (88111) 274/F4
Bell Ville, Argentina 143/D3
Bell Ville, Argentina 120/C6
Bellville, Georgia (30414) 217/H6
Bellville, Ohio (44813) 284/E4
Bellville, S. Africa 118/F6
Bellville, Texas (77418) 303/H8
Bellvue, Colo. (80512) 208/J1
Bellwald, Switzerland 39/F4
Bellwood, Ala. (36313) 195/G8
Bellwood, Ill. (60104) 222/B5
Bellwood, La. (†71468) 238/D3
Bellwood, Nebr. (68624) 264/G3
Bellwood, Pa. (16617) 294/F4
Belly (riv.), Alberta 182/D5
Belmar, N.J. (07719) 273/E3
Bélmez, Spain 33/D3
Belmond, Iowa (50421) 229/F3
Belmont, Ala. (†35450) 195/C5
Belmont, Calif. (94002) 204/J3
Belmont, Georgia (†30501) 217/E2
Belmont, Kansas (67014) 232/D4
Belmont, Ky. (40105) 237/K5
Belmont, La. (71406) 238/C3
Belmont○, Maine (†04915) 243/E7
Belmont, Manitoba 179/C5
Belmont○, Mass. (02178) 249/C6
Belmont, Miss. (38827) 256/H1
Belmont, Mont. (†59046) 262/G4
Belmont○, N.H. (03220) 268/E5
Belmont, N.Y. (14813) 276/E6
Belmont, N. Zealand 100/B2
Belmont, N.C. (28012) 281/H4
Belmont, Nova Scotia 168/E3
Belmont (co.), Ohio 284/J5
Belmont, Ohio (43718) 284/J5
Belmont, Ontario 177/C5
Belmont, Wash. (99104) 310/H3
Belmont, W. Va. (26134) 312/D4
Belmont, Wis. (53510) 317/F10
Belmonte, Brazil 132/G6
Belmonte, Portugal 33/C2
Belmonte, Spain 33/E3
Belmopan (cap.), Belize 146/K8
Belmopan (cap.), Belize 154/C2
Belmore, N.S. Wales 97/J4
Belmore, Ohio (45815) 284/B3
Belmullet, Ireland 17/B3
Bel-Nor, Mo. (†63101) 261/P2
Belo, W. Va. (†25661) 312/B7
Beloeil, Belgium 27/D7
Beloeil, Québec 172/D4
Belogorsk, U.S.S.R. 54/O4
Belogorsk, U.S.S.R. 48/N4
Belogradchik, Bulgaria 45/F4
Belo Horizonte, Brazil 2/G6
Belo Horizonte, Brazil 120/E4
Belo Horizonte, Brazil 132/F7
Belo Horizonte, Brazil 135/D1
Beloit, Ala. (†36759) 195/D6
Beloit, Kansas (67420) 232/D2
Beloit, Ohio (44609) 284/J4
Beloit, Wis. 188/J2
Beloit, Wis. (53511) 317/H10
Belomorsk, U.S.S.R. 48/D3
Belomorsk, U.S.S.R. 52/D2
Belorado, Spain 33/E1
Belorechensk, U.S.S.R. 52/E6
Beloretsk, U.S.S.R. 52/J4
Beloretsk, U.S.S.R. 48/F4
Belo-Tsiribihina, Madagascar 118/G3
Belovo, U.S.S.R. 48/J4
Beloye (lake), U.S.S.R. 48/D3
Beloye (lake), U.S.S.R. 52/E2
Belozersk, U.S.S.R. 52/E3
Belp, Switzerland 39/D3
Belpre, Kansas (67519) 232/C4
Belpre, Ohio (45714) 284/G7
Bel-Ridge, Mo. (†63101) 261/P2
Belshaw, Ind. (†46356) 227/C2
Belt, Mont. (59412) 262/E3
Belted (range), Nev. 266/E5
Belterra, Brazil 132/C3
Belton, Ky. (42324) 237/H6
Belton, Mo. (64012) 261/C5
Belton, S.C. (29627) 296/C2
Belton, Texas (76513) 303/G7
Beltra (lake), Ireland 17/C4
Beltrami (co.), Minn. 255/C2
Beltrami, Minn. (56517) 255/B3
Beltsville, Md. (20705) 245/G3
Bel'tsy, U.S.S.R. 7/G4
Bel'tsy, U.S.S.R. 52/C5
Belturbet, Ireland 17/G3
Beluga (lake), Alaska 196/B1
Belumut, Gunong (mt.), Malaysia 72/D7
Belush'ya Guba, U.S.S.R. 4/B7
Belush'ya Guba, U.S.S.R. 52/H1
Belva, W. Va. (26656) 312/D6
Belvedere, Calif. (94920) 204/H2
Belvedere, Georgia (†30032) 217/L1
Belvidere, Ill. (61008) 222/E1
Belvidere, Kansas (67015) 232/C4
Belvidere, Nebr. (68315) 264/G4
Belvidere, N.J. (07823) 273/C2
Belvidere, N.C. (27919) 281/S2
Belvidere, S. Dak. (57521) 298/G6
Belvidere, Tenn. (37306) 237/J10
Belvidere○, Vt. (05442) 268/B2
Belvidere (mt.), Vt. 268/B2
Belvidere Center, Vt. (05442) 268/B2
Belvidere Junction, Vt. (†05492) 268/B2
Belview, Minn. (56214) 255/C6
Belville, N.C. (†28451) 281/N6
Belvue, Kansas (66407) 232/F2
Belwood, N.C. (†28090) 281/F4
Belwood, Ontario 177/D4
Belyando (riv.), Queensland 88/H4
Belyando (riv.), Queensland 95/C4
Belyy (isl.), U.S.S.R. 4/B6
Belyy (isl.), U.S.S.R. 48/G2
Belzoni, Miss. (39038) 256/C4
Belzoni, Okla. (†74523) 288/R6
Bełżyce, Poland 47/F3
Bem, Mo. (†65066) 261/K6
Bembe, Angola 115/B5
Bemboka, N.S. Wales 97/E5
Bement, Ill. (61813) 222/E4
Bemersyde, Sask. 181/J5
Bemidji, Minn. (56601) 255/D3
Bemidji (lake), Minn. 255/D3
Bemis, S. Dak. (57215) 298/R4
Bemiss, Georgia (†31601) 217/F9
Bemmel, Netherlands 27/H5
Bemus Point, N.Y. (14712) 276/B6
Bena, Minn. (56626) 255/D3
Benabarre, Spain 33/G1
Bena-Dibele, Zaire 115/D4
Ben Alder (mt.), Scotland 15/D4
Benalla, Victoria 97/D5
Benalto, Alberta 182/C3
Benanee, N.S. Wales 97/B4
Benares (Varanasi), India 68/E3
Benavente, Spain 33/D1
Benavides, Texas (78341) 303/F10
Ben Avon, Pa. (†15202) 294/B6
Ben Avon (mt.), Scotland 15/E3
Ben Barvas (mt.), Scotland 15/B2
Benbecula (isl.), Scotland 15/A3
Benbecula (isl.), Scotland 10/C2
Benbrook, Texas (76126) 303/E2
Benbrook (lake), Texas 303/E3
Benchland, Mont. (†59462) 262/F3
Ben Cruachan (mt.), Scotland 15/C4
Bencubbin, W. Australia 92/B5
Bend, Oreg. 188/B2
Bend, Oreg. (97701) 291/F3
Bend, Texas (76824) 303/F7
Ben Dash (hill), Ireland 17/C6
Ben Davis (pt.), N.J. 273/C5
Bendel (state), Nigeria 106/F7
Bendemeer, N.S. Wales 97/F2
Bendena, Kansas (66008) 232/G2
Bender Beila, Somalia 115/K2
Bender Beila, Somalia 102/G4
Bender Cassim (Bosaso), Somalia 115/J1
Bendersville, Pa. (17306) 294/H6
Bendery, U.S.S.R. 52/C5
Bendigo, Australia 87/E9
Bendigo, Victoria 88/G7
Bendigo, Victoria 97/C5
Bendoc, Victoria 97/E5
Bendon, Mich. (†49643) 250/D4
Bendorf, W. Germany 22/B3
Bene Beraq, Israel 65/B3
Benedict (pond), Conn. 210/C1
Benedict, Kansas (66714) 232/G4
Benedict, Md. (20612) 245/M6
Benedict, Minn. (56436) 255/D3
Benedict, Nebr. (68316) 264/G3
Benedict (mt.), Newf. 166/C3
Benedict, N. Dak. (58716) 282/H4
Benedicta○, Maine (04733) 243/G4
Beneditinos, Brazil 132/F4
Benenitra, Madagascar 118/H4
Benešov, Czech. 41/C2
Benevean, Loch (lake), Scotland 15/D3
Benevento (prov.), Italy 34/E4
Benevento, Italy 34/E4
Benevolence, Georgia (31721) 217/C7
Benewah (co.), Idaho 220/B2
Benezett, Pa. (15821) 294/F3
Benfica, Portugal 33/A1
Benfleet, England 13/J8
Benga, Mozambique 118/E3
Bengal (bay) 54/K8
Bengal, Bay of (sea), Bangladesh 68/F5
Bengal, Bay of (sea) 2/P5
Bengal, Bay of (sea), Burma 72/B3
Bengal, Bay of (sea), India 68/F5
Bengal, Ind. (†46131) 227/F6
Bengal, Okla. (†74966) 288/R5
Ben Gardane, Tunisia 106/G2
Bengbis, Cameroon 115/B3
Bengbu (Pengpu), China 77/J5
Benge, Wash. (99105) 310/G4
Benggala (str.), Indonesia 85/A4
Benghazi, Libya 2/L4
Benghazi, Libya 102/D1
Benghazi (cap.), Libya 111/C1
Ben Ghnema, Jebel (mts.), Libya 111/C2
Bengkalis, Indonesia 85/C5
Bengkayang, Indonesia 85/E5
Bengkulu, Indonesia 85/C6
Bengo (dist.), Angola 115/B5
Bengough, Sask. 181/F6
Ben Griam More (mt.), Scotland 15/D2
Bengtsfors, Sweden 18/H7
Benguela (dist.), Angola 115/B6
Benguela, Angola 115/B6
Benguela, Angola 102/D6
Ben Guerdane (well), Mauritania 106/B3
Benguet (prov.), Philippines 82/C2
Benha, Egypt 111/J3
Benham, Ky. (40807) 237/R7
Benham, N.C. (†28621) 281/G2
Benhams, Va. (†24201) 307/D7
Ben Hee (mt.), Scotland 15/D2
Ben Hill (co.), Georgia 217/F7
Ben Hope (mt.), Scotland 15/D2
Ben Horn (mt.), Scotland 15/D2
Ben Hur, Va. (24218) 307/B7
Beni, El (dept.), Bolivia 136/C3
Beni (riv.), Bolivia 120/C4
Beni (riv.), Bolivia 136/B2
Beni, Zaire 115/E3
Beni Abbès, Algeria 106/D2
Benicarló, Spain 33/G2
Benicia, Calif. (94510) 204/K1
Benicito (riv.), Bolivia 136/C3
Beni Mazar, Egypt 111/J4
Beni Mellal, Morocco 106/C2
Beni Mellal, Morocco 102/B1
Benin 2/K5
Benin 102/C4
BENIN 106/E7
Benin (bight), Benin 106/E8
Benin (bight), Ghana 106/E8
Benin (bight), Nigeria 106/E8
Benin (bight), Togo 106/E8
Benin City, Nigeria 106/F7
Benin City, Nigeria 102/C4
Beni Ounif, Algeria 106/D2
Beni Saf, Algeria 106/D1
Beni Suef, Egypt 111/J3
Beni Suef, Egypt 102/E2
Beni Suef, Egypt 59/B4
Benito, Manitoba 179/A3
Beni Ulid, Libya 111/B1
Benjamín (isl.), Chile 138/D5
Benjamin, New Bruns. 170/D1
Benjamin (lake), Oreg. 291/G4
Benjamin, Texas (79505) 303/E4
Benjamin, Utah (†84660) 304/C3
Benjamín Aceval, Paraguay 144/C4
Benjamin Constant, Brazil 132/G9
Benjamin Constant, Brazil 120/B3
Benjamín Hill, Mexico 150/D1
Benkelman, Nebr. (69021) 264/C4
Ben Kilbreck (mt.), Scotland 15/D2
Ben Lawers (mt.), Scotland 15/D4
Benld, Ill. (62009) 222/D4
Ben Lomond, Ark. (71823) 202/B6
Ben Lomond, Calif. (95005) 204/K4
Ben Lomond, New Bruns. 170/E3
Ben Lomond (mt.), Scotland 15/D4
Ben Loyal (mt.), Scotland 15/D2
Ben Lui (mt.), Scotland 15/D4
Ben Macdhui (mt.), Scotland 15/E3
Ben Mhor (mt.), Scotland 15/A3
Ben More (mt.), Scotland 15/D4
Ben More (mt.), Scotland 15/B4
Ben More Assynt (mt.), Scotland 15/D2
Bennan (head), Scotland 15/C5
Bennane (head), Scotland 15/C5
Benndale, Miss. (†39450) 256/G9
Bennet, Nebr. (68317) 264/H4
Bennett, Br. Col. 184/J1
Bennett, W.A.C. (dam), Br. Col. 184/F2
Bennett, Colo. (80102) 208/L3
Bennett (peak), Colo. 208/G7
Bennett (creek), Idaho 220/C6
Bennett, Iowa (52721) 229/L5
Bennett, N.C. (27208) 281/K3
Bennett (lake), North. Terr. 93/B7
Bennett (co.), S. Dak. 298/F7
Bennett, Wis. (54815) 317/C3
Bennettsbridge, Ireland 17/G6
Bennetts Point, S.C. (†29446) 296/G6
Bennetts Switch, Ind. (†46901) 227/E3
Bennettsville, S.C. (29512) 296/H2
Bennettville, Minn. (†56431) 255/E4
Ben Nevis (mt.), Scotland 7/D3
Ben Nevis (mt.), Scotland 15/D4
Ben Nevis (mt.), Scotland 10/D2
Benning, D.C. (20019) 245/F5
Bennington, Idaho (†83254) 220/G7
Bennington, Ind. (47011) 227/G7
Bennington, Kansas (67422) 232/E2
Bennington, Nebr. (68007) 264/H3
Bennington○, N.H. (03442) 268/D5
Bennington, Okla. (74723) 288/P7
Bennington (co.), Vt. 268/A6
Bennington, Vt. (05201) 268/A6
Bennington○, Vt. (05201) 268/A6
Benns Church, Va. (†23430) 307/P7
Benoit, Miss. (38725) 256/C3
Benoit, Wis. (54816) 317/D3
Benom, Gunong (mt.), Malaysia 72/D7
Benoni, S. Africa 118/J6
Bensenville, Ill. (60106) 222/B5
Bensheim, W. Germany 22/C4
Benson, Ariz. (85602) 198/E7
Benson, Ill. (61516) 222/D3
Benson, La. (†71419) 238/C3
Benson, Minn. (56215) 255/C5
Benson, N.C. (27504) 281/N4
Benson (co.), N. Dak. 282/M3
Benson (Hollsopple), Pa. (15935) 294/E5
Benson, Sask. 181/J6
Benson○, Vt. (05731) 268/A4
Benson Landing, Vt. (†05731) 268/A4
Bens Run, W. Va. (26135) 312/D4
Bent (co.), Colo. 208/N7
Bent, N. Mex. (88314) 274/D5
Bent Creek, Va. (†24553) 307/L5
Benteng, Indonesia 85/F7
Bentham, England 13/E3
Bentheim, W. Germany 22/B2
Bentinck (isl.), Burma 72/C5
Bentinck (isl.), Queensland 88/F3
Bentinck (isl.), Queensland 95/A3
Bentiu, Sudan 111/E6
Bentley, Alberta 182/C3
Bentley, Ill. (†62321) 222/B3
Bentley, Iowa (†51559) 229/B6
Bentley, Kansas (67016) 232/E4
Bentley, La. (71407) 238/E3
Bentley, Mich. (48613) 250/E5
Bentley, N. Dak. (58522) 282/F7
Bentley, Okla. (†74525) 288/O6
Bentley Springs, Md. (21019) 245/M2
Bentleyville, Ohio (†44022) 284/J9
Bentleyville, Pa. (15314) 294/B5
Bentley with Arksey, England 13/F4
Bent Mountain, Va. (24059) 307/H6
Bento Gonçalves, Brazil 132/C10
Benton, Ala. (36785) 195/E6
Benton, Alberta 182/E4
Benton (co.), Ark. 202/B1
Benton, Ark. (72015) 202/E4
Benton, Calif. (93512) 204/G6
Benton, Ill. (62812) 222/E6
Benton (co.), Ind. 227/C3
Benton, Ind. (†46526) 227/F2
Benton (co.), Iowa 229/J4
Benton, Iowa (50835) 229/E7
Benton, Kansas (67017) 232/E4
Benton, Ky. (42025) 237/E7
Benton, La. (71006) 238/C1
Benton○, Maine (†04937) 243/D6
Benton (co.), Minn. 255/D5
Benton, Minn. (†55322) 255/F6
Benton (lake), Minn. 255/B6
Benton (co.), Miss. 256/F1
Benton, Miss. (39039) 256/D5
Benton (co.), Mo. 261/F6
Benton, Mo. (63736) 261/O8
Benton (lake), Mont. 262/E3
Benton, New Bruns. 170/C3
Benton○, N.H. (†03785) 268/D3
Benton, Ohio (44654) 284/G4
Benton (co.), Oreg. 291/D3
Benton, Pa. (17814) 294/K3
Benton (co.), Tenn. 237/E8
Benton, Tenn. (37307) 237/M10
Benton (co.), Wash. 310/F4
Benton, Wis. (53803) 317/F10
Benton City, Mo. (65232) 261/J4
Benton City, Wash. (99320) 310/F4
Bentong, Malaysia 72/D7
Benton Harbor, Mich. (49022) 250/C6
Benton Heights, Mich. (†49022) 250/C6
Bentonia, Miss. (39040) 256/D5
Benton Ridge, Ohio (45816) 284/C4
Bentonsport, Iowa (†52565) 229/K7
Bentonville, Ark. (72712) 202/B1
Bentonville, Ind. (47322) 227/G5
Bentonville, Ohio (45105) 284/C8
Bentonville, Va. (22610) 307/M3
Bent's Old Fort Nat'l Hist. Site, Colo. 208/M6
Benué (riv.), Cameroon 115/A2
Benue (state), Nigeria 106/F7
Benue (riv.), Nigeria 102/C4
Benue (riv.), Nigeria 106/F7
Ben Vorlich (mt.), Scotland 15/D4
Ben Vrackie (mt.), Scotland 15/E4
Benwee (head), Ireland 17/B3
Benwood, W. Va. (26031) 312/E2
Ben Wyvis (mt.), Scotland 15/D3
Benxi (Penki), China 77/K3
Benxi, China 54/O5
Benzie (co.), Mich. 250/C4
Benzonia, Mich. (49616) 250/D4
Beo, Indonesia 85/H5
Beograd (Belgrade) (cap.), Yugoslavia 45/E3
Beowawe, Nev. (89821) 266/E2
Beppu, Japan 81/E7
Bequia (isl.), St. Vin. & Grens. 156/G4
Beragh, N. Ireland 17/G2
Berar (reg.), India 68/D4
Berat, Albania 45/D5
Berau (bay), Indonesia 85/J6
Berber, Sudan 111/F4
Berber, Sudan 59/B6
Berber, Sudan 102/F3
Berbera, Somalia 115/J1
Berbera, Somalia 102/G3
Berberati, Cent. Afr. Rep. 102/D4
Berberati, Cent. Afr. Rep. 115/C3
Berbice (riv.), Guyana 131/B3
Berchem, Belgium 27/F6
Berchem-Sainte-Agathe, Belgium 27/B9
Bercher, Switzerland 39/C3
Berchtesgaden, W. Germany 22/E5
Berck, France 28/D2
Berclair, Texas (78107) 303/G9
Berdichev, U.S.S.R. 48/C5
Berdichev, U.S.S.R. 52/C5
Berdsk, U.S.S.R. 48/J4
Berdyansk, U.S.S.R. 7/H4
Berdyansk, U.S.S.R. 52/E5
Berea, Ky. (40403) 237/N5
Berea, Nebr. (†69301) 264/A2
Berea, N.C. (†27565) 281/M2
Berea, Ohio (44017) 284/G10
Berea, S.C. (29611) 296/C2
Berea, Spain 33/C1
Berea, W. Va. (26327) 312/E4
Bereda, Somalia 115/K1
Bereda, Somalia 102/H3
Beregovo, U.S.S.R. 52/B5
Berekum, Ghana 106/D7
Berenguela, Bolivia 136/A5
Berenice (ruins), Egypt 111/F3
Berens (riv.), Man. 162/G5
Berens (isl.), Manitoba 179/E2
Berens (riv.), Manitoba 179/F2
Berens (riv.), Ontario 175/A2
Berens River, Man. 162/G5
Berens River, Manitoba 179/F2
Beresford (lake), Fla. 212/E3
Beresford, New Bruns. 170/E1
Beresford, S. Dak. (57004) 298/R7
Beresford Lake, Manitoba 179/G4
Berești Tîrg, Romania 45/H2
Berettyó (riv.), Hungary 41/F3
Berettyóújfalu, Hungary 41/F3
Berezina (riv.), U.S.S.R. 52/C4
Bereznik, U.S.S.R. 52/F2
Berezniki, U.S.S.R. 7/K3
Berezniki, U.S.S.R. 48/F4
Berezniki, U.S.S.R. 52/J3
Berezovo, U.S.S.R. 48/G3
Berg, Norway 18/K2
Berg, Switzerland 39/H1
Berga, Algeria 106/E3
Berga, Spain 33/G1
Bergama, Turkey 63/B3
Bergama, Turkey 59/A2
Bergamo (prov.), Italy 34/B2
Bergamo, Italy 34/B2
Bergeijk, Netherlands 27/G6
Bergen (Mons), Belgium 27/E8
Bergen, E. Germany 22/E1
Bergen, Minn. (†56101) 255/D7
Bergen, Netherlands 27/F3
Bergen (co.), N.J. 273/E2
Bergen, N.Y. (14416) 276/E4
Bergen, N. Dak. (58792) 282/J3
Bergen, Norway 18/D6
Bergen, Norway 7/E2
Berg en Dal, Suriname 131/D3
Bergenfield, N.J. (07621) 273/C1
Bergen op Zoom, Netherlands 27/E5
Berger, Mo. (63014) 261/K5
Bergerac, France 28/D5
Bergholz, Ohio (43908) 284/J4
Bergisch Gladbach, W. Germany 22/B3
Bergland, Mich. (49910) 250/F1
Bergman, Ark. (72615) 202/E1
Bergoo, W. Va. (26298) 312/F6
Bergos (riv.), Turkey 63/C6
Bergshamra, Sweden 18/L7
Bergsjö, Sweden 18/K5
Bergstrom A.F.B., Texas 303/G7
Bergton, Va. (22811) 307/L3
Berguent, Morocco 106/D2
Bergum, Netherlands 27/H2
Bergumermeer (lake), Netherlands 27/J2
Bergün-Bravuogn, Switzerland 39/J3
Berhala (str.), Indonesia 85/C6
Berhampore, India 68/F4
Berhampur, India 68/F5
Berhida, Hungary 41/E3
Bering (sea) 2/A3

338 Bering

Bering (str.) 4/C18
Bering (strait) 54/W3
Bering (sea) 54/V4
Bering (sea) 146/A3
Bering (str.) 146/B3
Bering (str.), Alaska 188/C5
Bering (sea), Alaska 188/C6
Bering (glac.), Alaska 196/K2
Bering (sea), Alaska 196/D2
Bering (str.), Alaska 196/E1
Bering (isl.), U.S.S.R. 48/R4
Bering (sea), U.S.S.R. 48/S4
Bering (str.), U.S.S.R. 48/U3
Beringen, Belgium 27/G6
Bering Land Bridge Nat'l Preserve, Alaska 196/F1
Beringovskiy, U.S.S.R. 48/T3
Berino, N. Mex. (88024) 274/C6
Berja, Spain 33/E4
Berkåk, Norway 18/G5
Berkel, Netherlands 27/F5
Berkeley, Calif. 188/B3
Berkeley, Calif. (*94701) 204/J2
Berkeley, Ill. (60162) 222/B5
Berkeley, Mo. (63134) 261/P2
Berkeley (co.), S.C. 296/G5
Berkeley (co.), W. Va. 312/K4
Berkeley, W. Va. (†25401) 312/L4
Berkeley Heights○, N.J. (07922) 273/E2
Berkeley Lake, Georgia (†30136) 217/D3
Berkeley Springs (Bath), W. Va. (25411) 312/K3
Berken, Libya 111/B2
Berkey, Ohio (43504) 284/C2
Berkhamsted, England 13/G7
Berkhout, Netherlands 27/F3
Berkley, Iowa (†50220) 229/E5
Berkley○, Mass. (†02780) 249/K5
Berkley, Mich. (48072) 250/B6
Berkner (isl.), Ant. 2/G10
Berkner (isl.) 5/B16
Berkovitsa, Bulgaria 45/F4
Berks (co.), Pa. 294/K5
Berkshire, Conn. (†06482) 210/B3
Berkshire (co.), England 13/F6
Berkshire (co.), Mass. 249/B3
Berkshire (hills), Mass. 249/B4
Berkshire, N.Y. (13736) 276/H6
Berkshire○, Vt. (†05476) 268/B2
Berland (riv.), Alberta 182/A3
Berlanga de Duero, Spain 33/E2
Berleburg (Bad Berleburg), W. Germany 22/C3
Berlevåg, Norway 18/Q1
Berlin○, Conn. (06037) 210/E2
Berlin (cap.), E. Germany 7/F3
Berlin (cap.), E. Germany 2/K3
Berlin (dist.), E. Germany 22/F4
Berlin, East (cap.), E. Germany 22/F4
Berlin, Georgia (31722) 217/E8
Berlin, Ill. (†62670) 222/D4
Berlin, Md. (21811) 245/T7
Berlin○, Mass. (01503) 249/H3
Berlin (mt.), Nev. 266/D4
Berlin, N.H. 188/M2
Berlin, N.H. (03570) 268/E3
Berlin, N.J. (08009) 273/D4
Berlin, N.Y. (12022) 276/O5
Berlin, N. Dak. (58415) 282/O7
Berlin, Ohio (44610) 284/G4
Berlin (lake), Ohio 284/H4
Berlin, Okla. (†73662) 288/G4
Berlin, Pa. (15530) 294/E6
Berlin (pond), Vt. 268/B3
Berlin, W. Germany 7/F3
Berlin (West) (free city), W. Germany 22/E4
Berlin (West), W. Germany 22/E4
Berlin, W. Va. (†26452) 312/F4
Berlin, Wis. (54923) 317/H8
Berlin Center, Ohio (44401) 284/J3
Berlin Heights, Ohio (44814) 284/F3
Bermagui, N.S. Wales 97/F5
Bermeja (pt.), Argentina 143/D5
Bermejo (riv.), Argentina 120/C5
Bermejo (riv.), Argentina 143/E2
Bermejo (riv.), Bolivia 136/C8
Bermen (lake), Québec 174/D2
Bermeo, Spain 33/E1
Bermillo de Sayago, Spain 33/D2
Bermuda (isls.) 146/M6
Bermuda (isl.), (Br.) 2/F4
Bermuda, Ala. (†36438) 195/D8
BERMUDA 156/G3
Bermuda (isl.), Bermuda 156/H3
Bermuda, La. (†70558) 238/D3
Bern, Idaho (83220) 220/G7
Bern, Kansas (66408) 232/F2
Bern (canton), Switzerland 39/D2
Bern (cap.), Switzerland 7/E4
Bern (cap.), Switzerland 39/D3
Bernabé Rivera, Uruguay 145/B1
Bernadotte, Minn. (†56054) 255/D6
Bernalillo (co.), N. Mex. 274/C4
Bernalillo, N. Mex. (87004) 274/C3
Bernard, Iowa (52032) 229/M4
Bernardino de Sahagún, Mexico 150/M1
Bernardo, N. Mex. (†87028) 274/C4
Bernardo de Irigoyen, Argentina 143/F2
Bernardston○, Mass. (01337) 249/D2
Bernardsville, N.J. (07924) 273/D2
Bernasconi, Argentina 143/D4
Bernau bei Berlin, E. Germany 22/E2
Bernay, France 28/D3
Bernburg, E. Germany 22/D3
Berndorf, Austria 41/C3
Berne, Ind. (46711) 227/H3
Berne, N.Y. (12023) 276/M5
Berneray (isl.), Scotland 15/B2
Berneray (isl.), Scotland 15/A4
Berneray (isl.), Scotland 15/A3
Bernese Oberland (reg.), Switzerland 39/E3
Bernhards Bay, N.Y. (13028) 276/J4
Bernic (lake), Manitoba 179/G4
Bernice, La. (71222) 238/E1
Bernice, Okla. (74331) 288/S1
Bernic Lake, Manitoba 179/G4
Bernie, Mo. (63822) 261/M9
Bernier (bay), N.W. Terrs. 187/K2
Bernier (isl.), W. Australia 88/A4
Bernier (isl.), W. Australia 92/A4
Bernierville, Québec 172/F3
Bernina (pass), Italy 34/C1
Bernina, Piz (peak), Italy 34/B1
Bernina (mts.), Switzerland 39/J4
Bernina (pass), Switzerland 39/K4
Bernina (peak), Switzerland 39/J4
Bernina (riv.), Switzerland 39/J4
Bernkastel-Kues, W. Germany 22/B4
Bernstadt, Ky. (†40741) 237/N6
Bernville, Pa. (19506) 294/K5
Bero (riv.), Angola 115/B7
Beromünster, Switzerland 39/F2
Beroroha, Madagascar 118/G4
Beroun, Czech. 41/B2
Beroun, Minn. (55004) 255/F5
Berounka (riv.), Czech. 41/C2
Berovo, Yugoslavia 45/F5
Berre (lag.), France 28/F6
Berri, S. Australia 88/G6
Berri, S. Australia 94/G6
Berridale, N.S. Wales 97/E5
Berriedale, Scotland 15/E2
Berrien (co.), Georgia 217/F8
Berrien (co.), Mich. 250/C7
Berrien Springs, Mich. (49103) 250/C7
Berrigan, N.S. Wales 97/C4
Berrondo, Uruguay 145/C5
Berry, Ala. (35546) 195/C3
Berry (creek), Alberta 182/E4
Berry (isls.), Bahamas 156/B1
Berry (head), England 13/D7
Berry (trad. prov.) France 29
Berry, Ky. (41003) 237/N3
Berry, N.S. Wales 97/F4
Berry (head), Nova Scotia 168/G3
Berryessa (lake), Calif. 204/D5
Berry Hill, Tenn. (†37201) 237/H8
Berry Mills, New Bruns. 170/E2
Berrymoor, Alberta 182/C3
Berrysburg, Pa. (17005) 294/J4
Berry's Chapel, Tenn. (†37027) 237/H9
Berrys Lick, Ky. (†42268) 237/H6
Berryton, Georgia (30748) 217/B2
Berryton, Kansas (66409) 232/G3
Berryville, Ark. (72616) 202/C1
Berryville, Va. (22611) 307/M2
Berseba, Namibia 118/B5
Bertha, Minn. (56437) 255/C4
Berthier (co.), Québec 172/C3
Berthier (county), Québec 174/B3
Berthier-en-Bas, Québec 172/G3
Berthierville, Québec 172/D3
Berthold, N. Dak. (58718) 282/G3
Berthoud, Colo. (80513) 208/J2
Berthoud Pass, Colo. (†80438) 208/H3
Bertie (co.), N.C. 281/P2
Bertogne, Belgium 27/H8
Bertolínia, Brazil 132/F4
Bertoua, Cameroon 115/B3
Bertraghboy (bay), Ireland 17/A5
Bertram, Iowa (†52401) 229/K5
Bertram, Texas (78605) 303/F7
Bertrand, Cerro (mt.), Chile 138/D8
Bertrand, Mo. (63823) 261/O9
Bertrand, Nebr. (68927) 264/E4
Bertrand, New Bruns. 170/E1
Bertrandville, La. (†70040) 238/L7
Bertrix, Belgium 27/G9
Bertwell, Sask. 181/J3
Beru (atoll), Kiribati 87/H6
Bervie, Ontario 177/C3
Berwick, Ill. (61417) 222/C3
Berwick, Iowa (50032) 229/G5
Berwick, Kansas (†66534) 232/G2
Berwick, La. (70342) 238/H7
Berwick, Maine (03901) 243/B9
Berwick○, Maine (03901) 243/B9
Berwick, New Bruns. 170/E3
Berwick, N. Dak. (†58788) 282/K3
Berwick, Nova Scotia 168/D4
Berwick, Pa. (18603) 294/K3
Berwick (trad. co.), Scotland 15/B5
Berwick, Victoria 97/K6
Berwick-upon-Tweed, England 13/F2
Berwick-upon-Tweed, England 10/F3
Berwind, W. Va. (24815) 312/C8
Berwyn, Alberta 182/B1
Berwyn, Ill. (60402) 222/B6
Berwyn, Nebr. (68819) 264/E3
Berwyn, Pa. (19312) 294/L5
Berwyn (mts.), Wales 13/D5
Berwyn Heights, Md. (†20740) 245/G4
Beryl, Utah (84714) 304/A6
Beryl, W. Va. (†26726) 312/H4
Berzence, Hungary 41/D3
Besalampy, Madagascar 118/G3
Besançon, France 28/G4
Besançon, France 7/E4
Beşiktaş, Turkey 63/D6
Beşiri, Turkey 63/J4
Beskids, West (mts.), Czech. 41/E2
Beskids, East (mts.), Czech. 41/F1
Beskids (range), Poland 47/D4
Beslan, U.S.S.R. 52/F6
Besni, Turkey 63/G4
Besor (riv.), Israel 65/B5
Bessbrook, N. Ireland 17/J3
Bessèges, France 28/F5
Bessemer, Ala. 188/J4
Bessemer, Ala. (35020) 195/D4
Bessemer, Mich. (49911) 250/F2
Bessemer, Pa. (16112) 294/B4
Bessemer City, N.C. (28016) 281/G4
Bessie, Okla. (73622) 288/H4
Best, Texas (76931) 303/C6
Beswick, North. Terr. 88/E2
Beswick Aboriginal Reserve, North. Terr. 88/E2
Beswick Aboriginal Res., North. Terr. 93/C3
Beta, N.C. (†28779) 281/C4
Betanzos, Bolivia 136/C6
Betanzos, Spain 33/B1
Bétaré-Oya, Cameroon 115/B2
Bete Grise (bay), Mich. 250/B1
Bethalto, Ill. (62010) 222/B2
Bethanie, Namibia 118/B5
Bethany (res.), Calif. 204/L2
Bethany○, Conn. (†06501) 210/C3
Bethany, Ill. (61914) 222/E4
Bethany, Ind. (†46111) 227/E5
Bethany, La. (71007) 238/B2
Bethany, Manitoba 179/C4
Bethany, Minn. (†55910) 255/F6
Bethany, Mo. (64424) 261/E2
Bethany, Ohio (†45042) 284/B7
Bethany, Okla. (73008) 288/L3
Bethany, Ontario 177/F3
Bethany, Pa. (†18431) 294/M2
Bethany, Sask. 181/F3
Bethany, W. Va. (26032) 312/E2
Bethany Beach, Del. (19930) 245/T6
Bethel, Alaska 188/C6
Bethel, Alaska (99559) 196/F2
Bethel, Conn. (06801) 210/B3
Bethel○, Conn. (06801) 210/B3
Bethel, Del. (19931) 245/R6
Bethel, Ky. (40306) 237/O4
Bethel, Maine (04217) 243/B7
Bethel○, Maine (04217) 243/B7
Bethel, Minn. (55005) 255/E5
Bethel, Mo. (63434) 261/J3
Bethel, N.Y. (12720) 276/L7
Bethel, N.C. (27812) 281/P3
Bethel, Ohio (45106) 284/B8
Bethel, Okla. (74724) 288/S6
Bethel, Pa. (19507) 294/K5
Bethel, Vt. (05032) 268/B4
Bethel○, Vt. (05032) 268/B4
Bethel, Wis. (†54410) 317/F6
Bethel Acres, Okla. (†74801) 288/M4
Bethel Heights, Ark. (†72764) 202/B1
Bethel Island, Calif. (94511) 204/L1
Bethel Park, Pa. (15102) 294/B7
Bethelridge, Ky. (42516) 237/M6
Bethel Springs, Tenn. (38315) 237/D10
Bethel Town, Jamaica 158/G6
Bethera, S.C. (29430) 296/H5
Bethesda, Ark. (†72501) 202/G2
Bethesda, Md. (*20014) 245/E4
Bethesda, Ohio (43719) 284/H5
Bethesda, Wales 13/D4
Bethlehem, Conn. (06751) 210/C2
Bethlehem○, Conn. (06751) 210/C2
Bethlehem, Georgia (30620) 217/E3
Bethlehem, Ind. (47104) 227/G7
Bethlehem, Iowa (†50238) 229/G7
Bethlehem, Ky. (40007) 237/L4
Bethlehem, Md. (21609) 245/P6
Bethlehem, Miss. (†38659) 256/F1
Bethlehem○, N.H. (03574) 268/D3
Bethlehem, Pa. (*18015) 294/M4
Bethlehem, S. Africa 102/E7
Bethlehem, S. Africa 118/D5
Bethlehem, Virgin Is. (U.S.) 161/E4
Bethlehem, West Bank 65/C4
Bethlehem, W. Va. (†26003) 312/E2
Bethpage, N.Y. (11714) 276/R7
Bethpage, Tenn. (37022) 237/J7
Bethulie, S. Africa 118/D6
Bethune, Colo. (80805) 208/P4
Béthune, France 28/E2
Bethune, Sask. 181/F5
Bethune, S.C. (29009) 296/G3
Betijoque, Venezuela 124/C3
Betim, Brazil 135/D2
Betioky, Madagascar 118/G4
Betoota, Queensland 95/B5
Bet-Pak-Dala (des.), U.S.S.R. 48/H5
Bet Qama, Israel 65/B5
Betroka, Madagascar 118/H4
Bet She'an, Israel 65/D3
Bet Shemesh, Israel 65/B4
Betsiamites (riv.), Que. 162/J5
Betsiamites, Québec 174/D3
Betsiamites (riv.), Québec 174/C2
Betsiboka (riv.), Madagascar 118/H3
Betsy (riv.), Mich. 250/D4
Betsy Layne, Ky. (41605) 237/R5
Bette (peak), Libya 102/D2
Bette (peak), Libya 111/C3
Bettendorf, Iowa (52722) 229/N5
Betteravia, Calif. (†93454) 204/E9
Betterton, Md. (21610) 245/O3
Bettiah, India 68/E3
Bettlach, Switzerland 39/D2
Bettles, Alaska (†99726) 196/H1
Bettles Field, Alaska (99726) 196/H1
Bettsville, Ohio (44815) 284/D3
Bettyhill, Scotland 15/D2
Betul, India 68/D4
Betula, Pa. (†16749) 294/F2
Betwa (riv.), India 68/D4
Between, Georgia (†30655) 217/E3
Betws-y-Coed, Wales 13/D4
Betzdorf, W. Germany 22/B3
Beulah, Ala. (†36872) 195/H5
Beulah, Colo. (81023) 208/K6
Beulah, Manitoba 179/A4
Beulah, Mich. (49617) 250/C4
Beulah, Miss. (38726) 256/B3
Beulah, Mo. (65436) 261/J7
Beulah, N. Dak. (58523) 282/G5
Beulah, Oreg. (†97911) 291/J4
Beulah (res.), Oreg. 291/J4
Beulah, Victoria 97/B4
Beulah (lake), Wis. 317/J2
Belah, Wyo. (82712) 319/H1
Beulaker Wijde (lake), Netherlands 27/H3
Beulaville, N.C. (28518) 281/O5
Beuthen (Bytom), Poland 47/A3
Bevans, N.J. (†07851) 273/D1
Bevent, Wis. (†54440) 317/H6
Beveren, Belgium 27/E6
Beverin (peak), Switzerland 39/H3
Beverley, England 10/F4
Beverley, England 13/G4
Beverley, Sask. 181/C5
Beverley, W. Australia 92/B1
Beverly, C. Rica 154/F6
Beverly, Kansas (67423) 232/E2
Beverly, Ky. (40913) 237/P7
Beverly, Mass. (01915) 249/E5
Beverly, Mo. (†64079) 261/O4
Beverly, N.J. (08010) 273/D3
Beverly (lake), N.W. Terrs. 187/H3
Beverly, Ohio (45715) 284/G6
Beverly, Wash. (99321) 310/F4
Beverly, W. Va. (26253) 312/G5
Beverly Beach, Fla. (†32036) 212/E2
Beverly Hills, Calif. (*90210) 204/B10
Beverly Hills, Mich. (†48010) 250/B6
Beverly Shores, Ind. (46301) 227/C1
Beverwijk, Netherlands 27/F4
Bevier, Mo. (63532) 261/G3
Bevington, Iowa (50033) 229/F6
Bewdley, England 13/E5
Bewdley, England 10/F3
Bewdley, Ontario 177/F3
Bex, Switzerland 39/D4
Bexar, Ala. (†35570) 195/B2
Bexar (co.), Texas 303/F8
Bexhill, England 13/H7
Bexhill, England 10/G5
Bexley, England 13/H8
Bexley, England 10/C5
Bexley, Miss. (†39452) 256/G9
Bexley, Ohio (43209) 284/E6
Bey (mts.), Turkey 63/D4
Bey el Kebir, Wadi (dry riv.), Libya 111/B1
Beykoz, Turkey 63/D5
Beyla, Guinea 106/C7
Beylerbeyi, Turkey 63/D6
Beynon, Alberta 182/D4
Beyoğlu, Turkey 63/D6
Beypazarı, Turkey 59/B1
Beypazarı, Turkey 63/D2
Beyşehir, Turkey 59/B2
Beyşehir, Turkey 63/D4
Beyşehir (lake), Turkey 63/D4
Beytüşşebap, Turkey 63/K4
Bezanson, Alberta 182/A2
Bezhetsk, U.S.S.R. 52/E3
Béziers, France 7/E4
Béziers, France 28/E6
Bhadrak, India 68/F4
Bhadravati, India 68/D6
Bhadreswar, India 68/F1
Bhag, Pakistan 68/B3
Bhag, Pakistan 59/J4
Bhagalpur, India 68/F4
Bhaktapur, Nepal 68/F3
Bhaktapur, Nepal 68/F3
Bhamo, Burma 72/C1
Bhandara, India 68/E4
Bhandup, India 68/B7
Bhanjanagar, India 68/E4
Bharatpur, India 68/D3
Bharuch, India 68/C4
Bhatapara, India 68/E4
Bhatinda, India 68/C2
Bhatkal, India 68/C6
Bhatpara, India 68/F1
Bhavnagar, India 68/C4
Bhavnagar, India 54/J7
Bhawanipatna, India 68/E5
Bhera, Pakistan 68/C2
Bheri (riv.), Nepal 68/E3
Bhilai, India 68/E4
Bhilwara, India 68/C3
Bhima (riv.), India 68/D5
Bhimavaram, India 68/E5
Bhimunipatnam, India 68/E5
Bhind, India 68/D3
Bhinmal, India 68/C3
Bhir (Bir), India 68/D5
Bhiwandi, India 68/C5
Bhiwani, India 68/D3
Bhojpur, Nepal 68/F3
Bhopal, India 54/J7
Bhopal, India 68/D4
Bhor, India 68/C5
Bhubaneswar, India 68/F4
Bhuj, India 68/B4
Bhusawal, India 68/D4
Bhutan 2/P4
Bhutan 54/L7
BHUTAN 68/G3
Biafra (bight), Cameroon 115/A3
Biafra (bight), Equat. Guinea 115/A3
Biafra (bight), Nigeria 106/F8
Biak, Indonesia 85/K6
Biak (isl.), Indonesia 85/K6
Biała Podlaska, Poland 47/F3
Bia-Lła Podlaska (prov.), Poland 47/F3
Białogard, Poland 47/C1
Białystok (prov.), Poland 47/F2
Białystok, Poland 47/F2
Białystok, Poland 7/G3
Biancavilla, Italy 34/E6
Biarritz, France 28/C6
Bias, W. Va. (†25661) 312/B7
Biasca, Switzerland 39/H4
Biba, Egypt 111/J4
Bibai, Japan 81/L2
Bibala, Angola 115/B6
Bibb (co.), Ala. 195/D5
Bibb (co.), Georgia 217/E5
Bibb City, Georgia (†31901) 217/B5
Bibbenluke, N.S. Wales 97/E5
Biberach an der Riss, W. Germany 22/C4
Biberist, Switzerland 39/D2
Bible Grove, Ill. (62813) 222/E5
Bible Hill, Nova Scotia 168/E3
Bic, Québec 172/J1
Bic (isl.), Québec 172/J1
Bicas, Brazil 135/E2
Bicaz, Romania 45/G2
Bicester, England 13/F6
Biche (lake), Alberta 182/E2
Biche, Trin. & Tob. 161/B10
Bicheno, Tasmania 99/E3
Bickerdike, Alberta 182/B3
Bickerton (isl.), North. Terr. 93/E2
Bickerton West, Nova Scotia 168/G3
Bickleigh, Sask. 181/C4
Bickleton, Wash. (99322) 310/E5
Bickmore, W. Va. (25019) 312/D6
Bicknell, Ind. (47512) 227/C7
Bicknell, Utah (84715) 304/C5
Bicske, Hungary 41/E3
Bida, Nigeria 106/F7
Bidar, India 68/D5
Biddeford, Maine (04005) 243/B9
Biddeford, Maine 188/N2
Biddeford Pool, Maine (04006) 243/C9
Biddinghuizen, Netherlands 27/H4
Biddle, Mont. (59314) 262/L5
Biddu, West Bank 65/C4
Biddulph, England 13/H2
Bidean nam Bian (mt.), Scotland 15/D4
Bide Arm, Newf. 166/C3
Bideford, England 13/C6
Bideford, England 10/D5
Bidokht, Iran 66/L3
Bidon 5 (Poste Maurice Cordier), Algeria 106/E4
Bidwell, Ohio (45614) 284/F8
Bidyadhari (riv.), India 68/F2
Bié (dist.), Angola 115/C6
Bié, Angola 102/D6
Bié, Angola 115/C6
Bieber, Calif. (96009) 204/D2
Biebrza (riv.), Poland 47/F2
Biel, Switzerland 39/D2
Bielawa, Poland 47/C3
Bield, Manitoba 179/A3
Bieldside, Scotland 15/F3
Bielefeld, W. Germany 22/C2
Bieler (lake), N.W. Terrs. 187/L2
Bielersee (lake), Switzerland 39/D2
Biella, Italy 34/B2
Bielsko (prov.), Poland 47/D4
Bielsko-Biała, Poland 47/D4
Bielsk Podlaski, Poland 47/F2
Biencourt, Québec 172/J2
Bienfait, Sask. 181/J6
Bien Hoa, Vietnam 72/E5
Bienvenue, Fr. Guiana 131/E4
Bienville, Lac (lake), Que. 162/J4
Bienville (par.), La. 238/D2
Bienville, La. (71008) 238/D2
Bienville (lake), Québec 174/C2
Bière, Switzerland 39/B3
Bietigheim-Bissingen, W. Germany 22/C4
Bietschhorn (mt.), Switzerland 39/E4
Bièvre, Belgium 27/F9
Bièvres, France 28/A2
Big (isl.), Alberta 182/B5
Big (creek), Idaho 220/C4
Big (creek), Ind. 227/B8
Big (brook), Maine 243/E3
Big (lake), Maine 243/H5
Big (pond), Mass. 249/B4
Big (riv.), Mo. 261/L6
Big (lake), Mont. 262/G5
Big (mt.), Nev. 266/B1
Big (bay), Newf. 166/B2
Big (isl.), Newf. 166/B2
Big (riv.), Newf. 166/C3
Big (isl.), N.W. Terrs. 187/L3
Biga, Turkey 63/B2
Bigadiç, Turkey 63/C3
Bigalı, Turkey 63/B6
Big Annemessex (riv.), Md. 245/P8
Big Arm, Mont. (59910) 262/B3
Big Bald (mt.), New Bruns. 170/D1
Big Bar, Calif. (96010) 204/B3
Big Bar Creek, Br. Col. 184/F4
Big Basin, Calif. (†95006) 204/J4
Big Bay, Mich. (49808) 250/B2
Big Bay (pt.), Mich. 250/B2
Big Bay de Noc (bay), Mich. 250/C3
Big Bear City, Calif. (92314) 204/J9
Big Bear Lake, Calif. (92315) 204/J9
Big Beaver, Sask. 181/F6
Bigbee, Ala. (36510) 195/B7
Bigbee Valley, Miss. (39738) 256/H4
Big Bell, W. Australia 92/B4
Big Belt (mts.), Mont. 262/E4
Big Bend (dam), S. Dak. 298/K5
Bigbend, W. Va. (26136) 312/D5
Big Bend, Wis. (53103) 317/K2
Big Bend City, Minn. (†56262) 255/C5
Big Bend National Park, Texas (79834) 303/A8
Big Bend Nat'l Park, Texas 303/A8
Big Black (riv.), Maine 243/D2
Big Black (riv.), Miss. 256/C6
Big Black (creek), S.C. 296/G2
Big Black River, Manitoba 179/E1
Big Blue (riv.), Ind. 227/F5
Big Blue (riv.), Kansas 232/F1
Big Blue (riv.), Nebr. 264/H4
Big Boulder (creek), Idaho 220/B7
Big Bow, Kansas (67855) 232/A4
Big Bras d'Or, Nova Scotia 168/H2
Big Bureau (riv.), Ill. 222/D2
Big Burro (mts.), N. Mex. 274/A6
Bigbury (bay), England 13/C7
Big Cabin, Okla. (74332) 288/R1
Big Canoe (creek), Ala. 195/F2
Big Chimney, W. Va. (25302) 312/C6
Big Chino Wash (dry riv.), Ariz. 198/C3
Big Clifty, Ky. (42712) 237/J5
Big Coulee, Alberta 182/D2
Big Cove Tannery, Pa. (17212) 294/F6
Big Creek (lake), Ala. 195/B9
Big Creek, Calif. (93605) 204/F6
Big Creek, Idaho (†83677) 220/C4
Big Creek, Ky. (40914) 237/O6
Big Creek, Miss. (38914) 256/F3
Big Creek, W. Va. (25505) 312/B7
Big Cypress (swamp), Fla. 212/E5
Big Cypress Nat'l Preserve, Fla. 212/E5
Big Dry (creek), Mont. 262/K3
Big Eau Pleine (res.), Wis. 317/G6
Big Eddy, Br. Col. 184/H4
Big Elk (peak), Idaho 220/G6
Bigelow, Ark. (72016) 202/E3
Bigelow (brook), Conn. 210/G1
Bigelow (bight), Maine 243/C9
Bigelow (mt.), Maine 243/C5
Bigelow (bight), Mass. 249/M1
Bigelow, Minn. (56117) 255/C7
Bigelow, Mo. (64425) 261/B2
Big Falls, Minn. (56627) 255/E2
Big Falls, Wis. (54926) 317/H6
Big Flat, Ark. (72617) 202/F1
Big Flat (brook), N.J. 273/D1
Big Flats, N.Y. (14814) 276/G6
Bigfoot, Texas (78005) 303/F9
Big Fork, Ark. (71928) 202/B5
Bigfork, Minn. (56628) 255/E3
Big Fork (riv.), Minn. 255/E2
Bigfork, Mont. (59911) 262/C2
Big Four, W. Va. (†24853) 312/C8
Bigga, N.S. Wales 97/E4
Biggar, Sask. 162/F5
Biggar, Sask. 181/C3
Biggar, Scotland 10/E3
Biggar, Scotland 15/E5
Bigge (range), Queensland 95/D5
Bigge (isl.), W. Australia 92/D1
Biggers, Ark. (72413) 202/J1
Biggleswade, England 10/F4
Biggleswade, England 13/G5
Big Goose (creek), Wyo. 319/E1
Big Grizzly (creek), Colo. 208/G1
Biggs, Calif. (95917) 204/D4
Biggs, Oreg. (†97058) 291/G2
Biggs Field, Texas (†79908) 303/A10
Biggsville, Ill. (61418) 222/C3
Big Hole (mts.), Idaho 220/G6
Big Hole (riv.), Mont. 262/C5
Big Hole Nat'l Battlefield, Mont. 262/C5
Bighorn (riv.) 188/E2
Big Horn (dam), Alberta 182/B3
Bighorn (range), Alberta 182/B3
Big Horn (mts.), Ariz. 198/B5
Big Horn (co.), Mont. 262/J5
Bighorn, Mont. (59010) 262/J4
Bighorn (lake), Mont. 262/H5
Bighorn (riv.), Mont. 262/J5
Big Horn (co.), Wyo. 319/E1
Big Horn, Wyo. (82833) 319/E1
Bighorn (basin), Wyo. 319/D1
Bighorn (lake), Wyo. 319/D1
Bighorn (mts.), Wyo. 319/E1
Bighorn (riv.), Wyo. 319/D1
Bighorn Canyon Nat'l Rec. Area, Mont. 262/H5
Bighorn Canyon Nat'l Rec. Area, Wyo. 319/D1
Big Indian, N.Y. (12410) 276/M6
Big Iron (riv.), Mich. 250/F1
Big Isaac, W. Va. (†26426) 312/E4
Big Island, Ontario 177/G3
Big Island, Va. (24526) 307/K5
Big Lake, Alaska (†99687) 196/B1
Big Lake, Alaska (†99726) 196/J1
Big Lake, Minn. (55309) 255/E5
Big Lake, Texas (76932) 303/C6
Biglake, Wash. (†98273) 310/C2
Big Lake Ranch, Br. Col. 184/G4
Bigler, Pa. (16825) 294/F4
Biglerville, Pa. (17307) 294/H6
Big Lick, Tenn. (†38555) 237/L9
Big Lost (riv.), Idaho 220/E6
Big Moose, N.Y. (†13331) 276/L3
Big Moose (lake), N.Y. 276/L3
Big Muddy (riv.), Ill. 222/D6
Big Muddy (riv.), Mont. 262/M2
Big Muddy (lake), Sask. 181/G6
Big Muskego (lake), Wis. 317/L2
Bignona, Senegal 106/A6
Big Oak Flat, Calif. (95305) 204/E6
Big Otter (riv.), Va. 307/K6
Big Otter, W. Va. (25113) 312/D5
Big Pine, Calif. (93513) 204/G6
Big Pine (key), Fla. 212/E7
Big Pine (creek), Ind. 227/C3
Big Pine, N.C. (†28753) 281/D3
Big Piney, Mo. (65437) 261/H7
Big Piney, Wyo. (83113) 319/B3
Big Pipe (creek), Md. 245/K2
Big Plain, Ohio (†43140) 284/D6
Bigpoint, Miss. (†39567) 256/H9
Big Pond, Newf. 166/D2
Big Pond, Nova Scotia 168/H3
Big Pool, Md. (21711) 245/F2
Big Porcupine (creek), Mont. 262/J4
Big Prairie, Ohio (44611) 284/F4
Big Raccoon (creek), Ind. 227/C5
Big Rapids, Mich. (49307) 250/D5
Big Rib (riv.), Wis. 317/G5
Big Rideau (lake), Ontario 177/H3
Big River, Sask. 162/F5
Big River, Sask. 181/D2
Big Rock, Ill. (60511) 222/E2
Big Rock, Iowa (52725) 229/M5
Big Rock, Tenn. (37023) 237/F7
Big Rock, Va. (24603) 307/D6
Big Run, Pa. (15715) 294/E4
Big Sable (pt.), Mich. 250/C4
Big Sable (riv.), Mich. 250/C4
Big Sage (res.), Calif. 204/E2
Big Salmon (riv.), New Bruns. 170/E3
Big Sand (lake), Manitoba 179/H2
Big Sandy (riv.), Ariz. 198/B4
Big Sandy (creek), Colo. 208/N4
Big Sandy (riv.), Ky. 237/R4
Big Sandy (lake), Minn. 255/E4
Big Sandy, Mont. (59520) 262/G2
Big Sandy, Tenn. (38221) 237/E8
Big Sandy (riv.), Tenn. 237/E9
Big Sandy, Texas (75755) 303/J5
Big Sandy (riv.), W. Va. 312/A6
Big Sandy, Wyo. (†82923) 319/C3
Big Sandy (res.), Wyo. 319/C3
Big Sandy (riv.), Wyo. 319/C3
Big Sioux (riv.), Iowa 229/A3
Big Sioux (riv.), S. Dak. 188/G2
Big Sioux (riv.), S. Dak. 298/S7
Big Sky, Mont. (59716) 262/E5
Big Smoky (valley), Nev. 266/D4
Big Southern (butte), Idaho 220/E6

Blandburg 339

Big Spencer (mt.), Maine 243/E4
Big Spring, Georgia (†30240) 217/C5
Big Spring, Ky. (40106) 237/J5
Big Spring, Md. (21722) 245/G2
Big Spring, Tenn. (37323) 237/M10
Big Spring, Texas 188/F4
Big Spring, Texas (79720) 303/C5
Big Springs, Nebr. (69122) 264/B3
Big Springs, S. Dak. (†57001) 298/S8
Big Springs, W. Va. (26137) 312/D5
Big Star (lake), Mich. 250/C5
Bigstick (lake), Sask. 181/B5
Big Stone, Alberta 182/E4
Bigstone (lake), Manitoba 179/J3
Bigstone (pt.), Manitoba 179/E2
Bigstone (riv.), Manitoba 179/J3
Big Stone (co.), Minn. 255/B5
Big Stone (lake), Minn. 255/B5
Big Stone (lake), S. Dak. 298/R3
Big Stone City, S. Dak. (57216) 298/S3
Big Stone Gap, Va. (24219) 307/C7
Big Sur, Calif. (93920) 204/D7
Big Thicket Nat'l Preserve, Texas 303/K7
Big Thompson (riv.), Colo. 208/H2
Big Timber, Mont. (59011) 262/G5
Big Timber (creek), N.J. 273/C4
Big Tracadie (riv.), New Bruns. 170/E1
Bigtrails, Wyo. (†82442) 319/E2
Big Trout (lake), Ontario 177/F2
Big Trout (lake), Ontario 175/B2
Big Trout Lake, Ontario 175/C2
Big Valley, Alberta 182/D3
Big Walnut (creek), Ind. 227/D5
Big Walnut (creek), Ohio 284/E5
Big Wells, Texas (78830) 303/E9
Big Whiteshell Lake, Manitoba 179/G4
Big Wood (riv.), Idaho 220/D6
Bihać, Yugoslavia 45/B3
Bihar (state), India 68/F4
Bihar, India 68/F3
Biharamulo, Tanzania 115/F4
Biharkeresztes, Hungary 41/F3
Biharnagybajom, Hungary 41/F3
Bijagós (isls.), Guinea-Biss. 106/A6
Bijagós (isls.), Guinea-Biss. 102/A3
Bijapur, Karnataka, India 68/D5
Bijapur, Madhya Pradesh, India 68/E5
Bijar, Iran 66/E3
Bijeljina, Yugoslavia 45/D3
Bijelo Polje, Yugoslavia 45/D4
Bijiang, China 77/E6
Bijie, China 77/G6
Bijnor, India 68/D3
Bijou (creek), Colo. 208/L3
Bijou Hills, S. Dak. (†57310) 298/L6
Bikaner, India 54/J7
Bikaner, India 68/C3
Bikar (atoll), Marshall Is. 87/H4
Bikin, U.S.S.R. 48/O5
Bikini (atoll), Marshall Is. 87/G4
Bikoro, Zaire 115/C4
Bikoro, Zaire 102/D5
Bilaspur, India 68/E4
Bilauktaung (range), Burma 72/C4
Bilauktaung (range), Thailand 72/C4
Bilbao, Spain 33/E1
Bilbao, Spain 7/D4
Bileća, Yugoslavia 45/D4
Bilecik (prov.), Turkey 63/D2
Bilecik, Turkey 59/A1
Bilecik, Turkey 63/D2
Biłgoraj, Poland 47/F3
Bilibino, U.S.S.R. 4/C1
Bilibino, U.S.S.R. 48/R3
Bilin, Burma 72/C3
Bilina, Czech. 41/B1
Biliran (isl.), Philippines 82/E5
Bill, Wyo. (82631) 319/G2
Billate (riv.), Ethiopia 111/G6
Billerica○, Mass. (01821) 249/J2
Billings (lake), Conn. 210/H2
Billings, Mo. (65610) 261/F8
Billings, Mont. 146/H5
Billings, Mont. 188/E1
Billings, Mont. (*59101) 262/H5
Billings (co.), N. Dak. 282/D5
Billings, Okla. (74630) 288/M1
Billingsgate (isl.), Mass. 249/O5
Billingshurst, England 13/G6
Billingsley, Ala. (36006) 195/E5
Billiton (isl.), Indonesia 54/M10
Billiton (isl.), Indonesia 85/D6
Bill Williams (riv.), Ariz. 198/B4
Billy Clapp (lake), Wash. 310/F3
Bilma, Niger 102/D3
Bilma, Niger 106/G5
Biloela, Queensland 88/J4
Biloela, Queensland 95/D5
Biloku, Guyana 131/B5
Biloxi, Miss. 146/K6
Biloxi, Miss. 188/J4
Biloxi, Miss. (*39530) 256/G10
Biltine, Chad 111/D5
Biltine, Chad 102/D3
Biltmore Forest, N.C. (†28803) 281/E3
Bilwaskarma, Nicaragua 154/F3
Bilzen, Belgium 27/G7
Bim, W. Va. (25021) 312/C7
Biminis, The (isls.), Bahamas 156/B1
Bina-Itawa, India 68/D4
Binalbagan, Philippines 82/D5
Binalong, N.S. Wales 97/E4
Binboğa (mts.), Turkey 63/G3
Binbrook, Ontario 177/E4
Binche, Belgium 27/E8
Binda, N.S. Wales 97/E4
Bindloss, Alberta 182/E4
Bindoon, W. Australia 92/B1
Bindura, Zimbabwe 118/E3
Binéfar, Spain 33/G2
Binevenagh (mt.), N. Ireland 17/H1
Binford, N. Dak. (58416) 282/O4
Binga (mt.), Mozambique 118/E3
Bingara, N.S. Wales 97/F1
Bingen, Wash. (98605) 310/D5
Bingen, W. Germany 22/B4
Binger, Okla. (73009) 288/K4
Bingerville, Ivory Coast 106/D7
Bingham (co.), Idaho 220/F6
Bingham, Ill. (62011) 222/D4
Bingham, Maine (04920) 243/D5
Bingham○, Maine (04920) 243/D5
Bingham, Nebr. (69335) 264/B2
Bingham, N. Mex. (87815) 274/C5
Bingham, S.C. (†29565) 296/H3
Bingham Lake, Minn. (56118) 255/C7
Binghamton, N.Y. 188/L2
Binghamton, N.Y. (*13901) 276/J6
Bingöl (prov.), Turkey 63/J3
Bingöl (Çapakçur), Turkey 63/J3
Bingöl Dağları (mts.), Turkey 63/J3
Binhai, China 77/K5
Binh Long (An Loc), Vietnam 72/E5
Binh Son, Vietnam 72/F4
Binjai, Indonesia 85/B5
Binn, Switzerland 39/F4
Binnaway, N.S. Wales 97/E2
Binningen, Switzerland 39/D1
Binongko (isl.), Indonesia 85/G7
Binscarth, Manitoba 179/A4
Bintan (isl.), Indonesia 85/C5
Bintuhan, Indonesia 85/C6
Bintulu, Malaysia 85/E5
Binyamina, Israel 65/B2
Binyang, China 77/G7
Biobío (reg.), Chile 138/E1
Bío-Bío (riv.), Chile 138/E2
Biograd, Yugoslavia 45/B4
Bioko (isl.), Equat. Guinea 102/C4
Bioko (terr.), Equat. Guinea 115/A3
Bioko (isl.), Equat. Guinea 115/A3
Biola, Calif. (93606) 204/E7
Bippus, Ind. (46713) 227/F3
Bir, India 68/D5
Bira, U.S.S.R. 48/O5
Birag, Kuh-e (mts.), Iran 66/M7
Bir 'Ali, P.D.R. Yemen 59/E7
Birama (pt.), Cuba 158/G4
Birao, Cent. Afr. Rep. 115/D1
Biratnagar, Nepal 68/F3
Biratori, Japan 81/L2
Bir Bala, Iran 66/L8
Bir Bala, Iran 59/G4
Bircao, Somalia 115/H4
Birch (creek), Alaska 196/J1
Birch (hills), Alberta 182/A2
Birch (lake), Alberta 182/E3
Birch (mts.), Alberta 182/B5
Birch (riv.), Alberta 182/B5
Birch (creek), Idaho 220/F5
Birch (isl.), Manitoba 179/C2
Birch (lake), Minn. 255/G3
Birch (creek), Mont. 262/D2
Birch (lake), Sask. 181/C2
Birch (creek), Utah 304/B5
Birch (pt.), Wash. 310/C2
Birch Creek, Alaska (†99740) 196/J1
Birch Creek (valley), Idaho 220/E5
Birch Creek (res.), Mont. 262/D2
Birchdale, Minn. (56629) 255/D2
Birch Harbor, Maine (04613) 243/H7
Birch Hills, Sask. 181/F3
Birchip, Victoria 97/B4
Birch Island, Br. Col. 184/H4
Birchleaf, Va. (24220) 307/D6
Birch River, Manitoba 179/A2
Birch River, W. Va. (26610) 312/E6
Birch Run, Mich. (48415) 250/F5
Birchtown, Nova Scotia 168/C5
Birch Tree, Mo. (65438) 261/K9
Birchwood, Md. (†20021) 245/F5
Birchwood, Tenn. (37308) 237/M10
Birchwood, Wis. (54817) 317/C4
Birchy Bay, Newf. 166/D4
Bird (isl.), La. 238/M8
Bird (creek), Okla. 288/O1
Bird City, Kansas (67731) 232/A2
Bird Cove, Newf. 166/C3
Bird Island, Minn. (55310) 255/D6
Birds, Ill. (62415) 222/F5
Birdsboro, Pa. (19508) 294/L5
Birdseye, Ind. (47513) 227/D8
Birds Hill, Manitoba 179/F4
Birdsnest, Va. (23307) 307/S6
Birdsong, Ark. (†72386) 202/K3
Birdsville, Ky. (†42081) 237/D6
Birdsville, Queensland 88/F5
Birdsville, Queensland 95/A5
Birdtail, Manitoba 179/B4
Birdum, North. Terr. 93/C3
Birdwood, S. Australia 94/C7
Birecik, Turkey 63/H4
Bir el Khzaim (well), Mauritania 106/C4
Bireuen, Indonesia 85/B4
Bir Ganduz (well), Western Sahara 106/A4
Birganj, Nepal 68/F3
Bir Hakeim (ruins), Libya 111/D1
Birigui, Brazil 135/A2
Birjand, Iran 66/L4
Birjand, Iran 59/G3
Birjand, Iran 54/G6
Birken, Br. Col. 184/F5
Birkenfeld, Oreg. (97016) 291/D1
Birkenfeld, W. Germany 22/B4
Birkenhead, England 13/G2
Birkenhead, England 10/F2
Birkenhead, N. Zealand 100/B1
Birkenhead Lake Prov. Park, Br. Col. 184/F5
Birkerød, Denmark 21/F6
Birket Qârûn (lake), Egypt 111/J3
Bir Ksaib Ounane (well), Mali 106/C4
Birksgate (range), S. Australia 94/A2
Birlad, Romania 45/H2
Birlad (riv.), Romania 45/H2
Birmingham, Ala. 146/K6
Birmingham, Ala. 188/J4
Birmingham, Ala. 195/D3
Birmingham, England 7/D3
Birmingham, England 10/G3
Birmingham, England 13/F5
Birmingham, Iowa (52535) 229/K7
Birmingham, Mich. (*48008) 250/B6
Birmingham, Mo. (†64068) 261/R5
Birmingham, N.J. (08011) 273/D4
Birmingham, Ohio (44816) 284/F3
Birmingham, Pa. (†16686) 294/F4
Birmingham, Sask. 181/H5
Birmitrapur, India 68/E4
Bir Mogreïn, Mauritania 106/B3
Birnam, Scotland 15/E4
Birnamwood, Wis. (54414) 317/H6
Birney, Mont. (59012) 262/K5
Birnie, Manitoba 179/C4
Birnin Kebbi, Nigeria 106/E6
Birni-N'Konni, Niger 106/E6
Birni-N'Konni, Niger 102/C3
Bir Nzaran (well), Western Sahara 106/B4
Birobidzhan, U.S.S.R. 54/O5
Birobidzhan, U.S.S.R. 48/O5
Biron, Wis. (†54494) 317/G7
Bir Ounane (well), Mali 106/D4
Birqin, West Bank 65/C3
Birr, Ireland 17/F5
Birr, Ireland 10/B4
Birregurra, Victoria 97/B6
Birrie (riv.), N. S. Wales 88/H5
Birrie (riv.), N.S. Wales 97/D1
Birrimbah, North. Terr. 93/C3
Birrindudu, North. Terr. 93/A5
Birriwa, N.S. Wales 97/E3
Birs (riv.), Switzerland 39/D2
Birsay, Sask. 181/D4
Birsk, U.S.S.R. 52/J3
Birta, Ark. (†72853) 202/D3
Bir Taba, Egypt 59/B4
Bir Taba (well), Egypt 111/F2
Birtle, Manitoba 179/B4
Biru, China 77/D5
Biruaca, Venezuela 124/E4
Biruni, U.S.S.R. 48/G5
Biržai, U.S.S.R. 53/C2
Bir Zeit, West Bank 65/C4
Bisbee, Ariz. 188/E4
Bisbee, Ariz. (85603) 198/F7
Bisbee, N. Dak. (58317) 282/M2
Biscarrosse (lake), France 28/C5
Biscay (bay) 2/J3
Biscay (bay) 7/D4
Biscay (bay), France 28/B5
Biscay, Minn. (†55336) 255/D6
Biscay (bay), Spain 33/E1
Biscay Bay (riv.), Newf. 166/D2
Biscayne (bay), Fla. 212/F6
Biscayne (key), Fla. 212/B5
Biscayne Nat'l Park, Fla. 212/F6
Biscayne Park, Fla. (33152) 212/B4
Bisceglie, Italy 34/F4
Bischofshofen, Austria 41/B3
Bischofswerda, E. Germany 22/F3
Bischofszell, Switzerland 39/H1
Biscoe (isls.) 5/C15
Biscoe, Ark. (72017) 202/H4
Biscoe, N.C. (27209) 281/K4
Biscotasing, Ontario 177/J5
Biscotasing, Ontario 175/D3
Biscucuy, Venezuela 124/D3
Bisha, Saudi Arabia 59/D5
Bisha, Wadi (dry riv.), Saudi Arabia 59/D5
Bishiara (well), Libya 111/D3
Bisho (cap.), Ciskei, S. Africa 102/E8
Bishop, Calif. (93514) 204/G6
Bishop, Georgia (30621) 217/F3
Bishop, Md. (†21813) 245/S7
Bishop (creek), Nev. 266/F1
Bishop, Texas (78343) 303/G10
Bishop (creek), Utah 304/E3
Bishop, Va. (24604) 307/E6
Bishop Auckland, England 10/E3
Bishop Auckland, England 13/E3
Bishopbriggs, Scotland 15/B2
Bishop Hill, Ill. (61419) 222/C2
Bishopric, Sask. 181/F5
Bishop's Falls, Newf. 166/C4
Bishops Head, Md. (21611) 245/O7
Bishops Mitre (mt.), Newf. 166/B2
Bishop's Stortford, England 10/G5
Bishop's Stortford, England 13/H6
Bishopton, Québec 172/F4
Bishopton, Scotland 15/B2
Bishopville, Md. (21813) 245/T7
Bishopville, S.C. (29010) 296/G3
Bishri, Jebel el (mts.), Syria 63/H5
Biskra, Algeria 106/F2
Biskra, Algeria 102/C1
Biskupiec, Poland 47/E2
Bislig, Philippines 85/H4
Bislig, Philippines 82/F6
Bismarck, Ark. (71929) 202/D5
Bismarck, Ill. (61814) 222/F3
Bismarck, Mo. (63624) 261/L7
Bismarck (cap.), N. Dak. 146/H5
Bismarck (cap.), N. Dak. 188/G1
Bismarck (cap.), N. Dak. (58501) 282/J6
Bismarck (arch.), Papua N.G. 87/E6
Bismarck (arch.), Papua N.G. 86/B1
Bismarck (sea), Papua N.G. 86/B1
Bismarck (arch.), Papua N.G. 2/S6
Bismarck, W. Va. (†26739) 312/H4
Bismil, Turkey 63/J4
Bison (lake), Alberta 182/B1
Bison, Kansas (67520) 232/C3
Bison, Okla. (73720) 288/L2
Bison, S. Dak. (57620) 298/E2
Bispgården, Sweden 18/K5
Bissau (cap.), Guinea-Biss. 106/A6
Bissau (cap.), Guinea-Biss. 102/A3
Bissett, Manitoba 179/G4
Bistineau (lake), La. 238/D2
Bistrița, Romania 45/G2
Bita (riv.), Colombia 126/F5
Bitagron, Suriname 131/C3
Bitam, Gabon 115/B3
Bitburg, W. Germany 22/B4
Bitely, Mich. (49309) 250/D5
Bithlo, Fla. (†32801) 212/E3
Bitkine, Chad 111/C5
Bitlis (prov.), Turkey 63/J3
Bitlis, Turkey 63/J3
Bitlis, Turkey 59/D2
Bitola, Yugoslavia 45/E5
Bitola, Yugoslavia 7/G4
Bitonto, Italy 34/F4
Bitter (lakes), Egypt 111/K3
Bitter (lake), Sask. 181/B5
Bitter (creek), Wyo. 319/C4
Bitter Creek, Wyo. (†82901) 319/D4
Bitterfeld, E. Germany 22/E3
Bitterfontein, S. Africa 118/B6
Bittern (lake), Alberta 182/D3
Bittern Lake, Alberta 182/D3
Bitterroot (range) 188/D1
Bitterroot (range), Idaho 220/D3
Bitterroot (range), Mont. 262/B4
Bitterroot (riv.), Mont. 262/B4
Bitterroot (range), U.S. 146/G5
Bitti, Italy 34/B4
Bitumount, Alberta 182/E1
Bitung, Indonesia 85/H5
Biu, Nigeria 106/G6
Biu (plat.), Nigeria 106/G6
Bivalve, Md. (21814) 245/P7
Bivalve, N.J. (08301) 273/C5
Bivolari, Romania 45/H2
Biwa (lake), Japan 81/H6
Biwabik, Minn. (55708) 255/F3
Bixby, Minn. (55916) 255/E7
Bixby, Mo. (65439) 261/K7
Bixby, Okla. (74008) 288/P3
Biyang, China 77/H5
Biysk, U.S.S.R. 54/K4
Biysk, U.S.S.R. 48/J4
Bizcocho, Uruguay 145/B4
Bizerte, Tunisia 106/F1
Bizerte, Tunisia 102/C1
Bjargtangar (pt.), Iceland 21/A1
Bjelovar, Yugoslavia 45/C3
Bjerringbro, Denmark 21/C5
Bjorkdale, Sask. 181/H3
Bjørnafjorden (fjord), Norway 18/D6
Bjorne (pen.), N.W. Terrs. 187/K2
Bjornøya (isl.), Norway 18/D3
Blabon, N. Dak. (†58046) 282/P5
Blachly, Oreg. (97412) 291/D3
Black (sea) 2/L3
Black (sea) 54/E5
Black (sea) 7/H4
Black, Ala. (36314) 195/G8
Black (riv.), Alaska 196/K1
Black (mesa), Ariz. 198/E2
Black (mts.), Ariz. 198/A3
Black (riv.), Ariz. 198/E5
Black (riv.), Ark. 202/H2
Black (sea), Bulgaria 45/J4
Black (pond), Conn. 210/G1
Black (pt.), Conn. 210/G3
Black (mts.), England 13/D6
Black (creek), Fla. 212/E1
Black (head), Ireland 17/C5
Black (riv.), Jamaica 158/H6
Black (mt.), Ky. 237/R7
Black (lake), La. 238/D3
Black (pond), Maine 243/D3
Black (isl.), Manitoba 179/F3
Black (riv.), Manitoba 179/F4
Black (lake), Mich. 250/E3
Black (riv.), Mich. 250/E3
Black (riv.), Mich. 250/G5
Black (riv.), Minn. 255/D2
Black (creek), Miss. 256/F8
Black, Mo. (63625) 261/L7
Black (riv.), Mo. 261/L10
Black (mt.), N. Mex. 274/A6
Black (range), N. Mex. 274/B5
Black (lake), N.Y. 276/J1
Black (riv.), N.Y. 276/K3
Black (riv.), N.C. 281/N5
Black (riv.), Ohio 284/F3
Black (riv.), Ontario 177/E3
Black (sea), Romania 45/J4
Black (lake), Sask. 181/M2
Black (riv.), S.C. 296/H4
Black (sea), Turkey 63/E1
Black (sea), U.S.S.R. 48/D5
Black (sea), U.S.S.R. 52/D6
Black (creek), Vt. 268/B2
Black (riv.), Vt. 268/C2
Black (riv.), Vt. 268/B5
Black (riv.), Vietnam 72/D2
Black (mts.), Wales 13/D6
Black (for.), W. Germany 22/C4
Black (riv.), Wis. 317/E7
Black (riv.), Yukon 187/D3
Blackall, Australia 87/E8
Blackall, Queensland 88/H4
Blackall, Queensland 95/C5
Black Bear (creek), Okla. 288/M2
Blackberry (riv.), Conn. 210/B1
Blackbird, Del. (†19734) 245/R3
Blackbourne (pt.), Norfolk I. 88/L6
Black Branch, Nulhegan (riv.), Vt. 268/D2
Blackburn (mt.), Alaska 196/K2
Blackburn, England 13/H1
Blackburn, England 10/G1
Blackburn, La. (†71038) 238/D1
Blackburn, Mo. (65321) 261/F4
Blackburn, Okla. (74058) 288/N2
Blackburn, Ontario 177/J2
Blackburn, Scotland 15/C2
Black Butte (lake), Calif. 204/C4
Black Canyon City, Ariz. (85324) 198/C4
Black Canyon of the Gunnison Nat'l Mon., Colo. 208/D5
Black Creek, Br. Col. 184/E5
Black Creek, N.C. (27813) 281/O3
Black Creek, Wis. (54106) 317/K7
Black Diamond, Alberta 182/C4
Black Diamond, Wash. (98010) 310/D3
Blackduck, Minn. (56630) 255/D3
Black Duck (riv.), Ontario 175/C1
Black Eagle, Mont. (59414) 262/E3
Black Earth, Wis. (53515) 317/G9
Black Elster (riv.), E. Germany 22/E3
Blackey, Ky. (41804) 237/R6
Blackfalds, Alberta 182/D3
Blackfeet Ind. Res., Mont. 262/D2
Blackfoot, Alberta 182/E3
Blackfoot, Idaho (83221) 220/F6
Blackfoot (res.), Idaho 220/G7
Blackfoot (riv.), Idaho 220/G6
Blackfoot, Mont. (59415) 262/D2
Blackfoot (riv.), Mont. 262/C4
Blackford (co.), Ind. 227/G4
Blackford, Ky. (42403) 237/F6
Blackford, Scotland 15/E4
Black Forest, Colo. (80908) 208/K4
Blackfork, Ohio (45615) 284/E8
Black Fork, Mohican (riv.), Ohio 284/F4
Blackgum, Okla. (†74962) 288/S3
Black Hall, Conn. (†06371) 210/F3
Black Hawk, Colo. (80422) 208/J3
Blackhawk, Ind. (†47866) 227/C6
Black Hawk (co.), Iowa 229/J4
Black Hawk, Miss. (†38917) 256/E4
Black Hawk, S. Dak. (57718) 298/C5
Blackhead (bay), Newf. 166/D2
Blackhead Road, Newf. 166/D2
Black Hills (mts.) 188/F2
Black Hills (mts.), S. Dak. 298/B5
Blackie, Alberta 182/D4
Black Isle (pen.), Scotland 15/D3
Black Jack, Mo. (†63031) 261/R1
Black Lake (bayou), La. 238/D1
Black Lake, Québec 172/F3
Black Lake, Sask. 181/M2
Blackledge (riv.), Conn. 210/F2
Black Lick, Pa. (15716) 294/D4
Blacklock (pt.), Oreg. 291/C5
Black Mesa (mt.), Okla. 288/A1
Blackmore (mt.), Mont. 262/F5
Black Mountain, N.C. (28711) 281/E3
Black Oak, Ark. (72414) 202/K2
Black Oak, Ind. (†46406) 227/C1
Black Pine (mts.), Idaho 220/E7
Black Pine (peak), Idaho 220/E7
Black Pine (creek), S. Dak. 298/G6
Black Point, Calif. (†94947) 204/J1
Black Point, Conn. (†06357) 210/G3
Black Point, New Bruns. 170/D1
Blackpool, England 13/G1
Blackpool, England 10/F1
Blackridge, Va. (23916) 307/M7
Black River, Jamaica 158/H6
Black River, Jamaica 156/B3
Black River (bay), Jamaica 158/G6
Black River, Mich. (48721) 250/F4
Black River, New Bruns. 170/E3
Black River (pond), Newf. 166/C2
Black River, N.Y. (13612) 276/J3
Black River Bridge, New Bruns. 170/E2
Black River Falls, Wis. (54615) 317/E7
Black Rock, Ark. (72415) 202/H1
Black Rock (des.), Nev. 266/B2
Black Rock (range), Nev. 266/B1
Black Rock (pt.), R.I. 249/H8
Black Rock, Utah (†84751) 304/B5
Blacksburg, S.C. (29702) 296/D1
Blacksburg, Va. (24060) 307/H6
Blacks Fork, Green (riv.), Wyo. 319/C4
Blacks Harbour, New Bruns. 170/D3
Blackshear, Georgia (31516) 217/H8
Blackshear (lake), Georgia 217/E7
Blacksher, Ala. (†36507) 195/C8
Blacksod (bay), Ireland 17/A3
Black Springs, Ark. (†71960) 202/C5
Black Springs, Nev. (†89508) 266/B3
Black Squirrel (creek), Colo. 208/L5
Blackstairs (mt.), Ireland 17/H6
Blackstock, Ontario 177/F3
Blackstock, S.C. (29014) 296/E2
Blackstone○, Mass. (01504) 249/H4
Blackstone (riv.), Mass. 249/G3
Blackstone, Va. (23824) 307/N6
Blacksville, W. Va. (26521) 312/F3
Black Thunder (creek), Wyo. 319/G2
Black Tickle, Newf. 166/C3
Blackton, Ark. (†72069) 202/H4
Blacktown, N. S. Wales 88/K4
Blacktown, N.S. Wales 97/H3
Blackville, New Bruns. 170/E2
Blackville, S.C. (29817) 296/E5
Black Volta (riv.) 102/B3
Black Volta (riv.), Ghana 106/D6
Black Volta (riv.), Ivory Coast 106/D6
Black Volta (riv.), Upper Volta 106/D6
Black Warrior (riv.), Ala. 195/C5
Blackwater (riv.), England 13/H6
Blackwater (riv.), Fla. 212/B6
Blackwater, Ireland 17/J7
Blackwater (riv.), Ireland 10/B4
Blackwater (riv.), Ireland 17/D7
Blackwater (riv.), Ireland 17/H4
Blackwater, Mo. (65322) 261/G5
Blackwater (res.), N.H. 268/D5
Blackwater (riv.), N. Ireland 17/H3
Blackwater, Queensland 95/D4
Blackwater, Queensland 88/H4
Blackwater (res.), Scotland 15/D4
Blackwater, Va. (24221) 307/B7
Blackwater (riv.), Va. 307/J6
Blackwater (riv.), Va. 307/O6
Blackwell, Ark. (72019) 202/E3
Blackwell (brook), Conn. 210/H1
Blackwell, Okla. (74631) 288/M1
Blackwell, Texas (79506) 303/D5
Blackwell, Wis. (†54541) 317/J4
Blackwood (Ngunju) (cape), Indonesia 85/F8
Blackwood, N.J. (08012) 273/C4
Blackwood Terrace, N.J. (†08096) 273/C4
Bladen, Nebr. (68928) 264/F4
Bladen (co.), N.C. 281/M5
Bladenboro, N.C. (28320) 281/M5
Bladensburg, Md. (20710) 245/G4
Bladensburg, Ohio (43005) 284/F5
Blades, Del. (†19973) 245/R6
Bladon Springs, Ala. (36902) 195/B7
Bladworth, Sask. 181/E4
Blaeberry, Br. Col. 184/J4
Blaenavon, Wales 13/B6
Blagodarnoye, U.S.S.R. 52/F5
Blagoevgrad, Bulgaria 45/F5
Blagoveshchensk, U.S.S.R. 54/O4
Blagoveshchensk, U.S.S.R. 48/N4
Blagoveshchensk, U.S.S.R. 52/J4
Blain, France 28/C4
Blain, Pa. (17006) 294/H5
Blaine, Georgia (†30175) 217/C1
Blaine (co.), Idaho 220/D6
Blaine, Kansas (66410) 232/F2
Blaine, Ky. (41124) 237/R4
Blaine○, Maine (04734) 243/H2
Blaine, Mich. (†48032) 250/G5
Blaine, Minn. (†55433) 255/G5
Blaine, Miss. (38727) 256/C3
Blaine (co.), Mont. 262/G2
Blaine (co.), Nebr. 264/E3
Blaine, Ohio (43909) 284/J5
Blaine (co.), Okla. 288/K3
Blaine, Oreg. (†97108) 291/D2
Blaine, Tenn. (37709) 237/O8
Blaine, Wash. (98230) 310/C2
Blaine Lake, Sask. 181/D3
Blaine-Mars Hill, Maine (04734) 243/H2
Blainville, Québec 172/H4
Blair, Kansas (†66090) 232/H2
Blair, Nebr. (68008) 264/H3
Blair, Okla. (73526) 288/H5
Blair (co.), Pa. 294/F4
Blair, S.C. (29015) 296/E3
Blair, W. Va. (25022) 312/C7
Blair, Wis. (54616) 317/D7
Blair Athol, Queensland 95/C4
Blair Atholl, Scotland 10/E2
Blair Atholl, Scotland 15/E4
Blairgowrie and Rattray, Scotland 15/E4
Blairgowrie and Rattray, Scotland 10/E2
Blairmore, Alberta 182/C5
Blairs, Va. (24527) 307/K7
Blairsburg, Iowa (50034) 229/F4
Blairsden, Calif. (96103) 204/E4
Blairs Mills, Ky. (41402) 237/P4
Blairs Mills, Pa. (17213) 294/G5
Blairstown, Iowa (52209) 229/J5
Blairstown, Mo. (64726) 261/E5
Blairstown○, N.J. (07825) 273/C2
Blairsville, Georgia (30512) 217/E1
Blairsville, Pa. (15717) 294/D5
Blaisdell, N. Dak. (58720) 282/F3
Blaj, Romania 45/F2
Blake (pt.), Mich. 250/E1
Blakeley, Minn. (†56011) 255/E6
Blakeley, W. Va. (†25160) 312/D6
Blakely, Georgia (31723) 217/C8
Blakely, Pa. (18447) 294/F6
Blakesburg, Iowa (52536) 229/H7
Blakeslee, Ohio (43505) 284/A2
Blakeslee, Pa. (18610) 294/L3
Blaketown, Newf. 166/D2
Blalock, Ala. (†36773) 195/D6
Blalock, Georgia (†30525) 217/E1
Blalock (isl.), Wash. 310/F5
Blanc (cape) 2/J4
Blanc (mt.), France 7/E4
Blanc (mt.), France 28/G5
Blanc (mt.), Italy 34/A2
Blanc (cape), Mauritania 102/A2
Blanc (cape), Mauritania 106/A4
Blanc (cape), Tunisia 106/G1
Blanc (cape), Western Sahara 106/A4
Blanca (bay), Argentina 120/C6
Blanca (bay), Argentina 143/D4
Blanca (lag.), Chile 138/E10
Blanca (peak), Colo. 188/F3
Blanca, Colo. (81123) 208/H8
Blanca (peak), Colo. 208/H7
Blanca (pt.), C. Rica 154/F5
Blanca, Cordillera (mts.), Peru 128/D7
Blanch, N.C. (27212) 281/L2
Blanchard, Idaho (83804) 220/A1
Blanchard, Iowa (51630) 229/C7
Blanchard, La. (71009) 238/C1
Blanchard○, Maine (†04406) 243/D5
Blanchard, Mich. (49310) 250/D5
Blanchard, N. Dak. (58009) 282/R5
Blanchard (riv.), Ohio 284/C4
Blanchard, Okla. (73010) 288/L4
Blanchard, Pa. (16826) 294/G3
Blanchard, Wash. (†98232) 310/C2
Blanchardstown, Ireland 17/H5
Blanchardville, Wis. (53516) 317/G10
Blanche, Ky. (†40902) 237/O7
Blanche (riv.), Québec 172/E2
Blanche (lake), S. Australia 88/F5
Blanche (lake), S. Australia 94/F3
Blanche, Tenn. (†38488) 237/H10
Blanche (lake), W. Australia 88/C4
Blanche Marie (fall), Suriname 131/C3
Blanchester, Ohio (45107) 284/B7
Blanchisseuse, Trin. & Tob. 161/B10
Blanco (riv.), Argentina 143/C2
Blanco (riv.), Bolivia 136/D4
Blanco (lake), Chile 138/F10
Blanco (cape), C. Rica 154/E6
Blanco (peak), C. Rica 154/F6
Blanco (riv.), Mexico 150/Q2
Blanco, N. Mex. (87412) 274/B2
Blanco (creek), N. Mex. 274/F4
Blanco, Okla. (74528) 288/P5
Blanco (cape), Oreg. 188/A2
Blanco (cape), Oreg. 291/C5
Blanco (cape), Peru 128/B5
Blanco (riv.), Peru 128/F6
Blanco (co.), Texas 303/F8
Blanco, Texas (78606) 303/F7
Blanc-Sablon, Québec 174/F2
Bland, Mo. (65014) 261/J6
Bland (co.), Va. 307/F6
Bland, Va. (24315) 307/F6
Blandburg, Pa. (16619) 294/F4

340 Blandford

Blandford○, Mass. (01008) 249/C4
Blandford, Nova Scotia 168/D4
Blandford Forum, England 13/E7
Blandford Forum, England 10/E5
Blanding, Utah (84511) 304/E6
Blandinsville, Ill. (61420) 222/C3
Blandville, Ky. (42026) 237/D7
Blanefield, Scotland 15/B1
Blanes, Spain 33/H2
Blaney Park, Mich. (†49836) 250/D2
Blanford, Ind. (47831) 227/B5
Blankenberge, Belgium 27/C6
Blankenburg am Harz, E. Germany 22/D3
Blanket, Texas (76432) 303/F6
Blanquillo, Uruguay 145/D3
Blansko, Czech. 41/D2
Blanton, Ala. (†36872) 195/H5
Blanton, Fla. (†33525) 212/D3
Blantyre, Malawi 115/F7
Blantyre, Malawi 102/F6
Blantyre, Scotland 15/B2
Blarney, Ireland 10/B5
Blarney, Ireland 17/D8
Blas (peak), Switzerland 39/G3
Blasdell, N.Y. (14219) 276/C5
Blasket (isls.), Ireland 10/A4
Blasket (isls.), Ireland 17/A7
Blatná, Czech. 41/B2
Blato, Yugoslavia 45/C4
Blatten, Switzerland 39/E4
Blaubeuren, W. Germany 22/C4
Blauvelt, N.Y. (10913) 276/K8
Blåvands Huk (pt.), Denmark 21/A6
Blawenburg, N.J. (08504) 273/D3
Blawnox, Pa. (15238) 294/C6
Blaydon, England 10/F3
Blaydon, England 13/H3
Blaye, France 28/C5
Blayney, N.S. Wales 97/E3
Blaze (pt.), North. Terr. 88/D2
Blaze (pt.), North. Terr. 93/A2
Bleckley (co.), Georgia 217/F6
Bled, Yugoslavia 45/A2
Bledsoe (co.), Tenn. 237/L9
Bledsoe, Texas (79314) 303/A4
Bleecker, Ala. (†36874) 195/H5
Blekinge (co.), Sweden 18/J8
Blencoe, Iowa (51523) 229/A5
Blenheim, N. Zealand 100/D4
Blenheim, Ontario 177/C5
Blenheim, S.C. (29516) 296/H2
Blenker, Wis. (54415) 317/F6
Blennerhassett (isl.), Ohio 284/G7
Blerick, Netherlands 27/J6
Blesbok (riv.), S. Africa 118/J7
Blessing, Texas (77419) 303/H9
Blessington, Ireland 17/J5
Blevins, Ark. (71825) 202/C6
Blewett, Texas (†78801) 303/D8
Blida, Algeria 106/E1
Blida, Algeria 102/C1
Bligh (sound), N. Zealand 100/A6
Bligh Water (bay), Fiji 86/P10
Blind Channel, Br. Col. 184/E5
Blind River, Ont. 162/H6
Blind River, Ontario 177/J5
Blind River, Ontario 175/D3
Blinman, S. Australia 88/F6
Blinman, S. Australia 94/F4
Blinnenhorn (mt.), Switzerland 39/F4
Bliss, Idaho (83314) 220/D7
Bliss, N.Y. (14024) 276/D5
Blissfield, Mich. (49228) 250/F7
Blissfield, New Bruns. 170/D2
Blissfield, Ohio (43805) 284/G5
Blitar, Indonesia 85/K2
Blitchton, Georgia (†31308) 217/J6
Blocher, Ind. (47138) 227/F7
Block (isl.), R.I. 249/H8
Blocker, Okla. (74529) 288/P4
Block House, Nova Scotia 168/D4
Block Island (sound), N.Y. 276/S8
Block Island, R.I. (02807) 249/H8
Block Island (sound), R.I. 249/H8
Blockton, Iowa (50836) 229/D7
Blodgett, Mo. (63824) 261/O8
Blodgett, Oreg. (97326) 291/D3
Blodgett Landing, N.H. (†03255) 268/D5
Bloemendaal, Netherlands 27/E4
Bloemfontein, S. Africa 102/E7
Bloemfontein, S. Africa 118/C5
Blois, France 28/D4
Blokzijl, Netherlands 27/H3
Blomkest, Minn. (56216) 255/D6
Blonie, Poland 47/E2
Bloodroot (mt.), Vt. 268/B4
Bloodsworth (isl.), Md. 245/O8
Bloodvein (riv.), Manitoba 179/F3
Bloodvein (riv.), Ontario 175/A2
Bloodvein River, Manitoba 179/F3
Bloody Foreland (prom.), Ireland 17/E1
Bloody Foreland (prom.), Ireland 10/B3
Bloom, Kansas (67833) 232/C4
Bloom, N. Dak. (†58401) 282/N6
Blooming, Texas (75556) 303/L4
Bloom City, Wis. (54617) 317/E8
Bloomdale, Ohio (44817) 284/D3
Bloomer, Ark. (†72933) 202/B3
Bloomer, Wis. (54724) 317/D5
Bloomery, W. Va. (26817) 312/K4
Bloomfield, Sierra (mts.), Bolivia 136/D4
Bloomfield○, Conn. (06002) 210/E1
Bloomfield, Ind. (47424) 227/D6
Bloomfield, Iowa (52537) 229/J7
Bloomfield, Ky. (40008) 237/L5
Bloomfield, Mo. (63825) 261/M9
Bloomfield, Mont. (59315) 262/M3
Bloomfield, Nebr. (68718) 264/G2
Bloomfield, Newf. 166/D2
Bloomfield, N.J. (07003) 273/B2
Bloomfield, N. Mex. (87413) 274/A2
Bloomfield, Ontario 177/G4
Bloomfield (New Bloomfield), Pa. (17068) 294/H5
Bloomfield○, Vt. (†03590) 268/D2
Bloomfield Hills, Mich. (48013) 250/B6
Bloomfield Ridge, New Bruns. 170/D2
Bloomfield Station, New Bruns. 170/E3
Bloomingburg, N.Y. (12721) 276/L7
Bloomingburg, Ohio (43106) 284/D6
Bloomingdale, Georgia (31302) 217/K6
Bloomingdale, Ill. (60108) 222/A5
Bloomingdale, Ind. (47832) 227/C5
Bloomingdale, Mich. (49026) 250/C6
Bloomingdale, N.J. (07403) 273/E1
Bloomingdale, N.Y. (12913) 276/M2
Bloomingdale, Ohio (43910) 284/J5
Bloomingdale, Tenn. (37660) 237/R7
Bloomingdale, Wis. (†54667) 317/E8
Blooming Grove, Ind. (†47012) 227/G5
Blooming Grove, Pa. (†18428) 294/M3
Blooming Grove, Texas (76626) 303/H5
Bloomingport, Ind. (†47355) 227/G5
Blooming Prairie, Minn. (55917) 255/E7
Bloomington, Calif. (92316) 204/E10
Bloomington, Idaho (83223) 220/G7
Bloomington, Ill. 188/J2
Bloomington, Ill. (61701) 222/D3
Bloomington, Ind. (47401) 227/D6
Bloomington, Md. (21523) 245/B3
Bloomington, Minn. (55420) 255/G6
Bloomington, Nebr. (68929) 264/F4
Bloomington, Texas (77951) 303/H9
Bloomington, Wis. (53804) 317/E10
Bloomington Springs, Tenn. (38545) 237/K8
Blooming Valley, Pa. (†16335) 294/B2
Bloomsburg, Pa. (17815) 294/J3
Bloomsbury, Alberta 182/C2
Bloomsbury, N.J. (08804) 273/C2
Bloomsdale, Mo. (63627) 261/M6
Bloomville, N.Y. (13739) 276/L6
Bloomville, Ohio (44818) 284/D3
Blora, Indonesia 85/K2
Blossburg, Pa. (16912) 294/H2
Blossom, Texas (75416) 303/J4
Bloubergstrand, S. Africa 118/E6
Blount (co.), Ala. 195/E2
Blount (co.), Tenn. 237/O9
Blounts Creek, N.C. (27814) 281/P4
Blount Springs, Ala. (†35079) 195/E3
Blountstown, Fla. (32424) 212/A1
Blountsville, Ala. (35031) 195/E2
Blountsville, Ind. (†47360) 227/G4
Blountville, Tenn. (37617) 237/S7
Blowering (res.), N.S. Wales 97/E4
Blowing Rock, N.C. (28605) 281/F2
Bloxom, Va. (23308) 307/S5
Bludenz, Austria 41/A3
Blue, Ariz. (85922) 198/F5
Blue (riv.), Ariz. 198/F5
Blue (mt.), Colo. 208/B2
Blue (riv.), Colo. 208/G3
Blue (riv.), Ind. 227/E8
Blue (mts.), Jamaica 158/J6
Blue (mt.), Maine 243/C6
Blue (hills), Mass. 249/C8
Blue (creek), Nebr. 264/B3
Blue (mt.), New Bruns. 170/D1
Blue (mt.), N.H. 268/E2
Blue (mts.), N. S. Wales 88/H6
Blue (mts.), N. S. Wales 97/F3
Blue, Okla. (†74701) 288/O7
Blue (riv.), Okla. 288/O6
Blue (mts.), Oreg. 291/J3
Blue (mt.), Pa. 294/G5
Blue (creek), Utah 304/B2
Blue (lake), Utah 304/B4
Blue (lake), Wash. 310/F3
Blue (mts.), Wash. 310/H4
Blue Ash, Ohio (†45242) 284/C9
Blue Ball, Ark. (†72866) 202/C4
Blue Bell, S. Dak. (†57773) 298/C6
Bluebell, Utah (84007) 304/D3
Blueberry Creek, Br. Col. 184/J5
Blueberry Mountain, Alberta 182/A2
Blue Creek, Ohio (45616) 284/D8
Blue Creek, Utah (†84337) 304/B2
Bluecreek, Wash. (†99109) 310/H2
Blue Creek, W. Va. (25026) 312/D6
Blue Cypress (lake), Fla. 212/F4
Blue Diamond, Ky. (41718) 237/P6
Blue Earth (co.), Minn. 255/D6
Blue Earth, Minn. (56013) 255/D7
Blue Earth (riv.), Minn. 255/D7
Blue Eye, Ark. (65611) 202/D1
Blue Eye, Mo. (65611) 261/F9
Bluefield, Va. (24605) 307/F6
Bluefield, W. Va. 188/K3
Bluefield, W. Va. (24701) 312/D8
Bluefields, Jamaica 158/G6
Bluefields, Nicaragua 154/F4
Bluegrass, Ind. (†46939) 227/E3
Blue Grass, Iowa (52726) 229/M5
Blue Grass, Minn. (†56477) 255/C4
Blue Grass, Va. (24413) 307/J3
Blue Heron, Sask. 181/E2
Blue Hill, Maine (04614) 243/F7
Blue Hill○, Maine (04614) 243/F7
Blue Hill (bay), Maine 243/G7
Blue Hill, Nebr. (68930) 264/F4
Blue Hill Falls, Maine (04615) 243/F7
Blue Hills, Conn. (06112) 210/E1
Blue Island, Ill. (60406) 222/B6
Bluejacket, Okla. (74333) 288/R1
Blue Jay, Calif. (92317) 204/H9
Blue Joint (lake), Oreg. 291/H5
Blue Knob (mt.), Pa. 294/E5
Blue Lake, Calif. (95525) 204/A3
Blue Mesa (res.), Colo. 208/E5
Bluemont, Va. (22012) 307/N2
Blue Mound, Ill. (62513) 222/D4
Blue Mound, Kansas (66010) 232/H3
Blue Mound, Texas (†76101) 303/E2
Blue Mounds, Wis. (53517) 317/G9
Blue Mountain, Ala. (36201) 195/G3
Blue Mountain, Ark. (72826) 202/C3
Blue Mountain (lake), Ark. 202/C3
Blue Mountain (peak), Jamaica 158/K6
Blue Mountain (peak), Jamaica 156/C3
Blue Mountain, Miss. (38610) 256/G1
Blue Mountain (lake), N.Y. 276/M3
Blue Mountain Lake, N.Y. (12812) 276/M3
Blue Mountains, Australia 87/E9
Blue Mountains, N. S. Wales 88/J6
Blue Mountains, N.S. Wales 97/F3
Blue Nile (riv.) 102/F3
Blue Nile (Abay) (riv.), Ethiopia 111/G5
Blue Nile (prov.), Sudan 111/F5
Blue Nile (riv.), Sudan 59/B6
Blue Nile (riv.), Sudan 111/F5
Blue Nose (mt.), Idaho 220/D4
Bluenose (lake), N.W. Terrs. 187/G3
Blue Rapids, Kansas (66411) 232/F2
Blue Ridge, Alberta 182/C2
Blue Ridge, Georgia (30513) 217/D1
Blue Ridge (lake), Georgia 217/D1
Blue Ridge (mts.), Georgia 217/D1
Blue Ridge, Ind. (†46176) 227/F5
Blue Ridge (mts.), Md. 245/H3
Blue Ridge (mts.), N.C. 281/E3
Blue Ridge (mts.), S.C. 296/B1
Blue Ridge, Va. (24064) 307/J6
Blue Ridge (mts.), Va. 307/J6
Blue Ridge Manor, Ky. (†40201) 237/L2
Blue Ridge Summit, Pa. (17214) 294/G6
Blue River, Br. Col. 184/H4
Blue River, Colo. (†80424) 208/G4
Blue River, Oreg. (97413) 291/E3
Blue River, Wis. (53518) 317/E9
Blue Rock, Nova Scotia 168/D4
Blue Rock (Gaysport), Ohio (43720) 284/G6
Blue Sea Lake, Québec 172/A3
Bluesky, Alberta 182/A1
Blue Spring (hills), Utah 304/B1
Blue Springs, Ala. (†36017) 195/G7
Blue Springs, Miss. (38828) 256/G2
Blue Springs, Mo. (64015) 261/R6
Blue Springs, Nebr. (68318) 264/H4
Blue Stack (mts.), Ireland 17/E2
Bluestem (lake), Okla. 288/O1
Bluestone (lake), Va. 307/G5
Bluestone (lake), W. Va. 312/E7
Blue Sulphur Springs, W. Va. (†25545) 312/E7
Blue Summit, Mo. (†64101) 261/R5
Bluevale, Ontario 177/C4
Bluewater, N. Mex. (87005) 274/A3
Bluewater (creek), N. Mex. 274/B4
Bluewater (creek), N. Mex. 274/D6
Bluewater (lake), N. Mex. 274/A3
Bluff (cape), Newf. 166/C3
Bluff, N. Zealand 100/B7
Bluff, N.C. (†28743) 281/D3
Bluff, Utah (84512) 304/E6
Bluff City, Ark. (71722) 202/D6
Bluff City, Ill. (†62624) 222/E5
Bluff City, Kansas (67018) 232/E4
Bluff City, Tenn. (37618) 237/S8
Bluff Dale, Texas (76433) 303/F5
Bluffdale, Utah (†84065) 304/B3
Bluff Knoll (mt.), W. Australia 92/B6
Bluff Park, Ala. (35226) 195/E4
Bluffs, Ill. (62621) 222/C4
Bluffsprings, Fla. (†32535) 212/B5
Bluffton, Alberta 182/C3
Bluffton, Ark. (72827) 202/C4
Bluffton, Georgia (31724) 217/C7
Bluffton, Ind. (46714) 227/G3
Bluffton, Minn. (56518) 255/C4
Bluffton, Ohio (45817) 284/C4
Bluffton, S.C. (29910) 296/F7
Bluford, Ill. (62814) 222/E5
Blum, Texas (76627) 303/G5
Blumenau, Brazil 132/D9
Blumenau, Brazil 120/E5
Blumenfeld, Manitoba 179/D5
Blumenheim, Sask. 181/E3
Blumenhof, Sask. 181/D5
Blumenort, Manitoba 179/E5
Blumenort, Manitoba 179/F5
Blumenort, Sask. 181/D6
Blumenstein, Switzerland 39/E3
Blumenthal, Sask. 181/E3
Blümlisalp (mt.), Switzerland 39/E3
Blunt, S. Dak. (57522) 298/J4
Bly, Oreg. (97622) 291/F5
Blying (sound), Alaska 196/C1
Blyn, Wash. (†98382) 310/B3
Blyth, England 13/F2
Blyth, England 10/F3
Blyth, Ontario 177/C4
Blyth Bridge, Scotland 15/E5
Blythe, Calif. (92225) 204/L10
Blythe, Georgia (30805) 217/H4
Blythedale, Md. (†21904) 245/O2
Blythedale, Mo. (64426) 261/E2
Blythedale, Pa. (†15018) 294/C5
Blytheswood, Ontario 177/B5
Blytheville, Ark. 188/H3
Blytheville, Ark. (72315) 202/L2
Blytheville A.F.B., Ark. 202/K2
Blythewood, S.C. (29016) 296/E3
Bo, S. Leone 102/A4
Bo, S. Leone 106/B7
Boac, Philippines 82/C4
Boaco, Nicaragua 154/E4
Boa Esperança, Brazil 135/D2
Boalsburg, Pa. (16827) 294/G4
Boano (isl.), Indonesia 85/H6
Boa Nova, Brazil 132/B5
Board Camp, Ark. (71932) 202/B4
Boardman (riv.), Mich. 250/D4
Boardman, N.C. (†28438) 281/M6
Boardman, Ohio (44512) 284/J3
Boardman, Oreg. (97818) 291/H2
Boardman, Wis. (†54016) 317/A5
Boardmans Bridge, Conn. (†06776) 210/B2
Boas (riv.), N.W. Terrs. 187/K3
Boat Basin, Br. Col. 184/D5
Boat Harbour, Tasmania 99/B2
Boat of Garten, Scotland 15/E3
Boa Vista, Brazil 120/C2
Boa Vista, Brazil 132/H8
Boa Vista (isl.), C. Verde 106/B8
Boayan (isl.), Philippines 82/B5
Boaz, Ala. (35957) 195/F2
Boaz, Ky. (42027) 237/D7
Boaz, Mo. (†65631) 261/F8
Boaz, W. Va. (†26187) 312/D4
Boaz, Wis. (†53581) 317/E9
Bobadah, N.S. Wales 97/D3
Bobai, China 77/H7
Bobaomby (cape), Madagascar 102/G6
Bobaomby (Amber) (cape), Madagascar 118/H2
Bobare, Venezuela 124/D2
Bobbili, India 68/E5
Bobbitt, N.C. (†27544) 281/N2
Bobcaygeon, Ontario 177/F3
Bobigny, France 28/B1
Böblingen, W. Germany 22/C4
Bobo, Miss. (†38614) 256/C2
Bobo Dioulasso, Upper Volta 106/D6
Bobo Dioulasso, Upper Volta 102/B3
Bobon, Philippines 82/F7
Bobonaza (riv.), Ecuador 128/D3
Bobonong, Botswana 118/D4
Bobotov Kuk (mt.), Yugoslavia 45/D4
Bobr (riv.), Poland 47/B3
Bobrov, U.S.S.R. 52/F4
Bobruysk, U.S.S.R. 7/G3
Bobruysk, U.S.S.R. 52/C4
Bobruysk, U.S.S.R. 48/C4
Bobs (lake), Ontario 177/H3
Bobtown, Pa. (15315) 294/B6
Bobures, Venezuela 124/C3
Boby, Pic (mt.), Madagascar 118/H4
Bocabec, New Bruns. 170/C3
Boca Chica, Dom. Rep. 158/E6
Boca Chica (key), Fla. 212/E7
Boca Ciega (bay), Fla. 212/B3
Boca de Aroa, Venezuela 124/D2
Boca del Mangle, Venezuela 124/D2
Boca del Pao, Venezuela 124/F3
Boca del Pepé, Colombia 126/B5
Boca del Río, Mexico 150/Q2
Boca del Soco, Dom. Rep. 158/F6
Boca do Acre, Brazil 132/G10
Boca Grande, Fla. (33921) 212/D5
Boca Grande (key), Fla. 212/D7
Boca Grande (passage), Trin. & Tob. 161/A10
Boca Grande (gulf), Venezuela 124/H3
Bocaiúva, Brazil 132/E7
Bocaranga, Cent. Afr. Rep. 115/C2
Boca Raton, Fla. (*33432) 212/F5
Bocas del Toro, Panama 154/F6
Bocay, Nicaragua 154/E3
Bochnia, Poland 47/E4
Bocholt, Belgium 27/H6
Bocholt, W. Germany 22/B3
Bochov, Czech. 41/B1
Bochum, W. Germany 22/B3
Bock, Minn. (56313) 255/E5
Boco, Chile 138/F2
Boconó, Venezuela 124/C3
Boda, Cent. Afr. Rep. 115/C3
Bodalla, N.S. Wales 97/F5
Bodaybo, U.S.S.R. 54/N4
Bodaybo, U.S.S.R. 48/M4
Bodcaw, Ark. (†71858) 202/D6
Boddam, Scotland 15/G3
Boddington, W. Australia 92/B2
Bode, Iowa (50519) 229/E3
Bodega (bay), Calif. 204/B5
Bodega (head), Calif. 204/B5
Bodega Bay, Calif. (94923) 204/B5
Bodegraven, Netherlands 27/F4
Bodélé (depr.), Chad 102/D3
Bodélé (depr.), Chad 111/C4
Boden, Sweden 18/M4
Bodensee (Constance) (lake), Austria 41/A3
Bodensee (Constance) (lake), Switzerland 39/H1
Bodensee (Constance) (lake), W. Germany 22/C5
Boderg (lake), Ireland 17/E4
Bodfish, Calif. (93205) 204/G8
Bodhan, India 68/D5
Bodie (isl.), N.C. 281/T2
Bodinayakkanur, India 68/D6
Bodines, Pa. (17722) 294/H3
Bodio, Switzerland 39/G4
Bodkin (pt.), Md. 245/N4
Bodmin, England 13/C7
Bodmin, England 10/D5
Bodmin, Sask. 181/D2
Bodo, Alberta 182/E3
Bodø, Norway 18/J3
Bodø, Norway 7/F2
Bodrum, Turkey 63/B4
Bodrum, Turkey 59/A2
Bo Duc, Vietnam 72/E4
Bódvaszilas, Hungary 41/F2
Boelus, Nebr. (68820) 264/F3
Boende, Zaire 115/D4
Boerne, Texas (78006) 303/J10
Boeuf (lake), La. 238/J7
Boeuf (riv.), La. 238/G1
Boffa, Guinea 106/B6
Bog (lake), Maine 243/H6
Bogalusa, La. 188/H4
Bogalusa, La. (70427) 238/L5
Bogan (riv.), N.S. Wales 97/D2
Bogandé, Upper Volta 106/E6
Bogan Gate, N.S. Wales 97/D3
Bogantungan, Queensland 95/C4
Bogard, Mo. (64622) 261/E4
Bogart, Georgia (30622) 217/E3
Bogata, Texas (75417) 303/J4
Bogatynia, Poland 47/B3
Boğazlıyan, Turkey 63/F3
Bogen, W. Germany 22/E4
Bogenfels, Namibia 118/B5
Bogense, Denmark 21/D6
Boger City, N.C. (28092) 281/G4
Boggabilla, N.S. Wales 97/F1
Boggabri, N.S. Wales 97/F2
Boggeragh (mts.), Ireland 17/D7
Boggs, W. Va. (26299) 312/E6
Boggstown, Ind. (46110) 227/F5
Boggy (peak), Ant. & Bar. 161/D11
Boggy Creek, Manitoba 179/A3
Boggy Depot, Okla. (†74525) 288/O6
Bogia, Papua N.G. 85/B6
Bogie (riv.), Scotland 15/F3
Bognor Regis, England 13/G7
Bognor Regis, England 10/F5
Bogny-sur-Meuse, France 28/F3
Bogo, Philippines 82/E5
Bogon (riv.), N. S. Wales 88/H6
Bogong (mt.), Victoria 97/D5
Bogor, Indonesia 54/M10
Bogor, Indonesia 85/H2
Bogoslof (isl.), Alaska 196/E4
Bogotá (cap.), Colombia 126/D5
Bogotá (cap.), Colombia 120/B2
Bogotá (cap.), Colombia 2/F5
Bogota, Ill. (†62448) 222/E5
Bogota, N.J. (07603) 273/B2
Bogota, Tenn. (38007) 237/C8
Bogra, Bangladesh 68/F4
Boguchar, U.S.S.R. 52/F5
Bogue, Kansas (67625) 232/C2
Bogué, Mauritania 106/B5
Bogue Chitto, Miss. (39629) 256/D8
Bogue Chitto (riv.), Miss. 256/D8
Bogue Homo (lake), Miss. 256/F7
Boguszów-Gorce, Poland 47/B3
Bog Walk, Jamaica 158/J6
Bo Hai (gulf), China 77/J4
Boharm, Sask. 181/F5
Bohemian (for.), Czech. 41/B2
Bohemian (for.), W. Germany 22/E4
Bohemian-Moravian Heights (hills), Czech. 41/C2
Boherbue, Ireland 17/C7
Bohners Lake, Wis. (†53105) 317/K10
Bohodleh, Somalia 115/J2
Bohol (prov.), Philippines 82/E6
Bohol (isl.), Philippines 85/G4
Bohol (isl.), Philippines 82/E6
Bohol (sea), Philippines 82/E6
Bohol (str.), Philippines 82/D6
Böhönye, Hungary 41/D3
Bohu (Bagrax), China 77/C3
Boicourt, Kansas (†66075) 232/H3
Boiestown, New Bruns. 170/D2
Boiling Spring Lakes, N.C. (28461) 281/N7
Boiling Springs, N.C. (28017) 281/F4
Boiling Springs, Pa. (17007) 294/H5
Bois Blanc (isl.), Mich. 250/E3
Boischatel, Québec/J3
Boisdale, Nova Scotia 168/H2
Boisdale, Loch (inlet), Scotland 15/A3
Bois D'Arc, Mo. (65612) 261/F8
Bois-des-Filion, Québec 172/H4
Bois de Sioux (riv.), Minn. 255/B4
Bois de Sioux (riv.), S. Dak. 298/R1
Boise (co.), Idaho 220/C6
Boise (cap.), Idaho 146/G5
Boise (cap.), Idaho (*83701) 220/B6
Boise (cap.), Idaho 188/C2
Boise (mts.), Idaho 220/B6
Boise (riv.), Idaho 220/B6
Boise City, Okla. (73933) 288/B1
Boissevain, Man. 162/G6
Boissevain, Manitoba 179/C5
Boissevain, Va. (24606) 307/F6
Boistfort, Wash. (†98532) 310/B4
Boisvert (pt.), Québec 172/J1
Boizenburg an der Elbe, E. Germany 22/D2
Bojador (cape), W. Sahara 102/A2
Bojador (cape), Western Sahara 106/B3
Bojeador (cape), Philippines 82/C1
Bojnurd, Iran 66/K2
Bojnurd, Iran 59/G2
Bojonegoro, Indonesia 85/J2
Bokchito, Okla. (74726) 288/O6
Boké, Guinea 106/B6
Bokeelia, Fla. (33922) 212/D5
Bokel (cay), Belize 154/D2
Bokhara (riv.), N.S. Wales 97/D1
Bokhoma, Okla. (†71821) 288/S7
Boknafjord (fjord), Norway 18/D7
Boko, Congo 115/B4
Bokoro, Chad 111/C5
Bokoshe, Okla. (74930) 288/S4
Bokote, Zaire 115/D4
Bokpyin, Burma 72/C5
Boksburg, S. Africa 118/J6
Bokungu, Zaire 115/D4
Bol, Chad 111/B5
Bol, Chad 102/D3
Bolair, W. Va. (26288) 312/F6
Bolama, Guinea-Biss. 106/A6
Bolan (pass), Pakistan 68/B3
Bolangir, India 68/E4
Bolar, Va. (24414) 307/J4
Bolatusha, Miss. (†39160) 256/E5
Bolayır, Turkey 63/C5
Bolbec, France 28/D3
Bolckow, Mo. (64427) 261/C2
Boldersley, Denmark 21/C8
Bolding, Ark. (†71747) 202/F7
Boldman, Ky. (†41501) 237/R5
Boldon, England 13/J3
Bolduc, Québec 172/G4
Bole, China 77/B3
Bole, Ghana 106/D7
Boles, Ark. (72926) 202/B4
Bolesławiec, Poland 47/B3
Boley, Okla. (74829) 288/O4
Bolgatanga, Ghana 106/D6
Boli, China 77/M2
Boligee, Ala. (35443) 195/C5
Bolinao, Philippines 82/B2
Bolinao (cape), Philippines 82/B2
Bolinas, Calif. (94924) 204/H1
Boling, Texas (77420) 303/H8
Bolingbroke, Georgia (31004) 217/E5
Bolingbrook, Ill. (60439) 222/A6
Bolinger, Ala. (36903) 195/B7
Bolinger, La. (†71064) 238/C1
Bolívar, Argentina 143/D4
Bolívar, Bolivia 136/B3
Bolívar (dept.), Colombia 126/C3
Bolívar, Antioquia, Colombia 126/C5
Bolívar, Cauca, Colombia 126/B7
Bolívar (prov.), Ecuador 128/C3
Bolívar, Ecuador 128/C2
Bolivar (co.), Miss. 256/C3
Bolivar, Mo. (65613) 261/F7
Bolivar, N.Y. (14715) 276/D6
Bolivar, Ohio (44612) 284/G4
Bolivar, Pa. (15923) 294/D5
Bolívar, Peru 128/D6
Bolivar, Tenn. (38008) 237/C10
Bolivar (pen.), Texas 303/K8
Bolívar (state), Venezuela 124/F7
Bolívar, Cerro (mt.), Venezuela 124/G4
Bolívar, Pico (peak), Venezuela 124/C3
Bolivar, W. Va. (†25425) 312/L4
Bolivia 2/F6
Bolivia 120/C4
BOLIVIA 136
Bolivia, N.C. (28422) 281/N6
Bolkar (mts.), Turkey 63/F4
Bolkhov, U.S.S.R. 52/E4
Bolligen, Switzerland 39/E3
Bolling, Ala. (36007) 195/E7
Bolling A.F.B., D.C. 245/E5
Bollinger (co.), Mo. 261/M8
Bollington, England 10/G2
Bollington, England 13/H2
Bollnäs, Sweden 18/K6
Bollon, Queensland 95/C6
Bollon, Queensland 88/H5
Bollstabruk, Sweden 18/L5
Bolmen (lake), Sweden 18/H8
Bolobo, Zaire 115/C4
Bologna (prov.), Italy 34/C2
Bologna, Italy 34/C2
Bologna, Italy 7/F4
Bolognesi, Peru 128/F8
Bolognesi, Peru 128/F6
Bologoye, U.S.S.R. 52/D3
Bolomba, Zaire 115/C3
Bolonchén de Rejón, Mexico 150/O7
Bolondrón, Cuba 156/B2
Bolondrón, Cuba 158/D1
Bolovens (plat.), Laos 72/E4
Bolpebra, Bolivia 136/A2
Bolsena (lake), Italy 34/C3
Bol'shevik (isl.) U.S.S.R. 54/N2
Bol'shevik (isl.), U.S.S.R. 4/A4
Bol'shevik (isl.), U.S.S.R. 48/K2
Bol'shoy Lyakhov (isl.), U.S.S.R. 54/R2
Bol'shoy Lyakhovskiy (isl.), U.S.S.R. 48/P2
Bolsover, England 13/J2
Bolsters Mills, Maine (†04040) 243/B7
Bolsward, Netherlands 27/H2
Boltaña, Spain 33/F1
Boltigen, Switzerland 39/D3
Bolton○, Conn. (06040) 210/F1
Bolton, England 10/G2
Bolton, England 13/H2
Bolton○, Mass. (01740) 249/H3
Bolton, Miss. (39041) 256/D6
Bolton, N.C. (28423) 281/N6
Bolton○, Vt. (†05466) 268/B3
Bolton (mt.), Vt. 268/B3
Bolton Landing, N.Y. (12814) 276/N3
Bolu (prov.), Turkey 63/D2
Bolu, Turkey 59/B1
Bolu, Turkey 63/D2
Bolus (head), Ireland 17/A8
Bolvadin, Turkey 63/D3
Bolvanskiy Nos (cape), U.S.S.R. 52/K1
Bolvanskiy Nos (cape), U.S.S.R. 48/G2
Bolzano (Bolzen), Italy 34/C1
Bolzano, Italy 7/F4
Bolzano-Bozen (prov.), Italy 34/C1
Bolzen (Bolzano), Italy 34/C1
Boma, Zaire 102/D5
Boma, Zaire 115/B5
Bomaderry-Nowra, N.S. Wales 97/F4
Bomarton, Texas (†76380) 303/E4
Bomba (gulf), Libya 111/D1
Bombala, N.S. Wales 97/E5
Bombardopolis, Haiti 158/B5
Bombay, India 54/J8
Bombay, India 2/N5
Bombay (harb.), India 68/B7
Bombay, Minn. (†55946) 255/F6
Bombay, N.Y. (12914) 276/M1
Bomboma, Zaire 115/C3
Bom Conselho, Brazil 132/G5
Bom Despacho, Brazil 135/D1
Bom Despacho, Brazil 132/E7
Bomdila, India 68/G3
Bom Futuro, Brazil 120/C4
Bom Futuro, Brazil 132/A5
Bomi, China 77/E6
Bom Jesus, Brazil 132/E5
Bom Jesus da Lapa, Brazil 120/E4
Bom Jesus da Lapa, Brazil 132/F6
Bom Jesus do Itabapoana, Brazil 135/F2
Bomongo, Zaire 115/C3
Bomont, W. Va. (25030) 312/D6
Bomoseen, Vt. (05732) 268/A4
Bomoseen (lake), Vt. 268/A4
Bom Retiro, Brazil 132/D10
Bom Sucesso, Brazil 135/D2
Bomu (riv.), Cent. Afr. Rep. 102/E4
Bomu (riv.), Cent. Afr. Rep. 115/D3
Bomu (riv.), Zaire 115/D3
Bon (cape), Tunisia 102/D1
Bon (cape), Tunisia 106/G1
Bona (mt.), Alaska 196/K2
Bonabéri, Cameroon 115/A3
Bonacca (Guanaja) (isl.), Honduras 154/E2
Bon Accord, Alberta 182/D3
Bonaduz, Switzerland 39/H3
Bon Air, Ala. (35032) 195/F4
Bonair, Iowa (†52155) 229/J2
Bon Air, Tenn. (†38583) 237/L9
Bon Air, Va. (23235) 307/N5
Bonaire (isl.), Neth. Ant. 156/E4
Bonaire (isl.), Neth. Ant. 161/E9
Bonalbo, N.S. Wales 97/G1

Boyne City 341

Bonanza, Alberta 182/A2
Bonanza, Ark. (†72901) 202/B3
Bonanza, Colo. (†81155) 208/G6
Bonanza, Nicaragua 154/E4
Bonanza, Oreg. (97623) 291/F5
Bonanza, Utah (84008) 304/E3
Bonanza (peak), Wash. 310/E2
Bonao, Dom. Rep. 158/E6
Bonaparte, Iowa (52620) 229/K7
Bonaparte (lake), N.Y. 276/K2
Bonaparte (creek), Wash. 310/F2
Bonaparte (mt.), Wash. 310/F2
Bonaparte (arch.), W. Australia 88/C2
Bonaparte (arch.), W. Australia 92/D1
Bon Aqua, Tenn. (37025) 237/G9
Bonar Bridge, Scotland 15/D3
Bonaventure (cape), Newf. 166/D2
Bonaventure (co.), Québec 172/C2
Bonaventure (county), Québec 174/D3
Bonaventure, Québec 172/C2
Bonaventure (isl.), Québec 172/D1
Bonaventure (riv.), Québec 172/C1
Bonavista, Newf. 166/D2
Bonavista (bay), Newf. 166/D1
Bonavista (cape), Newf. 166/D1
Bonavista, Newf. 162/L6
Boncarbo, Colo. (81024) 208/K8
Bonchester Bridge, Scotland 15/F5
Boncourt, Switzerland 39/C2
Bond, Colo. (80423) 208/F3
Bond (co.), Ill. 222/D5
Bond, Ky. (40407) 237/N6
Bond, Miss. (39550) 256/F9
Bond (mt.), N.H. 268/E3
Bondeno, Italy 34/C2
Bond Falls (res.), Mich. 250/G2
Bondi (beach), N.S. Wales 97/K3
Bondiss, Alberta 182/D2
Bondo, Zaire 115/D3
Bondoukou, Ivory Coast 106/D7
Bondowoso, Indonesia 85/L2
Bondsville, Mass. (01009) 249/E4
Bonduel, Wis. (54107) 317/K6
Bondurant, Iowa (50035) 229/G5
Bondurant, Wyo. (82922) 319/B2
Bondville, Ill. (61815) 222/E3
Bondville, Ky. (40308) 237/M5
Bondville, Vt. (05340) 268/B5
Bondy, France 28/B1
Bône (Annaba), Algeria 106/F1
Bone, Idaho (†83401) 220/G6
Bone (gulf), Indonesia 54/O10
Bone (gulf), Indonesia 85/G7
Bone Cave, Tenn. (†38581) 237/L9
Bone Gap, Ill. (62815) 222/F5
Bo'ness, Scotland 10/C1
Bo'ness, Scotland 15/C1
Bonesteel, S. Dak. (57317) 298/M7
Bonet (riv.), Ireland 17/E3
Boneta, Utah (†84051) 304/D3
Bonete (dam), Uruguay 145/C3
Bonetraill, N. Dak. (†58801) 282/C3
Boneville, Georgia (30806) 217/G4
Bonfield, Ill. (60913) 222/E2
Bonfield, Ontario 177/E1
Bonfol, Switzerland 39/D2
Bong (range), Liberia 106/B7
Bongabong, Philippines 82/C4
Bongandanga, Zaire 115/D3
Bonggaw, Philippines 82/B8
Bongo (isl.), Philippines 82/D7
Bongor, Chad 111/C5
Bongor, Chad 102/D3
Bong Son (Hoai Nhon), Vietnam 72/F4
Bonham, Texas (75418) 303/H4
Bonhill, Scotland 15/B1
Bonhomme (isl.), Mo. 261/N2
Bon Homme (co.), S. Dak. 298/O7
Bonifacio, France 28/B7
Bonifacio (str.), France 28/B7
Bonifacio (str.), Italy 34/B4
Bonifay, Fla. (32425) 212/C5
Bönigen, Switzerland 39/E3
Bonilla, S. Dak. (†57348) 298/N4
Bonin (isls.), Japan 2/S4
Bonin (isls.), Japan 54/R7
Bonin (isls.), Japan 87/E3
Bonin (isls.), Japan 81/M3
Bonita, Ariz. (†85643) 198/E6
Bonita (pt.), Calif. 204/H2
Bonita, La. (71223) 238/G1
Bonita, Miss. (†39301) 256/G6
Bonita Springs, Fla. (33923) 212/E5
Bonlee, N.C. (27213) 281/L3
Bonn (cap.), W. Germany 7/E3
Bonn (cap.), W. Germany 22/B3
Bonne (bay), Newf. 166/C4
Bonneau, S.C. (29431) 296/H5
Bonner (co.), Idaho 220/B1
Bonners Ferry, Idaho (83805) 220/B1
Bonner Springs, Kansas (66012) 232/H2
Bonner-West Riverside, Mont. (59823) 262/C4
Bonnet (lake), Manitoba 179/G4
Bonnétable, France 28/D3
Bonnet Carré Spillway and Floodway, La. 238/N3
Bonne Terre, Mo. (63628) 261/L7
Bonnet Plume (riv.), Yukon 187/E3
Bonneville, France 28/G4
Bonneville (co.), Idaho 220/G6
Bonneville, Oreg. (97008) 291/F2
Bonneville (dam), Oreg. 291/E2
Bonneville (salt flats), Utah 304/A3
Bonneville (dam), Wash. 310/D5
Bonneville (lake), Wash. 310/D5
Bonneville, Wyo. (†82649) 319/E2
Bonneville (mt.), Wyo. 319/C3
Bonney Lake, Wash. (†98390) 310/C3
Bonnie, Ill. (62816) 222/E5
Bonnieville, Ky. (42713) 237/K6
Bonnots Mill, Mo. (65016) 261/J5
Bonny (res.), Colo. 208/P3
Bonny, Nigeria 106/F8
Bonny (bight), Nigeria 106/F8
Bonnybridge, Scotland 15/C1
Bonnyman, Ky. (41719) 237/P6
Bonnyrigg, N. S. Wales 88/K4
Bonnyrigg, N.S. Wales 97/H3
Bonnyrigg and Lasswade, Scotland 10/C1
Bonnyrigg and Lasswade, Scotland 15/D2
Bonny River, New Bruns. 170/D3
Bonnyville, Alberta 182/E2
Bono, Ark. (72416) 202/J2
Bono, Ohio (†43445) 284/D2
Bonorva, Italy 34/B4
Bonpas (creek), Ill. 222/F5
Bonpland (mt.), N. Zealand 100/A6
Bon Secour, Ala. (36511) 195/C10
Bon Secour (bay), Ala. 195/C10
Bonsecours, Québec 172/E4
Bonshaw, Pr. Edward I. 168/E2
Bonthain, Indonesia 85/F7
Bonthe, S. Leone 106/B7
Bontoc, Philippines 85/G2
Bontoc, Philippines 82/C2
Bon Wier, Texas (75928) 303/L7
Bonyhád, Hungary 41/E3
Boody, Ill. (62514) 222/D4
Book (cliffs), Utah 304/E4
Booker, Texas (79005) 303/D1
Booker T. Washington Nat'l Mon., Va. 307/J6
Boolaloo, W. Australia 92/B3
Booligal, N.S. Wales 97/C3
Boom, Belgium 27/E6
Boom, Tenn. (†38573) 237/L7
Boomer, N.C. (28606) 281/G2
Boomer, W. Va. (25031) 312/D6
Boomi, N. S. Wales 88/H5
Boomi, N.S. Wales 97/E1
Boon (pt.), Ant. & Bar. 161/E11
Boon, Mich. (49618) 250/D4
Boondall, Queensland 88/K2
Boone (co.), Ark. 202/D1
Boone, Colo. (81025) 208/L6
Boone (co.), Ill. 222/E1
Boone (co.), Ind. 227/E4
Boone (co.), Iowa 229/F5
Boone, Iowa (50036) 229/F4
Boone (co.), Ky. 237/M3
Boone, Ky. (†40403) 237/N5
Boone (co.), Mo. 261/H4
Boone (co.), Nebr. 264/F3
Boone, Nebr. (68625) 264/F3
Boone, N.C. (28607) 281/F2
Boone (lake), Tenn. 237/S8
Boone (co.), W. Va. 312/C6
Boone Grove, Ind. (46302) 227/C2
Boonesboro, Mo. (†65250) 261/G4
Boones Mill, Va. (24065) 307/J6
Boonesville, Va. (†22935) 307/L4
Booneville, Ark. (72927) 202/C3
Booneville, Ky. (41314) 237/O6
Booneville, Miss. (38829) 256/G1
Boonsboro, Md. (21713) 245/H2
Boonton, N.J. (07005) 273/E2
Boonton (res.), N.J. 273/E2
Boonville, Calif. (95415) 204/B5
Boonville, Ind. (47601) 227/C8
Boonville, Mo. (65233) 261/G5
Boonville, N.Y. (13309) 276/K4
Boonville, N.C. (27011) 281/H2
Boopi (riv.), Bolivia 136/B4
Boorooban, N.S. Wales 97/C4
Boorowa, N.S. Wales 97/E4
Boort, Victoria 97/B5
Booth, Ala. (36008) 195/E6
Boothbay, Maine (04537) 243/D8
Boothbay○, Maine (04537) 243/D8
Boothbay Harbor, Maine (04538) 243/D8
Boothia (pen.), Canada 4/B14
Boothia (gulf), Canada 4/B14
Boothia (pen.), N.W.T. 146/J2
Boothia (gulf), N.W.T. 146/J2
Boothia (isthmus), N.W.T. 162/G2
Boothia (pen.), N.W.T. 162/G1
Boothia (gulf), N.W.T. 162/G1
Boothia (gulf), N.W. Terrs. 187/K3
Boothia (pen.), N.W. Terrs. 187/J2
Boothville, La. (70038) 238/M8
Boothwyn, Pa. (19061) 294/L7
Bootle, England 10/E2
Bootle, England 13/G2
Booué, Gabon 115/B3
Bophuthatswana (bantustan), S. Africa 102/E7
Bophuthatswana (rep.), S. Africa 118/D5
Boppard, W. Germany 22/B3
Boquerón, Cuba 158/K4
Boquerón, Cuba 156/C3
Boquerón (dept.), Paraguay 144/B3
Boquerón, El (pass), Peru 128/E7
Boquerón, P. Rico 156/F1
Boquerón, P. Rico 161/A3
Boquerón (bay), P. Rico 161/A3
Boquilla del Carmen, Mexico 150/H2
Bor, Czech. 41/B2
Bor, Sudan 111/F6
Bor, Turkey 63/F4
Bor, U.S.S.R. 52/F3
Bor, Yugoslavia 45/E3
Bora-Bora (isl.), Fr. Poly. 87/L7
Borah (peak), Idaho 188/D2
Borah (peak), Idaho 220/E5
Borama, Somalia 115/H1
Borås, Sweden 7/F3
Borås, Sweden 18/H8
Borazjan, Iran 66/G6
Borazjan, Iran 59/F4
Borba, Brazil 120/D3
Borba, Brazil 132/H9
Borba, Portugal 33/C3
Borbón, Venezuela 124/F4
Borçka, Turkey 63/J2
Borculo, Netherlands 27/J4
Bordeaux, France 28/C5
Bordeaux, France 7/D4
Bordeaux, S.C. (†29835) 296/C4
Bordeaux (mt.), Virgin Is. (U.S.) 161/C4
Bordelonville, La. (71320) 238/G4
Borden (isl.), Canada 4/B15
Borden, Ind. (47106) 227/F8
Borden (isl.), N.W. Terrs. 187/G2
Borden (pen.), N.W. Terrs. 187/K2
Borden, Pr. Edward I. 168/E2
Borden, Sask. 181/D3
Borden, S.C. (29017) 296/G3
Borden (co.), Texas 303/C5
Borden, W. Australia 92/B6
Borden Shaft, Md. (†21532) 245/B2
Borden Springs, Ala. (†36262) 195/H3
Bordentown, N.J. (08505) 273/D3
Border, Minn. (†56623) 255/D2
Border, Wyo. (†83114) 319/B3
Borderland, W. Va. (25665) 312/B7
Borders (reg.), Scotland 15/E5
Bordertown, S. Australia 88/F7
Bordertown, S. Australia 94/G7
Bordighera, Italy 34/A3
Bordj Bou Arreridj, Algeria 106/E1
Bordj Fly Sainte Marie, Algeria 106/D3
Bordj Omar Driss, Algeria 106/F3
Bordj Omar Driss, Algeria 102/C2
Bordulac, N. Dak. (58417) 282/N5
Boreing, Ky. (†40740) 237/N6
Boreray (isl.), Scotland 15/A2
Boreray (isl.), Scotland 15/A3
Borgå, Finland 18/O6
Borge, Norway 18/H2
Borger, Netherlands 27/K3
Borger, Texas (79007) 303/C2
Borger, Texas 188/F3
Borgerhout, Belgium 27/E6
Borgholm, Sweden 18/K8
Borghorst, W. Germany 22/B2
Borgloon, Belgium 27/G7
Borgne (lake), La. 238/L7
Borgne (riv.), Switzerland 39/D4
Borgo, Italy 34/C1
Borgomanero, Italy 34/B2
Borgo San Lorenzo, Italy 34/C2
Borgworm (Waremme), Belgium 27/G7
Borikan, Laos 72/D3
Boring, Md. (21020) 245/L2
Boring, Oreg. (97009) 291/E2
Borinquen (pt.), P. Rico 156/F1
Borinquen (pt.), P. Rico 161/A1
Borislav, U.S.S.R. 52/B5
Borisoglebsk, U.S.S.R. 48/E4
Borisoglebsk, U.S.S.R. 52/F4
Borisov, U.S.S.R. 52/C4
Borisovka, U.S.S.R. 52/E4
Bo River Post, Sudan 111/E6
Borja, Peru 128/D5
Borja, Spain 33/F2
Borjas Blancas, Spain 33/G2
Borken, W. Germany 22/B3
Børkop, Denmark 21/C6
Borku, Chad 111/C4
Borkum, W. Germany 22/B2
Borkum (isl.), W. Germany 22/B2
Borlänge, Sweden 18/J6
Borna, E. Germany 22/E3
Borndiep (chan.), Netherlands 27/H2
Borne, Netherlands 27/K4
Borneo (isl.) 2/Q6
Borneo (isl.) 54/N9
Borneo (isl.), Indonesia 85/E5
Borneo (isl.), Malaysia 85/E5
Bornheim, W. Germany 22/B3
Bornholm (co.), Denmark 21/F9
Bornholm (isl.), Denmark 7/F3
Bornholm (isl.), Denmark 18/J9
Bornholm (isl.), Denmark 21/F9
Borno (state), Nigeria 106/G6
Bornova, Turkey 63/B3
Borocay (isl.), Philippines 82/D5
Borojó, Venezuela 124/C2
Boron, Calif. (93516) 204/H8
Borongan, Philippines 82/E5
Borot Kidod (well), Israel 65/C5
Borovichi, U.S.S.R. 52/D3
Borradaile, Alberta 182/E3
Borre, Norway 18/D4
Borrego Springs, Calif. (92004) 204/J10
Borris, Ireland 17/H6
Borris-in-Ossory, Ireland 17/F6
Borrisokane, Ireland 17/E6
Borrisoleigh, Ireland 17/E6
Borroloola, North. Terr. 88/F3
Borroloola, North. Terr. 93/E4
Borşa, Romania 45/G2
Borsod-Abaúj-Zemplén (co.), Hungary 41/F2
Bortala (Bole), China 77/B3
Borth, Wales 13/C5
Bort-les-Orgues, France 28/E5
Boruca, C. Rica 154/F6
Borujerd, Iran 59/E3
Borujerd, Iran 66/F4
Borup, Denmark 21/E7
Borup, Minn. (56519) 255/B3
Börzsöny (mts.), Hungary 41/E3
Borzya, U.S.S.R. 48/M4
Bosa, Italy 34/B4
Bosanska Dubica, Yugoslavia 45/C3
Bosanska Gradiška, Yugoslavia 45/C3
Bosanska Kostajnica, Yugoslavia 45/B3
Bosanska Krupa, Yugoslavia 45/C3
Bosanski Brod, Yugoslavia 45/D3
Bosanski Novi, Yugoslavia 45/C3
Bosanski Petrovac, Yugoslavia 45/C3
Bosanski Šamac, Yugoslavia 45/D3
Bosaso, Somalia 115/J1
Bosaso, Somalia 102/G3
Boscawen○, N.H. (03301) 268/D5
Bosch, van den (cape), Indonesia 85/J6
Bosco, La. (†71201) 238/F2
Boscobel, Wis. (53805) 317/E9
Bose, China 77/G7
Boshan, China 77/J4
Boskoop, Netherlands 27/F4
Boskovice, Czech. 41/D2
Bosler, Wyo. (82051) 319/G4
Bosna (riv.), Yugoslavia 45/D3
Bosnia and Hercegovina (rep.), Yugoslavia 45/C3
Boso (pen.), Japan 81/K6
Bosobolo, Zaire 115/D3
Bosporus (str.), Turkey 7/G4
Bosporus (str.), Turkey 59/A1
Bosporus (str.), Turkey 63/C2
Bosque (Bosque Farms), N. Mex. (87006) 274/C4
Bosque (co.), Texas 303/G6
Boss, Mo. (65440) 261/K7
Bossangoa, Cent. Afr. Rep. 102/D4
Bossangoa, Cent. Afr. Rep. 115/C2
Bossburg, Wash. (†99126) 310/H2
Bossé, New Bruns. 170/B1
Bossembele, Cent. Afr. Rep. 115/C2
Bossier (par.), La. 238/C1
Bossier City, La. (*71111) 238/C1
Bosso, Niger 106/G6
Bostan, Iran 66/F5
Bostan, Pakistan 68/B2
Bostanabad-e-Bala, Iran 66/E2
Bosten (Bagrax) Hu (lake), China 77/C3
Boston (mts.), Ark. 202/B2
Boston, England 13/G5
Boston, England 10/F4
Boston, Georgia (31626) 217/E9
Boston, Ind. (47324) 227/H5
Boston, Ky. (40107) 237/K5
Boston (cap.), Mass. 146/L5
Boston (cap.), Mass. 188/M2
Boston (cap.), Mass. (*02101) 249/D7
Boston (bay), Mass. 249/E6
Boston (harb.), Mass. 249/D7
Boston, Mo. (†64759) 261/D8
Boston, N.Y. (14025) 276/C5
Boston (mts.), Okla. 288/S3
Boston, Pa. (15135) 294/C7
Boston, Tenn. (†37064) 237/G9
Boston, Texas (75557) 303/K4
Boston, U.S. 2/F3
Boston, Va. (22713) 307/M3
Boston Bar, Br. Col. 184/G5
Boston Heights, Ohio (†44264) 284/J10
Bostonnais (co.), Québec 172/E2
Bostonnais, Grand Lac (lake), Québec 172/E2
Bostonnais (riv.), Québec 172/E2
Boston Nat'l Hist. Park, Mass. 249/D6
Bostwick, Fla. (32007) 212/E2
Bostwick, Georgia (30623) 217/E3
Bostwick, Nebr. (†68978) 264/F4
Boswell, Ark. (72516) 202/F1
Boswell, Br. Col. 184/J5
Boswell, Ind. (47921) 227/C3
Boswell, Okla. (74727) 288/P6
Boswell, Pa. (15531) 294/E5
Boswell Bay, Alaska (†99574) 196/J2
Boswil, Switzerland 39/F2
Bosworth, Mo. (64723) 261/F4
Bot (riv.), S. Africa 118/G7
Botany, N. S. Wales 88/L4
Botany (bay), N. S. Wales 88/L4
Botany, N.S. Wales 97/J4
Botany (bay), N.S. Wales 97/J4
Botene, Laos 72/D3
Botetourt (co.), Va. 307/J5
Botevgrad, Bulgaria 45/F4
Botha, Alberta 182/D3
Botha (riv.), Alberta 182/B1
Bothell, Wash. (98011) 310/B1
Bothnia (gulf) 7/G2
Bothnia (gulf), Finland 18/M5
Bothnia (gulf), Sweden 18/N4
Bothwell, Ontario 177/C5
Bothwell, Tasmania 99/C4
Bothwell, Utah (†84337) 304/B2
Botkins, Ohio (45306) 284/B5
Botna, Iowa (†51454) 229/C5
Botoşani, Romania 45/H2
Botrange (mt.), Belgium 27/J8
Botrivier, S. Africa 118/F7
Botsford, Conn. (06404) 210/C3
Botswana 2/L7
Botswana 102/E7
BOTSWANA 118/C4
Bottesford, England 13/G4
Bottineau (co.), N. Dak. 282/J2
Bottineau, N. Dak. (58318) 282/J2
Bottrel, Alberta 182/C4
Bottrop, W. Germany 22/B3
Botucatu, Brazil 135/B3
Botucatu, Brazil 132/D8
Botwood, Newf. 166/C4
Bouaflé, Ivory Coast 106/C7
Bouaké, Ivory Coast 102/B4
Bouaké, Ivory Coast 106/D7
Bouali, Cent. Afr. Rep. 115/C3
Bouar, Cent. Afr. Rep. 102/D4
Bouar, Cent. Afr. Rep. 115/C2
Bou Arfa, Morocco 106/D2
Bouca, Cent. Afr. Rep. 115/C2
Boucaut (bay), North. Terr. 93/D1
Boucherville, Québec 172/J4
Boucherville (isl.), Québec 172/J4
Bouches-du-Rhône (dept.), France 28/F6
Bouchette, Québec 172/A3
Bouckville, N.Y. (13310) 276/J5
Bou Djebeha, Mali 106/D5
Boudreau (bay), La. 238/M7
Boudreaux, La. (†70353) 238/J8
Boudreaux (lake), La. 238/J8
Boudry, Switzerland 39/C3
Boufarik, Algeria 106/E1
Bougainville (reef), 95/C2
Bougainville (reef), Coral Sea Is. Terr. 88/H3
Bougainville (isl.), Papua N.G. 87/F6
Bougainville (isl.), Papua N.G. 86/C2
Bougainville (str.), Papua N.G. 86/D2
Bougainville (str.), Solomon Is. 86/D2
Bougainville (cape), W. Australia 88/D2
Bougainville (cape), W. Australia 92/D1
Bougaroun (cape), Algeria 106/F1
Boughton (isl.), Pr. Edward I. 168/F2
Bougie (Béjaïa), Algeria 106/F1
Bougouni, Mali 106/C6
Bouillante, Guadeloupe 161/A6
Bouillon, Belgium 27/G9
Bou Izakarn, Morocco 106/C3
Boujad, Morocco 106/C2
Boula, Cent. Afr. Rep. 115/C3
Boulanger, Québec 172/E1
Boularderie (isl.), Nova Scotia 168/H2
Boulder, Australia 87/C9
Boulder, Colo. 188/E2
Boulder, Colo. 146/H6
Boulder (co.), Colo. 208/J2
Boulder, Colo. (*80301) 208/J2
Boulder (mts.), Idaho 220/D6
Boulder, Mont. (59632) 262/E4
Boulder (lake), N. Mex. 274/C2
Boulder, Utah (84716) 304/C6
Boulder (creek), Utah 304/C6
Boulder, W. Australia 88/C6
Boulder, Wyo. (82923) 319/C3
Boulder (lake), Wyo. 319/C3
Boulder City, Nev. (89005) 266/G7
Boulder Creek, Calif. (95006) 204/J4
Boulder Junction, Wis. (54512) 317/G3
Boulder-Kalgoorlie, W. Australia 92/C5
Boulevard, Calif. (92005) 204/J11
Boulevard Heights, Md. (†20027) 245/F5
Boulia, Queensland 95/A4
Boulia, Queensland 88/F4
Boulogne, Fla. (†32046) 212/E1
Boulogne-Billancourt, France 28/A2
Boulogne-sur-Mer, France 28/D2
Bouna, Ivory Coast 106/D7
Boundary, Alaska (†99732) 196/K2
Boundary (co.), Idaho 220/B1
Boundary (peak), Nev. 266/C5
Boundary (plat.), Sask. 181/B6
Boundary (bay), Wash. 310/C1
Boundary (dam), Wash. 310/H2
Boundary (lake), Wash. 310/H2
Boundary Bend, Victoria 97/B4
Bound Brook, N.J. (08805) 273/D2
Boundiali, Ivory Coast 106/C7
Boundji, Congo 115/C4
Boun Nua, Laos 72/D2
Bountiful, Utah (84010) 304/C3
Bounty (isls.), N. Zealand 87/H10
Bounty, Sask. 181/D4
Bourail, New Caled. 87/G8
Bourail, New Caled. 86/G4
Bourbon, Ill. (†61953) 222/E4
Bourbon, Ind. (46504) 227/E2
Bourbon (co.), Kansas 232/H4
Bourbon (co.), Ky. 237/N4
Bourbon, Miss. (†38756) 256/C4
Bourbon, Mo. (65441) 261/K6
Bourbonnais (trad. prov.), France 29
Bourbonnais, Ill. (60914) 222/F2
Bourem, Mali 106/E5
Bourg, La. (70343) 238/J7
Bourganeuf, France 28/D5
Bourg-des-Saintes, Guadeloupe 161/A7
Bourg-en-Bresse, France 28/F4
Bourgeois, New Bruns. 170/F2
Bourges, France 28/E4
Bourget, Ontario 177/J2
Bourg-Léopold (Leopoldsburg), Belgium 27/G6
Bourgoin-Jallieu, France 28/F5
Bourg Saint-Pierre, Switzerland 39/D5
Bourke, N. S. Wales 88/H6
Bourke, N.S. Wales 97/C2
Bourne, England 13/G5
Bourne, Mass. (02532) 249/M6
Bourne○, Mass. (02532) 249/M6
Bournedale, Mass. (†02532) 249/M5
Bournemouth, England 13/F7
Bournemouth, England 10/F5
Bourneville, Ohio (45617) 284/D7
Bou Saâda, Algeria 106/E1
Bouse, Ariz. (85325) 198/A5
Bouse Wash (dry riv.), Ariz. 198/A4
Boussac, France 28/D4
Bousso, Chad 111/C5
Boussu, Belgium 27/D8
Boutilimit, Mauritania 106/B5
Boutilimit, Mauritania 102/A3
Bouton, Iowa (50039) 229/E5
Boutte, La. (70039) 238/N4
Bouvard (cape), W. Australia 92/A2
Bouvet (isl.) 5/D1
Bouvetøya (Bouvet) (isl.) 5/D1
Boven Bolivia, Neth. Ant. 161/E8
Boves, Italy 34/A2
Bovey, Minn. (55709) 255/E3
Bovey Tracey, England 13/D7
Bovill, Idaho (83806) 220/B3
Bovina, Miss. (†39180) 256/C6
Bovina, Texas (79009) 303/A3
Bovril, Argentina 143/G5
Bow (riv.), Alberta 182/D4
Bow (riv.), Alta. 162/E5
Bow (lake), N.H. 268/E5
Bow, Wash. (98232) 310/C2
Bowbells, N. Dak. (58721) 282/F2
Bow City, Alberta 182/D4
Bowden, Alberta 182/C4
Bowden, Jamaica 158/K6
Bowden, W. Va. (26254) 312/G5
Bowdens, N.C. (28322) 281/M4
Bowdle, S. Dak. (57428) 298/K3
Bowdoin (lake), Mont. 262/J2
Bowdoinham○, Maine (04008) 243/D7
Bowdon, Georgia (30108) 217/B3
Bowdon, N. Dak. (58418) 282/L5
Bowdon Junction, Georgia (30109) 217/B3
Bowell, Alberta 182/E4
Bowen, Australia 87/E7
Bowen, Ill. (62316) 222/B3
Bowen, Ky. (40309) 237/O5
Bowen, Queensland 95/D3
Bowen, Queensland 88/H3
Bowen Island, Br. Col. 184/K3
Bowens, Md. (†20678) 245/M6
Bowerbank○, Maine (†04481) 243/E5
Bowers, Ind. (†47940) 227/D4
Bowers Beach, Del. (†19962) 245/S4
Bowers Mill, Mo. (†64848) 261/E8
Bowerston, Ohio (44695) 284/H5
Bowersville, Georgia (30516) 217/G2
Bowersville, Ohio (44695) 284/C6
Bowes, England 13/F3
Bowesmont, N. Dak. (58217) 282/R2
Bowie, Ariz. (85605) 198/F6
Bowie, Colo. (†81428) 208/D5
Bowie, Md. (20715) 245/L4
Bowie (creek), Miss. 256/E7
Bowie (co.), Texas 303/K4
Bowie, Texas (76230) 303/G4
Bow Island, Alberta 182/E5
Bowkan, Iran 66/E2
Bowlegs, Okla. (74830) 288/N4
Bowler, Wis. (54416) 317/J6
Bowling Green, Fla. (33834) 212/E4
Bowling Green, Ind. (47833) 227/D6
Bowling Green, Ky. (42101) 237/H7
Bowling Green, Ky. 188/J3
Bowling Green, Mo. (63334) 261/K4
Bowling Green, Ohio (43402) 284/C3
Bowling Green (cape), Queensland 88/H3
Bowling Green (cape), Queensland 95/C3
Bowling Green, S.C. (29703) 296/E1
Bowling Green, Va. (22427) 307/O4
Bowlus, Minn. (56314) 255/D5
Bowman, Calif. (95604) 204/C8
Bowman, Georgia (30624) 217/G2
Bowman (co.), N. Dak. 282/C7
Bowman, N. Dak. (58623) 282/D7
Bowman (bay), N.W.T. 162/J2
Bowman (bay), N.W. Terrs. 187/L3
Bowman (dam), Oreg. 291/G3
Bowman, S.C. (29018) 296/F5
Bowmansdale, Pa. (17008) 294/J5
Bowmanstown, Pa. (18030) 294/L4
Bowmansville, Pa. (17507) 294/L5
Bow Mills, N.H. (†03301) 268/D5
Bowmont, Idaho (†83651) 220/B6
Bowmore, Scotland 15/B5
Bowmore, Scotland 10/C3
Bowral, N.S. Wales 97/F4
Bowraville, N.S. Wales 97/G2
Bowring, Okla. (74009) 288/O1
Bowron Lake Prov. Park, Br. Col. 184/G3
Bowser, Br. Col. 184/H2
Bowser (lake), Br. Col. 184/C2
Bowsman, Manitoba 179/A2
Bowstring, Minn. (56631) 255/E3
Bowstring (lake), Minn. 255/E3
Boxborough○, Mass. (01719) 249/H3
Box Butte (co.), Nebr. 264/A2
Box Butte (res.), Nebr. 264/A2
Box Canyon (dam), Wash. 310/H2
Box Elder (creek), Colo. 208/K4
Box Elder, Mont. (59521) 262/F2
Boxelder (creek), Mont. 262/M5
Boxelder (creek), Mont. 262/H3
Box Elder, S. Dak. (57719) 298/D5
Boxelder (creek), S. Dak. 298/D5
Box Elder (co.), Utah 304/A2
Boxford, Mass. (01921) 249/L2
Boxford○, Mass. (01921) 249/L2
Box Hill, Victoria 97/J5
Box Hill, Victoria 88/L7
Boxholm, Iowa (50040) 229/E4
Bo Xian (Pohsien), China 77/J5
Boxley, Ark. (†72742) 202/D2
Boxmeer, Netherlands 27/H5
Box Springs, Georgia (31801) 217/C5
Boxtel, Netherlands 27/G5
Boyabat, Turkey 63/F2
Boyacá (dept.), Colombia 126/D5
Boyoma (Stanley) (falls), Zaire 102/E5
Boyoma (Stanley) (falls), Zaire 115/D3
Boyanup, W. Australia 92/A2
Boyce, La. (71409) 238/E4
Boyce, Va. (22620) 307/M2
Boyceville, Wis. (54725) 317/C5
Boyd, Ala. (†35470) 195/B5
Boyd, Fla. (†32347) 212/C1
Boyd (co.), Ky. 237/R4
Boyd, Minn. (56218) 255/C6
Boyd, Mont. (59013) 262/G5
Boyd (co.), Nebr. 264/F2
Boyd, Okla. (†73931) 288/E1
Boyd, Oreg. (†97021) 291/F2
Boyd, Texas (76023) 303/E1
Boyd, Wis. (54726) 317/E6
Boydell, Ark. (†71658) 202/H7
Boyden, Iowa (51234) 229/B2
Boyden Arbor, S.C. (†29128) 296/F3
Boyd Lake, Maine (†04463) 243/F5
Boyds, Md. (20720) 245/J4
Boyds, Wash. (99107) 310/G2
Boydton, Va. (23917) 307/M7
Boyer (riv.), Alberta 182/A5
Boyer, Iowa (†51448) 229/C4
Boyer (riv.), Iowa 229/B5
Boyer, W. Va. (†24915) 312/G5
Boyer Ahmediyeh and Kohkiluyeh (gov.), Iran 66/G5
Boyero, Colo. (80821) 208/N5
Boyers, Pa. (16020) 294/C3
Boyertown, Pa. (19512) 294/L5
Boyes, Mont. (59316) 262/M5
Boykin, Georgia (†31737) 217/C8
Boykin, S.C. (†29128) 296/F3
Boykins, Va. (23827) 307/O7
Boyle, Alberta 182/D2
Boyle, Ireland 17/E4
Boyle, Ireland 10/B3
Boyle (co.), Ky. 237/M5
Boyle, Miss. (38730) 256/C3
Boyleston, Ind. (†46057) 227/E4
Boylston○, Mass. (01505) 249/H3
Boylston, Nova Scotia 168/G3
Boyne (riv.), Ireland 17/J4
Boyne City, Mich. (49712) 250/E3

342 Boyne Falls

Boyne Falls, Mich. (49713) 250/E3
Boyne Lake, Alberta 182/E5
Boynton, Okla. (74422) 288/P3
Boynton Beach, Fla. (*33435) 212/F5
Boy River, Minn. (56632) 255/D3
Boysen (res.), Wyo. 319/D2
Boysen Bay, N.Y. (†13212) 276/H4
Boys Ranch, Texas (79010) 303/B2
Boys Town, Nebr. (68010) 264/H3
Boyuibe, Bolivia 136/D7
Bozcaada (isl.), Turkey 63/A3
Bozdoğan, Turkey 63/C4
Bozeman, Mont. 188/D1
Bozeman, Mont. (59715) 262/E5
Bozkır, Turkey 63/E4
Bozkurt, Turkey 63/F2
Bozman, Md. (21612) 245/N5
Bozoum, Cent. Afr. Rep. 115/C2
Bozova, Turkey 63/H4
Bozqush, Kuh-e (mts.), Iran 66/E2
Bozüyük, Turkey 59/B2
Bozüyük, Turkey 63/C3
Bra, Italy 34/A2
Brabant (prov.), Belgium 27/F7
Brabant Lake, Sask. 181/M3
Brač (isl.), Yugoslavia 45/C4
Bracadale, Loch (inlet), Scotland 15/B3
Bracciano, Italy 34/C3
Bracciano (lake), Italy 34/D3
Bracebridge, Ontario 177/E2
Braceville, Ill. (60407) 222/E2
Bracey, Va. (23919) 307/M7
Bräcke, Sweden 18/J5
Bracken (co.), Ky. 237/N3
Bracken, Sask. 181/C6
Brackendale, Br. Col. 184/F5
Brackenridge, Pa. (15014) 294/C4
Brackett, Wis. (†54742) 317/D6
Brackettville (canton), Texas 303/D8
Brackley, England 10/F4
Brackley, England 13/F5
Bracknell, England 13/G8
Bracknell, Tasmania 99/C3
Brackney, Pa. (18812) 294/K2
Brackwede, W. Germany 22/C3
Braço Maior do Araguaia (riv.), Brazil 132/D5
Braço Menor do Araguaia (riv.), Brazil 132/D6
Brad, Romania 45/F2
Bradbury, Calif. (91010) 204/D10
Braddock, N. Dak. (58524) 282/K6
Braddock, Pa. (15104) 294/C7
Braddock, Sask. 181/D5
Braddyville, Iowa (51631) 229/D7
Braden, Okla. (†74959) 288/S4
Braden, Tenn. (38010) 237/B10
Bradenton, Fla. (*33506) 212/D4
Bradenton Beach, Fla. (33510) 212/D4
Bradford, Ark. (72020) 202/G3
Bradford, England 13/J1
Bradford, England 10/H1
Bradford (co.), Fla. 212/D2
Bradford, Ill. (61421) 222/D2
Bradford, Ind. (47107) 227/E8
Bradford, Iowa (50041) 229/G3
Bradford, Ky. (†41043) 237/N3
Bradford, Maine (04410) 243/F5
Bradford○, Maine (04410) 243/F5
Bradford○, N.H. (03221) 268/D5
Bradford, Ohio (45308) 284/B5
Bradford, Ontario 177/E3
Bradford (co.), Pa. 294/J2
Bradford, Pa. (16701) 294/E2
Bradford, R.I. (02808) 249/H7
Bradford, Tenn. (38316) 237/D8
Bradford, Vt. (05033) 268/C3
Bradford○, Vt. (05033) 268/C3
Bradford Center, Maine (†04410) 243/F5
Bradford-on-Avon, England 13/E6
Bradfordsville, Ky. (40009) 237/L6
Bradgate, Iowa (50520) 229/E3
Bradley (co.), Ark. 202/F7
Bradley, Ark. (71826) 202/C7
Bradley, Calif. (93426) 204/E8
Bradley, Fla. (33835) 212/D4
Bradley, Georgia (†31032) 217/E4
Bradley, Ill. (60915) 222/F2
Bradley○, Maine (04411) 243/F6
Bradley, Miss. (†39759) 256/G4
Bradley, Ohio (†43917) 284/J5
Bradley, Okla. (73011) 288/L5
Bradley, S.C. (29819) 296/C3
Bradley, S. Dak. (57217) 298/O3
Bradley (co.), Tenn. 237/M10
Bradley, Wis. (†54487) 317/G4
Bradley Beach, N.J. (07720) 273/F3
Bradleyton, Ala. (†36041) 195/F7
Bradleyville, Mo. (65614) 261/F9
Bradner, Ohio (43406) 284/C3
Bradshaw, Nebr. (68319) 264/G4
Bradshaw, Texas (†79567) 303/D5
Bradshaw, W. Va. (24817) 312/C8
Bradwardine, Manitoba 179/B5
Bradwell, Sask. 181/E4
Brady (glac.), Alaska 196/M1
Brady, Mont. (59416) 262/E2
Brady, Nebr. (69123) 264/D3
Brady (mt.), S. Australia 94/D3
Brady, Texas (76825) 303/E6
Brady Lake, Ohio (44211) 284/H3
Bradyville, Tenn. (37026) 237/J9
Brae, Scotland 15/G2
Braedstrup, Denmark 21/C6
Braemar, Scotland 15/E3
Braemar, Scotland 10/E2
Braemar (dist.), Scotland 15/E3
Braemar, Tenn. (37658) 237/S8
Braeside, Ontario 177/H2
Braeside, W. Australia 92/C3
Braga (dist.), Portugal 33/B2
Braga, Portugal 7/D4
Braga, Portugal 33/B2
Bragado, Argentina 143/F7
Bragança, Brazil 120/E3
Bragança, Brazil 132/E3
Bragança (dist.), Portugal 33/C2
Bragança, Portugal 33/C2
Bragança Paulista, Brazil 135/C3
Bragança Paulista, Brazil 132/E8
Braggadocio, Mo. (63826) 261/N10
Bragg City, Mo. (63827) 261/N10
Bragg Creek, Alberta 182/C4
Braggs, Ala. (†36761) 195/E6
Braggs, Okla. (74423) 288/R3
Bragman's Bluff (Puerto Cabezas), Nicaragua 154/F3
Braham, Minn. (55006) 255/E5
Brahmaputra (riv.) 54/L7
Brahmaputra (riv.), Bangladesh 68/G3
Brahmaputra (riv.), India 68/G3
Braich-y-Pwll (prom.), Wales 10/D4
Braich-y-Pwll (prom.), Wales 13/C5
Braidwood, Ill. (60408) 222/E2
Braidwood, N.S. Wales 97/E4
Brăila, Romania 7/G4
Brăila, Romania 45/H3
Brăila (marshes), Romania 45/H3
Brainard, Nebr. (68626) 264/G3
Brainards, N.J. (08865) 273/C2
Braine-l'Alleud, Belgium 27/E7
Braine-le-Comte, Belgium 27/D7
Brainerd, Minn. 188/H1
Brainerd, Minn. (56401) 255/D4
Braintree○, Mass. (02184) 249/D8
Braintree (West Braintree), Vt. 268/B4
Braintree○, Vt. (†05669) 268/B4
Braintree and Bocking, England 13/H6
Braintree and Bocking, England 10/G5
Braithwaite, La. (70040) 238/P4
Brak, Libya 102/D2
Brak, Libya 111/B2
Brake, W. Germany 22/C2
Brakna (reg.), Mauritania 106/B5
Brakpan, S. Africa 118/J6
Bralorne, Br. Col. 184/F5
Braman, Okla. (74632) 288/M1
Bramber, Nova Scotia 168/D3
Bramberg am Wildkogel, Austria 41/B3
Bramble (bay), Queensland 95/E2
Bramming, Denmark 21/B7
Bramon, Venezuela 124/B4
Brampton, England 13/E3
Brampton, Mich. (49810) 250/B3
Brampton, N. Dak. (58010) 282/P7
Brampton, Ontario 177/J4
Bramsche, W. Germany 22/B2
Bramwell, W. Va. (24715) 312/D8
Bran (riv.), Scotland 15/D3
Brancepeth, Sask. 181/F2
Branch, Ark. (72928) 202/C3
Branch, La. (70516) 238/F6
Branch (co.), Mich. 250/D7
Branch, Mich. (49402) 250/D5
Branch, Minn. (†55056) 255/F5
Branch, Mo. (†65786) 261/G7
Branch, Newf. 166/D2
Branch (riv.), Newf. 166/C2
Branch, Wis. (54203) 317/L7
Branch Dale, Pa. (17923) 294/K4
Branchport, N.Y. (14418) 276/F5
Branchton, Pa. (16021) 294/C3
Branchville, Ala. (†35120) 195/F3
Branchville, Conn. (†06829) 210/B3
Branchville, Ind. (47514) 227/D8
Branchville, N.J. (07826) 273/D1
Branchville, S.C. (29432) 296/F5
Branchville, Va. (23828) 307/O7
Branco (riv.), Brazil 120/C2
Branco (riv.), Brazil 132/H8
Brandberg (mt.), Namibia 118/A4
Brande, Denmark 21/B6
Brandenburg, E. Germany 22/E2
Brandenburg (reg.), E. Germany 22/E2
Brandenburg, Ky. (40108) 237/J4
Brandon, Colo. (81026) 208/P6
Brandon, England 13/H5
Brandon, Fla. (33511) 212/D4
Brandon, Iowa (52210) 229/K4
Brandon (bay), Ireland 17/A7
Brandon (head), Ireland 17/A7
Brandon (mt.), Ireland 17/A7
Brandon, Man. 146/H4
Brandon, Man. 162/F6
Brandon, Manitoba 179/C5
Brandon, Minn. (56315) 255/C5
Brandon, Miss. (39042) 256/E6
Brandon, Nebr. (69102) 264/C4
Brandon, Ohio (†43050) 284/F5
Brandon, S. Dak. (57005) 298/R6
Brandon, Vt. (05733) 268/A4
Brandon○, Vt. (05733) 268/A4
Brandon, Wis. (53919) 317/J8
Brandon Gap (pass), Vt. 268/B4
Brandonville, W. Va. (26523) 312/G3
Brandreth (lake), N.Y. 276/L3
Brandsville, Mo. (65688) 261/J9
Brandt, Ohio (†45371) 284/B6
Brandt, S. Dak. (57218) 298/R4
Brandvlei, S. Africa 118/B6
Brandýs nad Labem-Stará Boleslavv, Czech. 41/C1
Brandy Station, Va. (22714) 307/N4
Brandywine, Md. (20613) 245/L6
Brandywine, W. Va. (26802) 312/H5
Branford, Conn. (06405) 210/D3
Branford○, Conn. (06405) 210/D3
Branford (harb.), Conn. 210/D4
Branford (riv.), Conn. 210/D3
Branford, Fla. (32008) 212/D2
Braniewo, Poland 47/D1
Brannock (isls.), Ireland 17/A5
Bransfield (str.) 5/C16
Branson, Colo. (81027) 208/M8
Branson, Mo. (65616) 261/F9
Brant, Alberta 182/D4
Brant, Mich. (48614) 250/E5
Brant, N.Y. (14027) 276/B5
Brant (lake), N.Y. 276/N3
Brant (county), Ontario 177/D4
Brant (lake), S. Dak. 298/R6
Brant Beach, N.J. (†08008) 273/E4
Brantford, Kansas (†66938) 232/E2
Brantford, N. Dak. (†58356) 282/N4
Brantford, Ontario 177/D4
Brant Lake, N.Y. (12815) 276/N3
Brantley, Ala. (36009) 195/F7
Brantley (co.), Georgia 217/J8
Brant Rock-Ocean Bluff, Mass. (02020) 249/M4
Brantville, New Bruns. 170/E1
Brantwood, Wis. (54513) 317/F4
Branxholm, Tasmania 99/D3
Branxholme, Victoria 97/A5
Branxton-Greta, N.S. Wales 97/F3
Bras d'Or, Nova Scotia 168/H2
Bras d'Or (lake), Nova Scotia 168/H3
Braselton, Georgia (30517) 217/E2
Brasfield, Ark. (†72017) 202/H4
Brashear, Mo. (63533) 261/H2
Brasher, Mo. (†63830) 261/N10
Brasher Falls-Winthrop, N.Y. (13613) 276/L1
Brasiléia, Brazil 132/G10
Brasília (cap.), Brazil 2/G6
Brasília (cap.), Brazil 120/E4
Brasília (cap.), Brazil 132/E6
Brasília de Minas, Brazil 132/F7
Braşov, Romania 45/G3
Braşov, Romania 7/G4
Brass, Nigeria 106/F8
Brass (isls.), Virgin Is. (U.S.) 161/A4
Brassey (range), W. Australia 92/C4
Brasstown Bald (mt.), Georgia 217/E1
Brassua (lake), Maine 243/D4
Braswell, Georgia (†30153) 217/C3
Brate, Norway 18/G7
Bratenahl, Ohio (†44101) 284/H9
Bratislava, Czech. 7/F4
Bratislava (city), Czech. 41/D2
Bratislava, Czech. 41/D2
Bratsk, U.S.S.R. 54/M4
Bratsk, U.S.S.R. 48/L4
Bratsk (res.), U.S.S.R. 48/L4
Brattleboro, Vt. (05301) 268/B6
Brattleboro○, Vt. (05301) 268/B6
Bratton, Sask. 181/D4
Braunau am Inn, Austria 41/B2
Braunlage, W. Germany 22/D3
Braunschweig (Brunswick), W. Germany 22/D2
Braunton, England 13/C6
Brava (isl.), C. Verde 106/B8
Brava, Somalia 115/H3
Brava, Somalia 102/G4
Brava (pt.), Uruguay 145/B7
Brave, Pa. (15316) 294/B6
Bravo (riv.), Chile 138/D7
Bravo (Grande) (riv.), Mexico 150/G2
Brawley, Calif. 188/C4
Brawley, Calif. (92227) 204/K11
Braxton, Miss. (39044) 256/D6
Braxton (co.), W. Va. 312/E5
Bray, Ireland 17/K5
Bray, Ireland 10/C4
Bray (head), Ireland 17/A8
Bray (isl.), N.W. Terrs. 187/L3
Bray, Okla. (73012) 288/L5
Braymer, Mo. (64624) 261/E3
Brayton, Iowa (50042) 229/D5
Brazeau (dam), Alberta 182/C3
Brazeau (mt.), Alberta 182/B3
Brazeau (riv.), Alberta 182/B3
Brazil 2/F6
Brazil 120/D4
BRAZIL 132, 135
Brazil, Ind. (47834) 227/C5
Brazil, Miss. (38963) 256/D2
Brazil, Tenn. (†38382) 237/C9
Brazilian Highlands (plat.), Brazil 120/E4
Brazilton, Kansas (†66743) 232/H4
Brazito, Mo. (†65101) 261/H6
Brazoria (co.), Texas 303/J8
Brazoria, Texas (77422) 303/J9
Brazos (peak), N. Mex. 274/C2
Brazos (co.), Texas 303/H7
Brazos (riv.), Texas 188/G4
Brazos (riv.), Texas 146/J6
Brazos (riv.), Texas 303/H7
Brazo Sur, Pilcomayo (riv.), Argentina 143/E1
Brazzaville (cap.), Congo 115/C4
Brazzaville (cap.), Congo 2/K6
Brazzaville (cap.), Congo 102/D5
Brčko, Yugoslavia 45/D3
Brda (riv.), Poland 47/C2
Brea, Calif. (92621) 204/D11
Breadalbane (dist.), Scotland 15/D4
Bread Loaf, Vt. (05753) 268/B4
Bread Loaf (mt.), Vt. 268/A3
Breakabeen, N.Y. (†12122) 276/M5
Breakeyville, Québec 172/J3
Breaks, Va. (24607) 307/D6
Breaksea (sound), N. Zealand 100/A6
Bream (bay), N. Zealand 100/E1
Breasclete, Scotland 15/B2
Breathitt (co.), Ky. 237/P5
Breau-Village, New Bruns. 170/F2
Breaux Bridge, La. (70517) 238/G6
Brebes, Indonesia 85/H2
Brébeuf, Québec 172/C3
Brébeuf (lake), Québec 172/G1
Brechin, Ontario 177/E3
Brechin, Scotland 10/E2
Brechin, Scotland 15/F4
Brecht, Belgium 27/F6
Breckenridge, Colo. (80424) 208/G4
Breckenridge, Mich. (48615) 250/E5
Breckenridge, Minn. (56520) 255/B4
Breckenridge, Mo. (64625) 261/E3
Breckenridge, Texas (76024) 303/F5
Breckenridge Hills, Mo. (†63114) 261/O2
Breckinridge (co.), Ky. 237/H5
Breckinridge, Okla. (73721) 288/L2
Brecknock (Brecon), Wales 13/D6
Brecksville, Ohio (44141) 284/H10
Břeclav, Czech. 41/D2
Brecon, Wales 13/D6
Brecon, Wales 10/E5
Brecon Beacons (mt.), Wales 13/D6
Brecon Beacons National Park, Wales 13/D6
Breda, Iowa (51436) 229/C4
Breda, Netherlands 27/F5
Bredasdorp, S. Africa 118/B6
Bredasdorp Nat'l Park, S. Africa 118/C6
Bredbo, N.S. Wales 97/E4
Bredbyn, Sweden 18/L5
Bredebro, Denmark 21/B7
Bredenbury, Sask. 181/K5
Bredene, Belgium 27/B6
Bredstedt, W. Germany 22/C1
Bree, Belgium 27/H6
Breed, Wis. (†54174) 317/K5
Breeden, W. Va. (25666) 312/B7
Breeding, Ky. (42715) 237/L7
Breedsville, Mich. (49027) 250/C6
Breese, Ill. (62230) 222/D5
Breesport, N.Y. (14816) 276/G6
Breezand, Netherlands 27/F3
Breezy Point, Minn. (†56472) 255/D4
Bregenz, Austria 41/A3
Bregovo, Bulgaria 45/F3
Breidhafjördhur (fjord), Iceland 7/B2
Breidhafjördhur (fjord), Iceland 21/B1
Breien, N. Dak. (58525) 282/H7
Breil-Brigels, Switzerland 39/H3
Breil-sur-Roya, France 28/G6
Breisach am Rhein, W. Germany 22/B4
Breisgau (reg.), W. Germany 22/B5
Breitenbach, Switzerland 39/E2
Breitenbush, Oreg. (†97342) 291/F3
Breithorn (mt.), Switzerland 39/E5
Breithorn (mt.), Switzerland 39/E4
Brejo, Brazil 132/F3
Bremanger (isl.), Norway 18/D6
Bremen, Ala. (35033) 195/E3
Bremen, Georgia (30110) 217/B3
Bremen, Ill. (†62233) 222/D6
Bremen, Ind. (46506) 227/E2
Bremen, Kansas (66412) 232/F2
Bremen, Ky. (42325) 237/G6
Bremen, N. Dak. (58319) 282/M4
Bremen, Ohio (43107) 284/F6
Bremen, Sask. 181/F3
Bremen, W. Germany 7/E3
Bremen (state), W. Germany 22/C2
Bremen, W. Germany 22/C2
Bremer (co.), Iowa 229/J3
Bremer, Iowa (†50677) 229/J3
Bremerhaven, W. Germany 22/C2
Bremerton, Wash. 188/B1
Bremerton, Wash. (98310) 310/A2
Bremervörde, W. Germany 22/C2
Bremgarten, Switzerland 39/F2
Bremo Bluff, Va. (23022) 307/M5
Bremond, Texas (76629) 303/H6
Brenham, Texas (77833) 303/H7
Brenner (pass), Austria 41/A3
Brenner (pass), Italy 34/C1
Brent, Ala. (35034) 195/D5
Brent, England 13/H8
Brent, England 10/B5
Brent, Ontario 177/F1
Brentford, S. Dak. (57429) 298/N3
Brenton (pt.), R.I. 249/J7
Brentwood, Ark. (†72959) 202/B2
Brentwood, Calif. (94513) 204/L2
Brentwood, England 10/C5
Brentwood, England 13/J8
Brentwood, Md. (20722) 245/F4
Brentwood, Mo. (63144) 261/P3
Brentwood○, N.H. (†03833) 268/E6
Brentwood, N.Y. (11717) 276/O9
Brentwood, Pa. (15227) 294/B7
Brentwood, Tenn. (37027) 237/H8
Brentwood Park, S. Africa 118/J6
Brereton Lake, Manitoba 179/G5
Bresaylor, Sask. 181/C3
Brescia (prov.), Italy 34/C2
Brescia, Italy 7/E4
Brescia, Italy 34/C2
Breskens, Netherlands 27/C6
Breslau (Wrocław), Poland 47/C3
Bressanone, Italy 34/C1
Bressay (isl.), Scotland 15/G2
Bressay (isl.), Scotland 10/G1
Bressuire, France 28/C4
Brest, France 7/D4
Brest, France 28/A3
Brest, Georgia (†31716) 217/D8
Brest, New Bruns. 170/E2
Brest, U.S.S.R. 7/G3
Brest, U.S.S.R. 48/C4
Brest, U.S.S.R. 52/B4
Bretaña, Peru 128/E5
Brethren, Mich. (49619) 250/D4
Breton, Alberta 182/C3
Breton (isls.), La. 238/M8
Breton (sound), La. 238/M7
Breton (cape), Nova Scotia 168/J3
Breton Cove, Nova Scotia 168/H2
Breton Woods, N.J. (08723) 273/E3
Brett (cape), N. Zealand 100/E1
Bretten, W. Germany 22/C4
Bretton Woods, N.H. (03575) 268/E3
Brevard (co.), Fla. 212/F3
Brevard, N.C. (28712) 281/D4
Breves, Brazil 132/D3
Brevig Mission, Alaska (99785) 196/E1
Brevik, Minn. (†56655) 255/D3
Brevoort (lake), Mich. 250/D3
Brevoort (isl.), N.W. Terrs. 187/M3
Brevort, Mich. (†49760) 250/E2
Brewarrina, N. S. Wales 88/H5
Brewarrina, N.S. Wales 97/D1
Brewer, Maine (04412) 243/F6
Brewer, Mo. (63775) 261/N7
Brewers, Ky. (†42025) 237/E7
Brewers Mills, New Bruns. 170/C2
Brewersville, Ind. (†47265) 227/F6
Brewerton, N.Y. (13029) 276/H4
Brewster (pond), Conn. 210/F2
Brewster, Kansas (67732) 232/A2
Brewster, Mass. (02631) 249/O5
Brewster○, Mass. (02631) 249/O5
Brewster (isls.), Mass. 249/E7
Brewster, Minn. (56119) 255/C7
Brewster, Nebr. (68821) 264/D3
Brewster (lake), N.S. Wales 97/D3
Brewster, N.Y. (10509) 276/N8
Brewster, Ohio (44613) 284/G4
Brewster, Cerro (mt.), Panama 154/H6
Brewster (co.), Texas 303/A8
Brewster, Wash. (98812) 310/F2
Brewton, Ala. (36426) 195/D8
Breynat, Alberta 182/D2
Brežice, Yugoslavia 45/B3
Brezina, Algeria 106/E2
Březnice, Czech. 41/B2
Breznik, Bulgaria 45/F4
Brezno, Czech. 41/E2
Bria, Cent. Afr. Rep. 102/E4
Bria, Cent. Afr. Rep. 115/D2
Briançon, France 28/G5
Brian Head, Utah (84719) 304/B6
Briar, Texas (†76023) 303/E1
Briar Creek, Pa. (†18603) 294/K3
Briare, France 28/E4
Briartown, Okla. (†74455) 288/R4
Briarwood, (†58102) 282/S6
Bribbaree, N.S. Wales 97/D3
Brice, Ohio (43109) 284/E6
Bricelyn, Minn. (56014) 255/E7
Brices Cross Roads Nat'l Battlefield Site, Miss.256/G2
Briceville, Tenn. (37710) 237/N8
Brí Chualann (Bray), Ireland 17/K5
Brick○, N.J. (08723) 273/E3
Brickaville (Vohibinany), Madagascar 118/H3
Brickerville, Pa. (†17543) 294/K5
Brickeys, Ark. (72320) 202/J4
Bricks, N.C. (†27891) 281/O2
Brickton, Nova Scotia 168/C4
Bridal Veil, Oreg. (97010) 291/E2
Bride (riv.), Ireland 17/E7
Bridesville, Br. Col. 184/H6
Bridge, Idaho (†83342) 220/E7
Bridge, Oreg. (†97458) 291/D4
Bridgeboro, Georgia (31705) 217/E8
Bridge City, Texas (77611) 303/L7
Bridgedale, New Bruns. 170/F3
Bridgeford, Sask. 181/E5
Bridgehampton, N.Y. (11932) 276/R9
Bridge Lake, Br. Col. 184/G4
Bridgeland, Utah (84012) 304/D3
Bridgend, Wales 13/A7
Bridgenorth, Ontario 177/F3
Bridge of Allan, Scotland 10/B1
Bridge of Allan, Scotland 15/C1
Bridge of Don, Scotland 15/F3
Bridge of Weir, Scotland 15/A2
Bridgeport, Ala. (35740) 195/G1
Bridgeport, Calif. (93517) 204/F5
Bridgeport, Conn. 188/M2
Bridgeport, Conn. (*06601) 210/C4
Bridgeport, Ill. (62417) 222/F5
Bridgeport, Kansas (67416) 232/E3
Bridgeport, Mich. (48722) 250/F5
Bridgeport, Nebr. (69336) 264/A3
Bridgeport, N.J. (08014) 273/C4
Bridgeport, N.Y. (13030) 276/J4
Bridgeport, Ohio (43912) 284/J5
Bridgeport, Okla. (†73047) 288/K3
Bridgeport, Oreg. (97819) 291/K3
Bridgeport, Pa. (19405) 294/M5
Bridgeport, Texas (76026) 303/G4
Bridgeport, Wash. (98813) 310/F3
Bridgeport, W. Va. (26330) 312/F4
Bridgeport, Wis. (†53821) 317/D9
Bridger, Mont. (59014) 262/H5
Bridgeton, Ind. (47836) 227/C5
Bridgeton, Mich. (†49327) 250/D5
Bridgeton, Mo. (63044) 261/O2
Bridgeton, N.J. (08302) 273/C5
Bridgeton, N.C. (28519) 281/R4
Bridgeton Terrace, Mo. (†63044) 261/O2
Bridgetown (cap.), Barbados 156/G4
Bridgetown (cap.), Barbados 161/B9
Bridgetown, Md. (†21640) 245/P4
Bridgetown, Nova Scotia 168/C4
Bridgetown, Ohio (†45211) 284/B9
Bridgetown, W. Australia 88/B6
Bridgetown, W. Australia 92/B6
Bridgeview, Ill. (60455) 222/B6
Bridgeville, Calif. (95526) 204/B3
Bridgeville, Del. (19933) 245/R6
Bridgeville, Nova Scotia 168/F3
Bridgeville, Pa. (15017) 294/B5
Bridgeville, Québec 172/D1
Bridgewater○, Conn. (06752) 210/B2
Bridgewater, Iowa (50837) 229/D6
Bridgewater○, Maine (04735) 243/H3
Bridgewater, Mass. (02324) 249/K5
Bridgewater○, Mass. (02324) 249/K5
Bridgewater○, N.H. (†03222) 268/D4
Bridgewater○, N.J. (08807) 273/D2
Bridgewater, N.Y. (13313) 276/K5
Bridgewater, N.S. 162/K7
Bridgewater, Nova Scotia 168/D4
Bridgewater, Pa. (15009) 294/B4
Bridgewater, S. Dak. (57319) 298/P6
Bridgewater, Tasmania 99/D4
Bridgewater○, Vt. (05034) 268/B4
Bridgewater (cape), Victoria 97/A6
Bridgewater, Va. (22812) 307/K4
Bridgewater Center, Vt. (†05034) 268/B4
Bridgewater Corners, Vt. (05035) 268/B4
Bridgman, Mich. (49106) 250/C7
Bridgnorth, England 13/E5
Bridgnorth, England 10/E4
Bridgton, Maine (04009) 243/B7
Bridgton○, Maine (04009) 243/B7
Bridgwater, England 10/E5
Bridgwater, England 13/E6
Bridlington, England 13/G3
Bridlington, England 10/F3
Bridlington (bay), England 13/G3
Bridport, England 13/E7
Bridport, England 10/E5
Bridport, Tasmania 99/D3
Bridport○, Vt. (05734) 268/A4
Brieg (Brzeg), Poland 47/C3
Brielle, Netherlands 27/E5
Brielle, N.J. (08730) 273/E3
Briensburg, Ky. (†42025) 237/E7
Brienz, Switzerland 39/F3
Brienzer Rothorn (mt.), Switzerland 39/F3
Brienzersee (lake), Switzerland 39/F3
Brier (isl.), Nova Scotia 168/B4
Brier, Wash. (†98036) 310/C3
Briercrest, Sask. 181/F5
Brierfield, Ala. (35035) 195/E4
Brier Hill, N.Y. (13614) 276/J1
Brig, Switzerland 39/F4
Brigantine, N.J. (08203) 273/E5
Brigantine (inlet), N.J. 273/E5
Brigden, Ontario 177/B5
Brigg, England 13/G4
Briggs, Texas (78608) 303/F7
Briggs Corner, New Bruns. 170/E2
Briggsdale, Colo. (80611) 208/L1
Briggsville, Ark. (72828) 202/C4
Briggsville, Wis. (53920) 317/H8
Brigham City, Utah 188/D2
Brigham City, Utah (84302) 304/C2
Brighowe, England 13/J1
Bright, Ind. (†45030) 227/H6
Bright, Victoria 97/D5
Brightlingsea, England 13/J6
Brightlingsea, England 10/G5
Brighton, Ala. (35020) 195/D4
Brighton, Colo. (80601) 208/K3
Brighton, England 10/F5
Brighton, England 13/G7
Brighton, Fla. (†33472) 212/E4
Brighton, Ill. (62012) 222/C4
Brighton, Ind. (†46746) 227/G1
Brighton, Iowa (52540) 229/K6
Brighton○, Maine (†04990) 243/D5
Brighton, Mich. (48116) 250/F6
Brighton, Mo. (65617) 261/F8
Brighton, Nova Scotia 168/C4
Brighton, Ohio (†44090) 284/F3
Brighton, Ontario 177/G3
Brighton, Oreg. (†97136) 291/C2
Brighton, S. Australia 88/D8
Brighton, S. Australia 94/A8
Brighton, Tasmania 99/D4
Brighton, Tenn. (38011) 237/B10
Brighton, Utah (†84101) 304/C3
Brighton, Victoria 97/J5
Brighton, Victoria 88/L7
Brighton, Wis. (†53139) 317/K3
Brightons, Scotland 15/C1
Brightsand (lake), Sask. 181/B2
Brights Grove, Ontario 177/B4
Brightshade, Ky. (40962) 237/O7
Brightstar, Ark. (†75556) 202/C7
Brightwood, D.C. (20011) 245/F4
Brightwood, Oreg. (97001) 291/E2
Brightwood, Va. (22715) 307/M4
Brignoles, France 28/G6
Brigus, Newf. 166/D2
Brihuega, Spain 33/E2
Brikama, Gambia 106/A6
Brill, Wis. (54818) 317/C4
Brilliant, Ala. (35548) 195/C2
Brilliant, Ohio (43913) 284/J5
Brillion, Wis. (54110) 317/L7
Brilon, W. Germany 22/C3
Brimfield, Ill. (61517) 222/D3
Brimfield, Ind. (46720) 227/G2
Brimfield○, Mass. (01010) 249/F4
Brimfield, Ohio (†44240) 284/H3
Brimley, Mich. (49715) 250/E2
Brimson, Minn. (55602) 255/F3
Brimson, Mo. (64642) 261/E2
Brimstone (hill), St. Chris.-Nevis 161/C10
Brinckerhoff, N.Y. (†12524) 276/N7
Brindakit, U.S.S.R. 48/O4
Brindisi (prov.), Italy 34/G4
Brindisi, Italy 7/F4
Brindisi, Italy 34/G4
Bringhurst, Ind. (46913) 227/E3
Brinkhaven, Ohio (43006) 284/F5
Brinkley, Ark. (72021) 202/H4
Brinkman, Okla. (†73673) 288/G4
Brinktown, Mo. (65443) 261/J6
Brinnon, Wash. (98320) 310/B3
Brinsmade, N. Dak. (58320) 282/M3
Brinson, Georgia (31725) 217/C9
Briny Breezes, Fla. (†33435) 212/G5
Brione, Switzerland 39/G4
Brioude, France 28/E5
Brisbane, Australia 2/S7
Brisbane, Calif. (94005) 204/J2
Brisbane (cap.), Queensland 95/D2
Brisbane (cap.), Queensland 88/K3
Brisbane (riv.), Queensland 88/J3
Brisbane (riv.), Queensland 95/D2
Brisbane Airport, Queensland 95/E2
Brisbane International Airport, Queensland 88/K2
Brisbane Water, N. S. Wales 88/J6
Brisbane Water, N.S. Wales 97/F3
Brisbin, Pa. (16620) 294/F4
Brisco, Br. Col. 184/J5
Briscoe (co.), Texas 303/C3
Briscoe, Texas (79011) 303/D2
Brisighella, Italy 34/C2
Brissago, Switzerland 39/G4
Bristol (bay), Alaska 188/C6
Bristol (bay), Alaska 146/B4
Bristol (bay), Alaska 196/F3
Bristol (lake), Calif. 204/K9
Bristol, Colo. (81028) 208/P6
Bristol, Conn. (06010) 210/D2
Bristol, England 13/E6
Bristol, England 7/D3
Bristol, England 10/E5
Bristol (chan.), England 13/C6
Bristol (chan.), England 10/E5
Bristol, Fla. (32321) 212/B1
Bristol, Georgia (31518) 217/H8
Bristol, Ind. (46507) 227/F1

Budaörs 343

Bristol, Maine (04539) 243/D8
Bristol○, Maine (04539) 243/D8
Bristol, Md. (†20820) 245/M5
Bristol (co.), Mass. 249/K5
Bristol, Mich. (†49688) 250/D4
Bristol, New Bruns. 170/C2
Bristol, N.H. (03222) 268/D4
Bristol○, N.H. (03222) 268/D4
Bristol, Pa. (19007) 294/N5
Bristol○, Pa. (19007) 294/N5
Bristol (co.), R.I. 249/J6
Bristol, R.I. (02809) 249/J6
Bristol, S. Dak. (57219) 298/O3
Bristol, Tenn. 188/K3
Bristol, Tenn. (37620) 237/S7
Bristol (bay), U.S. 4/D18
Bristol, Va. 188/K3
Bristol, Vt. (05443) 268/A3
Bristol○, Vt. (05443) 268/A3
Bristol (I.C.), Va. (24201) 307/D7
Bristol (chan.), Wales 13/C6
Bristol (chan.), Wales 10/E5
Bristol, W. Va. (26332) 312/F4
Bristolville, Ohio (44402) 284/J3
Bristow, Ind. (47515) 227/D8
Bristow, Iowa (50611) 229/H3
Bristow, Nebr. (68719) 264/F2
Bristow, Okla. (74010) 288/O3
Bristow, Va. (22013) 307/N3
Britannia Beach, Br. Col. 184/K2
British (mts.), Alaska 196/K1
British (mts.), Yukon 187/D3
British Columbia (prov.) 162/D4
BRITISH COLUMBIA 184
British Columbia (prov.), Canada 146/F4
British Indian Ocean Territory 2/N6
British Indian Ocean Territory 54/J10
British Isles 7/D3
Brits, S. Africa 118/D5
Britstown, S. Africa 118/C6
Britt, Iowa (50423) 229/F2
Britt, Minn. (55710) 255/F3
Britt, Ontario 177/D2
Brittany (trad. prov.), France 29
Brittany, La. (70718) 238/L3
Brittnau, Switzerland 39/E2
Britton, Mich. (49229) 250/F6
Britton, S. Dak. (57430) 298/O2
Brive-la-Gaillarde, France 28/D5
Briviesca, Spain 33/E1
Brno, Czech. 7/F4
Brno, Czech. 41/D2
Broa (inlet), Cuba 158/C1
Broach (Bharuch), India 68/C4
Broad (brook), Conn. 210/H2
Broad (creek), Del. 245/R6
Broad (riv.), N.C. 281/E4
Broad (sound), Queensland 88/H4
Broad (sound), Queensland 95/D4
Broad (bay), Scotland 15/B2
Broad (riv.), S.C. 296/F7
Broad (riv.), S.C. 296/E2
Broadacres, Oreg. (†97032) 291/A3
Broadacres, Sask. 181/B3
Broadalbin, N.Y. (12025) 276/M4
Broad Arrow, W. Australia 88/C6
Broad Arrow, W. Australia 92/C5
Broadback (riv.), Québec 174/B2
Broadbent, Oreg. (97414) 291/C4
Broad Brook, Conn. (06016) 210/E1
Broad Cove, Newf. 166/D2
Broad Cove, Nova Scotia 168/D4
Broaddus, Texas (75929) 303/K6
Broadfields, Ky. (†40201) 237/K2
Broadford, Ireland 17/C7
Broadford, Scotland 15/B3
Broadford, Victoria 97/C5
Broadford, Va. (24316) 307/E7
Broad Haven (harb.), Ireland 17/B3
Broadhurst, Georgia (†31545) 217/J8
Broadkill (riv.), Del. 245/S5
Broadland, S. Dak. (†57350) 298/N4
Broadlands, Ill. (61816) 222/E4
Broad Law (mt.), Scotland 15/E5
Broadmeadows, Victoria 88/L6
Broadmeadows, Victoria 97/H4
Broadstairs and Saint Peter's, England 13/J6
Broad Top, Pa. (16621) 294/F5
Broadus, Mont. (59317) 262/L5
Broad Valley, Manitoba 179/E4
Broadview, Ill. (60153) 222/B6
Broadview, Mont. (59015) 262/H4
Broadview, N. Mex. (88112) 274/F4
Broadview, Sask. 181/J5
Broadview Heights, Ohio (†44141) 284/H10
Broadview Park, Fla. (†33314) 212/B4
Broadwater (co.), Mont. 262/E4
Broadwater, Nebr. (69125) 264/B3
Broadway, N.J. (08808) 273/C2
Broadway, N.C. (27505) 281/L4
Broadway, Ohio (43007) 284/C5
Broadway, Va. (22815) 307/L3
Broadwell, Ill. (62623) 222/D3
Broager, Denmark 21/C8
Broc, Switzerland 39/D3
Brochet, Man. 162/F4
Brochet, Manitoba 179/H2
Brock (isl.), N.W.T. 162/M3
Brock, Nebr. (68320) 264/H4
Brock (isl.), N.W. Terrs. 187/G2
Brock, Sask. 181/C4
Brockdell, Tenn. (†37367) 237/L10
Brocken (mt.), E. Germany 22/D3
Brocket, Alberta 182/D5
Brocket, N. Dak. (58321) 282/O3
Brockington, Sask. 181/G2
Brockport, N.Y. (14420) 276/D4
Brockport, Pa. (15823) 294/E3
Brockton, Mass. (*02401) 249/K4
Brockton, Mont. (59213) 262/M2
Brockville, Ontario 177/J3
Brockway, Mont. (59214) 262/L3
Brockway, New Bruns. 170/C3
Brockway, Pa. (15824) 294/E3
Brocton, Ill. (61917) 222/F4
Brocton, N.Y. (14716) 276/B6
Broderick, Sask. 181/E4
Broderick-Bryte, Calif. (95605) 204/B8
Brodeur (pen.), Canada 4/B14
Brodeur (pen.), N.W.T. 146/K2
Brodeur (pen.), N.W.T. 162/H1
Brodeur (pen.), N.W. Terrs. 187/K2
Brodhead, Ky. (40409) 237/N6
Brodhead, Wis. (53520) 317/G10
Brodheadsville, Pa. (18322) 294/M4
Brodick, Scotland 15/C5
Brodick, Scotland 10/D3
Brodnax, Va. (23920) 307/N7
Brodnica, Poland 47/D2
Broek in Waterland, Netherlands 27/C4
Brogan, Oreg. (97903) 291/K3
Brohard, W. Va. (26138) 312/D4
Brohman, Mich. (49312) 250/D5
Brokaw, Wis. (54417) 317/G5
Broken (bay), N.S. Wales 97/F3
Broken Arrow, Okla. (74012) 288/P2
Broken Bow, Nebr. (68822) 264/E3
Broken Bow, Okla. (74728) 288/S7
Broken Bow (lake), Okla. 288/S6
Broken Hill, Australia 87/E9
Broken Hill, N. S. Wales 88/G6
Broken Hill, N.S. Wales 97/A3
Broken Hill (Kabwe), Zambia 115/E6
Brokensword, Ohio (†44820) 284/E4
Brokopondo (dist.), Suriname 131/D4
Brokopondo, Suriname 131/D3
Brome (co.), Québec 172/E4
Brome, Québec 172/E4
Brome (lake), Québec 172/E4
Bromer, Ind. (†47452) 227/E7
Bromhead, Sask. 181/H6
Bromide, Okla. (74530) 288/N6
Bromley, England 13/H8
Bromley, England 10/C5
Bromley, Ky. (†41016) 237/S2
Bromley (mt.), Vt. 268/B5
Bromont, Québec 172/E4
Brompton (lake), Québec 172/E4
Bromptonville, Québec 172/F4
Bromsgrove, England 13/E5
Bromyard, England 13/E5
Bronaugh, Mo. (64728) 261/C7
Bronco, Texas (†79355) 303/B4
Brønderslev, Denmark 18/F8
Brønderslev, Denmark 21/C3
Brønnøysund, Norway 18/G4
Brøns, Denmark 21/B7
Bronson, Fla. (32621) 212/D2
Bronson, Iowa (51007) 229/A4
Bronson, Kansas (66716) 232/H4
Bronson, Mich. (49028) 250/D7
Bronson (lake), Sask. 181/B2
Bronson, Texas (75930) 303/L6
Bronston, Ky. (42518) 237/M7
Bronte, Italy 34/E6
Bronte, Texas (76933) 303/D6
Bronwood, Georgia (31726) 217/D7
Bronx (co.), N.Y. 276/N9
Bronx (borough), N.Y. (*10401) 276/N9
Bronxville, N.Y. (10708) 276/O7
Brook, Ind. (47922) 227/C3
Brookdale, Calif. (95007) 204/J4
Brookdale, Manitoba 179/C4
Brookdale, Nova Scotia 168/D3
Brooke, Va. (22430) 307/O4
Brooke (co.), W. Va. 312/E2
Brookeborough, N. Ireland 17/G3
Brookeland, Texas (75931) 303/L6
Brooker, Fla. (32622) 212/D2
Brooke's Point, Philippines 82/A6
Brookeville, Md. (20729) 245/K4
Brookfield○, Conn. (06804) 210/B3
Brookfield, Georgia (31727) 217/F8
Brookfield, Ill. (60513) 222/B6
Brookfield, Mass. (01506) 249/F4
Brookfield○, Mass. (01506) 249/F4
Brookfield, Mo. (64628) 261/F3
Brookfield○, N.H. (†03872) 268/E4
Brookfield, N.Y. (13314) 276/K5
Brookfield, Nova Scotia 168/E3
Brookfield, Ohio (44403) 284/J3
Brookfield○, Vt. (05036) 268/B3
Brookfield, Wis. (53005) 317/K1
Brookfield Center, Conn. (06805) 210/B3
Brookford, N.C. (†28601) 281/G3
Brookhaven, Georgia (†30304) 217/K1
Brookhaven, Miss. (39601) 256/C7
Brookhaven, Pa. (19015) 294/M7
Brookhaven Nat'l Lab., N.Y. 276/P9
Brookings, Oreg. (97415) 291/C5
Brookings (co.), S. Dak. 298/R5
Brookings, S. Dak. (57006) 298/R5
Brookland, Ark. (72417) 202/J2
Brookland, D.C. (20017) 245/F4
Brooklawn, N.J. (08030) 273/B3
Brooklet, Georgia (30415) 217/J6
Brookley Air Force Base, Ala. 195/B9
Brooklin○, Maine (04616) 243/F7
Brookline○, Mass. (02146) 249/C7
Brookline○, N.H. (03033) 268/D6
Brookline○, Vt. (†05345) 268/B5
Brookline Station (Brookline), Mo. (65619) 261/F8
Brooklyn, Ala. (36429) 195/E8
Brooklyn○, Conn. (06234) 210/H1
Brooklyn, Georgia (†31814) 217/C6
Brooklyn (Lovejoy), Ill. (†62059) 222/A2
Brooklyn, Ill. (†62367) 222/C3
Brooklyn, Ind. (46111) 227/E5
Brooklyn, Iowa (52211) 229/J5
Brooklyn, Ky. (42209) 237/H6
Brooklyn, Md. (21225) 245/M4
Brooklyn, Mich. (49230) 250/E6
Brooklyn, Miss. (39425) 256/F8
Brooklyn, Newf. 166/D2
Brooklyn (borough), N.Y. (*11201) 276/N9
Brooklyn, Nova Scotia 168/D4
Brooklyn, Ohio (44144) 284/H9
Brooklyn, Pa. (18813) 294/L2
Brooklyn, Wash. (†98537) 310/B4
Brooklyn, Wis. (53521) 317/H10
Brooklyn Center, Minn. (55429) 255/G5
Brooklyn Heights, Ohio (†44131) 284/H9
Brooklyn Park, Minn. (†55444) 255/G5
Brookmere, Br. Col. 184/G5
Brookneal, Va. (24528) 307/L6
Brook Park, Minn. (55007) 255/F5
Brook Park, Ohio (44142) 284/G9
Brookport, Ill. (62910) 222/E6
Brooks (range), Alaska 146/C3
Brooks (range), Alaska 188/C5
Brooks (range), Alaska 196/G1
Brooks, Alberta 182/E4
Brooks (pen.), Br. Col. 184/D5
Brooks, Calif. (95606) 204/C5
Brooks (co.), Georgia 217/E9
Brooks, Georgia (30205) 217/D4
Brooks, Iowa (†50841) 229/D7
Brooks, Ky. (40109) 237/K4
Brooks○, Maine (04921) 243/E6
Brooks, Minn. (56715) 255/B3
Brooks, Mont. (†59457) 262/G3
Brooks, Oreg. (97305) 291/A3
Brooks (co.), Texas 303/F11
Brooks (range), U.S. 4/C17
Brooks, W. Va. (25957) 312/E7
Brooks, Wis. (53921) 317/G8
Brooks A.F.B., Texas 303/K11
Brooksburg, Ind. (†47250) 227/G7
Brooksby, Sask. 181/G2
Brookshire, Texas (77423) 303/J8
Brookside, Ala. (35036) 195/E3
Brookside, Colo. (†81212) 208/J6
Brookside, Del. (19711) 245/R2
Brookside, N.J. (07926) 273/D2
Brookside, Ohio (†43912) 284/J5
Brookside Village, Texas (77581) 303/J2
Brookston, Ind. (47923) 227/D3
Brookston, Minn. (55711) 255/F4
Brooksville, Ala. (†35031) 195/F2
Brooksville, Fla. (33512) 212/D3
Brooksville, Ky. (41004) 237/N3
Brooksville, Maine (04617) 243/F7
Brooksville○, Maine (04617) 243/F7
Brooksville, Miss. (39739) 256/G4
Brooksville, Okla. (†74873) 288/M4
Brookton, Georgia (†30501) 217/E2
Brookton, Maine (04413) 243/H4
Brookton, W. Australia 92/B2
Brooktondale, N.Y. (14817) 276/H6
Brookview, Md. (†21659) 245/P6
Brook Village, Nova Scotia 168/G2
Brookville, Ind. (47012) 227/G6
Brookville (lake), Ind. 227/G6
Brookville, Kansas (67425) 232/E3
Brookville, Mass. (†02343) 249/K4
Brookville, N.Y. (†11545) 276/R6
Brookville, Ohio (45309) 284/B6
Brookville, Pa. (15825) 294/D3
Brookwood, Ala. (35444) 195/D4
Broom, Loch (inlet), Scotland 15/C3
Broomall, Pa. (19008) 294/M6
Broome, Australia 87/C7
Broome (co.), N.Y. 276/J6
Broome, W. Australia 88/C3
Broome, W. Australia 92/C2
Broomfield, Colo. (80020) 208/J3
Broomhill, Manitoba 179/B5
Brooten, Minn. (56316) 255/C5
Brora, Scotland 15/E2
Brora (riv.), Scotland 15/D2
Brørup, Denmark 21/C7
Broseley, Mo. (63932) 261/M9
Brosna, Ireland 17/C7
Brosna (riv.), Ireland 17/F5
Brossard, Québec 172/H4
Brosseau, Alberta 182/E3
Brothers, Oreg. (97712) 291/G4
Brotherton, Tenn. (†38501) 237/L8
Brothertown, Wis. (†53014) 317/K7
Brou, France 28/D3
Brough (head), Scotland 15/E1
Brough Ness (prom.), Scotland 15/F2
Broughshane, N. Ireland 17/J2
Broughton, Ill. (62817) 222/E6
Broughton, Ohio (†45855) 284/B3
Broughton, Pa. (†15236) 294/B7
Broughton, Scotland 15/E5
Broughton Island, N.W. Terrs. 187/M3
Broumov, Czech. 41/D1
Brounland, W. Va. (†25314) 312/C6
Brouse, Br. Col. 184/J5
Broussard, La. (70518) 238/F6
Brouwershaven, Netherlands 27/D5
Brovst, Denmark 21/C3
Broward (co.), Fla. 212/F5
Browardale, Fla. (†33311) 212/B4
Browder, Ky. (42326) 237/H6
Browerville, Minn. (56438) 255/D4
Brown (co.), Ill. 222/C4
Brown (co.), Ind. 227/E6
Brown (co.), Kansas 232/G2
Brown (co.), Minn. 255/D6
Brown (co.), Nebr. 264/E2
Brown (lake), N.W. Terrs. 187/J3
Brown (co.), Ohio 284/C8
Brown (reefs), Philippines 85/F3
Brown (co.), S. Dak. 298/N2
Brown (co.), Texas 303/F6
Brown (Roan) (cliffs), Utah 304/E4
Brown (pt.), Wash. 310/A4
Brown, W. Va. (†26448) 312/F4
Brown (co.), Wis. 317/L7
Brownbranch, Mo. (65608) 261/G9
Brown City, Mich. (48416) 250/G5
Brown Deer, Wis. (53209) 317/L1
Browndell, Texas (†75931) 303/L7
Browne (bay), N.W. Terrs. 187/J2
Brownell, Kansas (67521) 232/C3
Browney (riv.), England 13/H3
Brownfield, Alberta 182/E3
Brownfield, Ill. (62911) 222/E6
Brownfield, Maine (04010) 243/B8
Brownfield○, Maine (04010) 243/B8
Brownfield, Miss. (†38683) 256/G1
Brownfield, Texas (79316) 303/B4
Browning, Ill. (62624) 222/C3
Browning, Mo. (64630) 261/F2
Browning, Mont. (59417) 262/C2
Browning, N.S. Wales 97/E4
Browning, Sask. 181/J6
Browning Entrance (str.), Br. Col. 184/B3
Brownington, Mo. (†64740) 261/E6
Brownington○, Vt. (†05860) 268/C2
Brownlee (dam), Idaho 220/B5
Brownlee, Nebr. (69126) 264/D2
Brownlee, Oreg. (†97840) 291/L3
Brownlee (dam), Oreg. 291/L3
Brownlee, Sask. 181/F5
Browns, Ala. (36724) 195/D6
Browns, Ill. (62818) 222/F5
Brown's (riv.), Vt. 268/A2
Brownsboro, Ala. (35741) 195/F1
Brownsboro, Oreg. (†97524) 291/E5
Brownsboro, Texas (75656) 303/J5
Brownsboro Farm, Ky. (†40201) 237/L1
Brownsburg, Ind. (46112) 227/E5
Brownsburg, Québec 172/C4
Brownsburg, Va. (24415) 307/K5
Brownsdale, Minn. (55918) 255/F7
Brownsdale, Newf. 166/D2
Browns Flat, New Bruns. 170/D3
Brown's Lake, Wis. (†53105) 317/K3
Browns Mills, N.J. (08015) 273/D4
Browns Spring, Mo. (†65610) 261/F9
Browns Summit, N.C. (27214) 281/K2
Brownstown, Ill. (62418) 222/E5
Brownstown, Ind. (47220) 227/F7
Browns Town, Jamaica 158/J6
Brownstown, Pa. (17508) 294/K5
Brownstown, Wash. (98920) 310/E4
Browns Valley, Ind. (†47933) 227/C5
Browns Valley, Minn. (56219) 255/B5
Browns Village, Fla. (†33142) 212/B4
Brownsville, Ind. (47325) 227/H5
Brownsville, Ky. (42210) 237/J6
Brownsville, Md. (21715) 245/H3
Brownsville, Minn. (55919) 255/G7
Brownsville, Miss. (†39041) 256/D6
Brownsville, Oreg. (97327) 291/E3
Brownsville, Pa. (15417) 294/C5
Brownsville, Tenn. (38012) 237/C9
Brownsville, Texas (*78520) 303/G12
Brownsville, Texas 188/G5
Brownsville, Texas 146/J7
Brownsville, Vt. (05037) 268/B5
Brownsville, Wash. (†98310) 310/A2
Brownsville, Wis. (53006) 317/J8
Brownton, Minn. (55312) 255/D6
Brownton, W. Va. (26334) 312/F4
Browntown, Va. (22610) 307/M3
Browntown, Wis. (53522) 317/G10
Brownvale, Alberta 182/B1
Brownville, Ala. (†35476) 195/C4
Brownville, Fla. (†33821) 212/E4
Brownville, Maine (04414) 243/E5
Brownville○, Maine (04414) 243/E5
Brownville, Nebr. (68321) 264/J4
Brownville, N.Y. (13615) 276/H3
Brownville Junction, Maine (04415) 243/E5
Brown Willy (mt.), England 13/C7
Brownwood, Texas (76801) 303/F6
Brownwood (lake), Texas 303/E6
Browse (isl.), W. Australia 88/C2
Browse (isl.), W. Australia 92/C1
Broxburn, Scotland 15/D1
Broxton, Georgia (31519) 217/G7
Broye (riv.), Switzerland 39/C3
Broyle (cape), Newf. 166/D2
Brozas, Spain 33/C3
Brozville, Miss. (†39095) 256/D4
Brtnice, Czech. 41/C2
Bruay-en-Artois, France 28/E2
Bruce, Alberta 182/E3
Bruce (mt.), Australia 87/C8
Bruce, Fla. (32455) 212/C6
Bruce, Miss. (38915) 256/F3
Bruce (mts.), N.W. Terrs. 187/L2
Bruce (county), Ontario 177/C3
Bruce (pen.), Ontario 177/C2
Bruce, S. Dak. (57220) 298/R5
Bruce (mt.), W. Australia 88/B4
Bruce (mt.), W. Australia 92/B3
Bruce, Wis. (54819) 317/D5
Bruce Crossing, Mich. (49912) 250/G2
Brucefield, Ontario 177/C4
Bruce Lake, Ontario 175/B2
Bruce Mines, Ontario 177/J5
Bruce Mines, Ontario 175/D3
Bruce Rock, W. Australia 88/B6
Bruce Rock, W. Australia 92/B5
Bruceton, Tenn. (38317) 237/E8
Bruceton Mills, W. Va. (26525) 312/G3
Brucetown, Va. (22622) 307/M2
Bruceville, Ind. (47516) 227/C7
Bruchsal, W. Germany 22/C4
Bruck an der Leitha, Austria 41/D2
Bruck an der Mur, Austria 41/C3
Bruderheim, Alberta 182/D3
Bruff, Ireland 17/D7
Bruges, Belgium 27/C6
Brugg, Switzerland 39/F2
Brugge (Bruges), Belgium 27/C6
Brühl, W. Germany 22/B3
Bruin, Ky. (41125) 237/P4
Bruin (cape), New Bruns. 170/G2
Bruin, Pa. (16022) 294/C3
Bruins, Ark. (†72348) 202/K4
Brûlé, Alberta 182/B3
Brule (riv.), Mich. 250/A3
Brule, Nebr. (69127) 264/C3
Brule, Nova Scotia 168/E3
Brûlé (lake), Québec 172/C3
Brûlé (lake), Québec 172/D2
Brule (co.), S. Dak. 298/L6
Brule (mt.), Switzerland 39/D4
Brule, Wis. (54820) 317/C2
Brumado, Brazil 120/E4
Brumado, Brazil 132/F6
Brumley, Mo. (65017) 261/H6
Brummen, Netherlands 27/J4
Brundidge, Ala. (36010) 195/G7
Bruneau, Idaho (83604) 220/C7
Bruneau (riv.), Idaho 220/C7
Brunei 2/Q5
Brunei 54/N9
BRUNEI 85/E4
Bruner, Mo. (65620) 261/F8
Brunete, Spain 33/F4
Brunette (isl.), Newf. 166/C4
Brunflo, Sweden 18/J5
Bruni, Texas (78344) 303/F10
Brunico, Italy 34/D1
Bruning, Nebr. (68322) 264/G4
Brunkild, Manitoba 179/E5
Brunner, N. Zealand 100/C5
Brunner (lake), N. Zealand 100/C5
Bruno, Ark. (72618) 202/E1
Bruno, Minn. (55712) 255/F4
Bruno, Nebr. (68014) 264/G3
Bruno, Sask. 181/F3
Brunot, Mo. (†63636) 261/M8
Brunsbüttel, W. Germany 22/C2
Brunson, S.C. (29911) 296/E6
Brunssum, Netherlands 27/J7
Brunsville, Iowa (51008) 229/A3
Brunswick (pen.), Chile 138/E10
Brunswick, Ga. 188/K4
Brunswick, Georgia (31520) 217/K8
Brunswick, Maine (04011) 243/C8
Brunswick○, Maine (04011) 243/C8
Brunswick, Md. (21716) 245/H3
Brunswick, Minn. (†55051) 255/E5
Brunswick, Miss. (†39180) 256/C5
Brunswick, Mo. (65236) 261/F4
Brunswick, Nebr. (68720) 264/G2
Brunswick (co.), N.C. 281/N6
Brunswick, N.C. (28424) 281/M6
Brunswick, Ohio (44212) 284/G3
Brunswick, Tenn. (38014) 237/B10
Brunswick, Victoria 88/K7
Brunswick, Victoria 97/H5
Brunswick (co.), Va. 307/N7
Brunswick (bay), W. Australia 88/C3
Brunswick, W. Germany 7/E3
Brunswick (bay), W. Australia 92/D1
Brunswick, W. Germany 22/D2
Brunswick Heads, N.S. Wales 97/G1
Brunswick Junction, W. Australia 92/A2
Bruntál, Czech. 41/D2
Bruree, Ireland 17/D7
Brus (lag.), Honduras 154/E2
Brusett, Mont. (59318) 262/J3
Brush, Colo. (80723) 208/M2
Brush Creek, Minn. (†56014) 255/E7
Brush Creek, Mo. (†65536) 261/G7
Brush Creek, Tenn. (38547) 237/J8
Brush Prairie, Wash. (98606) 310/C5
Brushton, N.Y. (12916) 276/L1
Brushy Prairie, Ind. (†46761) 227/G1
Brusio, Switzerland 39/K4
Brus Laguna, Honduras 154/E3
Brusly, La. (70719) 238/J2
Brusque, Brazil 132/D9
Brussels (cap.), Belgium 7/E3
Brussels, Ill. (62013) 222/C5
Brussels, Ontario 177/C4
Brussels, Wis. (54204) 317/L6
Bruthen, Victoria 97/D5
Brutus, Mich. (49716) 250/E3
Bruxelles, Manitoba 179/C5
Bruzual, Venezuela 124/D3
Bryan (co.), Georgia 217/K6
Bryan, Ohio (43506) 284/A3
Bryan (co.), Okla. 288/O7
Bryan, Texas 188/G4
Bryan, Texas (77801) 303/H7
Bryan (lake), Wash. 310/H4
Bryansk, U.S.S.R. 7/H3
Bryansk, U.S.S.R. 52/D4
Bryansk, U.S.S.R. 48/D4
Bryanston, Ontario 177/C4
Bryant, Ala. (35958) 195/G1
Bryant, Ark. (72022) 202/F4
Bryant, Fla. (33439) 212/F5
Bryant (lake), Fla. 212/E2
Bryant, Ill. (61519) 222/C3
Bryant, Ind. (47326) 227/G3
Bryant, Iowa (52727) 229/N5
Bryant, Okla. (†74437) 288/P4
Bryant, S. Dak. (57221) 298/P4
Bryant, Wis. (54418) 317/J5
Bryant Pond, Maine (04219) 243/B7
Bryantsburg, Ind. (†47250) 227/G7
Bryantsville, Ky. (40410) 237/M5
Bryantville, Mass. (02327) 249/L4
Bryce (mt.), Br. Col. 184/J4
Bryce Canyon, Utah (84717) 304/B6
Bryce Canyon Nat'l Park, Utah 304/B6
Bryceland, La. (71014) 238/E2
Bryceville, Fla. (32009) 212/D1
Bryn Athyn, Pa. (19009) 294/M5
Brynica (riv.), Poland 47/B4
Bryn Mawr, Pa. (19010) 294/M5
Brynmawr, Wales 10/E5
Brynmawr, Wales 13/B6
Bryn Mawr-Skyway, Wash. (†98101) 310/B2
Bryrup, Denmark 21/C5
Bryson, Texas (76027) 303/F4
Bryson City, N.C. (28713) 281/C4
Bryte-Broderick, Calif. (95605) 204/B8
Brzeg, Poland 47/C3
Brzeg Dolny, Poland 47/C3
Brzesko, Poland 47/E3
Brzozów, Poland 47/F4
B-Say-Tah, Sask. 181/G5
Bua Chum, Thailand 72/D4
Buad (isl.), Philippines 82/E5
Buba, Guinea-Biss. 106/B6
Bubali, Neth. Ant. 161/D10
Bubaque, Guinea-Biss. 106/A6
Bubendorf, Switzerland 39/E2
Bubikon, Switzerland 39/G2
Bubiyan (isl.), Kuwait 59/E4
Bucak, 63/D4
Bucaramanga, Colombia 120/B2
Bucaramanga, Colombia 126/D4
Bucareli (bay), Alaska 196/M2
Bucas Grande (isl.), Philippines 82/F6
Bucasia, Queensland 95/D4
Buccaneer (arch.), W. Australia 88/C3
Buccaneer (arch.), W. Australia 92/C2
Buchan (gulf), N.W. Terrs. 187/L2
Buchan (dist.), Scotland 15/F3
Buchanan, Georgia (30113) 217/B3
Buchanan (co.), Iowa 229/K4
Buchanan, Iowa (†52772) 229/L5
Buchanan, Ky. (†41129) 237/R4
Buchanan, Liberia 106/B7
Buchanan, Liberia 102/A4
Buchanan, Mich. (49107) 250/C7
Buchanan (co.), Mo. 261/C3
Buchanan, N.Y. (10511) 276/N8
Buchanan, N. Dak. (58420) 282/N5
Buchanan, Sask. 181/J4
Buchanan, Tenn. (38222) 237/E8
Buchanan (lake), Texas 303/F7
Buchanan (co.), Va. 307/D6
Buchanan, Va. (24066) 307/J5
Buchan Ness (prom.), Scotland 15/G3
Buchans, Newf. 166/C4
Bucharest (cap.), Romania 7/G4
Bucharest (cap.), Romania 2/L3
Bucharest (București) (cap.), Romania 45/G3
Buchegg (mts.), Switzerland 39/D2
Buchholz in der Nordheide, W. Germany 22/C2
Buchlyvie, Scotland 15/B1
Buchon (pt.), Calif. 204/D8
Buchs, Switzerland 39/H2
Buchtel, Ohio (45716) 284/F7
Buck (creek), Ind. 227/E8
Buck (creek), S.C. 296/J3
Buck (creek), Texas 303/D3
Buck (isl.), Virgin Is. (U.S.) 161/G3
Buck, W. Va. (†24935) 312/E7
Buckatunna, Miss. (39322) 256/G7
Buck Creek, Alberta 182/C3
Buck Creek, Ind. (47924) 227/D4
Bückeburg, W. Germany 22/C2
Buckeye, Ariz. (85326) 198/C5
Buckeye, Iowa (50043) 229/G4
Buckeye, La. (71321) 238/F4
Buckeye, N. Mex. (†88260) 274/F6
Buckeye (lake), Ohio 284/F6
Buckeye, W. Va. (24924) 312/F6
Buckeye Lake, Ohio (43008) 284/F6
Buckeystown, Md. (21717) 245/J3
Buckfastleigh, England 13/C7
Buckfield○, Maine (†04232) 243/C7
Buck Grove, Iowa (†51442) 229/C5
Buckhannon, W. Va. (26201) 312/F5
Buckhannon (riv.), W. Va. 312/F5
Buckhaven and Methil, Scotland 15/F4
Buckhaven and Methil, Scotland 10/E2
Buckhead, Georgia (30625) 217/F3
Buck Hollow (creek), Oreg. 291/G2
Buckholts, Texas (76518) 303/H7
Buckhorn (lake), Ky. 237/O6
Buckhorn, Mo. (†63655) 261/M8
Buckhorn, N. Mex. (88025) 274/A5
Buckhorn, Ontario 177/F3
Buckhorn (lake), Ontario 177/F3
Buckie, Scotland 15/E3
Buckie, Scotland 10/E2
Buckingham, Colo. (†80742) 208/L1
Buckingham, Conn. (†06033) 210/E2
Buckingham, England 13/G6
Buckingham, England 10/F5
Buckingham, Ill. (60917) 222/E2
Buckingham, Iowa (50612) 229/J4
Buckingham, Québec 172/B4
Buckingham, Texas (†75080) 303/H2
Buckingham (co.), Va. 307/L5
Buckingham, Va. (23921) 307/L5
Buckinghamshire (co.), England 13/G6
Buck Island (chan.), Virgin Is. (U.S.) 161/F3
Buck Island Reef Nat'l Mon., Virgin Is. (U.S.) 161/G3
Buck Lake, Alberta 182/C3
Buckland, Alaska (99727) 196/F1
Buckland, Conn. (06040) 210/E1
Buckland○, Mass. (01338) 249/C2
Buckland, Ohio (45819) 284/B4
Buckland, Québec 172/G3
Buckley, Ill. (60918) 222/F3
Buckley, Mich. (49620) 250/D4
Buckley, Wales 13/G2
Buckley, Wash. (98321) 310/C3
Bucklin, Kansas (67834) 232/C4
Bucklin, Mo. (64631) 261/G3
Buckman, Minn. (56317) 255/D5
Buckner, Ark. (71827) 202/D7
Buckner, Ill. (62819) 222/E6
Buckner, Ky. (40010) 237/L4
Buckner, Mo. (64016) 261/R5
Bucks, Ala. (36512) 195/B8
Bucks (co.), Pa. 294/M5
Bucksburn, Scotland 15/F3
Bucks Harbor, Maine (04618) 243/J6
Buckskin (mts.), Ariz. 198/B4
Buckskin, Ind. (47647) 227/C8
Bucksport, Maine (04416) 243/F6
Bucksport○, Maine (04416) 243/F6
Bucksport, S.C. (29527) 296/J4
Buckville, Ark. (71934) 202/D4
Bucoda, Mo. (†63876) 261/M10
Bucoda, Wash. (98530) 310/C4
Buco-Zau, Angola 115/B4
Buctouche, New Bruns. 170/F2
Buctouche (harb.), New Bruns. 170/F2
Buctouche (riv.), New Bruns. 170/F2
București (Bucharest) (cap.), Romania 45/G3
Bucyrus, Kansas (66013) 232/H3
Bucyrus, Mo. (65444) 261/H8
Bucyrus, N. Dak. (58624) 282/E7
Bucyrus, Ohio (44820) 284/E4
Bud, Ind. (†46131) 227/E6
Bud, W. Va. (24716) 312/D7
Buda, Ill. (61314) 222/D2
Buda, Texas (78610) 303/G7
Budafok, Hungary 41/E3
Budakeszi, Hungary 41/E3
Budaörs, Hungary 41/E3

344 Budapest

Budapest (city), Hungary 41/E3
Budapest (cap.), Hungary 41/E3
Budapest (cap.), Hungary 7/F4
Budaun, India 68/D3
Budd (lake), N.J. 273/D2
Budd Coast (reg.) 5/C6
Budd Lake, N.J. (07828) 273/D2
Buddon Ness (prom.), Scotland 15/F4
Bude (bay), England 13/C7
Bude, Miss. (39630) 256/C8
Bude-Stratton, England 13/C7
Budge-Budge, India 68/F2
Budgewoi Lake, N.S. Wales 97/F3
Budia, Spain 33/E2
Büdingen, W. Germany 22/C3
Budišov, Czech. 41/D2
Budjala, Zaire 115/C3
Budleigh Salterton, England 13/D7
Budrio, Italy 34/C2
Budva, Yugoslavia 45/D4
Buea, Cameroon 115/A3
Buechel, Ky. (40218) 237/K2
Buel (lake), Mass. 249/A4
Buellton, Calif. (93427) 204/E9
Buena, N.J. (08310) 273/D4
Buena, Wash. (98921) 310/E4
Buena Esperanza, Argentina 143/C3
Buena Park, Calif. (*90622) 204/D11
Buenaventura, Colombia 126/B6
Buenaventura, Colombia 120/B2
Buenaventura (bay), Colombia 126/B6
Buenaventura, Cuba 158/H3
Buenaventura, Mexico 150/F2
Buena Vista, Ala. (†36425) 195/D7
Buena Vista, Ark. (†71764) 202/D7
Buena Vista, Bolivia 136/D5
Buena Vista (lake), Calif. 204/F8
Buena Vista, Colo. (81211) 208/G5
Buenavista, Cuba 158/F2
Buenavista (bay), Cuba 158/F2
Buena Vista, Georgia (31803) 217/C6
Buena Vista (co.), Iowa 229/C3
Buena Vista, Miss. (†38851) 256/G3
Buena Vista, N. Mex. (87712) 274/D3
Buena Vista, Ohio (†45684) 284/D8
Buena Vista, Oreg. (†97351) 291/D3
Buena Vista, Paraguay 144/D5
Buenavista, Philippines 82/E6
Buena Vista, Sask. 181/F5
Buena Vista, Tenn. (38318) 237/E9
Buena Vista, Uruguay 145/E3
Buena Vista, Anzoátegui, Venezuela 124/F3
Buena Vista, Apure, Venezuela 124/D4
Buena Vista, Falcón, Venezuela 124/D2
Buena Vista (I.C.), Va. (24416) 307/K5
Buendía (res.), Spain 33/E2
Bueno (riv.), Chile 138/D3
Buenos Aires (lake) 120/B7
Buenos Aires (prov.), Argentina 143/D4
Buenos Aires (cap.), Argentina 120/C6
Buenos Aires (cap.), Argentina 143/H7
Buenos Aires (cap.), Argentina 2/F7
Buenos Aires (lake), Argentina 143/B6
Buenos Aires (lake), Chile 138/E6
Buenos Aires, Amazonas, Colombia 126/F9
Buenos Aires, Caquetá, Colombia 126/D7
Buenos Aires, C. Rica 154/F6
Buesaco, Colombia 126/B7
Buey Arriba, Cuba 158/H4
Bueyeros, N. Mex. (88412) 274/F3
Buffalo, Alberta 182/E4
Buffalo, Ala. (†36862) 195/H5
Buffalo (lake), Alberta 182/D3
Buffalo (riv.), Ark. 202/E2
Buffalo, Ill. (62515) 222/D4
Buffalo, Ind. (47925) 227/D3
Buffalo, Iowa (52728) 229/M6
Buffalo, Kansas (66717) 232/G4
Buffalo, Ky. (42716) 237/K6
Buffalo (bay), Manitoba 179/G5
Buffalo, Minn. (55313) 255/E5
Buffalo (riv.), Minn. 255/B4
Buffalo, Mo. (65622) 261/F7
Buffalo, Mont. (59418) 262/G4
Buffalo (co.), Nebr. 264/E4
Buffalo (creek), Nev. 266/B2
Buffalo, N.Y. 146/L5
Buffalo, N.Y. 188/L2
Buffalo, N.Y. (*14201) 276/B5
Buffalo, N. Dak. (58011) 282/R6
Buffalo, Ohio (43722) 284/G6
Buffalo, Okla. (73834) 288/G1
Buffalo, S.C. (29321) 296/D2
Buffalo (co.), S. Dak. 298/L5
Buffalo, S. Dak. (57720) 298/B2
Buffalo (creek), S. Dak. 298/F6
Buffalo (lake), S. Dak. 298/P2
Buffalo (riv.), Tenn. 237/F9
Buffalo, Texas (75831) 303/J6
Buffalo, W. Va. (25033) 312/C5
Buffalo (co.), Wis. 317/C7
Buffalo, Wis. (†54622) 317/C7
Buffalo, Wyo. (82834) 319/F1
Buffalo Bill (dam), Wyo. 319/C1
Buffalo Bill (res.), Wyo. 319/C1
Buffalo Center, Iowa (50424) 229/F2
Buffalo City, Ark. (†72653) 202/E1
Buffalo City, N.C. (†27931) 281/T3
Buffalo Creek, Br. Col. 184/G4
Buffalo Creek, Colo. (80425) 208/J4
Buffalo Fork, Snake (riv.), Wyo. 319/B2
Buffalo Gap, Sask. 181/F6
Buffalo Gap, S. Dak. (57722) 298/C6
Buffalo Gap, Texas (79508) 303/E5
Buffalo Grove, Ill. (†60090) 222/B5
Buffalo Head (hills), Alberta 182/B5
Buffalo Junction, Va. (24529) 307/L7
Buffalo Lake, Minn. (55314) 255/D6
Buffalo Lodge (lake), N. Dak. 282/J3
Buffalo Mills, Pa. (15534) 294/E6
Buffalo Narrows, Sask. 181/L3
Buffalo Nat'l River, Ark. 202/E1
Buffalo Pound Prov. Park, Sask. 181/F5
Buffalo River Junction, N.W. Terrs. 187/G3
Buffalo Valley, Tenn. (38548) 237/K8
Buffaloville, Ind. (47518) 227/D8
Buff Bay, Jamaica 158/K6
Buford, Alberta 182/D3
Buford, Georgia (30518) 217/D2
Buford, N. Dak. (†58853) 282/C3
Buford, Ohio (45110) 284/C7
Buford, Wyo. (82052) 319/G4
Bug (riv.) 7/G3
Bug (riv.), Poland 47/F2
Bug (riv.), U.S.S.R. 7/G4
Bug (riv.), U.S.S.R. 52/B4
Bug (riv.), U.S.S.R. 52/D5
Buga, Colombia 126/B6
Bugaboo Glacier Prov. Park, Br. Col. 184/J5
Bugak, Hungary 41/E3
Bugaldie, N.S. Wales 97/E2
Bugasong, Philippines 82/C5
Buggs Island (lake), N.C. 281/M1
Buggs Island (lake), Va. 307/L8
Bugiougio (isl.), Portugal 33/B2
Bugojno, Yugoslavia 45/C3
Bugrino, U.S.S.R. 52/G1
Bugsuk (isl.), Philippines 85/F4
Bugsuk (isl.), Philippines 82/A6
Bugt, China 77/K2
Bugui (pt.), Philippines 82/D4
Bugul'ma, U.S.S.R. 7/K3
Bugul'ma, U.S.S.R. 52/H4
Bugul'ma, U.S.S.R. 48/F4
Buguruslan, U.S.S.R. 52/H4
Buhl, Ala. (35446) 195/C4
Buhl, Idaho (83316) 220/D7
Buhl, Minn. (55713) 255/F3
Bühl, W. Germany 22/C4
Buhler, Kansas (67522) 232/E3
Buhuşi, Romania 45/H2
Buie, Loch (inlet), Scotland 15/C4
Buies, N.C. (†28377) 281/L5
Buies Creek, N.C. (27506) 281/M4
Buiksloot, Netherlands 27/C4
Builth Wells, Wales 13/D5
Builth Wells, Wales 10/E4
Buin, Chile 138/G4
Buin, Papua N.G. 86/C2
Buin (peak), Switzerland 39/K3
Buinsk, U.S.S.R. 52/G4
Bujalance, Spain 33/D4
Bujumbura (cap.), Burundi 102/F5
Bujumbura (cap.), Burundi 115/E4
Buka, Papua N.G. 87/F6
Buka (isl.), Papua N.G. 86/C2
Buka (passage), Papua N.G. 86/C2
Bukachacha, U.S.S.R. 48/M4
Bukama, Zaire 115/E5
Buka Passage, Papua N.G. 86/C2
Bukavu, Zaire 102/E5
Bukavu, Zaire 115/E4
Bukene, Tanzania 115/F4
Bukhara, U.S.S.R. 54/H5
Bukhara, U.S.S.R. 48/G5
Bukidnon (prov.), Philippines 82/E6
Bukittinggi, Indonesia 85/B6
Bükk (mts.), Hungary 41/F2
Bukoba, Tanzania 115/F4
Bukowno, Poland 47/C4
Bul, Kuh-e (mt.), Iran 66/H5
Bula, Indonesia 85/J6
Bula, Texas (79320) 303/B4
Bulacan (prov.), Philippines 82/C3
Bülach, Switzerland 39/G1
Bulahdelah, N.S. Wales 97/G3
Bulak (Bole), China 77/B3
Bulalakao, Philippines 82/C4
Bulan, Ky. (41722) 237/P6
Bulan, Philippines 82/D4
Bulancak, Turkey 63/H2
Bulanık, Turkey 63/K3
Bûlaq, Egypt 111/F2
Bûlaq, Egypt 59/B4
Bulawayo, Zimbabwe 118/D3
Bulawayo, Zimbabwe 102/E7
Buldan, Turkey 59/A2
Buldan, Turkey 63/C3
Buldibuyo, Peru 128/D7
Buldir (isl.), Alaska 196/J3
Bulgan, Mongolia 77/F2
Bulgan, Ömnögovĭ, Mongolia 77/F3
Bulgan, Hovd, Mongolia 77/D2
Bulgan, Bulgan, Mongolia 77/F2
Bulgaria 2/L3
Bulgaria 7/G4
BULGARIA 45/G4
Bulger, Pa. (15019) 294/B5
Bulgroo, Queensland 95/B5
Bulgroo, Queensland 88/G5
Bulhar, Somalia 115/H1
Buli, Indonesia 85/H5
Buliluyan (cape), Philippines 85/F4
Buliluyan (cape), Philippines 82/A6
Bulimba (creek), Queensland 95/E3
Bulkley (riv.), Br. Col. 184/D2
Bull, The (isl.), Ireland 17/A8
Bull (isl.), Newf. 166/D2
Bull (isl.), S.C. 296/H6
Bull (creek), S. Dak. 298/K6
Bull (creek), S. Dak. 298/C2
Bullard, Georgia (†31020) 217/F5
Bullard, Texas (75757) 303/J5
Bull Arm (inlet), Newf. 166/D2
Bullas, Spain 33/F4
Bulldog (isl.), Newf. 166/C3
Bulle, Switzerland 39/D3
Bullen (bay), Neth. Ant. 161/F8
Buller (riv.), N. Zealand 100/D4
Buller (mt.), Victoria 97/D5
Bullfinch, W. Australia 92/B5
Bull Harbour, Br. Col. 184/C5
Bullhead, S. Dak. (57621) 298/G2
Bullhead City-Riviera, Ariz. (86430) 198/A3
Bullitt (co.), Ky. 237/K5
Bull Lake (res.), Wyo. 319/C2
Bulloch (co.), Georgia 217/J6
Bullock (co.), Ala. 195/G6
Bullock, N.C. (27507) 281/M2
Bullock (creek), S.C. 296/E2
Bulloo (riv.), Queensland 88/G5
Bulloo (lake), Queensland 95/B6
Bulloo (riv.), Queensland 95/B6
Bulloo Downs, Queensland 88/G5
Bull Run (creek), Va. 307/N3
Bulls, N. Zealand 100/E4
Bulls (bay), S.C. 296/H6
Bull Savanna-Junction, Jamaica 158/H6
Bulls Bridge, Conn. (†06785) 210/B2
Bulls Gap, Tenn. (37711) 237/P8
Bull Shoals, Ark. (72619) 202/E1
Bull Shoals (lake), Ark. 202/E1
Bull Shoals (lake), Mo. 261/G10
Bully (creek), Oreg. 291/K3
Bulnes, Chile 138/E1
Bulo Burti, Somalia 115/J3
Bulolo, Papua N.G. 85/B7
Bulpitt, Ill. (62517) 222/D4
Buluan (lake), Philippines 82/E7
Bulukumba, Indonesia 85/G7
Bulun, U.S.S.R. 4/B3
Bulun, U.S.S.R. 48/N2
Bulungu, Zaire 115/C4
Bulusan, Philippines 82/E4
Bulusan (vol.), Philippines 82/D4
Bulyea, Sask. 181/G5
Bumba, Zaire 115/D3
Bumble Bee, Ariz. (†86301) 198/C4
Bumiayu, Indonesia 85/H2
Bumpass, Va. (23024) 307/N5
Bumping (lake), Wash. 310/D4
Bumpus Mills, Tenn. (37028) 237/F7
Bumthang, Bhutan 68/G3
Buna, Kenya 115/G3
Buna, Papua N.G. 85/C7
Buna, Texas (77612) 303/L7
Bunavista, Texas (†79007) 303/C2
Bunawan, Philippines 82/E6
Bunbeg-Derrybeg, Ireland 17/E1
Bunbury, Australia 87/B9
Bunbury, Pr. Edward I. 168/F2
Bunbury, W. Australia 88/B6
Bunbury, W. Australia 92/A2
Bunceton, Mo. (65237) 261/G5
Bunch, Iowa (†52552) 229/H7
Bunch, Okla. (74931) 288/S3
Bunche Park, Fla. (†33054) 212/B4
Bunclody-Carrickduff, Ireland 17/H6
Buncombe, Ill. (62912) 222/E6
Buncombe (co.), N.C. 281/D3
Buncrana, Ireland 17/G1
Buncrana, Ireland 10/C3
Bundaberg, Australia 87/E8
Bundaberg, Queensland 88/J4
Bundaberg, Queensland 95/D5
Bundanoon, N.S. Wales 97/F4
Bundarra, N.S. Wales 97/F2
Bünde, W. Germany 22/C2
Bundi, India 68/D3
Bundick (lake), La. 238/D5
Bundooma, North. Terr. 93/D8
Bundoora, Victoria 97/J4
Bundoran, Ireland 17/E3
Bunessan, Scotland 15/B4
Bunga (pt.), Philippines 82/E4
Bungalaut (chan.), Indonesia 85/B6
Bungay, England 10/G4
Bungay, England 13/J5
Bungee (brook), Conn. 210/G1
Bu Ngem, Libya 111/C1
Bungendore, N.S. Wales 97/E4
Bungo (str.), Japan 81/F7
Bunguran (Great Natuna) (isl.), Indonesia 85/D5
Bunguran (Natuna) (isls.), Indonesia 85/D5
Bunia, Zaire 115/E3
Bunia, Zaire 102/E4
Bunji, Pakistan 68/C1
Bunker, Mo. (63629) 261/K8
Bunker Group (isls.), Queensland 95/E4
Bunker Hill, Ill. (62014) 222/D4
Bunker Hill, Ind. (46914) 227/E3
Bunker Hill, Kansas (67626) 232/D3
Bunker Hill, Oreg. (†97420) 291/C4
Bunker Hill, W. Va. (25413) 312/K4
Bunker Hill Village, Texas (†77001) 303/J1
Bunkerville, Nev. (89007) 266/G6
Bunkeya, Zaire 115/E6
Bunkie, La. (71322) 238/F5
Bunn, N.C. (27508) 281/N3
Bunnell, Fla. (32010) 212/E2
Bunnlevel, N.C. (28323) 281/M4
Buntok, Indonesia 85/F6
Bunyala, Kenya 115/F3
Bünyan, Turkey 63/G3
Bunyan's Cove, Newf. 166/C2
Bunyu (isl.), Indonesia 85/F5
Buochs, Switzerland 39/F3
Buol, Indonesia 85/G5
Buq, Iran 66/M6
Bura, Kenya 115/H4
Bur Acaba, Somalia 115/H3
Bur Acaba, Somalia 102/G4
Buraida, Saudi Arabia 59/D4
Buraimi, Oman 59/G5
Buraimi, U.A.E. 59/G5
Buram, Sudan 111/E5
Burang, China 77/B5
Burao, Somalia 102/G4
Burao, Somalia 115/J2
Buras-Triumph, La. (70041) 238/L8
Burauen, Philippines 82/E5
Buraz, Turkey 63/B6
Burbank, Calif. (*91501) 204/C10
Burbank, Ill. (60459) 222/B6
Burbank, Ohio (44214) 284/F4
Burbank, Okla. (74633) 288/N1
Burbank, S. Dak. (57010) 298/R8
Burbank, Wash. (99323) 310/G4
Burchard, Minn. (†56115) 255/C6
Burchard, Nebr. (68323) 264/H4
Burcher, N.S. Wales 97/D3
Burchinal, Iowa (†50469) 229/G2
Burdekin (riv.), Queensland 88/H3
Burdekin (riv.), Queensland 95/C3
Burden, Kansas (67019) 232/F4
Burdett, Alberta 182/E5
Burdett, Kansas (67523) 232/C3
Burdett, N.Y. (14818) 276/G6
Burdette, Ark. (72321) 202/L2
Burdette, S. Dak. (†57476) 298/M4
Burdick, Kansas (66838) 232/F3
Burdur (prov.), Turkey 63/D4
Burdur, Turkey 59/A2
Burdur, Turkey 63/D4
Burdur (lake), Turkey 63/D4
Burdwan, India 68/F4
Bureå, Sweden 18/M4
Bureau (co.), Ill. 222/D2
Bureau, Ill. (61315) 222/D2
Burei, Ethiopia 111/G6
Büren, W. Germany 22/C3
Büren an der Aare, Switzerland 39/D2
Bürentsogt, Mongolia 77/H2
Burford (lake), N. Mex. 274/C2
Burford, Ontario 177/D4
Burfordville, Mo. (63739) 261/N8
Burgas, Bulgaria 45/H4
Burgas, Bulgaria 7/G4
Burg auf Fehmarn, W. Germany 22/D1
Burgaw, N.C. (28425) 281/N5
Burgaz (isl.), Turkey 63/D6
Burg bei Magdeburg, E. Germany 22/D2
Burgdorf, Switzerland 39/E2
Burgenland (prov.), Austria 41/D3
Burgeo, Newf. 166/C4
Burgersdorp, S. Africa 118/D6
Burgess, Mo. (†66756) 261/C7
Burgess, S.C. (†29576) 296/J4
Burgess, Va. (22432) 307/R5
Burgess (mt.), Yukon 187/D3
Burgess Hill, England 13/G7
Burgessville, Ontario 177/D4
Burgettstown, Pa. (15021) 294/A5
Burghausen, W. Germany 22/E4
Burghead, Scotland 10/E2
Burghead, Scotland 15/E3
Burghill, Ohio (44404) 284/J3
Burgin, Ky. (40310) 237/M5
Burgis, Sask. 181/J4
Bürglen, Thurgau, Switzerland 39/H1
Bürglen, Uri, Switzerland 39/G3
Burglengenfeld, W. Germany 22/D4
Burgoon, Ohio (43407) 284/D3
Burgos, Mexico 150/K4
Burgos (prov.), Spain 33/E1
Burgos, Spain 7/D4
Burgos, Spain 33/E1
Burg Stargard, E. Germany 22/E2
Burgsteinfurt, W. Germany 22/B2
Burgsvik, Sweden 18/K8
Burgundy (trad. prov.), France 29
Burhaniye, Turkey 63/B3
Burhanpur, India 68/D4
Buri, Brazil 135/B3
Buri (pen.), Ethiopia 111/H4
Burias (isl.), Philippines 82/D4
Burias (passage), Philippines 82/D4
Buribay, U.S.S.R. 52/J4
Burica (pt.), C. Rica 154/F6
Burica, Punta (cape), Panama 154/F6
Burien, Wash. (98166) 310/A2
Burin, Newf. 166/C4
Burin (pen.), Newf. 166/C4
Buriram, Thailand 72/D4
Buriti, Brazil 132/F3
Buriti Alegre, Brazil 132/D7
Buriti dos Lopes, Brazil 132/F3
Burj al Hattaba, Tunisia 106/F2
Burkburnett, Texas (76354) 303/F3
Burke (chan.), Br. Col. 184/D4
Burke (co.), Georgia 217/J4
Burke, Idaho (†83873) 220/C2
Burke, N.Y. (12917) 276/M1
Burke (co.), N.C. 281/F3
Burke (co.), N. Dak. 282/E2
Burke, S. Dak. (57523) 298/L7
Burke, Texas (75941) 303/K6
Burke○, Vt. (†05871) 268/D2
Burke (mt.), Vt. 268/D2
Burke, Va. (22015) 307/R3
Bürkelkopf (mt.), Switzerland 39/K3
Burkes Garden, Va. (24608) 307/F6
Burkesville, Ky. (42717) 237/L7
Burket, Ind. (46508) 227/F2
Burketown, Queensland 95/A3
Burketown, Queensland 88/F3
Burkett, Texas (76828) 303/E5
Burkettsville, Ohio (45310) 284/A5
Burkettville, Maine (04540) 243/E7
Burkeville, Texas (75932) 303/L7
Burkeville, Va. (23922) 307/M6
Burkittsville, Md. (21718) 245/H3
Burkley, Ky. (†42021) 237/C7
Burk's Falls, Ontario 177/E2
Burkville, Ala. (36725) 195/E6
Burleigh (co.), N. Dak. 282/J6
Burleson (co.), Texas 303/H7
Burleson, Texas (76028) 303/F3
Burley, Idaho (83318) 220/E7
Burley, Wash. (98322) 310/C3
Burlingame, Calif. (94010) 204/J2
Burlingame, Kansas (66413) 232/G3
Burlington, Colo. (80807) 208/P4
Burlington○, Conn. (06013) 210/D1
Burlington, Ill. (60109) 222/E1
Burlington, Ind. (46915) 227/E4
Burlington, Iowa (52601) 229/L7
Burlington, Iowa 188/H2
Burlington, Kansas (66839) 232/G3
Burlington, Ky. (41005) 237/R2
Burlington○, Maine (04417) 243/G5
Burlington○, Mass. (01803) 249/C5
Burlington, Mich. (49029) 250/D6
Burlington (co.), N.J. 273/D4
Burlington, N.J. (08016) 273/D3
Burlington, N.C. (27215) 281/K2
Burlington, N. Dak. (58722) 282/H3
Burlington, Ohio (†45680) 284/F9
Burlington, Okla. (73722) 288/K1
Burlington, Ontario 177/E4
Burlington, Pa. (18814) 294/J2
Burlington, Vt. (05401) 268/A3
Burlington, Vt. 146/L5
Burlington, Vt. 188/M2
Burlington, Wash. (98233) 310/C2
Burlington, W. Va. (26710) 312/J4
Burlington, Wis. (53105) 317/K10
Burlington, Wyo. (82411) 319/D1
Burlington Flats, N.Y. (13315) 276/K5
Burlington Junction, Mo. (64428) 261/B2
Burlison, Tenn. (38015) 237/B9
Burma 2/P4
Burma 54/L7
BURMA 72
Burmis, Alberta 182/C5
Burna, Ky. (42028) 237/E6
Burnaby, Br. Col. 184/K3
Burnaby (isl.), Br. Col. 184/B4
Burnet (co.), Texas 303/F7
Burnet, Texas (78611) 303/F7
Burnett, Minn. (†55727) 255/F4
Burnett (co.), Wis. 317/B4
Burnett, Wis. (53922) 317/J9
Burnettown, S.C. (†29834) 296/D5
Burnettsville, Ind. (47926) 227/D3
Burney, Calif. (96013) 204/D3
Burney (mt.), Chile 138/D9
Burney, Ind. (47222) 227/F6
Burneyville, Okla. (73430) 288/M7
Burnham, Ill. (†60601) 222/C6
Burnham○, Maine (04922) 243/E6
Burnham, Mo. (†65793) 261/J9
Burnham, Pa. (17009) 294/H4
Burnham-on-Crouch, England 13/H6
Burnham-on-Sea, England 13/D6
Burnie, Tasmania 99/B3
Burnie-Somerset, Tasmania 88/H8
Burning Springs, Ky. (40922) 237/O6
Burning Springs, W. Va. (26139) 312/D5
Burnips, Mich. (49314) 250/D6
Burnley, England 10/G1
Burnley, England 13/H1
Burnmouth, Scotland 15/F5
Burns, Colo. (80426) 208/F3
Burns, Kansas (66840) 232/F3
Burns, Miss. (†39153) 256/E6
Burns, N.S. Wales 97/A3
Burns, Oreg. (97720) 291/H4
Burns, Tenn. (37029) 237/G8
Burns, Wyo. (82053) 319/H4
Burns City, Ind. (47553) 227/D7
Burns Flat, Okla. (73624) 288/H4
Burns Harbor, Ind. (†46401) 227/C1
Burnside, Conn. (†06108) 210/E1
Burnside, Ill. (62318) 222/B3
Burnside, Iowa (50521) 229/E4
Burnside, Ky. (42519) 237/M6
Burnside, La. (70738) 238/L3
Burnside, Miss. (†39350) 256/F5
Burnside (riv.), N.W. Terrs. 187/G3
Burnside, Pa. (15721) 294/E4
Burnside, S. Australia 88/E8
Burnside, S. Australia 94/B8
Burnside, Suriname 131/C2
Burns Junction, Oreg. (†97902) 291/K5
Burns Lake, Br. Col. 162/D5
Burns Lake, Br. Col. 184/D3
Burnstad, N. Dak. (58526) 282/L7
Burnsville, Ala. (†36701) 195/E6
Burnsville, Ind. (†47201) 227/F6
Burnsville, Minn. (55337) 255/E6
Burnsville, Miss. (38833) 256/H1
Burnsville, New Bruns. 170/E1
Burnsville, N.C. (28714) 281/E3
Burnsville, Va. (24420) 307/J4
Burnsville, W. Va. (26335) 312/E5
Burnt (lakes), Alberta 182/C1
Burnt (lake), Newf. 166/B3
Burnt (riv.), Ontario 177/F3
Burnt (riv.), Oreg. 291/K3
Burnt (lake), Québec 174/E2
Burnt Cabins, Pa. (17215) 294/G5
Burnt Corn, Ala. (36431) 195/D7
Burnt House, W. Va. (26336) 312/D4
Burnt Island (lake), Ontario 177/F2
Burntisland, Scotland 15/D1
Burntisland, Scotland 10/C1
Burnt Islands, Newf. 166/C4
Burnt Point, Newf. 166/D2
Burnt Prairie, Ill. (62820) 222/E5
Burnt River, Ontario 177/F3
Burntroot (lake), Ontario 177/F2
Burntside (lake), Minn. 255/F3
Burntwood, England 13/F5
Burntwood, England 10/G2
Burntwood (riv.), Manitoba 179/J2
Burnwell, W. Va. (25034) 312/D6
Burqa, West Bank 65/C3
Burqin, China 77/C2
Burr (pond), Conn. 210/C1
Burr, Minn. (†56220) 255/B6
Burr, Nebr. (68324) 264/H4
Burr, Sask. 181/F3
Burra, S. Australia 94/F5
Burraboi, N.S. Wales 97/C4
Burramurra, North. Terr. 93/E6
Burray (isl.), Scotland 15/F2
Burrel, Albania 45/D5
Burren Junction, N.S. Wales 97/E2
Burriana, Spain 33/G3
Burringbar, N.S. Wales 97/G1
Burrinjuck (res.), N.S. Wales 97/E4
Burris, Wyo. (†82501) 319/C2
Burro (creek), Ariz. 198/B4
Burro (mts.), Mexico 150/J2
Burr Oak, Ind. (46509) 227/E2
Burr Oak, Iowa (52131) 229/K2
Burr Oak, Kansas (66936) 232/D2
Burr Oak, Mich. (49030) 250/D7
Burro-Burro (riv.), Guyana 131/B3
Burrow (head), Scotland 15/D6
Burrows, Ind. (46916) 227/E3
Burrows, Sask. 181/K5
Burr Ridge, Ill. (†60558) 222/B6
Burrsville, Md. (†21629) 245/P5
Burrton, Kansas (67020) 232/E3
Burrville, Conn. (†06790) 210/C1
Burrville, Tenn. (†37872) 237/M8
Burrville, Utah (†84701) 304/C5
Burrwood, La. (†70091) 238/M8
Burry Port, Wales 13/C6
Bursa (prov.), Turkey 63/C2
Bursa, Turkey 63/C2
Bursa, Turkey 59/A1
Bursa, Turkey 54/D5
Bur Sa'id (Port Said), Egypt 111/K2
Bur Said (Port Said), Egypt 59/B3
Burstall, Sask. 181/B5
Burt, Iowa (50522) 229/E2
Burt, Mich. (48417) 250/F5
Burt (lake), Mich. 250/E3
Burt (co.), Nebr. 264/H3
Burt, N.Y. (14028) 276/C4
Burt, N. Dak. (†58646) 282/F7
Burta, N.S. Wales 97/A3
Burt Lake, Mich. (49717) 250/E3
Burton, Br. Col. 184/H5
Burton (lake), Georgia 217/E1
Burton, Mich. (48507) 250/F6
Burton, Nebr. (†68778) 264/E2
Burton, New Bruns. 170/D3
Burton, Ohio (44021) 284/H3
Burton, S.C. (29902) 296/F7
Burton, Texas (77835) 303/H7
Burton, Wash. (98013) 310/C3
Burton, W. Va. (26562) 312/F3
Burtonport, Ireland 17/E2
Burtonport, Ireland 10/B3
Burton upon Trent, England 13/F5
Burton upon Trent, England 10/G2
Burtonville, Ky. (†41179) 237/P4
Burträsk, Sweden 18/M4
Burtrum, Minn. (56318) 255/D5
Burtts Corner, New Bruns. 170/D2
Buru (isl.), Indonesia 54/O10
Buru (isl.), Indonesia 85/H6
Buru (sea), Indonesia 85/H6
Burultokay (Fuhai), China 77/C2
Burundi 2/L6
Burundi 102/F5
BURUNDI 115/E4
Bururi, Burundi 115/F4
Burutu, Nigeria 106/F7
Burwash Landing, Yukon 187/D3
Burwell, Nebr. (68823) 264/E3
Burwell (mt.), Wyo. 319/C2
Burwood, N.S. Wales 88/K4
Burwood, N.S. Wales 97/J3
Bury, England 13/H2
Bury, England 10/G2
Bury, Québec 172/F4
Buryat A.S.S.R., U.S.S.R. 48/M4
Burye, Ethiopia 102/F3
Burye, Ethiopia 111/G5
Bury Saint Edmunds, England 13/H5
Bury Saint Edmunds, England 10/G4
Busby, Alberta 182/C3
Busby, Mont. (59016) 262/J5
Buseno, Switzerland 39/H4
Bush, Ill. (†62924) 222/D6
Bush, Ky. (40724) 237/O6
Bush, La. (70431) 238/L5
Buh (creek), Md. 245/J3
Bush (riv.), N. Ireland 17/H1
Bush (riv.), S.C. 296/D3
Bush City, Kansas (†66032) 232/G3
Bushehr (prov.), Iran 66/G6
Bushehr (Bushire), Iran 66/G6
Bushehr, Iran 59/F4
Bushell, Sask. 181/L2
Bushey, England 10/B5
Bushey, England 13/H7
Bushire, Iran 54/G7
Bushiribana, Neth. Ant. 161/E10
Bush Island, Nova Scotia 168/D4
Bushkill, Pa. (18324) 294/M3
Bushland, Texas (79012) 303/B2
Bushmills, N. Ireland 17/J1
Bushnell, Fla. (33513) 212/D3
Bushnell, Ill. (61422) 222/C3
Bushnell, Nebr. (69128) 264/A3
Bushnell, S. Dak. (†57276) 298/R5
Bushong, Kansas (66841) 232/F3
Bushton, Ill. (†61920) 222/E4
Bushton, Kansas (67427) 232/D3
Bushwood, Md. (20618) 245/L7
Bushyhead, Okla. (†74016) 288/P2
Bushy Park, Tasmania 99/C4
Busick, N.C. (†28714) 281/E3
Businga, Zaire 115/D3
Buskerud (co.), Norway 18/F6
Buskirk, Ky. (41406) 237/P5
Busko Zdrój, Poland 47/E3
Busra, Syria 63/G6
Busselton, W. Australia 88/A6
Busselton, W. Australia 92/A6
Busseron (creek), Ind. 227/C7
Bussee Woods (res.), Ill. 222/B5
Bussey, Iowa (50044) 229/H6
Bussigny-près-Lausanne, Switzerland 39/B3
Bussum, Netherlands 27/G4
Bustard (isls.), Ontario 177/C2
Busti, N.Y. (†14701) 276/B6
Bustinza, Argentina 143/F6
Busto Arsizio, Italy 34/B2
Busuanga (isl.), Philippines 82/B4
Busuanga (isl.), Philippines 85/F3
Busu-Djanoa, Zaire 115/D3
Büsum, W. Germany 22/C1
Buta, Zaire 102/E4
Buta, Zaire 115/D3
Buta-Ranquil, Argentina 143/C4
Butare, Rwanda 115/E4
Butaritari (atoll), Kiribati 87/H5
Butcher (isl.), India 68/B7
Bute (inlet), Br. Col. 184/E5
Bute (isl.), Scotland 15/C5
Bute (trad. co.), Scotland 15/A5
Bute (sound), Scotland 15/C5
Butedale, Br. Col. 184/C3
Butembo, Zaire 115/E3
Butembo, Zaire 102/E5
Butha, China 77/K2
Butiaba, Uganda 115/F3

Caltagirone 345

Butler (co.), Ala. 195/E7
Butler, Ala. (36904) 195/B6
Butler, Georgia (31006) 217/D5
Butler, Ill. (62015) 222/D4
Butler, Ind. (46721) 227/H2
Butler (co.), Iowa 229/H3
Butler (co.), Kansas 232/F4
Butler (co.), Ky. 237/H6
Butler, Ky. (41006) 237/N3
Butler, Md. (21023) 245/M2
Butler, Minn. (†56567) 255/C4
Butler (co.), Mo. 261/M9
Butler, Mo. (64730) 261/D6
Butler (co.), Nebr. 264/G3
Butler, N.J. (07405) 273/E2
Butler (co.), Ohio 284/A7
Butler, Ohio (44822) 284/F4
Butler, Okla. (73625) 288/H3
Butler (co.), Pa. 294/C4
Butler, Pa. (16001) 294/C4
Butler, S. Dak. (57222) 298/O3
Butler, Tenn. (37640) 237/T8
Butler (bay), Virgin Is. (U.S.) 161/E4
Butler, Wis. (53007) 317/K1
Butler Springs, Ala. (†36030) 195/E7
Butlerville, Ark. (†72176) 202/G4
Butlerville, Ind. (47223) 227/F6
Butlerville, Ohio (†45162) 284/B7
Butner, N.C. (27509) 281/M2
Bütschelegg (mt.), Switzerland 39/D3
Bütschwil, Switzerland 39/H2
Buttahatchee (riv.), Ala. 195/B3
Buttahatchee (riv.), Miss. 256/H3
Butte (co.), Calif. 204/D4
Butte (co.), Idaho 220/E6
Butte, Mont. 146/G5
Butte, Mont. 188/D1
Butte, Nebr. (68722) 264/F2
Butte (mts.), Nev. 266/F3
Butte, N. Dak. (58723) 282/J4
Butte (creek), Oreg. 291/G2
Butte (creek), Oreg. 291/B3
Butte (co.), S. Dak. 298/B4
Butte City, Calif. (95920) 204/C4
Butte City, Idaho (83213) 220/E6
Butte Des Morts, Wis. (†54901) 317/J7
Butte Falls, Oreg. (97522) 291/E5
Butter (creek), Oreg. 291/H2
Butterfield, Ark. (†72104) 202/E5
Butterfield, Minn. (56120) 255/D7
Butterfield, Mo. (65623) 261/E9
Butterfield (lake), N.Y. 276/J2
Butternut, Mich. (†48811) 250/E5
Butternut, Wis. (54514) 317/E3
Butternut (lake), Wis. 317/J4
Butter Pot Prov. Park, Newf. 166/D2
Butters, N.C. (28324) 281/M5
Butterworth, Malaysia 72/D6
Butterworth (Gcuwa), S. Africa 118/D6
Buttes, Switzerland 39/C3
Butte-Silver Bow County, Mont. (59701) 262/D5
Buttevant, Ireland 17/D7
Butteville, Oreg. (†97002) 291/A2
Butt of Lewis (prom.), Scotland 15/B2
Button (isls.), N.W. Terrs. 187/M3
Buttonwillow, Calif. (93206) 204/F8
Butts (co.), Georgia 217/E4
Buttzville, N.J. (07829) 273/D2
Buttzville, N. Dak. (†58054) 282/P6
Butuan, Philippines 82/E6
Butuan, Philippines 85/H4
Butuan, Philippines 54/O9
Butuan (bay), Philippines 82/E6
Butumi, U.S.S.R. 7/J4
Butung (isl.), Indonesia 54/O10
Butung (isl.), Indonesia 85/G6
Buturlinovka, U.S.S.R. 52/F4
Butzbach, W. Germany 22/C3
Bützow, E. Germany 22/E2
Buxtehude, W. Germany 22/C2
Buxton, England 10/G4
Buxton, England 13/J2
Buxton○, Maine (†04093) 243/C8
Buxton, N.C. (27920) 281/U4
Buxton, N. Dak. (58218) 282/R4
Buxton, Oreg. (97109) 291/D2
Buxton Center, Maine (†04093) 243/B8
Buy, U.S.S.R. 52/F3
Buyck, Minn. (55771) 255/F2
Buynaksk, U.S.S.R. 52/G6
Büyükada, Turkey 63/D6
Büyük Ağrı (Ararat) (mt.), Turkey 63/L3
Büyük Ağrı (Ararat) (mt.), Turkey 59/D2
Büyükanafarta, Turkey 63/B6
Büyükdere, Turkey 63/D5
Büyük Hasan Dağı, Turkey 63/E3
Büyük Menderes (riv.), Turkey 59/A2
Buzău, Romania 45/H3
Buzău (riv.), Romania 45/H3
Buzeima (well), Libya 111/D3
Buziaș, Romania 45/E3
Búzios (cape), Brazil 135/F3
Buzuluk, U.S.S.R. 52/H4
Buzuluk, U.S.S.R. 48/F4
Buzzard Roost (dam), S.C. 296/D3
Buzzards (bay), Mass. 249/L7
Buzzards Bay, Mass. (02532) 249/M5
Byala, Bulgaria 45/G4
Byala Slatina, Bulgaria 45/F4
Byam Martin (chan.), N.W. Terrs. 187/H2
Byam Martin (isl.), N.W. Terrs. 187/H2
Byars, Okla. (74831) 288/N5
Bybee, Tenn. (37713) 237/P8
Bydgoszcz (prov.), Poland 47/C2
Bydgoszcz, Poland 47/C2
Bydgoszcz, Poland 7/F3
Byemoor, Alberta 182/D4
Byers, Colo. (80103) 208/L3
Byers, Kansas (67021) 232/D4
Byers, Texas (76357) 303/F3
Byesville, Ohio (43723) 284/G6
Byfield, Mass. (01922) 249/L1
Byford, W. Australia 88/B2
Bygland, Minn. (†56723) 255/B3
Bygland, Norway 18/F7
Byhalia, Miss. (38611) 256/E1
Bykhov, U.S.S.R. 52/C4
Bylas, Ariz. (85530) 198/E5
Bylot (isl.), N.W.T. 146/L2
Bylot (isl.), N.W.T. 162/J1
Bylot (isl.), N.W. Terrs. 187/L2
Byng, Okla. (†74820) 288/N5
Byng Inlet, Ontario 177/D2
Byng Inlet, Ontario 175/D3
Bynum, Mont. (59419) 262/D3
Bynum (res.), Mont. 262/D2
Bynum, N.C. (27312) 281/L3
Bynumville, Mo. (†65281) 261/G3
Byram, Conn. (06830) 210/A4
Byram (pt.), Conn. 210/A4
Byram (riv.), Conn. 210/A4
Byram, Miss. (†39205) 256/D6
Byrd Station 5/A12
Byrdstown, Tenn. (38549) 237/L7
Byrnedale, Pa. (15827) 294/E3
Byrock, N.S. Wales 97/D2
Byromville, Georgia (31007) 217/E6
Byron, Calif. (94514) 204/L2
Byron (isl.), Chile 138/D7
Byron, Georgia (31008) 217/E5
Byron, Ill. (61010) 222/D1
Byron, Ind. (†46371) 227/C5
Byron, Maine (†04275) 243/B6
Byron○, Maine (†04275) 243/B6
Byron, Mich. (48418) 250/E6
Byron, Minn. (55920) 255/F6
Byron, Nebr. (68325) 264/G4
Byron (bay), Newf. 166/C3
Byron (cape), N. S. Wales 88/J5
Byron (cape), N.S. Wales 97/G1
Byron, N.Y. (14422) 276/D4
Byron, Okla. (73723) 288/K1
Byron (lake), S. Dak. 298/N4
Byron, Wis. (53009) 317/K8
Byron, Wyo. (82412) 319/D1
Byron Bay, N.S. Wales 97/G1
Byron Center, Mich. (49315) 250/D6
Byrum, Denmark 21/E3
Byskeälv (riv.), Sweden 18/L4
Bystřice nad Pernštejnem, Czech. 41/D2
Bystřice pod Hostýnem, Czech. 41/D2
Bystrzyca Kłodzka, Poland 47/C3
Bytča, Czech. 41/E2
Bytom, Poland 47/A3
Bytów, Poland 47/C1

C

Caacupé, Paraguay 144/B5
Caaguazú (dept.), Paraguay 144/D-E4
Caaguazú, Paraguay 144/D4
Caála, Angola 115/C6
Caamaño (sound), Br. Col. 184/C4
Caapucú, Paraguay 144/D5
Caatingas (for.), Brazil 120/E3
Caazapá (dept.), Paraguay 144/D-E5
Caazapá, Paraguay 144/D5
Caba, Philippines 82/C2
Cabadbaran, Philippines 82/E6
Cabaiguán, Cuba 158/E2
Cabalasan (mt.), Philippines 82/E5
Caballero, Paraguay 144/B5
Caballo, N. Mex. (87931) 274/B6
Caballo (res.), N. Mex. 274/B6
Caballo (creek), Wyo. 319/G1
Caballococha, Peru 128/G4
Caballones (chan.), Cuba 158/F3
Cabana, Peru 128/C7
Cabañaquinta, Spain 33/D1
Cabañas, Cuba 158/B1
Cabanatuan, Philippines 54/O8
Cabanatuan, Philippines 82/C3
Cabanatuan, Philippines 85/G2
Cabanes, Spain 33/F2
Cabano, Québec 172/J2
Cabarroquis, Philippines 82/C2
Cabarrus (co.), N.C. 281/H4
Cabazon, Calif. (92230) 204/J10
Cabbage Tree (creek), Queensland 95/D2
Cabedelo, Brazil 132/H4
Cabell (co.), W. Va. 312/B6
Cabery, Ill. (60919) 222/E3
Cabet, Pitons du (mt.), Martinique 161/C6
Cabeza del Buey, Spain 33/D3
Cabezas, Bolivia 136/D6
Cabezas, Cuba 158/D1
Cabildo, Chile 138/A9
Cabimas, Venezuela 120/B1
Cabimas, Venezuela 124/C2
Cabin Creek, W. Va. (25035) 312/C6
Cabinda (dist.), Angola 115/B5
Cabinda, Angola 115/B5
Cabinda, Angola 102/D5
Cabinet (mts.), Mont. 262/A2
Cabin John (creek), Md. 245/E4
Cabin John-Brookmont, Md. (20731) 245/E4
Cabins, W. Va. (26855) 312/H4
Cable, Minn. (†56301) 255/D5
Cable, Ohio (43009) 284/C5
Cable, Wis. (54821) 317/D3
Cabo Blanco, Peru 128/B5
Cabo Delgado (prov.), Mozambique 118/F2
Cabo Frio, Brazil 132/F8
Cabo Frio, Brazil 135/F3
Cabo Gracias a Dios, Nicaragua 154/F3
Cabonga (res.), Québec 174/B3
Cabool, Mo. (65689) 261/H8
Cabora Bassa (dam), Mozambique 118/E3
Caborn, Ind. (†47620) 227/B9
Cabo Rojo, P. Rico 161/A2
Cabo San Lucas, Mexico 150/E5
Cabot (str.) 162/K6
Cabot, Ark. (72023) 202/F4
Cabot (str.), Canada 146/N5
Cabot (lake), Newf. 166/B2
Cabot (str.), Newf. 166/B4
Cabot (mt.), N.H. 268/E2
Cabot (head), Ontario 177/C2
Cabot, Pa. (16023) 294/C4
Cabot, Vt. (05647) 268/C3
Cabot○, Vt. (05647) 268/C3
Cabo Vírgenes, Argentina 143/C7
Cabra, Spain 33/D4
Cabra de Santo Cristo, Spain 33/E4
Cabral, Dom. Rep. 158/D6
Cabral (lag.), Paraguay 144/A5
Cabrera, Dom. Rep. 158/E5
Cabrera (isl.), Spain 33/H3
Cabri, Sask. 181/C5
Cabri (lake), Sask. 181/B4
Cabrillo Nat'l Mon., Calif. 204/H11
Cabrits (isl.), Martinique 161/D7
Cabrón (cape), Dom. Rep. 158/F5
Cabruta, Venezuela 124/E4
Cabudare, Venezuela 124/D3
Cabugao, Philippines 82/C2
Cabulauan (isls.), Philippines 82/C5
Cabullones (pt.), P. Rico 161/C3
Caburai (mt.), Guyana 131/A3
Cabure, Venezuela 124/D2
Caçador, Brazil 132/D9
Cacahoatán, Mexico 150/N9
Čačak, Yugoslavia 45/E4
Caçapava, Brazil 135/D3
Caçapava do Sul, Brazil 132/C10
Cacapon (riv.), W. Va. 312/J4
Cáceres (lag.), Bolivia 136/G6
Cáceres, Brazil 132/B7
Cáceres, Brazil 120/D4
Cáceres, Colombia 126/C4
Cáceres (prov.), Spain 33/C3
Cáceres, Spain 33/C3
Cáceres, Spain 7/D5
Cachapoal (riv.), Chile 138/G5
Cache (riv.), Ark. 202/H3
Cache (riv.), Ill. 222/D6
Cache, Okla. (73527) 288/J5
Cache (creek), Okla. 288/K6
Cache (co.), Utah 304/C2
Cache Bay, Ontario 177/D1
Cache Creek, Br. Col. 184/G5
Cache Junction, Utah (84304) 304/C2
Cache la Poudre (riv.), Colo. 208/H1
Cacheu, Guinea-Biss. 106/A6
Cachi, Argentina 143/C2
Cachina, Quebrada (riv.), Chile 138/B5
Cachipo, Venezuela 124/G3
Cachoeira, Brazil 132/G6
Cachoeira de Itapemirim, Brazil 120/E5
Cachoeira do Arari, Brazil 132/D3
Cachoeira do Sul, Brazil 132/C10
Cachoeira do Sul, Brazil 120/D6
Cachoeiro de Itapemirim, Brazil 132/G8
Cachorras, Colombia 126/D8
Cachos (pt.), Chile 138/A6
Cachuela Esperanza, Bolivia 136/C2
Cachuma (lake), Calif. 204/F9
Cacocum, Cuba 158/H3
Cacocum, Cuba 156/C2
Cacolo, Angola 115/C6
Caconda, Angola 115/B6
Cacouna, Québec 172/H2
Cactus (range), Nev. 266/E5
Cactus (hills), Sask. 181/F5
Cactus, Texas (79013) 303/B1
Cactus Lake, Sask. 181/B3
Cacuri, Venezuela 124/F5
Cacuso, Angola 115/C5
Čadca, Czech. 41/E2
Caddo (riv.), Ark. 202/D5
Caddo (par.), La. 238/C1
Caddo (lake), La. 238/B1
Caddo (co.), Okla. 288/K4
Caddo, Okla. (74729) 288/O6
Caddo, Texas (76029) 303/F5
Caddo (lake), Texas 303/L5
Caddo Gap, Ark. (71935) 202/C5
Caddo Valley, Ark. (†71923) 202/D5
Caddy Lake, Manitoba 179/G5
Cade, La. (70519) 238/G6
Cadereyta Jiménez, Mexico 150/K4
Cades, S.C. (29518) 296/H4
Cades, Tenn. (†38358) 237/D9
Cades Cove, Tenn. (†37882) 237/O9
Cadet, Mo. (63630) 261/L6
Cadibarrawirracanna (lake), S. Australia 94/D3
Cadillac, Mich. (49601) 250/D4
Cadillac, Québec 174/B3
Cadillac, Sask. 181/D6
Cadiz, Calif. (92319) 204/K9
Cadiz (lake), Calif. 204/K9
Cadiz, Ind. (†47362) 227/G5
Cadiz, Ky. (42211) 237/F7
Cadiz, Ohio (43907) 284/J5
Cadiz, Philippines 82/D5
Cádiz (prov.), Spain 33/D4
Cádiz, Spain 33/C4
Cádiz, Spain 7/D5
Cádiz (gulf), Spain 33/C4
Cádizadiz (gulf), Portugal 33/C4
Cadogan, Alberta 182/E3
Cadogan○, Pa. (16212) 294/C4
Cadomin, Alberta 182/B3
Cadott, Wis. (54727) 317/D6
Cadotte (lake), Alberta 182/B1
Cadotte (riv.), Alberta 182/B1
Cadotte Lake, Alberta 182/B1
Cadron (creek), Ark. 202/F3
Caduruan (pt.), Philippines 82/D5
Cadwell, Georgia (31009) 217/G6
Cadyville, N.Y. (12918) 276/N1
Caen, France 28/C3
Caen, France 7/D4
Caerleon, Wales 13/B6
Caernarfon, Wales 13/C4
Caernarfon, Wales 10/D4
Caernarfon (bay), Wales 13/C4
Caernarfon (bay), Wales 10/D4
Caerphilly, Wales 13/B6
Caerphilly, Wales 10/E5
Caesar, Miss. (†39466) 256/E9
Caesarea, Ontario 177/F3
Caesars Head, S.C. (†29635) 296/B1
Caeté, Brazil 135/E1
Caetité, Brazil 132/F6
Cafayate, Argentina 143/C2
Cafelândia, Brazil 135/B2
Cagayan (prov.), Philippines 82/C1
Cagayan (isls.), Philippines 82/C6
Cagayan (isls.), Philippines 85/F4
Cagayan (riv.), Philippines 82/C2
Cagayancillo, Philippines 82/C6
Cagayan de Oro, Philippines 82/E6
Cagayan de Oro, Philippines 85/G4
Cagayan Sulu (isl.), Philippines 85/F4
Cagayan Sulu (isl.), Philippines 82/B7
Cagle, Tenn. (†37327) 237/L10
Cagles Mill (lake), Ind. 227/D6
Cagli, Italy 34/D3
Cagliari (prov.), Italy 34/B5
Cagliari, Italy 7/E5
Cagliari, Italy 34/B5
Cagliari (gulf), Italy 34/B5
Cagua (vol.), Philippines 82/D1
Cagua, Venezuela 124/E2
Caguán (riv.), Colombia 126/C7
Caguas, P. Rico 161/E2
Caguas, P. Rico 156/G1
Caha (mts.), Ireland 17/B8
Cahaba, Ala. (†36767) 195/D6
Cahaba (riv.), Ala. 195/D5
Cahabón, Guatemala 154/C3
Cahir, Ireland 10/B4
Cahir, Ireland 17/F7
Cahirciveen, Ireland 17/A8
Cahirciveen, Ireland 10/A5
Cahokia, Ill. (62206) 222/A3
Cahone, Colo. (81320) 208/B7
Cahore (pt.), Ireland 17/J6
Cahors, France 28/D5
Cahuapanas, Peru 128/D5
Cahuilla Ind. Res., Calif. 204/J10
Cahuinari (riv.), Colombia 126/E8
Cahuita (pt.), C. Rica 154/F6
Caiapônia, Brazil 132/C7
Caibarién, Cuba 158/F2
Caibarién, Cuba 156/B2
Caibiran, Philippines 82/E5
Caicara, Venezuela 124/G3
Caicara de Orinoco, Venezuela 124/E4
Caicedonia, Colombia 126/C5
Caicó, Brazil 120/F3
Caicó, Brazil 132/G4
Caicos (passage), Bahamas 156/D2
Caicos (bank), Turks & Caicos 156/D2
Caicos (isls.), Turks & Caicos 156/D2
Caicos (passage), Turks & Caicos 156/D2
Caile, Miss. (†38754) 256/C4
Cailloma, Peru 128/G10
Caillou (bay), La. 238/J8
Caimanera, Cuba 158/J4
Caimanera, Cuba 156/C3
Cain (creek), S. Dak. 298/N5
Cainde, Angola 115/B7
Cains (riv.), New Bruns. 170/D2
Cains Store, Ky. (42520) 237/M6
Cainsville, Mo. (64632) 261/E2
Cainsville, Tenn. (†37085) 237/J9
Caird Coast (reg.) 5/B17
Cairnbaan, Scotland 15/C4
Cairnbrook, Pa. (15924) 294/E5
Cairndow, Scotland 15/D4
Cairn Gorm (mt.), Scotland 15/E3
Cairngorm (mts.), Scotland 15/E3
Cairnryan, Scotland 15/D6
Cairns, Australia 87/E7
Cairns, Queensland 95/C3
Cairns, Queensland 88/H3
Cairnsmore (mt.), Scotland 15/D5
Cairn Toul (mt.), Scotland 15/E3
Cairo (cap.), Egypt 102/F2
Cairo (cap.), Egypt 111/J3
Cairo (cap.), Egypt 2/L4
Cairo, Egypt 59/B4
Cairo, Georgia (31728) 217/D9
Cairo, Ill. 188/J3
Cairo, Ill. (62914) 222/D6
Cairo, Kansas (†67035) 232/D4
Cairo, Mo. (65239) 261/H4
Cairo, Nebr. (68824) 264/F3
Cairo, N.Y. (12413) 276/M6
Cairo, Ohio (45820) 284/B4
Cairo, Okla. (†74538) 288/O5
Cairo, W. Va. (26337) 312/D4
Caissie (pt.), New Bruns. 170/F2
Caister-on-Sea, England 13/J5
Caistor, England 13/G4
Caithness (trad. co.), Scotland 15/B4
Caiundo, Angola 102/D6
Caiundo, Angola 115/C7
Caiza, Bolivia 136/C7
Cajabamba, Ecuador 128/C3
Cajabamba, Peru 128/C6
Cajacay, Peru 128/D8
Caja de Muertos (isl.), P. Rico 161/C3
Cajamarca (dept.), Peru 128/C6
Cajamarca, Peru 128/C6
Cajamarca, Peru 120/B3
Cajatambo, Peru 128/D8
Cajazeiras, Brazil 132/G4
Cajidiocan, Philippines 82/D4
Cajuata, Bolivia 136/B5
Cajuru, Brazil 135/C2
Čakovec, Yugoslavia 45/C2
Çal, Turkey 63/C3
Çala, Turkey 63/K2
Calabar, Nigeria 102/D4
Calabar, Nigeria 106/F7
Calabash, N.C. (†29566) 281/M7
Calabazar de Sagua, Cuba 158/E1
Calabogie, Ontario 177/H2
Calabozo, Venezuela 124/E3
Calabria (reg.), Italy 34/F5
Cala Burras (pt.), Spain 33/D4
Calaceite, Spain 33/G2
Calacoto, Bolivia 136/A5
Caladesi (isl.), Fla. 212/B2
Calafat, Romania 45/F3
Calafate, Argentina 143/B7
Calafquén (lake), Chile 138/E3
Calagnaan (isl.), Philippines 82/D5
Calagua (isls.), Philippines 82/D3
Calahoo, Alberta 182/D3
Calahorra, Spain 33/E1
Calais, Alberta 182/B2
Calais, France 28/D2
Calais, France 7/E3
Calais (Dover) (str.), France 28/D2
Calais, Maine 188/N1
Calais, Maine (04619) 243/J5
Calais○, Vt. (05648) 268/B3
Calama, Brazil 132/H10
Calama, Chile 120/C5
Calama, Chile 138/B3
Calamar, Bolívar, Colombia 126/C2
Calamar, Vaupés, Colombia 126/D7
Calamarca, Bolivia 136/A5
Calamba, Laguna, Philippines 82/C3
Calamba, Misamis Occ., Philippines 82/D6
Calamian Group (isls.), Philippines 85/F3
Calamian Group (isls.), Philippines 82/B4
Calamine, Ark. (72418) 202/H1
Calamocha, Spain 33/F2
Calamus, Iowa (52729) 229/M5
Calanasan, Philippines 82/C1
Calancasca (riv.), Switzerland 39/H4
Calanda, Spain 33/F2
Calang, Indonesia 85/B5
Calansho, Serir (des.), Libya 111/D2
Calansho Sand Sea (des.), Libya 111/D2
Calapan, Philippines 82/C4
Calapan, Philippines 85/G3
Calapooia (riv.), Oreg. 291/E3
Calapooya (mts.), Oreg. 291/E4
Călărași, Romania 45/H3
Calarcá, Colombia 126/C5
Calasparra, Spain 33/F3
Calatayud, Spain 33/F2
Calatorao, Spain 33/F2
Calauag, Philippines 82/D4
Calaveras (co.), Calif. 204/E5
Calaveras (res.), Calif. 204/L3
Calaveras (lake), Texas 303/K11
Calavite (cape), Philippines 82/C4
Calayan, Philippines 82/A2
Calayan (isl.), Philippines 82/A2
Calbayog, Philippines 82/E4
Calbe, E. Germany 22/D3
Calbuco, Chile 138/D4
Calca, Peru 128/G9
Calcasieu (par.), La. 238/D6
Calcasieu, La. (71433) 238/E4
Calcasieu (lake), La. 238/D7
Calcasieu (passage), La. 238/D7
Calcasieu (riv.), La. 238/E5
Calceta, Ecuador 128/C3
Calchaquí, Argentina 143/F5
Calcis, Ala. (†35178) 195/F4
Calcutta, India 68/F2
Calcutta, India 54/K7
Calcutta, India 2/P4
Calcutta, Ohio (43920) 284/J4
Calcutta, Suriname 131/C3
Caldas (dept.), Colombia 126/C5
Caldas da Rainha, Portugal 33/B3
Caldas Novas, Brazil 132/D7
Calder, Idaho (83808) 220/B2
Calder, Sask. 181/K4
Calder, Loch (lake), Scotland 15/E2
Caldera, Chile 120/B5
Caldera, Chile 138/A6
Calderas (bay), Dom. Rep. 158/D6
Calderas, Venezuela 124/C3
Calderwood, Tenn. (†37801) 237/N9
Caldicot, Wales 13/E6
Çaldıran, Turkey 63/K3
Caldwell, Ark. (72322) 202/J3
Caldwell, Idaho (83605) 220/B6
Caldwell, Idaho 188/C2
Caldwell, Kansas (67022) 232/E4
Caldwell (co.), Ky. 237/F6
Caldwell (par.), La. 238/F2
Caldwell (co.), Mo. 261/E3
Caldwell, N.J. (07006) 273/B2
Caldwell (co.), N.C. 281/F3
Caldwell, Ohio (43724) 284/G6
Caldwell (co.), Texas 303/G8
Caldwell, Texas (77836) 303/H7
Caldwell, W. Va. (24925) 312/F7
Caldwell, Wis. (†53149) 317/J2
Caldy (isl.), Wales 13/C6
Cale, Ark. (71828) 202/D6
Cale, Ind. (†47544) 227/D7
Caledon, N. Ireland 17/H3
Caledon, Ontario 177/E4
Caledon, S. Africa 118/G7
Caledonia, Ill. (61011) 222/E1
Caledonia, Mich. (49316) 250/D6
Caledonia, Minn. (55921) 255/G7
Caledonia, Miss. (39740) 256/H3
Caledonia, Mo. (63631) 261/L7
Caledonia, N.Y. (14423) 276/E5
Caledonia, N. Dak. (58219) 282/S5
Caledonia, Guysborough, Nova Scotia 168/F3
Caledonia, Queens, Nova Scotia 168/C4
Caledonia, Ohio (43314) 284/D4
Caledonia, Pa. (†15868) 294/F3
Caledonia (co.), Vt. 268/C2
Caledonia, Wis. (53108) 317/L2
Caledonian (canal), Scotland 15/D3
Calella, Spain 33/H2
Calenzana, France 28/B6
Calera, Ala. (35040) 195/E4
Calera, Okla. (74730) 288/O7
Calera de Tango, Chile 138/G4
Caleta Barquito, Chile 138/A6
Caleta Clarencia, Chile 138/E10
Caleta Olivia, Argentina 143/C6
Caleta Olivia, Argentina 120/C7
Caleta Pan de Azúcar, Chile 138/A5
Caleu, Chile 138/G2
Caleufú, Argentina 143/C4
Calexico, Calif. (92231) 204/K11
Calf of Man (isl.), I. of Man 13/C3
Calfsound, Scotland 15/F1
Calgary, Alberta 182/C4
Calgary, Alta. 162/E5
Calgary (cap.), Alta.. 146/G4
Calgary, Canada 2/D3
Calhan, Colo. (80808) 208/L4
Calheta, Portugal 33/A2
Calhoun (co.), Ala. 195/G3
Calhoun, Ala. (†36047) 195/F6
Calhoun (co.), Ark. 202/E6
Calhoun (co.), Fla. 212/D6
Calhoun (co.), Georgia 217/C7
Calhoun, Georgia (30701) 217/C1
Calhoun (co.), Ill. 222/C4
Calhoun, Ill. (62419) 222/E5
Calhoun (co.), Iowa 229/D4
Calhoun, Ky. (42327) 237/G5
Calhoun, La. (71225) 238/F2
Calhoun (co.), Mich. 250/D6
Calhoun (co.), Miss. 256/F3
Calhoun, Mo. (65323) 261/E6
Calhoun (co.), S.C. 296/F4
Calhoun, Tenn. (37309) 237/M10
Calhoun (co.), Texas 303/H9
Calhoun (co.), W. Va. 312/D5
Calhoun City, Miss. (38916) 256/F3
Calhoun Falls, S.C. (29628) 296/B3
Cali, Colombia 126/B6
Cali, Colombia 120/B2
Calicito, Cuba 158/H4
Calicoan (isl.), Philippines 82/E5
Calico Rock, Ark. (72519) 202/F1
Calicut (Kozhikode), India 68/D6
Caliente, Nev. (89008) 266/G5
Califon, N.J. (07830) 273/D2
California 188/B3
CALIFORNIA 204
California, Ky. (41007) 237/N3
California, Md. (20619) 245/M7
California (gulf), Mexico 146/G7
California (gulf), Mexico 150/D3
California, Mo. (65018) 261/H5
California, Pa. (15419) 294/C5
California, Trin. & Tob. 161/A11
California (state), U.S. 146/G6
California Aqueduct, Calif. 204/E7
California City, Calif. (93505) 204/H8
California Hot Springs, Calif. (93207) 204/G8
California Junction, Iowa (†51555) 229/B5
Calimete, Cuba 158/D1
Calio, N. Dak. (58322) 282/N2
Calion, Ark. (71724) 202/E7
Calipatria, Calif. (92233) 204/K10
Calistoga, Calif. (94515) 204/C5
Calixa-Lavallée, Québec 172/J4
Calkiní, Mexico 150/O6
Çalköy, Turkey 63/C3
Call, Texas (75933) 303/L7
Callabonna (lake), S. Australia 88/G5
Callabonna (lake), S. Australia 94/F3
Callafo, Ethiopia 111/H6
Callahan, Calif. (96014) 204/C2
Callahan, Fla. (32011) 212/E1
Callahan (co.), Texas 303/E5
Callalli, Peru 128/G10
Callan, Ireland 17/G7
Callan, Ireland 10/C4
Callander, Ont. 162/H6
Callander, Ontario 177/E1
Callander, Scotland 10/D2
Callander, Scotland 15/D4
Callands, Va. (24530) 307/J7
Callantsoog, Netherlands 27/F3
Callao, Mo. (63534) 261/G3
Callao (prov.), Peru 128/D9
Callao, Peru 128/D9
Callao, Peru 2/F6
Callao, Peru 120/B4
Callao, Utah (†84034) 304/A4
Callao, Va. (22435) 307/P5
Callapa, Bolivia 136/A5
Callaway, Minn. (56521) 255/C3
Callaway (co.), Mo. 261/J5
Callaway, Nebr. (68825) 264/D3
Callaway, Va. (24067) 307/H7
Calle Larga, Chile 138/G2
Callender, Iowa (50523) 229/E4
Callensburg, Pa. (16213) 294/D3
Calleuque, Chile 138/F5
Calliaqua, St. Vin. & Grens. 161/A9
Callicoon, N.Y. (12723) 276/K7
Callicoon Center, N.Y. (12724) 276/L7
Calliham, Texas (78007) 303/F9
Callimont, Pa. (†15552) 294/E6
Calling (lake), Alberta 182/D2
Callis, Somalia 115/J2
Callison, S.C. (29819) 296/C3
Callosa de Ensarriá, Spain 33/G3
Calloway, Fla. (32401) 212/D6
Calloway (co.), Ky. 237/E7
Calmar, Alberta 182/D3
Calmar, Iowa (52132) 229/K2
Calmer, Ark. (†71665) 202/F6
Calnali, Mexico 150/K6
Calne, England 13/F6
Calobre, Panama 154/G6
Caloosahatchee (riv.), Fla. 212/E5
Caloundra, Queensland 88/J5
Caloundra, Queensland 95/E5
Čalovo, Czech. 41/D3
Calpella, Calif. (95418) 204/B4
Calpet, Wyo. (†83123) 319/B3
Calpulálpan, Mexico 150/M1
Calstock, England 13/C7
Caltagirone, Italy 34/E6

Carseland 347

Cap (isl.), Philippines 82/C8
Cap (pt.), St. Lucia 161/G5
Capa, S. Dak. (57525) 298/H5
Capac, Mich. (48014) 250/G5
Capachica, Peru 128/H10
Çapakçur, Turkey 59/D2
Çapakçur, Turkey 63/J3
Cap-à-l'Aigle, Québec 172/G2
Capalonga, Philippines 82/D3
Capanaparo (riv.), Venezuela 124/E4
Capanema, Brazil 132/E3
Capannori, Italy 34/C3
Capão Bonito, Brazil 132/D9
Capão Bonito, Brazil 135/B4
Caparica, Portugal 33/A1
Caparo (riv.), Venezuela 124/C4
Capasin, Sask. 181/D2
Capatárida, Venezuela 124/C2
Capay, Calif. (95607) 204/C5
Cap-Bateau, New Bruns. 170/F1
Cap-Chat, Que. 162/K6
Cap-Chat, Québec 172/B1
Cap-Chat, Québec 174/D3
Cap-de-la-Madeleine, Québec 172/E3
Cap-des-Rosiers, Québec 172/D1
Cap d'Or (cape), Nova Scotia 168/D3
Cape (pen.), S. Africa 118/E7
Cape (pt.), S. Africa 118/F7
Cape (isl.), S.C. 296/J5
Cape Barren (isl.), Tasmania 88/H8
Cape Barren (isl.), Tasmania 99/E2
Cape Breton (isl.), N.S. 146/N5
Cape Breton (isl.), N.S. 162/K6
Cape Breton (co.), Nova Scotia 168/H3
Cape Breton (isl.), Nova Scotia 168/J2
Cape Breton Highlands Nat'l Park, Nova Scotia 168/H2
Cape Broyle, Newf. 166/D2
Cape Canaveral, Fla. (32920) 212/F3
Cape Carteret, N.C. (†28584) 281/P5
Cape Charles, Newf. 166/C3
Cape Charles, Va. (23310) 307/R6
Cape Coast, Ghana 106/D7
Cape Coast, Ghana 102/B4
Cape Cod (bay), Mass. 249/N5
Cape Cod (canal), Mass. 249/N5
Cape Cod Nat'l Seashore, Mass. 249/P5
Cape Coral, Fla. (33904) 212/E5
Cape Dorset, N.W.T. 162/J3
Cape Dorset, N.W. Terrs. 187/L3
Cape Dyer, N.W. Terrs. 187/M3
Cape Fanshaw, Alaska (†99833) 196/N1
Cape Fear (riv.), N.C. 188/L4
Cape Fear (riv.), N.C. 281/M5
Cape George, Nova Scotia 168/F3
Cape Girardeau (co.), Mo. 261/N8
Cape Girardeau, Mo. (63701) 261/08
Cape Girardeau, Mo. 188/H3
Cape Hatteras Nat'l Seashore, N.C. 281/T4
Cape Horn (mt.), Idaho 220/C5
Cape Krusenstern Nat'l Mon., Alaska 196/F1
Capel, W. Australia 92/A2
Capela, Brazil 132/G5
Cape Lisburne, Alaska (†99766) 196/E1
Capella, Queensland 95/D4
Capella (isls.), Virgin Is. (U.S.) 161/B5
Capelle, Netherlands 27/F5
Capelongo, Angola 115/C6
Cape Lookout Nat'l Seashore, N.C. 281/S5
Cape May (co.), N.J. 273/D5
Cape May, N.J. (08204) 273/D6
Cape May Coastguard Ctr., N.J. 273/D6
Cape May Court House, N.J. (08210) 273/D5
Cape May Point, N.J. (08212) 273/D6
Capenda-Camulemba, Angola 115/C5
Capenda-Camulemba, Angola 102/D5
Cape Neddick, Maine (03902) 243/B9
Cape Negro (isl.), Nova Scotia 168/C5
Cape North, Nova Scotia 168/H2
Cape of Good Hope (prov.), S. Africa 102/E8
Cape of Good Hope (prov.), S. Africa 118/C6
Cape Pole, Alaska (†99901) 196/M2
Cape Porpoise, Maine (04014) 243/C9
Cape Ray, Newf. 166/C4
Capers (isl.), S.C. 296/H6
Cape Sable (isl.), Nova Scotia 168/C5
Cape Saint Claire, Md. (21401) 245/N4
Cape Smith, N.W. Terrs. 187/L3
Capesterre, Basse-Terre, Guadeloupe 161/A7
Capesterre, Marie-Galante, Guadeloupe 161/B7
Cape Tormentine, New Bruns. 170/G2
Cape Town (cap.), S. Africa 2/L7
Cape Town (cap.), S. Africa 102/D8
Cape Town (cap.), S. Africa 118/E6
Cape Verde 2/H5
CAPE VERDE 106/A8
Capeville, Va. (23313) 307/R6
Cape Vincent, N.Y. (13618) 276/H2
Cape Yakataga, Alaska (99560) 196/K2
Cape York (pen.), Australia 87/E7
Cape York, Queensland 95/B1
Cape York (pen.), Queensland 88/G2
Cape York (pen.), Queensland 95/B2
Cap-Haïtien, Haiti 158/C5
Cap-Haïtien, Haiti 156/D3
Capiatá, Paraguay 144/B4
Capibara, Venezuela 124/E6
Capilla de Farruco, Uruguay 145/D3
Capim (riv.), Brazil 132/D3
Capinota, Bolivia 136/B5
Capira, Panama 154/G6
Capirenda, Bolivia 136/D7
Capistrano Beach, Calif. (92624) 204/H10
Capitan, N. Mex. (88316) 274/D5
Capitan (mts.), N. Mex. 274/D5
Capitan (peak), N. Mex. 274/D5
Capitán Aracena (isl.), Chile 138/E10
Capitán Bado, Paraguay 144/E3
Capitan Grande Ind. Res., Calif. 204/J11
Capitán Meza, Paraguay 144/E5
Capitán Pastene, Chile 138/D2
Capitán Ustarés, Cerro (mt.), Bolivia 136/E6
Capitol, Mont. (59319) 262/M5
Capitola, Calif. (95010) 204/K4
Capitola, Fla. (†32302) 212/B1
Capitol Heights, Md. (20743) 245/G5
Capitol Hill (cap.), No. Marianas 87/E4
Capitol Reef Nat'l Park, Utah 304/C5
Capiz (prov.), Philippines 82/D5
Caplan, Québec 172/C2
Capleville, Tenn. (†38101) 237/B10
Caplin Cove, Newf. 166/D2
Caplinger Mills, Mo. (65607) 261/E7
Čapljina, Yugoslavia 45/C4
Cap Lumière, New Bruns. 170/F2
Capon Bridge, W. Va. (26711) 312/K4
Capon Springs, W. Va. (26823) 312/K4
Capotoan (mt.), Philippines 82/E4
Cappahayden, Newf. 166/D2
Cappamore, Ireland 17/E6
Cappawhite, Ireland 17/E6
Cap-Pelé, New Bruns. 170/F2
Cappoquin, Ireland 17/F7
Capps, Ala. (†36353) 195/H8
Capraia (isl.), Italy 34/B3
Capreol, Ontario 175/D3
Capreol, Ontario 177/K5
Capri (isl.), Italy 34/E4
Capricorn (chan.), Queensland 95/D4
Capricorn Group (isls.), Queensland 88/J4
Capricorn Group (isls.), Queensland 95/E4
Caprivi Strip (reg.), Namibia 102/E6
Caprivi Strip (reg.), Namibia 118/C3
Caprock, N. Mex. (88213) 274/F5
Capron, Ill. (61012) 222/E1
Capron, Okla. (73725) 288/J1
Capron, Va. (23829) 307/07
Cap-Rouge, Québec 172/H3
Cap-Saint-Ignace, Québec 172/G2
Cap-Santé, Québec 172/F3
Cap-Seize, Québec 172/C1
Capshaw, Ala. (35742) 195/E1
Capstan (cape), Nova Scotia 168/D3
Capstick, Nova Scotia 168/H1
Captain Bermúdez, Argentina 143/F6
Captain Cook, Hawaii (96704) 218/G5
Captains Flat, N.S. Wales 97/E4
Captieux, France 28/C5
Captina (creek), Ohio 284/J6
Captiva, Fla. (33924) 212/D5
Captiva (isl.), Fla. 212/D5
Capua, Italy 34/E4
Capuchin (cape), Dominica 161/E5
Capulhuac de Mirafuentes, Mexico 150/K1
Capulin, Colo. (81124) 208/G8
Capulin, N. Mex. (88414) 274/F2
Capulin Mountain Nat'l Mon., N. Mex. 274/E2
Caputa, S. Dak. (57725) 298/D5
Caquetá (inten.), Colombia 126/C7
Caquetá (riv.), Colombia 120/B2
Caquetá (riv.), Colombia 126/E8
Caquiaviri, Bolivia 136/A5
Carabao (isl.), Philippines 82/D4
Carabelas, Argentina 143/F6
Carabobo (state), Venezuela 124/D2
Carabobo, Bolívar, Venezuela 124/H4
Carabobo, Carabobo, Venezuela 124/D3
Carabuco, Bolivia 136/A4
Caracal, Romania 45/G3
Caracaraí, Brazil 120/C2
Caracas (bay), Neth. Ant. 161/G9
Caracas (cap.), Venezuela 120/C2
Caracas (cap.), Venezuela 124/E2
Caracas (cap.), Venzuela 2/F5
Carache, Venezuela 124/C3
Caracollo, Bolivia 136/B5
Caraga, Philippines 82/F7
Caragabal, N.S. Wales 97/D3
Caraguatá, Uruguay 145/D3
Caraguatá (riv.), Uruguay 145/D3
Caraguatatuba, Brazil 135/D3
Caraguatay, Paraguay 144/B4
Carahue, Chile 138/D2
Carajás, Serra dos (range), Brazil 132/D4
Caramat, Ontario 177/H5
Caramat, Ontario 175/C3
Caramoan, Philippines 82/D4
Caranavi, Bolivia 136/B4
Carandaí, Brazil 135/E2
Carandaiti, Bolivia 136/D7
Carandotta, Queensland 95/A4
Carangola, Brazil 135/E2
Caransebeş, Romania 45/F3
Carapá (riv.), Paraguay 144/E4
Carapa, Venezuela 124/G3
Caraparaná (riv.), Colombia 126/D8
Caraparí, Bolivia 136/D7
Carapeguá, Paraguay 144/B5
Carapichaima, Trin. & Tob. 161/B10
Caraquet, New Bruns. 170/E1
Caraquet (isl.), New Bruns. 170/F1
Carás, Peru 128/D7
Caratasca, Honduras 154/F3
Caratasca (cays), Honduras 154/F2
Caratasca (lag.), Honduras 154/F3
Caratinga, Brazil 132/F7
Caratinga, Brazil 135/E1
Caratunk, Maine (04925) 243/C5
Caratunk○, Maine (04925) 243/C5
Carauari, Brazil 120/C3
Carauari, Brazil 132/G9
Caraúbas, Brazil 132/G4
Caravaca de la Cruz, Spain 33/E3
Caravaggio, Italy 34/B2
Caravelas, Brazil 132/G7
Caravelí, Peru 128/F10
Caravelle (pen.), Martinique 161/D6
Caraway, Ark. (72419) 202/K2
Carayaó, Paraguay 144/C4
Carazinho, Brazil 132/C10
Carballino, Spain 33/B1
Carballo, Spain 33/B1
Carberry, Manitoba 179/C5
Carbo, Mexico 150/D2
Carbon, Alberta 182/D4
Carbon (peak), Colo. 208/E5
Carbon, Ind. (47837) 227/C5
Carbon, Iowa (50839) 229/D6
Carbon (co.), Mont. 262/G5
Carbon (co.), Pa. 294/L4
Carbon, Texas (76435) 303/F5
Carbon (co.), Utah 304/D4
Carbon, W. Va. (25037) 312/D6
Carbon (co.), Wyo. 319/F4
Carbonado, Wash. (98323) 310/D3
Carbonara (cape), Italy 34/B5
Carbon Cliff, Ill. (61239) 222/C2
Carbondale, Alberta 182/D3
Carbondale, Colo. (81623) 208/E4
Carbondale, Ill. (62901) 222/D6
Carbondale, Kansas (66414) 232/G3
Carbondale, Ohio (45717) 284/F7
Carbondale, Pa. (18407) 294/L2
Carbonear, Newf. 166/D2
Carbon Hill, Ala. (35549) 195/D3
Carbon Hill, Ill. (†60416) 222/E2
Carbon Hill, Ohio (43111) 284/F7
Carbonia, Italy 34/B5
Carbonton, N.C. (†27330) 281/L3
Carbost, Scotland 15/B3
Carbury, Ireland 17/H5
Carbury, N. Dak. (58724) 282/J2
Carcagente, Spain 33/F3
Carcans (lake), France 28/C5
Carcarañá, Argentina 143/F6
Carcarañá (riv.), Argentina 143/F6
Carcassonne, France 28/D6
Carchi (prov.), Ecuador 128/C2
Carcoar, N.S. Wales 97/E3
Carcross, Yukon 187/E3
Çardak, Turkey 63/C6
Cardal, Uruguay 145/C5
Cardale, Manitoba 179/B4
Cárdenas, Cuba 158/D1
Cárdenas, Cuba 156/B2
Cárdenas (bay), Cuba 158/D1
Cárdenas, San Luis Potosí, Mexico 150/K6
Cárdenas, Tabasco, Mexico 150/N8
Cardenden, Scotland 15/D1
Cardiel (lake), Argentina 143/B6
Cardiff, Ala. (35041) 195/E3
Cardiff, Md. (21024) 245/N2
Cardiff, Wales 7/D3
Cardiff, Wales 13/B7
Cardiff, Wales 10/E5
Cardiff-by-the-Sea, Calif. (92007) 204/H10
Cardigan (mt.), N.H. 268/D4
Cardigan, Pr. Edward I. 168/F2
Cardigan (bay), Pr. Edward I. 168/F2
Cardigan, Wales 13/C5
Cardigan, Wales 10/D4
Cardigan (bay), Wales 10/D4
Cardigan (bay), Wales 13/C5
Cardin, Okla. (74335) 288/S1
Cardinal (lake), Alberta 182/B1
Cardinal, Manitoba 179/D5
Cardinal, Ontario 177/J3
Cardington, Ohio (43315) 284/E5
Cardona, Uruguay 145/B4
Cardoso (isl.), Brazil 135/C4
Cardozo, Uruguay 145/C3
Cardross, Sask. 181/F6
Cardston, Alberta 182/D5
Cardston, Alta. 162/E6
Cardville, Maine (04418) 243/F5
Cardwell, Mo. (63829) 261/M10
Cardwell, Mont. (59721) 262/E5
Cardwell, Queensland 95/C3
Cardwell, Va. (†23039) 307/N5
Carefree, Ariz. (85331) 198/C5
Carefree, Ind. (†47137) 227/E8
Carei, Romania 45/F2
Carén, Chile 138/A8
Carencro, La. (70520) 238/G6
Carentan, France 28/C3
Caretta, W. Va. (24821) 312/C8
Carey, Idaho (83320) 220/E6
Carey, Ohio (43316) 284/D4
Carey (lake), W. Australia 88/C5
Carey (lake), W. Australia 92/C5
Careywood, Idaho (83809) 220/B1
Cargill, Ontario 177/C3
Carhuás, Peru 128/D7
Cariaco, Venezuela 124/G2
Cariamanga, Ecuador 128/C5
Caribbean (sea) 2/F5
Caribbean (sea) 146/K8
Caribbean (sea) 156/B4
Caribbean (sea), Ant. & Bar. 156/B4
Caribbean (sea), Cayman Is. 156/B4
Caribbean (sea), Cuba 156/B4
Caribbean (sea), Dominica 156/B4
Caribbean (sea), Dom. Rep. 156/B4
Caribbean (sea), Grenada 156/B4
Caribbean (sea), Guadeloupe 156/B4
Caribbean (sea), Haiti 156/B4
Caribbean (sea), Jamaica 156/B4
Caribbean (sea), Martinique 156/B4
Caribbean (sea), Neth. Ant. 156/B4
Caribbean (sea), P. Rico 156/B4
Caribbean (sea), St. Chris.-Nevis 156/B4
Caribbean (sea), St. Lucia 156/B4
Caribbean (sea), St. Vin. & Grens. 156/B4
Caribbean (sea), Virgin Is. (Br.) 156/B4
Caribbean (sea), Virgin Is. (U.S.) 156/B4
Caribén, Venezuela 124/E4
Cariboo (mts.), Br. Col. 184/G3
Caribou (mts.), Alberta 182/B5
Caribou (co.), Idaho 220/G7
Caribou (mt.), Idaho 220/G6
Caribou (range), Idaho 220/G6
Caribou, Maine 188/N1
Caribou, Maine (04736) 243/G2
Caribou (riv.), Manitoba 179/J1
Caribou, Nova Scotia 168/F3
Caribou (isl.), Nova Scotia 168/F3
Caribou (isl.), Ontario 175/C3
Caribou (lake), Ontario 177/H4
Caribou (lake), Québec 172/D3
Caribou River, Nova Scotia 168/F3
Carib Reserve, Dominica 161/F6
Caribrod (Dimitrovgrad), Yugoslavia 45/F4
Carichic, Mexico 150/F2
Carievale, Sask. 181/K6
Carigara, Philippines 82/E5
Carignan, Québec 172/J4
Carignan (lake), Québec 172/E2
Carillon, Québec 172/C4
Carina, Queensland 88/K3
Carinda, N.S. Wales 97/D2
Cariñena, Spain 33/F2
Carinhanha, Brazil 132/E6
Carini, Italy 34/D5
Carinthia (prov.), Austria 41/B3
Caripe, Venezuela 124/G2
Caripito, Venezuela 124/G2
Cariquima, Chile 138/B2
Carirubana, Venezuela 124/C2
Carite (lake), P. Rico 161/E2
Cark (mt.), Ireland 17/F2
Carl, Georgia (30203) 217/E3
Carl Blackwell (lake), Okla. 288/M2
Carlea, Sask. 181/H2
Carleton, Mich. (48117) 250/F6
Carleton, Nebr. (68326) 264/G4
Carleton (co.), New Bruns. 170/C2
Carleton (mt.), New Bruns. 170/D1
Carleton, Nova Scotia 168/C4
Carleton (riv.), Nova Scotia 168/C4
Carleton, Québec 172/C2
Carleton Place, Ontario 177/H2
Carlile, Wyo. (82713) 319/H1
Carlin, Nev. (89822) 266/E2
Carlingford, Ireland 17/J3
Carlingford (inlet), Ireland 17/J3
Carlingford (mt.), Ireland 17/J3
Carlingford, New Bruns. 170/C2
Carlinville, Ill. (62626) 222/D4
Carlisle, Ark. (72024) 202/G4
Carlisle (bay), Barbados 161/B9
Carlisle, England 13/D3
Carlisle, England 10/E3
Carlisle, Ind. (47838) 227/C7
Carlisle, Iowa (50047) 229/G6
Carlisle (co.), Ky. 237/C7
Carlisle, Ky. (40311) 237/N4
Carlisle, La. (70042) 238/L7
Carlisle○, Mass. (01741) 249/J2
Carlisle, Minn. (56538) 255/B4
Carlisle, Miss. (39049) 256/C7
Carlisle, New Bruns. 170/C2
Carlisle, N.Y. (12031) 276/L5
Carlisle, Ohio (45005) 284/B6
Carlisle, Ontario 177/D4
Carlisle, Pa. (17013) 294/H5
Carlisle, S.C. (29031) 296/D2
Carl Junction, Mo. (64834) 261/C8
Carlock, Ill. (61725) 222/D3
Carlock, S. Dak. (†57533) 298/L7
Carloforte, Italy 34/B5
Carlos, Ind. (†47355) 227/G4
Carlos, Minn. (56319) 255/C5
Carlos Casares, Argentina 143/F7
Carlos Reyles, Uruguay 145/C4
Carlos Tejedor, Argentina 143/D4
Carlow (co.), Ireland 17/H6
Carlow, Ireland 17/H6
Carlow, Ireland 10/C4
Carloway, Scotland 15/B2
Carlowrie, Manitoba 179/E5
Carlowville, Ala. (†36761) 195/D6
Carl Sandburg Home Nat'l Hist. Site, N.C. 281/D4
Carlsbad, (92008) 204/H10
Carlsbad, N. Mex. 188/F4
Carlsbad, N. Mexico 146/H6
Carlsbad, N. Mex. (88220) 274/E6
Carlsbad, Texas (76934) 303/D6
Carlsbad Caverns Nat'l Park, N. Mex. 274/E6
Carlsbad Springs, Ontario 177/J2
Carlsborg, Wash. (98324) 310/B2
Carlshend, Mich. (49811) 250/B2
Carlstadt, N.J. (07072) 273/B2
Carlton, Ala. (36515) 195/C8
Carlton, Barbados 161/B8
Carlton, England 13/F5
Carlton, Georgia (30627) 217/F2
Carlton, Kansas (67429) 232/E3
Carlton (co.), Minn. 255/F4
Carlton, Minn. (55718) 255/F4
Carlton, N.Y. (†14411) 276/D4
Carlton, Oreg. (97111) 291/D2
Carlton, Pa. (16311) 294/C3
Carlton, Sask. 181/E3
Carlton, Texas (76436) 303/F6
Carlton, Wash. (98814) 310/F2
Carlton (pass), Wash. 310/D4
Carltonville, S. Africa 118/G7
Carluke, Scotland 15/E5
Carluke, Scotland 10/B1
Carlyle, Ill. (62231) 222/D5
Carlyle (lake), Ill. 222/D5
Carlyle, Kansas (66718) 232/G4
Carlyle, Mont. (59320) 262/M4
Carlyle, Sask. 181/J6
Carlyle Lake Resort, Sask. 181/J6
Carmacks, Yukon 187/E3
Carmagnola, Italy 34/A2
Carman, Ill. (61425) 222/B3
Carman, Man. 162/G6
Carman, Manitoba 179/D5
Carmangay, Alberta 182/D4
Carmanville, Newf. 166/D4
Carmarthen, Wales 13/C6
Carmarthen, Wales 10/D5
Carmarthen (bay), Wales 10/D5
Carmarthen (bay), Wales 13/C6
Carmaux, France 28/E5
Carmel, Calif. (93923) 204/D7
Carmel, Ind. (46032) 227/E5
Carmel (cape), Israel 65/B2
Carmel (mt.), Israel 65/C2
Carmel○, Maine (04419) 243/E6
Carmel○, N.Y. (10512) 276/N8
Carmel, Sask. 181/F3
Carmel (head), Wales 13/C4
Carmelo, Uruguay 145/A4
Carmelo, Venezuela 124/C2
Carmel Valley, Calif. (93924) 204/D7
Carmen, Ariz. (†85640) 198/D7
Carmen, Bolivia 136/B2
Carmen (riv.), Chile 138/B7
Carmen, C. Rica 154/F5
Carmen, Idaho (83462) 220/E4
Carmen (isl.), Mexico 150/D3
Carmen, Okla. (73726) 288/J1
Carmen, Bohol, Philippines 82/E6
Carmen, North Cotabato, Philippines 82/E7
Carmen, Uruguay 145/D4
Carmen de Areco, Argentina 143/F7
Carmen del Paraná, Paraguay 144/D5
Carmen de Patagones, Argentina 143/D5
Carmensa, Argentina 143/C4
Carmi, Br. Col. 184/H5
Carmi, Ill. (62821) 222/E5
Carmi (lake), Vt. 268/B2
Carmichael, Calif. (95608) 204/C8
Carmichael, Miss. (†39360) 256/G7
Carmichael, Sask. 181/C5
Carmichaels, Pa. (15320) 294/B6
Carmiel, Israel 65/C2
Carmila, Queensland 95/D4
Carmine, Texas (78932) 303/H7
Carmody Hills-Pepper Mill Village, Md. (†20028) 245/G5
Carmona, Spain 33/D4
Carnac, France 28/B4
Carnadero (creek), Calif. 204/L4
Carnamah, W. Australia 92/A5
Carnarvon, Australia 87/B8
Carnarvon, Iowa (51437) 229/C4
Carnarvon, Ontario 177/F2
Carnarvon (range), Queensland 95/D5
Carnarvon, S. Africa 118/C6
Carnarvon, W. Australia 88/A4
Carnarvon, W. Australia 92/A4
Carnation, Wash. (98014) 310/D3
Carnaxide, Portugal 33/A1
Carn Ban (mt.), Scotland 15/D3
Carndonagh, Ireland 17/G1
Carnduff, Sask. 181/K6
Carnegie, Georgia (†31740) 217/C7
Carnegie, Okla. (73015) 288/J4
Carnegie, Pa. (15106) 294/B7
Carnegie (lake), W. Australia 88/C5
Carnegie (lake), W. Australia 92/C4
Carn Eige (mt.), Scotland 15/C3
Carneiro, Kansas (†67425) 232/D3
Carnes, Miss. (†39455) 256/F8
Carnesville, Georgia (30521) 217/F2
Carnew, Ireland 17/H6
Carney, Mich. (49812) 250/B3
Carney, Okla. (74832) 288/N3
Carneys Point, N.J. (08069) 273/C4
Carnic Alps (mts.), Austria 41/B3
Carnic Alps (range), Italy 34/D1
Car Nicobar (isl.), India 68/G7
Carnlough, N. Ireland 17/K2
Carn More (mt.), Scotland 15/E3
Carnot, Cent. Afr. Rep. 115/C3
Carnoustie, Scotland 15/F4
Carnoustie, Scotland 10/E2
Carnsore (pt.), Ireland 10/C4
Carnsore (pt.), Ireland 17/J7
Carnwath (riv.), N.W. Terrs. 187/F3
Carnwath, Scotland 15/E5
Carnwood, Alberta 182/C3
Caro, Mich. (48723) 250/F5
Caroga Lake, N.Y. (12032) 276/L4
Carol City, Fla. (33055) 212/B4
Carolina, Ala. (†36420) 195/E8
Carolina, Brazil 132/E4
Carolina, P. Rico 161/E1
Carolina, R.I. (02812) 249/H7
Carolina Beach, N.C. (28428) 281/O6
Caroline, Alberta 182/C3
Caroline (isl.), Kiribati 87/M6
Caroline (co.), Md. 245/P5
Caroline, N.Y. (†14817) 276/H6
Caroline (isls.), Pac. Is. Terr. 87/E5
Caroline (isls.), Pacific Is. Terr. 2/S5
Caroline (co.), Va. 307/O4
Caroline, Wis. (54928) 317/J6
Carol Stream, Ill. (†60187) 222/A5
Caron, Sask. 181/F5
Caron Brook, New Bruns. 170/B1
Carondelet, Ecuador 128/C2
Caroni, Trin. & Tob. 161/B10
Caroní (riv.), Venezuela 120/C2
Caroní (riv.), Venezuela 124/G4
Carora, Venezuela 124/C2
Carouge, Switzerland 39/B4
Carp, Ind. (†47460) 227/D6
Carp, Minn. (†56623) 255/D2
Carp, Nev. (†89008) 266/G5
Carp, Ontario 177/H2
Carpathian (mts.) 7/G4
Carpathian (mts.), Romania 45/G2
Carpentaria (gulf) 88/F2
Carpentaria (gulf), Australia 87/D7
Carpentaria (gulf), North. Terr. 93/E3
Carpentaria (gulf), Queensland 95/A2
Carpenter (lake), Br. Col. 184/F5
Carpenter, Iowa (50426) 229/H2
Carpenter, Ky. (†40769) 237/O7
Carpenter, Miss. (39050) 256/C6
Carpenter (lake), N. Dak. 282/L2
Carpenter, Ohio (†47518) 284/F7
Carpenter, S. Dak. (57322) 298/O4
Carpenter, Wyo. (82054) 319/H4
Carpentersville, Ill. (60110) 222/E1
Carpentersville, N.J. (†08865) 273/C2
Carpenterville, Oreg. (†97415) 291/C5
Carpentras, France 28/F5
Carpertee (riv.), N.S. Wales 97/F3
Carpi, Italy 34/C2
Carpinteria, Calif. (93013) 204/F9
Carpio, N. Dak. (58725) 282/G3
Carp Lake, Mich. (49718) 250/E3
Carp Lake Prov. Park, Br. Col. 184/F3
Carr, Colo. (80612) 208/K1
Carra (lake), Ireland 17/C4
Carrabassett Valley○, Maine (†04947) 243/C5
Carrabelle, Fla. 212/B2
Carradale, Scotland 15/C5
Carragana, Sask. 181/J3
Carraguao (pt.), Cuba 158/B2
Carraipía, Colombia 126/D2
Carraizo (lake), P. Rico 161/E1
Carranglan, Philippines 82/C3
Carrantuohill (mt.), Ireland 10/B5
Carrantuohill (mt.), Ireland 17/B7
Carranza, Venustiano (res.), Mexico 150/J3
Carrao (riv.), Venezuela 124/G5
Carrara, Italy 34/C2
Carrasco, Uruguay 145/B7
Carrasquero, Venezuela 124/B2
Carrathool, N. S. Wales 88/G6
Carrathool, N.S. Wales 97/C4
Carrboro, N.C. (27510) 281/L3
Carrbridge, Scotland 15/E3
Carrera de Yeguas, Dom. Rep. 158/D6
Carrera Pinto, Chile 138/B6
Carreta (pt.), C. Rica 154/F6
Carreto, Panama 154/J6
Carriacou (isl.), Grenada 156/G4
Carrick, Manitoba 179/F5
Carrick (dist.), Scotland 15/D5
Carrickfergus (dist.), N. Ireland 17/K2
Carrickfergus, N. Ireland 10/D3
Carrickfergus, N. Ireland 17/K2
Carrickmacross, Ireland 10/C3
Carrickmacross, Ireland 17/H4
Carrick-on-Shannon, Ireland 17/F4
Carrick-on-Shannon, Ireland 10/C4
Carrick-on-Suir, Ireland 17/F7
Carrick-on-Suir, Ireland 10/C4
Carrier, Okla. (73727) 288/K2
Carriere, Miss. (39426) 256/E9
Carrier Mills, Ill. (62917) 222/E6
Carrigaholt, Ireland 17/B6
Carrigain (mt.), N.H. 268/E3
Carrigaline, Ireland 17/E8
Carrigallen, Ireland 17/F4
Carrigan (head), Ireland 17/D2
Carrigart, Ireland 17/F1
Carrigtwohill, Ireland 17/E8
Carrington, Mo. (†65251) 261/H5
Carrington, N. Dak. (58421) 282/M5
Carrión de los Condes, Spain 33/D1
Carrizal, Colombia 126/D1
Carrizal Bajo, Chile 138/A7
Carrizo (creek), Ariz. 198/E4
Carrizo (mts.), Ariz. 198/G2
Carrizo (creek), N. Mex. 274/F2
Carrizo (creek), Texas 303/A1
Carrizo Springs, Texas (78834) 303/E9
Carrizozo, N. Mex. (88301) 274/D5
Carroll (co.), Ark. 202/C1
Carroll (co.), Georgia 217/B3
Carroll (co.), Ill. 222/D1
Carroll (co.), Ind. 227/D3
Carroll (co.), Iowa 229/D4
Carroll, Iowa (51401) 229/D4
Carroll (co.), Ky. 237/L3
Carroll○, Maine (†04487) 243/G5
Carroll, Manitoba 179/B5
Carroll (lake), Manitoba 179/G3
Carroll (co.), Md. 245/K2
Carroll (co.), Miss. 256/E4
Carroll (co.), Mo. 261/F4
Carroll, Nebr. (68723) 264/G2
Carroll (co.), N.H. 268/E4
Carroll○, N.H. (†03595) 268/D3
Carroll, N.S. Wales 97/F2
Carroll (co.), Ohio 284/H4
Carroll, Ohio (43112) 284/E6
Carroll (co.), Tenn. 237/E9
Carroll (co.), Va. 307/G7
Carrolls, Wash. (98609) 310/C4
Carrolls Crossing, New Bruns. 170/D2
Carrollton, Ala. (35447) 195/B4
Carrollton, Georgia (30117) 217/C3
Carrollton, Ill. (62016) 222/C4
Carrollton, Iowa (†51440) 229/D5
Carrollton, Ky. (41008) 237/L3
Carrollton, Md. (†21157) 245/L2
Carrollton, Mich. (48724) 250/E5
Carrollton, Miss. (38917) 256/E4
Carrollton, Mo. (64633) 261/E4
Carrollton, Ohio (44615) 284/J4
Carrollton, Texas (*75006) 303/G2
Carrolltown, Pa. (15722) 294/E4
Carroll Valley, Pa. (†17320) 294/H6
Carron, Scotland 15/C1
Carron (riv.), Scotland 15/D3
Carron (riv.), Scotland 15/C3
Carron (riv.), Scotland 15/C1
Carron Valley (res.), Scotland 15/B1
Carrot (riv.), Sask. 181/J2
Carrot Creek, Alberta 182/B3
Carrothers, Ohio (44823) 284/D3
Carrot River, Sask. 181/H2
Carrowdore, N. Ireland 17/K2
Carrowkeel, Ireland 17/G1
Carrowmore (lake), Ireland 17/B3
Carrsville, Ky. (42030) 237/E6
Carrsville, Va. (23315) 307/P7
Carruthers, Sask. 181/B3
Carrville, Ala. (†36023) 195/G5
Carryduff, N. Ireland 17/K2
Carryville, Ark. (†72454) 202/K1
Çarşamba, Turkey 63/G2
Carseland, Alberta 182/D4

348 Carson

Carson, Ala. (†36548) 195/C8
Carson, Calif. (90745) 204/C11
Carson, Iowa (51525) 229/C6
Carson, Miss. (39427) 256/E7
Carson (lake), Nev. 266/C3
Carson (riv.), Nev. 266/B3
Carson (sink), Nev. 266/C3
Carson, N. Mex. (87517) 274/D2
Carson, N. Dak. (58529) 282/H7
Carson (co.), Texas 303/C2
Carson, Va. (23830) 307/O6
Carson, Wash. (98610) 310/D5
Carson City, Mich. (48811) 250/E5
Carson City (cap.), Nev. 146/G6
Carson City (cap.), Nev. 188/C3
Carson City (co.), Nev. 266/B3
Carson City (cap.), Nev. (89701) 266/B3
Carson Lake, Ark. (†72370) 202/K2
Carson Sink (depr.), Nev. 188/C3
Carsonville, Georgia (†31827) 217/D5
Carsonville, Mich. (48419) 250/G5
Carsphairn, Scotland 15/D5
Carstairs, Alberta 182/D4
Carswell A.F.B., Texas 303/E2
Cartagena, Chile 138/F3
Cartagena, Colombia 120/B1
Cartagena, Colombia 126/C2
Cartagena, Cuba 158/D2
Cartagena, Spain 7/D5
Cartagena, Spain 33/F4
Cartago, Calif. (93549) 204/G7
Cartago, Colombia 126/B5
Cartago, C. Rica 154/F6
Carta Valley, Texas (78835) 303/D8
Cartaxo, Portugal 33/B3
Cartecay, Georgia (†30540) 217/D1
Carter (co.), Ky. 237/P4
Carter, Ky. (41128) 237/P4
Carter (co.), Mo. 261/L9
Carter (co.), Mont. 262/M5
Carter, Mont. (59420) 262/E3
Carter (co.), Okla. 288/M6
Carter, Okla. (73627) 288/H4
Carter, S. Dak. (57526) 298/J7
Carter (co.), Tenn. 237/S8
Carter, Tenn. (†37643) 237/S8
Carter, Wis. (†54566) 317/J5
Carter, Wyo. (†82937) 319/B4
Carter Dome (mt.), N.H. 268/E3
Carteret, N.J. (07008) 273/E2
Carteret (co.), N.C. 281/R5
Carter Lake, Iowa (†68101) 229/B6
Carter Nine, Okla. (†74633) 288/N1
Carters, Georgia (30704) 217/C1
Carters (lake), Georgia 217/C1
Cartersburg, Ind. (46114) 227/E5
Cartersville, Georgia (30120) 217/C2
Cartersville, Iowa (†50469) 229/G2
Cartersville, Mont. (†59347) 262/K4
Cartersville, Okla. (74934) 288/S4
Cartersville, S.C. (†29161) 296/H3
Cartersville, Va. (23027) 307/M5
Carterton, N. Zealand 100/E4
Carterton and Black Bourton, England 13/F6
Carterville, Ill. (62918) 222/D6
Carterville, Mo. (64835) 261/D8
Carthage, Ark. (71725) 202/E5
Carthage, Ill. (62321) 222/B3
Carthage, Ind. (46115) 227/F5
Carthage, Maine (†04224) 243/C6
Carthage○, Maine (†04224) 243/C6
Carthage, Miss. (39051) 256/E5
Carthage, Mo. (64836) 261/D8
Carthage, N.Y. (13619) 276/J3
Carthage, N.C. (28327) 281/K4
Carthage, S. Dak. (57323) 298/O5
Carthage, Tenn. (37030) 237/K8
Carthage, Texas (75633) 303/K5
Cartier, Ontario 177/J5
Cartier (isl.), Terr. Ashmore and Cartier Is. 88/C2
Cartwright, Newf. 146/N4
Cartwright, Manitoba 179/C5
Cartwright, Newf. 166/C3
Cartwright, Newf. 162/L5
Cartwright, N. Dak. (58838) 282/C4
Caruai (riv.), Venezuela 124/H5
Caruaru, Brazil 132/G5
Carumás, Peru 128/G11
Carúpano, Venezuela 120/C1
Carúpano, Venezuela 124/G2
Carurú, Colombia 126/E7
Carutapera, Brazil 132/E3
Caruth, Mo. (†63857) 261/N10
Caruthers, Calif. (93609) 204/E7
Caruthersville, Mo. (63830) 261/N10
Carver○, Mass. (02330) 249/M5
Carver (co.), Minn. 255/E6
Carver, Minn. (55315) 255/E6
Carville, La. (70721) 238/K3
Carvoeiroeiro (cape), Portugal 33/B3
Cary, Ill. (60013) 222/E1
Cary○, Maine (†04465) 243/H4
Cary, Miss. (39054) 256/C5
Cary, N.C. (27511) 281/M3
Caryapundy (swamp), N.S. Wales 97/B1
Caryapundy (swamp), Queensland 95/B6
Carysbrook, Va. (23055) 307/M5
Carytown, Mo. (†64836) 261/D8
Caryville, Fla. (32427) 212/C6
Caryville, Mass. (02024) 249/J4
Caryville, Tenn. (37714) 237/N8
Casa, Ark. (72025) 202/D3
Casa Agapito, Colombia 126/D6
Casablanca, Chile 138/F3
Casablanca, Estero de (riv.), Chile 138/F3
Casablanca, Morocco 102/B1
Casablanca, Morocco 106/C2
Casablanca, Morocco 2/J4
Casa Blanca, N. Mex. (87007) 274/B4
Casa Branca, Brazil 135/C2
Casa Cruz (cape), Trin. & Tob. 161/B11
Casa Grande, Ariz. 188/D4
Casa Grande, Ariz. (85222) 198/D6
Casa Grande Nat'l Mon., Ariz. 198/D6
Casale Monferrato, Italy 34/B2
Casalmaggiore, Italy 34/C2
Casamance (riv.), Senegal 106/A6
Casanare (inten.), Colombia 126/B3
Casanare (riv.), Colombia 126/E4
Casanay, Venezuela 124/G2
Casa Nova, Brazil 132/F5
Casanova, Va. (22017) 307/N3
Casa Piedra, Texas (†79843) 303/C12
Casar, N.C. (28020) 281/F3
Casar de Cáceres, Spain 33/C3
Casas Grandes (riv.), Mexico 150/F1
Casas-Ibáñez, Spain 33/F3
Cascade (range) 188/B1
Cascade (range), Calif. 204/D1
Cascade, Colo. (80909) 208/K5
Cascade, Idaho (83611) 220/C5
Cascade (res.), Idaho 220/C5
Cascade, Iowa (52033) 229/L4
Cascade, Jamaica 158/G6
Cascade (co.), Mont. 262/E3
Cascade, Mont. (59421) 262/E3
Cascade, N.H. (†03581) 268/E3
Cascade (pt.), N. Zealand 100/B6
Cascade, Norfolk I. 88/L5
Cascade (bay), Norfolk I. 88/L5
Cascade (head), Oreg. 291/C2
Cascade (range), Oreg. 291/E4
Cascade, Seychelles 118/H5
Cascade (range), U.S. 146/F5
Cascade, Va. (24069) 307/J7
Cascade (pass), Wash. 310/D2
Cascade (range), Wash. 310/D4
Cascade (riv.), Wash. 310/D2
Cascade, W. Va. (26526) 312/G3
Cascade, Wis. (53011) 317/K8
Cascade Locks, Oreg. (97014) 291/E2
Cascade Summit, Oreg. (97425) 291/F4
Cascadia, Oreg. (97329) 291/E3
Cascais, Portugal 33/B3
Cascajal, Cuba 158/E1
Cascapédia (riv.), Québec 172/C1
Cascas, Peru 128/C6
Cascavel, Brazil 132/G4
Cascilla, Miss. (38920) 256/D3
Cascina-Navacchio, Italy 34/C3
Casco, Maine (04015) 243/B7
Casco○, Maine (04015) 243/B7
Casco (bay), Maine 243/C8
Casco, Wis. (54205) 317/L6
Cascorro, Cuba 158/H3
Cascumpeque (bay), Pr. Edward I. 168/E2
Caselton, Nev. (†89043) 266/G5
Case-Pilote, Martinique 161/C6
Caserta (prov.), Italy 34/E4
Caserta, Italy 34/E4
Caseville, Mich. (48725) 250/F5
Casey (key), Fla. 212/D4
Casey, Ill. (62420) 222/F4
Casey, Iowa (50048) 229/D5
Casey (co.), Ky. 237/M6
Casey, Québec 174/C3
Casey Creek, Ky. (42723) 237/L6
Caseyville, Ill. (62232) 222/B2
Caseyville, Ky. (†42459) 237/E5
Cash, Ark. (72421) 202/J2
Cashel, Ireland 17/F7
Cashel, Ireland 10/C4
Cashiers, N.C. (28717) 281/C4
Cashion, Ariz. (85329) 198/C5
Cashion, Okla. (73016) 288/L3
Cashmere, Wash. (98815) 310/E3
Cashmere, W. Va. (†24918) 312/E8
Cashton, Wis. (54619) 317/E8
Cashtown, Pa. (17310) 294/H6
Cashville, S.C. (†29388) 296/C2
Casigua, Falcón, Venezuela 124/C2
Casigua, Zulia, Venezuela 124/B3
Casiguran, Philippines 82/D2
Casiguran (sound), Philippines 82/C2
Casilda, Argentina 143/F6
Casilda, Cuba 158/E2
Casilda (pt.), Cuba 158/E2
Casino, N. S. Wales 88/J5
Casino, N.S. Wales 97/G1
Casiquiare, Brazo (riv.), Venezuela 124/E6
Casitas Springs, Calif. (†93001) 204/F9
Caslan, Alberta 182/D2
Čáslav, Czech. 41/C2
Casma, Peru 128/C7
Casma (riv.), Peru 128/C7
Casmalia, Calif. (93429) 204/E9
Casnovia, Mich. (49318) 250/D5
Caspar, Calif. (95420) 204/B4
Caspe, Spain 33/G2
Casper, Wyo. 188/E2
Casper, Wyo. 146/H5
Casper, Wyo. (82601) 319/F3
Casper (range), Wyo. 319/F3
Caspian (sea) 54/G5
Caspian (sea) 2/M3
Caspian (sea), Iran 66/G1
Caspian, Mich. (49915) 250/G2
Caspian (sea), U.S.S.R. 7/J4
Caspian (sea), U.S.S.R. 52/G6
Caspian (sea), U.S.S.R. 48/F6
Caspian (lake), Vt. 268/C2
Caspiana, La. (71015) 238/C2
Cass, Ark. (†72949) 202/C2
Cass (co.), Ill. 222/C4
Cass (co.), Ind. 227/E3
Cass, Ind. (†47882) 227/C6
Cass (co.), Iowa 229/D6
Cass (co.), Mich. 250/C7
Cass (riv.), Mich. 250/F5
Cass (co.), Minn. 255/D4
Cass (lake), Minn. 255/D3
Cass (co.), Mo. 261/D5
Cass (co.), Nebr. 264/H4
Cass (co.), N. Dak. 282/R5
Cass (co.), Texas 303/K4
Cass, W. Va. (24927) 312/G6
Cassadaga, Fla. (32706) 212/E3
Cassadaga, N.Y. (14718) 276/B6
Cassá de la Selva, Spain 33/H2
Cassai, Angola 115/D6
Cassamba, Angola 115/D6
Cassandra, Georgia (†30727) 217/B1
Cassandra, Pa. (15925) 294/E5
Cassano allo Ionio, Italy 34/F5
Cassatt, S.C. (29032) 296/G3
Cass City, Mich. (48726) 250/F5
Casscoe, Ark. (72026) 202/H4
Casselberry, Fla. (32707) 212/E3
Casselman (riv.), Md. 245/B2
Casselman, Ontario 177/J2
Casselman, Pa. (†15557) 294/D6
Casselman (riv.), Pa. 294/D6
Casselton, N. Dak. (58012) 282/R6
Cássia, Brazil 135/C2
Cassia (co.), Idaho 220/E7
Cassiar, Br. Col. 184/K2
Cassiar (mts.), Br. Col. 184/K2
Cassiar (mts.), Yukon 187/E3
Cassidy, Br. Col. 184/J3
Cassilis, N.S. Wales 97/E3
Cassils, Alberta 182/D4
Cassino, Italy 34/D4
Cassiporé (cape), Brazil 132/D2
Cassity, W. Va. (†26278) 312/F5
Cass Lake, Minn. (56633) 255/D3
Cassoday, Kansas (66842) 232/F3
Cassopolis, Mich. (49031) 250/C7
Casstown, Ohio (45312) 284/B5
Cassville, Georgia (30123) 217/C2
Cassville, Ind. (†46901) 227/E3
Cassville, Mo. (65625) 261/E9
Cassville, Pa. (16623) 294/G5
Cassville, W. Va. (26527) 312/F3
Cassville, Wis. (53806) 317/E10
Castagnola, Switzerland 39/G4
Castaic, Calif. (91310) 204/G9
Castalia, Iowa (52133) 229/K2
Castalia, New Bruns. 170/D4
Castalia, N.C. (27816) 281/O2
Castalia, Ohio (44824) 284/E3
Castalian Springs, Tenn. (37031) 237/J8
Castana, Iowa (51010) 229/B4
Castanhal, Brazil 120/E3
Castanhal, Brazil 132/E3
Castaños, Mexico 150/J3
Castelfranco Veneto, Italy 34/D2
Castel Gandolfo, Italy 34/F7
Casteljaloux, France 28/D5
Castella, Calif. (96017) 204/C2
Castellammare (gulf), Italy 34/D5
Castellammare del Golfo, Italy 34/D5
Castellammare di Stabia, Italy 34/E4
Castellane, France 28/G6
Castellanos, Uruguay 145/B6
Castelli, Buenos Aires, Argentina 143/H7
Castelli, Chaco, Argentina 143/D2
Castellón (prov.), Spain 33/G2
Castellón de la Plana, Spain 33/G2
Castellote, Spain 33/F2
Castelnaudary, France 28/E6
Castelo, Brazil 132/F8
Castelo Branco (dist.), Portugal 33/C3
Castelo Branco, Portugal 33/C3
Castelo de Vide, Portugal 33/C3
Castelo do Piauí, Brazil 132/F4
Castel San Pietro Terme, Italy 34/C2
Castelsarrasin, France 28/D6
Castelvetrano, Italy 34/D6
Casterton, Victoria 97/A5
Castiglione del Lago, Italy 34/C3
Castiglion Fiorentino, Italy 34/C3
Castile, N.Y. (14427) 276/D5
Castilletes, Venezuela 124/C2
Castillo, Cerro (mt.), Chile 138/E6
Castillo, Dom. Rep. 158/E5
Castillo de San Marcos Nat'l Mon., Fla. 212/E2
Castillos, Uruguay 145/F5
Castillos (lag.), Uruguay 145/F5
Castine○, Maine (04421) 243/F7
Castine, Ohio (45313) 284/A6
Castle (harb.), Bermuda 156/H2
Castle (mt.), Br. Col. 184/A2
Castle (peak), Colo. 208/F5
Castle (creek), Idaho 220/B7
Castle (peak), Idaho 220/D5
Castle (pt.), N. Zealand 100/F4
Castle, Okla. (74833) 288/O4
Castle (valley), Utah 304/D4
Castle A.F.B., Calif. 204/E6
Castlebar, Ireland 17/C4
Castlebar, Ireland 10/B4
Castlebay, Scotland 15/A4
Castlebellingham, Ireland 17/J4
Castleberry, Ala. (36432) 195/D8
Castleblayney, Ireland 10/C3
Castleblayney, Ireland 17/H3
Castlebridge, Ireland 17/J7
Castle Bruce, Dominica 161/F6
Castlecomer-Donaguile, Ireland 17/G6
Castlecomer-Donaguile, Ireland 10/C4
Castle Dale, Utah (84513) 304/D4
Castle Danger, Minn. (†56616) 255/G3
Castledawson, N. Ireland 17/H2
Castlederg, N. Ireland 17/F2
Castledermot, Ireland 17/H6
Castle Dome (mts.), Ariz. 198/A5
Castle Douglas, Scotland 15/E6
Castle Douglas, Scotland 10/D3
Castlefin, Ireland 17/F2
Castleford, Idaho (83321) 220/C7
Castlegar, Br. Col. 184/J5
Castlegregory, Ireland 10/B4
Castlegregory, Ireland 17/A7
Castle Hayne, N.C. (28429) 281/O6
Castle Hills, Texas (†78213) 303/J10
Castle Hot Springs, Ariz. (†85342) 198/C5
Castleisland, Ireland 17/B7
Castle Kennedy, Scotland 15/D6
Castlemaine, Victoria 97/C5
Castlemartyr, Ireland 17/E8
Castle Park, Mich. (†49423) 250/C6
Castlepollard, Ireland 17/G4
Castlerea, Ireland 17/D4
Castlerea, Ireland 10/B4
Castlereagh (riv.), N.S. Wales 97/E2
Castlereagh (dist.), N. Ireland 17/K2
Castle Rock, Colo. (80104) 208/K4
Castle Rock, Minn. (55010) 255/E6
Castle Rock, S. Dak. (†57760) 298/C4
Castle Rock, Utah (†82930) 304/C2
Castle Rock, Wash. (98611) 310/B4
Castle Rock (lake), Wis. 317/G8
Castle Shannon, Pa. (15234) 294/B7
Castleton, Ill. (61426) 222/D2
Castleton, Jamaica 158/J6
Castleton, Md. (†21034) 245/N2
Castleton, Ontario 177/F3
Castleton○, Vt. (05735) 268/A4
Castleton-on-Hudson, N.Y. (12033) 276/N5
Castletown, Ireland 17/F6
Castletown, I. of Man 13/C3
Castletown, Scotland 15/E2
Castletownbere, Ireland 17/B8
Castletownroche, Ireland 17/D7
Castletownshend, Ireland 17/C9
Castlewellan, N. Ireland 17/K3
Castlewood, S. Dak. (57223) 298/R4
Castlewood, Va. (24224) 307/D7
Castolon, Texas (†79852) 303/D12
Castor, Alberta 182/D3
Castor, La. (71016) 238/D2
Castorland, N.Y. (13620) 276/J3
Castres, France 28/E6
Castries (cap.), St. Lucia 156/G4
Castries (cap.), St. Lucia 161/G6
Castro, Brazil 135/B4
Castro, Brazil 132/D9
Castro, Chile 138/D4
Castro (co.), Texas 303/B3
Castro Alves, Brazil 132/G6
Castro Daire, Portugal 33/C2
Castro del Río, Spain 33/D4
Castrojeriz, Spain 33/E1
Castro Marim, Portugal 33/C4
Castropol, Spain 33/C1
Castrop-Rauxel, W. Germany 22/B3
Castroreale, Italy 34/E5
Castro-Urdiales, Spain 33/E1
Castro Valley, Calif. (94546) 204/K2
Castro Verde, Portugal 33/B4
Castrovillari, Italy 34/F5
Castroville, Calif. (95012) 204/D7
Castroville, Texas (78009) 303/J11
Castrovirreyna, Peru 128/E9
Castuera, Spain 33/D3
Casuarito, Colombia 126/G5
Casupá, Uruguay 145/D5
Caswell, Alaska (†99688) 196/B1
Caswell (co.), N.C. 281/L2
Caswell Beach, N.C. (†28461) 281/N7
Cat (isl.), Bahamas 146/L7
Cat (isl.), Bahamas 156/C1
Cat (isl.), Miss. 256/F10
Çat, Turkey 63/J3
Cat (isl.), Wis. 317/E1
Catacamas, Honduras 154/E3
Catacaos, Peru 128/B5
Catacocha, Ecuador 128/C5
Catadupa, Jamaica 158/H6
Cataguases, Brazil 135/E2
Catahoula (par.), La. 238/G3
Catahoula (lake), La. 238/F4
Cataingan, Philippines 82/E5
Çatak, Turkey 63/K4
Catalão, Brazil 132/D7
Çatalca, Turkey 63/C2
Cataldo, Idaho (83810) 220/B2
Catalina, Chile 138/B5
Catalina (pt.), Chile 138/F10
Catalina (isl.), Dom. Rep. 158/F6
Catalina, Newf. 166/D2
Catalone, Nova Scotia 168/H3
Catalonia (reg.), Spain 33/G2
Catalpa (creek), Miss. 256/G4
Çatalzeytin, Turkey 63/F1
Catamarca (prov.), Argentina 143/C2
Catamarca, Argentina 143/C2
Catamarca, Argentina 120/C5
Catamayo, Ecuador 128/C4
Catanauan, Philippines 82/D4
Catandica, Mozambique 118/E3
Catanduanes (prov.), Philippines 82/E4
Catanduanes (isl.), Philippines 82/E4
Catanduanes (isl.), Philippines 85/H3
Catanduva, Brazil 135/B2
Catanduva, Brazil 132/D8
Catania (prov.), Italy 34/E6
Catania, Italy 34/E6
Catania, Italy 7/F5
Cataño, P. Rico 156/G1
Cataño, P. Rico 161/D1
Catanzaro (prov.), Italy 34/F5
Catanzaro, Italy 34/F5
Cataouatche (lake), La. 238/N4
Cataract (creek), Ariz. 198/C3
Cataract, Ind. (†47460) 227/D6
Cataract (canyon), Utah 304/D5
Cataract, Wis. (54620) 317/E7
Catarama, Ecuador 128/C3
Cataricahua, Bolivia 136/B6
Catarina, Texas (78836) 303/E9
Catarman, Philippines 82/E4
Catarman (pt.), Philippines 82/F7
Catasauqua, Pa. (18032) 294/M4
Catastrophe (cape), S. Australia 88/F7
Catastrophe (cape), S. Australia 94/D6
Catatumbo (riv.), Colombia 126/D3
Catatumbo (riv.), Venezuela 124/B3
Cataula, Georgia (31804) 217/C5
Cataumet, Mass. (02534) 249/M6
Catawba (co.), N.C. 281/G3
Catawba, N.C. (28609) 281/G3
Catawba (lake), N.C. 281/G4
Catawba (riv.), N.C. 281/H5
Catawba, Ohio (43010) 284/C6
Catawba, S.C. (29704) 296/F2
Catawba (riv.), S.C. 296/F2
Catawba, Va. (24070) 307/H6
Catawba, W. Va. (†26554) 312/F3
Catawba, Wis. (54515) 317/E4
Catawba Island, Ohio (†43452) 284/E2
Catawissa, Mo. (63015) 261/L6
Catawissa, Pa. (17820) 294/K4
Cat Ba, Dao (isl.), Vietnam 72/E2
Catbalogan, Philippines 85/H3
Catbalogan, Philippines 82/E5
Cat Creek, Mont. (59017) 262/H3
Cateechee, S.C. (29629) 296/B2
Cateel, Philippines 85/H4
Cateel, Philippines 82/F7
Catemaco, Mexico 150/M7
Catemu, Chile 138/G2
Cater, Sask. 181/C2
Caterham and Warlingham, England 13/H8
Caterham and Warlingham, England 10/B6
Cates, Ind. (47927) 227/C4
Catete, Angola 115/B5
Catfish (lake), N.C. 281/P5
Catfish (lake), Ontario 177/F2
Catfish (creek), S.C. 296/J3
Cathance (lake), Maine 243/J6
Catharine, Kansas (67627) 232/C3
Catharine Lake, N.C. (†28754) 281/O5
Cathay, N. Dak. (58422) 282/M4
Cathedral (mt.), Texas 303/D12
Cathedral City, Calif. (92234) 204/J10
Cathedral Prov. Park, Br. Col. 184/H5
Catherine, Ala. (36728) 195/D6
Catherine (lake), Ark. 202/E5
Catheys Valley, Calif. (95306) 204/E6
Cathlamet, Wash. (98612) 310/B4
Cat Island (chan.), La. 238/M6
Cat Island (passage), La. 238/J8
Catlett, Va. (22019) 307/N3
Catlettsburg, Ky. (41129) 237/R4
Catlin, Ill. (61817) 222/F3
Catlin, Ind. (†47872) 227/C5
Catmon, Philippines 82/E5
Cato, Ark. (†72076) 202/F4
Cato (isl.), Australia 87/F8
Cato, Ind. (†47598) 227/C8
Cato, N.Y. (13033) 276/G4
Cato, Wis. (54206) 317/L7
Catoche (cape), Mexico 150/Q6
Catoctin (creek), Md. 245/H3
Catoctin Furnace, Md. (†21788) 245/J2
Catoctin Mt. Park, Md. 245/J2
Catolé do Rocha, Brazil 132/G4
Catonsville, Md. (21228) 245/M3
Catoosa (co.), Georgia 217/B1
Catoosa, Okla. (74015) 288/P2
Catriló, Argentina 143/D4
Catrimani, Brazil 132/H9
Catrine, Scotland 15/D5
Catron, Mo. (63833) 261/N9
Catron (co.), N. Mex. 274/A4
Catskill, N.Y. (12414) 276/N6
Catskill (mts.), N.Y. 276/L6
Cattaraugus (co.), N.Y. 276/C6
Cattaraugus, N.Y. (14719) 276/C6
Cattaraugus (creek), N.Y. 276/C6
Cattaraugus Ind. Res., N.Y. 276/C5
Catumbela, Angola 115/B6
Cauayan, Isabela, Philippines 82/C2
Cauayan, Negros Occ., Philippines 82/D6
Cauca (dept.), Colombia 126/B6
Cauca (riv.), Colombia 120/B2
Cauca (riv.), Colombia 126/C4
Caucagua, Venezuela 124/E2
Caucasia, Colombia 126/C4
Caucasus (mts.), U.S.S.R. 7/J4
Caucasus (mts.), U.S.S.R. 52/F6
Caucasus (mts.), U.S.S.R. 48/E5
Caucedo (cape), Dom. Rep. 158/E6
Caucete, Argentina 143/C3
Caucomgomoc (lake), Maine 243/D3
Caudete, Spain 33/F3
Caughnawaga, Québec 172/H4
Cauit (pt.), Philippines 82/F6
Cauldcleuch Head (mt.), Scotland 15/F5
Caulfield, Mo. (65626) 261/H9
Caulfield, Victoria 88/L7
Caulfield, Victoria 97/J5
Caulksville, Ark. (†72951) 202/C3
Caulonia, Italy 34/F5
Caúngula, Angola 115/C5
Cauquenes, Chile 138/A11
Caura (riv.), Venezuela 120/D2
Caura (riv.), Venezuela 124/F5
Causapscal, Québec 172/B2
Causeway, Ireland 17/B7
Causey, N. Mex. (88113) 274/F5
Causses (reg.), France 28/D5
Cauterets, France 28/C6
Cauthron, Ark. (†72958) 202/B4
Cauto (riv.), Cuba 158/H3
Cauto del Embarcadero, Cuba 158/H4
Cauto el Cristo, Cuba 158/J3
Cava de'Tirreni, Italy 34/E4
Cavaillon, France 28/F6
Cavaillon, Haiti 158/A6
Cavalier (co.), N. Dak. 282/N2
Cavalier, N. Dak. (58220) 282/P2
Cavalla (riv.), Liberia 106/C7
Cavalli (isls.), N. Zealand 100/E1
Cavallo (passage), Texas 303/H9
Cavally (riv.), Ivory Coast 106/C7
Cavan (co.), Ireland 17/G4
Cavan, Ireland 10/C4
Cavan, Ireland 17/G3
Cavan, Ontario 177/F3
Cavanaugh (lake), Wash. 310/D2
Cavari, Bolivia 136/B5
Cavarzere, Italy 34/D2
Cave City, Ark. (72521) 202/G2
Cave City, Ky. (42127) 237/K6
Cave Creek, Ariz. (85331) 198/D5
Cave Hill, Barbados 161/B9
Cave in Rock, Ill. (62919) 222/E6
Cave Junction, Oreg. (97523) 291/D5
Cavell, Sask. 181/C3
Cavendish, Alberta 182/E4
Cavendish, Idaho (†83550) 220/B3
Cavendish, Newf. 166/D2
Cavendish○, Vt. (05142) 268/B5
Cavergno, Switzerland 39/G4
Cave Spring, Georgia (30124) 217/B2
Cave Springs, Ark. (72718) 202/B1
Cavetown, Md. (21720) 245/H2
Caviana (isl.), Brazil 120/E2
Caviana (isl.), Brazil 132/D2
Cavili (isl.), Philippines 82/C6
Cavinas, Bolivia 136/B3
Cavite (prov.), Philippines 82/C3
Cavite, Philippines 82/C3
Cavite, Philippines 85/G3
Cavour, S. Dak. (57324) 298/N5
Cavour, Wis. (54516) 317/J4
Cawdor, Scotland 15/E3
Cawker City, Kansas (67430) 232/D2
Cawndilla (lake), N.S. Wales 97/A3
Cawnpore (Kanpur), India 68/E3
Cawood, Ky. (40815) 237/P7
Cawston, Br. Col. 184/H5
Cawston, England 13/J5
Caxambu, Brazil 135/D2
Caxias, Brazil 120/E3
Caxias, Brazil 132/F4
Caxias do Sul, Brazil 120/D5
Caxias do Sul, Brazil 132/D10
Caxito, Angola 115/B5
Çay, Turkey 63/D3
Cayacoa, Dom. Rep. 158/E6
Cayamas (cays), Cuba 158/C2
Cayambe, Ecuador 128/D3
Cayambe (mt.), Ecuador 128/D2
Cayasta, Argentina 143/F5
Cayastacito, Argentina 143/F5
Cayce, Ky. (†42041) 237/C7
Cayce, S.C. (29169) 296/E4
Çaycuma, Turkey 63/E2
Cayeli, Turkey 63/J2
Cayenne (cap.), Fr. Guiana 120/D2
Cayenne (cap.), Fr. Guiana 2/G5
Cayenne (dist.), Fr. Guiana 131/E3
Cayenne (cap.), Fr. Guiana 131/E3
Cayer, Manitoba 179/D3
Cayes Jacmel, Haiti 158/C6
Cayeux-sur-Mer, France 28/D2
Cayey, P. Rico 156/G1
Cayey, P. Rico 161/D2
Cayey, Sierra de (mts.), P. Rico 161/D2
Çayıralan, Turkey 63/F3
Çayırlı, Turkey 63/J3
Cayley, Alberta 182/D4
Cayman (isls.) 146/K8
Cayman Brac (isl.), Cayman Is. 156/B3
CAYMAN ISLANDS 156/B3
Cayo Costa (isl.), Fla. 212/D5
Cayon, St. Chris.-Nevis 161/C10
Cay Sal (bank), Bahamas 156/B2
Cayucos, Calif. (93430) 204/E8
Cayuga, Ind. (47928) 227/C5
Cayuga (co.), N.Y. 276/G4
Cayuga, N.Y. (13034) 276/G5
Cayuga (lake), N.Y. 276/G5
Cayuga, N. Dak. (58013) 282/R7
Cayuga, Texas (75832) 303/J6
Cayuga Heights, N.Y. (†14850) 276/H6
Cayuse, Oreg. (97821) 291/J2
Cayuta (creek), N.Y. 276/G6
Cazadero, Calif. (95421) 204/B5
Cazalla de la Sierra, Spain 33/D4
Cazaux (lake), France 28/C5
Cazenovia, N.Y. (13035) 276/J5
Cazenovia, Wis. (53924) 317/F8
Cazin, Yugoslavia 45/B3
Cazis, Switzerland 39/H3
Cazma (riv.), Yugoslavia 45/C3
Cazombo, Angola 115/D6
Cazones (gulf), Cuba 158/C2
Cazorla, Spain 33/E4
Cazorla, Venezuela 124/E3
Cazot, Uruguay 145/B6
Cazueleja, Cerro (mt.), Colombia 126/C6
Ceanannus Mór, Ireland 17/G4
Ceanannus Mór, Ireland 10/C4
Ceará (state), Brazil 132/G4
Ceará (Fortaleza), Brazil 132/G3
Ceará-Mirim, Brazil 132/H4
Ceará-Mirim, Brazil 120/F3
Cébaco (isl.), Panama 154/G7
Ceballos, Mexico 150/H3
Cebeci, Turkey 63/E3
Cebolla (creek), Colo. 208/E6
Cebolla, N. Mex. (87518) 274/C2
Cebollatí, Uruguay 145/F4
Cebollatí (riv.), Uruguay 145/F4
Cebreros, Spain 33/D2
Cebu (prov.), Philippines 82/D5
Cebu, Philippines 82/D5
Cebu, Philippines 85/G3
Cebu, Philippines 54/O8
Cebu, Philippines 2/R5
Cebu (isl.), Philippines 85/G3
Cebu (isl.), Philippines 82/D5
Cecelia, La. (70521) 238/G6
Cecil, Ala. (36013) 195/F6
Cecil, Ark. (72930) 202/C3
Cecil, Georgia (31627) 217/F8
Cecil (co.), Md. 245/P2
Cecil, Ohio (45821) 284/A3
Cecil, Oreg. (†97843) 291/H2
Cecil, Pa. (15321) 294/B5
Cecil, Wis. (54111) 317/K6
Cecil Field Naval Air Sta., Fla. 212/E1
Cecilia, Ky. (42724) 237/K5
Cecil Lake, Br. Col. 184/G2
Cecil M. Harden (lake), Ind. 227/C5
Cecilton, Md. (21913) 245/P3
Cecilville, Calif. (†96027) 204/B2
Cecina, Italy 34/C3

Changyŏn 349

Ceclavín, Spain 33/C3
Cedar (pt.), Ala. 195/B10
Cedar, Br. Col. 184/J3
Cedar (creek), Colo. 208/M1
Cedar (lake), Conn. 210/E3
Cedar (creek), Ind. 227/G2
Cedar (co.), Iowa 229/L5
Cedar, Iowa (52543) 229/H6
Cedar (riv.), Iowa 188/H2
Cedar (riv.), Iowa 229/K4
Cedar, Kansas (67628) 232/D2
Cedar (lake), Manitoba 179/B1
Cedar (pt.), Md. 245/N7
Cedar, Mich. (49621) 250/D4
Cedar (lake), Mich. 250/F4
Cedar (riv.), Minn. 255/F7
Cedar (co.), Mo. 261/E7
Cedar (co.), Nebr. 264/G2
Cedar (riv.), Nebr. 264/F3
Cedar (mt.), Nev. 266/D4
Cedar (creek), N.J. 273/E4
Cedar (creek), N. Dak. 282/G7
Cedar (pt.), Ohio 284/D2
Cedar (lake), Ontario 177/F1
Cedar (lake), Texas 303/B5
Cedar (mts.), Utah 304/B3
Cedar (isl.), Va. 307/S5
Cedar (riv.), Wash. 310/B2
Cedar Bluff, Ala. (35959) 195/G2
Cedar Bluff, Iowa (†52772) 229/L5
Cedar Bluff (res.), Kansas 232/C3
Cedarbluff, Miss. (39741) 256/G3
Cedar Bluff, Va. (24609) 307/E6
Cedar Bluffs, Kansas (†67749) 232/B2
Cedar Bluffs, Nebr. (68015) 264/H3
Cedar Breaks Nat'l Mon., Utah 304/B6
Cedar Brook, N.J. (08018) 273/D4
Cedarburg, Wis. (53012) 317/L9
Cedarbutte, S. Dak. (57527) 298/H6
Cedar City, Mo. (65022) 261/H5
Cedar City, Utah 188/D3
Cedar City, Utah (84720) 304/A6
Cedar Cove, Ala. (†35453) 195/D4
Cedar Creek, Ark. (†72950) 202/C4
Cedar Creek (peak), Idaho 220/E7
Cedar Creek (res.), Idaho 220/D7
Cedarcreek, Mo. (†65680) 261/G9
Cedar Creek, Nebr. (68016) 264/H3
Cedar Crest, N. Mex. (87008) 274/C3
Cedaredge, Colo. (81413) 208/D5
Cedar Falls, Iowa (50613) 229/H3
Cedar Falls, N.C. (27230) 281/K3
Cedar Falls, Wash. (†98045) 310/D3
Cedar Falls, Wis. (†54751) 317/C6
Cedar Fort, Utah (†84013) 304/B3
Cedar Gap, Mo. (†65746) 261/G8
Cedar Grove, Ant. & Bar. 161/E11
Cedar Grove, Fla. (†32401) 212/D6
Cedar Grove, Georgia (†30727) 217/L2
Cedar Grove, Ind. (47016) 227/H6
Cedar Grove, Md. (†20767) 245/K4
Cedar Grove○, N.J. (07009) 273/B2
Cedar Grove, N.C. (27231) 281/L2
Cedar Grove, Tenn. (38321) 237/D9
Cedar Grove, W. Va. (25039) 312/D6
Cedar Grove, Wis. (53013) 317/L8
Cedar Heights, Md. (†20027) 245/G5
Cedar Hill, N. Mex. (†87410) 274/B2
Cedar Hill, Tenn. (37032) 237/H7
Cedar Hill, Texas (75104) 303/G3
Cedar Hill Lakes, Mo. (63016) 261/L6
Cedar Hills, Oreg. (97225) 291/A2
Cedarhurst, N.Y. (11516) 276/P7
Cedar Island, N.C. (28520) 281/S5
Cedar Key, Fla. (32625) 212/C2
Cedar Knolls, N.J. (07927) 273/E2
Cedar Lake, Ind. (46303) 227/C2
Cedar Lake, Minn. (†56431) 255/E4
Cedar Mill, Oreg. (†97005) 291/A2
Cedar Mills, Minn. (55351) 255/D6
Cedar Mountain, N.C. (28718) 281/D4
Cedar Park, Texas (78613) 303/G7
Cedar Point, Ill. (61316) 222/D2
Cedar Point, Kansas (66843) 232/F3
Cedar Rapids, Iowa 188/H2
Cedar Rapids, Iowa (*52401) 229/K5
Cedar Rapids, Iowa 146/J5
Cedar Rapids, Nebr. (68627) 264/F3
Cedar River, Mich. (49813) 250/B3
Cedar Run, N.J. (†08092) 273/E4
Cedar Run, Pa. (17727) 294/H2
Cedar Springs, Georgia (31732) 217/C8
Cedar Springs, Mich. (49319) 250/D5
Cedar Springs, Mo. (†64744) 261/E7
Cedar Springs, Ontario 177/B5
Cedar Springs, Va. (†24368) 307/F7
Cedar Swamp (pond), Conn. 210/G2
Cedartown, Georgia (30125) 217/B2
Cedarvale, Br. Col. 184/C2
Cedar Vale, Kansas (67024) 232/F4
Cedarvale, N. Mex. (87009) 274/D4
Cedar Valley, Utah (84013) 304/B3
Cedarville, Ark. (72932) 202/B2
Cedarville, Calif. (96104) 204/E2
Cedarville, Ill. (61013) 222/D1
Cedarville, Ind. (†46741) 227/G2
Cedarville, Ky. (†41522) 237/S6
Cedarville, Md. (†20613) 245/L6
Cedarville, Mich. (49719) 250/E2
Cedarville, N.J. (08311) 273/C5
Cedarville, N.Y. (†13357) 276/K5
Cedarville, Ohio (45314) 284/C6
Cedarville, Va. (†22630) 307/M3
Cedarville, W. Va. (26611) 312/E5
Cedarwood Park, N.J. (†08723) 273/E3
Cedonia, Wash. (99137) 310/G2
Cedoux, Sask. 181/H6
Cedral, Mexico 150/J5
Cedros, Honduras 154/D3
Cedros (isl.), Mexico 146/G7
Cedros (isl.), Mexico 150/B2
Cedros, Trin. & Tob. 161/A11
Ceduna, S. Australia 88/E6
Ceduna, S. Australia 94/D5
Cee Vee, Texas (79223) 303/D3
Cefalù, Italy 34/E5
Cegléd, Hungary 41/E3
Ceglie Messapico, Italy 34/F4
Cehegín, Spain 33/F3
Ceiba, P. Rico 161/F2
Çekerek, Turkey 63/F2
Çekerek (riv.), Turkey 63/F3
Cela, Angola 115/C6
Celada Cué, Paraguay 144/D3
Celano, Italy 34/D3
Celanova, Spain 33/B1
Celaya, Mexico 150/J6
Celbridge, Ireland 17/H5
Celebes (sea) 54/O9
Celebes (isl.), Indonesia 54/N10
Celebes (isl.), Indonesia 2/R6
Celebes (Sulawesi) (isl.), Indonesia 85/G5
Celebes (sea), Indonesia 85/G5
Celebes (sea), Philippines 82/D8
Celendín, Peru 128/D6
Celerigna-Schlarigna, Switzerland 39/J3
Celeste, Texas (75423) 303/H4
Celestine, Ind. (47521) 227/D8
Celestún, Mexico 150/O6
Celica, Ecuador 128/B4
Céligny, Switzerland 39/B4
Çelikhan, Turkey 63/H3
Celilo, Oreg. (†97058) 291/G2
Celilo (lake), Oreg. 291/G2
Celilo (lake), Wash. 310/E5
Celina, Minn. (†55788) 255/E3
Celina, Ohio (45822) 284/A4
Celina, Tenn. (38551) 237/K7
Celina, Texas (75009) 303/H4
Celista, Br. Col. 184/H5
Celje, Yugoslavia 45/B2
Cella, Spain 33/F2
Cellar (head), Scotland 15/B2
Celldömölk, Hungary 41/D3
Celle, W. Germany 22/D2
Celorico da Beira, Portugal 33/C2
Celoron, N.Y. (14720) 276/B6
Cement, Okla. (73017) 288/K5
Cement City, Mich. (49233) 250/E6
Çemişkezek, Turkey 63/H3
Cemmaes (head), Wales 13/C5
Cenderawasih (bay), Indonesia 85/K6
Ceneri (mt.), Switzerland 39/G4
Cenia, Spain 33/G2
Census Bureau, Md. 245/F5
Centenary, Ind. (†47842) 227/B5
Centenary, S.C. (29519) 296/J3
Centennial (mts.), Idaho 220/F5
Centennial, Wyo. (82055) 319/F4
Centennial Wash (dry riv.), Ariz. 198/B5
Center, Colo. (81125) 208/G7
Center, Georgia (†30601) 217/F2
Center, Ind. (†46901) 227/E4
Center, Ky. (42214) 237/K6
Center (pond), Maine 243/E5
Center, Mo. (63436) 261/J3
Center, Nebr. (68724) 264/G2
Center, N. Dak. (58530) 282/H5
Center, Okla. (†74820) 288/N5
Center, S. Dak. (†57058) 298/P6
Center, Texas (75935) 303/K6
Center Barnstead, N.H. (03225) 268/E5
Center Belpre, Ohio (†45714) 284/G7
Centerbrook, Conn. (06409) 210/F3
Centerburg, Ohio (43011) 284/E5
Center City, Minn. (55012) 255/F5
Center Conway, N.H. (03813) 268/E4
Center Cross, Va. (22437) 307/P5
Centerdale, R.I. (02911) 249/H5
Centereach, N.Y. (11720) 276/O9
Centerfield, Utah (84622) 304/C4
Center Groton, Conn. (06340) 210/G3
Center Harbor○, N.H. (03226) 268/E4
Center Hill, Ark. (72143) 202/G3
Center Hill, Fla. (33514) 212/D3
Center Hill (lake), Tenn. 237/K9
Center Junction, Iowa (52212) 229/L4
Center Line, Mich. (48015) 250/B6
Center Lovell, Maine (04016) 243/B7
Center Montville, Maine (†04941) 243/E7
Center Moreland, Pa. (18657) 294/E7
Center Moriches, N.Y. (11934) 276/P9
Center Ossipee, N.H. (03814) 268/E4
Center Point, Ark. (71830) 202/C5
Centerpoint, Ind. (47840) 227/C6
Center Point, Iowa (52213) 229/K4
Center Point, La. (71323) 238/F4
Center Point, S. Dak. (†57070) 298/P7
Center Point, Texas (78010) 303/E8
Center Point, W. Va. (26339) 312/E4
Center Ridge, Ark. (72027) 202/E3
Center Rutland, Vt. (05736) 268/A4
Center Sandwich, N.H. (03227) 268/D4
Center Square, Ind. (†47043) 227/H7
Center Strafford, N.H. (03815) 268/E5
Centerton, Ark. (72719) 202/B1
Centerton, Ind. (46116) 227/E5
Centerton, N.J. (†08318) 273/C4
Centertown, Ky. (42328) 237/G6
Centertown, Mo. (65023) 261/H5
Centertown, Tenn. (†37110) 237/K9
Center Tuftonboro, N.H. (03816) 268/E4
Centerview, Mo. (64019) 261/E5
Center Village, Ohio (†43021) 284/E5
Centerville, Ark. (72829) 202/D3
Centerville, Del. (†19801) 245/R1
Centerville, Georgia (31028) 217/E5
Centerville, Ind. (47330) 227/H5
Centerville, Iowa (52544) 229/H7
Centerville, Kansas (66014) 232/H3
Centerville, Ky. (†41522) 237/S6
Centerville, La. (70522) 238/H7
Centerville○, Maine (†04623) 243/H6
Centerville, Mass. (02632) 249/N6
Centerville, Minn. (†55038) 255/E5
Centerville, Mo. (63633) 261/L8
Centerville, N.C. (†27549) 281/N2
Centerville, Ohio (45459) 284/B6
Centerville, Pa. (15417) 294/B6
Centerville, Pa. (16404) 294/C2
Centerville, S. Dak. (57014) 298/R7
Centerville, Tenn. (37033) 237/G9
Centerville, Texas (75833) 303/H6
Centerville, Utah (84014) 304/C3
Centerville, Wash. (98613) 310/D5
Centrahoma, Okla. (74534) 288/O5
Central, Ala. (36014) 195/F5
Central (sen. dist.), Alaska 196/H2
Central, Alaska (99730) 196/J1
Central, Ariz. (85531) 198/F6
Central, Cordillera (range), Bolivia 136/C6
Central, Cordillera (range), Colombia 126/C5
Central, Cordillera (range), Dom. Rep. 158/D5
Central, Idaho (†83241) 220/G7
Central, Ind. (47110) 227/E8
Central (Markazi) (prov.), Iran 66/G3
Central (dist.), Israel 65/B3
Central (prov.), Kenya 115/G4
Central, La. (†70723) 238/L3
Central, N. Mex. (88026) 274/A6
Central (dept.), Paraguay 144/D4
Central (Baganga), Philippines 82/F7
Central, Cordillera (range), P. Rico 161/C2
Central (reg.), Scotland 15/D4
Central, S.C. (29630) 296/B2
Central, Utah (†84701) 304/A6
Central, Utah (84722) 304/B5
Central Aboriginal Reserve, W. Australia 88/D4
Central Aboriginal Res., W. Australia 92/E3
Central African Republic 2/K5
Central African Republic 102/D4
CENTRAL AFRICAN REPUBLIC 115/C2
Central Aguirre, P. Rico 161/D3
Central Amancio Rodríguez, Cuba 158/G3
Central America 2/E5
Central América, Cuba 158/J4
Central Bedeque, Pr. Edward I. 168/E2
Central Blissville, New Bruns. 170/D3
Central Bolivia, Cuba 158/G2
Central Brasil, Cuba 158/G2
Central Bridge, N.Y. (12035) 276/M5
Central Butte, Sask. 181/E5
Central Cándido González, Cuba 158/G3
Central City, Ark. (†72923) 202/B3
Central City, Colo. (80427) 208/J3
Central City, Ill. (†62801) 222/D5
Central City, Iowa (52214) 229/K4
Central City, Ky. (42330) 237/G6
Central City, Nebr. (68826) 264/F3
Central City, Pa. (15926) 294/E5
Central City, S. Dak. (†57754) 298/B5
Central Colombia, Cuba 158/G3
Central Falls, R.I. (02863) 249/J5
Central Frank País, Cuba 158/K3
Central Greece and Euboea (reg.), Greece 45/F6
Central Guatemala, Cuba 158/J3
Central Haití, Cuba 158/G3
Centralhatchee, Georgia (†30217) 217/B4
Central Heights-Midland City, Ariz. (†85501) 198/E5
Centralia, Ill. (62801) 222/D5
Centralia, Iowa (†52068) 229/M4
Centralia, Kansas (66415) 232/F2
Centralia, Mo. (65240) 261/H4
Centralia, Okla. (74336) 288/R1
Centralia, Pa. (17927) 294/K4
Centralia, Texas (75834) 303/K6
Centralia, Wash. 188/B1
Centralia, Wash. (98531) 310/C4
Centralia, W. Va. (26612) 312/E5
Central Intelligence Agency (C.I.A.), Va. 307/S2
Central Islip, N.Y. (11722) 276/O9
Central Lake, Mich. (49622) 250/D3
Central Los Reynaldos, Cuba 158/J4
Central Loynaz Echevarría, Cuba 158/J3
Central Manuel Tames, Cuba 158/K4
Central Niágara, Cuba 158/B1
Central Pacolet, S.C. (†29372) 296/D2
Central Park, Wash. (98520) 310/B3
Central Patricia, Ontario 175/B2
Central Point, Oreg. (97502) 291/D5
Central Point, Va. (†22427) 307/O4
Central Saanich, Br. Col. 184/K3
Central Square, N.Y. (13036) 276/H4
Central Station, W. Va. (26340) 312/E4
Central Ural (mts.), U.S.S.R. 52/J2
Central Valley, Calif. (96019) 204/C3
Central Valley, N.Y. (10917) 276/M8
Central Village, Conn. (06332) 210/H2
Central Village, Mass. (02790) 249/K6
Central Wedge (mt.), North. Terr. 93/C7
Centre, Ala. (35960) 195/G2
Centre (co.), Pa. 294/G4
Centre Hall, Pa. (16828) 294/G4
Centre Island, N.Y. (†11771) 276/R6
Centre-Saint-Simon, New Bruns. 170/E1
Centreville, Ala. (35042) 195/D5
Centreville, Ill. (62206) 222/B3
Centreville, Md. (21617) 245/O4
Centreville, Mich. (49032) 250/D7
Centreville, Miss. (39631) 256/B8
Centreville, New Bruns. 170/C2
Centreville, Digby, Nova Scotia 168/B4
Centreville, Kings, Nova Scotia 168/D3
Centreville (Thurman), Ohio (†45685) 284/F8
Centuria, Wis. (54824) 317/A5
Centurión, Uruguay 145/F3
Century, Fla. (32535) 212/B5
Century, W. Va. (26214) 312/F4
Cephalonia (Kefallinía) (isl.), Greece 45/E6
Ceram (isl.), Indonesia 54/P10
Ceram (isl.), Indonesia 85/H6
Cerbat (mts.), Ariz. 198/A3
Cercal, Portugal 33/B4
Cerca la Source, Haiti 158/C5
Cereal, Alberta 182/E4
Ceredo, W. Va. (25507) 312/B6
Ceres, Argentina 143/D2
Ceres, Brazil 132/D6
Ceres, Brazil 120/E4
Ceres, Calif. (95307) 204/D6
Ceres, N.Y. (14721) 276/D6
Ceres, S. Africa 118/B6
Ceres, Va. (24318) 307/F6
Ceresco, Nebr. (68017) 264/H3
Céret, France 28/E6
Cereté, Colombia 126/C3
Cerf (lake), Québec 172/B3
Cerf (isl.), Seychelles 118/H5
Cerfontaine, Belgium 27/E8
Cerignola, Italy 34/E4
Çerkeş, Turkey 63/E2
Çerkezköy, Turkey 63/C2
Çermik, Turkey 63/H3
Cernavodă, Romania 45/J3
Cernier, Switzerland 39/C2
Cernobbio, Italy 34/B2
Cerralvo (isl.), Mexico 150/E4
Cerrillos, N. Mex. (87010) 274/D3
Cerrillos, Uruguay 145/A6
Cerrito, Paraguay 144/D5
Cerritos, Calif. (†90701) 204/C11
Cerritos, Mexico 150/J5
Cerro, N. Mex. (87519) 274/D2
Cerro Aconcagua (mt.) 120/C6
Cerro Alto (mt.), Texas 303/B10
Cêrro Azul, Brazil 135/B4
Cerro Azul, Mexico 150/L6
Cerro Azul, Peru 128/D9
Cerro Castillo, Chile 138/E9
Cerro Chato, Cerro Largo, Uruguay 145/F3
Cerro Chato, Rivera, Uruguay 145/D2
Cerro Chato, Treinta y Tres, Uruguay 145/D4
Cerro Colorado, Uruguay 145/D4
Cerro Corá, Paraguay 144/E3
Cerro de las Armas, Uruguay 145/B5
Cerro de las Cuentas, Uruguay 145/E3
Cerro de Pasco, Peru 120/B4
Cerro de Pasco, Peru 128/D8
Cerro de San Antonio, Colombia 126/C
Cerro Gordo, Ill. (61818) 222/E4
Cerro Gordo (co.), Iowa 229/G2
Cerro Gordo, N.C. (28430) 281/M6
Cerro Gordo (pt.), P. Rico 161/D1
Cerro Gordo, Tenn. (38322) 237/E10
Cerro Largo (dept.), Uruguay 145/E3
Cerro Manantiales, Chile 138/F10
Cerulean, Ky. (42215) 237/F7
Cervera, Spain 33/G2
Cervera del Río Alhama, Spain 33/E1
Cervera de Pisuerga, Spain 33/D1
Cerveteri, Italy 34/F4
Cervione, France 28/B6
Cesano, Italy 34/F6
César (dept.), Colombia 126/D3
César (riv.), Colombia 126/D2
Cesena, Italy 34/D2
Cesenatico, Italy 34/D2
Cēsis, U.S.S.R. 53/C2
Cēsis, U.S.S.R. 52/C3
Česká Kamenice, Czech. 41/C1
Česká Lípa, Czech. 41/C1
Česká Třebová, Czech. 41/D2
České Budějovice, Czech. 41/C2
Český Brod, Czech. 41/C1
Český Krumlov, Czech. 41/C2
Český Těšín, Czech. 41/E2
Çeşme, Turkey 63/B3
Céspedes, Cuba 158/G2
Cessford, Alberta 182/E4
Cessnock-Bellbird, N. S. Wales 88/J6
Cessnock-Bellbird, N.S. Wales 97/F3
Cestos (riv.), Liberia 106/C7
Cetinje, Yugoslavia 45/D4
Çetinkaya, Turkey 63/G3
Ceuta, Spain 106/C1
Ceuta, Spain 7/D5
Ceuta, Spain 102/B1
Ceuta, Spain 33/D5
Cévennes (mts.), France 28/E5
Cevio, Switzerland 39/G4
Cevizli, Turkey 63/D4
Ceyhan, Turkey 63/F4
Ceyhan (riv.), Turkey 63/F4
Ceyhan (riv.), Turkey 59/C2
Ceylanpınar, Turkey 63/H4
Ceylon (Sri Lanka) 54/K9
Ceylon, Minn. (56121) 255/D7
Ceylon, Sask. 181/G6
Chabás, Argentina 143/F6
Chaca, Chile 138/B1
Chacabuco, Argentina 143/F7
Chacabuco, Chile 138/G3
Chacachacare (isl.), Trin. & Tob. 161/A10
Chacahoula, La. (†70395) 238/J7
Chacalluta, Chile 138/A1
Chachacomani, Bolivia 136/A6
Chachapoyas, Peru 128/D6
Chachapoyas, Peru 120/B3
Chachoengsao, Thailand 72/D4
Chachro, Pakistan 68/C3
Chaco (prov.), Argentina 143/D2
Chaco (mesa), N. Mex. 274/B3
Chaco (riv.), N. Mex. 274/A2
Chaco (dept.), Paraguay 144/B-C2
Chaco Austral (reg.), Argentina 143/D2
Chaco Boreal (reg.), Paraguay 144/B2-3
Chaco Central (reg.), Argentina 143/D1
Chaco Culture Nat'l Hist. Park, N. Mex. 274/B2
Chacoma, Bolivia 136/A6
Chacon (cape), Alaska 196/N2
Chacon, N. Mex. (87713) 274/D2
Chacuaco (creek), Colo. 208/M8
Chad 2/K5
Chad 102/D3
Chad (lake) 102/D3
CHAD 111/C4
Chad (lake), Chad 111/C5
Chad (lake), Niger 106/G6
Chad (lake), Nigeria 106/G6
Chadan, U.S.S.R. 48/K4
Chadbourn, N.C. (28431) 281/M6
Chadron, Nebr. (69337) 264/B2
Chadwick, Ill. (61014) 222/D1
Chadwick, Mo. (65629) 261/G9
Chadwick Acres, N.C. (†28445) 281/P6
Chadwicks, N.Y. (13319) 276/K4
Chadyr-Lunga, U.S.S.R. 52/C5
Chaffee (co.), Colo. 208/G5
Chaffee, Mo. (63740) 261/N8
Chaffee, N.Y. (14030) 276/C5
Chaffee, N. Dak. (58014) 282/R6
Chaffers (isl.), Chile 138/D5
Chafurray, Colombia 126/D6
Chagai (hills), Afghanistan 68/A3
Chagai, Pakistan 59/H4
Chagai, Pakistan 68/A3
Chagai (hills), Pakistan 68/A3
Chagai (hills), Pakistan 59/H4
Chagda, U.S.S.R. 48/O4
Chaghcharan, Afghanistan 68/B2
Chagoda, U.S.S.R. 52/E3
Chagoness, Sask. 181/G3
Chagos (arch.), Br. Ind. Ocean Terr. 2/N6
Chagos (arch.), Br. Ind. Ocean Terr. 54/J10
Chagrin (riv.), Ohio 284/J8
Chagrin Falls, Ohio (44022) 284/J9
Chaguanas, Trin. & Tob. 161/B10
Chaguaramas, Trin. & Tob. 161/A10
Chaguaramas, Venezuela 124/E3
Chaguaya, Bolivia 136/C7
Chagulak (isl.), Alaska 196/D4
Chahal, Guatemala 154/C3
Chahar Borjak, Afghanistan 59/H3
Chahar Borjak, Afghanistan 68/A2
Chah Bahar, Afghanistan 59/H4
Chah Bahar, Iran 66/M8
Chahuites, Mexico 150/M8
Chai Badan, Thailand 72/D4
Chaibasa, India 68/F4
Chai Buri, Thailand 72/D3
Chainat, Thailand 72/D4
Chain-O-Lakes, Mo. (†65641) 261/E9
Chaira, Laguna (lake), Colombia 126/C7
Chaires, Fla. (†32302) 212/B1
Chaitén, Chile 138/E4
Chaiya, Thailand 72/C5
Chaiyaphum, Thailand 72/D4
Chajarí, Argentina 143/G5
Chajul, Guatemala 154/B3
Chake Chake, Tanzania 115/H5
Chala, Peru 128/E10
Chalais, Switzerland 39/E4
Chalatenango, El Salvador 154/C3
Chalchihuites, Mexico 150/G5
Chalco de Díaz Covarrubias, Mexico 150/M1
Chaleur (bay), New Bruns. 170/E1
Chaleur (bay), Québec 172/C2
Chaleur (bay), Québec 174/D3
Chalfont, Pa. (18914) 294/M5
Chalhuanca, Peru 128/F10
Chaling, China 77/H6
Chalk (creek), Utah 304/C3
Chalk River, Ontario 175/E3
Chalk River, Ontario 177/G1
Chalkyitsik, Alaska (99788) 196/K1
Challacollo, Bolivia 136/B6
Challana, Bolivia 136/A4
Challapata, Bolivia 136/B6
Challenger (mts.), N.W. Terrs. 187/L1
Challis, Idaho (83226) 220/D5
Chalviri (salt dep.), Bolivia 136/B8
Chalmers, Ind. (47929) 227/D3
Chalmette, La. (70043) 238/P4
Chalna Port, Bangladesh 68/F4
Chalonnes-sur-Loire, France 28/C4
Châlons-sur-Marne, France 28/F3
Chalon-sur-Saône, France 28/F4
Chaltel, Cerro (mt.), Chile 138/E8
Chalus, Iran 59/F2
Chalus, Iran 66/G2
Chalybeate, Miss. (38684) 256/G1
Chalybeate Springs, Georgia (†31816) 217/C5
Chalybeate Springs, N.C. (†27526) 281/M3
Cham, Switzerland 39/F2
Cham, W. Germany 22/E4
Chama, Colo. (81126) 208/J8
Chama, N. Mex. (87520) 274/C2
Chaman, Pakistan 68/B2
Chaman, Pakistan 59/J3
Chamba, India 68/D2
Chambal (riv.), India 68/D3
Chambas, Cuba 158/F2
Chamberino, N. Mex. (88027) 274/C6
Chamberlain (creek), Idaho 220/C4
Chamberlain (lake), Maine 243/E3
Chamberlain, Sask. 181/F5
Chamberlain, S. Dak. (57325) 298/L6
Chamberlain, Uruguay 145/C3
Chamberlin, La. (†70767) 238/J1
Chambers (co.), Ala. 195/H5
Chambers, Ariz. (86502) 198/F3
Chambers, Nebr. (68725) 264/F2
Chambers (co.), Texas 303/K8
Chambers (isl.), Wis. 317/M5
Chambersburg, Ill. (62323) 222/C4
Chambersburg, Ind. (†47454) 227/E7
Chambersburg, Ohio (†45631) 284/F8
Chambersburg, Pa. (17201) 294/G6
Chambéry, France 28/F5
Chambeshi (riv.), Zambia 115/F6
Chambeyron (mt.), France 28/G5
Chambeyron (mt.), Italy 34/A2
Chambi, Jebel (mt.), Tunisia 106/F2
Chamblee, Georgia (30341) 217/K1
Chambly (co.), Québec 172/J4
Chambly, Québec 172/J4
Chambord, France 28/D4
Chambord, Québec 172/E1
Chamdo (Qamdo), China 77/E5
Chame (pt.), Panama 154/H6
Chamela (bay), Mexico 150/G7
Chamical, Argentina 143/C3
Chamisal, N. Mex. (87521) 274/D2
Chamizal Nat'l Mem., Texas 303/A10
Chamizo, Uruguay 145/D5
Chamo (lake), Ethiopia 111/G6
Chamois, Mo. (65024) 261/J5
Chamonix-Mont-Blanc, France 28/G5
Chamoson, Switzerland 39/D4
Champ, Mo. (†63042) 261/O2
Champagne (trad. prov.), France 29
Champagne, Yukon 187/E3
Champaign, Ill. 188/J2
Champaign (co.), Ill. 222/E3
Champaign, Ill. (61820) 222/E3
Champaign (co.), Ohio 284/C5
Champasak, Laos 72/E4
Champdani, India 68/F1
Champerico, Guatemala 154/A3
Champéry, Switzerland 39/C4
Champex, Switzerland 39/D4
Champigny-sur-Marne, France 28/C2
Champion, Alberta 182/D4
Champion, Mich. (49814) 250/B2
Champion, Nebr. (69023) 264/C4
Champlain (lake) 188/M2
Champlain, N.Y. (12919) 276/N1
Champlain (lake), N.Y. 276/O1
Champlain (county), Québec 174/C3
Champlain (co.), Québec 172/E2
Champlain, Québec 172/E3
Champlain (lake), Québec 172/D4
Champlain (lake), Vt. 268/A2
Champlain, Va. (22438) 307/O4
Champlain Park, N.Y. (†12901) 276/O1
Champlin, Minn. (55316) 255/G5
Champney's West, Newf. 166/D2
Champotón, Mexico 150/O7
Chamusa, Sierra (mts.), Colombia 126/C6
Chamusca, Portugal 33/B3
Chan, Ko (isl.), Thailand 72/C5
Chana, Ill. (61015) 222/D2
Chañaral, Chile 120/B5
Chañaral, Chile 138/A6
Chañaral (isl.), Chile 138/A7
Chancay, Peru 128/D8
Chance, Ala. (36729) 195/C7
Chance, Ky. (†42728) 237/L7
Chance, Md. (21816) 245/P8
Chance Cove, Newf. 166/D2
Chance Cove (cape), Newf. 166/D2
Chance Harbour, New Bruns. 170/D3
Chancellor, Ala. (36316) 195/G8
Chancellor, Alberta 182/D4
Chancellor, S. Dak. (57015) 298/R7
Chancellorsville, Va. (†22401) 307/N4
Chanco, Chile 138/A11
Chancy, Switzerland 39/A4
Chandalar, Alaska (†99726) 196/J1
Chandalar (riv.), Alaska 196/J1
Chandalar, East Fork (riv.), Alaska 196/J1
Chandeleur (isls.), La. 238/N7
Chandeleur (sound), La. 238/M7
Chanderi, India 68/D4
Chandernagore, India 68/F1
Chandigarh (terr.), India 68/D2
Chandigarh, India 68/D2
Chandler, Ariz. (85224) 198/D5
Chandler, Ind. (47610) 227/C8
Chandler, Minn. (56122) 255/C7
Chandler, Okla. (74834) 288/N3
Chandler, Que. 162/K6
Chandler, Québec 174/E3
Chandler, Québec 172/D2
Chandler, Texas (75758) 303/J5
Chandler Springs, Ala. (†35160) 195/F4
Chandlers Valley, Pa. (16312) 294/D2
Chandlersville, Ohio (43727) 284/G6
Chandlerville, Ill. (62627) 222/C3
Chandmanĭ, Mongolia 77/E2
Chandolin, Switzerland 39/E4
Chandos (lake), Ontario 177/G3
Chandrapur, India 68/D5
Chaneysville, Pa. (†21530) 294/F6
Chang, Ko (isl.), Thailand 72/D4
Changane (riv.), Mozambique 118/E4
Changbaek-sanmaek (mts.), N. Korea 81/D2
Changchih (Changzhi), China 77/H4
Changchow (Zhangzhou), China 77/J7
Changchow (Changzhou), China 77/J5
Changchun, China 77/K3
Changchun, China 54/O5
Changchun, China 2/R3
Changde (Changteh), China 77/H6
Changde, China 54/N7
Change Islands, Newf. 166/D4
Changewater, N.J. (07831) 273/D2
Changhua, China 77/K7
Changhŭng, S. Korea 81/C6
Changji, China 77/C3
Changjiang, China 77/G8
Chang Jiang (Yangtze) (riv.), China 2/Q4
Chang Jiang (Yangtze) (riv.), China 54/N6
Chang Jiang (Yangtze) (riv.), China 77/K5
Changjin (res.), N. Korea 81/C3
Chang Khoeng, Thailand 72/C3
Changling, China 77/K3
Changsha, China 77/H6
Changsha, China 2/Q4
Changsha, China 54/N7
Changshun, China 77/G6
Changsŏng, S. Korea 81/C6
Changteh (Changde), China 77/H6
Changuinola, Panama 154/F6
Changwu, China 77/G4
Changyang, China 77/H5
Changyeh (Zhangye), China 77/F4
Changyŏn, N. Korea 81/B4

Chumbicha 351

Chesterfield, England 10/F4
Chesterfield, Idaho (†83217) 220/G7
Chesterfield, Ill. (62630) 222/D4
Chesterfield, Ind. (46017) 227/F4
Chesterfield (isl.), Madagascar 118/G3
Chesterfield○, Mass. (01012) 249/C3
Chesterfield, Mo. (63017) 261/N2
Chesterfield (isls.), New Caled. 87/F7
Chesterfield○, N.H. (03443) 268/C6
Chesterfield○, N.J. (†08505) 273/D3
Chesterfield (inlet), N.W.T. 146/J3
Chesterfield (inlet), N.W.T. 162/G2
Chesterfield (inlet), N.W. Terrs. 187/J3
Chesterfield (co.), S.C. 296/G2
Chesterfield, S.C. (29709) 296/G2
Chesterfield, Tenn. (†38351) 237/E9
Chesterfield (co.), Va. 307/N6
Chesterfield, Va. (23832) 307/N6
Chesterfield Inlet, N.W.T. 162/G3
Chesterfield Inlet, N.W. Terrs. 187/K3
Chester Gap, Va. (22623) 307/M3
Chester Heights, Pa. (19017) 294/L7
Chesterhill, Ohio (43728) 284/G6
Chester Hill, Pa. (†16866) 294/F4
Chesterland, Ohio (44026) 284/H2
Chester-le-Street, England 10/E3
Chester-le-Street, England 13/J3
Chester Morse (lake), Wash. 310/D3
Chesterton, Ind. (46304) 227/D1
Chestertown, Md. (21620) 245/O4
Chestertown, N.Y. (12817) 276/N3
Chesterville, Ill. (†61911) 222/E4
Chesterville, Maine (†04938) 243/C6
Chesterville○, Maine (†04938) 243/C6
Chesterville, Md. (†21651) 245/P3
Chesterville, Ohio (43317) 284/E5
Chesterville, Ontario 177/J2
Chesterville, Québec 172/F4
Chestnut, Ala. (†36425) 195/D7
Chestnut, Ill. (62518) 222/D3
Chestnut, La. (71017) 238/D2
Chestnut Hill, Conn. (†06249) 210/G2
Chestnut Mound, Tenn. (38552) 237/K8
Chest Springs, Pa. (16624) 294/E4
Chesuncook, Maine (†04478) 243/D3
Chesuncook (lake), Maine 243/E3
Cheswick, Pa. (15024) 294/C6
Cheswold, Del. (19936) 245/R4
Chetac (lake), Wis. 317/D4
Chetco (riv.), Oreg. 291/C5
Chetek, Wis. (54728) 317/C5
Chéticamp, Nova Scotia 168/G2
Chéticamp (isl.), Nova Scotia 168/G2
Chetlat (isl.), India 68/C6
Chetopa, Kansas (67336) 232/G4
Chetumal, Mexico 150/Q7
Chetumal (bay), Mexico 150/P8
Chetwynd, Br. Col. 184/G2
Chevak, Alaska (99563) 196/E2
Cheval Blanc (pt.), Haiti 158/B5
Chevelon (creek), Ariz. 198/E4
Cheverly, Md. (20785) 245/G4
Cheville (pass), Switzerland 39/D4
Cheviot (hills), England 13/E2
Cheviot, The (mt.), England 13/E2
Cheviot, N. Zealand 100/D5
Cheviot, Ohio (†45211) 284/B9
Cheviot (hills), Scotland 15/F5
Cheviot, The (mt.), Scotland 15/F5
Chevrolet, Ky. (40817) 237/P7
Chevy Chase, Md. (20815) 245/E4
Chevy Chase Section Four, Md. (†20015) 245/E4
Chewack (riv.), Wash. 310/E2
Chewalla, Tenn. (38393) 237/D10
Chewelah, Wash. (99109) 310/H2
Chewsville, Md. (21721) 245/H2
Chexbres, Switzerland 39/C3
Cheyenne (riv.) 188/F2
Cheyenne (co.), Colo. 208/O5
Cheyenne (co.), Kansas 232/A2
Cheyenne (co.), Nebr. 264/A3
Cheyenne, Okla. (73628) 288/G3
Cheyenne (riv.), S. Dak. 298/F4
Cheyenne (riv.), U.S. 146/H5
Cheyenne (cap.), Wyo. 146/H5
Cheyenne (cap.), Wyo. 188/E2
Cheyenne (cap.), Wyo. (82001) 319/H4
Cheyenne (riv.), Wyo. 319/H2
Cheyenne Bottoms (lake), Kansas 232/D3
Cheyenne River Ind. Res., S. Dak. 298/F4
Cheyenne Wells, Colo. (80810) 208/P5
Cheyne (bay), W. Australia 92/B6
Cheyney, Pa. (19319) 294/M6
Cheyres, Switzerland 39/C3
Chezacut, Br. Col. 184/F4
Chhatarpur, India 68/D4
Chhindwara, India 68/D4
Chi, Mae Nam (riv.), Thailand 72/D3
Chiai, China 77/K7
Chiambone, Somalia 115/H4
Chiang Dao, Thailand 72/C3
Chiange, Angola 115/B7
Chiang Khan, Thailand 72/D3
Chiang Mai, Thailand 72/C3
Chiang Mai, Thailand 54/L8
Chiang Rai, Thailand 72/C3
Chiang Saen, Thailand 72/C2
Chiapa de Corzo, Mexico 150/N8
Chiapas (state), Mexico 150/N8
Chiari, Italy 34/C2
Chiasso, Switzerland 39/G5
Chiatura, U.S.S.R. 52/F6
Chiautempan, Mexico 150/N1
Chiavari, Italy 34/B2
Chiba (pref.), Japan 81/P2
Chiba, Japan 81/P2
Chibabava, Mozambique 118/E4
Chibia, Angola 115/B7
Chiblow (lake), Ontario 177/A1
Chibougamau, Québec 174/C3
Chibougamau, Que. 162/J6
Chibukak (cape), Alaska 196/D2
Chibuto, Mozambique 118/E4
Chibwe, Zambia 115/E6
Chicago, Ill. 146/K5
Chicago, Ill. 188/J2
Chicago, Ill. (*60601) 222/C5
Chicago, North Branch (riv.), Ill. 222/B5
Chicago, U.S. 2/E3
Chicago Heights, Ill. (60411) 222/C6
Chicago Portage Nat'l Hist. Site, Ill. 222/B6
Chicago Ridge, Ill. (60415) 222/B6
Chicama, Peru 128/C6
Chicamacomico (riv.), Md. 245/P7
Chicamocha (riv.), Colombia 126/D4
Chicanán (riv.), Venezuela 124/H4
Chicapa (riv.), Angola 115/D5
Chicapa (riv.), Zaire 115/D5
Chic-Chocs (mts.), Québec 172/C1
Chichagof (isl.) Alaska 188/D6
Chichagof (isl.), Alaska 196/M1
Chichén-Itzá (ruin), Mexico 150/P6
Chichester, England 13/G7
Chichester, England 10/F5
Chichester○, N.H. (†03258) 268/E5
Chichester, N.Y. (12416) 276/M6
Chichi (isl.), Japan 87/E3
Chichi (isl.), Japan 81/M3
Chichibu, Japan 81/J5
Chichibu-Tama National Park, Japan 81/J6
Chichicaste, Honduras 154/E3
Chichicastenango, Guatemala 154/B3
Chichigalpa, Nicaragua 154/D4
Chichiriviche, Venezuela 124/D2
Chickalah, Ark. (†72833) 202/D3
Chickaloon, Alaska (†99645) 196/C1
Chickamauga, Georgia (30707) 217/B1
Chickamauga (lake), Tenn. 188/J3
Chickamauga (dam), Tenn. 237/L10
Chickamauga (lake), Tenn. 237/L10
Chickamauga and Chattanooga Nat'l Mil. Park, Georgia 217/B1
Chickamaw Beach, Minn. (†56474) 255/D4
Chickasaw, Ala. (36611) 195/B9
Chickasaw (co.), Iowa 229/J2
Chickasaw (co.), Miss. 256/G3
Chickasaw, Ohio (45826) 284/A5
Chickasawhay (riv.), Miss. 256/G7
Chickasaw Village, Natchez Trace Pkwy., Miss. 256/G2
Chickasha, Okla. 188/G4
Chickasha, Okla. (73018) 288/L4
Chickasha (lake), Okla. 288/K4
Chicken, Alaska (99732) 196/K2
Chiclana de la Frontera, Spain 33/C4
Chiclayo, Peru 128/C6
Chiclayo, Peru 120/B3
Chico (riv.), Argentina 120/C7
Chico (riv.), Argentina 143/C6
Chico (riv.), Argentina 143/C5
Chico, Calif. (95926) 204/D4
Chico, Mont. (†59027) 262/F5
Chico (riv.), Philippines 82/C2
Chico, Texas (76030) 303/G4
Chicoana, Argentina 143/C2
Chico Arroyo (creek), N. Mex. 274/B3
Chicopee, Kansas (†66762) 232/H4
Chicopee, Mass. (*01013) 249/D4
Chicopee (riv.), Mass. 249/D4
Chicora, Miss. (†39322) 256/G7
Chicora, Pa. (16025) 294/C4
Chicot (co.), Ark. 202/H7
Chicot, Ark. (†71640) 202/H7
Chicot (pt.), La. 238/M7
Chicoutimi, Que. 162/J6
Chicoutimi, Que. 146/L5
Chicoutimi (county), Québec 174/C2
Chicoutimi (co.), Québec 172/G1
Chicoutimi, Québec 172/G1
Chicoutimi, Québec 174/C3
Chicoutimi (riv.), Québec 172/F2
Chicoutimi-Nord, Québec 172/F1
Chicualacuala, Mozambique 118/E4
Chidambaram, India 68/E6
Chidester, Ark. (71726) 202/D6
Chidley (cape), Canada 146/M3
Chidley (cape), Newf. 166/B1
Chidley (cape), Newf. 162/K3
Chidley (cape), N.W. Terrs. 187/M3
Chidlow, W. Australia 88/B2
Chief Joseph (dam), Wash. 310/F3
Chiefland, Fla. (32626) 212/D2
Chiefs (pt.), Ontario 177/C3
Chiemsee (lake), W. Germany 22/E5
Chienti (riv.), Italy 34/D3
Chieri, Italy 34/A2
Chieti (prov.), Italy 34/E3
Chieti, Italy 34/E3
Chietla, Mexico 150/M2
Chièvres, Belgium 27/D7
Chifeng, China 77/J3
Chigasaki, Japan 81/O3
Chiginagak (mt.), Alaska 196/G3
Chignahuapan, Mexico 150/N1
Chignecto (bay), New Bruns. 170/F3
Chignecto (bay), Nova Scotia 168/D3
Chignecto (cape), Nova Scotia 168/C3
Chignecto (isth.), Nova Scotia 168/D3
Chignik, Alaska (†99613) 196/G3
Chignik (bay), Alaska 196/G3
Chignik Lagoon, Alaska (99565) 196/G3
Chignik Lake, Alaska (†99613) 196/G3
Chiguana, Bolivia 136/A7
Chigubo, Mozambique 118/E4
Chigwell, England 13/H8
Chigwell, England 10/C5
Chihuahua (state), Mexico 150/F2
Chihuahua, Mexico 150/F2
Chihuahua, Mexico 146/H7
Chikaskia (riv.), Kansas 232/E4
Chik Ballapur, India 68/D6
Chikmagalur, India 68/D6
Chilanga, Zambia 115/E7
Chilanko Forks, Br. Col. 184/E4
Chilapa de Álvarez, Mexico 150/K8
Chilas, Pakistan 68/C1
Chilas, Pakistan 59/K2
Chilca (Pucusana), Peru 128/D9
Chilcoot, Calif. (96105) 204/E4
Chilcotin (riv.), Br. Col. 184/E4
Childers, Queensland 88/J5
Childersburg, Ala. (35044) 195/F4
Childress (co.), Texas 303/D3
Childress, Texas (79201) 303/D3
Childs (lake), Manitoba 179/A3
Childs, Md. (21916) 245/P2
Childwold, N.Y. (12922) 276/L2
Chile 2/F7
Chile 120/B5
CHILE 138
Chile Chico, Chile 138/E6
Chilecito, Argentina 143/C2
Chiles, Colombia 126/A7
Chilete, Peru 128/C6
Chilga, Ethiopia 111/G5
Chilhowee, Mo. (64733) 261/E5
Chilhowee (mt.), Tenn. 237/O9
Chilhowie, Va. (24319) 307/E7
Chili, Ind. (46926) 227/F3
Chili, Wis. (54420) 317/F6
Chililabombwe, Zambia 115/E6
Chililabombwe, Zambia 102/E6
Chilili, N. Mex. (†87059) 274/C4
Chilka (lake), India 68/F5
Chilko (lake), Br. Col. 184/F4
Chilko (riv.), Br. Col. 184/E4
Chilkoot (pass), Alaska 196/M1
Chilkoot (pass), Br. Col. 184/J1
Chillán, Chile 120/B6
Chillán, Chile 138/A11
Chillicothe, Ill. (61523) 222/D3
Chillicothe, Iowa (52548) 229/J6
Chillicothe, Mo. (64601) 261/E3
Chillicothe, Ohio (45601) 284/E7
Chillicothe, Texas (79225) 303/E3
Chilliwack, Br. Col. 162/D6
Chilliwack, Br. Col. 184/M3
Chillum, Md. (20783) 245/F4
Chilmark○, Mass. (02535) 249/M7
Chilo, Ohio (45112) 284/B8
Chilocco, Okla. (74635) 288/M1
Chiloé (isl.), Chile 120/B7
Chiloé (isl.), Chile 138/D4
Chiloquin, Oreg. (97624) 291/F5
Chilpancingo de los Bravos, Mexico 150/K8
Chiltern (hills), England 13/G6
Chilton (co.), Ala. 195/E5
Chilton, Texas (76632) 303/G6
Chilton, Wis. (53014) 317/K7
Chiltonville, Mass. (†02360) 249/M5
Chilumba, Malawi 115/F6
Chilwa (lake), Malawi 115/G7
Chilwa (lake), Mozambique 118/F3
Chimacum, Wash. (98325) 310/C3
Chimaltenango, Guatemala 154/B3
Chimán, Panama 154/H6
Chimantá-tepuí (mt.), Venezuela 124/G5
Chimay, Belgium 27/E8
Chimayo, N. Mex. (87522) 274/D3
Chimbarongo, Chile 138/A10
Chimbay, U.S.S.R. 48/F5
Chimborazo (prov.), Ecuador 128/C3
Chimborazo (mt.), Ecuador 120/B3
Chimborazo (mt.), Ecuador 128/C3
Chimbote, Peru 120/B3
Chimbote, Peru 128/C7
Chimbote (bay), Peru 128/C7
Chimichaqua, Colombia 126/D3
Chimkent, U.S.S.R. 54/H5
Chimkent, U.S.S.R. 48/H5
Chimney Point, Vt. (†05491) 268/A3
Chimney Rock, Colo. (81127) 208/E8
Chimney Rock Nat'l Hist. Site, Nebr. 264/A3
Chimoio, Mozambique 118/E3
Chimoio, Mozambique 102/F6
Chin, Alberta 182/D5
Chin (state), Burma 72/B2
Chin (hills), Burma 72/B2
Chin (cape), Ontario 177/C2
China 2/P4
China 54/L6
CHINA 85
CHINA 77
China, Maine (04926) 243/E7
China○, Maine (04926) 243/E7
Chiná, Campeche, Mexico 150/O7
China, Nuevo León, Mexico 150/K4
Chinácota, Colombia 126/D4
China Gardens (dam), Wash. 310/J4
China Grove, Ala. (†36081) 195/G7
China Grove, N.C. (28023) 281/H3
China Grove, Texas (†78201) 303/K11
China Lake, Calif. (†93555) 204/H8
China Lake Naval Weapons Center, Calif. 204/H8
Chinameca, El Salvador 154/C4
Chinandega, Nicaragua 154/D4
Chinati (mts.), Texas 303/C12
Chinati (peak), Texas 303/C12
Chincha (isls.), Peru 128/D9
Chincha Alta, Peru 128/D9
Chincha Alta, Peru 120/B4
Chinchaga (riv.), Alberta 182/A5
Chinchilla, Pa. (18410) 294/F6
Chinchilla, Queensland 88/J5
Chinchilla de Monte-Aragón, Spain 33/F3
Chinchiná, Colombia 126/C5
Chinchón, Spain 33/G5
Chinchoua, Gabon 115/A4
Chinchow (Jinzhou), China 77/K3
Chincoteague (bay), Md. 245/S8
Chincoteague, Va. (23336) 307/T5
Chincoteague (bay), Va. 307/T4
Chincoteague (inlet), Va. 307/T5
Chinde, Mozambique 118/F3
Chinde, Mozambique 102/F6
Chindu, China 77/E5
Chindwin (riv.), Burma 72/B2
Chinese Camp, Calif. (95309) 204/E6
Chingleput, India 68/E6
Chingola, Zambia 115/E6
Chingola, Zambia 102/E6
Chinguar, Angola 115/C6
Chinguetti, Mauritania 106/B4
Chinhae, S. Korea 81/D6
Chiniak (cape), Alaska 196/H3
Chiñijo, Bolivia 136/A4
Chiniot, Pakistan 68/C2
Chinipas, Mexico 150/E3
Chinju, S. Korea 81/D6
Chinkapin Knob (mt.), Ark. 202/E2
Chinkiang (Zhenjiang), China 77/J5
Chinle, Ariz. (86503) 198/F2
Chinle (creek), Ariz. 198/F2
Chinle (valley), Ariz. 198/F2
Chinle (creek), Utah 304/E6
Chinle Wash (dry riv.), Ariz. 198/F2
Chino (valley), Ariz. 198/C3
Chino, Calif. (91710) 204/D10
Chinon, France 28/D4
Chinook, Alberta 182/E4
Chinook, Mont. (59523) 262/G2
Chinook (lake), Oreg. 291/F3
Chinook, Wash. (98614) 310/B4
Chinook (pass), Wash. 310/D4
Chinook Valley, Alberta 182/B1
Chino Valley, Ariz. (86323) 198/C4
Chinquapin, N.C. (28521) 281/O5
Chinsali, Zambia 115/F6
Chinsi (Jinxi), China 77/K3
Chintheche, Malawi 115/F6
Chinú, Colombia 126/C3
Chinwangtao (Qinhuangdao), China 77/K4
Chiny, Belgium 27/G9
Chioggia, Italy 34/D2
Chip (lake), Alberta 182/C3
Chipamanu (riv.), Bolivia 136/A2
Chipata, Zambia 115/F6
Chipata, Zambia 102/F6
Chipewyan (lake), Alberta 182/D1
Chipewyan (riv.), Alberta 182/D1
Chipewyan Lake, Alberta 182/D1
Chipindo, Angola 102/D6
Chipindo, Angola 115/C6
Chipinga, Zimbabwe 118/E4
Chipley, Fla. (32428) 212/D6
Chiplun, India 68/C5
Chipman, Alberta 182/D3
Chipman, New Bruns. 170/E2
Chipman (riv.), Sask. 181/M2
Chipoka, Malawi 115/F6
Chipola (riv.), Fla. 212/D6
Chipola, La. (†70441) 238/J5
Chippenham, England 13/E6
Chippenham, England 10/F5
Chippewa (co.), Mich. 250/E2
Chippewa (riv.), Mich. 250/E5
Chippewa (co.), Minn. 255/C5
Chippewa (riv.), Minn. 255/C5
Chippewa (riv.), Wis. 188/H1
Chippewa (co.), Wis. 317/D5
Chippewa (lake), Wis. 317/D4
Chippewa (riv.), Wis. 317/B7
Chippewa Falls, Wis. (54729) 317/D6
Chippewa Lake, Mich. (49320) 250/D5
Chipping Norton, England 13/F6
Chippis, Switzerland 39/E4
Chiputneticook (lakes), Maine 243/H4
Chiputneticook (lakes), New Bruns. 170/C3
Chiquián, Peru 128/D8
Chiquimula, Guatemala 154/C3
Chiquinquirá, Colombia 126/C5
Chiquita (lake), Argentina 120/C6
Chir (riv.), U.S.S.R. 52/F5
Chira (riv.) 120/A3
Chira (riv.), Ecuador 128/B5
Chirala, India 68/E5
Chirchik, U.S.S.R. 48/H5
Chireno, Texas (75937) 303/K6
Chirfa, Niger 106/G4
Chiri (mt.), S. Korea 81/C6
Chiribiquete, Sierra de (mts.), Colombia 126/D7
Chiricahua (mts.), Ariz. 198/F6
Chiricahua Nat'l Mon., Ariz. 198/F6
Chiriguaná, Colombia 126/D3
Chirikof (isl.), Alaska 196/G3
Chirinos, Peru 128/C5
Chiriquí (gulf), Panama 154/F7
Chiriquí (lag.), Panama 154/G6
Chiriquí Grande, Panama 154/F6
Chirk, Wales 13/D5
Chirnside, Scotland 15/F5
Chiromo, Malawi 115/F7
Chironico, Switzerland 39/G4
Chirpan, Bulgaria 45/G4
Chirripó Grande (mt.), C. Rica 154/F6
Chirundu, Zimbabwe 118/D3
Chisago (co.), Minn. 255/F5
Chisago City, Minn. (55013) 255/E5
Chisamba, Zambia 115/E6
Chisana, Alaska (†99566) 196/K2
Chisec, Guatemala 154/B3
Chisholm, Maine (†04239) 243/C7
Chisholm, Minn. (55719) 255/E3
Chisholm Mills, Alberta 182/C2
Chishui, China 77/G6
Chisimayu, Somalia 115/H4
Chisimayu, Somalia 102/G5
Chişineu Criş, Romania 45/E2
Chismville, Ark. (†72943) 202/C3
Chisos (mts.), Texas 303/A8
Chistochina, Alaska (†99586) 196/K2
Chistopol', U.S.S.R. 52/H3
Chiswick, Ontario 177/E1
Chita, U.S.S.R. 54/N4
Chita, U.S.S.R. 48/M4
Chitado, Angola 115/B7
Chitado, Namibia 118/A3
Chitek (lake), Manitoba 179/C2
Chitek (lake), Sask. 181/D2
Chitek Lake, Sask. 181/D2
Chitembo, Angola 115/C6
Chitina, Alaska (99566) 196/K2
Chitina (riv.), Alaska 196/K2
Chitipa, Malawi 115/F5
Chitorgarh, India 68/C4
Chitose, Japan 81/K2
Chitradurga, India 68/D6
Chitral, Pakistan 59/K2
Chitral, Pakistan 68/C1
Chitré, Panama 154/G7
Chittagong, Bangladesh 54/L7
Chittagong, Bangladesh 68/G4
Chittenango, N.Y. (13037) 276/J4
Chittenden (co.), Vt. 268/A3
Chittenden○, Vt. (05737) 268/B4
Chittenden (res.), Vt. 268/B4
Chittering, W. Australia 88/B6
Chittoor, India 68/D6
Chiumbe (riv.), Angola 115/D5
Chiva, Spain 33/F3
Chivacoa, Venezuela 124/D2
Chivapure (riv.), Venezuela 124/E4
Chivasso, Italy 34/A2
Chivato (mesa), N. Mex. 274/B3
Chivay, Peru 128/G10
Chive, Bolivia 136/A3
Chivilcoy, Argentina 143/F7
Chivilcoy, Argentina 120/C6
Chivington, Colo. (81031) 208/O6
Chiwawa (riv.), Wash. 310/E2
Chixoy (riv.), Guatemala 154/B2
Chizha, U.S.S.R. 52/F1
Chloe, W. Va. (25235) 312/D5
Chloride, Ariz. (86431) 198/A3
Chloride, Mo. (†63646) 261/L8
Chlumec, Czech. 41/C1
Choam Khsant, Cambodia 72/E4
Choapa, Chile 138/A9
Choapa (riv.), Chile 138/A9
Choate, Br. Col. 184/M3
Chobe (riv.), Botswana 118/C3
Chobe (riv.), Namibia 118/C3
Chobe Nat'l Park, Botswana 118/D3
Choc, St. Lucia 161/G5
Choc (bay), St. Lucia 161/G5
Chocalán, Chile 138/F4
Chocaya, Bolivia 136/B7
Choccolocco, Ala. (36254) 195/G3
Choceň, Czech. 41/D1
Choch'iwŏn, S. Korea 81/C5
Chocó (dept.), Colombia 126/B4
Chocó (bay), Colombia 126/B6
Chocolate (mts.), Ariz. 198/A5
Chocolate (mts.), Calif. 204/K10
Chocomán, Mexico 150/P2
Choconut, Pa. (†18818) 294/K2
Chocorua, N.H. (03817) 268/E4
Chocorua (mt.), N.H. 268/E4
Chocowinity, N.C. (27817) 281/P4
Choctaw (co.), Ala. 195/B6
Choctaw, Ala. (36905) 195/B6
Choctaw, Ark. (72028) 202/F2
Choctaw (co.), Miss. 256/F4
Choctaw (co.), Okla. 288/P6
Choctaw, Okla. (73020) 288/M3
Choctaw Bluff, Ala. (†36545) 195/C8
Choctawhatchee (riv.), Ala. 195/H8
Choctawhatchee (bay), Fla. 212/C6
Choctawhatchee (riv.), Fla. 212/C6
Choctaw Ind. Res., Miss. 256/F6
Chodov, Czech. 41/B1
Chodziez, Poland 47/C2
Choele-Choel, Argentina 143/C4
Choele-Choel, Argentina 120/C6
Choestoe, Georgia (†30512) 217/E1
Chofu, Japan 81/O2
Choiceland, Sask. 181/G2
Choiseul (sound), 143/E7
Choiseul, St. Lucia 161/F7
Choiseul (isl.), Solomon Is. 87/F6
Choiseul (isl.), Solomon Is. 86/D2
Choisy-le-Roi, France 28/B2
Choix, Mexico 150/E3
Chojna, Poland 47/B2
Chojnice, Poland 47/C2
Chojnów, Poland 47/B3
Chokai (mt.), Japan 81/J4
Choklo, Minn. (56221) 255/B5
Chokoloskee, Fla. (33925) 212/E6
Chokurdakh, U.S.S.R. 4/B2
Chokurdakh, U.S.S.R. 54/R2
Chokurdakh, U.S.S.R. 48/P2
Cholame, Calif. (93431) 204/E8
Cholet, France 28/C4
Choloma, Honduras 154/C3
Cholula de Rivadavia, Mexico 150/M1
Choluteca, Honduras 154/D4
Choluteca (riv.), Honduras 154/D4
Choma, Zambia 115/E7
Choma, Zambia 102/E6
Chomes, C. Rica 154/E5
Chomo Lhari (mt.), Bhutan 68/F3
Chomutov, Czech. 41/B1
Ch'ŏnan, S. Korea 81/C5
Chon Buri, Thailand 72/D4
Chonchi, Chile 138/D4
Ch'ŏnch'ŏn, N. Korea 81/C3
Chone, Ecuador 128/B3
Ch'ŏngjin, N. Korea 54/P5
Ch'ŏngjin, N. Korea 81/E3
Chŏngju, N. Korea 81/B4
Ch'ŏngju, S. Korea 81/C5
Chongqing (Chungking), China 77/G6
Chongqing, China 2/P4
Chongqing, China 54/M7
Chŏngŭp, S. Korea 81/C6
Chongyang, China 77/H6
Chongzuo, China 77/G7
Chŏnju, S. Korea 81/C6
Chon May, Vung (bay), Vietnam 72/F3
Chonos (arch.), Chile 120/B7
Chonos (arch.), Chile 138/D6
Chopin, La. (71412) 238/E4
Chopin (lake), Québec 172/B2
Choptank (riv.), Del. 245/P5
Choptank, Md. (†21655) 245/P6
Choptank (riv.), Md. 245/P6
Choquecota, Bolivia 136/A6
Chorley, England 10/G2
Chorley, England 13/G2
Chorleywood, England 13/G7
Chorleywood, England 10/A5
Choroni, Venezuela 124/E2
Choros (cape), Chile 138/A7
Choros, Los (riv.), Chile 138/A7
Chortitz, Sask. 181/D5
Chortkov, U.S.S.R. 52/B5
Ch'ŏrwŏn, S. Korea 81/C4
Chorzele, Poland 47/E2
Chorzów, Poland 47/B4
Ch'osan, N. Korea 81/C3
Choshi, Japan 81/K6
Chosica, Peru 128/D8
Chos-Malal, Argentina 143/C4
Choszczno, Poland 47/B2
Chota, Peru 128/C6
Choteau, Mont. (59422) 262/D3
Choteau (creek), S. Dak. 298/N7
Chotěboř, Czech. 41/C2
Choudrant, La. (71227) 238/F1
Chouteau (co.), Mont. 262/F3
Chouteau, Okla. (74337) 288/R2
Chovoreca, Cerro (mt.), Bolivia 136/F6
Chovoreca (mt.), Paraguay 144/C1
Chowan (co.), N.C. 281/R2
Chowan (riv.), N.C. 281/R2
Chowchilla, Calif. (93610) 204/E6
Choybalsan, Mongolia 54/N5
Choybalsan, Mongolia 77/J2
Chrastava, Czech. 41/C1
Chriesman, Texas (77838) 303/H7
Chrisman, Ill. (61924) 222/F4
Chrisney, Ind. (47611) 227/C8
Christchurch, England 10/F5
Christchurch, England 13/F7
Christchurch, N. Zealand 2/T8
Christchurch, N. Zealand 100/D5
Christian (sound), Alaska 196/M2
Christian (co.), Ill. 222/D4
Christian (co.), Ky. 237/F7
Christian (co.), Mo. 261/F9
Christian (cape), N.W. Terrs. 187/M2
Christian (isl.), Ontario 177/D3
Christian, W. Va. (†25135) 312/C7
Christiana, Del. (†19711) 245/R2
Christiana, Jamaica 158/H6
Christiana, Pa. (17509) 294/K6
Christiana, S. Africa 118/D5
Christiana, Tenn. (37037) 237/J9
Christiansburg, Ohio (45389) 284/C5
Christiansburg, Va. (24073) 307/H6
Christiansfeld, Denmark 21/C7
Christiansted, Virgin Is. (U.S.) 156/H2
Christiansted, Virgin Is. (U.S.) 161/F4
Christiansted Nat'l Hist. Site, Virgin Is. (U.S.) 161/F4
Christie, Okla. (†74965) 288/S3
Christina (lake), Alberta 182/E2
Christina (riv.), Alberta 182/E1
Christina (lake), Minn. 255/C4
Christina, Mont. (59423) 262/G3
Christina Lake, Br. Col. 184/H5
Christine, N. Dak. (58015) 282/S6
Christine, Texas (78012) 303/F9
Christmas, Ariz. (†85292) 198/E5
Christmas (isl.), Australia 54/M11
Christmas (isl.), Australia 2/Q6
Christmas, Fla. (32709) 212/E3
Christmas (isl.), Kiribati 87/L5
Christmas, Mich. (49862) 250/C2
Christmas (lake), Oreg. 291/G4
Christmas (riv.), W. Australia 88/D3
Christmas Creek, W. Australia 92/D2
Christmas Island, Nova Scotia 168/H3
Christopher, Ill. (62822) 222/D6
Christopher Lake, Sask. 181/F2
Christoval, Texas (76935) 303/D6
Chromo, Colo. (81128) 208/F8
Chrudim, Czech. 41/C2
Chrudimka (riv.), Czech. 41/C2
Chrysler, Ala. (†36550) 195/C8
Chryston, Scotland 15/C2
Chrzanów, Poland 47/D4
Chu (riv.), U.S.S.R. 48/H5
Chualar, Calif. (93925) 204/D7
Chüanchow (Quanzhou), China 77/J7
Chuathbaluk, Alaska (†99559) 196/G2
Chubbuck, Idaho (83202) 220/F7
Chubu-Sangaku National Park, Japan 81/H5
Chubut (prov.), Argentina 143/C5
Chubut (riv.), Argentina 120/C7
Chubut (riv.), Argentina 143/C5
Chuchi (lake), Br. Col. 184/E2
Chuchow (Zhuzhou), China 77/H6
Chuckey, Tenn. (37641) 237/R8
Chucunaque (riv.), Panama 154/J6
Chudleigh, Tasmania 99/C3
Chudovo, U.S.S.R. 52/D3
Chugach (isls.), Alaska 196/B2
Chugash (mts.), Alaska 196/C1
Chugiak, Alaska (99567) 196/C1
Chuginadak (isl.), Alaska 196/D4
Chuguchak (Tacheng), China 77/B2
Chugwater, Wyo. (82210) 319/H4
Chugwater (creek), Wyo. 319/H4
Chukai, Malaysia 72/D6
Chukchi (sea) 4/C18
Chukchi (sea) 54/W3
Chukchi (sea), Alaska 196/E1
Chukchi (pen.), U.S.S.R. 54/V3
Chukchi (pen.), U.S.S.R. 4/C18
Chukchi (pen.), U.S.S.R. 48/T3
Chukchi (sea), U.S.S.R. 48/T2
Chukchi Aut. Okr., U.S.S.R. 48/R3
Chukhloma, U.S.S.R. 52/F3
Chula, Ark. (†72857) 202/C4
Chula, Georgia (31733) 217/E7
Chula, Mo. (64635) 261/F3
Chula, Va. (†23002) 307/N6
Chu Lai, Vietnam 72/F4
Chula Vista, Calif. (*92010) 204/J11
Chulucanas, Peru 128/B5
Chulumani, Bolivia 136/B5
Chulym (riv.), U.S.S.R. 48/J4
Chuma, Bolivia 136/A4
Chumatien (Zhumadian), China 77/H5
Chumbicha, Argentina 143/C2

352 Chumikan

Chumikan, U.S.S.R. 48/O4
Chumphon, Thailand 72/C5
Chuna (riv.), U.S.S.R. 48/K4
Chunchi, Ecuador 128/C4
Ch'unch'ŏn, S. Korea 81/D5
Chunchula, Ala. (36521) 195/B9
Ch'ungju, S. Korea 81/C5
Chungking (Chongqing), China 77/G6
Chŭngsan, N. Korea 81/B4
Chungshan (Zhongshan), China 77/H7
Chunky, Miss. (39323) 256/G6
Chunya, Tanzania 115/F5
Chunya (riv.), U.S.S.R. 48/K3
Chupaca, Peru 128/E9
Chupadera (mesa), N. Mex. 274/C5
Chupara (pt.), Trin. & Tob. 161/B10
Chuquibamba, Peru 128/F10
Chuquibambilla, Peru 128/F9
Chuquicamata, Chile 138/B3
Chuquichambi, Bolivia 136/B5
Chuquisaca (dept.), Bolivia 136/C6
Chur, Switzerland 39/J3
Churachandpur, India 68/G4
Church, Iowa (†52151) 229/L2
Churchbridge, Sask. 181/J5
Church Creek, Md. (21622) 245/O6
Church Hill, Md. (21623) 245/O4
Church Hill, Miss. (39055) 256/B7
Church Hill, Tenn. (37642) 237/R7
Churchill (riv.) 162/G4
Churchill (pk.), Br. Col. 162/D4
Churchill (peak), Br. Col. 184/L2
Churchill (riv.), Canada 146/J4
Churchill, Man. 146/J4
Churchill, Man. 162/G4
Churchill (cape), Man. 162/G4
Churchill, Manitoba 179/K2
Churchill (cape), Manitoba 179/K2
Churchill (riv.), Manitoba 179/J2
Churchill (co.), Nev. 266/C3
Churchill (falls), Newf. 166/B3
Churchill (riv.), Newf. 166/B3
Churchill, Pa. (†15235) 294/C7
Churchill (riv.), Que. 162/K5
Churchill (riv.), Sask. 181/M3
Churchill, Victoria 97/D6
Churchill Falls, Newf. 166/B3
Churchman (mt.), W. Australia 92/B5
Church Point, La. (70525) 238/F6
Church Point, Nova Scotia 168/B4
Church's Ferry, N. Dak. (58325) 282/M3
Church Stretton, England 13/E5
Churchton, Md. (20733) 245/N5
Churchtown, Pa. (†17555) 294/L5
Church View, Va. (23032) 307/P5
Churchville, Md. (21028) 245/N2
Churchville, N.Y. (14428) 276/E4
Churchville, Va. (24421) 307/K4
Churchville, W. Va. (†26338) 312/E4
Churdan, Iowa (50050) 229/D4
Churfirsten (mt.), Switzerland 39/H2
Churín, Peru 128/D8
Churu, India 68/D3
Churubusco, Ind. (46723) 227/G2
Churubusco, N.Y. (12923) 276/N1
Churuguara, Venezuela 124/D2
Churwalden, Switzerland 39/J3
Chushul, India 68/D2
Chuska (mts.), N. Mex. 274/A2
Chusovoy, U.S.S.R. 52/J3
Chute-à-Blondeau, Ontario 177/K2
Chute-aux-Outardes, Québec 172/A1
Chute-des-Passes, Québec 174/C3
Chute-Saint-Philippe, Québec 172/B3
Chuvash A.S.S.R., U.S.S.R. 48/E4
Chuvash A.S.S.R., U.S.S.R. 52/G3
Chu Xian, China 77/J5
Chuxiong, China 77/F7
Chuy, Uruguay 145/F4
Chvalšiny, Czech. 41/C2
Ciales, P. Rico 161/C1
Ciamis, Indonesia 85/H2
Ciampino, Italy 34/F7
Cianjur, Indonesia 85/H2
Cibecue, Ariz. (85911) 198/E4
Cibola (co.), N.Mex. 274/B3
Cibolo, Texas (78108) 303/K10
Cibolo (creek), Texas 303/K11
Çiçekdagı, Turkey 63/F3
Cicero, Ill. (60650) 222/B5
Cicero, Ind. (46034) 227/E4
Cicero Dantas, Brazil 132/G5
Cicerone, W. Va. (†25243) 312/D5
Ciconsine (lake), Québec 172/D2
Cid, N.C. (†27292) 281/J3
Cide, Turkey 63/E2
Cidlina (riv.), Czech. 41/C1
Cidra, Cuba 158/D1
Cidra, P. Rico 161/D2
Ciechanów (prov.), Poland 47/E2
Ciechanów, Poland 47/E2
Ciechocinek, Poland 47/D2
Ciego de Ávila (prov.), Cuba 158/F2
Ciego de Ávila, Cuba 156/B2
Ciego de Ávila, Cuba 158/F2
Ciempozuelos, Spain 33/F5
Ciénaga, Colombia 120/B1
Ciénaga, Colombia 126/C2
Ciénaga de Oro, Colombia 126/C3
Cienfuegos (prov.), Cuba 158/E2
Cienfuegos, Cuba 156/B2
Cienfuegos, Cuba 146/K7
Cienfuegos, Cuba 158/D2
Cienfuegos (bay), Cuba 158/D2
Cieplice Sląskie-Zdrój, Poland 47/B3
Čierny Balog, Czech. 41/E2
Cieszyn, Poland 47/D4
Cieza, Spain 33/F3
Çifteler, Turkey 63/D3
Cifuentes, Spain 33/E2
Cigánd, Hungary 41/F2
Cihanbeyli, Turkey 63/E3
Cihuatlán, Mexico 150/G7
Cijara (res.), Spain 33/D3
Cijulang, Indonesia 85/H2
Cilacap, Indonesia 85/H2
Çıldır, Turkey 63/K2
Çıldır (lake), Turkey 63/K2
Cilleros, Spain 33/C2
Cilo Dağı (mt.), Turkey 63/K4
Cima, Calif. (92323) 204/K8
Cimahi, Indonesia 85/H2
Cimarron (riv.) 188/G3
Cimarron, Colo. (81220) 208/D6
Cimarron, Kansas (67835) 232/B4
Cimarron (riv.), Kansas 232/B4
Cimarron, N. Mex. (87714) 274/E2
Cimarron (riv.), N. Mex. 274/E2
Cimarron (co.), Okla. 288/A1
Cimarron, Okla. (73111) 288/L3
Cimarron (riv.), Okla. 288/N2
Cimin, Turkey 63/H3
Cimone (mt.), Italy 34/C2
Cîmpeni, Romania 45/F2
Cîmpia Turzii, Romania 45/F2
Cîmpina, Romania 45/H3
Cîmpulung, Romania 45/G3
Cîmpulung Moldovenesc, Romania 45/G2
Cinaruco (riv.), Colombia 126/F4
Cinaruco (riv.), Venezuela 124/D4
Cinca (riv.), Spain 33/G2
Cincinnati, Ark. (†72769) 202/B1
Cincinnati, Iowa (52549) 229/G7
Cincinnati, Ohio 146/K6
Cincinnati, Ohio (*45201) 284/B9
Cincinnati, Ohio 188/K3
Cincinnatus, N.Y. (13040) 276/H5
Cinclare, La. (†70767) 238/J2
Cinco, W. Va. (†25301) 312/D6
Cinco Balas (cays), Cuba 158/E3
Cinco Bayou, Fla. (†32548) 212/B6
Cinco Saltos, Argentina 143/C4
Cinderella, W. Va. (†25661) 312/B7
Cinderford, England 13/E6
Çine, Turkey 63/B4
Cinebar, Wash. (98533) 310/C4
Ciney, Belgium 27/G8
Cinnaminson○, N.J. (†08077) 273/B3
Cintalapa de Figueroa, Mexico 150/N8
Cinto (mt.), France 28/B6
Cipolletti, Argentina 143/C4
Circeo (cape), Italy 34/D4
Circle, Alaska (99733) 196/K1
Circle, Mont. (59215) 262/L3
Circle (butte), Utah 304/C6
Circle Back, Texas (†79371) 303/B3
Circle City, Mo. (†63846) 261/N9
Circle Pines, Minn. (55014) 255/G5
Circle Springs, Alaska (†99730) 196/K1
Circleville, Kansas (66416) 232/G2
Circleville, Ohio (43113) 284/D6
Circleville, Utah (84723) 304/B5
Circleville, W. Va. (26804) 312/H5
Circular (head), Tasmania 99/B2
Cirebon, Indonesia 85/H2
Cirebon, Indonesia 54/M10
Ciremay (mt.), Indonesia 85/H2
Cirencester, England 10/F5
Cirencester, England 13/E6
Cirque (mt.), Newf. 166/B2
Cisco, Georgia (30708) 217/C1
Cisco, Ill. (61830) 222/E3
Cisco, Texas (76437) 303/E5
Cisco, Utah (84515) 304/E5
Cisco Springs Wash (creek), Utah 304/E4
Ciskei (bantustan), S. Africa 102/E8
Cismont, Va. (†22947) 307/M4
Cisnădie, Romania 45/G3
Cisne (isls.), Honduras 154/F2
Cisne, Ill. (62823) 222/E5
Cisneros, Colombia 126/C4
Cisnes (riv.), Chile 138/E5
Cispus (pass), Wash. 310/D4
Cispus (riv.), Wash. 310/D4
Cissna Park, Ill. (60924) 222/F3
Citlaltépetl (mt.), Mexico 150/O2
Citra, Fla. (32627) 212/D2
Citronelle, Ala. (36522) 195/B8
Citrus (co.), Fla. 212/D3
Citrus Center, Fla. (†33471) 212/E5
Citrus Heights, Calif. (95610) 204/C8
Cittadella, Italy 34/C2
Città di Castello, Italy 34/C3
Cittanova, Italy 34/F5
City Mills, Mass. (†02056) 249/J4
City Point, Fla. (†32922) 212/F3
City Point, Wis. (†54466) 317/F7
City View, Ontario 177/J2
City View, S.C. (29611) 296/C2
Ciudad Acuña (Villa Acuña), Mexico 150/J2
Ciudad Altamirano, Mexico 150/J7
Ciudad Bolívar, Venezuela 120/C2
Ciudad Bolívar, Venezuela 124/G3
Ciudad Bolivia, Venezuela 124/C3
Ciudad Camargo, Chihuahua, Mexico 150/G3
Ciudad Camargo, Tamaulipas, Mexico 150/K3
Ciudad Darío, Nicaragua 154/D4
Ciudad del Carmen, Mexico 150/N7
Ciudad Delicias, Mexico 150/G2
Ciudad del Maíz, Mexico 150/K5
Ciudad de Nutrias, Venezuela 124/D3
Ciudad de Río Grande, Mexico 150/H5
Ciudadela, Spain 33/H2
Ciudad Guayana, Venezuela 120/C2
Ciudad Guayana, Venezuela 124/G3
Ciudad Guerrero, Mexico 150/F2
Ciudad Guzmán, Mexico 150/H7
Ciudad Hidalgo, Chiapas, Mexico 150/N9
Ciudad Hidalgo, Michoacán, Mexico 150/J7
Ciudad Juárez, Mexico 146/H6
Ciudad Juárez, Mexico 150/F1
Ciudad Lerdo, Mexico 150/H4
Ciudad Madero, Mexico 150/L5
Ciudad Mante, Mexico 150/K5
Ciudad Mendoza, Mexico 150/O2
Ciudad Miguel Alemán, Mexico 150/K3
Ciudad Obregón, Mexico 146/H7
Ciudad Obregón, Mexico 150/E3
Ciudad Ojeda, Venezuela 120/B2
Ciudad Ojeda, Venezuela 124/C2
Ciudad Piar (co.), Venezuela 124/G4
Ciudad Quesada, C. Rica 154/E5
Ciudad Real (prov.), Spain 33/D3
Ciudad Real, Spain 33/D3
Ciudad Río Bravo, Mexico 150/K4
Ciudad-Rodrigo, Spain 33/C2
Ciudad Satélite, Mexico 150/L1
Ciudad Serdán, Mexico 150/O2
Ciudad Valles, Mexico 150/K5
Ciudad Victoria, Mexico 150/K5
Civa (cape), Turkey 63/G2
Cividale del Friuli, Italy 34/D1
Civitavecchia, Italy 34/C3
Civitella del Tronto, Italy 34/D3
Civray, France 28/D4
Çivril, Turkey 63/C3
Cizre, Turkey 63/K4
Clachan, Scotland 15/C5
Clackamas (co.), Oreg. 291/E2
Clackamas, Oreg. (97015) 291/B2
Clackamas (riv.), Oreg. 291/E2
Clackmannan, Scotland 10/B1
Clackmannan, Scotland 15/C1
Clackmannan (trad. co.), Scotland 15/A5
Clacton, England 13/J6
Clacton, England 10/G5
Claflin, Kansas (67525) 232/D3
Claiborne, Ala. (36434) 195/D7
Claiborne (par.), La. 238/D1
Claiborne (lake), La. 238/E1
Claiborne, Md. (21624) 245/N5
Claiborne (co.), Miss. 256/C7
Claiborne (co.), Tenn. 237/O8
Clair, New Bruns. 170/B1
Clair, Sask. 181/G3
Claire (lake), Alberta 182/B5
Claire (lake), Alta. 162/E4
Claire City, S. Dak. (57224) 298/P2
Clairemont, Texas (†79518) 303/D4
Clair Engle (lake), Calif. 204/C3
Clairette, Texas (†76457) 303/F5
Clairfield, Tenn. (37715) 237/O7
Clairmont, Alberta 182/A2
Clairmont Springs, Ala. (†35160) 195/G4
Clairton, Pa. (15025) 294/C7
Clallam (co.), Wash. 310/B2
Clallam Bay, Wash. (98326) 310/A2
Clam (bay), Nova Scotia 168/F4
Clam (lake), Wis. 317/B4
Clam (riv.), Wis. 317/A4
Clamart, France 28/A2
Clamecy, France 28/E4
Clam Falls, Wis. (54825) 317/B4
Clam Gulch, Alaska (99568) 196/B1
Clam Lake, Wis. (54517) 317/E3
Clan Alpine (mts.), Nev. 266/D3
Clancy, Mont. (59634) 262/E4
Clandeboye, Manitoba 179/E4
Clandeboye, Ontario 177/C4
Clandonald, Alberta 182/E3
Clanton, Ala. (35045) 195/E5
Clanwilliam, Manitoba 179/C4
Clanwilliam, S. Africa 118/B6
Clapperton (isl.), Ontario 177/B1
Clara, Ireland 10/C4
Clara, Ireland 17/F5
Clara, Miss. (39324) 256/G7
Clara, Uruguay 145/D3
Clara Barton Nat'l Hist. Site, Md. 245/E4
Clara City, Minn. (56222) 255/C6
Claravale, North. Terr. 93/B3
Clare, Ill. (60111) 222/E1
Clare, Ind. (†46060) 227/F4
Clare, Iowa (50524) 229/E3
Clare (co.), Ireland 17/D6
Clare (isl.), Ireland 10/A4
Clare (isl.), Ireland 17/A4
Clare (riv.), Ireland 17/D5
Clare (co.), Mich. 250/E5
Clare, Mich. (48617) 250/E5
Clare, N.S. Wales 97/B3
Clare, S. Australia 94/F5
Claregalway, Ireland 17/D5
Claremont, Calif. (91711) 204/D10
Claremont, Ill. (62421) 222/F5
Claremont, Jamaica 158/J6
Claremont, Minn. (55924) 255/E6
Claremont, N.H. (03743) 268/C5
Claremont, N.C. (28610) 281/G3
Claremont, S. Dak. (57432) 298/N2
Claremont, Va. (23899) 307/P6
Claremore, Okla. (74017) 288/R2
Claremorris, Ireland 17/C4
Claremorris, Ireland 10/B4
Clarence (str.), Alaska 196/N2
Clarence (isl.), Chile 120/B8
Clarence (isl.), Chile 138/E10
Clarence, Iowa (52216) 229/M5
Clarence, La. (71414) 238/E3
Clarence, Mo. (63437) 261/H3
Clarence (riv.), N. S. Wales 88/J5
Clarence (riv.), N. S. Wales 97/G1
Clarence○, N.Y. (14031) 276/C5
Clarence (riv.), N. Zealand 100/E5
Clarence (str.), North. Terr. 88/E2
Clarence (str.), North. Terr. 93/B2
Clarence (cape), N.W. Terrs. 187/K2
Clarence (head), N.W. Terrs. 187/L2
Clarence, Pa. (16829) 294/G3
Clarence Bridge, N. Zealand 100/E5
Clarence Creek, Ontario 177/J2
Clarenceville, Québec 172/D4
Clarendon, Ark. (72029) 202/H4
Clarendon, New Bruns. 170/D3
Clarendon, N.C. (28432) 281/M6
Clarendon (lake), Ontario 177/G3
Clarendon, Pa. (16313) 294/D2
Clarendon (co.), S.C. 296/G4
Clarendon, Texas (79226) 303/C3
Clarendon○, Vt. (†05759) 268/A4
Clarendon Hills, Ill. (60514) 222/B6
Clarens, Switzerland 39/C4
Clarenville, Newf. 166/C2
Claresholm, Alberta 182/D4
Clariden (mt.), Switzerland 39/G3
Clarie Coast (reg.) 5/C7
Clarinda, Iowa (51632) 229/C7
Clarines, Venezuela 124/E3
Clarington, Ohio (43915) 284/J6
Clarington, Pa. (15828) 294/D3
Clarion, Iowa (50525) 229/F3
Clarión (isl.), Mexico 150/B7
Clarion, Mich. (†49796) 250/E3
Clarion (co.), Pa. 294/D3
Clarion, Pa. (16214) 294/D3
Clarion (riv.), Pa. 294/D3
Clarion River, East Branch (lake), Pa. 294/E2
Clarissa, Minn. (56440) 255/C4
Clarita, Okla. (74535) 288/O6
Clark (lake), Alaska 196/H2
Clark (co.), Ark. 202/D5
Clark, Colo. (80428) 208/F1
Clark (co.), Idaho 220/F5
Clark (co.), Ill. 222/F4
Clark (co.), Ind. 227/F8
Clark (co.), Kansas 232/C4
Clark (co.), Ky. 237/N4
Clark (co.), Mo. 261/J2
Clark, Mo. (65243) 261/H4
Clark (co.), Nev. 266/F6
Clark○, N.J. (07066) 273/A3
Clark, N.C. (†28560) 281/P4
Clark (buttes), N. Dak. 282/G7
Clark (co.), Ohio 284/C6
Clark, Ohio (43810) 284/G5
Clark (pt.), Ontario 177/C3
Clark, Pa. (16113) 294/B3
Clark (co.), S. Dak. 298/O4
Clark, S. Dak. (57225) 298/O4
Clark (co.), Wash. 310/C5
Clark (co.), Wis. 317/E6
Clark, Wyo. (†59008) 319/C1
Clark Canyon (res.), Mont. 262/D6
Clark Center, Ill. (†62441) 222/F4
Clarkdale, Ariz. (86324) 198/C4
Clarke (co.), Ala. 195/C7
Clarke (co.), Georgia 217/F3
Clarke (co.), Iowa 229/F6
Clarke (co.), Miss. 256/G6
Clarke (range), Queensland 95/C4
Clarke (isl.), Tasmania 99/E2
Clarke (co.), Va. 307/M2
Clarke City, Québec 174/D2
Clarkedale, Ark. (72325) 202/K3
Clarke's Beach, Newf. 166/D2
Clarkesville, Georgia (30523) 217/F1
Clarkfield, Minn. (56223) 255/C6
Clark Fork, Idaho (83811) 220/B1
Clark Fork (riv.), Mont. 188/D1
Clark Fork (riv.), Mont. 262/A3
Clark Hill (lake), Georgia 217/H3
Clark Hill (dam), S.C. 296/C4
Clark Hill (lake), S.C. 296/C4
Clarkia, Idaho (83812) 220/B2
Clark Island, Maine (†04859) 243/E8
Clarklake, Mich. (49234) 250/E6
Clarkrange, Tenn. (38553) 237/L8
Clarks, East Fork (riv.), Ky. 237/E7
Clarks, La. (71415) 238/F2
Clarks, Nebr. (68628) 264/G3
Clarksboro, N.J. (08020) 273/C4
Clarksburg, Calif. (95612) 204/B9
Clarksburg, Ind. (47225) 227/G6
Clarksburg, Md. (20734) 245/J4
Clarksburg, Mo. (65025) 261/G5
Clarksburg, N.J. (08510) 273/E3
Clarksburg, Ohio (43115) 284/D7
Clarksburg, Ontario 177/D3
Clarksburg, Tenn. (38324) 237/E9
Clarksburg, W. Va. 188/K3
Clarksburg, W. Va. (26301) 312/F4
Clarks Corner, Conn. (†06256) 210/G1
Clarksdale, Miss. 188/J4
Clarksdale, Miss. (38614) 256/D2
Clarksdale, Mo. (64430) 261/D3
Clarks Falls, Conn. (†06359) 210/H3
Clarks Fork, Yellowstone (riv.), Mont. 262/G6
Clarks Fork (riv.), Wyo. 319/C1
Clarks Green, Pa. (†18411) 294/F6
Clarks Grove, Minn. (56016) 255/E7
Clark's Harbour, Nova Scotia 168/C5
Clarks Hill, Ind. (47930) 227/D4
Clarks Hill, S.C. (29821) 296/C4
Clarks Mill, Maine (†04847) 243/B8
Clarks Mills, Pa. (16114) 294/B3
Clarkson, Ky. (42726) 237/J6
Clarkson, Miss. (†39752) 256/F3
Clarkson, Nebr. (68629) 264/G3
Clarkson, N.Y. (14430) 276/E4
Clarkson Valley, Mo. (†63017) 261/N3
Clarks Point, Alaska (99569) 196/G3
Clarks Summit, Pa. (18411) 294/F6
Clarkston, Georgia (30021) 217/L1
Clarkston, Mich. (48016) 250/F6
Clarkston, Scotland 15/B2
Clarkston, Utah (84305) 304/B2
Clarkston, Wash. (99403) 310/H4
Clark's Town, Jamaica 158/H6
Clarksville, Ark. (72830) 202/D3
Clarksville, Del. (19937) 245/T6
Clarksville, Fla. (32430) 212/D6
Clarksville, Ind. (47130) 227/F8
Clarksville, Iowa (50619) 229/H3
Clarksville, Md. (21029) 245/L4
Clarksville, Mich. (48815) 250/D6
Clarksville, Mo. (63336) 261/K4
Clarksville○, N.H. (†05902) 268/E1
Clarksville, N.Y. (12041) 276/M5
Clarksville, Ohio (45113) 284/C7
Clarksville (Clark), Pa. (16113) 294/B3
Clarksille, Pa. (15322) 294/B6
Clarksville, Tenn. 188/J3
Clarksville, Tenn. (37040) 237/G7
Clarksville, Texas (75426) 303/K4
Clarksville, Va. (23927) 307/L7
Clarkton, Mo. (63837) 261/M10
Clarkton, N.C. (28433) 281/M6
Clarno, Wis. (†53566) 317/G10
Claro (riv.), Bolivia 136/A3
Claro (riv.), Brazil 132/D7
Claro (riv.), Chile 138/G5
Claro, Switzerland 39/G4
Clashmoor, Sask. 181/H3
Clashmore, Ireland 17/F8
Clatonia, Nebr. (68328) 264/H4
Clatskanie, Oreg. (97016) 291/D1
Clatsop (co.), Oreg. 291/D1
Claud, Ala. (†36024) 195/F5
Claude, Texas (79019) 303/C2
Claudell, Kansas (†66951) 232/C2
Claudville, Va. (24076) 307/H7
Claudy, N. Ireland 17/G2
Claunch, N. Mex. (87011) 274/C4
Claussen, S.C. (†29501) 296/H3
Clausthal-Zellerfeld, W. Germany 22/D3
Claverack-Red Mills, N.Y. (12513) 276/N6
Claveria, Philippines 82/C1
Clavet, Sask. 181/E4
Clawson, Mich. (48017) 250/B6
Clawson, Utah (84516) 304/C4
Claxton, Georgia (30417) 217/J6
Clay (co.), Ala. 195/G4
Clay (co.), Ark. 202/K1
Clay, Calif. (†95638) 204/C9
Clay (creek), Colo. 208/O7
Clay (co.), Fla. 212/E2
Clay (co.), Georgia 217/B7
Clay (co.), Ill. 222/E5
Clay (co.), Ind. 227/C6
Clay (co.), Iowa 229/C2
Clay (co.), Kansas 232/E2
Clay (co.), Ky. 237/O6
Clay, Ky. (42404) 237/F6
Clay, La. (†71270) 238/E2
Clay (co.), Minn. 255/B4
Clay (co.), Miss. 256/G3
Clay (co.), Mo. 261/D4
Clay (co.), Nebr. 264/F4
Clay (co.), N.C. 281/B4
Clay (co.), S. Dak. 298/P8
Clay (co.), Tenn. 237/K7
Clay (co.), Texas 303/F4
Clay (hills), Utah 304/D6
Clay (co.), W. Va. 312/D6
Clay, W. Va. (25043) 312/D6
Claybank, Sask. 181/F5
Clay Bank, Va. (†23061) 307/P6
Clay Center, Kansas (67432) 232/E2
Clay Center, Nebr. (68933) 264/F4
Clay Center, Ohio (43408) 284/D2
Clay City, Ill. (62824) 222/E5
Clay City, Ind. (47841) 227/C6
Clay City, Ky. (40312) 237/O5
Claycomo, Mo. (†64119) 261/P5
Clay Cross, England 13/J2
Claydon, Sask. 181/B6
Clayhatchee, Ala. (†36322) 195/G8
Claymont, Del. (19703) 245/S1
Claymour, Ky. (†42220) 237/G7
Clayoquot (sound), Br. Col. 184/D5
Claypool, Ariz. (85532) 198/E5
Claypool, Ind. (46510) 227/F2
Claypool, Ky. (†42101) 237/J7
Claysburg, Pa. (16625) 294/F5
Clay Springs, Ariz. (†85934) 198/E4
Claysville, Ohio (43729) 284/G6
Claysville, Pa. (15323) 294/B5
Clayton, Ala. (36015) 195/G7
Clayton, Calif. (94517) 204/K2
Clayton, Del. (19938) 245/R3
Clayton (co.), Georgia 217/D3
Clayton, Georgia (30525) 217/F1
Clayton, Idaho (83227) 220/D5
Clayton, Ill. (62324) 222/B3
Clayton, Ind. (46118) 227/E5
Clayton (co.), Iowa 229/L3
Clayton, Iowa (†52049) 229/L3
Clayton, Kansas (67629) 232/B2
Clayton, La. (71326) 238/H3
Clayton (lake), Maine 243/D2
Clayton, Mich. (49235) 250/E7
Clayton, Miss. (†38626) 256/D1
Clayton, Mo. (63105) 261/P3
Clayton, N.J. (08312) 273/C4
Clayton, N. Mex. (88415) 274/F2
Clayton, N.Y. (13624) 276/H2
Clayton, N.C. (27520) 281/N3
Clayton, Ohio (45315) 284/B6
Clayton, Okla. (74536) 288/R5
Clayton, S. Dak. (†57332) 298/D7
Clayton, Victoria 97/J5
Clayton, Wash. (99110) 310/H3
Clayton, W. Va. (†24910) 312/E7
Clayton, Wis. (54004) 317/B5
Clayton Lake, Maine (04018) 243/E2
Claytonville, Ill. (60926) 222/F3
Claytor (lake), Va. 307/G6
Clayville, N.Y. (13322) 276/K5
Clayville, R.I. (02815) 249/H5
Clayville, S. Africa 118/H6
Clayville, Va. (†23139) 307/N6
Clear, Alaska (99704) 196/J2
Clear (cape), Alaska 196/D1
Clear (hills), Alberta 182/A1
Clear (creek), Ariz. 198/D4
Clear (lake), Calif. 188/B3
Clear (lake), Calif. 204/C4
Clear (lake), Iowa 229/G2
Clear (cape), Ireland 17/C9
Clear (cape), Ireland 17/B9
Clear (cape), Ireland 10/B5
Clear (isl.), Ireland 17/C9
Clear (lake), La. 238/D3
Clear (lake), Manitoba 179/C4
Clear (lake), Ontario 177/F3
Clear (lake), Ontario 177/G2
Clear (creek), Utah 304/B5
Clear (lake), Utah 304/B4
Clear (creek), Wyo. 319/F1
Clear Boggy (creek), Okla. 288/O6
Clearbrook, Br. Col. 184/L3
Clearbrook, Minn. (56634) 255/C3
Clear Brook, Va. (22624) 307/M2
Clear Creek, Calif. (†96039) 204/B2
Clear Creek (co.), Colo. 208/H3
Clear Creek, Ind. (47426) 227/E6
Clearcreek, Utah (†84538) 304/C4
Clear Creek, W. Va. (25044) 312/D7
Clearfield, Iowa (50840) 229/D7
Clearfield, Ky. (40313) 237/P4
Clearfield (co.), Pa. 294/F3
Clearfield, Pa. (16830) 294/F3
Clearfield, S. Dak. (57581) 298/K7
Clearfield, Utah (84015) 304/B2
Clear Fork (res.), Ohio 284/E4
Clear Fork, Mohican (riv.), Ohio 284/F4
Clear Fork, Brazos (riv.), Texas 303/D5
Clear Fork, Guyandotte (riv.), W. Va. 312/C7
Clear Hills, Alberta 182/B1
Clearlake, Calif. (95422) 204/C5
Clear Lake (res.), Calif. 204/D2
Clear Lake, Ind. (†46737) 227/H1
Clear Lake, Iowa (50428) 229/G2
Clear Lake, La. (†71414) 238/E3
Clear Lake, Minn. (55319) 255/E5
Clear Lake, S. Dak. (57226) 298/R4
Clearlake, Wash. (98235) 310/C2
Clear Lake, Wis. (54005) 317/B5
Clearlake Oaks, Calif. (95423) 204/C4
Clear Lake Shores, Texas (†77565) 303/K2
Clearmont, Mo. (64431) 261/C1
Clearmont, Wyo. (82835) 319/F1
Clear Ridge, Pa. (†17229) 294/F5
Clear Spring, Ind. (†47220) 227/E7
Clear Spring, Md. (21722) 245/G2
Clearview, Okla. (74835) 288/O4
Clearview, W. Va. (†26003) 312/E2
Clearview City, Kansas (66019) 232/G3
Clearville, Pa. (15535) 294/F6
Clearwater (riv.), Alberta 182/C4
Clearwater (riv.), Alberta 182/E1
Clearwater, Br. Col. 184/G4
Clearwater (lake), Br. Col. 184/G4
Clearwater (riv.), Br. Col. 184/G4
Clearwater, Fla. 188/K5
Clearwater, Fla. (*33515) 212/B2
Clearwater (co.), Idaho 220/C3
Clearwater, Idaho (83521) 220/C3
Clearwater (mts.), Idaho 220/C3
Clearwater (riv.), Idaho 220/B3
Clearwater, Kansas (67026) 232/E4
Clearwater, Manitoba 179/D5
Clearwater (co.), Minn. 255/C3
Clearwater, Minn. (55320) 255/D5
Clearwater (riv.), Minn. 255/C3
Clearwater (lake), Mo. 261/L8
Clearwater, Nebr. (68726) 264/F2
Clearwater (brook), New Bruns. 170/D2
Clearwater (riv.), Sask. 181/L3
Clearwater, S.C. (29822) 296/D4
Clearwater, Wash. (†98331) 310/A3
Clearwater Beach (isl.), Fla. 212/B2
Clearwater Lake, Minn. 255/E5
Clearwater Lake, Wis. (54518) 317/H4
Clearwater Lake Beach, Sask. 181/D5
Clearwater Lake Prov. Park, Manitoba 179/H3
Cleator Moor, England 13/D3
Cleburne (co.), Ala. 195/G3
Cleburne (co.), Ark. 202/F2
Cleburne, Texas 188/G4
Cleburne, Texas (76031) 303/G5
Cle Elum, Wash. (98922) 310/E3
Cle Elum (lake), Wash. 310/E3
Cleethorpes, England 13/H4
Cleethorpes, England 10/F4
Cleeves, Sask. 181/C2
Cleghorn, Iowa (51014) 229/B3
Cleghorn, Wis. (†54738) 317/C6
Clem, Georgia (†30117) 217/B3
Clemenceau, Ariz. (†86326) 198/C4
Clemenceau, Sask. 181/J3
Clément, Fr. Guiana 131/E4
Clemente (isl.), Chile 138/D6
Clementon, N.J. (08021) 273/D4
Clements, Calif. (95227) 204/C9
Clements, Kansas (66844) 232/F3
Clements, Md. (20624) 245/L7
Clements, Minn. (56224) 255/D6
Clementson, Minn. (56623) 255/D2
Clementsport, Nova Scotia 168/C4
Clementsvale, Nova Scotia 168/C4
Clementsville, N. Dak. (†58492) 282/O5
Clemmons, N.C. (27012) 281/J2
Clemons, Iowa (50051) 229/G4
Clemscot, Okla. (†73437) 288/L6
Clemson, S.C. (29631) 296/B2
Clendenin, W. Va. (25045) 312/D5
Clendening (lake), Ohio 284/H5
Cleopatra Needle (mt.), Philippines 82/B5
Cleora, Okla. (†74331) 288/S1
Cleo Springs, Okla. (73729) 288/K2
Clerf (riv.), Luxembourg 27/J8
Clermont, Fla. (32711) 212/E3
Clermont, France 28/E3
Clermont, Georgia (30527) 217/E2
Clermont, Iowa (52135) 229/K3
Clermont, Ky. (40110) 237/K5
Clermont, N.Y. (†12526) 276/N6
Clermont (co.), Ohio 284/B7
Clermont, Pa. (†16740) 294/E2
Clermont, Québec 172/G2
Clermont, Queensland 88/H4
Clermont, Queensland 95/C4
Clermont-Ferrand, France 7/E4
Clermont-Ferrand, France 28/E5
Clermont Harbor, Miss. (39551) 256/F10
Clervaux, Luxembourg 27/J8
Cleve, S. Australia 88/F6
Cleve, S. Australia 94/E5
Clevedon, England 13/D6
Cleveland, Ala. (35049) 195/E3
Cleveland (co.), Ark. 202/F6
Cleveland, Ark. (72030) 202/E3
Cleveland (co.), England 13/F3
Cleveland (hills), England 13/F3
Cleveland, Fla. (†33950) 212/E5
Cleveland, Georgia (30528) 217/E1
Cleveland, Minn. (56017) 255/E6
Cleveland, Miss. (38732) 256/C3

Coleman 353

Cleveland, Mo. (64734) 261/C5
Cleveland, Mont. (†59523) 262/G2
Cleveland, N. Mex. (87715) 274/D2
Cleveland, N.Y. (13042) 276/J4
Cleveland (co.), N.C. 281/F4
Cleveland, N.C. (27013) 281/H3
Cleveland, N. Dak. (58424) 282/M6
Cleveland, Ohio 188/K2
Cleveland, Ohio (*44101) 284/H9
Cleveland, Ohio 146/K5
Cleveland (co.), Okla. 288/M4
Cleveland, Okla. (74020) 288/O2
Cleveland, S.C. (29635) 296/C1
Cleveland, Tenn. (37311) 237/M10
Cleveland, Texas (77327) 303/K7
Cleveland, Utah (84518) 304/D4
Cleveland, Va. (24225) 307/D7
Cleveland, W. Va. (26215) 312/F5
Cleveland, Wis. (53015) 317/L8
Cleveland Heights, Ohio (44118) 284/H9
Cleveland-Hopkins Mun. Airport, Ohio 284/G9
Clevelândia do Norte, Brazil 132/D2
Cleveland Park, D.C. (20008) 245/E4
Clever, Mo. (65631) 261/F8
Cleves, Iowa (†50601) 229/G4
Cleves, Ohio (45002) 284/B9
Clew (bay), Ireland 17/B4
Clew (bay), Ireland 10/B4
Clewiston, Fla. (33440) 212/E5
Clichy, France 28/B1
Clicquot-Millis, Mass. (†02054) 249/A8
Clifden, Ireland 10/B4
Clifden, Ireland 17/B5
Cliff, N. Mex. (88028) 274/A6
Cliff (cape), Nova Scotia 168/E3
Cliff (creek), Utah 304/E3
Cliffdell, Wash. (†98937) 310/E4
Clifford, Ind. (47226) 227/F6
Clifford, Ky. (41208) 237/S4
Clifford (lake), Maine 243/H5
Clifford, Mich. (48727) 250/F5
Clifford, N. Dak. (58016) 282/R5
Clifford, Ontario 177/D4
Clifford, Pa. (18413) 294/L2
Clifford, Va. (24533) 307/K5
Clifford, Wis. (†54564) 317/F4
Cliffordvale, New Bruns. 170/C2
Cliffside, N.C. (28024) 281/F4
Cliffside Park, N.J. (07010) 273/C2
Clifftop, W. Va. (25822) 312/E6
Cliffwood, N.J. (07721) 273/E3
Clifton, Ariz. (85533) 198/F5
Clifton, Colo. (81520) 208/C4
Clifton, Idaho (83228) 220/F7
Clifton, Ill. (60927) 222/F3
Clifton, Kansas (66937) 232/E2
Clifton, La. (†70438) 238/K5
Clifton○, Maine (†04428) 243/G6
Clifton, New Bruns. 170/E1
Clifton, N.J. (*07011) 273/B2
Clifton, S.C. (29324) 296/D2
Clifton, Tenn. (38425) 237/F10
Clifton, Texas (76634) 303/G6
Clifton, W. Va. (25237) 312/B5
Clifton, Wis. (†54618) 317/F8
Clifton City, Mo. (†65348) 261/G5
Clifton Dartmouth Hardness, England 10/E5
Clifton Dartmouth Hardness, England 13/D7
Clifton Forge (I.C.), Va. (24422) 307/J5
Clifton Heights, Pa. (19018) 294/M7
Clifton Hill, Mo. (65244) 261/G4
Clifton Hills, S. Australia 94/F2
Clifton Mills, W. Va. (†26525) 312/G3
Clifton Park○, N.Y. (†12118) 276/N5
Clifton Springs, N.Y. (14432) 276/F4
Cliftonville, Miss. (†39739) 256/H4
Clifty, Ark. (†72756) 202/C1
Clifty (creek), Ind. 227/F6
Clifty, Ky. (42216) 237/G7
Clifty, Tenn. (†38583) 237/L9
Clifty, W. Va. (†25854) 312/E6
Climax, Colo. (80429) 208/G4
Climax, Georgia (31734) 217/D9
Climax, Kansas (67027) 232/F4
Climax, Ky. (40413) 237/N6
Climax, Mich. (49034) 250/D6
Climax, Minn. (56523) 255/B3
Climax, N.C. (27233) 281/K3
Climax, Sask. 181/C6
Climax Springs, Mo. (65324) 261/G6
Climbing Hill, Iowa (51015) 229/B4
Clinch (co.), Georgia 217/G9
Clinch (riv.), Tenn. 237/N9
Clinch (riv.), Va. 307/C7
Clinchburg, Va. (24321) 307/E7
Clinchco, Va. (24226) 307/D6
Clinchfield, Georgia (31013) 217/E6
Clinchmore, Tenn. (†37714) 237/N8
Clinchport, Va. (24244) 307/C7
Cline Settlement, Alberta 182/B3
Clingmans Dome (mt.), N.C. 281/C3
Clingmans Dome (mt.), Tenn. 237/P10
Clint, Texas (79836) 303/B10
Clinton, Ala. (35448) 195/C5
Clinton, Ark. (72031) 202/F2
Clinton, Br. Col. 184/G4
Clinton, Conn. (06413) 210/E3
Clinton○, Conn. (06413) 210/E3
Clinton (co.), Ill. 222/D5
Clinton, Ill. (61727) 222/E3
Clinton (co.), Ind. 227/E4
Clinton, Ind. (47842) 227/C5
Clinton (co.), Iowa 229/M5
Clinton, Iowa 188/J2
Clinton, Iowa (52732) 229/N5
Clinton (co.), Ky. 237/L7
Clinton, Ky. (42031) 237/D7
Clinton, La. (70722) 238/J5
Clinton, Maine (04927) 243/D6
Clinton○, Maine (04927) 243/D6
Clinton, Md. (20735) 245/G6
Clinton○, Mass. (01510) 249/H3
Clinton (co.), Mich. 250/E6
Clinton, Mich. (49236) 250/F6
Clinton, Minn. (56225) 255/B5
Clinton, Miss. (39056) 256/D6
Clinton (co.), Mo. 261/D3
Clinton, Mo. (64735) 261/E6
Clinton, Mont. (†59825) 262/C4
Clinton, Nebr. (†69343) 264/B2
Clinton, N.J. (08809) 273/D2
Clinton (res.), N.J. 273/E1
Clinton (co.), N.Y. 276/N1
Clinton, N.Y. (13323) 276/K4
Clinton, N. Zealand 100/B7
Clinton, N.C. (28328) 281/N5
Clinton (co.), Ohio 284/C7
Clinton, Ohio (44216) 284/G4
Clinton, Okla. (73601) 288/H3
Clinton, Ontario 177/C4
Clinton (co.), Pa. 294/G3
Clinton, Pa. (15026) 294/B5
Clinton, S.C. (29325) 296/D3
Clinton, Tenn. (37716) 237/N8
Clinton, Wash. (98236) 310/C3
Clinton, W. Va. (†26058) 312/E2
Clinton, Wis. (53525) 317/J10
Clinton-Colden (lake), N.W. Terrs. 187/H3
Clinton Corners, N.Y. (12514) 276/N7
Clinton Creek, Yukon 187/D3
Clintondale, N.Y. (12515) 276/M7
Clintondale, Pa. (†17751) 294/H3
Clinton Falls, Minn. (†55060) 255/E6
Clintonville, Conn. (†06473) 210/D3
Clintonville, Ky. (†40361) 237/N4
Clintonville, Pa. (16372) 294/C3
Clintonville, W. Va. (24928) 312/E7
Clintonville, Wis. (54929) 317/J6
Clintwood, Va. (24228) 307/D6
Clio, Ala. (36017) 195/G7
Clio, Iowa (50052) 229/G7
Clio, La. (†70462) 238/M2
Clio, Mich. (48420) 250/F5
Clio, S.C. (29525) 296/H2
Clio, W. Va. (25046) 312/D5
Clipper, Wash. (98244) 310/C2
Clipperton (isl.) 146/H8
Clipperton (isl.) 2/D5
Clisham (mt.), Scotland 15/B3
Clitherall, Minn. (56524) 255/C4
Clitheroe, England 13/H1
Clitheroe, England 10/G1
Clive, Alberta 182/D3
Clive, Iowa (50318) 229/F5
Clive, N. Zealand 100/F3
Cliza, Bolivia 136/C5
Cloan, Sask. 181/C3
Cloates (pt.), W. Australia 92/A3
Clode (sound), Newf. 166/D2
Cloe, Pa. (†15767) 294/E4
Cloghan, Ireland 17/F5
Clogh-Chatsworth, Ireland 17/G6
Clogheen, Ireland 17/F7
Clogher, N. Ireland 17/G3
Clogherhead, Ireland 17/J4
Cloghy, N. Ireland 17/K3
Clonakilty, Ireland 10/B5
Clonakilty, Ireland 17/D8
Clonakilty (bay), Ireland 17/D8
Clonaslee, Ireland 17/F5
Cloncurry, Australia 87/E8
Cloncurry, Queensland 95/B4
Cloncurry, Queensland 88/G4
Cloncurry (riv.), Queensland 95/B4
Clondalkin, Ireland 17/J5
Clonegal, Ireland 17/H6
Clones, Ireland 10/C3
Clones, Ireland 17/G3
Clonfert, Ireland 17/E5
Clonmany, Ireland 17/G1
Clonmel, Ireland 17/F7
Clonmel, Ireland 10/C4
Clonmellon, Ireland 17/H4
Clonroche, Ireland 17/H7
Clontarf, Minn. (56226) 255/C5
Clontuskert, Ireland 17/E4
Cloone, Ireland 17/F4
Cloppenburg, W. Germany 22/B2
Clopton, Ala. (36317) 195/G7
Cloquet, Minn. (55720) 255/F4
Cloquet (riv.), Minn. 255/F4
Cloridorme, Québec 172/D1
Clorinda, Argentina 143/E2
Closeburn, Scotland 15/E5
Closplint, Ky. (40927) 237/P7
Closter, N.J. (07624) 273/C1
Clothier, W. Va. (25047) 312/C7
Clotho, Minn. (†56347) 255/C4
Cloud (co.), Kansas 232/E2
Cloud (peak), Wyo. 319/E1
Cloud Chief, Okla. (†73632) 288/J4
Cloudcroft, N. Mex. (88317) 274/D6
Cloudland, Georgia (30709) 217/A1
Cloudy (bay), N. Zealand 100/E4
Cloudy, Okla. (74537) 288/R6
Cloughjordan, Ireland 17/E6
Cloughmills, N. Ireland 17/J2
Cloutierville, La. (71416) 238/E3
Clova, Québec 174/B3
Clover (creek), Oreg. 291/K3
Clover, S.C. (29710) 296/E1
Clover, Va. (24534) 307/L7
Clover, W. Va. (†25276) 312/D5
Clover Bar, Alberta 182/D3
Clover Bend, Ark. (†72433) 202/H2
Clover Bottom, Ky. (40447) 237/N5
Cloverdale, Ala. (35617) 195/C1
Cloverdale, Calif. (95425) 204/B5
Cloverdale, Ind. (46120) 227/D6
Cloverdale, Minn. (†55037) 255/F4
Cloverdale, Ohio (45827) 284/B3
Cloverdale, Oreg. (97112) 291/D2
Cloverdale, Va. (24077) 307/J6
Cloverland, Ind. (†47834) 227/C6
Cloverland, Wash. (†99402) 310/H4
Cloverleaf, Manitoba 179/F5
Clover Lick, W. Va. (†24979) 312/F6
Clover Pass, Alaska (†99901) 196/N2
Cloverport, Ky. (40111) 237/H5
Cloverton, Minn. (†55048) 255/F4
Clovis, Calif. (93612) 204/F7
Clovis, N.Mex. 188/F4
Clovis, N. Mex. (88101) 274/F4
Clovulin, Scotland 15/C4
Cloyne, Ireland 17/E8
Cloyne, Ontario 177/G3
Cluanie, Loch (lake), Scotland 15/C3
Club (isl.), Ontario 177/C2
Cluff Lake, Sask. 181/L2
Cluj-Napoca, Romania 45/F2
Cluj-Napoca, Romania 7/G4
Clun, England 10/E4
Clun, England 13/D6
Clune, Pa. (15727) 294/D4
Clunes, Victoria 97/B5
Cluny, Alberta 182/D4
Cluny, France 28/F4
Cluses, France 28/G4
Clusone-Fiorine, Italy 34/C2
Cluster Springs, Va. (24535) 307/L7
Clute, Texas (77531) 303/J9
Clutha (riv.), N. Zealand 100/B6
Clutier, Iowa (52217) 229/J4
Clwyd (co.), Wales 13/D4
Clyattville, Georgia (31604) 217/F9
Clyde, Alberta 182/D2
Clyde (lake), Alberta 182/E2
Clyde, Canada 4/B13
Clyde (riv.), Dominica 161/F6
Clyde, Kansas (66938) 232/E2
Clyde, Mo. (64432) 261/C2
Clyde, N.Y. (14433) 276/G4
Clyde, N.C. (28721) 281/D3
Clyde, N. Dak. (†58352) 282/N2
Clyde, N.W.T. 162/J1
Clyde (inlet), N.W.T. 162/K1
Clyde, N.W. Terrs. 187/M2
Clyde (inlet), N.W. Terrs. 187/M2
Clyde (riv.), Nova Scotia 168/C5
Clyde, Ohio (43410) 284/E3
Clyde (firth), Scotland 15/D5
Clyde (firth), Scotland 10/D3
Clyde (riv.), Scotland 10/E3
Clyde (riv.), Scotland 15/D5
Clyde (riv.), Tasmania 99/D4
Clyde, Texas (79510) 303/E5
Clyde (riv.), Vt. 268/C2
Clyde, Wash. (†99348) 310/G4
Clydebank, Scotland 15/B2
Clydebank, Scotland 10/A1
Clyde Hill, Wash. (†98004) 310/B2
Clyde Park, Mont. (59018) 262/F5
Clyde River, Nova Scotia 168/C5
Clyman, Wis. (53016) 317/J9
Clymer, N.Y. (14724) 276/A6
Clymer, Pa. (15728) 294/E4
Clymers, Ind. (†46947) 227/E3
Clyo, Georgia (31303) 217/K6
Cnoc May (mt.), Scotland 15/C5
Coachella, Calif. (92236) 204/J10
Coachella (canal), Calif. 204/K10
Coachford, Ireland 17/D8
Coahoma (co.), Miss. 256/C2
Coahoma, Miss. (38617) 256/C2
Coahoma, Texas (79511) 303/C5
Coahuila (state), Mexico 150/H3
Coakley, Ky. (†42782) 237/K6
Coal (creek), Ind. 227/C4
Coal, Mo. (†64735) 261/E6
Coal (co.), Okla. 288/O5
Coal (pt.), Oreg. 291/C5
Coal (butte), Utah 304/C5
Coal (creek), Wash. 310/G3
Coal (riv.), W. Va. 312/C6
Coal Bluff, Ind. (†47874) 227/C5
Coal Branch, New Bruns. 170/E2
Coalburn, Scotland 15/E5
Coal City, Ill. (60416) 222/E2
Coal City, Ind. (47427) 227/D6
Coal City, W. Va. (25823) 312/D7
Coalcomán de Matamoros, Mexico 150/H7
Coal Creek, Alaska (†99701) 196/K1
Coal Creek, Colo. (81221) 208/J6
Coal Creek, Ind. (†47932) 227/C4
Coal Creek, New Bruns. 170/E2
Coaldale, Alberta 182/D5
Coaldale, Colo. (81222) 208/H6
Coaldale, Nev. (†89049) 266/D4
Coaldale, Pa. (18218) 294/L4
Coaldale (Six Mile Run), Pa. (16679) 294/F5
Coalfield, Tenn. (37719) 237/N8
Coalfield, Wash. (†98055) 310/B2
Coal Fork, W. Va. (25306) 312/D6
Coalgate, Okla. (74538) 288/O5
Coal Grove, Ohio (†45638) 284/E9
Coal Harbour, Br. Col. 184/D5
Coal Hill, Ark. (72832) 202/C3
Coalhurst, Alberta 182/D5
Coaling, Ala. (35449) 195/D4
Coalinga, Calif. (93210) 204/E7
Coalisland, N. Ireland 17/H2
Coalmont, Br. Col. 184/G5
Coalmont, Colo. (80430) 208/F1
Coalmont, Ind. (47845) 227/C6
Coalmont, Tenn. (37313) 237/K10
Coalport, Pa. (16627) 294/E4
Coalridge, Mont. (†59219) 262/M2
Coal Run, Ky. (†41501) 237/R5
Coalspur, Alberta 182/B3
Coalton, Ill. (†62075) 222/D4
Coalton, Ohio (45621) 284/E7
Coalton, W. Va. (26257) 312/G5
Coal Valley, Alberta 182/B3
Coal Valley, Ill. (61240) 222/C2
Coalville, England 13/F5
Coalville, Iowa (†50501) 229/E4
Coalville, Utah (84017) 304/C3
Coalwood, Mont. (†59851) 262/L5
Coalwood, W. Va. (24824) 312/C8
Coambo, Angola 115/C5
Coamo, Angola 102/D5
Coamo, P. Rico 161/D2
Coamo, P. Rico 161/D3
Coamo (res.), P. Rico 161/D3
Coamo (riv.), P. Rico 161/D3
Coari, Brazil 120/C3
Coari, Brazil 132/H9
Coarsegold, Calif. (93614) 204/F6
Coast (mts.) 162/C4
Coast (ranges) 188/B2
Coast (mts.), Alaska 196/N1
Coast (mts.), Br. Col. 146/E4
Coast (mts.), Br. Col. 184/D3
Coast (ranges), Calif. 204/D7
Coast (prov.), Kenya 115/G4
Coast (ranges), Oreg. 291/D5
Coast (ranges), U.S. 146/F5
Coast (ranges), Wash. 310/B3
Coast Guard Academy, Conn. 210/G3
Coatbridge, Scotland 10/B1
Coatbridge, Scotland 15/C2
Coatepec, Mexico 150/P1
Coatepeque, Guatemala 154/A3
Coates, Minn. (†55068) 255/E6
Coatesville, Ind. (46121) 227/D5
Coatesville, Pa. (19320) 294/L5
Coatetelco, Mexico 150/L2
Coaticook, Québec 172/F4
Coatopa, Ala. (35450) 195/B6
Coats, Kansas (67028) 232/D4
Coats, N.C. (27521) 281/M4
Coats (isl.), N.W.T. 162/H3
Coats (isl.), N.W.T. 146/K3
Coats (isl.), N.W. Terrs. 187/K3
Coatsburg, Ill. (62325) 222/B3
Coats Land (reg.), Ant. 2/H10
Coats Land (reg.) 5/B17
Coatsville, Mo. (63535) 261/G1
Coatzacoalcos, Mexico 146/J8
Coatzacoalcos, Mexico 150/M7
Coatzingo, Mexico 150/N2
Cobalt, Conn. (06414) 210/E2
Cobalt, Idaho (83229) 220/D4
Cobalt, Ont. 162/H6
Cobalt, Ontario 177/K5
Cobalt, Ontario 175/D3
Cobalt City, Mo. (†63645) 261/M7
Cobán, Guatemala 154/B3
Cobar, N. S. Wales 88/H6
Cobar, N.S. Wales 97/C2
Cobargo, N.S. Wales 97/E5
Cobb (co.), Georgia 217/C3
Cobb, Georgia (31735) 217/E7
Cobb, Ky. (42405) 237/F6
Cobb (riv.), Minn. 255/E7
Cobb (isl.), Va. 307/S6
Cobb, Wis. (53526) 317/F10
Cobbadah, N.S. Wales 97/F2
Cobble Hill, Br. Col. 184/K3
Cobble Mountain (res.), Mass. 249/C4
Cobbs Creek, Va. (23035) 307/R6
Cobbtown, Georgia (30420) 217/H6
Cobden, Ill. (62920) 222/D6
Cobden, Minn. (†56085) 255/D6
Cobden, Ontario 177/H2
Cobden, Victoria 97/B6
Cobequid (bay), Nova Scotia 168/E3
Cóbh, Ireland 10/B5
Cóbh, Ireland 17/E8
Cobham (riv.), Manitoba 179/G1
Cobham (riv.), Ontario 175/A2
Cobija, Bolivia 136/A2
Cobija, Brazil 120/E4
Coble, Tenn. (†37033) 237/F9
Cobleskill, N.Y. (12043) 276/L5
Coboconk, Ontario 177/F3
Cobourg (pen.), North. Terr. 88/E2
Cobourg (pen.), North. Terr. 93/C1
Cobourg, Ontario 177/F4
Cobquecura, Chile 138/D1
Cobram, Victoria 97/C4
Cobre, Nev. (†89830) 266/G1
Cóbuè, Mozambique 118/F2
Coburg, Iowa (†51566) 229/C7
Coburg (isl.), N.W. Terrs. 187/L2
Coburg, Oreg. (97401) 291/E3
Coburg, Victoria 88/K7
Coburg, Victoria 97/H5
Coburg, W. Germany 22/D3
Coburn, Pa. (16832) 294/H4
Coburn, W. Va. (26562) 312/F3
Coca, Ecuador 128/D3
Cocachacra, Peru 128/G11
Cocagne, New Bruns. 170/F2
Cocagne (isl.), New Bruns. 170/F2
Cocagne (riv.), New Bruns. 170/F2
Cocagne Cape, New Bruns. 170/F2
Cocama, Peru 128/G8
Cocanada (Kakinada), India 68/E5
Cocani, Bolivia 136/B7
Cocapata, Bolivia 136/B5
Cocentaina, Spain 33/F3
Cochabamba (dept.), Bolivia 136/C5
Cochabamba, Bolivia 120/C4
Cochabamba, Bolivia 136/C5
Cochamó, Chile 138/E3
Coche (isl.), Venezuela 124/F2
Cocheco (riv.), N.H. 268/E5
Cochecton, N.Y. (12726) 276/K7
Cochem, W. Germany 22/B3
Cochenour, Ontario 175/B2
Cochetopa (creek), Colo. 208/F6
Cochimbo, Serra do (mts.), Brazil 132/C5
Cochin, Sask. 181/C2
Cochin-Alleppey, India 68/D6
Cochinos (bay), Cuba 158/D2
Cochise (co.), Ariz. 198/F7
Cochise, Ariz. (85606) 198/F6
Cochiti, N. Mex. (†87041) 274/C3
Cochituate, Mass. (01778) 249/A7
Cochituate (lake), Mass. 249/A7
Cochran, Georgia (31014) 217/F6
Cochran (co.), Texas 303/B4
Cochrane, Ala. (†35442) 195/B4
Cochrane, Alberta 182/C4
Cochrane (lake), Chile 138/E7
Cochrane, Cerro (mt.), Chile 138/E7
Cochrane (riv.), Manitoba 179/H2
Cochrane, Ont. 146/K5
Cochrane, Ont. 162/H6
Cochrane (terr. dist.), Ontario 177/J4
Cochrane (terr. dist.), Ontario 175/D2
Cochrane, Ontario 177/K5
Cochrane, Ontario 175/D3
Cochrane (riv.), Sask. 181/N2
Cochrane, Wis. (54622) 317/C7
Cochranton, Pa. (16314) 294/B2
Cochranville, Pa. (19330) 294/L6
Cockburn (chan.), Chile 138/E11
Cockburn (isl.), Ontario 177/A2
Cockburn, S. Australia 94/G5
Cockburn (sound), W. Australia 88/B2
Cockburn Harbour, Turks & Caicos 156/D2
Cockburnspath, Scotland 15/F5
Cocke (co.), Tenn. 237/P9
Cockenoe (isl.), Conn. 210/B4
Cockenzie and Port Seton, Scotland 15/D1
Cockermouth, England 13/D3
Cockermouth, England 10/E3
Cockeysville, Md. (21030) 245/M3
Cockrell Hill, Texas (75211) 303/G2
Cockrum, Miss. (†38632) 256/E1
Coclé del Norte, Panama 154/G6
Coco (chan.), Burma 72/B4
Coco (cay), Cuba 158/G1
Coco (riv.), Honduras 154/E3
Coco (chan.), India 68/G6
Coco (riv.), Nicaragua 154/E3
Coco, W. Va. (†25071) 312/D6
Cocoa, Fla. (32922) 212/F3
Cocoa Beach, Fla. (32931) 212/F3
Cocobeach, Gabon 115/B3
Cocodrie (lake), La. 238/E5
Cocolamus, Pa. (17014) 294/H4
Coconino (co.), Ariz. 198/C3
Coconino (plat.), Ariz. 198/C3
Coconut Creek, Fla. (†33060) 212/F5
Cocopah Ind. Res., Ariz. 198/A6
Cocorit, Mexico 150/E3
Cocos (isls.), Australia 2/P6
Cocos (isls.), Australia 54/L11
Cocos (isl.), C. Rica 146/K9
Cocos (isl.), Guam 86/K7
Cocos (bay), Trin. & Tob. 161/B10
Cocuy, Sierra Nevada del (mts.), Colombia 126/D4
Cod (cape), Mass. 146/M5
Cod (cape), Mass. 188/N2
Cod (cape), Mass. 249/O4
Cod (isl.), Newf. 166/B2
Codajás, Brazil 120/C3
Codajás, Brazil 132/H9
Coddle (harb.), Nova Scotia 168/G3
Codegua, Chile 138/G4
Codell, Kansas (67630) 232/C2
Coden, Ala. (36523) 195/B10
Codera (cape), Venezuela 124/F2
Coderre, Sask. 181/E5
Codesa, Alberta 182/B2
Codes Corner, Ontario 177/H3
Codette, Sask. 181/H2
Codfish (isl.), N. Zealand 100/A7
Codigua, Chile 138/F4
Codington (co.), S. Dak. 298/P4
Codó, Brazil 120/E3
Codó, Brazil 132/E4
Codorus, Pa. (17311) 294/J6
Codpa, Chile 138/B1
Codrington, Ant. & Bar. 156/G3
Codrington, Barbados 161/B8
Codroipo, Italy 34/D2
Codroy, Newf. 166/C4
Cody, Nebr. (69211) 264/C2
Cody, Wyo. (82414) 319/D1
Codys, New Bruns. 170/E3
Coe, Ind. (†47598) 227/C8
Coeburn, Va. (24230) 307/D7
Coe Hill, Ontario 177/G3
Coelemu, Chile 138/D1
Coello, Ill. (62825) 222/D6
Coen, Queensland 88/G2
Coen, Queensland 95/B2
Coeroeni (riv.), Suriname 131/C4
Coesfeld, W. Germany 22/B3
Coesse, Ind. (†46725) 227/G2
Coeur d'Alene, Idaho (83814) 220/B2
Coeur d'Alene, Idaho 188/C1
Coeur d'Alene (lake), Idaho 220/B2
Coeur d'Alene (mts.), Idaho 220/C2
Coeur d'Alene (riv.), Idaho 220/B2
Coevorden, Netherlands 27/K3
Coeymans, N.Y. (12045) 276/N6
Coffee (co.), Ala. 195/G8
Coffee (co.), Georgia 217/G8
Coffee (co.), Tenn. 237/J9
Coffee Creek, Mont. (59424) 262/F3
Coffeen, Ill. (62017) 222/D4
Coffee Springs, Ala. (36318) 195/G8
Coffeeville, Ala. (36524) 195/B7
Coffeeville (dam), Ala. 195/B7
Coffeeville, Miss. (38922) 256/E3
Coffey (co.), Kansas 232/G3
Coffey, Mo. (64636) 261/E2
Coffeyville, Kans. 188/G3
Coffeyville, Kansas (67337) 232/G4
Coffin (bay), S. Australia 94/D6
Coffin Bay (pen.), S. Australia 94/D6
Coffs Harbour, N. S. Wales 88/J6
Coffs Harbour, N.S. Wales 97/G2
Cofield, N.C. (27922) 281/R2
Cogan Station, Pa. (†17728) 294/H3
Cogar, Okla. (†73059) 288/K4
Cogdell, Georgia (31628) 217/G8
Cogealac, Romania 45/J3
Coggon, Iowa (52218) 229/L4
Coghinas (riv.), Italy 34/B4
Coglians (Hohe Warte) (mt.), Austria 41/B3
Cognac, France 28/C5
Cogolludo, Spain 33/E2
Cogotí, Chile 138/A8
Cogswell, N. Dak. (58017) 282/P7
Cogton, Philippines 82/E6
Cohagen, Mont. (59322) 262/K3
Cohansey (riv.), N.J. 273/C5
Cohasset, Ala. (36474) 195/E8
Cohasset○, Mass. (02025) 249/F7
Cohasset, Minn. (55721) 255/E3
Cohoctah, Mich. (48816) 250/F6
Cohocton, N.Y. (14826) 276/F5
Cohocton (riv.), N.Y. 276/F6
Cohoe, Alaska (†99669) 196/B1
Cohoes, N.Y. (12047) 276/N5
Cohoni, Bolivia 136/B5
Cohuna, Victoria 97/C4
Cohutta, Georgia (30710) 217/C1
Coiba, Isla de (isl.), Panama 154/F7
Coihaique, Chile 138/E6
Coihaique Alto, Chile 138/E6
Coihueco, Chile 138/A11
Coila, Miss. (38923) 256/E4
Coill Dubh, Ireland 17/H5
Coimbatore, India 54/J8
Coimbatore, India 68/D6
Coimbra (dist.), Portugal 33/B2
Coimbra, Portugal 7/D4
Coimbra, Portugal 33/B2
Coin, Iowa (51636) 229/C7
Coín, Spain 33/D4
Coinco, Chile 138/G5
Coinjock, N.C. (27923) 281/S2
Coipasa, Bolivia 136/A6
Coipasa (lake), Bolivia 136/B6
Coipasa (salt dep.), Bolivia 136/A6
Coire, Loch (lake), Scotland 15/D2
Cojata, Peru 128/H10
Cojedes (state), Venezuela 124/D3
Cojedes (riv.), Venezuela 124/D3
Cojimíes, Ecuador 128/B2
Cojoro, Venezuela 124/C2
Cojutepeque, El Salvador 154/C4
Cokato, Minn. (55321) 255/D5
Coke (co.), Texas 303/D6
Cokeburg, Pa. (15324) 294/B5
Cokedale, Colo. (81032) 208/K8
Coker, Ala. (35452) 195/C4
Cokercreek, Tenn. (37314) 237/N10
Coketon, W. Va. (†26292) 312/G4
Cokeville, Wyo. (83114) 319/B3
Colaba (pt.), India 68/B7
Colac, Victoria 88/G7
Colac, Victoria 97/B6
Colachel, India 68/D7
Colair (lake), India 68/E5
Colamus (riv.), Nebr. 264/E2
Colasay, Peru 128/C5
Colatina, Brazil 120/E4
Colatina, Brazil 132/F7
Colbeck (cape) 5/B10
Colbert (co.), Ala. 195/C1
Colbert, Georgia (30628) 217/F2
Colbert, Okla. (74733) 288/O7
Colbert, Wash. (99005) 310/H3
Colborne, Ontario 177/G4
Colbún, Chile 138/A11
Colburn, Idaho (83865) 220/B1
Colburn, Ind. (47931) 227/D3
Colby, Kansas (67701) 232/A2
Colby, Wash. (†98366) 310/A2
Colby, Wis. (54421) 317/F6
Colcamar, Peru 128/D6
Colchester, Conn. (06415) 210/F2
Colchester○, Conn. (06415) 210/F2
Colchester, England 13/H6
Colchester, England 10/G5
Colchester, Ill. (62326) 222/C3
Colchester (co.), Nova Scotia 168/E3
Colchester, Ontario 177/B6
Colchester○, Vt. (05446) 268/A2
Colcord, Okla. (74338) 288/S2
Colcord, W. Va. (25048) 312/D7
Cold (bay), Alaska 196/F4
Cold (lake), Alberta 182/E2
Cold (riv.), N.H. 268/C5
Cold Bay, Alaska (99571) 196/F3
Cold Brook, N.Y. (13324) 276/L4
Coldbrook Station, Nova Scotia 168/D3
Colden, N.Y. (14033) 276/C5
Coldingham, Scotland 15/F5
Cold Lake, Alberta 182/E2
Cold Spring, Ky. (41076) 237/T2
Cold Spring, Minn. (56320) 255/D5
Cold Spring, N.J. (†08204) 273/D6
Cold Spring (inlet), N.J. 273/D6
Cold Spring, N.Y. (10516) 276/N8
Coldspring (head), Nova Scotia 168/E3
Coldspring, Texas (77331) 303/J7
Cold Spring Harbor, N.Y. (11724) 276/R6
Cold Springs, Okla. (†73564) 288/J5
Coldstream, Br. Col. 184/H5
Cold Stream (pond), Maine 243/G5
Coldstream, New Bruns. 170/C2
Coldstream, Scotland 10/E3
Coldstream, Scotland 15/F5
Coldstream, Victoria 97/K4
Coldwater, Kansas (67029) 232/C4
Coldwater, Mich. (49036) 250/D7
Coldwater, Miss. (38618) 256/E1
Coldwater (riv.), Miss. 256/D1
Coldwater, Ohio (45828) 284/A5
Coldwater, Ontario 177/E3
Coldwater, Tenn. (†37334) 237/H10
Coldwater (creek), Texas 303/B1
Coldwater, W. Va. (†26411) 312/E4
Cole (co.), Mo. 261/H6
Cole (harb.), Nova Scotia 168/E4
Cole, Okla. (†73010) 288/L5
Colebrook○, Conn. (06021) 210/C1
Colebrook, N.H. (03576) 268/E2
Colebrook○, N.H. (03576) 268/E2
Colebrook, Ohio (†44034) 284/J2
Colebrook, Tasmania 99/D4
Colebrook River (lake), Conn. 210/C1
Cole Camp, Mo. (65325) 261/F6
Coleen (riv.), Alaska 196/K1
Colegrove, Pa. (†16749) 294/F2
Coleharbor, N. Dak. (58531) 282/H4
Coleman, Alberta 182/C5
Coleman, Alta. 162/E6
Coleman, Fla. (33521) 212/D3
Coleman, Georgia (31736) 217/C7
Coleman, Mich. (48618) 250/E5
Coleman, Okla. (73432) 288/O6
Coleman (riv.), Queensland 95/B2
Coleman (co.), Texas 303/E6
Coleman, Texas (76834) 303/E6

354 Coleman

Coleman, Wis. (54112) 317/L5
Coleman Falls, Va. (24536) 307/K6
Colemans Lake, Georgia (†30441) 217/H5
Çölemerik, Turkey 63/K4
Colerain, N.C. (27924) 281/R2
Coleraine, Minn. (55722) 255/E3
Coleraine (dist.), N. Ireland 17/H1
Coleraine, N. Ireland 17/H1
Coleraine, N. Ireland 10/C3
Coleraine, Québec 172/F4
Coleraine, Victoria 97/A5
Coleridge, Nebr. (68727) 264/G2
Coleridge (lake), N. Zealand 100/C5
Coleridge, N.C. (27234) 281/K3
Coles (co.), Ill. 222/E4
Coles, Miss. (†39638) 256/C8
Coles (pt.), Peru 128/G11
Colesberg, S. Africa 118/D6
Colesburg, Georgia (†31569) 217/J9
Colesburg, Iowa (52035) 229/L3
Colesburg, Ky. (†40150) 237/K5
Coles Island, New Bruns. 170/E3
Coles Point, Va. (22442) 307/P4
Colesville, Md. (20904) 245/K4
Colesville, N.J. (†07461) 273/D1
Coleta, Ill. (61017) 222/D2
Coleville, Calif. (96107) 204/F5
Coleville, Sask. 181/B4
Colfax, Calif. (95713) 204/E4
Colfax, Ill. (61728) 222/E3
Colfax, Ind. (46035) 227/D4
Colfax, Iowa (50054) 229/G5
Colfax, La. (71417) 238/E3
Colfax (co.), Nebr. 264/G3
Colfax (co.), N. Mex. 274/E2
Colfax, N. Dak. (58018) 282/S7
Colfax, Sask. 181/H6
Colfax, Wash. (99111) 310/H4
Colfax, Wis. (54730) 317/C6
Colgan, N. Dak. (†58844) 282/C2
Colgate, N. Dak. (†58046) 282/P5
Colgate (cape), N.W. Terrs. 187/J1
Colgate, Sask. 181/H6
Colgate, Wis. (53017) 317/K1
Colhué Huapí (lake), Argentina 143/C6
Co Lieu, Vietnam 72/E3
Colignan, Victoria 97/B4
Colijnsplaat, Netherlands 27/D5
Colima (state), Mexico 150/G7
Colima, Mexico 150/H7
Colina, Chile 138/G3
Colina (riv.), Chile 138/G3
Colinas, Brazil 132/F4
Colinet, Newf. 166/D2
Colington, N.C. (†27949) 281/T3
Colinton, Alberta 182/D2
Coll, Scotland 15/B2
Coll (isl.), Scotland 15/B4
Coll (isl.), Scotland 10/C2
Collaguasi, Chile 138/B3
Collamer, Ind. (†46787) 227/F2
Collarenebri, N.S. Wales 97/E1
Collbran, Colo. (81624) 208/C4
Colle di Val d'Elsa, Italy 34/C3
College, Alaska (99701) 196/J1
College Bridge, New Bruns. 170/F3
College City, Ark. (72476) 202/J1
College Corner, Ohio (45003) 284/A6
Collegedale, Tenn. (37315) 237/M10
College Grove, Tenn. (37046) 237/H9
College Heights, Alberta 182/D3
College Hill, Ky. (40416) 237/N5
College Hill, Miss. (†38655) 256/E2
College Mound, Mo. (†65247) 261/G3
College Park, Georgia (30337) 217/K2
College Park, Md. (20740) 245/G4
College Place, Wash. (99324) 310/G4
College Springs, Iowa (51637) 229/C7
College Station, Texas (77840) 303/H7
Collegeville, Ind. (47978) 227/C3
Collegeville, Minn. (56321) 255/D5
Collegeville, Pa. (19426) 294/M5
Colle Sestriere, Italy 34/A2
Colleton (co.), S.C. 296/F6
Collett, Ind. (†47371) 227/H4
Collette, New Bruns. 170/E2
Collettsville, N.C. (28611) 281/F3
Colley, Pa. (†18614) 294/K2
Colleyville, Texas (76034) 303/F2
Collie, Australia 87/B9
Collie, N.S. Wales 97/E2
Collie, W. Australia 88/B6
Collie, W. Australia 92/B2
Collier (co.), Fla. 212/E5
Collier (bay), W. Australia 88/C3
Collier (bay), W. Australia 92/C1
Colliers, Newf. 166/D2
Colliers, S.C. (†29838) 296/C4
Colliers, W. Va. (26035) 312/E2
Collierstown, Va. (†24450) 307/J5
Collierville, Tenn. (38017) 237/B10
Colliguay, Chile 138/F3
Collin (co.), Texas 303/H4
Collingdale, Pa. (19023) 294/N7
Collingswood, N.J. (08108) 273/B3
Collingsworth (co.), Texas 303/D3
Collingwood, N. Zealand 100/D4
Collingwood, Ontario 177/D3
Collingwood, Victoria 97/J5
Collingwood, Victoria 88/L7
Collingwood Corner, Nova Scotia 168/E3
Collins, Ark. (71634) 202/G6
Collins, Georgia (30421) 217/H6
Collins, Iowa (50055) 229/G5
Collins, Miss. (39428) 256/E7
Collins, Mo. (64738) 261/E7
Collins, Mont. (†59433) 262/E3
Collins, N.Y. (14034) 276/C6
Collins (head), Norfolk I. 88/L6
Collins, Ohio (44826) 284/E3
Collins, Ontario 177/G4
Collins (riv.), Tenn. 237/K9
Collins Bay, Ontario 177/H3
Collins Bay, Sask. 181/M2
Collins Center, N.Y. (14035) 276/C6
Collinston, La. (71229) 238/G1
Collinston, Utah (84306) 304/B2
Collinsville, Ala. (35961) 195/G2
Collinsville, Calif. (†94585) 204/L1
Collinsville, Conn. (06022) 210/D1
Collinsville, Ill. (62234) 222/B2
Collinsville, Mass. (†01826) 249/J2
Collinsville, Miss. (39325) 256/G6
Collinsville, Ohio (45004) 284/A6
Collinsville, Okla. (74021) 288/P2
Collinsville, Queensland 88/H4
Collinsville, Queensland 95/C4
Collinsville, Va. (24078) 307/J7
Collinwood, Tenn. (38450) 237/F10
Collipulli, Chile 138/E2
Collirene, Ala. (†36785) 195/E6
Collis, Minn. (†56236) 255/B5
Collison, Ill. (61831) 222/F3
Collista, Ky. (†41222) 237/R5
Collombey-Muraz, Switzerland 39/C4
Collon, Ireland 17/J4
Collon (mt.), Switzerland 39/D5
Collonge-Bellerive, Switzerland 39/B4
Collooney, Ireland 17/E3
Collpa, Bolivia 136/C6
Collyer, Kansas (67631) 232/B2
Colma, Calif. (94014) 204/J2
Colman, S. Dak. (57017) 298/R6
Colmar, France 28/G3
Colmar, Pa. (18915) 294/M5
Colmar Manor, Md. (†20722) 245/F4
Colmenar, Spain 33/D4
Colmenar de Oreja, Spain 33/G5
Colmenar Viejo, Spain 33/F4
Colmesneil, Texas (75938) 303/K7
Colmonell, Scotland 15/D5
Colne, England 10/G1
Colne, England 13/H1
Colne (riv.), England 10/B5
Colne (riv.), England 13/G8
Colne Valley, England 10/G2
Colne Valley, England 13/J2
Colo, Iowa (50056) 229/G4
Colo (riv.), N.S. Wales 97/F3
Cologne, Minn. (55322) 255/E6
Cologne, N.J. (08213) 273/D4
Cologne, W. Germany 7/E3
Cologne, W. Germany 22/B3
Coloma, Calif. (95613) 204/D5
Coloma, Mich. (49038) 250/C6
Coloma, Wis. (54930) 317/H7
Colombes, France 28/A1
Colombia 2/F5
Colombia 120/B2
COLOMBIA 126
Colombia, Colombia 126/C6
Colombo (cap.), Sri Lanka 54/J9
Colombo (cap.), Sri Lanka 2/N5
Colombo (cap.), Sri Lanka 68/D7
Colome, S. Dak. (57528) 298/K7
Colón, Buenos Aires, Argentina 143/F6
Colón, Entre Ríos, Argentina 143/G6
Colón, Colombia 120/B1
Colón, Colombia 126/B7
Colón, Cuba 158/D1
Colón, Cuba 156/B2
Colón, Archipiélago de (terr.), Ecuador 128/C8
Colón (mts.), Honduras 154/E3
Colón, Mexico 150/K6
Colon, Mich. (49040) 250/D7
Colon, Nebr. (68018) 264/H3
Colón, Pan. 146/K9
Colón, Panama 154/H6
Colón, Isla de (isl.), Panama 154/G6
Colón, Lavalleja, Uruguay 145/E4
Colón, Montevideo, Uruguay 145/B7
Colón, Venezuela 124/E6
Colona, Colo. (†81401) 208/D6
Colona, Ill. (61241) 222/C2
Colonarie, St. Vin. & Grens. 161/A9
Colonarie (pt.), St. Vin. & Grens. 161/A9
Colonel Light Gardens, S. Australia 88/D8
Colonel Light Gardens, S. Australia 94/A8
Colonia, N.J. (07067) 273/E2
Colonia (dept.), Uruguay 145/B5
Colonia, Uruguay 145/B5
Colonia Agraciada, Uruguay 145/A4
Colonia Arrué, Uruguay 145/B5
Colonia Artigas, Uruguay 145/B1
Colonia Concordia, Uruguay 145/A4
Colonia Elisa, Argentina 143/E2
Colonia Itacumbú, Uruguay 145/B1
Colonia Josefa, Argentina 143/D4
Colonia Las Heras, Argentina 143/C6
Colonia Lavalleja, Uruguay 145/C2
Colonial Beach, Va. (22443) 307/P4
Colonial Heights, Tenn. (37663) 237/R8
Colonial Heights (I.C.), Va. (23834) 307/O6
Colonial Nat'l Hist. Park, Va. 307/P6
Colonia Neuland, Paraguay 144/B3
Colonia Palma, Uruguay 145/B1
Colonia Pte. Stroessner, Paraguay 144/D3
Colonia Rossel y Rius, Uruguay 145/D4
Colonias, N. Mex. (†88435) 274/E3
Colonia San Alfredo, Paraguay 144/D3
Colonia Sgto. José E. Lopéz, Paraguay 144/D3
Colonia Valdense, Uruguay 145/B5
Colonia Yby Yu, Paraguay 144/E3
Colonie, N.Y. (†12201) 276/N5
Colonne (cape), Italy 34/F5
Colonsay, Sask. 181/F4
Colonsay (isl.), Scotland 10/C2
Colonsay (isl.), Scotland 15/B4
Colony, Kansas (66015) 232/G3
Colony, Mo. (†63563) 261/H2
Colony, Okla. (73021) 288/J4
Colony, Wyo. (†57717) 319/H1
Colora, Md. (21917) 245/O2
Colorada (lag.), Bolivia 136/A8
Colorado 188/E3
COLORADO 208
Colorado (riv.) 188/D4
Colorado (riv.), Argentina 2/F5
Colorado (riv.), Argentina 120/C6
Colorado (riv.), Argentina 143/D4
Colorado (riv.), Ariz. 198/A5
Colorado (riv.), Calif. 204/L8
Colorado (riv.), Colo. 208/A5
Colorado (riv.), Mexico 150/B1
Colorado, Arroyo (riv.), N. Mex. 274/B4
Colorado (co.), Texas 303/H8
Colorado (riv.), Texas 188/G4
Colorado (riv.), Texas 146/H6
Colorado (riv.), Texas 303/F7
Colorado (state), U.S. 146/H6
Colorado (riv.), U.S. 146/G6
Colorado (riv.), U.S. 2/D4
Colorado (riv.), Utah 304/E5
Colorado City, Ariz. (86021) 198/B2
Colorado City, Colo. (81019) 208/K6
Colorado City, Texas (79512) 303/C5
Colorado Nat'l Mon., Colo. 208/B4
Colorado River Aqueduct, Calif. 204/K10
Colorado River Ind. Res., Ariz. 198/A5
Colorado River Ind. Res., Calif. 204/L10
Colorados, Los (arch.), Cuba 158/A1
Colorado Springs, Colo. 146/H6
Colorado Springs, Colo. 188/F3
Colorado Springs, Colo. (*80901) 208/K5
Colored Hill, W. Va. (†24740) 312/D8
Colotlán, Mexico 150/H5
Colp, Ill. (62921) 222/D6
Colpoy (bay), Ontario 177/C3
Colpoys Bay, Ontario 177/C3
Colquechaca, Bolivia 136/B6
Colquiri, Bolivia 136/B5
Colquitt (co.), Georgia 217/E8
Colquitt, Georgia (31737) 217/C8
Colrain○, Mass. (01340) 249/D2
Colson, Ky. (†41858) 237/R6
Colstrip, Mont. (59323) 262/K5
Colt, Ark. (72326) 202/J3
Coltauco, Chile 138/F5
Colton, Calif. (92324) 204/E10
Colton, N.Y. (13625) 276/L1
Colton, Ohio (43510) 284/C3
Colton, Oreg. (97017) 291/B3
Colton, S. Dak. (57018) 298/P6
Colton, Utah (†84601) 304/C4
Colton, Wash. (99113) 310/H4
Coltons Point, Md. (20626) 245/M8
Colts Neck, N.J. (07722) 273/E3
Coluene (riv.), Brazil 120/D4
Columbia (riv.) 188/B1
Columbia, Ala. (36319) 195/H8
Columbia (glac.), Alaska 196/C1
Columbia (mt.), Alberta 182/B3
Columbia (co.), Ark. 202/D7
Columbia (lake), Br. Col. 184/K5
Columbia (mt.), Br. Col. 184/J4
Columbia (riv.), Br. Col. 184/H4
Columbia, Calif. (95310) 204/E5
Columbia (cape), Canada 4/A13
Columbia○, Conn. (06237) 210/F2
Columbia (co.), Fla. 212/D1
Columbia, Fla. (†32055) 212/D1
Columbia (co.), Georgia 217/H3
Columbia, Ill. (62236) 222/C5
Columbia, Iowa (50057) 229/G6
Columbia, Ky. (42728) 237/L6
Columbia, La. (71418) 238/F2
Columbia○, Maine (†04623) 243/H6
Columbia, Md. (21043) 245/L4
Columbia, Miss. (39429) 256/E8
Columbia, Mo. (65201) 261/H5
Columbia, Mo. 188/H3
Columbia, N.J. (07832) 273/C2
Columbia (co.), N.Y. 276/N6
Columbia, N.C. (27925) 281/S3
Columbia (cape), N.W.T. 162/N3
Columbia (cape), N.W. Terrs. 187/M1
Columbia (co.), Oreg. 291/D2
Columbia (riv.), Oreg. 291/G2
Columbia (co.), Pa. 294/K3
Columbia, Pa. (17512) 294/K5
Columbia (co.), S.C. 188/K4
Columbia (cap.), S.C. 146/K6
Columbia (cap.), S.C. (*29201) 296/F4
Columbia, S. Dak. (57433) 298/N2
Columbia, Tenn. 188/J3
Columbia, Tenn. (38401) 237/G9
Columbia (riv.), U.S. 146/F5
Columbia, Utah (†84501) 304/D4
Columbia, Va. (23038) 307/M5
Columbia (co.), Wash. 310/H4
Columbia (riv.), Wash. 310/B4
Columbia (co.), Wis. 317/H9
Columbia City, Ind. (46725) 227/G2
Columbia City, Oreg. (97018) 291/E2
Columbia Falls○, Maine (04623) 243/H6
Columbia Falls, Mont. (59912) 262/B2
Columbia Furnace, Va. (†22824) 307/L3
Columbia Heights, Minn. (55421) 255/G5
Columbia Heights, Wash. (†98632) 310/C4
Columbiana, Ala. (35051) 195/E4
Columbiana (co.), Ohio 284/J4
Columbiana, Ohio (44408) 284/J4
Columbia Road (res.), S. Dak. 298/N2
Columbia Station, Ohio (44028) 284/G10
Columbiaville, Mich. (48421) 250/F5
Columbine, Colo. (†80428) 208/E1
Columbretes (isls.), Spain 33/G3
Columbus (dam), Ala. 256/H3
Columbus, Ark. (71831) 202/C6
Columbus, Ga. 188/K4
Columbus, Ga. 146/K6
Columbus, Georgia (*31901) 217/C6
Columbus, Ill. (62328) 222/B4
Columbus, Ind. (47201) 227/E6
Columbus, Kansas (66725) 232/H4
Columbus, Ky. (42032) 237/C7
Columbus, Miss. 188/J4
Columbus, Miss. (39701) 256/H3
Columbus, Mont. (59019) 262/G5
Columbus, Nebr. (68601) 264/G3
Columbus, N.J. (08022) 273/D3
Columbus, N. Mex. (88029) 274/B7
Columbus (co.), N.C. 281/M6
Columbus, N.C. (28722) 281/E4
Columbus, N. Dak. (58727) 282/E2
Columbus (cap.), Ohio 188/K3
Columbus (cap.), Ohio 146/K6
Columbus (cap.), Ohio (*43201) 284/E6
Columbus, Pa. (16405) 294/C2
Columbus, Texas (78934) 303/H8
Columbus, Wis. (53925) 317/H9
Columbus A.F.B., Miss. 256/H3
Columbus City, Iowa (52737) 229/L6
Columbus Grove, Ohio (45830) 284/B4
Columbus Junction, Iowa (52738) 229/L6
Columbus Salt (marsh), Nev. 266/C4
Colusa (co.), Calif. 204/C4
Colusa, Calif. (95932) 204/C4
Colusa, Ill. (62329) 222/B3
Colver, Pa. (15927) 294/E4
Colville (riv.), Alaska 188/C5
Colville (riv.), Alaska 196/G1
Colville (cape), N. Zealand 100/E2
Colville (bay), N.W. Terrs. 187/K3
Colville (lake), N.W. Terrs. 187/F3
Colville, Wash. (99114) 310/H2
Colville (riv.), Wash. 310/H2
Colville Ind. Res., Wash. 310/G2
Colville Lake, N.W. Terrs. 187/F3
Colwell, Iowa (50620) 229/H2
Colwich, Kansas (67030) 232/E4
Colwyn, Pa. (†19023) 294/N7
Colwyn Bay, Wales 10/E4
Colwyn Bay, Wales 13/D4
Comacchio, Italy 34/D2
Comai, China 77/D6
Comal (co.), Texas 303/F8
Comala, Mexico 150/H7
Comalapa, Guatemala 154/B3
Comalapa, Nicaragua 154/E4
Comalcalco, Mexico 150/N7
Comanche (co.), Kansas 232/C4
Comanche, Mont. (†59015) 262/H4
Comanche (co.), Okla. 288/K5
Comanche, Okla. (73529) 288/L6
Comanche (co.), Texas 303/F5
Comanche, Texas (76442) 303/F6
Comandante Fontana, Argentina 143/D2
Comandante Luis Piedrabuena, Argentina 143/C6
Comaneşti, Romania 45/H2
Comarapa, Bolivia 136/C5
Comayagua, Honduras 154/D3
Combahee (riv.), S.C. 296/F6
Combarbalá, Chile 138/A8
Comber, N. Ireland 17/K2
Comber, Ontario 177/B5
Combermere (bay), Burma 72/B3
Combermere, Ontario 177/G2
Combine, Texas (†75159) 303/H3
Combined Locks, Wis. (54113) 317/K7
Comblain-au-Pont, Belgium 27/G8
Combourg, France 28/C3
Comboyne, N.S. Wales 97/G2
Combs, Ark. (72721) 202/C2
Combs, Ky. (41729) 237/P6
Comb Wash (creek), Utah 304/E6
Comeauville, Nova Scotia 168/B4
Come By Chance, Newf. 166/C2
Come-by-Chance, N.S. Wales 97/E2
Comendador, Dom. Rep. 158/C6
Comer, Ala. (†36053) 195/H6
Comer, Georgia (30629) 217/F2
Comeragh (mts.), Ireland 17/F7
Comerford (dam), N.H. 268/D3
Comerford (dam), Vt. 268/D3
Comerío, P. Rico 161/D2
Comet (riv.), Queensland 88/H4
Comet (riv.), Queensland 95/D5
Comfort, N.C. (28522) 281/O5
Comfort (cape), N.W. Terrs. 187/K3
Comfort, Texas (78013) 303/F7
Comfrey, Minn. (56019) 255/D6
Comilla, Bangladesh 68/G4
Comines, Belgium 27/B7
Comino (isl.), Malta 34/E7
Comins, Mich. (48619) 250/E4
Comiso, Italy 34/E6
Comitán de Domínguez, Mexico 150/O8
Comite, La. (†70739) 238/K1
Commack, N.Y. (11725) 276/O9
Commentry, France 28/E4
Commerce, Calif. (90040) 204/C10
Commerce, Georgia (30529) 217/E2
Commerce, Mo. (63742) 261/O8
Commerce, Okla. (74339) 288/R1
Commerce, Texas (75428) 303/J4
Commerce City, Colo. (80022) 208/K3
Commercial Point, Ohio (43116) 284/E6
Commercy, France 28/F3
Commewijne (dist.), Suriname 131/D3
Commewijne (riv.), Suriname 131/D3
Commiskey, Ind. (47227) 227/F7
Commissaires (lake), Québec 172/E1
Commissioner (isl.), Manitoba 179/E2
Committee (bay), N.W.T. 162/H2
Committee (bay), N.W. Terrs. 187/K3
Commodore, Pa. (15729) 294/D4
Commodore (reef), Philippines 85/F4
Commonwealth, Wis. (†54121) 317/K4
Communism (mt.), U.S.S.R. 54/J6
Communism (peak), U.S.S.R. 48/H6
Como, Colo. (80432) 208/H4
Como (prov.), Italy 34/B2
Como, Italy 7/E4
Como, Italy 34/B2
Como (lake), Italy 34/B1
Como, La. (†71295) 238/G2
Como, Miss. (38619) 256/E1
Como, N.C. (27818) 281/P1
Como, Tenn. (38223) 237/E8
Como, Texas (75431) 303/J4
Como, Wis. (†53147) 317/K10
Comodoro Rivadavia, Argentina 143/C6
Comodoro Rivadavia, Argentina 120/C7
Comoé (riv.), Ivory Coast 106/D7
Comoé (riv.), Upper Volta 106/D7
Comorin (cape), India 54/J9
Comorin (cape), India 2/N5
Comorin (cape), India 68/D7
Comoros 2/M6
Comoros 102/G6
COMOROS 118/G2
Comox, Br. Col. 184/H2
Compañero, Arroyo (creek), N. Mex. 274/B2
Compass Lake, Fla. (32448) 212/D6
Compeer, Alberta 182/E4
Compiègne, France 28/E3
Compostela, Mexico 150/G6
Comprida (isl.), Brazil 135/C4
Comptche, Calif. (95427) 204/B4
Compton, Calif. (*90220) 204/C11
Compton, Ill. (61318) 222/D2
Compton, Md. (20627) 245/M7
Compton (co.), Québec 172/F4
Compton, Québec 172/F4
Comrie, Scotland 15/E4
Comstock, Mich. (49041) 250/D6
Comstock, Minn. (56525) 255/B4
Comstock, Nebr. (68828) 264/E3
Comstock, N.Y. (12821) 276/O4
Comstock, Texas (78837) 303/C8
Comstock, Wis. (54826) 317/C5
Comstocks Bridge, Conn. (†06424) 210/F2
Comté (riv.), Fr. Guiana 131/E3
Comunidad, Venezuela 124/E6
Cona, China 77/D6
Conaica, Peru 128/E9
Conakry (cap.), Guinea 102/A4
Conanicut (isl.), R.I. 249/J6
Conara Junction, Tasmania 99/D3
Conargo, N.S. Wales 97/C4
Conasauga, Tenn. (37316) 237/M10
Conasauga (riv.), Tenn. 237/M11
Concarneau, France 28/A4
Conceição da Barra, Brazil 132/G7
Conceição do Araguaia, Brazil 132/D5
Conceição do Araguaia, Brazil 120/D3
Concepción, Corrientes, Argentina 143/E2
Concepción, Tucumán, Argentina 143/C2
Concepción, El Beni, Bolivia 136/B2
Concepción, Santa Cruz, Bolivia 136/D5
Concepción (lag.), Bolivia 136/E5
Concepción, Chile 138/D1
Concepción, Chile 120/B6
Concepción (chan.), Chile 138/D9
Concepción (bay), Mexico 150/D3
Concepción (dept.), Paraguay 144/D3
Concepción, Paraguay 144/D3
Concepción, Paraguay 120/D5
Concepción, Peru 128/E8
Concepcion, Texas (78349) 303/F10
Concepción de la Sierra, Argentina 143/E2
Concepción del Oro, Mexico 150/J4
Concepción del Uruguay, Argentina 143/G6
Concepción de María, Honduras 154/D4
Conception (pt.), Calif. 188/B4
Conception (pt.), Calif. 204/E9
Conception (bay), Newf. 166/D2
Conception Harbour, Newf. 166/D2
Conception Junction, Mo. (64434) 261/C2
Conchas (res.), N. Mex. 188/F3
Conchas (dam), N. Mex. 274/E3
Conchas (lake), N. Mex. 274/E3
Conchas (riv.), N. Mex. 274/E3
Conchas Dam, N. Mex. (88416) 274/E3
Conche, Newf. 166/C3
Conchi, Chile 138/B3
Conchillas, Uruguay 145/B5
Conchi Viejo, Chile 138/B3
Concho, Ariz. (85924) 198/F4
Concho, Okla. (73022) 288/L3
Concho (co.), Texas 303/E6
Conchos (riv.), Mexico 146/H7
Conchos (riv.), Mexico 150/G2
Concise, Switzerland 39/C3
Concón, Chile 138/F2
Conconully, Wash. (98819) 310/F2
Concord, Ark. (72523) 202/G2
Concord, Calif. (*94520) 204/K1
Concord, Del. (19973) 245/R6
Concord, Fla. (†32333) 212/B1
Concord, Georgia (30206) 217/D4
Concord, Ill. (62631) 222/C4
Concord, Ky. (41131) 237/P3
Concord○, Mass. (01742) 249/B6
Concord (riv.), Mass. 249/J2
Concord, Mich. (49237) 250/E6
Concord, Mo. (†63128) 261/P4
Concord, Nebr. (68728) 264/H2
Concord (cap.), N.H. 146/L5
Concord (cap.), N.H. 188/M2
Concord (cap.), N.H. (03301) 268/D5
Concord, N. S. Wales 88/K4
Concord, N.S. Wales 97/J3
Concord, N.C. (28025) 281/H4
Concord, Pa. (17217) 294/G5
Concord, Tenn. (37720) 237/N9
Concord○, Vt. (05824) 268/D3
Concord, Va. (24538) 307/K6
Concord, Wis. (†53066) 317/H1
Concordia, Argentina 143/G5
Concordia, Argentina 120/D6
Concórdia, Brazil 132/D9
Concordia, Honduras 154/D3
Concordia, Kansas (66901) 232/E2
Concordia, Ky. (†40157) 237/J4
Concordia (par.), La. 238/G4
Concordia, Mexico 150/G5
Concordia, Mo. (64020) 261/E5
Concordia, Peru 128/E5
Concordville, Pa. (19331) 294/M6
Concrete, N. Dak. (58221) 282/P2
Concrete, Wash. (98237) 310/D2
Con Cuong, Vietnam 72/E3
Conda, Idaho (83230) 220/G7
Condado, Cuba 158/E2
Condamine (riv.), Queensland 88/H5
Condamine (riv.), Queensland 95/D5
Condar, Colombia 126/D8
Conde, Brazil 132/G5
Conde, S. Dak. (57434) 298/N3
Condega, Nicaragua 154/D4
Condit, Ohio (†43074) 284/E5
Condo, Bolivia 136/B6
Condobolin, N.S. Wales 97/D3
Condobolin, N. S. Wales 88/H6
Condom, France 28/D6
Condon, Mont. (59826) 262/C3
Condon, Oreg. (97823) 291/G2
Condor, Alberta 182/C3
Cóndor, Cordillera del (range), Ecuador 128/C5
Cóndor, Cordillera del (range), Peru 128/C5
Condoto, Colombia 126/B5
Cone, Texas (79321) 303/C4
Conecuh (co.), Ala. 195/E8
Conecuh (riv.), Ala. 195/D8
Conegliano, Italy 34/D2
Conehatta, Miss. (39057) 256/F6
Conejos (co.), Colo. 208/G8
Conejos, Colo. (81129) 208/G8
Conejos (peak), Colo. 208/G8
Conejos (riv.), Colo. 208/G8
Conemaugh (riv.), Pa. 294/D5
Conemaugh River (lake), Pa. 294/D4
Conestee, S.C. (29636) 296/C2
Conestoga, Pa. (17516) 294/K6
Conesus, N.Y. (14435) 276/E5
Conesus (lake), N.Y. 276/E5
Conesville, Iowa (52739) 229/L6
Conesville, Ohio (43811) 284/G5
Conetoe, N.C. (27819) 281/O3
Conewango, N.Y. (†14726) 276/C6
Conewango (creek), N.Y. 276/B6
Conewango (creek), Pa. 294/D1
Confidence, Iowa (†52569) 229/G7
Confluence, Ky. (41730) 237/P6
Confluence, Pa. (15424) 294/D6
Confolens, France 28/D4
Confusion (range), Utah 304/A4
Confuso (riv.), Paraguay 144/C4
Cong, Ireland 17/C4
Congamond (lakes), Conn. 210/E1
Congamond (lakes), Mass. 249/D4
Congaree (riv.), S.C. 296/F4
Congaree Nat'l Mon., S.C. 296/F4
Conger, Minn. (56020) 255/E7
Conger (range), N.W. Terrs. 187/K1
Congerville, Ill. (61729) 222/D3
Conghua, China 77/H7
Congleton, England 13/H2
Congo 2/K6
Congo 102/D5
Congo (riv.) 102/D5
Congo (riv.) 2/L5
Congo (riv.), Angola 115/C4
CONGO 115/C3
Congo (riv.), Congo 115/C4
Congo, Ohio (†43730) 284/F6
Congo (riv.), Zaire 115/C4
Congonhas, Brazil 135/E2
Congress, Ariz. (85332) 198/C4
Congress, Ohio (†44287) 284/F4
Congress, Sask. 181/E6
Congress Heights, D.C. (20032) 245/F5
Cónico, Cerro (mt.), Argentina 143/B5
Cónico, Cerro (mt.), Chile 138/E4
Conimicut, R.I. (02889) 249/J6
Coningsby, England 13/G4
Coniston, North. Terr. 93/C7
Conjuror (bay), N.W. Terrs. 187/G3
Conklin, Alberta 182/E2
Conklin, Mich. (49403) 250/D5
Conley, Georgia (30027) 217/K2
Conn, Lough (lake), Ireland 10/B3
Conn (lake), Ireland 17/C3
Conn (lake), N.W. Terrs. 187/L2
Connacht (prov.), Ireland 17/C4
Connacht (trad. prov.), Ireland 17
Connah's Quay, Wales 13/G2
Connaught Heights, Sask. 181/G3
Conneaut, Ohio (44030) 284/J2
Conneaut Lake, Pa. (16316) 294/B2
Conneaut Lake Park, Pa. (16316) 294/B2
Conneautville, Pa. (16406) 294/A2
Connecticut 188/M2
Connecticut (riv.) 188/M2
CONNECTICUT 210
Connecticut (riv.), Conn. 210/E2
Connecticut (riv.), Mass. 249/D2
Connecticut (riv.), N.H. 268/B6
Connecticut (state), U.S. 146/L5
Connecticut (riv.), Vt. 268/C4
Connel, Scotland 15/C4
Connell, New Bruns. 170/C2
Connell, Wash. (99326) 310/G4
Connell Creek, Sask. 181/H2
Connellsville, Pa. (15425) 294/C5
Connellys Springs, N.C. (28612) 281/F3
Connelsville, Mo. (†63559) 261/G2
Connemara (dist.), Ireland 17/B5
Conner, Mont. (59827) 262/B5
Conner (mt.), North. Terr. 93/B8
Connersville, Ind. (47331) 227/G5
Connerville, Okla. (74836) 288/N6
Connétable (isls.), Fr. Guiana 131/F3
Connoquenessing, Pa. (16027) 294/B4
Connors, New Bruns. 170/B1
Conoble, N.S. Wales 97/C3
Conococheague (creek), Md. 245/G1
Cononbridge, Scotland 15/D3
Conover, N.C. (28613) 281/G3
Conover, Ohio (45317) 284/B5
Conover, Wis. (54519) 317/H3
Conowingo, Md. (21918) 245/O2
Conowingo (dam), Md. 245/O2
Conquerall Bank, Nova Scotia 168/D4
Conquest, Sask. 181/D4
Conquista, Bolivia 136/B2
Conrad, Alberta 182/D5
Conrad, Iowa (50631) 229/H4
Conrad, Mont. (59425) 262/D2
Conrad, Pa. (†16720) 294/G2
Conran, Mo. (63873) 261/N10
Conrath, Wis. (54731) 317/E5

Cyrenaica 357

Crossgar, N. Ireland 17/K3
Crosshaven, Ireland 17/E8
Crosshill, Scotland 15/D5
Cross Hill, S.C. (29332) 296/D3
Cross Junction, Va. (22625) 307/M2
Cross Keys, S.C. (†29379) 296/D2
Cross Lake, Manitoba 179/J3
Crosslake, Minn. (56442) 255/E4
Crossley (mt.), N. Zealand 100/D5
Crossmaglen, N. Ireland 17/H3
Crossmichael, Scotland 15/D6
Crossmolina, Ireland 17/C3
Crossnore, N.C. (28616) 281/F2
Cross Plains, Ind. (47017) 227/G7
Cross Plains, Tenn. (37049) 237/H7
Cross Plains, Texas (76443) 303/E5
Cross Plains, Wis. (53528) 317/G9
Cross River (state), Nigeria 106/F7
Cross Roads, Calif. (†92242) 204/L9
Crossroads, N. Mex. (88114) 274/F5
Cross Roads, Pa. (†17322) 294/J6
Cross Timbers, Mo. (65634) 261/F6
Crosstown, Mo. (†63775) 261/N7
Cross Village, Mich. (49723) 250/D3
Crossville, Ala. (35962) 195/G2
Crossville, Ill. (62827) 222/F5
Crossville, Tenn. (38555) 237/L9
Crosswicks, N.J. (08515) 273/D3
Crosswicks (creek), N.J. 273/D3
Croswell, Mich. (48422) 250/G5
Crotch (lake), Ontario 177/H3
Crothersville, Ind. (47229) 227/F7
Croton (Hartford), Ohio (43013) 284/E5
Crotone, Italy 34/F5
Croton Falls, N.Y. (10519) 276/N8
Croton-on-Hudson, N.Y. (10520) 276/N8
Crouch, Idaho (†83622) 220/B5
Crouseville, Maine (04738) 243/G2
Crow (creek), Colo. 208/L1
Crow (riv.), Minn. 255/F5
Crow, Oreg. (†97401) 291/D4
Crow (creek), S. Dak. 298/A4
Crow (creek), Wyo. 319/H4
Crow Agency, Mont. (59022) 262/J5
Crowborough, England 13/H6
Crow Creek Ind. Res., S. Dak. 298/L5
Crowder, Miss. (38622) 256/D2
Crowder, Okla. (74430) 288/P4
Crowduck (lake), Manitoba 179/G4
Crowdy (head), N.S. Wales 97/G2
Crowell, Texas (79227) 303/E4
Crowfoot, Alberta 182/D4
Crowheart, Wyo. (82512) 319/C2
Crow Ind. Res., Mont. 262/H5
Crowl (creek), N.S. Wales 97/C2
Crow Lake, S. Dak. (†57382) 298/M6
Crowle, England 13/G4
Crowley (lake), Calif. 204/G6
Crowley (co.), Colo. 208/M6
Crowley, Colo. (81033) 208/M6
Crowley, La. (70526) 238/F6
Crowley, Texas (76036) 303/E3
Crowley Lake, Calif. (93546) 204/G6
Crowley's Ridge (mt.), Ark. 202/J2
Crown, Minn. (†55005) 255/E5
Crown (mt.), Virgin Is. (U.S.) 161/A4
Crown City, Ohio (45623) 284/F8
Crown King, Ariz. (86333) 198/C4
Crown Point, Ind. (46307) 227/C2
Crownpoint, N. Mex. (87313) 274/A3
Crown Point, N.Y. (12928) 276/N3
Crown Prince Frederik (isl.), N.W. Terrs. 187/K3
Crownsville, Md. (21032) 245/M4
Crows Landing, Calif. (95313) 204/D6
Crowsnest (pass), Alberta 182/C5
Crowsnest, Br. Col. 184/K5
Crowsnest (pass), Br. Col. 184/K5
Crowville, La. (71230) 238/G2
Crow Wing (co.), Minn. 255/D4
Crow Wing (riv.), Minn. 255/D4
Croydon, England 13/H8
Croydon, England 10/B6
Croydon○, N.H. (†03753) 268/C5
Croydon (peak), N.H. 268/C5
Croydon, Queensland 88/G3
Croydon, Queensland 95/B3
Croydon, Utah (84018) 304/C2
Croydon, Victoria 88/M7
Croydon, Victoria 97/K5
Croydon Branch, Sugar (riv.), N.H. 268/C5
Crozet (isls.) 2/M8
Crozet, Va. (22932) 307/L4
Crozier (chan.), N.W. Terrs. 187/G2
Crozier, Va. (23039) 307/N5
Cruces, Cuba 158/E2
Cruces, Cuba 156/B2
Cruden Bay, Scotland 15/G3
Cruger, Miss. (38924) 256/D4
Cruillas, Mexico 150/K4
Crum (creek), Pa. 294/M7
Crum, W. Va. (25669) 312/B7
Crumlin, N. Ireland 17/J2
Crum Lynne, Pa. (19022) 294/M7
Crummies, Ky. (40821) 237/P7
Crump, Mich. (†48634) 250/E5
Crump (lake), Oreg. 291/H5
Crump, Tenn. (38327) 237/E10
Crumpton (pt.), Dominica 161/F5
Crumpton, Md. (21628) 245/P4
Crumrod, Ark. (72328) 202/H5
Crumstown, Ind. (†46554) 227/E1
Crusheen, Ireland 17/D6
Cruso, N.C. (†28716) 281/D4
Cruta, Honduras 154/F3
Crutchfield, Ky. (42034) 237/D7
Crutwell, Sask. 181/E2
Cruz (cape), Cuba 156/C3
Cruz (cape), Cuba 158/G4
Cruz Alta, Brazil 120/D5
Cruz Alta, Brazil 132/C10
Cruz Bay, Virgin Is. (U.S.) 161/C4
Cruz del Eje, Argentina 143/C3
Cruz del Eje, Argentina 120/C6
Cruz de Piedra, Uruguay 145/E3
Cruz de San Pedro, Uruguay 145/E2
Cruzeiro, Brazil 135/D3
Cruzeiro do Sol, Brazil 120/B3
Cruzeiro do Sul, Brazil 132/G10
Cruz Grande, Chile 138/A7
Crysler, Ontario 177/J2
Crystal (mts.), Congo 115/B4
Crystal (lake), Conn. 210/F1
Crystal (pond), Conn. 210/G1
Crystal (bay), Fla. 212/D3
Crystal (mts.), Gabon 115/B4
Crystal, Ind. (†47527) 227/D8
Crystal○, Maine (†04747) 243/G4
Crystal, Mich. (48818) 250/E5
Crystal (lake), Mich. 250/C4
Crystal, Minn. (†55428) 255/G5
Crystal, N.H. (†03591) 268/E2
Crystal (lake), N.H. 268/E5
Crystal, N. Mex. (†86504) 274/A2
Crystal, N. Dak. (58222) 282/P2
Crystal (lake), Vt. 268/C2
Crystal, W. Va. (†24747) 312/D8
Crystal Bay (Orono), Minn. (55323) 255/F5
Crystal Bay, Nev. (89402) 266/A3
Crystal Beach, Texas (77650) 303/K8
Crystal Brook, S. Australia 94/E5
Crystal City, Manitoba 179/C5
Crystal City, Mo. (63019) 261/M6
Crystal City, Texas (78839) 303/E9
Crystal Falls, Mich. (49920) 250/A2
Crystal Falls, Ontario 177/E1
Crystal Hill, Va. (24539) 307/L7
Crystal Lake, Conn. (†06066) 210/F1
Crystal Lake, Fla. (†32463) 212/D6
Crystal Lake, Ill. (60014) 222/E1
Crystal Lake, Iowa (50432) 229/F2
Crystal Lake Park, Mo. (†63101) 261/O3
Crystal Lakes, Ohio (†45341) 284/C6
Crystal River, Fla. (32629) 212/D3
Crystal Springs, Ark. (†71968) 202/D5
Crystal Springs (res.), Calif. 204/J3
Crystal Springs, Fla. (33524) 212/D3
Crystal Springs, Georgia (†30105) 217/B2
Crystal Springs, Kansas (†67058) 232/D4
Crystal Springs, Miss. (39059) 256/D7
Crystal Springs, N. Dak. (58427) 282/L6
Crystal Springs, Sask. 181/F3
Crystal Valley, Mich. (†49420) 250/C5
Csabrendek, Hungary 41/D3
Csákvár, Hungary 41/E3
Csanádpalota, Hungary 41/F3
Csenger, Hungary 41/G3
Csepel, Hungary 41/E3
Csepelsziget (isl.), Hungary 41/E3
Csepreg, Hungary 41/D3
Csongrád (co.), Hungary 41/F3
Csongrád, Hungary 41/F3
Csorna, Hungary 41/D3
Csorvás, Hungary 41/F3
Csurgó, Hungary 41/D3
Ctesiphon (ruins), Iraq 66/D4
Cúa, Venezuela 124/E2
Cuadro Nacional, Argentina 143/C3
Cuamba, Mozambique 118/F2
Cuando (riv.), Angola 115/C7
Cuando (riv.), Zambia 115/D7
Cuando Cubango (dist.), Angola 115/C7
Cuangar, Angola 115/C7
Cuango (riv.) 102/D5
Cuango, Angola 115/C5
Cuango (riv.), Angola 115/C5
Cuanza (riv.), Angola 102/D6
Cuanza (riv.), Angola 115/C5
Cuanza-Norte (dist.), Angola 115/B5
Cuanza-Sul (dist.), Angola 115/C6
Cuao (riv.), Venezuela 124/E5
Cua Rao, Vietnam 72/E3
Cuareim (riv.), Uruguay 145/B1
Cuaró, Uruguay 145/D2
Cuatrociénagas de Carranza, Mexico 150/H3
Cuatro Compañeros, Cuba 158/G3
Cuatro Ojos, Bolivia 136/D5
Cuauhtémoc, Mexico 150/F2
Cuautepec de Hinojosa, Mexico 150/K6
Cuautitlán de Romero Rubio, Mexico 150/L1
Cuautla Morelos, Mexico 150/L2
Cub (creek), Utah 304/C1
Cub (creek), Va. 307/L6
Cuba 2/E4
Cuba 146/L7
Cuba, Ala. (36907) 195/B6
CUBA 156/B2
CUBA 158
Cuba, Ill. (61427) 222/C3
Cuba, Ind. (†47460) 227/D6
Cuba, Kansas (66940) 232/E2
Cuba, Mo. (65453) 261/K6
Cuba, N. Mex. (87013) 274/B2
Cuba, N.Y. (14727) 276/D6
Cuba (chan.), N. Zealand 100/D7
Cuba, Ohio (45114) 284/C7
Cuba, Portugal 33/C3
Cuba City, Wis. (53807) 317/F10
Cubage, Ky. (40822) 237/O7
Cubagua (isl.), Venezuela 124/F2
Cuballing, W. Australia 92/B2
Cubango (riv.), Angola 102/D6
Cubango (riv.), Angola 115/C7
Cubango (riv.), Namibia 118/B3
Cubatão, Brazil 135/C3
Cube (mt.), N.H. 268/D4
Cubero, N. Mex. (87014) 274/B3
Cubiro, Venezuela 124/D3
Cub Run, Ky. (42729) 237/J6
Çubuk, Turkey 63/E2
Cubulco, Guatemala 154/B3
Cuchara, Colo. (81055) 208/J8
Cuchi, Angola 115/Ct
Cuchi, Angola 102/D6
Cuchillo, N. Mex. (87932) 274/B5
Cuchillo-Có, Argentina 143/D4
Cuchillo Negro (creek), N. Mex. 274/B5
Cuchivero, Venezuela 124/F4
Cuchivero (riv.), Venezuela 124/F4
Cuckfield, England 13/G6
Cuckfield, England 10/F5
Cucumber, W. Va. (24826) 312/C8
Cúcuta, Colombia 126/D4
Cúcuta, Colombia 120/B2
Cudahy, Calif. (90201) 204/C5
Cudahy, Wis. (53110) 317/M2
Cudal, N.S. Wales 97/E3
Cuddalore, India 68/E6
Cuddapah, India 68/D6
Cuddeback (lake), Calif. 204/H8
Cuddy, Pa. (15031) 294/B5
Cudgewa, Victoria 97/D5
Cudillero, Spain 33/C1
Cudjoe (key), Fla. 212/E7
Cudrefin, Switzerland 39/D3
Cudworth, Sask. 181/F3
Cue, W. Australia 88/B5
Cue, W. Australia 92/B4
Cuéllar, Spain 33/D2
Cuéllar-Baza, Spain 33/E4
Cuemaní (riv.), Colombia 126/D7
Cuenca, Ecuador 120/B3
Cuenca, Ecuador 128/C4
Cuenca (prov.), Spain 33/E2
Cuenca, Spain 33/E2
Cuenca, Sierra de (range), Spain 33/F3
Cuencamé de Ceniceros, Mexico 150/H4
Cuernavaca, Mexico 150/L2
Cuero, Texas (77954) 303/G8
Cuervo, N. Mex. (88417) 274/E3
Cuervo (creek), N. Mex. 274/E3
Cueto, Cuba 158/J3
Cuevas, Miss. (†39571) 256/F10
Cuevas del Almanzora, Spain 33/F4
Cuevas de Vinromá, Spain 33/F2
Cuevo, Bolivia 136/D7
Cufré, Uruguay 145/B5
Cuiabá, Brazil 120/D4
Cuiabá, Brazil 132/C6
Cuiabá (riv.), Brazil 132/B7
Cuicatlán, Mexico 150/L8
Cuicuina, Nicaragua 154/E4
Cuilapa, Guatemala 154/B3
Cuilapa Miravalles (vol.), C. Rica 154/E5
Cuilcagh (mt.), Ireland 17/F3
Cuilco, Guatemala 154/B3
Cuillin (hills), Scotland 15/B3
Cuillin (sound), Scotland 10/C2
Cuillin (sound), Scotland 15/B3
Cuilo, Angola 115/C5
Cuitlahuac, Mexico 150/P2
Cuito (riv.), Angola 115/C7
Cuito-Cuanavale, Angola 115/C7
Cuitzeo (lake), Mexico 150/J7
Cuivre (riv.), Mo. 261/N2
Cujmir, Romania 45/F3
Cukmantl, Czech. 41/D1
Çukur, Turkey 63/F3
Çukurca, Turkey 63/K4
Culaba, Philippines 82/E5
Cu Lao, Hon (isls.), Vietnam 72/F5
Culberson, N.C. (28903) 281/A4
Culberson (co.), Texas 303/C11
Culbertson, Mont. (59218) 262/M2
Culbertson, Nebr. (69024) 264/C4
Culcairn, N.S. Wales 97/D4
Culdaff, Ireland 17/G1
Culdaff (bay), Ireland 17/G1
Culdesac, Idaho (83524) 220/B3
Cul-de-Sac du Marin (bay), Martinique 161/D7
Culebra (creek), Colo. 208/H8
Culebra (peak), Colo. 208/J8
Culebra, P. Rico 161/G1
Culebra (isl.), P. Rico 161/G1
Culebra (isl.), P. Rico 156/G1
Culebras, Peru 128/C7
Culebrinas (riv.), P. Rico 161/A1
Culebrita (isl.), P. Rico 161/G2
Culemborg, Netherlands 27/G5
Culgoa (riv.), N.S. Wales 97/D1
Culgoa (riv.), Queensland 95/C6
Culiacán, Mexico 150/F4
Culiacán, Mexico 146/H7
Culion, Philippines 82/C5
Culion (isl.), Philippines 82/B5
Cullasaja, N.C. (†28734) 281/C4
Cullburra-Orient Point, N.S. Wales 97/F4
Cullen, La. (71021) 238/D1
Cullen, Sask. 181/J6
Cullen, Scotland 15/F3
Cullen, Va. (23934) 307/L6
Cullen Bullen, N.S. Wales 97/F3
Culleoka, Tenn. (38451) 237/G10
Cullera, Spain 33/F3
Cullin (lake), Ireland 17/C4
Cullison, Kansas (†67124) 232/D4
Cullman (co.), Ala. 195/E2
Cullman, Ala. (35055) 195/E2
Culloden, Georgia (31016) 217/D5
Culloden, W. Va. (25510) 312/B6
Cullom, Ill. (60929) 222/E3
Cullomburg, Ala. (36920) 195/B7
Cullompton, England 13/D7
Cullowhee, N.C. (28723) 281/C4
Cully, Switzerland 39/C4
Cullybackey, N. Ireland 17/J2
Culotte (lake), Québec 172/C2
Culp, Alberta 182/B2
Culp Creek, Oreg. (97427) 291/E4
Culpeper (co.), Va. 307/M3
Culpeper, Va. (22701) 307/M4
Culpepper (isl.), Ecuador 128/B8
Culpina, Bolivia 136/C7
Culross, Manitoba 179/E5
Culross, Scotland 10/B1
Culross, Scotland 15/C1
Culta, Bolivia 136/B6
Cults, Scotland 15/F3
Cultus (lake), Oreg. 291/F4
Cultus Lake, Br. Col. 184/M3
Culuene (riv.), Brazil 132/C6
Culver, Ind. (46511) 227/E2
Culver, Kansas (67435) 232/E3
Culver, Minn. (55727) 255/F4
Culver, Oreg. (97734) 291/F3
Culver (pt.), W. Australia 88/D6
Culver (pt.), W. Australia 92/D6
Culver City, Calif. (90230) 204/B10
Culverden, N. Zealand 100/D5
Culvers (lake), N.J. 273/D1
Culverton, Georgia (†31087) 217/G4
Cuma, Angola 115/B6
Cumaná, Venezuela 120/C2
Cumaná, Venezuela 124/F2
Cumanacoa, Venezuela 124/F2
Cumanayagua, Cuba 158/E2
Cumaria, Peru 128/F7
Cumback, Ind. (†47501) 227/C7
Cumbal, Colombia 126/B7
Cumberland (riv.) 188/J3
Cumberland (plat.), Ala. 195/F1
Cumberland, Br. Col. 184/E5
Cumberland (sound), Canada 4/C13
Cumberland (isl.), Georgia 217/K9
Cumberland (co.), Ill. 222/E4
Cumberland, Ind. (46229) 227/E5
Cumberland, Iowa (50843) 229/D6
Cumberland (co.), Ky. 237/L7
Cumberland, Ky. (40823) 237/R6
Cumberland (lake), Ky. 237/M7
Cumberland (mt.), Ky. 237/P7
Cumberland (riv.), Ky. 237/K8
Cumberland (co.), Maine 243/C8
Cumberland, Md. (21502) 245/D2
Cumberland, Md. 245/80
Cumberland, Md. 188/L3
Cumberland (basin), New Bruns. 170/F3
Cumberland (co.), N.J. 273/C5
Cumberland (co.), N.C. 281/M4
Cumberland, N.C. (28331) 281/M5
Cumberland (pen.), N.W.T. 162/K2
Cumberland (pen.), N.W. Terrs. 187/M3
Cumberland (sound), N.W.T. 146/N3
Cumberland (sound), N.W.T. 162/K2
Cumberland (sound), N.W. Terrs. 187/M3
Cumberland (co.), Nova Scotia 168/D3
Cumberland (basin), Nova Scotia 168/D3
Cumberland, Ohio (43732) 284/G6
Cumberland, Okla. (†73446) 288/N6
Cumberland, Ontario 177/J2
Cumberland (co.), Pa. 294/H5
Cumberland (isls.), Queensland 88/H4
Cumberland (isls.), Queensland 95/D4
Cumberland (bay), St. Vin. & Grens. 161/A8
Cumberland (lake), Sask. 181/J1
Cumberland (co.), Tenn. 237/L9
Cumberland (plat.), Tenn. 237/L9
Cumberland (riv.), Tenn. 237/K8
Cumberland (co.), Va. 307/M6
Cumberland, Va. (23040) 307/M6
Cumberland (mt.), Va. 307/B7
Cumberland, Wash. (†98022) 310/D3
Cumberland, Wis. (54829) 317/C4
Cumberland Bay, New Bruns. 170/E2
Cumberland Beach, Ontario 177/E3
Cumberland Center, Maine (04021) 243/C8
Cumberland Center○, Maine (04021) 243/C8
Cumberland City, Tenn. (37050) 237/F8
Cumberland Furnace, Tenn. (37051) 237/G8
Cumberland Gap, Tenn. (37724) 237/O8
Cumberland Gap Nat'l Hist. Park, Ky. 237/P7
Cumberland Gap Nat'l Hist. Park, Tenn. 237/O7
Cumberland Gap Nat'l Hist. Park, Va. 307/A7
Cumberland House, Sask. 181/J2
Cumberland Island Nat'l Seashore, Georgia 217/K9
Cumbernauld, Scotland 15/C1
Cumbre del Laudo (mt.), Argentina 143/C2
Cumbre Negra, Cerro (mt.), Argentina 143/C5
Cumbre Negra, Cerro (mt.), Chile 138/E5
Cumbria (co.), England 13/D3
Cumbrian (mts.), England 13/D3
Cumbum, India 68/D5
Cumby, Texas (75433) 303/J4
Cuming (co.), Nebr. 264/H3
Cummaquid, Mass. (02637) 249/N6
Cumming, Georgia (30130) 217/D2
Cumming, Iowa (50061) 229/F6
Cummings, Kansas (66016) 232/G2
Cummings, N. Dak. (58223) 282/S4
Cummings, S.C. (†29944) 296/E6
Cummingsville, Tenn. (†38583) 237/L9
Cummington○, Mass. (01026) 249/C3
Cummins, S. Australia 94/D6
Cumnock, N.S. Wales 97/E3
Cumnock, N.C. (27237) 281/L3
Cumnock and Holmhead, Scotland 10/D3
Cumnock and Holmhead, Scotland 15/D5
Cumpas, Mexico 150/E1
Çumra, Turkey 63/E4
Cuñapirú, Uruguay 145/D2
Cuñapirú, Arroyo (riv.), Uruguay 145/D2
Cunapo, Trin. & Tob. 161/B10
Cuñare, Colombia 126/D7
Cunaviche, Venezuela 124/E4
Cunco, Chile 138/E2
Cuncumén, Coquimbo, Chile 138/A9
Cuncumén, Santiago, Chile 138/F4
Cundeelee Aboriginal Reserve, W. Australia 88/C6
Cundeelee Aboriginal Res., W. Australia 92/C5
Cunderdin, W. Australia 92/B5
Cundiff, Ky. (42730) 237/L7
Cundinamarca (dept.), Colombia 126/C5
Cundiyo, N. Mex. (87522) 274/D3
Cunduacán, Mexico 150/N7
Cundys Harbor, Maine (04011) 243/D8
Cunene (riv.) 102/D6
Cunene (dist.), Angola 115/C7
Cunene (dam), Angola 115/B7
Cunene (riv.), Angola 115/B7
Cuneo (prov.), Italy 34/A2
Cuneo, Italy 34/A2
Çüngüş, Turkey 63/H3
Cunnamulla, Australia 87/E8
Cunnamulla, Queensland 95/C5
Cunnamulla, Queensland 88/H5
Cunningham, Kansas (67035) 232/D4
Cunningham, Ky. (42035) 237/D7
Cunningham, N.C. (†27343) 281/L1
Cunningham, Tenn. (37052) 237/G8
Cunningham, Wash. (99327) 310/G4
Cuorgnè, Italy 34/A2
Cupar, Sask. 181/G5
Cupar, Scotland 15/E4
Cupar, Scotland 10/E2
Cupertino, Calif. (95014) 204/K3
Cupica (gulf), Colombia 126/B4
Cupids, Newf. 166/D2
Ćuprija, Yugoslavia 45/E4
Cuprum, Idaho (†83612) 220/B4
Cupsuptic (riv.), Maine 243/B5
Cuquenán (riv.), Venezuela 124/H5
Cuquiari (riv.), Colombia 126/E7
Curaçá, Brazil 132/G5
Curaçao (isl.), Neth. Ant. 161/G7
Curaçao (isl.), Neth. Ant. 156/E4
Curacautín, Chile 138/E2
Curacaví, Chile 138/G3
Curahuara de Carangas, Bolivia 136/A5
Curahuara de Pacajes, Bolivia 136/A5
Curanilahue, Chile 138/D1
Curaray (riv.), Ecuador 128/D3
Curaumilla (pt.), Chile 138/E2
Curdsville, Ky. (42334) 237/G5
Curecanti Nat'l Rec. Area, Colo. 208/F6
Curepipe, Mauritius 118/G5
Curepto, Chile 138/A10
Curiapo, Venezuela 124/H3
Curiche, Bolivia 136/D6
Curicó, Chile 120/B6
Curicó, Chile 138/A10
Curieuse (isl.), Seychelles 118/H5
Curitiba, Brazil 132/D9
Curitiba, Brazil 120/F5
Curitiba, Brazil 135/B4
Curlew, Iowa (50527) 229/D3
Curlew (isls.), La. 238/M7
Curlew, Wash. (99118) 310/G2
Curlew (lake), Wash. 310/G2
Curlewis, N.S. Wales 97/F2
Curllsville, Pa. (16221) 294/D3
Curnamona, S. Australia 94/F4
Curragh, The, Ireland 17/H5
Curragh, The (racecourse), Ireland 10/C4
Currais Novos, Brazil 132/G4
Curran, Ill. (62632) 222/D4
Curran, Mich. (48728) 250/F4
Currant, Nev. (†89314) 266/F4
Currawilla, Queensland 95/B5
Current (riv.), Ark. 202/J1
Current (riv.), Mo. 261/K8
Currie, Minn. (56123) 255/C6
Currie, Nev. (†89301) 266/G2
Currie, N.C. (28435) 281/N6
Currie, Scotland 15/D2
Currie, Tasmania 99/A1
Currituck (co.), N.C. 281/S2
Currituck, N.C. (27929) 281/T2
Currituck (sound), N.C. 281/T2
Curry, Alaska (†99676) 196/J2
Curry (co.), N. Mex. 274/F4
Curry (co.), Oreg. 291/C5
Curryville, Mo. (63339) 261/K4
Curryville, Pa. (16631) 294/F5
Curtea de Argeș, Romania 45/G3
Curtice, Ohio (43412) 284/D2
Curtin, Oreg. (97428) 291/D4
Curtina, Uruguay 145/C3
Curtis, Ark. (71728) 202/D6
Curtis, La. (†71101) 238/C2
Curtis, Mich. (49820) 250/D2
Curtis, Nebr. (69025) 264/D4
Curtis, Okla. (†73852) 288/H2
Curtis (isl.), Queensland 88/J4
Curtis (isl.), Queensland 95/D4
Curtis, Wash. (98538) 310/B4
Curtis Group (isls.), Tasmania 99/C1
Curtiss, Wis. (54422) 317/F6
Curtis Station, Miss. (†38606) 256/D2
Curtisville, Ind. (†46036) 227/F4
Curuá (riv.), Brazil 132/C4
Curuçá, Brazil 132/E3
Curuguaty, Paraguay 144/E4
Curup, Indonesia 85/C6
Cururú, Bolivia 136/D4
Cururupu, Brazil 132/E3
Curutú (riv.), Venezuela 124/G5
Curuzú Cuatiá, Argentina 143/G5
Curuzú Cuatiá, Argentina 120/D5
Curve, Tenn. (†38063) 237/B9
Curvelo, Brazil 132/E7
Curwensville, Pa. (16833) 294/E4
Curwood (mt.), Mich. 250/A2
Cusachón (isl.), Colombia 126/D1
Cusco, Peru 120/B4
Cusco (dept.), Peru 128/F9
Cusco (Cuzco), Peru 128/F9
Cushendall, N. Ireland 17/J1
Cushing, Iowa (51018) 229/B4
Cushing○, Maine (04563) 243/E7
Cushing, Minn. (56443) 255/D4
Cushing, Nebr. (†68873) 264/F3
Cushing, Okla. (74023) 288/N3
Cushing, Texas (75760) 303/J6
Cushing, Wis. (54006) 317/A4
Cushman, Ark. (72526) 202/G2
Cushman, Mass. (01002) 249/D3
Cushman, Oreg. (†97439) 291/D4
Cushman (lake), Wash. 310/B3
Cusiana (riv.), Colombia 126/D5
Cusick, Wash. (99119) 310/H2
Cuslett, Newf. 166/C2
Cusset, France 28/E4
Cusseta, Ala. (36852) 195/H5
Cusseta, Georgia (31805) 217/C6
Cusson, Minn. (†55771) 255/F2
Custar, Ohio (43511) 284/C3
Custer (co.), Colo. 208/J6
Custer (co.), Idaho 220/D5
Custer, Ky. (40115) 237/J5
Custer, Mich. (49405) 250/C5
Custer (co.), Mont. 262/L4
Custer, Mont. (59024) 262/J4
Custer (co.), Nebr. 264/E3
Custer (co.), Okla. 288/H3
Custer (co.), S. Dak. 298/B6
Custer, S. Dak. (57730) 298/B6
Custer, Wash. (98240) 310/C2
Custer Battlefield Nat'l Mon., Mont. 262/J5
Custer City, Okla. (73639) 288/J3
Custer City, Pa. (16725) 294/E2
Custer Park, Ill. (60418) 222/E2
Cut Bank, Mont. (59427) 262/D2
Cut Bank (creek), Mont. 262/D2
Cut Bank (creek), N. Dak. 282/H2
Cutbank, Sask. 181/E4
Cutchogue-New Suffolk, N.Y. (11935) 276/P8
Cutervo, Peru 128/C6
Cuthbert, Georgia (31740) 217/C7
Cut Knife, Sask. 181/B3
Cutler, Calif. (93615) 204/F7
Cutler, Ill. (62238) 222/D5
Cutler, Ind. (46920) 227/D4
Cutler, Maine (04626) 243/J6
Cutler○, Maine (04626) 243/J6
Cutler, Ohio (45724) 284/G7
Cutler Ridge, Fla. (33157) 212/F6
Cutlerville, Mich. (49508) 250/D6
Cut Off, La. (70345) 238/K7
Cutra (lake), Ireland 17/D5
Cutral-Có, Argentina 143/C4
Cutshin, Ky. (41732) 237/P6
Cuttaburra (creek), N.S. Wales 97/C1
Cuttack, India 54/K7
Cuttack, India 68/F4
Cutten, Calif. (95534) 204/A3
Cuttingsville, Vt. (05738) 268/B4
Cuttyhunk, Mass. (02713) 249/L7
Cuttyhunk (isl.), Mass. 249/L7
Cuvier (isl.), N. Zealand 100/E2
Cuvier (cape), W. Australia 88/A4
Cuvier (cape), W. Australia 92/A4
Cuvo (riv.), Angola 115/B6
Cuxhaven, W. Germany 22/C2
Cuya, Chile 138/B2
Cuyabeno, Ecuador 128/E3
Cuyahoga (co.), Ohio 284/G3
Cuyahoga (riv.), Ohio 284/H10
Cuyahoga Falls, Ohio (*44221) 284/G3
Cuyahoga Heights, Ohio (†44101) 284/H9
Cuyama, Calif. (93214) 204/F9
Cuyama (riv.), Calif. 204/E8
Cuyapaipe Ind. Res., Calif. 204/J11
Cuyk, Netherlands 27/H5
Cuylerville, N.Y. (†14481) 276/E5
Cuyo, Philippines 82/C5
Cuyo (isl.), Philippines 82/C5
Cuyo (isls.), Philippines 82/C5
Cuyo (isls.), Philippines 85/G3
Cuyocuyo, Peru 128/H10
Cuyo East (passage), Philippines 82/C5
Cuyo West (passage), Philippines 82/C5
Cuyuna, Minn. (†56444) 255/E4
Cuyuna (range), Minn. 255/D4
Cuyuni (riv.) 120/C2
Cuyuni (riv.), Guyana 131/B2
Cuyuni (riv.), Venezuela 124/H4
Cuyu Tigni, Nicaragua 154/F3
Cuzco, Ind. (†47432) 227/D8
Cuzzart, W. Va. (26530) 312/H3
Čvrsnica (mt.), Yugoslavia 45/C4
Cwmamman, Wales 13/D6
Cwmbran, Wales 13/B6
Cyangugu, Rwanda 115/E4
Cyclades (isls.), Greece 45/G7
Cycle, N.C. (27015) 281/H2
Cyclone, Ind. (†46041) 227/E4
Cyclone, Pa. (16726) 294/E2
Cyclone, W. Va. (24827) 312/C7
Cygnet, Ohio (43413) 284/C3
Cygnet, Tasmania 99/C5
Cylinder, Iowa (50528) 229/D2
Cylon, Wis. (†54017) 317/B5
Cymric, Sask. 181/G4
Cynthia, Alberta 182/C3
Cynthiana, Ind. (47612) 227/B8
Cynthiana, Ky. (41031) 237/N4
Cynthiana, Ohio (45624) 284/D7
Cypert, Ark. (†72366) 202/J5
Cypress, Ala. (35454) 195/C5
Cypress (hills), Alberta 182/E5
Cypress (bayou), Ark. 202/F3
Cypress, Calif. (90630) 204/D11
Cypress, Fla. (32432) 212/A1
Cypress (lake), Fla. 212/E3
Cypress, Ill. (62923) 222/D6
Cypress, Ind. (†47708) 227/B9
Cypress (pond), Ind. 227/B8
Cypress, La. (71420) 238/D3
Cypress (hills), Sask. 181/B6
Cypress (lake), Sask. 181/B6
Cypress Gardens, Fla. (33880) 212/E3
Cypress Hills Prov. Park, Alberta 182/E5
Cypress Hills Prov. Park, Sask. 181/B6
Cypress Inn, Tenn. (38452) 237/F10
Cypress Prov. Park, Br. Col. 184/K3
Cypress Quarters, Fla. (†33472) 212/F4
Cypress River, Manitoba 179/D5
Cyprus 2/L4
Cyprus 54/E6
CYPRUS 59/B2
CYPRUS 63/E5
Cyrenaica (reg.), Libya 102/E1
Cyrenaica (reg.), Libya 111/D1

358 Cyrene

Cyrene (Shahat), Libya 111/D1
Cyrene, Mo. (†63334) 261/K4
Cyril, Okla. (73029) 288/K5
Cyrus, Minn. (56323) 255/C5
Czar, Alberta 182/E3
Czar, W. Va. (†26224) 312/F5
Czarna Białostocka, Poland 47/F2
Czarnków, Poland 47/C2
Czechoslovakia 2/K3
Czechoslovakia 7/F4
CZECHOSLOVAKIA 41
Czechowice-Dziedzice, Poland 47/D4
Czech Socialist Rep., Czech. 41/B1
Czeladź, Poland 47/B4
Czersk, Poland 47/D2
Częstochowa (prov.), Poland 47/D3
Częstochowa, Poland 47/D3
Częstochwa, Poland 7/F3
Człuchów, Poland 47/C2

D

Da'an (Talai), China 77/K2
Daaquam, Québec 172/H3
Dabajuro, Venezuela 124/C2
Dabakala, Ivory Coast 106/D7
Dabas, Hungary 41/E3
Daba Shan (range), China 77/G5
Dabeiba, Colombia 126/B4
Dabhoi, India 68/C4
Dabney, Ind. (†47023) 227/G6
Dabob (bay), Wash. 310/C3
Dabola, Guinea 106/B6
Dabou, Ivory Coast 106/D7
Daboya, Ghana 106/D7
Dąbrowa Górnicza, Poland 47/B3
Dąbrowa Tarnowska, Poland 47/E3
Dăbuleni, Romania 45/F4
Dacca (cap.), Bangladesh 54/L7
Dacca (cap.), Bangladesh 68/G4
Dachau, W. Germany 22/D4
Dačice, Czech. 41/C2
Dac Lac, Cao Nguyen (plat.), Vietnam 72/F4
Dacoma, Okla. (73731) 288/J1
Dacono, Colo. (80514) 208/K2
Dacre, Ontario 177/G2
Dacula, Georgia (30211) 217/E3
Dacusville, S.C. (†29640) 296/B2
Dadanawa, Guyana 131/B4
Daday, Turkey 63/E2
Dade (co.), Fla. 212/F6
Dade (co.), Georgia 217/A1
Dade (co.), Mo. 261/E8
Dade City, Fla. (33525) 212/D3
Dadeville, Ala. (36853) 195/G5
Dadeville, Mo. (65635) 261/E8
Dadra and Nagar Haveli (terr.), India 68/C4
Dads (lake), Nebr. 264/D2
Dadu, Pakistan 68/B3
Dadu, Pakistan 59/J4
Dăeni, Romania 45/J3
Daer (res.), Scotland 15/E5
Daet, Philippines 85/G3
Daet, Philippines 82/D3
Dafang, China 77/G6
Dafna, Israel 65/D1
Dafoe, Sask. 181/G4
Dafter, Mich. (49724) 250/E2
Dagabur, Ethiopia 111/H6
Dagana, Senegal 106/A5
Dagda, U.S.S.R. 53/D2
Dagelet (Ullŭng) (isl.), S. Korea 81/E5
Dagestan A.S.S.R., U.S.S.R. 48/E5
Dagestan A.S.S.R., U.S.S.R. 52/G6
Dagestanskiye Ogni, U.S.S.R. 52/G6
Daggett, Calif. (92327) 204/H9
Daggett, Mich. (49821) 250/B3
Daggett (co.), Utah 304/E3
Dagmar, Mont. (59219) 262/M2
Dagö (Hiiumaa) (isl.), U.S.S.R. 52/B3
Dagsboro, Del. (19930) 245/S6
Dagua, Colombia 126/B6
Daguan, China 77/F6
D'Aguilar (range), Tasmania 99/B4
Dagupan, Philippines 82/C2
Daguscahonda, Pa. (†15853) 294/E3
Dagus Mines, Pa. (15831) 294/E3
Dahab, Egypt 111/F2
Dahana (des.), Saudi Arabia 54/F7
Dahana (des.), Saudi Arabia 59/E4
Dahinda, Ill. (61428) 222/C3
Dahinda, Sask. 181/G6
Da Hingan Ling (Great Khingan) (range), China 54/O5
Da Hingan Ling (range), China 77/J3
Dahlak (arch.), Ethiopia 111/H4
Dahlak (arch.), Ethiopia 59/D6
Dahlak (isl.), Ethiopia 59/D6
Dahlak (isl.), Ethiopia 111/H4
Dahlem, W. Germany 22/E4
Dahlen, N. Dak. (58224) 282/P3
Dahlgren, Ill. (62828) 222/E5
Dahlgren, Va. (22448) 307/O4
Dahlia, N. Mex. (†87711) 274/D3
Dahlonega, Georgia (30533) 217/D1
Dahme, E. Germany 22/E3
Dai (mt.), Japan 81/F6
Dailekh, Nepal 68/E3
Dailey, Colo. (†80728) 208/O1
Dailly, Scotland 15/D5
Daimanji (mt.), Japan 81/F5
Daimiel, Spain 33/E3
Daingean, Ireland 17/G5
Daingerfield, Texas (75638) 303/K4
Daio (cape), Japan 81/H6
Daiquirí, Cuba 158/J4
Daireaux, Argentina 143/D4
Dairût, Egypt 111/J4
Dairy, Oreg. (97625) 291/F5
Dairy Flat-Redvale, N. Zealand 100/B1
Dairyland, Wis. (†54830) 317/B3
Daisen-Oki National Park, Japan 81/F6
Daisetsu (mt.), Japan 81/L2
Daisetsu-Zan National Park, Japan 81/L2
Daisetta, Texas (77533) 303/K7
Daisy, Ark. (†71950) 202/C5
Daisy, Georgia (30423) 217/J6
Daisy, Ky. (41733) 237/P6
Daisy, Mo. (63743) 261/N7
Daisy, Okla. (74540) 288/P5
Daisy, Wash. (†99167) 310/G2
Daito, Japan 81/J8
Daito (isls.), Japan 54/P7
Dajabón (prov.), Dom. Rep. 158/D5
Dajabón, Dom. Rep. 158/D5
Dajarra, Queensland 88/F4
Dajarra, Queensland 95/A4
Dakar (cap.), Senegal 2/J5
Dakar (cap.), Senegal 102/A3
Dakar (cap.), Senegal 106/A6
Dakhla (oasis), Egypt 111/E2
Dakhla (oasis), Egypt 59/A4
Dakhla, W. Sahara 102/A2
Dakhla, Western Sahara 106/A4
Dakoro, Niger 106/F6
Dakota, Georgia (†31714) 217/E7
Dakota, Ill. (61018) 222/D1
Dakota (co.), Minn. 255/E6
Dakota, Minn. (55925) 255/G7
Dakota (co.), Nebr. 264/H2
Dakota City, Iowa (50529) 229/E3
Dakota City, Nebr. (68731) 264/H2
Dal (riv.), Sweden 7/F2
Dala, Angola 115/D6
Dalaba, Guinea 106/B6
Dalälven (riv.), Sweden 18/K6
Dalaman (riv.), Turkey 63/C4
Dalandzadgad, Mongolia 77/G3
Dalanganem (isls.), Philippines 82/C5
Dalark, Ark. (†71923) 202/E5
Da Lat, Vietnam 72/F5
Dalavich, Scotland 15/C4
Dalbandin, Pakistan 68/A3
Dalbandin, Pakistan 59/H4
Dalbeattie, Scotland 10/E3
Dalbeattie, Scotland 15/E6
Dalbo, Minn. (55017) 255/E5
Dalby, Queensland 95/D5
Dalby, Queensland 88/J5
Dalby, Sweden 18/H6
Dalcahue, Chile 138/D4
Dalcour, La. (†70040) 238/P4
Dale (co.), Ala. 195/G8
Dale, Ill. (62829) 222/E6
Dale, Ind. (47523) 227/D8
Dale, Minn. (†56549) 255/B4
Dale, Norway 18/E6
Dale, Okla. (74838) 288/M4
Dale, Oreg. (97880) 291/J3
Dale, Pa. (†15901) 294/E5
Dale, S.C. (29914) 296/F6
Dale (mt.), W. Australia 88/B2
Dale (mt.), W. Australia 92/B1
Dale, Wis. (54931) 317/J7
Dale City, Va. (22193) 307/O3
Dale Hollow (lake), Ky. 237/L7
Dale Hollow (lake), Tenn. 237/L7
Dalemead, Alberta 182/D4
Dalen, Netherlands 27/K3
Daleside, S. Africa 118/H7
Daleville, Ala. (36322) 195/G8
Daleville, Ind. (47334) 227/F4
Daleville, Miss. (39326) 256/G5
Daleville, Va. (24083) 307/J6
Dale West, W. Australia 92/B2
Dalhart, Texas (79022) 303/B1
Dalhousie, New Bruns. 170/D1
Dalhousie (cape), N.W. Terrs. 187/E2
Dalhousie (mt.), Nova Scotia 168/E3
Dalhousie East, Nova Scotia 168/D4
Dalhousie Junction, New Bruns. 170/D1
Dalhousie West, Nova Scotia 168/C4
Dali, China 77/E6
Dalías, Spain 33/E4
Daliburgh, Scotland 15/A3
Dalizi, China 77/L3
Dalkeith, Ontario 177/K2
Dalkeith, Scotland 10/C1
Dalkeith, Scotland 15/D2
Dalkena, Wash. (†99156) 310/H2
Dall (isl.), Alaska 196/M2
Dall (mt.), Alaska 196/H2
Dallam (co.), Texas 303/B1
Dallas (co.), Ala. 195/D6
Dallas (co.), Ark. 202/E6
Dallas, Georgia (30132) 217/C3
Dallas (co.), Iowa 229/E5
Dallas, Iowa (50062) 229/G6
Dallas, Manitoba 179/E3
Dallas (co.), Mo. 261/F7
Dallas, N.C. (28034) 281/G4
Dallas, Oreg. (97338) 291/D3
Dallas, Pa. (18612) 294/E7
Dallas, Scotland 15/E3
Dallas, S. Dak. (57529) 298/K7
Dallas (co.), Texas 303/H5
Dallas, Texas (*75201) 303/G2
Dallas, Texas 188/G4
Dallas, Texas 146/J6
Dallas, U.S. 2/E4
Dallas, W. Va. (26036) 312/E2
Dallas, Wis. (54733) 317/C5
Dallas Center, Iowa (50063) 229/E5
Dallas City, Ill. (62330) 222/B3
Dallas Naval Air Sta., Texas 303/G2
Dallastown, Pa. (17313) 294/J6
Dalles, The, Oreg. (97058) 291/F2
Dalles, The (dam), Oreg. 291/F2
Dalles, The (dam), Wash. 310/D5
Dallesport, Wash. (98617) 310/D5
Dallol, Ethiopia 111/G5
Dallol Bosso (dry riv.), Niger 106/E6
Dalmaj, Hor (lake), Iraq 66/D4
Dalmally, Scotland 10/D2
Dalmally, Scotland 15/D4
Dalmatia, Pa. (17017) 294/J4
Dalmatia (reg.), Yugoslavia 45/C4
Dalmellington, Scotland 15/D5
Dalmellington, Scotland 10/D3
Dalmeny, Sask. 181/E3
Dal'negorsk, U.S.S.R. 48/O5
Dal'nerechensk, U.S.S.R. 48/O5
Daloa, Ivory Coast 106/C7
Daloa, Ivory Coast 102/B4
Dalroy, Alberta 182/D4
Dalry, Scotland 10/A1
Dalry, Scotland 15/D5
Dalrymple, Scotland 15/D5
Dalton, Ark. (72423) 202/H1
Dalton, Georgia (30720) 217/C1
Dalton, Ky. (†42445) 237/F6
Dalton○, Mass. (01226) 249/B3
Dalton, Mich. (†49445) 250/C5
Dalton, Minn. (56324) 255/C4
Dalton, Mo. (65246) 261/F4
Dalton, Nebr. (69131) 264/B3
Dalton○, N.H. (†03598) 268/D3
Dalton, N.Y. (14836) 276/E5
Dalton, N.C. (†27043) 281/J2
Dalton, Ohio (44618) 284/G4
Dalton, Pa. (18414) 294/L2
Dalton, Wis. (53926) 317/H8
Dalton City, Ill. (61925) 222/E4
Daltonganj, India 68/E4
Dalton Gardens, Idaho (†83814) 220/B2
Dalton-in-Furness, England 13/D3
Dalupiri (isl.), Philippines 82/A3
Dalwallinu, W. Australia 88/B6
Dalwallinu, W. Australia 92/B5
Dalwhinnie, Scotland 15/D4
Dalworthington Gardens, Texas (†76101) 303/F2
Daly (cape) 5/C4
Daly (riv.), North. Terr. 88/E2
Daly (riv.), North. Terr. 93/B2
Daly (bay), N.W. Terrs. 187/K3
Dalyat al-Karmel, Israel 65/B2
Daly City, Calif. (*94014) 204/H2
Daly River, North. Terr. 88/E2
Daly River, North. Terr. 93/B2
Daly River Aboriginal Reserve, North. Terr. 88/D2
Daly River Aboriginal Res., North. Terr. 93/A2
Dalyup, W. Australia 92/C6
Daly Waters, Australia 87/D7
Daly Waters, North. Terr. 88/E3
Daly Waters, North. Terr. 93/C4
Dalzell, Ill. (61320) 222/D2
Dalzell, S.C. (29040) 296/G3
Dam, Saudi Arabia 59/D5
Daman (dist.), India 68/C4
Damanhur, Egypt 111/J3
Damanhur, Egypt 59/A3
Damar (isl.), Indonesia 85/H7
Damar (isls.), Indonesia 85/H7
Damar, Kansas (67632) 232/C2
Damara, Cent. Afr. Rep. 115/C2
Damaraland (reg.), Namibia 118/B4
Damariscotta○, Maine (04543) 243/E7
Damariscotta-Newcastle, Maine (04543) 243/E7
Damascus, Ark. (72039) 202/F3
Damascus, Georgia (31741) 217/C8
Damascus, Md. (20750) 245/K3
Damascus, Ohio (44619) 284/J4
Damascus, Pa. (18415) 294/M2
Damascus (prov.), Syria 63/G6
Damascus (cap.), Syria 59/C3
Damascus (cap.), Syria 54/E6
Damascus (cap.), Syria 63/G6
Damascus, Va. (24236) 307/E7
Damavand, Iran 66/H3
Damavand (mt.), Iran 54/G6
Damavand (mt.), Iran 59/F2
Damavend (Demavend) (mt.), Iran 66/G3
Damazin (Ed Damazin), Sudan 111/F5
Damba, Angola 115/B5
Dam Doi, Vietnam 72/E5
Dame Marie, Haiti 158/A6
Dame Marie (cape), Haiti 158/A6
Dame Marie (cape), Haiti 156/C3
Dameron, Md. (20628) 245/N8
Dames Ferry, Georgia (†31046) 217/E4
Dames Quarter, Md. (21820) 245/P8
Damghan, Iran 59/F2
Damghan, Iran 66/J2
Damh, Loch (lake), Scotland 15/C3
Damietta, Egypt 102/F1
Damietta, Egypt 111/J3
Damietta, Egypt 59/B3
Damiya, Jordan 65/D3
Dammam, Saudi Arabia 59/F4
Dammastock (mt.), Switzerland 39/F3
Damme, Belgium 27/C6
Damodar (riv.), India 68/F4
Damoh, India 68/D4
Damongo, Ghana 106/D7
Dampier (str.), Indonesia 85/J6
Dampier (str.), Papua N.G. 86/B2
Dampier (str.), Papua N.G. 85/C7
Dampier, W. Australia 88/B4
Dampier (arch.), W. Australia 88/B4
Dampier, W. Australia 92/B3
Dampier (arch.), W. Australia 92/B3
Dampier Downs, W. Australia 92/C2
Dampier Land (reg.), W. Australia 88/C3
Dampier Land (reg.), W. Australia 92/C2
Damqut, P.D.R. Yemen 59/F6
Damvant, Switzerland 39/C2
Dan, Israel 65/D1
Dan (riv.), N.C. 281/L1
Dan (riv.), Va. 307/K7
Dana, Ill. (61321) 222/E3
Dana, Ind. (47847) 227/C5
Dana, Iowa (50064) 229/E4
Dana, Jordan 65/E5
Dana, Sask. 181/F3
Danakil (reg.), Ethiopia 111/H5
Danané, Ivory Coast 106/C7
Da Nang, Vietnam 72/E3
Da Nang, Vietnam 54/M8
Da Nang, Mui (cape), Vietnam 72/F3
Danao, Philippines 82/D5
Dana Point, Calif. (92629) 204/H10
Danba, China 77/F5
Danburg, Georgia (30668) 217/G3
Danbury, Conn. (06810) 210/B3
Danbury, Iowa (51019) 229/B4
Danbury, Nebr. (69026) 264/D4
Danbury○, N.H. (03230) 268/D4
Danbury, N.C. (27016) 281/J2
Danbury, Sask. 181/J4
Danbury, Texas (77534) 303/J8
Danbury, Wis. (54830) 317/B3
Danbury P.O. (South Danbury), N.H. (03230) 268/D5
Danby (lake), Calif. 204/K9
Danby○, Vt. (05739) 268/A5
Dancing (pt.), Manitoba 179/D2
Dancy, Ala. (†35442) 195/B4
Dancy, Miss. (†39751) 256/F3
Dancy, Wis. (†54455) 317/G6
Dancyville, Tenn. (†38069) 237/C10
Dand, Manitoba 179/B5
Dandaragan, W. Australia 88/B6
Dandaragan, W. Australia 92/A5
Dandenong, Victoria 97/K5
Dandenong, Victoria 88/M7
Dandenong (creek), Victoria 97/K5
Dandenong (mt.), Victoria 97/K5
Dandenong (creek), Victoria 88/M7
Danderyd, Sweden 18/H1
Dandong (Tantung), China 77/K3
Dandong, China 54/O5
Dandridge, Tenn. (37725) 237/O8
Dane (riv.), England 13/H2
Dane (co.), Wis. 317/H9
Dane, Wis. (53529) 317/G9
Daneborg, Greenl. 4/B10
Danford Lake, Québec 172/A4
Danforth, Ill. (60930) 222/E3
Danforth, Maine (04424) 243/H4
Danforth○, Maine (04424) 243/H4
Danger (Pukapuka) (atoll), Cook Is. 87/K7
Dangila, Ethiopia 111/G5
Dangrek (mts.), Cambodia 72/D4
Dangrek (Dong Rak) (mts.), Thailand 72/D4
Dangriga (Stann Creek), Belize 153/C2
Dania, Fla. (33004) 212/B4
Daniel (mt.), Wash. 310/D3
Daniel, Wyo. (83115) 319/B3
Daniel Boone, Ky. (†42442) 237/G6
Daniel-Johnson (dam), Québec 174/D2
Daniels, Md. (†21043) 245/L3
Daniels (co.), Mont. 262/L2
Daniels, W. Va. (25832) 312/D7
Daniel's Harbour, Newf. 166/C3
Danielson, Conn. (06239) 210/H1
Danielson Prov. Park, Sask. 181/E4
Danielstown, Guyana 131/B2
Danielsville, Georgia (30633) 217/F2
Danielsville, Pa. (18038) 294/M4
Danilov, U.S.S.R. 52/E3
Dankov, U.S.S.R. 52/E4
Danlí, Honduras 154/D3
Danmarkshavn, Greenl. 4/B10
Dannebrog, Nebr. (68831) 264/F3
Dannelly (res.), Ala. 195/D6
Dannemora, N.Y. (12929) 276/N1
Dannemora, Sweden 18/K6
Dannenberg, W. Germany 22/D2
Danner, Oreg. (†97910) 291/K5
Dannevirke, N. Zealand 100/F4
Dan Sai, Thailand 72/D3
Dansville, Mich. (48819) 250/E6
Dansville, N.Y. (14437) 276/E5
Dante (Hafun), Somalia 115/K1
Dante, S. Dak. (57329) 298/N7
Dante, Va. (24237) 307/D7
Danube (riv.) 7/G4
Danube (riv.), Austria 41/C2
Danube (riv.), Bulgaria 45/H4
Danube (riv.), Czech. 41/D3
Danube (riv.), Hungary 41/E3
Danube, Minn. (56230) 255/C6
Danube (delta), Romania 45/J3
Danube (riv.), Romania 45/H4
Danube (riv.), W. Germany 22/C4
Danube (riv.), Yugoslavia 45/E3
Danubyu, Burma 72/B3
Danvers, Ill. (61732) 222/D3
Danvers○, Mass. (01923) 249/D5
Danvers, Minn. (56231) 255/C5
Danvers, Mont. (59429) 262/G3
Danversport, Mass. (†01923) 249/E5
Danville, Ala. (35619) 195/D2
Danville, Ark. (72833) 202/D3
Danville, Calif. (94526) 204/K2
Danville, Georgia (31017) 217/F5
Danville, Ill. 188/J3
Danville, Ill. (61832) 222/F3
Danville, Ind. (46122) 227/D5
Danville, Iowa (52623) 229/L7
Danville, Kansas (67036) 232/E4
Danville, Ky. (40422) 237/M5
Danville, La. (†71008) 238/E2
Danville, Mo. (†63361) 261/J5
Danville○, N.H. (03819) 268/E6
Danville, Ohio (43014) 284/F5
Danville, Pa. (17821) 294/J4
Danville, Québec 172/E4
Danville○, Vt. (05828) 268/C3
Danville, Va. 188/L3
Danville, Va. 146/L6
Danville (I.C.), Va. (*24540) 307/J7
Danville, Wash. (99121) 310/G2
Danville, W. Va. (25053) 312/C6
Danville, Wis. (†53925) 317/J9
Dan Xian, China 77/G8
Danzig (Gdańsk), Poland 47/D1
Danzig (Gdańsk) (gulf), Poland 47/D1
Daocheng, China 77/F6
Dao Xian, China 77/H6
Dapa, Philippines 82/E6
Dapaong, Togo 106/E6
Daphne, Ala. (36526) 195/C9
Daphne, Sask. 181/G3
Dapitan, Philippines 82/D6
Dapoli, India 68/C5
Dapp, Alberta 182/C2
Da Qaidam, China 77/E4
Darab, Iran 59/G4
Darab, Iran 66/J6
Darabani, Romania 45/H1
Dar al Hamra, Saudi Arabia 59/C4
Daram (isl.), Philippines 82/E5
Daran, Iran 66/G4
Darbandikhan (dam), Iraq 66/D3
Darbhanga, India 68/F3
Darbun, Miss. (†39643) 256/D8
Darby (cape), Alaska 196/F2
Darby, Mont. (59829) 262/B4
Darby (creek), Ohio 284/D5
Darby, Pa. (19023) 294/M7
Darby (creek), Pa. 294/M6
Darby, Victoria 97/D6
Darbydale, Ohio (†43123) 284/D6
Darbyville, Ohio (†43164) 284/D6
D'Arcy, Br. Col. 184/F5
D'Arcy, Sask. 181/C4
Dardanelle, Ark. (72834) 202/D3
Dardanelle (lake), Ark. 202/D3
Dardanelles (str.), Turkey 7/G5
Dardanelles (str.), Turkey 59/A2
Dardanelles (str.), Turkey 63/B6
Darden, Tenn. (38328) 237/E9
Dare (co.), N.C. 281/T3
Dar-el-Beida (Casablanca), Morocco 106/C2
Darende, Turkey 63/G3
Dar es Salaam (cap.), Tanzania 102/F5
Dar es Salaam (cap.), Tanzania 2/M6
Dar es Salaam (cap.), Tanzania 115/G5
Dareton, N.S. Wales 97/B4
Daretown, N.J. (†08318) 273/C4
Darfur, Minn. (56022) 255/D6
Darfur, Northern (prov.), Sudan 111/D5
Darfur, Southern (prov.), Sudan 111/E5
Dargan, Md. (†25425) 245/H3
Dargaville, N. Zealand 100/D1
Dar Hamid (reg.), Sudan 111/F5
Darham Muminggan Lianheqi, China 77/H3
Darhan (Darkhan), Mongolia 77/G2
Darien○, Conn. (06820) 210/B4
Darien, Georgia (31305) 217/K8
Darien, Ill. (†60559) 222/B6
Darien, N.Y. (†14040) 276/D5
Darién (mts.), Panama 154/J6
Darien, Wis. (53114) 317/J10
Darien Center, N.Y. (14040) 276/D5
Dariense, Cordillera (range), Nicaragua 154/E4
Darjeeling, India 68/F3
Dark (head), St. Vin. & Grens. 161/A8
Darkan, W. Australia 92/B2
Dark Canyon (creek), N. Mex. 274/E6
Dark Cove, Newf. 166/D4
Darke (co.), Ohio 284/A5
Darkesville, W. Va. (†25428) 312/L4
Darkin (riv.), W. Australia 88/B2
Darlag, China 77/E5
Darling (river), Australia 87/E9
Darling, Miss. (38623) 256/D2
Darling (riv.), N. S. Wales 88/G6
Darling (riv.), N.S. Wales 97/B3
Darling (lake), N. Dak. 282/G2
Darling, Pa. (†19063) 294/L7
Darling (range), W. Australia 88/B6
Darling (range), W. Australia 92/A1
Darling Downs, Queensland 95/D5
Darlingford, Manitoba 179/D5
Darlington, Ala. (36730) 195/D7
Darlington, England 10/F3
Darlington, England 13/F3
Darlington, Fla. (†32464) 212/C5
Darlington, Idaho (83231) 220/E6
Darlington, Ind. (47940) 227/D4
Darlington, La. (70441) 238/J5
Darlington, Md. (21034) 245/N2
Darlington, Mo. (64438) 261/D2
Darlington, New Bruns. 170/D1
Darlington, Pa. (16115) 294/A4
Darlington (co.), S.C. 296/H3
Darlington, S.C. (29532) 296/H3
Darlington, Wis. (53530) 317/F10
Darlington Heights, Va. (23935) 307/L6
Darlington Point, N.S. Wales 97/C4
Darliston, Jamaica 158/H6
Darłowo, Poland 47/C1
Dar Masalit (reg.), Sudan 111/D5
Darmody, Sask. 181/E5
Darmstadt, Ill. (†62255) 222/D5
Darmstadt, Ind. (†47618) 227/B8
Darmstadt, W. Germany 22/C4
Darnell, La. (71231) 238/G1
Darnestown, Md. (†20760) 245/J4
Darnick, N.S. Wales 97/B3
Darnley (cape) 5/C4
Darnley (bay), N.W. Terrs. 187/F3
Daroca, Spain 33/F2
Darra, Queensland 88/K3
Darreh Gaz, Iran 66/L2
Darrington, Wash. (98241) 310/D2
Dar Rounga (reg.), Cent. Afr. Rep. 115/D2
Darrouzett, Texas (79024) 303/D1
Darrow, La. (70725) 238/K3
Darrtown, Ohio (†45056) 284/A7
Darsser Ort (pt.), E. Germany 22/E1
Dart (cape) 5/B12
Dart (riv.), England 13/D7
D'Artagnan, Québec 172/J3
Dartford, England 13/J8
Dartford, England 10/C5
Dartmoor, Victoria 97/A5
Dartmoor National Park, England 13/C7
Dartmouth (Clifton Dartmouth Hardness), England 10/E5
Dartmouth (Clifton Dartmouth Hardness), England 13/D7
Dartmouth○, Mass. (02714) 249/K6
Dartmouth, N.S. 162/K7
Dartmouth, Nova Scotia 168/E4
Dartmouth (riv.), Québec 172/D1
Darton, England 13/J2
Dartuch (cape), Spain 33/H3
Daru, Papua N.G. 87/E6
Daru, Papua N.G. 85/B7
Daruvar, Yugoslavia 45/C3
Darvel, Scotland 15/D5
Darwell, Alberta 182/C3
Darwen, England 10/G1
Darwen, England 13/H1
Darwin, Australia 2/R6
Darwin, Australia 87/D7
Darwin, Calif. (93522) 204/H7
Darwin (bay), Chile 138/D6
Darwin, Cordillera (mts.), Chile 138/D8
Darwin, Cordillera (mts.), Chile 138/E11
Darwin (Culpepper) (isl.), Ecuador 128/B8
Darwin, Ill. (†62477) 222/F4
Darwin, Minn. (55324) 255/D5
Darwin (cap.), North. Terr. 88/E2
Darwin (cap.), North. Terr. 93/B2
Darwin, Okla. (†74523) 288/P6
Das (isl.), U.A.E. 59/F4
Dash, Ben (hill), Ireland 17/C6
Dashan, Ras (mt.), Ethiopia 59/C7
Dashbalbar, Mongolia 77/H2
Dasher, Georgia (31601) 217/F9
Dashinchilen, Mongolia 77/F2
Dasht (riv.), Pakistan 68/A3
Dasht (riv.), Pakistan 59/H4
Dashtiari, Iran 66/M8
Dashtiari, Iran 59/H4
Dashwood, Br. Col. 184/H3
Dashwood, Ontario 177/C4
Dasol (bay), Philippines 82/B3
Dassel, Minn. (55325) 255/D5
Datça, Turkey 63/B4
Dateland, Ariz. (85333) 198/B6
Datia, India 68/D3
Datil, N. Mex. (87821) 274/B4
Datil (mts.), N. Mex. 274/B4
Datong, Qinghai, China 77/F4
Datong (Tatung), Shanxi, China 77/H3
Datto, Ark. (72424) 202/J1
Datu Piang, Philippines 82/E7
Daua (riv.), Kenya 115/H3
Daufuskie Island, S.C. (29915) 296/F7
Daugava (Western Dvina) (riv.), U.S.S.R. 53/D2
Daugavpils, U.S.S.R. 7/G3
Daugavpils, U.S.S.R. 53/D3
Daugavpils, U.S.S.R. 48/C4
Daugavpils, U.S.S.R. 52/C3
Daule, Ecuador 128/B3
Daulnay, New Bruns. 170/E1
Daun, W. Germany 22/B3
Daung Kyun (isl.), Burma 72/C4
Dauphin, Man. 162/F5
Dauphin, Manitoba 179/B3
Dauphin (lake), Manitoba 179/C3
Dauphin (riv.), Manitoba 179/D3
Dauphin (cape), Nova Scotia 168/H2
Dauphin (co.), Pa. 294/J5
Dauphin, Pa. (17018) 294/J5
Dauphin, St. Lucia 161/G5
Dauphiné (trad. prov.), France 29
Dauphin Island, Ala. (36528) 195/B10
Daus, Tenn. (†37327) 237/L10
Davangere, India 68/D6
Davant, La. (70046) 238/L7
Davao, Philippines 85/H4
Davao, Philippines 54/O9
Davao, Philippines 2/R5
Davao, Philippines 82/E7
Davao (gulf), Philippines 82/E7
Davao (gulf), Philippines 85/H4
Davao del Norte (prov.), Philippines 82/E7
Davao del Sur (prov.), Philippines 82/E7
Davao Oriental (prov.), Philippines 82/F7
Daveluyville, Québec 172/E3
Davenport, Calif. (95017) 204/K4
Davenport, Fla. (33837) 212/E3
Davenport, Iowa (*52801) 229/M5
Davenport, Iowa 188/H2
Davenport, Nebr. (68335) 264/G4
Davenport, N.Y. (13750) 276/L6
Davenport, N. Dak. (58021) 282/R6
Davenport (mt.), North. Terr. 93/B7
Davenport, Okla. (74026) 288/N3
Davenport, Va. (24239) 307/D6
Davenport, Wash. (99122) 310/G3
Daventry, England 13/F5
Davey, Nebr. (68336) 264/H4
Davey (riv.), Tasmania 99/B4
David (pt.), Grenada 161/D8
David, Ky. (41616) 237/R5
David, Panama 154/F6
David City, Nebr. (68632) 264/G3
Davidson (mts.), Alaska 196/K1
Davidson, Maine (†04782) 243/F4
Davidson (co.), N.C. 281/J3
Davidson, N.C. (28036) 281/H4
Davidson, Okla. (73530) 288/J6
Davidson, Sask. 181/E4
Davidson (co.), Tenn. 237/H8
Davidson (mts.), Yukon 187/D3
Davidsonville, Md. (21035) 245/M5
Davie, Fla. (33314) 212/B4
Davie (co.), N.C. 281/H3
Daviess (co.), Ind. 227/C7
Daviess (co.), Ky. 237/G5
Daviess (co.), Mo. 261/E3
Davik, Norway 18/D6
Davilla, Texas (76523) 303/G7
Davin, Sask. 181/H5
Daviot, Scotland 15/D3
Davis (str.) 2/G2
Davis (str.) 146/N3
Davis (str.) 4/C12
Davis (sea) 5/C5
Davis (dam), Ariz. 198/A3
Davis, Calif. (95616) 204/B8
Davis (isl.), Fla. 212/C3
Davis, Ill. (61019) 222/D1

360 Denton

Denton, England 13/H2
Denton, Georgia (31532) 217/G7
Denton, Kansas (66017) 232/G2
Denton, Ky. (41132) 237/R4
Denton, Md. (21629) 245/P5
Denton, Mo. (†63877) 261/N10
Denton, Mont. (59430) 262/G3
Denton, Nebr. (68339) 264/H4
Denton, N.C. (27239) 281/J3
Denton (co.), Texas 303/G4
Denton, Texas 188/G4
Denton, Texas (76201) 303/G4
D'Entrecasteaux (isls.), Papua N.G. 87/F6
D'Entrecasteaux (isls.), Papua N.G. 85/C7
D'Entrecasteaux (chan.), Tasmania 99/D5
D'Entrecasteaux (pt.), W. Australia 88/B7
D'Entrecasteaux (pt.), W. Australia 92/A6
Dents du Midi (mt.), Switzerland 39/C4
Dents Run, Pa. (†15832) 294/F3
Dentville, Miss. (†39059) 256/C7
Denver, Ark. (†72632) 202/D1
Denver (co.), Colo. 208/K3
Denver (cap.), Colo. (*80201) 208/K3
Denver (cap.), Colo. 188/F3
Denver (cap.), Colo. 146/H6
Denver, Ill. (†62321) 222/B3
Denver, Ind. (46926) 227/E3
Denver, Iowa (50622) 229/J3
Denver, Mo. (64441) 261/D2
Denver, N.C. (28037) 281/G3
Denver, Pa. (17517) 294/K5
Denver, Tenn. (37054) 237/F8
Denver, U.S. 2/D3
Denver City, Texas (79323) 303/B4
Denville○, N.J. (07834) 273/E2
Denzil, Sask. 181/B3
Deogarh, India 68/E4
Deoghar, India 68/F4
Deolali, India 68/C5
Deora, Colo. (†81054) 208/O7
Deoria, India 68/E3
De Panne, Belgium 27/B6
Depauville, N.Y. (13632) 276/H2
Depauw, Ind. (47115) 227/E8
De Peel (reg.), Netherlands 27/H6
Dependencias Federales (terr.), Venezuela 124/E2
De Pere, Wis. (54115) 317/K7
Depew, N.Y. (14043) 276/C5
Depew, Okla. (74028) 288/O3
De Peyster, N.Y. (13633) 276/K1
Depoe Bay, Oreg. (97341) 291/C3
Deport, Texas (75435) 303/J4
Deposit, N.Y. (13754) 276/K6
Dépôt Lézard, Fr. Guiana 131/E3
Depoy, Ky. (42336) 237/G6
Deptford○, N.J. (08096) 273/B4
Depue, Ill. (61322) 222/D2
Deputy, Ind. (47230) 227/F7
Dêqên, China 77/E6
De Queen, Ark. (71832) 202/B5
De Quincy, La. (70633) 238/D6
Der'a (prov.), Syria 63/G6
Der'a, Syria 63/G6
Dera Bugti, Pakistan 68/B3
Dera Bugti, Pakistan 59/J4
Dérac, Haiti 158/C5
Dera Ghazi Khan, Pakistan 68/C3
Dera Ghazi Khan, Pakistan 59/J3
Dera Ismail Khan, Pakistan 59/K3
Dera Ismail Khan, Pakistan 68/C2
Derbent, U.S.S.R. 7/J4
Derbent, U.S.S.R. 52/G6
Derby, Australia 87/C7
Derby, Conn. (06418) 210/C3
Derby, England 13/F5
Derby, England 10/F4
Derby, Ind. (47525) 227/D8
Derby, Iowa (50068) 229/G7
Derby, Kansas (67037) 232/E4
Derby, Maine (04425) 243/E5
Derby, Miss. (†39470) 256/E9
Derby, N.Y. (14047) 276/B5
Derby, Ohio (43117) 284/D6
Derby, Tasmania 99/D3
Derby, Texas (†78017) 303/E9
Derby (Derby Center), Vt. (05829) 268/C2
Derby○, Vt. (05829) 268/C2
Derby, W. Australia 88/C3
Derby, W. Australia 92/C2
Derby Line, Vt. (05830) 268/C2
Derbyshire (co.), England 13/F5
Derecske, Hungary 41/F3
Dereli, Turkey 63/H2
Derendingen, Switzerland 39/E2
Derg (lake), Ireland 17/E6
Derg (lake), Ireland 17/F2
Derg, Lough (lake), Ireland 10/B4
Derg (riv.), N. Ireland 17/F2
De Ridder, La. (70634) 238/D5
Derik, Turkey 63/J4
Dering Harbor, N.Y. (†11964) 276/R8
Derinkuyu, Turkey 63/F3
Derj, Libya 111/B1
Derma, Miss. (38839) 256/F3
Dermott, Ark. (71638) 202/H7
Derna, Libya 102/E1
Derna, Libya 111/D1
Dernic, Sask. 181/J4
Dernieres (isls.), La. 238/J8
Deroche, Br. Col. 184/L3
Deronda, Wis. (54008) 317/B5
De Rossett, Tenn. (†38583) 237/L9
Déroute (passage), Chan. Is. 13/F8
Derravaragh (lake), Ireland 17/G4
Derrinallum, Victoria 97/B5
Derry, La. (71421) 238/E3
Derry, N.H. (03038) 268/E6
Derry○, N.H. (03038) 268/E6
Derry, N. Mex. (87933) 274/B6
Derry, Pa. (15627) 294/D5
Derrygonnelly, N. Ireland 17/F3
Derryveagh (mts.), Ireland 17/E2
Derudeb, Sudan 111/G4
De Ruyter, N.Y. (13052) 276/J5
Dervaig, Scotland 15/B4
Derventa, Yugoslavia 45/C3
Dervock, N. Ireland 17/J1
Derwent, Alberta 182/E3
Derwent (riv.), England 13/H3
Derwent (riv.), England 13/G3
Derwent (riv.), England 10/F3
Derwent (riv.), Tasmania 99/C4
Derwent Bridge, Tasmania 99/C4
Derwood, Md. (20855) 245/K4
Desaguadero (riv.), Argentina 143/C3
Desaguadero, Bolivia 136/A5
Desaguadero (riv.), Bolivia 136/B5
Desaguadero, Peru 128/H11
De Salis (bay), N.W. Terrs. 187/F2
Des Allemands, La. (70030) 238/N4
Des Arc, Ark. (72040) 202/G4
Des Arc (bayou), Ark. 202/G3
Des Arc, Mo. (63636) 261/L8
Desatoya (mts.), Nev. 266/D3
Desbiens, Québec 172/E1
Des Bois (lake), N.W. Terrs. 187/F3
Desboro, Ontario 177/C3
Desborough, England 13/G5
Descanso, Calif. (92016) 204/J11
Deschaillons-sur-Saint-Laurent, Québec 172/E3
Deschambault, Québec 172/E3
Deschambault Lake, Sask. 181/M3
Descharme Lake, Sask. 181/L3
Deschênes, Québec 172/B4
Deschênes (lake), Québec 172/A4
Deschutes (co.), Oreg. 291/F4
Deschutes (riv.), Oreg. 291/G2
Deschutes (riv.), Wash. 310/C4
Deseado (riv.), Argentina 120/C7
Deseado (riv.), Argentina 143/C6
Deseado (cape), Chile 138/D10
Desemboque Seris, Mexico 150/C2
Desengaño (pt.), Argentina 143/C6
Desenzano del Garda, Italy 34/C2
Deseret, Utah (†84624) 304/B4
Deseronto, Ontario 177/G3
Desert (range), Nev. 266/F6
Desert (valley), Nev. 266/C1
Deserta Grande (isl.), Portugal 33/B2
Desertas (isl.), Portugal 102/A1
Desertas (isls.), Portugal 106/A2
Desertas (isls.), Portugal 33/A2
Desert Center, Calif. (92239) 204/K10
Desert Hot Springs, Calif. (92240) 204/J9
Desert View Highlands, Calif. (†93550) 204/G9
Desha (co.), Ark. 202/H6
Deshaies, Guadeloupe 161/A6
Deshler, Nebr. (68340) 264/G4
Deshler, Ohio (43516) 284/C3
Désirade, La (isl.), Guadeloupe 161/B6
Des Lacs, N. Dak. (58733) 282/G3
Des Lacs (riv.), N. Dak. 282/G3
Desloge, Mo. (63601) 261/M7
Desmarais, Alberta 182/D2
Desmaraisville, Québec 174/B3
Desmet, Idaho (83824) 220/B2
De Smet, S. Dak. (57231) 298/O5
Desmochados, Paraguay 144/C5
Des Moines (riv.) 188/H2
Des Moines (co.), Iowa 229/L7
Des Moines (cap.), Iowa 146/J5
Des Moines (cap.), Iowa 188/H2
Des Moines (cap.), Iowa (*50301) 229/G5
Des Moines (riv.), Iowa 229/J7
Des Moines (riv.), Minn. 255/C7
Des Moines (riv.), Mo. 261/J1
Des Moines, N. Mex. (88418) 274/F2
Des Moines, Wash. (98188) 310/B2
Desna (riv.), U.S.S.R. 52/D4
Desolación (isl.), Chile 120/B8
Desolación (isl.), Chile 138/D10
Desolation (canyon), Utah 304/E4
De Soto (co.), Fla. 212/E4
De Soto, Georgia (31743) 217/D7
De Soto, Ill. (62924) 222/D6
Desoto, Ind. (47302) 227/G4
De Soto, Iowa (50069) 229/E5
De Soto, Kansas (66018) 232/H3
De Soto (par.), La. 238/C2
De Soto (co.), Miss. 256/E1
De Soto, Miss. (†39360) 256/G7
De Soto, Mo. (63020) 261/L6
De Soto, Texas (75115) 303/G3
De Soto, Wis. (†54663) 317/D9
De Soto Nat'l Mem., Fla. 212/D4
Des Peres, Mo. (63131) 261/O3
Des Plaines, Ill. (*60016) 222/B5
Des Plaines (riv.), Ill. 222/A6
Dessa, Niger 106/E6
Dessalines, Haiti 158/C5
Dessau, E. Germany 22/E3
Dessel, Belgium 27/G6
Dessye, Ethiopia 102/G3
Dessye, Ethiopia 111/G5
Destelbergen, Belgium 27/D6
Destin, Fla. (32541) 212/C6
Destrehan, La. (70047) 238/N4
Destruction (isl.), Wash. 310/A3
Destruction Bay, Yukon 187/E3
Deta, Romania 45/E3
Detah, N.W. Terrs. 187/G3
Detlor, Ontario 177/G2
Detmold, W. Germany 22/C3
De Tour (passage), Mich. 250/E3
Detour (pt.), Mich. 250/C3
De Tour Village, Mich. (49725) 250/E3
Detrital Wash (dry riv.), Ariz. 198/A3
Detroit, Ala. (35552) 195/B2
Detroit, Ill. (62332) 222/C4
Detroit, Kansas (†67410) 232/E3
Detroit○, Maine (04929) 243/E6
Detroit, Mich. 146/K5
Detroit, Mich. 188/K2
Detroit, Mich. (*48201) 250/B7
Detroit (riv.), Mich. 250/B7
Detroit, Oreg. (97342) 291/E3
Detroit (lake), Oreg. 291/E3
Detroit, Texas (75436) 303/J4
Detroit, U.S. 2/E3
Detroit Beach, Mich. (†48161) 250/F7
Detroit Lakes, Minn. (56501) 255/C4
Dett, Zimbabwe 118/D3
Detva, Czech. 41/E2
De Twente (reg.), Netherlands 27/K4
Deuel (co.), Nebr. 264/B3
Deuel (co.), S. Dak. 298/R4
Deûle (riv.), Belgium 27/B7
Deurne, Belgium 27/F6
Deurne, Netherlands 27/H6
Deustua, Peru 128/G10
Deutsch Feistritz, Austria 41/C3
Deutschkreutz, Austria 41/D3
Deutsch Landsberg, Austria 41/C3
Deutsch Wagram, Austria 41/D2
Deux Frères, Les (isls.), Vietnam 72/E5
Deux-Montagnes (co.), Québec 172/C4
Deux-Montagnes, Québec 172/H4
Deux Montagnes (lake), Québec 172/C4
Deux Rivières, Ontario 177/F1
Deux-Sèvres (dept.), France 28/C4
Deva, Romania 45/F3
De Valls Bluff, Ark. (72041) 202/H4
Devault, Pa. (19432) 294/L5
Dévaványa, Hungary 41/F3
Devecser, Hungary 41/D3
Develi, Turkey 59/C2
Develi, Turkey 63/F3
Deventer, Netherlands 27/J4
Devenyns (lake), Québec 172/D2
Devereux, Georgia (†31087) 217/F4
Deveron (riv.), Scotland 15/F3
De View (bayou), Ark. 202/J3
Deville, La. (71328) 238/F4
Devil River (peak), N. Zealand 100/D4
Devils (isl.), Fr. Guiana 120/D2
Devil's (isl.), Fr. Guiana 131/E3
Devils (lake), N. Dak. 282/N3
Devils (riv.), Texas 303/D7
Devilsbit (mt.), Ireland 17/F6
Devil's Hole (Death Valley Nat'l Mon.), Nev. 266/E6
Devils Lake, N. Dak. 188/G1
Devils Lake, N. Dak. (58301) 282/N3
Devils Paw (mt.), Alaska 196/N1
Devils Postpile Nat'l Mon., Calif. 204/F6
Devils Slide, Utah (†84050) 304/C2
Devils Thumb (mt.), Br. Col. 184/A1
Devils Tower, Wyo. (82714) 319/H1
Devils Tower Nat'l Mon., Wyo. 319/H1
Devin, Bulgaria 45/G5
Devine, Texas (78016) 303/E8
Devizes, England 13/F6
Devizes, England 10/F5
Devol, Okla. (73531) 288/J6
Devola, Ohio (45750) 284/H7
De Volet (pt.), St. Vin. & Grens. 161/A8
Devon, Alberta 182/D3
Devon (isl.), Canada 4/B14
Devon, Conn. (†06460) 210/C4
Devon (co.), England 13/D7
Devon, Jamaica 158/H6
Devon, Kansas (†66701) 232/H4
Devon, Mont. (†59474) 262/E2
Devon (isl.), N.W.T. 162/M3
Devon (isl.), N.W.T. 146/K2
Devon (isl.), N.W. Terrs. 187/K2
Devondale, Ky. (†40201) 237/K2
Devonia, Tenn. (†37710) 237/N8
Devonport, Australia 87/E10
Devonport, N. Zealand 100/C1
Devonport, Tasmania 88/H8
Devonport, Tasmania 99/C3
Devrek, Turkey 63/D2
Devrekâni, Turkey 63/E2
Devrez (riv.), Turkey 63/E2
Dewar, Iowa (50623) 229/J3
Dewar, Okla. (74431) 288/P4
Dewart, Pa. (17730) 294/J3
Dewas, India 68/D4
Dewberry, Alberta 182/E3
Dewees (isl.), S.C. 296/H6
De Weese (plat.), Colo. 208/J6
Deweese, Nebr. (68934) 264/F4
Dewey, Ariz. (86327) 198/C4
Dewey, Ill. (61840) 222/E3
Dewey (lake), Ky. 237/R5
Dewey (co.), Okla. 288/H2
Dewey, Okla. (74029) 288/P1
Dewey (Culebra), P. Rico 161/G1
Dewey (co.), S. Dak. 298/G3
Dewey Park, Ill. (†62025) 222/B2
Deweyville, Texas (77614) 303/L7
Deweyville, Utah (84309) 304/B2
De Wijk, Netherlands 27/J3
De Winton, Alberta 182/C4
De Witt, Ark. (72042) 202/H5
De Witt (co.), Ill. 222/E3
Dewitt, Ill. (61735) 222/E3
De Witt, Iowa (52742) 229/N5
Dewitt, Ky. (†40935) 237/O7
De Witt, Mich. (48820) 250/E6
De Witt, Mo. (64639) 261/F4
De Witt, Nebr. (68341) 264/G4
DeWitt, N.Y. (13214) 276/H4
De Witt (co.), Texas 303/G9
Dewitt, Va. (23840) 307/N6
Dewittville, Québec 172/C4
Dewsbury, England 10/H2
Dewsbury, England 13/J1
Dewy Rose, Georgia (30634) 217/G2
Dexter (lake), Fla. 212/E2
Dexter, Georgia (31019) 217/G6
Dexter, Iowa (50070) 229/E5
Dexter, Kansas (67038) 232/F4
Dexter, Ky. (42036) 237/E7
Dexter, Maine (04930) 243/E5
Dexter○, Maine (04930) 243/E5
Dexter, Mich. (48130) 250/F6
Dexter, Minn. (55926) 255/F7
Dexter, Mo. (63841) 261/N9
Dexter, N. Mex. (88230) 274/E5
Dexter, N.Y. (13634) 276/H2
Dexter, Oreg. (97431) 291/E4
Dexter City, Ohio (45727) 284/G6
Dexterville, Wis. (†54466) 317/F7
Deyang, China 77/F5
Dey Dey (lake), S. Australia 88/E5
Dey Dey (lake), S. Australia 94/B3
DeYoung, Pa. (16728) 294/E2
Dez (riv.), Iran 59/E3
Dez (riv.), Iran 66/F4
De Zaan (riv.), Netherlands 27/B4
Dezful, Iran 59/E3
Dezful, Iran 54/F6
Dezful, Iran 66/F4
Dezhnev (cape), U.S.S.R. 4/C18
Dezhnev (cape), U.S.S.R. 48/T3
Dezhou (Tehchow), China 77/J4
Dezh Shahpur, Iran 66/E3
Dezh Shahpur, Iran 59/E2
Dhaba, Saudi Arabia 59/C4
Dhahiriya, West Bank 65/B5
Dhahran, Saudi Arabia 54/F7
Dhahran, Saudi Arabia 59/E4
Dhali, Cyprus 63/E5
Dhamar, Yemen Arab Rep. 59/D7
Dhamtari, India 68/E4
Dhanbad, India 68/F4
Dhangarhi, Nepal 68/E3
D'Hanis, Texas (78850) 303/E8
Dhank, Oman 59/G5
Dhankuta, Nepal 68/F3
Dhar, India 68/C4
Dharma, Saudi Arabia 59/E5
Dharmsala, India 68/D2
Dharwar-Hubli, India 68/C5
Dhaulagiri (mt.), Nepal 68/E3
Dhenkanal, India 68/E4
Dhidhimótikhon, Greece 45/H5
Dhikaia, Greece 45/H5
Dhimitsána, Greece 45/F7
Dhi Qar (gov.), Iraq 66/E5
Dhira', Jordan 65/D5
Dhofar (reg.), Oman 59/F6
Dholpur, India 68/D3
Dhomokós, Greece 45/F6
Dhond, India 68/C5
Dhoraji, India 68/C4
Dhubri, India 68/G3
Dhulia, India 68/C4
Dia (isl.), Greece 45/G8
Diable (pt.), Martinique 161/D5
Diablerets (mt.), Switzerland 39/D4
Diablo (canyon), Ariz. 198/D4
Diablo, Calif. (94528) 204/K2
Diablo, Sierra (mts.), Texas 303/C10
Diablo, Wash. (†98283) 310/D2
Diablo (dam), Wash. 310/D2
Diablo (lake), Wash. 310/D2
Diablotin, Morne (mt.), Dominica 161/E6
Diadema, Brazil 135/C3
Diagonal, Iowa (50845) 229/E7
Dial, Georgia (30536) 217/D1
Diamant, Rocher du (isl.), Martinique 161/C7
Diamante, Argentina 143/F6
Diamante (riv.), Argentina 143/C3
Diamantina, Brazil 132/F7
Diamantina (riv.), Queensland 88/G4
Diamantina (riv.), Queensland 95/B4
Diamantina Lakes, Queensland 95/B4
Diamantino, Brazil 132/B6
Diamond (lake), Conn. 210/F2
Diamond (head), Hawaii 218/C5
Diamond (peak), Idaho 220/E5
Diamond, Ind. (47874) 227/C5
Diamond, La. (†70083) 238/L7
Diamond, Mo. (64840) 261/D9
Diamond, Ohio (44412) 284/H3
Diamond, Oreg. (97722) 291/J4
Diamond (lake), Oreg. 291/E4
Diamond (peak), Oreg. 291/E4
Diamond, Pa. (†16354) 294/C2
Diamond, Virgin Is. (U.S.) 161/F4
Diamond, Wash. (†99111) 310/H4
Diamond (lake), Wash. 310/H2
Diamond Bluff, Wis. (†54014) 317/A6
Diamond City, Alberta 182/D5
Diamond City, Ark. (72644) 202/E1
Diamond Coast (reg.), Namibia 118/A5
Diamond Lake, Oreg. (97731) 291/E4
Diamond Point, N.Y. (12824) 276/N4
Diamond Springs, Calif. (95619) 204/D8
Diamondville, Wyo. (83116) 319/B4
Diana, W. Va. (26217) 312/F5
Dian Chi (lake), China 77/F7
Dianjiang, China 77/G5
Diano Marina, Italy 34/B3
Dianópolis, Brazil 132/E5
Diapaga, Upper Volta 106/E6
Dias Creek, N.J. (†08210) 273/D5
Diaz, Argentina 143/F6
Diaz, Ark. (72043) 202/H2
Dibaya, Zaire 115/D5
Dibaya-Lubue, Zaire 115/C4
Dibble, Okla. (73031) 288/L4
Dibeng, S. Africa 118/C5
D'Iberville, Miss. (†39532) 256/G10
Dibete, Botswana 118/D4
Diboll, Texas (75941) 303/K6
Dibrugarh, India 68/G3
Dibulla, Colombia 126/D2
Dickens, Iowa (51333) 229/C2
Dickens, Nebr. (69132) 264/C4
Dickens (pt.), R.I. 249/H8
Dickens (co.), Texas 303/D4
Dickens, Texas (79229) 303/D4
Dickenson (co.), Va. 307/D6
Dickerson, Md. (20753) 245/J4
Dickey, Georgia (†31746) 217/C7
Dickey (co.), N. Dak. 282/N7
Dickey, N. Dak. (58431) 282/N6
Dickeyville, Wis. (53808) 317/E10
Dickinson, Ala. (36436) 195/C7
Dickinson (co.), Iowa 229/C2
Dickinson (co.), Kansas 232/E3
Dickinson (co.), Mich. 250/B2
Dickinson, N. Dak. 188/F1
Dickinson, N. Dak. (58601) 282/E6
Dickinson, Pa. (17218) 294/H5
Dickinson, Texas (77539) 303/K3
Dickinson Center, N.Y. (12930) 276/M1
Dickson, Alberta 182/C3
Dickson, Okla. (†73401) 288/M6
Dickson (lake), Ontario 177/F2
Dickson (co.), Tenn. 237/G8
Dickson, Tenn. (37055) 237/G8
Dickson, W. Va. (†25535) 312/B6
Dickson City, Pa. (18519) 294/F7
Dicle, Turkey 63/J3
Dicle (riv.), Turkey 63/J4
Didam, Netherlands 27/J5
Didcot, England 13/F6
Dido, La. (†70656) 238/E5
Didsbury, Alberta 182/C4
Didsbury, Alta. 162/E5
Didyme, Québec 172/E1
Die, France 28/F5
Diébougou, Upper Volta 106/D6
Diefenbaker (lake), Sask. 181/E4
Diego de Almagro (isl.), Chile 138/D9
Diego Garcia (isl.), Br. Ind. Ocean Terr. 54/J10
Diego Lamas, Uruguay 145/C1
Diego Pérez (cay), Cuba 158/C2
Diégo-Suarez (Antsiranana), Madagascar 118/H2
Diehlstadt, Mo. (†63834) 261/N9
Diekirch, Luxembourg 27/J9
Dielsdorf, Switzerland 39/F1
Diemen, Netherlands 27/C5
Diemtigen, Switzerland 39/D3
Dien Bien Phu, Vietnam 72/D2
Diep (riv.), S. Africa 118/F6
Diepholz, W. Germany 22/C2
Diepoldsau, Switzerland 39/J2
Dieppe, France 28/D3
Dieppe, New Bruns. 170/F2
Dieppe Bay, St. Chris.-Nevis 161/C10
Dieren, Netherlands 27/J4
Dierks, Ark. (71833) 202/B5
Diessenhofen, Switzerland 39/G1
Diest, Belgium 27/F7
Dieterich, Ill. (62424) 222/E4
Dietikon, Switzerland 39/F2
Dietrich, Idaho (83324) 220/D7
Diever, Netherlands 27/J3
Diez y Nueve (19) de Abril, Uruguay 145/E5
Diez y Ocho (18) de Julio, Uruguay 145/F4
Dif, Somalia 115/H3
Diffa, Niger 106/G6
Differdange, Luxembourg 27/H9
Difficult, Tenn. (†37145) 237/K8
Difficult (mt.), Victoria 97/B5
Digboi, India 68/H3
Digby (co.), Nova Scotia 168/C4
Digby, Nova Scotia 168/C4
Digby Gut (chan.), Nova Scotia 168/C4
Digby Neck (pen.), Nova Scotia 168/B4
Digdeguash (riv.), New Bruns. 170/C3
Digges (isls.), N.W. Terrs. 187/L3
Diggins, Mo. (65636) 261/G8
Dighton, Kansas (67839) 232/B3
Dighton○, Mass. (02715) 249/K5
Dighton, Mich. (†49688) 250/D4
Digne, France 28/G5
Digoin, France 28/F4
Digor, Turkey 63/K2
Digos, Philippines 82/E7
Digul (riv.), Indonesia 85/K7
Dijon, France 28/F4
Dijon, France 7/E4
Dike, Iowa (50624) 229/H4
Dikhil, Djibouti 111/H5
Dikili, Turkey 63/B3
Diksmuide, Belgium 27/B6
Dikson, U.S.S.R. 4/B5
Dikson, U.S.S.R. 48/J2
Dikwa, Nigeria 106/G6
Dikwa, Nigeria 102/D3
Dilam, Saudi Arabia 59/E5
Dilbeek, Belgium 27/B9
Dildo, Newf. 166/D2
Dili, Indonesia 54/O10
Dili, Indonesia 85/H7
Dilia, N. Mex. (†87711) 274/D3
Diligent River, Nova Scotia 168/D3
Di Linh, Vietnam 72/F5
Dilke, Sask. 181/F5
Dilkon, Ariz. (†86047) 198/E3
Dilla, Ethiopia 111/G6
Dillabough, Sask. 181/J3
Dillard, Georgia (30537) 217/F1
Dillard, Mo. (65458) 261/K7
Dillard, Oreg. (97432) 291/D4
Dill City, Okla. (73641) 288/H4
Dille, W. Va. (26617) 312/E6
Dillenburg, W. Germany 22/C3
Diller, Nebr. (68342) 264/H4
Dilley, Oreg. (†97116) 291/A2
Dilley, Texas (78017) 303/E9
Dillia (dry riv.), Niger 106/G5
Dilliner, Pa. (15327) 294/B6
Dilling, Sudan 111/E5
Dillingen, W. Germany 22/B4
Dillingen an der Donau, W. Germany 22/D4
Dillingham, Alaska 188/C6
Dillingham, Alaska (99576) 196/G3
Dillon (riv.), Alberta 182/E2
Dillon, Colo. (80435) 208/H3
Dillon, Kansas (†67451) 232/E3
Dillon, Mont. (59725) 262/D5
Dillon (lake), Ohio 284/F5
Dillon (co.), S.C. 296/J3
Dillon, S.C. (29536) 296/J3
Dillonvale, Ohio (43917) 284/J5
Dillsboro, Ind. (47018) 227/G6
Dillsboro, N.C. (28725) 281/C4
Dillsburg, Pa. (17019) 294/J5
Dilltown, Pa. (15929) 294/E5
Dillwyn, Va. (23936) 307/M5
Dilolo, Zaire 115/D6
Dilsen, Belgium 27/H6
Dilworth, Minn. (56529) 255/B4
Dimas, Cuba 158/A2
Dimas, Mexico 150/F5
Dimashq (Damascus) (cap.), Syria 63/G6
Dimashq (Damascus) (cap.), Syria 59/C3
Dimbelenge, Zaire 115/D5
Dimbokro, Ivory Coast 106/D7
Dimboola, Victoria 97/B5
Dime Box, Texas (77853) 303/H7
Dimitrovgrad, Bulgaria 45/G4
Dimitrovgrad, U.S.S.R. 52/G4
Dimitrovgrad, U.S.S.R. 48/F4
Dimitrovgrad, Yugoslavia 45/F4
Dimlang (mt.), Nigeria 106/G7
Dimmit (co.), Texas 303/E9
Dimmitt, Texas (79027) 303/B3
Dimock, Pa. (18816) 294/L2
Dimock, S. Dak. (57331) 298/O7
Dimona, Israel 65/D4
Dimona (mt.), Israel 65/C5
Dimondale, Mich. (48821) 250/E6
Dimsdale, Alberta 182/A2
Dinagat, Philippines 82/E5
Dinagat (isl.), Philippines 85/H3
Dinagat (isl.), Philippines 82/E5
Dinagat (sound), Philippines 82/E5
Dinajpur, Bangladesh 68/F3
Dinan, France 28/B3
Dinant, Belgium 27/G8
Dinar, Kuh-e (mts.), Iran 66/G5
Dinar, Turkey 63/D3
Dinard, France 28/B3
Dinaric Alps (mts.), Yugoslavia 45/B3
Dinas Powis, Wales 13/B7
Dinder (riv.), Ethiopia 111/F5
Dinder (riv.), Sudan 59/B7
Dinder (riv.), Sudan 111/F5
Dindigul, India 68/D6
Dingalan (bay), Philippines 82/C3
Dingbian, China 77/G4
Dingess, W. Va. (25671) 312/B7
Dinggye, China 77/C6
Dinghai, China 77/K5
Dingle, Idaho (83233) 220/G7
Dingle, Ireland 10/A4
Dingle, Ireland 17/A7
Dingle (bay), Ireland 10/A4
Dingle (bay), Ireland 17/A7
Dingmans Ferry, Pa. (18328) 294/N3
Dingolfing, W. Germany 22/E4
Dinguiraye, Guinea 106/B6
Dingwall, Nova Scotia 168/H2
Dingwall, Scotland 15/D3
Dingwall, Scotland 10/D2
Dingxi, China 77/F4
Dingxing, China 77/H4
Dinh, Mui (cape), Vietnam 72/F5
Dinkelsbühl, W. Germany 22/D4
Dinnebito Wash (dry riv.), Ariz. 198/E3
Dinokwe, Botswana 118/D4
Dinorwic, Ontario 177/G5
Dinorwic, Ontario 175/B3
Dinosaur, Colo. (81610) 208/B2
Dinosaur Nat'l Mon., Colo. 208/B2
Dinosaur Nat'l Mon., Utah 304/E3
Dinsdale, Iowa (†50669) 229/H4
Dinsmore, Sask. 181/D4
Dinsor, Somalia 115/H3
Dinuba, Calif. (93618) 204/F7
Dinwiddie (co.), Va. 307/N6
Dinwiddie, Va. (23841) 307/N6
Dinxperlo, Netherlands 27/K5
Diogo (isl.), Philippines 82/B2
Dioila, Mali 106/C6
Diomede, Alaska (†99762) 196/E1
Diourbel, Senegal 106/A6
Diphu, India 68/G3
Dipilto, Cordillera (range), Nicaragua 154/D4
Diplo, Pakistan 68/B4
Dipolog, Philippines 82/D6
Dipper Harbour, New Bruns. 170/D3
Dir, Pakistan 68/C1
Dir, Pakistan 59/K2
Dire, Mali 106/D5
Direction (cape), Queensland 88/G2
Direction (cape), Queensland 95/B2
Dire Dawa, Ethiopia 102/G4
Dire Dawa, Ethiopia 111/H6
Diriamba, Nicaragua 154/D5
Dirico, Angola 115/D7
Dirico, Namibia 118/C3
Dirk Hartogs (isl.), Australia 87/B8
Dirk Hartogs (isl.), W. Australia 88/A5
Dirk Hartogs (isl.), W. Australia 92/A4
Dirksland, Netherlands 27/E5
Dirmil, Turkey 63/C4
Dirranbandi, Queensland 88/H5
Dirranbandi, Queensland 95/D6
Dirty Devil (riv.), Utah 304/D5
Disappointment (lake), Australia 87/C8
Disappointment (creek), Colo. 208/B7
Disappointment (isls.), Fr. Poly. 87/N7
Disappointment (lake), Newf. 166/B3
Disappointment (cape), Wash. 188/A1
Disappointment (cape), Wash. 310/A4
Disappointment (lake), W. Australia 88/C4
Disappointment (lake), W. Australia 92/C3
Discovery (bay) 88/E7
Discovery (bay), Victoria 97/A6
Discovery Bay, Jamaica 158/J5
Disentis-Mustér, Switzerland 39/G3
Dishman, Wash. (99213) 310/H3
Disko (isl.), Greenl. 4/C12

Dovray 361

Disko (isl.), Greenland 146/N3
Disko, Ind. (†46982) 227/E2
Disley, Sask. 181/F5
Dismal (riv.), Nebr. 264/C3
Dismal (Great) (swamp), N.C. 281/S1
Disney, Okla. (74340) 288/S2
Dison, Belgium 27/H7
Dispur, India 68/G3
Disputanta, Va. (23842) 307/O6
Disraeli (bay), N.W. Terrs. 187/L1
Disraëli, Québec 172/F4
Diss, England 13/J5
Diss, England 10/G4
Disston (lake), Fla. 212/E2
Disston, Oreg. (†97427) 291/E4
District Heights, Md. (20747) 245/G5
District of Columbia 146/L6
District of Columbia 188/L3
DISTRICT OF COLUMBIA 245
Distrito Especial, Colombia 126/C5
Distrito Federal, Argentina 143/H7
Distrito Federal, Mexico 150/L1
Distrito Federal, Venezuela 124/E2
Distrito Nacional, Dom. Rep. 158/E6
Disûq, Egypt 111/J3
Dittmer, Mo. (63023) 261/L6
Ditton (riv.), Québec 172/F4
Diu, India 68/C4
Diu (dist.), India 68/C4
Diuata (mts.), Philippines 82/E6
Divernon, Ill. (62530) 222/D4
Divide, Colo. (80814) 208/J5
Divide, Mont. (59727) 262/D5
Divide (co.), N. Dak. 282/C2
Dividing (creek), Md. 245/R8
Dividing Creek, N.J. (08315) 273/C5
Divino, Brazil 135/E2
Divinópolis, Brazil 132/E8
Divinópolis, Brazil 120/E5
Divinópolis, Brazil 135/D2
Divis (mt.), N. Ireland 17/J2
Divisa Nova, Brazil 135/C2
Division (peak), Nev. 266/B1
Divo, Ivory Coast 106/C7
Divriği, Turkey 63/H3
Divriği, Turkey 59/C2
Dix, Ill. (62830) 222/E5
Dix (riv.), Ky. 237/M5
Dix, Nebr. (69133) 264/A3
Dixfield, Maine (04224) 243/C6
Dixfield○, Maine (04224) 243/C6
Dix Hills, N.Y. (11746) 276/O9
Dixie, Ala. (†36420) 195/E8
Dixie (co.), Fla. 212/C2
Dixie, Georgia (31629) 217/E9
Dixie, Idaho (83525) 220/C4
Dixie, La. (†71107) 238/C1
Dixie, Wash. (99329) 310/G4
Dixie, W. Va. (25059) 312/D6
Dixie Inn, La. (†71055) 238/D1
Dixmont, Maine (04932) 243/E6
Dixmont○, Maine (04932) 243/E6
Dixmoor, Ill. (†60469) 222/C6
Dixmude (Diksmuide), Belgium 27/B6
Dixon, Calif. (95620) 204/B9
Dixon, Ill. (61021) 222/D2
Dixon, Iowa (52745) 229/M5
Dixon, Ky. (42409) 237/F5
Dixon, Miss. (†39350) 256/F5
Dixon, Mo. (65459) 261/H6
Dixon, Mont. (59831) 262/B3
Dixon (co.), Nebr. 264/H2
Dixon, Nebr. (68732) 264/H2
Dixon, N. Mex. (87527) 274/D2
Dixon, N.C. (†28445) 281/O5
Dixon, Ohio (†46773) 284/A4
Dixon, S. Dak. (57530) 298/L7
Dixon, Wyo. (82323) 319/E4
Dixon Entrance (chan.) 146/E4
Dixon Entrance (chan.), Alaska 196/M2
Dixon Entrance (chan.), Br. Col. 184/A3
Dixons Mills, Ala. (36736) 195/C6
Dixon Springs, Ill. (†62911) 222/E6
Dixon Springs, Tenn. (37057) 237/J8
Dixonville, Ala. (†36426) 195/E8
Dixonville, Alberta 182/B1
Dixonville, Pa. (15734) 294/D4
Dixville (peak), N.H. 268/E2
Dixville, Québec 172/F4
Dixville Notch, N.H. (†03576) 268/E2
Dixville Notch (pass), N.H. 268/E2
Diyadin, Turkey 63/K3
Diyala (heads), Iraq 66/D4
Diyala (riv.), Iraq 66/D4
Diyarbakır (prov.), Turkey 63/H4
Diyarbakır, Turkey 54/F6
Diyarbakır, Turkey 63/H4
Diyarbakır, Turkey 59/C2
Dizful (Dezful), Iran 66/F4
Dja (riv.), Cameroon 115/B3
Dja (riv.), Congo 115/B3
Djado (plat.) 102/D2
Djado, Niger 102/D2
Djado, Niger 106/G4
Djado (plat.), Niger 106/G4
Djakarta (Jakarta) (cap.), Indonesia 85/H1
Djakovica, Yugoslavia 45/E4
Djakovo, Yugoslavia 45/D3
Djambala, Congo 115/B4
Djambi (Jambi), Indonesia 85/C6
Djanet, Algeria 106/F4
Djanet, Algeria 102/C2
Djelfa, Algeria 106/E2
Djema, Cent. Afr. Rep. 115/E2
Djemaa, Algeria 106/F2
Djenné, Mali 102/B3
Djenné, Mali 106/D6
Djerba (isl.), Tunisia 106/G2
Djerid, Shott el (salt lake), Tunisia 106/F2
Djibo, Upper Volta 106/D6
Djibouti 2/L5
Djibouti 102/G3
DJIBOUTI 111/H5
Djibouti (cap.), Djibouti 111/H5
Djibouti (cap.), Djibouti 102/G3
Djokjakarta (Yogyakarta), Indonesia 85/J2
Djolu, Zaire 115/D3
Djouf, El (des.), Mauritania 106/C4
Djougou, Benin 106/E7
Djoum, Cameroon 115/B3
Djugu, Zaire 115/F3
D'Lo, Miss. (39062) 256/E7
Dmitriya Lapteva (str.), U.S.S.R. 4/B2
Dmitriya Lapteva (str.), U.S.S.R. 48/O2
Dneprodzerzhinsk, U.S.S.R. 7/H4
Dneprodzerzhinsk, U.S.S.R. 52/D5
Dnepropetrovsk, U.S.S.R. 7/H4
Dnepropetrovsk, U.S.S.R. 48/D5
Dnepropetrovsk, U.S.S.R. 52/D5
Dnieper (riv.), U.S.S.R. 7/H3
Dnieper (riv.), U.S.S.R. 48/D5
Dnieper (riv.), U.S.S.R. 52/D5
Dniester (riv.), U.S.S.R. 7/G4
Dniester (riv.), U.S.S.R. 52/C5
Dniester (riv.), U.S.S.R. 48/C5
Dno, U.S.S.R. 52/D3
Doaghbeg, Ireland 17/F1
Doaktown, New Bruns. 170/D2
Doans, Ind. (†47424) 227/D7
Doba, Chad 111/C6
Doba, Chad 102/D4
Dobbie (mt.), North. Terr. 93/E7
Dobbin (bay), N.W. Terrs. 187/L2
Dobbins A.F.B., Georgia 217/J1
Dobbs Ferry, N.Y. (10522) 276/O6
Dobbyn, Queensland 95/A3
Dobele, U.S.S.R. 53/B2
Döbeln, E. Germany 22/E3
Doberai (pen.), Indonesia 85/J6
Dobiegniew, Poland 47/B2
Doblas, Argentina 143/D4
Dobo, Indonesia 85/J7
Doboj, Yugoslavia 45/C3
Doboy (sound), Georgia 217/K8
Dobřany, Czech. 41/B2
Dobre Miasto, Poland 47/E2
Dobrich (Tolbukhin), Bulgaria 45/H4
Dobříš, Czech. 41/C2
Dobrush, U.S.S.R. 52/D4
Dobruška, Czech. 41/D1
Dobryanka, U.S.S.R. 52/J3
Dobšiná, Czech. 41/F2
Dobson, N.C. (27017) 281/H2
Doce (riv.), Brazil 135/E2
Doce (riv.), Brazil 132/F7
Doce Leguas (cays), Cuba 158/F3
Docker River, North. Terr. 93/A8
Docking, England 13/H5
Dock Junction (Arco), Georgia (†31520) 217/J8
Doctor Arroyo, Mexico 150/K5
Doctor Cecilio Báez, Paraguay 144/D4
Doctor Juan L. Mallorquín, Paraguay 144/E4
Doctor Juan Manuel Frutos, Paraguay 144/E4
Doctor M. Irala, Paraguay 144/E4
Doctor Pedro P. Peña, Paraguay 144/A3
Doctors Inlet, Fla. (32030) 212/E1
Doctortown, Georgia (†31545) 217/J7
Doddridge, Ark. (71834) 202/Ci
Doddridge (co.), W. Va. 312/E4
Dodds, Alberta 182/D3
Doddsville, Miss. (38736) 256/C3
Dodecanese (isls.), Greece 45/H8
Dodge (co.), Georgia 217/F6
Dodge, Mass. (†01507) 249/G4
Dodge (co.), Minn. 255/F7
Dodge (co.), Nebr. 264/H3
Dodge, Nebr. (68633) 264/H3
Dodge, N. Dak. (58625) 282/F5
Dodge, Texas (77334) 303/J7
Dodge (co.), Wis. 317/J9
Dodge, Wis. (54625) 317/D7
Dodge Center, Minn. (55927) 255/F6
Dodge City, Kans. 188/F3
Dodge City, Kansas (67801) 232/B4
Dodgeville, Wis. (53533) 317/F10
Dodgingtown, Conn. (†06470) 210/B3
Dodman (pt.), England 13/C7
Dodoma (reg.), Tanzania 115/G5
Dodoma, Tanzania 102/F5
Dodoma, Tanzania 115/G5
Dodsland, Sask. 181/C4
Dodson, La. (71422) 238/E2
Dodson, Mont. (59524) 262/H2
Dodson, Texas (79230) 303/D3
Doe (lake), Ontario 177/E2
Doe (bay), Wash. 310/C2
Doe Bay, Wash. (†98279) 310/C2
Doe Hill, Va. (24433) 307/K4
Doering, Wis. (†54435) 317/G5
Doerun, Georgia (31744) 217/E8
Doe Run, Mo. (63637) 261/M7
Doesburg, Netherlands 27/J4
Doetinchem, Netherlands 27/J5
Dog (pond), Conn. 210/C1
Dog (isl.), Fla. 212/B2
Dog (lake), Manitoba 179/D3
Dog (isl.), Newf. 166/B2
Dog (lake), Ontario 177/G5
Dogai Coring (lake), China 77/C5
Doğanbey, Turkey 63/D4
Doğanhisar, Turkey 63/D3
Doğansehir, Turkey 63/G3
Dog Creek, Br. Col. 184/G4
Dog Ear (creek), S. Dak. 298/K6
Döger, Turkey 63/D3
Dogo (isl.), Japan 81/F5
Dogondoutchi, Niger 106/E6
Dogondoutchi, Niger 102/C3
Dogpatch, Ark. (72648) 202/D1
Dog Pound, Alberta 182/C4
Dogskin (lake), Manitoba 179/G3
Doğubeyazıt, Turkey 63/K3
Dogwood (pt.), St. Chris.-Nevis 161/D11
Doha (cap.), Qatar 54/G7
Doha (cap.), Qatar 59/F4
Dohad, India 68/C4
Doheny, Québec 172/E2
Dohuk (gov.), Iraq 66/C2
Dohuk, Iraq 66/C2
Doi Inthanon (mt.), Thailand 72/C3
Doilungdêqên, China 77/C6
Doi Pha Hom Pok (mt.), Thailand 72/C2
Doi Pia Fai (mt.), Thailand 72/D4
Doische, Belgium 27/F8
Dois Córregos, Brazil 135/B3
Dois Irmãos, Serra (range), Brazil 132/F5
Dokkum, Netherlands 27/H2
Doksy, Czech. 41/C1
Dokterstuin, Neth. Ant. 161/F8
Dola, Ohio (45835) 284/C4
Dola, W. Va. (†26386) 312/F4
Dolan, Ind. (†47401) 227/E6
Doland, S. Dak. (57436) 298/N4
Dolan Springs, Ariz. (86441) 198/A3
Dolavon, Argentina 143/C5
Dolbeau, Québec 174/C3
Dolbeau, Québec 172/E1
Doldenhorn (mt.), Switzerland 39/E4
Dole, France 28/F4
Dolega, Panama 154/F6
Dolent (mt.), Switzerland 39/C5
Doles, Georgia (†31791) 217/E7
Dolgellau, Wales 13/D5
Dolgellau, Wales 10/E4
Dolgeville, N.Y. (13329) 276/L4
Dolgiy (isl.), U.S.S.R. 52/J1
Dolinsk, U.S.S.R. 48/P5
Dollar, Scotland 10/B1
Dollar, Scotland 15/E4
Dollar Bay, Mich. (49922) 250/G1
Dollard (bay), Netherlands 27/L2
Dollard, Sask. 181/C6
Dollard-des-Ormeaux, Québec 172/H4
Dollart (est.), W. Germany 22/B2
Dollarville, Mich. (†49868) 250/D2
Dolliver, Iowa (50531) 229/D2
Dolný Kubín, Czech. 41/E2
Dolo, Ethiopia 111/H7
Dolomite, Ala. (35061) 195/D4
Dolomite Alps (range), Italy 34/C1
Dolores, Argentina 143/E4
Dolores, Argentina 120/D6
Dolores (co.), Colo. 208/C7
Dolores, Colo. (81323) 208/C8
Dolores (riv.), Colo. 208/B5
Dolores, Guatemala 154/C2
Dolores, Philippines 82/E4
Dolores, Spain 33/F3
Dolores, Uruguay 145/A4
Dolores (riv.), Utah 304/E5
Dolores, Venezuela 124/D3
Dolores Hidalgo de la Independencia Nacional, Mexico 150/J6
Dolphin and Union (str.), N.W. Terrs. 187/G3
Dölsach, Austria 41/B3
Dolton, Ill. (60419) 222/C6
Dolton, S. Dak. (57023) 298/P7
Dom (mt.), Switzerland 39/E4
Domain, Manitoba 179/E5
Domanic, Turkey 63/C3
Domar (dry riv.), Chad 111/C4
Domat-Ems, Switzerland 39/H3
Domažlice, Czech. 41/B2
Dombås, Norway 18/F5
Dombe Grande, Angola 115/B6
Dombóvár, Hungary 41/E3
Dombrád, Hungary 41/F2
Dombresson, Switzerland 39/C2
Domburg, Netherlands 27/C5
Domburg, Suriname 131/D3
Dome, Ariz. (†85364) 198/A6
Dome Creek, Br. Col. 184/G3
Domeiko, Chile 138/A7
Domeyko, Cordillera (mts.), Chile 138/B4
Domínguez, Argentina 143/G6
Dominica 2/F5
Dominica 146/M8
DOMINICA 156/G4
DOMINICA 161/E7
Dominica (passage), Dominica 161/E5
Dominican Republic 2/F4
Dominican Republic 146/L8
DOMINICAN REPUBLIC 156/D3
DOMINICAN REPUBLIC 158
Dominion (lake), Newf. 166/B3
Dominion (cape), N.W. Terrs. 187/L3
Dominion, Nova Scotia 168/J2
Dominion City, Manitoba 179/E5
Domino, Newf. 166/C3
Dömitz, E. Germany 22/D2
Domjor, India 68/F1
Domleschg (valley), Switzerland 39/E2
Dommel (riv.), Netherlands 27/H6
Domo, Ethiopia 111/J6
Domodossola, Italy 34/A1
Dom Pedrito, Brazil 132/C10
Dompu, Indonesia 85/F7
Domremy, Sask. 181/F3
Domrémy-la-Pucelle, France 28/F3
Dom Silvério, Brazil 135/E2
Dömsöd, Hungary 41/E3
Domuyo (vol.), Argentina 143/B4
Don (riv.), England 10/F4
Don (riv.), England 13/F4
Don (riv.), Ontario 177/J4
Don (riv.), Scotland 15/F3
Don (riv.), Scotland 10/E2
Don (riv.), U.S.S.R. 7/J4
Don (riv.), U.S.S.R. 48/E5
Don (riv.), U.S.S.R. 52/F5
Dona Ana (Mutarara), Mozambique 118/F3
Dona Ana (co.), N. Mex. 274/C6
Dona Ana, N. Mex. (88032) 274/C6
Donabate, Ireland 17/J5
Donaghadee, N. Ireland 17/K2
Donahue, Iowa (52746) 229/M5
Donald, Br. Col. 184/J4
Donald, Oreg. (97020) 291/A3
Donald, Victoria 97/B5
Donald, Wash. (†98951) 310/E4
Donald, Wis. (†54433) 317/E5
Donalda, Alberta 182/D3
Donalds, S.C. (29638) 296/C3
Donaldson, Ark. (71941) 202/E5
Donaldson, Ind. (46513) 227/E2
Donaldson, Minn. (56720) 255/B2
Donaldson A.F.B., S.C. 296/C2
Donaldsonville, La. (70346) 238/K3
Donalsonville, Georgia (31745) 217/C8
Donansburg, Ky. (†42743) 237/K6
Donath, Switzerland 39/H3
Donatville, Alberta 182/D2
Donau (Danube) (riv.), Austria 41/D2
Donau (Danube) (riv.), W. Germany 22/C4
Donaueschingen, W. Germany 22/C5
Donauwörth, W. Germany 22/D4
Donavon, Sask. 181/D4
Donbar, Queensland 95/B3
Don Benito, Spain 33/C3
Doncaster, England 13/F4
Doncaster, England 10/F4
Doncaster, Md. (†20646) 245/K7
Doncaster and Templestowe, Victoria 88/L7
Doncaster and Templestowe, Victoria 97/J5
Dondo, Angola 115/B5
Dondo, Mozambique 118/F3
Dondra (head), Sri Lanka 68/E7
Dondra Head (cape), Sri Lanka 54/K9
Donegal (co.), Ireland 17/K2
Donegal, Ireland 10/B3
Donegal, Ireland 17/F2
Donegal (bay), Ireland 17/D3
Donegal (bay), Ireland 10/B3
Donegal (harb.), Ireland 17/E2
Donegal (pt.), Ireland 17/B6
Donegal, Pa. (15628) 294/D5
Donel, Honduras 154/E3
Doneraile, Ireland 17/D7
Doneraile, S.C. (†29532) 296/H3
Donets (riv.), U.S.S.R. 7/H4
Donets (riv.), U.S.S.R. 48/D5
Donets (riv.), U.S.S.R. 52/E5
Donetsk, U.S.S.R. 7/H4
Donetsk, U.S.S.R. 48/D5
Donetsk, U.S.S.R. 52/E5
Donga (riv.), Cameroon 115/B2
Donga, Nigeria 106/G7
Donga (riv.), Nigeria 106/G7
Dongara, W. Australia 92/A5
Dongchuan, China 77/F6
Dongen, Netherlands 27/F5
Dongfang, China 77/G8
Dongfanghong, China 77/M2
Donggala, Indonesia 85/F6
Dônghén, Laos 72/E3
Dong Hoi, Vietnam 72/E3
Dongio, Switzerland 39/H4
Dongning, China 77/M3
Dongo, Zaire 115/C3
Dongola, Ill. (62926) 222/D6
Dongola, Sudan 102/E3
Dongola, Sudan 59/B6
Dongola, Sudan 111/F4
Dongou, Congo 115/C3
Dong Rak (mts.), Thailand 72/D4
Dongsha (isl.), China 77/J7
Dongsheng, China 77/H4
Dongtai, China 77/K5
Dongting (lake), China 54/N7
Dongting Hu (riv.), China 77/H6
Dong Ujimqin, China 77/J2
Dongwe (riv.), Zambia 115/D6
Donie, Texas (75838) 303/H6
Doñihue, Chile 138/G5
Doniphan (co.), Kansas 232/G2
Doniphan, Mo. (63935) 261/L9
Doniphan, Nebr. (68832) 264/F4
Donji Vakuf, Yugoslavia 45/C3
Donkin, Nova Scotia 168/J2
Donley (co.), Texas 303/D2
Dønna (isl.), Norway 18/H3
Donna, Texas (78537) 303/F11
Donnacona, Québec 172/F3
Donnan, Iowa (52139) 229/K3
Donnellson, Ill. (62019) 222/D4
Donnellson, Iowa (52625) 229/K7
Donnelly, Alberta 182/B2
Donnelly, Idaho (83615) 220/B5
Donnelly, Minn. (56235) 255/B5
Donner (pass), Calif. 204/E4
Donner, La. (70352) 238/J7
Donner and Blitzen (riv.), Oreg. 291/J4
Donnybrook, N. Dak. (58734) 282/G2
Donnybrook, Queensland 95/D5
Donnybrook, W. Australia 92/A2
Donora, Pa. (15033) 294/C5
Donovan, Georgia (†31096) 217/G5
Donovan, Ill. (60931) 222/F3
Donsol, Philippines 82/D4
Donwell, Sask. 181/J4
Donzère, France 28/F5
Dooagh-Keel, Ireland 17/A4
Doole, Texas (76836) 303/E6
Dooling, Georgia (†31063) 217/E6
Doolittle (pond), Conn. 210/C1
Doolittle, Mo. (†65550) 261/J7
Doolittle Mills, Ind. (†47118) 227/D8
Dooly (co.), Georgia 217/E6
Doon, Iowa (51235) 229/A2
Doon, Ireland 17/E6
Doon, Loch (lake), Scotland 15/D5
Doon (riv.), Scotland 15/D5
Doonerak (mt.), Alaska 196/H1
Doonside, Sask. 181/K6
Door (pt.), La. 238/M6
Door (co.), Wis. 317/M6
Door (pen.), Wis. 317/M6
Doorn, Netherlands 27/G4
Doornik (Tournai), Belgium 27/C7
Doqa, Saudi Arabia 59/D6
Dor, Israel 65/B2
Dora, Ala. (35062) 195/D3
Dora, Mo. (65637) 261/H9
Dora, N. Mex. (88115) 274/F5
Dora, Oreg. (†97458) 291/D4
Dora (lake), W. Australia 88/C4
Dora (lake), W. Australia 92/C3
Dora Baltea (riv.), Italy 34/A2
Dorado, P. Rico 161/D1
Dora Lake, Minn. (†56661) 255/D3
Doran, Minn. (56530) 255/B4
Dora Riparia (riv.), Italy 34/A2
Doraville, Georgia (30340) 217/K1
D'Orbigny, Bolivia 136/D7
Dorbiljin (Emin), China 77/B2
Dorbod, China 77/K2
Dorcas, W. Va. (26835) 312/H5
Dorchester, England 10/E5
Dorchester, England 13/E7
Dorchester, Georgia (†31317) 217/K7
Dorchester, Ill. (62020) 222/D4
Dorchester, Iowa (52140) 229/L2
Dorchester (co.), Md. 245/O7
Dorchester, Mass. (†02122) 249/D7
Dorchester, Nebr. (68343) 264/G4
Dorchester, New Bruns. 170/F3
Dorchester○, N.H. (†03266) 268/D4
Dorchester, N.J. (08316) 273/D5
Dorchester (cape), N.W. Terrs. 187/L3
Dorchester, Ontario 177/C5
Dorchester (co.), Québec 172/C3
Dorchester (co.), S.C. 296/G5
Dorchester, S.C. (29437) 296/G5
Dorchester, Wis. (54425) 317/F5
Dorchester Crossing, New Bruns. 170/F2
Dordogne (dept.), France 28/D5
Dordogne (riv.), France 7/E4
Dordogne (riv.), France 28/D5
Dordrecht, Netherlands 27/F5
Doré (lake), Ontario 177/G2
Doré (lake), Sask. 181/L3
Dore Alps (mts.), France 28/E5
Doré Lake, Sask. 181/L4
Dorena, Mo. (†63845) 261/O9
Dorena, Oreg. (97434) 291/E4
Dorena (lake), Oreg. 291/E4
Dorenlee, Alberta 182/D3
Dores, Scotland 15/D3
Dores do Indaiá, Brazil 132/E7
Dorgali, Italy 34/B4
Dörgön Nuur (lake), Mongolia 77/D2
Dori, Mali 102/B3
Dori, Upper Volta 106/D6
Doring (riv.), S. Africa 118/B6
Dorintosh, Sask. 181/L4
Dorion, Ontario 177/H5
Dorion, Québec 172/C4
Dorking, England 13/G8
Dorking, England 10/F5
Dormont, Pa. (15216) 294/B7
Dornach, Switzerland 39/E2
Dornbirn, Austria 41/A3
Dornie, Scotland 15/C3
Dornoch, Scotland 10/D2
Dornoch, Scotland 15/D3
Dornoch (firth), Scotland 15/E3
Dornoch (firth), Scotland 10/E2
Dornod, Mongolia 77/H2
Dornogovĭ, Mongolia 77/G3
Dorog, Hungary 41/E3
Dorohoi, Romania 45/H2
Dorotea, Sweden 18/K4
Dorothy, Alberta 182/D4
Dorothy, Minn. (†56750) 255/B3
Dorothy, N.J. (08317) 273/D5
Dorothy, W. Va. (25060) 312/D7
Dorr (lake), Fla. 212/E2
Dorr, Mich. (49323) 250/D6
Dorrance, Kansas (67634) 232/D3
Dorre (isl.), W. Australia 88/A5
Dorre (isl.), W. Australia 92/A4
Dorreen, Br. Col. 184/C3
Dorrigo, N.S. Wales 97/G2
Dorris, Calif. (96023) 204/D2
Dorset (co.), England 13/E7
Dorset, Minn. (†56470) 255/D4
Dorset, Ohio (44032) 284/J2
Dorset○, Vt. (05251) 268/A5
Dorset (peak), Vt. 268/A5
Dorset Heights (hills), England 13/E7
Dorsey, Miss. (†38801) 256/H2
Dorsten, W. Germany 22/B3
Dortches, N.C. (†27801) 281/O2
Dortmund, W. Germany 7/E3
Dortmund, W. Germany 22/B3
Dorton, Ky. (41520) 237/R6
Dörtyol, Turkey 63/F4
Doruma, Zaire 115/E3
Dorval, Québec 172/H4
Dory Point, N.W. Terrs. 187/G3
Dos Bahías (cape), Argentina 143/D5
Dos Cabezas, Ariz. (†85643) 198/F6
Dos Caminos, Cuba 158/J4
Dos de Mayo, Peru 128/E6
Dos Hermanas, Spain 33/D4
Dos Palos, Calif. (93620) 204/E6
Dosquet, Québec 172/F3
Dos Reyes (pt.), Chile 138/A5
Dos Rios, Cuba 158/J4
Dosso, Niger 106/E6
Dossor, U.S.S.R. 48/F5
Dossville, Miss. (†39051) 256/F5
Doswell, Va. (23047) 307/N5
Dothan, Ala. 188/J4
Dothan, Ala. (*36303) 195/H8
Doti, Nepal 68/E3
Dot Klish (canyon), Ariz. 198/E2
Dot Lake, Alaska (99737) 196/K2
Dott, W. Va. (24721) 312/D8
Döttingen, Switzerland 39/F1
Doty, Wash. (98539) 310/B4
Douai, France 28/E2
Douala, Cameroon 115/B3
Douala, Cameroon 102/D4
Douarnenez, France 28/A3
Double Branches, Georgia (†30817) 217/H3
Double Mer (lake), Newf. 166/C3
Double Mountain Fork, Brazos (riv.), Texas 303/C4
Double Oak, Texas (†76226) 303/F1
Double Springs, Ala. (35553) 195/D2
Doubletop (peak), Wyo. 319/B2
Doubs (dept.), France 28/G4
Doubs (riv.), France 28/G4
Doubs, Md. (†21710) 245/J3
Doubs (riv.), Switzerland 39/C2
Doubtful (sound), N. Zealand 100/A6
Doubtless (bay), N. Zealand 100/D1
Doucette, Texas (79542) 303/K7
Douds, Iowa (52551) 229/J7
Doué-la-Fontaine, France 28/C4
Douentza, Mali 106/D6
Douentza, Mali 102/B3
Dougherty (co.), Georgia 217/D7
Dougherty, Iowa (50433) 229/G3
Dougherty, Okla. (73032) 288/M6
Dougherty, Texas (79231) 303/C4
Douglas, Ala. (35964) 195/F2
Douglas (mt.), Alaska 196/H3
Douglas, Ariz. 146/G6
Douglas, Ariz. 188/E4
Douglas, Ariz. (85607) 198/F7
Douglas (chan.), Br. Col. 184/C3
Douglas (co.), Colo. 208/K4
Douglas (creek), Colo. 208/B3
Douglas (bay), Dominica 161/E5
Douglas (co.), Georgia 217/C3
Douglas, Georgia (31533) 217/G7
Douglas (co.), Ill. 222/E4
Douglas, Ireland 17/D8
Douglas (cap.), I. of Man 13/C3
Douglas (cap.), I. of Man 10/D3
Douglas (co.), Kansas 232/G3
Douglas, Manitoba 179/C5
Douglas○, Mass. (†01516) 249/H4
Douglas, Mich. (49406) 250/C6
Douglas (co.), Minn. 255/C5
Douglas, Minn. (†55960) 255/F6
Douglas (co.), Mo. 261/G9
Douglas (mt.), Mont. 262/F5
Douglas (co.), Nebr. 264/H3
Douglas, Nebr. (68344) 264/H4
Douglas (co.), Nev. 266/B4
Douglas, N. Dak. (58735) 282/G4
Douglas, North. Terr. 93/B2
Douglas, Okla. (73733) 288/L2
Douglas, Ontario 177/H2
Douglas (pt.), Ontario 177/C3
Douglas (co.), Oreg. 291/D4
Douglas, Scotland 15/E5
Douglas, S. Africa 118/C5
Douglas (co.), S. Dak. 298/N7
Douglas (lake), Tenn. 237/P9
Douglas (co.), Wash. 310/F3
Douglas, Wash. (†98858) 310/F3
Douglas (co.), Wis. 317/C3
Douglas, Wyo. (82633) 319/G3
Douglas Harbour, New Bruns. 170/D3
Douglas Lake, Br. Col. 184/H5
Douglas Prov. Park, Sask. 181/E4
Douglass, Kansas (67039) 232/F4
Douglass, Texas (75943) 303/K6
Douglass Hills, Ky. (†40243) 237/L2
Douglassville, Pa. (19518) 294/L5
Douglastown, New Bruns. 170/E1
Douglastown, Québec 172/D1
Douglasville, Georgia (*30133) 217/C3
Doullens, France 28/E2
Doulus (head), Ireland 17/A8
Doumé, Cameroon 115/B3
Dounby, Scotland 15/E1
Doune, Scotland 15/D4
Dour, Belgium 27/D8
Dourados, Brazil 120/D5
Dourados, Brazil 132/C8
Douro (riv.), Portugal 7/D4
Douro (riv.), Portugal 33/B2
Douro (riv.), Spain 33/C2
Dousman, Wis. (53118) 317/J1
Douthat, Okla. (74341) 288/S1
Douville, Québec 172/D4
Dove (riv.), England 13/J2
Dove (creek), Utah 304/A2
Dove Creek, Colo. (81324) 208/A7
Dover, Ark. (72837) 202/D3
Dover (cap.), Del. 146/L6
Dover (cap.), Del. 188/L3
Dover (cap.), Del. (19901) 245/R4
Dover, England 7/E3
Dover, England 10/G5
Dover, England 13/J6
Dover (str.), England 13/J7
Dover (str.), England 10/G5
Dover, Fla. (33527) 212/D4
Dover, Georgia (30424) 217/J5
Dover, Idaho (83825) 220/B1
Dover, Ill. (61323) 222/D2
Dover, Ind. (†46052) 227/H6
Dover, Kansas (66420) 232/G3
Dover, Ky. (41034) 237/O3
Dover, Mass. (02030) 249/B7
Dover○, Mass. (02030) 249/B7
Dover, Minn. (55929) 255/F7
Dover, Mo. (64022) 261/E4
Dover, N.H. (03820) 268/F5
Dover, N.J. (07801) 273/D2
Dover, N.C. (28526) 281/P4
Dover, Ohio (44622) 284/G4
Dover (lake), Ohio 284/H4
Dover, Okla. (73734) 288/L3
Dover, Pa. (17315) 294/J6
Dover, Tasmania 99/C5
Dover, Tenn. (37058) 237/F8
Dover (pt.), W. Australia 88/D6
Dover (pt.), W. Australia 92/D6
Dover A.F.B., Del. 245/S4
Doverel, Georgia (†31742) 217/D7
Dover-Foxcroft, Maine (04426) 243/E5
Dover-Foxcroft○, Maine (04426) 243/E5
Dover Hill, Ind. (†47581) 227/D7
Dover Plains, N.Y. (12522) 276/O7
Dover South Mills, Maine (†04426) 243/E5
Dovesville, S.C. (29540) 296/H3
Dovey (riv.), Wales 10/D4
Dovey (riv.), Wales 13/D5
Dovns Klint (cliff), Denmark 21/D8
Dovray, Minn. (56125) 255/C6

362 Dovre

Dovre, Norway 18/F6
Dovrefjell (hills), Norway 18/F5
Dow (Xau) (lake), Botswana 118/C4
Dow, Ill. (62022) 222/C4
Dow, Okla. (†74547) 288/P5
Dowa, Malawi 115/F6
Dowagiac, Mich. (49047) 250/D6
Dow City, Iowa (51528) 229/B5
Dowell, Ill. (62927) 222/D6
Dowelltown, Tenn. (37059) 237/K8
Dowlatabad, Afghanistan 59/H3
Dowlatabad, Afghanistan 68/A2
Dowlatabad, Kerman, Iran 66/K6
Dowlatabad, Khorasan, Iran 66/M2
Dowlat Yar, Afghanistan 59/J3
Dowlat Yar, Afghanistan 68/B2
Dowling, Alberta 182/E4
Dowling (lake), Alberta 182/D4
Dowling, Mich. (49050) 250/D6
Dowling Park, Fla. (32060) 212/C1
Down (dist.), N. Ireland 17/K3
Downe, Sask. 181/C4
Downer, Minn. (†56514) 255/B4
Downers Grove, Ill. (60515) 222/A6
Downey, Calif. (*90240) 204/C11
Downey, Idaho (83234) 220/F7
Downey, Iowa (†52358) 229/L5
Downfall (creek), Queensland 95/D2
Downham Market, England 13/H5
Downham Market, England 10/G4
Downieville, Calif. (95936) 204/E4
Downing, Mo. (63536) 261/H2
Downing, Wis. (54734) 317/B5
Downings, Va. (†22460) 307/P5
Downingtown, Pa. (19335) 294/L5
Downpatrick (head), Ireland 17/C3
Downpatrick, N. Ireland 10/C3
Downpatrick, N. Ireland 17/K3
Downs, Ill. (61736) 222/E3
Downs, Kansas (67437) 232/D2
Downsville, La. (71234) 238/F1
Downsville, Md. (†21795) 245/G2
Downsville, N.Y. (13755) 276/L6
Downsville, Wis. (54735) 317/C6
Downton, England 13/F6
Dows, Iowa (50071) 229/F3
Dowshi, Afghanistan 59/J2
Dowshi, Afghanistan 68/B1
Doyle, Calif. (96109) 204/E3
Doyle, Georgia (†31803) 217/D6
Doyle, Tenn. (38559) 237/K9
Doylestown, Ohio (44230) 284/G4
Doylestown, Pa. (18901) 294/M5
Doylestown, Wis. (53928) 317/H9
Doyleville, Colo. (†81239) 208/F6
Doyline, La. (71023) 238/D1
Doyon, N. Dak. (58328) 282/O3
Dozen (isls.), Japan 81/F5
Dozier, Ala. (36028) 195/F7
Dozier, Texas (†79079) 303/D2
Dozois (res.), Québec 174/B3
Dra, Wadi (dry riv.), Morocco 106/C3
Drachten, Netherlands 27/J2
Dracut○, Mass. (01826) 249/J2
Drăgăneşti Olt, Romania 45/G3
Drăgăşani, Romania 45/F3
Dragonera (isl.), Spain 33/H3
Dragons Mouth (str.), Trin. & Tob. 156/F5
Dragons Mouth (str.), Trin. & Tob. 161/A10
Dragons Mouth (str.), Venezuela 124/H2
Dragoon, Ariz. (85609) 198/F6
Dragoon (mts.), Ariz. 198/F7
Draguignan, France 28/G6
Drain, Oreg. (97435) 291/D4
Drake (passage) 2/F8
Drake (passage) 5/C15
Drake (passage), Chile 138/E11
Drake, Colo. (80515) 208/J2
Drake, Mo. (†65066) 261/K6
Drake, N. Dak. (58736) 282/K4
Drake, Sask. 181/G4
Drakensberg (range), Lesotho 118/D6
Drakensberg (range), S. Africa 118/D6
Drakensberg (range), Swaziland 118/D6
Drakes (creek), Ky. 237/J7
Drakesboro, Ky. (42337) 237/H6
Drakes Branch, Va. (23937) 307/L7
Drakesville, Iowa (52552) 229/J7
Draketown, Georgia (†30179) 217/B3
Dráma, Greece 45/F5
Drammen, Norway 7/E3
Drammen, Norway 18/C4
Drance (riv.), Switzerland 39/D4
Drancy, France 28/B1
Drang, Ia (riv.), Cambodia 72/E4
Draper, S. Dak. (57531) 298/J6
Draper, Utah (84020) 304/C3
Draper, Va. (24324) 307/G7
Draper, Wis. (†54852) 317/E4
Draperstown, N. Ireland 17/H2
Draperstown, N. Ireland 10/C3
Drasco, Ark. (72530) 202/G2
Drau (riv.), Austria 41/C3
Drava (riv.) 7/F4
Dráva (riv.), Hungary 41/D3
Drava (riv.), Yugoslavia 45/C3
Dravosburg, Pa. (15034) 294/C7
Drawsko Pomorskie, Poland 47/B2
Drax Hall, Barbados 161/B8
Drayden, Md. (20630) 245/N8
Drayton, N. Dak. (58225) 282/R2
Drayton, Ontario 177/D4
Drayton Plains, Mich. (48020) 250/F6
Drayton Valley, Alberta 182/C3
Drenthe (prov.), Netherlands 27/K3
Dresbach, Minn. (55930) 255/G7
Dresden, E. Germany 7/F3
Dresden (dist.), E. Germany 22/E3
Dresden, E. Germany 22/E3
Dresden, Kansas (67635) 232/B2
Dresden○, Maine (04342) 243/D7
Dresden, Mo. (†65301) 261/F5
Dresden, N.Y. (14441) 276/F5
Dresden, N. Dak. (†58249) 282/O2
Dresden, Ohio (43821) 284/G5
Dresden, Ontario 177/B5
Dresden, Tenn. (38225) 237/D8
Dresden Station, N.Y. (†12887) 276/O3
Dresser, Wis. (54009) 317/A5
Dreux, France 28/D3
Drew (co.), Ark. 202/G6
Drew, Miss. (38737) 256/C3
Drew, Oreg. (†97484) 291/E5
Drewry, Ala. (†36460) 195/D8
Drewryville, Va. (23844) 307/O7
Drews (res.), Oreg. 291/G5
Drewsey, Oreg. (97904) 291/J4
Drewsville, N.H. (03604) 268/C5
Drexel, Mo. (64742) 261/C6
Drexel, N.C. (28619) 281/F3
Drexel Hill, Pa. (19026) 294/M6
Dreyfus, Ky. (40426) 237/N5
Drezdenko, Poland 47/B2
Driebergen, Netherlands 27/G4
Driffield, England 13/G3
Driffield, England 10/F4
Drift (creek), Oreg. 291/B3
Drifton, Pa. (18221) 294/L3
Driftwood, Okla. (†73722) 288/K1
Driftwood, Pa. (15832) 294/F3
Driggs, Ark. (†72943) 202/C3
Driggs, Idaho (83422) 220/G6
Drill, Va. (†24260) 307/E6
Drimoleague, Ireland 17/C8
Drin (riv.), Albania 45/E4
Drina (riv.), Yugoslavia 45/D3
Drinkwater, Sask. 181/F5
Dripping Springs, Texas (78620) 303/F7
Driscoll, N. Dak. (58532) 282/K6
Driscoll, Texas (78351) 303/G10
Drishane, Ireland 17/C7
Driskill (mt.), La. 238/E2
Drøbak, Norway 18/D4
Drobeta-Turnu Severin, Romania 45/F3
Drogenbos, Belgium 27/B10
Drogheda, Ireland 17/J4
Drogheda, Ireland 10/C4
Drogobych, U.S.S.R. 52/B5
Drogobych, U.S.S.R. 48/C5
Droichead Nua, Ireland 10/C4
Droichead Nua, Ireland 17/H5
Droitwich, England 13/E5
Dromahair, Ireland 17/E3
Drome (dept.), France 28/F5
Drome (riv.), France 28/F5
Dromore, Bainbridge, N. Ireland 17/J3
Dromore, Omagh, N. Ireland 17/G3
Dromore West, Ireland 17/D3
Dronfield, England 13/J2
Drongan, Scotland 15/D5
Dronne (riv.), France 28/D5
Dronninglund, Denmark 21/D3
Dronten (prov.), Netherlands 27/H4
Dronten, Netherlands 27/H3
Dropmore, Manitoba 179/A3
Drouin, Victoria 97/C6
Druid, Sask. 181/C4
Druif, Neth. Ant. 161/D10
Drum (hills), Ireland 17/F7
Drum (bay), La. 238/M7
Drum (inlet), N.C. 281/S5
Drumaness, N. Ireland 17/K3
Drumbeg, Scotland 15/C2
Drumbo, Ontario 177/D4
Drumcar, Ireland 17/J4
Drumconrath, Ireland 17/H4
Drumheller, Alberta 182/D4
Drumheller, Alta. 162/E5
Drumhill, N.C. (†27937) 281/R1
Drumkeerin, Ireland 17/E3
Drumlish, Ireland 17/F4
Drummond, Idaho (†83420) 220/G5
Drummond (isl.), Mich. 250/F2
Drummond, Mont. (59832) 262/D4
Drummond, New Bruns. 170/C1
Drummond (mt.), North. Terr. 93/E5
Drummond, Okla. (73735) 288/L2
Drummond (co.), Québec 172/E4
Drummond (range), Queensland 88/H4
Drummond (range), Queensland 95/C5
Drummond (lake), Va. 307/P7
Drummond, Wis. (54832) 317/D3
Drummond Island, Mich. (49726) 250/F3
Drummonds, Tenn. (38023) 237/A10
Drummondville, Québec 172/E4
Drummondville-Nord, Québec 172/E4
Drummondville-Sud, Québec 172/E4
Drummore, Scotland 15/D6
Drummoyne, N. S. Wales 88/K4
Drummoyne, N.S. Wales 97/J3
Drumnadrochit, Scotland 15/D3
Drumquin, N. Ireland 17/F2
Drumright, Okla. (74030) 288/N3
Drums, Pa. (18222) 294/K3
Drumshanbo, Ireland 17/E3
Drury, Mo. (65638) 261/H9
Druskininkai, U.S.S.R. 53/C3
Druten, Netherlands 27/H5
Druz, Jebel ed (mts.), Syria 63/G6
Druzhba, U.S.S.R. 48/J5
Druzhina, U.S.S.R. 48/P3
Drvar, Yugoslavia 45/C3
Dry (bay), Alaska 196/L3
Dry (creek), Ky. 237/R3
Dry (lake), N. Dak. 282/M3
Dry (riv.), North. Terr. 88/E3
Dry (riv.), North. Terr. 93/C3
Dry (creek), S. Dak. 298/G4
Dry (lake), S. Dak. 298/P3
Dry (creek), Wyo. 319/C2
Dryad, Wash. (†98532) 310/B4
Dryanovo, Bulgaria 45/G4
Dry Branch, Georgia (31020) 217/F5
Dry Cimarron (riv.), N. Mex. 274/F2
Dry Coal (creek), Utah 304/A6
Dry Cottonwood (creek), Wyo. 319/D1
Dry Creek, La. (70637) 238/D5
Dry Creek, W. Va. (25062) 312/D7
Dryden, Ark. (†72401) 202/J2
Dryden, Maine (04225) 243/C6
Dryden, Mich. (48428) 250/F6
Dryden, N.Y. (13053) 276/H6
Dryden, Ontario 177/G4
Dryden, Ontario 175/B3
Dryden, Texas (78851) 303/C7
Dryden, Va. (24243) 307/B7
Dryden, Wash. (98821) 310/E3
Dry Falls (dam), Wash. 310/F3
Dry Fork, Va. (24549) 307/K7
Dryfork, W. Va. (26263) 312/H5
Dry Fork (riv.), W. Va. 312/G5
Dry Fork (riv.), W. Va. 312/C8
Dry Fork, Cheyenne (riv.), Wyo. 319/G2
Dry Fork, Powder (riv.), Wyo. 319/F2
Dry Lake, Nev. (†89040) 266/G6
Drymen, Scotland 15/B1
Dry Mills, Maine (†04039) 243/C8
Dry Prong, La. (71423) 238/E3
Dry Ridge, Ky. (41035) 237/M3
Dry Run, Pa. (17220) 294/G5
Drysdale (riv.), W. Australia 88/D3
Drysdale (riv.), W. Australia 92/D1
Dry Tortugas (keys), Fla. 212/D7
Drytown, Calif. (95699) 204/C8
Dry Wood (lake), S. Dak. 298/P2
Dschang, Cameroon 115/A2
Duaca, Venezuela 124/D2
Duaringa, Queensland 95/D4
Duart, Ontario 177/C5
Duarte, Calif. (91010) 204/D10
Duarte (prov.), Dom. Rep. 158/E5
Duarte (peak), Dom. Rep. 158/D5
Dubach, La. (71235) 238/E1
Dubai, U.A.E. 59/F4
Dubawnt (lake), N.W.T. 162/F3
Dubawnt (lake), N.W.T. 146/H3
Dubawnt (lake), N.W. Terrs. 187/H3
Dubawnt (riv.), N.W.T. 162/F3
Dubawnt (riv.), N.W. Terrs. 187/H3
Du Bay (lake), Wis. 317/G6
Dubberly, La. (71024) 238/D1
Dubbo, N. S. Wales 88/H6
Dubbo, N.S. Wales 97/E3
Dubbs, Miss. (†38626) 256/D1
Dübendorf, Switzerland 39/G2
Dublin, Calif. (94566) 204/K2
Dublin, Georgia (31021) 217/G5
Dublin, Ind. (47335) 227/G5
Dublin (co.), Ireland 17/J5
Dublin (cap.), Ireland 7/D3
Dublin (cap.), Ireland 17/K5
Dublin (cap.), Ireland 10/C4
Dublin (bay), Ireland 10/C4
Dublin (bay), Ireland 17/J5
Dublin, Ky. (†42039) 237/D7
Dublin, Md. (†21154) 245/N2
Dublin, Mich. (†49689) 250/D4
Dublin, Miss. (38739) 256/C2
Dublin○, N.H. (03444) 268/C6
Dublin, N.C. (28332) 281/M5
Dublin, Ohio (43017) 284/D5
Dublin, Ontario 177/C4
Dublin, Pa. (18917) 294/M5
Dublin, Texas (76446) 303/F5
Dublin, Va. (24084) 307/G6
Dubna, U.S.S.R. 52/E4
Dubna, U.S.S.R. 52/E3
Dubnica nad Váhom, Czech. 41/E2
Dubno, U.S.S.R. 52/C4
Dubois, Idaho (83423) 220/F5
Dubois, Ill. (62831) 222/D5
Dubois (co.), Ind. 227/D8
Dubois, Ind. (47525) 227/D8
Du Bois, Nebr. (68345) 264/H4
DuBois, Pa. (15801) 294/E3
Dubois, Wyo. (82513) 319/C2
Duboistown, Pa. (†17701) 294/H3
Dubréka, Guinea 106/B7
Dubreuilville, Ontario 177/J5
Dubrovnik, Yugoslavia 45/C4
Dubreuilville, Ontario 175/D3
Dubuc, Sask. 181/J5
Dubuque (co.), Iowa 229/M4
Dubuque, Iowa 188/H2
Dubuque, Iowa (52001) 229/M3
Duchcov, Czech. 41/B1
Duchesne (co.), Utah 304/D3
Duchesne, Utah (84021) 304/D3
Duchesne (riv.), Utah 304/D3
Duchess, Alberta 182/E4
Duchess, Queensland 88/F4
Duchess, Queensland 95/A4
Ducie (isl.), Pitcairn Is. 87/O8
Duck (isls.), Maine 243/G7
Duck (lake), Mich. 250/F4
Duck (creek), Nev. 266/G3
Duck, N.C. (†27949) 281/T2
Duck (creek), Ohio 284/H6
Duck (isl.), Ontario 177/H4
Duck (isls.), Ontario 177/A2
Duck (riv.), Tenn. 237/F9
Duck, W. Va. (25063) 312/E5
Duck Bay, Manitoba 179/B2
Duck Hill, Miss. (38925) 256/E3
Duck Lake, Sask. 181/E3
Duck Lake Hist. Park, Sask. 181/E3
Duck Lake Post, Manitoba 179/J2
Duck Mountain Prov. Park, Manitoba 179/B3
Duck Mountain Prov. Park, Sask. 181/K4
Duck River, Tenn. (38454) 237/G9
Ducktown, Georgia (†30130) 217/D2
Ducktown, Tenn. (37326) 237/N10
Duckwater, Nev. (89314) 266/F4
Duclos, Québec 172/A4
Ducor, Calif. (93218) 204/G8
Ducos, Martinique 161/D6
Dudelange, Luxembourg 27/J10
Dudenville, Mo. (†64748) 261/D8
Duderstadt, W. Germany 22/D3
Dudhi, India 68/E4
Dudignac, Argentina 143/F7
Düdingen, Switzerland 39/D3
Dudinka, U.S.S.R. 54/K3
Dudinka, U.S.S.R. 4/B5
Dudinka, U.S.S.R. 48/J3
Dudley, England 13/E5
Dudley, England 10/G3
Dudley, Georgia (31022) 217/F5
Dudley○, Mass. (01570) 249/G4
Dudley, Mo. (63936) 261/M9
Dudley, N.C. (28333) 281/N4
Dudley, Pa. (16634) 294/F5
Dudley (lake), Québec 172/B3
Dudleytown, Ind. (†47274) 227/F7
Dudváh (riv.), Czech. 41/D2
Dudweiler, W. Germany 22/B4
Dueñas, Spain 33/D2
Duenweg, Mo. (64841) 261/D8
Duero (Douro) (riv.), Spain 33/C2
Due West, S.C. (29639) 296/C3
Duff, Sask. 181/H5
Duff, Tenn. (37729) 237/N8
Duffee, Miss. (†39337) 256/G6
Duffel, Belgium 27/F6
Dufferin (county), Ontario 177/D3
Duffield, Alberta 182/C3
Duffield, Va. (24244) 307/C7
Dufftown, Scotland 10/E2
Dufftown, Scotland 15/E3
Dufourspitze (mt.), Switzerland 39/E5
Dufresne, Manitoba 179/F5
Dufrost, Manitoba 179/F5
Dufur, Oreg. (97021) 291/F2
Dugald, Manitoba 179/F5
Dugger, Ind. (47848) 227/C6
Dugi Otok (isl.), Yugoslavia 45/B3
Dugspur, Va. (24325) 307/G7
Duguayville, New Bruns. 170/E1
Du Gué (riv.), Québec 174/C1
Dugway, Utah (84022) 304/B3
Dugway (range), Utah 304/A3
Dugway Proving Grounds, Utah 304/B3
Duhamel, Alberta 182/D3
Duhamel, Québec 172/B3
Duich, Loch (inlet), Scotland 15/C3
Duida, Cerro (mt.), Venezuela 124/F6
Duifken (pt.), Queensland 88/G2
Duifken (pt.), Queensland 95/B2
Duiker (pt.), S. Africa 118/E6
Duinain (riv.), Scotland 15/D3
Duirinish (dist.), Scotland 15/B3
Duisburg, W. Germany 22/B3
Duitama, Colombia 126/D5
Duiveland (isl.), Netherlands 27/D5
Duivendrecht, Netherlands 27/C5
Duke, Ala. (†36279) 195/G3
Duke (isl.), Alaska 196/N2
Duke, Mo. (65461) 261/H7
Duke, Okla. (73532) 288/G5
Duke Center, Pa. (16729) 294/F2
Dukedom, Tenn. (38226) 237/D8
Duke of Gloucester (isls.), Fr. Poly. 87/M8
Dukes (co.), Mass. 249/M7
Dukes, Mich. (†49885) 250/B2
Dukhan, Qatar 59/F4
Duki, Pakistan 68/B2
Dukla (pass), Czech. 41/F2
Dukla (pass), Poland 47/E4
Dukou, China 77/F6
Dulac, La. (70353) 238/J8
Dulah, N.C. (†28463) 281/M6
Dulan, China 77/E4
Dulce (riv.), Argentina 143/D2
Dulce (gulf), C. Rica 154/F6
Dulce, N. Mex. (87528) 274/B2
Duleek, Ireland 17/J4
Dulgalakh (riv.), U.S.S.R. 48/O3
Dülmen, W. Germany 22/B3
Dulunguin (pt.), Philippines 82/C7
Duluth, Georgia (30136) 217/D2
Duluth, Kansas (66421) 232/F2
Duluth, Minn. 146/J5
Duluth, Minn. 188/H1
Duluth, Minn. (*55801) 255/F4
Dulverton, England 13/D6
Duma, Syria 63/G6
Duma, West Bank 65/C3
Dumagasa (pt.), Philippines 82/C7
Dumaguete, Philippines 82/D6
Dumaguete, Philippines 85/G4
Dumanquilas (bay), Philippines 82/D7
Dumaran (isl.), Philippines 85/G3
Dumaran (isl.), Philippines 82/C5
Dumaresq (riv.), N.S. Wales 97/F1
Dumas, Ark. (71639) 202/H6
Dumas, Miss. (38625) 256/G1
Dumas, Sask. 181/J6
Dumas, Texas (79029) 303/C2
Dumbarton, New Bruns. 170/C3
Dumbarton, Scotland 10/A1
Dumbarton, Scotland 15/B1
Dum Dum, India 68/F1
Dume (pt.), Calif. 204/G10
Dumeir, Syria 63/G6
Dumfoundling (bay), Fla. 212/C4
Dumfries, New Bruns. 170/C3
Dumfries, Scotland 15/E5
Dumfries, Scotland 10/E3
Dumfries (trad. co.), Scotland, 15/B5
Dumfries, Va. (22026) 307/O3
Dumfries and Galloway (reg.), Scotland 15/E5
Dumlu, Turkey 63/J2
Dummer○, N.H. (†03588) 268/E2
Dummer, Sask. 181/G6
Dümmersee (lake), W. Germany 22/C2
Dumont, Iowa (50625) 229/H3
Dumont, Minn. (56236) 255/B5
Dumont, N.J. (07628) 273/C1
Dumont, Texas (79232) 303/D4
Dumont d'Urville Station 5/C7
Dumyât (Damietta), Egypt 111/J3
Dumyat (Damietta), Egypt 59/B3
Dun (isl.), Scotland 15/A2
Duna (Danube) (riv.), Hungary 41/E3
Dunaff (head), Ireland 17/F1
Dunaföldvár, Hungary 41/E3
Dunaharaszti, Hungary 41/E3
Dunajec (riv.), Czech. 41/F2
Dunajec (riv.), Poland 47/E4
Dunajská Streda, Czech. 41/D3
Dunakeszi, Hungary 41/E3
Dunalley, Tasmania 99/D4
Dunany (pt.), Ireland 17/J4
Dunaszekcsö, Hungary 41/E3
Dunaújváros, Hungary 41/E3
Dunav (Danube) (riv.), Bulgaria 45/H4
Dunavecse, Hungary 41/E3
Dunbar, Iowa (†50158) 229/H5
Dunbar, Nebr. (68346) 264/J4
Dunbar, Okla. (†74557) 288/P6
Dunbar, Pa. (15431) 294/C6
Dunbar, Scotland 10/E2
Dunbar, Scotland 15/F4
Dunbar, S.C. (†29525) 296/H2
Dunbar, W. Va. (25064) 312/C6
Dunbar, Wis. (54119) 317/K4
Dunbarton○, N.H. (†03301) 268/D5
Dunbarton (trad. co.), Scotland 15/A5
Dunbarton Center, N.H. (†03301) 268/D5
Dunbeath, Scotland 15/E2
Dunbeg, Scotland 15/C4
Dunblane, Sask. 181/D4
Dunblane, Scotland 15/E4
Dunblane, Scotland 10/D2
Dunbridge, Ohio (43414) 284/C3
Duncan, Ariz. (85534) 198/F6
Duncan, Br. Col. 184/J3
Duncan (riv.), Br. Col. 184/J5
Duncan (isls.), China 85/E2
Duncan, Ill. (†61559) 222/D3
Duncan (passage), India 68/G6
Duncan, Miss. (38740) 256/C2
Duncan, Nebr. (68634) 264/G3
Duncan, Okla. (73533) 288/L5
Duncan (lake), Québec 174/B2
Duncan, S.C. (29334) 296/C2
Duncan, W. Va. (25240) 312/C5
Duncan Falls, Ohio (43734) 284/G6
Duncannon, Ireland 17/H7
Duncannon, Pa. (17020) 294/H5
Duncans, Jamaica 158/H5
Duncans Bridge, Mo. (†63437) 261/H3
Duncansby (head), Scotland 15/F2
Duncansby (head), Scotland 10/E1
Duncansville, Pa. (16635) 294/F5
Duncanville, Ala. (35456) 195/D4
Duncanville, Texas (75116) 303/G3
Dunchurch, Ontario 177/E2
Duncombe, Iowa (50532) 229/E4
Duncombe (bay), Norfolk I. 88/L5
Dundaga, U.S.S.R. 53/B2
Dundalk, Ireland 17/H3
Dundalk, Ireland 10/C4
Dundalk (bay), Ireland 10/C4
Dundalk (bay), Ireland 17/J4
Dundalk, Md. (21222) 245/N3
Dundalk, Ontario 177/D3
Dundarrach, N.C. (†28386) 281/L5
Dundas (isl.), Br. Col. 184/B3
Dundas, Greenl. 4/B13
Dundas, Greenland 146/M2
Dundas, Ill. (62425) 222/E5
Dundas, Minn. (55019) 255/E6
Dundas (str.), North. Terr. 88/E2
Dundas (str.), North. Terr. 93/B1
Dundas (pen.), N.W. Terrs. 187/G2
Dundas, Ohio (45625) 284/E7
Dundas (county), Ontario 177/J2
Dundas, Ontario 177/D4
Dundas, Va. (23938) 307/M7
Dundas (lake), W. Australia 88/C6
Dundas (lake), W. Australia 92/C6
Dundee, Fla. (33838) 212/E3
Dundee (East and West Dundee), Ill. (60118) 222/E1
Dundee, Ind. (†47348) 227/F4
Dundee, Iowa (52038) 229/L3
Dundee, Ky. (42338) 237/H5
Dundee, Mich. (48131) 250/F7
Dundee, Minn. (56126) 255/C7
Dundee, Miss. (38626) 256/D1
Dundee, N.Y. (14837) 276/F5
Dundee, Oreg. (97115) 291/A2
Dundee, Scotland 7/D3
Dundee, Scotland 15/F4
Dundee, Scotland 10/E2
Dundee, S. Africa 118/E5
Dundee, Texas (76358) 303/F4
Dundgovĭ, Mongolia 77/G2
Dundon, W. Va. (†25043) 312/D6
Dundonald, Scotland 15/D5
Dundrum, N. Ireland 17/K3
Dundrum (bay), N. Ireland 17/K3
Dundurn, Sask. 181/E4
Dundy (co.), Nebr. 264/C4
Dune Acres, Ind. (†46304) 227/C1
Dunedin, Fla. (33528) 212/B2
Dunedin, N. Zealand 2/T8
Dunedin, N. Zealand 100/C6
Dunedoo, N.S. Wales 97/E3
Dunellen, N.J. (08812) 273/D2
Dunes (Westlake), Oreg. (†97493) 291/C4
Dunfanaghy, Ireland 17/F1
Dunfee, Ind. (†46802) 227/G2
Dunfermline, Ill. (61524) 222/D3
Dunfermline, Sask. 181/D3
Dunfermline, Scotland 15/D1
Dunfermline, Scotland 10/C1
Dungalear Station, N.S. Wales 97/D1
Dungannon (dist.), N. Ireland 17/H3
Dungannon, N. Ireland 17/H3
Dungannon, Ontario 177/C4
Dungannon, Va. (24245) 307/D7
Dungarpur, India 68/C4
Dungarvan, Ireland 10/C4
Dungarvan, Ireland 17/F7
Dungarvan (harb.), Ireland 10/C4
Dungarvan (harb.), Ireland 17/G7
Dungarvon (riv.), New Bruns. 170/D2
Dungeness (pt.), Argentina 143/C7
Dungeness (pt.), Chile 138/F10
Dungeness (prom.), England 13/J7
Dungeness (prom.), England 10/G5
Dungeness, Wash. (†98382) 310/B2
Dungiven, N. Ireland 17/H2
Dungloe, Ireland 17/E2
Dungog, N.S. Wales 97/F3
Dungu, Zaire 115/E3
Dungunab, Sudan 59/C5
Dungunab, Sudan 111/G3
Dunham, Québec 172/E4
Dunhua (Tunhwa), China 77/L3
Dunhuang, China 77/E3
Dunkeld, Queensland 95/D5
Dunkeld, Scotland 15/E4
Dunkeld, Victoria 97/B5
Dunkellin (riv.), Ireland 17/D5
Dunkerton, Iowa (50626) 229/J3
Dunkery (hill), England 13/D6
Dunkineely, Ireland 17/E2
Dunkirk (riv.), Alberta 182/D1
Dunkirk (Dunkerque), France 28/E2
Dunkirk, France 28/E2
Dunkirk, Ind. (47336) 227/G4
Dunkirk, N.Y. (14048) 276/B5
Dunkirk, Ohio (45836) 284/C4
Dunkley, Br. Col. 184/F3
Dunklin (co.), Mo. 261/M10
Dunkwa, Ghana 106/D7
Dún Laoghaire, Ireland 10/D4
Dún Laoghaire, Ireland 17/K5
Dunlap, Ill. (61525) 222/D3
Dunlap, Ind. (†46514) 227/F1
Dunlap, Iowa (51529) 229/B5
Dunlap, Kansas (66848) 232/F3
Dunlap, Tenn. (37327) 237/L10
Dunlavin, Ireland 17/H5
Dunleath, Sask. 181/K4
Dunleer, Ireland 17/J4
Dunleith, Miss. (†38756) 256/C4
Dunlow, W. Va. (25511) 312/B6
Dunloy, N. Ireland 17/J1
Dunmanus (bay), Ireland 17/B8
Dunmanway, Ireland 17/C8
Dunmanway, Ireland 10/B5
Dunmor, Ky. (42339) 237/G6
Dunmore, Alberta 182/E5
Dunmore, Ireland 17/D4
Dunmore, Pa. (18512) 294/F7
Dunmore (lake), Vt. 268/A4
Dunmore, W. Va. (24934) 312/G6
Dunmore East, Ireland 17/G7
Dunn, La. (71236) 238/G2
Dunn, N.C. (28334) 281/M4
Dunn (co.), N. Dak. 282/E5
Dunn, Texas (79516) 303/D5
Dunn (co.), Wis. 317/C6
Dunnamanagh, N. Ireland 17/G2
Dunn Center, N. Dak. (58626) 282/E5
Dunnegan, Mo. (65640) 261/E7
Dunnell, Minn. (56127) 255/D7
Dunnellon, Fla. (32630) 212/D2
Dunnet, Scotland 15/E2
Dunnet (bay), Scotland 15/E2
Dunnet (head), Scotland 10/E1
Dunnet (head), Scotland 15/E2
Dunnigan, Calif. (95937) 204/C5
Dunning, Nebr. (68833) 264/D3
Dunning, Scotland 15/E4
Dunn Loring, Va. (22027) 307/S2
Dunnottar, Manitoba 179/E4
Dunnottar, S. Africa 118/J6
Dunns, W. Va. (†25841) 312/D7
Dunnsville, Va. (22454) 307/P5
Dunnville, Ky. (42528) 237/M6
Dunnville, Ontario 177/E5
Du Noir (riv.), Wyo. 319/C2
Dunolly, Victoria 97/B5
Dunoon, Scotland 15/A2
Dunoon, Scotland 10/A1
Dunphy, Nev. (†89821) 266/E2
Dunragit, Scotland 15/D6
Dunrea, Manitoba 179/C5
Dunreith, Ind. (47337) 227/F5
Duns, Scotland 10/E3
Duns, Scotland 15/F5
Dunscore, Scotland 15/E5
Dunseith, N. Dak. (58329) 282/K2
Dunshaughlin, Ireland 17/H5
Dunsmuir, Calif. (96025) 204/C2
Dunstable, England 10/F5
Dunstable, England 13/G6
Dunstable○, Mass. (01827) 249/J2
Dunster, Br. Col. 184/G3
Duntochter, Scotland 15/B2
Dunure, Scotland 15/D5
Dunvegan, Nova Scotia 168/F4
Dunvegan, Scotland 15/B3
Dunvegan, Loch (inlet), Scotland 15/B3
Dunville, Newf. 166/D2
Dunwoody, Georgia (†30338) 217/K1
Duo, W. Va. (†25984) 312/E6
Duolun, China 77/J3
Duong Dong, Vietnam 72/D5
Du Page (co.), Ill. 222/E2
Du Page, East Branch (riv.), Ill. 222/A6
Du Page, West Branch (riv.), Ill. 222/A6
Du Page (riv.), Ill. 222/E2
Duparquet, Québec 174/B3
Duperow, Sask. 181/C4
Duplessis, La. (70728) 238/K2
Duplin (co.), N.C. 281/O5
Dupo, Ill. (62239) 222/A3
Du Pont, Georgia (31630) 217/G9
Dupont, Ind. (47231) 227/G7
Dupont, Ohio (45837) 284/B3
Dupont, Pa. (18641) 294/F7
Du Pont, Wash. (98327) 310/C3
Dupont Manor, Del. (†19901) 245/R4
Dupree, S. Dak. (57623) 298/F3
Dupuis Corner, New Bruns. 170/F2
Dupuy, Québec 174/B3
Dupuyer, Mont. (59432) 262/D2
Duque de Bragança, Angola 115/C5
Duque de Caxias, Brazil 135/E3
Duque de York (isl.), Chile 138/C9
Duquesne, Mo. (†64801) 261/D8
Duquesne, Pa. (15110) 294/C7
Duquette, Minn. (55729) 255/F4
Du Quoin, Ill. (62832) 222/D5
Duquoin, Kansas (†67058) 232/D4
Dura, West Bank 65/C4
Durack (range), W. Australia 88/D3
Durağan, Turkey 63/F2
Duran, N. Mex. (88319) 274/D4
Durance (riv.), France 28/F6

Eastsound 363

Durand, Georgia (†31830) 217/C5
Durand, Ill. (61024) 222/D1
Durand, Mich. (48429) 250/E6
Durand, Wis. (54736) 317/C6
Durango, Colo. 188/E3
Durango, Colo. (81301) 208/D8
Durango, Iowa (52039) 229/M3
Durango (state), Mexico 150/G4
Durango, Mexico 146/H7
Durango, Mexico 150/G4
Durango, Spain 33/E1
Duranillin, W. Australia 92/B2
Durant, Iowa (52747) 229/M5
Durant, Miss. (39063) 256/E4
Durant, Okla. 188/G4
Durant, Okla. (74701) 288/O6
Duratón (riv.), Spain 33/E2
Durazno (dept.), Uruguay 145/C3
Durazno, Uruguay 145/C4
Durazno, Grande del (range), Uruguay 145/D4
Durban, Manitoba 179/A3
Durban, S. Africa 2/L7
Durban, S. Africa 102/F7
Durban, S. Africa 118/E5
Durbanville, S. Africa 118/F6
Durbe, U.S.S.R. 53/A2
Durbin, Ind. (†46060) 227/F4
Durbin, N. Dak. (58023) 282/R6
Durbin, W. Va. (26264) 312/G5
Durbuy, Belgium 27/H8
Düren, W. Germany 22/B3
Durfee (hill), R.I. 249/G5
Durg, India 68/E4
Durgapur, India 68/F4
Durgerdam, Netherlands 27/C4
Durham, Ark. (†72701) 202/C2
Durham, Calif. (95938) 204/D4
Durham, Conn. (06422) 210/E3
Durham○, Conn. (06422) 210/E3
Durham (co.), England 13/F3
Durham, England 13/J3
Durham, England 10/F3
Durham, Kansas (67438) 232/E3
Durham, Mo. (63438) 261/J3
Durham, N.H. (03824) 268/F5
Durham○, N.H. (03824) 268/F5
Durham (pt.), N. Zealand 100/D7
Durham, N.C. 188/L3
Durham (co.), N.C. 281/M3
Durham, N.C. (*27701) 281/M2
Durham, Okla. (73642) 288/G3
Durham (reg. munic.), Ontario 177/F3
Durham, Ontario 177/D3
Durham, Oreg. (†97233) 291/A2
Durham Bridge, New Bruns. 170/D2
Durham Center, Conn. (†06422) 210/E3
Durham Downs, Queensland 95/B5
Durham-Sud, Québec 172/E4
Durhamville, N.Y. (13054) 276/J4
Duri, N.S. Wales 97/F2
Durkee, Oreg. (97905) 291/K3
Durness, Scotland 15/D2
Durnford (pt.), Western Sahara 106/A4
Dürnten, Switzerland 39/G2
Duror, Scotland 15/C4
Durrell, Newf. 166/D4
Dürrenroth, Switzerland 39/E2
Durrës (Durazzo), Albania 45/D5
Durrës, Albania 7/F4
Durrington, England 13/F6
Durrow, Laoighis, Ireland 17/G6
Durrow, Offaly, Ireland 17/F5
Dursey (isl.), Ireland 17/A8
Dursunbey, Turkey 63/C3
Duruh, Iran 59/H3
Duruh, Iran 66/M4
D'Urville (isl.), N. Zealand 100/D4
Duryea, Pa. (18642) 294/F7
Dusa Marreb, Somalia 115/J2
Dūsh, Egypt 59/B5
Dūsh, Egypt 111/F3
Dushan, China 77/G6
Dushanbe, U.S.S.R. 54/H6
Dushanbe, U.S.S.R. 2/N4
Dushanbe, U.S.S.R. 48/G6
Dushore, Pa. (18614) 294/K2
Dusky (sound), N. Zealand 100/A6
Duson, La. (70529) 238/F6
Düsseldorf, W. Germany 7/E3
Düsseldorf, W. Germany 22/B3
Dustin, Okla. (74839) 288/O4
Dusty, N. Mex. (87934) 274/B5
Dusty, Wash. (†99143) 310/H4
Dutch (creek), Ark. 202/C4
Dutch Cap (cay), Virgin Is. (U.S.) 161/A4
Dutchess (co.), N.Y. 276/N7
Dutch Flat, Calif. (95714) 204/E4
Dutch Harbor, Alaska (†99685) 196/E4
Dutch John, Utah (84023) 304/E3
Dutch Mills, Ark. (†72744) 202/B2
Dutch Neck, N.J. (†08550) 273/D3
Dutchtown, Mo. (63745) 261/N8
Dutton, Ala. (35744) 195/G1
Dutton, Ark. (†72760) 202/C2
Dutton (mt.), Conn. 210/C1
Dutton, Mont. (59433) 262/E3
Dutton, Ontario 177/C5
Dutton (mt.), Utah 304/B5
Duval (co.), Fla. 212/E1
Duval, Sask. 181/G4
Duval (co.), Texas 303/F10
Duvalierville, Haiti 158/C6
Duvall, Wash. (98019) 310/D3
Duvergé, Dom. Rep. 158/D6
Duvernay, Alberta 182/E3
Duwadami, Saudi Arabia 59/D5
Duxbury (pt.), Calif. 204/H2
Duxbury, Mass. (02332) 249/M4
Duxbury○, Mass. (02332) 249/M4
Duxbury○, Vt. (†05676) 268/B3
Duyun (Tuyün), China 77/G6
Düzce, Turkey 63/D2
Duzdab (Zahedan), Iran 66/M6
Dvina, (bay), U.S.S.R. 52/E2
Dvina, Northern (riv.), U.S.S.R. 4/C7
Dvina, Northern (riv.), U.S.S.R. 7/J2
Dvina, Northern (riv.), U.S.S.R. 48/E3
Dvina, Northern (riv.), U.S.S.R. 52/F2
Dvina, Western (riv.) U.S.S.R. 53/C2
Dvina, Western (riv.), U.S.S.R. 48/C4
Dvina, Western (riv.), U.S.S.R. 52/C3
Dvina, Western (riv.), U.S.S.R. 7/G3
Dvinsk (Daugavpils), U.S.S.R. 52/C3
Dvory nad Žitavou, Czech. 41/E3
Dvůr Králové nad Labem, Austria 41/C1
Dwale, Ky. (41621) 237/R5
Dwarka, India 68/B4
Dwellingup, W. Australia 92/B2
Dwight, Ill. (60420) 222/E2
Dwight, Kansas (66849) 232/F3
Dwight, Nebr. (68635) 264/G3
Dwight, N. Dak. (58024) 282/S7
Dwight, Ontario 177/F2
Dworshak (res.), Idaho 220/C3
Dwyer, N. Mex. (†88034) 274/B6
Dwyer, Wyo. (82211) 319/G3
Dyas, Ala. (†36507) 195/C9
Dyat'kovo, U.S.S.R. 52/D4
Dybvad, Denmark 21/D3
Dyce, Scotland 15/F3
Dyckesville, Wis. (†54217) 317/L6
Dycusburg, Ky. (42037) 237/E6
Dyer, Ark. (72935) 202/B3
Dyer, Ind. (46311) 227/C1
Dyer, Ky. (†40115) 237/J5
Dyer, Nev. (89010) 266/C5
Dyer (cape), N.W.T. 162/K2
Dyer (cape), N.W. Terrs. 187/M3
Dyer (co.), Tenn. 237/C8
Dyer, Tenn. (38330) 237/D8
Dyer Brook○, Maine (†04747) 243/G3
Dyersburg, Tenn. (38024) 237/C8
Dyersville, Iowa (52040) 229/L3
Dyess, Ark. (72330) 202/K2
Dyess A.F.B., Texas 303/D5
Dyfed, Wales 13/C6
Dyje (riv.), Czech. 41/D2
Dyke (lake), Newf. 166/A3
Dykh-Tau (mt.), U.S.S.R. 52/F6
Dyle (riv.), Belgium 27/F7
Dysart, Iowa (52224) 229/J4
Dysart, Sask. 181/H5
Dysartsville, N.C. (†28761) 281/F3
Dzamīn Üüd, Mongolia 77/H3
Dzaoudzi (cap.), France 118/H2
Dzavhan, Mongolia 77/E2
Dzavhan Gol (riv.), Mongolia 77/D2
Dzerzhinsk, U.S.S.R. 7/J3
Dzerzhinsk, U.S.S.R. 48/E4
Dzerzhinsk, U.S.S.R. 52/F3
Dzhalal-Abad, U.S.S.R. 48/H5
Dzhalilabad, U.S.S.R. 52/G7
Dzhalinda, U.S.S.R. 48/N4
Dzhambul, U.S.S.R. 54/J5
Dzhambul, U.S.S.R. 48/H5
Dzhankoy, U.S.S.R. 52/D5
Dzhelinda, U.S.S.R. 48/M2
Dzhetygara, U.S.S.R. 48/G4
Dzhezkazgan, U.S.S.R. 54/H5
Dzhezkazgan, U.S.S.R. 48/G5
Dzhugdzhur (range), U.S.S.R. 54/P4
Dzhugdzhur (range), U.S.S.R. 48/O4
Dzhul'fa, U.S.S.R. 52/G7
Dzhusaly, U.S.S.R. 48/G5
Działdowo, Poland 47/E2
Dzibalchén, Mexico 150/P7
Dzibichaltún (ruin), Mexico 150/P6
Dzidzantún, Mexico 150/P6
Dzierzoniów, Poland 47/C3
Dzilam de Bravo, Mexico 150/P6
Dzitbalché, Mexico 150/P6
Dzurh, Mongolia 77/E2
Dzüünharaa, Mongolia 77/G2
Dzuunmod, Mongolia 77/G2

E

Eabamet (lake), Ontario 175/C2
Eads, Colo. (81036) 208/O6
Eads, Tenn. (38028) 237/B10
Eadytown, S.C. (†29468) 296/G5
Eagan, Minn. (55111) 255/G6
Eagan, Tenn. (37730) 237/O7
Eagar, Ariz. (85925) 198/F4
Eagarville, Ill. (†62033) 222/D4
Eagle, Alaska 188/D5
Eagle, Alaska (99738) 196/K2
Eagle (creek), Ariz. 198/F5
Eagle (lake), Calif. 204/E3
Eagle (peak), Calif. 204/E2
Eagle (co.), Colo. 208/F3
Eagle, Colo. (81631) 208/F3
Eagle (riv.), Colo. 208/E3
Eagle, Idaho (83616) 220/B6
Eagle (creek), Ind. 227/E4
Eagle (lake), Iowa 229/F2
Eagle (creek), Ky. 237/M3
Eagle (lake), Maine 243/F1
Eagle (lake), Maine 243/E3
Eagle, Mich. (48822) 250/E6
Eagle (mt.), Minn. 255/G2
Eagle, Nebr. (68347) 264/H4
Eagle (riv.), Newf. 166/C3
Eagle, Ontario 177/C5
Eagle (lake), Ontario 177/F5
Eagle (lake), Ontario 177/E2
Eagle (creek), Oreg. 291/K3
Eagle (hills), Sask. 181/C3
Eagle (peak), Texas 303/C11
Eagle (mt.), Virgin Is. (U.S.) 161/E4
Eagle, Wis. (53119) 317/H2
Eagle (lake), Wis. 317/H2
Eagle (lake), Wis. 317/K3
Eagle (peak), Wyo. 319/B1
Eagle Bay, N.Y. (13331) 276/L3
Eagle Bend, Minn. (56446) 255/D4
Eagle Bridge, N.Y. (12057) 276/O5
Eagle Butte, S. Dak. (57625) 298/G4
Eagle City, Okla. (73658) 288/J3
Eagle Crags (mt.), Calif. 204/J8
Eagle Creek, Oreg. (97022) 291/E2
Eagle Grove, Iowa (50533) 229/F3
Eagle Harbor, Md. (†20608) 245/M6
Eagle Harbor, Mich. (49951) 250/A1
Eaglehawk, Victoria 97/C5
Eaglehill (creek), Sask. 181/D4
Eagle Lake, Fla. (33839) 212/E4
Eagle Lake, Maine (04739) 243/F1
Eagle Lake○, Maine (04739) 243/F1
Eagle Lake○, Minn. (56024) 255/E6
Eagle Lake, Ontario 177/F2
Eagle Lake, Texas (77434) 303/H8
Eagle Mills, Ark. (71729) 202/E6
Eagle Mountain, Calif. (92241) 204/K10
Eagle Mountain (lake), Texas 303/E2
Eagle Nest, N. Mex. (87718) 274/D2
Eagle Nest (lake), N. Mex. 274/D2
Eagle Pass, Texas (78852) 303/D9
Eagle Point, Oreg. (97524) 291/E5
Eagle River, Alaska (99577) 196/C1
Eagle River, Mich. (49924) 250/A1
Eagle River, Wis. (54521) 317/H4
Eagle Rock, Mo. (65641) 261/E9
Eagle Rock, Va. (24085) 307/J5
Eaglesfield, Scotland 15/E5
Eaglesham, Alberta 182/B2
Eaglesham, Scotland 15/D5
Eagles Mere, Pa. (17731) 294/J3
Eagle Springs, N.C. (27242) 281/K4
Eagleton Village, Tenn. (†37801) 237/O9
Eagletown, Ind. (†46074) 227/E4
Eagletown, Okla. (74734) 288/S6
Eagleville, Calif. (96110) 204/E2
Eagleville, Conn. (†06268) 210/F1
Eagleville, Mo. (64442) 261/D2
Eagleville, Tenn. (37060) 237/H9
Eakly, Okla. (73033) 288/K4
Ealing, England 13/H8
Ealing, England 10/B5
Ear (lake), Sask. 181/B3
Earby, England 13/H1
Eardley (lake), Manitoba 179/F2
Ear Falls, Ontario 175/B2
Earl (lake), Calif. 204/A2
Earl, N.C. (28038) 281/F4
Earl, Wis. (54833) 317/C4
Earle, Ark. (72331) 202/K3
Earle Naval Weapons Sta., N.J. 273/E3
Earleton, Fla. (32631) 212/D2
Earleville, Md. (21919) 245/P3
Earl Grey, Sask. 181/G5
Earlham, Iowa (50072) 229/E6
Earlimart, Calif. (93219) 204/F8
Earling, Iowa (51530) 229/C5
Earlington, Ky. (42410) 237/F6
Earl Park, Ind. (47942) 227/C3
Earlsboro, Okla. (74840) 288/N4
Earlston, Scotland 15/F5
Earlton, Kansas (†66720) 232/G4
Earlton, Ontario 177/K5
Earltown, Nova Scotia 168/E3
Earlville, Ill. (60518) 222/E2
Earlville, Iowa (52041) 229/L4
Earlville, N.Y. (13332) 276/J5
Early (co.), Georgia 217/C8
Early, Iowa (50535) 229/C4
Early Branch, S.C. (29916) 296/F6
Earlysville, Va. (22936) 307/M4
Earn, Loch (lake), Scotland 15/D4
Earn (riv.), Scotland 15/E4
Earnslaw (mt.), N. Zealand 100/B6
Earp, Calif. (92242) 204/L9
Earth, Texas (79031) 303/B3
Earthquake (lake), Mont. 262/E6
Easby, N. Dak. (†58249) 282/O2
Easington, England 13/J3
Easingwold, England 13/F3
Easky (lake), Ireland 17/E2
Easky, Ireland 17/D3
Easley, S.C. (29640) 296/B2
East (cape), Alaska 196/K4
East (riv.), Conn. 210/E3
East (pt.), Fla. 212/E6
East (bay), La. 238/M8
East (pt.), Mass. 249/E6
East (range), Nev. 266/D2
East (pt.), N.S. Wales 97/J2
East (riv.), N.Y. 276/N9
East (cape), N. Zealand 87/H9
East (cape), N. Zealand 100/G2
East (bay), Nova Scotia 168/H3
East (riv.), Nova Scotia 168/F3
East (lake), Oreg. 291/F4
East (pt.), Pr. Edward I. 168/G2
East (Dezhnev) (cape), U.S.S.R. 4/C18
East (pt.), Virgin Is. (U.S.) 161/G4
Eastaboga, Ala. (36260) 195/F3
Eastabuchie, Miss. (39436) 256/F8
East Albany, Vt. (†05820) 268/C2
East Alburg, Vt. (†05440) 268/A2
East Aldfield, Québec 172/A4
East Alligator (riv.), North. Terr. 93/C2
East Alton, Ill. (62024) 222/A2
East Andover, Maine (04226) 243/B6
East Andover, N.H. (03231) 268/D5
East Angus, Québec 172/F4
Eastanollee, Georgia (30538) 217/F1
East Arcadia, N.C. (†28434) 281/N6
East Arlington, Vt. (05252) 268/A5
East Arrow Park, Br. Col. 184/J5
East Aspetuck (riv.), Conn. 210/B2
East Aurora, N.Y. (14052) 276/C5
East Baldwin, Maine (04024) 243/B8
East Bangor, Pa. (18013) 294/M4
East Bank, W. Va. (25067) 312/D6
East Barnet, Vt. (†05821) 268/C3
East Barre-Graniteville, Vt. (05649) 268/C3
East Barrington, N.H. (03825) 268/F5
East Baton Rouge (par.), La. 238/K1
East Bay, Nova Scotia 168/H2
East Bay (hills), Nova Scotia 168/H3
East Bend, N.C. (27018) 281/H2
East Berbice-Corantyne (dist.), Guyana 131/C3
East Berkshire, Vt. (05447) 268/B2
East Berlin, Conn. (06023) 210/E2
East Berlin, Pa. (17316) 294/J6
East Bernard, Texas (77435) 303/H8
East Bernstadt, Ky. (40729) 237/N6
East Berwick, Pa. (†18603) 294/K3
East Bethany, N.Y. (14054) 276/D5
East Bethel, Minn. (†55005) 255/E5
East Bethel, Vt. (†05032) 268/B4
East Bloomfield, N.Y. (14443) 276/E5
East Blue Hill, Maine (04629) 243/G7
East Blythe, Calif. (†92225) 204/L10
East Boothbay, Maine (04544) 243/D8
Eastborough, Kansas (†67201) 232/E4
Eastbourne, England 13/H7
Eastbourne, England 10/G5
Eastbourne, N. Zealand 100/B3
East Brady, Pa. (16028) 294/C3
East Braintree, Manitoba 179/G5
East Braintree, Mass. (†02184) 249/D8
East Braintree, Vt. (†05060) 268/B3
East Branch, N.Y. (13756) 276/K7
East Branch, Rocky (riv.), Ohio 284/G10
East Brewster, Mass. (†02631) 249/O5
East Brewton, Ala. (36426) 195/E8
East Bridgewater○, Mass. (02333) 249/L4
East Brisbane, Queensland 88/K3
East Brisbane, Queensland 95/E3
East Brookfield, Mass. (01515) 249/G4
East Brookfield○, Mass. (01515) 249/G4
East Brookfield, Vt. (†05036) 268/C3
East Brooklyn, Conn. (†06239) 210/H1
East Broughton, Québec 172/F3
East Broughton Station, Québec 172/F3
East Brownfield, Maine (†04010) 243/B8
East Brunswick○, N.J. (08816) 273/E3
East Burke, Vt. (05832) 268/D2
East Butler, Pa. (16029) 294/C4
East Calais, Vt. (05650) 268/C3
East Calder, Scotland 15/D2
East Camden, Ark. (71701) 202/E6
East Canaan, Conn. (06024) 210/B1
East Candia, N.H. (03040) 268/E5
East Canton, Ohio (44730) 284/H4
East Canyon (res.), Utah 304/C3
East Cape Girardeau, Ill. (†62957) 222/D6
East Carbon, Utah (84520) 304/D4
East Carondelet, Ill. (62240) 222/A3
East Carroll (par.), La. 238/H1
East Chain, Minn. (†56031) 255/D7
East Charleston, Vt. (05833) 268/D2
Eastchester, N.Y. (10709) 276/P6
East Chester, Nova Scotia 168/D4
East Chevington, England 13/F2
East Chezzetcook, Nova Scotia 168/E4
East Chicago, Ind. (46312) 227/C1
East Chicago Heights, Ill. (†60411) 222/C6
East China (sea) 54/O7
East China (sea), China 77/L6
East China (sea), Japan 81/C8
East China (sea), S. Korea 81/C8
East Chop (pt.), Mass. 249/M7
East Claridon, Ohio (44033) 284/H2
East Cleveland, Ohio (44112) 284/H9
East Coast Bays, N. Zealand 100/B1
East Concord, Vt. (†05906) 268/D3
East Conemaugh, Pa. (15909) 294/E5
East Corinth, Maine (04427) 243/F5
East Corinth, Vt. (05040) 268/C3
East Cote Blanche (bay), La. 238/G7
East Coulée, Alberta 182/D4
East Craftsbury, Vt. (†05826) 268/C2
East Dedham, Mass. (02026) 249/C8
East Demerara-West Coast Berbice (dist.), Guyana 131/C2
East Dennis, Mass. (02641) 249/O5
East Dereham, England 13/H5
East Dereham, England 10/G4
East Derry, N.H. (03041) 268/E6
East Detroit, Mich. (48021) 250/B6
East Devils (lake), N. Dak. 282/N4
East Dixfield, Maine (04227) 243/C6
East Dixmont, Maine (†04932) 243/E6
East Dorset, Vt. (05253) 268/A5
East Douglas, Mass. (01516) 249/G4
East Dover, Vt. (05341) 268/B6
East Dublin, Georgia (31021) 217/G5
East Dubuque, Ill. (61025) 222/C1
East Duke, Okla. (†73532) 288/H5
East Dundee (Dundee), Ill. (†60118) 222/E1
East Durham, N.Y. (12423) 276/M6
East Eddington, Maine (04428) 243/F6
East Ellijay, Georgia (30539) 217/C1
East Ely, Nev. 266/G3
Eastend, Sask. 181/C6
Eastend, Virgin Is. (U.S.) 161/D4
East Enterprise, Ind. (47019) 227/H7
Easter (isl.), Chile 87/Q8
Easter (isl.), Chile 2/D7
Eastern (pt.), Conn. 210/G3
Eastern (Arabian) (des.), Egypt 111/F2
Eastern (prov.), Kenya 115/G4
Eastern (bay), Md. 245/N5
Eastern (pt.), Mass. 249/M2
Eastern (creek), N.S. Wales 97/H3
Eastern Channel (str.), Japan 81/D7
Eastern Ghats (mts.), India 68/D6
Eastern Samar (prov.), Philippines 82/E5
Eastern Scheldt (est.), Netherlands 27/D5
Eastern Taurus (mts.), Turkey 63/J3
Eastern Wolf (isl.), New Bruns. 170/D4
Easterville, Manitoba 179/C1
East Fairfield, Vt. (05448) 268/B2
East Falkland (isl.), 143/E7
East Falkland (isl.), Falk. Is. 120/D8
East Falmouth (Teaticket), Mass. (02536) 249/M6
East Farnham, Québec 172/E4
East Faxon, Pa. (†17701) 294/J3
East Feliciana (par.), La. 238/H5
East Ferry, Nova Scotia 168/B4
East Flanders (prov.), Belgium 27/D7
East Flat Rock, N.C. (28726) 281/E4
Eastford○, Conn. (06242) 210/G1
East Fork, Little Miami (riv.), Ohio 284/C7
East Fork, Green (riv.), Wyo. 319/C3
East Foxboro, Mass. (†02035) 249/K4
East Franklin, Maine (†04634) 243/G6
East Franklin, Vt. (†05457) 268/B2
East Freedom, Pa. (16637) 294/E5
East Freetown, Mass. (02717) 249/L5
East Friesland (reg.), W. Germany 22/B2
East Frisian (isls.), W. Germany 22/B2
East Gaffney, S.C. (†29340) 296/D1
East Galesburg, Ill. (61430) 222/C3
Eastgate, Nev. (†89406) 266/D3
East Georgia, Vt. (†05455) 268/A2
East Germantown (Pershing), Ind. (†47370) 227/G5
East Germany 7/F3
EAST GERMANY 22
East Gillespie, Ill. (†62033) 222/D4
East Glacier Park, Mont. (59434) 262/C2
East Glastonbury, Conn. (06025) 210/E2
East Grafton, N.H. (†03240) 268/D4
East Granby○, Conn. (06026) 210/E1
East Grand Forks, Minn. (56721) 255/B3
East Grand Rapids, Mich. (†49506) 250/D6
East Granville, Vt. (†05669) 268/B3
East Greenbush, N.Y. (12061) 276/N5
East Green Harbour, Nova Scotia 168/C5
East Greenville, Ohio (†44666) 284/G4
East Greenville, Pa. (18041) 294/L5
East Greenwich, R.I. (02818) 249/H6
East Grinstead, England 10/G5
East Grinstead, England 13/G6
Eastgulf, W. Va. (25835) 312/D7
East Gull Lake, Minn. (†56401) 255/D4
East Haddam○, Conn. (06423) 210/F3
Eastham○, Mass. (02642) 249/O5
East Hampstead, N.H. (03826) 268/E6
East Hampton, Conn. (06424) 210/E2
East Hampton○, Conn. (06424) 210/E2
Easthampton○, Mass. (01027) 249/D3
East Hampton, N.Y. (11937) 276/R9
East Hanover○, N.J. (07936) 273/E2
East Hardin, Ill. (†62031) 222/C4
East Hardwick, Vt. (05836) 268/C2
East Hartford○, Conn. (06108) 210/E1
East Hartland, Conn. (06027) 210/D1
East Harwich, Mass. (†02645) 249/O6
East Haven○, Conn. (06512) 210/D3
East Haven○, Vt. (05837) 268/D2
East Haverhill, N.H. (†03780) 268/D3
East Hazelcrest, Ill. (†60429) 222/C6
East Hebron, N.H. (03232) 268/D4
East Helena, Mont. (59635) 262/E4
East Hereford, Québec 172/F4
East Herkimer, N.Y. 276/L4
East Hickory, Pa. (16321) 294/D2
East Hills, N.Y. (†11576) 276/R7
East Hiram, Maine (†04041) 243/B8
East Hodge, La. (†71247) 238/E2
East Holden, Maine (04429) 243/F6
East Hope, Idaho (†83836) 220/B1
East Jackson, Maine (†04986) 243/E6
East Jamaica, Vt. (†05343) 268/B5
East Jordan, Mich. (49727) 250/D3
East Juliette, Georgia (†31046) 217/E4
East Keansburg, N.J. (07734) 273/E3
East Kelowna, Br. Col. 184/H5
East Kent, Conn. (†06785) 210/B2
East Kilbride, Scotland 15/B2
East Killingly, Conn. (06243) 210/H1
East Kingsford, Mich. (†49801) 250/A3
East Kingston○, N.H. (03827) 268/F6
East Knox, Maine (†04921) 243/E7
East Korea (bay), N. Korea 81/D4
East Lake, Mich. (49626) 250/C4
East Lake, Minn. (†55760) 255/E4
East Lake, N.C. (27931) 281/S3
Eastlake, Ohio (†44094) 284/J8
East Lake-Orient Park, Fla. (†33601) 212/C2
Eastland, Tenn. (†38583) 237/L9
Eastland (co.), Texas 303/F5
Eastland, Texas (76448) 303/F5
East Lansdowne, Pa. (†19050) 294/M7
East Lansing, Mich. (48823) 250/E6
East Laport, N.C. (†28723) 281/C4
East Las Vegas, Nev. (89112) 266/F6
East Laurinburg, N.C. (28352) 281/L5
East Lebanon, Maine (04027) 243/B9
East Lee, Mass. (†01238) 249/B3
Eastleigh, England 13/F7
Eastleigh, England 10/F5
East Lempster, N.H. (03605) 268/C5
East Limington, Maine (†04049) 243/B8
East Linton, Scotland 15/F5
East Litchfield, Conn. (†06759) 210/C1
East Livermore, Maine (04228) 243/C7
East Liverpool, Ohio (43920) 284/J4
East Loch (inlet), Hawaii 218/B3
East Loch Tarbert (inlet), Scotland 15/B3
East London, S. Africa 102/E8
East London, S. Africa 118/D6
East Longmeadow○, Mass. (01028) 249/E4
East Los Angeles, Calif. (90022) 204/C10
East Lowell, Maine (†04433) 243/G5
East Lyme○, Conn. (06333) 210/G3
East Lynn, Ill. (60932) 222/F3
East Lynn, W. Va. (25512) 312/B6
East Lynn (lake), W. Va. 312/B6
East Lynne, Mo. (64743) 261/D5
East Machias, Maine (04630) 243/J6
East Machias○, Maine (04630) 243/J6
East Machias (riv.), Maine 243/H6
East Madison, Maine (†04950) 243/D6
East Madison, N.H. (†03849) 268/E4
Eastmain, Que. 162/J5
Eastmain (riv.), Que. 146/L4
Eastmain (riv.), Que. 162/J5
Eastmain, Québec 174/B2
Eastmain (riv.), Québec 174/B2
Eastman, Georgia (31023) 217/F6
Eastman, Québec 172/E4
Eastman, Wis. (54626) 317/D9
East Marion, N.C. (†28752) 281/F3
East Meadow, N.Y. (11554) 276/R7
East Meredith, N.Y. (13757) 276/L6
East Middlebury, Vt. (05740) 268/A4
East Millcreek, Utah (84109) 304/C3
East Millinocket, Maine (04430) 243/F4
East Millinocket○, Maine (04430) 243/F4
East Millstone, N.J. (08873) 273/D3
East Milton, Mass. (†02186) 249/D7
East Mines, Nova Scotia 168/E3
East Moline, Ill. (61244) 222/C2
East Montpelier○, Vt. (05651) 268/B3
East Moriches, N.Y. (11940) 276/P9
East Morris, Conn. (†06763) 210/C2
East Murton, England 13/J3
East Musquash (lake), Maine 243/H5
East Naples, Fla. (†33962) 212/E5
East Newark, N.J. (†07100) 273/B2
East New Market, Md. (21631) 245/P6
East Newnan, Georgia (†30263) 217/C4
East New Portland, Maine (†04954) 243/D6
East Nishnabotna (riv.), Iowa 229/C6
East Northfield, Mass. (†01360) 249/E2
East Northport, N.Y. (11731) 276/O9
East Norton, Mass. (†02766) 249/K5
East Norwalk, Conn. (†06856) 210/B4
East Olympia, Wash. (98540) 310/B4
Easton, Calif. (93706) 204/F7
Easton○, Conn. (06612) 210/B4
Easton (res.), Conn. 210/B3
Easton, Ill. (62633) 222/D3
Easton, Kansas (66020) 232/G2
Easton, La. (†70586) 238/F5
Easton○, Maine (04740) 243/H2
Easton, Md. (21601) 245/O5
Easton○, Mass. (02334) 249/K4
Easton, Minn. (56025) 255/E7
Easton, Mo. (64443) 261/C3
Easton○, N.H. (†03580) 268/D3
Easton, Pa. (18042) 294/M4
Easton, Wash. (98925) 310/D3
Easton, Wis. (†53936) 317/G8
Eastondale, Mass. (†02375) 249/K4
East Orange, N.J. (*07017) 273/B2
East Orland, Maine (04431) 243/F6
East Orleans, Mass. (02643) 249/P5
East Otis, Mass. (01029) 249/B4
East Otisfield, Maine (†04270) 243/B7
East Otto, N.Y. (14729) 276/C6
Eastover, S.C. (29044) 296/F4
East Palatka, Fla. (32031) 212/E2
East Palestine, Ohio (44413) 284/J4
East Park (res.), Calif. 204/C4
East Parsonfield, Maine (04028) 243/B8
East Peacham, Vt. (†05821) 268/C3
East Pembroke, Mass. (†02359) 249/M4
East Pembroke, N.Y. (14056) 276/D5
East Peoria, Ill. (61611) 222/D3
East Pepperell, Mass. (01437) 249/H2
East Peru (Peru), Iowa (†50222) 229/F6
East Peru, Maine (04229) 243/C7
East Petersburg, Pa. (17520) 294/K5
East Pleasant Plain, Iowa (†52540) 229/K6
Eastpoint, Fla. (32328) 212/B2
East Point, Georgia (30344) 217/K2
East Point, Ky. (41216) 237/R5
East Point, La. (71025) 238/D2
East Poland, Maine (†04210) 243/C7
East Poplar, Sask. 181/F6
Eastport, Idaho (83826) 220/B1
Eastport, Maine 188/N2
Eastport, Maine (04631) 243/K6
Eastport, Mich. (49627) 250/D3
Eastport, Newf. 166/D1
Eastport, N.Y. (11941) 276/P9
East Poultney, Vt. (05741) 268/A4
East Prairie, Mo. (63845) 261/O9
East Preston, England 13/G7
East Prospect, Pa. (17317) 294/J6
East Providence, R.I. (02914) 249/J5
East Putnam, Conn. (†06260) 210/H1
East Randolph, N.Y. (14730) 276/C6
East Randolph, Vt. (05041) 268/B4
East Retford, England 13/G4
East Retford, England 10/F4
East Richford, Vt. (†05476) 268/B2
East Ridge, Tenn. (37412) 237/L11
Eastriggs, Scotland 15/E5
East Rindge, N.H. (†03461) 268/D6
East River, Conn. (†06443) 210/E3
East River Saint Marys, Nova Scotia 168/F3
East Riverside-Kingshurst, New Bruns. 170/E3
East Rochester, N.Y. (14445) 276/F4
East Rochester, Ohio (44625) 284/H4
East Rockaway, N.Y. (11518) 276/R7
East Rutherford, N.J. (07073) 273/B2
Eastry, England 13/J6
East Ryegate, Vt. (05042) 268/C3
East Saint Louis, Ill. 188/J3
East Saint Louis, Ill. (*62201) 222/A2
East Sandwich, Mass. (02537) 249/N6
East Saugus, Mass. (†01906) 249/D6
East Sebago, Maine (04029) 243/B8
East Selkirk, Manitoba 179/F4
East Shoal (lake), Manitoba 179/E4
East Siberian (sea), U.S.S.R. 4/B1
East Siberian (sea), U.S.S.R. 54/T2
East Siberian (sea), U.S.S.R. 48/S2
Eastside, Oreg. (97420) 291/C4
East Side, Pa. (18634) 294/L3
East Sister (peak), Idaho 220/C2
East Sister (isl.), Tasmania 99/E1
East Smithfield, Pa. (18817) 294/J2
Eastsound, Wash. (98245) 310/B2

364 East Sparta

East Sparta, Ohio (44626) 284/H4
East Spencer, N.C. (28039) 281/J3
East Springfield, N.Y. (13333) 276/L5
East Springfield, Pa. (16411) 294/A2
East Stone Gap, Va. (24246) 307/C7
East Stoneham, Maine (04231) 243/B7
East Stroudsburg, Pa. (18301) 294/M4
East Sullivan, Maine (†04607) 243/G6
East Sullivan, N.H. (03445) 268/C6
East Sumner, Maine (†04220) 243/C7
East Sussex (co.), England 13/H7
East Swan (riv.), Minn. 255/F3
East Swanzey, N.H. (03446) 268/C6
East Syracuse, N.Y. (13057) 276/H4
East Tawas, Mich. (48730) 250/F4
East Templeton, Mass. (01438) 249/G2
East Thermopolis, Wyo. (†82443) 319/D2
East Thetford, Vt. (05043) 268/C4
East Thompson, Conn. (†06255) 210/H1
East Tintic (creek), Utah 304/B4
East Tohopekaliga (lake), Fla. 212/E3
East Troy, Wis. (53120) 317/J2
East Union, Maine (†04862) 243/E7
Eastvale, Pa. (†15010) 294/B4
Eastvale, Texas (†75067) 303/G1
East Vassalboro, Maine (04935) 243/D7
East Verde (riv.), Ariz. 198/D4
Eastview, Tenn. (†38367) 237/D10
East View, W. Va. (†26301) 312/F4
East Village, Conn. (†06468) 210/C3
Eastville, Georgia (†30677) 217/E3
Eastville, Va. (23347) 307/R6
East Wakefield, N.H. (03830) 268/E4
East Walker (riv.), Nev. 266/B4
East Wallingford, Vt. (05742) 268/B5
East Walpole, Mass. (02032) 249/C8
East Wareham, Mass. (02538) 249/M5
East Washington, Pa. (†15301) 294/B5
East Waterboro, Maine (04030) 243/B8
East Waterford, Pa. (17021) 294/G5
East Wenatchee, Wash. (98801) 310/E3
East Weymouth, Mass. (†02189) 249/E8
East Whately, Mass. (†01373) 249/D3
East Williamson, N.Y. (14449) 276/F4
East Willington, Conn. (†06279) 210/G1
East Wilton, Maine (04234) 243/C6
East Windsor○, Conn. (†06088) 210/E1
East Windsor Hill, Conn. (06028) 210/E1
East Winn, Maine (†04495) 243/G5
East Wolfeboro, N.H. (†03894) 268/E4
Eastwood, Mich. (†49001) 250/D6
Eastwood, N.S. Wales 88/K4
Eastwood, N.S. Wales 97/J3
Eastwood, Ontario 177/D4
East Woodstock, Conn. (06244) 210/H1
East Worcester, N.Y. (12064) 276/L5
East York, Ontario 177/J4
Eaton, Colo. (80615) 208/K1
Eaton, Ill. (†62454) 222/F4
Eaton, Ind. (47338) 227/G4
Eaton, Maine (†04424) 243/H4
Eaton (co.), Mich. 250/E6
Eaton (Eaton Center)○, N.H. (03832) 268/E4
Eaton, N.Y. (13334) 276/J5
Eaton, Ohio (45320) 284/A6
Eaton, Tenn. (38331) 237/C9
Eaton Center, N.H. (03832) 268/E4
Eaton Estates, Ohio (†44035) 284/G3
Eatonia, Sask. 181/B4
Eaton Rapids, Mich. (48827) 250/E6
Eatonton, Georgia (31024) 217/F4
Eatontown, N.J. (07724) 273/E3
Eatonville, Fla. (32751) 212/E3
Eatonville, Wash. (98328) 310/C4
Eau Claire, Mich. (49111) 250/C6
Eau Claire, Pa. (16030) 294/C3
Eau Claire, Lac à l' (lake), Que. 162/J4
Eau Claire (lake), Québec 174/C1
Eau Claire, Wis. 188/H2
Eau Claire (co.), Wis. 317/D6
Eau Claire, Wis. (54701) 317/D6
Eau Claire (riv.), Wis. 317/D6
Eau Galle, Wis. (54737) 317/B6
Eauripik (atoll), Micronesia 87/E5
Ebal (mt.), Jordan 65/C3
Ebano, Mexico 150/K5
Ebb, Fla. (†32331) 212/C1
Ebb and Flow (lake), Manitoba 179/C3
Ebbw Vale, Wales 13/B6
Ebbw Vale, Wales 10/E5
Ebeltoft, Denmark 21/D5
Ebeltoft, Denmark 18/G8
Ebenezer, Miss. (39064) 256/D5
Ebenezer, Sask. 181/J4
Ebenfurth, Austria 41/D3
Eben Junction, Mich. (49825) 250/B2
Ebensburg, Pa. (15931) 294/E5
Ebensee, Austria 41/B3
Eberbach, W. Germany 22/C4
Ebersbach, E. Germany 22/F3
Eberswalde-Finow, E. Germany 22/E2
Ebetsu, Japan 81/K2
Ebingen, W. Germany 22/C4
Ebinur Hu (lake), China 77/B2
Ebnat-Kappel, Switzerland 39/H2
Eboli, Italy 34/E4
Ebolowa, Cameroon 102/D4
Ebolowa, Cameroon 115/B3
Ebon (atoll), Marshall Is. 87/G5
Ebony, Va. (23845) 307/N7
Ebor, Manitoba 179/A5
Ebrach, W. Germany 22/D4
Ebrié (lag.), Ivory Coast 106/D8
Ebro, Fla. (32437) 212/C6
Ebro, Minn. (†56621) 255/C3
Ebro (riv.), Spain 7/D4
Ebro (riv.), Spain 33/G2
Ecatepec de Morelos, Mexico 150/L1
Ecaussinnes, Belgium 27/E7
Ecclefechan, Scotland 15/E5
Eccles, W. Va. (25836) 312/D7
Ecclesville, Trin. & Tob. 161/B11
Eceabat, Turkey 63/B6
Echallens, Switzerland 39/C3
Echarate, Peru 128/F9
Echeconnee, Georgia (†31008) 217/E5
Echmiadzin, U.S.S.R. 52/F6
Echo, Ala. (†36360) 195/G8
Echo (cliffs), Ariz. 198/D2
Echo, La. (71330) 238/F4
Echo, Minn. (56237) 255/C6
Echo (lake), N.J. 273/E1
Echo, Oreg. (97826) 291/H2
Echo (lake), Tasmania 99/C4
Echo, Utah (84024) 304/C3
Echo (res.), Utah 304/C3
Echo (lake), Vt. 268/D2
Echo Bay, Ontario 177/J5
Echo Bay, Ontario 175/D3
Echola, Ala. (35457) 195/C4
Echo Lake, N.J. (†07435) 273/E1
Echo Lake, Nova Scotia 168/E4
Echols (co.), Georgia 217/G9
Echols, Ky. (42340) 237/H6
Echo Valley Prov. Park, Sask. 181/G5
Echt, Netherlands 27/H6
Echternach, Luxembourg 27/J9
Echuca, Victoria 97/C5
Echuca, Victoria 88/G7
Écija, Spain 33/D4
Eck, Loch (lake), Scotland 15/A1
Eckelson, N. Dak. (58432) 282/O6
Eckerman, Mich. (49728) 250/E2
Eckernförde, W. Germany 22/D1
Eckerty, Ind. (47116) 227/D8
Eckhart Mines, Md. (21528) 245/C2
Eckley, Colo. (80727) 208/P2
Eckman, N. Dak. (†58760) 282/H2
Eckman, W. Va. (24829) 312/C8
Eckville, Alberta 182/C3
Eclectic, Ala. (36024) 195/F5
Eclipse (harb.), Newf. 166/B2
Eclipse (sound), N.W. Terrs. 187/L2
Economy, Ind. (47339) 227/G5
Economy, Nova Scotia 168/D3
Economy, Pa. (†15005) 294/B4
Écorce (lake), Québec 172/A2
Écorces (riv.), Québec 172/F1
Ecorse, Mich. (48229) 250/B7
Écrins, Les (mt.), France 28/G5
Ecru, Miss. (38841) 256/F2
Ector (co.), Texas 303/B6
Ecuador 2/D6
Ecuador 120/B3
ECUADOR 128
Ecublens, Switzerland 39/B3
Ecum Secum, Nova Scotia 168/F3
Ecum Secum Bridge, Nova Scotia 168/F4
Edam, Sask. 181/C2
Edam-Volendam, Netherlands 27/G4
Eday (isl.), Scotland 10/E1
Eday (isl.), Scotland 15/F1
Edberg, Alberta 182/D3
Edcouch, Texas (78538) 303/G11
Edd, Ethiopia 111/H5
Edd, Ethiopia 59/D7
Ed Da'ein, Sudan 111/E5
Ed Damazin, Sudan 111/F5
Ed Damer, Sudan 111/F4
Ed Damer, Sudan 59/B6
Ed Damer, Sudan 102/F3
Ed Debba, Sudan 111/F4
Ed Debba, Sudan 59/B6
Edderton, Scotland 15/D3
Eddiceton, Miss. (39634) 256/C8
Eddington, Maine (†04428) 243/F6
Eddington○, Maine (†04428) 243/F6
Eddington, Pa. (19020) 294/N5
Eddleston, Scotland 15/E5
Eddontenajon, Br. Col. 184/K2
Eddrachillis (bay), Scotland 15/C2
Ed Dueim, Sudan 59/B7
Ed Dueim, Sudan 111/F5
Ed Dueim, Sudan 102/F3
Eddy (co.), N. Mex. 274/E6
Eddy (co.), N. Dak. 282/N4
Eddy, Texas (76524) 303/G6
Eddystone (rocks), England 13/C7
Eddystone (rocks), England 10/D5
Eddystone, Manitoba 179/C3
Eddystone, Pa. (†19013) 294/M7
Eddystone (pt.), Tasmania 88/H8
Eddystone (pt.), Tasmania 99/E2
Eddyville, Ill. (62928) 222/E6
Eddyville, Iowa (52553) 229/H6
Eddyville, Ky. (42038) 237/E6
Eddyville, Nebr. (68834) 264/E3
Eddyville, Oreg. (97343) 291/D3
Ede, Netherlands 27/H4
Ede, Nigeria 106/E7
Edéa, Cameroon 115/B3
Edelény, Hungary 41/F2
Edelstein, Ill. (61526) 222/D3
Eden, Ariz. (85535) 198/F6
Edén, Ecuador 128/E3
Eden (riv.), England 13/E3
Eden (riv.), England 10/E3
Eden, Georgia (31307) 217/K6
Eden, Idaho (83325) 220/D7
Eden, Ind. (†46140) 227/F5
Eden, Manitoba 179/C4
Eden, Md. (21822) 245/R7
Eden, Miss. (39065) 256/D5
Eden, Mont. (†59401) 262/E3
Eden, N.S. Wales 97/E5
Eden, N.Y. (14057) 276/C5
Eden, N.C. (27288) 281/K1
Eden (riv.), Scotland 15/F4
Eden, S. Dak. (57232) 298/P2
Eden, Texas (76837) 303/E6
Eden, Utah (84310) 304/C2
Eden○, Vt. (05652) 268/B2
Eden, Wis. (53019) 317/K8
Eden, Wyo. (82926) 319/C3
Edenburg, Sask. 181/E3
Edenburg, S. Africa 118/D5
Edendale, S. Africa 118/D5
Edenderry, Ireland 10/C4
Edenderry, Ireland 17/G5
Edenhope, Victoria 97/A5
Eden Mills, Ontario 177/D4
Eden Mills, Vt. (05653) 268/C2
Eden Prairie, Minn. (55344) 255/G6
Edenton, N.C. (27932) 281/R2
Edenton, Ohio (†45122) 284/C7
Edenvale, S. Africa 118/H6
Eden Valley, Minn. (55329) 255/D5
Eden Valley (res.), Wyo. 319/C3
Edenville, Mich. (48620) 250/E5
Edenwold, Sask. 181/G5
Eder (res.), W. Germany 22/C3
Eder (riv.), W. Germany 22/C3
Ederney and Kesh, N. Ireland 17/F2
Edgar (co.), Ill. 222/F4
Edgar, Mont. (59026) 262/H5
Edgar, Nebr. (68935) 264/F4
Edgar, Wis. (54426) 317/G6
Edgard, La. (70049) 238/M3
Edgar Springs, Mo. (65462) 261/J7
Edgarton, W. Va. (25672) 312/B7
Edgartown, Mass. (02539) 249/M7
Edgartown○, Mass. (02539) 249/M7
Edge (isl.), Norway 4/B8
Edgecliff, Texas (†76101) 303/E2
Edgecomb○, Maine (†04556) 243/D8
Edgecombe (co.), N.C. 281/O3
Edgecumbe (cape), Alaska 196/L1
Edgecumbe, N. Zealand 100/F2
Edgefield, La. (†71019) 238/D2
Edgefield (co.), S.C. 296/D4
Edgefield, S.C. (29824) 296/C4
Edge Hill, Georgia (†30810) 217/G4
Edgehill, Va. (†22485) 307/O4
Edgeley, N. Dak. (58433) 282/N7
Edgeley, Sask. 181/H5
Edgell (isl.), N.W. Terrs. 187/M3
Edgemere, Idaho (†83856) 220/B1
Edgemere, Md. (†21219) 245/N4
Edgemont, Ark. (72044) 202/F2
Edgemont, S. Dak. (57735) 298/B7
Edgemoor, Del. (†19801) 245/S1
Edgemoor, S.C. (29712) 296/E2
Edgemount, N.C. (28645) 281/F2
Edgeøya (isl.), Norway 18/D2
Edgerly, La. (†70668) 238/C6
Edgerton, Alberta 182/E3
Edgerton, Ind. (†46797) 227/H2
Edgerton, Kansas (66021) 232/H3
Edgerton, Minn. (56128) 255/B7
Edgerton, Mo. (64444) 261/C3
Edgerton, Ohio (43517) 284/A3
Edgerton, Va. (†23868) 307/N7
Edgerton, Wis. (53534) 317/H10
Edgerton, Wyo. (82635) 319/F2
Edgewater, Br. Col. 184/J5
Edgewater, Colo. (80214) 208/J3
Edgewater, Fla. (32032) 212/F3
Edgewater, N.J. (07020) 273/C2
Edgewater, Wis. (54834) 317/D4
Edgewater Park○, N.J. (†08010) 273/D3
Edgewood, Br. Col. 184/H5
Edgewood, Calif. (96094) 204/C2
Edgewood, Fla. (†32801) 212/E3
Edgewood, Ill. (62426) 222/E5
Edgewood, Ind. (†46011) 227/F4
Edgewood, Iowa (52042) 229/K3
Edgewood, Ky. (†41017) 237/S2
Edgewood, Md. (21040) 245/N3
Edgewood, N. Mex. (87015) 274/C3
Edgewood, Ohio (†44004) 284/J2
Edgewood, Pa. (†15218) 294/B7
Edgeworth, Pa. (†15143) 294/B4
Edgington, Ill. (†61284) 222/C2
Édhessa, Greece 45/F5
Edievale, N. Zealand 100/B6
Edina, Minn. (55424) 255/G5
Edina, Mo. (63537) 261/H2
Edinboro, Pa. (16412) 294/B2
Edinburg, Ill. (62531) 222/D4
Edinburg, Miss. (†39051) 256/F5
Edinburg, Mo. (†64683) 261/E2
Edinburg, N. Dak. (58227) 282/P3
Edinburg, Pa. (16116) 294/B3
Edinburg, Texas (78539) 303/F11
Edinburg, Va. (22824) 307/M3
Edinburgh, Ind. (46124) 227/E6
Edinburgh (cap.), Scotland 7/D3
Edinburgh (cap.), Scotland 15/D1
Edinburgh (cap.), Scotland 10/C1
Edingen (Enghien), Belgium 27/D7
Edirne (prov.), Turkey 63/B2
Edirne, Turkey 7/G4
Edirne, Turkey 63/B2
Edirne, Turkey 59/A1
Edison, Calif. (93220) 204/G8
Edison (lake), Calif. 204/F6
Edison, Georgia (31746) 217/C7
Edison, Nebr. (68936) 264/E4
Edison○, N.J. (*08817) 273/E2
Edison, Ohio (43320) 284/E4
Edison, Wash. (98246) 310/C2
Edison Nat'l Hist. Site, N.J. 273/A2
Edisto (isl.), S.C. 296/G6
Edisto (riv.), S.C. 296/G7
Edisto Beach, S.C. (†29438) 296/G7
Edisto Island, S.C. (29438) 296/G6
Edith, Georgia (†31631) 217/G9
Edithburgh, S. Australia 94/E6
Ediz Hook (pen.), Wash. 310/B2
Edjeleh, Algeria 106/F3
Edmeston, N.Y. (13335) 276/K5
Edmond, Kansas (67636) 232/C2
Edmond, Okla. (73034) 288/M3
Edmonds, Wash. (98020) 310/C3
Edmondson, Ark. (72332) 202/K3
Edmondt, Fr. Guiana 131/E3
Edmonson (co.), Ky. 237/J6
Edmonson, Texas (79032) 303/C3
Edmonston, Md. (†20781) 245/F4
Edmonton (cap.), Alberta 182/D3
Edmonton, Alta. 146/G4
Edmonton (cap.), Alta. 162/E5
Edmonton, Canada 2/D3
Edmonton, Ky. (42129) 237/K7
Edmonton Beach, Alberta 182/C3
Edmore, Mich. (48829) 250/E5
Edmore, N. Dak. (58330) 282/O3
Edmund, Sask. 181/H4
Edmund, Wis. (†53533) 317/F9
Edmunds, Maine (†04628) 243/J6
Edmunds, N. Dak. (†58746) 282/M5
Edmunds (co.), S. Dak. 298/L3
Edmundson, Mo. (†63101) 261/O2
Edmundston, N. Br. 162/K6
Edmundston, New Bruns. 170/B1
Edna, Ala. (†36922) 195/B6
Edna, Iowa (†51246) 229/A2
Edna, Kansas (67342) 232/G4
Edna, Texas (77957) 303/H9
Edna Bay, Alaska (†99901) 196/M2
Edo (riv.), Japan 81/P2
Edolo, Italy 34/C1
Edom, Texas (†75656) 303/J5
Edon, Ohio (43518) 284/A2
Édouard (lake), Québec 172/E2
Edrans, Manitoba 179/C4
Edray, W. Va. (†24954) 312/F6
Edremit, Turkey 63/B3
Edremit, Turkey 59/A2
Edremit (gulf), Turkey 63/B3
Edri, Libya 111/B2
Edsbyn, Sweden 18/J6
Edson, Alberta 182/B3
Edson, Alta. 162/E5
Edson, Kansas (67733) 232/A2
Eduardo Castex, Argentina 143/D4
Edwall, Wash. (99008) 310/H3
Edwand, Alberta 182/D2
Edward (lake) 102/E5
Edward, N.C. (27821) 281/R4
Edward (lake), Uganda 115/E4
Edward (lake), Zaire 115/E4
Edward MacDowell (res.), N.H. 268/D6
Edwards, Colo. (81632) 208/F3
Edwards (co.), Ill. 222/E5
Edwards, Ill. (61528) 222/D3
Edwards (riv.), Ill. 222/C2
Edwards (co.), Kansas 232/C4
Edwards (lake), La. 238/C2
Edwards, Miss. (39066) 256/C6
Edwards, Mo. (65326) 261/F6
Edwards, N.Y. (13635) 276/K2
Edwards (co.), Texas 303/D7
Edwards (plat.), Texas 303/C7
Edwards A.F.B., Calif. 204/H9
Edwardsburg, Mich. (49112) 250/C7
Edwardsport, Ind. (47528) 227/C7
Edwardsville, Ala. (36261) 195/H3
Edwardsville, Ill. (62025) 222/B2
Edwardsville, Ind. (†47150) 227/F8
Edwardsville, Kansas (66113) 232/H2
Edwardsville, Pa. (18704) 294/E7
Edward VII (pen.) 5/B11
Edward VIII (bay) 5/C4
Edwight, W. Va. (†25189) 312/C7
Edwin, Ala. (†36317) 195/H7
Edwin, Manitoba 179/D5
Edzell, Scotland 15/F4
Eefde, Netherlands 27/J4
Eek, Alaska (99578) 196/F2
Eeklo, Belgium 27/D6
Eel (riv.), Calif. 204/B4
Eel (riv.), Ind. 227/C6
Eel (riv.), Ind. 227/F3
Eel River Bridge, New Bruns. 170/F1
Eel River Crossing, New Bruns. 170/D1
Eems (riv.), Netherlands 27/K2
Eersterivier, S. Africa 118/F6
Efate (isl.), Vanuatu 87/G7
Eferding, Austria 41/B2
Effie, La. (71331) 238/F4
Effie, Minn. (56639) 255/E3
Effigy Mounds Nat'l Mon., Iowa 229/L2
Effingham (co.), Georgia 217/K6
Effingham (co.), Ill. 222/E4
Effingham, Ill. (62401) 222/E4
Effingham, Kansas (66023) 232/G2
Effingham, S.C. (29541) 296/H3
Effingham Falls, N.H. (†03814) 268/E4
Effort, Pa. (18330) 294/M4
Efland, N.C. (27243) 281/L2
Eflâni, Turkey 63/E2
Egadi (isls.), Italy 34/C6
Egan, Ill. (61026) 222/D1
Egan (range), Nev. 266/G4
Egan, S. Dak. (57024) 298/R6
Egaña, Uruguay 145/B4
Eganville, Ontario 177/G2
Egbert, Wyo. (†82053) 319/H4
Ege, Ind. (†46763) 227/G2
Egegik, Alaska (99579) 196/G3
Egeland, N. Dak. (58331) 282/M2
Eger, Hungary 41/F3
Egeria, W. Va. (†25902) 312/D7
Egernsund, Denmark 21/C8
Egerton (mt.), W. Australia 92/B4
Egg (isl.), Manitoba 179/E3
Egg (creek), N. Dak. 282/H3
Egg, Switzerland 39/G2
Eggenburg, Austria 41/C2
Eggertsville, N.Y. (†14226) 276/C5
Egg Harbor, Wis. (54209) 317/M5
Egg Harbor City, N.J. (08215) 273/D4
Egg Island (pt.), N.J. 273/C5
Eggiwil, Switzerland 39/E3
Egg Lagoon, Tasmania 99/A1
Eggleston, Va. (24086) 307/G6
Egham, England 13/G8
Egham, England 10/B5
Éghezée, Belgium 27/F7
Egilsay (isl.), Scotland 15/F1
Eglin A.F.B., Fla. 212/C6
Eglington (isl.), N.W.T. 162/L3
Eglinton (cape), N.W. Terrs. 187/M2
Eglinton (isl.), N.W. Terrs. 187/F2
Eglisau, Switzerland 39/G1
Eglon, W. Va. (26716) 312/G4
Egmond aan Zee, Netherlands 27/E3
Egmondville, Ontario 177/C4
Egmont (key), Fla. 212/D4
Egmont (cape), N. Zealand 100/D3
Egmont (mt.), N. Zealand 100/D3
Egmont (cape), Nova Scotia 168/H2
Egmont (bay), Pr. Edward I. 168/D2
Egmont (cape), Pr. Edward I. 168/D2
Egnach, Switzerland 39/H1
Egnar, Colo. (81325) 208/B7
Egremont, Alberta 182/D2
Egremont, England 13/D3
Eğridir, Turkey 63/D4
Eğridir (lake), Turkey 59/B2
Eğridir (lake), Turkey 63/D4
Egtved, Denmark 21/C6
Egvekinot, U.S.S.R. 48/S3
Egyek, Hungary 41/F3
Egypt 2/L4
Egypt 102/E2
EGYPT 111/E2
EGYPT 59/A4
Egypt, Georgia (†31329) 217/K6
Egypt, Miss. (†38860) 256/G3
Egypt Lake, Fla. (†33614) 212/C2
Eha Amufu, Nigeria 106/F7
Ehime (pref.), Japan 81/F7
Ehingen, W. Germany 22/C4
Ehrenberg (range), North. Terr. 93/B7
Ehrenburg, Ariz. (85334) 198/A5
Ehrenfeld, Pa. (†15956) 294/E5
Ehrhardt, S.C. (29081) 296/E5
Ehrwald, Austria 41/A3
Eiao (isl.), Fr. Poly. 87/M6
Eibar, Spain 33/E1
Eichstätt, W. Germany 22/D4
Eider (riv.), W. Germany 22/C1
Eidfjord, Norway 18/E6
Eidsfoss, Norway 18/C4
Eidson, Tenn. (37731) 237/P7
Eidsvold, Queensland 95/D5
Eidsvoll, Norway 18/G6
Eielson A.F.B., Alaska 196/J2
Eigenbrakel (Braine-l'Alleud), Belgium 27/E7
Eigersund, Norway 18/D7
Eigg (mt.), Nova Scotia 168/F3
Eigg (isl.), Scotland 15/B4
Eigg (isl.), Scotland 10/C2
Eigg (sound), Scotland 15/B4
Eight Degree (chan.), India 68/C7
Eighteen Mile (peak), Idaho 220/E5
Eight Mile (brook), Conn. 210/C3
Eight Mile (riv.), Conn. 210/F3
Eights Coast (reg.) 5/B14
Eighty Eight, Ky. (42130) 237/K7
Eighty Mile (beach), W. Australia 88/C3
Eighty Mile (beach), W. Australia 92/C2
Eijerlandsche Gat (str.), Netherlands 27/F2
Eil, Loch (lake), Scotland 15/C4
Eil, Somalia 115/J2
Eildon, Victoria 97/C5
Eildon (lake), Victoria 97/C5
Eileen, Ill. (†60416) 222/E2
Eileen (lake), N.W.T. 162/F3
Eilenburg, E. Germany 22/E3
Eilerts de Haan (mts.), Suriname 131/C4
Eina, Norway 18/G6
Einbeck, W. Germany 22/C3
Eindhoven, Netherlands 27/G6
'Ein Gedi, Israel 65/C5
'Ein Harod, Israel 65/C2
'Ein Netafim (well), Israel 65/D5
Einsiedeln, Switzerland 39/G2
Eirunepé, Brazil 132/G10
Eirunepé, Brazil 120/B3
Eisenach, E. Germany 22/D3
Eisenberg, E. Germany 22/D3
Eisenerz, Austria 41/C3
Eisenhower (mt.), Alberta 182/C4
Eisenhüttenstadt, E. Germany 22/F2
Eisenkappel-Vellach, Austria 41/C3
Eisenstadt, Austria 41/D3
Eiserfeld, W. Germany 22/C3
Eishort, Loch (inlet), Scotland 15/B3
Eisleben, E. Germany 22/D3
Eisling (mts.), Luxembourg 27/H9
Eitzen, Minn. (55931) 255/G7
Ejby, Denmark 21/C7
Ejea de los Caballeros, Spain 33/F1
Ejido, Venezuela 124/C3
Ejin, China 77/F3
Ejin Horo, China 77/G4
Ejutla de Crespo, Mexico 150/L8
Ekalaka, Mont. (59324) 262/M5
Ekenäs, Finland 18/N6
Ekeren, Belgium 27/E6
Eketahuna, N. Zealand 100/E4
Ekibastuz, U.S.S.R. 48/H4
Ekibin, Queensland 88/K3
Ekimchan, U.S.S.R. 48/O4
Ekin, Ind. (†46072) 227/E4
Ekonk, Conn. (†06384) 210/H2
Ekron, Ky. (40117) 237/J5
Eksjö, Sweden 18/J8
Ekuk, Alaska (†99569) 196/G3
Ekwan (riv.), Ont. 162/H5
Ekwan (riv.), Ontario 175/C2
Ekwok, Alaska (99580) 196/G3
El Aaiún (Laayoune), Morocco 102/A2
El Aaiún (Laayoune), Western Sahara 106/B3
El Abbasiya, Sudan 111/F5
El Abiar, Libya 111/D1
El Abiod Sidi Cheikh, Algeria 106/E2
El Agheila, Libya 111/C1
Elaine, Ark. (72333) 202/J5
El 'Al, Jordan 65/D4
El 'Alamein, Egypt 111/E1
El 'Alamein, Egypt 59/A3
El Almacén, Venezuela 124/G4
El Amparo de Apure, Venezuela 124/C4
Elams, N.C. (†23919) 281/O1
Elamton, Ky. (41420) 237/P5
Elamville, Ala. (†36311) 195/G7
Eland, Wis. (54427) 317/H6
El Ángel, Ecuador 128/C2
El Arahal, Spain 33/D4
El 'Arish, Egypt 59/B3
El 'Arish, Egypt 111/F1
El Asiento, Bolivia 136/B6
El Asnam, Algeria 106/E1
El Asnam, Algeria 102/C1
Elassón, Greece 45/F6
Elat, Israel 65/D6
Elath (Elat), Israel 65/D6
Elath, Israel 59/B4
El Athale (Itala), Somalia 115/J3
Elato (atoll), Micronesia 87/E5
El 'Atrun (oasis), Sudan 111/E4
El 'Auja, Israel 65/D5
Elâzığ (prov.), Turkey 63/H3
Elâzığ, Turkey 59/C2
Elâzığ, Turkey 63/H3
El Azizia, Libya 111/B1
El Azúcar (res.), Mexico 150/K3
Elba, Ala. (36323) 195/F8
Elba, Idaho (83326) 220/E7
Elba (isl.), Italy 7/E4
Elba (isl.), Italy 34/C3
Elba, Minn. (†55910) 255/F6
Elba, Nebr. (68835) 264/F3
Elba, N.Y. (14058) 276/D4
Elba, Ohio (45728) 284/H6
El Bab, Syria 63/G4
El Balqa (dist.), Jordan 65/D4
El Banco, Colombia 126/D3
El Barco, Spain 33/C1
El Barco de Ávila, Spain 33/D2
El Bardi, Libya 111/D1
El Barkat, Libya 111/B3
Elbasan, Albania 45/E5
El Baúl, Venezuela 124/D3
El Bawiti, Egypt 111/E2
El Bawiti, Egypt 102/E2
El Bawiti, Egypt 59/A4
El Bayadh, Algeria 106/E2
El Bayadh, Algeria 102/C1
Elbe (riv.) 7/F3
Elbe (riv.), E. Germany 22/D2
Elbe, Wash. (98330) 310/C4
Elbe (riv.), W. Germany 22/C2
El Beida, Yemen Arab Rep. 59/E7
El Beni (dept.), Bolivia 136/C3
Elberfeld, Ind. (47613) 227/C8
Elberon, Iowa (52225) 229/J4
Elberon, N.J. (07740) 273/F3
Elberon, Va. (23846) 307/P6
Elbert (mt.), Colo. 188/E3
Elbert (co.), Colo. 208/L4
Elbert, Colo. (80106) 208/L4
Elbert (mt.), Colo. 208/G4
Elbert (co.), Georgia 217/G2
Elbert, Texas (76359) 303/E4
Elbert, W. Va. (24830) 312/C8
Elberta, Ala. (36530) 195/C10
Elberta, Georgia (†31093) 217/E5
Elberta, Mich. (49628) 250/C4
Elberta, Utah (84626) 304/B4
Elberton, Georgia (30635) 217/G2
Elberton, Wash. (†99130) 310/H4
Elbeuf, France 28/D3
Elbing, Kansas (67041) 232/E3
Elbing (Elblag), Poland 47/D1
El Bira, West Bank 65/C4
Elbistan, Turkey 63/G3
Elbląg (prov.), Poland 47/D1
Elblag, Poland 47/D1
Elblag, Poland 7/F3
El Bolsón, Argentina 143/B5
Elbon, Pa. (†15823) 294/E3
El Bonillo, Spain 33/E3
El Boquerón (pass), Peru 128/E7
El Borma, Tunisia 106/F2
Elbow (riv.), Alberta 182/C4
Elbow (lake), Manitoba 179/G4
Elbow (lake), Minn. 255/C3
Elbow, Sask. 181/E4
Elbow Lake, Minn. (56531) 255/B5
Elbridge, N.Y. (13060) 276/G5
Elbridge, Tenn. (38227) 237/C8
El'brus (mt.), U.S.S.R. 48/E5
El'brus (mt.), U.S.S.R. 52/F6
El Buheyrat (prov.), Sudan 111/E6
El Bur, Somalia 115/J3
Elburg, Netherlands 27/H4
El Burgo de Osma, Spain 33/E2
Elburn, Ill. (60119) 222/E2
Elburz (mts.), Iran 59/F2
Elburz (mts.), Iran 66/G2
El Cajon, Calif. (*92020) 204/J11
El Callao, Venezuela 124/G4
El Calvario, Venezuela 124/E3
El Campo, Texas (77437) 303/H8
El Caney, Cuba 158/J4
El Carmen, El Beni, Bolivia 136/D3
El Carmen, Santa Cruz, Bolivia 136/F6
El Carmen, Ñuble, Chile 138/A11
El Carmen, O'Higgins, Chile 138/F5
El Carmen, Chocó, Colombia 126/B5
El Carmen, Nariño, Colombia 126/A6
El Carmen, Norte de Santander, Colombia 126/D3
El Carmen de Bolívar, Colombia 126/C3
El Carre, Ethiopia 111/H6
El Centro, Calif. 188/C4
El Centro, Calif. (92243) 204/K11
El Centro, Colombia 126/D4
El Cercado, Dom. Rep. 158/D6
El Cerrito, Calif. (94530) 204/J2
El Cerrito, Colombia 126/B6
El Cerro, Bolivia 136/E5
El Chaparro, Venezuela 124/F3
Elche, Spain 33/F3
Elche de la Sierra, Spain 33/E3
Elcho (isl.), North. Terr. 93/D1
Elcho, Wis. (54428) 317/H5
El Chocón (res.), Argentina 143/C4
Elcho Island Mission, North. Terr. 93/D1
El Choro, Bolivia 136/B6
El Chorro, Argentina 143/D1
Elco, Ill. (62929) 222/D6
El Cobre, Chile 138/A4
El Cobre, Cuba 158/J4
El Cocuy, Colombia 126/D4
El Convento, Chile 138/F4
El Corazón, Ecuador 128/C3
El Cristo, Venezuela 124/G4
El Cuey, Dom. Rep. 158/F6
El Cuy, Argentina 143/C4
Elda, Spain 33/F3
El Dara, Ill. (†62312) 222/B4

Elvira 365

Elde (riv.), E. Germany 22/D2
Elden (mt.), Ariz. 198/D3
El Der, Ethiopia 111/H6
Elderbank, Nova Scotia 168/E4
El Dere, Somalia 115/J3
El Dere, Somalia 102/G4
Elderon, Wis. (54429) 317/H6
Eldersburg, Md. (†21784) 245/L3
Eldersley, Sask. 181/H3
Eldersile, Scotland 15/B2
Eldersville, Pa. (15036) 294/A5
Elderton, Pa. (15736) 294/D4
El Diente (peak), Colo. 208/C7
El'dikan, U.S.S.R. 48/O3
Eldivan, Turkey 63/E2
El Diviso, Colombia 126/A7
El Djem, Tunisia 106/G1
El Djezair (Algiers) (cap.), Algeria 106/E1
El Djouf (des.) 102/B2
Eldon, Iowa (52554) 229/J7
Eldon, Mo. (65026) 261/G6
Eldon, Wash. (†98555) 310/B3
Eldora, Colo. (†80466) 208/H3
Eldora, Iowa (50627) 229/G4
Eldora, N.J. (†08270) 273/D5
Eldorado, Argentina 143/F2
El Dorado, Ark. 188/H4
El Dorado, Ark. (71730) 202/E7
Eldorado, Brazil 135/B4
El Dorado (co.), Calif. 204/E5
El Dorado, Calif. (95623) 204/C8
Eldorado (Fender), Georgia (†31794) 217/E8
Eldorado, Ill. (62930) 222/E6
Eldorado, Iowa (52175) 229/K2
El Dorado, Kansas (67042) 232/F4
Eldorado, Md. (†21659) 245/P6
Eldorado, Mexico 150/E4
Eldorado, Miss. (†39156) 256/C5
Eldorado, N.C. (†27371) 281/K4
Eldorado, Ohio (45321) 284/A6
Eldorado, Okla. (73537) 288/G6
Eldorado, Sask. 181/L2
Eldorado, Texas (76936) 303/D7
El Dorado, Venezuela 124/H4
Eldorado, Wis. (54932) 317/J8
El Dorado Hills, Calif. (95630) 204/C8
El Dorado Springs, Mo. (64744) 261/E7
Eldorendo, Georgia (†31737) 217/C8
Eldoret, Kenya 102/F4
Eldoret, Kenya 115/G3
Eldred, Ill. (62027) 222/C4
Eldred, Minn. (56532) 255/B3
Eldred, Pa. (16731) 294/F2
Eldridge, Ala. (35554) 195/C3
Eldridge, Iowa (52748) 229/M5
Eldridge, Mo. (65463) 261/G7
Eldridge, N. Dak. (58435) 282/N6
El Dulce Nombre, Honduras 154/E3
Eleanor, W. Va. (25070) 312/C5
Electra, Texas (76360) 303/F4
Electric (peak), Mont. 262/F6
Electric City, Wash. (99123) 310/F3
Electric Mills, Miss. (39329) 256/G5
Electron, Wash. (†98360) 310/C4
Eleele, Hawaii (96705) 218/C2
Elefantes (gulf), Chile 138/D6
Elek, Hungary 41/F3
Elektrostal', U.S.S.R. 7/H3
Elektrostal', U.S.S.R. 52/E3
El Empedrado, Venezuela 124/C3
Elena, Bulgaria 45/G4
Elephant (isl.) 5/D16
Elephant (riv.), Namibia 118/B5
Elephant (mt.), Texas 303/D12
Elephanta (isl.), India 68/B7
Elephant Butte, N. Mex. (87935) 274/B5
Elephant Butte (res.), N. Mex. 188/E4
Elephant Butte (res.), N. Mex. 274/B5
Eleroy, Ill. (61027) 222/D1
Eleşkirt, Turkey 63/K3
El Espinar, Spain 33/D2
El Estor, Guatemala 154/C3
Eleuthera (isl.), Bahamas 146/L7
Eleuthera (isl.), Bahamas 156/C1
Eleva, Wis. (54738) 317/D6
Eleven Mile Canyon (res.), Colo. 208/H5
Elevtheroúpolis, Greece 45/G5
El Faiyûm, Egypt 111/J3
El Faiyûm, Egypt 59/B4
El Faiyûm, Egypt 102/E2
El Fasher, Sudan 111/E5
El Fasher, Sudan 102/E3
El Fashn, Egypt 111/J4
El Ferrol, Spain 7/D4
Elfers, Fla. (33531) 212/D3
El Fifi, Sudan 111/D5
Elfin Cove, Alaska (99825) 196/M1
El Fogaha, Libya 111/C2
Elfrida, Ariz. (†85617) 198/F7
Elfros, Sask. 181/H4
El Fuerte, Mexico 150/E3
El Furat (riv.), Syria 63/H4
El Gallo, Nicaragua 154/E4
El Gatrun, Libya 111/B3
El Gatrun, Libya 102/D2
El Geneina, Sudan 111/D5
El Geneina, Sudan 102/E3
El Geteina, Sudan 111/F5
El Geteina, Sudan 59/B7
El Gezira, Libya 111/D2
El Gezira (prov.), Sudan 111/F5
Elgg, Switzerland 39/G2
El Gheria esh Sherqia, Libya 111/B1
El Ghor (reg.), Jordan 65/C6
Elgin, Ariz. (†85637) 198/E7
Elgin, Ill. 188/J2
Elgin, Ill. (60120) 222/E1
Elgin, Iowa (52141) 229/K3
Elgin, Kansas (†67361) 232/F4
Elgin, Manitoba 179/B5
Elgin, Minn. (55932) 255/F6
Elgin, Nebr. (68636) 264/F3
Elgin, Nev. (†89009) 266/G5
Elgin, New Bruns. 170/E3
Elgin, N. Dak. (58533) 282/G7
Elgin, Ohio (45838) 284/A4
Elgin, Okla. (73538) 288/K5
Elgin (county), Ontario 177/C5
Elgin, Ontario 177/H3
Elgin, Oreg. (97827) 291/K2
Elgin, Pa. (16413) 294/C2
Elgin, Scotland 10/E2
Elgin, Scotland 15/E3
Elgin, S.C. (29045) 296/F3
Elgin, Tenn. (37732) 237/M8
Elgin, Texas (78621) 303/G7
El Golea, Algeria 102/C1
El Goléa, Algeria 106/E2
Elgon (mt.) 102/F4
Elgon (mt.), Kenya 115/F3
Elgon (mt.), Uganda 115/F3
Elgood, W. Va. (24723) 312/E8
El Granada, Calif. (94018) 204/H3
El Guapo, Venezuela 124/F2
El Guayabo, Dom. Rep. 158/E5
El Hamad (des.), Iraq 59/D3
El Hammam, Egypt 111/E1
El Hammam, Egypt 59/A3
El Hamurre, Somalia 115/J2
El Haseke, Syria 59/D2
El Haseke, Syria 63/J4
El Hilla, Sudan 111/E5
El Huecu, Argentina 143/B4
El Husn, Jordan 65/D3
Eli, Nebr. (69213) 264/C2
Elias, Ky. (40186) 237/O6
Elida, N. Mex. (88116) 274/F5
Elida, Ohio (45807) 284/B4
Elie, Manitoba 179/E5
Elie and Earlsferry, Scotland 15/F4
Elihu, Ky. (42530) 237/M6
Elijah, Mo. (†65626) 261/H9
Elila (riv.), Zaire 115/E4
Elim, Alaska (99739) 196/F2
Elimsport, Pa. (†17810) 294/H3
El Indio, Texas (78860) 303/D9
Eling, England 13/F7
Elin Pelin, Bulgaria 45/F4
Eliot○, Maine (03903) 243/B9
Eliot (mt.), Newf. 166/B2
Elisa, Argentina 143/F5
Eliska, Ala. (†36480) 195/C8
El Iskandariya (Alexandria), Egypt 59/A3
El Iskandariya (Alexandria), Egypt 111/J2
Elista, U.S.S.R. 7/J4
Elista, U.S.S.R. 48/E5
Elista, U.S.S.R. 52/F5
Elizabeth, Ark. (72531) 202/F1
Elizabeth, Colo. (80107) 208/K4
Elizabeth, Georgia (30060) 217/J1
Elizabeth, Ill. (61028) 222/C1
Elizabeth, Ind. (47117) 227/F8
Elizabeth, La. (70638) 238/E5
Elizabeth (cape), Maine 243/C8
Elizabeth (isls.), Mass. 249/L7
Elizabeth, Minn. (56533) 255/B4
Elizabeth, Miss. (38742) 256/C4
Elizabeth (mt.), New Bruns. 170/D1
Elizabeth, N.J. (*07201) 273/B2
Elizabeth, Pa. (15037) 294/C5
Elizabeth, S. Australia 88/E7
Elizabeth, S. Australia 94/B7
Elizabeth, W. Va. (26143) 312/D4
Elizabeth City, N.C. (27909) 281/S2
Elizabethton, Tenn. (37643) 237/S8
Elizabethtown, Ill. (62931) 222/E6
Elizabethtown, Ind. (47232) 227/F6
Elizabethtown, Ky. (42701) 237/K5
Elizabethtown, N.Y. (12932) 276/N2
Elizabethtown, N.C. (28337) 281/M5
Elizabethtown, Ohio (†45052) 284/A9
Elizabethtown, Pa. (17022) 294/J5
Elizabethville, Pa. (17023) 294/J4
Elizaville, Ind. (†46052) 227/E4
Elizaville, Ky. (41037) 237/O4
Elizondo, Spain 33/F1
El Jadida, Morocco 102/B1
El Jadida, Morocco 106/C2
El Jauf, Libya 102/B1
El Jauf, Libya 111/D3
El Jicaral, Nicaragua 154/D4
El Jícaro, Nicaragua 154/E4
Elk (riv.), Ala. 195/D1
Elk (riv.), Br. Col. 184/K5
Elk, Calif. (95432) 204/B4
Elk (riv.), Colo. 208/F1
Elk (co.), Kansas 232/F4
Elk (riv.), Kansas 232/F4
Elk (isl.), Manitoba 179/F4
Elk (riv.), Md. 245/P3
Elk (lake), Mich. 250/D4
Elk, N. Mex. (†88210) 274/D6
Elk (creek), Okla. 288/H4
Elk (creek), Oreg. 291/E5
Elk (co.), Pa. 294/E3
Ełk, Poland 47/F2
Elk (creek), S. Dak. 298/C5
Elk (riv.), Tenn. 237/H10
Elk (ridge), Utah 304/E6
Elk, Wash. (99009) 310/H2
Elk (riv.), W. Va. 312/D6
Elkader, Iowa (52043) 229/L3
El Kamlin, Sudan 59/B7
El Karak (dist.), Jordan 65/E5
El Karak, Jordan 59/C3
El Karak, Jordan 65/E4
El Karnak, Egypt 111/F2
El Karnak, Egypt 59/B4
Elkatawa, Ky. (41322) 237/P5
Elk City, Idaho (83525) 220/C4
Elk City, Kansas (67344) 232/G4
Elk City (lake), Kansas 232/F4
Elk City, Okla. (73644) 288/G4
Elk City, Oreg. (†97391) 291/D3
Elk Creek, Calif. (95939) 204/C4
Elk Creek, Ky. (†40071) 237/L4
Elk Creek, Mo. (65464) 261/H8
Elk Creek, Nebr. (68348) 264/H4
Elk Creek, Va. (24326) 307/F7
Elk Creek, Wis. (†54747) 317/C7
El Kef, Tunisia 106/F1
El Kelaa des Srarhna, Morocco 106/C2
Elk Falls, Kansas (67345) 232/F4
Elkford, Br. Col. 184/K5
Elkfork, Ky. (41421) 237/P5
Elk Garden, Va. (†24266) 307/E7
Elk Garden, W. Va. (26717) 312/H4
Elk Grove, Calif. (95624) 204/B9
Elk Grove Village, Ill. (60007) 222/B5
El Khalil (Hebron), West Bank 65/C4
El Khandaq, Sudan 59/B6
El Khandaq, Sudan 111/E4
El Khârga, Egypt 111/F2
El Khârga, Egypt 102/E2
El Khârga, Egypt 59/B4
Elkhart, Ill. (62634) 222/D3
Elkhart, Ind. 188/J2
Elkhart (co.), Ind. 227/F1
Elkhart, Ind. (46514) 227/F1
Elkhart (riv.), Ind. 227/F1
Elkhart, Iowa (50073) 229/F5
Elkhart, Kansas (67950) 232/A4
Elkhart, Texas (75839) 303/J6
Elkhart Lake, Wis. (53020) 317/L8
Elkhead, Mo. (65753) 261/G8
Elk Horn, Iowa (51531) 229/C5
Elkhorn, Manitoba 179/A5
Elkhorn, Nebr. (68022) 264/H3
Elkhorn (riv.), Nebr. 264/G3
Elkhorn, W. Va. (24831) 312/D8
Elkhorn, Wis. (53121) 317/J10
Elkhorn City, Ky. (41522) 237/S6
Elkhovo, Bulgaria 45/H4
Elkhurst, W. Va. (†25043) 312/D6
Elkin, N.C. (28621) 281/H2
Elkins, Ark. (72727) 202/C1
Elkins, N. Mex. (†88101) 274/E5
Elkins, W. Va. (26241) 312/G5
Elkinsville, Ind. (†47448) 227/E6
Elk Island Nat'l Park, Alberta 182/D3
Elk Island Nat'l Pk., Alta 162/E5
El Kitta, Jordan 65/D3
Elk Lake, Ontario 177/K5
Elk Lake, Ontario 175/D3
Elk Lakes Prov. Park, Br. Col. 184/K5
Elkland, Mo. (65644) 261/F8
Elkland, Pa. (16920) 294/H1
Elk Mills, Md. (21920) 245/P2
Elkmont, Ala. (35620) 195/E1
Elkmont, Tenn. (†37862) 237/O9
Elk Mound, Wis. (54739) 317/C6
Elk Mountain, Wyo. (82324) 319/F4
Elk Neck, Md. (†21901) 245/P2
Elko, Br. Col. 184/K5
Elko, Georgia (31025) 217/E6
Elko, Minn. (55020) 255/E6
Elko, Nev. 188/C2
Elko, Nev. 146/G6
Elko (co.), Nev. 266/F1
Elko, Nev. (89801) 266/F2
Elko, S.C. (29826) 296/E5
Elk Park, N.C. (28622) 281/E2
Elk Point, Alberta 182/E3
Elk Point, S. Dak. (57025) 298/R8
Elkport, Iowa (52044) 229/L3
Elk Rapids, Mich. (49629) 250/D4
Elkridge, Md. (†21227) 245/M4
Elkridge, W. Va. (†24868) 312/D6
Elk River, Idaho (83827) 220/B3
Elk River, Minn. (55330) 255/E5
Elk Run Heights, Iowa (†50700) 229/J4
Elk Springs, Colo. (81633) 208/C2
Elkton, Alberta 182/C4
Elkton, Fla. (32033) 212/E2
Elkton, Ky. (42220) 237/G7
Elkton, Md. (21921) 245/P2
Elkton, Mich. (48731) 250/F5
Elkton, Minn. (55933) 255/F7
Elkton, Mo. (†65650) 261/F7
Elkton, Oreg. (97436) 291/D4
Elkton, S. Dak. (57026) 298/S5
Elkton, Tenn. (38455) 237/H10
Elkton, Va. (22827) 307/L4
Elk Valley, Tenn. (†37848) 237/N7
Elkview, W. Va. (25071) 312/C6
Elkville, Ill. (62932) 222/D6
Elkwater, Alberta 182/E5
Elkwater, W. Va. (†26273) 312/G5
Ellabell, Georgia (31308) 217/K6
El Ladhiqiya (Latakia), Syria 59/C2
El Ladhiqiya (Latakia), Syria 63/F5
El Lago, Texas (†77586) 303/K2
Ellamar, Alaska (†99695) 196/D1
Ellamore, W. Va. (26267) 312/F5
Ellaville, Fla. (†32060) 212/C1
Ellaville, Georgia (31806) 217/D6
Ellef Ringnes (isl.), Canada 4/B15
Ellef Ringnes (isl.), N.W.T. 146/H2
Ellef Ringnes (isl.), N.W.T. 162/M3
Ellef Ringnes (isl.), N.W. Terrs. 187/H2
Ellen (mt.), Utah 304/D5
Ellen (mt.), Vt. 268/B3
Ellenboro, N.C. (28040) 281/F4
Ellenboro, W. Va. (26346) 312/D4
Ellenboro, Wis. (†53813) 317/E10
Ellenburg Center, N.Y. (12934) 276/N1
Ellenburg Depot, N.Y. (12935) 276/N1
Ellendale, Del. (19941) 245/S5
Ellendale, Minn. (56026) 255/E7
Ellendale, N. Dak. (58436) 282/N7
Ellendale, Tasmania 99/C4
Ellendale, Tenn. (38029) 237/B10
Ellendale, W. Australia 92/D2
Ellensburg, Wash. (98926) 310/E3
Ellenton, Georgia (31747) 217/E8
Ellenville, N.Y. (12428) 276/M7
Ellenwood, Georgia (30049) 217/L2
Ellerbe, N.C. (28338) 281/K4
Ellershouse, Nova Scotia 168/D4
Ellerslie, Georgia (31807) 217/C5
Ellerslie, Md. (21529) 245/C2
Ellerslie, N. Zealand 100/C1
Ellerslie, Pr. Edward I. 168/D2
Ellerton, Barbados 161/B9
Ellerton, Md. (†21773) 245/H2
Ellery, Ill. (62833) 222/E5
Ellesmere (isl.), Canada 4/B14
Ellesmere (isl.), Canada 2/F1
Ellesmere, England 13/E5
Ellesmere (lake), N. Zealand 100/D5
Ellesmere (isl.), N.W.T. 146/K1
Ellesmere (isl.), N.W.T. 162/N3
Ellesmere (isl.), N.W. Terrs. 187/K2
Ellesmere Port, England 13/G2
Ellesmere Port, England 10/F2
Ellettsville, Ind. (47429) 227/D6
Ellezelles, Belgium 27/D7
El Libertador General Bernardo O'Higgins (reg.), Chile 138/A10
Ellice (riv.), N.W. Terrs. 187/H3
Ellicott City, Md. (21043) 245/L3
Ellicottville, N.Y. (14731) 276/C6
Ellijay, Georgia (30540) 217/C1
El Limón, Nicaragua 154/E4
Ellington○, Conn. (06029) 210/F1
Ellington, Mo. (63638) 261/L8
Ellington, N.Y. (14732) 276/B6
Ellington A.F.B., Texas 303/K2
Ellinwood, Kansas (67526) 232/D3
Elliot (lake), Manitoba 179/G2
Elliot, S. Africa 118/D6
Elliot Lake, Ontario 177/B1
Elliot Lake, Ontario 175/D3
Elliott, Ark. (†71701) 202/E7
Elliott (key), Fla. 212/F6
Elliott, Ill. (60933) 222/E3
Elliott, Iowa (51532) 229/C6
Elliott (co.), Ky. 237/P4
Elliott, Md. (21823) 245/P7
Elliott, Miss. (38926) 256/E3
Elliott, N. Dak. (58025) 282/P7
Elliott, North. Terr. 88/E3
Elliott, North. Terr. 93/C4
Elliott, S.C. (29046) 296/G3
Elliott, Tasmania 99/B3
Elliott (bay), Tasmania 99/B5
Elliottsburg, Pa. (17024) 294/H5
Elliottville, Ky. (40317) 237/P4
Ellis, Idaho (83235) 220/D5
Ellis (co.), Kansas 232/C3
Ellis, Kansas (67637) 232/C3
Ellis (pond), Maine 243/B6
Ellis (riv.), Maine 243/B6
Ellis (riv.), N.H. 268/E3
Ellis (co.), Okla. 288/G2
Ellis (co.), Texas 303/H5
El Lisan (pen.), Jordan 65/C5
Ellisburg, N.Y. (13636) 276/H3
Ellis Grove, Ill. (62241) 222/D5
Ellison Bay, Wis. (54210) 317/M5
Elliston, Mont. (59728) 262/D4
Elliston, Newf. 166/D2
Elliston, Ohio (43432) 284/D2
Elliston, S. Australia 88/E6
Elliston, S. Australia 94/D5
Elliston-Lafayette, Va. (24087) 307/H6
Ellisville, Ill. (61431) 222/C3
Ellisville, Miss. (39437) 256/F7
Ellisville, Mo. (†63011) 261/M3
Ellisville, Wis. (†54217) 317/L7
Ellon, Scotland 10/E2
Ellon, Scotland 15/F3
Elloree, S.C. (29047) 296/F4
Elloughton, England 13/G4
Ells (riv.), Alberta 182/D1
Ellscott, Alberta 182/D2
Ellsinore, Mo. (63937) 261/L9
Ellston, Iowa (50074) 229/E7
Ellsworth (hill), Conn. 210/B1
Ellsworth, Ill. (61737) 222/E3
Ellsworth, Iowa (50075) 229/F4
Ellsworth (co.), Kansas 232/D3
Ellsworth, Kansas (67439) 232/D3
Ellsworth, Maine (04605) 243/F6
Ellsworth, Mich. (49729) 250/D3
Ellsworth, Minn. (56129) 255/C7
Ellsworth, Nebr. (69340) 264/B2
Ellsworth○, N.H. (†03264) 268/D4
Ellsworth (lake), Okla. 288/K5
Ellsworth, Pa. (15331) 294/B5
Ellsworth, Wis. (54011) 317/A6
Ellsworth A.F.B., S. Dak. 298/C5
Ellsworth Land (reg.) 5/B14
Ellwangen, W. Germany 22/D4
Ellwood City, Pa. (16117) 294/B4
Elm (riv.), N. Dak. 282/R5
Elm (riv.), N. Dak. 282/N8
Elm (creek), S. Dak. 298/D4
Elm (riv.), S. Dak. 298/M2
Elm, Switzerland 39/H3
Elma, Iowa (50628) 229/J2
Elma, Manitoba 179/G5
Elma, N.Y. (14059) 276/C5
Elma, Wash. (98541) 310/B4
El Macao, Dom. Rep. 158/F6
El Madwar, Jordan 65/E3
El Mafraq, Jordan 65/E3
El Mahalla el Kubra, Egypt 111/J3
El Maitén, Argentina 143/B5
El Majdal, Jordan 65/D3
Elmalı, Turkey 63/C4
El Managil, Sudan 111/F5
El Mansûra, Egypt 111/K3
El Mansûra, Egypt 59/B3
El Manteco, Venezuela 124/G4
El Manzano, Chile 138/F5
El Ma'qil, Iraq 66/E5
El Marj, Libya 102/E1
El Marj, Libya 111/D1
El Marmol, Mexico 150/B2
Elm City, N.C. (27822) 281/O3
Elm Creek, Manitoba 179/E5
Elm Creek, Nebr. (68836) 264/E4
Elmdale, Kansas (66850) 232/F3
Elmdale, Minn. (†56314) 255/D5
Elmendorf, Texas (78112) 303/K11
Elmendorf A.F.B., Alaska 196/B1
Elmer, La. (71424) 238/E4
Elmer, Minn. (†55765) 255/F3
Elmer, Mo. (63538) 261/G3
Elmer, N.J. (08318) 273/C4
Elmer, Okla. (73539) 288/H6
Elmer City, Wash. (99124) 310/G2
Elm Fork, Trinity (riv.), Texas 303/G2
Elm Grove, La. (71051) 238/C2
Elm Grove, Wis. (53122) 317/K1
Elmhurst, Ill. (60126) 222/B5
Elmhurst, Pa. (18416) 294/F7
El Miamo, Venezuela 124/H4
El Milagro, Argentina 143/C3
Elmina, Ghana 106/D8
El Minya, Egypt 102/F2
El Minya, Egypt 59/B4
El Minya, Egypt 111/J4
Elmira, Ill. (†61483) 222/D2
Elmira, Mich. (49730) 250/E3
Elmira, Mo. (†64062) 261/D3
Elmira, N.Y. 188/L2
Elmira, N.Y. (*14901) 276/G6
Elmira, Ontario 177/D4
Elmira, Oreg. (97437) 291/D3
Elmira, Pr. Edward I. 168/F2
Elmira, W. Va. (26618) 312/E5
El Mirage, Ariz. (85335) 198/C5
Elmira Heights, N.Y. (14903) 276/G6
El Misti (mt.), Peru 128/G11
Elmo, Kansas (†67451) 232/E3
Elmo, Mo. (64445) 261/B1
Elmo, Mont. (59915) 262/B3
Elmo, Texas (75118) 303/H5
Elmo, Utah (84521) 304/D4
Elmo, Wyo. (†82327) 319/F4
Elmodel, Georgia (31748) 217/D8
Elmont, Kansas (†66603) 232/G2
Elmont, N.Y. (11003) 276/P7
El Monte, Calif. (*91731) 204/D10
El Monte, Chile 138/G4
Elmora, Pa. (15737) 294/E4
Elmore (co.), Ala. 195/F5
Elmore, Ala. (36025) 195/F5
Elmore (co.), Idaho 220/C6
Elmore, Minn. (56027) 255/D7
Elmore, Ohio (43416) 284/D3
Elmore City, Okla. (73035) 288/M5
El Morro, N. Mex. (†87321) 274/A3
El Morro Nat'l Mon., N. Mex. 274/A3
Elm Park, La. (†70775) 238/H5
El Mraïti (well), Mali 106/D5
El Mrayer (well), Mauritania 106/C4
El Mreïti (well), Mauritania 106/C4
Elmrock, Ky. (41624) 237/P6
Elmsdale, Nova Scotia 168/E4
Elmsdale, Pr. Edward I. 168/D2
Elmsford, N.Y. (10523) 276/O6
Elmshorn, W. Germany 22/C2
Elm Springs, Ark. (72728) 202/B1
Elm Springs, S. Dak. (57736) 298/D5
Elmsvale, Nova Scotia 168/E3
Elmvale, Ontario 177/E3
Elmville, Conn. (†06239) 210/H1
Elmwood, Conn. (06110) 210/D2
Elmwood, Ill. (61529) 222/D3
Elmwood, Mass. (02337) 249/L4
Elmwood, Nebr. (68349) 264/H4
Elmwood, Okla. (73935) 288/F1
Elmwood, Ontario 177/C3
Elmwood, Wis. (54740) 317/B6
Elmwood Park, Ill. (60635) 222/B5
Elmwood Park, N.J. (†07407) 273/B2
Elmwood Park, Wis. (†53401) 317/M3
Elmwood Place, Ohio (45216) 284/B9
Elmworth, Alberta 182/A2
Elne, France 28/E6
El Nido, Calif. (95317) 204/E6
El Nido, Philippines 82/B5
El Ñilhue, Chile 138/G2
Elnora, Alberta 182/D3
Elnora, Ind. (47529) 227/C7
El Obeid, Sudan 102/E3
El Obeid, Sudan 59/B7
El Obeid, Sudan 111/E5
Elobey (isls.), Equat. Guinea 115/A3
El Odaiya, Sudan 111/E5
Eloff, S. Africa 118/J6
Eloi (bay), La. 238/M7
Elon, Ala. (†35760) 195/F1
Elon College, N.C. (27244) 281/L2
Elora, Ontario 177/D4
Elora, Tenn. (37328) 237/J10
El Oro (prov.), Ecuador 128/C4
Elortondo, Argentina 143/F6
Elorza, Venezuela 124/D4
El Oso, Venezuela 124/H5
El Oued, Algeria 106/F2
Eloy, Ariz. (85231) 198/D6
El Pájaro, Colombia 126/D2
El Palmar, Chuquisaca, Bolivia 136/D7
El Palmar, Santa Cruz, Bolivia 136/D5
El Palmar, Tarija, Bolivia 136/D7
El Palmar, Venezuela 124/G4
El Pao, Anzoátegui, Venezuela 124/F3
El Pao, Bolívar, Venezuela 124/G3
El Pao, Cojedes, Venezuela 124/D3
El Paraíso, Colombia 126/C7
El Paraíso, Copán, Honduras 154/C3
El Paraíso, El Paraíso, Honduras 154/D4
El Pardo, Spain 33/F4
El Paso, Ark. (72045) 202/F3
El Paso (co.), Colo. 208/K5
El Paso, Ill. (61738) 222/D3
El Paso (co.), Texas 303/A10
El Paso, Texas 146/H6
El Paso, Texas 188/E4
El Paso, Texas (*79901) 303/A10
El Paso, U.S. 2/D4
El Pato, Colombia 126/C6
El Perú, Bolivia 136/B3
El Perú, Venezuela 124/H4
Elphin, Ireland 17/E4
Elphinstone, Manitoba 179/B4
El Pico, Bolivia 136/C4
El Pilar, Cuba 158/G3
El Pilar, Venezuela 124/G2
El Pintado, Argentina 143/D1
El Piquete, Argentina 143/D1
El Portal, Calif. (95318) 204/F6
El Portal, Fla. (†33101) 212/B4
El Portugués, Peru 128/C7
El Porvenir, Honduras 154/D3
El Porvenir, Mexico 150/G1
El Porvenir, N. Mex. (†87731) 274/D3
El Porvenir, Panama 154/H6
El Potosí, Mexico 150/J4
El Pozo, Dom. Rep. 158/E5
El Prado, N. Mex. (87529) 274/D2
El Progreso, Ecuador 128/C9
El Progreso, Guatemala 154/B3
El Progreso, Honduras 154/D3
El Puente, Santa Cruz, Bolivia 136/D5
El Puente, Tarija, Bolivia 136/C7
El Puerto de Santa María, Spain 33/C4
El Pun, Ecuador 128/D2
El Qâhira (Cairo) (cap.), Egypt 59/B4
El Qâhira (Cairo) (cap.), Egypt 111/J3
El Qantara, Egypt 111/K3
El Qantara, Egypt 59/B3
El Qasr, Egypt 111/E2
El Qasr, Egypt 59/A4
El Quadmus, Syria 63/F5
El Quebrachal, Argentina 143/D2
Elqui (riv.), Chile 138/A8
El Quisco, Chile 138/E3
El Quneitra (prov.), Syria 63/F6
El Quneitra, Syria 63/F6
El Quryatein, Syria 63/G5
El Quseir, Egypt 102/F2
El Quseir, Egypt 59/B4
El Quseir, Egypt 111/F2
El Quseir, Syria 63/G5
El Quweira, Jordan 65/E5
Elrama, Pa. (15038) 294/C5
El Rashid, Syria 63/H5
El Rashid, Syria 59/C2
El Rastro, Venezuela 124/E3
El Real de Santa María, Panama 154/J6
El Realejo, Nicaragua 154/D4
El Reno, Okla. (73036) 288/K3
El Rio, Calif. (†93030) 204/F9
El Rito, N. Mex. (87530) 274/C2
El Rito (riv.), N. Mex. 274/C2
Elrod, Ala. (35458) 195/C4
Elrod, Ind. (†47018) 227/G6
El Roque, Venezuela 124/E2
Elrosa, Minn. (56325) 255/C5
El Rosario, Estero (riv.), Chile 138/F3
El Rosario, Mexico 150/B1
Elrose, Sask. 181/D4
Elroy, Wis. (53929) 317/F8
Elsa, Texas (78543) 303/G11
Elsa, Yukon 187/E3
Elsah, Ill. (62028) 222/C5
El Salado, Dom. Rep. 158/F6
El Salto, Mexico 150/G5
El Salvador 2/E5
El Salvador 146/J8
El Salvador, C. Rica 154/F5
EL SALVADOR 154/C4
El Samán de Apure, Venezuela 124/D4
El Santo, Cuba 158/E1
Elsas, Ontario 175/D3
El Sauce, Nicaragua 154/D4
Elsberry, Mo. (63343) 261/L4
Elsburg, S. Africa 118/H6
El Segundo, Calif. (90245) 204/B11
El Seibo (prov.), Dom. Rep. 158/F6
El Seibo, Dom. Rep. 158/F6
Elsey, Mo. (†65633) 261/E9
Elsie, Mich. (48831) 250/E5
Elsie, Nebr. (69134) 264/C4
Elsie, Oreg. (†97138) 291/D2
Elsiesrivier, S. Africa 118/F6
Elsinore (lake), Calif. 204/E11
Elsinore, Utah (84724) 304/B5
Elsmere, Del. (†19801) 245/R2
Elsmere, Ky. (†41018) 237/R2
Elsmere, Nebr. (69135) 264/D2
Elsmore, Kansas (66732) 232/G4
El Socorro, Venezuela 124/F3
El Sollum (gulf), Egypt 111/E1
El Sombrero, Venezuela 124/E3
Elst, Netherlands 27/H5
Elster, Black (riv.), E. Germany 22/E3
Elster, White (riv.), E. Germany 22/E3
Elston, Ind. (†47901) 227/D4
Elstow, Sask. 181/E4
El Tabo, Chile 138/F3
El Tambo, Colombia 126/B6
El Teleno (mt.), Spain 33/C1
Eltham, N. Zealand 100/E3
Eltham, Victoria 97/J4
Eltham, Victoria 88/L6
El Tiemblo, Spain 33/D2
El Tigre, Venezuela 120/C2
El Tigre, Venezuela 124/F3
El Tocuyo, Venezuela 124/C3
El Tofo, Chile 138/A7
Elton, La. (70532) 238/E6
El'ton, U.S.S.R. 52/G5
Elton, W. Va. (25965) 312/E7
Elton, Wis. (54430) 317/J5
Eltopia, Wash. (99330) 310/G4
El Toro, Calif. (92630) 204/E11
El Toro (mt.), P. Rico 161/F2
El Toro, Venezuela 124/H3
El Toro Marine Air Sta., Calif. 204/D11
El Tránsito, Chile 138/B7
El Triunfo, Honduras 154/D4
El Tucuche (mt.), Trin. & Tob. 161/B10
El Tûr, Egypt 111/F2
El Tur, Egypt 59/B4
Eluru, India 68/E5
El' Uweinat, Libya 111/B2
Elva, Manitoba 179/A5
Elva, U.S.S.R. 53/D1
El Vado, N. Mex. (†87575) 274/C2
Elvas, Portugal 33/C3
Elvaston, Ill. (62334) 222/B3
Elverson, Pa. (19520) 294/L5
Elverum, Norway 18/G6
El Viejo, Nicaragua 154/D4
El Vigía, Venezuela 124/C3
El Vínculo, Venezuela 124/D1
Elvins, Mo. (63639) 261/L7
Elvira, Iowa (†52732) 229/N5

Fairhaven 367

Espada (pt.), Colombia 126/E1
Espada (pt.), Dom. Rep. 158/F6
Espagnol (pt.), St. Vin. & Grens. 161/A8
Espaillat (prov.), Dom. Rep. 158/E5
Espalion, France 28/E5
Española (isl.), Ecuador 128/C10
Espanola, Fla. (†32010) 212/E2
Espanola, N. Mex. (87532) 274/C3
Espanola, Ontario 177/J5
Espanola, Ontario 175/D3
Espanola, Wash. (†99022) 310/H3
Esparta, C. Rica 154/E5
Esparto, Calif. (95627) 204/C5
Espejo, Chile 138/G3
Espejo, Spain 33/D4
Espelkamp, W. Germany 22/C2
Espenberg (cape), Alaska 196/F1
Esperança, Brazil 132/G4
Esperance, Australia 87/C9
Esperance, N.Y. (12066) 276/M5
Esperance, W. Australia 88/C6
Esperance, W. Australia 92/C6
Esperance (bay), W. Australia 92/C6
Esperanza, Argentina 143/F5
Esperanza, Br. Col. 184/D5
Esperanza, Cuba 158/E2
Esperanza, Dom. Rep. 158/D5
Esperanza (mts.), Honduras 154/E3
Esperanza, Puebla, Mexico 150/O2
Esperanza, Sonora, Mexico 150/E3
Esperanza, Peru 128/G7
Esperanza, P. Rico 161/G2
Esperanza, Texas (†79841) 303/B11
Esperanza, Venezuela 124/E6
Espichel (cape), Portugal 33/B3
Espigão Mestre (Geral de Goiás) (range), Brazil 132/E6
Espinal, Colombia 126/C5
Espinhaço (mts.), Brazil 120/E4
Espinhaço, Serra do (range), Brazil 132/F7
Espinho, Portugal 33/B2
Espinillo, Argentina 143/E2
Espinillo (pt.), Uruguay 145/A7
Espino, Venezuela 124/F3
Espírito Santo (state), Brazil 132/F7
Espírito Santo (state), Brazil 135/F2
Espíritu Santo (isl.), Mexico 150/D4
Espiritu Santo (cape), Philippines 85/H3
Espiritu Santo (cape), Philippines 82/E4
Espiritu Santo (isl.), Vanuatu 87/G7
Espita, Mexico 150/Q6
Espiye, Turkey 63/H2
Esplanada, Brazil 132/G5
Espluga de Francolí, Spain 33/G2
Espoir (bay), Newf. 166/C4
Espoo, Finland 18/O6
Esposende, Portugal 33/B2
Esprit-Saint, Québec 172/J1
Espungabera, Mozambique 118/E4
Espy, Pa. (17815) 294/K4
Espyville Station, Pa. (16414) 294/B2
Esqueda, Mexico 150/E1
Esquel, Argentina 143/B5
Esquel, Argentina 120/B7
Esquimalt, Br. Col. 184/K4
Esquina, Argentina 143/G5
Esquipulas, Nicaragua 154/E4
Es Sahab, Jordan 65/E4
Es Salt, Jordan 65/D3
Es Salt, Jordan 59/C3
Essaouira, Morocco 106/B2
Essaouira, Morocco 102/A1
Essé, Cameroon 115/B3
Essen, Belgium 27/F6
Essen, W. Germany 7/E3
Essen, W. Germany 22/B3
Essendon, Victoria 88/K7
Essendon, Victoria 97/H5
Essequibo (riv.), Guyana 120/D2
Essequibo (riv.), Guyana 131/B3
Esserville, Va. (24274) 307/G2
Essex, Calif. (92332) 204/K9
Essex, Conn. (06426) 210/F3
Essex○, Conn. (06426) 210/F3
Essex (co.), England 13/H6
Essex, Ill. (60935) 222/E2
Essex, Iowa (51638) 229/C7
Essex, Md. (21221) 245/N3
Essex (co.), Mass. 249/L2
Essex, Mass. (01929) 249/L2
Essex○, Mass. (01929) 249/L2
Essex, Mo. (63846) 261/N9
Essex, Mont. (59916) 262/C2
Essex (co.), N.J. 273/E2
Essex (co.), N.Y. 276/N2
Essex, N.Y. (12936) 276/O2
Essex (county), Ontario 177/B5
Essex, Ontario 177/B5
Essex (co.), Vt. 268/D2
Essex○, Vt. (05451) 268/A2
Essex (co.), Va. 307/P5
Essex Fells, N.J. (07021) 273/B2
Essex Junction, Vt. (05452) 268/A3
Essexville, Mich. (48732) 250/F5
Es Sidr, Libya 111/C1
Essie, Ky. (40827) 237/P6
Essig, Minn. (56030) 255/D6
Essington, Pa. (19029) 294/M7
Esslingen am Neckar, W. Germany 22/C4
Essonne (dept.), France 28/E3
Es Sukhne, Jordan 65/E3
Es Sukhne, Syria 59/C3
Es Sukhne, Syria 63/H5
Es Suki, Sudan 59/B7
Es Suweida (prov.), Syria 63/G6
Es Suweida, Syria 59/C3
Es Suweida, Syria 63/G6
Est (pt.), Haiti 158/C4
Est (lake), Québec 172/H2
Estacada, Oreg. (97023) 291/E2
Estaca de Vares (pt.), Spain 33/C1
Estación Atlántida, Uruguay 145/B6
Estación Cuaró, Uruguay 145/C1
Estación J.J. Castro, Uruguay 145/C4
Estación José Ignacio, Uruguay 145/E5
Estación La Floresta, Uruguay 145/C7
Estación Lasala, Uruguay 145/C7
Estación Laureles, Uruguay 145/C2
Estación Margat, Uruguay 145/B6
Estación Migues, Uruguay 145/C6
Estación Pampa, Uruguay 145/C3
Estación Puma, Uruguay 145/D5
Estación Rincón, Uruguay 145/F3
Estación Sosa Díaz, Uruguay 145/C6
Estación Tapia, Uruguay 145/C6
Estación Villasboas, Uruguay 145/C4
Estación Yi, Uruguay 145/C4
Estados (isl.), Argentina 120/C8
Estados, Los (isl.), Argentina 143/D7
Estahbanat, Iran 59/F4
Estahbanat, Iran 66/J6
Estaire, Ontario 177/D1
Estampuis, Belgium 27/C7
Estância, Brazil 132/G5
Estância, Brazil 120/F4
Estancia, N. Mex. (87016) 274/D4
Estancia Caleta Josefina, Chile 138/F10
Estancia Laguna Blanca, Chile 138/E9
Estancia Morro Chico, Chile 138/E9
Estancia Punta Delgada, Chile 138/E9
Estancia San Gregorio, Chile 138/E9
Estancia Springhill (Cerro Manantiales), Chile 138/F10
Estanzuela, Uruguay 145/B5
Estanzuelas, El Salvador 154/C4
Estarca, Bolivia 136/C7
Estats (peak), Spain 33/G1
Estavayer-le-Lac, Switzerland 39/C3
Estcourt, S. Africa 118/D5
Este (pt.), Cuba 158/C3
Este, Italy 34/C2
Este (pt.), P. Rico 161/G2
Este (pt.), Uruguay 120/D6
Este (pt.), Uruguay 145/D6
Esteban Rams, Argentina 143/F5
Estelí, Nicaragua 154/D4
Estella, Spain 33/E1
Estelline, S. Dak. (57234) 298/R4
Estelline, Texas (79233) 303/D3
Estell Manor, N.J. (08319) 273/D5
Estepa, Spain 33/D4
Estepona, Spain 33/D4
Ester, Alaska (99725) 196/J2
Esterbrook, Wyo. (†82633) 319/G3
Estérel, Québec 172/C3
Esterhazy, Sask. 181/K5
Estero (bay), Calif. 204/D8
Estero (pt.), Calif. 204/D8
Estero, Fla. (33928) 212/E5
Estero (isl.), Fla. 212/E5
Estes Park, Colo. (80517) 208/J2
Este Sudeste (cays), Colombia 126/A10
Estevan, Sak. 162/F6
Estevan, Sask. 181/J6
Estevan Point, Br. Col. 184/D5
Estey, Mich. (†48652) 250/E5
Esther (isl.), Alaska 196/C1
Esther, Alberta 182/E4
Esther, La. (†70510) 238/F7
Esther, Mo. (†63601) 261/M7
Estherville, Iowa (51334) 229/D2
Estherwood, La. (70534) 238/F6
Estill (co.), Ky. 237/O5
Estill, Miss. (†38748) 256/C4
Estill, S.C. (29918) 296/E6
Estillfork, Ala. (35745) 195/F1
Estill Springs, Tenn. (37330) 237/J10
Estlin, Sask. 181/G5
Esto, Fla. (32425) 212/C5
Eston, England 13/F3
Eston, Sask. 162/F5
Eston, Sask. 181/C4
ESTONIA 53
Estonian S.S.R., U.S.S.R. 7/G3
Estonian S.S.R., U.S.S.R. 48/C4
Estonian S.S.R, U.S.S.R. 52/C3
Estoril, Portugal 33/B3
Estral Beach, Mich. (†48166) 250/F7
Estreito (res.), Brazil 135/C2
Estrela, Serra da (mts.), Portugal 33/C2
Estrella (riv.), Calif. 204/E8
Estremadura (reg.), Spain 33/C3
Estremoz, Portugal 33/C3
Estrondo, Serra do (range), Brazil 132/D4
Estuary, Sask. 181/B5
Esztergom, Hungary 41/E3
Etadunna, S. Australia 94/F3
Etalle, Belgium 27/H9
Étampes, France 28/E3
Étaples, France 28/D2
Etawah, India 68/D3
Etawney (lake), Manitoba 179/J2
Etchojoa, Mexico 150/E3
Ethan, S. Dak. (57334) 298/N6
Ethel, Ark. (72048) 202/H5
Ethel (mt.), Colo. 208/F1
Ethel, La. (70730) 238/H5
Ethel, Miss. (39067) 256/F4
Ethel, Mo. (63539) 261/G3
Ethel, Ontario 177/C4
Ethel, Wash. (98542) 310/C4
Ethel, W. Va. (25076) 312/C7
Ethelbert, Manitoba 179/B3
Ethel Creek, W. Australia 92/C3
Ethelsville, Ala. (35461) 195/B4
Ethelton, Sask. 181/G3
Ether, N.C. (27247) 281/K4
Ethete, Wyo. (82520) 319/D2
Ethiopia 2/L5
Ethiopia 102/F4
ETHIOPIA 59/C7
ETHIOPIA 111/G5
Ethridge, Mont. (59435) 262/D2
Ethridge, Tenn. (38456) 237/G10
Etive, Loch (inlet), Scotland 15/C4
Etiwanda, Calif. (91739) 204/E10
Etna, Calif. (96027) 204/C2
Etna, Ind. (†46725) 227/F2
Etna (vol.), Italy 7/F5
Etna (vol.), Italy 34/E6
Etna○, Maine (04434) 243/E6
Etna, N.H. (03750) 268/C4
Etna, Ohio (43018) 284/E6
Etna, Pa. (15223) 294/B6
Etna, Utah (†84313) 304/A2
Etna, Wyo. (83118) 319/A2
Etna Green, Ind. (46524) 227/E2
Etobicoke, Ontario 177/J4
Etoile, Ky. (42131) 237/K7
Etoile, Zaire 115/E6
Etolin (isl.), Alaska 196/N2
Etolin (str.), Alaska 196/E2
Etomami (riv.), Manitoba 179/F2
Etomami (riv.), Sask. 181/J3
Eton, England 10/F5
Eton, England 13/G8
Eton, Georgia (30724) 217/C1
Etosha Pan (salt pan), Namibia 118/B3
Etosha Salt Pan, Namibia 102/D6
Etoumbi, Congo 115/B3
Etowah (co.), Ala. 195/F2
Etowah, Ark. (72428) 202/K2
Etowah (riv.), Georgia 217/C2
Etowah, N.C. (28729) 281/D4
Etowah, Tenn. (37331) 237/M10
Étretat, France 28/D3
Etta, Miss. (38627) 256/F2
Etta (lake), N. Dak. 282/L6
Et Tafila, Jordan 65/E5
Et Taiyiba, Jordan 65/D2
Ettelbruck, Luxembourg 27/J9
Et Tell el Abyad, Syria 63/H4
Etten-Leur, Netherlands 27/F5
Etter, Minn. (†55033) 255/F6
Etterbeek, Belgium 27/B9
Etters, Pa. (17319) 294/J5
Etters Beach, Sask. 181/F4
Ettington, Sask. 181/F6
Ettlingen, W. Germany 22/C4
Ettrick, Scotland 15/E5
Ettrick, Va. (23803) 307/O6
Ettrick, Wis. (54627) 317/D7
Ettrick Pen (mt.), Scotland 15/E5
Etty, Ky. (41523) 237/R6
Etzatlán, Mexico 150/G6
Etzikom, Alberta 182/E5
Etzikom Coulee (riv.), Alberta 182/E5
Eu, France 28/D3
Euabalong, N.S. Wales 97/D3
Eubank, Ky. (42567) 237/M6
Euboea (Évvoia) (isl.), Greece 45/G6
Eucha, Okla. (74342) 288/S2
Eucha (lake), Okla. 288/S2
Eucla, W. Australia 92/E5
Euclid, Minn. (56722) 255/B3
Euclid, Ohio (44117) 284/J9
Eucumbene (lake), N.S. Wales 97/E5
Eucutta, Miss. (†39360) 256/G7
Eudora, Ark. (71640) 202/H7
Eudora, Kansas (66025) 232/G3
Eudora, Miss. (†38632) 256/D1
Eudora, Mo. (65645) 261/E7
Eufaula, Ala. (36027) 195/H7
Eufaula (Walter F. George Res.) (lake), Ala 195/H7
Eufaula (Walter F. George Res.) (lake), Georgia 217/B7
Eufaula (res.), Ohio 284/L4
Eufaula, Okla. (74432) 288/P4
Eufaula (lake), Okla. 288/P4
Eugene, Ind. (†47928) 227/B5
Eugene, Mo. (65032) 261/H6
Eugene, Oreg. 188/B2
Eugene, Oreg. 146/F5
Eugene, Oreg. (*97401) 291/D3
Eugene O'Neill Nat'l Hist. Site, Calif. 204/K2
Eugowra, N.S. Wales 97/E3
Euharlee, Georgia (†30120) 217/C2
Euless, Texas (76039) 303/F2
Eulo, Queensland 95/C6
Eulonia, Georgia (†31331) 217/K7
Eumungerie, N.S. Wales 97/E2
Eunice, La. (70535) 238/F6
Eunice, N. Mex. (88231) 274/F6
Eunola, Ala. (†36340) 195/G8
Eupen, Belgium 27/J7
Euphrates (riv.) 54/F6
Euphrates (riv.), Iran 59/E3
Euphrates (riv.), Iraq 59/E3
Euphrates (riv.), Iraq 66/D4
Euphrates (riv.), Syria 59/E3
Euphrates (El Furat) (riv.), Syria 63/H4
Euphrates (Fırat) (riv.), Turkey 63/G4
Eupora, Miss. (39744) 256/F3
Eure (dept.), France 28/D3
Eure (riv.), France 28/D3
Eure, N.C. (27935) 281/R2
Eure-et-Loir (dept.), France 28/D3
Eureka, Calif. 188/B2
Eureka, Calif. 146/F5
Eureka, Calif. (95501) 204/A3
Eureka, Canada 4/A14
Eureka, Colo. (†81433) 208/D7
Eureka (res.), Fla. 212/E2
Eureka, Ill. (61530) 222/D3
Eureka, Ind. (†47635) 227/C9
Eureka, Kansas (67045) 232/F4
Eureka, Mo. (63025) 261/M4
Eureka, Mont. (59917) 262/B2
Eureka (co.), Nev. 266/E3
Eureka, Nev. (89316) 266/E3
Eureka, N.C. (27830) 281/O3
Eureka, N.W.T. 146/K2
Eureka, N.W.T. 162/N3
Eureka, N.W. Terrs. 187/K2
Eureka (sound), N.W. Terrs. 187/K2
Eureka, Nova Scotia 168/F3
Eureka, S.C. (†29706) 296/E2
Eureka, S.C. (†29847) 296/D4
Eureka, S. Dak. (57437) 298/K2
Eureka, Utah (84628) 304/B4
Eureka, Wash. (†99348) 310/G4
Eureka, W. Va. (26144) 312/D4
Eureka Lodge, Alaska (†99588) 196/C1
Eureka Springs, Ark. (72632) 202/C1
Euroa, Victoria 97/C5
Europa (pt.), Gibraltar 33/D4
Europa (isl.), Réunion 102/G7
Europa (isl.), Réunion 118/G4
Europe 2/K3
Europoort, Netherlands 27/E5
Eusebio Ayala, Paraguay 144/B4
Euskirchen, W. Germany 22/B3
Eustace, Texas (75124) 303/H5
Eustis, Fla. (32726) 212/E3
Eustis, Maine (04936) 243/B5
Eustis○, Maine (04936) 243/B5
Eustis, Nebr. (69028) 264/D4
Euston, N.S. Wales 97/B4
Eutaw, Ala. (35462) 195/C5
Eutawville, S.C. (29048) 296/G5
Eutin, W. Germany 22/D1
Eutsuk (lake), Br. Col. 184/D3
Eva, Ala. (35621) 195/E2
Eva (lake), Alberta 182/B5
Eva, La. (†71354) 238/G4
Eva, Okla. (†73949) 288/C1
Eva, Tenn. (38333) 237/E8
Evadale, Texas (77615) 303/L7
Eva Downs, North. Terr. 93/D5
Évain, Québec 174/B3
Evan, Minn. (56238) 255/D6
Evan (lake), Québec 174/B2
Evandale, New Bruns. 170/D3
Evandale, Tasmania 99/D3
Evangeline (par.), La. 238/F5
Evangeline, La. (70537) 238/F6
Evangeline, New Bruns. 170/F1
Evans, Colo. (80620) 208/K2
Evans (mt.), Colo. 208/H3
Evans (co.), Georgia 217/J6
Evans, Georgia (30809) 217/H3
Evans, La. (70639) 238/D5
Evans (head), N.S. Wales 97/G1
Evans (str.), N.W.T. 162/H3
Evans (str.), N.W. Terrs. 187/K3
Evans, Wash. (99126) 310/H2
Evans, W. Va. (25241) 312/C5
Evansburg, Alberta 182/C3
Evans Center, N.Y. (†14006) 276/B5
Evans City, Pa. (16033) 294/B4
Evansdale, Iowa (50707) 229/J4
Evans Head, N.S. Wales 97/G1
Evans Mills, N.Y. (13637) 276/J2
Evansport, Ohio (43519) 284/B3
Evanston, Ill. (*60201) 222/B5
Evanston, Ind. (47531) 227/D8
Evanston, Wyo. 188/D2
Evanston, Wyo. (82930) 319/B4
Evansville (Bettles Field), Alaska (†99726) 196/H1
Evansville, Ark. (72729) 202/B2
Evansville, Ill. (62242) 222/D5
Evansville, Ind. 188/J3
Evansville, Ind. 146/K6
Evansville, Ind. (*47701) 227/C9
Evansville, Minn. (56326) 255/C4
Evansville, Miss. (†38676) 256/D1
Evansville, Pa. (19521) 294/L5
Evansville, Wis. (53536) 317/H10
Evansville, Wyo. (82636) 319/F3
Evant, Texas (76525) 303/G6
Evanton, Scotland 15/D3
Evart, Mich. (49631) 250/D5
Evarts, Ky. (40828) 237/P7
Evaton, S. Africa 118/H7
Evaz, Iran 66/J7
Eveleth, Minn. (55734) 255/F3
Evelyn, La. (†71052) 238/D3
Evendale, Ohio (†45201) 284/C9
Evening Shade, Ark. (72532) 202/G1
Evenki Aut. Okr., U.S.S.R. 48/K3
Evensk, U.S.S.R. 4/C1
Evensk, U.S.S.R. 48/Q3
Evensville, Tenn. (37332) 237/M9
Even Yehuda, Israel 65/B3
Everard (lake), S. Australia 88/E6
Everard (lake), S. Australia 94/D4
Everard (ranges), S. Australia 94/C2
Evere, Belgium 27/C9
Everest (mt.) 54/K7
Everest (mt.), China 77/C6
Everest, Kansas (66424) 232/G2
Everest (mt.), Nepal 68/F3
Everest, N. Dak. (†58023) 282/R6
Everett, Georgia (31536) 217/J8
Everett, Mass. (02149) 249/D6
Everett (mt.), Mass. 249/A4
Everett, New Bruns. 170/C1
Everett (dam), N.H. 268/D5
Everett (mts.), N.W. Terrs. 187/M3
Everett, Ontario 177/E3
Everett, Pa. (15537) 294/F5
Everett, Wash. 188/B1
Everett, Wash. (*98201) 310/C3
Everetts, N.C. (27825) 281/P3
Everettville, W. Va. (26533) 312/F3
Evergem, Belgium 27/D6
Everglades, The (swamp), Fla. 212/F6
Everglades, The (swamp), Fla. 188/K5
Everglades City, Fla. (33929) 212/E6
Everglades Nat'l Park, Fla. 212/F6
Evergreen, Ala. (36401) 195/E8
Evergreen, Colo. (80439) 208/J3
Evergreen, La. (71333) 238/F5
Evergreen, N.C. (28438) 281/M6
Evergreen, Va. (23939) 307/L6
Evergreen Park, Ill. (60642) 222/B6
Everly, Iowa (51338) 229/C2
Everman, Texas (76140) 303/F3
Everson, Pa. (15631) 294/C5
Everson, Wash. (98247) 310/C2
Eversonville, Mo. (†64688) 261/F3
Everton, Ark. (72633) 202/E1
Everton, Ind. (†47331) 227/G5
Everton, Mo. (65646) 261/E8
Evesham, England 10/E4
Evesham, England 13/F5
Evesham, Sask. 181/B3
Evington, Va. (24550) 307/K6
Evolène, Switzerland 39/D4
Évora (dist.), Portugal 33/C3
Évora, Portugal 7/D5
Évora, Portugal 33/C3
Évreux, France 28/D3
Évros (riv.), Greece 45/H5
Évry, France 28/E3
Évvoia (isl.), Greece 7/G5
Évvoia (isl.), Greece 45/G6
Ewa, Hawaii (96706) 218/A4
Ewab (Kai) (isls.), Indonesia 85/J7
Ewa Beach, Hawaii (96706) 218/A4
Ewan, N.J. (08025) 273/C4
Ewan, Wash. (99127) 310/H3
Ewaninga, North. Terr. 93/D7
Ewart, Iowa (†50171) 229/H5
Ewarton, Jamaica 156/C3
Ewarton, Jamaica 158/J6
Ewauna (lake), Oreg. 291/F5
Ewe, Loch (inlet), Scotland 15/C3
Ewell, Md. (21824) 245/O9
Ewen, Mich. (49925) 250/F2
Ewing, Ill. (62836) 222/E5
Ewing, Ky. (41039) 237/O4
Ewing, Mo. (63440) 261/J2
Ewing, Nebr. (68735) 264/F2
Ewing (mt.), North. Terr. 93/E7
Ewing, Va. (24248) 307/B7
Ewington, Ohio (45627) 284/F8
Ewo, Congo 115/B4
Exaltación, Bolivia 136/C3
Excel, Ala. (36439) 195/D8
Excel, Alberta 182/E4
Excello, Mo. (65247) 261/H3
Excello, Ohio (45042) 284/B7
Excelsior, Minn. (55331) 255/E6
Excelsior (mts.), Nev. 266/C4
Excelsior, Wis. (†53518) 317/E9
Excelsior Springs, Mo. (64024) 261/R4
Exchange, W. Va. (26619) 312/E5
Excursion Inlet, Alaska (†99826) 196/M1
Exe (riv.), England 13/D7
Exe (riv.), England 10/E5
Executive Committee (range) 5/B12
Exeland, Wis. (54835) 317/D4
Exeter, Calif. (93221) 204/F7
Exeter, Conn. (†06249) 210/F2
Exeter, England 13/D7
Exeter, England 10/E5
Exeter, Ill. (†62694) 222/C4
Exeter, Maine (04435) 243/E6
Exeter○, Maine (04435) 243/E6
Exeter, Mo. (65647) 261/D9
Exeter, Nebr. (68351) 264/G4
Exeter, N.H. (03833) 268/F6
Exeter○, N.H. (03833) 268/F6
Exeter (riv.), N.H. 268/E6
Exeter (sound), N.W. Terrs. 187/M3
Exeter, Ontario 177/C4
Exeter○, R.I. (02822) 249/H6
Exeter, Tasmania 99/C3
Exira, Iowa (50076) 229/D5
Exline, Iowa (52555) 229/H7
Exminster, England 13/D7
Exmoor National Park, England 13/D6
Exmore, Va. (23350) 307/S5
Exmouth, England 13/D7
Exmouth, England 10/E5
Exmouth, W. Australia 88/A4
Exmouth (gulf), W. Australia 88/A4
Exmouth, W. Australia 92/A3
Exmouth (gulf), W. Australia 92/A3
Expanse, Sask. 181/E6
Experiment, Georgia (30212) 217/D4
Exploits (riv.), Newf. 166/C4
Export, Pa. (15632) 294/C5
Exshaw, Alberta 182/C4
Extension, Br. Col. 184/J3
Extension, La. (71239) 238/G3
Exu, Brazil 132/G4
Exuma (cays), Bahamas 156/C1
Exuma (sound), Bahamas 156/C1
Eyasi (lake), Tanzania 115/F4
Eye, England 10/G4
Eye, England 13/J5
Eye (pen.), Scotland 15/B2
Eyebrow, Sask. 181/E5
Eyebrow (lake), Sask. 181/E5
Eyehill (creek), Sask. 181/B3
Eyemouth, Scotland 15/F5
Eyemouth, Scotland 10/F3
Eynesil, Turkey 63/H2
Eynhallow (sound), Scotland 15/E1
Eynort, Loch (inlet), Scotland 15/A3
Eyota, Minn. (55934) 255/F7
Eyre (lake), Australia 87/D8
Eyre (bay), Chile 138/D8
Eyre (mts.), N. Zealand 100/B6
Eyre (riv.), Queensland 88/F5
Eyre (lake), S. Australia 88/F5
Eyre (pen.), S. Australia 88/F6
Eyre (pen.), S. Australia 94/D5
Eyre, W. Australia 92/D6
Eyrecourt, Ireland 17/E5
Eyre North (lake), S. Australia 94/E3
Eyre South (lake), S. Australia 94/E3
Eysturoy (isl.), Denmark 21/B3
Eyüp, Turkey 63/D6
Ezel, Ky. (41425) 237/P5
Ezequiel Montes, Mexico 150/K6
Ezibider, Turkey 63/H2
Ezine, Turkey 63/B3
Ezna, Iran 66/F4
Ez Zababida, West Bank 65/C3
Ez Zarqa', Jordan 65/E3
Ez Zuetina, Libya 111/D1

F

Faaa, Fr. Poly. 86/S13
Fabens, Texas (79838) 303/B10
Faber (lake), N.W. Terrs. 187/G3
Faber, Va. (22938) 307/L5
Fabius, Ala. (35965) 195/G1
Fabius, N.Y. (13063) 276/J5
Fåborg, Denmark 21/D7
Fåborg, Denmark 18/G9
Fabriano, Italy 34/D3
Fabyan, Alberta 182/E3
Fabyan, Conn. (06245) 210/H1
Fabyan House, N.H. (†03595) 268/E3
Facatativá, Colombia 126/C5
Faceville, Georgia (†31717) 217/C9
Fachi, Niger 106/G5
Fackler, Ala. (35746) 195/G1
Factoryville, Pa. (18419) 294/L2
Facundo, Argentina 143/C6
Fada, Chad 111/D4
Fada-N'Gourma, Upper Volta 106/E6
Fadd, Hungary 41/E3
Faddeyevskiy (isl.), U.S.S.R. 4/B2
Faddeyevskiy (isl.), U.S.S.R. 48/P2
Faden, Newf. 166/A3
Faenza, Italy 34/C2
Faerøe (isls.), Den. 4/C10
Faerøe (isls.), Denmark 7/D2
Faerøe (isls.), Denmark 21/B2
FAERØE ISLANDS, Denmark 21/B2
Faerøe Islands, Denmark 21/B2
Fafan (riv.), Ethiopia 111/H6
Fafe, Portugal 33/B2
Fagan, Ky. (†40322) 237/O5
Făgăraş, Romania 45/G3
Fagernes, Norway 18/F6
Fagersta, Sweden 18/J6
Fagnano (lake), Argentina 143/C7
Fagnano (lake), Chile 138/F11
Faguibine (lake), Mali 106/D5
Fagundes, Brazil 132/G4
Fagus, Mo. (63938) 261/M9
Fahan, Ireland 17/G1
Fahrej (Iranshahr), Iran 66/M7
Fahrej (Iranshahr), Iran 59/H4
Faial (isl.), Portugal 33/B1
Faid, Saudi Arabia 59/D4
Faido, Switzerland 39/G4
Fainaven (mt.), Scotland 15/D2
Fair (head), N. Ireland 17/J1
Fair (isl.), Scotland 10/F1
Fairacres, N. Mex. (88033) 274/C6
Fairbank, Ariz. (85612) 198/E7
Fairbank, Iowa (50629) 229/K3
Fairbank, Md. (†21671) 245/N6
Fairbanks, Alaska 146/D3
Fairbanks, Alaska (99701) 196/J2
Fairbanks, Alaska 188/D5
Fairbanks, Fla. (†32601) 212/D2
Fairbanks, Ind. (47849) 227/B6
Fairbanks, La. (71240) 238/F1
Fairbanks, Maine (†04938) 243/C6
Fairbanks, Minn. (†55602) 255/G3
Fairbanks, U.S. 4/C17
Fairbanks, U.S. 2/C2
Fair Bluff, N.C. (28439) 281/M6
Fairborn, Ohio (45324) 284/B6
Fairburn, Georgia (30213) 217/J2
Fairburn, S. Dak. (57738) 298/C6
Fairbury, Ill. (61739) 222/E3
Fairbury, Nebr. (68352) 264/G4
Fairchance, Pa. (15436) 294/C6
Fairchild, Wis. (54741) 317/D6
Fairchild A.F.B., Wash. 310/H3
Fairdale, Ill. (†60146) 222/E1
Fairdale, Ky. (40118) 237/K4
Fairdale, N. Dak. (58229) 282/O3
Fairdealing, Mo. (63939) 261/L9
Fairfax, Ala. (36854) 195/H5
Fairfax, Calif. (94930) 204/H1
Fairfax, Iowa (52228) 229/K5
Fairfax, Manitoba 179/B5
Fairfax, Minn. (55332) 255/D6
Fairfax, Mo. (64446) 261/B2
Fairfax, Ohio (†45201) 284/C9
Fairfax, Okla. (74637) 288/N1
Fairfax, S.C. (29827) 296/E6
Fairfax, S. Dak. (57335) 298/M7
Fairfax○, Vt. (05454) 268/B2
Fairfax (co.), Va. 307/O3
Fairfax (I.C.), Va. (22030) 307/R3
Fairfax, Wash. (†98323) 310/C4
Fairfax Station, Va. (22039) 307/R3
Fairfield, Ala. (35064) 195/E4
Fairfield, Calif. (94533) 204/K1
Fairfield (co.), Conn. 210/B3
Fairfield○, Conn. (06430) 210/B4
Fairfield, Fla. (32634) 212/D2
Fairfield, Idaho (83327) 220/D6
Fairfield, Ill. (62837) 222/E5
Fairfield, Iowa (52556) 229/J6
Fairfield, Ky. (40020) 237/L5
Fairfield, Maine (04937) 243/D6
Fairfield○, Maine (04937) 243/D6
Fairfield, Mont. (59436) 262/D3
Fairfield, Nebr. (68938) 264/G4
Fairfield, New Bruns. 170/E3
Fairfield○, N.J. (07006) 273/A2
Fairfield, N. S. Wales 88/K4
Fairfield, N.S. Wales 97/H3
Fairfield, N. Zealand 100/C6
Fairfield, N.C. (27826) 281/S3
Fairfield, N. Dak. (58627) 282/D5
Fairfield (co.), Ohio 284/E6
Fairfield, Ohio (45014) 284/A7
Fairfield, Pa. (17320) 294/H6
Fairfield (co.), S.C. 296/E3
Fairfield, Tenn. (†37183) 237/J9
Fairfield, Texas (75840) 303/H6
Fairfield, Utah (†84013) 304/B3
Fairfield○, Vt. (05455) 268/B2
Fairfield (pond), Vt. 268/A2
Fairfield, Va. (24435) 307/K5
Fairfield, Wash. (99012) 310/H3
Fairfield Center, Maine (†04937) 243/D6
Fairford, Ala. (†36553) 195/B8
Fairford, Manitoba 179/D3
Fairgrange, Ill. (†61920) 222/E4
Fairgrove, Mich. (48733) 250/F5
Fair Grove, Mo. (65648) 261/F8W
Fair Harbour, Br. Col. 184/D5
Fairhaven○, Mass. (02719) 249/L6
Fair Haven, Mich. (48023) 250/G6
Fairhaven, Minn. (†55382) 255/D5
Fairhaven, New Bruns. 170/C4

368 Fair Haven

Fair Haven, N.J. (07701) 273/E3
Fair Haven, N.Y. (13064) 276/G4
Fairhaven, Ohio (†45003) 284/A6
Fair Haven, Vt. (05743) 268/A4
Fair Haven○, Vt. (05743) 268/A4
Fair Hill, Md. (†21921) 245/P2
Fairholme, Sask. 181/C2
Fairhope, Ala. (36532) 195/C10
Fairhope, Pa. (15538) 294/E6
Fairisle, New Bruns. 170/E1
Fair Isle (isl.), Scotland 15/F3
Fairland, Ind. (46126) 227/F5
Fairland, Okla. (74343) 288/S1
Fair Lawn, N.J. (07410) 273/B1
Fairlawn, Ohio (44313) 284/G3
Fairlawn, Va. (24141) 307/G6
Fairlee, Md. (†21620) 245/O4
Fairlee○, Vt. (05045) 268/C4
Fairless Hills, Pa. (19030) 294/N5
Fairlie, N. Zealand 100/C6
Fairlie, Scotland 15/D5
Fairlight, Sask. 181/K6
Fairmead, Calif. (†93610) 204/E6
Fairmont, Ill. (†62002) 222/A2
Fairmont, Minn. (56031) 255/D7
Fairmont, Mo. (†63474) 261/J2
Fairmont, Nebr. (68354) 264/G4
Fairmont, N.C. (28340) 281/L6
Fairmont, Okla. (73736) 288/L2
Fairmont, W. Va. 188/K3
Fairmont, W. Va. (26554) 312/F4
Fairmont City, Ill. (†62201) 222/B2
Fairmont Hot Springs, Br. Col. 184/J5
Fairmount, Georgia (30139) 217/C2
Fairmount, Ill. (61841) 222/F3
Fairmount, Ind. (46928) 227/F4
Fairmount, Md. (†21871) 245/P8
Fairmount, N. Dak. (58030) 282/S7
Fairmount, Sask. 181/B4
Fairmount Heights, Md. (†20027) 245/G5
Fair Oaks, Ark. (72397) 202/J3
Fair Oaks, Calif. (95628) 204/C8
Fair Oaks, Georgia (†30060) 217/J1
Fair Oaks, Ind. (47943) 227/C2
Fair Oaks, Okla. (†74080) 288/P2
Fair Plain, Mich. (49022) 250/C6
Fairplain, W. Va. (†25271) 312/C5
Fairplay, Colo. (80440) 208/H4
Fairplay, Ky. (42735) 237/L7
Fair Play, Mo. (65649) 261/E7
Fair Play, S.C. (29643) 296/A2
Fairpoint, Ohio (43927) 284/J5
Fairpoint, S. Dak. (†57785) 298/D4
Fairport, Iowa (†52761) 229/M6
Fairport, Kansas (†67665) 232/C2
Fairport, Mo. (64447) 261/D2
Fairport, N.Y. (14450) 276/F4
Fairport, Va. (†22539) 307/R5
Fairport Harbor, Ohio (44077) 284/H2
Fairton, N.J. (08320) 273/C5
Fairvale, New Bruns. 170/E3
Fairview, Ala. (35208) 195/E2
Fairview, Alberta 182/A1
Fairview, Ill. (61432) 222/B3
Fairview, Ind. (†46127) 227/G5
Fairview, Ind. (†47018) 227/G7
Fairview, Kansas (66425) 232/G2
Fairview, Ky. (†41101) 237/S2
Fairview, Ky. (42221) 237/G7
Fairview, Mich. (48621) 250/F4
Fairview, Mo. (64842) 261/D9
Fairview, Mont. (59221) 262/M3
Fairview, N.J. (07022) 273/C2
Fairview, N.Y. (†12601) 276/N7
Fairview, N.C. (28730) 281/D3
Fairview, Ohio (43736) 284/H5
Fairview, Okla. (73737) 288/J2
Fairview, Oreg. (97024) 291/B2
Fairview, Pa. (16415) 294/B1
Fairview, Pa. (†16041) 294/C3
Fairview, S. Dak. (57027) 298/R7
Fairview, Tenn. (37062) 237/G9
Fairview, Utah (84629) 304/C4
Fairview, W. Va. (26570) 312/F3
Fairview, Wyo. (83119) 319/B3
Fairview Heights, Ill. (62208) 222/B3
Fairview Park, Ind. (†47842) 227/C5
Fairview Park, Ohio (44126) 284/G9
Fairview-Sumach, Wash. (†98901) 310/E4
Fair Water, Wis. (53931) 317/J8
Fairway, Kansas (†66101) 232/H2
Fairweather (cape), Alaska 196/L1
Fairweather (mt.), Alaska 196/L1
Fairweather (mt.), Br. Col. 184/H1
Fairy Glen, Sask. 181/G2
Fais (isl.), Micronesia 87/E5
Faisalabad, Pakistan 54/J6
Faisalabad, Pakistan 59/K3
Faisalabad, Pakistan 68/C2
Faison, N.C. (28341) 281/N4
Faith, Minn. (†56584) 255/B3
Faith, N.C. (28041) 281/J3
Faith, S. Dak. (57626) 298/E4
Faithorn, Mich. (†49892) 250/B3
Faizabad-cum-Ayodhya, India 68/E3
Fajami, Syria 63/J5
Fajardo, P. Rico 161/F1
Fajardo (riv.), P. Rico 161/F1
Fajou (isl.), Guadeloupe 161/A6
Fakaofo (atoll), Tokelau Is. 87/J6
Fakarava (atoll), Fr. Poly. 87/M7
Fakenham, England 13/H5
Fakfak, Indonesia 85/J6
Fakılı, Turkey 63/F3
Fakse, Denmark 21/F7
Fakse (bay), Denmark 21/F7
Fakse Ladeplads, Denmark 21/F7
Falaise, France 28/C3
Falam, Burma 72/B2
Falama, West Bank 65/C3
Falcarragh, Ireland 17/E1
Fălciu, Romania 45/J2
Falcon, Ky. (41426) 237/P5
Falcon (lake), Manitoba 179/G5
Falcón (res.), Mexico 150/K3
Falcon, Miss. (38628) 256/D2
Falcon, N.C. (28342) 281/M4
Falcon (cape), Oreg. 291/C2
Falcon (res.), Texas 188/G5
Falcon (dam), Texas 303/E11
Falcon (res.), Texas 303/E11
Falcón (state), Venezuela 124/D2
Falcone (cape), Italy 34/B4
Falconer, N.Y. (14733) 276/B6
Falcon Heights, Minn. (55113) 255/G5
Falcon Heights, Oreg. (†97601) 291/F5
Falcon Lake, Manitoba 179/G5
Falémé (riv.), Mali 106/B6
Falémé (riv.), Senegal 106/B6
Faleolo, W. Samoa 86/L8
Falfurrias, Texas (78355) 303/F10
Falher, Alberta 182/B2
Falkenberg, Sweden 18/H8
Falkensee, E. Germany 22/E3
Falkenstein, E. Germany 22/E3
Falkirk, N. Dak. (†58577) 282/H5
Falkirk, Scotland 10/D3
Falkirk, Scotland 15/C1
Falkland (isls.) 2/G8
Falkland (isls.), 143/D7
Falkland (sound), 143/D7
Falkland, Br. Col. 184/H5
Falkland, N.C. (27827) 281/O3
Falkland, Scotland 15/E4
FALKLAND ISLANDS 143
Falkland Islands 120/D8
Falkner, Miss. (38629) 256/G1
Falknov (Sokolov), Czech. 41/B1
Falköping, Sweden 18/H7
Falkville, Ala. (35622) 195/E2
Fall (riv.), Kansas 232/G4
Falla, Cuba 158/F2
Fall Branch, Tenn. (37656) 237/R8
Fallbrook, Calif. (92028) 204/H10
Fall City, Wash. (98024) 310/D3
Fall Creek, Oreg. (97438) 291/E4
Fall Creek, Wis. (54742) 317/D6
Fallin, Scotland 15/C1
Falling Spring (Renick), W. Va. (†24966) 312/F6
Falling Waters, W. Va. (25419) 312/L3
Fallis, Okla. (†74881) 288/M3
Fall Mills, Tenn. (†37345) 237/J10
Fallon (co.), Mont. 262/M4
Fallon, Mont. (59326) 262/L4
Fallon, Nev. (89406) 266/C3
Fallon Ind. Res., Nev. 266/C3
Fallon Nav. Air Sta., Nev. 266/C3
Fall River, Kansas (67047) 232/G4
Fall River (lake), Kansas 232/F4
Fall River, Mass. 188/M2
Fall River, Mass. (*02720) 249/K6
Fall River, Nova Scotia 168/E4
Fall River (co.), S. Dak. 298/B7
Fall River, Tenn. (†38468) 237/G10
Fall River, Wis. (53932) 317/H9
Fall River Mills, Calif. (96028) 204/D3
Falls (riv.), Mass. 249/D2
Falls, Pa. (18615) 294/E6
Falls (co.), Texas 303/H6
Falls Church (I.C.), Va. (*22040) 307/S2
Falls City, Nebr. (68355) 264/J4
Falls City, Oreg. (97344) 291/D3
Falls City, Texas (78113) 303/G9
Falls Creek, Pa. (15840) 294/E3
Falls Mill, W. Va. (26620) 312/E5
Falls Mills, Va. (24613) 307/F6
Falls of Rough, Ky. (40119) 237/J5
Fallston, Md. (21047) 245/N2
Fallston, N.C. (28042) 281/G4
Falls Village, Conn. (06031) 210/B1
Fallsville, Ark. (†72861) 202/D2
Falmouth, Ant. & Bar. 161/E11
Falmouth, Ant. & Bar. 156/F3
Falmouth, England 10/D5
Falmouth, England 13/B7
Falmouth (bay), England 13/B7
Falmouth, Ind. (46127) 227/G5
Falmouth, Jamaica 158/H5
Falmouth, Jamaica 156/C3
Falmouth, Ky. (41040) 237/N3
Falmouth, Maine (04105) 243/C8
Falmouth○, Maine (04105) 243/C8
Falmouth, Mass. (*02540) 249/M6
Falmouth○, Mass. (*02540) 249/M6
Falmouth, Mich. (49632) 250/E4
Falmouth, Nova Scotia 168/D3
Falmouth, Va. (22401) 307/O4
False (bay), S. Africa 118/F7
False Detour (chan.), Mich. 250/F3
False Divi (pt.), India 68/E5
False Pass, Alaska (99583) 196/F4
Falso (cape), Dom. Rep. 158/C7
Falso (cape), Honduras 154/F3
Falso (cape), Mexico 150/D5
Falster (isl.), Denmark 21/F8
Fălticeni, Romania 45/H2
Falun, Kansas (67442) 232/E3
Falun, Sweden 18/J6
Falun, Sweden 7/F2
Falun, Wis. (†54840) 317/A4
Famagusta, Cyprus 63/F5
Famagusta, Cyprus 59/B3
Famagusta (bay), Cyprus 63/F5
Famaka, Sudan 111/F5
Famatina, Argentina 143/C2
Famatina, Sierra de (mts.), Argentina 143/C2
Family (lake), Manitoba 179/G3
Famoso, Calif. (†93280) 204/F8
Fan (lake), N. Dak. 282/L2
Fanad (head), Ireland 17/F1
Fancy Farm, Ky. (42039) 237/D7
Fancy Gap, Va. (24328) 307/G7
Fancy Prairie, Ill. (62637) 222/D4
Fandriana, Madagascar 118/H4
Fangak, Sudan 111/F6
Fang Xian, China 77/G5
Fangzheng, China 77/L2
Fannettsburg, Pa. (17221) 294/G5
Fannich, Loch (lake), Scotland 15/D3
Fannin (co.), Georgia 217/D1
Fannin, Miss. (†39042) 256/E6
Fannin (co.), Texas 303/H4
Fannin, Texas (77960) 303/G9
Fanning (isl.), Kiribati 87/L5
Fanning (isl.), Kiribati 2/B5
Fanning Springs (Suwannee River), Fla. (†32693) 212/D2
Fanny Bay, Br. Col. 184/H2
Fannystelle, Manitoba 179/E5
Fanø (isl.), Denmark 21/B7
Fanø (isl.), Denmark 18/F9
Fano, Italy 34/D3
Fanshawe, Okla. (74935) 288/S5
Fan Si Pan (mt.), Vietnam 72/D2
Fantasque (pt.), Haiti 158/B6
Fanwood, N.J. (07023) 273/E2
Fao, Iraq 66/F6
Faradje, Zaire 115/E3
Faradofay, Madagascar 102/G7
Faradofay, Madagascar 118/H5
Farafangana, Madagascar 102/G7
Farafangana, Madagascar 118/H4
Farâfra (oasis), Egypt 111/E2
Farâfra (oasis), Egypt 59/A4
Farah, Afghanistan 68/A2
Farah, Afghanistan 54/H6
Farah, Afghanistan 59/H3
Farah Rud (riv.) 54/H6
Farah Rud (riv.), Afghanistan 59/H3
Farah Rud (riv.), Afghanistan 68/A2
Farallon (isls.), Calif. 204/B6
Farallon de Pajaros (isl.), No. Marianas 87/E3
Farallons, The (gulf), Calif. 204/H2
Faranah, Guinea 106/B6
Farasan (isls.), Saudi Arabia 59/D6
Faraulep (atoll), Micronesia 87/E5
Farber, Mo. (63345) 261/J4
Farciennes, Belgium 27/E8
Fareham, England 10/F5
Fareham, England 13/F7
Farewell, Alaska (†99629) 196/H2
Farewell (cape), Greenl. 4/D12
Farewell (cape), Greenland 146/P4
Farewell (cape), Greenland 2/G3
Farewell (cape), N. Zealand 100/D4
Farfa, Italy 34/D3
Farfán, Ecuador 128/D2
Fargo, Ark. (†72021) 202/H4
Fargo, Georgia (31631) 217/G9
Fargo, Mich. (†48006) 250/G5
Fargo, N. Dak. 146/J5
Fargo, N. Dak. 188/G1
Fargo, N. Dak. (58102) 282/S6
Fargo, Okla. (73840) 288/G2
Fargo, Texas (†76384) 303/E3
Far Hills, N.J. (07931) 273/D2
Faribault, Minn. 188/H2
Faribault (co.), Minn. 255/D7
Faribault, Minn. (55021) 255/E6
Faridabad, India 68/D3
Faridpur, Bangladesh 68/F4
Fariman, Iran 66/L3
Farina, Ill. (62838) 222/E5
Farisita, Colo. (81037) 208/J7
Fariston, Ky. (†40741) 237/N6
Färjestaden, Sweden 18/K8
Farler, Ky. (41742) 237/P6
Farley, Iowa (52046) 229/L4
Farley, Mo. (64028) 261/O4
Farley, N. Mex. (†87747) 274/E2
Farlin, Iowa (50077) 229/E4
Farlington, Kansas (66734) 232/H4
Farm (riv.), Conn. 210/D3
Farmdale, Ohio (44417) 284/J3
Farmer, N.C. (27203) 281/K3
Farmer (isl.), N.W. Terrs. 187/K4
Farmer, Ohio (43520) 284/A3
Farmer, S. Dak. (57336) 298/O6
Farmer City, Ill. (61842) 222/E3
Farmers, Ky. (40319) 237/P4
Farmers Branch, Texas (75234) 303/G2
Farmersburg, Ind. (47850) 227/C6
Farmersburg, Iowa (52047) 229/L3
Farmersville, Ala. (36737) 195/E6
Farmersville, Calif. (93223) 204/F7
Farmersville, Ill. (62533) 222/D4
Farmersville, Mo. (†64683) 261/E3
Farmersville, Ohio (45325) 284/A6
Farmersville, Texas (75031) 303/H4
Farmerville, La. (71241) 238/F1
Farmhaven, Miss. (†39046) 256/E5
Farmill (riv.), Conn. 210/C3
Farmingdale, Maine (†04345) 243/D7
Farmingdale○, Maine (†04345) 243/D7
Farmingdale, N.J. (07727) 273/E3
Farmingdale, N.Y. (11735) 276/R7
Farmingdale, S. Dak. (†57725) 298/D6
Farmington, Ark. (72730) 202/B1
Farmington, Br. Col. 184/G2
Farmington, Calif. (95230) 204/E6
Farmington○, Conn. (06032) 210/D2
Farmington (riv.), Conn. 210/D1
Farmington, Del. (19942) 245/R5
Farmington, Georgia (30638) 217/F3
Farmington, Ill. (61531) 222/C3
Farmington, Iowa (52626) 229/K7
Farmington, Ky. (42040) 237/D7
Farmington, Maine (04938) 243/C6
Farmington○, Maine (04938) 243/C6
Farmington, Md. (†21911) 245/O2
Farmington, Mich. (*48024) 250/F6
Farmington, Minn. (55024) 255/E6
Farmington, Mo. (63640) 261/M7
Farmington, N.H. (03835) 268/E5
Farmington○, N.H. (03835) 268/E5
Farmington, N.M. 188/E3
Farmington, N. Mex. (87401) 274/A2
Farmington, N.C. (†27028) 281/H3
Farmington, Oreg. (†97123) 291/A2
Farmington, Tenn. (†37091) 237/H9
Farmington, Utah (84025) 304/C3
Farmington, Wash. (99128) 310/H3
Farmington, W. Va. (26571) 312/F3
Farmington, Wis. (†54020) 317/A5
Farmington Falls, Maine (04940) 243/C6
Farmington Hills, Mich. (48024) 250/F6
Farmland, Ind. (47340) 227/G4
Farmville, N.C. (27828) 281/O3
Farmville, Va. (23901) 307/M6
Farnam, Nebr. (69029) 264/D4
Farnams, Mass. (†01225) 249/B2
Farnborough, England 13/G8
Farner, Tenn. (37333) 237/N10
Farnham, England 13/G8
Farnham, England 10/F5
Farnham, N.Y. (14061) 276/B6
Farnham, Québec 172/E4
Farnham, Va. (22460) 307/P5
Farnhamville, Iowa (50538) 229/D4
Farnsworth, Texas (79033) 303/C1
Farnworth, England 13/H2
Faro, Brazil 132/B3
Faro (dist.), Portugal 33/B4
Faro, Portugal 7/D5
Faro, Portugal 33/B4
Fårö (isl.), Sweden 18/L8
Faro, Yukon 187/E3
Faro, Yukon 162/C3
Fårösund, Sweden 18/L8
Farquhar (cape), W. Australia 88/A4
Farquhar (cape), W. Australia 92/A3
Farr (bay) 5/C5
Farragut, Iowa (51639) 229/C7
Farrar, Georgia (†31085) 217/E4
Farrar, Iowa (†50161) 229/G5
Farrar, Mo. (63740) 261/N7
Farrar (riv.), Scotland 15/D3
Farrashband, Iran 66/G6
Farrell (lake), Alberta 182/D4
Farrell, Miss. (38630) 256/C2
Farrell, Pa. (16121) 294/A3
Farrellton, Québec 172/A4
Farris, Okla. (74542) 288/P6
Farrow, Alberta 182/D4
Farrukhabad-cum-Fatehgarh, India 68/D3
Fars (prov.), Iran 66/H6
Fársala, Greece 45/F6
Farsi, Afghanistan 68/A2
Farsi, Afghanistan 59/H3
Farsi (isl.), Iran 66/G7
Farsø, Denmark 21/C4
Farson, Iowa (†52563) 229/J6
Farson, Wyo. (82932) 319/C3
Farsund, Norway 18/E7
Fartak, Ras (cape), P.D.R. Yemen 59/F6
Farum, Denmark 21/F6
Farwell, Mich. (48622) 250/E5
Farwell, Minn. (56327) 255/C5
Farwell, Nebr. (68838) 264/F3
Farwell, Texas (79325) 303/A3
Fasa, Iran 66/H6
Fasa, Iran 59/F4
Fasano, Italy 34/F4
Fashoda (Kodok), Sudan 111/F6
Fassett, Québec 172/C4
Fastnet Rock (isl.), Ireland 17/B9
Fastov, U.S.S.R. 52/C4
Fatagar Tuting (cape), Indonesia 85/J6
Fatehpur, Rajasthan, India 68/C3
Fatehpur, Uttar Pradesh, India 68/E3
Fatih, Turkey 63/D6
Fátima, Portugal 33/B3
Fatsa, Turkey 63/G2
Fatshan (Foshan), China 77/H7
Fatuhiva (isl.), Fr. Poly. 87/N7
Faubush, Ky. (42532) 237/M6
Faucett, Mo. (64448) 261/C3
Faucilles (mts.), France 28/G3
Fauldhouse, Scotland 10/C1
Fauldhouse, Scotland 15/C2
Faulk (co.), S. Dak. 298/L3
Faulkner (co.), Ark. 202/F3
Faulkner, Iowa (†50601) 229/G3
Faulkner, Manitoba 179/D3
Faulkton, S. Dak. (57438) 298/L3
Faunsdale, Ala. (36738) 195/C6
Fauquier, Ontario 177/J5
Fauquier, Ontario 175/D3
Fauquier (co.), Va. 307/N3
Făurei, 45/H3
Faust, Alberta 182/C2
Favara, Italy 34/D6
Faversham, England 13/H6
Faversham, England 10/G5
Favignana (isl.), Italy 34/D6
Fawcett, Alberta 182/C2
Fawn (riv.), Ind. 227/G1
Fawn (riv.), Mich. 250/D7
Fawn (lake), Ont. 162/H5
Fawn (riv.), Ontario 175/C2
Fawn Grove, Pa. (17321) 294/J6
Fawnskin, Calif. (92333) 204/J9
Faxaflói (bay), Iceland 21/B1
Faxon, Okla. (73540) 288/J6
Fay, Ill. (†61285) 222/C2
Fay, Okla. (73646) 288/J3
Faya-Largeau, Chad 102/D3
Faya-Largeau, Chad 111/C4
Fayette (co.), Ala. 195/C3
Fayette, Ala. (35555) 195/C3
Fayette (co.), Georgia 217/C4
Fayette (co.), Ill. 222/D4
Fayette (co.), Ind. 227/G5
Fayette, Ind. (†46052) 227/E5
Fayette (co.), Iowa 229/K3
Fayette, Iowa (52142) 229/K3
Fayette (co.), Ky. 237/N4
Fayette○, Maine (†04349) 243/C7
Fayette, Miss. (39069) 256/B7
Fayette, Mo. (65248) 261/G4
Fayette (co.), Ohio 284/D6
Fayette, Ohio (43521) 284/B2
Fayette (co.), Pa. 294/C6
Fayette (co.), Tenn. 237/C10
Fayette (co.), Texas 303/H8
Fayette, Utah (84630) 304/C4
Fayette (co.), W. Va. 312/D6
Fayette City, Pa. (15438) 294/C5
Fayetteville, Ala. (†35150) 195/F4
Fayetteville, Ark. 188/H3
Fayetteville, Ark. (72701) 202/B1
Fayetteville, Georgia (30214) 217/C4
Fayetteville, Ill. (†62258) 222/D5
Fayetteville, Ind. (†47421) 227/D7
Fayetteville, Mo. (†64093) 261/E5
Fayetteville, N.Y. (13066) 276/J4
Fayetteville, N.C. 188/L3
Fayetteville, N.C. (*28301) 281/M4
Fayetteville, Ohio (45118) 284/C7
Fayetteville, Pa. (17222) 294/G6
Fayetteville, Tenn. (37334) 237/H10
Fayetteville, Texas (78940) 303/H8
Fayetteville, W. Va. (25840) 312/D6
Fayville, Mass. (01745) 249/H3
Faywood, N. Mex. (88034) 274/B6
Fdérik (Fort-Gouraud), Mauritania 106/B4
Feakle, Ireland 17/D6
Feale (riv.), Ireland 17/C7
Fear (cape), N.C. 188/L4
Fear (cape), N.C. 281/O7
Fearer, Md. (†21531) 245/A2
Fearns Springs, Miss. (†39339) 256/G4
Feather (riv.), Calif. 204/D4
Feather Falls, Calif. (95940) 204/D4
Featherston, N. Zealand 100/E4
Featherston, Okla. (†74561) 288/P4
Fécamp, France 28/D3
Fédala (Mohammedia), Morocco 106/C2
Federación, Argentina 143/G5
Federal, Alberta 182/E3
Federal, Wyo. (†82001) 319/G4
Federal Dam, Minn. (56641) 255/D3
Federal District, Brazil 132/E6
Federal Heights, Colo. (†80221) 208/J3
Federalsburg, Md. (21632) 245/P6
Federal Territory (state), Laos 72/D7
Fedora, S. Dak. (57337) 298/O5
Fedscreek, Ky. (41524) 237/S6
Feeagh (lake), Ireland 17/B4
Feeding Hills, Mass. (01030) 249/D4
Feeny, N. Ireland 17/H2
Feesburg, Ohio (45119) 284/B8
Fegyvernek, Hungary 41/F3
Fehérgyarmat, Hungary 41/G3
Fehmarn (str.), Denmark 21/E8
Fehmarn (isl.), W. Germany 22/D1
Fehmarn (str.), W. Germany 22/D1
Feia (lake), Brazil 135/F3
Feijó, Brazil 132/G10
Feilding, N. Zealand 100/E4
Feio (riv.), Brazil 135/B2
Feira, Portugal 33/B2
Feira (Luangwa), Zambia 115/E7
Feira de Santana, Brazil 132/G5
Feira de Santana, Brazil 120/F4
Fejér (co.), Hungary 41/E3
Fejø (isl.), Denmark 21/E8
Feke, Turkey 63/G4
Felanitx, Spain 33/H3
Felch, Mich. (49831) 250/B3
Felchville (Reading), Vt. (†05062) 268/B5
Felda, Fla. (33930) 212/E5
Feldbach, Austria 41/C3
Feldberg (mt.), W. Germany 22/C5
Feldkirch, Austria 41/A3
Feldkirchen in Kärnten, Austria 41/B3
Feliciano (riv.), Argentina 143/G5
Felicité (isl.), Seychelles 118/J5
Felicity, Ohio (45120) 284/B8
Felipe Carillo Puerto, Mexico 150/P7
Felipe Matiauda, Paraguay 144/D4
Felipe Yofré, Argentina 143/G4
Felix (cape), N.W. Terrs. 187/J3
Felixstowe, England 10/G5
Felixstowe, England 13/J6
Fellbach, W. Germany 22/C4
Felletin, France 28/E5
Felling, England 13/J3
Fellows, Calif. (93224) 204/F8
Fellowsville, W. Va. (†26410) 312/G4
Fellsburg, Kansas (67048) 232/C4
Fellsmere, Fla. (32948) 212/F4
Fels am Wagram, Austria 41/C2
Felsberg, Switzerland 39/H3
Felsenthal, Ark. (†71747) 202/F7
Felt, Idaho (83424) 220/G6
Felt, Okla. (73937) 288/A1
Felton, Ark. (†72360) 202/J4
Felton, Calif. (95018) 204/K4
Felton, Del. (19943) 245/R4
Felton, Georgia (30140) 217/B3
Felton, Minn. (56536) 255/B3
Felton, Pa. (17322) 294/J6
Feltre, Italy 34/C1
Felts Mills, N.Y. (13638) 276/J3
Feltwell, England 13/H5
Felty, Ky. (†40962) 237/O6
Femø (isl.), Denmark 21/E8
Femundsjø (lake), Norway 18/G5
Fence (riv.), Mich. 250/A2
Fence, Wis. (54120) 317/K4
Fence Lake, N. Mex. (87315) 274/A4
Fender, Georgia (†31794) 217/E8
Fenelon Falls, Ontario 177/F3
Fengcheng, China 77/K3
Fengjie, China 77/G5
Fengning, China 77/J3
Fengqing, China 77/E7
Fengtai, China 77/J5
Feng Xian, China 77/G5
Fengxiang, China 77/G5
Fengyang, China 77/H4
Fengzhen, China 77/H3
Fen He (riv.), China 77/H4
Fenholloway (riv.), Fla. 212/C1
Feni (isls.), Papua N.G. 86/C2
Fenimore (passage), Alaska 196/L4
Fenit, Ireland 17/B7
Fenn, Alberta 182/D3
Fenn, Idaho (83531) 220/B4
Fenner, Calif. (†92332) 204/K9
Fennimore, Wis. (53809) 317/E9
Fennville, Mich. (49408) 250/C6
Fenoarivo, Fianarantsoa, Madagascar 118/H4
Fenoarivo, Toamasina, Madagascar 118/H3
Fens, The (reg.), England 13/G5
Fenton (riv.), Conn. 210/G1
Fenton, Ill. (61251) 222/C2
Fenton, Iowa (50539) 229/E2
Fenton, La. (70640) 238/E6
Fenton, Mich. (48430) 250/F6
Fenton, Mo. (63026) 261/O4
Fenton, Sask. 181/F2
Fentress (co.), Tenn. 237/M8
Fenwick, Conn. (†06475) 210/F3
Fenwick, Mich. (48834) 250/D5
Fenwick, Nova Scotia 168/D3
Fenwick, W. Va. (26202) 312/E6
Fenwick Island, Del. (19944) 245/T7
Fenwood, Sask. 181/H4
Fenwood, Wis. (54431) 317/F6
Feodosiya, U.S.S.R. 52/D5
Ferbane, Ireland 17/F5
Ferdig, Mont. (59437) 262/E2
Ferdinand, Idaho (83526) 220/B3
Ferdinand, Ind. (47532) 227/D8
Ferdows, Iran 59/G3
Ferdows, Iran 66/K3
Ferfer, Somalia 115/J2
Fergana, U.S.S.R. 54/J6
Fergana, U.S.S.R. 48/H5
Fergus (riv.), Ireland 17/D6
Fergus (co.), Mont. 262/G3
Fergus, Mont. (59451) 262/H3
Fergus, Ontario 177/D4
Fergus Falls, Minn. (56537) 255/B4
Ferguson, Br. Col. 184/J5
Ferguson, Iowa (50078) 229/H5
Ferguson, Ky. (42533) 237/M6
Ferguson, Mo. (63135) 261/P2
Ferguson, N.C. (28624) 281/G2
Ferguson, W. Va. (†25511) 312/B6
Ferintosh, Alberta 182/D3
Ferkessédougou, Ivory Coast 106/D7
Ferlach, Austria 41/C3
Ferland, Ontario 177/H4
Ferland, Ontario 175/C2
Ferland, Québec 172/G1
Ferland, Sask. 181/D6
Ferlo (reg.), Senegal 106/B6
Fermanagh (dist.), N. Ireland 17/F3
Ferme-Neuve, Québec 172/B3
Fermeuse, Newf. 166/D2
Fermo, Italy 34/D3
Fermont, Québec 174/D2
Fermoselle, Spain 33/C2
Fermoy, Ireland 17/E7
Fermoy, Ireland 10/B4
Fernald, Iowa (†50201) 229/G4
Fernández, Argentina 143/D2
Fernandina (isl.), Ecuador 128/B9
Fernandina Beach, Fla. (32034) 212/E1
Fernando de la Mora, Paraguay 144/B4
Fernando Po (Bioko) (isl.), Equat. Guinea 102/C4
Fernando Po (Bioko) (isl.), Equat. Guinea 115/A3
Fernandópolis, Brazil 135/A2
Fernan Lake, Idaho (†83814) 220/B2
Fernbank, Ala. (35558) 195/B3
Fernberg, Queensland 88/K3
Ferndale, Calif. (95536) 204/A3
Ferndale, Md. (21061) 245/M4
Ferndale, Mich. (48220) 250/B6
Ferndale, Pa. (18921) 294/M4
Ferndale, Pa. (15905) 294/E5
Ferndale, Wash. (98248) 310/C2
Fernelmont, Belgium 27/F7
Ferness, Scotland 15/E3
Ferney, S. Dak. (57439) 298/N3
Fernie, Br. Col. 162/E6
Fernie, Br. Col. 184/K5
Fernley, Nev. (89408) 266/B3
Fern Ridge (lake), Oreg. 291/D3
Ferns, Ireland 17/J6
Fern Tree Gully, Victoria 97/K5
Fernwood, Idaho (83830) 220/B2
Fernwood, Miss. (39635) 256/D8
Fernwood, N.Y. (†12801) 276/N4
Fernwood, N.Y. (†13142) 276/H4
Ferolle (pt.), Newf. 166/C3
Ferrandina, Italy 34/F4
Ferrara (prov.), Italy 34/C2
Ferrara, Italy 7/F4
Ferrara, Italy 34/C2
Ferré (cape), Martinique 161/E7
Ferreira do Alentejo, Portugal 33/B3
Ferreira Gomes, Brazil 132/D2
Ferrellsburg, W. Va. (25513) 312/B6
Ferrelo (cape), Oreg. 291/C5
Ferrelview, Mo. (64163) 261/O4
Ferreñafe, Peru 128/C6
Ferriday, La. (71334) 238/G3
Ferrier, Alberta 182/C3
Ferrières, Belgium 27/H8
Ferris, Ill. (62336) 222/B3
Ferris, Texas (75125) 303/H3
Ferris (mts.), Wyo. 319/E3
Ferrisburg○, Vt. (05456) 268/A3
Ferrol (pen.), Peru 128/C7
Ferrol del Caudillo, Spain 33/B1
Ferron, Utah (84523) 304/C4
Ferron (creek), Utah 304/C4
Ferros, Brazil 132/F7
Ferrum, Va. (24088) 307/H7
Ferry, Guadeloupe 161/A6
Ferry, Mich. (49455) 250/C5
Ferry (co.), Wash. 310/G2
Ferryden, Scotland 15/F4
Ferryland, Newf. 166/D2
Ferryland (cape), Newf. 166/D2
Ferry Road, New Bruns. 170/E1
Ferrysburg, Mich. (49409) 250/C5
Ferryville, Wis. (54628) 317/D9
Fertigs, Pa. (†16364) 294/C3
Fertile, Iowa (50434) 229/G2
Fertile, Minn. (56540) 255/B3
Fertile, Sask. 181/K6
Fertilia, Italy 34/B4
Fertő tó (Neusiedler See) (lake), Austria 41/D3
Fertő tó (Neusiedler See) (lake), Hungary 41/D3
Fès (Fez), Morocco 106/D2
Fès, Morocco 102/B1

Fontaine 369

Feshi, Zaire 115/C5
Fessenden, N. Dak. (58438) 282/L4
Fesserton, Ontario 177/E3
Festina, Iowa (52143) 229/K2
Festus, Mo. (63028) 261/M6
Fetești, Romania 45/H3
Fethard, Tipperary, Ireland 17/F7
Fethard, Wexford, Ireland 17/H7
Fethiye, Turkey 63/C4
Fethiye, Turkey 59/A2
Fetlar (isl.), Scotland 15/G2
Fetlar (isl.), Scotland 10/H1
Feudal, Sask. 181/D4
Feuerkogel (mt.), Austria 41/B3
Feuerthalen, Switzerland 39/G1
Feuilles (riv.), Que. 162/J4
Feuilles (riv.), Que. 146/L4
Feuilles (riv.), Québec 174/C1
Feversham, Ontario 177/D3
Fevzipaşa, Turkey 63/G4
Feyzabad, Afghanistan 54/H6
Feyzabad, Afghanistan 59/K2
Feyzabad, Afghanistan 68/C1
Fezzan (reg.), Libya 102/D2
Fezzan (reg.), Libya 111/B2
Ffestiniog, Wales 10/E4
Ffestiniog, Wales 13/D5
Fiambalá, Argentina 143/C2
Fianarantsoa (prov.), Madagascar 118/H4
Fianarantsoa, Madagascar 102/G7
Fianarantsoa, Madagascar 118/H4
Fianga, Chad 111/C6
Fiat, Ind. (†47326) 227/G3
Fiatt, Ill. (61433) 222/C3
Fichtelberg (mt.), E. Germany 22/E3
Fichtelgebirge (range), W. Germany 22/D3
Fickle, Ind. (†46035) 227/D4
Ficklin, Georgia (†30673) 217/G3
Ficksburg, S. Africa 118/D5
Fidalgo (isl.), Wash. 310/C2
Fidelity, Ill. (62030) 222/C4
Fidenza, Italy 34/B2
Fieberbrunn, Austria 41/B3
Field, Br. Col. 184/J4
Field, Ky. (40934) 237/O7
Field, Ontario 177/E1
Fieldale, Va. (24089) 307/H7
Field Creek, Texas (†76869) 303/F7
Fielding, New Bruns. 170/C2
Fielding, Sask. 181/D3
Fielding, Utah (84311) 304/B2
Fieldon, Ill. (62031) 222/C4
Fields, La. (70641) 238/C5
Fields (lake), La. 238/J7
Fields, Oreg. (97710) 291/J5
Fieldsboro, N.J. (†08505) 273/D3
Fieldton, Texas (79326) 303/B3
Fier, Albania 45/D5
Fierro, N. Mex. (†88041) 274/A6
Fiesch, Switzerland 39/F4
Fiesole, Italy 34/C3
Fife (lake), Sask. 181/E6
Fife (reg.), Scotland 15/E4
Fife (trad. co.), Scotland 15/B5
Fife, Wash. (98424) 310/C3
Fife Lake, Mich. (49633) 250/D4
Fife Lake, Sask. 181/F6
Fife Ness (prom.), Scotland 15/F4
Fifield, N.S. Wales 97/D3
Fifield, Wis. (54524) 317/F4
Fifteenmile (creek), Oreg. 291/F2
Fifteenmile Arroyo (creek), N. Mex. 274/D4
Fifth (lake), Maine 243/H5
Fifth Cataract, Sudan 111/F4
Fifth Cataract, Sudan 59/B6
Fifth Cataract (dam), Sudan 102/F3
Fifty Lakes, Minn. (56448) 255/D4
Fiftysix, Ark. (72533) 202/F2
Fig (riv.), Newf. 166/B3
Figeac, France 28/D5
Figueira da Foz, Portugal 33/B2
Figueras, Spain 33/H1
Figuig, Morocco 102/B1
Figuig, Morocco 106/D2
Figuras (pt.), P. Rico 161/E3
Fiji 2/A6
Fiji 87/H8
FIJI 86/P11
Filadelfia, Bolivia 136/A2
Filadelfia, C. Rica 154/E5
Filadelfia, Paraguay 144/B3
Fil'akovo, Czech. 41/E2
Filbert, S.C. (†29745) 296/E1
Filbert, W. Va. (24835) 312/D8
Filchner Ice Shelf, Ant. 2/H10
Filchner Ice Shelf, Ant. 5/B16
Fil di Remia (peak), Switzerland 39/H4
File (hills), Sask. 181/H5
Filer, Idaho (83328) 220/D7
Filer City, Mich. (49634) 250/C4
Filey, England 13/G3
Filey, England 10/F3
Filiátes, Greece 45/E6
Filiatrá, Greece 45/E7
Filicudi (isl.), Italy 34/E5
Filingué, Niger 106/E6
Filion, Mich. (48432) 250/G5
Filippiás, Greece 45/E6
Filipstad, Sweden 18/H7
Filisur, Switzerland 39/J3
Filley, Nebr. (68357) 264/H4
Fillmore, Calif. (93015) 204/G9
Fillmore, Ill. (62032) 222/D4
Fillmore, Ind. (46128) 227/D5
Fillmore (co.), Minn. 255/F7
Fillmore, Minn. (†55990) 255/F7
Fillmore, Mo. (64449) 261/C2
Fillmore (co.), Nebr. 264/G4
Fillmore, N.Y. (14735) 276/D6
Fillmore, N. Dak. (58333) 282/L3
Fillmore, Okla. (†73450) 288/N6
Fillmore, Sask. 181/H6
Fillmore, Utah (84631) 304/B5
Filtu, Ethiopia 111/H6
Filyos (riv.), Turkey 63/D2
Fimi (riv.), Zaire 115/C4
Finale Emilia, Italy 34/C2
Finale Ligure, Italy 34/B2
Fiñana, Spain 33/E4
Fincastle, Ind. (†46172) 227/D5
Fincastle, Ky. (†40222) 237/L1
Fincastle, Va. (24090) 307/J6
Finch, Mont. (†59076) 262/K4
Finch, Ontario 177/J2
Finchburg, Ala. (†36444) 195/D7
Finchville, Ky. (40022) 237/L4
Findhorn, Scotland 15/E3
Findhorn (riv.), Scotland 15/E3
Fındıklı, Turkey 63/J2
Findlater, Sask. 181/F5
Findlay, Ill. (62534) 222/E4
Findlay, Ohio (45840) 284/C3
Findley Lake, N.Y. (14736) 276/A6
Findochty, Scotland 15/E3
Findon, Mont. (†59053) 262/F4
Fine, N.Y. (13639) 276/K2
Finesville, N.J. (†08865) 273/C2
Fingal, N. Dak. (58031) 282/P6
Fingal, Ontario 177/C5
Fingal, Tasmania 99/E3
Finger (lake), Ontario 175/B2
Finger, Tenn. (38334) 237/D10
Fingerville, S.C. (29338) 296/D1
Fingoè, Mozambique 118/E2
Finhaut, Switzerland 39/C4
Finike, Turkey 63/D4
Finistère (dept.), France 28/A3
Finisterre (cape), Spain 7/C4
Finisterre (cape), Spain 33/B1
Finke (riv.), North. Terr. 88/E5
Finke (riv.), North. Terr. 93/C8
Finke (riv.), S. Australia 94/C1
Finksburg, Md. (21048) 245/L3
Finland 2/L2
Finland 4/C8
Finland 7/G2
Finland (gulf) 7/G3
FINLAND 18
Finland (gulf), Finland 18/P7
Finland, Minn. (55603) 255/G3
Finland (gulf), U.S.S.R. 52/C3
Finland (gulf), U.S.S.R. 48/C4
Finland (gulf), U.S.S.R. 53/D1
Finlay (riv.), Br. Col. 162/D4
Finlay (riv.), Br. Col. 184/E1
Finlay (mts.), Texas 303/B10
Finlayson, Minn. (55735) 255/F4
Finley, Ky. (42736) 237/L6
Finley, N. S. Wales 88/H7
Finley, N.S. Wales 97/C4
Finley, N. Dak. (58230) 282/P4
Finley, Okla. (74543) 288/R6
Finley, Tenn. (38030) 237/B8
Finley, Wash. (†99336) 310/F4
Finleyson, Georgia (†31071) 217/F6
Finleyville, Pa. (15332) 294/B5
Finly, Ind. (46129) 227/F5
Finn (riv.), Ireland 17/F2
Finn (riv.), Ireland 17/G3
Finnegan, Alberta 182/E4
Finney (co.), Kansas 232/B3
Finnmark (co.), Norway 18/O2
Finschhafen, Papua N.G. 86/B2
Finschhafen, Papua N.G. 85/C7
Finspång, Sweden 18/J7
Finsteraarhorn (mt.), Switzerland 39/F3
Finstermünz (pass), Switzerland 39/K3
Finsterwalde, E. Germany 22/E3
Finstown, Scotland 15/E1
Fintona, N. Ireland 17/G3
Fintry, Scotland 15/B1
Fionn Loch (lake), Scotland 15/C3
Fir (riv.), Sask. 181/J2
Firat (riv.), Turkey 63/G4
Fircrest, Wash. (98466) 310/C3
Fire (isl.), Alaska 196/B1
Firebag (riv.), Alberta 182/E1
Firebaugh, Calif. (93622) 204/E7
Firebrick, Ky. (41137) 237/P3
Fireco, W. Va. (†25856) 312/D7
Fire Island National Seashore, N.Y. 276/P9
Firenze (Florence), Italy 34/C3
Fires (bay), Tasmania 99/E3
Firesteel (riv.), Mich. 250/G1
Firesteel, S. Dak. (57628) 298/G3
Firesteel (creek), S. Dak. 298/N6
Firestone, Colo. (80520) 208/K2
Firgrove, S. Africa 118/F6
Firmat, Argentina 143/F6
Firminy, France 28/F5
Fir Mountain, Sask. 181/E6
Firozabad, India 68/D3
Firozpur, India 68/C2
First (lake), New Bruns. 170/B1
First Cataract, Egypt 59/B5
First Connecticut (lake), N.H. 268/E1
First Eel (lake), New Bruns. 170/C3
Firstview, Colo. (†80810) 208/O5
Firth (riv.), Alaska 196/K1
Firth, Idaho (83236) 220/F6
Firth, Nebr. (68358) 264/H4
Firth (riv.), Yukon 187/D3
Firuzabad, Iran 66/H6
Firuzkuh, Iran 66/H3
Fischot Islands, Newf. 166/C3
Fish (creek), Ind. 227/H2
Fish (riv.), Maine 243/F2
Fish (riv.), Namibia 118/B5
Fish (creek), Ohio 284/A2
Fish (lake), Utah 304/C5
Fish (creek), W. Va. 312/E3
Fish Camp, Calif. (93623) 204/F6
Fish Creek (res.), Idaho 220/E6
Fish Creek (mts.), Nev. 266/D2
Fish Creek, Wis. (54212) 317/M5
Fisher, Ark. (72429) 202/J2
Fisher (isl.), Fla. 212/B5
Fisher, Ill. (61843) 222/E3
Fisher, La. (71426) 238/D4
Fisher (bay), Manitoba 179/E3
Fisher (riv.), Manitoba 179/E3
Fisher, Minn. (56723) 255/B3
Fisher (str.), N.W.T. 162/H3
Fisher (str.), N.W. Terrs. 187/K3
Fisher (lake), Nova Scotia 168/C4
Fisher, S. Australia 94/B4
Fisher (co.), Texas 303/D5
Fisher, W. Va. (26818) 312/H4
Fisher Bay, Manitoba 179/E3
Fisher Branch, Manitoba 179/E3
Fishermans (isl.), Va. 307/S6
Fishers, Ind. (46038) 227/E5
Fishers (isl.), N.Y. 276/S8
Fishers Island, N.Y. (06390) 276/R8
Fishersville, Va. (22939) 307/K4
Fisherville (South Grafton), Mass. (01560) 249/H4
Fishguard and Goodwick, Wales 13/B5
Fishguard and Goodwick, Wales 10/D4
Fish Haven, Idaho (83261) 220/G7
Fishing (lake), Manitoba 179/G2
Fishing (bay), Md. 245/O7
Fishing (creek), N.C. 281/O2
Fishing Creek, Md. (21634) 245/N7
Fishing Lake, Alberta 182/E3
Fishing Ships Harbour, Newf. 166/C3
Fishkill, N.Y. (12524) 276/N7
Fish River (lake), Maine 243/F2
Fishs Eddy, N.Y. (13774) 276/K8
Fish Springs (range), Utah 304/A4
Fishtail, Mont. (59028) 262/G5
Fishtoft, England 13/H5
Fishtrap, Ky. (41525) 237/S6
Fishtrap (lake), Ky. 237/S6
Fisk, Mo. (63940) 261/M9
Fiskdale, Mass. (01518) 249/F4
Fiske, Sask. 181/C4
Fiskeville, R.I. (02823) 249/H6
Fitch Bay, Québec 172/E4
Fitchburg, Mass. (01420) 249/G2
Fitchville, Conn. (06334) 210/G2
Fitchville, Ohio (†44851) 284/E3
Fithian, Ill. (61844) 222/F3
Fitler, Miss. (39070) 256/B5
Fittri (lake), Chad 111/C5
Fittstown, Okla. (74842) 288/N5
Fitzcarrald, Peru 128/G8
Fitzgerald, Alberta 182/C4
Fitzgerald, Georgia (31750) 217/F7
Fitzgerald, N.W.T. 162/E4
Fitzhugh (sound), Br. Col. 184/D4
Fitzhugh, Okla. (74843) 288/N5
Fitzmaurice (riv.), North. Terr. 93/B3
Fitzpatrick, Ala. (36029) 195/G6
Fitzpatrick, Georgia (†31044) 217/F5
Fitzroy (riv.), Australia 87/C7
Fitz Roy (Chaltel) (mt.), Chile 138/E8
Fitzroy, North. Terr. 93/B4
Fitzroy (riv.), Queensland 88/J4
Fitzroy (riv.), Queensland 95/D4
Fitzroy, Victoria 97/H5
Fitzroy, Victoria 88/L7
Fitzroy (riv.), W. Australia 88/C3
Fitzroy (riv.), W. Australia 92/D2
Fitzroy Crossing, W. Australia 88/D3
Fitzroy Crossing, W. Australia 92/D2
Fitzroy Harbour, Ontario 177/H2
Fitzwilliam○, N.H. (03447) 268/C6
Fitzwilliam (isl.), Ontario 177/C2
Fitzwilliam Depot, N.H. (03447) 268/C6
Fiume (Rijeka), Yugoslavia 45/B3
Fiumicino, Italy 34/F7
Five (isls.), Nova Scotia 168/D3
Five Fingers, New Bruns. 170/C1
Five Island (lake), Iowa 229/D2
Five Islands, Maine (04546) 243/D8
Five Islands, Nova Scotia 168/D3
Five Mile (riv.), Conn. 210/H1
Fivemile (creek), Oreg. 291/F2
Fivemile (pt.), Oreg. 291/C4
Fivemile (creek), Wyo. 319/D2
Fivemiletown, N. Ireland 17/G3
Five Points, Ala. (36855) 195/H4
Five Points, Fla. (32922) 212/D1
Five Points, Tenn. (38457) 237/G10
Five Stars, Guyana 131/A2
Fivizzano, Italy 34/B2
Fizi, Zaire 115/E4
Fjerritslev, Denmark 21/C3
Flagler, Colo. (80815) 208/N4
Flagler (co.), Fla. 212/E2
Flagler Beach, Fla. (32036) 212/E2
Flag Pond, Tenn. (37657) 237/R8
Flagstaff, Ariz. 146/G6
Flagstaff, Ariz. 188/D3
Flagstaff, Ariz. (86001) 198/D3
Flagstaff (lake), Maine 243/C5
Flagstaff (lake), Oreg. 291/H5
Flagtown, N.J. (08821) 273/D2
Flambeau (riv.), Wis. 317/E4
Flambeau Flowage (res.), Wis. 317/F3
Flamborough (head), England 13/G3
Flamborough (head), England 10/G3
Flamenco de San Pedro, Cuba 158/F3
Flaming Gorge (dam), Utah 304/E3
Flaming Gorge (res.), Utah 304/E3
Flaming Gorge (res.), Wyo. 319/C4
Flaming Gorge Nat'l Rec. Area, Utah 304/E2
Flaming Gorge Nat'l Rec. Area, Wyo. 319/C4
Flamingo (cay), Bahamas 156/C2
Flanagan, Ill. (61740) 222/E3
Flanagan (passage), Virgin Is. (Br.) 161/D4
Flanagan (passage), Virgin Is. (U.S.) 161/D4
Flanagin Town, Trin. & Tob. 161/B10
Flanders, Conn. (†06757) 210/B1
Flanders (trad. prov.) France 29
Flanders, N.J. (07836) 273/D2
Flanders, Ontario 175/B3
Flanders-Riverside, N.Y. (†11901) 276/P9
Flandreau, S. Dak. (57028) 298/R5
Flanigan, Nev. (†89501) 266/B2
Flannagan (res.), Va. 307/C6
Flannan (isls.), Scotland 15/A2
Flannan (isls.), Scotland 10/C1
Flasher, N. Dak. (58535) 282/H7
Flat, Ky. (41325) 237/O5
Flat, Mo. (†65550) 261/J7
Flat (isl.), Philippines 85/F3
Flat, Texas (76526) 303/G6
Flat (creek), Va. 307/M6
Flat (cays), Virgin Is. (U.S.) 161/A4
Flat Bay, Newf. 166/C4
Flatbrookville, N.J. (†07832) 273/D1
Flatbush, Alberta 182/C2
Flat Creek, Tenn. (†37160) 237/H10
Flat Creek-Wegra, Ala. (†35129) 195/D3
Flat Fork, Ky. (41427) 237/P5
Flatgap, Ky. (41219) 237/R5
Flathead (riv.), Br. Col. 184/K6
Flathead (co.), Mont. 262/B2
Flathead (lake), Mont. 188/D1
Flathead (lake), Mont. 262/C3
Flathead (riv.), Mont. 262/B2
Flatheand, North Fork (riv.), Mont. 262/B2
Flathead, South Fork (riv.), Mont. 262/C3
Flathead Ind. Res., Mont. 262/B3
Flatlands, New Bruns. 170/D1
Flat Lick, Ky. (40935) 237/O7
Flatonia, Texas (78941) 303/G8
Flat River, Mo. (63601) 261/M7
Flat Rock, Ala. (35966) 195/G1
Flat Rock, Ill. (62427) 222/F5
Flat Rock, Ind. (47234) 227/F6
Flatrock (creek), Ind. 227/F5
Flat Rock, Ky. (†42634) 237/M7
Flat Rock, Mich. (48134) 250/F6
Flat Rock, Newf. 166/D2
Flat Rock, N.C. (†27043) 281/E4
Flat Rock, Ohio (44828) 284/E3
Flats, N.C. (†28781) 281/B4
Flattery (cape), Br. Col. 162/D6
Flattery (cape), Queensland 88/H2
Flattery (cape), Queensland 95/C2
Flattery (cape), Wash. 146/F5
Flattery (cape), Wash. 188/A1
Flattery (cape), Wash. 310/A2
Flat Top, W. Va. (25841) 312/D7
Flatwillow (creek), Mont. 262/H4
Flatwood, Ala. (†36739) 195/C6
Flatwoods, Ky. (41139) 237/R4
Flatwoods, La. (71427) 238/E4
Flatwoods, Tenn. (38458) 237/F9
Flatwoods, W. Va. (26621) 312/E5
Flawil, Switzerland 39/H2
Flaxcombe, Sask. 181/B4
Flaxman (isl.), Alaska 196/J1
Flaxton, N. Dak. (58737) 282/F2
Flaxville, Mont. (59222) 262/L2
Fleet, Alberta 182/E3
Fleet, England 13/G8
Fleet, Loch (inlet), Scotland 15/D3
Fleetwood, England 10/E4
Fleetwood, England 13/D4
Fleetwood, Okla. (†73569) 288/L7
Fleetwood, Pa. (19522) 294/L5
Fleischmanns, N.Y. (12430) 276/L6
Flekkefjord, Norway 18/E7
Flémalle, Belgium 27/G7
Fleming, Colo. (80728) 208/O1
Fleming, Georgia (31309) 217/K7
Fleming (co.), Ky. 237/O4
Fleming, Mo. (†64077) 261/D4
Fleming, Pa. (19375) 294/G4
Fleming, Sask. 181/K5
Fleming-Neon, Ky. (41816) 237/R6
Flemingsburg, Ky. (41041) 237/O4
Flemington, Georgia (†31313) 217/K7
Flemington, Mo. (65650) 261/F7
Flemington, N.J. (08822) 273/D2
Flemington, Pa. (†17745) 294/G3
Flemington, W. Va. (26347) 312/F4
Flen, Sweden 18/K7
Flensburg, Minn. (56328) 255/D5
Flensburg, W. Germany 22/C1
Flers, France 28/C3
Flesherton, Ontario 177/D3
Flesk (riv.), Ireland 17/C7
Fleta, Ala. (†36043) 195/F6
Fletcher (pond), Mich. 250/F4
Fletcher, Mo. (63030) 261/L6
Fletcher, N.C. (28732) 281/E4
Fletcher, Ohio (45326) 284/B5
Fletcher, Okla. (73541) 288/K5
Fletcher○, Vt. (†05444) 268/B2
Fletschhorn (mt.), Switzerland 39/F4
Fleurance, France 28/D6
Fleur de Lys, Newf. 166/C3
Fleur-de-May (lake), Newf. 166/B3
Fleurier, Switzerland 39/C3
Fleurus, Belgium 27/E8
Flevoland Polders, Netherlands 27/G4
Flims, Switzerland 39/H3
Flinders (reefs), 95/D3
Flinders (riv.), Australia 87/E7
Flinders (reef), Coral Sea Is. Terr. 88/H3
Flinders (riv.), Queensland 88/G3
Flinders (riv.), Queensland 95/B3
Flinders (range), S. Australia 88/F6
Flinders (range), S. Australia 94/F4
Flinders (isl.), Tasmania 88/H7
Flinders (isl.), Tasmania 99/D1
Flinders (bay), W. Australia 88/A6
Flinders (bay), W. Australia 92/A6
Flin Flon, Man. 146/H4
Flin Flon, Manitoba 179/H3
Flin Flon, Man.-Sask. 162/F4
Flin Flon, Sask. 181/N4
Flint (riv.), Ga. 188/K4
Flint, Georgia (†31716) 217/D8
Flint (riv.), Georgia 217/D8
Flint, Ind. (†46703) 227/G1
Flint (isl.), Kiribati 87/L7
Flint, Mich. 146/K5
Flint, Mich. 188/K2
Flint, Mich. (*48501) 250/F5
Flint (riv.), Mich. 250/F5
Flint (lake), N.W. Terrs. 187/L3
Flint, Wales 13/G2
Flint City, Ala. (†35601) 195/D1
Flinthill, Mo. (63346) 261/L5
Flint Hill, Va. (22627) 307/M3
Flinton, Ontario 177/G3
Flint Rock (creek), S. Dak. 298/E3
Flintstone, Georgia (30725) 217/B1
Flintstone (lake), Manitoba 179/G4
Flintstone, Md. (21530) 245/D2
Flintville, Tenn. (37335) 237/H10
Flippen, Georgia (30215) 217/D3
Flippin, Ark. (72634) 202/E1
Flippin, Ky. (42132) 237/K7
Flix, Spain 33/G2
Flom, Minn. (56541) 255/B3
Flomaton, Ala. (36441) 195/D8
Flomot, Texas (79234) 303/D3
Flood, Br. Col. 184/M3
Floodwood, Minn. (55736) 255/E4
Flora, Ill. (62839) 222/E5
Flora, Ind. (46929) 227/E3
Flora, La. (71428) 238/D3
Flora, Miss. (39071) 256/D5
Flora, N. Dak. (†58348) 282/M4
Flora (riv.), North. Terr. 93/B3
Flora, Norway 18/D6
Flora, Oreg. (†97828) 291/K2
Florac, France 28/E5
Florahome, Fla. (32635) 212/E2
Floral, Ark. (72534) 202/G2
Florala, Ala. (36442) 195/F8
Floral City, Fla. (32636) 212/D3
Floral Park, N.Y. (*11001) 276/P7
Floraville, Queensland 95/B3
Flora Vista, N. Mex. (87415) 274/A2
Floreana (Sta. Maria), Ecuador 128/B10
Floreana (Santa María) (isl.), Ecuador 128/B10
Florence, Ala. 188/J4
Florence, Ala. (*35630) 195/C1
Florence, Ariz. (85232) 198/D5
Florence, Ark. (†71655) 202/G6
Florence (lake), Calif. 204/G6
Florence, Colo. (81226) 208/J6
Florence, Ill. (†62363) 222/C4
Florence, Ind. (47020) 227/H7
Florence (prov.), Italy 34/C3
Florence, Italy 7/F4
Florence, Italy 34/C3
Florence, Kansas (66851) 232/E3
Florence, Ky. (41042) 237/R2
Florence, Minn. (56130) 255/B6
Florence, Miss. (39073) 256/D6
Florence, Mo. (65329) 261/G5
Florence, Mont. (59833) 262/B4
Florence, N.Y. (†13316) 276/J4
Florence, N.C. (†28556) 281/R4
Florence, Nova Scotia 168/H2
Florence, Ontario 177/B5
Florence, Oreg. (97439) 291/C4
Florence, Pa. (†15021) 294/A5
Florence, S.C. 188/L4
Florence (co.), S.C. 296/H3
Florence, S.C. (29501) 296/H3
Florence, S. Dak. (57235) 298/P3
Florence (riv.), Tasmania 99/C4
Florence, Tenn. (†37130) 237/H9
Florence, Texas (76527) 303/G7
Florence, Vt. (05744) 268/A4
Florence (co.), Wis. 317/K4
Florence, Wis. (54121) 317/K4
Florence Junction, Ariz. (†85220) 198/D5
Florence-Roebling, N.J. (08518) 273/D3
Florenceville, New Bruns. 170/C2
Florencia, Colombia 126/C7
Florencia, Colombia 120/B2
Florencia, Cuba 158/F2
Florennes, Belgium 27/F8
Florenton, Minn. (†55792) 255/F3
Florenville, Belgium 27/G9
Flores, Las (riv.), Argentina 143/G7
Flores, Brazil 132/G4
Flores (isl.), Br. Col. 184/D5
Flores, Guatemala 154/C2
Flores (isl.), Indonesia 54/O10
Flores (isl.), Indonesia 85/G7
Flores (sea), Indonesia 2/Q6
Flores (sea), Indonesia 54/N10
Flores (sea), Indonesia 85/F7
Flores (isl.), Portugal 33/A1
Flores (dept.), Uruguay 145/C4
Flores (isl.), Uruguay 145/D5
Floresville, Texas (78114) 303/K11
Florey, Texas (†79714) 303/B5
Florham Park, N.J. (07932) 273/E2
Floriano, Brazil 132/F4
Floriano, Brazil 120/E3
Florianópolis, Brazil 132/E9
Florianópolis, Brazil 120/E5
Florida 188/K5
FLORIDA 212
Florida (strs.) 146/K7
Florida, Bolivia 136/D6
Florida, Cuba 158/G3
Florida (str.), Cuba 156/B1
Florida (bay), Fla. 188/K6
Florida (bay), Fla. 212/F6
Florida (cape), Fla. 212/F6
Florida (keys), Fla. 188/K6
Florida (keys), Fla. 212/E7
Florida (strs.), Fla. 188/K6
Florida (strs.), Fla. 212/F7
Florida○, Mass. (†01247) 249/B2
Florida, Mo. (†65283) 261/J4
Florida (mts.), N. Mex. 274/B7
Florida, N.Y. (10921) 276/M8
Florida, Ohio (†43545) 284/B3
Florida, P. Rico 161/C1
Florida (isls.), Solomon Is. 86/E3
Florida (state), U.S. 146/K7
Florida (dept.), Uruguay 145/D4
Florida, Uruguay 145/C5
Florida City, Fla. (33034) 212/F6
Florida Ridge, Fla. (†32960) 212/F4
Floridia, Italy 34/E6
Florien, La. (71429) 238/D4
Florin, Calif. (95828) 204/B8
Florin, Pa. (†17552) 294/J5
Flórina, Greece 45/E5
Floris, Iowa (52560) 229/J7
Florissant, Colo. (80816) 208/J5
Florissant, Mo. (*63031) 261/P1
Florissant Fossil Beds Nat'l Mon., Colo. 208/J5
Flossmoor, Ill. (60422) 222/B6
Flovilla, Georgia (30216) 217/E4
Flowerdale, Tasmania 99/B2
Floweree, Mont. (59440) 262/E3
Flower Mound, Texas (†75067) 303/F1
Flowerpot (isl.), Ontario 177/C2
Flowers (bay), Newf. 166/B2
Flowers Cove, Newf. 166/C3
Flowery Branch, Georgia (30542) 217/E2
Flowood, Miss. (†39201) 256/D6
Floyd (co.), Georgia 217/B2
Floyd, Georgia (30059) 217/J1
Floyd (co.), Ind. 227/F8
Floyd (co.), Iowa 229/H2
Floyd, Iowa (50435) 229/H2
Floyd (riv.), Iowa 229/A3
Floyd (co.), Ky. 237/R5
Floyd, La. (†71266) 238/H1
Floyd, N. Mex. (88118) 274/F4
Floyd (co.), Texas 303/C3
Floyd (co.), Va. 307/H7
Floyd, Va. (24091) 307/H7
Floydada, Texas (79235) 303/C3
Floyd Dale, S.C. (29542) 296/J3
Floyds Knobs, Ind. (47119) 227/F8
Fluchthorn (mt.), Switzerland 39/K3
Flüela (pass), Switzerland 39/J3
Flüelen, Switzerland 39/G3
Fluhberg (mt.), Switzerland 39/G2
Fluker, La. (70436) 238/K5
Flums, Switzerland 39/H2
Flushing, Mich. (48433) 250/F5
Flushing, Netherlands 27/C6
Flushing, Ohio (43977) 284/J5
Fluvanna, Texas (79517) 303/D5
Fluvanna (co.), Va. 307/M5
Fly, Ohio (45730) 284/H6
Fly (riv.), Papua N.G. 87/E6
Fly (riv.), Papua N.G. 85/A7
Fly Creek, N.Y. (13337) 276/K5
Flying H, N. Mex. (88322) 274/E5
Flying Shot, Alberta 182/A2
Flynns Lick, Tenn. (†38562) 237/K8
Foam Lake, Sask. 181/H4
Foard (co.), Texas 303/E3
Foça, Turkey 63/B3
Foča, Yugoslavia 45/D4
Fochabers, Scotland 15/E3
Focșani, Romania 45/H3
Foge (isl.), Nigeria 106/E6
Foggia (prov.), Italy 34/E4
Foggia, Italy 7/F4
Foggia, Italy 34/E4
Fogo (isl.), C. Verde 106/B8
Fogo, Newf. 166/D4
Fogo (isl.), Newf. 166/D4
Fogo (isl.), Newf. 162/L6
Fohnsdorf, Austria 41/C3
Föhr (isl.), W. Germany 22/C1
Foisy, Alberta 182/E3
Foix, France 28/D6
Foix (trad. prov.) France 29
Folcroft, Pa. (19032) 294/M7
Folda (fjord), Norway 18/J3
Folda (fjord), Norway 18/G4
Földeák, Hungary 41/F3
Földes, Hungary 41/F3
Foley, Ala. (36535) 195/C10
Foley, Fla. (†32347) 212/C1
Foley, Minn. (56329) 255/D5
Foley, Mo. (63347) 261/L4
Foley (isl.), N.W. Terrs. 187/L3
Foleyet, Ontario 177/J5
Foleyet, Ontario 175/D3
Folgares, Angola 115/C6
Foligno, Italy 34/D3
Folkestone, England 13/J6
Folkestone, England 10/G5
Folkston, Georgia (31537) 217/H9
Folkstone, N.C. (†28445) 281/O5
Follansbee, W. Va. (26037) 312/E2
Follett, Texas (79034) 303/D1
Föllinge, Sweden 18/J5
Folly Beach, S.C. (29439) 296/H6
Folsom, Calif. (95630) 204/C8
Folsom (lake), Calif. 204/C8
Folsom, La. (70437) 238/K5
Folsom, N.J. (†08037) 273/D4
Folsom, N. Mex. (88419) 274/F2
Folsom, Pa. (19033) 294/M7
Folsom, W. Va. (26348) 312/E4
Folsomville, Ind. (47614) 227/C8
Foltești, Romania 45/H3
Fomboni, Comoros 118/G2
Fomento, Cuba 158/E2
Fonda, Iowa (50540) 229/D3
Fonda, N.Y. (12068) 276/M5
Fonda, N. Dak. (†58366) 282/K2
Fond d'Or (bay), St. Lucia 161/G6
Fond-du-Lac (riv.), Sask. 162/F4
Fond du Lac, Sask. 181/L2
Fond du Lac (riv.), Sask. 181/M2
Fond du Lac, Wis. 188/J2
Fond du Lac (co.), Wis. 317/K8
Fond du Lac, Wis. (54935) 317/K8
Fond du Lac Ind. Res., Minn. 255/F4
Fonde, Ky. (40937) 237/O7
Fondi, Italy 34/D4
Fond-Lahaye, Martinique 161/C6
Fond-Saint-Denis, Martinique 161/C6
Fond Verrettes, Haiti 158/C6
Fonehill, Sask. 181/J4
Fongafale (cap.), Tuvalu 87/H6
Fonsagrada, Spain 33/C1
Fonseca, Colombia 126/D2
Fonseca (gulf), El Salvador 154/D4
Fonseca (gulf), Honduras 154/D4
Fonseca (gulf), Nicaragua 154/D4
Fontaine, New Bruns. 170/F2

Front 371

Foster (riv.), Sask. 181/M3
Foster (creek), S. Dak. 298/N4
Foster, W. Va. (25081) 312/C6
Foster, Wis. (†54758) 317/D6
Foster Center (Foster P.O.), R.I. (†02825) 249/H5
Foster City, Calif. (94404) 204/J2
Foster City, Mich. (49834) 250/B3
Fosters, Ala. (35463) 195/C4
Fosters, Mich. (†48415) 250/F5
Fosters Falls, Va. (24329) 307/G7
Fosterton, Sask. 181/C5
Foster Village, Hawaii (†96701) 218/B3
Fosterville, New Bruns. 170/C3
Fosterville, Tenn. (37063) 237/J9
Fostoria, Ala. (†36737) 195/E6
Fostoria, Iowa (51340) 229/C2
Fostoria, Kansas (66426) 232/F2
Fostoria, Mich. (48435) 250/F5
Fostoria, Ohio (44830) 284/D3
Fougamou, Gabon 115/A4
Fougères, France 28/C3
Fouke, Ark. (71837) 202/C7
Foul (bay), Egypt 111/G3
Foul (sound), Ireland 17/B5
Foula (isl.), Scotland 15/F2
Foula (isl.), Scotland 10/G1
Foules, La. (†71326) 238/G3
Foulness Island (pen.), England 13/J6
Foulpointe, Madagascar 118/H3
Foulweather (cape), Oreg. 291/C3
Foulwind (cape), N. Zealand 100/C4
Foumban, Cameroon 115/B2
Foumban, Cameroon 102/D4
Fountain, Ala. (36460) 195/D7
Fountain, Colo. (80817) 208/K5
Fountain (creek), Colo. 208/K5
Fountain, Fla. (32438) 212/D6
Fountain (co.), Ind. 227/C4
Fountain, Ind. (†47918) 227/C4
Fountain, Mich. (49410) 250/C4
Fountain, Minn. (55935) 255/F7
Fountain, N.C. (27829) 281/O3
Fountain City, Ind. (47341) 227/H5
Fountain City, Wis. (54629) 317/C7
Fountain Green, Ill. (†62321) 222/C3
Fountain Green, Utah (84632) 304/C4
Fountain Head, Md. (†21740) 245/G2
Fountain Head, Tenn. (†37148) 237/J7
Fountain Hill, Ark. (71642) 202/G7
Fountain Hill, Pa. (†18015) 294/L4
Fountain Inn, S.C. (29644) 296/C2
Fountain Run, Ky. (42133) 237/K7
Fountaintown, Ind. (46130) 227/F5
Fountain Valley, Calif. (92708) 204/D11
Four (peaks), Newf. 166/B2
Four Buttes, Mont. (59224) 262/L2
Fourche, Ariz. (†72016) 202/E4
Fourche LaFave (riv.), Ark. 202/D4
Four Corners, Oreg. (97301) 291/A3
Four Corners, Wyo. (82715) 319/H1
Four Falls, New Bruns. 170/C2
Four Hole Swamp (creek), S.C. 296/F5
Four Lakes, Wash. (99014) 310/H3
Fourmies, France 28/F2
Four Mile (riv.), Conn. 210/F3
Fourmile (lake), Oreg. 291/E5
Four Mountains (isls.), Alaska 196/E4
Fournier (cape), N. Zealand 100/E7
Fournier, Ontario 177/K2
Four Oaks, N.C. (27524) 281/M4
Four Paths, Jamaica 158/J6
Four Peaks (mt.), Ariz. 198/D5
Four States, W. Va. (26572) 312/F4
Fourteen Mile (pt.), Mich. 250/F1
Fourth (lake), Maine 243/H5
Fourth Cataract, Sudan 111/F4
Fourth Cataract, Sudan 59/B6
Fourth Cataract (dam), Sudan 102/F3
Foveaux (str.), N. Zealand 87/G10
Foveaux (str.), N. Zealand 100/A7
Fowler, Calif. (93625) 204/F7
Fowler, Colo. (81039) 208/L6
Fowler, Ill. (62338) 222/B3
Fowler, Ind. (47944) 227/C3
Fowler, Kansas (67844) 232/B4
Fowler, Mich. (48835) 250/E5
Fowlerton, Ind. (46930) 227/F4
Fowlerton, Texas (78021) 303/F9
Fowlerville, Mich. (48836) 250/F6
Fowlkes, Tenn. (38033) 237/C9
Fowlstown, Georgia (31752) 217/D9
Fowman, Iran 66/F2
Fowyang (Fuyang), China 77/J5
Fox (isls.), Alaska 196/E4
Fox, Ark. (72051) 202/F2
Fox (lake), Ill. 222/A4
Fox (riv.), Ill. 222/E5
Fox (riv.), Ill. 222/E2
Fox (riv.), Manitoba 179/K2
Fox, Mich. (†49813) 250/B3
Fox (isl.), New Bruns. 170/F1
Fox, Okla. (73435) 288/M6
Fox, Oreg. (97831) 291/H3
Fox (riv.), Wis. 317/K7
Fox (riv.), Wis. 317/K2
Foxboro, Mass. (02035) 249/J4
Foxboro○, Mass. (02035) 249/J4
Foxboro, Ontario 177/G3
Foxboro, Wis. (54836) 317/B2
Foxburg, Pa. (16036) 294/C3
Fox Chapel, Pa. (†15238) 294/C6
Fox Creek, Alberta 182/B2
Foxe (basin), Canada 4/C13
Foxe (basin), N.W.T. 146/L3
Foxe (basin), N.W.T. 162/J2
Foxe (basin), N.W. Terrs. 187/L3
Foxe (chan.), N.W.T. 162/H2
Foxe (chan.), N.W.T. 146/K3
Foxe (chan.), N.W. Terrs. 187/K3
Foxe (pen.), N.W.T. 146/L3
Foxe (pen.), N.W.T. 162/J3
Foxe (pen.), N.W. Terrs. 187/L3
Fox Farm, Wyo. (†82001) 319/H4
Foxfire, N.C. (†28373) 281/K4
Foxford, Ireland 17/C4
Foxford, Sask. 181/F2
Fox Glacier, N. Zealand 100/B5
Fox Harbour, Newf. 166/D2
Fox Harbour, Newf. 166/C3
Foxholm, N. Dak. (58738) 282/G3
Foxhome, Minn. (56543) 255/B4
Fox Lake, Alberta 182/B5
Fox Lake, Ill. (60020) 222/A4
Fox Lake, Wis. (53933) 317/J8
Foxon, Conn. (†06512) 210/D3
Foxpark, Wyo. (82057) 319/F4
Fox Point, Wis. (†53117) 317/M1
Fox River, Nova Scotia 168/D3
Fox River Grove, Ill. (60021) 222/A5
Foxton, Colo. (80441) 208/J4
Foxton, N. Zealand 100/E4
Fox Valley, Sask. 181/B5
Foxville, Md. (†21760) 245/H2
Foxwarren, Manitoba 179/A4
Foxwells, Va. (22578) 307/R5
Foxworth, Miss. (39483) 256/E8
Foyers, Scotland 15/D3
Foyil, Okla. (74031) 288/R2
Foyle (inlet), Ireland 17/G1
Foyle, Lough (inlet), Ireland 10/C3
Foyle (riv.), Ireland 17/G2
Foyle, Lough (inlet), N. Ireland 10/C3
Foyle (inlet), N. Ireland 17/G1
Foyle (riv.), N. Ireland 17/G2
Foynes, Ireland 10/B4
Foynes, Ireland 17/C6
Foz do Breu, Brazil 132/F10
Foz do Cunene, Angola 115/B7
Foz do Iguaçu, Brazil 132/C9
Frackville, Pa. (17931) 294/K4
Fraga, Spain 33/G2
Fragoso (cay), Cuba 158/F1
Fraile Muerto, Uruguay 145/E3
Frailes, Los (isl.), Dom. Rep. 158/C7
Fram, Paraguay 144/E5
Framboise, Nova Scotia 168/H3
Framboise Cove (bay), Nova Scotia 168/H3
Frame, W. Va. (25071) 312/C5
Frameries, Belgium 27/D8
Frametown, W. Va. (26623) 312/E5
Framingham○, Mass. (01701) 249/A7
Framingham Center, Mass. (01701) 249/J3
Framlingham, England 13/J5
Frampton, Québec 172/G3
Franca, Brazil 135/C2
Franca, Brazil 132/E8
Francavilla Fontana, Italy 34/F4
France 2/J3
France 7/E4
FRANCE 28
Francés (cape), Cuba 158/B2
Francés (cape), Cuba 158/A2
Frances (lake), Mont. 262/D2
Frances, Wash. (†98577) 310/B4
Frances (lake), Yukon 187/E3
Francestown○, N.H. (03043) 268/D6
Francés Viejo (cape), Dom. Rep. 158/E5
Francesville, Ind. (47946) 227/D3
Franceville, Gabon 115/B4
Franche Comté (trad. prov.), France 29
Francia, Uruguay 145/C3
Francis (lake), N.H. 268/E1
Francis, Okla. (74844) 288/N5
Francis, Sask. 181/H5
Francis, Utah (†84036) 304/C3
Francis Case (lake), S. Dak. 188/F2
Francis Case (lake), S. Dak. 146/J5
Francis Case (lake), S. Dak. 298/L7
Francisco, Ala. (†37345) 195/F1
Francisco, Ind. (47649) 227/B8
Francisco, N.C. (†27053) 281/J2
Francisco de Orellana, Peru 128/F4
Francisco I. Madero, Mexico 150/H4
Francis Creek, Wis. (54214) 317/L7
Francis E. Warren A.F.B., Wyo. 319/G4
Francistown, Botswana 118/D4
Francoeur, Québec 172/F3
Francois (lake), Br. Col. 162/D5
François (lake), Br. Col. 184/D3
François, Newf. 166/C4
François Lake, Br. Col. 184/D3
Franconia○, N.H. (03580) 268/D3
Franconia, Va. (22310) 307/S3
Franconian Jura (range), W. Germany 22/D4
Franconia Notch (pass), N.H. 268/D3
Franeker, Netherlands 27/H2
Frank, Alberta 182/C5
Frankel City, Texas (79737) 303/B5
Frankenberg-Eder, W. Germany 22/C3
Frankenmarkt, Austria 41/B3
Frankenmuth, Mich. (48734) 250/F5
Frankenthal, W. Germany 22/C4
Frankenwald (for.), W. Germany 22/D3
Frankewing, Tenn. (38459) 237/H10
Frankfield, Jamaica 158/H6
Frankford, Del. (19945) 245/S6
Frankford (Kilcormac), Ireland 17/F5
Frankford, Mo. (63441) 261/K4
Frankford, Ontario 177/G3
Frankford, W. Va. (24938) 312/F7
Frankfort, Ala. (†35653) 195/C1
Frankfort, Ill. (60423) 222/B6
Frankfort, Ind. (46041) 227/E4
Frankfort, Kansas (66427) 232/F2
Frankfort (cap.), Ky. (40601) 237/M4
Frankfort (cap.), Ky. 188/K3
Frankfort (cap.), Ky. 146/K6
Frankfort○, Maine (04438) 243/F6
Frankfort, Mich. (49635) 250/C4
Frankfort, N.Y. (13340) 276/K4
Frankfort, Ohio (45628) 284/D7
Frankfort, S. Dak. (57440) 298/N4
Frankfort Springs, Pa. (†15050) 294/A4
Frankfurt (dist.), E. Germany 22/F2
Frankfurt, W. Germany 7/E3
Frankfurt am Main, W. Germany 22/C3
Frankfurt an der Oder, E. Germany 22/F2
Frankland (cape), Tasmania 99/D1
Frankland (range), Tasmania 99/B4
Franklin (co.), Ala. 195/C2
Franklin, Ala. (36444) 195/G6
Franklin (pt.), Alaska 196/G1
Franklin, Ariz. (85534) 198/F6
Franklin (co.), Ark. 202/C2
Franklin, Ark. (72536) 202/G1
Franklin○, Conn. (†06254) 210/G2
Franklin (co.), Fla. 212/B2
Franklin (co.), Georgia 217/F2
Franklin, Georgia (30217) 217/B4
Franklin (co.), Idaho 220/G7
Franklin, Idaho (83237) 220/G7
Franklin (co.), Ill. 222/E5
Franklin, Ill. (62638) 222/C4
Franklin (co.), Ind. 227/G6
Franklin, Ind. (46131) 227/E6
Franklin (co.), Iowa 229/G3
Franklin, Iowa (†52625) 229/L7
Franklin (co.), Kansas 232/G3
Franklin, Kansas (66735) 232/H4
Franklin (co.), Ky. 237/M4
Franklin, Ky. (42134) 237/J7
Franklin (par.), La. 238/G2
Franklin, La. (70538) 238/G7
Franklin (co.), Maine 243/B5
Franklin, Maine (04634) 243/G6
Franklin○, Maine (04634) 243/G6
Franklin, Manitoba 179/C4
Franklin (co.), Mass. 249/D2
Franklin, Mass. (02038) 249/J4
Franklin○, Mass. (02038) 249/J4
Franklin, Mich. (48025) 250/B6
Franklin, Minn. (†55792) 255/F3
Franklin, Minn. (55333) 255/D6
Franklin (co.), Miss. 256/C8
Franklin (co.), Mo. 261/K6
Franklin, Mo. (65250) 261/G4
Franklin, Mont. (†59074) 262/G4
Franklin (co.), Nebr. 264/F4
Franklin, Nebr. (68939) 264/E4
Franklin (lake), Nev. 266/F2
Franklin, N.H. (03235) 268/D5
Franklin, N.J. (07416) 273/D1
Franklin (co.), N.Y. 276/M1
Franklin, N.Y. (13775) 276/K6
Franklin (co.), N.C. 281/N2
Franklin, N.C. (28734) 281/C4
Franklin (dist.), N.W.T. 162/H1
Franklin (bay), N.W. Terrs. 187/F2
Franklin (lake), N.W. Terrs. 187/J3
Franklin (mts.), N.W. Terrs. 187/F3
Franklin (str.), N.W. T. 162/G1
Franklin (str.), N.W. Terrs. 187/J2
Franklin (co.), Ohio 284/E5
Franklin, Ohio (45005) 284/B6
Franklin (co.), Pa. 294/G6
Franklin, Pa. (16323) 294/C3
Franklin, S. Dak. (†57042) 298/P6
Franklin, Tasmania 99/C5
Franklin (riv.), Tasmania 99/B4
Franklin (co.), Tenn. 237/J10
Franklin, Tenn. (37064) 237/H9
Franklin (co.), Texas 303/J4
Franklin, Texas (77856) 303/H7
Franklin (co.), Vt. 268/B2
Franklin○, Vt. (05457) 268/B2
Franklin (co.), Va. 307/J6
Franklin (I.C.), Va. (23851) 307/P7
Franklin (co.), Wash. 310/G4
Franklin, W. Va. (26807) 312/H5
Franklin, Wis. (53132) 317/L2
Franklin D. Roosevelt (lake), Wash. 310/G2
Franklin Falls (res.), N.H. 268/D4
Franklin Furnace, Ohio (45629) 284/E8
Franklin Grove, Ill. (61031) 222/D2
Franklin Lakes, N.J. (07417) 273/B1
Franklin Park, Ill. (60131) 222/B5
Franklin Park○, N.J. (†08823) 273/D3
Franklin River, Br. Col. 184/H3
Franklin Springs, Georgia (30639) 217/F2
Franklin Square, N.Y. (11010) 276/R7
Franklinton, La. (70438) 238/K5
Franklinton, N.C. (27525) 281/N2
Franklintown, Pa. (17323) 294/H5
Franklinville, N.J. (08322) 273/C4
Franklinville, N.Y. (14737) 276/D6
Franklinville, N.C. (27248) 281/K3
Franks (pond), Newf. 166/D2
Frankslake, Sask. 181/G5
Frankston, Texas (75763) 303/J5
Franksville, Wis. (53126) 317/M3
Frankton, Ind. (46044) 227/F4
Franktown, Colo. (80116) 208/K4
Franktown, Ontario 177/H2
Franktown, Va. (23354) 307/S6
Frankville, Ala. (36538) 195/B7
Frankville, Iowa (†52162) 229/K2
Frankville, Nova Scotia 168/G3
Frankville, Ontario 177/J2
Frannie, Wyo. (82423) 319/D1
Franquelin, Québec 172/B1
Franquia, Uruguay 145/B1
Franschhoek, S. Africa 118/F6
Fransfontein, Namibia 118/A4
Františkovy Lázně, Czech. 41/B1
Franz, Ontario 177/J5
Franz, Ontario 175/D3
Franz Josef Land (isls.), U.S.S.R. 2/L1
Franz Josef Land (isls.), U.S.S.R. 4/A7
Franz Josef Land (isls.), U.S.S.R. 48/F1
Frascati, Italy 34/F7
Fraser (isl.), Australia 87/F8
Fraser (riv.), Br. Col. 146/F4
Fraser (riv.), Br. Col. 162/D5
Fraser (lake), Br. Col. 184/E3
Fraser (riv.), Br. Col. 184/F4
Fraser, Colo. (80442) 208/H3
Fraser, Iowa (†50036) 229/E4
Fraser, Mich. (48026) 250/B6
Fraser, Minn. (†55719) 255/F3
Fraser (riv.), Newf. 166/B2
Fraser (isl.), Queensland 88/J4
Fraser (isl.), Queensland 95/E5
Fraserburgh, Scotland 15/G3
Fraserburgh, Scotland 10/E2
Fraserdale, Ontario 175/D3
Fraserdale, Ontario 177/J5
Fraser Lake, Br. Col. 184/E3
Fraser Mills, Br. Col. 184/K3
Fraser Reach (chan.), Br. Col. 184/C3
Frasertown, N. Zealand 100/F3
Fraserwood, Manitoba 179/E4
Frasnes-lez Anvaing, Belgium 27/D7
Frauenfeld, Switzerland 39/G1
Frauenkirchen, Austria 41/D3
Fray Bentos, Cuba 158/J3
Fray Bentos, Uruguay 145/A4
Fray Marcos, Uruguay 145/D5
Frazee, Minn. (56544) 255/C4
Frazer, Mont. (59225) 262/K2
Frazeysburg, Ohio (43822) 284/F5
Frazier Park, Calif. (93225) 204/F9
Fraziers Bottom, W. Va. (25082) 312/B5
Frechen, W. Germany 22/B3
Fred, Texas (77616) 303/K7
Freda, N. Dak. (†58569) 282/H7
Fredensborg, Denmark 21/F6
Fredensdal, Virgin Is. (U.S.) 161/F4
Frederic, Mich. (49733) 250/E4
Frederic, Wis. (54837) 317/B4
Frederica, Del. (19946) 245/S4
Fredericia, Denmark 21/C6
Fredericia, Denmark 18/F9
Frederick (sound), Alaska 196/N1
Frederick, Colo. (80530) 208/K2
Frederick, Ill. (62639) 222/C3
Frederick, Kansas (†67444) 232/D3
Frederick (co.), Md. 245/J3
Frederick, Md. (21701) 245/J3
Frederick, Okla. (73542) 288/H6
Frederick, S. Dak. (57441) 298/N2
Frederick (co.), Va. 307/M2
Fredericksburg, Ind. (47120) 227/E8
Fredericksburg, Iowa (50630) 229/J3
Fredericksburg, Ohio (44627) 284/G4
Fredericksburg, Pa. (17026) 294/J5
Fredericksburg, Pa. (†16335) 294/B2
Fredericksburg, Texas (78624) 303/E7
Fredericksburg (I.C.), Va. (*22401) 307/N4
Fredericks Hall, Va. (†23117) 307/N4
Frederickton, N.S. Wales 97/G2
Fredericktown, Mo. (63645) 261/M7
Fredericktown, Ohio (43019) 284/F5
Fredericktown, Pa. (15333) 294/C6
Fredericton, N. Br. 146/M5
Fredericton, N. Br. 162/K6
Fredericton (cap.), New Bruns. 170/D3
Fredericton Junction, New Bruns. 170/D3
Frederika, Iowa (50631) 229/J3
Frederik Hendrik (Kolepom) (isl.), Indonesia 85/K7
Frederiksberg (commune), Denmark 21/F6
Frederiksberg, Denmark 21/F6
Frederiksborg (co.), Denmark 21/E5
Frederikshåb, Greenl. 4/C12
Frederikshåb, Greenland 146/N3
Frederikshavn, Denmark 18/G8
Frederikshavn, Denmark 21/D3
Frederikssund, Denmark 21/E6
Frederiksted, Virgin Is. (U.S.) 161/E4
Frederiksted, Virgin Is. (U.S.) 156/G2
Frederiksvaerk, Denmark 21/E6
Frederiksvaerk, Denmark 18/G8
Frederik Willem IV (falls), Suriname 131/C4
Fredonia, Ala. (†31833) 195/H5
Fredonia, Ariz. (86022) 198/C2
Fredonia (Biscoe), Ark. (72017) 202/H4
Fredonia, Ind. (†47137) 227/E8
Fredonia, Iowa (†52738) 229/L6
Fredonia, Kansas (66736) 232/G4
Fredonia, Ky. (42411) 237/E6
Fredonia, N.Y. (14063) 276/B6
Fredonia, N. Dak. (58440) 282/M7
Fredonia, Pa. (16124) 294/B3
Fredonia, Texas (76842) 303/E7
Fredonia, Wis. (53021) 317/L8
Fredric, Iowa (†52531) 229/H6
Fredrika, Sweden 18/L4
Fredrikstad, Norway 18/D4
Freeborn (co.), Minn. 255/E7
Freeborn, Minn. (56032) 255/E7
Freeburg, Ill. (62243) 222/D5
Freeburg, Minn. (†55921) 255/G7
Freeburg, Mo. (65035) 261/J6
Freeburg, Pa. (17827) 294/H4
Freeburn, Ky. (41528) 237/S5
Freedhem, Minn. (†56345) 255/D4
Freedom, Calif. (95019) 204/L4
Freedom, Ind. (47431) 227/D6
Freedom, Ky. (†42157) 237/K7
Freedom○, Maine (04941) 243/E7
Freedom○, N.H. (03836) 268/E4
Freedom, Okla. (73842) 288/H1
Freedom, Pa. (15042) 294/B4
Freedom, Wyo. (83120) 319/B3
Freehold, N.J. (07728) 273/E3
Freehold, N.Y. (12431) 276/N6
Freel (peak), Calif. 204/F5
Freeland, Md. (21053) 245/M2
Freeland, Mich. (48623) 250/E5
Freeland, N.C. (28440) 281/N6
Freeland, Pa. (18224) 294/L3
Freeland, Wash. (98249) 310/C2
Freeland Park, Ind. (†47944) 227/C3
Freelandville, Ind. (47535) 227/C7
Freels (cape), Newf. 166/D3
Freelton, Ontario 177/D4
Freeman (riv.), Alberta 182/C2
Freeman, Ind. (†47460) 227/D6
Freeman (lake), Ind. 227/D3
Freeman, Mo. (64746) 261/C5
Freeman, S. Dak. (57029) 298/O7
Freeman, Wash. (99015) 310/H3
Freemansburg, Pa. (†18017) 294/M4
Freemanville, Ala. (†36502) 195/D8
Free Mason (isls.), La. 238/M7
Freemont, Calif. 188/B3
Freemont, Sask. 181/B3
Freeport, Bahamas 156/B1
Freeport, Fla. (32439) 212/C6
Freeport, Ill. 188/J2
Freeport, Ill. (61032) 222/D1
Freeport, Ind. (†46161) 227/F5
Freeport, Kansas (67049) 232/E4
Freeport, Maine (04032) 243/C8
Freeport○, Maine (04032) 243/C8
Freeport, Mich. (49325) 250/D6
Freeport, Minn. (56331) 255/D5
Freeport, N.Y. (11520) 276/R7
Freeport, Nova Scotia 168/B4
Freeport, Ohio (43973) 284/H5
Freeport, Pa. (16229) 294/C4
Freeport, Texas (77541) 303/J9
Freer, Texas (78357) 303/F10
Free Soil, Mich. (49411) 250/C4
Freestone (co.), Texas 303/H6
Freetown, Ant. & Bar. 161/E11
Freetown, Ind. (47235) 227/E7
Freetown, N.Y. (†11937) 276/R9
Freetown (cap.), S. Leone 102/A4
Freetown (cap.), S. Leone 106/B7
Free Union, Va. (22940) 307/L4
Freeville, N.Y. (13068) 276/H5
Freezeout (lake), Mont. 262/D3
Fregenal de la Sierra, Spain 33/C3
Fregene, Italy 34/F6
Freiberg, E. Germany 22/E3
Freiburg, W. Germany 7/E4
Freiburg im Breisgau, W. Germany 22/B5
Freidberg, Austria 41/D3
Freienbach, Switzerland 39/G2
Freire, Chile 138/E2
Freirina, Chile 138/A7
Freising, W. Germany 22/D4
Freistadt, Austria 41/C2
Freistatt, Mo. (65654) 261/E8
Freital, E. Germany 22/E3
Freixo de Espada à Cinta, Portugal 33/C2
Fréjus, France 28/G6
Fréjus (pass), France 28/G5
Fréjus (pass), Italy 34/A2
Frelighsburg, Québec 172/E4
Fremantle, Australia 2/Q7
Fremantle, Australia 87/B9
Fremantle, W. Australia 88/B6
Fremantle, W. Australia 92/A1
Fremington, England 13/C6
Fremont, Calif. (*94536) 204/K3
Fremont (peak), Calif. 204/H8
Fremont (co.), Colo. 208/J5
Fremont (co.), Idaho 220/G5
Fremont, Ind. (46737) 227/H1
Fremont (co.), Iowa 229/B7
Fremont, Iowa (52561) 229/H6
Fremont, Mich. (49412) 250/D5
Fremont, Mo. (63941) 261/K9
Fremont, Nebr. 188/G2
Fremont, Nebr. (68025) 264/H3
Fremont○, N.H. (03044) 268/E6
Fremont, N.C. (27830) 281/N3
Fremont, Ohio (43420) 284/D3
Fremont, Utah (84727) 304/C5
Fremont (isl.), Utah 304/B2
Fremont (riv.), Utah 304/C5
Fremont, Wis. (54940) 317/J7
Fremont (co.), Wyo. 319/D2
Fremont (lake), Wyo. 319/C3
Fremont (peak), Wyo. 319/C2
French, Argentina 143/F7
French (riv.), Conn. 210/H1
French (riv.), Ontario 177/D1
French (creek), Pa. 294/C2
French (creek), S. Dak. 298/C6
French (isl.), Victoria 97/C6
Frenchboro○, Maine (04635) 243/G7
French Broad (riv.), N.C. 281/D3
French Broad (riv.), Tenn. 237/R9
Frenchburg, Ky. (40322) 237/O5
French Camp, Miss. (39745) 256/F4
French Creek, W. Va. (26218) 312/F5
French Frigate (shoal), Hawaii 188/F6
French Frigate (shoals), Hawaii 87/K3
French Frigate (shoals), Hawaii 218/C6
Frenchglen, Oreg. (97736) 291/H5
French Guiana 2/G5
French Guiana 120/D2
FRENCH GUIANA 131/E3
French Lick, Ind. (47432) 227/D7
Frenchman (creek), Colo. 208/P1
Frenchman (bay), Maine 243/G7
Frenchman (riv.), Mont. 188/E1
Frenchman (riv.), Mont. 262/J1
Frenchman (creek), Nebr. 264/C4
Frenchman (riv.), Sask. 181/C6
Frenchman (cay), Virgin Is. (Br.) 161/C4
Frenchman Butte, Sask. 181/B2
Frenchman Flat (basin), Nev. 266/F6
Frenchmans Cap (mt.), Tasmania 99/B4
Frenchmans Island, Newf. 166/C3
Frenchpark, Ireland 17/E4
French Polynesia 87/L8
French River, Minn. (†55801) 255/G4
French River, Ontario 177/D1
French Settlement, La. (70733) 238/L2
Frenchton, W. Va. (26219) 312/F5
Frenchtown, Mont. (59834) 262/B3
Frenchtown, N.J. (08825) 273/C2
Frenchville, Maine (04745) 243/G1
Frenchville○, Maine (04745) 243/G1
Frenchville, Pa. (16836) 294/F3
Frenštát pod Radhoštěm, Czech. 41/E2
Fresco, Ivory Coast 106/C7
Fresh (pond), Mass. 249/C6
Freshford, Ireland 17/G6
Freshwater, Calif. (†95501) 204/B3
Freshwater (Guffey), Colo. (80820) 208/H5
Freshwater, England 13/F7
Freshwater, Newf. 166/D2
Fresia, Chile 138/D3
Fresillo, Mexico 146/H7
Fresnillo de González Echeverría, Mexico 150/H5
Fresno (co.), Calif. 204/E7
Fresno, Calif. 146/G6
Fresno, Calif. 188/C3
Fresno, Calif. (*93706) 204/F7
Fresno (riv.), Calif. 204/E7
Fresno, Colombia 126/C5
Fresno, Mont. (†59532) 262/G2
Fresno (res.), Mont. 262/F2
Fresno, Texas (77545) 303/J2
Freudenstadt, W. Germany 22/C4
Frew, Ky. (41744) 237/P6
Frewena, North. Terr. 93/D5
Frewsburg, N.Y. (14738) 276/B6
Freycinet (pen.), Tasmania 99/E4
Fria, Guinea 106/B6
Fria (cape), Namibia 102/D6
Fria (cape), Namibia 118/A3
Friant, Calif. (93626) 204/F7
Friant-Kern (canal), Calif. 204/F8
Friars Point, Miss. (38631) 256/C2
Frías, Argentina 143/D2
Fribourg (canton), Switzerland 39/D3
Fribourg, Switzerland 39/D3
Frick, Switzerland 39/E1
Friday Harbor, Wash. (98250) 310/B2
Fridley, Minn. (55432) 255/G5
Fried, N. Dak. (†58401) 282/N5
Friedberg, W. Germany 22/C3
Friedland, E. Germany 22/E2
Friedrichshafen, W. Germany 22/C5
Friedrichstadt, W. Germany 22/C1
Friend, Kansas (67845) 232/B3
Friend, Nebr. (68359) 264/G4
Friend, Oreg. (97021) 291/F2
Friendly, W. Va. (26146) 312/D3
Friendship, Ark. (71942) 202/E5
Friendship, Ind. (47021) 227/G7
Friendship, Maine (04547) 243/E7
Friendship○, Maine (04547) 243/E7
Friendship, Md. (20758) 245/M6
Friendship, N.Y. (14739) 276/D6
Friendship, Ohio (45630) 284/D8
Friendship, Tenn. (38034) 237/C9
Friendship, Wis. (53934) 317/G8
Friendship Hill Nat'l Hist. Site, Pa. 294/C6
Friendsville, Ill. (†62863) 222/F5
Friendsville, Md. (21531) 245/A2
Friendsville, Pa. (18818) 294/L2
Friendsville, Tenn. (37737) 237/N9
Friendswood, Texas (77546) 303/J2
Frienisberg (mt.), Switzerland 39/D2
Frierson, La. (71027) 238/C2
Fries, Va. (24330) 307/F7
Friesach, Austria 41/C3
Friesche Gat (chan.), Netherlands 27/J2
Friesland, Minn. (†55037) 255/E4
Friesland (prov.), Netherlands 27/H2
Friesland, Wis. (53935) 317/H8
Frigate (isl.), Seychelles 118/J5
Frigate Bay, St. Chris.-Nevis 161/C10
Frimley and Camberley, England 13/G8
Frink, Fla. (†32430) 212/D6
Frinton and Walton, England 10/G5
Frinton and Walton, England 13/J6
Frio (cape), Brazil 120/E5
Frio (cape), Brazil 135/F3
Frio (co.), Texas 303/E9
Frio (riv.), Texas 303/E8
Friockheim, Scotland 15/F4
Friol, Spain 33/C1
Friona, Texas (79035) 303/B3
Fripp (isl.), S.C. 296/G7
Frisches Haff (lag.), Poland 47/D1
Frisco, Colo. (80443) 208/G3
Frisco, N.C. (27936) 281/T4
Frisco, Pa. (†16117) 294/B4
Frisco, Texas (75034) 303/H4
Frisco City, Ala. (36445) 195/D8
Frisian (isls.) 7/E3
Frisian, North (isls.), Denmark 21/B7
Frisian, West (isls.), Netherlands 27/G2
Frisian, East (isls.), W. Germany 22/B2
Frisian, North (isls.), W. Germany 22/B1
Frissell (mt.), Conn. 210/B1
Fristoe, Mo. (†65355) 261/F6
Fritch, Texas (79036) 303/C2
Fritchton, Ind. (†47591) 227/C7
Fritz Creek, Alaska (†99603) 196/B2
Fritzlar, W. Germany 22/C3
Friuli-Venezia Giulia (reg.), Italy 34/D1
Frizzellburg, Md. (†21157) 245/K2
Frobisher (bay), N.W.T. 162/K3
Frobisher (bay), N.W. Terrs. 187/M3
Frobisher, Sask. 181/J6
Frobisher (lake), Sask. 181/L3
Frobisher Bay, N.W.T. 162/K3
Frobisher Bay, N.W. Terrs. 187/M3
Froelich, Iowa (†52047) 229/L2
Frog (lake), Alberta 182/E3
Frog Lake, Alberta 182/E3
Frogmore, S.C. (29920) 296/F7
Frogue, Ky. (†42714) 237/L7
Frohavet (bay), Norway 18/F5
Frohna, Mo. (63748) 261/N7
Frohnleiten, Austria 41/C3
Froid, Mont. (59226) 262/M2
Froidchapelle, Belgium 27/E8
Frolovo, U.S.S.R. 48/E5
Frolovo, U.S.S.R. 52/F5
Fromberg, Mont. (59029) 262/H5
Frome (lake), Australia 87/E9
Frome, England 10/E5
Frome, England 13/E6
Frome, Jamaica 158/G6
Frome (lake), S. Australia 88/G6
Frome (lake), S. Australia 94/G4
Front (range), Colo. 208/H1

372 Fronteira

Fronteira, Portugal 33/C3
Fronteiras, Brazil 132/F4
Frontenac, Kansas (66762) 232/H4
Frontenac, Minn. (55026) 255/F6
Frontenac, Mo. (†63101) 261/O3
Frontenac (county), Ontario 177/H3
Frontenac (co.), Québec 172/G4
Frontera, Mexico 150/N7
Frontier, Mich. (49239) 250/E7
Frontier (co.), Nebr. 264/D4
Frontier, N. Dak. (†58102) 282/S6
Frontier, Sask. 181/C6
Frontier, Wyo. (83121) 319/B4
Front Royal, Va. (22630) 307/M3
Frosinone (prov.), Italy 34/D4
Frosinone, Italy 34/D4
Frösö, Sweden 18/J5
Frost, La. (†70753) 238/L2
Frost, Minn. (56033) 255/D7
Frost, Texas (76641) 303/H5
Frost, W. Va. (†24954) 312/G6
Frostburg, Md. (21532) 245/C2
Frostproof, Fla. (33843) 212/E4
Froude, Sask. 181/H6
Frövi, Sweden 18/J7
Frøya (isl.), Norway 18/F5
Frozen (str.), N.W.T. 162/H2
Frozen (str.), N.W. Terrs. 187/K3
Fruita, Colo. (81521) 208/B4
Fruita, Utah (†84775) 304/C5
Fruitdale, Ala. (36539) 195/B8
Fruitdale, S. Dak. (57742) 298/B4
Fruitdale-Harbeck, Oreg. (†97526) 291/D5
Fruitgrove, Queensland 88/K3
Fruit Heights, Utah (†84037) 304/C2
Fruithurst, Ala. (36262) 195/G3
Fruitland, Idaho (83619) 220/B6
Fruitland, Iowa (52749) 229/L6
Fruitland, Md. (21826) 245/R7
Fruitland, Mo. (†63755) 261/N8
Fruitland, N. Mex. (87416) 274/A2
Fruitland, Tenn. (†38343) 237/D9
Fruitland, Utah (84027) 304/D3
Fruitland, Wash. (99129) 310/G2
Fruitland Park, Fla. (32731) 212/D3
Fruitland Park, Miss. (39577) 256/F9
Fruitport, Mich. (49415) 250/C5
Fruitvale, Br. Col. 184/J5
Fruitvale, Idaho (83620) 220/B5
Fruitvale, Tenn. (38336) 237/C9
Fruitvale, Wash. (†98901) 310/E4
Fruitville, Fla. (33578) 212/D4
Frunze, U.S.S.R. 54/J5
Frunze, U.S.S.R. 48/H5
Frutal, Brazil 135/B2
Frutigen, Switzerland 39/E3
Frutillar, Chile 138/D3
Fry, Georgia (37317) 217/D1
Fryburg, N. Dak. (†58622) 282/D6
Fryburg, Ohio (†45895) 284/B4
Fryburg, Pa. (16326) 294/D3
Fry Canyon, Utah (†84511) 304/D6
Frýdek-Místek, Czech. 41/E2
Frýdlant nad Ostravicí, Czech. 41/E2
Frýdlant v. Čechách, Czech. 41/C1
Frye, Maine (04235) 243/B6
Fryeburg, La. (†71039) 238/D2
Fryeburg, Maine (04037) 243/A7
Fryeburg○, Maine (04037) 243/A7
Fu'an, China 77/K6
Fuchu, Hiroshima, Japan 81/F6
Fuchu, Tokyo, Japan 81/O2
Fuding, China 77/K6
Fuengirola, Spain 33/D4
Fuensalida, Spain 33/D2
Fuente-Álamo, Spain 33/F4
Fuente de Cantos, Spain 33/C3
Fuentelapeña, Spain 33/D2
Fuente Obejuna, Spain 33/D3
Fuenterrabía, Spain 33/E1
Fuentesaúco, Spain 33/D2
Fuentes de Andalucía, Spain 33/D4
Fuentes de Oñoro, Spain 33/C2
Fuerte (isl.), Colombia 126/B3
Fuerte (riv.), Mexico 150/E3
Fuerte Bulnes, Chile 138/E10
Fuerte Olimpo, Argentina 120/D5
Fuerte Olimpo, Paraguay 144/C2
Fuerteventura (isl.), Spain 102/A2
Fuerteventura (isl.), Spain 106/B3
Fuerteventura (isl.), Spain 33/C4
Fuga (isl.), Philippines 82/A3
Fuglebjerg, Denmark 21/E7
Fugu, China 77/H4
Fuhai (Burultokay), China 77/C2
Fuik, Neth. Ant. 161/G9
Fujairah, U.A.E. 59/G4
Fuji, Japan 81/J6
Fuji (mt.), Japan 81/J6
Fuji (riv.), Japan 81/J6
Fujian (Fukien), China 77/J6
Fujieda, Japan 81/J6
Fuji-Hakone-Izu National Park, Japan 81/H6
Fujin, China 77/M2
Fujisawa, Japan 81/O3
Fukagawa, Japan 81/L2
Fukang, China 77/C3
Fukuchiyama, Japan 81/G6
Fukue, Japan 81/D7
Fukui (pref.), Japan 81/G5
Fukui, Japan 81/G5
Fukuoka (pref.), Japan 81/D7
Fukuoka, Japan 54/O6
Fukuoka, Japan 81/D7
Fukushima (pref.), Japan 81/K5
Fukushima, Japan 81/K5
Fukuyama, Japan 81/F6
Fulbourn, England 13/H5
Fulbright, Texas (75436) 303/J4
Fulda, Ind. (47536) 227/D8
Fulda, Minn. (56131) 255/C7
Fulda, Sask. 181/F3
Fulda, W. Germany 22/C3
Fulda (riv.), W. Germany 22/C3
Fulford, England 13/F4
Fulford Harbour, Br. Col. 184/K3
Fuling, China 77/G6
Fulks Run, Va. (22830) 307/L3
Fullarton, Trin. & Tob. 161/A11
Fullerton, Calif. (*92631) 204/D11
Fullerton, Ky. (†41175) 237/P3
Fullerton, La. (70642) 238/D4
Fullerton, Nebr. (68638) 264/F3
Fullerton, N. Dak. (58441) 282/O7
Fully, Switzerland 39/D4
Fulnek, Czech. 41/D2
Fulpmes, Austria 41/A3
Fulton, Ala. (36446) 195/C7
Fulton (co.), Ark. 202/G1
Fulton, Ark. (71838) 202/C6
Fulton (co.), Georgia 217/D3
Fulton (co.), Ill. 222/C3
Fulton, Ill. (61252) 222/C2
Fulton (co.), Ind. 227/E2
Fulton, Ind. (46931) 227/E3
Fulton, Iowa (†52060) 229/M4
Fulton, Kansas (66738) 232/H4
Fulton (co.), Ky. 237/C7
Fulton, Ky. (42041) 237/D7
Fulton, Mich. (49052) 250/D6
Fulton, Miss. (38843) 256/H2
Fulton, Mo. (65251) 261/J5
Fulton (co.), N.Y. 276/M4
Fulton, N.Y. (13069) 276/H4
Fulton (co.), Ohio 284/B2
Fulton, Ohio (43321) 284/E5
Fulton (co.), Pa. 294/F6
Fulton, S. Dak. (57340) 298/O6
Fulton, Tenn. (†38041) 237/B9
Fulton, Texas (78358) 303/H9
Fulton Chain (lakes), N.Y. 276/K3
Fultondale, Ala. (35068) 195/E3
Fultonham, Ohio (43738) 284/F6
Fultonville, N.Y. (12072) 276/M5
Fults, Ill. (62244) 222/C5
Fulwood, England 10/G1
Fulwood, England 13/G1
Funabashi, Japan 81/P2
Funafuti (atoll), Tuvalu 87/H6
Funchal (cap.), Madeira, Port. 102/A1
Funchal (dist.), Portugal 33/A2
Funchal (cap.), Madeira, Portugal 106/A2
Funchal, Portugal 33/A2
Fundación, Colombia 126/C2
Fundão, Portugal 33/C2
Fundy (bay) 162/K7
Fundy (bay), New Bruns. 170/E3
Fundy (bay), Nova Scotia 168/C3
Fundy Nat'l Park, New Bruns. 170/E3
Funhalouro, Mozambique 118/E4
Funing, China 77/K5
Funk, Nebr. (68940) 264/E4
Funk (isl.), Newf. 166/D4
Funkley, Minn. (†56630) 255/D3
Funkstown, Md. (21734) 245/H2
Funston, Georgia (31753) 217/E8
Funter, Alaska (†99801) 196/M1
Funtua, Nigeria 106/F6
Fuping, China 77/H4
Fuquay-Varina, N.C. (27526) 281/M3
Furancungo, Mozambique 118/E2
Furka (pass), Switzerland 39/F3
Furman, Ala. (36741) 195/E6
Furman, S.C. (29921) 296/E6
Furmanov, U.S.S.R. 52/F3
Furnace, Ky. (†40472) 237/O5
Furnace, Mass. (†01031) 249/F3
Furnace, Scotland 15/C4
Furnas (res.), Brazil 120/E5
Furnas (dam), Brazil 135/C2
Furnas (co.), Nebr. 264/E4
Furneaux Group (isls.), Australia 87/E9
Furneaux Group (isls.), Tasmania 88/H8
Furneaux Group (isls.), Tasmania 99/E1
Furnes (Veurne), Belgium 27/B6
Furness, Sask. 181/B2
Fury Creek, Br. Col. 184/K2
Fürstenberg, E. Germany 22/E2
Fürstenfeld, Austria 41/C3
Fürstenfeldbruck, W. Germany 22/D4
Fürstenwalde, E. Germany 22/F2
Fürth, W. Germany 22/D4
Furth im Wald, W. Germany 22/E4
Furukawa, Japan 81/K4
Fury and Hecla (str.), N.W.T. 162/H2
Fury and Hecla (str.), N.W. Terrs. 187/K3
Fusagasugá, Colombia 126/C5
Fushun, China 77/K3
Fushun, China 54/O5
Fusilier, Sask. 181/B4
Fusin (Fuxin), China 77/K3
Fusingchen (Simao), China 77/F7
Fusio, Switzerland 39/G4
Fusong, China 77/L3
Füssen, W. Germany 22/D5
Futa Jallon (mts.), Guinea 106/B6
Futaleufú, Chile 138/E4
Futrono, Chile 138/E3
Futuna (Hoorn) (isls.), Wallis and Futuna 87/J7
Fu Xian, Liaoning, China 77/K4
Fu Xian, Shaanxi, China 77/G4
Fuxin (Fusin), China 77/K3
Fuxin, China 54/O5
Fuyang (Fowyang), China 77/J5
Fuyu, Heilongjiang, China 77/K2
Fuyu, Jilin, China 77/L2
Fuyuan, Heilongjiang, China 77/M2
Fuyuan, Yunnan, China 77/F6
Fuyun, China 77/C2
Füzesabony, Hungary 41/F3
Füzesgyarmat, Hungary 41/F3
Fuzhou (Foochow), Fujian, China 77/J6
Fuzhou, Jiangxi, China 77/J6
Fuzhou, China 2/R4
Fuzhou, China 54/N7
Fyffe, Ala. (35971) 195/G2
Fylingdales, England 13/G3
Fyn (co.), Denmark 21/D7
Fyn (isl.), Denmark 21/D7
Fyn (isl.), Denmark 18/G9
Fyne, Loch (inlet), Scotland 10/D2
Fyne, Loch (inlet), Scotland 15/C5
Fyns Hoved (pt.), Denmark 21/D6
Fyvie, Scotland 15/F3
Fyzabad, Trin. & Tob. 161/A11

G

Gaastra, Mich. (49927) 250/G2
Gabarus, Nova Scotia 168/H3
Gabarus (bay), Nova Scotia 168/H3
Gabarus (cape), Nova Scotia 168/J3
Gabbettville, Georgia (†30240) 217/B5
Gabbs, Nev. (89409) 266/D4
Gabela, Angola 115/B6
Gabès, Tunisia 106/F2
Gabès, Tunisia 102/D1
Gabès (gulf), Tunisia 106/G2
Gabgaba, Wadi (dry riv.), Sudan 111/F3
Gable, S.C. (29051) 296/G4
Gabon 2/K6
Gabon 102/D4
GABON 115/B4
Gaborone (cap.), Botswana 2/L7
Gaborone (cap.), Botswana 118/D4
Gaborone (cap.), Botswana 102/E7
Gabras, Sudan 111/E5
Gabredarre, Ethiopia 111/H6
Gabriel (str.), N.W. Terrs. 187/M3
Gabrik (riv.), Iran 66/L7
Gabriola, Br. Col. 184/J3
Gabrovo, Bulgaria 45/G4
Gachalá, Colombia 126/D5
Gach Saran, Iran 59/F3
Gach Saran, Iran 66/G5
Gackle, N. Dak. (58442) 282/M6
Gacko, Yugoslavia 45/D4
Gadag-Betgeri, India 68/D5
Gäddede, Sweden 18/J4
Gadê, China 77/E5
Gadebusch, E. Germany 22/D2
Gadmen, Switzerland 39/F3
Gadsby, Alberta 182/D3
Gadsden, Ala. 188/J4
Gadsden, Ala. (*35901) 195/G2
Gadsden, Ariz. (85336) 198/A6
Gadsden (co.), Fla. 212/B1
Gadsden, S.C. (29052) 296/F4
Gadsden, Tenn. (38337) 237/D9
Gads Hill, Mo. (†63957) 261/L8
Gadston (pt.), Fla. 212/C3
Gadwal, India 68/D5
Gadyach, U.S.S.R. 52/D4
Găeşti, Romania 45/G3
Gaeta, Italy 34/D4
Gaeta (gulf), Italy 34/D4
Gaferut (isl.), Micronesia 87/E5
Gaffney, S.C. (29340) 296/D1
Gafsa, Tunisia 106/F2
Gagarin, U.S.S.R. 52/D3
Gage, Alberta 182/A1
Gage (co.), Nebr. 264/H4
Gage, N. Mex. (†88030) 274/A6
Gage, Okla. (73843) 288/G2
Gagetown, Mich. (48735) 250/F5
Gagetown, New Bruns. 170/D3
Gaggenau, W. Germany 22/C4
Gagnoa, Ivory Coast 102/B4
Gagnoa, Ivory Coast 106/C7
Gagnon, Que. 162/K5
Gagnon, Québec 174/D2
Gagnon (lake), Québec 172/B3
Gagny, France 28/C1
Gagra, U.S.S.R. 52/E6
Gahanna, Ohio (43230) 284/E5
Gaiba (lag.), Bolivia 136/F5
Gail, Saudi Arabia 59/E5
Gail, Texas (79738) 303/C5
Gaillac, France 28/D6
Gaillard (lake), Conn. 210/D3
Gaillard, Georgia (†31078) 217/D5
Gaima, Papua N.G. 85/B7
Gaiman, Argentina 143/C5
Gaines, Mich. (48436) 250/F6
Gaines, Pa. (16921) 294/G2
Gaines (co.), Texas 303/B5
Gainesboro, Tenn. (38562) 237/K8
Gainesboro, Va. (†22601) 307/M2
Gainestown, Ala. (36540) 195/C8
Gainesville, Ala. (35464) 195/B5
Gainesville (dam), Ala. 195/B5
Gainesville, Fla. 188/K5
Gainesville, Fla. (*32601) 212/D2
Gainesville, Georgia (30501) 217/E2
Gainesville, Mo. (65655) 261/G9
Gainesville, N.Y. (14066) 276/D5
Gainesville, Texas (76240) 303/G4
Gainesville, Va. (22065) 307/N3
Gainsborough, England 10/F4
Gainsborough, England 13/G4
Gainsborough, Sask. 181/K6
Gairdner (lake), Australia 87/D9
Gairdner (lake), S. Australia 88/F6
Gairdner (lake), S. Australia 94/D4
Gairloch, Scotland 15/C3
Gairloch, Loch (inlet), Scotland 15/C3
Gais, Switzerland 39/H2
Gaithersburg, Md. (20760) 245/K4
Gajdel, Czech. 41/E2
Gakona, Alaska (99586) 196/K2
Galadi, Ethiopia 111/J6
Galahad, Alberta 182/E3
Galana (riv.), Kenya 115/G4
Galand, Iran 66/J2
Galanta, Czech. 41/D2
Galápagos (isls.), Ecuador 2/E6
Galápagos (isls.), Ecuador 128/C8
Galashiels, Scotland 10/E3
Galashiels, Scotland 15/F5
Galata, Mont. (59444) 262/E2
Galata, Turkey 63/C6
Galaţi, Romania 7/G4
Galaţi, Romania 45/H3
Galatia, Ill. (62935) 222/E6
Galatia, Kansas (†67567) 232/D3
Galatina, Italy 34/G4
Galatone, Italy 34/F4
Galax (I.C.), Va. (24333) 307/G7
Galbally, Ireland 17/E7
Galbraith, La. (†71447) 238/E4
Galcaio, Somalia 102/G4
Galcaio, Somalia 115/J2
Galchutt, N. Dak. (58034) 282/S7
Gale, Ill. (62936) 222/D6
Gale (riv.), N.H. 268/D3
Galeana, Chihuahua, Mexico 150/F1
Galeana, Nuevo León, Mexico 150/J4
Galela, Indonesia 85/H5
Galen, Mont. (†59722) 262/D4
Galena, Alaska (99741) 196/G2
Galena, Ill. (61036) 222/C1
Galena, Ind. (†47119) 227/F8
Galena, Kansas (66739) 232/H4
Galena, Md. (21635) 245/P3
Galena, Mo. (65656) 261/F9
Galena, Ohio (43021) 284/E5
Galena Park, Texas (77547) 303/J1
Galeota (pt.), Trin. & Tob. 161/B11
Galera (pt.), Chile 138/D3
Galera (pt.), Ecuador 128/B2
Galera (pt.), Trin. & Tob. 161/C10
Galera (pt.), Trin. & Tob. 156/G5
Galesburg, Ill. 188/H2
Galesburg, Ill. (61401) 222/C3
Galesburg, Kansas (66740) 232/G4
Galesburg, Mich. (49053) 250/D6
Galesburg, N. Dak. (58035) 282/R5
Gales Creek, Oreg. (97117) 291/D2
Gales Ferry, Conn. (06335) 210/G3
Galestown, Md. (†19973) 245/P6
Galesville, Md. (20765) 245/M5
Galesville, Wis. (54630) 317/D7
Galeton, Colo. (80622) 208/K1
Galeton, Pa. (16922) 294/G2
Galetta, Ontario 177/H2
Galgenberg (hill), Netherlands 27/H4
Galguduud (prov.), Somalia 115/J2
Galiano, Br. Col. 184/K3
Galiano (isl.), Br. Col. 184/K3
Galice, Oreg. (†97532) 291/D5
Galich, U.S.S.R. 52/F3
Galicia (reg.), Spain 33/B1
Galien, Mich. (49113) 250/C7
Galilee, Sea of (lake), Israel 59/C3
Galilee, Sea of (Tiberias) (lake), Israel 65/D2
Galilee (reg.), Israel 65/C2
Galilee (lake), Queensland 95/C4
Galina (pt.), Jamaica 158/J6
Galion (bay), Martinique 161/D6
Galion, Ohio (44833) 284/E4
Galisteo, N. Mex. (87540) 274/D3
Galiuro (mts.), Ariz. 198/E6
Galivants Ferry, S.C. (29544) 296/J3
Gallabat, Sudan 111/G5
Gallan (head), Scotland 15/A2
Gallant, Ala. (35972) 195/F2
Gallarate, Italy 34/B2
Gallatin (co.), Ill. 222/E6
Gallatin (co.), Ky. 237/M3
Gallatin, Mo. (64640) 261/E3
Gallatin (co.), Mont. 262/E5
Gallatin (peak), Mont. 262/E5
Gallatin (riv.), Mont. 262/E5
Gallatin, Tenn. (37066) 237/H8
Gallatin Gateway, Mont. (59730) 262/E5
Gallaway, Tenn. (38036) 237/B10
Galle, Sri Lanka 54/J9
Galle, Sri Lanka 68/D7
Gallegos (riv.), Argentina 143/B7
Gallegos, N. Mex. (†87733) 274/F3
Galley (head), Ireland 17/D9
Gallia (co.), Ohio 284/F8
Galliano, La. (70354) 238/K8
Gallina, N. Mex. (87017) 274/C2
Gallinas (pt.), Colombia 120/B1
Gallinas (pt.), Colombia 126/E1
Gallinas (mts.), N. Mex. 274/B4
Gallinas (riv.), N. Mex. 274/E3
Gallion, Ala. (36742) 195/C6
Gallion, La. (†71223) 238/G1
Gallipoli, Italy 34/F4
Gallipoli, Turkey 59/A1
Gallipoli, Turkey 63/C5
Gallipolis, Ohio (45631) 284/F8
Gallipolis Ferry, W. Va. (25515) 312/B5
Gallitzin, Pa. (16641) 294/E4
Gällivare, Sweden 18/M3
Gallman, Miss. (39077) 256/D7
Gallo (pt.), Chile 138/E3
Gallo (mt.), Dom. Rep. 158/D5
Gällö, Sweden 18/J5
Galloo (isl.), N.Y. 276/H3
Galloway, Ark. (†72114) 202/F4
Galloway, Br. Col. 184/K5
Galloway (dist.), Scotland 15/D5
Galloway, Mull of (prom.), Scotland 15/D6
Galloway, Mull of (prom.), Scotland 10/D3
Galloway, W. Va. (26349) 312/F4
Galloway, Wis. (54432) 317/H6
Gallup, N. Mex. 188/E3
Gallup, N. Mex. (87301) 274/A3
Gallur, Spain 33/F2
Galole, Kenya 115/G4
Gal'on, Israel 65/B4
Galston, Scotland 10/D3
Galston, Scotland 15/D5
Galt, Calif. (95632) 204/C9
Galt, Iowa (50101) 229/F3
Galt, Mo. (64641) 261/F2
Galtee (mts.), Ireland 17/E7
Galtymore (mt.), Ireland 17/E7
Galva, Ill. (61434) 222/D2
Galva, Iowa (51020) 229/C3
Galva, Kansas (67443) 232/E3
Galván (mt.), Paraguay 144/C3
Galvarino, Chile 138/D2
Galveston, Ind. (46932) 227/E3
Galveston (co.), Texas 303/K8
Galveston, Texas 146/J7
Galveston, Texas 188/H5
Galveston, Texas (*77550) 303/L3
Galveston (bay), Texas 188/H5
Galveston (bay), Texas 303/L2
Galveston (isl.), Texas 303/K8
Gálvez, Argentina 143/F6
Galvez, La. (†70769) 238/L2
Gálvez, Spain 33/D3
Galvin, Wash. (98544) 310/B4
Galway (co.), Ireland 17/D5
Galway, Ireland 17/C5
Galway, Ireland 7/D3
Galway, Ireland 10/B4
Galway (bay), Ireland 17/C5
Galway (bay), Ireland 10/B4
Galway, N.Y. (12074) 276/N4
Gamaliel, Ky. (42140) 237/K7
Gamarra, Colombia 126/D3
Gamas Ab (riv.), Iran 66/E3
Gamay, Philippines 82/E4
Gamay (bay), Philippines 82/E4
Gamba, China 77/C6
Gambaga, Ghana 106/D6
Gambela, Ethiopia 111/F6
Gambell, Alaska (99742) 196/D2
Gamber, Md. (†21048) 245/L3
Gambia 2/J5
Gambia 102/A3
GAMBIA 106/A6
Gambia (riv.), Gambia 106/B6
Gambia (riv.), Senegal 106/B6
Gambier (isls.), Fr. Poly. 87/N8
Gambier, Ohio (43022) 284/F5
Gambo, Newf. 166/D4
Gamboma, Congo 115/C4
Gambos, Angola 115/B6
Gambrills, Md. (21054) 245/M4
Gamerco, N. Mex. (87317) 274/A3
Gaming, Austria 41/C3
Gamleby, Sweden 18/J8
Gammon (riv.), Manitoba 179/G3
Gammon (pt.), Mass. 249/N6
Gampel, Switzerland 39/E4
Gamu-Gofa (prov.), Ethiopia 111/G6
Gamvik, Norway 18/Q1
Ganado, Ariz. (86505) 198/F3
Ganado, Texas (77962) 303/H8
Ganale Dorya (riv.), Ethiopia 111/H6
Gananoque, Ontario 177/H3
Ganassi, Philippines 82/D7
Ganaveh, Iran 66/G6
Ganda, Angola 115/B6
Gandajika, Zaire 115/D5
Gandara, Philippines 82/E4
Gándara, Spain 33/C1
Gandava, Pakistan 68/B3
Gandava, Pakistan 59/J4
Gandeeville, W. Va. (25243) 312/D5
Gander, Newf. 166/D4
Gander (lake), Newf. 166/D4
Gander (riv.), Newf. 166/D4
Gander, Newf. 162/L6
Gandesa, Spain 33/G2
Gandhinagar, India 68/C4
Gandía, Spain 33/F3
Gandy, Nebr. (†69163) 264/D3
Gandy, Utah (†84728) 304/A4
Gandzha (Kirovabad), U.S.S.R. 52/G6
Ganga (Ganges) (riv.), India 68/F3
Gan Gan, Argentina 143/C5
Ganganagar, India 68/C3
Gangapur, India 68/D3
Gangara, Niger 106/F6
Gangaw, Burma 72/B2
Gangca, China 77/F4
Gangdisê Shan (range), China 77/B5
Ganges (riv.) 54/K7
Ganges (riv.) 2/P4
Ganges, Mouths of the (delta), Bangladesh 68/F3
Ganges (riv.), Bangladesh 68/F3
Ganges, Br. Col. 184/K3
Ganges, Mouths of the (delta), India 68/F4
Ganges (riv.), India 68/F3
Gangtok, India 68/F3
Gan He (riv.), China 77/K2
Gani, Indonesia 85/H6
Ganister, Pa. (†16693) 294/F5
Ganmain, N.S. Wales 97/D4
Gann (Brinkhaven), Ohio (†43006) 284/F5
Gannat, France 28/E4
Gannett, Idaho (†83313) 220/D6
Gannett (peak), Wyo. 188/D2
Gannett (peak), Wyo. 319/C2
Gannvalley, S. Dak. (57341) 298/L5
Ganquan, China 77/H4
Gans, Okla. (74936) 288/S4
Gänserndorf, Austria 41/D2
Gansevoort, N.Y. (12831) 276/N4
Ganshoren, Belgium 27/B9
Gansu (Kansu), China 77/E3
Gansville, La. (†71422) 238/E2
Gantt, Ala. (36038) 195/E8
Gantt, S.C. (†29609) 296/C2
Ganzhou (Kanchow), China 77/H6
Gao (mt.), Cent. Afr. Rep. 115/C2
Gao, Mali 102/C3
Gao, Mali 106/E5
Gao'an, China 77/H6
Gaolan, China 77/F4
Gaotai, China 77/F4
Gaoua, Upper Volta 106/D6
Gaoual, Guinea 106/B6
Gaoyou Hu (lake), China 77/J5
Gap, France 28/G5
Gap, Pa. (17527) 294/L6
Gap (creek), Sask. 181/B6
Gapan, Philippines 82/C3
Gapcreek, Ky. (†42603) 237/M7
Gap Mills, W. Va. (24941) 312/F7
Gar, China 77/B5
Gara (lake), Ireland 17/D4
Gara, Lough (lake), Ireland 10/B4
Garachiné, Panama 154/H6
Garad, Somalia 115/J2
Garadice (lake), Ireland 17/F3
Garah, N.S. Wales 97/E1
Garamba Nat'l Park, Zaire 115/E3
Garanhuns, Brazil 120/F3
Garanhuns, Brazil 132/G5
Garards Fort, Pa. (15334) 294/B6
Garbahaarrey, Somalia 115/H3
Garba Tula, Kenya 115/G3
Garber, Iowa (52048) 229/L3
Garber, Okla. (73738) 288/M2
Garberville, Calif. (95440) 204/B3
Garbosh, Kuh-e (mt.), Iran 66/G4
Garbsen, W. Germany 22/C2
Garça, Brazil 135/B3
Garcia, Colo. (81134) 208/J8
García de Sola (res.), Spain 33/D3
Garcitas, Venezuela 124/C3
Gard (dept.), France 28/F6
Gard (riv.), France 28/F5
Garda (lake), Italy 34/C2
Gardanne, France 28/F6
Gardar, N. Dak. (58234) 282/P2
Gardelegen, E. Germany 22/D2
Garden, Mich. (49835) 250/C3
Garden (isl.), Mich. 250/D3
Garden (pen.), Mich. 250/C3
Garden (co.), Nebr. 264/B3
Garden (isl.), W. Australia 88/A2
Garden (isl.), W. Australia 92/A1
Gardena, Calif. (*90747) 204/C11
Gardena, Idaho (†83629) 220/B5
Gardena, N. Dak. (58739) 282/J2
Garden City, Ala. (35070) 195/E2
Garden City, Georgia (31408) 217/K6
Garden City, Idaho (†83704) 220/B6
Garden City, Iowa (50102) 229/G4
Garden City, Kans. 188/F3
Garden City, Kansas (67846) 232/B4
Garden City, La. (70540) 238/H7
Garden City, Mich. (48135) 250/F6
Garden City, Minn. (56034) 255/D6
Garden City, Mo. (64747) 261/D5
Garden City, N.Y. (11530) 276/R7
Garden City, S. Dak. (57236) 298/O4
Garden City, Texas (79739) 303/C6
Garden City, Utah (84028) 304/C2
Garden City Beach, S.C. (29576) 296/K4
Gardendale, Ala. (35071) 195/E3
Garden Grove, Calif. (*92640) 204/D11
Garden Grove, Iowa (50103) 229/F7
Garden Home-Whitford, Oreg. (97223) 291/A2
Garden Island (bay), La. 238/M8
Garden Plain, Kansas (67050) 232/E4
Garden Prairie, Ill. (61038) 222/E1
Garden Reach, India 68/F2
Garden River, Alberta 182/B5
Gardenstown, Scotland 15/F3
Gardenton, Manitoba 179/F5
Garden Valley, Idaho (83622) 220/C5
Garden View, Pa. (†17701) 294/H3
Garden Village, Ontario 177/E1
Gardez, Afghanistan 59/J3
Gardez, Afghanistan 68/B2
Gardi, Georgia (†31545) 217/J7
Gardiner, Maine (04345) 243/D7
Gardiner, Mont. (59030) 262/F5
Gardiner, Oreg. (97441) 291/C4
Gardiner (dam), Sask. 181/D4
Gardiner, Wash. (98334) 310/B2
Gardiners (bay), N.Y. 276/R8
Gardiners (isl.), N.Y. 276/R8
Gardner (canal), Br. Col. 184/C3
Gardner, Colo. (81040) 208/J7
Gardner (lake), Conn. 210/G2
Gardner, Fla. (†33890) 212/E4
Gardner, Ill. (60424) 222/E2
Gardner, Kansas (66030) 232/H3
Gardner (isl.), Kiribati 87/J6
Gardner (lake), Maine 243/J6
Gardner, Mass. (01440) 249/G2
Gardner, N. Dak. (58036) 282/R5
Gardner, Tenn. (†38237) 237/D8
Gardner (mt.), Wash. 310/E2
Gardner Creek, New Bruns. 170/E3
Gardner Pinnacles (isls.), Hawaii 87/K3
Gardner Pinnacles (isls.), Hawaii 188/F6
Gardner Pinnacles (isls.), Hawaii 218/C6
Gardnerville, Nev. (89410) 266/B4
Gardo, Somalia 115/J2
Gardula, Ethiopia 111/G6
Gare Loch (inlet), Scotland 15/A1
Garelochhead, Scotland 15/A1
Garelochhead, Scotland 10/A1
Gareloi (isl.), Alaska 196/K4
Garessio, Italy 34/A2
Garfield, Ark. (72732) 202/C1
Garfield (co.), Colo. 208/C3
Garfield, Colo. (81227) 208/G5
Garfield, Georgia (30425) 217/H5
Garfield, Kansas (67529) 232/C3
Garfield, Ky. (40140) 237/J5
Garfield, Minn. (56332) 255/C5
Garfield (co.), Mont. 262/J3
Garfield (co.), Nebr. 264/F3
Garfield, N.J. (07026) 273/B2
Garfield, N. Mex. (87936) 274/B6
Garfield (co.), Okla. 288/L2
Garfield (co.), Utah 304/C6
Garfield (co.), Wash. 310/H4
Garfield, Wash. (99130) 310/H3
Garfield Heights, Ohio (44125) 284/J9
Gargaliánoi, Greece 45/E7
Gargunnock, Scotland 15/B1
Garibaldi, Br. Col. 184/F5
Garibaldi, Oreg. (97118) 291/D2
Garibaldi Prov. Park, Br. Col. 184/F5
Garies, S. Africa 118/B6
Garioch (dist.), Scotland 15/F3
Garissa, Kenya 115/G4
Garita, N. Mex. (88421) 274/E3
Garland, Ala. (†36456) 195/E7
Garland (co.), Ark. 202/D4

Ghemines 373

Garland, Ark. (71839) 202/C7
Garland, Kansas (66741) 232/H4
Garland, Maine (04939) 243/E5
Garland○, Maine (04939) 243/E5
Garland, Manitoba 179/B3
Garland, Nebr. (68360) 264/G4
Garland, N.C. (28441) 281/N5
Garland, Pa. (16416) 294/C2
Garland, Tenn. (†38019) 237/B9
Garland, Tex. 188/G4
Garland, Texas (*75040) 303/H2
Garland, Utah (84312) 304/B2
Garland, Wyo. (†82435) 319/D1
Garlandville, Miss. (†39345) 256/F6
Garlieston, Scotland 15/D6
Garlin, Ky. (†42728) 237/L6
Garmisch-Partenkirchen, W. Germany 22/D5
Garmouth, Scotland 15/E3
Garmsar, Iran 59/F2
Garmsar, Iran 66/H3
Garnavillo, Iowa (52049) 229/L3
Garneill, Mont. (59445) 262/G4
Garner, Ark. (72052) 202/G3
Garner, Iowa (50438) 229/F2
Garner (lake), Manitoba 179/G4
Garner, N.C. (27529) 281/M3
Garner, Mich. (†49762) 250/D2
Garnet, Mont. (†59832) 262/C4
Garnet (bay), N.W. Terrs. 187/L3
Garnett, Kansas (66032) 232/G3
Garnett, S.C. (29922) 296/E6
Garnish, Newf. 166/C4
Garoe, Somalia 115/J2
Garonne (riv.), France 7/D4
Garonne (riv.), France 28/C5
Garoua, Cameroon 102/D4
Garoua, Cameroon 115/B2
Garrabost, Scotland 15/B2
Garrard (co.), Ky. 237/M5
Garretson, S. Dak. (57030) 298/S6
Garrett, Ill. (†61913) 222/E4
Garrett, Ind. (46738) 227/G2
Garrett, Ky. (41630) 237/R6
Garrett (co.), Md. 245/A2
Garrett, Pa. (15542) 294/D6
Garrett, Wash. (†99362) 310/G4
Garrett, Wyo. (82058) 319/G3
Garrett Park, Md. (20766) 245/E3
Garretts Bend, W. Va. (†25523) 312/C6
Garrettsville, Ohio (44231) 284/H3
Garrick, Sask. 181/G2
Garrison, Iowa (52229) 229/J4
Garrison, Ky. (41141) 237/P3
Garrison, Md. (21055) 245/L3
Garrison, Minn. (56450) 255/E4
Garrison, Mo. (65657) 261/F9
Garrison, Mont. (59731) 262/D4
Garrison, Nebr. (68632) 264/G3
Garrison, N.Y. (10524) 276/N8
Garrison, N. Dak. (58540) 282/H4
Garrison (dam), N. Dak. 282/H5
Garrison, Texas (75946) 303/K6
Garrison, Utah (84728) 304/A5
Garrisonville, Va. (22463) 307/N4
Garron (pt.), N. Ireland 17/K1
Garrovillas, Spain 33/C3
Garry (lake), Canada 4/C14
Garry (lake), N.W.T. 162/G2
Garry (lake), N.W. Terrs. 187/H3
Garry, Loch (lake), Scotland 15/D3
Garry (riv.), Scotland 15/D4
Garryowen, Mont. (59031) 262/J5
Garsen, Kenya 115/G4
Garske, N. Dak. (†58382) 282/N3
Garson (lake), Alberta 182/E1
Garson, Manitoba 179/F4
Garstang, England 13/G1
Gartan (lake), Ireland 17/F2
Gartmore, Scotland 15/B1
Garulia, India 68/F1
Garut, Indonesia 85/H2
Garvagh, N. Ireland 17/H2
Garvan (isls.), Ireland 17/G1
Garvin, Minn. (56132) 255/C6
Garvin (co.), Okla. 288/M5
Garvin, Okla. (74736) 288/S7
Garwin, Iowa (50632) 229/H4
Garwolin, Poland 47/E3
Garwood, Mo. (†63965) 261/L8
Garwood, N.J. (07027) 273/E2
Garwood, Texas (77442) 303/H8
Gary, Ind. 146/K5
Gary, Ind. 188/J2
Gary, Ind. (*46401) 227/C1
Gary, Minn. (56545) 255/B3
Gary, S. Dak. (57237) 298/S4
Gary, Texas (75643) 303/K5
Gary, W. Va. (24836) 312/C8
Garyarsa (Gartok), China 77/B5
Garyarsa, China 54/K6
Garysburg, N.C. (27831) 281/O2
Garyville, La. (70051) 238/M3
Garza (co.), Texas 303/C4
Garzê, China 77/F5
Garzón, Colombia 126/C6
Garzón, Uruguay 145/E5
Garzón (lag.), Uruguay 145/E5
Gas, Kansas (66742) 232/G4
Gas (hills), Wyo. 319/E3
Gasan-Kuli, U.S.S.R. 48/F6
Gasburg, Va. (23857) 307/N7
Gas City, Ind. (46933) 227/F4
Gasconade (co.), Mo. 261/J6
Gasconade, Mo. (65036) 261/J5
Gasconade (riv.), Mo. 261/H7
Gascony (trad. prov.), France 29
Gascoyne (riv.), Australia 87/B8
Gascoyne, N. Dak. (58629) 282/D7
Gascoyne (riv.), W. Australia 88/A4
Gascoyne (riv.), W. Australia 92/B4
Gascoyne Junction, W. Australia 92/A4
Gash (Mareb) (riv.), Ethiopia 59/C7
Gash (riv.), Sudan 59/C6
Gashaka, Nigeria 106/G7
Gas Hills, Wyo. (82501) 319/E3
Gash Mareb (riv.), Ethiopia 111/G5
Gasht, Iran 66/M7
Gasker (isl.), Scotland 15/A3
Gaskiers, Newf. 166/D2
Gasmata, Papua N.G. 86/B2
Gaspar, Cuba 158/F2
Gaspar Hernández, Dom. Rep. 158/E5
Gasparilla (isl.), Fla. 212/D5
Gaspé, Que. 162/K6
Gaspé, Québec 172/D1
Gaspé, Québec 174/E3
Gaspé (bay), Québec 172/D1
Gaspé (cape), Québec 172/D1
Gaspé (pen.), Québec 172/D2
Gaspé-Est (county), Québec 174/E3
Gaspé-Est (co.), Québec 172/D1
Gaspé-Ouest (co.), Québec 172/C1
Gaspé-Ouest (county), Québec 174/D3
Gaspereau (riv.), New Bruns. 170/D2
Gaspereau (lake), Nova Scotia 168/D4
Gaspésie Prov. Park, Québec 174/D3
Gaspésie Prov. Park, Québec 172/C1
Gasport, N.Y. (14067) 276/C4
Gasque, Ala. (†36542) 195/C10
Gassan (mt.), Japan 81/J4
Gassaway, Tenn. (†37095) 237/K9
Gassaway, W. Va. (26624) 312/E5
Gassetts, Vt. (†05144) 268/B5
Gassville, Ark. (72635) 202/F1
Gaston, Ind. (47342) 227/G4
Gaston (co.), N.C. 281/G4
Gaston, N.C. (27832) 281/O1
Gaston (res.), N.C. 281/O2
Gaston, Oreg. (97119) 291/D2
Gaston, S.C. (29053) 296/E4
Gaston (lake), Va. 307/M8
Gastonburg, Ala. (†36728) 195/C6
Gastonia, N.C. 188/K3
Gastonia, N.C. (28052) 281/G4
Gastre, Argentina 143/C5
Gat, Israel 65/B4
Gata (cape), Cyprus 59/B3
Gata (cape), Cyprus 63/E5
Gata (cape), Spain 33/F4
Gata (mts.), Spain 33/C2
Gatchel, Ind. (†47586) 227/D8
Gatchina, U.S.S.R. 52/C3
Gate, Okla. (73844) 288/F1
Gate, Wash. (†98579) 310/B4
Gate City, Va. (24251) 307/C7
Gatehouse of Fleet, Scotland 10/E3
Gatehouse of Fleet, Scotland 15/D6
Gates, Nebr. (68839) 264/E3
Gates (co.), N.C. 281/R2
Gates, N.C. (27937) 281/R2
Gates, Oreg. (97346) 291/E3
Gates, Tenn. (38037) 237/C9
Gateshead, England 10/F3
Gateshead, England 13/J3
Gateshead (isl.), N.W. Terrs. 187/J2
Gates Mills, Ohio (44040) 284/J9
Gates of the Arctic Nat'l Park, Alaska 196/H1
Gates of the Arctic Nat'l Preserve, Alaska 196/H1
Gatesville, N.C. (27938) 281/R2
Gatesville, Texas (76528) 303/G6
Gateswood, Ala. (†36507) 195/C9
Gateway, Ark. (72733) 202/B1
Gateway, Colo. (81522) 208/B5
Gateway, Oreg. (†97741) 291/F3
Gateway Nat'l Rec. Area, N.J. 273/E2
Gateway Nat'l Rec. Area, N.Y. 276/M9
Gatewood, Mo. (63942) 261/K9
Gatico, Chile 138/A4
Gatineau (co.), Québec 172/B3
Gatineau (county), Québec 174/B3
Gatineau, Québec 172/B4
Gatineau (riv.), Québec 172/B3
Gatliff, Ky. (†40769) 237/O7
Gatlinburg, Tenn. (37738) 237/O9
Gatooma, Zimbabwe 118/D3
Gatooma, Zimbabwe 102/E6
Gatow, W. Germany 22/E4
Gatteville-le-Phare, France 28/C3
Gattman, Miss. (38844) 256/H3
Gatton, Queensland 88/J5
Gatton, Queensland 95/E5
Gatun (lake), Panama 154/G6
Gatzke, Minn. (56724) 255/C2
Gaucín, Spain 33/D4
Gauhati, India 68/G3
Gauhati, India 54/L7
Gauja (riv.), U.S.S.R. 53/C2
Gauley (riv.), W. Va. 312/D6
Gauley Bridge, W. Va. (25085) 312/D6
Gauley Mills, W. Va. (26240) 312/E6
Gaultois, Newf. 166/C4
Gausdale, Ky. (40906) 237/N7
Gause, Texas (77857) 303/H7
Gaussberg (mt.) 5/C5
Gautier, Miss. (39553) 256/G10
Gavater, Iran 59/H5
Gavater, Iran 66/M8
Gávdhos (isl.), Greece 45/F8
Gave de Pau (riv.), France 28/C6
Gavião, Portugal 33/C3
Gavins Point (dam), Nebr. 264/G2
Gavins Point (dam), S. Dak. 298/P8
Gaviota, Calif. (†93017) 204/E9
Gavkhuni (lake), Iran 59/F3
Gavkhuni (marsh), Iran 66/H4
Gävle, Sweden 7/F2
Gävle, Sweden 18/K6
Gävleborg (co.), Sweden 18/K6
Gawai, Burma 72/C1
Gawler, S. Australia 88/F6
Gawler (ranges), S. Australia 88/F6
Gawler, S. Australia 94/B6
Gawler (ranges), S. Australia 94/E5
Gawler (riv.), S. Australia 94/B6
Gay, Georgia (30218) 217/C4
Gay, Mich. (49928) 250/A1
Gay, U.S.S.R. 52/J4
Gay, W. Va. (25244) 312/C5
Gaya, India 68/F4
Gaya, Niger 106/E6
Gay Head○, Mass. (†02535) 249/L7
Gay Head (prom.), Mass. 249/L7
Gay Hill, Texas (†77833) 303/H7
Gayle, Jamaica 158/J6
Gaylesville, Ala. (35973) 195/G2
Gaylord, Kansas (67638) 232/D2
Gaylord, Mich. (49735) 250/E3
Gaylord, Minn. (55334) 255/D6
Gaylord, Oreg. (97458) 291/C5
Gaylord, Va. (†22611) 307/M2
Gaylordsville, Conn. (06755) 210/A2
Gayndah, Queensland 95/D5
Gayndah, Queensland 88/J5
Gayny, U.S.S.R. 52/H2
Gays, Ill. (61928) 222/E4
Gaysin, U.S.S.R. 52/C5
Gays Mills, Wis. (54631) 317/E9
Gaysport, Ohio (†43720) 284/G6
Gaysville, Vt. (05746) 268/B4
Gayville, S. Dak. (57031) 298/P8
Gaza, Cent. Afr. Rep. 115/C3
Gaza, Egypt 59/B3
Gaza, Gaza Strip 65/A5
Gaza, Iowa (†51245) 229/B2
Gaza (prov.), Mozambique 118/E4
Gaza, N.H. (†03269) 268/D4
GAZA STRIP 59/B3
Gaza Strip 65/A5
Gazelle, Calif. (96034) 204/C2
Gazelle (pen.), Papua N.G. 86/B2
Gaziantep (prov.), Turkey 63/G4
Gaziantep, Turkey 54/E6
Gaziantep, Turkey 63/G4
Gaziantep, Turkey 59/C2
Gazik, Iran 66/L4
Gazipaşa, Turkey 63/E4
Gbarnga, Liberia 106/C7
Gbarnga, Liberia 102/B4
Gbogo, Nigeria 106/F7
Gcuwa, S. Africa 118/D6
Gdańsk (prov.), Poland 47/D1
Gdańsk, Poland 7/F3
Gdańsk, Poland 47/D1
Gdov, U.S.S.R. 52/C3
Gdynia, Poland 7/F3
Gdynia, Poland 47/D1
Gearhart, Oreg. (97138) 291/C1
Geary (co.), Kansas 232/F3
Geary, New Bruns. 170/D3
Geary, Okla. (73040) 288/K3
Geashill, Ireland 17/G5
Geauga (co.), Ohio 284/H3
Gebe (isl.), Indonesia 85/H6
Gebeit Mine, Sudan 111/G3
Gebo, Wyo. (†82430) 319/D2
Gebze, Turkey 63/C2
Gedaref, Sudan 111/G5
Gedaref, Sudan 59/C7
Gedaref, Sudan 102/F3
Geddes, S. Dak. (57342) 298/M7
Gede (mt.), Indonesia 85/H2
Gedera, Israel 65/B4
Gedi (ruins), Kenya 115/G4
Gedinne, Belgium 27/F9
Gediz, Turkey 63/C3
Gediz (riv.), Turkey 63/C3
Gedo, Ethiopia 111/G6
Gedo (prov.), Somalia 115/H3
Gedser, Denmark 21/F8
Gedser Odde (pt.), Denmark 21/E8
Gedsted, Denmark 21/C4
Geebung, Queensland 88/K2
Geebung, Queensland 95/E2
Geel, Belgium 27/F6
Geelong, Victoria 88/L7
Geelong, Victoria 97/C6
Geelong West, Victoria 88/G7
Geelong West, Victoria 97/C6
Geelvink (Cenderawasih) (bay), Indonesia 85/K6
Geelvink (chan.), W. Australia 88/A5
Geelvink (chan.), W. Australia 92/A5
Geertruidenberg, Netherlands 27/F5
Geesthacht, W. Germany 22/D2
Geetingsville, Ind. (†46041) 227/D4
Geeveston, Tasmania 99/C5
Geff, Ill. (62842) 222/E5
Gê'gyai, China 77/B5
Geh, Iran 59/H4
Geh, Iran 66/L7
Gehua, Papua N.G. 85/C8
Geidam, Nigeria 106/G6
Geiger, Ala. (†35459) 195/B5
Geiger Heights, Wash. (†99219) 310/H3
Geikie (riv.), Sask. 181/M3
Geilo, Norway 18/F6
Geiranger, Norway 18/E5
Geislingen an der Steige, W. Germany 22/C4
Geismar, La. (70734) 238/K3
Geist (res.), Ind. 227/F5
Geistown, Pa. (15904) 294/E5
Geita, Tanzania 115/F4
Gejiu (Kokiu), China 77/F7
Gejiu, China 54/M7
Gela, Italy 34/E6
Gelang, Tanjong (pt.), Malaysia 72/D6
Geldenaken (Jodoigne), Belgium 27/F7
Gelderland (prov.), Netherlands 27/H4
Geldermalsen, Netherlands 27/G5
Geldern, W. Germany 22/B3
Geldrop, Netherlands 27/H6
Geleen, Netherlands 27/H7
Gelendzhik, U.S.S.R. 52/E6
Gelgia (riv.), Switzerland 39/J3
Gelibolu (Gallipoli), Turkey 63/C5
Gelidonya (cape), Turkey 59/B2
Gelidonya (cape), Turkey 63/D4
Gelligaer, Wales 13/A6
Gelnhausen, W. Germany 22/C3
Gelnica, Czech. 41/F2
Gelså (riv.), Denmark 21/C7
Gelsenkirchen, W. Germany 22/B3
Gelsted, Denmark 21/C7
Gelterkinden, Switzerland 39/E2
Gem, Alberta 182/D4
Gem (co.), Idaho 220/B6
Gem, Idaho (†83873) 220/C2
Gem, Ind. (†46140) 227/F5
Gem, Kansas (67734) 232/B2
Gem (lake), Manitoba 179/G4
Gem, W. Va. (26625) 312/E5
Gemas, Malaysia 72/D7
Gembloux-sur-Orneau, Belgium 27/F7
Gemena, Zaire 115/D3
Gemena, Zaire 102/E4
Gemerek, Turkey 63/G3
Gemert, Netherlands 27/H5
Gemlik, Turkey 63/D2
Gemmell, Minn. (†56660) 255/D3
Gemona, Italy 34/D1
Gemsa, Egypt 111/F2
Genç, Turkey 63/J3
Gendringen, Netherlands 27/J5
Gene Autry, Okla. (73436) 288/N6
Genemuiden, Netherlands 27/H3
General Acha, Argentina 143/C4
General Alvear, Buenos Aires, Argentina 143/F7
General Alvear, Mendoza, Argentina 143/C3
General Arenales, Argentina 143/F7
General Artigas, Paraguay 144/D5
General Belgrano, Argentina 143/G7
General Bravo, Mexico 150/K4
General Campos, Argentina 143/G5
General Cepeda, Mexico 150/J4
General Conesa, Argentina 143/C5
General Elizardo Aquino, Paraguay 144/D4
General Enrique Martínez, Uruguay 145/F4
General Eugenio A. Garay, Paraguay 144/A2
General Galarza, Argentina 143/C6
General Grant Grove Section (King's Canyon), Calif. 204/G7
General Güemes, Argentina 143/D1
General Guido, Argentina 143/E4
General José de San Martín, Argentina 143/E2
General Juan Madariaga, Argentina 143/E4
General Lagos, Chile 138/B1
General La Madrid, Argentina 143/D4
General Las Heras, Argentina 143/G7
General Lavalle, Argentina 143/E4
General Manuel Belgrano, Cerro (mt.), Argentina 143/C2
General Mitchell Field, Wis. 317/M2
General O'Brien, Argentina 143/F7
General Paz, Argentina 143/E2
General Paz, Argentina 143/H7
General Paz (lake), Chile 138/E5
General Pico, Argentina 143/D4
General Ramírez, Argentina 143/F6
General Roca, Argentina 143/C4
General Saavedra, Bolivia 136/D5
General San Martín, Argentina 143/D4
General San Martín, Argentina 143/G4
General Santos, Philippines 82/E7
General Terán, Mexico 150/K4
General Tinio, Philippines 82/C3
General-Toshevo, Bulgaria 45/H4
General Viamonte, Argentina 143/F7
General Villegas, Argentina 143/D4
Generoso (mt.), Switzerland 39/H5
Genesee, Idaho (83832) 220/B3
Genesee (co.), Mich. 250/F5
Genesee (co.), N.Y. 276/D4
Genesee (riv.), N.Y. 276/E5
Genesee, Pa. (16923) 294/G2
Genesee, Wis. (†53127) 317/J2
Genesee Depot, Wis. (53127) 317/J2
Geneseo, Ill. (61254) 222/C2
Geneseo, Kansas (67444) 232/D3
Geneseo, N.Y. (14454) 276/E5
Geneseo, N. Dak. (58037) 282/R7
Geneva (lake) 7/E4
Geneva (co.), Ala. 195/G8
Geneva, Ala. (36340) 195/G8
Geneva, Fla. (32732) 212/E3
Geneva (lake), France 28/G4
Geneva, Georgia (31810) 217/C5
Geneva, Idaho (83238) 220/G7
Geneva, Ill. (60134) 222/E2
Geneva, Ind. (46740) 227/H3
Geneva, Iowa (50633) 229/G3
Geneva, Ky. (†42406) 237/F5
Geneva, Minn. (56035) 255/E7
Geneva, Nebr. (68361) 264/G4
Geneva, N.Y. (14456) 276/G5
Geneva, Ohio (44041) 284/J2
Geneva, Pa. (16316) 294/B2
Geneva (Genève) (canton), Switzerland 39/B4
Geneva (Genève), Switzerland 39/B4
Geneva, Switzerland 7/E4
Geneva (lake), Switzerland 39/C4
Geneva, Texas (75947) 303/L6
Geneva (lake), Wis. 317/K10
Geneva-on-the-Lake, Ohio (44043) 284/H2
Genezin, Turkey 63/F3
Genichesk, U.S.S.R. 52/E5
Genil (riv.), Spain 33/D4
Genk, Belgium 27/H7
Gennargentu, Monti del (mt.), Italy 34/B5
Gennep, Netherlands 27/H5
Gennevilliers, France 28/B1
Genoa, Ark. (71840) 202/C7
Genoa, Colo. (80818) 208/N4
Genoa, Ill. (60135) 222/E1
Genoa (prov.), Italy 34/B2
Genoa, Italy 7/E4
Genoa, Italy 34/B2
Genoa (gulf), Italy 34/B2
Genoa, Nebr. (68640) 264/G3
Genoa, Nev. (89411) 266/B4
Genoa, N.Y. (13071) 276/G5
Genoa, Ohio (43430) 284/D2
Genoa, W. Va. (25517) 312/A6
Genoa, Wis. (54632) 317/D8
Genoa City, Wis. (53128) 317/K11
Genola, Minn. (†56364) 255/D5
Genola, Utah (†84655) 304/C4
Genova (Genoa), Italy 34/B2
Genovesa (isl.), Ecuador 128/C9
Gent (Ghent), Belgium 27/D6
Genthin, E. Germany 22/E2
Gentilly, France 28/B2
Gentilly, Minn. (†56716) 255/B3
Genting, Indonesia 85/D5
Gentofte, Denmark 21/F6
Gentry, Ark. (72734) 202/A1
Gentry (co.), Mo. 261/D2
Gentry, Mo. (64453) 261/D2
Gentryville, Ind. (47537) 227/C8
Gentryville, Mo. (†64402) 261/D2
Genzano di Roma, Italy 34/F7
Geographe (chan.), W. Australia 88/A4
Geographe (bay), W. Australia 92/A6
Geographe (chan.), W. Australia 92/A4
Geographical Center of North America, N. Dak. 282/K3
Geographical Center of U.S., S. Dak. 298/B4
George (isl.), 143/E7
George (lake), Fla. 212/E2
George, Iowa (51237) 229/B2
George (isl.), Manitoba 179/E2
George (lake), Manitoba 179/G4
George (co.), Miss. 256/G9
George (isl.), Newf. 166/C3
George (lake), N.S. Wales 97/E4
George (lake), N.Y. 276/N4
George (sound), N. Zealand 100/A6
George (lake), N. Dak. 282/L6
George (cape), Nova Scotia 168/G3
George (lake), Nova Scotia 168/B5
George (riv.), Que. 162/K4
George (riv.), Que. 146/M4
George (riv.), Québec 174/F2
George, S. Africa 118/C6
George (lake), Uganda 115/F4
George, Wash. (98824) 310/F3
George A.F.B., Calif. 204/H9
George B. Stevenson (dam), Pa. 294/G3
George Land (isl.), U.S.S.R. 4/B7
George Land (isl.), U.S.S.R. 48/E1
George Rogers Clark Nat'l Hist. Park, Ind. 227/B7
Georges (isls.), Maine 243/E8
Georges (riv.), N. S. Wales 88/K4
Georges (riv.), N.S. Wales 97/H4
Georges Brook, Newf. 166/D2
George's Cove, Newf. 166/C3
Georges Fork, Va. (†24228) 307/C6
Georges Mills, N.H. (03751) 268/C5
Georgetown, Ark. (72054) 202/G3
Georgetown, Calif. (95634) 204/E5
George Town (cap.), Cayman Is. 156/B3
Georgetown, Colo. (80444) 208/H3
Georgetown, Conn. (06829) 210/B4
Georgetown, Del. (19947) 245/S6
Georgetown, D.C. (20007) 245/E5
Georgetown, Fla. (32039) 212/E2
Georgetown, Gambia 106/A6
Georgetown, Georgia (31754) 217/B7
Georgetown (cap.), Guyana 2/G5
Georgetown (cap.), Guyana 131/C2
Georgetown (cap.), Guyana 120/D2
Georgetown, Idaho (83239) 220/G7
Georgetown, Ill. (61846) 222/F4
Georgetown, Ind. (47122) 227/F8
Georgetown, Ky. (40324) 237/M4
Georgetown, La. (71432) 238/F3
Georgetown, Maine (04548) 243/D8
Georgetown○, Maine (04548) 243/D8
George Town (Pinang), Malaysia 72/C6
George Town, Malaysia 54/M9
Georgetown, Mass. (01833) 249/L2
Georgetown○, Mass. (01833) 249/L2
Georgetown, Minn. (56546) 255/B3
Georgetown, Miss. (39078) 256/D7
Georgetown (lake), Mont. 262/C4
Georgetown, Ohio (45121) 284/C8
Georgetown, Pa. (15043) 294/A4
Georgetown, Pr. Edward I. 168/F2
Georgetown, Queensland 88/G3
Georgetown, Queensland 95/B3
Georgetown, St. Vin. & Grens. 161/A8
Georgetown, St. Vin. & Grens. 156/G4
Georgetown (co.), S.C. 296/J5
Georgetown, S.C. 188/L4
Georgetown, S.C. (29440) 296/J5
George Town, Tasmania 99/C3
George Town, Tasmania 88/H8
Georgetown, Tenn. (37336) 237/L10
Georgetown, Texas (78626) 303/G7
George V Coast (reg.) 5/C8
Georgeville, Minn. (†56312) 255/C5
Georgeville, Nova Scotia 168/F3
George Washington Carver Nat'l Mon., Mo. 261/D9
George Washington Birthplace Nat'l Mon., Va. 307/P4
George West, Texas (78022) 303/F9
Georgia 188/K4
GEORGIA 217
Georgia (str.), Br. Col. 184/J3
Georgia (state), U.S. 146/K6
Georgia○, Vt. (†05478) 268/A2
Georgia (str.), Wash. 310/B2
Georgia Center, Vt. (†05478) 268/A2
Georgian (bay), Ont. 162/H6
Georgian (bay), Ontario 177/D2
Georgian (bay), Ontario 175/D3
Georgiana, Ala. (36033) 195/E7
Georgian Bay Is. Nat'l Park, Ontario 177/C2D3
Georgian S.S.R., U.S.S.R. 7/J4
Georgian S.S.R., U.S.S.R. 52/F6
Georgian S.S.R., U.S.S.R. 48/D5
Georgiaville, R.I. (†02917) 249/H5
Georgina (riv.), North. Terr. 93/E6
Georgina (isl.), Ontario 177/E3
Georgina (riv.), Queensland 88/F4
Georgina (riv.), Queensland 95/A4
Georgiu-Dezh, U.S.S.R. 52/E4
Georgsmarienhütte, W. Germany 22/B2
Gera (dist.), E. Germany 22/D3
Gera, E. Germany 22/E3
Geraardsbergen, Belgium 27/D7
Gerald, Mo. (63037) 261/K6
Gerald, Sask. 181/K5
Geral de Goiás, Serra (range), Brazil 132/E6
Geraldine, Ala. (35974) 195/G2
Geraldine, Mont. (59446) 262/F3
Geraldine, N. Zealand 100/C6
Geraldton, Australia 87/B8
Geraldton, Ont. 162/H6
Geraldton, Ontario 177/H5
Geraldton, Ontario 175/C3
Geraldton, W. Australia 88/A5
Geraldton, W. Australia 92/A5
Gerar (dry riv.), Israel 65/B5
Gerber, Calif. (96035) 204/C3
Gerber (res.), Oreg. 291/F5
Gercüş, Turkey 63/J4
Gerdine (mt.), Alaska 196/A1
Gerede, Turkey 63/E2
Gereshk, Afghanistan 59/H3
Gereshk, Afghanistan 68/A2
Geretsried, W. Germany 22/D5
Gérgal, Spain 33/E4
Gerger, Turkey 63/H3
Gerik, Malaysia 72/D6
Gering, Nebr. (69341) 264/A3
Gerlach, Nev. (89412) 266/B2
Gerlachovka (mt.), Czech. 41/E2
Gerlogubi, Ethiopia 111/H6
Germania, Miss. (†39162) 256/C5
Germania, Pa. (16922) 294/G2
Germania, Wis. (†54968) 317/H8
Germano, Ohio (†43825) 284/J5
Germansen (lake), Br. Col. 184/E2
Germansen Landing, Br. Col. 184/E2
Germanton, N.C. (27019) 281/J2
Germantown, Ill. (62245) 222/D5
Germantown, Ky. (41044) 237/O3
Germantown, Md. (20767) 245/J4
Germantown, New Bruns. 170/F3
Germantown, N.Y. (12526) 276/N6
Germantown, Ohio (45327) 284/B6
Germantown, Tenn. (38138) 237/B10
Germantown, Wis. (53022) 317/K1
German Valley, Ill. (61039) 222/D1
Germany (East) 2/K3
Germany (West) 2/K3
GERMANY, EAST 22/E2
GERMANY, WEST 22
Germencik, Turkey 63/B4
Germersheim, W. Germany 22/C4
Germfask, Mich. (49836) 250/C2
Germiston, S. Africa 102/E7
Germiston, S. Africa 118/H6
Gerofit, Israel 65/D5
Gerolstein, W. Germany 22/B3
Gerona (prov.), Spain 33/H1
Gerona, Spain 33/H2
Geronimo, Ariz. (†85536) 198/F5
Geronimo, Okla. (73543) 288/K6
Gerpinnes, Belgium 27/F8
Gerpir (cape), Iceland 21/D1
Gerra, Switzerland 39/G4
Gerrardstown, W. Va. (25420) 312/K4
Gerringong, N.S. Wales 97/F4
Gerrish, N.H. (†03301) 268/D5
Gerry, N.Y. (14740) 276/B6
Gers (dept.), France 28/D6
Gers (riv.), France 28/D6
Gersau, Switzerland 39/G2
Gersfeld, W. Germany 22/C3
Gerster, Mo. (†64776) 261/E7
Gerty, Okla. (†74531) 288/O5
Gervais, Oreg. (97026) 291/A3
Gervasio, Uruguay 145/F4
Gêrzê, China 77/B5
Gerze, Turkey 63/F2
Geser, Indonesia 85/J6
Gesher, Israel 65/C2
Gesher Haziv, Israel 65/C1
Gessie, Ind. (†47974) 227/C4
Getafe, Spain 33/F4
Getaway, Ohio (†45675) 284/F9
Gettysburg, Ohio (45328) 284/A5
Gettysburg, Pa. (17325) 294/H6
Gettysburg, S. Dak. (57442) 298/K3
Gettysburg Nat'l Mil. Park, Pa. 294/H6
Getulio Vargas, Uruguay 145/F3
Getz Ice Shelf 5/B12
Geuda Springs, Kansas (67051) 232/E4
Geurie, N.S. Wales 97/E3
Gevar'am, Israel 65/B4
Gevaş, Turkey 63/K3
Gevgelija, Yugoslavia 45/F5
Gex, France 28/G4
Geyser, Mont. (59447) 262/F3
Geyserville, Calif. (95441) 204/B5
Geyve, Turkey 63/D2
Gezira, El (reg.), Sudan 111/F5
Ghabaghib, Syria 63/H5
Ghadames, Libya 102/D2
Ghadames, Libya 111/A2
Ghaghra (riv.), India 68/E3
Ghaida, P.D.R. Yemen 59/F6
Ghalla, Wadi el (dry riv.), Sudan 111/E5
Ghana 2/J5
Ghana 102/B4
GHANA 106/D7
Ghanzi, Botswana 118/C4
Ghard Abu Muharik (des.), Egypt 111/J4
Ghardaïa, Algeria 106/E2
Ghardaïa, Algeria 102/C1
Gharian, Libya 102/D1
Gharian, Libya 111/B1
Gharib, Jebel (mt.), Egypt 59/B4
Ghat, Libya 102/D2
Ghat, Libya 111/B3
Ghat Kopar, India 68/B7
Ghazaouet, Algeria 106/D2
Ghaziabad, India 68/D3
Ghazipur, India 68/E3
Ghazni, Afghanistan 68/B2
Ghazni, Afghanistan 59/J3
Ghea (riv.), India 68/F1
Gheen, Minn. (55740) 255/F3
Gheens, La. (70355) 238/K7
Ghemines, Libya 111/C1

374 Ghenghis Khan

Ghenghis Khan Wall (ruin), China 77/H2
Ghenghis Khan Wall (ruins), Mongolia 77/H2
Ghent, Belgium 27/D6
Ghent, Ky. (41045) 237/L3
Ghent, Minn. (56239) 255/C6
Ghent, N.Y. (12075) 276/N6
Ghent, W. Va. (25843) 312/D7
Gheorghe Gheorghiu-Dej, Romania 45/H2
Gheorghieni, Romania 45/G2
Gherla, Romania 45/G2
Ghimbi, Ethiopia 111/G6
Ghio, N.C. (†28345) 281/K5
Ghisonaccia, France 28/B7
Ghizar, Pakistan 68/C1
Gholson, Miss. (†39354) 256/G5
Ghost Dam, Alberta 182/C4
Ghost Lake, Alberta 182/C4
Ghurian, Afghanistan 68/A2
Ghurian, Afghanistan 59/H3
Giacomo (pass), Switzerland 39/G4
Gia Dinh, Vietnam 72/E5
Giannutri (isl.), Italy 34/C3
Giant's Causeway, N. Ireland 17/H1
Giarre, Italy 34/E6
Giatto, W. Va. (†24736) 312/D8
Gibara, Cuba 156/C2
Gibara, Cuba 158/J3
Gibbon, Minn. (55335) 255/D6
Gibbon, Nebr. (68840) 264/F4
Gibbon, Oreg. (†97810) 291/J2
Gibbons, Alberta 182/D3
Gibbonsville, Idaho (83463) 220/E4
Gibb River, W. Australia 92/D2
Gibbs, Mo. (63540) 261/H2
Gibbs, Sask. 181/G5
Gibbsboro, N.J. (08026) 273/B4
Gibbs City, Mich. (†49935) 250/G2
Gibbstown, N.J. (08027) 273/C4
Gibbsville, Wis. (†53085) 317/L8
Gibeon, Namibia 118/B5
Gibloux (mt.), Switzerland 39/D3
Gibraltar 7/D5
Gibraltar (str.) 2/J4
Gibraltar (str.) 102/B1
Gibraltar (str.) 7/D5
Gibraltar, 2/J4
GIBRALTAR 33
Gibraltar, 33/D4
Gibraltar (pt.), England 13/H4
Gibraltar, Mich. (48173) 250/F6
Gibraltar (str.), Morocco 106/C1
Gibraltar (str.), Spain 33/D5
Gibsland, La. (71028) 238/E1
Gibson (desert), Australia 87/C8
Gibson, Georgia (30810) 217/G4
Gibson (co.), Ind. 227/B8
Gibson, Iowa (50104) 229/J6
Gibson, La. (70356) 238/J7
Gibson, Miss. (†39730) 256/G3
Gibson, Mo. (63847) 261/M10
Gibson (res.), Mont. 262/D3
Gibson, N.C. (28343) 281/K5
Gibson, Pa. (18820) 294/L2
Gibson (co.), Tenn. 237/D9
Gibson, Tenn. (38338) 237/D9
Gibson, W. Australia 88/C6
Gibson, W. Australia 92/C6
Gibson (des.), W. Australia 88/C4
Gibson (des.), W. Australia 92/D3
Gibsonburg, Ohio (43431) 284/D3
Gibson City, Ill. (60936) 222/E3
Gibsonia, Pa. (15044) 294/B4
Gibsons, Br. Col. 184/K3
Gibson Station, Va. (†24248) 307/A7
Gibsonton, Fla. (33534) 212/C3
Gibsonville, N.C. (27249) 281/K2
Giddings, Texas (78942) 303/H7
Gideälv (riv.), Sweden 18/L5
Gideon, Mo. (63848) 261/N10
Gideon, Okla. (†74464) 288/R2
Gien, France 28/E4
Giese, Minn. (†56350) 255/E4
Giessendam-Hardinxveld, Netherlands 27/F5
Giethoorn, Netherlands 27/J3
Gif, France 28/E3
Gifan, Iran 66/K2
Giffard, Québec 172/J3
Giffnock, Scotland 15/B2
Gifford, Fla. (32960) 212/F4
Gifford, Ill. (61847) 222/E3
Gifford, Iowa (50259) 229/G4
Gifford (riv.), N.W. Terrs. 187/K2
Gifford, Scotland 15/F5
Gifford, S.C. (29923) 296/E6
Gifford, Wash. (99131) 310/G2
Gifhorn, W. Germany 22/D2
Gift Lake, Alberta 182/C2
Gifu (pref.), Japan 81/H6
Gifu, Japan 81/H6
Giganta, Sierra de la (mts.), Mexico 150/D4
Gigante, Colombia 126/C6
Gigha (isl.), Scotland 15/C5
Gigha (sound), Scotland 15/C5
Gig Harbor, Wash. (98335) 310/C3
Giglio (isl.), Italy 34/C3
Gijón, Spain 7/D4
Gijón, Spain 33/D1
Gil (isl.), Br. Col. 184/C3
Gila (riv.) 188/D4
Gila (co.), Ariz. 198/E5
Gila (mts.), Ariz. 198/A6
Gila (mts.), Ariz. 198/F5
Gila (riv.), Ariz. 198/B6
Gila, N. Mex. (88038) 274/A6
Gila (riv.), N. Mex. 274/A6
Gila (riv.), U.S. 146/G6
Gila Bend, Ariz. (85337) 198/C6
Gila Bend (mts.), Ariz. 198/B5
Gila Bend Ind. Res., Ariz. 198/C6
Gila Cliff Dwellings Nat'l Mon., N. Mex. 274/A5
Gila Hot Springs, N. Mex. (†88061) 274/A5
Gilan (prov.), Iran 66/F2
Gilan (reg.), Iran 66/F2
Gila River Ind. Res., Ariz. 198/C5
Gilat, Israel 65/B5
Gilbert, Ariz. (85234) 198/D5
Gilbert, Ark. (72636) 202/E2
Gilbert, Iowa (50105) 229/F4
Gilbert (isls.), Kiribati 2/T5
Gilbert (isls.), Kiribati 87/H6
Gilbert, La. (71336) 238/G2
Gilbert, Minn. (55741) 255/F3
Gilbert (riv.), Newf. 166/C3
Gilbert (riv.), Queensland 88/G3
Gilbert (riv.), Queensland 95/B3
Gilbert, S.C. (29054) 296/E4
Gilbert (peak), Utah 304/D3
Gilbert, W. Va. (25621) 312/C7
Gilberton, Pa. (17934) 294/K4
Gilbertown, Ala. (36908) 195/B7
Gilbert Plains, Manitoba 179/B3
Gilberts, Ill. (60136) 222/E1
Gilbertsville, Ky. (42044) 237/E7
Gilbertsville, N.Y. (13776) 276/K6
Gilbertville, Iowa (50634) 229/J4
Gilbertville, Mass. (01031) 249/F3
Gilbjerg Hoved (pt.), Denmark 21/F5
Gilboa, N.Y. (12076) 276/M6
Gilboa, Ohio (45847) 284/C3
Gilboa, W. Va. (26671) 312/E6
Gilbués, Brazil 132/E5
Gilby, N. Dak. (58235) 282/R3
Gilchrist (co.), Fla. 212/D2
Gilchrist (creek), Manitoba 179/F2
Gilchrist (lake), Manitoba 179/G2
Gilcrest, Colo. (80623) 208/K2
Gildford, Mont. (59525) 262/F2
Gilé, Mozambique 118/F3
Gilead, Conn. (†06232) 210/F2
Gilead, Ind. (†46951) 227/E3
Gilead○, Maine (†04217) 243/B7
Gilead, Nebr. (68362) 264/G4
Giles (co.), Tenn. 237/G10
Giles (co.), Va. 307/G6
Gilf Kebir (plat.), Egypt 111/E3
Gilford, Mich. (48736) 250/F5
Gilford○, N.H. (†03246) 268/E4
Gilford, N. Ireland 17/J3
Gilford Park, N.J. (†08753) 273/E4
Gilgai, N.S. Wales 97/F1
Gilgandra, N. S. Wales 88/H6
Gilgandra, N.S. Wales 97/E2
Gilgil, Kenya 115/G4
Gilgit, Pakistan 68/C1
Gilgit, Pakistan 59/K6
Gilgunnia, N.S. Wales 97/C3
Gill, Colo. (80624) 208/L2
Gill (lake), Ireland 17/E3
Gill○, Mass. (†01376) 249/D2
Gillam, Manitoba 179/K2
Gilleleje, Denmark 21/F5
Gilles (lake), S. Australia 94/E5
Gillespie, Ill. (62033) 222/D4
Gillespie, New Bruns. 170/C2
Gillespie (co.), Texas 303/F7
Gillett, Ark. (72055) 202/H5
Gillett, Pa. (16925) 294/J2
Gillett, Texas (78116) 303/G8
Gillett, Wis. (54124) 317/K6
Gillette, N.J. (07933) 273/E2
Gillette, Wyo. (82716) 319/G1
Gillett Grove, Iowa (51341) 229/C2
Gilleyville, La. 238/G2
Gillham, Ark. (71841) 202/B5
Gilliam, La. (71029) 238/C1
Gilliam, Mo. (65330) 261/F4
Gilliam (co.), Oreg. 291/G2
Gillies Bay, Br. Col. 184/H2
Gillingham, Dorset, England 13/E6
Gillingham, Kent, England 13/J8
Gillis (range), Nev. 266/C4
Gillisonville, S.C. (†29936) 296/E6
Gillsburg, Miss. (†39657) 256/C8
Gillsville, Georgia (30543) 217/E2
Gilly, Switzerland 39/B4
Gilman, Colo. (81634) 208/G3
Gilman, Conn. (06336) 210/G2
Gilman, Ill. (60938) 222/E3
Gilman, Ind. (†46001) 227/F4
Gilman, Iowa (50106) 229/H5
Gilman, Minn. (56333) 255/E5
Gilman, Vt. (05904) 268/D3
Gilman, Wis. (54433) 317/E5
Gilman City, Mo. (64642) 261/D2
Gilmanton○, N.H. (03237) 268/E5
Gilmanton, Wis. (54743) 317/C7
Gilmanton Iron Works, N.H. (03837) 268/E5
Gilmer (co.), Georgia 217/D1
Gilmer, Texas (75644) 303/J5
Gilmer (co.), W. Va. 312/E5
Gilmer, W. Va. (26350) 312/E4
Gilmore, Ark. (72339) 202/K3
Gilmore, Georgia (†30080) 217/J1
Gilmore City, Iowa (50541) 229/D3
Gilpin (co.), Colo. 208/H3
Gilroy, Calif. (95020) 204/D6
Gilson, Ill. (61436) 222/C3
Gilsum○, N.H. (03448) 268/C5
Gilt Edge, Tenn. (†38015) 237/B9
Giltner, Nebr. (68841) 264/F4
Gilze, Netherlands 27/F5
Gimel, Switzerland 39/B3
Gimie (mt.), St. Lucia 161/G6
Gimlet, Ky. (†41164) 237/P4
Gimli, Manitoba 179/F4
Gimo, Sweden 18/K6
Gingerland, St. Chris.-Nevis 161/D11
Gingin, W. Australia 92/A1
Gingoog, Philippines 82/E6
Gingoog (bay), Philippines 82/E6
Gings, Ind. (†46173) 227/G5
Ginir, Ethiopia 111/H6
Ginnosar, Israel 65/D2
Ginzo de Limia, Spain 33/C1
Gio, Hon (isl.), Vietnam 72/E3
Giohar, Somalia 102/G4
Giohar, Somalia 115/J3
Gioia del Colle, Italy 34/F4
Gioiosa Ionica, Italy 34/F5
Giornico, Switzerland 39/G4
Giovinazzo, Italy 34/F4
Gi-Paraná (riv.), Brazil 132/H10
Gippsland (reg.), Victoria 97/D6
Gipsy (lake), Alberta 182/E1
Gipsy, Mo. (63750) 261/M8
Gipsy, Pa. (15741) 294/E4
Giraltovce, Czech. 41/F2
Girard, (62640) 222/D4
Girard, Georgia (30426) 217/J4
Girard, Kansas (66743) 232/H4
Girard, La. (71244) 238/G2
Girard, Mich. (†49036) 250/E6
Girard, Ohio (44420) 284/J3
Girard, Pa. (16417) 294/B2
Girard, Texas (79518) 303/D4
Girardot, Colombia 126/C5
Girardville, Pa. (17935) 294/K4
Girardville, Québec 172/E1
Girdle Ness (prom.), Scotland 15/G3
Girdler, Ky. (40943) 237/O7
Girdletree, Md. (21829) 245/S8
Giresun (prov.), Turkey 63/H2
Giresun, Turkey 59/C1
Giresun, Turkey 63/H2
Girga, Egypt 59/B4
Girga, Egypt 111/F2
Girga, Egypt 102/F2
Giri (riv.), Zaire 115/C3
Girilambone, N.S. Wales 97/D2
Girón, Ecuador 128/C4
Gironde (dept.), France 28/C5
Gironde (riv.), France 28/C5
Giroux, Manitoba 179/F5
Girouxville, Alberta 182/B2
Girvan, Scotland 15/D5
Girvan, Scotland 10/D3
Girvin, Sask. 181/F4
Girvin, Texas (79740) 303/B6
Gisborne, N. Zealand 100/G3
Giscome, Br. Col. 184/F3
Gisenyi, Rwanda 115/E4
Gislaved, Sweden 18/H8
Gisors, France 28/D3
Gistel, Belgium 27/B6
Giswil, Switzerland 39/F3
Gitega, Burundi 115/F4
Giuba (riv.), Somalia 115/H3
Giubiasco, Switzerland 39/H4
Giulianova, Italy 34/E3
Giurgiu, Romania 45/G3
Giv'atayim, Israel 65/B3
Giv'at Brenner, Israel 65/B4
Giv'at Hayyim, Israel 65/B3
Give, Denmark 21/C6
Given, W. Va. (25245) 312/C5
Givet, France 28/F2
Givhans, S.C. (†29472) 296/G5
Givors, France 28/F5
Giza, Egypt 111/J3
Giza, Egypt 59/B4
Gizab, Afghanistan 59/J3
Gizab, Afghanistan 68/B2
Gizhiga (bay), U.S.S.R. 48/Q3
Gizo, Solomon Is. 86/D3
Gizycko, Poland 47/E1
Gjerlev, Denmark 21/D4
Gjerrild Klint (cliff), Denmark 21/D5
Gjirokastër, Albania 45/D5
Gjoa Haven, N.W.T. 162/G2
Gjoa Haven, N.W. Terrs. 187/J3
Gjøvik, Norway 18/G6
Gjøvik, Norway 7/E2
Glace Bay, N.S. 162/L6
Glace Bay, Nova Scotia 168/J2
Glacier (bay), Alaska 196/M1
Glacier, Br. Col. 184/J4
Glacier (co.), Mont. 262/C2
Glacier, Wash. (98244) 310/D2
Glacier (peak), Wash. 310/D2
Glacier Bay Nat'l Park, Alaska 196/M1
Glacier Bay Nat'l Preserve, Alaska 196/L1
Glacier Nat'l Park, Br. Col. 184/J4
Glacier Nat'l Park, Mont. 188/D1
Glacier Nat'l Park, Mont. 262/C2
Glacier Nat'l Pk., Br. Col. 162/D5
Gladbrook, Iowa (50635) 229/H4
Glade, Kansas (67639) 232/C2
Glade, La. (†71374) 238/G4
Gladehill, Va. (24092) 307/J7
Glade Park, Colo. (81523) 208/B5
Glades (co.), Fla. 212/E5
Glade Spring, Va. (24340) 307/E7
Glade Valley, N.C. (28627) 281/G2
Gladeville, Tenn. (37071) 237/J8
Gladewater, Texas (75647) 303/K5
Gladmar, Sask. 181/G6
Gladstone, Ill. (61437) 222/B3
Gladstone, Manitoba 179/D4
Gladstone, Mich. (49837) 250/C3
Gladstone, Mo. (64118) 261/P5
Gladstone, Nebr. (68363) 264/G4
Gladstone, N. Mex. (88422) 274/F2
Gladstone, N. Dak. (58630) 282/F6
Gladstone, Oreg. (97027) 291/B2
Gladstone, Queensland 88/J4
Gladstone, Queensland 95/D4
Gladstone, S. Australia 94/F5
Gladstone, Tasmania 99/D2
Gladstone, Va. (24553) 307/L5
Glad Valley, S. Dak. (57629) 298/F3
Gladwin (co.), Mich. 250/E4
Gladwin, Mich. (48624) 250/E5
Glady, W. Va. (26268) 312/G5
Gladys, Va. (24554) 307/K6
Glåma (riv.), Norway 7/F2
Glåma (riv.), Norway 18/G6
Glamis, Calif. (†92227) 204/K11
Glamis, Sask. 181/D4
Glamis, Scotland 15/F4
Glamoč, Yugoslavia 45/C3
Glamsbjerg, Denmark 21/D7
Glan, Philippines 85/G4
Glan, Philippines 82/E8
Glancy, Miss. (†39083) 256/C7
Gland, Switzerland 39/B4
Glandore, Ireland 17/C8
Glandore (harb.), Ireland 17/C9
Glandorf, Ohio (45848) 284/B3
Glâne (riv.), Switzerland 39/C3
Glanmire-Riverstown, Ireland 17/E8
Glanworth, Ireland 17/E7
Glärnisch (mt.), Switzerland 39/H2
Glarus (canton), Switzerland 39/H3
Glarus, Switzerland 39/H2
Glarus Alps (mts.), Switzerland 39/H3
Glasco, Kansas (67445) 232/E2
Glasco, N.Y. (12432) 276/M6
Glascock (co.), Georgia 217/G4
Glasford, Ill. (61533) 222/D3
Glasgo, Conn. (06337) 210/H2
Glasgow, Del. (†19711) 245/R2
Glasgow, Ill. (†62610) 222/C4
Glasgow, Ky. (42141) 237/J7
Glasgow, Mo. (65254) 261/G4
Glasgow, Mont. (59230) 262/K2
Glasgow, Pa. (16644) 294/E4
Glasgow, Scotland 7/D3
Glasgow, Scotland 10/B1
Glasgow, Scotland 15/B2
Glasgow, Va. (24555) 307/K5
Glasgow, W. Va. (25086) 312/D6
Glasier (lake), New Bruns. 170/A1
Glaslyn, Sask. 181/C2
Glas Maol (mt.), Scotland 15/E4
Glasnevin, Sask. 181/F6
Glass, Manitoba 179/F5
Glass (riv.), Scotland 15/D3
Glass (mts.), Texas 303/A7
Glassboro, N.J. (08028) 273/C4
Glasscock (co.), Texas 303/C6
Glasser, N.J. (07837) 273/D2
Glassport, Pa. (15045) 294/C7
Glasston, N. Dak. (58236) 282/R2
Glassville, New Bruns. 170/C2
Glastenbury (mt.), Vt. 268/A6
Glastonbury, Conn. (06033) 210/E2
Glastonbury○, Conn. (06033) 210/E2
Glastonbury, England 13/E6
Glastonbury, England 10/E5
Glatt (riv.), Switzerland 39/G2
Glattfelden, Switzerland 39/F1
Glauchau, E. Germany 22/E3
Glazier, Texas (79037) 303/D2
Glazov, U.S.S.R. 7/K3
Glazov, U.S.S.R. 52/H3
Gleason, Tenn. (38229) 237/D8
Gleason, Wis. (54435) 317/G5
Gleasondale, Mass. (01749) 249/J3
Gleeson, Ariz. (†85617) 198/F7
Gleichen, Alberta 182/D4
Gleisdorf, Austria 41/C3
Gleiwitz (Gliwice), Poland 47/A4
Glen (lake), Ireland 17/F1
Glen (lake), Mich. 250/C4
Glen, Minn. (†56431) 255/E4
Glen, Miss. (38846) 256/H1
Glen, Mont. (†59725) 262/D5
Glen, N.H. (03838) 268/E3
Glen (canyon), Utah 304/D6
Glen, W. Va. (25088) 312/D6
Glenada, Oreg. (†97439) 291/C4
Glenaire, Mo. (†64068) 261/R5
Glen Alice, Tenn. (†37854) 237/M9
Glen Allan, Miss. (38744) 256/B4
Glen Allen, Ala. (35559) 195/C3
Glenallen, Mo. (63751) 261/M8
Glen Allen, Va. (23060) 307/N5
Glen Almond, Québec 172/B4
Glen Alpine, N.C. (28628) 281/F3
Glenamaddy, Ireland 17/D4
Glen Arbor, Mich. (49636) 250/C4
Glenarden, Md. (†20801) 245/G4
Glen Arm, Md. (21057) 245/N3
Glenarm, N. Ireland 17/J2
Glenavon, Sask. 181/J5
Glen Avon Heights, Calif. (92509) 204/E10
Glenavy, N. Zealand 100/C6
Glenavy, N. Ireland 17/J2
Glen Bain, Sask. 181/E6
Glenbarr, Scotland 15/C5
Glenbeigh, Ireland 17/B7
Glenbeulah, Wis. (53023) 317/L8
Glenboro, Manitoba 179/C5
Glenbrook, Nev. (89413) 266/B3
Glenburn○, Maine (†04401) 243/F6
Glenburn, N. Dak. (58740) 282/H2
Glen Burnie, Md. (21061) 245/M4
Glenbush, Sask. 181/D2
Glen Campbell, Pa. (15742) 294/E4
Glen Canyon (dam), Ariz. 198/D2
Glen Canyon City, Utah (84741) 304/C6
Glen Canyon Nat'l Rec. Area, Ariz. 198/D1
Glen Canyon Nat'l Rec. Area, Utah 304/D6
Glencaple, Scotland 15/E5
Glen Carbon, Ill. (62034) 222/B2
Glencliff, N.H. (03238) 268/D4
Glencoe, Ala. (35905) 195/G3
Glencoe, Ill. (60022) 222/B5
Glencoe, Ky. (41046) 237/M3
Glencoe, La. (†70538) 238/G7
Glencoe, Minn. (55336) 255/D6
Glencoe, Mo. (63038) 261/M3
Glencoe, New Bruns. 170/D1
Glencoe, N. Mex. (88324) 274/D5
Glencoe, Ohio (43928) 284/J6
Glencoe, Okla. (74032) 288/M2
Glencoe, Ontario 177/C5
Glencoe, Pa. (15543) 294/E6
Glencoe, Scotland 15/C4
Glencoe, S. Africa 118/E5
Glencolumbkille, Ireland 17/D2
Glen Cove, Maine (04846) 243/E7
Glen Cove, N.Y. (11542) 276/R6
Glencross, S. Dak. (57630) 298/H3
Glendale, Ariz. (*85301) 198/C5
Glendale, Calif. 188/C4
Glendale, Calif. (*91201) 204/C10
Glendale, Fla. (†32433) 212/C5
Glendale, Ind. (†47558) 227/C7
Glendale, Kansas (†67425) 232/E3
Glendale, Ky. (42740) 237/K5
Glendale, Mass. (01229) 249/A3
Glendale, Mo. (63122) 261/P3
Glendale, Nev. (†89025) 266/G6
Glendale, N.H. (†03246) 268/E4
Glendale, Nova Scotia 168/G3
Glendale, Ohio (45246) 284/C9
Glendale, Oreg. (97442) 291/D5
Glendale (lake), Pa. 294/F4
Glendale, R.I. (02826) 249/H5
Glendale, S.C. (29346) 296/D2
Glendale, Utah (84729) 304/B6
Glen Dale, W. Va. (26038) 312/E3
Glendale, Wis. (†53209) 317/M1
Glendale Heights, Ill. (†60118) 222/A5
Glen Daniel, W. Va. (25844) 312/D7
Glen Dean, Ky. (40141) 237/J5
Glendevey, Colo. (†80485) 208/H1
Glendive, Mont. (59330) 262/M3
Glendo, Wyo. (82213) 319/G3
Glendo (res.), Wyo. 319/H3
Glendon, Alberta 182/E2
Glendon, N.C. (27251) 281/L4
Glendora, Calif. (91740) 204/D10
Glendora, Miss. (38928) 256/D3
Glendora, N.J. (08029) 273/B4
Glen Easton, W. Va. (26039) 312/E3
Glen Echo, Md. (20768) 245/E4
Glen Eden, N. Zealand 100/B1
Gleneden Beach, Oreg. (97388) 291/C3
Glen Elder, Kansas (67446) 232/D2
Glenelg, Md. (21737) 245/L3
Glenelg, Scotland 10/D2
Glenelg, Scotland 15/C3
Glenelg, S. Australia 88/D8
Glenelg, S. Australia 94/A8
Glenelg (riv.), Victoria 97/A5
Glenella, Manitoba 179/C4
Glen Ellyn, Ill. (60137) 222/A5
Glenevis, Alberta 182/C3
Glen Ewen, Sask. 181/K6
Glen Ferris, W. Va. (25090) 312/D6
Glenfield, N.Y. (13343) 276/K3
Glenfield, N. Zealand 100/B1
Glenfield, N. Dak. (58443) 282/N5
Glenfield, Pa. (†15143) 294/B6
Glen Flora, Texas (77443) 303/H8
Glen Flora, Wis. (54526) 317/E4
Glenford, Ohio (43739) 284/F6
Glen Gardner, N.J. (08826) 273/D2
Glengarriff, Ireland 17/C8
Glengarry, Mont. (†59457) 262/G3
Glengarry (county), Ontario 177/K2
Glengary, W. Va. (25421) 312/K4
Glenham, S. Dak. (57631) 298/J2
Glen Harbour, Sask. 181/G5
Glen Haven, Colo. (80532) 208/H2
Glen Haven, Mich. (†49621) 250/C4
Glen Haven, Wis. (53810) 317/E10
Glenhayes, W. Va. (25519) 312/A6
Glen Hedrick (Beaver), W. Va. (†25813) 312/D7
Glen Hope, Pa. (16645) 294/F4
Glen Innes, N. S. Wales 88/J5
Glen Innes, N.S. Wales 97/F1
Glen Jean, W. Va. (25846) 312/D7
Glen Kerr, Sask. 181/D5
Glenlea, Manitoba 179/E5
Glenlivet, New Bruns. 170/D1
Glenluce, Scotland 15/D6
Glen Lyn, Va. (24093) 307/G6
Glen Lyon, Pa. (18617) 294/E7
Glenmary, Tenn. (37740) 237/M8
Glenmere, Sask. 181/J5
Glen Miller, Ontario 177/G3
Glenmont, Ohio (44628) 284/F4
Glenmora, La. (71433) 238/E5
Glen More (dist.), Scotland 15/D3
Glenmorgan, Queensland 95/D5
Glenn (co.), Calif. 204/C4
Glenn, Georgia (30219) 217/B4
Glenn, Mich. (49416) 250/C6
Glennallen, Alaska (99588) 196/D1
Glenn Heights, Texas (†75115) 303/G3
Glennie, Mich. (48737) 250/F4
Glenns Ferry, Idaho (83623) 220/C7
Glenn Springs, S.C. (29347) 296/D2
Glennville, Calif. (93226) 204/G8
Glennville, Georgia (30427) 217/J7
Glenolden, Pa. (19036) 294/M7
Glenoma, Wash. (98336) 310/C4
Glenora, Br. Col. 184/K2
Glenorchy, Tasmania 88/H8
Glenorchy, Tasmania 99/D4
Glenormiston, Queensland 95/A4
Glen Park, N.Y. (†13601) 276/J3
Glenpool, Okla. (74033) 288/P3
Glen Raven, N.C. (27215) 281/L2
Glenreagh, N.S. Wales 97/G2
Glen Riddle, Pa. (19037) 294/L7
Glen Ridge, N.J. (07028) 273/B2
Glenrio, N. Mex. (88423) 274/F3
Glen Robertson, Ontario 177/K2
Glen Rock, N.J. (07452) 273/B1
Glen Rock, Pa. (17327) 294/J6
Glenrock, Wyo. (82637) 319/G3
Glen Rogers, W. Va. (25848) 312/D7
Glen Rose, Texas (76043) 303/G5
Glenrothes, Scotland 15/E4
Glen Roy, Ohio (†45692) 284/E7
Glen Saint Mary, Fla. (32040) 212/D1
Glens Falls, N.Y. (12801) 276/N4
Glens Fork, Ky. (42741) 237/L6
Glenshaw, Pa. (15116) 294/C6
Glenside, Pa. (19038) 294/M5
Glenside, Sask. 181/E4
Glenside-Churton Park, N. Zealand 100/B2
Glensted, Mo. (†65084) 261/G5
Glentana, Mont. (59240) 262/K2
Glenties, Ireland 10/B3
Glenties, Ireland 17/E2
Glentrool, Scotland 15/D5
Glentworth, Sask. 181/E6
Glen Ullin, N. Dak. (58631) 282/G6
Glenview, Ill. (60025) 222/B5
Glenview, Ky. (†40222) 237/K1
Glenview Nav. Air. Sta., Ill. 222/B5
Glenvil, Nebr. (68941) 264/F4
Glenville, Conn. (†06830) 210/A4
Glenville, Ireland 17/D7
Glenville, Minn. (56036) 255/E7
Glenville, N.C. (28736) 281/C4
Glenville, W. Va. (26351) 312/E5
Glen Walter, Ontario 177/K2
Glen White, W. Va. (25849) 312/D7
Glenwillow, Ohio (†44139) 284/J10
Glen Wilton, Va. (24438) 307/J5
Glenwood, Ala. (36034) 195/F7
Glenwood, Alberta 182/D5
Glenwood, Ark. (71943) 202/C5
Glenwood, Fla. (32722) 212/E2
Glenwood, Georgia (30428) 217/L1
Glenwood, Ill. (60425) 222/C6
Glenwood, Ind. (46133) 227/G5
Glenwood, Iowa (51534) 229/B6
Glenwood, Mich. (†49047) 250/C6
Glenwood, Minn. (56334) 255/C5
Glenwood, Mo. (63541) 261/G1
Glenwood, Newf. 166/D4
Glenwood, N.J. (07418) 273/D1
Glenwood, N. Mex. (88039) 274/A5
Glenwood, N.C. (28737) 281/F3
Glenwood, Oreg. (97120) 291/D2
Glenwood, Utah (84730) 304/C5
Glenwood, Va. (†24541) 307/K7
Glenwood, Wash. (98619) 310/D4
Glenwood, W. Va. (25520) 312/B5
Glenwood City, Wis. (54013) 317/B5
Glenwood Springs, Colo. (81601) 208/E4
Glezen, Ind. (†47567) 227/C8
Glidden, Iowa (51443) 229/D4
Glidden, Sask. 181/B4
Glidden, Wis. (54527) 317/E3
Glide, Oreg. (97443) 291/D4
Glin, Ireland 17/C6
Glis, Switzerland 39/E4
Glittertinden (mt.), Norway 7/E2
Glittertinden (mt.), Norway 18/F6
Gliwice, Poland 47/A4
Globe, Ariz. 188/D4
Globe, Ariz. (85501) 198/E5
Gloggnitz, Austria 41/D3
Głogów (Glogau), Poland 47/C3
Glomawr, Ky. (†41701) 237/P6
Glomfjord, Norway 18/J3
Gloria (bay), Cuba 158/G2
Glorieta, N. Mex. (87535) 274/D3
Glorioso (isls.), Réunion 118/H2
Glory, Minn. (†56431) 255/E4
Glory of Russia (cape), Alaska 196/D2
Glossop, England 13/J2
Glossop, England 10/G2
Gloster, La. (71030) 238/C2
Gloster, Miss. (39638) 256/B8
Glostrup, Denmark 21/F6
Gloucester, England 13/E6
Gloucester, England 10/E5
Gloucester, Mass. (01930) 249/M2
Gloucester (co.), New Bruns. 170/E1
Gloucester (co.), N.J. 273/C4
Gloucester, N.S. Wales 97/F2
Gloucester, N.C. (28528) 281/S5
Gloucester (cape), Papua N.G. 86/B2
Gloucester (co.), Va. 307/P6
Gloucester, Va. (23061) 307/P6
Gloucester City, N.J. (08030) 273/B3
Gloucester Junction, New Bruns. 170/E1
Gloucester Point, Va. (23062) 307/R6
Gloucestershire (co.), England 13/E6
Glouster, Ohio (45732) 284/F6
Glover (reef), Belize 154/D2
Glover, Mo. (63646) 261/L8
Glover (isl.), Newf. 166/C4
Glover, N. Dak. (†58474) 282/O7
Glover, Okla. (†74728) 288/S6
Glover○, Vt. (05839) 268/C2
Glovergap, W. Va. (†26585) 312/F3
Gloversville, N.Y. (12078) 276/M4
Glovertown, Newf. 166/C1
Gloverville, S.C. (29828) 296/D4
Głowno, Poland 47/D2
Głubczyce, Poland 47/C3
Glubokoye, U.S.S.R. 52/C3
Głuchołazy, Poland 47/C3
Glücksburg, W. Germany 22/C1
Gluckstadt, Miss. (†39110) 256/D5
Glückstadt, W. Germany 22/C2
Glukhov, U.S.S.R. 52/D4
Glumsø, Denmark 21/E7
Glyde (riv.), Ireland 17/H4
Glynco, Georgia (†31520) 217/J8
Glyncorrwg, Wales 13/D6
Glyndon, Md. (21071) 245/L3
Glyndon, Minn. (56547) 255/B4
Glyngøre, Denmark 21/C4
Glynn (co.), Georgia 217/J8
Glynn, La. (70736) 238/H5
Glynn, N. Ireland 17/K2
Gmünd, Carinthia, Austria 41/B3
Gmünd, Lower Austria, Austria 41/C2
Gmunden, Austria 41/B3
Gnadenhutten, Ohio (44629) 284/G5
Gnaw Bone, Ind. (†47448) 227/E6
Gnesta, Sweden 18/G2
Gniew, Poland 47/D2
Gniewkowo, Poland 47/D2
Gniezno, Poland 47/C2
Gnjilane, Yugoslavia 45/E4
Gnowangerup, W. Australia 88/B6
Gnowangerup, W. Australia 92/B6
Goa, Daman and Diu (terr.), India 68/C4
Goa (dist.), India 68/C5
Goalpara, India 68/G3
Goascorán, Honduras 154/D4
Goat Fell (mt.), Scotland 15/C5
Goat River, Br. Col. 184/K4
Goat Rock (dam), Ala. 195/H5
Goat Rock (lake), Ala. 195/H5
Goat Rock (dam), Georgia 217/B5
Goat Rock (lake), Georgia 217/B5
Goat Rocks (mts.), Wash. 310/D4
Goba, Ethiopia 111/H6
Goba, Ethiopia 102/G4
Goba, Mozambique 118/E5

Gramercy 375

Gobabis, Namibia 118/B4
Gobabis, Namibia 102/D7
Gobernador Crespo, Argentina 143/F5
Gobernador Gregores, Argentina 143/C6
Gobernador Mansilla, Argentina 143/G6
Gobi (des.) 54/M5
Gobi (des.), China 77/G3
Gobi (des.), Mongolia 77/G3
Goble, Oreg. (97048) 291/E1
Gobler, Mo. (63849) 261/N10
Gobles, Mich. (49055) 250/D6
Gobo, Japan 81/G7
Gobwen, Somalia 115/H4
Goch, W. Germany 22/B3
Go Cong, Vietnam 72/E5
Godahl, Minn. (†56081) 255/D6
Godalming, England 13/G8
Godalming, England 10/F5
Godavari (riv.), India 54/J8
Godavari (riv.), India 68/D5
Godbout, Québec 174/D3
Godbout, Québec 172/B1
Goddard, Kansas (67052) 232/E4
Godech, Bulgaria 45/F4
Goderich, Ontario 177/C4
Godfrey, Georgia (30650) 217/F4
Godfrey, Ill. (62035) 222/A2
Godhavn, Greenl. 4/C12
Godhavn, Greenland 146/N3
Godhra, India 68/C4
Gödöllő, Hungary 41/E3
Godoy Cruz, Argentina 143/C3
Gods (lake), Man. 162/G5
Gods (lake), Manitoba 179/K3
Gods (riv.), Man. 162/G4
Gods (riv.), Manitoba 179/K3
Gods Mercy (bay), N.W. Terrs. 187/K3
Gods River, Manitoba 179/K3
Godthåb (Nûk) (cap.), Greenl. 4/C12
Godthåb (Nûk) (cap.), Greenland 2/G2
Godthåb (Nûk) (cap.), Greenland 146/N3
Godwin, N.C. (28344) 281/M4
Godwin Austen (K2) (mt.), Pakistan 68/D1
Godwinsville, Georgia (†31023) 217/F6
Goehner, Nebr. (68364) 264/G4
Goéland (lake), Québec 174/B3
Goélands (lake), Québec 174/E1
Goeree (isl.), Netherlands 27/D5
Goes, Netherlands 27/D6
Goessel, Kansas (67053) 232/E3
Goetzville, Mich. (49736) 250/E2
Goff, Kansas (66428) 232/G2
Goff (creek), Okla. 288/C1
Goffstown○, N.H. (03045) 268/D5
Gogama, Ontario 175/D3
Gogama, Ontario 177/J5
Gogebic (co.), Mich. 250/F2
Gogebic (lake), Mich. 250/F2
Göggingen, W. Germany 22/D4
Gogrial, Sudan 111/E6
Goi, Ben (bay), Vietnam 72/F4
Goiana, Brazil 132/H4
Goiandira, Brazil 132/E7
Goiânia, Brazil 132/D7
Goiânia, Brazil 120/D4
Goiás (state), Brazil 132/D6
Goiás, Brazil 132/D6
Goiás, Brazil 120/D4
Goil, Loch (lake), Scotland 15/A1
Goin, Tenn. (†37825) 237/O8
Goirle, Netherlands 27/G5
Góis, Portugal 33/B2
Gojjam (prov.), Ethiopia 111/G5
Gökçe, Turkey 63/B2
Gökçeada (isl.), Turkey 59/A1
Gökçeada (isl.), Turkey 63/A2
Gökırmak (riv.), Turkey 63/F2
Göksu (riv.), Turkey 63/E4
Göksun, Turkey 63/G3
Gokteik, Burma 72/C2
Gol, Norway 18/F6
Gola (isl.), Ireland 17/E1
Golan Heights (reg.), West Bank 65/D1
Gölbaşı, Turkey 63/G4
Golborne, England 13/G2
Gol'chikha, U.S.S.R. 48/J2
Golconda, Ill. (62938) 222/E6
Golconda (ruins), India 68/D5
Golconda, Nev. (89414) 266/D2
Gölcük, Turkey 63/C2
Golčův Jeníkov, Czech. 41/C2
Gold (riv.), Nova Scotia 168/D4
Goldap, Poland 47/F1
Gold Bar, Wash. (98251) 310/D3
Gold Beach, Oreg. (97444) 291/C5
Goldbond, Va. (24094) 307/G6
Goldboro, Nova Scotia 168/G3
Gold Bridge, Br. Col. 184/F5
Gold Coast (reg.), Ghana 106/D8
Gold Coast, Queensland 95/E6
Gold Coast, Queensland 88/J5
Goldcreek, Mont. (59733) 262/D4
Golden, Br. Col. 184/J4
Golden, Colo. (80401) 208/J3
Golden, Idaho (†83530) 220/C4
Golden, Ill. g)62339) 222/B3
Golden, Ireland 17/F7
Golden, Miss. (38847) 256/H2
Golden, Mo. (65658) 261/E9
Golden, N. Mex. (†87047) 274/C3
Golden (bay), N. Zealand 100/D4
Golden, Okla. (74737) 288/S6
Golden (lake), Ontario 177/G2
Golden (lake), Wis. 317/H1
Golden Beach, Fla. (†33160) 212/C4
Golden City, Mo. (64748) 261/D8
Goldendale, Wash. (98620) 310/E5
Golden Ears Prov. Park, Br. Col. 184/L2
Golden Gate (chan.), Calif. 188/B3
Golden Gate (chan.), Calif. 204/H2
Golden Gate, Fla. (33999) 212/E5
Golden Gate, Ill. (62843) 222/E5
Golden Gate (range), Nev. 266/F5
Golden Gate Nat'l Rec. Area, Calif. 204/H2
Golden Grove, Jamaica 158/K6
Golden Hill, Md. (†21622) 245/O7
Golden Lake, Ontario 177/G2
Golden Meadow, La. (70357) 238/K8
Golden Prairie, Sask. 181/B5
Golden Rock, St. Chris.-Nevis 161/C10
Golden's Bridge, N.Y. (10526) 276/N8
Golden Shores, Ariz. (†86436) 198/A4
Golden Spike Nat'l Hist. Site, Utah 304/B2
Golden Vale (plain), Ireland 17/E7
Golden Valley, Minn. (55427) 255/G5
Golden Valley (co.), Mont. 262/G4
Golden Valley (co.), N. Dak. 282/C5
Goldenvalley, N. Dak. (58541) 282/F5
Golden Valley, Ontario 177/E2
Goldfield, Iowa (50542) 229/F3
Goldfield, Nev. 188/C3
Goldfield, Nev. (89013) 266/D5
Gold Hill, Ala. (†36879) 195/G5
Gold Hill, Nev. (†89440) 266/B3
Gold Hill, N.C. (28071) 281/J3
Gold Hill, Oreg. (97525) 291/D5
Goldonna, La. (71031) 238/D2
Gold Point, Nev. (†89013) 266/D5
Gold River, Br. Col. 184/D5
Goldsberry, Mo. (†63539) 261/G3
Goldsboro, Md. (21636) 245/P4
Goldsboro, N.C. 188/L3
Goldsboro, N.C. (27530) 281/O4
Goldsboro (Etters), Pa. (17319) 294/J5
Goldsby, Okla. (†73093) 288/L4
Goldsmith, Ind. (46045) 227/E4
Goldsmith, Texas (79741) 303/B5
Goldston, N.C. (27252) 281/L3
Goldstone (mt.), Idaho 220/E4
Goldsworthy, W. Australia 88/C4
Goldsworthy, W. Australia 92/B3
Goldthwaite, Texas (76844) 303/F6
Goldvein, Va. (22720) 307/N4
Goldville, Ala. (†35010) 195/G4
Göle, Turkey 63/K2
Goleniów, Poland 47/B2
Goleta, Calif. (93117) 204/F9
Golf, Fla. (†33444) 212/F5
Golf, Ill. (60029) 222/B5
Golfito, C. Rica 154/F6
Golf Manor, Ohio (†45201) 284/C9
Golfo Santa Clara, Mexico 150/B1
Gölhisar, Turkey 63/C4
Goliad (co.), Texas 303/G9
Goliad, Texas (77963) 303/G9
Gölköy, Turkey 63/G2
Golling an der Salzach, Austria 41/B3
Gölmarmara, Turkey 63/C3
Golmud (Golmo), China 77/D4
Golmud, China 54/L6
Golo (riv.), France 28/B6
Golo (isl.), Philippines 82/C4
Golovin, Alaska (99762) 196/F2
Golpayegan, Iran 59/F3
Golpayegan, Iran 66/G4
Gölpazarı, Turkey 63/D2
Golshan (Tabas), Iran 66/K4
Golspie, Scotland 15/E3
Goltry, Okla. (73739) 288/K1
Golts, Md. (21637) 245/P3
Gołub-Dobrzyn, Poland 47/D2
Golungo Alto, Angola 115/B5
Golva, N. Dak. (58632) 282/C6
Goma, Zaire 115/E4
Goma, Zaire 102/E5
Gombari, Zaire 115/E3
Gombe, Nigeria 106/G6
Gomel', U.S.S.R. 7/H3
Gomel', U.S.S.R. 48/D4
Gomel', U.S.S.R. 52/D4
Gomer, Ohio (45809) 284/B4
Gomera (isl.), Spain 106/A3
Gomera (isl.), Spain 33/B5
Gometra (isl.), Scotland 15/B4
Gomez, Fla. (†33455) 212/F4
Gómez Farías, Mexico 150/F2
Gómez Palacio, Mexico 150/G4
Gomishan, Iran 66/J2
Goms (valley), Switzerland 39/F4
Gona, Papua N.G. 85/C7
Gonabad, Iran 59/G3
Gonabad, Iran 66/L3
Gonaïves, Haiti 158/B5
Gonaïves, Haiti 156/D3
Gonâve (gulf), Haiti 158/B5
Gonâve (isl.), Haiti 158/B6
Gonâve (isl.), Haiti 156/D3
Gonbad-e Kavus, Iran 66/J2
Gonbadli, Iran 66/M2
Gönc, Hungary 41/F2
Gonda, India 68/E3
Gondal, India 68/C4
Gondar, Ethiopia 102/F3
Gondar, Ethiopia 59/C7
Gondar, Ethiopia 111/G5
Gondia, India 68/E4
Gondola Point, New Bruns. 170/D3
Gondomar, Portugal 33/B2
Gönen, Turkey 63/B2
Gonggar, China 77/D6
Gongga Shan (mt.), China 77/F6
Gonghe, China 77/F4
Gongliu, China 77/B3
Gongola (state), Nigeria 106/G7
Gongola (riv.), Nigeria 106/G6
Gongolgan, N.S. Wales 97/D2
Góngora (mt.), C. Rica 154/E5
Goñi, Uruguay 145/C4
Gonjo, China 77/E5
Gonvick, Minn. (56644) 255/C3
Gonzaga, Philippines 82/D1
Gonzales, Calif. (93926) 204/D7
Gonzales, La. (70737) 238/L2
Gonzales (co.), Texas 303/G8
Gonzales, Texas (78629) 303/G8
Gonzalez, Fla. (32560) 212/B6
González, Mexico 150/K5
González, Riacho (riv.), Paraguay 144/C3
Goobies, Newf. 166/D2
Goochland (co.), Va. 307/N5
Goochland, Va. (23063) 307/N5
Goodbee, La. (†70433) 238/K6
Goode (mt.), Alaska 196/C1
Goode, Va. (24556) 307/K6
Goodell, Iowa (50439) 229/F3
Goodenough (cape) 5/C7
Gooderham, Ontario 177/F3
Goodeve, Sask. 181/H4
Goodfare, Alberta 182/A2
Goodfellow A.F.B., Texas 303/D6
Goodfield, Ill. (61742) 222/D3
Good Harbor (bay), Mich. 250/D3
Good Hart, Mich. (49737) 250/D3
Good Hope, Ala. (†36024) 195/E2
Goodhope (bay), Alaska 196/F1
Good Hope, Georgia (30641) 217/E3
Good Hope, Ill. (61438) 222/C3
Good Hope, La. (†70079) 238/N3
Good Hope, Miss. (†39094) 256/E5
Good Hope, Ohio (43121) 284/D7
Good Hope (cape), S. Africa 102/D8
Good Hope (cape), S. Africa 2/K7
Good Hope (cape), S. Africa 118/E7
Goodhue (co.), Minn. 255/F6
Goodhue, Minn. (55027) 255/F6
Gooding (co.), Idaho 220/D6
Gooding, Idaho (83330) 220/D7
Goodland, Fla. (33933) 212/E6
Goodland, Ind. (47948) 227/C3
Goodland, Kansas (67735) 232/A2
Goodland, Minn. (55742) 255/E3
Goodlands, Manitoba 179/B5
Goodlettsville, Tenn. (37072) 237/H8
Goodlow, Br. Col. 184/G2
Good Luck, Md. (†20715) 245/G4
Goodman, Miss. (39079) 256/E5
Goodman, Mo. (63843) 261/C9
Goodman, Wis. (54125) 317/K4
Goodnews Bay, Alaska (99589) 196/F3
Goodnight, Texas (†79226) 303/C3
Goodnoe Hills, Wash. (†99356) 310/E5
Goodooga, N.S. Wales 97/D1
Good Pine, La. (†71342) 238/F3
Goodrich, Colo. (†80653) 208/M2
Goodrich, Mich. (48438) 250/F6
Goodrich, N. Dak. (58444) 282/K5
Goodrich, Texas (77335) 303/K7
Goodrich, Wis. (†54451) 317/G5
Goodridge, Alberta 182/E2
Goodridge, Minn. (56725) 255/C2
Goodsoil, Sask. 181/L4
Goodson, Mo. (65659) 261/F7
Good Spirit (lake), Sask. 181/J4
Goodspirit Lake Prov. Park, Sask. 181/J4
Goodspring, Tenn. (38460) 237/G10
Goodsprings, Ala. (35560) 195/D3
Goodsprings, Nev. (89019) 266/F7
Good Thunder, Minn. (56037) 255/D6
Goodview, Minn. (55027) 255/G6
Goodwater, Ala. (35072) 195/F4
Goodwater, Okla. (†74740) 288/S7
Goodwater, Sask. 181/H6
Goodway, Ala. (36449) 195/D8
Goodwell, Okla. (73939) 288/C1
Goodwin, Ark. (72340) 202/J4
Goodwin, S. Dak. (57238) 298/R4
Goodwins Mills, Maine (†04005) 243/B8
Goodwood, Ontario 177/E3
Goodwood, S. Africa 118/F6
Goodyear, Ariz. (85323) 198/C5
Gooik, Belgium 27/E7
Goole, England 10/F4
Goole, England 13/G4
Goolgowi, N.S. Wales 97/C3
Gooloogong, N.S. Wales 97/E3
Goomalling, W. Australia 88/B6
Goomalling, W. Australia 92/B1
Goombalie, N.S. Wales 97/C1
Goondiwindi, Queensland 88/H5
Goondiwindi, Queensland 95/D6
Goor, Netherlands 27/K4
Goose (lake) 188/B2
Goose (lake), Calif. 204/E1
Goose (creek), Idaho 220/E7
Goose (riv.), Newf. 166/B3
Goose (riv.), N. Dak. 282/P4
Goose (isl.), Nova Scotia 168/F4
Goose (isl.), Nova Scotia 168/G3
Goose (lake), Oreg. 291/G5
Goose (creek), Va. 307/J6
Goose (creek), Va. 307/N3
Goose Airport P.O. (Goose Bay), Newf. 162/K5
Goose Bay, Newf. 162/K5
Goose Bay, Newf. 146/M4
Goose Bay-Happy Valley, Newf. 166/B3
Gooseberry (creek), Wyo. 319/D1
Gooseberry Cove, Newf. 166/C2
Goose Cove, Newf. 166/C2
Goose Cove, Newf. 166/C3
Goose Cove, Nova Scotia 168/H2
Goose Creek (mts.), Idaho 220/E7
Goose Creek, Ky. (†40222) 237/L1
Goose Creek, S.C. (29445) 296/H6
Goose Lake, Iowa (52750) 229/N5
Gooseprairie, Wash. (†98937) 310/D4
Goose Rock, Ky. (40944) 237/O6
Goose Rocks Beach, Maine (†04046) 243/C9
Göppingen, W. Germany 22/C4
Góra, Poland 47/C3
Gorakhpur, India 68/E3
Gorchs, Argentina 143/G7
Gorda (pt.), Cuba 158/C2
Gorda (bank), Honduras 154/F3
Gorda (cay), Honduras 154/F3
Gorda (pt.), Nicaragua 154/F5
Gorda (pt.), Panama 154/H6
Gördes, Turkey 63/C3
Gordevio, Switzerland 39/G4
Gørding, Denmark 21/B7
Gordo, Ala. (35466) 195/C4
Gordola, Switzerland 39/G4
Gordon, Ala. (36343) 195/H8
Gordon (lake), Alberta 182/E1
Gordon (riv.), Br. Col. 184/H3
Gordon (isl.), Chile 138/E11
Gordon (co.), Georgia 217/C2
Gordon, Georgia (31031) 217/F5
Gordon, Kansas (†67010) 232/F4
Gordon, Nebr. (69343) 264/B2
Gordon, Ohio (45329) 284/B6
Gordon, Scotland 15/F5
Gordon, Tasmania 99/G5
Gordon (lake), Tasmania 99/C4
Gordon (riv.), Tasmania 99/B4
Gordon, Texas (76543) 303/F5
Gordon, W. Va. (25093) 312/C7
Gordon, Wis. (54838) 317/C3
Gordondale, Alberta 182/A2
Gordon Downs, W. Australia 92/E2
Gordon's Bay, S. Africa 118/F7
Gordonsburg, Tenn. (†38462) 237/F9
Gordonsville, Ala. (†36040) 195/E6
Gordonsville, Minn. (†56036) 255/E7
Gordonsville, Tenn. (38563) 237/K8
Gordonsville, Va. (22942) 307/M4
Gordonvale, Queensland 88/H3
Gordonvale, Queensland 95/C3
Gordonville, Mo. (63752) 261/N8
Gore (pt.), Alaska 196/C2
Goré, Chad 111/C6
Gore (range), Colo. 208/G3
Gore, Ethiopia 111/G6
Gore, Ethiopia 102/F4
Gore, N. Zealand 100/B7
Gore, Ohio (†43188) 284/F6
Gore, Okla. (74435) 288/R3
Gore (mt.), Vt. 268/D2
Gore, Va. (22637) 307/M2
Gore Bay, Ontario 177/B2
Gorebridge, Scotland 10/C1
Gorebridge, Scotland 15/D2
Goree, Texas (76363) 303/E4
Goregaon, India 68/B7
Görele, Turkey 63/H2
Gore Springs, Miss. (38929) 256/E3
Goreville, Ill. (62939) 222/E6
Gorey, Chan. Is. 13/F8
Gorey, Ireland 17/J6
Gorey, Ireland 10/C4
Gorgan, Iran 54/G6
Gorgan, Iran 59/F2
Gorgan (Gurgan), Iran 66/J2
Gorgan (riv.), Iran 66/J2
Gorgan (riv.), Iran 59/F2
Gorgas, Ala. (†35580) 195/D3
Gorgol (reg.), Mauritania 106/B5
Gorgona (isl.), Colombia 126/A6
Gorgona (isl.), Italy 34/B3
Gorham, Ill. (62940) 222/D6
Gorham, Kansas (67640) 232/D3
Gorham, Maine (04038) 243/C8
Gorham○, Maine (04038) 243/C8
Gorham, N.H. (03581) 268/E3
Gorham○, N.H. (03581) 268/E3
Gorham, N.Y. (14461) 276/F5
Gorham, N. Dak. (†58627) 282/D5
Gori, U.S.S.R. 52/F6
Gorin, Mo. (63543) 261/H2
Gorinchem, Netherlands 27/G5
Gorizia (prov.), Italy 34/D2
Gorizia, Italy 34/D2
Gorki, U.S.S.R. 52/D4
Gor'kiy, U.S.S.R. 2/M3
Gor'kiy, U.S.S.R. 7/J3
Gor'kiy, U.S.S.R. 48/E4
Gor'kiy, U.S.S.R. 52/F3
Gørlev, Denmark 21/E7
Gorlice, Poland 47/E4
Görlitz, E. Germany 22/F3
Görlitz, E. Germany 7/F3
Gorlitz, Sask. 181/J4
Gorlovka, U.S.S.R. 7/H4
Gorlovka, U.S.S.R. 52/E5
Gorman, Calif. (93243) 204/G9
Gorman, Tenn. (†37101) 237/F8
Gorman, Texas (76454) 303/F5
Gormania, W. Va. (26720) 312/H4
Gormanston, Ireland 17/J4
Gormanston, Tasmania 99/B4
Gorna Oryakhovitsa, Bulgaria 45/G4
Gornji Milanovac, Yugoslavia 45/D3
Gornji Vakuf, Yugoslavia 45/C4
Gorno-Altay Aut. Obl., U.S.S.R. 48/J4
Gorno-Altaysk, U.S.S.R. 48/J4
Gorno-Badakhshan Aut. Obl., U.S.S.R. 48/H6
Gornyak, U.S.S.R. 48/J4
Gorodets, U.S.S.R. 52/F3
Gorodok, U.S.S.R. 52/D3
Goroka, Papua N.G. 85/B7
Goroke, Victoria 97/A5
Gorong (isl.), Indonesia 85/J6
Gorong (isls.), Indonesia 85/J6
Gorongosa Nat'l Park, Mozambique 118/E3
Gorontalo, Indonesia 85/G5
Gorrahei, Ethiopia 111/H6
Gorredijk, Netherlands 27/J2
Gorrie, Ontario 177/C4
Gorst, Wash. (98337) 310/C3
Gort, Ireland 10/B4
Gort, Ireland 17/D5
Gortin, N. Ireland 17/G2
Gorum, La. (71434) 238/E4
Gorumna (isl.), Ireland 17/B5
Goryn' (riv.), U.S.S.R. 52/C4
Gorzów (prov.), Poland 47/B2
Gorzów Wielkopolski, Poland 47/B2
Gorzów Wielkopolski, Poland 7/F3
Göschenen, Switzerland 39/G3
Gose, Japan 81/J8
Gosen, Japan 81/J5
Goshen, Ala. (36035) 195/F7
Goshen, Ark. (72735) 202/C1
Goshen, Calif. (93227) 204/F7
Goshen○, Conn. (06756) 210/C1
Goshen (pt.), Conn. 210/G3
Goshen, Ind. (46526) 227/F1
Goshen, Ky. (40026) 237/K4
Goshen○, Mass. (01032) 249/C3
Goshen○, N.H. (03752) 268/C5
Goshen, N.J. (08218) 273/D5
Goshen, N.Y. (10924) 276/M8
Goshen, Nova Scotia 168/G3
Goshen, Ohio (45122) 284/B7
Goshen, Oreg. (97401) 291/D4
Goshen, Utah (84633) 304/C4
Goshen, Va. (24439) 307/K5
Goshen (co.), Wyo. 319/H4
Goshen Springs, Miss. (†39042) 256/E6
Goshogawara, Japan 81/K3
Goshute (mts.), Nev. 266/G2
Goshute Ind. Res., Nev. 266/G3
Goshute Ind. Res., Utah 304/A4
Gosier, Guadeloupe 161/B6
Goslar, W. Germany 22/D3
Gosnell, Ark. (†72315) 202/K2
Gosper (co.), Nebr. 264/E4
Gospić, Yugoslavia 45/B3
Gosport, Ala. (†36482) 195/C7
Gosport, England 13/F7
Gosport, England 10/F5
Gosport, Ind. (47433) 227/D6
Goss, Miss. (†39429) 256/E8
Gossau, Switzerland 39/H2
Gossville, N.H. (†03234) 268/E5
Gostivar, Yugoslavia 45/E5
Gostyń, Poland 47/C3
Gostynin, Poland 47/D2
Göta (canal), Sweden 18/J7
Göta (riv.), Sweden 18/H7
Gotebo, Okla. (73041) 288/J4
Göteborg, Sweden 7/F3
Göteborg, Sweden 18/G8
Göteborg och Bohus (co.), Sweden 18/G7
Gotha, E. Germany 22/D3
Gotham, Wis. (53540) 317/F9
Gothenburg, Nebr. (69138) 264/D4
Gothic (mesa), Ariz. 198/F2
Gotland (co.), Sweden 18/L8
Gotland (isl.), Sweden 7/F3
Gotland (isl.), Sweden 18/L8
Goto (isls.), Japan 81/D7
Goto (isls.), Neth. Ant. 161/D8
Gotse Delchev, Bulgaria 45/F5
Gotska Sandön (isl.), Sweden 18/L7
Gotsu, Japan 81/F6
Göttingen, W. Germany 22/D3
Gottwaldov, Czech. 41/D2
Götzis, Austria 41/A3
Goubere, Cent. Afr. Rep. 115/E2
Gouda, Netherlands 27/F4
Goudeau, La. (71338) 238/G5
Gough (lake), Alberta 182/D3
Gough, Georgia (30811) 217/H4
Gough (isl.), St. Helena 2/J8
Gouin (res.), Que. 162/J6
Gouin (res.), Québec 174/C3
Goulburn, N. S. Wales 88/J6
Goulburn, N.S. Wales 97/E4
Goulburn (isls.), North. Terr. 88/E2
Goulburn (isls.), North. Terr. 93/C1
Goulburn (riv.), Victoria 97/C5
Goulburn Island, North. Terr. 93/C1
Gould, Ark. (71643) 202/G6
Gould, Colo. (†80480) 208/G2
Gould, Okla. (73544) 288/G5
Gould, Québec 172/F4
Gould City, Mich. (49838) 250/D2
Goulding, Fla. (†32502) 212/B6
Goulds, Fla. (33170) 212/F6
Goulds, Newf. 166/D2
Gouldsboro, Maine (†04607) 243/H7
Gouldsboro○, Maine (†04607) 243/H7
Gouldsboro, Pa. (18424) 294/L3
Gouldtown, Sask. 181/D5
Goulimima, Morocco 106/C2
Goumbou, Mali 106/C6
Gounamitz (riv.), New Bruns. 170/C1
Goundam, Mali 106/D5
Goundam, Mali 102/B3
Gourara (oasis), Algeria 106/E3
Gourbeyre, Guadeloupe 161/A7
Gourdon, France 28/D5
Gouré, Niger 106/G6
Gourma-Rharous, Mali 106/D5
Gournay-en-Bray, France 28/D3
Gouro, Chad 111/C4
Gourock, Scotland 10/A1
Gourock, Scotland 15/A1
Gouveia, Portugal 33/C2
Gouverneur, N.Y. (13642) 276/K2
Gouvy, Belgium 27/H8
Gouyave, Grenada 161/C8
Gouyave, Grenada 156/F4
Govan, Sask. 181/G4
Govan, S.C. (†29843) 296/E5
Gove (co.), Kansas 232/B3
Gove, Kansas (67736) 232/B3
Gove (Nhulunbuy), North. Terr. 93/E2
Govena (cape), U.S.S.R. 48/R4
Govenlock, Sask. 181/B6
Governador Valadares, Brazil 132/F7
Governador Valadares, Brazil 120/E4
Government (mt.), Ariz. 198/C3
Government (peak), Mich. 250/F1
Government (creek), Utah 304/B3
Government Camp, Oreg. (97028) 291/F2
Governor (lake), Nova Scotia 168/F3
Govi-Altay, Mongolia 77/E3
Gowan, Minn. (†55736) 255/F4
Gowanda, N.Y. (14070) 276/B6
Gowd-e Zerreh (depr.), Afghanistan 59/H4
Gowen, Mich. (49326) 250/D5
Gowen, Okla. (74545) 288/R5
Gowensville, S.C. (†29356) 296/C1
Gower, Mo. (64454) 261/C3
Gower (isl.), N.S. Wales 97/J2
Gower (mt.), N.S. Wales 97/J2
Gower (pen.), Wales 13/C6
Gowna (lake), Ireland 17/G4
Gowran, Ireland 17/G6
Gowrie, Iowa (50543) 229/E4
Gowrie Park, Tasmania 99/C3
Goya, Argentina 120/D5
Goya, Argentina 143/G4
Goyave, Guadeloupe 161/A6
Goyder (riv.), North. Terr. 93/D2
Goyders (lag.), S. Australia 94/F2
Göynücek, Turkey 63/F2
Göynük, Turkey 63/D2
Goz Beïda, Chad 111/D5
Gozo (isl.), Malta 34/E6
Goz Regeb, Sudan 111/G4
Graaff-Reinet, S. Africa 118/C6
Graal-Müritz, E. Germany 22/E1
Graauw, Netherlands 27/E6
Grabill, Ind. (46741) 227/H2
Grabouw, S. Africa 118/F7
Grabs, Switzerland 39/H2
Gračac, Yugoslavia 45/B3
Gračanica, Yugoslavia 45/D3
Grace, Idaho (83241) 220/G7
Grace (mt.), Mass. 249/E2
Grace, Miss. (38745) 256/C5
Grace (pt.), R.I. 249/H8
Grace City, N. Dak. (58445) 282/N4
Gracefield, Québec 172/A3
Graceham, Md. (†21788) 245/J2
Gracemont, Okla. (73042) 288/K4
Graceton, Minn. (†56686) 255/D2
Graceton, Pa. (15743) 294/D4
Graceville, Fla. (32440) 212/D5
Graceville, Minn. (56240) 255/B5
Graceville, Queensland 88/K3
Gracewood, Georgia (30812) 217/H4
Gracey, Ky. (42232) 237/F7
Grächen, Switzerland 39/E4
Gracias, Honduras 154/C3
Gracias a Dios (cape), Nic. 146/K8
Gracias a Dios (cape), Nicaragua 154/F3
Graciosa (isl.), Portugal 33/C1
Gradačac, Yugoslavia 45/D3
Gradaús, Brazil 120/D3
Gradaús, Brazil 132/D4
Gradaús, Serra dos (range), Brazil 132/D4
Grado, Spain 33/D1
Grady, Ala. (36036) 195/F7
Grady, Ark. (71644) 202/G5
Grady (co.), Georgia 217/D9
Grady (isl.), Newf. 166/C3
Grady, N. Mex. (88120) 274/F4
Grady (co.), Okla. 288/L5
Grady, Okla. (73545) 288/L6
Gradyville, Ky. (42742) 237/L6
Graeagle, Calif. (96103) 204/E4
Graested, Denmark 21/F5
Graettinger, Iowa (51342) 229/D2
Graf, Iowa (†52039) 229/M3
Grafenau, W. Germany 22/E4
Grafenwöhr, W. Germany 22/D4
Graff, Mo. (65660) 261/H8
Graff-Reinet, S. Africa 102/E8
Graford, Texas (76045) 303/F5
Grafton, Australia 87/F8
Grafton (isls.), Chile 138/D10
Grafton, Ill. (62037) 222/C5
Grafton, Ind. (†47620) 227/B9
Grafton, Iowa (50440) 229/G2
Grafton○, Mass. (01519) 249/H4
Grafton, Nebr. (68365) 264/G4
Grafton, New Bruns. 170/C2
Grafton (co.), N.H. 268/D4
Grafton○, N.H. (03240) 268/D4
Grafton, N. S. Wales 88/J5
Grafton, N.S. Wales 97/G1
Grafton, N.Y. (12082) 276/N5
Grafton, N. Dak. (58237) 282/R3
Grafton, Ohio (44044) 284/F3
Grafton, Ontario 177/G4
Grafton○, Vt. (05146) 268/B5
Grafton, Va. (23692) 307/P6
Grafton, W. Va. (26354) 312/G4
Grafton, Wis. (53024) 317/L9
Grafton Center, N.H. (†03240) 268/D4
Graham, Ala. (36263) 195/H4
Graham (lake), Alberta 182/C1
Graham (co.), Ariz. 198/E6
Graham (mt.), Ariz. 198/F6
Graham (isl.), Br. Col. 184/A3
Graham (peak), Colo. 208/E8
Graham, Fla. (32042) 212/D2
Graham, Georgia (†31513) 217/H7
Graham (creek), Ind. 227/F7
Graham (co.), Kansas 232/C2
Graham, Ky. (42344) 237/G6
Graham (lake), Maine 243/G6
Graham, Mo. (64455) 261/C2
Graham (co.), N.C. 281/B4
Graham, N.C. (27253) 281/L2
Graham (isl.), N.W.T. 162/M3
Graham (isl.), N.W. Terrs. 187/J2
Graham, Okla. (73437) 288/M6
Graham, Ontario 175/B3
Graham, Ontario 177/G5
Graham, Texas (76046) 303/F4
Graham Bell (isl.), U.S.S.R. 4/A6
Graham Bell (isl.), U.S.S.R. 48/G1
Grahamdale, Manitoba 179/D3
Graham Land (reg.), Ant. 2/G9
Graham Land (reg.) 5/C15
Graham Reach (chan.), Br. Col. 184/C3
Grahamstown, S. Africa 102/E8
Grahamstown, S. Africa 118/D6
Grahamsville, N.Y. (12740) 276/L7
Grahn, Ky. (41142) 237/P4
Graian Alps (range), France 28/G5
Graian Alps (range), Italy 34/A2
Graiguenamanagh-Tinnahinch, Ireland 17/H6
Grain Coast (reg.), Liberia 106/B8
Grainfield, Kansas (67737) 232/B2
Grainger (co.), Tenn. 237/O8
Graingers, N.C. (†28501) 281/O4
Grainola, Okla. (†74652) 288/N1
Grainton, Nebr. (69169) 264/C4
Grain Valley, Mo. (64029) 261/S6
Grajaú, Brazil 132/E4
Grajaú (riv.), Brazil 132/E4
Grajewo, Poland 47/F2
Gram, Denmark 21/C7
Gramalote, Colombia 126/D4
Gramat, France 28/D5
Grambling, La. (71245) 238/E1
Gramercy, La. (70052) 238/M3

Guadalupe Bravo 377

Great Torrington, England 10/D5
Great Torrington, England 13/C7
Great Valley, N.Y. (14741) 276/C6
Great Victoria (des.) 88/D5
Great Victoria (desert), Australia 87/C8
Great Victoria (des.), S. Australia 94/B3
Great Victoria (des.), W. Australia 92/D5
Great Village, Nova Scotia 168/E3
Great Wall (ruins), China 54/N5
Great Wall (ruins), China 77/G4,J
Great Wass (isl.), Maine 243/J7
Great Western Tiers (mts.), Tasmania 99/C3
Great Yarmouth, England 13/J5
Great Yarmouth, England 10/G4
Great Zab (riv.), Iraq 66/C2
Grecco, Uruguay 145/B3
Grecia, C. Rica 154/E5
Greco (cape), Cyprus 63/F5
Gredos, Sierra de (range), Spain 33/D2
Greece 2/L4
Greece 7/G5
GREECE 45/F6
Greece, N.Y. (14616) 276/E4
Greeley, Colo. 188/F2
Greeley, Colo. (80631) 208/K2
Greeley, Iowa (52050) 229/L3
Greeley (co.), Kansas 232/A3
Greeley, Kansas (66033) 232/G3
Greeley (co.), Nebr. 264/F3
Greeley, Nebr. (68842) 264/F3
Greeley, Pa. (18425) 294/N3
Greeley (creek), Utah 304/B3
Greeleyville, S.C. (29056) 296/H4
Greely (fjord), N.W. Terrs. 187/K1
Greely, Ontario 177/J2
Green (bay) 188/J1
Green (riv.) 188/D3
Green (isl.), Ant. & Bar. 161/E11
Green (riv.), Colo. 208/A2
Green (isl.), Grenada 161/D8
Green (riv.), Ill. 222/D2
Green, Kansas (67447) 232/E2
Green (co.), Ky. 237/K6
Green (riv.), Ky. 237/G6
Green (isl.), Maine 243/F8
Green (riv.), Mass. 249/B2
Green, Mich. (†49953) 250/F1
Green (bay), Mich. 250/B4
Green (lake), Minn. 255/D5
Green (riv.), New Bruns. 170/B1
Green (cape), N.S. Wales 97/F5
Green (swamp), N.C. 281/N6
Green (riv.), N. Dak. 282/D5
Green (pt.), Nova Scotia 168/C5
Green (isl.), Ontario 177/A2
Green, Oreg. (†97470) 291/D4
Green (isls.), Papua N.G. 86/C2
Green (lake), Sask. 181/D1
Green (riv.), Tenn. 237/F10
Green (riv.), U.S. 146/H6
Green (riv.), Utah 304/D4
Green (mts.), Vt. 268/B4
Green (cay), Virgin Is. (U.S.) 161/F4
Green (lake), Wash. 310/A2
Green (riv.), Wash. 310/C3
Green (co.), Wis. 317/G10
Green (bay), Wis. 317/L6
Green (mt.), Wyo. 319/E3
Green (riv.), Wyo. 319/C4
Greenacres, Calif. (93308) 204/F8
Green Acres, Sask. 181/F2
Greenacres, Wash. (99016) 310/J3
Greenacres City, Fla. (33463) 212/F5
Greenan, Sask. 181/C4
Greenback, Tenn. (37742) 237/N9
Greenbackville, Va. (23356) 307/T5
Green Bank, N.J. (†08215) 273/D4
Greenbank, Wash. (98253) 310/C2
Green Bank, W. Va. (24944) 312/G6
Green Bay, N. Zealand 100/B1
Green Bay, Va. (23942) 307/M6
Green Bay, Wis. 188/J2
Green Bay, Wis. 146/J5
Green Bay, Wis. (*54301) 317/K6
Greenbelt, Md. (20770) 245/G4
Greenbelt Park, Md. 245/G4
Greenbrier, Ala. (†35758) 195/E1
Greenbrier, Ark. (72058) 202/F3
Greenbrier, Mo. (†63730) 261/M8
Greenbrier, Tenn. (37073) 237/H8
Greenbrier (co.), W. Va. 312/F7
Greenbrier (riv.), W. Va. 312/F6
Green Brook, N.J. (08812) 273/D2
Greenbush, Mass. (02040) 249/F8
Greenbush, Mich. (48738) 250/F4
Greenbush, Minn. (56726) 255/B2
Greenbush, Va. (23357) 307/S5
Green Camp, Ohio (43322) 284/D4
Greencastle, Ind. (46135) 227/D5
Greencastle, Ireland 17/H1
Green Castle, Mo. (63544) 261/G2
Greencastle, Pa. (17225) 294/G6
Green Center, Ind. (†46701) 227/G2
Green City, Mo. (63545) 261/F2
Green Court, Alberta 182/C2
Green Cove Springs, Fla. (32043) 212/E2
Greencreek, Idaho (83533) 220/B3
Green Creek, N.J. (08219) 273/D5
Greendale, Ind. (†47025) 227/H6
Greendale, Wis. (53129) 317/L2
Greendell, N.J. (07839) 273/D2
Greene (co.), Ala. 195/C5
Greene (co.), Ark. 202/J1
Greene (co.), Georgia 217/F3
Greene (co.), Ill. 222/C4
Greene (co.), Ind. 227/D6
Greene (co.), Iowa 229/E5
Greene, Iowa (50636) 229/H3
Greene○, Maine (04236) 243/C7
Greene (co.), Miss. 256/G8
Greene (co.), Mo. 261/F8
Greene (co.), N.Y. 276/M6
Greene, N.Y. (13778) 276/J6
Greene (co.), N.C. 281/O3
Greene, N. Dak. (†58787) 282/G2
Greene (co.), Ohio 284/C6
Greene (co.), Pa. 294/B6
Greene, R.I. (02827) 249/G6
Greene (co.), Tenn. 237/R8
Greene (co.), Va. 307/M4
Greenevers, N.C. (†28521) 281/O5
Greeneville, Tenn. (37743) 237/R8
Greenfield, Calif. (93927) 204/D7
Greenfield, Ill. (62044) 222/C4
Greenfield, Ind. (46140) 227/F5
Greenfield, Iowa (50849) 229/D6
Greenfield, Mass. (01301) 249/D2
Greenfield○, Mass. (01301) 249/D2
Greenfield, Minn. (†55373) 255/F5
Greenfield, Mo. (65661) 261/E8
Greenfield○, N.H. (03047) 268/D6
Greenfield, Nova Scotia 168/D4
Greenfield, Ohio (45123) 284/D7
Greenfield, Okla. (73043) 288/K3
Greenfield, S. Dak. (†57010) 298/R8
Greenfield, Tenn. (38230) 237/D8
Greenfield, Wis. (53220) 317/L2
Greenfield Hill, Conn. (†06430) 210/B4
Greenfield Park, Québec 172/J4
Greenford, Ohio (44422) 284/J4
Green Forest, Ark. (72638) 202/D1
Green Hall, Ky. (41328) 237/O6
Green Harbor, Mass. (02041) 249/M4
Green Haven, Md. (21122) 245/M4
Greenhills, Ohio (45218) 284/B9
Greenhorn, Oreg. (†97877) 291/J3
Green Island, Iowa (52051) 229/N4
Green Island, Jamaica 158/G6
Green Island, N.Y. (12183) 276/N5
Green Island, N. Zealand 100/C7
Greenisland, N. Ireland 17/K2
Green Island (bay), Philippines 82/B5
Green Island Cove, Newf. 166/C3
Green Isle, Minn. (55338) 255/E6
Green Lake, Maine (†04429) 243/F6
Green Lake, Sask. 181/L4
Green Lake (co.), Wis. 317/H8
Green Lake, Wis. (54941) 317/H8
Greenland 2/G2
Greenland 4/B12
Greenland 146/P2
Greenland (sea) 146/T2
Greenland (sea) 4/B10
Greenland, Ark. (72737) 202/B1
Greenland, Barbados 161/B8
Greenland, Colo. (†80118) 208/K4
Greenland, Mich. (49929) 250/G1
Greenland○, N.H. (03840) 268/F5
Greenlaw, Scotland 15/F5
Greenleaf, Idaho (83626) 220/B6
Greenleaf, Kansas (66943) 232/E2
Greenleaf, Minn. (†55355) 255/D6
Greenleaf, Oreg. (97445) 291/D3
Greenleaf, Wis. (54126) 317/L7
Greenleafton, Minn. (†55965) 255/F7
Greenlee (co.), Ariz. 198/F5
Green Lowther (mt.), Scotland 15/E5
Greenmount, Ky. (†40741) 237/N6
Greenmount, Md. (†21074) 245/L2
Green Mountain (res.), Colo. 208/G3
Green Mountain, Iowa (50637) 229/H4
Green Mountain, N.C. (28740) 281/E3
Green Mountain Falls, Colo. (80819) 208/K5
Green Oaks, Ill. (†60048) 222/B4
Greenock, Scotland 10/A1
Greenock, Scotland 15/A2
Greenore, Ireland 17/J4
Greenore (pt.), Ireland 17/J7
Greenough (mt.), Alaska 196/K1
Greenough, Georgia (†31716) 217/D8
Greenough, Mont. (59836) 262/C4
Green Peter (lake), Oreg. 291/E3
Green Pond, Ala. (35074) 195/D4
Green Pond, N.J. (07435) 273/E1
Green Pond, S.C. (29446) 296/F6
Greenport, N.Y. (11944) 276/P8
Green Ridge (mts.), 245/E2
Green Ridge, Mo. (65332) 261/F5
Green River (lake), Ky. 237/L6
Green River, Utah (84525) 304/D4
Green River (res.), Vt. 268/B2
Green River, Wyo. 188/E2
Green River, Wyo. (82935) 319/C4
Green River (mt.), Wyo. 319/C2
Green Rock, Ill. (†61241) 222/C2
Greens (peak), Ariz. 198/F4
Greensboro, Ala. (36744) 195/C5
Greensboro, Fla. (32330) 212/B1
Greensboro, Georgia (30642) 217/F3
Greensboro, Ind. (47344) 227/G5
Greensboro, Md. (21639) 245/P5
Greensboro, N.C. 146/L6
Greensboro, N.C. 188/K3
Greensboro, N.C. (*27401) 281/K2
Greensboro, Pa. (15338) 294/B6
Greensboro○, Vt. (05841) 268/C2
Greensburg, Ind. (47240) 227/G6
Greensburg, Kansas (67054) 232/C4
Greensburg, Ky. (42743) 237/K6
Greensburg, La. (70441) 238/J5
Greensburg, Mo. (†63531) 261/H2
Greensburg, Ohio (44232) 284/G4
Greensburg, Pa. (15601) 294/D5
Green Sea, S.C. (29545) 296/J3
Greens Farms, Conn. (06436) 210/B4
Greens Fork, Ind. (47345) 227/H5
Green's Harbour, Newf. 166/D2
Greenshields, Alberta 182/E3
Greenslopes, Queensland 88/K3
Greenslopes, Queensland 95/E3
Greenspond, Newf. 166/D4
Green Springs, Ohio (44836) 284/E3
Greenstone (pt.), Scotland 15/C3
Greenstreet, Sask. 181/A2
Green Sulphur Springs, W. Va. (25966) 312/E7
Greensville (co.), Va. 307/N7
Greentop, Mo. (63546) 261/H2
Greentown, Ind. (46936) 227/E4
Greentown, Ohio (44630) 284/H4
Greentree, Pa. (15242) 294/B7
Greenup, Ill. (62428) 222/E4
Greenup (co.), Ky. 237/R3
Greenup, Ky. (41144) 237/R3
Greenvale, Queensland 95/C3
Green Valley, Ariz. (85614) 198/D7
Green Valley, Ill. (61534) 222/D3
Green Valley, Minn. (†56258) 255/C6
Green Valley, Ontario 177/K2
Green Valley, Wis. (54127) 317/K6
Greenview, Calif. (96037) 204/B2
Greenview, Ill. (62642) 222/D3
Greenview, W. Va. (†25166) 312/C6
Green Village, N.J. (07935) 273/D2
Greenville, Ala. (36037) 195/E7
Greenville, Calif. (95947) 204/E3
Greenville, Del. (19807) 245/R1
Greenville, Fla. (32331) 212/C1
Greenville, Georgia (30222) 217/C4
Greenville, Ill. (62246) 222/D5
Greenville, Ind. (47124) 227/F8
Greenville, Iowa (51343) 229/C3
Greenville, Ky. (42345) 237/G6
Greenville, Liberia 106/C8
Greenville, Maine (04441) 243/D5
Greenville○, Maine (04441) 243/D5
Greenville, Mich. (48838) 250/D5
Greenville, Miss. 146/J6
Greenville, Miss. 188/H4
Greenville, Miss. (38701) 256/B4
Greenville, Mo. (63944) 261/M8
Greenville, N.H. (03048) 268/D6
Greenville○, N.H. (03048) 268/D6
Greenville, N.C. (27834) 281/P3
Greenville, Ohio (45331) 284/A5
Greenville, Pa. (16125) 294/B3
Greenville, R.I. (02828) 249/H5
Greenville, S.C. 146/K6
Greenville, S.C. 188/K4
Greenville (co.), S.C. 296/C2
Greenville, S.C. (*29601) 296/C2
Greenville, Texas 188/G4
Greenville, Texas (75401) 303/H4
Greenville, Utah (84731) 304/B5
Greenville, Va. (24440) 307/K5
Greenville, W. Va. (24945) 312/E7
Greenville, Wis. (54942) 317/J7
Greenville Junction, Maine (04442) 243/D5
Greenwald, Minn. (56335) 255/D5
Greenwater Lake, Sask. 181/H3
Greenwater Lake Prov. Park, Sask. 181/H3
Greenway, Ark. (72430) 202/K1
Greenway, Manitoba 179/C5
Greenway, S. Dak. (†57437) 298/K2
Greenwell Springs, La. (70739) 238/K1
Greenwich○, Conn. (06830) 210/A4
Greenwich (pt.), Conn. 210/A4
Greenwich, England 13/H8
Greenwich, England 10/B5
Greenwich (Kapingamarangi) (atoll), Micronesia 87/F5
Greenwich○, N.J. (08323) 273/C5
Greenwich, N.Y. (12834) 276/O4
Greenwich, Ohio (44837) 284/E3
Greenwich, Utah (84732) 304/B5
Greenwood, Ark. (72936) 202/B3
Greenwood, Br. Col. 184/H5
Greenwood, Calif. (95635) 204/E5
Greenwood, Del. (19950) 245/R5
Greenwood, Fla. (32443) 212/A1
Greenwood, Ind. (46142) 227/E5
Greenwood (co.), Kansas 232/F4
Greenwood, Ky. (†42634) 237/N7
Greenwood, La. (71033) 238/B2
Greenwood, Mass. (01880) 249/D6
Greenwood (lake), Minn. 255/G3
Greenwood, Miss. (38930) 256/D4
Greenwood, Mo. (64034) 261/R6
Greenwood, Nebr. (68366) 264/H3
Greenwood (lake), N.J. 273/E1
Greenwood, N.Y. (14839) 276/E6
Greenwood (lake), N.Y. 276/M8
Greenwood, S.C. 188/K4
Greenwood (co.), S.C. 296/C3
Greenwood, S.C. (29646) 296/C3
Greenwood (lake), S.C. 296/D3
Greenwood, S. Dak. (†57380) 298/N8
Greenwood, Va. (22943) 307/L4
Greenwood, W. Va. (26360) 312/E4
Greenwood, Wis. (54437) 317/E6
Greenwood Lake, N.Y. (10925) 276/M8
Greenwood Springs, Miss. (38848) 256/H3
Greer, Ariz. (85927) 198/F4
Greer, Idaho (†83544) 220/B3
Greer, Mo. (†65606) 261/K9
Greer, Ohio (†44628) 284/F4
Greer (co.), Okla. 288/G5
Greer, S.C. (29651) 296/C2
Greers Ferry, Ark. (†72067) 202/F2
Greers Ferry (lake), Ark. 202/G2
Greeson (lake), Ark. 202/C5
Gregg (co.), Texas 303/K5
Greggs, Georgia (†31620) 217/F8
Gregory, Ark. (72059) 202/H3
Gregory, Mich. (48137) 250/E6
Gregory (range), Queensland 95/B3
Gregory (riv.), Queensland 88/F3
Gregory (riv.), Queensland 95/A3
Gregory (lake), S. Australia 88/F5
Gregory (lake), S. Australia 94/F3
Gregory (co.), S. Dak. 298/L7
Gregory, S. Dak. (57533) 298/L7
Gregory (lake), W. Australia 92/C4
Gregory Landing, Mo. (†63435) 261/K2
Gregory's (sound), Ireland 17/B5
Greian (head), Scotland 15/A3
Greifensee (lake), Switzerland 39/G2
Greifswald, E. Germany 22/E1
Grein, Austria 41/C2
Greina (pass), Switzerland 39/G3
Greiz, E. Germany 22/E3
Grelton, Ohio (43523) 284/C3
Gremikha, U.S.S.R. 52/E1
Gremyachinsk, U.S.S.R. 52/J3
Grenå, Denmark 21/D5
Grenå, Denmark 18/G8
Grenada 2/F5
Grenada 146/M8
Grenada, Calif. (96038) 204/C2
GRENADA 161/D9
GRENADA 156/G4
Grenada (isl.), Grenada 156/G4
Grenada (co.), Miss. 256/E3
Grenada, Miss. (38901) 256/E3
Grenada (lake), Miss. 256/E3
Grenadier (isl.), N.Y. 276/H2
Grenadines (isls.), Grenada 156/G4
Grenadines (isls.), St. Vin. & Grens. 156/G4
Grenchen, Switzerland 39/D2
Grenfell, N.S. Wales 97/E3
Grenfell, Sask. 181/J5
Grenloch, N.J. (08032) 273/C4
Grenoble, France 7/E4
Grenoble, France 28/F5
Grenola, Kansas (67346) 232/F4
Grenora, N. Dak. (58845) 282/C2
Grenville (chan.), Br. Col. 184/C3
Grenville, Grenada 161/D8
Grenville (bay), Grenada 161/D8
Grenville, N. Mex. (88424) 274/F2
Grenville (county), Ontario 177/J3
Grenville, Québec 172/C4
Grenville (cape), Queensland 88/G2
Grenville (cape), Queensland 95/B1
Grenville, S. Dak. (57239) 298/O3
Grenville (pt.), Wash. 310/A3
Gresham, Nebr. (68367) 264/G3
Gresham, Oreg. (97030) 291/B2
Gresham, S.C. (29546) 296/J4
Gresham, Wis. (54128) 317/J6
Greshamville, Georgia (†30650) 217/F3
Gresik, Indonesia 85/K2
Gresston, Georgia (†31023) 217/F6
Greta-Branxton, N.S. Wales 97/F3
Greta East, N.S. Wales 97/F3
Gretna, Fla. (32332) 212/B1
Gretna, La. (70053) 238/O4
Gretna, Manitoba 179/E5
Gretna, Nebr. (68028) 264/H3
Gretna, Scotland 10/E3
Gretna, Scotland 15/E5
Gretna, Tasmania 99/D4
Gretna, Va. (24557) 307/K7
Grevelingen (str.), Netherlands 27/E5
Greven, W. Germany 22/B2
Grevená, Greece 45/E5
Grevenbroich, W. Germany 22/B3,
Grevenmacher, Luxembourg 27/J9
Grevesmühlen, E. Germany 22/D2
Greville (bay), Nova Scotia 168/D3
Grey (isls.), Newf. 166/C3
Grey (riv.), N. Zealand 100/C5
Grey (cape), North. Terr. 88/F2
Grey (cape), North. Terr. 93/E2
Grey (county), Ontario 177/D3
Grey (range), Queensland 88/G5
Grey (range), Queensland 95/B5
Grey Abbey, N. Ireland 17/K2
Greybull, Wyo. (82426) 319/E1
Greybull (riv.), Wyo. 319/D1
Greycliff, Mont. (59033) 262/G5
Grey Eagle, Minn. (56336) 255/D5
Grey Forest, Texas (†78201) 303/J10
Grey Islands, Newf. 166/C3
Greylock (mt.), Idaho 220/C6
Greylock (mt.), Mass. 249/B2
Greymouth, N. Zealand 100/C5
Greymouth, N. Zealand 87/G10
Grey River, Newf. 166/C4
Greys (riv.), Wyo. 319/B3
Greystone, Colo. (†81640) 208/B1
Greystone, Conn. (†06786) 210/C2
Greystone Park, N.J. (07950) 273/D2
Greystones-Delgany, Ireland 10/D4
Greystones-Delgany, Ireland 17/K5
Greytown, N. Zealand 100/E4
Greytown (San Juan del Norte), Nicaragua 154/F5
Greytown, S. Africa 118/E5
Grez-Doiceau, Belgium 27/F7
Gribbles Settlement, North. Terr. 93/B1
Gridley, Calif. (95948) 204/D4
Gridley (mt.), Conn. 210/B1
Gridley, Ill. (61744) 222/E3
Gridley, Kansas (66852) 232/G3
Gridone (mt.), Switzerland 39/G4
Griend (isl.), Netherlands 27/G2
Grier, N. Mex. (†88101) 274/F4
Gries am Brenner, Austria 41/A3
Griesheim, W. Germany 22/C4
Grieskirchen, Austria 41/B2
Griffin, Georgia (30223) 217/D4
Griffin, Ind. (47616) 227/B8
Griffin, Sask. 181/H6
Griffiss A.F.B., N.Y. 276/K4
Griffith, Ind. (46319) 227/C1
Griffith, N. S. 88/H6
Griffith, N.S. Wales 97/C4
Griffith (isl.), Ontario 177/D3
Griffithsville, W. Va. (25521) 312/B6
Griffithville, Ark. (72060) 202/G3
Grifton, N.C. (28530) 281/P4
Griggs (co.), N. Dak. 282/O5
Griggs, Okla. (†73949) 288/B1
Griggsville, Ill. (62340) 222/C4
Grigston, Kansas (†67871) 232/B3
Grijalva (riv.), Mexico 150/N7
Grim (cape), Tasmania 99/A2
Grimari, Cent. Afr. Rep. 115/C2
Grimbergen, Belgium 27/E7
Grimes, Ala. (†36350) 195/H8
Grimes, Calif. (95950) 204/C4
Grimes, Iowa (50111) 229/F5
Grimes, Okla. (†73628) 288/G4
Grimes (co.), Texas 303/J7
Grimesland, N.C. (27837) 281/P3
Griminish, Scotland 15/A3
Grimma, E. Germany 22/E3
Grimmen, E. Germany 22/E1
Grimms Landing, W. Va. (25095) 312/B5
Grimsby, England 13/G4
Grimsby, England 10/F4
Grimsby, Ontario 177/E4
Grimsel (pass), Switzerland 39/F3
Grímsey (isl.), Iceland 21/C1
Grimshaw, Alberta 182/B1
Grimsley, Tenn. (38565) 237/L2
Grimstad, Norway 18/F7
Grindelwald, Switzerland 39/E3
Grindrod, Br. Col. 184/H5
Grindsted, Denmark 21/B6
Grindstone, Maine (†04460) 243/F4
Grindstone (isl.), New Bruns. 170/F3
Grindstone (lake), Wis. 317/C4
Grind Stone City, Mich. (48467) 250/G4
Grindstone Prov. Rec. Park, Manitoba 179/F3
Grinnell, Iowa (50112) 229/H5
Grinnell, Kansas (67738) 232/B2
Grinnell (pen.), N.W. Terrs. 187/J2
Grippon, Guadeloupe 161/B6
Griqualand West (reg.), S. Africa 118/C5
Griquatown, S. Africa 118/C5
Grise Fiord, Canada 4/B13
Grise Fiord, N.W.T. 162/H1
Grise Fiord, N.W. Terrs. 187/K2
Gris-Nez (cape), France 28/D2
Grisons (Graubünden) (elec. div.), Switzerland 39/H3
Grissom A.F.B., Ind. 227/E3
Griswold, Iowa (51535) 229/C6
Griswold, Manitoba 179/B5
Griswoldville, Mass. (01345) 249/D2
Griva, U.S.S.R. 53/D3
Grizzly (bay), Calif. 204/K1
Grizzly Flats, Calif. (95636) 204/E5
Groais (isl.), Newf. 166/C3
Grobiņa, U.S.S.R. 53/A2
Grodno, U.S.S.R. 7/G3
Grodno, U.S.S.R. 48/C4
Grodno, U.S.S.R. 52/B4
Grodzisk Mazowiecki, Poland 47/E2
Grodzisk Wielkopolski, Poland 47/C2
Groenlo, Netherlands 27/K4
Groesbeck, Ohio (45239) 284/B9
Groesbeck, Texas (76642) 303/H6
Groesbeek, Netherlands 27/H5
Groix (isl.), France 28/B4
Grójec, Poland 47/E3
Grömitz, W. Germany 22/D1
Gronau, W. Germany 22/B2
Grondines, Québec 172/E3
Grong, Norway 18/H4
Grong Grong, N.S. Wales 97/D4
Groningen, Minn. (†55072) 255/E4
Groningen (prov.), Netherlands 27/K2
Groningen, Netherlands 27/K2
Groningen, Suriname 131/D2
Groninger Wad (sound), Netherlands 27/J2
Gronlid, Sask. 181/G2
Grønnedal, Greenl. 4/C12
Grono, Switzerland 39/H4
Groom, Texas (79039) 303/C2
Groomsport, N. Ireland 17/K2
Groot-Drakenstein, S. Africa 118/F6
Groote (isl.), North. Terr. 88/F2
Groote (riv.), S. Africa 118/C6
Groote Eylandt (isl.), Australia 87/D7
Groote Eylandt (isl.), North. Terr. 93/E3
Groote IJ Polder, Netherlands 27/B4
Grootfontein, Namibia 118/B3
Groot Sint Joris, Neth. Ant. 161/G9
Gros (pt.), Grenada 161/C8
Gros Islet, St. Lucia 161/G5
Gros Islet (bay), St. Lucia 161/G5
Grosmont (Island Lake), Alberta 182/D2
Gros Morne, Haiti 158/B5
Gros-Morne, Martinique 161/D6
Gros Morne (mt.), Newf. 166/C4
Gros-Morne, Québec 172/C1
Gros Morne Nat'l Park, Newf. 166/C4
Gros Piton (mt.), St. Lucia 161/G6
Gross, Nebr. (†68719) 264/F2
Grosse Ile, Mich. (48138) 250/B7
Grosse Isle, Manitoba 179/E4
Gross Emme (riv.), Switzerland 39/E2
Grossenbrode, W. Germany 22/D1
Grossenhain, E. Germany 22/E3
Grosse Pointe, Mich. (48236) 250/B7
Grosse Pointe Farms, Mich. (†48236) 250/B6
Grosse Pointe Park, Mich. (†48236) 250/B7
Grosse Pointe Shores, Mich. (†48236) 250/B6
Grosse Pointe Woods, Mich. (†48236) 250/B6
Grosser Arber (mt.), W. Germany 22/E4
Grosser Peilstein (mt.), Austria 41/C2
Grosses Coques, Nova Scotia 168/B4
Grosses-Roches, Québec 172/B1
Grosse Tete, La. (70740) 238/G6
Grosseto (prov.), Italy 34/C3
Grosseto, Italy 34/C3
Grossglockner (mt.), Austria 41/B3
Gross Litzner (mt.), Switzerland 39/K3
Grossräschen, E. Germany 22/E3
Grosssiegharts, Austria 41/C2
Grosswangen, Switzerland 39/F2
Grosvenor Dale, Conn. (06246) 210/H1
Gros Ventre (riv.), Wyo. 319/B2
Groswater (bay), Newf. 166/C3
Groton, Conn. (06340) 210/G3
Groton○, Conn. (06340) 210/G3
Groton, Mass. (01450) 249/H2
Groton○, Mass. (01450) 249/H2
Groton○, N.H. (†03241) 268/D4
Groton, N.Y. (13073) 276/H5
Groton, S. Dak. (57445) 298/N3
Groton○, Vt. (05046) 268/C3
Groton (lake), Vt. 268/C3
Groton Long (pt.), Conn. 210/H3
Groton Long Point, Conn. (†06340) 210/G3
Grottaferrata, Italy 34/F7
Grottaglie, Italy 34/F4
Grotto, Wash. (98288) 310/D3
Grottoes, Va. (24441) 307/L4
Grouard, Alberta 182/B2
Grouard Mission, Alberta 182/C2
Grouard Mission, Alta. 162/E4
Groundhog (riv.), Ontario 175/D3
Grouse (Lost River), Idaho (†83255) 220/E6
Grouse (mt.), N. Mex. 274/A5
Grouse (creek), Utah 304/A2
Grouse Creek, Utah (84313) 304/A2
Grouse Creek (mts.), Utah 304/A2
Grouw, Netherlands 27/H2
Grovania, Georgia (†31036) 217/E6
Grove, Maine (04638) 243/J5
Grove (lake), N. Dak. 282/L5
Grove, Okla. (74344) 288/S1
Grove Beach, Conn. (†06413) 210/E3
Grove Center, Ky. (†42437) 237/F5
Grove City, Fla. (33533) 212/D5
Grove City, Minn. (56243) 255/D5
Grove City, Ohio (43123) 284/D6
Grove City, Pa. (16127) 294/B3
Grovedale, Alberta 182/A2
Grove Hill, Ala. (36451) 195/C7
Groveland, Calif. (95321) 204/E6
Groveland, Fla. (32736) 212/E3
Groveland, Georgia (†31321) 217/J6
Groveland, Ind. (†46121) 227/D5
Groveland○, Mass. (01830) 249/L1
Groveland, N.Y. (14462) 276/E5
Groveoak, Ala. (35975) 195/F2
Grove Place, Virgin Is. (U.S.) 161/E4
Groveport, Ohio (43125) 284/E6
Grover, Colo. (80729) 208/L1
Grover, Mo. (63040) 261/M3
Grover, N.C. (28073) 281/G4
Grover, Pa. (17735) 294/J2
Grover, S.C. (29447) 296/F5
Grover, S. Dak. (†57201) 298/P4
Grover, Utah (†84773) 304/C5
Grover, Wyo. (83122) 319/B3
Grover City, Calif. (93433) 204/E8
Grover Hill, Ohio (45849) 284/B3
Grovertown, Ind. (46531) 227/D2
Groves, Texas (77619) 303/L8
Grovespring, Mo. (65662) 261/G8
Groveton, N.H. (03582) 268/D2
Groveton, Texas (75845) 303/J7
Groveton, Va. (†22306) 307/T3
Grovetown, Georgia (30813) 217/H4
Groveville, N.J. (†08601) 273/D3
Growler (mts.), Ariz. 198/B6
Groznyy, U.S.S.R. 7/J4
Groznyy, U.S.S.R. 48/E5
Groznyy, U.S.S.R. 52/G6
Grubbs, Ark. (72431) 202/H2
Grubišno Polje, Yugoslavia 45/C3
Grudovo, Bulgaria 45/H4
Grudziądz, Poland 47/D2
Gruenthal, Sask. 181/E3
Gruetli, Tenn. (37339) 237/K10
Gruinard (bay), Scotland 15/C3
Grulla, Texas (78548) 303/F11
Grünberg (Zielona Góra), Poland 47/B3
Grünburg, Austria 41/C3
Grundy (co.), Ill. 222/E2
Grundy (co.), Iowa 229/H4
Grundy (co.), Mo. 261/E2
Grundy (co.), Tenn. 237/K10
Grundy, Va. (24614) 307/D6
Grundy Center, Iowa (50638) 229/H4
Grunthal, Manitoba 179/F5
Gruver, Iowa (51344) 229/D2
Gruver, Texas (79040) 303/C1
Gruyères, Switzerland 39/D3
Gryazi, U.S.S.R. 52/F4
Gryazovets, U.S.S.R. 52/F3
Gryfice, Poland 47/B2
Gryfino, Poland 47/B2
Grygla, Minn. (56727) 255/C2
Gryon, Switzerland 39/D4
Grytviken 5/D17
Gstaad, Switzerland 39/D4
Gsteig, Switzerland 39/D4
Guacamaya, Colombia 126/C6
Guacamayo, Colombia 126/F6
Guacanayabo (gulf), Cuba 156/C2
Guacanayabo (gulf), Cuba 158/G4
Guacara, Venezuela 124/D2
Guachara, Venezuela 124/D4
Gu Achi, Ariz. (†85634) 198/C6
Guácimo, C. Rica 154/F5
Guacuí, Brazil 135/F2
Guadalajara, Mexico 2/D5
Guadalajara, Mexico 150/H6
Guadalajara, Mexico 146/H7
Guadalajara (prov.), Spain 33/E2
Guadalajara, Spain 33/E2
Guadalcanal (isl.), Solomon Is. 87/F7
Guadalcanal (isl.), Solomon Is. 86/D3
Guadalcanal, Spain 33/D3
Guadalimar (riv.), Spain 33/E3
Guadaloupe (isl.), Mexico 146/G7
Guadalquivir (riv.), Spain 7/D5
Guadalquivir (riv.), Spain 33/C4
Guadalupe, Potosí, Bolivia 136/B7
Guadalupe, Santa Cruz, Bolivia 136/C6
Guadalupe, Calif. (93434) 204/E9
Guadalupe (riv.), Calif. 204/K3
Guadalupe, Nuevo León, Mexico 150/K4
Guadalupe, Zacatecas, Mexico 150/H5
Guadalupe (co.), N. Mex. 274/E4
Guadalupe (mts.), N. Mex. 274/D6
Guadalupe, Peru 128/D5
Guadalupe, Spain 33/D3
Guadalupe, Sierra de (range), Spain 33/D3
Guadalupe (co.), Texas 303/G8
Guadalupe (mts.), Texas 303/C10
Guadalupe (peak), Texas 303/B10
Guadalupe (riv.), Texas 303/G8
Guadalupe Bravo, Mexico 150/F1

378 Guadalupe

Guadalupe Mts. Nat'l Park, Texas 303/C10
Guadalupe Victoria, Durango, Mexico 150/H4
Guadalupe Victoria, Puebla, Mexico 150/O1
Guadalupe y Calvo, Mexico 150/F3
Guadalupita, N. Mex. (87722) 274/D2
Guadarrama, Sierra de (range), Spain 33/E2
Guadarrama (riv.), Spain 33/F4
Guadarrama, Venezuela 124/D3
Guadeloupe (isl.) 146/M8
GUADELOUPE 161/A5
GUADELOUPE 156/F3
Guadeloupe (isl.), Guadeloupe 161/B6
Guadeloupe (isl.), Guadeloupe 156/F3
Guadeloupe (passage), Guadeloupe 161/A5
Guadeloupe Nat'l Park, Guadeloupe 161/A6
Guadiana (riv.) 7/D5
Guadiana (riv.), Portugal 33/C4
Guadiana (riv.), Spain 33/D3
Guadix, Spain 33/E4
Guafo (gulf), Chile 138/D5
Guafo (isl.), Chile 138/D5
Guage, Ky. (41329) 237/P5
Guaicanamar, Cuba 158/G3
Guaico, Trin. & Tob. 161/B10
Guaimaca, Honduras 154/D3
Guáimaro, Cuba 158/G3
Guaina, Venezuela 124/G5
Guainía (riv.) 120/C2
Guainía (comm.), Colombia 126/F6
Guainía (riv.), Colombia 126/F6
Guainía (riv.), Venezuela 124/E6
Guaira (dept.), Paraguay 144/D4
Guairá (falls), Paraguay 144/E4
Guaitecas (isls.), Chile 138/D5
Guajaba (cay), Cuba 158/G2
Guajará-Mirim, Brazil 132/H10
Guajará-Mirim, Brazil 120/C4
Guajataca (lake), P. Rico 161/B1
Guajira (pen.) 120/B1
Guajira, La (dept.), Colombia 126/D2
Guajira (pen.), Colombia 126/E1
Gualaca, Panama 154/F6
Gualaceo, Ecuador 128/C4
Gualala, Calif. (95445) 204/B5
Gualán, Guatemala 154/C3
Gualaquiza, Ecuador 128/C4
Guale, Ecuador 128/B3
Gualeguay, Argentina 143/G6
Gualeguay (riv.), Argentina 143/G5
Gualeguaychú, Argentina 143/G6
Gualpatanta, Honduras 154/E3
Guam (isl.) 87/E4
GUAM 86/K7
Guam (isl.), U.S. 2/S5
Guamal, Magdalena, Colombia 126/C3
Guamal, Meta, Colombia 126/D6
Guamblin (isl.), Chile 138/D5
Guamo, Cuba 158/H3
Guamote, Ecuador 128/C4
Guampí, Sierra de (mts.), Venezuela 124/F4
Guamúchil, Mexico 150/E4
Guana, Venezuela 124/G5
Guanabacoa, Cuba 158/C1
Guanabacoa, Cuba 156/B2
Guanabara (bay), Brazil 135/E3
Guanaceví, Mexico 150/G4
Guanahacabibes (gulf), Cuba 158/A2
Guanahacabibes (pen.), Cuba 158/A2
Guanaja, Honduras 154/E2
Guanaja (isl.), Honduras 154/E2
Guanajay, Cuba 158/B1
Guanajay, Cuba 156/A2
Guanajibo (pt.), P. Rico 161/A2
Guanajibo (riv.), P. Rico 161/A2
Guanajuato (state), Mexico 150/J6
Guanajuato, Mexico 150/J6
Guanambi, Brazil 120/E4
Guañape (isls.), Peru 128/C7
Guanare, Venezuela 124/D3
Guanare (riv.), Venezuela 124/D3
Guanare Viejo (riv.), Venezuela 124/D3
Guanarito, Venezuela 124/D3
Guandacol, Argentina 143/C2
Guane, Cuba 158/A2
Guane, Cuba 156/A2
Guangdong (Kwangtung) (prov.), China 77/H7
Guangnan, China 77/G7
Guangshan, China 77/J5
Guangxi Zhuangzu (Kwangsi Chuang Aut. Reg.), China 77/G7
Guangyuan, China 77/G5
Guangze, China 77/J6
Guangzhou (Canton), China 77/H7
Guangzhou (Canton), China 54/N7
Guánica, P. Rico 161/B3
Guánica, P. Rico 156/F1
Guánica (lake), P. Rico 161/B3
Guanipa (riv.), Venezuela 124/G3
Guaniquilla (pt.), P. Rico 161/A2
Guano, Ecuador 128/C3
Guano (creek), Oreg. 291/H5
Guano (lake), Oreg. 291/H5
Guanoco, Venezuela 124/G2
Guanta, Venezuela 124/F2
Guantánamo (prov.), Cuba 158/K4
Guantánamo, Cuba 146/L7
Guantánamo, Cuba 158/K4
Guantánamo, Cuba 156/C2
Guantánamo (bay), Cuba 158/J4
Guantánamo (bay), Cuba 156/C3
Guantánamo Bay U.S. Nav. Reserve, Cuba 158/K4
Guan Xian, China 77/F5
Guape, Colombia 126/D6
Guapí, Colombia 126/B6
Guapi (bay), Colombia 126/A6
Guápiles, C. Rica 154/F5
Guapo (bay), Trin. & Tob. 161/A11
Guaporé (riv.) 120/C4
Guaporé (riv.), Bolivia 136/C3
Guaporé (riv.), Brazil 132/H10
Guaqui, Bolivia 136/A5
Guarambaré, Paraguay 144/B5
Guaranda, Ecuador 128/C3
Guarapuava, Brazil 132/C9
Guaratinguetá, Brazil 135/D3
Guaratinguetá, Brazil 132/E8
Guarda (dist.), Portugal 33/C2
Guarda, Portugal 33/C2
Guardatinajas, Venezuela 124/E3
Guardiagrele, Italy 34/E3
Guardia Mitre, Argentina 143/D5
Guardian (bank), C. Rica 154/D6
Guardian, W. Va. (26221) 312/F5
Guareña, Spain 33/C3
Guarenésia, Brazil 135/C2
Guarero, Venezuela 124/B2
Guarico (pt.), Cuba 158/K3
Guárico (state), Venezuela 124/E3
Guarico, Venezuela 124/D3
Guárico (res.), Venezuela 124/E3
Guárico (riv.), Venezuela 124/E3
Guariquén, Venezuela 124/G2
Guarita, Honduras 154/C3
Guaro, Cuba 158/J3
Guarujá, Brazil 135/C4
Guarulhos, Brazil 135/C3
Guasave, Mexico 150/E4
Guasdualito, Venezuela 124/C4
Guasimal, Cuba 158/E2
Guasimal, Venezuela 124/D4
Guasipati, Venezuela 124/H4
Guastalla, Italy 34/C2
Guatemala 2/D5
Guatemala 146/J8
Guatemala (cap.), Guat. 146/J8
GUATEMALA 154/B3
Guatemala (cap.), Guatemala 154/B3
Guateque, Colombia 126/D5
Guatuaro (pt.), Trin. & Tob. 161/B11
Guaviare (riv.), Colombia 120/B2
Guaviare (riv.), Colombia 126/F6
Guaxupé, Brazil 135/C2
Guayabal, Cuba 158/G3
Guayabal (lake), P. Rico 161/C2
Guayabal, Amazonas, Venezuela 124/E6
Guayabal, Guárico, Venezuela 124/E3
Guayabero (riv.), Colombia 126/D6
Guayacán, Chile 138/A8
Guayaguayare, Trin. & Tob. 161/B11
Guayama (dist.), P. Rico 161/D2
Guayama, P. Rico 161/E3
Guayama, P. Rico 156/G1
Guayaneco (arch.), Chile 138/D7
Guayanés (pt.), P. Rico 161/F2
Guayanés (riv.), P. Rico 161/E2
Guayanilla, P. Rico 161/B3
Guayanilla, P. Rico 156/F1
Guayanilla (bay), P. Rico 161/B3
Guayape, Honduras 154/D3
Guayapo, Serranía (mts.), Venezuela 124/E5
Guayaquil, Ecuador 2/E6
Guayaquil, Ecuador 128/B4
Guayaquil, Ecuador 120/A3
Guayaquil (gulf), Ecuador 120/A3
Guayaquil (gulf), Ecuador 128/B4
Guayaquilaró (riv.), Argentina 143/G5
Guayaramerín, Bolivia 136/C2
Guayas (prov.), Ecuador 128/B4
Guayas (riv.), Ecuador 128/C4
Guaymas, Mexico 146/G7
Guaymas, Mexico 150/D3
Guaynabo, P. Rico 161/D1
Guayo (lake), P. Rico 161/B2
Guayos, Cuba 158/F2
Guayubín, Dom. Rep. 158/D5
Guazú-cuá, Paraguay 144/D5
Gubakha, U.S.S.R. 48/F4
Gubakha, U.S.S.R. 52/J3
Guban (reg.), Somalia 115/H1
Gubat, Philippines 82/E4
Gubbio, Italy 34/D3
Guben (Wilhelm-Pieck-Stadt), E. Germany 22/F3
Guben (Gubin), Poland 47/B3
Gubin, Poland 47/B3
Gubkin, U.S.S.R. 52/E4
Guckeen, Minn. (†56013) 255/D7
Gúdar, Sierra de (range), Spain 33/F2
Gudauta, U.S.S.R. 52/F6
Gudenå (riv.), Denmark 21/C5
Gudermes, U.S.S.R. 52/G6
Güdül, Turkey 63/E2
Gudur, India 68/D6
Guebwiller, France 28/G4
Guéckédou, Guinea 106/B7
Guelma, Algeria 106/F1
Guelph, N. Dak. (58447) 282/O7
Guelph, Ont. 162/H7
Guelph, Ontario 177/D4
Guelta de Zemmur (well), Western Sahara 106/B3
Guemar, Algeria 102/C1
Guemar, Algeria 106/F2
Güémez, Mexico 150/K5
Güeppí, Peru 128/E3
Guerara, Algeria 106/E2
Güere (riv.), Venezuela 124/F3
Guéréda, Chad 111/D5
Guéret, France 28/D4
Guerneville, Calif. (95446) 204/B5
Guernica y Luno, Spain 33/E1
Guernsey (isl.), Chan. Is. 13/E8
Guernsey (isl.), Chan. Is. 10/E6
Guernsey, Iowa (50172) 229/J5
Guernsey (co.), Ohio 284/H5
Guernsey, Sask. 181/F4
Guernsey, Wyo. (82214) 319/H3
Guernsey (res.), Wyo. 319/H3
Guerra, Texas (78360) 303/F11
Guerrero (state), Mexico 150/J8
Guerzim, Algeria 106/D3
Gueydan, La. (70542) 238/E6
Guffey, Colo. (80820) 208/H5
Gugerd, Kuh-e (mts.), Iran 66/H3
Guggisberg, Switzerland 39/D3
Gughe (mt.), Ethiopia 111/G6
Guiana (isl.), Ant. & Bar. 161/E11
Guiana Highlands (plat.) 120/C2
Guichi, China 77/J5
Guichón, Uruguay 145/B3
Guidder, Cameroon 115/B2
Guide, China 77/F4
Guide Rock, Nebr. (68942) 264/F4
Guidonia, Italy 34/F6
Guiglo, Ivory Coast 106/C7
Guihulngan, Philippines 82/D5
Güija (lake), El Salvador 154/C3
Güija (lake), Guatemala 154/C3
Guija, Mozambique 118/E4
Guijuelo, Spain 33/D2
Guilarte (mt.), P. Rico 161/B2
Guild, N.H. (03754) 268/C5
Guildford, England 13/G8
Guildford, England 10/F5
Guildford Junction, Tasmania 99/B3
Guildhall, Vt. (05905) 268/D2
Guilford, Conn. (06437) 210/E3
Guilford○, Conn. (06437) 210/E3
Guilford, Ind. (47022) 227/H6
Guilford, Maine (04443) 243/E5
Guilford○, Maine (04443) 243/E5
Guilford, Mo. (64457) 261/C2
Guilford, N.Y. (13780) 276/J6
Guilford (co.), N.C. 281/K3
Guilford○, Vt. (†05301) 268/B6
Guilin (Kweilin), China 77/G6
Guilin, China 54/N7
Guillaume-Delisle (lake), Québec 174/B1
Guimarães, Brazil 132/E3
Guimarães, Portugal 33/B2
Guimaras (isl.), Philippines 82/D5
Guimaras (str.), Philippines 82/D5
Guimba, Philippines 82/C3
Guin, Ala. (35563) 195/C3
Guinan, China 77/F4
Guinda, Calif. (95637) 204/C5
Guinea 2/J5
Guinea 102/A3
GUINEA 106/B6
Guinea (gulf) 2/K5
Guinea (gulf) 102/C4
Guinea (gulf), Benin 106/E8
Guinea (gulf), Ghana 106/E8
Guinea (gulf), Guinea-Biss. 106/E8
Guinea (gulf), Ivory Coast 106/E8
Guinea (gulf), Nigeria 106/E8
Guinea (gulf), Togo 106/E8
Guinea, Va. (†22580) 307/O4
Guinea-Bissau 2/H5
Guinea-Bissau 102/A3
GUINEA-BISSAU 106/A6
Güines, Cuba 158/C1
Güines, Cuba 156/B2
Guingamp, France 28/B3
Guion, Ark. (72540) 202/G2
Guionos (pt.), C. Rica 154/E6
Guiping, China 77/G7
Guipúzcoa (prov.), Spain 33/E1
Güira de Melena, Cuba 158/C1
Guiratinga, Brazil 132/C7
Guir Hamada (des.), Algeria 106/D2
Güiria, Venezuela 124/G2
Guisa, Cuba 158/H4
Guisanbourg, Fr. Guiana 131/F3
Guisborough, England 13/F3
Guise, France 28/E3
Guitiriz, Spain 33/C1
Guiuan, Philippines 82/E5
Guixi, China 77/J6
Gui Xian, China 77/G7
Guiyang (Kweiyang), Guizhou, China 77/G6
Guiyang, Hunan, China 77/H6
Guiyang, China 54/M7
Guizhou (Kweichow) (prov.), China 77/G6
Gujarat (state), India 68/C4
Gujranwala, Pakistan 59/K3
Gujranwala, Pakistan 68/C2
Gujrat, Pakistan 59/K3
Gujrat, Pakistan 68/C2
Gukovo, U.S.S.R. 52/F5
Gulang, China 77/F4
Gulargambone, N.S. Wales 97/E2
Gulbarga, India 68/D5
Gulbene, U.S.S.R. 53/D2
Gulch (cape), Newf. 166/B2
Gulen, Norway 18/D6
Gulf (co.), Fla. 212/D7
Gulf, N.C. (27256) 281/L3
Gulf Breeze, Fla. (32561) 212/B6
Gulf Crest, Ala. (†36521) 195/B8
Gulf Hammock, Fla. (32639) 212/D2
Gulf Harbors, Fla. (†33552) 212/D3
Gulf Island Nat'l Seashore, Fla. 212/B6
Gulf Islands Nat'l Seashore, Miss. 256/G10
Gulfport, Fla. (33737) 212/B3
Gulf Port, Ill. (†52601) 222/B3
Gulfport, Miss. 188/J4
Gulfport, Miss. (*39501) 256/F10
Gulf Shores, Ala. (36542) 195/C10
Gulf Stream, Fla. (†33444) 212/F5
Gulgong, N.S. Wales 97/E3
Gulian, China 77/K1
Gulin, China 77/G6
Gulistan, 48/G5
Gulja (Yining), China 77/B3
Gulkana, Alaska (†99586) 196/J2
Gull (lake), Alberta 182/C3
Gull (lake), Minn. 255/D4
Gull (isl.), Newf. 166/D2
Gullane, Scotland 15/F4
Gull Bay, Ontario 177/H5
Gull Bay, Ontario 175/C3
Gullfoot (lake), Ontario 177/F3
Gull Island, Newf. 166/D2
Gull Island (pt.), Newf. 166/C2
Gulliver, Mich. (49840) 250/D2
Gull Lake, Alberta 182/D3
Gull Lake, Sask. 181/C5
Gully, Minn. (56646) 255/C3
Gülnar, Turkey 63/E4
Gulnare, Colo. (81042) 208/K8
Gulnare, Ky. (41530) 237/S5
Gulquac (lake), New Bruns. 170/D2
Gulquac (riv.), New Bruns. 170/C2
Gülşehir, Turkey 63/F3
Gulu, Uganda 115/F3
Gulvain (mt.), Scotland 15/C4
Guma (Pishan), China 77/A4
Gumaca, Philippines 82/D4
Gumare, Botswana 118/C3
Gumbranch, Georgia (†31313) 217/J7
Gumel, Nigeria 106/F6
Gumeracha, S. Australia 94/C7
Gumma (pref.), Japan 81/J5
Gummersbach, W. Germany 22/B3
Gummi, Nigeria 106/F6
Gum Spring, Va. (23065) 307/N5
Gum Springs, Ark. (†71923) 202/D5
Gümüş, Turkey 63/F2
Gümüşhacıköy, Turkey 63/F2
Gümüşhane (prov.), Turkey 63/H2
Gümüşhane, Turkey 59/C1
Gümüşhane, Turkey 63/H2
Gun (cay), Bahamas 156/B1
Gun (lake), Mich. 250/D6
Guna, India 68/D4
Gunbower, Victoria 97/C4
Gundagai, N.S. Wales 97/D4
Gunderbooka (ranges), N.S. Wales 97/C2
Gündoğmuş, Turkey 63/D4
Güney, Turkey 63/C3
Gunflint Trail, Minn. (†55604) 255/F1
Gungu, Zaire 115/C5
Gunisao (lake), Manitoba 179/J3
Gunlock, Utah (84733) 304/A6
Gunn, Alberta 182/C3
Gunna (isl.), Scotland 15/B4
Gunnbjørn (mt.), Greenl. 4/C11
Gunn City, Mo. (†64760) 261/D5
Gunnedah, N. S. Wales 88/H6
Gunnedah, N.S. Wales 97/F2
Gunning, N.S. Wales 97/E4
Gunnison (co.), Colo. 208/E5
Gunnison, Colo. (81230) 208/E5
Gunnison (riv.), Colo. 208/C5
Gunnison (tunnel), Colo. 208/D6
Gunnison, Miss. (38746) 256/C3
Gunnison, Utah (84634) 304/C4
Gunnison (res.), Utah 304/C4
Gunnworth, Sask. 181/C4
Gunpowder (riv.), Md. 245/N3
Gunpowder, Queensland 95/A3
Gunpowder, Queensland 88/F3
Gunpowder Falls (creek), Md. 245/M2
Guntakal, India 68/D5
Gunter, Ontario 177/G3
Gunter, Oreg. (†97436) 291/D4
Gunter Air Force Base, Ala. 195/F6
Guntersville, Ala. (35976) 195/F2
Guntersville (dam), Ala. 195/F2
Guntersville (lake), Ala. 195/F2
Gunton, Manitoba 179/E4
Guntown, Miss. (38849) 256/G2
Guntur, India 54/K8
Guntur, India 68/D5
Gunungapi (isl.), Indonesia 85/H7
Günzburg, W. Germany 22/D4
Gunzenhausen, W. Germany 22/D4
Gurabo, P. Rico 161/E2
Gurais, India 68/D2
Gurdon, Ark. (71743) 202/D6
Gurgan (Gorgan), Iran 66/J2
Gurguéia (riv.), Brazil 132/E5
Guri, Venezuela 124/G4
Guri (dam), Venezuela 120/C2
Guri (res.), Venezuela 120/C2
Guri (res.), Venezuela 124/G4
Gurk, Austria 41/C3
Gurla Mandhada (mt.), China 77/B5
Gurley, Ala. (35748) 195/F1
Gurley, La. (†70730) 238/H5
Gurley, Nebr. (69141) 264/B3
Gurley, N.S. Wales 97/E1
Gurley, S.C. (†29569) 296/J3
Gurleyville, Conn. (†06268) 210/G1
Gurnee, Ill. (60031) 222/B4
Gurnet (pt.), Mass. 249/M4
Gurney, Wis. (54528) 317/F3
Gurneyville, Alberta 182/E2
Guro, Mozambique 118/E3
Gürpınar, Turkey 63/K3
Gurteen, Ireland 17/D3
Gurtnellen, Switzerland 39/G3
Gürün, Turkey 63/G3
Gurupá, Brazil 132/D3
Gurupi, Brazil 132/D5
Gurupi, Brazil 120/E4
Gurupi, Serra do (range), Brazil 132/E4
Gurupi (riv.), Brazil 132/E3
Gur'yev, U.S.S.R. 54/G5
Gur'yev, U.S.S.R. 48/F5
Gusau, Nigeria 106/F6
Gusau, Nigeria 102/C3
Gusher, Utah (84030) 304/E3
Gusinje, Yugoslavia 45/D4
Gusinoozersk, U.S.S.R. 48/L4
Gus'-Khrustal'nyy, U.S.S.R. 52/F3
Güssing, Austria 41/D3
Gustavo Díaz Ordaz, Mexico 150/K3
Gustavus, Alaska (99826) 196/M1
Gustavus, Ohio (†44417) 284/J3
Gustine, Calif. (95322) 204/D6
Gustine, Texas (76455) 303/F6
Guston, Ky. (40142) 237/J5
Güstrow, E. Germany 22/E2
Gütersloh, W. Germany 22/C3
Guthrie, Ind. (†47421) 227/D7
Guthrie (co.), Iowa 229/D5
Guthrie, Ky. (42234) 237/G7
Guthrie, Minn. (56451) 255/D3
Guthrie, Mo. (†65063) 261/H5
Guthrie, Okla. 188/G3
Guthrie, Okla. (73044) 288/M3
Guthrie, Texas (79236) 303/D4
Guthrie Center, Iowa (50115) 229/D5
Gutiérrez Zamora, Mexico 150/L6
Guttannen, Switzerland 39/F3
Guttenberg, Iowa (52052) 229/L3
Guttenberg, N.J. (07093) 273/C2
Guttingen, Switzerland 39/H1
Gu-Win, Ala. (†35563) 195/C3
Guy, Alberta 182/B2
Guy, Ark. (72061) 202/F3
Guyana 2/G5
Guyana 120/D2
GUYANA 131/B3
Guyandotte (riv.), W. Va. 312/B6
Guyang, China 77/G3
Guymon, Okla. (73942) 288/D1
Guyot (glac.), Alaska 196/K2
Guyot (mt.), N.C. 281/C3
Guyot (mt.), Tenn. 237/P9
Guyra, N.S. Wales 97/F2
Guys, Tenn. (38339) 237/D10
Guysborough (co.), Nova Scotia 168/F3
Guysborough, Nova Scotia 168/G3
Guysborough (riv.), Nova Scotia 168/G3
Guys Mills, Pa. (16327) 294/C2
Guysville, Ohio (45735) 284/G7
Guyton, Georgia (31312) 217/K6
Guyuan, China 77/G4
Guzmán (lake), Mexico 150/F1
Guzmán Blanco, Venezuela 124/E6
Guzmanes (cays), Cuba 158/B2
Gwa, Burma 72/B3
Gwaai, Zimbabwe 118/D3
Gwabegar, N.S. Wales 97/E2
Gwadabawa, Nigeria 106/F6
Gwadar, Pakistan 59/H5
Gwadar, Pakistan 68/A4
Gwalior, India 54/J7
Gwalior, India 68/D3
Gwanda, Zimbabwe 118/D4
Gwda (riv.), Poland 47/C2
Gweebarra (bay), Ireland 17/D2
Gweebarra (riv.), Ireland 17/D2
Gwelo, (Gweru) Zimbabwe 118/D3
Gwelo, Zimbabwe 102/F6
Gwent, Wales 13/D6
Gwersyllt, Wales 13/E4
Gwinn, Mich. (49841) 250/B2
Gwinner, N. Dak. (58040) 282/P7
Gwinnett (co.), Georgia 217/D2
Gwydir (riv.), N.S. Wales 97/E1
Gwynedd, Wales 13/C4
Gwynn, Va. (23066) 307/R5
Gwynne, Alberta 182/D3
Gwynneville, Ind. (46144) 227/F5
Gyaca, China 77/D6
Gyangzê, China 77/C6
Gyaring Co (lake), China 77/C5
Gyaring Hu (lake), China 77/E5
Gyasikan, Ghana 106/D7
Gyda (pen.), U.S.S.R. 54/J2
Gyda (pen.), U.S.S.R. 4/C6
Gyda, U.S.S.R. 48/H2
Gyda (pen.), U.S.S.R. 48/H2
Gydan (Kolyma) (range), U.S.S.R. 48/Q3
Gyirong, China 77/B6
Gylling, Denmark 21/D6
Gympie, Australia 87/F8
Gympie, Queensland 88/J5
Gympie, Queensland 95/E5
Gyobingauk, Burma 72/C3
Gyoma, Hungary 41/F3
Gyöngyös, Hungary 41/E3
Gyönk, Hungary 41/E3
Győr, Hungary 7/F4
Győr, Hungary 41/D3
Győr-Sopron (co.), Hungary 41/D3
Gypsum, Colo. (81637) 208/F3
Gypsum, Kansas (67448) 232/E3
Gypsum (lake), Manitoba 179/D3
Gypsum, Ohio (43433) 284/E2
Gypsumville, Manitoba 179/D3
Gyrfalcon (isls.), N.W. Terrs. 187/M4
Gyula, Hungary 41/F3

H

Haacht, Belgium 27/F7
Haag, Austria 41/C2
Haakon (co.), S. Dak. 298/F5
Haamstede, Netherlands 27/D5
Ha'apai Group (isls.), Tonga 87/J8
Haapajärvi, Finland 18/O5
Haapamäki, Finland 18/O5
Haapsalu, U.S.S.R. 53/B1
Haar, W. Germany 22/D4
Haarlem, Netherlands 27/F4
Haarlemmermeer (Hoofddorp), Netherlands 27/F4
Haarlemmermeer Polder, Netherlands 27/B5
Haast, N. Zealand 100/B5
Haast (pass), N. Zealand 100/B6
Haast (riv.), N. Zealand 100/B5
Haasts Bluff, North. Terr. 88/E4
Haasts Bluff, North. Terr. 93/B7
Haasts Bluff Aboriginal Reserve, North. Terr. 88/E5
Haasts Bluff Aboriginal Res., North. Terr. 93/B7
Hab (riv.), Pakistan 68/B3
Hab (riv.), Pakistan 59/J4
Habahe, China 77/C2
Habana, La (Havana) (prov.), Cuba 158/C1
Habana, Cuba 158/C1
Habay, Alberta 182/A5
Habay, Belgium 27/H9
Habban, P.D.R. Yemen 59/E7
Habbaniya, Iraq 59/D3
Habbaniya, Iraq 66/C4
Habbaniya, Hor al (lake), Iraq 66/C4
Habersham (co.), Georgia 217/E1
Habersham, Georgia (30544) 217/F1
Habersham, Tenn. (†37766) 237/N8
Habiganj, Bangladesh 68/G4
Habikino, Japan 81/J8
Habomai (isls.), Japan 81/N2
Habonim, Israel 65/B2
Haboro, Japan 81/K1
Hachenburg, W. Germany 22/B3
Hachinohe, Japan 81/K3
Hachioji, Japan 81/O2
Hachiro (lag.), Japan 81/J3
Hachita, N. Mex. (88040) 274/A7
Hacıbektaş, Turkey 63/F3
Hacienda Village, Fla. (†33301) 212/B4
Hacılar, Turkey 63/F3
Hack (mt.), S. Australia 94/F4
Hackberry, Ariz. (86411) 198/B3
Hackberry, La. (70645) 238/D7
Hackensack, Minn. (56452) 255/D4
Hackensack, N.J. (*07601) 273/B2
Hackensack (riv.), N.J. 273/C1
Hacker Valley, W. Va. (26222) 312/F5
Hacketstown, Ireland 17/H6
Hackett, Ark. (72937) 202/B3
Hacketts Cove, Nova Scotia 168/E4
Hackettstown, N.J. (07840) 273/D2
Hackleburg, Ala. (35564) 195/C2
Hackleman, Ind. (†46928) 227/F4
Hackney, England 13/H8
Hackney, England 10/B5
Hacksneck, Va. (23358) 307/S5
Hacoda, Ala. (†36442) 195/F8
Hadano, Japan 81/O3
Hadar, Nebr. (68738) 264/G2
Hadarba, Ras (cape), Sudan 111/G3
Hadashville, Manitoba 179/G5
Hadd, Ras al (cape), Oman 59/G5
Hadd, Ras al (cape), Oman 54/H7
Haddam○, Conn. (06438) 210/E3
Haddam, Kansas (66944) 232/E2
Haddam Neck, Conn. (†06424) 210/E2
Haddar, Saudi Arabia 59/E5
Haddington, Scotland 10/E3
Haddington, Scotland 15/F5
Haddix, Ky. (41331) 237/P6
Haddock, Georgia (31033) 217/F4
Haddonfield, N.J. (08033) 273/B3
Haddon Heights, N.J. (08035) 273/B3
Hadejia, Nigeria 106/G6
Hadejia (riv.), Nigeria 106/F6
Hadensville, Ky. (†42234) 237/G7
Hadera, Israel 65/B3
Hadera (dry riv.), Israel 65/B3
Haderslev, Denmark 21/C7
Haderslev, Denmark 18/F9
Hadhar, Iraq 66/C3
Hadhramaut (reg.), P.D.R. Yemen 54/F8
Hadhramaut (dist.), P.D.R. Yemen 59/E7
Hadhramaut, Wadi (dry riv.), P.D.R. Yemen 59/F7
Hadibu, P.D.R. Yemen 54/G8
Hadibu, P.D.R. Yemen 59/F7
Hadım, Turkey 63/E4
Haditha, Iraq 66/C3
Haditha, Iraq 59/D3
Hadiya, Saudi Arabia 59/C4
Hadleigh, England 13/H5
Hadley, Ind. (†46122) 227/D5
Hadley, Ky. (42235) 237/H6
Hadley○, Mass. (01035) 249/D3
Hadley, Minn. (56133) 255/C7
Hadley (bay), N.W. Terrs. 187/H2
Hadley, Pa. (16130) 294/B3
Hadley-Lake Luzerne, N.Y. (12835) 276/N4
Hadlock-Irondale, Wash. (98339) 310/C2
Hadlyme, Conn. (06439) 210/F3
Hadselfjorden (fjord), Norway 18/J2
Hadspen, Tasmania 99/D3
Hadsten, Denmark 21/C5
Hadsund, Denmark 21/D4
Haedo (range), Uruguay 145/C2
Haeju, N. Korea 81/B4
Haena, Hawaii (†96714) 218/C1
Haena (pt.), Hawaii 218/C1
Hafar al Batin, Saudi Arabia 59/E4
Haffe, Syria 63/G5
Hafford, Sask. 181/D3
Hafik, Turkey 63/G3
Haflong, India 68/G3
Hafnarfjördhur, Iceland 21/B2
Haft Gel, Iran 66/F5
Hafun, Somalia 115/K1
Hafun, Ras (cape), Somalia 115/K1
Hagaman, N.Y. (12086) 276/M5
Hagan, Georgia (30429) 217/J6
Hagar, Ontario 177/D1
Hagari (riv.), India 68/D6
Hagarstown, Ill. (62247) 222/D5
Hagarville, Ark. (72839) 202/D2
Hagemeister (isl.), Alaska 196/F3
Hagen, Sask. 181/F3
Hagen, W. Germany 22/B3
Hagenow, E. Germany 22/D2
Hagensborg, Br. Col. 184/D4
Hager City, Wis. (54014) 317/A6
Hagerman, Idaho (83332) 220/D7
Hagerman, N. Mex. (88232) 274/E5
Hagerstown, Ind. (47346) 227/G5
Hagerstown, Md. (21740) 245/G2
Hagerstown, Md. 188/L3
Hagfors, Sweden 18/H6
Hagi, Japan 81/E6
Ha Giang, Vietnam 72/E2
Hagley, Tasmania 99/C3
Hagood, S.C. (†29128) 296/F3
Hags (head), Ireland 17/B6
Hague, Fla. (†32601) 212/D2
Hague (cape), France 28/C3
Hague, The (cap.), Netherlands 7/E3
Hague, The (cap.), Netherlands 27/E4
Hague, N.Y. (12836) 276/N3
Hague, N. Dak. (58542) 282/L7
Hague, Sask. 181/E3
Hague, Va. (22469) 307/P4
Haguenau, France 28/G3
Haha (isl.), Japan 87/E3
Haha (isl.), Japan 81/M3
Ha! Ha! (lake), Qué. 172/G1

Hardesty 379

Ha! Ha! (riv.) Qué. 172/G1
Hahatonka, Mo. (†65020) 261/G7
Hahira, Georgia (31632) 217/F9
Hahndorf, S. Australia 94/C8
Hahnville, La. (70057) 238/N4
Hai, Iraq 59/E3
Hai, Iraq 66/E4
Haifa (dist.), Israel 65/C2
Haifa, Israel 65/B2
Haifa, Israel 59/B3
Haifa (bay), Israel 65/C2
Haifeng, China 77/J7
Haig (lake), Alberta 182/B1
Haight, Alberta 182/D3
Haigler, Nebr. (69030) 264/C4
Haikang, China 77/G7
Haikou (Hoihow), China 77/H7
Haikou, China 54/N8
Haiku, Hawaii (96708) 218/J2
Hail, Saudi Arabia 54/F7
Hail, Saudi Arabia 59/D4
Hailar, China 77/J2
Hailar He (riv.), China 77/K2
Haile, La. (†71260) 238/F1
Hailesboro, N.Y. (13645) 276/K2
Hailey, Idaho (83333) 220/D6
Haileybury, Ontario 177/K5
Haileybury, Ontario 175/D3
Haileyville, Okla. (74546) 288/P5
Hailong, China 77/L3
Hailsham, England 13/H7
Hailun, China 77/L2
Hailuoto, Finland 18/O4
Hailuoto (isl.), Finland 18/O4
Haina, Hawaii (96727) 218/H3
Hainan (isl.), China 2/Q5
Hainan (isl.), China 54/N8
Hainan (isl.), China 77/H8
Hainaut (prov.), Belgium 27/D7
Hainburg an der Donau, Austria 41/D2
Haines, Alaska (99827) 196/M1
Haines, Oreg. (97833) 291/J3
Hainesburg, N.J. (†07832) 273/C2
Haines City, Fla. (33844) 212/E3
Haines Junction, Yukon 187/E3
Haines Landing, Maine (†04447) 243/B6
Hainesport○, N.J. (08036) 273/D4
Hainesville, Ill. (†60030) 222/A4
Hainesville, N.J. (†07826) 273/D1
Hainfeld, Austria 41/C2
Haiphong, Vietnam 54/M7
Hairy Hill, Alberta 182/D3
Haiti 2/F5
Haiti 146/L8
HAITI 158
HAITI 156/D3
Haiwee, Calif. 204/H7
Haiya Junction, Sudan 59/C6
Haiya Junction, Sudan 111/G4
Haiyan, China 77/F4
Haiyang, China 77/K4
Haiyuan, China 77/G4
Hajara, Al (plain), Iraq 66/D5
Hajarain, P.D.R. Yemen 59/E6
Hajdú-Bihar (co.), Hungary 41/F3
Hajdúböszörmény, Hungary 41/F3
Hajdúdorog, Hungary 41/F3
Hajdúhadház, Hungary 41/F3
Hajdúnánás, Hungary 41/F3
Hajdúsámson, Hungary 41/F3
Hajdúszoboszló, Hungary 41/F3
Haji Ibraham (mt.), Iraq 66/D2
Hajja, Yemen Arab Rep. 59/D6
Hajnowka, Poland 47/F2
Hajós, Hungary 41/E3
Haka, Burma 72/B2
Hakalau, Hawaii (96710) 218/J4
Hakkâri (prov.), Turkey 63/K4
Hakkâri (Çölemerik), Turkey 63/K4
Hakkâri (mts.), Turkey 63/K4
Hakken (mt.), Japan 81/H6
Hakodate, Japan 81/K3
Hakodate, Japan 54/R5
Haku (mt.), Japan 81/H5
Hakui, Japan 81/H5
Hakusan National Park, Japan 81/H5
Hal (Halle), Belgium 27/E7
Halabja, Iraq 66/D3
Halachó, Mexico 150/O6
Halaib, Sudan 59/C5
Halaib, Sudan 111/G3
Halalii (lake), Hawaii 218/A2
Halaula, Hawaii 188/G5
Halawa, Hawaii, Hawaii (†96711) 218/G3
Halawa, Molokai, Hawaii (†96748) 218/H1
Halawa (bay), Hawaii 218/H1
Halawa (cape), Hawaii 218/H1
Halawa (stream), Hawaii 218/B3
Halawa Heights, Hawaii (†96701) 218/B3
Halberstadt, E. Germany 22/D3
Halbrite, Sask. 181/H6
Halbur, Iowa (51444) 229/D4
Halcon (mt.), Philippines 82/C4
Halcyon Dale, Georgia (†30467) 217/J5
Haldane, Ill. (†61030) 222/D1
Haldeman, Ky. (40329) 237/P4
Halden, Norway 18/G7
Haldensleben, E. Germany 22/D2
Haldimand, Ontario 177/E5
Haldimand-Norfolk (reg. munic.), Ontario 177/E5
Hale (co.), Ala. 195/C5
Hale, Argentina 143/F7
Hale, Colo. (80730) 208/P3
Hale, Camp, Colo. 208/G4
Hale, England 13/H2
Hale, Iowa (52230) 229/L4
Hale, Mich. (48739) 250/F4
Hale, Mo. (64643) 261/F3
Hale (riv.), North. Terr. 93/D8
Hale (co.), Texas 303/C3
Hale (mt.), W. Australia 92/B4
Haleakala (crater), Hawaii 218/K2
Haleakala Nat'l Park, Hawaii 218/K2
Haleb (Aleppo), Syria 59/C2
Haleb (Aleppo), Syria 63/G4
Haleburg, Ala. (†36319) 195/H8
Hale Center, Texas (79041) 303/C3
Haledon, N.J. (07508) 273/B1
Haleiwa, Hawaii (96712) 218/E1
Halen, Belgium 27/G7
Hales Corners, Wis. (53130) 317/K2
Halesowen, England 13/E5
Halesowen, England 10/G3
Hales Point, Tenn. (†38040) 237/B9
Halesworth, England 13/J5
Haley, N. Dak. (†58629) 282/D8
Haley Station, Ontario 177/H2
Haleyville, Ala. (35565) 195/C2
Haleyville, N.J. (†08349) 273/C5
Half Assini, Ghana 106/D8
Halfeti, Turkey 63/H4
Half Island Cove, Nova Scotia 168/G3
Half Moon (cay), Belize 154/D2
Halfmoon Bay, Alberta 182/C3
Halfmoon Bay, Br. Col. 184/J2
Half Moon Bay, Calif. (94019) 204/H3
Half Moon Bay (Oban), N. Zealand 100/B7
Half Moon Lake, Alberta 182/D2
Halford, Kansas (†67701) 232/B2
Halfway (riv.), Br. Col. 184/F2
Halfway, Ky. (42150) 237/J7
Halfway, Md. (†21740) 245/G2
Half Way, Mo. (65663) 261/F7
Halfway, Oreg. (97834) 291/K3
Halfway House, Hawaii (†96718) 218/H6
Halfway House, S. Africa 118/H6
Halfweg, Netherlands 27/B4
Halhul, West Bank 65/C4
Haliburton (county), Ontario 177/F2
Haliburton, Ontario 177/F2
Haliburton (lake), Ontario 177/F2
Halieli, Turkey 63/B6
Halifax, Canada 2/F3
Halifax, England 13/J1
Halifax, England 10/G1
Halifax (harb.), Grenada 161/C8
Halifax○, Mass. (02338) 249/L5
Halifax (co.), N.C. 281/O2
Halifax, N.C. (27839) 281/O2
Halifax (co.), Nova Scotia 168/E4
Halifax (cap.), N.S. 162/K7
Halifax (cap.), N.S. 146/M5
Halifax (cap.), Nova Scotia 168/E4
Halifax (harb.), Nova Scotia 168/E4
Halifax, Pa. (17032) 294/J5
Halifax (bay), Queensland 88/H3
Halifax (bay), Queensland 95/C3
Halifax○, Vt. (†05358) 268/B6
Halifax (co.), Va. 307/L7
Halifax, Va. (24558) 307/L7
Halifax Center, Vt. (†05358) 268/B6
Haliimaile, Hawaii (96787) 218/J2
Halil (riv.), Iran 59/G4
Halin, Somalia 115/J2
Halkett (cape), Alaska 196/H1
Halkirk, Alberta 182/D3
Halkirk, Scotland 10/E1
Halkirk, Scotland 15/E2
Hall (isl.), Alaska 196/D2
Hall (co.), Georgia 217/E2
Hall, Ind. (†46157) 227/D5
Hall, Ky. (†41840) 237/R6
Hall, Md. (†20716) 245/L5
Hall (isls.), Micronesia 87/F5
Hall, Mont. (59837) 262/C4
Hall (co.), Nebr. 264/F4
Hall (basin), N.W. Terrs. 187/M1
Hall (lake), N.W. Terrs. 187/K3
Hall (pen.), N.W.T. 162/K3
Hall (pen.), N.W. Terrs. 187/M3
Hall (riv.), Québec 172/C2
Hall (co.), Texas 303/D3
Hall, W. Va. (†26201) 312/F4
Halla (mt.), S. Korea 81/C7
Hallam, Nebr. (68368) 264/H4
Hallam, Victoria 97/K5
Halland (co.), Sweden 18/H8
Hallandale, Fla. (33009) 212/B4
Hallandale (riv.), Scotland 15/E2
Hallaniya (isl.), P.D.R. Yemen 59/G6
Hallau, Switzerland 39/F1
Hall Beach, N.W. Terrs. 187/K3
Hallboro, Manitoba 179/C4
Halle, Belgium 27/E7
Halle, E. Germany 7/F3
Halle (dist.), E. Germany 22/D3
Halle, E. Germany 22/D3
Halleck, Nev. (89824) 266/F2
Hällefors, Sweden 18/J7
Hallein, Austria 41/B3
Halle-Neustadt, E. Germany 22/D3
Hallett, Okla. (74034) 288/N2
Hallettsville, Texas (77964) 303/G8
Halley, Ark. (†71638) 202/H6
Halliday, N. Dak. (58636) 282/F5
Hallie, Wis. (†54729) 317/D6
Halligen (isls.), W. Germany 22/C1
Hall Meadow (brook), Conn. 210/C1
Hallock, Minn. (56728) 255/A2
Hallonquist, Sask. 181/D5
Hallowell, Kansas (66744) 232/H4
Hallowell, Maine (04347) 243/D7
Hall Park, Okla. (†73069) 288/M4
Halls (stream), N.H. 268/E1
Halls, Tenn. (38040) 237/C9
Halls (creek), Utah 304/D6
Hallsberg, Sweden 18/J7
Hallsboro, N.C. (28442) 281/M6
Halls Creek, Australia 87/C7
Halls Creek, W. Australia 88/D3
Halls Creek, W. Australia 92/D2
Halls Crossroads, Tenn. (37918) 237/O8
Hallson, N. Dak. (†58220) 282/P2
Halls Summit, Kansas (†66871) 232/G3
Hallstahammar, Sweden 18/K7
Hallstatt, Austria 41/B3
Hallstavik, Sweden 18/L6
Hallstead, Pa. (18822) 294/L2
Hall Summit, La. (71034) 238/D2
Hallsville, Ill. (†61727) 222/D3
Hallsville, Mo. (65255) 261/H4
Hallsville, Ohio (45633) 284/E7
Hallsville, Texas (75650) 303/K5
Hallton, Pa. (†15860) 294/E3
Halltown, Mo. (65664) 261/E8
Halltown, W. Va. (25423) 312/L4
Hallum, Netherlands 27/H2
Hallwilersee (lake), Switzerland 39/F2
Hallwood, Va. (23359) 307/S5
Halma, Minn. (56729) 255/B2
Halmahera (isl.), Indonesia 54/O9
Halmahera (isl.), Indonesia 85/H5
Halmahera (sea), Indonesia 85/H5
Halmstad, Sweden 18/H8
Halpine, Md. (†20852) 245/K4
Halq el Oued, Tunisia 106/G1
Hals, Denmark 21/D3
Halsell, Ala. (†36912) 195/B6
Halsey, Nebr. (69142) 264/D3
Halsey, Oreg. (97348) 291/D3
Halstad, Minn. (56548) 255/B3
Halstead, England 13/H6
Halstead, England 10/G5
Halstead, Kansas (67056) 232/E4
Haltdalen, Norway 18/G5
Haltemprice, England 13/G4
Haltemprice, England 10/F4
Haltern, W. Germany 22/B3
Haltiatunturi (mt.), Finland 18/M2
Haltom City, Texas (76117) 303/F2
Halton (reg. munic.), Ontario 177/E4
Halton Hills, Ontario 177/E4
Haltwhistle, England 13/E2
Halulu (lake), Hawaii 218/A2
Ham, Chad 111/C5
Ham, France 28/E3
Hama (prov.), Syria 63/G5
Hama, Syria 63/G5
Hama, Syria 59/C2
Hamada, Jebel (mt.), Egypt 59/B5
Hamada, Japan 81/E6
Hamadan (gov.), Iran 66/F3
Hamadan, Iran 66/F3
Hamadan, Iran 59/E3
Hamadan, Iran 54/F6
Hamamatsu, Japan 54/P6
Hamamatsu, Japan 81/H6
Hamar, N. Dak. (58336) 282/N4
Hamar, Norway 18/G6
Hamar, Saudi Arabia 59/E5
Hambantota, Sri Lanka 68/E7
Hamberg, N. Dak. (58337) 282/L4
Hamber Prov. Park, Br. Col. 184/H4
Hamblen (co.), Tenn. 237/P8
Hambleton, W. Va. (26269) 312/G4
Hamburg, Ark. (71646) 202/G7
Hamburg, Conn. (†06371) 210/F3
Hamburg, Ill. (62045) 222/C4
Hamburg, Iowa (51640) 229/B7
Hamburg, Mich. (48139) 250/F6
Hamburg, Minn. (55339) 255/D6
Hamburg, Miss. (†39661) 256/B7
Hamburg, N.J. (07419) 273/D1
Hamburg, N.Y. (14075) 276/C5
Hamburg, Pa. (19526) 294/L4
Hamburg, W. Germany 7/F3
Hamburg (state), W. Germany 22/D2
Hamburg, W. Germany 22/D2
Hamburg, Wis. (54438) 317/G5
Hamda, Saudi Arabia 59/D6
Hamden○, Conn. (06514) 210/D3
Hamden, N.Y. (13782) 276/K6
Hamden, Ohio (45634) 284/F7
Häme (prov.), Finland 18/O6
Hämeenlinna, Finland 18/O6
Hamel, Ill. (62046) 222/B2
Hamel, Minn. (55340) 255/F5
Hamel, Québec 172/G3
Hamelin Pool, W. Australia 88/A5
Hamelin Pool, W. Australia 92/A4
Hameln, W. Germany 22/C2
Hamer, Idaho (83425) 220/F6
Hamer, S.C. (29547) 296/J3
Hamersley (range), W. Australia 88/B4
Hamersley (range), W. Australia 92/B3
Hamersville, Ohio (45130) 284/C8
Hamhŭng, N. Korea 81/C4
Hami (Kumul), China 77/D3
Hami, China 54/L5
Hamill, S. Dak. (57534) 298/K6
Hamilton, Ala. (35570) 195/C2
Hamilton (lake), Ark. 202/D5
Hamilton (cap.), Bermuda 156/G3
Hamilton (mt.), Calif. 204/L3
Hamilton, Colo. (81638) 208/D2
Hamilton (co.), Fla. 212/D1
Hamilton, Georgia (31811) 217/C5
Hamilton (co.), Ill. 222/E5
Hamilton, Ill. (62341) 222/B3
Hamilton (co.), Ind. 227/E4
Hamilton, Ind. (46742) 227/H1
Hamilton (co.), Iowa 229/F4
Hamilton, Iowa (50116) 229/H6
Hamilton (co.), Kansas 232/A3
Hamilton, Kansas (66853) 232/F4
Hamilton○, Mass. (01936) 249/L2
Hamilton, Mich. (49419) 250/C6
Hamilton, Miss. (39746) 256/H3
Hamilton, Mo. (64644) 261/E3
Hamilton, Mont. (59840) 262/B4
Hamilton (co.), Nebr. 264/F4
Hamilton (inlet), Newf. 166/C3
Hamilton (inlet), Newf. 146/N4
Hamilton (inlet), Newf. 162/L5
Hamilton (sound), Newf. 166/D4
Hamilton (co.), N.Y. 276/L3
Hamilton, N.Y. (13346) 276/J5
Hamilton, N. Zealand 100/E2
Hamilton, N.C. (27840) 281/P3
Hamilton, N. Dak. (58238) 282/R2
Hamilton (co.), Ohio 284/A7
Hamilton, Ohio 188/K3
Hamilton, Ohio (*45011) 284/A7
Hamilton, Ont. 146/K5
Hamilton, Ont. 162/H7
Hamilton, Ontario 177/E4
Hamilton, Oreg. (†97856) 291/H3
Hamilton, Pa. (15744) 294/D4
Hamilton (riv.), Queensland 95/B4
Hamilton, R.I. (†02852) 249/J6
Hamilton, Scotland 15/C2
Hamilton, Scotland 10/B1
Hamilton, The (riv.), S. Australia 94/D2
Hamilton, The (riv.), S. Australia 88/E5
Hamilton, Tasmania 99/C4
Hamilton (co.), Tenn. 237/L10
Hamilton (co.), Texas 303/F6
Hamilton, Texas (76531) 303/G6
Hamilton, Victoria 88/G7
Hamilton, Victoria 97/B5
Hamilton, Va. (22068) 307/N2
Hamilton, Wash. (98255) 310/D2
Hamilton City, Calif. (95951) 204/C4
Hamilton Dome, Wyo. (82427) 319/D2
Hamilton Square-Mercerville, N.J. (08690) 273/D3
Hamilton-Wentworth (reg. munic.), Ontario 177/D4
Hamina, Finland 18/P6
Hamiota, Manitoba 179/B4
Ham Lake, Minn. (55304) 255/E5
Hamler, Ohio (43524) 284/B3
Hamlet, Ind. (46532) 227/D2
Hamlet, Nebr. (69031) 264/C4
Hamlet, N.Y. (†14138) 276/B6
Hamlet, N.C. (28345) 281/K5
Hamlet, N. Dak. (†58795) 282/E2
Hamlet, Ohio (†45102) 284/B8
Hamletsburg, Ill. (62944) 222/E6
Hamlin, Alberta 182/D2
Hamlin, Iowa (50117) 229/D5
Hamlin, Kansas (†66434) 232/G2
Hamlin, Ky. (42046) 237/E7
Hamlin○, Maine (†04785) 243/H1
Hamlin (lake), Mich. 250/C4
Hamlin, N.Y. (14464) 276/E4
Hamlin, Pa. (18427) 294/M3
Hamlin, Sask. 181/C3
Hamlin (co.), S. Dak. 298/P4
Hamlin, Texas (79520) 303/E5
Hamlin, W. Va. (25523) 312/B6
Hamm, W. Germany 22/B3
Hammamet (gulf), Tunisia 106/G1
Hammar, Hor al (lake), Iraq 66/E5
Hammarstrand, Sweden 18/J5
Hamme, Belgium 27/E6
Hammel, Denmark 21/C5
Hammelburg, W. Germany 22/C3
Hammer, S. Dak. (†57255) 298/R2
Hammerdal, Sweden 18/J5
Hammerfest, Norway 4/B9
Hammerfest, Norway 18/N1
Hammerfest, Norway 7/G1
Hammersmith, England 10/B5
Hammersmith, England 13/H8
Hammerum, Denmark 21/C5
Hammett, Idaho (83627) 220/C7
Hammon, Okla. (73650) 288/H3
Hammonasset (pt.), Conn. 210/E3
Hammonasset (res.), Conn. 210/E3
Hammonasset (riv.), Conn. 210/E3
Hammond, Ill. (61929) 222/E4
Hammond, Ind. (*46320) 227/B1
Hammond, Ky. (†40935) 237/O7
Hammond, La. (70401) 238/N1
Hammond, Minn. (55938) 255/F6
Hammond, Mo. (†65762) 261/G9
Hammond, Mont. (59332) 262/M5
Hammond (riv.), New Bruns. 170/E3
Hammond, N.Y. (13646) 276/J2
Hammond, Oreg. (97121) 291/C1
Hammond, Wis. (54015) 317/A6
Hammondsport, N.Y. (14840) 276/F6
Hammondsville, Ohio (43930) 284/J4
Hammondvale, New Bruns. 170/E3
Hammondville, Ala. (†35989) 195/G1
Hammonton, N.J. (08037) 273/D4
Hamnavoe, Scotland 15/G2
Ham-Nord, Québec 172/F4
Hamoa, Hawaii (†96713) 218/K2
Hamois, Belgium 27/G8
Hamont-Achel, Belgium 27/H6
Hampden, Maine (04444) 243/F6
Hampden○, Maine (04444) 243/F6
Hampden (co.), Mass. 249/D4
Hampden○, Mass. (01036) 249/E4
Hampden, Newf. 166/C4
Hampden, N. Zealand 100/C6
Hampden, N. Dak. (58338) 282/N2
Hampden, W. Va. (25623) 312/C7
Hampden Highlands, Maine (04445) 243/F6
Hampden-Sydney, Va. (23943) 307/L6
Hampshire (co.), England 13/F6
Hampshire, Ill. (60140) 222/E1
Hampshire (co.), Mass. 249/D3
Hampshire, Tenn. (38461) 237/G9
Hampshire (co.), W. Va. 312/J4
Hampshire, Wyo. (†82701) 319/H2
Hampstead, Dominica 161/E5
Hampstead, Md. (21074) 245/L2
Hampstead, New Bruns. 170/D3
Hampstead○, N.H. (03841) 268/E6
Hampstead, N.C. (28443) 281/O6
Hampstead, Québec 172/H4
Hampton, Ark. (71744) 202/F6
Hampton○, Conn. (06247) 210/G1
Hampton, Fla. (32044) 212/D2
Hampton, Georgia (30228) 217/D4
Hampton, Ill. (61256) 222/C2
Hampton, Iowa (50441) 229/G3
Hampton, Ky. (42047) 237/E6
Hampton, Minn. (55031) 255/E6
Hampton, Miss. (†38744) 256/B4
Hampton, Nebr. (68843) 264/G4
Hampton, New Bruns. 170/E3
Hampton, N.H. (03842) 268/F6
Hampton○, N.H. (03842) 268/F6
Hampton, N.J. (08827) 273/D2
Hampton, N.Y. (12837) 276/O3
Hampton, Nova Scotia 168/C4
Hampton, Oreg. (†97712) 291/G4
Hampton, Pa. (†17350) 294/H6
Hampton (co.), S.C. 296/E6
Hampton, S.C. (29924) 296/E6
Hampton, Tenn. (37658) 237/S8
Hampton (I.C.), Va. (*23601) 307/R6
Hampton Bays, N.Y. (11946) 276/R9
Hampton Beach, N.H. (03842) 268/F6
Hampton Falls○, N.H. (03844) 268/F6
Hampton Nat'l Hist. Site, Md. 245/M3
Hampton Park, Victoria 97/K6
Hampton Park, Victoria 88/M8
Hampton Roads (est.), Va. 307/R7
Hampton Springs, Fla. (†32347) 212/C1
Hamptonville, N.C. (27020) 281/H2
Hamrat esh Sheikh, Sudan 111/E5
Hamrin, Jabal (mts.), Iraq 66/D3
Hams Bluff (prom.), Virgin Is. (U.S.) 161/E3
Hams Fork (riv.), Wyo. 319/B4
Ham-Sud, Québec 172/F4
Hamton, Sask. 181/J4
Hamtramck, Mich. (48212) 250/B6
Hamur, Turkey 63/K3
Han (riv.), China 54/N6
Han (riv.), S. Korea 81/C5
Hana, Hawaii 188/F5
Hana, Hawaii (96713) 218/K2
Hanac, Turkey 63/K2
Hanaford (Logan), Ill. (†62856) 222/E6
Hanagita (peak), Alaska 196/K2
Hanahan, S.C. (29410) 296/H6
Hanakiya, Saudi Arabia 59/D5
Hanalei, Hawaii (96714) 218/C1
Hanalei (bay), Hawaii 218/C1
Hanalei (riv.), Hawaii 218/C1
Hanamaki, Japan 81/K4
Hanamalo (pt.), Hawaii 218/F7
Hanamaulu, Hawaii (96715) 218/C1
Hanapepe, Hawaii (96716) 218/C2
Hanapepe (bay), Hawaii 218/C2
Hanau, W. Germany 22/C3
Hanbogd, Mongolia 77/G3
Hanceville, Ala. (35077) 195/E2
Hancheng, China 77/H4
Hanchung (Hanzhong), China 77/G5
Hancock, Conn. (†06786) 210/C2
Hancock (co.), Georgia 217/G4
Hancock (co.), Ill. 222/B3
Hancock (co.), Ind. 227/F5
Hancock (co.), Iowa 229/F2
Hancock, Iowa (51536) 229/C6
Hancock (co.), Ky. 237/H5
Hancock (co.), Maine 243/G6
Hancock○, Maine (04640) 243/G6
Hancock, Md. (21750) 245/F2
Hancock○, Mass. (01237) 249/A2
Hancock, Mich. (49930) 250/G1
Hancock, Minn. (56244) 255/C5
Hancock (co.), Miss. 256/E10
Hancock, Mo. (†65452) 261/H7
Hancock○, N.H. (03449) 268/C6
Hancock (mt.), N.H. 268/D3
Hancock, N.Y. (13783) 276/K7
Hancock (co.), Ohio 284/C3
Hancock (co.), Tenn. 237/P7
Hancock○, Vt. (05748) 268/B4
Hancock (co.), W. Va. 312/E2
Hancock, W. Va. (25424) 312/K3
Hancock, Wis. (54943) 317/G7
Hancocks Bridge, N.J. (08038) 273/C4
Hand (co.), S. Dak. 298/L4
Handa (isl.), Scotland 15/C2
Handan (Hantan), China 77/H4
Handan, China 54/N6
Handel, Sask. 181/C3
Handeni, Tanzania 115/G5
Handies (peak), Colo. 208/E7
Handley, W. Va. (25102) 312/D6
Handlová, Czech. 41/E2
Handsom, Va. (23859) 307/O7
Handsworth, Sask. 181/J6
Haney, Br. Col. 184/L3
Hanford, Calif. (93230) 204/F7
Hanford Reservation, Wash. 310/F4
Hangayn Nuruu (mts.), Mongolia 77/E2
Hangchow (Hangzhou), China 77/J5
Hanggin, China 77/G4
Hanging Rock, Ohio (45635) 284/E8
Hangklip (cape), S. Africa 118/F7
Hangö, Finland 18/N7
Hangöudd (prom.), Finland 18/N7
Hangzhou (Hangchow), China 77/J5
Hangzhou, China 54/N6
Hangzhou Wan (bay), China 77/K5
Hanh, Mongolia 77/F1
Hani, Turkey 63/J3
Haniqra, Rosh (cape), Israel 65/C1
Hanish (isls.), Yemen Arab Rep. 59/D7
Hankinson, N. Dak. (58041) 282/S7
Hanko (Hangö), Finland 18/N7
Hanks, N. Dak. (†58856) 282/C2
Hanksville, Utah (84734) 304/D5
Hanle, India 68/D2
Hanley, Sask. 181/E4
Hanley Falls, Minn. (56245) 255/C6
Hanley Hills, Mo. (†63101) 261/P2
Hanlontown, Iowa (50444) 229/G2
Hanmer, N. Zealand 100/D5
Hann (mt.), W. Australia 92/D1
Hanna, Alberta 182/E4
Hanna, Alta. 162/E5
Hanna, Ind. (46340) 227/D2
Hanna, La. (71035) 238/D3
Hanna, Okla. (74845) 288/P4
Hanna, Utah (84031) 304/D3
Hanna, Wyo. (82327) 319/F4
Hanna City, Ill. (61536) 222/D3
Hannaford, N. Dak. (58448) 282/O5
Hannah, N. Dak. (58239) 282/N2
Hannah (bay), Ontario 175/D2
Hannawa Falls, N.Y. (13647) 276/L1
Hannibal, Mo. (63401) 261/K3
Hannibal, Mo. 188/H3
Hannibal, N.Y. (13074) 276/G4
Hannibal, Ohio (43931) 284/J6
Hannibal, Wis. (54439) 317/E5
Hanno, Japan 81/O2
Hannover, N. Dak. (58543) 282/H5
Hannover, W. Germany 7/E3
Hannover, W. Germany 22/C2
Hannuit (Hannut), Belgium 27/G7
Hannut, Belgium 27/G7
Hanöbukten (bay), Sweden 18/J9
Hanoi (cap.), Vietnam 2/Q4
Hanoi (cap.), Vietnam 54/M7
Hanover (isl.), Chile 120/B8
Hanover (isl.), Chile 138/D9
Hanover, Conn. (06350) 210/G2
Hanover, Ill. (61041) 222/C1
Hanover, Ind. (47243) 227/F7
Hanover, Kansas (66945) 232/F2
Hanover○, Maine (04237) 243/B7
Hanover, Md. (21201) 245/M4
Hanover○, Mass. (02339) 249/L4
Hanover, Mich. (49241) 250/E6
Hanover, Minn. (55341) 255/E5
Hanover, N.H. (03755) 268/C4
Hanover○, N.H. (03755) 268/C4
Hanover, N. Mex. (88041) 274/A6
Hanover, Ohio (†43055) 284/F5
Hanover, Ontario 177/C3
Hanover, Pa. (17331) 294/J6
Hanover (co.), Va. 307/N5
Hanover, Va. (23069) 307/O5
Hanover, W. Va. (24839) 312/C7
Hanover Park, Ill. (60103) 222/A5
Hanoverton, Ohio (44423) 284/J4
Hansboro, N. Dak. (58339) 282/M2
Hansell, Iowa (50640) 229/G3
Hansen, Idaho (83334) 220/D7
Hansford (co.), Texas 303/C1
Han Shui (riv.), China 77/H5
Hanska, Minn. (56041) 255/D6
Hans Lollik (isls.), Virgin Is. (U.S.) 161/B4
Hanson, Ky. (42413) 237/G6
Hanson, Mass. (02341) 249/L4
Hanson○, Mass. (02341) 249/L4
Hanson (bay), N. Zealand 100/E7
Hanson (riv.), North. Terr. 93/C6
Hanson, Okla. (†74955) 288/S4
Hanson (co.), S. Dak. 298/O6
Hansonville, Va. (†24266) 307/D7
Hanstholm, Denmark 21/B3
Hanston, Kansas (67849) 232/C3
Hansville, Wash. (98340) 310/C3
Hantan (Handan), China 77/H4
Hants (co.), Nova Scotia 168/D4
Hant's Harbour, Newf. 166/D2
Hantsport, Nova Scotia 168/D3
Hantzsch (riv.), N.W. Terrs. 187/L3
Hanumangarh, India 68/C3
Hanwood, N.S. Wales 97/C4
Hanyuan, China 77/F6
Hanzhong (Hanchung), China 77/G5
Hao (atoll), Fr. Poly. 87/N7
Haouach, Wadi (dry riv.), Chad 111/C4
Haparanda, Sweden 18/N4
Hapeville, Georgia (30354) 217/K2
Happy, Ky. (41746) 237/P6
Happy, Texas (79042) 303/C3
Happy Adventure, Newf. 166/D2
Happy Camp, Calif. (96039) 204/B2
Happy Jack, Ariz. (86024) 198/D4
Happy Jack, La. (†70083) 238/L7
Happy Valley, Oreg. (†97222) 291/B2
Happy Valley-Goose Bay, Newf. 166/B3
Haql, Saudi Arabia 59/C4
Harad, Saudi Arabia 59/E5
Harads, Sweden 18/M3
Harahan, La. (70123) 238/O4
Haraja, Saudi Arabia 59/D6
Haralson (co.), Georgia 217/B3
Haralson, Georgia (30229) 217/C4
Haramachi, Japan 81/K5
Harar (prov.), Ethiopia 111/H6
Harar, Ethiopia 111/H6
Harar, Ethiopia 102/G4
Harardera, Somalia 115/J3
Harare (Salisbury) (cap.), Zimbabwe 102/E6
Haraz, Chad 111/C5
Harbel, Liberia 106/B7
Harbeson, Del. (19951) 245/S6
Harbin, China 77/L2
Harbin, China 2/R3
Harbin, China 54/O5
Harbine, Nebr. (†68377) 264/G4
Harbinger, N.C. (27941) 281/T2
Harboør, Denmark 21/B4
Harbor, Oreg. (97415) 291/C5
Harbor Beach, Mich. (48441) 250/G5
Harbor City, Calif. (90710) 204/C11
Harborcreek, Pa. (16421) 294/C1
Harbor Springs, Mich. (49740) 250/D3
Harborton, Va. (23389) 307/S5
Harbor View, Ohio (43434) 284/C2
Harbour (isl.), Bahamas 156/C1
Harbour Breton, Newf. 166/C4
Harbour Deep, Newf. 166/C3
Harbour Grace, Newf. 166/D2
Harbour Grace, Newf. 162/L6
Harbour Main, Newf. 166/D2
Harbourton, N.J. (†08530) 273/D3
Harbourville, Nova Scotia 168/D3
Harburg-Wilhelmsburg, W. Germany 22/C2
Hårby, Denmark 21/D7
Harco, Ill. (†62935) 222/E6
Harcourt, Iowa (50544) 229/E4
Harcourt, New Bruns. 170/E2
Harcourt, Ontario 177/F2
Harcuvar (mts.), Ariz. 198/B5
Harda, India 68/D4
Hardangerfjord (fjord), Norway 18/D7
Hardangerfjorden (fjord), Norway 7/E3
Hardangervidda (plat.), Norway 18/E6
Hardaway, Ala. (36039) 195/G6
Hardburly, Ky. (41747) 237/P6
Hardee (co.), Fla. 212/E4
Hardee, Miss. (†39177) 256/C5
Hardeeville, S.C. (29927) 296/E7
Hardeman (co.), Tenn. 237/C10
Hardeman (co.), Texas 303/E3
Hardenberg, Netherlands 27/J3
Harden City, Okla. (74846) 288/N5
Harderwijk, Netherlands 27/H4
Hardesty, Okla. (73944) 288/D1

380 Hardieville

Hardieville, Alberta 182/D5
Hardin (co.), Ill. 222/E6
Hardin, Ill. (62047) 222/C4
Hardin (co.), Iowa 229/G4
Hardin (co.), Ky. 237/K5
Hardin, Ky. (42048) 237/E7
Hardin, Mo. (64035) 261/E4
Hardin, Mont. (59034) 262/J5
Hardin (co.), Ohio 284/C4
Hardin (co.), Tenn. 237/E10
Hardin (co.), Texas 303/K7
Harding (lake), Ala. 195/H5
Harding (lake), Georgia 217/B5
Harding, Manitoba 179/B5
Harding, Minn. (56364) 255/E4
Harding (co.), N. Mex. 274/F3
Harding (pt.), Nova Scotia 168/D5
Harding (co.), S. Dak. 298/B2
Harding, W. Va. (†26250) 312/G5
Harding Icefield, Alaska 196/C2
Hardingville, N.J. (†08343) 273/C4
Hardinsburg, Ind. (47125) 227/E8
Hardinsburg, Ky. (40143) 237/H5
Hardin Springs, Ky. (†42712) 237/J5
Hardinville, Ill. (†62449) 222/F5
Hardinxveld-Giessendam, Netherlands 27/G5
Hardisty, Alberta 182/E3
Hardisty (lake), N.W. Terrs. 187/G3
Hardman, Oreg. (†97836) 291/H2
Hardoi, India 68/E3
Hardshell, Ky. (41348) 237/P6
Hardt (mts.), W. Germany 22/C4
Hardtner, Kansas (67057) 232/D4
Hardwar, India 68/D2
Hardwick (Midway-Hardwick), Georgia (31034) 217/F4
Hardwick○, Mass. (01037) 249/F3
Hardwick, Minn. (56134) 255/B7
Hardwick, Vt. (05843) 268/C2
Hardwick○, Vt. (05843) 268/C2
Hardwick (lake), Vt. 268/C2
Hardwicke, New Bruns. 170/E1
Hardwicke Island, Br. Col. 184/E5
Hardwood Ridge, New Bruns. 170/D2
Hardy, Ark. (72542) 202/H1
Hardy (pen.), Chile 138/F11
Hardy, Iowa (50545) 229/E3
Hardy, Ky. (41531) 237/S5
Hardy, Miss. (†38901) 256/E3
Hardy, Nebr. (68943) 264/G4
Hardy, Okla. (†74641) 288/N1
Hardy, Sask. 181/G6
Hardy, Va. (24101) 307/J6
Hardy (co.), W. Va. 312/J4
Hardyville, Ky. (42746) 237/K6
Hare (bay), Newf. 166/C3
Hare (fjord), N.W. Terrs. 187/K1
Hare Bay, Newf. 166/D4
Harelbeke, Belgium 27/C7
Harfleur, France 28/D3
Harford (co.), Md. 245/N2
Harford, N.Y. (13784) 276/H6
Harford, Pa. (18823) 294/L2
Hargeysa, Somalia 115/H2
Hargeysa, Somalia 102/G4
Hargill, Texas (78549) 303/F11
Hargrave, Manitoba 179/A5
Hargwen, Alberta 182/B3
Har Hu (lake), China 77/E4
Hari (riv.), Indonesia 85/C6
Harib, Yemen Arab Rep. 59/E7
Haricha Hamada (des.), Mali 106/D4
Harim, Syria 63/G4
Harima (sea), Japan 81/G6
Harima, Jordan 65/D2
Haringey, England 10/B5
Haringey, England 13/H8
Haringvliet (str.), Netherlands 27/E5
Hariq, Saudi Arabia 59/E5
Harirud (riv.), Afghanistan 68/A1
Harirud (riv.), Afghanistan 59/H3
Hari Rud (riv.), Iran 66/M3
Haris, West Bank 65/C3
Harjavalta, Finland 18/M6
Harjo, Okla. (†74854) 288/N4
Harkaway, Victoria 97/K5
Harkers Island, N.C. (28531) 281/R5
Harkiko, Ethiopia 111/G4
Harlan, Ind. (46743) 227/H2
Harlan, Iowa (51537) 229/C5
Harlan, Kansas (67641) 232/D2
Harlan (co.), Ky. 237/P7
Harlan, Ky. (40831) 237/P7
Harlan (co.), Nebr. 264/E4
Harlan, Oreg. (†97343) 291/D3
Harlan County (lake), Nebr. 264/E5
Harlech, Wales 10/E4
Harlech, Wales 13/C5
Harlem, Fla. (33440) 212/F5
Harlem, Georgia (30814) 217/H4
Harlem, Mont. (59526) 262/H2
Harlem Springs, Ohio (44631) 284/J4
Harleston, England 13/J5
Harleton, Texas (75651) 303/K5
Hårlev, Denmark 21/F7
Harleyville, S.C. (29448) 296/G5
Harlingen, Netherlands 27/G2
Harlingen, N.J. (†08502) 273/D3
Harlingen, Texas (78550) 303/G11
Harlingen, Texas 188/G5
Harlow, England 13/H7
Harlow, N. Dak. (58340) 282/M3
Harlowton, Mont. (59036) 262/F4
Harman, W. Va. (26270) 312/G5
Harman-Maxie, Va. (24618) 307/D6
Harmans, Md. (21077) 245/M4
Harmattan, Alberta 182/C4
Harmon, Ill. (61042) 222/D2
Harmon (co.), Okla. 288/G5
Harmon, Okla. (73832) 288/G2
Harmonsburg, Pa. (16422) 294/B2
Harmony, Ark. (†72830) 202/D2
Harmony, Ind. (47853) 227/C5
Harmony, Maine (04942) 243/D6
Harmony○, Maine (04942) 243/D6
Harmony, Minn. (55939) 255/F7
Harmony, N.C. (28634) 281/H3
Harmony, Pa. (16037) 294/B4
Harmony, R.I. (02829) 249/H5
Harmony, W. Va. (25246) 312/D5
Harms, Tenn. (†37334) 237/H10
Harned, Ky. (40144) 237/J5
Harnett (co.), N.C. 281/M4
Harney (lake), Fla. 212/F3
Harney, Md. (†21787) 245/K2
Harney (co.), Oreg. 291/H4
Harney (lake), Oreg. 188/C2
Harney, Oreg. (†97720) 291/J4
Harney (lake), Oreg. 291/H4
Harney (peak), S. Dak. 298/B6
Härnösand, Sweden 18/L5
Haro, Spain 33/E1
Haro (str.), Wash. 310/B2
Harold, Fla. (32563) 212/B6
Harold, Ky. (41635) 237/R5
Harp (lake), Newf. 166/B2
Harper, Ill. (†61030) 222/D1
Harper, Iowa (52231) 229/J6
Harper (co.), Kansas 232/D4
Harper, Kansas (67058) 232/D4
Harper, Liberia 106/C8
Harper, Liberia 102/B4
Harper (co.), Okla. 288/G1
Harper, Oreg. (97906) 291/K4
Harper, Texas (78631) 303/E7
Harper, Wash. (†98366) 310/A2
Harper, W. Va. (25851) 312/D7
Harpers Ferry, Iowa (52146) 229/L2
Harpers Ferry, W. Va. (25425) 312/L4
Harpers Ferry Nat'l Hist. Park, Md. 245/G3
Harpers Ferry Nat'l Hist. Park, W. Va. 312/L4
Harpersville, Ala. (35078) 195/F4
Harperville, Miss. (39080) 256/E6
Harper Woods, Mich. (48225) 250/B6
Harpeth (riv.), Tenn. 237/G8
Harpster, Idaho (†83521) 220/C4
Harpster, Ohio (43323) 284/D4
Harpswell○, Maine (†04011) 243/D8
Harpswell Center, Maine (†04011) 243/D8
Harpursville, N.Y. (13787) 276/J6
Harput, Turkey 63/H3
Harquahala (mts.), Ariz. 198/B5
Harrah, Okla. (73045) 288/M4
Harrah, Wash. (98933) 310/E4
Harran, Turkey 63/H4
Harrell, Ark. (71745) 202/F7
Harrells, N.C. (28444) 281/N5
Harrellsville, N.C. (27942) 281/R2
Harricana (riv.), Québec 174/B3
Harriet, Ark. (72939) 202/E2
Harrietsfield, Nova Scotia 168/E4
Harrietta, Mich. (49638) 250/D4
Harriettsville, Ohio (†45745) 284/H6
Harrigan Cove, Nova Scotia 168/F4
Harriman, N.Y. (10926) 276/M8
Harriman, Oreg. (†97601) 291/E5
Harriman, Tenn. (37748) 237/M9
Harriman (res.), Vt. 268/B6
Harrington (sound), Bermuda 156/G3
Harrington, Del. (19952) 245/R5
Harrington○, Maine (04643) 243/H6
Harrington (lake), Maine 243/E4
Harrington, N.S. Wales 97/G2
Harrington, S. Dak. (†57551) 298/G7
Harrington, Wash. (99134) 310/G3
Harrington Harbour, Québec 174/F2
Harrington Park, N.J. (07640) 273/C1
Harris, Calif. (†95440) 204/B3
Harris (co.), Georgia 217/C5
Harris, Iowa (51345) 229/C2
Harris, Kansas (†66032) 232/G3
Harris, Mich. (49845) 250/B3
Harris, Minn. (55032) 255/F5
Harris, Mo. (64645) 261/F2
Harris, Okla. (†74740) 288/S7
Harris, Sask. 181/D4
Harris (dist.), Scotland 15/B3
Harris (dist.), Scotland 10/C2
Harris (sound), Scotland 15/A3
Harris (sound), Scotland 10/C2
Harris (lake), S. Australia 94/D4
Harris, Tenn. (†38261) 237/C8
Harris (co.), Texas 303/J8
Harrisburg, Ark. (72432) 202/J2
Harrisburg, Ill. (62946) 222/E6
Harrisburg, Ind. (†47331) 227/G5
Harrisburg, Mo. (65256) 261/H4
Harrisburg, Nebr. (69345) 264/A3
Harrisburg, N.C. (28075) 281/H4
Harrisburg, Ohio (43126) 284/D6
Harrisburg, Oreg. (97446) 291/D3
Harrisburg (cap.), Pa. 188/L2
Harrisburg (cap.), Pa. 146/L5
Harrisburg (cap.), Pa. (*17101) 294/H5
Harrisburg, S. Dak. (57032) 298/R7
Harrismith, S. Africa 118/D5
Harrison (bay), Alaska 196/H1
Harrison, Ark. (72601) 202/D1
Harrison (lake), Br. Col. 184/M2
Harrison, Georgia (31035) 217/G5
Harrison, Idaho (83833) 220/B2
Harrison, Ill. (†61072) 222/D1
Harrison (co.), Ind. 227/E8
Harrison (co.), Iowa 229/B5
Harrison (co.), Ky. 237/N4
Harrison○, Maine (04040) 243/B7
Harrison, Mich. (48625) 250/E4
Harrison (co.), Miss. 256/F10
Harrison (co.), Mo. 261/E2
Harrison, Mont. (59735) 262/E5
Harrison, Nebr. (69346) 264/A2
Harrison (cape), Newf. 166/C3
Harrison (cape), Newf. 162/L5
Harrison, N.J. (07029) 273/B2
Harrison, N.Y. (10528) 276/P6
Harrison (co.), Ohio 284/H5
Harrison, Ohio (45030) 284/A9
Harrison, S. Dak. (57344) 298/M7
Harrison, Tenn. (37341) 237/L10
Harrison (co.), Texas 303/K5
Harrison (co.), W. Va. 312/F4
Harrison, Wis. (†54435) 317/G5
Harrisonburg, La. (71340) 238/G3
Harrisonburg (I.C.), Va. (22801) 307/K4
Harrison Hot Springs, Br. Col. 184/M3
Harrison Valley, Pa. (16927) 294/G2
Harrisonville, Ill. (†62295) 222/C5
Harrisonville, Mo. (64701) 261/D5
Harrisonville, N.J. (08039) 273/C4
Harrisonville, Ohio (†45769) 284/F7
Harrisonville, Pa. (17228) 294/F6
Harriston, Miss. (39081) 256/C7
Harriston, Ontario 177/D4
Harristown, Ill. (62537) 222/D4
Harrisville, Ind. (†47390) 227/H4
Harrisville, Mich. (48740) 250/F4
Harrisville, Miss. (39082) 256/D7
Harrisville○, N.H. (03450) 268/C6
Harrisville, N.Y. (13648) 276/K2
Harrisville, Ohio (43974) 284/J5
Harrisville, Pa. (16038) 294/B3
Harrisville, R.I. (02830) 249/H5
Harrisville, Utah (†84401) 304/C2
Harrisville, W. Va. (26362) 312/E4
Harris Wash (creek), Utah 304/C6
Harrod, Ohio (45850) 284/C4
Harrodsburg, Ind. (47434) 227/D6
Harrodsburg, Ky. (40330) 237/M5
Harrods Creek, Ky. (40027) 237/K4
Harrogate, Br. Col. 184/J5
Harrogate, England 13/J1
Harrogate, England 10/F4
Harrogate-Shawanee, Tenn. (37752) 237/O8
Harrold, S. Dak. (57536) 298/K4
Harrold, Texas (76364) 303/F3
Harrop (lake), Manitoba 179/G2
Harrow, England 13/G8
Harrow, England 10/B5
Harrow, Ontario 177/B5
Harrow, Victoria 97/A5
Harrowby, Manitoba 179/A4
Harrowsmith, Ontario 177/H3
Harry Strunk (lake), Nebr. 264/D4
Harsens Island, Mich. (48028) 250/G6
Harshaw, Wis. (54529) 317/G4
Harstad, Norway 18/K2
Hart (lake), Fla. 212/E3
Hart (co.), Georgia 217/G2
Hart (co.), Ky. 237/K6
Hart, Mich. (49420) 250/C5
Hart (lake), Oreg. 291/H5
Hart (mt.), Oreg. 291/H5
Hart, Texas (79043) 303/B3
Hart (riv.), Yukon 187/E3
Hartbees (riv.), S. Africa 118/C5
Hartberg, Austria 41/C3
Harte, Manitoba 179/C4
Harte (mt.), Manitoba 179/A2
Hartell, Alberta 182/C4
Hartfield, Va. (23071) 307/R5
Hartford, Ala. (36344) 195/G8
Hartford (cape), Newf. 162/L5
Hartford, Ark. (72938) 202/B3
Hartford (co.), Conn. 210/D1
Hartford (cap.), Conn. 146/L5
Hartford (cap.), Conn. 188/M2
Hartford (cap.), Conn. (*06101) 210/E1
Hartford, Ill. (62048) 222/A2
Hartford, Iowa (50118) 229/G6
Hartford, Kansas (66854) 232/F3
Hartford, Ky. (42347) 237/H6
Hartford○, Maine (†04221) 243/C7
Hartford, Mich. (49057) 250/C6
Hartford, N.J. (†08057) 273/D4
Hartford, N.Y. (12838) 276/O4
Hartford, Ohio (†43013) 284/E5
Hartford, Ohio (44424) 284/J3
Hartford, S. Dak. (57033) 298/P6
Hartford, Tenn. (37753) 237/P9
Hartford○, Vt. (05047) 268/C4
Hartford, W. Va. (25247) 312/C4
Hartford, Wis. (53027) 317/K9
Hartford City, Ind. (47348) 227/G4
Harthill, Scotland 15/C2
Hartington, Nebr. (68739) 264/G2
Hartington, Ontario 177/H3
Hartland○, Conn. (†06091) 210/D1
Hartland, England 13/C7
Hartland (pt.), England 13/C6
Hartland (pt.), England 10/D5
Hartland, Maine (04943) 243/D6
Hartland○, Maine (04943) 243/D6
Hartland, Mich. (48029) 250/F6
Hartland, Minn. (56042) 255/E7
Hartland, New Bruns. 170/C2
Hartland○, Vt. (05048) 288/C4
Hartland, W. Va. (†25043) 312/D6
Hartland, Wis. (53029) 317/J1
Hartland Four Corners, Vt. (05049) 268/C4
Hartlepool, England 10/F3
Hartlepool, England 13/F3
Hartleton, Pa. (17829) 294/H4
Hartley, Iowa (51346) 229/C2
Hartley (co.), Texas 303/B2
Hartley, Texas (79044) 303/B2
Hartley, Zimbabwe 118/E3
Hartleyville, Alberta 182/D5
Hartline, Wash. (99135) 310/F3
Hartly, Del. (19953) 245/R4
Hartman, Ark. (72840) 202/C3
Hartman, Colo. (81043) 208/P6
Hartney, Manitoba 179/B5
Harts (pass), Wash. 310/E2
Harts, W. Va. (25524) 312/B6
Hartsburg, Ill. (62643) 222/D3
Hartsburg, Mo. (65039) 261/H5
Hartsdale, N.Y. (10530) 276/P6
Hartsel, Colo. (80449) 208/H4
Hartselle, Ala. (35640) 195/E2
Hartsfield, Georgia (31756) 217/E8
Hartsgrove, Ohio (†44085) 284/J2
Hartshorn, Mo. (65479) 261/J8
Hartshorne, Okla. (74547) 288/R5
Harts Range, North. Terr. 88/F4
Harts Range, North. Terr. 93/D7
Hartstown, Pa. (16131) 294/B2
Hartsville, Ind. (47244) 227/F6
Hartsville, Mass. (†01230) 249/B4
Hartsville, S.C. (29550) 296/G3
Hartsville, Tenn. (37074) 237/J8
Hartville, Mo. (65667) 261/G8
Hartville, Ohio (44632) 284/H4
Hartville, Wyo. (82215) 319/H3
Hartwell, Georgia (30643) 217/G2
Hartwell (dam), Georgia 217/G2
Hartwell (lake), Georgia 217/G2
Hartwell, Mo. (†64788) 261/E6
Hartwell (dam), S.C. 296/B3
Hartwell (lake), S.C. 296/A3
Hartwick, Iowa (52232) 229/J5
Hartwick, N.Y. (13348) 276/K5
Hartz (mt.), Tasmania 99/C5
Harug el Asued, El (mts.), Libya 111/C2
Haruniye, Turkey 63/G4
Har Us Nuur (lake), Mongolia 77/D2
Harvard (mt.), Colo. 208/G5
Harvard, Idaho (83834) 220/B3
Harvard, Ill. (60033) 222/E1
Harvard, Iowa (†50008) 229/G7
Harvard○, Mass. (01451) 249/H2
Harvard, Nebr. (68944) 264/F4
Harvel, Ill. (62538) 222/D4
Harvest, Ala. (35749) 195/E1
Harvester, Mo. (63303) 261/N2
Harvey, Ill. (60426) 222/B6
Harvey, Iowa (50119) 229/H6
Harvey (co.), Kansas 232/E3
Harvey, La. (70058) 238/O4
Harvey, Albert, New Bruns. 170/F3
Harvey, York, New Bruns. 170/D3
Harvey (lake), New Bruns. 170/C3
Harvey (mt.), New Bruns. 170/D3
Harvey, N. Dak. (58341) 282/L4
Harvey, W. Australia 88/B6
Harvey, W. Australia 92/A2
Harvey, W. Va. (25852) 312/D7
Harvey Cedars, N.J. (08008) 273/E4
Harveys (lake), Vt. 268/C3
Harveysburg, Ohio (45032) 284/C7
Harveys Lake, Pa. (18618) 294/E7
Harveyton, Ky. (†41718) 237/P6
Harveyville, Kansas (66431) 232/F3
Harviell, Mo. (63945) 261/M9
Harwich, England 13/J6
Harwich, England 10/G5
Harwich, Mass. (02645) 249/O6
Harwich○, Mass. (02645) 249/O6
Harwich Port, Mass. (02646) 249/O6
Harwinton, Conn. (06791) 210/C1
Harwinton○, Conn. (06791) 210/C1
Harwood, Mo. (64750) 261/D7
Harwood, N. Dak. (58042) 282/S6
Harwood, Ontario 177/F3
Harwood, Texas (78632) 303/G8
Harwood Heights, Ill. (60656) 222/B5
Harwood Island, N.S. Wales 97/G1
Harworth, England 13/F4
Haryana (state), India 68/D3
Harz (mts.), E. Germany 22/D3
Harz (mts.), W. Germany 22/D3
Harzgerode, E. Germany 22/D3
Hasa, Wadi el (dry riv.), Jordan 65/E5
Hasan Dağı, Büyük (mt.), Turkey 63/E3
Hasbrouck Heights, N.J. (07604) 273/B2
Hase (riv.), W. Germany 22/B2
Haseke (prov.), Syria 63/J4
Haselünne, W. Germany 22/B2
Hasenkamp, Argentina 143/F5
Hashtpar, Iran 66/F2
Haskeir (isl.), Scotland 15/A3
Haskell, Ark. (†72015) 202/E4
Haskell (co.), Kansas 232/B4
Haskell, N.J. (07420) 273/A1
Haskell (co.), Okla. 288/R4
Haskell, Okla. (74436) 288/P3
Haskell (co.), Texas 303/E4
Haskell, Texas (79521) 303/E4
Haskett, Manitoba 179/D5
Haskins, Iowa (†52201) 229/K6
Haskins, Ohio (43525) 284/C3
Haslach an der Mühl, Austria 41/C2
Hasle, Denmark 21/F8
Haslemere, England 13/G6
Haslemere, England 10/F5
Haslet, Texas (76052) 303/E2
Haslett, Mich. (48840) 250/E6
Haslev, Denmark 21/E7
Haslingden, England 13/H1
Hassa, Turkey 63/G4
Hassan, India 68/D6
Hassayampa (riv.), Ariz. 198/C5
Hasse, Texas (76456) 303/F6
Hassel (sound), N.W. Terrs. 187/J2
Hassel (isl.), Virgin Is. (U.S.) 161/B4
Hassell, N.C. (27841) 281/P3
Hasselt, Belgium 27/G7
Hasselt, Netherlands 27/J3
Hassfurt, W. Germany 22/D3
Hassi Messaoud, Algeria 106/F2
Hassi R'Mel, Algeria 106/E2
Hässleholm, Sweden 18/H8
Hassloch, W. Germany 22/C4
Haster, Scotland 15/E2
Hastière, Belgium 27/F8
Hastings, England 10/G5
Hastings, England 13/H7
Hastings, Fla. (32045) 212/E2
Hastings, Iowa (51540) 229/C6
Hastings, Mich. (49058) 250/D6
Hastings, Minn. (55033) 255/F6
Hastings, Nebr. 188/G2
Hastings, Nebr. (68901) 264/F4
Hastings, N. Zealand 100/F3
Hastings, N. Dak. (†58049) 282/O6
Hastings, Okla. (73548) 288/K6
Hastings (county), Ontario 177/G3
Hastings, Ontario 177/G3
Hastings, Pa. (16646) 294/E4
Hastings On Hudson, N.Y. (10706) 276/O6
Hasty, Ark. (72640) 202/D1
Hasty, Colo. (81044) 208/O6
Hasvik, Norway 18/M1
Haswell, Colo. (81045) 208/N6
Hat (peak), Calif. 204/E2
Hat (creek), S. Dak. 298/B7
Hatay (prov.), Turkey 63/G4
Hatay (Antakya), Turkey 63/G4
Hatboro, Pa. (19040) 294/M5
Hatch, N. Mex. (87937) 274/B6
Hatch, Utah (84735) 304/B6
Hatchechubbee, Ala. (36858) 195/H6
Hatcher, Georgia (†31754) 217/B7
Hatches Creek, North. Terr. 88/F4
Hatches Creek, North. Terr. 93/D6
Hatchet (mts.), N. Mex. 274/A7
Hatchett (pt.), Conn. 210/G3
Hatchie (riv.), Tenn. 237/B9
Hatchineha (lake), Fla. 212/E3
Haţeg, Romania 45/F3
Hatfield, Ark. (71945) 202/B5
Hatfield, England 13/H7
Hatfield, Ind. (47617) 227/C9
Hatfield, Ky. (†41514) 237/S5
Hatfield, Mass. (01038) 249/D3
Hatfield○, Mass. (01038) 249/D3
Hatfield, Minn. (56135) 255/B7
Hatfield, Mo. (64458) 261/D1
Hatfield, N.S. Wales 97/B3
Hatfield, Pa. (19440) 294/M5
Hatfield, Sask. 181/F4
Hatfield, Wis. (†54754) 317/E7
Hatfield Point, New Bruns. 170/E3
Hatgal, Mongolia 77/E1
Hathaway, Mont. (59333) 262/K4
Hatherleigh, Sask. 181/C2
Hathras, India 68/D3
Hatiba, Ras (cape), Saudi Arabia 59/C5
Ha Tien, Vietnam 72/E5
Hatillo, P. Rico 161/B1
Ha Tinh, Vietnam 72/E3
Hatira (mt.), Israel 65/B6
Hatley, Miss. (†38821) 256/H3
Hatley, Québec 172/F4
Hatley, Wis. (54440) 317/H6
Hato, Neth. Ant. 161/G8
Hato del Volcán, Panama 154/F6
Hato Mayor, Dom. Rep. 158/F6
Hato Rey, P. Rico 161/E1
Hatseva, Israel 65/D5
Hattem, Netherlands 27/H4
Hatteras (cape), N.C. 146/L6
Hatteras (cape), N.C. 188/M3
Hatteras, N.C. (27943) 281/T4
Hatteras (cape), N.C. 281/U4
Hatteras (inlet), N.C. 281/T4
Hatteras (isl.), N.C. 281/U4
Hatteras (cape), U.S. 2/F4
Hattiesburg, Miss. 188/H4
Hattiesburg, Miss. (39401) 256/F8
Hattieville, Ark. (72063) 202/E3
Hattieville, Belize 154/C2
Hatton, Ala. (†35672) 195/D1
Hatton, N. Dak. (58240) 282/R4
Hatton, Sask. 181/B5
Hatton, Scotland 15/G3
Hatton, Utah (†84637) 304/B5
Hatton, Wash. (99332) 310/G4
Hatuey, Cuba 158/G3
Hatvan, Hungary 41/E3
Hat Yai, Thailand 72/C6
Hatzic, Br. Col. 184/L3
Hau Bon, Vietnam 72/E4
Haubstadt, Ind. (47639) 227/B8
Haud (reg.), Ethiopia 111/J6
Haud (plat.), Somalia 115/J2
Haugan, Mont. (59842) 262/A3
Hauge, Norway 18/E7
Haugen, Wis. (54841) 317/C4
Haugesund, Norway 7/E3
Haugesund, Norway 18/D7
Haughton, La. (71037) 238/C1
Hauhungaroa (range), N. Zealand 100/E3
Haukivesi (lake), Finland 18/Q5
Haultain (riv.), Sask. 181/L3
Haunstetten, W. Germany 22/D4
Hauppauge, N.Y. (11787) 276/O9
Haura, P.D.R. Yemen 59/E7
Hauraki (gulf), N. Zealand 100/C1
Hauran, Wadi (dry riv.), Iraq 59/D3
Hauran, Wadi (dry riv.), Iraq 66/B4
Hauroko (lake), N. Zealand 100/A6
Hauru (pt.), Fr. Poly. 86/S12
Hauser, Idaho (†83854) 220/A2
Hauser (lake), Mont. 262/E4
Hauser, Oreg. (†97459) 291/C4
Hausstock (mt.), Switzerland 39/H3
Haut (isl.), Maine 243/G7
Haute (isl.), Nova Scotia 168/C3
Haute-Corse (dept.), France 28/B6
Haute-Garonne (dept.), France 28/D6
Haute-Loire (dept.), France 28/E5
Haute-Marne (dept.), France 28/F3
Hauterive, Québec 172/A1
Hauterive, Québec 174/D3
Hautes-Alpes (dept.), France 28/G5
Haute-Saône (dept.), France 28/G4
Haute-Savoie (dept.), France 28/G5
Hautes-Pyrénées (dept.), France 28/D6
Haute-Vienne (dept.), France 28/D5
Hautmont, France 28/F2
Haut-Rhin (dept.), France 28/G4
Hauts-de-Seine (dept.), France 28/A2
Haut-Zaïre (prov.), Zaire 115/E3
Hauula, Hawaii (96717) 218/E1
Havaco, W. Va. (24841) 312/C8
Havana, Ala. (35467) 195/C5
Havana, Ark. (72842) 202/D3
Havana (cap.), Cuba 156/A2
Havana (cap.), Cuba 2/E4
Havana (cap.), Cuba 146/K7
Havana (cap.), Cuba 158/C1
Havana, Fla. (32333) 212/B1
Havana, Ill. (62644) 222/D3
Havana, Kansas (67347) 232/G4
Havana, Minn. (†55060) 255/E6
Havana, N. Dak. (58043) 282/P8
Havana, Ohio (†44890) 284/E3
Havannah (chan.), New Caled. 86/H5
Havant and Waterloo, England 13/G7
Havasu (lake) 188/D4
Havasu (lake), Ariz. 198/A4
Havasu (lake), Calif. 204/L9
Havasu (lake), U.S. 146/G6
Havasupai Ind. Res., Ariz. 198/C2
Havdrup, Denmark 21/F6
Havel (riv.), E. Germany 22/E2
Havelange, Belgium 27/G8
Havelberg, E. Germany 22/D2
Havelock, Iowa (50546) 229/D3
Havelock, New Bruns. 170/E3
Havelock, N. Zealand 100/D4
Havelock, N.C. (28532) 281/P5
Havelock, N. Dak. (†58647) 282/E7
Havelock, Ontario 177/G3
Havelock North, N. Zealand 100/F3
Haven, Kansas (67543) 232/E4
Havensville, Kansas (66432) 232/F2
Haverford○, Pa. (19041) 294/M6
Haverfordwest, Wales 10/D5
Haverfordwest, Wales 13/B6
Haverhill, England 13/H5
Haverhill, Iowa (50120) 229/H5
Haverhill, Mass. (01830) 249/K1
Haverhill○, N.H. (03765) 268/C3
Haverhill, Ohio (45636) 284/E8
Havering, England 10/C5
Havering, England 13/J8
Haverstraw, N.Y. (10927) 276/M8
Havertown, Pa. (19083) 294/M6
Haviland, Kansas (67059) 232/C4
Haviland, Ohio (45851) 284/A3
Havillah, Wash. (†98855) 310/F2
Havířov, Czech. 41/E2
Havlíčkův Brod, Czech. 41/C2
Havran, Turkey 63/B3
Havre, Mont. 146/G5
Havre, Mont. 188/E1
Havre, Mont. (59501) 262/G2
Havre Boucher, Nova Scotia 168/G3
Havre de Grace, Md. (21078) 245/O2
Havre-Saint-Pierre, Québec 174/E2
Havre-St-Pierre, Que. 162/K5
Havsa, Turkey 63/B2
Havza, Turkey 63/F2
Haw (riv.), N.C. 281/K2
Hawaii 188/F5
HAWAII 218
Hawaii (co.), Hawaii 218/K7
Hawaii (isl.), Hawaii 87/L4
Hawaii (isl.), Hawaii 188/F6
Hawaii (isl.), Hawaii 218/H5
Hawaii (state), U.S. 2/B4
Hawaii (state), U.S. 87/K4
Hawaiian (isls.) 87/J3
Hawaii Kai, Hawaii (96825) 218/F2
Hawaii Nat'l Park, Hawaii (96718) 218/J6
Hawaii Volcanoes Nat'l Park, Hawaii 218/H6
Hawara, Jordan 65/D2
Hawarden, Iowa (51023) 229/A2
Hawarden, N. Zealand 100/D5
Hawarden, Sask. 181/E4
Hawarden, Wales 13/G2
Hawea (lake), N. Zealand 100/B6
Hawera, N. Zealand 100/E3
Hawes, England 13/E3
Hawesville, Ky. (42348) 237/H5
Hawi, Hawaii (96719) 218/G3
Hawick, Minn. (56246) 255/D5
Hawick, Scotland 10/E3
Hawick, Scotland 15/F5
Hawk (hills), Alberta 182/B1
Hawke (hills), Newf. 166/D2
Hawke (isl.), Newf. 166/C3
Hawke (riv.), Newf. 166/C3
Hawke (bay), N. Zealand 100/F3
Hawker, S. Australia 88/F6
Hawker, S. Australia 94/F4
Hawke's Bay, Newf. 166/C3
Hawkesbury (isl.), Br. Col. 184/C3
Hawkesbury, Ontario 177/K2
Hawkestone, Ontario 177/E3
Hawkeye, Iowa (52147) 229/J3
Hawkins, Mich. (†49677) 250/D5
Hawkins (co.), Tenn. 237/P8
Hawkins, Texas (75765) 303/J5
Hawkins, Wis. (54530) 317/E4
Hawkinsville, Georgia (31036) 217/E6
Hawk Junction, Ontario 175/D3
Hawk Junction, Ontario 177/J5
Hawk Point, Mo. (63349) 261/K5
Hawk Run, Pa. (16840) 294/F4
Hawks, Mich. (49743) 250/F3
Hawk Springs, Wyo. (82217) 319/H4
Hawley, Minn. (56549) 255/B4
Hawley, Pa. (18428) 294/M3
Hawley, Texas (79525) 303/E5
Hawleyville, Conn. (06440) 210/B3
Haworth, N.J. (07641) 273/C1
Haworth, Okla. (74740) 288/S7
Hawston, S. Africa 118/G7
Hawthorn, La. (†71446) 238/D4
Hawthorn, Pa. (16230) 294/D3
Hawthorn, Victoria 97/J5
Hawthorne, Calif. (90250) 204/C11
Hawthorne, Fla. (32640) 212/D2
Hawthorne, Nev. (89415) 266/C4
Hawthorne, N.J. (07507) 273/B2
Hawthorne, N.Y. (10532) 276/O6
Hawthorne, Victoria 88/L7
Hawthorne, Wis. (54842) 317/C3
Hawthorn Woods, Ill. (†60047) 222/B5
Haxby, England 13/F3
Haxtun, Colo. (80731) 208/O1
Hay (riv.) 162/E4
Hay (lake), Alberta 182/A5
Hay (riv.), Alberta 182/A5
Hay (riv.), Canada 146/G4
Hay, N. S. Wales 88/H6
Hay, N.S. Wales 97/C4
Hay (dry riv.), North. Terr. 88/F4
Hay (cape), North. Terr. 93/A3
Hay (dry riv.), North. Terr. 93/E7
Hay (lake), Ontario 177/F2

Hérouxville 381

Hay, Wales 10/E4
Hay, Wales 13/D5
Hay, Wash. (99136) 310/H4
Hayama, Japan 81/O3
Hayange, France 28/F3
Haycock, Alaska (†99762) 196/F1
Hayden, Ala. (35079) 195/E3
Hayden, Ariz. (85235) 198/E5
Hayden, Colo. (81639) 208/E2
Hayden, Idaho (†83835) 220/B2
Hayden (lake), Idaho 220/B2
Hayden, Ind. (47245) 227/F7
Hayden, Mo. (†65459) 261/H6
Hayden, N. Mex. (†88410) 274/F3
Hayden (peak), Utah 304/C3
Haydenburg, Tenn. (†38588) 237/K8
Hayden Lake, Idaho (83835) 220/B2
Haydenville, Mass. (01039) 249/C3
Haydenville, Ohio (43127) 284/F7
Hayes (mt.), Alaska 196/J2
Hayes (pen.), Greenl. 4/B13
Hayes, Jamaica 158/J6
Hayes, La. (70646) 238/E6
Hayes (riv.), Man. 162/G4
Hayes (riv.), Manitoba 179/K3
Hayes (co.), Nebr. 264/C4
Hayes (riv.), N.W. Terrs. 187/J3
Hayes, S. Dak. (57537) 298/H5
Hayes, Wis. (†54174) 317/J5
Hayes Center, Nebr. (69032) 264/C4
Hayesville, Iowa (52562) 229/J6
Hayesville, New Bruns. 170/D2
Hayesville, N.C. (28904) 281/B4
Hayesville, Ohio (44838) 284/F4
Hayesville, Oreg. (†97301) 291/A3
Hayfield, Iowa (50445) 229/F2
Hayfield, Minn. (55940) 255/F7
Hayfork, Calif. (96041) 204/B3
Hay Fork, Trinity (riv.), Calif. 204/B3
Hay Lakes, Alberta 182/D3
Hayle, England 13/B7
Haylow, Georgia (†31648) 217/G9
Haymana, Turkey 63/E3
Haymarket, Va. (22069) 307/N3
Hayne, N.C. (†28318) 281/M5
Haynes, Alberta 182/D3
Haynes, Ark. (72341) 202/J4
Haynes, N. Dak. (58637) 282/F8
Haynesville, La. (71038) 238/D1
Haynesville○, Maine (04446) 243/G4
Haynesville, Va. (22472) 307/P5
Hayneville, Ala. (36040) 195/E6
Hayrabolu, Turkey 63/B2
Hay River, N.W.T. 162/E3
Hay River, N.W.T. 146/G3
Hay River, N.W. Terrs. 187/G3
Hays, Alberta 182/E4
Hays, Kansas (67601) 232/C3
Hays, Mont. (59527) 262/H2
Hays, N.C. (28635) 281/G2
Hays (co.), Texas 303/F7
Haysi, Va. (24256) 307/D6
Hay Springs, Nebr. (69347) 264/B2
Haystack (mt.), Conn. 210/C1
Haystack (peak), Mont. 262/A3
Haystack (mt.), N.Y. 276/N2
Haystack (mt.), Vt. 268/B6
Haysville, Ind. (†47546) 227/D8
Haysville, Kansas (67060) 232/E4
Haysville, Pa. (†15143) 294/B4
Hayter, Alberta 182/E3
Hayti, Mo. (63851) 261/N10
Hayti, S. Dak. (57241) 298/P4
Hayti Heights, Mo. (†63851) 261/N10
Hayton, Wis. (†53014) 317/K7
Hayward, Calif. (*94541) 204/K2
Hayward (lake), Conn. 210/F2
Hayward, Minn. (56043) 255/E7
Hayward, Mo. (†63873) 261/N10
Hayward, Wis. (54843) 317/D3
Haywards-Manor Park, N. Zealand 100/B2
Haywood, Manitoba 179/D5
Haywood (co.), N.C. 281/C3
Haywood, N.C. (†27559) 281/L3
Haywood, Okla. (74548) 288/P5
Haywood (co.), Tenn. 237/C9
Haywood City, Mo. (†63736) 261/N9
Hazar (lake), Turkey 63/H3
Hazaran, Kuh-e (mt.), Iran 66/K6
Hazard, Ky. (41701) 237/P6
Hazard, Nebr. (68844) 264/F3
Hazardville, Conn. (06082) 210/E1
Hazaribagh, India 68/F4
Hazar Qadam, Afghanistan 59/J3
Hazar Qadam, Afghanistan 68/B2
Hazebrouck, France 28/E2
Hazel, Ky. (42049) 237/E7
Hazel, S. Dak. (57242) 298/P4
Hazel Cliffe, Sask. 181/J5
Hazel Crest, Ill. (60429) 222/B6
Hazeldean, New Bruns. 170/C2
Hazel Dell, Ill. (62430) 222/E4
Hazel Dell, Sask. 181/H4
Hazeldine, Alberta 182/E3
Hazel Green, Ala. (35750) 195/E1
Hazel Green, Ky. (41332) 237/O5
Hazelgreen, Mo. (†65556) 261/H7
Hazel Green, Wis. (53811) 317/F11
Hazel Grove and Bramhall, England 13/H2
Hazel Hill, Nova Scotia 168/G3
Hazelhurst, Ill. (†61064) 222/D2
Hazel Hurst, Pa. (16733) 294/E2
Hazelhurst, Wis. (54531) 317/G4
Hazel Park, Mich. (48030) 250/B6
Hazel Patch, Ky. (†40729) 237/N6
Hazelridge, Manitoba 179/F5
Hazelrigg, Ind. (†46052) 227/D4
Hazel Run, Minn. (56247) 255/C6
Hazelton, Br. Col. 162/D5
Hazelton, Br. Col. 184/D2
Hazelton (mts.), Br. Col. 184/C2
Hazelton, Idaho (83335) 220/E7
Hazelton, Kansas (67061) 232/D4
Hazelton, N. Dak. (58544) 282/K7
Hazelton, W. Va. (26535) 312*G3
Hazelton (peak), Wyo. 319/E1
Hazelwood, Ind. (†46118) 227/D5
Hazelwood, Mo. (*63042) 261/P2
Hazelwood, N.C. (28738) 281/C4
Hazen (bay), Alaska 196/E2
Hazen, Ark. (72064) 202/G4
Hazen, Nev. (89417) 266/C3
Hazen, N. Dak. (58545) 282/G5
Hazen (lake), N.W. Terrs. 187/L1
Hazen (str.), N.W. Terrs. 187/G2
Hazenmore, Sask. 181/D6
Hazerim, Israel 65/B5
Hazlehurst, Georgia (31539) 217/G7
Hazlehurst, Miss. (39083) 256/D7
Hazlet, N.J. (07730) 273/E3
Hazlet, Sask. 181/C5
Hazleton, Ind. (47640) 227/B8
Hazleton, Iowa (50641) 229/K3
Hazleton, Pa. (18201) 294/L4
Hazlett (lake), W. Australia 88/D4
Hazlettville, Del. (†19953) 245/R4
Hazor Hagelilit, Israel 65/D2
Hazro, Turkey 63/J3
Heacham, England 13/H5
Headford, Ireland 17/C5
Headland, Ala. (36345) 195/H8
Headlee, Ind. (†47960) 227/D3
Head of Amherst, Nova Scotia 168/E3
Head of Bay d'Espoir, Newf. 166/C4
Head of Bight (bay), S. Australia 94/B4
Head of Grassy, Ky. (41145) 237/P4
Head of Island, La. (†70462) 238/L2
Head of Jeddore, Nova Scotia 168/E4
Head of Millstream, New Bruns. 170/E3
Head of Saint Margarets Bay, Nova Scotia 168/E4
Headquarters, Idaho (83534) 220/C3
Headrick, Okla. (73549) 288/H5
Heads, The (prom.), Oreg. 291/C5
Heads of Ayr (cape), Scotland 15/D5
Head Waters, Va. (24442) 307/K4
Heafford Junction, Wis. (54532) 317/G4
Healdsburg, Calif. (95448) 204/B5
Healdton, Okla. (73438) 288/M6
Healdville, Vt. (05147) 268/B5
Healesville, Victoria 97/C5
Healing Springs, Ala. (†36558) 195/B7
Healing Springs, Va. (†24445) 307/J5
Healy, Alaska (99743) 196/H2
Healy, Kansas (67850) 232/B3
Healys, Va. (†23071) 307/R5
Heanor, England 13/F4
Heard (isl.), Australia 2/N8
Heard (co.), Georgia 217/B4
Hearne, Sask. 181/F5
Hearne, Texas (77859) 303/H7
Hearst (isl.) 5/B16
Hearst, Ont. 162/H6
Hearst, Ontario 177/J5
Hearst, Ontario 175/D3
Heart (lake), Alberta 182/E2
Heart (butte), N. Dak. 282/G6
Heart (riv.), N. Dak. 282/F6
Heart (lake), Wyo. 319/B1
Heart Butte, Mont. (59448) 262/C2
Heart River Settlement, Alberta 182/B2
Heart's Content, Newf. 166/D2
Heart's Delight, Newf. 166/D2
Heart's Desire, Newf. 166/D2
Hearts Hill, Sask. 181/B3
Heartwell, Nebr. (68945) 264/F4
Heartwellville, Vt. (†05350) 268/A6
Heaters, W. Va. (26627) 312/E5
Heath, Ala. (†36420) 195/F8
Heath, Alberta 182/E3
Heath (riv.), Bolivia 136/A3
Heath○, Mass. (01346) 249/C2
Heath, Mont. (†59457) 262/G3
Heath, Ohio (43055) 284/F5
Heath (riv.), Peru 128/H9
Heath (pt.), Québec 174/E3
Heathcote, Victoria 97/C5
Heatherton, Newf. 166/C4
Heatherton, Nova Scotia 168/G3
Heathhall, Scotland 15/E5
Heath Springs, S.C. (29058) 296/F2
Heath Steele, New Bruns. 170/D1
Heathsville, Va. (22473) 307/P5
Heaton, N. Dak. (58450) 282/L5
Heavener, Okla. (74937) 288/S5
Hebbardsville, Ky. (†42420) 237/G5
Hebbronville, Texas (78361) 303/F10
Hebbs Cross, Nova Scotia 168/D4
Hebburn, England 13/J3
Hebei (Hopei) (prov.), China 77/J4
Hebel, Queensland 95/C6
Heber, Ariz. (85928) 198/E4
Heber, Calif. (92249) 204/K11
Heber City, Utah (84032) 304/C3
Heber Springs, Ark. (72543) 202/G2
Hebert, La. (71436) 238/G2
Hébert (riv.), Nova Scotia 168/D3
Hébertville, Québec 172/F1
Hébertville-Station, Québec 172/F1
Hebgen (dam), Mont. 262/E6
Hebgen (lake), Mont. 262/E6
Hebi, China 77/H4
Hebo, Oreg. (97122) 291/D2
Hebrides, Inner (isls.), Scotland 10/C2
Hebrides, Inner (isls.), Scotland 15/B4
Hebrides, Outer (isls.), Scotland 10/C2
Hebrides, Outer (isls.), Scotland 15/A3
Hebrides (sea), Scotland 15/B3
Hebrides (sea), Scotland 10/C2
Hebron○, Conn. (06248) 210/F2
Hebron, Ill. (60034) 222/E1
Hebron, Ind. (46341) 227/C2
Hebron, Ky. (41048) 237/R2
Hebron○, Maine (04238) 243/C7
Hebron, Md. (21830) 245/R7
Hebron, Nebr. (68370) 264/G4
Hebron, Newf. 146/M4
Hebron, Newf. 162/K4
Hebron (fjord), Newf. 166/B2
Hebron○, N.H. (03241) 268/D4
Hebron, N. Dak. (58638) 282/G6
Hebron, Nova Scotia 168/B5
Hebron, Ohio (43025) 284/E6
Hebron, Texas (†75067) 303/G1
Hebron, West Bank 65/C4
Hebron, West Bank 59/C3
Hebron, W. Va. (26368) 312/D4
Hebron, Wis. (†53538) 317/J10
Hecate (str.), Br. Col. 162/C5
Hecate (str.), Br. Col. 146/E4
Hecate (str.), Br. Col. 184/B3
Hecelchakán, Mexico 150/O6
Heceta (isl.), Alaska 196/M2
Heceta (head), Oreg. 291/C3
Hechi, China 77/G7
Hechingen, W. Germany 22/C4
Hechuan (Hochwan), China 77/G5
Hecker, Ill. (62248) 222/D5
Hecla, Manitoba 179/F3
Hecla (isl.), Manitoba 179/F3
Hecla, S. Dak. (57446) 298/N2
Hecla Prov. Park, Manitoba 179/F3
Hector, Ark. (72843) 202/E3
Hector, Minn. (55342) 255/D6
Hector, N.Y. (14841) 276/G5
Hede, Sweden 18/H5
Hedemora, Sweden 18/K6
Hedenäset, Sweden 18/N3
Hedensted, Denmark 21/C6
Hedgesville, Mont. (†59078) 262/G4
Hedgesville, W. Va. (25427) 312/K3
Hedley, Br. Col. 184/G5
Hedley, Texas (79237) 303/D3
Hedmark (co.), Norway 18/G6
Hedon, England 13/G4
Hedrick, Iowa (52563) 229/J6
Hedville, Kansas (†67401) 232/E3
Hedwig Village, Texas (†77001) 303/H1
Heemskerk, Netherlands 27/F3
Heemstede, Netherlands 27/F4
Heer, Netherlands 27/H7
Heerde, Netherlands 27/H4
Heerenveen, Netherlands 27/H3
Heerhugowaard, Netherlands 27/F3
Heerlen, Netherlands 27/J7
Heesch, Netherlands 27/G5
Hefei (Hofei), China 77/J5
Hefei, China 54/N6
Heffley Creek, Br. Col. 184/G5
Heflin, Ala. (36264) 195/G3
Heflin, La. (71039) 238/D2
Hegang (Hokang), China 77/L2
Hegang, China 54/O5
Hegau (reg.), W. Germany 22/C5
Hegeler, Ill. (†61832) 222/F3
Hegins, Pa. (17938) 294/K4
Heiban, Sudan 111/F5
Heiberger, Ala. (†36756) 195/D5
Heide, W. Germany 22/C1
Heidelberg, Ky. (41333) 237/O5
Heidelberg, Minn. (†56071) 255/E6
Heidelberg, Miss. (39439) 256/F7
Heidelberg, Pa. (15106) 294/B7
Heidelberg, S. Africa 118/J7
Heidelberg, Victoria 97/J5
Heidelberg, Victoria 88/L7
Heidelberg, W. Germany 22/C4
Heiden, Switzerland 39/H2
Heidenau, E. Germany 22/E3
Heidenheim an der Brenz, W. Germany 22/D4
Heidenreichstein, Austria 41/C2
Heidrick, Ky. (40949) 237/O7
Heihe (Aihui) (Aigun), China 77/L1
Heijo (P'yŏngyang) (cap.), N. Korea 81/C4
Heil, N. Dak. (58546) 282/G7
Heilbron, S. Africa 118/D5
Heilbronn, W. Germany 22/C4
Heiligenblut, Austria 41/B3
Heiligenhafen, W. Germany 22/D1
Heiligenstadt, E. Germany 22/D3
Heilman, Ind. (†47523) 227/C8
Heilongjiang (Heilungkiang) (prov.), China 77/K2
Heilong Jiang (Amur) (riv.), China 77/L2
Heiloo, Netherlands 27/F3
Heilwood, Pa. (15745) 294/E4
Heimberg, Switzerland 39/E3
Heimdal, N. Dak. (58342) 282/L4
Heinola, Finland 18/P6
Heinola, Minn. (†56567) 255/C4
Heinsburg, Alberta 182/E3
Heinze Chaung (bay), Burma 72/C4
Heise, Idaho (†83443) 220/G6
Heiskell, Tenn. (37754) 237/O8
Heisler, Alberta 182/D3
Heislerville, N.J. (08324) 273/D5
Heisson, Wash. (98622) 310/C5
Heist-Knokke, Belgium 27/C6
Heist-op-den-Berg, Belgium 27/F6
Heizer, Kansas (†67530) 232/D3
Hejaz (reg.), Saudi Arabia 59/C4
Hejian, China 77/J4
Hejing, China 77/C3
Hekimhan, Turkey 63/G3
Hekla (mt.), Iceland 4/C11
Hekla (mt.), Iceland 7/C2
Hekla (vol.), Iceland 21/B1
Hekou, China 77/F7
Hel, Poland 47/D1
Hel (pen.), Poland 47/D1
Helan, China 77/G4
Heldens (pt.), St. Chris.-Nevis 161/C10
Helechawa, Ky. (41334) 237/P5
Helen, Georgia (30545) 217/E1
Helen, Md. (20635) 245/M7
Helen (lake), N. Dak. 282/K5
Helena, Ala. (35080) 195/E4
Helena, Ark. (72342) 202/J4
Helena, Calif. (96042) 204/B3
Helena, Georgia (31037) 217/G6
Helena, Mo. (64459) 261/C3
Helena (cap.), Mont. 146/G5
Helena (cap.), Mont. 188/D1
Helena (cap.), Mont. (59601) 262/E4
Helena (lake), Mont. 262/E4
Helena, N.Y. (13649) 276/L1
Helena, Ohio (43435) 284/D3
Helena, Okla. (73741) 288/K1
Helena, S.C. (†29108) 296/D3
Helensburgh, N.S. Wales 97/F4
Helensburgh, Scotland 10/A1
Helensburgh, Scotland 15/A1
Helen Springs, North. Terr. 93/C5
Helensville, N. Zealand 100/B1
Helenville, Wis. (53137) 317/J10
Helenwood, Tenn. (37755) 237/M8
Helez, Israel 65/B4
Helgoland (bay), W. Germany 22/C1
Helgoland (isl.), W. Germany 22/B1
Heliopolis, Egypt 111/J3
Helix, Oreg. (97835) 291/J2
Hellam, Pa. (17406) 294/J6
Hell Canyon (creek), S. Dak. 298/B6
Hellebaek, Denmark 21/F5
Hellendoorn, Netherlands 27/J4
Hellertown, Pa. (18055) 294/M4
Helles (cape), Turkey 63/B6
Hellevoetsluis, Netherlands 27/E5
Hellier, Ky. (41534) 237/S6
Hellín, Spain 33/F3
Hells (canyon), Idaho 220/B4
Hells Canyon (dam), Idaho 220/B4
Hells Canyon (dam), Oreg. 291/L2
Hells Canyon Nat'l Rec. Area, Idaho 220/B4
Hells Canyon Nat'l Rec. Area, Oreg. 291/K2
Hells Canyon Nat'l Rec. Area, Wash. 310/H5
Hells Half Acre, Wyo. (82601) 319/E2
Hell-Ville, Madagascar 102/G6
Hell-Ville, Madagascar 118/H2
Helm, Miss. (†38756) 256/C4
Helmand (riv.), Afghanistan 54/H6
Helmand (riv.), Afghanistan 59/J3
Helmand (riv.), Afghanistan 68/B2
Helmand (Sistan, Daryacheh-ye) (lake), Iran 66/M5
Helmer, Ind. (46744) 227/G1
Helmetta, N.J. (08828) 273/E3
Helmond, Netherlands 27/H6
Helmsburg, Ind. (47435) 227/E6
Helmsdale, Scotland 10/E1
Helmsdale, Scotland 15/E2
Helmsdale (riv.), Scotland 15/E2
Helmsley, England 13/G3
Helmstedt, W. Germany 22/D2
Helmville, Mont. (59843) 262/C4
Helotes, Texas (78023) 303/J10
Helper, Utah (84526) 304/D4
Helsenhorn (mt.), Switzerland 39/F4
Helsingborg, Sweden 18/H8
Helsingborg, Sweden 7/F3
Helsinge, Denmark 21/F6
Helsingør, Denmark 21/F6
Helsingør, Denmark 18/H8
Helsinki (cap.), Finland 18/O6
Helsinki (cap.), Finland 7/G2
Helsinki (cap.), Finland 2/L2
Helston, England 13/B7
Helston, England 10/D5
Helston, Manitoba 179/C4
Helton, Ky. (40840) 237/P7
Helton, N.C. (†28631) 281/G1
Heltonville, Ind. (47436) 227/E7
Helvecia, Argentina 143/F5
Helvetia, Pa. (†15848) 294/E3
Helvetia, W. Va. (26224) 312/F5
Helvick (head), Ireland 17/G7
Helwân, Egypt 59/B4
Helwân, Egypt 111/J3
Hemar (dry riv.), Israel 65/C5
Hemaruka, Alberta 182/E4
Hematite, Mo. (63047) 261/L6
Hemel Hempstead, England 10/F5
Hemel Hempstead, England 13/G7
Hemet, Calif. (92343) 204/H10
Hemford, Nova Scotia 168/C4
Hemingford, Nebr. (69348) 264/A2
Hemingway, S.C. (29554) 296/J4
Hemlock, Ind. (46937) 227/F4
Hemlock, Mich. (48626) 250/E5
Hemlock, N.Y. (14466) 276/E5
Hemlock (lake), N.Y. 276/E5
Hemlock, Ohio (43743) 284/F6
Hemlock (Eureka), S.C. (†29706) 296/E2
Hemlock Grove, Ohio (45738) 284/F7
Hemmingford, Québec 172/D4
Hemnes, Norway 18/J3
Hemphill (co.), Texas 303/D2
Hemphill, Texas (75948) 303/L6
Hemphill, W. Va. (24842) 312/C8
Hemple, Mo. (†64490) 261/D3
Hempstead (co.), Ark. 202/C6
Hempstead, N.Y. (*11550) 276/R7
Hempstead, Texas (77445) 303/J7
Hemse, Sweden 18/L8
Henagar, Ala. (35978) 195/G1
Henan (Honan) (prov.), China 77/H5
Henan, China 77/F5
Hen and Chickens (isls.), N. Zealand 100/E1
Henares (riv.), Spain 33/G4
Henbury, North. Terr. 93/C8
Hendaye, France 28/C6
Hendek, Turkey 63/D2
Henderson, Ala. (†36035) 195/F7
Henderson (co.), Ill. 222/C3
Henderson, Ill. (61439) 222/C2
Henderson (riv.), Ill. 222/C2
Henderson, Ind. (†46173) 227/F5
Henderson, Iowa (51541) 229/B6
Henderson (co.), Ky. 237/F5
Henderson, Ky. (42420) 237/F5
Henderson, La. (†70517) 238/G6
Henderson, Md. (21640) 245/P4
Henderson, Minn. (56044) 255/E6
Henderson, Nebr. (68371) 264/G4
Henderson, Nev. (89015) 266/G6
Henderson, N.Y. (13650) 276/H3
Henderson, N. Zealand 100/B1
Henderson (co.), N.C. 281/D4
Henderson, N.C. (27536) 281/N2
Henderson (isl.), Pitcairn Is. 87/O8
Henderson (co.), Tenn. 237/E9
Henderson, Tenn. (38340) 237/D10
Henderson (co.), Texas 303/J5
Henderson, Texas (75652) 303/K5
Henderson, W. Va. (25106) 312/B5
Hendersonville, N.C. (28739) 281/E4
Hendersonville, Pa. (15339) 294/B5
Hendersonville, S.C. (†29945) 296/F6
Hendersonville, Tenn. (37075) 237/H8
Hendley, Nebr. (68946) 264/D4
Hendon, Sask. 181/H3
Hendorabi (isl.), Iran 66/H7
Hendra, Queensland 88/K2
Hendricks (co.), Ind. 227/D5
Hendricks, Ky. (41441) 237/P5
Hendricks, Minn. (56136) 255/B6
Hendricks, W. Va. (26271) 312/G4
Hendrickson, Mo. (†63967) 261/M9
Hendrix, Okla. (74741) 288/O7
Hendrix Lake, Br. Col. 184/G4
Hendrum, Minn. (56550) 255/B3
Hendry (co.), Fla. 212/E5
Hendrysburg, Ohio (43744) 284/H5
Henefer, Utah (84033) 304/C2
Hengchun, China 77/K7
Hengduan Shan (mts.), China 77/E6
Hengelo, Gelderland, Netherlands 27/J4
Hengelo, Overijssel, Netherlands 27/K4
Hengshan, China 77/G4
Hengshui, China 77/J4
Heng Xian, China 77/G7
Hengyang, China 77/H6
Hengyang, China 54/N7
Henik (lakes), N.W. Terrs. 187/J3
Hénin-Beaumont, France 28/E2
Henjam (isl.), Iran 66/J7
Henlawson, W. Va. (25624) 312/B7
Henley, Mo. (65040) 261/H6
Henley and Grange, S. Australia 88/D8
Henley Harbour, Newf. 166/C3
Henley on Klip, S. Africa 118/H7
Henley-on-Thames, England 13/G8
Henlopen (cape), Del. 245/T5
Henlopen Acres, Del. (†19971) 245/T6
Henne, Denmark 21/B6
Hennebont, France 28/B4
Hennef, W. Germany 22/B3
Hennepin, Ill. (61327) 222/D2
Hennepin (co.), Minn. 255/E5
Hennepin, Okla. (73046) 288/M5
Hennessey, Okla. (73742) 288/L2
Hennigsdorf bei Berlin, E. Germany 22/E3
Henniker, N.H. (03242) 268/D5
Henniker○, N.H. (03242) 268/D5
Henning, Ill. (61848) 222/F3
Henning, Minn. (56551) 255/C4
Henning, Tenn. (38041) 237/B9
Henribourg, Sask. 181/F2
Henrico (co.), Va. 307/O6
Henrietta, Mo. (64036) 261/E4
Henrietta, N.Y. (14467) 276/E4
Henrietta, N.C. (28076) 281/F4
Henrietta, Texas (76365) 303/F4
Henrietta Maria (cape), Ont. 162/H4
Henrietta Maria (cape), Ontario 175/D1
Henriette, Minn. (55036) 255/E5
Henrieville, Utah (84736) 304/C6
Henry (co.), Ala. 195/H7
Henry (co.), Georgia 217/D4
Henry, Idaho (†83230) 220/G7
Henry (co.), Ill. 222/C2
Henry, Ill. (61537) 222/D2
Henry (co.), Ind. 227/G5
Henry (co.), Iowa 229/K6
Henry (co.), Ky. 237/L4
Henry (co.), Mo. 261/E6
Henry, Nebr. (69349) 264/A2
Henry (isl.), Nova Scotia 168/G3
Henry (co.), Ohio 284/B3
Henry, S.C. (†29554) 296/J4
Henry, S. Dak. (57243) 298/P4
Henry (co.), Tenn. 237/E8
Henry, Tenn. (38231) 237/E8
Henry (mts.), Utah 304/D6
Henry (co.), Va. 307/J7
Henry, Va. (24102) 307/J7
Henry (cape), Va. 307/R7
Henryetta, Okla. (74437) 288/O4
Henry House, Alberta 182/B3
Henry Kater (cape), N.W. Terrs. 187/M3
Henrys (lake), Idaho 220/G5
Henrys Fork, Snake (riv.), Idaho 220/G5
Henrys Fork, Green (riv.), Wyo. 319/C4
Henryton, Md. (21080) 245/L3
Henryville, Ind. (47126) 227/F7
Henryville, Pa. (18332) 294/M3
Henryville, Québec 172/D4
Henryville, Tenn. (†38483) 237/G10
Hensall, Ontario 177/C4
Hensel, N. Dak. (58241) 282/P2
Henshaw, Ky. (†42459) 237/F5
Hensies, Belgium 27/D8
Hensler, N. Dak. (58547) 282/H5
Hensley, Ark. (72065) 202/F4
Henson (creek), Md. 245/F6
Hentiy, Mongolia 77/H2
Henty, N.S. Wales 97/D4
Henzada, Burma 72/B3
Henzada, Burma 54/L8
Hepburn, Iowa (†51632) 229/C7
Hepburn, Ohio (†43326) 284/D4
Hepburn, Sask. 181/E3
Hephzibah, Georgia (30815) 217/H4
Hepler, Kansas (66746) 232/H4
Heppner, Oreg. (97836) 291/H2
Hepu (Hoppo), China 77/G7
Hepworth, Ontario 177/C3
Hepzibah, W. Va. (26369) 312/F4
Hequ, China 77/H4
Herald, Calif. (95638) 204/C9
Heralds (cays), 95/D3
Herat, Afghanistan 54/H6
Herat, Afghanistan 59/H3
Herat, Afghanistan 68/A2
Hérault (dept.), France 28/E6
Hérault (riv.), France 28/E6
Herbert, Ala. (†36401) 195/E8
Herbert (riv.), Queensland 88/H3
Herbert, Sask. 181/D5
Herbert Hoover Nat'l Hist. Site, Iowa 229/L5
Herbes (isl.), Ala. 195/B10
Herbeumont, Belgium 27/G9
Herb Lake, Manitoba 179/H3
Herborn, W. Germany 22/C3
Herbst, Ind. (†46952) 227/F3
Herbster, Wis. (54844) 317/D2
Herceg Novi, Yugoslavia 45/D4
Herchmer, Man. 162/G4
Herchmer, Manitoba 179/K2
Herculaneum, Mo. (63048) 261/M6
Hercules, Calif. (94547) 204/J1
Herd, Okla. (†74056) 288/O1
Heredia, C. Rica 154/E5
Hereford, Ariz. (85615) 198/E7
Hereford, Colo. (80732) 208/L1
Hereford, England 13/E5
Hereford, England 10/E4
Hereford, Md. (†21111) 245/M2
Hereford (inlet), N.J. 273/D5
Hereford, Oreg. (97837) 291/K3
Hereford, Pa. (18056) 294/L5
Hereford, S. Dak. (57743) 298/D5
Hereford, Texas (79045) 303/B3
Hereford and Worcester (co.), England 13/E5
Hérémence, Switzerland 39/D4
Herencia, Spain 33/E3
Herentals, Belgium 27/F6
Heretaunga-Pinehaven, N. Zealand 100/C2
Herford, W. Germany 22/C2
Hergiswil, Switzerland 39/F3
Héricourt, France 28/G4
Heringsdorf, E. Germany 22/F1
Herington, Kansas (67449) 232/E3
Heriot Bay, Br. Col. 184/E5
Herisau, Switzerland 39/H2
Herkimer, Kansas (66433) 232/F2
Herkimer (co.), N.Y. 276/L4
Herkimer, N.Y. (13350) 276/L4
Herlen Gol (Kerulen) (riv.), Mongolia 77/H2
Herlong, Calif. (96113) 204/E3
Herm (isl.), Chan. Is. 13/E8
Hermagor-Preseggersee, Austria 41/B3
Herman, Mich. (†49946) 250/A2
Herman, Minn. (56248) 255/B5
Herman, Nebr. (68029) 264/H3
Herman, Pa. (16039) 294/C4
Herman (lake), S. Dak. 298/P5
Herma Ness (prom.), Scotland 15/G2
Hermann, Mo. (65041) 261/K5
Hermannsburg, North. Terr. 88/E4
Hermannsburg, North. Terr. 93/C7
Hermansverk, Norway 18/E6
Hermansville, Mich. (49847) 250/B3
Hermantown, Minn. (†55811) 255/F4
Hermanus, S. Africa 118/G7
Hermanville, Miss. (39086) 256/C7
Hermidale, N.S. Wales 97/D2
Hermil, Lebanon 63/G5
Herminie, Pa. (15637) 294/C5
Hermiston, Oreg. (97838) 291/H2
Hermitage, Ark. (71647) 202/F7
Hermitage, Grenada 161/D8
Hermitage, Mo. (65668) 261/F7
Hermitage, Newf. 166/C4
Hermitage (bay), Newf. 166/C4
Hermitage Springs, Tenn. (†37150) 237/K7
Hermite (isls.), Chile 138/F11
Hermleigh, Texas (79526) 303/D5
Hermon, Ill. (†61458) 222/C3
Hermon○, Maine (†04401) 243/F6
Hermon, N.Y. (13652) 276/K2
Hermon (mt.), Syria 63/F6
Hermosa (peak), Colo. 208/D7
Hermosa, S. Dak. (57744) 298/C6
Hermosa Beach, Calif. (90254) 204/B11
Hermosillo, Mexico 146/G7
Hermosillo, Mexico 150/D2
Hermsdorf, W. Germany 22/E3
Hernád (riv.), Hungary 41/F2
Hernandarias, Argentina 143/F5
Hernandarias, Paraguay 144/E4
Hernández, Argentina 143/F6
Hernandez, N. Mex. (87537) 274/C2
Hernando, Argentina 143/D3
Hernando (co.), Fla. 212/D3
Hernando, Fla. (32642) 212/D3
Hernando, Miss. (38632) 256/E1
Herndon, Georgia (†30442) 217/H5
Herndon, Iowa (†50128) 229/E5
Herndon, Kansas (67739) 232/B2
Herndon, Ky. (42236) 237/G7
Herndon, Pa. (17830) 294/J4
Herndon, Va. (*22070) 307/O3
Herndon, W. Va. (24726) 312/D7
Herne, Belgium 27/E7
Herne, W. Germany 22/B3
Herning, Denmark 18/F8
Herning, Denmark 21/B5
Herod, Georgia (†31742) 217/D7
Herod, Ill. (62947) 222/E6
Heroica Caborca, Mexico 150/C1
Heroica Nogales, Mexico 150/D1
Heron (lake), Minn. 255/C7
Heron, Mont. (59844) 262/A2
Heron (isl.), New Bruns. 170/D1
Heron Bay, Ontario 177/H5
Heron Bay, Ontario 175/C3
Heron Lake, Minn. (56137) 255/C7
Hérouxville, Québec 172/E3

382 Herowabad

Herowabad, Iran 66/F2
Herradura, Argentina 143/E2
Herradura, Cuba 158/B1
Herreid, S. Dak. (57632) 298/K2
Herrera, Argentina 143/D2
Herrera del Duque, Spain 33/D3
Herrera de Pisuerga, Spain 33/D1
Herrero (pt.), Mexico 150/Q7
Herrick, Ill. (62431) 222/D4
Herrick, S. Dak. (57538) 298/L7
Herrick, Tasmania 99/D3
Herrick Center, Pa. (18430) 294/L2
Herrin, Ill. (62948) 222/E6
Herring Cove, Nova Scotia 168/E4
Herrings, N.Y. (13653) 276/J2
Herrington (lake), Ky. 237/M5
Herron, Mich. (49744) 250/F3
Herronton, Alberta 182/D4
Hersbruck, W. Germany 22/D4
Herschel, Sask. 181/C4
Herschel (isl.), Yukon 187/E3
Herscher, Ill. (60941) 222/E2
Herselt, Belgium 27/F6
Hersey, Mich. (49639) 250/D5
Hersey, Wis. (†54027) 317/B6
Hershey, Nebr. (69143) 264/D3
Hershey, Pa. (17033) 294/J5
Hersman, Ill. (†62353) 222/C4
Herstal, Belgium 27/H7
Hertel, Wis. (54845) 317/B4
Hertford, England 13/H7
Hertford, England 10/G5
Hertford (co.), N.C. 281/P2
Hertford, N.C. (27944) 281/S2
Hertfordshire (co.), England 13/G6
Hervás, Spain 33/D2
Herve, Belgium 27/H7
Hervey Bay, Queensland 88/J5
Hervey Bay, Queensland 95/E5
Hervey (bay), Queensland 88/J4
Hervey (bay), Queensland 95/E5
Herzberg, E. Germany 22/E3
Herzeliyya, Israel 65/B3
Herzogenbuchsee, Switzerland 39/E2
Herzogenburg, Austria 41/C2
Heshui, China 77/G4
Hesketh, Alberta 182/D4
Hesper, Iowa (†52101) 229/K2
Hesper, N. Dak. (†58348) 282/L4
Hesperange, Luxembourg 27/J9
Hesperia, Calif. (92345) 204/H9
Hesperia, Mich. (49421) 250/D5
Hespero, Alberta 182/C3
Hesperus, Colo. (81326) 208/C8
Hesperus (mt.), Colo. 208/C8
Hess, Okla. (†73539) 288/H6
Hess (riv.), Yukon 187/E3
Hesse (state), W. Germany 22/C3
Hessel, Mich. (49745) 250/E2
Hessmer, La. (71341) 238/F4
Hesston, Kansas (67062) 232/E3
Hesston, Pa. (16647) 294/F5
Hester, La. (70743) 238/L3
Hester, Okla. (†73554) 288/H5
Hesterville, Miss. (†39192) 256/E4
Hetch Hetchy (res.), Calif. 204/F6
Heth, Ark. (72346) 202/K3
Het IJ (est.), Netherlands 27/C4
Hetland, S. Dak. (57244) 298/P5
Hettick, Ill. (62649) 222/C4
Hettinger (co.), N. Dak. 282/E7
Hettinger, N. Dak. (58639) 282/E8
Hetton, England 13/J3
Hettstedt, E. Germany 22/D3
Heusden, Netherlands 27/G5
Heuvelland, Belgium 27/B7
Heuvelton, N.Y. (13654) 276/K1
Heves (co.), Hungary 41/F3
Heves, Hungary 41/F3
Heward, Sask. 181/H6
Hewins, Kansas (67024) 232/F4
Hewitt, Minn. (56453) 255/C4
Hewitt, N.J. (07421) 273/E1
Hewitt, Wis. (54441) 317/F6
Hewlett, N.Y. (11557) 276/P7
Hewlett Harbor, N.Y. (†11557) 276/P7
Hexham, England 13/E3
Hexham, England 10/E3
He Xian, China 77/H7
Hexigten, China 77/J3
Hext, Texas (76848) 303/E7
Heybeli (isl.), Turkey 63/D6
Heybridge, Tasmania 99/C3
Heyburn, Idaho (83336) 220/E7
Heyburn (res.), Okla. 288/O3
Heyden, Ontario 177/J5
Heyfield, Victoria 97/D6
Heyuan, China 77/H7
Heywood (chan.), Burma 72/B3
Heywood, England 13/H2
Heywood, Victoria 97/A6
Heyworth, Ill. (61745) 222/E3
Heze, China 77/J4
Hezuo, China 77/F5
Hialeah, Fla. 188/K5
Hialeah, Fla. (*33010) 212/B4
Hialeah Gardens, Fla. (†33010) 212/B4
Hiattville, Kansas (66747) 232/H4
Hiawassee, Georgia (30546) 217/E1
Hiawatha, Iowa (52233) 229/K4
Hiawatha, Kansas (66434) 232/G2
Hiawatha, Mich. (†49854) 250/C2
Hiawatha, Utah (84527) 304/D4
Hibbard, Ind. (†46511) 227/E2
Hibbing, Minn. 188/H1
Hibbing, Minn. (55746) 255/F3
Hibbs (pt.), Tasmania 99/B4
Hibernia, N.J. (07842) 273/E2
Hibuson (isl.), Philippines 82/E5
Hicacos (pen.), Cuba 158/D1
Hicacos (pt.), Cuba 158/D1
Hickam A.F.B., Hawaii 218/B4
Hickam Housing, Hawaii (96824) 218/B4
Hickman, Ark. (†72315) 202/L2
Hickman, Del. (†21629) 245/R5
Hickman (co.), Ky. 237/C7
Hickman, Ky. (42050) 237/C7
Hickman, Nebr. (68372) 264/H4
Hickman (co.), Tenn. 237/G9
Hickman, Tenn. (38567) 237/K8
Hickman's Harbour, Newf. 166/D2
Hickok, Kansas (†67880) 232/A4
Hickory, Ky. (42051) 237/D7
Hickory, Miss. (39332) 256/F6
Hickory (co.), Mo. 261/F7
Hickory, N.C. (28601) 281/G3
Hickory, Okla. (†73086) 288/N5
Hickory Corners, Mich. (49060) 250/D6
Hickory Creek, Texas (†75423) 303/F1
Hickory Flat, Ala. (†36274) 195/H4
Hickory Flat, Miss. (38633) 256/F1
Hickory Grove, S.C. (29717) 296/E2
Hickory Hills, Ill. (60457) 222/B6
Hickory Plains, Ark. (72066) 202/G3
Hickory Ridge, Ark. (72347) 202/J3
Hickory Valley, Tenn. (38042) 237/C10
Hickory Withe, Tenn. (38043) 237/B10
Hickox, Georgia (†31553) 217/H8
Hicks, La. (71437) 238/E4
Hickson, N. Dak. (†58047) 282/S6
Hickson, Ontario 177/D4
Hicksville, N.Y. (*11801) 276/R7
Hicksville, Ohio (43526) 284/A3
Hico, La. (†71235) 238/E1
Hico, Texas (76457) 303/F6
Hico, W. Va. (25854) 312/D6
Hida (riv.), Japan 81/H6
Hidalgo, Ill. (62432) 222/E4
Hidalgo, Ky. (42622) 237/M7
Hidalgo (state), Mexico 150/K6
Hidalgo, Coahuila, Mexico 150/K3
Hidalgo, Tamaulipas, Mexico 150/K4
Hidalgo (co.), N. Mex. 274/A7
Hidalgo (co.), Texas 303/F11
Hidalgo, Texas (78557) 303/F11
Hidalgo del Parral (Parral), Mexico 150/G3
Hidden Hills, Calif. (†91302) 204/B10
Hiddenite, N.C. (28636) 281/G3
Hiddensee (isl.), E. Germany 22/E1
Hieflau, Austria 41/C3
Hienghene, New Caled. 86/G4
Hierro (isl.), Spain 106/A3
Hierro (isl.), Spain 33/A5
Higashiosaka, Japan 81/J8
Higbee, Mo. (65257) 261/H4
Higden, Ark. (72067) 202/F2
Higdon, Ala. (35979) 195/G1
Higganum, Conn. (06441) 210/E2
Higgins (lake), Mich. 250/E4
Higgins, Texas (79046) 303/D1
Higgins Lake, Mich. (48627) 250/E4
Higginson, Ark. (72068) 202/G3
Higginsport, Ohio (45131) 284/C8
Higginsville, Mo. (64037) 261/E4
Higgston, Georgia (†30410) 217/G6
High, Iowa (†52203) 229/K5
High (isl.), Ireland 17/A4
High (isl.), Mich. 250/D3
High Atlas (ranges), Morocco 106/C2
High Bluff, Manitoba 179/D4
High Bridge, Ky. (40333) 237/M5
High Bridge, N.J. (08829) 273/D2
High Bridge, Wis. (54846) 317/E3
Highbury, W. Australia 92/B2
High Falls, N.Y. (12440) 276/M7
Highfalls, N.C. (27259) 281/K4
Highfield-Cascade, Md. (21753) 245/J2
Highfill, Ark. (†72734) 202/B1
Highgate, Jamaica 158/J6
Highgate, Ontario 177/C5
Highgate○, Vt. (†05459) 268/B2
Highgate Center, Vt. (05459) 268/B2
Highgate Falls, Vt. (†05459) 268/A2
Highgate Springs, Vt. (05460) 268/A2
Highgrove, Calif. (92507) 204/E10
High Hill, Mo. (63350) 261/K5
High Island, Texas (77623) 303/K8
Highland, Calif. (92346) 204/H9
Highland (lake), Conn. 210/C1
Highland (pt.), Fla. 212/E6
Highland, Ill. (62249) 222/D5
Highland, Ind. (46322) 227/B1
Highland, Kansas (66035) 232/G2
Highland (peak), Nev. 266/G5
Highland (lake), N.H. 268/C5
Highland, N.Y. (12528) 276/M7
Highland (co.), Ohio 284/C7
Highland, Ohio (45132) 284/C7
Highland (reg.), Scotland 15/D3
Highland, Utah (†84043) 304/C3
Highland (co.), Va. 307/J4
Highland, W. Va. (†26346) 312/D4
Highland, Wis. (53543) 317/F9
Highland Beach, Fla. (33431) 212/F5
Highland Beach, Md. (†21401) 245/M5
Highland Center, Iowa (52564) 229/J6
Highland City, Fla. (33846) 212/E4
Highland Falls, N.Y. (10928) 276/M8
Highland Heights, Ky. (41076) 237/T2
Highland Heights, Ohio (†44143) 284/J9
Highland Home, Ala. (36041) 195/F7
Highland Lake, Ala. (†35013) 195/F3
Highland Lake, Maine (†04082) 243/C8
Highland Lakes, N.J. (07422) 273/E1
Highland Park, Conn. (†06040) 210/F1
Highland Park, Fla. (32401) 212/E4
Highland Park, Ill. (60035) 222/B5
Highland Park, Mich. (48203) 250/B6
Highland Park, N.J. (08904) 273/D2
Highland Park, Pa. (†17044) 294/H4
Highland Park, Texas (†75201) 303/G2
Highlands (co.), Fla. 212/E4
Highlands, N.J. (07732) 273/F3
Highlands, N.C. (28741) 281/C4
Highlands, Texas (77562) 303/K1
Highland Springs, Va. (23075) 307/O5
Highland Village, Texas (†75205) 303/F1
Highlandville, Iowa (52149) 229/K2
Highlandville, Mo. (65669) 261/F9
High Level, Alberta 182/A5
Highmore, S. Dak. (57345) 298/L4
Highpine, Maine (†04090) 243/B9
High Plateaus (ranges), Algeria 106/D2
High Point, Fla. (†33515) 212/B3
Highpoint, Miss. (†39339) 256/F4
High Point, Mo. (65042) 261/G5
High Point (mt.), N.J. 273/D1
High Point, N.C. 188/K3
High Point, N.C. (*27260) 281/J3
High Prairie, Alberta 182/B2
Highridge, Alberta 182/D2
High Ridge, Mo. (63049) 261/M6
High River, Alberta 182/D4
High River, Alta. 162/E5
High Rock (creek), Nev. 266/B1
High Rock, N.C. (27239) 281/J3
High Rock (lake), N.C. 281/J3
High Rocky (pt.), Tasmania 99/B4
High Rolls-Mountain Park, N. Mex. (88325) 274/D5
High Shoals, N.C. (28077) 281/G4
Highspire, Pa. (17034) 294/J5
Highsplint, Ky. (†40828) 237/P7
High Springs, Fla. (32643) 212/D2
High Tatra (range), Poland 47/D4
Hightower, Ala. (†36264) 195/H3
Hightown, Va. (24444) 307/J4
Hightstown, N.J. (08520) 273/D3
Highway, Ky. (†42602) 237/L7
High Willhays (mt.), England 13/C7
Highwood (riv.), Alberta 182/C4
Highwood, Ill. (60040) 222/B5
Highwood, Mont. (59450) 262/F3
Highworth, England 13/F6
High Wycombe, England 13/G8
High Wycombe, England 10/F5
Higley, Ariz. (85236) 198/D5
Higuerote, Venezuela 124/F2
Higüey, Dom. Rep. 158/F6
Hiiraan (prov.), Somalia 115/J3
Hiiumaa (isl.), U.S.S.R. 7/G3
Hiiumaa (isl.), U.S.S.R. 52/B3
Hiiumaa (isl.), U.S.S.R. 53/B1
Hiiumaa (isl.), U.S.S.R. 48/C4
Híjar, Spain 33/F2
Hijuelas, Chile 138/F2
Hiko, Nev. (89017) 266/F5
Hikone, Japan 81/H6
Hikueru (atoll), Fr. Poly. 87/M7
Hikurangi, N. Zealand 100/E1
Hikurangi (mt.), N. Zealand 100/G2
Hiland, Wyo. (82638) 319/E2
Hiland Park, Fla. (32405) 212/C6
Hilbert, Wis. (54129) 317/K7
Hilbre, Manitoba 179/D3
Hilda, Alberta 182/E4
Hilda, S.C. (29813) 296/E5
Hildburghausen, E. Germany 22/D3
Hildebran, N.C. (28637) 281/F3
Hildebrand, Oreg. (†97625) 291/F5
Hilden, Nova Scotia 168/E3
Hildesheim, W. Germany 22/D2
Hildreth, Nebr. (68947) 264/E4
Hiles, Wis. (†54511) 317/J4
Hilgard (mt.), Utah 304/C5
Hilger, Mont. (59451) 262/G3
Hilham, Tenn. (38568) 237/L8
Hill (riv.), Minn. 255/C3
Hill (co.), Mont. 262/F2
Hill○, N.H. (03243) 268/D4
Hill (co.), Texas 303/G5
Hill (creek), Utah 304/E4
Hilla, Iraq 66/D4
Hilla, Iraq 59/D3
Hill A.F.B., Utah 304/C2
Hillaby (mt.), Barbados 161/B8
Hillandale, Md. (†20903) 245/F4
Hill Bank, Belize 154/C2
Hillburn, N.Y. (10931) 276/M8
Hill City, Idaho (83337) 220/D6
Hill City, Kansas (67642) 232/C2
Hill City, Minn. (55748) 255/E4
Hill City, S. Dak. (57745) 298/B6
Hill Country Village, Texas (†78232) 303/K10
Hill Creek Ext., Uintah and Ouray Ind. Res., Utah 304/E4
Hillcrest, Alberta 182/C5
Hillcrest, Ill. (†61244) 222/D2
Hillcrest, N.Y. (†10977) 276/K8
Hillcrest, Texas (†77511) 303/J3
Hillcrest Heights, Fla. (†33827) 212/E4
Hillcrest Heights, Md. (†20031) 245/F5
Hilldale, Utah (†84767) 304/A6
Hillegom, Netherlands 27/E4
Hillemann, Ark. (†72101) 202/H3
Hill End, N.S. Wales 97/E3
Hillerød, Denmark 18/H9
Hillerød, Denmark 21/F6
Hillers (mt.), Utah 304/D6
Hillham, Ind. (†47432) 227/D7
Hillhead, S. Dak. (†57270) 298/O2
Hillhouse, Miss. (†38720) 256/C2
Hilliard, Alberta 182/D3
Hilliard, Fla. (32046) 212/E1
Hilliard, Ohio (43026) 284/D5
Hilliards, Pa. (16040) 294/C3
Hilliardville, Fla. (†32327) 212/B1
Hillingdon, England 10/B5
Hillingdon, England 13/G8
Hillisburg, Ind. (46046) 227/E4
Hill Island (lake), N.W. Terrs. 187/H3
Hillman, Mich. (49746) 250/F3
Hillman, Minn. (56338) 255/E4
Hillman, New Bruns. 170/C2
Hillmond, Sask. 181/B2
Hill of Fearn, Scotland 15/D3
Hillridge, Manitoba 179/C3
Hillrose, Colo. (80733) 208/N2
Hills, Iowa (52235) 229/K5
Hills, Minn. (56138) 255/B7
Hillsboro, Ala. (35643) 195/D1
Hillsboro, Georgia (31038) 217/E4
Hillsboro, Ill. (62049) 222/D4
Hillsboro, Ind. (47949) 227/C4
Hillsboro, Iowa (52630) 229/K7
Hillsboro, Kansas (67063) 232/E3
Hillsboro, Ky. (41049) 237/O4
Hillsboro, Md. (21641) 245/P5
Hillsboro, Miss. (39087) 256/E6
Hillsboro, Mo. (63050) 261/L6
Hillsboro, N.H. (03244) 268/D5
Hillsboro○, N.H. (03244) 268/D5
Hillsboro, N. Mex. (88042) 274/B6
Hillsboro, N. Dak. (58045) 282/S5
Hillsboro, Ohio (45133) 284/C7
Hillsboro, Oreg. (97123) 291/A2
Hillsboro, Tenn. (37342) 237/K10
Hillsboro, Texas (76645) 303/G5
Hillsboro, Va. (22132) 307/N2
Hillsboro, W. Va. (24946) 312/F6
Hillsboro, Wis. (54634) 317/F8
Hillsboro Beach, Fla. (†33060) 212/F5
Hillsboro Lower Village, N.H. (†03244) 268/D5
Hillsborough, Calif. (94010) 204/J2
Hillsborough (co.), Fla. 212/D4
Hillsborough (bay), Fla. 212/C3
Hillsborough (canal), Fla. 212/F5
Hillsborough (riv.), Fla. 212/C2
Hillsborough, New Bruns. 170/F3
Hillsborough (co.), N.H. 268/D6
Hillsborough, N.C. (27278) 281/L2
Hillsborough, N. Ireland 17/J3
Hillsborough (bay), Pr. Edward I. 168/E2
Hillsboro Upper Village, N.H. (†03244) 268/D5
Hillsburgh, Ontario 177/D4
Hillsburn, Nova Scotia 168/C4
Hills Creek (lake), Oreg. 291/E4
Hillsdale, Ill. (61257) 222/C2
Hillsdale, Ind. (47854) 227/C5
Hillsdale, Kansas (66036) 232/H3
Hillsdale (co.), Mich. 250/E7
Hillsdale, Mich. (49242) 250/E7
Hillsdale, Mo. (†63101) 261/R2
Hillsdale, N.J. (07642) 273/B1
Hillsdale, N.Y. (12529) 276/O6
Hillsdale, Okla. (73743) 288/K1
Hillsdale, Ontario 177/E3
Hillsdale, Pa. (15746) 294/E4
Hillsdale, Wis. (54744) 317/C5
Hillsdale, Wyo. (82060) 319/H4
Hillsgrove, Pa. (18619) 294/J3
Hillsgrove, R.I. (†02887) 249/J6
Hillside, Ariz. (†86301) 198/B4
Hillside, Colo. (81232) 208/H6
Hillside, Ill. (60162) 222/B5
Hillside○, N.J. (07205) 273/B2
Hillside, Scotland 15/F4
Hillside, S. Dak. (†57328) 298/N7
Hillside Beach, Manitoba 179/F4
Hillsport, Ontario 175/C3
Hillsport, Ontario 177/H5
Hill Spring, Alberta 182/D5
Hillston, N.S. Wales 88/G6
Hillston, N.S. Wales 97/C3
Hillsview, S. Dak. (†57437) 298/L2
Hillsville, Pa. (16132) 294/A4
Hillsville, Va. (24343) 307/G7
Hillswick, Scotland 15/G2
Hilltonia, Georgia (30467) 217/J5
Hilltop, Ariz. (†85632) 198/F6
Hilltown, N. Ireland 17/J3
Hillview, Ill. (62050) 222/C4
Hillview, Minn. (†56477) 255/D4
Hillview, Newf. 166/D2
Hilmar-Irwin, Calif. (95324) 204/E6
Hilo, Hawaii 87/L4
Hilo, Hawaii (96720) 218/J5
Hilo, Hawaii 188/G6
Hilo (bay), Hawaii 218/J5
Hilongos, Philippines 82/E5
Hilshire Village, Texas (†77001) 303/J1
Hilt, Calif. (†96044) 204/C2
Hilterfingen, Switzerland 39/E3
Hilton (inlet) 5/B16
Hilton, Georgia (†31723) 217/C8
Hilton, Manitoba 179/C5
Hilton, N.Y. (14468) 276/E4
Hilton Beach, Ontario 177/J5
Hilton Head (isl.), S.C. 296/F7
Hilton Head Island, S.C. (29928) 296/F7
Hiltons, Va. (24258) 307/D7
Hilvan, Turkey 63/H4
Hilvarenbeek, Netherlands 27/G6
Hilversum, Netherlands 27/G4
Hima, Ky. (40951) 237/O6
Himachal Pradesh (state), India 68/D2
Himalaya (mts.) 54/L7
Himalaya (mts.), Bhutan 68/E2
Himalaya (mts.), China 77/C6
Himalaya (mts.), India 68/D2
Himalaya (mts.), Nepal 68/D2
Himanka, Finland 18/N5
Himeji, Japan 81/G6
Himi, Japan 81/H5
Himlerville (Beauty), Ky. (†41203) 237/S5
Himrod, N.Y. (14842) 276/F5
Himyar, Ky. (40952) 237/O7
Hinatuan, Philippines 82/F6
Hinchcliff, Miss. (†38646) 256/D2
Hinche, Haiti 158/C5
Hinche, Haiti 156/D3
Hinchinbrook (isl.), Alaska 196/D1
Hinchinbrook (isl.), Queensland 88/H3
Hinchinbrook (isl.), Queensland 95/C3
Hinchinbrook Entrance (chan.), Alaska 196/J3
Hinchliffe, Sask. 181/J3
Hinckley, England 10/F4
Hinckley, England 13/F5
Hinckley, Ill. (60520) 222/E2
Hinckley, Maine (04944) 243/D6
Hinckley, Minn. (55037) 255/E4
Hinckley, N.Y. (13352) 276/K4
Hinckley (res.), N.Y. 276/K4
Hinckley, Ohio (44233) 284/G3
Hinckley, Utah (84635) 304/B4
Hindeloopen, Netherlands 27/G3
Hindenburg (Zabrze), Poland 47/A4
Hinderwell, England 13/G3
Hindiya, Iraq 66/C4
Hindman, Ky. (41822) 237/R6
Hindmarsh, S. Australia 88/D8
Hindmarsh, S. Australia 94/A7
Hindmarsh (lake), Victoria 97/A5
Hinds (co.), Miss. 256/D6
Hinds, N. Zealand 100/C6
Hindsboro, Ill. (61930) 222/E4
Hindsville, Ark. (72738) 202/C1
Hindubagh, Pakistan 68/B2
Hindu Kush (mts.) 54/J6
Hindu Kush (mts.), Afghanistan 68/B1
Hindu Kush (mts.), Afghanistan 59/J2
Hindu Kush (mts.), India 68/C1
Hindu Kush (mts.), Pakistan 68/B1
Hindupur, India 68/D6
Hi-Nella, N.J. (†08083) 273/B4
Hines, Minn. (56647) 255/D3
Hines, Oreg. (97738) 291/H4
Hinesburg○, Vt. (05461) 268/A3
Hines Creek, Alberta 182/A1
Hines Creek, Alta. 162/E4
Hineston, La. (71438) 238/E4
Hinesville, Georgia (31313) 217/J7
Hinganghat, India 68/D4
Hingham, Mass. (02043) 249/E8
Hingham○, Mass. (02043) 249/E8
Hingham (bay), Mass. 249/E7
Hingham, Mont. (59528) 262/F2
Hingham, Wis. (53031) 317/K8
Hingoli, India 68/D5
Hinigaran, Philippines 82/D5
Hinis, Turkey 63/J3
Hinkley, Calif. (92347) 204/H9
Hinkston (creek), Ky. 237/N4
Hinlopenstreten (str.), Norway 18/C1
Hinnerup, Denmark 21/D5
Hinnøya (isl.), Norway 18/K2
Hino, Japan 81/O2
Hinojosa del Duque, Spain 33/D3
Hinsdale (co.), Colo. 208/E7
Hinsdale, Ill. (60521) 222/B6
Hinsdale○, Mass. (01235) 249/B3
Hinsdale, Mont. (59241) 262/K2
Hinsdale, N.H. (03451) 268/C6
Hinsdale○, N.H. (03451) 268/C6
Hinsdale, N.Y. (14743) 276/D6
Hinson, Fla. (†32333) 212/B1
Hinsonton, Georgia (†31779) 217/D8
Hinterrhein (riv.), Switzerland 39/H3
Hinton, Alberta 182/B3
Hinton, Iowa (51024) 229/A3
Hinton, Mo. (†65201) 261/H4
Hinton, Okla. (73047) 288/K4
Hinton, W. Va. (25951) 312/E7
Hintonville, Miss. (†39462) 256/F8
Hinwil, Switzerland 39/G2
Hinze, Miss. (†39108) 256/F4
Hippolytushoef, Netherlands 27/G3
Hipswell, England 13/F3
Hirakata, Japan 81/J7
Hiram, Georgia (30141) 217/C3
Hiram, Ky. (†40823) 237/P7
Hiram, Maine (04041) 243/B8
Hiram○, Maine (04041) 243/B8
Hiram, Mo. (63947) 261/M8
Hiram, Ohio (44234) 284/H3
Hirara, Japan 81/L7
Hirata, Japan 81/F6
Hiratsuka, Japan 81/O3
Hîrlău, Romania 45/H2
Hiroo, Japan 81/L2
Hirosaki, Japan 81/K3
Hiroshima (pref.), Japan 81/E6
Hiroshima, Japan 54/P6
Hiroshima, Japan 81/E6
Hirsch, Sask. 181/J6
Hirschberg (Jelenia Góra), Poland 47/B3
Hirson, France 28/F3
Hîrşova, Romania 45/J3
Hirtshals, Denmark 21/C2
Hisarönü, Turkey 63/E2
Hisban, Jordan 65/D4
Hisega, S. Dak. (†57701) 298/C5
Hiseville, Ky. (42152) 237/K6
Hisle, S. Dak. (†57577) 298/F7
Hispaniola (isl.) 146/L7
Hispaniola (isl.), Dom. Rep. 156/D2
Hispaniola (isl.), Haiti 156/D2
Hispaniola (isl.), W. Indies 156/D2
Hissar, India 68/D3
Hissop, Ala. (35081) 195/F5
Hit, Iraq 59/D3
Hit, Iraq 66/C4
Hitachi, Japan 81/K5
Hitachiota, Japan 81/K5
Hitchcock (lks), Conn. 210/D2
Hitchcock (co.), Nebr. 264/C4
Hitchcock, Okla. (73744) 288/K3
Hitchcock, Sask. 181/J6
Hitchcock, S. Dak. (57348) 298/M4
Hitchcock, Texas (77563) 303/K3
Hitchin, England 13/G6
Hitchin, England 10/F5
Hitchins, Ky. (41146) 237/R4
Hitchita, Okla. (74438) 288/P3
Hiteman, Iowa (†52531) 229/H6
Hitoyoshi, Japan 81/E7
Hitra (isl.), Norway 18/F5
Hitt, Mo. (†63555) 261/H1
Hitterdal, Minn. (56552) 255/B4
Hitzacker, W. Germany 22/D2
Hitzkirch, Switzerland 39/F2
Hivaoa (isl.), Fr. Poly. 87/N6
Hiwannee, Miss. (†39367) 256/G7
Hiwasse, Ark. (72739) 202/B1
Hiwassee (lake), N.C. 281/A4
Hiwassee (riv.), N.C. 281/A4
Hiwassee (riv.), Tenn. 237/O10
Hiwassee, Va. (24347) 307/G7
Hixon, Br. Col. 184/F3
Hixson, Tenn. (37343) 237/L10
Hixton, Wis. (54635) 317/E7
Hizan, Turkey 63/K3
Hjallerup, Denmark 21/C3
Hjälmaren (lake), Sweden 18/J7
Hjerm, Denmark 21/B5
Hjerting, Denmark 21/B6
Hjo, Sweden 18/J7
Hjørring, Denmark 18/F8
Hjørring, Denmark 21/C3
Hka, Nam (riv.), Burma 72/C2
Hkakabo Razi (mt.), Burma 72/C1
Hlinsko, Czech. 41/D2
Hlohovec, Czech. 41/D2
Hlučín, Czech. 41/E2
Hmawbi, Burma 72/C3
Hnúšťa-Likier, Czech. 41/E2
Ho, Ghana 106/E7
Hoa Binh, Vietnam 72/E2
Hoa Da, Vietnam 72/F5
Hoadley, Alberta 182/C3
Hoadly, Va. (†22191) 307/O3
Hoagland, Ind. (46745) 227/H3
Hoai Nhon, Vietnam 72/F4
Hoaksbergen, Netherlands 27/K4
Hoare (bay), N.W. Terrs. 187/M3
Hoback (peak), Wyo. 319/B2
Hoback (riv.), Wyo. 319/B2
Hobart, Australia 2/S8
Hobart, Ind. (46342) 227/C1
Hobart, N.Y. (13788) 276/L6
Hobart, Okla. (73651) 288/J5
Hobart (cap.), Tasmania 88/H8
Hobart (cap.), Tasmania 99/D4
Hobart, Wash. (98025) 310/D3
Hobbema, Alberta 182/D3
Hobbs, Ind. (46047) 227/F4
Hobbs (lake), Manitoba 179/G3
Hobbs, Md. (†21629) 245/P5
Hobbs, N. Mex. 188/F4
Hobbs, N. Mex. (88240) 274/F6
Hobbs Coast (reg.) 5/B12
Hobbs Island, Ala. (†35804) 195/F1
Hobbsville, N.C. (27946) 281/R2
Hoberg, Mo. (†65712) 261/E8
Hobe Sound, Fla. (33455) 212/F4
Hobgood, N.C. (27843) 281/P2
Hoboken, Belgium 27/E6
Hoboken, Georgia (31542) 217/H8
Hoboken, N.J. (07030) 273/C2
Hoboksar, China 77/C2
Hobro, Denmark 21/C4
Hobro, Denmark 18/F8
Hobson (lake), Br. Col. 184/H4
Hobson, Mont. (59452) 262/G4
Hobson City, Ala. (†36201) 195/G3
Hobsons (bay), Victoria 97/H5
Hobsons (bay), Victoria 88/L7
Hobucken, N.C. (28537) 281/S4
Hoburgen (cliff), Sweden 18/L8
Hochdorf, Switzerland 39/F2
Hochfeld, Manitoba 179/E5
Hochgolling (mt.), Austria 41/B3
Ho Chi Minh City, Vietnam 2/Q5
Ho Chi Minh City, Vietnam 54/M8
Hochwan (Hechuan), China 77/G5
Hochwang (mt.), Switzerland 39/J3
Hockaday, Mich. (†48624) 250/E4
Hockanum, Conn. (†06108) 210/E2
Hockanum (riv.), Conn. 210/E1
Hockenheim, W. Germany 22/C4
Hockerville, Okla. (†74363) 288/S1
Hockessin, Del. (19707) 245/R1
Hocking (co.), Ohio 284/F6
Hocking (riv.), Ohio 284/F7
Hockingport, Ohio (45739) 284/G7
Hockley (co.), Texas 303/B4
Hodaka (mt.), Japan 81/H5
Hodder (riv.), England 13/H1
Hoddesdon, England 13/H7
Hodeida, Yemen Arab Rep. 54/F8
Hodeida, Yemen Arab Rep. 59/D7
Hodgdon○, Maine (†04730) 243/H3
Hodge, La. (71247) 238/E2
Hodge, Mo. (†64096) 261/E4
Hodgeman (co.), Kansas 232/C3
Hodgen, Okla. (74939) 288/S5
Hodgenville, Ky. (42748) 237/K5
Hodges, Ala. (35571) 195/C2
Hodges, Mont. (†59353) 262/M4
Hodges, S.C. (29653) 296/C3
Hodge's Cove, Newf. 166/D2
Hodgesville, W. Va. (†26201) 312/F4
Hodgeville, Sask. 181/E5
Hodgkins, Ill. (60525) 222/B6
Hodgson, Manitoba 179/E3
Hodh (reg.), Mauritania 106/C5
Hod Hasharon, Israel 65/B3
Hodiyya, Israel 65/B4
Hódmezővásárhely, Hungary 41/F3
Hodonín, Czech. 41/D2
Hoehne, Colo. (81046) 208/L8
Hoei (Huy), Belgium 27/G8
Hoek, Netherlands 27/D6
Hoek van Holland (Hook of Holland), Netherlands 27/D4
Hoek van Holland (cape), Netherlands 27/D5
Hoensbroek, Netherlands 27/H7
Hoeryŏng, N. Korea 81/D2
Hoeselt, Belgium 27/G7
Hoey, Sask. 181/F3
Hof, W. Germany 22/D3
Hofei (Hefei), China 77/J5
Hoffman (mt.), Calif. 204/D2
Hoffman, Ill. (62250) 222/D5
Hoffman, Minn. (56339) 255/C5
Hoffman, N.C. (28347) 281/K4
Hoffman, Okla. (74439) 288/P4
Hoffman Estates, Ill. (60195) 222/A5
Hofgeismar, W. Germany 22/C3
Hofors, Sweden 18/K6
Hofs (glac.), Iceland 21/C1
Hofu, Japan 81/E6
Hofuf, Saudi Arabia 59/E4
Hofuf, Saudi Arabia 54/F7
Hog (isl.), Mich. 250/D3
Hog (isl.), Pr. Edward I. 168/E2
Hog (isl.), Va. 307/S6
Hogan, Mo. (†63646) 261/L7
Hogan (lake), Ontario 177/F2
Höganäs, Sweden 18/H8
Hogan Group (isls.), Tasmania 99/D1
Hogansburg, N.Y. (13655) 276/L1
Hogansville, Georgia (30230) 217/C4

Horwich 383

Hogarth (mt.), North. Terr. 93/E6
Hogatza, Alaska (99744) 196/G1
Hogeland, Mont. (59529) 262/H2
Hog Island (bay), Va. 307/S6
Hog River (Hogatza), Alaska (99744) 196/G1
Hogshead (pt.), Conn. 210/E3
Hőgyész, Hungary 41/E3
Hoh (head), Wash. 310/A3
Hoh (riv.), Wash. 310/A3
Hohenau, Paraguay 144/E5
Hohenau an der March, Austria 41/D2
Hohenberg, Austria 41/C3
Hohenems, Austria 41/A3
Hohenlinden, Miss. (†39751) 256/F3
Hohen Neuendorf, E. Germany 22/E2
Hohen Solms, La. (†70788) 238/K3
Hohenstollen (mt.), Switzerland 39/F3
Hohenwald, Tenn. (38462) 237/F9
Hohe Tauern (range), Austria 41/B3
Hohe Venn (plat.), Belgium 27/H8
Hohe Warte (mt.), Austria 41/B3
Hohhot (Huhehot), China 77/H3
Hohhot, China 54/N5
Hoh Ind. Res., Wash. 310/A3
Hohokam Pima Nat'l Mon., Ariz. 198/D5
Ho Ho Kus, N.J. (07423) 273/B1
Hoholitna (riv.), Alaska 196/G2
Hoh Xil Shan (mts.), China 77/C4
Hoi An, Vietnam 72/F4
Hoihow (Haikou), China 77/H7
Hoima, Uganda 115/F3
Hoisington, Kansas (67544) 232/D3
Hoi Xuan, Vietnam 72/E2
Højer, Denmark 21/B8
Højslev, Denmark 21/C4
Hokah, Minn. (55941) 255/G7
Hokang (Hegang), China 77/L2
Hoke (co.), N.C. 281/L4
Hokes Bluff, Ala. (35903) 195/G3
Hokianga (harb.), N. Zealand 100/D1
Hokitika, N. Zealand 100/C5
Hokkaido (pref.), Japan 81/K2
Hokkaido (isl.), Japan 2/S3
Hokkaido (isl.), Japan 54/R5
Hokkaido (isl.), Japan 81/L2
Holabird, S. Dak. (57540) 298/K4
Holbaek, Denmark 21/E6
Holbaek, Denmark 18/G9
Holbeach, England 10/F4
Holbeach, England 13/H5
Holbein, Sask. 181/E2
Holberg, Br. Col. 184/C5
Holbrook, Ariz. (86025) 198/E4
Holbrook, Idaho (83243) 220/F7
Holbrook, Iowa (†52325) 229/K5
Holbrook○, Mass. (02343) 249/D8
Holbrook, Nebr. (68948) 264/D4
Holbrook, N.S. Wales 97/D4
Holbrook, Oreg. (†97208) 291/A1
Holcomb, Ill. (61043) 222/D1
Holcomb, Kansas (67851) 232/B3
Holcomb, Miss. (38940) 256/D3
Holcomb, Mo. (63852) 261/N10
Holcomb, N.Y. (14469) 276/F5
Holcomb, W. Va. (26262) 312/E6
Holcombe, Wis. (54745) 317/D5
Holcombe Flowage (res.), Wis. 317/D5
Holden, Alberta 182/D3
Holden, La. (70744) 238/M1
Holden○, Mass. (01520) 249/G3
Holden, Mo. (64040) 261/E5
Holden, Utah (84636) 304/B4
Holden, W. Va. (25625) 312/B7
Holden Beach, N.C. (28462) 281/N7
Holdenville, Okla. (74848) 288/O4
Holder, Fla. (32645) 212/D3
Holderness (pen.), England 13/G4
Holderness○, N.H. (03245) 268/D4
Holdfast, Sask. 181/F5
Holdingford, Minn. (56340) 255/D5
Holdrege, Nebr. (68949) 264/E4
Holeby, Denmark 21/E8
Hølen, Norway 18/D4
Holešov, Czech. 41/D2
Holetown, Barbados 161/B8
Holgate, Ohio (43527) 284/B3
Holguín (prov.), Cuba 158/J3
Holguín, Cuba 146/L7
Holguín, Cuba 158/J3
Holguín, Cuba 156/C2
Holíč, Czech. 41/D2
Holice, Czech. 41/C1
Holiday Hills, Ill. (†60050) 222/A4
Holijsloot, Netherlands 27/C4
Holitna (riv.), Alaska 196/G2
Hollabrunn, Austria 41/D2
Holladay, Tenn. (38341) 237/E9
Holladay, Utah (84117) 304/C3
Hollam's Bird (isl.), Namibia 118/A4
Holland, Georgia (†30730) 217/B2
Holland, Ind. (47541) 227/C8
Holland, Iowa (50642) 229/H4
Holland, Ky. (42153) 237/J7
Holland, Manitoba 179/D5
Holland○, Mass. (†01550) 249/F4
Holland, Mich. (49423) 250/C6
Holland, Minn. (56139) 255/B6
Holland, Mo. (63853) 261/N10
Holland, N.Y. (14080) 276/C5
Holland, Ohio (43528) 284/C2
Holland, Texas (76534) 303/G7
Holland○, Vt. (†05830) 268/D2
Hollandale, Minn. (56045) 255/E7
Hollandale, Miss. (38748) 256/C4
Hollandale, Wis. (53544) 317/G10
Holland Centre, Ontario 177/D3
Hollandia (Jayapura), Indonesia 85/K6
Holland Landing, Ontario 177/E3
Holland Park, Queensland 88/K3
Holland Park, Queensland 95/E3
Holland Patent, N.Y. (13354) 276/K4
Hollandsburg, Ind. (†47872) 227/C5
Hollandstoun, Scotland 15/F1
Hollansburg, Ohio (45332) 284/A5
Hollenbeck (riv.), Conn. 210/B1
Hollenberg, Kansas (66946) 232/F2
Holley, N.Y. (14470) 276/D4
Holley, Oreg. (†97386) 291/E3
Hollick-Kenyon (plat.) 5/B13
Holliday, Mo. (65258) 261/H3
Holliday, Texas (76366) 303/F4
Hollidaysburg, Pa. (16648) 294/F5
Hollins, Ala. (35082) 195/F4
Hollins College, Va. (24020) 307/H6
Hollis, Ark. (†72857) 202/D4
Hollis, Kansas (†66901) 232/E2
Hollis○, N.H. (03049) 268/D6
Hollis, N.C. (†28040) 281/F4
Hollis, Okla. (73550) 288/G5
Hollis Center○, Maine (04042) 243/B8
Hollister, Calif. (95023) 204/D7
Hollister, Fla. (32047) 212/E2
Hollister, Idaho (†83301) 220/D7
Hollister, Mo. (65672) 261/F9
Hollister, N.C. (27844) 281/O2
Hollister, Okla. (73551) 288/J6
Hollister, Wis. (†54491) 317/J5
Holliston○, Mass. (01746) 249/A8
Holloman A.F.B., N. Mex. 274/C6
Holloway, Minn. (56249) 255/C5
Holloway, Ohio (43985) 284/H5
Hollowayville, Ill. (†61356) 222/D2
Hollow Creek, Ky. (†40228) 237/K4
Hollow Rock, Tenn. (38342) 237/E8
Hollsopple, Pa. (15935) 294/E5
Hollum, Netherlands 27/H2
Holly, Colo. (81047) 208/P6
Holly, Mich. (48442) 250/F6
Holly, Wash. (†98310) 310/C3
Holly Bluff, Miss. (39088) 256/C5
Holly Grove, Ark. (72069) 202/H4
Holly Hill, Fla. (32017) 212/E2
Holly Hill, S.C. (29059) 296/G5
Holly Oak, Del. (†19801) 245/S1
Holly Pond, Ala. (35083) 195/E2
Holly Ridge, La. (71248) 238/G2
Holly Ridge, Miss. (38749) 256/C4
Holly Ridge, N.C. (28445) 281/O6
Holly Shelter (swamp), N.C. 281/O6
Holly Springs, Ark. (71746) 202/E6
Holly Springs, Georgia (30142) 217/D2
Holly Springs, Miss. (38635) 256/E1
Holly Springs, N.C. (27540) 281/M3
Hollytree, Ala. (35751) 195/F1
Hollyville, Del. (†19951) 245/T6
Hollywood, Ala. (35752) 195/G1
Hollywood, Ark. (†71923) 202/D5
Hollywood, Calif. (90028) 204/C10
Hollywood, Fla. 188/K5
Hollywood, Fla. (*33020) 212/B4
Hollywood, Georgia (30523) 217/E1
Hollywood, La. (†70663) 238/D6
Hollywood, Md. (20636) 245/M7
Hollywood, Miss. (†38676) 256/D1
Hollywood, Mo. (†63821) 261/M10
Hollywood, S.C. (29449) 296/G6
Hollywood, W. Va. (†24983) 312/F7
Hollywood Park, Texas (†78201) 303/K10
Holman, N. Mex. (87723) 274/D2
Holman (isl.), N.W.T. 162/D1
Holman Island, Canada 4/B15
Holman Island, N.W. Terrs. 187/G2
Holmdel○, N.J. (07733) 273/E3
Holmen, Wis. (54636) 317/D8
Holmes (reef), 95/C3
Holmes (reef), Coral Sea Is. Terr. 88/H3
Holmes (co.), Fla. 212/C5
Holmes (creek), Fla. 212/D5
Holmes, Iowa (†50525) 229/F3
Holmes (co.), Miss. 256/D4
Holmes (co.), Ohio 284/G4
Holmes (mt.), Wyo. 319/B1
Holmes Beach, Fla. (33509) 212/D4
Holmes City, Minn. (56341) 255/C5
Holmeson, N.J. (†08526) 273/E3
Holmestrand, Norway 18/C4
Holmesville, Miss. (†39648) 256/D8
Holmesville, Nebr. (68374) 264/H4
Holmesville, New Bruns. 170/C2
Holmesville, Ohio (44633) 284/G4
Holmesville, Ontario 177/C4
Holmfield, Manitoba 179/C5
Holmfirth, England 13/J2
Holmquist, S. Dak. (†57274) 298/O3
Holmsbu, Norway 18/D4
Holmsund, Sweden 18/M5
Holmwood, La. (†70647) 238/D6
Holon, Israel 65/B3
Holopaw, Fla. (†32901) 212/E3
Holroyd, N.S. Wales 97/H3
Holroyd (riv.), Queensland 95/B2
Holstebro, Denmark 18/F8
Holstebro, Denmark 21/B5
Holsted, Denmark 21/B6
Holstein, Iowa (51025) 229/B4
Holstein, Mo. (63378) 261/K5
Holstein, Nebr. (68950) 264/F4
Holstein, Ontario 177/D3
Holsteinsborg, Greenl. 4/C12
Holston (riv.), Tenn. 237/O8
Holston, Va. (†24210) 307/D7
Holston, North Fork (riv.), Va. 307/D7
Holston Valley, Tenn. (†37620) 237/S7
Holsworthy, England 10/D5
Holsworthy, England 13/C7
Holt, Ala. (35404) 195/D4
Holt (dam), Ala. 195/D4
Holt, Calif. (95234) 204/D6
Holt, England 13/J5
Holt, Fla. (32564) 212/C6
Holt, Mich. (48842) 250/E6
Holt, Minn. (†56738) 255/B2
Holt (co.), Mo. 261/B2
Holt, Mo. (64048) 261/D4
Holt (co.), Nebr. 264/F2
Holte, Denmark 21/F6
Holter (lake), Mont. 262/D4
Holtland, Tenn. (†37034) 237/H9
Holton, Ind. (47023) 227/G6
Holton, Kansas (66436) 232/G2
Holton, La. (†70422) 238/K5
Holton, Mich. (49425) 250/C5
Holton, Newf. 166/C3
Holts Summit, Mo. (65043) 261/H5
Holtville, Ala. (†36022) 195/F5
Holtville, Calif. (92250) 204/K11
Holtville, New Bruns. 170/D2
Holtwood, Pa. (17532) 294/K6
Holualoa, Hawaii (96725) 218/G5
Holualoa, Hawaii 188/F6
Holwerd, Netherlands 27/H2
Holy (isl.), England 13/F2
Holy (isl.), England 10/F3
Holy (isl.), Scotland 15/C5
Holy (isl.), Wales 10/D4
Holy (isl.), Wales 13/C4
Holy City, Calif. (95026) 204/K4
Holy Cross, Alaska (99602) 196/G2
Holy Cross (mt.), Colo. 208/F4
Holy Cross, Iowa (52053) 229/L3
Holycross, Ireland 17/F6
Holy Cross, Wis. (†53004) 317/L9
Holyhead, Wales 10/D4
Holyhead, Wales 13/C4
Holy Loch (inlet), Scotland 15/A1
Holyoke, Colo. (80734) 208/P1
Holyoke, Mass. (01040) 249/D4
Holyoke (range), Mass. 249/D3
Holyoke, Minn. (55749) 255/F4
Holyrood, Kansas (67450) 232/D3
Holyrood, Newf. 166/D2
Holyrood (bay), Newf. 166/D2
Holyrood (pond), Newf. 166/D2
Holyroyd, N. S. Wales 88/K4
Holy Trinity, Ala. (36859) 195/H6
Holywell, Wales 13/G2
Holywood, N. Ireland 17/K2
Holzminden, W. Germany 22/C3
Homalin, Burma 72/B1
Homathko (riv.), Br. Col. 184/E4
Homayunshahr, Iran 66/G4
Hombori, Mali 106/D5
Hombori (mts.), Mali 106/D5
Homburg, W. Germany 22/B4
Home (bay) 162/K2
Home, Kansas (66438) 232/F2
Home (isl.), Newf. 166/B1
Home (bay), N.W. Terrs. 187/M3
Home, Pa. (15747) 294/D4
Homedale, Idaho (83628) 220/A6
Home Gardens, Calif. (†91720) 204/E11
Home Hill, Queensland 88/H3
Home Hill, Queensland 95/C3
Homeland, Calif. (92348) 204/H10
Homeland, Georgia (†31537) 217/H9
Home Place, La. (†70083) 238/L8
Homer, Alaska (99603) 196/B2
Homer, Georgia (30547) 217/F2
Homer, Ill. (61849) 222/F3
Homer, Ind. (46146) 227/F5
Homer, Ky. (†42276) 237/H7
Homer, La. (71040) 238/D1
Homer, Mich. (49245) 250/E6
Homer, Minn. (55942) 255/G6
Homer, Nebr. (68030) 264/H2
Homer, N.Y. (13077) 276/H5
Homer, Ohio (43027) 284/E5
Homer City, Pa. (15748) 294/D4
Homerville, Georgia (31634) 217/G8
Homerville, Ohio (44235) 284/F3
Homestead, Fla. (*33030) 212/F6
Homestead, Iowa (52236) 229/K5
Homestead, Mont. (59242) 262/M2
Homestead, Okla. (†73763) 288/K2
Homestead, Pa. (15120) 294/B7
Homestead, Queensland 95/C4
Homestead A.F.B., Fla. 212/F6
Homestead Nat'l Mon., Nebr. 264/H4
Homestown, Mo. (†63879) 261/N10
Hometown, Ill. (60456) 222/B6
Home Valley, Wash. (†98648) 310/D5
Homewood, Ala. (35209) 195/E4
Homewood, Calif. (95718) 204/E4
Homewood, Ill. (60430) 222/B6
Homewood, Kansas (†66095) 232/G3
Homewood, Manitoba 179/E5
Homewood, Miss. (†39152) 256/E6
Homewood, Pa. (15208) 294/B4
Homeworth, Ohio (44634) 284/J4
Hominy, Okla. (74035) 288/O2
Hominy Falls, W. Va. (†26651) 312/E6
Homochitto (riv.), Miss. 256/B8
Homoine, Mozambique 118/E4
Homonhon (isl.), Philippines 82/E5
Homosassa, Fla. (32646) 212/D3
Homosassa (isls.), Fla. 212/D3
Homosassa Springs, Fla. (32647) 212/D3
Homra, Hamada el (des.), Libya 111/B2
Homs, Libya 102/D1
Homs, Libya 111/B1
Homs (prov.), Syria 63/G5
Homs, Syria 59/C3
Homs, Syria 63/G5
Homs, Syria 54/E6
Hon, Ark. (†72958) 202/B4
Hon, Libya 102/D2
Hon, Libya 111/C2
Honaker, Va. (24260) 307/D6
Honan (Henan) (prov.), China 77/H5
Honaunau, Hawaii (96726) 218/G6
Honavar, India 68/C6
Honaz Dağı (mt.), Turkey 63/C4
Hon Chong, Vietnam 72/E5
Honda, Colombia 126/C5
Honda (bay), Cuba 158/B1
Honda (bay), Philippines 82/B6
Honda (bay), P. Rico 161/F2
Hondo (riv.), Belize 154/C1
Hondo, Japan 81/E7
Hondo (riv.), Mexico 150/P7
Hondo, N. Mex. (88336) 274/D5
Hondo, Texas (78861) 303/E8
Hondsrug (hills), Netherlands 27/K3
Honduras 2/E5
Honduras 146/K8
HONDURAS 154
Honduras (gulf) 146/K8
Honduras (gulf), Belize 154/D2
Honduras (gulf), Guatemala 154/D2
Honduras (cape), Honduras 154/D2
Honduras (gulf), Honduras 154/E2
Honea Path, S.C. (29654) 296/C3
Honegg (mt.), Switzerland 39/E3
Honeoye, N.Y. (14471) 276/F5
Honeoye (lake), N.Y. 276/F5
Honeoye Falls, N.Y. (14472) 276/F5
Honesdale, Pa. (18431) 294/M2
Honey (lake), Calif. 204/E3
Honey (creek), Ind. 227/C6
Honey (creek), Oreg. 291/G5
Honey Brook, Pa. (19344) 294/L5
Honey Creek, Ind. (†47356) 227/F4
Honey Creek, Iowa (51542) 229/B6
Honey Creek, Wis. (53138) 317/J3
Honeydale, New Bruns. 170/C3
Honeyford, N. Dak. (†58242) 282/R3
Honey Grove, Texas (75446) 303/J4
Honey Harbour, Ontario 177/E3
Honey Hill, S.C. (†29479) 296/H5
Honey Island, Texas (†77625) 303/K7
Honeymoon Bay, Br. Col. 184/J3
Honeyville, Utah (84314) 304/B2
Honeywood, Ontario 177/D3
Honfleur, France 28/D3
Honfleur, Québec 172/G3
Høng, Denmark 21/E7
Honga (riv.), Md. 245/O7
Hon Gai, Vietnam 72/E2
Hongch'ŏn, S. Korea 81/D5
Hong Kong 54/N7
Hong Kong, 2/Q4
HONG KONG 77
Hongliahe, China 77/E3
Hongor, Mongolia 77/H2
Hongshui He (riv.), China 77/G7
Hongsŏng, S. Korea 81/C5
Hongtong, China 77/H4
Honguedo (passage), Québec 174/E3
Hongwŏn, N. Korea 81/C3
Hongze Hu (lake), China 77/J5
Honiara (cap.), Solomon Is. 86/D3
Honiara (cap.), Solomon Is. 87/F6
Honiton, England 10/E5
Honiton, England 13/D7
Honjo, Japan 81/J4
Honnedaga (lake), N.Y. 276/L3
Honnelles, Belgium 27/D8
Honningsvag, Norway 18/O1
Honobia, Okla. (74549) 288/R5
Honohina, Hawaii (†96710) 218/J4
Honokaa, Hawaii 188/G5
Honokaa, Hawaii (96727) 218/H4
Honokahua, Hawaii (†96761) 218/H1
Honokohau, Hawaii, Hawaii (†96740) 218/G5
Honokohau, Maui, Hawaii (†96725) 218/J1
Honolulu (co.), Hawaii 218/D3
Honolulu (cap.), Hawaii 87/L3
Honolulu (cap.), Hawaii 188/F5
Honolulu (cap.), Hawaii (*96801) 218/C4
Honolulu (harb.), Hawaii 218/C4
Honolulu, U.S. 2/B5
Honolulu Int'l Airport, Hawaii 218/B4
Honomu, Hawaii (96728) 218/J4
Honor, Mich. (49640) 250/D4
Honoraville, Ala. (36042) 195/F7
Honouliuli, Hawaii (†96706) 218/A3
Honshu (isl.), Japan 2/S4
Honshu (isl.), Japan 54/P6
Honshu (isl.), Japan 81/J5
Honuapo, Hawaii (†96772) 218/H7
Hood, Calif. (95639) 204/B9
Hood (riv.), N.W. Terrs. 187/G3
Hood (mt.), Oreg. 291/F2
Hood (riv.), Oreg. 291/F2
Hood (co.), Texas 303/G5
Hood (canal), Wash. 310/B3
Hood River (co.), Oreg. 291/F2
Hood River, Oreg. (97031) 291/F2
Hoodsport, Wash. (98548) 310/B3
Hoofddorp (Haarlemmermeer), Netherlands 27/F4
Hoogeveen, Netherlands 27/J3
Hoogezand-Sappemeer, Netherlands 27/K2
Hooghly (riv.), India 68/F2
Hooghly-Chinsura, India 68/F1
Hoogkarspel, Netherlands 27/G3
Hoogstraten, Belgium 27/F6
Hook (head), Ireland 17/H7
Hook (isl.), Queensland 88/H4
Hook (isl.), Queensland 95/D4
Hookena, Hawaii (†96704) 218/G6
Hooker (co.), Nebr. 264/C3
Hooker, Okla. (73945) 288/D1
Hooker Creek, North. Terr. 88/E3
Hooker Creek, North. Terr. 93/B5
Hooker Creek Aboriginal Reserve, North. Terr. 93/B5
Hookersville, W. Va. (†26651) 312/E6
Hookerton, N.C. (28538) 281/O4
Hook of Holland, Netherlands 27/D4
Hooks, Texas (75561) 303/K4
Hooksett, N.H. (03106) 268/E5
Hooksett○, N.H. (03106) 268/E5
Hookstown, Pa. (15050) 294/B4
Hoolehua, Hawaii 188/F5
Hoolehua, Hawaii (96729) 218/G1
Hoonah, Alaska (99829) 196/M1
Hoonah (sound), Alaska 196/M1
Hoopa, Calif. (95546) 204/B2
Hoopa Valley Ind. Res., Calif. 204/A2
Hooper, Colo. (81136) 208/H7
Hooper (str.), Md. 245/O8
Hooper, Nebr. (68031) 264/H3
Hooper, Utah (84315) 304/B2
Hooper, Wash. (99333) 310/G4
Hooper Bay, Alaska (99604) 196/E2
Hooper Bay, Alaska 188/C5
Hoopersville, Md. (21642) 245/O7
Hoopeston, Ill. (60942) 222/F3
Hoople, N. Dak. (58243) 282/P2
Hooppole, Ill. (61258) 222/D2
Hoorn, Netherlands 27/G3
Hoorn (isls.), Wallis and Futuna 87/J7
Hoosac (mts.), Mass. 249/B2
Hoosac Tunnel, Mass. (†01339) 249/C2
Hoosic (riv.), Mass. 249/A1
Hoosic (riv.), Vt. 268/A6
Hoosick Falls, N.Y. (12090) 276/O5
Hoosier, Sask. 181/B4
Hoot Owl, Okla. (†74366) 288/R2
Hooven, Ohio (45033) 284/A9
Hoover, Ala. (†35216) 195/E4
Hoover (dam), Ariz. 198/A2
Hoover (dam), Nev. 266/G7
Hoover (res.), Ohio 284/E5
Hoover, S. Dak. (†57760) 298/C3
Hooversville, Pa. (15936) 294/E5
Hop (riv.), Conn. 210/F1
Hopa, Turkey 63/J2
Hopatcong, N.J. (07843) 273/D2
Hopatcong (lake), N.J. 273/D2
Hop Bottom, Pa. (18824) 294/L2
Hope, Alaska (99605) 196/C1
Hope (pt.), Alaska 196/E1
Hope (bay) 5/C16
Hope, Ark. (71801) 202/C6
Hope, Br. Col. 162/D6
Hope, Br. Col. 184/M3
Hope, Idaho (83836) 220/B1
Hope, Ind. (47246) 227/F6
Hope, Kansas (67451) 232/E3
Hope, Ky. (40334) 237/O4
Hope, Maine (04847) 243/E7
Hope○, Maine (04847) 243/E7
Hope, Mich. (48628) 250/E5
Hope, Minn. (56045) 255/E7
Hope, Mo. (†65061) 261/J5
Hope (lake), Newf. 166/B3
Hope, N.J. (07844) 273/D2
Hope, N. Mex. (88250) 274/E6
Hope, N. Dak. (58046) 282/P5
Hope (isl.), Norway 4/B8
Hope, R.I. (02831) 249/H6
Hope, Loch (lake), Scotland 15/D2
Hope Bay, Jamaica 158/K6
Hopedale, Ill. (61747) 222/D3
Hopedale, Mass. (01747) 249/H4
Hopedale○, Mass. (01747) 249/H4
Hopedale, Newf. 166/B2
Hopedale, Newf. 162/L4
Hopedale, Newf. 146/N4
Hopedale, Ohio (43976) 284/J5
Hopeful Heights, Ky. (†41018) 237/R2
Hope Hull, Ala. (36043) 195/F6
Hopei (Hebei) (prov.), China 77/J4
Hopeland, Pa. (17533) 294/K5
Hopelchén, Mexico 150/P7
Hopeman, Scotland 15/E3
Hope Mills, N.C. (28348) 281/M5
Hopen (isl.), Norway 18/E2
Hopes Advance (cape), Québec 174/F1
Hopeton, Okla. (73746) 288/J1
Hopeton, Va. (†23421) 307/S5
Hopetoun, Victoria 97/B4
Hopetoun, W. Australia 92/C6
Hopetown, Québec 172/D2
Hopetown, S. Africa 118/C5
Hopetown, W. Australia 88/C6
Hope Valley, R.I. (02832) 249/H6
Hope Valley (res.), S. Australia 88/E7
Hopeville, Iowa (†50174) 229/F7
Hopewell, Ala. (†36264) 195/H3
Hopewell, Jamaica 158/G5
Hopewell, Kansas (†67557) 232/D4
Hopewell, Md. (†21817) 245/P8
Hopewell, Miss. (†39059) 256/D7
Hopewell, N.J. (08525) 273/D3
Hopewell (isls.), N.W. Terrs. 187/L4
Hopewell, Nova Scotia 168/F3
Hopewell, Ohio (43746) 284/F6
Hopewell, Pa. (16650) 294/F5
Hopewell (I.C.), Va. (23860) 307/O6
Hopewell Cape, New Bruns. 170/F3
Hopewell Hill, New Bruns. 170/F3
Hopewell Junction, N.Y. (12533) 276/N7
Hopfgarten in Nordtirol, Austria 41/B3
Hopi (buttes), Ariz. 198/E3
Hopi Ind. Res., Ariz. 198/E2
Hopkins (co.), Ky. 237/F6
Hopkins, Mich. (49328) 250/D6
Hopkins, Minn. (55343) 255/G5
Hopkins, Mo. (64461) 261/C1
Hopkins (lake), North. Terr. 93/A8
Hopkins, S.C. (29061) 296/F4
Hopkins (co.), Texas 303/J4
Hopkins (riv.), Victoria 97/B5
Hopkins, Va. (†23421) 307/S5
Hopkins (lake), W. Australia 88/D4
Hopkins (lake), W. Australia 92/E4
Hopkinsville, Ky. (42240) 237/F7
Hopkinton, Iowa (52237) 229/L4
Hopkinton, Mass. (01748) 249/J4
Hopkinton○, Mass. (01748) 249/J4
Hopkinton○, N.H. (03301) 268/D5
Hopkinton, N.Y. (12940) 276/L1
Hopkinton○, R.I. (02833) 249/H7
Hopland, Calif. (95449) 204/B5
Hoppo (Hepu), China 77/G7
Hop River, Conn. (†06237) 210/F2
Hopwood, Pa. (15445) 294/C6
Hoquiam, Wash. 188/B1
Hoquiam, Wash. (98550) 310/A3
Horace, Kansas (†67879) 232/A3
Horace, N. Dak. (58047) 282/S6
Horasan, Turkey 63/K2
Horatio, Ark. (71842) 202/B3
Horatio, S.C. (29062) 296/F3
Horažd'ovice, Czech. 41/B2
Horche, Spain 33/E2
Horconcitos, Panama 154/F6
Hordaland (co.), Norway 18/E6
Horden, England 13/J4
Hordio, Somalia 115/K1
Hordville, Nebr. (68846) 264/G3
Horgen, Switzerland 39/G2
Hořice v Podkrkonoší, Czech. 41/C1
Horicon, Wis. (53032) 317/J9
Horine, Mo. (†63070) 261/M6
Horizon, Sask. 181/F6
Horley, England 13/H8
Hormigüeros, P. Rico 161/A2
Hormoz, Iran 66/J7
Hormoz (isl.), Iran 66/K7
Hormozgan (prov.), Iran 66/J7
Hormuz (str.), Iran 59/G4
Hormuz (str.), Iran 66/K7
Hormuz (str.), Oman 59/G4
Horn (cape) 2/F8
Horn, Austria 41/C2
Horn (cape), Chile 120/C8
Horn (cape), Chile 138/F11
Horn (cape), Iceland 7/B2
Horn (cape), Iceland 21/B1
Horn (head), Ireland 17/E1
Horn (isl.), Miss. 256/G10
Horn (mts.), N.W. Terrs. 187/G3
Horn (riv.), N.W. Terrs. 187/G3
Hornád (riv.), Czech. 41/F2
Hornaday (riv.), N.W. Terrs. 187/F3
Hornafjördhur (fjord), Iceland 21/D1
Horná Štubňa, Czech. 41/E2
Horn-Bad Meinberg, W. Germany 22/C3
Hornbeak, Tenn. (38232) 237/C8
Hornbeck, Alberta 182/B3
Hornbeck, La. (71439) 238/D4
Hornbrook, Calif. (96044) 204/C2
Hornby, N. Zealand 100/D5
Hornby (bay), N.W. Terrs. 187/G3
Hornby Island, Br. Col. 184/H2
Horncastle, England 13/G4
Horncastle, England 10/F4
Horndean, Manitoba 179/E5
Hörnefors, Sweden 18/L5
Hornell, N.Y. (14843) 276/E6
Hornepayne, Ontario 175/C3
Hornepayne, Ontario 177/J5
Horner, W. Va. (26372) 312/F5
Hornerstown, N.J. (†08514) 273/E3
Hornersville, Mo. (63855) 261/M10
Horn Hill, Ala. (†36467) 195/F8
Horní Benešov, Czech. 41/D2
Hornick, Iowa (51026) 229/A4
Horní Libina, Czech. 41/D2
Hornings Mills, Ontario 177/D3
Hornitos, Calif. (95325) 204/E6
Horn Lake, Miss. (38637) 256/D1
Hörnli (mt.), Switzerland 39/G2
Hornos, Falso (cape), Chile 138/F11
Hornsby, N. S. Wales 88/K3
Hornsby, N.S. Wales 97/J3
Hornsby, Tenn. (38044) 237/D10
Hornsea, England 13/G4
Hornsea, England 10/F4
Hornslandet (pen.), Sweden 18/K6
Hornslet, Denmark 21/D5
Horns Road, Nova Scotia 168/H2
Hornsund (bay), Norway 18/C2
Horntown, Va. (23395) 307/T5
Hořovice, Czech. 41/C2
Horqin Youyi Qianqi (Ulanhot), China 77/K2
Horqueta, Paraguay 144/D3
Horry (co.), S.C. 296/J4
Horse (lake), Calif. 204/E3
Horse (creek), Colo. 208/M5
Horse (creek), Fla. 212/E4
Horse (isls.), Newf. 166/C3
Horse (creek), Oreg. 291/F3
Horse (creek), Wyo. 319/H4
Horse (creek), Wyo. 319/B3
Horse Branch, Ky. (42349) 237/H6
Horse Cave, Ky. (42749) 237/K6
Horse Chops (head), Newf. 166/D2
Horse Creek, Calif. (96045) 204/C2
Horse Creek (res.), Colo. 208/N6
Horse Creek, Wyo. (82061) 319/G4
Horsefly, Br. Col. 184/G4
Horsefly (lake), Br. Col. 184/G4
Horsehead (lake), N. Dak. 282/L5
Horsehead (creek), S. Dak. 298/C7
Horseheads, N.Y. (14845) 276/G6
Horsens, Denmark 18/F9
Horsens, Denmark 21/C6
Horsens (fjord), Denmark 21/D6
Horseshoe (lake), Ariz. 198/D5
Horseshoe (pt.), Fla. 212/C2
Horseshoe (lake), Manitoba 179/G2
Horse Shoe (pt.), St. Chris.-Nevis 161/C11
Horseshoe (creek), Wyo. 319/G3
Horseshoe Beach, Fla. (32648) 212/C2
Horseshoe Bend, Ark. (72512) 202/G1
Horseshoe Bend, Idaho (83629) 220/B6
Horseshoe Bend Nat'l Mil. Park, Ala. 195/G5
Horseshoe Lake, Ontario 177/E2
Horse Shoe Run, W. Va. (26769) 312/G4
Horsetooth (res.), Colo. 208/J1
Horsham, England 10/F5
Horsham, England 13/G6
Horsham, Sask. 181/B5
Horsham, Victoria 97/B5
Horsham, Victoria 88/G7
Hørsholm, Denmark 21/F6
Horšovský Týn, Czech. 41/B2
Horst, Netherlands 27/H6
Horta (dist.), Portugal 33/A1
Horta, Portugal 33/B1
Hortaleza, Spain 33/G4
Horten, Norway 18/D4
Hortense, Georgia (31543) 217/J8
Hortensfjord (fjord), Norway 18/G4
Horton, Ala. (35980) 195/F2
Horton, Iowa (†50677) 229/J3
Horton, Kansas (66439) 232/G2
Horton, Mich. (49246) 250/E6
Horton, Mo. (64751) 261/D7
Horton (riv.), N.S. Wales 97/F2
Horton (riv.), N.W. Terrs. 187/F3
Horton, Oreg. (97448) 291/D3
Horton Bay, Mich. (†49712) 250/D3
Hortonia (lake), Vt. 268/A4
Hortonville, Ind. (†46069) 227/E4
Hortonville, Mass. (†02777) 249/K5
Hortonville, Wis. (54944) 317/J7
Hørve, Denmark 21/E6
Horwich, England 10/G2
Horwich, England 13/G2

384 Hoschton

Hoschton, Georgia (30548) 217/E2
Hoselaw, Alberta 182/E2
Hosenofu (well), Libya 111/D3
Hosford, Fla. (32334) 212/B1
Hoshab, Pakistan 68/A3
Hoshab, Pakistan 59/H4
Hoshangabad, India 68/D4
Hoskins, Nebr. (68740) 264/G2
Hosmer, Br. Col. 184/K5
Hosmer, S. Dak. (57448) 298/L2
Hospental, Switzerland 39/F3
Hospers, Iowa (51238) 229/B2
Hospet, India 68/D5
Hospital, Chile 138/G4
Hospital, Ireland 17/E7
Hospitalet, Spain 33/H2
Hosseina, Ethiopia 111/G6
Hosston, La. (71043) 238/C1
Hoste (isl.), Chile 120/B8
Hoste (isl.), Chile 138/F11
Hostinné, Czech. 41/C1
Hoswick, Scotland 15/G2
Hot, Thailand 72/C3
Hotan, China 77/B4
Hotan, China 54/K6
Hotan He (riv.), China 77/B4
Hotchkiss, Alberta 182/B1
Hotchkiss, Colo. (81419) 208/D5
Hotchkissville, Conn. (†06798) 210/C2
Hot Creek (range), Nev. 266/E4
Hot Creek (valley), Nev. 266/E4
Hotevilla, Ariz. (86030) 198/E3
Hotham (inlet), Alaska 196/F1
Hoting, Sweden 18/K4
Hot Lake, Oreg. (†97850) 291/K2
Hot Spring (co.), Ark. 202/E5
Hot Springs, Mont. (59845) 262/B3
Hot Springs (Truth or Consequences), N. Mex. (8790 274/B5
Hot Springs, N.C. (28743) 281/D3
Hot Springs, S. Dak. 188/F2
Hot Springs, S. Dak. (57747) 298/C7
Hot Springs, Va. (24445) 307/J4
Hot Springs (co.), Wyo. 319/D2
Hot Springs Cove, Br. Col. 184/D5
Hot Springs National Park, Ark. 188/H4
Hot Springs National Park, Ark. (71901) 202/D4
Hot Springs Nat'l Park, Ark. 202/D4
Hot Sulphur Springs, Colo. (80451) 208/H2
Hottah (lake), N.W.T. 162/E2
Hottah (lake), N.W. Terrs. 187/G3
Hottentot (bay), Namibia 118/A5
Hotton, Belgium 27/G8
Hou, Nam (riv.), Laos 72/D2
Houck, Ariz. (86506) 198/F3
Houcktown, Ohio (†45840) 284/C4
Houffalize, Belgium 27/H8
Houghton, Iowa (52631) 229/K7
Houghton, Maine (†04275) 243/B6
Houghton, Mich. 188/J1
Houghton (co.), Mich. 250/G1
Houghton, Mich. (49931) 250/G1
Houghton (lake), Mich. 250/E4
Houghton, N.Y. (14744) 276/D6
Houghton, S. Dak. (57449) 298/N2
Houghton Lake, Mich. (48629) 250/E4
Houghton Lake Heights, Mich. (48630) 250/E4
Houghton-le-Spring, England 13/J3
Houhoek, S. Africa 118/F7
Houlka, Miss. (38850) 256/G2
Houlton, Maine 188/N1
Houlton, Maine (04730) 243/H3
Houlton○, Maine (04730) 243/H3
Houlton, Wis. (†55082) 317/A5
Houma, China 77/H4
Houma, La. (70360) 238/J7
Houndé, Upper Volta 106/D6
Hounslow, England 13/G8
Hounslow, England 10/B5
Hourn, Loch (inlet), Scotland 15/C3
Housatonic (riv.), Conn. 210/C3
Housatonic, Mass. (01236) 249/A3
Housatonic (riv.), Mass. 249/A4
House (mt.), Alberta 182/C2
House (riv.), Alberta 182/D2
House, N. Mex. (88121) 274/F4
House (range), Utah 304/A4
House Springs, Mo. (63051) 261/L6
Houston (co.), Ala. 195/H8
Houston, Ala. (35572) 195/D2
Houston, Alaska (†99687) 196/B1
Houston, Ark. (72070) 202/E3
Houston, Br. Col. 184/D3
Houston, Del. (19954) 245/S5
Houston, Fla. (†32060) 212/D1
Houston (co.), Georgia 217/E6
Houston, Ind. (†47235) 227/E6
Houston (co.), Minn. 255/G7
Houston, Minn. (55943) 255/G7
Houston, Miss. (38851) 256/G3
Houston, Mo. (65483) 261/J8
Houston, Ohio (45333) 284/B5
Houston, Pa. (15342) 294/B5
Houston (co.), Tenn. 237/F8
Houston (co.), Texas 303/J6
Houston, Texas (*77001) 303/J2
Houston, Texas 188/G5
Houston, Texas 146/J7
Houston (lake), Texas 303/J8
Houston, U.S. 2/E4
Houston Acres, Ky. (†40201) 237/K2
Houstonia, Mo. (65333) 261/F5
Houston Lake, Mo. (†64152) 261/O5
Houston Ship (chan.), Texas 303/K2
Hout (bay), S. Africa 118/E6
Houtbaai, S. Africa 118/E6
Houtman Abrolhos (isls.), W. Australia 88/A5
Houtman Abrolhos (isls.), W. Australia 92/A5
Houtrak Polder, Netherlands 27/A4
Houtzdale, Pa. (16651) 294/F4
Hov, Denmark 21/D6
Hovd, Mongolia 77/D2
Hovd (Kobdo, Jirgalanta), Mongolia 77/D2
Hovd, Mongolia 54/L5
Hovd Gol (riv.), Mongolia 77/D2
Hove, England 13/G7
Hove, England 10/F5
Hoven, S. Dak. (57450) 298/K3
Hovenweep Nat'l Mon., Colo. 208/A8
Hovenweep Nat'l Mon., Utah 304/E6
Hoveyzeh, Iran 66/F5
Hoving, N. Dak. (†58060) 282/P7
Hovland, Minn. (55606) 255/G2
Hövsgöl, Mongolia 77/E1
Hövsgöl Nuur (lake), Mongolia 77/F1
Howar, Wadi (dry riv.), Sudan 111/E4
Howard (pass), Alaska 196/G1
Howard (co.), Ark. 202/C5
Howard, Colo. (81233) 208/H6
Howard, Georgia (31039) 217/D5
Howard (co.), Ind. 227/E4
Howard (co.), Iowa 229/J2
Howard, Kansas (67349) 232/F4
Howard (co.), Md. 245/L4
Howard (co.), Mo. 261/G4
Howard (co.), Nebr. 264/F3
Howard, New Bruns. 170/E2
Howard, Ohio (43028) 284/F5
Howard, Pa. (16841) 294/G3
Howard, S. Dak. (57349) 298/P5
Howard (co.), Texas 303/C5
Howard (creek), Texas 303/C7
Howard, Wis. (54303) 317/K6
Howard A. Hanson (res.), Wash. 310/D3
Howard City, Mich. (49329) 250/D5
Howard City (Boelus), Nebr. (68820) 264/F3
Howard Lake, Minn. (55349) 255/D5
Howards Grove-Millersville, Wis. (53081) 317/L8
Howards Ridge, Mo. (†65655) 261/H9
Howardstown, Ky. (40028) 237/K5
Howardsville, Va. (24562) 307/L5
Howardville, Mo. (†63869) 261/N9
Howden, England 13/G4
Howe (cape), Australia 87/F9
Howe (sound), Br. Col. 184/K2
Howe, Idaho (83244) 220/F6
Howe, Ind. (46746) 227/G1
Howe (cape), N. S. Wales 88/J7
Howe (cape), N.S. Wales 97/F5
Howe, Okla. (74940) 288/S5
Howe, Texas (75059) 303/H4
Howell, Ark. (72071) 202/H3
Howell, Georgia (†31636) 217/F9
Howell, Mich. (48843) 250/E6
Howell (co.), Mo. 261/J9
Howell○, N.J. (07731) 273/E3
Howell, Tenn. (†37334) 237/H10
Howell, Utah (84316) 304/B2
Howells, Nebr. (68641) 264/H3
Howes, S. Dak. (57748) 298/E4
Howesville, Ind. (†47438) 227/C6
Howesville, W. Va. (†26444) 312/G4
Howey In The Hills, Fla. (32737) 212/E3
Howick, N. Zealand 100/C1
Howick, Québec 172/D4
Howick, S. Africa 118/E5
Howison, Miss. (†39574) 256/F9
Howland, Maine (04448) 243/F5
Howland○, Maine (04448) 243/F5
Howland (isl.), Pacific 87/J5
Howland Ridge, New Bruns. 170/C2
Howley, Newf. 166/C4
Howlong, N.S. Wales 97/D4
Howrah, India 68/F2
Howrah, India 54/K7
Howser, Br. Col. 184/J5
Hoxeyville, Mich. (49641) 250/D4
Hoxie, Ark. (72433) 202/H1
Hoxie, Kansas (67740) 232/B2
Höxter, W. Germany 22/C3
Hoxud, China 77/C3
Hoy (isl.), Scotland 15/E2
Hoy (isl.), Scotland 10/E1
Hoy (sound), Scotland 15/E2
Hoyerswerda, E. Germany 22/F3
Hoylake, England 13/G2
Hoylake, England 10/F2
Hoyland Nether, England 13/J2
Hoyleton, Ill. (62803) 222/D5
Hoyos, Spain 33/C2
Hoyran (lake), Turkey 63/D3
Hoyt, Colo. (80641) 208/L2
Hoyt, Kansas (66440) 232/G2
Hoyt, New Bruns. 170/D3
Hoyt, Okla. (74440) 288/R4
Hoyt (peak), Utah 304/C3
Hoyt Lakes, Minn. (55750) 255/F3
Hoytsville, Utah (†84017) 304/C3
Hoytville, Ohio (43529) 284/C3
Hozat, Turkey 59/C2
Hozat, Turkey 63/H3
Hradec Králové, Czech. 41/C1
Hranice, Czech. 41/D2
Hrinova, Czech. 41/E2
Hron (riv.), Czech. 41/E2
Hronov, Czech. 41/D1
Hrubieszów, Poland 47/F3
Hrušovany, Czech. 41/D2
Hsewi, Burma 72/C2
Hsipaw, Burma 72/C2
Hsüchang (Xuchang), China 77/H5
Htawgaw, Burma 72/C1
Huacaraje, Bolivia 136/D3
Huacareta, Bolivia 136/C7
Huacaya, Bolivia 136/D7
Huachacalla, Bolivia 136/A6
Huachi, Bolivia 136/D4
Huachi, China 77/G4
Huachipato, Chile 138/D1
Huacho, Peru 120/B4
Huacho, Peru 128/D8
Huachuca (peak), Ariz. 198/E7
Huachuca City, Ariz. (85616) 198/E7
Huacrachuco, Peru 128/D7
Huade, China 77/H3
Huadian, China 77/L3
Hua Hin, Thailand 72/D4
Huahine (isl.), Fr. Poly. 87/L7
Huaibei, China 77/J5
Huaibin, China 77/H5
Huaide (Hwaiteh), China 77/K3
Huaiji, China 77/H7
Huainan, China 77/J5
Huainan, China 54/N6
Huairen, China 77/H4
Huajuapan de León, Mexico 150/L8
Hualaihué, Chile 138/E4
Hualalai (mt.), Hawaii 218/G5
Hualañé, Chile 138/A10
Hualapai (mts.), Ariz. 198/B4
Hualapai (peak), Ariz. 198/B3
Hualapai Ind. Res., Ariz. 198/B3
Hualgayoc, Peru 128/C6
Hualien, China 77/K7
Hualla, Peru 128/F9
Huallaga (riv.), Peru 120/B3
Huallaga (riv.), Peru 128/D5
Huallanca, Ancash, Peru 128/D7
Huallanca, Huánuco, Peru 128/D7
Huallen, Alberta 182/A2
Huamachuco, Peru 128/D6
Huamantla, Mexico 150/N1
Huambo (dist.), Angola 115/C6
Huambo, Angola 102/D6
Huambo, Angola 115/C6
Huambo, Angola 2/K6
Huanaqui, Bolivia 136/A7
Huanay, Bolivia 136/B4
Huancabamba, Peru 128/C5
Huancané, Bolivia 136/B6
Huancané, Peru 128/H10
Huancapi, Peru 128/E9
Huancavelica (dept.), Peru 128/E9
Huancavelica, Peru 120/B4
Huancavelica, Peru 128/E9
Huancayo, Peru 128/E9
Huancayo, Pru 120/B4
Huanchaca, Bolivia 136/B7
Huanchaca, Cerro (mt.), Bolivia 136/B7
Huanchaca, Serranía de (mts.), Bolivia 136/E4
Huanchaco, Peru 128/C7
Huanggang, China 77/J5
Huang He (riv.), China 2/Q4
Huang He (Hwang Ho) (riv.), China 54/N6
Huang He (Ma Qu) (riv.), China 77/F5
Huang He (Yellow) (riv.), China 77/J4
Huangling, China 77/G4
Huangliu, China 77/G8
Huangshi, China 77/J5
Huangzhong, China 77/F4
Huanqueros, Argentina 143/F5
Huanta, Peru 128/E9
Huánuco (dept.), Peru 128/D7
Huánuco, Peru 128/E7
Huánuco, Peru 120/B3
Huanuni, Bolivia 136/B6
Huanuni, Bolivia 120/C4
Huan Xian, China 77/G4
Huapai, N. Zealand 100/B1
Huapí (mts.), Nicaragua 154/E4
Huaquechula, Mexico 150/M2
Huara, Chile 138/B2
Huaral, Peru 128/D8
Huaráz, Peru 128/D7
Huaráz, Peru 120/B3
Huari, Bolivia 136/B6
Huari, Peru 128/D7
Huariaca, Peru 128/E8
Huarina, Bolivia 136/A5
Huarmey, Peru 128/C8
Huarochirí, Peru 128/D9
Huarocondo, Peru 128/F9
Huásabas, Mexico 150/E2
Huasaga (riv.), Peru 128/D4
Huascarán (mt.), Peru 120/B3
Huascarán (mt.), Peru 128/D7
Huasco, Chile 138/A7
Huasco (riv.), Chile 138/A7
Huatabampo, Mexico 150/D3
Huatunas (lag.), Bolivia 136/B3
Huatusco de Chicuellar, Mexico 150/P2
Huauchinango, Mexico 150/L6
Huaura, Peru 128/D8
Huautla de Jiménez, Mexico 150/L7
Huayabamba (riv.), Peru 128/D6
Huaylas, Peru 128/C7
Huayllas, Bolivia 136/C6
Hub, Miss. (†39429) 256/E8
Hubball, W. Va. (†25506) 312/B6
Hubbard, Iowa (50122) 229/G4
Hubbard (lake), Mich. 250/F4
Hubbard (co.), Minn. 255/D3
Hubbard, Minn. (†56470) 255/C4
Hubbard, Nebr. (68741) 264/J2
Hubbard, Ohio (44425) 284/J3
Hubbard, Oreg. (97032) 291/A3
Hubbard, Sask. 181/H4
Hubbard, Texas (76648) 303/H6
Hubbard Creek (lake), Texas 303/F5
Hubbard Lake, Mich. (49747) 250/F4
Hubbards, Nova Scotia 168/D4
Hubbardston○, Mass. (01452) 249/F3
Hubbardston, Mich. (48845) 250/E5
Hubbardstown, W. Va. (†25555) 312/A6
Hubbardsville, N.Y. (13355) 276/J5
Hubbardton○, Vt. (05749) 268/A4
Hubbart (pt.), Manitoba 179/K2
Hubbell, Mich. (49934) 250/A1
Hubbell, Nebr. (68375) 264/G4
Hubbell Trading Post Nat'l Hist. Site, Ariz. 198/F3
Hub City, Wis. (†53581) 317/F9
Hubei (Hupeh) (prov.), China 77/H5
Huberdeau, Québec 172/C4
Huber Heights, Ohio (45424) 284/B6
Hubert, N.C. (28539) 281/P5
Hubertus, Wis. (53033) 317/K1
Hubli-Dharwar, India 68/C5
Hubli-Dharwar, India 54/J8
Huch'ang, N. Korea 81/C3
Hückelhoven, W. Germany 22/B3
Hucknall, England 13/F4
Huddersfield, England 10/G2
Huddersfield, England 13/J2
Huddinge, Sweden 18/H1
Huddleston, Va. (24104) 307/K6
Huddy, Ky. (41535) 237/S5
Hudiksvall, Sweden 18/K6
Hudson (bay) 162/H3
Hudson (str.) 162/J3
Hudson (bay), Canada 2/E3
Hudson (str.), Canada 146/L3
Hudson (bay), Canada 146/K3
Hudson, Colo. (80642) 208/K2
Hudson, Fla. (33568) 212/D3
Hudson, Ill. (61748) 222/E3
Hudson, Ind. (46747) 227/G1
Hudson, Iowa (50643) 229/H4
Hudson, Kansas (67545) 232/D3
Hudson, Ky. (40145) 237/J5
Hudson○, Maine (04449) 243/F5
Hudson (bay), Manitoba 179/K2
Hudson, Md. (†21613) 245/N6
Hudson, Mass. (01749) 249/H3
Hudson○, Mass. (01749) 249/H3
Hudson, Mich. (49247) 250/E7
Hudson, N.H. (03051) 268/E6
Hudson○, N.H. (03051) 268/E6
Hudson (co.), N.J. 273/E2
Hudson (riv.), N.J. 273/C1
Hudson, N.Y. (12534) 276/N6
Hudson (riv.), N.Y. 276/N7
Hudson, N.C. (28638) 281/G3
Hudson (bay), N.W. Terrs. 187/K3
Hudson (str.), N.W. Terrs. 187/L3
Hudson, Ohio (44236) 284/H3
Hudson (lake), Okla. 288/R2
Hudson, Ontario 175/B2
Hudson, Ontario 177/G4
Hudson (bay), Ontario 175/D1
Hudson, Québec 172/C4
Hudson (bay), Québec 174/A1
Hudson (str.), Québec 174/F1
Hudson, S. Dak. (57034) 298/R7
Hudson, Wis. (54016) 317/A6
Hudson, Wyo. (82515) 319/D3
Hudson Bay, Sask. 181/J3
Hudson Falls, N.Y. (12839) 276/O4
Hudson Hope, Br. Col. 184/F2
Hudson Lake, Ind. (46552) 227/D1
Hudsons Bay, Alberta 182/E4
Hudsonville, Mich. (49426) 250/D6
Hudspeth (co.), Texas 303/B10
Hudwin (lake), Manitoba 179/G1
Hue, Vietnam 54/M8
Hue, Vietnam 72/E3
Hueco (mts.), N. Mex. 274/D6
Hueco (mts.), Texas 303/B10
Huedin, Romania 45/F2
Huehue, Hawaii (†96740) 218/G5
Huehuetenango, Guatemala 154/B3
Huehuetlán el Chico, Mexico 150/M2
Huejotzingo, Mexico 150/M1
Huejutla, Mexico 150/K6
Huelma, Spain 33/E4
Huelva (prov.), Spain 33/C4
Huelva, Spain 33/C4
Huelva, Spain 7/D5
Huelva (riv.), Spain 33/C4
Huentelauquén, Chile 138/A8
Huercal-Overa, Spain 33/F4
Huerfano (co.), Colo. 208/K7
Huerfano (riv.), Colo. 208/L7
Huesca (prov.), Spain 33/F1
Huesca, Spain 33/F1
Huéscar, Spain 33/E4
Huetamo, Mexico 150/J7
Huete, Spain 33/E2
Huetter, Idaho (†83854) 220/B2
Huey, Ill. (62252) 222/D5
Hueyotlipan de Hidalgo, Mexico 150/M1
Hueytown, Ala. (35020) 195/D4
Huff, N. Dak. (58555) 282/J6
Huffman, Ark. (†72315) 202/L2
Huffton, S. Dak. (†57432) 298/N2
Huger, S.C. (29450) 296/H5
Huggins, Mo. (65484) 261/H8
Hugh Butler (lake), Nebr. 264/D4
Hughenden, Alberta 182/E3
Hughenden, Australia 87/E8
Hughenden, Queensland 88/G4
Hughenden, Queensland 95/B4
Hughes, Alaska (99745) 196/H1
Hughes, Ark. (72348) 202/J4
Hughes (co.), Okla. 288/O4
Hughes, S. Australia 94/A4
Hughes (co.), S. Dak. 298/J5
Hughes (riv.), W. Va. 312/D4
Hughes Springs, Texas (75656) 303/K5
Hughestown, Pa. (†18640) 294/F7
Hughesville, Md. (20637) 245/L6
Hughesville, Mo. (65334) 261/F5
Hughesville, Pa. (17737) 294/J3
Hughson, Calif. (95326) 204/E6
Hughton, Sask. 181/D4
Hugh Town, England 13/A8
Hugo, Colo. (80821) 208/N4
Hugo, Minn. (55038) 255/E5
Hugo, Okla. (74743) 288/P7
Hugo (lake), Okla. 288/R6
Hugo Stroessner, Paraguay 144/C4
Hugoton, Kansas (67951) 232/A4
Huhehot (Hohhot), China 77/H3
Huiarau (range), N. Zealand 100/F3
Hŭich'ŏn, N. Korea 81/C3
Huila (dist.), Angola 115/B7
Huila (dept.), Colombia 126/C6
Huila (mt.), Colombia 120/B2
Huila, Nevado del (mt.), Colombia 126/C6
Huimanguillo, Mexico 150/N8
Huimin, China 77/J4
Huinca Renancó, Argentina 143/D3
Huining, China 77/G4
Huissen, Netherlands 27/H5
Huitzilán, Mexico 150/O1
Huitzuco de los Figueroa, Mexico 150/K7
Huixcolotla, Mexico 150/N2
Huixtepec, Mexico 150/L8
Huixtla, Mexico 150/N9
Huize, China 77/F6
Huizen, Netherlands 27/G4
Huizhou, China 77/H7
Hulaco, Ala. (†35087) 195/E2
Hulah (lake), Kansas 232/F5
Hulah, Okla. (†67333) 288/O1
Hulah (lake), Okla. 288/O1
Hulan, China 77/L2
Hulbert, Mich. (49748) 250/D2
Hulbert, Okla. (74441) 288/R3
Hulberton, N.Y. (14473) 276/D4
Hulett, Wyo. (82720) 319/H1
Hulin, China 77/M2
Hull, England 7/E3
Hull, England 10/F4
Hull, England 13/G4
Hull, Fla. (†33842) 212/E4
Hull, Georgia (30646) 217/F2
Hull, Ill. (62343) 222/B4
Hull, Iowa (51239) 229/A2
Hull (isl.), Kiribati 87/J6
Hull○, Mass. (02045) 249/E7
Hull, N. Dak. (†58542) 282/K7
Hull, Que. 162/J6
Hull (co.), Québec 172/B4
Hull, Québec 172/B4
Hulls Cove, Maine (04644) 243/G7
Hulopoe (bay), Hawaii 218/G2
Hulopoe Bay, Hawaii (†96763) 218/H2
Hulst, Netherlands 27/E6
Hultsfred, Sweden 18/K8
Hulun Nur (lake), China 77/J2
Huma, China 77/L1
Humacao (dist.), P. Rico 161/E2
Humacao, P. Rico 161/E2
Humacao, P. Rico 156/G1
Humacao (riv.), P. Rico 161/E2
Huma He (riv.), China 77/K1
Humahuaca, Argentina 143/C1
Humaitá, Bolivia 136/B2
Humaitá, Brazil 132/H10
Humaitá, Brazil 120/C3
Humaitá, Brazil 132/G10
Humaitá, Paraguay 144/C5
Humansdorp, S. Africa 118/C6
Humansville, Mo. (65674) 261/E7
Humarock, Mass. (02047) 249/M4
Humber (riv.), England 13/G4
Humber (riv.), England 10/G4
Humber (riv.), Newf. 166/C4
Humber (riv.), Ontario 177/J3
Humberside (co.), England 13/G4
Humberto, Argentina 143/F5
Humbird, Wis. (54746) 317/E6
Humble, Texas (*77338) 303/J7
Humble City, N. Mex. (†88240) 274/F6
Humboldt, Ariz. (86329) 198/C4
Humboldt (co.), Calif. 204/B3
Humboldt (bay), Calif. 204/A3
Humboldt (bay), Colombia 126/B4
Humboldt, Ill. (61931) 222/E4
Humboldt (co.), Iowa 229/E3
Humboldt, Iowa (50548) 229/E3
Humboldt, Kansas (66748) 232/G4
Humboldt, Minn. (56731) 255/A2
Humboldt, Nebr. (68376) 264/J4
Humboldt (co.), Nev. 266/C1
Humboldt, Nev. (*89418) 266/C2
Humboldt (range), Nev. 266/C2
Humboldt (riv.), Nev. 188/C2
Humboldt (riv.), Nev. 266/E2
Humboldt (sink), Nev. 266/C2
Humboldt (mt.), New Caled. 86/H4
Humboldt, Sask. 162/F5
Humboldt, Sask. 181/F3
Humboldt, S. Dak. (57035) 298/P6
Humboldt, Tenn. (38343) 237/D9
Humboldt Salt (marsh), Nev. 266/D3
Humbug (mt.), Oreg. 291/C5
Hume, Ill. (61932) 222/E4
Hume, Mo. (64752) 261/C6
Hume (res.), N.S. Wales 97/D4
Hume, N.Y. (14745) 276/D5
Hume, Sask. 181/H6
Hume (lake), Victoria 97/D4
Hume, Va. (22639) 307/N3
Humenné, Czech. 41/G2
Humeston, Iowa (50123) 229/G7
Humlum, Denmark 21/B4
Hummelstown, Pa. (17036) 294/J5
Hummock (isl.), Tasmania 99/D2
Humnoke, Ark. (72072) 202/G4
Humphrey (pt.), Alaska 196/K1
Humphrey, Ark. (72073) 202/G5
Humphrey, Idaho (†83446) 220/F5
Humphrey, Nebr. (68642) 264/G3
Humphreys (peak), Ariz. 198/D3
Humphreys, La. (†70356) 238/J7
Humphreys (co.), Miss. 256/C4
Humphreys, Mo. (64646) 261/F2
Humphreys, Okla. (†73521) 288/H5
Humphreys (co.), Tenn. 237/F8
Humpolec, Czech. 41/C2
Humptulips, Wash. (98552) 310/A3
Humptulips (riv.), Wash. 310/B3
Humpty Doo, North. Terr. 93/B2
Húnaflói (bay), Iceland 7/B2
Húnaflói (bay), Iceland 21/B1
Hunan (prov.), China 77/H6
Hunchun, China 77/M3
Hundested, Denmark 21/E6
Hundred, W. Va. (26575) 312/E3
Hunedoara, Romania 7/G4
Hunedoara, Romania 45/F3
Hünfeld, W. Germany 22/C3
Hungary 2/K3
Hungary 7/F4
HUNGARY 41
Hunger (mt.), Vt. 268/B3
Hungerford, Queensland 95/B6
Hŭngnam, N. Korea 54/O6
Hungry Horse, Mont. (59919) 262/C2
Hungry Horse (res.), Mont. 262/C2
Hungtow (isl.), China 77/K7
Hunjiang, China 77/L3
Hunmanby, England 13/G3
Hunnewell, Kansas (†67140) 232/E4
Hunnewell, Mo. (63443) 261/J3
Hunse (riv.), Netherlands 27/K3
Hunsrück (mts.), W. Germany 22/B4
Hunstanton, England 13/H5
Hunstanton, England 10/G4
Hunt, Ill. (†62480) 222/E4
Hunt (co.), Texas 303/H4
Hunt (mt.), Wyo. 319/E1
Hunte (riv.), W. Germany 22/C2
Hunter, Ark. (72074) 202/H3
Hunter (isl.), Br. Col. 184/C4
Hunter (peak), Idaho 220/D3
Hunter, Kansas (67452) 232/D2
Hunter, Mo. (†63943) 261/L9
Hunter (riv.), N.S. Wales 97/F3
Hunter, N.Y. (12442) 276/M6
Hunter (mt.), N.Y. 276/M6
Hunter (mts.), N. Zealand 100/A6
Hunter, N. Dak. (58048) 282/R5
Hunter, Okla. (74640) 288/L1
Hunter (isls.), Tasmania 88/G8
Hunter (isl.), Tasmania 99/A2
Hunter (isls.), Tasmania 99/B2
Hunterdon (co.), N.J. 273/D2
Hunter River, Pr. Edward I. 168/E2
Hunters, Wash. (99137) 310/G2
Hunters Creek Village, Texas (†77001) 303/J1
Hunters Hill, N. S. Wales 88/K4
Hunters Hill, N.S. Wales 97/J3
Huntersville, Ky. (†42602) 237/L7
Huntersville, Minn. (†56464) 255/D4
Huntersville, N.C. (28078) 281/H4
Huntersville, W. Va. (†24954) 312/G6
Huntertown, Ind. (46748) 227/G2
Hunterville, N. Zealand 100/E3
Hunting (riv.), N.C. 281/H2
Hunting (isl.), S.C. 296/G7
Huntingburg, Ind. (47542) 227/D8
Huntingdon, Br. Col. 184/L3
Huntingdon (isl.), Newf. 166/C3
Huntingdon (co.), Pa. 294/F5
Huntingdon, Pa. (16652) 294/G5
Huntingdon (co.), Québec 172/C4
Huntingdon, Québec 172/C4
Huntingdon, Tenn. (38344) 237/E8
Huntingdon and Godmanchester, England 13/G5
Huntingdon and Godmanchester, England 10/F4
Huntington, Ark. (72940) 202/B3
Huntington, Conn. (†06484) 210/C3
Huntington, England 13/G3
Huntington (co.), Ind. 227/G3
Huntington, Ind. (46750) 227/G3
Huntington (lake), Ind. 227/F3
Huntington, Iowa (†51334) 229/D2
Huntington○, Mass. (01050) 249/C4
Huntington (creek), Nev. 266/F2
Huntington, N.J. (†08865) 273/C2
Huntington, N.Y. (11743) 276/R6
Huntington, Oreg. (97907) 291/K3
Huntington, Texas (75949) 303/K6
Huntington, Utah (84528) 304/C4
Huntington (creek), Utah 304/C4
Huntington○, Vt. (05462) 268/B3
Huntington, Va. (†22301) 307/S3
Huntington, W. Va. 188/K3
Huntington, W. Va. (*25701) 312/A6
Huntington Beach, Calif. (*92646) 204/C11
Huntington Center, Vt. (†05462) 268/B3
Huntington Park, Calif. (90255) 204/C11
Huntington Station, N.Y. (11746) 276/R6
Huntingtown, Md. (20639) 245/M6
Hunting Valley, Ohio (†44022) 284/J9
Huntland, Tenn. (37345) 237/J10
Huntleigh, Mo. (†63101) 261/O3
Huntley, Ill. (60142) 222/E1
Huntley, Minn. (56047) 255/D7
Huntley, Mont. (59037) 262/H5
Huntley, Nebr. (68951) 264/E4
Huntley, Wyo. (82218) 319/H4
Huntly, N. Zealand 100/E2
Huntly, Scotland 10/E2
Huntly, Scotland 15/F3
Huntoon, Sask. 181/H6
Huntsburg, Ohio (44046) 284/H2
Hunts Inlet, Br. Col. 184/B3
Hunts Point, Nova Scotia 168/D5
Hunts Point, Wash. (†98004) 310/B2
Huntsville, Ala. 188/J4
Huntsville, Ala. (*35801) 195/E1
Huntsville, Ark. (72740) 202/C1
Huntsville, Conn. (†06031) 210/B1
Huntsville, Ind. (†47358) 227/F4
Huntsville, Ind. (†46064) 227/G4
Huntsville, Ky. (42251) 237/H6
Huntsville, Mo. (65259) 261/H4
Huntsville, Ohio (43324) 284/C5
Huntsville, Ontario 177/E2
Huntsville, Ontario 175/E3
Huntsville, Tenn. (37756) 237/N8
Huntsville, Texas (77340) 303/J7
Huntsville, Utah (84317) 304/C2
Huntsville, Wash. (†99328) 310/G4
Hunucmá, Mexico 150/O6
Hunza (Baltit), Pakistan 68/C1
Huocheng, China 77/B3
Huon (isls.), New Caled. 87/G7
Huon (gulf), Papua N.G. 87/E6
Huon (gulf), Papua N.G. 85/C7
Huon (pen.), Papua N.G. 86/A2
Huon (riv.), Tasmania 99/C5
Huong Khe, Vietnam 72/E3
Huonville-Ranelagh, Tasmania 99/C5
Huoshan, China 77/J5
Huot, Minn. (†56716) 255/B3
Huo Xian, China 77/H4
Hupei (Hubei) (prov.), China 77/H5
Hurbanovo, Czech. 41/E3
Hurd (cape), Ontario 177/C2
Hurdland, Mo. (63547) 261/H2
Hurdle Mills, N.C. (27541) 281/L2
Hurdsfield, N. Dak. (58451) 282/L5

Indianola 385

Hure, China 77/K3
Hureidha, P.D.R. Yemen 59/E6
Hurghada, Egypt 111/F2
Hurghada, Egypt 59/B4
Hurlburt, Fla. (†32548) 212/B6
Hurley, Miss. (39555) 256/H9
Hurley, Mo. (65675) 261/F9
Hurley, N. Mex. (88043) 274/A6
Hurley, N.Y. (12443) 276/M7
Hurley, S. Dak. (57036) 298/P7
Hurley, Va. (24620) 307/D6
Hurley, Wis. (54534) 317/F3
Hurleyville, N.Y. (12747) 276/L7
Hurlford, Scotland 15/D5
Hurlock, Md. (21643) 245/P6
Huron (lake) 146/K5
Huron (lake) 162/H7
Huron, Calif. (93234) 204/E7
Huron, Ind. (47437) 227/D7
Huron, Kansas (66038) 232/G2
Huron (lake), Mich. 188/K2
Huron (co.), Mich. 250/F5
Huron (bay), Mich. 250/A2
Huron (lake), Mich. 250/G4
Huron (riv.), Mich. 250/F6
Huron (co.), Ohio 284/E3
Huron, Ohio (44839) 284/E3
Huron (riv.), Ohio 284/E3
Huron (county), Ontario 177/C4
Huron (lake), Ontario 177/B3
Huron (lake), Ontario 175/D3
Huron, S. Dak. 188/G2
Huron, S. Dak. (57350) 298/N5
Huron, Tenn. (38345) 237/E9
Huron City, Mich. (†48467) 250/G4
Huron Mountain, Mich. (†49808) 250/B2
Huron Park, Ontario 177/C4
Huron River (pt.), Mich. 250/B2
Hurricane, Ala. (†36507) 195/C9
Hurricane (cliffs), Ariz. 198/B2
Hurricane (mt.), Mont. 262/D2
Hurricane, Utah (84737) 304/A6
Hurricane, W. Va. (25526) 312/C6
Hurricane Deck, Mo. (†65079) 261/G6
Hurricane Mills, Tenn. (37078) 237/F9
Hurst, Georgia (†30560) 217/D1
Hurst, Ill. (62949) 222/D6
Hurst, Texas (76053) 303/F2
Hurst, W. Va. (†26445) 312/E4
Hurstville, Iowa (†52060) 229/M4
Hurstville, N.S. Wales 88/K4
Hurstville, N.S. Wales 97/J4
Hurt, Va. (24563) 307/K6
Hürth, W. Germany 22/B3
Hurtsboro, Ala. (36860) 195/H6
Hurunui (riv.), N. Zealand 100/D5
Hurup, Denmark 21/B4
Húsavík, Iceland 21/C1
Husher, Wis. (†53108) 317/L2
Hushpuckena, Miss. (†38774) 256/C2
Huşi, Romania 45/J2
Husk, N.C. (28639) 281/F1
Huskisson, N.S. Wales 97/F4
Huslia, Alaska (99746) 196/G1
Huson, Mont. (59846) 262/B3
Hussar, Alberta 182/D4
Hustisford, Wis. (53034) 317/J9
Hustler, Wis. (54637) 317/F8
Hustontown, Pa. (17229) 294/F5
Hustonville, Ky. (40437) 237/M6
Hustopeče, Czech. 41/D2
Husum, Sweden 18/L5
Husum, Wash. (98623) 310/D5
Husum, W. Germany 22/C1
Hutchins (mt.), N.H. 268/E2
Hutchins, Texas (75141) 303/G3
Hutchins, Wis. (†54450) 317/H6
Hutchinson, Kans. 188/G3
Hutchinson, Kansas (67501) 232/D3
Hutchinson, Kansas 146/J6
Hutchinson, Minn. (55350) 255/D6
Hutchinson (co.), S. Dak. 298/O7
Hutchinson (co.), Texas 303/C2
Hutchinson, W. Va. (†26591) 312/F4
Huth, Yemen Arab Rep. 59/D6
Hutsonville, Ill. (62433) 222/F4
Hutt (riv.), N. Zealand 100/C2
Hüttenberg, Austria 41/C3
Hüttental, W. Germany 22/C3
Hutte Sauvage (lake), Québec 174/E1
Huttig, Ark. (71747) 202/F7
Hutto, Texas (78634) 303/G7
Hutton, La. (†71402) 238/D4
Hutton, Md. (†21550) 245/A3
Huttonsville, W. Va. (26273) 312/G5
Hutton Valley, Mo. (†65793) 261/J9
Huttwil, Switzerland 39/E2
Hutubi, China 77/C3
Huumula, Hawaii (†96743) 218/H5
Huutokoski, Finland 18/P5
Huwelijkszorg, Suriname 131/C2
Huxford, Ala. (36543) 195/D8
Hu Xian, China 77/G5
Huxley, Alberta 182/D4
Huxley, Iowa (50124) 229/F5
Huxley, Texas (†75973) 303/L6
Huy, Belgium 27/G8
Huyton-with-Roby, England 13/G2
Hvannadalshnúkur (mt.), Iceland 21/C1
Hvar (isl.), Yugoslavia 45/C4
Hvidbjerg, Denmark 21/B4
Hvide Sande, Denmark 21/A6
Hviding, Denmark 21/B7
Hvítá (riv.), Iceland 21/B1
Hwainan (Huainan), China 77/J5
Hwaiteh (Huaide), China 77/K3
Hwange (Wankie), Zimbabwe 118/D3
Hwang Ho (riv.), China 54/N6
Hwangju, N. Korea 81/C4
Hwangshih (Huangshi), China 77/J5
Hyak, Wash. (98068) 310/D3
Hyalite (peak), Mont. 262/E5
Hyannis, Mass. (02601) 249/N6
Hyannis, Nebr. (69350) 264/C3
Hyannis Port, Mass. (02647) 249/N6
Hyargas, Mongolia 77/D2
Hyargas Nuur (lake), Mongolia 77/D2
Hyas, Sask. 181/J4
Hyattstown, Md. (20734) 245/J3
Hyattsville, Md. (*20780) 245/F4
Hyattville, Wyo. (82428) 319/E1
Hybart, Ala. (36452) 195/D7
Hybord, Manitoba 179/C1
Hyco (riv.), N.C. 281/L2
Hyco (riv.), Va. 307/K8
Hydaburg, Alaska (99922) 196/M2
Hyde, England 13/H2
Hyde, England 10/G2
Hyde, N. Zealand 100/C6
Hyde (co.), N.C. 281/S3
Hyde, Pa. (16843) 294/F4
Hyde (co.), S. Dak. 298/K4
Hyden, Ky. (41749) 237/P6
Hyden, W. Australia 92/B6
Hyde Park, Mass. (02136) 249/C7
Hyde Park, N.Y. (12538) 276/N6
Hyde Park, Ontario 177/C4
Hyde Park, Pa. (15641) 294/D4
Hyde Park, Utah (84318) 304/C2
Hyde Park, Vt. (05655) 268/B2
Hyde Park○, Vt. (05655) 268/B2
Hyder, Alaska (99923) 196/P2
Hyderabad, India 2/N5
Hyderabad, India 68/D5
Hyderabad, India 54/J8
Hyderabad, Pakistan 68/B3
Hyderabad, Pakistan 59/J4
Hyderabad, Pakistan 54/H7
Hydesville, Calif. (95547) 204/B3
Hydetown, Pa. (16328) 294/C2
Hydeville, Vt. (05750) 268/A4
Hydraulic, Br. Col. 184/F4
Hydro, Okla. (73048) 288/J3
Hye, Texas (78635) 303/F7
Hyères, France 28/G6
Hyères (isls.), France 28/G6
Hyesan, N. Korea 81/D3
Hygiene, Colo. (80533) 208/J2
Hyland (riv.), Yukon 187/F3
Hylo, Alberta 182/D2
Hyltebruk, Sweden 18/H8
Hyman, S.C. (†29583) 296/H4
Hymer, Kansas (†66869) 232/F3
Hymera, Ind. (47855) 227/C6
Hyndman (peak), Idaho 220/D6
Hyndman, Pa. (15545) 294/E6
Hyner, Pa. (17738) 294/G3
Hynish (bay), Scotland 15/B4
Hyogo (pref.), Japan 81/H7
Hypoluxo, Fla. (†33460) 212/F5
Hyrra Banda, Cent. Afr. Rep. 115/D2
Hyrum, Utah (84319) 304/C2
Hyrynsalmi, Finland 18/Q4
Hysham, Mont. (59038) 262/J4
Hythe, Alberta 182/A2
Hythe, Alta. 162/E4
Hythe, England 10/G5
Hythe, England 13/H6
Hythe, Tasmania 99/C5
Hytop, Ala. (35753) 195/F1
Hyuga, Japan 81/E7
Hyvinkää, Finland 18/O6

I

Ia Drang (riv.), Vietnam 72/E4
Iaeger, W. Va. (24844) 312/C8
Ialomiţa (marshes), Romania 45/J3
Ialomiţa (riv.), Romania 45/H3
Iamonia (lake), Fla. 212/B1
Iantha, Mo. (64753) 261/D8
Iar Connacht (dist.), Ireland 17/C5
Iaşi, Romania 7/G4
Iaşi, Romania 45/H2
Iatan, Mo. (†64098) 261/C4
Iatt (lake), La. 238/E3
Iba, Philippines 85/F2
Iba, Philippines 82/B3
Ibadan, Nigeria 2/K5
Ibadan, Nigeria 102/C4
Ibadan, Nigeria 106/E7
Ibagué, Colombia 126/C5
Ibagué, Colombia 120/B2
Ibaiti, Brazil 135/A3
Ibapah, Utah (84034) 304/A3
Ibar (riv.), Yugoslavia 45/E4
Ibaraki (pref.), Japan 81/K5
Ibaraki, Japan 81/J7
Ibarra, Ecuador 128/D2
Ibarra, Ecuador 120/B2
Ibarreta, Argentina 143/D2
Ibb, Yemen Arab Rep. 59/D7
Ibbenbüren, W. Germany 22/B2
'Ibbin, Jordan 65/D3
Iberia (par.), La. 238/G7
Iberia, Mo. (65486) 261/H6
Iberia, Ohio (43325) 284/E4
Iberia, Peru 128/F5
Iberville (par.), La. 238/H6
Iberville, La. (70746) 238/K2
Iberville (co.), Québec 172/D4
Iberville, Québec 172/D4
Iberville, D' (lake), Québec 174/C1
Ibi, Nigeria 106/F7
Ibiá, Brazil 132/E7
Ibibobo, Bolivia 136/D7
Ibicaraí, Brazil 132/G6
Ibicuí (riv.), Brazil 132/C10
Ibicuy, Argentina 143/G6
Ibipetuba, Brazil 132/F5
Ibitinga, Brazil 135/B2
Ibiza, Spain 33/G3
Ibiza (isl.), Spain 7/E5
Ibiza (isl.), Spain 33/G3
Ibo, Bolivia 136/D7
Ibo, Mozambique 118/G2
Ibounzi (mt.), Gabon 115/B4
Ibra, Oman 59/G5
Ibra, Wadi (dry riv.), Sudan 111/D5
Ibrány, Hungary 41/F2
'Ibri, Oman 59/G5
Ibusuki, Japan 81/E8
Içá (riv.), Brazil 120/C3
Içá (riv.), Brazil 132/G9
Ica (dept.), Peru 128/E10
Ica, Peru 128/E10
Ica, Peru 120/B4
Ica (riv.), Peru 128/E10
Icabarú, Venezuela 124/H5
Icabarú (riv.), Venezuela 124/G5
Icacos (pt.), Trin. & Tob. 161/A11
Icaño, Catamarca, Argentina 143/C2
Icaño, Santiago del Estero, Argentina 143/D2
Icard, N.C. (28666) 281/G3
Ice Harbor (dam), Wash. 310/G4
Içel (prov.), Turkey 63/F4
Içel (Mersin), Turkey 63/F4
Iceland 2/J2
Iceland 7/C2
Iceland 4/C10
ICELAND 21/B1
Ichang (Yichang), China 77/H5
Ichchapuram, India 68/F5
Ichhapur, India 68/F1
Ichihara, Japan 81/P3
Ichikawa, Japan 81/P2
Ichilo (riv.), Bolivia 136/C5
Ichinohe, Japan 81/K3
Ichinomiya, Japan 81/H6
Ichinoseki, Japan 81/K4
Ichnya, U.S.S.R. 52/D4
Ichoa (riv.), Bolivia 136/C4
Ichoca, Bolivia 136/B5
Ichtegem, Belgium 27/B6
Ichun (Yichun), China 77/L2
Ichuña, Peru 128/G11
Icicle (creek), Wash. 310/E3
Ickesburg, Pa. (17037) 294/H5
Icla, Bolivia 136/C6
Içme, Turkey 63/H3
Icó, Brazil 132/G4
Iconium, Mo. (†64776) 261/E6
Icy (bay), Alaska 196/K3
Icy (cape), Alaska 196/F1
Icy (cape), Alaska 196/K3
Icy (pt.), Alaska 196/L1
Icy (str.), Alaska 196/M1
Ida (co.), Iowa 229/C4
Ida, La. (71044) 238/C1
Ida, Mich. (48140) 250/F7
Idabel, Okla. (74745) 288/S7
Ida Grove, Iowa (51445) 229/B4
Idaho 188/D2
IDAHO 220
Idaho (co.), Idaho 220/C4
Idaho, 202
Idaho, Ohio (45661) 284/D7
Idaho (state), U.S. 146/G5
Idaho City, Idaho (83631) 220/C6
Idaho Falls, Idaho 146/G5
Idaho Falls, Idaho 188/D2
Idaho Falls, Idaho (*83401) 220/F6
Idaho Springs, Colo. (80452) 208/H3
Idahue, Chile 138/F5
Idalia, Colo. (80735) 208/P3
Idalou, Texas (79329) 303/C4
Idana, Kansas (67432) 232/E2
Idanha, Oreg. (97350) 291/E3
Idanha-a-Nova, Portugal 33/C3
Idar-Oberstein, W. Germany 22/B4
Idaville, Ind. (47950) 227/D3
Idaville, Pa. (17337) 294/H5
Iddan, Somalia 115/J2
Iddesleigh, Alberta 182/E4
Ide, Japan 81/J7
Ideal, Georgia (31041) 217/D6
Ideal, S. Dak. (57541) 298/K6
Idehan Murzuk (des.), Libya 111/B2
Idehan Ubari (des.), Libya 111/B2
Idelès, Algeria 106/F4
Ider, Ala. (35981) 195/G1
Ider Gol (riv.), Mongolia 77/E2
Idfu, Egypt 111/F3
Idfu, Egypt 59/B5
Ídhi (mt.), Greece 45/G8
Ídhra, Greece 45/F7
Idi, Indonesia 85/B4
Idil, Turkey 63/J4
Idiofa, Zaire 115/C4
Idlewild, Mich. (49642) 250/D5
Idlewild, Tenn. (38346) 237/D8
Idleyld Park, Oreg. (97447) 291/D4
Idlib (prov.), Syria 63/G5
Idlib, Syria 63/G5
Idna, West Bank 65/B4
Idrigill (pt.), Scotland 15/B3
Idyllwild-Pine Cove, Calif. (92349) 204/J10
Ie (isl.), Japan 81/N6
Ieper, Belgium 27/B7
Ierápetra, Greece 45/G8
Iet, Somalia 115/H3
Ifakara, Tanzania 115/G5
Ifalik (atoll), Micronesia 87/E5
Ifanadiana, Madagascar 118/H4
Ife, Nigeria 106/E7
Iférouane, Niger 102/C3
Iférouane, Niger 106/F5
Iffley, Sask. 181/C3
Ifni, Morocco 106/B3
Ifni, Morocco 102/B2
Ifugao (prov.), Philippines 82/C2
Igal, Hungary 41/D3
Igara-Paraná (riv.), Colombia 126/D8
Igarapava, Brazil 135/C2
Igarapé-Miri, Brazil 132/D3
Igarka, U.S.S.R. 4/C5
Igarka, U.S.S.R. 54/K3
Igarka, U.S.S.R. 48/J3
Iğdır, Turkey 63/K3
Iggesund, Sweden 18/K6
Igis, Switzerland 39/J3
Igiugig, Alaska (†99613) 196/G3
Iglesias, Italy 34/B5
Igli, Algeria 106/D2
Igloo, S. Dak. (†57774) 298/B7
Igloolik, Canada 4/B14
Igloolik, N.W.T. 162/H2
Igloolik, N.W. Terrs. 187/K3
Iglosiatik (isl.), Newf. 166/B2
Ignace, Ont. 162/G6
Ignace, Ontario 175/B3
Ignace, Ontario 177/G5
Ignacio, Calif. (94947) 204/H1
Ignacio, Colo. (81137) 208/D8
Ignacio Agramonte, Cuba 158/G3
Ignacio de la Llave, Mexico 150/Q2
İğneada (cape), Turkey 63/C2
Igoumenitsa, Greece 45/E6
Igra, U.S.S.R. 52/H3
Igrim, U.S.S.R. 48/G3
Iguaçu (riv.) 120/D5
Iguaçu (riv.), Brazil 132/C9
Igualada, Spain 33/G2
Iguala de la Independencia, Mexico 150/K7
Iguape, Brazil 135/C4
Iguassú (falls) 120/D5
Iguatu, Brazil 120/F3
Iguatu, Brazil 132/G4
Iguazú (falls), Argentina 143/F2
Iguazú (falls), Brazil 132/C9
Iguazú (falls), Paraguay 144/E4
Iguazú Nat'l Park, Argentina 143/E2
Iguéla, Gabon 115/A4
Iguidi, Erg (des.), 102/B2
Iguidi, Erg (des.), Algeria 106/C3
Iguidi, Erg (des.), Mauritania 106/C3
Iheya (isl.), Japan 81/N6
Ihlen, Minn. (56140) 255/B7
Ihosy, Madagascar 118/H4
Ihu, Papua N.G. 85/B7
Ii (riv.), Finland 7/G2
Iida, Japan 81/H6
Iijoki (riv.), Finland 18/O4
Iisalmi, Finland 18/P5
Iizuka, Japan 81/E7
Ijamsville, Md. (21754) 245/J3
Ijebu-Ode, Nigeria 106/E7
IJist, Netherlands 27/H2
IJmeer (bay), Netherlands 27/C4
IJmuiden, Netherlands 27/E4
IJssel (riv.), Netherlands 27/J4
IJsselmeer (lake), Netherlands 27/G3
IJsselstein, Netherlands 27/F4
Ijuí, Brazil 132/C10
IJzendijke, Netherlands 27/D6
Ikaalinen, Finland 18/N6
Ikaría (isl.), Greece 45/G7
Ikast, Denmark 21/C5
Ikeda, Hokkaido, Japan 81/L2
Ikeda, Osaka, Japan 81/H7
Ikeja, Nigeria 106/E7
Ikela, Zaire 115/D4
Ikelemba, Congo 115/C3
Ikhtiman, Bulgaria 45/F4
Iki (isl.), Japan 81/D7
Ikom, Nigeria 106/F7
Ikoma, Japan 81/J8
Ikopa (riv.), Madagascar 118/H3
Ikpikpuk (riv.), Alaska 196/H1
Iksal, Israel 65/C2
Ikuno, Japan 81/G6
Ila, Georgia (30647) 217/F2
Ilagan, Philippines 82/C2
Ilam (gov.), Iran 66/E4
Ilam, Iran 66/E4
Ilam, Nepal 68/F3
Ilan, China 77/K7
Ilanskiy, U.S.S.R. 48/K4
Ilanz, Switzerland 39/H3
Ilaro, Nigeria 106/E7
Ilasco, Mo. (†63401) 261/K3
Ilava, Czech. 41/E2
Ilave, Peru 128/H11
Iława, Poland 47/D2
Ilderton, Ontario 177/C4
Île-à-la-Crosse, Sask. 181/L3
Île-à-la-Crosse (lake), Sask. 181/L3
Île-Bizard, Québec 172/H4
Ilebo, Zaire 115/D4
Île de France (trad. prov.), France, 29
Île-de-Montréal (co.), Québec 172/H4
Île des Chênes, Manitoba 179/F5
Île-Jésus (co.), Québec 172/H4
Ilek (riv.), U.S.S.R. 52/J4
Île-Perrot, Québec 172/G4
Îles (lake), Québec 172/B3
Ilesha, Nigeria 106/F7
Ilfeld, N. Mex. (87538) 274/D3
Ilfis (riv.), Switzerland 39/E3
Ilford, Manitoba 179/J2
Ilford, N.S. Wales 97/E3
Ilfracombe, England 10/D5
Ilfracombe, England 13/C6
Ilgaz, Turkey 63/E2
Ilgaz (mts.), Turkey 63/E2
Ilgın, Turkey 63/D3
Ilha Grande (bay), Brazil 135/D3
Ílhavo, Portugal 33/B2
Ilhéus, Brazil 120/F4
Ilhéus, Brazil 132/G6
Ili (riv.), U.S.S.R. 54/J5
Ili (riv.), U.S.S.R. 48/H5
Iliamna, Alaska (99606) 196/G3
Iliamna (lake), Alaska 188/C6
Iliamna (lake), Alaska 196/G3
Iliamna (vol.), Alaska 196/H2
Iliç, Turkey 63/H3
Ilıca, Turkey 63/J3
Iliff, Colo. (80736) 208/N1
Iligan, Philippines 82/E6
Iligan (bay), Philippines 82/E6
Ilin (isl.), Philippines 82/C4
Ilio (pt.), Hawaii 218/G1
Ilion, N.Y. (13357) 276/K5
Ilium (ruins), Turkey 63/B6
Ilkeston, England 13/F5
Ilkeston, England 10/F4
Illabo, N.S. Wales 97/D4
Illahe, Oreg. (†97406) 291/C5
Illampu, Nevada (mt.), Bolivia 136/A4
Illana (bay), Philippines 82/D7
Illana, Spain 33/E2
Illapel, Chile 138/A8
Ille-et-Vilaine (dept.), France 28/C3
Illéla, Niger 106/F6
Iller (riv.), W. Germany 22/D4
Illescas, Spain 33/D2
Illescas, Uruguay 145/D4
Ille-sur-Têt, France 28/E6
Illimani, Nevada (mt.), Bolivia 136/B5
Illinois 188/J3
ILLINOIS 222
Illinois (bayou), Ark. 202/D3
Illinois (riv.), Colo. 208/G1
Illinois (riv.), Ill. 188/H2
Illinois (riv.), Ill. 222/C4
Illinois (riv.), Okla. 288/S3
Illinois (riv.), Oreg. 291/D5
Illinois (state), U.S. 146/K6
Illinois - Mississippi (canal), Ill. 222/C2
Illiopolis, Ill. (62539) 222/D4
Illizi, Algeria 106/F3
Illizi, Algeria 102/C2
Illmo, Mo. (63754) 261/O8
Illnau, Switzerland 39/G2
Illora, Spain 33/E4
Illuka, N.S. Wales 97/G1
Il'men (lake), U.S.S.R. 7/H3
Il'men' (lake), U.S.S.R. 52/D3
Ilmenau, E. Germany 22/D3
Ilmenau (riv.), W. Germany 22/D2
Ilminster, England 13/D7
Ilo, Peru 128/G11
Ilobasco, El Salvador 154/C4
Ilocos Norte (prov.), Philippines 82/C1
Ilocos Sur (prov.), Philippines 82/C2
Iloilo (prov.), Philippines 82/D5
Iloilo, Philippines 85/G3
Iloilo, Philippines 82/D5
Iloilo, Philippines 54/O8
Iloilo (str.), Philippines 82/D5
Ilomantsi, Finland 18/R5
Ilorin, Nigeria 106/E7
Ilorin, Nigeria 102/C4
Ilpendam, Netherlands 27/C4
Ilsley, Ky. (†42408) 237/F6
Ilubabor (prov.), Ethiopia 111/F6
Ilūkste, U.S.S.R. 53/D3
Ilwaco, Wash. (98624) 310/A4
Iłża, Poland 47/E3
Imabari, Japan 81/F6
Imandra (lake), U.S.S.R. 48/D3
Imandra (lake), U.S.S.R. 52/D1
Imari, Japan 81/D7
Imataca, Serranía (mts.), Venezuela 124/H4
Imatra, Finland 18/Q6
Imazu, Japan 81/H6
Imbâba, Egypt 111/J3
Imbabura (prov.), Ecuador 128/C2
Imbaimadai, Guyana 131/A3
Imbert, Dom. Rep. 158/D5
Imbituba, Brazil 132/D10
Imbituva, Brazil 135/A4
Imbler, Oreg. (97841) 291/J2
Imboden, Ark. (72434) 202/H1
Imeri, Sierra (mts.), Venezuela 124/F7
Imese, Zaire 115/C3
Imi, Ethiopia 111/H6
Imías, Cuba 158/K4
Imilac, Chile 138/B4
Imishli, U.S.S.R. 52/G7
Imlay, Nev. (89418) 266/C2
Imlay, S. Dak. (†57780) 298/E6
Imlay City, Mich. (48444) 250/F5
Imlaystown, N.J. (08526) 273/D3
Imler, Pa. (16655) 294/E5
Immaculata, Pa. (19345) 294/L6
Immenstadt im Allgäu, W. Germany 22/C5
Immingham, England 13/G4
Immokalee, Fla. (33934) 212/E5
Imnaha, Oreg. (97842) 291/L2
Imnaha (riv.), Oreg. 291/L2
Imo (state), Nigeria 106/F7
Imogene, Iowa (51645) 229/C7
Imola, Italy 34/C2
Impach, Wash. (†99138) 310/G2
Imperatriz, Brazil 120/E3
Imperatriz, Brazil 132/E4
Imperia (prov.), Italy 34/B3
Imperia, Italy 34/B3
Imperial (dam), Ariz. 198/A6
Imperial (res.), Ariz. 198/A6
Imperial (co.), Calif. 204/K10
Imperial, Calif. (92251) 204/K11
Imperial (dam), Calif. 204/L11
Imperial (res.), Calif. 204/L10
Imperial (valley), Calif. 204/K10
Imperial (riv.), Chile 138/D2
Imperial, Mo. (63052) 261/M6
Imperial, Nebr. (69033) 264/C4
Imperial, Pa. (15126) 294/B5
Imperial, Peru 128/D9
Imperial, Sask. 181/F4
Imperial, Texas (79743) 303/B6
Imperial Beach, Calif. (92032) 204/H11
Imperial Mills, Alberta 182/E2
Impfondo, Congo 115/C3
Imphal, India 54/L7
Imphal, India 68/G4
Impora, Bolivia 136/C7
İmralı (isl.), Turkey 63/C2
İmranlı, Turkey 63/H2
İmroz (Gökçeada) (isl.), Turkey 63/A2
Imst, Austria 41/A3
Imuris, Mexico 150/D1
Imuruan (bay), Philippines 82/B5
Imuruk (basin), Alaska 196/E1
'Imwas, West Bank 65/B4
Ina, Ill. (62846) 222/E5
Ina, Japan 81/H6
Ina (riv.), Japan 81/H7
Inaha, Georgia (†31790) 217/E7
Inala, Queensland 88/K3
Inala, Queensland 95/D3
Inambari, Peru 128/H9
Inambari (riv.), Peru 128/H9
In Amenas, Algeria 106/F3
In Amguel, Algeria 106/E4
Inangahua Junction, N. Zealand 100/C4
Iñapari, Peru 128/H8
Inarajan, Guam 86/K7
Inari, Finland 18/P2
Inari (lake), Finland 7/G2
Inari (lake), Finland 18/P2
Inavale, Nebr. (68952) 264/F4
Inawashiro (lake), Japan 81/K5
In Azaoua (well), Niger 106/F4
Inca, Spain 33/H3
Incacamachi, Cerro (mt.), Bolivia 136/A6
Inca de Oro, Chile 138/B6
Incaguasi, Nevada (mt.), Chile 138/C6
Incahuasi, Cerro de (mt.), Argentina 143/C2
Ince (cape), Turkey 63/F1
Incekum (cape), Turkey 63/F4
Incesu, Turkey 63/F3
Inchard, Loch (inlet), Scotland 15/C2
Inchcape (Bell Rock) (isl.), Scotland 15/F4
Inchelium, Wash. (99138) 310/G2
Inchigeelagh, Ireland 17/C8
Inchiri (reg.), Mauritania 106/A5
Inchkeith, Sask. 181/J5
Inchkeith (isl.), Scotland 15/D1
Inchnadamph, Scotland 15/D2
Inch'ŏn, S. Korea 54/O6
Inch'ŏn, S. Korea 81/C5
Indaal, Loch (inlet), Scotland 15/B5
In Dagouber (well), Mali 106/D4
Indalsälven (riv.), Sweden 18/H5
Indawgyi (lake), Burma 72/C1
Indé, Mexico 150/G4
Independence (co.), Ark. 202/G2
Independence, Belize 154/C2
Independence, Calif. (93526) 204/H7
Independence, Ind. (†47918) 227/C4
Independence, Iowa (50644) 229/K4
Independence, Kansas (67301) 232/G4
Independence, Ky. (41051) 237/M3
Independence, La. (70443) 238/M1
Independence (lake), Mich. 250/B2
Independence, Minn. (†55359) 255/F5
Independence (lake), Minn. 255/F5
Independence, Miss. (38638) 256/E1
Independence, Mo. (*64050) 261/R5
Independence (mts.), Nev. 266/E1
Independence, Ohio (44131) 284/H9
Independence, Oreg. (97351) 291/D3
Independence, Va. (24348) 307/F7
Independence, W. Va. (26374) 312/G4
Independence, Wis. (54747) 317/D7
Independencia, Bolivia 136/B5
Independencia, Brazil 132/C6
Independencia (prov.), Dom. Rep. 158/D6
Independencia (bay), Peru 128/D10
Independencia (isl.), Peru 128/D10
Independencia, Venezuela 124/B4
Index, Wash. (98256) 310/D3
Index (peak), Wyo. 319/C1
India 2/N4
India 54/J7
INDIA 68/D4
Indiahoma, Okla. (73552) 288/J5
Indialantic, Fla. (32903) 212/F3
India Muerta (riv.), Uruguay 145/E4
Indian (ocean) 54/H10
Indian (ocean) 102/G7
Indian (mt.), Conn. 210/B1
Indian (pond), Conn. 210/A1
Indian (riv.), Del. 245/S6
Indian (riv.), Fla. 212/F3
Indian (creek), Idaho 220/C5
Indian (creek), Ind. 227/D6
Indian (creek), Ind. 227/E8
Indian (creek), Md. 245/G4
Indian (lake), Mich. 250/C2
Indian (stream), N.H. 268/E1
Indian (lake), N.Y. 276/M3
Indian (harb.), Nova Scotia 168/G3
Indian (lake), Ohio 284/C5
Indian (creek), S. Dak. 298/B4
Indian (creek), Utah 304/B5
Indian (creek), Utah 304/E5
Indiana 188/J3
INDIANA 227
Indiana (co.), Pa. 294/D4
Indiana, Pa. (15701) 294/D4
Indiana (state), U.S. 146/K6
Indiana Dunes Nat'l Lakeshore, Ind. 227/C1
Indianapolis (cap.), Ind. 146/K5
Indianapolis (cap.), Ind. 188/J3
Indianapolis (cap.), Ind. (*46201) 227/E5
Indian Bay, Manitoba 179/G5
Indian Beach, N.C. (†28575) 281/R5
Indian Brook, Nova Scotia 168/H2
Indian Cabins, Alberta 182/B4
Indian Creek, Fla. (†33139) 212/B4
Indian Creek, Ill. (†60069) 222/B4
Indian Harbour Beach, Fla. (†32901) 212/F3
Indian Head, Md. (20640) 245/K6
Indian Head, Sask. 162/F5
Indian Head, Sask. 181/H5
Indian Hill, Ohio (†45201) 284/C9
Indian Hills, Ky. (†40201) 237/K1
Indian Hills, N.C. (†28719) 281/C4
Indian Lake, N.Y. (12842) 276/M3
Indian Lake, Pa. (†15560) 294/E5
Indian Mills, W. Va. (24949) 312/E7
Indian Mound, Tenn. (37079) 237/F7
Indian Neck, Conn. (†06405) 210/D3
Indian Neck, Va. (23077) 307/O5
Indian Ocean 2/N6
Indian Ocean 5/C3
Indian Ocean, Indonesia 85/E8
Indian Ocean, S. Australia 94/E7
Indian Ocean, Tasmania 99/A4
Indian Ocean, Victoria 97/B6
Indian Ocean, W. Australia 92/A5
Indianola, Ill. 61850) 222/F4
Indianola, Iowa (50125) 229/F6

Kamienna Góra 389

Jones Creek, Texas (†77541) 303/J9
Jonesdale, Wis. (†53565) 317/F10
Jones Mills, Ark. (72105) 202/E5
Jones Mills, Pa. (15646) 294/D5
Jonesport, Maine (04649) 243/H6
Jonesport○, Maine (04649) 243/H6
Jones Springs, W. Va. (25427) 312/K4
Jonestown, Miss. (38639) 256/D2
Jonestown, Pa. (17038) 294/K5
Jonesville, Alaska (†99674) 196/B1
Jonesville, Ind. (47247) 227/F6
Jonesville, Ky. (41052) 237/M3
Jonesville, La. (71343) 238/G3
Jonesville, Mich. (49250) 250/E6
Jonesville, N.C. (28642) 281/H2
Jonesville, S.C. (29353) 296/D2
Jonesville, Vt. (05466) 268/B3
Jonesville, Va. (24263) 307/B7
Jonglei, Sudan 111/F6
Joniškis, U.S.S.R. 53/B2
Jönköping (co.), Sweden 18/H8
Jönköping, Sweden 18/H8
Jönköping, Sweden 7/F3
Jonquière, Que. 162/J6
Jonquière, Québec 172/F1
Jonquière, Québec 174/C3
Jonuta, Mexico 150/N7
Jonzac, France 28/C5
Joplin, Mo. (64801) 261/C8
Joplin, Mo. 146/J6
Joplin, Mo. 188/H3
Joplin, Mont. (59531) 262/F2
Joppa, Ala. (35087) 195/E2
Joppa, Ill. (62953) 222/E6
Joppa, Tenn. (†37861) 237/O8
Joppatowne, Md. (†21085) 245/N3
Jorat (mt.), Switzerland 39/C3
Jordan 2/L4
Jordan 54/E6
JORDAN 59/C3
Jordan (dam), Ala. 195/F5
Jordan (lake), Ala. 195/F5
Jordan, (creek) Idaho 220/A7
Jordan, Iowa (†50036) 229/F4
Jordan (riv.), Israel 65/D3
Jordan (riv.), Jordan 65/D3
Jordan, Minn. (55352) 255/E6
Jordan, Mont. (59337) 262/J3
Jordan, N.Y. (13080) 276/H4
Jordan, B. Everett (lake), N.C. 281/M3
Jordan (bay), Nova Scotia 168/C5
Jordan (lake), Nova Scotia 168/C4
Jordan (riv.), Nova Scotia 168/C5
Jordan (creek), Oreg. 291/K5
Jordan, S.C. (†29102) 296/G4
Jordan (riv.), Utah 304/C3
Jordan Falls, Nova Scotia 168/C5
Jordan River, Sask. 181/H2
Jordan Valley, Oreg. (97910) 291/K5
Jorge Montt (isl.), Chile 138/D9
Jorhat, India 68/G3
Jorm, Afghanistan 68/C1
Jorm, Afghanistan 59/K2
Jörn, Sweden 18/M4
Jornada del Muerto (valley), N. Mex. 274/C5
Jorquera (riv.), Chile 138/B6
Jõrva-Jaani, U.S.S.R. 53/D1
Jos, Nigeria 106/F7
Jos, Nigeria 102/C4
Jos (plat.), Nigeria 106/F7
Jose Abad Santos, Philippines 82/E8
José Agustín Palacios, Bolivia 136/B3
José Batlle y Ordóñez, Uruguay 145/D4
José Cardel, Mexico 150/Q1
José de San Martín, Argentina 143/B5
José Enrique Rodó, Uruguay 145/B4
José Ignacio (lag.), Uruguay 145/E5
José M. Micheo, Argentina 143/G7
Jose Panganiban, Philippines 82/D3
José Pedro Varela, Uruguay 145/E4
Joseph (lake), Newf. 166/B3
Joseph (lake), Ontario 177/E2
Joseph, Oreg. (97846) 291/K2
Joseph (creek), Oreg. 291/K2
Joseph, Utah (84739) 304/B5
Joseph Bonaparte (gulf) 88/D2
Joseph Bonaparte (gulf), Australia 87/C7
Joseph Bonaparte (gulf), North. Terr. 93/A3
Joseph Bonaparte (gulf), W. Australia 92/E1
Joseph City, Ariz. (86032) 198/E4
Josephine, Ala. (†36530) 195/C10
Josephine (co.), Oreg. 291/D5
Josephine, Pa. (15750) 294/D5
Joshinetsu-Kogen National Park, Japan 81/J5
Joshua (pt.), Conn. 210/E4
Joshua Tree, Calif. (92252) 204/J9
Joshua Tree Nat'l Mon., Calif. 204/J10
Jostedal, Norway 18/E6
Jostedalsbreen (glac.), Norway 18/E6
Jost Van Dyke (isl.), Virgin Is. (Br.) 161/C3
Jost Van Dyke (isl.), Virgin Is. (Br.) 156/G1
Joubert, S. Dak. (†57344) 298/M7
Jourdanton, Texas (78026) 303/F9
Joure, Netherlands 27/H3
Joussard, Alberta 182/B2
Joux (lake), Switzerland 39/B3
Jovellanos, Cuba 156/B2
Jovellanos, Cuba 158/D1
Joveyn (riv.), Iran 66/K2
Joy, Ill. (61260) 222/C2
Joy, Ky. (†42047) 237/E6
Joyce, La. (71440) 238/E3
Joyce, Wash. (98343) 310/B2
Joyce's Country (dist.), Ireland 17/B4
Joyo, Japan 81/J7
Juab (co.), Utah 304/A4
Juana Díaz, P. Rico 161/C2
Juan Aldama, Mexico 150/H4
Juan D. Jackson, Uruguay 145/C4
Juan de Fuca (str.) 146/F5
Juan de Fuca (str.), Br. Col. 162/D6
Juan de Fuca (str.), Br. Col. 184/J4
Juan de Fuca (str.), Wash. 188/A1
Juan de Fuca (str.), Wash. 310/A2
Juan de Mena, Paraguay 144/D4
Juan de Nova (isl.), Réunion 102/G6
Juan de Nova (isl.), Réunion 118/G3
Juan Fernández (isls.), Chile 2/E7
Juan Fernández (isls.), Chile 120/B6
Juangriego, Venezuela 124/G2
Juani (isl.), Tanzania 115/G5
Juanita, N. Dak. (58453) 282/N4
Juanita, Wash. (98033) 310/B1
Juanjuí, Peru 128/D6
Juan L. Lacaze, Uruguay 145/B5
Juan Stuven (isl.), Chile 138/D7
Juárez, Argentina 143/D4
Juárez, Mexico 150/J3
Juazeiro, Brazil 132/G5
Juàzeiro, Brazil 120/E3
Juazeiro do Norte, Brazil 132/F4
Juàzeiro do Norte, Brazil 120/F3
Juba, Sudan 111/F7
Juba, Sudan 102/F4
Jubail, Saudi Arabia 59/F4
Jubba, Saudi Arabia 59/D4
Jubbada Hoose (prov.), Somalia 115/H3
Jubbulpore (Jabalpur), India 68/D4
Jubilee (lake), W. Australia 88/D5
Juby (cape), Morocco 106/B3
Júcar (riv.), Spain 7/D5
Júcar (riv.), Spain 33/F3
Júcaro, Cuba 158/F2
Juchipila, Mexico 150/H6
Juchique de Ferrer, Mexico 150/Q1
Juchitán de Zaragoza, Mexico 150/M8
Jucuarán, El Salvador 154/C4
Jud, N. Dak. (58454) 282/N6
Juda, Wis. (53550) 317/H10
Judaea (reg.), Israel 65/B5
Judaea (reg.), Jordan 65/C4
Judas (pt.), C. Rica 154/E6
Judenburg, Austria 41/C3
Judibana, Venezuela 124/C2
Judique, Nova Scotia 168/G3
Judith (riv.), Mont. 262/G3
Judith (pt.), R.I. 249/J7
Judith Basin (co.), Mont. 262/F4
Judith Gap, Mont. (59453) 262/G4
Judson, Ind. (47856) 227/C5
Judson, Minn. (†56055) 255/D6
Judson, N. Dak. (†58563) 282/H6
Judsonia, Ark. (72081) 202/G3
Judyville, Ind. (†47993) 227/C4
Juelsminde, Denmark 21/D6
Juhu, India 68/B7
Juichin (Ruijin), China 77/J6
Juigalpa, Nicaragua 154/E4
Juist (isl.), W. Germany 22/B2
Juiz de Fora, Brazil 120/E5
Juiz de Fora, Brazil 135/E2
Juiz de Fora, Brazil 132/F8
Jujuy (prov.), Argentina 143/C1
Jujuy, Argentina 143/C1
Jujuy, Argentina 120/C5
Jukskei (riv.), S. Africa 118/H6
Julesburg, Colo. (80737) 208/P1
Juli, Peru 128/H11
Juliaca, Peru 120/B4
Juliaca, Peru 128/G10
Julia Creek, Queensland 88/G4
Julia Creek, Queensland 95/B4
Juliaetta, Idaho (83535) 220/B3
Julian, Calif. (92036) 204/J10
Julian, Nebr. (68379) 264/J4
Julian, N.C. (27283) 281/K3
Julian, Pa. (16844) 294/G4
Julian Alps (range), Italy 34/D1
Julianatop (mt.), Suriname 131/C4
Julianehåb, Greenl. 4/D12
Julianehåb, Greenland 2/G2
Julianehåb, Greenland 146/P3
Jülich, W. Germany 22/B3
Juliette, Georgia (31046) 217/E4
Juliff, Texas (†77583) 303/J3
Julio María Sanz, Uruguay 145/E4
Juliustown, N.J. (08042) 273/D3
Jullundur, India 68/D2
Jumbilla, Peru 128/C5
Jumbo, Okla. (†74523) 288/P6
Jumilla, Spain 33/F3
Jumla, Nepal 68/E3
Jumna (riv.), India 68/E3
Jump (riv.), Wis. 317/E5
Jumpertown, Miss. (†38829) 256/G1
Jumping Branch, W. Va. (25969) 312/E7
Jump River, Wis. (54434) 317/E5
Junagadh, India 68/B4
Junaina, Saudi Arabia 59/D5
Juncal, Argentina 143/F6
Juncos, P. Rico 161/E2
Juncos, P. Rico 156/G1
Junction, Ill. (62954) 222/E6
Junction, Texas (76849) 303/E7
Junction, Utah (84740) 304/B5
Junction, W. Va. (26824) 312/J4
Junction City, Ark. (71749) 202/E7
Junction City, Georgia (31812) 217/C5
Junction City, Ill. (†61601) 222/D5
Junction City, Kansas (66441) 232/E2
Junction City, Ky. (40440) 237/M5
Junction City, La. (71749) 238/E1
Junction City, Mo. (†63645) 261/M7
Junction City, Ohio (43748) 284/F6
Junction City, Oreg. (97448) 291/D3
Junction City, Wis. (54443) 317/G6
Jundah, Queensland 95/B5
Jundah, Queensland 88/G4
Jundiaí, Brazil 135/C3
Jundiaí, Brazil 132/E8
Juneau, Alaska 146/E4
Juneau (cap.), Alaska 188/E6
Juneau (cap.), Alaska (99801) 196/N1
Juneau, U.S. 4/D16
Juneau, U.S. 2/C3
Juneau (co.), Wis. 317/F8
Juneau, Wis. (53039) 317/J9
Juneda, Spain 33/G2
Junee, N.S. Wales 97/D4
June in Winter (lake), Fla. 212/E4
June Lake, Calif. (93529) 204/G6
June Park, Fla. (†32901) 212/F3
Jungar, China 77/H4
Jungfrau (mt.), Switzerland 39/E3
Jungfraujoch, Switzerland 39/E3
Junggar Pendi (desert basin), China 77/C2
Junglei (prov.), Sudan 111/F6
Juniata, Nebr. (68955) 264/F4
Juniata (co.), Pa. 294/H4
Juniata (riv.), Pa. 294/G5
Juniata Terrace, Pa. (†17044) 294/G4
Junín, Argentina 143/F7
Junín, Argentina 120/C6
Junín (dept.), Peru 128/E8
Junín, Peru 128/E8
Junín (lake), Peru 128/E8
Junín de los Andes, Argentina 143/B4
Junior, W. Va. (26275) 312/G5
Juniper (mts.), Ariz. 198/C3
Juniper (mt.), Colo. 208/C1
Juniper, Georgia (31801) 217/C6
Juniper, New Bruns. 170/C2
Juniper (creek), S.C. 296/H2
Junius, S. Dak. (†57042) 298/P6
Juniye, Lebanon 63/F5
Junlian, China 77/F6
Juno, Georgia (30534) 217/D2
Juno, North. Terr. 93/C5
Juno, Tenn. (†38351) 237/E9
Juno, Texas (76943) 303/C7
Juno Beach, Fla. (†33404) 212/F5
Junosuando, Sweden 18/N3
Juntura, Oreg. (97911) 291/K4
Jun Xian, China 77/H5
Juojärvi (lake), Finland 18/Q5
Jupiter, Fla. (33458) 212/F5
Jupiter, N.C. (28787) 281/D3
Jupiter Island, Fla. (†33455) 212/F4
Juquiá, Brazil 135/C4
Jur (riv.), Sudan 111/E6
Jura (dept.), France 28/F4
Jura (mts.), France 28/F4
Jura (isl.), Scotland 10/D3
Jura (isl.), Scotland 15/C5
Jura (sound), Scotland 15/C5
Jura (sound), Scotland 10/D3
Jura (canton), Switzerland /D2
Jura (mts.), Switzerland 39/B3
Juradó, Colombia 126/B4
Jurbarkas, U.S.S.R. 53/B3
Jurmala, U.S.S.R. 53/B2
Jurmala, U.S.S.R. 52/B3
Jurong, Singapore 72/E6
Juruá (riv.), Brazil 120/C3
Juruá (riv.), Brazil 132/G10
Juruá (riv.), Peru 128/F7
Juruena, Brazil 132/B6
Juruena (riv.), Brazil 120/D4
Juruena (riv.), Brazil 132/B5
Juruti, Brazil 132/B3
Juseplin, Venezuela 124/G3
Juskatla, Br. Col. 184/A3
Jussy, Switzerland 39/B4
Justice, Ill. (†60458) 222/B6
Justice, Manitoba 179/C4
Justice, W. Va. (24851) 312/C7
Justiceburg, Texas (79330) 303/C5
Justin, Texas (76247) 303/F1
Justus, Ohio (†44662) 284/G4
Jutaí (riv.), Brazil 132/G9
Jüterbog, E. Germany 22/E3
Jutiapa, Guatemala 154/B3
Jutiapa, Honduras 154/D3
Juticalpa, Honduras 154/D3
Jutland (pen.), Denmark 21/C5
Jutland (pen.), Denmark 18/F9
Jutland, N.J. (08809) 273/D2
Juuka, Finland 18/Q5
Juventud (municipio especial), Cuba 158/C2
Juventud (isl.), Cuba 146/K7
Juventud, Isla de la (Pines), Cuba 158/B3
Juventud (Pines) (isl.), Cuba 156/A2
Juwara, Oman 59/G6
Ju Xian, China 77/J4
Juye, China 77/J4
Jyderup, Denmark 21/E6
Jylland (Jutland) (pen.), Denmark 21/C5
Jyske Ås (hills), Denmark 21/D3
Jyväskylä, Finland 7/G2
Jyväskylä, Finland 18/O5

K

K2 (mt.) 54/J6
K2 (mt.), Pakistan 68/D1
Kaaawa, Hawaii (96730) 218/F1
Kaabong, Uganda 115/F3
Kaala (mt.), Hawaii 218/D1
Kaanapali, Hawaii (†96761) 218/H2
Kaba (Habahe), China 77/C2
Kaba, Hungary 41/F2
Kabacan, Philippines 82/E7
Kabaena (isl.), Indonesia 85/G7
Kabala, S. Leone 106/B7
Kabale, Uganda 115/E4
Kabalo, Zaire 115/E5
Kabambare, Zaire 115/E4
Kabardin-Balkar A.S.S.R., U.S.S.R. 48/E5
Kabardin-Balkar A.S.S.R., U.S.S.R. 52/F6
Kabare, Zaire 115/E4
Kabarega Nat'l Park, Uganda 115/F3
Kabasalan, Philippines 82/D7
Kabba, Nigeria 106/F7
Kabetogama, Minn. (†56669) 255/F2
Kabetogama (lake), Minn. 255/E2
Kabinakagami (riv.), Ontario 177/J5
Kabin Buri, Thailand 72/D4
Kabinda, Zaire 115/D5
Kabir Kuh (mts.), Iran 66/E4
Kabompo, Zambia 115/D6
Kabompo (riv.), Zambia 115/D6
Kabong, Malaysia 85/E5
Kabongo, Zaire 115/E5
Kabud Gonbad, Iran 66/L2
Kabul (cap.), Afghanistan 68/B2
Kabul (cap.), Afghanistan 59/J3
Kabul (cap.), Afghanistan 54/H6
Kabul (cap.), Afghanistan 2/N4
Kabul (riv.), Afghanistan 68/C2
Kabul (riv.), Afghanistan 59/K3
Kabul (riv.), Pakistan 68/C2
Kabunda, Zaire 115/E6
Kabwe, Zambia 102/E6
Kabwe, Zambia 115/E6
Kabylia (reg.), Algeria 106/E1
Kachemak, Alaska (†99663) 196/B2
Kachemak (bay), Alaska 196/B2
Kachess (lake), Wash. 310/D3
Kachin (state), Burma 72/C1
Kachug, U.S.S.R. 48/L4
Kaçkar Dağı (mt.), Turkey 63/J2
Kackley, Kansas (†66948) 232/E2
Kadaň, Czech. 41/B1
Kadan Kyun (isl.), Burma 72/C4
Kadavu (Kandavu) (isl.), Fiji 87/H7
Kadayanallur, India 68/D7
Kadei (riv.), Cameroon 115/C3
Kadei (riv.), Cent. Afr. Rep. 115/C3
Kadei (riv.), Congo 115/C3
Kadıköy, Turkey 63/D6
Kadina, S. Australia 88/F6
Kadina, S. Australia 94/F5
Kadınhanı, Turkey 63/E3
Kadiolo, Mali 106/C6
Kadiri, India 68/D6
Kadirli, Turkey 63/F4
Kadiyevka (Stakhanov), U.S.S.R. 52/E5
Kadmat (isl.), India 68/C6
Kadoka, S. Dak. (57543) 298/F6
Kadoma, Japan 81/J7
Kadoma (Gatooma), Zimbabwe 118/D3
Kadugli, Sudan 111/E5
Kadugli, Sudan 102/E3
Kaduna (state), Nigeria 106/F6
Kaduna, Nigeria 102/C3
Kaduna, Nigeria 106/F6
Kaduna (riv.), Nigeria 106/F7
Kadzherom, U.S.S.R. 52/J2
Kaech'ŏn, N. Korea 81/B4
Kaédi, Mauritania 106/B5
Kaédi, Mauritania 102/A3
Kaélé, Cameroon 115/B1
Kaena (pt.), Hawaii 218/D1
Kaeo, N. Zealand 100/D1
Kaesŏng, N. Korea 81/C4
Kaf, Saudi Arabia 59/C3
Kafan, U.S.S.R. 52/G7
Kafar Kanna, Israel 65/C2
Kaffa (prov.), Ethiopia 111/G6
Kaffrine, Senegal 106/A6
Kafia Kingi, Sudan 111/D6
Kafirévs (cape), Greece 45/G6
Kafr Yasif, Israel 65/C2
Kafue, Zambia 115/E7
Kafue (riv.), Zambia 115/E7
Kafue Nat'l Park, Zambia 115/E6
Kaga, Japan 81/H5
Kaga Bandoro, Cent. Afr. Rep. 115/C2
Kagalaska (isl.), Alaska 196/L4
Kagan, U.S.S.R. 48/G6
Kagawa (pref.), Japan 81/G6
Kagawong, Ontario 177/B2
Kagawong (lake), Ontario 177/B2
Kagera Nat'l Park, Rwanda 115/F4
Kağıthane, Turkey 63/D6
Kağızman, Turkey 63/K2
Kagoshima (pref.), Japan 81/E8
Kagoshima, Japan 81/E8
Kagoshima, Japan 54/O6
Kagoshima (bay), Japan 81/E8
Kagul, U.S.S.R. 52/C5
Kaguyak, Alaska (†99608) 196/H3
Kahakuloa, Hawaii (†96793) 218/J1
Kahala, Hawaii (†96801) 218/D5
Kahala (pt.), Hawaii 218/D1
Kahaluu, Hawaii (†96744) 218/E2
Kahama, Tanzania 115/F4
Kahana, Hawaii (†96717) 218/F1
Kahana (bay), Hawaii 218/F1
Kahayan (riv.), Indonesia 85/E6
Kahemba, Zaire 115/C5
Kahiltna (riv.), Alaska 196/B1
Kahlotus, Wash. (99335) 310/G4
Kah-Nee-Ta, Oreg. (†97761) 291/F3
Kahoka, Mo. (63445) 261/J2
Kahoolawe (isl.), Hawaii 188/F5
Kahoolawe (isl.), Hawaii 87/L4
Kahoolawe (isl.), Hawaii 218/H3
Kahouanne (isl.), Guadeloupe 161/A6
Kahramanmaraş (prov.), Turkey 63/G4
Kâhta, Turkey 63/H4
Kahuku, Hawaii (96731) 218/E1
Kahuku, Hawaii 188/F5
Kahuku (pt.), Hawaii 218/E1
Kahului, Hawaii (96732) 218/J2
Kahului, Hawaii 188/F5
Kahului (harb.), Hawaii 218/J1
Kai (isls.), Indonesia 85/J7
Kaiama, Nigeria 106/E7
Kaiapit, Papua N.G. 85/B7
Kaiapoi, N. Zealand 100/D5
Kaibab (plat.), Ariz. 198/C2
Kaibab Ind. Res., Ariz. 198/C2
Kaibito, Ariz. (86053) 198/D2
Kaibito (plat.), Ariz. 198/D2
Kaieteur (fall), Guyana 131/B3
Kaifeng, China 77/H5
Kaifeng, China 54/N6
Kaikohe, N. Zealand 100/D1
Kaikoura, N. Zealand 100/D5
Kaikoura (pen.), N. Zealand 100/E5
Kaikoura (range), N. Zealand 100/D5
Kaili, China 77/G6
Kailu, China 77/K3
Kailua (Kailua Kona), Hawaii, Hawaii (96740) 218/F5
Kailua, Oahu, Hawaii (96734) 218/F2
Kailua (bay), Hawaii 218/F2
Kailua (bay), Hawaii 218/F5
Kailua Kona, Hawaii (96740) 218/F5
Kaimana, Indonesia 85/J6
Kaimanawa (range), N. Zealand 100/E3
Kaimu, Hawaii (†96778) 218/J6
Kaimuki, Hawaii (96816) 218/D4
Kainaliu, Hawaii (†96750) 218/G5
Kainaliu, Hawaii 188/F6
Kainan (bay) 5/B10
Kaingaroa, N. Zealand 100/E7
Kainji (res.), Nigeria 106/E6
Kaipara (harb.), N. Zealand 100/D2
Kaipara (riv.), N. Zealand 100/A1
Kaiparowits (plat.), Utah 304/C6
Kaipokok (bay), Newf. 166/B2
Kaipokok (riv.), Newf. 166/B3
Kairouan, Tunisia 106/F1
Kairuku, Papua N.G. 85/B7
Kaiser, Mo. (65047) 261/G6
Kaiseregg (mt.), Switzerland 39/D3
Kaiserslautern, W. Germany 22/B4
Kaiserstuhl (mt.), W. Germany 22/B4
Kaitaia, N. Zealand 100/D1
Kaitangata, N. Zealand 100/C7
Kaitumälv (riv.), Sweden 18/M3
Kaiwi (chan.), Hawaii 218/E6
Kaiyuan, Liaoning, China 77/K3
Kaiyuan, Yunnan, China 77/F7
Kaiyuh (mts.), Alaska 196/G2
Kaizuka, Japan 81/H8
Kajaani, Finland 7/G2
Kajaani, Finland 18/P4
Kajabbi, Queensland 88/G3
Kajabbi, Queensland 95/A4
Kajiado, Kenya 115/G4
Kajok, Sudan 111/E6
Kaka, Cent. Afr. Rep. 115/E2
Kaka, Sudan 111/F5
Kakabeka Falls, Ontario 177/G5
Kakabeka Falls, Ontario 175/B3
Kakamega, Kenya 115/F3
Kake, Alaska (99830) 196/M1
Kakhk, Iran 66/L3
Kakhonak, Alaska (†99647) 196/H3
Kakhovka, U.S.S.R. 52/D5
Kakhovka (res.), U.S.S.R. 48/D5
Kakhovka (res.), U.S.S.R. 52/D5
Kakinada, India 54/K8
Kakinada, India 68/E5
Kakisa, N.W. Terrs. 187/G3
Kakkiviak (cape), Newf. 166/B1
Kakogawa, Japan 81/G6
Kaktovik, Alaska (99747) 196/K1
Kakwa (riv.), Alberta 182/A2
Kalaa-Kebira, Tunisia 106/F1
Kalabahi, Indonesia 85/G7
Kalabo, Zambia 115/D6
Kalach, U.S.S.R. 52/F4
Kalachinsk, U.S.S.R. 48/H4
Kalach-na-Donu, U.S.S.R. 52/F5
Kaladan (riv.), Burma 72/B2
Kaladar, Ontario 177/H3
Kalae, Hawaii (†96757) 218/G1
Ka Lae (cape), Hawaii 218/G7
Kalahari (des.) 102/E7
Kalahari (des.), Botswana 118/C4
Kalahari (des.), Namibia 118/C4
Kalahari Gemsbok Nat'l Park, S. Africa 118/C5
Kalaheo, Hawaii (96741) 218/C2
Kalajoki, Finland 18/N4
Kalajoki (riv.), Finland 18/O4
Kalakan, U.S.S.R. 48/M4
Kalaloch, Wash. (†98331) 310/A3
Kalam, Pakistan 68/C1
Kalama, Wash. (98625) 310/C4
Kalama (riv.), Wash. 310/C4
Kalámai, Greece 7/G5
Kalámai, Greece 45/F7
Kalamazoo, Mich. 188/J2
Kalamazoo (co.), Mich. 250/D6
Kalamazoo, Mich. (*49001) 250/D6
Kalamazoo (riv.), Mich. 250/C6
Kalambo (falls), Tanzania 115/F5
Kalambo (falls), Zambia 115/F5
Kalamo, Mich. (†49096) 250/D6
Kalampáka, Greece 45/E6
Kalamunda, W. Australia 88/B2
Kalan, Turkey 63/H3
Kalao (isl.), Indonesia 85/G7
Kalaoa, Hawaii (†96740) 218/G5
Kalaotoa (isl.), Indonesia 85/G5
Kalapana, Hawaii (†96778) 218/J6
Kalasin, Thailand 72/D3
Kalat (Qalat), Afghanistan 68/B2
Kalat (Qalat), Afghanistan 59/J3
Kalat, Pakistan 54/H7
Kalat, Pakistan 59/J4
Kalat, Pakistan 68/B3
Kalâtdlit-Nunât (Greenland) 4/B12
Kalâtdlit-Nunât (Greenland) 146/P2
Kalaupapa, Hawaii (96742) 218/G1
Kalaupapa (pen.), Hawaii 218/H1
Kalaupapa Nat'l Hist. Park, Hawaii 218/H1
Kalávrita, Greece 45/F6
Kalawao (co.), Hawaii 218/G1
Kalbarri, W. Australia 92/A4
Kale, Turkey 63/C4
Kalecik, Turkey 63/E2
Kaleden, Br. Col. 184/H5
Kalegauk (isl.), Burma 72/C4
Kalehe, Zaire 115/E4
Kaleida, Manitoba 179/D5
Kalemie, Zaire 115/E5
Kalemie, Zaire 102/E5
Kalemyo, Burma 72/B2
Kaleva, Mich. (49645) 250/C4
Kalevala, U.S.S.R. 52/D1
Kalewa, Burma 72/B2
Kalgan (Zhangjiakou), China 77/J3
Kalgin (isl.), Alaska 196/B1
Kalgoorlie, Australia 2/R7
Kalgoorlie, W. Australia 88/C6
Kalgoorlie, W. Australia 92/C5
Kalgoorlie-Boulder, W. Australia 92/C5
Kaliakra (cape), Bulgaria 45/J4
Kalianda, Indonesia 85/D7
Kalibo, Philippines 82/D5
Kalida, Ohio (45853) 284/B4
Kalihi, Hawaii (†96801) 218/C4
Kalihi (stream), Hawaii 218/C3
Kalihi Entrance (str.), Hawaii 218/B4
Kalihiwai, Hawaii (†96754) 218/C1
Kalima, Zaire 115/E4
Kalimantan (reg.), Indonesia 85/E5
Kálimnos, Greece 45/H7
Kálimnos (isl.), Greece 45/H7
Kalinga, Queensland 88/K2
Kalinga-Apayao (prov.), Philippines 82/C1
Kalinin, U.S.S.R. 7/H3
Kalinin, U.S.S.R. 48/D4
Kalinin, U.S.S.R. 52/E3
Kaliningrad, U.S.S.R. 7/G3
Kaliningrad, U.S.S.R. 48/B4
Kaliningrad, Kaliningrad, U.S.S.R. 52/B4
Kaliningrad, Moscow Oblast, U.S.S.R. 52/E3
Kalininsk, U.S.S.R. 52/F4
Kalinkovichi, U.S.S.R. 52/C4
Kalispel Ind. Res., Wash. 310/H2
Kalispell, Mont. 188/C1
Kalispell, Mont. (59901) 262/B2
Kalisz (prov.), Poland 47/D3
Kalisz, Poland 7/F3
Kalisz, Poland 47/D3
Kaliua, Tanzania 115/F5
Kalix, Sweden 18/N4
Kalixälv (riv.), Sweden 18/N3
Kalkaska (co.), Mich. 250/D4
Kalkaska, Mich. (49646) 250/D4
Kalkfeld, Namibia 118/B4
Kalkfontein, Botswana 118/C4
Kallaste, U.S.S.R. 53/D1
Kallavesi (lake), Finland 18/P5
Kallsjö (lake), Sweden 18/H5
Kalmalo, Nigeria 106/F6
Kalmar (co.), Sweden 18/K8
Kalmar, Sweden 7/F3
Kalmar, Sweden 18/K8
Kalmarsund (sound), Sweden 18/K8
Kalmthout, Belgium 27/F6
Kalmuck A.S.S.R., U.S.S.R. 52/F5
Kalmuck A.S.S.R., U.S.S.R. 48/E5
Kalmunai, Sri Lanka 68/E7
Kalmykovo, U.S.S.R. 48/F5
Kalo, Iowa (†50569) 229/E4
Kalocsa, Hungary 41/E3
Kalohi (chan.), Hawaii 218/G1
Kaloko-Honokohau Nat'l Hist. Park, Hawaii 218/F6
Kaloli (pt.), Hawaii 218/K5
Kalomo, Zambia 115/E7
Kalona, Iowa (52247) 229/K6
Kalpeni (isl.), India 68/C7
Kalpin, China 77/A3
Kalskag, Alaska (99607) 196/F2
Kaltag, Alaska (99748) 196/G2
Kaltbrunn, Switzerland 39/H2
Kaluaaha, Hawaii (†96748) 218/H1
Kaluga, U.S.S.R. 7/H3
Kaluga, U.S.S.R. 48/D4
Kaluga, U.S.S.R. 52/E4
Kalumburu Mission, W. Australia 88/D2
Kalumburu Mission, W. Australia 92/D1
Kalundborg, Denmark 21/D6
Kalundborg, Denmark 18/G9
Kalush, U.S.S.R. 52/B5
Kalutara, Sri Lanka 68/D7
Kalvarija, U.S.S.R. 53/B3
Kalvesta, Kansas (67856) 232/B3
Kalyan, India 68/C5
Kama, Burma 72/B3
Kama (res.), U.S.S.R. 52/J3
Kama (riv.), U.S.S.R. 7/K3
Kama (riv.), U.S.S.R. 52/H2
Kama, Zaire 115/E4
Kamaiki (pt.), Hawaii 218/H2
Kamaing, Burma 72/C1
Kamaishi, Japan 81/L4
Kamakou (peak), Hawaii 218/H1
Kamakura, Japan 81/O3
Kamakusa, Guyana 131/A3
Kamalino, Hawaii (†96769) 218/A2
Kamalo, Hawaii (†96748) 218/H1
Kaman, Turkey 63/E3
Kamaniskeg (lake), Ontario 177/G2
Kamanjab, Namibia 118/A3
Kamaran (isl.), P.D.R. Yemen 59/D6
Kamarang, Guyana 131/A3
Kamarhati, India 68/F1
Kamaria (falls), Guyana 131/B2
Kamas, Utah (84036) 304/C3
Kamay, Texas (76369) 303/F4
Kambalda, W. Australia 88/C6
Kambalda, W. Australia 92/C5
Kambia, S. Leone 106/B7
Kambove, Zaire 115/E6
Kambove, Zaire 102/E6
Kamchatka (pen.), U.S.S.R. 54/S4
Kamchatka (pen.), U.S.S.R. 2/T3
Kamchatka (pen.), U.S.S.R. 48/Q4
Kamela, Oreg. (†97859) 291/J2
Kamenets-Podol'skiy, U.S.S.R. 52/C5
Kamenice, Czech. 41/C2
Kamenjak (cape), Yugoslavia 45/A3
Kamenka, Archangel, U.S.S.R. 52/F1
Kamenka, Penza, U.S.S.R. 52/F4
Kamen'-na-Obi, U.S.S.R. 48/H4
Kamenskoye, U.S.S.R. 48/R3
Kamensk-Shakhtinskiy, U.S.S.R. 52/F5
Kamensk-Ural'skiy, U.S.S.R. 48/G4
Kamenz, E. Germany 22/F3
Kameoka, Japan 81/J7
Kames, Scotland 15/C5
Kamet (mt.), India 68/D2
Kamiah, Idaho (83536) 220/B3
Kamienna Góra, Poland 47/B3

Khachmas 391

Kazan-retto (Volcano) (isls.), Japan 81/M4
Kazatin, U.S.S.R. 52/C5
Kazbek (mt.), U.S.S.R. 52/F6
Kazerun, Iran 66/G6
Kazerun, Iran 59/F4
Kazhim, U.S.S.R. 52/H2
Kazimierza Wielka, Poland 47/E3
Kazımkarabekir, Turkey 63/E4
Kazincbarcika, Hungary 41/F2
Kazlu-Rūda, U.S.S.R. 53/B3
Kazumba, Zaire 115/D5
Kazvin (Qazvin), Iran 66/F2
Kbenhaven (co.), Denmark 21/F6
Kbenhavn (Copenhagen) (commune), Denmark 21/F6
Kdyně, Czech. 41/B2
Kéa, Greece 45/G7
Kéa (isl.), Greece 45/G7
Keaau, Hawaii 188/G6
Keaau, Hawaii (96749) 218/J5
Keady, N. Ireland 17/H3
Keahi (pt.), Hawaii 218/A4
Keahole (pt.), Hawaii 218/F5
Kealaikahiki (chan.), Hawaii 218/H3
Kealaikahiki (pt.), Hawaii 218/H3
Kealakekua, Hawaii (96750) 218/G5
Kealakekua (bay), Hawaii 218/F6
Kealia, Hawaii (†96704) 218/G6
Kealia, Kauai, Hawaii (96751) 218/D1
Keams Canyon, Ariz. (86034) 198/E3
Keanae, Hawaii (†96708) 218/K2
Keanapapa (pt.), Hawaii 218/G2
Keansburg, N.J. (07734) 273/E3
Kearney, Mo. (64060) 261/D4
Kearney, Nebr. 188/G2
Kearney (co.), Nebr. 264/F4
Kearney, Nebr. (68847) 264/E4
Kearney, Ontario 177/E2
Kearneysville, W. Va. (25430) 312/L4
Kearns, Utah (84118) 304/B3
Kearny, Ariz. (85237) 198/E5
Kearny (co.), Kansas 232/A3
Kearny, N.J. (07032) 273/B2
Kearny, Wyo. (†82832) 319/F1
Kearsarge, N.H. (03847) 268/E3
Kearsarge (mt.), N.H. 268/D5
Kearsarge, Pa. (†16501) 294/B1
Keasbey, N.J. (08832) 273/E2
Keatchie, La. (71046) 238/C2
Keating, Oreg. (†97814) 291/K3
Keating Summit, Pa. (16737) 294/F2
Keatley, Sask. 181/D3
Keaton, Ky. (41226) 237/P5
Keats, Kansas (†66502) 232/F2
Keats (mt.), W. Australia 92/A2
Keauhou, Hawaii (†96725) 218/F5
Keavy, Ky. (40737) 237/N6
Keawekaheka (pt.), Hawaii 218/F5
Keban, Turkey 63/H3
Kebang (mt.), S. Korea 81/D5
Ke Bao, Vietnam 72/E2
Kebbi (riv.), Nigeria 106/E6
Kebnekaise (mt.), Sweden 7/F2
Kebnekaise (mt.), Sweden 18/L3
Kebock (head), Scotland 15/B2
Kebumen, Indonesia 85/J2
Kecel, Hungary 41/E3
Kechi, Kansas (67067) 232/E4
Kechika (riv.), Br. Col. 184/L2
Keçiborlu, Turkey 63/D4
Kecskemét, Hungary 7/F4
Kecskemét, Hungary 41/E3
Kedah (state), Malaysia 72/D6
Kedainiai, U.S.S.R. 53/C3
Keddie, Calif. (95952) 204/E3
Kedges (strs), Md. 245/O8
Kedgwick, New Bruns. 170/C1
Kedgwick (riv.), New Bruns. 170/C1
Kedgwick Ouest, New Bruns. 170/C1
Kedgwick River, New Bruns. 170/C1
Kediri, Indonesia 85/K2
Kédougou, Senegal 106/B6
Kedron (brook), Queensland 95/D2
Kedzierzyn-Koźle, Poland 47/C3
Keechelus (lake), Wash. 310/D3
Keedysville, Md. (21756) 245/H3
Keefers, Br. Col. 184/G5
Keefton, Okla. (†74401) 288/R3
Keegan, Maine (†04785) 243/G1
Keego Harbor, Mich. (48030) 250/F6
Keehi (lag.), Hawaii 218/B4
Keel-Dooagh, Ireland 17/A4
Keele (riv.), N.W. Terrs. 187/F3
Keele (peak), Yukon 187/E3
Keeler, Calif. (93530) 204/H7
Keeler, Sask. 181/F5
Keeline, Wyo. (82220) 319/H3
Keeling (Cocos) (isls.), Australia 2/P6
Keeling, Va. (24566) 307/K7
Keels, Newf. 166/D1
Keelung, China 77/K6
Keenan, W. Va. (†24983) 312/F7
Keenan Siding, New Bruns. 170/E2
Keene, Calif. (93531) 204/G8
Keene, Ky. (40339) 237/M5
Keene, N.H. (03431) 268/C6
Keene, N.Y. (12942) 276/N2
Keene, N. Dak. (58847) 282/E4
Keene, Ohio (43828) 284/G5
Keene, Ontario 177/F3
Keene, Texas (76059) 303/G5
Keener, Ala. (†35954) 195/G2
Keenes, Ill. (62851) 222/E5
Keenesburg, Colo. (80643) 208/L2
Keene Valley, N.Y. (12943) 276/N2
Keensburg, Ill. (62852) 222/F5
Keeny (creek), Oreg. 291/K4
Keeper (hill), Ireland 17/E6
Keerweer (cape), Queensland 88/G2
Keerweer (cape), Queensland 95/B2
Keeseville, N.Y. (12944) 276/O2
Keesler A.F.B., Miss. 256/G10
Keetley, Utah (†84060) 304/C3
Keetmanshoop, Namibia 118/B5
Keetmanshoop, Namibia 102/D7
Keewatin, Minn. (55753) 255/E3
Keewatin (dist.), N.W.T. 162/G3
Keewatin (dist.), N.W. Terrs. 187/J3
Keewatin, Ontario 177/F5
Keewatin, Ontario 175/A3
Keewong, N.S. Wales 97/C3
Keezletown, Va. (22832) 307/L4
Kefallinía (isl.), Greece 45/E6
Kefar Blum, Israel 65/D1
Kefar Gil'adi, Israel 65/C1
Kefar Ruppin, Israel 65/D3
Kefar Sava, Israel 65/B3
Kefar Vitkin, Israel 65/B3
Kefar Zekhariya, Israel 65/B4
Keffi, Nigeria 106/F7
Keflavík, Iceland 21/B1
Kégashka, Québec 174/E2
Kegley, W. Va. (24731) 312/D8
Kegonsa (lake), Wis. 317/H10
Keg River, Alberta 182/A5
Kehl, W. Germany 22/B4
Kehoe, Ky. (†41144) 237/P4
Kehra, U.S.S.R. 53/C1
Keila, U.S.S.R. 53/C1
Keilor, Victoria 88/K7
Keilor, Victoria 97/H5
Keimoes, S. Africa 118/C5
Keirn, Miss. (†38924) 256/D4
Keiser, Ark. (72351) 202/K2
Keiss, Scotland 15/E2
Keitele (lake), Finland 18/O5
Keith (co.), Nebr. 264/C3
Keith, Scotland 10/E2
Keith, Scotland 15/F3
Keith, S. Australia 94/G7
Keith, W. Va. (†25148) 312/C6
Keith Arm (inlet), N.W. Terrs. 187/F3
Keithley Creek, Br. Col. 184/G4
Keithsburg, Ill. (61442) 222/B2
Keithville, La. (71047) 238/C2
Keizer, Oreg. (97303) 291/A3
Kejimkujik (lake), Nova Scotia 168/C4
Kejimkujik Nat'l Park, Nova Scotia 168/C4
Kekaa (pt.), Hawaii 218/H2
Kekaha, Hawaii (96752) 218/C2
Kekaha, Hawaii 188/E5
Kekertaluk (isl.), N.W. Terrs. 187/M3
Kékes (mt.), Hungary 41/E3
Kekoskee, Wis. (†53050) 317/J8
Kelang, Malaysia 72/D7
Kelantan (state), Malaysia 72/D6
Kelantan, Sungai (riv.), Malaysia 72/D6
Kelasa (str.), Indonesia 85/D6
Keldron, S. Dak. (57634) 298/F2
Keles, Turkey 63/C3
Kelfield, Sask. 181/C4
Kelford, N.C. (27847) 281/P2
Kelheim, W. Germany 22/D4
Kelkit, Turkey 63/H2
Kelkit (riv.), Turkey 59/C1
Kelkit (riv.), Turkey 63/G2
Kell, Ill. (62853) 222/E5
Kellé, Congo 115/B4
Keller (lake), N.W. Terrs. 187/F3
Keller, Texas (76248) 303/F2
Keller, Va. (23401) 307/S5
Keller, Wash. (99140) 310/G2
Kellerberrin, W. Australia 88/B6
Kellerberrin, W. Australia 92/B5
Kellerman, Ala. (35468) 195/D4
Kellerton, Iowa (50133) 229/E7
Kellerville, Texas (79057) 303/D2
Kellett (cape), N.W.T. 162/D1
Kellett (cape), N.W. Terrs. 187/F2
Kellett (str.), N.W. Terrs. 187/G2
Kellettville, Pa. (†16353) 294/D2
Kelley, Iowa (50134) 229/F5
Kelley (creek), Nev. 266/D1
Kelleys (isl.), Ohio 284/E2
Kelleys Island, Ohio (43438) 284/E2
Kelligrews, Newf. 166/D2
Kelliher, Minn. (56650) 255/D3
Kelliher, Sask. 181/H4
Kellnersville, Wis. (54215) 317/L7
Kellogg (mt.), Ariz. 198/E6
Kellogg, Idaho (83837) 220/B2
Kellogg, Iowa (50135) 229/H5
Kellogg, Minn. (55945) 255/G6
Kelloggsville, Ohio (†44048) 284/J2
Kelloselkä, Finland 18/Q3
Kells (Ceanannus Mór), Ireland 17/G4
Kells, Ireland 17/G6
Kells, N. Ireland 17/J2
Kelly, Georgia (31048) 217/E4
Kelly (creek), Idaho 220/C3
Kelly, Kansas (66446) 232/G2
Kelly, Ky. (†42240) 237/G7
Kelly, La. (71441) 238/F3
Kelly, N.C. (28448) 281/N6
Kelly, Wyo. (83011) 319/B2
Kelly A.F.B., Texas 303/J11
Kelly Lake, Br. Col. 184/G4
Kelly Lake, Minn. (55754) 255/F3
Kellys, N. Dak. (†58201) 282/R4
Kellysville, W. Va. (24732) 312/E8
Kellyton, Ala. (35089) 195/F5
Kellyville, Okla. (74039) 288/O3
Kelme, U.S.S.R. 53/B3
Kélo, Chad 111/C6
Kélo, Chad 102/D4
Kelowna, Br. Col. 146/G4
Kelowna, Br. Col. 162/E6
Kelowna, Br. Col. 184/H5
Kelsey, Alberta 182/D3
Kelsey, Minn. (55755) 255/F3
Kelsey Bay, Br. Col. 184/D5
Kelseyville, Calif. (95451) 204/C5
Kelso, Ark. (†71674) 202/H6
Kelso, Calif. (92351) 204/K8
Kelso, Mo. (63758) 261/O8
Kelso, Sask. 181/K6
Kelso, Scotland 10/E3
Kelso, Scotland 15/F5
Kelso, Tenn. (37348) 237/J10
Kelso, Wash. (98626) 310/C4
Kelstern, Sask. 181/E5
Kelston West, N. Zealand 100/B1
Keltie (cape) 5/C7
Keltner, Ky. (†42761) 237/K6
Kelton, S.C. (†29353) 296/D2
Kelty, Scotland 10/C1
Kelty, Scotland 15/D1
Keluang, Malaysia 72/D7
Kelvington, Sask. 181/H3
Kelwood, Manitoba 179/C4
Kem', U.S.S.R. 7/H2
Kem', U.S.S.R. 4/C8
Kem', U.S.S.R. 52/D2
Kem', U.S.S.R. 48/D3
Ké-Macina, Mali 106/C6
Kemah, Texas (77565) 303/K2
Kemah, Turkey 63/H3
Kemaliye, Turkey 63/H3
Kemalpaşa, Turkey 63/J2
Kemano, Br. Col. 184/D3
Kemasik, Malaysia 72/D6
Kembe, Cent. Afr. Rep. 115/D3
Kemble, Ontario 177/D3
Kemboma, Gabon 115/B3
Kemecse, Hungary 41/F2
Kemer, Turkey 63/D4
Kemerburgaz, Turkey 63/D5
Kemerovo, U.S.S.R. 54/K4
Kemerovo, U.S.S.R. 48/J4
Kemi, Finland 7/G2
Kemi, Finland 18/O4
Kemi (riv.), Finland 7/G2
Kemijärvi, Finland 18/P3
Kemijärvi (lake), Finland 18/Q3
Kemijoki (riv.), Finland 18/O3
Kemikli, Büyük (cape), Turkey 63/B6
Kemirhisar, Turkey 63/F4
Kemmerer, Wyo. (83101) 319/B4
Kemnay, Manitoba 179/B5
Kemnay, Scotland 15/F3
Kemp, Ill. (†61910) 222/E4
Kemp, Okla. (74747) 288/O7
Kemp, Texas (75143) 303/H5
Kemp (lake), Texas 303/E4
Kemp City (Hendrix), Okla. (†74741) 288/O7
Kemp Coast (reg.) 5/C3
Kemper (co.), Miss. 256/G5
Kemp Mill, Md. (†20901) 245/F3
Kempsey, N.S. Wales 88/J6
Kempsey, N.S. Wales 97/G2
Kempster, Wis. (54444) 317/H5
Kempston, England 13/G5
Kempt, Nova Scotia 168/C4
Kempt (lake), Québec 172/C2
Kempten, W. Germany 22/D5
Kempton, Ill. (60946) 222/E3
Kempton, Ind. (46049) 227/E4
Kempton, Md. (†26292) 245/A4
Kempton, N. Dak. (†58267) 282/P4
Kempton, Pa. (19529) 294/L4
Kempton, Tasmania 99/D4
Kempton Park, S. Africa 118/J6
Kemptown, Md. (†21770) 245/J3
Kemptown, Nova Scotia 168/E3
Kemptville, Nova Scotia 168/C4
Kemptville, Ontario 177/J2
Ken, Afghanistan 68/A2
Ken, Afghanistan 59/H3
Kenadsa, Algeria 106/D2
Kenai, Alaska (99611) 196/B1
Kenai (lake), Alaska 196/C1
Kenai (mt.), Alaska 196/C2
Kenai (pen.), Alaska 196/C2
Kenai Fjords Nat'l Park, Alaska 196/C3
Kenamu (riv.), Newf. 166/B3
Kenansville, Fla. (32739) 212/F4
Kenansville, N.C. (28349) 281/O5
Kenaston, N. Dak. (†58746) 282/F2
Kenaston, Sask. 181/E4
Kenbridge, Va. (23944) 307/M7
Kendal, Barbados 161/B8
Kendal, England 13/E3
Kendal, England 10/E3
Kendal, Indonesia 85/J2
Kendal, Sask. 181/H5
Kendall, Fla. (33156) 212/B5
Kendall (co.), Ill. 222/E2
Kendall, Kansas (67857) 232/A4
Kendall, N.S. Wales 97/G2
Kendall, N.Y. (14476) 276/E4
Kendall (cape), N.W. Terrs. 187/K3
Kendall (co.), Texas 303/F8
Kendall, Wash. (†98244) 310/C2
Kendall, Wis. (54638) 317/F8
Kendall Park, N.J. (08824) 273/D3
Kendallville, Ind. (46755) 227/G2
Kendallville, Iowa (†52136) 229/K2
Kendari, Indonesia 85/G6
Kendawangan, Indonesia 85/D6
Kendrapara, India 68/F4
Kendrick (peak), Ariz. 198/D3
Kendrick, Fla. (†32670) 212/D2
Kendrick, Idaho (83537) 220/B3
Kendrick, Okla. (74040) 288/N3
Kenduskeag○, Maine (04450) 243/E6
Kenedy (co.), Texas 303/G11
Kenedy, Texas (78119) 303/G9
Kenefic, Okla. (74748) 288/O6
Kenel, S. Dak. (†57642) 298/H2
Kenema, S. Leone 102/A4
Kenema, S. Leone 106/B7
Kenesaw, Nebr. (68956) 264/F4
Kengah (isls.), Indonesia 85/F7
Kenge, Zaire 115/C4
Keng Hkam, Burma 72/C2
Keng Tung, Burma 72/C2
Kenhardt, S. Africa 118/C5
Kenhorst, Pa. (†19607) 294/L5
Kéniéba, Mali 106/B6
Kenilworth, England 13/F5
Kenilworth, Ill. (60043) 222/B5
Kenilworth, N.J. (07033) 273/E2
Kenilworth, Ontario 177/D4
Kenilworth, Utah (84529) 304/D4
Keningau, Malaysia 85/F4
Kenitra, Morocco 102/B1
Kenitra, Morocco 106/C2
Kenli, China 77/J4
Kenly, N.C. (27542) 281/N3
Kenmare, Ireland 10/B5
Kenmare, Ireland 17/B8
Kenmare (riv.), Ireland 17/A8
Kenmare, N. Dak. (58746) 282/G2
Kenmore, N.Y. (14217) 276/C5
Kenmore, Queensland 88/J3
Kenmore, Scotland 15/E4
Kenmore, Wash. (98028) 310/B1
Kenna, N. Mex. (88122) 274/F5
Kenna, W. Va. (25248) 312/C5
Kennan, Wis. (54537) 317/F5
Kennard, Ind. (47351) 227/G5
Kennard, Nebr. (68034) 264/H3
Kennard, Pa. (†16125) 294/B3
Kennard, Texas (75847) 303/J6
Kennebago Lake, Maine (†04970) 243/B5
Kennebec (co.), Maine 243/D7
Kennebec (riv.), Maine 243/D7
Kennebec, S. Dak. (57544) 298/K6
Kennebecasis (bay), New Bruns. 170/E3
Kennebecasis (riv.), New Bruns. 170/E3
Kennebunk, Maine (04043) 243/B9
Kennebunk○, Maine (04043) 243/B9
Kennebunk Beach, Maine (†04043) 243/C9
Kennebunkport, Maine (04046) 243/C9
Kennebunkport○, Maine (04046) 243/C9
Kennedale, Texas (76060) 303/F3
Kennedy, Ala. (35574) 195/B3
Kennedy (Canaveral) (cape), Fla. 212/F3
Kennedy, Minn. (56733) 255/B2
Kennedy, N.Y. (14747) 276/B6
Kennedy (chan.), N.W.T. 162/N3
Kennedy (chan.), N.W. Terrs. 187/M1
Kennedy, Sask. 181/J5
Kennedy Center, D.C. 245/A5
Kennedy Entrance (str.), Alaska 196/H3
Kennedyville, Md. (21645) 245/P3
Kenner, La. (70062) 238/N4
Kennesaw, Georgia (30144) 217/C2
Kennesaw Mtn. Nat'l Battlefield Park, Georgia 217/J1
Kennet (riv.), England 13/F6
Kennetcook, Nova Scotia 168/E3
Kennetcook (riv.), Nova Scotia 168/E3
Kenneth, Ind. (†46947) 227/E3
Kenneth, Minn. (56147) 255/B7
Kenneth City, Fla. (33709) 212/B3
Kennett, Mo. (63857) 261/M10
Kennett Square, Pa. (19348) 294/L6
Kennewick, Wash. (99336) 310/F4
Kenney (dam), Br. Col. 184/E3
Kenney, Ill. (61749) 222/D3
Kennisis (lake), Ontario 177/F2
Keno, Oreg. (97627) 291/F5
Kenogami (riv.), Ont. 162/H6
Kenogami (riv.), Ontario 177/H4
Kenogami (riv.), Ontario 175/C2
Kénogami (lake), Québec 172/F1
Keno Hill, Yukon 187/E3
Kenoma, Mo. (†64759) 261/D8
Kenora (terr. dist.), Ont. 177/G5
Kenora (terr. dist.), Ont. 175/C2
Kenora, Ont. 146/J4
Kenora, Ont. 162/G5
Kenora, Ontario 175/B3
Kenora, Ontario 177/F4
Kenosee Park, Sask. 181/J6
Kenosha (co.), Wis. 317/K10
Kenosha, Wis. (*53140) 317/M3
Kenova, W. Va. (25530) 312/A6
Kensal, N. Dak. (58455) 282/N5
Kenscoff, Haiti 158/C6
Kensett, Ark. (72082) 202/G3
Kensett, Iowa (50448) 229/G2
Kensington, Calif. (†94701) 204/J2
Kensington, Conn. (06037) 210/D2
Kensington, Kansas (66951) 232/C2
Kensington, Md. (20795) 245/E4
Kensington, Minn. (56343) 255/C5
Kensington, N.S. Wales 97/J4
Kensington, Ohio (44427) 284/J4
Kensington, Pr. Edward I. 168/E2
Kensington and Chelsea, England 13/G8
Kensington and Chelsea, England 10/B5
Kensington and Norwood, S. Australia 88/E8
Kensington and Norwood, S. Australia 94/B8
Kent, Ala. (36045) 195/G5
Kent, Br. Col. 184/M3
Kent○, Conn. (06757) 210/B2
Kent (co.), Del. 245/R4
Kent (co.), England 13/H6
Kent, Ill. (61044) 222/D1
Kent, Ind. (†47250) 227/F7
Kent, Iowa (50850) 229/E7
Kent (co.), Md. 245/O3
Kent (isl.), Md. 245/N5
Kent (pt.), Md. 245/N5
Kent (co.), Mich. 250/D5
Kent, Minn. (56553) 255/B4
Kent (co.), New Bruns. 170/E2
Kent (pen.), N.W. Terrs. 187/H3
Kent, Ohio (44240) 284/H3
Kent (county), Ontario 177/B5
Kent, Oreg. (97033) 291/G2
Kent, Pa. (15752) 294/D4
Kent (co.), R.I. 249/H6
Kent (co.), Texas 303/D4
Kent, Texas (79855) 303/C11
Kent, Wash. (98031) 310/C3
Kentau, U.S.S.R. 48/G5
Kent Bridge, Ontario 177/B5
Kent City, Mich. (49330) 250/D5
Kent Furnace, Conn. (†06757) 210/B2
Kent Group (isls.), Tasmania 99/D1
Kent Junction, New Bruns. 170/E2
Kent Lake, New Bruns. 170/E2
Kentland, Ind. (47951) 227/C3
Kenton, Del. (19955) 245/R4
Kenton (co.), Ky. 237/M3
Kenton, Ky. (41053) 237/N3
Kenton, Manitoba 179/B5
Kenton, Mich. (49943) 250/G2
Kenton, Ohio (43326) 284/C4
Kenton, Okla. (73946) 288/A1
Kenton, Tenn. (38233) 237/C8
Kenton Vale, Ky. (†41011) 237/S2
Kents Hill, Maine (04349) 243/D7
Kents Store, Va. (23084) 307/M5
Kentuck, W. Va. (25249) 312/C5
Kentucky 188/J3
Kentucky (lake) 188/J3
KENTUCKY 237
Kentucky (dam), Ky. 237/E7
Kentucky (lake), Ky. 237/E8
Kentucky (riv.), Ky. 237/M3
Kentucky (lake), Tenn. 237/E8
Kentucky (state), U.S. 146/K6
Kentville, Nova Scotia 168/D3
Kentwood, La. (70444) 238/J5
Kentwood, Mich. (49508) 250/D6
Kenville, Manitoba 179/A3
Kenvir, Ky. (40847) 237/P7
Kenwood, Georgia (†30214) 217/D3
Kenwood, Okla. (†74365) 288/S2
Kenya 2/L5
Kenya 102/F4
KENYA 115/G3
Kenya (mt.), Kenya 102/F4
Kenya (mt.), Kenya 115/G4
Kenyon, Minn. (55946) 255/E6
Kenyon, R.I. (02836) 249/H7
Kenyonville, Conn. (†06281) 210/G1
Keo, Ark. (72083) 202/G4
Keokea, Hawaii, Hawaii (†96704) 218/G6
Keokea, Maui, Hawaii (†96790) 218/J2
Keokee, Va. (24265) 307/C7
Keokuk (co.), Iowa 229/J6
Keokuk, Iowa 188/H2
Keokuk, Iowa (52632) 229/L8
Keoma, Alberta 182/D4
Keomah, Iowa (†52577) 229/J6
Keomuku, Hawaii (†96763) 218/H2
Keonjhar, India 68/F4
Keosauqua, Iowa (52565) 229/J7
Keota, Colo. (†80729) 208/L1
Keota, Iowa (52248) 229/K6
Keota, Okla. (74941) 288/S4
Keowee (lake), S.C. 296/B2
Keowee (riv.), S.C. 296/B2
Kepez, Turkey 63/B6
Kepi, Indonesia 85/K7
Kępno, Poland 47/C3
Keppel (harb.), Singapore 72/F6
Kepsut, Turkey 63/C3
Kerala (state), India 68/D6
Kerama (isls.), Japan 81/M6
Kerang, Victoria 97/B4
Kerava, Finland 18/O6
Kerby, Oreg. (97531) 291/D5
Kerch', U.S.S.R. 7/H4
Kerch', U.S.S.R. 52/E5
Kerchoual, Mali 106/E5
Kerema, Papua N.G. 85/B7
Keremeos, Br. Col. 184/G5
Kerempe (cape), Turkey 63/E1
Keren, Ethiopia 59/C6
Keren, Ethiopia 111/G4
Kerens, Texas (75144) 303/H5
Kerens, W. Va. (26276) 312/G4
Keref', U.S.S.R. 52/D1
Kerguélen (isl.), 2/N8
Kerhonkson, N.Y. (12446) 276/M7
Kericho, Kenya 115/F4
Kerinci (mt.), Indonesia 85/C6
Keriya (Yutian), China 77/B4
Keriya He (riv.), China 77/B4
Keriya Shankou (pass), China 77/B4
Kerkdriel, Netherlands 27/G5
Kerkennah (isls.), Tunisia 106/G2
Kerkhoven, Minn. (56252) 255/C5
Kerki, U.S.S.R. 48/G6
Kérkira, Greece 45/D6
Kérkira (isl.), Greece 7/F5
Kérkira (isl.), Greece 45/D6
Kerkrade, Netherlands 27/J7
Kerlin, Ark. (†71753) 202/D7
Kerma, Sudan 111/F4
Kerma, Sudan 59/B6
Kermadec (isls.), N. Zealand 2/T7
Kermadec (isls.), N. Zealand 87/J9
Kerman, Calif. (93630) 204/E7
Kerman (prov.), Iran 66/K6
Kerman, Iran 54/G6
Kerman, Iran 59/G3
Kerman, Iran 66/K5
Kermanshah, Iran 54/F6
Kermanshah, Iran 59/E3
Kermanshah, Iran 66/E3
Kermanshahan (prov.), Iran 66/E3
Kerme (gulf), Turkey 63/B4
Kermit, Texas (79745) 303/B6
Kermit, W. Va. (25674) 312/B7
Kern (co.), Calif. 204/G8
Kern (riv.), Calif. 204/G8
Kernan, Ill. (†61364) 222/E2
Kernersville, N.C. (27284) 281/J2
Kerns, Switzerland 39/F3
Kernville, Calif. (93238) 204/G8
Kernville, Oreg. (†97367) 291/D3
Kérouané, Guinea 106/C7
Kerr (lake), Fla. 212/E2
Kerr, N.C. (†28444) 281/N5
Kerr, W. Scott (res.), N.C. 281/G2
Kerr, Robert S. (res.), Okla. 288/S4
Kerr (co.), Texas 303/E7
Kerrera (isl.), Scotland 15/C4
Kerrick, Minn. (55756) 255/F4
Kerrick, Texas (79051) 303/B1
Kerrobert, Sask. 181/C4
Kerrville, Tenn. (†38053) 237/B10
Kerrville, Texas (78028) 303/E7
Kerry (co.), Ireland 17/B7
Kerry (head), Ireland 17/A7
Kerry, Wales 13/D5
Kersey, Colo. (80644) 208/L2
Kersey, Ind. (†46310) 227/C3
Kersey, Pa. (15846) 294/E3
Kershaw (co.), S.C. 296/F3
Kershaw, S.C. (29067) 296/G2
Kersley, Br. Col. 184/F4
Kerteminde, Denmark 21/D7
Kerulen (riv.) 54/N5
Kerulen (riv.), Mongolia 77/H2
Kerwood, Ontario 177/C5
Kerzaz, Algeria 106/D3
Kerzers, Switzerland 39/D3
Kesagami (lake), Ontario 175/E2
Keşan, Turkey 63/B2
Keşap, Turkey 63/H2
Kesch (peak), Switzerland 39/J3
Kesennuma, Japan 81/K4
Kesgrave, England 13/J5
Kesh, N. Ireland 17/F3
Keshena, Wis. (54135) 317/J6
Keşiş Tepesi (mt.), Turkey 63/H3
Keskin, Turkey 63/E3
Keski-Suomi (prov.), Finland 18/O5
Kesley, Iowa (50649) 229/H3
Kessel, W. Va. (†26818) 312/H4
Kesten'ga, U.S.S.R. 52/D1
Kesteren, Netherlands 27/G5
Keswick, England 13/D3
Keswick, England 10/E3
Keswick, Iowa (50136) 229/J6
Keswick, New Bruns. 170/D3
Keswick (riv.), New Bruns. 170/C2
Keswick, Ontario 177/E3
Keswick, Va. (22947) 307/M4
Keswick Grove, N.J. (†08759) 273/E4
Keszthely, Hungary 41/D3
Keta, Ghana 106/E7
Ketapang, Indonesia 85/E6
Ketchen, Sask. 181/J3
Ketch Harbour, Nova Scotia 168/E4
Ketchikan, Alaska 146/E4
Ketchikan, Alaska 188/E6
Ketchikan, Alaska (99901) 196/N2
Ketchum, Idaho (83340) 220/D6
Ketchum, Okla. (74349) 288/R1
Kétegyháza, Hungary 41/F3
Kete Krachi, Ghana 106/E7
Kętrzyn, Poland 47/E1
Kettering, England 13/G5
Kettering, England 10/F4
Kettering, Ohio (45429) 284/B6
Kettering, Tasmania 99/D5
Kettle (riv.), Br. Col. 184/H5
Kettle (riv.), Minn. 255/F4
Kettle (pt.), Ontario 177/B4
Kettle (riv.), Wash. 310/G2
Kettle Falls, Wash. (99141) 310/H2
Kettleman City, Calif. (93239) 204/E7
Kettle River, Minn. (55757) 255/E4
Kettle River (range), Wash. 310/G2
Kettlersville, Ohio (45336) 284/B5
Kettle Valley, Br. Col. 184/H5
Keuka (lake), N.Y. 276/F5
Keuka Park, N.Y. (14478) 276/F5
Keuterville, Idaho (83538) 220/B3
Kevelaer, W. Germany 22/B3
Kevil, Ky. (42053) 237/D6
Kevin, Mont. (59454) 262/D2
Kevisville, Alberta 182/C4
Kew, Victoria 88/L7
Kew, Victoria 97/J5
Kewa, Wash. (†99138) 310/G2
Kewanee, Ill. (61443) 222/C2
Kewanee, Miss. (†39364) 256/H6
Kewanee, Mo. (63860) 261/N9
Kewanna, Ind. (46939) 227/E2
Kewaskum, Wis. (53040) 317/K8
Kewaunee (co.), Wis. 317/L6
Kewaunee, Wis. (54216) 317/M7
Keweenaw (co.), Mich. 250/A1
Keweenaw (bay), Mich. 250/A1
Keweenaw (pt.), Mich. 250/B1
Keweenaw Bay, Mich. (49944) 250/G1
Key, Ala. (†35960) 195/G2
Key (lake), Ireland 17/E3
Keya Paha (co.), Nebr. 264/E2
Keya Paha (riv.), Nebr. 264/D1
Keyapaha, S. Dak. (57545) 298/J7
Keya Paha (riv.), S. Dak. 298/K7
Key Biscayne, Fla. (33149) 212/B5
Key Colony Beach, Fla. (33051) 212/F7
Keyes, Calif. (95328) 204/E6
Keyes, Manitoba 179/C4
Keyes, Okla. (73947) 288/B1
Keyesport, Ill. (62253) 222/D5
Keyhole (res.), Wyo. 319/H1
Key Largo, Fla. (33037) 212/F6
Key Largo (key), Fla. 212/F6
Keymar, Md. (21757) 245/K2
Keynsham, England 13/E6
Keyport, N.J. (07735) 273/E3
Keyport, Wash. (98345) 310/A2
Keysbrook, W. Australia 88/B3
Keyser, W. Va. (26726) 312/J4
Keystone, Ind. (46759) 227/G3
Keystone, Iowa (52249) 229/J5
Keystone, Nebr. (69144) 264/C3
Keystone (res.), Ohio 284/K2
Keystone (lake), Okla. 288/O2
Keystone, S. Dak. (57751) 298/C6
Keystone, W. Va. (24852) 312/D8
Keystone Heights, Fla. (32656) 212/E2
Keystown, Sask. 181/F5
Keysville, Georgia (30816) 217/H4
Keysville, Va. (23947) 307/M6
Keytesville, Mo. (65261) 261/G4
Key Vaca (key), Fla. 212/E7
Key West, Fla. 146/K7
Key West, Fla. 188/K6
Key West, Fla. (33040) 212/E7
Key West Naval Air Sta., Fla. 212/E7
Kezar (lake), Maine 243/B7
Kezar (pond), Maine 243/B7
Kezar Falls, Maine (04047) 243/B8
Kežmarok, Czech. 41/F2
Khabake (Habahe), China 77/C2
Khabarovsk, U.S.S.R. 54/P5
Khabarovsk, U.S.S.R. 2/R3
Khabarovsk, U.S.S.R. 48/O5
Khabur (riv.), Syria 63/J5
Khabur (riv.), Syria 59/D2
Khachmas, U.S.S.R. 52/G6

Lead Mine 397

La Palma, El Salvador 154/C3
La Palma, Panama 154/H6
La Palma (isl.), Spain 102/A2
La Palma (isl.), Spain 106/A3
La Palma (isl.), Spain 33/A4
La Palma del Condado, Spain 33/C4
La Paloma, Uruguay 145/F5
La Pampa (prov.), Argentina 143/C4
La Paragua, Venezuela 124/G4
Laparan (isl.), Philippines 82/B8
Laparan (isls.), Philippines 82/B8
La Passe, Ontario 177/H2
La Patrie, Québec 172/F4
La Paz, Entre Rios, Argentina 143/G5
La Paz, Mendoza, Argentina 143/C3
La Paz (dept.), Bolivia 136/A4
La Paz (cap.), Bolivia 136/B5
La Paz (cap.), Bolivia 2/F6
La Paz (cap.), Bolivia 120/C4
La Paz, Honduras 154/D3
Lapaz, Ind. (46537) 227/E2
La Paz, Mexico 146/G7
La Paz, Bajo California Sur, Mexico 150/D5
La Paz, San Luis Potosí, Mexico 150/J5
La Paz (bay), Mexico 150/D4
La Paz, Philippines 82/E6
La Paz, Canelones, Uruguay 145/B6
La Paz, Colonia, Uruguay 145/B5
La Paz Central, Nicaragua 154/D4
La Paz de Oriente, Nicaragua 154/E5
La Pêche, Québec 172/B4
La Pedrera, Colombia 126/F8
La Pedrera, Uruguay 145/F5
Lapeer (co.), Mich. 250/F5
Lapeer, Mich. (48446) 250/F5
Lapel, Ind. (46051) 227/F4
La Pelada, Argentina 143/F5
La Pérade, Québec 172/E3
La Pérouse (str.) 54/R5
La Perouse, N.S. Wales 88/L4
La Perouse, N.S. Wales 97/J4
La Pérouse (str.), U.S.S.R. 48/P5
La Pesca, Mexico 150/L4
Lapeyrère (lake), Québec 172/E2
La Piedad Cavadas, Mexico 150/H6
Lapine, Ala. (36046) 195/F7
La Pine, Oreg. (97739) 291/F4
Lapinin (isl.), Philippines 82/E5
La Pintada, Panama 154/G6
Lapithos, Cyprus 63/E5
La Place, Ill. (61936) 222/E4
La Place, La. (70068) 238/N3
La Plaine, Dominica 161/F6
Lapland (reg.) 7/G2
Lapland (reg.), Finland 18/O2
Lapland (reg.), Norway 18/K2
Lapland (reg.), Sweden 18/M2
Lapland (reg.), U.S.S.R. 52/D1
La Plant, S. Dak. (57637) 298/H3
Laplante, New Bruns. 170/E1
La Plata (est.) 120/D6
La Plata, Argentina 143/H7
La Plata, Argentina 120/D6
La Plata, Río de (est.), Argentina 143/E4
La Plata, Colombia 126/C6
La Plata (co.), Colo. 208/D8
La Plata (peak), Colo. 208/G4
La Plata (riv.), Colo. 208/C8
La Plata, Md. (20646) 245/L6
La Plata, Mo. (63549) 261/H2
La Plata, N. Mex. (87418) 274/A2
La Plata (riv.), N. Mex. 274/A1
La Plume, Pa. (18440) 294/L2
La Pobla de Lillet, Spain 33/G1
La Pocatière, Québec 172/H2
La Poile, Newf. 166/C4
La Poile (bay), Newf. 166/C4
Lapoint, Utah (84039) 304/E3
La Pointe, Wis. (54850) 317/E2
La Porte, Calif. (95981) 204/D4
Laporte, Colo. (80535) 208/J1
LaPorte (co.), Ind. 227/D1
LaPorte, Ind. (46350) 227/D1
Laporte, Mich. (†48623) 250/E5
Laporte, Minn. (56461) 255/D3
Laporte, Pa. (18626) 294/K3
Laporte, Sask. 181/B4
La Porte, Texas (77571) 303/K2
La Porte City, Iowa (50651) 229/J4
Lappajärvi, Finland 18/O5
Lappajärvi (lake), Finland 18/O5
Lappeenranta, Finland 7/G2
Lappeenranta, Finland 18/P6
Lappi (prov.), Finland 18/P3
La Prairie, Ill. (62346) 222/B3
La Prairie, Minn. (†55744) 255/E3
Laprairie (co.), Québec 172/H4
La Prairie, Québec 172/J4
Laprida, Argentina 143/D4
La Protección, Honduras 154/D3
La Providence, Québec 172/E4
La Pryor, Texas (78872) 303/E9
Lâpseki, Turkey 63/C6
Laptev (sea), U.S.S.R. 4/B3
Laptev (sea), U.S.S.R. 54/O2
Laptev (sea), U.S.S.R. 48/N2
Lapua, Finland 18/N5
Lapuanjoki (riv.), Finland 18/N5
La Puebla, Spain 33/H3
La Puebla de Montalbán, Spain 33/D3
La Puente, Calif. (*91744) 204/D10
La Puerta, Cuba 158/H3
Lapu-Lapu, Philippines /E5
La Puntilla (cape), Ecuador 128/B4
La Purísima, Mexico 150/D3
La Push, Wash. (98350) 310/A3
Lapwai, Idaho (83540) 220/B3
Łapy, Poland 47/F2
Laqiya 'Umran (well), Sudan 111/E3
Laquey, Mo. (65534) 261/H7
La Quiaca, Argentina 143/C1
L'Aquila (prov.), Italy 34/D3
L'Aquila, Italy 34/D3
Lar, Iran 59/F4
Lar, Iran 66/J7
Lara (state), Venezuela 124/C2
Lara, Victoria 97/C6
Larabee, Pa. (†16731) 294/F2
Larache, Morocco 106/C1
Laracor, Ireland 17/H4
Larak (isl.), Iran 66/K7
La Rambla, Spain 33/D4
Laramie (mts.), Colo. 208/H1
Laramie (riv.), Colo. 208/H1
Laramie (co.), Wyo. 319/H4
Laramie, Wyo. 146/H5
Laramie, Wyo. 188/E2
Laramie, Wyo. (82070) 319/G4
Laramie (mts.), Wyo. 319/G3
Laramie (peak), Wyo. 319/G3
Laramie (riv.), Wyo. 319/G4
Laranjeiras do Sul, Brazil 132/C9
Larantuka, Indonesia 85/G7
Larat (isl.), Indonesia 85/J7
Larbert, Scotland 10/B1
Larbert, Scotland 15/C1
Lärbro, Sweden 18/L8
Larchmont, N.Y. (10538) 276/P7
Larchwood, Iowa (51241) 229/A2
Lardeau, Br. Col. 184/J5
Larder Lake, Ontario 175/E3
Larder Lake, Ontario 177/K5
L'Ardoise West, Nova Scotia 168/H3
La Rédemption, Québec 172/B2
Laredo (sound), Br. Col. 184/C4
Laredo, Mo. (64652) 261/E2
Laredo, Mont. (†59501) 262/G2
Laredo, Spain 33/E1
Laredo, Texas (*78040) 303/E10
Laredo, Texas 188/G5
Laredo, Texas 146/J7
La Reine, Québec 174/B3
Laren, Netherlands 27/G4
Larena, Philippines 82/D6
La Réole, France 28/C5
Lares, P. Rico 161/B2
Lares, P. Rico 156/F1
La Retuca, Chile 138/F3
Larew, W. Va. (†26537) 312/G4
Largentière, France 28/F5
Largo (cay), Cuba 158/D2
Largo (cay), Cuba 156/B2
Largo, Fla. (*33540) 212/B3
Largo (key), Fla. 212/F6
Largo, Md. (†20870) 245/G5
Largo, Cañon (creek), N. Mex. 274/B2
Largs, Scotland 15/A2
Largs, Scotland 10/A1
Lariat, Texas (79335) 303/B3
Larimer (co.), Colo. 208/H1
Larimer, Pa. (15647) 294/C5
Larimore, N. Dak. (58251) 282/P4
Larino, Italy 34/E4
La Rioja (prov.), Argentina 143/C2
La Rioja, Argentina 120/C5
La Rioja, Argentina 143/C2
La Rioja, Cuba 158/H3
Lárisa, Greece 45/F6
Lárisa, Greece 7/G5
Laristan (reg.), Iran 66/J7
La Rivière, Manitoba 179/D5
Lark, N. Dak. (58550) 282/H7
Larkana, Pakistan 59/J4
Larkana, Pakistan 68/B3
Larkhall, Scotland 10/B1
Larkhall, Scotland 15/E5
Lark Harbour, Newf. 166/C4
Larkinburg, Kansas (†66436) 232/G2
Larkinsville, Ala. (†35768) 195/F1
Larkspur, Calif. (94939) 204/H1
Larkspur, Colo. (80118) 208/K4
Larksville, Pa. (†18704) 294/E7
Larnaca, Cyprus 59/B3
Larnaca, Cyprus 63/E5
Larnaca (bay), Cyprus 63/E5
Larne (dist.), N. Ireland 17/K2
Larne, N. Ireland 17/K2
Larne, N. Ireland 10/D3
Lorne (inlet), N. Ireland 17/K2
Larned, Kansas (67550) 232/C3
La Robla, Spain 33/D1
La Roche, Switzerland 39/D3
La Roche-en-Ardenne, Belgium 27/G8
La Rochelle, France 7/D4
La Rochelle, France 28/C4
La Rochelle, Manitoba 179/F5
La Roche-sur-Yon, France 28/C4
La Roda, Spain 33/E3
La Romana (prov.), Dom. Rep. 158/F6
La Romana, Dom. Rep. 158/F6
La Romana, Dom. Rep. 156/E3
La Ronge, Sask. 181/L3
La Rose, Ill. (61541) 222/D3
Larose, La. (70373) 238/K7
Larouche, Québec 172/F1
Larrabee, Iowa (51029) 229/B3
Larrimah, North. Terr. 88/E3
Larrimah, North. Terr. 93/C3
Larroque, Argentina 143/F5
Larry's River, Nova Scotia 168/G3
Larsen (sound), N.W. Terrs. 187/J2
Larsen Bay, Alaska (99624) 196/H3
Larsen Ice Shelf, Ant. 2/F9
Larsen Ice Shelf, Ant. 5/C16
Larslan, Mont. (59244) 262/K2
Larsmont, Minn. (†55616) 255/G4
Larson, N. Dak. (58751) 282/E2
Larto, La. (71344) 238/G4
Larue (co.), Ky. 237/K5
La Rue, Ohio (43332) 284/D4
Laruns, France 28/C6
La Russell, Mo. (64848) 261/D8
Larvik, Norway 18/C4
Larwill, Ind. (46764) 227/F2
La Sal, Utah (84530) 304/E5
La Salle (co.), Ill. 222/E2
La Salle, Colo. (80645) 208/K2
La Salle (co.), Ill. 222/E2
La Salle, Ill. (61301) 222/E2
La Salle (par.), La. 238/F3
La Salle, Manitoba 179/E5
La Salle (riv.), Manitoba 179/E5
La Salle, Mich. (48145) 250/F7
La Salle, Minn. (56056) 255/D6
La Salle, Québec 172/H4
Lasalle (lake), Québec 172/E2
La Salle (co.), Texas 303/E9
Las Animas (co.), Colo. 208/L8
Las Animas, Colo. (81054) 208/N6
Las Animas (creek), N. Mex. 274/B5
Las Anod, Somalia 115/J2
La Sarraz, Switzerland 39/C3
La Sarre, Que. 162/J6
La Sarre, Québec 174/B3
Lasauces, Colo. (†81151) 208/H8
Las Aves (isls.), Venezuela 124/E2
Las Bonitas, Venezuela 124/F4
Las Breas, Chile 138/B7
Lasca, Ala. (†36784) 195/C6
Las Cabras, Chile 138/F5
Lascahobas, Haiti 156/D3
Lascahobas, Haiti 158/C6
Lascano, Uruguay 145/E4
Las Carreras, Bolivia 136/C7
Lascassas, Tenn. (37085) 237/J9
L'Ascension, Labelle, Québec 172/C3
L'Ascension, Lac-St-Jean-E., Québec 172/F1
L'Ascension-de-Patapédia, Québec 172/B2
Las Choapas, Mexico 150/M7
La Scie, Newf. 166/C4
Las Cruces, Chile 138/F3
Las Cruces, N. Mex. 146/H6
Las Cruces, N. Mex. 188/E4
Las Cruces, N. Mex. (88001) 274/C6
Las Dureh, Somalia 115/J1
La Selva Beach, Calif. (95076) 204/K4
La Serena, Chile 120/B5
La Serena, Chile 138/A8
La Seyne-sur-Mer, France 28/F6
Las Flores, Argentina 143/E4
Las Flores, Uruguay 145/D5
Las Hadas, Mexico 150/G7
Lashburn, Sask. 181/B2
Lash-e Joveyn, Afghanistan 68/A2
Lash-e Joveyn, Afghanistan 59/H3
Lashio, Burma 72/C2
Lashkar Gah, Afghanistan 68/A2
Lashkar Gah, Afghanistan 59/H3
La Sierra, Uruguay 145/D5
L'Asile, Haiti 158/B6
Las Juntas, Colombia 126/E6
Las Juntas, C. Rica 154/E5
Łask, Poland 47/D3
Lasker, N.C. (27848) 281/P2
La Skhirra, Tunisia 106/G2
Las Khoreh, Somalia 115/J1
Las Lajas, Argentina 143/B4
Las Lajitas, Venezuela 124/F4
Las Lomitas, Argentina 143/D1
Las Marias, P. Rico 161/B2
Las Martinas, Cuba 158/A2
Las Matas de Farfán, Dom. Rep. 158/D6
Las Matas de Farfán, Dom. Rep. 156/D3
Las Mercedes, Venezuela 124/E3
Las Navas del Marqués, Spain 33/D2
Lasne, Belgium 27/F7
Las Nieves, Mexico 150/G3
La Solana, Spain 33/E3
La Sorcière (mt.), St. Lucia 161/G6
La Souterraine, France 28/D4
Las Palmas, Argentina 143/E2
Las Palmas (cap.), Canary Is., 102/A2
Las Palmas, Panama 154/G6
Las Palmas (prov.), Spain 33/C4
Las Palmas de Gran Canaria, Spain 33/B4
Las Palmas de Gran Canaria, Spain 106/B3
Las Pampitas, Bolivia 136/C3
Las Parejas, Argentina 143/F6
Las Pedroñeras, Spain 33/E3
Las Petas, Bolivia 136/F5
La Spezia (prov.), Italy 34/B2
La Spezia, Italy 34/B2
La Spezia, Italy 7/E4
Las Piedras, Peru 128/H9
Las Piedras, P. Rico 161/E2
Las Piedras, Uruguay 145/B6
Las Piedras, Falcón, Venezuela 124/C2
Las Piedras, Zulia, Venezuela 124/B2
Las Plumas, Argentina 143/C5
Lasqueti Island, Br. Col. 184/J2
Las Rosas, Argentina 143/F6
Las Rosas, Mexico 150/N8
Lassen (co.), Calif. 204/E3
Lassen (peak), Calif. 204/D3
Lassen Volcanic Nat'l Park, Calif. 204/D3
L'Assomption (co.), Québec 172/D4
L'Assomption, Québec 172/D4
L'Assomption (riv.), Québec 172/D3
Las Tablas, N. Mex. (87541) 274/C2
Las Tablas, Panama 154/G7
Lastarria (vol.), Chile 138/B5
La Station-du-Coteau, Québec 172/C4
Last Chance (creek), Utah 304/C6
Las Termas, Argentina 143/D2
Last Mountain (lake), Sask. 181/F4
Las Toscas, Uruguay 145/E3
Lastoursville, Gabon 115/B4
Lastovo (Lagosta) (isl.), Yugoslavia 45/C4
Las Trincheras, Venezuela 124/F4
Las Truchas, Mexico 150/H7
Lastrup, Minn. (56344) 255/D4
Las Tunas (prov.), Cuba 158/H3
Las Varillas, Argentina 143/D3
Las Vegas, Nev. 146/G6
Las Vegas, Nev. 188/C3
Las Vegas, Nev. (*89101) 266/F6
Las Vegas (range), Nev. 266/F6
Las Vegas, N.Mex. 188/E3
Las Vegas, N. Mex. (87701) 274/D3
Las Vegas, Venezuela 124/D3
Las Yaras, Peru 128/G11
Las Yungas (reg.), Bolivia 136/B5
La Tabatière, Québec 174/F2
Latacunga, Ecuador 128/C3
La Tagua, Colombia 126/C8
Latah (co.), Idaho 220/B3
Latah, Wash. (99018) 310/H3
Latah (creek), Wash. 310/H3
Latakia (prov.), Syria 63/G5
Latakia, Syria 54/E6
Latakia, Syria 63/F5
Latakia, Syria 59/C2
La Taste, Grenada 161/D8
Latchford, Ontario 177/K5
Laterrière, Québec 172/F1
Latexo, Texas (75849) 303/J6
Latham, Ala. (†36579) 195/C8
Latham, Ill. (62543) 222/D4
Latham, Kansas (67072) 232/F4
Latham, Mo. (65050) 261/G5
Latham, N.Y. (12110) 276/N5
Latham, Ohio (45646) 284/D7
Latham, Tenn. (†38225) 237/D8
Lathrop, Calif. (95330) 204/D6
Lathrop, Mich. (†49880) 250/B2
Lathrop, Mo. (64465) 261/D3
La Tigra, Venezuela 124/H4
Latimer, Iowa (50452) 229/G3
Latimer, Kansas (†67449) 232/F3
Latimer (co.), Okla. 288/R5
Latimers (brook), Conn. 210/G3
Latina (prov.), Italy 34/D4
Latina, Italy 34/D4
La Tina, Peru 128/B5
Latium (Lazio) (reg.), Italy 34/D3
La Tola, Ecuador 128/C2
La Toma, Argentina 143/C3
Laton, Calif. (93242) 204/F7
Latorica (riv.), Czech. 41/F2
La Tortuga (isl.), Venezuela 124/F2
Latouche Treville (cape), W. Australia 88/C3
Latouche Treville (cape), W. Australia 92/C2
Latour, Mo. (64760) 261/D5
La Tour-de-Peilz, Switzerland 39/C4
La Tour-du-Pin, France 28/F5
Latourell Falls, Oreg. (†97060) 291/E2
La Trinidad, Nicaragua 154/D4
La Trinidad, Philippines 82/C2
La Trinidad, Venezuela 124/D3
La Trinidad de Arauca, Venezuela 124/D4
La Trinidad de Orichuna, Venezuela 124/D4
La Trinité, Martinique 161/D6
La Trinité-des-Monts, Québec 172/J1
Latrobe, Pa. (15650) 294/D5
Latrobe, Tasmania 99/C3
Latta, S.C. (29565) 296/J3
Lattimore, N.C. (28089) 281/F4
Lattingtown, N.Y. (†11560) 276/R6
Latty, Ohio (45855) 284/A3
La Tuque, Que. 162/J6
La Tuque, Québec 172/E2
La Tuque, Québec 174/C3
Latur, India 68/D5
LATVIA 53/B2
Latvian S.S.R., U.S.S.R. 7/G3
Latvian S.S.R., U.S.S.R. 52/B3
Latvian S.S.R., U.S.S.R. 48/C4
Lauca (riv.), Bolivia 136/A6
Lauca (riv.), Chile 138/B1
Lauchhammer, E. Germany 22/E3
Laud, Ind. (†46725) 227/G2
Laudat, Dominica 161/E6
Lauder, Manitoba 179/B5
Lauder, Scotland 10/E3
Lauder, Scotland 15/F5
Lauderdale (co.), Ala. 195/C1
Lauderdale, Minn. (†55101) 255/G5
Lauderdale (co.), Miss. 256/G6
Lauderdale, Miss. (39335) 256/G5
Lauderdale, Tasmania 99/D4
Lauderdale (co.), Tenn. 237/B9
Lauderdale-by-the-Sea, Fla. (33308) 212/C3
Lauderdale Lakes, Fla. (†33313) 212/B3
Lauderhill, Fla. (33313) 212/B3
Lauenburg an der Elbe, W. Germany 22/D2
Lauenen, Switzerland 39/D4
Lauf an der Pegnitz, W. Germany 22/D4
Läufelfingen, Switzerland 39/E2
Laufen, Switzerland 39/D2
Laufen, W. Germany 22/E5
Laufenburg, Switzerland 39/F1
Laughery (creek), Ind. 227/G6
Laughing Fish (pt.), Mich. 250/B2
Laughlin A.F.B., Texas 303/D8
Lau Group (isls.), Fiji 87/J7
Lauingen, W. Germany 22/D4
Launceston, England 13/C7
Launceston, England 10/D5
Launceston, Tasmania 99/C3
Launceston, Tasmania 88/H8
Laune (riv.), Ireland 17/B7
Launglon Bok (isls.), Burma 72/C4
La Unión, Chile 138/D3
La Unión, Colombia 126/B7
La Unión, El Salvador 154/D4
La Unión, Mexico 150/J8
La Union, N. Mex. (†88021) 274/C7
La Unión, Peru 128/D7
La Union (prov.), Philippines 82/C2
La Unión, Spain 33/F4
La Unión, Venezuela 124/E3
Laupahoehoe, Hawaii (96764) 218/J4
Laupen, Switzerland 39/D3
Lauperswil, Switzerland 39/E3
Laura, Ill. (61451) 222/D3
Laura, Ohio (45337) 284/B6
Laura, Queensland 88/G3
Laura, Queensland 95/C2
Laura, Sask. 181/D4
Laura, S. Australia 94/F5
La Urbana, Venezuela 124/E4
Laurel, Del. (19956) 245/R6
Laurel, Fla. (33545) 212/D4
Laurel, Ind. (47024) 227/G6
Laurel, Iowa (50141) 229/H5
Laurel (co.), Ky. 237/N6
Laurel, Md. (*20810) 245/L4
Laurel, Miss. 188/J4
Laurel, Miss. (39440) 256/F7
Laurel, Mont. (59044) 262/H5
Laurel, Nebr. (68745) 264/G2
Laurel, Oreg. (†97123) 291/A2
Laurel, Pa. (†17322) 294/K6
Laurel, Wash. (†98672) 310/D5
Laurel (mt.), W. Va. 312/G4
Laurel Bay, S.C. (29902) 296/F7
Laurel Bloomery, Tenn. (37680) 237/T7
Laureldale, Pa. (19605) 294/L5
Laurel Dale, W. Va. (†26743) 312/H4
Laureles, Paraguay 144/D5
Laurel Fork, Va. (24352) 307/G7
Laurel Hill, Fla. (32567) 212/C5
Laurel Hill, N.C. (28351) 281/K5
Laurel Hill (mt.), Pa. 294/D5
Laurel Park, N.C. (†28739) 281/D4
Laurel River (lake), Ky. 237/N6
Laurel Run, Pa. (†18701) 294/F7
Laurel Springs, N.J. (08021) 273/B4
Laurelton, Pa. (17835) 294/H4
Laurelville, Ohio (43135) 284/E7
Laurence G. Hanscom Field, Mass. 249/B6
Laurence Harbor, N.J. (08879) 273/E3
Laurencekirk, Scotland 10/E2
Laurencekirk, Scotland 15/F4
Laurens (co.), Georgia 217/G6
Laurens, Iowa (50554) 229/D3
Laurens, N.Y. (13796) 276/K5
Laurens (co.), S.C. 296/D2
Laurens, S.C. (29360) 296/C3
Laurentides, Québec 172/D4
Laurentides Prov. Park, Québec 174/C3
Laurentides Prov. Park, Québec 172/F2
Lauria, Italy 34/E4
Laurie (lake), Manitoba 179/A3
Laurie, Mo. (65038) 261/G6
Laurier, Manitoba 179/C4
Laurier, Wash. (99146) 310/G2
Laurier-Station, Québec 172/F3
Laurierville, Québec 172/F3
Laurieston, Scotland 15/D6
Laurin, Mont. (†59749) 262/D5
Laurinburg, N.C. (28352) 281/K5
Lauritsala, Finland 18/Q6
Laurium, Mich. (49913) 250/A1
Laurot (Laut Kecil) (isls.), Indonesia 85/E7
Lausanne, Switzerland 39/C3
Lauscha, E. Germany 22/D3
Laut (isl.), Indonesia 85/F6
Laut (North Natuna) (isl.), Indonesia 85/D5
Lautaro, Chile 138/E2
Lauterbach, W. Germany 22/C3
Lauterbrunnen, Switzerland 39/E3
Lauterique, Honduras 154/D4
Laut Kecil (isls.), Indonesia 85/E7
Lautoka, Fiji 86/P10
Lauwers (chan.), Netherlands 27/J1
Lauwers Zee (bay), Netherlands 27/J2
Lauzon, Québec 172/J3
Lava (lake), Oreg. 291/F4
Lava Beds Nat'l Mon., Calif. 204/D2
Lavaca, Ala. (36911) 195/B6
Lavaca, Ark. (72941) 202/B3
Lavaca (co.), Texas 303/H8
Lavaca (bay), Texas 303/H9
Lava Hot Springs, Idaho (83246) 220/F7
Laval, France 28/C3
Laval, Québec 172/H4
Laval (bay), Québec 172/J1
La Vale-Narrows Park, Md. (21502) 245/C2
Lavalette, W. Va. (25535) 312/B6
Lavalle, Argentina 143/G4
La Valle, Wis. (53941) 317/F8
Lavalleja (dept.), Uruguay 145/D5
Lavallette, N.J. (08735) 273/E4
Lavalley, Colo. (†81153) 208/J8
Lavaltrie, Québec 172/D4
Lavamünd, Austria 41/C3
Lavapié (pt.), Chile 138/D1
Lavaur, France 28/D6
La Vecilla de Curueño, Spain 33/D1
Laveen, Ariz. (85339) 198/C5
La Vega (prov.), Dom. Rep. 158/D6
La Vega, Dom. Rep. 158/E5
La Vega, Dom. Rep. 156/D3
La Vega, Spain 33/C1
La Vela (cape), Colombia 126/D1
La Vela de Coro, Venezuela 124/D2
Lavelanet, France 28/E6
Lavello, Italy 34/E4
Lavenham, Manitoba 179/D5
L'Avenir, Québec 172/E4
La Vergne, Tenn. (37086) 237/H9
La Verkin, Utah (84745) 304/A6
La Verne, Calif. (91750) 204/D10
Laverne, Okla. (73848) 288/G1
La Vernia, Texas (78121) 303/K11
Laverton, Australia 87/C8
Laverton, W. Australia 88/C5
Laverton, W. Australia 92/C5
La Veta, Colo. (81055) 208/J8
Lavey-Morcles, Switzerland 39/D4
Lavezares, Philippines 82/E4
La Victoria, Colombia 126/A7
La Victoria, Apure, Venezuela 124/D4
La Victoria, Apure, Venezuela 124/C4
La Victoria, Aragua, Venezuela 124/E2
Lavieille (lake), Ontario 177/F2
La Vieja (pt.), Chile 138/A11
Lavik, Norway 18/D6
Lavillette, New Bruns. 170/E1
Lavina, Mont. (59046) 262/H4
Lavinia, Manitoba 179/B4
Lavinia, Tenn. (38348) 237/D9
La Vista, Nebr. (†68046) 264/J3
Lavon (lake), Texas 303/H1
Lavongai (isl.), Papua N.G. 87/F6
Lavongai (isls.), Papua N.G. 86/B1
Lavonia, Georgia (30553) 217/F2
Lavos, Portugal 33/B2
Lavoy, Alberta 182/E3
Lavras, Brazil 132/E8
Lavras, Brazil 135/D2
Lávrion, Greece 45/G7
Lawa (riv.), Fr. Guiana 131/D4
Lawa (riv.), Suriname 131/D4
Lawai, Hawaii (96765) 218/C2
Lawang, Indonesia 85/K2
Lawen, Oreg. (97740) 291/J4
Lawler, Iowa (52154) 229/J2
Lawler, Minn. (†55760) 255/E4
Lawlers, W. Australia 92/C5
Lawley, Ala. (36793) 195/E5
Lawn, Newf. 166/C4
Lawn, Pa. (17041) 294/J5
Lawn, Texas (79530) 303/E5
Lawndale, Calif. (90260) 204/B11
Lawndale, Ill. (61751) 222/D3
Lawndale, Minn. (†56579) 255/B4
Lawndale, N.C. (28090) 281/F4
Lawnhill, Br. Col. 184/A3
Lawn Hill, Queensland 95/A3
Lawnside, N.J. (08045) 273/B3
Lawra, Ghana 106/D6
Lawrence (co.), Ala. 195/D1
Lawrence (co.), Ark. 202/H1
Lawrence (co.), Ill. 222/F5
Lawrence (co.), Ind. 227/E7
Lawrence, Ind. (46226) 227/E5
Lawrence, Kans. 188/G3
Lawrence, Kansas (66044) 232/G3
Lawrence (co.), Ky. 237/R4
Lawrence, Mass. 188/M2
Lawrence, Mass. (*01840) 249/K2
Lawrence, Mich. (49064) 250/C6
Lawrence (co.), Miss. 256/D7
Lawrence, Miss. (39336) 256/F6
Lawrence (co.), Mo. 261/E8
Lawrence, Nebr. (68957) 264/F4
Lawrence, N.Y. (11559) 276/P7
Lawrence, N. Zealand 100/B6
Lawrence, N.C. (†27886) 281/O2
Lawrence (co.), Ohio 284/E8
Lawrence (co.), Pa. 294/B4
Lawrence (co.), S. Dak. 298/B5
Lawrence (co.), Tenn. 237/G10
Lawrenceburg, Ind. (47025) 227/H6
Lawrenceburg, Ky. (40342) 237/M4
Lawrenceburg, Tenn. (38464) 237/G10
Lawrence Park○, Pa. (†16501) 294/C1
Lawrenceport, Ind. (†47446) 227/D7
Lawrence Station, New Bruns. 170/C3
Lawrencetown, Nova Scotia 168/C4
Lawrenceville, Georgia (30245) 217/D3
Lawrenceville, Ill. (62439) 222/F5
Lawrenceville, Ind. (†47041) 227/H6
Lawrenceville○, N.J. (08648) 273/D3
Lawrenceville, N.Y. (12949) 276/L1
Lawrenceville, Ohio (†45501) 284/C6
Lawrenceville, Pa. (16929) 294/H2
Lawrenceville, Québec 172/E4
Lawrenceville, Va. (23868) 307/N7
Lawson, Ark. (71750) 202/F7
Lawson, Colo. (†80452) 208/H3
Lawson, Mo. (64062) 261/D4
Lawson, Sask. 181/E5
Lawsonville, N.C. (27022) 281/J2
Lawtell, La. (70550) 238/F5
Lawtey, Fla. (32058) 212/D1
Lawton, Ind. (†46996) 227/D2
Lawton, Iowa (51030) 229/A4
Lawton, Kansas (66752) 232/H4
Lawton, Ky. (41153) 237/P4
Lawton, Mich. (49065) 250/D6
Lawton, N. Dak. (58345) 282/O3
Lawton, Okla. 146/J6
Lawton, Okla. 188/G4
Lawton, Okla. (73501) 288/K5
Lawton, Pa. (18828) 294/K2
Lawton, W. Va. (25863) 312/E7
Lawtonka (lake), Okla. 288/K5
Lawu (mt.), Indonesia 85/J2
Lax, Georgia (†31650) 217/F8
Lax, Switzerland 39/F4
Laxå, Sweden 18/J7
Laxey, I. of Man 13/C3
Laxford, Loch (inlet), Scotland 15/C2
Lay (dam), Ala. 195/E5
Lay (lake), Ala. 195/F4
Lay (pt.), Alaska 196/F1
Lay, Colo. (†81625) 208/D2
Lay, Mui (cape), Vietnam 72/E3
Layang Layang, Malaysia 72/E5
Layland, W. Va. (25864) 312/E7
Layopolis (Sand Fork), W. Va. (†26430) 312/E5
Layou (riv.), Dominica 161/E6
Layou, St. Vin. & Grens. 161/A9
Laysan (isl.), Hawaii 87/J3
Laysan (isl.), Hawaii 188/E6
Laysan (isl.), Hawaii 218/B5
Laysville, Conn. (†06371) 210/F3
Layton, Fla. (†33050) 212/F7
Layton, N.J. (07851) 273/D1
Layton, Utah (84041) 304/C2
Laytonsville, Md. (20760) 245/K4
Laytonville, Calif. (95454) 204/B4
Laytown-Bettystown-Mornington, Ireland 17/J4
Lazarev Station, Ant. 5/C1
Lazdijai, U.S.S.R. 53/B3
Lazear, Colo. (81420) 208/D5
Lazi, Philippines 82/D6
Łaziska Górne, Poland 47/A4
Lazy Lake, Fla. (†33301) 212/B3
Lea (riv.), England 13/G6
Lea (co.), N. Mex. 274/F6
Leaburg, Oreg. (97401) 291/E3
Leach, Okla. (74351) 288/S2
Leach, Tenn. (38349) 237/E9
Leachville, Ark. (72438) 202/K2
Leacross, Sask. 181/H2
Lead, S. Dak. 188/F2
Lead, S. Dak. (57754) 298/B5
Leadbetter (pt.), Wash. 310/A4
Leader, Minn. (56462) 255/D4
Leader, Sask. 181/B5
Lead Hill, Ark. (72644) 202/D1
Leadington, Mo. (†63640) 261/M7
Leadmine (brook), Conn. 210/C1
Lead Mine, W. Va. (†26290) 312/G4

Lingshan 399

Leti (isls.), Indonesia 85/H7
Leticia, Colombia 126/F10
Leticia, Colombia 120/B3
L'Etivaz, Switzerland 39/D4
Letka, U.S.S.R. 52/H3
Leto, Fla. (†33614) 212/C2
Letohatchee, Ala. (36047) 195/E6
Leton, La. (†71072) 238/D1
Letona, Ark. (72085) 202/G3
Letong, Indonesia 85/D5
Le Touquet-Paris-Plage, France 28/D2
Letpadan, Burma 72/C3
Le Tréport, France 28/D2
Letsôk-aw Kyun (isl.), Burma 72/C5
Lette, N.S. Wales 97/B4
Letterkenny, Ireland 10/B3
Letterkenny, Ireland 17/F2
Letterkenny Army Depot, Pa. 294/G6
Lettermullan (isl.), Ireland 17/B5
Letts, Ind. (†47240) 227/F6
Letts, Iowa (52754) 229/L6
Lettsworth, La. (70753) 238/G5
Leucadia, Calif. (92024) 204/H10
Leucate (mts.), France 28/E6
Leuchars, Scotland 15/F4
Leuk, Switzerland 39/E4
Leukerbad, Switzerland 39/E4
Leupp, Ariz. (86035) 198/E3
Leurbost, Scotland 15/B2
Leuser (mt.), Indonesia 85/B5
Leuven, Belgium 27/F7
Leuze-en-Hainaut, Belgium 27/D7
Levádhia, Greece 45/F6
Levallois-Perret, France 28/A1
Levan, Utah (84639) 304/C4
Levanger, Norway 18/G5
Levant, Kansas (67743) 232/A2
Levant○, Maine (04456) 243/F6
Levanzo (isl.), Italy 34/D5
Levasy, Mo. (64066) 261/S5
Le Vauclin, Martinique 161/D6
Levee, Ky. (†40337) 237/O5
Level, Md. (†21078) 245/O2
Level Green, Ky. (†40456) 237/N6
Level Land, S.C. (†29655) 296/C3
Levelland, Texas (79336) 303/B4
Levelock, Alaska (99625) 196/G3
Level Plains, Ala. (†36322) 195/G8
Levels, W. Va. (25431) 312/J4
Leven, Scotland 10/E2
Leven, Scotland 15/F4
Leven, Loch (inlet), Scotland 15/D4
Leven (lake), Scotland 15/E4
Leven (riv.), Tasmania 99/B3
Leveque (cape), Australia 87/C7
L'Evêque (cape), N. Zealand 100/D7
Lévêque (cape), W. Australia 88/C3
Lévêque (cape), W. Australia 92/C2
Leverburgh, Scotland 15/B3
Le Verdon-sur-Mer, France 28/C5
Leverett○, Mass. (01054) 249/E3
Levering, Mich. (49755) 250/E3
Leverkusen, W. Germany 22/B3
Levesque, New Bruns. 170/C1
Levice, Czech. 41/E2
Levick (mt.) 5/B8
Levie, France 28/B7
Le Vigan, France 28/E5
Levin, N. Zealand 100/E4
Lévis (co.), Québec 172/J3
Lévis, Québec 172/J3
Lévis, Québec 174/C3
Levisa Fork (riv.), Va. 307/C5
Levítha (isl.), Greece 45/H7
Levittown, N.Y. (11756) 276/R7
Levittown, Pa. (*19053) 294/N5
Levittown, P. Rico 161/D1
Levkás, Greece 45/E6
Levkás (isl.), Greece 45/E6
Levoča, Czech. 41/F2
Lévrier (bay), Mauritania 106/A4
Levuka, Fiji 87/H7
Levukaa, Fiji 86/Q10
Levy (co.), Fla. 212/D2
Levy (lake), Fla. 212/D2
Levy, N. Mex. (†87752) 274/E2
Lewe, Burma 72/B3
Lewellen, Nebr. (69147) 264/B3
Lewes, Del. (19958) 245/T5
Lewes, England 13/H7
Lewes, England 10/G5
Lewis, Colo. (81327) 208/B8
Lewis (isl.), Fla. 212/B3
Lewis (co.), Idaho 220/B3
Lewis, Ind. (47858) 227/C6
Lewis, Iowa (51544) 229/C6
Lewis, Kansas (67552) 232/C4
Lewis (co.), Ky. 237/P3
Lewis, Manitoba 179/F5
Lewis (lake), Manitoba 179/G2
Lewis (co.), Mo. 261/J2
Lewis, Mo. (†64735) 261/E6
Lewis (range), Mont. 262/C2
Lewis (co.), N.Y. 276/K3
Lewis, N.Y. (12950) 276/N2
Lewis (dist.), Scotland 15/B2
Lewis (dist.), Scotland 10/C1
Lewis, Butt of (prom.), Scotland 15/B2
Lewis, Butt of (prom.), Scotland 10/C1
Lewis, S.C. (†29706) 296/E2
Lewis (co.), Tenn. 237/F9
Lewis (creek), Vt. 268/A3
Lewis (co.), Wash. 310/C4
Lewis (riv.), Wash. 310/C5
Lewis (co.), W. Va. 312/E4
Lewis, Wis. (54851) 317/B4
Lewis (lake), Wyo. 319/B1
Lewis and Clark (co.), Mont. 262/D3
Lewis and Clark (lake), Nebr. 264/G2
Lewis and Clark (lake), S. Dak. 298/O8
Lewis and Clark Village, Mo. (†64484) 261/C3
Lewisberry, Pa. (17339) 294/J5
Lewisburg, Ky. (42256) 237/G6
Lewisburg, La. (†70525) 238/F6
Lewisburg, Ohio (45338) 284/A6
Lewisburg, Pa. (17837) 294/J4
Lewisburg, Tenn. (37091) 237/H10
Lewisburg, W. Va. (24901) 312/E7
Lewis Center, Ohio (43035) 284/D5
Lewis Creek, Ind. (†47234) 227/F6
Lewisetta, Va. (22505) 307/R4
Lewisham, England 10/B5
Lewisham, England 13/H8
Lewis Hill (mt.), Newf. 166/C4
Lewisport, Ky. (42351) 237/H5
Lewisporte, Newf. 166/C4
Lewis Run, Pa. (16738) 294/E2
Lewis Smith (dam), Ala. 195/D3
Lewis Smith (lake), Ala. 195/D2
Lewiston, Calif. (96052) 204/C3
Lewiston, Idaho 188/C1
Lewiston, Idaho (83501) 220/A3
Lewiston, Maine 188/N2
Lewiston, Maine (04240) 243/C7
Lewiston, Mich. (49756) 250/E4
Lewiston, Minn. (55952) 255/G7
Lewiston, Nebr. (68380) 264/H4
Lewiston, N.Y. (14092) 276/B4
Lewiston, N.C. (27849) 281/P2
Lewiston, Utah (84320) 304/C2
Lewiston, Vt. (†05055) 268/C4
Lewistown, Ill. (61542) 222/C3
Lewistown, Md. (21701) 245/J2
Lewistown, Mo. (63452) 261/J2
Lewistown, Mont. (59457) 262/G3
Lewistown, Ohio (43333) 284/C5
Lewistown, Pa. (17044) 294/G4
Lewisville, Ark. (71845) 202/C7
Lewisville, Idaho (83431) 220/F6
Lewisville, Ind. (47352) 227/G5
Lewisville, Minn. (56060) 255/D7
Lewisville, Ohio (43754) 284/H6
Lewisville (Ulysses), Pa. (16948) 294/G2
Lewisville, Pa. (19351) 294/L6
Lewisville, Texas (*75067) 303/G1
Lewisville (lake), Texas 303/G1
Lewvan, Sask. 181/H5
Lexa, Ark. (72355) 202/J4
Lexie, Miss. (†39667) 256/D8
Lexington, Ala. (35648) 195/D1
Lexington, Ark. (†72153) 202/F2
Lexington, Georgia (30648) 217/F3
Lexington, Ill. (61753) 222/E3
Lexington, Ind. (47138) 227/F7
Lexington, Ky. (*40501) 237/N4
Lexington, Ky. 146/K6
Lexington, Ky. 188/K3
Lexington○, Mass. (02173) 249/B6
Lexington, Mich. (48450) 250/G5
Lexington, Minn. (†55014) 255/G5
Lexington, Miss. (39095) 256/D4
Lexington, Mo. (64067) 261/E4
Lexington, Nebr. (68850) 264/E4
Lexington, N.Y. (12452) 276/M6
Lexington, N.C. (27292) 281/J3
Lexington, Ohio (44904) 284/E4
Lexington, Okla. (73051) 288/M4
Lexington, Oreg. (97839) 291/H2
Lexington (co.), S.C. 296/E4
Lexington, S.C. (29072) 296/E4
Lexington, Tenn. (38351) 237/E9
Lexington, Texas (78947) 303/G7
Lexington (I.C.), Va. (24450) 307/J5
Lexington Blue Grass Army Depot, Ky. 237/N5
Lexington Park, Md. (20653) 245/M7
Lexsy, Georgia (†30401) 217/H6
Leyba, N. Mex. (87542) 274/D3
Leyburn, England 13/F3
Leyden○, Mass. (†01301) 249/D2
Leye, China 77/G7
Leyland, England 13/G1
Leyland, England 10/F1
Leyond (riv.), Manitoba 179/F3
Leysin, Switzerland 39/C4
Leyte (prov.), Philippines 82/E5
Leyte (isl.), Philippines 54/O8
Leyte (gulf), Philippines 82/E5
Leyte (isl.), Philippines 85/H3
Leyte (isl.), Philippines 82/E5
Lezajsk, Poland 47/F3
Lezama, Argentina 143/H7
Lézarde (riv.), Martinique 161/D6
Lezhë, Albania 45/D5
Lézignan-Corbières, France 28/E6
Lezuza, Spain 33/E3
L'gov, U.S.S.R. 52/E4
Lhanbryde, Scotland 15/E3
Lhari, China 77/D5
Lhasa, China 77/D6
Lhasa, China 2/P4
Lhasa, China 54/L7
Lhazê (Lhatse), China 77/C6
Lhazhong, China 77/C5
Lhokseumawe, Indonesia 85/B4
Lhorong, China 77/E5
Lhozhag, China 77/D6
Lhünzê, China 77/D6
Lhünzhub, China 77/D5
Liancheng, China 77/J6
Lianga, Philippines 82/E6
Lianga (bay), Philippines 82/F6
Lianping, China 77/H7
Lian Xian, China 77/H7
Lianyungang (Lienyünkang), China 77/J5
Lianyungang, China 54/N6
Liao (riv.), China 54/O5
Liaodong Bandao (pen.), China 77/K3
Liao He (riv.), China 77/K3
Liaoning (prov.), China 77/K3
Liaoyang, China 77/K3
Liaoyuan, China 77/K3
Liard (riv.) 162/D3
Liard (riv.), Br. Col. 184/L2
Liard (riv.), Canada 146/F3
Liard (riv.), N.W. Terrs. 187/F4
Liard (riv.), Yukon 187/E3
Liard River, Br. Col. 184/L2
Libáň, Czech. 41/C1
Líbano, Colombia 126/C5
Libau, Manitoba 179/F4
Libby, Minn. (†55760) 255/E4
Libby, Mont. (59923) 262/A2
Libenge, Zaire 115/C3
Liberal, Kansas (67901) 232/B4
Liberal, Mo. (64762) 261/D7
Liberal, Oreg. (†97042) 291/B3
Liberdade, Brazil 135/D3
Liberec, Czech. 41/C1
Liberia 2/J5
Liberia 102/B4
LIBERIA 106/C7
Liberia, C. Rica 154/E5
Liberta, Ant. & Bar. 161/E11
Libertad, Belize 154/C1
Libertad, Uruguay 145/C5
Libertad, Barinas, Venezuela 124/D3
Libertad, Cojedes, Venezuela 124/D3
Liberty, Ariz. (†85326) 198/C5
Liberty (co.), Fla. 212/B1
Liberty (co.), Georgia 217/J7
Liberty, Ill. (62347) 222/B4
Liberty, Ind. (47353) 227/H5
Liberty, Kansas (67351) 232/G4
Liberty, Ky. (42539) 237/M6
Liberty, Maine (04949) 243/E7
Liberty○, Maine (04949) 243/E7
Liberty (lake), Md. 245/L3
Liberty, Miss. (39645) 256/C8
Liberty, Mo. (64068) 261/R5
Liberty (co.), Mont. 262/E2
Liberty, Nebr. (68381) 264/H4
Liberty (mt.), N.H. 268/D3
Liberty, N.Y. (12754) 276/L7
Liberty, N.C. (27298) 281/K3
Liberty, Pa. (16930) 294/H2
Liberty, Pa. (†15100) 294/C7
Liberty, Sask. 181/F4
Liberty, S.C. (29657) 296/B2
Liberty, Tenn. (37095) 237/K8
Liberty (co.), Texas 303/K7
Liberty, Texas (77575) 303/K7
Liberty, Wash. (†98922) 310/E3
Liberty, W. Va. (25124) 312/C5
Liberty Center, Ind. (46766) 227/G3
Liberty Center, Iowa (50145) 229/F6
Liberty Center, Ohio (43532) 284/B3
Liberty Corner, N.J. (07938) 273/D2
Liberty Grove, Md. (†21918) 245/O2
Liberty Hill, Conn. (†06249) 210/G2
Liberty Hill, La. (†71008) 238/E2
Liberty Hill, S.C. (29074) 296/F3
Liberty Lake, Wash. (99019) 310/J3
Liberty Mills, Ind. (46946) 227/F2
Liberty Pole, Wis. (†54665) 317/D8
Libertytown, Md. (21762) 245/J3
Libertyville, Ala. (†36420) 195/F8
Libertyville, Ill. (60048) 222/B4
Libertyville, Iowa (52567) 229/K7
Libiaz, Poland 47/D3
Libin, Belgium 27/G9
Libochovice, Czech. 41/B1
Libon, Philippines 82/D4
Libong, Ko (isl.), Thailand 72/C6
Libourne, France 28/C5
Libramont-Chevigny, Belgium 27/G9
Library, Pa. (15129) 294/B7
Libres, Mexico 150/O1
Libreville (cap.), Gabon 2/K6
Libreville (cap.), Gabon 115/A3
Libreville (cap.), Gabon 102/C4
Libuse, La. (71348) 238/F4
Libya 2/K4
Libya 102/D2
LIBYA 111/B2
Libyan (des.) 102/E2
Libyan (des.), Egypt 111/E2
Libyan (plat.), Egypt 111/E1
Libyan (des.), Libya 111/D2
Libyan (plat.), Libya 111/D1
Libyan (des.), Sudan 111/E3
Licancábur, Cerro (mt.), Chile 138/B4
Licantén, Chile 138/A10
Licata, Italy 34/D6
Lice, Turkey 63/J3
Lichfield, England 13/F5
Lichfield, England 10/G2
Lichinga, Mozambique 102/F6
Lichinga, Mozambique 118/F2
Lichtenberg, E. Germany 22/F4
Lichtenfels, W. Germany 22/D3
Lichtenrade, W. Germany 22/F4
Lichterfelde, W. Germany 22/E4
Lichtervelde, Belgium 27/C6
Lick (creek), Tenn. 237/R8
Lick Creek, Ill. (†62912) 222/D6
Licking, North Fork (riv.), Ky. 237/O3
Licking, South Fork (riv.), Ky. 237/N3
Licking (riv.), Ky. 237/N3
Licking, Mo. (65542) 261/J8
Licking (co.), Ohio 284/F5
Licking (riv.), Ohio 284/F5
Licking (creek), Pa. 294/F6
Licosa (cape), Italy 34/E4
Lida, Ky. (†40741) 237/O6
Lida (lake), Minn. 255/C4
Lida, U.S.S.R. 52/C4
Lidcombe, N.S. Wales 97/J3
Liddel Water (riv.), Scotland 15/F5
Lidderdale, Iowa (51452) 229/D4
Liddes, Switzerland 39/D5
Liddon (gulf), N.W. Terrs. 187/G4
Lidgerwood, N. Dak. (58053) 282/R7
Lidice, Czech. 41/C1
Lidingö, Sweden 18/H1
Lidköping, Sweden 18/H7
Lido di Ostia, Italy 34/F7
Lido di Venezia, Italy 34/D2
Lidzbark, Poland 47/D2
Lidzbark Warmiński, Poland 47/E1
Liebenthal, Kansas (67553) 232/C3
Liebenthal, Sask. 181/B5
Liechtensteig, Switzerland 39/H2
Liechtenstein 7/F4
LIECHTENSTEIN 39/J2
Liedekerke, Belgium 27/D7
Liége (riv.), Alberta 182/D1
Liège (prov.), Belgium 27/H7
Liège, Belgium 7/E3
Liège, Belgium 27/H7
Liegnitz (Legnica), Poland 47/C3
Lieksa, Finland 18/R5
Lienyünkang (Lianyungang), China 77/J5
Lienz, Austria 41/B3
Liepāja, U.S.S.R. 7/F3
Liepāja, U.S.S.R. 53/A2
Liepāja, U.S.S.R. 48/B4
Liepāja, U.S.S.R. 52/B3
Lier, Belgium 27/F6
Lierneux, Belgium 27/H8
Lierre (Lier), Belgium 27/F6
Liestal, Switzerland 39/E2
Liévin, France 28/E2
Lièvre (riv.), Québec 172/B4
Lièvres (isl.), Québec 172/H2
Liezen, Austria 41/C3
Liffey (riv.), Ireland 17/H5
Liffey (riv.), Ireland 10/C4
Lifford, Ireland 10/C3
Lifford, Ireland 17/F2
Lifu (isl.), New Caled. 87/G8
Lifu (isl.), New Caled. 86/H4
Ligao, Philippines 82/D4
Līgatne, U.S.S.R. 53/C2
Liggett, Ky. (†40831) 237/P7
Lightfoot, Va. (23090) 307/P6
Lighthouse (pt.), Fla. 212/B2
Light House (pt.), Mich. 250/D3
Lighthouse Point, Fla. (33064) 212/F5
Lightning (creek), Oreg. 291/L2
Lightning (creek), Wyo. 319/G2
Lightning Ridge, N.S. Wales 97/E1
Lightsville, Ohio (†45362) 284/A5
Lignite, N. Dak. (58752) 282/F2
Ligon, Ky. (41646) 237/R6
Ligonha (riv.), Mozambique 118/F3
Ligonier, Ind. (46767) 227/F2
Ligonier, Pa. (15658) 294/D5
Liguria (reg.), Italy 34/B2
Ligurian (sea), Italy 34/B3
Lihir Group (isls.), Papua N.G. 86/C1
Lihou (cays), Coral Sea Is. Terr. 88/J3
Lihue, Hawaii (96766) 218/C2
Lihue, Hawaii 188/E5
Lihula, U.S.S.R. 53/C1
Lijiang, China 77/F6
Likasi, Panda-, Zaire 115/E6
Likati, Zaire 115/D3
Likely, Br. Col. 184/G4
Likely, Calif. (96116) 204/E2
Likhoslavl', U.S.S.R. 52/E3
Likouala (riv.), Congo 115/C3
Lila (lake), N.Y. 276/L2
Lilac, Sask. 181/D3
Lilbourn, Mo. (63862) 261/N9
Lilburn, Georgia (30247) 217/D3
Lileah, Tasmania 99/B2
L'Île-Rousse, France 28/B6
Liles (pt.), Chile 138/F2
Lilesville, N.C. (28091) 281/K5
Lilienfeld, Austria 41/C3
Lille, France 7/E3
Lille, France 28/E2
Lille, Maine (04749) 243/G1
Lilleå (riv.), Denmark 21/B5
Lille Baelt (chan.), Denmark 21/C7
Lillehammer, Norway 18/F6
Lillesand, Norway 18/F7
Lillestrøm, Norway 18/E3
Lillian, Ala. (36549) 195/D10
Lillie, La. (71256) 238/E1
Lilliesleaf, Scotland 15/F5
Lillington, N.C. (27546) 281/M4
Lillinonah (lake), Conn. 210/B3
Lilliwaup, Wash. (98555) 310/B3
Lillo, Spain 33/E3
Lillooet, Br. Col. 162/D5
Lillooet, Br. Col. 184/G5
Lillooet (riv.), Br. Col. 184/F5
Lilly Baelt (chan.), Denmark 21/C7
Lilly, Georgia (31051) 217/E6
Lilly, Ill. (†61755) 222/D3
Lilly, Pa. (15938) 294/E5
Lilly Chapel, Ohio (†43162) 284/D6
Lillydale, Victoria 97/J4
Lilongwe (cap.), Malawi 2/L6
Lilongwe (cap.), Malawi 102/F6
Lilongwe (cap.), Malawi 115/F6
Liloy, Philippines 82/D6
Lily, Ky. (40740) 237/N6
Lily, S. Dak. (57250) 298/O3
Lily, Wis. (54445) 317/J5
Lilydale, Minn. (†55050) 255/G5
Lily Dale, N.Y. (14752) 276/B6
Lilydale, Tasmania 99/D3
Lily Plain, Sask. 181/E2
Lim (fjord), Denmark 18/E8
Lim (riv.), Yugoslavia 45/D4
Lima, Ill. (62348) 222/B3
Lima (isls.), Indonesia 85/F7
Lima, Pulau (isl.), Malaysia 72/F6
Lima, Mont. (59739) 262/D6
Lima (res.), Mont. 262/D6
Lima, N.Y. (14485) 276/E5
Lima, Ohio (*45801) 284/B4
Lima, Ohio 188/K2
Lima (New Lima), Okla. (†74858) 288/O4
Lima, Paraguay 144/D3
Lima, Pa. (†19037) 294/L7
Lima (dept.), Peru 128/D8
Lima (cap.), Peru 2/F6
Lima (cap.), Peru 120/B4
Lima (cap.), Peru 128/D8
Lima (riv.), Portugal 33/B2
Lima (pt.), P. Rico 161/F2
Lima Center, Wis. (†53190) 317/J10
Limache, Chile 138/F2
Lima Duarte, Brazil 135/E2
Limal, Bolivia 136/C8
Limanowa, Poland 47/E4
Limarí (riv.), Chile 138/A8
Limasawa (isl.), Philippines 82/E6
Limassol, Cyprus 59/B3
Limassol, Cyprus 63/E5
Limavady (dist.), N. Ireland 17/H1
Limavady, N. Ireland 10/C3
Limavady, N. Ireland 17/H1
Limaville, Ohio (44640) 284/H4
Limay (riv.), Argentina 120/C6
Limay (riv.), Argentina 143/C4
Limbach-Oberfrohna, E. Germany 22/E3
Limbani, Peru 128/H10
Limbaži, U.S.S.R. 53/C2
Limbé, Haiti 158/C5
Limbourg, Belgium 27/J7
Limbunya, North. Terr. 93/B4
Limburg (prov.), Belgium 27/G7
Limburg (Limbourg), Belgium 27/J7
Limburg (prov.), Netherlands 27/H6
Limburg an der Lahn, W. Germany 22/C3
Lime, Oreg. (†97907) 291/K3
Limedsforsen, Sweden 18/H6
Limeira, Brazil 132/E8
Limeira, Brazil 135/C3
Lime Kiln, Md. (†21701) 245/J3
Limekilns, Scotland 15/D1
Limenária, Greece 45/G5
Limerick (co.), Ireland 17/D7
Limerick, Ireland 17/D6
Limerick, Ireland 10/B4
Limerick, Ireland 7/D3
Limerick○, Maine (04048) 243/B8
Limerick, Sask. 181/E6
Limeridge, Wis. (53942) 317/F9
Lime Rock, Conn. (†06039) 210/B1
Lime Springs, Iowa (52155) 229/J2
Limestone (co.), Ala. 195/E1
Limestone, Ark. (72628) 202/D2
Limestone, Fla. (†33865) 212/E4
Limestone, Maine (04750) 243/H2
Limestone○, Maine (04750) 243/H2
Limestone, Mont. (†59028) 262/F5
Limestone, N.Y. (14753) 276/C6
Limestone, Tenn. (37681) 237/R8
Limestone (co.), Texas 303/H6
Lime Village, Alaska (†99673) 196/G2
Limfjorden (fjord), Denmark 21/D4
Limfjorden (fjord), Denmark 21/A4
Limington, Maine (04049) 243/B8
Limington○, Maine (04049) 243/B8
Limmat (riv.), Switzerland 39/F2
Limmen (bight), North. Terr. 88/F2
Limmen (bight), North. Terr. 93/D3
Limmen Bight (riv.), North. Terr. 88/F3
Limmen Bight (riv.), North. Terr. 93/D4
Límni, Greece 45/F6
Límnos (isl.), Greece 45/G6
Limoeiro, Brazil 132/H4
Limoeiro do Norte, Brazil 132/G4
Limoges, France 7/E4
Limoges, France 28/D5
Limoges, Ontario 177/J2
Limon, Colo. (80828) 208/M4
Limón, C. Rica 146/K8
Limón, C. Rica 154/F6
Limón, Honduras 154/E3
Limonade, Haiti 158/C5
Limonar, Cuba 158/D1
Limoquije, Bolivia 136/C4
Limousin (trad. prov.), France, 29
Limousin (reg.), France 28/D5
Limoux, France 28/E6
Limpio, Paraguay 144/B4
Limpopo (riv.) 102/E7
Limpopo (riv.), Botswana 118/D4
Limpopo (riv.), Mozambique 118/E4
Limpopo (riv.), S. Africa 118/D4
Lim Rock, Ala. (†35776) 195/F1
Linapacan (isl.), Philippines 82/B5
Linapacan (str.), Philippines 82/B5
Linard (peak), Switzerland 39/K3
Linares, Chile 138/A11
Linares, Chile 120/B6
Linares, Mexico 150/K4
Linares, Spain 33/E3
Linares, Spain 7/D5
Linaria, Alberta 182/C2
Lincang, China 77/E7
Linch, Wyo. (82640) 319/F2
Lincklaen, N.Y. (†13052) 276/J5
Lincoln (sea) 146/M1
Lincoln (sea) 4/A12
Lincoln, Ala. (35096) 195/F3
Lincoln, Argentina 143/F7
Lincoln (co.), Ark. 202/G6
Lincoln, Ark. (72744) 202/B2
Lincoln, Calif. (95648) 204/B8
Lincoln (isl.), China 85/E2
Lincoln (co.), Colo. 208/M5
Lincoln (mt.), Colo. 208/G4
Lincoln, Del. (19960) 245/S5
Lincoln, England 13/G4
Lincoln, England 10/F4
Lincoln (co.), Georgia 217/H3
Lincoln (co.), Idaho 220/D6
Lincoln, Ill. (62656) 222/D3
Lincoln, Ind. (†46994) 227/E3
Lincoln, Iowa (50652) 229/H4
Lincoln (co.), Kansas 232/D2
Lincoln, Kansas (67455) 232/D2
Lincoln (co.), Ky. 237/M6
Lincoln (par.), La. 238/E1
Lincoln (co.), Maine 243/D7
Lincoln, Maine (04457) 243/G5
Lincoln○, Maine (04457) 243/G5
Lincoln○, Mass. (01773) 249/B6
Lincoln, Mich. (48742) 250/F4
Lincoln (co.), Minn. 255/B6
Lincoln (co.), Miss. 256/D8
Lincoln (co.), Mo. 261/L4
Lincoln, Mo. (65338) 261/F6
Lincoln (co.), Mont. 262/A2
Lincoln, Mont. (59639) 262/D4
Lincoln (co.), Nebr. 264/D4
Lincoln (cap.), Nebr. 146/J5
Lincoln (cap.), Nebr. 188/G2
Lincoln (cap.), Nebr. (*68501) 264/H4
Lincoln (co.), Nev. 266/F5
Lincoln○, N.H. (03251) 268/D3
Lincoln (mt.), N.H. 268/D3
Lincoln (co.), N. Mex. 274/D5
Lincoln, N. Mex. (88338) 274/D5
Lincoln (co.), N.C. 281/G3
Lincoln, N. Dak. (†58501) 282/J6
Lincoln (sea), N.W. Terrs. 187/M1
Lincoln (co.), Okla. 288/N3
Lincoln, Ontario 177/E4
Lincoln (co.), Oreg. 291/D3
Lincoln, Pa. (†15037) 294/C7
Lincoln (co.), S. Dak. 298/R7
Lincoln (co.), Tenn. 237/H10
Lincoln, Texas (78948) 303/H7
Lincoln (creek), Utah 30r/C2
Lincoln○, Vt. (†05443) 268/B3
Lincoln (co.), Wash. 310/G3
Lincoln, Wash. (99147) 310/G3
Lincoln (co.), W. Va. 312/B6
Lincoln (co.), Wis. 317/G5
Lincoln (co.), Wyo. 319/B3
Lincoln Beach, Oreg. (†97341) 291/C3
Lincoln Boyhood Nat'l Mem., Ind. 227/C8
Lincoln Center, Maine (04458) 243/G5
Lincoln Center, Mass. (01773) 249/B6
Lincoln City, Ind. (47552) 227/C8
Lincoln City, Oreg. (97367) 291/C3
Lincoln Gap (pass), Vt. 268/B3
Lincoln Heights, Ohio (†45201) 284/C9
Lincolnia, Va. (†22313) 307/S3
Lincoln Park, Colo. (†81212) 208/J6
Lincoln Park, Georgia (†30286) 217/D5
Lincoln Park, Mich. (48146) 250/B7
Lincoln Park, N.J. (07035) 273/A1
Lincolnshire (co.), England 13/G4
Lincolnshire, Ill. (†60015) 222/B5
Lincolnton, Georgia (30817) 217/G3
Lincolnton, N.C. (28092) 281/G4
Lincoln University, Pa. (19352) 294/L6
Lincolnville, Ind. (†46992) 227/F3
Lincolnville, Kansas (66858) 232/F3
Lincolnville, Maine (04849) 243/E7
Lincolnville○, Maine (04849) 243/E7
Lincolnville, Nova Scotia 168/G3
Lincolnville, S.C. (†29483) 296/G6
Lincolnville Center, Maine (04850) 243/E7
Lincoln Wolds (hills), England 13/G4
Lincolnwood, Ill. (†60645) 222/B5
Lincroft, N.J. (07738) 273/E3
L'Incudine (mt.), France 28/B7
Lind, Wash. (99341) 310/G4
Linda, Calif. (†95901) 204/D4
Lindale, Alberta 182/C3
Lindale, Georgia (30147) 217/B2
Lindale, Texas (75771) 303/J5
Lindau, W. Germany 22/C5
Lindberg, Alberta 182/E3
Linden, Ala. (36748) 195/C6
Linden, Alberta 182/D4
Linden, Ariz. (†85901) 198/E4
Linden, Calif. (95236) 204/D5
Linden, Guyana 131/L2
Linden, Ind. (47955) 227/D4
Linden, Iowa (50146) 229/E5
Linden, Mich. (48451) 250/F6
Linden, N.J. (07036) 273/A3
Linden, N.C. (28356) 281/M4
Linden (mts.), Switzerland 39/F2
Linden, Tenn. (37096) 237/F9
Linden, Texas (75563) 303/K4
Linden, Va. (22642) 307/M3
Linden, W. Va. (25256) 312/D5
Linden, Wis. (53553) 317/F10
Linden Beach, Ontario 177/B6
Lindenhurst, Ill. (†60046) 222/B4
Lindenhurst, N.Y. (11757) 276/O9
Lindenwold, N.J. (08021) 273/B4
Lindenwood, Ill. (61049) 222/D1
Lindesberg, Sweden 18/J7
Lindesnes (cape), Norway 7/E3
Lindesnes (cape), Norway 18/E8
Lindi (reg.), Tanzania 115/G5
Lindi, Tanzania 102/F5
Lindi, Tanzania 115/G5
Lindi (riv.), Zaire 115/E3
Lindisfarne (Holy) (dist.), England 13/F2
Lindisfarne (Holy) (isl.), England 10/F3
Lindley, N.Y. (14858) 276/F6
Lindon, Colo. (80740) 208/N3
Lindon, Utah (†84062) 304/C3
Lindos, Greece 45/J7
Lindrith, N. Mex. (87029) 274/C2
Lindsay, Calif. (93247) 204/F7
Lindsay, La. (†70748) 238/H5
Lindsay, Mont. (59339) 262/L3
Lindsay, Nebr. (68644) 264/G3
Lindsay, Okla. (73052) 288/L5
Lindsay, Ontario 177/F3
Lindsborg, Kansas (67456) 232/E3
Lindsey, Ohio (43442) 284/D3
Lindsey, Wis. (†54449) 317/F6
Lindside, W. Va. (24951) 312/E8
Lindstrom, Minn. (55045) 255/F5
Line (isls.) 2/B6
Line (isls.), Pacific 87/K5
Lineboro, Md. (21088) 245/L2
Linesville, Pa. (16424) 294/A2
Lineville, Ala. (36266) 195/G4
Lineville, Iowa (50147) 229/G7
Linfen, China 77/H4
Linfield, Pa. (19468) 294/L5
Linganore (creek), Md. 245/J3
Lingao, China 77/G8
Lingayen, Philippines 85/F2
Lingayen, Philippines 82/C2
Lingayen (gulf), Philippines 82/C2
Lingen, W. Germany 22/B2
Lingga (arch.), Indonesia 85/D5
Lingga (isl.), Indonesia 85/D6
Lingle, Wyo. (82223) 319/H3
Linglestown, Pa. (17112) 294/J5
Lingling, China 77/H6
Lingo, N. Mex. (88123) 274/F5
Lingqui, China 77/H4
Lingshan, China 77/G7

400 Lingshui

Lingshui, China 77/H8
Linguère, Senegal 106/B5
Lingwu, China 77/G4
Linhai, China 77/K6
Linhares, Brazil 132/F7
Linhe, China 77/G3
Linière, Québec 172/G3
Linkebeek, Belgium 27/C10
Linköping, Sweden 18/K7
Linköping, Sweden 7/F3
Linkou, China 77/M2
Linkwood, Md. (21835) 245/P6
Linlithgow, Scotland 10/B1
Linlithgow, Scotland 15/C1
Linn (co.), Iowa 229/K4
Linn (co.), Kansas 232/H3
Linn, Kansas (66953) 232/E2
Linn (co.), Mo. 261/F3
Linn, Mo. (65051) 261/J5
Linn (co.), Oreg. 291/E3
Linn, Texas (78563) 303/F11
Linn, W. Va. (26384) 312/E4
Linn Creek, Mo. (65052) 261/G6
Linndale, Ohio (†44101) 284/G9
Linneus○, Maine (†04730) 243/H3
Linneus, Mo. (64653) 261/F3
Linn Grove, Ind. (46769) 227/H3
Linn Grove, Iowa (51033) 229/C3
Linnhe, Loch (inlet), Scotland 10/D2
Linnhe, Loch (inlet), Scotland 15/C4
Linnsburg, Ind. (†47933) 227/D5
Linntown, Pa. (†17837) 294/J4
Lino Lakes, Minn. (†55038) 255/G5
Linosa (isl.), Italy 34/D7
Linqing (Lintsing), China 77/J4
Lins, Brazil 132/D8
Lins, Brazil 135/B2
Linstead, Jamaica 158/J6
Linter, Belgium 27/G7
Linth (riv.), Switzerland 39/G3
Linthal, Switzerland 39/H3
Linthicum Heights, Md. (21090) 245/M4
Lintlaw, Sask. 181/H3
Linton, Georgia (†31087) 217/F4
Linton, Ind. (47441) 227/C6
Linton, Ky. (†42211) 237/F7
Linton, N. Dak. (58552) 282/K7
Linville, La. (71257) 238/F1
Linville, N.C. (28646) 281/F2
Linville, Va. (22834) 307/L3
Linville Falls, N.C. (28647) 281/F3
Linwood, Georgia (†30728) 217/B1
Linwood, Ind. (†46001) 227/F4
Linwood, Kansas (66052) 232/G2
Linwood, Ky. (†42765) 237/K6
Linwood, Md. (21764) 245/K2
Linwood, Mass. (01525) 249/H4
Linwood, Mich. (48634) 250/F5
Linwood, Nebr. (68036) 264/H3
Linwood, N.J. (08221) 273/D5
Linwood, N.C. (27299) 281/J3
Linwood, Ontario 177/D4
Linwood, Pa. (19061) 294/L7
Linwood, Scotland 15/B2
Linxi, China 77/J3
Linxia (Linsia), China 77/F4
Linyi, China 77/J4
Linz, Austria 7/F4
Linz, Austria 41/C2
Linze, China 77/F4
Linzee (cape), Nova Scotia 168/G2
Lionel, Scotland 15/B2
Lionel Town, Jamaica 158/J7
Lions (gulf) 7/E4
Lions (gulf), France 28/F6
Lion's Bay, Br. Col. 184/K3
Lion's Head, Ontario 177/C2
Lipa, Philippines 82/C4
Lipan, Texas (76462) 303/F5
Lipari, Italy 34/E5
Lipari (isl.), Italy 34/E5
Lipari (isls.), Italy 34/E5
Lipetsk, U.S.S.R. 7/H3
Lipetsk, U.S.S.R. 48/E4
Lipetsk, U.S.S.R. 52/E4
Lípez, Cordillera de (range), Bolivia 136/B8
Liping, China 77/G6
Lipník nad Bečvou, Czech. 41/D2
Lipno (res.), Czech. 41/C2
Lipno, Poland 47/D2
Lipoa (pt.), Hawaii 218/H1
Lipova, Romania 45/E2
Lippe (riv.), W. Germany 22/C3
Lippstadt, W. Germany 22/C3
Lipscomb, Ala. (35020) 195/E4
Lipscomb (co.), Texas 303/D1
Lipscomb, Texas (79056) 303/D1
Lipton, Sask. 181/H5
Liptovský Hrádok, Czech. 41/E2
Liptovský Mikuláš, Czech. 41/E2
Lipu, China 77/H7
Lira, Uganda 115/F3
Lircay, Peru 128/E9
Liri (riv.), Italy 34/D4
Liria, Spain 33/F3
Lisala, Zaire 115/D3
Lisbellaw, N. Ireland 17/K2
Lisbon○, Conn. (06351) 210/G2
Lisbon, Ill. (†60541) 222/E2
Lisbon, Ind. (†46755) 227/G2
Lisbon, Iowa (52253) 229/L5
Lisbon, La. (71048) 238/E1
Lisbon○, Maine (04250) 243/C7
Lisbon, Md. (21765) 245/K3
Lisbon, Mo. (†65254) 261/G4
Lisbon, N.H. (03585) 268/D3
Lisbon○, N.H. (03585) 268/D3
Lisbon, N.Y. (13658) 276/K1
Lisbon, N. Dak. (58054) 282/P7
Lisbon, Ohio (44432) 284/J4
Lisbon (dist.), Portugal 33/A1
Lisbon (cap.), Portugal 2/J4
Lisbon (cap.), Portugal 7/D5
Lisbon (Lisboa) (cap.), Portugal 33/A1
Lisbon Falls, Maine (04252) 243/D7
Lisbon-Lisbon Center, Maine (04250) 243/C7
Lisburn, Alberta 182/C3
Lisburn (dist.), N. Ireland 17/J2
Lisburn, N. Ireland 10/D3
Lisburn, N. Ireland 17/J2
Lisburne (cape), Alaska 196/E1
Lisburne (pen.), Alaska 196/E1
Liscannor (bay), Ireland 17/B6
Liscarroll, Ireland 17/D7
Lisco, Nebr. (69148) 264/B3
Liscomb, Iowa (50148) 229/H4
Liscomb (isl.), Nova Scotia 168/G4
Lisdoonvarna, Ireland 17/C5
Lishi, China 77/H4
Lishui, China 77/K6
Lisianski (isl.), Hawaii 188/E6
Lisianski (isl.), Hawaii 87/J3
Lisianski (isl.), Hawaii 218/B5
Lisichansk, U.S.S.R. 52/E5
Lisieux, France 28/D3
Lisieux, Sask. 181/E6
Liskeard, England 13/C7
Liskeard, England 10/D5
Lisle, Ill. (60532) 222/A6
Lisle, N.Y. (13797) 276/H6
Lisle, Ontario 177/E3
L'Islet (co.), Québec 172/G2
L'Islet, Québec 172/G2
L'Islet-sur-Mer, Québec 172/G2
L'Isle-Verte, Québec 172/G1
Lisman, Ala. (36912) 195/B6
Lisman, Ky. (†42404) 237/F6
Lismore, Australia 87/F8
Lismore, Ireland 10/B4
Lismore, Ireland 17/F7
Lismore, La. (†71343) 238/G3
Lismore, Minn. (56155) 255/B7
Lismore, N. S. Wales 88/J5
Lismore, N.S. Wales 97/G1
Lismore (isl.), Scotland 15/C4
Lisnaskea, N. Ireland 17/G3
Lišov, Czech. 41/C2
Lispeszentadorján, Hungary 41/D3
Lisse, Netherlands 27/F4
Lista (pen.), Norway 18/E7
Lister (mt.) 5/B8
Listie, Pa. (15549) 294/D5
Listowel, Ireland 17/C7
Listowel, Ireland 10/B4
Listowel, Ontario 177/D4
Litang, China 77/F6
Litani (riv.), Fr. Guiana 131/D4
Litani (riv.), Lebanon 63/F6
Litani (riv.), Suriname 131/D4
Litchfield (co.), Conn. 210/B1
Litchfield, Conn. (06759) 210/C2
Litchfield○, Conn. (06759) 210/C2
Litchfield, Ill. (62056) 222/D4
Litchfield○, Maine (04350) 243/D7
Litchfield, Mich. (49252) 250/E6
Litchfield, Minn. (55355) 255/D5
Litchfield, Nebr. (68852) 264/E3
Litchfield○, N.H. (†03051) 268/E6
Litchfield, North. Terr. 93/B2
Litchfield, Ohio (44253) 284/F3
Litchfield Park, Ariz. (85340) 198/C5
Litchville, N. Dak. (58461) 282/O6
Lith, Netherlands 27/G5
Litherland, England 13/G2
Litherland, England 10/F2
Lithgow, Australia 87/F9
Lithgow, N. S. Wales 88/J6
Lithgow, N.S. Wales 97/F3
Lithia, Va. (24066) 307/J6
Lithia Springs, Georgia (30057) 217/C3
Lithium, Mo. (†63775) 261/N7
Lithonia, Georgia (30058) 217/D3
Lithopolis, Ohio (43136) 284/E6
LITHUANIA 53/B3
Lithuanian S.S.R., U.S.S.R. 7/G3
Lithuanian S.S.R., U.S.S.R. 48/C4
Lithuanian S.S.R., U.S.S.R. 52/B3
Lititz, Pa. (17543) 294/K5
Litókhoron, Greece 45/F5
Litoměřice, Czech. 41/C1
Litomyšl, Czech. 41/D2
Litovel, Czech. 41/D2
Littau, Switzerland 39/F2
Littcarr, Ky. (41834) 237/R6
Little (riv.), Ala. 195/G2
Little (riv.), Ala. 195/C8
Little (riv.), Ark. 202/B6
Little (riv.), Conn. 210/G2
Little (riv.), Conn. 210/H1
Little (riv.), Ind. 227/G3
Little (riv.), La. 238/F3
Little (riv.), Mass. 249/C4
Little (riv.), New Bruns. 170/D2
Little (riv.), N.C. 281/N3
Little (riv.), N.C. 281/L4
Little (riv.), Okla. 288/R6
Little (riv.), Oreg. 291/E4
Little (riv.), S.C. 296/D3
Little (riv.), S.C. 296/C3
Little (riv.), Vt. 268/B3
Little (inlet), Va. 307/S6
Little (riv.), Va. 307/N5
Little (riv.), Va. 307/H7
Little Alföld (plain), Hungary 41/D3
Little America, Ant. 2/B10
Little America 5/B10
Little America, Wyo. (82929) 319/C4
Little Andaman (isl.), India 68/G6
Little Arkansas (riv.), Kansas 232/E3
Little Barrier (isl.), N. Zealand 100/E2
Little Bay de Noc (bay), Mich. 250/B3
Little Bay Islands, Newf. 166/C4
Little Beaver (creek), Kansas 232/A2
Little Beaver (creek), Ohio 284/J4
Little Bighorn (riv.), Mont. 262/J5
Little Birch (lake), Manitoba 179/E3
Little Birch, W. Va. (26629) 312/E5
Little Bitterroot (lake), Mont. 262/B2
Little Black (riv.), Maine 243/E1
Little Black, Wis. (†54451) 317/F5
Little Blue (riv.), Kansas 232/E1
Little Blue (riv.), Nebr. 264/H5
Little Boars Head, N.H. (†03871) 268/F6
Little Bow (riv.), Alberta 182/D4
Little Britain, Ontario 177/F3
Little Brook, Nova Scotia 168/B4
Little Brosna (riv.), Ireland 17/E5
Little Buffalo Lake, Alberta 182/B1
Little Bullhead, Manitoba 179/F3
Little Butter (creek), Oreg. 291/H2
Little Cadotte (riv.), Alberta 182/B1
Little Cape, New Bruns. 170/F2
Little Catalina, Newf. 166/D2
Little Cayman (isl.), Cayman Is. 156/B3
Little Cedar, Iowa (50454) 229/H2
Little Chief, Okla. (†74637) 288/N1
Little Choptank (riv.), Md. 245/N6
Little Chute, Wis. (54140) 317/K7
Little Coco (isl.), Burma 72/B4
Little Colorado (riv.), Ariz. 188/D3
Little Colorado (riv.), Ariz. 198/D3
Little Compton○, R.I. (02837) 249/K6
Little Corn (isl.), Nicaragua 154/F4
Little Creek, Del. (19961) 245/S4
Little Creek, La. (†71371) 238/F3
Little Creek (peak), Utah 304/B6
Little Current, Ontario 177/B2
Little Current (riv.), Ontario 175/C2
Little Deep (creek), N. Dak. 282/G2
Little Deer Isle, Maine (†04627) 243/F7
Little Diomede (isl.), Alaska 196/E1
Little Dover, Nova Scotia 168/G3
Little Dry (creek), Mont. 262/K3
Little Eagle, S. Dak. (57639) 298/H2
Little Egg (harb.), N.J. 273/E4
Little Egg (inlet), N.J. 273/E5
Little Elkhart (riv.), Ind. 227/F1
Little Falls, Minn. (56345) 255/D5
Little Falls○, N.J. (07424) 273/B2
Little Falls, N.Y. (13365) 276/L4
Little Falls-South Windham, Maine (04082) 243/C8
Little Farms, La. (†70123) 238/N4
Little Ferry, N.J. (07643) 273/B2
Littlefield, Ariz. (86432) 198/B2
Littlefield, Texas (79339) 303/B4
Little Flock, Ark. (†72712) 202/B1
Littlefork, Minn. (56653) 255/E2
Little Fork (riv.), Minn. 255/E2
Little Genesee, N.Y. (14754) 276/D6
Little Girl (pt.), Mich. 250/E1
Little Goose (dam), Wash. 310/G4
Little Grand Rapids, Manitoba 179/G2
Little Gunpowder Falls (creek), Md. 245/M2
Littlehampton, England 13/G7
Littlehampton, England 10/F5
Little Harbour, Nova Scotia 168/D5
Little Heart's Ease, Newf. 166/D2
Little Hocking, Ohio (45742) 284/G7
Little Humboldt (riv.), Nev. 266/D1
Little Inagua (isl.), Bahamas 156/D2
Little Kai (isl.), Indonesia 85/J7
Little Kanawha (riv.), W. Va. 312/D5
Little Knife (riv.), N. Dak. 282/F3
Little Lake, Calif. (93542) 204/H8
Little Lake, Mich. (49833) 250/B2
Little Laramie (riv.), Wyo. 319/G4
Little London, Jamaica 158/G6
Little Lorraine, Nova Scotia 168/J3
Little Lost (riv.), Idaho 220/E5
Littlelot, Tenn. (†38454) 237/G9
Little Lynches (riv.), S.C. 296/G3
Little Madawaska (riv.), Maine 243/G2
Little Makin (atoll), Kiribati 87/H5
Little Manitou (lake), Sask. 181/F4
Little Marais, Minn. (55611) 255/G3
Little Marsh, Pa. (16931) 294/H2
Little Meadows, Pa. (18830) 294/K2
Little Mecatina (riv.), Newf. 166/B3
Little Medicine Bow (riv.), Wyo. 319/F3
Little Miami (riv.), Ohio 284/B6
Little Minch (sound), Scotland 10/C2
Little Minch (sound), Scotland 15/B3
Little Missouri (riv.) 188/F1
Little Missouri (riv.), Ark. 202/D6
Little Missouri (riv.), Mont. 262/M5
Little Missouri (riv.), N. Dak. 282/D4
Little Missouri (riv.), S. Dak. 298/B1
Little Missouri (riv.), Wyo. 319/H1
Littlemore, England 13/F6
Little Moreau (riv.), S. Dak. 298/G3
Little Mountain, S.C. (29075) 296/E3
Little Muddy (riv.), N. Dak. 282/C3
Little Muddy (creek), Wyo. 319/B4
Little Muskingum (riv.), Ohio 284/H6
Little Narrows, Nova Scotia 168/H3
Little Nicobar (isl.), India 68/G7
Little Orleans, Md. (21766) 245/E2
Little Owyhee (riv.), Idaho 220/B7
Little Paint Branch (riv.), Md. 245/F4
Little Para (riv.), S. Australia 88/D7
Little Para (riv.), S. Australia 94/B7
Little Patuxent (riv.), Md. 245/L4
Little Pee Dee (riv.), N.C. 281/L6
Little Pee Dee (riv.), S.C. 296/J4
Little Pigeon (creek), Ind. 227/C9
Little Plymouth, Va. (23091) 307/P5
Little Popo Agie (riv.), Wyo. 319/D3
Littleport, England 13/H5
Littleport, Iowa (52055) 229/L3
Little Powder (riv.), Wyo. 319/G1
Little Prairie, Wis. (†53119) 317/H2
Little Red (riv.), Ark. 202/G3
Little River, Ala. (36550) 195/C8
Little River (co.), Ark. 202/B6
Littleriver, Calif. (95456) 204/B4
Little River, Kansas (67457) 232/E3
Little River, N. Zealand 100/D5
Little River, Nova Scotia 168/B4
Little River (harb.), Nova Scotia 168/B5
Little River, S.C. (29566) 296/K4
Little River (inlet), S.C. 296/L4
Little Rock (cap.), Ark. 188/H4
Little Rock (cap.), Ark. 146/J6
Little Rock (cap.), Ark. (*72201) 202/F4
Little Rock, Iowa (51243) 229/B2
Little Rock, Minn. (†56373) 255/D5
Little Rock (creek), Minn. 255/C7
Little Rock, Miss. (39337) 256/F5
Little Rock, S.C. (29567) 296/J3
Littlerock, Wash. (98556) 310/B4
Little Rock A.F.B., Ark. 202/F4
Little Sable (pt.), Mich. 250/C5
Little Saint Bernard (pass), France 28/G5
Little Saint George (isl.), Fla. 212/B2
Little Salmon (riv.), Idaho 220/B4
Little Salt (lake), Utah 304/A6
Little Sandy (creek), Wyo. 319/C3
Little Sauk, Minn. (56346) 255/D5
Little Sevogle (riv.), New Bruns. 170/D1
Little Shawmut, Ala. (†36876) 195/H5
Little Sheep (creek), Oreg. 291/K2
Little Shippegan, New Bruns. 170/F1
Little Silver, N.J. (07739) 273/F3
Little Sioux, Iowa (51545) 229/B5
Little Sioux (riv.), Iowa 229/B3
Little Sitkin (isl.), Alaska 196/K4
Little Smoky, Alberta 182/B2
Little Smoky (riv.), Alberta 182/B2
Little Smoky (valley), Nev. 266/E4
Little Southwest Miramichi (riv.), New Bruns. 170/D2
Little Spokane (riv.), Wash. 310/H3
Littlestown, Pa. (17340) 294/H6
Little Suamico, Wis. (54141) 317/L6
Little Summer (isl.), Mich. 250/C3
Little Tallahatchie (riv.), Miss. 256/D2
Little Tennessee (riv.), N.C. 281/B4
Little Tennessee (riv.), Tenn. 237/N10
Little Thunder (creek), Wyo. 319/G2
Little Tinicum (isl.), Pa. 294/M7
Little Tobago (isl.), Virgin Is. (Br.) 161/B3
Little Tobique (riv.), New Bruns. 170/C1
Littleton, Colo. (*80120) 208/K3
Littleton, Ill. (61452) 222/C3
Littleton, Iowa (†50648) 229/K3
Littleton, Ireland 17/F6
Littleton○, Maine (†04760) 243/H3
Littleton○, Mass. (01460) 249/H2
Littleton, N.H. (03561) 268/D3
Littleton○, N.H. (03561) 268/D3
Littleton, N.C. (27850) 281/O2
Littleton, Va. (†23890) 307/O7
Littleton, W. Va. (26581) 312/F3
Littleton Common, Mass. (†01460) 249/J2
Little Traverse (bay), Mich. 250/D3
Little Trout River (pond), Newf. 166/C4
Little Tupper (lake), N.Y. 276/L2
Little Valley, N.Y. (14755) 276/C6
Little Vermilion (riv.), Ind. 227/B5
Littleville, Ala. (†35653) 195/C1
Little Wabash (riv.), Ill. 222/E5
Little Weiser (riv.), Idaho 220/B5
Little White (riv.), S. Dak. 298/H7
Little Wood (riv.), Idaho 220/D6
Little Yenisey (riv.), U.S.S.R. 48/K4
Little York, Ill. (61453) 222/C2
Little York, Ind. (47139) 227/F7
Little York, N.J. (08834) 273/C2
Little Zab (riv.), Iraq 66/C3
Lituya (bay), Alaska 196/L1
Litvínov, Czech. 41/B1
Liuba, China 77/G5
Liukang Tenggaja (isls.), Indonesia 85/F7
Liuli, Tanzania 115/F6
Liuzhou (Liuchow), China 77/G7
Liuzhou, China 54/M7
Līvāni, U.S.S.R. 53/D2
Livelong, Sask. 181/C2
Lively (isl.), 143/E7
Lively, Va. (22507) 307/P5
Livengood, Alaska (†99701) 196/J1
Live Oak, Calif. (†95073) 204/K4
Live Oak, Calif. (95953) 204/D4
Live Oak, Fla. (32060) 212/D1
Live Oak (co.), Texas 303/F9
Live Oak, Texas (†78201) 303/K10
Liveringa, W. Australia 88/C3
Liveringa, W. Australia 92/D2
Livermore, Calif. (94550) 204/L2
Livermore, Colo. (80536) 208/J1
Livermore, Iowa (50558) 229/E3
Livermore, Ky. (42352) 237/G5
Livermore, Maine (04253) 243/C7
Livermore○, Maine (04253) 243/C7
Livermore (mt.), Texas 303/C11
Livermore Falls, Maine (04254) 243/C7
Livermore Falls○, Maine (04254) 243/C7
Livermore Falls, N.H. (†03264) 268/D4
Liverpool (swamp), Bolivia 136/D4
Liverpool, England 10/F2
Liverpool, England 13/G2
Liverpool (bay), England 13/D4
Liverpool, Ill. (61543) 222/C3
Liverpool, N. S. Wales 88/K4
Liverpool, N.S. Wales 97/H4
Liverpool (range), N.S. Wales 97/F2
Liverpool, N.Y. (13088) 276/H4
Liverpool (bay), N.W. Terrs. 187/E2
Liverpool (cape), N.W. Terrs. 187/L2
Liverpool, Nova Scotia 168/D4
Liverpool (bay), Nova Scotia 168/D5
Liverpool, Pa. (17045) 294/H4
Liverpool, Texas (77577) 303/J3
Liverpool, W. Va. (25257) 312/C5
Livia, Ky. (†42376) 237/G5
Livigno, Italy 34/C1
Livingston, Ala. (35470) 195/B5
Livingston, Calif. (95334) 204/E6
Livingston, Guatemala 154/C3
Livingston (co.), Ill. 222/E3
Livingston, Ill. (62058) 222/D5
Livingston (co.), Ky. 237/E6
Livingston, Ky. (40445) 237/N6
Livingston (par.), La. 238/L2
Livingston, La. (70754) 238/L1
Livingston (co.), Mich. 250/F6
Livingston (co.), Mo. 261/E3
Livingston, Mont. 188/D1
Livingston, Mont. (59047) 262/F5
Livingston○, N.J. (07039) 273/E2
Livingston (co.), N.Y. 276/E5
Livingston, Scotland 15/C2
Livingston, Scotland 10/C1
Livingston, S.C. (29076) 296/E4
Livingston, Tenn. (38570) 237/L8
Livingston, Texas (77351) 303/K7
Livingston (lake), Texas 303/K7
Livingston, Wis. (53554) 317/E10
Livingstone (range), Alberta 182/C4
Livingstone (falls), Zaire 115/B5
Livingstone, Zambia 115/E7
Livingstone, Zambia 102/E6
Livingstonia, Malawi 115/F6
Livingston Manor, N.Y. (12758) 276/L7
Livingstonville, N.Y. (†12122) 276/M6
Livno, Yugoslavia 45/C4
Livny, U.S.S.R. 52/E4
Livona, N. Dak. (58501) 282/K6
Livonia, Ind. (†47108) 227/E7
Livonia, La. (70755) 238/G5
Livonia, Mich. (*48150) 250/F6
Livonia, Mo. (63551) 261/G1
Livonia, N.Y. (14487) 276/E5
Livonia, Pa. (†16872) 294/H4
Livorno (Leghorn), Italy 34/C3
Livry-Gargan, France 28/C1
Liwale, Tanzania 115/G5
Li Xian, China 77/H6
Lixoúrion, Greece 45/E6
Lizard, The (pen.), England 13/B8
Lizard (pt.), England 10/D6
Lizard (pt.), England 13/B8
Lizella, Georgia (31052) 217/E5
Lizemores, W. Va. (25125) 312/D6
Lizton, Ind. (46149) 227/D5
Ljubinje, Yugoslavia 45/D4
Ljubljana, Yugoslavia 45/B3
Ljubljana, Yugoslavia 7/F4
Ljubuški, Yugoslavia 45/C4
Ljugarn, Sweden 18/L8
Ljungan (riv.), Sweden 18/K5
Ljungby, Sweden 18/J8
Ljusdal, Sweden 18/J6
Ljusna (riv.), Sweden 7/F2
Ljusnan (riv.), Sweden 18/H5
Ljusne, Sweden 18/K6
Llagostera, Spain 33/H2
Llaima (vol.), Chile 138/E2
Llallagua, Bolivia 136/B6
Llallagua, Bolivia 120/C4
Llamara, Salar de (salt dep.), Chile 138/B3
Llanarth, Wales 13/C5
Llancanelo (lag.), Argentina 143/C4
Llancanelo, Salina y Laguna (salt dep.), Argentina 143/C4
Llandeilo, Wales 13/C6
Llandovery, Wales 13/D5
Llandovery, Wales 10/D5
Llandrindod Wells, Wales 10/E4
Llandrindod Wells, Wales 13/D5
Llandudno, Wales 13/D4
Llandudno, Wales 10/E4
Llandybie, Wales 13/C6
Llandyssul, Wales 13/C5
Llanelli, Wales 13/C6
Llanelli, Wales 10/D5
Llanes, Spain 33/D1
Llanfair Caereinion, Wales 13/D5
Llanfairfechan, Wales 13/D4
Llanfyllin, Wales 10/E4
Llanfyllin, Wales 13/D5
Llangefni, Wales 13/C4
Llangollen, Wales 13/D5
Llangollen, Wales 10/E4
Llanguicke, Wales 13/D6
Llanidloes, Wales 13/D5
Llanidloes, Wales 10/E4
Llanllyfni, Wales 13/C4
Llannon, Wales 13/C6
Llano, N.Mex. (87543) 274/D2
Llano (co.), Texas 303/F7
Llano, Texas (78643) 303/F7
Llano (riv.), Texas 303/D7
Llano Estacado (Staked) (plain), N. Mex. 274/F5
Llano Estacado (plain), Texas 303/B4
Llanon, Wales 13/C5
Llanos (plain) 120/B2
Llanos (plains), Colombia 126/D5
Llanquera, Bolivia 136/A6
Llanquihue (lake), Chile 138/E3
Llanrhaeadr, Wales 13/D5
Llanrhystyd, Wales 13/C5
Llanrian, Wales 13/B6
Llanrwst, Wales 13/D4
Llanrwst, Wales 10/E4
Llantrisant, Wales 13/A7
Llantwit Major, Wales 13/A7
Llanwnog, Wales 13/D5
Llanwrtyd Wells, Wales 13/D5
Llata, Peru 128/D7
Llay-Llay, Chile 138/G2
Llera de Canales, Mexico 150/K5
Llerena (pt.), C. Rica 154/F6
Llerena, Spain 33/C3
Lleyn (pen.), Wales 13/C5
Llica, Bolivia 136/A6
Llico, Chile 138/A10
Llivia, Spain 33/G1
Llobregat (riv.), Spain 33/H2
Llodio, Spain 33/E1
Llolleo, Chile 138/F4
Llorente, Philippines 82/E5
Lloyd, Fla. (32337) 212/C1
Lloyd (res.), Ga. 188/K4
Lloyd, Ky. (41156) 237/R3
Lloyd, Mont. (59535) 262/G2
Lloyd Harbor, N.Y. (†11743) 276/R6
Lloydminster, Alberta 182/E3
Lloydminster, Alta.-Sask. 162/E5
Lloydminster, Sask. 181/A2
Lluchmayor, Spain 33/H3
Lluidas Vale, Jamaica 158/J6
Llullaillaco (mt.) 120/C5
Llullaillaco (vol.), Argentina 143/C1
Llullaillaco (vol.), Chile 138/B5
Lluta (riv.), Chile 138/B1
Llwchwr, Wales 13/D6
Loa (riv.), Chile 120/C5
Loa (riv.), Chile 138/B3
Loa, Utah (84747) 304/C5
Loachapoka, Ala. (36865) 195/G5
Loami, Ill. (62661) 222/D4
Loange (riv.), Angola 115/C5
Loange (riv.), Zaire 115/C5
Loanhead, Scotland 10/C1
Loanhead, Scotland 15/D2
Lobatse, Botswana 118/D5
Löbau, E. Germany 22/F3
Lobaye (riv.), Cent. Afr. Rep. 115/C2
Lobdell, La. (†70767) 238/J1
Lobeco, S.C. (29931) 296/F6
Lobelia, W. Va. (†24946) 312/F6
Lobelville, Tenn. (37097) 237/F9
Lobenstein, E. Germany 22/D3
Loberia, Argentina 143/E4
Lobethal, S. Australia 94/C7
Łobez, Poland 47/B2
Lobito, Angola 115/B6
Lobito, Angola 102/D6
Lobitos, Peru 128/B5
Lobo, Philippines 82/C4
Lobo (cay), P. Rico 161/G1
Lobos, Argentina 143/G7
Lobos (pt.), Chile 138/A3
Lobos (cape), Mexico 150/C2
Lobos (pt.), Mexico 150/D3
Lobos (isl.), Uruguay 145/E6
Lobos de Afuera (isls.), Peru 128/B6
Lobos de Tierra (isl.), Peru 128/B6
Lobster (lake), Maine 243/E4
Locarno, Switzerland 39/G4
Locate, Mont. (†59336) 262/L4
Lochaber, Nova Scotia 168/F3
Lochaber (dist.), Scotland 15/D4
Lochailort, Scotland 15/C4
Lochaline, Scotland 15/C4
Lochans, Scotland 15/D6
Locharbriggs, Scotland 15/E5
Lochawe, Scotland 15/C4
Lochboisdale, Scotland 15/A3
Lochbuie, Colo. (†80601) 208/K2
Lochcarron, Scotland 10/D2
Lochcarron, Scotland 15/C3
Lochearnhead, Scotland 15/D4
Lochem, Netherlands 27/J4
Lochend, Scotland 15/D3
Loches, France 28/D4
Lochgelly, Scotland 10/C1
Lochgelly, Scotland 15/D1
Lochgelly, W. Va. (25866) 312/D6
Lochgilphead, Scotland 10/D2
Lochgilphead, Scotland 15/C4
Lochgoilhead, Scotland 15/D4
Lochindorb (lake), Scotland 15/E3
Lochinver, Scotland 10/D1
Lochinver, Scotland 15/C2
Lochloosa, Fla. (32662) 212/E2
Lochloosa (lake), Fla. 212/D2
Loch Lynn Heights, Md. (†21550) 245/A3
Lochmaben, Scotland 10/E3
Lochmaben, Scotland 15/E5
Lochmaddy, Scotland 15/A3
Lochmere, N.H. (03252) 268/D5
Lochnagar (mt.), Scotland 15/E4
Lochore, Scotland 15/D1
Lochranza, Scotland 15/C5
Loch Raven (res.), Md. 245/M3
Lochristi, Belgium 27/D6
Lochsa (riv.), Idaho 220/C3
Lochwinnoch, Scotland 15/A2
Lochy, Loch (lake), Scotland 15/D3
Lochy, Loch (lake), Scotland 10/D2
Lock, S. Australia 94/D5
Lockatong (creek), N.J. 273/C3
Lockbourne, Ohio (43137) 284/E6
Locke, Calif. (†95690) 204/B9
Locke, N.Y. (13092) 276/H5
Locke (mt.), Texas 303/D11
Lockeford, Calif. (95237) 204/C9
Locke Mills, Maine (04255) 243/B7
Lockeport, Nova Scotia 168/C5
Lockerbie, Scotland 10/E3
Lockerbie, Scotland 15/E5
Lockesburg, Ark. (71846) 202/B6
Lockhart, Ala. (36455) 195/F8
Lockhart, Minn. (†56510) 255/B3
Lockhart (mt.), Mont. 262/D3
Lockhart, N.S. Wales 97/D4
Lockhart (riv.), N.W. Terrs. 187/H3
Lockhart, S.C. (29364) 296/E2
Lockhart, Texas (78644) 303/G8
Lock Haven, Pa. (17745) 294/H3
Lockington, Ohio (†45356) 284/B5
Lockland, Ohio (45215) 284/C9
Lockney, Texas (79241) 303/C3
Lockney, W. Va. (25258) 312/E5
Lockport, Ill. (60441) 222/B6
Lockport, Ky. (40036) 237/M4
Lockport, La. (70374) 238/K7
Lockport, Manitoba 179/F4
Lockport, N.Y. (14094) 276/C4
Lockridge, Iowa (52635) 229/K7
Lock Springs, Mo. (64654) 261/E3
Lockwood, Mo. (65682) 261/E8
Lockwood, Sask. 181/G4
Lockwood, W. Va. (†26651) 312/D6
Loc Ninh, Vietnam 72/E5
Loco, Okla. (73442) 288/L6
Loco Hills, N. Mex. (88255) 274/F6

Locumba, Peru 128/G11
Locumba (riv.), Peru 128/G11
Locust, N.C. (28097) 281/J4
Locust Bayou, Ark. (†71701) 202/E6
Locust Fork, Ala. (35097) 195/E3
Locust Fork (riv.), Ala. 195/E3
Locust Grove, Ark. (72550) 202/G2
Locust Grove, Georgia (30248) 217/D4
Locust Grove, N.Y. (†11791) 276/R6
Locust Grove, Ohio (†45660) 284/D8
Locust Grove, Okla. (74352) 288/R2
Locust Hill, Ky. (40151) 237/J5
Locustville, Va. (23404) 307/S5
Lod (Lydda), Israel 65/B4
Loda, Ill. (60948) 222/E3
Lodar, P.D.R. Yemen 59/E7
Loddon, England 13/J5
Loddon (riv.), Victoria 97/B5
Loddon (riv.), Victoria 88/G7
Lodève, France 28/E6
Lodeynoye Pole, U.S.S.R. 52/D2
Lodge (creek), Mont. 262/G1
Lodge (creek), Sask. 181/B6
Lodge, S.C. (29082) 296/F5
Lodge Bay, Newf. 166/C3
Lodge Grass, Mont. (59050) 262/J5
Lodge Hill, Barbados 161/B8
Lodgepole, Alberta 182/C3
Lodge Pole, Mont. (†59524) 262/H2
Lodgepole, Nebr. (69149) 264/B3
Lodgepole (creek), Nebr. 264/A3
Lodgepole, S. Dak. (57640) 298/D2
Lodgepole (creek), Wyo. 319/H2
Lodgepole (creek), Wyo. 319/H4
Lodi, Calif. 188/B3
Lodi, Calif. (95240) 204/C9
Lodi, Italy 34/B2
Lodi, Miss. (†39767) 256/E3
Lodi, Mo. (63950) 261/M8
Lodi, N.J. (07644) 273/B2
Lodi, N.Y. (14860) 276/G5
Lodi, Ohio (44254) 284/F3
Lodi (cape), Tasmania 99/E3
Lodi, Texas (75564) 303/K5
Lodi, Wis. (53555) 317/G9
Lødingen, Norway 18/J2
Lodja, Zaire 102/E5
Lodja, Zaire 115/D4
Lodosa, Spain 33/E1
Lodrino, Switzerland 39/G4
Lodwar, Kenya 115/G3
Łódź (prov.), Poland 47/D3
Łódź (city), Poland 47/D3
Łódź, Poland 7/F3
Łódź, Poland 47/D3
Loei, Thailand 72/D3
Loen, Norway 18/E6
Lofer, Austria 41/B3
Lofoten (isls.), Norway 4/C9
Lofoten (isls.), Norway 7/F2
Lofoten (isls.), Norway 18/H2
Loftus, England 13/G3
Loftus, England 10/F3
Lofty (mt.), S. Australia 88/E8
Lofty (mt.), S. Australia 94/B8
Lofty (range), Tasmania 99/B3
Logan, Ala. (35098) 195/E2
Logan (lake), Alberta 182/E2
Logan (co.), Ark. 202/C3
Logan (mt.), Canada 4/C17
Logan (co.), Colo. 208/N1
Logan (co.), Ill. 222/D3
Logan, Ill. (62856) 222/E6
Logan, Ind. (†45030) 227/H6
Logan, Iowa (51546) 229/B5
Logan (co.), Kansas 232/A3
Logan, Kansas (67646) 232/C2
Logan (co.), Ky. 237/H7
Logan, Mont. (†59741) 262/E5
Logan (co.), Nebr. 264/D3
Logan (creek), Nebr. 264/H2
Logan, N. Mex. (88426) 274/F3
Logan (co.), N. Dak. 282/L7
Logan, N. Dak. (†58701) 282/H3
Logan (co.), Ohio 284/C5
Logan, Ohio (43138) 284/F6
Logan (co.), Okla. 288/M3
Logan, Okla. (73849) 288/F1
Logan, Oreg. (†97405) 291/B2
Logan, Utah (84321) 304/C2
Logan, Utah 188/D2
Logan (mt.), Wash. 310/E2
Logan (co.), W. Va. 312/C7
Logan, W. Va. (25601) 312/B7
Logan (mt.), Yukon 162/B3
Logan (mt.), Yukon 187/D3
Logan (mts.), Yukon 187/F3
Logandale, Nev. (89021) 266/G6
Logan Internat'l Airport, Mass. 249/D7
Logan Lake, Br. Col. 184/G5
Logan Martin (lake), Ala. 195/F4
Logansport, Ind. (46947) 227/E3
Logansport, Ky. (42258) 237/H6
Logansport, La. (71049) 238/C3
Loganton, Pa. (17747) 294/H3
Loganville, Georgia (30249) 217/E3
Loganville, Pa. (17342) 294/J6
Loganville, Wis. (53943) 317/F9
Loge (riv.), Angola 115/B5
Loggieville, New Bruns. 170/E1
Log Lane Village, Colo. (†80701) 208/M2
Logone (riv.) 102/D3
Logone (riv.), Cameroon 115/C2
Logone (riv.), Chad 111/C5
Logroño (prov.), Spain 33/E1
Logroño, Spain 7/D4
Logroño, Spain 33/E1
Logrosán, Spain 33/D3
Logsden, Oreg. (97357) 291/D3
Løgstør, Denmark 21/C4
Løgstør, Denmark 18/F8
Løgstør Bredning (fjord), Denmark 21/C4
Løgumkloster, Denmark 21/B7
Lohals, Denmark 21/D7
Lohardaga, India 68/E4
Lohatlha, S. Africa 118/C5
Lohman, Mo. (65053) 261/H5
Lohman, Mont. (†59523) 262/G2
Lohn, Texas (76852) 303/E6
Löhne, W. Germany 22/C2
Loho (Luohe), China 77/H5
Lohr am Main, W. Germany 22/C4
Lohrville, Iowa (51453) 229/D4
Lohrville, Wis. (†54970) 317/H7
Loica, Chile 138/F4
Loi-kaw, Burma 72/C3
Loi Leng (mt.), Burma 72/C2
Loimaa, Finland 18/N6
Loir (riv.), France 28/D4
Loire (dept.), France 28/F5
Loire (riv.), France 7/E4
Loire (riv.), France 28/C4
Loire-Atlantique (dept.), France 28/C4
Loiret (dept.), France 28/E4
Loir-et-Cher (dept.), France 28/D4
Loíza, P. Rico 161/E1
Loíza Aldea, P. Rico 161/E1
Loja (prov.), Ecuador 128/C4
Loja, Ecuador 128/C4
Loja, Ecuador 120/B3
Loja, Spain 33/D4
Løjt Kirkeby, Denmark 21/C7
Loka, Sudan 111/F7
Lokeren, Belgium 27/D6
Lokitaung, Kenya 115/G3
Lokka (res.), Finland 18/Q3
Løkken, Denmark 21/C3
Løkken, Norway 18/F5
Lokoja, Nigeria 106/F7
Lokolama, Zaire 115/D4
Lokoro (riv.), Zaire 115/C4
Lököshása, Hungary 41/F3
Lokossa, Benin 106/E7
Loksa, U.S.S.R. 53/C1
Loks Land (isl.), N.W. Terrs. 187/M3
Lol (dry riv.), Sudan 111/E6
Lola, Ky. (42059) 237/E6
Loleta, Calif. (95551) 204/A3
Lolgorien, Kenya 115/G4
Lolita, Texas (77971) 303/H9
Lolland (isl.), Denmark 18/G9
Lolland (isl.), Denmark 21/E8
Lollie, Georgia (30433) 217/G6
Lolo (creek), Idaho 220/C3
Lolo (pass), Idaho 220/D3
Lolo, Mont. (59847) 262/B4
Lolo (pass), Mont. 262/B4
Lolo Hot Springs, Mont. (†59847) 262/B4
Lom, Bulgaria 45/F4
Lom (riv.), Cameroon 115/B2
Lom, Norway 18/F6
Loma, Colo. (81524) 208/B4
Loma, Mont. (59460) 262/F3
Loma, N. Dak. (†58311) 282/O2
Loma, Mansa (lag.), S. Leone 106/B7
Loma Alta, Bolivia 136/B2
Loma Bonita, Mexico 150/M7
Loma Linda, Calif. (92354) 204/F10
Loma Mar, Calif. (94021) 204/J3
Lomami (riv.), Zaire 115/D4
Loman, Minn. (56654) 255/E2
Loma Plata, Paraguay 144/C3
Lomas, Peru 128/E10
Lomas de Zamora, Argentina 143/G7
Lomax, Ala. (†35045) 195/E5
Lomax, Ill. (61454) 222/B3
Lomax, Texas (†77571) 303/K2
Lombard, Ill. (60148) 222/B5
Lombarda, Serra (mts.), Brazil 132/D2
Lombardville, Ill. (†61421) 222/D2
Lombardy (reg.), Italy 34/B2
Lombardy, S. Africa 118/H6
Lombez, France 28/D6
Lomblen (isl.), Indonesia 85/G7
Lombok (isl.), Indonesia 54/N10
Lombok (isl.), Indonesia 85/F7
Lombok (str.), Indonesia 85/E7
Lomé (cap.), Togo 102/C4
Lomé (cap.), Togo 106/E7
Lomela, Zaire 115/D4
Lomela (riv.), Zaire 115/D4
Lometa, Texas (76853) 303/F6
Lomié, Cameroon 115/B3
Lomira, Wis. (53048) 317/J8
Lo Miranda, Chile 138/G5
Lomita, Calif. (90717) 204/C11
Lommel, Belgium 27/G6
Lomnice, Czech. 41/C2
Lomond, Alberta 182/D4
Lomond, Loch (lake), Nova Scotia 168/H3
Lomond, Loch (lake), Scotland 15/D4
Lomond, Loch (lake), Scotland 10/A1
Lompoc, Calif. (93436) 204/E9
Lom Sak, Thailand 72/D3
Łomża (prov.), Poland 47/F2
Łomża, Poland 47/F2
Lonaconing, Md. (21539) 245/C2
Loncoche, Chile 138/D2
Loncopué, Argentina 143/B4
London, Ark. (72847) 202/D3
London, Greater, England 13/H8
London (cap.), England 7/D3
London (cap.), England 10/B5
London (cap.), England 13/H8
London, Ind. (†46126) 227/F5
London, Ky. (40741) 237/N6
London, Minn. (56061) 255/E7
London, Ohio (43140) 284/C6
London, Ont. 146/K5
London, Ont. 162/H7
London, Ontario 177/C5
London, Texas (76854) 303/E7
London (cap.), U.K. 2/J3
London, Wis. (†53523) 317/H9
Londonderry (isl.), Chile 138/E11
Londonderry○, N.H. (03053) 268/E6
Londonderry, N. Ireland 7/D3
Londonderry (dist.), N. Ireland 17/G2
Londonderry, N. Ireland 10/C3
Londonderry, N. Ireland 17/G2
Londonderry, Nova Scotia 168/E3
Londonderry, Ohio (45647) 284/E7
Londonderry○, Vt. (05148) 268/B5
Londonderry (cape), W. Australia 88/D2
Londonderry (cape), W. Australia 92/D1
Londonderry Station, Nova Scotia 168/E3
London Mills, Ill. (61544) 222/C3
Londontowne, Md. (†21035) 245/M4
Londrina, Brazil 132/D8
Londrina, Brazil 120/D5
Lone (mt.), Mont. 262/E5
Lone (mt.), Nev. 266/D4
Lone Butte, Br. Col. 184/G4
Lone Cedar, W. Va. (†26153) 312/C4
Lone Cone (mt.), Colo. 208/C7
Lone Elm, Kansas (†66039) 232/G3
Lone Grove, Okla. (73443) 288/M6
Lone Jack, Mo. (64070) 261/S6
Lonely (lake), Manitoba 179/C3
Lonely (isl.), Ontario 177/C2
Lone Mountain, Tenn. (†37879) 237/O8
Lone Oak, Georgia (†30230) 217/C4
Lone Oak, Ky. (42001) 237/D6
Lone Oak, Texas (75453) 303/H5
Lone Pine, Alberta 182/C2
Lone Pine, Calif. (93545) 204/H7
Lone Pine (peak), Idaho 220/D5
Lonepine, La. (†71367) 238/F5
Lonepine, Mont. (59848) 262/B3
Lone Prairie, Br. Col. 184/G2
Lone Rock, Iowa (50559) 229/E2
Lonerock, Oreg. (†97823) 291/H2
Lone Rock, Sask. 181/A2
Lone Rock, Wis. (53556) 317/F9
Lone Star, S.C. (29077) 296/F4
Lone Tree (creek), Colo. 208/K1
Lone Tree, Iowa (52755) 229/L6
Lonetree, N. Dak. (†58718) 282/G3
Lonetree, Wyo. (82936) 319/B4
Lone Wolf, Okla. (73655) 288/H5
Long, Alaska (†99768) 196/E2
Long (isl.), Alaska 196/M2
Long (isl.), Ant. & Bar. 161/E11
Long (isl.), Bahamas 146/L7
Long (cay), Bahamas 156/C2
Long (isl.), Bahamas 156/C2
Long (bay), Barbados 161/B9
Long (mt.), Conn. 210/B2
Long (pond), Conn. 210/H3
Long (key), Fla. 212/F7
Long (key), Fla. 212/B3
Long (pond), Fla. 212/D2
Long (co.), Georgia 217/J7
Long (bay), Jamaica 158/H7
Long (lake), Maine 243/E2
Long (lake), Maine 243/G1
Long (lake), Maine 243/B7
Long (pond), Maine 243/E5
Long (pond), Maine 243/D6
Long (pond), Maine 243/C4
Long (lake), Manitoba 179/G4
Long (pt.), Manitoba 179/D1
Long (pt.), Manitoba 179/D4
Long (isl.), Martinique 161/D6
Long (isl.), Mass. 249/E7
Long (pond), Mass. 249/L5
Long (pt.), Mass. 249/O4
Long (lake), Mich. 250/F3
Long (lake), Minn. 255/D4
Long (lake), Minn. 255/F3
Long, Miss. (†38828) 256/C4
Long (valley), Nev. 266/B1
Long (isl.), New Bruns. 170/D3
Long (lake), New Bruns. 170/D1
Long (isl.), Newf. 166/C2
Long (isl.), Newf. 166/D2
Long (lake), Newf. 166/A3
Long (lake), Newf. 166/B3
Long (pt.), Newf. 166/C4
Long (mt.), N.H. 268/E2
Long (beach), N.J. 273/E4
Long (isl.), N.Y. 188/M2
Long (isl.), N.Y. 276/P9
Long (lake), N.Y. 276/M2
Long (isl.), N. Zealand 100/A7
Long (lake), N.C. 281/P5
Long (lake), N. Dak. 282/K6
Long (lake), N. Dak. 282/J4
Long (lake), N. Dak. 282/L2
Long (isl.), Nova Scotia 168/B4
Long (lake), Ontario 177/H5
Long (lake), Ontario 175/C3
Long (pt.), Ontario 177/D5
Long (isl.), Papua N.G. 85/B7
Long (isl.), Papua N.G. 86/A2
Long (creek), Sask. 181/H6
Long, Loch (inlet), Scotland 10/A1
Long, Loch (inlet), Scotland 15/D4
Long (lake), S. Dak. 298/L2
Long (pt.), Tasmania 99/E3
Long (str.), U.S.S.R. 48/S2
Long (pt.), Virgin Is. (U.S.) 161/B4
Long (pt.), Virgin Is. (U.S.) 161/E4
Long (isl.), Wash. 310/A4
Long (lake), Wash. 310/H3
Long (reef), W. Australia 92/D1
Long (lake), Wis. 317/C4
Longa, Angola 115/C6
Longa (isl.), Scotland 15/C3
Longaví, Chile 138/A11
Long Bay, Jamaica 158/K6
Long Beach, Br. Col. 184/E5
Long Beach, Calif. 146/F6
Long Beach, Calif. 188/C4
Long Beach, Calif. (*90801) 204/C11
Long Beach (pen.), Conn. 210/C4
Long Beach, Ind. (†46360) 227/D1
Long Beach, Minn. (†56334) 255/C5
Long Beach, Miss. (39560) 256/F10
Long Beach (isl.), N.J. 273/E4
Long Beach, N.Y. (11561) 276/R7
Long Beach, N.C. (28461) 281/N7
Long Beach, Ontario 177/E5
Long Beach, Wash. (98631) 310/A4
Longbenton, England 13/J3
Longboat (key), Fla. 212/D4
Longboat Key, Fla. (33548) 212/D4
Long Bottom, Ohio (45743) 284/G7
Long Branch, N.J. (07740) 273/F3
Longbranch, Wash. (98351) 310/C3
Longchuan, China 77/J7
Long Cove, Maine (†04857) 243/E8
Long Creek, Oreg. (97856) 291/H3
Longcreek, S.C. (29658) 296/A2
Longdale, Okla. (73755) 288/K2
Longde, China 77/G4
Long Eaton, England 13/F5
Long Eddy, N.Y. (12760) 276/K7
Long Falls (dam), Maine 243/C5
Longfellow (mts.), Maine 243/B6
Longford (co.), Ireland 17/F4
Longford, Ireland 10/C4
Longford, Ireland 17/F4
Longford, Kansas (67458) 232/E2
Longford, Ontario 177/E3
Longford, Tasmania 99/C3
Longford, Virgin Is. (U.S.) 161/F4
Long Green, Md. (21092) 245/M3
Long Grove, Ill. (60047) 222/B5
Long Grove, Iowa (52756) 229/M5
Long Harbour, Newf. 166/D2
Long Hill, Conn. (†06611) 210/C3
Longhua, China 77/J3
Longhui, China 77/H6
Longido, Tanzania 115/G4
Longiram, Indonesia 85/F5
Long Island (sound), Conn. 210/C4
Long Island (bay), Ireland 17/B9
Long Island, Kansas (67647) 232/C2
Long Island (sound), N.Y. 276/P9
Longisland, N.C. (28648) 281/H3
Long Island, Tenn. (†37662) 237/S7
Long Island, Va. (24569) 307/K6
Longjiang, China 77/K2
Long Key, Fla. (33001) 212/F7
Longkou, China 77/J4
Longlac, Ontario 177/H5
Longlac, Ontario 175/C3
Long Lake, Mich. (48743) 250/F4
Long Lake, Minn. (55356) 255/F5
Long Lake, N.Y. (12847) 276/L3
Longlake, S. Dak. (57457) 298/L2
Long Lake, Wis. (54542) 317/J4
Long Lane, Mo. (65590) 261/G7
Longleaf, La. (71448) 238/E4
Long Meadow (pond), Conn. 210/C2
Longmeadow○, Mass. (01106) 249/D4
Longmire, Wash. (98397) 310/D4
Longmont, Colo. 188/E2
Longmont, Colo. (80501) 208/J2
Longnan, China 77/J7
Longnawan, Indonesia 85/F5
Long Neck (pt.), Conn. 210/B4
Long Pine, Nebr. (69217) 264/E2
Long Point, Ill. (61333) 222/E3
Long Point, Nova Scotia 168/G3
Long Point (bay), Ontario 177/D5
Long Point Beach, Ontario 177/D5
Long Pond, Maine (†04945) 243/C4
Long Pond, Pa. (18334) 294/L3
Longport, N.J. (08403) 273/D5
Long Prairie, Minn. (56347) 255/D5
Long Prairie (riv.), Minn. 255/D4
Long Range (mts.), Newf. 166/C4
Long Rapids, Mich. (†49753) 250/F3
Longreach, Australia 87/E8
Long Reach (inlet), New Bruns. 170/D3
Longreach, Queensland 88/G4
Longreach, Queensland 95/B4
Long Reef (pt.), N.S. Wales 97/K3
Longridge, England 13/H1
Longridge, England 10/G1
Longs (peak), Colo. 208/H2
Longs, S.C. (29568) 296/K4
Long Sault, Ontario 177/K2
Longshan, China 77/G6
Long Siding, Minn. (†55371) 255/E5
Long Society, Conn. (†06360) 210/G2
Long Spruce, Manitoba 179/K2
Longstreet, La. (71050) 238/B2
Longton, Kansas (67352) 232/F4
Longtown, Miss. (†38665) 256/D1
Longtown, Mo. (†63775) 261/N7
Longtown, S.C. (†29130) 296/F3
Longueuil, Québec 172/J4
Long Valley, N.J. (07853) 273/D2
Longvalley, S. Dak. (57547) 298/F7
Longview, Ala. (†35137) 195/E4
Longview, Alberta 182/C4
Longview, Colo. (†80135) 208/J4
Longview, Ill. (61852) 222/E4
Longview, Miss. (†39759) 256/G4
Longview, N.C. (28601) 281/F3
Longview, Texas 188/G4
Longview, Texas (*75601) 303/K5
Longview, Wash. 188/B1
Longview, Wash. (98632) 310/B4
Longville, La. (70652) 238/D5
Longville, Minn. (56655) 255/D4
Longwood, Fla. (32750) 212/E3
Longwood, Mo. (†65301) 261/F5
Longwood, N.C. (28452) 281/M7
Longwood Park, N.C. (†28345) 281/K5
Longworth, Br. Col. 184/G3
Longworth, Texas (†79604) 303/D5
Longwy, France 28/F3
Long Xian, China 77/G5
Long Xuyen, Vietnam 72/E5
Longyan, China 77/J6
Longyearbyen, Norway 18/D2
Longyearbyen, Norway 4/B8
Longzhen (Lungchen), China 77/L2
Loni Beach, Manitoba 179/F4
Lonigo, Italy 34/C2
Lonneker, Netherlands 27/K4
Lonoke (co.), Ark. 202/G4
Lonoke, Ark. (72086) 202/G4
Lonquimay, Chile 138/E2
Lonsdale, Ark. (72087) 202/E4
Lonsdale, Minn. (55046) 255/E6
Lonsdale, R.I. (†02864) 249/J5
Lons-le-Saunier, France 28/F4
Lonton, Burma 72/B1
Lontzen, Belgium 27/H9
Looe, England 13/C7
Loogootee, Ind. (47553) 227/D7
Lookeba, Okla. (73053) 288/K4
Lookingglass (riv.), Mich. 250/E6
Lookout (mt.), Ala. 195/G2
Lookout (ridge), Alaska 196/G1
Lookout, Calif. (96054) 204/D2
Lookout (mt.), Idaho 220/F5
Lookout (mt.), Idaho 220/D5
Lookout, Ky. (41542) 237/S6
Lookout (pt.), Md. 245/N8
Lookout (cape), N.C. 188/L4
Lookout (cape), N.C. 281/S5
Lookout, Okla. (†73842) 288/H1
Lookout (cape), Oreg. 188/B1
Lookout (cape), Oreg. 291/C2
Lookout, Pa. (†18417) 294/M2
Lookout, W. Va. (25868) 312/E6
Lookout, Wyo. (†82051) 319/G4
Lookout Mountain, Georgia (†30741) 217/B1
Lookout Mountain, Tenn. (37350) 237/L11
Lookout Point (lake), Oreg. 291/E4
Looma, Alberta 182/D3
Loomis, Calif. (95650) 204/C8
Loomis, Nebr. (68958) 264/E4
Loomis, Sask. 181/C6
Loomis, S. Dak. (57360) 298/N6
Loomis, Wash. (98827) 310/F2
Loomis, Wis. (†54157) 317/K5
Loon (lake), Alberta 182/C1
Loon (riv.), Alberta 182/C1
Loon (lake), Maine 243/D3
Loon (lake), Ontario 177/F3
Loon (creek), Sask. 181/G4
Loon (lake), Wash. 310/H2
Looneyville, W. Va. (25259) 312/D5
Loon Lake, Alberta 182/C1
Loon Lake, Maine (†04970) 243/B5
Loon Lake, N.Y. (†12968) 276/M1
Loon Lake, Sask. 181/B2
Loon Lake, Wash. (99148) 310/H2
Loon op Zand, Netherlands 27/G5
Loon Strait, Manitoba 179/F3
Loop (head), Ireland 17/A6
Loop (head), Ireland 10/A4
Loop, Texas (79342) 303/B5
Loos, Br. Col. 184/G3
Loosahatchie (riv.), Tenn. 237/B10
Loose Creek, Mo. (65054) 261/J5
Lo Ovalle, Chile 138/F3
Looxahoma, Miss. (†38668) 256/E1
Looz (Borgloon), Belgium 27/G7
Lopatka (cape), U.S.S.R. 54/S4
Lopatka (cape), U.S.S.R. 48/Q4
Lop Buri, Thailand 72/D4
Lopeno, Texas (78564) 303/E11
Lopez (pt.), Calif. 204/D7
Lopez (cape), Gabon 102/C5
Lopez (cape), Gabon 115/A4
Lopez, Pa. (18628) 294/K3
Lopez, Wash. (98261) 310/C2
Lopez (isl.), Wash. 310/C2
Lopi, Congo 115/C3
Lop Nor (Lop Nur) (lake), China 77/D3
Lopnur (Yuli), China 77/C3
Lop Nur (lake), China 54/L5
Lopphavet (bay), Norway 18/M1
Lora, Hamun-i- (swamp), Pakistan 68/B3
Lora, Hamun-i- (swamp), Pakistan 59/J4
Lora del Río, Spain 33/D4
Lorado, W. Va. (25630) 312/C7
Lorain (co.), Ohio 284/F3
Lorain, Ohio (*44052) 284/F3
Loraine, Ill. (62349) 222/B3
Loraine, N. Dak. (58761) 282/G2
Loraine, Texas (79532) 303/D5
Loraine, Wis. (†54825) 317/B4
Loralai, Pakistan 68/B2
Loralai, Pakistan 59/J3
Loramie (lake), Ohio 284/B5
Loranger, La. (70446) 238/N1
Lorca, Spain 33/F4
Lord Howe (isl.), Australia 87/G9
Lord Howe (isl.), Australia 2/T7
Lord Howe (isl.), N.S. Wales 97/J2
Lord Howe (Ontong Java) (isl.), Solomon Is. 87/G6
Lord Howe (Ontong Java) (isl.), Solomon Is. 86/D2
Lord Mayor (bay), N.W. Terrs. 187/J3
Lordsburg, N. Mex. (88045) 274/A6
Lords Point, Conn. (†06378) 210/H3
Lordstown, Ohio (†44481) 284/J3
Lords Valley, Pa. (†18428) 294/M3
Loreauville, La. (70552) 238/G6
Loreburn, Sask. 181/E4
Lore City, Ohio (43755) 284/H6
Lorena, Brazil 135/D3
Lorena, Miss. (†39153) 256/F6
Lorengau, Papua N.G. 86/A1
Lorengau, Papua N.G. 87/E6
Lo-Reninge, Belgium 27/B7
Lorentz, W. Va. (†26201) 312/F4
Lorenzo, Idaho (†83442) 220/G6
Lorenzo, Texas (79343) 303/C4
Lorenzo Geyres, Uruguay 145/B3
Lorestan (Luristan) (governorate), Iran 66/F4
Loreto, Bolivia 136/C4
Loreto, Colombia 126/E9
Loreto, Ecuador 128/D3
Loreto, Baja California, Mexico 150/D4
Loreto, Zacatecas, Mexico 150/J5
Loreto, Paraguay 144/D3
Loreto (dept.), Peru 128/E5
Loreto, Agusan del Sur, Philippines 82/E6
Loreto, Surigao del Norte, Philippines 82/E5
Loretta, Kansas (†67520) 232/C3
Loretta, Wis. (54852) 317/E4
Lorette, Manitoba 179/F5
Loretteville, Québec 172/H3
Loretto, Ky. (40037) 237/L5
Loretto, Mich. (49852) 250/B3
Loretto, Minn. (55357) 255/F5
Loretto, Nebr. (68646) 264/F3
Loretto, Pa. (15940) 294/E4
Loretto, Tenn. (38469) 237/G10
Loretto, Va. (22509) 307/O4
Lorian (swamp), Kenya 115/G3
Lorica, Colombia 126/C3
Lorida, Fla. (33857) 212/E4
Lorient, France 7/D4
Lorient, France 28/B4
L'Orignal, Ontario 177/K2
Lorimor, Iowa (50149) 229/E6
Lőrinci, Hungary 41/E3
Loring, Mont. (59537) 262/J2
Loring, Ontario 177/D2
Loring A.F.B., Maine 243/H2
Loris, S.C. (29569) 296/K3
Lorlie, Sask. 181/H5
Lorman, Miss. (39096) 256/B7
Lorne, New Bruns. 170/D1
Lorne, Nova Scotia 168/F3
Lorne (dist.), Scotland 15/C4
Lorne (firth), Scotland 10/D2
Lorne (firth), Scotland 15/C4
Loros (pt.), Chile 138/E3
Lörrach, W. Germany 22/B5
Lorrain (riv.), Martinique 161/D5
Lorraine (trad. prov.), France 29
Lorraine, Kansas (67459) 232/D3
Lorraine, N.Y. (13659) 276/J3
Lorraine, Québec 172/H4
Lorrainville, Québec 174/B3
Lorrha, Ireland 17/E5
Lort (riv.), W. Australia 88/C6
Lorton, Nebr. (68382) 264/H4
Lorton, Va. (22079) 307/O3
Lorze (riv.), Switzerland 39/F2
Los (isls.), Guinea 106/B7
Losada (riv.), Colombia 126/C6
Los Alamitos, Calif. (90720) 204/D11
Los Alamos, Calif. (93440) 204/E9
Los Alamos, N. Mex. 188/E3
Los Alamos (co.), N. Mex. 274/C3
Los Alamos, N. Mex. (87544) 274/C3
Los Alerces Nat'l Park, Argentina 143/C5
Los Algodones, Mexico 150/B1
Los Altos, Calif. (94022) 204/K3
Los Altos Hills, Calif. (94022) 204/J3
Los Amates, Guatemala 154/C3
Los Andes, Chile 138/B9
Los Andes, Colombia 126/B7
Los Angeles, Calif. 146/G6
Los Angeles, Calif. 188/C4
Los Angeles (co.), Calif. 204/G9
Los Angeles, Calif. (*90001) 204/C10
Los Ángeles, Chile 138/D1
Los Angeles, Chile 120/B6
Los Angeles, Texas (78051) 303/F9
Los Angeles, U.S. 2/D4
Los Angeles Aqueduct, Calif. 204/G8
Los Antiguos, Argentina 143/B6
Losantville, Ind. (47354) 227/G4
Los Arabos, Cuba 158/E1
Los Arroyos, Cuba 158/A2
Los Banos, Calif. (93635) 204/E6
Los Barcos (pt.), Cuba 158/B2
Los Canarreos (arch.), Cuba 158/C2
Los Castillos, Venezuela 124/G3
Los Choros (riv.), Chile 138/A7
Los Colorados (arch.), Cuba 158/A1
Los Conquistadores, Argentina 143/G5
Los Coyotes Ind. Res., Calif. 204/J10
Los Cusis, Bolivia 136/D4
Los Estados (isl.), Argentina 143/D7
Los Frailes (isl.), Dom. Rep. 158/C7
Los Fresnos, Texas (78566) 303/G11
Los Gatos, Calif. (95030) 204/K4
Los Glaciares Nat'l Park, Argentina 143/B6
Loshan (Leshan), China 77/F6
Los Hermanos (isls.), Venezuela 124/F2
Łosice, Poland 47/F2
Los Indios, Cuba 158/B2
Lošinj (isl.), Yugoslavia 45/B3
Los Lagos (reg.), Chile 138/D3
Los Lagos, Chile 138/D3
Los Llanos, Dom. Rep. 158/F6
Los Loros, Chile 138/B6
Los Lunas, N. Mex. (87031) 274/C4
Los Menucos, Argentina 143/C5
Los Mochis, Mexico 150/E4
Los Molinos, Calif. (96055) 204/D3
Los Monjes (isls.), Venezuela 124/C1
Los Muermos, Chile 138/D3
Los Navalmorales, Spain 33/D3
Los Navalucillos, Spain 33/D3
Los Negros, Cuba 158/F2
Løsning, Denmark 21/C6
Los Novillos, Uruguay 145/D2
Los Ojos, N. Mex. (87551) 274/C2
Los Olivos, Calif. (93441) 204/E9
Los Olmos (creek), Texas 303/F10
Los Olmos (creek), Texas 303/F11
Los Osos-Baywood Park, Calif. (†93402) 204/E8
Los Palacios, Cuba 158/B1
Los Palacios, Cuba 156/A2
Los Perales de Tapihue, Chile 138/F3
Los Pinos (riv.), Colo. 208/G8
Los Ranchos De Albuquerque, N. Mex. (†87101) 274/C3
Los Reyes de Salgado, Mexico 150/H7
Los Ríos (prov.), Ecuador 128/C3
Los Roques (isls.), Venezuela 124/E2
Los Santos, Panama 154/G7
Los Santos de Maimona, Spain 33/C3
Los Sauces, Chile 138/D2
Losser, Netherlands 27/L4
Lossiemouth and Branderburgh, Scotland 15/E3
Lossiemouth and Branderburgh, Scotland 10/E2
Lost (riv.), Calif. 204/D1

402 Lost

Lost (riv.), Ind. 227/D7
Lost (riv.), Minn. 255/C3
Lost (riv.), Oreg. 291/F5
Lost (creek), Utah 304/C5
Lostallo, Switzerland 39/H4
Lostant, Ill. (61334) 222/D2
Los Taques, Venezuela 124/C2
Lost Cabin, Wyo. (†82642) 319/E2
Lost City, W. Va. (26810) 312/J5
Lost Creek, Ky. (41348) 237/P6
Lost Creek, Wash. (†99180) 310/H2
Lost Creek, W. Va. (26385) 312/F4
Los Teques, Venezuela 120/C2
Los Teques, Venezuela 124/E2
Los Testigos (isls.), Venezuela 124/G2
Lost Hills, Calif. (93249) 204/F8
Lostine, Oreg. (97857) 291/K2
Lost Island (lake), Iowa 229/D2
Lost Nation, Iowa (52254) 229/M5
Lost River, Idaho (†83255) 220/E6
Lost River (range), Idaho 220/E5
Lost River, W. Va. (26811) 312/J5
Lost Springs, Kansas (66859) 232/E3
Lost Springs, Wyo. (82224) 319/G3
Lost Trail (pass), Idaho 220/E4
Lost Trail (pass), Mont. 262/B5
Lostwood, N. Dak. (†58784) 282/F3
Los Vilos, Chile 138/A9
Los Yébenes, Spain 33/E3
Lot (dept.), France 28/D5
Lot (riv.), France 28/D5
Lota, Chile 138/D1
Lotagipi Swamp (plain), Sudan 111/F6
Lotbinière (co.), Québec 172/F3
Lotbinière, Québec 172/F3
Lot-et-Garonne (dept.), France 28/D5
Lothair, Ky. (†41701) 237/P6
Lothair, Mont. (59461) 262/E2
Lothian, Md. (20820) 245/M5
Lothian (reg.), Scotland 15/E5
Lothain (trad. co.), Scotland 15/A5
Loto, Zaire 115/D4
Lötschberg (tunnel), Switzerland 39/E4
Lotsee, Okla. (†74063) 288/O2
Lott, Texas (76656) 303/H6
Lottie, Ala. (†36552) 195/C8
Lottie, La. (70756) 238/G5
Lottsville, Pa. (†16402) 294/D2
Lotus, Calif. (95651) 204/C8
Lotzwil, Switzerland 39/E2
Louang Namtha, Laos 72/D2
Louangphrabang, Laos 72/D3
Louangphrabang, Laos 54/M7
Louann, Ark. (71751) 202/E7
Loubomo, Congo 115/B4
Loubomo, Congo 102/D5
Loudéac, France 28/B3
Loudima, Congo 115/B4
Loudon○, N.H. (03301) 268/E5
Loudon (co.), Tenn. 237/N9
Loudon, Tenn. (37774) 237/N9
Loudonville, Ohio (44842) 284/F4
Loudoun (co.), Va. 307/N2
Loudun, France 28/D4
Louellen, Ky. (40853) 237/P7
Louga, Senegal 106/A5
Loughborough, England 13/F5
Loughborough, England 10/F4
Loughbrickland, N. Ireland 17/J3
Lougheed, Alberta 182/E3
Lougheed (isl.), N.W. Terrs. 187/H2
Loughman, Fla. (33858) 212/E3
Loughrea, Ireland 17/E5
Loughrea, Ireland 10/B4
Loughros More (bay), Ireland 17/D2
Louin, Miss. (39338) 256/F6
Louisa (co.), Iowa 229/L6
Louisa, Ky. (41230) 237/R4
Louisa, La. (†70538) 238/G7
Louisa (lake), Ontario 177/F2
Louisa (co.), Va. 307/N5
Louisa, Va. (23093) 307/M4
Louisbourg, Nova Scotia 168/J3
Louisbourg Nat'l Hist. Park, Nova Scotia 168/J3
Louisburg, Kansas (66053) 232/H3
Louisburg, Minn. (56254) 255/B5
Louisburg, Mo. (65685) 261/F7
Louisburg, N.C. (27549) 281/N2
Louisburgh, Ireland 17/B4
Louis Creek, Br. Col. 184/H4
Louisdale, Nova Scotia 168/G3
Louise (lake), Alaska 196/C1
Louise (isl.), Br. Col. 184/B4
Louise, Miss. (39097) 256/C5
Louise (lake), Québec 172/C4
Louise, Texas (77455) 303/H8
Louiseville, Québec 172/E3
Louisiade (arch.), Papua N.G. 87/F7
Louisiade (arch.), Papua N.G. 85/D8
Louisiana 188/H4
LOUISIANA 238
Louisiana (pt.), La. 238/C7
Louisiana, Mo. (63353) 261/K4
Louisiana (state), U.S. 146/J6
Louis Trichardt, S. Africa 118/E4
Louisville, Ala. (36048) 195/G7
Louisville, Colo. (80027) 208/J3
Louisville, Georgia (30434) 217/H4
Louisville, Ill. (62858) 222/E5
Louisville, Kansas (66450) 232/F2
Louisville, Ky. (*40201) 237/J2
Louisville, Ky. 146/K6
Louisville, Miss. (39339) 256/G4
Louisville, Nebr. (68037) 264/H3
Louisville, Ohio (44641) 284/H4
Louisville, Tenn. (37777) 237/N9
Louisville, Ky. 188/J3
Louis XIV (pt.), Que. 162/H5
Louis XIV (pt.), Québec 174/B2
Loukhi, U.S.S.R. 52/D1
Loulé, Portugal 33/B4
Louny, Czech. 41/B1
Loup (co.), Nebr. 264/E3
Loup (riv.), Nebr. 264/F3
Loup (riv.), Québec 172/H2
Loup City, Nebr. (68853) 264/E3
Lourdes, France 28/C6
Lourdes, Newf. 166/C4
Lourdes, N. Mex. (†87701) 274/D3
Lourdes, Québec 172/F3
Louriçal, Portugal 33/B3
Lourinhã, Portugal 33/B3
Lousã, Portugal 33/B2
Lousana, Alberta 182/D3
Louth, England 13/H4
Louth, England 10/F4
Louth (co.), Ireland 17/J4
Louth, Ireland 17/J4
Louth, N.S. Wales 97/C2
Loutrá Aidhipsoú, Greece 45/F6
Louvain (Leuven), Belgium 27/F7
Louvale, Georgia (31814) 217/C6
Louviers, Colo. (80131) 208/K4
Louviers, France 28/D3
Lövånger, Sweden 18/M4
Lovango (cay), Virgin Is. (U.S.) 161/C4
Lovat' (riv.), U.S.S.R. 52/D3
Love, Miss. (†38632) 256/D1
Love (co.), Okla. 288/M7
Love, Sask. 181/G2
Lovech, Bulgaria 45/G4
Lovejoy, Georgia (30250) 217/D4
Lovejoy, Ill. (62059) 222/A2
Lovelaceville, Ky. (42060) 237/D7
Lovelady, Texas (75851) 303/J6
Loveland, Colo. 188/E2
Loveland, Colo. (80537) 208/J2
Loveland, Iowa (†51555) 229/B6
Loveland, Ohio (45140) 284/D9
Loveland, Okla. (73553) 288/J6
Lovell, Maine (04051) 243/B7
Lovell○, Maine (04051) 243/B7
Lovell, Okla. (†73028) 288/L2
Lovell, Wyo. (82431) 319/D1
Lovells, Mich. (†49738) 250/E4
Lovelock, Nev. (89419) 266/C2
Lovely, Ky. (41231) 237/S5
Lovenia (mt.), Utah 304/D3
Love Point, Md. (†21617) 245/N4
Loverna, Sask. 181/B4
Loves Park, Ill. (61111) 222/E1
Lovett, Georgia (†31021) 217/G5
Lovett, Ind. (†47265) 227/F7
Lovettsville, Va. (22080) 307/N2
Love Valley, N.C. (28677) 281/H3
Loveville, Md. (20656) 245/M7
Lovewell, Kansas (†66942) 232/D2
Lovewell (res.), Kansas 232/D2
Lovilia, Iowa (50150) 229/H6
Loving, N. Mex. (88256) 274/E6
Loving (co.), Texas 303/A6
Lovingston, Va. (22949) 307/L5
Lovington, Ill. (61937) 222/E4
Lovington, N. Mex. (88260) 274/F6
Lovisa, Finland 18/P6
Lövö, Hungary 41/D3
Lovosice, Czech. 41/C1
Lóvua, Angola 115/D5
Low (cape), N.W.T. 162/H3
Low (cape), N.W. Terrs. 187/K3
Low, Québec 172/B4
Lowa (riv.), Zaire 115/E4
Low Bush River, Ontario 177/K5
Low Bush River, Ontario 175/E3
Lowden, Iowa (52255) 229/L5
Lowder, Ill. (62662) 222/A4
Lowe Farm, Manitoba 179/E5
Lowell, Ark. (72745) 202/B1
Lowell, Fla. (32663) 212/D2
Lowell, Idaho (†83539) 220/C3
Lowell (lake), Idaho 220/B6
Lowell, Ind. (46356) 227/C2
Lowell, Iowa (†52645) 229/L7
Lowell, Maine (†04433) 243/F5
Lowell○, Maine (†04433) 243/F5
Lowell, Mass. 188/M2
Lowell, Mass. (*01850) 249/J2
Lowell, Mich. (49331) 250/D6
Lowell, N.C. (28098) 281/G4
Lowell, Ohio (45744) 284/H6
Lowell, Oreg. (97452) 291/E4
Lowell○, Vt. (05847) 268/C2
Lowell, W. Va. (†24910) 312/E7
Lowell, Wis. (53557) 317/J9
Lowell Nat'l Hist. Park, Mass. 249/J2
Lowellville, Ohio (44436) 284/J3
Lower Alkali (lake), Calif. 204/E2
Lower Argyle, Nova Scotia 168/C5
Lower Arrow (lake), Br. Col. 184/H5
Lower Austria (prov.), Austria 41/C2
Lower Bank, N.J. (†08215) 273/E4
Lower Barneys River, Nova Scotia 168/F3
Lower Brule, S. Dak. (57548) 298/K5
Lower Brule Ind. Res., S. Dak. 298/K5
Lower Burrell, Pa. (15068) 294/C4
Lower Cabot, Vt. (†05658) 268/C3
Lower California (pen.), Mexico 2/D4
Lower California (pen.), Mexico 146/G7
Lower California (pen.), Mexico 150/C3
Lower Cloverdale, New Bruns. 170/F2
Lower Crab (creek), Wash. 310/F4
Lower Derby, New Bruns. 170/E2
Lower Durham, New Bruns. 170/D2
Lower East Pubnico, Nova Scotia 168/C5
Lower Elwah Ind. Res., Wash. 310/B2
Lower Engadine (valley), Switzerland 39/K3
Lower Goose Creek (res.), Idaho 220/D7
Lower Granite (lake), Idaho 220/A3
Lower Granite (dam), Wash. 310/H4
Lower Granite (lake), Wash. 310/H4
Lower Hainesville, New Bruns. 170/C2
Lower Hutt, N. Zealand 100/B2
Lower Island Cove, Newf. 166/D2
Lower Kalskag, Alaska (99626) 196/F2
Lower Kars, New Bruns. 170/E3
Lower Klamath (lake), Calif. 204/D2
Lower Lake, Calif. (95457) 204/C5
Lower L'Ardoise, Nova Scotia 168/H3
Lower Marlboro, Md. (†20836) 245/M6
Lower Matecumbe (key), Fla. 212/F7
Lower Millstream, New Bruns. 170/E3
Lower Montague, Pr. Edward I. 168/F2
Lower Monumental (dam), Wash. 310/G4
Lower Monumental (lake), Wash. 310/G4
Lower New York (bay), N.J. 273/E2
Lower Nicola, Br. Col. 184/G5
Lower Ohio, Nova Scotia 168/C5
Lower Paia, Hawaii (†96779) 218/J1
Lower Peach Tree, Ala. (36751) 195/C7
Lower Post, Br. Col. 184/K1
Lower Red (lake), Minn. 255/C3
Lower Red Rock (lake), Mont. 262/E6
Lower Rhine (riv.), Netherlands 27/H5
Lower Roach (pond), Maine 243/E4
Lower Saint Mary (lake), Mont. 262/C2
Lower Salem, Ohio (45745) 284/H6
Lower Sapin, New Bruns. 170/F2
Lower Saranac (lake), N.Y. 276/M2
Lower Saxony (state), W. Germany 22/C2
Lower Southampton, New Bruns. 170/C2
Lower South River, Nova Scotia 168/F3
Lower Sysladobsis (lake), Maine 243/G5
Lower Tonsina, Alaska (†99566) 196/J2
Lower Tunguska (riv.), U.S.S.R. 54/L3
Lower Tunguska (riv.), U.S.S.R. 48/K3
Lower Waterford, Vt. (05848) 268/D3
Lower Wedgeport, Nova Scotia 168/C5
Lower West Pubnico, Nova Scotia 168/C5
Lower Woods Harbour, Nova Scotia 168/C5
Lowery, Ala. (†36453) 195/F8
Lowery (lake), Fla. 212/E3
Lowes, Ky. (42061) 237/D7
Lowestoft, England 13/J5
Lowestoft, England 10/G4
Lowesville, Va. (22951) 307/K5
Lowgap, N.C. (27024) 281/H1
Łowicz, Poland 47/D2
Lowland, N.C. (28552) 281/S4
Lowman, Idaho (83637) 220/C5
Lowmansville, Ky. (41232) 237/R5
Low Moor, Iowa (52757) 229/N5
Lowmoor, Va. (24457) 307/J5
Lowndes (co.), Ala. 195/E6
Lowndes (co.), Georgia 217/F9
Lowndes (co.), Miss. 256/H4
Lowndes, Mo. (63951) 261/M8
Lowndesboro, Ala. (36752) 195/E6
Lowndesville, S.C. (29659) 296/B3
Lowpoint, Ill. (61545) 222/D3
Low Rocky (pt.), Tasmania 99/B4
Lowry, Minn. (56349) 255/C5
Lowry, S. Dak. (†57472) 298/K3
Lowry, Va. (24570) 307/K6
Lowry A.F.B., Colo. 208/K3
Lowry City, Mo. (64763) 261/E6
Lowrys, S.C. (†29706) 296/E2
Lowther (isl.), N.W. Terrs. 187/J2
Lowville, N.Y. (13367) 276/J3
Low Wassie, Mo. (†65588) 261/K9
Loxahatchee, Fla. (33470) 212/F5
Loxley, Ala. (36551) 195/C9
Loxton, S. Australia 94/G6
Loxton North, S. Australia 94/G6
Loyal, Okla. (73756) 288/K3
Loyal, Loch (lake), Scotland 15/D2
Loyal, Wis. (54446) 317/E6
Loyalhanna, Pa. (15661) 294/D5
Loyalist, Alberta 182/E4
Loyall, Ky. (40854) 237/P7
Loyalton, Calif. (96118) 204/E4
Loyalton, Pa. (†17048) 294/J4
Loyalton, S. Dak. (†57471) 298/L3
Loyalty (isls.), New Caled. 87/G8
Loyalty (isls.), New Caled. 86/H4
Loyang (Luoyang), China 77/H5
Loyd, Wis. (†53924) 317/F9
Loyne, Loch (lake), Scotland 15/C3
Loysburg, Pa. (16659) 294/F5
Loysville, Pa. (17047) 294/H5
Lozeau (lake), Newf. 166/B3
Lozère (dept.), France 28/E5
Loznica, Yugoslavia 45/D3
Lozovaya, U.S.S.R. 52/E5
Lua (riv.), Zaire 115/C3
Luacano, Angola 115/D6
Luachimo, Angola 115/D5
Lualaba (riv.), Zaire 102/E5
Lualaba (riv.), Zaire 115/E4
Lua Makika (mt.), Hawaii 218/J3
Lu'an, China 77/J5
Luana, Iowa (52156) 229/K2
Luana (pt.), Jamaica 158/G6
Luanchuan, China 77/H5
Luanda (dist.), Angola 115/B5
Luanda (cap.), Angola 2/K6
Luanda (cap.), Angola 115/B5
Luanda (cap.), Angola 102/D5
Luang, Thale (lag.), Thailand 72/D6
Luang (mt.), Thailand 72/C5
Luang Prabang (Loungphrabang), Laos 72/D3
Luangwa (Feira), Zambia 115/E7
Luangwa (riv.), Zambia 115/F6
Luanshya, Zambia 115/E6
Luanshya, Zambia 102/E6
Luao, Angola 115/D6
Luapula (riv.), Zaire 115/E6
Luapula (riv.), Zambia 115/E6
Luarca, Spain 33/C1
Luashi, Zaire 115/D6
Luba, Equat. Guinea 115/A3
Lubaczów, Poland 47/F3
Lubań, Poland 47/B3
Lubāna (lake), U.S.S.R. 53/D2
Lubang, Philippines 82/C4
Lubang (isls.), Philippines 85/F3
Lubang (isls.), Philippines 82/B4
Lubango, Angola 115/B6
Lubango, Angola 102/D6
Lubartów, Poland 47/F3
Lubawa, Poland 47/D2
Lübben, E. Germany 22/E3
Lübbenau, E. Germany 22/F3
Lubbock (co.), Texas 303/C4
Lubbock, Texas 146/H6
Lubbock, Texas (*79401) 303/C4
Lubbock, Texas 188/F4
Lubec, Maine (04652) 243/K6
Lubec○, Maine (04652) 243/K6
Lübeck, W. Germany 7/E3
Lübeck, W. Germany 22/D2
Lubeck, W. Va. (†26101) 312/C4
Lubefu, Zaire 115/D4
Lubero, Zaire 115/E4
L'ubica, Czech. 41/F2
Lubicon (lake), Alberta 182/C1
Lubien Kujawski, Poland 47/D2
Lubilash (riv.), Zaire 115/D5
Lublin, Poland 47/C3
Lublin (prov.), Poland 47/F3
Lublin, Poland 47/F3
Lublin, Poland 7/G3
Lublin, Wis. (54447) 317/E5
Lubliniec, Poland 47/D3
Lubny, U.S.S.R. 52/D4
Luboń, Poland 47/C2
Lubrín, Spain 33/F4
Lubsko, Poland 47/B3
Lubuagan, Philippines 82/C2
Lubudi, Zaire 115/E5
Lubuklinggau, Indonesia 85/C6
Lubuksikaping, Indonesia 85/B5
Lubumbashi, Zaire 2/L6
Lubumbashi, Zaire 115/E6
Lubumbashi, Zaire 102/E6
Lubutu, Zaire 115/E4
Lübz, E. Germany 22/D2
Lucama, N.C. (27851) 281/N3
Lucan, Minn. (56255) 255/C6
Lucan, Ontario 177/C4
Luc An Chau, Vietnam 72/E2
Lucan-Doddsborough, Ireland 17/J5
Lucas (co.), Iowa 229/G6
Lucas, Iowa (50151) 229/G6
Lucas, Kansas (67648) 232/D2
Lucas, Ky. (42156) 237/K7
Lucas, Mich. (†49657) 250/D4
Lucas (co.), Ohio 284/C2
Lucas, Ohio (44843) 284/F4
Lucas, S. Dak. (57549) 298/L7
Lucas, Texas (†75069) 303/H1
Lucas E. de Peña, Dom. Rep. 158/D5
Lucas González, Argentina 143/G6
Lucasville, Ohio (45648) 284/E8
Lucban, Philippines 82/C3
Lucca (prov.), Italy 34/C3
Lucca, Italy 34/C3
Lucca, N. Dak. (†58027) 282/P6
Luce (co.), Mich. 250/D2
Luce, Minn. (†56573) 255/C4
Luce (bay), Scotland 10/D3
Luce (bay), Scotland 15/D6
Lucea, Jamaica 158/G5
Lucedale, Miss. (39452) 256/G9
Lucena, Philippines 85/G3
Lucena, Philippines 82/C4
Lucena, Spain 33/D4
Lucena del Cid, Spain 33/F2
Lučenec, Czech. 41/E2
Lucens, Switzerland 39/C3
Lucera, Italy 34/E4
Lucerna, Peru 128/H9
Lucerne, Calif. (95458) 204/C4
Lucerne, Colo. (80646) 208/K2
Lucerne, Ind. (46950) 227/E3
Lucerne, Mo. (64655) 261/F2
Lucerne, Québec 172/B4
Lucerne (Luzern) (canton), Switzerland 39/F2
Lucerne, Switzerland 39/F2
Lucerne (lake), Switzerland 39/F3
Lucerne, Wash. (†98816) 310/E2
Lucerne, Wyo. (†82443) 319/D2
Lucernemines, Pa. (15754) 294/D4
Lucerne Valley, Calif. (92356) 204/J9
Lucero (lake), N. Mex. 274/C6
Luceville, Québec 172/J1
Luchow (Luzhou), China 77/G6
Lüchow, W. Germany 22/D2
Lucia, Calif. (†93920) 204/D7
Lucie (riv.), Suriname 131/C4
Lucien, Miss. (39646) 256/C7
Lucien, Okla. (73757) 288/M2
Lucile, Georgia (†31723) 217/C8
Lucile, Idaho (83542) 220/B4
Lucile, Ky. (†41171) 237/P4
Lucinda, Pa. (16235) 294/D3
Lucira, Angola 115/B6
Luck, Wis. (54853) 317/B4
Luckau, E. Germany 22/E3
Luckenwalde, E. Germany 22/E2
Lucketts, Va. (†22075) 307/N2
Luckey, Ohio (43443) 284/D3
Lucknow, India 68/E3
Lucknow, India 54/K7
Lucknow, Ontario 177/C4
Lucky, La. (†71008) 238/E2
Lucky Lake, Sask. 181/D5
Lucky Peak (lake), Idaho 220/B6
Luçon, France 28/C4
Lucrecia (cape), Cuba 158/J3
Lucy, La. (†70049) 238/M3
Lucy, Tenn. (†38053) 237/B10
Lucy Creek, North. Terr. 93/E7
Lüda (Lüta), China 77/K4
Lüda, China 2/R4
Lüda, China 54/O6
Ludden, N. Dak. (58462) 282/O7
Ludell, Kansas (67744) 232/B2
Lüdenscheid, W. Germany 22/B3
Lüderitz, Namibia 118/A5
Lüderitz, Namibia 102/D7
Lüderitz (bay), Namibia 118/A5
Ludhiana, India 54/J6
Ludhiana, India 68/D2
Ludington, Mich. (49431) 250/C5
Ludlow, Calif. (†92365) 204/J9
Ludlow, England 10/E4
Ludlow, England 13/E5
Ludlow, Ill. (60949) 222/E3
Ludlow, Ky. (41016) 237/S2
Ludlow○, Maine (†04730) 243/G3
Ludlow○, Mass. (01056) 249/E4
Ludlow, Miss. (39098) 256/E5
Ludlow, Mo. (64656) 261/E3
Ludlow, New Bruns. 170/D2
Ludlow, Pa. (16333) 294/E2
Ludlow, S. Dak. (57755) 298/C2
Ludlow, Vt. (05149) 268/B5
Ludlow○, Vt. (05149) 268/B5
Ludlow (mt.), Vt. 268/B5
Ludlow Center, Mass. (†01056) 249/E4
Ludlow Falls, Ohio (45339) 284/B6
Ludowici, Georgia (31316) 217/J7
Luduş, Romania 45/G2
Ludvika, Sweden 18/J6
Ludville, Georgia (†30175) 217/C2
Ludwigsburg, W. Germany 22/C4
Ludwigshafen am Rhein, W. Germany 22/C4
Ludwigslust, E. Germany 22/D2
Ludza, U.S.S.R. 53/D2
Lue, N.S. Wales 97/E3
Luebbering, Mo. (63061) 261/L6
Luebo, Zaire 115/D5
Lueders, Texas (79533) 303/E5
Luella, Georgia (†30248) 217/D4
Luena, Angola 115/C6
Luepa, Venezuela 124/H5
Lüeyang, China 77/G5
Lufeng, China 77/J7
Lufira (riv.), Zaire 115/E5
Lufkin, Texas (75901) 303/K6
Luga, U.S.S.R. 52/C3
Luga, U.S.S.R. 48/D4
Lugano, Switzerland 39/G4
Lugano (lake), Switzerland 39/H5
Luganville, Vanuatu 87/G7
Lugareño, Cuba 158/G3
Lugenda (riv.), Mozambique 118/F2
Lugerville, Wis. (†54555) 317/E4
Lugnaquillia (mt.), Ireland 17/J5
Lugo, Italy 34/D2
Lugo (prov.), Spain 33/C1
Lugo, Spain 33/C1
Lugoff, S.C. (29078) 296/F3
Lugoj, Romania 45/F3
Luhaiya, Yemen Arab Rep. 59/D6
Luiana, Angola 115/D7
Luiana, Angola 102/E6
Luik (Liège), Belgium 27/H7
Łuilaka (riv.), Zaire 115/C4
Luimneach (Limerick), Ireland 10/B4
Luimneach (Limerick), Ireland 17/D6
Luina, Tasmania 99/B3
Luing (isl.), Scotland 15/C4
Luís Correia, Brazil 132/F3
Luis de Saboya, Cerro (mt.), Chile 138/F11
Luishia, Zaire 115/E6
Luitpold Coast (reg.) 5/B17
Luiza, Zaire 115/D5
Luján, Argentina 143/G7
Lujiang, China 77/J5
Lukachukai, Ariz. (86507) 198/F2
Lukachukai (mts.), Ariz. 198/F2
Lukapa, Angola 115/D5
Luke, Md. (21540) 245/B3
Luke A.F.B., Ariz. 198/C5
Lukenie (riv.), Zaire 115/D4
Lukeville, Ariz. (85341) 198/C7
Lukolela, Equateur, Zaire 115/C4
Lukolela, Kasai-Oriental, Zaire 115/D5
Lukovit, Bulgaria 45/G4
Łuków, Poland 47/F3
Lukuga (riv.), Zaire 115/E5
Lukula, Zaire 115/B5
Lukulu, Zambia 115/D6
Lula, Georgia (30554) 217/E2
Lula, Miss. (38644) 256/C2
Lula, Okla. (†74825) 288/O5
Lule (riv.), Sweden 7/G2
Luleå, Sweden 7/G2
Luleå, Sweden 18/N4
Luleälv (riv.), Sweden 18/M4
Lüleburgaz, Turkey 63/B2
Lules, Argentina 143/C2
Luling, La. (70070) 238/N4
Luling, Texas (78648) 303/G8
Lulu, Fla. (32061) 212/D1
Lulua (riv.), Zaire 115/D5
Lum, Mich. (48452) 250/F5
Lumajang, Indonesia 85/K2
Lumajangdong Co (lake), China 77/B5
Lumbala, Angola 115/D6
Lumber (riv.), N.C. 281/L6
Lumber (riv.), S.C. 296/J3
Lumber Bridge, N.C. (28357) 281/L5
Lumber City, Georgia (31549) 217/G7
Lumber City, Pa. (†16833) 294/E4
Lumberport, W. Va. (26386) 312/F4
Lumberton, Miss. (39455) 256/E8
Lumberton, N.J. (08048) 273/D4
Lumberton, N. Mex. (87547) 274/C2
Lumberton, N.C. (28358) 281/L5
Lumberton, Texas (†77656) 303/K7
Lumberville, Pa. (18933) 294/N5
Lumbo, Mozambique 118/G3
Lumbrales, Spain 33/C2
Lumbrein, Switzerland 39/H3
Lumby, Br. Col. 184/H5
Lumding, India 68/G3
Lummen, Belgium 27/G7
Lummi (isl.), Wash. 310/C2
Lummi Ind. Res., Wash. 310/C2
Lummi Island, Wash. (98262) 310/C2
Lumphat, Cambodia 72/E4
Lumpkin (co.), Georgia 217/D1
Lumpkin, Georgia (31815) 217/C6
Lumsden, Newf. 166/D4
Lumsden, N. Zealand 100/B6
Lumsden, Sask. 181/G5
Lumsden, Scotland 15/F3
Lumsden Beach, Sask. 181/F5
Lumut, Malaysia 72/D6
Luna, Ark. (†71653) 202/H7
Luna (co.), N. Mex. 274/B6
Luna, N. Mex. (87824) 274/A5
Luna Pier, Mich. (48157) 250/F7
Luncarty, Scotland 15/E4
Lund, Br. Col. 184/E5
Lund, Idaho (†83241) 220/G7
Lund, Nev. (89317) 266/F4
Lund, Sweden 18/H9
Lund, Utah (†84720) 304/A5
Lundale, W. Va. (25631) 312/C7
Lunda Norte (dist.), Angola 115/C5
Lundar, Manitoba 179/D4
Lunda Sul (dist.), Angola 115/D5
Lundazi, Zambia 115/F6
Lundbreck, Alberta 182/C5
Lundby, Denmark 21/E7
Lundell, Ark. (†72367) 202/H5
Lunderskov, Denmark 21/C7
Lundi (riv.), Zimbabwe 118/E4
Lunds Corner, Mass. (02745) 249/L6
Lundsvalley, N. Dak. (†58724) 282/E3
Lundy (isl.), England 13/C6
Lundy (isl.), England 10/D5
Lune (riv.), England 13/E3
Lüneburg, W. Germany 22/D2
Lüneburger Heide (dist.), W. Germany 22/C2
Lunel, France 28/E6
Lünen, W. Germany 22/B3
Lunenburg, Mass. (01462) 249/H2
Lunenburg○, Mass. (01462) 249/H2
Lunenburg, N.S. 162/K7
Lunenburg (co.), Nova Scotia 168/D4
Lunenburg, Nova Scotia 168/D4
Lunenburg (bay), Nova Scotia 168/D4
Lunenburg○, Vt. (05906) 268/D3
Lunenburg (co.), Va. 307/M7
Lunenburg, Va. (23952) 307/M7
Lunéville, France 28/G3
Lung (riv.), Ireland 17/D4
Lungchen (Longzhen), China 77/L2
Lungdo, China 77/B5
Lungern, Switzerland 39/F3
Lungi, S. Leone 106/B7
Lungleh, India 68/G4
Lungwebungu (riv.), Angola 115/D6
Lungwebungu (riv.), Zambia 115/D6
Luni (riv.), India 68/C3
Luninets, U.S.S.R. 52/C4
Luning, Nev. (89420) 266/C4
Lunita, La. (†70661) 238/C6
Lunsford, Ark. (†72437) 202/K2
Luocheng, China 77/G7
Luodian, China 77/G6
Luoding, China 77/H7
Luohe, China 77/H5
Luoyang (Loyang), China 77/H5
Luoyang, China 54/N6
Luozi, Zaire 115/B5
Lupeni, Romania 45/F3
Luperón, Dom. Rep. 158/D5
Lupon, Philippines 82/E7
Lupton, Ariz. (86508) 198/F3
Lupton, Mich. (48635) 250/F4
Lupus, Mo. (†65046) 261/H5
Luputa, Zaire 115/D5
Luqu, China 77/F5
Luque, Paraguay 144/B4
Luquillo, P. Rico 161/F1
Luquillo, Sierra de (mts.), P. Rico 161/E2
Lurah (riv.), Afghanistan 68/B2
Lurah (riv.), Afghanistan 59/J3
Luray, Kansas (67649) 232/D2
Luray, Mo. (63453) 261/J2
Luray, S.C. (29932) 296/E6
Luray, Tenn. (38352) 237/D9
Luray, Va. (22835) 307/M3
Lure, France 28/G4
Lurgan, N. Ireland 17/J3
Luribay, Bolivia 136/B5
Lurín, Peru 128/D9
Lúrio, Mozambique 118/G2
Lúrio (riv.), Mozambique 118/F2
Luristan (Lorestan) (gov.), Iran 66/F4
Lurton, Ark. (†72856) 202/D2
Lusaka (cap.), Zambia 115/E7
Lusaka (cap.), Zambia 102/E6
Lusaka (cap.), Zambia 2/L6
Lusambo, Zaire 102/E5
Lusambo, Zaire 115/D4
Lusatia (reg.), E. Germany 22/F3
Lusby, Md. (20657) 245/N7
Luseland, Sask. 181/B3
Lushi, China 77/H5
Lushnje, Albania 45/D5
Lushoto, Tanzania 115/G4
Lushton, Nebr. (†68371) 264/G4
Lushui, China 77/E6
Lüshun, China 77/K4
Lusk, Ireland 17/J4
Lusk, Wyo. (82225) 319/H3
Luso, Angola 102/E6
Luss, Scotland 15/A1
Lustenau, Austria 41/A3
Lustre, Mont. (59225) 262/K2
Lut, Dasht-e (des.), Iran 59/G3
Lut, Dasht-e (des.), Iran 66/L5
Lüta (Lüda), China 77/K4
Lutcher, La. (70071) 238/L3
Lutesville, Mo. (63762) 261/M8
Luther, Iowa (50152) 229/F5
Luther, Mich. (49656) 250/D4
Luther, Mont. (59051) 262/G5
Luther, Okla. (73054) 288/M3
Luther, Tenn. (†37869) 237/P8
Luthern, Switzerland 39/E2
Luthersburg, Pa. (15848) 294/E3
Luthersville, Georgia (30251) 217/C4
Lutherville-Timonium, Md. (21093) 245/M3
Lutie, Okla. (†74578) 288/R5
Luton, England 13/G6
Luton, England 10/F5
Luton, Iowa (†51052) 229/A4
Lutry, Switzerland 39/C3

Magaguadavic 403

Lutsen, Minn. (55612) 255/F2
Lutsk, U.S.S.R. 7/G3
Lutsk, U.S.S.R. 52/B4
Lutsk, U.S.S.R. 48/C4
Luttrell, Tenn. (37779) 237/O8
Lutts, Tenn. (38471) 237/F10
Lutz, Fla. (33549) 212/D3
Lützelflüh, Switzerland 39/E3
Lützow-Holm (bay) 5/C3
Luuq, Somalia 115/H3
Luverne, Ala. (36049) 195/F7
Lu Verne, Iowa (50560) 229/E3
Luverne Minn. (56156) 255/B7
Luverne, N. Dak. (58056) 282/P5
Luvua (riv.), Zaire 115/E5
Luwingu, Zambia 115/E6
Luwuk, Indonesia 85/G6
Lux, Miss. (†39401) 256/F8
Luxembourg 7/E4
Luxembourg (prov.), Belgium 27/G9
LUXEMBOURG 27/J9
Luxembourg (cap.), Luxembourg 27/J9
Luxemburg, Iowa (52056) 229/L3
Luxemburg, Minn. (†56301) 255/D5
Luxemburg, Wis. (54217) 317/L6
Luxeuil-les-Bains, France 28/G4
Luxi, China 77/E7
Luxi, China 77/F7
Luxor, Egypt 102/F2
Luxor, Egypt 59/B4
Luxor, Egypt 111/F2
Luxora, Ark. (72358) 202/K2
Luz, Brazil 135/D1
Luz (isl.), Chile 138/D6
Luza, U.S.S.R. 52/G2
Luzein, Switzerland 39/J3
Luzern (canton), Switzerland 39/F2
Luzern (Lucerne), Switzerland 39/F2
Luzerne, Iowa (52257) 229/J5
Luzerne, Mich. (48636) 250/E4
Luzerne (co.), Pa. 294/L3
Luzerne, Pa. (18709) 294/E7
Luzhai, China 77/G7
Luzhi, China 77/G6
Luzhou (Luchow), China 77/G6
Luziânia, Brazil 132/E7
Luzilândia, Brazil 132/F3
Lužnice (riv.), Czech. 41/C2
Luzon (isl.), Philippines 2/R5
Luzon (isl.), Philippines 54/O8
Luzon (isl.), Philippines 82/C3
Luzon (isl.), Philippines 85/G2
Luzon (sea), Philippines 82/B4
Luzon (str.), Philippines 82/A2
Luz-Saint-Sauveur, France 28/C6
L'vov, U.S.S.R. 7/G4
L'vov, U.S.S.R. 48/C4
L'vov (Lwów), U.S.S.R. 52/B5
Lyakhov (isls.), U.S.S.R. 4/B3
Lyal (isl.), Ontario 177/C3
Lyallpur (Faisalabad), Pakistan 68/C2
Lyallpur (Faisalabad), Pakistan 59/K3
Lyalta, Alberta 182/D4
Lyatkhovskiye (isls.), U.S.S.R. 48/O2
Lybster, Scotland 10/E1
Lybster, Scotland 15/E2
Lycan, Colo. (†81054) 208/P7
Lycksele, Sweden 18/L4
Lycoming, N.Y. (13093) 276/H3
Lycoming (co.), Pa. 294/H3
Lycoming (creek), Pa. 294/H3
Lydall ville, Conn. (†06040) 210/F1
Lydd, England 13/H7
Lydda, Israel 65/B4
Lydenburg, S. Africa 118/E4
Lydia, Minn. (†55352) 255/E6
Lydia, S.C. (29079) 296/G3
Lydia Mills, S.C. (29325) 296/D3
Lydick, Ind. (†46601) 227/E1
Lyell (mt.), Alberta 182/B4
Lyell (isl.), Br. Col. 184/B4
Lyell (mt.), Br. Col. 184/J4
Lyell (mt.), Tasmania 99/B4
Lyerly, Georgia (30730) 217/B2
Lyford, Ind. (†47874) 227/C5
Lyford, Texas (78569) 303/G11
Lykens, Pa. (17048) 294/J4
Lyle, Minn. (55953) 255/F7
Lyle, Wash. (98635) 310/D5
Lyles, Tenn. (37098) 237/G9
Lyleton, Manitoba 179/A5
Lyman, Miss. (†39501) 256/F10
Lyman, Nebr. (69352) 264/A3
Lyman○, N.H. (†03585) 268/D3
Lyman, S.C. (29365) 296/C2
Lyman (co.), S. Dak. 298/J6
Lyman, Utah (84749) 304/C5
Lyman, Wash. (98263) 310/D2
Lyman, Wyo. (82937) 319/B4
Lyme (bay), England 13/D7
Lyme (bay), England 10/E5
Lyme○, N.H. (03768) 268/C4
Lyme Center, N.H. (03769) 268/C4
Lyme Regis, England 13/E7
Lyme Regis, England 10/E5
Lymington, England 10/F5
Lymington, England 13/F7
Lymm, England 13/H2
Lymm, England 10/G2
Lyn, Ontario 177/J3
Łyna (riv.), Poland 47/E1
Lynbrook, N.Y. (11563) 276/P7
Lynch, Ky. (40855) 237/R7
Lynch, Md. (21646) 245/O3
Lynch, Nebr. (68746) 264/F2
Lynchburg, Mo. (65543) 261/H7
Lynchburg, N. Dak. (†58023) 282/R6
Lynchburg, Ohio (45142) 284/C7
Lynchburg, S.C. (29080) 296/G3
Lynchburg, Tenn. (37352) 237/J10
Lynchburg, Va. 188/L3
Lynchburg, Va. 146/K6
Lynchburg (I.C.), Va. (*24501) 307/K6
Lynches (riv.), S.C. 296/H3
Lynch Station, Va. (24571) 307/K6
Lynd, Minn. (56157) 255/C6
Lynd, Queensland 95/C3
Lyndeborough○, N.H. (†03082) 268/D6
Lynden, Ontario 177/D4
Lynden, Wash. (98264) 310/C2
Lyndhurst○, N.J. (07071) 273/B2
Lyndhurst, N.S. Wales 97/E3
Lyndhurst, Ohio (44124) 284/J9
Lyndhurst, Ontario 177/H3
Lyndhurst, S. Australia 88/F6
Lyndhurst, S. Australia 94/E4
Lyndoch, S. Australia 94/C6
Lyndon, Ill. (61261) 222/D2
Lyndon, Kansas (66451) 232/G3
Lyndon, Ohio (45649) 284/D7
Lyndon○, Vt. (05849) 268/C2
Lyndon, W. Australia 92/A3
Lyndon B. Johnson Nat'l Hist. Site, Texas 303/F7
Lyndon B. Johnson Space Ctr., Texas 303/K2
Lyndon Center, Vt. (05850) 268/C2
Lyndon Station, Wis. (53944) 317/F8
Lyndonville, N.Y. (14098) 276/D4
Lyndonville, Vt. (05851) 268/D2
Lyndora, Pa. (16045) 294/B4
Lynedoch, Ontario 177/D5
Lyness, Scotland 15/E2
Lyngby, Denmark 21/F6
Lynhurst, Ontario 177/C5
Lynn, Ala. (35575) 195/C2
Lynn, Ark. (72440) 202/H2
Lynn, Ind. (47355) 227/H4
Lynn, Mass. (*01901) 249/D6
Lynn, N.C. (28750) 281/E4
Lynn (co.), Texas 303/C4
Lynn, Wis. (†54436) 317/F6
Lynn Canal (inlet), Alaska 196/M1
Lynn Center, Ill. (61262) 222/C2
Lynn Creek, Miss. (†39739) 256/G4
Lynndyl, Utah (84640) 304/B4
Lynnfield○, Mass. (01940) 249/D5
Lynnfield Center (Lynnfield P.O.), Mass. (†01940) 249/C5
Lynn Grove, Ky. (42062) 237/E7
Lynn Haven, Fla. (32444) 212/C6
Lynn Lake, Man. 162/G4
Lynn Lake, Man. 146/H4
Lynn Lake, Manitoba 179/H2
Lynnview, Ky. (†40201) 237/K4
Lynnville, Ill. (†62650) 222/C4
Lynnville, Ind. (47619) 227/C8
Lynnville, Iowa (50153) 229/H5
Lynnville, Ky. (42063) 237/D7
Lynnville, Tenn. (38472) 237/G10
Lynnwood, Wash. (98036) 310/C3
Lynton, England 10/E5
Lynton, England 13/D6
Lynwood, Calif. (90262) 204/C11
Lynwood, Ill. (†60411) 222/C6
Lynx (lake), N.W. Terrs. 187/H3
Lynxville, Wis. (54640) 317/D9
Lyon, France 7/E4
Lyon, France 28/F5
Lyon (co.), Iowa 229/A2
Lyon (co.), Kansas 232/F3
Lyon (co.), Ky. 237/E6
Lyon (co.), Minn. 255/C6
Lyon, Miss. (38645) 256/D2
Lyon (co.), Nev. 266/B3
Lyon (inlet), N.W. Terrs. 187/K3
Lyon, Loch (lake), Scotland 15/D4
Lyon (riv.), Scotland 15/D4
Lyon Mountain, N.Y. (12952) 276/N1
Lyonnais (trad. prov.) France 29
Lyons, Colo. (80540) 208/J2
Lyons, Georgia (30436) 217/H6
Lyons, Ill. (60534) 222/B6
Lyons, Ind. (47443) 227/C7
Lyons, Kansas (67554) 232/D3
Lyons, Ky. (†40051) 237/K5
Lyons, Mich. (48851) 250/E6
Lyons, Nebr. (68038) 264/H3
Lyons, N.J. (07939) 273/D2
Lyons, N.Y. (14489) 276/F4
Lyons, Ohio (43533) 284/B2
Lyons, Oreg. (97358) 291/E3
Lyons (Lyon Station), Pa. (19536) 294/L5
Lyons, S. Dak. (57041) 298/R6
Lyons (riv.), W. Australia 88/B4
Lyons (riv.), W. Australia 92/A4
Lyons, Wis. (53148) 317/K10
Lyons Brook, Nova Scotia 168/F3
Lyons Falls, N.Y. (13368) 276/K3
Lyons Plain, Conn. (†06880) 210/B4
Lyon Station, Pa. (19536) 294/L5
Lyra (reef), Papua N.G. 86/C1
Lys (riv.), Belgium 27/B7
Lys (riv.), France 28/E2
Lysaker, Norway 18/D3
Lysá nad Labem, Czech. 41/C1
Lysander, N.Y. (13094) 276/H4
Lysekil, Sweden 18/G7
Lysite, Wyo. (82642) 319/E2
Lyss, Switzerland 39/D2
Lyster, Québec 172/F3
Lys'va, U.S.S.R. 7/K3
Lys'va, U.S.S.R. 48/F4
Lys'va, U.S.S.R. 52/J3
Lytham Saint Anne's, England 13/G1
Lytham Saint Anne's, England 10/F1
Lytle, Texas (78052) 303/J11
Lyttelton, N. Zealand 100/D5
Lytton, Br. Col. 184/G5
Lytton, Iowa (50561) 229/D4
Lyubertsy, U.S.S.R. 52/E3
Lyubotin, U.S.S.R. 52/E4
Lyudinovo, U.S.S.R. 52/D4

M

Ma'ad, Jordan 65/D2
Maalaea, Hawaii (†96753) 218/J2
Maalaea (bay), Hawaii 218/J2
Ma'alot-Tarshiha, Israel 65/C1
Ma'an (dist.), Jordan 65/D5
Ma'an, Jordan 65/E5
Ma'an, Jordan 59/C3
Ma'anshan, China 77/J5
Maarianhamina (Mariehamn), Finland 18/M7
Maarssen, Netherlands 27/F4
Maas (riv.), Netherlands 27/G5
Maasbree, Netherlands 27/H6
Maaseik, Belgium 27/H6
Maasin, Philippines 82/E5
Maasmechelen, Belgium 27/H7
Maassluis, Netherlands 27/E5
Maastricht, Netherlands 27/H7
Maatsuyker (isls.), Tasmania 99/C5
Mababe (depr.), Botswana 118/C3
Mabalane, Mozambique 118/E4
Mabank, Texas (75147) 303/H5
Mabaruma, Guyana 131/B1
Mabay, Cuba 158/H4
Mabel (lake), Br. Col. 184/H5
Mabel, Minn. (55954) 255/G7
Mabelvale, Ark. (72103) 202/F4
Maben, Miss. (39750) 256/F3
Maben, W. Va. (25870) 312/D7
Maberly, Ontario 177/H3
Mabie, W. Va. (26278) 312/F5
Mabille (lake), Newf. 166/B3
Mabini, Philippines 82/E6
Mablethorpe and Sutton, England 13/H4
Mablethorpe and Sutton, England 10/G4
Mableton, Georgia (30059) 217/J1
Mabote, Mozambique 118/E4
Mabou, Nova Scotia 168/G2
Mabou (harb.), Nova Scotia 168/G2
Mabou Highlands (hills), Nova Scotia 168/G2
Mabrouk, Mali 106/D5
Mabscott, W. Va. (25871) 312/D7
Mabton, Wash. (98935) 310/E4
Macá (mt.), Chile 138/D5
Macachín, Argentina 143/D4
Macaé, Brazil 135/F3
Macaé, Brazil 132/F8
Macaíba, Brazil 132/H4
Macajalar (bay), Philippines 82/E6
Macalister, Br. Col. 184/F4
Macaloge, Mozambique 118/F2
MacAlpine (lake), N.W. Terrs. 187/H3
Macamic, Québec 174/B3
Macan (isls.), Indonesia 85/G7
Macanao (pen.), Venezuela 124/F2
Maçao, Portugal 33/B3
Macao (Macau) 77
Macapá, Brazil 120/D2
Macapá, Brazil 132/D2
Macará, Ecuador 128/C5
Macaranaima, Colombia 126/E7
Macarena, Serranía de La (mts.), Colombia 126/D6
Macareo Santo Niño, Venezuela 124/H3
Macarthur, Victoria 97/A6
Macas, Ecuador 128/D4
Macassar, S. Africa 118/F6
Macau 54/N7
Macau, Brazil 120/F3
Macau, Brazil 132/G4
MACAU (MACAO) 77
Macau (Macao) (cap.), Macau 77/H7
Macau 2/Q4
Macaúbas, Brazil 132/F6
Macaya (mt.), Haiti 158/A6
Macbeth, S.C. (†29431) 296/H5
Maccan, Nova Scotia 168/D3
Maccarese, Italy 34/F6
Macclenny, Fla. (32063) 212/D1
Maccles (lake), Newf. 166/C1
Macclesfield, England 10/G2
Macclesfield, England 13/H2
Macclesfield, N.C. (27852) 281/O3
Macdiarmid, Ontario 177/H5
MacDill A.F.B., Fla. 212/C3
Macdoel, Calif. (96058) 204/D2
Macdona, Texas (78054) 303/J11
Macdonald, Manitoba 179/D4
Macdonald (lake), North. Terr. 93/B7
Macdonald (lake), W. Australia 88/D4
Macdonald (lake), W. Australia 92/E3
Macdonaldton, Pa. (†15530) 294/E6
Macdonnell (ranges), Australia 87/D8
Macdonnell (ranges), North. Terr. 88/E4
Macdonnell (ranges), North. Terr. 93/C7
Macdowall, Sask. 181/E2
Macduff, Scotland 10/E2
Macduff, Scotland 15/F3
Mace, Ind. (†47933) 227/D4
Mace, W. Va. (†26281) 312/F6
Macedon, N.Y. (14502) 276/F4
Macedonia, Ark. (†71753) 202/D7
Macedonia, Conn. (†06757) 210/A2
Macedonia (reg.), Greece 45/E5
Macedonia, Ill. (62860) 222/E5
Macedonia, Iowa (51549) 229/C6
Macedonia, Ohio (44056) 284/J10
Macedonia (rep.), Yugoslavia 45/E5
Maceió, Brazil 120/F3
Maceió, Brazil 132/H5
Macel, Miss. (†38950) 256/D3
Macenta, Guinea 102/B4
Macenta, Guinea 106/C7
Maceo, Cuba 158/H3
Maceo, Ky. (42355) 237/H5
Macerata (prov.), Italy 34/D3
Macerata, Italy 34/D3
Maces (bay), New Bruns. 170/D3
Maces Bay, New Bruns. 170/D3
Macfarlan, W. Va. (26148) 312/D4
Macfarlane (lake), S. Australia 88/F6
Macfarlane (lake), S. Australia 94/E5
Macgillicuddy's Reeks (mts.), Ireland 17/B7
MacGregor, Manitoba 179/D5
MacGregor's Bay, Ontario 177/G2
Mach, Pakistan 59/J4
Mach, Pakistan 68/B3
Macha, Bolivia 136/B6
Machacamarca, Bolivia 136/B5
Machachi, Ecuador 128/C3
Machado, Brazil 135/C2
Machakos, Kenya 115/G4
Machala, Ecuador 120/B3
Machala, Ecuador 128/B4
Machalí, Chile 138/G5
Machalilla, Ecuador 128/B3
Machaneng, Botswana 118/D4
Machanga, Mozambique 118/F4
Machareti, Bolivia 136/D7
Machattie (lake), Queensland 88/G5
Machattie (lake), Queensland 95/B5
Machaze, Mozambique 118/E4
Machelen, Belgium 27/C9
Macheng, China 77/J5
Machers, The (pen.), Scotland 15/D6
Machias, Maine (04654) 243/J6
Machias○, Maine (04654) 243/J6
Machias (bay), Maine 243/J6
Machias (riv.), Maine 243/H6
Machias (riv.), Maine 243/F2
Machias-Lime Lake, N.Y. (14101) 276/D6
Machiasport, Maine (04655) 243/H6
Machiasport○, Maine (04655) 243/H6
Machias Seal (isl.), Maine 243/J7
Machico, Portugal 33/A2
Machida, Japan 81/O2
Machilipatnam, India 68/E5
Machipongo, Va. (23405) 307/S6
Machiques, Venezuela 124/B3
Macho, Arroyo del (creek), N. Mex. 274/D5
Machrihanish, Scotland 15/C5
Machupicchu, Peru 128/F9
Machupo (riv.), Bolivia 136/C3
Machynlleth, Wales 13/D5
Machynlleth, Wales 10/D4
Macia, Mozambique 118/E4
Maciel, Argentina 143/F6
Maciel, Paraguay 144/D5
Maciel, Arroyo (riv.), Uruguay 145/C4
Macina (depr.), Mali 106/D6
Macintyre (riv.), N. S. Wales 88/J5
Macintyre (riv.), N.S. Wales 97/E1
Macintyre (riv.), Queensland 95/D6
Mack, Colo. (81525) 208/B4
Mack, Ohio (†45202) 284/B9
MacKay, Alberta 182/C3
MacKay (riv.), Alberta 182/D1
Mackay, Australia 87/F8
Mackay (lake), Australia 87/D8
Mackay, Idaho (83251) 220/E6
Mackay (res.), Idaho 220/E6
Mackay (lake), North. Terr. 88/D4
Mackay (lake), North. Terr. 93/A7
MacKay (lake), N.W. Terrs. 187/G3
Mackay, Queensland 88/H4
Mackay, Queensland 95/D4
Mackay (lake), W. Australia 92/E3
Mackenzie, Guyana 131/B3
Mackenzie, Br. Col. 184/F2
Mackenzie, Br. Col. 184/F2
Mackenzie (bay), Canada 4/B16
Mackenzie (mts.), Canada 4/C16
Mackenzie (mts.), Canada 146/E3
Mackenzie (riv.), Canada 2/C2
Mackenzie (riv.), Canada 4/C16
Mackenzie, Mo. (†63101) 261/P3
Mackenzie (dist.), N.W.T. 162/E3
Mackenzie (bay), N.W. Terrs. 187/E3
Mackenzie (mts.), N.W. Terrs. 187/E3
Mackenzie (riv.), N.W.T. 162/C2
Mackenzie (riv.), N.W.T. 146/F3
Mackenzie (riv.), N.W. Terrs. 187/F3
Mackenzie (bay), Yukon 162/C2
Mackenzie (bay), Yukon 187/E3
Mackenzie (mts.), Yukon 187/E3
Mackenzie King (isl.), Canada 4/B15
Mackenzie King (isl.), N.W.T. 162/M3
Mackenzie King (isl.), N.W. Terrs. 187/G2
Mackey, Ind. (47654) 227/C8
Mackeys, N.C. (†27970) 281/R3
Mackeyville, Pa. (17750) 294/H3
Mackinac (co.), Mich. 250/D2
Mackinac (isl.), Mich. 250/E3
Mackinac (str.), Mich. 250/E3
Mackinac Island, Mich. (49757) 250/E3
Mackinaw, Ill. (61755) 222/D3
Mackinaw (riv.), Ill. 222/E3
Mackinaw City, Mich. (49701) 250/E3
Macklin, Sask. 181/A3
Macks, Ark. (72113) 202/H2
Macksburg, Iowa (50155) 229/E6
Macksburg, Ohio (45746) 284/G6
Macks Creek, Mo. (65786) 261/G7
Macks Inn, Idaho (83433) 220/G5
Macksville, Kansas (67557) 232/D4
Macksville, N.S. Wales 97/G2
Mackville, Ky. (40040) 237/L5
Maclean, N.S. Wales 97/G1
Maclean (str.), N.W. Terrs. 187/H2
Maclear, S. Africa 118/D6
Maclear (cape), S. Africa 118/F7
Macmillan (pass), N.W. Terrs. 187/F3
Macmillan (pass), Yukon 187/F3
Macmillan (riv.), Yukon 187/E3
Macnean (lake), Ireland 17/F3
Macnean (lake), N. Ireland 17/F3
MacNutt, Sask. 181/K4
Macomb, Ill. (61455) 222/C3
Macomb (co.), Mich. 250/G6
Macomb, Okla. (74852) 288/M4
Macomer, Italy 34/B4
Macomia, Mozambique 118/F2
Macon (co.), Ala. 195/G6
Mâcon, France 28/F4
Macon, Ga. 188/K4
Macon, Ga. 146/K6
Macon (co.), Georgia 217/D6
Macon, Georgia (*31201) 217/E5
Macon (co.), Ill. 222/E4
Macon, Ill. (62544) 222/E4
Macon (bayou), La. 238/H1
Macon, Miss. (39341) 256/G4
Macon (co.), Mo. 261/G3
Macon, Mo. (63552) 261/H3
Macon, Nebr. (†68939) 264/E4
Macon (co.), N.C. 281/B4
Macon, N.C. (27551) 281/N2
Macon, Ohio (†45171) 284/C8
Macon (co.), Tenn. 237/J7
Macon, Tenn. (38048) 237/B10
Macondo, Angola 115/D6
Macorís (cape), Dom. Rep. 158/E5
Macosquin, N. Ireland 17/H1
Macotera, Spain 33/D2
Macouba, Martinique 161/C5
Macoun, Sask. 181/H6
Macoupin (co.), Ill. 222/D4
Macoupin (riv.), Ill. 222/C4
Macouria, Fr. Guiana 131/E3
Macquarie (riv.), N. S. Wales 88/H6
Macquarie (lake), N.S. Wales 97/F3
Macquarie (riv.), N.S. Wales 97/D2
Macquarie (harb.), Tasmania 88/G8
Macquarie (harb.), Tasmania 99/B4
Macquarie (riv.), Tasmania 99/D3
Mac-Robertson Land (reg.) 5/B4
Macroom, Ireland 10/B5
Macroom, Ireland 17/C8
Macrorie, Sask. 181/E4
Mactan (isl.), Philippines 82/E5
Mactaquac (lake), New Bruns. 170/C3
MacTier, Ontario 177/E2
Macumba (riv.), S. Australia 88/F5
Macumba, The (riv.), S. Australia 94/E2
Macungie, Pa. (18062) 294/L4
Macurijes (pt.), Cuba 158/F3
Macuro, Venezuela 124/H2
Macusani, Peru 128/G10
Macuspana, Mexico 150/N8
Macuto, Venezuela 124/E2
Macwahoc○, Maine (†04451) 243/G4
Macy, Ind. (46951) 227/E3
Macy, Nebr. (68039) 264/H2
Mad (riv.), Calif. 204/B3
Mad (riv.), Conn. 210/C2
Mad (riv.), Conn. 210/C1
Mad (riv.), N.H. 268/D4
Mad (riv.), Ohio 284/C6
Mad (riv.), Vt. 268/B3
Ma'daba, Jordan 65/D4
Madadi, Chad 111/D4
Madagascal (pond), Maine 243/G5
Madagascar 2/M6
Madagascar 102/G7
MADAGASCAR 118/H3
Madaket, Mass. (†02554) 249/O7
Madama, Niger 106/G4
Madame (isl.), Nova Scotia 168/H3
Madang, Papua N.G. 85/B6
Madang, Papua N.G. 87/E6
Madaoua, Niger 106/F6
Madaras, Hungary 41/E3
Madaripur, Bangladesh 68/G4
Madauk, Burma 72/C3
Madawaska, Maine (04756) 243/G1
Madawaska○, Maine (04756) 243/G1
Madawaska (co.), New Bruns. 170/B1
Madawaska (riv.), New Bruns. 170/B1
Madawaska, Ontario 177/F2
Madawaska (riv.), Ontario 177/G2
Madawaska (riv.), Québec 172/J2
Madbury○, N.H. (†03820) 268/F5
Maddela, Philippines 82/C2
Madden, Alberta 182/C4
Madden, Miss. (39109) 256/F5
Maddock, N. Dak. (58348) 282/L4
Maddy, Loch (inlet), Scotland 15/A3
Madeira (riv.), Brazil 2/F6
Madeira (riv.), Brazil 120/C3
Madeira (riv.), Brazil 132/A4
Madeira, Ohio (45243) 284/C9
Madeira (isl.), Portugal 33/A2
Madeira (isl.), Portugal 106/A2
Madeira (isls.), Portugal 2/H4
Madeira (isls.), Portugal 102/A1
Madeira (isls.), Portugal 33/A2
Madeira (isls.), Portugal 106/A2
Madeira Beach, Fla. (33738) 212/B3
Madeira Park, Br. Col. 184/J2
Madeleine (cape), Québec 172/D1
Madelia, Minn. (56062) 255/D6
Madeline, Calif. (96119) 204/E2
Madeline (isl.), Wis. 317/E2
Maden, Turkey 63/H3
Madera (co.), Calif. 204/F6
Madera, Calif. (93637) 204/E7
Madera, Mexico 150/E2
Madera, Pa. (16661) 294/F4
Madera Canyon, Ariz. (†85637) 198/E7
Madh, India 68/B7
Madhubani, India 68/F3
Madhya Pradesh (state), India 68/D4
Madidi (riv.), Bolivia 136/A3
Madill, Okla. (73446) 288/N6
Madinat ash Sha'b, P.D.R. Yemen 59/E7
Madinat el-Thawra, Syria 63/H5
Madingo-Kayes, Congo 115/B4
Madingou, Congo 115/B4
Madirovalo, Madagascar 118/H3
Madison (co.), Ala. 195/E1
Madison, Ala. (35758) 195/E1
Madison (co.), Ark. 202/C1
Madison, Ark. (72359) 202/J4
Madison, Calif. (95653) 204/D5
Madison, Conn. (06443) 210/E3
Madison○, Conn. (06443) 210/E3
Madison (co.), Fla. 212/C1
Madison, Fla. (32340) 212/C1
Madison (co.), Georgia 217/F2
Madison, Georgia (30650) 217/F3
Madison (co.), Idaho 220/G6
Madison (co.), Ill. 222/D5
Madison, Ill. (62060) 222/A2
Madison (co.), Ind. 227/F4
Madison, Ind. (47250) 227/G7
Madison (co.), Iowa 229/E6
Madison, Kansas (66860) 232/F3
Madison (co.), Ky. 237/N5
Madison (par.), La. 238/H2
Madison, Maine (04950) 243/D6
Madison○, Maine (04950) 243/D6
Madison, Md. (21648) 245/O6
Madison, Minn. (56256) 255/B5
Madison (co.), Miss. 256/D5
Madison, Miss. (39110) 256/D6
Madison (co.), Mo. 261/M8
Madison, Mo. (65263) 261/H4
Madison (co.), Mont. 262/D5
Madison (riv.), Mont. 262/E5
Madison (co.), Nebr. 264/G3
Madison, Nebr. (68748) 264/G3
Madison○, N.H. (03849) 268/E4
Madison (mt.), N.H. 268/E3
Madison, N.J. (07940) 273/E2
Madison (co.), N.Y. 276/J5
Madison, N.Y. (13402) 276/J5
Madison (co.), N.C. 281/D3
Madison, N.C. (27025) 281/J2
Madison (co.), Ohio 284/D6
Madison, Ohio (44057) 284/H2
Madison, Sask. 181/B4
Madison, S.C. (29693) 296/A2
Madison, S.C. (†29829) 296/D4
Madison, S. Dak. (57042) 298/P6
Madison (lake), S. Dak. 298/P6
Madison (co.), Tenn. 237/D9
Madison (co.), Texas 303/J6
Madison (co.), Va. 307/M4
Madison, Va. (22727) 307/M4
Madison, W. Va. (25130) 312/C6
Madison (cap.), Wis. 146/K5
Madison (cap.), Wis. 188/H2
Madison (cap.), Wis. (*53701) 317/H9
Madison, Wyo. (†82190) 319/B1
Madison (plat.), Wyo. 319/B1
Madisonburg, Ohio (†44691) 284/G4
Madison Heights, Mich. (48071) 250/B6
Madison Heights, Va. (24572) 307/K6
Madison Lake, Minn. (56063) 255/E6
Madisonville, Ky. (42431) 237/F6
Madisonville, La. (70447) 238/K6
Madisonville, Tenn. (37354) 237/N9
Madisonville, Texas (77864) 303/J7
Madiun, Indonesia 85/K2
Madley (mt.), W. Australia 92/C4
Madoc, Mont. (†59222) 262/L2
Madoc, Ontario 177/G3
Mado Gashi, Kenya 115/G3
Madoi, China 77/E4
Madona, U.S.S.R. 53/C2
Madona, U.S.S.R. 52/C3
Madonna, Md. (†21161) 245/M2
Madraka, Ras (cape), Oman 59/G6
Madran, New Bruns. 170/E1
Madras, India 68/E6
Madras, India 54/K8
Madras, India 2/P5
Madras, Oreg. (97741) 291/F3
Madre (lag.), Mexico 150/L4
Madre (lag.), Texas 188/G5
Madre (lag.), Texas 303/G11
Madre de Dios (riv.) 120/C4
Madre de Diós (riv.), Bolivia 136/A3
Madre de Dios (isl.), Chile 120/B8
Madre de Dios (isl.), Chile 138/D8
Madre de Dios (dept.), Peru 128/G8
Madre de Dios, Peru 128/G9
Madre de Dios (riv.), Peru 128/G9
Madre del Sur, Sierra (mts.), Mexico 150/K8
Madre Occidental, Sierra (mts.), Mexico 150/F3
Madre Oriental, Sierra (mts.), Mexico 150/J4
Madrid, Ala. (36348) 195/H8
Madrid, Iowa (50156) 229/F5
Madrid○, Maine (†04966) 243/B6
Madrid, Nebr. (69150) 264/C4
Madrid, N. Mex. (†87010) 274/C3
Madrid, N.Y. (13660) 276/K1
Madrid (prov.), Spain 33/E2
Madrid (cap.), Spain 7/D4
Madrid (cap.), Spain 33/F4
Madrid (cap.), Spain 2/J4
Madridejos, Spain 33/E3
Madrigal de las Altas Torres, Spain 33/D2
Madrigalejo, Spain 33/D3
Madrisahorn (mt.), Switzerland 39/J3
Madroñera, Spain 33/D3
Madsen, Ontario 175/B2
Madugula, India 68/E5
Madura (isl.), Indonesia 54/N10
Madura (isl.), Indonesia 85/K2
Madura (str.), Indonesia 85/K2
Madura, W. Australia 92/D5
Madurai, India 54/J9
Madurai, India 68/D7
Madvar, Kuh-e (mt.), Iran 59/F3
Madvar, Kuh-e (mt.), Iran 66/F3
Maebashi, Japan 81/J5
Mae Hong Son, Thailand 72/C3
Mae Klong, Mae Nam (riv.), Thailand 72/C4
Mael, Norway 18/F6
Maella, Spain 33/G2
Maeser, Utah (†84078) 304/E3
Maesteg, Wales 13/D6
Maestra, Sierra (mts.), Cuba 158/H4
Maevatanana, Madagascar 118/H3
Maeystown, Ill. (62256) 222/C5
Mafeking, Manitoba 179/B2
Mafeking (Mafikeng), S. Africa 118/C5
Mafeteng, Lesotho 118/D5
Maffin (bay), Indonesia 85/K6
Maffra, Victoria 97/D5
Mafia (isl.), Tanzania 102/G5
Mafia (isl.), Tanzania 115/H5
Mafikeng (Mafeking), S. Africa 118/C5
Mafra, Brazil 132/D9
Mafra, Portugal 33/B3
Magadan, U.S.S.R. 2/S3
Magadan, U.S.S.R. 54/R4
Magadan, U.S.S.R. 48/P4
Magadi, Kenya 115/G4
Magadino, Switzerland 39/G4
Magaguadavic, New Bruns. 170/C3
Magaguadavic (lake), New Bruns. 170/C3
Magaguadavic (riv.), New Bruns. 170/C3

404 Magalia

Magalia, Calif. (95954) 204/D4
Magaliesburg, S. Africa 118/G6
Magallanes (reg.), Chile 138/E10
Magallanes (Magellan) (str.), Chile 138/D10
Magallanes, Philippines 82/D4
Magallenes (Magellan) (str.), Argentina 143/C7
Magangué, Colombia 126/C3
Maganoy, Philippines 82/E7
Mağara, Turkey 63/G3
Magarabomba, Cuba 158/G2
Magaria, Niger 106/F6
Magazine, Ark. (72943) 202/C3
Magazine (mt.), Ark. 202/C3
Magdagachi, U.S.S.R. 48/N4
Magdala, Ethiopia 111/G5
Magdalen (isls.), Que. 162/K6
Magdalena, Argentina 143/H7
Magdalena, Bolivia 136/C3
Magdalena (isl.), Chile 138/D5
Magdalena (dept.), Colombia 126/C3
Magdalena (riv.), Colombia 120/B2
Magdalena (riv.), Colombia 126/C3
Magdalena (bay), Mexico 150/C4
Magdalena, N. Mex. (87825) 274/B4
Magdalena (mts.), N. Mex. 274/B4
Magdalena de Kino, Mexico 150/D1
Magdeburg, E. Germany 7/F3
Magdeburg (dist.), E. Germany 22/D2
Magdeburg, E. Germany 22/D2
Magdelaine (cays), Coral Sea Is. Terr. 88/H3
Magé, Brazil 135/E3
Magee, Miss. (39111) 256/E7
Magee, Island (pen.), N. Ireland 17/K2
Magelang, Indonesia 85/J2
Magellan (str.) 120/C8
Magellan (str.) 2/F8
Magellan (str.), Argentina 143/C7
Magellan (str.), Chile 138/D10
Magen, Israel 65/A5
Magens (bay), Virgin Is. (U.S.) 161/B4
Magerøya (isl.), Norway 18/P1
Magerrain (mt.), Switzerland 39/H2
Magetan, Indonesia 85/K2
Maggia, Switzerland 39/G4
Maggia (riv.), Switzerland 39/G4
Maggie Valley, N.C. (28751) 281/C3
Maggiore (lake), Fla. 212/B3
Maggiore (lake), Italy 34/B1
Maggiore (lake), Switzerland 39/G5
Maggotty, Jamaica 158/H6
Maghâgha, Egypt 59/B4
Maghâgha, Egypt 111/J4
Maghama, Mauritania 102/A3
Maghama, Mauritania 106/B5
Maghera, N. Ireland 17/H2
Magherafelt (dist.), N. Ireland 17/H2
Magherafelt, N. Ireland 10/C3
Magherafelt, N. Ireland 17/H2
Magic (res.), Idaho 220/D6
Magilligan (pt.), N. Ireland 17/H1
Maglaj, Yugoslavia 45/D3
Magley, Ind. (†46733) 227/G3
Maglie, Italy 34/G4
Magna, Utah (84044) 304/B3
Magna Bay, Br. Col. 184/H4
Magness, Ark. (72553) 202/H2
Magnet, Ark. (†72104) 202/E5
Magnet, Ind. (47555) 227/D8
Magnet, Manitoba 179/C3
Magnet, Nebr. (68749) 264/G2
Magnetawan, Ontario 177/E2
Magnetawan (riv.), Ontario 177/D2
Magnetic Springs, Ohio (43036) 284/D5
Magnitogorsk, U.S.S.R. 54/H4
Magnitogorsk, U.S.S.R. 48/G4
Magnolia, Ala. (36754) 195/C6
Magnolia, Ark. (71753) 202/D7
Magnolia, Del. (19962) 245/R4
Magnolia, Ill. (61336) 222/D2
Magnolia, Iowa (51550) 229/B5
Magnolia, Minn. (56158) 255/B7
Magnolia, Miss. (39652) 256/D8
Magnolia, N.J. (08049) 273/B3
Magnolia, N.C. (28453) 281/O5
Magnolia, Ohio (44643) 284/H4
Magnolia, Texas (77355) 303/J7
Magnolia, W. Va. (†25422) 312/K3
Magnolia Springs, Ala. (36555) 195/C10
Màgoé, Mozambique 118/E3
Magoffin (co.), Ky. 237/P5
Magog, Québec 172/E4
Magpie, Québec 174/E2
Magpie (lake), Québec 174/E2
Magrath, Alberta 182/D5
Magude, Mozambique 118/E5
Maguindanao (prov.), Philippines 82/E7
Maguse (lake), N.W. Terrs. 187/J3
Magwe (div.), Burma 72/B2
Magwe, Burma 72/B2
Mahabad, Iran 59/E2
Mahabad, Iran 66/D2
Mahabaleshwar, India 68/C5
Mahabo, Madagascar 118/G4
Mahaena, Fr. Poly. 86/T13
Mahaffey, Pa. (15757) 294/E4
Mahagi, Zaire 115/F3
Mahaica, Guyana 131/C2
Mahaicony Village, Guyana 131/C2
Mahajamba (bay), Madagascar 118/H2
Mahajanga (prov.), Madagascar 118/H3
Mahajanga, Madagascar 102/G6
Mahakam (riv.), Indonesia 85/F6
Mahalapye, Botswana 118/D4
Mahalapye, Botswana 102/E7
Mahalasville, Ind. (†46151) 227/E6
Mahallat, Iran 66/G4
Mahan, Iran 66/K5
Mahanadi (riv.), India 68/E4
Mahanoro, Madagascar 118/H3
Mahanoy City, Pa. (17948) 294/K4
Maharashtra (state), India 68/C5
Maha Sarakham, Thailand 72/D3
Mahaska (co.), Iowa 229/H6
Mahaska, Kansas (66955) 232/E2
Mahaxai, Laos 72/E3
Mahbubnagar, India 68/D5
Mahdia, Guyana 131/B3
Mahdia, Tunisia 106/G1
Mahe, India 68/D6
Mahé (isl.), Seychelles 118/H5
Mahébourg, Mauritius 118/G5
Mahenge, Tanzania 115/G5
Maheno, N. Zealand 100/C6
Maher, Colo. (81421) 208/D5
Maheshkhali, Bangladesh 68/G4
Mahia (pen.), N. Zealand 100/G3
Mahim, India 68/C5
Mahim (bay), India 68/B7
Mahkonce, Minn. (†56557) 255/C3
Mahlaing, Burma 72/B2
Mahmudiye, Turkey 63/D3
Mahnomen (co.), Minn. 255/C3
Mahnomen, Minn. (56557) 255/C3
Maho (bay), Virgin Is. (U.S.) 161/C4
Mahoba, India 68/D3
Mahomet, Ill. (61853) 222/E3
Mahón, Spain 33/J3
Mahone (bay), Nova Scotia 168/D4
Mahone Bay, Nova Scotia 168/D4
Mahoning (co.), Ohio 284/J4
Mahood (lake), Br. Col. 184/G4
Mahopac, N.Y. (10541) 276/N8
Mahout, Dominica 161/E6
Mahto, S. Dak. (57643) 298/H2
Mahtomedi, Minn. (55115) 255/F5
Mahtowa, Minn. (55762) 255/F4
Mahukona, Hawaii (†96719) 218/G3
Mahuva, India 68/C4
Mahwah○, N.J. (07430) 273/E1
Maia, Portugal 33/B2
Maicao, Colombia 126/D2
Maicuru (riv.), Brazil 132/C2
Maida, N. Dak. (58255) 282/O2
Maida, Yemen Arab Rep. 59/D6
Maidan, Iraq 66/D3
Maidan, Iraq 59/E3
Maidani, Ras (cape), Iran 59/G4
Maiden, N.C. (28650) 281/G3
Maidenhead, England 10/F5
Maidenhead, England 13/G8
Maiden Rock, Wis. (54750) 317/B6
Maidens, The (isls.), N. Ireland 17/K2
Maidens, Scotland 15/D5
Maidens, Va. (23102) 307/N5
Maidstone, England 13/J8
Maidstone, England 10/G5
Maidstone, Ontario 177/B5
Maidstone, Sask. 181/B2
Maidstone○, Vt. (†05905) 268/D2
Maidstone (lake), Vt. 268/D2
Maidsville, W. Va. (26541) 312/F3
Maiduguri, Nigeria 106/G6
Maiduguri, Nigeria 102/D3
Maienfeld, Switzerland 39/J2
Maigatari, Nigeria 106/F6
Maigualida, Sierra (range), Venezuela 124/F4
Maigue (riv.), Ireland 17/D6
Maihara, Japan 81/G6
Maili, Hawaii (†96792) 218/D2
Maillard, Québec 172/G2
Ma'in, Jordan 65/D4
Main (passage), La. 238/M8
Main (riv.), N. Ireland 17/J2
Main (chan.), Ontario 177/C2
Main (str.), Singapore 72/F6
Main (riv.), W. Germany 22/C4
Main-à-Dieu, Nova Scotia 168/J3
Main Barrier (range), N. S. Wales 88/G6
Main Barrier (range), N.S. Wales 97/A2
Main Brook, Newf. 166/C3
Main Centre, Sask. 181/D5
Mai-Ndombe (lake), Zaire 115/C4
Maine 188/N1
MAINE 243
Maine (gulf) 188/N2
Maine (gulf) 162/K7
Maine (trad. prov.), France, 29
Maine (riv.), Ireland 17/C7
Maine (gulf), Mass. 249/M2
Maine, N.Y. (13802) 276/H6
Maine (state), U.S. 146/M5
Maine-et-Loire (dept.), France 28/C4
Mainesburg, Pa. (16932) 294/J2
Mainé-Soroa, Niger 106/G6
Maineville, Ohio (45039) 284/C9
Maingard (lake), Québec 172/G1
Maingkwan, Burma 72/C1
Mainit, Philippines 82/E6
Mainit (lake), Philippines 82/E6
Mainland, Orkney Is. (isl.), Scotland 10/E1
Mainland, Shetland Is. (isl.), Scotland 10/G1
Mainland (isl.), Scotland 15/G2
Mainland (isl.), Scotland 15/E1
Mainling, China 77/D6
Mainoru, North. Terr. 93/C3
Mainstream, Maine (†04942) 243/D6
Maintirano, Madagascar 118/G3
Main Topsail (mt.), Newf. 166/C4
Mainz, W. Germany 22/C4
Maio (isl.), C. Verde 106/B8
Maipo (vol.), Argentina 143/C3
Maipo (riv.), Chile 138/F4
Maipú, Argentina 143/E4
Maipú, Chile 138/G3
Maipú (vol.), Chile 138/B10
Maipures, Colombia 126/F5
Maiquetía, Venezuela 120/C1
Maiquetía, Venezuela 124/E2
Mairana, Bolivia 136/D6
Maisí, Cuba 158/K4
Maisí (cape), Cuba 158/K4
Maisí (cape), Cuba 156/D2
Maison de Pierre (lake), Québec 172/C3
Maisonnette, New Bruns. 170/E1
Maisons-Alfort, France 28/B2
Maisons-Laffitte, France 28/A1
Maïssade, Haiti 158/C5
Maitencillo, Chile 138/A8
Maitland, Australia 87/F9
Maitland, Fla. (32751) 212/E3
Maitland, Mo. (64466) 261/B2
Maitland, N. S. Wales 88/J6
Maitland, N.S. Wales 97/F3
Maitland, Annapolis, Nova Scotia 168/C4
Maitland, Hants, Nova Scotia 168/E3
Maitland, Ontario 177/J3
Maitland, S. Australia 94/E6
Maitum, Philippines 82/E7
Maize, Kansas (67101) 232/E4
Maíz Grande (Great Corn) (isl.), Nicaragua 154/F4
Maizhokunggar, China 77/D6
Maíz Pequeña (Little Corn) (isl.), Nicaragua 154/F4
Maizuru, Japan 81/G6
Majagua, Cuba 158/F2
Majagual, Colombia 126/C3
Majalengka, Indonesia 85/H2
Majene, Indonesia 85/F6
Majenica, Ind. (†46750) 227/F3
Majes (riv.), Peru 128/F11
Majestic, Ky. (41547) 237/S5
Maji, Ethiopia 111/G6
Majma'a, Saudi Arabia 59/D4
Majoli, Suriname 131/D4
Major (co.), Okla. 288/K2
Major, Sask. 181/B4
Majorca (isl.), Spain 7/E5
Majorca (isl.), Spain 33/H3
Majorsville, W. Va. (†26036) 312/F3
Majunga, Madagascar 118/H3
Majuro (atoll) (cap.), Marshall Is. 87/H5
Makaha, Hawaii (†96792) 218/D2
Makaha (pt.), Hawaii 218/B1
Makah Ind. Res., Wash. 310/A2
Makahuena (pt.), Hawaii 218/C2
Makaiwa, Hawaii (†96763) 218/H2
Makakilo, Hawaii (96706) 218/E2
Makale, Ethiopia 102/F3
Makale, Ethiopia 111/G5
Makallé, Argentina 143/E2
Makanda, Ill. (62958) 222/D6
Makanza, Zaire 115/C3
Makapala, Hawaii (†96711) 218/G3
Makapuu (pt.), Hawaii 218/F2
Makara Beach, N. Zealand 100/A2
Makara-Ohariu, N. Zealand 100/A3
Makari, Cameroon 115/B1
Makaroff, Manitoba 179/A3
Makarov, U.S.S.R. 48/P5
Makarska, Yugoslavia 45/C4
Makar'yev, U.S.S.R. 52/F3
Makassar (Ujung Pandang), Indonesia 85/F7
Makassar (str.), Indonesia 54/N10
Makassar (str.), Indonesia 85/F6
Makatea (isl.), Fr. Poly. 87/L7
Makawao, Hawaii (96768) 218/K2
Makaweli, Hawaii (96769) 218/B2
Makena, Hawaii (†96790) 218/J2
Makeni, S. Leone 102/A4
Makeni, S. Leone 106/B7
Makepeace, Alberta 182/D4
Makeyevka, U.S.S.R. 7/H4
Makeyevka, U.S.S.R. 52/E5
Makgadikgadi (salt pan), Botswana 102/E7
Makgadikgadi (salt pan), Botswana 118/D3
Makhachkala, U.S.S.R. 7/J4
Makhachkala, U.S.S.R. 48/E5
Makhachkala, U.S.S.R. 52/G6
Makharadze, U.S.S.R. 52/F6
Makhmur, Iraq 66/C3
Makiki, Hawaii (96822) 218/C4
Makin (Butaritari) (atoll), Kiribati 87/H5
Makinak, Manitoba 179/C4
Makinen, Minn. (55763) 255/F3
Makinsk, U.S.S.R. 48/H4
Makinson (inlet), N.W. Terrs. 187/L2
Makkovik, Newf. 166/C2
Makkovik (cape), Newf. 166/C2
Makkum, Netherlands 27/G2
Makó, Hungary 41/F3
Makokou, Gabon 115/B3
Makoti, N. Dak. (58756) 282/G4
Makoua, Congo 115/C3
Maków Mazowiecki, Poland 47/E2
Makran (reg.), Iran 66/M8
Makteïr (des.), Mauritania 106/B4
Maku, Iran 66/D1
Makubetsu, Japan 81/L2
Makumbako, Tanzania 115/G5
Makurazaki, Japan 81/O3
Makurdi, Nigeria 102/C4
Makurdi, Nigeria 106/F7
Makushin (vol.), Alaska 196/E4
Makwa, Sask. 181/C2
Makwa (lake), Sask. 181/B1
Makwa (riv.), Sask. 181/B1
Mal, Mauritania 106/B5
Mala, Punta (cape), Panama 154/H7
Malå, Sweden 18/L4
Malabang, Philippines 82/D7
Malabar, Fla. (32950) 212/F3
Malabar (hill), India 68/B7
Malabar (pt.), India 68/B7
Malabar Coast (reg.), India 68/C6
Malabo (cap.), Equat. Guinea 102/C4
Malabo (cap.), Equat. Guinea 115/A3
Malabrigo, Argentina 143/F4
Mal Abrigo, Uruguay 145/C5
Malabungan, Philippines 82/A6
Malacca (str.) 54/M9
Malacca (str.), Indonesia 85/C5
Malacca (Melaka), Malaysia 72/D7
Malacca (str.), Malaysia 72/D7
Malacky, Czech. 41/D2
Malad (riv.), Idaho 220/F7
Malad, India 68/B6
Malad (creek), India 68/B7
Malad (riv.), Utah 304/B1
Malad City, Idaho (83252) 220/F7
Maladers, Switzerland 39/J3
Málaga, Colombia 126/D4
Malaga, N.J. (08328) 273/C4
Malaga, N. Mex. (88263) 274/E6
Malaga, Ohio (43757) 284/H6
Málaga (prov.), Spain 33/D4
Málaga, Spain 7/D5
Málaga, Spain 33/D4
Malaga, Wash. (98828) 310/E3
Malagash, Nova Scotia 168/E3
Malagash (pt.), Nova Scotia 168/E3
Malagón, Spain 33/E3
Malagueta (bay), Cuba 158/H3
Malahide, Ireland 17/J5
Malaita (isl.), 86/E3
Malaita (isl.), Solomon Is. 87/G6
Malakal, Sudan 111/F6
Malakal, Sudan 102/F4
Malakanagiri, India 68/E5
Malakand, Pakistan 68/C2
Malakand, Pakistan 59/K3
Malakoff, France 28/A2
Malakoff, Texas (75148) 303/H5
Malakwa, Br. Col. 184/H5
Malalag, Philippines 82/E7
Malamir (Izeh), Iran 66/F5
Malang, Indonesia 54/N10
Malang, Indonesia 85/K2
Malange (dist.), Angola 115/C6
Malange, Angola 102/D5
Malange, Angola 115/C5
Malangka (cape), Indonesia 85/G5
Malans, Switzerland 39/J3
Malanville, Benin 106/E6
Mälaren (lake), Sweden 18/G1
Malargüe, Argentina 120/C6
Malargüe, Argentina 143/C4
Malartic, Québec 174/B3
Malaspina (glac.), Alaska 196/K3
Malaspina (str.), Br. Col. 184/J2
Malatya (prov.), Turkey 63/H3
Malatya, Turkey 59/C2
Malatya, Turkey 54/E6
Malatya, Turkey 63/H3
Malawi 2/L6
Malawi 102/F6
MALAWI 115/F6
Malawi (Nyasa) (lake), Malawi 115/F6
Malay (pen.), Malaysia 72/D6
Malay (pen.), Malaysia 85/B4
Malay (pen.), Thailand 72/D6
MALAYA, MALAYSIA 72
Malaya (reg.), Malaysia 54/M9
Malaya (reg.), Malaysia 72/E6
Malaya Vishera, U.S.S.R. 52/D3
Malaybalay, Philippines 82/E6
Malayer, Iran 66/F3
Malaysia 2/Q5
Malaysia 54/M9
MALAYSIA 85/D4
Malazgirt, Turkey 63/K3
Malbaie (riv.), Québec 172/G2
Malbon, Queensland 95/B4
Malbork (Marienburg), Poland 47/D1
Malchinersee (lake), E. Germany 22/E2
Malchow, E. Germany 22/E2
Malcolm, Ala. (36556) 195/B8
Malcolm, Nebr. (68402) 264/H4
Malcom, Iowa (50157) 229/H5
Maldegem, Belgium 27/C6
Malden, Ill. (61337) 222/D2
Malden, Ind. (†46383) 227/C2
Malden (isl.), Kiribati 87/L6
Malden, Mass. (02148) 249/D6
Malden, Mo. (63863) 261/M9
Malden, New Bruns. 170/G2
Malden, Wash. (99149) 310/H3
Malden, W. Va. (25306) 312/C6
Maldives 2/N5
MALDIVES 68
Maldives 54/J9
Maldives (isls.) 68/C7
Maldon, England 10/G5
Maldon, England 13/H8
Maldon, Victoria 97/C5
Maldonado (pt.), Mexico 150/K8
Maldonado (dept.), Uruguay 145/E5
Maldonado, Uruguay 145/D6
Male (cap.), Maldives 54/J9
Male (cap.), Maldives 2/N5
Maléa (cape), Greece 45/F7
Malebo (Stanley Pool) (lake), Zaire 115/C4
Malegaon, India 54/J7
Malegaon, India 68/C4
Malekula (isl.), Vanuatu 87/G7
Malema, Mozambique 118/F2
Malemba-Nkulu, Zaire 115/E5
Malente, W. Germany 22/D1
Maler Kotla, India 68/D2
Malesus, Tenn. (†38301) 237/D9
Malgobek, U.S.S.R. 52/F6
Malhão da Estrela (mt.), Portugal 33/C2
Malheur (lake), Oreg. 188/C2
Malheur (co.), Oreg. 291/K4
Malheur (lake), Oreg. 291/J4
Malheur (riv.), Oreg. 291/J4
Mali 2/J5
Mali 102/B2
Mali (riv.), Burma 72/C1
Mali, Guinea 106/B6
MALI 106/D5
Malibu, Calif. (90265) 204/B10
Malignant Cove, Nova Scotia 168/F3
Maligne (lake), Alberta 182/B3
Mali Kyun (isl.), Burma 72/C4
Malili, Indonesia 85/G6
Malin, Ireland 17/G1
Malin (head), Ireland 17/F1
Malin (head), Ireland 10/C3
Malin, Oreg. (97632) 291/F5
Malin, U.S.S.R. 52/C4
Malinau, Indonesia 85/F5
Malindang (mt.), Philippines 82/D6
Malindi, Kenya 102/B2
Malindi, Kenya 115/H4
Malines (Mechelen), Belgium 27/F6
Malinta, Ohio (43535) 284/B3
Malita, Philippines 82/E7
Maliwun, Burma 72/C5
Malkapur, India 68/D4
Malkara, Turkey 63/B2
Malkiya, Israel 65/D1
Malko Tŭrnovo, Bulgaria 45/H4
Mallacoota, Victoria 97/E5
Mallaig, Alberta 182/E2
Mallaig, Scotland 10/D2
Mallaig, Scotland 15/C4
Mallanganee, N.S. Wales 97/G1
Mallard, Iowa (50562) 229/D3
Mallawi, Egypt 111/J4
Mallawi, Egypt 59/B4
Mallén, Spain 33/F2
Malleray, Switzerland 39/D2
Mallet Creek, Ohio (†44256) 284/G3
Malling, Denmark 21/D5
Mallnitz, Austria 41/B3
Malloa, Chile 138/G5
Malloch (cape), N.W. Terrs. 187/H2
Mallorca (Majorca) (isl.), Spain 33/H3
Mallory, N.Y. (13103) 276/H4
Mallory, W. Va. (25634) 312/C7
Mallorytown, Ontario 177/J3
Mallow, Ireland 17/D7
Mallow, Ireland 10/B4
Malmanoury, Fr. Guiana 131/E3
Malmberget, Sweden 18/M3
Malmédy, Belgium 27/J8
Malmesbury, England 13/E6
Malmesbury, S. Africa 118/B6
Malmköping, Sweden 18/F1
Malmo, Minn. (†56431) 255/E4
Malmo, Nebr. (68040) 264/H3
Malmö, Sweden 7/F3
Malmö, Sweden 18/H9
Malmöhus (co.), Sweden 18/H9
Malmok (mt.), Neth. Ant. 161/E8
Malmstrom A.F.B., Mont. 262/E3
Malo, Wash. (99150) 310/G2
Maloca, Brazil 132/C4
Maloca, Brazil 120/D3
Maloelap (atoll), Marshall Is. 87/H5
Malolos, Philippines 82/C3
Malone, Fla. (32445) 212/A1
Malone, Ky. (41451) 237/P5
Malone, N.Y. (12953) 276/M1
Malone, Texas (76660) 303/H6
Malone, Wash. (98559) 310/B4
Maloneton, Ky. (41158) 237/R3
Maloney (res.), Nebr. 264/D3
Malonton, Manitoba 179/E4
Malott, Wash. (98829) 310/F2
Maloy, Iowa (50852) 229/F7
Malpartida de Cáceres, Spain 33/C3
Malpartida de Plasencia, Spain 33/C2
Malpelo (isl.), Colombia 120/A2
Malpeque (bay), Pr. Edward I. 168/E2
Malta 2/K4
Malta 7/F5
Malta, Colo. (†80461) 208/G4
Malta, Idaho (83342) 220/E7
Malta, Ill. (60150) 222/E2
Malta (chan.), Italy 34/E6
MALTA 34
Malta (isl.), Malta 34/E7
Malta, Mont. (59538) 262/J2
Malta, Ohio (43758) 284/G6
Malta Bend, Mo. (65339) 261/F4
Maltahöhe, Namibia 118/B4
Maltepe, Turkey 63/D6
Malters, Switzerland 39/F2
Malton, England 13/G3
Malton, England 10/F3
Maltrata, Mexico 150/O2
Malung, Sweden 18/H6
Malvaglia, Switzerland 39/H4
Malvan, India 68/C5
Malvern, Ala. (36349) 195/G8
Malvern, Ark. (72104) 202/E5
Malvern, England 13/E5
Malvern, England 10/E4
Malvern, Iowa (51551) 229/B7
Malvern, Jamaica 158/H6
Malvern, Ohio (44644) 284/H4
Malvern, Pa. (19355) 294/L5
Malvern, Victoria 88/L7
Malvern, Victoria 97/J5
Malverne, N.Y. (11565) 276/R7
Malvina, Miss. (†38769) 256/C3
Malvinas (Falkland) (isls.), 143/D7
Malyye Karmakuly, U.S.S.R. 52/H1
Mama, U.S.S.R. 48/M4
Mamala (bay), Hawaii 218/B4
Mamalu (bay), Hawaii 218/K3
Mamanguape, Brazil 132/H4
Mamaroneck, N.Y. (10543) 276/P7
Mambahenauhan (isl.), Philippines 82/B7
Mambajao, Philippines 82/E6
Mambasa, Zaire 115/E3
Mamberamo (riv.), Indonesia 85/K6
Mambrui, Kenya 115/H4
Mamburao, Philippines 82/C4
Ma-Me-O Beach, Alberta 182/D3
Mamer, Luxembourg 27/H9
Mamers, France 28/D3
Mamers, N.C. (27552) 281/L4
Mamfé, Cameroon 115/A2
Mamie, N.C. (27952) 281/T2
Mamiña, Chile 138/B2
Mammoth, Ariz. (85618) 198/E6
Mammoth, Utah (†84628) 304/B4
Mammoth (creek), Utah 304/B6
Mammoth, W. Va. (25132) 312/D6
Mammoth Cave Nat'l Park, Ky. 237/J6
Mammoth Hot Springs (Yellowstone Nat'l Park), Wyo. (†82190) 319/B1
Mammoth Lakes, Calif. (93546) 204/G6
Mammoth Spring, Ark. (72554) 202/G1
Mamoré (riv.), Bolivia 120/C4
Mamoré (riv.), Bolivia 136/C2
Mamou, Guinea 106/B6
Mamou, La. (70554) 238/F5
Mampong, Ghana 106/D7
Mamry, Jezioro (lake), Poland 47/E1
Mamuju, Indonesia 85/F6
Man (isl.), I. of Man 13/C3
Man, Ivory Coast 106/C7
Man, Ivory Coast 102/B4
Man, W. Va. (25635) 312/C7
Mana, Fr. Guiana 131/E3
Mana (riv.), Fr. Guiana 131/E3
Mana (isl.), N. Zealand 100/B2
Manabí (prov.), Ecuador 128/B3
Manacacías (riv.), Colombia 126/D6
Manacapuru, Brazil 120/C3
Manacapuru, Brazil 132/H9
Manacas, Cuba 158/E1
Manacle (pt.), England 13/C7
Manacor, Spain 33/H3
Manado, Indonesia 54/O9
Manado, Indonesia 85/G5
Manage, Belgium 27/E7
Managua (cap.), Nic. 146/K8
Managua (cap.), Nicaragua 154/D4
Managua (lake), Nicaragua 154/E4
Manah, Oman 59/G5
Manahawkin, N.J. (08050) 273/E4
Manaia, N. Zealand 100/E3
Manakara, Madagascar 118/H4
Manakara, Madagascar 102/G7
Manakha, Yemen Arab Rep. 59/D6
Manakin-Sabot, Va. (23103) 307/N5
Manalapan, N.J. (†07746) 273/E3
Manama (cap.), Bahrain 59/F4
Manana (isl.), Hawaii 218/F2
Mananara, Madagascar 118/J3
Mananara (riv.), Madagascar 118/H4
Mananbao (riv.), Madagascar 118/G3
Mananjary, Madagascar 118/H4
Mananjary, Madagascar 102/G7
Manannah, Minn. (†56243) 255/D5
Manapire (riv.), Venezuela 124/E3
Manapouri (lake), N. Zealand 100/A6
Manaqil, Sudan 59/B7
Manar, Jebel (mt.), Yemen Arab Rep. 59/D7
Manare, Colombia 126/E4
Manas, China 77/C3
Manas He (riv.), China 77/C3
Manas Hu (lake), China 77/C2
Manasquan, N.J. (08736) 273/E3
Manasquan (riv.), N.J. 273/E3
Manassa, Colo. (81141) 208/H8
Manassas, Georgia (30438) 217/H6
Manassas (I.C.), Va. (22110) 307/O3
Manassas Nat'l Battlefield Park, Va. 307/K3
Manassas Park (I.C.), Va. (22110) 307/O3
Manatee (co.), Fla. 212/D4
Manatee (riv.), Fla. 212/D4
Manatí, Cuba 158/H3
Manatí, P. Rico 156/G1
Manatí, P. Rico 161/C1
Manaus, Brazil 2/F6
Manaus, Brazil 120/D3
Manaus, Brazil 132/H9
Manavgat, Turkey 63/D4
Manawa, Wis. (54949) 317/J7
Manay, Philippines 82/F7
Mancelona, Mich. (49659) 250/E4
Mancha, La (reg.), Spain 33/E3
Manchac (passage), La. 238/N2
Manchaca, Texas (78652) 303/G7
Mancha Real, Spain 33/E4
Manchaug, Mass. (01526) 249/G4
Manche (dept.), France 28/C3
Manche, La (English) (chan.), France 28/B3
Manchester, Ala. (†35501) 195/D3
Manchester, Calif. (95459) 204/B5
Manchester, Conn. (06040) 210/E1
Manchester○, Conn. (06040) 210/E1
Manchester, Greater (co.), England 13/H2
Manchester, England 7/D3
Manchester, England 10/G2
Manchester, England 13/H2
Manchester, Georgia (31816) 217/C5
Manchester, Ill. (62663) 222/C4
Manchester, Ind. (†47001) 227/H6
Manchester, Iowa (52057) 229/L3
Manchester, Kansas (67463) 232/E2
Manchester, Ky. (40962) 237/O6
Manchester○, Maine (04351) 243/D7
Manchester, Md. (21102) 245/L2
Manchester○, Mass. (01944) 249/F5
Manchester, Mich. (48158) 250/E6
Manchester, Minn. (56064) 255/E7
Manchester, Mo. (63011) 261/O3
Manchester, N.H. 188/M2
Manchester, N.H. (*03101) 268/E6
Manchester, N.Y. (14504) 276/F5
Manchester, Ohio (45144) 284/C8
Manchester, Okla. (73758) 288/L1
Manchester, Pa. (17345) 294/J5
Manchester, S. Dak. (†57353) 298/O5
Manchester, Tenn. (37355) 237/J10
Manchester, Vt. (05254) 268/A5
Manchester○, Vt. (05254) 268/A5
Manchester, Wash. (98353) 310/A2
Manchester, Wis. (†53946) 317/J8
Manchester Center, Vt. (05255) 268/A5
Manchester Depot, Vt. (†05254) 268/B5
Manchioneal, Jamaica 158/K6
Manchouli (Manzhouli), China 77/J2
Máncora, Peru 128/B5
Mancos, Colo. (81328) 208/C8
Mancos (riv.), Colo. 208/B8
Manda, Tanzania 115/F6
Mandabe, Madagascar 118/G4
Mandah, Mongolia 77/G3
Mandal, Norway 18/E7
Mandalay (div.), Burma 72/B2
Mandalay, Burma 54/L7
Mandalay, Burma 72/C2

Mariano Roque Alonso **405**

Mandalgovĭ, Mongolia 77/G2
Mandali, Iraq 66/D4
Mandal-Ovoo, Mongolia 77/F3
Mandalya (gulf), Turkey 63/B4
Mandan, N. Dak. 188/F1
Mandan, N. Dak. (58554) 282/J6
Mandaon, Philippines 82/D4
Mandar (cape), Indonesia 85/F6
Mandaree, N. Dak. (58757) 282/E4
Mandaue, Philippines 82/E5
Mandeb, Bab el (str.), Saudi Arabia 59/D7
Mandeb, Bab el (str.), Yemen Arab Rep. 59/D7
Mandera, Kenya 115/H3
Manderson, S. Dak. (57756) 298/D7
Manderson, Wyo. (82432) 319/E1
Mandeville, Ark. (†75501) 202/C7
Mandeville, Jamaica 158/H6
Mandeville, La. (70448) 238/L6
Mandi, India 68/D2
Mandié, Mozambique 118/E3
Mandimba, Mozambique 118/F2
Mandinga, Panama 154/H6
Mandioré (lag.), Bolivia 136/F6
Mandla, India 68/E4
Mándok, Hungary 41/G2
Mandritsara, Madagascar 118/H3
Mand Rud (riv.), Iran 59/F4
Mand Rud (riv.), Iran 66/G6
Mandsaur, India 68/C4
Mandurah, W. Australia 88/B3
Mandurah, W. Australia 92/A2
Manduria, Italy 34/F4
Mandvi, India 68/B4
Manele (bay), Hawaii 218/H2
Manele Bay, Hawaii (†96763) 218/H2
Manendragarh, India 68/E4
Manes, Mo. (†65711) 261/H8
Manfalût, Egypt 111/J4
Manfalût, Egypt 59/B4
Manfred, N. Dak. (58465) 282/L4
Manfredonia, Italy 34/F4
Manfredonia (gulf), Italy 34/F4
Manga, Brazil 132/E6
Manga, Uruguay 145/B7
Mangai, Zaire 115/C4
Mangaia (isl.), Cook Is. 87/L8
Mangakino, N. Zealand 100/E3
Mangalia, Romania 45/J4
Mangalore, India 54/J8
Mangalore, India 68/C6
Mangareva (isl.), Fr. Poly. 87/N8
Mangaweka, N. Zealand 100/E3
Mangere (isl.), N. Zealand 100/E7
Mangerton (mt.), Ireland 17/C8
Mangham, La. (71259) 238/G2
Mangkalihat (cape), Indonesia 85/F5
Manglaralto, Ecuador 128/B3
Mangle (pt.), Cuba 158/J3
Manglillo (pt.), P. Rico 161/B3
Mangnai, China 77/D4
Mango, Fla. (33550) 212/D4
Mango, Togo 106/E6
Mangochi, Malawi 115/G6
Mangoky (riv.), Madagascar 102/G7
Mangoky (riv.), Madagascar 118/G4
Mangole (isl.), Indonesia 85/H6
Mangonui, N. Zealand 100/D1
Mangoro (riv.), Madagascar 118/H3
Mangotsfield, England 10/E5
Mangotsfield, England 13/E6
Mangrol, India 68/B4
Mangsee (isls.), Philippines 82/A7
Mangualde, Portugal 33/C2
Mangueigne, Chad 111/D5
Mangueira (lag.), Brazil 132/D11
Manguera Azul, Uruguay 145/D4
Mangui, China 77/K1
Manguito, Cuba 158/D1
Mangum, Okla. (73554) 288/G5
Mangyshlak (pen.), U.S.S.R. 48/F5
Manhan (riv.), Mass. 249/D4
Manhasset, N.Y. (11030) 276/P7
Manhattan, Ill. (60442) 222/F2
Manhattan, Ind. (†46171) 227/D5
Manhattan, Kansas (66502) 232/F2
Manhattan, Mont. (59741) 262/E5
Manhattan, Nev. (89022) 266/E4
Manhattan (borough), N.Y. (*10001) 276/M9
Manhattan (isl.), N.Y. 276/M9
Manhattan Beach, Calif. (90266) 204/B11
Manhattan Beach, Minn. (56463) 255/E4
Manhay, Belgium 27/H8
Manheim, Pa. (17545) 294/K5
Manheim, W. Va. (26403) 312/G4
Manhiça, Mozambique 118/E5
Man Hpang, Burma 72/C2
Manhuaçu, Brazil 132/F8
Manhuaçu, Brazil 135/E2
Manhumirim, Brazil 135/E2
Maní, Colombia 126/D5
Maniamba, Mozambique 102/F6
Maniamba, Mozambique 118/F2
Manibridge, Manitoba 179/J2
Manica (prov.), Mozambique 118/E4
Manica, Mozambique 118/E3
Manicani (isl.), Philippines 82/E5
Manicaragua, Cuba 158/E2
Manicoré, Brazil 120/C3
Manicoré, Brazil 132/H9
Manicouagan, Québec 174/D2
Manicouagan (pt.), Québec 172/B1
Manicouagan (res.), Québec 174/D2
Manicouagan (riv.), Que. 162/K5
Manicouagan (riv.), Québec 174/D2
Manifest, La. (†71340) 238/G3
Manifold (cape), Queensland 88/J4
Manifold (cape), Queensland 95/D4
Manigotagan, Manitoba 179/F3
Manigotagan (lake), Manitoba 179/G4
Manigotagan (riv.), Manitoba 179/G3
Manigouche, Québec 174/C3
Manihiki (atoll), Cook Is. 87/K7
Manila, Ala. (†36586) 195/C7
Manila, Ark. (72442) 202/K2
Manila (prov.), Philippines 82/C3
Manila (cap.), Philippines 2/R5
Manila (cap.), Philippines 85/G3
Manila (cap.), Philippines 82/C3
Manila (cap.), Philippines 54/N8
Manila (bay), Philippines 82/C3
Manila, Utah (84046) 304/E3
Manildra, N.S. Wales 97/E3
Manilla, Ind. (46150) 227/F5
Manilla, Iowa (51454) 229/C5
Manilla, N.S. Wales 97/F2
Maningrida, North. Terr. 93/C2
Manipa (str.), Indonesia 85/H6
Manipur (riv.), Burma 72/B2
Manipur (state), India 68/G4
Manisa (prov.), Turkey 63/B3
Manisa, Turkey 63/B3
Manisa, Turkey 59/A2
Manistee, Mich. 188/J2
Manistee (co.), Mich. 250/C4
Manistee, Mich. (49660) 250/C4
Manistee (riv.), Mich. 250/C4
Manistique, Mich. (49854) 250/C3
Manistique (lake), Mich. 250/D2
Manistique (riv.), Mich. 250/C2
Manito, Ill. (61546) 222/D3
Manito (lake), Sask. 181/B3
Manitoba (prov.) 162/G5
Manitoba (prov.), Canada 146/J4
MANITOBA 179
Manitoba (lake), Man. 146/H4
Manitoba (lake), Man. 162/G5
Manitoba (lake), Manitoba 179/D4
Manitou, Ky. (42436) 237/F6
Manitou, Manitoba 179/D5
Manitou (isl.), Mich. 250/B1
Manitou, N. Dak. (†58776) 282/E3
Manitou, Okla. (73555) 288/J5
Manitou (lake), Ontario 177/C2
Manitou (lake), Québec 172/C3
Manitou Beach, Sask. 181/F4
Manitoulin (terr. dist.), Ontario 175/D3
Manitoulin (terr. dist.), Ontario 177/B2
Manitoulin (isl.), Ont. 162/H6
Manitoulin (isl.), Ontario 175/D3
Manitoulin (isl.), Ontario 177/B2
Manitou Springs, Colo. (80829) 208/J5
Manitouwadge, Ontario 177/H5
Manitouwadge, Ontario 175/C3
Manitowaning, Ontario 177/C2
Manitowish, Wis. (†54547) 317/F3
Manitowoc (co.), Wis. 317/L7
Manitowoc, Wis. (54220) 317/L7
Maniwaki, Québec 174/B3
Maniwaki, Québec 172/B3
Manizales, Colombia 126/C5
Manizales, Colombia 120/B2
Manja, Jordan 65/D4
Manja, Madagascar 118/G4
Manjacaze, Mozambique 118/E5
Manjimup, W. Australia 88/B6
Manjimup, W. Australia 92/B6
Mankato, Kansas (66956) 232/D2
Mankato, Minn. 188/H2
Mankato, Minn. (56001) 255/E6
Mankono, Ivory Coast 106/C7
Mankota, Sask. 181/D6
Manley, Nebr. (68403) 264/H4
Manley Hot Springs, Alaska (99756) 196/H2
Manlius, Ill. (61338) 222/D2
Manlius, N.Y. (13104) 276/J5
Manlleu, Spain 33/H1
Manly, Iowa (50456) 229/G2
Manly, N. S. Wales 88/L4
Manly, N. S. Wales 97/K3
Manly, N.C. (†28387) 281/L4
Manly, Queensland 88/L2
Manmad, India 68/C4
Manmanoc (mt.), Philippines 82/C2
Mann (riv.), North. Terr. 93/D2
Manna, Indonesia 85/C6
Mannahill, S. Australia 94/F5
Mannar (gulf) 54/J9
Mannar (gulf), India 68/D7
Mannar, Sri Lanka 68/E7
Mannar (gulf), Sri Lanka 68/D7
Mannargudi, India 68/E6
Mannboro, Va. (23105) 307/N6
Männedorf, Switzerland 39/G2
Mannersdorf am Leithagebirge, Austria 41/D3
Manners Sutton, New Bruns. 170/D3
Mannford, Okla. (74044) 288/O2
Mannheim, W. Germany 7/E4
Mannheim, W. Germany 22/C4
Manning, Alberta 182/B1
Manning, Ark. (71757) 202/E5
Manning, Iowa (51455) 229/C5
Manning, Kansas (†67871) 232/B3
Manning (riv.), N.S. Wales 97/F2
Manning, N. Dak. (58642) 282/E5
Manning (cape), N.W. Terrs. 187/F2
Manning (str.), Solomon Is. 86/D2
Manning, S.C. (29102) 296/G4
Manning Prov. Park, Br. Col. 184/G5
Mannington, Ky. (†42217) 237/G6
Mannington, W. Va. (26582) 312/F3
Männlifluh (mt.), Switzerland 39/E3
Manns Choice, Pa. (15550) 294/E6
Manns Harbor, N.C. (27953) 281/T3
Mannsville, Ky. (42758) 237/L6
Mannsville, N.Y. (13661) 276/H3
Mannsville, Okla. (73447) 288/N6
Mannu (riv.), Italy 34/B5
Mannum, S. Australia 94/F6
Mannville, Alberta 182/E3
Mano (riv.), Liberia 106/B7
Mano (riv.), S. Leone 106/B7
Manoa, Bolivia 136/C1
Manokin, Md. (21836) 245/P8
Manokin (riv.), Md. 245/P8
Manokotak, Alaska (99628) 196/G3
Manokwari, Indonesia 85/J6
Manola, Alberta 182/C2
Manombo, Madagascar 118/G4
Manomet, Mass. (02345) 249/M5
Manomet (pt.), Mass. 249/N5
Manono, Zaire 115/E5
Manono, Zaire 102/E5
Manor, Georgia (31550) 217/G8
Manor, Pa. (15665) 294/C5
Manor, Sask. 181/K6
Manor, Texas (78653) 303/G7
Manorhamilton, Ireland 17/E3
Manori, India 68/B6
Manori (creek), India 68/B7
Manorville, N.Y. (11949) 276/P9
Manorville, Pa. (16238) 294/C4
Manosque, France 28/G6
Manotick, Ontario 177/J2
Manouane, Québec 172/C2
Manouane (lake), Québec 174/C2
Manp'o, N. Korea 81/B3
Manquin, Va. (23106) 307/O5
Manra (Sydney) (isl.), Kiribati 87/K6
Manresa, Spain 33/G2
Mansa, Zambia 115/E6
Mansa, Zambia 102/E6
Mansalay, Philippines 82/C4
Mansavillagra, Uruguay 145/D4
Manseau, Québec 172/E3
Mansel (isl.), N.W.T. 162/H3
Mansel (isl.), N.W.T. 146/K3
Mansel (isl.), N.W. Terrs. 187/K3
Mansel'ka (mts.), U.S.S.R. 52/C1
Mansfield, Ark. (72944) 202/B3
Mansfield○, Conn. (†06250) 210/F1
Mansfield, England 13/K2
Mansfield, England 10/F4
Mansfield, Georgia (30255) 217/E4
Mansfield, Ill. (61854) 222/E3
Mansfield, Ind. (†47872) 227/C5
Mansfield, La. (71052) 238/C2
Mansfield, Mass. (02048) 249/J4
Mansfield○, Mass. (02048) 249/J4
Mansfield, Minn. (†56009) 255/E7
Mansfield, Mo. (65704) 261/G8
Mansfield, Ohio 188/K2
Mansfield, Ohio (*44901) 284/F4
Mansfield, Pa. (16933) 294/H2
Mansfield, S. Dak. (57460) 298/N3
Mansfield, Tenn. (38236) 237/E8
Mansfield, Texas (76063) 303/F3
Mansfield (mt.), Vt. 268/B2
Mansfield, Victoria 97/D5
Mansfield, Wash. (98830) 310/F3
Mansfield Center, Conn. (06250) 210/G1
Mansfield Depot, Conn. (06251) 210/F1
Mansfield Woodhouse, England 13/F4
Mansilla de las Mulas, Spain 33/D1
Manso (riv.), Brazil 132/C6
Manso (riv.), Chile 138/E4
Manson, Ind. (†46041) 227/D4
Manson, Iowa (50563) 229/D3
Manson, Manitoba 179/A4
Manson, N.C. (27553) 281/N2
Manson, Wash. (98831) 310/E3
Manson Creek, Br. Col. 184/E2
Mansonville, Québec 172/E4
Mansura, La. (71350) 238/G4
Manta, Ecuador 128/B3
Manta, Ecuador 120/A3
Manta (bay), Ecuador 128/B3
Mantachie, Miss. (38855) 256/H2
Mantador, N. Dak. (58058) 282/R7
Mantagao (lake), Manitoba 179/E3
Mantagao (riv.), Manitoba 179/E3
Mantalingajan (mt.), Philippines 82/A6
Mantario, Sask. 181/B4
Mantaro (riv.), Peru 128/E8
Mantas (well), Niger 106/E5
Manteca, Calif. (95336) 204/D6
Mantecal, Apure, Venezuela 124/D4
Mantecal, Bolívar, Venezuela 124/F4
Mantee, Miss. (39751) 256/F3
Manteigas, Portugal 33/C2
Manteno, Ill. (60950) 222/F2
Manteo, N.C. (27954) 281/T3
Manter, Kansas (67862) 232/A4
Mantes-la-Jolie, France 28/D3
Manti, Utah (84642) 304/C4
Mantiqueira (range), Brazil 135/D3
Manto, Honduras 154/D3
Mantoloking, N.J. (08738) 273/E3
Manton, Calif. (96059) 204/D3
Manton, Mich. (49663) 250/D4
Manton, R.I. (†02904) 249/J5
Mantorville, Minn. (55955) 255/F6
Mänttä, Finland 18/O6
Mantua, Ala. (35472) 195/C4
Mantua, Cuba 158/A2
Mantua (prov.), Italy 34/C2
Mantua, Italy 34/C2
Mantua○, N.J. (08051) 273/C4
Mantua, Ohio (44255) 284/H3
Mantua, Utah (†84302) 304/C2
Mantua, Va. (†22030) 307/S3
Manturovo, U.S.S.R. 52/F3
Manú, Peru 128/G9
Manú (riv.), Peru 128/G8
Manua (isls.), Amer. Samoa 87/K7
Manuae (atoll), Cook Is. 87/K7
Manuel Benavides, Mexico 150/H2
Manuelito, N. Mex. (†86506) 274/A3
Manuel Rodríguez (isl.), Chile 138/D10
Manuels, New Bruns. 170/F1
Manuels, Newf. 166/D2
Manui (isl.), Indonesia 85/G6
Manukan, Philippines 82/D6
Manukau, N. Zealand 100/C1
Manukau (harb.), N. Zealand 100/B1
Manulla, Ireland 17/C4
Manumuskin (riv.), N.J. 273/D5
Manunui, N. Zealand 100/E3
Manuripi (riv.), Bolivia 136/B2
Manus (isl.), Papua N.G. 87/E6
Manus (isl.), Papua N.G. 86/A1
Manutuke, N. Zealand 100/F3
Manvel, N. Dak. (58256) 282/R3
Manvel, Texas (77578) 303/J3
Manville, N.J. (08835) 273/D2
Manville, R.I. (02838) 249/H5
Manville, Wyo. (82227) 319/H3
Many, La. (71449) 238/C3
Manyara (lake), Tanzania 115/G4
Manyas, Turkey 63/B3
Manyberries, Alberta 182/E5
Manych-Gudilo (lake), U.S.S.R. 52/F5
Many Farms, Ariz. (86538) 198/F2
Manyoni, Tanzania 115/G5
Manzai, Pakistan 59/K3
Manzanar, Chile 138/F2
Manzanares, Spain 33/E3
Manzanares (riv.), Spain 33/F4
Manzanillo, Cuba 158/H4
Manzanillo, Cuba 156/C2
Manzanillo (bay), Dom. Rep. 158/C5
Manzanillo (bay), Haiti 158/C5
Manzanillo, Mexico 150/G7
Manzanillo, Mexico 146/H8
Manzanillo (pt.), Panama 154/H6
Manzanita, Oreg. (97130) 291/C2
Manzanita Ind. Res., Calif. 204/J11
Manzano, N. Mex. (†87016) 274/C4
Manzano (mts.), N. Mex. 274/C4
Manzano (peak), N. Mex. 274/C4
Manzanola, Colo. (81058) 208/M6
Manzhouli (Manchouli), China 77/J2
Manzini, Swaziland 118/E5
Mao, Chad 111/C5
Mao, Dom. Rep. 158/D5
Maoke (mts.), Indonesia 85/K6
Maoming (Mowming), China 77/H7
Mapai, Mozambique 118/E4
Mapararí, Venezuela 124/D2
Mapastepec, Mexico 150/N9
Mapes, N. Dak. (58349) 282/O3
Mapia (isls.), Indonesia 85/J5
Mapimí, Mexico 150/G4
Mapimí (depr.), Mexico 150/G3
Mapire, Venezuela 124/F4
Mapiri, Bolivia 136/B4
Mapiripán, Laguna (lake), Colombia 126/E6
Maple (peak), Ariz. 198/F5
Maple (riv.), Mich. 250/E5
Maple (lake), Minn. 255/B3
Maple (riv.), Minn. 255/E7
Maple (riv.), N. Dak. 282/O8
Maple (riv.), N. Dak. 282/R6
Maple (creek), Sask. 181/B5
Maple (riv.), S. Dak. 298/M1
Maple, Wis. (54854) 317/C2
Maple Bay, Br. Col. 184/K3
Maple Bay, Minn. (†56736) 255/B3
Maple City, Kansas (67102) 232/F4
Maple City, Mich. 250/D4
Maple Creek, Sask. 162/F6
Maple Creek, Sask. 181/B6
Maple Falls, Wash. (98266) 310/D2
Maple Grove, Minn. (†55369) 255/G5
Maple Grove, Ontario 177/F4
Maple Grove, Québec 172/H4
Maple Heights, Ohio (44137) 284/H9
Maple Hill, Iowa (50564) 229/D2
Maple Hill, Kansas (66507) 232/F2
Maple Hill, N.C. (28454) 281/O5
Maple Island, Minn. (†55082) 255/F7
Maple Lake, Minn. (55358) 255/D5
Maple Park, Ill. (60151) 222/E2
Maple Plain, Minn. (55359) 255/F5
Maple Rapids, Mich. (48853) 250/E5
Maple Ridge, Br. Col. 184/L3
Maple River, Iowa (†51401) 229/D4
Maples, Ind. (†46802) 227/H2
Maples, Mo. (†65542) 261/J7
Maple Shade○, N.J. (08052) 273/B3
Maplesville, Ala. (36750) 195/E5
Mapleton, Iowa (51034) 229/B4
Mapleton, Kansas (66754) 232/H3
Mapleton○, Maine (04757) 243/G2
Mapleton, Mich. (†49684) 250/D4
Mapleton, Minn. (56065) 255/E7
Mapleton, N.C. (†27855) 281/P2
Mapleton, N. Dak. (58059) 282/R6
Mapleton, Oreg. (97453) 291/C3
Mapleton (Mapleton Depot), Pa. (17052) 294/F5
Mapleton, Utah (†84663) 304/C3
Mapleton, Wis. (†53066) 317/J1
Mapleton Depot, Pa. (17052) 294/F5
Maple Valley, Wash. (98038) 310/C3
Mapleview, Minn. (†55912) 255/E7
Mapleview, New Bruns. 170/C2
Mapleville, Md. (†21713) 245/H2
Mapleville, R.I. (02839) 249/H5
Maplewood, La. (†70663) 238/D6
Maplewood, Minn. (55109) 255/G5
Maplewood, Mo. (63143) 261/P3
Maplewood, N.H. (†03574) 268/D3
Maplewood○, N.J. (07040) 273/E2
Maplewood, Ohio (45340) 284/B5
Maplewood, Wis. (54226) 317/M6
Mapocho (riv.), Chile 138/G3
Mapoon Mission Station, Queensland 88/G2
Mapoon Mission Station, Queensland 95/B1
Maporal, Venezuela 124/C4
Mapos (Amazones), Cuba 158/F2
Mappsville, Va. (23407) 307/T5
Mapuera (riv.), Brazil 132/B3
Maputo (city) (prov.), Mozambique 118/E5
Maputo (prov.), Mozambique 118/E5
Maputo (cap.), Mozambique 2/L7
Maputo (cap.), Mozambique 118/E5
Maputo (cap.), Mozambique 102/F7
Maqatin (ruins), P.D.R. Yemen 59/E7
Maqên, China 77/F5
Maqna, Saudi Arabia 59/C4
Ma Qu (Huang He) (riv.), China 77/F5
Maquapit (lake), New Bruns. 170/D3
Maqueda (chan.), Philippines 82/D3
Maquela do Zombo, Angola 102/D5
Maquela do Zombo, Angola 115/C5
Maquereau (pt.), Québec 172/D2
Maquinchao, Argentina 143/C5
Maquoketa, Iowa (52060) 229/M4
Maquon, Ill. (61458) 222/C3
Mar (mts.), Brazil 120/E5
Mar (range), Brazil 135/C4
Mar, Serra do (range), Brazil 132/E9
Mar (dist.), Scotland 15/F3
Mara, Guyana 131/C3
Mara (reg.), Tanzania 115/F4
Marabá, Brazil 132/D4
Marabá, Brazil 120/E3
Marabahan, Indonesia 85/E6
Marabella, Trin. & Tob. 161/A11
Maracá (isl.), Brazil 120/E2
Maracá (isl.), Brazil 132/D2
Maracaibo, Venezuela 124/C2
Maracaibo, Venezuela 120/B1
Maracaibo (lake), Venezuela 120/B2
Maracaibo (lake), Venezuela 124/C3
Maracaju, Brazil 132/C8
Maracas (bay), Trin. & Tob. 161/C10
Maracay, Venezuela 124/E2
Maracay, Venezuela 120/C2
Marada, Libya 111/D2
Maradi, Niger 106/F6
Maradi, Niger 102/C3
Maragheh, Iran 59/E2
Maragheh, Iran 66/E2
Maragogipe, Brazil 132/G6
Maraira (pt.), Philippines 82/C1
Marajó (est.), Brazil 120/E2
Marajó (isl.), Brazil 120/E3
Marajó (bay), Brazil 132/E2
Marajó (isl.), Brazil 132/D3
Maralal, Kenya 115/G3
Maralinga, S. Australia 88/E6
Maralwexi (Bachu), China 77/A4
Maramag, Philippines 82/E7
Maramec, Okla. (74045) 288/N2
Marampa, S. Leone 106/B7
Marana, Ariz. (85238) 198/D6
Marand, Iran 59/E2
Marand, Iran 66/D1
Marandellas, Zimbabwe 118/E3
Marang, Malaysia 72/D6
Maranguape, Brazil 132/G3
Maranhão (state), Brazil 132/E4
Maranoa (riv.), Queensland 95/C5
Marañón (riv.), Peru 120/B3
Marañón (riv.), Peru 128/E5
Marapanim, Brazil 132/E3
Maras (mt.), Indonesia 85/D6
Maraş, Turkey 59/C2
Maraş (Kahramanmaraş), Turkey 63/G4
Marathon, Fla. (33050) 212/E7
Marathón, Greece 45/G6
Marathon, Iowa (50565) 229/C3
Marathon, N.Y. (13803) 276/J6
Marathon, Ohio (45145) 284/C7
Marathon, Ont. 162/H6
Marathon, Ontario 177/H5
Marathon, Ontario 175/C3
Marathon, Texas (79842) 303/A7
Marathon (co.), Wis. 317/G6
Marathon, Wis. (54448) 317/G6
Maratua (isl.), Indonesia 85/F5
Maravillas, Bolivia 136/B2
Maravillas (creek), Texas 303/A7
Marawi, Philippines 85/G4
Marawi, Philippines 82/E6
Marbach, Switzerland 39/E3
Marbach am Neckar, W. Germany 22/C4
Marbella, Spain 33/D4
Marble, Ark. (72746) 202/C1
Marble, Colo. (†81623) 208/E4
Marble, Minn. (55764) 255/E3
Marble, N.C. (28905) 281/B4
Marble (isl.), N.W.T. 162/G3
Marble (isl.), N.W. Terrs. 187/J3
Marble Bar, Australia 87/C8
Marble Bar, W. Australia 88/B4
Marble Bar, W. Australia 92/C3
Marble Canyon, Ariz. (86036) 198/D2
Marble Canyon Nat'l Mon., Ariz. 198/D2
Marble City, Okla. (74945) 288/S3
Marble Dale, Conn. (06777) 210/B2
Marble Falls, Texas (78654) 303/F7
Marblehead, Ill. (†62301) 222/B4
Marblehead○, Mass. (01945) 249/E7
Marblehead (neck), Mass. 249/E7
Marblehead, Ohio (†43440) 284/E2
Marble Hill, Georgia (30148) 217/D2
Marble Hill, Mo. (63764) 261/N8
Marblemount, Wash. (98267) 310/D2
Marble Rock, Iowa (50653) 229/H3
Marbleton, Québec 172/F4
Marbleton, Wyo. (†83113) 319/B3
Marble Valley, Ala. (†35150) 195/F4
Marburg an der Lahn, W. Germany 22/C3
Marbury, Ala. (36051) 195/E5
Marbury, Md. (20658) 245/K6
Marcala, Honduras 154/C3
Marcali, Hungary 41/D3
Marcapata, Peru 128/G9
Marcelin, Sask. 181/E3
Marceline, Mo. (64658) 261/F3
Marcell, Minn. (56657) 255/E3
Marcella, Ark. (72555) 202/G2
Marcella, N.J. (†07866) 273/E2
Marcelline, Ill. (†62376) 222/B3
Marcellus, Mich. (49067) 250/D6
Marcellus, N.Y. (13108) 276/H5
Marcelville, New Bruns. 170/E2
March (riv.), Austria 41/D2
March, England 10/G4
March, England 13/H5
March A.F.B., Calif. 204/E11
Marchand, Manitoba 179/F5
Marche, Ark. (†72114) 202/F4
Marche (trad. prov.) France 29
Marche (reg.), Italy 34/D3
Marche-en-Famenne, Belgium 27/G8
Marchegg, Austria 41/D2
Marchena (isl.), Ecuador 128/B9
Marchena, Spain 33/D4
Marchfield, Barbados 161/B9
Marchigüe, Chile 138/F5
Marchin, Belgium 27/G8
Mar Chiquita (lake), Argentina 143/D3
Marchwell, Sask. 181/K5
Marco (Marco Island), Fla. (33937) 212/E6
Marco (isl.), Fla. 212/E6
Marco, Ind. (†47443) 227/C7
Marco, La. (†71447) 238/E3
Marcola, Oreg. (97454) 291/E3
Marcona, Peru 128/E10
Marcos Juárez, Argentina 143/D3
Marcus, Iowa (51035) 229/B3
Marcus (isl.), Japan 87/F3
Marcus, S. Dak. (57757) 298/E4
Marcus, Wash. (99151) 310/H2
Marcus Baker (mt.), Alaska 196/C1
Marcus Hook, Pa. (19061) 294/L7
Marcy, N.Y. (13403) 276/K4
Marcy (mt.), N.Y. 276/N2
Mardan, Pakistan 68/C2
Mardan, Pakistan 59/K3
Mardela Springs, Md. (21837) 245/P7
Mar del Plata, Argentina 143/E4
Mar del Plata, Argentina 120/D6
Mardin (prov.), Turkey 63/J4
Mardin, Turkey 63/J4
Mardin, Turkey 59/D2
Maré (isl.), New Caled. 87/G8
Mare (isl.), New Caled. 86/J4
Mareb (riv.), Ethiopia 59/C7
Marechal Deodoro, Brazil 132/H5
Maree, Loch (lake), Scotland 10/D2
Maree, Loch (lake), Scotland 15/C3
Mareeba, Queensland 95/C3
Mareeba, Queensland 88/G3
Mare Island Navy Yard, Calif. 204/J1
Marengo (co.), Ala. 195/C6
Marengo, Ala. (†36736) 195/C6
Marengo, Ill. (60152) 222/E1
Marengo, Ind. (47140) 227/E8
Marengo, Iowa (52301) 229/J5
Marengo, Ohio (43334) 284/E5
Marengo, Sask. 181/B4
Marengo, Wash. (†99004) 310/G3
Marengo, Wis. (54855) 317/E3
Marenisco, Mich. (49947) 250/F2
Marennes, France 28/C5
Mareth, Tunisia 106/F2
Marettimo (isl.), Italy 34/C6
Marfa, Texas (79843) 303/C12
Marfield, N.S. Wales 97/C3
Marfrance, W. Va. (25975) 312/E6
Margai Caka (lake), China 77/C4
Marganets, U.S.S.R. 52/E5
Margao, India 68/C5
Margaree, Nova Scotia 168/G2
Margaree (isl.), Nova Scotia 168/F4
Margaree Centre, Nova Scotia 168/H2
Margaree Forks, Nova Scotia 168/G2
Margaree Harbour, Nova Scotia 168/G2
Margaree Valley, Nova Scotia 168/H2
Margaret, Ala. (35112) 195/F3
Margaret (lake), Alberta 182/B5
Margaret, Manitoba 179/C5
Margaret, Texas (†79227) 303/E3
Margaret (riv.), W. Australia 88/D3
Margaret River, W. Australia 88/A6
Margaret River, W. Australia 92/A6
Margaret River Station, W. Australia 92/D2
Margaretsville, Nova Scotia 168/C3
Margaretville, N.Y. (12455) 276/L6
Margarita, Argentina 143/F5
Margarita (isl.), Venezuela 120/C1
Margarita (isl.), Venezuela 124/F2
Margate, England 13/J6
Margate, England 10/G5
Margate, Fla. (33063) 212/F5
Margate, S. Africa 118/E6
Margate, Tasmania 99/D4
Margate City, N.J. (08402) 273/E5
Margento, Colombia 126/C4
Margerum, Ala. (†35616) 195/B1
Margherita (Jamama), Somalia 115/H3
Margherita (mt.), Uganda 115/E3
Margherita (mt.), Zaire 102/E4
Margherita (mt.), Zaire 115/E3
Margie, Minn. (56658) 255/E2
Margo, Sask. 181/H4
Margos, Peru 128/D8
Margosatubig, Philippines 82/D7
Margow, Dasht-e (des.), Afghanistan 59/H3
Margow, Dasht-e (des.), Afghanistan 68/A2
Margraten, Netherlands 27/H7
Margret, Georgia (†30536) 217/D1
Margrethe (lake), Mich. 250/E4
Marguerite (bay) 5/C15
Maria (isl.), Fr. Poly. 87/L8
Maria (creek), Ind. 227/C7
Maria, Québec 172/C2
Maria (isls.), St. Lucia 161/G7
Maria (isl.), Tasmania 99/E4
Mari A.S.S.R., U.S.S.R. 52/G3
Mari A.S.S.R., U.S.S.R. 48/E4
María Albina, Uruguay 145/E4
María Cleófas (isl.), Mexico 150/F6
María Elena, Chile 138/B3
Mariager, Denmark 21/D4
Mariager, Denmark 18/G8
Mariager (fjord), Denmark 21/D4
Mariah Hill, Ind. (47556) 227/D8
María Madre (isl.), Mexico 150/F6
María Magdalena (isl.), Mexico 150/F6
Marian (lake), Fla. 212/E4
Marian (lake), N.W. Terrs. 187/G3
Marian, Queensland 88/H4
Marian, Queensland 95/D4
Mariana, Brazil 135/E2
Mariana Lake, Alberta 182/D2
Marianao, Cuba 158/C1
Marianao, Cuba 156/A2
Marianas, Northern 87/E4
Mariana Trench 87/E4
Marianna, Ark. (72360) 202/J4
Marianna, Fla. (32446) 212/A1
Marianna, Pa. (15345) 294/B5
Mariano I. Loza, Argentina 143/G4
Mariano Roque Alonso, Paraguay 144/A4

McKinley 407

Matadi, Zaire 102/D5
Matador, Sask. 181/D5
Matador, Texas (79244) 303/D3
Matagalpa, Nicaragua 154/E4
Matagami, Québec 174/B3
Matagami (lake), Québec 174/B3
Matagorda (co.), Texas 303/H9
Matagorda, Texas (77457) 303/J9
Matagorda (bay), Texas 188/G5
Matagorda (bay), Texas 303/H9
Matagorda (isl.), Texas 303/H9
Matagorda (pen.), Texas 303/J9
Matagorda Isl. Bombing and Gunnery Range, Texas 303/H9
Matakana (isl.), N. Zealand 100/F2
Matala (dam), Angola 115/B6
Matam, Senegal 106/B5
Matamoras, Pa. (18336) 294/N3
Matamoros, Mexico 146/J7
Matamoros, Coahuila, Mexico 150/H4
Matamoros, Tamaulipas, Mexico 150/L4
Matane (co.), Québec 172/B1
Matane (county), Québec 174/D3
Matane, Québec 174/D3
Matane, Québec 172/B1
Matane (riv.), Québec 172/B1
Matane Prov. Park, Québec 172/B1
Matanuska (riv.), Alaska 196/C1
Matanza, Colombia 126/D4
Matanzas (prov.), Cuba 158/D1
Matanzas, Cuba 146/K7
Matanzas, Cuba 158/C1
Matanzas, Cuba 156/B2
Matanzas (bay), Cuba 158/D1
Matanzas (inlet), Fla. 212/E2
Mata Palacio, Dom. Rep. 158/F6
Matapalo (cape), C. Rica 154/F6
Matapan (Tainaron) (cape), Greece 45/F7
Matapédia (county), Québec 174/D3
Matapédia (co.), Québec 172/B2
Matapédia, Québec 172/B2
Matapédia (lake), Québec 172/B1
Matapédia (riv.), Québec 172/B2
Mataquito (riv.), Chile 138/A10
Matara, Sri Lanka 68/E7
Mataram, Indonesia 85/F7
Matarani, Peru 120/B4
Matarani, Peru 128/F11
Mataranka, North. Terr. 93/C3
Matarinao (bay), Philippines 82/E5
Mataró, Spain 33/H2
Matatiele, S. Africa 118/D6
Matatindoc (pt.), Philippines 82/D6
Mataura, N. Zealand 100/B7
Mataura (riv.), N. Zealand 100/B6
Mata Utu (cap.), Wallis and Futuna 87/J7
Matawai, N. Zealand 100/F3
Matawan, Minn. (†56072) 255/E7
Matawan, N.J. (07747) 273/E3
Matawin (lake), Québec 172/C3
Matawin (riv.), Québec 172/D3
Mateare, Nicaragua 154/D4
Mateguá, Bolivia 136/D3
Matehuala, Mexico 150/J5
Matelot, Trin. & Tob. 161/B10
Matera (prov.), Italy 34/F4
Matera, Italy 34/F4
Maternillos (pt.), Cuba 158/H2
Mátészalka, Hungary 41/G3
Matetsi, Zimbabwe 118/D3
Mateur, Tunisia 106/F1
Matewan, W. Va. (25678) 312/B7
Matfield Green, Kansas (66862) 232/F3
Mather, Manitoba 179/C5
Mather, Wis. (54641) 317/F7
Mather A.F.B., Calif. 204/C8
Matherville, Ill. (61263) 222/C2
Matherville, Miss. (†39360) 256/G7
Matheson, Colo. (80830) 208/M4
Matheson, Ontario 177/K5
Matheson Island, Manitoba 179/E3
Mathews, Ala. (36052) 195/F6
Mathews (lake), Calif. 204/E11
Mathews, La. (70375) 238/J7
Mathews (co.), Va. 307/R6
Mathews, Va. (23109) 307/R6
Mathias, W. Va. (26812) 312/J5
Mathinna, Tasmania 99/E3
Mathis, Texas (78368) 303/G9
Mathiston, Miss. (39752) 256/F3
Mathoura, N.S. Wales 97/C4
Mathura, India 68/D3
Mati, Philippines 85/H4
Mati, Philippines 82/F7
Matías Romero, Mexico 150/M8
Matinenda (lake), Ontario 177/B1
Matinicus, Maine (04851) 243/F8
Matinicus Rock (isl.), Maine 243/F8
Matlock, England 10/F4
Matlock, England 13/J2
Matlock, Iowa (51244) 229/A2
Matlock, Wash. (98560) 310/B3
Matoaca, Va. (23803) 307/N6
Matoaka, W. Va. (24736) 312/D8
Matochkin Shar (str.), U.S.S.R. 48/F2
Mato Grosso (state), Brazil 132/B6
Mato Grosso, Brazil 120/D4
Mato Grosso, Brazil 132/B6
Mato Grosso (plat.), Brazil 120/D4
Mato Grosso, Planalto de (plat.), Brazil 132/B6
Mato Grosso do Sul (state), Brazil 132/C7
Matopos, Zimbabwe 118/D4
Matosinhos, Portugal 33/B2
Matoury, Fr. Guiana 131/E3
Mátra (mts.), Hungary 41/E3
Matrah, Oman 54/G7
Matrah, Oman 59/G5
Matrei in Osttirol, Austria 41/B3
Matruh, Egypt 59/A3
Matsqui, Br. Col. 184/L3
Matsu (Mazu) (isl.), China 77/K6
Matsubara, Japan 81/H8
Matsue, Japan 81/F6
Matsumae, Japan 81/J3
Matsumoto, Japan 81/H5
Matsusaka, Japan 81/H6
Matsuto, Japan 81/H5
Matsuyama, Japan 81/F7
Matsuyama, Japan 54/P6
Matt, Switzerland 39/H3
Mattabesset (riv.), Conn. 210/E2
Mattagami (riv.), Ontario 175/D3
Mattagami (riv.), Ontario 177/J5
Mattamiscontis (lake), Maine 243/F4
Mattamuskeet (lake), N.C. 281/S3
Mattapan, Mass. (02126) 249/C7
Mattapoisett, Mass. (02739) 249/L6
Mattapoisett○, Mass. (02739) 249/L6
Mattaponi, Va. (23110) 307/P5
Mattaponi (riv.), Va. 307/O5
Mattaponi Ind. Res., Va. 307/P5
Mattawa, Ont. 162/J6
Mattawa, Ontario 177/F1
Mattawa, Ontario 175/E3
Mattawa, Wash. (99344) 310/F4
Mattawamkeag○, Maine (04459) 243/G5
Mattawamkeag (lake), Maine 243/G4
Mattawamkeag (riv.), Maine 243/G4
Mattawan, Mich. (49071) 250/D6
Mattawana, Pa. (17054) 294/G5
Mattawoman (creek), Md. 245/K6
Matterhorn (mt.), Switzerland 39/E4
Mattersburg, Austria 41/D3
Matteson, Ill. (60443) 222/B6
Matthew, Ky. (41454) 237/P5
Matthews, Georgia (30818) 217/H4
Matthews, Ind. (46957) 227/F4
Matthews, Mo. (63857) 261/N9
Matthews, N.C. (28105) 281/H4
Matthews Ridge, Guyana 131/B2
Mattice, Ontario 175/D3
Mattice, Ontario 177/J5
Mattighofen, Austria 41/B2
Mattituck, N.Y. (11952) 276/P9
Mattoon, Ill. (61938) 222/E4
Mattoon, Wis. (54450) 317/J5
Mattson, Miss. (38758) 256/C2
Matu, Venezuela 124/F4
Matucana, Peru 128/D8
Matuku (isl.), Fiji 86/Q11
Matún, Cuba 158/D2
Matura, Trin. & Tob. 161/B10
Matura (bay), Trin. & Tob. 161/B10
Maturín, Venezuela 120/C2
Maturín, Venezuela 124/G3
Matutum (mt.), Philippines 82/E7
Matutum (mt.), Philippines 85/G4
Matveyev (isl.), U.S.S.R. 52/J1
Mau, India 68/E3
Mauá, Brazil 135/C3
Mauá, Mozambique 118/F2
Maubeuge, France 28/F2
Ma-ubin, Burma 72/B3
Mauch Chunk (Jim Thorpe), Pa. (18229) 294/L4
Mauchline, Scotland 15/D5
Mauckport, Ind. (47142) 227/E8
Maud, Ala. (†35616) 195/B1
Maud, Ky. (40042) 237/L5
Maud, Miss. (†38626) 256/D1
Maud, Ohio (†45069) 284/B7
Maud, Okla. (74854) 288/N4
Maud, Scotland 15/F3
Maud, Texas (75567) 303/K4
Maude, N.S. Wales 97/C4
Maudlow, Mont. (59714) 262/E4
Mauerkirchen, Austria 41/B2
Maués, Brazil 132/B3
Maués, Brazil 120/D3
Maués-Açu (riv.), Brazil 132/B4
Mauganville, Md. (21767) 245/H2
Mauger (cay), Belize 154/D2
Maugerville, New Bruns. 170/D3
Maui (co.), Hawaii 218/J1
Maui (isl.), Hawaii 87/L3
Maui (isl.), Hawaii 188/F5
Maui (isl.), Hawaii 218/J2
Mauk, Georgia (31058) 217/D6
Mauke (isl.), Cook Is. 87/L8
Mauldin, S.C. (29662) 296/C2
Maule (reg.), Chile 138/A11
Maule (riv.), Chile 138/A11
Mauléon-Licharre, France 28/C6
Maullín, Chile 138/D4
Maullín (riv.), Chile 138/D3
Maumakeogh (mt.), Ireland 17/C3
Maumee (riv.), Ind. 227/H2
Maumee (bay), Mich. 250/F7
Maumee, Ohio (43537) 284/C2
Maumee (bay), Ohio 284/D2
Maumee (riv.), Ohio 284/A3
Maumelle (lake), Ark. 202/E4
Maumere, Indonesia 85/G7
Maumturk (mts.), Ireland 17/B5
Maun, Botswana 118/C4
Maunabo, P. Rico 161/E3
Mauna Kea (mt.), Hawaii 87/L4
Mauna Kea (mt.), Hawaii 188/G6
Mauna Kea (mt.), Hawaii 218/H4
Maunaloa, Hawaii (96770) 218/G1
Mauna Loa (mt.), Hawaii 188/G6
Mauna Loa (mt.), Hawaii 218/G6
Maunalua (bay), Hawaii 218/F2
Maunawili, Hawaii (†96744) 218/F2
Maungaturoto, N. Zealand 100/E1
Maungdaw, Burma 72/B2
Maunie, Ill. (62861) 222/E5
Maupin, Oreg. (97037) 291/F2
Maurepas, La. (70449) 238/M2
Maurepas (lake), La. 238/M2
Maurertown, Va. (22644) 307/L3
Mauriac, France 28/E5
Maurice, Iowa (51036) 229/A3
Maurice, La. (70555) 238/F6
Maurice (riv.), N.J. 273/C4
Maurice (lake), S. Australia 88/E5
Maurice (lake), S. Australia 94/B3
Mauricetown, N.J. (08325) 273/D5
Mauricio Hirsch, Argentina 143/F7
Maurine, S. Dak. (†57626) 298/E3
Mauritania 2/J4
Mauritania 102/A3
MAURITANIA 106/B5
Mauritius 2/M6
MAURITIUS 118/G5
Maury, N.C. (28554) 281/O4
Maury (co.), Tenn. 237/G9
Maury (riv.), Va. 307/K5
Maury City, Tenn. (38050) 237/C9
Mauston, Wis. (53948) 317/F8
Mautern in Steiermark, Austria 41/C3
Mauthausen, Austria 41/C2
Mauthen-Kötschach, Austria 41/B3
Mauvoisin (dam), Switzerland 39/D4
Mavaca (riv.), Venezuela 124/F6
Maverick, Ariz. (†85920) 198/F5
Maverick (co.), Texas 303/D9
Mavila, Peru 128/H8
Mavillette, Nova Scotia 168/B4
Mavinga, Angola 115/D7
Mavora (mt.), N. Zealand 100/B6
Mavqi'im, Israel 65/B4
Mawai, Malaysia 72/F5
Mawbanna, Tasmania 99/B2
Mawer, Sask. 181/E5
Mawkmai, Burma 72/C2
Mawlaik, Burma 72/B2
Mawlu, Burma 72/C1
Mawson 5/C4
Max, Minn. (56659) 255/D3
Max, Nebr. (69037) 264/C4
Max, N. Dak. (58759) 282/H4
Maxbass, N. Dak. (58760) 282/H2
Maxcanú, Mexico 150/O6
Maxeys, Georgia (30671) 217/F3
Maxie, La. (†70526) 238/F6
Maxie, Miss. (†39458) 256/F9
Máximo Gómez, Ciego de Ávila, Cuba 158/F2
Máximo Gómez, Matanzas, Cuba 158/D1
Máximo Paz, Argentina 143/F6
Maxinkuckee, Ind. (†46511) 227/E2
Maxinkuckee (lake), Ind. 227/E2
Maxixe, Mozambique 118/F4
Max Meadows, Va. (24360) 307/G6
Maxstone, Sask. 181/F6
Maxton, N.C. (28364) 281/L5
Maxville, Mont. (59858) 262/C4
Maxville, Ontario 177/K2
Maxwell, Calif. (95955) 204/C4
Maxwell, Ind. (46154) 227/F5
Maxwell, Iowa (50161) 229/G5
Maxwell, Nebr. (69151) 264/D3
Maxwell, New Bruns. 170/C3
Maxwell, N. Mex. (87728) 274/E2
Maxwell (bay), N.W. Terrs. 187/K2
Maxwell, Tenn. (†37306) 237/J10
Maxwell Air Force Base, Ala. 195/F6
Maxwelton, Queensland 88/G4
May, Idaho (83253) 220/E5
May (cape), N.J. 188/M3
May (cape), N.J. 273/C6
May, Okla. (73851) 288/G1
May, Isle of (isl.), Scotland 15/F4
May, Texas (76857) 303/F5
Maya (mts.), Belize 154/C2
Maya (riv.), U.S.S.R. 54/P4
Maya (riv.), U.S.S.R. 48/O4
Maya Beach, Belize 154/C2
Mayaguana (isl.), Bahamas 146/L7
Mayaguana (isl.), Bahamas 156/D2
Mayaguana (passage), Bahamas 156/D2
Mayagüez (dist.), P. Rico 161/B2
Mayagüez, P. Rico 161/A2
Mayagüez, P. Rico 156/F1
Mayagüez (bay), P. Rico 161/A2
Mayajigua, Cuba 158/F2
Mayáls, Spain 33/G2
Mayarí, Cuba 158/J3
Mayarí Arriba, Cuba 158/J4
Mayaro, Trin. & Tob. 161/B11
Mayaro (bay), Trin. & Tob. 161/B11
Maybee, Mich. (48159) 250/F6
Maybell, Colo. (81640) 208/C2
Mayberry, Md. (†21157) 245/K2
Maybeury, W. Va. (24861) 312/D8
Maybole, Scotland 10/D3
Maybole, Scotland 15/D5
Maybrook, N.Y. (12543) 276/M8
Mayburg, Pa. (†16347) 294/D2
Maydena, Tasmania 99/C4
Mayen, W. Germany 22/B3
Mayenne (dept.), France 28/C3
Mayenne, France 28/C3
Mayenne (riv.), France 28/C4
Mayer, Ariz. (86333) 198/C4
Mayer, Chile 138/E7
Mayer, Minn. (55360) 255/E6
Mayersville, Miss. (39113) 256/B5
Mayerthorpe, Alberta 182/C3
Mayes (co.), Okla. 288/R2
Mayesville, S.C. (29104) 296/G4
Mayetta, Kansas (66509) 232/G2
Mayetta, N.J. (†08092) 273/E4
Mayfair, Sask. 181/D2
Mayfield, Georgia (31087) 217/G4
Mayfield, Kansas (67103) 232/E4
Mayfield, Ky. (42066) 237/D7
Mayfield (creek), Ky. 237/C7
Mayfield, N.Y. (12117) 276/M4
Mayfield, Ohio (44124) 284/J9
Mayfield, Okla. (73656) 288/G4
Mayfield, Pa. (18433) 294/L2
Mayfield, Scotland 15/C2
Mayfield, Utah (84643) 304/C4
Mayfield (lake), Wash. 310/C4
Mayfield Heights, Ohio (44124) 284/J9
Mayflower, Ark. (72106) 202/F4
Mayger, Oreg. (97016) 291/D1
Mayhew, Miss. (39753) 256/G4
Mayhill, N. Mex. (88339) 274/D6
Maykop, U.S.S.R. 7/H4
Maykop, U.S.S.R. 48/D5
Maykop, U.S.S.R. 52/F6
Mayland, Tenn. (†38555) 237/L8
Maylene, Ala. (35114) 195/E4
Maymont, Sask. 181/D3
Maymyo, Burma 72/C2
Mayna, La. (†71343) 238/G4
Maynard, Ark. (72444) 202/J1
Maynard, Iowa (50655) 229/K3
Maynard○, Mass. (01754) 249/J3
Maynard, Minn. (56260) 255/C6
Maynardville, Tenn. (37807) 237/O8
Mayne, Br. Col. 184/K3
Maynooth, Ireland 17/H5
Maynooth, Ontario 177/G2
Mayo, Canada 4/C16
Mayo, Fla. (32066) 212/C1
Mayo (co.), Ireland 17/C4
Mayo, Md. (21106) 245/M5
Mayo (riv.), Peru 128/D6
Mayo (bay), Philippines 82/F7
Mayo, S.C. (29368) 296/D1
Mayo, Yukon 187/E3
Mayo, Yukon 162/C3
Mayo (lake), Yukon 187/E3
Mayodan, N.C. (27027) 281/K2
Mayon (vol.), Philippines 82/D4
Mayor (isl.), N. Zealand 100/F2
Mayor (cape), Spain 33/E1
Mayor Martínez, Paraguay 144/C5
Mayor Pablo Lagerenza, Paraguay 144/B1
MAYOTTE 118/G2
Mayotte (isl), France 102/G6
Mayoworth, Wyo. (†82639) 319/F2
May Park, Oreg. (†97850) 291/J2
May Pen, Jamaica 158/J6
Mayport Naval Air Sta., Fla. 212/E1
Mayrhofen, Austria 41/A3
Mays, Ind. (46155) 227/G5
Maysan (gov.), Iraq 66/E5
Maysel, W. Va. (25133) 312/D5
Mays Landing, N.J. (08330) 273/D5
Mays Lick, Ky. (41055) 237/O3
Maysville, Ark. (72747) 202/A1
Maysville, Georgia (30558) 217/E2
Maysville, Iowa (†52773) 229/M5
Maysville, Ky. (41056) 237/O3
Maysville, Mo. (64469) 261/D3
Maysville, N.C. (28555) 281/P5
Maysville, Okla. (73057) 288/M5
Maysville, W. Va. (26833) 312/H4
Maytiguid (isl.), Philippines 82/B5
Maytown, Ky. (41455) 237/O5
Mayumba, Gabon 115/A4
Mayuram, India 68/D6
Mayview, Mo. (64071) 261/E4
Mayville, Mich. (48744) 250/F5
Mayville, N.Y. (14757) 276/A6
Mayville, N. Dak. (58257) 282/R4
Mayville, Oreg. (97830) 291/G2
Mayville, Wis. (53050) 317/K9
Maywood, Calif. (90201) 204/C10
Maywood, Ill. (60153) 222/B5
Maywood, Mo. (63454) 261/J3
Maywood, Nebr. (69038) 264/D4
Maywood, N.J. (07607) 273/B2
Maywood Park, Oreg. (97220) 291/B2
Maza, N. Dak. (†58324) 282/M3
Mazabuka, Zambia 115/E7
Mazabuka, Zambia 102/E6
Mazagan (El Jadida), Morocco 106/C2
Mazagão, Brazil 132/D3
Mazama, Wash. (98833) 310/E2
Mazamet, France 28/E6
Mazán, Peru 128/F4
Mazana (lake), Québec 172/C2
Mazana (riv.), Québec 172/C2
Mazandaran (prov.), Iran 66/H2
Mazangano, Uruguay 145/E3
Mazapil, Mexico 150/J4
Mazara del Vallo, Italy 34/D6
Mazar-e Sharif, Afghanistan 59/J2
Mazar-e Sharif, Afghanistan 68/B1
Mazarrón, Spain 33/F4
Mazaruni (riv.), Guyana 131/A2
Mazaruni-Potaro (dist.), Guyana 131/A2
Mazatán, Mexico 150/E2
Mazatenango, Guatemala 154/B3
Mazatlán, Mexico 146/H7
Mazatlán, Mexico 150/F5
Mazatzal (peak), Ariz. 198/D4
Mažeikiai, U.S.S.R. 53/A2
Mazenod, Sask. 181/E6
Mazeppa, Alberta 182/D4
Mazeppa, Minn. (55956) 255/F6
Mazgirt, Turkey 63/H3
Mazıdağı, Turkey 63/J4
Mazie, Okla. (74353) 288/R2
Mazinaw (lake), Ontario 177/G3
Mazirbe, U.S.S.R. 53/B2
Mazocruz, Peru 128/H11
Mazoe (riv.), Mozambique 118/E3
Mazoe, Zimbabwe 118/E3
Mazoe (riv.), Zimbabwe 118/E3
Mazomanie, Wis. (53560) 317/G9
Mazon, Ill. (60444) 222/E2
Mazra', Israel 65/C5
Mazu (Matsu) (isl.), China 77/K6
Mazzarino, Italy 34/E6
Mbabane (cap.), Swaziland 118/E5
Mbabane (cap.), Swaziland 102/F7
Mbaïki, Cent. Afr. Rep. 115/C3
Mbakou (res.), Cameroon 115/B2
Mbala, Zambia 102/F5
Mbala, Zambia 115/F5
Mbale, Uganda 115/F3
Mbale, Uganda 102/F4
Mbalmayo, Cameroon 115/B3
Mbamba Bay, Tanzania 115/G6
Mbandaka, Zaire 115/C3
Mbandaka, Zaire 102/D5
Mbanza Congo, Angola 115/B5
Mbanza-Ngungu, Zaire 102/D5
Mbanza-Ngungu, Zaire 115/C5
Mbaracayú, Cordillera de (mts.), Paraguay 144/E3
Mbarangandu (riv.), Tanzania 115/G5
Mbarara, Uganda 115/F4
Mbemkuru (riv.), Tanzania 115/G5
Mbengga (isl.), Fiji 86/Q11
Mbéré (riv.), Cameroon 115/B2
Mbéré (riv.), Cent. Afr. Rep. 115/B2
Mbéré (riv.), Chad 111/C6
Mbeya (reg.), Tanzania 115/F5
Mbeya, Tanzania 102/F5
Mbeya, Tanzania 115/F5
M'Bigou, Gabon 115/B4
Mbinda, Congo 115/B4
Mbini, Equat. Guinea 115/A3
Mbocayaty, Paraguay 144/C5
M'Bour, Senegal 106/A6
M'Bout, Mauritania 106/B5
Mbres, Cent. Afr. Rep. 115/D2
M'Bridge (riv.), Angola 115/B5
Mbuji-Mayi, Zaire 102/E5
Mbuji-Mayi, Zaire 115/D5
Mbulu, Tanzania 115/G4
Mburucuyá, Argentina 143/E2
Mbuyapey, Paraguay 144/D5
McAdam, New Bruns. 170/C3
McAdams, Miss. (39107) 256/E4
McAdoo, Pa. (18237) 294/L4
McAdoo, Texas (79243) 303/D4
McAfee, N.J. (07428) 273/D1
McAlester, Okla. 188/G4
McAlester, Okla. (74501) 288/P5
McAlester (lake), Okla. 288/P4
McAllister, N. Mex. (88427) 274/F4
McAlisterville, Pa. (17049) 294/H4
McAllaster, Kansas (†67755) 232/A3
McAllen, Texas 188/G5
McAllen, Texas (78501) 303/F11
McAllister, Mont. (59740) 262/E5
McAllister, Wis. (†54177) 317/L5
McAlpin, Fla. (32062) 212/D1
McAndrews, Ky. (41543) 237/S5
McArthur, Calif. (96056) 204/D2
McArthur, Ohio (45651) 284/F7
McArthur River, North. Terr. 88/F3
McAuley, Manitoba 179/A4
McBain, Mich. (49657) 250/D4
McBaine, Mo. (†65201) 261/H5
McBean, Georgia (†30908) 217/J4
McBee, S.C. (29101) 296/G3
McBride, Br. Col. 184/G3
McBride, Miss. (†39144) 256/C7
McBride, Mo. (63776) 261/N7
McBride, Okla. (†74441) 288/N7
McBride Lake, Sask. 181/J3
McBrides, Mich. (48852) 250/D5
McCabe, Mont. (59245) 262/M2
McCain, N.C. (28361) 281/L4
McCall, Idaho (83638) 220/C5
McCall, La. (†70346) 238/K3
McCalla, Ala. (35111) 195/E4
McCall Creek, Miss. (39647) 256/C7
McCallsburg, Iowa (50154) 229/G4
McCallum, Newf. 166/C4
McCamey, Texas (79752) 303/B6
McCammon, Idaho (83250) 220/F7
McCanna, N. Dak. (58253) 282/P3
McCarley, Miss. (38943) 256/E3
McCarr, Ky. (41544) 237/S5
McCarthy, Alaska (†99566) 196/K2
McCaskill, Ark. (71847) 202/C6
McCauley (isl.), Br. Col. 184/B3
McCaulley, Texas (79534) 303/E5
McCausland, Iowa (52758) 229/M5
McCaysville, Georgia (30555) 217/D1
McChord A.F.B., Wash. 310/C3
McClain (co.), Okla. 288/L5
McClave, Colo. (81057) 208/O6
McCleary, Wash. (98557) 310/B3
McClellan A.F.B., Calif. 204/B8
McClelland (lake), Alberta 182/E1
McClelland, Ark. (†72006) 202/H3
McClelland, Iowa (51548) 229/B6
McClellanville, S.C. (29458) 296/H5
McCloud, Calif. (96057) 204/C2
McCloud, Tenn. (†37857) 237/R8
McClure (lake), Calif. 204/E6
McClure, Ill. (62957) 222/D6
McClure, Ohio (43534) 284/C3
McClure, Pa. (17841) 294/H4
McClure, Va. (24269) 307/D6
McClusky, N. Dak. (58463) 282/K4
McColl, S.C. (29570) 296/H2
McComb, Miss. (39648) 256/D8
McComb, Ohio (45858) 284/C3
McConaughy, C. W. (lake), Nebr. 264/C3
McCondy, Miss. (38854) 256/G3
McCone (co.), Mont. 262/L3
McConnell, Ill. (61050) 222/D1
McConnell, Manitoba 179/B4
McConnell, Tenn. (†38237) 237/D8
McConnell A.F.B., Kansas 232/E4
McConnells, S.C. (29726) 296/E2
McConnellsburg, Pa. (17233) 294/F6
McConnellsville, N.Y. (13401) 276/J4
McConnelsville, Ohio (43756) 284/G6
McCook, Nebr. (69001) 264/D4
McCook (co.), S. Dak. 298/P6
McCool, Miss. (39108) 256/F4
McCool Junction, Nebr. (68401) 264/G4
McCord, Sask. 181/E6
McCordsville, Ind. (46055) 227/F5
McCorkle, W. Va. (†25564) 312/C6
McCormick (co.), S.C. 296/C4
McCormick, S.C. (29835) 296/C4
McCoy, Colo. (80463) 208/F3
McCoy (head), New Bruns. 170/E3
McCoy, Oreg. (†97338) 291/D2
McCoy (creek), Oreg. 291/J2
McCoy, Va. (24111) 307/G6
McCoy A.F.B., Fla. 212/E3
McCoysburg, Ind. (†47978) 227/C3
McCracken, Kansas (67556) 232/C3
McCracken (co.), Ky. 237/D6
McCrea, Pa. (†17241) 294/H5
McCreary (co.), Ky. 237/N7
McCreary, Manitoba 179/C4
McCrory, Ark. (72101) 202/H3
McCulloch (co.), Texas 303/E6
McCullom Lake, Ill. (†60050) 222/E1
McCullough, Ala. (36552) 195/D8
McCune, Kansas (66753) 232/G4
McCurtain (co.), Okla. 288/S6
McCurtain, Okla. (74944) 288/R4
McCutchenville, Ohio (44844) 284/D4
McDade, Texas (78650) 303/G7
McDaniel, Md. (21647) 245/N5
McDaniels, Ky. (40152) 237/J5
McDavid, Fla. (32568) 212/B5
McDermitt, Nev. (89421) 266/D1
McDermott, Ohio (45652) 284/D8
McDonald (isls.), Australia 2/N8
McDonald, Kansas (67745) 232/A2
McDonald (co.), Mo. 261/D9
McDonald (lake), Mont. 262/B2
McDonald, N. Mex. (88262) 274/F5
McDonald, N.C. (28340) 281/L5
McDonald, Ohio (44437) 284/J3
McDonald, Pa. (15057) 294/B5
McDonald, Tenn. (37353) 237/M10
McDonalds Corners, Ontario 177/H3
McDonnell, Queensland 95/B1
McDonough (lake), Conn. 210/D1
McDonough, Del. (†19709) 245/R3
McDonough, Georgia (30253) 217/D4
McDonough (co.), Ill. 222/C3
McDonough, N.Y. (13801) 276/J5
McDougal, Ark. (72441) 202/K1
McDougall (lake), New Bruns. 170/D3
McDowell, Ala. (†35450) 195/C5
McDowell, Ky. (41647) 237/R6
McDowell (co.), N.C. 281/E3
McDowell, Va. (24458) 307/J4
McDowell (co.), W. Va. 312/C8
McDowell, W. Va. (24858) 312/D8
McDuffie (co.), Georgia 217/H4
McElhattan, Pa. (17748) 294/H3
McElmo (creek), Colo. 208/B8
McElmo (creek), Utah 304/E6
McEwen, Tenn. (37101) 237/F8
McFadden, Wyo. (82080) 319/F4
McFall, Mo. (64657) 261/D2
McFarlan, N.C. (28102) 281/J5
McFarland, Calif. (93250) 204/F8
McFarland, Kansas (66501) 232/F2
McFarland, Mich. (†49880) 250/B2
McFarland, Wis. (53558) 317/H10
McFarlane (riv.), Sask. 181/L2
McGaffey, N. Mex. (†87316) 274/A3
McGaheysville, Va. (22840) 307/L4
McGee, Sask. 181/C4
McGees Mills, Pa. (15755) 294/E4
McGehee, Ark. (71654) 202/H6
McGill, Nev. (89318) 266/G3
McGivney, New Bruns. 170/D2
McGloughlin (peak), Mont. 262/C4
McGrath, Alaska 188/C5
McGrath, Alaska (99627) 196/H2
McGrath, Minn. (56350) 255/E4
McGraw, N.Y. (13101) 276/H5
McGraw Brook, New Bruns. 170/D2
McGrawsville, Ind. (†46911) 227/E3
McGregor (lake), Alberta 182/D4
McGregor, Br. Col. 184/G3
McGregor (riv.), Br. Col. 184/G3
McGregor, Iowa (52157) 229/L2
McGregor, Minn. (55760) 255/E4
McGregor (lake), Mont. 262/B3
McGregor, N. Dak. (58755) 282/D2
McGregor, Ontario 177/B5
McGregor, Texas (76657) 303/G6
McGrew, Nebr. (69353) 264/A3
McGuffey, Ohio (45859) 284/C4
McGuire (mt.), Idaho 220/D4
McGuire A.F.B., N.J. 273/D3
McHenry (co.), Ill. 222/E1
McHenry, Ill. (60050) 222/E1
McHenry, Ky. (42354) 237/H6
McHenry, Miss. (39561) 256/F9
McHenry (co.), N. Dak. 282/J3
McHenry, N. Dak. (58464) 282/N4
McHenry Shores, Ill. (†60050) 222/E1
Mchinga, Tanzania 115/H5
Mchinji, Malawi 115/F6
McIlwraith (range), Queensland 95/B2
McIndoe Falls, Vt. (05050) 268/C3
McIntire, Iowa (50455) 229/H2
McIntosh, Ala. (36553) 195/B8
McIntosh, Fla. (32664) 212/D2
McIntosh (co.), Georgia 217/K7
McIntosh, Georgia (†31320) 217/K7
McIntosh, Minn. (56556) 255/C3
McIntosh, N. Mex. (87032) 274/D4
McIntosh (co.), N. Dak. 282/L7
McIntosh (co.), Okla. 288/P4
McIntosh, Ontario 177/F4
McIntosh, Ontario 175/B3
McIntosh, S. Dak. (57641) 298/G2
McIntyre, Georgia (31054) 217/F5
McIvor, Mich. (†48748) 250/F4
McKague, Sask. 181/G3
McKamie, Ark. (†71860) 202/C7
McKay (lake), Manitoba 179/C2
McKay (res.), Oreg. 291/J2
McKean (co.), Pa. 294/E2
McKean, Pa. (16426) 294/B2
McKeand (riv.), N.W. Terrs. 187/M3
McKee (creek), Ill. 222/C4
McKee, Ky. (40447) 237/O6
McKee City, N.J. (†08232) 273/D5
McKeesport, Pa. 188/L2
McKeesport, Pa. (*15130) 294/C7
McKees Rocks, Pa. (15136) 294/B7
McKellar, Ontario 177/D2
McKendrick, New Bruns. 170/D1
McKenna, Wash. (98558) 310/C4
McKenney, Va. (23872) 307/N7
McKenzie, Ala. (36456) 195/E7
McKenzie (co.), N. Dak. 282/D4
McKenzie, N. Dak. (58553) 282/K6
McKenzie, South Fork (riv.), Oreg. 291/E3
McKenzie, Tenn. (38201) 237/E8
McKenzie Bridge, Oreg. (97401) 291/E3
McKerrow, Ontario 177/C1
McKinlay, Queensland 95/B4
McKinlay, Queensland 88/G4
McKinley, Ala. (†36743) 195/C6
McKinley (mt.), Alaska 146/C3
McKinley (mt.), Alaska 188/D5
McKinley (mt.), Alaska 196/H2
McKinley, Cuba 158/B2
McKinley, Minn. (55761) 255/F3
McKinley (co.), N. Mex. 274/A3
McKinley (mt.), U.S. 4/C17

408 McKinley

McKinley, Wyo. (†82633) 319/G3
McKinley Park, Alaska (99755) 196/J2
McKinleyville, Calif. (95521) 204/A3
McKinney (lake), Kansas 232/A3
McKinney, Ky. (40448) 237/M6
McKinney, Texas (75069) 303/H4
McKinnon, Georgia (†31545) 217/J8
McKinnon, Tenn. (†37175) 237/F8
McKinnon, Wyo. (82938) 319/C4
McKittrick, Calif. (93251) 204/F8
McKittrick, Mo. (65056) 261/J5
McLain, Miss. (39456) 256/G8
McLane, Pa. (†16426) 294/B2
McLaughlin, Alberta 182/E3
McLaughlin, S. Dak. (57642) 298/H2
McLaurin, Miss. (†39401) 256/F8
McLean (co.), Ill. 222/E3
McLean, Ill. (61754) 222/D3
McLean (co.), Ky. 237/G5
McLean, Nebr. (68747) 264/G2
McLean, N.Y. (13102) 276/H5
McLean (co.), N. Dak. 282/G4
McLean, Sask. 181/G5
McLean, Texas (79057) 303/D2
McLean, Va. (*22101) 307/S2
McLeansboro, Ill. (62859) 222/E5
McLelan (str.), Newf. 166/B1
McLemoresville, Tenn. (38235) 237/D9
McLennan, Alberta 182/B2
McLennan (co.), Texas 303/G6
McLeod (riv.), Alberta 182/B3
McLeod (co.), Minn. 255/D6
McLeod, Mont. (59052) 262/G5
McLeod, N. Dak. (58057) 282/R7
McLeod (bay), N.W. Terrs. 187/G3
McLeod (lake), W. Australia 88/A4
McLeod (lake), W. Australia 92/A4
McLeod Lake, Br. Col. 184/F2
McLeod River, Alberta 182/B3
M'Clintock, Manitoba 179/K2
M'Clintock (chan.), N.W.T. 146/H2
M'Clintock (chan.), N.W.T. 162/F1
M'Clintock (bay), N.W. Terrs. 187/K1
M'Clintock (chan.), N.W. Terrs. 187/H2
McLoud, Okla. (74851) 288/M4
McLoughlin (mt.), Oreg. 291/E5
McLoughlin House Nat'l Hist. Site, Oreg. 291/B2
McLouth, Kansas (66054) 232/G2
McLure, Br. Col. 184/H4
M'Clure (str.), Canada 4/B15
M'Clure (cape), N.W.T. 162/D1
M'Clure (str.), N.W.T. 146/F2
M'Clure (str.), N.W.T. 162/E1
M'Clure (cape), N.W. Terrs. 187/F2
M'Clure (str.), N.W. Terrs. 187/G2
McMahon, Sask. 181/D5
McMechen, W. Va. (26040) 312/E3
McMillan, Mich. (49853) 250/D2
McMillan (lake), N.Mex. 188/F4
McMillan (lake), N. Mex. 274/E6
McMillan, Okla. (73445) 288/M6
McMinn (co.), Tenn. 237/M10
McMinnville, Oreg. (97128) 291/D2
McMinnville, Tenn. (37110) 237/K9
McMorran, Sask. 181/C4
McMullen (co.), Texas 303/F9
McMunn, Manitoba 179/G5
McMurdo (sound), Ant. 2/A10
McMurdo (sound) 5/B9
McMurdo, Br. Col. 184/J4
McMurray, Wash. (†98273) 310/C2
McNab, Alberta 182/D5
McNab, Ark. (†71838) 202/C6
McNabb, Ill. (61335) 222/D2
McNair, Texas (†77520) 303/K1
McNairy (co.), Tenn. 237/D10
McNairy, Tenn. (†38315) 237/D10
McNamee, New Bruns. 170/D2
McNary, Ariz. (85930) 198/F4
McNary, La. (†71433) 238/E5
McNary, Oreg. (97858) 291/H2
McNary (dam), Oreg. 291/H2
McNary, Texas (79839) 303/B11
McNary (dam), Wash. 310/F5
McNaughton, Wis. (54543) 317/H4
McNeal, Ariz. (85617) 198/F7
McNeil, Ark. (71752) 202/D7
McNeill, Miss. (39457) 256/E9
McNulty, Oreg. (†97053) 291/E2
McNutt (isl.), Nova Scotia 168/C5
McPhadyen (riv.), Newf. 166/A3
McPhail (riv.), Manitoba 179/F2
McPherson (co.), Kansas 232/E3
McPherson, Kansas (67460) 232/E3
McPherson (co.), Nebr. 264/C3
McPherson (range), N.S. Wales 97/G1
McPherson (co.), S. Dak. 298/L2
McQuady, Ky. (40153) 237/H5
McRae, Alberta 182/E2
McRae, Ark. (72102) 202/G3
McRae, Georgia (31055) 217/G6
McRoberts, Ky. (41835) 237/R6
McShan, Ala. (35471) 195/B4
McSherrystown, Pa. (17344) 294/H6
McTaggart, Sask. 181/H6
McTavish, Manitoba 179/E5
McTavish Arm (inlet), N.W. Terrs. 187/G3
McVeigh, Ky. (41546) 237/S5
McVeytown, Pa. (17051) 294/G4
McVicar Arm (inlet), N.W. Terrs. 187/F3
McVille, N. Dak. (58254) 282/O4
McWhorter, W. Va. (26401) 312/F4
McWilliams, Ala. (36753) 195/D7
Meacham (lake), N.Y. 276/M1
Meacham, Oreg. (97859) 291/J2
Meacham, Sask. 181/F3
Mead (lake) 188/D3
Mead (lake), Ariz. 198/A2
Mead, Colo. (80542) 208/K2
Mead, Nebr. (68041) 264/H3
Mead (lake), Nev. 266/G6
Mead, Okla. (73449) 288/O7
Mead (lake), U.S. 146/G6
Mead, Wash. (99021) 310/H3
Meade (riv.), Alaska 196/G1
Meade (peak), Idaho 220/G7
Meade (co.), Kansas 232/B4
Meade, Kansas (67864) 232/B4
Meade (co.), Ky. 237/J5
Meade (co.), S. Dak. 298/D5
Meador, W. Va. (†25678) 312/B7
Meadow (creek), Idaho 220/C4
Meadow (mt.), Md. 245/B2
Meadow (lake), Sask. 181/C1
Meadow, S. Dak. (57644) 298/E2
Meadow, Texas (79345) 303/B4
Meadow, Utah (84644) 304/B5
Meadow (riv.), W. Va. 312/E6
Meadow Bluff, W. Va. (24958) 312/E7
Meadow Bridge, W. Va. (25976) 312/E7
Meadowbrook, Ill. (†62010) 222/B2
Meadowbrook, W. Va. (26404) 312/F4
Meadow Creek, W. Va. (25977) 312/E7
Meadow Grove, Nebr. (68752) 264/G2
Meadow Lake, Sask. 181/C1
Meadow Lake Prov. Park, Sask. 181/K4
Meadowlands, Minn. (55765) 255/F3
Meadow Lands, Pa. (15347) 294/B5
Meadow Portage, Manitoba 179/C3
Meadows, Idaho (†83654) 220/B5
Meadows, Ill. (†61726) 222/E3
Meadows, Md. (†20870) 245/G5
Meadows, N.H. (03587) 268/E3
Meadows, S. Australia 94/B8
Meadows of Dan, Va. (24120) 307/H7
Meadow Vale, Ky. (†40201) 237/L1
Meadow Valley, Calif. (95956) 204/D4
Meadow Valley Wash (riv.), Nev. 266/G5
Meadowview-Emory, Va. (24361) 307/D7
Meadow Vista, N. Mex. (†79901) 274/C7
Meadville, Miss. (39653) 256/C8
Meadville, Mo. (64659) 261/F3
Meadville, Pa. 188/L2
Meadville, Pa. (16335) 294/B2
Meaford, Ontario 177/D3
Meagher (co.), Mont. 262/F4
Meaghers Grant, Nova Scotia 168/E4
Meakan (mt.), Japan 81/L2
Mealhada, Portugal 33/B2
Meally, Ky. (41234) 237/R5
Mealy (lake), Newf. 166/C3
Meander, Tasmania 99/C3
Meander River, Alberta 182/A5
Meanook, Alberta 182/D2
Means, Ky. (40346) 237/O5
Meansville, Georgia (30256) 217/D4
Meares (cape), Oreg. 291/C2
Mearim (riv.), Brazil 132/E4
Mearns, Alberta 182/D3
Mears, Mich. (49436) 250/C5
Meath (co.), Ireland 17/H4
Meathas Truim, Ireland 17/G4
Meath Park, Sask. 181/F2
Meaux, France 28/E3
Mebane, N.C. (27302) 281/L2
Mecca, Calif. (92254) 204/K10
Mecca, Ind. (47860) 227/C5
Mecca (cap.), Saudi Arabia 2/M4
Mecca (cap.), Saudi Arabia 59/C5
Mecca (cap.), Saudi Arabia 54/F7
Mechanic Falls, Maine (04256) 243/C7
Mechanic Falls○, Maine (04256) 243/C7
Mechanicsburg, Ill. (62545) 222/D4
Mechanicsburg, Ind. (†47356) 227/G5
Mechanicsburg, Ohio (43044) 284/D5
Mechanicsburg, Pa. (17055) 294/H5
Mechanicsburg, Va. (†24315) 307/G6
Mechanicstown, Ohio (44651) 284/H4
Mechanicsville, Conn. (06252) 210/H1
Mechanicsville, Georgia (30040) 217/L1
Mechanicsville, Iowa (52306) 229/L5
Mechanicsville, Md. (20659) 245/M7
Mechanicsville, Va. (23111) 307/O5
Mechanicville, N.Y. (12118) 276/N5
Mechelen, Belgium 27/F6
Mecheria, Algeria 106/D2
Mechernich, W. Germany 22/B3
Mecidiye, Turkey 63/B5
Mecitözü, Turkey 63/F2
Mecklenburg (bay), E. Germany 22/D1
Mecklenburg (reg.), E. Germany 22/E2
Mecklenburg, N.Y. (14863) 276/G6
Mecklenburg (co.), N.C. 281/H4
Mecklenburg (co.), Va. 307/M7
Mecklenburg (bay), W. Germany 22/D1
Meckling, S. Dak. (57044) 298/R8
Meconta, Mozambique 118/F3
Mecosta (co.), Mich. 250/D5
Mecosta, Mich. (49332) 250/D5
Mecoya, Bolivia 136/C8
Mecsek (mts.), Hungary 41/D3
Mecúfi, Mozambique 118/G2
Mecula, Mozambique 118/F2
Medain Salih, Saudi Arabia 59/C4
Medan, Indonesia 54/L9
Medan, Indonesia 85/B5
Médanos, Buenos Aires, Argentina 143/D4
Médanos, Entre Ríos, Argentina 143/G6
Médanos (isth.), Venezuela 124/D2
Medanosa (pt.), Argentina 143/D6
Medaryville, Ind. (47957) 227/D2
Meddybemps○, Maine (04657) 243/J5
Meddybemps (lake), Maine 243/J5
Médéa, Algeria 106/E1
Medel (mt.), Switzerland 39/D2
Medellín, Colombia 120/B2
Medellín, Colombia 126/C4
Medellín de Bravo, Mexico 150/Q2
Medemblik, Netherlands 27/G3
Médenine, Tunisia 106/F2
Méderdra, Mauritania 106/A5
Mederville, Iowa (†52043) 229/K3
Medetsiz Tepe (mt.), Turkey 63/F4
Medfield, Mass. (02052) 249/B8
Medfield○, Mass. (02052) 249/B8
Medford, Maine (†04453) 243/F5
Medford○, Maine (†04453) 243/F5
Medford, Mass. (02155) 249/C6
Medford, Minn. (55049) 255/E6
Medford, N.J. (08055) 273/D4
Medford, Okla. (73759) 288/L1
Medford, Oreg. 188/B2
Medford, Oreg. 146/F5
Medford, Oreg. (97501) 291/E5
Medford, Wis. (54451) 317/F5
Medford Center, Maine (†04453) 243/F5
Medford Lakes, N.J. (08055) 273/D4
Medgidia, Romania 45/J3
Medgun (creek), N.S. Wales 97/E1
Media, Ill. (61460) 222/C3
Media, Pa. (*19063) 294/L7
Media Agua, Argentina 143/C3
Media Luna, Cuba 158/G4
Mediapolis, Iowa (52637) 229/L6
Mediaş, Romania 45/G2
Medical Lake, Wash. (99022) 310/H3
Medical Springs, Oreg. (97860) 291/K2
Medicine (lake), Mont. 262/M2
Medicine (creek), Nebr. 264/D4
Medicine (creek), S. Dak. 298/J6
Medicine Bow (range), Colo. 208/G1
Medicine Bow, Wyo. (82329) 319/F4
Medicine Bow (range), Wyo. 319/F4
Medicine Bow (riv.), Wyo. 319/F3
Medicine Creek (dam), Nebr. 264/D4
Medicine Hat, Alberta 182/E4
Medicine Hat, Alta. 146/H4
Medicine Hat, Alta. 162/E5
Medicine Knoll (creek), S. Dak. 298/J5
Medicine Lake, Minn. (55441) 255/G5
Medicine Lake, Mont. (59247) 262/M2
Medicine Lodge (creek), Idaho 220/F5
Medicine Lodge, Kansas (67104) 232/D4
Medicine Lodge (riv.), Kansas 232/D4
Medicine Mound, Texas (†79252) 303/E3
Medicine Park, Okla. (73557) 288/J5
Medill, Mo. (†63445) 261/J2
Medina, Colombia 126/D5
Medina (Hamel), Minn. (†55340) 255/F5
Medina, N.Y. (14103) 276/D4
Medina, N. Dak. (58467) 282/M6
Medina (co.), Ohio 284/G3
Medina, Ohio (44256) 284/G3
Medina, Saudi Arabia 54/F7
Medina, Saudi Arabia 59/D5
Medina, Tenn. (38355) 237/D9
Medina (co.), Texas 303/E8
Medina, Texas (78055) 303/E8
Medina (lake), Texas 303/E8
Medina (riv.), Texas 303/J11
Medina, Wash. (98039) 310/B2
Medinaceli, Spain 33/E2
Medina del Campo, Spain 33/D2
Medina de Rioseco, Spain 33/D2
Medina-Sidonia, Spain 33/D4
Mediodía, Colombia 126/D8
Mediterranean (sea) 2/K4
Mediterranean (sea) 7/E5
Mediterranean (sea), Algeria 106/E1
Mediterranean (sea), Egypt 111/E1
Mediterranean (sea), France 28/E7
Mediterranean (sea), Italy 34/B6
Mediterranean (sea), Libya 111/C1
Mediterranean (sea), Morocco 106/D1
Mediterranean (sea), Tunisia 106/F1
Medix Run, Pa. (†15868) 294/F3
Medjerda (riv.), Algeria 106/F1
Medjerda (riv.), Tunisia 106/F1
Medley, Fla. (†33101) 212/B4
Medley, W. Va. (26734) 312/H4
Mednogorsk, U.S.S.R. 52/J4
Mednogorsk, U.S.S.R. 48/F4
Médoc (reg.), France 28/C5
Médog, China 77/E6
Medon, Tenn. (38356) 237/D10
Medora, Ill. (62063) 222/C4
Medora, Ind. (47260) 227/E7
Medora, Kansas (67558) 232/E3
Medora, Manitoba 179/B5
Medora, N. Dak. (58645) 282/C6
Médouneu, Gabon 115/B3
Medstead, Sask. 181/C2
Meductic, New Bruns. 170/C3
Medveditsa (riv.), U.S.S.R. 52/F4
Medvezh'yegorsk, U.S.S.R. 48/D3
Medvezh'yegorsk, U.S.S.R. 52/D2
Medway (riv.), England 13/H6
Medway○, Maine (04460) 243/G4
Medway○, Mass. (02053) 249/J4
Medway (harb.), Nova Scotia 168/D4
Medway (riv.), Nova Scotia 168/C4
Medzilaborce, Czech. 41/F2
Meeandah, Queensland 88/K2
Meehan, Miss. (†39301) 256/G6
Meekatharra, Australia 87/B8
Meekatharra, W. Australia 88/B5
Meekatharra, W. Australia 92/B4
Meeker, Colo. (81641) 208/D2
Meeker, La. (71346) 238/F4
Meeker (co.), Minn. 255/D5
Meeker, Ohio (†43302) 284/D4
Meeker, Okla. (74855) 288/N4
Meeks, Georgia (†31049) 217/G5
Meeks Bay, Calif. (†95730) 204/E5
Meelpaeg (lake), Newf. 166/C4
Meerane, E. Germany 22/E3
Meerhout, Belgium 27/G6
Meers, Okla. (73558) 288/J5
Meersburg, W. Germany 22/C5
Meerssen, Netherlands 27/H7
Meerut, India 54/J7
Meerut, India 68/D3
Meeteetse, Wyo. (82433) 319/D1
Meeting (lake), Sask. 181/D2
Meeting Creek, Alberta 182/D3
Mega, Ethiopia 111/G7
Mega (isl.), Indonesia 85/C6
Megalópolis, Greece 45/E7
Mégantic (co.), Québec 172/F3
Mégantic (lake), Québec 172/G4
Mégara, Greece 45/F6
Megargel, Ala. (36457) 195/D8
Megargel, Texas (76370) 303/F4
Meggett, S.C. (29460) 296/G6
Meghalaya (state), India 68/G3
Megiddo, Israel 65/C2
Mehama, Oreg. (97384) 291/E3
Mehan, Okla. (†74074) 288/M2
Meherrin (riv.), N.C. 281/P1
Meherrin, Va. (23954) 307/M6
Meherrin (riv.), Va. 307/M7
Mehetia (isl.), Fr. Poly. 87/M7
Mehlville, Mo. (†63129) 261/P4
Mehoopany, Pa. (18629) 294/K2
Mehran, Iran 66/E4
Mehran (riv.), Iran 59/F4
Mehran (riv.), Iran 66/J7
Mehsana, India 68/C4
Mehun-sur-Yèvre, France 28/E4
Meifa, P.D.R. Yemen 59/E7
Meiganga, Cameroon 115/B2
Meighen (isl.), N.W.T. 162/M3
Meighen (isl.), N.W. Terrs. 187/H1
Meigle, Scotland 15/E4
Meigs, Georgia (31765) 217/D8
Meigs (co.), Ohio 284/F7
Meigs (co.), Tenn. 237/M9
Meikle (riv.), Alberta 182/A1
Meiktila, Burma 72/B2
Meilen, Switzerland 39/G2
Meiners Oaks-Mira Monte, Calif. (93023) 204/F9
Meiningen, E. Germany 22/D3
Meire Grove, Minn. (†56352) 255/C5
Meiringen, Switzerland 39/F3
Meiron (mt.), Israel 65/C1
Meise, Belgium 27/E7
Meissen, E. Germany 22/E3
Mei Xian, China 77/J7
Mejillones, Chile 120/B5
Mejillones, Chile 138/A4
Mejillones del Sur (bay), Chile 138/A4
Mekambo, Gabon 115/B3
Mekerrhane, Sebkha (salt lake), Algeria 106/E3
Mekili, Libya 111/D1
Mékinac (lake), Québec 172/E2
Mekinock, N. Dak. (58258) 282/R4
Meknès, Morocco 102/B1
Meknès, Morocco 106/C2
Mekong (riv.) 54/M8
Mekong (riv.) 2/Q4
Mekong (riv.), Burma 72/D2
Mekong (riv.), Cambodia 72/E4
Mekong (Lancang Jiang) (riv.), China 77/F7
Mekong (riv.), Laos 72/D3
Mekong (riv.), Thailand 72/E3
Mekong, Mouths of the (delta), Vietnam 72/E5
Mekoryuk, Alaska (99630) 196/E2
Melaka (state), Malaysia 72/D7
Melaka, Malaysia 54/M9
Melaka, Malaysia 72/D7
Melanesia (reg.), Pacific 87/E5
Melaval, Sask. 181/E6
Melba, Idaho (83641) 220/B6
Melber, Ky. (42069) 237/D7
Melbern, Ohio (†43506) 284/A3
Melbeta, Nebr. (69355) 264/A3
Melbourne, Ark. (72556) 202/G1
Melbourne, Australia 2/R7
Melbourne, Australia 87/E9
Melbourne, Fla. 188/K5
Melbourne, Fla. (*32901) 212/F3
Melbourne, Iowa (50162) 229/G5
Melbourne, Ky. (41059) 237/T2
Melbourne, Mo. (†64642) 261/E2
Melbourne (isl.), N.W. Terrs. 187/H3
Melbourne, Ontario 177/C5
Melbourne, Québec 172/E4
Melbourne (cap.), Victoria 88/H7
Melbourne (cap.), Victoria 97/H5
Melbourne, Wash. (†98563) 310/B4
Melbourne Airport, Victoria 88/K7
Melbourne Beach, Fla. (32951) 212/F3
Melby, Minn. (56351) 255/C4
Melcher, Honduras 154/D3
Melcher, Iowa (50163) 229/G6
Melchor (isl.), Chile 138/D6
Melchor Múzquiz, Mexico 150/H3
Melchor Ocampo, Mexico 150/H4
Melchor Ocampo del Balsas, Mexico 150/H8
Melder, La. (71451) 238/E4
Meldorf, W. Germany 22/C1
Meldrim, Georgia (31318) 217/K6
Meldrum Bay, Ontario 177/A2
Meldrum Creek, Br. Col. 184/F4
Meleb, Manitoba 179/E4
Melenki, U.S.S.R. 52/F3
Meleuz, U.S.S.R. 52/J4
Mélèzes (riv.), Québec 174/C1
Melfa, Va. (23410) 307/S5
Melfi, Chad 111/C5
Melfi, Italy 34/E4
Melfort, Sask. 162/F5
Melfort, Sask. 181/G3
Melfort, Loch (inlet), Scotland 15/C4
Melgaço, Portugal 33/B1
Melgar de Fernamental, Spain 33/D1
Melide, Switzerland 39/G5
Meligalá, Greece 45/F7
Melilla, Spain 106/D1
Melilla, Spain 102/B1
Melilla, Spain 7/D5
Melimoyu (mt.), Chile 138/D5
Melinca, Chile 138/D5
Melincué, Argentina /F6
Melipilla, Chile 138/F4
Melita, Manitoba 179/A5
Melitopol', U.S.S.R. 7/H4
Melitopol', U.S.S.R. 52/D5
Melitota, Md. (†21620) 245/O4
Melk, Austria 41/C2
Melkbosstrand, S. Africa 118/E6
Melksham, England 13/E6
Melksham, England 10/E5
Mellansel, Sweden 18/L5
Melle, W. Germany 22/C2
Mellen, Wis. (54546) 317/E3
Mellerud, Sweden 18/H7
Mellette (co.), S. Dak. 298/H6
Mellette, S. Dak. (57461) 298/N3
Mellingen, Switzerland 39/F2
Mellott, Ind. (47958) 227/C4
Mellwood, Ark. (72367) 202/H5
Melmore, Ohio (44845) 284/D3
Mělník, Czech. 41/C1
Melo, Uruguay 120/D6
Melo, Uruguay 145/E3
Melocheville, Québec 172/C4
Melozitna (riv.), Alaska 196/H1
Melrhir, Chott (salt lake), Algeria 106/F2
Melrose, Conn. (06049) 210/E1
Melrose, Fla. (32666) 212/D2
Melrose, Iowa (52569) 229/G7
Melrose, La. (71452) 238/E3
Melrose, Md. (†21102) 245/L2
Melrose, Mass. (02176) 249/D6
Melrose, Minn. (56352) 255/D5
Melrose, Mont. (59743) 262/D5
Melrose, New Bruns. 170/F2
Melrose, Newf. 166/D2
Melrose, N. Mex. (88124) 274/F4
Melrose, N.S. Wales 97/D3
Melrose, Ohio (45861) 284/B3
Melrose, Oreg. (†97470) 291/D4
Melrose, Scotland 15/F5
Melrose, Scotland 10/E3
Melrose, Wis. (54642) 317/E7
Melrose Park, Fla. (†33301) 212/B4
Melrose Park, Ill. (*60160) 222/B5
Melrose Park, N.Y. (†13021) 276/G5
Melrude, Minn. (55766) 255/F3
Mels, Switzerland 39/H2
Melsetter, Zimbabwe 118/E3
Melstone, Mont. (59054) 262/H4
Melsungen, W. Germany 22/C3
Melton, Victoria 97/C5
Melton Hill (lake), Tenn. 237/N9
Melton Mowbray, England 10/F4
Melton Mowbray, England 13/G5
Meltonville, Iowa (†50472) 229/G2
Melun, France 28/E3
Melut, Sudan 111/F5
Melvaig, Scotland 15/C3
Melvern, Kansas (66510) 232/G3
Melvern (lake), Kansas 232/G3
Melvern Square, Nova Scotia 168/C3
Melvich, Scotland 15/E2
Melville (isl.), Australia 87/D7
Melville (isl.), Canada 4/B15
Melville (pen.), Canada 4/C14
Melville (bay), Greenl. 4/B13
Melville, La. (71353) 238/G5
Melville, Mont. (59055) 262/F4
Melville (pen.), N.W.T. 146/K3
Melville (pen.), N.W.T. 162/H2
Melville (isl.), N.W.T. 146/G2
Melville (isl.), N.W.T. 162/E1
Melville (lake), N.W.T. 162/L5
Melville (lake), Newf. 166/C3
Melville, N.Y. (11746) 276/O9
Melville, N. Dak. (†58421) 282/M5
Melville (isl.), N.W. Terrs. 187/G2
Melville (pen.), N.W. Terrs. 187/K3
Melville (isl.), North. Terr. 88/E2
Melville (bay), North. Terr. 88/F2
Melville (bay), North. Terr. 93/E2
Melville (isl.), North. Terr. 93/B1
Melville (cape), Queensland 88/G2
Melville (cape), Queensland 95/C2
Melville, Sask. 162/F5
Melville, Sask. 181/J5
Melville, W. Australia 92/A1
Melvin, Ala. (36913) 195/B7
Melvin, Ill. (60952) 222/E3
Melvin, Iowa (51350) 229/B2
Melvin, Lough (lake), Ireland 10/B3
Melvin (lake), Ireland 17/E3
Melvin, Mich. (48454) 250/G5
Melvin, Minn. (†56540) 255/B3
Melvin, Lough (lake), N. Ireland 10/B3
Melvin, Texas (76858) 303/E6
Melvina, Wis. (54619) 317/E8
Melvindale, Mich. (48122) 250/B7
Melvin Mills, N.H. (†03278) 268/D5
Melvin Village, N.H. (03850) 268/E4
Mélykút, Hungary 41/E3
Memaliaj, Albania 45/D5
Memba, Mozambique 118/G2
Membij, Syria 63/G4
Memel (Klaipeda), U.S.S.R. 52/B3
Memel (Klaipeda), U.S.S.R. 53/A3
Memmingen, W. Germany 22/D5
Mempawah, Indonesia 85/D5
Memphis, Ala. (†35442) 195/B4
Memphis (ruins), Egypt 111/J3
Memphis, Fla. (†33561) 212/D4
Memphis, Ind. (47143) 227/F8
Memphis, Mich. (48041) 250/G6
Memphis, Miss. (†38680) 256/D1
Memphis, Mo. (63555) 261/H2
Memphis, Nebr. (68042) 264/H3
Memphis, Tenn. 146/K6
Memphis, Tenn. 188/J3
Memphis, Tenn. (*38101) 237/B10
Memphis, Texas (79245) 303/D3
Memphis Naval Air Sta., Tenn. 237/B10
Memphremagog (lake), Québec 172/E4
Memphremagog (lake), Vt. 268/C1
Memramcook, New Bruns. 170/F2
Mena, Ark. (71953) 202/B4
Menafra, Uruguay 145/B3
Menahga, Minn. (56464) 255/C4
Menai (str.), Wales 13/C4
Menai Bridge, Wales 13/C4
Menaik, Alberta 182/D3
Ménaka, Mali 106/E5
Menan, Idaho (83434) 220/F6
Menands, N.Y. (†12201) 276/N5
Menarandra (riv.), Madagascar 118/H4
Menard (co.), Ill. 222/D3
Menard (co.), Texas 303/E7
Menard, Texas (76859) 303/E7
Menasalbas, Spain 33/D3
Menasha, Wis. (54952) 317/J7
Mencué, Argentina 143/C5
Mendak, Saudi Arabia 59/D5
Mende, France 28/E5
Mendenhall (cape), Alaska 196/E3
Mendenhall, Miss. (39114) 256/E7
Menderes, Büyük (riv.), Turkey 59/A2
Menderes, Büyük (riv.), Turkey 63/C4
Mendes, Georgia (†30427) 217/H7
Méndez, Ecuador 128/C4
Mendham, N.J. (07945) 273/D2
Mendham, Sask. 181/B5
Mendi, Ethiopia 111/G6
Mendi, Papua N.G. 85/B7
Mendip (hills), England 13/E6
Mendocino (cape), Calif. 146/F5
Mendocino (cape), Calif. 188/A2
Mendocino (co.), Calif. 204/B4
Mendocino, Calif. (95460) 204/B4
Mendocino (cape), Calif. 204/A3
Mendon, Ill. (62351) 222/B3
Mendon○, Mass. (01756) 249/H4
Mendon, Mich. (49072) 250/D7
Mendon, Mo. (64660) 261/F3
Mendon, N.Y. (14506) 276/E4
Mendon, Ohio (45862) 284/A4
Mendon, Utah (84325) 304/B2
Mendon○, Vt. (†05701) 268/B4
Mendooran, N.S. Wales 97/E2
Mendota, Calif. (93640) 204/E7
Mendota, Ill. (61342) 222/D2
Mendota, Minn. (55050) 255/G5
Mendota, Va. (24270) 307/D7
Mendota (lake), Wis. 317/H9
Mendota Heights, Minn. (†55050) 255/G6
Mendoza (prov.), Argentina 143/C4
Mendoza, Argentina 120/C6
Mendoza, Argentina 143/C3
Mendoza (riv.), Argentina 143/C3
Mendoza, Cuba 158/A2
Mendoza, Peru 128/D6
Mendoza, Uruguay 145/C5
Mendrisio, Switzerland 39/G5
Mene de Mauroa, Venezuela 124/C2
Mene Grande, Venezuela 124/C3
Menemen, Turkey 63/B3
Menemsha, Mass. (02552) 249/L7
Menen, Belgium 27/C7
Meneses, Cuba 158/F2
Menfi, Italy 34/D6
Menfro, Mo. (63765) 261/N7
Mengcheng, China 77/J5
Mengen, Turkey 63/D2
Menggala, Indonesia 85/D6
Menghai, China 77/E7
Mengla, China 77/F7
Mengshan, China 77/H7
Mengzi, China 77/F7
Menifee, Ark. (72107) 202/E3
Menifee (co.), Ky. 237/O5
Menihek, Newf. 166/A3
Menihek (lakes), Newf. 166/A3
Menin (Menen), Belgium 27/C7
Menindee, N.S. Wales 97/B3
Menindee (lake), N.S. Wales 97/B3
Meningie, S. Australia 94/F6
Menisino, Manitoba 179/F5
Menistouc (lake), Newf. 166/A3
Menlo, Georgia (30731) 217/B2
Menlo, Iowa (50164) 229/E5
Menlo, Kansas (67746) 232/B2
Menlo, Wash. (98561) 310/B4
Menlo Park, Calif. (94025) 204/J3
Menlo Park, N.J. (08837) 273/E2
Menneval, New Bruns. 170/C1
Menno, S. Dak. (57045) 298/P7
Meno, Okla. (73760) 288/K2
Menoken, N. Dak. (58558) 282/J6
Menominee, Ill. (†61025) 222/C1
Menominee (co.), Mich. 250/B3
Menominee, Mich. (49858) 250/B3
Menominee (riv.), Mich. 250/B3
Menominee (co.), Wis. 317/J5
Menominee (riv.), Wis. 317/L5
Menominee Ind. Res., Wis. 317/J5
Menomonee Falls, Wis. (53051) 317/K1
Menomonie, Wis. (54751) 317/C6
Menongue, Angola 115/C6
Menorca (Minorca) (isl.), Spain 33/J2
Mentasta (pass), Alaska 196/K2
Mentasta Lake, Alaska (†99586) 196/K2
Mentawai (isls.), Indonesia 54/L10
Mentawai (isls.), Indonesia 85/B6
Mentmore, N. Mex. (87319) 274/A3
Menton, France 28/G6
Mentone, Ala. (35984) 195/G1
Mentone, Calif. (92359) 204/H9
Mentone, Ind. (46539) 227/E2
Mentone, Texas (79754) 303/D10
Mentor, Kansas (67465) 232/E3
Mentor, Ky. (†41060) 237/N3
Mentor, Minn. (56736) 255/B3
Mentor, Ohio (44060) 284/H2
Mentor-on-the-Lake, Ohio (44060) 284/G2
Menunketesuck (riv.), Conn. 210/E3
Menye, Turkey 63/C3
Menyuan, China 77/F4
Menzel Bourguiba, Tunisia 106/F1
Menzel Temime, Tunisia 106/G1
Menzie, Manitoba 179/B4
Menzies, W. Australia 88/C5
Menzies, W. Australia 92/C5
Menzingen, Switzerland 39/G2
Menznau, Switzerland 39/E2
Meoquí, Mexico 150/G2
Meota, Sask. 181/C2
Meppel, Netherlands 27/J3
Meppen, W. Germany 22/B2
Mequineza (res.), Spain 33/F2
Mequon, Wis. (53092) 317/L1
Mera, Ecuador 128/C3
Mera (riv.), Switzerland 39/E2
Merabéllou (gulf), Greece 45/H8
Meraïa (reg.), Mauritania 106/C5
Meråker, Norway 18/G5
Meramangye (lake), S. Australia 94/C3
Meramec (riv.), Mo. 261/N3
Merano, Italy 34/C1
Merasheen (isl.), Newf. 166/C2

Miguelete 409

Merauke, Indonesia 85/K7
Merbein, Victoria 97/A4
Mercaderes, Colombia 126/B7
Mercara, India 68/D6
Merced (co.), Calif. 204/E6
Merced, Calif. (95340) 204/E6
Merced (riv.), Calif. 204/E6
Mercedario, Cerro (mt.), Argentina 143/B3
Mercedes, Buenos Aires, Argentina 143/G7
Mercedes, San Luis, Argentina 143/C3
Mercedes, Argentina 120/C6
Mercedes, Corrientes, Argentina 143/G4
Mercedes, Texas (78570) 303/F12
Mercedes, Uruguay 120/D6
Mercedes, Uruguay 145/B4
Merceditas, Chile 138/B7
Mercer (co.), Ill. 222/C2
Mercer (co.), Ky. 237/M5
Mercer○, Maine (04957) 243/D6
Mercer (co.), Mo. 261/E2
Mercer, Mo. (64661) 261/F2
Mercer (co.), N.J. 273/D3
Mercer, N. Zealand 100/E2
Mercer (co.), N. Dak. 282/G5
Mercer, N. Dak. (58559) 282/J5
Mercer (co.), Ohio 284/A4
Mercer, Ohio (†45862) 284/A4
Mercer (co.), Pa. 294/B3
Mercer, Pa. (16137) 294/B3
Mercer, Tenn. (38392) 237/D10
Mercer (co.), W. Va. 312/D8
Mercer, Wis. (54547) 317/F3
Mercer Island (city), Wash. (98040) 310/B2
Mercersburg, Pa. (17236) 294/G6
Mercerville-Hamilton Square, N.J. (08619)273/D3
Merchantville, N.J. (08109) 273/B3
Merchtem, Belgium 27/E7
Mercier, Bolivia 136/B2
Mercier, Kansas (†66439) 232/G2
Mercier, Québec 172/H4
Mercier (dam), Québec 172/A3
Mercoal, Alberta 182/B3
Mercury, Nev. (89023) 266/E6
Mercury (bay), N. Zealand 100/F2
Mercury (isls.), N. Zealand 100/F2
Mercury, Texas (†76872) 303/E6
Mercy (bay), N.W. Terrs. 187/G2
Mercy (cape), N.W. Terrs. 187/M3
Mere, England 13/E6
Meredith, Colo. (81642) 208/F4
Meredith (lake), Colo. 208/M6
Meredith, N.H. (03253) 268/D4
Meredith○, N.H. (03253) 268/D4
Meredith Center, N.H. (†03253) 268/D4
Meredosia, Ill. (62665) 222/C4
Merefa, U.S.S.R. 52/E5
Meregh, Somalia 115/J3
Merelbeke, Belgium 27/D7
Merevari (riv.), Venezuela 124/F5
Mergui, Burma 54/L8
Mergui, Burma 72/C4
Mergui (arch.), Burma 72/C5
Meriç, Turkey 63/B2
Meriç (riv.), Turkey 63/B2
Merid, Sask. 181/B4
Mérida, Mexico 146/J7
Mérida, Mexico 150/P6
Mérida, Spain 7/D5
Mérida, Spain 33/C3
Mérida (state), Venezuela 124/C3
Mérida, Venezuela 120/B2
Mérida, Venezuela 124/C3
Mérida, Cordillera de (range), Venezuela 124/C3
Meriden, Conn. (06450) 210/D2
Meriden, Iowa (51037) 229/B3
Meriden, Kansas (66512) 232/G2
Meriden, Minn. (56067) 255/E6
Meriden, N.H. (03770) 268/C4
Meriden, Wyo. (82081) 319/H4
Meridian, Georgia (31319) 217/K8
Meridian, Idaho (83642) 220/B6
Meridian, Miss. 146/K6
Meridian, Miss. 188/J4
Meridian, Miss. (39301) 256/G6
Meridian, N.Y. (13113) 276/H4
Meridian, Okla. (73058) 288/M3
Meridian, Texas (76665) 303/G6
Meridian Naval Air Sta., Miss. 256/G5
Meridianville, Ala. (35759) 195/F1
Merigold, Miss. (38759) 256/C3
Merigomish, Nova Scotia 168/F3
Merigomish (harb.), Nova Scotia 168/F3
Merimbula, N.S. Wales 97/F5
Merín (lag.), Uruguay 145/F4
Merino, Colo. (80741) 208/N2
Merino, Victoria 97/A5
Merino Jarpa (isl.), Chile 138/D7
Merinos, Uruguay 145/C3
Merino Village, Mass. (†01570) 249/G4
Merion Station, Pa. (19066) 294/M6
Merir (isl.), Belau 87/D5
Meriwether (co.), Georgia 217/C4
Meriwether Lewis Park, Natchez Trace Pkwy., Tenn. 237/G10
Merj 'Uyun, Lebanon 63/F6
Mérk, Hungary 41/G3
Merkel, Texas (79536) 303/E5
Merksem, Belgium 27/E6
Merksplas, Belgium 27/F6
Merlin, Ontario 177/B5
Merlin, Oreg. (97532) 291/D5
Merlo, Argentina 143/G7
Mermentau, La. (70556) 238/E6
Mermentau (riv.), La. 238/E7
Merna, Nebr. (68856) 264/E3
Merna, Wyo. (†83115) 319/B3
Meroe (ruins), Sudan 111/F4
Merom, Ind. (47861) 227/B6
Merowe, Sudan 111/F4
Merowe, Sudan 59/B6
Merredin, W. Australia 88/B6
Merredin, W. Australia 92/B5
Merri (riv.), Victoria 88/L7
Merriam, Ind. (†46701) 227/G2
Merriam, Kansas (66203) 232/H3
Merrick (co.), Nebr. 264/F3
Merrick, N.Y. (11566) 276/R7
Merrick (mt.), Scotland 15/D5
Merrickville, Ontario 177/J3
Merricourt, N. Dak. (58469) 282/N7
Merrifield, Minn. (56465) 255/D4
Merrifield (bay), Newf. 166/B2
Merrifield, N. Dak. (†58201) 282/R4
Merrifield, Va. (22116) 307/S3
Merrill (pass), Alaska 196/H2
Merrill, Iowa (51038) 229/A3
Merrill, Mich. (48637) 250/E5
Merrill, Miss. (†39452) 256/G9
Merrill, N.Y. (12955) 276/N1
Merrill, Oreg. (97633) 291/F5
Merrill, Wis. (54452) 317/G5
Merrillan, Wis. (54754) 317/E7
Merrillville, Georgia (†31792) 217/E9
Merrillville, Ind. (46410) 227/C2
Merrimac, Ky. (†40009) 237/L6
Merrimac○, Mass. (01860) 249/L1
Merrimac, W. Va. (†25661) 312/B7
Merrimac, Wis. (53561) 317/G9
Merrimack (riv.), Mass. 249/K1
Merrimack (co.), N.H. 268/D5
Merrimack○, N.H. (03054) 268/D6
Merrimack (riv.), N.H. 268/D5
Merrimacport, Mass. (†01860) 249/L1
Merriman, Nebr. (69218) 264/C2
Merrimon, N.C. (†28516) 281/R5
Merrionette Park, Ill. (†60601) 222/B6
Merritt, Br. Col. 162/D5
Merritt, Br. Col. 184/G5
Merritt (isl.), Fla. 212/F3
Merritt, Ill. (†62650) 222/C4
Merritt, Mich. (49667) 250/D4
Merritt (res.), Nebr. 264/D2
Merritt, Wash. (†98826) 310/E3
Merritt Island, Fla. (32952) 212/F3
Merriwa, N.S. Wales 97/F3
Merriwagga, N.S. Wales 97/C3
Merriweather, Mich. (49947) 250/F1
Mer Rouge, La. (71261) 238/G1
Merrow, Conn. (06251) 210/F1
Merry Hill, N.C. (27957) 281/R2
Merrymeeting (lake), N.H. 268/E5
Merry Oaks, N.C. (†27559) 281/L3
Merryville, La. (70653) 238/D5
Mersa Fatma, Ethiopia 111/H5
Mersá Matrûh, Egypt 111/E1
Mersa Matrûh, Egypt 102/E1
Mersch, Luxembourg 27/J9
Mersea (dist.), England 13/J6
Merseburg, E. Germany 22/D3
Mersey (riv.), England 10/F2
Mersey (riv.), England 13/G2
Mersey (riv.), Nova Scotia 168/C4
Mersey (riv.), Tasmania 99/C3
Merseyside (co.), England 13/G2
Mershon, Georgia (31551) 217/H8
Mersin, Turkey 63/F4
Mersin, Turkey 59/B2
Mersin, Turkey 54/E6
Mersing, Malaysia 72/E7
Mērsrags, U.S.S.R. 53/B2
Mertert, Luxembourg 27/J9
Merthyr Tydfil, Wales 13/A6
Merthyr Tydfil, Wales 10/E5
Mértola, Portugal 33/C4
Merton, England 10/B5
Merton, England 13/H8
Merton, Wis. (53056) 317/K1
Mertz Glacier Tongue 5/C8
Mertzon, Texas (76941) 303/C6
Mertztown, Pa. (19539) 294/L4
Meru, Kenya 115/G3
Meru (mt.), Tanzania 115/G4
Merv (Mary), U.S.S.R. 48/F8
Merville, Br. Col. 184/E5
Mervin, Sask. 181/C2
Merwin, Mo. (†64723) 261/C6
Merwin (lake), Wash. 310/C5
Merzifon, Turkey 63/F2
Merzig, W. Germany 22/B4
Mesa, Ariz. 146/G6
Mesa, Ariz. 188/D4
Mesa, Ariz. (*85201) 198/D5
Mesa (co.), Colo. 208/B5
Mesa, Colo. (81005) 208/C4
Mesa, Idaho (83643) 220/B5
Mesa, Miss. (†39667) 256/D8
Mesa, Wash. (99343) 310/G4
Mesabi (range), Minn. 255/E3
Mesa Bolívar, Venezuela 124/C3
Mesachie Lake, Br. Col. 184/J3
Mesa del Seri, Mexico 150/D2
Mesagne, Italy 34/G4
Mesai (riv.), Colombia 126/D7
Mesará (gulf), Greece 45/G8
Mesa Verde National Park, Colo. (81330) 208/C8
Mesa Verde Nat'l Park, Colo. 208/C8
Mescalero, N. Mex. (88340) 274/D5
Mescalero (ridge), N. Mex. 274/F6
Mescalero (valley), N. Mex. 274/F5
Mescalero Apache Ind. Res., N. Mex. 274/D5
Meschede, W. Germany 22/C3
Mesena, Georgia (30819) 217/G4
Meservey, Iowa (50457) 229/G3
Meshed, Iran 54/G6
Meshed, Iran 66/L2
Meshed, Iran 59/H2
Meshed-i-Sar (Babol Sar), Iran 66/H2
Meshik, Alaska (†99579) 196/G3
Meshoppen, Pa. (18630) 294/L2
Meshra er Req, Sudan 111/E6
Mesic, N.C. (†28515) 281/R4
Mesick, Mich. (49668) 250/D4
Mesilla, N. Mex. (88046) 274/C6
Mesilla Park, N. Mex. (88047) 274/C6
Mesita, Colo. (81142) 208/H8
Meskanaw, Sask. 181/F3
Meskene, Syria 63/H5
Meskene, Syria 59/C2
Mesocco, Switzerland 39/H4
Mesolóngion, Greece 45/E6
Mesopotamia (reg.), Iraq 66/B3
Mesopotamia (reg.), Iraq 59/D3
Mesopotamia, Ohio (44439) 284/J3
Mesquite, Nev. (89024) 266/G6
Mesquite, N. Mex. (88048) 274/C6
Mesquite, Texas (*75149) 303/H2
Messancy, Belgium 27/H9
Messina (prov.), Italy 34/E5
Messina, Italy 34/E5
Messina, Italy 7/F5
Messina (str.), Italy 34/E6
Messina, S. Africa 118/D4
Messines, Québec 172/B3
Messíni, Greece 45/E7
Messíni (gulf), Greece 45/E7
Mesta (riv.), Bulgaria 45/F5
Mestre, Italy 34/D2
Mesudiye, Turkey 63/F4
Meta (riv.) 120/B2
Meta (dept.), Colombia 126/D6
Meta (riv.), Colombia 126/E5
Meta, Ky. (41501) 237/S5
Meta, Mo. (65058) 261/H6
Meta (riv.), Venezuela 124/E4
Metabetchouan, Québec 172/F1
Métabetchouane (riv.), Québec 172/F1
Metairie, La. (*70001) 238/O4
Metaline, Wash. (99152) 310/H2
Metaline Falls, Wash. (99153) 310/H2
Metamma, Ethiopia 111/G5
Metamora, Ill. (61548) 222/D3
Metamora, Ind. (47030) 227/G6
Metamora, Mich. (48455) 250/F6
Metamora, Ohio (43540) 284/C2
Metán, Argentina 143/D2
Metangula, Mozambique 118/F2
Metapán, El Salvador 154/C3
Métascouac (lake), Québec 172/F2
Metasville, Georgia (†30673) 217/G3
Metauro (riv.), Italy 34/D3
Metcalf, Georgia (†31792) 217/E9
Metcalf, Ill. (61940) 222/F4
Metcalfe (co.), Ky. 237/K7
Metcalfe, Miss. (38760) 256/B4
Metcalfe, Ontario 177/J2
Metchin (riv.), Newf. 166/B3
Metchosin, Br. Col. 184/K4
Metea, Ind. (†46950) 227/E3
Metedeconk (riv.), N.J. 273/E3
Meteghan, Nova Scotia 168/B4
Meteghan Centre, Nova Scotia 168/B4
Meteghan River, Nova Scotia 168/B4
Meteor (crater), Ariz. 198/E3
Metepec, Mexico 150/M2
Methlick, Scotland 15/F3
Methow, Wash. (98834) 310/E2
Methow (riv.), Wash. 310/E2
Methuen○, Mass. (01844) 249/K2
Methven, N. Zealand 100/C5
Methven, Scotland 15/E4
Metica (riv.), Colombia 126/D6
Metigoshe (lake), N. Dak. 282/K2
Metinic (isl.), Maine 243/E8
Metinota, Sask. 181/C2
Metiskow, Alberta 182/E3
Métis-sur-Mer, Québec 172/A1
Metlakatla, Alaska (99926) 196/N2
Metlakatla, Br. Col. 184/B3
Metlatonoc, Mexico 150/K8
Metlili Chaamba, Algeria 106/E2
Meto (bayou), Ark. 202/H5
Metolius, Oreg. (†97741) 291/F3
Metolius (riv.), Oreg. 291/F3
Metompkin (inlet), Va. 307/T5
Metompkin (isl.), Va. 307/T5
Metonga (lake), Wis. 317/J4
Metropolis, Ill. (62960) 222/E6
Metropolitan, Mich. (†49381) 250/A3
Métsovon, Greece 45/E6
Mettawa, Ill. (†60048) 222/B4
Mettawee (riv.), Vt. 268/A5
Metter, Georgia (30439) 217/H6
Mettet, Belgium 27/F8
Mettler, Calif. (93307) 204/G8
Metuchen, N.J. (08840) 273/E2
Metula, Israel 65/D1
Metz, France 7/E4
Metz, France 28/G3
Metz, Ind. (†46703) 227/H1
Metz, Mich. (†49776) 250/F3
Metz, Mo. (64765) 261/C6
Metz, W. Va. (26585) 312/F3
Metzger, Oreg. (†97223) 291/A2
Metzingen, W. Germany 22/C4
Meudon, France 28/A2
Meulaboh, Indonesia 85/B5
Meulebeke, Belgium 27/C7
Meung-sur-Loire, France 28/D4
Meurthe-et-Moselle (dept.), France 28/G3
Meuse (riv.), Belgium 27/F8
Meuse (dept.), France 28/F3
Meuse (riv.), France 28/F3
Meuselwitz, E. Germany 22/E3
Mexia, Ala. (36458) 195/D8
Mexia, Texas (76667) 303/H6
Mexiana (isl.), Brazil 132/D2
Mexicali, Mexico 150/B1
Mexicali, Mexico 146/G6
Mexican Hat, Utah (84531) 304/E6
Mexican Springs, N. Mex. (87320) 274/A3
Mexico 2/D4
MEXICO 150
Mexico 146/H7
Mexico (gulf) 188/J5
Mexico (gulf) 2/E4
Mexico (gulf) 146/K7
Mexico (gulf), Ala. 195/E10
Mexico (gulf), Cuba 158/A1
Mexico (gulf), Fla. 212/C4
Mexico, Ind. (46958) 227/E3
Mexico, Ky. (†42411) 237/E6
Mexico (gulf), La. 238/F8
Mexico, Maine (04257) 243/B6
Mexico○, Maine (04257) 243/B6
México (state), Mexico 150/K7
Mexico (gulf), Mexico 150/N4
Mexico, Mo. (65265) 261/J4
Mexico, N.Y. (13114) 276/H4
Mexico, Pa. (17056) 294/H4
Mexico (gulf), Texas 303/K9
Mexico Beach, Fla. (32410) 212/D6
Mexico City (cap.), Mexico 150/L1
Mexico City (cap.), Mexico 146/J7
Mexico City (cap.), Mexico 2/E5
Meyadin, Syria 59/C3
Meyadin, Syria 63/J5
Meybod, Iran 66/J4
Meydani, Ras-e (cape), Iran 59/G4
Meydani, Ras-e (cape), Iran 66/L8
Meyer, Iowa (†50455) 229/H2
Meyers Chuck, Alaska (99903) 196/N2
Meyersdale, Pa. (15552) 294/E6
Meyers Lake, Ohio (†44701) 284/H4
Meyerton, S. Africa 118/H7
Meymaneh, Afghanistan 68/A1
Meymaneh, Afghanistan 54/H6
Meymaneh, Afghanistan 59/H2
Meyrin, Switzerland 39/B4
Meyronne, Sask. 181/E6
Mezcala (riv.), Mexico 150/J8
Mezen', U.S.S.R. 4/C7
Mezen', U.S.S.R. 7/J2
Mezen' (riv.), U.S.S.R. 7/J2
Mezen', U.S.S.R. 48/E3
Mezen', U.S.S.R. 52/F1
Mezen' (bay), U.S.S.R. 52/F1
Mezen' (riv.), U.S.S.R. 52/G1
Mezen' (riv.), U.S.S.R. 48/E3
Mézenc (mt.), France 28/E5
Mezhdurechenskiy, U.S.S.R. 48/G4
Mezhdusharskiy (isl.), U.S.S.R. 52/G1
Meziadin (lake), Br. Col. 184/C2
Mézin, France 28/D5
Mezőberény, Hungary 41/F3
Mezőcsát, Hungary 41/F3
Mezőfalva, Hungary 41/E3
Mezőhegyes, Hungary 41/F3
Mezőkovácsháza, Hungary 41/F3
Mezőkövesd, Hungary 41/F3
Mezőszilas, Hungary 41/E3
Mezőtúr, Hungary 41/F3
Mezquital, Mexico 150/G5
Mezquital (riv.), Mexico 150/G5
Mhor, Loch (lake), Scotland 15/D3
Mhow, India 68/D4
Miacatlán, Mexico 150/K2
Miahuatlán de Porfirio Díaz, Mexico 150/L8
Miajadas, Spain 33/D3
Miami, Ariz. (85539) 198/E5
Miami, Fla. 188/K5
Miami, Fla. 146/K7
Miami, Fla. (*33101) 212/B5
Miami (canal), Fla. 212/F5
Miami (riv.), Fla. 212/B5
Miami (co.), Ind. 227/E3
Miami, Ind. (46959) 227/E3
Miami (co.), Kansas 232/H3
Miami, Manitoba 179/D5
Miami, Mo. (65344) 261/F4
Miami, N. Mex. (87729) 274/E2
Miami (co.), Ohio 284/B5
Miami, Okla. (74354) 288/S1
Miami, Texas (79059) 303/D2
Miami, U.S. 2/F4
Miami Beach, Fla. 188/L5
Miami Beach, Fla. (33139) 212/C5
Miami Lakes, Fla. (†33101) 212/B4
Miamisburg, Ohio (45342) 284/B6
Miami Shores, Fla. (33153) 212/B4
Miami Springs, Fla. (33166) 212/B5
Miamitown, Ohio (45041) 284/A9
Miamiville, Ohio (45147) 284/D9
Miandowab, Iran 66/E2
Miandrivazo, Madagascar 118/G3
Mianeh, Iran 59/E2
Mianeh, Iran 66/E2
Mianus, Conn. (†06830) 210/A4
Mianus (riv.), Conn. 210/A4
Mianwali, Pakistan 68/C2
Mianwali, Pakistan 59/K3
Mianyang, Hubei, China 77/H5
Mianyang, Sichuan, China 77/G5
Mianzhu, China 77/F5
Miass, U.S.S.R. 48/G4
Miastko, Poland 47/C2
Miazal, Ecuador 128/D4
Mica, Wash. (99023) 310/H3
Mica Creek, Br. Col. 184/H4
Micanopy, Fla. (32667) 212/D2
Micawber, Okla. (†74882) 288/N3
Micay, Colombia 126/B6
Micco, Fla. (†32960) 212/F4
Miccosukee, Fla. (32309) 212/B1
Miccosukee (lake), Fla. 212/B1
Michael, I. of Man 13/C3
Michael (lake), Newf. 166/C3
Michalovce, Czech. 41/G2
Michaud (pt.), Nova Scotia 168/H3
Michelago, N.S. Wales 97/E4
Michelson (mt.), Alaska 196/K1
Michelstadt, W. Germany 22/C4
Miches, Dom. Rep. 158/F6
Michiana, Mich. (†49117) 250/C7
Michiana Shores, Ind. (†49117) 227/D1
Michichi, Alberta 182/D4
Michie, Tenn. (38357) 237/E10
Michigamme, Mich. (49861) 250/B2
Michigamme (lake), Mich. 250/A2
Michigamme (res.), Mich. 250/B2
Michigamme (riv.), Mich. 250/A2
Michigan 188/J1
Michigan (lake) 188/J2
Michigan (lake), Ill. 222/F1
Michigan (lake), Ind. 227/C1
MICHIGAN 250/80
Michigan (lake), Mich. 250/B5
Michigan, N. Dak. (58259) 282/O3
Michigan (state), U.S. 146/K5
Michigan (lake), U.S. 146/K5
Michigan (isl.), Wis. 317/F2
Michigan (lake), Wis. 317/M9
Michigan Bar, Calif. (†95683) 204/C8
Michigan Center, Mich. (49254) 250/E6
Michigan City, Ind. (46360) 227/C1
Michigan City, Miss. (38647) 256/F1
Michigantown, Ind. (46057) 227/E4
Michigan Valley, Kansas (†66528) 232/G3
Michipicoten (isl.), Ontario 177/H5
Michipicoten (isl.), Ontario 175/C3
Michipicoten River, Ontario 177/H5
Michipicoten River, Ontario 175/C3
Michoacán (state), Mexico 150/H7
Michurin, Bulgaria 45/H4
Michurinsk, U.S.S.R. 52/F4
Michurinsk, U.S.S.R. 48/E4
Mickleton, N.J. (08056) 273/C4
Micotrin (mt.), Dominica 161/F6
Micoua, Québec 174/D3
Micoud, St. Lucia 161/G6
Micro, N.C. (27555) 281/N3
Micronesia, Federated States of 87/F5
Micronesia (reg.), Pacific 87/E4
Midale, Sask. 181/H6
Midas, Nev. (†89414) 266/E1
Middelburg, Netherlands 27/C6
Middelburg, C. of Good Hope, S. Africa 118/D6
Middelburg, Transvaal, S. Africa 118/D5
Middelfart, Denmark 21/C7
Middelfart, Denmark 18/G9
Middelharnis, Netherlands 27/E5
Middelkerke, Belgium 27/B6
Middelvlei, S. Africa 118/G7
Middenmeer, Netherlands 27/F3
Middle (riv.), Conn. 210/F1
Middle (pt.), Fla. 212/E6
Middle, Iowa (52307) 229/K5
Middle (riv.), Minn. 255/B2
Middle Alkali (lake), Calif. 204/E2
Middle Andaman (isl.), India 68/G6
Middle Arm, Newf. 166/C4
Middle Atlas (ranges), Morocco 106/C2
Middle Bass, Ohio (43446) 284/E2
Middle Bass (isl.), Ohio 284/E2
Middle Beaver (creek), Colo. 208/P4
Middleboro, Mass. (02346) 249/L5
Middleboro○, Mass. (02346) 249/L5
Middleboro (McKean), Pa. (16426) 294/B2
Middlebourne, W. Va. (26149) 312/E3
Middlebranch, Ohio (44652) 284/H4
Middlebro, Manitoba 179/G5
Middlebrook, Va. (24459) 307/K4
Middleburg, Fla. (32068) 212/E1
Middleburg, Ky. (42541) 237/M6
Middleburg, Md. (21768) 245/K2
Middleburg, N.C. (27556) 281/N2
Middleburg, Ohio (43336) 284/C5
Middleburg, Pa. (17842) 294/H4
Middleburg, Va. (22117) 307/N3
Middleburgh, N.Y. (12122) 276/M5
Middleburg Heights, Ohio (†44017) 284/G10
Middlebury○, Conn. (06762) 210/C2
Middlebury, Ind. (46540) 227/F1
Middlebury, Vt. (05753) 268/A3
Middlebury○, Vt. (05753) 268/A3
Middlebury Center, Pa. (16935) 294/H2
Middlebury Gap (pass), Vt. 268/B4
Middlebush, N.J. (08874) 273/D3
Middlechurch, Manitoba 179/E4
Middle Concho (riv.), Texas 303/C6
Middledam, Maine (†04216) 243/B6
Middle Falls, N.Y. (12848) 276/O4
Middlefield○, Conn. (06455) 210/E2
Middlefield○, Mass. (01243) 249/B3
Middlefield, Ohio (44062) 284/H3
Middle Fork (peak), Idaho 220/D5
Middlefork, Ind. (†46039) 227/E4
Middle Fork, Powder (riv.), Wyo. 319/F2
Middlegate, Norfolk Is. 88/L6
Middle Granville, N.Y. (12849) 276/O4
Middlegrove, Ill. (61549) 222/C3
Middle Grove, Mo. (†65263) 261/H4
Middle Haddam, Conn. (06456) 210/E2
Middle Harbour (creek), N. S. Wales 88/K3
Middle Harbour (creek), N.S. Wales 97/J3
Middle Hope, N.Y. (12550) 276/M7
Middle Inlet, Wis. (54148) 317/K5
Middle Lake, Sask. 181/F3
Middle Loch (inlet), Hawaii 218/A3
Middle Loup (riv.), Nebr. 264/D3
Middlemarch, N. Zealand 100/B6
Middle Musquodoboit, Nova Scotia 168/E3
Middle Patuxent (riv.), Md. 245/L3
Middle Piney (creek), Wyo. 319/B3
Middle Point, Ohio (45863) 284/B4
Middleport, N.Y. (14105) 276/C4
Middleport, Ohio (45760) 284/F7
Middleport, Pa. (17953) 294/K4
Middle River, Md. (21220) 245/N3
Middle River, Minn. (56737) 255/B2
Middle River, Nova Scotia 168/G2
Middle Saranac (lake), N.Y. 276/M2
Middlesboro, Ky. (40965) 237/O7
Middlesboro, Ky. 188/K3
Middlesbrough, England 7/D3
Middlesbrough, England 13/F3
Middlesbrough, England 10/F3
Middlesex (co.), Conn. 210/E3
Middlesex (co.), Mass. 249/J3
Middlesex (co.), N.J. 273/E3
Middlesex, N.J. (08846) 273/E2
Middlesex, N.Y. (14507) 276/F5
Middlesex, N.C. (27557) 281/N3
Middlesex (county), Ontario 177/C4
Middlesex○, Vt. (†05602) 268/B3
Middlesex (co.), Va. 307/R5
Middle Stewiacke, Nova Scotia 168/E3
Middleton (isl.), Alaska 196/J3
Middleton, England 13/H2
Middleton, England 10/G2
Middleton, Georgia (†30635) 217/G2
Middleton, Idaho (83644) 220/B6
Middleton○, Mass. (01949) 249/K2
Middleton, Mich. (48856) 250/E5
Middleton○, N.H. (†03887) 268/E5
Middleton, Nova Scotia 168/C4
Middleton, Tenn. (38052) 237/D10
Middleton, Wis. (53562) 317/G9
Middletown, Calif. (95461) 204/C5
Middletown, Conn. (06457) 210/E2
Middletown, Del. (19709) 245/R3
Middletown, Ill. (62666) 222/D3
Middletown, Ind. (47356) 227/F4
Middletown, Iowa (52638) 229/L7
Middletown, Ky. (40243) 237/L2
Middletown, Md. (21769) 245/J3
Middletown, Mo. (63359) 261/J4
Middletown○, N.J. (07748) 273/E3
Middletown, N.Y. (10940) 276/L8
Middletown, N.C. (†27824) 281/T4
Middletown, N. Ireland 17/H3
Middletown, Ohio (45042) 284/A6
Middletown, Pa. (17057) 294/J5
Middletown○, R.I. (02840) 249/J6
Middletown, Va. (22645) 307/M2
Middletown Springs○, Vt. (05757) 268/A5
Middle Valley, N.J. (†07853) 273/D2
Middleville, Mich. (49333) 250/D6
Middleville, N.J. (07855) 273/D1
Middleville, N.Y. (13406) 276/K4
Middleville, Ontario 177/H2
Middle Water, Texas (†79022) 303/B2
Middleway, W. Va. (†25430) 312/K4
Middlewich, England 13/H2
Middlewich, England 10/G2
Middlewood, Nova Scotia 168/D4
Midfield, Ala. (35228) 195/E4
Midgic Station, New Bruns. 170/F3
Mid Glamorgan, Wales 13/D6
Midhurst, Ontario 177/E3
Midian (dist.), Saudi Arabia 59/C4
Midkiff, W. Va. (25540) 312/B6
Midland, Ark. (72945) 202/B3
Midland, Ind. (47445) 227/C6
Midland, La. (70557) 238/F6
Midland, Md. (21542) 245/C2
Midland (co.), Mich. 250/E5
Midland, Mich. (48640) 250/E5
Midland, N.C. (28107) 281/J4
Midland, Ohio (45148) 284/C7
Midland, Ontario 177/D3
Midland, Oreg. (97634) 291/F5
Midland, Pa. (15059) 294/A4
Midland, S. Dak. (57552) 298/G5
Midland, Tex. 188/F4
Midland (co.), Texas 303/B6
Midland, Texas (*79701) 303/C6
Midland, Va. (22728) 307/N3
Midland City, Ala. (36350) 195/H8
Midland Park, N.J. (07432) 273/B1
Midlandvale, Alberta 182/D4
Midleton, Ireland 17/E8
Midleton, Ireland 10/B5
Midlothian, Ill. (60445) 222/B6
Midlothian (trad. co.), Scotland 15/B5
Midlothian, Texas (76065) 303/G5
Midlothian, Va. (23113) 307/N6
Midnapore, India 68/F4
Midnight, Miss. (39115) 256/C4
Midnight (lake), Sask. 181/C2
Midongy Atsimo, Madagascar 118/H4
Midvale, Idaho (83645) 220/B5
Midvale, Ohio (44653) 284/H5
Midvale, Utah (84047) 304/B3
Midville, Georgia (30441) 217/H5
Midway (isls.) 188/E6
Midway, Ala. (36053) 195/H6
Midway, Br. Col. 184/H6
Midway, Del. (†19971) 245/T6
Midway, Fla. (32343) 212/B1
Midway, Georgia (31320) 217/K7
Midway, Ind. (†47635) 227/C8
Midway, Ky. (40347) 237/M4
Midway (Sedalia), Ohio (†43151) 284/D6
Midway, Pa. (15060) 294/B5
Midway, Tenn. (37809) 237/P8
Midway (isls.), U.S. 87/J3
Midway, Utah (84049) 304/C3
Midway City, Calif. (92655) 204/D11
Midway Park, N.C. (28544) 281/O5
Midwest, Wyo. (82643) 319/F2
Midwest City, Okla. (73110) 288/M4
Midyat, Turkey 63/J4
Midye, Turkey 63/C2
Mid Yell, Scotland 15/G2
Midzhur (mt.), Bulgaria 45/F4
Midzhur (mt.), Yugoslavia 45/F4
Mie (pref.), Japan 81/H6
Miechów, Poland 47/E3
Międzychód, Poland 47/B2
Międzylesie, Poland 47/C3
Międzyrzec Podlaski, Poland 47/F3
Międzyrzecz, Poland 47/B2
Mielec, Poland 47/E3
Mier, Ind. (†46919) 227/F3
Mier, Mexico 150/K3
Miercurea Ciuc, Romania 45/G2
Mieres, Spain 33/D1
Miesso, Ethiopia 111/H6
Miesso, Ethiopia 102/G4
Miesville, Minn. (†55033) 255/F6
Miette, Alberta 182/B3
Mifflin, Ohio (†44805) 284/F4
Mifflin (co.), Pa. 294/G4
Mifflin, Pa. (17058) 294/H4
Mifflin, Wis. (†53580) 317/F10
Mifflinburg, Pa. (17844) 294/H4
Mifflintown, Pa. (17059) 294/H4
Miflin, Ala. (†36530) 195/C10
Migdal, Israel 65/C2
Migdal Ha 'Emeq, Israel 65/C2
Mignon, Ala. (†35150) 195/F4
Migori, Kenya 115/F4
Miguel Alves, Brazil 132/F4
Miguel Auza, Mexico 150/H4
Miguel de la Borda, Panama 154/G6
Miguelete, Uruguay 145/B5

Monomoy 411

Mirjaveh, Pakistan 59/H4
Mirnyy 5/C5
Mirnyy, U.S.S.R. 54/N3
Mirnyy, U.S.S.R. 48/M3
Mirpur, Pakistan 68/C2
Mirpur Khas, Pakistan 68/B3
Mirror, Alberta 182/D3
Mirror Lake, N.H. (03853) 268/E4
Mirtóön (sea), Greece 45/F7
Miryang, S. Korea 81/D6
Mirzapur-cum-Vindhyachal, India 68/E4
Misamis Occidental (prov.), Philippines 82/D6
Misamis Oriental (prov.), Philippines 82/E6
Misantla, Mexico 150/P1
Misawa, Japan 81/K3
Miscou (isl.), New Bruns. 170/F1
Miscou (pt.), New Bruns. 170/F1
Miscou Centre, New Bruns. 170/F1
Miscouche, Pr. Edward I. 168/D2
Miscou Harbour, New Bruns. 170/F1
Misenheimer, N.C. (28109) 281/J4
Misery (bay), Mich. 250/G1
Misery (riv.), Mich. 250/G1
Misery (mt.), St. Chris.-Nevis 161/C10
Misgar, Pakistan 68/C1
Misha'ab, Ras (cape), Saudi Arabia 59/E4
Mishagua, Peru 128/F8
Mishan, China 77/M2
Mishaum (pt.), Mass. 249/L6
Mishawaka, Ind. (46544) 227/E1
Misheguk (mt.), Alaska 196/F1
Mishicot, Wis. (54228) 317/L7
Mishmar Hanegev, Israel 65/B5
Mishmar Hayarden, Israel 65/D1
Mishmi (hills), India 68/H3
Misima (isl.), Papua N.G. 85/C8
Misiones (prov.), Argentina 143/F2
Misiones (dept.), Paraguay 144/D5
Miskitos (cays), Nicaragua 154/F3
Miskolc, Hungary 41/F2
Miskolc, Hungary 7/G4
Misool (isl.), Indonesia 85/J6
Mispec, New Bruns. 170/E3
Mispillion (riv.), Del. 245/S5
Misquah (hills), Minn. 255/F2
Missanabie, Ontario 177/J5
Missanabie, Ontario 175/D3
Missaukee (co.), Mich. 250/D4
Missi Falls, Manitoba 179/J2
Missinaibi (riv.), Ont. 162/H6
Missinaibi (lake), Ontario 175/D3
Missinaibi (riv.), Ontario 177/J5
Missinaibi (riv.), Ontario 175/D2
Mission, Br. Col. 184/L3
Mission, Kansas (66205) 232/H2
Mission (range), Mont. 262/C3
Mission, S. Dak. (57555) 298/H7
Mission, Texas (78572) 303/F11
Mission Beach, Alberta 182/C3
Mission City, Br. Col. 184/L3
Mission Hill, S. Dak. (57046) 298/P8
Mission Ridge, S. Dak. (57557) 298/H4
Mission Viejo, Calif. (92691) 204/D11
Missisa (lake), Ontario 175/D2
Missisquoi (co.), Québec 172/D4
Missisquoi (riv.), Vt. 268/B2
Mississagi (riv.), Ontario 177/A1
Mississagi (str.), Ontario 177/A2
Mississauga, Ontario 177/J4
Mississinewa (lake), Ind. 227/F3
Mississinewa (riv.), Ind. 227/F3
Mississippi 188/J4
MISSISSIPPI 256
Mississippi (riv.) 188/H4
Mississippi (sound), Ala. 195/B10
Mississippi (co.), Ark. 202/K2
Mississippi (riv.), Ark. 202/H7
Mississippi (riv.), Ill. 222/C5
Mississippi (riv.), Iowa 229/L7
Mississippi (riv.), Ky. 237/A10
Mississippi (delta), La. 146/K7
Mississippi (delta), La. 188/J5
Mississippi (delta), La. 238/M8
Mississippi (riv.), La. 238/H3
Mississippi (sound), La. 238/M6
Mississippi (riv.), Minn. 255/D4
Mississippi (riv.), Miss. 256/A8
Mississippi (sound), Miss. 256/G10
Mississippi (co.), Mo. 261/O9
Mississippi (riv.), Mo. 261/L4
Mississippi (lake), Ontario 177/H2
Mississippi (riv.), Tenn. 237/A10
Mississippi (state), U.S. 146/K6
Mississippi (riv.), U.S. 2/E4
Mississippi (riv.), U.S. 146/J6
Mississippi (riv.), Wis. 317/D10
Mississippi River Gulf Outlet (canal), La. 238/L7
Mississippi State, Miss. (39762) 256/G4
Missoula, Mont. 146/G5
Missoula, Mont. 188/D1
Missoula (co.), Mont. 262/C3
Missoula, Mont. (*59801) 262/C4
Missouri 188/H3
MISSOURI 261
Missouri (riv.) 188/H3
Missouri (riv.), Iowa 229/A4
Missouri (riv.), Kansas 232/G1
Missouri (riv.), Mo. 261/H5
Missouri (riv.), Mont. 262/L3
Missouri (riv.), Nebr. 264/H3
Missouri (riv.), N. Dak. 282/H5
Missouri (riv.), S. Dak. 298/P8
Missouri (state), U.S. 146/J6
Missouri (riv.), U.S. 2/D3
Missouri (riv.), U.S. 146/J5
Missouri Branch, W. Va. (†25511) 312/A7
Missouri City, Mo. (64072) 261/R5
Missouri City, Texas (77459) 303/J2
Missouri Coteau (hills), Sask. 181/F5
Missouri Valley, Iowa (51555) 229/B5
Mist, Ark. (†71646) 202/G7
Mist, Oreg. (97016) 291/D1
Mistake (bay), N.W. Terrs. 187/J3
Mistake Creek, North. Terr. 93/A4
Mistaken (pt.), Newf. 166/D2
Mistassibi (riv.), Que. 162/J5
Mistassibi (riv.), Québec 174/C3
Mistassini (lake), Que. 162/J5
Mistassini (lake), Que. 146/L4
Mistassini (terr.), Québec 174/B2
Mistassini, Québec 172/E1
Mistassini, Québec 174/C3
Mistassini (Baie-du-Poste), Québec 174/C2
Mistassini (lake), Québec 174/C2
Mistastin (lake), Newf. 166/B2
Mistastin (riv.), Newf. 166/B2
Mistatim, Sask. 181/K3
Mistehae (lake), Alberta 182/C2
Mistelbach an der Zaya, Austria 41/D2
Misteriosa (bank), Cayman Is. 156/A3
Misti, El (mt.), Peru 120/B4
Misti, El (mt.), Peru 128/G11
Mistinippi (lake), Newf. 166/B3
Miston, Tenn. (38056) 237/B8
Mistretta, Italy 34/E6
Misty Fjords Nat'l Mon., Alaska 196/N2
Misurata, Libya 102/D1
Misurata, Libya 111/C1
Mita (pt.), Mexico 150/G6
Mitaka, Japan 81/O2
Mitcham, S. Australia 88/D8
Mitcham, S. Australia 94/B8
Mitchell (lake), Ala. 188/J4
Mitchell (dam), Ala. 195/E5
Mitchell (lake), Ala. 195/F5
Mitchell, Ark. (†72583) 202/G1
Mitchell (co.), Georgia 217/D8
Mitchell, Georgia (30820) 217/G4
Mitchell, Ind. (47446) 227/E7
Mitchell (co.), Iowa 229/H2
Mitchell, Iowa (†50461) 229/H2
Mitchell (co.), Kansas 232/D2
Mitchell, La. (71453) 238/C3
Mitchell, Nebr. (69357) 264/A3
Mitchell (co.), N.C. 281/E2
Mitchell (mt.), N.C. 188/K3
Mitchell (mt.), N.C. 281/E3
Mitchell, Ontario 177/C4
Mitchell, Oreg. (97750) 291/G3
Mitchell, Queensland 88/H5
Mitchell, Queensland 95/C5
Mitchell (riv.), Queensland 88/G3
Mitchell (riv.), Queensland 95/B2
Mitchell, S. Dak. 188/G2
Mitchell, S. Dak. (57301) 298/N6
Mitchell (creek), S. Dak. 298/G5
Mitchell (co.), Texas 303/D5
Mitchell (riv.), Victoria 97/D5
Mitchell Bay, Ontario 177/B5
Mitchell Heights, W. Va. (†25601) 312/B7
Mitchells, Va. (22729) 307/N4
Mitchellsburg, Ky. (40452) 237/M5
Mitchellsville, Ill. (†62946) 222/E6
Mitchellton, Sask. 181/F6
Mitchellville, Ark. (†71639) 202/H6
Mitchellville, Iowa (50169) 229/G5
Mitchellville, Tenn. (37119) 237/J7
Mitchelstown, Ireland 10/B4
Mitchelstown, Ireland 17/E7
Mitchelton, Queensland 88/J2
Mitchelton, Queensland 95/D2
Mitchinamécus (res.), Québec 172/C2
Mithi, Pakistan 68/C4
Míthimna, Greece 45/G6
Mitiaro, Cook Is. 87/L8
Mitilíni, Greece 45/H6
Mitkof (isl.), Alaska 196/N2
Mitla (ruin), Mexico 150/M8
Mito, Japan 81/K5
Mitrofania (isl.), Alaska 196/G3
Mitsamiouli, Comoros 118/G2
Mitsinjo, Madagascar 118/H3
Mitsue, Alberta 182/C2
Mitsukaido, Japan 81/P2
Mittagong, N.S. Wales 97/F4
Mitta Mitta (riv.), Victoria 97/D5
Mittenwald, W. Germany 22/D5
Mittersill, Austria 41/B3
Mittie, La. (70654) 238/E5
Mittweida, E. Germany 22/E3
Mitú, Colombia 126/E7
Mitú, Colombia 120/B2
Mituas, Colombia 126/F6
Mitwaba, Zaire 115/E5
Mitzic, Gabon 115/B3
Miura, Japan 81/O3
Miura (pen.), Japan 81/O3
Mivtahim, Israel 65/A5
Mix, La. (†70760) 238/G5
Miyagi (pref.), Japan 81/K4
Miyako, Japan 81/L4
Miyako (isl.), Japan 81/L7
Miyako (isls.), Japan 81/L7
Miyakonojo, Japan 81/E8
Miyazaki (pref.), Japan 81/E8
Miyazaki, Japan 81/E8
Miyazu, Japan 81/G6
Miyoshi, Japan 81/F6
Mizan Teferi, Ethiopia 111/G6
Mizda, Libya 111/B1
Mize, Georgia (†30577) 217/F2
Mize, Miss. (39116) 256/E7
Mizen (head), Ireland 10/A5
Mizen (head), Ireland 17/B9
Mizen (head), Ireland 17/K6
Mizhi, China 77/H4
Mizil, Romania 45/H3
Mizo (hill), India 68/G4
Mizoram (terr.), India 68/G4
Mizpah, Minn. (56660) 255/D3
Mizpah, N.J. (08342) 273/D5
Mizpe Ramon, Israel 65/D5
Mizque, Bolivia 136/C5
Mizque (riv.), Bolivia 136/C6
Mizusawa, Japan 81/K4
Mjölby, Sweden 18/J7
Mkokotoni, Tanzania 115/G5
Mkushi, Zambia 115/E6
Mladá Boleslav, Czech. 41/C1
Mladá Vožice, Czech. 41/C2
Mława, Poland 47/E2
Mljet (isl.), Yugoslavia 45/C4
Mmabatho (cap.), Bophuthatswana, S. Africa 102/E7
Mmabatho, S. Africa 118/D5
Mnichovo Hradiště, Czech. 41/C1
Mo, Norway 7/F2
Mo, Norway 18/J3
Moa, Cuba 158/K3
Moa (riv.), Guinea 106/B7
Moa (isl.), Indonesia 85/H7
Moa (riv.), S. Leone 106/B7
Moab, Utah (84532) 304/E5
Moak Lake, Manitoba 179/J2
Moala (isl.), Fiji 86/Q11
Moama, N.S. Wales 97/C5
Moamba, Mozambique 118/E5
Moanalua (stream), Hawaii 218/B3
Moanda, Gabon 115/B4
Moanda, Zaire 115/B5
Moapa, Nev. (89025) 266/G6
Moapa River Ind. Res., Nev. 266/G6
Moar (lake), Manitoba 179/G2
Moark, Ark. (†72422) 202/J1
Moate, Ireland 17/F5
Moatsville, W. Va. (26405) 312/G4
Mobara, Japan 81/K6
Mobaye, Cent. Afr. Rep. 115/D3
Mobayi-Mbongo, Zaire 115/D3
Mobayi-Mbongo, Zaire 102/E4
Mobeetie, Texas (79061) 303/D2
Moberly, Br. Col. 184/J4
Moberly (lake), Br. Col. 184/F2
Moberly, Mo. (65270) 261/G4
Moberly, Mo. 188/H3
Moberly Lake, Br. Col. 184/G2
Mobile, Ala. 146/K6
Mobile, Ala. 188/J4
Mobile (bay), Ala. 188/J5
Mobile (co.), Ala. 195/B9
Mobile, Ala. (*36601) 195/B9
Mobile (bay), Ala. 195/B10
Mobile (pt.), Ala. 195/B10
Mobile (riv.), Ala. 195/C9
Mobile, Ariz. (†85239) 198/C5
Mobile, Newf. 166/D2
Mobile Big (pond), Newf. 166/D2
Mobjack, Va. (23118) 307/R6
Mobjack (bay), Va. 307/R6
Mobridge, S. Dak. (57601) 298/J2
Mobuto Sese Seko (lake) 102/F4
Mobuto Sese Seko (lake), Uganda 115/F3
Mobuto Sese Seko (lake), Zaire 115/F3
Moca, Dom. Rep. 156/D3
Moca, Dom. Rep. 158/D5
Moca, P. Rico 161/A1
Mocajuba, Brazil 132/D3
Moçambique, Mozambique 118/G3
Moçambique, Mozambique 102/F6
Moçâmedes (dist.), Angola 115/B7
Moçâmedes, Angola 102/D6
Moçâmedes, Angola 115/B7
Mocanaqua, Pa. (18655) 294/K3
Moccasin, Ariz. (†86022) 198/C2
Moccasin, Mont. (59462) 262/F3
Mocha (isl.), Chile 138/B2
Mocha, Yemen Arab Rep. 59/D7
Moc Hoa, Vietnam 72/E5
Mochudi, Botswana 118/D4
Mochudi, Botswana 102/E7
Mocímboa da Praia, Mozambique 118/G2
Mociu, Romania 45/G2
Mocksville, N.C. (27028) 281/H3
Moclips, Wash. (98562) 310/A3
Moco (mt.), Angola 115/C6
Mocoa, Colombia 126/B7
Mococa, Brazil 135/C2
Mocodome (cape), Nova Scotia 168/G3
Mocomoco, Bolivia 136/A4
Mocoretá, Argentina 143/G5
Mocorito, Mexico 150/F4
Moctezuma, San Luis Potosí, Mexico 150/J5
Moctezuma, Sonora, Mexico 150/E2
Moctezuma (riv.), Mexico 150/K6
Mocuba, Mozambique 118/F3
Modale, Iowa (51556) 229/B5
Modane, France 28/G5
Modasa, India 68/C4
Modderfontein, S. Africa 118/H6
Mode, Ill. (62444) 222/E4
Model, Colo. (81059) 208/L8
Modena (prov.), Italy 34/C2
Modena, Italy 7/F4
Modena, Italy 34/C2
Modena, Utah (84753) 304/A6
Modena, Wis. (†54755) 317/C7
Modeste, La. (70376) 238/K3
Modesto, Calif. 188/B3
Modesto, Calif. (*95350) 204/D6
Modesto, Ill. (62667) 222/D4
Modest Town, Va. (23412) 307/T5
Modica, Italy 34/E6
Mödling, Austria 41/D2
Modoc (co.), Calif. 204/E2
Modoc, Georgia (†30401) 217/H5
Modoc, Ill. (62261) 222/C5
Modoc, Ind. (47358) 227/G4
Modoc, Kansas (67866) 232/A3
Modoc, S.C. (29838) 296/C4
Modoc Point, Oreg. (†97624) 291/F5
Modra, Czech. 41/D2
Modriča, Yugoslavia 45/D3
Modrý Kameň, Czech. 41/E2
Mo Duc, Vietnam 72/F4
Moe, Victoria 88/H7
Moe, Victoria 97/D6
Moen (isl.), Micronesia 87/F5
Moencopi (plat.), Ariz. 198/D3
Moengo, Suriname 131/D3
Moenkopi, Ariz. (†86045) 198/D2
Moenkopi Wash (dry riv.), Ariz. 198/D2
Moerai, Fr. Poly. 87/L8
Moerdijk, Netherlands 27/F5
Moerewa, N. Zealand 100/E1
Moësa (riv.), Switzerland 39/H4
Moeskroen (Mouscron), Belgium 27/C7
Moffat (co.), Colo. 208/C1
Moffat, Colo. (81143) 208/H6
Moffat, Scotland 15/E5
Moffat, Scotland 10/E3
Moffet (peak), N. Zealand 100/B6
Moffett, Okla. (74946) 288/S4
Moffett Nav. Air Sta., Calif. 204/K3
Moffit, N. Dak. (58560) 282/K6
Mogadiscio (prov.), Somalia 115/J3
Mogadishu (cap.), Somalia 2/M5
Mogadishu (cap.), Somalia 102/G4
Mogadishu (cap.), Somalia 115/J3
Mogador (Essaouira), Morocco 106/B2
Mogadore, Ohio (44260) 284/H3
Mogadouro, Portugal 33/C2
Mogami (riv.), Japan 81/K4
Mogaung, Burma 72/C1
Møgeltønder, Denmark 21/B8
Mogi das Cruzes, Brazil 132/E9
Mogi das Cruzes, Brazil 135/C3
Mogi Guaçu (riv.), Brazil 135/C2
Mogi-Guaçu, Brazil 135/C3
Mogilev, U.S.S.R. 7/G3
Mogilev, U.S.S.R. 52/C4
Mogilev, U.S.S.R. 48/D4
Mogilev-Podol'skiy, U.S.S.R. 52/C5
Mogil Mogil, N.S. Wales 97/E1
Mogilno, Poland 47/C2
Mogi-Mirim, Brazil 135/C3
Mogincual, Mozambique 118/G3
Mogocha, U.S.S.R. 48/N4
Mogok, Burma 72/C2
Mogollon (plat.), Ariz. 198/D4
Mogollon, N. Mex. (†88039) 274/A5
Mogollon (mts.), N. Mex. 274/A5
Mogollon Baldy (peak), N. Mex. 274/A5
Mogollon Rim (cliffs), Ariz. 198/D4
Mogororo, Chad 111/D5
Mogotes (pt.), Argentina 143/E4
Moguer, Spain 33/C4
Mohács, Hungary 41/E4
Mohaka (riv.), N. Zealand 100/F3
Mohaleshoek, Lesotho 118/D6
Mohall, N. Dak. (58761) 282/G2
Mohammadia, Algeria 106/D1
Mohammedia, Morocco 106/C2
Mohave (co.), Ariz. 198/A3
Mohave (lake), Ariz. 198/A3
Mohave (mts.), Ariz. 198/A4
Mohave (lake), Nev. 266/G7
Mohawk (mts.), Ariz. 198/B6
Mohawk (mt.), Conn. 210/B1
Mohawk, Ind. (†46140) 227/F5
Mohawk, Mich. (49950) 250/A1
Mohawk (riv.), N.H. 268/E2
Mohawk (lake), N.J. 273/D1
Mohawk, N.Y. (13407) 276/L4
Mohawk (riv.), N.Y. 276/L5
Mohawk, Oreg. (†97477) 291/E3
Mohawk, Tenn. (37810) 237/P8
Mohawk, W. Va. (24862) 312/C7
Mohe, China 77/K1
Mohegan, Conn. (†06382) 210/G3
Mohéli (isl.), Comoros 102/G6
Mohéli (isl.), Comoros 118/G2
Mohelnice, Czech. 41/D2
Mohenjo Daro (ruins), Pakistan 68/B3
Moher (cliffs), Ireland 17/B6
Mohican (cape), Alaska 196/E2
Mohican (riv.), Ohio 284/F4
Mohill, Ireland 17/F4
Mohler, Wash. (99154) 310/G3
Möhlin, Switzerland 39/E1
Mohn, Kapp (cape), Norway 18/E1
Mohnton, Pa. (19540) 294/L5
Mohnyin, Burma 72/C1
Moho, Peru 128/H10
Mohoro, Tanzania 115/G5
Mohrsville, Pa. (19541) 294/K5
Moi, Norway 18/E7
Moidart (dist.), Scotland 15/C4
Moiese, Mont. (59824) 262/B3
Moiliili, Hawaii (96828) 218/C4
Moinești, Romania 45/H2
Moingona, Iowa (†50036) 229/F4
Moira, N.Y. (12957) 276/M1
Moîrai, Greece 45/G8
Moirones, Uruguay 145/E2
Mõisaküla, U.S.S.R. 53/C1
Moise (riv.), Que. 146/M4
Moisés Ville, Argentina 143/E5
Moisie (riv.), Que. 162/K5
Moisie, Québec 174/D2
Moisie (riv.), Québec 174/D2
Moissac, France 28/D5
Moïssala, Chad 111/C6
Moitaco, Venezuela 124/F4
Mojácar, Spain 33/F4
Mojave, Calif. (93501) 204/G8
Mojave (des.), Calif. 204/H9
Mojave (riv.), Calif. 204/J9
Mojo, Bolivia 136/C7
Mojocoya, Bolivia 136/C6
Mojokerto, Indonesia 85/K2
Mokane, Mo. (65059) 261/J5
Mokapu, Hawaii (†96734) 218/F2
Mokapu (pen.), Hawaii 218/F2
Mokau (riv.), N. Zealand 100/E3
Mokelumne (riv.), Calif. 204/C9
Mokelumne Hill, Calif. (95245) 204/E5
Mokena, Ill. (60448) 222/B6
Mokil (atoll), Micronesia 87/G5
Moknine, Tunisia 106/G1
Mokohinau (isl.), N. Zealand 100/E1
Mokokchung, India 68/G3
Mokolo, Cameroon 115/B1
Mokp'o, S. Korea 81/C6
Moksha (riv.), U.S.S.R. 52/F4
Mokuauia (isl.), Hawaii 218/E1
Mokuaweoweo (crater), Hawaii 218/H6
Mokuhooniki (isl.), Hawaii 218/J1
Mokuleia, Hawaii (†96791) 218/D1
Mol, Belgium 27/G6
Mola di Bari, Italy 34/F4
Molalla, Oreg. (97038) 291/B3
Molalla (riv.), Oreg. 291/B3
Moland, Minn. (†55946) 255/E6
Molanosa, Sask. 181/M4
Moláoi, Greece 45/F7
Molare (peak), Switzerland 39/G3
Mold, Wales 13/G2
Moldau (Vltava) (riv.), Czech. 41/C2
Moldava nad Bodvou, Czech. 41/F2
Moldavian S.S.R., U.S.S.R. 7/G4
Moldavian S.S.R., U.S.S.R. 52/C5
Moldavian S.S.R., U.S.S.R. 48/C5
Molde, Norway 18/E5
Moldova Nouă, Romania 45/E3
Moldoveanul (mt.), Romania 45/G3
Mole (riv.), England 13/H8
Môle (cape), Haiti 158/B5
Mole Creek, Tasmania 99/C3
Molega (lake), Nova Scotia 168/D4
Molena, Georgia (30258) 217/D4
Molenbeek-Saint-Jean, Belgium 27/B9
Molepolole, Botswana 118/C4
Molepolole, Botswana 102/E7
Môle Saint Nicolas, Haiti 158/B5
Molfetta, Italy 34/F4
Molina, Chile 138/A10
Molina, Colo. (81646) 208/D4
Molina, Spain 33/E2
Molinas, Argentina 143/C2
Moline, Ill. 188/J2
Moline, Ill. (61265) 222/C2
Moline, Kansas (67353) 232/F4
Moline, Manitoba 179/B4
Moline, Mich. (49335) 250/D6
Moline Acres, Mo. (†63101) 261/R2
Molinicos, Spain 33/E3
Molinière (pt.), Grenada 161/C8
Molino, Fla. (32577) 212/B6
Molinos (pt.), P. Rico 161/G1
Moliro, Zaire 115/E5
Molise (reg.), Italy 34/E4
Mollebjerg (mt.), Denmark 21/C6
Mollendo, Peru 120/B4
Mollendo, Peru 128/F11
Mollerusa, Spain 33/G2
Molles (pt.), Chile 138/A9
Mollis, Switzerland 39/H2
Mölln, W. Germany 22/D2
Mollusk, Va. (22517) 307/P5
Mollys Falls (pond), Vt. 268/C3
Mölndal, Sweden 18/H8
Moloaa, Hawaii (†96703) 218/D1
Molodechno, U.S.S.R. 48/C4
Molodechno, U.S.S.R. 52/C4
Molokai (isl.), Hawaii 87/L3
Molokai (isl.), Hawaii 188/F5
Molokai (isl.), Hawaii 218/G1
Molokini (isl.), Hawaii 218/J2
Molong, N.S. Wales 97/E3
Molopo (riv.), Botswana 118/C5
Molopo (riv.), S. Africa 118/C5
Molotov (Perm'), U.S.S.R. 52/J3
Moloundou, Cameroon 115/C3
Molson (lake), Manitoba 179/J3
Molson, Wash. (†98844) 310/F2
Molt, Mont. (59057) 262/H5
Molteno, S. Africa 118/D6
Molucca (isls.), Indonesia 54†/O10
Molucca (sea), Indonesia 54/O10
Molucca (sea), Indonesia 85/H6
Moluccas (isls.), Indonesia 85/H6
Molunkus (lake), Maine 243/G4
Moma, Mozambique 118/F3
Mombasa, Kenya 115/G4
Mombasa, Kenya 102/G5
Mombetsu, Japan 81/L1
Mombo, Tanzania 115/G4
Momchilgrad, Bulgaria 45/G5
Momence, Ill. (60954) 222/F2
Momeyer, N.C. (†27856) 281/N3
Momignies, Belgium 27/E8
Momostenango, Guatemala 154/B3
Mompog (passage), Philippines 82/D4
Mompós, Colombia 126/C3
Mon (state), Burma 72/C3
Mon (riv.), Burma 72/B2
Møn (isl.), Denmark 21/F8
Møn (isl.), Denmark 18/H9
Mona (passg.) 146/M8
Mona, Cyprus 63/E5
Mona (passage), Dom. Rep. 156/E3
Mona (passage), Dom. Rep. 158/F6
Mona (isl.), P. Rico 156/E3
Mona (passage), P. Rico 156/E3
Mona (passage), P. Rico 161/A2
Mona, Utah (84645) 304/C4
Mona (res.), Utah 304/C4
Monaca, Pa. (15061) 294/B4
Monach (isls.), Scotland 15/A3
Monach (sound), Scotland 15/A3
Monaco 7/E4
MONACO 28/G6
Monadhliath (mts.), Scotland 15/D3
Monadnock (mt.), N.H. 268/C6
Monagas (state), Venezuela 124/G3
Monaghan (co.), Ireland 17/H3
Monaghan, Ireland 10/C3
Monaghan, Ireland 17/G3
Monahans, Texas (79756) 303/B6
Monango, N. Dak. (58471) 282/N7
Monapo, Mozambique 118/G2
Monar, Loch (lake), Scotland 15/C3
Monarch, Alberta 182/D5
Monarch, Mont. (59463) 262/F3
Monarch Mills, S.C. (†29379) 296/D2
Monarda, Maine (†04776) 243/G4
Monaro (range), N.S. Wales 97/E5
Monashee (mts.), Br. Col. 184/H4
Monasterevan, Ireland 17/H5
Monastery, Nova Scotia 168/G3
Monastir, Tunisia 106/G1
Monatélé, Cameroon 115/B3
Mona Vale, N.S. Wales 88/L3
Mona Vale, N.S. Wales 97/K2
Monaville, W. Va. (25636) 312/B7
Monavullagh (mts.), Ireland 17/F7
Monbetsu, Japan 81/L2
Moncalieri, Italy 34/A2
Monção, Portugal 33/B1
Moncayo (mt.), Spain 33/F2
Moncayo, Sierra de (range), Spain 33/F2
Monchegorsk, U.S.S.R. 7/H2
Monchegorsk, U.S.S.R. 48/C3
Monchegorsk, U.S.S.R. 52/D1
Mönchengladbach, W. Germany 22/B3
Monches, Wis. (†53029) 317/J1
Monchique, Portugal 33/B4
Monchique, Serra de (mts.), Portugal 33/B4
Monción, Dom. Rep. 158/D5
Moncks Corner, S.C. (29461) 296/G5
Monclo, W. Va. (†25183) 312/C7
Monclova, Mexico 146/H7
Monclova, Mexico 150/J3
Monclova, Ohio (43542) 284/C2
Moncouche (lake), Québec 172/G1
Moncton, N. Br. 146/M5
Moncton, N. Br. 162/K6
Moncton, New Bruns. 170/F2
Moncure, N.C. (27559) 281/L3
Mondamin, Iowa (51557) 229/B5
Monday (riv.), Paraguay 144/E4
Mondego (cape), Portugal 33/B2
Mondego (riv.), Portugal 33/B2
Mondéjar, Spain 33/E2
Mondonac (lake), Québec 172/D2
Mondoñedo, Spain 33/C1
Mondovi, Wis. (54755) 317/C6
Mondovì Breo, Italy 34/A2
Mondragon, Philippines 85/H3
Mondragon, Philippines 82/E4
Mondsee, Austria 41/B3
Moneague, Jamaica 158/J6
Monee, Ill. (60449) 222/F2
Monero, N. Mex. (†87547) 274/C2
Monessen, Pa. (15062) 294/C5
Monesterio, Spain 33/C3
Moneta, Iowa (51352) 229/C2
Moneta, Va. (24121) 307/J6
Moneta, Wyo. (†82601) 319/E2
Monett, Mo. (65708) 261/E9
Monetta, S.C. (29105) 296/D4
Monette, Ark. (72447) 202/K2
Money (isl.), China 85/E2
Money, Miss. (38945) 256/D3
Moneygall, Ireland 17/F6
Moneymore, N. Ireland 17/H2
Monfalcone, Italy 34/D2
Monforte, Portugal 33/C3
Monforte, Spain 33/C1
Monga, Zaire 115/D3
Mongalla, Sudan 111/F6
Mong Cai, Vietnam 72/E2
Möng Hsat, Burma 72/C2
Monghyr, India 68/F3
Möng Maü, Burma 72/C3
Möng Mit, Burma 72/C2
Mongo, Chad 111/C5
Mongo, Chad 102/D3
Mongo, Ind. (46771) 227/G1
Mongolia 2/P3
Mongolia 54/M5
Mongoumba, Cent. Afr. Rep. 115/C3
Möng Pan, Burma 72/C2
Möng Si, Burma 72/C2
Möng Tön, Burma 72/C2
Möng Tung, Burma 72/C2
Mongu, Zambia 102/E6
Mongu, Zambia 115/D7
Monhegan○, Maine (04852) 243/E8
Monhegan (isl.), Maine 243/E8
Mönhhaan, Mongolia 77/H2
Moniac, Georgia (†31646) 217/H9
Moniaive, Scotland 10/D3
Moniaive, Scotland 15/E5
Monica, Ill. (†61559) 222/D3
Monico, Wis. (54549) 317/H4
Monida, Mont. (†59739) 262/D6
Monie, Md. (†21853) 245/P8
Monifieth, Scotland 15/F4
Moniquirá, Colombia 126/D5
Moniteau (co.), Mo. 261/G5
Monitor, Alberta 182/E4
Monitor, Ind. (†47901) 227/D4
Monitor (range), Nev. 266/E4
Monitor, Oreg. (†97072) 291/B3
Monitor, Wash. (98836) 310/E3
Monivea, Ireland 17/D5
Monkayo, Philippines 82/E7
Monkey (pt.), Nicaragua 154/F5
Monkey (hill), St. Chris.-Nevis 161/C10
Monkey River Town, Belize 154/C2
Mońki, Poland 47/F2
Monkoto, Zaire 115/D4
Monkton, Md. (21111) 245/M2
Monkton, Ontario 177/C4
Monkton○, Vt. (05469) 268/A3
Monkton Ridge, Vt. (†05473) 268/A3
Monmouth, Ill. (61462) 222/C3
Monmouth, Ind. (†46733) 227/H3
Monmouth, Iowa (52309) 229/M4
Monmouth, Maine (04259) 243/D7
Monmouth○, Maine (04259) 243/D7
Monmouth (co.), N.J. 273/E3
Monmouth, Oreg. (97361) 291/D3
Monmouth, Wales 13/E6
Monmouth, Wales 10/E5
Monmouth Beach, N.J. (07750) 273/F3
Monmouth Junction, N.J. (08852) 273/D3
Monnickendam, Netherlands 27/C4
Mono (riv.), Benin 106/E7
Mono (lake), Calif. 188/C3
Mono (co.), Calif. 204/F5
Mono (lake), Calif. 204/G5
Mono (riv.), Togo 106/E7
Monocacy (riv.), Md. 245/J3
Monocacy Nat'l Battlefield, Md. 245/J3
Mono Lake, Calif. (†93541) 204/F5
Monolith, Calif. (†93561) 204/G8
Monólithos, Greece 45/H7
Monomonac (lake), Mass. 249/G2
Monomoy (isl.), Mass. 249/O6

412 Monomoy

Monomoy (pt.), Mass. 249/O6
Monon, Ind. (47959) 227/D3
Monona (co.), Iowa 229/B4
Monona, Iowa (52159) 229/L2
Monona, Wis. (53716) 317/H9
Monongah, W. Va. (26554) 312/F4
Monongahela, Pa. (15063) 294/B5
Monongahela (riv.), Pa. 294/C6
Monongahela (riv.), W. Va. 312/G3
Monongalia (co.), W. Va. 312/F3
Monopoli, Italy 34/F4
Monor, Hungary 41/E3
Monos (isl.), Trin. & Tob. 161/A10
Monóvar, Spain 33/F3
Monoville, Tenn. (37121) 237/K8
Monowi, Nebr. (†68746) 264/F2
Monreal del Campo, Spain 33/F2
Monreale, Italy 34/D5
Monroe (co.), Ala. 195/D7
Monroe (co.), Ark. 202/H4
Monroe, Ark. (72108) 202/H4
Monroe○, Conn. (06468) 210/C3
Monroe (co.), Fla. 212/E7
Monroe (lake), Fla. 212/E3
Monroe (co.), Georgia 217/E4
Monroe, Georgia (30655) 217/E3
Monroe (co.), Ill. 222/C5
Monroe (co.), Ind. 227/D6
Monroe, Ind. (46772) 227/H3
Monroe (lake), Ind. 227/E6
Monroe (co.), Iowa 229/H7
Monroe, Iowa (50170) 229/G5
Monroe (co.), Ky. 237/K7
Monroe, La. 188/H4
Monroe, La. 146/J6
Monroe, La. (*71201) 238/F1
Monroe○, Maine (04951) 243/E6
Monroe (co.), Mich. 250/F7
Monroe, Mich. (48161) 250/F7
Monroe (co.), Miss. 256/H3
Monroe (co.), Mo. 261/H3
Monroe, Nebr. (68647) 264/G3
Monroe○, N.H. (03771) 268/C3
Monroe (mt.), N.H. 268/E3
Monroe○, N.J. (07434) 273/E3
Monroe (co.), N.Y. 276/E4
Monroe, N.Y. (10950) 276/M8
Monroe, N.C. (28110) 281/J5
Monroe (co.), Ohio 284/H6
Monroe, Ohio (45050) 284/B7
Monroe, Okla. (74947) 288/S4
Monroe, Oreg. (97456) 291/D3
Monroe (co.), Pa. 294/M3
Monroe (Monroeton), Pa. (18832) 294/J2
Monroe, S. Dak. (57047) 298/P7
Monroe (co.), Tenn. 237/N10
Monroe, Tenn. (38573) 237/L8
Monroe, Utah (84754) 304/B5
Monroe (peak), Utah 304/B5
Monroe, Va. (24574) 307/K6
Monroe, Wash. (98272) 310/D3
Monroe (co.), W. Va. 312/E7
Monroe (co.), Wis. 317/E8
Monroe, Wis. (53566) 317/G10
Monroe Bridge, Mass. (01350) 249/C2
Monroe Center, Ill. (61052) 222/E1
Monroe City, Ind. (47557) 227/C7
Monroe City, Mo. (63456) 261/J3
Monroe P.O. (Stepney), Conn. (06468) 210/B3
Monroeton, Pa. (18832) 294/J2
Monroeville, Ala. (36460) 195/D7
Monroeville, Ind. (46773) 227/H3
Monroeville, N.J. (08343) 273/C4
Monroeville, Ohio (44847) 284/E3
Monroeville, Pa. (15146) 294/C7
Monrovia, Ala. (†35804) 195/E1
Monrovia, Calif. (91016) 204/D10
Monrovia, Ind. (46157) 227/E5
Monrovia (cap.), Liberia 106/B7
Monrovia (cap.), Liberia 2/J5
Monrovia (cap.), Liberia 102/A4
Monrovia, Md. (21770) 245/J3
Mons, Belgium 27/E8
Monsanto, Portugal 33/C2
Monschau, W. Germany 22/B3
Monse, Wash. (†98812) 310/F2
Monsefú, Peru 128/C6
Monselice, Italy 34/C2
Monserrate (isl.), Mexico 150/D4
Monsey, N.Y. (10952) 276/J8
Møns Klint (cliff), Denmark 21/F8
Monson○, Maine (04464) 243/E5
Monson, Mass. (01057) 249/E4
Monson○, Mass. (01057) 249/E4
Mönsterås, Sweden 18/K8
Montagu, S. Africa 118/C6
Montague (isl.), Alaska 196/D1
Montague (str.), Alaska 196/D1
Montague, Calif. (96064) 204/C2
Montague○, Mass. (01351) 249/E2
Montague (isl.), Mexico 150/B1
Montague, Mich. (49437) 250/C5
Montague, Mont. (†59442) 262/F3
Montague, N.J. (†07851) 273/D1
Montague, N.C. (†28435) 281/N6
Montague, Pr. Edward I. 168/F2
Montague (co.), Texas 303/G4
Montague, Texas (76251) 303/G4
Montague (sound), W. Australia 88/C2
Montague (sound), W. Australia 92/D1
Montague City, Mass. (†01351) 249/D2
Montalba, Texas (75853) 303/J6
Montalbán, Spain 33/F2
Montalcino, Italy 34/C3
Mont Alto, Pa. (17237) 294/G6
Montalto Uffugo, Italy 34/E5
Montalvão, Portugal 33/C3
Montalvo, Calif. (93003) 204/F9
Montana 188/E1
MONTANA 262
Montana, Alaska (†99676) 196/B1
Montaña, La (reg.), Peru 128/F8
Montana, Switzerland 39/D4
Montana (state), U.S. 146/H5
Montana Mines, W. Va. (26586) 312/F3
Montánchez, Spain 33/D3
Montanja di Reij, Neth. Ant. 161/G9
Montara, Calif. (94037) 204/H3
Montargil, Portugal 33/B3
Montargis, France 28/E3
Montauban, France 28/D5
Montauban, Québec 172/E3
Montauk, N.Y. (11954) 276/S8
Montauk (pt.), N.Y. 276/S8
Montbard, France 28/F4
Montbéliard, France 28/G4
Mont Belvieu, Texas (77580) 303/L1
Montblanch, Spain 33/G2
Montbrison, France 28/F5
Montbrook, Fla. (†32696) 212/D2
Montcalm (co.), Mich. 250/D5
Montcalm (co.), Québec 172/C3
Montcalm (county), Québec 174/B3
Mont-Carmel, Québec 172/H2
Montceau-les-Mines, France 28/F4
Mont Cenis (tunnel), France 28/G5
Mont Cenis (tunnel), Italy 34/A2
Montcerf, Québec 172/A3
Montclair, Calif. (91763) 204/D10
Montclair, N.J. (*07042) 273/B2
Montclare, S.C. (†29532) 296/H3
Montcoal, W. Va. (25135) 312/D7
Mont-de-Marsan, France 28/C6
Montdidier, France 28/E3
Mont-Dore, France 28/E5
Monteagle, Tenn. (37356) 237/K10
Monteagudo, Bolivia 136/D6
Monte Alegre, Brazil 132/C3
Montealegre del Castillo, Spain 33/F3
Monte Alegre de Minas, Brazil 132/D7
Monte Aprazível, Brazil 135/A2
Monte Azul, Brazil 132/F6
Monte Bello (isls.), Australia 87/B8
Montebello, Calif. (90640) 204/C10
Montebello, Québec 172/B4
Monte Bello (isls.), W. Australia 88/A4
Monte Bello (isls.), W. Australia 92/A3
Montebelluna, Italy 34/D2
Monte Carlo, Monaco 28/G6
Monte Caseros, Argentina 143/G5
Montecito, Calif. (93103) 204/F9
Monte Comán, Argentina 143/C3
Monte Creek, Br. Col. 184/G5
Montecristi (prov.), Dom. Rep. 158/D5
Monte Cristi, Dom. Rep. 156/D2
Montecristi, Dom. Rep. 158/C5
Montecristi, Ecuador 128/B3
Monte Cristo, Bolivia 136/E4
Montecristo (isl.), Italy 34/C3
Monte Cristo (range), Nev. 266/D4
Monte Dourado, Brazil 132/C2
Montefiascone, Italy 34/D3
Montefrío, Spain 33/D4
Montego (bay), Jamaica 158/G5
Montego Bay, Jamaica 158/H5
Montego Bay, Jamaica 156/B3
Montego Bay (pt.), Jamaica 158/G5
Montegut, La. (70377) 238/J8
Montehermoso, Spain 33/C2
Monteiro, Brazil 132/G4
Monteith, Iowa (†50115) 229/D5
Montejinnie, North. Terr. 93/C4
Monte Lake, Br. Col. 184/G5
Montélimar, France 28/F5
Montelindo (riv.), Paraguay 144/C3
Montellano, Spain 33/D4
Montello, Nev. (89830) 266/G1
Montello, Wis. (53949) 317/H8
Montemayor (plat.), Argentina 143/C5
Montemorelos, Mexico 150/K4
Montemor-o-Novo, Portugal 33/B3
Montemor-o-Velho, Portugal 33/B2
Monte Ne, Ark. (†72756) 202/B1
Montenegro, Brazil 132/D10
Montenegro, Chile 138/G2
Montenegro (rep.), Yugoslavia 45/D4
Monte Patria, Chile 138/A8
Monte Plata, Dom. Rep. 158/E6
Montepuez, Mozambique 118/F2
Montepulciano, Italy 34/C3
Monte Quemado, Argentina 143/D2
Monte Real, Brazil 132/A5
Monterey, Ala. (†36030) 195/E7
Monterey, Calif. 188/B3
Monterey (bay), Calif. 188/B3
Monterey (co.), Calif. 204/D7
Monterey, Calif. (93940) 204/D7
Monterey (bay), Calif. 204/K4
Monterey, Ind. (46960) 227/D2
Monterey, Ky. (†40359) 237/M4
Monterey, La. (71354) 238/G4
Monterey○, Mass. (01245) 249/B4
Monterey, Tenn. (38574) 237/L8
Monterey, Va. (24465) 307/K4
Monterey, Wis. (†53066) 317/J1
Monterey Park, Calif. (91754) 204/C10
Montería, Colombia 120/B2
Montería, Colombia 126/B3
Monte Rio, Calif. (95462) 204/B5
Montero, Bolivia 136/D5
Monteros, Argentina 143/C2
Monterotondo, Italy 34/F6
Monterrey, Mexico 2/D4
Monterrey, Mexico 146/J7
Monterrey, Mexico 150/J4
Monterville, W. Va. (26282) 312/F5
Montes, Uruguay 145/D5
Montesano, Wash. (98563) 310/B4
Monte Sant'Angelo, Italy 34/F4
Monte Santo, Brazil 132/G5
Montes Claros, Brazil 120/E4
Montes Claros, Brazil 132/E7
Monte Sereno, Calif. (95030) 204/K4
Montevallo, Ala. (35115) 195/E4
Montevallo, Mo. (†64767) 261/D7
Montevarchi, Italy 34/C3
Montevideo, Minn. (56265) 255/C6
Montevideo (dept.), Uruguay 145/B7
Montevideo (cap.), Uruguay 145/B7
Montevideo (cap.), Uruguay 120/D6
Montevideo (cap.), Uruguay 143/G4
Monteview, Idaho (83435) 220/F6
Monte Vista, Colo. (81144) 208/G7
Montezuma (co.), Colo. 208/B8
Montezuma, Colo. (†80435) 208/H3
Montezuma (peak), Colo. 208/F8
Montezuma, Georgia (31063) 217/E6
Montezuma, Ind. (47862) 227/C5
Montezuma, Iowa (50171) 229/H5
Montezuma, Kansas (67867) 232/B4
Montezuma, N. Mex. (87731) 274/D3
Montezuma, Ohio (45866) 284/A4
Montezuma, Tenn. (†38340) 237/D10
Montezuma (creek), Utah 304/E6
Montezuma Castle Nat'l Mon., Ariz. 198/D4
Montezuma Creek, Utah (84534) 304/E6
Montfoort, Netherlands 27/G4
Montfort, France 28/C3
Montfort, Wis. (53569) 317/E10
Montgomery (cap.), Ala. 188/J4
Montgomery (cap.), Ala. 146/K6
Montgomery (co.), Ala. 195/F6
Montgomery (cap.), Ala. (*36101) 195/F6
Montgomery (co.), Ark. 202/C4
Montgomery (co.), Georgia 217/G6
Montgomery (co.), Ill. 222/D4
Montgomery, Ill. (60538) 222/E2
Montgomery (co.), Ind. 227/D4
Montgomery, Ind. (47558) 227/C7
Montgomery (co.), Iowa 229/C6
Montgomery, Iowa (51353) 229/C2
Montgomery (co.), Kansas 232/G4
Montgomery (co.), Ky. 237/O4
Montgomery, La. (71454) 238/E3
Montgomery (co.), Md. 245/J4
Montgomery, Mich. (49255) 250/E7
Montgomery, Minn. (56069) 255/E6
Montgomery (co.), Miss. 256/E4
Montgomery (co.), Mo. 261/K5
Montgomery (co.), N.Y. 276/M5
Montgomery, N.Y. (12549) 276/M7
Montgomery (co.), N.C. 281/K4
Montgomery (co.), Ohio 284/B6
Montgomery, Ohio (45242) 284/C9
Montgomery (co.), Pa. 294/M5
Montgomery, Pa. (17752) 294/H3
Montgomery (co.), Tenn. 237/G8
Montgomery (co.), Texas 303/J7
Montgomery, Texas (77356) 303/J7
Montgomery○, Vt. (05470) 268/B2
Montgomery (co.), Va. 307/H6
Montgomery, Wales 13/D5
Montgomery, Wales 10/E4
Montgomery, W. Va. (25136) 312/D6
Montgomery Center, Vt. (05471) 268/B2
Montgomery City, Mo. (63361) 261/K5
Monthey, Switzerland 39/C4
Monticello, Ark. (71655) 202/G6
Monticello, Fla. (32344) 212/C1
Monticello, Georgia (31064) 217/E4
Monticello, Ill. (61856) 222/E3
Monticello, Ind. (47960) 227/D3
Monticello, Iowa (52310) 229/L4
Monticello, Ky. (42633) 237/M7
Monticello○, Maine (04760) 243/H3
Monticello, Minn. (55362) 255/E5
Monticello, Miss. (39654) 256/D7
Monticello, Mo. (63457) 261/J2
Monticello, N. Mex. (87939) 274/B5
Monticello, N.Y. (12701) 276/L7
Monticello, Ohio (†45887) 284/B4
Monticello, S.C. (29106) 296/E3
Monticello, Utah (84535) 304/E6
Monticello, Wis. (53570) 317/G10
Mont Ida, Kansas (†66091) 232/G3
Montier, Mo. (65546) 261/J8
Montigny-les-Metz, France 28/G3
Montigny-le-Tilleul, Belgium 27/E8
Montijo, Panama 154/G6
Montijo (gulf), Panama 154/G7
Montijo, Portugal 33/B3
Montijo, Spain 33/C3
Montilla, Spain 33/D4
Montjoie (lake), Québec 172/B3
Mont-Joli, Que. 162/K6
Mont-Joli, Québec 174/D3
Mont-Joli, Québec 172/J1
Mont-Laurier, Que. 162/J6
Mont-Laurier, Québec 172/B3
Mont-Laurier, Québec 174/B3
Mont-Louis, Québec 172/C1
Montluçon, France 28/E4
Montmagny (co.), Québec 172/G3
Montmagny, Québec 174/C3
Montmagny, Québec 172/G3
Montmartre, Sask. 181/H5
Montmédy, France 28/F3
Montmorenci, Ind. (47962) 227/D4
Montmorenci, S.C. (29839) 296/D4
Montmorency (co.), Mich. 250/E3
Montmorency, Québec 172/J3
Montmorency (riv.), Québec 172/F2
Montmorency, Victoria 97/J4
Montmorency No. 1 (co.), Québec 172/F2
Montmorency No. 2 (co.), Québec 172/G3
Montmorency No. I (county), Québec 174/C3
Montmorillon, France 28/D4
Mont Nebo, Sask. 181/E2
Montney, Br. Col. 184/G2
Monto, Queensland 95/D5
Monto, Queensland 88/J4
Montoire-sur-le-Loir, France 28/D4
Montoro, Spain 33/D3
Montosa (mesa), N. Mex. 274/E3
Montour, Idaho (83617) 220/B6
Montour, Iowa (50173) 229/H5
Montour (co.), Pa. 294/J3
Montour Falls, N.Y. (14865) 276/G6
Montoursville, Pa. (17754) 294/J3
Montowese, Conn. (†06473) 210/D3
Montoya, N. Mex. (†88401) 274/F3
Montoz (mt.), Switzerland 39/D2
Montpelier, Idaho 188/D2
Montpelier, Idaho (83254) 220/G7
Montpelier, Ind. (47359) 227/G3
Montpelier, Iowa (52759) 229/M6
Montpelier, Jamaica 158/H6
Montpelier, La. (†70422) 238/M1
Montpelier, Miss. (39754) 256/G3
Montpelier, N. Dak. (58472) 282/N6
Montpelier, Ohio (43543) 284/A2
Montpelier (cap.), Vt. (05602) 268/B3
Montpelier (cap.), Vt. 146/L5
Montpelier (cap.), Vt. 188/M2
Montpellier, France 7/E4
Montpellier, France 28/E6
Montpellier, Québec 172/B4
Montréal, Canada 2/F3
Montreal (riv.), Mich. 250/F1
Montreal, Mo. (65591) 261/G7
Montréal, Que. 146/L5
Montréal, Que. 162/J7
Montréal, Québec 172/H4
Montreal (lake), Sask. 181/F1
Montreal, Wis. (54550) 317/F3
Montreal (riv.), Wis. 317/F2
Montréal-Est, Québec 172/J4
Montreal Lake, Sask. 181/F1
Montréal-Nord, Québec 172/H4
Montreal River Harbor, Ontario 177/J5
Montreat, N.C. (28757) 281/E3
Montreuil, Pas-de-Calais, France 28/D2
Montreuil, Seine-Saint-Denis, France 28/B2
Montreux, Switzerland 39/C4
Montricher, Switzerland 39/B3
Mont-Rolland, Québec 172/C4
Montrose, Ala. (36559) 195/C9
Montrose, Ark. (71658) 202/H7
Montrose, Br. Col. 184/J5
Montrose (co.), Colo. 208/C6
Montrose, Colo. (81401) 208/D6
Montrose, Georgia (31065) 217/F5
Montrose, Ill. (62445) 222/E4
Montrose, Iowa (52639) 229/L7
Montrose, Kansas (†66956) 232/D2
Montrose, La. (†71457) 238/D3
Montrose, Md. (†20850) 245/K4
Montrose, Mich. (48457) 250/F5
Montrose, Minn. (55363) 255/E5
Montrose, Miss. (†39338) 256/F6
Montrose, Mo. (64770) 261/E6
Montrose, Pa. (18801) 294/L2
Montrose, Scotland 10/E2
Montrose, Scotland 15/F4
Montrose, S. Dak. (57048) 298/P6
Montrose, Victoria 97/K5
Montrose, W. Va. (26283) 312/G4
Montrose-La Crescenta, Calif. (91214) 204/C10
Montross, Va. (22520) 307/P4
Montrouge, France 28/B2
Mont-Royal, Québec 172/H4
Monts (pt.), Québec 172/B1
Mont-Saint-Hilaire, Québec 172/D4
Mont-Saint-Michel, France 28/C3
Mont-Saint-Michel, Québec 172/B3
Mont-Saint-Pierre, Québec 172/C1
MONTSERRAT 156/G3
Montserrat (mt.), Spain 33/G2
Montsinéry, Fr. Guiana 131/E3
Mont-Tremblant, Québec 172/C3
Mont-Tremblant Prov. Park, Québec 172/C3
Mont-Tremblant Prov. Park, Québec 174/C3
Montvale, N.J. (07645) 273/B1
Montvale, Va. (24122) 307/J6
Montverde, Fla. (32756) 212/E3
Mont Vernon○, N.H. (03057) 268/D6
Montville, Conn. (06353) 210/G3
Montville○, Conn. (06353) 210/G3
Montville, Maine (†04941) 243/E7
Montville○, Maine (†04941) 243/E7
Montville, Mass. (†01255) 249/B4
Montville○, N.J. (07045) 273/E2
Montville, Ohio (44064) 284/H2
Montz, La. (†70068) 238/M3
Monument, Colo. (80132) 208/K4
Monument (peak), Idaho 220/B4
Monument, Kansas (67747) 232/A2
Monument, N. Mex. (88265) 274/F6
Monument, Oreg. (97864) 291/H3
Monument (valley), Utah 304/D6
Monument Beach, Mass. (02553) 249/M6
Monument Valley, Utah (84536) 304/D6
Monywa, Burma 72/B2
Monza, Italy 34/B2
Monze, Zambia 115/E7
Monzón, Spain 33/G2
Mooar, Iowa (†52632) 229/L8
Moodie (isl.), N.W. Terrs. 187/M3
Moodus, Conn. (06469) 210/F2
Moodus (res.), Conn. 210/F2
Moody, Ala. (†35125) 195/F3
Moody, Maine (04054) 243/B9
Moody, Mo. (65770) 261/J9
Moody (co.), S. Dak. 298/R5
Moody, Texas (76557) 303/G6
Moody A.F.B., Georgia 217/F9
Moodys, Okla. (74444) 288/S2
Moodyville, Tenn. (†38549) 237/L7
Mooers, N.Y. (12958) 276/N1
Mooka, Japan 81/K5
Mooleyville, Ky. (40154) 237/H4
Mooloo Downs, W. Australia 92/B4
Moomin (creek), N.S. Wales 97/E1
Moon (lake), Calif. 204/E2
Moon (lake), Nebr. 264/E2
Moon, Okla. (†71821) 288/S7
Moonachie, N.J. (†07070) 273/B2
Moonah (creek), Queensland 95/A4
Moonbeam, Ontario 177/J5
Mooncoin, Ireland 17/G7
Moonie (riv.), N.S. Wales 97/E1
Moonie, Queensland 95/D5
Moon Run, Pa. (†15244) 294/B5
Moonta, S. Australia 94/E5
Moora, W. Australia 88/B6
Moora, W. Australia 92/B5
Moorabbin, Victoria 88/L7
Moorabbin, Victoria 97/J5
Moorcroft, Wyo. (82721) 319/H1
Moore, Idaho (83255) 220/E6
Moore, Mont. (59464) 262/G4
Moore (dam), N.H. 268/D3
Moore (res.), N.H. 268/D3
Moore (co.), N.C. 281/L4
Moore, Okla. (73160) 288/M4
Moore, S.C. (29369) 296/D2
Moore (co.), Tenn. 237/J10
Moore (co.), Texas 303/C2
Moore, Texas (78057) 303/E9
Moore, Utah (†84523) 304/C5
Moore (dam), Vt. 268/D3
Moore (res.), Vt. 268/D3
Moore (lake), W. Australia 88/B5
Moore (lake), W. Australia 92/B5
MOOREA, Fr. Poly. 86/S13
Moorea (isl.), Fr. Poly. 87/L7
Moorea (isl.), Fr. Poly. 86/S13
Moorefield, Ark. (†72501) 202/G2
Moorefield, Ind. (†47043) 227/G7
Moorefield, Ky. (40350) 237/O4
Moorefield, Nebr. (69039) 264/D4
Moorefield, Ontario 177/D4
Moorefield, W. Va. (26836) 312/J4
Moore Haven, Fla. (33471) 212/E5
Mooreland, Ind. (47360) 227/G5
Mooreland, Okla. (73852) 288/H2
Moore Park, Manitoba 179/C4
Mooresboro, N.C. (28114) 281/F4
Moores Bridge, Ala. (†35458) 195/C4
Mooresburg, Tenn. (37811) 237/P8
Moores Creek, Ky. (40453) 237/O6
Moores Creek Nat'l Battlefield, N.C. 281/N6
Moores Hill, Ind. (47032) 227/G6
Moores Mills, New Bruns. 170/C3
Moorestown, Mich. (49651) 250/D4
Moorestown, N.J. (08057) 273/B3
Mooresville, Ala. (35649) 195/E1
Mooresville, Ind. (46158) 227/E5
Mooresville, Mo. (64664) 261/E3
Mooresville, N.C. (28115) 281/H3
Mooreton, N. Dak. (58061) 282/S7
Moore Town, Jamaica 158/K6
Mooretown, Ontario 177/B5
Mooreville, Miss. (38857) 256/G2
Moorfoot (hills), Scotland 15/E5
Moorhead, Iowa (51558) 229/B5
Moorhead, Minn. 188/G1
Moorhead, Minn. (56560) 255/B4
Moorhead, Miss. (38761) 256/C4
Mooringsport, La. (71060) 238/B1
Moorland, Iowa (50566) 229/E4
Moorland, Ky. (†40223) 237/L2
Moorman, Ky. (42357) 237/G6
Moorooka, Queensland 88/K3
Moorooka, Queensland 95/D3
Mooroopna, Victoria 97/C5
Moorpark, Calif. (93021) 204/G9
Moorreesburg, S. Africa 118/B6
Moorslede, Belgium 27/B7
Moosburg an der Isar, W. Germany 22/D4
Moose (creek), Idaho 220/D3
Moose (pond), Maine 243/B7
Moose (riv.), Maine 243/D4
Moose (isl.), Manitoba 179/E3
Moose (riv.), Minn. 255/C2
Moose (riv.), N.Y. 276/K3
Moose (mt.), Sask. 181/J6
Moose (riv.), Vt. 268/D2
Moose (lake), Wis. 317/E3
Moose (lake), Wis. 317/F3
Moose, Wyo. (83012) 319/B2
Moose Creek, Ontario 177/K2
Moose Factory, Ontario 175/D2
Moosehead, Maine (†04478) 243/D4
Moosehead (lake), Maine 243/D4
Mooseheart, Ill. (60539) 222/E2
Moose Heights, Br. Col. 184/F3
Moosehorn, Manitoba 179/D3
Moose Jaw, Sask. 146/H4
Moose Jaw, Sask. 162/F6
Moose Jaw, Sask. 181/F5
Moose Jaw (riv.), Sask. 181/G5
Moose Lake, Manitoba 179/H3
Moose Lake, Minn. (55767) 255/F4
Mooseland, Nova Scotia 168/F4
Mooseleuk (stream), Maine 243/F2
Mooselookmeguntic (lake), Maine 243/B6
Moose Mountain (creek), Sask. 181/J6
Moose Mountain Prov. Park, Sask. 181/J6
Moose Pass, Alaska (99631) 196/C1
Moose Range, Sask. 181/H2
Moose River○, Maine (†04945) 243/C4
Moose River, Ontario 175/D2
Moosic, Pa. (18507) 294/F7
Moosilauke (mt.), N.H. 268/D3
Moosomin, Sask. 162/F5
Moosomin, Sask. 181/K5
Moosonee, Ont. 162/H5
Moosonee, Ont. 146/K4
Moosonee, Ontario 175/D2
Moosup, Conn. (06354) 210/H2
Moosup (riv.), Conn. 210/H2
Mopang (lake), Maine 243/H6
Mopeia, Mozambique 118/F3
Mopti, Mali 102/B3
Mopti, Mali 106/D6
Moqatta, Sudan 59/C7
Moqor, Afghanistan 68/B2
Moqor, Afghanistan 59/J3
Moquah, Wis. (†54806) 317/D2
Moquegua (dept.), Peru 128/G11
Moquegua, Peru 120/B4
Moquegua, Peru 128/G11
Mór, Hungary 41/E3
Mora, Cameroon 115/B1
Mora, India 68/B7
Mora, La. (71455) 238/E4
Mora, Minn. (55051) 255/E5
Mora, Mo. (65345) 261/F5
Mora (co.), N. Mex. 274/E3
Mora, N. Mex. (87732) 274/D3
Mora (riv.), N. Mex. 274/E3
Mora, Portugal 33/B3
Mora, Spain 33/E3
Mora, Sweden 18/J6
Moradabad, India 54/J7
Moradabad, India 68/D3
Mora de Rubielos, Spain 33/F2
Morado, Quebrado (riv.), Chile 138/A6
Morafenobe, Madagascar 118/G3
Morąg, Poland 47/E2
Moraga, Calif. (94556) 204/K2
Moraine, Ohio (†45439) 284/B6
Moraleda (chan.), Chile 138/D5
Morales, Guatemala 154/C3
Morales, Peru 128/D6
Moramanga, Madagascar 118/H3
Moramanga, Madagascar 102/G6
Moran, Ind. (†46041) 227/D4
Moran, Kansas (66755) 232/G4
Moran, Mich. (49760) 250/E2
Moran, Texas (76464) 303/E5
Moran, Wyo. (83013) 319/B2
Moranbah, Queensland 95/C9
Morane (isl.), Fr. Poly. 87/N8
Morant (pt.), Jamaica 156/C3
Morant Bay, Jamaica 158/K7
Morar, Scotland 15/C4
Morar, Loch (lake), Scotland 15/C4
Morat (lake), Switzerland 39/D3
Morata de Tajuña, Spain 33/G4
Moratalla, Spain 33/E3
Morattico, Va. (22523) 307/P5
Moratuwa, Sri Lanka 68/D7
Morava (riv.), Czech. 41/D2
Morava (riv.), Yugoslavia 45/E3
Moravia, Iowa (52571) 229/H7
Moravia, N.Y. (13118) 276/H5
Moravian Falls, N.C. (28654) 281/G2
Moravská Třebová, Czech. 41/D2
Moravské Budějovice, Czech. 41/D2
Morawa, W. Australia 88/B5
Morawa, W. Australia 92/B5
Morawhanna, Guyana 120/D2
Morawhanna, Guyana 131/B1
Moray (firth), Scotland 7/D3
Moray (firth), Scotland 15/E3
Moray (firth), Scotland 10/E2
Moray (trad. co.), Scotland 15/A5
Morazán, Honduras 154/D3
Morbihan (dept.), France 28/B4
Mörbylånga, Sweden 18/K8
Morden, Man. 162/G6
Morden, Manitoba 179/D5
Mordialloc, Victoria 97/J6
Mordialloc, Victoria 88/L7
Mordvinian A.S.S.R., U.S.S.R. 52/G4
Mordvinian A.S.S.R., U.S.S.R. 48/E4
More, Loch (lake), Scotland 15/E2
More, Loch (lake), Scotland 15/D2
Morea, Victoria 97/A5
Moreau (riv.), S. Dak. 298/G3
Moreauville, La. (71355) 238/G4
Morebattle, Scotland 15/F5
Morecambe, Alberta 182/E3
Morecambe (bay), England 10/oe3
Morecambe (bay), England 13/D3
Moree, N. S. Wales 88/H5
Moree, N.S. Wales 97/E1
Morehead, Kansas (†66776) 232/G4
Morehead, Ky. (40351) 237/P4
Morehead City, N.C. (28557) 281/R5
Morehouse (par.), La. 238/G1
Morehouse, Mo. (63868) 261/N9
Moreland, Ark. (72849) 202/E3
Moreland, Georgia (30259) 217/C4
Moreland, Idaho (83256) 220/F6
Moreland Hills, Ohio (†44022) 284/J9
Morelia, Mexico 150/J7
Morelia, Mexico 146/H8
Morella, Queensland 95/B4
Morell, Pr. Edward I. 168/F2
Morella, Queensland 88/G4
Morella, Spain 33/F2
Morelos (state), Mexico 150/K7
Morelos, Mexico 150/J2
Morelos Cañada, Mexico 150/O2
Morena, India 68/D3
Morena, Sierra (mts.), Spain 7/D5
Morena, Sierra (range), Spain 33/E3
Morenci, Ariz. (85540) 198/F5
Morenci, Mich. (49256) 250/E7
Moreni, Romania 45/G3
Moreno, Bolivia 136/B2
Moreno, Calif. (92360) 204/H10
Moreno (bay), Chile 138/A4
Møre og Romsdal (co.), Norway 18/E5
Mores (creek), Idaho 220/C6
Moresby, Br. Col. 184/B3
Moresby (isl.), Br. Col. 184/B4
Moreton (isl.), Queensland 88/J5
Moreton (bay), Queensland 88/K2
Moreton (bay), Queensland 95/E5
Moreton (isl.), Queensland 95/E5
Moretonhampstead, England 13/C7
Moreton-in-Marsh, England 13/F6
Moretown○, Vt. (05660) 268/B3
Morewood, Ontario 177/J2
Morgan (co.), Ala. 195/E2
Morgan (co.), Colo. 208/M2
Morgan (pt.), Conn. 210/D4
Morgan (co.), Georgia 217/F3
Morgan, Georgia (31766) 217/C7
Morgan (co.), Ill. 222/C4
Morgan (co.), Ind. 227/E6
Morgan (co.), Ky. 237/P5
Morgan, Ky. (†41040) 237/N3
Morgan, Minn. (56266) 255/D6
Morgan (co.), Mo. 261/G6
Morgan, Mo. (†65706) 261/G7
Morgan (co.), Ohio 284/G6
Morgan (co.), Tenn. 237/M8
Morgan, Texas (76671) 303/G5
Morgan (co.), Utah 304/C2
Morgan, Utah (84050) 304/C2
Morgan○, Vt. (05853) 268/D2
Morgan (co.), W. Va. 312/K3
Morgan Center, Vt. (05854) 268/D2
Morgan City, La. (70380) 238/H7
Morgan City, Miss. (38946) 256/D4

414 Mount Washington

Mount Washington○, Mass. (†12517) 249/A4
Mount Wellington, N. Zealand 100/C1
Mount Willing, Ala. (†36012) 195/E6
Mount Wolf, Pa. (17347) 294/J5
Mount Zion, Georgia (30150) 217/B3
Mount Zion, Ill. (62549) 222/E4
Mount Zion, Ind. (†46792) 227/G3
Mount Zion, Iowa (†52565) 229/K7
Mount Zion, W. Va. (26151) 312/D5
Moura, Portugal 33/C3
Moura, Queensland 95/D5
Moura, Queensland 88/J4
Mourão, Portugal 33/C3
Mourdi (depr.), Chad 111/D4
Mourne (Newry and Mourne) (dist.), N. Ireland17/J3
Mourne (mts.), N. Ireland 17/J3
Mourne (riv.), N. Ireland 17/G2
Mouscron, Belgium 27/C7
Moussoro, Chad 111/C5
Mouthcard, Ky. (41548) 237/S6
Mouth of Wilson, Va. (24363) 307/F7
Moutier, Switzerland 39/D2
Moûtiers, France 28/G5
Mouton (isl.), Nova Scotia 168/D5
Mouydir (mts.), Algeria 106/E3
Moville, Iowa (51039) 229/A4
Moville, Ireland 17/G1
Mowbray, Manitoba 179/D5
Mowdok Mual (mt.), Bangladesh 68/G4
Moweaqua, Ill. (62550) 222/E4
Mower (co.), Minn. 255/F7
Mowming (Maoming), China 77/H7
Mowrystown, Ohio (45155) 284/C7
Moxahala, Ohio (43761) 284/F6
Moxee City, Wash. (98936) 310/E4
Moxico (dist.), Angola 115/D6
Moxie (lake), Maine 243/D5
Moxley, Georgia (†30477) 217/H5
Moy (riv.), Ireland 17/C3
Moy, N. Ireland 17/H3
Moyale, Ethiopia 111/G7
Moyale, Kenya 115/G3
Moyamba, S. Leone 106/B7
Moycullen, Ireland 17/C5
Moyers, Okla. (74557) 288/P6
Moyers, W. Va. (26813) 312/H6
Moyeuvre-Grande, France 28/G3
Moygashel, N. Ireland 17/H3
Moyie, Br. Col. 184/K5
Moyie (riv.), Idaho 220/B1
Moyie Springs, Idaho (83845) 220/B1
Moyle (dist.), N. Ireland 17/J1
Moynalty, Ireland 17/H4
Moyo, Uganda 115/F3
Moyobamba, Peru 120/B3
Moyobamba, Peru 128/D6
Moyock, N.C. (27958) 281/S1
Moyogalpa, Nicaragua 154/E5
Moyu (Karakax), China 77/A4
Moza Illit, Israel 65/C4
Mozambique 2/L6
Mozambique 102/F6
Mozambique (chan.) 2/L7
Mozambique (chan.) 102/G6
Mozambique (pt.), La. 238/M7
Mozambique (chan.), Madagascar 118/G3
MOZAMBIQUE 118/E4
Mozambique (chan.), Mozambique 118/G3
Mozart, Sask. 181/G4
Mozer, W. Va. (†26866) 312/H5
Mozhaysk, U.S.S.R. 52/E3
Mozhga, U.S.S.R. 52/H3
Mozier, Ill. (62070) 222/C4
Mozyr', U.S.S.R. 48/C4
Mozyr', U.S.S.R. 52/C4
Mpanda, Tanzania 115/F5
Mpika, Zambia 115/F6
Mporokoso, Zambia 115/F5
M'Pouya, Congo 115/C4
Mpraeso, Ghana 106/D7
Mpulungu, Zambia 115/F5
Mpwapwa, Tanzania 115/G5
Mrągowo, Poland 47/E2
Msaken, Tunisia 106/G1
M'Sila, Algeria 106/E1
Msta (riv.), U.S.S.R. 52/D3
Mtakuja, Tanzania 115/F5
Mtsensk, U.S.S.R. 52/E4
Mtwara (reg.), Tanzania 115/G5
Mtwara-Mikindani, Tanzania 102/G6
Mtwara-Mikindani, Tanzania 115/H6
Mu (riv.), Burma 72/B2
Mualama, Mozambique 118/F3
Muang Hinboun, Laos 72/E3
Muang Kènthao, Laos 72/D3
Muang Khammouan, Laos 72/E3
Muang Không, Laos 72/E4
Muang Khôngxédôn, Laos 72/E4
Muang Khoua, Laos 72/D2
Muang May, Laos 72/E4
Muang Ou Tai, Laos 72/D2
Muang Pak-Lay, Laos 72/D3
Muang Paktha, Laos 72/D2
Muang Pakxan, Laos 72/D2
Muang Phin, Laos 72/E3
Muang Sing, Laos 72/D2
Muang Tahoi, Laos 72/E3
Muang Vangviang, Laos 72/D3
Muang Vapi, Laos 72/E4
Muang Xaignabouri (Sayaboury), Laos 72/D3
Muang Xay, Laos 72/D3
Muang Xépôn, Laos 72/E3
Muang Xon, Laos 72/D2
Muar, Malaysia 72/D7
Muarabungo, Indonesia 85/C6
Muarasiberut, Indonesia 85/B6
Muaratewe, Indonesia 85/F6
Muari, Ras (cape), Pakistan 68/B4
Muari, Ras (cape), Pakistan 59/J5
Mubarraz, Saudi Arabia 59/E4
Mubende, Uganda 115/F3
Mubi, Nigeria 106/G6
Muchanes, Bolivia 136/B4
Mücheln, E. Germany 22/D3
Muck (isl.), Scotland 10/C2
Muck (isl.), Scotland 15/B4
Muckamore, N. Ireland 17/J2
Muckle Flugga (isl.), Scotland 15/G2
Muckleshoot Ind. Res., Wash. 310/C3
Muckno (lake), Ireland 17/H3
Muco (riv.), Colombia 126/E5
Mucojo, Mozambique 118/G2
Mucope, Angola 115/B7
Mucuchachí, Venezuela 124/C3
Mucuchíes, Venezuela 124/C3
Mucugê, Brazil 132/F6
Mucur, Turkey 63/F3
Mucurapo, Trin. & Tob. 161/A10
Mucuri, Brazil 132/G7
Mucuripe (pt.), Brazil 132/G3
Mucusso, Angola 115/D7
Mud (lake), Idaho 220/F6
Mud (riv.), Ky. 237/H7
Mud (lake), La. 238/D7
Mud (lake), Minn. 255/C2
Mud (lake), Minn. 255/B5
Mud (riv.), Minn. 255/C2
Mud (isl.), Nova Scotia 168/B5
Mud (creek), Okla. 288/L6
Mud (creek), Oreg. 291/K2
Mud (creek), S. Dak. 298/N3
Mud (lake), S. Dak. 298/R2
Mud, W. Va. (†25565) 312/C6
Mud (riv.), W. Va. 312/B6
Mudanjiang (Mutankiang), China 77/M3
Mudanjiang, China54/O5
Mudan Jiang (riv.), China 77/L3
Mudanya, Turkey 63/C2
Mudauwara, Jordan 59/C4
Mud Bay, Br. Col. 184/H2
Mud Butte, S. Dak. (57758) 298/D4
Muddy (creek), Colo. 208/E4
Muddy (brook), Conn. 210/H1
Muddy (pond), Conn. 210/G1
Muddy (riv.), Conn. 210/D3
Muddy, Ill. (62965) 222/E6
Muddy (mts.), Nev. 266/G6
Muddy (creek), N. Dak. 282/G6
Muddy (pt.), St. Chris.-Nevis 161/C10
Muddy (lake), Sask. 181/B3
Muddy (creek), Utah 304/A2
Muddy (creek), Utah 304/C4
Muddy (creek), Wyo. 319/F3
Muddy (creek), Wyo. 319/D2
Muddy (mt.), Wyo. 319/F3
Muddy Boggy (creek), Okla. 288/O5
Mudge (pond), Conn. 210/B1
Mudgee, N. S. Wales 88/J6
Mudgee, N.S. Wales 97/E3
Mudhnib, Saudi Arabia 59/D4
Mudjatik (riv.), Sask. 181/L3
Mud Lake, Idaho (†83450) 220/F6
Mud Lake, Newf. 166/B3
Mud Lake (res.), S. Dak. 298/N2
Mud Mountain (lake), Wash. 310/D3
Mudon, Burma 72/C3
Mudug (prov.), Somalia 115/J2
Mudurnu, Turkey 63/D2
Muecate, Mozambique 118/F2
Mueda, Mozambique 118/F2
Muenster, Sask. 181/F3
Muenster, Texas (76252) 303/G4
Muerto, Mar (lag.), Mexico 150/N9
Muezerskiy, U.S.S.R. 52/D2
Muff, Ireland 17/G1
Mufulira, Zambia 115/E6
Mufulira, Zambia 102/E6
Muge, Portugal 33/B3
Mugford (cape), Newf. 166/B2
Mughar, Israel 65/C2
Muğla (prov.), Turkey 63/C4
Muğla, Turkey 59/A2
Muğla, Turkey 63/C4
Muglad, Sudan 111/E5
Muhammad, Ras (cape), Egypt 59/B4
Muhammad, Ras (cape), Egypt 111/F2
Muhammad Qol, Sudan 59/C5
Muhammad Qol, Sudan 111/G3
Muharraq, Bahrain 59/F4
Mühldorf am Inn, W. Germany 22/E4
Muhlenberg (co.), Ky. 237/G6
Mühlhausen (Thomas-Müntzer-Stadt), E. Germany 22/D3
Mühlviertel (reg.), Austria 41/C2
Muhu (isl.), U.S.S.R. 53/B1
Mui Bai Bung (pt.), Vietnam 54/M9
Muiden, Netherlands 27/G4
Muinebeag, Ireland 17/H6
Muir (glac.), Alaska 196/M1
Muir, Mich. (48860) 250/D5
Muir, Pa. (17957) 294/J4
Muirkirk, Md. (†20705) 245/L4
Muirkirk, Scotland 15/E5
Muir of Ord, Scotland 15/D3
Muiron (isls.), W. Australia 88/A4
Muiron (isls.), W. Australia 92/A3
Muir Woods Nat'l Mon., Calif. 204/H2
Muizenberg, S. Africa 118/E7
Muju, S. Korea 81/C6
Mukachevo, U.S.S.R. 52/B5
Mukah, Malaysia 85/E5
Mukalla, P.D.R. Yemen 54/F8
Mukalla, P.D.R. Yemen 59/E7
Mukdahan, Thailand 72/E3
Mukden, Bolivia 136/A2
Mukden (Shenyang), China 77/K3
Mukilteo, Wash. (98275) 310/C3
Mukinbudin, W. Australia 92/B5
Muko, Japan 81/J7
Muko (isl.), Japan 81/M3
Muko (riv.), Japan 81/H7
Mukutawa (lake), Manitoba 179/G2
Mukutawa (riv.), Manitoba 179/E1
Mukwonago, Wis. (53149) 317/J2
Mula, Spain 33/F3
Mulaló, Ecuador 128/C3
Mulanje (mt.), Malawi 102/F6
Mulanje (mts.), Malawi 115/G7
Mulatos, Colombia 126/B3
Mulberry (creek), Ala. 195/E5
Mulberry, Ark. (72947) 202/B2
Mulberry (riv.), Ark. 202/C2
Mulberry, Calif. (†95926) 204/D4
Mulberry, Fla. (33860) 212/E4
Mulberry, Ind. (46058) 227/D4
Mulberry, Kansas (66756) 232/H4
Mulberry, Ohio (†45150) 284/B7
Mulberry, Tenn. (37359) 237/H10
Mulberry Fork (riv.), Ala. 195/E3
Mulberry Grove, Ill. (62262) 222/D5
Mulchatna (riv.), Alaska 196/G2
Mulchén, Chile 138/E1
Mulde (riv.), E. Germany 22/E3
Muldon, Miss. (†39730) 256/G3
Muldoon, Texas (78949) 303/G8
Muldraugh, Ky. (40155) 237/J5
Muldrow, Okla. (74948) 288/S4
Mule (mts.), Ariz. 198/E7
Mule (creek), Kansas 232/C4
Mule Creek, N. Mex. (88051) 274/A5
Mule Creek, Wyo. (†57735) 319/H2
Muleculus, Nicaragua 154/E4
Mulegé, Mexico 150/C3
Mulegns, Switzerland 39/J3
Muleshoe, Texas (79347) 303/B3
Mulgrave, Nova Scotia 168/G3
Mulgrave (lake), Nova Scotia 168/F3
Mulhacén (mt.), Spain 33/E4
Mulhall, Okla. (73063) 288/M2
Mülheim an der Ruhr, W. Germany 22/B3
Mulhouse, France 7/E4
Mulhouse, France 28/G4
Mulhurst, Alberta 182/D3
Muli, China 77/F6
Muli (str.), Indonesia 85/K7
Mulino, Oreg. (97042) 291/B2
Mulinu'u (cape), W. Samoa 86/L8
Mulkear (riv.), Ireland 17/E6
Mull (head), Scotland 15/F2
Mull (head), Scotland 15/F1
Mull (isl.), Scotland 10/D2
Mull (isl.), Scotland 15/C4
Mull (sound), Scotland 15/C4
Mullagh, Ireland 17/H4
Mullaghareirk (mts.), Ireland 17/C7
Mullaghearn (mt.), N. Ireland 17/G2
Mullaghmore, Ireland 17/D3
Mullaittivu, Sri Lanka 68/E7
Mullaley, N.S. Wales 97/E2
Mullan, Idaho (83846) 220/C2
Mullardoch, Loch (lake), Scotland 15/C3
Mullen, Nebr. (69152) 264/C2
Mullens, W. Va. (25882) 312/D7
Müller (mts.), Indonesia 85/E5
Mullet (key), Fla. 212/D4
Mullett (lake), Mich. 250/E3
Mullett Lake, Mich. (49761) 250/E3
Mullewa, W. Australia 88/B5
Mullewa, W. Australia 92/A5
Müllheim, Switzerland 39/G1
Müllheim, W. Germany 22/B5
Mullica (riv.), N.J. 273/D4
Mullica Hill, N.J. (08062) 273/C4
Mulliken, Mich. (48861) 250/E6
Mullin, Texas (76864) 303/F6
Mullinahone, Ireland 17/F7
Mullinavat, Ireland 17/G7
Mullingar, Ireland 10/C4
Mullingar, Ireland 17/G4
Mullingar, Sask. 181/D2
Mullins, S.C. (29574) 296/J3
Mullinville, Kansas (67109) 232/C4
Mullion, England 13/B7
Mull of Galloway (prom.), Scotland 15/D6
Mull of Kintyre (prom.), Scotland 15/C5
Mull of Oa (prom.), Scotland 15/B5
Mullumbimby, N.S. Wales 97/G1
Mulobezi, Zambia 115/E7
Mulongo, Zaire 115/E5
Mulroy (bay), Ireland 17/F1
Multan, Pakistan 54/J6
Multan, Pakistan 68/C2
Multan, Pakistan 59/K3
Multnomah (co.), Oreg. 291/E2
Mulund, India 68/B6
Mulungushi (dam), Zambia 115/E6
Mulvane, Kansas (67110) 232/E4
Mulvihill, Manitoba 179/D4
Mulwala, N.S. Wales 97/D4
Mumbwa, Zambia 115/E6
Mumford, N.Y. (14511) 276/E4
Mümliswil-Ramiswil, Switzerland 39/E2
Mumra, U.S.S.R. 52/G5
Mun, Mae Nam (riv.), Thailand 72/D4
Muna (isl.), Indonesia 85/G7
Muna, Mexico 150/P6
Munbura, Queensland 95/C2
Munbura, Queensland 88/G2
Müncheberg, E. Germany 22/F2
München (Munich), W. Germany 22/D4
Münchenbuchsee, Switzerland 39/E2
Muncho Lake, Br. Col. 184/L2
Muncho Lake Prov. Park, Br. Col. 184/L2
Muncie, Ill. (61857) 222/F3
Muncie, Ind. 188/J2
Muncie, Ind. (*47302) 227/G4
Muncy, Pa. (17756) 294/J3
Muncy Valley, Pa. (17758) 294/J3
Munda, Solomon Is. 86/D3
Mundabullangana, W. Australia 92/B3
Mundare, Alberta 182/D3
Mundaring (res.), W. Australia 88/B2
Munday, Texas (76371) 303/E4
Mundelein, Ill. (60060) 222/A4
Munden, Kansas (66959) 232/E2
Münden, W. Germany 22/C3
Mundesley, England 13/J5
Mundijong, W. Australia 88/B3
Mundijong, W. Australia 92/A2
Mundiwindi, W. Australia 92/B3
Mundo Novo, Brazil 132/F5
Mundrabilla, W. Australia 92/E5
Mundubbera, Queensland 88/J5
Munera, Spain 33/E3
Munford, Ala. (36268) 195/F3
Munford, Tenn. (38058) 237/B10
Munfordville, Ky. (42765) 237/J6
Mungbere, Zaire 115/E3
Munger, Mich. (48747) 250/F5
Mungindi, N.S. Wales 97/E1
Mungindi, Queensland 95/D6
Munguba, Brazil 132/C2
Munhall, Pa. (15120) 294/C7
Munhango, Angola 115/C6
Munich, N. Dak. (58352) 282/N2
Munich, W. Germany 7/F4
Munich, W. Germany 22/D4
Munising, Mich. (49862) 250/C2
Munith, Mich. (49259) 250/E6
Munjor, Kansas (†67601) 232/C3
Munku-Sardyk (mt.), Mongolia 77/F1
Munnerlyn, Georgia (†30830) 217/H5
Munning (pt.), N. Zealand 100/E7
Munnsville, N.Y. (13409) 276/J4
Muñoz Gamero (pen.), Chile 138/D10
Munro (mt.), Tasmania 99/E2
Munroe Falls, Ohio (44262) 284/H3
Münsingen, Switzerland 39/E3
Munson, Alberta 182/D4
Munson, Fla. (†32570) 212/B5
Munson, Pa. (16860) 294/F4
Munsonville, N.H. (03457) 268/C5
Munster, Ind. (46321) 227/B1
Munster (prov.), Ireland 17/D7
Munster (trad. prov.), Ireland 17
Munster, Ontario 177/J2
Münster, Switzerland 39/F4
Münster, W. Germany 22/B3
Munsungan (lake), Maine 243/E3
Muntendam, Netherlands 27/K2
Muntok, Indonesia 85/D6
Munuscong (lake), Mich. 250/E2
Muojärvi (lake), Finland 18/R4
Muong Khuong, Vietnam 72/E2
Muonio (riv.) 7/G2
Muonio, Finland 18/O3
Muonio (riv.), Finland 18/M2
Muonioälv (riv.), Sweden 18/M2
Muota (riv.), Switzerland 39/G3
Muotathal, Switzerland 39/G3
Muqaddam, Wadi (dry riv.), Sudan 111/F4
Muqdadiyah, Iraq 66/D4
Muqdisho (Mogadishu) (cap.), Somalia 115/J3
Muqdisho (Mogadishu) (cap.), Somalia 102/G4
Muqeible, Israel 65/C2
Muqui, Brazil 132/F8
Mur (riv.), Austria 41/C3
Mur (riv.), Yugoslavia 45/B2
Mura (riv.), Hungary 41/D3
Muradiye, Turkey 63/K3
Murakami, Japan 81/J4
Murallón, Cerro (mt.), Argentina 143/B6
Murallón, Cerro (mt.), Chile 138/D8
Murarrie, Queensland 88/K2
Murashi, U.S.S.R. 52/G3
Murat, France 28/E5
Murat (riv.), Turkey 59/C2
Murat (riv.), Turkey 63/H3
Murat Dağı (mt.), Turkey 63/C3
Murau, Austria 41/C3
Murbat, Oman 59/G6
Murchison, N. Zealand 100/D4
Murchison (range), North. Terr. 93/D6
Murchison (falls), Uganda 115/F3
Murchison (riv.), W. Australia 88/B5
Murchison (mt.), W. Australia 92/B4
Murchison (riv.), W. Australia 92/B4
Murchison Downs, W. Australia 88/B5
Murcia (prov.), Spain 33/F4
Murcia, Spain 7/D5
Murcia, Spain 33/F4
Murcia (reg.), Spain 33/F3
Murderers (creek), Oreg. 291/H3
Murderkill (riv.), Del. 245/R5
Murdo, S. Dak. (57559) 298/H6
Murdochville, Québec 172/C1
Murdock, Fla. (33938) 212/D4
Murdock, Ill. (61941) 222/E4
Murdock, Kansas (67111) 232/E4
Murdock, Minn. (56271) 255/C5
Murdock, Nebr. (68407) 264/H4
Muren (Mörön), Mongolia 77/F2
Mureş (riv.), Romania 45/E2
Muret, France 28/D6
Muretto (pass), Switzerland 39/J4
Murfreesboro, Ark. (71958) 202/C5
Murfreesboro, N.C. (27855) 281/R2
Murfreesboro, Tenn. (37130) 237/J9
Murg (riv.), Switzerland 39/G1
Murgab, U.S.S.R. 48/H6
Murgab (riv.), U.S.S.R. 48/G6
Murghab (riv.), Afghanistan 59/H2
Murgon, Queensland 88/J5
Murgon, Queensland 95/D5
Murgoo, W. Australia 92/B4
Muri, Switzerland 39/F2
Muriaé, Brazil 135/E2
Muriaé, Brazil 132/F8
Murias de Paredes, Spain 33/C1
Muri bei Bern, Switzerland 39/E3
Muriel (lake), Alberta 182/E2
Murindó, Colombia 126/B4
Müritzsee (lake), E. Germany 22/E2
Murjek, Sweden 18/M3
Murl, Ky. (†42633) 237/M7
Murle, Ethiopia 111/G6
Murmansk, U.S.S.R. 7/H2
Murmansk, U.S.S.R. 2/L2
Murmansk, U.S.S.R. 4/C8
Murmansk, U.S.S.R. 48/D3
Murmansk, U.S.S.R. 52/D1
Murnau, W. Germany 22/D5
Murnpeowie, S. Australia 94/F3
Murom, U.S.S.R. 52/F3
Murongo, Tanzania 115/F4
Muroran, Japan 81/K2
Muros, Spain 33/B1
Muroto, Japan 81/G7
Muroto (pt.), Japan 81/G7
Murphy, Idaho (83650) 220/B6
Murphy, Miss. (†38748) 256/C4
Murphy, Mo. (†63088) 261/O4
Murphy, N.C. (28906) 281/B4
Murphy, Oreg. (97533) 291/D5
Murphy (isl.), S.C. 296/J5
Murphy, Texas (†75074) 303/H1
Murphys, Calif. (95247) 204/E5
Murphysboro, Ill. (62966) 222/D6
Murphytown, W. Va. (†26142) 312/D4
Murra Murra, Queensland 95/C6
Murray (riv.) 88/G6
Murray (river), Australia 87/E9
Murray (riv.), Br. Col. 184/G3
Murray (co.), Georgia 217/C1
Murray, Idaho (83874) 220/C2
Murray, Ind. (†46714) 227/G3
Murray, Iowa (50174) 229/F6
Murray, Ky. (42071) 237/E7
Murray (co.), Minn. 255/C6
Murray, Nebr. (68409) 264/J4
Murray (riv.), N.S. Wales 97/A4
Murray (co.), Okla. 288/M6
Murray (lake), Okla. 288/M6
Murray (lake), Papua N.G. 85/B7
Murray (riv.), S. Australia 94/F6
Murray (lake), S.C. 188/K4
Murray (lake), S.C. 296/D4
Murray, Utah (84107) 304/C3
Murray, Utah 188/D2
Murray (riv.), Victoria 97/A4
Murray (bay), Victoria 88/H7
Murray (riv.), W. Australia 92/A2
Murray Bridge, S. Australia 88/F7
Murray Bridge, S. Australia 94/F6
Murray City, Ohio (43144) 284/F6
Murray Corner, New Bruns. 170/G2
Murray Downs, North. Terr. 93/D6
Murray Harbour, Pr. Edward I. 168/F2
Murray Lake Hills, Tenn. (37416) 237/L10
Murray River, Pr. Edward I. 168/F2
Murraysville, W. Va. (26153) 312/C4
Murrayville, Georgia (30564) 217/E2
Murrayville, Ill. (62668) 222/C4
Murrayville, Victoria 97/A4
Murree, Pakistan 68/C2
Murrells Inlet, S.C. (29576) 296/K4
Mürren, Switzerland 39/E3
Murrieta, Calif. (92362) 204/H10
Murringo, N.S. Wales 97/E4
Murrumbidgee (riv.), N. S. Wales 88/H6
Murrumbidgee (riv.), N.S. Wales 97/C4
Murrumburrah, N.S. Wales 97/E4
Murrupula, Mozambique 118/F3
Murrurundi, N.S. Wales 97/F2
Murrysville, Pa. (15668) 294/C5
Murska Sobota, Yugoslavia 45/B2
Murtaröl (peak), Switzerland 39/K3
Murtaugh, Idaho (83344) 220/D7
Murten, Switzerland 39/D3
Murtle (lake), Br. Col. 184/H4
Murtoa, Victoria 97/B5
Murud, India 68/C5
Murupara, N. Zealand 100/F3
Mururoa (isl.), Fr. Poly. 87/M8
Murwara, India 68/E4
Murwillumbah, N. S. Wales 88/J5
Murwillumbah, N.S. Wales 97/G1
Muryo (mt.), Indonesia 85/J2
Mürz (riv.), Austria 41/C3
Murzuk, Libya 102/D2
Murzuk, Libya 111/B2
Mürzzuschlag, Austria 41/C3
Muş (prov.), Turkey 63/J3
Muş, Turkey 63/J3
Muş, Turkey 59/D2
Musa Khel Bazar, Pakistan 59/K3
Musa Khel Bazar, Pakistan 68/B2
Musala (mt.), Bulgaria 45/F4
Musan, N. Korea 81/D2
Musandam, Ras (cape), Oman 59/G4
Musashino, Japan 81/O2
Muscadine, Ala. (36269) 195/H3
Muscat (cap.), Oman 54/G7
Muscat (cap.), Oman 2/M4
Muscat (cap.), Oman 59/G5
Muscatatuck (riv.), Ind. 227/E7
Muscatine (co.), Iowa 229/L5
Muscatine, Iowa 188/H2
Muscatine, Iowa (52761) 229/L6
Muscle Shoals, Ala. (35660) 195/C1
Muscoda, Wis. (53573) 317/F9
Muscogee (co.), Georgia 217/C6
Musconetcong (beach), N.J. 273/C2
Muscongus (bay), Maine 243/E8
Muscotah, Kansas (66058) 232/G2
Muscoy, Calif. (92405) 204/E10
Muse, Okla. (74949) 288/S5
Musella, Georgia (31066) 217/E5
Musgrave (ranges), Australia 87/D8
Musgrave, Queensland 95/B2
Musgrave (range), S. Australia 88/E5
Musgrave (ranges), S. Australia 94/B2
Musgrave Harbour, Newf. 166/D4
Musgravetown, Newf. 166/C2
Mushaboom, Nova Scotia 168/F4
Mushandike Nat'l Park, Zimbabwe 118/D4
Mushie, Zaire 102/D5
Mushie, Zaire 115/C4
Musi (riv.), Indonesia 85/C6
Musidora, Alberta 182/E3
Muskeg (bay), Manitoba 179/G6
Muskeg (bay), Minn. 255/C2
Muskeget (chan.), Mass. 249/N7
Muskeget (isl.), Mass. 249/N7
Muskego, Wis. (53150) 317/K2
Muskegon (co.), Mich. 250/C5
Muskegon, Mich. 188/J2
Muskegon, Mich. (*49440) 250/C5
Muskegon (riv.), Mich. 250/C5
Muskegon Heights, Mich. (49444) 250/C5
Muskeg River, Alberta 182/A3
Muskingum (co.), Ohio 284/G5
Muskingum (riv.), Ohio 284/G6
Muskogee, Okla. 188/H3
Muskogee (co.), Okla. 288/R3
Muskogee, Okla. (74401) 288/R3
Muskoka (dist. munic.), Ontario 177/E3
Muskoka (lake), Ontario 177/E2
Muskrat (creek), Wyo. 319/E2
Muskwa (lake), Alberta 182/C1
Muskwa (riv.), Alberta 182/C1
Muskwa (riv.), Br. Col. 184/M2
Muslimiya, Syria 63/G4
Musmar, Sudan 111/G4
Musoma, Tanzania 115/F4
Musoma, Tanzania 102/F5
Musquacook (lakes), Maine 243/E2
Musquash (harb.), New Bruns. 170/D3
Musquodoboit (riv.), Nova Scotia 168/E4
Musquodoboit Harbour, Nova Scotia 168/E4
Mussau (isl.), Papua N.G. 86/B1
Musselburgh, Scotland 15/D2
Musselburgh, Scotland 10/C1
Musselshell (riv.) 188/E1
Musselshell (co.), Mont. 262/H4
Musselshell, Mont. (59059) 262/H4
Musselshell (riv.), Mont. 262/J3
Mustafakemalpaşa, Turkey 63/C3
Mustahil, Ethiopia 111/H6
Müstair, Switzerland 39/K3
Mustang, Nepal 68/E3
Mustang, Okla. (73064) 288/L4
Mustang (creek), Texas 303/A1
Mustang (isl.), Texas 303/G10
Mustang Draw (dry riv.), Texas 303/B5
Musters (lake), Argentina 143/C6
Mustinka (riv.), Minn. 255/B5
Mustoe, Va. (24468) 307/J4
Mustvee, U.S.S.R. 53/D1
Muswellbrook, N. S. Wales 88/J6
Muswellbrook, N.S. Wales 97/F3
Mût, Egypt 111/E2
Mût, Egypt 59/A4
Mût, Egypt 102/E2
Mut, Turkey 63/E4
Mutankiang (Mudanjiang), China 77/M3
Mutarara (Dona Ana), Mozambique 118/F3
Mutare (Umtali), Zimbabwe 118/E3
Muthanna (gov.), Iraq 66/D5
Muthill, Scotland 15/E4
Muting, Indonesia 85/K7
Mutki, Turkey 63/J3
Mutrie, Sask. 181/H5
Mutsamudu, Comoros 118/G2
Mutshatsha, Zaire 115/D6
Mutsu, Japan 81/K3
Mutsu (bay), Japan 81/K3
Muttaburra, Queensland 95/C4
Muttalip, Turkey 63/D3
Muttenz, Switzerland 39/E1
Muttler (mt.), Switzerland 39/K3
Mutton (isl.), Ireland 17/B6
Mutton Bird (isl.), N.S. Wales 97/J2
Muttonville, Mich. (†48062) 250/G6
Mutual, Ohio (†43078) 284/C5
Mutual, Okla. (73853) 288/H2
Mutum, Brazil 135/F1
Mu Us Shamo (des.), China 77/G4
Muwailih, Saudi Arabia 59/C4
Muwale, Tanzania 115/F5
Muxima, Angola 115/B5
Muy Muy, Nicaragua 154/E4
Muy Muy Viejo, Nicaragua 154/E4
Muynak, U.S.S.R. 48/F5
Muyumba, Zaire 115/E5
Muzaffarabad, Pakistan 68/C2
Muzaffarnagar, India 68/D3
Muzaffarpur, India 68/E3
Muzambinho, Brazil 135/C2
Muzo, Colombia 126/D5
Muzon (cape), Alaska 196/M2
Muztag (mt.), China 77/B4
Muztagata (mt.), China 77/A4
Mvadhi-Ousyé, Gabon 115/B3
M'Vouti, Congo 115/B4
Mwadingusha, Zaire 115/E6
Mwadui, Tanzania 115/F4
Mwanza, Malawi 115/F7
Mwanza (reg.), Tanzania 115/F4
Mwanza, Tanzania 115/F4
Mwanza, Tanzania 102/F5
Mwanza, Zaire 115/E5
Mwaya, Tanzania 115/F5
Mweelrea (mt.), Ireland 17/B4
Mweenish (isl.), Ireland 17/B5
Mweka, Zaire 115/D4
Mwene-Ditu, Zaire 115/D5
Mwenga, Zaire 115/E4
Mweru (lake) 102/E5
Mweru (lake), Zaire 115/E5
Mweru (lake), Zambia 115/E5
Mwesi, Tanzania 115/F5
Mwinilunga, Zambia 115/D6
Mya, Wadi (dry riv.), Algeria 106/E2
Myakka (riv.), Fla. 212/D4
Myakka City, Fla. (33551) 212/D4
Myall (lake), N.S. Wales 97/G3
Myanaung, Burma 72/B3
Myaungmya, Burma 72/B3
Myebon, Burma 72/B2
Myers, Ky. (†40311) 237/O4
Myers, Mont. (†59038) 262/J4
Myerstown, Pa. (17067) 294/K5
Myersville, Md. (21773) 245/H3
Myingyan, Burma 72/B2
Myitkyina, Burma 54/L7
Myitkyina, Burma 72/C1
Myitnge, Burma 72/C2
Myitnge (riv.), Burma 72/C2
Myjava, Czech. 41/D2
Mylo, N. Dak. (†58317) 282/L2
Mymensingh (Nasirabad), Bangladesh 68/G4
Mynyddislwyn, Wales 13/B6
Myohaung, Burma 72/B2
Myohyang (mt.), N. Korea 81/C3
Myŏngch'ŏn, N. Korea 81/D3

Naturaliste 415

Myra, Texas (76253) 303/G4
Myra, W. Va. (25544) 312/B6
Myricks, Mass. (†02780) 249/K5
Myrnam, Alberta 182/E3
Myrtle, Idaho (†83540) 220/B3
Myrtle, Manitoba 179/E5
Myrtle, Minn. (56070) 255/E7
Myrtle, Miss. (38650) 256/F1
Myrtle, Mo. (65778) 261/K9
Myrtle (lake), N. Dak. 282/L5
Myrtle Beach, S.C. (29577) 296/K4
Myrtle Beach A.F.B., S.C. 296/K4
Myrtle Creek, Oreg. (97457) 291/D4
Myrtleford, Victoria 97/D5
Myrtle Grove, Fla. (32506) 212/B6
Myrtle Grove, La. (†70083) 238/K7
Myrtle Point, Oreg. (97458) 291/C4
Myrtlewood, Ala. (36763) 195/C6
Mysen, Norway 18/G7
Myślenice, Poland 47/E4
Myślibórz, Poland 47/B2
Mysłowice, Poland 47/C4
Mysore, India 68/D6
Mysore, India 54/J8
Mys Shmidta, U.S.S.R. 4/C1
Mys Shmidta, U.S.S.R. 48/T3
Mystery Lake, Manitoba 179/J2
Mystic, Conn. (06355) 210/H3
Mystic (riv.), Conn. 210/H3
Mystic, Georgia (31769) 217/F7
Mystic, Iowa (52574) 229/H7
Mystic (lake), Mass. 249/C6
Mystic (riv.), Mass. 249/C6
Mystic, S. Dak. (†57778) 298/B5
Mystic Islands, N.J. (08087) 273/E4
Myszków, Poland 47/D3
My Tho, Vietnam 72/E5
Mytishchi, U.S.S.R. 52/E3
Myton, Utah (84052) 304/D3
M'zab (oasis), Algeria 106/E2
Mže (riv.), Czech. 41/B2
Mzimba, Malawi 115/F6
Mzimba, Malawi 102/F6

N

Naab (riv.), W. Germany 22/E4
Naafkopf (mt.), Switzerland 39/J2
Naaldwijk, Netherlands 27/E4
Naalehu, Hawaii (96772) 218/H7
Naalehu, Hawaii 188/G6
Naantali, Finland 18/M6
Naarden, Netherlands 27/G4
Naas, Ireland 10/C4
Naas, Ireland 17/H5
Naba, Burma 72/B1
Nababeep, S. Africa 118/B5
Nabari, Kiribati 87/J6
Nabb, Ind. (47147) 227/F7
Nabburg, W. Germany 22/E4
Naberezhnye Chelny, U.S.S.R. 52/H3
Nabesna, Alaska (†99764) 196/K2
Nabeul, Tunisia 106/G1
Nabiac, N.S. Wales 97/G3
Nabire, Indonesia 85/K6
Nablus (Nabulus), West Bank 65/C3
Nabnasset, Mass. (01861) 249/J2
Nabua, Philippines 82/D4
Nacala, Mozambique 118/G2
Nacala, Mozambique 102/G6
Nacaome, Honduras 154/D4
Naches, Wash. (98937) 310/E4
Naches (pass), Wash. 310/D3
Naches (riv.), Wash. 310/E4
Nachikatsuura, Japan 81/H7
Nachingwea, Tanzania 115/G6
Náchod, Czech. 41/D1
Nachusa, Ill. (61057) 222/D2
Nachvak (fjord), Newf. 166/B2
Nacimiento (riv.), Calif. 204/D8
Nacimiento, Chile 138/D1
Nacimiento (mts.), N. Mex. 274/C3
Nacimiento (peak), N. Mex. 274/C2
Nacka, Sweden 18/H1
Nackawic, New Bruns. 170/C2
Nacmine, Alberta 182/D4
Naco, Ariz. (85620) 198/E7
Naco, Mexico 150/D1
Nacogdoches (co.), Texas 303/K6
Nacogdoches, Texas (75961) 303/J6
Nacozari, Mexico 150/E1
Nacunday, Paraguay 144/E5
Nadadores, Mexico 150/H3
Nadawah, Ala. (†36726) 195/D7
Nadeau, Mich. (49863) 250/B3
Nadi, Fiji 86/P10
Nadi, Fiji 87/H7
Nadiad, India 68/C4
Nădlac, Romania 45/E2
Nador, Morocco 106/D1
Nádudvar, Hungary 41/F3
Nadvoitsy, U.S.S.R. 52/D2
Nadym, U.S.S.R. 48/H3
Nadym (riv.), U.S.S.R. 48/H3
Naestved, Denmark 21/E7
Naestved, Denmark 18/G9
Naf, Idaho (83342) 220/E7
Näfels, Switzerland 39/H2
Nafenen, Switzerland 39/H3
Naft-e Shah, Iran 66/D4
Naft Kaneh, Iraq 66/D3
Naga, Philippines 85/G3
Naga, Philippines 54/O8
Naga, Philippines 82/D4
Nagahama, Ehime, Japan 81/F7
Nagahama, Shiga, Japan 81/H6
Nagai (isl.), Alaska 196/F4
Nagaland (state), India 68/G3
Nagambie, Victoria 97/C5
Nagano (pref.), Japan 81/J5
Nagano, Japan 81/J5
Nagaoka, Kyoto, Japan 81/J7
Nagaoka, Niigata, Japan 81/J5
Nagaokakyo, Japan 81/J7
Nagapattinam, India 68/E6
Nagar, Pakistan 68/D1
Nagarote, Nicaragua 154/D4
Nagar Parkar, Pakistan 68/C4
Nagarzê, China 77/C6
Nagasaki (pref.), Japan 81/D7
Nagasaki, Japan 54/O6
Nagasaki, Japan 81/D7
Nagato, Japan 81/E6
Nagaur, India 68/C3
Nagawicka (lake), Wis. 317/J1
Nagele, Netherlands 27/H3
Nagercoil, India 68/D7
Nagina, India 68/D3
Nagishot, Sudan 111/F7
Nagles (mts.), Ireland 17/E7
Nago, Japan 81/N6
Nagold, W. Germany 22/C4
Nagorno-Karabakh Aut. Obl., U.S.S.R. 48/E5
Nagorno-Karabakh Aut. Obl., U.S.S.R. 52/G7
Nagornyy, U.S.S.R. 48/N4
Nagoya, Japan 81/H6
Nagoya, Japan 2/R4
Nagoya, Japan 54/P6
Nagpur, India 54/J7
Nagpur, India 68/D4
Nagqu, China 77/D5
Nags Head, N.C. (27959) 281/T3
Nagua, Dom. Rep. 158/E5
Naguabo, P. Rico 161/F2
Naguabo, P. Rico 156/G1
Nagyatád, Hungary 41/D3
Nagybajom, Hungary 41/D3
Nagyecsed, Hungary 41/G3
Nagyhalász, Hungary 41/F2
Nagykálló, Hungary 41/F3
Nagykanizsa, Hungary 41/D3
Nagykáta, Hungary 41/E3
Nagykőrös, Hungary 41/E3
Nagyszénás, Hungary 41/F3
Naha, Japan 54/O7
Naha, Japan 81/N6
Nahan, India 68/D2
Nahang (riv.), Iran 66/N7
Nahanni Butte, N.W. Terrs. 187/F3
Nahanni Nat'l Park, N.W.T. 162/D3
Nahanni Nat'l Park, N.W. Terrs. 187/F3
Nahant○, Mass. (01908) 249/E6
Nahant (bay), Mass. 249/E6
Nahariyya, Israel 65/C1
Nahavand, Iran 59/E3
Nahavand, Iran 66/F3
Nahcotta, Wash. (98537) 310/A4
Nahhalin, West Bank 65/C4
Nahiku, Hawaii (†96713) 218/K2
Nahma, Mich. (49864) 250/C3
Nahmakanta (lake), Maine 243/E4
Nahuel Huapí (lake), Argentina 120/B7
Nahuel Huapí (lake), Argentina 143/B5
Nahuel Huapí Nat'l Park, Argentina 143/B5
Nahunta, Georgia (31553) 217/H8
Naica, Mexico 150/G2
Naicam, Sask. 181/G3
Naihati, India 68/F1
Nailsworth, England 13/E6
Naiman, China 77/K3
Na'in, Iran 66/H4
Na'in, Iran 59/F3
Nain, Jamaica 158/H6
Nain, Newf. 166/B2
Nain, Newf. 162/K4
Naini Tal, India 68/D3
Nainpur, India 68/E4
Naipo (isl.), Colombia 126/F6
Nairn, La. (†70082) 238/L8
Nairn, Ontario 177/C1
Nairn, Scotland 15/E3
Nairn, Scotland 10/E2
Nairn (trad. co.), Scotland 15/B5
Nairn (riv.), Scotland 15/D3
Nairne, S. Australia 94/C8
Nairobi, Kenya 115/G4
Nairobi (cap.), Kenya 2/L6
Nairobi (cap.), Kenya 115/G4
Nairobi (cap.), Kenya 102/F5
Naivasha, Kenya 115/G4
Najafabad, Iran 59/F3
Najafabad, Iran 66/G4
Najayo Abajo, Dom. Rep. 158/E6
Najin, N. Korea 81/E2
Najran (Aba as Sa'ud), Saudi Arabia 59/D6
Naka (riv.), Japan 81/K5
Nakalele (pt.), Hawaii 218/J1
Nakaminato, Japan 81/K5
Nakamti, Ethiopia 102/F4
Nakamti, Ethiopia 111/G6
Nakamura, Japan 81/F7
Nakasato, Japan 81/K3
Nakatane, Japan 81/E8
Nakatsu, Japan 81/E7
Na Keal, Loch (inlet), Scotland 15/B4
Naked (isl.), Alaska 196/D1
Nakfa, Ethiopia 111/G4
Nakhichevan', U.S.S.R. 7/J5
Nakhichevan', U.S.S.R. 48/E6
Nakhichevan', U.S.S.R. 52/F7
Nakhichevan' A.S.S.R., U.S.S.R. 52/F7
Nakhichevan' A.S.S.R., U.S.S.R. 48/E6
Nakhodka, U.S.S.R. 54/P5
Nakhodka, U.S.S.R. 48/O5
Nakhon Nayok, Thailand 72/D4
Nakhon Pathom, Thailand 72/C4
Nakhon Phanom, Thailand 72/D3
Nakhon Ratchasima, Thailand 72/D4
Nakhon Ratchasima, Thailand 54/M8
Nakhon Sawan, Thailand 72/D4
Nakhon Si Thammarat, Thailand 54/M9
Nakhon Si Thammarat, Thailand 72/D5
Nakina, N.C. (28455) 281/M6
Nakina, Ont. 162/H5
Nakina, Ontario 177/H4
Nakina, Ontario 175/C2
Nakło nad Notecia, Poland 47/C2
Naknek, Alaska (99633) 196/G3
Naknek (lake), Alaska 196/G3
Nakonde, Zambia 115/F5
Nakop, Namibia 118/B5
Nakskov, Denmark 21/E8
Nakskov, Denmark 18/G9
Naktong (riv.), S. Korea 81/D6
Nakuru, Kenya 102/F5
Nakuru, Kenya 115/G4
Nakusp, Br. Col. 184/J5
Nal, Pakistan 59/J4
Nal, Pakistan 68/B3
Nal (riv.), Pakistan 59/J4
Nal (riv.), Pakistan 68/B3
Nalate, Turkey 63/G4
Nalayh (Nalaikha), Mongolia 77/G2
Nalcayec (isl.), Chile 138/D6
Nal'chik, U.S.S.R. 7/J4
Nal'chik, U.S.S.R. 48/E5
Nal'chik, U.S.S.R. 52/F6
Nalgonda, India 68/D5
Nallen, W. Va. (26680) 312/E6
Nallıhan, Turkey 63/D2
Nalut, Libya 111/B1
Namacurra, Mozambique 118/F3
Namak, Daryacheh-ye (salt lake), Iran 59/F3
Namak, Daryacheh-ye (salt lake), Iran 66/G3
Namaka, Alberta 182/D4
Namaksar (salt lake), Afghanistan 59/H3
Namaksar (salt lake), Afghanistan 68/A2
Namaksar (lake), Iran 66/M4
Namaksar (salt lake), Iran 59/H3
Namakzar-e Shahdad (salt lake), Iran 59/G3
Namakzar-e Shahdad (salt lake), Iran 66/L5
Namanga, Kenya 115/G4
Namangan, U.S.S.R. 48/H5
N'amaniya, Iraq 66/D4
Namapa, Mozambique 118/F2
Namaqualand (reg.), S. Africa 118/B5
Namarrói, Mozambique 118/F3
Namasagali, Uganda 115/F3
Namasigüe, Honduras 154/D4
Namatanai, Papua N.G. 87/F6
Namatanai, Papua N.G. 86/C1
Nambe, N. Mex. (†87501) 274/D3
Nambour, Queensland 88/J5
Nambour, Queensland 95/E5
Nambucca Heads, N.S. Wales 97/G2
Nam Co (lake), China 77/D5
Nam Dinh, Vietnam 72/E2
Namekagon (lake), Wis. 317/D3
Namekagon (riv.), Wis. 317/C3
Namen (Namur), Belgium 27/F8
Námestovo, Czech. 41/E2
Nametil, Mozambique 118/F3
Namhkam, Burma 72/C2
Namib (des.), Namibia 118/A3
Namibia 2/K7
Namibia 102/D7
Namibia (des.) 102/D6
NAMIBIA (SOUTH-WEST AFRICA) 118/B3
Naminga, U.S.S.R. 48/M4
Namiquipa, Mexico 150/F2
Namlan, Burma 72/C2
Namlea, Indonesia 85/H6
Namoi (riv.), N. S. Wales 88/H6
Namoi (riv.), N.S. Wales 97/E2
Namonuito (atoll), Micronesia 87/E5
Namorik (atoll), Marshall Is. 87/G5
Nampa, Alberta 182/B1
Nampa, Idaho 146/G5
Nampa, Idaho (83651) 220/B6
Nampa, Idaho 188/C2
Nampala, Mali 106/C5
Namp'o, N. Korea 81/B4
Nampo-Shoto (isls.), Japan 81/M3
Nampula (prov.), Mozambique 118/F2
Nampula, Mozambique 118/F3
Nampula, Mozambique 102/F6
Namsen (riv.), Norway 18/H4
Namsos, Norway 7/F2
Namsos, Norway 18/G4
Nam Tram, Mui (cape), Vietnam 72/F4
Namtu, Burma 72/C2
Namu, Br. Col. 184/D4
Namuac, Philippines 82/C1
Namuli, Serra (mt.), Mozambique 118/F3
Namuno, Mozambique 118/F2
Namur (lake), Alberta 182/D1
Namur (prov.), Belgium 27/F8
Namur, Belgium 27/F8
Namur, Québec 172/C4
Namutoni, Namibia 118/B3
Namwala, Zambia 115/E6
Namwŏn, S. Korea 81/C6
Namysłów, Poland 47/C3
Namzha Parwa (mt.), China 77/E6
Nan, Thailand 72/D3
Nan, Mae Nam (riv.), Thailand 72/D3
Nanacamilpa, Mexico 150/M1
Nana Candundo, Angola 115/D6
Nanafalia, Ala. (36764) 195/B6
Nanaimo, Br. Col. 146/F5
Nanaimo, Br. Col. 162/D6
Nanaimo, Br. Col. 184/J3
Nanakuli, Hawaii (96792) 218/D2
Nanao, Japan 81/H5
Nanay (riv.), Peru 128/E4
Nancagua, Chile 138/F6
Nance (co.), Nebr. 264/F3
Nanchang, China 77/J6
Nanchang, China 54/N7
Nancheng, China 77/J6
Nanchong (Nanchung), China 77/G5
Nanchong, China 54/M6
nan Clar, Loch (lake), Scotland 15/D2
Nancowry (isl.), India 68/G7
Nancy, France 28/G3
Nancy, France 7/E4
Nancy, Ky. (42544) 237/M6
Nanda Devi (mt.), India 68/D2
Nandaime, Nicaragua 154/E5
Nander, India 68/D5
Nandi (Nadi), Fiji 87/H7
Nando, Uruguay 145/F3
Nandurbar, India 68/C4
Nandyal, India 68/D5
Nanga-Eboko, Cameroon 115/B3
Nanga Parbat (mt.), Pakistan 68/D1
Nangapinoh, Indonesia 85/E6
Nangatayap, Indonesia 85/E6
Nangnim-sanmaek (range), N. Korea 81/C3
Nangong, China 77/H4
Nangqên, China 77/E5
Nang Rong, Thailand 72/D4
Nangwarry, S. Australia 94/G7
Nang Xian, China 77/D6
Nanika (dam), Br. Col. 184/D3
Nanika (lake), Br. Col. 184/D3
Nanisivik, N.W. Terrs. /K2
Nanjemoy, Md. (20662) 245/K7
Nanjing (Nanking), China 77/J5
Nanjing, China 2/Q4
Nanjing, China 54/N6
Nanking (Nanjing), China 77/J5
Nankoku, Japan 81/F7
Nan Ling (mts.), China 77/H6
Nannine, W. Australia 92/B4
Nanning, China 77/G7
Nanning, China 54/M7
Nannup, W. Australia 92/B6
Nanoose Bay, Br. Col. 184/J3
Nanortalik, Greenl. 4/D12
Nanpan Jiang (riv.), China 77/F7
Nanping, China 77/J6
Nansei Shoto (Ryukyu) (isls.), Japan 81/M6
Nansen (sound), N.W. Terrs. 187/J1
Nanson, N. Dak. (58354) 282/L2
Nantahala, N.C. (†28702) 281/B4
Nantahala (lake), N.C. 281/B4
Nantai (mt.), Japan 81/J5
Nantasket Beach, Mass. (†02045) 249/E7
Nanterre, France 28/A1
Nantes, France 28/C4
Nantes, France 7/D4
Nantes, Québec 172/F4
Nanticoke (riv.), Del. 245/R6
Nanticoke, Md. (21840) 245/P7
Nanticoke (riv.), Md. 245/P7
Nanticoke, Ontario 177/E5
Nanticoke, Pa. (18634) 294/E7
Nanton, Alberta 182/D4
Nantong, China 77/K5
Nantua, France 28/F4
Nantucket (co.), Mass. 249/O7
Nantucket, Mass. (02554) 249/O7
Nantucket○, Mass. (02554) 249/O7
Nantucket (isl.), Mass. 188/N2
Nantucket (isl.), Mass. 249/O8
Nantucket (sound), Mass. 249/N6
Nanty Glo, Pa. (15943) 294/E5
Nantyglo and Blaina, Wales 13/B6
Nanuet, N.Y. (10954) 276/K8
Nanuktok (isls.), Newf. 166/C2
Nanuku (passage), Fiji 86/R10
Nanumea (atoll), Tuvalu 87/H6
Nanuque, Brazil 132/F7
Nanuque, Brazil 120/E4
Nanxiong, China 77/H6
Nanyang, China 77/H5
Nanyuki, Kenya 115/G3
Nanzhang, China 77/H5
Nanzhao, China 77/H5
Nao (cape), Spain 33/G3
Naococane (lake), Québec 174/C2
Naolinco de Victoria, Mexico 150/P1
Naomi, Ky. (†42544) 237/M6
Náousa, Greece 45/F5
Napa, Calif. 188/B3
Napa (co.), Calif. 204/C5
Napa, Calif. (94558) 204/C5
Napadogan, New Bruns. 170/D2
Napa Junction, Calif. (†94590) 204/J1
Napakiak, Alaska (99634) 196/F2
Napaktok (bay), Newf. 166/B2
Napanee, Ontario 177/G3
Napanoch, N.Y. (12458) 276/M7
Napaskiak, Alaska (99559) 196/F2
Napata (ruins), Sudan 111/F4
Napavine, Wash. (98565) 310/C4
Napè, Laos 72/E3
Naper, Nebr. (68755) 264/E2
Naperville, Ill. (60540) 222/A6
Napf (mt.), Switzerland 39/E3
Napier, Ky. (†40851) 237/P7
Napier, N. Zealand 100/F3
Napier, N. Zealand 87/H9
Napier (mt.), North Terr. 93/A4
Napier, W. Va. (26631) 312/E5
Napier Field, Ala. (36303) 195/H8
Napierville (co.), Québec 172/D4
Napierville, Québec 172/D4
Napili-Honokowai, Hawaii (†96761) 218/H1
Napinka, Manitoba 179/B5
Naplate, Ill. (†61350) 222/E2
Naples, Fla. (*33940) 212/E5
Naples, Idaho (83847) 220/B1
Naples, Ill. (62669) 222/C4
Naples (prov.), Italy 34/E4
Naples, Italy 7/F4
Naples, Italy 34/E4
Naples○, Maine (04055) 243/B8
Naples, N.Y. (14512) 276/F5
Naples, S. Dak. (†57271) 298/O4
Naples, Texas (75568) 303/K4
Naples Park, Fla. (†33940) 212/E5
Napo (riv.) 120/B3
Napo, China 77/G7
Napo (prov.), Ecuador 128/D3
Napo (riv.), Ecuador 128/D3
Napo (riv.), Peru 128/F4
Napoleon, Ind. (47034) 227/G6
Napoleon, Mich. (49261) 250/E6
Napoleon, Mo. (64074) 261/E4
Napoleon, N. Dak. (58561) 282/L6
Napoleon, Ohio (43545) 284/B3
Naponee, Nebr. (68960) 264/E4
Nappa Merri, Queensland 95/B5
Nappan, Nova Scotia 168/D3
Nappanee, Ind. (46550) 227/F2
Napperby, North. Terr. 93/C7
Napton, Mo. (65346) 261/F4
Naqa (ruins), Sudan 111/F4
Nara (pref.), Japan 81/J8
Nara, Japan 81/J8
Nara, Mali 106/C5
Naracoopa, Tasmania 99/B1
Naracoorte, S. Australia 88/F7
Naracoorte, S. Australia 94/G7
Naradhan, N.S. Wales 97/D3
Naramata, Br. Col. 184/H5
Naranja, Fla. (33032) 212/F6
Naranjal (riv.), Ecuador 128/C4
Naranjito, Honduras 154/C3
Naranjito, P. Rico 161/D1
Naranjos, Mexico 150/L6
Naraq, Iran 66/G3
Narashino, Japan 81/P2
Narathiwat, Thailand 72/D6
Nara Visa, N. Mex. (88430) 274/F3
Narayanganj, Bangladesh 68/G4
Narayanpet, India 68/D5
Narberth, Pa. (19072) 294/M6
Narberth, Wales 13/C6
Narbonne, France 28/E6
Narcissa, Okla. (†74354) 288/S1
Narcisse, Manitoba 179/E4
Narcondam (isl.), India 68/G6
Narcoossee, Fla. (†32769) 212/E3
Nardin, Okla. (74646) 288/M1
Nardò, Italy 34/F4
Naré, Argentina 143/F5
Nare, Colombia 126/C4
Narellan, N.S. Wales 97/F3
Nares (str.) 146/L2
Nares (str.), N.W.T. 162/N3
Nares (str.), N.W. Terrs. 187/L2
Narew (riv.), Poland 47/E2
Naricual, Venezuela 124/F2
Narinda, Madagascar 118/H3
Nariño (dept.), Colombia 126/B7
Nariva (swamp), Trin. & Tob. 161/B10
Narka, Kansas (66960) 232/E2
Narmada (riv.), India 54/J7
Narmada (riv.), India 68/D4
Narman, Turkey 63/J2
Narnaul, India 68/D3
Narni, Italy 34/D3
Naro, Italy 34/D6
Narodnaya (mt.), U.S.S.R. 7/K2
Narodnaya (mt.), U.S.S.R. 48/G3
Narodnaya (mt.), U.S.S.R. 52/J1
Narok, Kenya 115/G4
Narooma, N.S. Wales 97/F5
Narrabeen, N. S. Wales 88/L3
Narrabeen, N. S. Wales 97/K3
Narrabri, N. S. Wales 88/J6
Narrabri, N.S. Wales 97/E2
Narragansett, R.I. (02882) 249/J7
Narragansett○, R.I. (02882) 249/J7
Narragansett (bay), R.I. 249/J6
Narran (lake), N.S. Wales 97/D1
Narran (riv.), N. S. Wales 97/D1
Narrandera, N. S. Wales 88/H6
Narrandera, N.S. Wales 97/D4
Narre Warren North, Victoria 97/K5
Narrogin, W. Australia 88/B6
Narrogin, W. Australia 92/B2
Narromine, N.S. Wales 88/H6
Narromine, N.S. Wales 97/E3
Narrows, Ky. (42358) 237/H5
Narrows, Oreg. (†97721) 291/H4
Narrows, The (str.), St. Chris.-Nevis 161/D11
Narrows, The (str.), Virgin Is. (Br.) 161/C4
Narrows, The (str.), Virgin Is. (U.S.) 161/C4
Narrows, Va. (24124) 307/G6
Narrowsburg, N.Y. (12764) 276/L7
Narrows Park-La Vale, Md. (†21502) 245/C2
Narsimhapur, India 68/D4
Narsinghgarh, India 68/D4
Narssaq, Greenl. 4/C12
Naruna, Va. (24576) 307/L6
Narva, U.S.S.R. 52/C3
Narva, U.S.S.R. 53/E1
Narva (res.), U.S.S.R. 53/D1
Narvik, Norway 4/C9
Narvik, Norway 7/F2
Narvik, Norway 18/K2
Nary, Minn. (†56601) 255/D3
Nar'yan-Mar, U.S.S.R. 4/C7
Nar'yan-Mar, U.S.S.R. 7/K2
Nar'yan-Mar, U.S.S.R. 48/F3
Nar'yan-Mar, U.S.S.R. 52/H1
Naryn, U.S.S.R. 48/H5
Nasarawa, Nigeria 106/F7
Năsăud, Romania 45/G2
Naseby, N. Zealand 100/C6
Naseby, Sask. 181/C3
Naselle, Wash. (98638) 310/B4
Naselle (riv.), Wash. 310/B4
Nash (stream), N.H. 268/E2
Nash (co.), N.C. 281/O2
Nash, N. Dak. (58264) 282/P3
Nash, Okla. (73761) 288/K1
Nash, Texas (75569) 303/K4
Nashawena (isl.), Mass. 249/L7
Nash Creek, New Bruns. 170/D1
Nashoba, Okla. (74558) 288/R6
Nashotah, Wis. (53058) 317/J1
Nashport, Ohio (43830) 284/F5
Nashua, Iowa (50658) 229/J3
Nashua (riv.), Mass. 249/H3
Nashua, Minn. (56565) 255/B4
Nashua, Mont. (59248) 262/K2
Nashua, N.H. 188/M2
Nashua, N.H. (03060) 268/D6
Nashville, Ark. (71852) 202/C6
Nashville, Georgia (31639) 217/F8
Nashville, Ill. (62263) 222/D5
Nashville, Ind. (47448) 227/E6
Nashville, Kansas (67112) 232/D4
Nashville, Mich. (49073) 250/D6
Nashville, Mo. (†64855) 261/D8
Nashville, N.C. (27856) 281/O3
Nashville, Ohio (44661) 284/F4
Nashville, Oreg. (†97370) 291/D3
Nashville (cap.), Tenn. 146/K6
Nashville (cap.), Tenn. 188/J3
Nashville (cap.), Tenn. (*37201) 237/H8
Nashwaak (riv.), New Bruns. 170/D2
Nashwaak Bridge, New Bruns. 170/D2
Nashwaak Village, New Bruns. 170/D2
Nashwauk, Minn. (55769) 255/E3
Našice, Yugoslavia 45/C3
Nasielsk, Poland 47/E2
Näsijärvi (lake), Finland 18/O6
Nasik, India 68/C5
Nasik, India 54/J8
Nasir, Sudan 111/F6
Nasirabad, Bangladesh 68/G4
Nasirabad, India 68/C3
Naskaupi (riv.), Newf. 166/B3
Naso (pt.), Philippines 82/C5
Nason, Ill. (†62816) 222/D5
Nasonville, R.I. (†02830) 249/H5
Nasratabad (Zabol), Iran 59/H3
Nasratabad (Zabol), Iran 66/M5
Nass (riv.), Br. Col. 184/C2
Nassau (cap.), Bahamas 146/L7
Nassau (cap.), Bahamas 156/C1
Nassau (bay), Chile 120/C8
Nassau (bay), Chile 138/F11
Nassau (isl.), Cook Is. 87/K7
Nassau, Del. (19969) 245/T6
Nassau (co.), Fla. 212/E1
Nassau (riv.), Fla. 212/E1
Nassau (sound), Fla. 212/E1
Nassau, Minn. (56272) 255/B5
Nassau (co.), N.Y. 276/N9
Nassau, N.Y. (12123) 276/N5
Nassau Bay, Texas (†77598) 303/K2
Nassawadox, Va. (23413) 307/S6
Nassawango (creek), Md. 245/S8
Nasser (lake), Egypt 102/F2
Nasser (lake), Egypt 111/F3
Nasser (lake), Egypt 59/F3
Nassereith, Austria 41/A3
Nässjö, Sweden 18/J8
Nassogne, Belgium 27/G8
Nasty (creek), S. Dak. 298/C2
Nasu (mt.), Japan 81/J5
Nata, Botswana 118/D4
Natá, Panama 154/G6
Natagaima, Colombia 126/C6
Natal, Brazil 2/H6
Natal, Brazil 132/H4
Natal, Brazil 120/F3
Natal, Br. Col. 184/K5
Natal (prov.), S. Africa 102/F7
Natal (prov.), S. Africa 118/E5
Natalbany, La. (70451) 238/N1
Natalia, Texas (78059) 303/J11
Natalicio Talavera, Paraguay 144/D4
Natanz, Iran 59/F3
Natanz, Iran 66/H4
Natashquan (riv.) 162/K5
Natashquan (riv.), Newf. 166/B3
Natashquan, Québec 174/E3
Natashquan (riv.), Québec 174/E2
Natashquan-Est (riv.), Newf. 166/B3
Natchaug (riv.), Conn. 210/G1
Natchez, Ala. (†36425) 195/D7
Natchez, La. (71456) 238/D3
Natchez, Miss. 188/H4
Natchez, Miss. (39120) 256/B7
Natchitoches (par.), La. 238/D3
Natchitoches, La. (71457) 238/D3
Naters, Switzerland 39/E4
Natewa (bay), Fiji 86/Q10
Nathalia, Victoria 97/C5
Nathalie, Va. (24577) 307/L7
Nathan, Mich. (†49821) 250/B3
Nathrop, Colo. (81236) 208/H5
Natick○, Mass. (01760) 249/A7
Natick, R.I. (†02887) 249/H6
Natimuk, Victoria 97/A5
Nation (riv.), Br. Col. 184/F2
National Agricultural Research Center, Md. 245/G3
National Capital Region (Manila) (prov.), Philippines 82/C3
National City, Calif. (92050) 204/J11
National City, Mich. (48748) 250/F4
National Gardens, Fla. (†32074) 212/E2
National Mills, Manitoba 179/A2
National Mine, Mich. (49865) 250/B2
National Park, N.J. (08063) 273/B3
National Park, Switzerland 39/K3
National Reactor Testing Sta. (U.S.A.E.C), Idaho 220/F6
National Stock Yards, Ill. (62071) 222/A2
Natitingou, Benin 106/E6
Natividade, Brazil 132/E5
Natmauk, Burma 72/B2
Natoma, Kansas (67651) 232/D2
Natron (lake), Kenya 115/G4
Natron (lake), Tanzania 115/G4
Natrona (co.), Wyo. 319/F3
Natrona, Wyo. (82646) 319/F2
Natrona Heights, Pa. (15065) 294/C4
Nattavaara, Sweden 18/M3
Natuna (isls.), Indonesia 54/M9
Natuna (isls.), Indonesia 85/D5
Natural Bridge, Ala. (35577) 195/C2
Natural Bridge, N.Y. (13665) 276/K2
Natural Bridge, Va. (24578) 307/J5
Natural Bridges Nat'l Mon., Utah 304/E6
Natural Bridge Station, Va. (24579) 307/K5
Natural Dam, N.Y. (†13642) 276/J2
Naturaliste (cape), Tasmania 99/E2
Naturaliste (cape), W. Australia 88/A6
Naturaliste (chan.), W. Australia 88/A5
Naturaliste (cape), W. Australia 92/A6

416 Naturaliste

Naturaliste (chan.), W. Australia 92/A4
Natural Steps, Ark. (†72135) 202/F4
Naturita, Colo. (81422) 208/B6
Naubinway, Mich. (49762) 250/D2
Naucalpan de Juárez, Mexico 150/L1
Nauders, Austria 41/A3
Nauen, E. Germany 22/E2
Naugatuck, Conn. (06770) 210/C3
Naugatuck (riv.), Conn. 210/C3
Naugatuck, W. Va. (25685) 312/B7
Nauhcampatépetl (mt.), Mexico 150/O1
Naujan (lake), Philippines 82/C4
Naujoji-Akmene, U.S.S.R. 53/B2
Naumburg, E. Germany 22/D3
Na'ur, Jordan 65/D4
Nauru 2/T6
Nauru 87/G6
Naushon (isl.), Mass. 249/L7
Naustdal, Norway 18/E6
Nauta, Peru 128/F5
Nautla, Mexico 150/L6
Nauvoo, Ala. (35578) 195/D3
Nauvoo, Ill. (62354) 222/B3
Nauwigewauk, New Bruns. 170/E3
Nava, Mexico 150/J2
Nava del Rey, Spain 33/D2
Navajo (co.), Ariz. 198/E3
Navajo, Ariz. (86509) 198/F3
Navajo (creek), Ariz. 198/D2
Navajo (peak), Colo. 208/F8
Navajo (res.), Colo. 208/E8
Navajo, Mont. (†59222) 262/M2
Navajo, N. Mex. (87328) 274/A3
Navajo (dam), N. Mex. 274/B2
Navajo (res.), N. Mex. 274/B2
Navajo (mt.), Utah 304/D6
Navajo Ind. Res., Ariz. 198/D2
Navajo Ind. Res., N. Mex. 274/A2
Navajo Ind. Res., Utah 304/D7
Navajo Nat'l Mon., Ariz. 198/E2
Navajo Ord. Depot, Ariz. 198/D3
Naval Academy, U.S., Md. 245/N5
Naval Air Sta., La. 238/O4
Naval Air Station, Calif. 204/J2
Naval Air Station, Va. 307/R7
Naval Base, S.C. 296/H6
Navalcarnero, Spain 33/F4
Naval Medical Center, Md. 245/E4
Navalmoral de la Mata, Spain 33/D3
Naval Submarine Base, Conn. 210/G3
Naval Support Ctr., Wash. 310/B1
Naval Weapons Center, Md. 245/F3
Naval Yard, D.C. 245/F5
Navan (An Uaimh), Ireland 17/H4
Navan, Ontario 177/J2
Navarin (cape), U.S.S.R. 4/C18
Navarin (cape), U.S.S.R. 48/T3
Navarino (isl.), Chile 138/F11
Navarino, Wis. (54108) 317/J6
Navarra (prov.), Spain 33/F1
Navarre, Kansas (67469) 232/E3
Navarre, Ohio (44662) 284/H4
Navarro, Argentina 143/G7
Navarro, Calif. (95463) 204/B4
Navarro (riv.), Calif. 204/B4
Navarro (co.), Texas 303/H5
Navasota, Texas (77868) 303/J7
Navasota (riv.), Texas 303/H7
Navassa, N.C. (†28404) 281/O6
Navassa (isl.), Virgin Is. (U.S.) 156/C3
Naver, Loch (lake), Scotland 15/D2
Naver (riv.), Scotland 15/D2
Navesink, N.J. (07752) 273/E3
Navesink (riv.), N.J. 273/E3
Navia (riv.), Spain 33/C1
Navidad, Chile 138/A10
Navidad (riv.), Texas 303/H8
Navin, Manitoba 179/F5
Navoi, U.S.S.R. 48/G6
Navojoa, Mexico 150/E3
Navolato, Mexico 150/E4
Návpaktos, Greece 45/F6
Návplion, Greece 45/F7
Navrongo, Ghana 106/D6
Navsari, India 68/C4
Navy Board (inlet), N.W. Terrs. 187/K2
Navy Yard City, Wash. (†98310) 310/A2
Nawabganj, Bangladesh 68/F4
Nawabshah, Pakistan 68/B3
Nawabshah, Pakistan 59/J4
Nawiliwili (bay), Hawaii 218/D2
Naxera, Va. (23122) 307/R6
Náxos, Greece 45/G7
Náxos (isl.), Greece 45/G7
Naya, Colombia 126/B6
Nayarit (state), Mexico 150/G6
Nayarit, Sierra (mts.), Mexico 150/G5
Nay Band, Iran 59/F4
Nay Band, Iran 59/G3
Nay Band, Bushehr, Iran 66/H7
Nay Band, Khorasan, Iran 66/K4
Naylor, Georgia (31641) 217/F9
Naylor, Mo. (63953) 261/L9
Nayoro, Japan 81/L1
Naytahwaush, Minn. (56566) 255/C3
Nazaré, Brazil 132/G6
Nazaré, Portugal 33/B3
Nazareth, Belgium 27/D7
Nazareth, Israel 65/C2
Nazareth, Pa. (18064) 294/M4
Nazareth, Texas (79063) 303/B3
Nazarovo, U.S.S.R. 48/K4
Nazas, Mexico 150/G4
Nazas (riv.), Mexico 150/G4
Nazca, Peru 128/E10
Naze, The (prom.), England 13/J6
Naze, Japan 81/O5
Nazerat 'Illit, Israel 65/C2
Nazilli, Turkey 63/C4
Nazko, Br. Col. 184/F3
Nazret, Ethiopia 111/G6
Nazret, Ethiopia 102/F4
Nazyvayevsk, U.S.S.R. 48/H4
Ncheu (Ntcheu), Malawi 115/F6
Ndalatando, Angola 115/B5
Ndele, Cent. Afr. Rep. 115/D2
N'Dendé, Gabon 115/B4
Ndeni (isl.), Solomon Is. 87/G7
N'Djamena (cap.), Chad 111/C5
N'Djamena (cap.), Chad 2/K5
N'Djamena (cap.), Chad 102/D3
N'Djolé, Gabon 115/B4
N'Dogo (lag.), Gabon 115/B4
Ndola, Zambia 115/E6
Ndola, Zambia 102/E6
Nead, Ind. (†46970) 227/E3
Neagh (lake), N. Ireland 17/J2
Neagh, Lough (lake), N. Ireland 10/C3
Neah Bay, Wash. (98357) 310/A2
Neal, Kansas (66863) 232/F4
Neale (lake), North. Terr. 88/D4
Neale (lake), North. Terr. 93/A8
Neales, The (riv.), S. Australia 94/E3
Neales, The (riv.), S. Australia 88/F5
Neápolis, Greece 45/F7
Neapolis, Ohio (43547) 284/C3
Near (isls.), Alaska 196/H3
Neath, Wales 10/E5
Neath, Wales 13/D6
Neavitt, Md. (21652) 245/N6
Nebikon, Switzerland 39/F2
Nebish, Minn. (†56667) 255/D3
Nebit-Dag, U.S.S.R. 48/F6
Neblina, Pico da (peak), Brazil 132/G8
Neblina (Phelps) (peak), Venezuela 124/E7
Nebo (mt.), Ark. 202/D3
Nebo, Ill. (62355) 222/C4
Nebo (mt.), Jordan 65/D4
Nebo, Ky. (42441) 237/F6
Nebo, La. (†71342) 238/F3
Nebo, Mo. (65471) 261/H7
Nebo (mt.), Utah 304/C4
Nebo, W. Va. (25141) 312/D5
Nebraska 188/F2
NEBRASKA 264
Nebraska, Ind. (47262) 227/F6
Nebraska (state), U.S. 146/J5
Nebraska City, Nebr. (68410) 264/J4
Necedah, Wis. (54646) 317/F7
Nechako (riv.), Br. Col. 184/E3
Neche, N. Dak. (58265) 282/P2
Neches, Texas (75779) 303/J6
Neches (riv.), Texas 303/K6
Nechí (riv.), Colombia 126/C4
Neckar (riv.), W. Germany 22/C4
Neckarsulm, W. Germany 22/C4
Neck City, Mo. (†64755) 261/C8
Necker (isl.), Hawaii 87/K3
Necker (isl.), Hawaii 188/F6
Necker (isl.), Hawaii 218/D6
Necochea, Argentina 143/E4
Necochea, Argentina 120/D6
Nectar, Ala. (†35049) 195/E3
Necum Teuch (harb.), Nova Scotia 168/F4
Ned, Ky. (41355) 237/P6
Neded, Czech. 41/D2
Nederland, Colo. (80466) 208/H3
Nederland, Texas (77627) 303/K8
Nedgera (creek), N.S. Wales 97/E2
Nedlands, W. Australia 88/B2
Nedlands, W. Australia 92/A1
Neeb, Sask. 181/C1
Neebish (isl.), Mich. 250/E2
Neede, Netherlands 27/K4
Needham, Ala. (36915) 195/B7
Needham, Ind. (46162) 227/E5
Needham○, Mass. (02192) 249/B7
Needham Heights, Mass. (02194) 249/B7
Needle (mt.), Wyo. 319/C1
Needles, Calif. 188/C4
Needles, Calif. (92363) 204/L9
Needles (pt.), N. Zealand 100/E2
Needmore, Ind. (†47421) 227/E7
Needmore, N.C. (†28713) 281/B4
Needmore, Pa. (17238) 294/F6
Needmore, W. Va. (†26801) 312/J4
Needville, Texas (77461) 303/J8
Neelin, Manitoba 179/C5
Neely, Miss. (39461) 256/G8
Neely Henry (lake), Ala. 195/F3
Neelys Landing, Mo. (†63755) 261/O7
Neelyton, Pa. (17239) 294/G5
Neelyville, Mo. (63954) 261/M9
Ñeembucú (dept.), Paraguay 144/C-D5
Neenah, Wis. (54956) 317/J7
Neepawa, Manitoba 179/C4
Neerlandia, Alberta 182/C2
Neerpelt, Belgium 27/G6
Neeses, S.C. (29107) 296/E4
Nee Soon, Singapore 72/F6
Nee so Pah (res.), Colo. 208/D6
Neffs, Ohio (43940) 284/J5
Neffs Mills, Pa. (†16669) 294/G4
Nefta, Tunisia 106/F2
Neftekamsk, U.S.S.R. 52/J3
Nefteyugansk, U.S.S.R. 48/H3
Nefud (des.), Saudi Arabia 54/F7
Nefud (des.), Saudi Arabia 59/D4
Nefud Dahi (des.), Saudi Arabia 59/D5
Nefusa, Jebel (mts.), Libya 111/B1
Nefyn, Wales 13/C5
Negara, Indonesia 85/E7
Negaunee, Mich. (49866) 250/B2
Negba, Israel 65/B4
Negelli, Ethiopia 111/G6
Negeri Sembilan (state), Malaysia 72/D7
Negev (reg.), Israel 65/D5
Negley, Ohio (44441) 284/J4
Negomane, Mozambique 118/F2
Negombo, Sri Lanka 68/D7
Negotin, Yugoslavia 45/F3
Negra, Cordillera (mts.), Peru 128/D7
Negra (pt.), Peru 128/B6
Negra (pt.), P. Rico 161/G2
Negra (lag.), Uruguay 145/F5
Negra (range), Uruguay 145/D2
Negrais (cape), Burma 72/B3
Negreet, La. (71460) 238/C4
Negreiros, Chile 138/B2
Negreşti, Romania 45/H2
Negril, Jamaica 158/G6
Negrillos, Bolivia 136/A6
Negritos, Peru 128/B5
Negro (riv.) 2/F5
Negro (cape), Angola 115/B7
Negro (riv.), Argentina 120/C6
Negro (riv.), Argentina 143/D4
Negro (riv.), Bolivia 136/D4
Negro (riv.), Brazil 120/C3
Negro (riv.), Brazil 132/H9
Negro (riv.), Colombia 126/G7
Negro (riv.), Paraguay 144/C4
Negro (bay), Somalia 115/J2
Negro (riv.), Uruguay 120/D6
Negro, Arroyo (riv.), Uruguay 145/B3
Negro (riv.), Uruguay 145/B4
Negro (riv.), Venezuela 124/E7
Negro Bay, Virgin Is. (U.S.) 161/E4
Negros (isl.), Philippines 54/O9
Negros (isl.), Philippines 85/G4
Negros (isl.), Philippines 82/D6
Negros Occidental (prov.), Philippines 82/D6
Negros Oriental (prov.), Philippines 82/D6
Neguac, New Bruns. 170/E1
Nehalem, Oreg. (97131) 291/D2
Nehalem (riv.), Oreg. 291/D2
Nehawka, Nebr. (68413) 264/H4
Nehbandan, Iran 59/G3
Nehbandan, Iran 66/L5
Nehe, China 77/L2
Neheim-Hüsten, W. Germany 22/C3
Neiafu, Tonga 87/J7
Neiba, Dom. Rep. 158/D6
Neiba, Dom. Rep. 156/D3
Neiba (bay), Dom. Rep. 158/D6
Neiba, Sierra de (mts.), Dom. Rep. 158/D6
Neiber, Wyo. (†82401) 319/D2
Neidpath, Sask. 181/D5
Neiges (lake), Québec 172/F2
Neigette, Québec 172/J1
Neihart, Mont. (59465) 262/F4
Neijiang (Neikiang), China 77/G6
Neilburg, Sask. 181/B3
Neillsville, Wis. (54456) 317/E6
Neil's Harbour, Nova Scotia 168/H2
Neilston, Scotland 15/B2
Neilton, Wash. (98566) 310/B3
Nei Monggol (Inner Mongolian Aut. Reg.), China 77/H3
Neis Beach, Sask. 181/E2
Neisse (riv.), E. Germany 22/F3
Neisse (Nysa), Poland 47/C3
Neisse (riv.), Poland 47/B3
Neiva, Colombia 120/B2
Neiva, Colombia 126/C6
Nejanilini (lake), Manitoba 179/J1
Nejd (reg.), Saudi Arabia 59/D4
Nejdek, Czech. 41/B1
Nejo, Ethiopia 111/G6
Nekoma, Kansas (67559) 232/C3
Nekoma, N. Dak. (58355) 282/O2
Nekoosa, Wis. (54457) 317/G7
Neksø, Denmark 18/J9
Neksø, Denmark 21/F9
Nelagoney, Okla. (†74056) 288/O1
Nelas, Portugal 33/C2
Nelchina, Alaska (†99588) 196/C1
Nelidovo, U.S.S.R. 52/D3
Neligh, Nebr. (68756) 264/G2
Nel'kan, U.S.S.R. 48/O4
Nellie, Ohio (†43844) 284/F5
Nellis, W. Va. (25142) 312/C6
Nellis A.F.B., Nev. 266/F6
Nellis Air Force Range and AEC Nuclear Testing Sit, Nev. 266/E5
Nelliston, N.Y. (13410) 276/L5
Nellore, India 54/K8
Nellore, India 68/E6
Nellysford, Va. (22958) 307/L5
Nelma, Wis. (†49935) 317/J3
Nelse, Ky. (41550) 237/R6
Nelson (isl.), Alaska 196/E2
Nelson, Argentina 143/F5
Nelson, Ariz. (†86434) 198/B3
Nelson, Br. Col. 162/E6
Nelson, Br. Col. 184/J5
Nelson (str.), Chile 138/D9
Nelson, England 13/H1
Nelson, England 10/G1
Nelson, Georgia (30151) 217/D2
Nelson, Ill. (61058) 222/D2
Nelson (co.), Ky. 237/K5
Nelson, Ky. (†42330) 237/G6
Nelson (riv.), Man. 146/J4
Nelson (riv.), Man. 162/G4
Nelson (riv.), Manitoba 179/J2
Nelson, Minn. (56355) 255/C5
Nelson, Mo. (65347) 261/F4
Nelson (res.), Mont. 262/J2
Nelson, Nebr. (68961) 264/F4
Nelson, Nev. (†89046) 266/G7
Nelson (creek), Nev. 266/G2
Nelson○, N.H. (†03457) 268/C5
Nelson, N. Zealand 87/H10
Nelson, N. Zealand 100/D4
Nelson (co.), N. Dak. 282/O4
Nelson, Pa. (16940) 294/H2
Nelson (cape), Victoria 97/A6
Nelson (co.), Va. 307/L5
Nelson, Wis. (54756) 317/C7
Nelson Forks, Br. Col. 184/M2
Nelson Head (prom.), N.W. Terrs. 187/F2
Nelson House, Manitoba 179/J2
Nelson Lagoon, Alaska (†99571) 196/F3
Nelson-Miramichi, New Bruns. 170/E2
Nelsonville, Ark. (†72569) 202/H1
Nelsonville, Ky. (†40051) 237/K5
Nelsonville, N.Y. (10516) 276/N8
Nelsonville, Ohio (45764) 284/F7
Nelsonville, Wis. (54458) 317/H7
Nelspruit, S. Africa 118/E5
Néma, Mauritania 106/C5
Néma, Mauritania 102/B3
Nemacolin, Pa. (15351) 294/B6
Nemadji (riv.), Minn. 255/F4
Nemaha, Iowa (50567) 229/C3
Nemaha (co.), Kansas 232/F2
Nemaha (riv.), Kansas 232/G1
Nemaha (co.), Nebr. 264/J4
Nemaha, Nebr. (68414) 264/J4
Neméa, Greece 45/F7
Nemi, Italy 34/F7
Nemiskam, Alberta 182/E5
Nemo, S. Dak. (57759) 298/B5
Nemours, France 28/E3
Nemrut Dağı (mt.), Turkey 63/J3
Nemunas (Niemen) (riv.), U.S.S.R. 53/A3
Nemuro, Japan 81/M2
Nemuro (str.), Japan 81/M1
Nen (riv.), China 54/O5
Nenagh, Ireland 10/B4
Nenagh, Ireland 17/E6
Nenagh (riv.), Ireland 17/E6
Nenana, Alaska (99760) 196/J2
Nendaz, Switzerland 39/D4
Nene (riv.), England 10/F4
Nene (riv.), England 13/H5
Nenets Aut. Okr., U.S.S.R. 48/F3
Nenets Aut. Okr., U.S.S.R. 52/H1
Nenjiang, China 77/L2
Nen Jiang (riv.), China 77/K2
Nenzel, Nebr. (69219) 264/C2
Neodesha, Kansas (66757) 232/G4
Neoga, Ill. (62447) 222/E4
Neola, Iowa (51559) 229/B6
Neola, Utah (84053) 304/D3
Neola, W. Va. (24961) 312/F7
Neon-Fleming, Ky. (41840) 237/R6
Néon Karlóvasi, Greece 45/H7
Neopit, Wis. (54150) 317/J6
Neópolis, Brazil 132/G5
Neosho (riv.) 188/G3
Neosho (co.), Kansas 232/G4
Neosho (riv.), Kansas 232/G4
Neosho, Mo. (64850) 261/D9
Neosho (riv.), Okla. 288/R1
Neosho, Wis. (53059) 317/J9
Neosho Falls, Kansas (66758) 232/G3
Neosho Rapids, Kansas (66864) 232/F3
Neotsu, Oreg. (97364) 291/C2
Nepa, U.S.S.R. 48/L4
Nepal 2/P4
Nepal 54/K7
NEPAL 68/E3
Nepalganj, Nepal 68/E3
Nepaug (res.), Conn. 210/D1
Nepaug (riv.), Conn. 210/C1
Nepean (isl.), Norfolk I. 88/L6
Nephi, Utah (84648) 304/C4
Nephin (mt.), Ireland 17/C3
Nephin Beg (mt.), Ireland 17/B3
Nephton, Ontario 177/G3
Nepisiguit (bay), New Bruns. 170/E1
Nepisiguit (lakes), New Bruns. 170/D1
Nepisiguit (riv.), New Bruns. 170/D1
Nepomuk, Czech. 41/B2
Neponset, Ill. (61345) 222/D2
Neponset, Mass. (†02122) 249/D7
Neponset (riv.), Mass. 249/C8
Nepton, Ky. (†41039) 237/O4
Neptune○, N.J. (07753) 273/E3
Neptune, Ohio (†45822) 284/A4
Neptune (isls.), S. Australia 94/D6
Neptune Beach, Fla. (32233) 212/E1
Neptune City, N.J. (07753) 273/E3
Nera (riv.), Italy 34/D3
Nérac, France 28/D5
Nerekhta, U.S.S.R. 52/F3
Nerepis (riv.), New Bruns. 170/D3
Neresheim, W. Germany 22/D4
Nereta, U.S.S.R. 53/C2
Neretva (riv.), Yugoslavia 45/D4
Neriquinha, Angola 115/D7
Nerja, Spain 33/E4
Nerka (lake), Alaska 196/G3
Ñermete (pt.), Peru 128/B5
Nerpio, Spain 33/E3
Nerstrand, Minn. (55053) 255/E6
Nerva, Spain 33/C4
Neryungri, U.S.S.R. 48/N4
Nes (Neskaupstadhur), Iceland 21/D1
Nes, Netherlands 27/H2
Nesbit, Miss. (38651) 256/D1
Nesbitt, Manitoba 179/C5
Nescopeck, Pa. (18635) 294/K3
Nesebūr, Bulgaria 45/H4
Neshanic Station, N.J. (†08853) 273/D3
Nesher, Israel 65/C2
Neshkoro, Wis. (54960) 317/H8
Neshoba (co.), Miss. 256/F5
Neshoba, Miss. (39365) 256/F5
Neskaupstadhur, Iceland 7/C2
Neskaupstadhur, Iceland 21/D1
Neskowin, Oreg. (97149) 291/D2
Nesmith, S.C. (29580) 296/H5
Nespelem, Wash. (99155) 310/G2
Nesquehoning, Pa. (18240) 294/L4
Ness (co.), Kansas 232/C3
Ness, Loch (lake), Scotland 15/D3
Ness, Loch (lake), Scotland 10/D2
Ness (riv.), Scotland 15/D3
Ness City, Kansas (67560) 232/C3
Nesselrode (mt.), Alaska 196/N1
Nesselwang, W. Germany 22/D5
Nesslau, Switzerland 39/H2
Neston, England 13/G2
Neston, England 10/F2
Nestor, Trin. & Tob. 161/B10
Nestor Falls, Ontario 177/F5
Nestor Falls, Ontario 175/B3
Nestoria, Mich. (†49861) 250/A2
Nestórion, Greece 45/E5
Nestorville, W. Va. (†26380) 312/G4
Néstos (riv.), Greece 45/G5
Nestow, Alberta 182/D2
Nesttun, Norway 18/D6
Nestucca (riv.), Oreg. 291/D2
Nesvady, Czech. 41/E3
Nes Ziyyona, Israel 65/B4
Net (riv.), Mich. 250/G2
Netanya, Israel 65/B3
Netarts, Oreg. (97143) 291/C2
Netawaka, Kansas (66516) 232/G2
Netcong, N.J. (07857) 273/D2
Nethe (riv.), Belgium 27/F6
Netherhill, Sask. 181/C4
Netherlands 2/K3
Netherlands 7/E3
NETHERLANDS 27/G4
Netherlands Antilles 120/C1
Netherlands Antilles 146/M8
NETHERLANDS ANTILLES 161
NETHERLANDS ANTILLES 156/E4
Nethy Bridge, Scotland 15/E3
Netivot, Israel 65/B5
Netolice, Czech. 41/C2
Netstal, Switzerland 39/H2
Nett (lake), Minn. 255/E2
Nettie, W. Va. (26681) 312/E6
Nettilling (lake), Canada 4/C13
Nettilling (fjord), N.W. Terrs. 187/M3
Nettilling (lake), N.W. Terrs. 187/L3
Nett Lake, Minn. (55772) 255/E2
Nett Lake Ind. Res., Minn. 255/E2
Nettleham, England 13/G4
Nettleton, Miss. (38858) 256/G2
Nettuno, Italy 34/D4
Netzahualcóyotl, Mexico 150/L1
Neuanlage, Sask. 181/E3
Neuberg an der Mürz, Austria 41/C3
Neubert, Tenn. (†37901) 237/O9
Neubois, Québec 172/F3
Neubrandenburg (dist.), E. Germany 22/E2
Neubrandenburg, E. Germany 22/E2
Neuburg an der Donau, W. Germany 22/D4
Neuchâtel (canton), Switzerland 39/C3
Neuchâtel, Switzerland 39/C3
Neuchâtel (lake), Switzerland 39/C3
Neudorf, Sask. 181/J5
Neuenegg, Switzerland 39/D3
Neuenhagen bei Berlin, E. Germany 22/F4
Neufchâteau, Belgium 27/G9
Neufchâteau, France 28/F3
Neufchâtel-en-Bray, France 28/D3
Neugersdorf, E. Germany 22/F3
Neuhausen am Rheinfall, Switzerland 39/G1
Neuhorst, Sask. 181/E3
Neuilly-sur-Seine, France 28/A1
Neu-Isenburg, W. Germany 22/C3
Neumarkt am Wallersee, Austria 41/B3
Neumarkt in der Oberpfalz, W. Germany 22/D4
Neumarkt in Steiermark, Austria 41/C3
Neumünster, W. Germany 22/C1
Neunkirch, Switzerland 39/F1
Neunkirchen, Austria 41/C3
Neunkirchen, W. Germany 22/B4
Neuquén (prov.), Argentina 143/C4
Neuquén, Argentina 143/C4
Neuquén, Argentina 120/C6
Neuquén (riv.), Argentina 143/C4
Neuruppin, E. Germany 22/E2
Neuse, N.C. (27561) 281/M3
Neuse (riv.), N.C. 281/R5
Neusiedl am See, Austria 41/D3
Neusiedler See (lake), Austria 41/D3
Neusiedler See (lake), Hungary 41/D3
Neuss, W. Germany 22/B3
Neustadt, E. Germany 22/D3
Neustadt, Ontario 177/D3
Neustadt (Titisee-Neustadt), W. Germany 22/C5
Neustadt an der Aisch, W. Germany 22/D4
Neustadt an der Weinstrasse, W. Germany 22/B4
Neustadt bei Coburg, W. Germany 22/D3
Neustadt-Glewe, E. Germany 22/D2
Neustadt in Holstein, W. Germany 22/D1
Neustift im Stubaital, Austria 41/A3
Neustrelitz, E. Germany 22/E2
NEUTRAL ZONE 59/E4
Neutral Zone 54/F7
Neu-Ulm, W. Germany 22/D4
Neuville, Québec 172/F3
Neuwerk (isl.), W. Germany 22/C2
Neuwied, W. Germany 22/B3
Neva, Tenn. (†37689) 237/T8
Nevada 188/C3
NEVADA 266
Nevada (co.), Ark. 202/D6
Nevada (co.), Calif. 204/E4
Nevada, Sierra (mts.), Calif. 204/E4
Nevada, Iowa (50201) 229/G5
Nevada, Mo. (64772) 261/D7
Nevada, Ohio (44849) 284/D4
Nevada, Sierra (mts.), Spain 33/E4
Nevada (state), U.S. 146/G6
Nevada City, Calif. (95959) 204/D4
Nevatim, Israel 65/B5
Nevel', U.S.S.R. 52/D3
Nevele, Belgium 27/D6
Nevel'sk, U.S.S.R. 48/P5
Nevers, France 28/E4
Neversink (res.), N.Y. 276/L7
Nevertire, N.S. Wales 97/D2
Nevesinje, Yugoslavia 45/D4
Neville, Ohio (45156) 284/B8
Neville, Sask. 181/D6
Nevils, Georgia (†30458) 217/J6
Nevinnomyssk, U.S.S.R. 52/F6
Nevinville, Iowa (50856) 229/D6
Nevis, Alberta 182/D3
Nevis, Minn. (56467) 255/D4
Nevis (isl.), St. Chris.-Nevis 161/D11
Nevis (isl.), St. Chris.-Nevis 156/F3
Nevis (peak), St. Chris.-Nevis 161/D11
Nevis, Loch (inlet), Scotland 15/C3
Nevisdale, Ky. (40754) 237/N7
Nevşehir (prov.), Turkey 63/F3
Nevşehir, Turkey 59/B2
Nevşehir, Turkey 63/F3
New (riv.), Belize 154/C2
New (riv.), Calif. 204/K11
New (for.), England 13/F6
New (riv.), Fla. 212/D1
New (riv.), Fla. 212/B1
New (riv.), Guyana 131/C4
New, South Fork (riv.), N.C. 281/G2
New (riv.), N.C. 281/O5
New (riv.), S.C. 296/E6
New (inlet), Va. 307/S6
New (riv.), Va. 307/F8
New (riv.), W. Va. 312/E7
New Abbey, Scotland 15/E6
New Agat, Guam 86/K7
Newagen, Maine (04552) 243/D8
Newala, Tanzania 115/G6
New Albany, Ind. 188/J3
New Albany, Ind. (47150) 227/F8
New Albany, Kansas (66759) 232/G4
New Albany, Miss. (38652) 256/G2
New Albany, Ohio (43054) 284/E5
New Albany, Pa. (18833) 294/J2
New Albin, Iowa (52160) 229/L2
Newald, Wis. (54551) 317/J4
New Alexandria, Ohio (†43938) 284/J5
New Alexandria, Pa. (15670) 294/C5
Newalla, Okla. (74857) 288/M4
New Alluwe, Okla. (74049) 288/R1
New Almaden, Calif. (95042) 204/L4
New Almelo, Kansas (67652) 232/B2
New Amsterdam, Guyana 120/D2
New Amsterdam, Guyana 131/B2
New Amsterdam, Ind. (†47110) 227/E8
New Amsterdam, Wis. (†54636) 317/C8
New Angledool, N.S. Wales 97/E1
Newark, Ark. (72562) 202/H2
Newark, Calif. (94560) 204/K3
Newark, Del. (19711) 245/P2
Newark, England 13/G4
Newark, England 10/F4
Newark, Ill. (60541) 222/E2
Newark, Md. (21841) 245/S7
Newark, Mo. (63458) 261/H2
Newark, N.J. 188/L2
Newark, N.J. (*07101) 273/B2
Newark (bay), N.J. 273/B2
Newark, N.Y. (14513) 276/G4
Newark, Ohio (43055) 284/F5
Newark, S. Dak. (†57453) 298/O2
Newark, Texas (76071) 303/E1
Newark○, Vt. (†05871) 268/D2
Newark, W. Va. (†26143) 312/D4
Newark Int'l Airport, N.J. 273/B2
Newark Valley, N.Y. (13811) 276/H6
Newarthill, Scotland 15/C2
New Athens, Ill. (62264) 222/D5
New Athens, Ohio (43981) 284/H5
New Auburn, Minn. (55366) 255/D6
New Auburn, Wis. (54757) 317/D5
New Augusta, Miss. (39462) 256/F8
Newaygo (co.), Mich. 250/D5
Newaygo, Mich. (49337) 250/D5
New Baden, Ill. (62265) 222/D5
New Baltimore, Mich. (48047) 250/G6
New Baltimore, N.Y. (12124) 276/N6
New Baltimore, Pa. (15553) 294/E6
New Baltimore, Va. (†22186) 307/N3
New Bavaria, Ohio (43548) 284/B3
New Beaver, Pa. (†16141) 294/B4
New Bedford, Ill. (61346) 222/D2
New Bedford, Mass. 188/N2
New Bedford, Mass. (*02740) 249/K6
New Bedford, Ohio (†43824) 284/G5
New Bedford, Pa. (16140) 294/A3
New Bellsville, Ind. (†47448) 227/E6
Newberg, Oreg. (97132) 291/A2
New Berlin, Ill. (62670) 222/D4
New Berlin, N.Y. (13411) 276/K5
New Berlin, Pa. (17855) 294/J4
New Berlin, Wis. (53151) 317/K2
Newbern, Ala. (36765) 195/C5
Newbern, Ind. (†47201) 227/F6
New Bern, N.C. 188/L4
New Bern, N.C. (28560) 281/P4
Newbern, Tenn. (38059) 237/C8
Newberne, W. Va. (26409) 312/E4
Newberry, Fla. (32669) 212/D2
Newberry, Ind. (47449) 227/C7
Newberry, Mich. (49868) 250/D2
Newberry (co.), S.C. 296/D3
Newberry, S.C. (29108) 296/D3
Newberry Springs, Calif. (92365) 204/J9
New Bethlehem, Pa. (16242) 294/D3
Newbiggin-by-the-Sea, England 13/F2
New Blaine, Ark. (72851) 202/D3
Newbliss, Ireland 17/G3
New Bloomfield, Mo. (65063) 261/J5
New Bloomfield, Pa. (17068) 294/H5
New Bloomington, Ohio (43341) 284/D4
New Bonaventure, Newf. 166/D2
Newborn, Georgia (30262) 217/E3
Newboro, Ontario 177/H3
New Boston, Ill. (61272) 222/B2
New Boston, Mich. (48164) 250/F6
New Boston, Mo. (63557) 261/G3
New Boston○, N.H. (03070) 268/D6
New Boston, Ohio (45662) 284/E8
New Boston, Texas (75570) 303/K4
New Bothwell, Manitoba 179/F5
New Braintree○, Mass. (01531) 249/F3
New Braunfels, Texas (78130) 303/K10
New Bremen, N.Y. (13412) 276/K3
New Bremen, Ohio (45869) 284/B5
Newbridge (Droichead Nua), Ireland 17/H5
New Bridge, Oreg. (†97870) 291/K3
New Brigden, Alberta 182/E4
New Brighton, Minn. (55112) 255/G5
New Brighton, Pa. (15066) 294/B4
New Britain, Conn. (*06050) 210/E2
New Britain (isl.), Papua N.G. 87/F6
New Britain (isl.), Papua N.G. 85/C7
New Britain (isl.), Papua N.G. 86/B2

N'Gounié 417

New Britain, Pa. (18901) 294/M5
New Brockton, Ala. (36351) 195/G8
Newbrook, Alberta 182/D2
New Brunswick (prov.) 162/K6
New Brunswick (prov.), Canada 146/M5
NEW BRUNSWICK 170
New Brunswick, N.J. (*08901) 273/E3
New Buena Vista, Pa. (†15550) 294/E5
New Buffalo, Mich. (49117) 250/C7
New Buffalo, Pa. (17069) 294/H5
Newburg, Ark. (72556) 202/G1
Newburg, Iowa (†50135) 229/H5
Newburg, Md. (20664) 245/L7
Newburg, Mo. (65550) 261/J7
Newburg, N. Dak. (58762) 282/J2
Newburg, Pa. (17240) 294/G5
Newburg (La Jose), Pa. (†15753) 294/E4
Newburg, W. Va. (26410) 312/G4
Newburg, Wis. (53060) 317/K9
Newburgh, Ind. (47630) 227/C9
Newburgh○, Maine (†04445) 243/F6
Newburgh, N.Y. 188/M2
Newburgh, N.Y. (12550) 276/M7
Newburgh, Ontario 177/H3
Newburgh, Scotland 10/E2
Newburgh, Grampian, Scotland 15/G3
Newburgh, Fife, Scotland 15/E4
Newburgh Heights, Ohio (†44101) 284/H9
New Burlington, Ind. (†47302) 227/G4
New Burlington, Ohio (†45201) 284/B9
New Burnside, Ill. (62967) 222/E6
Newbury, England 13/F6
Newbury, England 10/F5
Newbury○, Mass. (01950) 249/L1
Newbury○, N.H. (03255) 268/C5
Newbury, Ohio (44065) 284/H3
Newbury, Ontario 177/C5
Newbury, Vt. (05051) 268/C3
Newbury○, Vt. (05051) 268/C3
Newburyport, Mass. (01950) 249/L1
New Bussa, Nigeria 106/E6
New Caledonia (isl.) 2/T7
NEW CALEDONIA 86
New Caledonia 87/G8
New Caledonia (isl.), New Caled. 87/G8
New Caledonia (isl.), New Caled. 86/G4
New Cambria, Kansas (67470) 232/E3
New Cambria, Mo (63558) 261/G3
New Canaan○, Conn. (06840) 210/B4
New Canton, Ill. (62356) 222/B4
New Canton, Va. (23123) 307/M5
New Carlisle, Ind. (46552) 227/E1
New Carlisle, Ohio (45344) 284/C6
New Carlisle, Québec 172/D2
New Carlisle, Québec 174/E3
New Carrollton, Md. (20784) 245/G4
New Castile (reg.), Spain 33/E3
Newcastle, Australia 2/S7
Newcastle, Calif. (95658) 204/C8
New Castle, Colo. (81647) 208/E3
New Castle (co.), Del. 245/R2
New Castle, Del. (19720) 245/R2
New Castle, Ind. (47362) 227/G5
Newcastle, Ireland 10/B4
Newcastle, Ireland 17/D7
New Castle, Ky. (40050) 237/L4
Newcastle○, Maine (04553) 243/D7
Newcastle, N. Br. 162/K6
Newcastle, N. S. Wales 88/J6
Newcastle, Nebr. (68757) 264/H2
Newcastle, New Bruns. 170/E2
New Castle○, N.H. (03854) 268/F5
Newcastle, N.S. Wales 97/F3
Newcastle, N. Ireland 10/D3
Newcastle, N. Ireland 17/J3
Newcastle (creek), North. Terr. 93/C4
New Castle, Ohio (†43843) 284/F5
Newcastle, Okla. (73065) 288/L4
Newcastle, Ontario 177/F4
New Castle, Pa. 188/K2
New Castle, Pa. (*16101) 294/B3
Newcastle, St. Chris.-Nevis 161/D11
Newcastle, S. Africa 118/E5
Newcastle, Texas (76372) 303/F4
Newcastle, Utah (84756) 304/A6
New Castle, Va. (24127) 307/H5
Newcastle, Wyo. (82701) 319/H2
Newcastle Creek, New Bruns. 170/D2
Newcastle-Damariscotta, Maine (04553) 243/E7
Newcastle Emlyn, Wales 13/C5
Newcastleton, Scotland 15/F5
Newcastle-under-Lyme, England 13/E4
Newcastle-under-Lyme, England 10/E4
Newcastle upon Tyne, England 7/D3
Newcastle upon Tyne, England 10/E3
Newcastle upon Tyne, England 13/H3
Newcastle Waters, North. Terr. 93/C4
New Centerville, Pa. (†15557) 294/D6
New Chelsea, Newf. 166/D2
New Chicago, Ind. (†46342) 227/C1
New Church, Va. (23415) 307/S5
New Cinema, Br. Col. 184/F3
New City, N.Y. (10956) 276/K8
New Columbia, Pa. (17856) 294/H3
New Columbus, Pa. (†17878) 294/K3
Newcomb, N. Mex. (†87325) 274/A2
Newcomb, N.Y. (12852) 276/M3
Newcomb, Tenn. (37819) 237/N7
Newcomerstown, Ohio (43832) 284/G5
New Concord, Ky. (42076) 237/E7
New Concord, Ohio (43762) 284/G6
New Cordell (Cordell), Okla. (†73632) 288/H4
New Corydon, Ind. (†47326) 227/H3
New Court, Mo. (†63452) 261/J2
New Creek, W. Va. (26743) 312/J4
New Cumberland, Pa. (17070) 294/J5
New Cumberland, W. Va. (26047) 312/E2
New Cumnock, Scotland 15/D5
Newdale, Idaho (83436) 220/G6
Newdale, Manitoba 179/B4
New Dayton, Alberta 182/D5
New Deal, Texas (79350) 303/C4
New Deer, Scotland 15/F3
Newdegate, W. Australia 92/B6
New Delhi (cap.), India 2/N4
New Delhi, India 54/J7
New Delhi (cap.), India 68/D3
New Denmark, New Bruns. 170/C1
New Denver, Br. Col. 184/J5
New Diggings, Wis. (†61075) 317/F10
New Douglas, Ill. (62074) 222/D5
New Dover, Ohio (†43040) 284/D5
New Durham○, N.H. (03855) 268/E5
New Eagle, Pa. (15067) 294/B5
New Edinburg, Ark. (71660) 202/F6
New Effington, S. Dak. (57255) 298/R2
New Egypt, N.J. (08533) 273/E3
Newell, Ala. (36270) 195/H4
Newell (lake), Alberta 182/E4
Newell, Iowa (50568) 229/D3
Newell, S. Dak. (57760) 298/C4
Newell, W. Va. (26050) 312/E1
New Ellenton, S.C. (29809) 296/D5
Newellton, La. (71357) 238/H2
Newellton, Nova Scotia 168/C5
New England (range), N.S. Wales 97/F1
New England, N. Dak. (58647) 282/E6
New England, W. Va. (26154) 312/C4
Newenham (cape), Alaska 196/F3
New Enterprise, Pa. (16664) 294/F5
New Era, La. (†71354) 238/G4
New Era, Mich. (49446) 250/C5
New Era, Oreg. (†97013) 291/B2
New Yam, Israel 65/B2
Newe Zohar, Israel 65/C5
New Fairfield○, Conn. (06810) 210/B3
Newfane, N.Y. (14108) 276/C4
Newfane, Vt. (05345) 268/B6
Newfane○, Vt. (05345) 268/B6
Newfield, Maine (04056) 243/B8
Newfield○, Maine (04056) 243/B8
Newfield, N.J. (08344) 273/D4
Newfield, N.Y. (14867) 276/G6
Newfields○, N.H. (03856) 268/F5
New Fish Creek, Alberta 182/B2
New Florence, Mo. (63363) 261/K5
New Florence, Pa. (15944) 294/D5
Newfolden, Minn. (56738) 255/B2
New Fork (lakes), Wyo. 319/C2
Newfound (lake), N.H. 268/D4
Newfoundland (prov.) 162/L5
Newfoundland (isl.) 162/L6
Newfoundland (prov.), Canada 146/M4
Newfoundland (isl.), Canada 2/G3
Newfoundland, Ky. (41162) 237/P4
NEWFOUNDLAND 166
Newfoundland (isl.), Newf. 166/C4
Newfoundland (isl.), Newf. 146/N5
Newfoundland, N.J. (07435) 273/D1
Newfoundland, Pa. (18445) 294/M3
Newfoundland (mts.), Utah 304/A2
New Franken, Wis. (54229) 317/L6
New Frankfort, Mo. (65349) 261/F4
New Franklin, Mo. (65274) 261/G4
New Freedom, Pa. (17349) 294/J6
New Freeport, Pa. (15352) 294/B6
New Galilee, Pa. (16141) 294/A4
New Galloway, Scotland 10/D3
New Galloway, Scotland 15/D5
Newgate, Br. Col. 184/K5
New Georgia (isl.), Solomon Is. 87/F6
New Georgia (isl.), Solomon Is. 86/D3
New Germantown, Pa. (17071) 294/G5
New Germany, Minn. (55367) 255/E6
New Germany, Nova Scotia 168/D4
New Glarus, Wis. (53574) 317/G10
New Glasgow, Nova Scotia 168/F3
New Glasgow, Québec 172/D4
New Gloucester, Maine (04260) 243/C8
New Gloucester○, Maine (04260) 243/C8
New Goshen, Ind. (47863) 227/B5
New Gretna, N.J. (08224) 273/E4
New Guinea (isl.) 2/S6
New Guinea (isl.) 54/P10
New Guinea (isl.) 87/E6
New Guinea (isl.), Papua N.G. 86/B2
Newgulf, Texas (77462) 303/J8
Newhalem, Wash. (†98283) 310/D2
Newhalen, Alaska (†99606) 196/H3
Newhall, Calif. (91321) 204/G9
Newhall, Iowa (52315) 229/K5
Newhall, W. Va. (24866) 312/C8
Newham, England 13/H8
Newham, England 10/B5
New Hamburg, Mo. (†63736) 261/O8
New Hamburg, Ontario 177/D4
New Hampshire 188/M2
NEW HAMPSHIRE 268
New Hampshire, Ohio (45870) 284/C4
New Hampshire (state), U.S. 146/L5
New Hampton, Iowa (50659) 229/J2
New Hampton, Mo. (64471) 261/D2
New Hampton○, N.H. (03256) 268/D4
New Hampton, N.J. (†08827) 273/D2
New Hanover (co.), N.C. 281/O6
New Hanover (Lavongai) (isl.), Papua N.G. 87/F6
New Hanover (isl.), Papua N.G. 86/B1
New Harbor, Maine (04554) 243/E8
New Harbour, Newf. 166/C4
New Harbour, Newf. 166/D2
New Harbour, Nova Scotia 168/G3
New Harmony, Ind. (47631) 227/B8
New Harmony, Utah (84757) 304/A6
New Hartford, Conn. (06057) 210/C1
New Hartford○, Conn. (06057) 210/C1
New Hartford, Iowa (50660) 229/H3
New Hartford, Mo. (63364) 261/K4
New Hartford, N.Y. (13413) 276/K4
New Haven, Conn. 188/M2
New Haven (co.), Conn. 210/D3
New Haven, Conn. (*06501) 210/D3
New Haven (harb.), Conn. 210/D3
Newhaven, England 10/F5
Newhaven, England 13/H7
New Haven, Ill. (62867) 222/E6
New Haven, Ind. (46774) 227/H2
New Haven, Ky. (40051) 237/K5
New Haven, Mich. (48048) 250/G6
New Haven, Mo. (63068) 261/K5
New Haven, N.Y. (13121) 276/H4
New Haven, Nova Scotia 168/H2
New Haven, Ohio (44850) 284/E3
New Haven○, Vt. (05472) 268/A3
New Haven, W. Va. (25265) 312/C5
New Haven, Wyo. (†82720) 319/H1
New Hazelton, Br. Col. 184/D2
New Hebrides (Vanuatu) 87/G7
Newhebron, Miss. (39140) 256/D7
New Hill, N.C. (27562) 281/M3
New Holland, Georgia (†30501) 217/E2
New Holland, Ill. (62671) 222/D3
New Holland, N.C. (27885) 281/S4
New Holland, Ohio (43145) 284/D6
New Holland, Pa. (17557) 294/K5
New Holland, S. Dak. (57364) 298/M7
New Holstein, Wis. (53061) 317/K8
New Home, Texas (79383) 303/C4
New Hope, Ala. (35760) 195/F1
Newhope, Ark. (71959) 202/C5
New Hope, Ky. (40052) 237/L5
New Hope, Minn. (†55428) 255/G5
New Hope, Ohio (†45320) 284/A6
New Hope, Pa. (18938) 294/N5
New Hope, Tenn. (†37380) 237/K11
New Hope, Va. (24469) 307/L4
New Horse Springs, N. Mex. (†87821) 274/A5
New Houlka (Houlka), Miss. (38850) 256/G2
New Hradec, N. Dak. (58648) 282/E5
New Hyde Park, N.Y. (11040) 276/P7
New Iberia, La. (70560) 238/G6
Newington○, Conn. (06111) 210/E2
Newington, Georgia (30446) 217/J5
Newington○, N.H. (†03801) 268/F5
Newington, Ontario 177/K2
Newington, Va. (22122) 307/S3
New Ipswich○, N.H. (03071) 268/D6
New Ireland (isl.), Papua N.G. 87/F6
New Ireland (isl.), Papua N.G. 86/B1
New Jersey 188/M3
NEW JERSEY 273
New Jersey, New Bruns. 170/E1
New Jersey (state), U.S. 146/L5
New Johnsonville, Tenn. (37134) 237/E8
New Kensington, Pa. (15068) 294/C4
New Kent (co.), Va. 307/P5
New Kent, Va. (23124) 307/P5
Newkirk, N. Mex. (88431) 274/E3
Newkirk, Okla. (74647) 288/N1
New Knoxville, Ohio (45871) 284/B5
New Laguna, N. Mex. (87038) 274/B4
New Lancaster, Kansas (†66040) 232/H3
Newland, Ind. (†47978) 227/C2
Newland, N.C. (28657) 281/F2
New Lebanon, Ind. (47864) 227/C6
New Lebanon, N.Y. (12125) 276/O6
New Lebanon, Ohio (45345) 284/B6
New Lebanon, Pa. (†16145) 294/B3
New Leipzig, N. Dak. (58562) 282/G7
New Lenox, Ill. (60451) 222/B6
New Lexington, Ohio (43764) 284/F6
New Liberty, Iowa (52765) 229/M5
New Liberty, Ky. (40355) 237/M3
New Lima, Okla. (74884) 288/O4
New Limerick○, Maine (04761) 243/G3
Newlin, Texas (†79245) 303/D3
New Lisbon, Ind. (47366) 227/G5
New Lisbon, N.J. (08064) 273/D4
New Lisbon, Wis. (53950) 317/F8
New Liskeard, Ont. 162/H6
New Liskeard, Ontario 177/K5
New Liskeard, Ontario 175/E3
Newllano, La. (71461) 238/D4
New London, Ark. (†71765) 202/F7
New London, Conn. 188/M2
New London (co.), Conn. 210/G2
New London, Conn. (06320) 210/G3
New London, Ind. (†46979) 227/E4
New London, Iowa (52645) 229/L7
New London, Minn. (56273) 255/C5
New London, Mo. (63459) 261/K3
New London, N.H. (03257) 268/D5
New London○, N.H. (03257) 268/D5
New London, N.C. (28127) 281/J4
New London, Ohio (44851) 284/F3
New London (bay), Pr. Edward I. 168/E2
New London, Texas (75682) 303/K5
New London, Wis. (54961) 317/J7
New Lothrop, Mich. (48460) 250/F5
New Lowell, Ontario 177/E3
New Lyme, Ohio (44066) 284/J2
New Lynn, N. Zealand 100/B1
New Madison, Ohio (45346) 284/A6
New Madrid (co.), Mo. 261/N9
New Madrid, Mo. (63869) 261/O9
Newmains, Scotland 15/C2
Newman, Calif. (95360) 204/D6
Newman, Ill. (61942) 222/B6
Newman, Ky. (†42301) 237/G5
Newman (sound), Newf. 166/D2
Newman, W. Australia 88/B4
Newman (lake), Wash. 310/H3
Newman, W. Australia 92/B3
New Manchester, W. Va. (26056) 312/E1
Newman Grove, Nebr. (68758) 264/G3
Newman Lake, Wash. (99025) 310/J3
Newmans Cove, Newf. 166/D2
New Marion, Ind. (†47023) 227/G6
New Market, Ala. (35761) 195/F1
Newmarket, England 13/H5
Newmarket, England 10/G4
New Market, Ind. (47965) 227/D5
New Market, Iowa (51646) 229/D7
Newmarket, Ireland 10/B4
Newmarket, Ireland 17/C7
Newmarket, Jamaica 158/H6
New Market, Md. (21774) 245/J3
New Market, Minn. (55054) 255/E6
New Market, Mo. (†64439) 261/C4
Newmarket, New Bruns. 170/D3
Newmarket, N.H. (03857) 268/F5
Newmarket○, N.H. (03857) 268/F5
New Market, Ohio (†45133) 284/C7
Newmarket, Ontario 177/E3
Newmarket, Queensland 88/K2
Newmarket, Queensland 95/D2
Newmarket, Scotland 15/B2
New Market, Tenn. (37820) 237/O8
New Market, Va. (22844) 307/L3
Newmarket-on-Fergus, Ireland 17/D6
New Marlborough○, Mass. (†01230) 249/B4
New Martinsburg, Ohio (†43160) 284/D7
New Martinsville, W. Va. (26155) 312/E3
New Maryland, New Bruns. 170/D3
New Matamoras, Ohio (45767) 284/J6
New Meadows, Idaho (83654) 220/B4
New Melle, Mo. (63365) 261/L5
New Memphis, Ill. (62266) 222/D5
Newmerella, Victoria 97/E5
New Mexico 188/E4
NEW MEXICO 274
New Mexico (state), U.S. 146/H6
New Miami, Ohio (45011) 284/A7
New Middleton, Tenn. (†38563) 237/J8
New Middletown, Ind. (47160) 227/E8
New Middletown, Ohio (44442) 284/J4
New Milford, Conn. (06776) 210/B2
New Milford○, Conn. (06776) 210/B2
New Milford, N.J. (07646) 273/B1
New Milford, Ohio (†44272) 284/H3
New Milford, Pa. (18834) 294/L2
Newmill, Scotland 15/E3
New Mills, England 13/J2
New Mills, England 10/G2
Newmilns and Greenholm, Scotland 15/D5
New Milton, W. Va. (26411) 312/E4
New Minas, Nova Scotia 168/D3
New Minden, Ill. (†62263) 222/D5
New Mount Pleasant, Ind. (†47371) 227/G4
New Munich, Minn. (56356) 255/D5
Newnan, Georgia (30263) 217/C4
Newnans (lake), Fla. 212/D2
New Norcia, W. Australia 92/A5
New Norfolk, Tasmania 88/H8
New Norfolk, Tasmania 99/C4
New Norway, Alberta 182/D3
New Offenburg, Mo. (63661) 261/M7
New Orleans, La. 188/H5
New Orleans, La. 146/K7
New Orleans, La. (*70101) 238/O4
New Orleans, U.S. 2/E4
New Osgoode, Sask. 181/H3
New Oxford, Pa. (17350) 294/H6
New Palestine, Ind. (46163) 227/F5
New Pallas, Ireland 17/E6
New Paltz, N.Y. (12561) 276/M7
New Paris, Ind. (46553) 227/F2
New Paris, Ohio (45347) 284/A6
New Paris, Pa. (15554) 294/E5
New Pass (range), Nev. 266/D3
New Pekin, Ind. (†47165) 227/F7
New Perlican, Newf. 166/D2
New Petersburg, Ohio (†45123) 284/D7
New Philadelphia, Ill. (†61459) 222/C3
New Philadelphia, Ind. (†47167) 227/F7
New Philadelphia, Ohio (44663) 284/G5
New Philadelphia, Pa. (17959) 294/K4
New Pine Creek, Oreg. (97635) 291/G5
New Pitsligo, Scotland 15/F3
New Pittsburg, Ohio (†44691) 284/F4
New Plymouth, Idaho (83655) 220/B6
New Plymouth, N. Zealand 100/D3
New Plymouth, Ohio (45654) 284/F7
New Point, Ind. (47263) 227/G6
New Point, Mo. (64473) 261/B2
Newport, Ark. (72112) 202/H2
Newport, Del. (19804) 245/R2
Newport, England 13/F7
Newport, England 13/E5
Newport, England 10/F5
Newport, Ind. (47966) 227/C5
Newport, Mayo, Ireland 17/C4
Newport, Tipperary, Ireland 17/E6
Newport, Ky. (*41071) 237/S2
Newport, Ky. 188/K3
Newport, Maine (04953) 243/E6
Newport○, Maine (04953) 243/E6
Newport, Md. (†20622) 245/L7
Newport, Minn. (55055) 255/F6
Newport, Miss. (†38641) 256/D1
Newport, Nebr. (68759) 264/E2
New Port, Neth. Ant. 161/G9
Newport, N.H. (03773) 268/C5
Newport○, N.H. (03773) 268/C5
Newport, N.J. (08345) 273/C5
Newport, N.Y. (13416) 276/K4
Newport, N.C. (28570) 281/R5
Newport, Nova Scotia 168/E3
Newport, Ohio (†43140) 284/C6
Newport, Ohio (45768) 284/H7
Newport, Oreg. (97365) 291/C3
Newport, Pa. (17074) 294/H5
Newport, Québec 172/D2
Newport, R.I. 188/M2
Newport (co.), R.I. 249/K6
Newport, R.I. (02840) 249/J7
Newport, Tenn. (37821) 237/P9
Newport, Texas (76254) 303/F4
Newport, Vt. (05855) 268/C2
Newport○, Vt. (05855) 268/C2
Newport, Va. (24128) 307/H6
Newport, Wales 10/E5
Newport, Dyfed, Wales 13/C5
Newport, Gwent, Wales 13/B6
Newport, Wash. (99156) 310/H2
Newport Beach, Calif. (*92660) 204/D11
Newport Center, Vt. (05857) 268/C2
New Portland, Maine (04954) 243/C6
New Portland○, Maine (04954) 243/C6
Newport News, Va. 188/L3
Newport News (I.C.), Va. (*23601) 307/P6
Newport-on-Tay, Scotland 15/F4
Newport Pagnell, England 13/G5
New Port Richey, Fla. (*33552) 212/D3
New Prague, Minn. (56071) 255/E6
New Preston, Conn. (06777) 210/B2
New Providence (isl.), Bahamas 156/C1
New Providence (Borden), Ind. (†47106) 227/F8
New Providence, Iowa (50206) 229/G4
New Providence, N.J. (07974) 273/E2
New Providence, Pa. (17560) 294/K6
New Prue (Prue), Okla. (†74060) 288/O2
Newquay, England 10/D5
Newquay, England 13/B7
New Quay, Wales 10/D4
New Quay, Wales 13/C5
New Raymer, Colo. (80742) 208/M1
New Richland, Minn. (56072) 255/E7
New Richmond, Ind. (47967) 227/D4
New Richmond, Ohio (45157) 284/B8
New Richmond, Québec 172/C2
New Richmond, Wis. (54017) 317/A5
New Riegel, Ohio (44853) 284/D3
New River, N.C. (28540) 281/O5
New River (inlet), N.C. 281/P6
New River, Tenn. (†37755) 237/M8
New River, Va. (24129) 307/G6
New River Beach, New Bruns. 170/D3
New Road, Nova Scotia 168/E4
New Roads, La. (70760) 238/G5
New Rochelle, N.Y. (*10801) 276/P7
New Rockford, N. Dak. (58356) 282/N4
New Romney, England 13/J7
New Ross, Ind. (47968) 227/D5
New Ross, Ireland 10/C4
New Ross, Ireland 17/H7
New Ross, Nova Scotia 168/D4
Newry, Maine (04261) 243/B6
Newry○, Maine (04261) 243/B6
Newry, N. Ireland 17/J3
Newry, N. Ireland 10/C3
Newry, North. Terr. 93/A3
Newry, Pa. (16665) 294/F5
Newry, S.C. (29665) 296/B2
New Salem, Ill. (62357) 222/C4
New Salem, Ind. (†46173) 227/G5
New Salem, Kansas (†67156) 232/F4
New Salem○, Mass. (01355) 249/E2
New Salem, N. Dak. (58563) 282/G6
New Salem, Nova Scotia 168/D3
New Salem, Ohio (†43148) 284/E6
New Salem, Pa. (15468) 294/C6
New Salem (Delmont), Pa. (†15626) 294/D5
New Salisbury, Ind. (47161) 227/E8
New Sarepta, Alberta 182/D3
New Sarpy, La. (70078) 238/N4
New Schwabenland (reg.) 5/B1
New Scone, Scotland 15/E4
New Sharon, Iowa (50207) 229/H6
New Sharon○, Maine (04955) 243/C6
New Sharon, N.J. (†08691) 273/D3
New Shoreham (Block Island)○, R.I. (†02807) 249/H8
New Siberian (isls.), U.S.S.R. 54/R2
New Siberian (isls.), U.S.S.R. 4/B2
New Siberian (isls.), U.S.S.R. 2/S2
New Siberian (isls.), U.S.S.R. 48/P2
New Site, Ala. (†35010) 195/G4
New Site, Miss. (38859) 256/H1
New Smyrna Beach, Fla. (32069) 212/F2
Newsoms, Va. (23874) 307/O7
New South Wales, /H6
New South Wales (state), Australia 87/E9
NEW SOUTH WALES 97
New Spadra, Ark. (†72830) 202/C3
New Square, N.Y. (†10901) 276/K8
New Stanton, Pa. (15672) 294/C5
New Straitsville, Ohio (43766) 284/F6
New Strawn (Strawn), Kansas (66839) 232/G3
New Stuyahok, Alaska (99636) 196/G3
New Sweden, Maine (04762) 243/G2
New Sweden○, Maine (04762) 243/G2
New Tazewell, Tenn. (37825) 237/O8
Newtok, Alaska (99681) 196/F2
Newton, Ala. (36352) 195/G8
Newton (co.), Ark. 202/D2
Newton (co.), Georgia 217/E3
Newton, Georgia (31770) 217/D8
Newton, Ill. (62448) 222/E5
Newton (co.), Ind. 227/C3
Newton, Iowa 188/H2
Newton, Iowa (50208) 229/H5
Newton, Kansas (67114) 232/E3
Newton, Mass. (†02158) 249/C7
Newton (co.), Miss. 256/F6
Newton, Miss. (39345) 256/F6
Newton (co.), Mo. 261/D9
Newton○, N.H. (03858) 268/E6
Newton, N.J. (07860) 273/D1
Newton, N.C. (28658) 281/G3
Newton, Québec 172/C4
Newton, Scotland 15/E5
Newton (co.), Texas 303/L7
Newton, Texas (75966) 303/L7
Newton, Utah (84327) 304/C2
Newton, W. Va. (25266) 312/D5
Newton Abbot, England 13/D7
Newton Abbot, England 10/E5
Newton Center, Mass. (02159) 249/C7
Newton Falls, N.Y. (13666) 276/K2
Newton Falls, Ohio (44444) 284/J3
Newtongrange, Scotland 15/D2
Newton Grove, N.C. (28366) 281/N4
Newton Hamilton, Pa. (17075) 294/G5
Newton Highlands, Mass. (02161) 249/C7
Newtonia, Mo. (64853) 261/D9
Newton Junction, N.H. (03859) 268/E6
Newton-le-Willows, England 13/H2
Newton Lower Falls, Mass. (†02162) 249/B7
Newton Mearns, Scotland 15/B2
Newton Mills, Nova Scotia 168/F3
Newtonmore, Scotland 15/D3
Newton Siding, Manitoba 179/D5
Newton Stewart, Scotland 10/D3
Newton Stewart, Scotland 15/D6
Newtonsville, Ohio (45158) 284/B7
Newton Upper Falls, Mass. (†02164) 249/C7
Newtonville, Ind. (47632) 227/D8
Newtonville, Mass. (02160) 249/C7
Newtonville, N.J. (08346) 273/D4
Newtown, Conn. (06470) 210/B3
Newtown○, Conn. (06470) 210/B3
Newtown, Ind. (47969) 227/C4
Newtown, Ky. (†40324) 237/N4
Newtown, Mo. (64667) 261/F2
Newtown, New Bruns. 170/E3
Newtown, Newf. 166/D4
Newtown, N.S. Wales 97/C6
New Town, N. Dak. (58763) 282/F4
Newtown, Ohio (45244) 284/C10
Newtown, Pa. (18940) 294/N5
New Town, S.C. (†29536) 296/J3
Newtown, Victoria 97/C6
Newtown, Wales 13/D5
Newtown, Wales 10/E4
Newtownabbey (dist.), N. Ireland 17/J2
Newtownabbey, N. Ireland 17/K2
Newtownards, N. Ireland 17/K2
Newtownbutler, N. Ireland 17/G3
Newtown Forbes, Ireland 17/F4
Newtownhamilton, N. Ireland 17/H3
Newtownmountkennedy, Ireland 17/J5
Newtown Saint Boswells, Scotland 15/F5
Newtownsandes, Ireland 17/C6
Newtown Square○, Pa. (19073) 294/L6
Newtownstewart, N. Ireland 17/G2
New Trenton, Ind. (47035) 227/H6
New Trier, Minn. (†55031) 255/F6
New Tripoli, Pa. (18066) 294/L4
New Troy, Mich. (49119) 250/C7
New Tulsa, Okla. (†74080) 288/P2
Newtyle, Scotland 15/E4
New Ulm, Minn. (56073) 255/D6
New Ulm, Texas (78950) 303/H8
New Underwood, S. Dak. (57761) 298/D5
New Vernon, N.J. (07976) 273/D2
New Victoria, Nova Scotia 168/H2
New Vienna, Iowa (52065) 229/L3
New Vienna, Ohio (45159) 284/C7
Newville, Ala. (36353) 195/H8
Newville, Ind. (†46721) 227/H2
Newville, Pa. (17241) 294/H5
Newville, W. Va. (26632) 312/E5
New Vineyard○, Maine (04956) 243/C6
New Virginia, Iowa (50210) 229/F6
New Washington, Ind. (47162) 227/F7
New Washington, Ohio (44854) 284/E4
New Washington, Philippines 82/D5
New Waterford, Nova Scotia 168/J2
New Waterford, Ohio (44445) 284/J4
New Waverly, Ind. (46961) 227/E3
New Waverly, Texas (77358) 303/J7
New Westminster, Br. Col. 162/D6
New Westminster, Br. Col. 184/K3
New Weston, Ohio (45348) 284/A5
New Whiteland, Ind. (46184) 227/E5
New Wilmington, Pa. (16142) 294/B3
New Winchester, Ind. (†46122) 227/D5
New Winchester, Ohio (†44820) 284/D4
New Windsor, England 13/G8
New Windsor, England 10/F5
New Windsor, Ill. (61465) 222/C2
New Windsor, Md. (21776) 245/K2
New Windsor, N.Y. (12550) 276/N8
New Witten, S. Dak. (†57584) 298/K7
New Woodstock, N.Y. (13122) 276/J5
New World (isl.), Newf. 166/C4
New York 188/L2
NEW YORK 276
New York, N.Y. 146/L5
New York, N.Y. 188/M2
New York (co.), N.Y. 276/M9
New York, N.Y. (*10001) 276/M9
New York (state), U.S. 146/L5
New York, U.S. 2/F3
New York Mills, Minn. (56567) 255/C4
New York Mills, N.Y. (13417) 276/K4
New York State Barge (canal), N.Y. 276/C4
New Zealand 2/T8
New Zealand 87/G9
NEW ZEALAND 100
New Zion, New Bruns. 170/D2
New Zion, S.C. (29111) 296/H4
Ney, Ohio (43549) 284/B3
Neyagawa, Japan 81/J7
Neyland, Wales 13/B6
Neyriz, Iran 66/J6
Neyshabur, Iran 59/G2
Neyshabur, Iran 66/L2
Nezhin, U.S.S.R. 52/D4
Nez Perce (co.), Idaho 220/B3
Nezperce, Idaho (83543) 220/B3
Nez Perce Nat'l Hist. Park, Idaho 220/B-C3
Nezwar (mt.), Iran 66/H3
Ngabang, Indonesia 85/D5
N'gage, Angola 115/C5
Ngage, Angola 102/D5
Ngahere, N. Zealand 100/C5
Ngami (lake), Botswana 118/C4
Ngamiland (reg.), Botswana 118/C3
Ngamring, China 77/C6
Ngangla Ringco (lake), China 77/B5
Ngangzê Co (lake), China 77/C5
Ngao, Thailand 72/D3
Ngaoundéré, Cameroon 115/B2
Ngaoundéré, Cameroon 102/D4
Ngapara, N. Zealand 100/C6
Ngara, Tanzania 115/F4
Ngaruawahia, N. Zealand 100/E2
Ngatapa, N. Zealand 100/F3
Ngatik (atoll), Micronesia 87/F5
Ngau (isl.), Fiji 86/Q10
Ngauruhoe (mt.), N. Zealand 100/E3
Ngawi, Indonesia 85/K2
Nghia Lo, Vietnam 72/D2
Ngiva, Angola 102/D6
Ngiva, Angola 115/C7
Ngoc Linh (mt.), Vietnam 72/E4
Ngom Qu (riv.), China 77/E5
Ngong, Kenya 115/G4
Ngoring Hu (lake), China 77/E4
Ngorongoro (crater), Tanzania 115/F4
N'Gounié (riv.), Congo 115/B4

418 N'Gounié

N'Gounié (riv.), Gabon 115/B4
Ngourou, Cent. Afr. Rep. 115/D2
N'Guigmi, Niger 106/G6
Ngulu (atoll), Micronesia 87/D5
Ngunju (cape), Indonesia 85/F8
Ngunza, Angola 102/D6
Ngunza, Angola 115/B6
Nguru, Nigeria 102/D3
Nguru, Nigeria 106/G6
Nhâmundá (riv.), Brazil 120/D3
Nhamundá (riv.), Brazil 132/B3
Nharêa, Angola 115/C6
Nharêa, Angola 102/D6
Nha Trang, Vietnam 72/F4
Nha Trang, Vietnam 54/M8
Nhava-Sheva, India 68/B7
Nhill, Victoria 88/G7
Nhill, Victoria 97/A5
Nhulunbuy, North. Terr. 88/F2
Nhulunbuy, North. Terr. 93/E2
Ni (riv.), Va. 307/N4
Niafunké, Mali 106/D5
Niagara (co.), N.Y. 276/C4
Niagara (riv.), N.Y. 276/B4
Niagara, N. Dak. (58266) 282/P4
Niagara (reg. munic.), Ontario 177/E4
Niagara (riv.), Ontario 177/E4
Niagara, Wis. (54151) 317/K4
Niagara Falls, N.Y. 188/K2
Niagara Falls, N.Y. (*14301) 276/C4
Niagara Falls, Ont. 162/J7
Niagara Falls, Ontario 177/E4
Niagara-on-the-Lake, Ontario 177/E4
Niamey (cap.), Niger 2/K5
Niamey (cap.), Niger 102/C3
Niamey (cap.), Niger 106/E6
Niangara, Zaire 115/E3
Niangua, Mo. (65713) 261/G8
Niantic, Conn. (06357) 210/G3
Niantic (riv.), Conn. 210/G3
Niantic, Ill. (62551) 222/D4
Niarada, Mont. (59852) 262/B3
Niari (riv.), Congo 115/B4
Nias (isl.), Indonesia 54/L9
Nias (isl.), Indonesia 85/B5
Niassa (prov.), Mozambique 118/F2
Nibbe, Mont. (†59088) 262/H4
Nibe, Denmark 21/C4
Nibe, Denmark 18/F8
Nibley, Utah (†84321) 304/C2
Nicaragua 2/E5
Nicaragua 146/K8
Nicaragua (lake), Nic. 146/K8
NICARAGUA 154/E4
Nicaragua (lake), Nicaragua 154/E5
Nicaro, Cuba 158/J3
Nicasio, Calif. (94946) 204/H1
Nicastro, Italy 34/F5
Nicatous (lake), Maine 243/G5
Nice, France 7/E4
Nice, France 28/G6
Niceville, Fla. (32578) 212/C6
Nichinan, Japan 81/E8
Nichol (isl.), Nova Scotia 168/F4
Nicholas (chan.), Cuba 156/B2
Nicholas (chan.), Cuba 158/E1
Nicholas (co.), Ky. 237/N4
Nicholas (co.), W. Va. 312/E6
Nicholas Denys, New Bruns. 170/D1
Nicholasville, Ky. (40356) 237/N5
Nicholls, Georgia (31554) 217/G7
Nichols, Conn. (†06611) 210/C4
Nichols, Fla. (33863) 212/E4
Nichols, Iowa (52766) 229/L6
Nichols, Minn. (†56431) 255/E4
Nichols, N.Y. (13812) 276/H6
Nichols, S.C. (29581) 296/J3
Nichols, Wis. (54152) 317/K6
Nichols Hills, Okla. (†73116) 288/L3
Nicholson (riv.) 88/F3
Nicholson, Br. Col. 184/J4
Nicholson, Georgia (30565) 217/F2
Nicholson, Miss. (39463) 256/E10
Nicholson, Port (inlet), N. Zealand 100/B3
Nicholson (riv.), North. Terr. 93/E5
Nicholson, Pa. (18446) 294/L2
Nicholson (riv.), Queensland 95/A3
Nicholson, W. Australia 92/E2
Nicholsville, Ala. (†36784) 195/C6
Nicholville, N.Y. (12965) 276/L1
Nickel Centre, Ontario 175/D3
Nickel Centre, Ontario 177/D1
Nickelsville, Va. (24271) 307/D7
Nickerie (dist.), Suriname 131/C3
Nickerie (riv.), Suriname 131/C3
Nickerson, Kansas (67561) 232/D3
Nickerson, Minn. (†55797) 255/F4
Nickerson, Nebr. (68044) 264/H3
Nicobar (isls.), India 54/L9
Nicobar (isls.), India 68/G7
Nicodemus, Kansas (†67625) 232/C2
Nicola, Br. Col. 184/G5
Nicolaus, Calif. (95659) 204/B8
Nicolet (co.), Québec 172/E3
Nicolet, Québec 172/E3
Nicolet (lake), Québec 172/F4
Nicolet (riv.), Québec 172/E3
Nicollet (co.), Minn. 255/D6
Nicollet, Minn. (56074) 255/D6
Nicoma Park, Okla. (73066) 288/M4
Nicomen Island, Br. Col. 184/L3
Nico Pérez, Uruguay 145/D4
Nicosia (cap.), Cyprus 63/E5
Nicosia (cap.), Cyprus 59/B2
Nicosia (cap.), Cyprus 54/E6
Nicosia, Italy 34/E6
Nicoya, C. Rica 154/E5
Nicoya (gulf), C. Rica 154/E6
Nicoya (pen.), C. Rica 154/E6
Nictau, New Bruns. 170/C1
Nictaux, Nova Scotia 168/D4
Nidau, Switzerland 39/D2
Nidd (riv.), England 10/F3
Nidwalden (canton), Switzerland 39/F3
Nidzica, Poland 47/E2
Niebüll, W. Germany 22/C1
Niederbipp, Switzerland 39/E2
Niedere Tauern (range), Austria 41/B3
Niederurnen, Switzerland 39/G2
Nielsville, Minn. (56568) 255/B3
Niemba, Zaire 115/E5
Niemen (riv.), U.S.S.R. 7/G3
Niemen (riv.), U.S.S.R. 52/B4
Niemen (riv.), U.S.S.R. 53/A3
Nienburg, W. Germany 22/C3
Nieuport (Nieuwpoort), Belgium 27/B6
Nieuw-Amsterdam, Suriname 131/D2
Nieuw-Buinen, Netherlands 27/K3
Nieuwegein, Netherlands 27/G4
Nieuwendam, Netherlands 27/C4
Nieuwe-Pekela, Netherlands 27/L2
Nieuweschans, Netherlands 27/L2
Nieuwkoop, Netherlands 27/F4
Nieuw-Nickerie, Suriname 120/D2
Nieuw-Nickerie, Suriname 131/C2
Nieuwpoort, Belgium 27/B6
Nieuw-Schoonebeek, Netherlands 27/L3
Nieuwveld (range), S. Africa 118/C6
Nieves, Mexico 150/H5
Nièvre (dept.), France 28/E4
Nigadoo, New Bruns. 170/E1
Niğde (prov.), Turkey 63/F4
Niğde, Turkey 59/B2
Niğde, Turkey 63/F4
Nigel, S. Africa 118/J7
Niger 2/K5
Niger 102/C3
Niger (riv.) 2/K5
Niger (riv.) 102/C4
Niger (riv.), Benin 106/E6
Niger (riv.), Guinea 106/C6
Niger (riv.), Mali 106/D5
NIGER 106/F5
Niger (riv.), Niger 106/E6
Niger (state), Nigeria 106/F7
Niger (delta), Nigeria 106/F8
Niger (riv.), Nigeria 106/F7
Nigeria 2/K5
Nigeria 102/C4
NIGERIA 106/F6
Nightcaps, N. Zealand 100/B6
Nighthawk, Wash. (†98855) 310/F2
Nightingale, Alberta 182/D4
Nightingale (mts.), Nev. 266/B2
Nightingale (Bach Long Vi) (isl.), Vietnam 72/F2
Nightmute, Alaska (99690) 196/F2
Nigrita, Greece 45/F5
Nigua (riv.), P. Rico 161/D2
Nihoa (isl.), Hawaii 87/K3
Nihoa (isl.), Hawaii 188/F6
Nihoa (isl.), Hawaii 218/D6
Nii (isl.), Japan 81/J6
Niigata (pref.), Japan 81/J5
Niigata, Japan 54/P6
Niigata, Japan 81/J5
Niihama, Japan 81/F6
Niihau (isl.), Hawaii 87/K3
Niihau (isl.), Hawaii 188/E5
Niihau (isl.), Hawaii 218/A2
Niimi, Japan 81/F6
Niitsu, Japan 81/J5
Nijar, Spain 33/E4
Nijkerk, Netherlands 27/H4
Nijmegen, Netherlands 27/H5
Nijvel (Nivelles), Belgium 27/E7
Nijverdal, Netherlands 27/J4
Nikel', U.S.S.R. 52/C1
Nikep, Md. (21546) 245/C2
Nikki, Benin 106/E7
Nikko National Park, Japan 81/J5
Nikolai, Alaska (99691) 196/H2
Nikolayev, U.S.S.R. 7/H4
Nikolayev, U.S.S.R. 48/D5
Nikolayev, U.S.S.R. 52/D5
Nikolayevsk, U.S.S.R. 2/S3
Nikolayevsk, U.S.S.R. 4/D2
Nikolayevsk, U.S.S.R. 54/P4
Nikolayevsk, U.S.S.R. 52/G4
Nikolayevsk-na-Amure, U.S.S.R. 48/P4
Nikol'sk, U.S.S.R. 52/G3
Nikol'sk, U.S.S.R. 52/G4
Nikolski, Alaska (99638) 196/E4
Nikol'skoye, U.S.S.R. 48/R4
Nikopol, Bulgaria 45/G4
Nikopol', U.S.S.R. 52/D5
Niksar, Turkey 63/G2
Nikshahr, Iran 59/H4
Nikshahr, Iran 66/L7
Nikšić, Yugoslavia 45/D4
Nikumaroro (Gardner) (isl.), Kiribati 87/J6
Nila (isl.), Indonesia 85/H7
Nilahue, Chile 138/E6
Niland, Calif. (92257) 204/K10
Nilaveli, Sri Lanka 68/E7
Nile (riv.) 2/L5
Nile (riv.) 102/F2
Nile (riv.), Egypt 111/F2
Nile (riv.), Egypt 59/B4
Nile (prov.), Sudan 111/F4
Nile (riv.), Sudan 59/B6
Nile (riv.), Sudan 111/F4
Niles, Ill. (60648) 222/B5
Niles, Kansas (†67480) 232/E2
Niles, Mich. (49120) 250/C7
Niles, Ohio (44446) 284/J3
Ni'lin, West Bank 65/C4
Nilópolis, Brazil 135/E3
Nilwood, Ill. (62672) 222/D4
Nimach, India 68/D4
Nimba (lag.), Guinea 106/C7
Nimba (lag.), Ivory Coast 106/C7
Nimba (lag.), Liberia 106/C7
Nîmes, France 28/F6
Nîmes, France 7/E4
Nimmitabel, N.S. Wales 97/E5
Nimmons, Ark. (72461) 202/K1
Nimnyrskiy, U.S.S.R. 48/N4
Nimrod, Ark. (†72126) 202/D4
Nimrod (lake), Ark. 202/D4
Nimrod, Minn. (56478) 255/D4
Nimule, Sudan 111/F7
Nin (bay), Philippines 82/D4
Nin, Yugoslavia 45/B3
Ninaview, Colo. (†81054) 208/N7
Ninawa (gov.), Iraq 66/B3
Nine Degree (chan.), India 68/C7
Ninemile (pt.), Mich. 250/E3
Nine Mile (creek), Utah 304/D4
Nine Mile Falls, Wash. (99026) 310/H3
Nine Mile River, Nova Scotia 168/E3
Ninepipe (res.), Mont. 262/C3
Nine Times, S.C. (†29685) 296/B2
Ninette, Manitoba 179/C5
Ninety Mile (beach), N. Zealand 100/D1
Ninety Mile (beach), Victoria 97/D6
Ninety Six, S.C. (29666) 296/C3
Ninety Six Nat'l Hist. Site, S.C. 296/C3
Nineveh (ruins), Iraq 66/C2
Nineveh, N.Y. (13813) 276/J6
Nineveh, Pa. (15353) 294/B6
Ninfas (pt.), Argentina 143/D5
Ninga, Manitoba 179/C5
Ning'an, China 77/L3
Ningbo (Ningpo), China 77/K6
Ningbo, China 54/O7
Ningde, China 77/K6
Ningdu, China 77/J6
Ninghua, China 77/J6
Ningpo (Ningbo), China 77/K6
Ningsia (Yinchuan, Yinchwan), China 77/G4
Ningsia Hui Aut. Reg. (Ningxia Huizu), China 77/F3
Ningwu, China 77/H4
Ningxia Huizu (Ningsia Hui Aut. Reg.), China 77/F3
Ning Xian, China 77/G4
Ninh Binh, Vietnam 72/E3
Ninigo Group (isls.), Papua N.G. 87/E6
Ninilchik, Alaska (99639) 196/B1
Ninini (pt.), Hawaii 218/D2
Ninnekah, Okla. (73067) 288/L5
Ninnescah (riv.), Kansas 232/E4
Ninnis Glacier Tongue, Ant. 5/C8
Ninole, Hawaii (96773) 218/J4
Ninove, Belgium 27/D7
Nioaque, Brazil 132/C8
Niobe, N.Y. (14758) 276/B6
Niobe, N. Dak. (†58746) 282/F2
Niobrara (riv.), Nebr. 188/F2
Niobrara, Nebr. (68760) 264/G2
Niobrara (riv.), Nebr. 264/E2
Niobrara (co.), Wyo. 319/H2
Niobrara (riv.), Wyo. 319/J3
Niono, Mali 106/C6
Nioro, Mali 106/C5
Nioro, Mali 102/B3
Nioro-du-Rip, Senegal 106/A6
Niort, France 28/C4
Niota, Ill. (62358) 222/B3
Niota, Tenn. (37826) 237/M9
Niotaze, Kansas (67355) 232/F4
Nipani, India 68/C5
Nipawin, Sask. 181/H2
Nipawin Prov. Park, Sask. 181/G1
Nipe (bay), Cuba 158/J3
Nipigon, Ont. 162/H6
Nipigon (lake), Ont. 146/K5
Nipigon (lake), Ont. 162/H6
Nipigon, Ontario 177/H5
Nipigon, Ontario 175/C3
Nipigon (lake), Ontario 175/C3
Nipigon (lake), Ontario 177/H5
Nipinnawasee, Calif. (†93601) 204/F6
Nipishish (lake), Newf. 166/B3
Nipissing (terr. dist.), Ontario 177/F2
Nipissing (terr. dist.), Ontario 175/E3
Nipissing, Ontario 177/E1
Nipissing (lake), Ontario 177/E1
Nipissing (lake), Ontario 175/E3
Nipomo, Calif. (93444) 204/E8
Nippers Harbour, Newf. 166/C4
Nipton, Calif. (92364) 204/K8
Niquelândia, Brazil 132/D6
Ñiquén, Chile 138/E1
Niquero, Cuba 158/G4
Niquero, Cuba 156/C2
Niquivil, Argentina 143/C3
Nirgua, Venezuela 124/D2
Nirmal, India 68/D5
Nirvana, Mich. (†49642) 250/D5
Nir Yitzhaq, Israel 65/A5
Niš, Yugoslavia 7/G4
Niš, Yugoslavia 45/F4
Nisa, Portugal 33/C3
Nisab, P.D.R. Yemen 59/E7
Nisab, Saudi Arabia 59/D4
Nisbet, Pa. (17759) 294/H3
Niscemi, Italy 34/E6
Nishapur (Neyshabur), Iran 66/L2
Nishino (isl.), Japan 81/M3
Nishinomiya, Japan 81/H8
Nishinoomote, Japan 81/E8
Nísiros (isl.), Greece 45/H7
Niskayuna, N.Y. (†12301) 276/N5
Nisko, Poland 47/E3
Nisku, Alberta 182/D3
Nisland, S. Dak. (57762) 298/C4
Nisqually, Wash. (†98501) 310/C3
Nisqually (riv.), Wash. 310/C4
Nisqually Ind. Res., Wash. 310/C4
Nissan (isl.), Papua N.G. 86/C2
Nissum (fjord), Denmark 21/A5
Nisswa, Minn. (56468) 255/D4
Niterói, Brazil 132/F8
Niterói, Brazil 120/E5
Niterói, Brazil 135/E3
Nith (riv.), Scotland 15/E5
Nith (riv.), Scotland 10/E3
Nitil, Jordan 65/D4
Nitinat, Br. Col. 184/H3
Nitinat (lake), Br. Col. 184/H3
Niton Junction, Alberta 182/C3
Nitra, Czech. 41/E2
Nitra (riv.), Czech. 41/E2
Nitro, W. Va. (25143) 312/C6
Nitta Yuma, Miss. (38763) 256/C4
Nittedal, Norway 18/D3
Niuafo'ou (isl.), Tonga 87/J7
Niuatoputapu (isl.), Tonga 87/J7
Niue (isl.) 87/K7
Niue (isl.), N. Zealand 2/A6
Niutao (atoll), Tuvalu 87/H6
Nivala, Finland 18/O5
Nive (riv.), Tasmania 99/C4
Nivelles, Belgium 27/E7
Nivernais (trad. prov.), France 29
Niverville, Manitoba 179/F5
Niwot, Colo. (80544) 208/J2
Nixa, Mo. (65714) 261/F8
Nixburg, Ala. (36058) 195/F5
Nixon, Nev. (89424) 266/B3
Nixon, N.J. (08817) 273/E2
Nixon, Texas (78140) 303/G8
Nixonville, S.C. (†29526) 296/K4
Niya (Minfeng), China 77/B4
Nizamabad, India 68/D5
Nizao, Dom. Rep. 158/E6
Nizhnekamsk, U.S.S.R. 7/K3
Nizhnekamsk, U.S.S.R. 52/H3
Nizhneudinsk, U.S.S.R. 48/K4
Nizhnevartovsk, U.S.S.R. 48/H3
Nizhneyansk, U.S.S.R. 48/O3
Nizhniy Lomov, U.S.S.R. 52/F4
Nizhniy Novgorod (Gor'kiy), U.S.S.R. 52/F3
Nizhniy Tagil, U.S.S.R. 54/H4
Nizhniy Tagil, U.S.S.R. 48/G4
Nizhnyaya Pesha, U.S.S.R. 52/G1
Nizina, Alaska (†99566) 196/K2
Nizip, Turkey 63/G4
Nizwa, Oman 59/G5
Nizza Monferrato, Italy 34/B2
Nizzanim, Israel 65/B4
Njombe, Tanzania 115/F5
Njombe (riv.), Tanzania 115/F5
Nkambe, Cameroon 115/B2
Nkayi, Congo 115/B4
Nkhata Bay, Malawi 115/F6
Nkhotakota, Malawi 115/F6
N'Komi (lag.), Gabon 115/A4
Nkongsamba, Cameroon 115/B3
Nkongsamba, Cameroon 102/D4
Nmai (riv.), Burma 72/C1
Nnewi, Nigeria 106/F7
Noah, Tenn. (†37355) 237/J9
Noakhali, Bangladesh 68/G4
Noank, Conn. (06340) 210/G3
Noatak, Alaska (99761) 196/F1
Noatak (riv.), Alaska 196/F1
Noatak Nat'l Preserve, Alaska 196/F1
Nobel, Ontario 177/D2
Nobeoka, Japan 81/E7
Noble, Georgia (†30728) 217/B1
Noble, Ill. (62868) 222/E5
Noble (co.), Ind. 227/G2
Noble, Iowa (†52641) 229/K6
Noble, La. (71462) 238/C3
Noble, Mo. (65715) 261/G9
Noble (co.), Ohio 284/G6
Noble (co.), Okla. 288/M2
Noble, Okla. (73068) 288/M4
Nobleboro◯, Maine (04555) 243/D7
Nobleford, Alberta 182/D5
Noble Lake, Ark. (†71601) 202/G5
Nobles (co.), Minn. 255/C7
Noblesville, Ind. (46060) 227/F4
Nobleton, Fla. (33554) 212/D3
Nobleton, Ontario 177/J3
Noboribetsu, Japan 81/K2
Nocatee, Fla. (33864) 212/E4
Noccundra, Queensland 95/B5
Nocera Inferiore, Italy 34/E4
Nochistlán, Mexico 150/H6
Nocona, Texas (76255) 303/G4
Noctor, Ky. (41357) 237/P5
Noda, Japan 81/P2
Nodaway, Iowa (50857) 229/D7
Nodaway (riv.), Iowa 229/D7
Nodaway (co.), Mo. 261/C2
Nodaway, Mo. (†64421) 261/C3
Node, Wyo. (82228) 319/H3
Nodine, Minn. (†55925) 255/G7
Noel, Mo. (64854) 261/D9
Noel, Nova Scotia 168/E3
Noel Road, Nova Scotia 168/E3
Noelville, Ontario 177/D1
Nogal, N. Mex. (88341) 274/D5
Nogal (reg.), Somalia 115/J2
Nogales, Ariz. 188/D4
Nogales, Ariz. (85621) 198/E7
Nogales, Chile 138/F2
Nogales, Mexico 150/P2
Nogamut, Alaska (†99668) 196/G2
Nogata, Japan 81/E7
Nogent-le-Rotrou, France 28/D3
Nogent-sur-Seine, France 28/E3
Nogoa (riv.), Queensland 88/H4
Nogoa (riv.), Queensland 95/C5
Nogoyá, Argentina 143/F6
Nógrád (co.), Hungary 41/E3
Nohili (pt.), Hawaii 218/B1
Nohkú (pt.), Mexico 150/Q7
Noinville, New Bruns. 170/E2
Noir (isl.), Chile 138/E11
Noires (mts.), Dom. Rep. 158/C5
Noires (mts.), Haiti 158/C5
Noirmont (mt.), Switzerland 39/B4
Noirmoutier (isl.), France 28/B4
Noisy-le-Sec, France 28/B1
Nojima (cape), Japan 81/K6
Nokesville, Va. (22123) 307/N3
Nokhowch, Kuh-e (mt.), Iran 66/M7
Nokia, Finland 18/N6
Nok Kundi, Pakistan 68/A3
Nok Kundi, Pakistan 59/H4
Nokomis, Ala. (†36502) 195/D8
Nokomis, Fla. (33555) 212/D4
Nokomis, Ill. (62075) 222/D4
Nokomis, Sask. 181/F4
Nokou, Chad 111/B5
Nola, Ark. (†72838) 202/C4
Nola, Cent. Afr. Rep. 115/C3
Nola, Miss. (†39665) 256/D7
Nolan (co.), Texas 303/D5
Nolan, W. Va. (25687) 312/B7
Nolichucky (riv.), N.C. 281/E2
Nolichucky (riv.), Tenn. 237/R8
Nolin, Ky. (†42776) 237/K5
Nolin (lake), Ky. 237/K6
Nolin (riv.), Ky. 237/J6
Nolinsk, U.S.S.R. 52/H3
Nollesemic (lake), Maine 243/F4
Noma, Fla. (32452) 212/C5
Nomans Land (isl.), Mass. 249/L7
Nombre de Dios, Mexico 150/G5
Nome, Alaska 146/B3
Nome, Alaska (99762) 196/E2
Nome, Alaska 188/C5
Nome, Alaska 2/A2
Nome, N. Dak. (58062) 282/P6
Nome, U.S. 4/C18
Nomgon, Mongolia 77/G3
Nominingue, Québec 172/B3
Nominingue (lake), Québec 172/B3
Nomoi (isls.), Micronesia 87/F5
Nonacho (lake), N.W.T. 162/F3
Nonacho (lake), N.W. Terrs. 187/H3
Nonamesset (isl.), Mass. 249/M6
Nondalton, Alaska (99640) 196/G2
Nong Het, Laos 72/E3
Nong Khai, Thailand 72/D3
Nong Lahan (lake), Thailand 72/D3
Nonoava, Mexico 150/F3
Nonouti (atoll), Kiribati 87/H6
Nonquitt, Mass. (02748) 249/L6
Nonsan, S. Korea 81/C5
Nontron, France 28/D5
Nooksack, Wash. (98276) 310/C2
Nooksack (riv.), Wash. 310/C2
Noonan, N. Dak. (58765) 282/D2
Noord (pt.), Neth. Ant. 161/F8
Noord (pt.), Neth. Ant. 161/D8
Noord di Salinja, Neth. Ant. 161/E8
Noordwijk, Netherlands 27/E4
Noorvik, Alaska (99763) 196/F1
Nootka, Br. Col. 184/D5
Nootka (isl.), Br. Col. 184/D5
Nootka (sound), Br. Col. 184/D5
Nopalucan de la Granja, Mexico 150/O1
Nopeming, Minn. (†55810) 255/F4
Nopiming Prov. Park, Manitoba 179/G4
Nóqui, Angola 115/B5
Noquochoke P.O. (Westport), Mass. (02790) 249/K6
Nora, Ill. (61059) 222/D1
Nora, Nebr. (68962) 264/G4
Nora, Sask. 181/H3
Nora, S. Dak. (†57001) 298/R8
Nora, Sweden 18/J7
Nora, Va. (24272) 307/D6
Noranda, Que. 162/J6
Noranda, Québec 174/B3
Noranside, Queensland 95/A4
Nora Springs, Iowa (50458) 229/H2
Norbeck, S. Dak. (†57480) 298/L3
Norberg, Sweden 18/K6
Norberto de la Riestra, Argentina 143/G7
Norbertville, Québec 172/F3
Norborne, Mo. (64668) 261/E4
Norcatur, Kansas (67653) 232/B2
Norco, Calif. (91760) 204/E11
Norco, La. (70079) 238/N3
Norcross, Georgia (*30071) 217/D3
Norcross, Maine (†04462) 243/F4
Norcross, Minn. (56274) 255/B5
Nord (dept.), France 28/E2
Nord, Greenl. 4/A10
Nord (pt.), Guadeloupe 161/B7
Nord (dept.), Haiti 158/C5
Nord (riv.), Québec 172/C4
Nordaustlandet (isl.), Norway 18/D1
Nordborg, Denmark 21/C7
Nordby, Århus, Denmark 21/D5
Nordby, Ribe, Denmark 21/B7
Norddeich, W. Germany 22/B2
Nordegg, Alberta 182/B3
Nordegg (riv.), Alberta 182/C3
Norden, Nebr. (†68778) 264/D2
Norden, W. Germany 22/B2
Nordenham, W. Germany 22/C2
Norderney, W. Germany 22/B2
Norderney (isl.), W. Germany 22/B2
Norderstedt, W. Germany 22/D2
Nord-Est (bay), Guadeloupe 161/B6
Nordfjord (fjord), Norway 18/E6
Nordhausen, E. Germany 22/D3
Nordheim, Texas (78141) 303/G9
Nordhorn, W. Germany 22/B2
Nordin, New Bruns. 170/E1
Nordjylland (co.), Denmark 21/D4
Nordkapp (cape), Norway 7/G1
Nordkapp (pt.), Norway 18/C1
Nordkinn (headland), Norway 18/Q1
Nordkinn (pen.), Norway 18/P1
Nordland (co.), Norway 18/J3
Nordland, Wash. (98358) 310/C2
Nordli, Norway 18/H4
Nördlingen, W. Germany 22/D4
Nordmaling, Sweden 18/L5
Nordman, Idaho (83848) 220/B1
Nord-Ostsee (canal), W. Germany 22/C1
Nord-Ouest (dept.), Haiti 158/B5
Nordstrand (isl.), W. Germany 22/C1
Nord-Trøndelag (co.), Norway 18/H4
Nordvik-Ugol'naya, U.S.S.R. 4/B4
Nordvik-Ugol'naya, U.S.S.R. 48/M2
Nore (riv.), Ireland 10/C4
Nore (riv.), Ireland 17/G7
Norene, Tenn. (37136) 237/J8
Norfield, Miss. (†39629) 256/C8
Norfolk (isl.), Australia 2/T7
Norfolk◯, Conn. (06058) 210/C1
Norfolk (co.), England 13/H5
Norfolk (co.), Mass. 249/K4
Norfolk◯, Mass. (02056) 249/J4
Norfolk, Nebr. 188/G2
Norfolk, Nebr. (68701) 264/G2
Norfolk, N.Y. (13667) 276/K1
Norfolk (bay), Tasmania 99/D4
Norfolk, Va. 188/L3
Norfolk, Va. 146/L6
Norfolk (I.C.), Va. (*23501) 307/R7
Norfolk Island, /L5
Norfolk Island (terr.), Australia 87/G8
Norfork, Ark. (72658) 202/F1
Norfork (lake), Ark. 202/F1
Norfork (lake), Mo. 261/H10
Norg, Netherlands 27/J2
Norge, Okla. (†73018) 288/K4
Norge, Va. (23127) 307/P6
Norglenwold, Alberta 182/C3
Noril'sk, U.S.S.R. 2/P2
Noril'sk, U.S.S.R. 54/L3
Noril'sk, U.S.S.R. 4/B5
Noril'sk, U.S.S.R. 48/J3
Norland, Fla. (†33169) 212/B4
Norland, Ontario 177/F3
Norlina, N.C. (27563) 281/N2
Norma, N.J. (08347) 273/C4
Norma, N. Dak. (58766) 282/G2
Norma, Tenn. (†37827) 237/N8
Normal, Ill. (61761) 222/E3
Normalville, Pa. (15469) 294/D5
Norman, Ark. (71960) 202/C5
Norman, Ind. (47264) 227/E7
Norman (co.), Minn. 255/B3
Norman, Nebr. (68963) 264/F4
Norman (cape), Newf. 166/C3
Norman, N.C. (28367) 281/K4
Norman (lake), N.C. 281/H3
Norman, Okla. (*73069) 288/M4
Norman (riv.), Queensland 88/G3
Norman (creek), Queensland 95/D3
Norman (riv.), Queensland 95/B3
Norman (isl.), Virgin Is. (Br.) 161/D4
Normanby, Queensland 88/K2
Normand (lake), Québec 172/D2
Normandale, Ontario 177/D5
Normandin, Québec 172/E1
Normandy (trad. prov.), France 29
Normandy, Mo. (63121) 261/R2
Normandy (riv.), Queensland 95/C2
Normandy, Tenn. (37360) 237/J10
Normandy, Texas (78852) 303/D9
Normandy Beach, N.J. (08739) 273/E3
Normandy Park, Wash. (†98100) 310/A2
Normangee, Texas (77871) 303/H6
Norman Park, Georgia (31771) 217/E8
Norman's Cove, Newf. 166/D2
Normanton, Australia 87/E7
Normanton, Queensland 95/B3
Normanton, Queensland 88/G3
Normantown, Georgia (†30474) 217/H6
Normantown, W. Va. (25267) 312/E5
Norman Wells, Canada 4/C16
Norman Wells, N.W.T. 146/F3
Norman Wells, N.W.T. 162/D2
Norman Wells, N.W. Terrs. 187/F3
Normétal, Québec 174/B3
Noroton, Conn. (†06820) 210/B4
Noroton Heights, Conn. (†06820) 210/B4
Norphlet, Ark. (71759) 202/E7
Norquay, Sask. 181/J4
Ñorquincó, Argentina 143/B5
Norrbotten (co.), Sweden 18/L3
Nørre Åby, Denmark 21/C7
Nørre Alslev, Denmark 21/E8
Nørre Broby, Denmark 21/D7
Nørre Nebel, Denmark 21/B6
Nørre Snede, Denmark 21/C6
Nørre Vorupør, Denmark 21/B4
Norridge, Ill. (†60656) 222/B5
Norridgewock, Maine (04957) 243/D6
Norridgewock◯, Maine (04957) 243/D6
Norris, Wis. (†54414) 317/H6
Norris, Ill. (61553) 222/C3
Norris, Miss. (†39074) 256/F6
Norris, Mont. (59745) 262/E5
Norris, S.C. (29667) 296/B2
Norris, S. Dak. (57560) 298/G7
Norris (lake), Tenn. 188/K3
Norris, Tenn. (37828) 237/N8
Norris (dam), Tenn. 237/N8
Norris (lake), Tenn. 237/O8
Norris, Wyo. (†82190) 319/B1
Norris Arm, Newf. 166/C4
Norris City, Ill. (62869) 222/E6
Norris Point, Newf. 166/C4
Norristown, Ark. (†72801) 202/D3
Norristown, Georgia (30447) 217/H5
Norristown, Ind. (†47234) 227/F6
Norristown, Pa. (*19401) 294/M5
Norrisville, Md. (†21161) 245/N2
Norrköping, Sweden 7/F3
Norrköping, Sweden 18/K7
Norrsundet, Sweden 18/K6
Norrtälje, Sweden 18/L7
Norseland, Minn. (†56082) 255/D6
Norseman, W. Australia 88/C6
Norseman, W. Australia 92/C6
Norsjö, Sweden 18/L4
Norte (pt.), Argentina 143/D5
Norte (chan.), Brazil 120/E2
Norte (chan.), Brazil 132/D2
Norte, Serra do (range), Brazil 132/B5
Norte del Cabo San Antonio (pt.), Argentina 143/E4
Norte de Santander (dept.), Colombia 126/D3
North (sea) 2/K3
North (sea) 7/E3
North (cape), Alaska 196/L4
North (pt.), Barbados 161/B8
North (sea), Belgium 27/D4
North (rocks), Bermuda 156/H2
North (sea), Denmark 21/B9
North (sea), England 13/J4
North (sea), France 28/E1
North (cape), Ice. 4/C11
North (Horn) (cape), Iceland 21/B1
North (sound), Ireland 17/B5
North (isls.), La. 238/M7
North (pass), La. 238/N8
North (pt.), La. 238/M8
North (pt.), Md. 245/N4

Northwood 419

North (riv.), Mass. 249/D2
North (riv.), Mass. 249/L4
North (chan.), Mich. 250/F2
North (pt.), Mich. 250/F3
North (lake), Minn. 255/F1
North (sea), Netherlands 27/E3
North (lake), New Bruns. 170/C3
North (riv.), Newf. 166/C3
North (riv.), Newf. 166/B2
North (isl.), N. Zealand 87/H9
North (cape), N. Zealand 87/H9
North (cape), N. Zealand 100/D1
North (isl.), N. Zealand 100/F1
North (lake), N. Dak. 282/J3
North (chan.), N. Ireland 10/D3
North (chan.), N. Ireland 17/K1
North (Nordkapp) (cape), Norway 7/G1
North (cape), Norway 4/B8
North (cape), N.S. 162/K6
North (cape), Nova Scotia 168/H1
North (mt.), Nova Scotia 168/D3
North (chan.), Ontario 177/A1
North (chan.), Ontario 175/D3
North (mt.), Pa. 294/K3
North (pt.), Pr. Edward I. 168/E1
North (chan.), Scotland 10/D3
North (chan.), Scotland 15/C5
North (sound), Scotland 15/G4
North (sound), Scotland 15/F1
North (isl.), Seychelles 118/H5
North, S.C. (29112) 296/E4
North (inlet), S.C. 296/J5
North (isl.), S.C. 296/J5
North (pt.), Tasmania 99/E1
North (creek), Utah 304/C6
North (lake), Utah 304/B2
North (riv.), Wash. 310/B4
North (sea), W. Germany 22/B2
North (riv.), W. Va. 312/J4
North (lake), Wis. 317/J1
North Abington, Mass. (02351) 249/L4
North Acton, Mass. (†01720) 249/J2
North Adams, Mass. (01247) 249/B2
North Adams, Mich. (49262) 250/E7
Northallerton, England 10/F3
Northallerton, England 13/F3
Northam, England 13/C6
Northam, W. Australia 88/B6
Northam, W. Australia 92/B1
NORTH AMERICA 146
North America 2/C4
North Amherst, Mass. (01059) 249/E3
North Amity, Maine (04465) 243/H4
Northampton, England 13/F5
Northampton, England 10/F4
Northampton, Mass. (01060) 249/D3
Northampton (co.), N.C. 281/P2
Northampton (co.), Pa. 294/M4
Northampton, Pa. (18067) 294/M4
Northampton (co.), Va. 307/S6
Northampton, W. Australia 88/A5
Northampton, W. Australia 92/A5
Northamptonshire (co.), England 13/G5
North Andaman (isl.), India 68/G6
North Andover○, Mass. (01845) 249/K2
North Anna (riv.), Va. 307/M4
North Anson, Maine (04958) 243/D6
North Apollo, Pa. (15673) 294/D4
North Arlington, N.J. (07032) 273/B2
North Arm (inlet), N.W. Terrs. 187/G3
North Asheboro, N.C. (†27203) 281/K3
North Ashford, Conn. (†06282) 210/G1
North Aspy (riv.), Nova Scotia 168/H2
North Atlantic Ocean 2/H3
North Attleboro○, Mass. (*02760) 249/J5
North Augusta, Ontario 177/J3
North Augusta, S.C. (29841) 296/C5
North Aulatsivik (isl.), Newf. 166/B2
North Aurora, Ill. (60542) 222/E2
North Avondale, Colo. (†81022) 208/L6
North Ballachulish, Scotland 15/C4
North Baltimore, Ohio (45872) 284/C3
North Bangor, N.Y. (12966) 276/M1
North Barrington, Ill. (†60010) 222/A5
North Bass (isl.), Ohio 284/E2
North Battleford, Sask. 146/H4
North Battleford, Sask. 162/F5
North Battleford, Sask. 181/C3
North Bay, N.Y. (13123) 276/J4
North Bay, Ont. 146/L5
North Bay, Ont. 162/J6
North Bay, Ontario 177/E1
North Bay, Ontario 175/E3
North Bay, Wis. (†53401) 317/M3
North Bay Ingonish (bay), Nova Scotia 168/H2
North Bay Village, Fla. (33141) 212/B4
North Beach, Md. (20831) 245/N6
North Belgrade, Maine (†04963) 243/D7
North Bellingham, Mass. (†02019) 249/J4
North Bend, Br. Col. 184/G5
North Bend, Nebr. (68649) 264/H3
North Bend, Ohio (45052) 284/B9
North Bend, Oreg. (97459) 291/C4
North Bend, Pa. (17760) 294/G3
North Bend, Wash. (98045) 310/D3
North Bend, Wis. (†54642) 317/D7
North Bennington, Vt. (05257) 268/A6
North Bergen○, N.J. (07047) 273/B2
North Berwick, Maine (03906) 243/B9
North Berwick○, Maine (03906) 243/B9
North Berwick, Scotland 15/F4
North Berwick, Scotland 10/E2
North Beveland (isl.), Netherlands 27/D5
North Billerica, Mass. (01862) 249/J2
North Bloomfield, Conn. (†06002) 210/E1
North Bloomfield, Ohio (44450) 284/J3
North Bonneville, Wash. (98639) 310/C5
North Borneo (Sabah) (state), Malaysia 85/F3
Northboro, Iowa (51647) 229/C7
Northborough, Mass. (01532) 249/H3
Northborough○, Mass. (01532) 249/H3
North Boston, N.Y. (14110) 276/C5
North Bourke, N.S. Wales 97/C2
North Brabant (prov.), Netherlands 27/F5
North Braddock, Pa. (15104) 294/C7
North Bradford, Maine (†04410) 243/F5
North Bradley, Mich. (†48618) 250/E5
Northbranch, Kansas (†66936) 232/D2
North Branch, Md. (†21502) 245/D2
North Branch, Mich. (48461) 250/F5
North Branch, Minn. (55056) 255/F5
North Branch, N.H. (†03440) 268/D5
North Branch, N.J. (08876) 273/D2
North Branch Oromocto (riv.), New Bruns. 170/D3
North Branford○, Conn. (06471) 210/E3
North Brentwood, Md. (†20722) 245/F4
Northbridge○, Mass. (01534) 249/H4
North Bridgton, Maine (04057) 243/B7
Northbrook, Ill. (60062) 222/B5
North Brook, Ontario 177/G3
North Brookfield, Mass. (01535) 249/F3
North Brookfield○, Mass. (01535) 249/F3
North Brooksville, Maine (†04617) 243/F7
North Brunswick○, N.J. (08902) 273/D3
North Bruny (isl.), Tasmania 99/D5
North Buena Vista, Iowa (52066) 229/L3
North Calais, Vt. (†05648) 268/C3
North Caldwell, N.J. (†07006) 273/B2
North Calling Lake, Alberta 182/D2
North Canadian (riv.) 188/G3
North Canadian (riv.), Okla. 288/K3
North Canton, Conn. (06059) 210/D1
North Canton, Georgia (†30114) 217/C2
North Canton, Ohio (44720) 284/H4
North Cape (Nordkapp) (pt.), Norway 18/P1
North Cape May, N.J. (08204) 273/C6
North Caribou (lake), Ontario 175/B2
North Carolina 188/L3
NORTH CAROLINA 281
North Carolina (state), U.S. 146/K6
North Carrizo (creek), Colo. 208/N8
North Carrizo (riv.), Okla. 288/A1
North Carrollton, Miss. (38947) 256/E3
North Carter (mt.), N.H. 268/E3
North Carver, Mass. (02355) 249/L5
North Cascades Nat'l Park, Wash. 310/D2
North Catasauqua, Pa. (†18032) 294/L4
North Charleston, S.C. (29406) 296/G6
North Charlestown, N.H. (†03603) 268/C5
North Chatham, Mass. (02650) 249/O6
North Chatham, N.H. (†04058) 268/E3
North Chelmsford, Mass. (01863) 249/J2
North Chesterville, Maine (†04938) 243/C6
North Chicago, Ill. (60064) 222/B4
North Chichester, N.H. (†03263) 268/E5
North Chili, N.Y. (14514) 276/E4
North City (Coello), Ill. (†62825) 222/E5
North Clarendon, Vt. (05759) 268/B4
Northcliffe, W. Australia 92/B6
North Cohasset, Mass. (†02025) 249/F7
North Colebrook, Conn. (†06021) 210/C1
North College Hill, Ohio (45239) 284/B9
North Collins, N.Y. (14111) 276/C5
North Concho (riv.), Texas 303/C6
North Concord, Vt. (05858) 268/D3
North Conway, N.H. (03860) 268/E3
North Cooking Lake, Alberta 182/D3
North Cotabato (prov.), Philippines 82/E7
Northcote, Minn. (†56728) 255/A2
Northcote, N. Zealand 100/B1
Northcote, Victoria 88/L7
Northcote, Victoria 97/J5
North Cove, N.C. (†28752) 281/F3
North Cove, Wash. (†98590) 310/A4
North Cowichan, Br. Col. 184/J3
North Creek, N.Y. (15853) 276/M3
North Crossett, Ark. (71635) 202/G7
North Cutler, Maine (†04626) 243/J6
North Dakota 188/F1
NORTH DAKOTA 282
North Dakota (state), U.S. 146/H5
North Dandalup, W. Australia 88/B3
North Danger (reef), Philippines 85/E3
North Danville, Vt. (†05819) 268/C3
North Dartmouth, Mass. (02747) 249/K6
North Dexter, Maine (†04930) 243/E5
North Dighton, Mass. (02764) 249/K5
North Dixmont, Maine (†04932) 243/E6
North Down (dist.), N. Ireland 17/K2
North Downs (hills), England 13/G6
North Eagle Butte, S. Dak. (†57625) 298/G3
Northeast (cape), Alaska 196/E2
North East (pt.), Jamaica 158/K6
Northeast (pass), La. 238/M8
North East, Md. (21901) 245/P2
North East, Pa. (16428) 294/C1
North East Breakers, Bermuda 156/H2
North East Cape Fear (riv.), N.C. 281/O4
North East Carry, Maine (†04441) 243/D4
North-Eastern (prov.), Kenya 115/G3
Northeast Foreland (pen.), Greenl. 4/A10
North Eastham, Mass. (02651) 249/O5
Northeast Harbor, Maine (04662) 243/G7
Northeast Land (isl.), Norway 4/B8
North East Margaree (riv.), Nova Scotia 168/H2
North Easton, Mass. (02356) 249/K4
North East Polder, Netherlands 27/H3
North East Providence (chan.), Bahamas 156/C1
North Edisto (riv.), S.C. 296/G6
North Edwards, Calif. (93523) 204/H8
North Egremont, Mass. (01252) 249/A4
Northeim, W. Germany 22/C3
North English, Iowa (52316) 229/J5
North Enid, Okla. (†73701) 288/L2
Northern (dist.), Israel 65/C2
Northern (head), New Bruns. 170/D4
Northern (prov.), Sudan 111/E3
Northern Cheyenne Ind. Res., Mont. 262/K5
Northern Dvina (riv.), U.S.S.R. 52/F2
Northern Dvina (riv.), U.S.S.R. 48/E3
Northern Indian (lake), Manitoba 179/J2
NORTHERN IRELAND 17
NORTHERN IRELAND 10/C3
Nottoway (riv.), Va. 307/O7
Notukeu (creek), Sask. 181/D6
Notus, Idaho (83656) 220/B6
Nouadhibou, Mauritania 106/A4
Nouadhibou, Mauritania 102/A2
Nouakchott (cap.), Mauritania 106/A5
Nouakchott (cap.), Mauritania 102/A3
Nouakchott (cap.), Mauritania 2/J5
Nouméa (cap.), New Caled. 87/G8
Nouméa (cap.), New Caledonia 2/T7
Nouméa (cap.), New Caled. 86/H5
Nounan, Idaho (†83254) 220/G7
Noup (head), Scotland 15/E1
Noupoort, S. Africa 118/C6
Nouveau-Comptoir, Québec 174/B2
Northern Ireland, U.K. 7/D3
Northern Marianas 87/E4
Northern Marianas, U.S. 2/S5
Northern Peninsula Aboriginal Reserve, Queensland 88/G2
Northern Peninsula Aboriginal Res., Queensland 95/B1
Northern Samar (prov.), Philippines 82/E4
Northern Sporades (isls.), Greece 45/F6
Northern Territory, 88/E3
NORTHERN TERRITORY 93
Northern Territory (terr.), Australia 87/D7
North Esk (riv.), Scotland 15/F4
North Esk (riv.), Tasmania 99/D3
North Fairfield, Ohio (44855) 284/E3
North Falmouth, Mass. (02556) 249/M6
North Ferrisburg, Vt. (05473) 268/A3
Northfield, Conn. (06778) 210/C2
Northfield, Ill. (60093) 222/B5
Northfield, Ky. (†40201) 237/K1
Northfield○, Maine (†04654) 243/H6
Northfield, Mass. (01360) 249/E2
Northfield○, Mass. (01360) 249/E2
Northfield, Minn. (55057) 255/E6
Northfield○, N.H. (†03276) 268/D5
Northfield, N.J. (08225) 273/D5
Northfield, Ohio (44067) 284/J10
Northfield, Texas (79246) 303/D3
Northfield, Vt. (05663) 268/B3
Northfield○, Vt. (05663) 268/B3
Northfield, Wis. (†54635) 317/D7
Northfield Falls, Vt. (05664) 268/B3
Northfield Farms, Mass. (†01360) 249/E2
Northfield-Tilton, N.H. (†03276) 268/D5
Northfleet, England 10/C5
Northfleet, England 13/J8
North Fond du Lac, Wis. (†54935) 317/J8
Northford, Conn. (06472) 210/D3
North Foreland (prom.), England 10/G5
North Foreland (prom.), England 13/J6
North Fork, Calif. (93643) 204/F6
North Fork, Frenchman (creek), Colo. 208/O1
North Fork, Gunnison (riv.), Colo. 208/D5
North Fork, Smoky Hill (riv.), Colo. 208/P4
North Fork, Idaho (83466) 220/D4
North Fork (riv.), Idaho 220/B7
North Fork, Flathead (riv.), Mont. 262/B2
North Fork, Little Humboldt (riv.), Nev. 266/D1
North Fork, Grand (riv.), N. Dak. 282/E8
Northfork, W. Va. (24868) 312/D8
North Fork, Powder (riv.), Wyo. 319/F2
North Fork, Shoshone (riv.), Wyo. 319/C1
North Fork, Wind (riv.), Wyo. 319/C2
North Fort Myers, Fla. (33903) 212/E5
North Foster, R.I. (†02857) 249/H5
North Fourchu, Nova Scotia 168/H3
North Fox (isl.), Mich. 250/D3
North Franklin, Conn. (06254) 210/G2
North Freedom, Wis. (53951) 317/G9
North Friars (bay), St. Chris.-Nevis 161/D10
North Friesland (reg.), W. Germany 22/C1
North Frisian (isls.), Denmark 21/B7
North Frisian (isls.), W. Germany 22/B1
North Fryeburg, Maine (04058) 243/B7
North Galiano, Br. Col. 184/K3
North Garden, Va. (22959) 307/L5
Northgate, N. Dak. (58767) 282/F2
Northgate, Sask. 181/J6
Northglenn, Colo. (80233) 208/K3
North Gorham, Maine (†04075) 243/B8
North Gosforth, England 13/J3
North Gower, Ontario 177/J2
North Grafton, Mass. (01536) 249/H4
North Granby, Conn. (06060) 210/D1
North Grant, Nova Scotia 168/G3
North Grosvenor Dale, Conn. (06255) 210/H1
North Groton, N.H. (†03266) 268/D4
North Grove, Ind. (†46911) 227/F3
North Guilford, Conn. (†06437) 210/E3
North Hadley, Mass. (†01035) 249/D3
North Haledon, N.J. (07508) 273/B1
North Hampton○, N.H. (03862) 268/F6
North Hampton, Ohio (45349) 284/C5
North Hanover, Mass. (†02339) 249/L4
North Hansel (mts.), Utah 304/B2
North Harbour, Newf. 166/D2
North Harlowe, N.C. (†28532) 281/R5
North Hartland, Vt. (05052) 268/C4
North Hartsville, S.C. (†29550) 296/G3
North Harwich, Mass. (†02645) 249/O6
North Hatfield, Mass. (01066) 249/D3
North Hatley, Québec 172/F4
North Haven○, Conn. (06473) 210/D3
North Haven, Maine (04853) 243/F7
North Haven○, Maine (04853) 243/F7
North Haverhill, N.H. (03774) 268/D3
North Havre, Mont. (†59501) 262/G2
North Hayden, Ind. (†46356) 227/B2
North Head, New Bruns. 170/D4
North Henderson, Ill. (61466) 222/C2
North Hero, Vt. (05474) 268/A2
North Highlands, Calif. (95660) 204/B8
North High Shoals, Georgia (†30645) 217/F3
North Hills, W. Va. (†26101) 312/D4
North Hodge, La. (†71247) 238/E2
North Holland (prov.), Netherlands 27/F3
North Holland (canal), Netherlands 27/C4
North Hollywood, Calif. (*91601) 204/B10
North Hornell, N.Y. (†14843) 276/E6
North Horr, Kenya 115/G3
North Hudson, N.Y. (12855) 276/N3
North Hudson, Wis. (†54016) 317/A5
North Hyde Park, Vt. (05665) 268/B2
North Hykeham, England 13/G4
North Industry, Ohio (44707) 284/H4
North Inishkea (isl.), Ireland 17/A3
North Java, N.Y. (14113) 276/D5
North Jay, Maine (04262) 243/C6
North Johns, Ala. (35086) 195/D4
North Judson, Ind. (46366) 227/D2
North Kansas City, Mo. (64116) 261/P5
North Kedgwick (riv.), New Bruns. 170/C1
North Kent, Conn. (†06757) 210/B1
North Kent (isl.), N.W. Terrs. 187/J2
North Kingstown○, R.I. (02852) 249/J6
North Kingsville, Ohio (44068) 284/J2
North Knife (lake), Manitoba 179/J2
North Knife Lake, Manitoba 179/J2
North Korea 54/O5
North La Junta, Colo. (†81050) 208/N7
Northlake, Ill. (60164) 222/B5
Northlake, Texas (75238) 303/F1
North Lake, Wis. (53064) 317/J1
North Lakhimpur, India 68/G3
Northland, Mich. (49869) 250/B2
Northland, Wis. (†54945) 317/H6
North Landgrove, Vt. (†05148) 268/B5
North Laramie (riv.), Wyo. 319/G3
North Las Vegas, Nev. (89030) 266/F6
North Lauderdale, Fla. (†33063) 212/B3
North Lawrence, N.Y. (12967) 276/L1
North Lawrence, Ohio (44666) 284/G4
North Leeds, Maine (04263) 243/C7
North Lewisburg, Ohio (43060) 284/C5
North Liberty, Ind. (46554) 227/E1
North Liberty, Iowa (52317) 229/K5
North Lima, Ohio (44452) 284/J4
North Limington, Maine (†04049) 243/B8
North Little Rock, Ark. (*72114) 202/F4
North Livermore, Maine (†04254) 243/C7
North Loup, Nebr. (68859) 264/F3
North Loup (riv.), Nebr. 264/E3
North Lovell, Maine (†04231) 243/B7
North Lubec, Maine (†04652) 243/J6
North Luconia (shoals), Philippines 85/E4
North Madison, Conn. (†06443) 210/E3
North Madison, Ohio (†44057) 284/H2
North Magnetic Pole (dist.) 162/F1
North Magnetic Pole, Canada 4/B15
North Magnetic Pole, N.W. Terrs. 187/H2
North Manchester, Ind. (46962) 227/F3
North Manitou, Mich. (†49654) 250/C3
North Manitou (isl.), Mich. 250/C3
North Mankato, Minn. (56001) 255/D6
North Marshfield, Mass. (02059) 249/M4
North Merritt (isl.), Fla. 212/F3
North Miami, Fla. (33161) 212/B4
North Miami, Okla. (74358) 288/R1
North Miami Beach, Fla. (33161) 212/C4
North Middleboro, Mass. (02346) 249/L5
North Middletown, Ky. (40357) 237/N4
North Minch (sound), Scotland 10/D1
North Minch (sound), Scotland 15/B3
North Montpelier, Vt. (05666) 268/C3
Northmoor, Mo. (†64152) 261/P5
North Motton, Tasmania 99/C3
North Mountain, W. Va. (†25427) 312/K3
North Muskegon, Mich. (49445) 250/C5
North Myrtle Beach, S.C. (29582) 296/K4
North Naples, Fla. (33940) 212/E5
North Natuna (isl.), Indonesia 85/D4
North Negril (pt.), Jamaica 158/G6
North Newport, N.H. (†03773) 268/C5
North New Portland, Maine (04961) 243/C6
North New River (canal), Fla. 212/F5
North Newry, Maine (†04261) 243/B6
North Newton, Kansas (67117) 232/E3
North Oaks, Minn. (†55101) 255/G5
North Ogden, Utah (†84404) 304/C2
North Olmsted, Ohio (44070) 284/G9
Northome, Minn. (56661) 255/D3
North Ossetian A.S.S.R., U.S.S.R. 48/E5
North Ossetian A.S.S.R., U.S.S.R. 52/F6
North Oxford, Mass. (01537) 249/G4
North Pacific (ocean) 87/F4
North Pacific Ocean 2/B5
North Pacific Ocean 2/T4
North Pagai (isl.), Indonesia 85/C6
North Palm Beach, Fla. (33403) 212/F5
North Park, Ill. (†61111) 222/D1
North Parsonfield, Maine (†04047) 243/A8
North Pease (riv.), Texas 303/D3
North Pekin, Ill. (†61554) 222/D3
North Pembroke, Mass. (02358) 249/M4
North Pender Island, Br. Col. 184/K3
North Penobscot, Maine (†04476) 243/F7
North Perry, Maine (†04667) 243/J5
North Perry, Ohio (†44081) 284/H2
North Petherton, England 13/D6
North Pine, Br. Col. 184/G2
North Plain, Conn. (†06371) 210/F3
North Plainfield, N.J. (07060) 273/E2
North Plains, Oreg. (97133) 291/A2
North Platte (riv.) 188/F2
North Platte (riv.), Colo. 208/G1
North Platte, Nebr. 188/F2
North Platte, Nebr. (69101) 264/D3
North Platte (riv.), Nebr. 264/B3
North Platte (riv.), U.S. 146/H5
North Platte (riv.), Wyo. 319/H3
North Plymouth, Mass. (02360) 249/L5
North Pole 4/A1
North Pole 2/F1
North Pole, Alaska (99705) 196/J2
North Pole (brook), New Bruns. 170/D1
North Pomfret, Vt. (05053) 268/B4
Northport, Ala. (35476) 195/C4
North Port, Fla. (33595) 212/D4
Northport○, Maine (†04849) 243/E7
Northport, Mich. (49670) 250/D3
Northport, Nebr. (†69336) 264/B3
Northport, N.Y. (11768) 276/O9
Northport, Nova Scotia 168/E3
Northport, Wash. (99157) 310/H2
North Portal, Sask. 181/J6
North Potomac, Md. (†20857) 245/K4
North Powder, Oreg. (97867) 291/K2
North Pownal, Vt. (05260) 268/A6
North Prairie, Wis. (53153) 317/J2
North Providence○, R.I. (02908) 249/J5
North Pulaski, Va. (†24301) 307/G6
North Randall, Ohio (†44101) 284/H9
North Randolph, Vt. (†05061) 268/B4
North Raymond, Maine (†04274) 243/C8
North Reading○, Mass. (01864) 249/C5
North Redington Beach, Fla. (†33708) 212/B3
North Redwood, Minn. (56275) 255/D6
North Renous (riv.), New Bruns. 170/D2
North Rhine-Westphalia (state), W. Germany 22/B3
North Richland Hills, Texas (76118) 303/F2
Northridge, Ohio (45414) 284/B6
North Ridgeville, Ohio (44039) 284/F3
North Rim, Ariz. (86052) 198/C2
North River, Newf. 166/D2
North River, N.Y. (12856) 276/M3
North River, N. Dak. (†58102) 282/S6
North River, Nova Scotia 168/D4
North Riverside, Ill. (60546) 222/B5
North Robinson, Ohio (44856) 284/E4
North Ronaldsay (firth), Scotland 15/F1
North Ronaldsay (isl.), Scotland 15/F1
North Ronaldsay (isl.), Scotland 10/E1
Northrop, Minn. (56075) 255/D7
North Rose, N.Y. (14516) 276/G4
North Roxboro, N.C. (†27573) 281/L2
North Royalton, Ohio (44133) 284/H10
North Rustico, Pr. Edward I. 168/E2
North Saanich, Br. Col. 184/K3
North Saint Paul, Minn. (55109) 255/G5
North Salem, Ind. (46165) 227/D5
North Salem, N.H. (03073) 268/E6
North Salt Lake, Utah (†84010) 304/C3
North Sandwich, N.H. (03259) 268/E4
North San Juan, Calif. (95960) 204/E4
North Santiam (riv.), Oreg. 291/E3
North Saskatchewan (riv.) (dist.) 162/E5
North Saskatchewan (riv.), Alberta 182/E3
North Saskatchewan (riv.), Canada 146/G4
North Saskatchewan (riv.), Sask. 181/D3
North Scituate, Mass. (02060) 249/F8
North Scituate, R.I. (02857) 249/H5
North Sea (canal), Netherlands 27/F4
North Seal (riv.), Manitoba 179/H2
North Searsmont, Maine (†04973) 243/E7
North Sentinel (isl.), India 68/G6
North Sevogle (riv.), New Bruns. 170/D1
North Shapleigh, Maine (04060) 243/B8
North Shoal (lake), Manitoba 179/E4
North Shore, Wis. 317/M1
Northside, N.C. (27564) 281/M2
Northside, Sask. 181/F2
North Sioux City, S. Dak. (57049) 298/R8
North Skunk (riv.), Iowa 229/H5
North Somercotes, England 10/G4
North Somercotes, England 13/H4
North Somers, Conn. (†06071) 210/F1
North Spectacle (lake), Conn. 210/B2
North Spirit Lake, Ontario 175/B2
North Springfield, Pa. (16430) 294/A1
North Springfield, Vt. (05150) 268/B5
North Springfield, Va. (22151) 307/S3
North Star, Alberta 182/B1
North Star, Mich. (48862) 250/E5
North Star, Ohio (45350) 284/A5
North Stonington○, Conn. (06359) 210/H3
North Stratford, N.H. (03590) 268/D2
North Sunderland, England 13/F2
North Sutton, N.H. (03260) 268/D5
North Swansea, Mass. (†02777) 249/K5
North Sydney, N. S. Wales 88/L4
North Sydney, N.S. Wales 97/J3
North Sydney, Nova Scotia 168/H2
North Syracuse, N.Y. (13212) 276/H4
North Taranaki (bight), N. Zealand 100/D3
North Tarrytown, N.Y. (10591) 276/O6
North Terre Haute, Ind. (47805) 227/C5
North Thetford, Vt. (05054) 268/C4
North Thompson (riv.), Br. Col. 184/G4
North Tidworth, England 13/F6
North Tiverton, R.I. (†02722) 249/K6
North Tolsta, Scotland 15/B2
Northton, Scotland 15/B3
North Tonawanda, N.Y. (14120) 276/C4
North Trap (isl.), N. Zealand 100/B7
North Troy, Vt. (05859) 268/C2
North Truchas (peak), N. Mex. 274/D3
North Truro, Mass. (02652) 249/O4
North Tunbridge, Vt. (†05077) 268/C4
North Turner, Maine (04266) 243/C7
North Twin (mt.), N.H. 268/D3
North Tyne (riv.), England 13/E2
North Uist (isl.), Scotland 15/A3
North Uist (isl.), Scotland 10/C2
Northumberland (co.), England 13/E2
Northumberland (co.), New Bruns. 170/D2
Northumberland (str.), New Bruns. 170/F2
Northumberland○, N.H. (†03582) 268/D2
Northumberland (str.), Nova Scotia 168/E2
Northumberland (county), Ontario 177/G3
Northumberland (co.), Pa. 294/J4
Northumberland, Pa. (17857) 294/J4
Northumberland (str.), Pr. Edward I. 168/D2
Northumberland (isls.), Queensland 95/D4
Northumberland (cape), S. Australia 94/F8
Northumberland (co.), Va. 307/R5
Northumberland National Park, England 13/E2
North Umpqua (riv.), Oreg. 291/E4
North Ural (mts.), U.S.S.R. 52/K1
North Utica (Utica), Ill. (†61373) 222/E2
North Uxbridge, Mass. (01538) 249/H4
Northvale, N.J. (07647) 273/F1
North Vancouver, Br. Col. 162/D6
North Vancouver, Br. Col. 184/K3
North Vassalboro, Maine (04962) 243/D7
North Vernon, Ind. (47265) 227/F6
Northview, Mo. (†65706) 261/G8
Northville, Conn. (†06776) 210/B2
Northville, Mich. (48167) 250/F6
Northville, N.Y. (12134) 276/M4
Northville, S. Dak. (57465) 298/M3
North Wabasca (lake), Alberta 182/D1
North Wakefield, N.H. (†03872) 268/E4
North Waldoboro, Maine (†04572) 243/E7
North Wales, Pa. (19454) 294/M5
North Walpole, N.H. (†03608) 268/C5
North Walsham, England 13/J5
North Walsham, England 10/G4
North Waltham, Mass. (02154) 249/B6
North Warren, Pa. (†16365) 294/D2
North Washington, Iowa (50661) 229/J2
North Waterboro, Maine (04061) 243/B8
North Waterford, Maine (04267) 243/B7
Northway, Alaska (99764) 196/K2
North Wayne, Maine (†04284) 243/C7
North Weare, N.H. (†03281) 268/D5
North Webster, Ind. (46555) 227/F2
Northwest (pt.), Fla. 212/E6
North West (dist.), Guyana 131/A2
North West (pt.), Jamaica 158/G5
North West (cape), Australia 87/B8
North West (cape), W. Australia 88/A4
North West (cape), W. Australia 92/A3
North-West Aboriginal Reserve, S. Australia 88/E5
North-West Aboriginal Res., W. Australia 92/E4
North West Arm (inlet), Newf. 166/D2
North West Brook, Newf. 166/C2
North West Brook (riv.), Newf. 166/D2
North Westchester, Conn. (06474) 210/F2
Northwestern (sen. dist.), Alaska 196/E2
North-West Frontier (prov.), Pakistan 68/C2
North West Gander (riv.), Newf. 166/C4
North Westminster, Vt. (†05101) 268/B5
Northwest Miramichi (riv.), New Bruns. 170/D1
Northwest Oromocto (riv.), New Bruns. 170/D3
North Westport, Mass. (02790) 249/K6
North West Providence (chan.), Bahamas 156/B1
North West River, Newf. 166/B3
Northwest Territories 162/E2
Northwest Territories (prov.), Canada 146/G3
NORTHWEST TERRITORIES 187
Northwest Upsalquitch (riv.), New Bruns. 170/D1
North Weymouth, Mass. (02191) 249/D8
North Whitefield, Maine (04353) 243/D7
Northwich, England 13/H2
Northwich, England 10/G2
North Wilbraham, Mass. (†01095) 249/E4
North Wildwood, N.J. (08260) 273/D6
North Wilkesboro, N.C. (28659) 281/G2
North Williston, Vt. (†05495) 268/A3
North Wilton, Conn. (†06897) 210/B4
North Windham, Conn. (06256) 210/G1
North Windham, Maine (04062) 243/C8
North Wolcott, Vt. (†05680) 268/C2
Northwood, Iowa (50459) 229/G2
Northwood○, N.H. (03261) 268/E5
Northwood, N. Dak. (58267) 282/P4

422 Old Washington

Old Washington, Ohio (43768) 284/H5
Oldwick, N.J. (08858) 273/D2
Old Wives, Sask. 181/E5
Old Wives (lake), Sask. 181/E5
Old Woman (creek), Wyo. 319/H3
Olean, Mo. (65064) 261/G6
Olean, N.Y. (14760) 276/D6
O'Leary (peak), Ariz. 198/D3
O'Leary, Pr. Edward I. 168/D2
Olecko, Poland 47/F1
Oleiros, Portugal 33/B3
Olëkma (riv.), U.S.S.R. 48/N4
Olëkminsk, U.S.S.R. 48/N3
Olema, Calif. (94950) 204/H1
Olenegorsk, U.S.S.R. 52/D1
Olenek, U.S.S.R. 4/C4
Olenëk (riv.), U.S.S.R. 54/N3
Olënek, U.S.S.R. 48/M3
Olënek (bay), U.S.S.R. 48/N2
Olënek (riv.), U.S.S.R. 48/M3
Olentangy (riv.), Ohio 284/D4
Oléron (isl.), France 28/C5
Oleśnica, Poland 47/C3
Olesno, Poland 47/D3
Oleta, Okla. (74751) 288/R6
Olex, Oreg. (†97812) 291/G2
Oley, Pa. (19547) 294/L5
Olga, N. Dak. (†58221) 282/O2
Olga (mt.), North. Terr. 93/B8
Olga, Wash. (98279) 310/C2
Ölgiy (Ulegei), Mongolia 77/C2
Ølgod, Denmark 21/B6
Olha, Manitoba 179/B4
Olhão, Portugal 33/C4
Oliena, Italy 34/B4
Olifants (riv.), Mozambique 118/D4
Olifants (riv.), S. Africa 118/D4
Olimar, Uruguay 145/E3
Olimar Grande (riv.), Uruguay 145/E4
Olímpia, Brazil 135/B2
Olin, Iowa (52320) 229/L5
Olin, Ky. (†40447) 237/N6
Olin, N.C. (28660) 281/H3
Olinda, Brazil 120/F3
Olinda, Brazil 132/H4
Olinda, Calif. (96007) 204/C3
Olinda, Victoria 97/K5
Oliva, Argentina 143/D3
Oliva, Spain 33/F3
Oliva de la Frontera, Spain 33/C3
Olivais, Portugal 33/A1
Olivar Alto, Chile 138/G5
Olivares, Cerro de (mt.), Argentina 143/B3
Olivares, Cerro de (mt.), Chile 138/B8
Olive, Mont. (59343) 262/L5
Olive, Okla. (†74030) 288/O2
Olive Branch, Ill. (62969) 222/D6
Olive Branch, Miss. (38654) 256/E1
Olive Branch, Ohio (†45103) 284/D10
Olive Hill, Ky. (41164) 237/P4
Olivehill, Tenn. (38475) 237/E10
Oliveira, Brazil 135/D2
Olivenza, Spain 33/C3
Oliver (dam), Ala. 195/J5
Oliver, Br. Col. 184/H5
Oliver, Georgia (30449) 217/J5
Oliver (dam), Georgia 217/B6
Oliver (lake), Georgia 217/B5
Oliver, Ind. (†47620) 227/B8
Oliver (co.), N. Dak. 282/H5
Oliver, Pa. (15472) 294/C6
Oliver, Wis. (†54880) 317/B2
Oliver Springs, Tenn. (37840) 237/N8
Olivet, Ill. (†61846) 222/F4
Olivet, Kansas (†66856) 232/G3
Olivet, Md. (†20657) 245/N7
Olivet, Mich. (49076) 250/E6
Olivet, S. Dak. (57052) 298/O7
Olivet, Wis. (†54767) 317/B6
Olivette, Mo. (63124) 261/O2
Olivia, Minn. (56277) 255/C6
Olivia, N.C. (28368) 281/L4
Olivier, La. (†70560) 238/G7
Olivone, Switzerland 39/G3
Olkusz, Poland 47/D3
Olla, La. (71465) 238/F3
Ollachea, Peru 128/G9
Ollagüe (vol.), Bolivia 136/B7
Ollagüe, Chile 120/C5
Ollagüe, Chile 138/B3
Ollantaytambo, Peru 128/F9
Ollie, Iowa (52576) 229/J6
Ollon, Switzerland 39/D4
Olmedo, Spain 33/D2
Olmitz, Kansas (67564) 232/D3
Olmos, Peru 128/C5
Olmos Park, Texas (78212) 303/F8
Olmstead, Ky. (42265) 237/H7
Olmsted, Ill. (62970) 222/D6
Olmsted (co.), Minn. 255/F7
Olmsted Falls, Ohio (44138) 284/G9
Olmstedville, N.Y. (12857) 276/N3
Olmué, Chile 138/F2
Olney, Ill. (62450) 222/E5
Olney, Md. (20832) 245/K4
Olney, Mo. (63370) 261/K4
Olney, Mont. (59927) 262/B2
Olney, Okla. (†74538) 288/O6
Olney, Oreg. (†97103) 291/D1
Olney, Texas (76374) 303/F4
Olney Springs, Colo. (81062) 208/M6
Olofström, Sweden 18/J8
Oloh, Miss. (†39482) 256/E8
Olomouc, Czech. 7/F4
Olomouc, Czech. 41/D2
Olonets, U.S.S.R. 52/D2
Olongapo, Philippines 82/C3
Oloron-Sainte-Marie, France 28/C6
Olot, Spain 33/H1
Olowalu, Hawaii (†96761) 218/H2
Oloy (range), U.S.S.R. 48/R3
Olpe, Kansas (66865) 232/F3
Olsa (riv.), Austria 41/C3
Olsburg, Kansas (66520) 232/F2
Olst, Netherlands 27/J4
Olsztyn (prov.), Poland 47/E2
Olsztyn, Poland 7/G3
Olsztyn, Poland 47/E2
Olsztynek, Poland 47/E2
Olt (riv.), Romania 7/G4
Olt (riv.), Romania 45/G3
Olta, Argentina 143/C3
Olten, Switzerland 39/E2
Oltenița, Romania 45/H3
Olton, Texas (79064) 303/B3
Oltu, Turkey 63/J2
Olur, Turkey 63/K2
Olustee, Fla. (32072) 212/D1
Olustee (riv.), Fla. 212/D1
Olustee, Okla. (73560) 288/H5
Olutanga (isl.), Philippines 82/D7
Olutanga (isl.), Philippines 85/G4
Olvera, Spain 33/D4
Olvey, Ark. (†72601) 202/E1
Olwampi (cape), China 77/K7
Olympia (isls.), Greece 45/E7
Olympia, Ky. (40358) 237/O4
Olympia (cap.), Wash. 146/F5
Olympia (cap.), Wash. 188/B1
Olympia (cap.), Wash. (*98501) 310/C3
Olympia Fields, Ill. (60461) 222/B6
Olympian Village, Mo. (†63050) 261/M6
Olympic (mts.), Wash. 310/B3
Olympic Nat'l Park, Wash. 188/A1
Olympic Nat'l Park, Wash. 310/B3
Olympic Valley, Calif. (95730) 204/E4
Olympus (mt.), Greece 45/F5
Olympus (mt.), Wash. 310/B3
Olyphant, Ark. (72020) 202/H3
Olyphant, Pa. (18447) 294/F7
Olyphic, N.C. (†28463) 281/M7
Olyutorskiy (cape), U.S.S.R. 54/U4
Olyutorskiy (cape), U.S.S.R. 48/S4
Oma (cape), Japan 81/K3
Oma, Miss. (†39654) 256/D7
Omagari, Japan 81/K4
Omagh (dist.), N. Ireland 17/G2
Omagh, N. Ireland 10/C3
Omagh, N. Ireland 17/G2
Omaguas, Peru 128/F5
Omaha, Ala. (†36274) 195/H4
Omaha, Ark. (72662) 202/D1
Omaha (beach), France 28/C3
Omaha, Georgia (31821) 217/C6
Omaha, Ill. (62871) 222/E6
Omaha, Nebr. 188/G2
Omaha, Nebr. 146/J5
Omaha, Nebr. (*68101) 264/J3
Omaha Ind. Res., Nebr. 264/H2
Omak, Wash. (98841) 310/F2
Omak (lake), Wash. 310/F2
Oman 2/M5
Oman 54/G8
Oman (gulf) 54/G7
Oman (gulf), Iran 59/G5
Oman (gulf), Iran 66/M8
OMAN 59/G6
Oman (gulf), Oman 59/G5
Oman (reg.), Oman 59/G5
Oman (gulf), U.A.E. 59/G5
Omar, W. Va. (25638) 312/C7
Omaruru, Namibia 118/B4
Omas, Peru 128/D9
Omatako (riv.), Namibia 118/B3
Omate, Peru 128/G11
Ombai (str.), Indonesia 85/H7
Omboué, Gabon 115/A4
Ombrone (riv.), Italy 34/C3
Ombúes de Lavalle, Uruguay 145/B4
Ombúes de Oribe, Uruguay 145/C4
Omdurman, Sudan 102/F3
Omdurman, Sudan 59/B6
Omdurman, Sudan 111/F4
Omega, Georgia (31775) 217/E8
Omega, Ind. (†46030) 227/F4
Omega, Ohio (†45690) 284/E7
Omega, Okla. (73764) 288/K3
Omemee, N. Dak. (†58739) 282/K2
Omemee, Ontario 177/F3
Omena, Mich. (49674) 250/D3
Omeo, Victoria 97/D5
'Omer, Israel 65/B5
Omer, Mich. (48749) 250/F4
Ömerli, Turkey 63/J4
Omerville, Québec 172/E4
Ometepe (isl.), Nicaragua 154/E5
Ometepec, Mexico 150/K8
Omey (isl.), Ireland 17/A5
Omineca (mts.), Br. Col. 184/E2
Omineca (riv.), Br. Col. 184/E2
Omiš, Yugoslavia 45/C4
Omiya, Japan 81/O2
Ommaney (cape), Alaska 196/M2
Ommanney (bay), N.W. Terrs. 187/H2
Omme (riv.), Denmark 21/B6
Ommen, Netherlands 27/J3
Ömnögovĭ, Mongolia 77/F3
Omø (isl.), Denmark 21/E7
Omo (riv.), Ethiopia 111/G6
Omoa, Honduras 154/C3
Omolon (riv.), U.S.S.R. 54/S3
Omolon (riv.), U.S.S.R. 4/C1
Omolon (riv.), U.S.S.R. 48/Q3
Omoloy (riv.), U.S.S.R. 48/O3
Omono (riv.), Japan 81/J4
Ompah, Ontario 177/H2
Omps, W. Va. (†25411) 312/K4
Omro, Wis. (54963) 317/J7
Omsk, U.S.S.R. 54/J4
Omsk, U.S.S.R. 2/N3
Omsk, U.S.S.R. 48/H4
Omsukchan, U.S.S.R. 48/Q3
Omu, Japan 81/L1
Omura, Bonin Is., Japan 81/M3
Omura, Nagasaki, Japan 81/E7
Omurtag, Bulgaria 45/H4
Omuta, Japan 81/E7
Omutninsk, U.S.S.R. 48/F4
Omutninsk, U.S.S.R. 52/H3
Ona, Fla. (33865) 212/E4
Ona, W. Va. (25545) 312/B6
Onaga, Kansas (66521) 232/F2
Onagawa, Japan 81/K4
Onaka, S. Dak. (57466) 298/L3
Onalaska, Texas (77360) 303/J7
Onalaska, Wash. (98570) 310/C4
Onalaska, Wis. (54650) 317/D8
Onaman (lake), Ontario 177/H4
Onamia, Minn. (56359) 255/E4
Onancock, Va. (23417) 307/S5
Onangué (lake), Gabon 115/A4
Onanole, Manitoba 179/C4
Onaping Falls, Ontario 177/J5
Onaping Falls, Ontario 175/D3
Onaqui, Utah (†84080) 304/B3
Onarga, Ill. (60955) 222/F3
Onawa, Iowa (51040) 229/A4
Onawa, Maine (†04464) 243/E5
Onawa (lake), Maine 243/E5
Onaway, Idaho (†83855) 220/B3
Onaway, Mich. (49765) 250/E3
Onchan, I. of Man 13/C3
Onchiota, N.Y. (12968) 276/M2
Oncócua, Angola 115/B7
Onda, Spain 33/F3
Ondangua, Namibia 118/B3
Ondava (riv.), Czech. 41/F2
Ondo (state), Nigeria 106/F7
Ondo, Nigeria 106/F7
Öndörhaan (Undur Khan), Mongolia 77/G2
Öndörhaan, Mongolia 54/N5
Öndverdharnes (mt.), Iceland 21/A1
O'Neals, Calif. (93645) 204/F6
Oneco, Conn. (06373) 210/H2
Oneco, Fla. (33558) 212/D4
Onefour, Alberta 182/E5
Onega, U.S.S.R. 7/H2
Onega (lake), U.S.S.R. 7/H2
Onega (riv.), U.S.S.R. 7/H2
Onega, U.S.S.R. 52/E2
Onega, U.S.S.R. 48/D3
Onega (bay), U.S.S.R. 52/E2
Onega (lake), U.S.S.R. 48/D3
Onega (lake), U.S.S.R. 52/E2
Onega (riv.), U.S.S.R. 48/D3
Onega (riv.), U.S.S.R. 52/E2
Onego, W. Va. (26886) 312/H5
One Hundred and Fifty Mile House, Br. Col. 184/G4
One Hundred Mile House, Br. Col. 184/G4
Onehunga, N. Zealand 100/B1
Oneida, Ark. (72369) 202/J5
Oneida (co.), Idaho 220/F7
Oneida, Ill. (61467) 222/C2
Oneida, Iowa (†52057) 229/L3
Oneida, Kansas (66522) 232/G2
Oneida, Ky. (40972) 237/O6
Oneida (co.), N.Y. 276/J4
Oneida, N.Y. (13421) 276/J4
Oneida (lake), N.Y. 276/J4
Oneida, Pa. (18242) 294/K4
Oneida, Tenn. (37841) 237/N7
Oneida (co.), Wis. 317/G4
Oneida, Wis. (54155) 317/K7
O'Neill, Nebr. (68763) 264/F2
Onekama, Mich. (49675) 250/C4
Oneonta, Ala. (35121) 195/E3
Oneonta, N.Y. (13820) 276/K6
One Tree Hill, N. Zealand 100/B1
Ong, Nebr. (68452) 264/G4
Ongjin, N. Korea 81/B5
Ongniud, China 77/J3
Ongole, India 68/E5
Ongwediva, Namibia 118/B3
Onhaye, Belgium 27/F8
Oni, U.S.S.R. 52/F6
Onida, S. Dak. (57564) 298/K4
Onilahy (riv.), Madagascar 118/G4
Onima, Neth. Ant. 161/E8
Onion Lake, Sask. 181/B2
Onitsha, Nigeria 106/F7
Onitsha, Nigeria 102/C4
Onkaparinga (riv.), S. Australia 88/D8
Onkaparinga (riv.), S. Australia 94/B8
Onkivesi (lake), Finland 18/P5
Onley, Va. (23418) 307/S5
Only, Tenn. (37140) 237/F9
Ono, Calif. (†96001) 204/C3
Ono, Japan 81/H6
Ono (riv.), Japan 81/E7
Ono, Pa. (17077) 294/J5
Onoda, Japan 81/E6
Onomea, Hawaii (†96781) 218/J4
Onomichi, Japan 81/F6
Onon, Mongolia 77/H2
Onondaga, Mich. (49264) 250/E6
Onondaga (co.), N.Y. 276/H5
Onondaga Ind. Res., N.Y. 276/H5
Onota (lake), Mass. 249/A3
Onoto, Venezuela 124/F3
Onotoa (atoll), Kiribati 87/H6
Onoway, Alberta 182/C3
Onrusrivier, S. Africa 118/G7
Onset, Mass. (02558) 249/M6
Onslow, Australia 87/B8
Onslow, Iowa (52321) 229/M4
Onslow (co.), N.C. 281/P5
Onslow (bay), N.C. 281/P6
Onslow, W. Australia 88/B4
Onslow, W. Australia 92/A3
Onsŏng, N. Korea 81/E2
Onsted, Mich. (49265) 250/E6
Onstwedde, Netherlands 27/K2
Ontake (mt.), Japan 81/H6
Ontario (prov.) 162/H5
Ontario (lake) 146/L5
Ontario (lake) 162/J7
Ontario, Calif. (*91761) 204/D10
Ontario (prov.), Canada 146/K4
Ontario, Ind. (†46746) 227/G1
Ontario, Iowa (†50010) 229/F4
Ontario (lake), N.Y. 188/L2
Ontario (co.), N.Y. 276/F5
Ontario, N.Y. (14519) 276/F4
Ontario (lake), N.Y. 276/F3
Ontario, Ohio (44862) 284/E4
ONTARIO 177
Ontario (lake), Ontario 177/G4
Ontario, Oreg. (97914) 291/K3
Ontario, Wis. (54651) 317/E8
Onteniente, Spain 33/F3
Onton, Ky. (†42455) 237/G5
Ontonagon (co.), Mich. 250/F1
Ontonagon, Mich. (49953) 250/F1
Ontonagon (riv.), Mich. 250/G1
Ontonagon Ind. Res., Mich. 250/F1
Ontong Java (isl.), Solomon Is. 87/G6
Ontong Java (isls.), Solomon Is. 86/D2
Onverwacht, Suriname 131/D3
Onward, Ind. (46967) 227/E3
Onward, Miss. (†39159) 256/C5
Onycha, Ala. (†36467) 195/F8
Onyx, Ark. (†72860) 202/D4
Onyx, Calif. (93255) 204/G8
Oobagooma, W. Australia 92/D2
Oodnadatta, Australia 87/D8
Oodnadatta, S. Australia 88/E5
Oodnadatta, S. Australia 94/D2
Ookala, Hawaii (96774) 218/J4
Oola, Ireland 17/E6
Ooldea, S. Australia 94/B4
Oolitic, Ind. (47451) 227/E7
Oologah, Okla. (74053) 288/P2
Oologah (lake), Okla. 288/P1
Ooltewah, Tenn. (37363) 237/M10
Oona River, Br. Col. 184/C3
Oosterwolde, Netherlands 27/J2
Oostanaula, Georgia (†30701) 217/B1
Oostanaula (riv.), Georgia 217/B2
Oostburg, Netherlands 27/C6
Oostburg, Wis. (53070) 317/L8
Oostende (Ostend), Belgium 27/B6
Oosterend, Netherlands 27/G2
Oosterhout, Netherlands 27/F5
Oostkamp, Belgium 27/C6
Oostmahorn, Netherlands 27/J2
Oost-Vlieland, Netherlands 27/F2
Oostzaan, Netherlands 27/C4
Oostzaan Polder, Netherlands 27/B4
Ootacamund, India 68/D6
Ootmarsum, Netherlands 27/K4
Ootsa (lake), Br. Col. 184/D3
Ootsa Lake, Br. Col. 184/E3
Oozewekwun, Manitoba 179/B5
Opal, Alberta 182/D3
Opal, S. Dak. (57765) 298/D4
Opal, Wyo. (83124) 319/B4
Opala, Zaire 115/D4
Opal Cliffs, Calif. (†95060) 204/K4
Opa Locka, Fla. (33054) 212/B4
Opalton, Queensland 95/B4
Opari, Sudan 111/F7
Oparino, U.S.S.R. 52/G3
Opasatika, Ontario 177/J5
Opasatika, Ontario 175/D3
Opatija, Yugoslavia 45/A3
Opatów, Poland 47/E3
Opava, Czech. 41/E2
Opazatika (riv.), Ontario 175/D3
Opdyke, Ill. (62872) 222/E5
Opelika, Ala. (36801) 195/H5
Opelousas, La. (70570) 238/G5
Opeongo (lake), Ontario 177/F2
Opfikon, Switzerland 39/G2
Opheim, Ill. (61468) 222/C2
Opheim, Mont. (59250) 262/K2
Ophir, Alaska 196/G2
Ophir, Colo. (81426) 208/D7
Ophir, Oreg. (97464) 291/C5
Ophir, Utah (†84074) 304/B3
Opihikao, Hawaii (†96778) 218/K6
Opinaca (riv.), Que. 162/J5
Opinaca (riv.), Québec 174/B2
Opine, Ala. (†36784) 195/C7
Opinnagau (riv.), Ontario 175/D2
Opiscotéo (lake), Québec 174/D2
Opladen, W. Germany 22/B3
Opochka, U.S.S.R. 52/C3
Opoco, Bolivia 136/B6
Opoczno, Poland 47/E3
Opole, Minn. (†56340) 255/D5
Opole (prov.), Poland 47/C3
Opole, Poland 47/C3
Opolis, Kansas (66760) 232/H4
Oporto (Porto) (dist.), Portugal 33/B2
Oporto (Porto), Portugal 33/B2
Opotiki, N. Zealand 100/F3
Opp, Ala. (36467) 195/F8
Oppdal, Norway 18/F5
Oppeln, Poland 47/C3
Oppelo, Ark. (†72110) 202/E3
Oppenheim, W. Germany 22/C4
Oppland (co.), Norway 18/F6
Opportunity, Wash. (99214) 310/H3
Oppy, Ky. (†25685) 237/S5
Optima, Okla. (73948) 288/D1
Optima (lake), Okla. 288/D1
Opua, N. Zealand 100/D1
Opunake, N. Zealand 100/D3
Opuntia (lake), Sask. 181/C4
Opwijk, Belgium 27/F7
'Oqair, Saudi Arabia 59/E4
Oquawka, Ill. (61469) 222/C3
Oquossoc, Maine (04964) 243/B6
Ora, Ind. (46968) 227/D2
Ora, Miss. (†39428) 256/E7
Ora, S.C. (29371) 296/D2
Oracabessa, Jamaica 158/J5
Oracle, Ariz. (85623) 198/E6
Oradea, Romania 7/G4
Oradea, Romania 45/E2
Oradell, N.J. (07649) 273/B1
Oradell (res.), N.J. 273/B1
Orai, India 68/D3
Oraibi, Ariz. (86039) 198/E3
Oraibi Wash (dry riv.), Ariz. 198/E3
Oral, S. Dak. (57766) 298/C7
Oran, Algeria 106/D1
Oran, Algeria 102/B1
Oran, Iowa (50664) 229/J3
Oran, Mo. (63771) 261/N8
Orange (riv.) 2/K7
Orange (riv.) 102/D7
Orange, Australia 87/E9
Orange (riv.), Botswana 118/B5
Orange (cape), Brazil 132/D1
Orange (co.), Calif. 204/H10
Orange, Calif. (*92666) 204/D11
Orange○, Conn. (06477) 210/C3
Orange (co.), Fla. 212/E3
Orange, Fla. (†32321) 212/B1
Orange (lake), Fla. 212/D2
Orange, France 28/F5
Orange, Georgia (†30114) 217/D2
Orange (co.), Ind. 227/E7
Orange, Ind. (†47343) 227/G5
Orange, Mass. (01364) 249/E2
Orange○, Mass. (01364) 249/E2
Orange (canal), Netherlands 27/K3
Orange○, N.H. (†03741) 268/D4
Orange, N.J. (*07050) 273/B2
Orange, N.S. Wales 88/H6
Orange, N.S. Wales 97/E3
Orange (co.), N.Y. 276/M8
Orange (co.), N.C. 281/L2
Orange, Ohio (†44101) 284/J9
Orange (riv.), S. Africa 118/B5
Orange (mts.), Suriname 131/D4
Orange (co.), Texas 303/L7
Orange, Texas (77630) 303/L7
Orange (butte), Utah 304/D5
Orange (co.), Vt. 268/C3
Orange○, Vt. (†05649) 268/C3
Orange (co.), Va. 307/M4
Orange, Va. (22960) 307/M4
Orange Beach, Ala. (36561) 195/C10
Orangeburg, N.Y. (10962) 276/K8
Orangeburg (co.), S.C. 296/F5
Orangeburg, S.C. (29115) 296/F4
Orange City, Fla. (32763) 212/E3
Orange City, Iowa (51041) 229/A2
Orange Cove, Calif. (93646) 204/F7
Orangedale, Nova Scotia 168/G3
Orange Free State (prov.), S. Africa 102/E7
Orange Free State (prov.), S. Africa 118/D5
Orange Grove, Miss. (†39501) 256/H10
Orange Grove, Texas (78372) 303/F10
Orange Hill, St. Vin. & Grens. 161/A8
Orange Lake, Fla. (32681) 212/D2
Orange Park, Fla. (32073) 212/E1
Orange Springs, Fla. (32682) 212/E2
Orangeville, Ill. (61060) 222/D1
Orangeville, Ind. (†47452) 227/D7
Orangeville, Mich. (†49344) 250/D6
Orangeville, Ohio (44453) 284/J3
Orangeville, Ontario 177/D4
Orangeville, Pa. (17859) 294/K3
Orangeville, Utah (84537) 304/C4
Orange Walk Town, Belize 154/C1
Oranienburg, E. Germany 22/E2
Oranjemund, Namibia 102/D7
Oranjemund, Namibia 118/B5
Oranjestad (cap.), Aruba, Neth. Ant. 161/D10
Oranjestad, Neth. Ant. 156/D4
Oranmore, Ireland 17/D5
Orapa, Botswana 118/D4
Oras, Philippines 82/E4
Orăștie, Romania 45/F3
Orava (res.), Czech. 41/E2
Orava (riv.), Czech. 41/E2
Orava (res.), Poland 47/D4
Oraville, Ill. (62971) 222/D6
Oravița, Romania 45/E3
Orb (riv.), France 28/E6
Orbe, Switzerland 39/C3
Orbe (riv.), Switzerland 39/C3
Orbetello, Italy 34/C3
Órbigo (riv.), Spain 33/D1
Orbisonia, Pa. (17243) 294/G5
Orbost, Victoria 88/H7
Orbost, Victoria 97/E5
Örbyhus, Sweden 18/K6
Orca, Alaska (†99574) 196/J2
Orcadia, Sask. 181/J4
Orcas (isl.), Wash. 310/C2
Orcera, Spain 33/E3
Orchard, Colo. (80649) 208/L2
Orchard, Iowa (50460) 229/H2
Orchard, Nebr. (68764) 264/F2
Orchard Beach, Md. (†21122) 245/M4
Orchard Hill, Georgia (30266) 217/D4
Orchard Lake, Mich. (48033) 250/F6
Orchard Mesa, Colo. (†81501) 208/C4
Orchard Park, N.Y. (14127) 276/C5
Orchards, Wash. (98662) 310/C5
Orchard Valley, Wyo. (†82001) 319/H4
Orchid, Fla. (†32970) 212/F4
Orchid, Va. (†23117) 307/N5
Orchy (riv.), Scotland 15/D4
Orcotuna, Peru 128/E8
Orcutt, Calif. (93454) 204/E9
Orcuttville, Conn. (†06076) 210/F1
Ord (mt.), Ariz. 198/D5
Ord (riv.), Australia 87/C7
Ord, Nebr. (68862) 264/F3
Ord (riv.), W. Australia 88/D3
Ord (mt.), W. Australia 92/D2
Ord (riv.), W. Australia 92/E2
Órdenes, Spain 33/B1
Orderville, Utah (84758) 304/B6
Ordoqui, Argentina 143/F7
Ordos (reg.), China 77/G4
Ord River, W. Australia 92/E2
Ordu (prov.), Turkey 63/G2
Ordu, Turkey 59/C1
Ordu, Turkey 63/G2
Ordway, Colo. (81063) 208/M6
Ordway, S. Dak. (†57433) 298/N2
Ordzhonikidze, U.S.S.R. 7/J4
Ordzhonikidze, U.S.S.R. 48/E5
Ordzhonikidze, U.S.S.R. 52/F6
Orealla, Guyana 131/C3
Örediv (riv.), Sweden 18/L4
Oreana, Idaho (83659) 220/B6
Oreana, Ill. (62554) 222/E4
Oreana, Nev. (†89419) 266/C2
Orebank, Tenn. (†37660) 237/R7
Örebro (co.), Sweden 18/J7
Örebro, Sweden 7/F3
Örebro, Sweden 18/J7
Ore City, Texas (75683) 303/K5
Oregon 188/B2
OREGON 291
Oregon, Ill. (61061) 222/D1
Oregon (co.), Mo. 261/K9
Oregon, Mo. (64473) 261/B2
Oregon (inlet), N.C. 281/U3
Oregon, Ohio (43616) 284/D2
Oregon (creek), Oreg. 291/K5
Oregon (state), U.S. 146/F5
Oregon, Wis. (53575) 317/H10
Oregon Caves Nat'l Mon., Oreg. 291/D5
Oregon City, Oreg. 188/B1
Oregon City, Oreg. (97045) 291/B2
Oregon Dunes Nat'l Rec. Area, Oreg. 291/C4
Oregonia, Ohio (45054) 284/B7
Öregrund, Sweden 18/L6
Orel, U.S.S.R. 7/H3
Orel, U.S.S.R. 52/E4
Orel, U.S.S.R. 48/D4
Orellana, Peru 128/E6
Orellana la Vieja, Spain 33/D3
Orem, Utah (84057) 304/C3
Orenburg, U.S.S.R. 7/K3
Orenburg, U.S.S.R. 48/F4
Orenburg, U.S.S.R. 52/J4
Orenco, Oreg. (†97123) 291/A2
Orense (prov.), Spain 33/C1
Orense, Spain 33/C1
Orense, Spain 7/D4
Orestes, Ind. (46063) 227/F4
Orestías, Greece 45/H5
Øresund (sound), Denmark 21/F6
Öresund (sound), Denmark 18/H9
Öresund (sound), Sweden 18/H9
Oreti (riv.), N. Zealand 100/B6
Oretta, La. (†70660) 238/D5
Orewa, N. Zealand 100/E2
Orford○, N.H. (03777) 268/C4
Orford, Tasmania 99/D4
Orford Ness (prom.), England 13/J5
Orfordville, N.H. (†03777) 268/C4
Orfordville, Wis. (53576) 317/H10
Organ, N. Mex. (88052) 274/C6
Organabo, Fr. Guiana 131/E3
Organ Pipe Cactus Nat'l Mon., Ariz. 198/C6
Órgãos (range), Brazil 135/E3
Orgas, W. Va. (25148) 312/C6
Orgaz, Spain 33/E3
Orgeyev, U.S.S.R. 52/C5
Orhaneli, Turkey 63/C3
Orhangazi, Turkey 63/C2
Orhon Gol (riv.), Mongolia 77/F2
Oria, Spain 33/E4
Orick, Calif. (95555) 204/A2
Orient, Ill. (62874) 222/E6
Orient, Iowa (50858) 229/E6
Orient○, Maine (04471) 243/H4
Orient, N.Y. (11957) 276/R8
Orient (pt.), N.Y. 276/R8
Orient, Ohio (43146) 284/D6
Orient, S. Dak. (57467) 298/L4
Orient, Wash. (99160) 310/G2
Orienta, Okla. (73765) 288/J2
Oriental, Cordillera (range), Bolivia 136/C5
Oriental, Cordillera (range), Colombia 126/D5
Oriental, Cordillera (range), Dom. Rep. 158/F6
Oriental, Mexico 150/O1
Oriental, N.C. (28571) 281/R4
Oriental, Cordillera (range), Peru 128/H10
Oriental Mindoro (prov.), Philippines 82/C4
Orihuela, Spain 33/F3
Orihvesi (lake), Finland 18/Q5
Orillia, Ontario 177/E3
Orin, Wash. (†99114) 310/H2
Orin, Wyo. (†82633) 319/G3
Orinda, Calif. (94563) 204/J2
Orinoca, Bolivia 136/B6
Orinoco (riv.) 120/C2
Orinoco (riv.) 2/F5
Orinoco (riv.), Colombia 126/G5
Orinoco (delta), Venezuela 120/C2
Orinoco (delta), Venezuela 124/H3
Orinoco (riv.), Venezuela 124/G3
Oriole, Md. (21848) 245/P8
Orion, Ala. (†36081) 195/F7
Orion, Alberta 182/E5
Orion, Ill. (61273) 222/C2
Oriska, N. Dak. (58063) 282/P6
Oriskany, N.Y. (13424) 276/K4
Oriskany, Va. (24130) 307/J5
Oriskany Falls, N.Y. (13425) 276/J5
Orissa (state), India 68/E5
Oristano, Italy 34/B5
Oristano (gulf), Italy 34/B5
Orituco (riv.), Venezuela 124/E3
Oriximiná, Brazil 132/C3
Orizaba, Mexico 146/J8
Orizaba, Mexico 150/P2
Orizaba (Citlaltépetl) (mt.), Mexico 150/O2
Órjiva, Spain 33/E4
Orkanger, Norway 18/F5
Örkény, Hungary 41/E3
Orkney, Sask. 181/D6
Orkney (islands area), Scotland 15/E1
Orkney (trad. co.), Scotland 15/B4
Orkney (isls.), Scotland 7/D3
Orkney (isls.), Scotland 15/F1
Orkney (isls.), Scotland 10/E1
Orla, Texas (79770) 303/D10
Orland, Calif. (95963) 204/C4
Orland, Ind. (46776) 227/G1
Orland, Maine (04472) 243/F6
Orland○, Maine (04472) 243/F6
Orlândia, Brazil 135/C2
Orlando, Fla. 146/K7
Orlando, Fla. 188/K5
Orlando, Fla. (*32801) 212/E3
Orlando, Ky. (40460) 237/N6

Owyhee 423

Orlando, Okla. (73073) 288/M2
Orlando, W. Va. (26412) 312/E5
Orland Park, Ill. (60462) 222/B6
Orleães, Brazil 132/D10
Orléanais (trad. prov.) France 29
Orleans, Calif. (95556) 204/B2
Orléans, France 7/E4
Orléans, France28/D3
Orleans, Ind. (47452) 227/D7
Orleans, Iowa, (†51360) 229/C2
Orleans, (par.), La. 238/L6
Orleans, Mass. (02653) 249/O5
Orleans○, Mass. (02653) 249/O5
Orleans, Minn. (56743) 255/B2
Orleans, Nebr.(68966) 264/E4
Orleans (co.), N.Y. 276/D4
Orleans Ontario 177/J2
Orléans (isl.) Québec 172/F3
Orleans (co.), Vt. 268/C2
Orleans, Vt. (05860) 268/C2
Orleans Cross Roads, W. Va. (†25422) 312/K3
Orléansville (El Asnam), Algeria 106/E1
Orlice (riv.), Czech. 41/D1
Orlická (res.), Czech. 41/C2
Orlinda, Tenn. (37141) 237/H7
Orlová, Czech. 41/E2
Orly, France 28/B2
Orma, W. Va. (25268) 312/D5
Ormara, Pakistan 59/J4
Ormara, Pakistan 68/A3
Orme, Tenn. (35740) 237/K10
Ormea, Italy 34/A2
Ormiston, Sask. 181/F6
Ormoc, Philippines 82/E5
Ormoc (bay), Philippines 82/E5
Ormond Beach, Fla. (32074) 212/E2
Ormond-by-the-Sea, Fla. (32074) 212/E2
Ormont-Dessus, Switzerland 39/D4
Ormsby, Minn. (56162) 255/D7
Ormsby, Pa. (16741) 294/E2
Ormskirk, England 10/F2
Ormskirk, England 13/G2
Ormstown, Québec 172/D4
Orne (dept.), France 28/C3
Orne (riv.), France 28/C3
Orneta, Poland 47/E1
Ornö (isl.), Sweden 18/J2
Örnsköldsvik, Sweden 18/L5
Orobayaya, Bolivia 136/D3
Orocovis, P. Rico 161/C2
Orocué, Colombia 126/E5
Orofino, Idaho (83544) 220/B3
Orofino (creek), Idaho 220/C3
Oro Grande, Calif. (92368) 204/H9
Orogrande, Idaho (†83525) 220/C4
Orogrande, N. Mex. (88342) 274/D6
Orohena (mt.), Fr. Poly. 86/T13
Oro Ingenio, Bolivia 136/C7
Oroluk (atoll), Micronesia 87/F5
Oromocto, New Bruns. 170/D3
Oromocto (lake), New Bruns. 170/C3
Oromocto (riv.), New Bruns. 170/D3
Oron, Israel 65/C6
Oron, Nigeria 106/F8
Orona (Hull) (isl.), Kiribati 87/J6
Orondo, Wash. (98843) 310/E3
Orongorongo (riv.), N. Zealand 100/B3
Oron-la-Ville, Switzerland 39/C3
Orono, Maine (04473) 243/F6
Orono○, Maine (04473) 243/F6
Orono, Minn. (†55323) 255/F5
Oronoco, Minn. (55960) 255/F6
Oronogo, Mo. (64855) 261/D8
Oronsay (isl.), Scotland 15/B4
Orontes (riv.), Syria 59/C2
Orontes (riv.), Syria 63/G5
Oropesa, Spain 33/D3
Oropuche (riv.), Trin. & Tob. 161/B10
Oroqen, China 77/K1
Oroquieta, Philippines 85/G4
Oroquieta, Philippines 82/D6
Orosei (gulf), Italy 34/B4
Orosháza, Hungary 41/F3
Orosi, Calif. (93647) 204/F7
Oroszlány, Hungary 41/E3
Orote (pen.), Guam 86/K7
Orotina, C. Rica 154/E6
Orotukan, U.S.S.R. 48/Q3
Orovada, Nev. (89425) 266/D1
Oro Valley, Ariz. (†85704) 198/E6
Oroville, Calif. (95965) 204/D4
Oroville (lake), Calif. 204/D4
Oroville, Wash. (98844) 310/F2
Orozco, Cuba 158/B1
Orpha, Wyo. (†82633) 319/G3
Orr, Minn. (55771) 255/F2
Orr, N. Dak. (†58244) 282/P3
Orr, Okla. (†73456) 288/M6
Orrefors, Sweden 18/J8
Orrick, Mo. (64077) 261/D4
Orrin, N. Dak. (58359) 282/K3
Orrin (riv.), Scotland 15/D3
Orrington, Maine (04474) 243/F6
Orrington○, Maine (04474) 243/F6
Orroroo, S. Australia 94/F5
Orrs Island, Maine (04066) 243/D8
Orrstown, Pa. (17244) 294/G5
Orrtanna, Pa. (17353) 294/H6
Orrum, N.C. (28369) 281/L6
Orrville, Ala. (36767) 195/D6
Orrville, Ohio (44667) 284/G4
Orrville, Ontario 177/E2
Orsa, Sweden 18/J6
Orsainville, Québec 172/H3
Orsha, U.S.S.R. 7/G3
Orsha, U.S.S.R. 52/C4
Orsières, Switzerland 39/D4
Orsk, U.S.S.R. 7/K3
Orsk, U.S.S.R. 48/F4
Orsk, U.S.S.R. 52/J4
Orson, Pa. (18449) 294/M2
Orsonnens, Switzerland 39/D3
Orşova, Romania 45/F3
Ørsted, Denmark 21/D5
Orta, Turkey 63/E2
Ortaca, Turkey 63/C4
Ortakaraviran, Turkey 63/E4
Ortaköy, Çorum, Turkey 63/F2
Ortaköy, Niğde, Turkey 63/F3
Ortega, Colombia 126/C6
Ortegal (cape), Spain 33/B1
Orteguaza (riv.), Colombia 126/C7
Orthez, France 28/C6
Ortigueira, Spain 33/C1
Orting, Wash. (98360) 310/C3
Ortiz, Colo. (†81120) 208/H8
Ortiz, Mexico 150/D2
Ortiz, Venezuela 124/E3
Ortles (range), Italy 34/C1
Ortley, S. Dak. (57256) 298/P3
Ortoire (riv.), Trin. & Tob. 161/B11
Ortón (riv.), Bolivia 136/B2
Ortona, Italy 34/E3
Ortonville, Mich. (48462) 250/F6
Ortonville, Minn. (56278) 255/B5
Oruro (dept.), Bolivia 136/A6
Oruro, Bolivia 120/C4
Oruro, Bolivia 136/B5
Oruzgan (Hazar Qadam), Afghanistan 68/B2
Orvieto, Italy 34/D3
Orville, Ky. (40057) 237/M4
Orviston, Pa. (16864) 294/G3
Orwell, N.Y. (13426) 276/J3
Orwell, Ohio (44076) 284/J2
Orwell○, Vt. (05760) 268/A4
Orwigsburg, Pa. (17961) 294/K4
Oryakhovo, Bulgaria 45/F4
Or Yehuda, Israel 65/B4
Orzesze, Poland 47/A4
Orzysz, Poland 47/E2
Osa, U.S.S.R. 52/J3
Osage (riv.) 188/H3
Osage, Ark. (†72638) 202/D1
Osage, Iowa (50461) 229/H2
Osage (co.), Kansas 232/G3
Osage, Minn. (56570) 255/C4
Osage (co.), Mo. 261/J6
Osage (riv.), Mo. 261/E6
Osage (co.), Okla. 288/O1
Osage, Okla. (74054) 288/O2
Osage, Sask. 181/H6
Osage, W. Va. (26543) 312/F3
Osage, Wyo. (82723) 319/H2
Osage Beach, Mo. (65065) 261/G6
Osage City, Kansas (66523) 232/G3
Osage Ind. Res., Okla. 288/O1
Osaka (pref.), Japan 81/J8
Osaka, Japan 2/R4
Osaka, Japan 54/P6
Osaka, Japan 81/J8
Osaka (bay), Japan 81/H8
Osakis, Minn. (56360) 255/C5
Osasco, Brazil 135/C3
Osawatomie, Kansas (66064) 232/H3
Osborn, Miss. (†39759) 256/G3
Osborn, Mo. (64474) 261/D3
Osborn, S.C. (†29426) 296/G6
Osborne (co.), Kansas 232/D2
Osborne, Kansas (67473) 232/D2
Osborne, Pa. (†15143) 294/B4
Osbornsville, N.J. (08723) 273/E3
Osburn, Idaho (83849) 220/B2
Oscar, Fr. Guiana 131/E4
Oscar, La. (70762) 238/H5
Oscar, Okla. (73561) 288/L7
Oscarville, Alaska (†99559) 196/F2
Osceola, Ark. (72370) 202/K2
Osceola (co.), Fla. 212/E3
Osceola, Ind. (46561) 227/E1
Osceola (co.), Iowa 229/B2
Osceola, Iowa (50213) 229/F6
Osceola (co.), Mich. 250/D5
Osceola, Mo. (64776) 261/E6
Osceola, Nebr. (68651) 264/G3
Osceola (mt.), N.H. 268/E3
Osceola, N.Y. (†13316) 276/J3
Osceola, Pa. (16942) 294/H2
Osceola, S. Dak. (†57353) 298/O5
Osceola, Wis. (54020) 317/A5
Osceola Mills, Pa. (16666) 294/F4
Oschatz, E. Germany 22/E3
Oschersleben, E. Germany 22/D2
Oscoda (co.), Mich. 250/E4
Oscoda, Mich. (48750) 250/F4
Oscura (mts.), N. Mex. 274/C5
Oscuro, N. Mex. (†88301) 274/C5
Ösel (Saaremaa) (isl.), U.S.S.R. 52/B3
Osgood, Ind. (47037) 227/G6
Osgood, Mo. (†63556) 261/F2
Osgood, Ohio (45351) 284/A5
Osgoode, Ontario 177/J2
Osh, U.S.S.R. 54/J5
Osh, U.S.S.R. 48/H5
Osha (peak), N. Mex. 274/C4
Oshawa, Ontario 177/F4
Oshikango, Namibia 118/A3
O-Shima (isl.), Japan 81/J6
Oshkosh, Nebr. (69154) 264/B3
Oshkosh, Wis. 188/J2
Oshkosh, Wis. (54901) 317/J8
Oshnoviyeh, Iran 66/D2
Oshogbo, Nigeria 102/C4
Oshogbo, Nigeria 106/F7
Oshoto, Wyo. (82724) 319/G1
Oshtoran Kuh (mt.), Iran 66/F4
Oshwe, Zaire 115/C4
Osierfield, Georgia (†31798) 217/F7
Osijek, Yugoslavia 7/F4
Osijek, Yugoslavia 45/D3
Osimo, Italy 34/D3
Osipenko (Berdyansk), U.S.S.R. 52/E5
Osipovichi, U.S.S.R. 52/C4
Oskaloosa, Iowa (52577) 229/H6
Oskaloosa, Iowa 188/H2
Oskaloosa, Kansas (66066) 232/G2
Oskaloosa, Mo. (†66711) 261/D7
Oskarshamn, Sweden 18/K8
Oskélanéo, Québec 174/C3
Oslavany, Czech. 41/D2
Osler, Sask. 181/E3
Oslo, Minn. (56744) 255/A2
Oslo (city), Norway 18/D3
Oslo (cap.), Norway 2/K2
Oslo (cap.), Norway 7/F2
Oslo (cap.), Norway 18/D3
Oslofjord (fjord), Norway 18/D4
Osmanabad, India 68/D5
Osmancık, Turkey 63/F2
Osmaneli, Turkey 63/D2
Osmaniye, Turkey 63/G4
Osmond, Nebr. (68765) 264/G2
Osnabrock, N. Dak. (58269) 282/O2
Osnabrück, W. Germany 22/C2
Osnaburgh House, Ontario 175/B2
Oso, Wash. (98223) 310/D2
Osogna, Switzerland 39/H4
Osorno, Chile 120/B7
Osorno, Chile 138/D3
Osorno, Spain 33/D1
Osoyoos, Br. Col. 184/H5
Osoyoos (lake), Wash. 310/F1
Ospino, Venezuela 124/D3
Osprey (reef), 95/C2
Osprey, Fla. (33559) 212/D4
Osprey (reef), Queensland 88/H2
Oss, Netherlands 27/H5
Ossa, Serra da (mts.), Portugal 33/C3
Ossa (mt.), Tasmania 88/H8
Ossa (mt.), Tasmania 99/C3
Ossabaw (isl.), Georgia 217/K7
Ossabaw (sound), Georgia 217/K7
Osse (riv.), Nigeria 106/F7
Osseo, Mich. (49266) 250/E7
Osseo, Minn. (55369) 255/G5
Osseo, Wis. (54758) 317/D6
Ossian, Ind. (46777) 227/G3
Ossian, Iowa (52161) 229/K2
Ossineke, Mich. (49766) 250/F4
Ossining, N.Y. (10562) 276/N8
Ossipee○, N.H. (03864) 268/E4
Ossipee (lake), N.H. 268/E4
Ossipee (mts.), N.H. 268/E4
Ossipee (riv.), N.H. 268/F4
Ossokmanuan (res.), Newf. 166/B3
Ostashkov, U.S.S.R. 52/D3
Oste (riv.), W. Germany 22/C2
Osteen, Fla. (32764) 212/E3
Ostend, Belgium 27/B6
Osterburg, Pa. (16667) 294/E5
Österdalälven (riv.), Sweden 18/H6
Osterdock, Iowa (†52035) 229/L3
Östergötland (co.), Sweden 18/J7
Osterholz-Scharmbeck, W. Germany 22/C2
Osterode am Harz, W. Germany 22/D3
Östersund, Sweden 7/F2
Östersund, Sweden 18/J5
Osterville, Mass. (02655) 249/N6
Øster Vrå, Denmark 21/D3
Osterwick, Manitoba 179/D5
Østfold (co.), Norway 18/G7
Östhammar, Sweden 18/L6
Ostia Antica, Italy 34/F7
Ostrander, Minn. (55961) 255/F7
Ostrander, Ohio (43061) 284/D5
Ostrava, Czech. 7/F4
Ostrava, Czech. 41/E2
Ostróda, Poland 47/D2
Ostrogozhsk, U.S.S.R. 48/D4
Ostrogozhsk, U.S.S.R. 52/E4
Ostrołęka (prov.), Poland 47/E2
Ostrołęka, Poland 47/E2
Ostrov, Czech. 41/B1
Ostrov, U.S.S.R. 52/C3
Ostrowiec Świętokrzyski, Poland 47/E3
Ostrów Mazowiecka, Poland 47/E2
Ostrów Wielkopolski, Poland 47/C3
Ostrzeszów, Poland 47/C3
Ostuni, Italy 34/F4
O'Sullivan (dam), Wash. 310/F4
Osŭm (riv.), Bulgaria 45/G4
Osumi (isls.), Japan 81/E8
Osumi (pen.), Japan 81/E8
Osumi (str.), Japan 81/E8
Osuna, Spain 33/D4
Oswaldtwistle, England 13/H1
Oswayo, Pa. (16915) 294/G2
Oswegatchie, N.Y. (13670) 276/K2
Oswegatchie (riv.), N.Y. 276/K2
Oswego, Ill. (60543) 222/E2
Oswego, Ind. (†46538) 227/F2
Oswego, Kansas (67356) 232/G4
Oswego, Mont. (59251) 262/L2
Oswego (riv.), N.J. 273/E4
Oswego, N.Y. 188/L2
Oswego (co.), N.Y. 276/H4
Oswego, N.Y. (13126) 276/G4
Oswego (riv.), N.Y. 276/H4
Oswego, S.C. (29121) 296/G3
Oswestry, England 10/E4
Oswestry, England 13/E5
Oświęcim, Poland 47/D3
Osyka, Miss. (39657) 256/D8
Ota, Japan 81/J5
Otago (harb.), N. Zealand 100/C6
Otago (pen.), N. Zealand 100/C6
Otahuhu, N. Zealand 100/C1
Otaki, N. Zealand 100/E4
Otakine (mt.), Japan 81/K5
Otaru, Japan 81/K2
Otautau, N. Zealand 100/B7
Otava (riv.), Czech. 41/B2
Otavalo, Ecuador 128/C2
Otavi, Namibia 118/B3
Otawara, Japan 81/K5
O.T. Downs, North Terr. 93/D4
Oteen, N.C. (28805) 281/E3
Otego, N.Y. (13825) 276/K6
Otematata, N. Zealand 100/B6
Otero (co.), Colo. 208/M7
Otero (co.), N. Mex. 274/D6
Othello, Wash. (99344) 310/F4
Otho, Iowa (50569) 229/E4
Oti (riv.), Ghana 106/E7
Oti (riv.), Togo 106/E7
Oti (riv.), Upper Volta 106/E7
Otira, N. Zealand 100/C5
Otis, Colo. (80743) 208/O2
Otis, Ind. (46367) 227/D1
Otis, Kansas (67565) 232/C3
Otis, La. (71466) 238/E4
Otis○, Mass. (01253) 249/B4
Otis (res.), Mass. 249/B4
Otis, N. Mex. (†88220) 274/E6
Otis, Oreg. (97368) 291/D2
Otis, Québec 172/G1
Otis A.F.B., Mass. 249/M6
Otisco, Ind. (47163) 227/F7
Otisco, Minn. (56077) 255/E7
Otisco (lake), N.Y. 276/H5
Otisfield, Maine (†04270) 243/B7
Otisfield○, Maine (†04270) 243/B7
Otish (mts.), Québec 174/C2
Otis Orchards-East Farms, Wash. (99027) 310/H3
Otisville, Mich. (48463) 250/F5
Otisville, N.Y. (10963) 276/L8
Otjiwarongo, Namibia 102/D7
Otjiwarongo, Namibia 118/B4
Otley, Iowa (50214) 229/G6
Oto, Iowa (51044) 229/B4
Otoe (co.), Nebr. 264/H4
Otoe, Nebr. (68417) 264/H4
Otofuke, Japan 81/L2
Otog, China 77/G4
Otorohanga, N. Zealand 100/E3
Otoskwin (riv.), Ontario 175/B2
Otra (riv.), Norway 18/E7
Otrabanda, Neth. Ant. 161/F9
Otradnyy, U.S.S.R. 52/H4
Otranto (str.), Albania 45/D5
Otranto, Iowa (†50472) 229/H2
Otranto, Italy 34/G4
Otranto (str.), Italy 34/G5
Otsego (co.), Mich. 250/E3
Otsego, Mich. (49078) 250/D6
Otsego (lake), Mich. 250/E4
Otsego (co.), N.Y. 276/K5
Otsego (lake), N.Y. 276/L5
Otsego, Ohio (†43762) 284/G5
Otsego Lake, Mich. (†49735) 250/E4
Otselic (riv.), N.Y. 276/J5
Otsu, Japan 81/J7
Otta, Norway 18/F6
Ottauquechee (riv.), Vt. 268/B4
Ottawa (riv.) 162/J6
Ottawa (cap.), Canada 2/F3
Ottawa (cap.), Canada 146/L5
Ottawa (cap.), Canada 162/J6
Ottawa (riv.), Canada 146/L5
Ottawa, Ill. (61350) 222/E2
Ottawa (co.), Kansas 232/E2
Ottawa, Kansas (66067) 232/G3
Ottawa (co.), Mich. 250/C6
Ottawa, Minn. (†56058) 255/E6
Ottawa (isls.), N.W.T. 146/K4
Ottawa (isls.), N.W.T. 162/H4
Ottawa (isls.), N.W. Terrs. 187/K4
Ottawa (co.), Ohio 284/D2
Ottawa, Ohio (45875) 284/B3
Ottawa (co.), Okla. 288/S1
Ottawa (cap.), Canada, Ontario 177/J2
Ottawa (riv.), Ontario 175/E3
Ottawa (riv.), Ontario 177/H2
Ottawa (riv.), Québec 172/B4
Ottawa (riv.), Québec 174/B3
Ottawa Beach, Mich. (†49423) 250/C6
Ottawa-Carleton (reg. munic.), Ontario 177/J2
Ottawa Hills, Ohio (†43601) 284/C2
Ottawa Lake, Mich. (49267) 250/F7
Otter (isl.), Alaska 196/D3
Otter (lakes), Alberta 182/B1
Otter, Mont. (59062) 262/K5
Otter (creek), Utah 304/C5
Otter (creek), Utah 304/C2
Otter (creek), Vt. 268/A3
Otterbein, Ind. (47970) 227/C4
Otterburne, Manitoba 179/E5
Otterburn Park, Québec 172/D4
Otter Creek, Fla. (32683) 212/D2
Otter Creek, Maine (04665) 243/G7
Otter Creek (res.), Utah 304/C5
Otter Lake, Mich. (48464) 250/F5
Otterlo, Netherlands 27/H4
Otterøya (isl.), Norway 18/E5
Otter River, Mass. (†01440) 249/F2
Otter Rock, Oreg. (97369) 291/C3
Otter Tail (co.), Minn. 255/C4
Ottertail, Minn. (56571) 255/C4
Otter Tail (lake), Minn. 255/C4
Otter Tail (riv.), Minn. 255/B4
Otterup, Denmark 21/D7
Otterville, Ill. (†62052) 222/C4
Otterville, Iowa (†50644) 229/K3
Otterville, Mo. (65348) 261/G5
Otterville, Ontario 177/D5
Ottery Saint Mary, England 13/D7
Ottery Saint Mary, England 10/E5
Otthon, Sask. 181/J4
Ottleys (creek), N.S. Wales 97/F1
Otto, Ind. (†47162) 227/G7
Otto, Mo. (63052) 261/M6
Otto, N.Y. (14766) 276/C6
Otto, N.C. (28763) 281/C4
Otto (fjord), N.W. Terrs. 187/K1
Otto, Wyo. (82434) 319/D1
Ottosen, Iowa (50570) 229/E3
Ottoville, Ohio (45876) 284/B4
Ottsville, Pa. (18942) 294/M5
Ottumwa, Iowa 188/H2
Ottumwa, Iowa (52501) 229/J6
Ottumwa, S. Dak. (57565) 298/G5
Otumba de Gómez Farías, Mexico 150/M1
Otuquis (riv.), Bolivia 136/F6
Otuzco, Peru 128/C6
Otway (bay), Chile 138/D10
Otway (sound), Chile 138/E10
Otway, Ohio (45657) 284/D8
Otway (cape), Victoria 97/B6
Otway (cape), Victoria 88/G7
Otwell, Ark. (†72401) 202/J2
Otwell, Ind. (47564) 227/C8
Otwock, Poland 47/E2
Ötztal Alps (mts.), Austria 41/A3
Ötztal Alps (range), Italy 34/C1
Ou, Nam (riv.), Laos 72/D2
Ouachita (riv.) 188/H4
Ouachita (co.), Ark. 202/E6
Ouachita, Ark. (†71263) 202/E6
Ouachita (lake), Ark. 202/C4
Ouachita (mts.), Ark. 202/B4
Ouachita (riv.), Ark. 202/E7
Ouachita (par.), La. 238/F2
Ouachita (riv.), La. 238/F1
Ouachita (mts.), Okla. 288/R5
Ouadane, Mauritania 106/B4
Ouadda, Cent. Afr. Rep. 115/D2
Ouagadougou (cap.), Upper Volta 106/D6
Ouagadougou (cap.), Upper Volta 102/B3
Ouahigouya, Upper Volta 106/D6
Ouahigouya, Upper Volta 102/B3
Oualata, Mauritania 106/C5
Ouallene, Algeria 106/E4
Ouanaminthe, Haiti 158/C5
Ouanary, Fr. Guiana 131/F3
Ouanda Djallé, Cent. Afr. Rep. 115/D2
Ouango, Cent. Afr. Rep. 115/D3
Ouaqui, Fr. Guiana 131/D4
Ouarane (reg.), Mauritania 106/B4
Ouareau (lake), Québec 172/D3
Ouareau (riv.), Québec 172/D3
Ouargla, Algeria 106/F2
Ouargla, Algeria 102/C1
Ouarzazate, Morocco 106/C2
Ouchy, Switzerland 39/C4
Oud-Beijerland, Netherlands 27/E5
Ouddorp, Netherlands 27/D5
Oudenaarde, Belgium 27/D7
Oudenbosch, Netherlands 27/E5
Oudenburg, Belgium 27/B6
Oude-Pekela, Netherlands 27/K2
Oudeschild, Netherlands 27/F2
Oude-Tonge, Netherlands 27/E5
Oudewater, Netherlands 27/F4
Oudtshoorn, S. Africa 102/E8
Oudtshoorn, S. Africa 118/C6
Oud-Turnhout, Belgium 27/F6
Oued Zem, Morocco 106/C2
Ouelle (riv.), Québec 172/H2
Ouellette, Maine (†04743) 243/G1
Ouémé (riv.), Benin 106/E7
Ouessant (isl.), France 28/A3
Ouesso, Congo 115/C3
Ouest (dept.), Haiti 158/C6
Ouest (pt.), Haiti 158/B4
Ouest (pt.), Haiti 158/B6
Ouezzane, Morocco 106/C2
Oughter (lake), Ireland 17/G3
Oughterard, Ireland 17/C5
Ouham (riv.), Cent. Afr. Rep. 115/C2
Ouham (riv.), Chad 111/C6
Ouidah, Benin 106/E7
Oujaf, Mauritania 106/C5
Oujda, Morocco 106/D2
Oujda, Morocco 102/B1
Oujeft, Mauritania 106/B4
Oulainen, Finland 18/O4
Ouled Djellal, Algeria 106/F2
Oullins, France 28/F5
Oulu (prov.), Finland 18/P4
Oulu, Finland 7/G2
Oulu, Finland 18/O4
Oulu (lake), Finland 7/G2
Oulujärvi (lake), Finland 18/P4
Oulujoki (riv.), Finland 18/O4
Oum Chalouba, Chad 111/D4
Oum el Asel (well), Mali 106/D4
Oum Hadjer, Chad 102/E3
Oum Hadjer, Chad 111/D5
Ounas (riv.), Finland 7/G2
Ounasjoki (riv.), Finland 18/O3
Oundle, England 13/G5
Oungre, Sask. 181/H6
Ounianga-Kébir, Chad 111/D4
Oupeye, Belgium 27/H7
Oupu, China 77/L1
Our (riv.), Luxembourg 27/J9
Our (riv.), W. Germany 22/B3
Ouray (co.), Colo. 208/D6
Ouray, Colo. (81427) 208/D6
Ouray (peak), Colo. 208/G6
Ouray, Utah (†84026) 304/E3
Ourinhos, Brazil 132/D8
Ourinhos, Brazil 135/B3
Ourique, Portugal 33/B4
Ouro Fino, Brazil 132/E8
Ouro Fino, Brazil 135/C3
Ouro Preto, Brazil 132/F8
Ouro Preto, Brazil 135/E2
Ourthe (riv.), Belgium 27/G8
Ouse (riv.), England 13/G6
Ouse (riv.), England 13/G4
Ouse, Tasmania 99/C4
Ouse (riv.), Tasmania 99/C4
Ousley, Georgia (†31601) 217/F9
Outagamie (co.), Wis. 317/K7
Outardes (riv.), Québec 174/D2
Outer (isl.), Wis. 317/F1
Outer Harbor, S. Australia 94/A7
Outer Hebrides (isls.), Scotland 15/A3
Outer Santa Barbara (passage), Calif. 204/G10
Outing, Minn. (56662) 255/E4
Outjo, Namibia 118/B4
Outjo, Namibia 102/D7
Outlook, Mont. (59252) 262/M2
Outlook, Sask. 181/E4
Outlook, Wash. (98938) 310/E4
Outokumpu, Finland 18/Q5
Outram, Sask. 181/H6
Outremont, Québec 172/H4
Ouyen, Victoria 88/G7
Ouyen, Victoria 97/B4
Ouzinkie, Alaska (99644) 196/H3
Ovacık, Çankırı, Turkey 63/E2
Ovacık, İçel, Turkey 63/E4
Ovacık, Tunceli, Turkey 63/H3
Ovalau (isl.), Fiji 86/Q10
Ovalle, Chile 120/B6
Ovalle, Chile 138/A8
Ovamboland (reg.), Namibia 118/B3
Ovando, Mont. (59854) 262/C3
Ovar, Portugal 33/B2
Ovens (riv.), Victoria 97/D5
Overall, Tenn. (†37130) 237/J9
Overbrook, Kansas (66524) 232/G3
Overbrook, Okla. (73453) 288/M6
Overflakkee (isl.), Netherlands 27/E5
Overflow (bay), Manitoba 179/A1
Overflowing (riv.), Manitoba 179/A1
Overflowing (riv.), Sask. 181/K2
Overflowing River, Manitoba 179/A1
Overgaard, Ariz. (85933) 198/E4
Overhills, N.C. (28370) 281/L4
Overijse, Belgium 27/F7
Overijssel (prov.), Netherlands 27/J4
Overisel, Mich. (†49423) 250/C6
Överkalix, Sweden 18/N3
Overland, Mo. (63114) 261/O2
Overland Park, Kansas (66204) 232/H3
Overlea, Md. (21206) 245/N3
Overloon, Netherlands 27/H5
Overly, N. Dak. (58360) 282/K2
Overpelt, Belgium 27/G6
Overstreet, Fla. (32453) 212/D6
Overton, Nebr. (68863) 264/E4
Overton, Nev. (89040) 266/G6
Overton, Pa. (†18833) 294/K2
Overton (co.), Tenn. 237/L8
Overton, Texas (75684) 303/K5
Övertorneå, Sweden 18/N3
Överum, Sweden 18/K7
Ovett, Miss. (39464) 256/F8
Ovid, Colo. (80744) 208/P1
Ovid, Idaho (83260) 220/G7
Ovid, Mich. (48866) 250/E5
Ovid, N.Y. (14521) 276/G5
Oviedo, Dom. Rep. 158/D7
Oviedo, Fla. (32765) 212/E3
Oviedo (prov.), Spain 33/C1
Oviedo, Spain 33/C1
Oviedo, Spain 7/D4
Ovilla, Texas (†76065) 303/G2
Ovoca (riv.), Ireland 17/J6
Övörhangay, Mongolia 77/F2
Øvre-Sirdal, Norway 18/E7
Ovruch, U.S.S.R. 52/C4
Ovtrup, Denmark 21/B6
Owaka, N. Zealand 100/B7
Owando, Congo 115/C4
Owando, Congo 102/D5
Owaneco, Ill. (62555) 222/D4
Owanka, S. Dak. (57767) 298/D5
Owasa, Iowa (†50627) 229/G4
Owasco, N.Y. (13130) 276/G5
Owasco (lake), N.Y. 276/G5
Owase, Japan 81/H6
Owassa, Ala. (†36401) 195/E8
Owassa (lake), N.J. 273/D1
Owasso, Okla. (74055) 288/P2
Owatonna, Minn. (55060) 255/E6
Owbeh, Afghanistan 68/A2
Owbeh, Afghanistan 59/H3
Owego, N.Y. (13827) 276/H6
Owel (lake), Ireland 17/G4
Owen (co.), Ind. 227/D6
Owen (co.), Ky. 237/M3
Owen (mt.), N. Zealand 100/D4
Owen (chan.), Ontario 177/C2
Owen (sound), Ontario 177/D3
Owen, Wis. (54460) 317/F6
Owen (lake), Wis. 317/D3
Owendale, Alberta 182/D5
Owendale, Mich. (48754) 250/F5
Owendo, Gabon 115/A3
Owen Falls (dam), Uganda 115/F3
Owenga, N. Zealand 100/E7
Owenkillew (riv.), N. Ireland 17/G2
Owenmore (riv.), Ireland 17/D3
Owenmore (riv.), Ireland 17/B3
Owens (lake), Calif. 188/C3
Owens (lake), Calif. 204/H7
Owens (peak), Calif. 204/H8
Owens (riv.), Calif. 204/G6
Owensboro, Ky. (42301) 237/G5
Owensboro, Ky. 188/J3
Owensburg, Ind. (47453) 227/D7
Owens Cross Roads, Ala. (35763) 195/E1
Owen Sound, Ont. 162/H7
Owen Sound, Ontario 177/D3
Owensville, Ark. (†72087) 202/E4
Owensville, Ind. (47665) 227/B8
Owensville, Mo. (65066) 261/K6
Owensville, Ohio (45160) 284/B7
Owenton, Ky. (40359) 237/M3
Owenton, Va. (†23077) 307/O5
Owerri, Nigeria 106/F7
Owey (isl.), Ireland 17/D1
Owia (bay), St. Vin. & Grens. 161/A8
Owikeno (lake), Br. Col. 184/D4
Owings, Md. (20836) 245/M6
Owings, S.C. (†29645) 296/C2
Owings Mills, Md. (21117) 245/L3
Owingsville, Ky. (40360) 237/O4
Owl (creek), Colo. 208/K1
Owl (riv.), Manitoba 179/K2
Owl (creek), S. Dak. 298/B4
Owl, North Fork (creek), Wyo. 319/D2
Owl Creek (mts.), Wyo. 319/D2
Owl River, Alberta 182/E2
Owlseye, Alberta 182/E2
Owls Head○, Maine (04854) 243/F7
Owo, Nigeria 106/F7
Owosso, Mich. (48867) 250/E5
Owraman, Iran 66/E3
Owsley (co.), Ky. 237/O6
Owyhee (riv.) 188/C2
Owyhee (co.), Idaho 220/B7
Owyhee (mts.), Idaho 220/B6
Owyhee, East Fork (riv.), Idaho 220/B7
Owyhee, Nev. (89832) 266/F1
Owyhee (riv.), Nev. 266/E1
Owyhee (dam), Oreg. 291/K4
Owyhee (lake), Oreg. 291/K4
Owyhee (mts.), Oreg. 291/K4
Owyhee, North Fork (riv.), Oreg. 291/K5
Owyhee (riv.), Oreg. 291/K5

Ox (Slieve Gamph) (mts.), Ireland 17/D3
Oxapampa, Peru 128/E8
Oxbow (dam), Idaho 220/B5
Oxbow○, Maine (04764) 243/G3
Oxbow, Oreg. (97840) 291/L2
Oxbow (dam), Oreg. 291/L3
Oxbow, Sask. 181/J6
Oxelösund, Sweden 18/K7
Oxford, Ala. (36203) 195/G3
Oxford, Ark. (72565) 202/G1
Oxford○, Conn. (06483) 210/C3
Oxford, England 13/F6
Oxford, England 10/F5
Oxford, Fla. (32684) 212/D3
Oxford, Georgia (30267) 217/E3
Oxford, Idaho (†83263) 220/F7
Oxford, Ind. (47971) 227/C3
Oxford, Iowa (52322) 229/K5
Oxford, Kansas (67119) 232/E4
Oxford, La. (†71052) 238/C3
Oxford (co.), Maine 243/B7
Oxford, Maine (04270) 243/B7
Oxford○, Maine (04270) 243/B7
Oxford (lake), Manitoba 179/J3
Oxford, Md. (21654) 245/O6
Oxford, Mass. (01540) 249/G4
Oxford○, Mass. (01540) 249/G4
Oxford, Mich. (48051) 250/F6
Oxford, Miss. (38655) 256/F2
Oxford, Nebr. (68967) 264/E4
Oxford, N.J. (07863) 273/C2
Oxford, N.Y. (13830) 276/J6
Oxford, N. Zealand 100/D5
Oxford, N.C. (27565) 281/M2
Oxford, Nova Scotia 168/E3
Oxford, Ohio (45056) 284/A6
Oxford, Pa. (19363) 294/K6
Oxford, W. Va. (†26456) 312/E4
Oxford, Wis. (53952) 317/H8
Oxford House, Manitoba 179/J3
Oxford Junction, Iowa (52323) 229/M4
Oxford Junction, Nova Scotia 168/E3
Oxford Mills, Iowa (†52323) 229/L5
Oxford Mills, Ontario 177/J3
Oxfordshire (co.), England 13/F6
Oxkutzcab, Mexico 150/P6
Oxley, N.S. Wales 97/C4
Oxley (creek), Queensland 95/D3
Oxly, Mo. (63955) 261/L9
Oxnard, Calif. (93030) 204/F9
Oxnard A.F.B., Calif. 204/F9
Oxon Hill, Md. (20745) 245/F6
Oxon Run (riv.), Md. 245/F5
Oxton, Scotland 15/F5
Oxtongue Lake, Ontario 177/E2
Oyabe, Japan 81/H5
Oyahue (vol.), Chile 138/C3
Oyama, Br. Col. 184/H5
Oyama, Japan 81/J5
Oyapock (riv.) 120/D2
Oyapock (riv.), Brazil 132/C2
Oyapock (riv.), Fr. Guiana 131/E4
Oyem, Gabon 102/D4
Oyem, Gabon 115/B3
Oyen, Alberta 182/E4
Oyens, Iowa (51045) 229/A3
Oykel (riv.), Scotland 15/D3
Oykel Bridge, Scotland 15/D3
Oylen, Minn. (†56481) 255/D4
Oymyakon, U.S.S.R. 4/C2
Oymyakon, U.S.S.R. 48/O3
Oyo, Congo 115/C4
Oyo (state), Nigeria 106/E7
Oyo, Nigeria 106/E7
Oyón, Peru 128/D8
Oyonnax, France 28/F4
Oyster (bay), Tasmania 88/H8
Oyster (bay), Tasmania 99/E4
Oyster, Va. (23419) 307/S6
Oyster Bay, N.Y. (11771) 276/R6
Oyster River (pt.), Conn. 210/D4
Oysterville, Wash. (98641) 310/A4
Özalp, Turkey 63/K3
Ozamiz, Philippines 82/D6
Ozan, Ark. (71855) 202/C6
Ozark (mts.) 188/H3
Ozark, Ala. (36360) 195/G8
Ozark, Ark. (72949) 202/C3
Ozark (lake), Ark. 202/C3
Ozark (plat.), Ark. 202/C1
Ozark (res.), Ark. 202/C3
Ozark, Ill. (62972) 222/E6
Ozark (co.), Mo. 261/H9
Ozark, Mo. (65721) 261/F8
Ozark (plat.), Mo. 261/E9
Ozark Nat'l Scenic Riverways, Mo. 261/K8
Ozarks, Lake of the (lake), Mo. 261/F6
Ozaukee (co.), Wis. 317/L9
Ozawkie, Kansas (66070) 232/G2
Ózd, Hungary 41/F2
Ozernovskiy, U.S.S.R. 48/Q4
Ozernoy (cape), U.S.S.R. 48/R4
Ozette, Wash. (†98326) 310/A2
Ozette (lake), Wash. 310/A2
Ozette Ind. Res., Wash. 310/A2
Ozieri, Italy 34/B4
Ozona, Fla. (33560) 212/D3
Ozona, Texas (76943) 303/C7
Ozone, Ark. (72854) 202/D2
Ozone, Tenn. (37842) 237/M9
Ozorków, Poland 47/D3
Ozu, Japan 81/F7
Ozuluama, Mexico 150/L6
Ozumba de Alzate, Mexico 150/M1

P

Pa-an, Burma 72/C3
Paarden (bay), Neth. Ant. 161/D10
Paarl, S. Africa 102/D8
Paarl, S. Africa 118/F6
Paauhau, Hawaii (96775) 218/H4
Paauilo, Hawaii (96776) 218/H4
Paavola, Finland 18/O4
Pabbay (isl.), Scotland 15/A4
Pabbay (isl.), Scotland 15/A3
Pabianice, Poland 47/D3
Pablo, Mont. (59855) 262/B3
Pabna, Bangladesh 68/F4
Pabos, Québec 172/D2
Pabos-Mills, Québec 172/D2
Pabrade, U.S.S.R. 53/C3
Pacajá Grande (riv.), Brazil 132/D4
Pacaraimã, Serra da (mts.), Brazil 132/H8
Pacaraima, Sierra (mts.), Venezuela 124/G5
Pacasmayo, Peru 128/C6
Pace, Fla. (32570) 212/B6
Pace, Miss. (38764) 256/C3
Pachaug, Conn. (†06351) 210/H2
Pachaug (pond), Conn. 210/H2
Pachaug (riv.), Conn. 210/H2
Pacheco, Calif. (94553) 204/K1
Pachino, Italy 34/E6
Pachitea (riv.), Peru 128/E7
Pachiza, Peru 128/D6
Pachmarhi, India 68/D4
Pacho, Colombia 126/C5
Pachuca de Soto, Mexico 150/K6
Pachuta, Miss. (39347) 256/G6
Pacific (ocean) 54/T5
Pacific (ocean) 146/E6
Pacific, Mo. (63069) 261/L5
Pacific (co.), Wash. 310/B4
Pacific, Wash. (98047) 310/C3
Pacifica, Calif. (94044) 204/H2
Pacific Beach, Calif. (92109) 204/H11
Pacific Beach, Wash. (98571) 310/A3
Pacific City, Oreg. (97135) 291/C2
Pacific Grove, Calif. (93950) 204/C7
Pacific Heights, Hawaii (†96801) 218/C4
Pacific Islands, Terr. of the 87/F5
Pacific Islands, Territory of the 2/S5
Pacific Junction, Iowa (51561) 229/B6
Pacific Palisades, Hawaii (†96782) 218/E2
Pacific Rim Nat'l Park, Br. Col. 184/E6
Pacitan, Indonesia 85/J2
Pack (riv.), Idaho 220/B1
Pack (creek), Utah 304/E5
Packanack Lake, N.J. (07470) 273/B1
Packertown, Ind. (†46510) 227/F2
Packerville, Conn. (†06331) 210/H2
Packington, Québec 172/J2
Packsville, W. Va. (25151) 312/C7
Packwaukee, Wis. (53953) 317/G8
Packwood, Iowa (52580) 229/J6
Packwood, Wash. (98361) 310/D4
Paco, Philippines 82/C2
Pacoa, Colombia 126/E7
Paço de Arcos, Portugal 33/A1
Pacoima, Calif. (91331) 204/B10
Pacolet, S.C. (29372) 296/D2
Pacolet (riv.), S.C. 296/D1
Pacolet Mills, S.C. (29373) 296/D2
Pacov, Czech. 41/C2
Pacsa, Hungary 41/D3
Pacsan (mt.), Philippines 82/C2
Pactolus, N.C. (†27834) 281/P3
Padada, Philippines 82/E7
Padang, Indonesia 54/L10
Padang, Indonesia 85/B6
Padangpanjang, Indonesia 85/B6
Padangsidempuan, Indonesia 85/B5
Padany, U.S.S.R. 52/D2
Padborg, Denmark 21/C8
Padcaya, Bolivia 136/C7
Paddle Prairie, Alberta 182/A5
Paddock Lake, Wis. (†53168) 317/K10
Paddockwood, Sask. 181/F2
Paden, Miss. (38861) 256/H1
Paden, Okla. (74860) 288/N3
Paden City, W. Va. (26159) 312/D3
Paderborn, W. Germany 22/C3
Padgett, S.C. (†29481) 296/F5
Padiham, England 13/H1
Padilla, Bolivia 136/C6
Padilla, Mexico 150/K5
Padilla (creek), N. Mex. 274/D5
Padilla (bay), Wash. 310/C2
Padloping (isl.), N.W.T. 162/K2
Padloping (isl.), N.W. Terrs. 187/M3
Padre (isl.), Texas 188/G5
Padre (isl.), Texas 303/G10
Padre Island Nat'l Seashore, Texas 303/G11
Padre Las Casas, Dom. Rep. 158/D6
Padrón, Spain 33/B1
Padroni, Colo. (80745) 208/N1
Padstow, England 10/D5
Padstow, England 13/B7
Padua (prov.), Italy 34/C2
Padua, Italy 7/F4
Padua, Italy 34/C2
Padua, Minn. (†56378) 255/C5
Paducah, Ky. (42001) 237/D6
Paducah, Ky. 146/K6
Paducah, Ky. 188/J3
Paducah, Texas (79248) 303/D4
Padul, Spain 33/E4
Paekam, N. Korea 81/D3
Paektu (mt.), N. Korea 81/D3
Paeroa, N. Zealand 100/E2
Páez, Colombia 126/C6
Pafúri, Mozambique 118/E4
Pag, Yugoslavia 45/B3
Pag (isl.), Yugoslavia 45/B3
Pagadian, Philippines 82/D7
Pagalungan, Philippines 82/E7
Pagan, Burma 72/B2
Pagan (isl.), No. Marianas 87/E4
Page, Ariz. (86040) 198/D2
Page (co.), Iowa 229/C7
Page, Nebr. (68766) 264/F2
Page, N. Dak. (58064) 282/P5
Page, Okla. (†74939) 288/S5
Page (co.), Va. 307/M3
Page, W. Va. (25152) 312/D6
Page City, Kansas (†67764) 232/A2
Pagedale, Mo. (†63101) 261/P2
Pageland, S.C. (29728) 296/G2
Pago (bay), Guam 86/K7
Pagoda (peak), Colo. 208/E2
Pago Pago (Cap.), Amer. Samoa 86/N9
Pago Pago (cap.), Amer. Samoa 87/J7
Pagosa Junction, Colo. (†81147) 208/E8
Pagosa Springs, Colo. (81147) 208/E8
Pagoua (bay), Dominica 161/F6
Paguate, N. Mex. (87040) 274/B3
Pagwa River, Ontario 177/J5
Pagwa River, Ontario 175/D3
Pahala, Hawaii 188/G6
Pahala, Hawaii (96777) 218/H6
Pahang (state), Malaysia 72/D7
Pahang, Sungai (riv.), Malaysia 72/D7
Pahaska, Wyo. (82414) 319/C1
Pahiatua, N. Zealand 100/F4
Pahlevi (Enzeli), Iran 59/E2
Pahlevi (Enzeli), Iran 66/F2
Pahoa, Hawaii (96778) 218/J5
Pahokee, Fla. (33476) 212/F5
Pahranagat (range), Nev. 266/F5
Pahrock (range), Nev. 266/F5
Pah-rum (peak), Nev. 266/B2
Pahrump, Nev. (89041) 266/E6
Pahrump (valley), Nev. 266/F6
Pahsimeroi (riv.), Idaho 220/E5
Pahute (mesa), Nev. 266/E5
Paia, Hawaii (96779) 218/J2
Paicheng (Baicheng), China 77/K2
Paicines, Calif. (95043) 204/D7
Paide, U.S.S.R. 53/C1
Paige, Texas (78659) 303/G7
Paihia, N. Zealand 100/D1
Paihuano, Chile 138/B8
Paiján, Peru 128/C6
Päijänne (lake), Finland 18/O6
Pailin, Cambodia 72/D4
Paillaco, Chile 138/D3
Pailolo (chan.), Hawaii 218/H1
Paimboeuf, France 28/C4
Paimpol, France 28/B3
Painan, Indonesia 85/C6
Paincourt, Ontario 177/B5
Paincourtville, La. (70391) 238/K3
Paine, Chile 138/G4
Paine, Cerro (mt.), Chile 138/D9
Painesdale, Mich. (49955) 250/G1
Painesville, Ohio (44077) 284/H2
Painswick, Ontario 177/E3
Paint (lake), Manitoba 179/J2
Paint (riv.), Mich. 250/A2
Paint (creek), Ohio 284/D7
Paint, Pa. (†15963) 294/E5
Paint Bank, Va. (24131) 307/H5
Paint Branch (riv.), Md. 245/F4
Painted (des.), Ariz. 198/D2
Painted Desert Section (Petrified Forest), Ariz. 198/F3
Painted Post, N.Y. (14870) 276/F6
Painted Rock (dam), Ariz. 198/C5
Painter, Ala. (†35962) 195/F2
Painter, Va. (23420) 307/S5
Painter Ridge (hills), Conn. 210/B2
Painters Hill, Fla. (†32036) 212/E2
Paintersville, Ohio (†45335) 284/C6
Paint Lick, Ky. (40461) 237/N5
Paint Lick (riv.), Ky. 237/M5
Paint Rock, Ala. (35764) 195/F1
Paint Rock (riv.), Ala. 195/F1
Paint Rock, Texas (76866) 303/E6
Paintsville, Ky. (41240) 237/R5
Paipa, Colombia 126/D5
Paipote, Chile 138/B6
Paipote, Quebrada de (riv.), Chile 138/B6
Paisley, Ontario 177/C3
Paisley, Oreg. (97636) 291/G5
Paisley, Scotland 10/A1
Paisley, Scotland 15/B2
Paita, Peru 128/B5
Paita (bay), Peru 128/B5
Paiute Ind. Res., Calif. 204/G6
Pajala, Sweden 18/N3
Paján, Ecuador 128/B3
Pajarito (creek), N. Mex. 274/A2
Pajaro, Calif. (†95076) 204/D7
Pájaros (isls.), Chile 138/A7
Pakanbaru, Indonesia 54/M9
Pakanbaru, Indonesia 85/C5
Pakaraima (mts.), Guyana 131/A3
Pakawau, N. Zealand 100/D4
Pakchan (riv.), Burma 72/C5
Pakchan (riv.), Thailand 72/C5
Pakch'ŏn, N. Korea 81/B4
Pakenham, Ontario 177/H2
Pakhoi (Beihai), China 77/G7
Pakistan 2/N4
Pakistan 54/H7
PAKISTAN 59/J4
PAKISTAN 68/B3
Pakokku, Burma 72/B2
Pakowki (lake), Alberta 182/E5
Paks, Hungary 41/E3
Pakwach, Uganda 115/F3
Pakxé, Laos 72/E4
Pala, Chad 111/B6
Palacios, Texas (77465) 303/H9
Palafrugell, Spain 33/H2
Palagruža (Pelagosa) (isl.), Yugoslavia 45/C4
Pala Ind. Res., Calif. 204/H10
Palamós, Spain 33/H2
Palana, U.S.S.R. 54/S4
Palana, U.S.S.R. 48/R4
Palanan, Philippines 82/D2
Palanan, Philippines 85/G2
Palanan (bay), Philippines 82/D2
Palanda, Ecuador 128/C5
Palanga, U.S.S.R. 53/A3
Palangkaraya, Indonesia 85/E6
Palanpur, India 68/C4
Palaoa (pt.), Hawaii 218/G2
Palapag, Philippines 82/E4
Palapye, Botswana 118/D4
Palas de Rey, Spain 33/C1
Palatine, Ill. (60067) 222/B5
Palatka, Ark. (†72422) 202/J1
Palatka, Fla. (32077) 212/E2
Palau (Belau) 87/D5
Palauli (bay), W. Samoa 86/L8
Palaumerak, Indonesia 85/G1
Palaw, Burma 72/C4
Palawan (prov.), Philippines 82/B6
Palawan (isl.), Philippines 2/Q5
Palawan (isl.), Philippines 54/N8
Palawan (isl.), Philippines 85/F4
Palawan (isl.), Philippines 82/B6
Palawan (passage), Philippines 85/F4
Palawan (passage), Philippines 82/A6
Palaya, Bolivia 136/A6
Palayan, Philippines 82/C3
Palayankottai, India 68/D7
Palazzolo Acreide, Italy 34/E6
Palca, Bolivia 136/A5
Palco, Kansas (67657) 232/C2
Paldiski, U.S.S.R. 53/B1
Paldiski, U.S.S.R. 52/B3
Paleleh, Indonesia 85/G5
Palembang, Indonesia 54/M10
Palembang, Indonesia 85/D6
Palena, Chile 138/E5
Palena (lake), Chile 138/E5
Palena (riv.), Chile 138/D5
Palencia (prov.), Spain 33/D1
Palencia, Spain 33/D2
Palenque (pt.), Dom. Rep. 158/E6
Palenque, Mexico 150/O8
Palenque (ruin), Mexico 150/O8
Palenville, N.Y. (12463) 276/M6
Palermo, Calif. (95968) 204/D4
Palermo (prov.), Italy 34/D5
Palermo, Italy 7/F5
Palermo, Italy 34/D5
Palermo○, Maine (04354) 243/E7
Palermo, N.J. (†08226) 273/D5
Palermo, N. Dak. (58769) 282/F3
Palermo, Uruguay 145/D4
Palestina, Chile 138/B4
Palestine, Ala. (†36252) 195/H3
Palestine, Ark. (72372) 202/J4
Palestine, Ill. (62451) 222/F4
Palestine, Ind. (†46508) 227/F2
Palestine, Ohio (45352) 284/A5
Palestine, Texas 188/H4
Palestine, Texas (75801) 303/J6
Palestine, W. Va. (26160) 312/D4
Palestrina, Italy 34/F7
Paletwa, Burma 72/B2
Palghat, India 68/D6
Palha, Mar da (bay), Portugal 33/A1
Pali, India 68/C4
Palidoro, Italy 34/F6
Paliocabe (Payocabe), Chile 138/F4
Palisade, Colo. (81526) 208/C4
Palisade, Minn. (56469) 255/E4
Palisade, Nebr. (69040) 264/C4
Palisade, Nev. (†89822) 266/E2
Palisades, Idaho (83437) 220/G6
Palisades (res.), Idaho 220/G6
Palisades, N.J. 273/C1
Palisades, N.Y. (10964) 276/K8
Palisades, Wash. (98845) 310/E3
Palisades (res.), Wyo. 319/A2
Palisades Park, N.J. (07650) 273/C2
Paliseul, Belgium 27/G9
Palizada, Mexico 150/O7
Palk (str.), India 68/D7
Palk (str.), Sri Lanka 68/D7
Pallamallawa, N.S. Wales 97/F1
Palling, Br. Col. 184/D3
Palliser (bay), N. Zealand 100/C3
Palliser (cape), N. Zealand 100/E4
Pall Mall, Tenn. (38577) 237/M7
Palm (beach), Neth. Ant. 161/D10
Palma (bay), Alaska 196/L1
Palma, Mozambique 118/G2
Palma, Spain 7/E5
Palma, Spain 33/H3
Palma (bay), Spain 33/H3
Palma del Río, Spain 33/D4
Palma di Montechiaro, Italy 34/D6
Palmarejo, Venezuela 124/C2
Palmares, Brazil 132/H5
Palmares, C. Rica 154/F6
Palmarito, Apure, Venezuela 124/D4
Palmarito, Guárico, Venezuela 124/F3
Palmarito, Mérida, Venezuela 124/C3
Palmarola (isl.), Italy 34/D4
Palmas (cape) 102/B4
Palmas, Brazil 132/C9
Palmas (cape), Liberia 106/C8
Palmas Altas (pt.), P. Rico 161/C1
Palma Soriano, Cuba 158/J4
Palm Bay, Fla. (32905) 212/F3
Palm Beach, Fla. 188/L5
Palm Beach (co.), Fla. 212/F5
Palm Beach, Fla. (33480) 212/G4
Palm Beach Gardens, Fla. (†33403) 212/F5
Palm Beach Shores, Fla. (†33404) 212/G5
Palm City, Fla. (33490) 212/F4
Palm Coast, Fla. (32037) 212/E2
Palmdale, Calif. (93550) 204/G9
Palmdale, Fla. (33944) 212/E5
Palm Desert, Calif. (92260) 204/J10
Palmeira, Brazil 132/D9
Palmeira, Brazil 135/B4
Palmeira das Missões, Brazil 132/C9
Palmeiras, Brazil 132/F6
Palmeirinhas (pt.), Angola 115/B5
Palmer, Alaska (99645) 196/C1
Palmer, Alaska 188/D5
Palmer (arch.) 5/C15
Palmer, Ill. (62556) 222/D4
Palmer, Ind. (†46307) 227/C2
Palmer, Iowa (50571) 229/D3
Palmer, Kansas (66962) 232/E2
Palmer, Mass. (01069) 249/E4
Palmer○, Mass. (01069) 249/E4
Palmer, Mich. (49871) 250/B2
Palmer, Nebr. (68864) 264/F3
Palmer (head), N. Zealand 100/B3
Palmer, P. Rico 161/F1
Palmer (riv.), Queensland 95/B2
Palmer, Sask. 181/E6
Palmer, Tenn. (37365) 237/K10
Palmer, Wash. (98048) 310/D3
Palmer (lake), Wash. 310/F2
Palmer Lake, Colo. (80133) 208/J4
Palmer Land (reg.), Ant. 2/F9
Palmer Land (reg.), Ant. 5/B15
Palmer Rapids, Ontario 177/G2
Palmers, Minn. (†55801) 255/G4
Palmers Crossing, Miss. (†39401) 256/F8
Palmer Station, Ant. 5/C15
Palmerston (atoll), Cook Is. 87/K7
Palmerston, N. Zealand 100/C6
Palmerston, Ontario 177/D4
Palmerston North, N. Zealand 87/H10
Palmerston North, N. Zealand 100/E4
Palmersville, Tenn. (38241) 237/D8
Palmerton, Pa. (18071) 294/L4
Palmerville, Queensland 95/B3
Palmetto, Fla. (33561) 212/D4
Palmetto, Georgia (30268) 217/C3
Palmetto, La. (71358) 238/G5
Palmetto (pt.), St. Chris.-Nevis 161/C10
Palm Harbor, Fla. (33563) 212/D3
Palmi, Italy 34/E5
Palmiet (riv.), S. Africa 118/F7
Palmilla, Chile 138/F6
Palmillas (pt.), Dom. Rep. 158/F6
Palmillas, Mexico 150/K5
Palmira, Colombia 120/B2
Palmira, Colombia 126/B6
Palmira, Cuba 158/E2
Palmitas, Uruguay 145/B4
Palmito de la Virgen (isl.), Mexico 150/F5
Palmito del Verde (isl.), Mexico 150/F5
Palm River-Clair Mel, Fla. (33619) 212/C3
Palms, Mich. (48465) 250/G5
Palms, Isle of (isl.), S.C. 296/H6
Palm Shores, Fla. (†32901) 212/F3
Palm Springs, Calif. 188/C4
Palm Springs, Calif. (92262) 204/J10
Palm Springs, Fla. (33460) 212/F5
Palmyra, Ill. (62674) 222/C4
Palmyra, Ind. (47164) 227/E8
Palmyra○, Maine (04965) 243/E6
Palmyra, Mich. (49268) 250/E7
Palmyra, Mo. (63461) 261/J3
Palmyra, Nebr. (68418) 264/H4
Palmyra, N.J. (08065) 273/B3
Palmyra, N.Y. (14522) 276/F4
Palmyra (atoll), Pacific 87/K5
Palmyra, Pa. (17078) 294/J5
Palmyra (ruin), Syria 59/C3
Palmyra (Tadmor) (ruins), Syria 63/H5
Palmyra, Tenn. (37142) 237/G8
Palmyra (isl.), U.S. 2/A5
Palmyra, Va. (22963) 307/M5
Palmyra, Wis. (53156) 317/H2
Palmyras (pt.), India 68/F4
Palnackie, Scotland 15/E6
Palni, India 68/D6
Palo, Iowa (52324) 229/K4
Palo, Mich. (48870) 250/E5
Palo, Minn. (†55705) 255/F3
Palo, Philippines 82/E5
Palo Alto, Calif. 188/B3
Palo Alto, Calif. (*94301) 204/K3
Palo Alto, Cuba 158/F3
Palo Alto (co.), Iowa 229/D2
Palo Alto (lake), Iowa 229/D2
Palo Bola, Mexico 150/D4
Palo Duro (creek), Texas 303/B2
Palo Duro (creek), Texas 303/C1
Paloemeu (riv.), Suriname 131/D4
Palolo (stream), Hawaii 218/D4
Paloma, Ill. (62359) 222/B3
Palomar (mt.), Calif. 204/J10
Palomas, Mexico 150/F1
Palomas, Uruguay 145/B2
Palombara Sabina, Italy 34/F6
Palometas, Bolivia 136/D5
Palompon, Philippines 82/E5
Palo Pinto (co.), Texas 303/F5
Palo Pinto, Texas (76072) 303/F5
Palopo, Indonesia 85/F6
Palos (cape), Spain 33/F4
Palo Santo, Argentina 143/E2
Palo Seco, P. Rico 161/D1
Palo Seco, Trin. & Tob. 161/A11
Palos Heights, Ill. (60463) 222/B6
Palos Hills, Ill. (60465) 222/B6
Palos Park, Ill. (60464) 222/B6
Palos Verdes Estates, Calif. (90274) 204/B11
Palotás, Hungary 41/E3
Palourde (lake), La. 238/H7
Palouse (riv.), Idaho 220/B3
Palouse, Wash. (99161) 310/H4
Palouse (riv.), Wash. 310/G4
Palo Verde, Ariz. (85343) 198/C5
Palo Verde, Calif. (92266) 204/L10
Palpa, Nepal 68/E3
Palpa, Peru 128/E10
Palsagua, Nicaragua 154/E4
Palsen (riv.), Manitoba 179/G2
Palu, Indonesia 85/F6
Palu, Turkey 63/H3
Paluan, Philippines 82/C4
Pama, Upper Volta 106/E6
Pamangkat, Indonesia 85/D5
Pamar, Colombia 126/E8
Pambrun, Sask. 181/D6
Pambula, N.S. Wales 97/E5
Pamekasan, Indonesia 85/L2
Pameungpeuk, Indonesia 85/H2
Pamiers, France 28/D6
Pamir (plat.) 54/J6
Pamlico (sound), N.C. 188/L3
Pamlico (co.), N.C. 281/R4
Pamlico (riv.), N.C. 281/R4
Pamlico (sound), N.C. 281/S4
Pampa, Texas 188/F3
Pampa, Texas (79065) 303/D2
Pampa Aullagas, Bolivia 136/B6
Pampachiri, Peru 128/F10
Pampacolca, Peru 128/F10
Pampa de la Salina (salt dep.), Argentina 143/C3
Pampa de las Salinas, Argentina 143/C3
Pampa de la Tres Hermanas (plain), Argentina 143/C6
Pampa del Infierno, Argentina 143/D2
Pampa Grande, Bolivia 136/D5
Pampanga (prov.), Philippines 82/C3
Pampas (plain), Argentina 120/C6
Pampas (plain), Argentina 143/D4
Pampas, Peru 128/E9
Pampas (riv.), Peru 128/E9
Pampilhosa da Serra, Portugal 33/C3
Pamplico, S.C. (29583) 296/H4
Pamplin, Va. (23958) 307/L6
Pamplona, Colombia 126/D4
Pamplona, Spain 33/F1
Pamplona, Spain 7/D4
Pamunkey (riv.), Va. 307/O5
Pamunkey Ind. Res., Va. 307/P5
Pana, Ill. (62557) 222/D4
Panabá, Mexico 150/P6
Panabo, Philippines 82/E7
Panaca, Nev. (89042) 266/G5
Panacachi, Bolivia 136/B6
Panacea, Fla. (32346) 212/B1
Panache (lake), Ontario 177/C1
Panagyurishte, Bulgaria 45/F4
Panaitan (isl.), Indonesia 85/C7
Panaji, India 68/C5
Panama 2/E5
Panama 146/K9
Panama (canal) 2/E5
Panama, Ill. (62077) 222/D4
Panama, Iowa (51562) 229/B5
Panama, Nebr. (68419) 264/H4
Panama, N.Y. (14767) 276/A6
Panama, Okla. (74951) 288/S4
Panamá (cap.), Pan. 146/L9
Panama (canal), Pan. 146/L8
Panamá (gulf), Pan. 146/L9
PANAMA 154/G6
Panamá (cap.), Panama 154/H6
Panama (gulf), Panama 154/H7
Panama City, Fla. 188/K4
Panama City, Fla. (*32401) 212/C6
Panama City Beach, Fla. (32407) 212/C6
Panamint (range), Calif. 204/H7
Panamint (valley), Calif. 204/H7
Panao, Peru 128/E7
Panaon (isl.), Philippines 82/E5
Panarea (isl.), Italy 34/E5
Panaro (riv.), Italy 34/C2
Panarukan, Indonesia 85/K2
Panay (isl.), Philippines 54/O8
Panay (isl.), Philippines 85/G3
Panay (isl.), Philippines 82/D5
Pancake (range), Nev. 266/F4
Pančevo, Yugoslavia 45/E3
Panchor, Malaysia 72/F5
Panchur, India 68/F2
Panciu, Romania 45/H3
Panda, Mozambique 118/E4
Pandale, Texas (76944) 303/C7
Panda-Likasi, Zaire 115/E6
Panda-Likasi, Zaire 102/E6
Pandan, Antique, Philippines 82/C5
Pandan, Catanduanes, Philippines 82/E3
Pan de Azúcar, Quebrado (riv.), Chile 138/B5
Pan de Azúcar, Uruguay 145/D5
Pandeglang, Indonesia 85/G1
Pandharpur, India 68/D5
Pandi Pandi, S. Australia 94/F2
Pando (dept.), Bolivia 136/B2
Pando, Cerro (mt.), Panama 154/F6
Pando, Uruguay 145/B6
Pando (riv.), Uruguay 145/B6
Pandora, Ohio (45877) 284/C4
Pandrup, Denmark 21/C3
Panevežys, U.S.S.R. 52/B3
Panevežys, U.S.S.R. 53/C3
Panfilov, U.S.S.R. 48/H5
Pangai, Tonga 87/J7
Pangala, Congo 115/B4
Pangalanes (canal), Madagascar 118/H4
Pangani, Tanzania 115/G5
Pangani (riv.), Tanzania 115/G4
Panganiban, Philippines 82/E4
Pangasinan (prov.), Philippines 82/C3
Pangburn, Ark. (72121) 202/G3
Pangi, Zaire 115/E4
Pangkalanberandan, Indonesia 85/B5
Pangkalanbuun, Indonesia 85/E6
Pangkalpinang, Indonesia 85/D6
Pangkor, Pulau (isl.), Malaysia 72/D6
Panglao (isl.), Philippines 82/D6
Pangman, Sask. 181/G6
Pangnirtung, Canada 4/C13
Pangnirtung, N.W.T. 162/K2
Pangnirtung, N.W. Terrs. 187/M3
Pangong Tso (lake), India 68/D2
Pangsau (pass), Burma 72/C1
Panguipulli, Chile 138/E2
Panguitch, Utah (84759) 304/B6
Panguitch (creek), Utah 304/B6
Pangutaran, Philippines 82/C7
Pangutaran (isl.), Philippines 82/C7
Pangutaran Group (isls.), Philippines 82/C7
Pangutaran Group (isls.), Philippines 85/G4
Panhandle, Texas (79068) 303/C2
Paniau (peak), Hawaii 218/A2
Panié (mt.), New Caled. 86/G4
Panihati, India 68/F1
Panipat, India 68/D3
Paniqui, Philippines 82/C3
Panj (riv.), Afghanistan 68/C1

Pátzcuaro 425

Panjab, Afghanistan 68/B2
Panjab, Afghanistan 59/J3
Panjang, Hon (Hon Tho Chau) (isl.), Vietnam 72/D5
Panjgur, Pakistan 68/A3
Panjgur, Pakistan 59/H4
Panjim, India 54/J8
Panjim (Panaji), India 68/C5
Pankow, E. Germany 22/F3
Pankshin, Nigeria 106/F7
P'anmunjŏm, N. Korea 81/C5
P'anmunjŏm, S. Korea 81/C5
Panmure (isl.), Pr. Edward I. 168/F2
Panna, India 68/E4
Pannawonica, W. Australia 92/B3
Pannonhalma, Hungary 41/D3
Panny (riv.), Alberta 182/C1
Panola, Ala. (35477) 195/B5
Panola, Ill. (†61738) 222/E3
Panola (co.), Miss. 256/E2
Panola, Okla. (74559) 288/R5
Panola (co.), Texas 303/K5
Panora, Iowa (50216) 229/E5
Panorama Park, Iowa (†52722) 229/N5
Panquehue, Chile 138/G2
Panruti, India 68/D6
Pansey, Ala. (36370) 195/H8
Pantanal (reg.), Brazil 120/D4
Pantar (isl.), Indonesia 85/G7
Pantego, N.C. (27860) 281/R3
Pantego, Texas (76013) 303/F2
Pantelleria, Italy 34/C6
Pantelleria (isl.), Italy 7/F5
Pantelleria (isl.), Italy 34/D6
Pantha, Burma 72/B2
Panther (creek), Idaho 220/D4
Panther (creek), Ky. 237/G5
Panther, W. Va. (24872) 312/C8
Panther Burn, Miss. (38765) 256/C4
Panthersville, Georgia (†30032) 217/L1
Pantin, France 28/B1
Pantoja, Peru 128/E3
Panton○, Vt. (†05491) 268/A3
Pánuco, Mexico 150/K6
Pánuco (riv.), Mexico 150/K5
Panuke (lake), Nova Scotia 168/D4
Pan Xian, China 77/G6
Panyam, Nigeria 106/F7
Panzós, Guatemala 154/C3
Pao (riv.), Venezuela 124/D3
Pao (riv.), Venezuela 124/F3
Paoki (Baoji), China 77/G5
Paola, Italy 34/E5
Paola, Kansas (66071) 232/H3
Paoli, Colo. (80746) 208/P1
Paoli, Ind. (47454) 227/E7
Paoli, Okla. (73074) 288/M5
Paoli, Pa. (19301) 294/M5
Paoli, Wis. (†53508) 317/G10
Paonia, Colo. (81428) 208/D5
Paopao (bay), Fr. Poly. 86/S12
Paoting (Baoding), China 77/J4
Paotow (Baotou), China 77/G3
Paoua, Cent. Afr. Rep. 115/C2
Paoy Pet, Cambodia 72/D4
Papa, Hawaii (†96704) 218/G6
Pápa, Hungary 41/D3
Papaaloa, Hawaii (96780) 218/J4
Papagaio (riv.), Brazil 132/B6
Papagayo (gulf), C. Rica 154/E5
Papago Ind. Res., Ariz. 198/C6
Papaikou, Hawaii 188/G6
Papaikou, Hawaii (96781) 218/J5
Papakura, N. Zealand 100/E2
Papallacta, Ecuador 128/D3
Papanoa, Mexico 150/J8
Papantla de Olarte, Mexico 150/L6
Papar, Malaysia 85/F4
Papara, Fr. Poly. 86/S13
Papa Stour (isl.), Scotland 10/G1
Papa Stour (isl.), Scotland 15/F2
Papatoetoe, N. Zealand 100/C1
Papa Westray (isl.), Scotland 15/F1
Papa Westray (isl.), Scotland 10/E1
Papeete (cap.), Fr. Polynesia 2/B6
Papeete (cap.), Fr. Poly. 86/S13
Papeete (cap.), Fr. Poly. 87/M7
Papelón, Venezuela 124/D3
Papenburg, W. Germany 22/B2
Papenoo, Fr. Poly. 86/T12
Papetoai, Fr. Poly. 86/S12
Paphos, Cyprus 63/E5
Papillion, Nebr. (68046) 264/J3
Papineau, Ill. (60956) 222/F3
Papineau (lake), Ontario 177/G2
Papineau (co.), Québec 172/B4
Papineau (lake), Québec 172/C4
Papineauville, Québec 172/C4
Paposo, Chile 138/A5
Papradno, Czech. 41/E2
Paps, The (mt.), Ireland 17/C7
Paps of Jura (mt.), Scotland 15/C5
Papua (gulf), Papua N.G. 87/E6
Papua New Guinea 2/S6
PAPUA NEW GUINEA 86/B1
PAPUA NEW GUINEA 85/B7
Papua New Guinea 87/E6
Papudo, Chile 138/A9
Papun, Burma 72/C3
Papunáua (riv.), Colombia 126/E6
Papunya, North. Terr. 93/B7
Papurí (riv.), Colombia 126/F7
Paquera, C. Rica 154/E6
Paquette, Québec 172/F4
Paquetville, New Bruns. 170/E1
Pará (state), Brazil 132/C4
Pará (Belém), Brazil 132/E3
Pará (est.), Brazil 120/E3
Pará (riv.), Brazil 132/D3
Para (dist.), Suriname 131/D3
Paraburdoo, W. Australia 88/B4
Paraburdoo, W. Australia 92/B3
Paracale, Philippines 82/D3
Paracas (pen.), Peru 128/D9
Paracatu, Brazil 132/E7
Paracatu (riv.), Brazil 132/E7
Paracel (isls.), China 85/E2
Parachilna, S. Australia 88/F6
Parachilna, S. Australia 94/F4
Parachute, Colo. 208/C4
Paraćin, Yugoslavia 45/E4
Parada Esperanza, Uruguay 145/B3
Parada Liebigs, Uruguay 145/A4
Parada Rivas, Uruguay 145/B2
Parade, S. Dak. (57647) 298/G3
Pará de Minas, Brazil 132/E7
Pará de Minas, Brazil 135/D1
Paradip, India 68/F4
Paradis, La. (70080) 238/M4
Paradise, Ariz. (†85632) 198/F7
Paradise, Calif. (95969) 204/D4
Paradise, Guyana 131/C3
Paradise, Kansas (67658) 232/D2
Paradise, Mich. (49768) 250/D2
Paradise (lake), Mich. 250/E3
Paradise, Mo. (†64089) 261/D4
Paradise, Mont. (59856) 262/B3
Paradise, Newf. 166/D2
Paradise (riv.), Newf. 166/C3
Paradise, Nova Scotia 168/C4
Paradise (lake), Nova Scotia 168/C4
Paradise, Pa. (17562) 294/K5
Paradise, Texas (76073) 303/G5
Paradise, Utah (84328) 304/C2
Paradise, W. Va. (†25124) 312/C5
Paradise Hill, Okla. (†74435) 288/R3
Paradise Hill, Sask. 181/B2
Paradise Inn, Wash. (98398) 310/D4
Paradise River, Newf. 166/C3
Paradise Valley, Alberta 182/E3
Paradise Valley, Ariz. (85253) 198/D5
Paradise Valley, Nev. (89119) 266/F6
Paradise Valley, Nev. (89426) 266/D1
Paradise Valley, Wyo. (†82601) 319/F3
Paradisino (peak), Switzerland 39/K4
Paradiso, Switzerland 39/G5
Paradox, Colo. (81429) 208/B6
Paragon, Ind. (46166) 227/D6
Paragonah, Utah (84760) 304/B6
Paragould, Ark. (72450) 202/J1
Paraguá (riv.), Bolivia 136/E4
Paragua (riv.), Venezuela 124/G4
Paraguaçu (riv.), Brazil 120/F4
Paraguaçu (riv.), Brazil 132/F6
Paraguaçu Paulista, Brazil 132/D8
Paraguai (riv.) 120/D4
Paraguai (riv.), Brazil 132/B8
Paraguaipoa, Venezuela 124/C2
Paraguaná (pen.), Venezuela 124/C1
Paraguarí (dept.), Paraguay 144/D4-5
Paraguay 2/F7
Paraguay 120/D5
PARAGUAY 144
Paraguay (riv.), Argentina 143/E1
Paraguay (riv.), Bolivia 136/F7
Paraguay (riv.), Paraguay 144/D4
Paraíba (state), Brazil 132/G4
Paraíba (riv.), Brazil 120/E5
Paraíba (riv.), Brazil 135/E2
Paraíba do Sul, Brazil 135/E3
Parainen, Finland 18/M6
Paraíso, C. Rica 154/F6
Paraíso, Dom. Rep. 158/D7
Paraíso, Mexico 150/N7
Paraíso de Chabasquén, Venezuela 124/D3
Parakou, Benin 106/E7
Parallel, Kansas (†66933) 232/F2
Paraloma, Ark. (†71846) 202/B6
Paramaribo (dist.), Suriname 131/D2
Paramaribo (cap.), Suriname 131/D2
Paramaribo (cap.), Suriname 2/G5
Paramaribo (cap.), Suriname 120/D2
Paramithía, Greece 45/E6
Paramonga, Peru 128/C8
Paramount, Calif. (90723) 204/C11
Paramus, N.J. (07652) 273/B1
Paramushir (isl.) 54/S5
Paramushir (isl.), U.S.S.R. 48/Q4
Paran (dry riv.), Israel 65/D5
Paraná (riv.) 2/G7
Paraná (riv.) 120/D5
Paraná, Argentina 143/F5
Paraná, Argentina 120/D6
Paraná (riv.), Argentina 143/E2
Paraná (state), Brazil 132/D9
Paraná (state), Brazil 135/B4
Paranã, Brazil 132/E6
Paranã (riv.), Brazil 132/C8
Paranã (riv.), Brazil 132/E6
Paranaguá, Brazil 120/E5
Paranaguá, Brazil 132/E9
Paranaguá, Brazil 135/B4
Paranaíba, Brazil 132/D7
Paranam, Suriname 131/D3
Paranapanema (riv.), Brazil 132/C8
Paranapanema (riv.), Brazil 135/B3
Paranapiacaba (range), Brazil 135/B4
Paranatinga (riv.), Brazil 120/D4
Paranatinga (riv.), Brazil 132/C6
Parang, Maguindanao, Philippines 82/E7
Parang, Sulu, Philippines 82/C8
Parao (riv.), Uruguay 145/E3
Paraparaumu, N. Zealand 100/E4
Parapetí (riv.), Bolivia 136/D6
Para Station, N.S. Wales 97/B3
Parati, Brazil 135/D3
Paratinga, Brazil 132/F6
Paray-le-Monial, France 28/F4
Parbhani, India 68/D5
Parchim, E. Germany 22/D2
Parchman, Miss. (38738) 256/D3
Parchment, Mich. (49004) 250/D6
Parczew, Poland 47/F3
Pardee (res.), Calif. 204/C9
Pardee, Va. (†24285) 307/C6
Pardeeville, Wis. (53954) 317/H8
Pardes Hanna-Karkur, Israel 65/B2
Parding, China 77/C5
Pardo (riv.), Brazil 132/D8
Pardo (riv.), Brazil 132/F6
Pardo (riv.), Brazil 135/B2
Pardo (riv.), Brazil 132/C8
Pardoe, Pa. (†16137) 294/B3
Pardoo, W. Australia 92/B3
Pardubice, Czech. 41/C1
Pare, Indonesia 85/K2
Parece Vela (isl.), Japan 54/P7
Parece Vela (isl.), Japan 87/D3
Parecis (mts.), Brazil 120/C4
Parecis, Serra dos (range), Brazil 132/B6
Paredes de Nava, Spain 33/D1
Paredones, Chile 138/A10
Parent, Québec 174/C3
Pareora, N. Zealand 100/C6
Parepare, Indonesia 85/F6
Parguera, P. Rico 161/A3
Parham, Ant. & Bar. 161/E11
Parham, Ontario 177/H3
Parhams, La. (†71343) 238/G4
Paria (gulf) 120/C1
Paria (plat.), Ariz. 198/D2
Paria (riv.), Ariz. 198/D1
Paria, Bolivia 136/B5
Paria (gulf), Trin. & Tob. 156/G5
Paria (gulf), Trin. & Tob. 161/A11
Paria (riv.), Utah 304/B6
Paria (gulf), Venezuela 124/H2
Paria (pen.), Venezuela 124/G2
Pariaguán, Venezuela 124/F3
Pariaman, Indonesia 85/B6
Paricutín (vol.), Mexico 150/H7
Parida (isl.), Panama 154/F6
Parika, Guyana 131/B2
Parikkala, Finland 18/Q6
Parima, Sierra (mts.), Venezuela 124/F6
Parinacochas (lake), Peru 128/F10
Parinacota, Cerro (mt.), Chile 138/B1
Parinari, Peru 128/E5
Pariñas (pt.), Peru 128/B5
Parintins, Brazil 120/D3
Parintins, Brazil 132/B3
Paris, Ark. (72855) 202/C3
Paris (city) (dept.), France 28/B2
Paris (cap.), France 2/J3
Paris (cap.), France 7/E4
Paris (cap.), France 28/B2
Paris, Idaho (83261) 220/G7
Paris, Ill. (61944) 222/F4
Paris, Iowa (†52214) 229/K4
Paris, Ky. (40361) 237/N4
Paris○, Maine (04271) 243/B7
Paris, Mich. (49338) 250/D5
Paris, Miss. (38949) 256/F2
Paris, Mo. (65275) 261/J4
Paris, Ohio (44669) 284/H4
Paris, Ontario 177/D4
Paris, Tenn. (38242) 237/E8
Paris, Texas (75460) 303/J4
Paris, Texas 188/G4
Paris, Va. (22130) 307/N3
Paris Crossing, Ind. (47270) 227/F7
Parish, N.Y. (13131) 276/H4
Parish, Uruguay 145/C3
Parishville, N.Y. (13672) 276/L1
Parisville, Mich. (†48470) 250/G5
Parisville, Québec 172/F3
Parita, Panama 154/G6
Parita (bay), Panama 154/G6
Park (co.), Colo. 208/H4
Park (range), Colo. 208/F1
Park (riv.), Conn. 210/E2
Park, Kansas (67751) 232/B2
Park (co.), Mont. 262/F5
Park (riv.), N. Dak. 282/R3
Park (dist.), Scotland 15/B2
Park (co.), Wyo. 319/C1
Parkano, Finland 18/N6
Parkbeg, Sask. 181/E5
Park City, Ill. (†60085) 222/B4
Park City, Kansas (†67201) 232/E4
Park City, Ky. (42160) 237/J6
Park City, Mont. (59063) 262/H5
Park City, Utah (84060) 304/C3
Parkdale, Ark. (71661) 202/H7
Parkdale, Colo. (†81212) 208/H6
Parkdale, Oreg. (97041) 291/F2
Parkdale, Pr. Edward I. 168/E2
Parke (co.), Ind. 227/C5
Parker, Ariz. (85344) 198/A4
Parker (dam), Ariz. 198/A4
Parker, Colo. (80134) 208/K4
Parker, Fla. (32401) 212/C6
Parker, Idaho (83438) 220/G6
Parker, Kansas (66072) 232/H3
Parker, Pa. (16049) 294/C3
Parker, S. Dak. (57053) 298/P7
Parker (lake), S. Dak. 298/P3
Parker (co.), Texas 303/G5
Parker, Texas (†75069) 303/H1
Parker, Wash. (98939) 310/E4
Parker City, Ind. (47368) 227/G4
Parker Dam, Calif. (92267) 204/L9
Parkersburg, Ill. (62452) 222/F5
Parkersburg, Ind. (†47954) 227/D5
Parkersburg, Iowa (50665) 229/H3
Parkersburg, W. Va. 188/K3
Parkersburg, W. Va. (26101) 312/D4
Parkers Cove, Newf. 166/D4
Parkers Cove, Nova Scotia 168/C4
Parkers Lake, Ky. (42634) 237/M7
Parkers Prairie, Minn. (56361) 255/C4
Parkertown, N.J. (†08087) 273/E4
Parkerview, Sask. 181/H4
Parkerville, Kansas (†66846) 232/F3
Parkes, N. S. Wales 88/H6
Parkes, N.S. Wales 97/E3
Parkesburg, Pa. (19365) 294/L6
Park Falls, Wis. (54552) 317/F4
Park Forest, Ill. (60466) 222/B6
Park Forest South, Ill. (60466) 222/F2
Park Hall, Md. (20667) 245/N8
Park Hill, Okla. (74451) 288/R3
Parkhill, Ontario 177/C4
Park Hills, Ky. (†41011) 237/S2
Parkin, Ark. (72373) 202/J3
Parkland, Alberta 182/D4
Parkland, Fla. (†33441) 212/F5
Parkland, Okla. (†74824) 288/N3
Parkland, Wash. (98444) 310/C3
Parkman○, Maine (†04443) 243/D5
Parkman, Ohio (44080) 284/H3
Parkman, Sask. 181/K6
Parkman, Wyo. (82838) 319/E1
Park Place, Oreg. (†97045) 291/B2
Park Rapids, Minn. (56470) 255/D4
Park Rapids, Wash. (†99114) 310/H2
Park Ridge, Ill. (60068) 222/B5
Park Ridge, N.J. (07656) 273/B1
Park Ridge, Wis. (†54481) 317/H6
Park River, N. Dak. (58270) 282/P3
Parks, Ariz. (86018) 198/C3
Parks, Ark. (72950) 202/B4
Parks, La. (70582) 238/G6
Parks, Nebr. (69041) 264/C4
Parkside, Pa. (†19013) 294/M7
Parkside, Sask. 181/E2
Parksley, Va. (23421) 307/S5
Parkston, S. Dak. (57366) 298/O7
Parksville, Br. Col. 184/J3
Parksville, Ky. (40464) 237/M5
Parksville, N.Y. (12768) 276/L7
Parksville, S.C. (29844) 296/C4
Parkton, Md. (21120) 245/M2
Parkton, N.C. (28371) 281/M5
Park Valley, Utah (84329) 304/A2
Parkview (mt.), Colo. 208/G2
Parkville, Md. (21234) 245/M3
Parkville, Mo. (64152) 261/O5
Parkville, Pa. (†17331) 294/J6
Parkville, Victoria 97/H5
Parkway, Mo. (64130) 261/L6
Parkway Village, Ky. (†40201) 237/J2
Parkwood, N.C. (27707) 281/M3
Parlakhemundi, India 68/E5
Parlier, Calif. (93648) 204/F7
Parlin, Colo. (81239) 208/F6
Parlin (pond), Maine 243/C4
Parma, Idaho (83660) 220/B6
Parma (prov.), Italy 34/C2
Parma, Italy 7/E4
Parma, Italy 34/C2
Parma (riv.), Italy 34/C2
Parma, Mich. (49269) 250/E6
Parma, Mo. (63870) 261/N9
Parma, Ohio (44129) 284/H9
Parmachenee (lake), Maine 243/B5
Parma Heights, Ohio (†44130) 284/G9
Parmana, Venezuela 124/F4
Parmele, N.C. (27861) 281/P3
Parmelee, S. Dak. (57566) 298/G7
Parmer (co.), Texas 303/B3
Parnaguá, Brazil 132/E5
Parnaíba, Brazil 132/F3
Parnaíba, Brazil 120/E3
Parnaíba (riv.), Brazil 120/E3
Parnaíba (riv.), Brazil 132/F3
Parnamirim, Brazil 132/F4
Parnassus (mt.), Greece 45/F6
Parnassus, N. Zealand 100/D5
Parndana, S. Australia 94/E6
Parnell, Iowa (52325) 229/J5
Parnell, Mo. (64475) 261/C2
Pärnu, U.S.S.R. 7/G3
Pärnu, U.S.S.R. 53/C1
Pärnu, U.S.S.R. 52/C3
Pärnu, U.S.S.R. 48/C4
Paro, Bhutan 68/F3
Paron, Ark. (72132) 202/E4
Paroo (riv.), N. S. Wales 88/G5
Paroo (chan.), N. S. Wales 97/B2
Paroo (riv.), N. S. Wales 97/C1
Paroo (riv.), Queensland 95/C6
Paropamisus (mts.), Afghanistan 59/H3
Paropamisus (range), Afghanistan 68/A2
Páros (isl.), Greece 45/G7
Parow, S. Africa 118/F6
Parowan, Utah (84761) 304/B6
Parpan, Switzerland 39/J3
Parr, Ind. (†47978) 227/C2
Parr, S.C. (29066) 296/E3
Parral, Chile 138/A11
Parral, Mexico 150/G3
Parral, Ohio (†44622) 284/G4
Parramatta, N. S. Wales 88/K4
Parramatta (riv.), N. S. Wales 88/K4
Parramatta, N.S. Wales 97/H3
Parramatta (riv.), N.S. Wales 97/J3
Parramore (isl.), Va. 307/S5
Parran, Md. (†20639) 245/M6
Parras de la Fuente, Mexico 150/H4
Parratah, Tasmania 99/D4
Parrett (riv.), England 13/E6
Parrish, Ala. (35580) 195/D3
Parrish, Fla. (33564) 212/D4
Parrish, Wis. (†54435) 317/H5
Parris Island Marine Base, S.C. 296/F7
Parrott, Georgia (31777) 217/D7
Parrott, Va. (24132) 307/G6
Parrottsville, Tenn. (37843) 237/P8
Parrsboro, Nova Scotia 168/D3
Parry (isls.), N.W.T. 146/G2
Parry (chan.), N.W.T. 146/G2
Parry (chan.), N.W.T. 162/E-H1
Parry (bay), N.W. Terrs. 187/K3
Parry (cape), N.W. Terrs. 187/F2
Parry (chan.), N.W. Terrs. 187/G2
Parry (isls.), N.W. Terrs. 187/G2
Parry (pen.), N.W. Terrs. 187/F2
Parry (isl.), Ontario 177/D2
Parry (sound), Ontario 177/D2
Parry, Sask. 181/G6
Parry Sound, Ont. 162/J6
Parry Sound (terr. dist.), Ontario 175/E3
Parry Sound, Ontario 175/D3
Parry Sound, Ontario 177/D2
Parseierspitze (mt.), Austria 41/A3
Parshall, Colo. (80468) 208/G2
Parshall, N. Dak. (58770) 282/F4
Parsippany-Troy Hills○, N.J. (07054) 273/E2
Parsnip (riv.), Br. Col. 184/F3
Parson, Br. Col. 184/J4
Parsons, Kans. 188/G3
Parsons, Kansas (67357) 232/G4
Parsons, Tenn. (38363) 237/E9
Parsons, W. Va. (26287) 312/G4
Parsonsburg, Md. (21849) 245/R7
Parson's Pond, Newf. 166/C3
Partanna, Italy 34/D6
Partapgarh, India 68/C4
Parthenay, France 28/C4
Partinico, Italy 34/D6
Partizansk, U.S.S.R. 48/O5
Partizánske, Czech. 41/E2
Partlow, Va. (22534) 307/N4
Partridge, Kansas (67566) 232/D4
Partridge (riv.), Minn. 255/G3
Partridge (bay), Newf. 166/C3
Partridge (pt.), Newf. 166/C3
Partry (mts.), Ireland 17/C4
Paru (riv.), Brazil 132/C3
Paru de Oeste (riv.), Brazil 120/D3
Paru de Oeste (riv.), Brazil 132/B3
Paruro, Peru 128/F9
Parvatipuram, India 68/E5
Parys, S. Africa 118/D5
Pas, De (riv.), Québec 174/D1
Pasadena, Calif. 188/C4
Pasadena, Calif. (*91101) 204/C10
Pasadena, Md. (21122) 245/M4
Pasadena, Newf. 166/C4
Pasadena, Texas (*77501) 303/J2
Pasado (cape), Ecuador 128/B3
Pasaje, Ecuador 128/C4
Pa Sak, Mae Nam (riv.), Thailand 72/D4
Pasangkayu, Indonesia 85/F6
Pasargadae (ruins), Iran 66/H5
Pasatiempo, Calif. (†95060) 204/K4
Pasawng, Burma 72/C3
Pasayten (riv.), Wash. 310/E2
Pascagoula, Miss. (39567) 256/G10
Pascagoula (riv.), Miss. 256/G9
Pascalis, Québec 174/B3
Paşcani, Romania 45/H2
Paschall, N.C. (†27589) 281/N1
Pasco (co.), Fla. 212/D3
Pasco (dept.), Peru 128/E8
Pasco, Wash. (99301) 310/F4
Pascoag, R.I. (02859) 249/H5
Pascola, Mo. (63871) 261/N10
Pascua (riv.), Chile 138/D7
Pas-de-Calais (dept.), France 28/E2
Pasewalk, E. Germany 22/F2
Pasighat, India 68/G3
Pasinler, Turkey 63/J3
Pasión (riv.), Guatemala 154/B2
Paskenta, Calif. (96074) 204/C4
Pasłek, Poland 47/D1
Pasley (bay), N.W. Terrs. 187/J2
Pasni, Pakistan 68/A3
Pasni, Pakistan 54/H7
Pasni, Pakistan 59/H4
Paso Ataques, Uruguay 145/D2
Paso Barreto, Paraguay 144/D3
Paso de Andrés Pérez, Uruguay 145/B3
Paso de Indios, Argentina 143/C5
Paso de la Laguna, Salto, Uruguay 145/B2
Paso de la Laguna, Tacuarembó, Uruguay 145/D3
Paso de las Piedras, Uruguay 145/C2
Paso del Borracho, Uruguay 145/D2
Paso del Cerro, Uruguay 145/C2
Paso de León, Uruguay 145/B1
Paso del Horno, Uruguay 145/C2
Paso de Los Libres, Argentina 143/E2
Paso de los Toros, Uruguay 145/C3
Paso del Parque, Uruguay 145/B2
Paso de Ovejas, Mexico 150/Q2
Paso de Patria, Paraguay 144/C5
Paso de Ramos, Uruguay 145/C1
Paso de Uleste, Uruguay 145/B3
Paso Flores, Argentina 143/C5
Paso Hondo, Uruguay 145/B4
Paso Potrero, Uruguay 145/C2
Pasorapa, Bolivia 136/C6
Paso Real, Honduras 154/E3
Paso Robles, Calif. (93446) 204/E8
Paspébiac, Québec 172/D2
Pasqua, Sask. 181/F5
Pasque (isl.), Mass. 249/L7
Pasquia (hills), Sask. 181/J2
Pasquia (riv.), Sask. 181/K2
Pasquotank (co.), N.C. 281/S2
Pass (creek), Wyo. 319/F4
Passaconaway (mt.), N.H. 268/E4
Passadumkeag○, Maine (04475) 243/F5
Passage (isl.), Mich. 250/E1
Passage East, Ireland 17/G7
Passagem Franca, Brazil 132/E4
Passage West, Ireland 17/E8
Passage West, Ireland 10/B5
Passaic, Mo. (64777) 261/D6
Passaic (co.), N.J. 273/E1
Passaic, N.J. (07055) 273/E2
Passaic (riv.), N.J. 273/E2
Passamaquoddy (bay), Maine 243/J5
Passamaquoddy (bay), New Bruns. 170/C3
Passamaquoddy Ind. Res., Maine 243/J6
Passau, W. Germany 22/E4
Pass Christian, Miss. (39571) 256/F10
Passero (cape), Italy 7/F5
Passero (cape), Italy 34/E6
Passes (lake), Québec 172/F2
Passi, Philippines 82/D5
Passo Fundo, Brazil 120/D5
Passo Fundo, Brazil 132/D10
Passos, Brazil 132/E8
Passos, Brazil 135/C2
Passumpsic, Vt. (05861) 268/D3
Passumpsic (riv.), Vt. 268/D2
Pastaza (riv.) 120/B3
Pastaza (prov.), Ecuador 128/D3
Pastaza (riv.), Ecuador 128/D4
Pastaza (riv.), Peru 128/D5
Pasto, Colombia 120/B2
Pasto, Colombia 126/B7
Pastol (bay), Alaska 196/F2
Pastora (peak), Ariz. 198/F2
Pastos Bons, Brazil 132/E4
Pastrana, Spain 33/E2
Pastura, N. Mex. (88435) 274/E4
Pasuquin, Philippines 82/C1
Pasuruan, Indonesia 85/K2
Pasvalys, U.S.S.R. 53/C2
Pasvikelv (riv.), Norway 18/Q2
Paswegin, Sask. 181/H4
Pásztó, Hungary 41/E3
Pata, Bolivia 136/A4
Patacamaya, Bolivia 136/B5
Patagonia (reg.), Argentina 120/C7
Patagonia (reg.), Argentina 143/C5
Patagonia, Ariz. (85624) 198/E7
Pataguanset (lake), Conn. 210/G3
Pataha, Wash. (†99347) 310/H4
Pataha (creek), Wash. 310/H4
Patan, India 68/C4
Patapédia (riv.), New Bruns. 170/C1
Patapédia (riv.), Québec 172/B2
Patapsco, Md. (†21048) 245/L2
Patapsco (riv.), Md. 245/M4
Pataskala, Ohio (43062) 284/E5
Pataz, Peru 128/D6
Patchewollock, Victoria 97/A4
Patch Grove, Wis. (53817) 317/D10
Patchogue, N.Y. (11772) 276/P9
Patea, N. Zealand 100/E3
Paternion, Austria 41/B3
Paterno, Italy 34/E6
Pateros, Wash. (98846) 310/E2
Pateros (lake), Wash. 310/F2
Paterson, N.J. 188/M2
Paterson, N.J. (*07501) 273/B2
Paterson, Wash. (99345) 310/F5
Patesville, Ky. (†42364) 237/H5
Pathankot, India 68/D2
Pathfinder (res.), Wyo. 188/E2
Pathfinder (res.), Wyo. 319/F3
Pathiu, Thailand 72/C5
Pathlow, Sask. 181/G3
Pati (pt.), Guam 86/K6
Pati, Indonesia 85/J2
Patía, Colombia 126/B6
Patía (riv.), Colombia 126/B6
Patiala, India 68/D2
Patillas, P. Rico 161/E2
Patillas (lake), P. Rico 161/E2
Pativilca (riv.), Peru 128/D8
Patmos, Ark. (†71801) 202/C7
Pátmos (isl.), Greece 45/H7
Patna, India 54/K7
Patna, India 68/F3
Patna, Scotland 15/D5
Patnanongan (isl.), Philippines 82/D3
Patnos, Turkey 63/K3
Patoka, Ill. (62875) 222/D5
Patoka, Ind. (47666) 227/B8
Patoka (riv.), Ind. 227/C8
Paton, Iowa (50217) 229/E4
Patos, Brazil 120/F3
Patos, Brazil 132/G4
Patos (lake), Brazil 120/D6
Patos (lag.), Brazil 132/D10
Patos de Minas, Brazil 120/E4
Patos de Minas, Brazil 132/E7
Patoutville, La. (†70544) 238/G7
Patquía, Argentina 143/C3
Pátrai, Greece 7/G5
Pátrai, Greece 45/E6
Patricia, Alberta 182/E4
Patricia, S. Dak. (†57551) 298/G7
Patricia, Texas (79352) 303/B5
Patricio Lynch (isl.), Chile 138/D7
Patrick, Neth. Ant. 161/F8
Patrick, S.C. (29584) 296/G2
Patrick (co.), Va. 307/H7
Patrick A.F.B., Fla. 212/F3
Patricksburg, Ind. (47455) 227/D6
Patrick's Cove, Newf. 166/C2
Patrick Springs, Va. (24133) 307/H7
Patrickswell, Ireland 17/D6
Patriot, Ind. (47038) 227/H7
Patriot, Ohio (45658) 284/F8
Patrocínio, Brazil 132/E7
Patronville, Ind. (†47635) 227/C9
Patroon, Texas (75967) 303/L6
Patsaliga (creek), Ala. 195/F7
Patsburg, Ala. (†36049) 195/F7
Patta (isl.), Kenya 115/H4
Pattani, Thailand 72/D6
Patten, Maine (04765) 243/F4
Patten○, Maine (04765) 243/F4
Pattenburg, N.J. (†08802) 273/C2
Patterson, Ark. (72123) 202/H3
Patterson, Calif. (95363) 204/D6
Patterson, Georgia (31557) 217/H8
Patterson, Idaho (†83253) 220/E5
Patterson, Ill. (62078) 222/C4
Patterson, Iowa (50218) 229/F6
Patterson, La. (70392) 238/H7
Patterson (pt.), Mich. 250/D3
Patterson, Mo. (63956) 261/L8
Patterson, N.Y. (12563) 276/N7
Patterson, N.C. (28661) 281/F3
Patterson, Edward A. (lake), N. Dak. 282/E6
Patterson, Ohio (45843) 284/C4
Patterson, Va. (24633) 307/D6
Patterson (creek), W. Va. 312/J4
Patterson Creek, W. Va. (26746) 312/J3
Pattersonville, N.Y. (12137) 276/M5
Patti, Italy 34/E5
Pattison, Miss. (39144) 256/C7
Patton, Mo. (63662) 261/M8
Patton, Pa. (16668) 294/E4
Pattonsburg, Mo. (64670) 261/D2
Patuanak, Sask. 181/L3
Patuca, Honduras 154/E3
Patuca (pt.), Honduras 154/E3
Patuca (riv.), Honduras 154/E3
Patuha (mt.), Indonesia 85/H2
Pătulele, Romania 45/F3
Patutahi, N. Zealand 100/F3
Patuxent (riv.), Md. 245/M7
Patuxent River Nav. Air Test Ctr., Md. 245/N7
Patzau, Wis. (†54836) 317/B3
Pátzcuaro, Mexico 150/J7

426 Pátzcuaro

Pátzcuaro (lake), Mexico 150/J7
Pau, France 28/C6
Pau, France 7/D4
Paucarbamba, Peru 128/E9
Paucartambo, Cusco, Peru 128/G9
Paucartambo, Pasco, Peru 128/E8
Paudash (lake), Ontario 177/F3
Pau dos Ferros, Brazil 132/G4
Pauillac, France 28/C5
Paukaa, Hawaii (†96781) 218/J5
Paul, Ala. (36469) 195/E8
Paul, Idaho (83347) 220/E7
Paul (isl.), Newf. 166/B2
Paul (stream), Vt. 268/D2
Paulatuk, N.W.T. 162/D2
Paulatuk, N.W. Terrs. 187/F3
Paulaya (riv.), Honduras 154/E3
Paulden, Ariz. (86334) 198/C4
Paulding (co.), Georgia 217/C3
Paulding, Miss. (39348) 256/F6
Paulding (co.), Ohio 284/A3
Paulding, Ohio (45879) 284/A3
Paulette, Miss. (39349) 256/H4
Paulina, La. (70763) 238/L3
Paulina, Oreg. (97751) 291/G3
Paulina (lake), Oreg. 291/F4
Pauline, Kansas (66619) 232/G3
Pauline, Nebr. (†68941) 264/F4
Pauline, S.C. (29374) 296/D2
Pauline Kill (riv.), N.J. 273/D1
Paul Isnard, Fr. Guiana 131/D3
Paulistana, Brazil 132/F4
Paullina, Iowa (51046) 229/B3
Paulo Afonso, Brazil 120/F3
Paulo Afonso, Brazil 132/G5
Paulo Afonso (falls), Brazil 120/F3
Paulo de Faria, Brazil 135/B2
Paulsboro, N.J. (08066) 273/C4
Paul Smiths, N.Y. (12970) 276/M2
Paul Spur, Ariz. (†85607) 198/F7
Pauls Valley, Okla. (73075) 288/M5
Paungassi, Manitoba 179/G2
Paungde, Burma 72/B3
Pauni, India 68/E4
Paunsaugunt (plat.), Utah 304/B6
Paupack, Pa. (18451) 294/M3
Paute, Ecuador 128/C4
Pauto (riv.), Colombia 126/E5
Pauwalu (pt.), Hawaii 218/K2
Pauwela, Hawaii (†96708) 218/K2
Pavant (mts.), Utah 304/B5
Pavia (prov.), Italy 34/B2
Pavia, Italy 34/B2
Pavilion (key), Fla. 212/E6
Pavilion, N.Y. (14525) 276/D5
Pavillion, Wyo. (82523) 319/D2
Pāvilosta, U.S.S.R. 53/A2
Pāvilosta, U.S.S.R. 52/B3
Pavlodar, U.S.S.R. 54/J4
Pavlodar, U.S.S.R. 48/H4
Pavlof (bay), Alaska 196/F3
Pavlof (vol.), Alaska 196/F3
Pavlograd, U.S.S.R. 52/E5
Pavlovo, U.S.S.R. 52/F3
Pavo, Georgia (31778) 217/E9
Pavón, Colombia 126/D6
Pavullo nel Frignano, Italy 34/C2
Pawcatuck, Conn. (06379) 210/H3
Pawcatuck (riv.), Conn. 210/H3
Pawcatuck (riv.), R.I. 249/G7
Pawhuska, Okla. (74056) 288/O1
Pawlet○, Vt. (05761) 268/A5
Pawleys Island, S.C. (29585) 296/J5
Pawling, N.Y. (12564) 276/N7
Pawn, Nam (riv.), Burma 72/C2
Pawnee (creek), Colo. 208/M1
Pawnee, Ill. (62558) 222/D4
Pawnee (co.), Kansas 232/C3
Pawnee (riv.), Kansas 232/B3
Pawnee (co.), Nebr. 264/H4
Pawnee (co.), Okla. 288/N2
Pawnee, Okla. (74058) 288/N2
Pawnee City, Nebr. (68420) 264/H4
Pawnee Rock, Kansas (67567) 232/D3
Pawpaw, Ill. (61353) 222/E2
Paw Paw, Mich. (49079) 250/D6
Paw Paw (riv.), Mich. 250/C6
Paw Paw, W. Va. (25434) 312/K3
Paw Paw Lake, Mich. (†49038) 250/C6
Pawtuckaway (pond), N.H. 268/E5
Pawtucket, R.I. (*02860) 249/J5
Pax, W. Va. (25904) 312/D7
Paxico, Kansas (66526) 232/F2
Paxoí (isl.), Greece 45/D6
Paxson, Alaska (99737) 196/J2
Paxton, Fla. (32538) 212/C5
Paxton, Ill. (60957) 222/E3
Paxton, Ind. (47865) 227/C6
Paxton○, Mass. (01612) 249/G3
Paxton, Nebr. (69155) 264/C3
Paxville, S.C. (29102) 296/G4
Payakumbuh, Indonesia 85/C6
Paya Lebar, Singapore 72/F6
Payerne, Switzerland 39/C3
Payette (co.), Idaho 220/B5
Payette, Idaho (83661) 220/B5
Payette (lake), Idaho 220/C4
Payette (mts.), Idaho 220/B5
Payette (riv.), Idaho 220/B6
Payne, Georgia (†31201) 217/E5
Payne, Minn. (†55765) 255/F3
Payne, Ohio (45880) 284/A3
Payne (co.), Okla. 288/N2
Payne (lake), Que. 162/J4
Payne (lake), Québec 174/E1
Payneham, S. Australia 88/E8
Payneham, S. Australia 94/B7
Paynes, Miss. (†38920) 256/D3
Paynes Creek, Calif. (96080) 204/D3
Payne's Find, W. Australia 92/B5
Paynesville, Ind. (†47250) 227/F7
Paynesville, Mich. (†49912) 250/G2
Paynesville, Minn. (56362) 255/D5
Paynesville, Mo. (63371) 261/L4
Payneville, Ky. (40157) 237/J5
Paynton, Sask. 181/B2
Paysandú (dept.), Uruguay 145/B3
Paysandú, Uruguay 145/A3
Paysandú, Uruguay 120/D6
Payson, Ariz. (85541) 198/D4
Payson, Ill. (62360) 222/B4
Payson, Utah (84651) 304/C3
Pay-Yer (mt.), U.S.S.R. 52/K1
Pazanan, Iran 66/F5
Pazar, Rize, Turkey 63/J2
Pazar, Tokat, Turkey 63/G2
Pazarcık, Turkey 63/G4
Pazardzhik, Bulgaria 45/G4
Pazaryeri, Turkey 63/C3
Paz de Ariporo, Colombia 126/E5
Paz de Río, Colombia 126/D4
Pazña, Bolivia 136/B6
Pea (riv.), Ala. 195/F8
Peabody, Kansas (66866) 232/E3
Peabody, Ky. (40974) 237/O6
Peabody, Mass. (01960) 249/E5
Peace (riv.), Alberta 182/B1
Peace (riv.), Alta. 162/E4
Peace (riv.), Br. Col. 162/D4
Peace (riv.), Br. Col. 184/G2
Peace (riv.), Canada 146/G4
Peace (riv.), Fla. 212/E4
Peace Dale-Wakefield, R.I. (02883) 249/J7
Peace Garden, Manitoba 179/C5
Peace River, Alberta 182/B1
Peace River, Alta. 146/G4
Peace River, Alta. 162/E4
Peace Valley, Mo. (65788) 261/J9
Peach (co.), Georgia 217/E5
Peacham○, Vt. (05862) 268/C3
Peach Bottom, Pa. (17563) 294/K6
Peachland, Br. Col. 184/G5
Peachland, N.C. (28133) 281/J5
Peach Orchard, Ark. (72453) 202/J1
Peach Springs, Ariz. (86434) 198/B3
Peachtree (creek), Georgia 217/K1
Peachtree, North Fork (creek), Georgia 217/L1
Peachtree City, Georgia (30269) 217/C4
Peacock, Alberta 182/D4
Peacock, Mich. (†49938) 250/D4
Peacock, Texas (79542) 303/D4
Peahi, Hawaii (†96708) 218/K2
Peak, The (mt.), England 13/J2
Peak (range), Queensland 95/C4
Peak, S.C. (29122) 296/E3
Peak District National Park, England 13/F4
Peak Hill, N.S. Wales 97/E3
Peak Hill, W. Australia 92/B4
Peaks, Va. (†23069) 307/O5
Peale (mts.), Idaho 220/G7
Peale (mt.), Utah 304/E5
Peapack-Gladstone, N.J. (07977) 273/D2
Pear, W. Va. (†25955) 312/E7
Pearblossom, Calif. (93553) 204/H9
Pearce, Alberta 182/D5
Pearce, Ariz. (85625) 198/F7
Pearcy, Ark. (71964) 202/D5
Peard (bay), Alaska 196/G1
Pea Ridge, Ark. (72751) 202/B1
Pea Ridge Nat'l Mil. Park, Ark. 202/B1
Pearisburg, Va. (24134) 307/G6
Pearl (riv.) 188/J4
Pearl (harb.), Hawaii 188/F5
Pearl (harb.), Hawaii 218/A3
Pearl, Idaho (†83616) 220/B6
Pearl, Ill. (62361) 222/C4
Pearl (riv.), La. 238/L5
Pearl, Miss. (39208) 256/D6
Pearl (riv.), Miss. 256/D8
Pearl (cays), Nicaragua 154/F4
Pearl (creek), S. Dak. 298/N5
Pearl, Texas (†76528) 303/F6
Pearland, Texas (77581) 303/J2
Pearl and Hermes (reef), Hawaii 188/E5
Pearl and Hermes (atoll), Hawaii 218/B5
Pearl Beach, Mich. (48052) 250/G6
Pearl City, Hawaii (96782) 218/B3
Pearl City, Ill. (61062) 222/D1
Pearl Harbor Naval Station, Hawaii 218/B3
Pearlington, Miss. (39572) 256/E10
Pearl Lake, Québec 172/E2
Pearl River, La. (70452) 238/L6
Pearl River (co.), Miss. 256/E9
Pearl River, N.Y. (10965) 276/K8
Pearsall, Texas (78061) 303/E9
Pearse (canal), Alaska 196/N2
Pearson, Ark. (†72131) 202/F3
Pearson, Georgia (31642) 217/G8
Pearson, Okla. (†74826) 288/N4
Pearson, Wis. (54462) 317/H5
Peary (chan.), N.W.T. 162/M3
Peary (chan.), N.W. Terrs. 187/H2
Peary Land (reg.), Greenl. 4/A11
Peary Land (reg.), Greenland 146/Q1
Pease, Minn. (56363) 255/E5
Pease (riv.), Texas 303/D3
Pease A.F.B., N.H. 268/F5
Peasleeville, N.Y. (†12972) 276/N1
Peason, La. (†71429) 238/D4
Pebane, Mozambique 118/F3
Pebble (isl.), 143/E7
Pebble Beach, Calif. (93953) 204/C7
Pebworth, Ky. (41359) 237/O5
Peć, Yugoslavia 45/E4
Peçanha, Brazil 132/F7
Pecan Island, La. (†70548) 238/F7
Pecan Point, Ark. (†72350) 202/L3
Pecatonica, Ill. (61063) 222/D1
Pecatonica (riv.), Wis. 317/H11
Peccia, Switzerland 39/G4
Pechea, Romania 45/H3
Pechenga, U.S.S.R. 4/C8
Pechenga, U.S.S.R. 48/D2
Pechenga, U.S.S.R. 52/D1
Pechora, U.S.S.R. 7/K2
Pechora (riv.), U.S.S.R. 4/C7
Pechora (riv.), U.S.S.R. 7/K2
Pechora, U.S.S.R. 48/F3
Pechora, U.S.S.R. 52/J1
Pechora (bay), U.S.S.R. 52/H1
Pechora (riv.), U.S.S.R. 52/H1
Pechora (riv.), U.S.S.R. 48/F3
Pechora (sea), U.S.S.R. 52/H1
Pecica, Romania 45/E2
Peck, Idaho (83545) 220/B3
Peck, Kansas (67120) 232/E4
Peck, La. (†71368) 238/G3
Peck, Mich. (48466) 250/G5
Peckerwood (lake), Ark. 202/G4
Peckham, Okla. (74647) 288/M1
Pecks Mill, W. Va. (25547) 312/B7
Peconic, N.Y. (11958) 276/P8
Peconic (bay), N.Y. 276/R9
Pecos (riv.) 188/F4
Pecos, N. Mex. (87552) 274/D3
Pecos (riv.), N. Mex. 274/E5
Pecos (co.), Texas 303/B7
Pecos, Texas (79772) 303/D10
Pecos (riv.), Texas 303/C7
Pecos (riv.), U.S. 146/H6
Pecos Nat'l Mon., N. Mex. 274/D3
Pécs, Hungary 7/F4
Pécs, Hungary 41/E3
Pécsvárad, Hungary 41/E3
Peculiar, Mo. (64078) 261/D5
Pedasí, Panama 154/G7
Pedder (lake), Tasmania 99/B4
Pedee, Oreg. (†97361) 291/D3
Pedernal, Argentina 143/G5
Pedernales, Salar de (salt dep.), Chile 138/B5
Pedernales (prov.), Dom. Rep. 158/D7
Pedernales, Dom. Rep. 158/C7
Pedernales, Ecuador 128/B2
Pedernales (riv.), Texas 303/F7
Pedernales, Venezuela 124/G3
Pederneiras, Brazil 135/B3
Pedlar Mills, Va. (†24574) 307/K5
Pedley, Alberta 182/B3
Pedley, Calif. (†92509) 204/E10
Pedra Azul, Brazil 132/F6
Pedraza, Colombia 126/C2
Pedregal, Venezuela 124/C2
Pedreiras, Brazil 132/E4
Pedrera, Uruguay 145/C6
Pedricktown, N.J. (08067) 273/C4
Pedrika, S. Australia 94/D2
Pedro (bank), Jamaica 156/B3
Pedro (cays), Jamaica 156/C3
Pedro, Ohio (45659) 284/E8
Pedro, S. Dak. (†57729) 298/E5
Pedro (pt.), Sri Lanka 68/E6
Pedro Afonso, Brazil 132/E5
Pedro Antonio de los Santos, Mexico 150/Q7
Pedro Bay, Alaska (99647) 196/H3
Pedro Betancourt, Cuba 158/D1
Pedro Chico, Colombia 126/E7
Pedro de Valdivia, Chile 138/B4
Pedro Díaz Colodrero, Argentina 143/G5
Pedro Juan Caballero, Argentina 120/D5
Pedro Juan Cabellero, Paraguay 144/E3
Pedro Luro, Argentina 143/D4
Pedro Montoya, Mexico 150/K6
Pedro Segundo, Brazil 132/F4
Peduyim, Israel 65/B5
Peebles, Ohio (45660) 284/D8
Peebles, Sask. 181/J5
Peebles, Scotland 10/E3
Peebles (trad. co.), Scotland 15/B5
Peebles, Scotland 15/E5
Pee Dee, N.C. (†28091) 281/K5
Pee Dee (riv.), N.C. 281/J4
Peedee, S.C. (29586) 296/H3
Pee Dee (riv.), S.C. 296/H2
Peekskill, N.Y. (10566) 276/N8
Peeksville, Wis. (†54514) 317/E3
Peel (riv.) 162/C2
Peel, I. of Man 10/D3
Peel, I. of Man 13/C3
Peel (sound), N.W.T. 162/G1
Peel, New Bruns. 170/C2
Peel (sound), N.W. Terrs. 187/J2
Peel (reg. munic.), Ontario 177/E4
Peel (inlet), W. Australia 92/A2
Peel (riv.), Yukon 187/E3
Peel Fell (mt.), England 13/E2
Peel Fell (mt.), Scotland 15/F5
Pe Ell, Wash. (98572) 310/B4
Peene (riv.), E. Germany 22/E2
Peenemünde, E. Germany 22/E1
Peer, Belgium 27/G6
Peera Peera Poolanna (lake), S. Australia 94/F2
Peerless (lake), Alberta 182/C1
Peerless, Mont. (59253) 262/L2
Peerless, Sask. 181/L4
Peerless Lake, Alberta 182/C1
Peerless Park, Mo. (†63088) 261/N4
Peers, Alberta 182/B3
Peers, Mo. (†63357) 261/K5
Peery (lake), N.S. Wales 97/B2
Peesane, Sask. 181/H3
Peetz, Colo. (80747) 208/N1
Peever, S. Dak. (57257) 298/R2
Pefferlaw, Ontario 177/E3
Pegarah, Tasmania 99/B1
Pegasus (bay), N. Zealand 100/D5
Pegasus, Port (inlet), N. Zealand 100/A7
Peggs, Okla. (74452) 288/R2
Pegnitz, W. Germany 22/D4
Pego, Spain 33/F3
Pegram, Tenn. (37143) 237/H8
Pegu (div.), Burma 72/C3
Pegu, Burma 54/L8
Pegu, Burma 72/C3
Pegun (isl.), Indonesia 85/J5
Pegu Yoma (mts.), Burma 72/B3
Pehan (Bei'an), China 77/L2
Pehuajó, Argentina 143/D4
Pehuajó, Argentina 120/C6
Peine, W. Germany 22/D2
Peiplin, Poland 47/D2
Peipus (lake), U.S.S.R. 7/G3
Peipus (lake), U.S.S.R. 53/D1
Peipus (lake), U.S.S.R. 48/C4
Peipus (lake), U.S.S.R. 52/C3
Peixe, Brazil 132/D6
Pei Xian, China 77/J5
Pejepscot, Maine (04067) 243/D8
Pejivalle, C. Rica 154/F6
Pekalongan, Indonesia 85/J2
Pekan, Malaysia 72/D7
Pekan Nanas, Malaysia 72/E5
Pekelmeer (lake), Neth. Ant. 161/E9
Pekin, Ill. (61554) 222/D3
Pekin, Ind. (47165) 227/E7
Pekin, N. Dak. (58361) 282/O4
Peking (cap.), People's Rep. of China 54/N5
Peking (cap.), People's Rep. of China 2/Q3
Peking (Beijing) (cap.), People's Rep. of China 77/J3
Pekisko, Alberta 182/C4
Pelabuhan Ratu (bay), Indonesia 85/G2
Pelagie (isls.), Italy 34/D7
Pelagosa (Palagruža) (isl.), Yugoslavia 45/C4
Pelahatchie, Miss. (39145) 256/E6
Peleaga (mt.), Romania 45/F3
Pelechuco, Bolivia 136/A4
Peleduy, U.S.S.R. 48/M4
Pelée (vol.), Martinique 161/C5
Pelée (vol.), Martinique 156/G4
Pelee (pt.), Ontario 177/B6
Peleihari, Indonesia 85/E6
Peleliu (isl.), Belau 87/D5
Peleng (isl.), Indonesia 85/G6
Pelequén, Chile 138/G5
Pelham, Ala. (35124) 195/E4
Pelham, Georgia (31779) 217/D8
Pelham○, Mass. (†01002) 249/E3
Pelham○, N.H. (03076) 268/E6
Pelham, N.Y. (10803) 276/O7
Pelham, N.Y. (†10803) 276/O7
Pelham, N.C. (27311) 281/L1
Pelham, Ontario 177/E4
Pelham, Queensland 95/B3
Pelham, Tenn. (37366) 237/K10
Pelhřimov, Czech. 41/C2
Pelican, Alaska (99832) 196/M1
Pelican (lake), Alberta 182/D2
Pelican (mt.), Alberta 182/D2
Pelican (mts.), Alberta 182/D2
Pelican (isl.), Barbados 161/B9
Pelican, La. (71063) 238/C3
Pelican (bay), Manitoba 179/B2
Pelican (lake), Manitoba 179/C5
Pelican (lake), Manitoba 179/B2
Pelican (lake), Minn. 255/C4
Pelican (lake), Minn. 255/D4
Pelican (lake), Minn. 255/F2
Pelican (riv.), Minn. 255/B4
Pelican (riv.), Minn. 255/F2
Pelican (lake), Nebr. 264/D2
Pelican (lake), Sask. 181/E5
Pelican (lake), Wis. 317/H4
Pelican Lake, Wis. (54463) 317/H4
Pelican Lakes (Breezy Point), Minn. (†56472) 255/D4
Pelican Narrows, Sask. 181/N3
Pelican Portage, Alberta 182/D2
Pelican Rapids, Manitoba 179/B2
Pelican Rapids, Minn. (56572) 255/B4
Pelileo, Ecuador 128/C3
Pelion, S.C. (29123) 296/E4
Pelkie, Mich. (49958) 250/G1
Pelkosenniemi, Finland 18/P3
Pella, Iowa (50219) 229/H6
Pella, Wis. (†54950) 317/J6
Pell City, Ala. (35125) 195/F3
Pellegrini, Argentina 143/D4
Pelletier Mills, New Bruns. 170/B1
Pell Lake, Wis. (53157) 317/K10
Pello, Finland 18/O3
Pellston, Mich. (49769) 250/E3
Pellville, Ky. (42364) 237/H5
Pellworm (isl.), W. Germany 22/C1
Pelly (bay), N.W. Terrs. 187/J3
Pelly (lake), N.W. Terrs. 187/H3
Pelly, Sask. 181/K4
Pelly (riv.), Yukon 162/C3
Pelly (mts.), Yukon 187/E3
Pelly (riv.), Yukon 187/E3
Pelly Bay, N.W.T. 162/G2
Pelly Bay, N.W. Terrs. 187/K3
Pelly Crossing, Yukon 187/E3
Peloncillo (mts.), Ariz. 198/F6
Peloncillo (mts.), N. Mex. 274/A6
Pelopónnisos (reg.), Greece 45/F7
Pelotas, Brazil 120/D6
Pelotas, Brazil 132/C10
Pelsor, Ark. (72856) 202/D2
Pelzer, Ind. (†47601) 227/C8
Pelzer, S.C. (29669) 296/B2
Pemadumcook (lake), Maine 243/E4
Pemalang, Indonesia 85/J2
Pemaquid, Maine (04558) 243/E8
Pematangsiantar, Indonesia 54/L9
Pematangsiantar, Indonesia 85/B5
Pemba, Mozambique 118/G2
Pemba, Mozambique 102/F6
Pemba (reg.), Tanzania 115/H5
Pemba (isl.), Tanzania 102/G5
Pemba (isl.), Tanzania 115/H5
Pemberton, Br. Col. 184/F5
Pemberton, Minn. (56078) 255/E7
Pemberton, N.J. (08068) 273/D4
Pemberton, Ohio (45353) 284/B5
Pemberton, W. Australia 92/A6
Pemberton, W. Va. (25905) 312/D7
Pemberville, Ohio (43450) 284/C3
Pembina (riv.), Alberta 182/C3
Pembina (hills), Manitoba 179/D5
Pembina (riv.), Manitoba 179/C5
Pembina (co.), N. Dak. 282/P2
Pembina, N. Dak. (58271) 282/R2
Pembina (riv.), N. Dak. 282/O1
Pembine, Wis. (54156) 317/L4
Pembrey, Wales 13/C6
Pembroke, Georgia (31321) 217/J6
Pembroke, Ill. (†60944) 222/F2
Pembroke, Ky. (42266) 237/G7
Pembroke, Maine (04666) 243/J6
Pembroke○, Maine (04666) 243/J6
Pembroke○, Mass. (02359) 249/L4
Pembroke○, N.H. (†03275) 268/E5
Pembroke, N.C. (28372) 281/L5
Pembroke, Ont. 162/J6
Pembroke, Ontario 177/G2
Pembroke, Ontario 175/E3
Pembroke, Va. (24136) 307/G6
Pembroke, Wales 13/C6
Pembroke, Wales 10/D5
Pembroke Park, Fla. (†33023) 212/B4
Pembroke Pines, Fla. (33024) 212/B4
Pembrokeshire Coast National Park, Wales 13/C6
Pembuang (riv.), Indonesia 85/E6
Pemigewasset, East Branch (riv.), N.H. 268/D3
Pemigewasset (riv.), N.H. 268/D4
Pemiscot (co.), Mo. 261/N10
Pemuco, Chile 138/E1
Peñablanca, Chile 138/F2
Pena Blanca, N. Mex. (87041) 274/C3
Penafiel, Portugal 33/B2
Peñafiel, Spain 33/E2
Peñaflor, Chile 138/G4
Peñal, Trin. & Tob. 161/B11
Peñalara (mt.), Spain 33/E2
Penalosa, Kansas (67121) 232/D4
Penalva, Brazil 132/E3
Penamacor, Portugal 33/C2
Penápolis, Brazil 135/A2
Peñaranda de Bracamonte, Spain 33/D2
Pen Argyl, Pa. (18072) 294/M4
Peñarroya (peak), Spain 33/F2
Peñarroya-Pueblonuevo, Spain 33/D3
Penarth, Wales 13/B7
Penas (gulf), Chile 120/B7
Penas (gulf), Chile 138/D7
Peñas (cape), Spain 33/D1
Penasco, N. Mex. (87553) 274/D2
Peña Vieja (mt.), Spain 33/D1
Penbrook, Pa. (17103) 294/J5
Pencarrow (head), N. Zealand 100/B3
Pence, Ind. (47973) 227/C4
Pence, Wis. (54553) 317/F3
Pencer, Minn. (56746) 255/D2
Pence Springs, W. Va. (24962) 312/E7
Pencil Bluff, Ark. (71965) 202/C4
Penco, Chile 138/D1
Pendant d'Oreille, Alberta 182/E5
Pendé (riv.), Cent. Afr. Rep. 115/C2
Pendé (riv.), Chad 111/C6
Pendembu, S. Leone 106/B7
Pender, Nebr. (68047) 264/H2
Pender (co.), N.C. 281/O5
Pendergrass, Georgia (30567) 217/E2
Pendleton, Camp, Calif. 204/H10
Pendleton, Ind. (46064) 227/F5
Pendleton (co.), Ky. 237/N3
Pendleton, N.Y. (†14094) 276/C4
Pendleton, N.C. (27862) 281/P2
Pendleton, Oreg. 188/C1
Pendleton, Oreg. (97801) 291/J2
Pendleton, S.C. (29670) 296/B2
Pendleton (co.), W. Va. 312/H5
Pendleton Bay, Br. Col. 184/E3
Pendletons, Va. (23117) 307/N5
Pend Oreille (riv.), Br. Col. 184/J6
Pend Oreille (lake), Idaho 188/C1
Pend Oreille (lake), Idaho 220/B1
Pend Oreille (mt.), Idaho 220/B1
Pend Oreille (riv.), Idaho 220/A1
Pend Oreille (co.), Wash. 310/H2
Pend Oreille (riv.), Wash. 310/H2
Pendroy, Mont. (59467) 262/D2
Pendryl, Alberta 182/C3
Penedo, Brazil 132/G5
Penetanguishene, Ontario 177/D3
Penfield, Georgia (30658) 217/F3
Penfield, Ill. (61862) 222/F3
Penfield, N.Y. (14526) 276/F4
Penfield, Pa. (15849) 294/E3
Penganga (riv.), India 68/D5
Penge, Zaire 115/D5
Penghu (Pescadores) (isls.), China 77/J7
Pengilly, Minn. (55775) 255/E3
Penglai, China 77/K4
Pengpu (Bengbu), China 77/J5
Pengshui, China 77/G6
Penguin, Tasmania 99/C3
Penhold, Alberta 182/D3
Penhook, Va. (24137) 307/J7
Penibética, Sistema (range), Spain 33/E4
Peniche, Portugal 33/B3
Penicuik, Scotland 10/C1
Penicuik, Scotland 15/D2
Peninsula (pt.), Mich. 250/C3
Peninsula (pt.), N.Y. 276/H3
Peninsula, Ohio (44264) 284/G3
Peñíscola, Spain 33/G2
Penitente, Serra do (range), Brazil 132/E5
Pénjamo, Mexico 150/J6
Penk (riv.), England 10/G2
Penki (Benxi), China 77/K3
Penmaenmawr, Wales 13/C4
Penmarch (pt.), France 28/A4
Penn, N. Dak. (58362) 282/M3
Penn, Pa. (15675) 294/C5
Pennant (pt.), Nova Scotia 168/E4
Pennant, Sask. 181/C5
Penndel, Pa. (19047) 294/N5
Penne, Italy 34/D3
Pennell (mt.), Utah 304/D6
Penner (riv.), India 68/D6
Penney Farms, Fla. (32079) 212/E2
Pennfield, New Bruns. 170/D3
Penn Hills○, Pa. (15235) 294/C7
Penniac, New Bruns. 170/D2
Pennine Alps (range), Italy 34/A2
Pennine Alps (range), Switzerland 39/D5
Pennine Chain (range), England 13/E3
Pennington, Ala. (36916) 195/B6
Pennington (co.), Minn. 255/B2
Pennington, Minn. (56663) 255/D3
Pennington, N.J. (08534) 273/D3
Pennington (co.), S. Dak. 298/C6
Pennington, Texas (75856) 303/J6
Pennington Gap, Va. (24277) 307/C7
Pennline, Pa. (†16424) 294/A2
Pennock, Minn. (56279) 255/C5
Penn Run, Pa. (15765) 294/D4
Pennsauken○, N.J. (08110) 273/B3
Pennsauken (creek), N.J. 273/B3
Pennsboro, Mo. (†65752) 261/E8
Pennsboro, W. Va. (26415) 312/E4
Pennsburg, Pa. (18073) 294/M5
Pennsdale, Pa. (17761) 294/J3
Penns Grove, N.J. (08069) 273/C4
Penns Park, Pa. (18943) 294/N5
Pennsuco, Fla. (†33010) 212/B4
Pennsville, N.J. (08070) 273/C4
Pennsville, Ohio (43770) 284/G6
Pennsylvania 188/L2
PENNSYLVANIA 294
Pennsylvania (state), U.S. 146/L5
Pennsylvania Furnace, Pa. (16865) 294/G4
Pennville, Ind. (47369) 227/G4
Pennville, Pa. (†17331) 294/J6
Penn Wynne, Pa. (†19151) 294/M6
Penny, Br. Col. 184/G3
Penny (str.), N.W. Terrs. 187/J2
Penn Yan, N.Y. (14527) 276/F5
Penobscot (co.), Maine 243/F5
Penobscot, Maine (04476) 243/F7
Penobscot○, Maine (04476) 243/F7
Penobscot (bay), Maine 243/F7
Penobscot (lake), Maine 243/C4
Penobscot (riv.), Maine 243/F5
Penobscot Ind. Res., Maine 243/F6
Penobsquis, New Bruns. 170/E3
Penokee, Kansas (67659) 232/C2
Penola, S. Australia 88/G7
Penola, S. Australia 94/G7
Peñón (pt.), P. Rico 161/B1
Peñón Blanco, Mexico 150/H4
Penong, S. Australia 88/E6
Penong, S. Australia 94/C4
Penonomé, Panama 154/G6
Penpont, Scotland 15/E5
Penrhyn (Tongareva) (atoll), Cook Is. 87/L6
Penrith, England 10/E3
Penrith, England 13/E3
Penrith, N. S. Wales 88/J6
Penrith, N.S. Wales 97/F3
Penrod, Ky. (42365) 237/G6
Penrose, Colo. (81240) 208/K6
Penrose, N.C. (28766) 281/D4
Penryn, Calif. (95663) 204/C8
Penryn, England 13/B7
Pensacola, Fla. 146/K6
Pensacola, Fla. 188/J4
Pensacola, Fla. (*32501) 212/B6
Pensacola (bay), Fla. 212/B6
Pensacola, Okla. (†74301) 288/R2
Pensacola N.A.S., Fla. 212/B6
Pensamiento, Bolivia 136/E4
Pensaukee, Wis. (†54153) 317/L6
Pense, Sask. 181/G5
Penshurst, Victoria 97/B5
Pentagon, Va. 307/T3
Penthalaz, Switzerland 39/C3
Penticton, Br. Col. 184/H5
Pentland (firth), Scotland 10/E1
Pentland (firth), Scotland 15/E2
Pentland (hills), Scotland 15/D2
Penton, Miss. (†38664) 256/D1
Pentress, W. Va. (26544) 312/F3
Pentwater, Mich. (49449) 250/C5
Peñuelas, Chile 138/F3
Peñuelas (lake), Chile 138/F2
Peñuelas, P. Rico 161/B2
Penwell, Texas (79776) 303/B6
Penyu (isls.), Indonesia 85/H7
Penza, U.S.S.R. 7/J3
Penza, U.S.S.R. 52/G4
Penza, U.S.S.R. 48/E4
Penzance, England 10/D5
Penzance, England 13/B7
Penzance, Sask. 181/F4
Penzberg, W. Germany 22/D5
Penzhina (bay), U.S.S.R. 48/R3
Peoa, Utah (84061) 304/C3
Peonan (pt.), Manitoba 179/D3
Peoples, Ky. (40467) 237/N6
Peoria, Alberta 182/A2
Peoria, Ariz. (85345) 198/C5
Peoria, Ill. 188/J2
Peoria, Ill. 146/K5
Peoria (co.), Ill. 222/D3
Peoria, Ill. (*61601) 222/D3
Peoria, Iowa (†50219) 229/H6
Peoria, Kansas (†66067) 232/G3
Peoria, Miss. (†39645) 256/C8
Peoria, Ohio (†43067) 284/D5
Peoria, Okla. (†66713) 288/S1
Peoria Heights, Ill. (61614) 222/D3
Peosta, Iowa (52068) 229/M4
Peotone, Ill. (60468) 222/F2
Pep, N. Mex. (†88115) 274/F5
Pepacton (res.), N.Y. 276/L6
Pepe (cape), Cuba 158/B3
Pepeekeo, Hawaii (96783) 218/J4
Pepeekeo (pt.), Hawaii 218/J4
Pepel, S. Leone 106/B7
Pepin (lake), Minn. 255/F6
Pepin (co.), Wis. 317/C6
Pepin, Wis. (54759) 317/B7
Pepin (lake), Wis. 317/B7
Pepperell, Mass. (01463) 249/H2
Pepperell○, Mass. (01463) 249/H2
Pepper Pike, Ohio (†44124) 284/J9
Pepperwood, Calif. (†95569) 204/A3
Peqin, Albania 45/D5
Pequabuck, Conn. (06781) 210/C2
Pequabuck (riv.), Conn. 210/D2
Pequaming, Mich. (†49946) 250/A2
Pequannock○, N.J. (07440) 273/B1

428 Piedmont

Piedmont (lake), Ohio 284/H5
Piedmont, Okla. (73078) 288/L3
Piedmont, S.C. (29673) 296/C2
Piedmont, S. Dak. (57769) 298/C5
Piedmont, W. Va. (26750) 312/H4
Piedmont, Wyo. (†82933) 319/B4
Piedra, Calif. (93649) 204/F7
Piedra (riv.), Colo. 208/E8
Piedra Blanca, Dom. Rep. 158/E6
Piedrabuena, Spain 33/D3
Piedrahita, Spain 33/D2
Piedras, Las (riv.), Peru 128/G8
Piedras Blancas (pt.), Calif. 204/D8
Piedras Coloradas, Uruguay 145/B3
Piedras Negras, Mexico 146/H7
Piedras Negras, Coahuila, Mexico 150/J2
Piedras Negras, Veracruz, Mexico 150/Q2
Piedra Sola, Uruguay 145/C3
Piekary Śląskie, Poland 47/B4
Pieksämäki, Finland 18/P5
Pielinen (lake), Finland 18/Q5
Pieman (riv.), Tasmania 99/B3
Piendamó, Colombia 126/B6
Pierce, Colo. (80650) 208/K1
Pierce, Fla. (†33860) 212/E4
Pierce (co.), Georgia 217/H8
Pierce, Idaho (83546) 220/C3
Pierce, Ky. (†42743) 237/K6
Pierce (pond), Maine 243/C5
Pierce (co.), Nebr. 264/G2
Pierce, Nebr. (68767) 264/G2
Pierce (co.), N. Dak. 282/K3
Pierce (co.), Wash. 310/C3
Pierce, W. Va. (†26292) 312/H4
Pierce (co.), Wis. 317/B6
Pierce City, Mo. (65723) 261/E8
Piercefield, N.Y. (12973) 276/L2
Pierceland, Sask. 181/K4
Pierceton, Ind. (46562) 227/F2
Pierceville, Ind. (†47031) 227/G6
Pierceville, Kansas (67868) 232/B4
Piermont○, N.H. (03779) 268/C4
Piermont, N.Y. (10968) 276/K8
Pierowall, Scotland 15/E1
Pierpont, Ohio (44082) 284/J2
Pierpont, S. Dak. (57468) 298/O3
Pierre (bayou), Miss. 256/C7
Pierre (cap.), S. Dak. 146/J5
Pierre (cap.), S. Dak. 188/F2
Pierre (cap.), S. Dak. (57501) 298/J5
Pierrefonds, Québec 172/H4
Pierrepont Manor, N.Y. (13674) 276/J3
Pierreville, Québec 172/E3
Pierron, Ill. (62273) 222/D5
Pierson, Fla. (32080) 212/E2
Pierson, Iowa (51048) 229/B3
Pierson, Manitoba 179/A5
Pierson, Mich. (49339) 250/D5
Pierson Station, Ill. (†61929) 222/E4
Pierz, Minn. (†56364) 255/D5
Piešťany, Czech. 41/D2
Pietarsaari (Jakobstad), Finland 18/N5
Pieterlen, Switzerland 39/D2
Pietermaritzburg (cap.), Natal, S. Africa 102/F7
Pietermaritzburg, S. Africa 118/E5
Pietersburg, S. Africa 102/F7
Pietersburg, S. Africa 118/D4
Pie Town, N. Mex. (87827) 274/A4
Pietrasanta, Italy 34/B3
Piet Retief, S. Africa 118/D5
Pietrosul (mt.), Romania 45/G2
Pigeon (creek), Ala. 195/E7
Pigeon (lake), Alberta 182/D3
Pigeon, Guadeloupe 161/A6
Pigeon (creek), Ind. 227/C8
Pigeon (riv.), Ind. 227/F1
Pigeon (riv.), Manitoba 179/F2
Pigeon, Mich. (48755) 250/F5
Pigeon (riv.), Mich. 250/D7
Pigeon (riv.), Mich. 250/E3
Pigeon (riv.), Minn. 255/G2
Pigeon (riv.), N.C. 281/C3
Pigeon (isl.), St. Lucia 161/G5
Pigeon, W. Va. (25155) 312/D5
Pigeon (creek), W. Va. 312/B7
Pigeon Cove, Mass. (01966) 249/M2
Pigeon Creek, Ala. (†36037) 195/E7
Pigeon Falls, Wis. (54760) 317/D7
Pigeon Forge, Tenn. (37863) 237/O9
Pigeon Hill, New Bruns. 170/F1
Pigeonroost, Ky. (†40962) 237/O6
Pigg (riv.), Va. 307/J7
Piggott, Ark. (72454) 202/K1
Pignon, Haiti 158/C5
Pigs (Cochinos) (bay), Cuba 158/B2
Pigüé, Argentina 143/D4
Piippola, Finland 18/P4
Pija, Sierra de (mts.), Honduras 154/D3
Pijijiapan, Mexico 150/N9
Pik, Iran 66/G3
Pike (co.), Ala. 195/G7
Pike (co.), Ark. 202/C5
Pike (co.), Georgia 217/D4
Pike (co.), Ill. 222/C4
Pike (co.), Ind. 227/C8
Pike (co.), Ky. 237/S6
Pike (riv.), Minn. 255/F3
Pike (co.), Miss. 256/D8
Pike (co.), Mo. 261/K4
Pike, N.H. (03780) 268/C3
Pike, N.Y. (14130) 276/D5
Pike (co.), Ohio 284/D7
Pike (co.), Pa. 294/M3
Pike, W. Va. (†26346) 312/D4
Pike Bay, Ontario 177/C3
Pike City, Ark. (†71940) 202/C5
Pike Lake, Sask. 181/E4
Pike Road, Ala. (36064) 195/F6
Pike Road, N.C. (27860) 281/R3
Pikes (peak), Colo. 188/E3
Pikes (peak), Colo. 208/J5
Pikes Peak, Ind. (†47201) 227/E6
Pikesville, Md. (21208) 245/M3
Piketberg, S. Africa 118/B6
Piketon, Ohio (45661) 284/E7
Pike View, Ky. (42770) 237/K6
Pikeville, Ind. (†47590) 227/C8
Pikeville, Ky. (41501) 237/S6
Pikeville, N.C. (27863) 281/N4
Pikeville, Tenn. (37367) 237/L9
Pikol'skiy, U.S.S.R. 48/G5
Pikwitonei, Manitoba 179/J3
Pila, Argentina 143/H7
Piła (prov.), Poland 47/C2
Piła, Poland 47/C2
Pilão Arcado, Brazil 132/F5
Pilar, Argentina 143/F5
Pilar, Brazil 132/H5
Pilar, Paraguay 120/D5
Pilar, Paraguay 144/C5
Pilas (isl.), Philippines 82/C7
Pilate, Haiti 158/C5
Pilatus (mt.), Switzerland 39/F2
Pilaya (riv.), Bolivia 136/C7
Pilcomayo (riv.) 120/C5
Pilcomayo (riv.), Argentina 143/E1
Pilcomayo (riv.), Bolivia 136/D7
Pilcomayo (riv.), Paraguay 144/C4
Pilger, Nebr. (68768) 264/G2
Pilger, Sask. 181/F3
Pilgrim, Ky. (41250) 237/S5
Pili, Philippines 82/D4
Pilibhit, India 68/D3
Pilica (riv.), Poland 47/D3
Pilis, Hungary 41/E3
Pilisvörösvár, Hungary 41/E3
Pillager, Minn. (56473) 255/D4
Pillar (pt.), Calif. 204/H3
Pillar (cape), Tasmania 88/H8
Pillar (cape), Tasmania 99/E5
Pillar (pt.), Wash. 310/A2
Pillaro, Ecuador 128/C3
Pilliga, N.S. Wales 97/E2
Pillow, Pa. (17080) 294/J4
Pillsbury (lake), Calif. 204/C4
Pillsbury, N. Dak. (58065) 282/P5
Pillsbury (sound), Virgin Is. (U.S.) 161/B4
Pilmaiquén (riv.), Chile 138/D3
Pilón, Cuba 158/H4
Pílos, Greece 45/E7
Pilot (peak), Idaho 220/C6
Pilot (peak), Idaho 220/C4
Pilot, Ky. (†40380) 237/O5
Pilot (peak), Nev. 266/C4
Pilot, Va. (24138) 307/H6
Pilot Butte, Sask. 181/G5
Pilot Butte (res.), Wyo. 319/D2
Pilote (riv.), Martinique 161/D7
Pilot Grove, Iowa (52648) 229/L7
Pilot Grove, Minn. (†56027) 255/D7
Pilot Grove, Mo. (65276) 261/G5
Pilot Knob (mt.), Idaho 220/C4
Pilot Knob, Ind. (†47118) 227/E8
Pilot Knob, Mo. (63663) 261/L7
Pilot Mound, Iowa (50223) 229/F4
Pilot Mound, Manitoba 179/D5
Pilot Mound, Minn. (†55923) 255/F7
Pilot Mountain, N.C. (27041) 281/J2
Pilotos, Cuba 158/B1
Pilot Point, Alaska (99649) 196/G3
Pilot Point, Texas (76258) 303/H4
Pilot Rock, Oreg. (97868) 291/J2
Pilot Station, Alaska (99650) 196/F2
Pilottown, La. (70081) 238/M8
Pilsen, Wis. (†54217) 317/L7
Piltene, U.S.S.R. 53/A2
Piltown, Ireland 17/G7
Pima (co.), Ariz. 198/D6
Pima, Ariz. (85543) 198/F6
Pimenta, Brazil 135/D2
Pimentel, Dom. Rep. 158/E5
Pimentel, Peru 128/B6
Pimento, Ind. (47866) 227/C6
Pimichín, Venezuela 124/E6
Pimmit, Va. (22043) 307/S2
Pina, Spain 33/F2
Pinal (co.), Ariz. 198/D6
Pinal (peak), Ariz. 198/E5
Pinaleno (mts.), Ariz. 198/F6
Pinamalayan, Philippines 82/C4
Pinang (Penang) (state), Malaysia 72/D6
Pinang (George Town), Malaysia 72/C6
Pinang, Pulau (isl.), Malaysia 72/C6
Pınarbaşı, Turkey 63/G3
Pinar del Río (prov.), Cuba 158/A2
Pinar del Río, Cuba 146/K7
Pinar del Río, Cuba 156/A2
Pinar del Río, Cuba 158/B2
Pınarhisar, Turkey 63/B2
Piñas, Ecuador 128/C4
Piñas (pt.), Panama 154/H7
Pinatubo (mt.), Philippines 82/C3
Pinawa, Manitoba 179/G4
Pinch, W. Va. (25156) 312/D6
Pinchbeck, England 13/G5
Pincher Creek, Alberta 182/D5
Pincher Creek, Br. Col. 162/E6
Pincher Station, Alberta 182/C5
Pinchi (lake), Br. Col. 184/E3
Pinckard, Ala. (36371) 195/G8
Pinckney, Mich. (48169) 250/F6
Pinckneyville, Ill. (62274) 222/D5
Pinckneyville, Miss. (†39669) 256/B8
Pinconning, Mich. (48650) 250/F5
Pincota, Romania 45/E2
Pincourt, Québec 172/D4
Pińczów, Poland 47/E3
Pindall, Ark. (72669) 202/E1
Pindamonhangaba, Brazil 135/D3
Pindi Gheb, Pakistan 68/C2
Pindo (riv.), Ecuador 128/D3
Píndus (mts.), Greece 45/E6
Pine, Ariz. (85544) 198/D4
Pine (riv.), Br. Col. 184/G2
Pine (creek), Calif. 204/D3
Pine, Colo. (80470) 208/J4
Pine (brook), Conn. 210/E2
Pine (isl.), Fla. 212/D5
Pine (pt.), Fla. 212/C2
Pine, Idaho (†83647) 220/C6
Pine (mt.), Ky. 237/O7
Pine (lake), Mich. 250/F4
Pine (riv.), Mich. 250/D4
Pine (riv.), Mich. 250/E5
Pine (co.), Minn. 255/F4
Pine, Mo. (†63935) 261/K9
Pine (creek), Nev. 266/E2
Pine (cape), Newf. 166/D2
Pine (riv.), N.H. 268/E4
Pine (creek), Oreg. 291/L3
Pine (creek), Oreg. 291/J4
Pine (creek), Pa. 294/H2
Pine (creek), Utah 304/C6
Pine (creek), Wash. 310/H3
Pine (lake), Wis. 317/J1
Pine Alcove (creek), Utah 304/D6
Pine Apple, Ala. (36768) 195/E7
Pine Bank, Pa. (15354) 294/B6
Pine Beach, N.J. (08741) 273/E4
Pine Bluff, Ark. 188/H4
Pine Bluff, Ark. (*71601) 202/F5
Pinebluff, N.C. (28373) 281/K4
Pine Bluff Arsenal, Ark. 202/F5
Pine Bluffs, Wyo. (82082) 319/H4
Pine Brook, N.J. (07058) 273/E2
Pine Bush, N.Y. (12566) 276/M7
Pine City, Ark. (†72069) 202/H4
Pine City, Minn. (55063) 255/F5
Pine City, Wash. (†99170) 310/H3
Pinecliffe, Colo. (80471) 208/J3
Pine Creek (pt.), Conn. 210/C4
Pinecreek, Minn. (†56753) 255/C2
Pine Creek, North. Terr. 88/E2
Pine Creek, North. Terr. 93/C2
Pine Creek (lake), Okla. 288/R6
Pinecrest, Calif. (95364) 204/F5
Pinedale, Ariz. (85934) 198/E4
Pinedale, Calif. (93650) 204/F7
Pinedale, Wyo. (82941) 319/C3
Pine Dock, Manitoba 179/F3
Pine Falls, Manitoba 179/F4
Pine Flat (lake), Calif. 204/F7
Pine Forest (range), Nev. 266/C1
Pinega, U.S.S.R. 52/F2
Pinega (riv.), U.S.S.R. 52/G2
Pine Grove, Ark. (†71763) 202/E6
Pine Grove, Georgia (†31513) 217/H7
Pine Grove, Ky. (40470) 237/N5
Pine Grove, La. (70453) 238/J5
Pine Grove, Pa. (17963) 294/K4
Pine Grove (res.), Pa. 294/K6
Pine Grove, W. Va. (26419) 312/E3
Pine Grove Furnace, Pa. (†17324) 294/H5
Pine Grove Mills, Pa. (16868) 294/G4
Pine Hall, N.C. (27042) 281/K2
Pinehaven (Heretaunga-Pinehaven), N. Zealand 100/C2
Pine Hill, Ala. (36769) 195/C7
Pine Hill, Ky. (40364) 237/N6
Pine Hill, N.J. (08021) 273/D4
Pine Hill, N.Y. (12465) 276/M6
Pine Hills, Fla. (32808) 212/E3
Pine House, Sask. 181/M3
Pinehurst (lake), Alberta 182/E2
Pinehurst, Georgia (31070) 217/E6
Pinehurst, Idaho (83850) 220/B2
Pinehurst, Mass. (01866) 249/B5
Pinehurst, N.C. (28374) 281/K4
Pine Island (sound), Fla. 212/D5
Pine Island, Minn. (55963) 255/F6
Pine Island, N.Y. (10969) 276/L8
Pine Knoll Shores, N.C. (†28557) 281/R5
Pine Knot, Ky. (42635) 237/M7
Pine Lake, Alberta 182/B4
Pine Lake, Georgia (30072) 217/D3
Pine Lake, Ind. (†46350) 227/D1
Pine Lake Prov. Park, Sask. 181/E4
Pineland, Fla. (33945) 212/D5
Pineland, S.C. (29934) 296/E6
Pineland, Texas (75968) 303/L6
Pinelands, S. Africa 118/F6
Pine Lawn, Mo. (†63120) 261/R2
Pine Level, Ala. (36065) 195/F6
Pine Level, N.C. (27568) 281/N4
Pinellas (co.), Fla. 212/D4
Pinellas (pt.), Fla. 212/C3
Pinellas Park, Fla. (33565) 212/B3
Pine Log (creek), Fla. 212/C6
Pine Log, Georgia (30152) 217/C2
Pine Meadow, Conn. (06061) 210/D1
Pine Mountain, Georgia (31822) 217/C5
Pineola, N.C. (28662) 281/F2
Pineora, Georgia (†31312) 217/K6
Pine Orchard, Conn. (†06405) 210/D3
Pine Park, Georgia (†31728) 217/D9
Pine Plains, N.Y. (12567) 276/N7
Pine Point, Maine (†04074) 243/C8
Pine Point, N.W. Terrs. 187/G3
Pine Prairie, La. (70576) 238/E5
Piñera, Uruguay 145/C3
Pine Ridge, Ark. (71961) 202/C4
Pine Ridge, Miss. (†39120) 256/B7
Pineridge, S.C. (†29169) 296/E4
Pine Ridge, S. Dak. (57770) 298/E7
Pine Ridge Ind. Res., S. Dak. 298/D7
Pine River, Manitoba 179/B3
Pine River, Minn. (56474) 255/D4
Pine River, Wis. (54965) 317/H7
Pinerolo, Italy 34/A2
Pines (Isla de la Juventud) (isl.), Cuba 158/B3
Pines (isl.), Cuba 156/A2
Pines (isl.), New Caled. 87/G8
Pines, New Caled. 86/H5
Pines (lake), N.J. 273/B1
Pine Springs, Texas (†88220) 303/C10
Pinetop, Ariz. (85935) 198/F4
Pinetops, N.C. (27864) 281/O3
Pinetown, N.C. (27865) 281/R3
Pinetown, S. Africa 118/E6
Pinetta, Fla. (32350) 212/C1
Pine Valley, Br. Col. 184/F2
Pine Valley, Calif. (92062) 204/J11
Pine Valley, N.J. (†08021) 273/C4
Pine Valley, N.Y. (14872) 276/G6
Pine Valley, Utah (†84722) 304/A6
Pineview, Georgia (31071) 217/F6
Pineview, N.C. (†27330) 281/L4
Pine Village, Ind. (47975) 227/C4
Pineville, Ark. (72566) 202/F1
Pineville, Ky. (40977) 237/O7
Pineville, La. (71360) 238/F4
Pineville, Miss. (†39079) 256/F6
Pineville, Mo. (64856) 261/D9
Pineville, N.C. (28134) 281/H4
Pineville, S.C. (29468) 296/H5
Pineville, W. Va. (24874) 312/C7
Pinewood, Minn. (56664) 255/C3
Pinewood, S.C. (29125) 296/G4
Piney, Ark. (†72847) 202/D3
Piney (isl.), Fla. 212/B1
Piney (pt.), Fla. 212/C2
Piney, Manitoba 179/F5
Piney Flats, Tenn. (37686) 237/S8
Piney Fork, Ohio (43941) 284/J5
Piney Park, Mo. (†63077) 261/L6
Piney Point, Md. (20674) 245/M8
Piney Point Village, Texas (†77001) 303/J1
Piney River, Va. (22964) 307/L5
Piney Woods, Miss. (39148) 256/D6
Ping, Mae Nam (riv.), Thailand 72/C3
Pingdingshan, China 77/H5
Pingelap (atoll), Micronesia 87/G5
Pingelly, W. Australia 88/B6
Pingelly, W. Australia 92/B2
Pingelly West, W. Australia 92/B2
Pinger (pt.), N.W. Terrs. 187/K3
Pingguo, China 77/G7
Pingjiang, China 77/H6
Pingle, China 77/H7
Pingliang, China 77/G4
Pingluo, China 77/G4
Pingquan, China 77/J3
Pingree, Idaho (83262) 220/F6
Pingree, N. Dak. (58476) 282/N5
Pingtan (isl.), China 77/K6
Pingtung, China 77/K7
Pingwu, China 77/F5
Pingxiang, Guangxi Zhuangzu, China 77/G7
Pingxiang, Jiangxi, China 77/H6
Pingyang, China 77/K6
Pinhal, Brazil 135/C3
Pinheiro, Brazil 132/E3
Pinheiro, Brazil 120/E3
Pinhel, Portugal 33/C2
Piniós (riv.), Greece 45/E6
Pinjarra, W. Australia 88/B6
Pinjarra, W. Australia 92/A2
Pink (cliffs), Ariz. 198/E4
Pink, Okla. (†74873) 288/M4
Pinkafeld, Austria 41/C3
Pinke Gat (chan.), Netherlands 27/H2
Pinkham, Sask. 181/B4
Pinkham Notch (pass), N.H. 268/E3
Pink Hill, N.C. (28572) 281/O4
Pink Mountain, Br. Col. 184/F1
Pinkstaff, Ill. (†62439) 222/F5
Pinnacle, N.C. (27043) 281/J2
Pinnacles Nat'l Mon., Calif. 204/D7
Pinnaroo, S. Australia 88/G7
Pinnaroo, S. Australia 94/G6
Pinneberg, W. Germany 22/C2
Pinnebog, Mich. (†48445) 250/F5
Pinney's (beach), St. Chris.-Nevis 161/D11
Pinola, Miss. (39149) 256/E7
Pinole, Calif. (94564) 204/J1
Pinon, Ariz. (86510) 198/E2
Pinon, Colo. (†81001) 208/K6
Pinon, N. Mex. (88344) 274/D6
Pinopolis, S.C. (29469) 296/G5
Pinopolis (dam), S.C. 296/G5
Pinos (riv.), Colo. 208/D8
Pinos, Rio de los (riv.), N. Mex. 274/B2
Pinos Altos, N. Mex. (88053) 274/A6
Pinos-Puente, Spain 33/E4
Pinquén, Peru 128/G9
Pinrang, Indonesia 85/F6
Pins (pt.), Ontario 177/C5
Pinsk, U.S.S.R. 48/C4
Pinsk, U.S.S.R. 52/C4
Pinson, Ala. (35126) 195/E3
Pinson, Tenn. (38366) 237/D10
Pinta (isl.), Ecuador 128/B9
Pintada, N. Mex. (†88435) 274/D4
Pintada Arroyo (creek), N. Mex. 274/E4
Pintado, Artigas, Uruguay 145/C1
Pintado, Florida, Uruguay 145/C4
Pintados, Chile 138/B2
Pintados, Salar de (salt dep.), Chile 138/B2
Pintendre, Québec 172/J3
Pinto, Chile 138/A11
Pinto, Md. (21556) 245/C2
Pinto (creek), Sask. 181/D6
Pintura, Utah (84720) 304/A6
Pintuyan, Philippines 82/E6
Pintwater (range), Nev. 266/F6
Pinware (riv.), Newf. 166/C3
Pinware River, Newf. 166/C3
Pinyon (peak), Idaho 220/C5
Pinzón (isl.), Ecuador 128/B9
Pioche, Nev. (89043) 266/G5
Piombino, Italy 34/C3
Pioneer (mts.), Idaho 220/D6
Pioneer, Iowa (†50541) 229/E3
Pioneer, La. (71266) 238/H1
Pioneer, Mo. (†65734) 261/E9
Pioneer, Ohio (43554) 284/A2
Pioneer, Tenn. (37847) 237/N8
Pioner (isl.), U.S.S.R. 48/J2
Pionerskiy, U.S.S.R. 48/G3
Pionki, Poland 47/E3
Piopio, N. Zealand 100/E3
Piopolis, Québec 172/F4
Piotrków (prov.), Poland 47/D3
Piotrków Trybunalski, Poland 47/D3
Piove di Sacco, Italy 34/C2
Pipe (creek), Ind. 227/F4
Piper (peak), Nev. 266/D5
Piper City, Ill. (60959) 222/E3
Piper City, Kansas (66109) 232/H2
Pipersville, Pa. (18947) 294/M5
Piperton, Tenn. (†38017) 237/B10
Pipe Spring Nat'l Mon., Ariz. 198/C2
Pipestem (riv.), N. Dak. 282/M5
Pipestem, W. Va. (25979) 312/E7
Pipestone, Manitoba 179/B5
Pipestone (creek), Manitoba 179/A5
Pipestone (co.), Minn. 255/B6
Pipestone, Minn. (56164) 255/B7
Pipestone (riv.), Ontario 175/B2
Pipestone (creek), Sask. 181/K6
Pipestone (riv.), Sask. 181/L2
Pipestone Nat'l Mon., Minn. 255/B6
Pipinas, Argentina 143/H7
Pipinui (pt.), N. Zealand 100/B2
Pipmuacan (res.), Québec 174/D3
Piqan (Shanshan), China 77/D3
Piqua, Kansas (66761) 232/G4
Piqua, Ohio (45356) 284/B5
Piquete, Brazil 135/D3
Piquiri (riv.), Brazil 132/C7
Piquiri (riv.), Brazil 132/C9
Piracanjuba, Brazil 132/D7
Piracicaba, Brazil 120/E5
Piracicaba, Brazil 135/C3
Piracicaba, Brazil 132/E8
Piracuruca, Brazil 132/F3
Piraí do Sul, Brazil 132/D9
Piraí do Sul, Brazil 135/B4
Piraiévs, Greece 7/G5
Piraiévs (Piraeus), Greece 45/F7
Piraju, Brazil 135/B3
Pirajuba, Brazil 135/B1
Pirajuí, Brazil 135/B2
Pirámide, Cerro (mt.), Chile 138/D8
Piran, Yugoslavia 45/A3
Pirané, Argentina 143/E2
Pirapora, Brazil 120/E4
Pirapora, Brazil 132/E7
Piraraja, Uruguay 145/E4
Pirassununga, Brazil 135/C2
Pirata (mt.), P. Rico 161/F2
Piraúba, Brazil 135/E2
Piray (riv.), Bolivia 136/D5
Pirayú, Paraguay 144/B5
Pirdop, Bulgaria 45/G4
Pirenópolis, Brazil 132/D6
Pires do Rio, Brazil 132/D7
Pírgos, Greece 45/E7
Piriápolis, Uruguay 145/D5
Piribebuy, Paraguay 144/B5
Piribebuy (riv.), Paraguay 144/B4
Piripiri, Brazil 132/F4
Píritu, Anzoátegui, Venezuela 124/F2
Píritu, Falcón, Venezuela 124/D2
Píritu, Portuguesa, Venezuela 124/D3
Pirmasens, W. Germany 22/B4
Pirna, E. Germany 22/E3
Pirongia (mt.), N. Zealand 100/E3
Pirot, Yugoslavia 45/F4
Piru, Calif. (93040) 204/G9
Piru, Indonesia 85/H6
Piryatin, U.S.S.R. 52/D4
Piryí, Greece 45/G6
Pisa (prov.), Italy 34/C3
Pisa, Italy 34/C3
Pisac, Peru 128/G9
Pisagua, Chile 138/A2
Piscadera (bay), Neth. Ant. 161/F9
Piscataqua (riv.), Maine 243/B9
Piscataqua (riv.), N.H. 268/F5
Piscataquis (co.), Maine 243/E4
Piscataquis (riv.), Maine 243/E5
Piscataquog (riv.), N.H. 268/D5
Piscataway, Md. (†20735) 245/L6
Piscataway (creek), Md. 245/G6
Piscataway○, N.J. (08854) 273/D2
Piscataway Park, Md. 245/K6
Piscatosine (lake), Québec 172/B3
Pisco, Peru 128/D9
Pisco, Peru 120/B4
Pisco (bay), Peru 128/D9
Pisco (riv.), Peru 128/D9
Piseco, N.Y. (12139) 276/L4
Piseco (lake), N.Y. 276/M4
Písek, Czech. 41/C2
Pisek, N. Dak. (58273) 282/P3
Pisgah, Ala. (35765) 195/G1
Pisgah, Iowa (51564) 229/B5
Pisgah, Md. (20640) 245/K6
Pisgah Forest, N.C. (28768) 281/D4
Pishan (Guma), China 77/A4
Pishin, Iran 66/M7
Pishin, Pakistan 68/B2
Pishin, Pakistan 59/J3
Pishkun (res.), Mont. 262/D3
Pisinimo, Ariz. (85634) 198/C6
Pismo Beach, Calif. (93449) 204/E8
Piso Firme, Bolivia 136/D3
Pisoniano, Italy 34/F6
Pissis (mt.), Argentina 143/C2
Pistakee (lake), Ill. 222/A4
Pistapaug (pond), Conn. 210/E3
Pisticci, Italy 34/F4
Pistoia (prov.), Italy 34/C2
Pistoia, Italy 34/C2
Pistolet (bay), Newf. 166/C3
Pistol River, Oreg. (97444) 291/C5
Pisz, Poland 47/E2
Pit (riv.), Calif. 204/D2
Pitalito, Colombia 126/B7
Pitangui, Brazil 135/D1
Pitarpunga (lake), N.S. Wales 97/B4
Pitcairn (isl.) 87/O8
Pitcairn (isl.), (Br.) 2/C7
Pitcairn, Pa. (15140) 294/C5
Pitch (lake), Trin. & Tob. 161/A11
Piteå, Sweden 18/M4
Piteälv (riv.), Sweden 18/M4
Pitești, Romania 45/G3
Pitești, Romania 7/G4
Píthion, Greece 45/H5
Pithiviers, France 28/E3
Pitiquito, Mexico 150/D1
Pitkas Point, Alaska (†99658) 196/F2
Pitkin (co.), Colo. 208/F4
Pitkin, Colo. (81241) 208/F5
Pitkin, La. (70656) 238/E5
Pitlochry, Scotland 15/E4
Pitlochry, Scotland 10/E2
Pitman, N.J. (08071) 273/C4
Pitman, Sask. 181/G5
Pitmedden, Scotland 15/F3
Pitogo, Philippines 82/C4
Piton des Neiges (mt.), Réunion 118/G5
Pitrufquén, Chile 138/D2
Pitsburg, Ohio (45358) 284/A6
Pitt (isl.), Br. Col. 184/C3
Pitt (lake), Br. Col. 184/L2
Pitt, Minn. (56665) 255/D2
Pitt (isl.), N. Zealand 100/E7
Pitt (str.), N. Zealand 100/E7
Pitt (co.), N.C. 281/P3
Pittenweem, Scotland 15/F4
Pitti (isl.), India 68/C6
Pittman Center, Tenn. (†37738) 237/P9
Pitt Meadows, Br. Col. 184/L3
Pittock, Pa. (†15136) 294/B7
Pitts, Ark. (†72421) 202/J2
Pitts, Georgia (31072) 217/E7
Pittsboro, Ind. (46167) 227/D5
Pittsboro, Miss. (38951) 256/F3
Pittsboro, N.C. (27312) 281/L3
Pittsburg, Calif. (94565) 204/L1
Pittsburg, Georgia (†30084) 217/L1
Pittsburg, Ill. (62974) 222/E6
Pittsburg, Ind. (†46923) 227/D3
Pittsburg, Kansas (66762) 232/H4
Pittsburg, Ky. (40755) 237/N6
Pittsburg, Mo. (65724) 261/F7
Pittsburg○, N.H. (03592) 268/E1
Pittsburg (co.), Okla. 288/P5
Pittsburg, Okla. (74560) 288/P5
Pittsburg, Texas (75686) 303/J4
Pittsburgh, Pa. 146/K5
Pittsburgh, Pa. 188/L2
Pittsburgh, Pa. (*15201) 294/B7
Pittsfield, Ill. (62363) 222/C4
Pittsfield, Maine (04967) 243/E6
Pittsfield○, Maine (04967) 243/E6
Pittsfield, Mass. 188/M2
Pittsfield, Mass. (01201) 249/A3
Pittsfield, N.H. (03263) 268/E5
Pittsfield○, N.H. (03263) 268/E5
Pittsfield, Pa. (16340) 294/D2
Pittsfield○, Vt. (05762) 268/B4
Pittsford, Mich. (49271) 250/E7
Pittsford, N.Y. (14534) 276/E4
Pittsford, Vt. (05763) 268/A4
Pittsford○, Vt. (05763) 268/A4
Pittston○, Maine (†04345) 243/D7
Pittston, Pa. (*18640) 294/F7
Pittstown, N.J. (08867) 273/C2
Pittsview, Ala. (36871) 195/H6
Pittsville, Md. (21850) 245/S7
Pittsville, Mo. (†64040) 261/E5
Pittsville, Va. (24139) 307/K7
Pittsville, Wis. (54466) 317/F7
Pittsylvania (co.), Va. 307/K7
Pittville, Calif. (†96056) 204/D2
Pittwood, Ill. (†60970) 222/F3
Piúí, Brazil 132/E8
Piúí, Brazil 135/D2
Piura (dept.), Peru 128/B5
Piura, Peru 120/A3
Piura, Peru 128/B5
Piura (riv.), Peru 128/B5
Piute (co.), Utah 304/B5
Piute (res.), Utah 304/B5
Pivijay, Colombia 126/C2
Pixley, Calif. (93256) 204/F8
Piyas (lake), S. Dak. 298/P2
Pizacoma, Peru 128/H11
Pizarro, Colombia 126/B5
Pizol (peak), Switzerland 39/H3
Place, Ky. (†40734) 237/N7
Placentia, Calif. (92670) 204/D11
Placentia, Newf. 166/C2
Placentia (bay), Newf. 166/C2
Placentia (sound), Newf. 166/C2
Placer (co.), Calif. 204/E4
Placer, Philippines 82/E6
Placerville, Calif. (95667) 204/C8
Placerville, Colo. (81430) 208/D6
Placerville, Idaho (83666) 220/C6
Placetas, Cuba 158/E2
Placid (lake), Fla. 212/E4
Placid (lake), N.Y. 276/N2
Placida, Fla. (33946) 212/D5
Placilla, Chile 138/F6
Placilla de Caracoles, Chile 138/B4
Placilla de Peñuelas, Chile 138/F2
Placitas, N. Mex. (87043) 274/C3
Plad, Mo. (†65764) 261/G7
Pladda (isl.), Scotland 15/C5
Plaffeien, Switzerland 39/D3
Plahn, Liberia 106/C7
Plain, Wash. (†98826) 310/E3
Plain, Wis. (53577) 317/F9
Plain City, Ohio (43064) 284/D5
Plain City, Utah (†84401) 304/B2
Plain Dealing, La. (71064) 238/C1
Plainfield, Ark. (†71740) 202/D7
Plainfield, Conn. (06374) 210/H2
Plainfield○, Conn. (06374) 210/H2
Plainfield, Georgia (31073) 217/F6
Plainfield, Ill. (60544) 222/A6
Plainfield, Ind. (46168) 227/E5
Plainfield, Iowa (50666) 229/J3
Plainfield○, Mass. (01070) 249/C2
Plainfield○, N.H. (03781) 268/C4
Plainfield, N.J. (*07060) 273/E2
Plainfield, Ohio (43836) 284/G5
Plainfield, Vt. (05667) 268/C3
Plainfield○, Vt. (05667) 268/C3
Plainfield, Wis. (54966) 317/G7
Plains, Georgia (31780) 217/D6
Plains, Kansas (67869) 232/B4
Plains, Mont. (59859) 262/B3
Plains, Pa. (†18701) 294/F7
Plains, Texas (79355) 303/B4
Plainsboro, N.J. (08536) 273/D3

Search Books: [By Keyword ▾] [_____] [**Find Book**]   **> Advanced Search**

Home > Search Results

0843712511, 0843712511 , Hardcover

You Searched For: **Keywords:**   0843712511 NOT ("print on demand" OR "printed on demand"), **ISBN:**   0843712511

5 Results (Displaying results 1 - 5)   Page: **[1]**   Sort Results By: [Lowest Total Price ▾]

Condition
All Conditions
  New Books
  Used Books

Binding
All Bindings
  Hardcover
  Softcover

Collectible Attributes
  First Edition
  Signed Copy
  Dust Jacket (3)
  Seller-Supplied Images
  Not Printed On Demand

Free Shipping
  Free US Shipping (2)

Bookseller Location
All Locations
  Select a Country

Bookseller Rating
All Booksellers
      and up
      and up
      and up

Search Within These Results: [_____] [Go]   **> Edit Your Search**

1.

Ambassador World Atlas
Hammond Incorporated
Bookseller: Wonder Book
(Frederick, MD, U.S.A.)
Bookseller Rating: ★★★★★
Quantity Available: 1
ISBN: 9780843712513

Price: US$ 5.56
Convert Currency

Shipping: FREE
Within U.S.A.
Destination, Rates & Speeds

[⬚ **Add to Basket**]

Book Description: Hammond World Atlas Corp. Book Condition: Very Good. . Good dust jacket. Bookseller Inventory # wpf15950n

Bookseller & Payment Information | More Books from this Seller

---

2.

Ambassador World Atlas
Hammond
Bookseller: P&S Antiques and Books
(Dallas, TX, U.S.A.)
Bookseller Rating: ★★★★☆
Quantity Available: 1
ISBN: 0843712511 / 0-8437-1251-1

Price: US$ 2.00
Convert Currency

Shipping: US$ 3.99
Within U.S.A.
Destination, Rates & Speeds

[⬚ **Add to Basket**]

Book Description: Union, New Jersey, U.S.A.: Hammond World Atlas Corp, 1984. Hardcover. Book Condition: Very Good. Bookseller Inventory # ABE-8351388677

Bookseller & Payment Information | More Books from this Seller | Ask Bookseller a Question

---

3.

Ambassador World Atlas
Hammond Incorporated
Bookseller: ExtremelyReliable
(Richmond, TX, U.S.A.)
Bookseller Rating: ★★★★★
Quantity Available: 1
ISBN: 0843712511 / 0-8437-1251-1

Price: US$ 4.76
Convert Currency

Shipping: US$ 4.99
Within U.S.A.
Destination, Rates & Speeds

[⬚ **Add to Basket**]

Book Description: Hammond World Atlas Corp. Hardcover. Book Condition: Used: Very Good. Bookseller Inventory # SONG0843712511

Bookseller & Payment Information | More Books from this Seller | Ask Bookseller a Question

---

4.

Hammond Ambassador World Atlas
Hammond Incorporated
Bookseller: MW Books Ltd
(New York, NY, U.S.A.)
Bookseller Rating: ★★★★★
Quantity Available: 2
ISBN: 0843712511 / 0-8437-1251-1

Price: US$ 36.13
Convert Currency

Shipping: FREE
Within U.S.A.
Destination, Rates & Speeds

[⬚ **Add to Basket**]

Book Description: Maplewood, N. J. : Hammond Incorporated, 1984. New Edition. New Final Census Edition including Zip Codes. Description: 1 atlas (xvi, 484 p.) : col. Ill. , col. Maps ; 32 cm. Subjects: Atlases. Notes: Includes indexes. Abundantly map illustrated. An exceptional copy; fine in an equally fine dw. Particularly and surprisingly well-preserved; tight, bright, clean and especially sharp-cornered. Literally as new. 3 Kg. 484 pp. Bookseller Inventory # 80829

Bookseller & Payment Information | More Books from this Seller | Ask Bookseller a Question

---

5.

Hammond Ambassador World Atlas
Hammond Incorporated
Bookseller: MW Books Ltd.
(Galway, ., Ireland)
Bookseller Rating: ★★★★★
Quantity Available: 2
ISBN: 0843712511 / 0-8437-1251-1

Add to Basket

Price: US$ 34.40
Convert Currency

Shipping: US$ 10.62
From Ireland to U.S.A.
Destination, Rates & Speeds

Book Description: Maplewood, N. J. : Hammond Incorporated, 1984. New Edition. New Final Census Edition including Zip Codes. Description: 1 atlas (xvi, 484 p.) : col. Ill. , col. Maps ; 32 cm. Subjects: Atlases. Notes: Includes indexes. Abundantly map illustrated. An exceptional copy; fine in an equally fine dw. Particularly and surprisingly well-preserved; tight, bright, clean and especially sharp-cornered. Literally as new. 3 Kg. 484 pp. Bookseller Inventory # 80829

Bookseller & Payment Information | More Books from this Seller | Ask Bookseller a Question

---

5 Results (Displaying results 1 - 5)   Page: **[1]**   Sort Results By: Lowest Total Price

---

Create a Want
Tell us what you're looking for and once a match is found, we'll inform you by e-mail.

> Create a Want

BookSleuth
Can't remember the title or the author of a book? Our BookSleuth is specially designed for you.

> Visit BookSleuth

Help with Search
> Search Tips
> Glossary of Terms
> Set your own Search Preferences

GuidedNavigation by ENDECA

  UK Books | UK Textbooks   Deutsche Bücher   Livres en français   Libri in Italiano   Libros en español   Australia & New Zealand Books   Canada Books

Find a Book
How AbeBooks Works
Advanced Search
ISBN List
Author List
Title List
New & Used Textbooks
Bestselling Textbooks
Bestselling Authors
Bestselling Titles
Used Books
ISBN Search

Account
Your Account
Sign On/Off
View Basket

Services
Sell Books
AbeBooks HomeBase®
Affiliate Program

Company
Company Information
Contact Us
Careers
Privacy & Security
Designated Agent

Community
Blog
Forums
BookSleuth
GiftSleuth
Newsletters
Features Archive
More...

Help
Order Tracking
Shipping Information
Payment Options
Returns
More...

AbeBooks Companies
BookFinder.com
FillZ.com
ZVAB.com

Follow AbeBooks on Twitter   Visit our Facebook Page   See us on YouTube   Read our Blog

Rangeley 433

Quay (co.), N. Mex. 274/F3
Quay, N. Mex. (88433) 274/F4
Quay, Okla. (†74085) 288/N2
Quchan, Iran 66/L2
Quchan, Iran 59/G2
Quealy, Wyo. (†82901) 319/C4
Queanbeyan, N. S. Wales 88/H7
Queanbeyan, N.S. Wales 97/E4
Québec (prov.) 162/J5
QUÉBEC 172
Québec, Canada 2/F3
Québec (prov.), Que. 146/L4
Québec (cap.), Que. 146/L5
Québec (cap.) Que. 162/J6
Québec (co.), Québec 172/F3
Québec (county), Québec 174/C3
Québec (cap.), Québec 172/H3
Québec (cap.), Québec 174/C3
Queeck, Tenn. (38579) 237/K9
Quebracho, Uruguay 145/B2
Quebracho Coto, Argentina 143/D2
Quebrada de Alvarado, Chile 138/F2
Quebradillas, P. Rico 161/B1
Quechee, Vt. (05059) 268/C4
Quechisla, Bolivia 136/C7
Quecholac, Mexico 150/O2
Quecreek, Pa. (15555) 294/D5
Quedlinburg, E. Germany 22/D3
Queen (cape), N.W. Terrs. 187/L3
Queen, Pa. (16670) 294/E5
Queen Anne, Md. (21657) 245/O5
Queen Annes (co.), Md. 245/P4
Queenborough, England 13/H6
Queenborough, England 10/G5
Queen Charlotte (isls.), Br. Col. 146/E4
Queen Charlotte (isls.), Br. Col. 162/C5
Queen Charlotte, Br. Col. 184/A3
Queen Charlotte (isls.), Br. Col. 184/B3
Queen Charlotte (sound), Br. Col. 184/C4
Queen Charlotte (str.), Br. Col. 184/D5
Queen Charlotte (sound), N.W.T. 162/D5
Queen City, Mo. (63561) 261/H2
Queen City, Texas (75572) 303/L4
Queen Creek, Ariz. (85242) 198/D5
Queen Elizabeth (isls.), Canada 2/C2
Queen Elizabeth (isls.), Canada 4/B15
Queen Elizabeth (isls.), N.W.T. 146/G2
Queen Elizabeth (isls.), N.W.T. 162/M3
Queen Elizabeth (isls.), N.W. Terrs. 187/H1
Queen Mary Coast (reg.) 5/C5
Queen Maud (mts.) 5/A12
Queen Maud (gulf), N.W.T. 162/F2
Queen Maud (gulf), N.W. Terrs. 187/H3
Queen Maud Land (reg.), Ant. 2/K10
Queen Maud Land (reg.) 5/B1
Queens (sound), Br. Col. 184/C4
Queen's (co.), New Bruns. 170/D3
Queens (co.), N.Y. 276/N9
Queens (borough), N.Y. (*11101) 276/N9
Queens (chan.), N.W. Terrs. 187/J2
Queens (co.), Nova Scotia 168/C4
Queens (co.), Pr. Edward I. 168/E2
Queens, W. Va. (†26237) 312/F5
Queensberry (mt.), Scotland 15/E5
Queenscliff, Victoria 97/C6
Queensferry, Scotland 10/C1
Queensferry, Scotland 15/D1
Queen Shoals, W. Va. (†25045) 312/D6
Queensland, 88/G4
QUEENSLAND 95
Queensland (state), Australia 87/E8
Queensport, Nova Scotia 168/G3
Queenstown, Alberta 182/D4
Queenstown, Guyana 131/B2
Queenstown (Cóbh), Ireland 10/B5
Queenstown (Cóbh), Ireland 17/E8
Queenstown, Md. (21658) 245/O5
Queenstown, New Bruns. 170/D3
Queenstown, N. Zealand 100/B6
Queenstown, S. Africa 102/E8
Queenstown, S. Africa 118/D6
Queenstown, Tasmania 99/B4
Queenstown, Tasmania 88/H8
Queensville, Ind. (†47265) 227/F6
Queets, Wash. (†98331) 310/A3
Queets (riv.), Wash. 310/A3
Queilén, Chile 138/D4
Queimadas, Brazil 132/F5
Quela, Angola 115/C5
Quelimane, Mozambique 118/F3
Quelimane, Mozambique 102/F6
Quelpart (Cheju) (isl.), S. Korea 81/C7
Queluz, Portugal 33/A1
Quemado (pt.), Cuba 158/K4
Quemado, N. Mex. (87829) 274/A4
Quemado, Texas (78877) 303/D9
Quemado de Güines, Cuba 158/E1
Quemchi, Chile 138/D4
Quemoy (Jinmen) (isl.), China 77/J7
Quemú-Quemú, Argentina 143/D4
Quenemo, Kansas (66528) 232/G3
Quentin, Miss. (39647) 256/C8
Quepos, C. Rica 154/E6
Quequay Chico (riv.), Uruguay 145/B3
Quequay Grande (riv.), Uruguay 145/B3
Que Que, Zimbabwe 118/D3
Que Que, Zimbabwe 102/E6
Quequén, Argentina 143/E4
Querecotillo, Peru 128/B5
Querétaro (state), Mexico 150/J6
Querétaro, Mexico 146/J7
Querétaro, Mexico 150/J6
Quesada, Spain 33/E4
Queshan, China 77/H5
Quesnel, Br. Col. 162/D5
Quesnel (lake), Br. Col. 162/D5
Quesnel, Br. Col. 184/F4
Quesnel (lake), Br. Col. 184/G4
Quesnel (riv.), Br. Col. 184/F4
Quesnel (lake), Manitoba 179/G4
Questa, N. Mex. (87556) 274/D2
Queteña, Bolivia 136/B8
Quetico Prov. Park, Ontario 175/B3
Quetico Prov. Park, Ontario 177/G5
Quetta, Pakistan 54/H6
Quetta, Pakistan 59/J3
Quetta, Pakistan 68/B2
Queule, Chile 138/D2
Quevedo, Ecuador 128/C3
Quévy, Belgium 27/D8
Quezaltenango, Guatemala 154/B3
Quezaltepeque, Guatemala 154/C3
Quezon (prov.), Philippines 82/C3
Quibala, Angola 115/C6
Quibaxe, Angola 115/B5
Quibdó, Colombia 126/B5
Quiberon, France 28/B4
Quibor, Venezuela 124/D3
Quicacha, Peru 128/F10
Quick, Br. Col. 184/D3
Quick, W. Va. (25045) 312/D6
Quicksand, Ky. (41363) 237/P5
Quicksburg, Va. (22847) 307/L3
Quiebra Hacha, Cuba 158/B1
Quiévrain, Belgium 27/D8
Quigley, Alberta 182/E1
Quiindy, Paraguay 144/B5
Quijotoa, Ariz. (†85634) 198/C6
Quilalí, Nicaragua 154/E4
Quilán (cape), Chile 138/D4
Quilán (isl.), Chile 138/D5
Quilca, Peru 128/F11
Quilcene, Wash. (98376) 310/B3
Quilchena, Br. Col. 184/G5
Quilengues, Angola 115/B6
Quilicura, Chile 138/G3
Quill (lakes), Sask. 181/G4
Quillabamba, Peru 128/F9
Quillacas, Bolivia 136/B6
Quillacollo, Bolivia 136/B5
Quillacollo, Bolivia 120/C4
Quillagua, Chile 138/B3
Quillaicillo, Chile 138/A8
Quillan, France 28/E6
Quillayute Ind. Res., Wash. 310/A3
Quilleco, Chile 138/E1
Quill Lake, Sask. 181/G3
Quillota, Chile 138/F2
Quilon, India 68/D7
Quilpie, Queensland 88/G5
Quilpie, Queensland 95/C5
Quilpué, Chile 138/F2
Quimby, Iowa (51049) 229/B3
Quimby, Maine (04770) 243/F2
Quime, Bolivia 136/B5
Quimili, Argentina 143/D2
Quimper, France 28/A4
Quimperlé, France 28/B4
Quinault, Wash. (98575) 310/B3
Quinault (lake), Wash. 310/B3
Quinault (riv.), Wash. 310/A3
Quinault Ind. Res., Wash. 310/A3
Quinby, S.C. (†29501) 296/H3
Quinby, Va. (23423) 307/S5
Quinby (inlet), Va. 307/S6
Quince Mil, Peru 128/G9
Quincy, Calif. (95971) 204/E4
Quincy, Fla. (32351) 212/B1
Quincy, Ill. 188/H3
Quincy, Ill. (62301) 222/B4
Quincy, Ind. (47456) 227/D6
Quincy, Kansas (†66870) 232/F4
Quincy, Ky. (41166) 237/P3
Quincy, Mass. (02169) 249/D7
Quincy (bay), Mass. 249/D7
Quincy, Mich. (49082) 250/E7
Quincy, Miss. (†38848) 256/H3
Quincy, Mo. (65735) 261/F6
Quincy, N.H. (†03266) 268/D4
Quincy, Ohio (43343) 284/C5
Quincy, Wash. (98848) 310/F3
Quincy, W. Va. (†25015) 312/C6
Quindío (dept.), Colombia 126/C5
Quinebaug, Conn. (06262) 210/H1
Quinebaug (riv.), Conn. 210/H2
Quinebaug (riv.), Mass. 249/F4
Quines, Argentina 143/C3
Quinhagak, Alaska (99655) 196/F3
Qui Nhon, Vietnam 72/F4
Qui Nhon, Vietnam 54/M8
Quiniluban (isls.), Philippines 82/C5
Quinlan, Okla. (†73852) 288/J2
Quinlan, Texas (75474) 303/H5
Quinn (riv.), Nev. 266/D1
Quinn, S. Dak. (57775) 298/E5
Quinn Canyon (range), Nev. 266/F4
Quinnesec, Mich. (49876) 250/A3
Quinnimont, W. Va. (25910) 312/D7
Quinnipiac, Conn. (†06492) 210/D3
Quinnipiac (riv.), Conn. 210/D3
Quinta de Tilcoco, Chile 138/G5
Quintana de la Serena, Spain 33/D3
Quintanar de la Orden, Spain 33/E3
Quintana Roo (state), Mexico 150/P7
Quintay, Chile 138/F3
Quinter, Kansas (67752) 232/B2
Quintero, Chile 138/F2
Quinto (riv.), Argentina 143/D3
Quinto, Spain 33/F2
Quinto, Switzerland 39/G3
Quinton, Ky. (†42518) 237/M7
Quinton, N.J. (08072) 273/C4
Quinton, Okla. (74561) 288/R4
Quinton, Sask. 181/G4
Quinton, Va. (23141) 307/O5
Quinwood, W. Va. (25981) 312/E6
Quinzau, Angola 115/B5
Quionga, Mozambique 118/G2
Quipapá, Brazil 132/G5
Quirey, Colombia 126/F5
Quirihue, Chile 138/E1
Quirindi, N.S. Wales 97/F2
Quirino (prov.), Philippines 82/C2
Quirino, Philippines 82/C2
Quiriquire, Venezuela 124/G3
Quirke (lake), Ontario 177/B1
Quiroga, Argentina 143/F7
Quiroga, Bolivia 136/C6
Quiroga, Spain 33/C1
Quirusillas, Bolivia 136/D6
Quisiro, Venezuela 124/C2
Quispamsis, New Bruns. 170/E3
Quissanga, Mozambique 118/G2
Quissett, Mass. (†02540) 249/M6
Quissico, Mozambique 118/F4
Quitaque, Texas (79255) 303/C3
Quitasueño (bank), Colombia 126/A8
Quitilipi, Argentina 143/D2
Quitman, Ark. (72131) 202/F3
Quitman (co.), Georgia 217/B7
Quitman, Georgia (31643) 217/E9
Quitman, La. (71268) 238/E2
Quitman (co.), Miss. 256/D2
Quitman, Miss. (39355) 256/G6
Quitman, Mo. (†64428) 261/C2
Quitman, Texas (75783) 303/J5
Quitman (mts.), Texas 303/B11
Quito (cap.), Ecuador 2/F6
Quito (cap.), Ecuador 128/C3
Quito (cap.), Ecuador 120/B2
Quixadá, Brazil 120/F3
Quixadá, Brazil 132/G4
Quixeramobim, Brazil 132/F4
Qujing, China 77/F6
Qulin, Mo. (63961) 261/M9
Qum, Iran 54/G6
Qum (Qom), Iran 59/F3
Qum (Qom), Iran 66/G3
Qumar He (riv.), China 77/D4
Qumarlêb, China 77/D5
Qumeim, Jordan 65/D2
Qunfidha, Saudi Arabia 59/D6
Quogue, N.Y. (11959) 276/P9
Quoich (riv.), N.W. Terrs. 187/J3
Quoich, Loch (lake), Scotland 15/C3
Quonnipaug (lake), Conn. 210/E3
Quorn, S. Australia 88/F6
Quorn, S. Australia 94/F5
Quryat, Oman 59/G5
Qusaiba, Saudi Arabia 59/D4
Quteife, Syria 63/G6
Qu Xian, Sichuan, China 77/G5
Qu Xian, Zhejiang, China 77/J6
Qüxü, China 77/D6
Quyon, Québec 172/A4
Quyquyó, Paraguay 144/D5

R

Raab (riv.), Austria 41/C3
Raabs an der Thaya, Austria 41/C2
Raahe, Finland 18/O4
Raalte, Netherlands 27/J4
Ra'anana, Israel 65/B3
Raanes (pen.), N.W. Terrs. 187/K2
Raasay (isl.), Scotland 15/C3
Raasay (sound), Scotland 15/B3
Rab, Yugoslavia 45/B3
Rab (isl.), Yugoslavia 45/B3
Rába (riv.), Hungary 41/D3
Raba, Indonesia 85/F7
Rabat (cap.), Morocco 2/J4
Rabat (cap.), Morocco 106/C2
Rabat (cap.), Morocco 102/B1
Rabaul, Papua N.G. 87/F6
Rabaul, Papua N.G. 86/B2
Rabbit (riv.), Mich. 250/D6
Rabbit (isl.), N.S. Wales 97/J2
Rabbit (creek), S. Dak. 298/E3
Rabbit Ears (peak), Colo. 208/G2
Rabbit Ears (range), Colo. 208/F2
Rabbithash, Ky. (†41091) 237/M3
Rabbit Lake, Sask. 181/D2
Rabbit Lake, Sask. 181/M2
Rabigh, Saudi Arabia 59/C5
Rabinal, Guatemala 154/B3
Rabka, Poland 47/D4
Rabocheostrovsk, U.S.S.R. 52/D1
Rabun, Ala. (†36507) 195/C8
Rabun (co.), Georgia 217/F1
Rabun (lake), Georgia 217/E1
Rabun Gap, Georgia (30568) 217/F1
Raccoon (pt.), Fla. 212/D3
Raccoon, Ind. (†46172) 227/D5
Raccoon (riv.), Iowa 229/D4
Raccoon (pt.), La. 238/H8
Raccoon (creek), N.J. 273/C4
Raccoon (creek), Ohio 284/F8
Race (pt.), Mass. 249/N4
Race (cape), Newf. 166/D2
Race (cape.), Newf. 146/N5
Race (cape), Newf. 162/L6
Raceland, Ky. (41169) 237/R3
Raceland, La. (70394) 238/J7
Racepond, Georgia (†31537) 217/H8
Rachel, W. Va. (26587) 312/F3
Rach Gia, Vietnam 72/E5
Racibórz, Poland 47/C3
Racine, Minn. (55967) 255/F7
Racine, Mo. (64858) 261/C9
Racine, Ohio (45771) 284/G8
Racine, Québec 172/E4
Racine, W. Va. (25165) 312/C6
Racine, Wis. 188/J2
Racine (co.), Wis. 317/K10
Racine, Wis. (*53401) 317/M3
Ráckeve, Hungary 41/E3
Rackham, Manitoba 179/B4
Raco, Mich. (49778) 250/E2
Racola, Mo. (†63630) 261/L8
Radama (isls.), Madagascar 118/H2
Rădăuţi, Romania 45/G2
Radbuza (riv.), Czech. 41/B2
Radcliff, Ky. (40160) 237/K5
Radcliff, Ohio (45670) 284/F7
Radcliffe, England 13/H2
Radcliffe, Iowa (50230) 229/G4
Radeberg, E. Germany 22/E3
Radebeul, E. Germany 22/E3
Radenthein, Austria 41/B3
Rader, Tenn. (†37743) 237/R8
Radersburg, Mont. (59641) 262/E4
Radford (I.C.), Va. (24141) 307/G6
Radhanpur, India 68/C4
Radiant, Va. (22732) 307/M4
Radisson, Québec 174/B2
Radisson, Sask. 181/D3
Radisson, Wis. (54867) 317/D4
Radium, Colo. (80472) 208/G3
Radium, Kansas (67571) 232/D3
Radium, Minn. (56749) 255/B2
Radium Hill, S. Australia 88/G6
Radium Hill, S. Australia 94/G5
Radium Hot Springs, Br. Col. 184/J5
Radium Springs, N. Mex. (88054) 274/B6
Radkersburg, Austria 41/C3
Radley, Ind. (†46938) 227/F4
Radnice, Czech. 41/B2
Radnor, Ind. (†46923) 227/D3
Radnor, Ohio (43066) 284/D5
Radnor (for.), Wales 13/D5
Radnor, W. Va. (25556) 312/A6
Radolfzell, W. Germany 22/C5
Radom, Ill. (62876) 222/D5
Radom (prov.), Poland 47/E3
Radom, Poland 7/G3
Radom, Poland 47/E3
Radomir, Bulgaria 45/F4
Radomsko, Poland 47/D3
Radoviš, Yugoslavia 45/F5
Radstadt, Austria 41/B3
Radviliškis, U.S.S.R. 53/B3
Radville, Sask. 162/F6
Radville, Sask. 181/G6
Radway, Alberta 182/D2
Radziejów, Poland 47/D2
Radzyń Podlaski, Poland 47/F3
Rae (isth.), N.W.T. 162/H2
Rae (isth.), N.W. Terrs. 187/K3
Rae (riv.), N.W. Terrs. 187/G3
Rae (str.), N.W. Terrs. 187/J3
Rae-Edzo, N.W.T. 162/E3
Rae-Edzo, N.W. Terrs. 187/G3
Raeford, N.C. (28376) 281/L5
Rae Lake, N.W. Terrs. 187/G3
Raeren, Belgium 27/J7
Raeside (lake), W. Australia 88/C5
Raeside (lake), W. Australia 92/C5
Raetihi, N. Zealand 100/E3
Raeville, Nebr. (68656) 264/F3
Rafaela, Argentina 143/F5
Rafaela, Argentina 120/C6
Rafah, Gaza Strip 65/A5
Rafai, Cent. Afr. Rep. 115/D2
Rafidiya, West Bank 65/C3
Rafsanjan, Iran 59/G3
Rafsanjan, Iran 66/K5
Raft (riv.), Idaho 220/E7
Raft (riv.), Utah 304/A1
Raft River (mts.), Utah 304/A2
Rafz, Switzerland 39/G1
Raga, Sudan 111/E6
Ragan, Nebr. (68969) 264/E4
Ragang (vol.), Philippines 82/E7
Ragay (gulf), Philippines 82/D4
Ragged (isl.), Bahamas 156/C2
Ragged (pt.), Barbados 161/C8
Ragged (isl.), Maine 243/F8
Ragged (lake), Maine 243/E4
Ragged (isls.), Newf. 166/C2
Raglan, N. Zealand 100/E2
Raglan (harb.), N. Zealand 100/E2
Ragland, Ala. (35131) 195/F3
Ragley, La. (70657) 238/D5
Rago, Kansas (67128) 232/D4
Ragsdale, Ind. (47573) 227/C7
Ragusa (prov.), Italy 34/E6
Ragusa, Italy 34/E6
Ragusa (Dubrovnik), Yugoslavia 45/C4
Raha, Indonesia 85/G6
Rahaeng (Tak), Thailand 72/C3
Rahan, Ireland 17/F5
Rahimyar Khan, Pakistan 68/C3
Rahotu, N. Zealand 100/D3
Rahue (riv.), Chile 138/D3
Rahway, N.J. (*07065) 273/E2
Raiatea (isl.), Fr. Poly. 87/L7
Raices, Argentina 143/G6
Raichur, India 68/D5
Raiford, Fla. (32083) 212/D1
Raigarh, India 68/E4
Railley (mt.), Mont. 262/C3
Railroad (valley), Nev. 266/F4
Railroad, Pa. (17355) 294/J6
Railroad Canyon (res.), Calif. 204/E11
Railton, Tasmania 99/C3
Rainbow (lake), Alberta 182/A5
Rainbow (plat.), Ariz. 198/D2
Rainbow, Conn. (†06095) 210/E1
Rainbow (mt.), Idaho 220/C4
Rainbow (lake), Maine 243/E4
Rainbow, Victoria 97/A4
Rainbow Bridge Nat'l Mon., Utah 304/C6
Rainbow City, Ala. (35901) 195/F3
Rainbow Lake, Alberta 182/A5
Rainelle, W. Va. (25962) 312/E7
Rainier, Alberta 182/D4
Rainier, Oreg. (97048) 291/E1
Rainier (mt.), Wash. 188/B1
Rainier, Wash. (98576) 310/C4
Rainier (mt.), Wash. 310/D4
Rains, S.C. (29589) 296/J3
Rains (co.), Texas 303/J5
Rainsboro, Ohio (45165) 284/C7
Rainsburg, Pa. (†15522) 294/F6
Rainsville, Ala. (35986) 195/G2
Rainsville, Ind. (†47918) 227/C4
Rainsville, N. Mex. (87736) 274/D2
Rainy (riv.), Minn. 188/H1
Rainy (lake), Minn. 188/H1
Rainy (lake), Minn. 255/E2
Rainy (riv.), Minn. 255/D2
Rainy (lake), Ont. 162/G6
Rainy (lake), Ontario 177/G5
Rainy (lake), Ontario 175/B3
Rainy River, Ont. 162/G6
Rainy River (terr. dist.), Ontario 177/G5
Rainy River (terr. dist.), Ontario 175/B3
Rainy River, Ontario 175/A3
Rainy River, Ontario 177/F5
Raipur, India 54/K7
Raipur, India 68/E4
Raisin, Calif. (93652) 204/E7
Raisin (riv.), Mich. 250/F7
Raisio, Finland 18/M6
Raith, Ontario 175/C3
Raith, Ontario 177/G5
Raivavae (isl.), Fr. Poly. 87/M8
Raja Ampat Group (isls.), Indonesia 85/H6
Rajahmundry, India 68/E5
Rajang (riv.), Malaysia 85/E5
Rajapalaiyam, India 68/D7
Rajapur, India 68/C5
Rajasthan (state), India 68/C3
Rajec, Czech. 41/E2
Rajgarh, India 68/D4
Rajka, Hungary 41/D3
Rajkot, India 54/H7
Rajkot, India 68/C4
Rajnandgaon, India 68/E4
Rajpipla, India 68/C4
Rajpur, India 68/F2
Rajpura, India 68/D2
Rajshahi, Bangladesh 68/F4
Rakahanga (atoll), Cook Is. 87/K7
Rakaia, N. Zealand 100/C5
Rakaia (riv.), N. Zealand 100/C5
Rakamaz, Hungary 41/F2
Rakan, Ras (cape), Qatar 59/F4
Rakaposhi (mt.), Pakistan 68/C1
Rakaposhi (mt.), Pakistan 59/K2
Rakata (isl.), Indonesia 85/C7
Rake, Iowa (50465) 229/F2
Rakhov, U.S.S.R. 52/B5
Rakino (isl.), N. Zealand 100/C1
Rakitu (isl.), N. Zealand 100/E2
Rakkestad, Norway 18/G7
Rakof (isls.), Alaska 196/M1
Rákospalota, Hungary 41/E3
Rakovník, Czech. 41/B1
Rakvere, U.S.S.R. 53/D1
Rakvere, U.S.S.R. 52/C3
Raleigh, Fla. (†32696) 212/D2
Raleigh, Georgia (†30293) 217/C5
Raleigh, Ill. (62977) 222/E6
Raleigh, Ind. (†46173) 227/G5
Raleigh, Miss. (39153) 256/F6
Raleigh, Newf. 166/C3
Raleigh (cap.), N.C. 146/L6
Raleigh (cap.), N.C. 188/L3
Raleigh (cap.), N.C. (*27601) 281/M3
Raleigh (bay), N.C. 281/S5
Raleigh, N. Dak. (58564) 282/H7
Raleigh, Tenn. (38128) 237/B10
Raleigh (co.), W. Va. 312/D7
Raleigh, W. Va. (25911) 312/D7
Ralik Chain (isls.), Marshall Is. 87/G5
Ralls (co.), Mo. 261/J3
Ralls, Texas (79357) 303/C4
Ralph, Ala. (35480) 195/C4
Ralph, Mich. (49877) 250/B2
Ralph, Sask. 181/H6
Ralph, S. Dak. (57650) 298/C2
Ralphton, Pa. (†15563) 294/D5
Ralston, Alberta 182/E4
Ralston, Iowa (51459) 229/D4
Ralston, Nebr. (68127) 264/J3
Ralston, N.J. (†07945) 273/D2
Ralston, Okla. (74650) 288/N2
Ralston, Pa. (17763) 294/H2
Ralston, Tenn. (†38237) 237/D8
Ralston, Wash. (†99169) 310/G4
Ralston, Wyo. (82440) 319/D1
Ram (head), Virgin Is. (U.S.) 161/C5
Rama, Nicaragua 154/E4
Rama, Sask. 181/H4
Ramadi, Iraq 59/D3
Ramadi, Iraq 66/C4
Ramage, W. Va. (25166) 312/C7
Ramah, Colo. (80832) 208/L4
Ramah (bay), Newf. 166/B2
Ramah, N. Mex. (87321) 274/A3
Ramallah, West Bank 65/C4
Ramallo, Argentina 143/F6
Ramapo (riv.), N.J. 273/E1
Ramat Gan, Israel 65/B3
Ramat Hasharon, Israel 65/B3
Rambi (isl.), Fiji 86/R10
Ramblewood, N. J. (†08054) 273/D4
Rambouillet, France 28/D3
Rame, Israel 65/C2
Ramea, Newf. 166/C4
Ramea (isls.), Newf. 166/C4
Ramechhap, Nepal 68/F3
Ramelton, Ireland 17/F1
Ramer, Ala. (36069) 195/F6
Ramer, Tenn. (38367) 237/D10
Rameswarem, India 68/D7
Ramey, Minn. (†56329) 255/E5
Ramey, Pa. (16671) 294/F4
Ramey A.F.B., P. Rico 161/A1
Ramhormoz, Iran 66/F5
Ramhurst, Georgia (†30705) 217/C1
Ramiers (isl.), Martinique 161/C6
Ramla, Israel 65/B4
Ramm, Jebel (mt.), Jordan 65/D5
Ramme, Denmark 21/B4
Rammun, West Bank 65/C4
Ramnäs, Sweden 18/J7
Ramon (mt.), Israel 65/D5
Ramon, N. Mex. (†88136) 274/D4
Ramona, Calif. (92065) 204/J10
Ramona, Kansas (67475) 232/E3
Ramona, Okla. (74061) 288/P1
Ramona, S. Dak. (57054) 298/P5
Ramón Castilla, Peru 128/G5
Ramón de las Yaguas, Cuba 158/J4
Ramón Santana, Dom. Rep. 158/F6
Ramón Trigo, Uruguay 145/E3
Ramor (lake), Ireland 17/G4
Ramore, Ontario 177/K5
Ramos (riv.), Mexico 150/G4
Ramos Arizpe, Mexico 150/J4
Ramosch, Switzerland 39/K3
Ramotswa, Botswana 118/C4
Rampart, Alaska (99767) 196/H1
Ramparts (riv.), N.W. Terrs. 187/E3
Rampur, Him. Pradesh, India 68/D2
Rampur, Uttar Pradesh, India 68/D3
Ramree (isl.), Burma 72/B3
Ramsar, Iran 66/G2
Ramsay, Mich. (49959) 250/F2
Ramsay, Mont. (59748) 262/D4
Ramsay, Ontario 177/J5
Ramsbottom, England 13/H2
Ramsele, Sweden 18/K5
Ramsen, Switzerland 39/G1
Ramseur, N.C. (27316) 281/K3
Ramsey, England 10/F4
Ramsey, England 13/G5
Ramsey, Ill. (62080) 222/D4
Ramsey, Ind. (47166) 227/E8
Ramsey, I. of Man 13/C3
Ramsey, I. of Man 10/D3
Ramsey (bay), I. of Man 13/C3
Ramsey (co.), Minn. 255/E5
Ramsey, Minn. (†55303) 255/E5
Ramsey, N.J. (07446) 273/B1
Ramsey (co.), N. Dak. 282/N3
Ramsey (mt.), Tasmania 99/B3
Ramsey (isl.), Wales 13/B6
Ramsgate, England 10/G5
Ramsgate, England 13/J6
Ramsjö, Sweden 18/J5
Ramu (riv.), Papua N.G. 85/B7
Ramunia, Tanjong (pt.), Malaysia 72/F6
Ramville (isl.), Martinique 161/D6
Rana (fjord), Norway 18/H3
Rana (riv.), Norway 18/J3
Ranau, Malaysia 85/F4
Ranburne, Ala. (36273) 195/H3
Rancagua, Chile 138/G5
Rancagua, Chile 120/B6
Ranches of Taos, N. Mex. (87557) 274/D2
Ranchester, Wyo. (82839) 319/E1
Ranchi, India 68/F4
Rancho Cordova, Calif. (95670) 204/C8
Rancho Cucamonga, Calif. (91730) 204/E10
Rancho Mirage, Calif. (92270) 204/J10
Rancho Palos Verdes, Calif. (90274) 204/B11
Rancho Santa Clarita, Calif. (†91321) 204/G9
Rancho Santa Fe, Calif. (92067) 204/H10
Rancho Veloz, Cuba 158/D1
Ranchuelo, Cuba 158/E2
Ranchwood Manor, Okla. (†73160) 288/L4
Ranco (lake), Chile 138/E3
Rancocas, N.J. (08073) 273/D3
Rancocas (creek), N.J. 273/D3
Rand, Colo. (80473) 208/G2
Randalia, Iowa (52164) 229/K3
Randall, Iowa (50231) 229/F4
Randall, Kansas (66963) 232/D2
Randall, Minn. (56475) 255/D4
Randall (co.), Texas 303/C2
Randall (mt.), W. Australia 88/B3
Randallstown, Md. (21133) 245/L3
Randalstown, N. Ireland 17/J2
Randburg, S. Africa 118/H6
Randers, Denmark 18/G8
Randers, Denmark 21/C5
Randfontein, S. Africa 118/G6
Randle, Wash. (98377) 310/D4
Randleman, N.C. (27317) 281/K3
Randles, Mo. (†63740) 261/N8
Randlett, Okla. (73562) 288/K6
Randlett, Utah (84063) 304/E3
Randolph (co.), Ala. 195/H4
Randolph, Ala. (36792) 195/E5
Randolph, Ariz. (85243) 198/D6
Randolph (co.), Ark. 202/H1
Randolph (co.), Georgia 217/C7
Randolph (co.), Ill. 222/D5
Randolph (co.), Ind. 227/G4
Randolph, Iowa (51649) 229/B7
Randolph, Kansas (66554) 232/F2
Randolph○, Maine (†04345) 243/D7
Randolph, Md. (†20853) 245/K4
Randolph○, Mass. (02368) 249/D8
Randolph, Minn. (55065) 255/E6
Randolph, Miss. (38864) 256/F2
Randolph (co.), Mo. 261/G3
Randolph, Mo. (†64101) 261/P5
Randolph, Nebr. (68771) 264/G2
Randolph○, N.H. (03593) 268/E3
Randolph○, N.J. (†07801) 273/D2
Randolph, N.Y. (14772) 276/C6
Randolph (co.), N.C. 281/K3
Randolph, Ohio (44265) 284/H3
Randolph, Utah (84064) 304/C2
Randolph, Vt. (05060) 268/B4
Randolph○, Vt. (05060) 268/B4
Randolph, Va. (23962) 307/L7
Randolph (co.), W. Va. 312/G5
Randolph, Wis. (53956) 317/H8
Randolph A.F.B., Texas 303/K10
Randolph Center, Vt. (05061) 268/B4
Random (isl.), Newf. 166/D2
Random (sound), Newf. 166/D2
Random Lake, Wis. (53075) 317/K8
Randsburg, Calif. (93554) 204/H8
Randwick, N. S. Wales 88/L4
Randwick, N.S. Wales 97/J3
Ranelagh, Tasmania 99/C4
Ranfurly, Alberta 182/E3
Ranfurly, N. Zealand 100/B6
Rangamati, Bangladesh 68/G4
Rangasa (cape), Indonesia 85/F6
Rangatira (isl.), N. Zealand 100/E7
Range, Ala. (36473) 195/D8
Range (creek), Utah 304/D4
Rangeley, Maine (04970) 243/B6

434 Rangeley

Rangeley○, Maine (04970) 243/B6
Rangeley (lake), Maine 243/B6
Rangely, Colo. (81648) 208/B2
Ranger, Georgia (30734) 217/C2
Ranger (peak), Idaho 220/D3
Ranger, N.C. (†28906) 281/A4
Ranger, Sask. 181/D2
Ranger, Texas (76470) 303/F5
Ranger, W. Va. (25557) 312/B6
Rangiauria (Pitt) (isl.), N. Zealand 100/E7
Rangiora, N. Zealand 100/D5
Rangiroa (atoll), Fr. Poly. 87/M7
Rangitaiki (riv.), N. Zealand 100/F3
Rangitata (riv.), N. Zealand 100/C5
Rangitikei (riv.), N. Zealand 100/E3
Rangitoto (isl.), N. Zealand 100/C1
Rangkasbitung, Indonesia 85/G2
Rangoon (div.), Burma 72/C3
Rangoon (cap.), Burma 2/P5
Rangoon (cap.), Burma 54/L8
Rangoon (cap.), Burma 72/C3
Rangoon, W. Va. (†26238) 312/F4
Rangpur, Bangladesh 68/F3
Rania, Iraq 66/D2
Ranier, Minn. (56668) 255/E2
Ranken (riv.), North. Terr. 93/E6
Rankin, Ill. (60960) 222/F3
Rankin (co.), Miss. 256/E6
Rankin, Pa. (†15104) 294/C7
Rankin, Texas (79778) 303/B6
Rankine Store, North. Terr. 93/E5
Rankin Inlet, N.W. Terrs. 187/J3
Rankins Springs, N.S. Wales 97/D3
Rankweil, Austria 41/A3
Ranlo, N.C. (28052) 281/G4
Rannoch (dist.), Scotland 15/D4
Rannoch, Loch (lake), Scotland 10/D2
Rannoch, Loch (lake), Scotland 15/D4
Ranong, Thailand 72/C5
Ransiki, Indonesia 85/J6
Ransom, Ill. (60470) 222/E2
Ransom, Kansas (67572) 232/C3
Ransom (co.), N. Dak. 282/P7
Ransom, Pa. (18653) 294/F7
Ransomville, N.Y. (14131) 276/C4
Ranson, W. Va. (25438) 312/L4
Rantauprapat, Indonesia 85/C5
Rantekombola (mt.), Indonesia 85/F6
Rantis, West Bank 65/C3
Rantoul, Ill. (61866) 222/E3
Rantoul, Kansas (66079) 232/G3
Ranua, Finland 18/P4
Ranui, N. Zealand 100/B1
Ranum, Denmark 21/C4
Ranya, Wadi (dry riv.), Saudi Arabia 59/D5
Rao Co (mt.), Laos 72/E3
Rao Co (mt.), Vietnam 72/E3
Raohe, China 77/M2
Raoui, Erg er (des.), Algeria 106/D3
Raoul (isl.), N. Zealand 87/J8
Raoul (cape), Tasmania 99/D5
Rapa (isl.), Fr. Poly. 87/M8
Rapallo, Italy 34/B2
Rapa Nui (Easter) (isl.), Chile 87/Q8
Rapch (riv.), Iran 66/L8
Rapel, Chile 138/F4
Rapel (riv.), Chile 138/F4
Rapelje, Mont. (59067) 262/G5
Raper (cape), N.W.T. 162/K2
Raper (cape), N.W. Terrs. 187/M3
Raphine, Va. (24472) 307/K5
Raphoe, Ireland 17/F2
Rapid (riv.), Mich. 250/B2
Rapid (riv.), Minn. 255/D2
Rapidan, Va. (22733) 307/M4
Rapidan (riv.), Va. 307/M4
Rapid City, Manitoba 179/B4
Rapid City, Mich. (49676) 250/D4
Rapid City, S. Dak. 146/H5
Rapid City, S. Dak. 188/F2
Rapid City, S. Dak. (57701) 298/C5
Rapide-Blanc, Québec 174/C3
Rapides (par.), La. 238/E4
Rapide Taureau (dam), Québec 172/D3
Rapid River, Mich. (49878) 250/C3
Rapids City, Ill. (61278) 222/C2
Rapid View, Sask. 181/C1
Răpina, U.S.S.R. 53/D1
Raposos, Brazil 135/E2
Rappahannock (co.), Va. 307/M3
Rappahannock (riv.), Va. 307/P4
Rapperswil, Switzerland 39/G2
Rápulo (riv.), Bolivia 136/C4
Rapu-Rapu (isl.), Philippines 82/E4
Raqqa (El Rashid), Syria 63/H5
Raquette (lake), N.Y. 276/L3
Raquette (riv.), N.Y. 276/L1
Raquette Lake, N.Y. (13436) 276/L3
Raraka (atoll), Fr. Poly. 87/M7
Rarden, Ohio (45671) 284/D8
Rardin, Ill. (61948) 222/E4
Raritan, Ill. (61471) 222/C3
Raritan, N.J. (08869) 273/D2
Raritan (bay), N.J. 273/E3
Raritan (riv.), N.J. 273/D2
Raroia (atoll), Fr. Poly. 87/M7
Raron, Switzerland 39/E4
Rarotonga (isl.), Cook Is. 87/K8
Rasa (isl.), Philippines 82/B6
Ra's al Khafji, Saudi Arabia 59/E4
Ras al Khaimah, U.A.E. 59/G4
Rasar, Tenn. (†37878) 237/O9
Ras Asèr (cape), Somalia 102/H3
Ras Dashan (mt.), Ethiopia 102/F3
Ras Dashan (mt.), Ethiopia 111/G5
Raseiniai, U.S.S.R. 53/B3
Ra's en Naqb, Jordan 65/E5
Ras Ghârib, Egypt 111/F2
Rashad, Sudan 111/F5
Ras Hafun (cape), Somalia 102/H3
Rasharkin, N. Ireland 17/J2
Rasheiya, Lebanon 63/F6
Rashid (Rosetta), Egypt 111/J2
Rashid (Rosetta), Egypt 59/B3
Rashid (prov.), Syria 63/H5
Rasht, Iran 59/E2
Rasht, Iran 54/G6
Rasht, Iran 66/F2
Rask, Iran 66/M7
Raška, Yugoslavia 45/E4
Ras Lanuf, Libya 111/C1
Rason (lake), W. Australia 88/C5
Rason (lake), W. Australia 92/D5
Rasskazovo, U.S.S.R. 52/F4
Ras Tanura, Saudi Arabia 59/F4
Rastatt, W. Germany 22/C4
Rastede, W. Germany 22/C2
Rat (isls.), Alaska 196/K4
Rat (riv.), Manitoba 179/F5
Ratak Chain (isls.), Marshall Is. 87/G5
Ratangarh, India 68/C3
Rat Buri, Thailand 72/C4
Ratcliff, Ark. (72951) 202/C3
Ratcliff, Texas (75858) 303/J6
Ratcliffe, Sask. 181/G6
Rathangan, Ireland 17/G5
Rathbun, Iowa (52545) 229/H7
Rathbun (lake), Iowa 229/G7
Rathcoole, Ireland 17/J5
Rathcormac, Ireland 17/E7
Rathdowney, Ireland 17/F6
Rathdrum, Idaho (83858) 220/A2
Rathdrum, Ireland 17/J6
Rathedaung, Burma 72/B2
Rathenow, E. Germany 22/E2
Rathfriland, N. Ireland 17/J3
Rathgormuck, Ireland 17/F7
Rathkeale, Ireland 17/D7
Rathkeale, Ireland 10/B4
Rathlin (isl.), N. Ireland 10/C3
Rathlin (isl.), N. Ireland 17/J1
Rathlin (sound), N. Ireland 17/J1
Rathlin O'Birne (isl.), Ireland 17/C2
Rathluirc, Ireland 10/B4
Rathluirc, Ireland 17/D7
Rathmore, Ireland 17/J5
Rathmullen, Ireland 17/F1
Rathnew-Merrymeeting, Ireland 17/J6
Rathowen, Ireland 17/F4
Rathvilly, Ireland 17/H6
Rathwell, Manitoba 179/D5
Ratibor (Racibórz), Poland 47/C3
Ratingen, W. Germany 22/B3
Ratio, Ark. (†72333) 202/J5
Ratlam, India 68/C4
Ratliff City, Okla. (73081) 288/M6
Ratnagiri, India 68/C5
Ratnapura, Sri Lanka 68/D7
Ratoath, Ireland 17/J5
Raton, N. Mex. 188/F3
Raton, N. Mex. (87740) 274/E2
Rats (riv.), Québec 172/D2
Rattan, Okla. (74562) 288/R6
Ratten, Austria 41/C3
Rattlesnake (creek), Kansas 232/D4
Rattlesnake (creek), Ohio 284/C7
Rattlesnake (creek), Oreg. 291/K5
Rattlesnake (hills), Wyo. 319/E3
Rattlesnake (range), Wyo. 319/E3
Rattray (head), Scotland 15/G3
Rättvik, Sweden 18/J6
Ratzeburg, W. Germany 22/D2
Raub, Ind. (47976) 227/C3
Raub, Malaysia 72/D7
Raub, N. Dak. (58774) 282/F4
Rauch, Argentina 143/E4
Rauch, Minn. (†55740) 255/E3
Raukumara (range), N. Zealand 100/F3
Raul Leoni (dam), Venezuela 124/G4
Raul Soares, Brazil 135/E2
Rauma, Finland 18/M6
Rauma (riv.), Norway 18/F5
Raunds, England 13/G5
Raung (mt.), Indonesia 85/L2
Raurkela, India 68/F4
Rausu, Japan 81/M1
Rauville, S. Dak. (†57201) 298/P3
Ravalli (co.), Mont. 262/B4
Ravalli, Mont. (59863) 262/B3
Ravanna, Ark. (†75556) 202/C7
Ravanna, Mo. (†64673) 261/E2
Ravar, Iran 59/G3
Ravar, Iran 66/K5
Ravelo, Bolivia 136/C6
Ravels, Belgium 27/G6
Raven, Va. (24639) 307/E6
Ravena, N.Y. (12143) 276/N6
Ravencliff, W. Va. (25913) 312/C7
Ravendale, Calif. (96123) 204/E3
Ravenden, Ark. (72459) 202/H1
Ravenden Springs, Ark. (72460) 202/H1
Ravenel, S.C. (29470) 296/G6
Ravenna (prov.), Italy 34/D2
Ravenna, Italy 34/D2
Ravenna, Ky. (40472) 237/O5
Ravenna, Mich. (49451) 250/D5
Ravenna, Nebr. (68869) 264/E4
Ravenna, Ohio (44266) 284/H3
Ravenna, Texas (75476) 303/H4
Raven Rock, W. Va. (†26170) 312/D4
Ravensburg, W. Germany 22/C5
Ravenscrag, Sask. 181/C6
Ravensdale, Wash. (98051) 310/D3
Ravenshoe, Queensland 88/H3
Ravenshoe, Queensland 95/C3
Ravensthorpe, W. Australia 88/C6
Ravensthorpe, W. Australia 92/B6
Ravenswood, W. Va. (26164) 312/C5
Ravenwood, Mo. (64479) 261/C2
Ravi (riv.), Pakistan 68/C2
Ravia, Okla. (73455) 288/N6
Ravine, Pa. (17966) 294/K4
Ravinia, S. Dak. (57357) 298/N7
Ravne na Koroškem, Yugoslavia 45/B2
Rawalpindi, Pakistan 54/J6
Rawalpindi, Pakistan 68/C2
Rawalpindi, Pakistan 59/K3
Rawa Mazowiecka, Poland 47/E3
Rawdon, Québec 172/D3
Rawene, N. Zealand 100/D2
Rawhide (creek), Wyo. 319/G1
Rawhide (creek), Wyo. 319/H3
Rawi, Ko (isl.), Thailand 72/C6
Rawicz, Poland 47/C3
Rawlings, Md. (21557) 245/C2
Rawlings, Va. (23876) 307/N7
Rawlinna, W. Australia 88/C6
Rawlinna, W. Australia 92/D5
Rawlins (co.), Kansas 232/A2
Rawlins, Wyo. 188/E2
Rawlins, Wyo. (82301) 319/E4
Rawson, Argentina 120/C7
Rawson, Buenos Aires, Argentina 143/F7
Rawson, Chubut, Argentina 143/D5
Rawson, N. Dak. (†58831) 282/C4
Rawson, Ohio (45881) 284/C4
Rawtenstall, England 13/H1
Rawtenstall, England 10/G2
Raxaul, India 68/E3
Ray (mts.), Alaska 196/H1
Ray, Ill. (†62681) 222/C3
Ray, Ind. (46737) 227/H1
Ray, Minn. (56669) 255/E2
Ray (co.), Mo. 261/E4
Ray (cape), Newf. 166/C4
Ray (cape), Newf. 162/K6
Ray, N. Dak. (58849) 282/D3
Ray, Ohio (45672) 284/E7
Raya (mt.), Indonesia 85/E6
Rayagada, India 68/E5
Rayak, Lebanon 63/G6
Raybon, Georgia (†31553) 217/H8
Rayborn, Mo. (†65703) 261/H8
Raychikhinsk, U.S.S.R. 48/N5
Ray City, Georgia (31645) 217/F8
Ray Hubbard (lake), Texas 303/H2
Rayland, Ohio (43943) 284/J5
Rayle, Georgia (30660) 217/G3
Rayleigh, Br. Col. 184/G5
Rayleigh, England 13/J8
Raymer (New Raymer), Colo. (80742) 208/M1
Raymond, Alberta 182/D5
Raymond, Alta. 162/E6
Raymond, Calif. (93653) 204/F6
Raymond, Idaho (†83114) 220/G7
Raymond, Ill. (62560) 222/D4
Raymond, Ind. (†45056) 227/H6
Raymond, Iowa (50667) 229/J4
Raymond, Kansas (67573) 232/D3
Raymond, Maine (04071) 243/B8
Raymond○, Maine (04071) 243/B8
Raymond, Minn. (56282) 255/C5
Raymond, Miss. (39154) 256/D6
Raymond, Mont. (59256) 262/M2
Raymond, Nebr. (68428) 264/H4
Raymond, N.H. (03077) 268/E5
Raymond○, N.H. (03077) 268/E5
Raymond, Ohio (43067) 284/C5
Raymond, S. Dak. (57258) 298/O4
Raymond, Wash. (98577) 310/B4
Raymond, Wis. (†53126) 317/L2
Raymond City, W. Va. (†25159) 312/C6
Raymond Terrace, N.S. Wales 97/F3
Raymondville, Mo. (65555) 261/J8
Raymondville, N.Y. (13678) 276/L1
Raymondville, Texas (78580) 303/G11
Raymore, Mo. (64083) 261/D5
Raymore, Sask. 181/G4
Rayne, La. (70578) 238/F6
Raynesford, Mont. (59469) 262/F3
Raynham○, Mass. (02767) 249/K5
Raynham, N.C. (†28340) 281/L5
Raynham Center, Mass. (02768) 249/K5
Rayón, San Luis Potosí, Mexico 150/K6
Rayón, Sonora, Mexico 150/D2
Rayong, Thailand 72/D4
Rays (lake), Idaho 220/F6
Rays Crossing, Ind. (†46176) 227/F5
Rayside-Balfour, Ontario 177/K5
Raystown (lake), Pa. 294/F5
Raystown Branch, Juniata (riv.), Pa. 294/F5
Raysut (Risut), Oman 59/F6
Raytown, Mo. (64133) 261/P6
Rayville, La. (71269) 238/G2
Rayville, Mo. (64084) 261/E4
Raywick, Ky. (40060) 237/L5
Razan, Iran 66/F3
Razaza (res.), Iraq 66/C4
Razdan, U.S.S.R. 52/G6
Razgrad, Bulgaria 45/H4
Razlog, Bulgaria 45/F5
Ré (isl.), France 28/C4
Rea, Mo. (64480) 261/C2
Reader, Ark. (71726) 202/D6
Reader, W. Va. (26167) 312/E3
Readfield, Maine (04355) 243/D7
Readfield○, Maine (04355) 243/D7
Readfield, Wis. (54969) 317/J7
Reading, England 13/G8
Reading, England 10/F5
Reading, Kansas (66868) 232/F3
Reading○, Mass. (01867) 249/C5
Reading, Mich. (49274) 250/E7
Reading, Minn. (56165) 255/C7
Reading, Ohio (45215) 284/C9
Reading, Pa. 188/L2
Reading, Pa. (*19601) 294/L5
Reading○, Vt. (05062) 268/B5
Readington, N.J. (08870) 273/D2
Readland, Ark. (71664) 202/H7
Readlyn, Iowa (50668) 229/J3
Readlyn, Sask. 181/F6
Readsboro, Vt. (05350) 268/B6
Readsboro○, Vt. (05350) 268/B6
Reads Landing, Minn. (55968) 255/F6
Reads Mill, Ala. (†36279) 195/G3
Readstown, Wis. (54652) 317/E9
Readsville, Mo. (†65067) 261/J5
Readville, Mass. (02137) 249/C8
Ready, Ky. (†42721) 237/J6
Readyville, Tenn. (37149) 237/J9
Reagan, Okla. (†73460) 288/N6
Reagan, Tenn. (38368) 237/E9
Reagan (co.), Texas 303/C6
Reagan, Texas (76680) 303/H6
Real, Cordillera (range), Bolivia 136/A5
Real (co.), Texas 303/E8
Real de San Carlos, Uruguay 145/A5
Realitos, Texas (78376) 303/F10
Realp, Switzerland 39/F3
Reamstown, Pa. (17567) 294/K5
Reao (atoll), Fr. Poly. 87/N7
Reardan, Wash. (99029) 310/H3
Reasnor, Iowa (50232) 229/G5
Reaville, N.J. (†08822) 273/D3
Reay, Scotland 15/E2
Rebecca, Georgia (31783) 217/E7
Rebecca (lake), W. Australia 88/C6
Rebecca (lake), W. Australia 92/C5
Rebecq, Belgium 27/E7
Rebersburg, Pa. (16872) 294/H4
Rebiana (oasis), Libya 111/D3
Rebiana Sand Sea (des.), Libya 111/D3
Reboledo, Uruguay 145/D4
Rebun (isl.), Japan 81/K1
Recanati, Italy 34/D3
Recherche (arch.), Australia 87/C9
Recherche (arch.), W. Australia 88/C6
Recherche (arch.), W. Australia 92/C6
Rechitsa, U.S.S.R. 52/C4
Rechnitz, Austria 41/D3
Rechthalten, Switzerland 39/D3
Recife, Brazil 132/H5
Recife, Brazil 120/F3
Recife, Brazil 2/H6
Reckingen, Switzerland 39/F4
Recklinghausen, W. Germany 22/B3
Recluse, Wyo. (82725) 319/G1
Reconquista, Argentina 143/F4
Recreo, Argentina 143/C2
Rector, Ark. (72461) 202/K1
Rectortown, Va. (22140) 307/N3
Recuay, Peru 128/D7
Red (riv.) 146/J5
Red (riv.) 188/H4
Red (sea) 2/L4
Red (sea) 54/E7
Red (riv.) 54/M7
Red (sea) 102/F2
Red (riv.), Ark. 202/C6
Red (mt.), Conn. 210/B1
Red (sea), Egypt 111/G3
Red (sea), Ethiopia 111/H4
Red (riv.), Idaho 220/C4
Red (riv.), Ky. 237/G7
Red (riv.), Ky. 237/O5
Red (riv.), La. 238/G4
Red (riv.), Manitoba 179/F4
Red (lake), Minn. 188/H1
Red (isl.), Newf. 166/C2
Red (bay), N. Ireland 17/K1
Red, North Fork (riv.), Okla. 288/H4
Red (riv.), Okla. 288/R7
Red (lake), Ontario 175/B2
Red (sea), Saudi Arabia 59/C5
Red (lake), S. Dak. 298/L6
Red (sea), Sudan 111/G3
Red (riv.), Tenn. 237/G7
Red (riv.), Texas 303/F3
Red (riv.), U.S. 146/J6
Red (riv.), Utah 304/D3
Red (riv.), Vietnam 72/E2
Red (pt.), Virgin Is. (U.S.) 161/D4
Red (sea), Yemen Arab Rep. 59/C5
Reda, Poland 47/D1
Redang, Pulau (isl.), Malaysia 72/D6
Redange, Luxembourg 27/H9
Red Ash, Va. (24640) 307/E6
Red Bank, New Bruns. 170/E2
Red Bank, N.J. (07701) 273/E3
Redbank (creek), Pa. 294/E3
Red Bank, Tenn. (37415) 237/L10
Red Banks, Miss. (38661) 256/F1
Red Bay, Ala. (35582) 195/B2
Red Bay, Fla. (†32455) 212/C6
Red Bay, Newf. 166/C3
Red Bay, Ontario 177/C3
Red Beach, Maine (04670) 243/J5
Red Bird, Mo. (†65014) 261/J6
Redbird, Okla. (74458) 288/P3
Red Bluff, Calif. (96080) 204/C3
Red Bluff (lake), N. Mex. 274/E7
Red Bluff (lake), Texas 188/F4
Red Bluff (lake), Texas 303/A6
Red Boiling Springs, Tenn. (37150) 237/K7
Redbridge, England 13/H8
Redbridge, England 10/C5
Red Bud, Ill. (62278) 222/D5
Redbush, Ky. (41251) 237/P5
Redby, Minn. (56670) 255/D3
Redcar, England 10/F3
Redcar, England 13/F3
Red Cedar (riv.), Wis. 317/C5
Red Chute (bayou), La. 238/C1
Redcliff, Alberta 182/E4
Red Cliff, Colo. (81649) 208/G4
Red Cliff, Wis. (†54814) 317/E2
Redcliffe, Queensland 95/E5
Red Cliffe, Queensland 88/J5
Red Cliff Ind. Res., Wis. 317/E2
Red Cliffs, Victoria 97/B4
Redcloud (peak), Colo. 208/E6
Red Cloud, Nebr. (68970) 264/F4
Red Creek, N.Y. (13143) 276/G4
Red Creek, W. Va. (26289) 312/H4
Redcrest, Calif. (95569) 204/A3
Red Deer, Alberta 182/D3
Red Deer (lake), Alberta 182/D3
Red Deer (riv.), Alberta 182/D4
Red Deer, Alta. 146/H4
Red Deer, Alta. 162/E5
Red Deer (lake), Manitoba 179/A2
Red Deer (riv.), Manitoba 179/A2
Red Deer (riv.), Sask. 181/K3
Red Deer (riv.), Sask. 181/A5
Red Deer Hill, Sask. 181/F2
Reddell, La. (70580) 238/F5
Redden, Del. (†19947) 245/S5
Red Devil, Alaska (99656) 196/G2
Reddick, Fla. (32686) 212/D2
Reddick, Ill. (60961) 222/E2
Redding, Calif. 146/F5
Redding, Calif. 188/B2
Redding, Calif. (96001) 204/C3
Redding○, Conn. (06875) 210/B3
Redding, Iowa (50860) 229/E7
Redding Ridge, Conn. (06876) 210/B3
Reddington, Ind. (†47274) 227/F6
Redditch, England 13/E5
Redditch, England 10/G3
Redearth Creek, Alberta 182/C1
Red Elm, S. Dak. (†57623) 298/F3
Redeye (riv.), Minn. 255/D4
Red Feather Lakes, Colo. (80545) 208/H1
Redfield, Ark. (72132) 202/F5
Redfield, Iowa (50233) 229/E5
Redfield, Kansas (66769) 232/H4
Redfield, N.Y. (13437) 276/J3
Redfield, Sask. 181/D2
Redfield, S. Dak. (57469) 298/N4
Redfish (lake), Idaho 220/D5
Redford, Mo. (63665) 261/L8
Redford, Texas (79846) 303/C12
Red Fork, Powder (riv.), Wyo. 319/F2
Redgranite, Wis. (54970) 317/J7
Redhead, Trin. & Tob. 161/B10
Red Head Cove, Newf. 166/D2
Red Hill (mt.), Hawaii 218/K2
Red Hill, Pa. (18076) 294/L5
Red Hook, N.Y. (12571) 276/N7
Redhouse, Ky. (†40475) 237/N5
Red House, Nev. (†89414) 266/D2
Red House, Va. (23963) 307/L6
Red House, W. Va. (25168) 312/C5
Redig, S. Dak. (57776) 298/C3
Red Indian (lake), Newf. 166/C4
Redington, Nebr. (†69336) 264/A3
Redington Beach, Fla. (33708) 212/B3
Redington Shores, Fla. (†33708) 212/B3
Red Jacket, W. Va. (25692) 312/B7
Redkey, Ind. (47373) 227/G4
Redlake, Minn. (56671) 255/C3
Red Lake (co.), Minn. 255/B3
Red Lake (riv.), Minn. 255/B2
Red Lake, Ont. 162/G6
Red Lake, Ontario 175/B2
Red Lake Falls, Minn. (56750) 255/B3
Red Lake Ind. Res., Minn. 255/C2
Red Lake Road, Ontario 177/G5
Red Lake Road, Ontario 175/B2
Redland, Alberta 182/D4
Redland, Oreg. (†97045) 291/B2
Redlands, Calif. (92373) 204/H9
Red Level, Ala. (36474) 195/E8
Red Lick, Miss. (†39096) 256/B7
Red Lion, Del. (†19701) 245/R2
Red Lion, N.J. (08088) 273/D4
Red Lion, Ohio (†45005) 284/B7
Red Lion, Pa. (17356) 294/J6
Red Lodge, Mont. (59068) 262/G5
Redman, Mich. (†48468) 250/G5
Red Mesa, Colo. (†81326) 208/C8
Redmon, Ill. (61949) 222/F4
Redmond, Oreg. (97756) 291/F3
Redmond, Utah (84652) 304/C4
Redmond, Wash. (98052) 310/B1
Red Mountain, Calif. (93558) 204/H8
Red Oak, Georgia (30272) 217/J2
Red Oak, Iowa (51566) 229/C6
Red Oak, Mich. (†49756) 250/E4
Red Oak, N.C. (27868) 281/N2
Red Oak, Okla. (74563) 288/R5
Red Oak, Texas (75154) 303/H5
Red Oak, Va. (23964) 307/L7
Red Oaks Mill, N.Y. (†12601) 276/N7
Redon, France 28/C4
Redonda (isl.), Ant. & Bar. 156/F3
Redondela, Spain 33/B1
Redondo, Portugal 33/C3
Redondo, Wash. (98054) 310/C3
Redondo Beach, Calif. (*90277) 204/B11
Redoubt (vol.), Alaska 196/H2
Redowl, S. Dak. (57777) 298/D4
Red Owl (creek), S. Dak. 298/E4
Redpa, Tasmania 99/A2
Red Pass, Br. Col. 184/H4
Redridge, Mich. (†49931) 250/G1
Red River (par.), La. 238/D2
Red River, N. Mex. (87558) 274/D2
Red River, Nova Scotia 168/H2
Red River, S.C. (†29730) 296/F2
Red River (co.), Texas 303/J4
Red River Hot Springs, Idaho (†83525) 220/C4
Red River of the North (riv.) 188/G1
Red River of the North (riv.), Minn. 255/A2
Red River of the North (riv.), N. Dak. 282/S4
Red Rock, Ariz. (85245) 198/D6
Red Rock, Br. Col. 184/F3
Red Rock (lake), Iowa 229/G6
Red Rock (lakes), Mont. 262/E6
Red Rock (riv.), Mont. 262/D6
Redrock, N. Mex. (88055) 274/A6
Red Rock, Okla. (74651) 288/M2
Red Rock, Ontario 177/H5
Red Rock, Ontario 175/C3
Red Rock, Texas (78662) 303/G8
Red Scaffold (creek), S. Dak. 298/F4
Red Sea (prov.), Sudan 111/G4
Red Sea Hills (mts.), Sudan 59/C5
Red Springs, N.C. (28377) 281/L5
Red Springs, Texas (76378) 303/E4
Redstar, W. Va. (25914) 312/D7
Redstone, Br. Col. 184/F4
Redstone, Colo. (†81623) 208/E4
Redstone, Mont. (59257) 262/M2
Redstone, N.H. (†03813) 268/E3
Redstone (riv.), N.W. Terrs. 187/F3
Redstone (lake), Ontario 177/F2
Redstone (creek), S. Dak. 298/O5
Redstone Arsenal, Ala. 195/E1
Red Sucker Lake, Manitoba 179/K3
Red Sulphur Springs, W. Va. (†24963) 312/E7
Redtop, Minn. (†56342) 255/E4
Redvale, Colo. (81431) 208/B6
Redvers, Sask. 181/K6
Red Volta (riv.), Ghana 106/D6
Red Volta (riv.), Upper Volta 106/D6
Redwater, Alberta 182/D3
Redwater (riv.), Mont. 262/L3
Redwater (creek), S. Dak. 298/A4
Redway, Calif. (95560) 204/B3
Red Willow, Alberta 182/D3
Red Willow (co.), Nebr. 264/D4
Redwine, Ky. (†41477) 237/P4
Red Wine (riv.), Newf. 166/B3
Red Wing, Colo. (81066) 208/J7
Redwing, Kansas (†67544) 232/D3
Red Wing, Minn. (55066) 255/F6
Redwood (co.), Minn. 255/C6
Redwood (riv.), Minn. 255/C6
Redwood, Miss. (39156) 256/C6
Redwood, N.Y. (13679) 276/J2
Redwood City, Calif. (*94061) 204/J3
Redwood Estates-Chemeketa Park, Calif. (95044) 204/K4
Redwood Falls, Minn. (56283) 255/C6
Redwood Nat'l Park, Calif. 204/A2
Redwood Valley, Calif. (95470) 204/B4
Ree, Lough (lake), Ireland 10/B4
Ree (lake), Ireland 17/F5
Reece, Kansas (†67045) 232/F4
Reece City, Ala. (†35954) 195/G2
Reed, Ark. (71670) 202/H6
Reed, Ky. (42451) 237/G5
Reed, Okla. (73563) 288/G5
Reed (mt.), Québec 174/D2
Reed City, Mich. (49677) 250/D5
Reeder, Manitoba 179/A4
Reeder, N. Dak. (58649) 282/E7
Reedley, Calif. (93654) 204/F7
Reedpoint, Mont. (59069) 262/G5
Reeds, Mo. (64859) 261/D8
Reedsburg (res.), Mich. 250/E4
Reedsburg, Ohio (†44691) 284/F4
Reedsburg, Wis. (53959) 317/G8
Reeds Ferry, N.H. (†03054) 268/D6
Reedsport, Oreg. (97467) 291/C4
Reeds Spring, Mo. (65737) 261/F9
Reedsville, Ohio (45772) 284/G7
Reedsville, Pa. (17084) 294/G4
Reedsville, W. Va. (26547) 312/G3
Reedsville, Wis. (54230) 317/L7
Reedville, Oreg. (†97005) 291/A2
Reedville, Va. (22539) 307/R5
Reedy (lake), Fla. 212/E4
Reedy (riv.), S.C. 296/C2
Reedy, W. Va. (25270) 312/D5
Reedy (creek), W. Va. 312/D5
Reedyville, Ky. (†42275) 237/H6
Reef (bay), Virgin Is. (U.S.) 161/C4
Reefton, N. Zealand 100/C5
Ree Heights, S. Dak. (57371) 298/L4
Reelfoot (lake), Tenn. 237/C8
Reelsville, Ind. (46171) 227/D5
Reeman, Mich. (†49412) 250/D5
Reese, Mich. (48757) 250/F5
Reese (riv.), Nev. 266/D3
Reese A.F.B., Texas 303/B4
Reeseville, Wis. (53579) 317/J9
Reesville, Ohio (45166) 284/C7
Reeves, La. (70658) 238/D5
Reeves (co.), Texas 303/D11
Reeves Knob (mt.), Ark. 202/E2
Reevesville, Ill. (†62943) 222/E6
Reevesville, S.C. (29471) 296/F5
Refahiye, Turkey 63/H3
Refa'i, Iraq 66/E5
Reform, Ala. (35481) 195/C4
Reform, Miss. (39757) 256/F4
Refton, Pa. (17568) 294/K6
Refuge Cove, Br. Col. 184/E5
Refugio (isl.), Chile 138/D5
Refugio (co.), Texas 303/G9
Refugio, Texas (78377) 303/G9
Rega (riv.), Poland 47/B2
Regal, Minn. (†56312) 255/D5
Regan, N. Dak. (58477) 282/K5
Regen, W. Germany 22/E4
Regen (riv.), W. Germany 22/E4
Regeneração, Brazil 132/F4
Regensburg, W. Germany 7/F4
Regensburg, W. Germany 22/E4
Regensdorf, Switzerland 39/F2
Regent, Manitoba 179/B5
Regent, N. Dak. (58650) 282/E7
Reger, Mo. (†63556) 261/F2
Reggane, Algeria 106/D3
Regge (riv.), Netherlands 27/K4
Reggio, La. (†70085) 238/L7
Reggio di Calabria (prov.), Italy 34/E5
Reggio di Calabria, Italy 7/F5
Reggio di Calabria, Italy 34/E5
Reggio nell'Emilia (prov.), Italy 34/C2
Reggio nell'Emilia, Italy 34/C2
Reghin, Romania 45/G2
Régina, Fr. Guiana 131/E3
Regina, Mont. (59539) 262/J3
Regina, N. Mex. (87046) 274/B2
Regina (cap.), Sask. 162/F5
Regina (cap.), Sask. 146/H4
Regina (cap.), Sask. 181/G5
Regina Beach, Sask. 181/F5
Register, Georgia (30452) 217/J6
Registro, Brazil 135/C4
Regla, Cuba 158/C1
Regnitz (riv.), W. Germany 22/D4
Reguengos de Monsaraz, Portugal 33/C3
Regway, Sask. 181/G6
Rehau, W. Germany 22/D3
Rehoboth, Ala. (†36720) 195/D6
Rehoboth○, Mass. (02769) 249/K5
Rehoboth, Namibia 118/B4
Rehoboth, Namibia 102/D7
Rehoboth, N. Mex. (87322) 274/A3
Rehoboth, Va. (†23974) 307/M7
Rehoboth Beach, Del. (19971) 245/T6
Rehovot, Israel 65/B4
Rehrersburg, Pa. (19550) 294/K5
Reichenau an der Rax, Austria 41/C3
Reichenbach, E. Germany 22/E3
Reichenbach im Kandertal, Switzerland 39/E3

Reid, Md. (†21740) 245/H2
Reid (lake), S. Dak. 298/O3
Reid (rocks), Tasmania 99/B1
Reid, W. Australia 92/E5
Reiden, Switzerland 39/F2
Reids Grove, Md. (†21869) 245/P6
Reidsville, Georgia (30453) 217/H6
Reidsville, N.C. (27320) 281/K2
Reidville, S.C. (29375) 296/C2
Reigate, England 13/H8
Reigate, England 10/F5
Reile's Acres, N. Dak. (†58078) 282/S6
Reily, Ohio (45060) 284/A7
Re'im, Israel 65/A5
Reims, France 7/E4
Reims, France 28/E3
Reina Adelaida (arch.), Chile 120/B8
Reina Adelaida (arch.), Chile 138/D9
Reinach in Aargau, Switzerland 39/F2
Reinach in Baselland, Switzerland 39/E2
Reinbeck, Iowa (50669) 229/H4
Reindeer (lake) 162/F4
Reindeer (lake), Canada 146/H4
Reindeer (isl.), Manitoba 179/E2
Reindeer (lake), Manitoba 179/H2
Reindeer (lake), Sask. 181/N3
Reindeer (riv.), Sask. 181/M3
Reinersville, Ohio (43756) 284/G6
Reinfeld, W. Germany 22/D2
Reinga (cape), N. Zealand 100/D1
Reinland, Manitoba 179/E5
Reinosa, Spain 33/D1
Reisaelv (riv.), Norway 18/M2
Reisduoddarhal'di (Haltiatunturi), Norway 18/M2
Reiss, Scotland 15/E2
Reisterstown, Md. (21136) 245/L3
Reitz, S. Africa 118/D5
Rejaf, Sudan 111/F7
Reliance, Md. (†19973) 245/P6
Reliance, N.W. Terrs. 187/H3
Reliance, S. Dak. (57569) 298/K6
Reliance, Tenn. (37369) 237/N10
Reliance, Va. (22649) 307/M3
Reliance, Wyo. (82943) 319/C4
Relief, Ky. (41463) 237/P5
Relizane, Algeria 106/E1
Reloncaví (bay), Chile 138/D4
Remada, Tunisia 106/F2
Remagen, W. Germany 22/B3
Remanso, Brazil 132/F5
Remates, Cuba 158/A2
Rembang, Indonesia 85/K2
Rembert, S.C. (29128) 296/G3
Rembrandt, Iowa (50576) 229/C3
Rembrandt, Manitoba 179/E4
Remedios, Colombia 126/C4
Remedios, Cuba 156/B2
Remedios, Cuba 158/E2
Remedios (pt.), El Salvador 154/B4
Remer, Minn. (56672) 255/E3
Remerton, Georgia (31601) 217/F9
Remich, Luxembourg 27/J9
Reminderville, Ohio (†44202) 284/J10
Remington, Ind. (47977) 227/C3
Remington, Ohio (†45202) 284/C9
Remington, Va. (22734) 307/N3
Rémire, Fr. Guiana 131/E3
Rémire (isls.), Fr. Guiana 131/F3
Remiremont, France 28/G3
Remlap, Ala. (35133) 195/E3
Remmel (mt.), Wash. 310/E2
Remo, Br. Col. 184/C3
Remolino, Colombia 126/C2
Remote, Oreg. (97468) 291/D5
Remscheid, W. Germany 22/B3
Remsen, Iowa (51050) 229/B3
Remsen, N.Y. (13438) 276/K4
Remus, Mich. (49340) 250/D5
Remus, Okla. (†74801) 288/N4
Remy, La. (†70763) 238/L3
Rena, Ark. (†72956) 202/B3
Rena, Norway 18/G6
Reñaca, Chile 138/F2
Renaix (Ronse), Belgium 27/D7
Rena Lara, Miss. (38767) 256/C2
Renan, Switzerland 39/C2
Renault, Ill. (62279) 222/C5
Renca, Chile 138/G3
Rencona, N. Mex. (†87562) 274/D3
Rencontre East, Newf. 166/C4
Rend (lake), Ill. 222/E5
Rendeux, Belgium 27/H8
Rendova (isl.), Solomon Is. 86/D3
Rendsburg, W. Germany 22/C1
Rendville, Ohio (†43730) 284/F6
Renens, Switzerland 39/C3
Renews, Newf. 166/D2
Renforth, New Bruns. 170/E3
Renfrew, Ont. 162/J6
Renfrew (county), Ontario 177/G2
Renfrew (county), Ontario 175/E3
Renfrew, Ontario 177/H2
Renfrew, Ontario 175/E3
Renfrew, Pa. (16053) 294/C4
Renfrew, Scotland 10/A1
Renfrew, Scotland 15/B2
Renfrew (trad. co.), Scotland 15/A5
Renfroe, Ala. (†35160) 195/F4
Renfroe, Georgia (†31805) 217/C6
Renfroe, Miss. (†39051) 256/F5
Renfrow, Okla. (†73759) 288/L1
Rengam, Malaysia 72/E5
Rengat, Indonesia 85/C6
Rengo, Chile 138/G5
Reni, U.S.S.R. 52/C5
Renick, Mo. (65278) 261/H4
Renick, W. Va. (24966) 312/F6
Renigunta, India 68/E6
Renish (pt.), Scotland 15/B3
Renk, Sudan 111/F5
Renkum, Netherlands 27/H5
Renmark, S. Australia 88/G6
Renmark, S. Australia 94/G5
Rennell (isl.), Solomon Is. 87/F7
Rennell (isl.), Solomon Is. 86/E3
Renner, S. Dak. (57055) 298/R6
Rennert, N.C. (†28386) 281/L5
Rennes, France 7/D4
Rennes, France 28/C3
Rennie, Manitoba 179/G5
Rennie (lake), N.W. Terrs. 187/H3
Renno, S.C. (†29325) 296/D2
Reno, Alberta 182/B2
Reno, Georgia (†31728) 217/D9
Reno, Ill. (†62086) 222/D5
Reno (co.), Kansas 232/D4
Reno (lake), Minn. 255/C5
Reno, Nev. 146/G6
Reno, Nev. 188/C3
Reno, Nev. (*89501) 266/B3
Reno, Ohio (45773) 284/H7
Reno, Texas (†76020) 303/E2
Reno Beach, Ohio (†43412) 284/D2
Renous, New Bruns. 170/E2
Renous (riv.), New Bruns. 170/D2
Renova, Miss. (†38732) 256/C3
Renovo, Pa. (17764) 294/G3
Renown, Sask. 181/F4
Rensburg, S. Africa 118/J7
Rensselaer, Ind. (47978) 227/C3
Rensselaer, Mo. (†63401) 261/J3
Rensselaer (co.), N.Y. 276/O5
Rensselaer, N.Y. (12144) 276/N5
Rensselaer Falls, N.Y. (13680) 276/K1
Rentchler, Ill. (†62220) 222/B3
Rentiesville, Okla. (74459) 288/R4
Renton, Scotland 15/A1
Renton, Wash. (98055) 310/B2
Rentz, Georgia (31075) 217/G6
Renville (co.), Minn. 255/C6
Renville, Minn. (56284) 255/C6
Renville (co.), N. Dak. 282/G2
Renwer, Manitoba 179/B2
Renwick, Iowa (50577) 229/E3
Répcelak, 41/D3
Repentigny, Québec 172/J4
Replete, W. Va. (†26222) 312/F5
Repos (lake), Québec 172/C2
Repton, Ala. (36475) 195/D8
Republic, Ala. (†35203) 195/E3
Republic (co.), Kansas 232/E2
Republic, Kansas (66964) 232/E2
Republic, Mich. (49879) 250/B2
Republic, Mo. (65738) 261/E8
Republic, Ohio (44867) 284/D3
Republic, Wash. (99166) 310/G2
República Dominicana, Cuba 158/F2
Republican (riv.) 188/F2
Republican (riv.), Colo. 208/P3
Republican (riv.), Kansas 232/E2
Republican (riv.), Nebr. 264/G5
Republican City, Nebr. (68971) 264/E4
Republican Grove, Va. (24585) 307/K7
Repulse (bay), Queensland 88/H4
Repulse Bay, Canada 4/C14
Repulse Bay, N.W.T. 162/H2
Repulse Bay, N.W. Terrs. 187/K3
Requa, Calif. (†95548) 204/A2
Requegua, Chile 138/G5
Requena, Peru 128/F5
Requena, Spain 33/F3
Requínoa, Chile 138/G5
Rera, Brazil 132/A1
Resaca, Georgia (30735) 217/C1
Reşadiye, Turkey 63/G2
Research, Victoria 97/J4
Reseda, Calif. (91335) 204/B10
Resende, Brazil 135/D3
Resende, Portugal 33/B2
Reserve, Kansas (66529) 232/G2
Reserve, La. (70084) 238/M3
Reserve, Mont. (59258) 262/M2
Reserve, N. Mex. (87830) 274/A5
Reserve, Sask. 181/J3
Reserve, Wis. (†54876) 317/D4
Reserve Mines, Nova Scotia 168/H2
Resht (Rasht), Iran 66/F2
Reshui, China 77/E4
Resistencia, Argentina 143/E2
Resistencia, Argentina 120/D5
Reşiţa, Romania 45/E3
Resolute, Canada 4/B14
Resolute Bay, N.W.T. 162/G1
Resolute Bay, N.W. Terrs. 187/J2
Resolution (isl.), N.W.T. 146/M3
Resolution (isl.), N.W.T. 162/K3
Resolution (isl.), N. Zealand 100/A6
Resolution (isl.), N.W. Terrs. 187/M3
Resolution Island, N.W. Terrs. 187/M3
Resort, Loch (inlet), Scotland 15/A2
Resource, Sask. 181/G3
Respenda de la Peña, Spain 33/D1
Restauración, Dom. Rep. 158/D5
Rest Haven, Georgia (†30518) 217/E2
Restigouche (co.), New Bruns. 170/C1
Restigouche (riv.), New Bruns. 170/C1
Restigouche, Québec 172/C2
Reston, Manitoba 179/A5
Reston, Va. (22090) 307/R2
Restoule, Ontario 177/E1
Restoule (lake), Ontario 177/E1
Restrepo, Colombia 126/D5
Reszel, Poland 47/E1
Retalhuleu, Guatemala 154/B3
Retamosa, Uruguay 145/E4
Rethel, France 28/F3
Réthimnon, Greece 45/G8
Retie, Belgium 27/G6
Retiro, Chile 138/A11
Retlaw, Alberta 182/D4
Rétság, Hungary 41/E3
Retsil, Wash. (98378) 310/A2
Retsof, N.Y. (14539) 276/E5
Retz, Austria 41/D2
Reubens, Idaho (83548) 220/B3
Réunion (isl.), (Fr.) 2/M7
RÉUNION 118/F5
Reus, Spain 33/G2
Reusel, Netherlands 27/G6
Reuss (riv.), Switzerland 39/F2
Reutlingen, W. Germany 22/C4
Reutte, Austria 41/A3
Reva, S. Dak. (57651) 298/C2
Revadim, Israel 65/B4
Reveille (peak), Nev. 266/E5
Reveille (range), Nev. 266/E4
Revel, France 28/E6
Revel (Tallinn), U.S.S.R. 52/B3
Revelo, Ky. (42638) 237/N7
Revelstoke, Br. Col. 162/E5
Revelstoke, Br. Col. 184/J5
Reventazón, Peru 128/B6
Revenue, Sask. 181/B3
Revere, Mass. (02151) 249/D6
Revere, Minn. (56166) 255/C6
Revere, Mo. (63465) 261/J2
Revere, N. Dak. (†58484) 282/O5
Revere, W. Va. (†26158) 312/E5
Reverie, Tenn. (38062) 237/A9
Revillagigedo (chan.), Alaska 196/N2
Revillagigedo (isl.), Alaska 196/N2
Revillagigedo (isls.), Mexico 146/G8
Revillagigedo (isls.), Mexico 2/D5
Revillagigedo (isls.), Mexico 150/C7
Revillo, S. Dak. (57259) 298/R3
Révin, France 28/F3
Revivim, Israel 65/D5
Revúca, Czech. 41/E2
Revuelto (creek), N. Mex. 274/F3
Rew, Pa. (16744) 294/F2
Rewa, India 68/E4
Reward, Sask. 181/B3
Rewataya (reef), Indonesia 85/F7
Rewey, Wis. (53580) 317/F10
Rex, N.C. (28378) 281/M5
Rex, Oreg. (†97132) 291/A2
Rexburg, Idaho (83440) 220/G6
Rexford, Kansas (67753) 232/B2
Rexford, Mont. (59930) 262/A2
Rexton, Mich. (†49734) 250/D2
Rexton, New Bruns. 170/F2
Rexville, Ind. (†47250) 227/G7
Rexville, N.Y. (14877) 276/E6
Rey, Iran 59/F2
Rey, Iran 66/G3
Rey (isl.), Panama 154/H6
Rey Bouba, Cameroon 115/B2
Reydell, Ark. (72133) 202/G5
Reydon, Okla. (73660) 288/G3
Reyes, Bolivia 136/B4
Reyes (pt.), Calif. 204/B6
Reyhanlı, Turkey 63/G4
Reykjanestá (cape), Iceland 7/B2
Reykjanestá (cape), Iceland 21/A2
Reykjavík (cap.), Iceland 4/C11
Reykjavík (cap.), Iceland 2/J2
Reykjavík (cap.), Iceland 21/B1
Reykjavík (cap.), Iceland 7/B2
Reynaud, Sask. 181/F3
Reyno, Ark. (72462) 202/J1
Reynolds, Georgia (31076) 217/D5
Reynolds (creek), Idaho 220/B6
Reynolds, Ill. (61279) 222/C2
Reynolds, Ind. (47980) 227/D3
Reynolds (co.), Mo. 261/L8
Reynolds, Mo. (63666) 261/K8
Reynolds, Nebr. (68429) 264/G4
Reynolds, N. Dak. (58275) 282/R4
Reynolds Bridge, Conn. (†06787) 210/C2
Reynoldsburg, Ohio (43068) 284/E6
Reynolds Station, Ky. (42368) 237/H5
Reynoldsville, Pa. (15851) 294/D3
Reynosa, Mexico 150/K3
Rezaiyeh (Urmia), Iran 66/D2
Reza'iyeh (Urmia), Iran 59/D2
Rezé, France 28/C4
Rēzekne, U.S.S.R. 52/C3
Rēzekne, U.S.S.R. 53/D2
Rhaetian Alps (range), Switzerland 39/J4
Rhame, N. Dak. (58651) 282/C7
Rhätikon (mts.), Liecht. 39/J2
Rhätikon (mts.), Switzerland 39/J2
Rhayader, Wales 13/D5
Rhea (creek), Oreg. 291/H2
Rhea (co.), Tenn. 237/M9
Rheatown, Tenn. (†37641) 237/R8
Rheda-Wiedenbrück, W. Germany 22/C3
Rheden, Netherlands 27/J4
Rheims (Reims), France 28/E4
Rhein, Sask. 181/J4
Rheinau, Switzerland 39/G1
Rheine, W. Germany 22/B2
Rheineck, Switzerland 39/J2
Rheinfeld, Sask. 181/D5
Rheinfelden, Switzerland 39/E1
Rheinfelden, W. Germany 22/B5
Rheinsberg, E. Germany 22/E2
Rheinwaldhorn (mt.), Switzerland 39/G4
Rhems, S.C. (†29440) 296/H4
Rhenen, Netherlands 27/H5
Rhéris, Wadi (dry riv.), Morocco 106/D2
Rheydt, W. Germany 22/B3
Rhine (riv.) 7/E4
Rhine (riv.), Austria 41/A3
Rhine (riv.), France 28/G3
Rhine, Georgia (31077) 217/F7
Rhine (riv.), Liecht. 39/J2
Rhine (riv.), Netherlands 27/J5
Rhine (riv.), Switzerland 39/J2
Rhine (riv.), W. Germany 22/B3
Rhinebeck, N.Y. (12572) 276/N7
Rhinecliff, N.Y. (12574) 276/N7
Rhineland, Mo. (65069) 261/J5
Rhineland, Sask. 181/D5
Rhinelander, Wis. (54501) 317/H4
Rhineland-Palatinate (state), W. Germany 22/B4
Rhinns, The (pen.), Scotland 15/C6
Rhinns (pt.), Scotland 15/B5
Rhino Camp, Uganda 115/F3
Rhir, Wadi (dry riv.), Algeria 106/F2
Rhir (cape), Morocco 106/B2
Rho, Italy 34/B2
Rhode Island 188/M2
RHODE ISLAND 249
Rhode Island (isl.), R.I. 249/J6
Rhode Island (sound), R.I. 249/J7
Rhode Island (state), U.S. 146/M5
Rhodell, W. Va. (25915) 312/D7
Rhodes (Ródhos), Greece 45/J7
Rhodes (isl.), Greece 7/G5
Rhodes (isl.), Greece 45/H7
Rhodes (peak), Idaho 220/D3
Rhodes, Iowa (50234) 229/G5
Rhodes, Mich. (48652) 250/E5
Rhodes Inyanga Nat'l Park, Zimbabwe 118/E3
Rhodes Point, Md. (21858) 245/O9
Rhodhiss, N.C. (28667) 281/F3
Rhododendron, Oreg. (97073) 291/F2
Rhodope (mts.), Bulgaria 45/G5
Rhodope (mts.), Greece 45/G5
Rhome, Texas (76078) 303/E1
Rhön (mts.), E. Germany 22/D3
Rhön (mts.), W. Germany 22/D3
Rhondda, Wales 13/A6
Rhondda, Wales 10/E5
Rhône (dept.), France 28/F5
Rhône (riv.), France 7/E4
Rhône (riv.), France 28/F5
Rhône (riv.), Switzerland 39/D4
Rhosllanerchrugog, Wales 13/D4
Rhu, Scotland 15/A1
Rhu Coigeach (cape), Scotland 15/C2
Rhyl, Wales 13/D4
Rhymney, Wales 13/A6
Rhymney (riv.), Wales 13/B6
Rhynie, Scotland 15/F3
Rhyolite (Ghost Town), Nev. (†89003) 266/E6
Riachão, Brazil 132/E4
Riachuelo, Uruguay 145/B5
Rialto, Calif. (92376) 204/E10
Riana, Tasmania 99/B3
Riaño, Spain 33/D1
Riau (arch.), Indonesia 85/C5
Riaza, Spain 33/E2
Rib (mt.), Wis. 317/G6
Ribadavia, Spain 33/B1
Ribadeo, Spain 33/C1
Ribamar, Brazil 132/F3
Ribas do Rio Pardo, Brazil 132/C8
Ribat Qila, Pakistan 68/A3
Ribat Qila, Pakistan 59/H4
Ribáuè, Mozambique 118/F3
Ribble (riv.), England 10/E4
Ribble (riv.), England 13/E4
Ribe (co.), Denmark 21/B7
Ribe, Denmark 21/B7
Ribe, Denmark 18/F9
Ribeira, Brazil 135/B4
Ribeira (riv.), Brazil 135/B4
Ribeira Brava, Portugal 33/A2
Ribeira de Iguape, Brazil 135/C4
Ribeira de Pena, Portugal 33/C2
Ribeira Grande, C. Verde 106/B7
Ribeirão Preto, Brazil 120/E5
Ribeirão Preto, Brazil 135/C2
Ribeirão Preto, Brazil 132/E8
Ribera, N. Mex. (87560) 274/D3
Ribérac, France 28/D5
Riberach an der Riss, W. Germany 22/C4
Riberalta, Bolivia 136/C2
Riberalta, Bolivia 120/C4
Rib Falls, Wis. (†54426) 317/G6
Ribla, Kuh-e (riv.), Iran 66/J6
Rib Lake, Wis. (54470) 317/F5
Ribnitz-Damgarten, E. Germany 22/E1
Ribstone, Alberta 182/E3
Říčany u Prahy, Czech. 41/C2
Ricaurte, Colombia 126/A7
Riccarton, N. Zealand 100/D5
Rice, Calif. (†92280) 204/L9
Rice (co.), Kansas 232/D3
Rice, Kansas (66965) 232/E2
Rice (co.), Minn. 255/E6
Rice, Minn. (56367) 255/D5
Rice (lake), Minn. 255/E4
Rice (mt.), N.H. 268/E2
Rice (lake), Ontario 177/F3
Rice, Texas (75155) 303/H5
Rice, Va. (23966) 307/M6
Rice, Wash. (99167) 310/G2
Riceboro, Georgia (31323) 217/K7
Rice Lake, Wis. (54868) 317/C5
Rices Landing, Pa. (15357) 294/C6
Riceton, Sask. 181/G5
Ricetown, Ky. (41364) 237/O6
Riceville, Iowa (50466) 229/H2
Riceville, Pa. (16432) 294/C2
Riceville, Tenn. (37370) 237/M10
Rich, Miss. (38662) 256/D2
Rich (cape), Ontario 177/D3
Rich (co.), Utah 304/C2
Richard, Sask. 181/D3
Richard City, Tenn. (†37380) 237/K11
Richard Collinson (inlet), N.W. Terrs. 187/G2
Richards, Iowa (†50579) 229/D4
Richards, Mo. (64778) 261/D7
Richards (isl.), N.W. Terrs. 187/E3
Richards Bay, S. Africa 118/E5
Richards Gebaur A.F.B., Mo. 261/P6
Richards Landing, Ontario 177/J5
Richardson (riv.), Alberta 182/C5
Richardson, Ky. (41253) 237/R5
Richardson (lakes), Maine 243/B6
Richardson (co.), Nebr. 264/J4
Richardson (isls.), N.W. Terrs. 187/G3
Richardson (mts.), N.W. Terrs. 187/E3
Richardson, Sask. 181/G5
Richardson, Texas (75080) 303/G2
Richardson, W. Va. (†26151) 312/D5
Richardson (mts.), Yukon 187/E3
Richardsons Landing, Tenn. (†38023) 237/B10
Richardsville, Ky. (42270) 237/J6
Richardsville, New Bruns. 170/D1
Richard Toll, Senegal 106/A5
Richardton, N. Dak. (58652) 282/F6
Richburg, N.Y. (14774) 276/D6
Richburg, S.C. (29729) 296/E2
Rich Creek, Va. (24147) 307/G6
Richdale, Alberta 182/E4
Riche (pt.), Newf. 166/C3
Richelieu, Ky. (42271) 237/H7
Richelieu (co.), Québec 172/D4
Richelieu, Québec 172/D4
Richer, Manitoba 179/F5
Richey, Mont. (59259) 262/L3
Richfield, Idaho (83349) 220/D6
Richfield, Kansas (67953) 232/A4
Richfield, Minn. (55423) 255/G5
Richfield, N.C. (28137) 281/J4
Richfield, Nova Scotia 168/C4
Richfield, Ohio (44286) 284/G3
Richfield, Pa. (17086) 294/H4
Richfield, Utah (84701) 304/B5
Richfield, Wis. (53076) 317/K1
Richfield Springs, N.Y. (13439) 276/K5
Richford, N.Y. (13835) 276/H6
Richford, Vt. (05476) 268/B2
Richford○, Vt. (05476) 268/B2
Richford, Wis. (†54930) 317/H7
Rich Fountain, Mo. (65070) 261/J6
Richgrove, Calif. (93261) 204/F8
Rich Hill, Mo. (64779) 261/D6
Richhill, N. Ireland 17/H3
Richibucto, New Bruns. 170/E2
Richibucto (harb.), New Bruns. 170/F2
Richibucto (riv.), New Bruns. 170/E2
Richibucto Village, New Bruns. 170/F2
Rich Lake, Alberta 182/E2
Richland, Fla. (†33599) 212/D3
Richland, Georgia (31825) 217/C6
Richland (co.), Ill. 222/E5
Richland, Ind. (47634) 227/C9
Richland (creek), Ind. 227/D6
Richland, Iowa (52585) 229/K6
Richland, Kansas (†66409) 232/G3
Richland (par.), La. 238/G2
Richland, Mich. (49083) 250/D6
Richland, Miss. (†39218) 256/D6
Richland, Mo. (65556) 261/H7
Richland (co.), Mont. 262/M3
Richland, Mont. (59260) 262/K2
Richland, Nebr. (68657) 264/G3
Richland, N.J. (08350) 273/D5
Richland, N.Y. (13144) 276/H3
Richland (co.), N. Dak. 282/R7
Richland (co.), Ohio 284/E4
Richland, Oreg. (97870) 291/K3
Richland, Pa. (17087) 294/K5
Richland (co.), S.C. 296/F4
Richland, S.C. (29675) 296/A2
Richland, S. Dak. (†57025) 298/R8
Richland (creek), Tenn. 237/G10
Richland, Texas (76681) 303/H6
Richland, Wash. 188/B1
Richland, Wash. (99352) 310/F4
Richland (co.), Wis. 317/F9
Richland Balsam (mt.), N.C. 281/D4
Richland Center, Wis. (53581) 317/F9
Richland Hills, Texas (76118) 303/F2
Richland-Kennewick, Wash. 310/80
Richlands, N.C. (28574) 281/O5
Richlands, Va. (24641) 307/E6
Richland Springs, Texas (76871) 303/F6
Richlandtown, Pa. (18955) 294/M5
Richlea, Sask. 181/C4
Richmond, Ala. (†36761) 195/D6
Richmond, Ark. (†71822) 202/B6
Richmond, Br. Col. 184/K3
Richmond, Calif. (*94801) 204/J1
Richmond, England 13/F3
Richmond, England 10/E3
Richmond (co.), Georgia 217/H4
Richmond, Ill. (60071) 222/E1
Richmond, Ind. (47374) 227/H5
Richmond, Iowa (52247) 229/K6
Richmond, Jamaica 158/J6
Richmond, Kansas (66080) 232/G3
Richmond, Ky. (40475) 237/N5
Richmond, La. (†71282) 238/H2
Richmond, Maine (04357) 243/D7
Richmond○, Maine (04357) 243/D7
Richmond○, Mass. (01254) 249/A3
Richmond, Mich. (48062) 250/G6
Richmond, Minn. (56368) 255/D5
Richmond, Mo. (64085) 261/D4
Richmond○, N.H. (†03470) 268/C6
Richmond (range), N.S. Wales 97/G1
Richmond (riv.), N.S. Wales 97/G1
Richmond (co.), N.Y. 276/M9
Richmond (Staten Island) (borough), N.Y. 276/M9
Richmond, N. Zealand 100/D4
Richmond (range), N. Zealand 100/D4
Richmond (co.), N.C. 281/K4
Richmond (co.), Nova Scotia 168/H3
Richmond (Grand River), Ohio (†44045) 284/H2
Richmond, Ohio (43944) 284/J5
Richmond, Ontario 177/J2
Richmond (co.), Québec 172/E4
Richmond, Québec 172/E4
Richmond, Queensland 88/G4
Richmond, Queensland 95/B4
Richmond (peak), St. Vin. & Grens. 161/A8
Richmond, S. Africa 118/C6
Richmond, Tasmania 99/D4
Richmond, Texas (77469) 303/J8
Richmond, Utah (84333) 304/C2
Richmond, Vt. (05477) 268/A3
Richmond○, Vt. (05477) 268/A3
Richmond, Victoria 88/L7
Richmond, Victoria 97/J5
Richmond (cap.), Va. 188/L3
Richmond (cap.), Va. 146/L6
Richmond (co.), Va. 307/P5
Richmond (cap.) (I.C.), Va. (*23201) 307/O5
Richmond Beach-Innis Arden, Wash. (98160) 310/A1
Richmond Corner, Maine (†04357) 243/D7
Richmond Corner, New Bruns. 170/C2
Richmond Dale, Ohio (45673) 284/E7
Richmond Furnace, Mass. (01254) 249/A3
Richmond Heights, Fla. (†33158) 212/F6
Richmond Heights, Mo. (63117) 261/P3
Richmond Heights, Ohio (44143) 284/H9
Richmond Highlands, Wash. (†98133) 310/A1
Richmond Hill, Georgia (31324) 217/K7
Richmond Hill, Ontario 177/J4
Richmond Nat'l Battlefield Park, Va. 307/O6
Richmond upon Thames, England 10/B5
Richmond upon Thames, England 13/H8
Richmondville, N.Y. (12149) 276/M5
Richmond-Windsor, N.S. Wales 97/F3
Richmound, Sask. 181/B5
Rich Mountain, Ark. (†71953) 202/B4
Rich Square, N.C. (27869) 281/P2
Richterswil, Switzerland 39/G2
Richthofen (mt.), Colo. 208/G2
Richton, Miss. (39476) 256/G8
Richton Park, Ill. (60471) 222/B6
Richvale, Calif. (95974) 204/D4
Richvalley, Ind. (†46992) 227/F3
Richview, Ill. (62877) 222/D5
Richville, Mich. (48758) 250/F5
Richville, Minn. (56576) 255/C4
Richville, N.Y. (13681) 276/K2
Richwood, La. (†71201) 238/F2
Richwood, Minn. (56577) 255/C4
Richwood, N.J. (08074) 273/C4
Richwood, Ohio (43344) 284/D5
Richwood, W. Va. (26261) 312/F6
Richwood, Wis. (†53094) 317/J9
Richwoods, Mo. (63071) 261/L6
Rickardsville, Iowa (†52039) 229/M3
Rickenbacker Air Force Base, Ohio 284/E6
Ricketts, Iowa (51460) 229/B4
Ricketts (pt.), Victoria 97/J6
Ricketts (pt.), Victoria 88/L8
Rickman, Tenn. (38580) 237/L8
Rickmansworth, England 13/G8
Rickmansworth, England 10/A5
Rickreall, Oreg. (97371) 291/D3
Ricla, Spain 33/F2
Rico, Colo. (81332) 208/C7
Ricobayo (res.), Spain 33/D2
Ricse, Hungary 41/G2
Ridderkerk, Netherlands 27/F5
Riddle, Idaho (†89832) 220/B7
Riddle, Oreg. (97469) 291/D5
Riddlesburg, Pa. (16672) 294/F5
Riddleton, Tenn. (37151) 237/J8
Riddleville, Georgia (†31018) 217/G5
Riddon, Loch (inlet), Scotland 15/C5
Rideau (lake), Ontario 177/H3
Riderwood, Ala. (†36904) 195/B6
Ridge, Md. (20680) 245/N8
Ridge, Mont. (†59314) 262/M5
Ridgecrest, Calif. (93555) 204/H8
Ridgecrest, La. (†71334) 238/G3
Ridgedale, Mo. (65739) 261/F9
Ridgedale, Sask. 181/H2
Ridge Farm, Ill. (61870) 222/F4
Ridgefield, Conn. (06877) 210/B3
Ridgefield○, Conn. (06877) 210/B3
Ridgefield, N.J. (07657) 273/B2
Ridgefield, Wash. (98642) 310/C5
Ridgefield Park, N.J. (07660) 273/B2
Ridgeland, Miss. (39157) 256/D6
Ridgeland, S.C. (29936) 296/E7
Ridgeland, Wis. (54763) 317/B5
Ridgeley, W. Va. (26753) 312/J3
Ridgely, Md. (21660) 245/P5
Ridgely, Mo. (†64444) 261/C4
Ridgely, Tenn. (38080) 237/B8
Ridgeside, Tenn. (†37401) 237/L10
Ridge Spring, S.C. (29129) 296/D4
Ridgetop, Tenn. (37152) 237/H8
Ridgetown, Ontario 177/C5
Ridgeview, S. Dak. (57652) 298/H3
Ridgeville, Georgia (†31331) 217/K8
Ridgeville, Ind. (47380) 227/G4
Ridgeville, Manitoba 179/E5
Ridgeville, S.C. (29472) 296/G5
Ridgeville Corners, Ohio (43555) 284/B3
Ridgeway, Iowa (52165) 229/K2
Ridgeway, Minn. (†55943) 255/G7
Ridgeway, Mo. (64481) 261/D2
Ridgeway, N.C. (27570) 281/N2
Ridgeway, Ohio (43345) 284/C4
Ridgeway, S.C. (29130) 296/F3
Ridgeway, Va. (24148) 307/J7
Ridgeway, W. Va. (25440) 312/K4
Ridgeway, Wis. (53582) 317/F10
Ridgeway Branch, Toms (riv.), N.J. 273/E3
Ridgewood, N.J. (*07450) 273/B1
Ridgley, Tasmania 99/B3
Ridgway, Colo. (81432) 208/D6
Ridgway, Ill. (62979) 222/E6
Ridgway, Pa. (15853) 294/E3
Ridi, Nepal 68/E3
Riding (mt.), Manitoba 179/B4
Riding Mountain, Manitoba 179/C4
Riding Mountain Nat'l Park, Man. 162/F5
Riding Mountain Nat'l Park, Manitoba 179/B4
Ridley, Tenn. (†38474) 237/G9
Ridley Park, Pa. (19078) 294/M7
Ridott, Ill. (61067) 222/D1
Ridotto, Iowa (†50546) 229/D3
Ried im Innkreis, Austria 41/B2
Riegelsville, N.J. (†08865) 273/C2
Riegelsville, Pa. (18077) 294/M4
Riegelwood, N.C. (28456) 281/N6
Riehen, Switzerland 39/E1
Rienzi, Miss. (38865) 256/G1
Riesa, E. Germany 22/E3
Riesco (isl.), Chile 138/E10
Riesel, Texas (76682) 303/H6
Riesi, Italy 34/E6
Rietavas, U.S.S.R. 53/A3
Rietberg, W. Germany 22/C3
Rietfontein, Namibia 118/C4
Rieth, Oreg. (†97801) 291/J2
Rieti (prov.), Italy 34/D3
Rieti, Italy 34/D3
Rif, Er (range), Morocco 106/D2

436 Riffelalp

Riffelalp, Switzerland 39/E5
Rifle, Colo. (81650) 208/D3
Rifle (creek), Colo. 208/D3
Rifle (riv.), Mich. 250/E4
Rifle (lake), Wash. 310/C4
Rifstangi (cape), Iceland 21/C1
Rift Valley (prov.), Kenya 115/G3
Riga (lake), Conn. 210/B1
Riga, U.S.S.R. 2/L3
Riga, U.S.S.R. 7/G3
Riga (gulf), U.S.S.R. 7/G3
Riga (cap.), U.S.S.R. 53/C2
Riga, U.S.S.R. 48/C4
Riga, U.S.S.R. 52/B3
Riga (gulf), U.S.S.R. 52/B3
Riga (gulf), U.S.S.R. 53/B2
Riga (gulf), U.S.S.R. 48/C4
Rigan, Iran 66/L6
Rigaud, Québec 172/C4
Rigby, Idaho (83442) 220/F6
Rigdon, Ind. (†46928) 227/F4
Rigestan (reg.), Afghanistan 59/H3
Riggins, Idaho (83549) 220/B4
Riggisberg, Switzerland 39/E3
Rigi (mt.), Switzerland 39/F2
Rigo, Papua N.G. 85/C7
Rigolet, Newf. 166/C3
Rigolet, Newf. 162/L5
Rig Rig, Chad 111/B5
Rigside, Scotland 15/E5
Riihimäki, Finland 18/O6
Riiser-Larsen (pen.), Ant. 2/L9
Riiser-Larsen (pen.) 5/C2
Rijeka, Yugoslavia 45/B3
Rijeka, Yugoslavia 7/F4
Rijen, Netherlands 27/F5
Rijnsburg, Netherlands 27/F4
Rijssen, Netherlands 27/J4
Rijswijk, Netherlands 27/E4
Rikitea, Fr. Poly. 87/N8
Rikuchu-Kaigan National Park, Japan 81/L4
Rikuzentakata, Japan 81/K4
Riley, Ind. (47871) 227/C6
Riley (co.), Kansas 232/F2
Riley, Kansas (66531) 232/F2
Riley, Ky. (†40328) 237/L5
Riley, Maine (†04262) 243/C6
Riley, Oreg. (97758) 291/H4
Riley Brook, New Bruns. 170/C1
Rileysburg, Ind. (†47932) 227/B4
Rillito, Ariz. (85246) 198/D6
Rillton, Pa. (15678) 294/C5
Rima (riv.), Niger 106/F6
Rima (riv.), Nigeria 106/F6
Rima, Wadi (dry riv.), Saudi Arabia 59/D4
Rimac (riv.), Peru 128/D9
Rimal, Ar (des.), Saudi Arabia 59/F5
Rimatara (isl.), Fr. Poly. 87/L8
Rimavská Sobota, Czech. 41/E2
Rimbey, Alberta 182/C3
Rimbo, Sweden 18/L7
Rimersburg, Pa. (16248) 294/D3
Rimini, Italy 34/D2
Rimini, S.C. (29131) 296/G4
Rîmnicu Sărat, Romania 45/H3
Rîmnicu Vîlcea, Romania 45/G3
Rimouski, Que. 162/K6
Rimouski (co.), Québec 172/J1
Rimouski (county), Québec 174/D3
Rimouski, Québec 172/J1
Rimouski, Québec 174/D3
Rimouski (riv.), Québec 172/J1
Rimouski-Est, Québec 172/J1
Rimpfischhorn (mt.), Switzerland 39/E4
Rimrock, Ariz. (86335) 198/D4
Rimrock (lake), Wash. 310/D4
Rimutaka (range), N. Zealand 100/B3
Rinard, Ill. (62878) 222/E5
Rinard, Iowa (50587) 229/D4
Rincón, Cerro (mt.), Argentina 143/C1
Rincon (peak), Ariz. 198/E6
Rincón, Cerro (mt.), Chile 138/C4
Rincón, Dom. Rep. 158/E5
Rincón (bay), Dom. Rep. 158/F5
Rincon, Georgia (31326) 217/K6
Rincon, Neth. Ant. 161/E8
Rincon, N. Mex. (87940) 274/C6
Rincón (pt.), Panama 154/G6
Rincón, P. Rico 161/A1
Rincón (bay), P. Rico 161/D3
Rinconada, Argentina 143/C1
Rinconada San Martín, Chile 138/G2
Rincón de Romos, Mexico 150/H5
Rindge○, N.H. (03461) 268/C6
Riner, Va. (24149) 307/H6
Rineyville, Ky. (40162) 237/K5
Ringarooma, Tasmania 99/D3
Ringarooma (bay), Tasmania 99/D2
Ringe, Denmark 21/D7
Ringebu, Norway 18/G6
Ringelspitz (mt.), Switzerland 39/H3
Ringerike, Norway 18/C3
Ringgold, Georgia (30736) 217/B1
Ringgold (co.), Iowa 229/E7
Ringgold, La. (71068) 238/D2
Ringgold, Md. (†21783) 245/H2
Ringgold, Nebr. (†69167) 264/D3
Ringgold, Texas (76261) 303/G4
Ringgold, Va. (24586) 307/K7
Ringim, Nigeria 106/F6
Ringkøbing (co.), Denmark 21/B5
Ringkøbing, Denmark 18/E8
Ringkøbing, Denmark 21/A5
Ringkøbing (fjord), Denmark 21/B6
Ringling, Mont. (59642) 262/F4
Ringling, Okla. (73456) 288/L6
Ringmer, England 13/H7
Ringoes, N.J. (08551) 273/D3
Ringold, Okla. (74754) 288/R6
Ringsted, Denmark 21/E7
Ringsted, Iowa (50578) 229/D2
Ringtown, Pa. (17967) 294/K4
Ringvassøy (isl.), Norway 18/L2
Ringwood, England 13/F7
Ringwood, Ill. (60072) 222/E1
Ringwood, N.J. (07456) 273/E1
Ringwood, N.C. (†27823) 281/O2
Ringwood, North. Terr. 93/D7
Ringwood, Okla. (73768) 288/K2
Ringwood, Victoria 88/M7
Ringwood, Victoria 97/K5
Rinn (lake), Ireland 17/F4
Rinteln, W. Germany 22/C2
Rio, Ill. (61472) 222/C2
Rio, La. (†70427) 238/L5
Rio, W. Va. (26755) 312/J4
Rio, Wis. (53960) 317/H9
Rio Arriba (co.), N. Mex. 274/B2
Riobamba, Ecuador 128/C3
Riobamba, Ecuador 120/B3
Río Blanco, Chile 138/B9
Rio Blanco (co.), Colo. 208/C3
Rio Blanco, Colo. (†81650) 208/C3
Río Blanco, P. Rico 161/F2
Rio Bonito, Brazil 135/E3
Rio Branco, Brazil 120/C3
Rio Branco, Brazil 132/G10
Río Branco, Uruguay 145/F3
Rio Brazos (riv.), N. Mex. 274/C2
Rio Brilhante, Brazil 132/C8
Río Bueno, Chile 138/D3
Rio Bueno, Jamaica 158/H5
Río Caribe, Venezuela 124/G2
Río Cauto, Cuba 158/H4
Rio Chama (riv.), N. Mex. 274/C2
Río Chico, Venezuela 124/F2
Río Cisnes, Chile 138/E5
Rio Claro, Brazil 132/E8
Rio Claro, Brazil 135/C3
Rio Claro, Trin. & Tob. 161/B11
Río Claro, Venezuela 124/D3
Río Colorado, Argentina 120/C6
Río Colorado, La Pampa, Argentina 143/D4
Río Colorado, Río Negro, Argentina 143/D4
Rio Creek, Wis. (54231) 317/L6
Río Cuarto, Argentina 143/D3
Río Cuarto, Argentina 120/C6
Rio de Janeiro (state), Brazil 135/E3
Rio de Janeiro (state), Brazil 132/F8
Rio de Janeiro, Brazil 2/G7
Rio de Janeiro, Brazil 120/E5
Rio de Janeiro, Brazil 135/E3
Rio de Janeiro, Brazil 132/F8
Rio Dell, Calif. (95562) 204/A3
Río de Oro, Colombia 126/D3
Rio do Sul, Brazil 132/D9
Rio Felix (riv.), N. Mex. 274/E5
Río Gallegos, Argentina 120/C8
Río Gallegos, Argentina 143/C7
Rio Grande (riv.) 2/D4
Rio Grande (riv.) 146/H7
Rio Grande (riv.) 188/F5
Río Grande, Argentina 143/C7
Río Grande, Bolivia 136/B7
Rio Grande, Brazil 120/D6
Rio Grande, Brazil 132/D11
Rio Grande (co.), Colo. 208/G7
Rio Grande (res.), Colo. 208/E7
Rio Grande (riv.), Colo. 208/H8
Rio Grande, N.J. (08242) 273/D5
Rio Grande (riv.), N. Mex. 274/C5
Rio Grande, Ohio (45674) 284/F8
Río Grande, P. Rico 161/E1
Rio Grande (riv.), Texas 303/D9
Rio Grande City, Texas (78582) 303/F11
Rio Grande do Norte (state), Brazil 132/G4
Rio Grande do Sul (state), Brazil 132/C10
Rio Grande Pyramid (mt.), Colo. 208/E7
Rio Grande Wild and Scenic River, Texas 303/B8
Riohacha, Colombia 120/B1
Riohacha, Colombia 126/D2
Rio Hondo, Guatemala 154/C3
Rio Hondo (riv.), N. Mex. 274/E5
Rio Hondo, Texas (78583) 303/G11
Rioja, Peru 128/D6
Río Lagartos, Mexico 150/P6
Rio Linda, Calif. (95673) 204/B8
Rio Maior, Portugal 33/B3
Rio Mulato, Bolivia 136/B6
Río Muni (terr.), Equat. Guinea 115/B3
Rion, S.C. (29132) 296/E3
Riondel, Br. Col. 184/J5
Río Negro (prov.), Argentina 143/C5
Rio Negro, Brazil 132/D9
Río Negro, Chile 138/D3
Rionegro, Antioquia, Colombia 126/C4
Rionegro, Santander, Colombia 126/D4
Río Negro (dept.), Uruguay 145/B3
Río Negro (res.), Uruguay 145/D3
Rionero in Vulture, Italy 34/E4
Rio Pardo, Brazil 132/C10
Rio Pardo de Minas, Brazil 132/F6
Rio Penasco (riv.), N. Mex. 274/E6
Río Piedras, P. Rico 161/E1
Rio Pomba, Brazil 135/E2
Rio Puerco (riv.), N. Mex. 274/C4
Rio Rancho, N. Mex. (87124) 274/C3
Rio Real, Brazil 132/G5
Rio Rico, Ariz. (85621) 198/E7
Rio Salado (riv.), N. Mex. 274/B4
Río San Juan, Dom. Rep. 158/E5
Río Seco, Cuba 158/A2
Río Segundo, Argentina 143/D3
Riosucio, Caldas, Colombia 126/C5
Riosucio, Chocó, Colombia 126/B4
Río Tercero, Argentina 143/D3
Río Tigre, Ecuador 128/D4
Rio Tinto, Brazil 132/H4
Río Tocuyo, Venezuela 124/C2
Riou (lake), Sask. 181/M2
Rio Verde, Brazil 132/D7
Río Verde, Brazil 120/D4
Río Verde, Chile 138/E10
Rioverde, Mexico 150/J6
Rio Verde de Mato Grosso, Brazil 132/C7
Rio Vista, Calif. (94571) 204/L1
Riparia, Wash. (†99359) 310/G4
Riparius, N.Y. (12862) 276/M3
Ripley, Calif. (92272) 204/L10
Ripley, England 13/F4
Ripley, Ill. (†62353) 222/C3
Ripley (co.), Ind. 227/G6
Ripley○, Maine (†04930) 243/E5
Ripley, Miss. (38663) 256/G1
Ripley (co.), Mo. 261/L9
Ripley, N.Y. (14775) 276/A6
Ripley, Ohio (45167) 284/C8
Ripley, Okla. (74062) 288/N2
Ripley, Ontario 177/C3
Ripley, Tenn. (38063) 237/B9
Ripley, W. Va. (25271) 312/C5
Riplinger, Wis. (†54479) 317/E6
Ripoll, Spain 33/H1
Ripon, Calif. (95366) 204/D6
Ripon, England 10/F3
Ripon, England 13/F3
Ripon, Québec 172/B4
Ripon, Wis. (54971) 317/J8
Rippey, Iowa (50235) 229/E5
Ripplemead, Va. (24150) 307/G6
Ripples, New Bruns. 170/D3
Rippon, W. Va. (25441) 312/L4
Rippowam (riv.), Conn. 210/A4
Ripton○, Vt. (05766) 268/A4
Ririe, Idaho (83443) 220/G6
Risafe, Syria 63/H5
Risalpur Cantonment, Pakistan 68/C2
Risaralda (dept.), Colombia 126/B5
Risca, Wales 13/B6
Risco, Mo. (63874) 261/N9
Rishiri (isl.), Japan 81/K1
Rishon Le Ziyyon, Israel 65/B4
Rishra, India 68/F1
Rising City, Nebr. (68658) 264/G3
Rising Fawn, Georgia (30738) 217/A1
Rising Star, Texas (76471) 303/F5
Rising Sun, Ind. (47040) 227/H7
Rising Sun, Md. (21911) 245/O2
Risingsun, Ohio (43457) 284/C3
Rising Sun, Wis. (†54628) 317/D9
Risle (riv.), France 28/D3
Rison, Ark. (71665) 202/F6
Risør, Norway 18/F7
Risoux (mt.), Switzerland 39/B3
Ristigouche (riv.), Québec 172/B2
Ristijärvi, Finland 18/Q4
Rita Blanca (creek), Texas 303/B2
Ritchey, Mo. (†64844) 261/D9
Ritchie, Md. (†20027) 245/G5
Ritchie (co.), W. Va. 312/D4
Ritchies (arch.), India 68/G6
Ritidian (pt.), Guam 86/K6
Ritner, Ky. (42639) 237/M7
Ritter, Oreg. (97872) 291/H3
Ritter, S.C. (29488) 296/F6
Rittman, Ohio (44270) 284/G4
Ritzville, Wash. (99169) 310/G3
Rivadavia, Mendoza, Argentina 143/C3
Rivadavia, Salta, Argentina 143/D1
Rivadavia, San Juan, Argentina 143/C3
Rivadavia, Chile 138/A7
Riva del Garda, Italy 34/C2
Rivanna (riv.), Va. 307/M5
Rivas, Nicaragua 154/E5
Riva San Vitale, Switzerland 39/G5
Rive-de-Gier, France 28/F5
Rivera, Switzerland 39/G4
Rivera (dept.), Uruguay 145/D2
Rivera, Uruguay 145/D1
Rivera, Uruguay 120/D6
Riverbank, Calif. (95367) 204/E6
River Bourgeois, Nova Scotia 168/H3
River Cess, Liberia 106/C7
Rivercourse, Alberta 182/E3
Riverdale, Calif. (93656) 204/E7
Riverdale, Georgia (*30274) 217/K2
Riverdale, Ill. (60627) 222/C6
Riverdale, Iowa (†52722) 229/N5
Riverdale, Kansas (†67152) 232/E4
Riverdale, Md. (20840) 245/F4
Riverdale, Mich. (48877) 250/E5
Riverdale, Nebr. (68870) 264/E4
Riverdale, N.H. (†03045) 268/D5
Riverdale, N.J. (07457) 273/A1
Riverdale, N. Dak. (58565) 282/H4
Riverdale Heights, Md. (†20840) 245/G4
River de Chute, New Bruns. 170/C2
River Denys, Nova Scotia 168/G3
River Edge, N.J. (07661) 273/B1
River Falls, Ala. (36476) 195/E8
River Falls, Wis. (54022) 317/A6
River Forest, Ill. (60305) 222/B5
River Forest, Ind. (†46011) 227/F4
River Glade, New Bruns. 170/E3
River Grove, Ill. (60171) 222/B5
River Grove, Oreg. (†97223) 291/B2
Riverhead, Newf. 166/D2
Riverhead, N.Y. (11901) 276/P9
Riverhead, N. Zealand 100/B1
River Hébert, Nova Scotia 168/D3
River Heights, Utah (†84321) 304/C2
River Hills, Manitoba 179/G4
River Hills, Wis. (†53201) 317/M1
Riverhurst, Sask. 181/E5
Riverina (reg.), N. S. Wales 88/H7
Riverina (reg.), N.S. Wales 97/C4
River John, Nova Scotia 168/E3
River Jordan, Br. Col. 184/J3
Riverland, Fla. (†33301) 212/B4
Riverlea, Ohio (†43085) 284/D5
Rivermines, Mo. (†63601) 261/L7
Rivero (isl.), Chile 138/D6
River Oaks, Texas (77019) 303/E2
River of Ponds, Newf. 166/C3
River of Ponds (lake), Newf. 166/C3
Riverport, Nova Scotia 168/D4
River Rouge, Mich. (48218) 250/B7
Rivers (inlet), Br. Col. 184/D4
Rivers, Manitoba 179/B4
Rivers (state), Nigeria 106/F8
Rivers (lake), Sask. 181/F6
Riversdale, Jamaica 158/J6
Riversdale, S. Africa 118/H7
Riversdale, S. Africa 118/C6
Riverside, Ala. (35135) 195/F3
Riverside, Calif. 188/C4
Riverside (co.), Calif. 204/J10
Riverside, Calif. (*92501) 204/E11
Riverside (res.), Colo. 208/L2
Riverside, Conn. (06878) 210/A4
Riverside, Georgia (†30759) 217/B2
Riverside, Georgia (†31768) 217/E8
Riverside, Ill. (60546) 222/B6
Riverside, Ind. (†47918) 227/C4
Riverside, Iowa (52327) 229/K6
Riverside, Ky. (42272) 237/J6
Riverside, Md. (†20662) 245/K7
Riverside, Mass. (†01376) 249/D2
Riverside, Mich. (49084) 250/C6
Riverside, Mo. (64168) 261/O5
Riverside○, N.J. (08075) 273/B3
Riverside, N.Y. (†14830) 276/F6
Riverside, N. Dak. (†58078) 282/S6
Riverside, Oreg. (97917) 291/J4
Riverside, Pa. (17868) 294/J4
Riverside, R.I. (02915) 249/J5
Riverside, Sask. 181/G6
Riverside, Texas (77367) 303/J7
Riverside, Utah (84334) 304/B2
Riverside, Wash. (98849) 310/F2
Riverside, Wyo. (†82325) 319/F4
Riverside-Albert, New Bruns. 170/F3
Riverside Stage Stop, Ariz. (85237) 198/D5
Rivers Inlet, Br. Col. 184/D4
River Sioux, Iowa (†51545) 229/B5
Riverstown, Ireland 17/E3
Riverton, Conn. (06065) 210/D1
Riverton, Ill. (62561) 222/D4
Riverton, Ind. (†47861) 227/B6
Riverton, Iowa (51650) 229/B7
Riverton, Kansas (66770) 232/H4
Riverton, La. (†71418) 238/F2
Riverton, Man. 162/G5
Riverton, Manitoba 179/E3
Riverton, Minn. (†56455) 255/D4
Riverton, Nebr. (68972) 264/F4
Riverton, N.J. (08077) 273/B3
Riverton, N. Zealand 100/B7
Riverton, Nova Scotia 168/F3
Riverton, Oreg. (†97423) 291/C4
Riverton, Utah (84065) 304/B3
Riverton, Vt. (05668) 268/B3
Riverton, Va. (22651) 307/M3
Riverton, Wash. (†98188) 310/B2
Riverton, W. Va. (26814) 312/H5
Riverton, Wyo. (82501) 319/D2
Riverton Heights, Wash. (98188) 310/B2
Rivervale, Ark. (72377) 202/K2
River Vale○, N.J. (07675) 273/B1
River Valley, Ontario 177/D1
Riverview, Ala. (†36426) 195/D8
River View, Ala. (36872) 195/H5
Riverview, Fla. (33569) 212/D4
Riverview, Mich. (48192) 250/B7
Riverview, Mo. (†63101) 261/R2
Riverview, New Bruns. 170/F2
Riverville, Va. (†24553) 307/L5
Riverwood, Ky. (†40222) 237/K1
Riverwoods, Ill. (†60015) 222/B5
Rives, Mo. (63875) 261/M10
Rives, Tenn. (38253) 237/C8
Rives Junction, Mich. (49277) 250/E6
Rivesville, W. Va. (26588) 312/F3
Riviera (reg.), France 28/G6
Riviera, Texas (78379) 303/G10
Riviera Beach, Fla. (33404) 212/G5
Riviera Beach, Md. (†21061) 245/N4
Riviera-Bullhead, Ariz. (86440) 198/A3
Rivière-à-Claude, Québec 172/C1
Rivière-à-Pierre, Québec 172/E3
Rivière-au-Renard, Québec 172/D1
Rivière-au-Tonnerre, Québec 174/D2
Rivière-Bleue, Québec 172/J2
Rivière-Bois-Clair, Québec 172/F3
Rivière-du-Loup, Que. 162/K6
Rivière-du-Loup (co.), Québec 172/H2
Rivière-du-Loup, Québec 174/D3
Rivière-du-Loup, Québec 172/H2
Rivière-du-Moulin, Québec 172/G1
Rivière-du-Portage, New Bruns. 170/F1
Rivière-Éternité, Québec 172/G1
Rivière-la-Madeleine, Québec 172/C1
Rivière-Matawin, Québec 172/E3
Rivière-Ouelle, Québec 172/G2
Rivière-Pentecôte, Québec 174/D3
Rivière-Pilote, Martinique 161/D7
Rivière-Portneuf, Québec 172/H1
Rivière-Port-Daniel, Québec 172/D2
Rivière-Saint-Paul, Québec 174/F2
Rivière-Salée, Martinique 161/D7
Rivière-Trois-Pistoles, Québec 172/J1
Rivière-Verte, New Bruns. 170/B1
Rivière-Verte, Québec 172/H2
Riwaka, N. Zealand 100/D4
Riwoqê, China 77/E5
Rixeyville, Va. (22737) 307/M3
Rixford, Pa. (16745) 294/F2
Riyadh (cap.), Saudi Arabia 2/M4
Riyadh (cap.), Saudi Arabia 54/F7
Riyadh (cap.), Saudi Arabia 59/E5
Riyan, P.D.R. Yemen 59/E7
Rizal (prov.), Philippines 82/C3
Rize (prov.), Turkey 63/J2
Rize, Turkey 59/D1
Rize, Turkey 63/J2
Rizokarpasso, Cyprus 63/F5
Rjukan, Norway 18/F7
Roa, Norway 18/G6
Roa, Spain 33/E2
Roachdale, Ind. (46172) 227/D5
Road (bay), Virgin Is. (Br.) 161/D3
Roadside, Scotland 15/F4
Roadstown, N.J. (†08302) 273/C5
Road Town (cap.), Virgin Is. (Br.) 161/D3
Road Town (cap.), Virgin Is. (Br.) 156/H1
Roag, Loch (inlet), Scotland 15/B2
Roan (creek), Colo. 208/C4
Roan (plat.), Colo. 208/B3
Roan, Norway 18/G4
Roan (isl.), Scotland 15/D2
Roan (cliffs), Utah 304/E4
Roane (co.), Tenn. 237/M9
Roane (co.), W. Va. 312/D5
Roan Mountain, Tenn. (37687) 237/S8
Roann, Ind. (46974) 227/F3
Roanne, France 28/E4
Roanoke (riv.) 188/L3
Roanoke, Ala. (36274) 195/H4
Roanoke, Ill. (61561) 222/D3
Roanoke, Ind. (46783) 227/G3
Roanoke, La. (70581) 238/E6
Roanoke, Mo. (†65230) 261/G4
Roanoke (isl.), N.C. 281/T3
Roanoke (riv.), N.C. 281/P2
Roanoke, Texas (76262) 303/F1
Roanoke, Va. 146/L6
Roanoke, Va. 188/K3
Roanoke (co.), Va. 307/H6
Roanoke (I.C.), Va. (*24001) 307/H6
Roanoke (riv.), Va. 307/N8
Roanoke, W. Va. (26423) 312/F5
Roanoke Rapids, N.C. (27870) 281/O2
Roaring (brook), Conn. 210/F1
Roaring (brook), Conn. 210/E2
Roaring Branch, Pa. (17765) 294/J2
Roaring Fork, Colorado (riv.), Colo. 208/E4
Roaring Gap, N.C. (28668) 281/H2
Roaring River, N.C. (28669) 281/G2
Roaring Spring, Pa. (16673) 294/F5
Roaring Springs, Texas (79256) 303/D4
Roaringwater (bay), Ireland 17/B9
Roark, Ky. (40979) 237/P6
Roatán, Honduras 154/D2
Roatán (isl.), Honduras 154/D2
Roba, Ala. (†36089) 195/G6
Robards, Ky. (42452) 237/F5
Robat Karim, Iran 66/G3
Robb, Alberta 182/B3
Robben (isl.), S. Africa 118/E6
Robbins, Calif. (95676) 204/B8
Robbins, Ill. (60472) 222/B6
Robbins, N.C. (27325) 281/K4
Robbins (isl.), Tasmania 99/B2
Robbins, Tenn. (37852) 237/M8
Robbinsdale, Minn. (55422) 255/G5
Robbinston, Maine (04671) 243/J5
Robbinston○, Maine (04671) 243/J5
Robbinsville, N.J. (08691) 273/D3
Robbinsville, N.C. (28771) 281/B4
Robe (mt.), N.S. Wales 97/A2
Robe, S. Australia 94/F7
Robe, Wash. (†98252) 310/D2
Robeline, La. (71469) 238/D3
Roberdel, N.C. (†28379) 281/K5
Robersonville, N.C. (27871) 281/P3
Robert (isl.), China 85/E2
Robert, La. (70455) 238/N1
Robert (harb.), Martinique 161/D6
Roberta, Georgia (31078) 217/D5
Roberta, Okla. (†74701) /K7
Robert Lee, Texas (76945) 303/D6
Roberto Payán, Colombia 126/A7
Roberts, Idaho (83444) 220/F6
Roberts, Ill. (60962) 222/E3
Roberts, Mont. (59070) 262/G5
Roberts (co.), S. Dak. 298/P2
Roberts (co.), Texas 303/D2
Roberts, Wis. (54023) 317/A6
Robert's Arm, Newf. 166/C4
Robertsburg, W. Va. (25172) 312/C5
Roberts Creek, Br. Col. 184/J3
Robertsdale, Ala. (36567) 195/C9
Robertsdale, Pa. (16674) 294/F5
Roberts Field Int'l Airport, Liberia 106/C7
Robertsfors, Sweden 18/M4
Robertsganj, India 68/E4
Robertson (co.), Ky. 237/N3
Robertson, S. Africa 118/C6
Robertson (co.), Tenn. 237/H7
Robertson (co.), Texas 303/H6
Robertson, Wyo. (82944) 319/B4
Robertsonville, Québec 172/F3
Robertsport, Liberia 102/A4
Robertsport, Liberia 106/B7
Robertstown, Georgia (†30545) 217/E1
Robertsville, Conn. (†06098) 210/C1
Robertsville, Ohio (44670) 284/H4
Robertville, New Bruns. 170/E1
Roberval, Que. 162/J6
Roberval, Québec 174/C3
Roberval, Québec 172/E1
Robeson (co.), N.C. 281/L5
Robeson (chan.), N.W. Terrs. 187/M1
Robesonia, Pa. (19551) 294/K5
Robichaud, New Bruns. 170/F2
Robinhood, Sask. 181/C2
Robins, Iowa (52328) 229/K4
Robins, Ohio (†43723) 284/H6
Robins A.F.B., Georgia 217/F5
Robinson, Ill. (62454) 222/F5
Robinson, Iowa (†52330) 229/K4
Robinson, Kansas (66532) 232/G2
Robinson, Ky. (41082) 237/N4
Robinson, N. Dak. (58478) 282/L5
Robinson (riv.), North. Terr. 93/E4
Robinson, Pa. (15949) 294/D5
Robinson (lake), S.C. 296/G3
Robinson (ranges), W. Australia 92/B4
Robinson Creek, Ky. (41560) 237/S6
Robinson Crusoe (isl.), Chile 120/B6
Robinson River, North. Terr. 93/E4
Robinsons, Maine (†04734) 243/H3
Robinsonville, Miss. (38664) 256/D1
Robinsonville, New Bruns. 170/C1
Robinvale, Victoria 97/B4
Robles, Colombia 126/D2
Roblin, Manitoba 179/A3
Roblin, Ontario 177/G3
Roboré, Bolivia 136/F6
Roboré, Bolivia 120/D4
Rob Roy, Ind. (†47918) 227/C4
Robsart, Sask. 181/B6
Robson (mt.), Br. Col. 162/D5
Robson, Br. Col. 184/J5
Robson (mt.), Br. Col. 184/H3
Robstown, Texas (78380) 303/G10
Roby, Mo. (65557) 261/H7
Roby, Texas (79543) 303/D5
Roca, Nebr. (68430) 264/H4
Roca (cape), Portugal 33/B3
Rocafuerte, Ecuador 128/B3
Rocanville, Sask. 181/K5
Roca Partida (isl.), Mexico 150/C7
Roca que Vela (cay), Colombia 126/B8
Rocas (isl.), Brazil 120/F3
Rocas de Santo Domingo, Chile 138/F4
Roccastrada, Italy 34/C3
Rocha (dept.), Uruguay 145/E4
Rocha, Uruguay 145/E5
Rocha (lag.), Uruguay 145/E5
Rochdale, England 13/H2
Rochdale, England 10/G2
Rochdale, Mass. (01542) 249/G4
Roche, Switzerland 39/C4
Rochechouart, France 28/D5
Rochefort, Belgium 27/G8
Rochefort, France 28/C4
Roche Harbor, Wash. (98250) 310/B2
Rochelle, Georgia (31079) 217/F7
Rochelle, Ill. (61068) 222/D2
Rochelle, Texas (76872) 303/E6
Rochelle, Wyo. (†82701) 319/H2
Rochelle Park○, N.J. (07662) 273/B2
Roche Percé, Sask. 181/J6
Rocheport, Mo. (65279) 261/H5
Rocher River, N.W.T. 162/E3
Rocher River, N.W. Terrs. 187/G3
Rochert, Minn. (56578) 255/C4
Rochester, Alberta 182/D2
Rochester, England 13/J8
Rochester, England 10/G5
Rochester, Ill. (62563) 222/D4
Rochester, Ind. (46975) 227/E2
Rochester, Iowa (†52772) 229/L5
Rochester, Ky. (42273) 237/H6
Rochester○, Mass. (02770) 249/L6
Rochester, Mich. (48063) 250/F6
Rochester, Minn. 188/H2
Rochester, Minn. (55901) 255/F6
Rochester, N.H. (03867) 268/E5
Rochester, N.Y. 188/L2
Rochester, N.Y. 146/L5
Rochester, N.Y. (*14601) 276/E4
Rochester, Ohio (†44090) 284/F3
Rochester, Pa. (15074) 294/B4
Rochester, Texas (79544) 303/E4
Rochester○, Vt. (05767) 268/B4
Rochester, Victoria 97/C5
Rochester, Wash. (98579) 310/C4
Rochester, Wis. (53167) 317/K3
Rochester Mills, Pa. (15771) 294/D4
Rochford, S. Dak. (57778) 298/B5
Rochfort Bridge, Alberta 182/C3
Rochon Sands, Alberta 182/D3
Rociada, N. Mex. (87742) 274/D3
Rock (creek), Idaho 220/F7
Rock (creek), Ill. 222/D2
Rock (riv.), Ill. 222/C2
Rock (riv.), Iowa 229/A2
Rock, Kansas (67131) 232/F4
Rock (lake), Manitoba 179/C5
Rock (creek), Md. 245/K4
Rock, Mass. (†02346) 249/L5
Rock, Mich. (49880) 250/B2
Rock (co.), Minn. 255/B7
Rock (riv.), Minn. 255/B7
Rock (creek), Mont. 262/C4
Rock (co.), Nebr. 264/E2
Rock (creek), Nev. 266/E2
Rock (creek), Oreg. 291/E4
Rock (creek), Oreg. 291/G2
Rock (creek), Oreg. 291/H3
Rock (creek), S. Dak. 298/O6
Rock (creek), Wash. 310/H3
Rock (lake), Wash. 310/H3
Rock (co.), Wis. 317/H10
Rock (riv.), Wis. 317/J9
Rockall (isl.), Scotland 7/C3
Rockaway, N.J. (07866) 273/D2
Rockaway, Oreg. (97136) 291/C2
Rockaway Beach, Mo. (65740) 261/F9
Rock Bluff, Fla. (†32321) 212/B1
Rockbridge, Ill. (62081) 222/C4
Rockbridge, Mo. (65741) 261/H9
Rockbridge, Ohio (43149) 284/E6
Rockbridge (co.), Va. 307/K5
Rockbridge, Wis. (†53581) 317/F9
Rockcastle (co.), Ky. 237/N6
Rockcastle (riv.), Ky. 237/N6
Rock Castle, W. Va. (25272) 312/C5
Rock Cave, W. Va. (26234) 312/F5
Rock City, Ill. (61070) 222/D1
Rockcliffe Park, Ontario 177/J2
Rockcorry, Ireland 17/H3
Rock Creek, Br. Col. 184/H6
Rock Creek, Kansas (†66512) 232/G2
Rock Creek, Minn. (55067) 255/F5
Rock Creek, Ohio (44084) 284/J2
Rock Creek, Yukon 187/E3
Rockdale (co.), Georgia 217/D3
Rockdale, Ill. (60436) 222/E2
Rockdale, N. S. Wales 88/K4
Rockdale, N.S. Wales 97/J4
Rockdale, Texas (76567) 303/G7
Rockdale, Wis. (†53523) 317/J10
Rock Dell, Minn. (†55920) 255/F7
Rockerville, S. Dak. (†57701) 298/C6
Rockfall, Conn. (06481) 210/E2
Rock Falls, Ill. (61071) 222/D2
Rock Falls, Iowa (50467) 229/G2
Rock Falls, Wis. (54764) 317/C6
Rockfield, Ind. (46977) 227/D3
Rockfield, Ky. (42274) 237/J7
Rockfield, Wis. (53077) 317/L1
Rockfish, N.C. (†28302) 281/L5
Rockford, Ala. (35136) 195/F5
Rockford, Idaho (†83221) 220/F6
Rockford, Ill. 146/K5
Rockford, Ill. 188/J2
Rockford, Ill. (*61101) 222/D1
Rockford, Iowa (50468) 229/H2
Rockford, Mich. (49341) 250/D5

Rosston 437

Rockford, Minn. (55373) 255/F5
Rockford, N.C. (27044) 281/H2
Rockford, Ohio (45882) 284/A4
Rockford, Sask. 181/J3
Rockford, Tenn. (37853) 237/O9
Rockford, Wash. (99030) 310/H3
Rock Forest, Québec 172/F4
Rock Glen, Pa. (18246) 294/K4
Rockglen, Sask. 181/F6
Rock Grove, Ill. (†61070) 222/D1
Rock Hall, Md. (21661) 245/O4
Rockham, S. Dak. (57470) 298/M4
Rockhampton, Australia 2/S7
Rockhampton, Australia 87/F8
Rockhampton, Queensland 88/H4
Rockhampton, Queensland 95/D4
Rockhampton Downs, North. Terr. 93/D5
Rockhaven, Sask. 181/B3
Rock Hill, Mo. (†63119) 261/P3
Rock Hill, S.C. 188/K4
Rock Hill, S.C. (29730) 296/E2
Rockholds, Ky. (40759) 237/N7
Rockingham, Georgia (†31510) 217/H7
Rockingham (co.), N.H. 268/E5
Rockingham (co.), N.C. 281/K2
Rockingham, N.C. (28379) 281/K5
Rockingham○, Vt. (†05101) 268/B5
Rockingham (co.), Va. 307/L4
Rockingham, W. Australia 88/B2
Rockingham, W. Australia 92/A2
Rock Island, Ill. 188/J2
Rock Island (co.), Ill. 222/C2
Rock Island, Ill. (61201) 222/C2
Rock Island, Okla. (†74932) 288/T4
Rock Island, Québec 172/E4
Rock Island, Tenn. (38581) 237/K9
Rock Island, Texas (77470) 303/H8
Rock Island, Wash. (†98801) 310/E3
Rock Island (dam), Wash. 310/E3
Rock Island Arsenal, Ill. 222/C2
Rocklake, N. Dak. (58365) 282/M2
Rockland, Conn. (†06443) 210/E3
Rockland, Del. (19732) 245/R1
Rockland, Idaho (83271) 220/F7
Rockland, Maine (04841) 243/E7
Rockland○, Mass. (02370) 249/L4
Rockland, Mich. (49960) 250/G1
Rockland (co.), N.Y. 276/M8
Rockland, Ontario 177/J2
Rockland, Texas (75970) 303/K6
Rockland, Wis. (54653) 317/D8
Rocklands (res.), Victoria 97/B5
Rockledge, Fla. (32955) 212/F3
Rockledge, Georgia (30454) 217/G6
Rockledge, Pa. (†19101) 294/M5
Rockleigh, N.J. (07647) 273/C1
Rocklin, Calif. (95677) 204/B8
Rockmart, Georgia (30153) 217/B2
Rock Mills, Ala. (36274) 195/H4
Rock Oak, W. Va. (†26756) 312/J4
Rock Point, Md. (20682) 245/L7
Rockport, Ark. (†72104) 202/E5
Rockport, Calif. (†95488) 204/B4
Rockport, Ill. (62370) 222/B4
Rockport, Ind. 227/C9
Rockport, Ky. (42369) 237/H6
Rockport, Maine (04856) 243/F7
Rockport○, Maine (04856) 243/F7
Rockport○, Mass. (01966) 249/M2
Rockport, Miss. (†39083) 256/D7
Rock Port, Mo. (64482) 261/B2
Rockport, Texas (78382) 303/H9
Rockport (lake), Utah 304/C3
Rockport, Wash. (98283) 310/D2
Rockport, W. Va. (26169) 312/C4
Rock Rapids, Iowa (51246) 229/A2
Rock River, Wyo. (82083) 319/G4
Rock Run, Ala. (†36272) 195/G2
Rocks, Md. (†21084) 245/N2
Rocks (pt.), N. Zealand 100/C4
Rock Springs, Mont. (59312) 262/K4
Rocksprings, Texas (78880) 303/D8
Rock Springs, Wis. (53961) 317/F8
Rock Springs, Wyo. 146/H5
Rock Springs, Wyo. 188/E2
Rock Springs, Wyo. (82901) 319/C4
Rockstone, Guyana 131/B2
Rockton, Ill. (61072) 222/E1
Rockvale, Colo. (81244) 208/J6
Rockvale, Mont. (†59080) 262/H5
Rockvale, Tenn. (37153) 237/J9
Rock Valley, Iowa (51247) 229/A2
Rockville, Conn. (†06066) 210/F1
Rockville, Ind. (47872) 227/C5
Rockville, Maine (†04841) 243/E7
Rockville, Md. (*20850) 245/K4
Rockville, Mass. (†02054) 249/A8
Rockville, Minn. (56369) 255/D5
Rockville, Mo. (64780) 261/D6
Rockville, Nebr. (68871) 264/F3
Rockville, Nova Scotia 168/B5
Rockville, R.I. (02873) 249/G6
Rockville, S.C. (†29487) 296/G6
Rockville, Utah (84763) 304/A6
Rockville, Va. (23146) 307/N5
Rockville, Wis. (†53820) 317/E10
Rockville Centre, N.Y. (*11570) 276/R7
Rockwall (co.), Texas 303/H5
Rockwall, Texas (75087) 303/H5
Rockwell, Iowa (50469) 229/G3
Rockwell, N.C. (28138) 281/J3
Rockwell City, Iowa (50579) 229/D4
Rockwood, Ala. (†35653) 195/C2
Rockwood, Ill. (62280) 222/D6
Rockwood, Maine (04478) 243/D4
Rockwood, Mich. (48173) 250/F6
Rockwood, Ontario 177/D4
Rockwood, Pa. (15557) 294/D6
Rockwood, Tenn. (37854) 237/M9
Rockwood, Texas (76873) 303/E6
Rocky (mts.) 162/D4
Rocky (mts.) 146/F4
Rocky (mts.) 188/E3
Rocky (mts.), Alberta 182/BC4
Rocky (mts.), Br. Col. 184/F2
Rocky (mts.), Canada 4/D16
Rocky (mts.), Colo. 208/F1
Rocky (mts.), Idaho 220/D1
Rocky (lake), Maine 243/J6
Rocky (mts.), Mont. 262/D4
Rocky (bay), Newf. 166/C3
Rocky (riv.), Newf. 166/D2
Rocky (mts.), N. Mex. 274/C1
Rocky (pt.), Norfolk I. 88/K6
Rocky (riv.), N.C. 281/H4
Rocky (riv.), Ohio 284/G9
Rocky, Okla. (73661) 288/J4
Rocky (riv.), S.C. 296/B3
Rocky (cape), Tasmania 99/B2
Rocky (mts.), Wash. 310/H2
Rocky (mts.), Wyo. 319/C1
Rocky (mts.), Yukon 187/F4
Rocky Bottom, S.C. (†29685) 296/B1
Rocky Boy, Mont. (†59521) 262/G2
Rocky Boy's Ind. Res., Mont. 262/G2
Rocky Comfort, Mo. (64861) 261/D9
Rocky Face, Georgia (30740) 217/C1
Rockyford, Alberta 182/D4
Rocky Ford, Colo. (81067) 208/M6
Rocky Ford, Georgia (30455) 217/J5
Rocky Fork (lake), Ohio 284/D7
Rocky Gap, Va. (24366) 307/F6
Rocky Gorge (res.), Md. 245/L4
Rocky Harbour, Newf. 166/C4
Rocky Hill○, Conn. (06067) 210/E2
Rocky Hill, Ky. (42163) 237/J6
Rocky Hill, N.J. (08553) 273/D3
Rocky Lane, Alberta 182/B5
Rocky Mount, Georgia (†30251) 217/C4
Rocky Mount, La. (†71064) 238/C1
Rocky Mount, Mo. (65072) 261/G6
Rocky Mount, N.C. 188/L3
Rocky Mount, N.C. (27801) 281/O3
Rocky Mount, Va. (24151) 307/J7
Rocky Mountain Arsenal, Colo. 208/K3
Rocky Mountain House, Alberta 182/C3
Rocky Mountain House, Alta. 162/E5
Rocky Mountain Nat'l Park, Colo. 208/H2
Rocky Point, N.C. (28457) 281/O6
Rocky Point, Wash. (†98626) 310/A2
Rockypoint, Wyo. (†82721) 319/G1
Rocky Rapids, Alberta 182/C3
Rocky Reach (dam), Wash. 310/E3
Rocky Ridge (mt.), Idaho 220/C3
Rocky Ridge, Ohio (43458) 284/D2
Rocky River, Ohio (44116) 284/G9
Rodanthe, N.C. (27968) 281/U3
Rodarte, N. Mex. (87561) 274/D2
Rodas, Cuba 158/E2
Rødby, Denmark 21/E8
Rødby, Denmark 18/G9
Roddickton, Newf. 166/C3
Rødding, Denmark 21/B7
Roddy, Tenn. (†37381) 237/M9
Rødekro, Denmark 21/C7
Roden, Netherlands 27/J2
Rodeo, Calif. (94572) 204/J1
Rodeo, Mexico 150/G4
Rodeo, N. Mex. (88056) 274/A7
Roderfield, W. Va. (24881) 312/C8
Roderick (isl.), Br. Col. 184/C4
Rodessa, La. (71069) 238/B1
Rodez, France 28/E5
Ródhos, Greece 45/J7
Roding (riv.), England 13/J7
Rodinga, North. Terr. 93/D8
Rødkaersbro, Denmark 21/C5
Rodman, Iowa (50580) 229/D2
Rodman, N.Y. (13682) 276/J3
Rodman, S.C. (†29706) 296/E2
Rodney, Mich. (49342) 250/D5
Rodney, Miss. (†39096) 256/B7
Rodney, Ontario 177/C5
Rodney Village, Del. (19901) 245/R4
Rodrigues, Brazil 132/F10
Rodríguez, Uruguay 145/C5
Rødvig, Denmark 21/F7
Roe, Ark. (72134) 202/H4
Roe (riv.), N. Ireland 17/H1
Roebling-Florence, N.J. (08554) 273/D3
Roebourne, W. Australia 88/B4
Roebourne, W. Australia 92/B3
Roebuck (bay), W. Australia 88/C3
Roebuck (bay), W. Australia 92/C2
Roebuck Plains, W. Australia 92/C2
Roeland Park, Kansas (†66205) 232/H2
Roer (riv.), Netherlands 27/J6
Roermond, Netherlands 27/J6
Roeselare, Belgium 27/C7
Roes Welcome (sound), N.W.T. 162/H2
Roes Welcome (sound), N.W. Terrs. 187/K3
Roff, Okla. (74865) 288/N5
Rogachev, U.S.S.R. 52/D4
Rogagua (lake), Bolivia 136/B3
Rogaguado (lake), Bolivia 136/C3
Rogaland (co.), Norway 18/E7
Rogatica, Yugoslavia 45/D4
Roger Mills (co.), Okla. 288/G3
Rogers, Ark. (72756) 202/B1
Rogers, Br. Col. 184/J4
Rogers (lake), Calif. 204/H9
Rogers, Conn. (06263) 210/H1
Rogers (lake), Conn. 210/F3
Rogers, La. (†71342) 238/F3
Rogers, Minn. (55374) 255/E5
Rogers, Nebr. (68659) 264/H3
Rogers, N. Mex. (88132) 274/F5
Rogers, N. Dak. (58479) 282/O5
Rogers, Ohio (44455) 284/J4
Rogers (co.), Okla. 288/P2
Rogers, Texas (76569) 303/G7
Rogers (mt.), Va. 307/E7
Rogers City, Mich. (49779) 250/F3
Rogerson, Idaho (83302) 220/D7
Rogers Springs, Tenn. (†38052) 237/D10
Rogersville, Ala. (35652) 195/D1
Rogersville, Mo. (65742) 261/G8
Rogersville, New Bruns. 170/E2
Rogersville, Pa. (15359) 294/B6
Rogersville, Tenn. (37857) 237/P8
Roger Williams Nat'l Mem., R.I. 249/J5
Roggen, Colo. (80652) 208/L2
Roggwil, Switzerland 39/E2
Rogliano, France 28/B6
Rogozno, Poland 47/C2
Rogue (riv.), Oreg. 291/C5
Rogue River, Oreg. (97537) 291/D5
Roha, India 68/C5
Rohnert Park, Calif. (94928) 204/C5
Rohnerville, Calif. (†95540) 204/B3
Rohrbach in Oberösterreich, Austria 41/B2
Rohrersville, Md. (21779) 245/H3
Rohri, Pakistan 68/B3
Rohtak, India 68/C5
Rohwer, Ark. (71666) 202/H6
Roi Et, Thailand 72/D4
Roja, U.S.S.R. 53/B2
Rojas, Argentina 143/F7
Rojo (cape), Mexico 150/L6
Rojo (cape), P. Rico 161/A3
Rojo (cape), P. Rico 156/F1
Rokan (riv.), Indonesia 85/C5
Rokeby, Sask. 181/J4
Rokiškis, U.S.S.R. 53/C2
Rokycany, Czech. 41/B2
Rokytnice nad Jizerou, Czech. 41/C1
Rola Co (lake), China 77/C4
Roland, Ark. (72135) 202/E4
Roland, Iowa (50236) 229/F4
Roland, Manitoba 179/D5
Roland, Okla. (74954) 288/S4
Røldal, Norway 18/E7
Roldán, Argentina 143/F6
Rolecha, Chile 138/D4
Rolesville, N.C. (27571) 281/N3
Rolette (co.), N. Dak. 282/L2
Rolette, N. Dak. (58366) 282/L2
Roleystone, W. Australia 88/B2
Rolfe, Iowa (50581) 229/D3
Roll, Ariz. (85347) 198/A6
Rolla, Ark. (†72104) 202/E5
Rolla, Br. Col. 184/G2
Rolla, Kansas (67954) 232/A4
Rolla, Mo. (65401) 261/J7
Rolla, N. Dak. (58367) 282/L2
Rollag, Minn. (†56549) 255/B4
Rolle, Switzerland 39/B4
Rollingbay, Wash. (98061) 310/A2
Rollingdam, New Bruns. 170/C3
Rolling Fields, Ky. (†40201) 237/K2
Rolling Fork (riv.), Ky. 237/L5
Rolling Fork, Miss. (39159) 256/C5
Rolling Hills, Alberta 182/E4
Rolling Hills, Calif. (90274) 204/B11
Rolling Hills, Ky. (†40201) 237/L1
Rolling Hills Estates, Calif. (90274) 204/B11
Rolling Meadows, Ill. (60008) 222/A5
Rolling Prairie, Ind. (46371) 227/D1
Rollingstone, Minn. (55969) 255/G6
Rollins, Mont. (59931) 262/B3
Rollo (bay), Pr. Edward I. 168/F2
Rolphton, Ontario 177/G1
Roma, Australia 87/E8
Roma (Rome) (cap.), Italy 34/F6
Roma, Queensland 88/H5
Roma, Queensland 95/D5
Roma, Sweden 18/L8
Romain (cape), S.C. 296/J6
Romaine (riv.), Newf. 166/B3
Romaine (riv.), Que. 162/K5
Romaine, Québec 174/E2
Romaine (riv.), Québec 174/E2
Roma-Los Saenz, Texas (78584) 303/E11
Roman, Romania 45/H2
Romance, Ark. (72136) 202/F3
Romance, Sask. 181/G3
Romance, W. Va. (25175) 312/C5
Romang, Argentina 143/F4
Romang (isl.), Indonesia 85/H7
Romania 2/L3
Romania 7/G4
ROMANIA 45/F3
Romano (cay), Cuba 158/G2
Romano (cay), Cuba 156/C2
Romano (cape), Fla. 212/E6
Romanshorn, Switzerland 39/H1
Romans-sur-Isère, France 28/F5
Romanzof (cape), Alaska 196/E2
Rombauer, Mo. (63962) 261/M9
Romblon (prov.), Philippines 82/D4
Romblon, Philippines 82/D4
Romblon (isl.), Philippines 82/D4
Rome, Ga. 188/K4
Rome, Georgia (30161) 217/B2
Rome, Ill. (61562) 222/D3
Rome, Ind. (47574) 227/D9
Rome, Iowa (52642) 229/K7
Rome (prov.), Italy 34/F6
Rome (cap.), Italy 7/F4
Rome (cap.), Italy 34/F6
Rome (cap.), Italy 2/K3
Rome○, Maine (†04957) 243/D6
Rome, Miss. (38768) 256/C3
Rome, N.Y. 188/M2
Rome, N.Y. (13440) 276/J4
Rome (Stout), Ohio (†45684) 284/D8
Rome, Ohio (44085) 284/J2
Rome, Oreg. (†97910) 291/K5
Rome, Pa. (18837) 294/K2
Rome, Wis. (†53178) 317/H1
Rome City, Ind. (46784) 227/G1
Romeo, Colo. (81148) 208/G8
Romeo, Mich. (48065) 250/F6
Romeoville, Ill. (60441) 222/B6
Romeroville, N. Mex. (†87701) 274/D3
Romeville, La. (†70723) 238/L3
Romilly-sur-Seine, France 28/E3
Romney, Ind. (47981) 227/D4
Romney, W. Va. (26757) 312/J4
Romny, U.S.S.R. 52/D4
Rømø, Denmark 21/B7
Rømø (isl.), Denmark 21/B7
Rømø (isl.), Denmark 18/F9
Romont, Switzerland 39/C3
Romorantin-Lanthenay, France 28/D4
Romsdalsfjorden (fjord), Norway 18/E5
Romsey, England 10/F5
Romsey, England 13/F6
Romulus, Mich. (48174) 250/F6
Romulus, N.Y. (14541) 276/G5
Ron, Vietnam 72/E3
Ron, Mui (cape), Vietnam 72/E3
Rona (isl.), Scotland 15/B3
Ronald, Wash. (98940) 310/E3
Ronan, Mont. (59864) 262/C3
Ronay (isl.), Scotland 15/A3
Roncador, Serra do (range), Brazil 132/D5
Roncador (cays), Colombia 126/B9
Ronceverte, W. Va. (24970) 312/F7
Ronciglione, Italy 34/C3
Ronda, N.C. (28670) 281/H2
Ronda, Spain 33/D4
Rønde, Denmark 21/D5
Ronde (isl.), Grenada 161/D7
Rondeau Prov. Park, Ontario 177/C5
Rondo, Ark. (†72355) 202/J4
Rondônia (terr.), Brazil 132/H10
Rondônia, Brazil 132/H10
Rondonópolis, Brazil 120/D4
Rondout (res.), N.Y. 276/M7
Rondu, Pakistan 68/D1
Rong, Koh (isl.), Cambodia 72/D5
Rong'an, China 77/G6
Ronge, Lac La (lake), Sask. 162/F4
Ronge, La (lake), Sask. 181/M3
Rongelap (atoll), Marshall Is. 87/G4
Rongjiang, China 77/G6
Rong Kwang, Thailand 72/D3
Rong Xian, China 77/H7
Ronju (mt.), Fr. Poly. 86/T13
Ronkonkoma, N.Y. (11779) 276/O9
Rønne, Denmark 21/F9
Rønne, Denmark 18/J9
Ronneby, Minn. (†56324) 255/E5
Ronneby, Sweden 18/J8
Ronne Entrance (inlet) 5/B15
Ronne Ice Shelf, Ant. 2/F10
Ronne Ice Shelf 5/B15
Ronse, Belgium 27/D7
Ronuro (riv.), Brazil 132/C6
Roodepoort, S. Africa 118/H6
Roodhouse, Ill. (62082) 222/C4
Roof Butte (mt.), Ariz. 198/F2
Rooi, Neth. Ant. 161/E8
Rooks (co.), Kansas 232/C2
Roopville, Georgia (30170) 217/B4
Roosendaal, Netherlands 27/F5
Roosevelt (isl.), Ant. 2/A10
Roosevelt (isl.) 5/A10
Roosevelt (res.), Ariz. 188/D4
Roosevelt, Ariz. (85545) 198/D5
Roosevelt (riv.), Brazil 120/C3
Roosevelt (riv.), Brazil 132/A5
Roosevelt, La. (†71276) 238/H1
Roosevelt, Minn. (56673) 255/C2
Roosevelt (co.), Mont. 262/L2
Roosevelt, N.J. (08555) 273/E3
Roosevelt (co.), N. Mex. 274/F4
Roosevelt, N.Y. (11575) 276/R7
Roosevelt, Okla. (73564) 288/J5
Roosevelt, Texas (76874) 303/D7
Roosevelt, Utah (84066) 304/D3
Roosevelt, Wash. (99356) 310/E5
Roosevelt Campobello Int'l Park, New Bruns. 170/D4
Roosevelt City, Ala. (35020) 195/E4
Roosevelt Park, Mich. (49444) 250/C5
Roosevelt Road Naval Res., P. Rico 161/F2
Roosville, Br. Col. 184/K5
Root (riv.), Minn. 255/G7
Rootstown, Ohio (44272) 284/H3
Roper, N.C. (27970) 281/R3
Roper (riv.), North. Terr. 88/E3
Roper (riv.), North. Terr. 93/C3
Roper River, North. Terr. 93/D3
Roper River Mission, North. Terr. 88/E2
Roper Valley, North. Terr. 93/D3
Ropesville, Texas (79358) 303/B4
Roque Bluffs○, Maine (†04654) 243/H6
Roque González de Santa Cruz, Paraguay 144/B5
Roque Pérez, Argentina 143/G7
Roquetas, Spain 33/G2
Rora (head), Scotland 15/E2
Roraima (mt.) 120/C2
Roraima (terr.), Brazil 132/H8
Roraima (mt.), Guyana 131/A3
Roraima (mt.), Venezuela 124/H5
Rørby, Denmark 21/E6
Rorketon, Manitoba 179/C3
Røros, Norway 18/G5
Rorschach, Switzerland 39/H2
Rosa, Ala. (†35049) 195/E3
Rosa (cape), Ecuador 128/B10
Rosa (mt.), Italy 34/A1
Rosa, La. (71364) 238/G5
Rosa, Manitoba 179/F5
Rosa (mt.), Switzerland 39/E5
Rosaire, Québec 172/G3
Rosaireville, New Bruns. 170/E2
Rosalia, Kansas (67132) 232/F4
Rosalia, Wash. (99170) 310/H3
Rosalie, Dominica 161/F6
Rosalie, Nebr. (68055) 264/H2
Rosalina, Paraguay 144/D3
Rosalind, Alberta 182/D3
Rosamond, Calif. (93560) 204/G9
Rosamond (lake), Calif. 204/G9
Rosamond, Ill. (62083) 222/D4
Rosamorada, Mexico 150/G5
Rosapenna, Ireland 17/F1
Rosario, Argentina 143/F6
Rosario, Argentina 120/C6
Rosário, Brazil 132/E3
Rosario, Chile 138/F5
Rosario (cay), Cuba 158/C2
Rosario, Sinaloa, Mexico 150/G5
Rosario, Sonora, Mexico 150/E3
Rosario, Paraguay 144/D4
Rosario, P. Rico 161/A2
Rosario, Uruguay 145/B5
Rosario, Venezuela 124/B2
Rosario (str.), Wash. 310/C2
Rosario de la Frontera, Argentina 143/D2
Rosario de Lerma, Argentina 143/C1
Rosario del Tala, Argentina 143/G6
Rosário do Sul, Brazil 132/C10
Rosário Oeste, Brazil 132/C6
Rosas, Spain 33/H1
Rosas (gulf), Spain 33/H1
Rosati, Mo. (†65559) 261/J6
Rosa Zárate, Ecuador 128/C2
Rosburg, Wash. (98643) 310/B4
Rosbys Rock, W. Va. (†26041) 312/E3
Roscoe, Ill. (61073) 222/D1
Roscoe, Minn. (56371) 255/D5
Roscoe, Mo. (64781) 261/E7
Roscoe, Mont. (59071) 262/G5
Roscoe, Nebr. (†69153) 264/C3
Roscoe, N.Y. (12776) 276/L7
Roscoe, Pa. (15477) 294/C5
Roscoe, S. Dak. (57471) 298/L3
Roscoe, Texas (79545) 303/D5
Roscoff, France 28/A3
Roscommon (co.), Ireland 17/E4
Roscommon, Ireland 10/B4
Roscommon, Ireland 17/E4
Roscommon (co.), Mich. 250/E4
Roscommon, Mich. (48653) 250/E4
Roscrea, Ireland 10/B4
Roscrea, Ireland 17/F6
Rose (peak), Ariz. 198/F5
Rose (pt.), Br. Col. 184/B3
Rose (pt.), Martinique 161/D6
Rose, Nebr. (68772) 264/E2
Rose, N.Y. (14542) 276/G4
Rose (riv.), North. Terr. 93/D2
Rose, Okla. (74364) 288/R2
Roseau (cap.), Dominica 156/G4
Roseau (cap.), Dominica 161/E7
Roseau (riv.), Dominica 161/E7
Roseau (co.), Minn. 255/C2
Roseau, Minn. (56751) 255/C2
Roseau (riv.), Minn. 255/B2
Roseau (riv.), St. Lucia 161/G6
Roseau River, Manitoba 179/F5
Roseaux, Haiti 158/A6
Rosebank, Manitoba 179/D5
Roseberry, Br. Col. 184/J5
Rosebery, Tasmania 99/B3
Rose Blanche, Newf. 166/C4
Roseboom, N.Y. (13450) 276/L5
Roseboro, N.C. (28382) 281/N5
Rosebud, Alberta 182/D4
Rosebud (riv.), Alberta 182/D4
Rose Bud, Ark. (72137) 202/F3
Rosebud, Mo. (63091) 261/K6
Rosebud (co.), Mont. 262/K4
Rosebud, Mont. (59347) 262/K4
Rosebud (creek), Mont. 262/K4
Rosebud, S. Dak. (57570) 298/H7
Rosebud, Texas (76570) 303/G7
Rosebud (creek), Utah 304/A2
Rosebud Ind. Res., S. Dak. 298/H7
Roseburg, Oreg. (97470) 291/D4
Rosebush Mich. (48878) 250/E5
Rose City, Mich. (48654) 250/E4
Rose Creek, Minn. (55970) 255/F7
Rosedale, Ind. (47874) 227/C5
Rosedale, La. (70772) 238/G6
Rosedale, Md. (21237) 245/M3
Rosedale, Miss. (38769) 256/B3
Rosedale, Okla. (†74831) 288/M5
Rosedale, Tenn. (†37381) 237/N8
Rosedale, Va. (24280) 307/E7
Rosedale, W. Va. (26636) 312/E5
Rosefield, La. (†71435) 238/G3
Roseglen, N. Dak. (58775) 282/G4
Rosehearty, Scotland 15/F3
Rosehill, Ala. (†36028) 195/F8
Rose Hill, Barbados 161/B8
Rose Hill, Ill. (†62448) 222/E4
Rose Hill, Iowa (52586) 229/J6
Rose Hill, Kansas (67133) 232/E4
Rose Hill, Ky. (†40330) 237/M5
Rose Hill, Miss. (39356) 256/F6
Rose Hill, N.C. (28458) 281/N5
Rose Hill, Va. (24281) 307/B7
Roseisle, Manitoba 179/D5
Rose Lake, Br. Col. 184/E3
Roseland, Ark. (72463) 202/K2
Roseland, Fla. (32957) 212/F4
Roseland, Ind. (†46601) 227/E1
Roseland, Kansas (†66773) 232/H4
Roseland, La. (70456) 238/J5
Roseland, Minn. (†56216) 255/C6
Roseland, Nebr. (68973) 264/F4
Roseland, N.J. (07068) 273/A2
Roseland, Va. (22967) 307/K5
Roselawn, Ind. (†46310) 227/C2
Roselle, Ill. (60172) 222/A5
Roselle, N.J. (07203) 273/B2
Roselle Park, N.J. (07204) 273/A2
Rose Lodge, Oreg. (97372) 291/D3
Rose Lynn, Alberta 182/E4
Rosemark, Tenn. (38053) 237/B10
Rosemary, Alberta 182/E4
Rosemead, Calif. (91770) 204/C10
Rosemère, Québec 172/H4
Rosemont, Ill. (60018) 222/B5
Rosemont, Md. (†21758) 245/H3
Rosemont, N.J. (08556) 273/D3
Rosemont, Pa. (19010) 294/M5
Rosemount, Minn. (55068) 255/E6
Rosemount, Ohio (†45662) 284/D8
Rosen, Minn. (†56212) 255/B5
Rosenberg, Texas (77471) 303/J8
Rosendale, Minn. (†56243) 255/D5
Rosendale, Mo. (64483) 261/C2
Rosendale, N.Y. (12472) 276/M7
Rosendale, Wis. (54974) 317/J8
Rosenfeld, Manitoba 179/E5
Rosengart, Manitoba 179/E5
Rosenhayn, N.J. (08352) 273/C5
Rosenheim, W. Germany 22/D5
Rosenhof, Sask. 181/D5
Rosenlaui, Switzerland 39/F3
Rosenort, Manitoba 179/E5
Rosepine, La. (70659) 238/D5
Rose Prairie, Br. Col. 184/G2
Roseray, Sask. 181/C5
Roseto, Pa. (18013) 294/M4
Rosetown, Sask. 162/F5
Rosetown, Sask. 181/D4
Rosetta, Egypt 111/J2
Rosetta, Egypt 59/B3
Rosetta, Miss. (†39633) 256/B8
Rosette, Utah (†84329) 304/A2
Rose Valley, Pa. (†19065) 294/L7
Rose Valley, Sask. 181/H3
Roseville, Calif. (95678) 204/B8
Roseville, Ill. (61473) 222/C3
Roseville, Mich. (48066) 250/B6
Roseville, Minn. (55113) 255/G5
Roseville, Ohio (43777) 284/F6
Roseville, Pa. (†16933) 294/H2
Roseway (riv.), Nova Scotia 168/C4
Rosewood, North. Terr. 93/A4
Rosewood, Ohio (43070) 284/C5
Rosewood Heights, Ill. (†62024) 222/B2
Roseworthy, S. Australia 94/B6
Roshage (cape), Denmark 18/F8
Rosharon, Texas (77583) 303/J3
Rosh Ha 'Ayin, Israel 65/B3
Rosholt, S. Dak. (57260) 298/R2
Rosholt, Wis. (54473) 317/H6
Rosh Pinna, Israel 65/D2
Rosice, Czech. 41/D2
Rosiclare, Ill. (62982) 222/E6
Rosie, Ark. (72571) 202/G2
Rosier, Georgia (†30434) 217/H5
Rosignano Marittimo, Italy 34/C3
Rosignol, Guyana 131/C2
Rosine, Ky. (42370) 237/H6
Roşiori de Vede, Romania 45/G3
Rositsa, Bulgaria 45/H4
Roskilde (co.), Denmark 21/E6
Roskilde, Denmark 21/E6
Roskilde, Denmark 18/G9
Roslavl', U.S.S.R. 52/D4
Roslev, Denmark 21/B4
Roslin, Ontario 177/G3
Roslin, Tenn. (†38556) 237/M8
Roslyn, N.Y. (11576) 276/R6
Roslyn, S. Dak. (57261) 298/P2
Roslyn, Wash. (98941) 310/E3
Rosman, N.C. (28772) 281/D4
Rosmaninhal, Portugal 33/C3
Røsnaes (pen.), Denmark 21/D6
Rosneath, Scotland 15/A1
Rosneath, Scotland 10/A1
Ross (isl.), Ant. 2/T10
Ross (sea), Ant. 2/A10
Ross (isl.) 5/B9
Ross (sea) 5/B10
Ross, Calif. (94957) 204/H1
Ross, Iowa (†50025) 229/D5
Ross, Manitoba 179/F5
Ross (isl.), Manitoba 179/J3
Ross, Minn. (56753) 255/C2
Ross (isl.), New Bruns. 170/D4
Ross, N. Zealand 100/C5
Ross (pt.), Norfolk I. 88/L6
Ross, N. Dak. (58776) 282/E3
Ross (co.), Ohio 284/D7
Ross, Ohio (45061) 284/B9
Ross, Tasmania 99/D4
Ross (dam), Wash. 310/D2
Ross (lake), Wash. 310/D2
Rossa, Switzerland 39/H4
Rossall (pt.), England 13/D4
Rossan (pt.), Ireland 10/B3
Ross and Cromarty (trad. co.), Scotland 15/A5
Rossano, Italy 34/F5
Rossarden, Tasmania 99/D3
Ross Barnett (res.), Miss. 256/D6
Ross Bay Junction, Newf. 166/A3
Rossbear (lake), Alberta 182/C1
Rossburg, Ohio (45362) 284/A5
Rossburn, Manitoba 179/B4
Rosscarbery, Ireland 17/C8
Rosscarbery (bay), Ireland 10/B5
Rosscarbery (bay), Ireland 17/D9
Rosseau, Ontario 177/E2
Rosseau (lake), Ontario 177/E2
Rossel (isl.), Papua N.G. 85/D8
Rossendale, Manitoba 179/D5
Rosser, Manitoba 179/E4
Rosses (bay), Ireland 17/D1
Rosses Point, Ireland 17/D3
Rossford, Ohio (43460) 284/C2
Ross Fork, Mont. (†59457) 262/G3
Ross Ice Shelf, Ant. 2/A11
Ross Ice Shelf 5/A10
Rossie, Iowa (51356) 229/C2
Rossie, N.Y. (†13646) 276/J2
Rossignol (lake), Nova Scotia 168/C4
Rossing, Namibia 118/B4
Rossiter, Pa. (15772) 294/E4
Rosskeeragh (pt.), Ireland 17/D3
Ross Lake Nat'l Rec. Area, Wash. 310/E2
Rossland, Br. Col. 162/E6
Rossland, Br. Col. 184/H6
Rosslare, Ireland 10/C4
Rosslare, Ireland 17/J7
Rosslare (bay), Ireland 17/J7
Rosslare Harbour (Ballygeary), Ireland 17/J7
Rosslau, E. Germany 22/E3
Rosslyn Farms, Pa. (†15106) 294/B7
Rosslyn Village, Ontario 177/G5
Rosslyn Village, Ontario 175/C3
Rossmore, W. Va. (25643) 312/C7
Rossmoyne, Ohio (45236) 284/C9
Rosso, Mauritania 106/A5
Rosso, Mauritania 102/A3
Ross of Mull (pen.), Scotland 15/B4
Ross-on-Wye, England 10/E5
Ross-on-Wye, England 13/E6
Rossosh', U.S.S.R. 52/E4
Rossport, Ontario 177/H5
Ross River, Yukon 187/E3
Rosstock (mt.), Switzerland 39/G3
Rosston, Ark. (71858) 202/D6
Rosston, Ind. (†46077) 227/E4
Rosston, Okla. (73855) 288/G1

S

Sainte-Marguerite 439

Saas, Switzerland 39/J3
Saas Fee, Switzerland 39/E4
Saba (isl.), Neth. Ant. 156/F3
Saba (isl.), Virgin Is. (U.S.) 161/A4
Šabac, Yugoslavia 45/D3
Sabadell, Spain 7/E4
Sabadell, Spain 33/H2
Sabae, Japan 81/H5
Sabah (state), Malaysia 2/Q5
Sabah (state), Malaysia 85/F4
Sabah (reg.), Malaysia 54/N9
Sábalo, Cuba 158/A2
Sabana, Cuba 158/K4
Sabana (arch.), Cuba 158/E1
Sabana de la Mar, Dom. Rep. 156/E3
Sabana de la Mar, Dom. Rep. 158/F5
Sabana Grande, Dom. Rep. 158/E6
Sabanagrande, Honduras 154/D4
Sabana Grande, P. Rico 161/B2
Sabanalarga, Colombia 126/C2
Sabana Seca, P. Rico 161/D1
Sabancuy, Mexico 150/O7
Sabaneta, Dom. Rep. 158/D5
Sabaneta, Barinas, Venezuela 124/D3
Sabaneta, Falcón, Venezuela 124/D2
Sabang, Celebes, Indonesia 85/F5
Sabang, Weh, Indonesia 85/B4
Şabanözü, Turkey 63/E2
Sabará, Brazil 135/E1
Sabattus, Maine (04280) 243/C7
Sabattus○, Maine (04280) 243/C7
Sabaudia, Italy 34/D4
Sabaya, Bolivia 136/A6
Saberi, Hamun-e (lake), Iran 66/M5
Sabetha, Kansas (66534) 232/G2
Sabi (riv.), Zimbabwe 118/E3
Sabile, U.S.S.R. 53/B2
Sabillasville, Md. (21780) 245/J2
Sabin, Minn. (56580) 255/B4
Sabina, Ohio (45169) 284/C7
Sabinal (cay), Cuba 158/H2
Sabinal, Texas (78881) 303/E8
Sabinas, Mexico 150/J3
Sabinas (riv.), Mexico 150/J3
Sabinas Hidalgo, Mexico 150/J3
Sabine (riv.) 188/H4
Sabine (mt.) 5/B9
Sabine (par.), La. 238/C3
Sabine (lake), La. 238/C7
Sabine (passage), La. 238/C7
Sabine (riv.), La. 238/C5
Sabine (pen.), N.W. Terrs. 187/H2
Sabine (co.), Texas 303/L6
Sabine, Texas (†77640) 303/L8
Sabine (lake), Texas 303/L8
Sabine (riv.), Texas 303/L7
Sabine Pass, Texas (77655) 303/L8
Sabinópolis, Brazil 132/F7
Sabinoso, N. Mex. (†87746) 274/E3
Sabinov, Czech. 41 F2
Sabinsville, Pa. (16943) 294/G2
Sabir, Jebel (mt.), Yemen Arab Rep. 59/D7
Sabirabad, U.S.S.R. 52/G6
Sabkha, Syria 63/H5
Sablayan, Philippines 82/C4
Sable (cape), Fla. 188/K5
Sable (cape), Fla. 212/E6
Sable (cape), N.S. 146/M5
Sable (isl.), N.S. 146/N5
Sable (cape), N.S. 162/K7
Sable (isl.), N.S. 162/L7
Sable (cape), Nova Scotia 168/C5
Sable (isl.), Nova Scotia 168/J5
Sable (riv.), Ontario 177/B1
Sable (riv.), Québec 174/D1
Sable River, Nova Scotia 168/C5
Sables (lake), Québec 172/B3
Sables (lake), Québec 172/H1
Sablé-sur-Sarthe, France 28/C4
Sabougla, Miss. (†38955) 256/F3
Sabra (cape), Indonesia 85/J6
Sabrathaa, Libya 111/B1
Sabrina Coast (reg.) 5/C6
Sabtang, Philippines 82/B2
Sabtang (isl.), Philippines 82/B2
Sabugal, Portugal 33/C2
Sabula, Iowa (52070) 229/N4
Sabula, Mo. (†63620) 261/L8
Sabula, Pa. (†15801) 294/E3
Sabya, Saudi Arabia 59/D6
Sabzevar, Iran 54/G6
Sabzevar, Iran 59/G2
Sabzevar, Iran 66/K2
Sabzvaran, Iran 66/K6
Sabzvaran, Iran 59/G4
Sac (co.), Iowa 229/C4
Sac (riv.), Mo. 261/E7
Sacaba, Bolivia 136/C5
Sacaca, Bolivia 136/B6
Sacajawea (peak), Oreg. 291/K2
Sacajawea (lake), Wash. 310/G4
Sácama, Colombia 126/D4
Sacandaga (lake), N.Y. 276/L3
Sac and Fox Ind. Res., Iowa 229/H5
Sacapulas, Guatemala 154/B3
Sacaton, Ariz. (85247) 198/D5
Sacavém, Portugal 33/A1
Sac City, Iowa (50583) 229/C4
Sacedón, Spain 33/E2
Săcele, Romania 45/G3
Sac-Fox-Iowa Ind. Res., Kansas 232/G2
Sacheen (lake), Wash. 310/H2
Sachem (head), Conn. 210/E4
Sachem Head, Conn. (†06437) 210/E3
Sachigo (riv.), Ont. 162/G5
Sachigo (riv.), Ontario 175/B2
Sachojere, Bolivia 136/C4
Sachse, Texas (†75040) 303/H2
Sachseln, Switzerland 39/F3
Sachs Harbour, Canada 4/B16
Sachs Harbour, N.W.T. 162/D1
Sachs Harbour, N.W. Terrs. 187/F2
Sackets (harb.), N.Y. 276/H3
Sackets Harbor, N.Y. (13685) 276/H3
Säckingen, W. Germany 22/C5
Sackville, New Bruns. 170/F3
Sackville, Nova Scotia 168/E4
Saco, Ala. (†36081) 195/G7
Saco, Maine (04072) 243/C8
Saco (riv.), Maine 243/B8
Saco, Mo. (†63645) 261/M8
Saco, Mont. (59261) 262/J2
Saco (riv.), N.H. 268/E3
Sacol (isl.), Philippines 82/D7
Sacramento, Brazil 132/D7
Sacramento, Brazil 135/C1
Sacramento (cap.), Calif. 146/F6
Sacramento (cap.), Calif. 188/B3
Sacramento (riv.), Calif. 188/B3
Sacramento (co.), Calif. 204/D5
Sacramento (cap.), Calif. (*95801) 204/B8
Sacramento (riv.), Calif. 204/D5
Sacramento, Ky. (42372) 237/G6
Sacramento, N. Mex. (88347) 274/D6
Sacramento (mts.), N. Mex. 274/D6
Sacramento Army Depot, Calif. 204/B8
Sacramento Wash (dry riv.), Ariz. 198/A4
Sacratif (cape), Spain 33/E4
Sacré-Coeur-de-Saguenay, Québec 172/H1
Sacred Heart, Minn. (56285) 255/C6
Sacul, Texas (75788) 303/K6
Sádaba, Spain 33/F1
Sadani, Tanzania 115/G5
Saddle (hills), Alberta 182/A2
Saddle, Ark. (†72554) 202/G1
Saddle (mt.), Idaho 220/F6
Saddle (mt.), Idaho 220/D3
Saddle (riv.), N.J. 273/B1
Saddle (mts.), Wash. 310/E4
Saddle Brook○, N.J. (07662) 273/B1
Saddle Mountain, Okla. (†73023) 288/J5
Saddle River, N.J. (07458) 273/B1
Saddlestring, Wyo. (82840) 319/F1
Saddleworth, England 13/J2
Saddleworth, England 10/G2
Sa Dec, Vietnam 72/E5
Sadhoowa, Trin. & Tob. 161/B11
Sadieville, Ky. (40370) 237/M4
Sadij (riv.), Iran 66/L8
Sadiya, India 68/H3
Sa'diya, Iraq 66/D3
Sa'diya, Hor (lake), Iraq 66/E4
Sadlers Village, St. Chris.-Nevis 161/C10
Sadlersville, Tenn. (37154) 237/G7
Sado (isl.), Japan 81/J4
Sado (riv.), Portugal 33/B3
Sadon, Burma 72/C1
Sadorus, Ill. (61872) 222/E4
Saeby, Denmark 18/G8
Saeby, Denmark 21/D3
Saegertown, Pa. (16433) 294/B2
Saetermoen, Norway 18/L2
Saetermoen, Norway 18/L2
Safad (Zefat), Israel 65/C2
Safaniya, Ras (cape), Saudi Arabia 59/E4
Šafárikovo, Czech. 41/F2
Safata (bay), W. Samoa 86/M9
Safe, Mo. (†65559) 261/J6
Safety Harbor, Fla. (33572) 212/B2
Säffle, Sweden 18/H7
Safford, Ala. (36773) 195/D6
Safford, Ariz. (85546) 198/F6
Saffordville, Kansas (†66869) 232/F3
Saffron Walden, England 10/G4
Saffron Walden, England 13/H5
Safi, Jordan 65/E5
Safi, Morocco 102/B1
Safi, Morocco 106/C2
Safidar, Kuh-e (mt.), Iran 59/F4
Safidar, Kuh-e (mt.), Iran 66/H6
Safid Rud (riv.), Iran 66/F2
Safien, Switzerland 39/H3
Safita, Syria 63/G5
Safonovo, U.S.S.R. 52/D3
Safranbolu, Turkey 63/E2
Safut, Jordan 65/D3
Saga, China 77/B6
Saga (pref.), Japan 81/E7
Saga, Japan 81/E7
Sagadahoc (co.), Maine 243/D7
Sagaing (div.), Burma 72/B1
Sagaing, Burma 72/B2
Sagami (bay), Japan 81/O3
Sagami (riv.), Japan 81/O2
Sagami (sea), Japan 81/J6
Sagamihara, Japan 81/O2
Sagamore, Mass. (02561) 249/M5
Sagamore, Pa. (16250) 294/D4
Sagamore Hill Nat'l Hist. Site, N.Y. 276/R6
Sagamore Hills, Ohio (†44067) 284/J10
Saganaga (lake), Minn. 255/H2
Saganaga (lake), Ontario 175/B3
Sagar, India 68/D4
Sagavanirktok (riv.), Alaska 196/J1
Sagay, Camiguin, Philippines 82/E6
Sagay, Negros Occ., Philippines 82/D5
Sage, Ark. (72573) 202/G1
Sage (creek), Mont. 262/F2
Sage (mt.), Virgin Is. (Br.) 161/D4
Sage, Wyo. (†83101) 319/B4
Sagemace (bay), Manitoba 179/B3
Sagerton, Texas (79548) 303/E4
Sageville, Iowa (†52001) 229/M3
Sag Harbor, N.Y. (11963) 276/R8
Saginaw, Ala. (35137) 195/E4
Saginaw, Mich. 188/K2
Saginaw (bay), Mich. 188/K2
Saginaw (co.), Mich. 250/E5
Saginaw, Mich. (*48601) 250/F5
Saginaw (bay), Mich. 250/F5
Saginaw (riv.), Mich. 250/F5
Saginaw, Minn. (55779) 255/F4
Saginaw, Mo. (64864) 261/C8
Saginaw, Oreg. (97472) 291/E4
Saginaw, Texas (76179) 303/E2
Sagle, Idaho (83860) 220/B1
Saglek (bay), Newf. 166/B2
Saglek (fjord), Newf. 166/B2
Saglouc, Que. 162/J3
Saglouc, Québec 174/E1
Sagnay, Philippines 82/D4
Sagola, Mich. (49881) 250/B2
Saguache (co.), Colo. 208/G6
Saguache, Colo. (81149) 208/G6
Saguache (creek), Colo. 208/F6
Sagua de Tánamo, Cuba 158/K3
Sagua la Grande, Cuba 156/B2
Sagua la Grande, Cuba 158/E1
Sagua la Grande (riv.), Cuba 158/E1
Saguaro (lake), Ariz. 198/D5
Saguaro Nat'l Mon., Ariz. 198/E6
Saguenay (county), Québec 174/D2
Saguenay (co.), Québec 172/H1
Saguenay (riv.), Québec 174/C3
Saguenay (riv.), Québec 172/G1
Saguia el Hamra (dry riv.), Western Sahara 106/B3
Sagunto, Spain 33/F3
Sa'gya, China 77/C6
Sahagún, Colombia 126/C3
Sahagún, Spain 33/D1
Sahand, Kuh-e (mt.), Iran 66/E2
Sahara (desert) 2/J4
Sahara (des.) 102/C2
Sahara (des.), Algeria 106/E4
Sahara (des.), Chad 111/C3
Sahara (des.), Egypt 111/E3
Sahara (des.), Libya 111/C3
Sahara (des.), Mali 106/D4
Sahara (des.), Mauritania 106/C4
Sahara (des.), Niger 106/F4
Sahara (des.), Sudan 111/E3
Saharan Atlas (ranges), Algeria 106/E2
Saharanpur, India 68/D3
Saharsa, India 68/F3
Şahinli, Turkey 63/C6
Sahiwal, Pakistan 68/C2
Sahiwal, Pakistan 59/K3
Sahuaripa, Mexico 150/E2
Sahuarita, Ariz. (85629) 198/E7
Sahuayo de Díaz, Mexico 150/H7
Šahy, Czech. 41/E2
Saïda, Algeria 106/E2
Saida, Lebanon 63/F6
Sa'idabad, Iran 66/J6
Sa'idabad, Iran 59/G4
Saïdia, Morocco 106/D2
Saidor, Papua N.G. 85/B7
Saidu, Pakistan 68/C2
Saignelégier, Switzerland 39/D2
Saigo, Japan 81/F5
Saigon (Ho Chi Minh City), Vietnam 54/M8
Saihut, P.D.R. Yemen 54/G8
Saihut, P.D.R. Yemen 59/F6
Saikai National Park, Japan 81/D7
Saiki, Japan 81/E7
Sailes, La. (†71028) 238/D2
Sailor (creek), Idaho 220/C7
Sailor Springs, Ill. (62879) 222/E5
Saimaa (lake), Finland 18/Q6
Saimbeyli, Turkey 63/G4
Sain Alto, Mexico 150/H5
Sain-ni, N. Korea 81/B4
Saint Abbs, Scotland 15/F5
Saint Abbs (head), Scotland 15/F5
Saint-Adalbert, Québec 172/H3
Saint-Adelme, Québec 172/B1
Saint-Adelphe, Québec 172/E3
Saint Adolphe, Manitoba 179/E5
Saint-Adolphe, Québec 172/F2
Saint-Adolphe-d'Howard, Québec 172/C4
Saint-Adrien, Québec 172/F4
Saint-Affrique, France 28/E6
Saint-Agapitville, Québec 172/F3
Saint Agatha○, Maine (04772) 243/G1
Saint Agnes, England 13/B7
Saint-Aimé-des-Lacs, Québec 172/G2
Saint-Alban, Québec 172/E3
Saint Albans, England 13/H7
Saint Albans, England 10/F5
Saint Alban's (head), England 13/F7
Saint Albans○, Maine (04971) 243/E6
Saint Albans, Mo. (63073) 261/L5
Saint Alban's, Newf. 166/C4
Saint Albans, Vt. (05478) 268/A2
Saint Albans○, Vt. (05478) 268/A2
Saint Albans, W. Va. (25177) 312/C6
Saint Albans Bay, Vt. (05481) 268/A2
Saint Albert, Alberta 182/D3
Saint Albert, Ontario 177/J2
Saint-Albert, Québec 172/E3
Saint-Alexandre, Québec 172/D4
Saint-Alexandre-de-Kamouraska, Québec 172/H2
Saint-Alexis, Québec 172/D4
Saint-Alexis-de-Matapédia, Québec 172/B2
Saint-Alexis-des-Monts, Québec 172/D3
Saint Almo, New Bruns. 170/C2
Saint Alphonse, Manitoba 179/C5
Saint-Alphonse, Québec 172/D4
Saint Alphonse de Clare, Nova Scotia 168/B4
Saint-Alphonse-de-Caplan, Québec 172/C2
Saint-Amable, Québec 172/J4
Saint-Amand-Mont-Rond, France 28/E4
Saint Amant, La. (70774) 238/L2
Saint Ambroise, Manitoba 179/E4
Saint-Ambroise, Québec 172/F1
Saint-Anaclet, Québec 172/J1
Saint-André (cape), Madagascar 118/G3
Saint-André, New Bruns. 170/C1
Saint-André, Québec 172/B2
Saint-André, Réunion 118/G5
Saint-André-Avellin, Québec 172/B4
Saint-André-de-Kamouraska, Québec 172/H2
Saint-André-du-Lac-Saint-Jean, Québec 172/E1
Saint-André-Est, Québec 172/C4
Saint Andrew (pt.), Fla. 212/D6
Saint Andrew (sound), Georgia 217/K9
Saint Andrew (lake), Manitoba 179/E3
Saint Andrew (mt.), St. Vin. & Grens. 161/A9
Saint Andrews, New Bruns. 170/C3
Saint Andrew's, Newf. 166/C4
Saint Andrews, Nova Scotia 168/F3
Saint Andrews (chan.), Nova Scotia 168/H2
Saint Andrews, Scotland 15/F4
Saint Andrews, Scotland 10/E2
Saint Andrews (bay), Scotland 15/F4
Saint Andrews, S.C. (29407) 296/G6
Saint Andrews, Tenn. (37372) 237/K10
Saint-Anicet, Québec 172/C4
Saint Ann, Mo. (63074) 261/O2
Saint Anne, Chan. Is. 13/E8
Saint Anne, Ill. (60964) 222/F2
Saint Anns (bay), Nova Scotia 168/H2
Saint Anns, Ontario 177/E4
Saint Ann's Bay, Jamaica 156/C3
Saint Ann's Bay, Jamaica 158/J5
Saint-Anselme, Québec 172/F3
Saint Ansgar, Iowa (50472) 229/H2
Saint Anthony, Idaho (83445) 220/G6
Saint Anthony, Ind. (47575) 227/D8
Saint Anthony, Iowa (50239) 229/G4
Saint Anthony, Minn. (†56307) 255/D5
Saint Anthony, Minn. (55414) 255/G5
Saint Anthony, Newf. 166/C3
Saint Anthony, N. Dak. (58566) 282/H6
Saint-Antoine, New Bruns. 170/F2
Saint-Antoine, Québec 172/H4
Saint-Antoine-Abbé, Québec 172/D4
Saint-Antoine-sur-Richelieu, Québec 172/D4
Saint-Antonin, Québec 172/H2
Saint-Antonin-Noble-Val, France 28/D5
Saint Arnaud, Victoria 97/B5
Saint-Arsène, Québec 172/H2
Saint Arthur, New Bruns. 170/D1
Saint-Astier, France 28/D5
Saint-Athanase, Québec 172/H2
Saint-Aubert, Québec 172/G2
Saint Aubin, Chan. Is. 13/E8
Saint-Aubin-Sauges, Switzerland 39/C3
Saint Augustin (riv.), Newf. 166/C3
Saint-Augustin, Québec 172/G4
Saint-Augustin, Québec 174/F2
Saint-Augustin (riv.), Québec 174/F2
Saint-Augustin-de-Québec, Québec 172/E3
Saint Augustine, Fla. 188/K5
Saint Augustine, Fla. 146/K7
Saint Augustine, Fla. (32084) 212/E2
Saint Augustine, Ill. (61474) 222/C3
Saint Augustine, Md. (†21915) 245/P3
Saint Augustine Beach, Fla. (32084) 212/E2
Saint Austell (bay), England 13/C7
Saint Austell-with-Fowey, England 13/C7
Saint Austell with Fowey, England 10/D5
Saint-Barnabé, Québec 172/D4
Saint-Barthélemy (isl.), Guadeloupe 156/F3
Saint-Barthélemy, Québec 172/D3
Saint Basile, New Bruns. 170/B1
Saint-Basile-le-Grand, Québec 172/J4
Saint-Basile-Sud, Québec 172/F3
Saint Bees (head), England 13/D3
Saint Benedict, Kansas (†66538) 232/F2
Saint Benedict, La. (70457) 238/K5
Saint Benedict, Oreg. (97373) 291/B3
Saint Benedict, Pa. (15773) 294/E4
Saint Benedict, Sask. 181/F3
Saint-Benjamin, Québec 172/G3
Saint-Benoît, Réunion 118/G5
Saint-Benoît-Labre, Québec 172/G3
Saint Bernard, Ala. (35138) 195/E2
Saint Bernard (par.), La. 238/L7
Saint Bernard, La. (70085) 238/L7
Saint Bernard, Nova Scotia 168/B4
Saint Bernard, Ohio (45217) 284/B9
Saint-Bernard, Québec 172/F3
Saint Bernard, Great (pass), Switzerland 39/D5
Saint-Bernard-sur-Mer, Québec 172/G2
Saint Bernice, Ind. (47875) 227/C5
Saint Bethlehem, Tenn. (37155) 237/G7
Saint Blaise, Québec 172/E4
Saint-Blaise, Switzerland 39/D2
Saint-Bonaventure-de-Yamaska, Québec 172/E4
Saint-Boniface-de-Shawinigan, Québec 172/D3
Saint Bonifacius, Minn. (55375) 255/F5
Saint Brendan's, Newf. 166/D4
Saint Brides, Alberta 182/E2
Saint Bride's, Newf. 166/C2
Saint Brides (bay), Wales 10/D5
Saint Brides (bay), Wales 13/B6
Saint-Brieuc, France 28/B3
Saint Brieux, Sask. 181/G3
Saint-Bruno, Québec 172/F1
Saint-Bruno-de-Montarville, Québec 172/J4
Saint-Calais, France 28/D4
Saint-Calixte-de-Kilkenny, Québec 172/D4
Saint-Camille, Québec 172/F4
Saint-Camille-de-Bellechasse, Québec 172/G3
Saint-Casimir, Québec 172/E3
Saint Catharine, Mo. (64677) 261/G3
Saint Catharines, Ontario 177/E4
Saint Catherine, Fla. (†33513) 212/D3
Saint Catherine (mt.), Grenada 161/D8
Saint Catherine (lake), Vt. 268/A5
Saint Catherines (isl.), Georgia 217/K7
Saint Catherines (sound), Georgia 217/K7
Saint-Céré, France 28/D5
Saint-Cergue, Switzerland 39/B4
Saint-Césaire, Québec 172/D4
Saint-Chamond, France 28/F5
Saint Charles, Ark. (72140) 202/H5
Saint Charles, Idaho (83272) 220/G7
Saint Charles, Ill. (60174) 222/E2
Saint Charles, Iowa (50240) 229/F6
Saint Charles, Ky. (42453) 237/F6
Saint Charles (par.), La. 238/K7
Saint Charles, Mich. (48655) 250/E5
Saint Charles, Minn. (55972) 255/F7
Saint Charles (co.), Mo. 261/M2
Saint Charles, Mo. (63301) 261/N1
Saint-Charles, New Bruns. 170/F2
Saint Charles, Ontario 177/D1
Saint-Charles, Bellechasse, Québec 172/G3
Saint Charles, S.C. (29134) 296/G3
Saint Charles, S. Dak. (57571) 298/L7
Saint Charles, Va. (24282) 307/B7
Saint-Charles-de-Mandeville, Québec 172/D3
Saint-Charles-Garnier, Québec 172/J1
Saint-Charles-sur-Richelieu, Québec 172/D4
SAINT CHRISTOPHER-NEVIS 156/F3
SAINT CHRISTOPHER (SAINT KITTS)-NEVIS 161/D11
Saint Christopher (isl.), St. Chris.-Nevis 156/F3
Saint Christopher (isl.), St. Chris.-Nevis 161/D10
Saint Chrysostom, Pr. Edward I. 168/E2
Saint-Chrysostome, Québec 172/D4
Saint Clair (co.), Ala. 195/F3
Saint Clair, Ala. (36774) 195/E6
Saint Clair, Georgia (†30816) 217/H4
Saint Clair (co.), Ill. 222/D5
Saint Clair (lake), Mich. 188/K2
Saint Clair (co.), Mich. 250/G6
Saint Clair, Mich. (48079) 250/G6
Saint Clair (lake), Mich. 250/G6
Saint Clair (riv.), Mich. 250/G6
Saint Clair, Minn. (56080) 255/E6
Saint Clair (co.), Mo. 261/E6
Saint Clair, Mo. (63077) 261/K6
Saint Clair (lake), Ontario 177/B5
Saint Clair (riv.), Ontario 177/B5
Saint Clair, Pa. (17970) 294/K4
Saint Clair (lake), Tasmania 99/C4
Saint Clair Beach, Ontario 177/B5
Saint Clair Shores, Mich. (*48080) 250/B6
Saint Clair Springs, Ala. (†35146) 195/F3
Saint Clairsville, Ohio (43950) 284/J5
Saint Clairsville, Pa. (16676) 294/F5
Saint-Claude, France 28/F4
Saint-Claude, Guadeloupe 161/A7
Saint Claude, Manitoba 179/D5
Saint-Claude, Québec 172/F4
Saint Clears, Wales 13/C6
Saint-Clément, Québec 172/H2
Saint Clements, Ontario 177/D4
Saint-Cléophas, Québec 172/D3
Saint-Clet, Québec 172/C4
Saint Cloud, Fla. (32769) 212/E3
Saint Cloud, France 28/A2
Saint Cloud, Minn. 188/H1
Saint Cloud, Minn. (56301) 255/D5
Saint Cloud, Wis. (53079) 317/K8
Saint Columb Major, England 13/B7
Saint Combs, Scotland 15/G3
Saint-Côme, Québec 172/D3
Saint-Constant, Québec 172/H4
Saint Croix (riv.) 188/H1
Saint Croix, Ind. (47576) 227/D8
Saint Croix (riv.), Maine 243/J5
Saint Croix (riv.), Minn. 255/F5
Saint Croix, New Bruns. 170/C3
Saint Croix (riv.), New Bruns. 170/C3
Saint Croix, Nova Scotia 168/E4
Saint Croix (isl.), Virgin Is. (U.S.) 156/H2
Saint Croix (isl.), Virgin Is. (U.S.) 161/G4
Saint Croix (co.), Wis. 317/B5
Saint Croix (lake), Wis. 317/A6
Saint Croix (riv.), Wis. 317/A4
Saint Croix Falls, Wis. (54024) 317/A5
Saint Croix Flowage (res.), Wis. 317/C3
Saint Croix Isl. Nat'l Mon., Maine 243/J5
Saint-Cuthbert, Québec 172/D3
Saint-Cyprien, Québec 172/J2
Saint-Cyrille, Québec 172/E4
Saint-Cyrille-de-L'Islet, Québec 172/G3
Saint Cyrus, Scotland 15/F4
Saint-Damase, Québec 172/B1
Saint-Damase-des-Aulnaies, Québec 172/C2
Saint-Damien-de-Brandon, Québec 172/D3
Saint-Damien-de-Buckland, Québec 172/G3
Saint David, Ariz. (85630) 198/E7
Saint David, Ill. (61563) 222/C3
Saint David, Maine (04773) 243/G1
Saint-David, Québec 172/J3
Saint-David-de-Falardeau, Québec 172/F1
Saint-David-d'Yamaska, Québec 172/E4
Saint Davids (isl.), Bermuda 156/H2
Saint David's, Wales 13/B6
Saint David's (head), Wales 10/D5
Saint David's (head), Wales 13/B6
Saint-Denis, France 28/B1
Saint-Denis, Québec 172/D4
Saint-Denis (cap.), Réunion 118/F5
Saint Denis, Sask. 181/F3
Saint-Denis-de-la-Bouteillerie, Québec 172/G2
Saint-Didace, Québec 172/D3
Saint-Dié, France 28/G3
Saint-Dizier, France 28/F3
Saint-Dominique, Québec 172/E4
Saint-Donat-de-Montcalm, Québec 172/C3
Saint-Donat-de-Rimouski, Québec 172/J1
Saint Donatus, Iowa (52071) 229/M4
Sainte-Adèle, Québec 172/C4
Sainte Agathe, Manitoba 179/E5
Sainte-Agathe, Québec 172/F3
Sainte-Agathe-des-Monts, Québec 172/C3
Sainte-Agnes-de-Charlevoix, Québec 172/G2
Sainte Amélie, Manitoba 179/C4
Sainte-Anastasie, Québec 172/F3
Sainte-Angèle-de-Mérici, Québec 172/J1
Sainte Anne (lake), Alberta 182/C3
Sainte-Anne, Guadeloupe 161/B6
Sainte Anne, Manitoba 179/F5
Sainte-Anne, Martinique 161/D7
Sainte-Anne, New Bruns. 170/E1
Sainte-Anne (lake), Québec 172/H2
Sainte-Anne (riv.), Québec 172/C1
Sainte-Anne (riv.), Québec 172/G2
Sainte-Anne (riv.), Québec 172/F3
Sainte Anne (isl.), Seychelles 118/H5
Sainte-Anne-de-Beaupré, Québec 172/F2
Sainte-Anne-de-Bellevue, Québec 172/H4
Sainte-Anne-de-Kent, New Bruns. 170/F2
Sainte-Anne-de-Madawaska, New Bruns. 170/B1
Sainte-Anne-des-Monts, Québec 172/C1
Sainte-Anne-des-Plaines, Québec 172/H4
Sainte-Anne-du-Lac, Québec 172/B3
Sainte-Apolline, Québec 172/G3
Sainte-Aurélie, Québec 172/G3
Sainte-Béatrix, Québec 172/D3
Sainte-Bernadette, Québec 172/G1
Sainte-Blandine, Québec 172/J1
Sainte-Brigide, Québec 172/D4
Sainte-Catherine, Québec 172/F3
Sainte-Cécile-de-Frontenac, Québec 172/G4
Sainte-Cécile-de-Masham, Québec 172/A4
Sainte-Claire, Québec 172/G3
Sainte-Clothilde-de-Horton, Québec 172/E4
Sainte-Croix, Québec 172/F3
Sainte-Croix, Switzerland 39/B3
Sainte-Édouard-de-Kent, New Bruns. 170/F2
Sainte-Édouard-de-Maskinongé, Québec 172/D3
Sainte-Édouard-de-Napierville, Québec 172/D4
Saint Edward, Nebr. (68660) 264/G3
Saint Edward, Pr. Edward I. 168/D2
Sainte-Edwidge, Québec 172/F4
Sainte-Élisabeth, Québec 172/D3
Sainte-Émélie-de-l'Énergie, Québec 172/D3
Sainte-Eulalie, Québec 172/E3
Sainte-Euphémie, Québec 172/G3
Sainte-Famille-d'Aumond, Québec 172/B3
Sainte-Famille-d'Orléans, Québec 172/G3
Sainte-Félicité, Québec 172/B1
Sainte-Flavie, Québec 172/J1
Sainte-Florence, Québec 172/B2
Sainte-Foy, Québec 172/H3
Sainte-Françoise, Québec 172/H1
Sainte-Geneviève, Manitoba 179/F5
Sainte Genevieve (co.), Mo. 261/M7
Sainte Genevieve, Mo. (63670) 261/M6
Sainte-Geneviève, Québec 172/H4
Sainte-Geneviève-de-Batiscan, Québec 172/E3
Sainte-Hedwidge-de-Roberval, Québec 172/E1
Sainte-Hélène-de-Bagot, Québec 172/E4
Sainte-Hélène-de-Kamouraska, Québec 172/H2
Sainte-Hénédine, Québec 172/F3
Sainte-Julie-de-Verchères, Québec 172/J4
Sainte-Julienne, Québec 172/D4
Sainte-Julie-Station, Québec 172/F3
Sainte-Justine, Québec 172/G3
Sainte-Justine-de-Newton, Québec 172/C4
Saint Eleanors, Pr. Edward I. 168/E2
Sainte-Éleuthère, Québec 172/H2
Saint Elias (mt.), Alaska 188/D5
Saint Elias (cape), Alaska 196/K3
Saint Elias (mt.), Alaska 196/K2
Saint Elias (mts.), Alaska 196/L2
Saint Elias (mt.), Yukon 162/B3
Saint Elias (mt.), Yukon 187/D3
Saint Elias (mts.), Yukon 187/E3
Saint-Élie, Fr. Guiana 131/E3
Saint-Élie, Québec 172/E3
Saint Elizabeth, Mo. (65075) 261/H6
Saint Elmo, Ala. (36568) 195/B10
Saint Elmo, Colo. (†81236) 208/G5
Saint Elmo, Ill. (62458) 222/E4
Sainte-Éloi, Québec 172/H1
Sainte-Louise, Québec 172/G2
Sainte-Luce, Martinique 161/D7
Sainte-Luce, Québec 172/J1
Sainte-Lucie-de-Beauregard, Québec 172/H3
Sainte-Lucie-de-Doncaster, Québec 172/C3
Saint-Elzéar, Québec 172/F3
Saint-Elzéar-de-Bonaventure, Québec 172/C2
Sainte-Marguerite, Guadeloupe 161/B6
Sainte-Marguerite-de-Dorchester, Québec 172/G3
Sainte-Marguerite-Marie, Québec 172/B2
Sainte-Marguerite (riv.), Québec 172/G1
Sainte-Marguerite Nord-Est (riv.), Québec 172/H1
Sainte-Marguerite (riv.), Québec 174/D2

Seminoe 445

Scapa, Alberta 182/D4
Scapa Flow (chan.), Scotland 15/E2
Scapa Flow (chan.), Scotland 10/E1
Scappoose, Oreg. (97056) 291/E2
Scarba (isl.), Scotland 15/C4
Scarboro, Barbados 161/B9
Scarboro, Georgia (†30442) 217/J5
Scarborough, England 10/F3
Scarborough, England 13/G3
Scarborough, Maine (04074) 243/C8
Scarborough○, Maine (04074) 243/C8
Scarborough, Ontario 177/K4
Scarborough, Trin. & Tob. 156/G5
Scarbro, W. Va. (25917) 312/D7
Scarinish, Scotland 15/B4
Scarp (isl.), Scotland 15/A2
Scarriff, Ireland 17/E6
Scarriff (isl.), Ireland 17/A8
Scarsdale, N.Y. (10583) 276/P6
Scarth, Manitoba 179/B5
Scarville, Iowa (50473) 229/F2
Scatarie (isl.), Nova Scotia 168/J2
Scavaig, Loch (inlet), Scotland 15/B3
Sceaux, France 28/A2
Scenic, S. Dak. (57780) 298/D6
Scenic, Wash. (†98288) 310/D3
Sceptre, Sask. 181/B5
Schaal, Ark. (†71851) 202/C6
Schaalsee (lake), E. Germany 22/D2
Schaalsee (lake), W. Germany 22/D2
Schaan, Liecht. 39/H2
Schaefferstown, Pa. (17088) 294/K5
Schaerbeek, Belgium 27/C9
Schaffer, Mich. (49882) 250/B3
Schaffhausen (canton), Switzerland 39/G1
Schaffhausen, Switzerland 39/G1
Schagen, Netherlands 27/F3
Schaghticoke, N.Y. (12154) 276/N5
Schaller, Iowa (51053) 229/C4
S-chanf, Switzerland 39/J3
Schangnau, Switzerland 39/E3
Schänis, Switzerland 39/H2
Scharans, Switzerland 39/J3
Schärding, Austria 41/B2
Scharhörn (isl.), W. Germany 22/C2
Schattdorf, Switzerland 39/G3
Schaumburg, Ill. (60194) 222/A5
Schawana, Wash. (†99321) 310/F4
Schefferville, Que. 146/L4
Schefferville, Que. 162/K5
Schefferville, Québec 174/D2
Scheibbs, Austria 41/C2
Scheinfeld, W. Germany 22/D4
Schelde (Scheldt) (riv.), Belgium 27/C7
Scheldt (riv.), Belgium 27/C7
Schell City, Mo. (64783) 261/D6
Schell Creek (range), Nev. 266/G3
Schellsburg, Pa. (15559) 294/E5
Schellville, Calif. (†95476) 204/J1
Schenectady, N.Y. 188/M2
Schenectady (co.), N.Y. 276/M5
Schenectady, N.Y. (*12301) 276/M5
Schenevus, N.Y. (12155) 276/L5
Schererville, Ind. (46375) 227/C2
Scherhorn (mt.), Switzerland 39/G3
Schertz, Texas (78154) 303/K10
Scherzingen, Switzerland 39/H1
Schesaplana (mt.), Switzerland 39/J2
Scheveningen, Netherlands 27/E4
Schichallion (mt.), Scotland 15/D4
Schiedam, Netherlands 27/E5
Schiermonnikoog, Netherlands 27/J1
Schiermonnikoog (isl.), Netherlands 27/J1
Schiers, Switzerland 39/J3
Schijndel, Netherlands 27/G5
Schiller Park, Ill. (60176) 222/B5
Schinznach-Dorf, Switzerland 39/F2
Schio, Italy 34/C2
Schiphol, Netherlands 27/B5
Schkeuditz, E. Germany 22/E3
Schladming, Austria 41/B3
Schlater, Miss. (38952) 256/D3
Schlei (inlet), W. Germany 22/C1
Schleicher (co.), Texas 303/D7
Schleitheim, Switzerland 39/G1
Schleswig, Iowa (51461) 229/B4
Schleswig, W. Germany 22/C1
Schleswig-Holstein (state), W. Germany 22/C1
Schleusingen, E. Germany 22/D3
Schley (co.), Georgia 217/D6
Schley, Minn. (†56633) 255/D3
Schlieren, Switzerland 39/F2
Schliersee, W. Germany 22/D5
Schlitz, W. Germany 22/C3
Schlüchtern, W. Germany 22/C3
Schmalkalden, E. Germany 22/D3
Schmölln, E. Germany 22/E3
Schnecksville, Pa. (18078) 294/L4
Schneeberg, E. Germany 22/E3
Schneeberg (mt.), W. Germany 22/D3
Schnee Eifel (plat.), Belgium 27/J8
Schneidemühl (Piła), Poland 47/C2
Schneider, Ind. (46376) 227/C2
Schnellville, Ind. (47580) 227/D8
Schoelcher, Martinique 161/C6
Schoenchen, Kansas (67667) 232/C3
Schoenfeld, Sask. 181/D5
Schoen Lake Prov. Park, Br. Col. 184/E5
Schofield, Wis. (54476) 317/H6
Schofield Barracks, Hawaii (96786) 218/E2
Schoharie (co.), N.Y. 276/M5
Schoharie, N.Y. (12157) 276/M5
Schoharie (creek), N.Y. 276/M6
Schoharie (res.), N.Y. 276/M6
Scholle, N. Mex. (†87036) 274/C4
Scholls, Oreg. (†97123) 291/A2
Schomberg, Ontario 177/J3
Schönberg, E. Germany 22/D2
Schönberg, W. Germany 22/D1
Schönebeck, E. Germany 22/D2
Schöneberg, W. Germany 22/E4
Schöneiche, E. Germany 22/E2
Schönenwerd, Switzerland 39/E2
Schongau, W. Germany 22/D5
Schöningen, W. Germany 22/D2
Schoodic (lake), Maine 243/F5
Schoolcraft (co.), Mich. 250/C2
Schoolcraft, Mich. (49087) 250/D6
Schoolcraft (riv.), Minn. 255/C3
Schooleys Mountain, N.J. (07870) 273/D2
School Hill, Wis. (†53042) 317/L8
Schoonhoven, Netherlands 27/F5
Schoten, Belgium 27/F6
Schottegat (bay), Neth. Ant. 161/G9
Schouten (isls.), Indonesia 85/K6
Schouten (isls.), Papua N.G. 85/B6
Schouten (isl.), Tasmania 99/E4
Schouwen (isl.), Netherlands 27/D5
Schramberg, W. Germany 22/C4
Schram City, Ill. (†62049) 222/D4
Schreckhorn (mt.), Switzerland 39/F3
Schreiber, Ontario 177/H5
Schreiber, Ontario 175/C3
Schrems, Austria 41/C2
Schriever, La. (70395) 238/J7
Schroeder, Minn. (55613) 255/G3
Schroon (lake), N.Y. 276/N3
Schroon (riv.), N.Y. 276/N3
Schroon Lake, N.Y. (12870) 276/N3
Schruns, Austria 41/A3
Schübelbach, Switzerland 39/G2
Schulenburg, Texas (78956) 303/H8
Schuler, Alberta 182/E4
Schull, Ireland 10/B5
Schull, Ireland 17/B8
Schulter, Okla. (74460) 288/P3
Schultz (lake), N.W. Terrs. 187/J3
Schumacher, Ontario 175/D3
Schüpfheim, Switzerland 39/F3
Schurz, Nev. (89427) 266/C4
Schussenried, W. Germany 22/C4
Schuyler (co.), Ill. 222/C3
Schuyler (co.), Mo. 261/G2
Schuyler, Nebr. (68661) 264/G3
Schuyler (co.), N.Y. 276/G6
Schuyler, Va. (22969) 307/L5
Schuyler Lake, N.Y. (13457) 276/L5
Schuylerville, N.Y. (12871) 276/N4
Schuylkill (co.), Pa. 294/K4
Schuylkill (riv.), Pa. 294/M5
Schuylkill Haven, Pa. (17972) 294/K4
Schwaan, E. Germany 22/E2
Schwabach, W. Germany 22/D4
Schwäbisch Gmünd, W. Germany 22/C4
Schwäbisch Hall, W. Germany 22/C4
Schwalmstadt, W. Germany 22/C3
Schwanden, Switzerland 39/H2
Schwandorf im Bayern, W. Germany 22/E4
Schwaner (mts.), Indonesia 85/E6
Schwarzach im Pongau, Austria 41/B3
Schwarzenburg, Switzerland 39/D3
Schwarzhorn (mt.), Switzerland 39/E4
Schwarzhorn (mt.), Switzerland 39/F3
Schwarzwald (Black) (for.), W. Germany 22/C4
Schwatka (mts.), Alaska 196/G1
Schwaz, Austria 41/A3
Schwechat, Austria 41/D2
Schwedt, E. Germany 22/F2
Schweidnitz (Świdnica), Poland 47/C3
Schweinfurt, W. Germany 22/D3
Schwelm, W. Germany 22/B3
Schwenksville, Pa. (19473) 294/L5
Schwerin (dist.), E. Germany 22/D2
Schwerin, E. Germany 22/D2
Schwerinersee (lake), E. Germany 22/D2
Schwertberg, Austria 41/C2
Schwetzingen, W. Germany 22/C4
Schwyz (canton), Switzerland 39/G2
Schwyz, Switzerland 39/G2
Sciacca, Italy 34/D6
Scicli, Italy 34/E6
Science Hill, Ky. (42553) 237/M6
Scilly (isls.), England 13/A7
Scilly (isls.), England 10/C6
Scio, N.Y. (14880) 276/E6
Scio, Ohio (43988) 284/H5
Scio, Oreg. (97374) 291/E3
Sciota, Ill. (61475) 222/C3
Sciota, Pa. (18354) 294/M4
Scioto (co.), Ohio 284/D8
Scioto (riv.), Ohio 284/D8
Sciotodale, Ohio (†45662) 284/E8
Scioto Furnace, Ohio (45677) 284/E8
Scipio, Ind. (47273) 227/F6
Scipio, Ind. (†45053) 227/H6
Scipio, Okla. (†74501) 288/P4
Scipio, Utah (84656) 304/B4
Scircleville, Ind. (46066) 227/E4
Scitico, Conn. (†06036) 210/E1
Scituate, Mass. (02066) 249/F8
Scituate○, Mass. (02066) 249/F8
Scituate (res.), R.I. 249/H5
Sclater, Manitoba 179/B3
Scobey, Miss. (38953) 256/E3
Scobey, Mont. (59263) 262/L2
Scofield, Utah (†84526) 304/C4
Scofield (res.), Utah 304/C4
Scollard, Alberta 182/D4
Scone, N.S. Wales 97/F3
Scooba, Miss. (39358) 256/G5
Scopi (mt.), Switzerland 39/G3
Scopus, Mo. (63762) 261/N8
Scoresby (sound), Greenl. 4/B10
Scoresbysund, Greenl. 4/B10
Scotch Grove, Iowa (52331) 229/L4
Scotch Plains○, N.J. (07076) 273/E2
Scotchtown, Nova Scotia 168/H2
Scotch Village, Nova Scotia 168/E3
Scotfield, Alberta 182/E4
Scotia (sea) 2/G8
Scotia (sea) 5/D16
Scotia, Calif. (95565) 204/A3
Scotia, Nebr. (68875) 264/F3
Scotia, N.Y. (12302) 276/N5
Scotia, S.C. (29939) 296/E6
SCOTLAND 15
SCOTLAND 10/D2
Scotland, Ark. (72141) 202/E2
Scotland○, Conn. (06264) 210/G2
Scotland, Georgia (31083) 217/G6
Scotland, Ind. (47457) 227/D7
Scotland, Md. (20687) 245/N8
Scotland (co.), Mo. 261/H2
Scotland (co.), N.C. 281/L5
Scotland, Ontario 177/D4
Scotland, Pa. (17254) 294/G6
Scotland, S. Dak. (57059) 298/O7
Scotland, Texas (76379) 303/F4
Scotland, U.K. 7/D3
Scotland Neck, N.C. (27874) 281/P2
Scotlandville, La. (70807) 238/J1
Scots (bay), Nova Scotia 168/D3
Scots Bay, Nova Scotia 168/D3
Scotsburn, Nova Scotia 168/F3
Scotsguard, Sask. 181/C6
Scotstown, Ireland 17/H3
Scotstown, Québec 172/F4
Scotsville, Nova Scotia 168/G2
Scott (isl.), Ant. 2/A9
Scott (isl.), Ant. 5/C10
Scott (co.), Ark. 202/B4
Scott, Ark. (72142) 202/F4
Scott (cape), Br. Col. 162/D5
Scott (cape), Br. Col. 184/C5
Scott (isls.), Br. Col. 184/C5
Scott (riv.), Calif. 204/B2
Scott, Georgia (31095) 217/G5
Scott (co.), Ill. 222/C4
Scott (co.), Ind. 227/F7
Scott, Ind. (†46746) 227/F1
Scott (co.), Iowa 229/M5
Scott (co.), Kansas 232/B3
Scott (co.), Ky. 237/M4
Scott, La. (70583) 238/F6
Scott (co.), Minn. 255/E6
Scott (co.), Miss. 256/E6
Scott, Miss. (38772) 256/B3
Scott (co.), Mo. 261/N8
Scott, Ohio (45886) 284/A4
Scott (mt.), Okla. 288/K5
Scott, Sask. 181/C3
Scott (lake), Sask. 181/M2
Scott (co.), Tenn. 237/M8
Scott (co.), Va. 307/C7
Scott A.F.B., Ill. 222/B3
Scott City, Kansas (67871) 232/B3
Scott City, Mo. (63780) 261/O8
Scottdale, Georgia (30079) 217/L1
Scottdale, Pa. (15683) 294/C5
Scott-Jonction, Québec 172/F3
Scottland, Ill. (†61924) 222/F4
Scotts (head), Dominica 161/E7
Scotts, N.C. (28699) 281/H3
Scottsbluff, Nebr. 188/F2
Scottsbluff, Nebr. 146/H5
Scotts Bluff (co.), Nebr. 264/A3
Scottsbluff, Nebr. (69361) 264/A3
Scotts Bluff Nat'l Mon., Nebr. 264/A3
Scottsboro, Ala. (35768) 195/F1
Scottsburg, Ind. (47170) 227/F7
Scottsburg, Ky. (†42445) 237/F6
Scottsburg, Oreg. (97473) 291/D4
Scottsburg, Va. (24589) 307/L7
Scottsdale, Ariz. (*85251) 198/D5
Scottsdale, Tasmania 99/D3
Scotts Hill, N.C. (†28401) 281/O6
Scotts Hill, Tenn. (38374) 237/E10
Scotts Mills, Oreg. (97375) 291/B3
Scottsmoor, Fla. (32775) 212/F3
Scotts Ridge (hills), Conn. 210/A3
Scott Station, Ant. 5/B9
Scotts Valley, Calif. (95060) 204/K4
Scottsville, Ark. (†72843) 202/D3
Scottsville, Kansas (67477) 232/D2
Scottsville, Ky. (42164) 237/J7
Scottsville, N.Y. (14546) 276/E4
Scottsville, Va. (24590) 307/L5
Scottville, Ill. (62683) 222/C4
Scottville, Mich. (49454) 250/C5
Scoudouc, New Bruns. 170/F2
Scourie, Scotland 15/C2
Scout Lake, Sask. 181/F6
Scrabster, Scotland 15/E2
Scraggly (lake), Maine 243/H5
Scraggly (lake), Maine 243/F3
Scranage, Ala. (†36552) 195/C8
Scranton, Ark. (72863) 202/C3
Scranton, Iowa (51462) 229/D4
Scranton, Kansas (66537) 232/G3
Scranton, Ky. (40373) 237/O5
Scranton, N.Y. (†14075) 276/C5
Scranton, N.C. (27875) 281/S4
Scranton, N. Dak. (58653) 282/D7
Scranton, Pa. 188/L2
Scranton, Pa. 146/L5
Scranton, Pa. (*18501) 294/F7
Scranton, S.C. (29591) 296/H4
Scraper, Okla. (†74359) 288/S2
Screven (co.), Georgia 217/J5
Screven, Georgia (31560) 217/H7
Scriba, N.Y. (†13827) 276/H4
Scribner, Nebr. (68057) 264/H3
Scridain, Loch (inlet), Scotland 15/B4
Scugog (lake), Ontario 177/F3
Scullin, Okla. (†73086) 288/N5
Scunthorpe, England 10/F4
Scunthorpe, England 13/G4
Scuol, Switzerland 39/K3
Scurdie Ness (prom.), Scotland 15/F4
Scurrival (pt.), Scotland 15/A3
Scurry (co.), Texas 303/D5
Scurry, Texas (75158) 303/H5
Scusciuban, Somalia 115/J1
Scutari (lake), Albania 45/D4
Scutari (lake), Yugoslavia 45/D4
Scyrene, Ala. (†36436) 195/C7
Sea (isls.), Georgia 217/K9
Sea (isls.), S.C. 296/G7
Seabeck, Wash. (98380) 310/C3
Seaboard, N.C. (27876) 281/O1
Seabold, Wash. (†98110) 310/A1
Sea Breeze, N.Y. (†14617) 276/F4
Sea Bright, N.J. (07760) 273/F3
Seabrook○, N.H. (03874) 268/F6
Seabrook, N.J. (08302) 273/C5
Seabrook, S.C. (29940) 296/F6
Seabrook (isl.), S.C. 296/G6
Seabrook, Texas (77586) 303/K2
Seabrook-Lanham, Md. (20801) 245/G4
Sea Cliff, N.Y. (11579) 276/R6
Seadrift, Texas (77983) 303/H9
Seaford, Del. (19973) 245/R6
Seaford, England 10/G5
Seaford, England 13/H7
Seaford, N.Y. (11783) 276/R7
Seaford, Va. (23696) 307/R6
Seaforth, Minn. (56287) 255/C6
Seaforth, Ontario 177/C4
Seaforth, Loch (inlet), Scotland 15/B3
Sea Girt, N.J. (08750) 273/E3
Seagoville, Texas (75159) 303/H3
Seagraves, Texas (79359) 303/B5
Seagrove, N.C. (27341) 281/K3
Seaham, England 10/F3
Seaham, England 13/J3
Seahorse (lake), Newf. 166/A3
Seahorse (pt.), N.W. Terrs. 187/L3
Seahurst, Wash. (98062) 310/A2
Sea Island, Georgia (31561) 217/K8
Sea Isle City, N.J. (08243) 273/D5
Seal (isl.), Maine 243/F8
Seal (riv.), Man. 162/G4
Seal (riv.), Manitoba 179/J2
Seal (lake), Newf. 166/B3
Seal (isl.), Nova Scotia 168/B5
Seal (isl.), S. Africa 118/F7
Sea Lake, Victoria 97/B4
Seal Beach, Calif. (90740) 204/C11
Seal Cove, Maine (04674) 243/G7
Seal Cove, New Bruns. 170/D4
Seal Cove, Newf. 166/C4
Seal Cove, Newf. 166/C3
Seale, Ala. (36875) 195/H6
Sealevel, N.C. (28577) 281/S5
Seal Harbor, Maine (04675) 243/G7
Seal Rock, Oreg. (97376) 291/C3
Sealston, Va. (22547) 307/O4
Sealy, Texas (77474) 303/H8
Seaman, Ohio (45679) 284/C8
Seamer, England 13/G3
Sea Pines, S.C. (†29928) 296/F7
Sea Ranch Lakes, Fla. (†33301) 212/C3
Searchlight, Nev. (89046) 266/F7
Searchmont, Ontario 177/J5
Searcy (co.), Ark. 202/E2
Searcy, Ark. (72143) 202/G3
Searight, Ala. (†36028) 195/F8
Searles, Ala. (†35468) 195/D4
Searles (lake), Calif. 204/H8
Searles, Minn. (56084) 255/D6
Sears, Mich. (49679) 250/D5
Searsboro, Iowa (50242) 229/H5
Searsburg○, Vt. (†05363) 268/A6
Searsmont, Maine (04973) 243/E7
Searsmont○, Maine (04973) 243/E7
Searsport, Maine (04974) 243/F7
Searsport○, Maine (04974) 243/F7
Seascale, England 10/E2
Seascale, England 13/D3
Seaside, Calif. (93955) 204/D7
Seaside, Oreg. (97138) 291/D2
Seaside Heights, N.J. (08751) 273/E4
Seaside Park, N.J. (08752) 273/E4
Seaton, England 13/D7
Seaton, Ill. (61476) 222/C2
Seaton Valley, England 13/J3
Seatonville, Ill. (61359) 222/D2
Seat Pleasant, Md. (20027) 245/G5
Seattle, U.S. 2/C3
Seattle, Wash. 146/F5
Seattle, Wash. 188/B1
Seattle, Wash. (*98101) 310/A2
Seaview, Wash. (98644) 310/A4
Seaward Kaikouras (range), N. Zealand 100/D5
Seawell, Barbados 161/B9
Seba, Indonesia 85/G8
Seba Beach, Alberta 182/C3
Sebago (lake), Maine 243/B8
Sebago Lake, Maine (04075) 243/B8
Sebastian (co.), Ark. 202/B3
Sebastian, Fla. (32958) 212/F4
Sebastian (cape), Oreg. 291/C5
Sebastián Vizcaíno (bay), Mexico 150/B2
Sebasticook (lake), Maine 243/E6
Sebastopol, Calif. (95472) 204/C5
Sebastopol, Miss. (39359) 256/F5
Sebastopol, Victoria 97/B5
Sebatik (isl.), Indonesia 85/F5
Sebatik (isl.), Malaysia 85/F5
Sebec, Maine (04481) 243/E5
Sebec○, Maine (04481) 243/E5
Sebec Lake, Maine (04482) 243/E5
Sebec Station, Maine (†04426) 243/E5
Sebeka, Minn. (56477) 255/C4
Seben, Turkey 63/D2
Sebeş, Romania 45/F3
Sebes Körös (riv.), Hungary 41/F3
Sebewaing, Mich. (48759) 250/F5
Sebha, Libya 102/D2
Sebha, Libya 111/B2
Şebinkarahisar, Turkey 63/H2
Sebiş, Romania (2) 45/F2
Sebnitz, E. Germany 22/F3
Seboeis○, Maine (04484) 243/F5
Seboeis (lake), Maine 243/F5
Seboeis (riv.), Maine 243/F3
Seboomook, Maine (†04478) 243/D4
Seboomook (lake), Maine 243/D4
Seboruco, Venezuela 124/B3
Sebou (riv.), Morocco 106/C2
Seboyeta, N. Mex. (87055) 274/B3
Sebree, Ky. (42455) 237/F6
Sebrell, Va. (†23837) 307/O7
Sebring, Fla. (33870) 212/E4
Sebring, Ohio (44672) 284/H4
Sebringville, Ontario 177/C4
Sebuku (bay), Indonesia 85/F5
Secane, Pa. (†19018) 294/M7
Secas (isls.), Panama 154/G7
Secaucus, N.J. (07094) 273/B2
Secesh (riv.), Idaho 220/C4
Sechelt, Br. Col. 184/J2
Sechura, Peru 128/B5
Sechura (bay), Peru 128/B5
Seco, Ky. (41849) 237/R6
Second (lake), N.H. 268/E1
Second Cataract, Sudan 59/B5
Second Cataract, Sudan 111/F3
Secondcreek, W. Va. (24974) 312/F7
Second Mesa, Ariz. (86043) 198/E3
Secor, Ill. (61771) 222/D3
Sečovce, Czech. 41/F2
Secretan, Sask. 181/E5
Secretary, Md. (21664) 245/P6
Secretary (isl.), N. Zealand 100/A6
Section, Ala. (35771) 195/G1
Secunderabad, India 68/D5
Sécure (riv.), Bolivia 136/C4
Security-Widefield, Colo. (80911) 208/K5
Sedalia, Alberta 182/E4
Sedalia, Colo. (80135) 208/K4
Sedalia, Ind. (46067) 227/E4
Sedalia, Ky. (42079) 237/D7
Sedalia, Mo. (65301) 261/F5
Sedalia, Mo. 188/H3
Sedalia, Ohio (43151) 284/D6
Sedalia, S.C. (†29379) 296/D2
Sedan, France 28/F3
Sedan, Ind. (†46793) 227/G2
Sedan, Kansas (67361) 232/F4
Sedan, Minn. (56380) 255/C5
Sedan, N. Mex. (88436) 274/F2
Sedano, Spain 33/E1
Sedbergh (co.), England 10/E3
Sedbergh, England 13/E3
Seddon, N. Zealand 100/E4
Seddonville, N. Zealand 100/C4
Seddülbahir, Turkey 63/B6
Sede Boqer, Israel 65/D5
Sederot, Israel 65/B4
Sedgewick, Alberta 182/E3
Sedgewickville, Mo. (63781) 261/N7
Sedgwick, Ark. (72465) 202/J2
Sedgwick (co.), Colo. 208/P1
Sedgwick, Colo. (80749) 208/O1
Sedgwick (co.), Kansas 232/E4
Sedgwick, Kansas (67135) 232/E4
Sedgwick○, Maine (04676) 243/F7
Sedhiou, Senegal 106/A6
Sedili Kechil, Tanjong (pt.), Malaysia 72/F5
Sedlčany, Czech. 41/C2
Sedley, Sask. 181/H5
Sedley, Va. (23878) 307/P7
Sedom, Israel 65/D5
Sedona, Ariz. (86336) 198/D4
Sedot Yam, Israel 65/B3
Sedro-Woolley, Wash. (98284) 310/C2
Šeduva, U.S.S.R. 53/B3
Seebe, Alberta 182/C4
Seebert, W. Va. (24975) 312/F6
Seechelt (inlet), Br. Col. 184/J2
Seechelt (pen.), Br. Col. 184/J2
Seeheim, Namibia 118/B5
Seeis, Namibia 118/B4
Seekonk○, Mass. (02771) 249/J5
Seeley, Calif. (92273) 204/K11
Seeley, Wis. (†54843) 317/D3
Seeley Lake, Mont. (59868) 262/C3
Seeleys Bay, Ontario 177/H3
Seelyville, Ind. (47878) 227/C6
Seelyville, Pa. (18431) 294/M2
Seesen, W. Germany 22/D3
Seewis im Prättigau, Switzerland 39/J2
Seez (riv.), Switzerland 39/H2
Şefaatli, Turkey 63/F3
Seferihisar, Turkey 63/B3
Seffner, Fla. (33584) 212/D4
Sefrou, Morocco 106/D2
Sefton, N. Zealand 100/D5
Seg (lake), U.S.S.R. 52/D2
Segamat, Malaysia 72/D7
Segarcea, Romania 45/F3
Segezha, U.S.S.R. 52/D2
Segezha, U.S.S.R. 48/D3
Segnes (pass), Switzerland 39/H3
Segni, Italy 34/F7
Segorbe, Spain 33/F3
Ségou, Mali 106/C6
Ségou, Mali 102/B3
Segovia, Colombia 126/C4
Segovia (Coco) (riv.), Honduras 154/E3
Segovia (Coco) (riv.), Nicaragua 154/E3
Segovia (prov.), Spain 33/D2
Segovia, Spain 33/D2
Segré, France 28/C4
Segre (riv.), Spain 33/G2
Segreganset, Mass. (02773) 249/K5
Seguam (isl.), Alaska 196/D4
Seguam (passage), Alaska 196/D4
Séguéla, Ivory Coast 106/C7
Seguí, Argentina 143/F6
Seguin, Kansas (†67740) 232/B2
Séguin (lake), Québec 172/B2
Seguin, Texas (78155) 303/G8
Segula (isl.), Alaska 196/K4
Segundo, Colo. (81070) 208/K8
Segura (riv.), Spain 33/F3
Sehore, India 68/D4
Sehwan, Pakistan 59/J4
Sehwan, Pakistan 68/B3
Seiad Valley, Calif. (96086) 204/B2
Seibert (lake), Alberta 182/E2
Seibert, Colo. (80834) 208/O4
Seibo, Dom. Rep. 156/E3
Seil (isl.), Scotland 15/C4
Seiland (isl.), Norway 18/N1
Seiling, Okla. (73663) 288/J2
Sein (isl.), France 28/A3
Seinäjoki, Finland 18/N5
Seine (riv.), France 7/E4
Seine (bay), France 28/C3
Seine (riv.), France 28/D3
Seine (riv.), Ontario 175/B3
Seine-et-Marne (dept.), France 28/E3
Seine-Saint-Denis (dept.), France 28/C1
Seistan (reg.), Iran 66/M5
Seixal, Portugal 33/A1
Seiyun, P.D.R. Yemen 59/E6
Sejerø (isl.), Denmark 21/E6
Sejny, Poland 47/F1
Seke-Banza, Zaire 115/B5
Sekenke, Tanzania 115/F4
Se Khong (riv.), Cambodia 72/E4
Se Khong (riv.), Laos 72/E4
Sekiu, Wash. (98381) 310/A2
Sekkane, Erg (des.), Mali 106/D4
Sekondi, Ghana 106/D8
Selah, Wash. (98942) 310/E4
Selama, Malaysia 72/D6
Selangor (state), Malaysia 72/D7
Selaphum, Thailand 72/E3
Selaru (isl.), Indonesia 85/J7
Selatan (cape), Indonesia 85/E6
Selawik, Alaska (99770) 196/G1
Selawik (lake), Alaska 196/F1
Selayar (isl.), Indonesia 85/G7
Selb, W. Germany 22/E3
Selby, England 13/F4
Selby, S. Dak. (57472) 298/J3
Selby, Victoria 97/K5
Selby-on-the-Bay, Md. (†21037) 245/N5
Selbyville, Del. (19975) 245/S7
Selbyville, W. Va. (26236) 312/F5
Selçuk, Turkey 63/B3
Selden, Kansas (67757) 232/B2
Seldom, Newf. 166/D4
Seldovia, Alaska (99663) 196/B2
Sele (riv.), Italy 34/E4
Selebi-Pikwe, Botswana 118/D4
Selemdzha (riv.), U.S.S.R. 48/O4
Selemiya, Syria 63/G5
Selendi, Turkey 63/C3
Selenga (riv.) 54/M5
Selenge, Mongolia 77/G2
Selenge, Mongolia 77/F2
Selenge (Selenga) Mörön (riv.), Mongolia 77/G2
Sélestat, France 28/G3
Selfridge, N. Dak. (58568) 282/J7
Sélibaby, Mauritania 106/B5
Seligman, Ariz. (86337) 198/B3
Seligman, Mo. (65745) 261/D9
Selim, Turkey 63/K2
Selima (oasis), Sudan 111/E3
Selima (oasis), Sudan 59/A5
Selimiye, Turkey 63/B4
Selinsgrove, Pa. (17870) 294/J4
Selje, Norway 18/D5
Selkirk (mts.), Br. Col. 184/J4
Selkirk (mts.), Idaho 220/B1
Selkirk, Kansas (67873) 232/A3
Selkirk, Man. 162/G5
Selkirk, Manitoba 179/F4
Selkirk (isl.), Manitoba 179/C1
Selkirk, Mich. (†48661) 250/E4
Selkirk, Scotland 10/E3
Selkirk, Scotland 15/F5
Selkirk (trad. co.) Scotland 15/B5
Sella, Bolivia 136/C7
Selle (peak), Haiti 158/C6
Selleck, Wash. (†98051) 310/D3
Sellers, Ala. (†36046) 195/F6
Sellers, S.C. (29592) 296/H3
Sellersburg, Ind. (47172) 227/F8
Sellersville, Pa. (18960) 294/M5
Sells, Ariz. (85634) 198/D7
Sells, Georgia (†30548) 217/E2
Sellye, Hungary 41/D4
Selma, Ala. 188/J4
Selma, Ala. (36701) 195/E6
Selma, Ark. (†71670) 202/G6
Selma, Calif. (93662) 204/F7
Selma, Ind. (47383) 227/G4
Selma, Iowa (52588) 229/J7
Selma, Miss. (†39120) 256/B7
Selma, N.C. (27576) 281/N3
Selma, Ohio (45364) 284/C6
Selma, Oreg. (97538) 291/D5
Selma, Texas (†78201) 303/K10
Selma, Va. (24474) 307/J5
Selmah, Nova Scotia 168/E3
Selman, Okla. (73856) 288/H1
Selmer, Tenn. (38375) 237/D10
Selmont, Ala. (†36701) 195/E6
Selous (mt.), Yukon 187/E3
Selsey, England 13/G7
Selsey Bill (prom.), England 13/G7
Selukwe, Zimbabwe 118/E3
Selva, Argentina 143/D2
Selvas (for.), Brazil 120/C3
Selvin, Ind. (†47523) 227/C8
Selway (riv.), Idaho 220/C3
Selwyn (lake), N.W. Terrs. 187/H4
Selwyn, Queensland 95/B4
Selwyn (range), Queensland 95/B4
Selwyn (lake), Sask. 181/M2
Selwyn, W. Va. (†25674) 312/B7
Selwyn (mts.), Yukon 187/E3
Selz, N. Dak. (58373) 282/L4
Seman, Ala. (†36092) 195/F5
Semans, Sask. 181/G4
Semara, W. Sahara 102/A2
Semara, Western Sahara 106/B3
Semarang, Indonesia 54/N10
Semarang, Indonesia 85/J2
Sematan, Malaysia 85/D5
Sembé, Congo 115/B3
Sembrancher, Switzerland 39/D4
Şemdinli, Turkey 63/L4
Semenov, U.S.S.R. 52/F3
Semeru (mt.), Indonesia 85/K2
Semichi (isls.), Alaska 196/J3
Semidi (isls.), Alaska 196/G3
Semiluki, U.S.S.R. 52/E4
Semily, Czech. 41/C1
Seminary, Miss. (39479) 256/E7
Seminoe (res.), Wyo. 188/E2

446 Seminoe

Seminoe (mts.), Wyo. 319/E3
Seminoe (res.), Wyo. 319/F3
Seminoe Dam, Wyo. (†82334) 319/E3
Seminole, Ala. (36574) 195/D10
Seminole (co.), Fla. 212/E3
Seminole, Fla. (33542) 212/B3
Seminole (lake), Fla. 212/B1
Seminole (co.), Georgia 217/C9
Seminole (lake), Georgia 217/B9
Seminole (co.), Okla. 288/N4
Seminole, Okla. (74868) 288/N4
Seminole, Pa. (16253) 294/D4
Seminole, Texas (79360) 303/B5
Seminole Ind. Res., Fla. 212/F5
Seminole Ind. Res., Fla. 212/E4
Semipalatinsk, U.S.S.R. 54/K4
Semipalatinsk, U.S.S.R. 48/H4
Semirara (isls.), Philippines 82/C5
Semisopochnoi (isl.), Alaska 196/K4
Semitau, Indonesia 85/E5
Semmering (pass), Austria 41/C3
Semmes, Ala. (36575) 195/B9
Semnan (governorate), Iran 66/J3
Semnan, Iran 59/F2
Semnan, Iran 66/H3
Semois (riv.), Belgium 27/G9
Semora, N.C. (27343) 281/L2
Sempach, Switzerland 39/F2
Sempach (lake), Switzerland 39/F2
Semporna, Malaysia 85/F5
Semsales, Switzerland 39/C3
Semur-en-Auxois, France 28/F4
Sen, Stoeng (riv.), Cambodia 72/E4
Sena, Bolivia 136/B2
Sena, N. Mex. (87568) 274/D3
Senador Pompeu, Brazil 132/G4
Senai, Malaysia 72/F5
Sena Madureira, Brazil 132/G10
Senanga, Zambia 115/D7
Senate, Sask. 181/B6
Senath, Mo. (63876) 261/M10
Senatobia, Miss. (38668) 256/E1
Sendai, Japan 54/R6
Sendai, Kagoshima, Japan 81/E8
Sendai, Miyagi, Japan 81/K4
Senec, Czech. 41/D2
Seneca, Ill. (61360) 222/E2
Seneca, Kansas (66538) 232/F2
Seneca, Miss. (†39455) 256/F8
Seneca, Mo. (64865) 261/C9
Seneca, Nebr. (69161) 264/D2
Seneca, N. Mex. (88437) 274/F2
Seneca (co.), N.Y. 276/G5
Seneca (lake), N.Y. 276/G5
Seneca (riv.), N.Y. 276/G5
Seneca (co.), Ohio 284/D3
Seneca, Oreg. (97873) 291/J3
Seneca, S.C. (29678) 296/A2
Seneca (riv.), S.C. 296/B2
Seneca, S. Dak. (57473) 298/L3
Seneca, Wis. (54654) 317/E9
Seneca Falls, N.Y. (13148) 276/G5
Seneca Gardens, Ky. (†40201) 237/K2
Senécal (lake), Newf. 166/B3
Senecaville, Ohio (43780) 284/H6
Senecaville (lake), Ohio 284/H6
Senegal 2/J5
Senegal 102/A3
Seegal (riv.) 102/A3
Senegal (riv.), Mali 106/B5
Senegal (riv.), Mauritania 106/B5
SENEGAL 106/A5
Senegal (riv.), Senegal 106/B5
Senekal, S. Africa 118/D5
Seney, Iowa (†51031) 229/A3
Seney, Mich. (49883) 250/C2
Senftenberg, E. Germany 22/F3
Sengiley, U.S.S.R. 52/G4
Senguerr (riv.), Argentina 143/B6
Senhor do Bonfim, Brazil 120/F4
Senhor do Bonfim, Brazil 132/F5
Senica, Czech. 41/D2
Senigallia, Italy 34/D3
Senirkent, Turkey 63/D3
Senj, Yugoslavia 45/B3
Senja (isl.), Norway 7/F2
Senja (isl.), Norway 18/K2
Şenkaya, Turkey 63/K2
Senlac, Sask. 181/B3
Senlis, France 28/E3
Senmonoron, Cambodia 72/E4
Sennar, Sudan 59/B7
Sennar, Sudan 111/F5
Sennar, Sudan 102/F3
Sennar (dam), Sudan 59/B7
Sennar (dam), Sudan 111/F5
Senne (riv.), Belgium 27/E7
Sennestadt, W. Germany 22/C3
Senneterre, Québec 174/B3
Senneville, Québec 172/G4
Senoia, Georgia (30276) 217/C4
Sens, France 28/E3
Sense (riv.), Switzerland 39/D3
Sensuntepeque, El Salvador 154/C4
Sent, Switzerland 39/K3
Senta, Yugoslavia 45/D3
Sentery, Zaire 115/E5
Sentinel, Alberta 182/C5
Sentinel, Ariz. (†85333) 198/B6
Sentinel (butte), N. Dak. 282/C6
Sentinel, Okla. (73664) 288/H4
Sentinel Butte, N. Dak. (58654) 282/C6
Senyavin (isls.), Micronesia 87/F5
Seo de Urgel, Spain 33/G1
Seon, Switzerland 39/F2
Seoni, India 68/D4
Seoul (cap.), S. Korea 2/R4
Seoul (cap.), S. Korea 54/O6
Seoul (cap.), S. Korea 81/C5
Separ, N. Mex. (†88045) 274/A6
Sepetiba (bay), Brazil 135/D3
Sepik (riv.), Papua N.G. 85/B6
Sępólno Krajeńskie, Poland 47/C2
Septentrional, Cordillera (range), Dom. Rep. 158/D5
Sept-Îles, Que. 146/M4
Sept-Îles (Seven Is.), Que. 162/K5
Sept-Îles, Québec 174/D2
Septimer (pass), Switzerland 39/J4
Sepulga (riv.), Ala. 195/E7
Sepulveda, Calif. (91343) 204/B10
Sequatchie (co.), Tenn. 237/L10
Sequatchie, Tenn. (37374) 237/K10
Sequatchie (riv.), Tenn. 237/L10
Sequeira, Uruguay 145/C1
Sequeros, Spain 33/C2
Sequim, Wash. (98382) 310/B2
Sequoia Nat'l Park, Calif. 204/G7
Sequoyah (co.), Okla. 288/S3
Sera (isl.), Indonesia 85/J7
Serafimovich, U.S.S.R. 52/F5
Serafina, N. Mex. (87569) 274/D3
Seraing, Belgium 27/G7
Serakhs, U.S.S.R. 48/G6
Serampore, India 68/F1
Serang, Indonesia 85/G1
Serangoon, Singapore 72/F6
Serasan (isl.), Indonesia 85/E5
Serbia (rep.), Yugoslavia 45/E3
Serçiler, Turkey 63/C6
Serdobol (Sortavala), U.S.S.R. 52/D2
Serdobsk, U.S.S.R. 52/F4
Sered', Czech. 41/D2
Şereflikoçhisar, Turkey 63/E3
Seremban, Malaysia 72/D7
Serena, Ill. (60549) 222/E2
Serengeti Nat'l Park, Tanzania 115/F4
Serenje, Zambia 115/F6
Sergach, U.S.S.R. 52/F3
Sergeant, Pa. (†16735) 294/E2
Sergeant Bluff, Iowa (51054) 229/A4
Sergeantsville, N.J. (08557) 273/D3
Sergeya Kirova (isls.), U.S.S.R. 48/J2
Sergipe (state), Brazil 132/G5
Seria, Brunei 85/E5
Serian, Malaysia 85/E5
Sérifos (isl.), Greece 45/G7
Sérigny (riv.), Québec 174/D1
Serik, Turkey 63/D4
Seringapatam, India 68/D6
Sermata (isl.), Indonesia 85/H7
Serón, Spain 33/E4
Serós, Spain 33/G2
Serov, U.S.S.R. 54/H4
Serov, U.S.S.R. 48/G4
Serowe, Botswana 118/D4
Serowe, Botswana 102/E7
Serpa, Portugal 33/C4
Serpa Pinto, Angola 102/D6
Serpentine (lake), New Bruns. 170/D1
Serpentine (lakes), S. Australia 88/D5
Serpentine (lakes), S. Australia 94/A3
Serpentine (riv.), W. Australia 88/B3
Serpents Mouth (passage), Trin. & Tob. 156/G5
Serpents Mouth (passage), Trin. & Tob. 161/A11
Serpents Mouth (passage), Venezuela 124/H3
Serpukhov, U.S.S.R. 7/H3
Serpukhov, U.S.S.R. 48/D4
Serpukhov, U.S.S.R. 52/E4
Serra do Navio, Brazil 132/C2
Sérrai, Greece 7/G4
Sérrai, Greece 45/F5
Serrana (bank), Colombia 126/B9
Serra Namuli (mt.), Mozambique 102/F6
Serranilla (bank), Colombia 126/B8
Serra Talhada, Brazil 132/G4
Serres, France 28/F5
Serrinha, Brazil 120/F4
Serrinha, Brazil 132/G5
Sertã, Portugal 33/B3
Sertânia, Brazil 132/G5
Sertãozinho, Brazil 135/B2
Serua (isl.), Indonesia 85/H7
Serui, Indonesia 85/K6
Serule, Botswana 118/D4
Sérvia, Greece 45/F5
Servia, Ind. (46980) 227/F3
Servia, W. Va. (†26623) 312/E5
Service Creek, Oreg. (†97874) 291/G3
Serviceton, Victoria 97/A5
Sêrxü, China 77/E5
Se San (riv.), Vietnam 72/E4
Sese (isls.), Uganda 115/F4
Sesegenaga (lake), Ontario 177/G4
Sesfontein, S. Africa 118/J6
Sesheke, Zambia 115/E7
Sesimbra, Portugal 33/B3
Sesser, Ill. (62884) 222/D5
Sessums, Miss. (39758) 256/G4
Sesto Fiorentino, Italy 34/C3
Sestri Levante, Italy 34/B2
Sesvenna (peak), Switzerland 39/K3
Sète, France 28/E6
Sete Lagoas, Brazil 120/E4
Sete Lagoas, Brazil 132/E7
Sete Quedas (falls) 120/D5
Sete Quedas (falls), Brazil 132/C9
Sete Quedas, (Grande) (isl.), Brazil 132/C8
Seth, W. Va. (25181) 312/C6
Sétif, Algeria 106/F1
Sétif, Algeria 102/C1
Setit (riv.), Sdan 111/G5
Seto, Japan 81/H6
Setonaikai National Park, Japan 81/H7
Seton Portage, Br. Col. 184/F5
Setouchi, Japan 81/O5
Settat, Morocco 106/C2
Settebagni, Italy 34/F6
Setté-Cama, Gabon 115/A4
Settecamini, Italy 34/F6
Setting (lake), Manitoba 179/H3
Settle, England 13/E3
Settsu, Japan 81/J8
Setúbal (dist.), Portugal 33/B3
Setúbal, Portugal 7/D5
Setúbal, Portugal 33/B3
Setúbal (bay), Portugal 33/B3
Seul (lake), Ontario 177/G4
Seul (lake), Ontario 175/B2
Seul Choix (pt.), Mich. 250/D3
Seuzach, Switzerland 39/G1
Sevan (lake), U.S.S.R. 7/J4
Sevan (lake), U.S.S.R. 52/G6
Sevaruyo, Bolivia 136/B6
Sevastopol', U.S.S.R. 7/H4
Sevastopol', U.S.S.R. 48/D5
Sevastopol', U.S.S.R. 52/D6
Sevelen, Switzerland 39/H2
Seven (heads), Ireland 17/D8
Seven Corners, Va. (22044) 307/S3
Seven Devils (res.), Ark. 202/G6
Seven Devils (mts.), Idaho 220/B4
Seven Hills, Ohio (†44131) 284/H9
Seven Hogs, The (isls.), Ireland 17/A7
Seven Islands (bay), Newf. 166/B2
Seven Islands (Sept-Îles), Québec 174/D2
Seven Mile, Ohio (45062) 284/A7
Sevenmile (creek), Ohio 284/A6
Seven Mile Ford, Va. (24373) 307/E7
Sevenoaks, England 13/J8
Sevenoaks, England 10/C6
Seven Persons, Alberta 182/E5
Seven Rivers (riv.), N. Mex. 274/E6
Seven Sisters, Texas (†78357) 303/F9
Seven Sisters Falls, Manitoba 179/G4
Seven Springs, N.C. (28578) 281/O4
Seven Springs, Pa. (†15557) 294/D6
Seventy Mile House, Br. Col. 184/G4
Seven Valleys, Pa. (17360) 294/J6
Severance, Colo. (80546) 208/K1
Severance, Kansas (66081) 232/G2
Severn (riv.), England 13/E6
Severn (riv.), England 10/E5
Severn, Md. (21144) 245/M4
Severn (riv.), Md. 245/N4
Severn (riv.), N.S. Wales 97/F1
Severn, N.C. (27877) 281/P2
Severn (riv.), Ont. 146/J4
Severn (riv.), Ont. 162/G5
Severn (lake), Ontario 175/B2
Severn (riv.), Ontario 177/E3
Severn (riv.), Ontario 175/B2
Severn, Mouth of the (est.), Wales 13/B7
Severn (riv.), Wales 13/E5
Severna Park, Md. (21146) 245/M4
Severnaya Zemlya (isls.), U.S.S.R. 4/A4
Severnaya Zemlya (isls.), U.S.S.R. 54/M1
Severnaya Zemlya (isls.), U.S.S.R. 2/P1
Severnaya Zemlya (isls.), U.S.S.R. 48/L1
Severnyy, U.S.S.R. 52/K1
Severobaykal'sk, U.S.S.R. 48/M4
Severočeský (reg.), Czech. 41/C1
Severodonetsk, U.S.S.R. 52/E5
Severodvinsk, U.S.S.R. 7/H2
Severodvinsk, U.S.S.R. 48/E3
Severodvinsk, U.S.S.R. 52/E2
Severo-Kuril'sk, U.S.S.R. 48/Q4
Severomoravský (reg.), Czech. 41/D2
Severomorsk, U.S.S.R. 52/D1
Severoural'sk, U.S.S.R. 48/G3
Severo-Yeniseysk, U.S.S.R. 48/K3
Severy, Kansas (67137) 232/F4
Sevier (co.), Ark. 202/B6
Sevier, N.C. (†28752) 281/E3
Sevier (co.), Tenn. 237/O9
Sevier (co.), Utah 304/C5
Sevier, Utah (84766) 304/B5
Sevier (lake), Utah 188/D3
Sevier (riv.), Utah 188/D3
Sevier (des.), Utah 304/B4
Sevier (lake), Utah 304/A5
Sevier (riv.), Utah 304/B4
Sevier, East Fork (riv.), Utah 304/B6
Sevier Bridge (res.), Utah 304/C4
Sevierville, Tenn. (37862) 237/P9
Sevilla, Colombia 126/C5
Sevilla (prov.), Spain 33/D4
Seville, Fla. (32090) 212/E2
Seville, Georgia (31084) 217/E7
Seville, Ohio (44273) 284/G3
Seville, Spain 7/D5
Seville, Spain 33/D4
Sevlievo, Bulgaria 45/G4
Sèvres, France 28/A2
Sewal, Iowa (52589) 229/G7
Sewalls Point, Fla. (†33457) 212/F4
Sewanee, Tenn. (37375) 237/K10
Seward, Alaska 146/C3
Seward, Alaska 188/D6
Seward, Alaska (99664) 196/C1
Seward (pen.), Alaska 146/C3
Seward (pen.), Alaska 196/E1
Seward (co.), Kansas 232/B4
Seward, Kansas (67577) 232/D3
Seward (co.), Nebr. 264/G4
Seward, Nebr. (68434) 264/H4
Seward, Okla. (†73044) 288/M3
Seward, Pa. (15954) 294/E5
Seward, U.S. 4/D17
Seward (pen.), U.S. 4/C18
Sewaren, N.J. (07077) 273/E2
Sewart A.F.B., Tenn. 237/J8
Sewell, Br. Col. 184/A3
Sewell, Ky. (†41385) 237/P5
Sewell, N.J. (08080) 273/C4
Sewickley, Pa. (15143) 294/B4
Sexsmith, Alberta 182/A2
Sexton, Ind. (†46173) 227/G5
Sexton, Iowa (†50483) 229/E2
Sextons Creek, Ky. (40983) 237/O6
Sextonville, Wis. (53584) 317/F9
Seybaplaya, Mexico 150/O7
Seychelles 2/M6
SEYCHELLES 118/H5
Seydhisfjördhur, Iceland 21/D1
Seydişehir, Turkey 63/D4
Seyfe (lake), Turkey 63/F3
Seyhan (riv.), Turkey 63/F4
Seyhan (riv.), Turkey 59/C2
Seyitgazi, Turkey 63/D3
Seym (riv.), U.S.S.R. 52/D4
Seymour (canal), Alaska 196/N1
Seymour (inlet), Br. Col. 184/D4
Seymour○, Conn. (06483) 210/C3
Seymour, Ill. (61875) 222/E3
Seymour, Ind. (47274) 227/F7
Seymour, Iowa (52590) 229/G7
Seymour, Mo. (65746) 261/G8
Seymour, Tenn. (37865) 237/O9
Seymour, Texas (76380) 303/E4
Seymour (lake), Vt. 268/D2
Seymour, Victoria 88/H7
Seymour, Victoria 97/C5
Seymour, Wis. (54165) 317/K6
Seymour Johnson A.F.B., N.C. 281/O4
Seymourville, La. (†70764) 238/J2
Seymourville, Manitoba 179/F3
Seyppel, Ark. (†72348) 202/K4
Sézanne, France 28/E3
Sezze, Italy 34/D4
Sfax, Tunisia 106/G2
Sfax, Tunisia 102/D1
Sfîntu Gheorghe, Romania 45/G3
Sfîntu Gheorghe, Romania 45/J3
's-Gravenbrakel (Braine-le-Comte), Belgium 27/D7
's Gravendeel, Netherlands 27/E5
's Gravenhage (The Hague) (cap.), Netherlands 27/E4
's Gravenzande, Netherlands 27/E4
Sgurr a Choire Ghlais (mt.), Scotland 15/D3
Sgurr Alasdair (mt.), Scotland 15/B3
Sgurr Mor (mt.), Scotland 15/C3
Sgurr na Ciche (mt.), Scotland 15/C3
Sgurr na Lapaich (mt.), Scotland 15/C3
Shaanxi (Shensi) (prov.), China 77/G5
Shaba (prov.), Zaire 115/E5
Shabani, Zimbabwe 102/E7
Shabani, Zimbabwe 118/E4
Shabasha, Sudan 59/B7
Shabbona, Ill. (60550) 222/E2
Shabeellaha Dhexe (prov.), Somalia 115/J3
Shabeellaha Hoose (prov.), Somalia 115/H3
Shabla, Bulgaria 45/J4
Shabo, Newf. 166/A3
Shabogamo (lake), Newf. 166/A3
Shabunda, Zaire 115/E4
Shabwa, P.D.R. Yemen 59/E6
Shache (Yarkand), China 77/A4
Shache, China 54/J6
Shackelford (co.), Texas 303/E5
Shackleton, Sask. 181/C5
Shackleton Ice Shelf, Ant. 2/P9
Shackleton Ice Shelf, Ant. 5/C5
Shade, Ohio (45776) 284/G7
Shadegan, Iran 66/F5
Shade Gap, Pa. (17255) 294/G5
Shadehill, S. Dak. (57653) 298/E2
Shadehill (res.), S. Dak. 298/E2
Shadeland, Ind. (†47901) 227/C4
Shader, Scotland 15/B2
Shadrinsk, U.S.S.R. 48/G4
Shady Bend, Kansas (†67455) 232/D2
Shady Cove, Oreg. (97539) 291/E5
Shady Dale, Georgia (31085) 217/E4
Shady Grove, Ala. (†36036) 195/F7
Shady Grove, Fla. (32357) 212/C1
Shady Grove, Ky. (†42064) 237/F6
Shady Grove, Pa. (17256) 294/G6
Shady Point, Okla. (74956) 288/S4
Shady Side, Md. (20867) 245/M5
Shadyside, Ohio (43947) 284/J6
Shady Valley, Tenn. (37688) 237/T7
Shafer (lake), Ind. 227/D3
Shafer, Minn. (55074) 255/F5
Shafter, Calif. (93263) 204/F8
Shafter, Nev. (†89835) 266/G2
Shafter, Texas (79850) 303/C12
Shaftesbury, England 13/E6
Shaftesbury, England 10/E5
Shaftsbury○, Vt. (05262) 268/A6
Shageluk, Alaska (99665) 196/G2
Shag Harbour, Nova Scotia 168/C5
Shahabad, Iran 66/E3
Shahat, Libya 102/E1
Shahat, Libya 111/D1
Shahbandar, Pakistan 68/B4
Shahdad, Iran 59/G3
Shahdad, Iran 66/K5
Shahdol, India 68/E4
Shahi, Iran 66/H2
Shahin Dezh, Iran 66/E2
Shahistan (Saravan), Iran 66/N7
Shah Jahan, Kuh-e (mts.), Iran 66/L2
Shahjahanpur, India 68/E3
Shah Juy, Afghanistan 59/J3
Shahpur, Iran 66/D1
Shahrakht, Iran 66/M4
Shahreza, Iran 59/F3
Shahreza, Iran 66/H4
Shahr Kord, Iran 66/G4
Shahrud, Iran 59/G2
Shahrud, Iran 66/J2
Shahsavar, Iran 59/F2
Shahsavar, Iran 66/G2
Shaibara (isl.), Saudi Arabia 59/C4
Sha'ib Hisb, Wadi (dry riv.), Iraq 66/C5
Shaikh Sa'ad, Iraq 66/E4
Shaikh Shu'aib (isl.), Iran 66/H7
Shaikh Shu'aib (isl.), Iran 59/F4
Shailerville, Conn. (†06438) 210/E3
Shajapur, India 68/D4
Shakawe, Botswana 118/C3
Shaker Heights, Ohio (44120) 284/H9
Shakespeare, Ontario 177/D4
Shakhtinsk, U.S.S.R. 48/H5
Shakhty, U.S.S.R. 7/J4
Shakhty, U.S.S.R. 48/E5
Shakhty, U.S.S.R. 52/F5
Shakhun'ya, U.S.S.R. 52/G3
Shaki, Nigeria 106/E7
Shâkir (isl.), Egypt 59/B4
Shakopee, Minn. (55379) 255/F6
Shakopee (creek), Minn. 255/C5
Shaktoolik, Alaska (99771) 196/F2
Shalalth, Br. Col. 184/F5
Shaler (mts.), N.W. Terrs. 187/G2
Shalimar, Fla. (32579) 212/C6
Shallala, Wadi esh (dry riv.), Jordan 65/D2
Shallotte, N.C. (28459) 281/N7
Shallow (lake), Maine 243/E3
Shallowater, Texas (79363) 303/B4
Shallow Lake, Ontario 177/C3
Shallow Water, Kansas (†67871) 232/B3
Sham, Jebel (mt.), Oman 59/G5
Shamattawa, Manitoba 179/K2
Shamattawa (riv.), Ontario 175/C2
Shambaugh, Iowa (51651) 229/D7
Shambe, Sudan 111/F6
Shamil, Iran 66/K7
Shammar, Jebel (plat.), Saudi Arabia 59/D4
Shamokin, Pa. (17872) 294/J4
Shamokin Dam, Pa. (17876) 294/J4
Shamrock, Fla. (†32628) 212/C2
Shamrock, Okla. (74068) 288/N3
Shamrock, Sask. 181/E5
Shamrock, Texas (79079) 303/D2
Shamrock Lakes, Ind. (†47348) 227/G4
Shamva, Zimbabwe 118/E3
Shan (state), Burma 72/C2
Shan (plat.), Burma 72/C2
Shanagolden, Ireland 17/C6
Shandan, China 77/F4
Shandon, Calif. (93461) 204/E8
Shandong (Shantung) (prov.), China 77/J4
Shangani (riv.), Zimbabwe 118/D3
Shangdu, China 77/H3
Shanghai, China 2/R4
Shanghai, China 54/O6
Shanghai, China 77/K5
Shanghai, Va. (23158) 307/P5
Shanghai, W. Va. (†25427) 312/K4
Shanghang, China 77/J6
Shangnan, China 77/H5
Shangqui (Shangkiu), China 77/J5
Shangrao (Shangjao), China 77/J6
Shangshui, China 77/J5
Shang Xian, China 77/H5
Shangzhi, China 77/L2
Shaniko, Oreg. (97057) 291/G3
Shanks, W. Va. (26761) 312/J4
Shanksville, Pa. (15560) 294/E5
Shannock, R.I. (02875) 249/H7
Shannon, Georgia (30172) 217/B2
Shannon (isl.), Greenl. 4/B10
Shannon, Ill. (61078) 222/D1
Shannon, Mouth of the (est.), Ireland 17/B6
Shannon (riv.), Ireland 10/B4
Shannon (riv.), Ireland 17/E6
Shannon, Miss. (38868) 256/G2
Shannon (co.), Mo. 261/K8
Shannon, New Bruns. 170/E3
Shannon, N. Zealand 100/E4
Shannon, N.C. (28386) 281/L5
Shannon, Québec 172/F3
Shannon (co.), S. Dak. 298/D7
Shannon (lake), Wash. 310/D2
Shannon Airport, Ireland 17/D6
Shannon Bridge, Ireland 17/F5
Shannon City, Iowa (50861) 229/E7
Shannondale, Ind. (†47933) 227/D4
Shannon Hills, Ark. (†72103) 202/F4
Shannontown, S.C. (†29150) 296/G4
Shannonville, Ontario 177/G3
Shanshan (Piqan), China 77/D3
Shansi (Shanxi) (prov.), China 77/H4
Shantar (isls.), U.S.S.R. 54/P4
Shantar (isls.), U.S.S.R. 48/O4
Shantou (Swatou), China 77/J7
Shantou, China 54/N7
Shantung (Shandong) (prov.), China 77/J4
Shanty Bay, Ontario 177/E3
Shanxi (Shansi) (prov.), China 77/H4
Shanyang, China 77/G5
Shanyin, China 77/H4
Shaoguan (Shiukwan), China 77/H7
Shaowu, China 77/J6
Shaoxing (Shaohing), China 77/K5
Shaoyang, China 77/H6
Shap, England 13/E3
Shapinsay (isl.), Scotland 15/F1
Shapio (lake), Newf. 166/B3
Shapleigh, Maine (04076) 243/B8
Shapleigh○, Maine (04076) 243/B8
Shaqlawa, Iraq 66/D2
Shaqra, Saudi Arabia 54/F7
Shaqra, Saudi Arabia 59/D4
Sharafkhaneh, Iran 66/D1
Sharbatat, Ras (cape), Oman 59/G6
Sharbot Lake, Ontario 177/H3
Shari (riv.) 102/D4
Shari (riv.), Cent. Afr. Rep. 115/C2
Shari (riv.), Chad 111/C5
Shari, Japan 81/M2
Sharifabad, Iran 66/L2
Sharjah, U.A.E. 59/F4
Shark (pt.), Fla. 212/E6
Shark (bay), W. Australia 88/A5
Shark (bay), W. Australia 92/A4
Shark Bay, W. Australia 88/A5
Sharkey (co.), Miss. 256/C5
Sharlyk, U.S.S.R. 52/H4
Sharon○, Conn. (06069) 210/B1
Sharon, Georgia (30664) 217/G3
Sharon, Kansas (67138) 232/D4
Sharon, Mass. (02067) 249/K4
Sharon○, Mass. (02067) 249/K4
Sharon, Miss. (39163) 256/E5
Sharon○, N.H. (†03458) 268/D6
Sharon, N. Dak. (58277) 282/P4
Sharon, Ohio (43781) 284/G6
Sharon, Okla. (73857) 288/H2
Sharon, Pa. (16146) 294/B3
Sharon, S.C. (29742) 296/E2
Sharon, Tenn. (38255) 237/D8
Sharon○, Vt. (05065) 268/C4
Sharon, W. Va. (25182) 312/D6
Sharon, Wis. (53585) 317/J11
Sharon Center, Ohio (44274) 284/G3
Sharon Grove, Ky. (42280) 237/G7
Sharon Hill, Pa. (19079) 294/N7
Sharon Springs, Kansas (67758) 232/A3
Sharon Springs, N.Y. (13459) 276/L5
Sharon Valley, Conn. (†06069) 210/B1
Sharonville, Ohio (45241) 284/C9
Sharp (co.), Ark. 202/G1
Sharpe, Kansas (†66871) 232/G3
Sharpe (lake), S. Dak. 298/J5
Sharpe Army Depot, Calif. 204/D6
Sharpes, Fla. (32959) 212/F3
Sharples, W. Va. (25183) 312/C7
Sharps (isl.), Md. 245/N6
Sharps, Va. (22548) 307/P5
Sharpsburg, Georgia (30277) 217/C4
Sharpsburg, Iowa (50862) 229/D7
Sharpsburg, Ky. (40374) 237/O4
Sharpsburg, Md. (21782) 245/G3
Sharpsburg, N.C. (27878) 281/O3
Sharpsburg, Pa. (15215) 294/B6
Sharps Chapel, Tenn. (37866) 237/O8
Sharpsville, Ind. (46068) 227/E4
Sharpsville, Pa. (16150) 294/A3
Sharptown, Md. (21861) 245/R6
Sharptown, N.J. (†08098) 273/C4
Shar'ya, U.S.S.R. 48/E4
Shar'ya, U.S.S.R. 52/G3
Shashe, Botswana 118/D4
Shashe (riv.), Botswana 118/D4
Shashe (riv.), Zimbabwe 118/D4
Shashi (Shasi), China 77/H5
Shasta (res.), Calif. 188/B2
Shasta (mt.), Calif. 188/B2
Shasta (co.), Calif. 204/C3
Shasta, Calif. (96087) 204/C3
Shasta (dam), Calif. 204/C3
Shasta (lake), Calif. 204/C3
Shasta (mt.), Calif. 204/C2
Shasta (riv.), Calif. 204/C2
Shati, Wadi esh (dry riv.), Libya 111/B2
Shatra, Iraq 66/E5
Shatt-al-'Arab (riv.), 66/E4
Shattuc, Ill. (62283) 222/D5
Shattuck, Okla. (73858) 288/G2
Shattuckville, Mass. (01369) 249/D2
Shauck, Ohio (43349) 284/E4
Shaughnessy, Alberta 182/D5
Shaunavon, Sask. 162/F6
Shaunavon, Sask. 181/C6
Shavano Park, Texas (†78201) 303/J10
Shaver Lake, Calif. (93664) 204/F6
Shavers Fork (riv.), W. Va. 312/G5
Shave Ziyyon, Israel 65/B2
Shaw, Kansas (†66733) 232/G4
Shaw, La. (†71373) 238/G4
Shaw, Minn. (†55717) 255/F3
Shaw, Miss. (38773) 256/C3
Shaw (mt.), N.H. 268/E4
Shaw, Oreg. (†97325) 291/A3
Shaw A.F.B., S.C. 296/F4
Shawan, China 77/B3
Shawanese, Pa. (18654) 294/E7
Shawano (co.), Wis. 317/J6
Shawano, Wis. (54166) 317/J6
Shawano (lake), Wis. 317/K6
Shawboro, N.C. (27973) 281/S2
Shawbost, Scotland 15/B2
Shawbridge, Québec 172/C4
Shawinigan, Que. 162/J6
Shawinigan, Québec 174/C3
Shawinigan, Québec 172/E3
Shawinigan (riv.), Québec 172/E3
Shawinigan-Sud, Québec 172/E3
Shaw Island, Wash. (98286) 310/B2
Shawmut, Ala. (36876) 195/H5
Shawmut, Maine (04975) 243/D6
Shawmut, Mont. (59078) 262/G4
Shawmut, Pa. (†15823) 294/E3
Shawnee, Colo. (80475) 208/H4
Shawnee (co.), Kansas 232/G2
Shawnee, Kansas (*66202) 232/H2
Shawnee, Ohio (43782) 284/F6
Shawnee, Okla. 188/G3
Shawnee, Okla. (74801) 288/N4
Shawnee, Wyo. (82229) 319/G3
Shawnee Hills, Ohio (43065) 284/D5
Shawnee on Delaware, Pa. (18356) 294/N3
Shawneetown, Ill. (62984) 222/E6
Shawnigan Lake, Br. Col. 184/J3
Shawomet, R.I. (†02886) 249/J6
Shawsheen Village, Mass. (01810) 249/K2
Shawshine (riv.), Mass. 249/K2
Shawsville, Md. (†21161) 245/M2
Shawsville, Va. (24162) 307/H6
Shawville, Québec 172/A4
Shay Gap, W. Australia 92/C3
Shayib, Jebel (mt.), Egypt 59/B4
Shay Juy, Afghanistan 68/B2
Shchekino, U.S.S.R. 52/E4
Shchel'yayur, U.S.S.R. 52/H1
Shchigry, U.S.S.R. 52/E4
Shchuchinsk, U.S.S.R. 48/H4
Sheakleyville, Pa. (16151) 294/B3
Sheaville, Oreg. (†97910) 291/K4
Shebandowan, Ontario 177/G5
Sheberghan, Afghanistan 54/H6
Sheberghan, Afghanistan 68/B1
Sheberghan, Afghanistan 59/H2
Sheboygan, Wis. 188/J2
Sheboygan (co.), Wis. 317/L8
Sheboygan, Wis. (53081) 317/L8
Sheboygan Falls, Wis. (53085) 317/L8
Shedd, Oreg. (97377) 291/D3
Shedden, Ontario 177/C5
Shediac, New Bruns. 170/F2
Shediac (isl.), New Bruns. 170/F2
Shediac Bridge, New Bruns. 170/F2
Sheeffry (hills), Ireland 17/B4
Sheelin (lake), Ireland 17/G4
Sheenjek (riv.), Alaska 196/K1
Sheep (mt.), Colo. 208/E6
Sheep (mt.), Mont. 262/C2
Sheep (range), Nev. 266/F6
Sheep (creek), Oreg. 291/L2

Sieradz 447

Sheep (creek), Utah 304/E3
Sheep Creek, Alberta 182/A2
Sheep Haven (harb.), Ireland 17/F1
Sheeps (head), Ireland 17/B8
Sheepscott, Maine (†04579) 243/D7
's Heerenberg, Netherlands 27/J5
Sheerness, Alberta 182/E4
Sheet (harb.), Nova Scotia 168/F4
Sheet Harbour, Nova Scotia 168/F4
Shefar'am, Israel 65/C2
Shefayim, Israel 65/B3
Sheffield, Ala. (35660) 195/C1
Sheffield, England 7/D3
Sheffield, England 10/F4
Sheffield, England 13/J2
Sheffield, Ill. (61361) 222/D2
Sheffield, Iowa (50475) 229/G3
Sheffield○, Mass. (01257) 249/A4
Sheffield, Mont. (†59347) 262/K4
Sheffield, New Bruns. 170/D3
Sheffield, Ohio (†44052) 284/F3
Sheffield, Pa. (16347) 294/D2
Sheffield, Tasmania 99/C3
Sheffield, Texas (79781) 303/B7
Sheffield○, Vt. (05866) 268/C2
Sheffield Lake, Ohio (44054) 284/F3
Shefford (co.), Québec 172/E4
Sheguiandah, Ontario 177/C2
Sheho, Sask. 181/H4
Shehy (mts.), Ireland 17/C8
Sheikh Sa'id, Yemen Arab Rep. 59/D7
Sheila, New Bruns. 170/F1
Sheki, U.S.S.R. 52/G6
Shelagh (riv.), Iran 66/M5
Shelagskiy (cape), U.S.S.R. 48/R2
Shelbiana, Ky. (41562) 237/R6
Shelbina, Mo. (63468) 261/H3
Shelburn, Ind. (47879) 227/C6
Shelburne, N.H. (†03581) 268/E3
Shelburne○, N.H. (†03581) 268/E3
Shelburne (co.), Nova Scotia 168/C5
Shelburne, Nova Scotia 168/C5
Shelburne, Ontario 177/D3
Shelburne○, Vt. (05482) 268/A3
Shelburne (pond), Vt. 268/A3
Shelburne Falls, Mass. (01370) 249/D2
Shelby (co.), Ala. 195/E4
Shelby, Ala. (35143) 195/E4
Shelby (co.), Ill. 222/E4
Shelby (co.), Ind. 227/F5
Shelby, Ind. (46377) 227/C2
Shelby (co.), Iowa 229/C5
Shelby, Iowa (51570) 229/C5
Shelby (co.), Ky. 237/L4
Shelby, Mich. (49455) 250/C5
Shelby, Miss. (38774) 256/C3
Shelby (co.), Mo. 261/H3
Shelby, Mont. (59474) 262/E2
Shelby, Nebr. (68662) 264/G3
Shelby, N.C. (28150) 281/G4
Shelby (co.), Ohio 284/B5
Shelby, Ohio (44875) 284/E4
Shelby (co.), Tenn. 237/B10
Shelby (co.), Texas 303/K6
Shelby Center, N.Y. (†14103) 276/D4
Shelbyville, Ill. (62565) 222/E4
Shelbyville (lake), Ill. 222/E4
Shelbyville, Ind. (46176) 227/F6
Shelbyville, Ky. (40065) 237/L4
Shelbyville, Mo. (63469) 261/H3
Shelbyville, Tenn. (37160) 237/H10
Shelbyville, Texas (75973) 303/L6
Sheldahl, Iowa (50243) 229/F5
Sheldon, Ill. (60966) 222/F3
Sheldon, Iowa (51201) 229/B2
Sheldon, Minn. (†55921) 255/G7
Sheldon, Mo. (64784) 261/D7
Sheldon, N. Dak. (58068) 282/P6
Sheldon, S.C. (29941) 296/F6
Sheldon, Texas (†77001) 303/K1
Sheldon○, Vt. (05483) 268/B2
Sheldon, Wis. (54766) 317/D5
Sheldon Junction, Vt. (†05483) 268/B2
Sheldon Point, Alaska (99666) 196/E2
Sheldon Springs, Vt. (05485) 268/A2
Sheldonville, Mass. (02070) 249/J4
Shelekhov (gulf), U.S.S.R. 54/S3
Shelekhov (gulf), U.S.S.R. 48/Q4
Shelikof (str.), Alaska 196/H3
Shell (pt.), Fla. 212/B1
Shell (riv.), Minn. 255/C4
Shell (creek), N. Dak. 282/F3
Shell, Loch (inlet), Scotland 15/B3
Shell (lake), Wis. 317/C4
Shell, Wyo. (82441) 319/E1
Shell (creek), Wyo. 319/E1
Shellbrook, Sask. 162/F5
Shellbrook, Sask. 181/E2
Shelley, Br. Col. 184/F3
Shelley, Idaho (83274) 220/F6
Shellharbour, N.S. Wales 97/F4
Shell Knob, Mo. (65747) 261/E9
Shell Lake, Sask. 181/D2
Shell Lake, Wis. (54871) 317/C4
Shellman, Georgia (31786) 217/C7
Shellmouth, Manitoba 179/A4
Shell Rock, Iowa (50670) 229/H3
Shellsburg, Iowa (52332) 229/K4
Shelltown, Md. (†21838) 245/R9
Shelly, Minn. (56581) 255/B3
Shelmerdine, N.C. (†27834) 281/P4
Shelocta, Pa. (15774) 294/D4
Shelter (isl.), N.Y. 276/R8
Shelton, Conn. (06484) 210/C3
Shelton, Nebr. (68876) 264/F4
Shelton, S.C. (†29015) 296/E3
Shelton, Wash. (98584) 310/B3
Shemakha, U.S.S.R. 52/G6
Shemogue, New Bruns. 170/F2
Shemya (isl.), Alaska 196/J3
Shemya Air Force Base, Alaska 196/J3
Shenandoah, Iowa (51601) 229/C7
Shenandoah, Pa. (17976) 294/K4
Shenandoah (co.), Va. 307/L3
Shenandoah, Va. (22849) 307/L4
Shenandoah (mt.), Va. 307/K3
Shenandoah (riv.), Va. 307/N2
Shenandoah (riv.), W. Va. 312/K4
Shenandoah Junction, W. Va. (25442) 312/L4
Shenandoah Nat'l Park, Va. 307/L3
Shenango, Pa. (†16125) 294/A3
Shenango River (lake), Pa. 294/B3
Shendam, Nigeria 106/F7
Shendi, Sudan 59/B6
Shendi, Sudan 102/F3
Shendi, Sudan 111/F4
Shëngjin, Albania 45/D5
Sheng Xian, China 77/K6
Shenipsit (lake), Conn. 210/F1
Shenkursk, U.S.S.R. 52/F2
Shenkursk, U.S.S.R. 48/E3
Shenmu, China 77/G4
Shennington, Wis. (†54618) 317/F7
Shennongjia, China 77/H5
Shensi (Shaanxi) (prov.), China 77/G5
Shenyang (Mukden), China 77/K3
Shenyang, China 54/O5
Shenyang, China 2/R3
Sheopur, India 68/D3
Shepard, Alberta 182/D4
Shepardsville, Ind. (47880) 227/B5
Shepaug (dam), Conn. 210/B3
Shepaug (riv.), Conn. 210/B2
Shepetovka, U.S.S.R. 52/C4
Shepherd, Mich. (48883) 250/E5
Shepherd, Mont. (59079) 262/H5
Shepherd (bay), N.W. Terrs. 187/J3
Shepherd, Texas (77371) 303/K7
Shepherdstown, W. Va. (25443) 312/L4
Shepherdsville, Ky. (40165) 237/K4
Shepody, New Bruns. 170/F3
Shepody (bay), New Bruns. 170/F3
Sheppard A.F.B., Texas 303/F3
Shepparton, Victoria 88/G7
Shepparton, Victoria 97/C5
Sheppey (isl.), England 13/J6
Sheppton, Pa. (18248) 294/K4
Shepshed, England 13/F5
Shepton Mallet, England 13/E6
Shepton Mallet, England 10/E5
Sheqi, China 77/H5
Sherack, Minn. (†56722) 255/B2
Sherard, Miss. (38669) 256/C2
Sherard (cape), N.W. Terrs. 187/L2
Sherborn○, Mass. (01770) 249/A8
Sherborne, England 10/E5
Sherborne, England 13/E7
Sherbro (isl.), S. Leone 106/B7
Sherbrooke, Nova Scotia 168/G3
Sherbrooke (lake), Nova Scotia 168/D4
Sherbrooke (riv.), Nova Scotia 168/D4
Sherbrooke, Que. 162/J7
Sherbrooke (co.), Québec 172/E4
Sherbrooke, Québec 172/E4
Sherburn, Minn. (56171) 255/D7
Sherburne (co.), Minn. 255/E5
Sherburne, N.Y. (13460) 276/K5
Shercock, Ireland 17/G4
Shereik, Sudan 111/F4
Sheridan, Ark. (72150) 202/F5
Sheridan, Calif. (95681) 204/D5
Sheridan, Colo. (†80110) 208/J3
Sheridan, Ill. (60551) 222/E2
Sheridan, Ind. (46069) 227/E4
Sheridan (co.), Kansas 232/B2
Sheridan, Maine (04775) 243/F2
Sheridan, Mich. (48884) 250/D5
Sheridan, Mo. (64486) 261/C1
Sheridan (co.), Mont. 262/M2
Sheridan, Mont. (59749) 262/D5
Sheridan (co.), Nebr. 264/B2
Sheridan, N.Y. (14135) 276/B5
Sheridan (co.), N. Dak. 282/K4
Sheridan, Oreg. (97378) 291/D2
Sheridan, W. Va. (†25506) 312/B6
Sheridan, Wis. (†54981) 317/H7
Sheridan, Wyo. 188/E2
Sheridan, Wyo. 146/H5
Sheridan (co.), Wyo. 319/F1
Sheridan, Wyo. (82801) 319/F1
Sheridan Lake, Colo. (81071) 208/P6
Sheringham, England 13/J5
Sheringham, England 10/G4
Sherkin (isl.), Ireland 17/C9
Sherman (mt.), Colo. 208/G4
Sherman○, Conn. (06784) 210/B2
Sherman, Ill. (62684) 222/D4
Sherman (co.), Kansas 232/A2
Sherman, Kansas (†67356) 232/H4
Sherman, Ky. (†41035) 237/M3
Sherman, Maine (†04777) 243/G4
Sherman○, Maine (†04777) 243/G4
Sherman, Mich. (†49668) 250/D4
Sherman, Miss. (38869) 256/G2
Sherman, Mo. (63078) 261/N3
Sherman (co.), Nebr. 264/F3
Sherman (res.), Nebr. 264/E3
Sherman, N. Mex. (†88057) 274/B6
Sherman, N.Y. (14781) 276/A6
Sherman (inlet), N.W. Terrs. 187/J3
Sherman (co.), Oreg. 291/G2
Sherman, S. Dak. (57060) 298/S6
Sherman (co.), Texas 303/C1
Sherman, Texas (75090) 303/H4
Sherman, Texas 188/G4
Sherman, W. Va. (26173) 312/C5
Sherman City, Mich. (†48632) 250/D5
Sherman Mills, Maine (04776) 243/G4
Shermans Dale, Pa. (17090) 294/H5
Sherman Station, Maine (04777) 243/F4
Sherrard, Ill. (61281) 222/C2
Sherrard, W. Va. (†26003) 312/E3
Sherridon, Man. 162/G4
Sherridon, Manitoba 179/H3
Sherrill, Ark. (72152) 202/F5
Sherrill, Iowa (52073) 229/M3
Sherrill, N.Y. (13461) 276/J4
Sherrington, Québec 172/D4
Sherrodsville, Ohio (44675) 284/H4
Sherry, Wis. (†54454) 317/G6
's Hertogenbosch, Netherlands 27/G5
Sherwood, Ark. (72116) 202/F4
Sherwood (pt.), Conn. 210/B4
Sherwood (for.), England 13/F4
Sherwood, Mich. (49089) 250/D6
Sherwood, N. Dak. (58782) 282/G2
Sherwood, Ohio (43556) 284/A3
Sherwood, Okla. (†74728) 288/S6
Sherwood, Oreg. (97140) 291/A2
Sherwood, Pr. Edward I. 168/E2
Sherwood, Tenn. (37376) 237/K10
Sherwood, Texas (†76941) 303/D6
Sherwood, Wis. (54169) 317/K7
Sherwood Park, Alberta 182/D3
Sheslay (riv.), Br. Col. 184/J2
Shetek (lake), Minn. 255/C6
Shetland (islands area), Scotland 15/F2
Shetland (isls.), Scotland 7/D2
Shetland (isls.), Scotland 10/G1
Shetland (isls.), Scotland 15/G2
Shetucket (riv.), Conn. 210/G2
Shevchenko, U.S.S.R. 54/G5
Shevchenko, U.S.S.R. 48/F5
Shevlin, Manitoba 179/A3
Shevlin, Minn. (56676) 255/C3
Sheyenne, N. Dak. (58374) 282/M4
Sheyenne (riv.), N. Dak. 188/G1
Sheyenne (riv.), N. Dak. 282/O6
Sheykh Sho'eyb (isl.), Iran 66/H7
Shiant (isls.), Scotland 15/B3
Shiant (sound), Scotland 15/B3
Shiawassee (co.), Mich. 250/E6
Shiawassee (riv.), Mich. 250/E5
Shibam, P.D.R. Yemen 59/E6
Shibata, Japan 81/J5
Shibetsu, Japan 81/M2
Shibin el Kom, Egypt 111/J3
Shibogama (lake), Ontario 175/C2
Shickley, Nebr. (68436) 264/G4
Shickshinny, Pa. (18655) 294/K3
Shideler, Ind. (†47338) 227/G4
Shidler, Okla. (74652) 288/N1
Shiel, Loch (lake), Scotland 10/D2
Shiel, Loch (lake), Scotland 15/C4
Shieldaig, Scotland 15/C3
Shields, Kansas (67874) 232/B3
Shields (riv.), Mont. 262/F4
Shields, N. Dak. (58569) 282/H7
Shieldsville, Minn. (†55021) 255/E6
Shifnal, England 13/E5
Shiga (pref.), Japan 81/J7
Shigatse (Xigazê), China 77/C6
Shigawake, Québec 172/D2
Shihezi (Shihhotzu), China 77/C3
Shihr, P.D.R. Yemen 59/E7
Shijak, Albania 45/D5
Shijiazhuang (Shihkiachwang), China 77/J4
Shijiazhuang, China 54/N6
Shikarpur, Pakistan 68/B3
Shikarpur, Pakistan 59/J4
Shikoku, Japan 54/P6
Shikoku (isl.), Japan 2/R4
Shikoku (isl.), Japan 81/F7
Shikotan (isl.), Japan 81/N2
Shikotsu (lake), Japan 81/K2
Shikotsu-Toya National Park, Japan 81/K2
Shilbottle, England 13/F2
Shildon, England 13/F3
Shilka (riv.), U.S.S.R. 54/N4
Shilka, U.S.S.R. 48/M4
Shillelagh, Ireland 17/J6
Shillelagh, Ireland 10/C4
Shillington, Pa. (19607) 294/K5
Shillong, India 68/G3
Shilo, Manitoba 179/C5
Shiloh, Ala. (†35979) 195/G2
Shiloh, Ala. (†36754) 195/C6
Shiloh, Georgia (31826) 217/C5
Shiloh, Ill. (†62220) 222/B3
Shiloh, N.J. (08353) 273/C5
Shiloh, Ohio (44878) 284/E4
Shiloh, S.C. (†29080) 296/G4
Shiloh, Tenn. (38376) 237/E10
Shiloh, Va. (22549) 307/O4
Shiloh Nat'l Mil. Park, Tenn. 237/E10
Shilovo, U.S.S.R. 52/F4
Shimabara, Japan 81/E7
Shimamoto, Japan 81/J7
Shimane (pref.), Japan 81/F6
Shimane (pen.), Japan 81/F6
Shimanovsk, U.S.S.R. 48/N4
Shimbir Berris (mt.), Somalia 115/J1
Shimizu, Japan 81/J6
Shimoda, Japan 81/J6
Shimoga, India 68/D6
Shimokita (pen.), Japan 81/K3
Shimonoseki, Japan 81/E6
Shin (falls), Scotland 15/D3
Shin, Loch (lake), Scotland 15/D2
Shin, Loch (lake), Scotland 10/D1
Shin (riv.), Scotland 15/D3
Shinano (riv.), Japan 81/J5
Shinas, Oman 59/G5
Shindand, Afghanistan 59/H3
Shindand, Afghanistan 68/A2
Shindler, S. Dak. (†57101) 298/R7
Shiner, Texas (77984) 303/G8
Shingbwiyang, Burma 72/B1
Shinglehouse, Pa. (16748) 294/F2
Shingler, Georgia (†31781) 217/E7
Shingle Springs, Calif. (95682) 204/C8
Shingleton, Mich. (49884) 250/C2
Shingu, Japan 81/H7
Shining Tree, Ontario 177/J5
Shinjo, Japan 81/K4
Shinko (riv.), Cent. Afr. Rep. 115/D2
Shinnecock Ind. Res., N.Y. 276/R9
Shinnston, W. Va. (26431) 312/F4
Shin Pond, Maine (†04765) 243/F3
Shinrone, Ireland 17/F5
Shinyanga (reg.), Tanzania 115/F4
Shinyanga, Tanzania 115/F4
Shinyanga, Tanzania 102/F5
Shiocton, Wis. (54170) 317/K7
Shiogama, Japan 81/K4
Shiono (cape), Japan 81/H7
Ship (isl.), Miss. 256/G10
Ship Bottom, N.J. (08008) 273/E4
Ship Harbour, Newf. 166/D2
Ship Harbour, Nova Scotia 168/F4
Shiping, China 77/F7
Shipki (pass), India 68/D2
Shipman, Ill. (62685) 222/C4
Shipman, Sask. 181/F2
Shipman, Va. (22971) 307/L5
Shippan (pt.), Conn. 210/A4
Shippegan, New Bruns. 170/F1
Shippegan (gully), New Bruns. 170/F1
Shippegan (bay), New Bruns. 170/E1
Shippensburg, Pa. (17257) 294/H5
Shippenville, Pa. (16254) 294/D3
Shiprock, N. Mex. (87420) 274/A2
Ship Rock (peak), N. Mex. 274/A2
Shipshaw (riv.), Québec 172/F1
Shipshewana, Ind. (46565) 227/F1
Ship Shoal (isl.), Va. 307/S6
Shipston on Stour, England 13/F5
Shiqian, China 77/G6
Shiqma (riv.), Israel 65/B4
Shiquan, China 77/G5
Shiquanhe, China 77/A5
Shiragami (cape), Japan 81/J3
Shirakawa, Japan 81/K5
Shirane (mt.), Japan 81/H6
Shirane (mt.), Japan 81/J5
Shiranuka, Japan 81/M2
Shiraz, Iran 54/G7
Shiraz, Iran 66/H6
Shiraz, Iran 59/F4
Shire (riv.), Malawi 115/G7
Shire (riv.), Mozambique 118/E3
Shiretoko (cape), Japan 81/M1
Shiriya (cape), Japan 81/K3
Shir Kuh (mt.), Iran 59/F3
Shir Kuh (mt.), Iran 66/J5
Shirland, Ill. (61079) 222/D1
Shirley, Ark. (72153) 202/F2
Shirley, Ill. (61772) 222/E3
Shirley, Ind. (47384) 227/F5
Shirley, Mass. (01464) 249/H2
Shirley○, Mass. (01464) 249/H2
Shirley, Mo. (†63664) 261/L7
Shirley, W. Va. (26434) 312/E4
Shirley (basin), Wyo. 319/F3
Shirley Basin, Wyo. (82615) 319/F3
Shirley Center, Mass. (01465) 249/H2
Shirley City (Woodburn), Ind. (†46797) 227/H2
Shirley Mills, Maine (04485) 243/D5
Shirley Mills○, Maine (04485) 243/D5
Shirleysburg, Pa. (17260) 294/G5
Shiro, Texas (77876) 303/J7
Shiroishi, Japan 81/K4
Shirvan, Iran 59/G2
Shirvan, Iran 66/K2
Shirvan (riv.), Iran 66/E3
Shishaldin (vol.), Alaska 196/E4
Shishmaref, Alaska (99772) 196/E1
Shithatha, Iraq 59/D3
Shithatha, Iraq 66/C4
Shitike (creek), Oreg. 291/F3
Shiukwan (Shaoguan), China 77/H7
Shively, Calif. (†95565) 204/B3
Shively, Ky. (40216) 237/K4
Shivers, Miss. (39164) 256/E7
Shivpuri, India 68/D3
Shivwits (plat.), Ariz. 198/B2
Shivwits Ind. Res., Utah 304/A6
Shiyan, China 77/H5
Shizuishan (Shihsuishan), China 77/G4
Shizunai, Japan 81/L2
Shizuoka (pref.), Japan 81/H6
Shizuoka, Japan 54/P6
Shizuoka, Japan 81/H6
Shkodër, Albania 7/F4
Shkodër, Albania 45/D5
Shoa (prov.), Ethiopia 111/G6
Shoal (riv.), Fla. 212/C6
Shoal (creek), Ill. 222/D5
Shoal (lake), Manitoba 179/B4
Shoal (lake), Manitoba 179/G5
Shoal (riv.), Manitoba 179/B2
Shoal (bay), Newf. 166/D2
Shoal (bay), Nova Scotia 168/F4
Shoal (creek), Tenn. 237/F10
Shoal (creek), Utah 304/A6
Shoal Branch, Wading (riv.), N.J. 273/D4
Shoal Cove, Newf. 166/C3
Shoal Harbour, Newf. 166/C2
Shoalhaven (riv.), N.S. Wales 97/E4
Shoal Lake, Manitoba 179/B4
Shoals, Ind. (47581) 227/D7
Shoals (isls.), N.H. 268/F6
Shoals, N.C. (†27043) 281/J2
Shoals, W. Va. (25562) 312/B6
Shoals Junction, S.C. (29638) 296/C3
Shoalwater (bay), Queensland 88/J4
Shoalwater (cape), Wash. 310/A4
Shoalwater Ind. Res., Wash. 310/B4
Shobara, Japan 81/F6
Shobonier, Ill. (62885) 222/D5
Shock, W. Va. (26638) 312/D5
Shoemakersville, Pa. (19555) 294/K4
Shoffner, Ark. (†72112) 202/H2
Shohola, Pa. (18458) 294/N3
Sholapur, India 54/J8
Sholapur, India 68/D5
Sholes, Nebr. (†68771) 264/G2
Shona (isl.), Scotland 15/C4
Shongaloo, La. (71072) 238/D1
Shonkin, Mont. (59476) 262/F3
Shonto, Ariz. (86054) 198/E2
Shonto (plat.), Ariz. 198/E2
Shook, Mo. (63963) 261/M8
Shooting Creek, N.C. (†28904) 281/B4
Shopiere, Wis. (†53525) 317/H10
Shop Springs, Tenn. (†37184) 237/J8
Shorapur, India 68/D5
Shoreacres, Br. Col. 184/J5
Shore Acres, N.J. (†08723) 273/E3
Shore Acres, Texas (†77571) 303/K2
Shoreham, Mich. (†49085) 250/C6
Shoreham, Minn. (†56501) 255/C4
Shoreham, N.Y. (11786) 276/P8
Shoreham○, Vt. (05770) 268/A4
Shoreham-by-Sea, England 13/G7
Shoreham-by-Sea, England 10/F5
Shoreview, Minn. (†55112) 255/G5
Shorewood, Ill. (60435) 222/E2
Shorewood, Minn. (†55331) 255/F5
Shorewood, Wis. (53211) 317/M1
Shorewood Hills, Mich. (†49125) 250/C7
Shorewood Hills, Wis. (†53701) 317/G9
Short, Okla. (†72955) 288/S3
Short Beach, Conn. (†06405) 210/D3
Short Creek, Ohio (43989) 284/J5
Shortdale, Manitoba 179/A3
Shorter, Ala. (36075) 195/G6
Shorterville, Ala. (36373) 195/H7
Short Falls, N.H. (†03234) 268/E5
Short Hills, N.J. (07078) 273/E2
Shortland (isls.), Solomon Is. 86/D2
Shortleaf, Ala. (†36732) 195/C6
Shortsville, N.Y. (14548) 276/F5
Shoshone, Calif. (92384) 204/J8
Shoshone (co.), Idaho 220/B2
Shoshone, Idaho (83352) 220/D7
Shoshone (falls), Idaho 220/D7
Shoshone (mt.), Nev. 266/E6
Shoshone (mts.), Nev. 266/D3
Shoshone (range), Nev. 266/E2
Shoshone (lake), Wyo. 319/B1
Shoshone (riv.), Wyo. 319/D1
Shoshong, Botswana 118/D4
Shoshoni, Wyo. (82649) 319/D2
Shostka, U.S.S.R. 52/D4
Shotley, England 13/J6
Shotts, Scotland 15/C2
Shouldice, Alberta 182/D4
Shoultes, Wash. (†98270) 310/C2
Shouns, Tenn. (†37683) 237/T8
Shoup, Idaho (83469) 220/D4
Shoval, Israel 65/B5
Shovel Lake, Minn. (†55785) 255/E4
Showak, Sudan 111/G5
Showell, Md. (21862) 245/T7
Show Low, Ariz. (85901) 198/F4
Shoyna, U.S.S.R. 52/F1
Shpola, U.S.S.R. 52/D5
Shreve, Ohio (44676) 284/F4
Shreveport, La. 146/J6
Shreveport, La. 188/H4
Shreveport, La. (*71101) 238/C2
Shrewsbury, England 13/E5
Shrewsbury, England 10/E4
Shrewsbury○, Mass. (01545) 249/H3
Shrewsbury, Mo. (†63101) 261/P3
Shrewsbury, N.J. (07701) 273/E3
Shrewsbury, Pa. (17361) 294/J6
Shrewsbury○, Vt. (†05738) 268/B4
Shrule, Ireland 17/C4
Shuangcheng, China 77/L2
Shuangliao, China 77/K3
Shuangyashan, China 77/M2
Shubenacadie, Nova Scotia 168/E3
Shubenacadie (lake), Nova Scotia 168/E4
Shubenacadie (riv.), Nova Scotia 168/E3
Shubert, Nebr. (68437) 264/J4
Shubuta, Miss. (39360) 256/G7
Shue (creek), S. Dak. 298/N5
Shu'eib, Wadi (dry riv.), Jordan 65/D4
Shueyville, Iowa (†52401) 229/K5
Shu'fat, West Bank 65/C4
Shuicheng, China 77/G6
Shuksan (mt.), Wash. 310/D2
Shulan, China 77/L3
Shulerville, S.C. (29480) 296/H5
Shullsburg, Wis. (53586) 317/F10
Shumagin (isls.), Alaska 196/G4
Shumen, Bulgaria 45/H4
Shumerlya, U.S.S.R. 52/G3
Shumway, Ill. (62461) 222/E4
Shunat Nimrin, Jordan 65/D4
Shunchang, China 77/J6
Shungnak, Alaska (99773) 196/G1
Shungopavy (Shongopovi), Ariz. (†86043)198/E3
Shunk, Pa. (17768) 294/J2
Shunock (riv.), Conn. 210/H3
Shuo Xian, China 77/H4
Shuqaiq, Saudi Arabia 59/D6
Shuqra, P.D.R. Yemen 59/E7
Shuqualak, Miss. (39361) 256/G5
Shur (riv.), Iran 66/J7
Shusf, Iran 66/L5
Shush, Iran 66/F4
Shushan, N.Y. (12873) 276/O4
Shushenskoye, U.S.S.R. 48/K4
Shushtar, Iran 66/F4
Shushtar, Iran 59/E3
Shuswap (lake), Br. Col. 162/E5
Shuswap (lake), Br. Col. 184/H4
Shutesbury○, Mass. (01072) 249/E3
Shuttle Meadow (res.), Conn. 210/D2
Shutty Bench, Br. Col. 184/J5
Shuweika, West Bank 65/C3
Shuya, U.S.S.R. 52/F3
Shuyak (isl.), Alaska 196/H3
Shwebo, Burma 72/B2
Shwegyin, Burma 72/C3
Shweli (riv.), Burma 72/C2
Shwenyaung, Burma 72/C2
Shyok, India 68/D2
Si (riv.), China 54/N7
Siahan (mts.), Pakistan 59/H4
Siahan (range), Pakistan 68/A3
Siah Kuh (mt.), Iran 66/L3
Siak (riv.), Indonesia 85/C5
Siaksriinderapura, Indonesia 85/C5
Siakwan (Xiaguan), China 77/E6
Sialkot, Pakistan 68/C2
Sialkot, Pakistan 59/K3
Siam (Thailand) (gulf), Thailand 72/D5
Sian (Xi'an), China 77/G5
Siangfan (Xiangfan), China 77/H5
Siangtan (Xiangtan), China 77/H6
Siapa (riv.), Venezuela 124/E7
Siargao (isl.), Philippines 85/H4
Siargao (isl.), Philippines 82/F6
Siasconset, Mass. (02564) 249/P7
Siasi, Philippines 82/C8
Siasi (isl.), Philippines 82/C8
Siátista, Greece 45/E5
Siaton, Philippines 82/D6
Siaton (pt.), Philippines 82/D6
Siau (isl.), Indonesia 85/H5
Šiauliai, U.S.S.R. 7/G3
Šiauliai, U.S.S.R. 53/B3
Šiauliai, U.S.S.R. 52/B3
Šiauliai, U.S.S.R. 48/C4
Sib, Iran 66/N7
Sibalom, Philippines 82/C5
Sibanicú, Cuba 158/G3
Sibay (isl.), Philippines 82/C5
Sibay, U.S.S.R. 52/J4
Sibbald, Alberta 182/E4
Šibenik, Yugoslavia 45/C4
Siberia, Ind. (47582) 227/D8
Siberia (reg.), U.S.S.R. 4/C2
Siberia (reg.), U.S.S.R. 2/P2
Siberia (reg.), U.S.S.R. 54/M4
Siberia (reg.), U.S.S.R. 48/M3
Sibert, Ky. (†40962) 237/O6
Siberut (isl.), Indonesia 54/L10
Siberut (isl.), Indonesia 85/B6
Siberut (str.), Indonesia 85/B6
Sibi, Pakistan 68/B3
Sibi, Pakistan 59/J4
Sibiti, Congo 115/B4
Sibiu, Romania 7/G4
Sibiu, Romania 45/G3
Sibley, Ill. (61773) 222/E3
Sibley, Iowa (51249) 229/B2
Sibley, La. (71073) 238/D1
Sibley (co.), Minn. 255/D6
Sibley, Miss. (39165) 256/B8
Sibley, Mo. (64088) 261/S5
Sibley, N. Dak. (†58429) 282/P5
Sibley Prov. Park, Ontario 175/C3
Sibley Prov. Park, Ontario 177/H5
Sibolga, Indonesia 85/B5
Siboney, Cuba 158/J4
Sibsagar, India 68/H3
Sibu, Malaysia 85/E5
Sibu, Malaysia 54/N9
Sibube, C. Rica 154/F6
Sibuco, Philippines 82/C7
Sibuguey (bay), Philippines 82/D7
Sibundoy, Colombia 126/B7
Sibut, Cent. Afr. Rep. 115/C2
Sibutu (passage), Philippines 85/F4
Sibutu (passage), Philippines 82/B8
Sibutu Group (isls.), Philippines 82/B8
Sibuyan (isl.), Philippines 85/G3
Sibuyan (isl.), Philippines 82/D4
Sibuyan (sea), Philippines 82/D4
Sibuyan (sea), Philippines 85/G3
Sicamous, Br. Col. 184/H5
Sicasica, Bolivia 136/B5
Siccus (riv.), S. Australia 88/F6
Sichuan (Szechwan) (prov.), China 77/F5
Sicily (reg.), Italy 34/D6
Sicily (isl.), Italy 7/F5
Sicily (isl.), Italy 34/E6
Sicily (str.), Italy 34/D6
Sicily Island, La. (71368) 238/G3
Sicklerville, N.J. (08081) 273/D4
Sico (riv.), Honduras 154/E3
Sicuani, Peru 128/G10
Šid, Yugoslavia 45/D3
Sidamo (prov.), Ethiopia 111/G7
Siddipet, India 68/D5
Sideby, Finland 18/M5
Side Lake, Minn. (55781) 255/E3
Sidell, Ill. (61876) 222/F4
Siderno, Italy 34/F5
Sidewood, Sask. 181/C5
Sidheros (cape), Greece 45/H8
Sidhi, India 68/E4
Sidhirókastron, Greece 45/F5
Sidhpur, India 68/C4
Sidi Barrani, Egypt 111/E1
Sidi Barrani, Egypt 59/A3
Sidi Bel-Abbès, Algeria 106/D1
Sidi Bel Abbes, Algeria 102/C1
Sidi Ifni, Morocco 106/C2
Sidi Kacem, Morocco 106/C2
Siding Springs, N.S. Wales 97/E2
Sidlaw (hills), Scotland 15/E4
Sidley (mt.) 5/B12
Sidmouth, England 13/D7
Sidmouth, England 10/E5
Sidmouth (cape), Queensland 95/C2
Sidnaw, Mich. (49961) 250/G2
Sidney, Ark. (72577) 202/G1
Sidney, Br. Col. 184/K3
Sidney, Ill. (61877) 222/E3
Sidney, Ind. (46566) 227/F2
Sidney, Iowa (51652) 229/B7
Sidney○, Maine (†04330) 243/D7
Sidney, Manitoba 179/C5
Sidney, Mich. (48885) 250/D5
Sidney, Mont. (59270) 262/M3
Sidney, Nebr. (69162) 264/B3
Sidney, N.Y. (13838) 276/K6
Sidney, Ohio (45365) 284/B5
Sidney Center, N.Y. (13839) 276/K6
Sidney Lanier (lake), Georgia 217/D2
Sidoharjo, Indonesia 85/K2
Sidon, Ark. (†72137) 202/G3
Sidon (Saida), Lebanon 63/F6
Sidon, Miss. (38954) 256/D4
Sidonia, Tenn. (†38255) 237/D8
Sidra (gulf) 102/D1
Sidra (gulf), Libya 111/C1
Siedlce (prov.), Poland 47/F2
Siedlce, Poland 47/F2
Siegas, New Bruns. 170/C1
Siegburg, W. Germany 22/B3
Siegen, W. Germany 22/C3
Siemianowice Śląskie, Poland 47/B4
Siemiatycze, Poland 47/F2
Siempang, Cambodia 72/E4
Siemreab, Cambodia 72/D4
Siena (prov.), Italy 34/C3
Siena, Italy 34/C3
Sienyang (Xianyang), China 77/G5
Sieper, La. (71472) 238/E4
Sieradz (prov.), Poland 47/D3

Songhua Hu 449

Skull Valley Ind. Res., Utah 304/B3
Skuna (riv.), Miss. 256/F2
Skungamaug (riv.), Conn. 210/F1
Skunk (riv.), Iowa 229/K6
Skuteč, Czech. 41/D2
Skutskär, Sweden 18/K6
Skwentna, Alaska (99667) 196/B1
Skwentna (riv.), Alaska 196/A1
Skwierzyna, Poland 47/B2
Skye, Isle of (isl.), Scotland 15/B3
Skye (isl.), Scotland 10/C2
Skykomish, Wash. (98288) 310/D3
Skykomish (riv.), Wash. 310/D3
Skyland, N.C. (28776) 281/D4
Skylight (mt.), N.Y. 276/M2
Skyline, Minn. (†56001) 255/D6
Skyring (bay), Chile 138/E10
Skytop, Pa. (18357) 294/M3
Sky Valley, Georgia (30525) 217/F1
Slab Fork, W. Va. (25920) 312/D7
Slade, Ky. (40376) 237/O5
Sládečkovce, Czech. 41/D2
Slag (bay), Neth. Ant. 161/D8
Slagelse, Denmark 21/E7
Slagelse, Denmark 18/G9
Slagle, La. (71475) 238/D4
Slakow, Poland 47/B4
Slamannan, Scotland 15/C2
Slamet (mt.), Indonesia 85/J2
Slana, Alaska 196/K2
Slaná (riv.), Czech. 41/F2
Slane, Ireland 17/H4
Slanesville, W. Va. (25444) 312/K4
Slaney (riv.), Ireland 17/H7
Slangerup, Denmark 21/E6
Slangkop (pt.), S. Africa 118/E7
Slănic, Romania 45/G3
Slantsy, U.S.S.R. 52/C3
Slaný, Czech. 41/C1
Slate (mt.), Ariz. 198/D3
Slate (riv.), Colo. 208/E5
Slate (creek), Idaho 220/B4
Slate (isls.), Ontario 175/C3
Slate (riv.), Va. 307/L5
Slate, W. Va. (†26143) 312/D4
Slate (creek), Wyo. 319/C3
Slatedale, Pa. (18079) 294/L4
Slater, Colo. (81653) 208/E1
Slater, Iowa (50244) 229/F5
Slater, Mo. (65349) 261/G4
Slater, Wyo. (82201) 319/H4
Slater-Marietta, S.C. (29683) 296/C1
Slatersville, R.I. (02876) 249/H4
Slate Run, Pa. (17769) 294/H3
Slaterville Springs, N.Y. (14881) 276/H6
Slate Spring, Miss. (38955) 256/F3
Slatina, Romania 45/G3
Slatington, Pa. (18080) 294/L4
Slaton, Texas (79364) 303/C4
Slaughter, La. (70777) 238/H5
Slaughter Beach, Del. (†19963) 245/S5
Slaughters, Ky. (42456) 237/F6
Slaughterville, Okla. (†73051) 288/M4
Slave (riv.) 162/E3
Slave (riv.), Alberta 182/C5
Slave (riv.), Canada 146/G3
Slave (riv.), N.W. Terrs. 187/G3
Slave Coast (reg.), Benin 106/E7
Slave Coast (reg.), Nigeria 106/E7
Slave Coast (reg.), Togo 106/E7
Slave Lake, Alberta 182/C2
Slavgorod, U.S.S.R. 48/H4
Slavkov, Czech. 41/D2
Slavonia (reg.), Yugoslavia 45/C3
Slavonska Požega, Yugoslavia 45/C3
Slavonski Brod, Yugoslavia 45/D3
Slavuta, U.S.S.R. 52/C4
Slavyansk, U.S.S.R. 52/E5
Slavyansk-na-Kubani, U.S.S.R. 52/E5
Sławno, Poland 47/C1
Slayden, Miss. (†38642) 256/F1
Slayden, Tenn. (37165) 237/G8
Slayton, Minn. (56172) 255/C7
Sleaford, England 13/G5
Sleaford, England 10/F4
Sleat (dist.), Scotland 15/C3
Sleat (pt.), Scotland 15/B4
Sleat (sound), Scotland 15/C3
Sledge, Miss. (38670) 256/D2
Sleeper, Mo. (†65536) 261/G7
Sleeping Bear Dunes Nat'l Lakeshore, Mich. 250/C4
Sleeping Deer (mt.), Idaho 220/D5
Sleepy Creek, W. Va. (†25411) 312/K3
Sleepy Eye, Minn. (56085) 255/D6
Sleepy Eye (creek), Minn. 255/C6
Sleepy Hollow, Ill. (†60118) 222/E1
Sleetmute, Alaska (99668) 196/G2
Sleeve (lake), Manitoba 179/E3
Slemish (mt.), N. Ireland 17/J2
Slemon (lake), Manitoba 179/G1
Slemp, Ky. (41763) 237/P6
Slick, Okla. (74071) 288/O3
Slickford, Ky. (†42633) 237/M7
Slickville, Pa. (15684) 294/C5
Slide (mt.), N.Y. 276/L6
Slidell, La. (70458) 238/L6
Sliedrecht, Netherlands 27/F5
Sliema, Malta 34/E7
Slieve Anierin (mt.), Ireland 17/F3
Slieve Aughty (mts.), Ireland 17/D5
Slieve Beagh (mt.), N. Ireland 17/G3
Slieve Bernagh (mt.), Ireland 17/D6
Slieve Bloom (mts.), Ireland 17/F5
Slieve Callan (mt.), Ireland 17/C6
Slieve Car (mt.), Ireland 17/B3
Slieve Donard (mt.), N. Ireland 10/D3
Slieve Donard (mt.), N. Ireland 17/K3
Slieve Elva (mt.), Ireland 17/C5
Slievefelim (mts.), Ireland 17/E6
Slieve Gamph (mts.), Ireland 17/D3
Slieve Gullion (mt.), N. Ireland 17/J3
Slieve League (mt.), Ireland 17/D2
Slieve Mishkish (mts.), Ireland 17/B8
Slievenaman (mt.), Ireland 17/F7
Sligo (co.), Ireland 17/D3
Sligo, Ireland 17/E3
Sligo, Ireland 10/B3
Sligo (bay), Ireland 10/B3
Sligo (bay), Ireland 17/D3
Sligo, La. (†71037) 238/C2
Sligo, Pa. (16255) 294/C3
Slinger, Wis. (53086) 317/K9
Slipper (isl.), N. Zealand 100/F2
Slippery Rock, Pa. (16057) 294/B3
Slite, Sweden 18/L8
Sliven, Bulgaria 45/H4
Sliven, Bulgaria 7/G4
Sloan, Iowa (51055) 229/A4
Sloan, Nev. (†89114) 266/F7
Sloan, N.Y. (†14201) 276/C5
Sloans Valley, Ky. (42555) 237/N7
Sloat, Calif. (†96103) 204/E4
Sloatsburg, N.Y. (10974) 276/M8
Slobodskoy, U.S.S.R. 48/E4
Slobodskoy, U.S.S.R. 52/H3
Slobozia, Romania 45/H3
Slocan, Br. Col. 184/J5
Slocan (lake), Br. Col. 184/J5
Slocan Park, Br. Col. 184/J5
Slochteren, Netherlands 27/K2
Slocomb, Ala. (36375) 195/G8
Slocum, R.I. (02877) 249/H6
Slocum, Texas (†75839) 303/J6
Slonim, U.S.S.R. 52/B4
Slope (co.), N. Dak. 282/C7
Slot, The (chan.), Solomon Is. 86/D3
Sloten, Friesland, Netherlands 27/H3
Sloten, North Holland, Netherlands 27/B5
Sloterdijk, Netherlands 27/B4
Slotermeer (lake), Netherlands 27/H3
Slough, England 13/G8
Sloughhouse, Calif. (95683) 204/C8
Slovak Socialist Rep., Czech. 41/E2
Slovenia (rep.), Yugoslavia 45/B2
Slovenské Rudohorie (mts.), Czech. 41/E2
Słubice, Poland 47/B2
Sluis, Netherlands 27/C6
Słupca, Poland 47/D2
Słupia (riv.), Poland 47/C1
Słupsk (prov.), Poland 47/C1
Słupsk, Poland 47/C1
Słupsk, Poland 7/F3
Slutsk, U.S.S.R. 52/C4
Slyne (head), Ireland 10/A4
Slyne (head), Ireland 17/A5
Slyudyanka, U.S.S.R. 48/L4
Smackover, Ark. (71762) 202/E7
Smale, Ark. (†72021) 202/H4
Small, Idaho (†83423) 220/F5
Small (cape), Maine 243/D8
Small Isles (isls.), Scotland 15/B4
Small Point, Maine (04567) 243/D8
Smallwood (res.), Newf. 166/B3
Smallwood (res.), Newf. 146/M4
Smallwood (res.), Newf. 162/K5
Smarr, Georgia (31086) 217/E5
Smarts (mt.), N.H. 268/C4
Smartt, Tenn. (37378) 237/K9
Smartville, Calif. (95977) 204/D4
Smeaton, Sask. 181/G2
Smederevo, Yugoslavia 45/E3
Smederevska Palanka, Yugoslavia 45/E3
Smedjebacken, Sweden 18/J6
Smela, U.S.S.R. 52/D5
Smelterville, Idaho (83868) 220/B2
Smerwick (harb.), Ireland 17/A7
Smethport, Pa. (16749) 294/F2
Smicksburg, Pa. (16256) 294/D4
Smilax, Ky. (41764) 237/P6
Smilde, Netherlands 27/K3
Smiley, Sask. 181/B4
Smiley, Texas (78159) 303/G8
Smiltene, U.S.S.R. 53/C2
Smith (bay), Alaska 196/H1
Smith, Alberta 182/D2
Smith (sound), Br. Col. 184/C4
Smith (riv.), Calif. 204/A2
Smith (creek), Idaho 220/B1
Smith (co.), Kansas 232/D2
Smith (isl.), Md. 245/O8
Smith (co.), Miss. 256/E6
Smith (riv.), Mont. 262/E3
Smith, Nev. (89430) 266/B4
Smith (sound), Newf. 166/D2
Smith (isl.), N.C. 281/O7
Smith (basin), N.W.T. 162/N3
Smith (cape), N.W.T. 162/H3
Smith (bay), N.W. Terrs. 187/L2
Smith (cape), N.W. Terrs. 187/L3
Smith (sound), N.W. Terrs. 187/L2
Smith (cape), Ontario 177/C2
Smith (riv.), Oreg. 291/D4
Smith (creek), S. Dak. 298/L6
Smith (co.), Tenn. 237/J8
Smith (co.), Texas 303/J5
Smith (isl.), Va. 307/S6
Smith (riv.), Va. 307/J7
Smith Arm (inlet), N.W. Terrs. 187/F3
Smithboro, Ill. (62284) 222/D5
Smithburg, N.J. (†07728) 273/E3
Smithburg, W. Va. (26436) 312/E4
Smith Center, Kansas (66967) 232/D2
Smith Creek (valley), Nev. 266/D3
Smith Creek, W. Va. (†26807) 312/H5
Smithdale, Miss. (39664) 256/C8
Smithers, Br. Col. 146/F4
Smithers, Br. Col. 162/D5
Smithers, Br. Col. 184/D3
Smithers, W. Va. (25186) 312/D6
Smithfield, Ill. (61477) 222/C3
Smithfield, Ky. (40068) 237/L4
Smithfield○, Maine (04978) 243/D6
Smithfield, Nebr. (68976) 264/E4
Smithfield, N.C. (27577) 281/N3
Smithfield, Ohio (43948) 284/J5
Smithfield, Ontario 177/G3
Smithfield, Pa. (15478) 294/C6
Smithfield, Texas (†76180) 303/F2
Smithfield, Utah (84335) 304/C2
Smithfield, Va. (23430) 307/P7
Smithfield, W. Va. (26437) 312/E4
Smith Hill, Manitoba 179/C5
Smithland, Iowa (51056) 229/B4
Smithland, Ky. (42081) 237/E6
Smithmill, Pa. (16680) 294/F4
Smith Mills, Ky. (42457) 237/F5
Smith Mountain (lake), Va. 307/J6
Smithonia, Georgia (†30628) 217/F2
Smithport (lake), La. 238/C2
Smith River, Calif. (95567) 204/A2
Smiths, Ala. (36877) 195/H5
Smithsburg, Md. (21783) 245/H2
Smiths Cove, Nova Scotia 168/C4
Smiths Creek, Mich. (48074) 250/G6
Smiths Creek, New Bruns. 170/E3
Smiths Falls, Ontario 177/H3
Smiths Ferry, Idaho (†83611) 220/C5
Smiths Fork (riv.), Wyo. 319/B3
Smiths Grove, Ky. (42171) 237/J6
Smithshire, Ill. (61478) 222/C3
Smiths Station, Miss. (†39066) 256/C6
Smithton, Ark. (†71743) 202/D6
Smithton, Ill. (62285) 222/C5
Smithton, Mo. (65350) 261/F5
Smithton, Pa. (15479) 294/C5
Smithton, Tasmania 99/A2
Smithton, Tasmania 88/H8
Smith Town, Ky. (†42647) 237/M7
Smithtown, N.H. (†03874) 268/F6
Smithtown, N.Y. (11787) 276/O9
Smithtown-Gladstone, N.S. Wales 97/G2
Smith Valley, Ind. (†46142) 227/E5
Smithville, Ark. (72466) 202/H1
Smithville, Georgia (31787) 217/D7
Smithville, Ind. (47458) 227/D6
Smithville, Miss. (38870) 256/H2
Smithville, Mo. (64089) 261/D4
Smithville, N.J. (†08060) 273/D4
Smithville, N.J. (08201) 273/E5
Smithville, Ohio (44677) 284/G4
Smithville, Okla. (74957) 288/S6
Smithville, Ontario 177/E4
Smithville, Tenn. (37166) 237/K9
Smithville, Texas (78957) 303/G7
Smithville, W. Va. (26178) 312/D4
Smithville Flats, N.Y. (13841) 276/J6
Smithwick, S. Dak. (57782) 298/C7
Smoaks, S.C. (29481) 296/F5
Smoke Bend, La. (†70346) 238/K3
Smoke Creek (des.), Nev. 266/B2
Smoke Hole, W. Va. (†26866) 312/H5
Smokey Burn, Sask. 181/H2
Smoky (riv.), Alberta 182/A2
Smoky (riv.), Alta. 162/E5
Smoky (mts.), Idaho 220/D6
Smoky (cape), N.S. Wales 97/G2
Smoky (lake), N. Dak. 282/K3
Smoky (cape), Nova Scotia 168/H2
Smoky Bay, S. Australia 88/E6
Smoky Bay, S. Australia 94/D5
Smoky Hill (riv.) 188/G3
Smoky Hill (riv.), Colo. 208/P5
Smoky Hill, North Fork (riv.), Kansas 232/A2
Smoky Hill (riv.), Kansas 232/C3
Smoky Junction, Tenn. (†37827) 237/N8
Smoky Lake, Alberta 182/D2
Smøla (isl.), Norway 18/E5
Smolan, Kansas (67479) 232/E3
Smolensk, U.S.S.R. 7/H3
Smolensk, U.S.S.R. 48/D4
Smolensk, U.S.S.R. 52/D4
Smolyan, Bulgaria 45/G5
Smoot, W. Va. (24977) 312/E7
Smoot, Wyo. (83126) 319/B3
Smooth Rock Falls, Ontario 177/J5
Smooth Rock Falls, Ontario 175/D3
Smugglers Notch (pass), Vt. 268/B2
Smuts, Sask. 181/F3
Smyadovo, Bulgaria 45/H4
Smyer, Ala. (†36727) 195/B7
Smyrna, Del. (19977) 245/R3
Smyrna (res.), Del. 245/R3
Smyrna, Georgia (30080) 217/K1
Smyrna, Mich. (48887) 250/D5
Smyrna, N.Y. (13464) 276/J5
Smyrna, N.C. (28579) 281/R5
Smyrna, S.C. (29743) 296/E1
Smyrna, Tenn. (37167) 237/H9
Smyrna (Izmir), Turkey 63/B3
Smyrna, Wash. (†99357) 310/F4
Smyrna Mills, Maine (04780) 243/G3
Smyrna Mills○, Maine (04780) 243/G3
Smyth (co.), Va. 307/E7
Snaefell (mt.), I. of Man 13/C3
Snaefell (mt.), I. of Man 10/D3
Snake (riv.) 188/C1
Snake (riv.), Idaho 220/A3
Snake (riv.), Minn. 255/E3
Snake (riv.), Minn. 255/E4
Snake (riv.), Nebr. 264/C2
Snake (mts.), Nev. 266/F1
Snake (range), Nev. 266/G3
Snake (riv.), Oreg. 291/K3
Snake (creek), S. Dak. 298/F4
Snake (creek), S. Dak. 298/F5
Snake (creek), S. Dak. 298/M3
Snake (riv.), U.S. 146/G5
Snake (isl.), Victoria 97/D6
Snake (riv.), Wash. 310/G4
Snake (riv.), Wyo. 319/B2
Snake Creek (canal), Fla. 212/B4
Snake Indian (riv.), Alberta 182/A3
Snake River (plain), Idaho 220/D7
Snake River (range), Idaho 220/G6
Snake River, Wash. (†99301) 310/G4
Snare (riv.), N.W. Terrs. 187/G3
Snare Lake, N.W. Terrs. 187/G3
Snares, The (isls.), N. Zealand 100/A7
Snåsa, Norway 18/H4
Snåsavatn (lake), Norway 18/H4
Snead, Ala. (35952) 195/F2
Sneads, Fla. (32460) 212/B1
Sneads Ferry, N.C. (28460) 281/P5
Snedsted, Denmark 21/B4
Sneedville, Tenn. (37869) 237/P7
Sneek, Netherlands 27/H2
Sneekermeer (lake), Netherlands 27/H2
Sneem, Ireland 17/B8
Sneeuwkop (mt.), S. Africa 118/F6
Sneffels (mt.), Colo. 208/D7
Snegamook (lake), Newf. 166/B3
Snell, Va. (22553) 307/N4
Snelling, Calif. (95369) 204/E6
Snelling, S.C. (†29812) 296/E5
Snellville, Georgia (30278) 217/D3
Snezhnogorsk, U.S.S.R. 48/J3
Śniardwy, Jezioro (lake), Poland 47/E2
Sniečkus, U.S.S.R. 53/D3
Snina, Czech. 41/G2
Snipe (lake), Alberta 182/B2
Snipe Lake, Sask. 181/B4
Snizort, Loch (inlet), Scotland 15/B3
Snohomish (co.), Wash. 310/D2
Snohomish, Wash. (98290) 310/D3
Snohomish (riv.), Wash. 310/C3
Snoqualmie, Wash. (†98065) 310/D3
Snoqualmie (pass), Wash. 310/D3
Snoqualmie (riv.), Wash. 310/D3
Snoqualmie Falls, Wash. (†98065) 310/D3
Snover, Mich. (48472) 250/G5
Snow, Okla. (74567) 288/R6
Snow (mt.), Vt. 268/B6
Snow (peak), Wash. 310/G2
Snowball, Ark. (†72650) 202/E2
Snowbird (lake), N.W. Terrs. 187/H3
Snow Camp, N.C. (27349) 281/L3
Snowden, N.C. (†27929) 281/S2
Snowden, Sask. 181/G2
Snowdon (mt.), Wales 13/D4
Snowdon (mt.), Wales 10/D4
Snowdonia Nat'l Park, Wales 13/D4
Snowdoun, Ala. (†36104) 195/F6
Snowdrift, N.W.T. 162/E3
Snowdrift, N.W. Terrs. 187/G3
Snowfield (peak), Wash. 310/D2
Snowflake, Ariz. (85937) 198/E4
Snowflake, Manitoba 179/D5
Snow Hill, Ala. (36778) 195/E7
Snow Hill, Ark. (†71751) 202/E7
Snow Hill, Md. (21863) 245/S8
Snow Hill, N.C. (28580) 281/O4
Snow Lake, Ark. (72379) 202/H5
Snow Lake, Man. 162/G5
Snow Lake, Manitoba 179/H3
Snowmass, Colo. (81654) 208/E4
Snowshoe (lake), Manitoba 179/G4
Snow Shoe, Pa. (16874) 294/G3
Snowtown, S. Australia 94/E5
Snowville, N.H. (†03849) 268/E4
Snowville, Utah (84336) 304/B2
Snow Water (lake), Nev. 266/G2
Snowy (mts.), N.S. Wales 97/E5
Snowy (riv.), N.S. Wales 97/E5
Snowy (riv.), Victoria 88/H7
Snug, Tasmania 99/D5
Snyder, Ark. (†71658) 202/G7
Snyder, Colo. (80750) 208/M2
Snyder, Mo. (†65286) 261/F3
Snyder, Nebr. (68664) 264/H3
Snyder, Okla. (73566) 288/J5
Snyder (co.), Pa. 294/H4
Snyder, Texas (79549) 303/D5
Snydertown, Pa. (17877) 294/J4
So (isl.), S. Korea 81/C6
Soalala, Madagascar 118/H3
Soalara, Madagascar 118/G4
Soanierana-Ivongo, Madagascar 118/H3
Soap (lake), Wash. 310/F3
Soap Lake, Wash. (98851) 310/F3
Soasiu, Indonesia 85/H5
Soatá, Colombia 126/D4
Soay (isl.), Scotland 15/A2
Soay (isl.), Scotland 15/B3
Sobat (riv.), Sudan 111/F6
Sober (isl.), Nova Scotia 168/F4
Soběslav, Czech. 41/C2
Sobieski, Minn. (†56345) 255/D5
Sobieski, Wis. (54171) 317/L6
Sobotka, Czech. 41/C1
Sobral, Brazil 120/E3
Sobral, Brazil 132/G3
Sobrance, Czech. 41/G2
Soca, Uruguay 145/C6
Sochaczew, Poland 47/E2
Soche (Shache), China 77/A4
Sochi, U.S.S.R. 7/H4
Sochi, U.S.S.R. 48/D5
Sochi, U.S.S.R. 52/E6
Social Circle, Georgia (30279) 217/E3
Society (isls.), Fr. Poly. 87/L7
Society Hill, Ala. (†36801) 195/H6
Society Hill, S.C. (29593) 296/H2
Socompa (vol.), Chile 138/B4
Socorro, Brazil 135/C3
Socorro, Colombia 126/D4
Socorro (isl.), Mexico 150/D7
Socorro, N. Mex. 188/E4
Socorro (co.), N. Mex. 274/C5
Socorro, N. Mex. (87801) 274/C4
Socotra (isl.), P.D.R. Yemen 54/G8
Socotra (isl.), P.D.R. Yemen 2/M5
Socotra (isl.), P.D.R. Yemen 59/F7
Socuéllamos, Spain 33/E3
Soda (lake), Calif. 204/K8
Soda (plains), India 68/D1
Soda, Jebel es (mts.), Libya 111/C2
Soda Creek, Br. Col. 184/F4
Sodankylä, Finland 18/P3
Soda Plains, Pakistan 68/D1
Soda Springs, Calif. (95728) 204/E4
Soda Springs, Idaho (83276) 220/G7
Sodaville, Oreg. (†97355) 291/E3
Soddu, Ethiopia 111/G6
Soddy-Daisy, Tenn. (37319) 237/L10
Söderhamn, Sweden 18/K6
Söderköping, Sweden 18/K7
Södermanland (co.), Sweden 18/K7
Södertälje, Sweden 18/G1
Sodiri, Sudan 111/E5
Sodus, Mich. (49126) 250/C6
Sodus, N.Y. (14551) 276/G4
Sodus Point, N.Y. (14555) 276/G4
Soe, Indonesia 85/G7
Soest, Netherlands 27/G4
Soest, W. Germany 22/C3
Soesterberg, Netherlands 27/G4
Soeurs (isl.), Québec 172/J4
Sofala (prov.), Mozambique 118/E3
Sofia (cap.), Bulgaria 7/G4
Sofia (cap.), Bulgaria 45/F4
Sofia (riv.), Madagascar 118/H3
Sofkee, Georgia (†31201) 217/E5
Soft Shell, Ky. (41853) 237/P6
Sogamoso, Colombia 126/D5
Sogamoso (riv.), Colombia 126/D4
Soğanlı (mts.), Turkey 63/H2
Soğanlı (riv.), Turkey 63/E2
Sognafjorden (fjord), Norway 18/D6
Sognefjorden (fjord), Norway 7/E2
Sogn og Fjordane (co.), Norway 18/E6
Sogod, Philippines 82/E5
Sogod (bay), Philippines 82/E5
Söğüt, Turkey 63/D3
Söğüt (lake), Turkey 63/D4
Sog Xian, China 77/D5
Soh, Iran 66/G4
Sohâg, Egypt 111/F2
Sohâg, Egypt 59/B4
Sohâg, Egypt 102/F2
Soham, N. Mex. (†87565) 274/D3
Sohar, Oman 59/G5
Sŏhŭng, N. Korea 81/C4
Soignies, Belgium 27/D7
Sointula, Br. Col. 184/D5
Soissons, France 28/E3
Soka, Japan 81/O2
Sokch'o, S. Korea 81/D4
Söke, Turkey 63/B4
Söke, Turkey 59/A2
Sokna, Libya 111/C2
Sokodé, Togo 106/E7
Sokol, U.S.S.R. 52/F3
Sokol, U.S.S.R. 48/E4
Sokółka, Poland 47/F2
Sokolo, Mali 106/C6
Sokolov, Czech. 41/B1
Sokołów Podlaski, Poland 47/F2
Sokota, Ethiopia 111/G5
Sokoto (state), Nigeria 106/F6
Sokoto, Nigeria 102/C3
Sokoto, Nigeria 106/F6
Sokoto (riv.), Nigeria 106/E6
Sola, Cuba 158/G2
Solana Beach, Calif. (92075) 204/H11
Solander (isl.), N. Zealand 100/A7
Solano (co.), Calif. 204/D5
Solano (pt.), Colombia 126/B4
Solano, N. Mex. (87746) 274/E3
Solano, Philippines 82/C2
Solano, Venezuela 124/E6
Solbad Hall in Tirol, Austria 41/A3
Solca, Romania 45/G2
Soldado (pt.), P. Rico 161/G2
Soldier, Iowa (51572) 229/B5
Soldier, Kansas (66540) 232/G2
Soldier, Ky. (41173) 237/P4
Soldier Pond, Maine (04781) 243/F1
Soldiers Cove, Nova Scotia 168/H3
Soldiers Grove, Wis. (54655) 317/E9
Soldier Summit, Utah (†84601) 304/C4
Soldotna, Alaska (99669) 196/B1
Soledad, Argentina 143/F5
Soledad, Calif. (93960) 204/D7
Soledad, Colombia 126/C2
Soledad, Venezuela 124/G3
Soledad de Doblado, Mexico 150/Q2
Soledad Díez Gutiérrez, Mexico 150/J5
Soleduck (riv.), Wash. 310/A3
Solen, N. Dak. (58570) 282/J7
Solent (chan.), England 13/F7
Solentiname (isls.), Nicaragua 154/E5
Soleure (Solothurn) (canton), Switzerland 39/E2
Solgohachia, Ark. (72156) 202/E3
Solhan, Turkey 63/J3
Soligalich, U.S.S.R. 52/F3
Soligorsk, U.S.S.R. 52/C4
Solihull, England 13/F5
Solihull, England 10/G3
Solikamsk, U.S.S.R. 7/K3
Solikamsk, U.S.S.R. 48/F3
Solikamsk, U.S.S.R. 52/J3
Sol'-Iletsk, U.S.S.R. 52/J4
Solingen, W. Germany 22/B3
Solís, Uruguay 145/D5
Solís de Mataojo, Uruguay 145/D5
Solitary (isl.), N.S. Wales 97/G1
Sollefteå, Sweden 18/K5
Sollentuna, Sweden 18/H1
Sóller, Spain 33/H3
Søllested, Denmark 21/E8
Solna, Sweden 18/H1
Solo (Surakarta), Indonesia 85/J2
Solo, Mo. (65564) 261/J8
Sologne (reg.), France 28/E4
Solok, Indonesia 85/C6
Sololá, Guatemala 154/B3
Solomon (sea) 87/F6
Solomon, Alaska (†99762) 196/F2
Solomon, Ariz. (85551) 198/F6
Solomon, Kansas (67480) 232/E3
Solomon (riv.), Kansas 232/E2
Solomon (isls.), Pacific 87/F6
Solomon (isls.), Papua N.G. 86/C3
Solomon (sea), Papua N.G. 85/C7
Solomon (isls.), Solomon Is. 86/C3
Solomon (sea), Solomon Is. 86/D3
Solomon Islands 2/T6
SOLOMON ISLANDS 86/D2
Solomon Islands 87/G6
Solomons, Md. (20688) 245/N7
Solon, China 77/K2
Solon, Ind. (†47111) 227/F7
Solon, Iowa (52333) 229/L5
Solon○, Maine (04979) 243/D6
Solon, Ohio (44139) 284/J9
Solon Springs, Wis. (54873) 317/C3
Solor (isl.), Indonesia 85/G7
Solothurn (elec. div.), Switzerland 39/E2
Solothurn (Soleure), Switzerland 39/E2
Solovetskiye (isls.), U.S.S.R. 52/E1
Solsberry, Ind. (47459) 227/D6
Solsgirth, Manitoba 179/B4
Solsona, Philippines 82/C1
Solsona, Spain 33/G2
Solt, Hungary 41/E3
Šolta (isl.), Yugoslavia 45/C4
Soltau, W. Germany 22/C2
Soltvadkert, Hungary 41/E3
Soluk, Libya 111/D1
Solund, Norway 18/D6
Solvang, Calif. (93463) 204/E9
Solvay, N.Y. (13209) 276/H4
Sölvesborg, Sweden 18/J9
Solway (firth), England 13/D3
Solway, Minn. (56678) 255/C3
Solway (firth), Scotland 10/D3
Solway (firth), Scotland 15/E6
Solwezi, Zambia 115/E6
Soma, Japan 81/K5
Soma, Turkey 63/B3
Somabula, Zimbabwe 118/D3
Somalia 2/M5
Somalia 102/G4
SOMALIA 115/J2
Sombor, Yugoslavia 45/D3
Sombra, Ontario 177/B5
Sombrerete, Mexico 150/H5
Sombrero (chan.), India 68/G7
Sombrero (isl.), St. Chris.-Nevis 156/F3
Somerdale, N.J. (08083) 273/B4
Somers, Conn. (06071) 210/F1
Somers○, Conn. (06071) 210/F1
Somers, Iowa (50586) 229/E4
Somers, Mont. (59932) 262/B2
Somers, Wis. (53171) 317/M3
Somerset, (22972) 307/M4
Somerset (isl.), Bermuda 156/G3
Somerset (isl.), Canada 4/B14
Somerset, Colo. (81434) 208/E5
Somerset (co.), England 13/E6
Somerset, Ind. (46984) 227/F3
Somerset, Ky. (42501) 237/M6
Somerset, La. (†71357) 238/H2
Somerset (co.), Maine 243/C4
Somerset, Manitoba 179/D5
Somerset (co.), Md. 245/R8
Somerset, Md. (†20015) 245/E4
Somerset○, Mass. (02725) 249/K5
Somerset (co.), N.J. 273/D2
Somerset, N.Y. (†14012) 276/C4
Somerset (isl.), N.W.T. 146/J2
Somerset (isl.), N.W.T. 162/G1
Somerset (isl.), N.W. Terrs. 187/J2
Somerset, Nova Scotia 168/D3
Somerset, Ohio (43783) 284/F6
Somerset (co.), Pa. 294/D6
Somerset, Pa. (15501) 294/D6
Somerset, Texas (78069) 303/J11
Somerset (res.), Vt. 268/A5
Somerset, Wis. (54025) 317/A5
Somerset East, S. Africa 118/D6
Somerset West, S. Africa 118/F6
Somers Point, N.J. (08244) 273/D5
Somersville, Conn. (06072) 210/F1
Somersworth, N.H. (03878) 268/F5
Somerton, Ariz. (85350) 198/A6
Somerton, England 13/E6
Somerton, Ohio (43784) 284/H6
Somervell (co.), Texas 303/G5
Somerville, Ala. (35670) 195/E2
Somerville, Ind. (47683) 227/C8
Somerville○, Maine (†04341) 243/D7
Somerville, Mass. (02143) 249/C6
Somerville, New Bruns. 170/C2
Somerville, N.J. (08876) 273/D2
Somerville, Ohio (45064) 284/A6
Somerville, Tenn. (38068) 237/C10
Somerville, Texas (77879) 303/H7
Somes (isl.), N. Zealand 100/B2
Someş (riv.), Romania 45/F2
Somesbar, Calif. (95568) 204/B2
Somesville (Mount Desert), Maine (†04660) 243/G7
Somme (dept.), France 28/E3
Somme (riv.), France 28/D2
Somme, Sask. 181/J3
Somme-Leuze, Belgium 27/G8
Sommen (lake), Sweden 18/J8
Sömmerda, E. Germany 22/D3
Somogy (co.), Hungary 41/D3
Somonauk, Ill. (60552) 222/E2
Somotillo, Nicaragua 154/D4
Somoto, Nicaragua 154/D4
Somvix, Switzerland 39/G3
Son (riv.), India 68/E3
Son, Norway 18/D4
Son, Con (isls.), Vietnam 72/E5
Soná, Panama 154/G6
Sonaguera, Honduras 154/D3
Sŏnch'ŏn, N. Korea 81/B4
Sønderborg, Denmark 21/C8
Sønderborg, Denmark 18/G9
Sønderho, Denmark 21/B7
Sønderjylland (co.), Denmark 21/C7
Sønder Nissum, Denmark 21/A5
Sønder Omme, Denmark 21/B6
Sondershausen, E. Germany 22/D3
Søndersø, Denmark 21/D7
Sondheimer, La. (71276) 238/H1
Søndre Strømfjord, Greenl. 4/C12
Sondrio (prov.), Italy 34/B1
Sondrio, Italy 34/B1
Sonepur, India 68/E4
Sonestown, Pa. (17770) 294/K3
Song Ba (riv.), Vietnam 72/F4
Song Ca (riv.), Vietnam 72/E3
Song Cai (riv.), Vietnam 72/E4
Song Cau, Vietnam 72/F4
Song Da (Black) (riv.), Vietnam 72/E2
Songea, Tanzania 115/G6
Songea, Tanzania 102/F6
Song Hong (Red) (riv.), Vietnam 72/E2
Songhua (riv.), China 54/P5
Songhua Hu (lake), China 77/L3

Songhua Jiang (Sungari) (riv.), China 77/M2
Songkhla, Thailand 54/L9
Songkhla, Thailand 72/D6
Songnim, N. Korea 81/B4
Songo, Angola 115/C5
Songo, Angola 102/D5
Songo, Mozambique 118/E3
Songololo, Zaire 115/B5
Songololo, Zaire 102/D5
Songpan, China 77/F5
Songxi, China 77/J6
Son Ha, Vietnam 72/F4
Sonid Youqi, China 77/H3
Sonid Zuoqi, China 77/H3
Son La, Vietnam 72/D2
Sonmiani, Pakistan 68/B3
Sonmiani, Pakistan 59/J4
Sonneberg, E. Germany 37/H3
Sonnehorn (mt.), Switzerland 39/F4
Sonnette, Mont. (59348) 262/L5
Sonningdale, Sask. 181/D3
Sono (riv.), Brazil 132/E5
Sonobe, Japan 81/J7
Sonoita, Ariz. (85637) 198/E7
Sonoma (co.), Calif. 204/C3
Sonoma, Calif. (95476) 204/C5
Sonoma (range), Nev. 266/D2
Sonora (state), Mexico 150/D2
Sonora, Calif. (95370) 204/E6
Sonora, Ky. (42776) 237/K5
Sonora (state), Mexico 150/D2
Sonora (riv.), Mexico 150/D2
Sonora, Nova Scotia 168/G3
Sonora, Texas (76950) 303/D7
Sonoyta, Mexico 150/C1
Sonqor, Iran 66/E3
Sonseca, Spain 33/D3
Sonsón, Colombia 126/C5
Sonsorol, El Salvador 154/C4
Sonsorol (isl.), Belau 87/D5
Sontag, Miss. (39665) 256/D7
Son Tay, Vietnam 72/E2
Sonthofen, W. Germany 37/G5
Sonvico, Switzerland 39/G4
Soochow (Suzhou), China 77/K5
Sooke, Br. Col. 184/J4
Sopachuy, Bolivia 136/C6
Sopas, Arroyo (riv.), Uruguay 145/C2
Sopchoppy, Fla. (32358) 212/B1
Soper, Okla. (74759) 288/P6
Soperton, Georgia (30457) 217/G6
Sopetrán, Colombia 126/C4
Sophia, Ind. (27350) 281/K3
Sophia, W. Va. (25921) 312/D7
Sophie, Fr. Guiana 131/E4
Sopi (cape), Indonesia 85/H5
Sopot, Poland 47/D1
Sopron, Hungary 41/D3
Soquel, Calif. (95073) 204/K4
Sora, Italy 34/D4
Sorah, Pakistan 68/B3
Sorata, Bolivia 136/A4
Sorbas, Spain 33/E4
Sorcière, La (mt.), St. Lucia 161/G6
Sorel, Québec 172/D4
Sorell (cape), Tasmania 99/B4
Sorell (lake), Tasmania 99/B4
Sorell-Midway Point, Tasmania 99/D4
Sorento, Ill. (62086) 222/D5
Soresina, Italy 34/C2
Sorgun, Turkey 63/F3
Soria (prov.), Spain 33/E2
Soria, Spain 33/E2
Soriano (dept.), Uruguay 145/B4
Soriano, Uruguay 145/A4
Sorikmerapi (mt.), Indonesia 85/B5
Sérkapp (pt.), Norway 18/C2
Soré, Denmark 21/E7
Sorocaba, Brazil 132/B8
Sorocaba, Brazil 120/E5
Sorocaba, Brazil 132/E5
Sorochinsk, U.S.S.R. 52/H4
Sorol (atoll), Micronesia 87/D5
Sorong, Indonesia 54/P10
Sorong, Indonesia 85/H3
Soroti, Uganda 117/B3
Söröya (isl.), Norway 7/G1
Soréya (isl.), Norway 18/N1
Sorrento, Br. Col. 184/H5
Sorrento, Fla. (32776) 212/E3
Sorrento, Italy 34/E4
Sorrento, La. (70778) 238/L3
Sorrento○, Maine (04677) 243/G7
Sorsele, Sweden 18/K4
Sorsogon (prov.), Philippines 82/E4
Sorsogon, Philippines 82/E4
Sorsogon, Philippines 85/G3
Sort, Spain 33/G1
Sortavala, U.S.S.R. 48/C3
Sortavala, U.S.S.R. 52/C5
Sér-Tréndelag (co.), Norway 18/G5
Sorum, S. Dak. (57654) 298/D3
Sosan, S. Korea 81/B4
Sos del Rey Católico, Spain 33/F1
Sosnogorsk, U.S.S.R. 52/K2
Sosnogorsk, U.S.S.R. 48/F3
Sosnovka, U.S.S.R. 52/F4
Sosnovo-Ozerskoye, U.S.S.R. 48/M4
Sosnowiec, Poland 47/B4
Soso, Miss. (39480) 256/F7
Sosúa, Dom. Rep. 158/E5
Sosumav, Madagascar 118/H2
Sotkamo, Finland 18/Q4
Soto la Marina, Mexico 150/L4
Sotomayor, Bolivia 136/C6
Sotrondio, Spain 33/D1
Sotteville-lès-Rouen, France 28/D3
Sotuta, Mexico 150/P6
Souanké, Congo 115/B3
Soubey, Switzerland 39/F3
Soudan, Ark. (†72360) 202/J4
Soudan, Minn. (55782) 255/F3
Soudan, North. Terr. 93/E6

Souderton, Pa. (18964) 294/M5
Souf (oasis), Algeria 106/F2
Souflion, Greece 45/H5
Soufrière, Dominica 161/E7
Soufrière (bay), Dominica 161/E7
Soufrière, St. Lucia 161/F6
Soufrière (mt.), Guadeloupe 161/A7
Soufrière, St. Lucia 156/G4
Soufrière (bay), St. Lucia 161/F6
Soufrière (mt.), St. Vin. & Grens. 161/A8
Souhegan (riv.), N.H. 268/D6
Souillac, Mauritius 118/G5
Souk Ahras, Algeria 106/F1
Soul (lake), Manitoba 179/C2
Soulanges (co.), Québec 172/C4
Sounding (creek), Alberta 182/E4
Sourdeaunahunk (lake), Maine 243/F3
Sourdough, Alaska (†99586) 196/J2
Soure, Brazil 132/D3
Soure, Portugal 33/B2
Souris, Man. 162/F6
Souris, Manitoba 179/B5
Souris (riv.), Manitoba 179/B5
Souris (riv.), N. Dak. 188/F1
Souris, N. Dak. (58783) 282/J2
Souris (riv.), N. Dak. 282/J2
Souris, P.E.I. 166/E2
Souris (riv.), Sask. 181/H6
Souris, Pr. Edward I. 168/F2
Sour Lake, Texas (77659) 303/K7
Sousa, Brazil 120/F3
Sousel, Portugal 33/C3
Sousse, Tunisia 102/D1
Sousse, Tunisia 106/G1
Soustons, France 28/C6
South, Ala. (†36474) 195/E8
South (pt.), Barbados 161/B9
South (riv.), Georgia 217/K2
South (sound), Ireland 17/C5
South, Ky. (42777) 237/J6
South (pt.), La. 238/M8
South (riv.), Mass. 249/D2
South (bay), Mich. 250/C2
South (chan.), Mich. 250/F4
South (pt.), Mich. 250/F4
South (isl.), N. Zealand 87/G10
South (cape), N. Zealand 100/A7
South (isl.), N. Zealand 100/B5
South (riv.), N.C. 281/M4
South (bay), N.W. Terrs. 187/K3
South (riv.), Ontario 177/C2
South (mt.), Pa. 294/H6
South (isl.), S.C. 296/F3
South (cape), Tasmania 99/C5
South Acton, Maine (†04027) 243/B8
South Acton, Mass. (†01720) 249/J3
South Acworth, N.H. (03607) 268/C5
South Addison, Maine (†04606) 243/H6
South Africa 2/L7
South Africa 102/E7
SOUTH AFRICA 118/C5
South Alexandria, N.H. (†03222) 268/D4
South Allan, Sask. 181/E4
South Alligator (riv.), North. Terr. 88/E2
South Alligator (riv.), North. Terr. 93/C2
Southam, N. Dak. (†58327) 282/N3
South Amana, Iowa (52334) 229/J5
South Amboy, N.J. (08879) 273/E3
South America 2/D6
South Amherst, Mass. (†01002) 249/E3
South Amherst, Ohio (†44001) 284/F3
Southampton, England 7/D3
Southampton, England 10/F5
Southampton, England 13/J8
Southampton○, Mass. (01073) 249/C4
Southampton, N.Y. (11968) 276/R9
Southampton (isl.), N.W.T. 162/H2
Southampton (cape), N.W. Terrs. 187/K3
Southampton (isl.), N.W. Terrs. 187/K3
Southampton, Nova Scotia 168/D3
Southampton, Ontario 177/C3
Southampton (co.), Va. 307/O7
South Andaman (isl.), India 68/G6
South Anna (riv.), Va. 307/N5
Southard, Okla. (73770) 288/K2
South Ashburnham, Mass. (01466) 249/G2
South Athol, Mass. (01331) 249/F2
South Atlantic Ocean 2/J6
South Aulatsivik (isl.), Newf. 166/B2
South Australia 88/F6
South Australia (state), Australia 87/D8
Southaven, Miss. (38671) 256/E1
South Bancroft, Maine (†04424) 243/G4
Southbank, Br. Col. 184/E3
South Barre, Mass. (01074) 249/F3
South Barre, Vt. (05670) 268/B3
South Barrington, Ill. (†60010) 222/A5
South Barwon, Victoria 97/C6
South Bay (isl.), Ohio 284/E2
South Bay Aqueduct, Calif. 204/L2
South Baymouth, Ontario 177/B2
Southbeach, Oreg. (97366) 291/C3
South Belmar, N.J. (†07719) 273/E3
South Beloit, Ill. (61080) 222/E1
South Bend, Ind. 188/J2
South Bend, Ind. (†46601) 227/E1
South Bend, Nebr. (68058) 264/H4
South Bend, Texas (76081) 303/F5
South Bend, Wash. (98586) 310/B4
South Bennettsville, S.C. (†29512) 296/H2
South Bentinck Arm (inlet), Br. Col. 184/D4
South Berlin, Mass. (01549) 249/H3
South Berwick, Maine (03908) 243/B9
South Berwick○, Maine (03908) 243/B9

South Bethany, Del. (†19930) 245/T6
South Bethlehem, N.Y. (12161) 276/N5
South Bethlehem, Pa. (†16242) 294/D4
South Beveland (isl.), Netherlands 27/D6
South Bloomfield, Ohio (†43103) 284/D6
South Bloomingville, Ohio (43152) 284/E7
South Boardman, Mich. (49680) 250/D4
South Bolton, Québec 172/E4
Southborough, England 13/H8
Southborough○, Mass. (01772) 249/H3
South Boston (I.C.), Québec 307/L7
South Boston (pt.) (†47167) 227/H7
South Bound Brook, N.J. (08880) 273/E2
South Braintree, Mass. (†02185) 249/D8
South Branch, Mich. (48761) 250/E4
South Branch, Minn. (†56081) 255/D7
South Branch, N. Bruns. 170/F2
South Branch, Newf. 166/B4
South Branch, N.J. (†08876) 273/D2
South Branch Oromocto (riv.), New Bruns. 170/D3
Southbridge, Mass. (01550) 249/G4
Southbridge○, Mass. (01550) 249/G4
Southbridge, N. Zealand 100/D5
South Bridgton, Maine (†04009) 243/B8
South Bristol○, Maine (04568) 243/D8
South Britain, Conn. (06487) 210/B3
South Broadway, Wash. (†98901) 310/E4
South Brook, Green Bay Dist., Newf. 166/C4
South Brook, Humber Dist., Newf. 166/C4
South Brookfield, Nova Scotia 168/D4
South Brooksville, Maine (†04617) 243/F7
South Brunswick○, N.J. (†08852) 273/E3
South Bruny (isl.), Tasmania 99/D5
South Burlington, Vt. (05401) 268/A3
South Burro (mt.), Utah 304/D3
Southbury○, Conn. (06488) 210/C3
South Calling Lake, Alberta 182/D2
South Canaan, Conn. (†06031) 210/B1
South Carolina 188/K4
SOUTH CAROLINA 296
South Carolina (state), U.S. 146/K6
South Carrollton, Ky. (42374) 237/H6
South Carthage, Tenn. (†37030) 237/K8
South Carver, Mass. (02366) 249/M5
South Casco, Maine (04077) 243/B8
South Central (sen. dist.), Alaska 196/G3
South Charleston, Ohio (45368) 284/C6
South Charleston, W. Va. (25303) 312/C4
South Chatham, Mass. (02659) 249/O6
South Chatham, N.H. (†04037) 268/E3
South Cheyenne (riv.), Wyo. 319/H2
South Chicago Heights, Ill. (60411) 222/D6
South China (sea) 54/N8
South China (sea) 2/Q5
South China (sea), China 77/J7
South China (sea), Indonesia 85/D4
South China (sea), Malaysia 85/D4
South China (sea), Philippines 85/D4
South China (sea), Philippines 82/B3
South China (sea), Vietnam 72/F4
South Cle Elum, Wash. (98943) 310/D3
South Cleveland, Tenn. (37311) 237/M10
South Clinton, Tenn. (37716) 237/N8
South Coffeyville, Okla. (74072) 288/P1
South Colby, Wash. (98384) 310/A2
South Colton, N.Y. (13687) 276/L1
South Congaree, S.C. (†29169) 296/E4
South Connellsville, Pa. (15425) 294/C4
South Corning, N.Y. (14830) 276/F6
South Cotabato (prov.), Philippines 82/E7
South Coventry (Coventry), Conn. (†06238) 210/F1
South Cow (creek), Calif. 204/C3
South Dakota 188/F2
SOUTH DAKOTA 298
South Dakota (state), U.S. 146/H5
South Danbury, N.H. (†03230) 268/D5
South Danville, Ill. (38881) 268/E6
South Dartmouth, Mass. (02748) 249/L6
South Dayton, N.Y. (14138) 276/C6
South Daytona, Fla. (32021) 212/F2
South Deerfield, Mass. (01373) 249/D3
South Deerfield, N.H. (03037) 268/E5
South Dennis, Mass. (02660) 249/O6
South Dennis, N.J. (08245) 273/D5
South Dorset, Vt. (05263) 268/A5
South Dos Palos, Calif. (93665) 204/E7
South Downs (hills), England 13/G7
South Dum Dum, India 68/F2
South Duxbury, Mass. (†02332) 249/M4
Southeast (cape), Alaska 196/E2
South East (cape), Australia 87/E10
Southeast (pt.), Jamaica 158/K6
South East (pass), La. 238/M8
South East (cape), Tasmania 88/H8
South East (pt.), Victoria 97/D6
SOUTHEAST ASIA 85
Southeastern (sen. dist.), Alaska 196/L3
Southeast Loch (inlet), Hawaii 218/B3
Southeast Upsalquitch (riv.), New Bruns. 170/D1
South Effingham, N.H. (03882) 268/E4
South Egremont, Mass. (01258) 249/A4
South Elgin, Ill. (60177) 222/C4
South Eliot, Maine (†03903) 243/B9
South El Monte, Calif. (91733) 204/C10
Southend, Scotland 15/C5
Southend-on-Sea, England 10/G5

Southend-on-Sea, England 13/H6
South English, Iowa (52335) 229/J6
Southern (dist.), Israel 65/B5
Southern Alps (range), N. Zealand 100/C5
Southern Cross, Mont. (†59711) 262/C4
Southern Cross, W. Australia 88/E6
Southern Cross, W. Australia 92/B5
Southern Harbour, Newf. 166/C2
Southern Indian (lake), Man. 162/G4
Southern Indian (lake), Man. 146/J4
Southern Indian (lake), Manitoba 179/H2
Southern Leyte (prov.), Philippines 82/E5
Southern Pines, N.C. (28387) 281/L4
Southern Ute Ind. Res., Colo. 208/D8
Southesk (riv.), Scotland 15/F4
Southesk Tablelands, W. Australia 92/D3
Southey, Sask. 181/G5
South Fallsburg, N.Y. (12779) 276/L7
Southfield, Mass. (†01259) 249/B4
Southfield, Mich. (*48034) 250/F6
Southfields, N.Y. (10975) 276/M8
South Flomaton, Fla. (†36441) 212/B5
Southford, Conn. (†06488) 210/C3
South Foreland (prom.), England 13/J6
South Fork, Colo. (81154) 208/F7
South Fork, Frenchman, Colo. 208/01
South Fork, Mo. (65776) 261/J9
South Fork, Flathead (riv.), Mont. 262/C3
South Fork, Humboldt (riv.), Nev. 266/F2
South Fork, Owyhee (riv.), Nev. 266/E1
South Fork, Pa. (15956) 294/E5
South Fork, Sask. 181/C6
South Fork, Powder (riv.), Wyo. 319/F2
South Fork, Shoshone (riv.), Wyo. 319/C1
South Foster, R.I. (†02857) 249/H5
South Fowl (lake), Minn. 255/G1
South Fox (isl.), Mich. 250/D3
South Friars (bay), St. Chris.-Nevis 161/C10
South Fulton, Tenn. (†42041) 237/D8
South Gate, Calif. (90280) 204/C11
South Gate, Ky. (41071) 237/T2
South Gate, Md. (†21113) 245/M4
South Gate, Mich. (48195) 250/F6
South Georgia (isl.) 2/H8
South Georgia (isl.), Ant. 5/D17
South Gifford, Mo. (†63549) 261/G2
South Glamorgan, Wales 13/A7
South Glastonbury, Conn. (06073) 210/E2
South Glens Falls, N.Y. (†12801) 276/N4
South Goldsboro, N.C. (†27530) 281/N4
South Grafton, Mass. (01560) 249/H4
South Greenfield, Mo. (65752) 261/E8
South Groveland, Mass. (†01830) 249/L2
South Hadley○, Mass. (†01075) 249/D4
South Hadley Falls, Mass. (01075) 249/D4
Southhampton (isl.), N.W.T. 146/K3
Southhampton, N.H. (†01913) 268/F5
South Hanover, Mass. (†02339) 249/L4
South Harbour, Nova Scotia 168/H2
South Harpswell, Maine (04079) 243/C8
South Harwich, Mass. (02661) 249/O6
South Haven, Kansas (67143) 232/E4
South Haven, Mich. (49090) 250/C6
South Haven, Minn. (55382) 255/D5
South Haven, Nova Scotia 168/H2
South Hazelton, Br. Col. 184/D2
South Heart, N. Dak. (58655) 282/D6
South Heights, Pa. (15081) 294/B4
South Hero○, Vt. (†05486) 268/A2
South Hill, Va. (23970) 307/M7
South Hiram, Maine (04080) 243/B8
South Holland, Ill. (60473) 222/C6
South Holland (prov.), Netherlands 27/E5
South Holston (lake), Tenn. 237/S7
South Holston (lake), Va. 307/F7
South Hope, Maine (†04862) 243/E7
South Houston, Texas (77587) 303/J2
South Hutchinson, Kansas (†67501) 232/D3
South Indian Lake, Manitoba 179/H2
Southington○, Conn. (06489) 210/D2
South International Falls, Minn. (56679) 255/E2
South Irvine, Ky. (†40336) 237/N5
South Jacksonville, Ill. (†62650) 222/C4
South Jordan, Utah (†84065) 304/B3
South Junction, Manitoba 179/G5
South Junction, Oreg. (†97037) 291/F3
South Kedgwick (riv.), New Bruns. 170/B1
South Kensington, Md. (†20795) 245/E4
South Kent, Conn. (06785) 210/B2
South Killingly, Conn. (†06239) 210/H1
South Knife (riv.), Manitoba 179/J2
South Knife Lake, Manitoba 179/J2
South Korea 54/O6
South La Grange, Maine (†04453) 243/F5
Southlake, Texas (76051) 303/F2
South Lake Tahoe, Calif. (95705) 204/F5
South Lancaster, Mass. (01561) 249/H3
South Laurel, Md. (†20810) 245/L4
South Lead Hill, Ark. (†72644) 202/D1
South Lebanon, Maine (†03901) 243/A9
South Lebanon, Ohio (45065) 284/B7
South Lee, Mass. (01260) 249/A3
South Lee, N.H. (†03042) 268/E5
South Liberty, Maine (†04949) 243/E7

South Lincoln, Maine (†04457) 243/F5
South Lincoln, Vt. (†05443) 268/B3
South Londonderry, Vt. (05155) 268/B5
South Loup (riv.), Nebr. 264/E3
South Luconia (shoal), Philippines 85/G4
South Lunenburg, Vt. (05908) 268/D3
South Lyme, Conn. (06376) 210/F3
South Lyndeboro, N.H. (03082) 268/D6
South Lynnfield, Mass. (†01940) 249/D5
South Lyon, Mich. (48178) 250/F6
South Magnetic Pole, Ant. 2/B9
South Magnetic Pole, Ant. 5/C8
South Maitland, Nova Scotia 168/E3
South Manitou, Mich. (†49654) 250/C3
South Manitou (isl.), Mich. 250/C3
South Mansfield, La. (†71052) 238/C3
South Marsh (isl.), Md. 245/O8
South Mayo (riv.), Va. 307/H7
South Medford, Oreg. (†97501) 291/E5
South Melbourne, Victoria 97/J5
South Melbourne, Victoria 88/K7
South Merrimack, N.H. (03083) 268/D6
South Miami, Fla. (33143) 212/B5
South Miami Heights, Fla. (†33157) 212/F6
South Middleboro, Mass. (02346) 249/L5
South Milford, Ind. (46786) 227/G1
South Mills, N.C. (27976) 281/S2
South Milwaukee, Wis. (53172) 317/M2
South Molton, England 10/E5
South Molton, England 13/D6
South Monmouth, Maine (†04259) 243/D7
South Monroe, Mich. (†48161) 250/F7
South Mound, Kansas (†67357) 232/G4
South Mountain, Ontario 177/J3
South Mountain, Pa. (17261) 294/H6
South Nahanni (riv.), N.W. Terrs. 187/F3
South Naknek, Alaska (99670) 196/G3
South Natick, Mass. (†01760) 249/A7
South Natuna (isls.), Indonesia 85/D5
South Negril (pt.), Jamaica 158/B3
South Negril (pt.), Jamaica 156/B3
South New Berlin, N.Y. (13843) 276/K5
South Newbury, N.H. (03272) 268/D5
South Newbury, Vt. (05066) 268/C3
South Newfane, Vt. (05351) 268/B6
South Newport, Georgia (†31323) 217/K7
South New River (canal), Fla. 212/F5
South Norfolk, Conn. (†06058) 210/C1
South Norwalk, Conn. (06850) 210/B4
South Nyack, N.Y. (10960) 276/K8
South Ogden, Utah (†84403) 304/C2
South Ohio, Nova Scotia 168/B5
South Olive, Ohio (43724) 284/G6
South Orange○, N.J. (07079) 273/A2
South Orkney (isls.) 2/G9
South Orkney (isls.), Ant. 5/C16
South Orleans, Mass. (02662) 249/O5
South Oromocto (lake), New Bruns. 170/D4
South Oroville, Calif. (†95965) 204/D4
South Orrington, Maine (04474) 243/F6
South Ossetian Aut. Obl., U.S.S.R. 48/E5
South Ossetian Aut. Obl., U.S.S.R. 52/F6
South Otselic, N.Y. (13155) 276/J5
South Pacific (sea) 87/H8
South Pacific Ocean 2/C8
South Padre Island, Texas (78597) 303/G11
South Pagai (isl.), Indonesia 85/C6
South Para (riv.), S. Australia 94/C7
South Paris, Maine (04281) 243/C7
South Pasadena, Calif. (91030) 204/C10
South Pasadena, Fla. (†33707) 212/B3
South Pass City, Wyo. (82520) 319/D3
South Patrick Shores, Fla. (†32901) 212/F3
South Pekin, Ill. (61564) 222/D3
South Pender Island, Br. Col. 184/K3
South Penobscot, Maine (†04476) 243/F7
South Perry, Ohio (†43135) 284/E6
South Perth, W. Australia 88/B2
South Perth, W. Australia 92/A1
South Philipsburg, Pa. (†16866) 294/F4
South Piney (creek), Wyo. 319/B3
South Pittsburg, Tenn. (37380) 237/K10
South Pittsfield, N.H. (†03263) 268/E5
South Plainfield, N.J. (07080) 273/E2
South Plains, Texas (79258) 303/C3
South Platte (riv.) 188/F2
South Platte (riv.), Colo. 208/N1
South Platte (riv.), Nebr. 264/C3
South Platte (riv.), U.S. 146/G5
South Point (isl.), Md. 245/O9
South Pole 2/E11
South Pole, Ant. 5/A4
South Pomfret, Vt. (05067) 268/B4
South Porcupine, Ontario 177/D2
Southport, Conn. (06490) 210/B4
Southport, England 10/F2
Southport, England 13/G1
Southport, Fla. (†32401) 212/C6
Southport, Ind. (†46201) 227/E5
Southport, Maine (04569) 243/D8
Southport○, Maine (04538) 243/D8
Southport, N.Y. (†14901) 276/G6
Southport, N.C. (28461) 281/N7
South Portland, Maine (04106) 243/C8
South Portsmouth, Ky. (41174) 237/P3
South Prairie, Wash. (98385) 310/D3
South Pugwash, Nova Scotia 168/E3
South Range, Mich. (49963) 250/G1
South Range, Wis. (54874) 317/B20
South Renous (riv.), New Bruns. 170/D2
South Renovo, Pa. (†17764) 294/G3
South River (peak), Colo. 208/F7

South River, Newf. 166/D2
South River, N.J. (08882) 273/E3
South River, Ontario 177/E2
South Rockwood, Mich. (46179) 250/F7
South Ronaldsay (isl.), Scotland 10/E1
South Ronaldsay (isl.), Scotland 15/F2
South Roxana, Ill. (62087) 222/B2
South Royalston, Mass. (†01331) 249/F2
South Royalton, Vt. (05068) 268/C4
South Russell, Ohio (†44022) 284/H3
South Ryegate, Vt. (05069) 268/C3
South Sacramento, Calif. (†95823) 204/B8
South Saint Paul, Minn. (55075) 255/G6
South Salem, Ohio (45681) 284/D7
South Salt Lake, Utah (84115) 304/C3
South Sandisfield, Mass. (†01255) 249/B4
South Sandwich (isls.) 2/H8
South Sandwich (isls.), Ant. 5/D17
South Sanford, Maine (†04073) 243/B9
South San Francisco, Calif. (94080) 204/J2
South Santiam (riv.), Oreg. 291/E3
South Saskatchewan (riv.), Alberta 182/E4
South Saskatchewan (riv.), Canada 146/G4
South Saskatchewan (riv.), Sask. 181/C5
South Seabrook, N.H. (†03874) 268/F6
South Seal (riv.), Manitoba 179/J2
South Seaville, N.J. (08246) 273/D5
South Sevogle (riv.), New Bruns. 170/D1
South Shaftsbury, Vt. (†05262) 268/A6
South Shetland (isls.) 2/F9
South Shetland (isls.), Ant. 5/C15
South Shields, England 13/J3
South Shields, England 10/F3
South Shore, Ky. (41175) 237/R3
South Shore, S. Dak. (57263) 298/P3
Southside, Ala. (†35901) 195/F3
Southside, Tenn. (37171) 237/G8
Southside Place, Texas (†77001) 303/J2
South Sioux City, Nebr. (68776) 264/H2
South Skunk (riv.), Iowa 229/H6
South Slocan, Br. Col. 184/J5
South Solon, Ohio (43153) 284/C6
South Spectacle (lake), Conn. 210/B2
South Stoddard, N.H. (†03464) 268/C5
South Strafford, Vt. (05070) 268/C4
South Suburban, India 68/F2
South Sudbury, Mass. (†01776) 249/J3
South Superior, Wyo. (†82945) 319/D4
South Sutton, N.H. (03273) 268/D5
South Sydney, N. S. Wales 97/J3
South Sydney, N. S. Wales 97/J3
South Taft, Calif. (93268) 204/F8
South Tamworth, N.H. (03883) 268/E4
South Taranaki (bight), N. Zealand 100/D3
South Thomaston○, Maine (04858) 243/E7
South Toms River, N.J. (08753) 273/E4
South Trap (isl.), N. Zealand 100/B7
South Tucson, Ariz. (85713) 198/D6
South Tunnel, Tenn. (†37066) 237/K8
South Twin (mt.), N.H. 268/D3
South Tyne (riv.), England 13/E3
South Uist (isl.), Scotland 10/C2
South Uist (isl.), Scotland 15/A3
South Umpqua (riv.), Oreg. 291/E4
South Union, Ky. (42283) 237/H7
South Union, Maine (†04864) 243/E7
South Venice, Fla. (33595) 212/D4
South Vienna, Ohio (45369) 284/C6
Southville, Mass. (†01772) 249/H3
South Wabasca (lake), Alberta 182/D2
South Wadesboro, N.C. (†28170) 281/J5
South Waldoboro, Maine (†04572) 243/E7
South Wallingford, Vt. (05773) 268/A5
South Walpole, Mass. (†02071) 249/K4
South Wanatah, Ind. (†46390) 227/D2
Southwark, England 13/H8
Southwark, England 13/H8
South Warren, Maine (†04864) 243/E7
South Waterford, Maine (04081) 243/B7
South Waverly, Pa. (†18840) 294/J2
South Wayne, Wis. (53587) 317/G10
South Weare, N.H. (†03281) 268/D5
South Webster, Ohio (45682) 284/E8
South Weldon, N.C. (†27890) 281/O2
South Wellfleet, Mass. (02663) 249/P5
South Wellington, Br. Col. 184/J3
Southwest (pass), La. 238/L8
Southwest (head), New Bruns. 170/D4
South West (brook), Newf. 166/C2
South West (cape), Tasmania 88/G7
South West (cape), Tasmania 99/B5
Southwest (cape), Virgin Is. (U.S.) 161/K4
South-West Africa (Namibia) 2/K6
South-West Africa (Namibia) 102/D7
South West Arm (inlet), Newf. 166/D2
South West City, Mo. (64863) 261/D9
Southwest Harbor, Maine (04679) 243/G7
Southwest Harbor○, Maine (04679) 243/G7
South West Margaree (riv.), Nova Scotia 168/G2
Southwest Miramichi (riv.), New Bruns. 170/D2
South Westport, Mass. (02790) 249/K6
South West Port Mouton, Nova Scotia 168/D5
South West Rocks, N.S. Wales 97/G2
South Weymouth, Mass. (†02190) 249/E8
South Whitley, Ind. (46787) 227/F2
Southwick, Idaho (†83537) 220/B3
Southwick○, Mass. (01077) 249/C4
South Williamson, Ky. (†25661) 237/S5
South Williamsport, Pa. (17701) 294/J3

Starogard Gdański 451

South Willington, Conn. (06265) 210/F1
South Wilmington, Ill. (60474) 222/E2
South Wilton, Conn. (†06897) 210/B4
South Windham, Conn. (06266) 210/G2
South Windham (Little Falls-South Windham), Maine (04082) 243/C8
South Windham, Vt. (†05359) 268/B5
South Windsor○, Conn. (06074) 210/E1
Southwold, England 13/J5
Southwold, England 10/G4
South Wolf (isl.), Newf. 166/C3
South Wolfeboro, N.H. (†03894) 268/E4
South Woodbury, Vt. (†05681) 268/C3
South Woodstock, Conn. (06267) 210/G1
South Woodstock, Vt. (05071) 268/B4
Southworth, Wash. (98386) 310/A2
South Worthington, Mass. (†01098) 249/C3
South Yadkin (riv.), N.C. 281/H3
South Yarmouth, Mass. (02664) 249/O6
South Yorkshire (co.), England 13/F4
South Zanesville, Ohio (43701) 284/F6
Sovata, Romania 45/G2
Sovereign, Sask. 181/D4
Sovetsk, U.S.S.R. 7/J3
Sovetsk, U.S.S.R. 52/G3
Sovetsk (Tilsit), U.S.S.R. 52/B4
Sovetskaya Gavan', U.S.S.R. 54/R5
Sovetskaya Gavan', U.S.S.R. 48/P5
SOVIET UNION (U.S.S.R.) 48
Sowerby Bridge, England 13/H1
Sowerby Bridge, England 10/G2
Soweto, S. Africa 118/H6
Soya (pt.), Japan 81/L1
Soyhières, Switzerland 39/D2
Soyo, Angola 115/B5
Soyo, Angola 102/D5
Sozopol, Bulgaria 45/H4
Spa, Belgium 27/H8
Spades, Ind. (†47041) 227/G6
Spain 2/J3
Spain 7/D4
SPAIN 33
Spalding, England 13/G5
Spalding, England 10/F4
Spalding (co.), Georgia 217/D4
Spalding, Mich. (49886) 250/B3
Spalding, Mo. (†63401) 261/J3
Spalding, Nebr. (68665) 264/F3
Spalding, Sask. 181/G3
Spaldings, Jamaica 158/H6
Spallumcheen, Br. Col. 184/H5
Spanaway, Wash. (98387) 310/C3
Spandau, W. Germany 22/E3
Spangle, Wash. (99031) 310/H3
Spangler, Pa. (15775) 294/E4
Spaniard's Bay, Newf. 166/D2
Spanish (head), I. of Man 13/C3
Spanish, Ontario 177/J5
Spanish (riv.), Ontario 177/C1
Spanishburg, W. Va. (25922) 312/D8
Spanish Fork, Utah (84660) 304/C3
Spanish Fork (riv.), Utah 304/C3
Spanish Fort, Ala. (36527) 195/C9
Spanish Fort, Texas (†76255) 303/G4
Spanish Lake, Mo. (†63138) 261/R1
Spanish Ship Bay, Nova Scotia 168/G4
Spanish Town, Jamaica 158/J6
Spanish Town, Jamaica 156/C3
Sparkill, N.Y. (10976) 276/K8
Sparkman, Ark. (71763) 202/E6
Sparks, Georgia (31647) 217/F8
Sparks, Kansas (†66035) 232/G2
Sparks, Nebr. (69220) 264/D2
Sparks, Nev. 188/C3
Sparks, Nev. (89431) 266/B3
Sparks, Okla. (74869) 288/N3
Sparks (lake), Oreg. 291/F3
Sparksville, Ky. (42778) 237/L6
Sparland, Ill. (61565) 222/D2
Sparlingville, Mich. (†48060) 250/G6
Sparr, Fla. (32690) 212/D2
Sparrow Bush, N.Y. (12780) 276/L8
Sparrows Point, Md. (21219) 245/N4
Sparta, Georgia (31087) 217/F4
Sparta, Greece 45/F7
Sparta, Ill. (62286) 222/D5
Sparta, Ky. (41086) 237/M3
Sparta, Mich. (49345) 250/D5
Sparta, Mo. (65753) 261/F9
Sparta○, N.J. (07871) 273/D1
Sparta, N.C. (28675) 281/G1
Sparta, Ohio (43350) 284/E5
Sparta, Ontario 177/C5
Sparta, Oreg. (†97870) 291/K3
Sparta, Tenn. (38583) 237/K9
Sparta, Va. (22552) 307/O4
Sparta, Wis. (54656) 317/E8
Spartanburg, Ind. (†47355) 227/H4
Spartanburg, S.C. 188/K4
Spartanburg (co.), S.C. 296/D2
Spartanburg, S.C. (*29301) 296/C1
Spartansburg, Pa. (16434) 294/C2
Spartivento (cape), Italy 34/B5
Spartivento (cape), Italy 34/F6
Sparwood, Br. Col. 184/K5
Spassk-Dal'niy, U.S.S.R. 48/O5
Spátha (cape), Greece 45/F8
Spaulding, Ill. (†62561) 222/D4
Spavinaw, Okla. (74366) 288/R2
Spavinaw (lake), Okla. 288/S2
Spean (riv.), Scotland 15/D4
Spean Bridge, Scotland 15/D4
Spear (cape), New Bruns. 170/G2
Spear (cape), Newf. 166/D2
Spearfish, S. Dak. (57783) 298/B5
Spearman, Texas (79081) 303/C1
Spearsville, Ind. (†46181) 227/E6
Spearsville, La. (71277) 238/E1
Spearville, Kansas (67876) 232/C4
Spectacle (lakes), Conn. 210/B2
Specter (range), Nev. 266/E6
Speculator, N.Y. (12164) 276/M3
Spedden, Alberta 182/E2
Spednik (lake), New Bruns. 170/C3
Speed, Ind. (47172) 227/F8
Speed, Kansas (†67639) 232/C2
Speed, N.C. (27881) 281/P3
Speedway, Ind. (46224) 227/E5
Speedwell, Tenn. (37870) 237/O8
Speedwell, Va. (24374) 307/F8
Speer (mt.), Switzerland 39/H2
Speers, Sask. 181/D3
Speightstown, Barbados 161/B8
Speightstown, Barbados 156/G4
Speigner, Ala. (†36025) 195/F5
Spelterville, Ind. (†47808) 227/C5
Spelve, Loch (inlet), Scotland 15/C4
Spenard, Alaska (99503) 196/C1
Spenborough, England 13/J1
Spence Bay, N.W. Terrs. 187/J3
Spencer (cape), Alaska 196/L1
Spencer (pt.), Alaska 196/E1
Spencer (lake), Alberta 182/E2
Spencer (gulf), Australia 87/D9
Spencer, Idaho (†83423) 220/F5
Spencer (co.), Ind. 227/C9
Spencer, Ind. (47460) 227/D6
Spencer, Iowa (51301) 229/C2
Spencer (co.), Ky. 237/L4
Spencer, La. (71278) 238/F1
Spencer (pond), Maine 243/D4
Spencer (stream), Maine 243/C5
Spencer, Mass. (01562) 249/F3
Spencer○, Mass. (01562) 249/F3
Spencer, Nebr. (68777) 264/F2
Spencer (cape), New Bruns. 170/E3
Spencer, N.Y. (14883) 276/H6
Spencer, N.C. (28159) 281/H3
Spencer, Ohio (44275) 284/F3
Spencer, Okla. (73084) 288/M3
Spencer (creek), Oreg. 291/E5
Spencer (gulf), S. Australia 88/F6
Spencer (cape), S. Australia 88/F7
Spencer (cape), S. Australia 94/E6
Spencer (gulf), S. Australia 94/E6
Spencer, S. Dak. (57374) 298/O6
Spencer, Tenn. (38585) 237/L9
Spencer, Va. (24165) 307/J7
Spencer, W. Va. (25276) 312/D5
Spencer, Wis. (54479) 317/F6
Spencerburg, Mo. (†63441) 261/K4
Spencerport, N.Y. (14559) 276/E4
Spencers Island, Nova Scotia 168/D3
Spencerville, Ind. (46788) 227/G2
Spencerville, Ohio (45887) 284/B4
Spencerville, Okla. (74760) 288/R6
Spencerville, Ontario 177/J3
Spences Bridge, Br. Col. 184/G5
Spennymoor, England 13/F3
Spennymoor, England 10/F3
Spenser (mts.), N. Zealand 100/D5
Sperling, Manitoba 179/E5
Sperrin (mts.), N. Ireland 17/G2
Sperry, Iowa (52650) 229/L7
Sperry, Okla. (74073) 288/P2
Sperryville, Va. (22740) 307/M3
Spessart (range), W. Germany 22/C4
Spétsai, Greece 45/F7
Spey (riv.), Scotland 10/E2
Spey (riv.), Scotland 15/E3
Speyer, W. Germany 22/C4
Sphinx (mt.), Mont. 262/E5
Spiceland, Ind. (47385) 227/F5
Spicer, Minn. (56288) 255/C5
Spicer (isls.), N.W. Terrs. 187/L3
Spicewood, Texas (78669) 303/F7
Spickard, Mo. (64679) 261/F2
Spiddal, Ireland 17/C5
Spider (lake), Maine 243/E3
Spider (lake), Wis. 317/D3
Spiekeroog (isl.), W. Germany 22/B2
Spies, N.C. (†27325) 281/K4
Spiez, Switzerland 39/E3
Spili, Greece 45/G8
Spillimacheen, Br. Col. 184/J5
Spillville, Iowa (52168) 229/J2
Spilsby, England 13/H4
Spin Buldak, Afghanistan 68/B2
Spin Buldak, Afghanistan 59/J3
Spindale, N.C. (28160) 281/F4
Spink (co.), S. Dak. 298/N4
Spink, S. Dak. (†57010) 298/R8
Spinnerstown, Pa. (18968) 294/M5
Spirit (lake), Idaho 220/B2
Spirit (lake), Iowa 229/C2
Spirit (lake), S. Dak. 298/O4
Spirit (lake), Wash. 310/C4
Spirit, Wis. (†54513) 317/F5
Spirit Lake, Idaho (83869) 220/A2
Spirit Lake, Iowa (51360) 229/C2
Spirit River, Alberta 182/A2
Spirit River, Alta. 162/E4
Spiritwood, N. Dak. (58481) 282/N6
Spiritwood, Sask. 181/D2
Spiro, Okla. (74959) 288/S4
Spišská Belá, Czech. 41/F2
Spišská Nová Ves, Czech. 41/F2
Spital am Pyhrn, Austria 41/C3
Spithead (chan.), England 13/F7
Spitsbergen (isl.), Norway 4/B9
Spitsbergen (isl.), Norway 18/C2
Spittal an der Drau, Austria 41/B3
Spitz, Austria 41/C2
Spivey, Kansas (67142) 232/D4
Splendora, Texas (77372) 303/J7
Split (lake), Manitoba 179/J2
Split (cape), Nova Scotia 168/D3
Split, Yugoslavia 7/F4
Split, Yugoslavia 45/C4
Split Lake, Manitoba 179/J2
Split Rock, Wis. (†54486) 317/H6
Splügen (pass), Italy 34/B1
Splügen, Switzerland 39/H3
Splügen (pass), Switzerland 39/H3
Spofford, N.H. (03462) 268/C6
Spofford, Texas (78877) 303/D8
Spokane, Mo. (65754) 261/F9
Spokane, Wash. 146/G5
Spokane, Wash. 188/C1
Spokane (co.), Wash. 310/H3
Spokane, Wash. (*99201) 310/H3
Spokane (mt.), Wash. 310/H3
Spokane (riv.), Wash. 310/H3
Spokane Ind. Res., Wash. 310/G3
Spöl (riv.), Switzerland 39/F2
Spoleto, Italy 34/D3
Spoon (riv.), Ill. 222/C3
Spooner, Wis. (54801) 317/B4
Spot (pond), Mass. 249/C6
Spotswood, N.J. (08884) 273/E3
Spotsylvania (co.), Va. 307/N4
Spotsylvania, Va. (22553) 307/N4
Spotted (range), Nev. 266/F6
Spotted Horse, Wyo. (†82831) 319/G1
Spottsville, Ky. (42458) 237/G5
Spottswood, Va. (24475) 307/K5
Spotville, Ark. (†71753) 202/D7
Spragge, Ontario 177/J5
Sprague, Ala. (36076) 195/F6
Sprague, Manitoba 179/G5
Sprague, Nebr. (68438) 264/H4
Sprague (riv.), Oreg. 291/F5
Sprague, Wash. (99032) 310/G3
Sprague (lake), Wash. 310/G3
Sprague River, Oreg. (97639) 291/F5
Spragueville, Iowa (52074) 229/N4
Spratly (isl.), Philippines 85/E4
Spratt, Mich. (†49753) 250/F3
Spray (mts.), Alberta 182/C4
Spray, Oreg. (97874) 291/H3
Spray Lakes, Alberta 182/C4
Spraytown, Ind. (†47228) 227/E6
Spread Eagle, Wis. (†54121) 317/K4
Spreckelsville, Hawaii (96779) 218/J1
Spree (riv.), E. Germany 22/F3
Spreewald (for.), E. Germany 22/F3
Spremberg, E. Germany 22/F3
Sprent, Tasmania 99/C3
Sprigg, W. Va. (25693) 312/B7
Sprimont, Belgium 27/H8
Spring (riv.), Ark. 202/H1
Spring (creek), Nev. 266/D2
Spring (mts.), Nev. 266/F6
Spring (valley), Nev. 266/G3
Spring (creek), N. Dak. 282/E5
Spring (creek), S. Dak. 298/J2
Spring (creek), S. Dak. 298/C6
Spring, Texas (*77373) 303/J7
Spring Arbor, Mich. (49283) 250/E6
Spring Bay, Ill. (†61601) 222/D3
Spring Bay, Ontario 177/B2
Springbok, S. Africa 118/B5
Springboro, Ohio (45066) 284/B6
Springboro, Pa. (16435) 294/B2
Springbrook, Iowa (52075) 229/N4
Spring Brook, N. Dak. (58850) 282/D3
Springbrook, Ontario 177/G3
Springbrook, Oreg. (†97132) 291/A2
Springbrook, Wis. (54875) 317/C4
Spring City, Mo. (†64801) 261/C9
Spring City, Pa. (19475) 294/L5
Spring City, Tenn. (37381) 237/M9
Spring City, Utah (84662) 304/C4
Spring Coulée, Alberta 182/D5
Spring Creek, Pa. (16436) 294/D2
Spring Creek, Tenn. (38378) 237/D9
Spring Creek, W. Va. (†24966) 312/F7
Springdale, Ark. (72764) 202/B1
Springdale, Iowa (†52776) 229/L5
Springdale, Mont. (59082) 262/F5
Springdale, Newf. 166/C4
Springdale, Ohio (45246) 284/B9
Springdale, Pa. (15144) 294/C6
Springdale, S.C. (†29720) 296/F2
Springdale, S.C. (29169) 296/E4
Springdale, Utah (84767) 304/B6
Springdale, Wash. (99173) 310/H2
Springe, W. Germany 22/C2
Springer (mt.), Georgia 217/D1
Springer (lake), Ill. 222/E4
Springer, N. Mex. (87747) 274/E2
Springer, Okla. (73458) 288/M6
Springerton, Ill. (62887) 222/E5
Springerville, Ariz. (85938) 198/F4
Springfield, Ark. (72157) 202/E3
Springfield, Colo. (81073) 208/O8
Springfield, Fla. (32401) 212/D6
Springfield, Georgia (31329) 217/K6
Springfield, Idaho (83277) 220/F6
Springfield (cap.), Ill. 146/J6
Springfield (cap.), Ill. 188/H3
Springfield (cap.), Ill. (*62701) 222/D4
Springfield (lake), Ill. 222/D4
Springfield, Ind. (†47638) 227/B8
Springfield, Ky. (40069) 237/L5
Springfield, La. (70462) 238/M2
Springfield○, Maine (04487) 243/G5
Springfield, Mass. 188/M2
Springfield, Mass. (*01101) 249/D4
Springfield, Mich. (49015) 250/D6
Springfield, Minn. (56087) 255/C6
Springfield, Mo. (*65801) 261/F8
Springfield, Mo. 188/H3
Springfield, Mo. 146/J6
Springfield, Nebr. (68059) 264/H3
Springfield, King's, New Bruns. 170/E3
Springfield, York, New Bruns. 170/C2
Springfield○, N.H. (†03284) 268/C4
Springfield○, N.J. (07081) 273/E2
Springfield, Nova Scotia 168/D4
Springfield, Ohio 188/K2
Springfield, Ohio (*45501) 284/C6
Springfield, Ontario 177/C5
Springfield, Oreg. (97477) 291/E3
Springfield○, Pa. (19064) 294/M7
Springfield, Queensland 88/G5
Springfield, Queensland 95/B5
Springfield, S.C. (29146) 296/E4
Springfield, S. Dak. (57062) 298/N8
Springfield, Tenn. (37172) 237/H8
Springfield, Vt. (05156) 268/B5
Springfield○, Vt. (05156) 268/B5
Springfield, Va. (*22150) 307/S3
Springfield, W. Va. (26763) 312/J4
Springfield Armory Nat'l Hist. Site, Mass. 249/D4
Springford, Ontario 177/D5
Spring Garden, Ala. (36275) 195/G3
Spring Garden, Calif. (95971) 204/D4
Spring Garden, Ill. (†62846) 222/E5
Spring Green, Wis. (53588) 317/G9
Spring Grove, Ill. (60081) 222/E1
Spring Grove, Ind. (†47374) 227/H5
Spring Grove, Minn. (55974) 255/G7
Spring Grove, Pa. (17362) 294/J6
Spring Grove, Va. (23881) 307/P6
Spring Hall, Barbados 161/B8
Springhaven, Nova Scotia 168/C5
Spring Hill, Ark. (†71801) 202/C6
Spring Hill, Iowa (†50125) 229/F6
Spring Hill, Kansas (66083) 232/H3
Springhill, La. (71075) 238/D1
Spring Hill, Minn. (†56352) 255/D5
Springhill, Nova Scotia 168/E3
Spring Hill, Tenn. (37174) 237/H9
Springhill Junction, Nova Scotia 168/D3
Springhills, Ohio (†43357) 284/C5
Springholm, Scotland 15/E5
Spring Hope, N.C. (27882) 281/N3
Springhouse, Br. Col. 184/G4
Spring Lake, Ind. (†46140) 227/F5
Spring Lake, Mich. (49456) 250/C5
Spring Lake, Minn. (†55056) 255/E5
Spring Lake, Minn. (56680) 255/E3
Spring Lake, N.J. (07762) 273/F3
Spring Lake, N.C. (28390) 281/M4
Springlake, Texas (79082) 303/B3
Spring Lake, Wis. (†54960) 317/H8
Spring Lake Heights, N.J. (†07762) 273/E3
Spring Lake Park, Minn. (†55432) 255/E5
Springlee, Ky. (†40201) 237/K2
Spring Lick, Ky. (42779) 237/H6
Spring Mills, Pa. (16875) 294/G4
Spring Mills, S.C. (†29067) 296/F2
Spring Park, Minn. (55384) 255/F5
Spring Place, Georgia (†30705) 217/C1
Springport, Ind. (47386) 227/G4
Springport, Mich. (49284) 250/E6
Spring Ridge, La. (†71047) 238/B2
Springs, S. Africa 118/J6
Springside, Sask. 181/J4
Springstein, Manitoba 179/E5
Springsure, Queensland 95/D5
Springton (res.), Pa. 294/L6
Springtown, Ark. (72767) 202/B1
Springtown, Texas (76082) 303/G5
Springvale, Georgia (31788) 217/C7
Springvale, Maine (04083) 243/B9
Springvale, Victoria 88/L7
Springvale, Victoria 97/J5
Spring Valley, Ala. (†35674) 195/C1
Spring Valley, Ill. (61362) 222/D2
Spring Valley, Minn. (55975) 255/F7
Spring Valley, N.Y. (10977) 276/K8
Spring Valley, Ohio (45370) 284/C6
Spring Valley, Sask. 181/F6
Spring Valley, Texas (†77001) 303/J1
Spring Valley, Wis. (54767) 317/B6
Springview, Nebr. (68778) 264/E2
Springville, Ala. (35146) 195/E3
Springville, Calif. (93265) 204/G7
Springville, Ind. (47462) 227/D7
Springville, Iowa (52336) 229/L4
Springville, La. (†70754) 238/L2
Springville, Miss. (†38863) 256/F2
Springville, N.Y. (14141) 276/C5
Springville, Pa. (18844) 294/L2
Springville, Tenn. (38256) 237/E8
Springville, Utah (84663) 304/C3
Springwater, N.Y. (14560) 276/E5
Springwater, Sask. 181/C4
Springwood, Va. (†24066) 307/J5
Sproat Lake, Br. Col. 184/H3
Sprott, Ala. (36779) 195/D5
Sprowston, England 13/J5
Spruce (isl.), Manitoba 179/B1
Spruce, Mich. (48762) 250/F4
Spruce (mt.), Vt. 268/C3
Spruce Creek, Pa. (16683) 294/F4
Sprucedale, Ontario 177/E2
Spruce Grove, Alberta 182/D3
Spruce Home, Sask. 181/F2
Spruce Knob (mt.), W. Va. 312/G5
Spruce Knob-Seneca Rocks Nat'l Rec. Area, W. Va. 312/H5
Spruce Lake, Sask. 181/B2
Spruce Pine, Ala. (35585) 195/C2
Spruce Pine, N.C. (28777) 281/E3
Spruce Run (res.), N.J. 273/D2
Spruce View, Alberta 182/C3
Spruce Woods, Manitoba 179/C5
Spruce Woods Prov. Park, Manitoba 179/C5
Sprule, Ky. (40986) 237/O7
Spry (harb.), Nova Scotia 168/F4
Spry Harbour, Nova Scotia 168/F4
Spur, Texas (79370) 303/D4
Spurgeon, Ind. (47584) 227/C8
Spurlockville, W. Va. (25565) 312/B6
Spurn (head), England 13/H4
Spurn (head), England 10/G4
Spurr (mt.), Alaska 196/B1
Spur Tree, Jamaica 158/H6
Spuzzum, Br. Col. 184/G5
Spy (pond), Mass. 249/C6
Spy Hill, Sask. 181/K5
Squam (lake), N.H. 268/E4
Squamish, Br. Col. 184/F5
Squa Pan, Maine (†04732) 243/G2
Squa Pan (lake), Maine 243/G2
Square (lake), Maine 243/G1
Square Butte, Mont. (†59442) 262/F3
Square Islands, Newf. 166/C3
Squatec, Québec 172/J2
Squatec (lake), Québec 172/J2
Squaw (creek), Idaho 220/B5
Squaw (peak), Idaho 220/D4
Squaw (creek), Oreg. 291/F3
Squaw (creek), S. Dak. 298/B3
Squaw Harbor, Alaska (†99661) 196/F3
Squaw Lake, Minn. (56681) 255/D3
Squaw Rapids, Sask. 181/H2
Squibnocket (pt.), Mass. 249/M7
Squillace (gulf), Italy 34/F5
Squinzano, Italy 34/G4
Squire, W. Va. (24884) 312/C8
Squires, Mo. (65755) 261/G9
Squires Mem. Park, Newf. 166/C4
Squirrel, Idaho (83447) 220/G5
Sragen, Indonesia 85/J2
Sre Ambel, Cambodia 72/D5
Srebrenica, Yugoslavia 45/D3
Srednekolymsk, U.S.S.R. 4/C2
Srednekolymsk, U.S.S.R. 48/Q3
Sre Khtum, Cambodia 72/E4
Śrem, Poland 47/C2
Sremska Mitrovica, Yugoslavia 45/D3
Srepok (riv.), Cambodia 72/E4
Sretensk, U.S.S.R. 54/N4
Sretensk, U.S.S.R. 48/M4
Srikakulam, India 68/E5
Sri Lanka 54/K9
SRI LANKA (CEYLON) 68/E7
Srinagar, India 68/D2
Srinagar, India 54/J6
Srivardhan, India 68/C5
Środa Śląska, Poland 47/C3
Środa Wielkopolska, Poland 47/C2
Staaten (riv.), Queensland 88/G3
Staaten (riv.), Queensland 95/B3
Staatsburg, N.Y. (12580) 276/N7
Stab, Ky. (42557) 237/N6
Stacks (mts.), Ireland 17/B7
Stacy, Minn. (55079) 255/E5
Stacy, N.C. (28581) 281/S5
Stacy, Va. (24616) 307/E6
Stacyville, Iowa (50476) 229/H2
Stacyville, Maine (04782) 243/F4
Stacyville○, Maine (04782) 243/F4
Stade, W. Germany 22/C2
Staden, Belgium 27/B7
Stadskanaal, Netherlands 27/L3
Stadthagen, W. Germany 22/C2
Stäfa, Switzerland 39/G2
Staffa (isl.), Scotland 15/B4
Staffelstein, W. Germany 22/D3
Staffhorst, W. Germany 22/C2
Stafford○, Conn. (06075) 210/F1
Stafford, England 10/G2
Stafford, England 13/E5
Stafford (lake), Fla. 212/D2
Stafford (co.), Kansas 232/D3
Stafford, Kansas (67578) 232/D4
Stafford, N.Y. (14143) 276/D5
Stafford, Ohio (43786) 284/H6
Stafford, Okla. (†73601) 288/H3
Stafford, Queensland 88/K2
Stafford, Queensland 95/D2
Stafford, Texas (77477) 303/J2
Stafford (co.), Va. 307/O4
Stafford, Va. (22554) 307/O4
Staffordshire (co.), England 13/E5
Stafford Springs, Conn. (06076) 210/F1
Staffordsville, Ky. (41256) 237/R5
Staffordville, Conn. (06077) 210/G1
Staffordville, N.J. (†08092) 273/E4
Staines (pen.), Chile 138/D9
Staines, England 10/B5
Staines, England 13/G8
Stainville, Tenn. (†37710) 237/N8
Staked (Llano Estacado) (plain), N. Mex. 274/F5
Staked (Llano Estacado) (plain), Texas 303/B4
Stakhanov, U.S.S.R. 52/E5
Stalden, Switzerland 39/E4
Staley, N.C. (27355) 281/K3
Stalham, England 13/J5
Stalheim, Norway 18/E6
Stalin, Albania 45/D5
Stalingrad (Volgograd), U.S.S.R. 7/J4
Stalingrad (Volgograd), U.S.S.R. 48/E5
Stalingrad (Volgograd), U.S.S.R. 52/F5
Stallings, N.C. (†28079) 281/H4
Stallo, Miss. (†39350) 256/F5
Stallworthy (cape), N.W. Terrs. 187/J1
Stalowa Wola, Poland 47/F3
Stalwart, Mich. (49789) 250/E2
Stalwart, Sask. 181/F4
Stambaugh, Mich. (49964) 250/G2
Stamford, Conn. (*06901) 210/A4
Stamford, England 13/G5
Stamford, England 10/F4
Stamford, Nebr. (68977) 264/E4
Stamford, N.Y. (12167) 276/L6
Stamford, Queensland 88/G4
Stamford, Texas (79553) 303/E5
Stamford (lake), Texas 303/E4
Stamford○, Vt. (05352) 268/A6
Stampa, Switzerland 39/J4
Stamping Ground, Ky. (40379) 237/M4
Stampriet, Namibia 118/B4
Stamps, Ark. (71860) 202/D7
Stanardsville, Va. (22973) 307/L4
Stanberry, Mo. (64489) 261/C2
Stanbridge-Est, Québec 172/D4
Stanchfield, Minn. (55080) 255/E5
Standard, Alberta 182/D4
Standard, Calif. (95373) 204/E6
Standard, Ill. (61363) 222/D2
Standard, La. (†71465) 238/F3
Standard City, Ill. (62686) 222/D4
Standerton, S. Africa 118/D5
Standfast (pt.), Ant. & Bar. 161/E11
Standing Rock, Ala. (36878) 195/H4
Standing Rock Ind. Res., N. Dak. 282/J7
Standish, Calif. (96128) 204/E3
Standish, Maine (04084) 243/B8
Standish○, Maine (04084) 243/B8
Standish, Mich. (48658) 250/F5
Standish-with-Langtree, England 13/G2
Stand Off, Alberta 182/D5
Stanfield, Ariz. (85272) 198/C6
Stanfield, N.C. (28163) 281/J4
Stanfield, Oreg. (97875) 291/H2
Stanford, Calif. (94305) 204/J3
Stanford, Ill. (61774) 222/D3
Stanford, Ind. (47463) 227/D6
Stanford, Ky. (40484) 237/M5
Stanford, Mont. (59479) 262/F3
Stanfordville, N.Y. (12581) 276/N7
Stangelville, Wis. (†54208) 317/L7
Stanger, S. Africa 118/E5
Stanhope, England 13/E3
Stanhope, Iowa (50246) 229/F4
Stanhope, N.J. (07874) 273/D2
Stanhope, Pr. Edward I. 168/E2
Stanhope, Québec 172/F4
Stanislaus (co.), Calif. 204/D6
Stanke Dimitrov, Bulgaria 45/F4
Stanley, England 13/H3
Stanley (cap.), Falk. Is. 120/D8
Stanley (cap.), Falk. Is. 143/E7
Stanley, Idaho (83278) 220/D5
Stanley, Iowa (50671) 229/K3
Stanley, Kansas (†66223) 232/H3
Stanley, Ky. (42375) 237/G5
Stanley, La. (†71049) 238/C3
Stanley, New Bruns. 170/D2
Stanley, N. Mex. (87056) 274/D3
Stanley, N.Y. (14561) 276/F5
Stanley, N.C. (28164) 281/G4
Stanley, N. Dak. (58784) 282/F3
Stanley (mt.), North. Terr. 93/B7
Stanley, Nova Scotia 168/E3
Stanley, Okla. (†74536) 288/R5
Stanley, Scotland 15/E4
Stanley (co.), S. Dak. 298/H5
Stanley, Tasmania 99/B2
Stanley (mt.), Tasmania 99/A1
Stanley, Va. (22851) 307/L3
Stanley, Wis. (54768) 317/E6
Stanley (falls), Zaire 102/E5
Stanley (falls), Zaire 115/D3
Stanley Pool (lake), Zaire 115/C4
Stanleytown, Va. (24168) 307/H7
Stanleyville, N.C. (†27045) 281/J2
Stanly (co.), N.C. 281/J4
Stanmore, Alberta 182/E4
Stannards, N.Y. (†14895) 276/E6
Stann Creek Town, Belize 154/C2
Stanovoy (range), U.S.S.R. 54/O4
Stanovoy (range), U.S.S.R. 48/N4
Stans, Switzerland 39/F3
Stanstead (co.), Québec 172/F4
Stanstead Plain, Québec 172/F4
Stanthorpe, Queensland 88/J5
Stanthorpe, Queensland 95/D6
Stanton, Ala. (36790) 195/E5
Stanton, Calif. (90680) 204/D11
Stanton, England 13/H5
Stanton, Iowa (51573) 229/C7
Stanton (co.), Kansas 232/A4
Stanton, Ky. (40380) 237/O5
Stanton, Mich. (48888) 250/D5
Stanton, Miss. (†39120) 256/B7
Stanton, Mo. (63079) 261/K6
Stanton (co.), Nebr. 264/G3
Stanton, Nebr. (68779) 264/G3
Stanton, N.J. (08885) 273/D2
Stanton, N. Dak. (58571) 282/H5
Stanton, Tenn. (38069) 237/C10
Stanton, Texas (79782) 303/C5
Stantonsburg, N.C. (27883) 281/O3
Stantonville, Tenn. (38379) 237/E10
Stanwood, Iowa (52337) 229/L5
Stanwood, Mich. (49346) 250/D5
Stanwood, Wash. (98292) 310/C2
Stanzel, Iowa (†50849) 229/E6
Staphorst, Netherlands 27/J3
Staplehurst, Nebr. (68439) 264/G4
Staples, Minn. (56479) 255/D4
Staples, Ontario 177/B5
Stapleton, Ala. (36578) 195/C9
Stapleton, Georgia (30823) 217/H4
Stapleton, Nebr. (69163) 264/D3
Stapylton (bay), N.W. Terrs. 187/G3
Star, Alberta 182/D3
Star, Idaho (83669) 220/B6
Star (lake), Minn. 255/C4
Star, Miss. (39167) 256/D6
Star, N.C. (27356) 281/K4
Star, Texas (76880) 303/F6
Starachowice, Poland 47/E3
Stará L'ubovňa, Czech. 41/F2
Staraya Russa, U.S.S.R. 52/D3
Stara Zagora, Bulgaria 7/G4
Stara Zagora, Bulgaria 45/G4
Starbuck (isl.), Kiribati 87/L6
Starbuck, Manitoba 179/E5
Starbuck, Minn. (56381) 255/C5
Starbuck, Wash. (99359) 310/G4
Star City, Ark. (71667) 202/G6
Star City, Ind. (46985) 227/D3
Star City, Sask. 181/G3
Star City, W. Va. (26505) 312/F3
Staré Město, Czech. 41/D2
Stargard Szczeciński, Poland 47/B2
Stargo, Ariz. (†85540) 198/F5
Starhill, La. (†70748) 238/H5
Stark (co.), Ill. 222/D2
Stark, Kansas (66775) 232/G4
Stark, Minn. (†55032) 255/E5
Stark, Mont. (†59846) 262/B3
Stark○, N.H. (03582) 268/E2
Stark (co.), N. Dak. 282/E6
Stark (co.), Ohio 284/H4
Stark City, Mo. (64866) 261/D9
Starke, Fla. (32091) 212/D2
Starke (co.), Ind. 227/D2
Starkey, Oreg. (†97850) 291/J2
Star Keys (isls.), N. Zealand 100/E7
Starks, La. (70661) 238/C6
Starks○, Maine (†04980) 243/D6
Starks, Wis. (†54501) 317/H4
Starksboro○, Vt. (05487) 268/A3
Starkville, Colo. (81074) 208/L8
Starkville, Miss. (39759) 256/G4
Starkweather, N. Dak. (58377) 282/N3
Star Lake, N.Y. (13690) 276/K2
Star Lake, Wis. (54561) 317/G3
Starlight, Ind. (†47119) 227/F8
Starnberg, W. Germany 22/D4
Starnbergersee (lake), W. Germany 22/D5
Starodub, U.S.S.R. 52/D4
Starogard Gdański, Poland 47/D2

452 Star Prairie

Star Prairie, Wis. (54026) 317/A5
Starr, S.C. (29684) 296/B3
Starr (co.), Texas 303/F11
Starr King (mt.), N.H. 268/E3
Starrucca, Pa. (18462) 294/M2
Start, La. (71279) 238/G2
Start (pt.), Scotland 15/F1
Star Tannery, Va. (22654) 307/L2
Startex, S.C. (29377) 296/C2
Startup, Wash. (98293) 310/D3
Starvation (res.), Utah 304/D3
Stary Sacz, Poland 47/E4
Staryy Oskol, U.S.S.R. 52/E4
Staser, Ind. (†47539) 227/B8
Stassfurt, E. Germany 22/D3
Staszów, Poland 47/E3
State Center, Iowa (50247) 229/G5
State College, Pa. (16801) 294/G4
State Line, Idaho (†83854) 220/A2
State Line, Ind. (47982) 227/C4
State Line, Mass. (01261) 249/A3
State Line, Miss. (39362) 256/G8
State Line, Pa. (17263) 294/G6
Staten (Los Estados) (isl.), Argentina 143/D7
Staten (isl.), N.Y. 276/M9
Staten Island (borough), N.Y. (*10301) 276/M9
Statenville, Georgia (31648) 217/G9
State Road, N.C. (28676) 281/H2
Statesboro, Georgia (30458) 217/J6
Statesville, N.C. (28677) 281/H3
Statesville, Tenn. (†37184) 237/J8
Statham, Georgia (30666) 217/E3
Static, Tenn. (†38549) 237/L7
Station Camp, Ky. (†40336) 237/N5
Statts Mills, W. Va. (25279) 312/C5
Statue of Liberty Nat'l Mon., N.J. 273/B2
Statue of Liberty Nat'l Mon., N.Y. 276/M9
Staunton, Ill. (62088) 222/D5
Staunton, Ind. (47881) 227/C6
Staunton (I.C.), Va. (24401) 307/K4
Staunton (Roanoke) (riv.), Va. 307/K6
Stavanger, Norway 18/D7
Stavanger, Norway 7/E3
Stave (lake), Br. Col. 184/L3
Staveley, England 13/K2
Stavelot, Belgium 27/H8
Stavely, Alberta 182/D4
Staveren, Netherlands 27/G3
Stavern, Norway 18/D4
Stavropol', U.S.S.R. 7/J4
Stavropol', U.S.S.R. 52/F5
Stavropol', U.S.S.R. 48/E5
Stavrós, Greece 45/F5
Stawell, Victoria 97/B5
Stayner, Ontario 177/E3
Stayton, Oreg. (97383) 291/E3
Stead, Manitoba 179/F4
Stead, N. Mex. (88438) 274/F2
Steamboat, Ariz. (†86505) 198/F3
Steamboat (mt.), Idaho 220/C4
Steamboat Rock, Iowa (50672) 229/G4
Steamboat Springs, Colo. (80477) 208/F2
Steamburg, N.Y. (14783) 276/C6
Stearns, Ky. (42647) 237/N7
Stearns (co.), Minn. 255/D5
Stebbins, Alaska (99671) 196/F2
Steckborn, Switzerland 39/G1
Stecoah, N.C. (†28771) 281/B4
Stedman, N.C. (28391) 281/M4
Steedman, S.C. (†29070) 296/E4
Steeds, N.C. (†27341) 281/K4
Steel (mt.), Idaho 220/C6
Steele, Ala. (35987) 195/F3
Steele (co.), Minn. 255/E7
Steele, Mo. (63877) 261/N10
Steele (co.), N. Dak. 282/P4
Steele, N. Dak. (58482) 282/L6
Steele City, Nebr. (68440) 264/G4
Steele Narrows Hist. Park, Sask. 181/B2
Steele's (pt.), Norfolk I. 88/L5
Steeles Tavern, Va. (24476) 307/K5
Steeleville, Ill. (62288) 222/D6
Steelman, Sask. 181/J6
Steelmanville, N.J. (†08270) 273/D5
Steelton, Pa. (17113) 294/J5
Steelville, Mo. (65565) 261/K7
Steen, Minn. (56173) 255/B7
Steen, Sask. 181/H3
Steenbergen, Netherlands 27/E5
Steenkool, Indonesia 85/J6
Steenokkerzeel, Belgium 27/C9
Steen River, Alberta 182/B4
Steens, Miss. (39766) 256/H3
Steens (mt.), Oreg. 291/J5
Steensby (inlet), N.W. Terrs. 187/L2
Steenwijk, Netherlands 27/J3
Steep (pt.), W. Australia 88/A5
Steep (pt.), W. Australia 92/A4
Steep Falls, Maine (04085) 243/B8
Steep Rock, Manitoba 179/D3
Ştefăneşti, Romania 45/H2
Stefanie (lake), Ethiopia 111/G7
Stefansson (isl.), N.W.T. 162/F1
Stefansson (isl.), N.W. Terrs. 187/H2
Steffenville, Mo. (63470) 261/J3
Steffisburg, Switzerland 39/E3
Stege, Denmark 21/F8
Stege, Denmark 18/H9
Steger, Ill. (60475) 222/F2
Stehekin, Wash. (98852) 310/E2
Steigerwald (for.), W. Germany 22/D4
Steilacoom, Wash. (98388) 310/C3
Stein, Switzerland 39/E1
Steinach, Austria 41/A3
Steinach, E. Germany 22/D3
Stein am Rhein, Switzerland 39/G1
Steinauer, Nebr. (68441) 264/H4
Steinbach, Manitoba 179/F5
Steinhatchee, Fla. (32359) 212/C2
Steinhausen, Namibia 118/B4
Steinhuder Meer (lake), W. Germany 22/C2
Steinkjer, Norway 18/G4
Steinneset (cape), Norway 18/E2
Stekene, Belgium 27/E6
Stella, Mo. (64867) 261/D9
Stella, Nebr. (68442) 264/J4
Stella, N.C. (28582) 281/P5
Stella, Wash. (†98632) 310/B4
Stellarton, Nova Scotia 168/F3
Stellenbosch, S. Africa 118/F6
Steller (mt.), Alaska 196/K2
Stelvio (pass), Switzerland 39/K3
Stem, N.C. (27581) 281/M2
Stendal, E. Germany 22/D2
Stendal, Ind. (47585) 227/C8
Stenen, Sask. 181/J4
Stenhousemuir, Scotland 15/C1
Stenlille, Denmark 21/E6
Stennett, Iowa (†51566) 229/C6
Stenstrup, Denmark 21/D7
Stenungsund, Sweden 18/G7
Stepanakert, U.S.S.R. 48/E6
Stepanakert, U.S.S.R. 52/G7
Stepaside, Ireland 17/J5
Stephan, S. Dak. (57346) 298/K5
Stephen, Minn. (56757) 255/A2
Stephenfield, Manitoba 179/D5
Stephens (passage), Alaska 196/N1
Stephens, Ark. (71764) 202/E7
Stephens (isl.), Br. Col. 184/B3
Stephens (co.), Georgia 217/F1
Stephens, Georgia (30667) 217/F3
Stephens (isl.), N. Zealand 100/D4
Stephens (co.), Okla. 288/L6
Stephens (co.), Texas 303/F5
Stephensburg, Ky. (42781) 237/J5
Stephensburg, N.J. (†07865) 273/D2
Stephens City, Va. (22655) 307/M2
Stephen's Creek, N.S. Wales 97/A2
Stephenson (co.), Ill. 222/D1
Stephenson, Mich. (49887) 250/B3
Stephensport, Ky. (40170) 237/H5
Stephentown, N.Y. (12168) 276/O5
Stephenville, Newf. 166/C4
Stephenville, Newf. 162/L6
Stephenville, Texas (76401) 303/F5
Stephenville Crossing, Newf. 166/C4
Stepney, Conn. (†06468) 210/B3
Stepovak (bay), Alaska 196/G3
Steprock, Ark. (72159) 202/G3
Steptoe, Wash. (99174) 310/H3
Sterling, Alaska (99672) 196/B1
Sterling, Colo. 188/F2
Sterling, Colo. (80751) 208/N1
Sterling (res.), Colo. 208/N1
Sterling○, Conn. (06377) 210/H2
Sterling, Georgia (†31520) 217/K8
Sterling, Idaho (83279) 220/F6
Sterling, Ill. (61081) 222/D2
Sterling, Kansas (67579) 232/D3
Sterling○, Mass. (01564) 249/G3
Sterling, Mich. (48659) 250/E4
Sterling, Nebr. (68443) 264/H4
Sterling, N. Dak. (58572) 282/K6
Sterling, Ohio (44276) 284/G4
Sterling, Okla. (73567) 288/K5
Sterling, Pa. (18463) 294/M3
Sterling (co.), Texas 303/C6
Sterling, Utah (84665) 304/C4
Sterling, Va. (22170) 307/O2
Sterling City, Texas (76951) 303/D6
Sterling Heights, Mich. (48077) 250/B6
Sterling Run, Pa. (†15832) 294/F3
Sterlington, La. (71280) 238/F1
Sterlitamak, U.S.S.R. 7/K3
Sterlitamak, U.S.S.R. 48/F4
Sterlitamak, U.S.S.R. 52/J4
Šternberg, E. Germany 22/D2
Šternberk, Czech. 41/D2
Sterrett, Ala. (35147) 195/F4
Stet, Mo. (64680) 261/E4
Stetson○, Maine (04488) 243/E6
Stetsonville, Wis. (54480) 317/F5
Stettin (Szczecin), Poland 47/B2
Stettler, Alberta 182/D3
Stettler, Alta. 162/E5
Stettyn (mt.), S. Africa 118/G6
Steuben (co.), Ind. 227/G1
Steuben, Maine (04680) 243/H6
Steuben○, Maine (04680) 243/H6
Steuben, Mich. (†49854) 250/C2
Steuben (co.), N.Y. 276/F6
Steuben, Wis. (54657) 317/E9
Steubenville, Ohio 188/K2
Steubenville, Ohio (43952) 284/J5
Steve, Ark. (†72857) 202/D4
Stevenage, England 13/G6
Stevenage, England 10/F5
Stevens (co.), Kansas 232/A4
Stevens (co.), Minn. 255/B5
Stevens (creek), S.C. 296/C4
Stevens (co.), Wash. 310/H2
Stevens (pass), Wash. 310/D3
Stevensburg, Va. (22741) 307/N4
Stevenson, Ala. (35772) 195/G1
Stevenson, Conn. (06491) 210/C3
Stevenson (lake), Manitoba 179/J3
Stevenson, The (riv.), S. Australia 94/D2
Stevenson, Wash. (98648) 310/C5
Stevenson Entrance (str.), Alaska 196/H3
Stevens Point, Wis. (54481) 317/G7
Stevens Pottery, Georgia (31088) 217/F5
Stevenston, Scotland 15/D5
Stevenstown, Wis. (†54636) 317/D7
Stevens Village, Alaska (99774) 196/J1
Stevensville, Md. (21666) 245/N5
Stevensville, Mich. (49127) 250/C6
Stevensville, Mont. (59870) 262/C4
Stevns Klint (cliff), Denmark 21/F7
Steward, Ill. (60553) 222/D2
Stewardson, Ill. (62463) 222/E4
Stewart, Ala. (35484) 195/C5
Stewart, Br. Col. 162/D4
Stewart, Br. Col. 184/C2
Stewart (isl.), Chile 138/E11
Stewart (co.), Georgia 217/C6
Stewart, Minn. (55385) 255/D6
Stewart, Miss. (39767) 256/F4
Stewart (isl.), N. Zealand 87/G10
Stewart (isl.), N. Zealand 100/A7
Stewart (cape), North. Terr. 93/D1
Stewart, Ohio (45778) 284/G7
Stewart (co.), Tenn. 237/F7
Stewart, Tenn. (37175) 237/F8
Stewart (riv.), Yukon 162/C3
Stewart (riv.), Yukon 187/E3
Stewart Crossing, Yukon 187/E3
Stewarton, Scotland 15/D5
Stewart River, Yukon 187/D3
Stewart River, Yukon 162/B3
Stewarts Point, Calif. (95480) 204/B5
Stewartstown○, N.H. (†03576) 268/E2
Stewartstown, N. Ireland 17/H2
Stewartstown, Pa. (17363) 294/K6
Stewartsville, Ind. (47636) 227/B8
Stewartsville, Mo. (64490) 261/C3
Stewartsville, N.J. (08886) 273/C2
Stewartsville, Ohio (43960) 284/J6
Stewart Town, Jamaica 158/H6
Stewart Valley, Sask. 181/D5
Stewartville, Ala. (†35150) 195/F4
Stewartville, Minn. (55976) 255/F7
Stewiacke, Nova Scotia 168/E3
Stewiacke (riv.), Nova Scotia 168/E3
Steyer, Md. (†21550) 245/A3
Steyr, Austria 41/C2
Stia, Italy 34/C3
Stickney, Ill. (60402) 222/B6
Stickney, New Bruns. 170/C2
Stickney, S. Dak. (57375) 298/M6
Stickney, W. Va. (25188) 312/D7
Stidham, Okla. (74461) 288/P4
Stiens, Netherlands 27/H2
Stigler, Okla. (74462) 288/R4
Stikine (riv.), Alaska 196/N2
Stikine (str.), Alaska 196/N2
Stikine (riv.), Br. Col. 162/C4
Stikine (riv.), Br. Col. 184/B1
Stiles, Iowa (†52537) 229/J7
Stiles, Wis. (54172) 317/L6
Stilesville, Ind. (46180) 227/D5
Stilis, Greece 45/F6
Still (riv.), Conn. 210/B3
Still (riv.), Conn. 210/C1
Still (riv.), Conn. 210/G1
Stillman Valley, Ill. (61084) 222/D1
Stillmore, Georgia (30464) 217/H6
Still Pond, Md. (21667) 245/O3
Still River, Mass. (01467) 249/H3
Stillwater, Ky. (†41301) 237/O5
Stillwater, Maine (04489) 243/F6
Stillwater (riv.), Mass. 249/G3
Stillwater, Minn. (55082) 255/F5
Stillwater (co.), Mont. 262/G5
Stillwater (riv.), Mont. 262/G5
Stillwater, Nev. (†89406) 266/C3
Stillwater (range), Nev. 266/C3
Stillwater, N.J. (07875) 273/D1
Stillwater, N.Y. (12170) 276/N5
Stillwater, Ohio (44679) 284/H5
Stillwater (riv.), Ohio 284/B5
Stillwater, Okla. (74074) 288/N2
Stillwater, Pa. (17878) 294/K3
Stillwater (res.), R.I. 249/C2
Stillwell, Ill. (†62380) 222/B3
Stillwell, Ind. (46351) 227/D1
Stilson, Georgia (30415) 217/J6
Stilwell, Kansas (66085) 232/H3
Stilwell, Okla. (74960) 288/S3
Stimson (mt.), Mont. 262/C2
Stinchar (riv.), Scotland 15/D5
Stinesville, Ind. (47464) 227/D6
Stinnett, Texas (79083) 303/C2
Stinson Beach, Calif. (94970) 204/H2
Stinson Lake, N.H. (03274) 268/D4
Stintino, Italy 34/B4
Štip, Yugoslavia 45/F5
Stiring-Wendel, France 28/G3
Stirling, Alberta 182/D5
Stirling, N.J. (07980) 273/E2
Stirling (creek), North. Terr. 88/D3
Stirling (creek), North. Terr. 93/A4
Stirling, Ontario 177/G3
Stirling, Scotland 10/B1
Stirling, Scotland 15/C1
Stirling (trad. co.), Scotland 15/A5
Stirling, W. Australia 88/B2
Stirling, W. Australia 92/A1
Stirling City, Calif. (95978) 204/D4
Stirling North, S. Australia 94/E5
Stirling Station, North. Terr. 93/C6
Stirrat, W. Va. (25645) 312/C7
Stirum, N. Dak. (58069) 282/P7
Stites, Idaho (83552) 220/C3
Stittsville, Ontario 177/J2
Stittville, N.Y. (13469) 276/K4
Stitzer, Wis. (53825) 317/E10
Stockbridge, Georgia (30281) 217/D3
Stockbridge, Mass. (01262) 249/A3
Stockbridge○, Mass. (01262) 249/A3
Stockbridge, Mich. (49285) 250/E6
Stockbridge○, Vt. (05772) 268/B4
Stockbridge, Wis. (53088) 317/K7
Stockbridge Ind. Res., Wis. 317/J6
Stockdale, Ohio (45683) 284/E8
Stockdale, Texas (78160) 303/G8
Stockerau, Austria 41/D2
Stockertown, Pa. (18083) 294/M4
Stockett, Mont. (59480) 262/E3
Stockham, Nebr. (†68818) 264/F4
Stockholm○, Maine (04783) 243/G1
Stockholm, N.J. (07460) 273/D1
Stockholm, Sask. 181/J5
Stockholm, S. Dak. (57264) 298/R3
Stockholm (co.), Sweden 18/L7
Stockholm (cap.), Sweden 2/K3
Stockholm (cap.), Sweden 7/F3
Stockholm (cap.), Sweden 18/G1
Stockholm, Wis. (54769) 317/B7
Stockhorn (mt.), Switzerland 39/E3
Stockland, Ill. (60967) 222/F3
Stockley, Del. (†19947) 245/S6
Stockport, England 13/H2
Stockport, England 10/G2
Stockport, Iowa (52651) 229/K7
Stockport, Ohio (43787) 284/G6
Stocksbridge, England 13/J2
Stockton, Ala. (36579) 195/C9
Stockton, Calif. 188/B3
Stockton, Calif. (*95201) 204/D6
Stockton, Georgia (31649) 217/G9
Stockton, Ill. (61085) 222/C1
Stockton, Iowa (52769) 229/M5
Stockton, Kansas (67669) 232/C2
Stockton, Manitoba 179/C5
Stockton, Md. (21864) 245/S8
Stockton, Minn. (55988) 255/G6
Stockton, Mo. (65785) 261/E7
Stockton (lake), Mo. 261/E7
Stockton, N.J. (08559) 273/D3
Stockton, N.Y. (14784) 276/B6
Stockton (plat.), Texas 303/B7
Stockton, Utah (84071) 304/B3
Stockton (isl.), Wis. 317/F2
Stockton-on-Tees, England 13/F3
Stockton-on-Tees, England 10/F3
Stockton Springs, Maine (04981) 243/F7
Stockton Springs○, Maine (04981) 243/F7
Stockville, Nebr. (69042) 264/D4
Stockwell, Ind. (47983) 227/D4
Stoco, Ontario 177/G3
Stod, Czech. 41/B2
Stoddard (co.), Mo. 261/N9
Stoddard○, N.H. (03464) 268/C5
Stoddard, Wis. (54658) 317/D8
Stoeng Treng, Cambodia 72/E4
Stoer (pt.), Scotland 15/C2
Stoholm, Denmark 21/C5
Stoke-on-Trent, England 13/E4
Stoke-on-Trent, England 10/E4
Stokes (bay), Chile 138/D10
Stokes (co.), N.C. 281/J2
Stokes, N.C. (27884) 281/P3
Stokes (pt.), Tasmania 99/A1
Stokes Bay, Ontario 177/C2
Stokesdale, N.C. (27357) 281/K2
Stolac, Yugoslavia 45/D4
Stolberg, W. Germany 22/B3
Stolp (Słupsk), Poland 47/C1
Ston, Yugoslavia 45/C4
Stone (co.), Ark. 202/F2
Stone, England 10/E4
Stone, England 13/E5
Stone, Idaho (83280) 220/F7
Stone, Ky. (41567) 237/S5
Stone (co.), Miss. 256/F9
Stone (co.), Mo. 261/F9
Stone (mts.), N.C. 281/E2
Stone (mts.), Tenn. 237/T8
Stone Bank, Wis. (†53066) 317/J1
Stonebluff, Ind. (†47987) 227/C4
Stonebluff, Okla. (†74436) 288/P3
Stoneboro, Pa. (16153) 294/B3
Stoneboro, S.C. (†29058) 296/F2
Stone City, Iowa (†52205) 229/L4
Stonecliffe, Ontario 177/G1
Stone Creek, Ohio (43840) 284/G5
Stonefort, Ill. (62987) 222/E6
Stonega, Va. (24285) 307/C7
Stoneham, Colo. (80754) 208/M1
Stoneham○, Mass. (02180) 249/C6
Stoneham, Québec 172/F4
Stone Harbor, N.J. (08247) 273/D5
Stonehaven, Scotland 10/E2
Stonehaven, Scotland 15/F4
Stonehenge (ruins), England 13/F6
Stonehenge, Queensland 95/B5
Stonehenge, Queensland 88/G4
Stonehenge, Sask. 181/F6
Stonehouse, Scotland 15/D5
Stone Lake, Wis. (54876) 317/C4
Stone Mountain, Georgia (*30083) 217/D3
Stone Mountain Prov. Park, Br. Col. 184/L2
Stone Park, Ill. (†60160) 222/B5
Stoner, Br. Col. 184/F3
Stones (riv.), Tenn. 237/H9
Stones River Nat'l Battlefield, Tenn. 237/H9
Stoneville, Miss. (38776) 256/C4
Stoneville, N.C. (27048) 281/K2
Stoneville, S. Dak. (57784) 298/D4
Stonewall, Ark. (72468) 202/J1
Stonewall, Georgia (†30291) 217/J2
Stonewall, La. (71078) 238/C2
Stonewall, Manitoba 179/E4
Stonewall, Miss. (39363) 256/G6
Stonewall, N.C. (28583) 281/R4
Stonewall, Okla. (74871) 288/O5
Stonewall (co.), Texas 303/D4
Stonewall, Texas (78671) 303/F7
Stonewood, W. Va. (26301) 312/F4
Stoney Creek, Ontario 177/E4
Stoney Point, Ontario 177/B5
Stonington, Colo. (81075) 208/P8
Stonington, Conn. (06378) 210/H3
Stonington○, Conn. (06378) 210/H3
Stonington, Ill. (62567) 222/D4
Stonington○, Maine (04681) 243/F7
Stonington, Mich. (†49878) 250/C3
Stono (inlet), S.C. 296/H6
Stony (riv.), Alaska 196/G2
Stony (isl.), Newf. 166/C3
Stony (brook), N.J. 273/D3
Stony (ranges), N.S. Wales 97/B2
Stony (isl.), N.Y. 276/H3
Stony (pt.), N.Y. 276/H3
Stony (lake), Ontario 177/E2
Stony (lake), Ontario 177/G3
Stony (head), Tasmania 99/C2
Stony (creek), Va. 307/N6
Stony (riv.), W. Va. 312/H4
Stony Beach, Sask. 181/F5
Stony Bottom, W. Va. (24979) 312/F6
Stony Brook, N.Y. (11790) 276/O9
Stony Creek, Conn. (†06405) 210/D3
Stony Creek, N.Y. (12878) 276/M4
Stony Creek, Va. (23882) 307/N7
Stonyford, Calif. (95979) 204/C4
Stony Gorge (res.), Calif. 204/C4
Stony Island, Nova Scotia 168/C5
Stony Lake, Mich. (49455) 250/C5
Stony Mountain, Manitoba 179/E4
Stony Plain, Alberta 182/C3
Stony Point, N.Y. (10980) 276/M8
Stony Point, N.C. (28678) 281/G3
Stony Rapids, Sask. 181/M2
Stony River, Alaska (†99557) 196/G2
Stony Tunguska (riv.), U.S.S.R. 54/L3
Stony Tunguska (riv.), U.S.S.R. 48/K3
Stony Wold, N.Y. (†12968) 276/M1
Storå (riv.), Denmark 21/B5
Stora Lulevatten (lake), Sweden 18/L3
Storden, Minn. (56174) 255/C6
Store Baelt (chan.), Denmark 18/G9
Store Baelt (chan.), Denmark 21/D6
Store Heddinge, Denmark 21/F7
Store-Heddinge, Denmark 18/H9
Stor-Elvdal, Norway 18/G6
Støren, Norway 18/F5
Storey (co.), Nev. 266/B3
Storeys Creek, Tasmania 99/D3
Storeytown, New Bruns. 170/D2
Storfjorden (fjord), Norway 18/D2
Storjorm (lake), Sweden 18/J4
Storkerson (bay), N.W. Terrs. 187/F2
Storla, S. Dak. (†57359) 298/M6
Storm (lake), Iowa 229/C3
Storm (bay), Tasmania 99/D5
Storm Lake, Iowa (50588) 229/C3
Stormont (county), Ontario 177/K2
Stornoway, Québec 172/F4
Stornoway, Sask. 181/K4
Stornoway, Scotland 15/B2
Stornoway, Scotland 10/C1
Stornoway (harb.), Scotland 15/B2
Storøya (isl.), Norway 18/E1
Storozhevsk, U.S.S.R. 52/H2
Storr, The (mt.), Scotland 15/B3
Storrs, Conn. (06268) 210/F1
Storsjön (lake), Sweden 18/J5
Storstrøm (co.), Denmark 21/E7
Stort (riv.), England 13/H7
Storthoaks, Sask. 181/K6
Storuman, Sweden 18/K4
Storuman (lake), Sweden 18/K4
Storvik, Sweden 18/K6
Story, Ind. (†47448) 227/E6
Story (co.), Iowa 229/G4
Story, Wyo. (82842) 319/F1
Story City, Iowa (50248) 229/F4
Stosch (isl.), Chile 138/C8
Stotesbury, Mo. (64786) 261/C7
Stotesbury, W. Va. (†25921) 312/D7
Stotts City, Mo. (65756) 261/E8
Stottville, N.Y. (12172) 276/N6
Stoughton○, Mass. (02072) 249/K4
Stoughton, Sask. 181/J6
Stoughton, Wis. (53589) 317/H10
Stoumont, Belgium 27/H8
Stour (riv.), England 13/J6
Stour (riv.), England 13/H6
Stour (riv.), England 13/E7
Stour (riv.), England 10/G4
Stourbridge, England 13/E5
Stourbridge, England 10/G3
Stourport-on-Severn, England 10/G3
Stourport-on-Severn, England 13/E5
Stout, Iowa (50673) 229/H3
Stout, Ohio (45684) 284/D8
Stout (lake), Ontario 175/B2
Stoutland, Mo. (65567) 261/G7
Stoutsville, Mo. (65283) 261/J3
Stoutsville, Ohio (43154) 284/E6
Stovall, Miss. (38672) 256/C2
Stovall, N.C. (27582) 281/M2
Stover, Mo. (65078) 261/G6
Støvring, Denmark 21/C4
Stow○, Maine (†04058) 243/A7
Stow○, Mass. (01775) 249/H3
Stow (creek), N.J. 273/C5
Stow, Ohio (44224) 284/H3
Stow, Scotland 15/F5
Stowe, Pa. (19464) 294/L5
Stowe, Vt. (05672) 268/B3
Stowe○, Vt. (05672) 268/B3
Stowmarket, England 13/J5
Stowmarket, England 10/G4
Stowport, Tasmania 99/B3
Stoy, Ill. (62464) 222/F5
Stoystown, Pa. (15563) 294/E5
Strabane (dist.), N. Ireland 17/G2
Strabane, N. Ireland 17/G2
Strabane, N. Ireland 10/C3
Strachan, Scotland 15/F3
Strachur Bay, Scotland 15/C4
Stradbally, Laoighis, Ireland 17/G5
Stradbally, Waterford, Ireland 17/F7
Strafford, Mo. (65757) 261/F8
Strafford (co.), N.H. 268/E5
Strafford○, N.H. (03884) 268/E5
Strafford○, Vt. (05072) 268/C4
Straffordville, Ontario 177/D5
Strahan, Iowa (†51540) 229/B7
Strahan, Tasmania 99/B4
Strait (butte), Utah 304/C6
Straits, N.C. (†28579) 281/S5
Straits Pond, Mass. (†02045) 249/F7
Straitsville, Conn. (†06770) 210/C3
Strakonice, Czech. 41/B2
Stralsund, E. Germany 22/E1
Strand, S. Africa 118/F7
Strandburg, S. Dak. (57265) 298/R3
Strandby, Denmark 21/D3
Strandquist, Minn. (56758) 255/B2
Strang, Nebr. (68444) 264/G4
Strang, Okla. (74367) 288/R2
Strange Creek, W. Va. (26639) 312/E5
Strangford, N. Ireland 17/K3
Strangford (inlet), N. Ireland 17/K3
Strängnäs, Sweden 18/F1
Stranraer, Sask. 181/C4
Stranraer, Scotland 10/D3
Stranraer, Scotland 15/C6
Strasbourg, France 28/H3
Strasbourg, France 7/E4
Strasbourg, Sask. 181/G4
Strasburg, Colo. (80136) 208/L3
Strasburg, Ill. (62465) 222/E4
Strasburg, Mo. (64090) 261/D5
Strasburg, N. Dak. (58573) 282/K7
Strasburg, Ohio (44680) 284/G4
Strasburg, Pa. (17579) 294/K6
Strasburg, Va. (22657) 307/M3
Strassburg, Austria 41/C3
Stratford, Calif. (93266) 204/F7
Stratford○, Conn. (06497) 210/C4
Stratford (pt.), Conn. 210/C4
Stratford, Iowa (50249) 229/F4
Stratford○, N.H. (†03590) 268/D2
Stratford, N.J. (08084) 273/B4
Stratford, N.Y. (13470) 276/L4
Stratford, N. Zealand 100/E3
Stratford, Okla. (74872) 288/M5
Stratford, Ontario 177/C4
Stratford, S. Dak. (57474) 298/N3
Stratford, Texas (79084) 303/C1
Stratford, Va. (22558) 307/P4
Stratford, Wash. (98853) 310/F3
Stratford, Wis. (54484) 317/F6
Stratford-Centre, Québec 172/F4
Stratford-upon-Avon, England 13/F5
Stratford-upon-Avon, England 10/F4
Strathalbyn, S. Australia 94/F6
Stratham○, N.H. (03885) 268/F5
Strathaven, Scotland 15/D5
Strathbogie (dist.), Scotland 15/F3
Strathclair, Manitoba 179/B4
Strathclyde (reg.), Scotland 15/C4
Strathcona, Minn. (56759) 255/B2
Strathcona Prov. Park, Br. Col. 184/E5
Strathfield, N. S. Wales 88/K4
Strathfield, N.S. Wales 97/J3
Strathfoyle, N. Ireland 17/G1
Strathgordon, Tasmania 99/C4
Strathlorne, Nova Scotia 168/G2
Strathmere, N.J. (08248) 273/D5
Strathmoor Village, Ky. (†40201) 237/J2
Strathmore, Alberta 182/D4
Strathmore, Calif. (93267) 204/F7
Strathmore, N.J. (†07747) 273/E3
Strathmore, Scotland 15/E4
Strathnaver, Br. Col. 184/F3
Strathpeffer, Scotland 15/D3
Strathroy, Ontario 177/C5
Strathspey (dist.), Scotland 15/E3
Strathy (pt.), Scotland 15/E2
Strathy (pt.), Scotland 10/D1
Strathyre, Scotland 15/D4
Strattanville, Pa. (16258) 294/D3
Stratton, Colo. (80836) 208/O4
Stratton, Maine (04982) 243/B5
Stratton, Nebr. (69043) 264/C4
Stratton, Ohio (43961) 284/J4
Stratton, Ontario 177/F5
Stratton, Ontario 175/B3
Stratton○, Vt. (†05360) 268/B5
Stratton (mt.), Vt. 268/B5
Straubing, W. Germany 22/E4
Straubville, N. Dak. (58070) 282/O7
Straughn, Ind. (47387) 227/G5
Strausberg, E. Germany 22/F2
Strausstown, Pa. (19559) 294/K5
Straw, Mont. (†59418) 262/G4
Strawberry, Ark. (72469) 202/H2
Strawberry (lake), N. Dak. 282/J4
Strawberry (res.), Utah 304/C3
Strawberry (riv.), Utah 304/D3
Strawberry Plains, Tenn. (37871) 237/O8
Strawberry Point, Iowa (52076) 229/K3
Strawn, Ill. (61775) 222/E3
Strawn, Kansas (66839) 232/G3
Strawn, Texas (76475) 303/F5
Strayhorn, Miss. (†38665) 256/D1
Strážnice, Czech. 41/D2
Streaky (bay), S. Australia 88/E6
Streaky (bay), S. Australia 94/C5
Streaky Bay, S. Australia 88/E6
Streaky Bay, S. Australia 94/D5
Streamstown, Alberta 182/E3
Streamwood, Ill. (60103) 222/A5
Streator, Ill. (61364) 222/E2
Středočeský (reg.), Czech. 41/C2
Středoslovenský (reg.), Czech. 41/E2
Street, England 10/E5
Street, England 13/E6
Street, Md. (21154) 245/N2
Streeter, N. Dak. (58483) 282/M6
Streeter, Texas (†76856) 303/E7
Streetman, Texas (75859) 303/H6
Streetsboro, Ohio (44240) 284/H3
Strehaia, Romania 45/F3
Stresa, Italy 34/B2
Stretford, England 13/H2
Stretford, England 10/G2
Streymoy (isl.), Denmark 21/B3
Strezhevoy, U.S.S.R. 48/H3
Střibro, Czech. 41/B2
Strichen, Scotland 15/F3
Strickler, Ark. (†72774) 202/B2
Strike, C.J. (res.), Idaho 220/C7
Strimón (gulf), Greece 45/G5
Stringer, Miss. (39481) 256/F7
Stringtown, Miss. (38777) 256/C3
Stringtown, Okla. (74569) 288/P6
Stripe (lake), Sask. 181/C4
Striven, Loch (inlet), Scotland 15/A2
Stroeder, Argentina 143/D5
Strofádhes (isls.), Greece 45/E7
Stroh, Ind. (46789) 227/G1
Strokestown, Ireland 17/E4
Stroma (isl.), Scotland 15/E2
Stromboli (isl.), Italy 34/E5
Strome, Alberta 182/E3
Stromeferry, Scotland 15/C3
Stromness, Scotland 10/E1
Stromness, Scotland 15/E2
Stromsburg, Nebr. (68666) 264/G3
Strömstad, Sweden 18/G7
Strömsund, Sweden 18/K5
Stronach, Mich. (49681) 250/C4
Strong, Ark. (71765) 202/F7
Strong○, Maine (04983) 243/C6

Surfside Beach 453

Strong (riv.), Miss. 256/D7
Strong City, Kansas (66869) 232/F3
Strong City, Okla. (73665) 288/G3
Strongfield, Sask. 181/E4
Stronghurst, Ill. (61480) 222/C3
Strongs, Mich. (49790) 250/E2
Strongs, Miss. (†39730) 256/G3
Strongsville, Ohio (44136) 284/G10
Stronsay (firth), Scotland 15/F1
Stronsay (isl.), Scotland 10/E1
Stronsay (isl.), Scotland 15/F1
Strontian, Scotland 15/C4
Stropkov, Czech. 41/F2
Stroud, Ala. (†36855) 195/H4
Stroud, England 13/E6
Stroud, England 10/E5
Stroud, N.S. Wales 97/G3
Stroud, Okla. (74079) 288/N3
Stroud, Ontario 177/E3
Stroudsburg, Pa. (18360) 294/M4
Struan, Sask. 181/D3
Struan, Scotland 15/B3
Struble, Iowa (51057) 229/A3
Struer, Denmark 21/B5
Struer, Denmark 18/F8
Struga, Yugoslavia 45/E5
Strum, Wis. (54770) 317/D6
Struma (riv.), Bulgaria 45/F5
Strumble (head), Wales 13/B5
Strumica, Yugoslavia 45/F5
Strunk, Ky. (42649) 237/N7
Struthers, Ohio (44471) 284/J3
Stryker, Mont. (59933) 262/B2
Stryker, Ohio (43557) 284/B3
Strykersville, N.Y. (14145) 276/C5
Strzegom, Poland 47/C3
Strzelce Krajeńskie, Poland 47/B2
Strzelce Opolskie, Poland 47/D3
Strzelecki (creek), S. Australia 88/G5
Strzelecki (creek), S. Australia 94/G3
Strzelecki (mt.), Tasmania 99/D2
Strzelin, Poland 47/C3
Strzelno, Poland 47/D2
Strzyzów, Poland 47/E4
Stuart (isl.), Alaska 196/F2
Stuart (lake), Br. Col. 184/E3
Stuart, Fla. (33494) 212/F4
Stuart, Iowa (50250) 229/E6
Stuart, Nebr. (68780) 264/E2
Stuart, Okla. (74570) 288/O5
Stuart (range), S. Australia 94/D3
Stuart, Va. (24171) 307/H7
Stuart (mt.), Wash. 310/E3
Stuartburn, Manitoba 179/F5
Stuart Island, Br. Col. 184/E5
Stuarts Draft, Va. (24477) 307/L4
Stuart Town, N.S. Wales 97/E3
Stubbekøbing, Denmark 21/F8
Stubbenkammer (pt.), E. Germany 22/E1
Stub Hill (mt.), N.H. 268/E1
Stuckey, S.C. (29554) 296/H4
Studénka, Czech. 41/D2
Studley, Kansas (67759) 232/B2
Studley, Va. (23162) 307/O5
Stukely-Sud, Québec 172/E4
Stump (lake), N. Dak. 282/O4
Stumptown, W. Va. (25280) 312/E5
Stumpy Point, N.C. (27978) 281/T3
Stupino, U.S.S.R. 52/E4
Stura (riv.), Italy 34/A2
Sturbridge, Mass. (01566) 249/F4
Sturbridge○, Mass. (01566) 249/F4
Sturdivant, Mo. (63782) 261/M8
Sturgeon (lake), Alberta 182/B2
Sturgeon (bay), Manitoba 179/E3
Sturgeon (riv.), Mich. 250/C2
Sturgeon (riv.), Minn. 255/F3
Sturgeon, Mo. (65284) 261/H4
Sturgeon (lake), Ontario 177/G5
Sturgeon, Pa. (15082) 294/B5
Sturgeon, Pr. Edward I. 168/F2
Sturgeon (riv.), Sask. 181/E2
Sturgeon Bay, Wis. (54235) 317/M6
Sturgeon Falls, Ont. 162/H6
Sturgeon Falls, Ontario 175/E3
Sturgeon Falls, Ontario 177/E1
Sturgeon Heights, Alberta 182/B2
Sturgeon Lake, Minn. (55783) 255/F4
Sturgeon Point, Ontario 177/F3
Sturgeon Weir, Sask. 181/N4
Sturgis, Ky. (42459) 237/F5
Sturgis, Mich. (49091) 250/D7
Sturgis, Miss. (39769) 256/G4
Sturgis, Sask. 181/J4
Sturgis, S. Dak. (57785) 298/B5
Štúrovo, Czech. 41/E3
Sturt (mt.), N.S. Wales 97/A1
Sturt (plain), North. Terr. 93/C4
Sturt (des.), Queensland 88/G5
Sturt (des.), Queensland 95/B3
Sturt (riv.), S. Australia 88/D8
Sturt (des.), S. Australia 94/G3
Sturt (riv.), S. Australia 94/B8
Sturt (creek), W. Australia 88/D3
Sturt (creek), W. Australia 92/D2
Sturtevant, Wis. (53177) 317/M3
Stutsman (co.), N. Dak. 282/M5
Stutterheim, S. Africa 118/D6
Stuttgart, Ark. (72160) 202/H4
Stuttgart, Kansas (67670) 232/C2
Stuttgart, W. Germany 7/E4
Stuttgart, W. Germany 22/C4
Styria (prov.), Austria 41/C3
Suai, Malaysia 85/E5
Suakin, Sudan 102/F3
Suakin, Sudan 59/C6
Suakin, Sudan 111/G4
Suakin (arch.), Sudan 111/G4
Suamico, Wis. (54173) 317/K6
Suao, China 77/K7
Suapi, Bolivia 136/B4
Suapure (riv.), Venezuela 124/E4
Suaqui, Mexico 150/E2
Suárez (riv.), Colombia 126/D4
Subang, Indonesia 85/H2
Subata, U.S.S.R. 53/D2
Subei, China 77/E4
Subeihi, Jordan 65/D3
Subh, Jebel (mt.), Saudi Arabia 59/C5
Subiaco, Ark. (72865) 202/C3
Subiaco, W. Australia 88/B2
Subi Besar (isl.), Indonesia 85/D5
Subic (bay), Philippines 82/C3
Sublett (mts.), Idaho 220/E7
Sublett, Ky. (41470) 237/P5
Sublette, Ill. (61367) 222/D2
Sublette, Kansas (67877) 232/B4
Sublette, Mo. (†63546) 261/G2
Sublette (co.), Wyo. 319/C3
Subligna, Georgia (†30747) 217/B1
Sublimity, Oreg. (97385) 291/E3
Subotica, Yugoslavia 7/F4
Subotica, Yugoslavia 45/D2
Subtle, Ky. (42129) 237/L7
Sucarnochee, Miss. (†39352) 256/H5
Sucarnoochee (creek), Miss. 256/G5
Succasunna, N.J. (07876) 273/D2
Success, Ark. (72470) 202/J1
Success, Mo. (65570) 261/H8
Success, Sask. 181/D5
Succor (creek), Oreg. 291/K4
Suceava, Romania 45/G2
Suchedniów, Poland 47/E3
Suches, Bolivia 136/A4
Suches (riv.), Bolivia 136/A4
Suches, Georgia (30572) 217/E1
Suchitoto, El Salvador 154/C4
Süchow (Xuzhou), China 77/J5
Sucia (bay), P. Rico 161/A3
Sucia (isl.), Wash. 310/C2
Sucio (riv.), Colombia 126/B4
Suck (riv.), Ireland 17/E5
Sucre (cap.), Bolivia 2/F6
Sucre (cap.), Bolivia 120/C4
Sucre (cap.), Bolivia 136/C6
Sucre (dept.), Colombia 126/C3
Sucre, Bolívar, Colombia 126/C3
Sucre, Caquetá, Colombia 126/C7
Sucre, Ecuador 128/B3
Sucre (state), Venezuela 124/G2
Sucre, Venezuela 124/D3
Sucúa, Ecuador 128/C4
Sucuriju, Brazil 132/D2
Sud (dept.), Haiti 158/A6
Sud (chan.), Haiti 158/B6
Suda (riv.), U.S.S.R. 52/E3
Sudak, U.S.S.R. 52/E6
Sudan 2/L5
Sudan 102/E3
SUDAN 111/E4
SUDAN 59/B6
Sudan (reg.) 102/D3
Sudan (reg.), Benin 106/E6
Sudan (reg.), Chad 111/C5
Sudan (reg.), Mali 106/D6
Sudan (reg.), Niger 106/F6
Sudan (reg.), Nigeria 106/F6
Sudan (reg.), Sudan 111/E5
Sudan, Texas (79371) 303/B3
Sudan (reg.), Upper Volta 106/D6
Sudbury, England 10/G4
Sudbury, England 13/H5
Sudbury○, Mass. (01776) 249/A6
Sudbury (res.), Mass. 249/H3
Sudbury (riv.), Mass. 249/A6
Sudbury, Ont. 162/H6
Sudbury, Ont. 146/K5
Sudbury (reg. munic.), Ontario 175/D3
Sudbury (terr. dist.), Ontario 175/D3
Sudbury (terr. dist.), Ontario 177/J5
Sudbury (reg. munic.), Ontario 177/K6
Sudbury, Ontario 177/K5
Sudbury, Ontario 175/D3
Sudbury○, Vt. (†05733) 268/A4
Sudd (swamp), Sudan 102/F4
Sudd (swamp), Sudan 111/F6
Suddie, Guyana 131/B2
Sudeten (mts.), Czech. 41/C1
Sudeten (range), Poland 47/B3
Sudhuroy (isl.), Denmark 21/B3
Sudirman (range), Indonesia 85/K6
Sudith, Ky. (40381) 237/O4
Sudlersville, Md. (21668) 245/P4
Sue (riv.), Sudan 111/E6
Sueca, Spain 33/F3
Suemez (isl.), Alaska 196/M2
Suez (canal) 2/L4
Suez, Egypt 111/K3
Suez, Egypt 59/B4
Suez, Egypt 102/F2
Suez (canal), Egypt 102/F1
Suez (canal), Egypt 111/K3
Suez (canal), Egypt 59/B3
Suez (gulf), Egypt 111/F2
Suez (gulf), Egypt 59/B4
Suf, Jordan 65/D3
Sufeina, Saudi Arabia 59/D5
Sufers, Switzerland 39/H3
Suffern, N.Y. (10901) 276/J8
Suffield, Alberta 182/E4
Suffield, Conn. (06078) 210/E1
Suffield○, Conn. (06078) 210/E1
Suffield, Ohio (†44260) 284/H3
Suffolk (co.), England 13/H5
Suffolk (co.), Mass. 249/K3
Suffolk, Mont. (†59451) 262/G3
Suffolk (co.), N.Y. 276/P9
Suffolk (I.C.), Va. (*23432) 307/P7
Sufian, Iran 66/E1
Sugar (creek), Ind. 227/B4
Sugar (creek), Ind. 227/F5
Sugar (creek), Ind. 227/C5
Sugar (isl.), Mich. 250/E2
Sugar (riv.), N.H. 268/C5
Sugar (creek), Pa. 294/J2
Sugar (riv.), Wis. 317/H10
Sugar Bush, Wis. (†54961) 317/J7
Sugarbush Hill (mt.), Wis. 317/J4
Sugar City, Colo. (81076) 208/M6
Sugar City, Idaho (83448) 220/G6
Sugar Creek, Mo. (64054) 261/R5
Sugarcreek, Ohio (44681) 284/G5
Sugar Creek, Pa. (†16323) 294/C3
Sugar Grove, Ark. (†72927) 202/C3
Sugar Grove, Ill. (60554) 222/E2
Sugar Grove, Ohio (43155) 284/E6
Sugargrove, Pa. (16350) 294/D1
Sugar Grove, Va. (24375) 307/E7
Sugar Grove, W. Va. (26815) 312/H5
Sugar Hill, Georgia (†30518) 217/E2
Sugar Hill○, N.H. (03585) 268/D3
Sugar Island, Mich. (†49783) 250/E2
Sugar Land, Texas (77478) 303/J8
Sugarloaf (key), Fla. 212/E7
Sugarloaf (hill), Hawaii 218/C4
Sugarloaf (mt.), Ireland 17/B8
Sugarloaf (pt.), N. S. Wales 88/J6
Sugarloaf (passage), N.S. Wales 97/J1
Sugarloaf (pt.), N.S. Wales 97/G3
Sugarloaf P.O. (Big Bear City), Calif. (92314) 204/J9
Sugar Notch, Pa. (18706) 294/E7
Sugartown, La. (70662) 238/D5
Sugar Tree, Tenn. (38380) 237/E9
Sugar Tree Ridge, Ohio (45133) 284/C7
Sugar Valley, Georgia (30746) 217/C1
Sugbai (passage), Philippines 82/C8
Sugden, Okla. (†73565) 288/L6
Suggsville, Ala. (†36482) 195/C7
Sühbaatar, Mongolia 77/H2
Sühbaatar (Sukhe Bator), Mongolia 77/G1
Sühbaatar, Mongolia 54/M5
Suheli Par (atoll), India 68/C6
Suhl (dist.), E. Germany 22/D3
Suhl, E. Germany 22/D3
Suhr, Switzerland 39/F2
Şuhut, Turkey 63/D3
Sui, Pakistan 68/B3
Suiattle (riv.), Wash. 310/D2
Suichang, China 77/J6
Suide, China 77/G4
Suifenhe, China 77/M3
Suihua, China 77/L2
Suijiang, China 77/F6
Suileng, China 77/L2
Suining, China 77/G5
Suipacha, Argentina 143/G7
Suipacha, Bolivia 136/C7
Suir (riv.), Ireland 10/C4
Suir (riv.), Ireland 17/G7
Suisun (bay), Calif. 204/K1
Suisun City, Calif. (94585) 204/K1
Suit, N.C. (28906) 281/A4
Suita, Japan 81/J7
Suitland-Silver Hill, Md. (†20746) 245/F5
Sui Xian, China 77/H5
Suizhong, China 77/K3
Sukabumi, Indonesia 85/H2
Sukadana, Indonesia 85/E6
Sukagawa, Japan 81/K5
Sukhana, U.S.S.R. 48/M3
Sukhinichi, U.S.S.R. 52/E4
Sukhona (riv.), U.S.S.R. 52/F2
Sukhothai, Thailand 72/D3
Sukhumi, U.S.S.R. 7/H4
Sukhumi, U.S.S.R. 52/F6
Sukhumi, U.S.S.R. 48/D5
Suk, Sudan 111/F5
Sukkertoppen, Greenl. 4/C12
Sukkur, Pakistan 54/H7
Sukkur, Pakistan 59/J4
Sukkur, Pakistan 68/B3
Sükösd, Hungary 41/E3
Sukumo, Japan 81/F7
Sul (chan.), Brazil 120/E2
Sul (chan.), Brazil 132/D2
Sula (isls.), Indonesia 54/O10
Sula (isls.), Indonesia 85/H6
Sula, Mont. (59871) 262/B5
Sulaco, Honduras 154/D3
Sulaco (riv.), Honduras 154/D3
Sulaiman (range), Pakistan 68/C3
Sulaimaniya (gov.), Iraq 66/D3
Sulaimaniya, Iraq 59/E2
Sulaimaniya, Iraq 66/D3
Sulaiyil, Saudi Arabia 59/E5
Sulakyurt, Turkey 63/E2
Sulanheer, Mongolia 77/G3
Sulawesi (isl.), Indonesia 85/G6
Sulechów, Poland 47/B2
Sulęcin, Poland 47/B2
Sulgen, Switzerland 39/H1
Sulina, Romania 45/J3
Sulitelma (mt.), Sweden 18/K3
Sulitjelma, Norway 18/K3
Sulitjelma (mt.), Norway 18/J3
Sullana, Peru 128/B5
Sullana, Peru 120/A3
Sulligent, Ala. (35586) 195/B3
Sullivan (lake), Alberta 182/D3
Sullivan, Ill. (61951) 222/E4
Sullivan (co.), Ind. 227/C6
Sullivan, Ind. (47882) 227/C6
Sullivan, Ky. (42460) 237/E6
Sullivan, Maine (†04689) 243/G6
Sullivan○, Maine (†04689) 243/G6
Sullivan (co.), Mo. 261/F2
Sullivan, Mo. (63080) 261/K6
Sullivan (co.), N.H. 268/C5
Sullivan○, N.H. (†03445) 268/C5
Sullivan (co.), N.Y. 276/L7
Sullivan, Ohio (44880) 284/F3
Sullivan (co.), Pa. 294/J3
Sullivan (co.), Tenn. 237/S7
Sullivan (lake), Wash. 310/H2
Sullivan, W. Va. (†25847) 312/D7
Sullivan, Wis. (53178) 317/H1
Sullivan Gardens, Tenn. (†37660) 237/R8
Sullivan Mines, Québec 174/B3
Sullivans Island, S.C. (29482) 296/H6
Sully, Iowa (50251) 229/H5
Sully, Québec 172/H2
Sully (co.), S. Dak. 298/J4
Sulmona, Italy 34/D3
Sulphide, Ontario 177/G3
Sulphur (riv.), Ark. 202/B7
Sulphur, Ind. (47174) 227/E8
Sulphur, Ky. (40070) 237/L4
Sulphur, La. (70663) 238/D6
Sulphur, Nev. (†89445) 266/C2
Sulphur, Okla. (73086) 288/N5
Sulphur (creek), S. Dak. 298/D4
Sulphur (riv.), Texas 303/J4
Sulphur City, Ark. (†72701) 202/B2
Sulphur Creek, Tasmania 99/C3
Sulphur Draw (dry riv.), Texas 303/B4
Sulphur Fork, Red (riv.), Tenn. 237/H8
Sulphur Rock, Ark. (72579) 202/H2
Sulphur Spring (valley), Ariz. 198/F6
Sulphur Spring (range), Nev. 266/E3
Sulphur Springs, Ala. (†30738) 195/G1
Sulphur Springs, Ark. (72768) 202/B1
Sulphur Springs, Ind. (47388) 227/G4
Sulphur Springs, Iowa (†50588) 229/C3
Sulphur Springs, Mo. (63083) 261/M6
Sulphur Springs, Ohio (44881) 284/E4
Sulphur Springs, Texas (75482) 303/J4
Sulphur Springs (creek), Texas 303/B4
Sulphur Well, Ky. (42129) 237/K6
Sultan, Ontario 175/D3
Sultan, Ontario 177/J5
Sultan (mts.), Turkey 63/D3
Sultan, Wash. (98294) 310/D3
Sultan (riv.), Wash. 310/D3
Sultanabad (Kashmar), Iran 66/L3
Sultandağı, Turkey 63/D3
Sultanhanı, Turkey 63/E3
Sultan Kudarat (prov.), Philippines 82/E7
Sulu (prov.), Philippines 82/C7
Sulu (arch.), Philippines 54/O9
Sulu (sea), Philippines 54/N9
Sulu (arch.), Philippines 82/B8
Sulu (arch.), Philippines 85/G4
Sulu (sea), Philippines 85/G4
Sulu (sea), Philippines 82/B6
Suluan (isl.), Philippines 82/F5
Suluova, Turkey 63/F2
Sulz, Switzerland 39/F1
Sulzbach, W. Germany 22/B4
Sulzbach-Rosenberg, W. Germany 22/D4
Sulzberger (bay) 5/B11
Sulzfluh (mt.), Switzerland 39/J2
Sumami Auma, Brazil 132/B4
Sumampa, Argentina 143/D2
Sumas, Wash. (98295) 310/C2
Sumatra, Fla. (32335) 212/B1
Sumatra (isl.), Indonesia 2/P6
Sumatra (isl.), Indonesia 54/L9
Sumatra (isl.), Indonesia 85/B5
Sumatra, Mont. (59083) 262/J4
Sumava Resorts, Ind. (46379) 227/C2
Sumba (isl.), Indonesia 54/N11
Sumba (isl.), Indonesia 85/F7
Sumba (str.), Indonesia 85/F7
Sumbawa (isl.), Indonesia 54/N11
Sumbawa (isl.), Indonesia 85/F7
Sumbawa Besar, Indonesia 85/F7
Sumbawanga, Tanzania 115/F5
Sumbay, Peru 128/G10
Sumbilca, Peru 128/D8
Sumbing (mt.), Indonesia 85/J2
Sumburgh (head), Scotland 15/G2
Sumedang, Indonesia 85/H2
Sümeg, Hungary 41/D3
Sumenep, Indonesia 85/L2
Sumgait, U.S.S.R. 7/J4
Sumgait, U.S.S.R. 52/G6
Sumidero, Cuba 158/A2
Sumiswald, Switzerland 39/E2
Sumiton, Ala. (35148) 195/D3
Summan (plat.), Saudi Arabia 59/E4
Summer (isl.), Mich. 250/C3
Summer (lake), Oreg. 188/C2
Summer (lake), Oreg. 291/G5
Summerberry, Sask. 181/J5
Summerdale, Ala. (36580) 195/C10
Summerfield, Ala. (†36701) 195/E5
Summerfield, Fla. (32691) 212/D2
Summerfield, Ill. (62289) 222/D5
Summerfield, Kansas (66541) 232/F2
Summerfield, La. (71079) 238/E1
Summerfield, Mo. (†65013) 261/J6
Summerfield, N.C. (27358) 281/K2
Summerfield, Ohio (43788) 284/H6
Summerfield, Okla. (74966) 288/S5
Summerfield, Texas (79085) 303/B3
Summerford, Newf. 166/C4
Summerford, Ohio (†43140) 284/D6
Summer Hill, Ill. (62372) 222/C4
Summerhill, Pa. (15958) 294/E5
Summer Isles (isls.), Scotland 15/C2
Summer Lake, Oreg. (97640) 291/G5
Summerland, Br. Col. 184/G5
Summerland, Calif. (93067) 204/F9
Summerland, Miss. (†39168) 256/F7
Summerland Key, Fla. (33042) 212/E7
Summers, Ark. (72769) 202/A2
Summers (co.), W. Va. 312/E7
Summerset, Iowa (†50125) 229/F6
Summer Shade, Ky. (42166) 237/K7
Summerside, Pr. Edward I. 168/E2
Summersville, Ky. (42782) 237/K6
Summersville, Mo. (65571) 261/J8
Summersville, Ohio (†43344) 284/D5
Summersville, W. Va. (26651) 312/E6
Summersville (lake), W. Va. 312/E6
Summerton, S.C. (29148) 296/G4
Summertown, Georgia (30466) 217/H5
Summertown, Tenn. (38483) 237/G10
Summerville, Georgia (30747) 217/B2
Summerville, La. (†71465) 238/F3
Summerville, Newf. 166/D2
Summerville, Oreg. (97876) 291/K2
Summerville, Pa. (15864) 294/D3
Summerville, S.C. (29483) 296/G5
Summerville Centre, Nova Scotia 168/D5
Summit, Ala. (†35031) 195/F2
Summit, Alaska (†99729) 196/J2
Summit, Ark. (72677) 202/E1
Summit (co.), Colo. 208/G4
Summit (peak), Colo. 208/F8
Summit (lake), Iowa 229/E6
Summit, Miss. (39666) 256/D8
Summit (lake), Nev. 266/C1
Summit, N.J. (07901) 273/E2
Summit (co.), Ohio 284/G3
Summit (creek), Oreg. 291/J3
Summit, Québec 172/E2
Summit, R.I. (†02827) 249/H6
Summit, S.C. (†29054) 296/E4
Summit, S. Dak. (57266) 298/P3
Summit (co.), Utah 304/D3
Summit, Utah (84772) 304/B6
Summit-Argo, Ill. (60501) 222/B6
Summit Bridge, Del. (†19709) 245/R2
Summit City, Calif. (96089) 204/C3
Summit City, Mich. (†49649) 250/D4
Summit Hill, Pa. (18250) 294/L4
Summit Lake, Wis. (54485) 317/H5
Summit Lake Ind. Res., Nev. 266/B1
Summit Point, W. Va. (25446) 312/K4
Summitville, Ind. (46070) 227/F4
Summitville, Iowa (†52632) 229/K8
Summitville, N.Y. (12781) 276/L7
Summitville, Ohio (43962) 284/J4
Summitville, Tenn. (37382) 237/K9
Summum, Ill. (†61501) 222/C3
Sumner (str.), Alaska 196/M2
Sumner, Georgia (31789) 217/E7
Sumner, Ill. (62466) 222/F5
Sumner, Iowa (50674) 229/J3
Sumner (co.), Kansas 232/E4
Sumner○, Maine (†04292) 243/C7
Sumner, Mich. (48889) 250/E5
Sumner, Miss. (38957) 256/D3
Sumner, Mo. (64681) 261/F3
Sumner, Nebr. (68878) 264/E4
Sumner (dam), N. Mex. 274/E4
Sumner (lake), N. Mex. 274/E4
Sumner (lake), N. Zealand 100/D5
Sumner, Oreg. (†97420) 291/C4
Sumner (co.), Tenn. 237/J8
Sumner, Wash. (98390) 310/C3
Sumner-East Sumner, Maine (04232) 243/C7
Sumoto, Japan 81/G6
Šumperk, Czech. 41/D1
Sumprabum, Burma 72/C1
Sumpter, Ark. (†71647) 202/F7
Sumpter, Oreg. (97877) 291/J3
Sumrall, Miss. (39482) 256/E8
Sumter (co.), Ala. 195/B5
Sumter, Ala. (†35086) 195/D4
Sumter (co.), Fla. 212/D3
Sumter (co.), Georgia 217/D6
Sumter (co.), S.C. 296/G4
Sumter, S.C. (29150) 296/G4
Sumterville, Ala. (†35460) 195/B5
Sumy, U.S.S.R. 7/H3
Sumy, U.S.S.R. 52/E4
Sumy, U.S.S.R. 48/D4
Sun, La. (70463) 238/L5
Sun (riv.), Mont. 262/D3
Sunagawa, Japan 81/K2
Sunapee○, N.H. (03782) 268/C5
Sunapee (lake), N.H. 268/C5
Sunart, Loch (inlet), Scotland 15/C4
Sunbeam, Colo. (†81640) 208/C1
Sunbeam, Idaho (†83278) 220/D5
Sunbright, Tenn. (37872) 237/M8
Sunburg, Minn. (56289) 255/C5
Sunburst, Mont. (59482) 262/E2
Sunbury, Iowa (†52778) 229/M5
Sunbury (co.), New Bruns. 170/D3
Sunbury, N.C. (27979) 281/R2
Sunbury, Ohio (43074) 284/E5
Sunbury, Pa. (17801) 294/J4
Sunbury, Victoria 97/C5
Sunbury-on-Thames, England 13/G8
Sunbury-on-Thames, England 10/B6
Sunchales, Argentina 143/F5
Suncho Corral, Argentina 143/D2
Sunch'ŏn, N. Korea 81/B4
Sunch'ŏn, S. Korea 81/C6
Sun City, Ariz. (*85351) 198/C5
Sun City, Calif. (92381) 204/F11
Sun City, Fla. (33586) 212/D4
Sun City, Kansas (67143) 232/D4
Sun City Center, Fla. (†33570) 212/C3
Suncook, N.H. (03275) 268/D5
Suncook (lakes), N.H. 268/E5
Suncook (riv.), N.H. 268/E5
Sunda (isls.), Indonesia 54/L10
Sunda (str.), Indonesia 54/M10
Sunda (str.), Indonesia 85/C7
Sundahl, Minn. (†56545) 255/B3
Sundance, Wyo. (82729) 319/H1
Sundarbans (reg.), Bangladesh 68/F4
Sundarbans (reg.), India 68/F4
Sundargarh, India 68/E4
Sunday (riv.), Maine 243/B6
Sundbyberg, Sweden 18/G1
Sunderland, England 13/J3
Sunderland, England 10/F3
Sunderland○, Mass. (01375) 249/D3
Sunderland, Ontario 177/E3
Sunderland○, Vt. (†05250) 268/A5
Sundown, Manitoba 179/F5
Sundown, Texas (79372) 303/B4
Sundra, S. Africa 118/J6
Sundre, Alberta 182/C4
Sundridge, Ontario 177/E2
Sundsvall, Sweden 18/K5
Sundsvall, Sweden 7/F2
Sunfield, Ill. (†62832) 222/D5
Sunfield, Mich. (48890) 250/D6
Sunfish Lake, Minn. (†55075) 255/E6
Sunflower, Ala. (36581) 195/B8
Sunflower (mt.), Kansas 232/A2
Sunflower (co.), Miss. 256/C3
Sunflower, Miss. (38778) 256/C3
Sunflower (riv.), Miss. 256/C5
Sungaipenuh, Indonesia 85/C6
Sungai Petani, Malaysia 72/C6
Sungurlu, Turkey 63/F2
Sunland, Calif. (91040) 204/C10
Sunland Gardens, Fla. (†33450) 212/F4
Sunman, Ind. (47041) 227/G6
Sunndalsøra, Norway 18/F5
Sunne, Sweden 18/H7
Sunnybrae, Nova Scotia 168/F3
Sunnybrook, Alberta 182/C3
Sunny Corner, New Bruns. 170/E2
Sunnydale, Wash. (†98101) 310/B2
Sunny Isles, Fla. (33160) 212/C4
Sunnymead, Calif. (92388) 204/F11
Sunnynook, Alberta 182/E4
Sunny Point Mil. Ocean Term., N.C. 281/O6
Sunnyside, Fla. (32461) 212/C6
Sunny Side, Georgia (30284) 217/D4
Sunnyside, Ill. (†60050) 222/A4
Sunnyside, New Bruns. 170/D1
Sunnyside, Newf. 166/D2
Sunnyside, Utah (84539) 304/D4
Sunnyside, Wash. (98944) 310/F4
Sunnyslope, Alberta 182/D4
Sunny South, Ala. (36780) 195/C7
Sunnyvale, Calif. (*94086) 204/K3
Sunnyvale, Texas (†75149) 303/H2
Sunny Valley, Oreg. (97478) 291/D5
Sunol, Calif. (94586) 204/L2
Sunol, Nebr. (†69149) 264/B3
Sun Prairie, Wis. (53590) 317/H9
Sunray, Texas (79086) 303/C1
Sunrise, Fla. (33313) 212/B4
Sunrise, Wyo. (†82215) 319/H3
Sunrise Beach, Mo. (65079) 261/G6
Sunrise Manor, Nev. (†89110) 266/F6
Sunrise Ridge, Ill. (†60097) 222/E1
Sunrise Valley, Br. Col. 184/G2
Sun River, Mont. (59483) 262/E3
Sunsas, Serranía de (mts.), Bolivia 136/F5
Sunset, Ark. (†72364) 202/K3
Sunset (peak), Idaho 220/E6
Sunset, La. (70584) 238/F6
Sunset, Maine (04683) 243/F7
Sunset, S.C. (29685) 296/B2
Sunset, Texas (79407) 303/G4
Sunset, Utah (†84015) 304/B2
Sunset Beach, Calif. (90742) 204/C11
Sunset Beach, Hawaii (†96712) 218/E1
Sunset Beach, N.C. (28459) 281/N7
Sunset Crater Nat'l Mon., Ariz. 198/D3
Sunset Hills, Mo. (†63101) 261/O4
Sunset Hills, Va. (22090) 307/R2
Sunset House, Alberta 182/B2
Sunset Prairie, Br. Co. 184/G2
Sunshine, La. (†70776) 238/K2
Sunshine, Maine (†04627) 243/G7
Sunshine, Victoria 88/K7
Sunshine, Victoria 97/H5
Sunspot, N. Mex. (88349) 274/D6
Suntar, U.S.S.R. 48/M3
Suntrana, Alaska (†99743) 196/J2
Sun Valley, Idaho (83353) 220/D6
Sun Valley, Nev. (†89431) 266/B3
Sun Valley, Sask. 181/F5
Sunyani, Ghana 106/D7
Sunzu (mt.), Zambia 115/F5
Suo (sea), Japan 81/E7
Suolahti, Finland 18/O5
Suomussalmi, Finland 18/Q4
Suonenjoki, Finland 18/P5
Suong, Cambodia 72/E5
Suoyarvi, U.S.S.R. 52/D2
Supai, Ariz. (86435) 198/C2
Supe, Peru 128/D8
Superb, Sask. 181/B4
Superior (lake) 162/G-H6
Superior (lake) 146/K5
Superior (lake) 188/J1
Superior, Ariz. (85273) 198/D5
Superior, Colo. (†80027) 208/J3
Superior, Iowa (51363) 229/D2
Superior (lag.), Mexico 150/M9
Superior (lake), Mich. 250/C2
Superior (lake), Minn. 255/G3
Superior, Mont. (59872) 262/B3
Superior, Nebr. (68978) 264/F4
Superior (lake), Ontario 177/H5
Superior (lake), Ontario 175/C3
Superior, Wis. 188/H1
Superior, Wis. (54880) 317/C2
Superior (lake), Wis. 317/F1
Superior, Wyo. (82945) 319/D4
Superior Village, Wis. (†54880) 317/B2
Superstition (mts.), Ariz. 198/D5
Suphan Buri, Thailand 72/C4
Süphan Dağı (mt.), Turkey 59/D2
Süphan Dağı (mt.), Turkey 63/K3
Supiori (isl.), Indonesia 85/K6
Supply, N.C. (28462) 281/N6
Supreme, La. (†70372) 238/K4
Supung (res.), N. Korea 81/B3
Suqian, China 77/J5
Suquamish, Wash. (98392) 310/A1
Sur (pt.), Calif. 204/D7
Sur, Lebanon 63/F6
Sur, Oman 59/G5
Sura, Ras (cape), Somalia 115/J1
Sura (riv.), U.S.S.R. 52/G4
Surab, Pakistan 68/B3
Surab, Pakistan 59/J4
Surabaya, Indonesia 54/N10
Surabaya, Indonesia 85/K2
Surada, India 68/E5
Surahammar, Sweden 18/J7
Surakarta, Indonesia 54/N10
Surakarta, Indonesia 85/J2
Šurany, Czech. 41/E2
Surat, India 54/J7
Surat, India 68/C4
Surat, Queensland 88/H5
Suratgarh, India 68/C3
Surat Thani, Thailand 72/C5
Sur del Cabo San Antonio (pt.), Argentina 143/E4
Surdulica, Yugoslavia 45/F4
Surendranagar, India 68/C4
Suresnes, France 28/A2
Suretka, C. Rica 154/F6
Surette Island, Nova Scotia 168/B5
Surf, Calif. (†93436) 204/E9
Surf City, N.J. (08008) 273/E4
Surf City, N.C. (28445) 281/O6
Surfside, Fla. (33154) 212/B4
Surfside Beach, S.C. (29577) 296/K4

454 Surgidero de Batabanó

Surgidero de Batabanó, Cuba 156/A2
Surgidero de Batabanó, Cuba 158/C1
Surgoinsville, Tenn. (37873) 237/R8
Surgut, U.S.S.R. 48/H3
Surigao, Philippines 82/E6
Surigao, Philippines 85/H4
Surigao (str.), Philippines 82/E6
Surigao del Norte (prov.), Philippines 82/F5
Surigao del Sur (prov.), Philippines 82/F6
Surimena, Colombia 126/D6
Surin, Thailand 72/D4
Suriname 2/G5
Suriname 120/D2
SURINAME 131/C3
Suriname (dist.), Suriname 131/D3
Suriname (riv.), Suriname 131/D3
Suring, Wis. (54174) 317/K5
Suripa, Venezuela 124/D4
Suripá (riv.), Venezuela 124/C4
Surire, Salar de (salt dep.), Chile 138/B2
Sürmene, Turkey 63/J2
Surprise, Ariz. (85345) 198/C5
Surprise, Ind. (†47228) 227/E7
Surprise, Nebr. (68667) 264/G3
Surrency, Georgia (31563) 217/H7
Surrey, Br. Col. 184/K3
Surrey (co.), England 13/G6
Surrey, N. Dak. (58785) 282/H3
Surry◯, Maine (04684) 243/F7
Surry◯, N.H. (03431) 268/C5
Surry (co.), N.C. 281/H2
Surry (co.), Va. 307/P6
Surry, Va. (23883) 307/P6
Surry Mountain (lake), N.H. 268/C5
Sursee, Switzerland 39/F2
Surtsey (isl.), Iceland 21/B2
Sürüç, Turkey 63/H4
Surud Ad (mt.), Somalia 115/J1
Suruga (bay), Japan 81/J6
Surup, Philippines 82/F7
Surveyor, W. Va. (25932) 312/D7
Surwakwima (fall), Guyana 131/A2
Susâ (riv.), Denmark 21/E7
Susa (ruins), Iran 66/F4
Susa, Italy 34/A2
Susa, Libya 111/D1
Susa Creek, Alberta 182/A3
Susaki, Japan 81/F7
Susan (riv.), Calif. 204/D3
Susan, Va. (23163) 307/R6
Susangerd, Iran 59/E3
Susangerd, Iran 66/F5
Susank, Kansas (67580) 232/D3
Susanville, Calif. (96130) 204/E3
Susch, Switzerland 39/K3
Suşehri, Turkey 63/H2
Sušice, Czech. 41/B2
Susie, Ky. (†42633) 237/M7
Susitna, Alaska (†99501) 196/B1
Susitna (riv.), Alaska 196/B1
Susquehanna (riv.), Md. 245/N1
Susquehanna (riv.), N.Y. 276/H6
Susquehanna (co.), Pa. 294/L2
Susquehanna, Pa. (18847) 294/L2
Susquehanna (riv.), Pa. 294/K6
Susquehanna, West Branch (riv.), Pa. 294/G3
Susques, Argentina 143/C1
Sussex (co.), Del. 245/S6
Sussex, East (co.), England 13/H7
Sussex, West (co.), England 13/G7
Sussex, New Bruns. 170/E3
Sussex (co.), N.J. 273/D1
Sussex, N.J. (07461) 273/D1
Sussex (co.), Va. 307/O7
Sussex, Va. (23884) 307/O7
Sussex, Wis. (53089) 317/K1
Sussex, Wyo. (†82639) 319/F2
Sussex Corner, New Bruns. 170/E3
Sussex Inlet, N.S. Wales 97/F4
Susten (pass), Switzerland 39/G3
Sustenhorn (mt.), Switzerland 39/G3
Sustut (riv.), Br. Col. 184/D2
Susuman, U.S.S.R. 4/C2
Susuman, U.S.S.R. 54/R3
Susuman, U.S.S.R. 48/P3
Susurluk, Turkey 63/C3
Susuz, Turkey 63/K2
Sütçüler, Turkey 63/D4
Sutherland, Iowa (51058) 229/B3
Sutherland, Nebr. (69165) 264/C3
Sutherland (res.), Nebr. 264/C3
Sutherland, N. S. Wales 88/K5
Sutherland, N.S. Wales 97/J4
Sutherland (trad. co.), Scotland 15/A4
Sutherland Springs, Texas (78161) 303/K11
Sutherlin, Oreg. (97479) 291/D4
Sutherlin, Va. (24594) 307/O7
Sutlej (riv.) 54/J6
Sutlej (riv.), India 68/C3
Sutlej (riv.), Pakistan 68/C3
Sutlej (riv.), Pakistan 59/K4
Sutter (co.), Calif. 204/D4
Sutter, Calif. (95982) 204/D4
Sutter Creek, Calif. (95685) 204/C9
Suttle, Ala. (†36701) 195/D5
Sutton, Alaska (99674) 196/C1
Sutton, England 13/H8
Sutton, England 10/B6
Sutton, Mass. (†01527) 249/G4
Sutton, Nebr. (68979) 264/G4
Sutton◯, N.H. (†03260) 268/D5
Sutton, N. Dak. (58484) 282/O5
Sutton, Ontario 177/E3
Sutton (lake), Ontario 175/D2
Sutton (riv.), Ontario 175/D2
Sutton, Québec 172/E4
Sutton (co.), Texas 303/D7
Sutton◯, Vt. (05867) 268/C2
Sutton, W. Va. (26601) 312/E5
Sutton (lake), W. Va. 312/F5
Sutton Bridge, England 13/H5
Sutton in Ashfield, England 10/F4
Sutton in Ashfield, England 13/K2
Suttons Bay, Mich. (49682) 250/D3
Suttor (riv.), Queensland 88/H4
Suttor (riv.), Queensland 95/C4
Suttsu, Japan 81/J2
Sutwik (isl.), Alaska 196/G3
Suure-Jaani, U.S.S.R. 53/C1
Suva (cap.), Fiji 87/H7
Suva (cap.), Fiji 2/T6
Suva (Cap.), Fiji 86/Q11
Suvarlı, Turkey 63/G4
Suwa, Japan 81/H6
Suwaiq, Oman 59/G5
Suwaiqiya, Hor as (lake), Iraq 66/D4
Suwałki (prov.), Poland 47/F1
Suwałki, Poland 47/F1
Suwanee, Georgia (30174) 217/D2
Suwannaphum, Thailand 72/D4
Suwannee (co.), Fla. 212/C1
Suwannee, Fla. (32692) 212/C2
Suwannee (riv.), Fla. 212/C2
Suwannee (sound), Fla. 212/C2
Suwannee (riv.), Georgia 217/G10
Suwannee River (Fanning Springs), Fla. (†32693) 212/D2
Suwanose (isl.), Japan 81/O4
Suwar, Syria 63/J5
Suwarrow (atoll), Cook Is. 87/K7
Suweilih, Jordan 65/D3
Suweima, Jordan 65/D4
Suwŏn, S. Korea 81/C5
Su Xian, China 77/J5
Suzhou (Soochow), China 77/K5
Suzhou, China 54/O6
Suzu, Japan 81/H5
Suzu (pt.), Japan 81/H5
Suzuka, Japan 81/H6
Suzzara, Italy 34/C2
Svalbard (isls.), Norway 2/J2
Svalbard (isls.), Norway 4/B9
Svalbard (isls.), Norway 18/C3
Svaneke, Denmark 21/F8
Svanstein, Sweden 18/N3
Svanvik, Norway 18/R2
Svárov, Czech. 41/C1
Svay Rieng, Cambodia 72/E5
Svea, Minn. (56290) 255/C6
Sveagruva, Norway 18/D2
Sveg, Sweden 18/J5
Svelvik, Norway 18/D4
Švenčionis, U.S.S.R. 53/D3
Svendborg, Denmark 18/G9
Svendborg, Denmark 21/D7
Svenljunga, Sweden 18/H8
Svensen, Oreg. (†97103) 291/D1
Svenstavik, Sweden 18/H5
Sverdlovsk, U.S.S.R. 2/N3
Sverdlovsk, U.S.S.R. 54/H4
Sverdlovsk, U.S.S.R. 48/F4
Sverdrup (isls.), N.W.T. 146/J2
Sverdrup (chan.), N.W. Terrs. 187/J1
Sverdrup (isls.), N.W. Terrs. 187/J2
Svetlogorsk, U.S.S.R. 52/C4
Svetlograd, U.S.S.R. 52/F5
Svetlyy, U.S.S.R. 52/A4
Svetozarevo, Yugoslavia 45/E4
Svidník, Czech. 41/F2
Svilajnac, Yugoslavia 45/E3
Svilengrad, Bulgaria 45/G5
Svinninge, Denmark 21/E6
Svir' (riv.), U.S.S.R. 52/D2
Svishtov, Bulgaria 45/G4
Svitava (riv.), Czech. 41/D2
Svitavy, Czech. 41/D2
Svobodnyy, U.S.S.R. 54/O4
Svobodnyy, U.S.S.R. 48/N4
Svolvaer, Norway 18/J2
Svratka (riv.), Czech. 41/D2
Swabian Jura (range), W. Germany 22/C4
Swadlincote, England 10/G2
Swadlincote, England 13/F5
Swaffham, England 13/H5
Swaffham, England 10/G4
Swaim, Ala. (†35764) 195/F1
Swain (co.), N.C. 281/B3
Swain (reefs), Queensland 88/J4
Swain (reefs), Queensland 95/E4
Swains (isl.), Amer. Samoa 87/K7
Swainsboro, Georgia (30401) 217/H5
Swakop (riv.), Namibia 118/B4
Swakopmund, Namibia 118/A4
Swakopmund, Namibia 102/D7
Swale (riv.), England 13/F3
Swale (riv.), England 10/F3
Swale (isl.), Newf. 166/D1
Swaledale, Iowa (50477) 229/G3
Swalwell, Alberta 182/D4
Swampscott◯, Mass. (01907) 249/E6
Swan (hills), Alberta 182/C2
Swan (riv.), Alberta 182/C2
Swan (Cisne) (isls.), Honduras 154/F2
Swan, Iowa (50252) 229/G6
Swan (lake), Manitoba 179/B2
Swan (lake), Manitoba 179/D5
Swan (riv.), Manitoba 179/A3
Swan (lake), Minn. 255/D6
Swan (lake), Mont. 262/C3
Swan (lake), Nebr. 264/B3
Swan (riv.), Sask. 181/J3
Swan (creek), S. Dak. 298/J3
Swan (lake), S. Dak. 298/K3
Swan (lake), S. Dak. 298/O3
Swan (isl.), Tasmania 99/E2
Swan (lake), Utah 304/B4
Swan, W. Australia 88/B2
Swan (riv.), W. Australia 92/A1
Swanage, England 10/F5
Swanage, England 13/E7
Swan Creek, Ill. (†61473) 222/C3
Swandale, W. Va. (†25043) 312/E5
Swan Hill, Victoria 88/G7
Swan Hill, Victoria 97/B4
Swan Hills, Alberta 182/C2
Swanington, Ind. (†47944) 227/C3
Swanlake, Idaho (83281) 220/F7
Swan Lake, Manitoba 179/D5
Swan Lake, Miss. (38958) 256/D3
Swan Lake, Mont. (59911) 262/C3
Swanlinbar, Ireland 17/F3
Swannanoa, N.C. (28778) 281/E3
Swan Plain, Sask. 181/K3
Swanquarter, N.C. (27885) 281/S4
Swan River, Man. 162/F5
Swan River, Manitoba 179/A2
Swan River, Minn. (55784) 255/E3
Swansboro, N.C. (28584) 281/P5
Swanscombe, England 10/C5
Swanscombe, England 13/J8
Swansea, Ill. (62221) 222/B3
Swansea◯, Mass. (02777) 249/K5
Swansea, S.C. (29160) 296/E4
Swansea, Tasmania 99/D4
Swansea, Wales 7/D3
Swansea, Wales 13/C6
Swansea, Wales 10/D5
Swansea (bay), Wales 13/D6
Swansea Center, Mass. (†02777) 249/K5
Swans Island, Maine (04685) 243/G7
Swans Island◯, Maine (04685) 243/G7
Swanson (lake), Nebr. 264/D4
Swanson, Sask. 181/D4
Swanton, Md. (21561) 245/A3
Swanton, Nebr. (68445) 264/H4
Swanton, Ohio (43558) 284/C2
Swanton, Vt. (05488) 268/A2
Swanton◯, Vt. (05488) 268/A2
Swan Valley, Idaho (83449) 220/G6
Swan View, W. Australia 88/B2
Swanville◯, Maine (†04915) 243/E6
Swanville, Minn. (56382) 255/D5
Swanwick, Ill. (62290) 222/D5
Swanzey◯, N.H. (†03431) 268/C6
Swarthmore, Pa. (19081) 294/M7
Swartswood, N.J. (07877) 273/D1
Swartswood (lake), N.J. 273/D1
Swartz, La. (71281) 238/G1
Swartz Creek, Mich. (48473) 250/F6
Swarzędz, Poland 47/C2
Swatara, Minn. (55785) 255/E4
Swatara, Pa. (17111) 294/J5
Swatow (Shantou), China 77/J7
Swayzee, Ind. (46986) 227/F4
Swaziland 2/L7
Swaziland 102/F7
SWAZILAND 118/E5
Swea City, Iowa (50590) 229/E2
Sweatman, Miss. (†38925) 256/E3
Swedeboro, Mo. (65572) 261/H7
Swedeburg, Nebr. (†68066) 264/H3
Sweden 2/K2
Sweden 4/D9
Sweden 7/F2
SWEDEN 18
Sweden, Maine (†04040) 243/B7
Sweden◯, Maine (†04040) 243/B7
Swedesboro, N.J. (08085) 273/C4
Swedesburg, Iowa (52652) 229/L6
Sweeden, Ky. (42285) 237/J6
Sween, Loch (inlet), Scotland 15/C5
Sweeny, Texas (77480) 303/J8
Sweet, Idaho (83670) 220/B6
Sweet Bay, Newf. 166/D2
Sweet Briar, Va. (24595) 307/K5
Sweet Chalybeate, Va. (†24426) 307/H5
Sweet Grass (co.), Mont. 262/G5
Sweetgrass, Mont. (59484) 262/E2
Sweet Home, Ark. (72164) 202/F4
Sweet Home, Oreg. (97386) 291/E3
Sweet Home, Texas (77987) 303/H8
Sweet Lake, La. (†70601) 238/D7
Sweetser, Ind. (46987) 227/F3
Sweet Springs, Mo. (65351) 261/F5
Sweet Springs, W. Va. (24980) 312/F7
Sweet Valley, Pa. (18656) 294/K3
Sweet Water, Ala. (36782) 195/C6
Sweetwater, Fla. (†33144) 212/B5
Sweetwater, Nebr. (†68844) 264/E3
Sweetwater (lake), N. Dak. 282/N3
Sweetwater, Okla. (73666) 288/G4
Sweetwater, Tenn. (37874) 237/N9
Sweetwater, Texas 188/F4
Sweetwater, Texas (79556) 303/D5
Sweetwater (co.), Wyo. 319/D4
Sweetwater (riv.), Wyo. 319/D3
Sweetwater Creek, Fla. (†33614) 212/B2
Swellendam, S. Africa 118/C6
Swenson, Texas (†79502) 303/D4
Swett, S. Dak. (†57551) 298/E7
Świdnica, Poland 47/C3
Świdnik, Poland 47/F3
Świdwin, Poland 47/B2
Świebodzice, Poland 47/C3
Świebodzin, Poland 47/B2
Świecie, Poland 47/D2
Świętochłowice, Poland 47/A4
Swift (riv.), Maine 243/B6
Swift (riv.), Mass. 249/E4
Swift (co.), Minn. 255/C5
Swift, Minn. (56682) 255/C2
Swift (creek), Va. 307/O6
Swift Creek (res.), Wash. 310/C4
Swift Current, Newf. 166/C2
Swift Current, Sask. 146/H4
Swift Current, Sask. 162/F5
Swift Current, Sask. 181/D5
Swift Current (creek), Sask. 181/D5
Swifterbant, Netherlands 27/H3
Swift Falls, Minn. (†56215) 255/C5
Swifton, Ark. (72471) 202/H2
Swiftown, Miss. (38959) 256/D4
Swift River, Yukon 187/E3
Swifts Creek, Victoria 97/D5
Swiftwater, N.H. (†03785) 268/D3
Swilly (inlet), Ireland 17/F1
Swilly, Lough (inlet), Ireland 10/C3
Swilly (riv.), Ireland 17/F2
Swinburne (cape), N.W. Terrs. 187/J2
Swindon, England 10/F5
Swindon, England 13/F6
Swinemünde (Świnoujście), Poland 47/A2
Swinford, Ireland 17/C4
Swink, Colo. (81077) 208/M7
Swink, Okla. (74761) 288/R6
Swinomish Ind. Res., Wash. 310/C2
Świnoujście (Swinemünde), Poland 47/B1
Swinton, Scotland 15/F5
Swisher, Iowa (52338) 229/K5
Swisher (co.), Texas 303/C3
Swiss, W. Va. (26690) 312/D6
Swisshome, Oreg. (97480) 291/D3
Swissvale, Pa. (15218) 294/C7
Switz City, Ind. (47465) 227/C6
Switzer, Ky. (†40379) 237/M4
Switzer, W. Va. (25647) 312/B7
Switzerland 2/K3
Switzerland 7/E4
Switzerland, Fla. (†32043) 212/E1
Switzerland (co.), Ind. 227/G7
Switzerland, S.C. (†29936) 296/E7
SWITZERLAND 39
Swona (isl.), Scotland 15/E2
Swords, Ireland 17/J5
Swords Creek, Va. (24649) 307/E6
Sybille (creek), Wyo. 319/G4
Sybouts, Sask. 181/G6
Sycamore, Ala. (35149) 195/F4
Sycamore, Georgia (31790) 217/E7
Sycamore, Ill. (60178) 222/E2
Sycamore, Ind. (†46936) 227/F4
Sycamore, Kansas (67363) 232/G4
Sycamore, Mo. (65758) 261/H9
Sycamore, Ohio (44882) 284/D4
Sycamore, Pa. (15364) 294/B6
Sycamore, S.C. (29846) 296/E5
Sycan (riv.), Oreg. 291/F5
Syców, Poland 47/C3
Sydenham, Ontario 177/H3
Sydenham (riv.), Ontario 177/B5
Sydney, Australia 2/S7
Sydney, Australia 87/F9
Sydney (isl.), Kiribati 87/K6
Sydney (cap.), N. S. Wales 88/L4
Sydney (bay), Norfolk I. 88/L6
Sydney, N. Dak. (†58401) 282/N6
Sydney, Nova Scotia 168/H2
Sydney, N.S. 162/K6
Sydney, N.S. 146/N5
Sydney (harb.), Nova Scotia 168/H2
Sydney Mines, Nova Scotia 168/H2
Sydney River, Nova Scotia 168/H2
Sykeston, N. Dak. (58486) 282/M5
Sykesville, Md. (21784) 245/K3
Sykesville, Pa. (15865) 294/E3
Syktyvkar, U.S.S.R. 7/K2
Syktyvkar, U.S.S.R. 48/F3
Syktyvkar, U.S.S.R. 52/H2
Sylacauga, Ala. (35150) 195/F4
Sylhet, Bangladesh 68/G4
Sylt (isl.), W. Germany 22/C1
Sylva, N.C. (28779) 281/C4
Sylvan, Oreg. (†97201) 291/B2
Sylvan, Pa. (†17236) 294/G6
Sylvan (lake), Wash. 310/G3
Sylvan Beach, N.Y. (13157) 276/J4
Sylvan Grove, Kansas (67481) 232/D2
Sylvania, Ala. (35988) 195/G1
Sylvania, Georgia (30467) 217/J5
Sylvania, Ind. (†47985) 227/C5
Sylvania, Ohio (43560) 284/C2
Sylvania, Pa. (16945) 294/J2
Sylvania, Sask. 181/G3
Sylvan Lake, Alberta 182/C3
Sylvan Lake, Mich. (†48053) 250/F6
Sylvarena, Miss. (39153) 256/F6
Sylvatus, Va. (†24343) 307/G7
Sylvester, Georgia (31791) 217/E7
Sylvester (lake), North. Terr. 93/D5
Sylvester, Texas (79560) 303/D5
Sylvester, W. Va. (25193) 312/C6
Sylvia, Kansas (67581) 232/D4
Sylvia, Tenn. (†37055) 237/G8
Symco, Wis. (†54949) 317/J6
Symerton, Ill. (†60481) 222/F2
Symmes (creek), Ohio 284/F8
Symonds, Miss. (†38769) 256/C3
Syosset, N.Y. (11791) 276/R6
Syracuse, Ind. (46567) 227/F2
Syracuse (prov.), Italy 34/E6
Syracuse, Italy 7/F5
Syracuse, Italy 34/E6
Syracuse, Kansas (67878) 232/A3
Syracuse, Mo. (65354) 261/G5
Syracuse, Nebr. (68446) 264/H4
Syracuse, N.Y. 188/L2
Syracuse, N.Y. (*13201) 276/H4
Syracuse, Ohio (45779) 284/G7
Syracuse, Utah (†84041) 304/B2
Syrdar'ya (riv.), U.S.S.R. 2/N3
Syrdar'ya (riv.), U.S.S.R. 54/H5
Syrdar'ya (riv.), U.S.S.R. 48/G5
Syre, Minn. (†56584) 255/B3
Syria 2/L4
Syria 54/E6
SYRIA 63/G5
SYRIA 59/C3
Syria, Va. (22743) 307/M4
Syriam, Burma 72/C3
Syrian (des.), Iraq 66/B4
Syrian (El Hamad) (des.), Iraq 59/D3
Syrte, Libya 102/D1
Syrte, Libya 111/C1
Sysladobsis, Lower (lake), Maine 243/G5
Sysola (riv.), U.S.S.R. 52/H2
Sysslebäck, Sweden 18/H6
Syzran', U.S.S.R. 7/J3
Syzran', U.S.S.R. 48/E4
Syzran', U.S.S.R. 52/G4
Szabadszállás, Hungary 41/E3
Szabolcs-Szatmár (co.), Hungary 41/G3
Szamotuły, Poland 47/C2
Szarvas, Hungary 41/F3
Százhalombatta, Hungary 41/E3
Szczebrzeszyn, Poland 47/F3
Szczecin (prov.), Poland 47/B2
Szczecin, Poland 7/F3
Szczecin, Poland 47/B2
Szczecinek, Poland 47/C2
Szczytno, Poland 47/E2
Szechwan (Sichuan) (prov.), China 77/F5
Szécsény, Hungary 41/E2
Szeged, Hungary 41/E3
Szeged, Hungary 7/F4
Szeghalom, Hungary 41/F3
Szegvár, Hungary 41/F3
Székesfehérvár, Hungary 41/E3
Szekszárd, Hungary 41/E3
Szendrő, Hungary 41/F2
Szentendre, Hungary 41/E3
Szentendreisziget (isl.), Hungary 41/E3
Szentes, Hungary 41/F3
Szentgotthárd, Hungary 41/D3
Szentlőrinc, Hungary 41/E3
Szeping (Siping), China 77/K3
Szerencs, Hungary 41/F2
Szigetvár, Hungary 41/D3
Szikszó, Hungary 41/F2
Szil, Hungary 41/D3
Szirák, Hungary 41/E3
Szolnok (co.), Hungary 41/F3
Szolnok, Hungary 41/F3
Szombathely, Hungary 41/D3
Szprotawa, Poland 47/B3
Sztum, Poland 47/D2
Szubin, Poland 47/C2
Szydłowiec, Poland 47/E3

T

Taal (lake), Philippines 82/C4
Tab, Hungary 41/E3
Tab, Ind. (†47917) 227/C4
Taba, Bir, Egypt 59/B4
Tabacal (pt.), Cuba 158/H4
Tabacundo, Ecuador 128/C2
Tabaquite, Trin. & Tob. 161/B11
Tabar (isls.), Papua N.G. 86/C1
Tabarka, Tunisia 106/F1
Tabas, Iran 59/G3
Tabas, Iran 66/L4
Tabas, Iran 66/K4
Tabasará (mts.), Panama 154/G6
Tabasco (state), Mexico 150/N7
Tabasco, Mexico 150/H6
Tabask, Kuh-e (mt.), Iran 66/G6
Tabas-Masina (Tabas), Iran 59/H3
Tabb, Va. (23602) 307/R6
Tabelbala, Algeria 106/D3
Taber, Alberta 182/E5
Taberg, N.Y. (13471) 276/J4
Tabernacle, St. Chris.-Nevis 161/C10
Tabernash, Colo. (80478) 208/H3
Tabernes de Valldigna, Spain 33/G3
Taberville, Mo. (64787) 261/E6
Tabiang, Kiribati 87/G6
Tabiona, Utah (84072) 304/D3
Tabiteuea (atoll), Kiribati 87/H6
Tablas (cape), Chile 138/A9
Tablas (isl.), Philippines 82/D4
Tablas (str.), Philippines 82/C4
Table (mt.), Nev. 266/C3
Table (bay), Newf. 166/C3
Table (bay), S. Africa 118/E6
Table (mt.), S. Africa 118/E6
Table (peak), Wyo. 319/B2
Table Grove, Ill. (61482) 222/C3
Tableland, Trin. & Tob. 161/B11
Tableland Station, W. Australia 92/D2
Tabler, Okla. (†73018) 288/L4
Table Rock (riv.), Ark. 202/D1
Table Rock (res.), Mo. 261/E9
Table Rock, Nebr. (68447) 264/H4
Tablers Station, W. Va. (†25428) 312/K4
Taboada, Spain 33/C1
Taboga (isl.), Panama 154/H6
Tábor, Czech. 41/C2
Tabor, Iowa (51653) 229/B7
Tabor (mt.), Israel 65/C2
Tabor, Minn. (†56712) 255/B2
Tabor, N.J. (07878) 273/E2
Tabor, S. Dak. (57063) 298/O8
Tabor (mt.), Vt. 268/B5
Tabora (reg.), Tanzania 115/F5
Tabora, Tanzania 115/F5
Tabora, Tanzania 102/F5
Tabor City, N.C. (28463) 281/M6
Tabou, Ivory Coast 106/C8
Tabriz, Iran 54/F6
Tabriz, Iran 66/D2
Tabriz, Iran 59/E2
Tabuk, Philippines 82/C2
Tabusintac, New Bruns. 170/E1
Tabusintac (gully), New Bruns. 170/F1
Tabusintac (riv.), New Bruns. 170/E1
Täby, Sweden 18/H1
Tacajó, Cuba 158/J3
Tacámbaro de Codallos, Mexico 150/J7
Tacaná, Guatemala 154/A3
Tacaná (vol.), Guatemala 154/A3
Tacarigua, Trin. & Tob. 161/B10
Taché (lake), Québec 172/J1
Tachen (Taizhou) (isls.), China 77/K6
Tacheng (Qoqek), China 77/B2
Tachikawa, Japan 81/O2
Tachina, Ecuador 128/C2
Táchira (state), Venezuela 124/C4
Tachov, Czech. 41/B2
Tacloban, Philippines 82/E5
Tacloban, Philippines 85/H3
Tacna, Ariz. (85352) 198/B6
Tacna (dept.), Peru 128/G11
Tacna, Peru 128/G11
Tacna, Peru 120/B4
Tacobamba, Bolivia 136/C6
Tacoma, Va. (†24230) 307/C7
Tacoma, Wash. 146/F5
Tacoma, Wash. 188/B1
Tacoma, Wash. (*98401) 310/C3
Tacoma Park, S. Dak. (†57433) 298/N2
Taconic, Conn. (06079) 210/B1
Taconic (mts.), Mass. 249/A2
Taconite, Minn. (55786) 255/E3
Taconite Harbor, Minn. (†55613) 255/H3
Tacopaya, Bolivia 136/B5
Tacora (vol.), Chile 138/B1
Tacotalpa, Mexico 150/N8
Tacuaras, Paraguay 144/C5
Tacuarembó (dept.), Uruguay 145/D3
Tacuarembó, Uruguay 145/D2
Tacuarembó (riv.), Uruguay 145/D2
Tacuarí (riv.), Uruguay 145/E3
Tacuatí, Paraguay 144/D3
Tacutu (riv.), Brazil 132/B2
Tadcaster, England 13/K1
Tademaït (plat.), Algeria 102/C2
Tademaït, Plateau du (plat.), Algeria 106/E3
Tadine, New Caled. 86/H4
Tadjnout Hagguerete (well), Mali 106/D4
Tadjoura, Djibouti 111/H5
Tadley, England 13/F6
Tadmor (Palmyra) (ruin), Syria 59/C3
Tadmore, Sask. 181/J4
Tadmur, Syria 59/C3
Tadmur, Syria 63/H5
Tadó, Colombia 126/B5
Tadoule (lake), Manitoba 179/J2
Tadoussac, Que. 162/J6
Tadoussac, Québec 174/C3
Tadoussac, Québec 172/H1
Tadzhik S.S.R., U.S.S.R. 54/H6
Tadzhik S.S.R., U.S.S.R. 48/H6
Taebaek (mt.), S. Korea 81/D5
Taedong (riv.), N. Korea 81/C4
Taegu, S. Korea 54/O6
Taegu, S. Korea 81/D6
Taejŏn, S. Korea 54/O6
Taejŏn, S. Korea 81/C5
Tafalla, Spain 33/F1
Tafassasset, Wadi (dry riv.), Algeria 106/F4
Tafassasset, Wadi (dry riv.), Niger 106/F4
Tafers, Switzerland 39/D3
Taff (riv.), Wales 13/B7
Tafí Viejo, Argentina 120/C5
Tafí Viejo, Argentina 143/C2
Taft, Calif. (93268) 204/F8
Taft, Fla. (32809) 212/E3
Taft, Iran 66/J5
Taft, La. (†70057) 238/N4
Taft, Okla. (74463) 288/R3
Taft, Philippines 82/E5
Taft, Tenn. (38488) 237/H10
Taft, Texas (78390) 303/G9
Taftan, Kuh-e (mt.), Iran 66/M6
Taftan, Kuh-e (mt.), Iran 59/H4
Taftsville, Vt. (05073) 268/C4
Taftville, Conn. (06380) 210/G2
Tagab, Afghanistan 59/J3
Tagab, Afghanistan 68/B2
Taga Dzong, Bhutan 68/G3
Taganrog, U.S.S.R. 7/H4
Taganrog, U.S.S.R. 52/E5
Taganrog, U.S.S.R. 48/D5
Tagant (reg.), Mauritania 106/B5
Tagapula (isl.), Philippines 82/E4
Tagawa, Japan 81/E7
Tagaytay, Philippines 82/C3
Tagbilaran, Philippines 82/E6
Taghit, Algeria 106/D2
Taghmon, Ireland 17/H7
Tagish (lake), Br. Col. 184/J1
Tagish, Yukon 187/E3
Tagliamento (riv.), Italy 34/D1
Tagolo (pt.), Philippines 82/D6
Tagolo (pt.), Philippines 85/G4
Tagoloan, Philippines 82/E6
Tagomago (isl.), Spain 33/G3
Tagounite, Morocco 106/C3
Tagua, Bolivia 136/B6
Taguatinga, Brazil 120/E4
Taguatinga, Fed. Dist., Brazil 132/D6
Taguatinga, Goiás, Brazil 132/E6
Tague (bay), Virgin Is. (U.S.) 161/G4
Tagula (isl.), Papua N.G. 85/C8
Tagum, Philippines 82/E7
Tagus (riv.) 7/D5
Tagus, N. Dak. (†58720) 282/G3
Tagus (riv.), Portugal 33/B3
Tagus (riv.), Spain 33/D3
Tahaa (isl.), Fr. Poly. 87/L7
Tahakopa, N. Zealand 100/B7
Tahan, Gunong (mt.), Malaysia 72/D6
Tahat (mt.), Algeria 102/C2
Tahat (mt.), Algeria 106/F4
Tahawus, N.Y. (12879) 276/M2
Tahiryuak (lake), N.W. Terrs. 187/G2
Tahiti (isl.), Fr. Polynesia 2/B6
TAHITI, Fr. Poly. 86/S13
Tahiti (isl.), Fr. Poly. 87/L7
Tahiti (isl.), Fr. Poly. 86/S13
Tahlequah, Okla. (74464) 288/R3
Tahma (riv.), Turkey 63/G3
Tahoe (lake) 188/C3
Tahoe (lake), Calif. 204/F4
Tahoe (lake), Nev. 266/B3
Tahoe City, Calif. (95730) 204/E4
Tahoka, Texas (79373) 303/C4
Taholah, Wash. (98587) 310/A3
Tahoma, Calif. (95733) 204/E4
Tahoua, Niger 102/C3
Tahoua, Niger 106/F6
Tahquamenon (falls), Mich. 250/D2
Tahquamenon (riv.), Mich. 250/D2
Tahsis, Br. Col. 184/D5
Tahta, Egypt 59/B4
Tahta, Egypt 111/F2
Tahtsa (lake), Br. Col. 184/D3
Tahua, Bolivia 136/B3
Tahuamanu (riv.), Bolivia 136/A2
Tahuamanu, Peru 128/H8
Tahuamanu (riv.), Peru 128/H8
Tahulandang (isl.), Indonesia 85/H5
Tahuna, Indonesia 85/G5
Tahuya, Wash. (98588) 310/B3
Tai'an, China 77/J4
Taiarapu (pen.), Fr. Poly. 86/T13
Taiban, N. Mex. (88134) 274/F4
Taibus, China 77/J3
Taichow (Taizhou), China 77/K5

Taurianova 455

Taichung, China 77/K7
Taichung, Taiwan 54/O7
Taieri (riv.), N. Zealand 100/C7
Taif, Saudi Arabia 54/F7
Taif, Saudi Arabia 59/D5
Taigu, China 77/H4
Taihape, N. Zealand 100/E3
Taihe, China 77/J6
Tai Hu (lake), China 77/J5
Tailem Bend, S. Australia 88/F7
Tailem Bend, S. Australia 94/F6
Tailfingen, W. Germany 22/C4
Taima, Saudi Arabia 59/C4
Tain, Scotland 15/D3
Tain, Scotland 10/D2
Tainan, China 77/J7
Tainaron (cape), Greece 7/G5
Tainaron (cape), Greece 45/F7
Taintor, Iowa (50253) 229/H6
Taipei, China 77/K7
Taipei (cap.), Rep. of China 54/O7
Taipei (cap.), Rep. of China 2/R4
Taiping, Malaysia 72/D6
Taitao (pen.), Chile 120/B7
Taitao (cape), Chile 138/D6
Taitao (pen.), Chile 138/D6
Taits Gap, Ala. (†35121) 195/F3
Taitung, China 77/K7
Taivalkoski, Finland 18/P4
Taiwan 54/N7
Taiwan 2/R4
Taiwan (str.) 54/N7
Taiwan (isl.) 54/N7
Taiwan, China 77/K7
Taiwan (Formosa) (isl.), China 77/K7
Taiwan (Formosa) (str.), China 77/J7
Taiyuan, China 77/H4
Taiyuan, China 54/N6
Taizhou (Tachen) (isls.), China 77/K6
Taizhou (Taichow), China 77/K5
Ta'izz, Yemen Arab Rep. 54/F8
Ta'izz, Yemen Arab Rep. 59/D7
Tajimi, Japan 81/H6
Tajique, N. Mex. (87057) 274/C4
Tajo (Tagus) (riv.), Spain 33/D3
Tajrish, Iran 66/G3
Tajumulco (vol.), Guatemala 154/B3
Tak, Thailand 72/C3
Takaishi, Japan 81/H8
Takaka, N. Zealand 100/D4
Takalar, Indonesia 85/F7
Takama, Guyana 131/C3
Takamatsu, Japan 81/F6
Takaoka, Japan 81/H5
Takapau, N. Zealand 100/F4
Takapuna, N. Zealand 100/B1
Takarazuka, Japan 81/H7
Takaroa (atoll), Fr. Poly. 87/M7
Takasaki, Japan 81/J5
Takatsuki, Japan 81/J7
Takayama, Japan 81/H5
Takefu, Japan 81/G6
Takeshima (isls.), Japan 81/F5
Takestan, Iran 66/F2
Takev, Cambodia 72/E5
Takhiatash, U.S.S.R. 48/F5
Takhta-Bazar, U.S.S.R. 48/G6
Takikawa, Japan 81/K2
Takingeun, Indonesia 85/B5
Takitimu (mts.), N. Zealand 100/A6
Takkaze (riv.), Ethiopia 111/G5
Takla (lake), Br. Col. 184/D2
Takla Makan (des.), China 54/K6
Takla Makan (Taklimakan Shamo) (des.), China 77/B4
Taklimakan Shamo (des.), China 77/B4
Tako, Sask. 181/B3
Takoma Park, Md. (20912) 245/F4
Takoradi, Ghana 106/D8
Takoradi-Sekondi, Ghana 102/B4
Taksimo, U.S.S.R. 48/M4
Taku (glac.), Alaska 196/N1
Taku (riv.), Alaska 196/N1
Taku (riv.), Br. Col. 184/J2
Takua Pa, Thailand 72/C5
Takutu (riv.), Guyana 131/B4
Tala, Mexico 150/H6
Tala, Uruguay 145/D5
Talab (riv.), Iran 59/H4
Talab (riv.), Iran 66/N6
Talab (riv.), Pakistan 68/A3
Talagante, Chile 138/G4
Talai (Da'an, Dalai), China 77/K2
Talak (reg.), Niger 106/E5
Talala, Okla. (74080) 288/P1
Talamanca (range), C. Rica 154/F6
Talangbetutu, Indonesia 85/C6
Talara, Peru 128/B5
Talara, Peru 120/A3
Talaud (isls.), Indonesia 54/O9
Talaud (isls.), Indonesia 85/H5
Talavera de la Reina, Spain 33/D2
Talawe (mt.), Papua N.G. 86/B2
Talbert, Ky. (41377) 237/P6
Talbingo, N.S. Wales 97/E4
Talbot, Alberta 182/E3
Talbot (isl.), Fla. 212/E1
Talbot (co.), Georgia 217/C5
Talbot, Ind. (47984) 227/C3
Talbot (co.), Md. 245/O5
Talbot (inlet), N.W. Terrs. 187/L2
Talbot (cape), W. Australia 88/D2
Talbot (cape), W. Australia 92/D1
Talbott, Tenn. (37877) 237/P8
Talbotton, Georgia (31827) 217/C5
Talca, Chile 138/A11
Talca, Chile 120/B6
Talca (pt.), Chile 138/E3
Talcahuano, Chile 138/D1
Talcahuano, Chile 120/B6
Talcán (isl.), Chile 138/D4
Talco, Texas (75487) 303/K4
Talcott (range), Conn. 210/D1
Talcott, W. Va. (24981) 312/E7
Talcottville, Conn. (†06066) 210/F1
Taldy-Kurgan, U.S.S.R. 54/J5
Taldy-Kurgan, U.S.S.R. 48/H5
Taleh, Somalia 115/J2
Talent, Oreg. (97540) 291/E5
Talgar, U.S.S.R. 48/H5
Talgarth, Wales 13/D5
Tali (Dali), China 77/E6
Taliabu (isl.), Indonesia 85/G6
Taliaferro (co.), Georgia 217/G3
Talibon, Philippines 82/E5
Talihina, Okla. (74571) 288/S5
Talina, Bolivia 136/B7
Tali Post, Sudan 111/F6
Talisayan, Philippines 82/E6
Talisheek, La. (70464) 238/L5
Talita, Uruguay 145/D4
Tal Kaif, Iraq 66/C2
Talkeetna, Alaska (99676) 196/B1
Talkeetna (mts.), Alaska 196/J2
Talkheh (riv.), Iran 66/E1
Talking Rock, Georgia (30175) 217/D1
Tallaboa, P. Rico 161/B3
Talladega (co.), Ala. 195/F4
Talladega, Ala. (35160) 195/F4
Talladega Springs, Ala. (†35150) 195/F4
Tallaght, Ireland 17/J5
Tallahaga (creek), Miss. 256/F4
Tallahala (creek), Miss. 256/F7
Tallahassee (cap.), Fla. 146/K6
Tallahassee (cap.), Fla. 188/K4
Tallahassee (cap.), Fla. (*32301) 212/B1
Tallahatchie (co.), Miss. 256/D3
Tallahatchie (riv.), Miss. 256/D3
Tallahatta Springs, Ala. (†36784) 195/C7
Tallangatta, Victoria 97/D5
Tallant, Okla. (†74002) 288/O1
Tallapoosa (co.), Ala. 195/G5
Tallapoosa (riv.), Ala. 195/G4
Tallapoosa, Georgia (30176) 217/B3
Tallapoosa, Mo. (63878) 261/N9
Tallassee, Ala. (36078) 195/G5
Tallinn, U.S.S.R. 7/G3
Tallinn (cap.), U.S.S.R. 53/C1
Tallinn, U.S.S.R. 48/C4
Tallinn, U.S.S.R. 52/B3
Tallmadge, Ohio (44278) 284/H3
Tallman, N.Y. (10982) 276/J8
Tallman, Sask. 181/E3
Tallmansville, W. Va. (26237) 312/F5
Tallow, Ireland 17/F7
Tallula, Ill. (62688) 222/D4
Tallulah, La. (71282) 238/H2
Tallulah Falls, Georgia (30573) 217/F1
Talma, Ind. (†46975) 227/E2
Talmage, Kansas (67482) 232/E2
Talmage, Nebr. (68448) 264/H4
Talmage, Sask. 181/H6
Talmage, Utah (84073) 304/D3
Talmo, Georgia (30575) 217/E2
Talmo, Kansas (†66935) 232/E2
Talmoon, Minn. (56637) 255/E3
Talodi, Sudan 111/F5
Talofofo (bay), Guam 86/K7
Taloga, Okla. (73667) 288/J2
Talon (lake), Ontario 177/E1
Taloqan, Afghanistan 68/B1
Taloqan, Afghanistan 59/J2
Talpa, Texas (76882) 303/E6
Talpa de Allende, Mexico 150/G6
Talparo, Trin. & Tob. 161/B10
Talquin (lake), Fla. 212/B1
Talsi, U.S.S.R. 53/B2
Taltal, Chile 138/A5
Taltal, Chile 120/B5
Taltal, Quebrada de (riv.), Chile 138/B5
Taltson (riv.), N.W. Terrs. 187/G3
Talvik, Norway 18/N2
Talyawalka (creek), N.S. Wales 97/B2
Talyawalka Ana Branch, Darling (riv.), N.S. Wales 97/B3
Tama (co.), Iowa 229/H4
Tama, Iowa (52339) 229/H5
Tama (riv.), Japan 81/O2
Tamaha, Okla. (†74462) 288/S4
Tamaki (str.), N. Zealand 100/C1
Tamale, Ghana 102/B4
Tamale, Ghana 106/D7
Tamalpais (mt.), Calif. 204/H1
Tamana (mt.), Trin. & Tob. 161/B10
Tamanrasset, Algeria 106/F4
Tamanrasset, Algeria 102/C2
Tamanrasset, Wadi (dry riv.), Algeria 106/E4
Tamaqua, Pa. (18252) 294/L4
Tamar (riv.), England 13/C7
Tamar (riv.), England 10/D5
Tamar (riv.), Tasmania 99/D3
Támara, Colombia 126/D5
Tamarac, Fla. (†33321) 212/B3
Tamarac (riv.), Minn. 255/A2
Tamarack, Idaho (†83654) 220/B5
Tamarack (isl.), Manitoba 179/F3
Tamarack, Minn. (55787) 255/E4
Tamarack (riv.), Minn. 255/D2
Tamarack, Pa. (†17729) 294/G3
Tamarite de Litera, Spain 33/G2
Tamaro (mt.), Switzerland 39/G4
Tamaroa, Ill. (62888) 222/D5
Tamarugal, Pampa del (plain), Chile 138/B3
Tamási, Hungary 41/E3
Tamassee, S.C. (29686) 296/A2
Tamatama, Venezuela 124/F6
Tamatave (Toamasina), Madagascar 118/H3
Tamaulipas (state), Mexico 150/K4
Tamaya, Chile 138/A8
Tamayo, Dom. Rep. 158/D5
Tamazula, Mexico 150/F4
Tamazulapan del Progreso, Mexico 150/L8
Tamazunchale, Mexico 150/K6
Tambacounda, Senegal 106/B6
Tambar Springs, N.S. Wales 97/E2
Tambelan (isls.), Indonesia 85/D5
Tamberias, Argentina 143/C3
Tambey, U.S.S.R. 48/G2
Tambo (riv.), Peru 128/G11
Tambo, Queensland 88/H4
Tambo, Queensland 95/C5
Tambo de Mora, Peru 128/D9
Tambo Grande, Peru 128/B5
Tambohorano, Madagascar 118/G3
Tambopata (riv.), Peru 128/H9
Tambores, Uruguay 145/C2
Tamboril, Dom. Rep. 158/D5
Tamboritha (mt.), Victoria 97/D5
Tambov, U.S.S.R. 7/J3
Tambov, U.S.S.R. 52/F4
Tambov, U.S.S.R. 48/E4
Tambura, Sudan 111/E6
Tamchakett, Mauritania 106/B5
Tame, Colombia 126/E4
Tame (riv.), England 10/G3
Tâmega (riv.), Portugal 33/C2
Tamentit, Algeria 106/D3
Tamiahua, Mexico 150/L6
Tamiami (canal), Fla. 212/E6
Tamil Nadu (state), India 68/D6
Tamin (gov.), Iraq 66/D3
Tamina (riv.), Switzerland 39/H3
Tamins, Switzerland 39/H3
Tamise (Temse), Belgium 27/E6
Tam Ky, Vietnam 72/F4
Tammisaari (Ekenäs), Finland 18/N6
Tamms, Ill. (62988) 222/D6
Tammun, West Bank 65/C3
Tamo, Ark. (71644) 202/G5
Tamora, Nebr. (†68434) 264/G4
Tampa, Fla. 188/K5
Tampa, Fla. 146/K7
Tampa (bay), Fla. 188/K5
Tampa, Fla. (*33601) 212/C2
Tampa (bay), Fla. 212/D4
Tampa, Kansas (67483) 232/E3
Tampere, Finland 7/G2
Tampere, Finland 18/N6
Tampico, Ill. (61283) 222/D2
Tampico, Ind. (†47220) 227/F7
Tampico, Mexico 146/J7
Tampico, Mexico 150/L5
Tampico, Mont. (†59230) 262/K2
Tampico, Wash. (†98901) 310/E4
Tampoc (riv.), Fr. Guiana 131/E4
Tam Quan, Vietnam 72/F4
Tamra, Saudi Arabia 59/E5
Tams, W. Va. (25933) 312/D7
Tamsagbulag, Mongolia 77/J2
Tamsagout, Mauritania 106/C4
Tamshiyacu, Peru 128/F5
Tamsweg, Austria 41/B3
Tamuin, Mexico 150/K6
Tamuning, Guam 86/K7
Tamworth, Australia 87/E9
Tamworth, England 13/F5
Tamworth, England 10/G3
Tamworth○, N.H. (03886) 268/E4
Tamworth, N.S. Wales 88/J6
Tamworth, N.S. Wales 97/F2
Tamworth, Ontario 177/H3
Tamyang, S. Korea 81/C6
Tana (lake), Ethiopia 102/F3
Tana (lake), Ethiopia 111/G5
Tana (riv.), Finland 18/P2
Tana (riv.), Kenya 102/G5
Tana (riv.), Kenya 115/G4
Tana, Norway 18/Q1
Tana (riv.), Norway 18/P1
Tanabe, Kyoto, Japan 81/J7
Tanabe, Wakayama, Japan 81/G7
Tanacross, Alaska (99776) 196/K2
Tanafjord (fjord), Norway 18/Q1
Tanaga (isl.), Alaska 196/K4
Tanaga (vol.), Alaska 196/K4
Tanahgrogot, Indonesia 85/F6
Tanahmerah, Indonesia 85/K7
Tanah Merah, Malaysia 72/D6
Tanamá (riv.), P. Rico 161/B1
Tanami (des.), North. Terr. 88/E3
Tanami, North. Terr. 93/A5
Tanami (des.), North. Terr. 93/C5
Tánamo, Cuba 158/J3
Tan An, Vietnam 72/E5
Tanana, Alaska 188/D5
Tanana, Alaska (99777) 196/H1
Tanana (riv.), Alaska 146/D3
Tanana (riv.), Alaska 188/D5
Tanana (riv.), Alaska 196/J2
Tananarive (Antananarivo) (cap.), Madagascar 118/H3
Tanaro (riv.), Italy 34/B2
Tanch'ŏn, N. Korea 81/D3
Tancook Island, Nova Scotia 168/D4
Tanda, India 68/E3
Tandag, Philippines 82/F6
Tandil, Argentina 143/E4
Tandil, Argentina 120/D6
Tando Adam, Pakistan 68/B3
Tando Allahyar, Pakistan 68/B3
Tandou (lake), N.S. Wales 97/A3
Tandragee, N. Ireland 17/J3
Tanega (isl.), Japan 81/E8
Taney (co.), Mo. 261/F9
Taneycomo (lake), Mo. 261/F9
Taneytown, Md. (21787) 245/K2
Taneyville, Mo. (65759) 261/F9
Tanezrouft (des.), Algeria 102/C2
Tanezrouft (des.), Algeria 106/E4
Tang, Kas (isl.), Cambodia 72/D5
Tanga (isls.), Papua N.G. 86/C1
Tanga (reg.), Tanzania 115/G5
Tanga, Tanzania 115/G4
Tanga, Tanzania 102/F5
Tangainony, Madagascar 118/H4
Tangalla, Sri Lanka 68/E7
Tanganyika (lake) 102/F5
Tanganyika (lake), Burundi 115/E5
Tanganyika (lake), Tanzania 115/E5
Tanganyika (lake), Zaire 115/E5
Tanganyika (lake), Zambia 115/E5
Tangent (pt.), Alaska 196/H1
Tangent, Alberta 182/B2
Tangent, Oreg. (97389) 291/D3
Tangerang, Indonesia 85/G1
Tangermünde, E. Germany 22/D2
Tanggula Shan (range), China 77/D5
Tangier, Ind. (47985) 227/C5
Tangier (sound), Md. 245/P8
Tangier (Tanger), Morocco 106/C1
Tangier, Morocco 102/B1
Tangier, Nova Scotia 168/F4
Tangier (riv.), Nova Scotia 168/F4
Tangier, Okla. (†73801) 288/G2
Tangier, Va. (23440) 307/R5
Tangier (isl.), Va. 307/R5
Tangier (sound), Va. 307/S5
Tangipahoa (par.), La. 238/K5
Tangipahoa, La. (70465) 238/J5
Tangipahoa (riv.), La. 238/N1
Tangra Yumco (lake), China 77/C5
Tangshan, China 77/J4
Tangshan, China 54/N5
Tangub, Philippines 82/D6
Tangyanika (lake) 2/L6
Tangyuan, China 77/L2
Tanimbar (isls.), Indonesia 54/P10
Tanimbar (isls.), Indonesia 85/J7
Tanjay, Philippines 82/D6
Tanjore (Thanjavur), India 68/D6
Tanjungbalai, Indonesia 85/C5
Tanjungkarang, Indonesia 54/M10
Tanjungkarang, Indonesia 85/C7
Tanjungpandan, Indonesia 85/D6
Tanjungpinang, Indonesia 85/C5
Tanjungpriok, Indonesia 85/H1
Tanjungpura, Indonesia 85/B5
Tanjungredeb, Indonesia 85/F5
Tanjungselor, Indonesia 85/F5
Tanna (isl.), Vanuatu 87/H7
Tanner, Ala. (35671) 195/E1
Tanner, W. Va. (26179) 312/E5
Tannersville, N.Y. (12485) 276/M6
Tannersville, Pa. (18372) 294/M3
Tannis (bay), Denmark 21/D2
Tannu-Ola (range), Mongolia 77/D1
Tannu-Ola (range), U.S.S.R. 48/K5
Tanon (str.), Philippines 82/D6
Tanout, Niger 106/F6
Tanque Verde, Ariz. (†85701) 198/E6
Tanta, Egypt 111/J3
Tanta, Egypt 59/B3
Tantallon, Sask. 181/K5
Tantalus (mt.), Hawaii 218/D4
Tan-Tan, Morocco 106/B3
Tantoyuca, Mexico 150/L6
Tantung (Dandong), China 77/K3
Tanumshede, Sweden 18/G7
Tanunda, S. Australia 94/C6
Tanzania 2/L6
Tanzania 102/F5
TANZANIA 115/F5
Tao, Ko (isl.), Thailand 72/C5
Tao'an, China 77/K2
Taole, China 77/G4
Taongi (atoll), Marshall Is. 87/G4
Taopi, Minn. (55977) 255/F7
Taormina, Italy 34/E6
Taos, Mo. (†65101) 261/H5
Taos (co.), N. Mex. 274/D2
Taos, N. Mex. (87571) 274/D2
Taos Pueblo, N. Mex. (†87571) 274/D2
Taoudenni, Mali 106/D4
Taoudenni, Mali 102/B2
Taourirt, Algeria 106/E3
Taourirt, Morocco 106/D2
Taouz, Morocco 106/D2
Taoyuan, China 77/K6
Tapa, U.S.S.R. 53/C1
Tapacarí, Bolivia 136/B5
Tapachula, Mexico 150/N9
Tapajós (riv.), Brazil 2/G6
Tapajós (riv.), Brazil 120/D3
Tapajós (riv.), Brazil 132/B4
Tapaktuan, Indonesia 85/B5
Tapalquén, Argentina 143/E4
Tapanahoni (riv.), Suriname 131/D4
Tapani (lake), Québec 172/B3
Tapanui, N. Zealand 100/B6
Tapaz, Philippines 82/D5
Tapera do Jeronimo, Brazil 132/C2
Tapeta, Liberia 106/C7
Tapi, Mae Nam (riv.), Thailand 72/C5
Tapiantana Group (isls.), Philippines 82/D7
Tapiche (riv.), Peru 128/E6
Taping (riv.), Burma 72/C1
Tápiószele, Hungary 41/E3
Tapirapecó, Sierra (mts.), Venezuela 124/F7
Tapiutan (isl.), Philippines 82/B5
Tapoco, N.C. (28780) 281/A4
Tapolca, Hungary 41/D3
Tappahannock, Va. (22560) 307/O5
Tappan (lake), N.J. 273/C1
Tappan, N.Y. (10983) 276/K8
Tappan (lake), Ohio 284/H5
Tappen, N. Dak. (58487) 282/L6
Tappi (cape), Japan 81/K3
Tapti (riv.), India 68/D4
Tapul (isl.), Philippines 82/C8
Tapul Group (isls.), Philippines 85/G4
Tapul Group (isls.), Philippines 82/C8
Taputapu (cape), Amer. Samoa 86/N9
Taquari (riv.), Brazil 132/C7
Taquaritinga, Brazil 132/D8
Taquaritinga, Brazil 135/B2
Tar (riv.), N.C. 281/O3
Tara (hill), Ireland 17/H4
Tara, Ontario 177/C3
Tara (isl.), Philippines 82/C4
Tara, Queensland 95/D5
Tara, Queensland 88/J5
Tara, U.S.S.R. 48/H4
Tara (riv.), Yugoslavia 45/D4
Tarabuco, Bolivia 136/C6
Tarabulus, Lebanon 63/F5
Tarabulus, Lebanon 59/C3
Taradale, N. Zealand 100/F3
Taraira (riv.), Colombia 126/F8
Tarairi, Bolivia 136/D7
Tarakan, Indonesia 54/N9
Tarakan, Indonesia 85/F5
Taralga, N.S. Wales 97/E4
Tarama (isl.), Japan 81/L7
Tarancón, Spain 33/E3
Tarangire Nat'l Park, Tanzania 115/G4
Taranna, Tasmania 99/D5
Taransay (isl.), Scotland 15/A3
Taranto (prov.), Italy 34/F4
Taranto, Italy 34/F4
Taranto, Italy 7/F4
Taranto (gulf), Italy 7/F5
Taranto (gulf), Italy 34/F5
Tarapacá (reg.), Chile 138/B2
Tarapacá, Chile 138/B2
Tarapacá, Colombia 126/F9
Tarapaya, Bolivia 136/B6
Tarapoto, Peru 120/B3
Tarapoto, Peru 128/D6
Tarare, France 28/F5
Tararua (range), N. Zealand 100/E4
Tarascon, France 28/F6
Tarasp, Switzerland 39/K3
Tarata, Bolivia 136/C5
Tarata, Peru 128/H11
Tarauacá, Brazil 132/G10
Tarauaca, Brazil 120/C3
Taravao (bay), Fr. Poly. 86/T13
Taravao (isth.), Fr. Poly. 86/T13
Tarawa (atoll), Kiribati 87/H5
Tarazona, Spain 33/E2
Tarazona de la Mancha, Spain 33/F3
Tarbat Ness (prom.), Scotland 15/E3
Tarbert, Ireland 17/C6
Tarbert, Strathclyde, Scotland 15/C5
Tarbert, W. Isles, Scotland 15/B3
Tarbert, East Loch (inlet), Scotland 15/B3
Tarbert, Loch (inlet), Scotland 15/B5
Tarbert, West Loch (inlet), Scotland 15/C5
Tarbert, West Loch (inlet), Scotland 15/A3
Tarbes, France 7/E4
Tarbes, France 28/D6
Tarbolton, Scotland 15/D5
Tarboro, Georgia (†31568) 217/J8
Tarboro, N.C. (27886) 281/O3
Tarbot, Nova Scotia 168/H2
Tarcoola, S. Australia 88/E6
Tarcoola, S. Australia 94/D4
Tarcutta, N.S. Wales 97/D4
Tardienta, Spain 33/F2
Tardošked, Czech. 41/E2
Taree, N.S. Wales 88/J6
Taree, N.S. Wales 97/G2
Tärendö, Sweden 18/N3
Tarentum, Pa. (15084) 294/C4
Tarfaya, Morocco 106/B3
Tarfaya, Morocco 102/A2
Tar Heel, N.C. (28392) 281/M5
Tarhuna, Libya 102/D1
Tarhuna, Libya 111/B1
Tariana, Colombia 126/F7
Táriba, Venezuela 124/B4
Tarifa, Spain 33/D4
Tariff, W. Va. (25281) 312/D5
Tariffville, Conn. (06081) 210/D1
Tarija (riv.), Argentina 143/D1
Tarija (dept.), Bolivia 136/D7
Tarija, Bolivia 120/C5
Tarija, Bolivia 136/C7
Tarija, Rio Grande de (riv.), Bolivia 136/C8
Tariku (riv.), Indonesia 85/K6
Tarim (riv.), China 54/K5
Tarim, P.D.R. Yemen 59/E6
Tarim He (riv.), China 77/B3
Tarim Pendi (basin), China 77/B4
Tar Island, Alberta 182/E1
Taritatu (riv.), Indonesia 85/K6
Tarkio, Mo. (64491) 261/B2
Tarkio, Mont. (†59872) 262/B4
Tarko-Sale, U.S.S.R. 48/H3
Tarkwa, Ghana 106/D7
Tarlac (prov.), Philippines 82/C3
Tarlac, Philippines 82/C3
Tarlac, Philippines 85/G2
Tarland, Scotland 15/F3
Tarleton (lake), N.H. 268/D4
Tarlton, Ohio (43156) 284/E6
Tarlton, Tenn. (†37301) 237/K9
Tarlton Downs, North. Terr. 93/E7
Tarm, Denmark 21/B6
Tarma, Peru 128/E8
Tarn (dept.), France 28/E6
Tarn (riv.), France 28/E6
Tarna (riv.), Hungary 41/F3
Tärnaby, Sweden 18/J4
Tarnak (riv.), Afghanistan 68/B2
Tårnby, Denmark 21/F6
Tarn-et-Garonne (dept.), France 28/D5
Tarnobrzeg (prov.), Poland 47/E3
Tarnobrzeg, Poland 47/E3
Tarnopol, Sask. 181/F3
Tarnov, Nebr. (68642) 264/G3
Tarnów (prov.), Poland 47/E4
Tarnów, Poland 7/G3
Tarnów, Poland 47/E4
Tarnowskie Góry, Poland 47/A3
Tarom, Iran 66/J6
Tarom, Iran 59/G4
Taroom, Queensland 95/D5
Tarouca, Portugal 33/C2
Taroudannt, Morocco 106/C2
Taroudant, Morocco 102/A2
Tarpa, Hungary 41/G2
Tarpon Springs, Fla. (*33589) 212/D3
Tarqui, Peru 128/E3
Tarquinia, Italy 34/C3
Tarqumiya, West Bank 65/C4
Tarragona (prov.), Spain 33/G2
Tarragona, Spain 33/G2
Tarragona, Spain 7/E4
Tarraleah, Tasmania 99/C4
Tarrant (co.), Texas 303/G5
Tarrant City, Ala. (35217) 195/E3
Tarrants, Mo. (†63334) 261/K4
Tarrasa, Spain 33/G2
Tárrega, Spain 33/G2
Tarryall (creek), Colo. 208/H4
Tarrytown, Georgia (30470) 217/H6
Tarrytown, N.Y. (10591) 276/O6
Tarsney Lakes, Mo. (†64063) 261/R6
Tarsus, Turkey 59/C2
Tarsus, Turkey 63/F4
Tart, China 77/D4
Tartagal, Argentina 143/D1
Tartagal, Argentina 120/C5
Tartas, France 28/C6
Tartu, U.S.S.R. 7/G3
Tartu, U.S.S.R. 53/D1
Tartu, U.S.S.R. 48/C4
Tartu, U.S.S.R. 52/C3
Tartus (prov.), Syria 63/G5
Tartus, Syria 63/F5
Tarutung, Indonesia 85/B5
Tarver, Georgia (†31648) 217/G9
Tarzan, Texas (79783) 303/B5
Tarzana, Calif. (91356) 204/B10
Täsch, Switzerland 39/E4
Tasco, Kansas (†67740) 232/B2
Tashauz, U.S.S.R. 48/F5
Tashk (lake), Iran 59/F4
Tashk (lake), Iran 66/J6
Tashkent, U.S.S.R. 54/H5
Tashkent, U.S.S.R. 2/N3
Tashkent, U.S.S.R. 48/G5
Tasikmalaya, Indonesia 85/H2
Tasisuak (lake), Newf. 166/B2
Taşkent, Turkey 63/E4
Taşköprü, Turkey 63/F2
Taşlıçay, Turkey 63/K3
Tasman (sea) 2/S7
Tasman (sea) 87/G9
Tasman (sea) 88/J7
Tasman (sea), N.S. Wales 97/F5
Tasman (bay), N. Zealand 100/D4
Tasman (mt.), N. Zealand 100/C5
Tasman (mts.), N. Zealand 100/D4
Tasman (sea), N. Zealand 100/B4
Tasman (pen.), Tasmania 88/H8
Tasman (head), Tasmania 99/D5
Tasman (pen.), Tasmania 99/E5
Tasman (sea), Tasmania 99/E4
Tasman (sea), Victoria 97/F5
Tasmania, 87/H8
Tasmania (state), Australia 87/E10
TASMANIA 99
Tasmania (isl.), Australia 2/S8
Tăşnad, Romania 45/F2
Taşova, Turkey 63/F4
Tassili N'Ahagger (plat.), Algeria 106/E4
Tassili N'Ajjer (plat.), Algeria 106/F3
Tåstrup, Denmark 21/F6
Tasu, Br. Col. 184/A4
Taşucu (gulf), Turkey 63/E4
Taswell, Ind. (47175) 227/D8
Tata, Hungary 41/E3
Tataa (pt.), Fr. Poly. 86/S13
Tatabánya, Hungary 41/E3
Tatahouine, Tunisia 106/G2
Tatalrose, Br. Col. 184/D3
Tatamagouche, Nova Scotia 168/E3
Tatamba, Solomon Is. 86/D3
Tatamy, Pa. (18085) 294/M4
Tatar (str.), U.S.S.R. 54/R5
Tatar (str.), U.S.S.R. 48/P4
Tatar A.S.S.R., U.S.S.R. 52/G3
Tatar A.S.S.R., U.S.S.R. 48/F4
Tatarsk, U.S.S.R. 48/H4
Tate, Georgia (30177) 217/D2
Tate (co.), Miss. 256/E1
Tate, Sask. 181/G4
Tateville, Ky. (42558) 237/M7
Tateyama, Japan 81/K6
Tathlina (lake), N.W. Terrs. 187/G3
Tathlith, Saudi Arabia 59/D6
Tathra, N.S. Wales 97/F5
Tati (riv.), Botswana 118/D4
Tatitlek, Alaska (99677) 196/D1
Tatla Lake, Br. Col. 184/E4
Tatlatui (lake), Br. Col. 184/D2
Tatlayoko (lake), Br. Col. 184/E4
Tatnam (cape), Manitoba 179/K2
Tatnum (cape), Man. 162/G4
Tatoosh (isl.), Wash. 310/A2
Tatra, High (mts.), Czech. 41/E2
Tatra, High (range), Poland 47/D4
Tatta, Pakistan 59/J5
Tatta, Pakistan 68/B4
Tattnall (co.), Georgia 217/J6
Tatuí, Brazil 135/C3
Tatum, N. Mex. (88267) 274/F5
Tatum, S.C. (29594) 296/H2
Tatum, Texas (75691) 303/K5
Tatums, Okla. (73087) 288/M6
Tatung (Datong), China 77/H3
Tatura, Victoria 97/C5
Tatvan, Turkey 63/K3
Taubaté, Brazil 132/E8
Taubaté, Brazil 135/D3
Tauber (riv.), W. Germany 22/C4
Täuffelen, Switzerland 39/D2
Taumarunui, N. Zealand 100/E3
Taum Sauk (mt.), Mo. 261/L7
Taung, S. Africa 118/C5
Taungdwingyi, Burma 72/C2
Taunggyi, Burma 72/C2
Taungthonton (mt.), Burma 72/B1
Taungup, Burma 72/B3
Taunton, England 13/D6
Taunton, England 10/E5
Taunton, Mass. (02780) 249/K5
Taunton (riv.), Mass. 249/K5
Taunton, Minn. (56291) 255/B6
Taunus (range), W. Germany 22/C3
Taupo, N. Zealand 100/F3
Taupo (lake), N. Zealand 100/F3
Tauq, Iraq 66/D3
Taurage, U.S.S.R. 53/B3
Taurage, U.S.S.R. 52/B3
Tauranga, N. Zealand 100/F2
Taureau (res.), Québec 172/D3
Taurianova, Italy 34/E5

Trousdale 459

Toronto, Canada 2/F3
Toronto, Iowa (52343) 229/M5
Toronto, Kansas (66777) 232/G4
Toronto (lake), Kansas 232/F4
Toronto (res.), N.Y. 276/L7
Toronto, Ohio (43964) 284/J5
Toronto (cap.), Ont. 146/K5
Toronto (cap.), Ont. 162/H7
Toronto (metro. munic.), Ontario 177/K4
Toronto (cap.), Ontario 177/K4
Toronto, S. Dak. (57268) 298/R4
Toropalca, Bolivia 136/B7
Toropets, U.S.S.R. 52/D3
Tororo, Uganda 115/F3
Torote (riv.), Spain 33/G4
Torotoro, Bolivia 136/C6
Torpedo, Pa. (†16340) 294/D2
Torphins, Scotland 15/F3
Torpoint, England 13/C7
Torquay (Torbay), England 13/D7
Torquay, Sask. 181/H6
Torquemada, Spain 33/D1
Torr (head), N. Ireland 17/K1
Torrance, Calif. 188/C4
Torrance, Calif. (*90501) 204/C11
Torrance (co.), N. Mex. 274/D4
Torrance, Ontario 177/E3
Torrance, Pa. (15779) 294/D5
Torre, Cerro de la (mt.), Chile 138/E4
Torre Annunziata, Italy 34/E4
Torreblanca, Spain 33/G2
Torrecilla (lag.), P. Rico 161/E1
Torre del Greco, Italy 34/E4
Torre de Moncorvo, Portugal 33/C2
Torredonjimeno, Spain 33/D4
Torre Gaia, Italy 34/F6
Torrejón (res.), Spain 33/D3
Torrejoncillo, Spain 33/C3
Torrejón de Ardoz, Spain 33/G4
Torrelaguna, Spain 33/E2
Torrelavega, Spain 33/D1
Torremaggiore, Italy 34/E4
Torremolinos, Spain 33/D4
Torrens (riv.) 88/E7
Torrens (lake), Australia 87/D9
Torrens (isl.), S. Australia 88/D7
Torrens (lake), S. Australia 88/F6
Torrens (lake), S. Australia 94/E4
Torrens (riv.), S. Australia 94/C7
Torrente, Spain 33/F3
Torreón, Mexico 146/H7
Torreón, Mexico 150/H4
Torreon, N. Mex. (87061) 274/C4
Torre-Pacheco, Spain 33/F4
Torres (strait) 87/E7
Torres (str.), Papua N.G. 85/A7
Torres (str.), Queensland 88/G2
Torres (str.), Queensland 95/B1
Torres (isls.), Vanuatu 87/G7
Torres Martinez Ind. Res., Calif. 204/J10
Torres Novas, Portugal 33/B3
Torres Vedras, Portugal 33/B3
Torrevieja, Spain 33/F4
Torrey, Utah (84775) 304/C5
Torridge (riv.), England 13/C7
Torridon, Loch (inlet), Scotland 15/C3
Torriente, Cuba 158/D1
Torrijos, Philippines 82/D4
Torrijos, Spain 33/D2
Tørring, Denmark 21/C6
Torringford, Conn. (†06790) 210/C1
Torrington, Alberta 182/D4
Torrington, Conn. (06790) 210/C1
Torrington, Wyo. (82240) 319/H3
Torroella de Montgrí, Spain 33/H1
Torrowangee, N.S. Wales 97/A2
Torrox, Spain 33/E4
Torsby, Sweden 18/H6
Tors Cove, Newf. 166/D2
Torshälla, Sweden 18/K7
Tórshavn, Denmark 7/D2
Tórshavn (cap.), Faerøe Is., Denmark 21/A3
Tortilla Flat, Ariz. (85290) 198/D5
Tortola (isl.), Virgin Is. (Br.) 161/D3
Tortola (isl.), Virgin Is. (Br.) 156/H1
Tórtolas, Cerro de las (mt.), Chile 138/B8
Tortona, Italy 34/B2
Tortorici, Italy 34/E6
Tortosa, Spain 33/G2
Tortosa (cape), Spain 33/G2
Tortue (chan.), Haiti 158/C5
Tortue (Tortuga) (isl.), Haiti 156/D2
Tortue (Tortuga) (isl.), Haiti 158/C4
Tortuga (isl.), Haiti 158/C4
Tortuga (isl.), Haiti 156/D2
Tortugas (gulf), Colombia 126/B6
Tortuguero (lag.), P. Rico 161/D1
Tortuguilla (pt.), Cuba 158/K4
Tortum, Turkey 63/J2
Torud, Iran 59/F2
Torud, Iran 66/J3
Torul, Turkey 63/H2
Toruń (prov.), Poland 47/D2
Toruń, Poland 7/F3
Toruń, Poland 47/D2
Torunos, Venezuela 124/C3
Tõrva, U.S.S.R. 53/C1
Tory (isl.), Ireland 17/E1
Tory (isl.), Ireland 10/B3
Tory (sound), Ireland 17/E1
Torysa (riv.), Czech. 41/F2
Torzhok, U.S.S.R. 52/D3
Tosa, Japan 81/F7
Tosa (bay), Japan 81/F7
Tosashimizu, Japan 81/F7
Toson Hu (lake), China 77/E4
Töss (riv.), Switzerland 39/G1
Tostado, Argentina 143/D2
Toston, Mont. (59643) 262/E4
Tosu, Japan 81/E7
Tosya, Turkey 63/F2
Tota, Laguna de (lake), Colombia 126/D5
Totana, Spain 33/F4
Tótkomlós, Hungary 41/F3
Tot'ma, U.S.S.R. 48/E4
Tot'ma, U.S.S.R. 52/F3
Totnes, England 13/D7
Totnes, England 10/E5
Totnes, Sask. 181/C4
Totness, Suriname 131/C3
Toto, Ind. (†46534) 227/D2
Totoket, Conn. (†06405) 210/D3
Totonicapán, Guatemala 154/B3
Totora, Cochabamba, Bolivia 136/C5
Totora, Oruro, Bolivia 136/A5
Totoral, Chile 138/A6
Totoral, Quebrada (riv.), Chile 138/A6
Totoral, Uruguay 145/C3
Totowa, N.J. (07512) 273/B1
Totoya (isl.), Fiji 86/R11
Tottenham, N.S. Wales 97/D3
Tottenham, Ontario 177/E3
Tottori (pref.), Japan 81/G6
Tottori, Japan 81/G6
Touat (oasis), Algeria 106/E3
Touba, Ivory Coast 106/C7
Touba, Senegal 106/A6
Toubkal, Jebel (mt.), Morocco 102/B1
Toubkal, Jebel (mt.), Morocco 106/C2
Touchet, Wash. (99360) 310/G4
Touchet (riv.), Wash. 310/G4
Touchwood (lake), Alberta 182/E2
Touchwood (hills), Sask. 181/G4
Toufourine (well), Mali 106/C4
Tougaloo, Miss. (39174) 256/D6
Tougan, Upper Volta 106/D6
Touggourt, Algeria 106/F2
Touggourt, Algeria 102/C1
Toughkenamon, Pa. (19374) 294/L6
Tougué, Guinea 106/B6
Touila (well), Algeria 106/C3
Touila (well), Mauritania 106/C3
Toukoto, Mali 106/C6
Toul, France 28/F3
Touladi, Grand Lac (lake), Québec 172/J1
Toulnustouc (riv.), Québec 174/D2
Toulon, France 7/E4
Toulon, France 28/F6
Toulon, Ill. (61483) 222/D2
Toulouse, France 7/E4
Toulouse, France 28/D6
Toumodi, Ivory Coast 106/D7
Toungo, Nigeria 106/G7
Toungoo, Burma 72/C3
Touraine (trad. prov.), France 29
Tourakom, Laos 72/D3
Tourbis (lake), Québec 172/C2
Tourcoing, France 28/E2
Tour d'Ai (mt.), Switzerland 39/C4
Tourelle, Québec 172/C1
Tournai, Belgium 27/C7
Tournavista, Peru 128/E7
Tournon, France 28/F5
Tournus, France 28/F4
Touros, Brazil 132/H4
Touro Synagogue Nat'l Hist. Site, R.I. 249/J7
Tours, France 28/D4
Tours, France 7/E4
Tourville, Québec 172/H2
Toutes Aides, Manitoba 179/C3
Toutle, Wash. (98649) 310/C4
Toutle, North Fork (riv.), Wash. 310/C4
Toutle, South Fork (riv.), Wash. 310/C4
Toužim, Czech. 41/B1
Töv, Mongolia 77/G2
Tovar, Venezuela 124/C3
Tovey, Ill. (62570) 222/D4
Towaco, N.J. (07082) 273/E2
Towada, Japan 81/K3
Towada (lake), Japan 81/K3
Towada-Hachimantai National Park, Japan 81/K3
Towakaima, Guyana 131/B2
Towanda, Ill. (61776) 222/E3
Towanda, Kansas (67144) 232/E4
Towanda, Pa. (18848) 294/J2
Towanda (creek), Pa. 294/J2
Towaoc, Colo. (81334) 208/B8
Towcester, England 13/F5
Tower, Mich. (49792) 250/E3
Tower, Minn. (55790) 255/F3
Tower, Wyo. (†82190) 319/B1
Tower City, N. Dak. (58071) 282/P6
Tower City, Pa. (17980) 294/J4
Tower Hamlets, England 13/H8
Tower Hill, Ill. (62571) 222/E4
Tower Lakes, Ill. (†60010) 222/A4
Towers of Silence, India 68/B7
Tow Law, England 13/H4
Town (creek), Ala. 195/C1
Town (creek), Md. 245/E2
Town and Country, Mo. (†63101) 261/O3
Town and Country, Wash. (†99218) 310/H3
Town Creek, Ala. (35672) 195/D1
Towner, Colo. (81080) 208/P6
Towner (co.), N. Dak. 282/M2
Towner, N. Dak. (58788) 282/K3
Townley, Ala. (35587) 195/D3
Town of Pines, Ind. (†46360) 227/D1
Town Point, Md. (†21915) 245/P3
Towns (co.), Georgia 217/E1
Towns, Georgia (†31055) 217/G7
Townsend, Del. (19734) 245/R3
Townsend, Georgia (31331) 217/J7
Townsend, Mass. (01469) 249/H2
Townsend○, Mass. (01469) 249/H2
Townsend, Mont. (59644) 262/E4
Townsend (inlet), N.J. 273/D5
Townsend, Tenn. (37882) 237/O9
Townsend, Va. (23443) 307/R6
Townsend, Wis. (54175) 317/K5
Townsend Harbor, Mass. (†01469) 249/G2
Townsends Inlet, N.J. (†08243) 273/D5
Townshend○, Vt. (05353) 268/B5
Townsville, Australia 2/S6
Townsville, Australia 87/E7
Townsville, N.C. (27584) 281/N1
Townsville, Queensland 88/H3
Townsville, Queensland 95/C3
Townville, Pa. (16360) 294/C2
Townville, S.C. (29689) 296/B2
Towot, Sudan 111/F6
Towraghondi, Afghanistan 68/A1
Towson, Md. (21204) 245/M3
Towuti (lake), Indonesia 85/G6
Towy (riv.), Wales 13/D6
Towy (riv.), Wales 10/E5
Toxey, Ala. (36921) 195/B7
Toya (lake), Japan 81/K2
Toyah, Texas (79785) 303/D11
Toyah (creek), Texas 303/D11
Toyah (lake), Texas 303/A6
Toyahvale, Texas (79786) 303/D11
Toyama (pref.), Japan 81/H5
Toyama, Japan 81/H5
Toyama (bay), Japan 81/H5
Toyohashi, Japan 81/H6
Toyonaka, Japan 81/J7
Toyooka, Japan 81/G6
Toyota, Japan 81/H6
Tozeur, Tunisia 106/F2
Trabzon (prov.), Turkey 63/H2
Trabzon, Turkey 54/E5
Trabzon, Turkey 63/H2
Trabzon, Turkey 59/C1
Tracadie, New Bruns. 170/F1
Tracadie, Nova Scotia 168/G3
Tracadie (bay), Pr. Edward I. 168/F2
Trachselwald, Switzerland 39/E2
Tracy, Calif. (95376) 204/D6
Tracy, Conn. (†06492) 210/D2
Tracy, Iowa (50256) 229/H6
Tracy, Ky. (†42123) 237/K7
Tracy, Minn. (56175) 255/C6
Tracy, Mo. (64079) 261/C4
Tracy, New Bruns. 170/D3
Tracy, Québec 172/D3
Tracy Arm (inlet), Alaska 196/N1
Tracy City, Tenn. (37387) 237/K10
Tracyton, Wash. (98393) 310/A2
Trade, Tenn. (37691) 237/T8
Trade Lake, Wis. (†54837) 317/A4
Tradespark, Scotland 15/E3
Tradesville, S.C. (†29720) 296/F2
Tradewater (riv.), Ky. 237/F6
Trading (bay), Alaska 196/B1
Trading Post, Kansas (†66075) 232/H3
Traer, Iowa (50675) 229/J4
Traer, Kansas (†67749) 232/B2
Trafalgar, Ind. (46181) 227/E6
Trafalgar, Nova Scotia 168/F3
Trafalgar (cape), Spain 33/C4
Trafaria, Portugal 33/A1
Trafford, Ala. (35172) 195/E3
Trafford, Pa. (15085) 294/C5
Traghen, Libya 111/B2
Traiguén, Chile 138/D2
Traiguén (isl.), Chile 138/D6
Trail, Br. Col. 162/E6
Trail, Br. Col. 146/G4
Trail, Br. Col. 184/J6
Trail, Minn. (56684) 255/C3
Trail, Oreg. (97541) 291/E5
Trail City, S. Dak. (57657) 298/H3
Trail Creek, Ind. (†46360) 227/D1
Traill (isl.), Greenl. 4/B10
Traill (co.), N. Dak. 282/R5
Traîne (lake), Québec 172/D2
Trainer, Pa. (†19013) 294/L7
Traiskirchen, Austria 41/D2
Trakai, U.S.S.R. 53/C3
Tralake, Miss. (38757) 256/C4
Tralee, Ireland 10/B4
Tralee, Ireland 17/B7
Tralee (bay), Ireland 17/B7
Tramán-tepuí (mt.), Venezuela 124/G5
Tramelan, Switzerland 39/D2
Trammel, Va. (24289) 307/D6
Tramore, Ireland 10/C4
Tramore, Ireland 17/G7
Tramore (bay), Ireland 17/G7
Trampas, N. Mex. (87576) 274/D2
Tramperos (creek), N. Mex. 274/F2
Tramping (lake), Sask. 181/C3
Tramping Lake, Sask. 181/B3
Tranås, Sweden 18/J7
Trancoso, Portugal 33/C2
Tranebjerg, Denmark 21/D6
Tranebjerg (mt.), Denmark 21/C6
Tranent, Scotland 15/F5
Trang, Thailand 72/C6
Trangan (isl.), Indonesia 85/J7
Trangie, N.S. Wales 97/D3
Trani, Italy 34/F4
Tranquebar, India 68/E6
Tranqueras, Uruguay 145/D2
Tranqui (isl.), Chile 138/D4
Tranquility, N.J. (07879) 273/D2
Tranquillity, Calif. (93668) 204/E7
Transantarctic (mts.) 5/B17
Trans-Carpathian Oblast, U.S.S.R. 52/B5
Transfer, Pa. (16154) 294/A3
Transkei (aut. rep.), S. Africa 102/E8
Transkei (aut. rep.), S. Africa 118/D6
Transquaking (riv.), Md. 245/P7
Transvaal (prov.), S. Africa 102/E7
Transvaal (prov.), S. Africa 118/D4
Transylvania, La. (71286) 238/H1
Transylvania (co.), N.C. 281/D4
Transylvanian Alps (mts.), Romania 45/G3
Trapani (prov.), Italy 34/D5
Trapani, Italy 7/F5
Trapani, Italy 34/D5
Trap Falls (res.), Conn. 210/C3
Traphill, N.C. (28685) 281/H2
Trappe, Md. (21673) 245/O6
Trappers (lake), Colo. 208/E3
Traralgon, Victoria 97/D6
Traralgon, Victoria 88/H7
Trarza (reg.), Mauritania 106/A5
Trasimeno (lake), Italy 34/D3
Traskwood, Ark. (72167) 202/E5
Trat, Thailand 72/D4
Traun, Austria 41/C2
Traun (riv.), Austria 41/C2
Traun See (lake), Austria 41/B3
Traunstein, W. Germany 22/E5
Travancore (reg.), India 68/D7
Travelers Rest, S.C. (29690) 296/C2
Travellers (lake), N.S. Wales 97/B3
Travellers Rest, Ky. (†41314) 237/O6
Travemünde, W. Germany 22/D2
Travers, Alberta 182/D4
Travers (res.), Alberta 182/D4
Traverse (bay), Manitoba 179/F4
Traverse (isl.), Mich. 250/A1
Traverse (pt.), Mich. 250/A1
Traverse (co.), Minn. 255/B5
Traverse, Minn. (†56082) 255/D6
Traverse (lake), Minn. 255/B5
Traverse (lake), S. Dak. 298/R2
Traverse City, Mich. 188/K2
Traverse City, Mich. (49684) 250/D4
Tra Vinh (Phu Vinh), Vietnam 72/E5
Travis (co.), Texas 303/G7
Travis (lake), Texas 303/G7
Travis A.F.B., Calif. 204/L1
Travnik, Yugoslavia 45/C3
Trawbreaga (bay), Ireland 17/F1
Traynor, Sask. 181/C3
Traytown, Newf. 166/D1
Trbovlje, Yugoslavia 45/B2
Treadway, Tenn. (37883) 237/P8
Treasure (isl.), Fla. 212/B3
Treasure (co.), Mont. 262/J4
Treasure Island, Fla. (33740) 212/B3
Treasury (isls.), Solomon Is. 86/C2
Treaty, Ind. (†46992) 227/F3
Trebbia (riv.), Italy 34/B2
Třebíč, Czech. 41/C2
Trebinje, Yugoslavia 45/D4
Trebišov, Czech. 41/F2
Trebizond (Trabzon), Turkey 63/H2
Trebloc, Miss. (38875) 256/G3
Třeboň, Czech. 41/C2
Trece Martires, Philippines 82/C3
Tredegar, Wales 13/B6
Treece, Kansas (66778) 232/H4
Treelon, Sask. 181/C6
Trees, La. (71081) 238/B1
Treesbank, Manitoba 179/C5
Tregaron, Wales 13/D5
Tregaron, Wales 10/E4
Tregarva, Sask. 181/G5
Trego (co.), Kansas 232/C3
Trego, Mont. (59934) 262/B2
Trego, Wis. (54888) 317/C4
Treherne, Manitoba 179/D5
Treig, Loch (lake), Scotland 15/D4
Treinta y Tres (dept.), Uruguay 145/E4
Treinta y Tres, Uruguay 145/E4
Trelew, Argentina 143/C5
Trelleborg, Sweden 18/H9
Tremadoc (bay), Wales 10/D4
Tremadoc (prom.), Wales 13/C5
Tremblant (lake), Québec 172/C3
Trembleur (lake), Br. Col. 184/E3
Trementina, N. Mex. (88439) 274/E3
Tremiti (isls.), Italy 34/E3
Tremont, Ill. (61568) 222/D3
Tremont, Maine (†04653) 243/G7
Tremont○, Maine (†04653) 243/G7
Tremont, Miss. (38876) 256/H2
Tremont, Pa. (17981) 294/K4
Tremont City, Ohio (45372) 284/C5
Tremonton, Utah (84337) 304/B2
Tremp, Spain 33/G1
Trempealeau (co.), Wis. 317/D7
Trempealeau, Wis. (54661) 317/C8
Trempealeau (riv.), Wis. 317/C7
Trenary, Mich. (49891) 250/C2
Trenčín, Czech. 41/E2
Trenel, Argentina 143/D4
Trenggalek, Indonesia 85/K2
Trenque Lauquen, Argentina 143/D4
Trent (riv.), England 13/G4
Trent (riv.), England 10/F4
Trent (riv.), N.C. 281/P4
Trent, Oreg. (†97431) 291/E4
Trent, S. Dak. (57065) 298/R6
Trent, Texas (79561) 303/D5
Trente et un Milles (lake), Québec 172/B3
Trentham, Manitoba 179/F5
Trentham Cliffs, N.S. Wales 97/B4
Trentino-Alto Adige (reg.), Italy 34/C1
Trento (prov.), Italy 34/C1
Trento, Italy 34/C1
Trenton, Ala. (35774) 195/F1
Trenton, Ark. (†72374) 202/J5
Trenton, Fla. (32693) 212/D2
Trenton, Georgia (30752) 217/A1
Trenton, Ill. (62293) 222/D5
Trenton, Iowa (†52641) 229/K6
Trenton, Ky. (42286) 237/G7
Trenton, Maine (†04605) 243/G7
Trenton○, Maine (†04605) 243/G7
Trenton, Md. (†21155) 245/L2
Trenton, Mich. (48183) 250/B7
Trenton, Miss. (†39153) 256/E6
Trenton, Mo. (64683) 261/E2
Trenton, Nebr. (69044) 264/D4
Trenton (cap.), N.J. 146/L5
Trenton (cap.), N.J. 188/M2
Trenton (cap.), N.J. (*08601) 273/D3
Trenton, N.C. (28585) 281/P4
Trenton, N. Dak. (58853) 282/C3
Trenton, Nova Scotia 168/F3
Trenton, Ohio (45067) 284/B7
Trenton, Ontario 177/G3
Trenton, S.C. (29847) 296/D4
Trenton, Tenn. (38382) 237/D9
Trenton, Texas (75490) 303/H4
Trenton, Utah (84338) 304/B2
Trent Woods, N.C. (†28560) 281/P4
Trepassey, Newf. 166/D2
Treptow, E. Germany 22/F4
Tres Árboles, Uruguay 145/C3
Tres Arroyos, Argentina 143/D4
Tres Arroyos, Argentina 120/C6
Tres Bocas, Uruguay 145/B2
Tresckow, Pa. (18254) 294/K4
Tresco (isl.), England 13/A8
Três Corações, Brazil 132/E8
Três Corações, Brazil 135/D2
Tres Cruces, Nevado (mt.), Chile 138/B6
Tres Esquinas, Colombia 126/C7
Treshnish (isls.), Scotland 15/B4
Tres Islas, Uruguay 145/E3
Três Lagoas, Brazil 120/D5
Três Lagoas, Brazil 132/C8
Três Marias (res.), Brazil 120/E4
Tres Montes (cape), Chile 120/B7
Tres Montes (cape), Chile 138/C7
Tres Montes (gulf), Chile 138/D6
Tres Montes (pen.), Chile 138/C6
Tres Palmas, Colombia 126/B3
Trespassey (bay), Newf. 166/D2
Tres Picos, Cerro (mt.), Argentina 143/B5
Tres Piedras, N. Mex. (87577) 274/D2
Tres Pinos, Calif. (95075) 204/D7
Três Pontas, Brazil 135/D2
Tres Puntas (cape), Argentina 120/C7
Tres Puntas (cape), Argentina 143/D6
Tres Puntas (cape), Guatemala 154/C3
Três Rios, Brazil 135/E3
Três Rios, Brazil 132/F8
Tres Ritos, N. Mex. (†87579) 274/D2
Třešť, Czech. 41/C2
Treuchtlingen, W. Germany 22/D4
Treungen, Norway 18/F7
Treutlen (co.), Georgia 217/G6
Trevelin, Argentina 143/B5
Trevett, Maine (04571) 243/D8
Treviglio, Italy 34/B2
Treviño, Spain 33/E1
Treviso (prov.), Italy 34/D2
Treviso, Italy 34/D2
Trevlac, Ind. (†47448) 227/E6
Trevorton, Pa. (17881) 294/J4
Trevose (head), England 13/B7
Trévoux, France 28/F5
Treynor, Iowa (51575) 229/B6
Treyvaux, Switzerland 39/D3
Trezevant, Tenn. (38258) 237/D8
Trhové Sviny, Czech. 41/C2
Triabunna, Tasmania 99/D4
Triadelphia (lake), Md. 245/L4
Triadelphia, W. Va. (26059) 312/E2
Triana, Ala. (†35758) 195/E1
Triangle, Alberta 182/B2
Triangle, Va. (22172) 307/O3
Triángulo Este (isl.), Mexico 150/N6
Triángulo Oeste (isl.), Mexico 150/N6
Tribbett, Miss. (38779) 256/C4
Tribbey, Okla. (†74852) 288/M4
Triberg im Schwarzwald, W. Germany 22/C4
Tribune, Kansas (67879) 232/A3
Tribune, Sask. 181/H6
Tricase, Italy 34/G5
Trichur, India 68/D6
Trida, N.S. Wales 97/C3
Tridell, Utah (84076) 304/E3
Trident, Mont. (59752) 262/E5
Trident (peak), Nev. 266/C1
Trieben, Austria 41/C3
Trier, W. Germany 22/B4
Triesen, Liecht. 39/H2
Trieste (prov.), Italy 34/E2
Trieste, Italy 34/E2
Trieste, Italy 7/F4
Trieste (gulf), Italy 34/D2
Trigal, Bolivia 136/C6
Trigg (co.), Ky. 237/F7
Triglav (mt.), Yugoslavia 45/A2
Trigueros, Spain 33/C4
Tríkkala, Greece 45/E6
Tri Lakes, Ind. (†46725) 227/G2
Trilby, Fla. (33593) 212/D3
Trilla, Ill. (62469) 222/E4
Trillick, N. Ireland 17/G3
Trim, Ireland 17/H4
Trim, Ireland 10/C4
Trimble, Ill. (†62454) 222/F4
Trimble (co.), Ky. 237/L3
Trimble, Ky. (42559) 237/M6
Trimble, Mo. (64492) 261/D4
Trimble, Ohio (45782) 284/F7
Trimble, Tenn. (38259) 237/C8
Trim Cane (creek), Miss. 256/G4
Trimmis, Switzerland 39/J3
Trimont, Minn. (56176) 255/D7
Trin, Switzerland 39/H3
Trinchera, Colo. (81081) 208/M8
Trinchera (peak), Colo. 208/J8
Trinchera (riv.), Colo. 208/H8
Trincheras, Mexico 150/D1
Trincomalee, Sri Lanka 54/K9
Trincomalee, Sri Lanka 68/E7
Trindade, Brazil 132/D7
Třinec, Czech. 41/E2
Tring, England 13/G7
Tring, England 10/F5
Tring-Jonction, Québec 172/F3
Trinidad (isl.), Argentina 143/D4
Trinidad, Bolivia 120/C4
Trinidad, Bolivia 136/C4
Trinidad, Calif. (95570) 204/A2
Trinidad (head), Calif. 204/A2
Trinidad (gulf), Chile 138/D8
Trinidad, Colombia 126/E5
Trinidad, Colo. 146/H6
Trinidad, Colo. 188/F3
Trinidad, Colo. (81082) 208/L8
Trinidad, Cuba 158/E2
Trinidad, Cuba 156/B2
Trinidad, Honduras 154/C3
Trinidad, Paraguay 144/E5
Trinidad, Texas (75163) 303/J5
Trinidad (isl.), Trin. & Tob. 156/G5
Trinidad (isl.), Trin. & Tob. 161/A9
Trinidad, Uruguay 145/B4
Trinidad, Wash. (†98848) 310/F3
Trinidad and Tobago 2/G5
Trinidad and Tobago 146/N8
TRINIDAD and TOBAGO 161
TRINIDAD and TOBAGO 156/G5
Trinity, Ala. (35673) 195/D1
Trinity (isls.), Alaska 196/H3
Trinity (co.), Calif. 204/B3
Trinity (riv.), Calif. 204/B3
Trinity (mt.), Idaho 220/C6
Trinity, Ky. (†41179) 237/O3
Trinity (range), Nev. 266/C2
Trinity, Newf. 166/D4
Trinity, Newf. 166/D2
Trinity (bay), Newf. 166/D2
Trinity (bay), Queensland 88/H3
Trinity (bay), Queensland 95/C3
Trinity (co.), Texas 303/J6
Trinity, Texas (75862) 303/J7
Trinity (bay), Texas 303/L2
Trinity (riv.), Texas 188/G4
Trinity (riv.), Texas 303/H5
Trinity, West Fork (riv.), Texas 303/G2
Trinity Center, Calif. (96091) 204/C2
Trinity Springs, Ind. (†47581) 227/D7
Trinity Ville, Jamaica 158/K6
Trinkitat, Sudan 111/G4
Trinkitat, Sudan 59/C6
Trino, Italy 34/B2
Trinway, Ohio (43842) 284/F5
Trio, S.C. (29595) 296/H5
Trion, Georgia (30753) 217/B1
Triplet, Va. (23886) 307/N7
Triplett, Mo. (65286) 261/F4
Tripoli, Iowa (50676) 229/J3
Tripoli (Tarabulus), Lebanon 59/C3
Tripoli (Tarabulus), Lebanon 63/F5
Tripoli (cap.), Libya 2/K4
Tripoli (cap.), Libya 102/D1
Tripoli (cap.), Libya 111/B1
Tripoli, Wis. (54564) 317/G4
Tripolis, Greece 45/F7
Tripolitania (reg.), Libya 102/D1
Tripolitania (reg.), Libya 111/B1
Tripp (co.), S. Dak. 298/K7
Tripp, S. Dak. (57376) 298/N7
Tripura (state), India 68/G4
Trischen (isl.), W. Germany 22/C1
Tristan da Cunha (isl.), St. Helena 2/J7
Triste (gulf), Venezuela 124/D2
Triton (isl.), China 85/E2
Triumph, Ill. (61371) 222/E2
Triumph-Buras, La. (†70041) 238/L8
Triune, Tenn. (†37014) 237/H9
Trivandrum, India 54/J9
Trivandrum, India 68/D7
Trivoli, Ill. (61569) 222/D3
Trnava, Czech. 41/D2
Trobriand (isls.), Papua N.G. 87/F6
Trobriand (isls.), Papua N.G. 85/C7
Trochu, Alberta 182/D4
Troense, Denmark 21/D7
Trofaiach, Austria 41/C3
Trogir, Yugoslavia 45/C4
Troisdorf, W. Germany 22/B3
Trois-Pistoles, Québec 172/H1
Trois Pitons, Morne (mt.), Dominica 161/E6
Trois-Ponts, Belgium 27/H8
Trois-Rivières, Guadeloupe 161/A7
Trois-Rivières (riv.), Haiti 158/B5
Trois-Rivières, Que. 162/J6
Trois-Rivières, Que. 146/L5
Trois-Rivières, Que. 172/E3
Trois-Rivières-Ouest, Québec 172/E3
Trois-Saumons, Québec 172/G2
Troistorrents, Switzerland /C4
Troisvierges, Luxembourg 27/J9
Troitsa (lake), Br. Col. 184/D3
Troitsk, U.S.S.R. 48/G4
Troitsko-Pechorsk, U.S.S.R. 52/J2
Trojan, S. Dak. (†57754) 298/B5
Trollhättan, Sweden 18/H7
Trombay, India 68/B7
Trombetas (riv.), Brazil 132/B3
Tromie (riv.), Scotland 15/D4
Trommald, Minn. (†56455) 255/D4
Troms (co.), Norway 18/L2
Tromsø, Norway 4/B9
Tromsø, Norway 7/F2
Tromsø, Norway 18/L2
Trona, Calif. (93562) 204/H8
Tronador (mt.), Argentina 143/B5
Tronador, Cerro (mt.), Chile 138/E3
Trondheim, Norway 7/F2
Trondheim, Norway 18/F5
Trondheimsfjorden (fjord), Norway 7/F2
Trondheimsfjorden (fjord), Norway 18/G5
Troodos (mt.), Cyprus 63/E5
Troon, Scotland 10/D3
Troon, Scotland 15/D5
Tropic, Utah (84776) 304/B6
Trosa, Sweden 18/K7
Trosky, Minn. (56177) 255/B7
Trossachs, Sask. 181/G6
Trossachs, The, (valley), Scotland 15/D4
Trostan (mt.), N. Ireland 17/J1
Trotternish (dist.), Scotland 15/B3
Trotters, N. Dak. (58657) 282/C5
Trotwood, Ohio (45426) 284/B6
Trou Bonbon, Haiti 158/A6
Trou du Nord, Haiti 158/C5
Troup (co.), Georgia 217/B4
Troup (head), Scotland 15/F3
Troup, Texas (75789) 303/J5
Troupsburg, N.Y. (14885) 276/F6
Trousdale, Kansas (†67059) 232/C4
Trousdale, Okla. (†74878) 288/M4

Upper Fairmount 461

Twelvepole (creek), W. Va. 312/A6
Twentynine Palms, Calif. (92277) 204/K9
Twentynine Palms Marine Base, Calif. 204/J9
Twig, Minn. (55791) 255/F4
Twiggs (co.), Georgia 217/F5
Twila, Ky. (†40873) 237/P7
Twillingate, Newf. 166/C4
Twin (lakes), Conn. 210/B1
Twin (falls), Idaho 220/D7
Twin (lakes), Maine 243/F4
Twin (lakes), Wash. 310/G2
Twin Bridges, Mont. (59754) 262/D5
Twin Brooks, S. Dak. (57269) 298/R3
Twin City, Georgia (30471) 217/H5
Twin Falls (co.), Idaho 220/D7
Twin Falls, Idaho (83301) 220/D7
Twin Falls, Idaho 188/C2
Twin Falls, Idaho 146/G5
Twin Falls, Newf. 166/B3
Twin Hills, Alaska (†99576) 196/F3
Twining, Mich. (48766) 250/F4
Twin Lake, Mich. (49457) 250/C5
Twin Lakes, Calif. (†95060) 204/K4
Twin Lakes, Colo. (81251) 208/G4
Twin Lakes (res.), Colo. 208/G4
Twin Lakes, Minn. (56089) 255/E7
Twin Lakes, Wis. (53181) 317/K11
Twin Mountain, N.H. (03595) 268/D3
Twin Oaks, Mo. (†63088) 261/N3
Twin Peaks, Calif. (92391) 204/H9
Twin Peaks (mt.), Idaho 220/D5
Twin Rocks, Oreg. (†97136) 291/C2
Twin Rocks, Pa. (15960) 294/E4
Twinsburg, Ohio (44087) 284/J10
Twin Sisters (mt.), Wash. 310/D2
Twin Valley, Minn. (56584) 255/B3
Twisp, Wash. (98856) 310/E2
Twisp (pass), Wash. 310/E2
Twisp (riv.), Wash. 310/E2
Twitchell (res.), Calif. 204/E9
Two Arm (bay), Alaska 196/C2
Two Butte (creek), Colo. 208/N7
Two Buttes, Colo. (81084) 208/P7
Two Buttes (res.), Colo. 208/O7
Twodot, Mont. (59085) 262/F4
Twofold (bay), N.S. Wales 97/F5
Two Harbors, Minn. (55616) 255/G3
Two Hearted (riv.), Mich. 250/D2
Two Hills, Alberta 182/E3
Two Rivers (riv.), Minn. 255/A1
Two Rivers (res.), N. Mex. 274/E5
Two Rivers, Wis. (54241) 317/M7
Two Water (creek), Utah 304/E4
Twynholm, Scotland 15/D6
Tyaskin, Md. (21865) 245/P7
Tybee Island, Georgia (31328) 217/L6
Tybee Roads (chan.), S.C. 296/F7
Tychy, Poland 47/B4
Tye, Texas (79563) 303/E5
Tye River, Va. (22975) 307/L5
Tygart (lake), W. Va. 312/G4
Tygart Valley (riv.), W. Va. 312/F5
Tyger (riv.), S.C. 296/D2
Tygh Valley, Oreg. (97063) 291/F2
Tyler, Ala. (36785) 195/E6
Tyler (lake), Conn. 210/B1
Tyler, Minn. (56178) 255/B6
Tyler, Mo. (†63877) 261/N10
Tyler, N. Dak. (†58075) 282/S7
Tyler, Pa. (†15849) 294/F3
Tyler (co.), Texas 303/K7
Tyler, Texas 188/H4
Tyler, Texas (*75701) 303/J5
Tyler, Wash. (†99004) 310/H3
Tyler (co.), W. Va. 312/E4
Tylersburg, Pa. (16361) 294/D3
Tylersville, Pa. (17773) 294/G4
Tylertown, Miss. (39667) 256/D8
Tylerville, Conn. (†06438) 210/F3
Tym (riv.), U.S.S.R. 48/J3
Tymovskoye, U.S.S.R. 48/P4
Týn, Czech. 41/C2
Tynagh, Ireland 17/E5
Tynan, Texas (78391) 303/G9
Tynda, U.S.S.R. 48/N4
Tyndall, Manitoba 179/F4
Tyndall, S. Dak. (57066) 298/O8
Tyndall A.F.B., Fla. 212/C6
Tyndrum, Scotland 15/D4
Tyne (riv.), England 13/F3
Tyne (riv.), England 10/F3
Tyne (riv.), Scotland 15/F5
Tyne and Wear (co.), England 13/H3
Tynemouth, England 13/J3
Tynemouth, England 10/F3
Tyner, Ind. (46572) 227/E2
Tyner, Ky. (40486) 237/O6
Tyner, N.C. (27980) 281/R2
Tyner, Sask. 181/C4
Tyne Valley, Pr. Edward I. 168/E2
Tyngsboro○, Mass. (01879) 249/J2
Tynset, Norway 18/G5
Tyntynder South, Victoria 97/B4
Tyonek, Alaska (99682) 196/B1
Tyra (cays), Nicaragua 154/F4
Tyre (Sur), Lebanon 63/F6
Tyrifjord (lake), Norway 18/C3
Tyringham○, Mass. (01264) 249/A4
Tyrnyauz, U.S.S.R. 52/F6
Tyro, Kansas (67364) 232/G4
Tyro, Miss. (†38668) 256/E1
Tyro, Va. (22976) 307/K5
Tyrol (Tirol) (prov.), Austria 41/A3
Tyrone, Colo. (†81059) 208/L8
Tyrone, Georgia (30290) 217/C4
Tyrone, Ky. (†40342) 237/M4
Tyrone, Mo. (†65564) 261/J8
Tyrone, N. Mex. (88065) 274/A6
Tyrone, Okla. (73951) 288/D1
Tyrone, Pa. (16686) 294/F4
Tyronza, Ark. (72386) 202/K3
Tyronza (riv.), Ark. 202/K2
Tyrrell (co.), N.C. 281/S3
Tyrrell (lake), Victoria 97/B4
Tyrrellspass, Ireland 17/G5
Tyrrhenian (sea) 7/F4
Tyrrhenian (sea), Italy 34/C4
Tysnes, Norway 18/D6
Tyson, Vt. (†05149) 268/B5
Tyson Wash (dry riv.), Ariz. 198/A5
Ty Ty, Georgia (31795) 217/E8
Tyumen, U.S.S.R. 54/H4
Tyumen', U.S.S.R. 48/G4
Tyung (riv.), U.S.S.R. 48/M3
Tyvan, Sask. 181/H5
Tywyn, Wales 13/C5
Tywyn, Wales 10/D4
Tzaneen, S. Africa 118/E4
Tzekung (Zigong), China 77/F6
Tzepo (Zibo), China 77/J4
Tzucabab, Mexico 150/P7

U

Uahuka (isl.), Fr. Poly. 87/N6
Uanda, Queensland 95/C4
Uanle Uen, Somalia 115/H3
Uanle Uen, Somalia 102/G4
Uapou (isl.), Fr. Poly. 87/M6
Uatumã (riv.), Brazil 132/B3
Uaupés (riv.), Brazil 132/G9
Ub, Yugoslavia 45/E3
Ubá, Brazil 135/E2
Ubá, Brazil 132/F8
Übach-Palenberg, W. Germany 22/B3
Ubaíra, Brazil 132/G6
Ubaitaba, Brazil 132/G6
Ubaiyidh, Wadi (dry riv.), Iraq 66/B5
Ubangi (riv.) 102/D4
Ubangi (riv.), Cent. Afr. Rep. 115/C3
Ubangi (riv.), Congo 115/C3
Ubangi (riv.), Zaire 115/C3
Ubari, Libya 102/D2
Ubari, Libya 111/B2
Ubaté, Colombia 126/D5
Ubatuba, Brazil 135/D3
Ubay, Philippines 82/E5
Ube, Japan 81/E6
Úbeda, Spain 33/E3
Uberaba (lag.), Bolivia 136/G5
Uberaba, Brazil 120/E4
Uberaba, Brazil 132/D7
Uberaba, Brazil 135/C1
Uberlândia, Brazil 120/E4
Uberlândia, Brazil 132/E7
Überlingen, W. Germany 22/C5
Ubina, Bolivia 136/B7
Ubinas, Peru 128/G11
Ubly, Mich. (48475) 250/G5
Ubombo, S. Africa 118/E5
Ubon, Thailand 54/M8
Ubon, Thailand 72/E4
Ubrique, Spain 33/D4
Ubundu, Zaire 115/E4
Ucayali (dept.), Peru 128/E6
Ucayali (riv.), Peru 2/F6
Ucayali (riv.), Peru 120/B3
Ucayali (riv.), Peru 128/F5
Uccle, Belgium 27/B9
Uch, Pakistan 68/B3
Uchaly, U.S.S.R. 7/K3
Uchaly, U.S.S.R. 52/J4
Ucharonidge, North. Terr. 93/D4
Uchee, Ala. (†36858) 195/H6
Uchiura (bay), Japan 81/K2
Uchiza, Peru 128/D7
Uch Turfan (Wushi), China 77/A3
Uckange, France 28/G3
Ücker (riv.), E. Germany 22/E2
Uckfield, England 10/G5
Uckfield, England 13/H7
Ucluelet, Br. Col. 184/E6
Ucon, Idaho (83454) 220/F6
Ucross, Wyo. (†82835) 319/F1
Ucumasi, Bolivia 136/B6
Uda (riv.), U.S.S.R. 48/O4
Udaipur, India 68/C4
Udall, Kansas (67146) 232/E4
Udaypur, India 54/J7
Uddevalla, Sweden 18/G7
Uddingston, Scotland 15/B2
Uddjaur (lake), Sweden 18/L4
Udell, Iowa (52593) 229/H7
Uden, Netherlands 27/H5
Udhampur, India 68/D2
Udine (prov.), Italy 34/D1
Udine, Italy 34/D2
Udine, Italy 7/F4
Udipi, India 68/C6
Udmurt A.S.S.R., U.S.S.R. 48/F4
Udmurt A.S.S.R., U.S.S.R. 52/H3
Udon Thani, Thailand 54/M8
Udon Thani, Thailand 72/D3
Udora, Ontario 177/E3
Ueckermünde, E. Germany 22/F2
Ueda, Japan 81/J5
Uehling, Nebr. (68063) 264/H3
Uele (riv.) 102/E4
Uele (riv.), Zaire 115/E3
Uelen, U.S.S.R. 54/V3
Uelen, U.S.S.R. 4/C18
Uelen, U.S.S.R. 48/T3
Uelzen, W. Germany 22/D2
Uen (isl.), New Caled. 86/H5
Uetendorf, Switzerland 39/E3
Uetersen, W. Germany 22/C2
Ufa, U.S.S.R. 2/M3
Ufa, U.S.S.R. 7/K3
Ufa, U.S.S.R. 48/F4
Ufa, U.S.S.R. 52/J4
Ufa (riv.), U.S.S.R. 52/J3
Ugab (riv.), Namibia 118/A4
Uganda 2/L5
Uganda 102/F4
UGANDA 115/F3
Ugashik, Alaska (†99649) 196/G3
Ugashik (lakes), Alaska 196/G3
Ugie (riv.), Scotland 15/G3
Ugljar, Spain 33/E4
Ugjoktok (bay), Newf. 166/B2
Uglegorsk, U.S.S.R. 48/P5
Uglich, U.S.S.R. 52/E3
Ugo, Japan 81/K4
Ugod, Hungary 41/D3
Uherské Hradiště, Czech. 41/D2
Uherský Brod, Czech. 41/D2
Úhlava (riv.), Czech. 41/B2
Uhlířské Janovice, Czech. 41/C2
Uhrichsville, Ohio (44683) 284/H5
Uig, Scotland 10/C2
Uig, Highland, Scotland 15/B3
Uig, W. Isles, Scotland 15/A2
Uige (dist.), Angola 115/B5
Uige, Angola 115/C5
Uiju, N. Korea 81/B3
Uinkaret (plat.), Ariz. 198/B2
Uinta (mts.), Utah 304/D3
Uinta (riv.), Utah 304/D3
Uinta (co.), Wyo. 319/B4
Uintah (co.), Utah 304/E3
Uintah, Utah (†84401) 304/C2
Uintah and Ouray Ind. Res., Utah 304/D3
Ŭisŏng, S. Korea 81/D5
Uitenhage, S. Africa 102/E8
Uitenhage, S. Africa 118/C6
Uithoorn, Netherlands 27/F4
Uithuizen, Netherlands 27/K2
Uitkijk, Suriname 131/D3
Uivak (cape), Newf. 166/B2
Ujelang (atoll), Marshall Is. 87/F5
Újfehértó, Hungary 41/F3
Uji, Honduras 154/F3
Uji, Japan 81/J7
Ujiji (Kigoma-Ujiji), Tanz. 115/E4
Ujjain, India 68/D4
Újpest, Hungary 41/E3
Újszász, Hungary 41/F2
Ujung Pandang, Indonesia 54/N10
Ujung Pandang, Indonesia 85/F7
Ukasiksalik (isl.), Newf. 166/B2
Ukhta, U.S.S.R. 48/F3
Ukiah, Calif. (95482) 204/B4
Ukiah, Oreg. (97880) 291/J2
Ukkel (Uccle), Belgium 27/B9
Ukmerge, U.S.S.R. 53/C3
Ukmerge, U.S.S.R. 52/C3
Ukrainian S.S.R., U.S.S.R. 7/G4
Ukrainian S.S.R., U.S.S.R. 48/C5
Ukrainian S.S.R., U.S.S.R. 52/D5
Ula, Turkey 63/C4
Ulaanbaatar (Ulan Bator) (cap.), Mongolia 77/G2
Ulaanbaatar (cap.), Mongolia 54/M5
Ulaanbaatar (cap.), Mongolia 2/Q3
Ulaangom (Ulangom), Mongolia 77/D2
Ulaangom, Mongolia 54/L5
Ulah, N.C. (†27203) 281/K3
Ulak (isl.), Alaska 196/K4
Ulan, China 77/E4
Ulanhot (Horquin Youyi Qianqi), China 77/K2
Ulan-Ude, U.S.S.R. 54/M4
Ulan-Ude, U.S.S.R. 2/Q3
Ulan-Ude, U.S.S.R. 48/L4
Ulapes, Argentina 143/C3
Ulaş, Turkey 63/G3
Ulchin, S. Korea 81/D5
Ulcinj, Yugoslavia 45/D5
Uldum, Denmark 21/C6
Ulegei (Ölgiy), Mongolia 77/C2
Ulen, Ind. (†46052) 227/E4
Ulen, Minn. (56585) 255/B3
Uler, W. Va. (25282) 312/D5
Ulfborg, Denmark 21/B5
Ulhasnagar, India 68/C5
Uliastay (Jibhalanta), Mongolia 77/E2
Uliastay, Mongolia 54/L5
Ulindi (riv.), Zaire 115/E4
Ulithi (atoll), Micronesia 87/D4
Ulla (riv.), Spain 33/B1
Ulladulla, N.S. Wales 97/F4
Ullapool, Scotland 10/D2
Ullapool, Scotland 15/C3
Ulla Ulla, Bolivia 136/A4
Ulldecona, Spain 33/G2
Ullensvang, Norway 18/E6
Ullin, Ill. (62992) 222/D6
Ulloma, Bolivia 136/A5
Ullŭng (isl.), S. Korea 81/E5
Ulm, Ark. (72170) 202/H4
Ulm, Mont. (59485) 262/E3
Ulm, W. Germany 22/C4
Ulm, Wyo. (†82835) 319/F1
Ulman, Mo. (65083) 261/H6
Ulmarra, N.S. Wales 97/G1
Ulmer, Iowa (51464) 229/D4
Ulmer, S.C. (29849) 296/E5
Ulongue, Mozambique 118/E2
Ulricehamn, Sweden 18/H8
Ulrichen, Switzerland 39/F3
Ulriksfors, Sweden 18/K5
Ulrum, Netherlands 27/J2
Ulsan, S. Korea 81/D6
Ulster (part) (prov.), Ireland 17/G2
Ulster (trad. prov.), Ireland 17/K8
Ulster (co.), N.Y. 276/M7
Ulster (part) (prov.), N. Ireland 17/G2
Ulster, Pa. (18850) 294/J2
Ulster Spring, Jamaica 158/H6
Última Esperanza (sound), Chile 138/E9
Ulúa (riv.), Honduras 154/D3
Ulubat (lake), Turkey 63/C2
Ulubey, Turkey 63/C3
Uluborlu, Turkey 63/D3
Uludağ (mt.), Turkey 63/C3
Uludere, Turkey 63/K4
Ulugan (bay), Philippines 82/B5
Ulughchat (Wuqia), China 77/A4
Ulukışla, Turkey 63/F4
Ulumalu, Hawaii (†96708) 218/K2
Ulu Muztag (mt.), China 77/C4
Ulundi, S. Africa 118/E5
Ulungur He (riv.), China 77/C2
Ulungur Hu (lake), China 77/C2
Ulupalakua, Hawaii (†96790) 218/J2
Ulus, Turkey 63/E2
Ulutau (mts.), U.S.S.R. /G5
Ulu Tiram, Malaysia 72/F5
Ulva (isl.), Scotland 15/B4
Ulverston, England 13/D3
Ulverston, England 10/E3
Ulverstone, Tasmania 99/C3
Ulvik, Norway 18/E6
Ulvila, Finland 18/N6
Ul'yanovsk, U.S.S.R. 7/J3
Ul'yanovsk, U.S.S.R. 48/E4
Ul'yanovsk, U.S.S.R. 52/G4
Ulysses, Kansas (67880) 232/A4
Ulysses, Ky. (†41232) 237/R5
Ulysses, Nebr. (68669) 264/G3
Ulysses, Pa. (16948) 294/G2
Umag, Yugoslavia 45/A3
Umala, Bolivia 136/B5
Umán, Mexico 150/P6
Uman', U.S.S.R. 52/D5
Umanun (pt.), Philippines 82/F6
Umapine, Oreg. (97881) 291/J2
Umarkot, Pakistan 59/J4
Umatilla, Fla. (32784) 212/E3
Umatilla (co.), Oreg. 291/J2
Umatilla, Oreg. (97882) 291/H2
Umatilla (lake), Oreg. 291/G2
Umatilla (riv.), Oreg. 291/H2
Umatilla (lake), Wash. 310/E5
Umatilla Army Depot, Oreg. 291/H2
Umatilla Ind. Res., Oreg. 291/J2
Umba, U.S.S.R. 52/D1
Umbagog (lake), Maine 243/A6
Umbagog (lake), N.H. 268/E2
Umbakumba, North. Terr. 93/E3
Umbarger, Texas (79091) 303/B3
Umbeara, North. Terr. 93/C8
Umbertide, Italy 34/D3
Umboi (isl.), Papua N.G. 86/A2
Umbrail (peak), Switzerland 39/K3
Umbría, Colombia 126/B7
Umbria (reg.), Italy 34/D3
Umcalcus (lake), Maine 243/G3
Ume (riv.), Sweden 7/F2
Umeå, Sweden 7/F2
Umeå, Sweden 18/M5
Umeälv (riv.), Sweden 18/L4
Umiakovik (lake), Newf. 166/B2
Umiat, Alaska (†99701) 196/H1
Umikoa, Hawaii (†96776) 218/H4
Um Jauza, Jordan 65/D3
Umm al Qaiwain, U.A.E. 59/G4
Umm el Abid, Libya 111/C2
Umm el Fahm, Israel 65/C2
Umm Hajar, Ethiopia 111/G5
Umm Keddada, Sudan 111/E5
Umm Lajj, Saudi Arabia 59/C4
Umm Qasr, Iraq 66/E5
Umm Ruwaba, Sudan 111/F5
Umm Ruwaba, Sudan 102/F3
Umm Ruwaba, Sudan 59/B7
Umm Sa'id, Qatar 59/F5
Umnak (isl.), Alaska 196/E4
Umnak (passage), Alaska 196/E4
Umnak (isl.), U.S. 4/D18
Umpire, Ark. (71971) 202/B5
Umpqua, Oreg. (97486) 291/D4
Umpqua (riv.), Oreg. 291/D4
Umrer, India 68/D4
Umsaskis (lake), Maine 243/E2
Umtali, Zimbabwe 102/F6
Umtali, Zimbabwe 118/E3
Umtata, S. Africa 118/D6
Umtata (cap.), Transkei, S. Africa 102/E8
Umurbey, Turkey 63/C6
Umvukwe (range), Zimbabwe 118/E3
Umvuma, Zimbabwe 118/D3
Umzimbuvu, S. Africa 118/D6
Umzinto, S. Africa 118/E6
Una (mt.), N. Zealand 100/D5
Una (riv.), Yugoslavia 45/C3
Unadilla, Georgia (31091) 217/E6
Unadilla, Nebr. (68454) 264/H4
Unadilla, N.Y. (13849) 276/K6
Unadilla (riv.), N.Y. 276/K5
Unaí, Brazil 132/E7
Unaka, N.C. (28908) 281/A4
Unaka (mts.), N.C. 281/E2
Unaka (mts.), Tenn. 237/S8
Unalakleet, Alaska (99684) 196/G2
Unalakleet, Alaska 188/C5
Unalaska, Alaska 188/C6
Unalaska, Alaska (99685) 196/E4
Unalaska (isl.), Alaska 196/E4
Unalaska (isl.), U.S. 4/D18
Unare (riv.), Venezuela 124/F3
Uncas, Okla. (†74601) 288/M1
Uncastillo, Spain 33/F1
Uncasville, Conn. (06382) 210/G3
Uncertain, Texas (†75661) 303/K5
Uncía, Bolivia 136/B6
Uncompahgre (peak), Colo. 208/E6
Uncompahgre (plat.), Colo. 208/B5
Uncompahgre (riv.), Colo. 208/D5
Underbool, Victoria 97/A4
Underhill, Manitoba 179/B5
Underhill○, Vt. (05489) 268/B2
Underhill, Wis. (54176) 317/K6
Underhill Center, Vt. (05490) 268/B2
Underwood, Ind. (47177) 227/F7
Underwood, Iowa (51576) 229/B6
Underwood, Minn. (56586) 255/C4
Underwood, N. Dak. (58576) 282/H5
Underwood, Ontario 177/C3
Underwood, Wash. (98651) 310/D5
Undu (pt.), Fiji 86/R10
Undzha (riv.), U.S.S.R. 52/F3
Unecha, U.S.S.R. 52/D4
Uneeda, W. Va. (25205) 312/C6
Unga (isl.), Alaska 196/F3
Ungalik, Alaska (†99684) 196/F2
Ungarie, N.S. Wales 97/D3
Ungava (bay), Canada 146/M4
Ungava (bay), N.W.T. 162/K4
Ungava (bay), N.W. Terrs. 187/M4
Ungava (bay), Québec 174/F1
Ungava (pen.), Que. 146/L3
Ungava (pen.), Que. 162/J3
Ungava (pen.), Québec 174/E1
Ungeny, U.S.S.R. 52/C5
Unger, W. Va. (25447) 312/K4
Unggi, N. Korea 81/E2
União, Brazil 132/F4
União da Vitória, Brazil 132/D9
União dos Palmares, Brazil 132/H5
Unicoi (mts.), N.C. 281/A4
Unicoi (co.), Tenn. 237/S8
Unicoi, Tenn. (37692) 237/S8
Unicoi (mts.), Tenn. 237/N10
Uničov, Czech. 41/D2
Unimak (isl.), Alaska 188/C6
Unimak (bight), Alaska 196/F4
Unimak (isl.), Alaska 196/E4
Unimak (passage), Alaska 196/F4
Unimak (isl.), U.S. 4/D18
Unini, Peru 128/F8
Union, Ala. (†35462) 195/C5
Union (mt.), Ariz. 198/C4
Union (co.), Ark. 202/E7
Union, Ark. (†72576) 202/G1
Union○, Conn. (†06076) 210/G1
Union (co.), Fla. 212/D1
Union (co.), Georgia 217/E1
Union, Grenada 161/D8
Union (co.), Ill. 222/D6
Union, Ill. (60180) 222/E1
Union (co.), Ind. 227/H5
Union, Ind. (†47540) 227/C8
Union (co.), Iowa 229/E7
Union, Iowa (50258) 229/G4
Union (co.), Ky. 237/F5
Union, Ky. (41091) 237/M3
Union (par.), La. 238/F1
Union, La. (†70723) 238/L3
Union, Maine (04862) 243/E7
Union○, Maine (04862) 243/E7
Union, West Branch (riv.), Maine 243/G6
Union (co.), Miss. 256/F2
Union, Miss. (39365) 256/F5
Union, Mo. (63084) 261/L6
Union, Nebr. (68455) 264/J4
Union, N.H. (03887) 268/E5
Union (co.), N.J. 273/E2
Union○, N.J. (07083) 273/A2
Union (lake), N.J. 273/C5
Union (co.), N. Mex. 274/F2
Union (co.), N.C. 281/H4
Union, N. Dak. (58279) 282/O2
Union (co.), Ohio 284/D5
Union, Ohio (45322) 284/B6
Union, Ontario 177/C5
Union (co.), Oreg. 291/J2
Union, Oreg. (97883) 291/K2
Unión, Paraguay 144/D4
Union (co.), Pa. 294/H4
Union (isl.), St. Vin. & Grens. 156/G4
Union (co.), S.C. 296/D2
Union, S.C. (29379) 296/D2
Union (co.), S. Dak. 298/R8
Union (co.), Tenn. 237/O8
Unión, Uruguay 145/B7
Union, Wash. (98592) 310/B3
Union (lake), Wash. 310/B2
Union, W. Va. (24983) 312/E7
Union Bay, Br. Col. 184/H2
Union Beach, N.J. (07735) 273/E3
Union Bridge, Md. (21791) 245/K2
Union Center, S. Dak. (57787) 298/D4
Union Center, Wis. (53962) 317/F8
Union Church, Miss. (39668) 256/C7
Union City, Calif. (94587) 204/K2
Union City, Conn. (†06770) 210/C2
Union City, Georgia (30291) 217/J2
Union City, Ind. (47390) 227/H4
Union City, Mich. (49094) 250/D6
Union City, N.J. (07087) 273/C2
Union City, Ohio (†47390) 284/A5
Union City, Okla. (73090) 288/L4
Union City, Pa. (16438) 294/C2
Union City, Tenn. (38261) 237/C8
Union Creek, Oreg. (†97536) 291/E5
Uniondale, Ind. (46791) 227/G3
Uniondale, N.Y. (11553) 276/R7
Union Dale, Pa. (18470) 294/M2
Unión de Reyes, Cuba 158/C1
Unión de Tula, Mexico 150/G7
Union Furnace, Ohio (43158) 284/F7
Union Gap, Wash. (98903) 310/E4
Union Grove, Ala. (35175) 195/E2
Union Grove, N.C. (28689) 281/H2
Union Grove, Wis. (53182) 317/L3
Union Hall, Va. (24176) 307/J6
Unión Hidalgo, Mexico 150/M8
Union Hill, Ill. (60969) 222/E2
Union Hill, N.Y. (14563) 276/F4
Union Level, Va. (23973) 307/M7
Union Mills, Ind. (46382) 227/D2
Union Mills, Md. (†21157) 245/K2
Union Mills, N.C. (28167) 281/F3
Union of Soviet Socialist Republics 2/L2
Union of Soviet Socialist Republics 4/C2
Union of Soviet Socialist Republics 54/L3
Union of Soviet Socialist Republics 7/H2
UNION OF SOVIET SOCIALIST REPUBLICS 48
UNION OF SOVIET SOCIALIST REPUBLICS, EUROPEAN 52
Union Pier, Mich. (49129) 250/C7
Union Point, Georgia (30669) 217/F3
Unionport, Ind. (†47340) 227/G4
Unionport, Ohio (43966) 284/J5
Union Springs, Ala. (36089) 195/G6
Union Springs, N.Y. (13160) 276/G5
Union Star, Ky. (40171) 237/H5
Union Star, Mo. (64494) 261/C2
Uniontown, Ala. (36786) 195/D6
Uniontown, Ark. (72955) 202/B2
Uniontown, Ind. (†47515) 227/D
Uniontown, Kansas (66779) 232/G4
Uniontown, Ky. (42461) 237/F5
Uniontown, Md. (21157) 245/K2
Uniontown, Mo. (63783) 261/N7
Uniontown, Ohio (44685) 284/H4
Uniontown, Pa. (15401) 294/C6
Uniontown, Wash. (99179) 310/H4
Union Village, Vt. (†05075) 268/C4
Unionville, Conn. (06085) 210/D1
Unionville, Georgia (†31794) 217/F8
Unionville, Ill. (†61270) 222/E6
Unionville, Ind. (47468) 227/E6
Unionville, Iowa (52594) 229/H7
Unionville, Maine (†04622) 243/H6
Unionville, Md. (21792) 245/K3
Unionville, Mich. (48767) 250/F5
Unionville, Mo. (63565) 261/G2
Unionville, Nev. (†89418) 266/C2
Unionville, N.Y. (10988) 276/L8
Unionville, N.C. (†28110) 281/J4
Unionville, Ohio (44088) 284/J2
Unionville (Fleming), Pa. (19375) 294/G4
Unionville, Tenn. (37180) 237/H9
Unionville, Va. (22567) 307/N4
Unionville Center, Ohio (43077) 284/D5
Uniopolis, Ohio (45888) 284/B4
United, Pa. (15689) 294/D5
United Arab Emirates 2/M4
United Arab Emirates 54/G7
UNITED ARAB EMIRATES 59/F5
UNITED KINGDOM 10
United Kingdom 2/J3
United Kingdom 7/D3
United States 2/D4
United States 146/H5
United States 4/C17
UNITED STATES 188
U.S. Capitol, D.C. 245/F5
U.S.S. Arizona Memorial, Hawaii 218/B3
U.S. Nav. Air Sta., Virgin Is. (U.S.) 161/A4
U.S. Naval Base, Va. 307/R7
Unity○, Maine (04988) 243/E6
Unity, Md. (†20729) 245/K4
Unity, Mo. (64063) 261/R6
Unity○, N.H. (†03743) 268/C5
Unity, Ohio (†44413) 284/J4
Unity, Oreg. (97884) 291/J3
Unity, Sask. 181/B3
Unity, Wis. (54488) 317/F6
Unityville, Pa. (17774) 294/K3
Unityville, S. Dak. (†57058) 298/P6
Universal, Ind. (47884) 227/C5
Universal City, Texas (78148) 303/K10
University, Fla. (33620) 212/C2
University, N.C. (†27701) 281/L2
University City, Mo. (63130) 261/P3
University City, Mo. 188/H3
University Heights, Iowa (†52240) 229/K5
University Heights, Ohio (44118) 284/H9
University Park, Iowa (52595) 229/H6
University Park, Md. (†20740) 245/F4
University Park, N. Mex. (88003) 274/C6
University Park, Texas (†75205) 303/G2
Unley, S. Australia 88/D8
Unley, S. Australia 94/B8
Unnao, India 68/E3
Uno, Manitoba 179/B4
Unsan, N. Korea 81/C4
Unst (isl.), Scotland 15/G2
Unst (isl.), Scotland 10/H1
Unstrut (riv.), E. Germany 22/D3
Unterägeri, Switzerland 39/G2
Unteriberg, Switzerland 39/G2
Unterkulm, Switzerland 39/F2
Untermann (mt.), Utah 304/E3
Untersee (lake), Switzerland 39/H1
Unterseen, Switzerland 39/E3
Untervaz, Switzerland 39/H3
Unterwalden (reg.), Switzerland 39/F3
Unuk (riv.), Alaska 196/N2
Unuk (riv.), Br. Col. 184/B2
Ünye, Turkey 59/C1
Ünye, Turkey 63/G2
Unzen (mt.), Japan 81/D7
Unzen-Amakusa National Park, Japan 81/D7
Uozu, Japan 81/H5
Upalco, Utah (†84007) 304/D3
Upata, Venezuela 124/G3
Upemba (lake), Zaire 115/E5
Upemba Nat'l Park, Zaire 115/E5
Upernavik, Greenl. 4/B12
Uphall, Scotland 15/C1
Upham, New Bruns. 170/E3
Upham, N. Dak. (58789) 282/J2
Upía (riv.), Colombia 126/D5
Úpice, Czech. 41/C1
Upington, S. Africa 102/E7
Upington, S. Africa 118/C5
Upland, Calif. (91786) 204/E10
Upland, Ind. (46989) 227/F4
Upland, Kansas (†67431) 232/E2
Upland, Nebr. (68981) 264/F4
Upland, Pa. (†19013) 294/L7
Upolu (pt.), Hawaii 218/G3
Upolu (isl.), W. Samoa 87/J7
Upolu (isl.), W. Samoa 86/M8
Upolu (isl.), W. Samoa 86/M8
Upper Alkali (lake), Calif. 204/E2
Upper Amherst Cove, Newf. 166/D2
Upper Ammonoosuc (riv.), N.H. 268/E2
Upper Arlington, Ohio (43221) 284/D6
Upper Arrow (lake), Br. Col. 184/H5
Upper Austria (prov.), Austria 41/B2
Upper Black Eddy, Pa. (18972) 294/N4
Upper Blackville, New Bruns. 170/E2
Upper Buctouche, New Bruns. 170/F2
Upper Chateaugay (lake), N.Y. 276/M1
Upperco, Md. (21155) 245/L2
Upper Dam, Maine (†04293) 243/B6
Upper Darby○, Pa. (*19082) 294/M6
Upper Des Lacs (lake), N. Dak. 282/F2
Upper Engadine (valley), Switzerland 39/J4
Upper Fairmount, Md. (21867) 245/P8

V

464 Victoria Land

Victoria Land (reg.), Ant. 2/T10
Victoria Land (reg.) 5/B8
Victoria River Downs, North. Terr. 88/E3
Victoria River Downs, North. Terr. 93/B4
Victoria Road, Ontario 177/F3
Victorias, Philippines 82/D5
Victoriaville, Québec 172/F3
Victoria West, S. Africa 118/C6
Victorica, Argentina 143/C4
Victorino, Colombia 126/F6
Victorino, Venezuela 124/E6
Victor Rosales, Mexico 150/H5
Victorville, Calif. (92392) 204/H9
Victory, Ky. (40767) 237/N6
Victory, Wis. (54663) 317/D9
Victory Mills (Victory), N.Y. (12884) 276/N4
Vicuña, Chile 138/A8
Vicuña Mackenna, Argentina 143/D3
Vida, Mo. (†65401) 261/J7
Vida, Mont. (59274) 262/L3
Vida, Oreg. (97488) 291/E3
Vidal, Calif. (92280) 204/L9
Vidal Gormaz (isl.), Chile 138/D9
Vidalia, Georgia (30474) 217/H6
Vidalia, La. (71373) 238/G3
Videbaek, Denmark 21/B5
Videle, Romania 45/G3
Vidette, Georgia (†30830) 217/H4
Vidigueira, Portugal 33/C3
Vidin, Bulgaria 45/F4
Vidisha, India 68/D4
Vidor, Texas (77662) 303/L7
Vidora, Sask. 181/B6
Vidrine, La. (†70586) 238/F5
Viechtach, W. Germany 22/E4
Viedma, Argentina 143/D5
Viedma, Argentina 120/C7
Viedma (lake), Argentina 120/B7
Viedma (lake), Argentina 143/B6
Vieille Case, Dominica 161/E5
Vieira de Leiria, Portugal 33/B3
Vieja, Sierra (mts.), Texas 303/C11
Viella, Spain 33/G1
Vielsalm, Belgium 27/H8
Vienna (city), Austria 41/D2
Vienna (cap.), Austria 41/D2
Vienna (cap.), Austria 7/F4
Vienna, Georgia (31092) 217/E6
Vienna, Ill. (62995) 222/E6
Vienna, Ind. (†47170) 227/F7
Vienna, La. (†71270) 238/E1
Vienna○, Maine (04360) 243/D6
Vienna, Md. (21869) 245/P7
Vienna, Mo. (65582) 261/H6
Vienna, N.J. (07880) 273/D2
Vienna, Ohio (44473) 284/J3
Vienna, Ontario 177/D5
Vienna, S. Dak. (57271) 298/O4
Vienna, Va. (22180) 307/R2
Vienna, W. Va. (26105) 312/D4
Vienne (dept.), France 28/D4
Vienne, France 28/F5
Vienne (riv.), France 28/D4
Vientiane (Viangchan) (cap.), Laos 72/D3
Vientiane (cap.), Laos 54/M8
Vieques (pt.), P. Rico 161/E3
Vieques, P. Rico 156/G1
Vieques (Isabel Segunda), P. Rico 161/G2
Vieques (isl.), P. Rico 161/G2
Vieques (isl.), P. Rico 156/G1
Vieques (passage), P. Rico 161/F2
Vieques (sound), P. Rico 161/G2
Vierge (pt.), St. Lucia 161/G6
Vierkant (pt.), Neth. Ant. 161/E8
Viersen, W. Germany 22/B3
Vierzon, France 28/D4
Viesca, Mexico 150/H4
Vietnam 2/Q5
Vietnam 54/M8
VIETNAM 72
Vieux Desert (lake), Mich. 250/G2
Vieux Desert (lake), Wis. 317/J3
Vieux-Fort, Guadeloupe 161/B7
Vieux-Fort (pt.), Guadeloupe 161/A7
Vieux Fort, St. Lucia 156/G4
Vieux Fort, St. Lucia 161/G7
Vieux Fort (riv.), St. Lucia 161/G6
Vieux-Habitants, Guadeloupe 161/A7
Vievis, U.S.S.R. 53/C3
Viewpark, Scotland 15/C2
Vieytes, Argentina 143/H7
Vig, Denmark 21/E6
Viga, Philippines 82/E4
Vigan, Philippines 85/F2
Vigan, Philippines 82/C2
Vigevano, Italy 34/B2
Vigia, Brazil 132/E3
Vigía (cay), Colombia 126/A10
Vignemale (mt.), France 28/C6
Vigo (co.), Ind. 227/C6
Vigo, Spain 7/D4
Vigo, Spain 33/B1
Vigrestad, Norway 18/D7
Vigsø (bay), Denmark 21/B3
Viipuri (Vyborg), U.S.S.R. 52/C2
Vijayawada, India 54/K8
Vijayawada, India 68/D5
Vijosë (riv.), Albania 45/D5
Vik, Norway 18/E6
Viking, Alberta 182/E3
Viking (lake), Manitoba 179/G3
Viking, Minn. (56760) 255/B2
Vikna (isls.), Norway 18/G4
Vila (cap.), Vanuatu 87/G7
Vila Arminda Monteiro, Indonesia 85/H7
Vilacaya, Bolivia 136/C6
Vila de Maganja, Mozambique 118/F3
Vila de Sena, Mozambique 118/E3
Vila do Bispo, Portugal 33/B4
Vila do Conde, Portugal 33/B2
Vila do Porto, Portugal 33/D2
Vila Fontes, Mozambique 118/E3
Vilafranca del Penedès, Spain 33/G2
Vila Franca de Xira, Portugal 33/B3
Vila Guilherme Capelo, Angola 115/B5
Vilaine (riv.), France 28/C4
Viļaka, U.S.S.R. 53/D2
Vilanculos, Mozambique 118/E4
Vila Nova de Foz Côa, Portugal 33/C2
Vila Nova de Gaia, Portugal 33/B2
Vila Nova de Milfontes, Portugal 33/B4
Vila Nova do Seles, Angola 115/B6
Vila Paiva de Andrada, Mozambique 118/E3
Vila Pouca de Aguiar, Portugal 33/C2
Vila Real (dist.), Portugal 33/C2
Vila Real, Portugal 33/C2
Vila Real de Santo António, Portugal 33/C4
Vilar Formoso, Portugal 33/C2
Vilas, Colo. (81087) 208/P8
Vilas, N.C. (28692) 281/F2
Vilas, S. Dak. (†57349) 298/O6
Vilas (co), Wis. 317/G3
Vila Salazar, Indonesia 85/H7
Vila Velha, Brazil 132/D2
Vila Velha Argolas, Brazil 132/F8
Vila Velha de Ródão Portugal 33/C3
Vila Verde, Portugal 33/B2
Vila Viçosa, Portugal 33/C3
Vilcabamba, Cordillera (mts.), Peru 128/F9
Vilcanota (mt.), Peru 128/G10
Vildbjerg, Denmark 21/B5
Vildo, Tenn. (†38075) 237/C10
Vileyka, U.S.S.R. 52/C4
Vilhelmina, Sweden 18/K4
Vilhena, Brazil 132/H10
Viliya (riv.), U.S.S.R. 53/C3
Viljandi, U.S.S.R. 53/C1
Vilkija, U.S.S.R. 53/B3
Vil'kitskogo (str.), U.S.S.R. 4/B4
Vil'kitskogo (str.), U.S.S.R. 48/L2
Villa, Switzerland 39/H3
Villa Abecia, Bolivia 136/C7
Villa Acuña, Mexico 150/J2
Villa Alemana, Chile 138/F2
Villa Alhué, Chile 138/G4
Villa Altagracia, Dom. Rep. 158/E6
Villa Amazónica, Colombia 126/B7
Villa Ana, Argentina 143/E2
Villa Ángela, Argentina 143/D2
Villa Atamisqui, Argentina 143/D2
Villa Atuel, Argentina 143/C3
Villa Bella, Bolivia 136/C2
Villablino, Spain 33/C1
Villa Bruzual, Venezuela 124/D3.
Villabruzzi (Johar), Somalia 115/J3
Villa Bustos, Argentina 143/C2
Villa Cañas, Argentina 143/F6
Villacañas, Spain 33/E3
Villacarriedo, Spain 33/D1
Villacarrillo, Spain 33/E3
Villach, Austria 41/B3
Villacidro, Italy 34/B5
Villa Cisneros (Dakhla), W. Sahara 102/A2
Villa Cisneros (Dakhla), Western Sahara 106/A4
Villa Clara, Argentina 143/G5
Villa Clara (prov.), Cuba 158/E1
Villa Constitución, Argentina 143/F6
Villa Cuauhtémoc, Mexico 150/L5
Villada, Spain 33/D1
Villa Darwin, Uruguay 145/B4
Villa de Cos, Mexico 150/H5
Villa de Cura, Venezuela 124/E2
Villa de Guadalupe Hidalgo, Mexico 150/L1
Villa del Cerro, Uruguay 145/A7
Villa del Rosario, Argentina 143/D3
Villa de María, Argentina 143/D2
Villa de San Antonio, Honduras 154/D3
Villa Diego, Argentina 143/F6
Villadiego, Spain 33/D1
Villa Dolores, Argentina 143/C3
Villa Elisa, Argentina 143/G6
Villa E. Viscarra, Bolivia 136/C6
Villafamés, Spain 33/G2
Villa Federal, Argentina 143/G5
Villa Florida, Paraguay 144/D5
Villa Franca, Paraguay 144/C5
Villafranca, Spain 33/F1
Villafranca del Bierzo, Spain 33/C1
Villafranca del Cid, Spain 33/F2
Villafranca de los Barros, Spain 33/C3
Villafranca di Verona, Italy 34/C2
Villa Frontado, Venezuela 124/G2
Villa Frontera, Mexico 150/J3
Villa García, Mexico 150/J5
Villagarcía, Spain 33/B1
Village, Ark. (71769) 202/D7
Village, N.S. Wales 97/J2
Village-Blier, Québec 172/H2
Village-des-Aulnaies, Québec 172/G2
Village Mills, Texas (77663) 303/K7
Villa General Pérez, Bolivia 136/A4
Villa General Ramírez, Argentina 143/F6
Villa General Roca, Argentina 143/C3
Village-Saint-Laurent, New Bruns. 170/E1
Villagran, Mexico 150/K4
Villa Grove, Colo. (81155) 208/G6
Villa Grove, Ill. (61956) 222/E4
Villaguay, Argentina 143/G5
Villa Guillermina, Argentina 143/D2
Villa Hayes, Paraguay 144/A4
Villahermosa, Mexico 146/J8
Villahermosa, Mexico 150/N8
Villahermosa, Spain 33/E3
Villa Hidalgo, Durango, Mexico 150/G3
Villa Hidalgo, Sonora, Mexico 150/E1
Villa Hills, Ky. (†41017) 237/R2
Villa Huidobro, Argentina 143/D3
Villa Industrial, Chile 138/B1
Villa Ingavi, Bolivia 136/D7
Villajoyosa, Spain 33/F3
Villa Krause, Argentina 143/C3
Villalba, P. Rico 161/C2
Villalba, Spain 33/C1
Villalbín, Paraguay 144/D5
Villaldama, Mexico 150/J3
Villalon, Philippines 82/E5
Villalón de Campos, Spain 33/D1
Villalpando, Spain 33/D2
Villa Mantero, Argentina 143/G6
Villa María, Argentina 143/D3
Villa María, Argentina 120/C6
Villa María Grande, Argentina 143/F5
Villa Martín, Bolivia 136/B7
Villa Matamoros, Mexico 150/G3
Villamil, Ecuador 128/B9
Villa Montes, Bolivia 120/C5
Villa Montes, Bolivia 136/D7
Villanova, Pa. (19085) 294/M6
Villanow, Georgia (†30728) 217/B1
Villa Nueva, Argentina 143/C3
Villanueva, Colombia 126/D2
Villanueva, Mexico 150/H5
Villanueva, N. Mex. (87583) 274/D3
Villanueva de Córdoba, Spain 33/D3
Villanueva del Arzobispo, Spain 33/E3
Villanueva de la Serena, Spain 33/D3
Villanueva de los Infantes, Spain 33/E3
Villanueva y Geltrú, Spain 33/G2
Villány, Hungary 41/E4
Villa Ocampo, Argentina 143/D2
Villa Oliva, Paraguay 144/C5
Villa Orías, Bolivia 136/C6
Villa Park, Calif. (92667) 204/D11
Villa Park, Ill. (60181) 222/B5
Villar, Bolivia 136/C6
Villa Ranchaero, S. Dak. (†57701) 298/C5
Villarcayo, Spain 33/E1
Villard, Minn. (56385) 255/C5
Villar del Arzobispo, Spain 33/F3
Villareal, Philippines 82/E5
Villa Regina, Argentina 143/C4
Villa Rica, Georgia (30180) 217/C3
Villa Ridge, Ill. (62996) 222/D6
Villa Riva, Dom. Rep. 158/E5
Villa Rosario, Colombia 126/D4
Villarreal de los Infantes, Spain 33/G3
Villarrica, Chile 138/E2
Villarrica (lake), Chile 138/E2
Villarrica, Paraguay 120/D5
Villarrica, Paraguay 144/C5
Villarrobledo, Spain 33/E3
Villarrubia de los Ojos, Spain 33/E3
Villas, N.J. (08251) 273/D5
Villasana de Mena, Spain 33/E1
Villa San Agustín, Argentina 143/C3
Villa San José, Argentina 143/G6
Villa San Martín, Argentina 143/D2
Villa Serrano, Bolivia 136/C6
Villa Tasso, Fla. (†32548) 212/C6
Villa Tunari, Bolivia 136/C5
Villa Unión, Argentina 143/C2
Villa Unión, Coahuila, Mexico 150/J2
Villa Unión, Durango, Mexico 150/H5
Villa Unión, Sinaloa, Mexico 150/F5
Villa Vaca Guzmán, Bolivia 136/D6
Villaverde, Spain 33/F4
Villavicencio, Colombia 120/B2
Villavicencio, Colombia 126/D5
Villa Vicente Guerrero, Mexico 150/N1
Villaviciosa, Spain 33/D1
Villawood, N. S. Wales 88/K4
Villawood, N.S. Wales 97/H3
Villa y Puerto del Son, Spain 33/B1
Villazón, Bolivia 120/C5
Villazón, Bolivia 136/C7
Ville Bonheur, Haiti 158/C6
Villefranche, France 28/G6
Villefranche-de-Lauragais, France 28/D6
Villefranche-de-Rouergue, France 28/E5
Villefranche-sur-Saône, France 28/F4
Villegreen, Colo. (81088) 208/M8
Villejuif, France 28/B2
Ville-Marie, Québec 174/B3
Villemomble, France 28/C1
Villena, Spain 33/F3
Villeneuve, Québec 172/J3
Villeneuve, Switzerland 39/C4
Villeneuve-Saint-Georges, France 28/E3
Villeneuve-sur-Lot, France 28/D5
Ville Platte, La. (70586) 238/F5
Villeroy, Québec 172/F3
Villeta, Colombia 126/C5
Villeta, Paraguay 144/A5
Villeurbanne, France 28/F5
Villiers (lake), Québec 172/C2
Villiersdorp, S. Africa 118/G6
Villingen-Schwenningen, W. Germany 22/C4
Villisca, Iowa (50864) 229/C7
Villupuram, India 68/D6
Vilna, Alberta 182/E2
Vilna, U.S.S.R. 7/G3
Vilna (Vilnius) (cap.), U.S.S.R. 53/C3
Vilna (Vilnius), U.S.S.R. 52/C4
Vilna (Vilnius), U.S.S.R. 48/C4
Vilnius (Vilna) (cap.), U.S.S.R. 53/C3
Vilonia, Ark. (72173) 202/F3
Vils, Austria 41/A3
Vilvoorde, Belgium 27/F7
Vilvorde (Vilvoorde), Belgium 27/F7
Vilyuy (range), U.S.S.R. 48/M3
Vilyuy (res.), U.S.S.R. 48/M3
Vilyuy (riv.), U.S.S.R. 48/L3
Vilyuy (riv.), U.S.S.R. 54/N3
Vilyuysk, U.S.S.R. 48/N3
Vimianzo, Spain 33/B1
Vimioso, Portugal 33/C2
Vimmerby, Sweden 18/J8
Vimperk, Czech. 41/B2
Vimy, Alberta 182/D2
Vimy Ridge, Ark. (†72002) 202/F4
Vina, Ala. (35593) 195/B2
Vina, Calif. (96092) 204/D4
Viña del Mar, Chile 120/B6
Viña del Mar, Chile 138/F2
Viñales, Cuba 156/A2
Viñales, Cuba 158/A1
Vinalhaven○, Maine (04863) 243/F7
Vinalhaven (isl.), Maine 243/F7
Vinaroz, Spain 33/G2
Vincennes (bay) 5/C6
Vincennes, France 28/B2
Vincennes, Ind. (47591) 227/C7
Vincennes, Iowa (†52619) 229/K7
Vincent, Ala. (35178) 195/F4
Vincent, Ark. (†72327) 202/K3
Vincent, Iowa (50594) 229/E3
Vincent (pt.), Norfolk I. 88/L5
Vincent, Ohio (45784) 284/G7
Vincentown, N.J. (08088) 273/D4
Vinces, Ecuador 128/C3
Vinchina, Argentina 143/C2
Vinchos, Peru 128/E9
Vindelälven (riv.), Sweden 18/L4
Vindeln, Sweden 18/L4
Vinderup, Denmark 21/B5
Vindhya (range), India 68/D4
Vinegar Bend, Ala. (36584) 195/B8
Vine Grove, Ky. (40175) 237/K5
Vineland, Colo. (†81001) 208/K6
Vineland, N.J. (08360) 273/C5
Vinemont, Ala. (35179) 195/E2
Vineyard (sound), Mass. 249/L7
Vineyard Haven, Mass. (02568) 249/M7
Vinh, Vietnam 72/E3
Vinh, Vietnam 54/M8
Vinhais, Portugal 33/C2
Vinh Long, Vietnam 72/E5
Vinh Yen, Vietnam 72/E2
Vining, Iowa (52348) 229/J5
Vining, Kansas (†66937) 232/E2
Vining, Minn. (56588) 255/C4
Vinings, Georgia (†30080) 217/K1
Vinita, Okla. (74301) 288/R1
Vinita Park, Mo. (†63101) 261/P2
Vinkovci, Yugoslavia 45/D3
Vinland, Kansas (†66006) 232/G3
Vinnitsa, U.S.S.R. 7/G4
Vinnitsa, U.S.S.R. 52/C5
Vinnitsa, U.S.S.R. 48/C5
Vinogradov, U.S.S.R. 52/B5
Vinson, Okla. (73571) 288/G5
Vinson Massif (mt.) 5/B14
Vinsulla, Br. Col. 184/G5
Vint Hill Farms Mil. Res., Va. 307/N3
Vinton, Iowa (52349) 229/J4
Vinton, La. (70668) 238/C6
Vinton (co.), Ohio 284/E7
Vinton, Ohio (45686) 284/F8
Vinton, Va. (24179) 307/J6
Vintondale, Pa. (15961) 294/E5
Vinukonda, India 68/D5
Viola, Ark. (72583) 202/G1
Viola, Del. (19979) 245/R4
Viola, Idaho (83872) 220/B3
Viola, Ill. (61486) 222/C2
Viola, Iowa (52350) 229/L4
Viola, Kansas (67149) 232/E4
Viola, Ky. (†42051) 237/D7
Viola, Minn. (55980) 255/F6
Viola, Mo. (†65747) 261/E9
Viola, N.Y. (†10901) 276/J8
Viola, Tenn. (37394) 237/K9
Viola, Wis. (54664) 317/E8
Violet, La. (70092) 238/P4
Violet Grove, Alberta 182/C3
Violet Hill, Ark. (72584) 202/G1
Violette Brook, New Bruns. 170/C1
Violet Valley Aboriginal Reserve, W. Australia 88/D3
Viqueque, Indonesia 85/H7
Virac, Philippines 82/E4
Virago (sound), Br. Col. 184/A3
Virajpet, India 68/D6
Viramgam, India 68/C4
Viranşehir, Turkey 63/H4
Virden, Ill. (62690) 222/D4
Virden, Manitoba 179/A5
Virden, N. Mex. (†88055) 274/A6
Vire, France 28/C3
Virgelle, Mont. (†59460) 262/F2
Virgie, Ky. (41572) 237/R6
Virgil, Kansas (66870) 232/F4
Virgil, S. Dak. (57379) 298/N5
Virgilina, Va. (24598) 307/L7
Virgin (mts.), Ariz. 198/B2
Virgin (riv.), Ariz. 198/B2
Virgin (mts.), Nev. 266/G6
Virgin (peak), Nev. 266/G6
Virgin (riv.), Nev. 266/G6
Virgin (creek), S. Dak. 298/H3
Virgin, Utah (84779) 304/A6
Virgin (riv.), Utah 304/A6
Virgin, East Fork (riv.), Utah 304/B6
Virgin (str.), Virgin Is. (U.S.) 161/A4
Virgin Gorda (isl.), Virgin Is. (Br.) 156/H1
Virginia 188/L3
VIRGINIA 307
Virginia (key), Fla. 212/B5
Virginia, Idaho (†83234) 220/F7
Virginia, Ill. (62691) 222/C4
Virginia, Ireland 17/G4
Virginia, Minn. 188/H1
Virginia, Minn. (55792) 255/F3
Virginia, Nebr. (68458) 264/H4
Virginia (range), Nev. 266/B3
Virginia, S. Australia 94/B7
Virginia (state), U.S. 146/L6
Virginia Beach, Va. 188/L3
Virginia Beach (I.C.), Va. (*23450) 307/S7
Virginia City, Mont. (59755) 262/E5
Virginia City, Nev. (89440) 266/B3
Virginia Dale, Colo. (80548) 208/J1
Virginia Gardens, Fla. (†33166) 212/B5
Virginiatown, Ontario 177/K5
Virginiatown, Ontario 175/E3
Virgin Islands (U.S.) 146/M8
VIRGIN ISLANDS (U.S.) 161
VIRGIN ISLANDS (U.S.) 156/H1
VIRGIN ISLANDS (Br.) 161
VIRGIN ISLANDS (British) 156/H1
Virgin Isls. Nat'l Park, Virgin Is. (U.S.) 161/C4
Virginville, W. Va. (†26035) 312/F2
Virochey, Cambodia 72/E4
Viroinval, Belgium 27/F8
Viroqua, Wis. (54665) 317/D8
Virovitica, Yugoslavia 45/C3
Virserum, Sweden 18/J8
Virton, Belgium 27/H9
Virtsu, U.S.S.R. 53/B1
Virú, Peru 128/C7
Virunga (range), Rwanda 115/E4
Virunga (range), Uganda 115/E4
Virunga, Zaire 115/E5
Virunga (range), Zaire 115/E4
Virunga Nat'l Park, Uganda 115/F4
Virunga Nat'l Park, Zaire 115/E4
Vis (isl.), Yugoslavia 45/C4
Visakhapatnam, India 54/K8
Visakhapatnam, India 68/E5
Visalia, Calif. 188/C3
Visalia, Calif. (93277) 204/F7
Visalia, Ky. (†41063) 237/N3
Visayan (sea), Philippines 82/D5
Visayan (sea), Philippines 85/G3
Visby, Sweden 18/L8
Visby, Sweden 7/F3
Viscondé dos Rio Branco, Brazil 135/E2
Viscount, Sask. 181/F4
Viscount Melville (sound), Canada 4/B15
Viscount Melville (sound), N.W.T. 162/E1
Viscount Melville (sound), N.W.T. 146/H2
Viscount Melville (sound), N.W. Terrs. 187/G2
Visé, Belgium 27/H7
Višegrad, Yugoslavia 45/D4
Viseu, Brazil 132/E3
Viseu (dist.), Portugal 33/C2
Viseu, Portugal 33/C2
Vişeul de Sus, Romania 45/F2
Vishera (riv.), U.S.S.R. 52/J2
Vishoek, S. Africa 118/E7
Vislanda, Sweden 18/H8
Visnagar, India 68/C4
Viso (mt.), Italy 34/A2
Visoko, Yugoslavia 45/D4
Visp, Switzerland 39/E4
Visp (riv.), Switzerland 39/E4
Vissoie, Switzerland 39/E4
Vista, Calif. (92083) 204/H10
Vista, Manitoba 179/B4
Vista, Mo. (64789) 261/E7
Vista Hermosa, Cuba 158/G3
Vistula, Ind. (†46507) 227/F1
Vistula (riv.), Poland 7/F3
Vistula (riv.), Poland 47/D2
Vistula (spit), Poland 47/D1
Vit (riv.), Bulgaria 45/G4
Vita, Manitoba 179/F5
Vitali (isl.), Philippines 82/D7
Vitebsk, U.S.S.R. 7/H3
Vitebsk, U.S.S.R. 52/C3
Vitebsk, U.S.S.R. 48/D4
Viterbo (prov.), Italy 34/C3
Viterbo, Italy 34/C3
Vitiaz (str.), Papua N.G. 85/B7
Vitiaz (str.), Papua N.G. 86/A2
Vitichi, Bolivia 136/C7
Vitigudino, Spain 33/C2
Viti Levu (isl.), Fiji 87/H7
Viti Levu (isl.), Fiji 86/P11
Vitim (riv.), U.S.S.R. 54/N4
Vitim (riv.), U.S.S.R. 48/M4
Vitimskiy, U.S.S.R. 48/M4
Vítkov, Czech. 41/D2
Vitor, Quebrado (riv.), Chile 138/A1
Vitor, Peru 128/G11
Vitor (riv.), Peru 128/F11
Vitória, Brazil 120/F5
Vitória, Brazil 132/G8
Vitoria, Spain 33/E1
Vitoria, Spain 7/D4
Vitória da Conquista, Brazil 120/E4
Vitória da Conquista, Brazil 132/F6
Vitória de Santo Antão, Brazil 132/G4
Vitória de Sto. Antao, Brazil 120/F3
Vitré, France 28/C3
Vitry-le-François, France 28/F3
Vitry-sur-Seine, France 28/B2
Vittangi, Sweden 18/M3
Vittel, France 28/F3
Vittoria, Italy 34/E6
Vittoria, Ontario 177/D5
Vittorio Veneto, Italy 34/D1
Vitu (isls.), Papua N.G. 86/B2
Vivero, Spain 33/C1
Vivian, La. (71082) 238/B1
Vivian, S. Dak. (57576) 298/J6
Vivian, W. Va. (24891) 312/D8
Vivorillo (cays), Honduras 154/F3
Vixen, La. (†71418) 238/F2
Vizagapatam (Visakhapatnam), India 68/E5
Vizcaino (cape), Calif. 204/B4
Vizcaya (prov.), Spain 33/E1
Vize, Turkey 63/B2
Vizianagaram, India 68/E5
Vizille, France 28/F5
Vizinga, U.S.S.R. 52/G2
Viziru, Romania 45/H3
Vizovice, Czech. 41/D2
Vizzini, Italy 34/E6
Vlaardingen, Netherlands 27/E5
Vladimir, U.S.S.R. 7/J3
Vladimir, U.S.S.R. 48/D4
Vladimir, U.S.S.R. 52/F3
Vladimir-Volynskiy, U.S.S.R. 52/B4
Vladivostok, U.S.S.R. 54/P5
Vladivostok, U.S.S.R. 2/R3
Vladivostok, U.S.S.R. 48/O5
Vlagtwedde, Netherlands 27/L3
Vlasenica, Yugoslavia 45/D3
Vlašim, Czech. 41/C2
Vleteren, Belgium 27/B7
Vlieland (isl.), Netherlands 27/F2
Vliestroom (str.), Netherlands 27/G2
Vliets, Kansas (66545) 232/F2
Vlijmen, Netherlands 27/G5
Vlissingen (Flushing), Netherlands 27/C6
Vlorë, Albania 45/D5
Vltava (riv.), Czech. 41/C2
Voca, Texas (76887) 303/E7
Vöcklabruck, Austria 41/B2
Voda, Kansas (†67631) 232/C2
Vodl (lake), U.S.S.R. 52/E2
Vodňany, Czech. 41/C2
Vogar, Manitoba 179/D4
Vogel Center, Mich. (†49657) 250/E4
Vogelkop (Doberai) (pen.), Indonesia 85/J6
Vogelsberg (mts.), W. Germany 22/C3
Voghera, Italy 34/B2
Voglers Cove, Nova Scotia 168/D4
Voh, New Caled. 86/G4
Vohibinany, Madagascar 118/H3
Vohimarina (Vohémar), Madagascar 118/J2
Vohimena (cape), Madagascar 102/G7
Vohimena (cape), Madagascar 118/G5
Vohipeno, Madagascar 118/H4
Voi, Kenya 115/G4
Voi, Kenya 102/F5
Voil, Loch (lake), Scotland 15/D4
Voiron, France 28/F5
Voisey (bay), Newf. 166/B2
Voitsberg, Austria 41/C3
Voïvis (lake), Greece 45/F6
Vojens, Denmark 21/C7
Vojmsjön (lake), Sweden 18/J4
Vojnice, Czech. 41/E3
Vojvodina (aut. prov.), Yugoslavia 45/D3
Volador, Colombia 126/C3
Volant, Pa. (16156) 294/B3
Volary, Czech. 41/B2
Volborg, Mont. (59351) 262/L5
Volcano, Calif. (95689) 204/E5
Volcano, Hawaii (96785) 218/J6
Volcano (isls.), Japan 87/E3
Volcano (isls.), Japan 81/M4
Volda, Norway 18/E5
Volendam-Edam, Netherlands 27/G4
Volga, Iowa (52077) 229/L3
Volga, S. Dak. (57071) 298/R5
Volga (riv.), U.S.S.R. 7/J4
Volga (riv.), U.S.S.R. 2/M3
Volga (riv.), U.S.S.R. 48/E5
Volga (riv.), U.S.S.R. 52/G5
Volga, W. Va. (26238) 312/F4
Volga-Don (canal), U.S.S.R. 52/F5
Volgodonsk, U.S.S.R. 52/F5
Volgograd, U.S.S.R. 2/M3
Volgograd, U.S.S.R. 7/J4
Volgograd, U.S.S.R. 48/E5
Volgograd, U.S.S.R. 52/F5
Volgograd (res.), U.S.S.R. 52/G5
Volin, S. Dak. (57072) 298/P8
Völkermarkt, Austria 41/C3
Volkhov, U.S.S.R. 52/D3
Volkhov (riv.), U.S.S.R. 52/D3
Völklingen, W. Germany 22/B4
Volkovysk, U.S.S.R. 52/B4
Volksrust, S. Africa 118/D5
Volney, Mich. (†49309) 250/D5
Volney, Va. (24379) 307/F7
Volochanka, U.S.S.R. 48/K2
Vologda, U.S.S.R. 7/J3
Vologda, U.S.S.R. 48/E4
Vologda, U.S.S.R. 52/F3
Vólos, Greece 7/G5
Vólos, Greece 45/F6
Vol'sk, U.S.S.R. 7/J3
Vol'sk, U.S.S.R. 52/G4
Volta (lake), Ghana 102/B4
Volta (lake), Ghana 106/D7
Volta (riv.), Ghana 102/C4
Volta (riv.), Ghana 106/E7
Volta Grande (res.), Brazil 135/B1
Voltaire, N. Dak. (58792) 282/J3
Volta Redonda, Brazil 120/E5
Volta Redonda, Brazil 132/E8
Volta Redonda, Brazil 135/D3
Volterra, Italy 34/C3
Volturno (riv.), Italy 34/E4
Voluntown○, Conn. (06384) 210/H2
Volusia (co.), Fla. 212/E2
Vólvi (lake), Greece 45/F5
Volyně, Czech. 41/B2
Volyn Oblast, U.S.S.R. 52/C4
Volzhsk, U.S.S.R. 52/G3
Volzhskiy, U.S.S.R. 7/J4
Volzhskiy, U.S.S.R. 52/G5
Vom, Nigeria 106/F7
Vona, Colo. (80861) 208/O4
Vonda, Sask. 181/F3
Vónitsa, Greece 45/E6
Vonore, Tenn. (37885) 237/N9
Von Ormy, Texas (78073) 303/J11
Voorburg, Netherlands 27/E4
Voorhees○, N.J. (†08043) 273/B3
Voorheesville, N.Y. (12186) 276/M5
Voorhies, Iowa (†50643) 229/J4
Voorne (isl.), Netherlands 27/D5
Voorst, Netherlands 27/J4
Vopnafjördhur (fjord), Iceland 21/D1
Vorab (mt.), Switzerland 39/H3
Vorarlberg (prov.), Austria 41/A3
Vorbasse, Denmark 21/B6
Vorden, Netherlands 27/J4
Vordernberg, Austria 41/C3
Vorderrhein (riv.), Switzerland 39/G3

Wamic 465

Vordingborg, Denmark 21/E7
Vordingborg, Denmark 18/G9
Vorgod (riv.), Denmark 21/B6
Vorkuta, U.S.S.R. 4/C6
Vorkuta, U.S.S.R. 7/L2
Vorkuta, U.S.S.R. 52/K1
Vorkuta, U.S.S.R. 48/G3
Vormsi (isl.), U.S.S.R. 53/B1
Vorona (riv.), U.S.S.R. 52/F4
Voronezh, U.S.S.R. 7/H3
Voronezh, U.S.S.R. 52/E4
Voronezh, U.S.S.R. 48/E4
Voroshilovgrad, U.S.S.R. 7/H4
Voroshilovgrad, U.S.S.R. 52/E5
Voroshilovgrad, U.S.S.R. 48/E5
Vorskla (riv.), U.S.S.R. 52/E4
Vorst (Forest), Belgium 27/B9
Võrtsjärv (lake), U.S.S.R. 53/D1
Võru, U.S.S.R. 52/C2
Võru, U.S.S.R. 53/D2
Vosges (dept.), France 28/G3
Vosges (mts.), France 28/G3
Voskresensk, U.S.S.R. 52/E3
Voss, N. Dak. (58280) 282/R3
Voss, Norway 18/E6
Vossburg, Miss. (39366) 256/F7
Vostochnyy, U.S.S.R. 48/O5
Vostok (isl.), Kiribati 2/B6
Vostok (isl.), Kiribati 87/L7
Votamo (riv.), Venezuela 124/F6
Votice, Czech. 41/C2
Votkinsk, U.S.S.R. 48/F4
Votkinsk, U.S.S.R. 52/H3
Votuporanga, Brazil 135/B2
Vouvry, Switzerland 39/C4
Voúxa (cape), Greece 45/F8
Vouziers, France 28/F3
Voyageurs Nat'l Park, Minn. 255/F2
Voy-Vozh, U.S.S.R. 48/F3
Voy-Vozh, U.S.S.R. 52/H2
Vozhe (lake), U.S.S.R. 52/F2
Vozhega, U.S.S.R. 52/F2
Vozhma, U.S.S.R. 52/G3
Voznesensk, U.S.S.R. 52/D5
Vrå, Denmark 21/C3
Vráble, Czech. 41/E2
Vracov, Czech. 41/D2
Vrangelya (isl.), U.S.S.R. 54/U2
Vranje, Yugoslavia 45/F4
Vranov nad Teplou, Czech. 41/F2
Vratsa, Bulgaria 45/F4
Vrbas, Yugoslavia 45/D3
Vrbas (riv.), Yugoslavia 45/C3
Vrbno pod Pradědem, Czech. 41/D1
Vrbovce, Czech. 41/D1
Vrbové, Czech. 41/D2
Vrchlabí, Czech. 41/C1
Vrede, S. Africa 118/D5
Vredenburg, S. Africa 118/B6
Vredenburgh, Ala. (36481) 195/D7
Vredendal, S. Africa 118/B6
Vreed-en-Hoop, Guyana 131/B2
Vresse-sur-Semois, Belgium 27/F9
Vriezenveen, Netherlands 27/K4
Vrondádhes, Greece 45/G6
Vršac, Yugoslavia 45/E3
Vrútky, Czech. 41/E2
Vryburg, S. Africa 118/C5
Vryheid, S. Africa 118/E5
Vsetín, Czech. 41/D2
Vsevidof (mt.), Alaska 196/E4
Vuadens, Switzerland 39/C3
Vučitrn, Yugoslavia 45/E4
Vught, Netherlands 27/G5
Vukovar, Yugoslavia 45/D3
Vulcan, Alberta 182/D4
Vulcan, Mich. (49892) 250/B3
Vulcan, Mo. (63675) 261/L8
Vulcan, W. Va. (25697) 312/B7
Vulcano (isl.), Italy 34/E5
Vu Liet, Vietnam 72/E3
Vung Tau, Vietnam 72/E5
Vuollerim, Sweden 18/M3
Vuolvojaure (lake), Sweden 18/L3
Vuotso, Finland 18/P2
Vya, Nev. (†96104) 266/B1
Vyatka (riv.), U.S.S.R. 52/H3
Vyatskiye Polyany, U.S.S.R. 52/H3
Vyazemskiy, U.S.S.R. 48/O5
Vyaz'ma, U.S.S.R. 52/D3
Vyborg, U.S.S.R. 7/G2
Vyborg, U.S.S.R. 52/C2
Vyborg, U.S.S.R. 48/C3
Vychegda (riv.), U.S.S.R. 52/G2
Východočeský (reg.), Czech. 41/C1
Východoslovenský (reg.), Czech. 41/F2
Vyg (lake), U.S.S.R. 52/E2
Vyksa, U.S.S.R. 52/F3
Vym' (riv.), U.S.S.R. 52/H2
Vyshniy Volochek, U.S.S.R. 7/H2
Vyshniy Volochek, U.S.S.R. 52/D3
Vyshniy Volochek, U.S.S.R. 48/D4
Vyškov, Czech. 41/D2
Vysoké Mýto, Czech. 41/D2
Vysoké Tatry, Czech. 41/F2
Vyšší Brod, Czech. 41/C2
Vytegra, U.S.S.R. 52/E2

W

Wa, Ghana 106/D6
Waal (riv.), Netherlands 27/G5
Waalre, Netherlands 27/G6
Waalwijk, Netherlands 27/F5
Waarschoot, Belgium 27/D6
Waas (mt.), Utah 304/E5
Waasis, New Bruns. 170/D3
Wabamun, Alberta 182/C3
Waban, Mass. (†02168) 249/B7
Wabana, Newf. 166/D2
Wabaningo, Mich. (49463) 250/C5
Wabasca, Alberta 182/D2
Wabasca (riv.), Alberta 182/C1
Wabasca (riv.), Alta. 162/E4
Wabash (riv.) 188/J3
Wabash, Ark. (72389) 202/J5
Wabash (co.), Ill. 222/F5
Wabash (riv.), Ill. 222/F5
Wabash (co.), Ind. 227/F3
Wabash, Ind. (46992) 227/F3
Wabash (riv.), Ind. 227/B7
Wabash, Ohio (†45822) 284/A4
Wabash (riv.), Ohio 284/A5
Wabasha (co.), Minn. 255/F6
Wabasha, Minn. (55981) 255/G6
Wabasso, Fla. (32970) 212/F4
Wabasso, Minn. (56293) 255/C6
Wabatawangang (lake), Minn. 255/D3
Wabaunsee (co.), Kansas 232/F3
Wabaunsee, Kansas (†66547) 232/F2
Wabbaseka, Ark. (72175) 202/G5
Wabeno, Wis. (54566) 317/J5
Wabi (riv.), Ethiopia 111/H6
Wabigoon, Ontario 175/B3
Wabigoon, Ontario 177/G5
Wabi Shebelle (riv.) 102/G4
Wabi Shebelle (riv.), Ethiopia 111/H6
Wabowden, Manitoba 179/J3
Wąbrzeźno, Poland 47/D2
Wabuk (pt.), Ontario 175/D1
Wabush, Newf. 166/A3
Wabush, Newf. 162/K5
Wabuska, Nev. (†89447) 266/B3
Waccamaw (lake), N.C. 281/N6
Waccamaw (riv.), N.C. 281/M7
Waccamaw (riv.), S.C. 296/J5
Waccasassa (bay), Fla. 212/D2
Waccasassa (riv.), Fla. 212/D2
Wachapreague, Va. (23480) 307/S5
Wachapreague (inlet), Va. 307/T6
Wachtebeke, Belgium 27/D6
Wachusett (mt.), Mass. 249/G3
Wachusett (res.), Mass. 249/G3
Wacissa, Fla. (32361) 212/B1
Waco, Georgia (30182) 217/B3
Waco, Ky. (40385) 237/N5
Waco, Mo. (63869) 261/C8
Waco, Nebr. (68460) 264/G4
Waco, N.C. (28169) 281/G4
Waco, Texas 188/G4
Waco, Texas 146/J6
Waco, Texas (*76701) 303/G6
Waconda (lake), Kansas 232/D2
Waconia, Minn. (55387) 255/E6
Wadai (reg.), Chad 111/D5
Waddamana, Tasmania 99/C4
Waddan, Libya 102/D2
Waddan, Libya 111/C2
Waddell, Ariz. (85355) 198/C5
Waddenzee (sound), Netherlands 27/G2
Waddington (mt.), Br. Col. 162/D5
Waddington (mt.), Br. Col. 184/E4
Waddington, N.Y. (13694) 276/K1
Waddy, Ky. (40076) 237/L4
Wade, Miss. (†39567) 256/G9
Wade (lake), Newf. 166/A3
Wade, N.C. (28395) 281/M4
Wade, Ohio (†74723) 288/O7
Wadebridge, England 13/C7
Wade-Hampton, S.C. (†29607) 296/C2
Wadena, Ind. (†47944) 227/C3
Wadena, Iowa (52169) 229/K3
Wadena (co.), Minn. 255/D4
Wadena, Minn. (56482) 255/C4
Wadena, Sask. 181/H4
Wädenswil, Switzerland 39/G2
Wadesboro, La. (†70454) 238/M2
Wadesboro, N.C. (28170) 281/J5
Wadestown, W. Va. (26589) 312/F3
Wadesville, Ind. (47638) 227/B8
Wadeville, N.C. (†27306) 281/J4
Wadhams, N.Y. (12990) 276/N2
Wadi Dra, Morocco 102/B2
Wadi es Sir, Jordan 65/D4
Wadi Halfa, Sudan 111/F3
Wadi Musa, Jordan 65/E5
Wading (riv.), N.J. 273/D4
Wading River, N.Y. (11792) 276/P9
Wadley, Ala. (36276) 195/G4
Wadley, Georgia (30477) 217/H5
Wadmalaw (isl.), S.C. 296/G6
Wad Medani, Sudan 111/F5
Wad Medani, Sudan 59/B7
Wad Medani, Sudan 102/F3
Wadowice, Poland 47/D4
Wadsworth, Ala. (†36022) 195/E5
Wadsworth, Ill. (60083) 222/B4
Wadsworth, Nev. (89442) 266/B3
Wadsworth, Ohio (44281) 284/G3
Wadsworth, Texas (77483) 303/J9
Waelder, Texas (78959) 303/G8
Wagait Aboriginal Res., North. Terr. 93/B2
Wagarville, Ala. (36585) 195/B8
Wagener, S.C. (29164) 296/E4
Wageningen, Netherlands 27/H5
Wageningen, Suriname 131/C3
Wager (bay), N.W.T. 146/J3
Wager (bay), N.W.T. 162/G2
Wager (bay), N.W. Terrs. 187/K3
Wagga Wagga, Australia 87/E9
Wagga Wagga, N. S. Wales 88/H7
Wagga Wagga, N.S. Wales 97/D4
Waggoner, Ill. (62572) 222/D4
Waggrakine, W. Australia 92/A5
Wagin, W. Australia 88/B6
Wagin, W. Australia 92/B2
Wagner, Alberta 182/C2
Wagner, Mont. (59543) 262/H2
Wagner, S. Dak. (57380) 298/N7
Wagoner (co.), Okla. 288/P3
Wagoner, Okla. (74467) 288/R3
Wagon Mound, N. Mex. (87752) 274/E2
Wagontire, Oreg. (†97720) 291/H4
Wagon Wheel Gap, Colo. (†81130) 208/F7
Wagram, N.C. (28396) 281/L5
Wągrowiec, Poland 47/C2
Wah, Pakistan 68/C2
Wahai, Indonesia 85/H6
Wahalak, Miss. (†39358) 256/G5
Wahiawa, Hawaii (96786) 218/E2
Wahiawa, Hawaii 188/F5
Wahkiacus, Wash. (98670) 310/D5
Wahkiakum (co.), Wash. 310/B4
Wahkon, Minn. (56386) 255/E4
Wahlern, Switzerland 39/D3
Wahoo, Nebr. (68066) 264/H3
Wahpeton, Iowa (†51360) 229/C2
Wahpeton, N. Dak. 188/G1
Wahpeton, N. Dak. (58075) 282/S7
Wahsatch, Utah (†82930) 304/C2
Wah Wah (mts.), Utah 304/A5
Wahwashkesh (lake), Ontario 177/D2
Wahweap (creek), Utah 304/C6
Wai, Poulo (isls.), Vietnam 72/E4
Waiakoa, Hawaii (†96788) 218/J2
Waialae, Hawaii (96816) 218/D4
Waialeale (mt.), Hawaii 218/C1
Waialee, Hawaii (†96731) 218/E1
Waialua, Hawaii 188/F5
Waialua, Molokai, Hawaii (†96748) 218/H1
Waialua, Oahu, Hawaii (96791) 218/E1
Waianae, Hawaii (96792) 218/D2
Waiau, N. Zealand 100/D5
Waiau (riv.), N. Zealand 100/A6
Waidhofen an der Thaya, Austria 41/C2
Waidhofen an der Ybbs, Austria 41/C3
Waidsboro, Va. (†24088) 307/J7
Waigama, Indonesia 85/H6
Waigeo (isl.), Indonesia 85/J5
Waihee, Hawaii (†96793) 218/J2
Waiheke (isl.), N. Zealand 100/E2
Waihi, N. Zealand 100/E2
Waikabubak, Indonesia 85/F7
Waikanae, N. Zealand 100/E4
Waikane, Hawaii (†96744) 218/F2
Waikapu, Hawaii (†96793) 218/J2
Waikaremoana (lake), N. Zealand 100/F3
Waikari, N. Zealand 100/D5
Waikato (riv.), N. Zealand 100/E2
Waikawa, N. Zealand 100/B7
Waikerie, S. Australia 94/F6
Waikii, Hawaii (†96743) 218/H4
Waikiki (canton), Hawaii (96815) 218/C4
Waikiki (beach), Hawaii 218/C4
Waikouaiti, N. Zealand 100/C6
Wailau, Hawaii (†96748) 218/H1
Wailea, Hawaii (†96710) 218/J4
Wailea, Maui, Hawaii (†96790) 218/J2
Wailua, Hawaii (†96746) 218/D2
Wailuku, Hawaii (96793) 218/J2
Wailuku, Hawaii 188/F5
Wailuku (riv.), Hawaii 218/J5
Waimakariri (riv.), N. Zealand 100/D5
Waimalu, Hawaii (†96701) 218/B3
Waimanalo, Hawaii (96795) 218/F2
Waimanalo Bch., Hawaii (†96795) 218/F2
Waimangaroa, N. Zealand 100/C4
Waimate, N. Zealand 100/C6
Waimea (Kamuela), Hawaii, (†96743) 218/G3
Waimea, Kauai, Hawaii (96796) 218/B2
Waimea, Oahu, Hawaii (†96712) 218/E1
Waimea (bay), Hawaii 218/B2
Waimea (riv.), Hawaii 218/C2
Waimes, Belgium 27/J8
Wainaku, Hawaii (†96720) 218/J5
Wainfleet, Ontario 177/E4
Wainfleet All Saints, England 13/H4
Waingapu, Indonesia 85/G7
Waini (riv.), Guyana 131/B2
Wainiha, Hawaii (†96714) 218/C1
Wainiha (riv.), Hawaii 218/C1
Wainuiomata, N. Zealand 100/B3
Wainui-o-mata (riv.), N. Zealand 100/B3
Wainwright, Alaska (99782) 196/F1
Wainwright, Alberta 182/E3
Wainwright, Ohio (44686) 284/G5
Wainwright, Okla. (74468) 288/R3
Wainwright, U.S. 4/B18
Waiohinu, Hawaii (†96772) 218/G7
Waipa (riv.), N. Zealand 100/E2
Waipahu, Hawaii 188/F5
Waipahu, Hawaii (96797) 218/A3
Waipara, N. Zealand 100/D5
Waipawa, N. Zealand 100/F3
Waipio, Hawaii (†96758) 218/H3
Waipio (bay), Hawaii 218/H3
Waipio (pen.), Hawaii 218/A3
Waipio (pt.), Hawaii 218/A4
Waipio Acres, Hawaii (†96786) 218/E2
Waipiro Bay, N. Zealand 100/G3
Waipukurau, N. Zealand 100/F4
Wairau (riv.), N. Zealand 100/D4
Wairoa, N. Zealand 100/F3
Wairoa (riv.), N. Zealand 100/E1
Waitakere, N. Zealand 100/B1
Waitakere (range), N. Zealand 100/A1
Waitaki (riv.), N. Zealand 100/C6
Waitangi, N. Zealand 100/D7
Waitara, N. Zealand 100/E3
Waite○, Maine (04492) 243/H5
Waite Hill, Ohio (†44094) 284/H2
Waitemata (harb.), N. Zealand 100/B1
Waite Park, Minn. (56387) 255/D5
Waiteville, W. Va. (24984) 312/F8
Waitotara, N. Zealand 100/E3
Waits (riv.), Vt. 268/C3
Waitsburg, Wash. (99361) 310/G4
Waitsfield○, Vt. (05673) 268/B3
Waits River, Vt. (†05076) 268/C3
Waitville, Sask. 181/F3
Waiuku, N. Zealand 100/E2
Waiyevu, Fiji 86/R10
Wajabula, Indonesia 85/H5
Wajima, Japan 81/H5
Wajir, Kenya 115/H3
Wajir, Kenya 102/F4
Waka, Ethiopia 111/G6
Waka, Texas (79093) 303/D1
Waka, Zaire 115/D3
Wakarusa, Ind. (46573) 227/F1
Wakarusa, Kansas (66546) 232/G3
Wakasa, Japan 81/G6
Wakasa (bay), Japan 81/G6
Wakatipu (lake), N. Zealand 100/B6
Wakaw, Sask. 181/F3
Wakaw Lake, Sask. 181/F3
Wakayama (pref.), Japan 81/G6
Wakayama, Japan 54/P6
Wakayama, Japan 81/G6
Wakde (isl.), Indonesia 85/K6
Wake (co.), N.C. 281/M3
Wake (isl.), Pacific 87/G4
WaKeeney, Kansas (67672) 232/C2
Wakefield, England 10/F4
Wakefield, England 13/J2
Wakefield, Kansas (67487) 232/E2
Wakefield, La. (70784) 238/H5
Wakefield○, Mass. (01880) 249/C5
Wakefield, Mich. (49968) 250/F2
Wakefield, Nebr. (68784) 264/H2
Wakefield○, N.H. (†03872) 268/F4
Wakefield, Ohio (45687) 284/E8
Wakefield, Va. (23888) 307/O7
Wakefield-Peace Dale, R.I. (*02879) 249/J7
Wake Forest, N.C. (27587) 281/M3
Wakema, Burma 72/B3
Wakeman, Ohio (44889) 284/F3
Wakenda, Mo. (64687) 261/F4
Wake Village, Texas (75501) 303/K4
Wakita, Okla. (73771) 288/L1
Wakkanai, Japan 81/K1
Wakonda, S. Dak. (57073) 298/P7
Wakool, N.S. Wales 97/C4
Wakopa, Manitoba 179/C5
Wakpala, S. Dak. (57658) 298/H2
Wakulla (co.), Fla. 212/B1
Wakulla, Fla. (†32327) 212/B1
Wakwekobi (lake), Ontario 177/A1
Wala, Kuh-i- (mt.), Afghanistan 59/H3
Walbridge, Ohio (43465) 284/C2
Wałbrzych (prov.), Poland 47/C3
Wałbrzych, Poland 47/C3
Walcha, N.S. Wales 97/F2
Walchensee (lake), W. Germany 22/D5
Walcheren (isl.), Netherlands 27/C5
Walcott, Ark. (72474) 202/J1
Walcott, Br. Col. 184/D3
Walcott (lake), Idaho 220/E7
Walcott, Iowa (52773) 229/M5
Walcott, N. Dak. (58077) 282/R6
Walcott, Wyo. (82335) 319/F4
Walcourt, Belgium 27/F8
Wałcz, Poland 47/C2
Wald, Switzerland 39/G2
Waldeck, Sask. 181/D5
Walden, Colo. (80480) 208/G1
Walden, Georgia (†31201) 217/E5
Walden, Ky. (40768) 237/N7
Walden (pond), Mass. 249/A6
Walden, N.Y. (12586) 276/M7
Walden, Ontario 175/D3
Walden, Ontario 177/J5
Walden, Tenn. (†37377) 237/L10
Walden○, Vt. (†05873) 268/C3
Waldenburg, Ark. (72475) 202/J2
Waldenburg (Wałbrzych), Poland 47/C3
Waldenburg, Switzerland 39/E2
Walden Heights, Vt. (†05873) 268/C3
Waldersee, Manitoba 179/D4
Waldheim, E. Germany 22/E3
Waldheim, La. (†70433) 238/L5
Waldheim, Sask. 181/E3
Waldia, Ethiopia 111/G5
Waldkirch, Switzerland 39/H2
Waldkirch, W. Germany 22/B4
Waldkraiburg, W. Germany 22/E4
Waldo, Ala. (†35150) 195/F4
Waldo, Ark. (71770) 202/D7
Waldo, Br. Col. 184/K5
Waldo, Fla. (32694) 212/D2
Waldo, Kansas (67673) 232/D2
Waldo (co.), Maine 243/E6
Waldo○, Maine (†04915) 243/E7
Waldo, Ohio (43356) 284/D5
Waldo (lake), Oreg. 291/E4
Waldo, Wis. (53093) 317/L8
Waldoboro, Maine (04572) 243/E7
Waldoboro○, Maine (04572) 243/E7
Waldorf, Md. (20601) 245/L6
Waldorf, Minn. (56091) 255/E7
Waldport, Oreg. (97394) 291/C3
Waldron, Ark. (72958) 202/B4
Waldron, Ind. (46182) 227/F6
Waldron, Kansas (67150) 232/D4
Waldron, Mich. (49288) 250/E7
Waldron, Mo. (64092) 261/O5
Waldron, Sask. 181/J5
Waldron, Wash. (98297) 310/B2
Waldrup, Miss. (†39422) 256/F7
Waldsassen, W. Germany 22/E3
Waldshut-Tiengen, W. Germany 22/C5
Waldwick, N.J. (07463) 273/B1
Waldwick, Wis. (†53565) 317/G10
Walensee (lake), Switzerland 39/H2
Walenstadt, Switzerland 39/H2
Wales, Alaska (99783) 196/E1
Wales, Alaska 188/C5
Wales○, Mass. (01081) 249/F4
Wales, Minn. (†55616) 255/G3
Wales, N. Dak. (58281) 282/N2
Wales (isl.), N.W. Terrs. 187/K3
Wales, Tenn. (†38478) 237/G10
Wales, U.K. 7/D3
Wales, Utah (84667) 304/C4
WALES 13
WALES, Wales 10/E4
Wales, Wis. (53183) 317/J1
Walesboro, Ind. (†47201) 227/F6
Waleska, Georgia (30183) 217/D2
Walford, Iowa (52351) 229/K5
Walford, Ontario 177/B1
Walgett, N. S. Wales 88/H6
Walgett, N.S. Wales 97/E2
Walgreen Coast (reg.) 5/B13
Walhachin, Br. Col. 184/G5
Walhalla, Mich. (49458) 250/C5
Walhalla, N. Dak. (58282) 282/P2
Walhalla, S.C. (29691) 296/A2
Walhonding, Ohio (43843) 284/F5
Walikale, Zaire 115/E4
Walker (co.), Ala. 195/D3
Walker (creek), Ariz. 198/F2
Walker (mt.), Ark. 202/E2
Walker (co.), Georgia 217/B1
Walker, Iowa (52352) 229/K4
Walker, Kansas (67674) 232/C3
Walker, Ky. (40997) 237/O7
Walker, La. (70785) 238/L1
Walker, Mich. (49504) 250/D6
Walker, Minn. (56484) 255/D3
Walker, Mo. (64790) 261/D7
Walker (lake), Nev. 188/C3
Walker (lake), Nev. 266/C4
Walker (riv.), Nev. 266/C3
Walker, N.Y. (†14468) 276/E4
Walker (bay), N.W. Terrs. 187/G2
Walker, Oreg. (†97426) 291/D4
Walker, S. Dak. (57659) 298/G2
Walker (isl.), Tasmania 99/B2
Walker (co.), Texas 303/J7
Walker (creek), Va. 307/F6
Walker, W. Va. (26180) 312/D4
Walkerburn, Scotland 15/F5
Walker Mill, Md. (†20023) 245/F5
Walker River Ind. Res., Nev. 266/C3
Walker Springs, Ala. (36586) 195/C7
Walkerston, Queensland 88/H4
Walkerston, Queensland 95/D4
Walkersville, Md. (21793) 245/J3
Walkersville, W. Va. (26447) 312/F5
Walkerton, Ind. (46574) 227/E2
Walkerton, Ontario 177/C3
Walkerton, Va. (23177) 307/O5
Walkertown, N.C. (27051) 281/J2
Walkerville, Mich. (49459) 250/C5
Walkerville, Mont. (59701) 262/D4
Walkerville, S. Australia 88/E8
Wall○, N.J. (07719) 273/E3
Wall, Pa. (†15148) 294/C5
Wall, S. Dak. (57790) 298/E6
Wall, Texas (76957) 303/D6
Wallace, Ala. (†36426) 195/D8
Wallace (mt.), Alberta 182/C2
Wallace, Calif. (95254) 204/C9
Wallace, Idaho (83873) 220/C2
Wallace, Ind. (47988) 227/C5
Wallace (co.), Kansas 232/A3
Wallace, Kansas (67761) 232/A3
Wallace, La. (†70049) 238/M3
Wallace (lake), La. 238/C2
Wallace, Mich. (49893) 250/B3
Wallace, Nebr. (69169) 264/C4
Wallace, N.Y. (14890) 276/E6
Wallace, N.C. (28466) 281/N5
Wallace, Nova Scotia 168/E3
Wallace (harb.), Nova Scotia 168/E3
Wallace, S.C. (29596) 296/H2
Wallace, S. Dak. (57272) 298/P3
Wallace, W. Va. (26448) 312/E4
Wallaceburg, Ontario 177/B5
Wallace Lake, Manitoba 179/G3
Wallaceton, Pa. (16876) 294/F4
Wallacetown, Ontario 177/C5
Wallaga (prov.), Ethiopia 111/G6
Wallal Station, W. Australia 92/C2
Walland, Tenn. (37886) 237/O9
Wallaroo, S. Australia 94/E5
Wallasey, England 13/G2
Wallasey, England 10/F2
Walla Walla, N.S. Wales 97/D4
Walla Walla (riv.), Oreg. 291/J1
Walla Walla, Wash. 188/C1
Walla Walla (co.), Wash. 310/G4
Walla Walla, Wash. (99362) 310/G4
Walla Walla (riv.), Wash. 310/G4
Wallback, W. Va. (25285) 312/D5
Wallburg, N.C. (27373) 281/J3
Walldürn, W. Germany 22/C4
Walled Lake, Mich. (48088) 250/F6
Wallen, Ind. (†46802) 227/G2
Wallendbeen, N.S. Wales 97/E4
Wallenpaupack (lake), Pa. 294/M3
Waller (co.), Texas 303/J8
Wallerawang, N.S. Wales 97/F3
Wallerville, Miss. (†38652) 256/G2
Wallibu, St. Vin. & Grens. 161/A8
Walling, Tenn. (38587) 237/K9
Wallingford, Conn. (06492) 210/D3
Wallingford○, Conn. (06492) 210/D3
Wallingford, England 13/F6
Wallingford, Iowa (51365) 229/D2
Wallingford, Ky. (41093) 237/O4
Wallingford, Pa. (19086) 294/L7
Wallingford, Vt. (05773) 268/B5
Wallingford○, Vt. (05773) 268/B5
Wallington, N.J. (07057) 273/B2
Wallins Creek, Ky. (40873) 237/O7
Wallis (lake), N.S. Wales 97/G3
Wallis, Texas (77485) 303/H8
Wallis (isls.), Wallis and Futuna 87/J7
Wallis and Futuna 87/J7
Wallisellen, Switzerland 39/G2
Wallisville, Texas (77597) 303/L1
Wallkill (riv.), N.J. 273/D1
Wallkill, N.Y. (12589) 276/M7
Wallkill (riv.), N.Y. 276/L8
Wall Lake, Iowa (51466) 229/C4
Wallo (prov.), Ethiopia 111/H5
Wallonia, Ky. (†42405) 237/F7
Walloon (lake), Mich. 250/E3
Walloon Lake, Mich. (49796) 250/E3
Wallops (isl.), Va. 307/T5
Wallowa (co.), Oreg. 291/K2
Wallowa, Oreg. (97885) 291/K2
Wallowa (mts.), Oreg. 291/K2
Wallowa (riv.), Oreg. 291/K2
Wallpack Center, N.J. (07881) 273/D1
Walls, Miss. (38680) 256/D1
Walls, Scotland 15/G2
Wallsburg, Utah (84082) 304/C3
Wallsend, England 13/J3
Wallula (lake), Oreg. 291/H1
Wallula, Wash. (99363) 310/G4
Wallula (lake), Wash. 310/F4
Walney, Isle of (isl.), England 13/D3
Walney, Isle of (isl.), England 10/E3
Walnut, Calif. (91789) 204/D10
Walnut (creek), Calif. 204/K1
Walnut, Ill. (61376) 222/D2
Walnut, Iowa (51577) 229/C6
Walnut, Kansas (66780) 232/G4
Walnut (creek), Kansas 232/B3
Walnut (riv.), Kansas 232/E4
Walnut, Miss. (38683) 256/G1
Walnut, N.C. (28753) 281/D3
Walnut, Pa. (†17082) 294/G4
Walnut (creek), Texas 303/F3
Walnut Bottom, Pa. (17266) 294/H5
Walnut Canyon Nat'l Mon., Ariz. 198/D3
Walnut Cove, N.C. (27052) 281/J2
Walnut Creek, Calif. (*94595) 204/K2
Walnut Creek, N.C. (†27530) 281/O4
Walnut Creek, Ohio (44687) 284/G4
Walnut Grove, Ala. (35990) 195/F2
Walnut Grove, Calif. (95690) 204/B9
Walnut Grove, Georgia (†30209) 217/E3
Walnut Grove, Ill. (†61470) 222/C3
Walnut Grove, Ky. (42563) 237/M6
Walnut Grove, Minn. (56180) 255/C6
Walnut Grove, Miss. (39189) 256/F5
Walnut Grove, Mo. (65770) 261/F8
Walnut Hill, Ark. (†71826) 202/C7
Walnut Hill, Fla. (32568) 212/B5
Walnut Hill, Ill. (62893) 222/E5
Walnut Hill, Maine (†04021) 243/C8
Walnutport, Pa. (18088) 294/L4
Walnut Ridge, Ark. (72476) 202/J1
Walnut Springs, Texas (76690) 303/G5
Walpole, Mass. (02081) 249/B8
Walpole○, Mass. (02081) 249/B8
Walpole○, N.H. (03608) 268/C5
Walpole (isl.), Ontario 177/B5
Walpole, Sask. 181/K6
Walpole, W. Australia 92/B6
Walrus (isl.), Alaska 196/E3
Walrus (isls.), Alaska 196/F3
Walsall, England 10/G4
Walsall, England 13/E5
Walsenburg, Colo. (81089) 208/K7
Walsh, Alberta 182/E5
Walsh, Colo. (81090) 208/P8
Walsh (co.), N. Dak. 282/P3
Walsh, Queensland 95/B3
Walshville, Ill. (62091) 222/D4
Walsingham, England 13/H5
Walsingham (cape), N.W.T. 162/K2
Walsingham (cape), N.W. Terrs. 187/M3
Walsrode, W. Germany 22/C2
Walston, Pa. (15781) 294/D4
Walstonburg, N.C. (27888) 281/O3
Walterboro, S.C. (29488) 296/F6
Walter F. George (dam), Ala. 195/H7
Walter F. George (res.), Ala. 195/H7
Walter F. George (dam), Georgia 217/B7
Walter F. George (res.), Georgia 217/B7
Walterhill, Tenn. (†37130) 237/J9
Walter Reed Army Med. Ctr., D.C. 245/E4
Walter Reed Army Med. Ctr Annex, Md. 245/E4
Walters, La. (71374) 238/G3
Walters, Minn. (56092) 255/E7
Walters, Okla. (73572) 288/K6
Walters Falls, Ontario 177/D3
Waltershausen, E. Germany 22/D3
Waltersville, Ky. (†40312) 237/N5
Waltersville, Miss. (†39180) 256/C6
Walterville, Oreg. (97489) 291/E3
Walthall (co.), Miss. 256/D8
Walthall, Miss. (39771) 256/F3
Waltham○, Maine (†04605) 243/G6
Waltham, Mass. (02154) 249/B6
Waltham, Minn. (55982) 255/F7
Waltham○, Vt. (†05491) 268/A3
Waltham Forest, England 13/H8
Waltham Forest, England 10/B5
Waltham Holy Cross, England 13/H7
Waltham Holy Cross, England 10/B5
Walthill, Nebr. (68067) 264/H2
Walthourville, Georgia (31333) 217/J7
Waltman, Wyo. (†82648) 319/E2
Walton (co.), Fla. 212/C6
Walton, Fla. (†33457) 212/F4
Walton (co.), Georgia 217/E3
Walton, Ind. (46994) 227/E3
Walton, Kansas (67151) 232/E3
Walton, Ky. (41094) 237/M3
Walton, Nebr. (68461) 264/H4
Walton, N.Y. (13856) 276/K6
Walton, Nova Scotia 168/E3
Walton, Ontario 177/C4
Walton, Oreg. (97490) 291/D3
Walton, W. Va. (25286) 312/D5
Walton and Weybridge, England 13/G8
Walton and Weybridge, England 10/B6
Walton Hills, Ohio (†44146) 284/J10
Walton-le-Dale, England 13/G1
Walton-le-Dale, England 10/F1
Waltonville, Ill. (62894) 222/D5
Waltreak, Ark. (†72833) 202/C4
Waltz, Mich. (†48164) 250/F6
Walum, N. Dak. (†58448) 282/O5
Walupt (lake), Wash. 310/D4
Walvis (bay), S. Africa 118/A4
Walvis Bay, S. Africa 2/K7
Walvis Bay, S. Africa 102/D7
Walvis Bay, S. Africa 118/A4
Walworth, N.Y. (14568) 276/F4
Walworth (co.), S. Dak. 298/J3
Walworth (co.), Wis. 317/J10
Walworth, Wis. (53184) 317/J10
Walzenhausen, Switzerland 39/J2
Wamac, Ill. (†62801) 222/D5
Wamba, Kenya 115/G3
Wamba, Nigeria 106/F7
Wamba, Zaire 115/E3
Wamego, Kansas (66547) 232/F2
Wamel, Netherlands 27/H5
Wamena, Indonesia 85/K6
Wamgumbaug (lake), Conn. 210/F1
Wami (riv.), Tanzania 115/G5
Wamic, Oreg. (97063) 291/F2

Westernport 467

Waver (Wavre), Belgium 27/F7
Waverley, Mass. (02179) 249/B6
Waverley, N. S. Wales 88/L4
Waverley, N.S. Wales 97/K3
Waverley, N. Zealand 100/E3
Waverley, Nova Scotia 168/E4
Waverley, Ontario 177/E3
Waverley, Victoria 97/J5
Waverley, Victoria 88/L7
Waverley Downs, N.S. Wales 97/B1
Waverly, Ala. (36879) 195/G5
Waverly, Fla. (33877) 212/E4
Waverly, Georgia (31565) 217/J8
Waverly, Ill. (62692) 222/D4
Waverly, Iowa (50677) 229/J3
Waverly, Kansas (66871) 232/G3
Waverly, Ky. (42462) 237/F5
Waverly, La. (71232) 238/H2
Waverly, Minn. (55390) 255/E5
Waverly, Mo. (64096) 261/E4
Waverly, Nebr. (68462) 264/H4
Waverly, N.Y. (14892) 276/G7
Waverly, Ohio (45690) 284/D7
Waverly, S. Dak. (57202) 298/R3
Waverly, Tenn. (37185) 237/F8
Waverly, Va. (23890) 307/O6
Waverly, Wash. (99039) 310/H3
Waverly, W. Va. (26184) 312/D4
Waverly Hall, Georgia (31831) 217/C5
Waves, N.C. (27982) 281/U3
Wavre, Belgium 27/F7
Wawa (riv.), Nicaragua 154/E3
Wawa, Ontario 175/C3
Wawa, Ontario 177/J5
Wawaka, Ind. (46794) 227/F2
Wawanesa, Manitoba 179/C5
Wawasee, Ind. (†46567) 227/F2
Wawasee (lake), Ind. 227/F2
Wawayanda (lake), N.J. 273/E1
Waweig, New Bruns. 170/C3
Wawina, Minn. (55794) 255/E3
Wawota, Sask. 181/J6
Wawpecong, Ind. (†46901) 227/F3
Wax, Ky. (42787) 237/J6
Waxahachie, Texas (75165) 303/H5
Waxhaw, N.C. (28173) 281/H5
Way, Miss. (†39046) 256/E5
Way (lake), W. Australia 88/C5
Way (lake), W. Australia 92/C4
Wayagamac (lake), Québec 172/E2
Wayan, Idaho (83285) 220/G7
Wayatinah, Tasmania 99/C4
Waycross, Ga. 188/K4
Waycross, Georgia (31501) 217/H8
Wayerton, New Bruns. 170/E1
Wayland, Iowa (52654) 229/K6
Wayland, Ky. (41666) 237/R6
Wayland○, Mass. (01778) 249/A7
Wayland, Mich. (49348) 250/D6
Wayland, Mo. (63472) 261/J2
Wayland, N.Y. (14572) 276/E5
Wayland, Ohio (44285) 284/H3
Waymansville, Ind. (†47201) 227/E6
Waymart, Pa. (18472) 294/M2
Wayne, Ala. (†36763) 195/C6
Wayne, Alberta 182/D4
Wayne (co.), Georgia 217/J7
Wayne (co.), Ill. 222/E5
Wayne, Ill. (60184) 222/E2
Wayne (co.), Ind. 227/G5
Wayne (co.), Iowa 229/G7
Wayne, Kansas (†66930) 232/E2
Wayne (co.), Ky. 237/M7
Wayne, Maine (04284) 243/D7
Wayne○, Maine (04284) 243/D7
Wayne (co.), Mich. 250/F6
Wayne, Mich. (48184) 250/F6
Wayne (co.), Miss. 256/G7
Wayne (co.), Mo. 261/L8
Wayne (co.), Nebr. 264/G2
Wayne, Nebr. (68787) 264/G2
Wayne○, N.J. (07470) 273/A1
Wayne (co.), N.Y. 276/F4
Wayne, N.Y. (14893) 276/F6
Wayne (co.), N.C. 281/N4
Wayne (co.), Ohio 284/G4
Wayne, Ohio (43466) 284/C3
Wayne, Okla. (73095) 288/M5
Wayne (co.), Pa. 294/M2
Wayne, Pa. (19087) 294/M6
Wayne (co.), Tenn. 237/F10
Wayne (co.), Utah 304/C5
Wayne (co.), W. Va. 312/B6
Wayne, W. Va. (25570) 312/B6
Wayne City, Ill. (62895) 222/E5
Waynesboro, Georgia (30830) 217/J4
Waynesboro, Miss. (39367) 256/G7
Waynesboro, Pa. (17268) 294/G6
Waynesboro, Tenn. (38485) 237/F10
Waynesboro (I.C.), Va. (22980) 307/K4
Waynesburg, Ky. (40489) 237/M6
Waynesburg, Ohio (44688) 284/H4
Waynesburg, Pa. (15370) 294/B6
Waynesfield, Ohio (45896) 284/C4
Waynesville, Georgia (31566) 217/J8
Waynesville, Ill. (61778) 222/D3
Waynesville, Ind. (†47201) 227/F6
Waynesville, Mo. (65583) 261/H7
Waynesville, N.C. (28786) 281/D4
Waynesville, Ohio (45068) 284/B6
Waynetown, Ind. (47990) 227/C4
Waynoka, Okla. (73860) 288/J1
Wayside, Georgia (†31032) 217/E4
Wayside, Kansas (†67301) 232/G4
Wayside, Miss. (38780) 256/C4
Wayside, Texas (79094) 303/C3
Wayside, Wis. (†54126) 317/L7
Wayzata, Minn. (55391) 255/G5
Wazirabad, Pakistan 59/K3
We (isl.), Indonesia 85/B4
Wé, New Caled. 86/H4
Weagamow Lake, Ontario 175/B2
Weakley (co.), Tenn. 237/D8
Weald, The (reg.), England 13/H6
Wear (riv.), England 13/F3
Wear (riv.), England 10/F3
Weare○, N.H. (03281) 268/D5
Weare P.O. (North Weare), N.H. (03281) 268/D5
Weatherby, Mo. (64497) 261/D3
Weatherby Lake, Mo. (†64152) 261/O5
Weatherford, Okla. (73096) 288/J4
Weatherford, Texas (76086) 303/G5
Weatherly, Pa. (18255) 294/L4
Weathers, Okla. (†74560) 288/P5
Weathersby, Miss. (†39114) 256/E7
Weatogue, Conn. (06089) 210/D1
Weaubleau, Mo. (65774) 261/F7
Weaver, Ala. (36277) 195/G3
Weaver (riv.), England 13/G2
Weaver (lake), Manitoba 179/F2
Weaver, Minn. (†55958) 255/G6
Weaver, New Bruns. 170/E2
Weaver, N. Dak. (†58352) 282/N2
Weaverville, Calif. (96093) 204/B3
Weaverville, N.C. (28787) 281/D3
Webb, Ala. (36376) 195/H8
Webb, Iowa (51366) 229/D3
Webb (lake), Maine 243/C6
Webb, Miss. (38966) 256/D3
Webb (bay), Newf. 166/B2
Webb, Sask. 181/C5
Webb (co.), Texas 303/E10
Webb, Texas (†76010) 303/F3
Webb City, Ark. (†72949) 202/C3
Webb City, Mo. (64870) 261/C8
Webb City, Okla. (74654) 288/N1
Webber, Kansas (66970) 232/D2
Webbers Falls, Okla. (74470) 288/R3
Webbers Falls (res.), Okla. 288/R3
Webberville, Mich. (48892) 250/E6
Webb Lake, Wis. (54892) 317/B3
Webbs Cross Roads, Ky. (42652) 237/L6
Webbville, Ky. (41180) 237/R4
Webbwood, Ontario 177/C1
Webequie, Ontario 175/C2
Weber (co.), Utah 304/B2
Weber (riv.), Utah 304/C3
Weber City, Va. (24251) 307/C7
Webi Shabelle (riv.), Somalia 115/H3
Webster, Fla. (33597) 212/D3
Webster (co.), Georgia 217/C6
Webster, Ind. (47392) 227/H5
Webster (co.), Iowa 229/E4
Webster, Iowa (52355) 229/J6
Webster (res.), Kansas 232/C2
Webster (co.), Ky. 237/F5
Webster, Ky. (40176) 237/J5
Webster (par.), La. 238/D1
Webster (brook), Maine 243/E3
Webster, Mass. (01570) 249/G4
Webster○, Mass. (01570) 249/G4
Webster (lake), Mass. 249/G4
Webster, Minn. (55088) 255/E6
Webster (co.), Miss. 256/F3
Webster (co.), Mo. 261/G8
Webster (co.), Nebr. 264/F4
Webster○, N.H. (†03301) 268/D5
Webster, N.Y. (14580) 276/F4
Webster, N.C. (28788) 281/C4
Webster, N. Dak. (58382) 282/N3
Webster, Pa. (15087) 294/C5
Webster, S. Dak. (57274) 298/P3
Webster, Texas (77598) 303/K2
Webster (co.), W. Va. 312/F6
Webster, Wis. (54893) 317/B4
Webster City, Iowa (50595) 229/F4
Webster Groves, Mo. (63119) 261/P3
Webster Mills, Pa. (†17233) 294/F6
Webster Springs, W. Va. (26288) 312/F6
Websterville, Vt. (05678) 268/B3
Wecota, S. Dak. (57480) 298/L3
Weda, Indonesia 85/H5
Wedau, Papua N.G. 85/C7
Weddel (isl.), 143/D7
Weddell (sea), Ant. 2/H10
Weddell (sea) 5/C16
Wedderburn, Oreg. (97491) 291/C5
Wedderburn, Victoria 97/B5
Weddington, Ark. (†72701) 202/B1
Wedel, W. Germany 22/C2
Wedgefield, S.C. (29168) 296/F4
Wedgeport, Nova Scotia 168/C5
Wedgeworth, Ala. (†36776) 195/C5
Wedowee, Ala. (36278) 195/H4
Weed, Calif. (96094) 204/C2
Weed, N. Mex. (88354) 274/D6
Weed (hills), Sask. 181/J5
Weed Heights, Nev. (89443) 266/B4
Weedon-Centre, Québec 172/F4
Weedsport, N.Y. (13166) 276/G4
Weedville, Pa. (15868) 294/F3
Weehawken○, N.J. (07087) 273/C2
Week (isls.), Chile 138/D10
Weekapaug, R.I. (02891) 249/G7
Weekes, Sask. 181/J3
Weeki Wachee, Fla. (†33512) 212/D3
Weeks, La. (†70569) 238/G7
Weeks, Nev. (†89447) 266/B3
Weeks (isl.), N. Zealand 100/B1
Weeksbury, Ky. (41667) 237/R6
Weeks Mills, Maine (04361) 243/E7
Weeksville, N.C. (27909) 281/S2
Weems, Va. (22576) 307/R5
Weeping Water, Nebr. (68463) 264/J4
Weert, Netherlands 27/H6
Weesatche, Texas (77993) 303/G9
Weesen, Switzerland 39/H2
Weesp, Netherlands 27/C5
Weethalle, N.S. Wales 97/D3
Wee Waa, N.S. Wales 97/E1
Wegdahl, Minn. (†56265) 255/C6
Weggis, Switzerland 39/F2
Węgorzewo, Poland 47/E1
Wegra-Flat Creek, Ala. (†35129) 195/D3
Węgrów, Poland 47/E2
Weichang, China 77/J3
Weida, E. Germany 22/D3
Weiden in der Oberpfalz, W. Germany 22/D4
Weidman, Mich. (48893) 250/D5
Weifang, China 77/J4
Weihai (Weihaiwei), China 77/K4
Wei He (riv.), China 77/G5
Weilburg, W. Germany 22/C3
Weilheim im Oberbayern, W. Germany 22/D5
Weimar, E. Germany 22/D3
Weimar, Texas (78962) 303/H8
Weinan, China 77/H5
Weiner, Ark. (72479) 202/J2
Weinert, Texas (76388) 303/E4
Weinfelden, Switzerland 39/H1
Weingarten, W. Germany 22/C5
Weinheim, W. Germany 22/C4
Weining, China 77/F6
Weinsberg, W. Germany 22/C4
Weipa, Queensland 88/G1
Weipa, Queensland 95/B2
Weippe, Idaho (83553) 220/C3
Weir (lake), Fla. 212/E2
Weir, Kansas (66781) 232/H4
Weir, Miss. (39772) 256/F4
Weirdale, Sask. 181/F2
Weirgor, Wis. (†54835) 317/D4
Weir River, Manitoba 179/J2
Weirsdale, Fla. (32695) 212/D3
Weirton, W. Va. (26062) 312/E2
Weirwood, Va. (23484) 307/S6
Weisburg, Ind. (†47041) 227/H6
Weiser, Idaho (83672) 220/B5
Weiser (riv.), Idaho 220/B5
Weishan, China 77/F6
Weismes (Waimes), Belgium 27/J8
Weiss (lake), Ala. 195/G2
Weiss (lake), Georgia 217/A2
Weissenburg im Bayern, W. Germany 22/D4
Weissenfels, E. Germany 22/D3
Weissensee, E. Germany 22/F3
Weissenstein (mts.), Switzerland 39/D2
Weisserstein (mt.), Belgium 27/J8
Weissert, Nebr. (68880) 264/E3
Weisshorn (mt.), Switzerland 39/J3
Weisshorn (mt.), Switzerland 39/E4
Weissmies (mt.), Switzerland 39/F4
Weisswasser, E. Germany 22/F3
Weitchpec, Calif. (†95546) 204/B2
Weitensfeld-Flattnitz, Austria 41/B3
Weitra, Austria 41/C2
Weixi, China 77/E6
Weixin, China 77/F6
Weiz, Austria 41/C3
Wejh, Saudi Arabia 59/C4
Wejh, Saudi Arabia 54/E7
Wejherowo, Poland 47/D1
Welaka, Fla. (32093) 212/E2
Welbekend, S. Africa 118/J6
Welch, Okla. (74369) 288/R1
Welch, Texas (79377) 303/B5
Welch, W. Va. (24801) 312/C8
Welches, Oreg. (†97067) 291/E2
Welchman Hall, Barbados 161/B8
Welchville, Maine (†04270) 243/C7
Welcome, La. (†70086) 238/L3
Welcome, Md. (20693) 245/K7
Welcome, Minn. (56181) 255/D7
Welcome, N.C. (27374) 281/J3
Welcome, Ontario 177/F4
Welcome All, Georgia (†30304) 217/J2
Weld (co.), Colo. 208/L1
Weld○, Maine (04285) 243/C6
Weld (range), W. Australia 92/B4
Welda, Kansas (66091) 232/G3
Weldon, Ark. (72177) 202/H3
Weldon, Calif. (93283) 204/G8
Weldon, Ill. (61882) 222/E3
Weldon, Iowa (50264) 229/F7
Weldon, New Bruns. 170/F3
Weldon, N.C. (27890) 281/O2
Weldon, Sask. 181/F2
Weldon, Texas (75863) 303/J6
Weldona, Colo. (80653) 208/M2
Weldon Spring Heights, Mo. (†63301) 261/M2
Weleetka, Okla. (74880) 288/O4
Welford, Queensland 95/C5
Welkom, S. Africa 102/E7
Welkom, S. Africa 118/D5
Welland (riv.), England 13/G5
Welland (riv.), England 10/F4
Welland, Ontario 177/E5
Welland (canal), Ontario 177/E5
Wellandport, Ontario 177/E4
Wellborn, Fla. (32094) 212/D1
Wellersburg, Pa. (15564) 294/E6
Wellesley (isls.), Australia 87/D7
Wellesley○, Mass. (02181) 249/B7
Wellesley, Ontario 177/D4
Wellesley (isls.), Queensland 88/F3
Wellesley (isls.), Queensland 95/A3
Wellesley Hills, Mass. (02181) 249/B7
Wellfleet○, Mass. (02667) 249/O5
Wellfleet (harb.), Mass. 249/O5
Wellfleet, Nebr. (69170) 264/D4
Wellford, S.C. (29385) 296/C2
Wellin, Belgium 27/G8
Welling, Alberta 182/D5
Welling, Okla. (74471) 288/S3
Wellingborough, England 13/G5
Wellingborough, England 10/F4
Wellington, Ala. (36279) 195/G3
Wellington (isl.), Chile 120/B7
Wellington (isl.), Chile 138/D8
Wellington, Colo. (80549) 208/K1
Wellington, England 13/D7
Wellington, England 10/E5
Wellington, Ill. (60973) 222/F3
Wellington, Kansas (67152) 232/E4
Wellington, Ky. (†40201) 237/K2
Wellington, Ky. (40387) 237/O5
Wellington○, Maine (04990) 243/D5
Wellington, Mo. (64097) 261/E4
Wellington, Nev. (89444) 266/B4
Wellington, N.S. Wales 97/E3
Wellington (cap.), N. Zealand 2/T8
Wellington (cap.), N. Zealand 87/H10
Wellington (cap.), N. Zealand 100/A3
Wellington (bay), N.W. Terrs. 187/H3
Wellington (chan.), N.W.T. 162/G1
Wellington (chan.), N.W. Terrs. 187/J2
Wellington, Nova Scotia 168/E4
Wellington, Ohio (44090) 284/F3
Wellington (county), Ontario 177/D4
Wellington, Ontario 177/G4
Wellington, Pr. Edward I. 168/D2
Wellington, S. Africa 118/B6
Wellington, Texas (79095) 303/D3
Wellington, Utah (84542) 304/D4
Wellington (lake), Victoria 97/D6
Wellington, Va. (†22308) 307/T3
Wellman, Iowa (52356) 229/K6
Wellman (lake), Manitoba 179/B3
Wellman, Texas (79378) 303/B5
Wellpinit, Wash. (99040) 310/G3
Wells, Br. Col. 184/G3
Wells, England 13/E6
Wells, England 10/E5
Wells (co.), Ind. 227/G3
Wells, Kansas (67488) 232/E2
Wells, Maine (04090) 243/B9
Wells○, Maine (04090) 243/B9
Wells, Mich. (49894) 250/B3
Wells, Minn. (56097) 255/E7
Wells, Nev. (89835) 266/G1
Wells, N.Y. (12190) 276/M4
Wells (co.), N. Dak. 282/L4
Wells, Texas (75976) 303/J6
Wells○, Vt. (05774) 268/A5
Wells (riv.), Vt. 268/C3
Wells (dam), Wash. 310/F3
Wells (lake), W. Australia 88/C5
Wells (lake), W. Australia 92/C4
Wells Beach, Maine (04090) 243/B9
Wellsboro, Ind. (†46382) 227/D1
Wellsboro, Pa. (16901) 294/H2
Wells Bridge, N.Y. (13859) 276/K6
Wellsburg, Iowa (50680) 229/H4
Wellsburg, N.Y. (14894) 276/G6
Wellsburg, N. Dak. (†58341) 282/L4
Wellsburg, W. Va. (26070) 312/E2
Wellsford, N. Zealand 100/E2
Wells Gray Prov. Park, Br. Col. 184/H4
Wells-next-the-Sea, England 13/H5
Wells-next-the-Sea, England 10/G4
Wells River, Vt. (05081) 268/C3
Wellston, Mich. (49689) 250/D4
Wellston, Mo. (63112) 261/R2
Wellston, Ohio (45692) 284/F7
Wellston, Okla. (74881) 288/M3
Wellsville, Kansas (66092) 232/G3
Wellsville, Mo. (63384) 261/K4
Wellsville, N.Y. (14895) 276/E6
Wellsville, Ohio (43968) 284/J4
Wellsville, Pa. (17365) 294/J5
Wellsville, Utah (84339) 304/C2
Wellton, Ariz. (85356) 198/A6
Wellwood, Manitoba 179/C4
Wels, Austria 41/C2
Welsford, New Bruns. 170/D3
Welsford, Nova Scotia 168/E3
Welsh, La. (70591) 238/E6
Welshfield, Ohio (†44021) 284/H3
Welshpool, New Bruns. 170/D4
Welshpool, Wales 10/E4
Welshpool, Wales 13/D5
Welton, Iowa (52774) 229/M5
Welty, Okla. (74882) 288/O3
Welwyn, England 13/H7
Welwyn, England 10/F5
Welwyn, Sask. 181/K5
Wem, England 13/E5
Wembere (riv.), Tanzania 115/F4
Wembley, Alberta 182/A2
Wemmel, Belgium 27/B9
Wemyss Bay, Scotland 15/A2
Wenamu (riv.), Guyana 131/A2
Wenas (creek), Wash. 310/E4
Wenasoga, Miss. (†38834) 256/G1
Wenatchee, Wash. 188/B1
Wenatchee, Wash. (98801) 310/E3
Wenatchee (lake), Wash. 310/E3
Wenatchee (mts.), Wash. 310/E3
Wenatchee (riv.), Wash. 310/E3
Wenchi, Ghana 106/D7
Wenchow (Wenzhou), China 77/J6
Wendel, Calif. (96136) 204/E3
Wendel, W. Va. (26450) 312/F4
Wendell, Idaho (83355) 220/D7
Wendell○, Mass. (01379) 249/E2
Wendell, Minn. (56590) 255/B4
Wendell, N.H. (03783) 268/C5
Wendell, N.C. (27591) 281/N3
Wendell Depot, Mass. (01380) 249/E2
Wenden, Ariz. (85357) 198/B5
Wendeng, China 77/K4
Wendover, England 13/G7
Wendover, Ontario 177/J2
Wendover, Utah (84083) 304/A3
Wendover, Wyo. (†82214) 319/H3
Wendron, England 13/B7
Wendte, S. Dak. (†57532) 298/H5
Wenham○, Mass. (01984) 249/L2
Wenling, China 77/K6
Wenlock (riv.), Queensland 88/G2
Wenman (isl.), Ecuador 128/B8
Wenona, Georgia (†31015) 217/E7
Wenona, Ill. (61377) 222/E2
Wenona, Md. (21870) 245/P8
Wenona, N.C. (†27860) 281/R3
Wenonah, Ill. (†62075) 222/D4
Wenonah, N.J. (08090) 273/C4
Wenquan, Qinghai, China 77/D5
Wenquan, Xinjiang Uygur, China 77/B3
Wenshan, China 77/F7
Wensum (riv.), England 13/J5
Wentworth, Mo. (64873) 261/D8
Wentworth○, N.H. (03282) 268/D4
Wentworth (lake), N.H. 268/E4
Wentworth, N.S. Wales 97/B4
Wentworth, N.C. (27375) 281/K2
Wentworth, Nova Scotia 168/E3
Wentworth, S. Dak. (57075) 298/R6
Wentworth, Wis. (54894) 317/C2
Wentworths Location○, N.H. (†03579) 268/E2
Wentzville, Mo. (63385) 261/L5
Wen Xian, China 77/G5
Wenzhou (Wenchow), China 77/J6
Wenzhou, China 54/N7
Weogufka, Ala. (35183) 195/F4
Weohyakapka (lake), Fla. 212/E4
Weott, Calif. (95571) 204/A3
Wepawaug (riv.), Conn. 210/C3
Wequetequock, Conn. (†02891) 210/H3
Werdau, E. Germany 22/E3
Werder, E. Germany 22/E2
Werner Lake, Ontario 175/A2
Wernersville, Pa. (19565) 294/K5
Wernigerode, E. Germany 22/D3
Werra (riv.), E. Germany 22/D3
Werra (riv.), W. Germany 22/D3
Werribee, Victoria 88/G7
Werrimull, Victoria 97/A4
Werris Creek, N.S. Wales 97/F2
Wertheim, W. Germany 22/C4
Wervik, Belgium 27/B7
Wesco, Mo. (65586) 261/K7
Wesel, W. Germany 22/B3
Weser (riv.), Germany 7/E3
Weser (riv.), W. Germany 22/C2
Weskan, Kansas (67762) 232/A3
Weslaco, Texas (78596) 303/F11
Weslemkoon (lake), Ontario 177/G2
Wesley, Ark. (72773) 202/C1
Wesley, Dominica 161/F5
Wesley, Georgia (†30401) 217/H6
Wesley, Iowa (50483) 229/E2
Wesley, Maine (04686) 243/H6
Wesley○, Maine (04686) 243/H6
Wesley Vale, Tasmania 99/C3
Wesleyville, Newf. 166/D4
Wesleyville, Pa. (16510) 294/C1
Wes-Rand, S. Africa 118/G6
Wessel (isls.), Australia 87/D7
Wessel (cape), North. Terr. 88/F2
Wessel (cape), North. Terr. 93/E1
Wessel (isls.), North. Terr. 88/F2
Wessel (isls.), North. Terr. 93/E1
Wessington, S. Dak. (57381) 298/M5
Wessington Springs, S. Dak. (57382) 298/M5
Wesson, Ark. (†71749) 202/E7
Wesson, Miss. (39191) 256/D7
West (riv.), Conn. 210/D3
West (riv.), Conn. 210/E3
West, Iowa (52357) 229/J5
West (bay), La. 238/M8
West (isl.), Mass. 249/L6
West (riv.), Mass. 249/H4
West, Miss. (39192) 256/E4
West (isls.), New Bruns. 170/D4
West (cape), N. Zealand 100/A6
West (bay), Nova Scotia 168/G3
West (pt.), Nova Scotia 168/H5
West (riv.), Nova Scotia 168/F3
West (pt.), Pr. Edward I. 168/D2
West (pt.), Tasmania 99/A2
West, Texas (76691) 303/G6
West (bay), Texas 303/K3
West (riv.), Vt. 268/B5
West Acton, Mass. (01720) 249/H3
West Alexander, Pa. (15376) 294/B5
West Alexandria, Ohio (45381) 284/A6
West Allis, Wis. (53214) 317/L1
West Alton, Mo. (63386) 261/M5
West Alton, N.H. (†03246) 268/E4
West Amboy, N.Y. (†13493) 276/J4
West Arichat, Nova Scotia 168/G3
West Ashford, Conn. (†06251) 210/G1
West Aspetuck (riv.), Conn. 210/B2
West Athens, Maine (†04912) 243/D6
West Augusta, Va. (24485) 307/K4
West Avon, Conn. (†06001) 210/D1
West Baden Springs, Ind. (47469) 227/D7
West Baines (riv.), North. Terr. 93/A4
West Baldwin, Maine (04091) 243/B8
Westbank, Br. Col. 184/H5
WEST BANK 59/C3
WEST BANK 65/C3
West Bank (reg.), 65/C3
West Baraboo, Wis. (†53913) 317/G9
West Barnet, Vt. (05870) 268/C3
West Barns, Scotland 15/F5
West Barnstable, Mass. (02668) 249/N6
West Barrington, R.I. (†02806) 249/J5
West Bath○, Maine (†04530) 243/D8
West Baton Rouge (par.), La. 238/H6
West Bay, Fla. (32437) 212/C6
West Bay, Nova Scotia 168/G3
West Bay Road, Nova Scotia 168/G3
West Bend, Iowa (50597) 229/D3
Westbend, Ky. (40388) 237/N5
West Bend, Sask. 181/H4
West Bend, Wis. (53095) 317/K9
West Bengal (state), India 68/F4
West Berkshire, Vt. (†05450) 268/B2
West Berlin, Mass. (†01503) 249/H3
West Berlin, N.J. (08091) 273/D4
West Bethel, Maine (04286) 243/B7
West Blocton, Ala. (35184) 195/D4
West Bloomfield, Wis. (†54983) 317/J7
Westboro, Mo. (64498) 261/B2
Westboro, Ohio (†45148) 284/C7
Westboro, Wis. (54490) 317/F5
Westborough, Mass. (01581) 249/H3
Westborough○, Mass. (01581) 249/H3
West Bountiful, Utah (†84087) 304/B3
Westbourne, Manitoba 179/D4
Westbourne, Tenn. (†37766) 237/O7
West Boxford, Mass. (01885) 249/K2
West Boylston○, Mass. (01583) 249/G3
West Braintree, Vt. (†05669) 268/B4
West Branch (res.), Conn. 210/C1
West Branch, Iowa (52358) 229/L5
West Branch, Farmington (riv.), Mass. 249/B4
West Branch, Mich. (48661) 250/E4
West Branch, Rocky (riv.), Ohio 284/G10
West Brattleboro, Vt. (05301) 268/B6
West Brentwood, N.H. (†03848) 268/E6
West Brewster, Mass. (†02631) 249/O5
Westbridge, Br. Col. 184/H5
West Bridgewater○, Mass. (02379) 249/K4
West Bridgewater, Vt. (†05034) 268/B4
West Bridgford, England 13/F5
West Bromwich, England 13/F5
West Bromwich, England 10/G3
Westbrook, Conn. (06498) 210/F3
Westbrook○, Conn. (06498) 210/F3
Westbrook, Maine (04092) 243/C8
Westbrook, Minn. (56183) 255/C6
West Brook, Nova Scotia 168/D3
Westbrook, Texas (79565) 303/C5
West Brookfield, Mass. (01585) 249/F4
West Brookfield○, Mass. (01585) 249/F4
West Brooklyn, Ill. (61378) 222/D2
West Brooksville, Maine (†04617) 243/F7
West Brownsville, Pa. (15417) 294/C5
West Buechel, Ky. (†40218) 237/K2
West Burke, Vt. (05871) 268/C2
West Burlington, Iowa (52655) 229/L7
West Burra (isl.), Scotland 15/G2
Westbury, England 10/E5
Westbury, England 13/E6
Westbury, N.Y. (11590) 276/R7
Westbury, Tasmania 99/C3
West Buxton, Maine (04093) 243/B8
Westby, Mont. (59275) 262/M2
Westby, Wis. (54667) 317/E8
West Calder, Scotland 15/C2
West Caldwell, N.J. (07006) 273/A2
West Campton, N.H. (03228) 268/D4
West Canaan, N.H. (03741) 268/C4
West Cape May, N.J. (†08204) 273/D6
West Carroll (par.), La. 238/H1
West Carrollton, Ohio (45449) 284/B6
West Carthage, N.Y. (†13619) 276/J3
West Charleston, Vt. (05872) 268/C2
West Chatham, Mass. (02669) 249/O6
West Chazy, N.Y. (12992) 276/N1
West Chelmsford, Mass. (†01824) 249/J2
Westchester, Conn. (†06474) 210/F2
Westchester, Ill. (60153) 222/B5
West Chester, Iowa (52359) 229/K6
Westchester (co.), N.Y. 276/N8
West Chester, Ohio (45069) 284/C9
West Chester, Pa. (19380) 294/L6
West Chesterfield, Mass. (01084) 249/C3
Westchester Station, Nova Scotia 168/E3
West Chicago, Ill. (60185) 222/A5
West Chop (pt.), Mass. 249/M7
West City, Ill. (†62812) 222/E5
Westcliffe, Colo. (81252) 208/H6
West College Corner, Ind. (†47353) 227/H5
West Columbia, S.C. (29169) 296/E4
West Columbia, Texas (77486) 303/J8
West Columbia, W. Va. (25287) 312/B5
West Concord, Mass. (†01742) 249/A6
West Concord, Minn. (55985) 255/F6
West Corinth, Vt. (†05039) 268/C3
West Cornwall, Conn. (06796) 210/B1
West Cornwall, Vt. (†05753) 268/A4
West Cote Blanche (bay), La. 238/G7
Westcott, Alberta 182/C4
Westcott Cove (bay), Conn. 210/A4
West Covina, Calif. (*91790) 204/D10
Westcreek, Colo. (†80135) 208/J4
West Creek, N.J. (08092) 273/E4
West Crossett, Ark. (†71635) 202/F7
West Cummington, Mass. (†01026) 249/B3
West Danville, Vt. (05873) 268/C3
West Dean, England 13/E6
West Demerara-Essequibo Coast (dist.), Guyana 131/B2
West Dennis, Mass. (02670) 249/O6
West Deptford○, N.J. (†08086) 273/B3
West Des Moines, Iowa (50318) 229/F5
West Dover, Nova Scotia 168/E4
West Dover, Vt. (05356) 268/B6
West Dublin, Nova Scotia 168/D4
West Dudley, Mass. (†01550) 249/F4
West Dummerston, Vt. (05357) 268/B6
West Dundee (Dundee), Ill. (†60118) 222/E1
West Eau Gallie, Fla. (32935) 212/F3
West Elizabeth, Pa. (15088) 294/C5
West Elkton, Ohio (45070) 284/A6
West Elmira, N.Y. (†14901) 276/G6
West Eminence, Mo. (†65466) 261/J8
Westend, Calif. (†93562) 204/H8
West End, N.C. (27376) 281/K4
West End, Sask. 181/J5
West End, Virgin Is. (Br.) 161/C4
West End-Cobb Town, Ala. (†36201) 195/G3
Westend Saltpond (lag.), Virgin Is. (U.S.) 161/E4
West Enfield, Maine (04493) 243/F5
West Epping, N.H. (†03042) 268/E5
Wester Eems (chan.), Netherlands 27/K1
Westerland, W. Germany 22/C1
Westerlo, Belgium 27/F6
Westerlo, N.Y. (12193) 276/M6
Westerly, R.I. (02891) 249/G7
Westerly○, R.I. (02891) 249/G7
Western (prov.), Kenya 115/G3
Western, Nebr. (68464) 264/G4
Western (head), Nova Scotia 168/D5
Western Australia 88/B5
WESTERN AUSTRALIA 92
Western Australia (state), Australia 87/C8
Western Bay, Newf. 166/D2
Western Channel (str.), Japan 81/D6
Western Dvina (riv.), U.S.S.R. 53/C2
Western Dvina (riv.), U.S.S.R. 52/C3
Western Dvina (riv.), U.S.S.R. 48/C4
Western Ghats (mts.), India 68/C5
Western Grove, Ark. (72685) 202/D1
Western Institute, Tenn. (38074) 237/C10
Western Isles (islands area), Scotland 15/A3
Westernport, Md. (21562) 245/B3

Willow Springs 469

White City, Sask. 181/G5
Whiteclay, Nebr. (69365) 264/B2
White Cliffs, N.S. Wales 97/B2
White Cloud, Ind. (†47112) 227/E8
White Cloud, Kansas (66094) 232/G2
White Cloud, Mich. (49349) 250/D5
White Coomb (mt.), Scotland 15/E5
White Cottage, Ohio (43791) 284/F6
Whitecourt, Alberta 182/C2
White Deer, Pa. (17887) 294/J3
White Deer, Texas (79097) 303/C2
White Earth, Minn. (56591) 255/C3
White Earth, N. Dak. (58794) 282/E3
White Earth (riv.), N. Dak. 282/E3
White Earth Ind. Res., Minn. 255/C3
White Elster (riv.), E. Germany 22/E3
Whiteface (riv.), Minn. 255/F3
Whiteface, N.H. (†03259) 268/E4
Whiteface (mt.), N.H. 268/E4
Whiteface (mt.), N.Y. 276/N2
Whiteface, Texas (79379) 303/B4
White Face (mt.), Vt. 268/B2
Whitefield, Maine (04362) 243/D7
Whitefield○, Maine (04362) 243/D7
Whitefield, N.H. (03598) 268/D3
Whitefield○, N.H. (03598) 268/D3
Whitefield, Okla. (74472) 288/R4
Whitefish (bay), Mich. 250/E2
Whitefish (pt.), Mich. 250/E2
Whitefish (riv.), Mich. 250/C2
Whitefish (lake), Minn. 255/D4
Whitefish, Mont. (59937) 262/B2
Whitefish (lake), Mont. 262/B2
Whitefish Falls, Ontario 177/C1
Whitefish Point, Mich. (†49768) 250/E2
Whiteflat, Texas (†79234) 303/D3
Whiteford, Md. (21160) 245/N2
White Fox, Sask. 181/H2
White Fox (riv.), Sask. 181/G2
Whitegate, Ireland 17/E8
White Gull (creek), Sask. 181/G2
White Hall, Ala. (†36040) 195/E6
Whitehall, Ark. (†72432) 202/J3
White Hall, Ark. (71602) 202/F5
White Hall, Georgia (†30601) 217/F3
White Hall, Ill. (62092) 222/C4
Whitehall, Ind. (†47401) 227/D6
Whitehall, La. (†70462) 238/M2
White Hall, Md. (21161) 245/M2
Whitehall, Mich. (49461) 250/C5
Whitehall, Mont. (59759) 262/D5
Whitehall, N.Y. (12887) 276/O3
Whitehall, Ohio (43213) 284/E6
Whitehall, Pa. (†15234) 294/B7
Whitehall, Scotland 15/F1
White Hall, S.C. (†29945) 296/F6
White Hall, Va. (22987) 307/L4
Whitehall, Wis. (54773) 317/D7
White Handkerchief (cape), Newf. 166/B2
Whitehaven, England 13/D3
Whitehaven, England 10/E3
Whitehaven, Md. (21873) 245/P7
Whitehaven (harb.), Nova Scotia 168/G3
White Haven, Pa. (18661) 294/L3
White Head, New Bruns. 170/D4
White Head (isl.), New Bruns. 170/D4
Whitehead, N. Ireland 17/K2
Whitehead, Nova Scotia 168/G3
White Heath, Ill. (61884) 222/E3
Whitehills, Scotland 15/F3
White Horn, Tenn. (†37711) 237/R8
Whitehorse, Canada 4/C16
Whitehorse, Canada 2/C3
Whitehorse, S. Dak. (57661) 298/H3
Whitehorse (cap.), Yukon 187/E3
Whitehorse (cap.), Yukon 162/C3
Whitehorse (cap.), Yukon 146/E3
White Horse Lake, N. Mex. (87073) 274/B3
Whitehouse, Ky. (41269) 237/R5
Whitehouse, N.J. (08888) 273/D2
Whitehouse, Ohio (43571) 284/C2
White House, Tenn. (37188) 237/H8
White House Station, N.J. (08889) 273/D2
White Iron (lake), Minn. 255/G3
White Knob (mts.), Idaho 220/E6
White Lake, N.C. (28337) 281/M5
White Lake, Ontario 177/H2
White Lake, S. Dak. (57383) 298/M6
White Lake, Wis. (54491) 317/J5
Whiteland, Ind. (46184) 227/E5
Whitelaw, Alberta 182/A1
Whitelaw, Wis. (54247) 317/L7
Whiteman A.F.B., Mo. 261/E5
Whitemark, Tasmania 99/D2
White Marsh, Md. (21162) 245/N3
White Meadow Lake, N.J. (†07866) 273/D2
White Mills, Ky. (42788) 237/J5
White Mills, Pa. (18473) 294/M2
White Mountain, Alaska (99784) 196/F2
White Mountains Nat'l Rec. Area, Alaska 196/J1
Whitemouth, Manitoba 179/G5
Whitemouth (lake), Manitoba 179/G5
Whitemouth (riv.), Manitoba 179/G5
Whitemud (riv.), Alberta 182/A1
Whiten (head), Scotland 15/D2
White Nile (riv.) 2/L5
White Nile (riv.) 102/F4
White Nile (prov.), Sudan 111/F5
White Nile (riv.), Sudan 111/F5
White Nile (riv.), Sudan 59/B7
White Oak (lake), Ark. 202/D6
White Oak, Georgia (31568) 217/J8
White Oak, Md. (†20901) 245/F3
Whiteoak, Mo. (63880) 261/M10
White Oak, N.C. (28399) 281/M5
Whiteoak (swamp), N.C. 281/P5
Whiteoak (creek), Ohio 284/C7
White Oak, Okla. (†74301) 288/R1
White Oak, Pa. (15131) 294/C7
White Oak, S.C. (29176) 296/E3
Whiteoak (creek), Tenn. 237/F8
White Oak, Texas (75693) 303/K5
White Oaks, Conn. (†06488) 210/C2
White Oaks, N. Mex. (†88301) 274/D5
White Owl, S. Dak. (57792) 298/E4
White Partridge (lake), Ontario 177/G2
White Pass, Wash. (†98937) 310/D4
White Pigeon, Mich. (49099) 250/D7
White Pine, Mich. (49971) 250/F1
Whitepine, Mont. (†59874) 262/A3
White Pine (co.), Nev. 266/F3
White Pine (range), Nev. 266/F3
White Pine, Tenn. (37890) 237/P8
White Pines, Calif. (†95223) 204/E5
White Plains, Ala. (†36862) 195/G3
White Plains, Georgia (30678) 217/F4
White Plains, Ky. (42464) 237/G6
White Plains, Md. (20695) 245/L6
White Plains, N.Y. (*10601) 276/P6
White Plains, N.C. (27031) 281/H2
White Plains, Va. (23893) 307/N7
White Pond, S.C. (29854) 296/D5
White Post, Va. (22663) 307/M2
White Quartz Hill, North. Terr. 93/D7
White Rapids, New Bruns. 170/E2
Whiteriver, Ariz. (85941) 198/E5
White River, Ont. 162/H6
White River, Ontario 175/C3
White River, Ontario 177/J5
White River, S. Dak. (57579) 298/H6
White River (lake), Texas 303/C4
White River Junction, Vt. (05001) 268/C4
White Rock, Br. Col. 184/K3
White Rock (creek), Kansas 232/D2
White Rock, N. Mex. (87544) 274/C3
Whiterock, N.C. (†28753) 281/D3
White Rock, S.C. (29177) 296/E3
White Rock, S. Dak. (†57260) 298/R2
White Rock (creek), Texas 303/G2
Whiterocks, Utah (84085) 304/E3
White Russian S.S.R., U.S.S.R. 7/G3
White Russian S.S.R., U.S.S.R. 52/C4
White Russian S.S.R., U.S.S.R. 48/C4
Whites, Wash. (†98541) 310/B3
Whitesail (lake), Br. Col. 184/D3
White Salmon, Wash. (98672) 310/D5
White Salmon (riv.), Wash. 310/D4
White Sands (des.), N. Mex. 274/C5
White Sands Missile Range, N. Mex. (88002) 274/C6
White Sands Missile Range, N. Mex. 274/C5
White Sands Nat'l Mon., N. Mex. 274/C6
Whitesbog, N.J. (†08015) 273/E4
Whitesboro, N.J. (08252) 273/D5
Whitesboro, N.Y. (13492) 276/K4
Whitesboro, Okla. (74577) 288/S5
Whitesboro, Texas (76273) 303/H4
Whitesburg, Georgia (30185) 217/B4
Whitesburg, Ky. (41858) 237/R6
Whitesburg, Tenn. (37891) 237/P8
Whites Chapel, Ala. (†35094) 195/F3
Whites City, N. Mex. (88268) 274/E6
Whites Creek, W. Va. (†25530) 312/A6
White Settlement, Texas (76108) 303/E2
Whiteshell Prov. Park, Manitoba 179/G4
White Shield, N. Dak. (†58534) 282/G4
Whiteshore (lake), Sask. 181/C3
Whiteside (chan.), Chile 138/E10
Whiteside (co.), Ill. 222/D2
Whiteside, Mo. (63387) 261/K4
Whiteside, Tenn. (37396) 237/K10
Whites Lake, Nova Scotia 168/E4
Whiteson, Oreg. (†97128) 291/D2
White Springs, Fla. (32096) 212/D1
Whitestone, Georgia (30186) 217/C1
White Stone, Va. (22578) 307/R5
Whitestown, Ind. (46075) 227/E5
White Sulphur Springs, Georgia (†31822) 217/C5
White Sulphur Springs, La. (†71371) 238/F3
White Sulphur Springs, Mont. (59645) 262/E4
White Sulphur Springs, W. Va. (24986) 312/F7
Whitesville, Georgia (†31833) 217/C5
Whitesville, Ky. (42378) 237/H5
Whitesville, Mo. (†64480) 261/C2
Whitesville, N.J. (†08701) 273/E3
Whitesville, N.Y. (14897) 276/E6
Whitesville, W. Va. (25209) 312/C6
Whiteswan (lakes), Sask. 181/F1
White Swan, Wash. (98952) 310/E4
Whitetail, Mont. (59276) 262/L2
Whitetop, Va. (24292) 307/E7
Whiteville, La. (71376) 238/F5
Whiteville, N.C. (28472) 281/M6
Whiteville, Tenn. (38075) 237/C10
White Volta (riv.) 102/B4
White Volta (riv.), Ghana 106/D6
White Volta (riv.), Upper Volta 106/D6
Whitewater, Colo. (81527) 208/C5
Whitewater (bay), Fla. 212/F6
Whitewater, Ind. (†47374) 227/H5
Whitewater (riv.), Ind. 227/H6
Whitewater, Kansas (67154) 232/E4
Whitewater, Manitoba 179/B5
Whitewater (lake), Manitoba 179/B5
Whitewater, Mo. (63785) 261/N8
Whitewater, Mont. (59544) 262/J2
Whitewater, Wis. (53190) 317/J10
Whitewater Baldy (mt.), N. Mex. 274/A5
Whitewood, Sask. 181/J5
Whitewood, S. Dak. (57793) 298/B5
Whitewood (creek), S. Dak. 298/B4
Whitewood, Va. (24657) 307/E6
Whitewright, Texas (75491) 303/H4
Whitfield, Ala. (†36925) 195/B6
Whitfield (co.), Georgia 217/B1
Whitfield, Miss. (39193) 256/E6
Whitford, Alberta 182/D3
Whitharral, Texas (79380) 303/B4
Whithorn, Scotland 10/D3
Whithorn, Scotland 15/D6
Whitianga, N. Zealand 100/E2
Whiting, Ind. (46394) 227/C1
Whiting, Iowa (51063) 229/A4
Whiting, Kansas (66552) 232/G2
Whiting○, Maine (04691) 243/J6
Whiting, Mo. (†63845) 261/O9
Whiting, N.J. (08759) 273/E4
Whiting○, Vt. (05778) 268/A4
Whiting, Wis. (†54481) 317/H7
Whiting Bay, Scotland 15/C5
Whiting Field Naval Air Sta., Fla. 212/B6
Whitingham○, Vt. (05361) 268/B6
Whitinsville, Mass. (01588) 249/H4
Whitkow, Sask. 181/D3
Whitla, Alberta 182/E5
Whitlash, Mont. (59545) 262/E2
Whitley (co.), Ind. 227/F2
Whitley (co.), Ky. 237/N7
Whitley Bay, England 13/J3
Whitley City, Ky. (42653) 237/N7
Whitleyville, Tenn. (38588) 237/K8
Whitlock, Tenn. (†38242) 237/E8
Whitman○, Mass. (02382) 249/L4
Whitman (riv.), Mass. 249/G2
Whitman, Nebr. (69366) 264/C2
Whitman, N. Dak. (58283) 282/O3
Whitman (co.), Wash. 310/H4
Whitman Mission Nat'l Hist. Site, Wash. 310/G4
Whitmer, W. Va. (26296) 312/G5
Whitmire, S.C. (29178) 296/D3
Whitmore, Calif. (96096) 204/D3
Whitmore Lake, Mich. (48189) 250/F6
Whitmore Village, Hawaii (†96786) 218/E1
Whitnel, N.C. (28645) 281/F3
Whitney (riv.), Calif. 188/C3
Whitney (mt.), Calif. 204/G7
Whitney (lake), Conn. 210/D3
Whitney, Nebr. (69367) 264/A2
Whitney, New Bruns. 170/E2
Whitney, Ontario 177/F2
Whitney, Pa. (15693) 294/D5
Whitney, S.C. (29303) 296/D1
Whitney, Texas (76692) 303/G6
Whitney Point, N.Y. (13862) 276/J6
Whitney Point (lake), N.Y. 276/J6
Whitneyville, Conn. (06517) 210/D3
Whitneyville○, Maine (04692) 243/H6
Whitsett, Texas (78075) 303/F9
Whitsunday (isl.), Queensland 88/H4
Whitsunday (isl.), Queensland 95/D4
Whitt, Texas (76090) 303/G5
Whittaker, Mich. (48190) 250/F6
Whittemore, Iowa (50598) 229/E2
Whittemore, Mich. (48770) 250/F4
Whitten, Iowa (50269) 229/H4
Whittier, Alaska (99693) 196/C1
Whittier, Calif. (*90601) 204/D11
Whittier, Iowa (52360) 229/K4
Whittier, N.C. (28789) 281/C4
Whittle (cape), Québec 174/F2
Whittlesea, Victoria 97/C5
Whittlesey, England 13/G5
Whittlesey, Wis. (†54451) 317/F5
Whitton, N.S. Wales 97/C4
Whitwell, Tenn. (37397) 237/K10
Wholdaia (lake), N.W. Terrs. 187/H3
Why, Ariz. (85321) 198/C6
Whyalla, Australia 87/D9
Whyalla, S. Australia 94/E5
Whycocomagh, Nova Scotia 168/G3
Whyjonta, N.S. Wales 97/B1
Wiarton, Ontario 177/C3
Wiau (lake), Alberta 182/E2
Wiawso, Ghana 106/D7
Wiay (isl.), Scotland 15/A3
Wibaux (co.), Mont. 262/M4
Wibaux, Mont. (59353) 262/M3
Wichabai, Guyana 131/B4
Wichita, Kans. 188/G3
Wichita (co.), Kansas 232/A3
Wichita, Kansas 146/J6
Wichita, Kansas (*67201) 232/E4
Wichita (mts.), Okla. 288/J5
Wichita (co.), Texas 303/F3
Wichita (riv.), Texas 303/F4
Wichita Falls, Texas 146/H6
Wichita Falls, Texas (*76301) 303/F4
Wichita Falls, Texas 188/G4
Wick, Iowa (†50240) 229/F6
Wick, Scotland 10/E1
Wick, Scotland 15/E2
Wick (riv.), Scotland 15/E2
Wick, W. Va. (26185) 312/E4
Wickahoney (creek), Idaho 220/C7
Wickatunk, N.J. (07765) 273/E3
Wicked (pt.), Manitoba 179/D2
Wickenburg, Ariz. (85358) 198/C5
Wickepin, W. Australia 92/B2
Wickersham, Wash. (†98284) 310/C2
Wickes, Ark. (71973) 202/B5
Wickes, Mont. (†59638) 262/D4
Wickett, Texas (79788) 303/A6
Wickham, New Bruns. 170/D3
Wickham, Québec 172/E4
Wickham (cape), Tasmania 99/A1
Wickham, W. Australia 92/B3
Wickiup (res.), Oreg. 291/F4
Wickliffe, Ky. (42087) 237/C7
Wickliffe, Ohio (44092) 284/J9
Wicklow (co.), Ireland 17/J5
Wicklow, Ireland 10/C4
Wicklow, Ireland 17/K6
Wicklow (head), Ireland 17/K6
Wicklow (head), Ireland 10/D4
Wicklow (mts.), Ireland 17/J6
Wicklow, New Bruns. 170/C2
Wicksburg, Ala. (†36352) 195/G8
Wicomico (co.), Md. 245/R7
Wicomico, Md. (†20611) 245/L7
Wicomico (riv.), Md. 245/R7
Wicomico (riv.), Md. 245/L7
Wicomico Church, Va. (22579) 307/R5
Wiconisco, Pa. (17097) 294/J4
Wide (chan.), Chile 138/D8
Wide (bay), Papua N.G. 86/C2
Wide (bay), Queensland 95/E5
Wideman, Ark. (72585) 202/G1
Widemouth, W. Va. (†24736) 312/D8
Widen, W. Va. (25211) 312/E6
Widener, Ark. (72394) 202/J3
Widewater, Alberta 182/C2
Widgiemooltha, W. Australia 88/C6
Widgiemooltha, W. Australia 92/C5
Widnes, England 10/F2
Widnes, England 13/G2
Widnoon, Pa. (16261) 294/D4
Więcbork, Poland 47/C2
Wiederkehr Village, Ark. 202/C3
Wiehl, W. Germany 22/B3
Wiek, E. Germany 22/E1
Wieliczka, Poland 47/E3
Wieluń, Poland 47/D3
Wien (Vienna) (cap.), Austria 41/D2
Wiener Neustadt, Austria 41/D3
Wieprz (riv.), Poland 47/F3
Wierden, Netherlands 27/K4
Wieringermeer Polder, Netherlands 27/G3
Wierum, Netherlands 27/H2
Wieruszów, Poland 47/D3
Wiesbaden, W. Germany 7/E3
Wiesbaden, W. Germany 22/B3
Wiese (isl.), U.S.S.R. 4/B6
Wiese (isl.), U.S.S.R. 48/H2
Wiesmoor, W. Germany 22/B2
Wigan, England 13/G2
Wigan, England 10/G2
Wiggins, Colo. (80654) 208/L2
Wiggins, Miss. (39577) 256/F9
Wiggins, S.C. (†29446) 296/F6
Wight (isl.), England 13/F7
Wight (isl.), England 10/F5
Wigston, England 13/F5
Wigton, England 13/D3
Wigtown, Scotland 10/D3
Wigtown, Scotland 15/D6
Wigtown (trad. co.), Scot. 15/A5
Wigtown (bay), Scotland 10/D3
Wigtown (bay), Scotland 15/D6
Wijhe, Netherlands 27/J4
Wijk bij Duurstede, Netherlands 27/G5
Wijk en Aalburg, Netherlands 27/F5
Wikel, W. Va. (†24945) 312/E7
Wikieup, Ariz. (85360) 198/B4
Wikwemikong, Ontario 177/C2
Wil, Switzerland 39/H2
Wilawana, Pa. (†18840) 294/J2
Wilbarger (co.), Texas 303/E3
Wilber, Nebr. (68465) 264/G4
Wilberforce, Ontario 177/F3
Wilbert, Minn. (†56031) 255/D7
Wilbraham, Mass. (01095) 249/E4
Wilbraham○, Mass. (01095) 249/E4
Wilbur, Ind. (†46151) 227/D5
Wilbur, Ky. (†41124) 237/R5
Wilbur, Oreg. (97494) 291/D4
Wilbur, Wash. (99185) 310/G3
Wilbur, W. Va. (26459) 312/E4
Wilbur Park, Mo. (†63101) 261/P3
Wilburton, Kansas (†67950) 232/A4
Wilburton, Okla. (74578) 288/R5
Wilcannia, N. S. Wales 88/G6
Wilcannia, N.S. Wales 97/B2
Wilchingen, Switzerland 39/F1
Wilcox (co.), Ala. 195/D7
Wilcox, Fla. (†32693) 212/D2
Wilcox (co.), Georgia 217/F7
Wilcox, Mo. (†64468) 261/C2
Wilcox, Nebr. (68982) 264/E4
Wilcox, Pa. (15870) 294/E2
Wilcox, Sask. 181/G5
Wilczek Land (isl.), U.S.S.R. 4/B6
Wilczek Land (isl.), U.S.S.R. 48/G1
Wild Ammonoosuc (riv.), N.H. 268/D3
Wildbad im Schwarzwald, W. Germany 22/C4
Wildcat (creek), Ind. 227/E4
Wild Cat, Ky. (40998) 237/O6
Wild Cherry, Ark. (†72576) 202/F1
Wild Cove, Newf. 166/C3
Wilder, Idaho (83676) 220/A6
Wilder, Minn. (56184) 255/C7
Wilder (dam), N.H. 268/C4
Wilder, Tenn. (38589) 237/L8
Wilder, Vt. (05088) 268/C4
Wilder (dam), Vt. 268/C4
Wilderness, Va. (†22553) 307/N4
Wilders, Ky. (†41071) 237/S2
Wildersville, Tenn. (38388) 237/E9
Wilderswil, Switzerland 39/E3
Wildervank, Netherlands 27/K2
Wilderville, Oreg. (97543) 291/D5
Wildeshausen, W. Germany 22/C2
Wild Goose, Ontario 177/H5
Wild Goose, Ontario 175/C3
Wildhaus, Switzerland 39/H2
Wildhay (riv.), Alberta 182/B3
Wildhorn (mt.), Switzerland 39/D4
Wild Horse, Colo. (80862) 208/N5
Wild Horse (res.), Nev. 266/E1
Wildhorse (creek), Okla. 288/L5
Wildie, Ky. (40492) 237/N6
Wildomar, Calif. (92395) 204/H10
Wildon, Austria 41/C3
Wildorado, Texas (79098) 303/B2
Wild Rice (lake), Minn. 255/F4
Wild Rice (riv.), Minn. 255/B3
Wild Rice, N. Dak. (†58047) 282/S6
Wild Rice (riv.), N. Dak. 282/R7
Wildrose, N. Dak. (58795) 282/D2
Wild Rose, Wis. (54984) 317/H7
Wildspitze (mt.), Austria 41/A3
Wildstrubel (mt.), Switzerland 39/E4
Wildsville, La. (71377) 238/G3
Wildwood, Alberta 182/C3
Wildwood, Fla. (32785) 212/D3
Wildwood, Minn. (†56643) 255/E3
Wildwood, N.J. (08260) 273/D6
Wildwood Crest, N.J. (08260) 273/D6
Wileville, Nova Scotia 168/D4
Wiley, Colo. (81092) 208/O6
Wiley, Georgia (30581) 217/F1
Wiley (creek), Oreg. 291/E3
Wiley City, Wash. (98906) 310/E4
Wiley Ford, W. Va. (26767) 312/J3
Wileyville, W. Va. (26186) 312/E3
Wilfred, Ind. (†47879) 227/C6
Wilhelm (mt.), Papua N.G. 85/B7
Wilhelm II Coast (reg.) 5/C5
Wilhelmina (canal), Netherlands 27/G6
Wilhelmina (mts.), Suriname 131/C4
Wilhelm-Pieck-Stadt, E. Germany 22/F3
Wilhelmsburg, Austria 41/C2
Wilhelmshaven, W. Germany 22/B2
Wilkes (co.), Georgia 217/G3
Wilkes (co.), N.C. 281/G2
Wilkes (lake), Ontario 177/F1
Wilkes-Barre, Pa. 188/L2
Wilkes-Barre, Pa. (*18701) 294/F7
Wilkesboro, N.C. (28697) 281/G2
Wilkes Land (reg.), Ant. 2/R10
Wilkes Land (reg.) 5/B7
Wilkeson, Wash. (98396) 310/D3
Wilkesville, Ohio (45695) 284/F7
Wilke, Sask. 181/C3
Wilkin (co.), Minn. 255/B4
Wilkins, Nev. (†89835) 266/G1
Wilkinsburg, Pa. (15221) 294/C7
Wilkinson (co.), Georgia 217/F5
Wilkinson, Ind. (46186) 227/F5
Wilkinson, Minn. (†56633) 255/D3
Wilkinson (co.), Miss. 256/B8
Wilkinson, Miss. (†39669) 256/B8
Wilkinson (lakes), S. Australia 94/C3
Wilkinson, W. Va. (25653) 312/B7
Wilkinsonville, Mass. (01590) 249/G4
Will (co.), Ill. 222/F2
Willacoochee, Georgia (31650) 217/G8
Willacy (co.), Texas 303/G11
Willamette (riv.), Oreg. 291/A3
Willamette, Middle Fork (riv.), Oreg. 291/E4
Willamina, Oreg. (97396) 291/D2
Willandra Billabong (creek), N.S. Wales 97/C3
Willapa, Wash. (†98577) 310/B4
Willapa (bay), Wash. 310/A4
Willard, Kansas (†66601) 232/G2
Willard, Mich. (†48611) 250/E5
Willard, Mo. (65781) 261/F8
Willard, Mont. (59354) 262/M4
Willard, N. Mex. (87063) 274/D4
Willard, N.Y. (14588) 276/G5
Willard, N.C. (28478) 281/O5
Willard, Ohio (44890) 284/E3
Willard, Utah (84340) 304/C2
Willard, Wis. (54493) 317/E6
Willards, Md. (21874) 245/S7
Willaumez (pen.), Papua N.G. 86/B2
Willaura, Victoria 97/B5
Willcox, Ariz. (85643) 198/F6
Willebroek, Belgium 27/E6
Willems (canal), Netherlands 27/G5
Willemstad, Netherlands 27/F5
Willemstad (cap.), Neth. Ant. 161/F9
Willemstad (cap.), Neth. Ant. 156/E4
Willen, Manitoba 179/A4
Willernie, Minn. (55090) 255/G5
Willeroo, North. Terr. 93/B3
Willette, Tenn. (†37150) 237/K8
Willey, Iowa (†51401) 229/D5
Willey House, N.H. (†03812) 268/E3
William (riv.), Sask. 181/L2
William Creek, S. Australia 94/E3
William H. Taft Nat'l Hist. Site, Ohio 284/C10
William L. Springer (lake), Ill. 222/E4
Williams, Ariz. (86046) 198/C3
Williams, Calif. (95987) 204/C4
Williams, Ind. (47470) 227/D7
Williams, Iowa (50271) 229/F3
Williams, Minn. (56686) 255/D2
Williams (co.), N. Dak. 282/C3
Williams (co.), Ohio 284/A2
Williams, Okla. (†74932) 288/T4
Williams, Oreg. (97544) 291/D5
Williams, S.C. (29493) 296/F5
Williams, W. Australia 92/B2
Williams (riv.), W. Va. 312/F6
Williams A.F.B., Ariz. 198/D5
Williams Bay, Wis. (53191) 317/J10
Williamsboro, N.C. (†27536) 281/M2
Williamsburg, Colo. (†81226) 208/J6
Williamsburg, Iowa (52361) 229/J5
Williamsburg, Kansas (66095) 232/G3
Williamsburg, Ky. (40769) 237/N7
Williamsburg, Md. (21674) 245/P6
Williamsburg○, Mass. (01096) 249/C3
Williamsburg, Mich. (49690) 250/D4
Williamsburg, Mo. (63388) 261/J5
Williamsburg, New Bruns. 170/D2
Williamsburg, N. Mex. (87942) 274/B5
Williamsburg, Ohio (45176) 284/B7
Williamsburg, Ontario 177/J3
Williamsburg, Pa. (16693) 294/F5
Williamsburg (co.), S.C. 296/H4
Williamsburg (I.C.), Va. (23185) 307/P6
Williamsburg, W. Va. (24991) 312/F7
Williamsfield, Ill. (61489) 222/C3
Williamsfield, Jamaica 158/H6
Williamsfield, Ohio (44093) 284/J2
Williamsford, Ontario 177/D3
Williamsford, Tasmania 99/B3
Williams Fork, Colorado (riv.), Colo. 208/G3
Williams Fork, Yampa (riv.), Colo. 208/E2
Williams Harbour, Newf. 166/C3
Williams Lake, Br. Col. 162/D5
Williams Lake, Br. Col. 184/F4
Williamson, Georgia (30292) 217/D4
Williamson (co.), Ill. 222/E6
Williamson, Ill. (†62088) 222/D5
Williamson, Iowa (50272) 229/G6
Williamson, N.Y. (14589) 276/F4
Williamson (riv.), Oreg. 291/E5
Williamson (co.), Tenn. 237/H9
Williamson (co.), Texas 303/G7
Williamson, W. Va. (25661) 312/B7
Williamsport, Ind. (47993) 227/C4
Williamsport, Ky. (41271) 237/R5
Williamsport, Md. (21795) 245/G2
Williamsport, Newf. 166/C3
Williamsport, Ohio (43164) 284/D6
Williamsport, Pa. 188/L2
Williamsport, Pa. (17701) 294/H3
Williamsport, Tenn. (38487) 237/G9
Williamston, Mich. (48895) 250/E6
Williamston, N.C. (27892) 281/R3
Williamston, S.C. (29697) 296/B2
Williamstown, Kansas (†66073) 232/G2
Williamstown, Ky. (41097) 237/M3
Williamstown, Mass. (01267) 249/B2
Williamstown○, Mass. (01267) 249/B2
Williamstown, Mo. (63473) 261/J2
Williamstown, New Bruns. 170/C2
Williamstown, N.J. (08094) 273/D4
Williamstown, N.Y. (13493) 276/J4
Williamstown, Ontario 177/K2
Williamstown, Pa. (17098) 294/J4
Williamstown, S. Australia 94/C7
Williamstown○, Vt. (05679) 268/B3
Williamstown, Victoria 97/H5
Williamstown, Victoria 88/K7
Williamstown, W. Va. (26187) 312/C4
Williamsville, Ill. (62693) 222/D4
Williamsville, Miss. (†39090) 256/F4
Williamsville, Mo. (63977) 261/L9
Williamsville, N.Y. (14221) 276/C5
Williamsville, Vt. (05362) 268/B6
Williamsville, Va. (24487) 307/J4
Willies (range), Queensland 95/C6
Williford, Ark. (72482) 202/H1
Willimantic, Conn. (06226) 210/G2
Willimantic (riv.), Conn. 210/F1
Willimantic, Maine (†04443) 243/E5
Willimantic○, Maine (†04443) 243/E5
Willingboro○, N.J. (08046) 273/D3
Willingdon, Alberta 182/E3
Willington○, Conn. (†06279) 210/F1
Willington, S.C. (29852) 296/C4
Willis (islets), Australia 87/F7
Willis (isls.), Coral Sea Is. Terr. 88/J3
Willis, Kansas (66435) 232/G2
Willis, Mich. (48191) 250/F6
Willis, Okla. (†73439) 288/N7
Willis, Texas (77378) 303/J7
Willis, Va. (24380) 307/H7
Willis (riv.), Va. 307/M5
Willisau, Switzerland 39/F2
Willisburg, Ky. (40078) 237/L5
Williston (lake), Br. Col. 162/D4
Williston (lake), Br. Col. 184/F2
Williston, Fla. (32696) 212/D2
Williston, N. Dak. 188/F1
Williston, N. Dak. (58801) 282/C3
Williston, S.C. (29853) 296/E5
Williston, Tenn. (38076) 237/C10
Williston○, Vt. (05495) 268/A3
Williston Park, N.Y. (11596) 276/R7
Willisville, Ark. (71864) 202/D6
Willisville, Ill. (62997) 222/D6
Willisville, Ontario 177/C1
Willis Wharf, Va. (23486) 307/S5
Williton, England 13/D6
Willits, Calif. (95490) 204/B4
Willmar, Minn. (56201) 255/C5
Willmar, Sask. 181/J6
Willmathsville, Mo. (†63546) 261/G2
Willmore Wilderness Prov. Park, Alberta 182/A3
Willoughby (bay), Ant. & Bar. 161/E11
Willoughby, N. S. Wales 88/K3
Willoughby, N.S. Wales 97/J3
Willoughby, Ohio (44094) 284/J8
Willoughby, Vt. (†05822) 268/C2
Willoughby (lake), Vt. 268/D2
Willoughby Hills, Ohio (†44094) 284/J9
Willow, Alaska (99688) 196/B1
Willow, Ark. (†72084) 202/E5
Willow (creek), Calif. 204/E3
Willow (creek), Idaho 220/G6
Willow (riv.), Minn. 255/E4
Willow (creek), Mont. 262/E2
Willow, Okla. (73673) 288/G4
Willow (creek), Oreg. 291/H2
Willow (creek), Oreg. 291/K3
Willow (creek), S. Dak. 298/C4
Willow (creek), Utah 304/E4
Willow (res.), Wis. 317/F4
Willow (creek), Wyo. 319/F2
Willow (lake), Wyo. 319/C2
Willow Bend, W. Va. (24992) 312/F7
Willow Branch, Ind. (46187) 227/F5
Willowbrook, Ill. (†60521) 222/B6
Willowbrook, Kansas (†67501) 232/D3
Willowbrook, Sask. 181/J4
Willow Bunch, Sask. 181/F6
Willow Bunch (lake), Sask. 181/F6
Willow City, N. Dak. (58384) 282/K2
Willow City, Texas (78675) 303/F7
Willow Creek, Calif. (95573) 204/B3
Willow Creek, Mont. (59760) 262/E5
Willow Creek (res.), Mont. 262/E5
Willowcreek, Oreg. (†97918) 291/K3
Willow Creek, Sask. 181/B6
Willowdale, Oreg. (†97741) 291/G3
Willow Grove, Del. (†19934) 245/R4
Willow Grove, New Bruns. 170/E3
Willow Grove, Pa. (19090) 294/M5
Willow Hill, Ill. (62480) 222/E5
Willow Hill, Pa. (17271) 294/G5
Willowick, Ohio (44094) 284/J8
Willow Island, Nebr. (69171) 264/D4
Willowlake (riv.), N.W. Terrs. 187/F3
Willow Lake, S. Dak. (57278) 298/O4
Willowmore, S. Africa 118/C6
Willowra, North. Terr. 93/C6
Willow Ranch, Calif. (96108) 204/E2
Willow River, Br. Col. 184/F3
Willow River, Minn. (55795) 255/F4
Willows, Calif. (95988) 204/C4
Willows, Md. (†20732) 245/M6
Willows, Sask. 181/F6
Willow Springs, Ill. (60480) 222/B6

472 Yamatotakada

Yamatotakada, Japan 81/J8
Yamba, N.S. Wales 97/G1
Yambah, North. Terr. 93/C7
Yambio, Sudan 111/E7
Yambio, Sudan 102/E4
Yambol, Bulgaria 45/H4
Yambou (head), St. Vin. & Grens. 161/A9
Yambrasbamba, Peru 128/D5
Yamdena (isl.), Indonesia 85/J7
Yamethin, Burma 72/C2
Yamhill (co.), Oreg. 291/D2
Yamhill, Oreg. (97148) 291/D2
Y'Ami (isl.), Philippines 82/B2
Yamma Yamma (lake), Queensland 88/G5
Yamma Yamma (lake), Queensland 95/B5
Yampa, Colo. (80483) 208/F2
Yampa (riv.), Colo. 208/B2
Yamparaéz, Bolivia 136/C6
Yampi Sound, W. Australia 88/C3
Yampi Sound, W. Australia 92/C2
Yamsk, U.S.S.R. 48/Q4
Yamun, West Bank 65/C3
Yamuna (Jumna) (riv.), Pakistan 68/E3
Yamzho Yumco (lake), China 77/C6
Yan, Nigeria 106/G7
Yana, U.S.S.R. 54/P3
Yana (riv.), U.S.S.R. 4/C3
Yana (riv.), U.S.S.R. 48/O3
Yanac, Victoria 97/A5
Yanacachi, Bolivia 136/B5
Yanahuanca, Peru 128/D8
Yanam, India 68/E5
Yan'an (Yenan), China 77/G4
Yanaoca, Peru 128/G10
Yanaul, U.S.S.R. 52/J3
Yancannia, N.S. Wales 97/B2
Yancey, Ky. (†40831) 237/P7
Yancey (co.), N.C. 281/E3
Yanceyville, N.C. (27379) 281/L2
Yancheng, China 77/K5
Yanchi, China 77/G4
Yanco, N.S. Wales 97/D4
Yandé (isl.), New Caled. 86/F4
Yandeyarra Aboriginal Reserve, W. Australia 88/B4
Yandina, Solomon Is. 86/D3
Yandoon, Burma 72/B3
Yanfolila, Mali 106/C6
Yanga, Mexico 150/P2
Yangambi, Zaire 115/D3
Yangambi, Zaire 102/E4
Yangcheng, China 77/H4
Yangchow (Yangzhou), China 77/J5
Yangchüan (Yangquan), China 77/H4
Yangchun, China 77/H7
Yangdŏk, N. Korea 81/C4
Yanggao, China 77/H3
Yanggu, S. Korea 81/C4
Yangjiang, China 77/H7
Yangquan (Yangchüan), China 77/H4
Yangshan, China 77/H7
Yang Sin, Chu (mt.), Vietnam 72/F4
Yangtze (riv.), China 54/N6
Yangtze (riv.), China 2/Q4
Yangtze (Chang Jiang) (riv.), China 77/K5
Yangyang, S. Korea 81/D4
Yangzhou (Yangchow), China 77/J5
Yanhuqu, China 77/B5
Yanji (Yenki), China 77/L3
Yankee Fork, Salmon (riv.), Idaho 220/D5
Yankee Lake, Ohio (†44403) 284/J3
Yankeetown, Fla. (32698) 212/D2
Yankeetown, Ind. (†47630) 227/C9
Yanko (creek), N.S. Wales 97/C4
Yankton, S. Dak. 188/G2
Yankton (co.), S. Dak. 298/P7
Yankton, S. Dak. (57078) 298/P8
Yanqi, China 77/C3
Yanrey, W. Australia 92/A3
Yantabulla, N.S. Wales 97/C1
Yantai (Chefoo), China 77/K4
Yantai, China 54/O6
Yantara, N.S. Wales 97/B1
Yantara (lake), N.S. Wales 97/B1
Yantic, Conn. (06389) 210/G2
Yantic (riv.), Conn. 210/G2
Yantis, Texas (75497) 303/J5
Yantley, Ala. (36924) 195/B6
Yanush, Okla. (†74574) 288/R5
Yao, Japan 81/J8
Yaoundé (cap.), Cameroon 2/K5
Yaoundé (cap.), Cameroon 102/D4
Yaoundé (cap.), Cameroon 115/B3
Yap (isl.), Micronesia 87/D5
Yapacani (riv.), Bolivia 136/C5
Yapei, Ghana 106/D7
Yapen (isl.), Indonesia 85/K6
Yapen (str.), Indonesia 85/K6
Yapraklı, Turkey 63/E2
Yaque del Norte (riv.), Dom. Rep. 158/D5
Yaque del Sur (riv.), Dom. Rep. 158/D6
Yaqui, Mexico 150/D3
Yaqui (riv.), Mexico 146/H7
Yaqui (riv.), Mexico 150/D2
Yaquina, Oreg. (†97365) 291/C3
Yara, Cuba 158/H4
Yaracuy (state), Venezuela 124/D2
Yaraka, Queensland 95/C5
Yaraligöz Daği (mt.), Turkey 59/B1
Yaraligöz Daği (mt.), Turkey 63/E2
Yaransk, U.S.S.R. 52/G3
Yarbo, Ala. (†36558) 195/B7
Yarbo, Sask. 181/K5
Yarboutenda, Senegal 106/B6
Yarda, Chad 111/C4
Yardley, Pa. (19067) 294/N5
Yardville, N.J. (08620) 273/D3
Yare (riv.), England 13/J5
Yare (riv.), England 10/G4
Yarega, U.S.S.R. 52/H2
Yaretas de Vizcachas, Cerro (mt.), Chile 138/G3
Yarí, Colombia 126/D7
Yarí (riv.), Colombia 126/D8
Yarim, Yemen Arab Rep. 59/D7
Yaritagua, Venezuela 124/D2
Yarkand (Shache), China 77/A4
Yarkand (riv.), China 54/K6
Yarkant He (riv.), China 77/A4
Yarker, Ontario 177/H3
Yarle (lakes), S. Australia 94/B4
Yarmouth, Iowa (52660) 229/L6
Yarmouth, Maine (04096) 243/C8
Yarmouth◯, Maine (04096) 243/C8
Yarmouth◯, Mass. (02675) 249/O6
Yarmouth, N.S. 162/K7
Yarmouth (co.), Nova Scotia 168/C5
Yarmouth, Nova Scotia 168/B5
Yarmouth (sound), Nova Scotia 168/B5
Yarmouth Port, Mass. (02675) 249/N6
Yarmuk (riv.), Israel 65/D2
Yarnell, Ariz. (85362) 198/C4
Yaroslavl', U.S.S.R. 7/H3
Yaroslavl', U.S.S.R. 48/D4
Yaroslavl', U.S.S.R. 52/E3
Yarqon (riv.), Israel 65/B3
Yarra (riv.), Victoria 97/C5
Yarra (riv.), Victoria 88/L6
Yarram, Victoria 97/D6
Yarrawonga, Victoria 97/C5
Yarrow, Br. Col. 184/M3
Yarrow, Mo. (†63501) 261/G2
Yarrow (riv.), Scotland 15/E5
Yarrowitch, N.S. Wales 97/F2
Yarrow Point, Wash. (†98004) 310/B2
Yartsevo, U.S.S.R. 48/J4
Yartsevo, U.S.S.R. 52/D3
Yarumal, Colombia 126/C4
Yaruu, Mongolia 77/E2
Yas (isl.), U.A.E. 59/F5
Yasawa Group (isls.), Fiji 86/P10
Yásica Abajo, Dom. Rep. 158/E5
Yasin, Pakistan 59/K2
Yasin, Pakistan 68/C1
Yasnyy, U.S.S.R. 52/J4
Yasothon, Thailand 72/D4
Yass, N.S. Wales 97/E4
Yasuj, Iran 66/G5
Yasun (cape), Turkey 63/G2
Yata (riv.), Bolivia 136/C3
Yatabe, Japan 81/P2
Yatağan, Turkey 63/C4
Yataity, Paraguay 144/C5
Yateley, England 13/G8
Yates (dam), Ala. 195/G5
Yates (co.), N.Y. 276/F5
Yates Center, Kansas (66783) 232/G4
Yates City, Ill. (61572) 222/C3
Yatesville, Georgia (31097) 217/D5
Yathkyed (lake), N.W.T. 162/F3
Yathkyed (lake), N.W. Terrs. 187/J3
Yatina, Bolivia 136/C7
Yatsushiro, Japan 81/E7
Yatta, West Bank 65/C5
Yatton, England 13/E6
Yatua (riv.), Venezuela 124/E7
Yauca, Peru 128/E10
Yauco, P. Rico 161/B2
Yauco, P. Rico 156/F1
Yauco (lake), P. Rico 161/B2
Yauli, Peru 128/D8
Yaúna Moloca, Colombia 126/E8
Yaupi, Ecuador 128/D4
Yaupon Beach, N.C. (†28461) 281/N7
Yauri, Peru 128/G10
Yautepec, Mexico 150/L2
Yauyos, Peru 128/E9
Yava, Ariz. (†86301) 198/C4
Yavapai (co.), Ariz. 198/C4
Yavapai Ind. Res., Ariz. 198/C4
Yavaraté, Colombia 126/F7
Yavari (riv.) 120/B3
Yavari (riv.), Peru 128/G5
Yavaros, Mexico 150/E3
Yavero (riv.), Peru 128/F9
Yavita, Venezuela 124/E6
Yavne, Israel 65/B4
Yavne'el, Israel 65/D2
Yawata, Japan 81/J7
Yawatahama, Japan 81/F7
Yawkey, W. Va. (25573) 312/C6
Yawri (bay), S. Leone 106/B7
Ya Xian, China 77/G8
Yaxley, England 13/G5
Yayladağı, Turkey 63/F5
Yazd (governorate), Iran 66/J5
Yazd (Yezd), Iran 66/J5
Yazd, Iran 59/F3
Yazd, Iran 54/G6
Yazdan, Iran 66/M4
Yazdan, Iran 59/H3
Yazd-e Khvasat, Iran 66/H5
Yazoo (co.), Miss. 265/D5
Yazoo (riv.), Miss. 188/H4
Yazoo (riv.), Miss. 256/C5
Yazoo City, Miss. (39194) 256/D5
Ybbs an der Donau, Austria 41/C2
Ybycuí, Paraguay 144/B5
Ybytymí, Paraguay 144/B5
Yding Skovhøj (mt.), Denmark 21/C6
Ye, Burma 72/C4
Yea, Victoria 97/C5
Yeaddiss, Ky. (41777) 237/P6
Yeadon, Pa. (19050) 294/N7
Yeager, Okla. (†74848) 288/O4
Yeagertown, Pa. (17099) 294/G4
Yebbi-Bou, Chad 111/C3
Yecheng, China 77/A4
Yecla, Spain 33/F3
Yécora, Mexico 150/E2
Yecuatla, Mexico 150/P1
Yeddo, Ind. (†47952) 227/C4
Yeeda River, W. Australia 92/C2
Yeelirrie, W. Australia 92/C4
Yefremov, U.S.S.R. 52/E4
Yegros, Paraguay 144/D5
Yeguas (pt.), P. Rico 161/F3
Yehualtepec, Mexico 150/O2
Yehud, Israel 65/B3
Yei, Sudan 111/F7
Yelabuga, U.S.S.R. 52/H3
Yelan', U.S.S.R. 52/F4
Yelcho (lake), Chile 138/E4
Yelets, U.S.S.R. 7/H3
Yelets, U.S.S.R. 48/D4
Yelets, U.S.S.R. 52/E4
Yelimané, Mali 106/B5
Yelizavety (cape), U.S.S.R. 54/R4
Yelizavety (cape), U.S.S.R. 48/P4
Yelizovo, U.S.S.R. 48/Q4
Yell (co.), Ark. 202/D3
Yell (isl.), Scotland 15/G2
Yell (isl.), Scotland 10/G1
Yell (sound), Scotland 15/G2
Yellamanchili, India 68/E5
Yelleq, Jebel (mt.), Egypt 59/B3
Yellow (sea) 54/O6
Yellow (Huang He) (riv.), China 77/J4
Yellow (sea), China 77/K4
Yellow (creek), Colo. 208/C3
Yellow (riv.), Fla. 212/B6
Yellow (riv.), Ind. 227/D2
Yellow (brook), N.J. 273/E3
Yellow (sea), N. Korea 81/B6
Yellow (creek), Ohio 284/J4
Yellow (sea), S. Korea 81/B6
Yellow (creek), Tenn. 237/F8
Yellow (creek), W. Va. 312/E1
Yellow (lake), Wis. 317/B4
Yellow (riv.), Wis. 317/F7
Yellow Bluff, Ala. (†36769) 195/C7
Yellowbud, Ohio (†45601) 284/D7
Yellowcreek, N.C. (†28771) 281/A4
Yellow Creek, Sask. 181/F3
Yellow Dog (riv.), Mich. 250/B2
Yellow Grass, Sask. 181/H6
Yellowhead (pass), Alberta 182/A3
Yellowhead (pass), Br. Col. 184/H4
Yellow Jacket, Colo. (81335) 208/B7
Yellowknife, Canada 4/C15
Yellowknife, Canada 2/D2
Yellowknife, N.W.T. 146/G3
Yellowknife (cap.), N.W.T. 162/E3
Yellowknife (cap.), N.W. Terrs. 187/G3
Yellowknife (riv.), N.W. Terrs. 187/G3
Yellow Medicine (co.), Minn. 255/B6
Yellow Pine, Ala. (36588) 195/B8
Yellow Pine, Idaho (83677) 220/C4
Yellow Pine, La. (†71039) 238/D2
Yellow Spring, W. Va. (26865) 312/J4
Yellow Springs, Md. (†21701) 245/H3
Yellow Springs, Ohio (45387) 284/C6
Yellowstone (riv.) 188/E1
Yellowstone (co.), Mont. 262/H4
Yellowstone (riv.), Mont. 262/M3
Yellowstone (riv.), N. Dak. 282/B4
Yellowstone (riv.), U.S. 146/H5
Yellowstone (lake), Wyo. 188/E2
Yellowstone (lake), Wyo. 319/B1
Yellowstone (riv.), Wyo. 319/B1
Yellowstone Nat'l Park, Idaho 262/F6
Yellowstone Nat'l Park, Mont. 262/F6
Yellowstone Nat'l Park, Wyo. (82190) 31/B1
Yellowstone Nat'l Park, Wyo. 188/E2
Yellowstone Nat'l Park, Wyo. 319/B1
Yellville, Ark. (72687) 202/E1
Yelm, Wash. (98597) 310/C4
Yelverton (bay), N.W. Terrs. 187/K1
Yelwa, Nigeria 106/F6
Yemassee, S.C. (29945) 296/F6
Yemen, People's Dem. Rep. of 2/M5
Yemen, People's Democratic Republic of 54/F8
YEMEN, PEOPLE'S DEM. REPUBLIC OF, 59/E7
YEMEN ARAB REP. 59/D7
Yemen Arab Republic 2/M5
Yemen Arab Republic 54/F8
Yemetsk, U.S.S.R. 52/F2
Yenakiyevo, U.S.S.R. 52/E5
Yenan (Yan'an), China 77/G4
Yenangyaung, Burma 72/B2
Yen Bai, Vietnam 72/E2
Yenbo, Saudi Arabia 54/E7
Yenbo, Saudi Arabia 59/C5
Yenda, N.S. Wales 97/D4
Yendi, Ghana 106/D7
Yengisar, China 77/A4
Yenice, Çanakkale, Turkey 63/B3
Yenice, İçel, Turkey 63/F4
Yenice, Zonguldak, Turkey 63/E2
Yeniceoba, Turkey 63/E3
Yeniköy, Çanakkale, Turkey 63/B6
Yeniköy, Çanakkale, Turkey 63/C5
Yeniköy, İstanbul, Turkey 63/D6
Yenimahalle, Turkey 63/E3
Yenişehir, Turkey 63/C2
Yenisey (riv.), U.S.S.R. 4/C5
Yenisey (riv.), U.S.S.R. 2/P2
Yenisey (riv.), U.S.S.R. 54/K3
Yenisey (riv.), U.S.S.R. 48/J3
Yeniseysk, U.S.S.R. 54/L4
Yeniseysk, U.S.S.R. 48/K4
Yenki (Yanji), China 77/L3
Yen Minh, Vietnam 72/E2
Yentai (Yantai), China 77/K4
Yentna (riv.), Alaska 196/A1
Yeo (lake), W. Australia 88/D5
Yeo (lake), W. Australia 92/D5
Yeola, India 68/C4
Yeoman, Ind. (47997) 227/D3
Yeotmal, India 68/D4
Yeoval, N.S. Wales 97/E3
Yeovil, England 10/E5
Yeovil, England 13/E7
Yeppoon, Queensland 95/D4
Yeppoon, Queensland 88/J4
Yerevan (Erivan), U.S.S.R. 52/F6
Yericaño, Venezuela 124/F5
Yerington, Nev. (89447) 266/B4
Yerington Ind. Res., Nev. 266/B3
Yerkesik, Turkey 63/C4
Yerköy, Turkey 63/F3
Yerlisu, Turkey 63/C5
Yermak, U.S.S.R. 48/H4
Yermentau, 48/H4
Yermo, Calif. (92398) 204/J9
Yeroham, Israel 65/B6
Yerolimín, Greece 45/F7
Yeronga, Queensland 95/D3
Yeronga, Queensland 88/K3
Yerseke, Netherlands 27/E6
Yershov, U.S.S.R. 52/G4
Yesagyo, Burma 72/B2
Yeshbum, P.D.R. Yemen 59/E7
Yesil', 48/G4
Yeşilhisar, Turkey 63/F3
Yeşilırmak (riv.), Turkey 63/G2
Yeşilköy, Turkey 63/D6
Yeşilova, Burdur, Turkey 63/C4
Yeşilova, Niğde, Turkey 63/E3
Yeşilyurt, Turkey 63/H3
Yeso, N. Mex. (88136) 274/E4
Yeso (creek), N. Mex. 274/E4
Yesodot, Israel 65/B4
Yessentuki, U.S.S.R. 52/F6
Yessey, U.S.S.R. 48/L3
Yeste, Spain 33/E3
Yesud Hama'ala, Israel 65/D1
Yetholm, Scotland 15/F5
Yetman, N.S. Wales 97/F1
Yettem, Calif. (93670) 204/F7
Yetter, Iowa (51433) 229/D4
Ye-u, Burma 72/B2
Yeu (isl.), France 28/B4
Yevlakh, U.S.S.R. 52/G6
Yevpatoria, U.S.S.R. 52/D5
Ye Xian, China 77/K4
Yeysk, U.S.S.R. 52/E5
Ygatimí, Paraguay 144/E4
Yhú, Paraguay 144/E4
Yi (riv.), Uruguay 145/B4
Yialousa, Cyprus 63/E5
Yiannitsá, Greece 45/F5
Yibin (Ipin), China 77/F6
Yibin, China 54/M7
Yibug Caka (lake), China 77/C5
Yichang (Ichang), China 77/H5
Yichun, Heilongjiang, China 77/L2
Yichun, Jiangxi, China 77/H6
Yidu, Hubei, China 77/H5
Yidu, Shandong, China 77/J4
Yiftah, Israel 65/D1
Yığılca, Turkey 63/D2
Yıldızeli, Turkey 63/G3
Yiliang, China 77/F7
Yinchuan (Ningsia, Yinchwan), China 77/G4
Yinchuan, China 54/M6
Yingjiang, China 77/E7
Yingkou (Yinkow), China 77/K3
Yingshan, Hubei, China 77/H5
Yingshan, Sichuan, China 77/G5
Yining, China 77/B3
Yining, China 54/K5
Yinjiang, China 77/G6
Yin Shan (mts.), China 77/G3
Yirga-Alam, Ethiopia 102/F4
Yirga Alam, Ethiopia 111/G6
Yirka, Israel 65/C2
Yirol, Sudan 111/F6
Yirrkala, North. Terr. 93/E2
Yishan, China 77/G7
Yithion, Greece 45/F7
Yiwu (Aratürük), China 77/D3
Yiyang, China 77/H6
Ylikitka (lake), Finland 18/Q3
Ylitornio, Finland 18/O3
Ylivieska, Finland 18/O4
Ymir, Br. Col. 184/J5
Ynys Môn (Anglesey) (ridge), Wales 13/C4
Ynys Môn (Anglesey) (isl.), Wales 10/D4
Yoakum (co.), Texas 303/B4
Yoakum, Texas (77995) 303/G8
Yocalla, Bolivia 136/B6
Yocemento, Kansas (†67601) 232/C3
Yockanookany (riv.), Miss. 256/E5
Yoco, Venezuela 124/G2
Yocón, Honduras 154/D3
Yocum, Ky. (41478) 237/P5
Yoder, Colo. (80864) 208/L5
Yoder, Ind. (46798) 227/G3
Yoder, Kansas (67585) 232/E4
Yoder, Wyo. (82244) 319/H4
Yodo (riv.), Japan 81/J7
Yog (pt.), Philippines 82/E3
Yogyakarta, Indonesia 54/M10
Yogyakarta, Indonesia 85/J2
Yoho Nat'l Park, Br. Col. 162/E5
Yoho Nat'l Park, Br. Col. 184/J4
Yoichi, Japan 81/K2
Yojoa (lake), Honduras 154/D3
Yokadouma, Cameroon 115/B3
Yokawa, Japan 81/H7
Yokena, Miss. (†39180) 256/C6
Yokkaichi, Japan 81/H6
Yoko, Cameroon 115/B2
Yokohama, Japan 2/R4
Yokohama, Japan 81/O3
Yokohama, Japan 54/R6
Yokosuka, Japan 81/O3
Yokote, Japan 81/K4
Yola, Nigeria 106/G7
Yola, Nigeria 102/D4
Yolla, Tasmania 99/B3
Yolo (co.), Calif. 204/D5
Yolo, Calif. (95697) 204/B8
Yolyn, W. Va. (25654) 312/C7
Yona, Guam 86/K7
Yonago, Japan 81/F6
Yonaguni (isl.), Japan 81/K7
Yoncalla, Oreg. (97499) 291/D4
Yonezawa, Japan 81/K5
Yongamp'o, N. Korea 81/B4
Yongchang, China 77/F4
Yŏngch'ŏn, S. Korea 81/D6
Yongchuan, China 77/G6
Yongdeng, China 77/F4
Yŏngdŏk, S. Korea 81/D5
Yonges Island, S.C. (29494) 296/G6
Yonghe, China 77/H4
Yŏnghŭng, N. Korea 81/C4
Yŏngju, S. Korea 81/D5
Yongning, China 77/G4
Yongren, China 77/F6
Yongxin, China 77/H6
Yongxing, China 77/H6
Yonkers, Georgia (†31014) 217/F6
Yonkers, N.Y. (*10701) 276/O6
Yonne (dept.), France 28/E4
Yonne (riv.), France 28/E3
Yono, Japan 81/O2
Yopal, Colombia 126/D5
Yorba Linda, Calif. (92686) 204/D11
Yorito, Honduras 154/D3
York, Ala. (36925) 195/B6
York (cape), Australia 2/S6
York (cape), Australia 87/E7
York, England 13/F4
York, England 10/F4
York (cape), Greenl. 4/B13
York, Ky. (41184) 237/P3
York (co.), Maine 243/B9
York, Maine (03909) 243/B9
York◯, Maine (03909) 243/B9
York (co.), Nebr. 264/G4
York, Nebr. (68467) 264/G4
York (co.), New Bruns. 170/C3
York, N.Y. (14592) 276/E5
York, N. Dak. (58386) 282/L3
York (reg. munic.), Ontario 177/E4
York, Ontario 177/J4
York, Pa. 188/L3
York (co.), Pa. 294/J6
York, Pa. (*17401) 294/J6
York (riv.), Québec 172/D1
York (cape), Queensland 88/G2
York (cape), Queensland 95/B1
York (co.), S.C. 296/E2
York, S.C. (29745) 296/E1
York (co.), Va. 307/P6
York (riv.), Va. 307/P6
York, W. Australia 88/B6
York, W. Australia 92/B1
York (sound), W. Australia 88/C2
York (sound), W. Australia 92/D1
York, Wis. (†54758) 317/D7
York Beach, Maine (03910) 243/B9
Yorke (pen.), S. Australia 88/F7
Yorke (pen.), S. Australia 94/E6
Yorketown, S. Australia 88/F6
Yorketown, S. Australia 94/E6
York Factory, Man. 162/G4
York Factory, Manitoba 179/K2
York Harbor, Maine (03911) 243/B9
York Haven, Pa. (17370) 294/J5
York Landing, Man. 146/J4
York Landing, Manitoba 179/J2
Yorklyn, Del. (19736) 245/R1
Yorkshire, North (co.), England 13/F3
Yorkshire, South (co.), England 13/F4
Yorkshire, West (co.), England 13/J1
Yorkshire, N.Y. (14173) 276/D5
Yorkshire, Ohio (45388) 284/B5
Yorkshire Dales National Park, England 13/E3
York Springs, Pa. (17372) 294/H6
Yorkton, Sask. 146/H4
Yorkton, Sask. 162/F5
Yorkton, Sask. 181/J4
Yorktown, Ark. (71678) 202/G5
Yorktown, Ind. (47396) 227/G4
Yorktown, Iowa (51656) 229/C7
Yorktown, N.J. (†08098) 273/C4
Yorktown, Texas (78164) 303/G9
Yorktown, Va. (23690) 307/R6
Yorktown Heights, N.Y. (10598) 276/N8
Yorkville, Ill. (60560) 222/E2
Yorkville, Ind. (†47022) 227/H6
Yorkville, N.Y. (13495) 276/K4
Yorkville, Ohio (43971) 284/J5
Yorkville, Tenn. (38389) 237/C8
Yoro, Honduras 154/D3
Yoron (isl.), Japan 81/N6
Yorosso, Mali 106/C6
Yosemite, Ky. (42566) 237/M6
Yosemite National Park, Calif. (95389) 204/F6
Yosemite Nat'l Park, Calif. 188/C3
Yosemite Nat'l Park, Calif. 204/F6
Yoshino (riv.), Japan 81/G6
Yoshino-Kumano National Park, Japan 81/H7
Yoshkar-Ola, U.S.S.R. 7/J3
Yoshkar-Ola, U.S.S.R. 52/G3
Yoshkar-Ola, U.S.S.R. 48/E4
Yost, Utah (†84329) 304/A2
Yŏsu, S. Korea 81/C6
Yotala, Bolivia 136/C6
Yotaú, Bolivia 136/D5
Yotvata, Israel 65/D5
Youanmi, W. Australia 92/B5
Youbou, Br. Col. 184/J3
Youghal, Ireland 10/B5
Youghal, Ireland 17/F8
Youghal (bay), Ireland 10/C5
Youghal (bay), Ireland 17/F8
Youghiogheny (riv.), Md. 245/A3
Youghiogheny (dam), Pa. 294/D6
Youghiogheny River (lake), Md. 245/A2
Youghiogheny River (lake), Pa. 294/D6
Young, Ariz. (85554) 198/D4
Young, N. S. Wales 88/H6
Young, N.S. Wales 97/E4
Young (cape), N. Zealand 100/D7
Young (mt.), North. Terr. 93/D3
Young, Sask. 181/F4
Young (co.), Texas 303/F4
Young, Uruguay 145/B3
Young America, Ind. (46998) 227/E3
Young America, Minn. (55397) 255/E6
Youngcane, Georgia (†30512) 217/D1
Young Cove, Nova Scotia 168/C4
Young Harris, Georgia (30582) 217/E1
Youngs Cove, New Bruns. 170/E3
Youngs Creek, Ind. (†47454) 227/D8
Youngs Creek, Ky. (†40759) 237/N7
Youngstown, Alberta 182/E4
Youngstown, Fla. (32466) 212/D6
Youngstown, Ind. (†47808) 227/C6
Youngstown, N.Y. (14174) 276/C4
Youngstown, Ohio (*44501) 284/J3
Youngstown, Ohio 188/K2
Youngsville, La. (70592) 238/G6
Youngsville, N. Mex. (87064) 274/C2
Youngsville, N.Y. (12791) 276/L7
Youngsville, N.C. (27596) 281/N2
Youngsville, Pa. (16371) 294/D2
Youngtown, Ariz. (85363) 198/C5
Youngwood, Pa. (15697) 294/D5
Yountville, Calif. (94599) 204/C5
Youshashan, China 77/D4
Youssoufia, Morocco 106/C2
Youyang, China 77/G6
Yozgat (prov.), Turkey 63/F3
Yozgat, Turkey 59/B2
Yozgat, Turkey 63/F3
Ypacaraí, Paraguay 144/B5
Ypané, Paraguay 144/B5
Ypané (riv.), Paraguay 144/D3
Ypé Jhú, Paraguay 144/E3
Ypoá (lake), Paraguay 144/B5
Ypres (Ieper), Belgium 27/B7
Ypsilanti, Georgia (†31827) 217/D5
Ypsilanti, Mich. (48197) 250/F6
Ypsilanti, N. Dak. (58497) 282/N6
Yreka, Calif. 188/B2
Yreka, Calif. (96097) 204/C2
Yser (riv.), Belgium 27/B7
Yssingeaux, France 28/F5
Ystad, Sweden 18/H9
Ystradgynlais, Wales 13/D6
Ythan (riv.), Scotland 15/F3
Yuan (riv.), China 54/M7
Yuan Jiang (riv.), China 77/H6
Yuanling, China 77/G6
Yuanmou, China 77/F6
Yuanping, China 77/H4
Yuba (co.), Calif. 204/D4
Yuba (riv.), Calif. 204/D4
Yuba, Okla. (†74721) 288/O7
Yuba, Wis. (54672) 317/F8
Yuba City, Calif. (95991) 204/D4
Yubari, Japan 81/L2
Yubetsu, Japan 81/L1
Yucaipa, Calif. (92399) 204/J9
Yucatán (chan.) 146/K7
Yucatán (state), Mexico 150/P6
Yucatán (pen.), Mexico 146/K7
Yucatán (pen.), Mexico 150/P7
Yucca, Ariz. (86438) 198/A4
Yucca Flat (basin), Nev. 266/E6
Yucca House Nat'l Mon., Colo. 208/B8
Yucca Valley, Calif. (92284) 204/J9
Yuci (Yütze), China 77/H4
Yudu, China 77/J6
Yuendumu, North. Terr. 93/B7
Yuexi, China 77/F6
Yueyang, China 77/H6
Yug (riv.), U.S.S.R. 52/G2
Yugorskiy (pen.), U.S.S.R. 52/K1
Yugoslavia 2/K3
Yugoslavia 7/F4
YUGOSLAVIA 45/C3
Yuhuan (isl.), China 77/K6
Yukon (riv.) 2/B2
Yukon (riv.) 146/C3
Yukon (riv.) 4/C17
Yukon (riv.), Alaska 188/C5
Yukon (riv.), Alaska 196/F2
Yukon, Mo. (65589) 261/J8
Yukon, Okla. (73099) 288/L3
Yukon, Pa. (15698) 294/C5
Yukon (riv.), Yukon 162/C3
Yukon (riv.), Yukon 187/E3
Yukon-Charley Rivers Nat'l Preserve, Alaska 196/K2
Yukon Territory 162/C3
Yukon Territory (terr.), Canada 146/E3
YUKON TERRITORY 187
Yüksekova, Turkey 63/L4
Yukuhashi, Japan 81/E7
Yule (riv.), W. Australia 92/B3
Yulee, Fla. (32097) 212/E1
Yuli (Lopnur), China 77/C3
Yulin, Guangxi Zhuangzu, China 77/G7
Yulin, Shanxi, China 77/G4
Yuma, Ariz. 188/D4
Yuma, Ariz. 146/G6
Yuma (co.), Ariz. 198/A5
Yuma, Ariz. (85364) 198/A6
Yuma (des.), Ariz. 198/A6
Yuma (co.), Colo. 208/P2
Yuma, Colo. (80759) 208/O2
Yuma (bay), Dom. Rep. 158/F6
Yuma, Tenn. (38390) 237/E9
Yuma Ind. Res., Calif. 204/L11
Yuma Marine Corps Air Sta., Ariz. 198/A6
Yuma Proving Ground, Ariz. 198/A6
Yumbel, Chile 138/E1
Yumbo, Colombia 126/B6
Yumen, China 77/E4
Yumen, China 54/L6
Yumenzhen, China 77/E3
Yumin, China 77/B2
Yumurtalık, Turkey 63/F4
Yuna (riv.), Dom. Rep. 158/E5
Yuna, W. Australia 92/A5
Yunak, Turkey 63/D3
Yunan, China 77/H7
Yunaska (isl.), Alaska 196/D4
Yuncheng, China 77/H4
Yungas, Las (reg.), Bolivia 136/B5
Yungay, Chile 138/E1
Yungkia (Wenzhou), China 77/J6
Yunguyo, Peru 128/H11
Yunnan (prov.), China 77/F7
Yunta, S. Australia 94/F5
Yunxi, China 77/G5
Yunxiao, China 77/J7
Yunyang, China 77/G5
Yupukari, Guyana 131/B4

Zzyzx 473

Yura, Bolivia 136/B7
Yuraguanal, Cuba 158/G2
Yurga, U.S.S.R. 48/J4
Yurimaguas, Peru 128/E5
Yuruá (riv.), Peru 128/F7
Yuruari (riv.), Venezuela 124/H4
Yurungkax He (riv.), China 77/A4
Yur'yevets, U.S.S.R. 52/F3
Yuscarán, Honduras 154/D4
Yushan (isls.), China 77/K6
Yü Shan (mt.), China 77/K7
Yushu, Jilin, China 77/L3
Yushu, Qinghai, China 77/E5
Yusufeli, Turkey 63/J2
Yutan, Nebr. (68073) 264/H3
Yutian, Hebei, China 77/J4
Yutian, Xinjiang Uygur, China 77/B4
Yuty, Paraguay 144/D5
Yütze (Yuci), China 77/H4
Yuxi, China 77/F7
Yu Xian, China 77/H4
Yuzawa, Japan 81/K4
Yuzhno-Kuril'sk, U.S.S.R. 48/P5
Yuzhno-Sakhalinsk, U.S.S.R. 54/R5
Yuzhno-Sakhalinsk, U.S.S.R. 48/P5
Yvelines (dept.), France 28/D3
Yverdon, Switzerland 39/C3
Yvetot, France 28/D3
Yvoir, Belgium 27/F8
Yvonand, Switzerland 39/C3
Ywathit, Burma 72/C3

Z

Zaachila, Mexico 150/L8
Zaandam (Zaanstad), Netherlands 27/B4
Zaandijk, Netherlands 27/B4
Zabaykal'sk, U.S.S.R. 48/M5
Zabid, Yemen Arab Rep. 59/D7
Ząbki, Poland 47/E2
Ząbkowice, Poland 47/B3
Ząbkowice Śląskie, Poland 47/C3
Žabljak, Yugoslavia 45/D4
Zabol, Iran 59/H3
Zabol, Iran 66/M5
Zabré, Upper Volta 106/D6
Zábřeh, Czech. 41/D2
Zabrze, Poland 7/F3
Zabrze, Poland 47/A4
Zacapa, Guatemala 154/C3
Zacapoaxtla, Mexico 150/O1
Zacapu, Mexico 150/J7
Zacatecas (state), Mexico 150/H5
Zacatecas, Mexico 150/H5
Zacatecoluca, El Salvador 154/C4
Zacatelco, Mexico 150/N1
Zacatepec, Mexico 150/L2
Zacatlán, Mexico 150/N1
Zach, Tenn. (†38320) 237/E8
Zachariah, Ky. (41396) 237/O5
Zachary, La. (70791) 238/K1
Zachow, Wis. (54182) 317/K6
Zacoalco de Torres, Mexico 150/H6
Zadar, Yugoslavia 45/B3
Zadetkyi Kyun (isl.), Burma 72/C5
Zadi, Burma 72/C4
Zadoi, China 77/E5
Zafra, Spain 33/C3
Żagań, Poland 47/B3
Žagare, U.S.S.R. 53/B2
Zagarolo, Italy 34/F7
Zagazig, Egypt 59/B3
Zagazig, Egypt 111/K3
Zagheh, Iran 66/F4
Zagora, Morocco 106/C2
Zagorsk, U.S.S.R. 7/H3
Zagorsk, U.S.S.R. 52/E3
Zagreb, Yugoslavia 7/F4
Zagreb, Yugoslavia 45/C3
Zagros (mts.), Iran 59/E3
Zagros (mts.), Iran 66/E4
Zagyva (riv.), Hungary 41/F3
Zahedan, Iran 59/H4
Zahedan, Iran 66/M6
Zahedan, Iran 54/G7
Zahl, N. Dak. (58856) 282/C2
Zahle, Lebanon 63/F6
Záhony, Hungary 41/G2
Zahran, Saudi Arabia 59/D6
Zaidín, Spain 33/G2
Zaire 2/K6
Zaire 102/E5
ZAIRE 115/D4
Zaire (Congo) (riv.) 102/E4
Zaire (dist.), Angola 115/B5
Zaire (Congo) (riv.), Zaire 115/C4
Zaječar, Yugoslavia 45/E4
Zakamensk, U.S.S.R. 48/L4
Zakho, Iraq 66/C2
Zákinthos, Greece 45/E7
Zákinthos (Zante) (isl.), Greece 45/E7
Zako, Cent. Afr. Rep. 115/D2
Zakopane, Poland 47/D4
Zala (co.), Hungary 41/D3
Zala (riv.), Hungary 41/D3
Zalaegerszeg, Hungary 41/D3
Zalamea de la Serena, Spain 33/D3
Zalamea la Real, Spain 33/C4
Zalaszentgrót, Hungary 41/D3
Zalău, Romania 45/F2
Zaleski, Ohio (45698) 284/F7
Zalim, Saudi Arabia 59/D5
Zalingei, Sudan 111/D5
Zalma, Mo. (63787) 261/N8
Zaltbommel, Netherlands 27/G5
Zalun, Burma 72/B3
Zama (lake), Alberta 182/A5
Zama, Miss. (†39090) 256/F5
Zambales (prov.), Philippines 82/C3
Žamberk, Czech. 41/D1
Zambezi (riv.) 2/L6
Zambezi (riv.) 102/E6
Zambezi (riv.), Angola 115/D6
Zambezi (riv.), Mozambique 118/E3
Zambezi (riv.), Namibia 118/C3
Zambezi, Zambia 115/D6
Zambezi (riv.), Zambia 115/D7
Zambezi (riv.), Zimbabwe 118/E3
Zambézia (prov.), Mozambique 118/F3
Zambia 2/L6
Zambia 102/E6
ZAMBIA 115/E7
Zamboanga, Philippines 85/G4
Zamboanga, Philippines 82/C7
Zamboanga, Philippines 54/N9
Zamboanga del Norte (prov.), Philippines 82/D6
Zamboanga del Sur (prov.), Philippines 82/D7
Zambrów, Poland 47/E2
Zamora, Calif. (95698) 204/C5
Zamora, Ecuador 128/C5
Zamora (riv.), Ecuador 128/B4
Zamora (prov.), Spain 33/D2
Zamora, Spain 33/D2
Zamora-Chinchipe (prov.), Ecuador 128/C5
Zamora de Hidalgo, Mexico 150/H7
Zamość (prov.), Poland 47/F3
Zamość, Poland 47/F3
Zams, Austria 41/A3
Zamtang, China 77/F5
Zanaga, Congo 115/B4
Zanda, China 77/A5
Zanderij, Suriname 131/D3
Zanderij, Suriname 120/D2
Zandvoort, Netherlands 27/E4
Zanesfield, Ohio (43360) 284/C5
Zanesville, Ind. (46799) 227/G3
Zanesville, Ohio 188/K3
Zanesville, Ohio (43701) 284/G6
Zanja de Lira, Venezuela 124/E3
Zanjan (governorate), Iran 66/F2
Zanjan, Iran 59/E2
Zanjan, Iran 66/K5
Zanjan (riv.), Iran 66/F2
Zanoni, Mo. (65784) 261/H9
Zante (Zákinthos), Greece 45/E7
Zanthus, W. Australia 92/C5
Zanzibar, Tanzania 102/F5
Zanzibar, Tanzania 115/G5
Zanzibar (isl.), Tanzania 2/M6
Zanzibar (isl.), Tanzania 102/F5
Zanzibar (isl.), Tanzania 115/G5
Zanzibar Mjini (reg.), Tanzania 115/G5
Zanzibar Shambani North (reg.), Tanzania 115/G5
Zanzibar Shambani South (reg.), Tanzania 115/G5
Zao (mt.), Japan 81/K5
Zaouiet Kounta, Algeria 106/D3
Zaoyang, China 77/H5
Zaozernyy, U.S.S.R. 48/K4
Zaozhuang, China 77/J5
Zap, N. Dak. (58580) 282/G5
Západočeský (reg.), Austria 41/B2
Západoslovenský (reg.), Austria 41/D2
Zapala, Argentina 143/B6
Zapala, Argentina 120/B6
Zapaleri, Cerro (mt.), Argentina 143/C1
Zapaleri, Cerro (mt.), Bolivia 136/B8
Zapaleri, Cerro (mt.), Chile 138/C4
Zapallar, Chile 138/A9
Zapata (pen.), Cuba 158/C2
Zapata (co.), Texas 303/E11
Zapata, Texas (78076) 303/E11
Zapata Occidental (swamp), Cuba 158/D2
Zapata Oriental (swamp), Cuba 158/D2
Zapatera (isl.), Nicaragua 154/E5
Zapatoca, Colombia 126/D4
Zapatosa, Ciénaga de (swamp), Colombia 126/D3
Zapicán, Uruguay 145/E4
Zapiga, Chile 138/B2
Zapolyarnyy, U.S.S.R. 52/D1
Zaporozh'ye, U.S.S.R. 7/H4
Zaporozh'ye, U.S.S.R. 48/D5
Zaporozh'ye, U.S.S.R. 52/E5
Zapotillo, Ecuador 128/B5
Zapucay, Uruguay 145/D2
Zapug, China 77/B5
Za Qu (riv.), China 77/E5
Zara, Turkey 59/C1
Zara, Turkey 63/G3
Zara (Zadar), Yugoslavia 45/B3
Zarafshan, 48/G5
Zaragoza, Colombia 126/C4
Zaragoza, Chihuahua, Mexico 150/F1
Zaragoza, Coahuila, Mexico 150/J2
Zaragoza, Puebla, Mexico 150/O1
Zaragoza (prov.), Spain 33/F2
Zaragoza (Saragossa), Spain 33/F2
Zarand, Iran 59/G3
Zarand, Iran 66/H6
Zaranj, Afghanistan 68/A2
Zaranj, Afghanistan 59/H3
Zarasai, U.S.S.R. 53/C3
Zárate, Argentina 143/G6
Zaraza, Venezuela 124/F3
Zard Kuh (mt.), Iran 66/F4
Zarembo (isl.), Alaska 196/N2
Zarephath, N.J. (08890) 273/D2
Zaria, Nigeria 106/F6
Zaria, Nigeria 102/C3
Zarineh (riv.), Iran 66/E2
Zărnești, Romania 45/G3
Zarqa' (riv.), Jordan 65/D3
Zarqam, Iran 66/H6
Zaruma, Ecuador 128/C4
Zarumilla, Peru 128/B4
Zary, Poland 47/B3
Zarzal, Colombia 126/B5
Zarza la Mayor, Spain 33/C3
Zarzis, Tunisia 106/G2
Zarzis, Tunisia 102/D1
Zaskar (mts.), India 68/D2
Zastron, S. Africa 118/D6
Žatec, Czech. 41/B1
Zavala (co.), Texas 303/E9
Zavalla, Argentina 143/F6
Zavalla, Texas (75980) 303/K6
Zavdi'el, Israel 65/B4
Zaventem, Belgium 27/C9
Zavitinsk, U.S.S.R. 48/O4
Zawi, Zimbabwe 118/D3
Zawia, Libya 102/D1
Zawia, Libya 111/B1
Zawiercie, Poland 47/D3
Zayandeh (riv.), Iran 66/H4
Zayar, China 77/B3
Zaysan, U.S.S.R. 48/J5
Zaysan (lake), U.S.S.R. 54/K5
Zaysan (lake), U.S.S.R. 48/J5
Zayü, China 77/E6
Zaza del Medio, Cuba 158/F2
Zázrivá, Czech. 41/E2
Zbąszyń, Poland 47/B2
Zbiroh, Czech. 41/B2
Zborov, Czech. 41/F2
Žd'ár nad Sázavou, Czech. 41/C2
Zduńska Wola, Poland 47/D3
Zealand (Sjaelland) (isl.), Den. 21/E6
Zealand, New Bruns. 170/D2
Zealandia, Sask. 181/D4
Zearing, Iowa (50278) 229/G4
Zeballos, Br. Col. 184/D5
Zebdani, Syria 63/G6
Zebirget (isl.), Egypt 59/C5
Zebulon, Georgia (30295) 217/D4
Zebulon, Ky. (†41501) 237/S5
Zebulon, N.C. (27597) 281/N3
Zedelgem, Belgium 27/C6
Zeebrugge, Belgium 27/C6
Zeehan, Tasmania 99/B3
Zeeland, Mich. (49464) 250/D6
Zeeland (prov.), Netherlands 27/D6
Zeeland, N. Dak. (58581) 282/L8
Ze'elim, Israel 65/A5
Zeerust, S. Africa 118/D5
Zeewolde, Netherlands 27/G4
Zefat, Israel 65/C2
Zegharta, Lebanon 63/G5
Zegrzyńskie (lake), Poland 47/E2
Zehdenick, E. Germany 22/E2
Zehner, Sask. 181/G5
Zeigler, Ill. (62999) 222/D6
Zeila, Somalia 115/H1
Zeil am Main, W. Germany 22/D4
Zeist, Netherlands 27/G4
Zeitz, E. Germany 22/E3
Zekiah Swamp (riv.), Md. 245/L7
Zêkog, China 77/F5
Zele, Belgium 27/E6
Zelenoborskiy, U.S.S.R. 52/D1
Zelenodol'sk, U.S.S.R. 52/G3
Zelenokumsk, U.S.S.R. 52/F6
Zelienople, Pa. (16063) 294/B4
Želiezovce, Czech. 41/E2
Zell, S. Dak. (57483) 298/M4
Zell, Luzern, Switzerland 39/E2
Zell, Zürich, Switzerland 39/G2
Zell, W. Germany 22/B4
Zella, Libya 102/D2
Zella, Libya 111/C2
Zella-Mehlis, E. Germany 22/D3
Zell am See, Austria 41/B3
Zell am Ziller, Austria 41/A3
Zellersee (lake), Switzerland 39/G1
Zellwood, Fla. (32798) 212/E3
Zelma, Sask. 181/F4
Zelow, Poland 47/D3
Zelten, Jebel (mts.), Libya 111/D2
Zeltweg, Austria 41/C3
Zelzate, Belgium 27/D6
Zemio, Cent. Afr. Rep. 115/D2
Zemongo, Cent. Afr. Rep. 115/E2
Zemple, Minn. (†56636) 255/E3
Zempoala, Mexico 150/Q1
Zemst, Belgium 27/E7
Zenas, Ind. (†47223) 227/G6
Zenda, Kansas (67159) 232/D4
Zeneta, Sask. 181/J5
Zenia, Calif. (95495) 204/B3
Zenica, Yugoslavia 45/C3
Zenith, Ill. (†62899) 222/E5
Zenith, Kansas (†67578) 232/D4
Zenith, W. Va. (†24951) 312/F7
Zenith-Saltwater, Wash. (†98101) 310/C3
Zenjan (Zanjan), Iran 66/F2
Zenobia (peak), Colo. 208/B1
Zenon Park, Sask. 181/H2
Zenoria, La. (†71371) 238/F3
Zent, Ark. (†72021) 202/H4
Zenta (Senta), Yugo. 45/D3
Zeona, S. Dak. (57795) 298/D3
Žepče, Yugoslavia 45/D3
Zepernick, E. Germany 22/F3
Zephyr, Ontario 177/E3
Zephyr, Texas (76890) 303/F6
Zephyr Cove, Nev. (89448) 266/A3
Zephyrhills, Fla. (33599) 212/D3
Zepp, Va. (†22654) 307/L3
Zerbst, E. Germany 22/E3
Zereh, Gowd-e (depr.), Afghanistan 68/A3
Zermatt, Switzerland 39/E4
Zernez, Switzerland 39/K3
Zernograd, U.S.S.R. 52/F5
Zessfontein, Namibia 118/A3
Zêtang, China 77/D6
Zetland (trad. co.), Scot. 15/B4
Zeulenroda, E. Germany 22/D3
Zeven, W. Germany 22/C2
Zevenaar, Netherlands 27/J5
Zevenbergen, Netherlands 27/E5
Zeya, U.S.S.R. 48/N4
Zeya (riv.), U.S.S.R. 48/N4
Zeytinburnu, Turkey 63/D6
Zeytindağ, Turkey 63/B3
Zgierz, Poland 47/D3
Zgorzelec, Poland 47/B3
Zhanang, China 77/D6
Zhanghei, China 77/J3
Zhangjiakou (Kalgan), China 77/J3
Zhangjiakou, China 54/N5
Zhangping, China 77/J6
Zhangye (Changyeh), China 77/F4
Zhangye, China 54/M6
Zhangzhou (Changchow), China 77/J7
Zhanjiang (Chankiang), China 77/H7
Zhanjiang, China 54/N7
Zhanyi, China 77/F6
Zhaodong, China 77/K2
Zhaojue, China 77/F6
Zhaoqing, China 77/H7
Zhaosu, China 77/B3
Zhaotong (Chaotung), China 77/F6
Zhari Namco (lake), China 77/C5
Zhashui, China 77/G5
Zhatay, U.S.S.R. 48/O3
Zhaxi Co (lake), China 77/C5
Zhdanov, U.S.S.R. 7/H4
Zhdanov, U.S.S.R. 48/D5
Zhdanov, U.S.S.R. 52/E5
Zhejiang (Chekiang) (prov.), China 77/K6
Zhelaniye (cape), U.S.S.R. 48/H2
Zheleznodorozhnyy, U.S.S.R. 52/H2
Zheleznogorsk, U.S.S.R. 52/E4
Zheleznogorsk-Ilimskiy, U.S.S.R. 48/L4
Zhenba, China 77/G5
Zheng'an, China 77/G6
Zhenglan, China 77/J3
Zhengzhou (Chengchow), China 77/H5
Zhengzhou, China 54/N6
Zhenjiang (Chinkiang), China 77/J5
Zhenxiong, China 77/F6
Zhenyuan, China 77/G6
Zhido, China 77/E5
Zhigalovo, U.S.S.R. 48/L4
Zhigansk, U.S.S.R. 4/C3
Zhigansk, U.S.S.R. 54/N3
Zhigansk, U.S.S.R. 48/N3
Zhigulevsk, U.S.S.R. 52/G4
Zhi Qu (Tongtian He) (riv.), China 77/E5
Zhirnovsk, U.S.S.R. 52/G4
Zhitomir, U.S.S.R. 7/G3
Zhitomir, U.S.S.R. 48/C4
Zhitomir, U.S.S.R. 52/C4
Zhlobin, U.S.S.R. 52/D4
Zhmerinka, U.S.S.R. 52/C5
Zhob (riv.), Pakistan 59/J3
Zhob (riv.), Pakistan 68/B2
Zhodino, U.S.S.R. 52/C4
Zhongba, China 77/B6
Zhongdian, China 77/F6
Zhongning, China 77/G4
Zhongshan (Chungshan), China 77/H7
Zhongwei, China 77/F4
Zhoushan (arch.), China 77/K5
Zhovtnevoye, U.S.S.R. 52/D5
Zhuanghe, China 77/K4
Zhucheng, China 77/J4
Zhukovka, U.S.S.R. 52/D4
Zhumadian (Chumatien), China 77/H5
Zhushan, China 77/G5
Zhuzhou (Chuchow), China 77/H6
Zhuzhou, China 54/N7
Zia Pueblo, N. Mex. (†87053) 274/C3
Žiar nad Hronom, Czech. 41/E2
Zibak, Afghanistan 59/K2
Zibak, Afghanistan 68/C1
Zibo (Tzepo), China 77/J4
Zibo, China 54/N6
Zichang, China 77/G4
Židlochovice, Czech. 41/D2
Ziebach (co.), S. Dak. 298/F4
Ziębice, Poland 47/C3
Ziel (mt.), North. Terr. 88/E4
Ziel (mt.), North. Terr. 93/C7
Zielona Góra (prov.), Poland 47/B3
Zielona Góra, Poland 47/B3
Zierikzee, Netherlands 27/D5
Zifta, Egypt 111/J3
Zigong (Tzekung), China 77/F6
Ziguei, Chad 111/C5
Zigui, China 77/H5
Ziguinchor, Senegal 106/A6
Ziguinchor, Senegal 102/A3
Zihuatanejo, Mexico 150/J8
Zikhron Ya'aqov, Israel 65/B2
Zilbir (riv.), Iran 66/D1
Zile, Turkey 59/C1
Zile, Turkey 63/G2
Zilfi, Saudi Arabia 59/E4
Žilina, Czech. 41/E2
Zillah, Wash. (98953) 310/E4
Zillis-Reischen, Switzerland 39/H3
Zilupe, U.S.S.R. 53/D2
Zilwaukee, Mich. (†48601) 250/F5
Zim, Minn. (55799) 255/F3
Zima, U.S.S.R. 48/L4
Zimatlán de Álvarez, Mexico 150/L8
Zimbabwe 2/L6
Zimbabwe 102/E6
ZIMBABWE 118/D4
Zimbabwe Nat'l Park, Zimbabwe 118/E4
Zimmerdale, Kansas (†67117) 232/E3
Zimmerman, La. (†71409) 238/E4
Zimmerman, Minn. (55398) 255/E5
Zimnicea, Romania 45/G4
Zimnitsa, Bulgaria 45/H4
Zinal, Switzerland 39/E4
Zinc, Ark. (†72601) 202/E1
Zinder, Niger 106/F6
Zinder, Niger 102/C3
Zingren, China 77/G6
Zingst, E. Germany 22/E1
Zinhui, China 77/H7
Zinjibar, P.D.R. Yemen 59/E7
Zinnik (Soignies), Belgium 27/D7
Zion, Ark. (72589) 202/G1
Zion, Ill. (60099) 222/F1
Zion, Md. (†21901) 245/P2
Zion, Mo. (†63645) 261/M8
Zion, N.J. (†08853) 273/D3
Zion, S.C. (†29574) 296/J3
Zion Hill, St. Chris.-Nevis 161/D11
Zion National Park, Utah (84767) 304/B6
Zion Nat'l Park, Utah 304/A6
Zionsville, Ind. (46077) 227/E5
Zionville, N.C. (28698) 281/F2
Zipaquirá, Colombia 126/D5
Zippori, Israel 65/C2
Zirc, Hungary 41/D3
Žirje (isl.), Yugoslavia 45/B4
Zirkel (mt.), Colo. 208/F1
Zirko (isl.), U.A.E. 59/F5
Zirl, Austria 41/A3
Zirndorf, W. Germany 22/D4
Zistersdorf, Austria 41/D2
Zitácuaro, Mexico 150/J7
Zittau, E. Germany 22/F3
Zitterwald (plat.), Belgium 27/J8
Zivarık, Turkey 63/E3
Ziwa Magharibi (West Lake) (reg.), Tanzania 115/F4
Ziyang, China 77/F5
Ziz, Wadi (dry riv.), Morocco 106/D2
Zizers, Switzerland 39/J3
Zlaté Moravce, Czech. 41/E2
Zlatograd, Bulgaria 45/G5
Zlatoust, U.S.S.R. 54/G4
Zlatoust, U.S.S.R. 48/F4
Zlín (Gottwaldov), Czech. 41/D2
Zliten, Libya 111/C1
Złocieniec, Poland 47/C2
Złotoryja, Poland 47/C3
Złotów, Poland 47/C2
Žlutice, Czech. 41/B1
Znamenka, U.S.S.R. 52/D5
Żnin, Poland 47/C2
Znojmo, Czech. 41/D2
Zoar (lake), Conn. 210/C3
Zoar, Ohio (44697) 284/H4
Zoarville, Ohio (44698) 284/H4
Zofingen, Switzerland 39/F2
Zogang, China 77/E5
Zohreh (riv.), Iran 66/F5
Zoigê, China 77/F5
Zolfo Springs, Fla. (33890) 212/E4
Zollikofen, Switzerland 39/E3
Zollikon, Switzerland 39/G2
Zolotonosha, U.S.S.R. 52/D5
Zomba, Malawi 115/G7
Zomba, Malawi 102/F6
Zonderend (riv.), S. Africa 118/G6
Zongo, Bolivia 136/B5
Zongo, Zaire 115/C3
Zongolica, Mexico 150/P2
Zonguldak (prov.), Turkey 63/D2
Zonguldak, Turkey 63/D2
Zonguldak, Turkey 59/B1
Zonhoven, Belgium 27/G6
Zoo Baba (well), Niger 106/G5
Zook, Kansas (†67550) 232/C3
Zorbatiya, Iraq 66/D4
Zorita, Spain 33/D3
Zorritos, Peru 128/B4
Zortman, Mont. (59546) 262/H3
Zottegem, Belgium 27/D7
Zouar, Chad 111/C3
Zouîrât, Mauritania 106/B4
Zoutkamp, Netherlands 27/J2
Zrenjanin, Yugoslavia 45/E3
Zuata, Venezuela 124/F3
Zuata (riv.), Venezuela 124/F3
Zububa, West Bank 65/C2
Zucchero (mt.), Switzerland 39/G4
Zudáñez, Bolivia 136/C6
Zug (canton), Switzerland 39/G2
Zug, Switzerland 39/G2
Zugdidi, U.S.S.R. 52/F6
Zugersee (lake), Switzerland 39/F2
Zugspitze (mt.), Austria 41/A3
Zugspitze (mt.), W. Germany 22/D5
Zuidelijke IJsselmeerpolders (prov.), Netherlands 27/H4
Zuienkerke, Belgium 27/C6
Zuila, Libya 111/C2
Zújar, Spain 33/E4
Zújar (res.), Spain 33/D3
Zula, Ethiopia 111/G4
Zula, Ethiopia 59/C6
Zula, Ky. (†42603) 237/M7
Zulia (state), Venezuela 124/B2
Zulia (riv.), Venezuela 124/B3
Zülpich, W. Germany 22/B3
Zulu, Ind. (†46773) 227/H2
Zulueta, Cuba 158/E2
Zululand (reg.), S. Africa 118/E5
Zumba, Ecuador 128/C5
Zumbo, Mozambique 118/E3
Zumbro (riv.), Minn. 255/F6
Zumbro Falls, Minn. (55991) 255/F6
Zumbrota, Minn. (55992) 255/F6
Zumpango del Río, Mexico 150/J8
Zumpango de Ocampo, Mexico 150/L1
Zundert, Netherlands 27/F6
Zungeru, Nigeria 106/F7
Zunhua, China 77/J3
Zuni (riv.), Ariz. 198/F4
Zuni, N. Mex. (87327) 274/A3
Zuni (mts.), N. Mex. 274/A3
Zuni (riv.), N. Mex. 274/A3
Zuni, Va. (23898) 307/P7
Zuni Ind. Res., N. Mex. 274/A3
Zunyi (Tsunyi), China 77/G6
Zunyi, China 54/M7
Zuoz, Switzerland 39/J3
Zuqar (isl.), Yemen Arab Rep. 59/D7
Zurabad, Iran 66/M3
Zurich, Kansas (67676) 232/C2
Zurich, Mont. (59547) 262/G2
Zurich, Ontario 177/C4
Zürich (canton), Switzerland 39/G2
Zürich, Switzerland 39/F2
Zürich, Switzerland 7/E4
Zürichsee (lake), Switzerland 39/G2
Zuromin, Poland 47/E2
Zurzach, Switzerland 39/F1
Zushi, Japan 81/O3
Zutphen, Netherlands 27/J4
Zuweiza, Jordan 65/D4
Zuyevka, U.S.S.R. 52/H3
Zvolen, Czech. 41/E2
Zvornik, Yugoslavia 45/D3
Zwai (lake), Ethiopia 111/G6
Zwanenburg, Netherlands 27/A4
Zwara, Libya 111/B1
Zwart (riv.), S. Africa 118/G7
Zwartsluis, Netherlands 27/H3
Zweibrücken, W. Germany 22/B4
Zweisimmen, Switzerland 39/D3
Zwelitsha, S. Africa 118/D6
Zwenkau, E. Germany 22/E3
Zwettl-Niederösterreich, Austria 41/C2
Zwickau, E. Germany 22/E3
Zwijndrecht, Netherlands 27/E5
Zwingle, Iowa (52079) 229/M4
Zwischenahn, W. Germany 22/B2
Zwoleń, Poland 47/E3
Zwolle, La. (71486) 238/C3
Zwolle, Netherlands 27/J3
Zychlin, Poland 47/D2
Żyrardów, Poland 47/E2
Zyryanka, U.S.S.R. 4/C2
Zyryanka, U.S.S.R. 54/S3
Zyryanka, U.S.S.R. 48/Q3
Zyryanovsk, U.S.S.R. 48/J5
Żywiec, Poland 47/D4
Zzyzx, Calif. (†92309) 204/J8

GEOGRAPHICAL TERMS

A. = Arabic Burm. = Burmese Camb. = Cambodian Ch. = Chinese Czech. = Czechoslovakian Dan. = Danish Du. = Dutch Finn. = Finnish Fr. = French Ger. = German Ice. = Icelandic It. = Italian Jap. = Japanese Mong. = Mongol Nor. = Norwegian Per. = Persian Port. = Portuguese Russ. = Russian Sp. = Spanish Sw. = Swedish Turk. = Turkish

Å	Nor., Sw.	Stream
Aas	Dan., Nor.	Hills
Abajo	Sp.	Lower
Ada, Adasi	Turk.	Island
Altipiano	It.	Plateau
Altiplano	Sp.	Plateau
Alv, Alf, Elf	Sw.	River
Arrecife	Sp.	Reef
Asa	Nor., Sw.	Hill
Asaga	Turk.	Lower
Austral	Sp.	Southern
Baai	Du.	Bay
Bab	Arabic	Gate or Strait
Bahia	Sp.	Bay
Bahr	Arabic	Marsh, Lake, Sea, River
Baia	Port.	Bay
Baie	Fr.	Bay, Gulf
Baizo	Port.	Low
Bakke	Dan.	Hill
Bana	Jap.	Cape
Bañados	Sp.	Marshes
Band	Per.	Mt. Range
Bandao	Ch.	Peninsula
Bandar	Per.	Harbor
Barra	Sp.	Reef
Bel	Turk.	Pass
Belt	Ger.	Strait
Ben	Gaelic	Mountain
Bera	Du.	Mountain
Berg	Ger., Du.	Mountain
Bir	Arabic	Well
Boca	Sp.	Gulf, Inlet
Boğhaz	Turk.	Strait
Bolshoi, Bolshaya	Russ.	Big
Bolson	Sp.	Depression
Bong	Korean	Mountain
Boreal	Sp.	Northern
Breen	Nor.	Glacier
Bro	Dan., Nor., Sw.	Bridge
Bucht	Ger.	Bay
Bugt	Dan.	Bay
Bukhta	Russ.	Bay
Bukit	Malay	Hill, Mountain
Bukt	Nor., Sw.	Bay, Gulf
Burnu, Burun	Turk.	Cape, Point
By	Dan., Nor., Sw.	Town
Cabo	Port., Sp.	Cape
Campos	Port.	Plains
Canal	Port., Sp.	Channel
Cap, Capo	Fr., It.	Cape
Cataratas	Sp.	Falls
Catena	It.	Mt. Range
Catingas	Port.	Open Woodlands
Cayos	Sp.	Islands
Central, Centrale	Fr., It.	Middle
Cerrito, Cerro	Sp.	Hill
Cerros	Sp.	Hills, Mountains
Chai	Turk.	River
Chott	Arabic	Salt Lake
Ciénaga	Sp.	Swamp
Ciudad	Sp.	City
Col	Fr.	Pass
Cordillera	Sp.	Mt. Range, Mts.
Côte	Fr.	Coast
Csatoria	Magyar	Canal
Cuchilla	Sp.	Mt. Range
Curiche	Sp.	Swamp
Dağ, Dağı	Turk.	Mountain, Peak
Dağlari	Turk.	Mt. Range
Dal	Nor., Sw.	Valley
Dar	Arabic	Land
Dar'ya	Russ.	River
Daryacheh	Per.	Marshy Lake
Dasht	Per.	Desert, Plain
Deniz, Denizi	Turk.	Sea, Lake
Desierto	Sp.	Desert
Détroit	Fr.	Strait
Djeziret	Arabic, Turk.	Island
Do	Korean	Island
Doi	Thai	Mountain
Eiland	Du.	Island
Elv	Dan., Nor.	River
Embalse	Sp.	Reservoir
Emi	Berber	Mountain
Erg	Arabic	Dune, Desert
Eski	Turk.	Old
Est, Este	Fr., Port., Sp.	East
Estero	Sp.	Estuary, Creek
Estrecho, Estreito	Sp., Port.	Strait
Etang	Fr.	Pond, Lagoon, Lake
Feng	Ch.	Mountain
Fiume	It.	River
Fjäll	Sw.	Mountain
Fjeld, Fjell	Nor.	Hills, Mountain
Fjord	Dan., Nor., Sw.	Fiord
Fleuve	Fr.	River
Fljót	Ice.	Stream
Fluss	Ger.	River
Fors	Sw.	Waterfall
Fos, Foss	Dan., Nor.	Waterfall
Gamla	Nor.	Old
Gamle	Dan.	Old
Gata	Jap.	Lake
Gawa	Jap.	River
Gebel	Arabic	Mountain
Gebergte	Du.	Mt. Range
Gebirge	Ger.	Mt. Range
Gobi	Mongol	Desert
Goe	Jap.	Pass
Gol	Mongol, Turk.	Lake, Stream
Golf	Ger., Du.	Gulf
Golfe	Fr.	Gulf
Golfo	Sp., It., Port.	Gulf
Gölü	Turk.	Lake
Gora	Russ.	Mountain
Grand, Grande	Fr., Sp.	Big
Groot	Du.	Big
Gross	Ger.	Big
Grosso	It., Port.	Big
Guba	Russ.	Bay, Gulf
Gunto	Jap.	Archipelago
Gunung	Malay	Mountain
Hai	Ch.	Sea
Haixia	Ch.	Strait
Halbinsel	Ger.	Peninsula
Hamáda, Hammada	Arabic	Rocky Plateau
Hamn	Sw.	Harbor
Hamún	Per.	Marsh
Hanto	Jap.	Peninsula
Has, Hassi	Arabic	Well
Hav	Dan., Nor., Sw.	Sea, Ocean
Havet	Nor.	Bay
Havn	Dan., Nor.	Harbor
Havre	Fr.	Harbor
He	Ch.	River, Stream
Higashi, Higasi	Jap.	East
Hochebene	Ger.	Plateau
Hoek	Du.	Cape
Hoku	Jap.	North
Holm	Dan., Nor., Sw.	Island
Hory	Czech.	Mountains
Hoved	Dan., Nor.	Cape, Promontory
Hu	Ch.	Lake
Huang	Ch.	Yellow
Huk	Dan., Nor., Sw.	Point
Hus, Huus	Dan., Nor., Sw.	House
Idehan	Arabic	Desert
Ile	Fr.	Island
Ilet	Fr.	Islet
Ilot	Fr.	Islet
Indre	Dan., Nor.	Inner
Inferieur, Inferiore	Fr., It.	Lower
Inner, Inre	Sw.	Inner
Insel	Ger.	Island
Irmak	Turk.	River
Isla	Sp.	Island
Isola	It.	Island
Jabal, Jebel	Arabic	Mountains
Järvi	Finn.	Lake
Jaure	Sw.	Lake
Jiang	Ch.	River, Stream
Jima	Jap.	Island
Joki	Finn.	River
Kaap	Du.	Cape
Kabir, Kebir	Arabic	Big
Kai	Jap.	Sea
Kaikyo	Jap.	Strait
Kami	Turk.	Upper
Kanaal	Du.	Canal
Kanal	Russ., Ger.	Canal, Channel
Kao	Thai	Mountain
Kap, Kapp	Nor., Sw., Ice.	Cape
Kaupunki	Finn.	Town
Kawa	Jap.	River
Khao	Thai	Mountain
Khrebet	Russ.	Mt. Range
Kita	Jap.	North
Klein	Du., Ger.	Small
Klint	Dan.	Promontory
Kô	Jap.	Lake
Ko	Thai	Island
Koh	Camb., Khmer	Island
Kop	Du.	Peak, Head
Köping	Sw.	Market, Borough
Körfez, Körfezi	Turk.	Gulf
Kosa	Russ.	Spit
Kosui	Jap.	Lake
Kraal	Du.	Native Village
Kuchuk	Turk.	Small
Kuh, Kuhha	Per.	Mt. Range, Mts.
Kul	Sinkiang Turki	Lake
Kum	Turk.	Desert
Kuro	Jap.	Black
Laag	Du.	Low
Lac	Fr.	Lake
Lago	Port., Sp., It.	Lake
Lagoa	Port.	Lagoon
Laguna	Sp.	Lagoon
Lagune	Fr.	Lagoon
Lahti	Finn.	Bay, Bight
Län	Sw.	County
Liedao	Ch.	Islands, Archipelago
Lilla	Sw.	Small
Lille	Dan., Nor.	Small
Ling	Ch.	Mountain
Llanos	Sp.	Plains
Mae Nam	Thai	River
Mali, Malaya	Russ.	Small
Man	Korean	Bay
Mar	Sp., Port.	Sea
Mare	It.	Sea
Medio	Sp.	Middle
Meer	Du.	Lake
Meer	Ger.	Sea
Mer	Fr.	Sea
Meridionale	It.	Southern
Meseta	Sp.	Plateau
Middelst, Midden	Du.	Middle
Minami	Jap.	Southern
Mis	Russ.	Cape
Misaki	Jap.	Cape
Mittel	Ger.	Middle
Mont	Fr.	Mountain
Montagne	Fr.	Mountain
Montaña	Sp.	Mountains
Monte	Sp., It., Port.	Mountain
More	Russ.	Sea
Mörön	Mong.	Stream
Morro	Port., Sp.	Mountain, Promontory
Morue	Fr.	Hill
Moyen	Fr.	Middle
Muang	Siamese	Town
Mui	Vietnamese	Cape, Point
Mys	Russ.	Cape
Nada	Jap.	Sea
Naka	Jap.	Middle
Nam	Burm., Lao	River
Namakzar	Per.	Salt Waste
Nan	Jap.	South
Nes	Nor.	Cape, Point
Nevado	Sp.	Snow-covered Peak
Nieder	Ger.	Lower
Nishi, Nisi	Jap.	West
Nizhni, Nizhnyaya	Russ.	Lower
Njarga	Finn.	Peninsula, Promontory
Nong	Thai	Lake
Noord	Du.	North
Nord	Fr., Ger.	North
Norte	Sp., It., Port.	North
Nos	Russ.	Cape
Novi, Novaya	Russ.	New
Nur, Nuur	Ch., Mong.	Lake
Nuruu	Mong.	Mountains
Nusa	Malay	Island
Ny, Nya	Nor., Sw.	New
O	Jap.	Big
ö	Nor., Sw.	Island
Ober	Ger.	Upper
Occidental, Occidentale	Sp., It.	Western
Odde	Dan.	Point
Oeste	Port.	West
Ooster	Du.	Eastern
Opper, Over	Du.	Upper
Oriental	Sp., Fr.	Eastern
Orientale	It.	Eastern
Orta	Turk.	Middle
Ost	Ger.	East
Ostrov	Russ.	Island
Ouest	Fr.	West
öy	Nor.	Island
Ozero	Russ.	Lake
Pampa	Sp.	Plain
Pas	Fr.	Channel, Strait
Paso	Sp.	Pass
Passo	It., Port.	Pass
Peña	Sp.	Rock, Mountain
Pendi	Ch.	Basin
Penisola	It.	Peninsula
Pequeño	Sp.	Small
Pereval	Russ.	Pass
Peski	Russ.	Desert
Petit, Petite	Fr.	Small
Phu	Lao, Annamese	Mtn.
Pic	Fr.	Mountain
Piccolo	It.	Small
Pico	Port., Sp.	Mountain, Peak
Pik	Russ.	Mountain, Peak
Piton	Fr.	Mountain, Peak
Planalto	Port.	Plateau
Plato	Russ.	Plateau
Pointe	Fr.	Point
Poluostrov	Russ.	Peninsula
Ponta	Port.	Point
Presa	Sp.	Reservoir
Presqu'île	Fr.	Peninsula
Proliv	Russ.	Strait
Pulou, Pulo	Malay	Island
Punt	Du.	Point
Punta	Sp., It., Port.	Point
Qiryat	Hebrew	City, Settlement
Qum	Turk.	Desert
Qundao	Ch.	Islands
Rada	Sp.	Inlet
Rade	Fr.	Bay, Inlet
Ras	Arabic	Cape
Reka	Russ.	River
Retto	Jap.	Archipelago
Ria	Sp.	Estuary
Río	Sp.	River
Rivier, Rivière	Du., Fr.	River
Rud	Per.	River
Sai	Jap.	West
Saki	Jap.	Cape
Salar, Salina	Sp.	Salt Deposit
Salto	Sp., Port.	Falls
San	Jap., Korean	Hill
Sanmaek	Korean	Mt. Range
Schiereiland	Du.	Peninsula
Se	Camb., Khmer	River
See	Ger.	Sea, Lake
Selvas	Sp., Port.	Woods, Forest
Seno	Sp.	Bay, Gulf
Serra	Port.	Mts.
Serranía	Sp.	Mts.
Seto	Jap.	Strait
Settentrionale	It.	Northern
Severni, Severnaya	Russ.	North
Shamo	Ch.	Desert
Shan	Ch., Jap.	Hill, Mts.
Shankou	Ch.	Pass
Shatt	Arabic	River
Shima	Jap.	Island
Shimo	Jap.	Lower
Shin	Jap.	Land
Shiro	Jap.	White
Shoto	Jap.	Islands
Si	Ch.	West
Sierra	Sp.	Mt. Range, Mts.
Sjö	Nor., Sw.	Lake, Sea
Sok, Suk, Souk	Arabic	Market
Song	Annamese	River
Sopka	Russ.	Volcano
Spitze	Ger.	Mt. Peak
Sredni, Srednyaya	Russ.	Middle
Stad	Dan., Nor., Sw.	City
Stari, Staraya	Russ.	Old
Step	Russ.	Treeless Plain
Straat	Du.	Strait
Strasse	Ger.	Strait
Stretto	It.	Strait
Ström	Dan., Nor., Sw.	Sound
Stung	Camb., Khmer	River
Su	Turk.	River
Sud, Süd	Sp., Fr., Ger.	South
Suido	Jap.	Strait, Channel
Sul	Port.	South
Sund	Dan., Nor., Sw.	Sound
Sungei	Malay	River
Supérieur	Fr.	Upper
Superior, Superiore	Sp., It.	Upper
Sur	Sp.	South
Suyu	Turk.	River
Ta	Ch.	Big
Tafelland	Du.	Plateau
Tagh	Turk.	Mt. Range
Take	Jap.	Peak, Ridge
Takht	Arabic	Lower
Tal	Ger.	Valley
Tanjung	Malay	Cape, Point
Tell	Arabic	Hill
Thale	Thai	Sea, Lake
Tind	Nor.	Peak
Tō	Jap.	East
To	Jap.	Island
Toge	Jap.	Pass
Trask	Finn.	Lake
Tugh	Somali	Dry River
Ujung	Malay	Point
Umi	Jap.	Bay
Unter	Ger.	Lower
Ura	Jap.	Inlet
Uul	Mong.	Mountain
Val	Fr.	Valley
Vatn	Nor.	Lake
Vecchio	It.	Old
Veld	Du.	Plain, Field
Velho	Port.	Old
Verkhni	Russ.	Upper
Vesi	Finn.	Lake
Viejo	Sp.	Old
Vik	Nor., Sw.	Bay
Vishni, Vishnyaya	Russ.	High
Vodokhranilishche	Russ.	Reservoir
Volcán	Sp.	Volcano
Vostochni, Vostochnaya	Russ.	East, Eastern
Wadi	Arabic	Dry River
Wald	Ger.	Forest
Wan	Jap.	Bay
Westersch	Du.	Western
Wüste	Ger.	Desert
Yama	Jap.	Mountain
Yug, Yuzhni, Yuzhnaya	Russ.	South, Southern
Zaki	Jap.	Cape
Zaliv	Russ.	Bay, Gulf
Zangbo	Tibetan	River, Stream
Zapadni, Zapadnaya	Russ.	Western
Zee	Du.	Sea
Zemlya	Russ.	Land
Zizhiqu	Ch.	Autonomous Region
Zuid	Du.	South

MAP PROJECTIONS

by Erwin Raisz

Our earth is rotating around its *axis* once a day. The two end points of its axis are the *poles;* the line circling the earth midway between the poles is the *equator.* The arc from either of the poles to the equator is divided into 90 *degrees.* The distance, expressed in degrees, from the equator to any point is its *latitude* and circles of equal latitude are the *parallels.* On maps it is customary to show parallels of evenly-spaced degrees such as every fifth or every tenth.

The equator is divided into 360 degrees. Lines circling from pole to pole through the degree points on the equator are called *meridians.* They are all equal in length but by international agreement the meridian passing through the Greenwich Observatory in London has been chosen as *prime meridian.* The distance, expressed in degrees, from the prime meridian to any point is its *longitude.* While meridians are all equal in length, parallels become shorter and shorter as they approach the poles. Whereas one degree of latitude represents everywhere approximately 69 miles, one degree of longitude varies from 69 miles at the equator to nothing at the poles.

Each degree is divided into 60 minutes and each minute into 60 seconds. One minute of latitude equals a nautical mile.

The map is flat but the earth is nearly spherical. Neither a rubber ball nor any part of a rubber ball may be flattened without stretching or tearing unless the part is very small. To present the curved surface of the earth on a flat map is not difficult as long as the areas under consideration are small, but the mapping of countries, continents, or the whole earth requires some kind of *projection.* Any regular set of parallels and meridians upon which a map can be drawn makes a map projection. Many systems are used.

In any projection only the parallels or the meridians or some other set of lines can be *true* (the same length as on the globe of corresponding scale); all other lines are too long or too short. Only on a globe is it possible to have both the parallels and the meridians true. The scale given on a flat map cannot be true everywhere. The construction of the various projections begins usually with laying out the parallels or meridians which have true lengths.

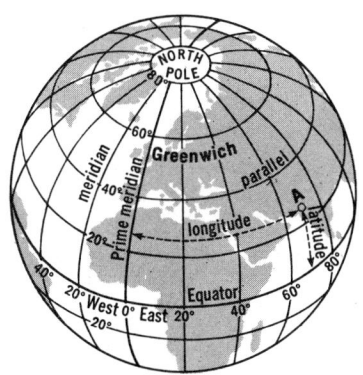

RECTANGULAR PROJECTION — This is a set of evenly-placed meridians and horizontal parallels. The central or *standard parallel* and all meridians are true. All other parallels are either too long or too short. The projection is used for simple maps of small areas, as city plans, etc.

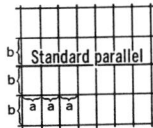

Rectangular Projection

MERCATOR PROJECTION — In this projection the meridians are evenly-spaced vertical lines. The parallels are horizontal, spaced so that their length has the same relation to the meridians as on a globe. As the meridians converge at higher latitudes on the globe, while on the map they do not, the parallels have to be drawn also farther and farther apart to maintain the correct relationship. When every very small area has the same shape as on a globe we call the projection *conformal.* The most interesting quality of this projection is that all *compass directions* appear as straight lines. For this reason it is generally used for marine charts. It is also frequently used for world maps in spite of the fact that the high latitudes are very much exaggerated in size. Only the equator is true to scale; all other parallels and meridians are too long. The Mercator projection did *not* derive from projecting a globe upon a cylinder.

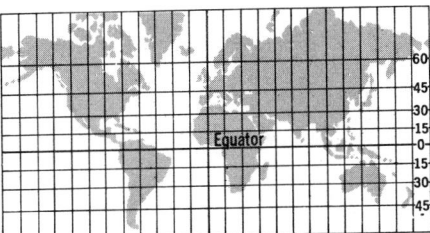

Mercator Projection

SINUSOIDAL PROJECTION — The parallels are truly-spaced horizontal lines. They are divided truly and the connecting curves make the meridians. It does not make a good world map because the outer regions are distorted, but the

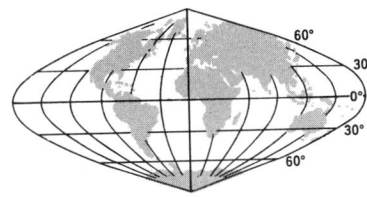

Sinusoidal Projection

central portion is good and this part is often used for maps of Africa and South America. Every part of the map has the same area as the corresponding area on the globe. It is an *equal-area* projection.

MOLLWEIDE PROJECTION — The meridians are equally-spaced ellipses; the parallels are horizontal lines spaced so that every belt of latitude should have the same area as on a globe. This projection is popular for world maps, especially in European atlases.

GOODE'S INTERRUPTED PROJECTIONS—Only the good central part of the Mollweide or sinusoidal (or both) projection is used and the oceans are cut. This makes an equal-area map with little distortion of shape. It is commonly used for world maps.

ECKERT PROJECTIONS — These are similar to the sinusoidal or the Mollweide projections, but the poles are shown as lines half the length of the equator. There are several variants; the meridians are either sine curves or ellipses; the parallels are horizontal and spaced either evenly or so as to make the projection equal area. Their use for world maps is increasing. The figure shows the elliptical equal-area variant.

CONIC PROJECTION — The original idea of the conic projection is that of capping the globe by a cone upon which both the parallels and meridians are projected from the center of the globe. The cone is then cut open and laid flat. A cone can be made tangent to any chosen *standard parallel.*

The actually-used conic projection is a modification of this idea. The radius of the standard parallel is obtained as above. The meridians are straight radiating lines spaced truly on the standard parallel. The parallels are concentric circles spaced at true distances. All parallels except the standard are too long. The projection is used for maps of countries in middle latitudes, as it presents good shapes with small scale error.

There are several variants: The use of *two standard parallels,* one near the top, the other near the bottom of the map, reduces the scale error. In the *Albers projection* the parallels are spaced unevenly, to make the projection equal-area. This is a good projection for the United States. In the *Lambert conformal conic projection* the parallels are spaced so that any small quadrangle of the grid should have the same shape as on the globe. This is the best projection for air-navigation charts as it has relatively straight azimuths.

An *azimuth* is a great-circle direction reckoned clockwise from north. A *great-circle direction* points to a place along the shortest line on the earth's surface. This is not the same as compass direction. The center of a great circle is the center of the globe.

BONNE PROJECTION — The parallels are laid out exactly as in the conic projection. All parallels are divided truly and the connecting curves make the meridians. It is an equal-area projection. It is used for maps of the northern continents, as Asia, Europe, and North America.

POLYCONIC PROJECTION — The central meridian is divided truly. The parallels are non-concentric circles, the radii of which are obtained by drawing tangents to the globe as though the globe were covered by several cones rather than by only one. Each parallel is divided truly and the connecting curves make the meridians. All meridians except the central one are too long. This projection is used for large-scale topographic sheets — less often for countries or continents.

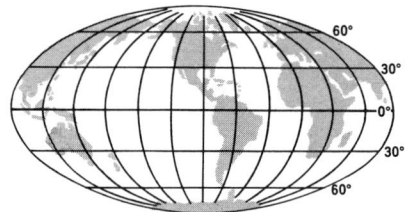

Mollweide Projection

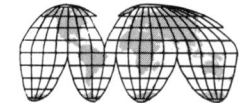

Goode's Interrupted Projection

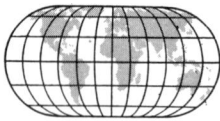

Eckert Projection

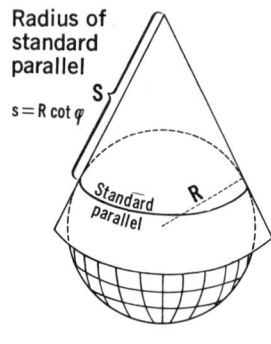

Radius of standard parallel

$s = R \cot \varphi$

Conic Projection

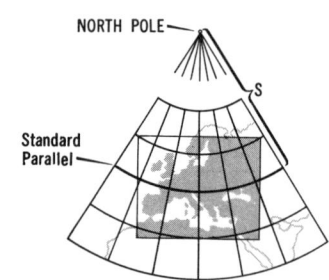

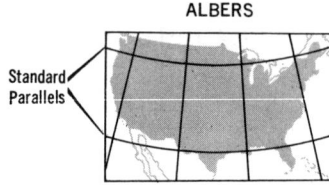

ALBERS

Albers Projection

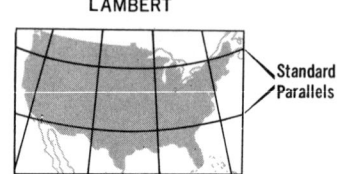

LAMBERT

Lambert Conformal Conic Projection

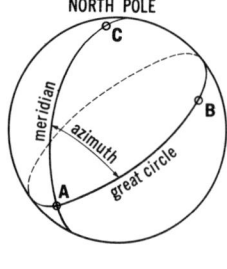

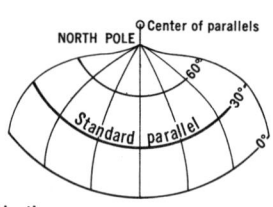

Bonne Projection

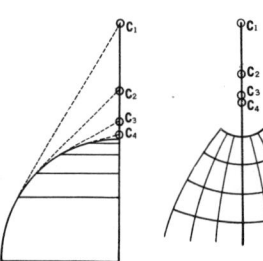

Polyconic Projection

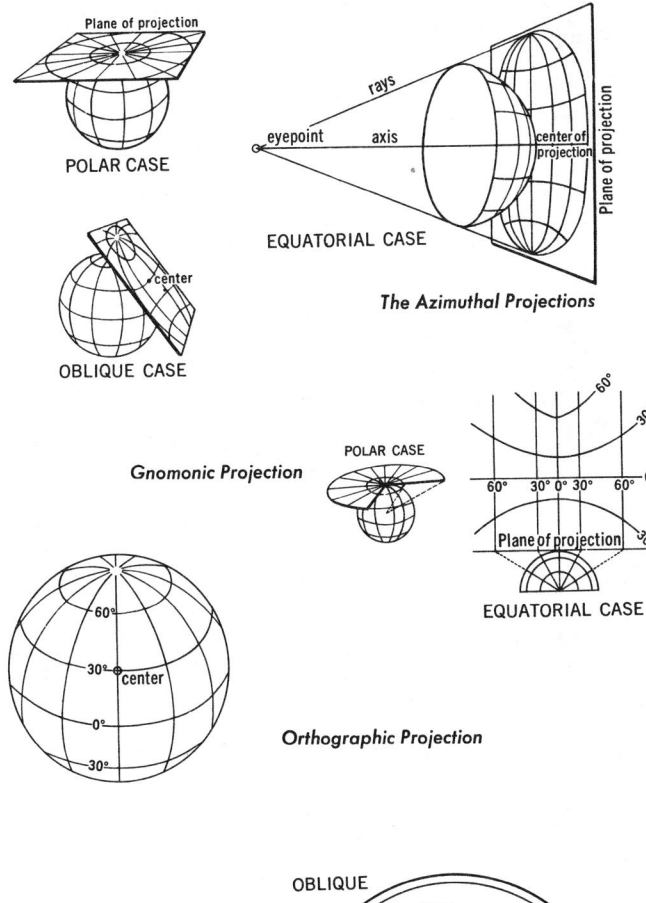

POLAR CASE

EQUATORIAL CASE

The Azimuthal Projections

OBLIQUE CASE

Gnomonic Projection

POLAR CASE

EQUATORIAL CASE

Orthographic Projection

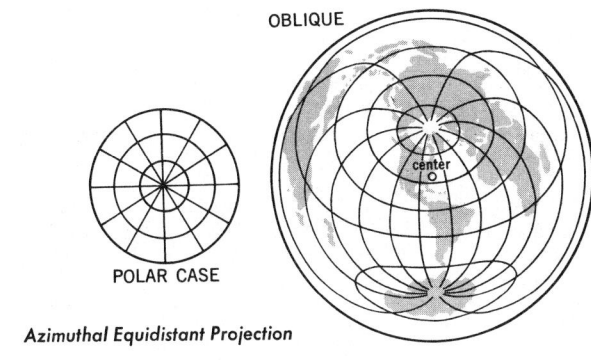

OBLIQUE

POLAR CASE

Azimuthal Equidistant Projection

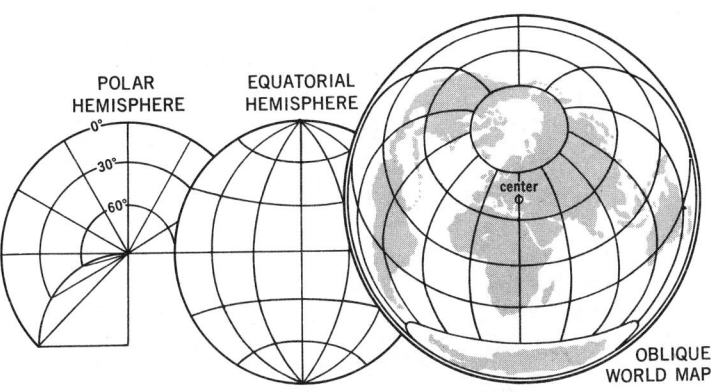

POLAR HEMISPHERE

EQUATORIAL HEMISPHERE

OBLIQUE WORLD MAP

Lambert Azimuthal Equal-Area Projection

THE AZIMUTHAL PROJECTIONS — In this group a part of the globe is projected from an eyepoint onto a plane. The eyepoint can be at different distances, making different projections. The plane of projection can be tangent at the equator, at a pole, or at any other point on which we want to focus attention. The most important quality of all azimuthal projections is that they show every point at its true direction (azimuth) from the center point, and all points equally distant from the center point will be equally distant on the map also.

GNOMONIC PROJECTION — This projection has the eyepoint at the center of the globe Only the central part is good; the outer regions are badly distorted. Yet the projection has one important quality, all great circles being shown as straight lines. For this reason it is used for laying out the routes for long range flying or trans-oceanic navigation.

ORTHOGRAPHIC PROJECTION — This projection has the eyepoint at infinite distance and the projecting rays are parallel. The polar or equatorial varieties are rare but the oblique case became very popular on account of its visual quality. It looks like a picture of a globe. Although the distortion on the peripheries is extreme, we see it correctly because the eye perceives it not as a map but as a picture of a three-dimensional globe. Obviously only a hemisphere (half globe) can be shown.

Some azimuthal projections do not derive from the actual process of projecting from an eyepoint, but are arrived at by other means:

AZIMUTHAL EQUIDISTANT PROJECTION — This is the only projection in which every point is shown both at true great-circle direction and at true distance from the center point, but all other directions and distances are distorted. The principle of the projection can best be understood from the polar case. Most polar maps are in this projection. The oblique case is used for radio direction finding, for earthquake research, and in long-distance flying. A separate map has to be constructed for each central point selected.

LAMBERT AZIMUTHAL EQUAL-AREA PROJECTION—The construction of this projection can best be understood from the polar case. All three cases are widely used. It makes a good polar map and it is often extended to include the southern continents. It is the most common projection used for maps of the Eastern and Western Hemispheres, and it is a good projection for continents as it shows correct areas with relatively little distortion of shape. Most of the continent maps in this atlas are in this projection.

IN THIS ATLAS, on almost all maps, parallels and meridians have been marked because they are useful for the following:

(a) They show the north-south and east-west directions which appear on many maps at oblique angles especially near the margins.

(b) With the help of parallels and meridians every place can be exactly located; for instance, New York City is at 41° N and 74° W on any map.

(c) They help to measure distances even in the distorted parts of the map. The scale given on each map is true only along certain lines which are specified in the foregoing discussion for each projection. One degree of latitude equals nearly 69 statute miles or 60 nautical miles. The length of one degree of longitude varies (1° long. = 1° lat. × cos lat.).

WORLD STATISTICAL TABLES

Elements of the Solar System

	Mean Distance from Sun: in Miles	in Kilometers	Period of Revolution around Sun	Period of Rotation on Axis	Equatorial Diameter: in Miles	in Kilometers	Surface Gravity (Earth = 1)	Mass (Earth = 1)	Mean Density (Water = 1)	Number of Satellites
MERCURY	35,990,000	57,900,000	87.97 days	59 days	3,032	4,880	0.38	0.055	5.5	0
VENUS	67,240,000	108,200,000	224.70 days	243 days†	7,523	12,106	0.90	0.815	5.25	0
EARTH	93,000,000	149,700,000	365.26 days	23h 56m	7,926	12,755	1.00	1.00	5.5	1
MARS	141,730,000	228,100,000	687.00 days	24h 37m	4,220	6,790	0.38	0.107	4.0	2
JUPITER	483,880,000	778,700,000	11.86 years	9h 50m	88,750	142,800	2.87	317.9	1.3	16
SATURN	887,130,000	1,427,700,000	29.46 years	10h 14m	74,580	120,020	1.32	95.2	0.7	17
URANUS	1,783,700,000	2,870,500,000	84.01 years	10h 49m†	31,600	50,900	0.93	14.6	1.3	5
NEPTUNE	2,795,500,000	4,498,800,000	164.79 years	15h 48m	30,200	48,600	1.23	17.2	1.8	3
PLUTO	3,667,900,000	5,902,800,000	247.70 years	6.39 days (?)	1,500	2,400	0.03 (?)	0.01(?)	0.7(?)	1

†Retrograde motion

Facts About the Sun

Equatorial diameter	865,000 miles	1,392,000 kilometers
Period of rotation on axis	25-35 days*	
Orbit of galaxy	every 225 million years	
Surface gravity (Earth = 1)	27.8	
Mass (Earth = 1)	333,000	
Density (Water = 1)	1.4	
Mean distance from Earth	93,000,000 miles	149,700,000 kilometers

*Rotation of 25 days at Equator, decreasing to about 35 days at the poles.

Facts About the Moon

Equatorial diameter	2,160 miles	3,476 kilometers
Period of rotation on axis	27 days, 7 hours, 43 minutes	
Period of revolution around Earth (sidereal month)	27 days, 7 hours, 43 minutes	
Phase period between new moons (synodic month)	29 days, 12 hours, 44 minutes	
Surface gravity (Earth = 1)	0.16	
Mass (Earth = 1)	0.0123	
Density (Water = 1)	3.34	
Maximum distance from Earth	252,710 miles	406,690 kilometers
Minimum distance from Earth	221,460 miles	356,400 kilometers
Mean distance from Earth	238,860 miles	384,400 kilometers

Dimensions of the Earth

	Area in Sq. Miles	Sq. Kilometers
Superficial area	197,751,000	512,175,090
Land surface	57,970,000	150,142,300
Water surface	139,781,000	362,032,790

	Miles	Kilometers
Equatorial circumference	24,902	40,075
Polar circumference	24,860	40,007
Equatorial diameter	7,926.68	12,756.4
Polar diameter	7,899.99	12,713.4
Equatorial radius	3,963.34	6,378.2
Polar radius	3,949.99	6,356.7
Volume of the Earth	2.6×10^{11} cubic miles	10.84×10^{11} cubic kilometers
Mass or weight	6.6×10^{21} short tons	6.0×10^{21} metric tons
Maximum distance from Sun	94,600,000 miles	152,000,000 kilometers
Minimum distance from Sun	91,300,000 miles	147,000,000 kilometers

The Continents

	Area in: Sq. Miles	Sq. Km.	Percent of World's Land
Asia	17,128,500	44,362,815	29.5
Africa	11,707,000	30,321,130	20.2
North America	9,363,000	24,250,170	16.2
South America	6,875,000	17,806,250	11.8
Antarctica	5,500,000	14,245,000	9.5
Europe	4,057,000	10,507,630	7.0
Australia	2,966,136	7,682,300	5.1

Oceans and Major Seas

	Area in: Sq. Miles	Sq. Km.	Greatest Depth in: Feet	Meters
Pacific Ocean	64,186,000	166,241,700	36,198	11,033
Atlantic Ocean	31,862,000	82,522,600	28,374	8,648
Indian Ocean	28,350,000	73,426,500	25,344	7,725
Arctic Ocean	5,427,000	14,056,000	17,880	5,450
Caribbean Sea	970,000	2,512,300	24,720	7,535
Mediterranean Sea	969,000	2,509,700	16,896	5,150
Bering Sea	875,000	2,266,250	15,800	4,800
Gulf of Mexico	600,000	1,554,000	12,300	3,750
Sea of Okhotsk	590,000	1,528,100	11,070	3,370
East China Sea	482,000	1,248,400	9,500	2,900
Sea of Japan	389,000	1,007,500	12,280	3,740
Hudson Bay	317,500	822,300	846	258
North Sea	222,000	575,000	2,200	670
Black Sea	185,000	479,150	7,365	2,245
Red Sea	169,000	437,700	7,200	2,195
Baltic Sea	163,000	422,170	1,506	459

Major Ship Canals

	Length in: Miles	Kms.	Minimum Feet	Depth in: Meters
Volga-Baltic, U.S.S.R.	225	362	—	—
Baltic-White Sea, U.S.S.R.	140	225	16	5
Suez, Egypt	100.76	162	42	13
Albert, Belgium	80	129	16.5	5
Moscow-Volga, U.S.S.R.	80	129	18	6
Volga-Don, U.S.S.R.	62	100	—	—
Göta, Sweden	54	87	10	3
Kiel (Nord-Ostsee), W. Ger.	53.2	86	38	12
Panama Canal, Panama	50.72	82	41.6	13
Houston Ship, U.S.A.	50	81	36	11

Largest Islands

	Area in: Sq. Mi.	Sq. Km.		Area in: Sq. Mi.	Sq. Km.		Area in: Sq. Mi.	Sq. Km.
Greenland	840,000	2,175,600	South I., New Zealand	58,393	151,238	Hokkaido, Japan	28,983	75,066
New Guinea	305,000	789,950	Java, Indonesia	48,842	126,501	Banks, Canada	27,038	70,028
Borneo	290,000	751,100	North I., New Zealand	44,187	114,444	Ceylon, Sri Lanka	25,332	65,610
Madagascar	226,400	586,376	Newfoundland, Canada	42,031	108,860	Tasmania, Australia	24,600	63,710
Baffin, Canada	195,928	507,454	Cuba	40,533	104,981	Svalbard, Norway	23,957	62,049
Sumatra, Indonesia	164,000	424,760	Luzon, Philippines	40,420	104,688	Devon, Canada	21,331	55,247
Honshu, Japan	88,000	227,920	Iceland	39,768	103,000	Novaya Zemlya (north isl.), U.S.S.R.	18,600	48,200
Great Britain	84,400	218,896	Mindanao, Philippines	36,537	94,631	Marajó, Brazil	17,991	46,597
Victoria, Canada	83,896	217,290	Ireland	31,743	82,214	Tierra del Fuego, Chile & Argentina	17,900	46,360
Ellesmere, Canada	75,767	196,236	Sakhalin, U.S.S.R.	29,500	76,405	Alexander, Antarctica	16,700	43,250
Celebes, Indonesia	72,986	189,034	Hispaniola, Haiti & Dom. Rep.	29,399	76,143			

Principal Mountains of the World

Mountain	Feet	Meters
Everest, Nepal-China	29,028	8,848
Godwin Austen (K2), Pakistan-China	28,250	8,611
Kanchenjunga, Nepal-India	28,208	8,598
Lhotse, Nepal-China	27,923	8,511
Makalu, Nepal-China	27,824	8,481
Dhaulagiri, Nepal	26,810	8,172
Nanga Parbat, Pakistan	26,660	8,126
Annapurna, Nepal	26,504	8,078
Gasherbrum, Pakistan-China	26,740	8,068
Nanda Devi, India	25,645	7,817
Rakaposhi, Pakistan	25,550	7,788
Kamet, India	25,447	7,756
Gurla Mandhada, China	25,355	7,728
Kongur Shan, China	25,325	7,719
Tirich Mir, Pakistan	25,230	7,690
Gongga Shan, China	24,790	7,556
Muztagata, China	24,757	7,546
Communism Peak, U.S.S.R.	24,599	7,498
Pobeda Peak, U.S.S.R.	24,406	7,439
Chomo Lhari, Bhutan-China	23,997	7,314
Muztag, China	23,891	7,282
Cerro Aconcagua, Argentina	22,831	6,959
Ojos del Salado, Chile-Argentina	22,572	6,880
Bonete, Chile-Argentina	22,541	6,870
Tupungato, Chile-Argentina	22,310	6,800
Pissis, Argentina	22,241	6,779
Mercedario, Argentina	22,211	6,770
Huascarán, Peru	22,205	6,768
Llullaillaco, Chile-Argentina	22,057	6,723
Nevada Ancohuma, Bolivia	21,489	6,550
Illampu, Bolivia	21,276	6,485
Chimborazo, Ecuador	20,561	6,267
McKinley, Alaska	20,320	6,194
Logan, Canada (Yukon)	19,524	5,951
Cotopaxi, Ecuador	19,347	5,897
Kilimanjaro, Tanzania	19,340	5,895
El Misti, Peru	19,101	5,822
Pico Cristóbal Colón, Colombia	19,029	5,800
Huila, Colombia	18,865	5,750
Citlaltépetl (Orizaba), Mexico	18,855	5,747
El'brus, U.S.S.R.	18,510	5,642
Damavand, Iran	18,376	5,601
St. Elias, Alaska-Canada (Yukon)	18,008	5,489
Vilcanota, Peru	17,999	5,486
Popocatépetl, Mexico	17,887	5,452
Dykhtau, U.S.S.R.	17,070	5,203
Kenya, Kenya	17,058	5,199
Ararat, Turkey	16,946	5,165
Vinson Massif, Antarctica	16,864	5,140
Margherita (Ruwenzori), Africa	16,795	5,119
Kazbek, U.S.S.R.	16,512	5,033
Puncak Jaya, Indonesia	16,503	5,030
Tyree, Antarctica	16,289	4,965
Blanc, France	15,771	4,807
Klyuchevskaya Sopka, U.S.S.R.	15,584	4,750
Fairweather (Br. Col., Canada)	15,300	4,663
Dufourspitze (Mte. Rosa), Italy-Switzerland	15,203	4,634
Ras Dashan, Ethiopia	15,157	4,620
Matterhorn, Switzerland	14,691	4,478
Whitney, California, U.S.A.	14,494	4,418
Elbert, Colorado, U.S.A.	14,433	4,399
Rainier, Washington, U.S.A.	14,410	4,392
Shasta, California, U.S.A.	14,162	4,350
Pikes Peak, Colorado, U.S.A.	14,110	4,301
Finsteraarhorn, Switzerland	14,022	4,274
Mauna Kea, Hawaii, U.S.A.	13,796	4,205
Mauna Loa, Hawaii, U.S.A.	13,677	4,169
Jungfrau, Switzerland	13,642	4,158
Cameroon, Cameroon	13,350	4,069
Grossglockner, Austria	12,457	3,797
Fuji, Japan	12,389	3,776
Cook, New Zealand	12,349	3,764
Etna, Italy	11,053	3,369
Kosciusko, Australia	7,310	2,228
Mitchell, North Carolina, U.S.A.	6,684	2,037

Longest Rivers of the World

River	Length in: Miles	Length in: Kms.
Nile, Africa	4,145	6,671
Amazon, S. Amer.	3,915	6,300
Chang Jiang (Yangtze), China	3,900	6,276
Mississippi-Missouri-Red Rock, U.S.A.	3,741	6,019
Ob'Irtysh-Black Irtysh, U.S.S.R.	3,362	5,411
Yenisey-Angara, U.S.S.R.	3,100	4,989
Huang He (Yellow), China	2,877	4,630
Amur-Shilka-Onon, Asia	2,744	4,416
Lena, U.S.S.R.	2,734	4,400
Congo (Zaire), Africa	2,718	4,374
Mackenzie-Peace-Finlay, Canada	2,635	4,241
Mekong, Asia	2,610	4,200
Missouri-Red Rock, U.S.A.	2,564	4,125
Niger, Africa	2,548	4,101
Paraná-La Plata, S. Amer.	2,450	3,943
Mississippi, U.S.A.	2,348	3,778
Murray-Darling, Australia	2,310	3,718
Volga, U.S.S.R.	2,194	3,531
Madeira, S. Amer.	2,013	3,240
Purus, S. Amer.	1,995	3,211
Yukon, Alaska-Canada	1,979	3,185
St. Lawrence, Canada-U.S.A.	1,900	3,058
Rio Grande, Mexico-U.S.A.	1,885	3,034
Syrdar'ya-Naryn, U.S.S.R.	1,859	2,992
São Francisco, Brazil	1,811	2,914
Indus, Asia	1,800	2,897
Danube, Europe	1,775	2,857
Salween, Asia	1,770	2,849
Brahmaputra, Asia	1,700	2,736
Euphrates, Asia	1,700	2,736
Tocantins, Brazil	1,677	2,699
Xi (Si), China	1,650	2,655
Amudar'ya, Asia	1,616	2,601
Nelson-Saskatchewan, Canada	1,600	2,575
Orinoco, S. Amer.	1,600	2,575
Zambezi, Africa	1,600	2,575
Paraguay, S. Amer.	1,584	2,549
Kolyma, U.S.S.R.	1,562	2,514
Ganges, Asia	1,550	2,494
Ural, U.S.S.R.	1,509	2,428
Japurá, S. Amer.	1,500	2,414
Arkansas, U.S.A.	1,450	2,334
Colorado, U.S.A.-Mexico	1,450	2,334
Negro, S. Amer.	1,400	2,253
Dnieper, U.S.S.R.	1,368	2,202
Orange, Africa	1,350	2,173
Irrawaddy, Burma	1,325	2,132
Brazos, U.S.A.	1,309	2,107
Ohio-Allegheny, U.S.A.	1,306	2,102
Kama, U.S.S.R.	1,262	2,031
Red, U.S.A.	1,222	1,966
Don, U.S.S.R.	1,222	1,967
Columbia, U.S.A.-Canada	1,214	1,953
Saskatchewan, Canada	1,205	1,939
Peace-Finlay, Canada	1,195	1,923
Tigris, Asia	1,181	1,901
Darling, Australia	1,160	1,867
Angara, U.S.S.R.	1,135	1,827
Sungari, Asia	1,130	1,819
Pechora, U.S.S.R.	1,124	1,809
Snake, U.S.A.	1,000	1,609
Churchill, Canada	1,000	1,609
Pilcomayo, S. Amer.	1,000	1,609
Magdalena, Colombia	1,000	1,609
Uruguay, S. Amer.	994	1,600
Platte-N. Platte, U.S.A.	990	1,593
Ohio, U.S.A.	981	1,578
Pecos, U.S.A.	926	1,490
Oka, U.S.S.R.	918	1,477
Canadian, U.S.A.	906	1,458
Colorado, Texas, U.S.A.	894	1,439
Dniester, U.S.S.R.	876	1,410

Principal Natural Lakes

Lake	Area in: Sq. Miles	Area in: Sq. Km.	Max. Depth in: Feet	Max. Depth in: Meters
Caspian Sea, U.S.S.R.-Iran	143,243	370,999	3,264	995
Lake Superior, U.S.A.-Canada	31,820	82,414	1,329	405
Lake Victoria, Africa	26,724	69,215	270	82
Aral Sea, U.S.S.R.	25,676	66,501	256	78
Lake Huron, U.S.A.-Canada	23,010	59,596	748	228
Lake Michigan, U.S.A.	22,400	58,016	923	281
Lake Tanganyika, Africa	12,650	32,764	4,700	1,433
Lake Baykal, U.S.S.R.	12,162	31,500	5,316	1,620
Great Bear Lake, Canada	12,096	31,328	1,356	413
Lake Nyasa (Malawi), Africa	11,555	29,928	2,320	707
Great Slave Lake, Canada	11,031	28,570	2,015	614
Lake Erie, U.S.A.-Canada	9,940	25,745	210	64
Lake Winnipeg, Canada	9,417	24,390	60	18
Lake Ontario, U.S.A.-Canada	7,540	19,529	775	244
Lake Ladoga, U.S.S.R.	7,104	18,399	738	225
Lake Balkhash, U.S.S.R.	7,027	18,200	87	27
Lake Maracaibo, Venezuela	5,120	13,261	100	31
Lake Chad, Africa	4,000-10,000	10,360-25,900	25	8
Lake Onega, U.S.S.R.	3,710	9,609	377	115
Lake Eyre, Australia	3,500-0	9,000-0	—	—
Lake Titicaca, Peru-Bolivia	3,200	8,288	1,000	305
Lake Nicaragua, Nicaragua	3,100	8,029	230	70
Lake Athabasca, Canada	3,064	7,936	400	122
Reindeer Lake, Canada	2,568	6,651	—	—
Lake Turkana (Rudolf), Africa	2,463	6,379	240	73
Issyk-Kul', U.S.S.R.	2,425	6,281	2,303	702
Lake Torrens, Australia	2,230	5,776	—	—
Vänern, Sweden	2,156	5,584	328	100
Nettilling Lake, Canada	2,140	5,543	—	—
Lake Winnipegosis, Canada	2,075	5,374	38	12
Lake Mobutu Sese Seko (Albert), Africa	2,075	5,374	160	49
Kariba Lake, Zambia-Zimbabwe	2,050	5,310	295	90
Lake Nipigon, Canada	1,872	4,848	540	165
Lake Mweru, Zaire-Zambia	1,800	4,662	60	18
Lake Manitoba, Canada	1,799	4,659	12	4
Lake Taymyr, U.S.S.R.	1,737	4,499	85	26
Lake Khanka, China-U.S.S.R.	1,700	4,403	33	10
Lake Kioga, Uganda	1,700	4,403	25	8

Foreign City Weather

Two figures are given for each of the months, thus 88/73. The first figure is the average daily high temperature (°F) and the second is the average daily low temperature (°F) for the month. The boldface figures indicate the average number of days with rain for each month.

City	January	February	March	April	May	June	July	August	September	October	November	December
ABIDJAN, Ivory Coast	88/73 **3**	90/75 **4**	90/75 **6**	90/75 **9**	88/75 **16**	85/73 **18**	83/73 **8**	82/71 **7**	83/73 **8**	85/74 **13**	87/74 **13**	88/74 **6**
ACAPULCO, Mexico	85/70 **0**	87/70 **0**	87/70 **0**	87/71 **1**	89/74 **4**	89/76 **15**	89/75 **11**	89/75 **14**	88/75 **18**	88/74 **12**	88/72 **4**	87/70 **1**
ACCRA, Ghana	87/73 **1**	88/75 **2**	88/76 **4**	88/76 **6**	87/75 **9**	84/74 **10**	81/73 **4**	80/71 **3**	81/73 **4**	85/74 **6**	87/75 **3**	88/75 **2**
ADDIS ABABA, Ethiopia	75/43 **2**	76/47 **4**	77/49 **8**	77/50 **10**	77/50 **10**	74/49 **20**	69/50 **28**	70/51 **27**	72/49 **21**	75/45 **3**	73/43 **2**	73/41 **2**
ALGIERS, Algeria	59/49 **11**	61/49 **9**	63/52 **9**	68/55 **5**	73/59 **5**	78/65 **3**	83/70 **1**	85/71 **1**	81/69 **4**	74/63 **7**	66/56 **11**	60/51 **12**
AMSTERDAM, Netherlands	40/34 **19**	41/34 **15**	46/37 **13**	52/43 **14**	60/50 **12**	65/55 **12**	69/59 **14**	68/59 **14**	64/56 **15**	56/48 **18**	47/41 **19**	41/35 **19**
ANKARA, Turkey	39/24 **8**	42/26 **8**	51/31 **7**	63/40 **7**	73/49 **7**	78/53 **5**	86/59 **2**	87/59 **1**	78/52 **3**	69/44 **5**	57/37 **6**	43/29 **9**
APIA, Western Samoa	86/75 **22**	85/76 **19**	86/76 **19**	86/75 **14**	85/74 **12**	85/74 **7**	85/74 **7**	84/75 **5**	84/74 **11**	85/75 **14**	86/74 **16**	85/74 **19**
ATHENS, Greece	54/42 **7**	55/43 **6**	60/46 **5**	67/52 **3**	77/60 **3**	85/67 **2**	90/72 **1**	90/72 **1**	83/66 **2**	74/60 **4**	64/52 **6**	57/46 **7**
BAGHDAD, Iraq	60/39 **4**	64/42 **3**	71/48 **4**	85/57 **3**	97/67 **1**	105/73 **0**	110/76 **0**	110/76 **0**	104/70 **0**	92/61 **1**	77/51 **3**	64/42 **5**
BALI, Indonesia	88/74 **19**	88/74 **14**	88/74 **13**	88/74 **7**	88/73 **5**	87/71 **3**	87/70 **1**	87/70 **1**	89/71 **1**	90/73 **2**	90/75 **6**	88/74 **14**
BANGKOK, Thailand	89/68 **1**	91/72 **1**	93/75 **3**	95/77 **3**	93/77 **9**	91/76 **10**	90/76 **13**	90/76 **13**	89/76 **15**	88/75 **14**	87/72 **5**	87/68 **1**
BARCELONA, Spain	56/42 **5**	57/44 **7**	61/47 **7**	64/51 **8**	71/57 **8**	77/63 **5**	81/69 **4**	82/69 **5**	78/65 **7**	71/58 **8**	62/50 **7**	57/44 **6**
BEIRUT, Lebanon	62/51 **15**	63/51 **12**	66/54 **9**	72/58 **5**	78/64 **2**	84/74 **12**	83/73 **11**	84/74 **11**	84/74 **9**	85/74 **9**	85/73 **12**	85/73 **15**
BELFAST, Northern Ireland	45/34 **22**	47/34 **18**	49/35 **20**	53/39 **18**	59/43 **17**	64/49 **10**	66/51 **18**	65/51 **20**	62/48 **17**	55/42 **19**	50/37 **21**	46/35 **25**
BELGRADE, Yugoslavia	37/27 **8**	41/27 **6**	53/35 **7**	64/45 **9**	74/53 **9**	79/58 **9**	84/61 **6**	83/60 **7**	76/55 **6**	65/47 **8**	52/39 **7**	40/30 **9**
BERLIN, Germany	35/26 **10**	38/27 **8**	46/32 **9**	55/38 **9**	65/46 **8**	70/51 **9**	74/55 **10**	72/54 **10**	66/48 **8**	55/41 **8**	43/33 **8**	37/29 **11**
BIARRITZ, France	54/40 **10**	52/38 **11**	63/43 **11**	63/44 **11**	69/53 **11**	72/56 **10**	80/66 **7**	77/61 **7**	77/58 **9**	74/55 **11**	58/44 **12**	53/41 **14**
BOGOTA, Colombia	67/48 **6**	68/49 **7**	67/50 **13**	67/51 **20**	67/51 **17**	65/51 **16**	64/50 **18**	65/50 **16**	66/49 **13**	66/50 **20**	66/50 **16**	66/49 **15**
BOMBAY, India	83/67 **1**	83/67 **1**	86/72 **1**	89/76 **1**	91/80 **1**	89/79 **14**	85/77 **21**	85/76 **19**	85/76 **13**	89/76 **3**	89/73 **1**	87/69 **1**
BONN, West Germany	39/30 **7**	37/26 **6**	50/35 **7**	58/39 **14**	67/46 **13**	69/52 **19**	73/56 **16**	72/55 **17**	67/50 **16**	58/45 **16**	47/37 **15**	44/36 **15**
BRASILIA, Brazil	80/65 **17**	81/64 **20**	82/64 **7**	82/62 **10**	79/56 **5**	77/52 **0**	78/51 **2**	82/55 **0**	87/60 **2**	82/64 **16**	82/66 **17**	78/64 **16**
BRINDISI, Italy	55/43 **10**	57/43 **6**	60/45 **5**	65/50 **5**	73/57 **5**	80/64 **2**	84/68 **1**	84/69 **3**	80/65 **4**	70/58 **8**	64/52 **10**	58/46 **8**
BUCHAREST, Romania	33/20 **6**	38/24 **6**	51/33 **6**	63/41 **6**	74/51 **8**	81/58 **9**	86/61 **7**	86/60 **5**	76/53 **5**	65/44 **5**	49/35 **6**	37/26 **6**
BUDAPEST, Hungary	35/26 **7**	40/28 **6**	51/36 **7**	62/44 **8**	72/52 **9**	78/57 **8**	82/61 **7**	81/59 **6**	74/53 **7**	61/45 **8**	47/37 **8**	38/31 **9**
BUENOS AIRES, Argentina	85/63 **7**	83/63 **6**	79/60 **7**	72/53 **8**	64/47 **7**	57/41 **7**	57/42 **8**	60/43 **9**	64/46 **8**	69/50 **8**	76/56 **9**	82/61 **8**
CAIRO, Egypt	65/47 **1**	69/48 **1**	75/52 **1**	83/57 **1**	91/63 **1**	95/68 **0**	96/70 **0**	95/71 **0**	90/68 **0**	86/65 **1**	78/58 **1**	68/50 **1**
CALCUTTA, India	80/55 **1**	84/59 **1**	93/69 **2**	97/75 **3**	96/77 **7**	92/79 **13**	89/79 **18**	89/78 **18**	90/78 **13**	89/74 **6**	84/64 **1**	79/55 **1**
CAPE TOWN, South Africa	78/60 **3**	79/60 **2**	77/58 **3**	72/53 **6**	67/49 **9**	65/46 **9**	63/45 **10**	64/46 **9**	65/49 **7**	70/52 **5**	73/55 **3**	76/58 **3**
CARACAS, Venezuela	75/56 **6**	79/56 **2**	79/58 **3**	81/60 **4**	80/62 **9**	78/62 **14**	78/61 **15**	79/61 **15**	80/61 **13**	79/61 **12**	77/60 **13**	78/58 **10**
CHARLOTTE AMALIE, Virgin Islands	82/73 **18**	81/72 **13**	82/73 **12**	83/74 **13**	85/76 **15**	86/77 **15**	87/78 **16**	88/78 **19**	87/78 **17**	87/77 **18**	85/76 **19**	83/74 **18**
COLOMBO, Sri Lanka	86/72 **7**	87/72 **2**	88/74 **8**	88/76 **14**	87/79 **19**	85/77 **17**	85/77 **12**	85/77 **11**	85/75 **13**	85/75 **19**	85/73 **16**	85/72 **10**
COPENHAGEN, Denmark	36/29 **9**	36/28 **7**	41/31 **8**	50/37 **9**	61/44 **8**	67/51 **8**	72/55 **9**	69/54 **12**	63/49 **8**	53/42 **9**	43/35 **10**	38/32 **11**
DARWIN, Australia	90/77 **20**	90/77 **18**	91/77 **17**	92/76 **6**	91/73 **1**	88/69 **1**	87/67 **0**	89/70 **0**	91/74 **2**	93/77 **5**	94/78 **10**	92/78 **15**
DJAKARTA, Indonesia	84/74 **18**	84/74 **17**	86/74 **15**	87/75 **11**	87/75 **9**	87/74 **7**	87/73 **5**	87/73 **4**	88/74 **5**	87/74 **8**	86/74 **12**	85/74 **14**
DUBLIN, Ireland	47/35 **13**	47/35 **11**	51/36 **10**	54/38 **11**	59/42 **11**	65/48 **11**	67/51 **13**	67/51 **13**	63/47 **12**	57/43 **12**	51/38 **12**	47/36 **13**
EDINBURGH, Scotland	43/35 **18**	43/35 **15**	47/36 **15**	50/39 **16**	55/43 **15**	62/48 **15**	65/52 **17**	64/52 **17**	60/48 **16**	53/44 **18**	47/39 **18**	44/36 **17**
FLORENCE, Italy	49/35 **9**	53/36 **9**	60/40 **7**	68/46 **7**	75/53 **9**	84/58 **5**	89/63 **4**	88/62 **4**	81/58 **6**	69/51 **9**	58/42 **10**	50/37 **9**
GENEVA, Switzerland	39/29 **10**	43/30 **9**	51/35 **10**	58/41 **11**	66/48 **12**	73/55 **11**	77/58 **9**	76/57 **10**	69/52 **10**	58/44 **11**	47/37 **11**	40/31 **10**
GUAYAQUIL, Ecuador	88/70 **20**	87/71 **25**	88/72 **24**	89/71 **14**	88/68 **9**	87/68 **4**	84/67 **2**	86/65 **0**	87/66 **2**	86/68 **3**	88/68 **4**	88/70 **10**
HAMBURG, West Germany	35/28 **12**	37/30 **10**	42/33 **10**	51/39 **11**	60/47 **9**	67/53 **10**	69/56 **12**	67/55 **13**	63/51 **10**	53/44 **11**	44/36 **11**	38/31 **12**
HAMILTON, Bermuda	68/58 **14**	68/57 **12**	68/57 **12**	71/59 **9**	76/64 **9**	81/69 **9**	85/73 **10**	86/74 **13**	84/72 **10**	79/69 **12**	74/63 **13**	70/60 **15**
HAVANA, Cuba	79/65 **6**	79/65 **4**	81/67 **4**	84/69 **4**	86/72 **7**	88/74 **10**	89/75 **9**	89/75 **10**	88/75 **11**	85/73 **11**	81/69 **7**	79/67 **6**
HELSINKI, Finland	27/17 **11**	26/15 **8**	32/22 **8**	43/31 **8**	55/41 **8**	63/49 **9**	71/57 **8**	66/55 **12**	57/46 **11**	45/37 **12**	37/30 **11**	31/22 **11**
HONG KONG	64/56 **4**	63/55 **5**	67/60 **7**	75/67 **8**	82/74 **13**	85/78 **18**	87/78 **17**	87/78 **15**	85/77 **12**	81/73 **6**	74/65 **2**	68/59 **3**
JERUSALEM, Israel	55/41 **9**	56/42 **11**	65/46 **3**	73/50 **3**	81/57 **1**	85/60 **1**	87/63 **0**	87/64 **0**	85/62 **1**	81/59 **4**	70/53 **4**	59/45 **7**
JOHANNESBURG, South Africa	78/58 **12**	77/58 **11**	75/55 **9**	72/50 **4**	66/43 **3**	62/39 **1**	63/39 **1**	68/43 **1**	73/48 **2**	77/53 **7**	77/55 **10**	78/57 **11**
KARACHI, Pakistan	77/55 **1**	79/58 **1**	85/67 **1**	90/73 **1**	93/79 **1**	93/82 **1**	91/81 **2**	88/79 **2**	88/77 **1**	91/72 **1**	87/64 **1**	80/57 **1**
KINGSTON, Jamaica	86/67 **3**	86/67 **3**	86/68 **2**	87/70 **3**	87/72 **4**	89/74 **5**	90/73 **4**	90/73 **7**	89/73 **6**	88/73 **9**	87/71 **5**	87/69 **4**
LAGOS, Nigeria	88/74 **2**	89/77 **3**	89/78 **7**	89/77 **10**	87/76 **16**	85/74 **20**	83/74 **16**	82/73 **10**	83/74 **14**	85/74 **16**	88/75 **7**	88/75 **2**
LA PAZ, Bolivia	63/43 **21**	63/43 **18**	64/42 **16**	65/40 **9**	64/37 **5**	62/34 **2**	62/33 **2**	63/35 **4**	64/38 **9**	66/40 **9**	67/42 **11**	65/42 **18**

Foreign City Weather

City	January	February	March	April	May	June	July	August	September	October	November	December
LAS PALMAS, Canary Is.	70/58 8	71/58 5	71/59 5	71/61 3	73/62 1	75/65 1	77/67 1	79/70 1	79/69 1	79/67 5	76/64 7	72/60 8
LENINGRAD, USSR	23/12 17	24/12 15	33/18 13	45/31 11	58/42 12	66/51 12	71/57 13	66/53 15	57/45 14	45/37 15	34/27 17	26/18 18
LIMA, Peru	82/66 9	83/67 4	83/66 10	80/63 7	74/60 1	68/58 1	67/57 1	66/56 2	68/57 1	71/58 1	74/60 1	78/62 1
LISBON, Portugal	56/46 9	58/47 8	61/49 10	64/52 7	69/56 6	75/60 2	79/63 1	80/64 1	76/62 4	69/57 7	62/52 10	57/47 10
LIVERPOOL, England	44/36 18	44/36 13	48/38 13	52/41 14	58/46 14	63/51 13	66/55 13	65/55 16	61/51 15	55/46 17	48/41 17	45/37 18
LONDON, England	44/35 17	45/35 13	51/47 11	56/40 14	63/45 13	69/51 11	73/55 13	72/54 13	67/51 13	58/44 14	49/39 16	45/36 16
MADRID, Spain	47/33 9	51/35 9	57/40 11	64/44 9	71/50 9	80/57 6	87/62 3	86/62 2	77/56 6	66/48 8	54/40 10	48/35 9
MANILA, Philippines	86/69 6	88/69 3	91/71 4	93/73 4	93/75 12	91/75 17	88/75 24	87/75 23	88/75 22	88/74 19	87/72 14	86/70 11
MARACAIBO, Venezuela	90/73 1	90/73 1	91/74 1	92/76 1	92/77 1	93/77 0	94/76 5	94/77 4	94/77 6	92/76 7	91/76 8	91/75 2
MARSEILLE, France	53/38 10	52/37 8	55/38 8	59/41 10	65/46 10	72/52 9	78/58 6	83/61 4	82/61 5	76/57 7	67/50 10	59/43 11
MELBOURNE, Australia	78/57 9	78/57 8	75/55 9	68/51 13	62/47 14	57/44 16	56/42 17	59/43 17	63/46 15	67/48 14	71/51 13	75/54 11
MEXICO CITY, Mexico	66/42 4	69/43 5	75/47 4	77/51 14	78/54 17	76/55 21	73/53 27	73/54 27	74/53 23	70/50 13	68/46 6	66/43 4
MILAN, Italy	40/29 7	47/33 6	56/38 6	66/46 6	72/54 9	80/61 6	84/64 6	82/63 7	76/58 6	64/49 7	51/39 7	42/33 7
MONTEVIDEO, Uruguay	83/62 6	82/61 5	78/59 5	71/53 6	64/48 6	59/43 5	58/43 6	58/43 6	63/46 6	68/49 6	74/54 6	79/59 7
MOSCOW, USSR	21/9 11	23/10 9	32/17 8	47/31 9	65/44 9	73/51 10	76/55 12	72/52 12	61/43 9	46/34 11	31/23 10	23/13 9
MUNICH, West Germany	33/23 10	37/25 9	45/31 10	54/37 13	63/45 13	69/51 14	72/54 14	71/53 13	64/48 11	53/40 10	42/31 9	36/26 11
NAIROBI, Kenya	77/54 5	79/55 6	77/57 11	75/58 16	72/56 17	70/53 9	69/51 6	70/52 7	75/52 6	76/55 8	74/56 15	74/55 11
NAPLES, Italy	54/42 11	55/43 11	60/46 6	67/50 6	73/56 6	81/62 3	86/67 1	86/67 3	81/63 6	72/56 9	63/49 11	57/45 11
NASSAU, Bahamas	77/65 6	77/64 6	79/66 5	81/69 6	84/71 9	87/74 12	88/75 14	89/76 14	88/75 15	85/73 13	81/70 9	79/67 6
NEW DELHI, India	70/44 2	75/49 2	87/58 1	97/68 1	105/79 2	102/83 4	96/81 8	93/79 8	93/75 4	93/65 1	84/52 1	73/46 1
NICE, France	56/40 8	56/41 8	59/45 8	64/49 7	69/56 8	76/62 5	81/66 2	81/66 5	77/62 6	70/55 7	62/48 7	58/43 8
NOUMEA, New Caledonia	86/72 10	85/73 12	85/72 16	83/70 13	79/66 15	77/64 13	76/62 13	76/61 12	78/63 8	80/65 7	83/68 7	86/70 6
ODESSA, USSR	28/22 7	31/26 4	39/32 5	52/41 6	67/55 6	74/62 7	79/65 6	78/65 5	68/56 4	57/47 5	43/35 5	33/27 6
OSLO, Norway	30/20 8	32/20 7	40/25 7	50/34 7	62/43 7	69/51 8	73/56 10	69/53 11	60/45 8	49/37 10	37/29 9	31/24 10
PALERMO, Sicily, Italy	58/47 14	60/47 10	62/49 7	67/53 5	83/59 5	82/66 1	86/71 1	87/72 1	83/69 4	75/62 10	67/55 9	61/50 11
PALMA, Majorca, Spain	57/42 8	59/43 8	62/45 8	66/49 5	73/55 5	80/61 3	84/66 1	87/67 2	81/64 6	74/57 8	65/50 9	59/44 10
PAPEETE, Tahiti	89/72 16	89/72 16	89/72 17	89/72 10	87/70 10	86/69 8	86/68 5	86/68 6	86/69 6	87/70 9	88/71 13	88/72 14
PARIS, France	42/32 15	45/33 13	52/36 15	60/41 14	67/47 13	73/52 11	76/55 12	75/55 12	69/50 11	59/44 14	49/38 15	43/33 17
PEKING, China	35/15 3	41/20 3	53/30 3	68/44 4	80/56 4	88/65 9	89/71 13	87/69 11	80/58 7	69/44 4	50/30 2	37/19 2
PHNOM PENH, Cambodia	87/70 1	90/72 1	93/74 3	94/76 6	92/76 14	91/76 15	89/76 16	89/76 17	89/76 19	87/75 17	86/74 7	86/71 4
PORT-AU-PRINCE, Haiti	87/68 3	88/68 5	87/69 7	89/71 11	90/72 13	92/73 8	94/74 7	93/73 11	91/73 12	90/72 12	88/71 7	87/69 3
PORT OF SPAIN, Trinidad	85/67 14	86/67 8	87/67 8	88/69 7	89/70 10	87/71 17	87/70 20	87/71 21	88/71 18	88/71 16	87/70 17	86/69 16
PRAGUE, Czechoslovakia	34/25 12	38/28 11	45/33 13	55/40 12	65/49 13	72/55 14	74/58 14	73/57 12	65/52 11	54/44 11	41/35 12	34/29 13
RANGOON, Burma	89/65 1	92/67 1	96/71 1	97/76 2	92/77 14	86/76 23	85/76 26	85/76 25	86/76 20	88/76 10	88/73 8	88/67
RIO DE JANEIRO, Brazil	84/73 13	85/73 11	83/72 12	80/69 10	77/65 10	76/64 7	75/63 7	76/64 7	75/65 11	77/65 11	79/68 13	82/71 14
ROME, Italy	54/39 8	56/39 7	62/42 5	68/46 6	74/55 4	82/60 3	88/64 2	88/64 3	83/61 6	73/53 9	63/46 8	56/41 9
SAIGON (HO CHI MINH CITY), Vietnam	89/70 2	91/71 1	93/74 4	95/76 4	92/76 16	89/75 21	88/75 23	88/75 21	88/74 21	88/74 20	87/73 11	87/71 7
SAN JUAN, Puerto Rico	80/70 20	80/70 15	81/70 15	82/72 14	84/74 16	85/75 17	85/75 19	85/76 20	86/75 18	85/75 18	84/73 19	81/72 21
SANTIAGO, Chile	85/53 0	84/52 0	80/49 11	74/45 5	65/41 5	58/37 6	59/37 6	62/39 5	66/42 3	72/45 3	78/48 1	80/51 3
SÃO PAULO, Brazil	81/63 19	82/64 17	81/62 15	78/58 10	73/54 10	71/51 8	71/49 6	73/51 8	74/54 11	76/57 13	79/59 14	80/61 13
SEOUL, South Korea	32/15 8	37/20 6	47/29 7	62/41 8	72/51 10	80/61 10	84/70 16	87/71 13	78/59 9	67/45 7	51/32 9	37/20 9
SEVILLE, Spain	59/41 8	62/44 9	67/48 8	73/51 8	80/57 5	89/63 2	96/67 1	97/68 1	89/64 3	78/57 5	67/49 6	60/44 8
SHANGHAI, China	46/33 6	47/34 9	55/40 9	66/50 9	77/59 9	82/67 13	90/74 12	90/74 12	82/66 11	74/57 4	63/45 6	53/36 6
SINGAPORE, Singapore	86/73 17	88/73 11	88/75 14	88/75 15	89/75 15	88/75 13	88/75 13	88/75 14	87/75 14	87/74 16	87/74 18	87/74 19
SOFIA, Bulgaria	34/22 6	39/25 6	51/32 8	62/41 8	70/49 11	76/54 9	82/57 7	82/56 6	74/50 8	63/42 7	50/35 7	37/26 7
STOCKHOLM, Sweden	31/23 8	31/22 7	37/26 7	45/32 6	57/41 8	65/49 7	70/55 10	66/53 10	58/46 8	48/39 9	38/31 9	35/30 9
SYDNEY, Australia	78/65 14	78/73 13	76/63 14	71/58 14	66/52 12	61/48 12	60/46 12	63/48 11	67/51 12	71/56 12	74/60 12	77/63 13
TAIPEI, Taiwan, China	66/54 9	65/53 13	70/57 12	77/63 14	83/69 12	89/73 13	92/76 10	91/75 12	88/73 10	81/67 9	75/62 7	69/57 8
TEHRAN, Iran	45/27 4	50/32 4	59/39 5	71/49 3	82/58 7	93/66 1	99/72 1	97/71 1	90/64 1	76/53 1	63/43 3	51/33 4
TEL AVIV, Israel	63/48 10	65/48 8	67/50 9	74/54 2	81/60 1	84/65 0	87/69 0	87/70 0	86/68 1	84/64 2	77/59 7	66/52 11
TOKYO, Japan	47/29 5	48/31 6	54/36 10	63/46 10	71/54 10	76/63 12	83/70 10	86/72 7	79/66 12	69/55 11	60/43 7	52/33 5
VALPARAISO, Chile	72/56 1	72/56 1	70/54 1	67/52 1	63/50 5	60/48 7	60/47 7	61/47 5	62/48 2	65/50 7	69/52 1	71/54 1
VENICE, Italy	43/33 6	46/35 5	54/41 6	63/49 5	71/57 8	78/64 8	82/67 5	82/67 5	78/62 5	65/52 7	54/43 7	46/37 7
VIENNA, Austria	34/26 8	38/28 7	47/34 7	57/41 9	66/50 9	71/56 9	75/59 9	73/58 10	66/52 7	55/44 8	44/36 8	37/30 9
WELLINGTON, New Zealand	69/56 10	69/56 9	67/54 11	63/51 13	58/47 16	55/44 17	53/42 18	54/43 17	57/46 15	60/48 14	63/50 13	67/54 12
ZURICH, Switzerland	48/14 11	52/15 11	62/22 14	70/32 14	77/39 14	83/47 15	86/51 15	84/49 14	78/42 11	68/32 14	57/25 12	49/16 13

U.S. City Weather

City	Record Temperature High (F°)	Record Temperature Low (F°)	Annual Average: Precip. (Water equiv.) (in.)	Annual Average: Snow and Sleet (in.)	Annual Average: Wind Speed (mph)	First Freeze Date 32 F° or less Average	First Freeze Date 32 F° or less Earliest on record	Last Freeze Date 32 F° or less Average	Last Freeze Date 32 F° or less Latest on record	Elevation of Station (feet)
Albany	104	—28	36.46	65.7	8.8	Oct. 13	Sept. 23	Apr. 27	May 20	292
Albuquerque	105	—17	8.33	10.7	9.0	Oct. 29	Oct. 11	Apr. 16	May 18	5,314
Atlanta	103	— 9	48.66	1.5	9.1	Nov. 12	Oct. 24	Mar. 24	Apr. 15	1,034
Baltimore	107	— 7	41.62	21.9	9.5	Oct. 26	Oct. 8	Apr. 15	May 11	155
Birmingham	107	—10	53.46	1.2	7.4	Nov. 10	Oct. 17	Mar. 17	Apr. 21	630
Bismarck	114	—45	16.15	38.4	10.6	Sept. 22	Sept. 6	May 11	May 30	1,660
Boise	111	—23	11.97	21.7	9.0	Oct. 12	Sept. 9	May 6	May 31	2,868
Boston	104	—18	41.55	41.9	12.6	Nov. 7	Oct. 5	Apr. 8	May 3	29
Buffalo	99	—21	35.19	88.6	12.3	Oct. 25	Sept. 23	Apr. 30	May 24	706
Burlington, Vt.	101	—30	32.54	78.4	8.8	Oct. 3	Sept. 13	May 10	May 24	340
Charleston, W. Va.	108	—24	43.66	28.8	6.5	Oct. 28	Sept. 29	Apr. 18	May 11	951
Charlotte	104	— 5	45.00	5.6	7.6	Nov. 4	Oct. 15	Apr. 2	Apr. 16	769
Cheyenne	100	—38	14.48	52.0	13.3	Sept. 27	Aug. 25	May 18	June 18	6,141
Chicago	105	—23	33.47	40.7	10.3	Oct. 26	Sept. 25	Apr. 20	May 14	623
Cincinnati	102	—19	40.40	23.2	9.1	Oct. 25	Sept. 28	Apr. 15	May 25	877
Cleveland	103	—19	34.15	51.5	10.8	Nov. 2	Sept. 29	Apr. 21	May 14	805
Columbia, S.C.	107	— 2	45.23	1.8	6.9	Nov. 3	Oct. 4	Mar. 30	Apr. 21	225
Columbus, Ohio	106	—20	36.98	27.7	8.7	Oct. 31	Oct. 7	Apr. 16	May 9	833
Concord, N.H.	102	—37	38.13	64.1	6.7	Sept. 24	Sept. 13	May 17	June 6	346
Dallas-Ft. Worth, Tex.	112	— 8	32.11	2.7	11.1	Nov. 21	Oct. 27	Mar. 16	Apr. 13	596
Denver	105	—30	14.60	60.1	9.0	Oct. 14	Sept. 16	May 2	May 28	5,332
Des Moines	110	—30	31.49	33.2	11.1	Oct. 10	Sept. 28	Apr. 20	May 11	963
Detroit	105	—24	31.49	31.7	10.2	Oct. 21	Sept. 23	Apr. 23	May 12	626
El Paso	109	— 8	8.47	4.4	9.6	Nov. 11	Oct. 31	Mar. 13	Apr. 11	3,916
Great Falls	107	—49	14.83	57.7	13.1	Sept. 26	Sept. 7	May 14	June 8	3,657
Hartford	102	—26	43.00	53.1	9.0	Oct. 15	Sept. 27	Apr. 22	May 10	179
Houston	108	5	47.07	0.4	7.6	Dec. 11	Oct. 25	Feb. 5	Mar. 27	108
Indianapolis	107	—25	39.98	21.3	9.7	Oct. 22	Sept. 27	Apr. 23	May 27	808
Jackson	107	— 5	50.96	0.8	7.7	Nov. 8	Oct. 9	Mar. 18	Apr. 25	331
Jacksonville	105	10	51.75	Trace	8.6	Dec. 16	Nov. 3	Feb. 6	Mar. 31	31
Juneau	90	—22	53.95	109.1	8.5	Oct. 21	Sept. 9	Apr. 22	June 8	24
Kansas City, Mo.	113	—22	36.66	19.7	10.2	Oct. 26	Sept. 30	Apr. 7	May 6	1,025
Little Rock	110	—13	48.17	5.3	8.2	Nov. 15	Oct. 23	Mar. 16	Apr. 13	265
Los Angeles	110	23	11.94	Trace	7.4	—	Dec. 9	—	Jan. 21	104
Louisville	107	—20	42.94	17.3	8.4	Oct. 25	Oct. 15	Apr. 10	Apr. 19	488
Memphis	106	—13	48.74	5.7	9.2	Nov. 5	Oct. 17	Mar. 20	Apr. 15	284
Miami	100	26	59.21	—	9.1	—	—	—	Feb. 6	12
Milwaukee	105	—25	30.18	45.2	11.8	Oct. 23	Sept. 20	Apr. 25	May 27	693
Minneapolis-St. Paul	108	—34	26.62	45.8	10.6	Oct. 13	Sept. 3	Apr. 29	May 24	838
Mobile	104	— 1	63.26	0.4	9.3	Dec. 12	Nov. 15	Feb. 17	Mar. 20	221
Nashville	107	—15	46.61	10.9	7.9	Oct. 31	Oct. 7	Apr. 3	Apr. 24	605
New Orleans	102	7	58.93	0.2	8.4	Dec. 3	Nov. 11	Feb. 15	Apr. 8	30
New York City	106	—15	43.56	29.1	9.4	Nov. 12	Oct. 19	Apr. 7	Apr. 24	87
Norfolk	105	2	45.22	7.2	10.6	Nov. 21	Nov. 7	Mar. 22	Apr. 14	30
Oklahoma City	113	—17	31.71	9.2	12.9	Nov. 7	Oct. 7	Apr. 1	May 3	1,304
Omaha	114	—32	28.48	32.5	10.9	Oct. 20	Sept. 24	Apr. 14	May 11	982
Philadelphia	106	—11	41.18	20.3	9.6	Nov. 17	Oct. 19	Mar. 30	Apr. 20	28
Phoenix	118	16	7.41	Trace	6.1	Dec. 11	Nov. 4	Jan. 27	Mar. 3	1,107
Pittsburgh	103	—20	36.21	45.5	9.4	Oct. 20	Oct. 10	Apr. 21	May 4	1,225
Portland, Me.	103	—39	42.15	74.3	8.8	Sept. 27	Sept. 17	May 12	May 31	63
Portland, Ore.	107	— 3	37.98	7.5	7.8	Dec. 1	Oct. 26	Feb. 25	May 4	39
Providence	104	—17	40.90	37.8	10.8	Oct. 26	Oct. 3	Apr. 14	Apr. 24	62
Reno	106	—19	7.65	26.8	6.4	Oct. 2	Aug. 30	May 14	June 25	4,400
Richmond	107	—12	43.77	14.3	7.6	Nov. 8	Oct. 5	Apr. 2	May 11	177
Sacramento	115	17	17.33	Trace	8.3	Dec. 11	Nov. 4	Jan. 24	Mar. 14	25
St. Louis	115	—23	36.70	17.8	9.5	Oct. 20	Sept. 28	Apr. 15	May 10	564
Salt Lake City	107	—30	15.63	58.1	8.7	Nov. 1	Sept. 25	Apr. 12	Apr. 30	4,227
San Francisco	106	20	18.88	Trace	10.5	—	Dec. 11	—	Jan. 21	18
Seattle	100	0	40.30	15.2	9.3	Dec. 1	Oct. 19	Feb. 23	Apr. 3	450
Spokane	108	—30	16.19	54.0	8.7	Oct. 12	Sept. 13	Apr. 20	May 16	2,365
Washington, D.C.	106	—15	40.00	16.8	9.2	Nov. 10	Oct. 2	Mar. 29	May 12	65
Wichita	114	—22	30.06	16.3	12.6	Nov. 1	Sept. 27	Apr. 5	Apr. 21	1,340
Wilmington, Del.	107	—15	43.63	20.1	9.1	Oct. 26	Sept. 27	Apr. 18	May 9	80

SOURCE: National Climatic Center

U.S. City Weather

AVERAGE MONTHLY TEMPERATURES (in °F)

City	Jan.	Feb.	Mar.	April	May	June	July	Aug.	Sept.	Oct.	Nov.	Dec.	ANNUAL
Albany	23.0°	23.7°	33.5°	46.5°	58.4°	67.7°	72.5°	70.2°	62.7°	51.4°	39.7°	27.7°	48.1°
Albuquerque	34.5	39.5	46.3	54.8	63.8	73.3	77.1	75.1	68.4	56.8	43.9	35.1	55.7
Atlanta	43.5	45.6	52.6	61.3	69.6	76.4	78.5	77.8	73.1	62.9	52.0	44.7	61.5
Baltimore	33.2	35.0	42.6	53.6	63.1	72.1	76.8	75.3	68.5	57.3	46.0	36.4	55.0
Birmingham	45.6	47.1	55.0	62.9	70.7	77.8	79.9	79.6	75.2	64.6	53.4	46.3	63.2
Bismarck	8.1	12.2	25.3	42.9	54.6	64.1	70.6	68.5	57.9	45.7	28.6	15.4	41.1
Boise	29.9	35.5	42.3	49.6	57.8	65.4	74.5	72.5	62.7	52.3	40.6	32.1	51.3
Boston	28.9	29.1	36.9	46.9	57.7	67.0	72.6	70.7	64.0	54.2	43.5	32.6	50.3
Buffalo	25.1	24.5	32.3	43.3	54.6	64.7	70.3	68.9	62.6	51.8	40.0	29.5	47.3
Burlington, Vt.	18.0	18.4	29.3	42.6	55.2	64.8	69.7	67.3	59.6	48.8	36.6	23.3	44.5
Charleston, W. Va.	36.6	38.0	46.0	56.0	64.8	72.3	76.0	74.8	69.3	58.0	46.7	38.2	56.4
Charlotte	42.0	43.9	51.0	60.0	68.9	76.0	78.7	77.4	72.2	61.6	50.9	43.1	60.5
Cheyenne	26.1	27.7	32.4	41.4	51.0	61.0	67.7	66.4	57.3	46.4	35.2	28.6	45.1
Chicago	24.7	27.1	36.4	47.8	58.2	68.4	73.8	72.5	65.6	54.5	40.4	29.4	49.9
Cincinnati	30.8	33.6	41.7	53.5	63.3	71.9	75.5	74.2	67.3	56.3	43.6	34.4	53.9
Cleveland	27.5	27.8	35.9	47.0	58.3	67.9	72.2	70.6	64.6	53.8	41.6	31.3	49.9
Columbia, S.C.	46.6	48.1	55.1	63.5	71.9	78.5	80.8	79.9	75.1	64.5	54.4	47.2	63.8
Columbus, Ohio	29.4	30.8	40.0	51.1	61.9	70.9	74.8	72.9	66.6	55.0	42.3	32.4	52.3
Concord, N.H.	21.3	22.8	31.9	44.4	56.2	64.9	70.0	67.3	59.7	49.2	37.5	25.6	45.9
Dallas-Ft. Worth, Tex.	45.6	48.8	56.9	65.2	72.7	80.9	84.5	84.6	77.8	67.8	56.1	47.7	65.7
Denver	30.1	32.8	38.7	47.4	56.7	66.6	72.6	71.3	62.6	51.6	39.6	32.3	50.2
Des Moines	20.8	24.7	36.3	50.4	61.5	71.1	76.1	73.7	65.3	54.2	38.5	26.1	49.9
Detroit	25.3	25.8	34.5	46.7	58.1	68.2	73.0	71.1	64.2	53.1	40.1	29.5	49.2
El Paso	44.7	49.3	55.6	63.8	72.2	80.8	81.9	80.2	74.8	64.7	52.5	45.2	63.8
Great Falls	21.2	26.1	31.4	43.3	53.3	60.9	69.7	67.9	57.6	48.3	34.8	27.1	45.1
Hartford	27.1	27.7	36.9	47.9	59.0	67.9	73.1	70.9	63.7	53.3	42.1	30.4	50.0
Houston	53.2	54.6	62.0	67.9	74.3	79.8	82.4	81.3	77.5	70.2	59.6	55.5	68.2
Indianapolis	28.5	30.8	40.1	52.0	62.5	71.8	75.7	73.7	66.9	55.5	42.0	31.9	52.6
Jackson	48.4	50.9	57.3	65.3	72.6	79.6	81.8	81.5	76.9	66.5	55.7	49.5	65.5
Jacksonville	55.0	56.6	61.8	67.5	73.7	78.5	80.4	80.1	77.1	68.9	60.6	54.9	67.9
Juneau	22.2	27.3	31.2	38.4	46.4	52.8	55.5	54.1	49.0	41.5	32.0	26.9	39.8
Kansas City, Mo.	29.7	33.1	43.2	55.5	65.3	74.7	79.5	78.0	70.0	59.1	44.7	33.6	55.6
Little Rock	41.7	44.8	52.9	62.5	70.1	78.2	81.3	80.5	74.1	63.8	51.9	43.8	62.1
Los Angeles	54.6	55.9	56.9	59.3	62.1	64.9	68.3	69.5	68.5	65.2	60.4	56.4	61.8
Louisville	34.7	36.8	45.6	56.3	66.0	74.6	78.3	76.8	70.4	58.9	46.4	37.2	56.9
Memphis	41.3	44.1	52.2	62.1	70.5	78.2	81.2	80.0	74.1	63.5	51.6	43.6	61.9
Miami	67.5	68.0	71.3	74.9	78.0	80.9	82.2	82.7	81.6	77.8	72.3	68.5	75.5
Milwaukee	20.9	23.2	32.6	44.3	54.3	64.5	70.7	69.7	62.5	51.5	37.7	26.1	46.5
Minneapolis-St. Paul	13.2	16.7	29.6	45.7	57.9	67.8	73.1	70.7	61.5	50.0	33.0	19.5	44.9
Mobile	51.9	54.4	60.1	67.1	74.3	80.3	81.8	81.5	78.1	68.9	58.9	53.1	67.6
Nashville	39.1	41.0	49.5	59.5	68.2	76.3	79.4	78.3	72.2	61.1	48.9	41.1	59.6
New Orleans	54.3	56.5	61.7	68.9	75.4	80.8	82.2	82.0	78.8	70.7	60.7	55.6	69.0
New York City	32.3	32.7	40.6	51.1	61.9	70.9	76.1	74.6	68.0	58.0	46.7	35.7	54.1
Norfolk	41.6	42.3	48.8	57.4	66.7	74.7	78.6	77.5	72.4	62.2	52.1	43.6	59.8
Oklahoma City	37.2	40.8	49.8	60.2	68.2	77.0	81.4	81.1	73.7	62.7	49.4	39.9	60.1
Omaha	22.0	26.5	37.5	51.7	62.7	72.3	77.4	75.1	66.3	55.0	39.3	27.5	51.1
Philadelphia	33.1	33.8	41.6	52.2	63.0	71.8	76.6	74.7	68.4	57.5	46.2	36.2	54.6
Phoenix	51.6	55.4	60.5	67.7	76.0	85.2	90.8	89.0	83.6	71.7	59.8	52.4	70.3
Pittsburgh	30.7	31.3	39.9	51.1	62.0	70.6	74.6	72.8	66.6	55.2	43.2	33.6	52.7
Portland, Me.	22.4	23.4	32.3	42.8	53.2	62.4	68.2	66.6	59.6	49.6	38.6	26.9	45.5
Portland, Ore.	38.5	43.0	45.9	50.6	57.0	60.2	65.8	65.3	62.7	54.0	45.7	41.1	52.5
Providence	29.4	29.3	37.6	47.5	57.8	66.9	72.7	71.0	63.9	54.0	43.4	32.6	50.5
Reno	31.8	36.6	41.2	47.4	54.9	62.5	70.2	68.5	60.7	50.9	41.0	33.4	49.9
Richmond	38.0	39.4	46.9	56.9	66.1	74.0	77.6	76.1	69.9	58.9	48.7	39.7	57.7
Sacramento	44.9	49.8	53.1	58.1	64.5	70.8	75.4	74.3	71.6	63.4	52.9	45.7	60.4
St. Louis	31.7	34.8	44.3	56.1	65.9	75.1	79.3	77.5	70.1	59.0	45.3	35.3	56.2
Salt Lake City	28.0	33.2	40.7	49.0	58.3	68.1	77.2	75.4	65.1	53.1	40.5	31.4	51.7
San Francisco	48.0	50.9	52.9	54.6	57.3	60.3	61.5	62.0	62.9	60.0	54.3	49.3	56.2
Seattle	38.2	42.2	43.9	48.1	55.0	59.9	64.4	63.8	59.6	51.8	44.6	40.5	51.0
Spokane	26.8	31.7	39.4	47.6	55.8	62.5	70.2	68.7	59.5	48.7	37.0	30.4	48.2
Washington, D.C.	36.1	37.7	45.7	56.1	65.8	74.3	78.4	76.9	70.3	59.6	48.4	38.4	57.3
Wichita	31.6	35.2	44.7	56.3	65.4	75.3	80.3	79.3	70.9	59.6	45.2	35.0	56.5
Wilmington, Del.	32.6	33.1	41.9	52.2	62.7	71.4	76.0	74.1	67.9	56.8	45.7	35.2	54.2

SOURCE: National Climatic Center (data based on normals for 1936-1975)

TABLES OF AIRLINE DISTANCES

All Distances in Statute Miles

Between Principal Cities of the World

FROM/TO	Azores	Bagdad	Berlin	Bombay	Buenos Aires	Callao	Cairo	Cape Town	Chicago	Istanbul	Guam	Honolulu	Juneau	London	Los Angeles	Melbourne	Mexico City	Montreal	New Orleans	New York	Panama	Paris	Rio de Janeiro	San Francisco	Santiago	Seattle	Shanghai	Singapore	Tokyo	Wellington
Azores	....	3906	2148	5930	5385	4825	3325	5670	3305	2880	8985	7421	4715	1562	5034	12190	4584	2548	3718	2604	3918	1617	4312	5114	5718	4720	7324	8338	7370	11475
Bagdad	3906	....	2040	2022	8215	8618	785	4923	6490	1085	6380	8445	6180	2568	7695	8150	8155	5814	7212	6066	7807	2385	7012	7521	8876	6848	4468	4443	5242	9782
Berlin	2148	2040	....	3947	7411	6937	1823	5949	4458	1068	7158	7384	4638	575	5849	9992	6119	3776	5182	4026	5902	540	6246	5744	7842	5121	5323	6226	5623	11384
Bombay	5930	2022	3947	....	9380	10530	2698	5133	8144	3043	4831	8172	6992	4526	8810	6140	9818	7582	8952	7875	9832	4391	8438	8523	10127	7830	3219	2425	4247	7752
Buenos Aires	5385	8215	7411	9380	....	1982	7428	4332	5598	7638	10516	7653	7964	6919	6148	7336	4609	5619	4902	5295	3319	6891	1230	6487	731	6956	12295	9940	11601	6341
Callao	4825	8618	6937	10530	1982	....	7870	6195	3765	7666	9760	5993	5806	6376	4155	8196	2619	3954	2990	3633	1450	6455	2400	4500	1548	4964	10760	11700	9740	6696
Cairo	3325	785	1823	2698	7428	7870	....	4476	6231	780	7175	8925	6352	2218	7675	8720	7807	5502	6862	5701	7230	2020	6242	7554	8100	6915	5290	5152	6005	10360
Cape Town	5670	4923	5949	5133	4332	6195	4476	....	8551	5210	8918	11655	10382	5975	10165	6510	8620	7975	8390	7845	7090	5732	3850	10340	5080	10305	8179	6025	9234	7149
Chicago	3305	6490	4458	8144	5598	3765	6231	8551	....	5530	7510	4315	2310	4015	1741	9837	1690	750	827	727	2320	4219	5320	1875	5325	1753	7155	9475	6410	8465
Istanbul	2880	1085	1068	3043	7638	7666	780	5210	5530	....	7015	8200	5665	1540	6895	9189	7160	4825	6220	5060	6797	1390	6420	6770	8230	6124	5084	5440	5649	10790
Guam	8985	6380	7158	4831	10516	9760	7175	8918	7510	7015	....	3896	5225	7605	6255	3497	7690	7840	7895	8115	9220	7675	11710	5952	9946	5785	1945	2990	1596	4206
Honolulu	7421	8445	7384	8172	7653	5993	8925	11655	4315	8200	3896	....	2825	7320	2620	5581	3846	4992	4305	5051	5347	7525	8400	2407	6935	2707	5009	6874	3940	4676
Juneau	4715	6180	4638	6992	7964	5806	6352	10382	2310	5665	5225	2825	....	4496	1835	8162	3210	2647	2860	2874	4456	4700	7611	1530	7320	870	4968	7375	4117	7501
London	1562	2568	575	4526	6919	6376	2218	5975	4015	1540	7605	7320	4496	....	5496	10590	5605	3370	4656	3500	5310	210	5747	5440	7275	4850	5841	6818	6050	11790
Los Angeles	5034	7695	5849	8810	6148	4155	7675	10165	1741	6895	6255	2620	1835	5496	....	8098	1445	2468	1695	2466	3025	5711	6330	345	5595	961	6598	8955	5600	6806
Melbourne	12190	8150	9992	6140	7336	8196	8720	6510	9837	9189	3497	5581	8162	10590	8098	....	8599	10553	9455	10541	9211	10500	8340	7970	7130	8330	4967	3768	5172	1655
Mexico City	4584	8155	6119	9818	4609	2619	7807	8620	1690	7160	7690	3846	3210	5605	1445	8599	....	2247	940	2110	1532	5800	4810	1870	4122	2339	8120	10495	7190	7003
Montreal	2548	5814	3776	7582	5619	3954	5502	7975	750	4825	7840	4992	2647	3370	2468	10553	2247	....	1390	340	2545	3490	5110	2557	5461	2309	7141	9280	6546	9206
New Orleans	3718	7212	5182	8952	4902	2990	6862	8390	827	6220	7895	4305	2860	4656	1695	9455	940	1390	....	1161	1600	4846	4798	1960	4553	2137	7830	10255	6993	7950
New York	2604	6066	4026	7875	5295	3633	5701	7845	727	5060	8115	5051	2874	3500	2466	10541	2110	340	1161	....	2211	3600	4810	2606	5134	2440	7460	9617	6846	9067
Panama	3918	7807	5902	9832	3319	1450	7230	7090	2320	6797	9220	5347	4456	5310	3025	9211	1532	2545	1600	2211	....	5440	3311	3349	3000	3680	9430	11800	8560	7580
Paris	1617	2385	540	4391	6891	6455	2020	5762	4219	1390	7675	7525	4700	210	5711	10500	5800	3490	4846	3600	5440	....	5710	5680	7300	5080	5855	6730	6132	11865
Rio de Janeiro	4312	7012	6246	8438	1230	2400	6242	3850	5320	6420	11710	8400	7611	5747	6330	8340	4810	5110	4798	4810	3311	5710	....	6655	1852	6945	11510	9875	11600	7510
San Francisco	5114	7521	5744	8523	6487	4500	7554	10340	1875	6770	5952	2407	1530	5440	345	7970	1870	2557	1960	2606	3349	5680	6655	....	5960	692	6245	8440	5250	6800
Santiago	5718	8876	7842	10127	731	1548	8100	5080	5325	8230	9946	6935	7320	7275	5595	7130	4122	5461	4553	5134	3000	7300	1852	5960	....	6466	11850	10270	10850	5925
Seattle	4720	6848	5121	7830	6956	4964	6915	10305	1753	6124	5785	2707	870	4850	961	8330	2339	2309	2137	2440	3680	5080	6945	692	6466	....	5780	8200	4863	7310
Shanghai	7324	4468	5323	3219	12295	10760	5290	8179	7155	5084	1945	5009	4968	5841	6598	4967	8120	7141	7830	7460	9430	5855	11510	6245	11850	5780	....	2395	1095	6080
Singapore	8338	4443	6226	2425	9940	11700	5152	6025	9475	5440	2990	6874	7375	6818	8955	3768	10495	9280	10255	9617	11800	6730	9875	8440	10270	8200	2395	....	3350	5360
Tokyo	7370	5242	5623	4247	11601	9740	6005	9234	6410	5649	1596	3940	4117	6050	5600	5172	7190	6546	6993	6846	8560	6132	11600	5250	10850	4863	1095	3350	....	5730
Wellington	11475	9782	11384	7752	6341	6696	10360	7149	8465	10790	4206	4676	7501	11790	6806	1655	7003	9206	7950	9067	7580	11865	7510	6800	5925	7310	6080	5360	5730	......

Between Principal Cities of Europe

	Amsterdam	Athens	Baku	Barcelona	Belgrade	Berlin	Brussels	Bucharest	Budapest	Cologne	Copenhagen	Istanbul	Dresden	Dublin	Frankfort	Hamburg	Leningrad	Lisbon	London	Lyon	Madrid	Marseilles	Milan	Moscow	Munich	Oslo	Paris	Riga	Rome	Sofia	Stockholm	Toulouse	Warsaw	Vienna	Zurich
Amsterdam	....	1340	2218	770	875	365	105	1100	710	128	381	1360	385	468	228	232	1090	1140	220	458	912	627	517	1325	415	568	257	820	808	1073	695	625	673	580	375
Athens	1340	....	1395	1160	500	1112	1292	460	698	1200	1320	350	1022	1765	1113	1250	1535	1770	1476	1100	1463	1025	900	1388	925	1610	1300	1310	650	335	1495	1215	990	795	1000
Baku	2218	1395	....	2427	1487	1867	2240	1220	1562	2127	1980	1070	1837	2490	2055	2020	1570	3050	2435	2238	2742	2238	2028	1175	1912	2118	2335	1590	1900	1360	1862	2425	1555	1700	2050
Barcelona	770	1160	2427	....	998	925	658	1210	924	692	1085	1380	860	919	665	910	1740	610	707	327	316	211	450	1852	648	1330	518	1440	530	1072	1410	156	1150	830	513
Belgrade	875	500	1487	998	....	618	850	295	205	750	840	502	530	1327	652	760	1165	1555	1040	752	1235	750	540	1160	475	1112	890	855	440	231	1005	930	510	300	590
Berlin	365	1112	1867	925	618	....	401	798	425	300	225	1068	95	815	268	165	815	1410	575	601	1149	730	570	995	310	520	540	520	730	810	503	815	320	322	410
Brussels	105	1292	2240	658	850	401	....	1110	700	110	475	1345	407	480	198	301	1175	998	202	352	807	521	435	1392	372	672	170	900	730	945	793	515	720	568	312
Bucharest	1100	460	1220	1210	295	798	1110	....	295	982	970	272	725	1560	890	950	1080	1842	1285	1025	1518	1020	819	920	725	1245	1152	870	700	194	1080	1210	580	520	855
Budapest	710	698	1562	924	205	425	700	295	....	590	629	650	345	1176	504	572	965	1515	900	680	1214	718	476	965	350	920	770	685	500	395	820	883	342	128	498
Cologne	128	1200	2127	692	750	300	110	982	590	....	400	1240	292	585	93	228	1090	1126	308	370	875	528	390	1285	282	635	250	805	675	945	722	875	602	460	259
Copenhagen	381	1320	1960	1085	840	225	475	970	629	400	....	1240	315	768	412	180	708	1520	590	760	1272	906	720	970	520	303	634	453	948	1010	330	962	415	538	595
Istanbul	1360	350	1070	1380	502	1068	1345	272	650	1240	1240	....	995	1830	1150	1222	1292	2005	1540	1238	1690	1205	1030	1180	975	1505	1390	1115	840	315	1340	1400	852	790	1090
Dresden	385	1022	1837	860	530	95	407	725	345	292	315	995	....	852	236	238	885	1380	592	540	1100	655	435	1200	227	620	523	585	630	730	598	762	325	235	342
Dublin	468	1765	2490	919	1327	815	480	1560	1176	585	768	1830	852	....	671	668	1440	1015	300	720	902	875	880	1728	855	786	480	1210	1175	1525	1010	761	1130	1040	768
Frankfort	228	1113	2055	665	652	268	198	890	504	93	412	1150	236	671	....	250	1075	1160	392	350	888	492	323	1240	193	675	295	780	698	860	730	560	550	370	193
Hamburg	232	1250	2020	910	760	165	301	950	572	228	180	1222	238	668	250	....	880	1301	448	580	1098	730	570	1100	378	445	459	600	810	954	502	780	462	460	432
Leningrad	1090	1535	1570	1740	1165	815	1175	1080	965	1090	708	1292	885	1440	1075	880	....	2235	1300	1420	1980	1540	1315	391	1100	670	1335	300	1440	1218	435	1635	640	975	1225
Lisbon	1140	1770	3050	610	1555	1410	998	1842	1515	1126	1520	2005	1380	1015	1160	1301	2235	....	975	850	313	810	1350	430	1208	1690	890	1940	1150	1685	1848	640	1700	1415	1058
London	220	1476	2435	707	1040	575	202	1285	900	308	590	1540	592	300	392	448	1300	975	....	455	777	620	595	1540	526	720	210	1035	890	1235	885	550	890	762	480
Lyon	458	1100	2238	327	752	601	352	1025	680	370	760	1238	540	720	350	580	1420	850	455	....	577	170	210	1560	352	1005	248	1122	462	928	1080	228	850	562	206
Madrid	912	1463	2742	316	1235	1149	807	1518	1214	875	1272	1690	1100	902	888	1098	1980	313	777	557	....	394	728	2120	910	1474	645	1670	840	1385	1598	344	1410	1110	765
Marseilles	627	1025	2238	211	750	730	521	1020	718	528	906	1205	655	875	492	730	1540	810	620	170	394	....	238	1642	445	1165	410	1238	372	895	1225	196	950	620	318
Milan	517	900	2028	450	540	570	435	819	476	390	720	1030	435	880	323	570	1315	1350	595	210	728	238	....	1408	215	1000	400	1010	295	715	1020	400	705	385	137
Moscow	1325	1388	1175	1852	1160	995	1392	920	965	1285	970	1180	1200	1728	1240	1100	391	430	1540	1560	2120	1642	1408	....	1220	1030	1538	520	1462	1100	770	1770	710	1028	1350
Munich	415	925	1912	648	475	310	372	725	350	282	520	975	227	855	193	378	1100	1208	526	352	910	445	215	1220	....	810	425	800	430	672	811	570	500	222	158
Oslo	568	1610	2118	1330	1112	520	672	1245	920	635	303	1505	620	786	675	445	670	1690	720	1005	1474	1165	1000	1030	810	....	830	531	1242	1295	267	1140	653	835	869
Paris	257	1300	2335	518	890	540	170	1152	770	250	634	1390	523	480	295	459	1335	890	210	248	645	410	400	1538	425	830	....	1050	690	1080	950	431	845	770	295
Riga	820	1310	1590	1440	855	520	900	870	685	805	453	1115	585	1210	780	600	300	1940	1035	1122	1670	1238	1010	520	800	531	1050	....	1155	985	276	1335	350	685	930
Rome	808	650	1900	530	440	730	730	700	500	675	948	840	630	1175	698	810	1440	1150	890	462	840	372	295	1462	430	1242	690	1155	....	545	1220	569	810	470	421
Sofia	1073	335	1360	1072	231	810	945	194	395	945	1010	315	730	1525	860	954	1218	1685	1235	928	1385	895	715	1100	672	1295	1080	985	545	....	1170	1080	662	500	780
Stockholm	695	1495	1862	1410	1005	503	793	1080	820	722	330	1340	598	1010	730	502	435	1848	885	1080	1598	1225	1020	770	811	267	950	276	1220	1170	....	1281	500	770	908
Toulouse	625	1215	2425	156	930	815	515	1210	883	875	962	1400	762	761	560	780	1635	640	550	228	344	196	400	1770	570	1140	431	1335	569	1080	1281	....	1062	725	425
Warsaw	673	990	1555	1150	510	320	720	580	342	602	415	852	325	1130	550	462	640	1700	890	850	1410	950	705	710	500	653	845	350	810	662	500	1062	....	345	640
Vienna	580	795	1700	830	300	322	568	520	128	460	538	790	235	1040	370	460	975	1415	762	562	1110	620	385	1028	222	835	770	685	470	500	770	725	345	....	365
Zurich	375	1000	2050	513	590	410	312	855	498	259	595	1090	342	768	193	432	1225	1058	480	206	765	318	137	1350	158	869	295	930	421	780	908	425	640	365	....